DIRECTORS AND THEIR FILMS

DIRECTORS AND THEIR FILMS

A Comprehensive Reference, 1895–1990

by

Brooks Bushnell

McFarland & Company, Inc., Publishers
Jefferson, North Carolina, and London

British Library Cataloguing-in-Publication data are available

Library of Congress Cataloguing-in-Publication Data

Bushnell, Brooks, 1961–
    Directors and their films : a comprehensive reference, 1895–1990 /
by Brooks Bushnell.
     p. cm.
   ISBN 0-89950-766-2 (lib. bdg. : 40# alk. paper) ∞
   1. Motion picture producers and directors—Credits. 2. Motion
pictures—Catalogs. I. Title.
PN1998.B85 1993
791.43′0233′0922—dc20
                                           92-56633
                                              CIP

Manufactured in the United States of America

McFarland & Company, Inc., Publishers
 Box 611, Jefferson, North Carolina 28640

Acknowledgments

I would like to thank these people
for their kind help and support:
David Canfield,
Karin Fenz,
Harry Geduld,
Madoka Igeta,
Christina Ilioaia,
Ron Norman,
Mike Parrish
Margaret Siwko-Bajon

Contents

Introduction

This book is an international listing of director credits for more than 108,000 film titles. It is divided into two parts, the first of which is in alphabetical order by director name and the second of which is in alphabetical order by film title. (Movies made for television have been excluded unless they received some sort of theatrical release.)

In the director listings, films for a given director are listed in order of year. If two or more films by the same director have the same year, they are listed in alphabetical order for that year. Alternate titles for the same film are separated by a dot (or "bullet") and are in alphabetical order; all the known titles for a film are listed before the year is indicated. For films made before 1900, all four digits of the year are shown. For films made after 1899, the digits "19" are omitted from the year. An asterisk (*) following the year indicates a codirecting credit.

Where possible, the year shown is the year in which the film was completed. Most commonly, it's the year in which the film was released in the country it was made. For some of the foreign films, the year shown is the year in which the film was released in the United States.

Last names that begin "Mc" are alphabetized as if they began "Mac" and abbreviations such as "Dr." and "Mr." are alphabetized as if spelled out.

When articles such as "a," "an" and "the" are the first word in a film title, they will be found at the end of the title in the film listings and were not taken into consideration when the titles were alphabetized. The following is a list of foreign language articles that were handled in the same way.

al	il
as	l'
az	la
das	las
de	le
den	les
der	lo
det	los
die	lu
een	o (sometimes "ho")
egy	op
ein	os
eine	ta
ek	to
el	um
en	uma
enas	un
et	un'
ett	una
gli	une
ha'	uno
het	yr
i	

Because alphabetization in this book is word by word, "Dead Line, The" comes about 66 places before "Deadline, The" in the film listings. So, if you aren't finding the title you're after, it may be because it begins with a compound word where you would expect two words, or because it begins with two words where you would expect a compound word.

I. Directors, Showing Films

A, Da Three Monks 81

Aaberg, Lasse see Åberg, Lasse

Aagaard, Sigfred I Morgen Er Det Slut 88

Aagren, Gösta see Ågren, Gösta

Aaltonen, Veikko The Final Arrangement • Tilinteko 87

Aaron, Paul A Different Story 78; A Force of One 79; Deadly Force 83; Home Front • Morgan Stewart's Coming Home 85*; Maxie 85

Abadie, Alfred C. Weary Willie Kidnaps the Child 04*

Abashidze, Dodo The Legend of Suram Fortress • The Legend of the Suram Fortress • Legenda Suramskoi Kreposti 84*; Arabeski na Temu Pirosmani • Arabesques on the Pirosmani Theme 85*; Ashik Kerib • Traveling Artists 88*

Abbas, Khwaja Ahmad Children of the Earth • Dharti ke Lal 46; The Lost Child • Munna 54; Journey Beyond Three Seas • Khazdeni za Tri Morya • Pardesi • The Traveller 57*; The City and the Dream • Shehar aur Sapna 63; The Celestial Palace 66; Saat Hindustani 70; Do Boond Pani 72

Abbe, Derwin The Great Adventures of Captain Kidd 53*

Abbe, James E. Home Talent 21*

Abbott, Charles The Fighting Texan 37; The Adventures of the Masked Phantom 39

Abbott, George Half Way to Heaven 29; Why Bring That Up? 29; Manslaughter 30; The Sea God 30; The Cheat 31; My Sin 31; Secrets of a Secretary 31; Stolen Heaven 31; Too Many Girls 40; The Pajama Game 57*; Damn Yankees • What Lola Wants • Whatever Lola Wants 58*

Abbott, Norman The Last of the Secret Agents? 66

Abdelsalam, Shadi El Mumia • The Night of Counting the Years 69

Abdrashitov, Vadim Parad Planyet • Parade of the Planets 84; Plumbum ili Opasnaya Igra • Plumbum, or A Dangerous Game 86

Abe, Yutaka The Woman Who Touched the Legs 26

Abel, Alan Is There Sex After Death? 71*; The Faking of the President 76*

Abel, Alfred Narkose 29; Glückliche Reise 33; Alles um eine Frau 35

Abel, Jeanne Is There Sex After Death? 71*; The Faking of the President 76*

Abel, Robert Elvis on Tour 72*; Let the Good Times Roll 73*

Åberg, Lasse Charter Trip II—Snow Roller • Sällskapsresan II—Snow Roller 85; S.O.S.—En Segel Sällskapsresan 88

Abey, Dennis Gollocks, There's Plenty of Room in New Zealand 74; Never Too Young to Rock 75

Abeysekara, Tissa Viragaya • The Way of the Lotus 87

Abou Seif, Salah see Abu Saif, Salah

Aboulouakar, Mohamed Hadda 86

Abraham, John Amma Ariyan • Report to Mother 86

Abrahams, Derwin Border Vigilantes 41; Secrets of the Wasteland 41; Both Barrels Blazing • The Yellow Streak 45; By Whose Hand? • Rustlers of the Badlands 45; Decoy • Rough Ridin' Justice 45; Northwest Trail 45; The Return of the Durango Kid • Stolen Time 45; Chick Carter, Detective 46; Drifting Along 46; The Fighting Frontiersman • Golden Lady 46; Frontier Gunlaw • Menacing Shadows 46; The Haunted Mine 46; Hop Harrigan 46; Son of the Guardsman 46; The Forger • Prairie Raiders 47; Riders of the Lone Star 47; The Schemer • Swing the Western Way 47; Smoky River Serenade • The Threat 47; South of the Chisholm Trail 47; The Stranger from Ponca City 47; Cowboy Cavalier 48; Docks of New Orleans 48; The Rangers Ride 48; Tex Granger 48; Mississippi Rhythm 49; The Girl from San Lorenzo 50; Whistling Hills 51

Abrahams, Edward The Pit 62

Abrahams, Jim Airplane! 80*; Top Secret! 84*; Ruthless People 86*; Big Business 88; Welcome Home, Roxy Carmichael 90

Abramowicz, Myriam As If It Were Yesterday 80

Abramson, Hans The Serpent 66; Relations 72

Abramson, Ivan Should a Woman Divorce? 14; The Concealed Truth 15; The Unwelcome Wife 15; The City of Illusion 16; The Faded Flower 16; Forbidden Fruit 16; The Girl Who Did Not Care • The Sex Lure 16; Her Surrender 16; The Immortal Flame 16; Enlighten Thy Daughter 17; One Law for Both 17; Moral Suicide 18; The Echo of Youth 19; Someone Must Pay 19; A Child for Sale 20; The Wrong Woman 20; The Bride's Confession 21; Mother Eternal 21; Wildness of Youth 22; I Am the Man 24; Meddling Women 24; Lying Wives 25

Abruzzese, Alberto Anemia 86*

Absalov, Melo Granny General 86

Abu Saif, Salah Always in My Heart • Daiman fi Kalbi 47; The Avenger • El Muntakem 47; The Adventures of Antar and Abla • Mughammarat Antar wa Abla 48; Shariah el Bahlawane • Street of the Puppet Show 49; The Falcon • El Sakr 50; El Hub Bahdala • Love Is a Scandal 51; Laka Yom Ya Zalem • Your Day Will Come 51; Foreman Hassan • El Osta Hassen 52; Raya and Sekina 53; The Monster • El Wahsh 54; Chabab Emraa • A Woman's Youth 56; El Fatawa • The Tough 56; The Empty Pillow • El Wessada el Khalia 57; La Anam • No Tomorrow 57; The Barred Road • El Tarik el Masdud 58; Mugarem fi Ijaza • Thief on Holiday 58; Agony of Love • Lawet el Hub 59; Ana Hurra • I'm Free 59; Bayn el Samaa wa el Ard • Between Heaven and Earth 59; Bint Sabatashar • A Girl of Seventeen 59; Bedaya wa Nehayat • The Beginning and the End 60; La Tutfi el Shems • The Sun Will Never Set 61; Letter from an Unknown Woman • Ressalah min Emraa Maghoola

62; Cairo 30 66; The Second Wife • El Zawga el Sania 67; El Cadia 68 • Case 68 68; Awdit el Roh • The Return of the Spirit 69; Al Bedaya • Satan's Empire 86

Abuladze, Tenghiz Dimitri Arakishvili 52*; Our Palace 53*; The Georgian State Dancing Company 54*; Lurdzha Magdany • Magdana's Donkey • Magdan's Donkey 55*; Chuzhie Deti • Somebody Else's Children • Someone Else's Children • Stepchildren 58*; I, Grandmother, Illiko & Illarion • Me, Grandma, Iliko and Hillarion • Ya, Babushka, Illiko & Illarion 63; The Entreaty • Molba • The Plea • The Prayer • Supplication 67; A Necklace for My Beloved 72; An Open Air Museum 73; Drevo Zhelanya • The Miracle Tree • The Tree of Wishes • The Wishing Tree 76; Confession • Monanieba • Pokayaniye • Pokjaniye • Repentance 84

Abzalov, Malis Armon 88

Achard, Marcel Jean de la Lune 48; The Paris Waltz • La Valse de Paris 49

Achternbusch, Herbert Der Junge Monch • The Young Monk 78; Das Gespenst 83; Die Fohnforscher 85; Heal Hitler • Heilt Hitler 86; Wohin? 88

Acin, Jovan The Concrete Rose 75; Bal na Vodi • Dancing on Water • Hey Babu Riba 86

Ackeren, Robert van see Van Ackeren, Robert

Ackerman, Justin Beneath the Angka, A Story of the Khmer Rouge 82

Ackland, Rodney Lady Be Kind 41; Thursday's Child 42

Acomba, David Slipstream 73; Hank Williams: The Show He Never Gave 82

Acosta, Ivan Amigos 86

Acres, Birt Charge of the Uhlans 1895; The Derby 1895; Inauguration of the Kiel Canal by Kaiser Wilhelm II 1895; Oxford and Cambridge Boat Race • Oxford-Cambridge Boat Race 1895; Sea Waves at Dover 1895; Shoeblack at Work in a London Street 1895; Smith and Machinery at Work 1895; Tom Merry, Lightning Cartoonist 1895; The Arrest of a Pickpocket 1896; The Boxing Kangaroo 1896; Boxing Match • Boxing Match, or Glove Contest 1896; Dancing Girls 1896; Golfing Extraordinary • Golfing Extraordinary, Five Gentlemen 1896; Landing at Low Tide 1896; Pierrot and Pierrette 1896; A Surrey Garden 1896; Three Burlesque Dancers 1896; An Unfriendly Call 1897

Adam, Michal Bat see Bat-Adam, Michal

Adam, Raymond Komba, Dieu des Pygmees • Komba, Lord of the Pygmies 85

Adams, Catlin Sticky Fingers 88

Adams, Doug Blackout 88

Adamson, Al Two Tickets to Terror 64; Blood of Ghastly Horror • The Fiend with the Atomic Brain • The Fiend with the Electronic Brain • The Fiend with the Synthetic Brain • The Love Maniac • The Man with the Synthetic Brain • Psycho à Go-Go! 65; Blood of Dracula's Castle • Dracula's Castle 67*; The Female Bunch • A

Time to Run 69*; Five Bloody Days to Tombstone • Five Bloody Graves • Gun Riders • Lonely Man 69; Satan's Sadist • Satan's Sadists 69; Blood of Frankenstein • Dracula vs. Frankenstein • They're Coming to Get You 70; Creatures of the Prehistoric Planet • Creatures of the Red Planet • The Flesh Creatures • Flesh Creatures of the Red Planet • Horror Creatures of the Prehistoric Planet • Horror Creatures of the Red Planet • Horror of the Blood Monsters • Space Mission of the Lost Planet • Vampire Men of the Lost Planet 70*; The Fakers • Hell's Bloody Devils • Operation M • Smashing the Crime Syndicate • Swastika Savages 70; The Blood Seekers 71; The Brain of Blood • The Creature's Revenge 71; Last of the Comancheros 71; Angels' Wild Women 72; The Naughty Stewardesses 73; The Dynamite Brothers 74; Girls for Rent 74; Blazing Stewardesses 75; Jessie's Girls • Wanted Women 75; Stud Brown 75; Black Heat 76; Beyond the Living • Hospital of Terror • Nurse Sherri 77; Black Samurai 77; Cinderella 2000 77; Death Dimension 78; Sunset Cove 78; Freeze Bomb 80; Carnival Magic 82

Adamson, Victor The Lone Rider 22; Ace of Cactus Range 24*; Compassion 27; Sagebrush Politics 30; The Fighting Cowboy 33; Boss Cowboy 34; Circle Canyon 34; Lightning Range 34; The Pecos Dandy 34*; Range Riders 34; Rawhide Romance 34

Adar, Rafi Gloves • Kfafot 87

Ad Castillo, Celso Nympha 70; Kill Barbara with Panic • Patayin Mo sa Sindak si Barbara 73; Burlesk Queen 77

Adcook, W. Fighting Jim Grant 23

Addiss, Jus The Cry Baby Killer 58

Adelman, Joseph A Continental Girl 15; Where Is My Father? 16

Adidge, Pierre Joe Cocker, Mad Dogs and Englishmen • Mad Dogs and Englishmen 70; Elvis on Tour 72*

Adler, Joseph Mayhem • Scream, Baby, Scream 69; Revenge Is My Destiny 71; Sammy Somebody 76; Convention Girls 78

Adler, Lou Up in Smoke 78; Ladies and Gentlemen…The Fabulous Stains 81

Adlon, Percy Céleste 81; Five Last Days • The Last Five Days • Letzte Fünf Tage 82; Die Schaukel • The Swing 83; Sugarbaby • Zuckerbaby 84; Bagdad Cafe • Out of Rosenheim 87; Rosalie Goes Shopping 89

Adlum, Ed Invasion of the Blood Farmers 72

Adolfi, John G. A Child of God 15; A Man and His Mate 15; Alicia of the Orphans • The Ragged Princess 16; Caprice of the Mountains 16; Little Miss Happiness 16; The Man Inside 16; Merely Mary Ann 16; The Mischief Maker 16; A Modern Thelma 16; The Sphinx 16; A Child of the Wild 17; A Modern Cinderella 17; Patsy 17; Small Town Girl 17; The Cavell Case • The Woman the Germans Shot 18; The Heart of a Girl 18; Queen of the Sea 18; Who's Your Brother? 19; The Little 'Fraid Lady 20; The Wonder Man 20; The Darling of the Rich 22; The Little Red Schoolhouse 23; Chalk Marks 24; What Shall I Do? 24; Before Midnight 25; Big Pal 25; The Phantom Express 25; The Scarlet West 25; The Checkered Flag 26; Husband Hunters 27; What Happened to Father 27; The Devil's Skipper 28; The Little Snob 28; The Midnight Taxi 28; Prowlers of the Sea • Sea Prowlers 28; Sinner's Parade 28; Evidence 29; Fancy Baggage 29; In the Headlines 29; The Show of Shows 29; College Lovers 30; Dumbbells in Ermine 30; Recaptured Love 30; Sinner's Holiday 30; Alexander Hamilton 31; Compromised • We Three 31; The Millionaire 31; A Successful Calamity 31; Central Park 32; The Man Who Played God • The Silent Voice 32; The Adopted Father • The Working Man 33; The King's Vacation 33; Voltaire 33

Adolphson, Edvin Brokiga Blad 31; The Count of the Monk's Bridge • The Count of the Old Town • Munkbrogreven 34*; Cleared for Action • Klart til Drabbning 37

Adreon, Franklin Canadian Mounties vs. Atomic Invaders • Missile Base at Taniak 53; Commando Cody 53*; The Man with the Steel Whip 54; Target, Sea of China • Trader Tom of the China Seas 54; The Claw Monsters • Panther Girl of the Congo 55; King of the Carnival 55; No Man's Woman 55; The Man Is Armed 56; Terror at Midnight 56; Hell's Crossroads 57; The Nun and the Sergeant 62; Cyborg 2087 66; Dimension 4 • Dimension 5 66

Adrian, Michael Herowork 77

Aegal, W. S. Quel Maledetto Giorno della Resa dei Conti 71

Af Hällström, Roland Noita Palaa Elämään • The Witch • The Witch Returns to Life 52

Afrić, Vjekoslav Slavica 47

Aga-Mirzayev, Mukhtar Grubaya Posadka • Rough Landing 87

Agabra, Edmon Caravan pour Zagora • Le Secret des Hommes Bleus • El Secreto de los Hombres Azules 60*

Agadati, B. This Is the Land 36

Agadzhanova-Shutko, Nina Dva, Bouldej, Dva • Dva-Buldi-Dva • The Great Buldis • Two-Buldi-Two 29*

Ågård, Sigfred see Aagaard, Sigfred

Agashidze, David see Abashidze, Dodo

Aggarwal, K. C. Aakhri Nischay 88

Agha, Jalal Goonj 89

Aghion, Gabriel La Scarlatine • Scarlet Fever 83

Aghte, Arend A Chick for Cairo • Küken für Kairo 85

Agosti, Silvano N.P. • N.P.—The Secret 68; Fit to Be Untied • Matti da Slegare • Nessuno o Tutti, Matti da Slegare 74*; Another Day • Quartiere 87

Agostini, Philippe Ordinations 54; Le Naïf aux Quarante Enfants 57; Tu Es Pierre 58; The Carmelites • Le Dialogue des Carmélites 59*; Rencontres 61; La Soupe aux Poulets 63; La Petite Fille et la Recherche du Printemps 71; Grandeur Nature • Life Size • Love Doll • Tamaño Natural 73*

Agrama, Frank Dawn of the Mummy 81*

Agranenko, Z. Bessmertnyi Garnizon • The Immortal Garrison 56*; Leningrad Symphony 58

Agras, John see García Agraz, José Luis

Agraz, José Luis García see García Agraz, José Luis

Agraz, Joseph Louis see García Agraz, José Luis

Ågren, Gösta Ballad 68

Agresti, Alejandro El Hombre Que Ganó la Razón • The Man Who Gained Reason 86; El Amor Es una Mujer Gorda • Love Is a Fat Woman 87

Aguerre, Roberto Elogio della Pazzia • In Praise of Folly 86

Aguilar, Rolando Madres del Mundo 36; Esos Hombres 37; Glorious Nights • Noches de Gloria 38; Los Millónes de Chaflan 38; La Canción del Milagro • The Miracle Song 40; Fury in Paradise 55*

Aguirre, Javier Cemetery Girls • Count Dracula's Great Love • Dracula's Great Love • Dracula's Virgin Lovers • El Gran Amor del Conde Drácula • Vampire Playgirls 72; The Hunchback of the Morgue • El Jorobado de la Morgue 72

Agustsson, Agust Maya 82*

Ah Mon, Lawrence see Lawrence, Ah Mon

Ahearn, Charlie Wild Style 82

A'Hiller, Lejaren The Devil's Angel 20

Ahlberg, Mac I, a Woman 66

Ahlin, Per Resan till Melonia • Voyage to Melonia 87

Ahmed, Dara Pratidan 88

Ahmed, Sultan Daata 89

Ahrne, Marianne Near and Far 76; A Matter of Life and Death • Pa Liv och Dod 86

Ahuja, Ramesh Tamacha 88

Ainsworth, John The Bay of St. Michel • Operation Mermaid • Pattern for Plunder 63; Hell Is Empty 63*

Aitken, Doug Big Wheels and Sailor 80

Aitken, Tom Trotter on the Trot 20

Aivasian, Agassi The Lit Lantern • Sashshennyi Fonar • Zazzennyj Fonar 83

Ajvazjan, Agasi see Aivasian, Agassi

Akalaitis, JoAnne Dead End Kids • Dead End Kids: A Story of Nuclear Power 86

Akarasainee, Pisarn The Last Song 87

Akasaka, Chogi The Brain from Outer Space 59*

Akasaka, Koreyoshi The Atomic Rulers of the World • Attack of the Flying Saucers • Supergiant II 57*

Akat, Lütfü Damga 47; Unutulan Sır 47; Vurun Kahpeye 48; İngiliz Kemal Lawrens'e Karşı 49; Kaatil 53; Beyaz Mendil 55; Ak Altın 57

Akerman, Chantal Blow Up My City • Saute Ma Ville 68; L'Enfant Aimé • The Loved Child 71; La Chambre • The Room 72; Hotel Monterey 72; Hanging Out in

Yonkers • Hanging Out, Yonkers • Yonkers, Hanging Out 73; Le 15/18 73*; I...You...He...She • Je Tu Il Elle 74; Jeanne Dielman • Jeanne Dielman, 23 Quai du Commerce, 1080 Bruxelles 75; News from Home • Nuit et Jour 76; The Meetings of Anna • Les Rendez-Vous d'Anna 78; Dis-Moi • Tell Me 80; All Night Long • Toute Une Nuit 82; Les Années 80 • The Eighties • The Golden Eighties 83; L'Homme à la Valise • Man with a Suitcase 83; On Tour with Pina Bausch 83; I'm Hungry, I'm Cold • J'Ai Faim, J'Ai Froid 84; Letters Home 86; Seven Women, Seven Sins 87*; American Stories • Histoires d'Amérique 88; Un Jour Pina M'à Demandé 88; Window Shopping 88

Akhadov, Valeri A Sánta Dervis 87*

Akkad, Moustapha The Message • Mohammad, Messenger of God • Al Risalah 76; Lion of the Desert • Omar Mukhtar 79

Akomfrah, John Testament 88

Alamehzadeh, Reza The Guests of the Hotel Astoria 89

Alarcón, Sebastián The Jaguar • Yaguar 87

Alazraki, Benito Raíces • The Roots 55; Los Amantes 56; Ladros de Niños 57; Café Colón 58; Inferno de Almas 58; La Tijera d'Oro 58; Curse of the Doll People • Devil Doll Men • Muñecos Infernales 60*; Espiritismo • Spiritism 61; Frankenstein, el Vampiro y Cía. • Frankenstein, el Vampiro y Compañía • Frankenstein, the Vampire and Co. 61; Los Pistoleros 61; The Time and the Touch 62

Alba, Rafael Moreno see Moreno Alba, Rafael

Alberini, Filoteo Il Sacco di Roma • The Sacking of Rome 14

Albert, Al see Albertini, Adalberto

Albert, Ronnie The Amorous Sex • Sweet Beat 59

Albertini, Adalberto The Twilight Avengers • I Vendicatori dell'Ave Maria 70

Albicocco, Jean-Gabriel La Fille aux Yeux d'Or • The Girl with the Golden Eyes 61; Le Rat d'Amérique 62; Le Grand Meaulnes • The Wanderer 67; L'Amour au Féminin 68*; Le Cœur Fou 70; Le Petit Matin 71

Albin, Hans Der Chef Wünscht Keine Zeugen • The Chief Wants No Survivors • No Survivors Please 63*; Games of Desire 68

Alcazar, Rafael No Hagas Planes con Marga 88

Alcocer, Santos Scandal, Inc. 56; Hothead 63; The Drifters • Hallucination Generation 66; Only a Coffin • The Orgies of Dr. Orloff • Sólo un Ataúd 66; Blind Man's Bluff • Blind Man's Buff • Cauldron of Blood • El Coleccionista de Cadáveres • The Corpse Collectors • Death Comes from the Dark • The Shrinking Corpse 67; Who Says I Can't Ride a Rainbow? 71; Hooch 77

Alcoriza, Luis Los Jóvenes • The Young Ones 60; The Pearl of Tlayucán • The Pearls of St. Lucía • The Pearly Tlayucán

• Tlayucán 61; A Morte Espreita no Mar • Tiburoneros 62; Always Further On • Tarahumara 64; El Gangster 64; Safo 64; Jogo Perigoso • Juego Peligroso 66*; La Puerta 68; Mecánica Nacional 71; Fe, Esperanza y Caridad 73*; Presagio 74; Las Fuerzas Vivas 75; Tac-Tac 81; Terror and Black Lace • Terror y Encajes Negro 86; Lo Que Importa Es Vivir (El Amante Eficaz) 87

Alda, Alan The Four Seasons 81; Sweet Liberty 86; A New Life 88; Betsy's Wedding 90

Alderman, Thomas S. The Severed Arm 73

Alderson, John In Your Garden 38

Aldis, Will Stealing Home 88*

Aldrich, Hank Robin 79

Aldrich, Robert The Big Leaguer 53; Apache 54; Vera Cruz 54; World for Ransom 54; The Big Knife 55; Kiss Me Deadly 55; Attack! 56; Autumn Leaves 56; The Garment Center • The Garment Jungle 57*; Ten Seconds to Hell 58; The Angry Hills 59; The Last Days of Sodom and Gomorrah • Sodom and Gomorrah • Sodoma e Gomorra • Sodome et Gomorrhe 61*; The Last Sunset 61; What Ever Happened to Baby Jane? 62; Four for Texas 63; Hush...Hush, Sweet Charlotte 64; The Flight of the Phoenix 65; The Dirty Dozen 67; The Killing of Sister George 68; The Legend of Lylah Clare 68; Suicide Run • Too Late the Hero 69; The Grissom Gang 70; Ulzana's Raid 72; Emperor of the North • The Emperor of the North Pole 73; The Longest Yard • The Mean Machine 74; Hustle 75; The Choirboys 77; Twilight's Last Gleaming 77; The Frisco Kid • No Knife 79; ...All the Marbles • The California Dolls 81

Aldridge, Sidney The Adventures of Willie Woodbine and Lightning Larry — A Joyride to the Cannibal Islands 15

Alea, Tomás Gutiérrez see Gutiérrez Alea, Tomás

Alessandrini, Goffredo La Diga di Maghmod 29; La Segretaria Privata 31; Seconda B 34; Don Bosco 35; Cavalleria 36; Between Two Worlds • Una Donna Fra Due Mondi 37; Luciano Serra Pilota 38; La Vedova 38; Abuna Messias 39*; Caravaggio 40; Il Ponte di Vetro 40; Nozze di Sangue 41; Giarabub 42; Noi Vivi • We the Living 42; Chi l'Ha Visto? 43; Lettere a Sottemente 43; Furia 46; L'Ebreo Errante • The Wandering Jew 47; Lo Sparviero del Nilo 49; Rapture 50; Sangue sul Sagrato 50; Anita Garibaldi • Camicie Rosse • Red Shirts 51*; Los Amantes del Desierto • Gli Amanti del Deserto • The Desert Warrior • La Figlia dello Sceicco 58*

Alexander, Donald Monkey Into Man 41*

Alexander, Harald Der Videopirat 85

Alexander, Hilton Streets of Hong Kong 79

Alexander, Jack Operation Manhunt 54

Alexander, Michael Nosey Dobson 77; The Adman 80

Alexander, Peter The Divine Mr. J 74

Alexander, William That Man of Mine 47

Alexandersson, Håkan The Laundry • Tvätten 85; Never Travel on a One-Way Ticket • Res Aldrig på Enkel Biljett 87; Spårvagn till Havet • A Tram to the Sea 87

Alexandre, Robert Cloistered 36

Alexandrov, Grigori October • Oktyabar • Oktyabr' • Ten Days That Shook the World 27*; The General Line • Generalnaya Linya • Old and New • The Old and the New • Staroye i Novoye 29*; Romance Sentimentale 30*; Woman's Weal, Woman's Woe • Women's Crusade 31; Que Viva Mexico! 32*; The Internationale 33; Jazz Comedy • Jolly Fellows • Moscow Laughs • Vesyolye Rebyata 34; The Circus • Cirk 36; Report of Comrade Stalin on Proposed Constitution of the U.S.S.R. to the Eighth Extraordinary Congress of the Soviets 37; May First • Maja 38; Volga-Volga 38; Bright Path • The Bright Road • Svetlyi Put • Tanya 40; Film Report on the War No. 4 41; A Family • Odna Semya • One Family 43; The Caspians • Kaspichy • Men of the Caspian • Those from the Caspian 44; Spring • Vesna 47; Meeting on the Elbe • Vstrecha na Elbe 49; Glinka • Kompozitor Glinka • Man of Music 52; Chelovek Cheloveku • Man to Man 58; Russian Souvenir • Russkii Suvenir 60; Lenin in Poland • Lenin in Polsce 61; Before October • Pered Oktyabre 65; Lenin in Switzerland • Lenin v Shveitzarii 66; Star and Lyra 73

Alexeïeff, Alexander Night on a Bare Mountain • Night on Bald Mountain • Une Nuit sur le Mont Chauve 33*; La Belle au Bois Dormant 35*; Lingner Werke 35*; Opta Empfangt 35*; L'Orchestre Automatique 35*; Parade des Chapeaux 36*; Le Trône de France 36*; La Crème Simon 37*; L'Eau d'Évian 37*; Franck Aroma 37*; Grands Feux 37*; Huilor 37*; Les Vêtements Sigrand 37*; Balatum 38*; Les Cigarettes Bastos 38*; Les Fonderies Martin 38*; Les Oranges de Jaffa 38*; Cenpa 39*; Les Gaines Roussel 39*; Gulf Stream 39*; En Passant 43*; Fumées 51*; Masques 52*; Esso 54*; Nocturne 54*; Pure Beauté 54*; Rimes 54*; Le Buisson Ardent 55*; The Earth's Cap • La Sève de la Terre 55*; Bain d'X • Bendix 56*; Osram 56*; Quatre Temps 56*; Cent pour Cent 57*; Constance 57*; Anonyme 58*; Automation 58*; La Dauphine Java 60*; Divertissement 60*; À Propos de Jivago 62*; Le Nez • The Nose 63*; L'Eau 66*; Pictures at an Exhibition • Tableaux d'une Exposition 72*; L'Écran d'Épingles 73*; Three Themes • Trois Thèmes 79*

Alfarjani, Mohamed Ali Alshazhia • Shrapnel 87

Alfaro, Emilio Hay Unos Tipos Abajo • There Are Some Guys Downstairs 85*

Alfaro, Italo Sentivano...uno Strano, Eccitante, Pericoloso Puzzo di Dollari 73

Alfredson, Hans False As Water • Falsk

Som Vatten 85; Jim and the Pirates • Jim och Piraterna Blom 87; Vargens Tid 88

Algar, James The Adventures of Ichabod and Mr. Toad • Ichabod and Mr. Toad 49*; Beaver Valley 50; The Living Desert 53; The Vanishing Prairie 54; The African Lion 55; Secrets of Life 56; White Wilderness 57; Jungle Cat 59; The Legend of Lobo 62

Algier, Sidney Silver Devil • Wild Horse 31*

Ali, Muzaffar Anjuman 87

Ali, Sheikh Niamat Affliction • Dahan 86

Aliprandi, Marcello The Girl of Tin • La Ragazza di Latta • The Tin Girl 70; Sussurri nel Buio • Un Sussurro nel Buio • A Whisper in the Dark 76; Morte in Vaticano • Vatican Conspiracy 81

Alk, Howard Janis 74*

Allahyari, Houchang Borderline 88

Allan, Anthony Havelock see *Havelock-Allan, Anthony*

Alland, William Macbeth 48*; Look in Any Window 61

Allégret, Marc Voyage au Congo 26*; Papoul 29; Le Blanc et le Noir 30*; J'Ai Quelque Chose à Vous Dire 30; La Meilleure Bobonne 30; Les Amants de Minuit 31*; Attaque Nocturne 31; Mam'zelle Nitouche 31; La Petite Chocolatière 31; Fanny 32; L'Hôtel du Libre-Échange 33*; Lac aux Dames 34; Sans Famille 34; Zou Zou 34; Les Beaux Jours 35; Les Amants Terribles 36; Aventure à Paris 36; Razumov • Sous les Yeux d'Occident 36; La Dame de Malacca 37; Gribouille • Heart of Paris 37; Orage 37; The Curtain Rises • Entrée des Artistes 38; Le Corsaire 39; Jeunes Filles de France 40*; Parade en Sept Nuits 41; L'Arlésienne 42; La Belle Aventure • Twilight 42; Félicie Nanteuil • Histoire Comique 42; Les Petites du Quai aux Fleurs 43; Lunégarde 44; Pétrus 46; Blanche Fury 47; Maria Chapdelaine • The Naked Heart 49; Blackmailed 50; André Gide • Avec André Gide 51; La Damoiselle et Son Revenant 51; Jean Coton 52; L'Occultisme et la Magie 52; L'Amante di Paride • Eterna Femmina • Eternal Woman • The Face That Launched a Thousand Ships • Femmina • Helen of Troy • Love of Three Queens • Loves of Three Queens 53*; Le Film de Jean 53; Julietta 53; Futures Vedettes • Joy of Loving • School for Love • Sweet Sixteen 54; L'Amant de Lady Chatterley • Lady Chatterley's Lover 55; En Effeuillant la Marguerite • Mademoiselle Striptease • Please, Mr. Balzac • While Plucking the Daisy 56; L'Amour Est un Jeu • Ma Femme, Ma Gosse et Moi 57; Be Beautiful But Shut Up • Blonde for Danger • Sois Belle et Tais-Toi 57; Un Drôle de Dimanche • Sunday Encounter 58; Les Affreux 59; Les Démons de Minuit • Midnight Folly 61*; Of Beds and Broads • Le Parigine • Les Parisiennes • Tales of Paris 62*; L'Abominable Homme des Douanes 63; Expo 1900 • Exposition 1900 66; Lumière 66;

Début de Siècle 68; La Grande-Bretagne et les États-Unis de6 à 1900 68; Jeunesse de France 68; Le Bal du Comte d'Orgel 69; Europe Continentale Avant 1900 69; Europe Méridionale au Temps des Rois 69

Allégret, Yves Prix et Profits 32; Ténériffe 32; Le Gagnant 35; Vous N'Avez Rien à Déclarer? 36*; L'Émigrante 38*; The Girls of France • Jeune Fille de France 38; Tobie Est un Ange 41; Les Deux Timides • Jeunes Timides 42; La Boîte aux Rêves 43*; Les Démons de l'Aube 45; Dédée • Dédée d'Anvers • Woman of Antwerp 47; Riptide • Une Si Jolie Petite Plage • Such a Pretty Little Beach 48; The Cheat • Manèges • The Wanton 49; Les Miracles N'Ont Lieu Qu'une Fois 50; Nez de Cuir 51; Les Sept Péchés Capitaux • I Sette Peccati Capitali • The Seven Deadly Sins 51*; Desperate Decision • La Jeune Folle 52; Mam'zelle Nitouche 53; Les Orgueilleux • The Proud and the Beautiful • The Proud Ones 53; Oasis 54; La Meilleure Part 55; Méfiez-Vous Fillettes • Young Girls Beware 57; Quand la Femme S'en Mêle 57; L'Ambitieuse • The Climbers 58; La Fille de Hambourg • The Girl from Hamburg • Port of Desire 58; La Chien de Pique 60; Germinal 62; Konga Yo • Terreur sur la Savane 62; Johnny Banco • Johnny Banco—Geliebter Taugenichts 66; L'Invasion 70; Orzowei 75; Mords Pas, On T'Aime 76

Allen, A. K. see *Greek, Janet*

Allen, Corey Pinocchio 71; Thunder and Lightning 77; Avalanche 78

Allen, David The Dungeonmaster 85*

Allen, Ethan Safe at Home 41

Allen, Fred Freighters of Destiny 31; Beyond the Rockies 32; Ghost Valley 32; The Hawk • Ride Him Cowboy 32; Partners 32; The Saddle Buster 32; The Fighting Phantom • The Mysterious Rider 33; Thugs with Dirty Mugs 39*

Allen, Frederick J. His Unknown Rival 15

Allen, Irving Forty Boys and a Song 42; Strange Voyage 45; Avalanche 46; Climbing the Matterhorn 47; High Conquest 47; 16 Fathoms Deep 48; Chase of Death 49; Slaughter Trail 51

Allen, Irwin The Sea Around Us 51; The Animal World 56; The Story of Mankind 57; The Lost World 60; Voyage to the Bottom of the Sea 61; Five Weeks in a Balloon 62; City Beneath the Sea • One Hour to Doomsday 70; The Poseidon Adventure 72*; The Towering Inferno 74*; The Swarm 78; Beyond the Poseidon Adventure 79

Allen, James Burndown 89

Allen, Johannes The Young Have No Time 59

Allen, Lewis The Uninvited 43; Our Hearts Were Young and Gay 44; Those Endearing Young Charms 45; The Unseen 45; The Imperfect Lady • Mrs. Loring's Secret 46; The Perfect Marriage 46; Desert Fury 47; Sealed Verdict 48; So Evil My Love 48; Appointment with Danger 49; At

Sword's Point • Sons of the Musketeers 49; Chicago Deadline 49; Valentino 51; Suddenly 54; A Bullet for Joey 55; Illegal 55; Another Time, Another Place 58; Whirlpool 59; Decision at Midnight 65

Allen, Penny Property 79

Allen, Russell The Roaring Forties • Robes of Sin 24; The Valley of Hate 24

Allen, Woody What's Up Tiger Lily? 66*; Take the Money and Run 69; Bananas 71; Everything You Always Wanted to Know About Sex* (*but were afraid to ask) 72; Sleeper 73; Love and Death 75; Annie Hall • Annie Hall: A Nervous Romance 77; Interiors 78; Manhattan 79; Stardust Memories 80; A Midsummer Night's Sex Comedy 82; Zelig 83; Broadway Danny Rose 84; The Purple Rose of Cairo 85; Hannah and Her Sisters 86; Radio Days 86; September 87; Another Woman 88; Crimes and Misdemeanors 89; New York Stories 89*; Alice 90

Allensworth, Carl A Pilgrimage for Peace, Pope Paul VI Visits America 66

Allio, René Les Âmes Mortes • Dead Souls 60; The Haystack • La Meule 62; The Shameless Old Lady • La Vieille Dame Indigne 64; The Other One • L'Une et l'Autre 67; Pierre et Paul 68; Les Camisards 70; Rude Journée pour la Reine 73; Moi Pierre Rivière • Moi, Pierre Rivière, Ayant Égorgé Ma Mère, Ma Sœur et Mon Frère 76; Retour à Marseille 80

Allouache, Merzak Un Amour à Paris • A Romance in Paris 87

Almeida, Paulo Sérgio de see *De Almeida, Paulo Sérgio*

Almendros, Nestor A Common Confusion • Una Confusión Cotidiana 50*; Improper Conduct • Mauvaise Conduite 84*; Nadie Escuchaba • Nobody Listened 88*

Almereyda, Michael Twister 88

Almodóvar, Pedro La Caída de Sódoma 74; Dos Putas, o Historia de Amor Que Termina en Boda 74; Homenaje 75; El Sueño 75; El Estrella 76; Complementos 77; Sexo Va 77; Folle, Folle, Fólleme, Tim 78; Salomé 78; Pepi, Luci & Bom • Pepi, Luci, Bom and Other Girls Like Mom • Pepi, Luci, Bom y Otras Chicas del Montón 80; Laberinto de Pasiones • Labyrinth of Passion 82; Dark Habits • Entre Tinieblas 83; ¿Qué He Hecho Yo para Merecer Esto? • What Have I Done to Deserve This!? 84; Trayler para Amantes de lo Prohibido 85; Law of Desire • La Ley del Deseo 86; Matador 86; Mujeres al Borde de un Ataque de Nervios • Women on the Verge of a Nervous Breakdown 88; ¡Átame! • Tie Me Up! Tie Me Down! 90

Almond, Paul Backfire 61; Isabel 68; Act of the Heart 70; Journey 72; Final Assignment 80; Prep School • Ups and Downs 81; Captive Hearts 87

Alonzo, John A. Citizens' Band • FM 78

Alov, Alexander Taras Shevchenko 51*; Restless Youth • Trevozhnaya Molodost • Turbulent Youth 54*; Pavel Korchagin 56*; Veter • The Wind 58*; Mir

Amico, Gianni Tropici • Tropics 68
Amiel, Jon Queen of Hearts 89; Tune in Tomorrow... 90
Amiguet, Jean-François La Méridienne 88
Amin, Ruhul A Kind of English 86
Amina, Mohammed Lakhdar Yasmina 61*; Les Fusils de la Liberté 62*
Amir, Gideon Behind Enemy Lines • P.O.W. The Escape 86
Amiradzibi, H. Christmas Eve • Przedświateczny Wieczór 66*
Ammann, Peter The Red Train 73
Ammar, Abdel-Latif Ben see Ben Ammar, Abdel-Latif
Amo, Antonio del see Del Amo, Antonio
Amoureux, Yves Le Beauf 87
Amram, Robert The Mini Affair 68; Sentinels of Silence 72; Sky High 75; The Late Great Planet Earth 77; Pacific Challenge 77
Amurri, Franco The Pony Express Boy • Il Ragazzo del Pony Express 86; Da Grande 87; Flashback 90
Amy, George She Had to Say Yes 33*; Granny Get Your Gun 39; Kid Nightingale 39; Gambling on the High Seas 40
Amyes, Julian Hell in Korea • A Hill in Korea 56; Miracle in Soho 57; Great Expectations 81; Jane Eyre 83
Anand, Tinnu Shahenshah 88
Anda, Gilberto de see De Anda, Gilberto
Anda, Raúl de see De Anda, Raúl
Anders, Allison Border Radio 87*
Anders, Christian Love Camp 81
Anders, Jan Threes, Ménage à Trois 68
Anderson, Andy Positive I.D. 86
Anderson, Barbara Boyd see Boyd-Anderson, Barbara
Anderson, Broncho Billy see Anderson, Gilbert M.
Anderson, C. T. The Police Dog 14; The Police Dog Gets Piffles in Bad 15; The Police Dog No. 2 15; The Police Dog No. 3 15; The Police Dog No. 4 15; The Police Dog No. 5 15; The Police Dog to the Rescue 15; The Police Dog in the Park 16; The Police Dog on the Wire 16; The Police Dog Turns Nurse 16; Working Out with the Police Dog 16; The Pinkerton Pup's Portrait 18
Anderson, Clyde see Aured, Carlos
Anderson, Gerry Crossroads to Crime 60
Anderson, Gilbert M. Raffles, the American Cracksman 05; An Awful Skate 07; The Bandit King 07; The Bandit Makes Good 07; Ben Gets a Duck and Is Ducked 07; Western Justice 07; The Best Man Wins 09; The Black Sheep 09; The Heart of a Cowboy 09; The Indian Trailer 09; Judgment 09; Mexican's Gratitude 09; The Spanish Girl 09; A Tale of the West 09; Away Out West 10; Bronco Billy's Redemption 10; The Cowboy and the Squaw 10; The Desperado 10; The Flower of the Ranch 10; The Forest Ranger 10; An Outlaw's Sacrifice 10; Pals of the Range 10; The Pony Express Rider 10; The Silent

Message 10; Take Me Out to the Ball Game 10; Under Western Skies 10; Western Chivalry 10; Across the Plains 11; The Border Ranger 11; Bronco Billy's Adventure 11; The Cowboy Coward 11; The Faithful Indian 11; The Lucky Card 11; The Outlaw and the Child 11; Alkali Bests Bronco Billy 12; Alkali Ike's Boarding House 12; Bronco Billy Outwitted 12; An Indian's Friendship 12; The Smuggler's Daughter 12; Alkali Ike's Misfortunes 13; Bronco Billy's Oath 13; The Three Gamblers 13; Bronco Billy's Indian Romance 14; The Calling of Jim Barton 14; Andy of the Royal Mounted 15; Bronco Billy's Marriage 15; Bronco Billy's Vengeance 15; His Regeneration 15; Bronco Billy and the Revenue Agent 16; Vera the Medium 16; Shootin' Mad 18; Ashes 22; The Greater Duty 22
Anderson, J. L. Jessica • Miss Jessica Is Pregnant • Spring Night, Summer Night 67
Anderson, James M. Echo of Applause 46; Those Were the Days 46; Return Fare to Laughter 50; Made for Laughs 52; All in Good Fun 56; Crazy Days 62
Anderson, John J. Avalon 88
Anderson, John Murray King of Jazz 30*
Anderson, Kenneth M. The Girth of a Nation 18; Hocking the Kaiser 18; Me and Gott 18; Oh What a Beautiful Dream 18; Power Pro and Con 18; Truths on the War in Slang 18
Anderson, Laurie Home of the Brave 86
Anderson, Lindsay Meet the Pioneers 48; Idlers That Work 49; Three Installations 52; Trunk Conveyor 52; Wakefield Express 52; O Dreamland 53; Thursday's Children 53*; The Children Upstairs 54; Green and Pleasant Land 54; Henry 54; Energy First 55; Foot and Mouth 55; A Hundred Thousand Children 55; Twenty Pounds a Ton 55; Every Day Except Christmas 57; March to Aldermaston 59*; This Sporting Life 62; The White Bus 66; Raz, Dwa, Trzy • The Singing Lesson 67; If... 68; O Lucky Man! 72; In Celebration 74; Britannia Hospital 81; Foreign Skies 86; The Whales of August 87
Anderson, Marion Clayton The Crowning Experience 60
Anderson, Martyn Flying Fox in a Freedom Tree 89
Anderson, Max Treasure at the Mill 57
Anderson, Michael Private Angelo 49*; Waterfront • Waterfront Women 50; Hell Is Sold Out 51; Night Was Our Friend 51; Dial 17 52; The House of the Arrow 52; Will Any Gentleman...? 53; The Dam Busters 54; 1984 55; Around the World in 80 Days 56; Battle Hell • Escape of the Amethyst • Yangtse Incident 56; Chase a Crooked Shadow 58; Shake Hands with the Devil 59; The Wreck of the Mary Deare 59; All the Fine Young Cannibals 60; The Naked Edge 61; Ashiya Kara no Hikō • Flight from Ashiya 63; Monsieur Cognac • Wild and Wonderful 63; Code Name: Operation Crossbow • The Great

Spy Mission • Operation Crossbow • Operazione Crossbow 64; Eye of the Devil • Thirteen 66*; The Quiller Memorandum 66; The Shoes of the Fisherman 68; The Devil's Imposter • Pope Joan 72; Conduct Unbecoming 75; Doc Savage • Doc Savage: The Man of Bronze • The Man of Bronze 75; Logan's Run 75; Killer Whale • Orca • Orca...Killer Whale • Orca the Killer Whale 76*; Avenging Spirit • Dominique • Dominique Is Dead 77; Bells • The Calling • Murder by Phone 81; Second Time Lucky 84; Separate Vacations 86; La Boutique de l'Orfèvre • The Jeweller's Shop 88; Millennium 89
Anderson, Robert The Feeling of Rejection 48
Anderson, Robert Cindy and Donna 71; The Young Graduates 71; The Hoax 72
Anderson, Will A Day in the Life of a Dog 17; Young Nick Carter Detectiff 17
Andersson, Roy Giliap 76
Andjaparidze, Marie Three Tales of Chekhov 61*
Andolfi, Marco Antonio La Croce dalle Sette Pietre • The Cross of the Seven Stones • The Cross with the Seven Stones 86
Andonov, Metodi The Goat Horn 72
Andra, Fern Eine Motte Flog zum Licht 15; Ernst Ist das Leben 16
Andrade, Joaquim Pedro de see De Andrade, Joaquim Pedro
András, Ferenc The Great Generation • A Nagy Generáció 86; Vadon • The Wilderness 89
André, Raoul Man and Child 57; Les Clandestines • Vice Dolls 61; The Hideout 61; Marchandes d'Illusions • Nights of Shame 61; Walls of Fear 62; Ladies First 63
Andreacchio, Mario Fair Game 86; The Dreaming 88
Andréani, Henri Faust 10; Messaline 10*; Moïse Sauvé des Eaux 10; Absalon 12; La Fille de Jephté 13; La Reine de Saba 13; L'Homme Qui Assassina 17; Mimi Trottin 22; Ziska la Danseuse Espionne 22; L' Autre Aile 24; Flamenca la Gitane 28; La Pente 28
Andrei, Frédéric Paris Midnight • Paris Minuit 86
Andrei, Marcello The Eye of the Needle • La Smania Andosso 63; El Macho 77
Andrei, Yannik Beyond Fear 77
Andreievsky, Alexander Gibel Sensaty • Loss of Feeling 35
Andreou, Errikos Make Me a Woman • The Sisters 69
Andrés, Luis San see San Andrés, Luis
Andrews, Charles Pirates of the Sky 27
Andrews, David The Sea Children 73
Andrews, Del Galloping Fish 24; Judgment of the Storm 24; No Man's Law 25; The Ridin' Streak 25; Ridin' the Wind 25*; That Devil Quemado 25; The Wild Bull's Lair 25; Collegiate 26; Is That Nice? 26; Man Rustlin' 26; The Timid Terror 26; The Yellow Back 26; Ain't Love Funny? 27; A Hero on Horseback 27; The Rawhide Kid 28; The Wild West Show 28

Andrews, Martin Machiste in King Solomon's Mines 64

Andreyev, Piotr Shadowman 88

Andrien, Jean-Jacques Droeven • The Endless Land of Alexis • Le Grand Paysage d'Alexis Droeven 81

Andrieux, Roger Mr. Brown 72; The Little Siren • La Petite Sirène 80; Envoyez les Violons 88

Andrus, Malon Ace of Cactus Range 24*

Angel, Jack Teenage Teasers 82

Angel, Mikel The Love Butcher 75*

Angelidi, Antoinetta Topos 85

Angelis, Fabrizio de see De Angelis, Fabrizio

Angelis, Nato de see De Angelis, Nato

Angelis, Vertunio de see De Angelis, Vertunio

Angell, Robert Vintage '28 53

Angelo, Edmond Breakdown 53

Angelopoulos, Theodoros The Broadcast • I Ekpombi • L'Émission • The Transmission 68; Anaparastassis • Reconstitution • Reconstruction • Reconstruction of a Crime 70; Days of 36 • Jours de 36 • I Meres tou 36 72; O Thassios • The Travelling Players • Les Voyages des Comédiens 75; The Hunters • The Huntsmen • I Kinigi 77; Alexander the Great • O Meg' Alexandros 80; Athens, 1982 82; Journey to Cythera • Taxidi sta Kithira • Taxidi stin Kythira • Voyage to Cythera 84; The Beekeeper • O Melissokomos 86; Landscape in the Mist • Topio stin Omichli 88

Angelucci, Gian Franco Honey 81

Anger, Kenneth Who Has Been Rocking My Dream Boat? 41; Prisoner of Mars 42; Tinsel Tree 42; The Nest 43; Escape Episode 44; Drastic Demise 45; Fireworks 47; Puce Moment 49; La Lune des Lapins • Rabbit's Moon 50; Eaux d'Artifice 53; Le Jeune Homme et la Mort 53; Inauguration of the Pleasure Dome • Lord Shiva's Dream 54; Thelema Abbey 55; The Story of O 61; Scorpio Rising 63; Kustom Kar Kommandos 64; Invocation of My Demon Brother 69; Psychedelirium 69; Rabbit's Moon 71; Lucifer Rising 80; He Stands in a Desert Counting the Seconds of His Life 85

Ängstfeld, Axel Krieg und Frieden • War and Peace 82*

Angus, Robert The Candidate • Party Girls for the Candidate 64

An-hua, Hsu see Hui, Ann

Anhua, Xu see Hui, Ann

Anker Gudrun • Suddenly a Woman 63

Annakin, Ken Cooks 42; London—1942 42; A Ride with Uncle Joe 43; Black Diamonds 44; Combined Cadets 44; The New Crop 44; A Farm in the Fens 45; Make Fruitful the Land 45; Pacific Thrust 45; Three Cadets 45; English Criminal Justice 46; It Began on the Clyde 46; The West Riding 46; Broken Journey 47; Holiday Camp 47; Turn It Out 47; The Facts of Life • Quartet 48*; Here Come the Huggetts 48; Miranda 48; Vote for Huggett 48; The Huggetts Abroad 49; Landfall

49; Double Confession 50; Trio 50*; Hotel Sahara 51; Outpost in Malaya • The Planter's Wife • White Blood 52; Robin Hood • The Story of Robin Hood • The Story of Robin Hood and His Merrie Men 52*; The Sword and the Rose • When Knighthood Was in Flower 53; Land of Fury • The Seekers 54; You Know What Sailors Are 54; Value for Money 55; Loser Takes All 56; Three Men in a Boat 56; Across the Bridge 57; Elephant Gun • Nor the Moon by Night 58; Banner in the Sky • Third Man on the Mountain 59; The Swiss Family Robinson 60; A Coming-Out Party • A Very Important Person 61; The Hellions 61; Crooks Anonymous 62; The Fast Lady 62; The Longest Day 62*; The Informers • The Snout • Underworld Informers 63; The Battle of the Bulge 65; Those Magnificent Men in Their Flying Machines • Those Magnificent Men in Their Flying Machines, or How I Flew from London to Paris in 25 Hours and 11 Minutes 65*; The Long Duel 66; The Biggest Bundle of Them All 67; Monte Carlo or Bust! • Quei Temerari sulle Loro Pazze, Scatenate, Scalcinate Carriole • Those Daring Young Men in Their Jaunty Jalopies 68*; The Call of the Wild • Il Richiamo della Foresta • White Fang 72; Paper Tiger 74; Behind the Iron Mask • The Fifth Musketeer 77; Cheaper to Keep Her 80; The Pirate Movie 82; The New Adventures of Pippi Longstocking 88

Annaud, Jean-Jacques Black and White in Color • La Victoire en Chantant 76; Coup de Tête • Hothead 79; Quest for Fire 81; Der Name der Rose • The Name of the Rose 86; The Bear • L'Ours 88

Annensky, I. The Elusive Jan • Neulovimyi Yan 42*; Marriage 45; The Anna Cross 54; The Sailor from the Comet 59

Annett, Paul The Beast Must Die • Black Werewolf 74; Never Never Land 80; And the Walls Came Tumbling Down 84; The Girl from Mani 86

Anouilh, Jean Le Voyageur Sans Bagage 43; Deux Sous de Violettes 51

Ansara, Martha The Pursuit of Happiness 87

Anselmo, Carlos Men of Brazil 60*

Anspaugh, David Best Shot • Hoosiers 86; Fresh Horses 88

Anstey, Edgar Granton Trawler 33*; 6.30 Collection 33*; Uncharted Waters 33; BBC: Droitwich 34*; Eskimo Village 34; So This Is London 34*; Dinner Hour • Enough to Eat • Nutrition 35; Housing Problems 35*

Antalffy, Alexander Das Rätsel von Bangalor 17*

Antamoro, Giulio Christus 17; The Passion of St. Francis 32

Antel, Frank see Antel, Franz

Antel, Franz The Bandit and the Princess 62; Naughty Nymphs 74; Casanova and Co. • The Rise and Rise of Casanova • Sex on the Run • Some Like It Cool 76

Anthony, Joseph The Rainmaker 56;

The Matchmaker 58; Career 59; All in a Night's Work 61; The Captive City • La Città Prigionera • The Conquered City 62; Tomorrow 72

Anthony, Len Fright House 90

Antoine, André The Corsican Brothers • Les Frères Corses 16; Le Coupable 17; Israël 18; Les Travailleurs de la Mer 18; Mademoiselle de la Seiglière 20; Quatre-vingt-Treize 21; La Terre 21; L'Alouette et la Mésange 22; L'Arlésienne 22

Anton, Amerigo see Boccia, Tanio

Anton, Karl Das Mädel von der Reeperbahn 31; Der Fall des Oberst Redl 32; Criez-Le sur les Toits • Shout It from the Housetops 35; Letzte Rose 36; Weisse Sklaven 37; Mit Versiegelter Order • Under Sealed Orders 38; The Avenger • Der Rächer 60

Antonelli, John Jack Kerouac's America • Kerouac 85

Antonini, Alfredo The Young Guns 56; I Bury the Living 58; Face of Fire 59; I Pascoli Rossi • Red Pastures 63; Massacre at Grand Canyon • Massacro al Grande Canyon 64*; Show Down • The Tramplers • Gli Uomini dal Passo Pesante 66*; Dracula's Dog • Zoltan, Hound of Dracula 77; She Came to the Valley 79; Ghoulies II 88

Antonio, Emile de see De Antonio, Emile

Antonio, Lauro O Vestido Cor de Fogo 86

Antonioni, Michelangelo Gente del Po 47; N.U. • Nettezza Urbana 48; Oltre l'Oblio 48; Roma-Montevideo 48; Superstizione 48; L'Amorosa Menzogna 49; Bomarzo 49; Ragazze in Bianco 49; Chronicle of a Love • Cronaca di un Amore • Story of a Love Affair 50; La Funivia del Faloria 50; Sette Canne e un Vestito 50; La Villa dei Mostri 50; I Nostri Figli • The Vanquished • I Vinti 52; Amore in Città • Love in the City 53*; Camille Without Camellias • The Lady Without Camellias • La Signora Senza Camelie • The Woman Without Camellias 53; Le Amiche • The Girl Friends 55; The Cry • Il Grido • The Outcry 57; Nel Segno di Roma • La Regina del Deserto • Sign of the Gladiator 58*; Tempest • La Tempesta 58*; The Adventure • L'Avventura 59; The Night • La Notte 60; The Eclipse • L'Eclisse 62; Le Désert Rouge • Il Deserto Rosso • The Red Desert 64; Three Faces of a Woman • I Tre Volti 64*; Blow-Up 66; Zabriskie Point 69; China • Chung Kuo • La Cina 72; The Passenger • Profession: Reporter • Professione: Reporter 74; Il Mistero di Oberwald • The Mystery of Oberwald • The Oberwald Mystery 79; Identification of a Woman • Identificazione di una Donna 82

Apfel, Oscar Aida 11*; The Passerby 12; The Bells 13; The Fight for Right 13; Her Rosary 13; The Squaw Man • The White Man 13*; Brewster's Millions 14*; The Call of the North 14*; The Circus Man 14; The Ghost Breaker 14*; The Last Volunteer 14; The Lost Paradise 14; The Making of Bobby Burnit 14; The Man on the Box 14*;

The Master Mind 14*; Ready Money 14; After Five 15; The Broken Law 15; Cameo Kirby 15; Kilmeny 15; The Little Gypsy 15; Peer Gynt 15; Snobs 15; A Soldier's Oath 15; Battle of Hearts 16; The End of the Trail 16; Fighting Blood 16; The Fires of Conscience 16; Hoodman Blind • Man of Sorrow 16; The Man from Bitter Roots 16; The Hidden Children 17; A Man's Man 17; The Price of Her Soul 17; The Grouch 18; The Interloper 18; Merely Players 18; Tinsel 18; To Him That Hath 18; The Turn of the Card 18; An Amateur Widow 19; Bringing Up Betty 19; Crook of Dreams 19; The Little Intruder 19; Mandarin's Gold 19; Me and Captain Kid 19; The Oakdale Affair 19; Phil-for-Short 19; The Roughneck 19; The Steel King 19; Ten Nights in a Bar Room 21; Auction of Souls 22; The Lion's Mouse 22; The Man Who Paid 22; The Wolf's Fangs 22; Bulldog Drummond 23; In Search of a Thrill 23; A Man's Man 23; The Social Code 23; The Heart Bandit • The Heart of a Bandit 24; Trail of the Law 24; Borrowed Finery 25; Sporting Chance 25; The Thoroughbred 25; The Call of the Klondike 26; The Last Alarm 26; Midnight Limited 26; Perils of the Coast Guard 26; Race Wild 26; Somebody's Mother 26; Cheaters 27; Code of the Cow Country 27; When Seconds Count 27

Apostolof, Stephen C. Fugitive Girls 75
Appleby, Basil Sunday in the Park 56*
Applegate, Chad see Wood, Sam
Applegate, Roy All for a Girl 15
Apted, Michael Soldier in Skirts • The Triple Echo 72; Stardust 74; The Squeeze 77; Stronger Than the Sun 77; Agatha 78; Coal Miner's Daughter 79; Continental Divide 81; Kipperbang • P'Tang Yang Kipperbang 82; Gorky Park 83; Firstborn 84; 28 Up 84; Bring On the Night 85; Critical Condition 87; Gorillas in the Mist 88; The Long Way Home 89; Class Action 90
Aragón, Manuel Gutiérrez see Gutiérrez Aragón, Manuel
Araiza, Raúl El Maleficio II • The Spell II 86
Araki, Gregg Three Bewildered People in the Night 87
Arakon, A. Conquest of Constantinople 54
Aranda, Vicente The Blood-Spattered Bride • The Blood-Splattered Bride • Bloody Fiancée • La Novia Ensangrentada • 'Til Death Do Us Part • Till Death Us Do Part 69; Tiempo de Silencio • Time of Silence 86; El Lute—Camina o Revienta • El Lute—Forge On or Die 87; El Lute II • Mañana Seré Libre 88
Aratow, Paul Lucifer's Women 78
Arau, Alfonso The Barefoot Eagle 67; Calzonzín Inspector 74; Mojado Power 80; Chido Guan 84
Aravindan, G. Chidambaram 86; Once Somewhere • Oridath 86
Arbuckle, Fatty see Arbuckle, Roscoe
Arbuckle, Roscoe The Alarm 14*; A

Brand New Hero 14*; Fatty Again 14; Fatty and Minnie He-Haw 14*; Fatty and the Heiress 14*; Fatty's Debut 14*; Fatty's Finish 14; Fatty's Gift 14*; Fatty's Jonah Day 14*; Fatty's Magic Pants 14*; Fatty's Wine Party 14*; An Incompetent Hero 14; Leading Lizzie Astray 14*; The Sea Nymphs 14; Shotguns That Kick 14; The Sky Pirate 14*; That Minstrel Man 14; Those Country Kids 14; Those Happy Days 14; Zipp the Dodger 14; Fatty and Mabel at the San Diego Exposition 15; Fatty and Mabel Viewing the World's Fair at San Francisco • Mabel and Fatty Viewing the World's Fair at San Francisco 15*; Fatty and Mabel's Simple Life • Mabel and Fatty's Simple Life 15*; Fatty and the Broadway Stars 15*; Fatty's Chance Acquaintance 15; Fatty's Faithful Fido 15*; Fatty's New Role 15*; Fatty's Plucky Pup • Foiled by Fido 15; Fatty's Reckless Fling 15; Fatty's Tintype Tangle • Fido's Tintype Tangle 15; Fickle Fatty's Fall 15; Mabel and Fatty's Married Life 15; Mabel and Fatty's Wash Day 15*; Mabel, Fatty and the Law 15; Miss Fatty's Seaside Lovers 15; That Little Band of Gold 15; The Village Scandal 15; When Love Took Wings 15; Bright Lights • The Lure of Broadway 16; A Cream Puff Romance • A Reckless Romeo 16; Fatty and Mabel Adrift 16; He Did and He Didn't • Love and Lobsters 16; His Alibi 16; His Wife's Mistake 16; The Moonshiners 16; The Other Man 16; The Waiter's Ball 16; The Butcher Boy 17; Coney Island • Fatty at Coney Island 17; A Country Hero 17; His Wedding Night 17; Oh Doctor! 17; The Rough House 17; The Bell Boy 18; The Cook 18; Good Night Nurse 18; Moonshine 18; Out West • The Sheriff 18; Back Stage 19; A Desert Hero 19; The Garage 19; The Hayseed 19; Love 19; The Fighting Dude 25; The Movies 25; The Tourist 25; Cleaning Up 26; Fool's Luck 26; His Private Life 26; My Stars 26; The Red Mill 26; Special Delivery 27; Up a Tree 30; Won by a Neck 30; The Back Page 31; Beach Pajamas 31; Honeymoon Trio 31; The Lure of Hollywood 31; Marriage Rows 31; Smart Work 31; The Tamale Vendor 31; Up Pops the Duke 31; Windy Riley Goes to Hollywood 31; Anybody's Goat 32; Bridge Wives 32; Gigolettes 32; Hollywood Luck 32; It's a Cinch 32; Keep Laughing 32; Moonlight and Cactus 32; Mother's Holiday 32; Niagara Falls 32

Arcady, Alexandre Hold-Up 85; L'Été Dernier à Tanger • Last Summer in Tangiers 87
Arcand, Denys Seul ou avec d'Autres 62*; On Est au Coton 70; La Maudite Galette 72; Québec: Duplessis et Après... 72; Rejeanne Padovani 72; Gina 75; Le Confort et l'Indifférence 82; Le Crime d'Ovide Plouffe • The Crime of Ovide Plouffe • Les Plouffe 84*; Le Déclin de l'Empire Américain • The Decline of the American Empire 86; Jésus de Montréal • Jesus of Montreal 89

Arcelin, Jacques Bitter Cane 84
Arch, Albert H. Piccadilly Nights 30
Archainbaud, George As Man Made Her 17; The Awakening 17; The Brand of Satan 17; Diamonds and Pearls 17; The Iron Ring 17; A Maid of Belgium 17; Yankee Pluck 17; The Cross Bearer 18; The Divine Sacrifice 18; The Love Cheat 18; The Trap 18; A Damsel in Distress 19; In Walked Mary 20; Marooned Hearts 20; The Pleasure Seekers 20; The Shadow of Rosalie Byrnes 20; What Women Want 20; The Wonderful Chance 20; Clay Dollars 21; The Girl from Nowhere 21; Handcuffs or Kisses 21; The Man of Stone 21; The Miracle of Manhattan 21; Evidence 22; One Week of Love 22; The Power of a Lie 22; Under Oath 22; The Common Law 23; Cordelia the Magnificent 23; The Midnight Guest 23; Christine of the Hungry Heart 24; The Flaming Forties 24*; For Sale 24; The Mirage 24; The Plunderer 24; Shadow of the Desert • The Shadow of the East • Single Wives 24; The Storm Daughter 24; Enticement 25; The Necessary Evil 25; Scarlet Saint 25; What Fools Men 25; Men of Steel 26; Puppets 26; The Silent Lover 26; Easy Pickings 27; Night Life 27; Bachelor's Paradise 28; George Washington Cohen 28; The Grain of Dust 28; Ladies of the Night Club 28; The Man in Hobbles 28; The Tragedy of Youth 28; A Woman Against the World 28; The Broadway Hoofer • Dancing Feet 29; Broadway Scandals 29; The College Coquette 29; Two Men and a Maid 29; The Voice Within 29; Alias French Gertie • Love Finds a Way 30; Framed 30; Shooting Straight 30; The Silver Horde 30; The Lady Refuses 31; Three Who Loved 31; Cardigan's Last Case • State's Attorney 32; The Lost Squadron 32; Men of Chance 32; The Penguin Pool Murder • The Penguin Pool Mystery 32; Thirteen Women 32; After Tonight • Sealed Lips 33; The Big Brain • Enemies of Society 33; Keep 'Em Rolling 34; Murder on the Blackboard 34; My Marriage 35; Thunder in the Night 35; Hideaway Girl 36; The Return of Sophie Lang 36; Blonde Trouble 37; Clarence 37; Hotel Haywire 37; Thrill of a Lifetime 37; Boy Trouble 38; Campus Confessions • Fast Play 38; Her Jungle Love 38; Thanks for the Memory 38; Night Work 39; Rhythm Romance • Some Like It Hot 39; Comin' Round the Mountain 40; Untamed 40; Opened by Mistake 41; Flying with Music 42; False Colors 43; Hoppy Serves a Writ 43; The Kansan • Wagon Wheels 43; The Woman of the Town 43; The Young in Heart 43; Alaska 44; The Big Bonanza 44; Mystery Man 44; Texas Masquerade 44; Girls of the Big House 45; The Devil's Playground 46; Fool's Gold 46; Unexpected Guest 46; The Crime Doctor's Vacation • The Millerson Case 47; Dangerous Venture 47; Hoppy's Holiday 47; King of the Wild Horses 47; Marauders 47; Borrowed Trouble 48; The Dead Don't Dream 48; False Paradise 48; Silent Conflict 48;

Sinister Journey 48; Strange Gamble 48; Border Treasure 50; Hunt the Man Down 50; Apache Country 52; Barbed Wire • False News 52; Blue Canadian Rockies 52; Night Stage to Galveston 52; The Old West 52; Wagon Team • Wagon Train 52; Goldtown Ghost Raiders • Goldtown Ghost Raiders 53; Last of the Pony Riders 53; On Top of Old Smoky 53; Pack Train 53; Saginaw Trail 53; Winning of the West 53

Archer, Ted Django 2 — Il Grande Ritorno 88

Archibald, James The Enigma Variations 70

Archibugi, Francesca Mignon e Partita 88

Arconti, Carlos see *Alazraki, Benito*

Arcos, Luis de los see *De los Arcos, Luis*

Ardavin, César Lazarillo • El Lazarillo de Tormes 59

Ardavin, Eusebio El Agua en el Suelo • Water in the Ground 35; Vidas Rotas 35

Arden, Jane The Other Side of the Underneath 72; Anti-Clock 80*

Ardolino, Emile He Makes Me Feel Like Dancin' 83; Dirty Dancing 87; Chances Are 89; 3 Men and a Little Lady 90

Arecha, Juan Cano Caso Cerrado 85

Arehn, Mats Maria 75; The Assignment 76; Buddies • Dödspolare 85; About Love • Om Kärlek 87; Istanbul • Istanbul, Keep Your Eyes Open 90

Argento, Dario Probabilità Zero 68*; The Bird with the Crystal Plumage • The Bird with the Glass Feathers • The Gallery Murders • Das Geheimnis der Schwarzen Handschuhe • The Phantom of Terror • L'Uccello dalle Piume di Cristallo 69; The Cat o' Nine Tails • Il Gatto a Nove Code 70; Four Flies on Grey Velvet • Four Patches of Grey Velvet • Quatre Mouches de Velours Gris • Quattro Mosche di Velluto Grigio 71; Le Cinque Giornate 73; Deep Red • Deep Red Hatchet Murders • Dripping Deep Red • The Hatchet Murders • Profondo Rosso • The Sabre Tooth Tiger 75; Suspiria 76; Inferno 78; Sotto gli Occhi dell'Assassino • Tenebrae • Unsane 82; Creepers • Phenomena 84; Opera 87; Due Occhi Diabolici • Two Evil Eyes 90*

Argüello, Iván Mujeres de la Frontera • Women of the Frontier 87

Argyle, John That's His Weakness 30; The Last Tide 31; Paradise Alley 31; The Final Reckoning 32; Smilin' Along 32; Send for Paul Temple 46; The Hills of Donegal 47; Holiday Island 51; Sunshine in Attica 52; The Land Is Green 58

Arias, Alfredo Fuegos 87

Arias, Bernardo El Inquisidor • The Inquisitor 75

Arikawa, Sadamasa The Phoenix • War of the Wizards 83*

Arino, Luis Los Días del Cometa 89

Aristarain, Adolfo La Parte del León 78; La Playa del Amor 79; La Discoteca del Amor 80; Tiempo de Revancha • A Time for Revenge 81; Últimos Días de la Víctima 82; The Stranger 87

Arizal The Stabilizer 87

Arkatov, Alexander The Bloody East 15; Tale of Priest Pankrati 18*

Arkin, Alan Little Murders 70; Fire Sale 77

Arkless, Robert The Man Who Would Not Die • Target in the Sun 75

Arkush, Allan Hollywood Boulevard 76*; Deathsport 78*; Rock 'n' Roll High School 79; Heartbeeps 81; Get Crazy 83; Caddyshack II 88

Arliss, Leslie The Farmer's Wife 40*; The Team 41; The Night Has Eyes • Terror House 42; The Man in Grey 43; A Lady Surrenders • Love Story 44; The Wicked Lady 45; A Man About the House 47; Idol of Paris 48; Saints and Sinners 48; The Woman's Angle 52; Forever My Heart 54*; Miss Tulip Stays the Night 55; See How They Run 55; Danger List 57; Dearth of a Salesman 57; Insomnia Is Good for You 57; Man with a Dog 58

Armendariz, Montxo Twenty-Seven Hours • 27 Horas 86

Armfield, Neil Twelfth Night 86

Armiñán, Jaime de see *De Armiñán, Jaime*

Armitage, George Private Duty Nurses 71; Hit Man 72; Vigilante Force 76; Miami Blues 89

Armstrong, Charles The Sporting Mice 09; Votes for Women, A Caricature 09; The Clown and His Donkey 10; Ta-Ta, Come Again 11; Isn't It Wonderful? 14; Armstrong's Trick War Incidents 15

Armstrong, Gillian Roof Needs Mowing 71; Gretel 73; One Hundred a Day 73; Satdee Night 73; Smokes and Lollies 75; The Singer and the Dancer 76; My Brilliant Career 78; A Busy Kind of Bloke 80; Fourteen's Good, Eighteen's Better 80; Touch Wood 80; Starstruck 82; Having a Go 83; Not Just a Pretty Face 83; Mrs. Soffel 84; High Tide 87; Bingo, Bridesmaids and Braces 88

Armstrong, Michael Austria 1700 • Brenn Hexe Brenn • Burn, Witch, Burn • Hexen Bis aufs Blut Gequält • Mark of the Devil • Satan 69; The Dark • The Haunted House of Horror • Horror House 69; The Image 69

Armstrong, R. Dale The Crucifix of Destiny 20; False Women 21

Arner, Gwen My Champion 81

Arnett, James The Mackintosh Man 73*

Arnfred, Morten Himmel og Helvede 88

Arnold, Jack With These Hands 50; The Challenge 51; World Affairs Are Your Affairs 51; Girls in the Night • Life After Dark 53; The Glass Web 53; It Came from Outer Space 53; The Creature from the Black Lagoon 54; The Man from Bitter Ridge 55; Red Sundown 55; Revenge of the Creature 55; Tarantula 55; This Island Earth 55*; Outside the Law 56; The Incredible Shrinking Man 57; The Lady Takes a Flyer 57; Man in the Shadow • Pay the Devil 57; The Tattered Dress 57; High School Confidential! • Young Hellions 58; Monster on the Campus 58; The Space

Children 58; The Mouse That Roared 59; No Name on the Bullet 59; Bachelor in Paradise 61; A Global Affair 63; The Lively Set 64; Hello Down There • Sub-a-Dub-Dub 68; Black Eye 73; The Black Bounty Killer • Boss • Boss Nigger 74; The Bunny Caper • The Games Girls Play • Sex Play 74; The Swiss Conspiracy 75; Marilyn: The Untold Story 80*; When the Snow Bled 81

Arnold, John The Passing Stranger 54

Arnold, Newton Hands of a Stranger 62; Blood Thirst 65; Allan Quatermain and the Lost City of Gold 85*; Bloodsport 87

Arnold, Vinton see *Arnold, Jack*

Arnshtam, Lev Ankara, Heart of Turkey • Ankara, Serdtsye Turkiye • The Soviets Greet New Turkey 34*; Girl Friends • Podrugi • Three Women 36; Zoya 44; Glinka • The Great Glinka 46; The Ballet of Romeo and Juliet • Romeo and Juliet 55*; A Lesson in History 57*; Five Days, Five Nights 61

Arnstam, Leo see *Arnshtam, Lev*

Aron, E. Pesni Abaya • Song of Abaya 45*

Aronov, Grigori Sedmoi Sputnik 68*

Aronovitch, Simon Torpedo Bombers • Torpidonostci 86

Aronson, Jerry The Divided Trail 80*

Arora, Prakash Boot Polish 58

Arrabal, Fernando Viva la Muerte 71; Guérnica 76; The Emperor of Peru • Odyssey of the Pacific 81

Artaud, E. The Dancer and the King 14

Artenstein, Isaac Break of Dawn 87

Arthur, Daniel V. The Great Diamond Robbery 14

Arthur, George M. Crooks Can't Win 28

Arthur, Karen Legacy 75; The Cage • The Mafu Cage • My Sister, My Love 78; Lady Beware 87

Arthur, Robert Alan see *Aurthur, Robert Alan*

Artigot, Raúl El Monte de las Brujas • Witches' Mountain 70

Arvat, Caterina The Pretty Things 66*

Arvedson, Ragnar The Coast's Happy Cavaliers • Kustens Glada Kavaljerer 39

Arzner, Dorothy Fashions for Women 27; Get Your Man 27; Ten Modern Commandments 27; Manhattan Cocktail 28; Charming Sinners • The Constant Wife 29*; The Wild Party 29; Anybody's Woman 30; Behind the Makeup 30*; Paramount on Parade 30*; Sarah and Son 30; Honor Among Lovers 31; Working Girls 31; Merrily We Go to… • Merrily We Go to Hell 32; Christopher Strong 33; Lady of the Boulevards • Nana 34; Craig's Wife 35; The Bride Wore Red 37; The Last of Mrs. Cheyney 37*; Dance, Girl, Dance 40; First Comes Courage 43

Asagaroff, Georg Eva and the Grasshopper 28; Escaped from Hell 29; Der Tolle Bomberg 35

Ascott, Anthony see *Carmineo, Giuliano*

Asgari-Nasab, Manoochehr Beyond the Mist 86

Ash, Dan Madigan's Millions • El Millón de Madigan • El Testamento de Madigan • Un Dollaro per 7 Vigliacchi 67*

Ashby, Hal The Landlord 70; Harold and Maude 71; The Last Detail 73; Shampoo 75; Bound for Glory 76; Coming Home 77; The Hamster of Happiness • Hamsters of Happiness • Second-Hand Hearts 78; Being There 79; Lookin' to Get Out 81; Let's Spend the Night Together • Time Is on Our Side 82; Neil Simon's The Slugger's Wife • The Slugger's Wife 84; 8 Million Ways to Die 86

Ashcroft, Ronnie The Astounding She-Monster • Mysterious Invader 57

Ashe, Richard Track of the Moon Beast 76

Ashe, Robert Attack on a Picquet • Surprising a Picket 1899; The Battle of Glencoe 1899; The Bombardment of Mafeking 1899; British Capturing a Maxim Gun 1899; Nurses Attending the Wounded • Nurses on the Battlefield 1899; Shooting a Boer Spy 1899; The Victory 1899; Wrecking an Armoured Train 1899

Asher, Billy Where Ambition Leads 19

Asher, Robert Follow a Star 59; The Bulldog Breed 60; Make Mine Mink 60; Maid for Murder • She'll Have to Go 61; On the Beat 62; A Stitch in Time 63; The Early Bird 65; The Intelligence Men • Spylarks 65; Press for Time 66

Asher, William Leather Gloves • Loser Take All 48*; Mobs, Inc. 56; The Shadow on the Window 56; The 27th Day 56; Beach Party 63; Johnny Cool 63; Muscle Beach Party 63; Bikini Beach 64; Beach Blanket Bingo 65; How to Stuff a Wild Bikini 65; Fireball 500 66; Butcher, Baker, Nightmare Maker • Momma's Boy • Night Warning • Nightmare Maker • Thrilled to Death 81; Movers and Shakers 85

Ashley, Arthur The Guardian 17; The Marriage Market 17; Rasputin the Black Monk 17; Shall We Forgive Her? 17; The Beautiful Mrs. Reynolds 18; Broken Ties 18; Oh Mary Be Careful! 21

Ashley, Helmut see Ashley, Helmuth

Ashley, Helmuth Murder Party 61; The Puzzle of the Red Orchid • The Secret of the Red Orchid 62; Operation Hong Kong 64; No Time to Die 84*

Ashley, Ray The Little Fugitive 53*

Ashwood, Terry Elizabeth Is Queen 53

Askarian, Dan Komitas 88

Askey, David Take Me High 73

Askoldov, Alexander Commissar • Komissar 67

Aslanian, Samson Torment 86*

Asquith, Anthony Shooting Stars 27*; Princess Priscilla's Fortnight • Priscillas Fahrt ins Glück • The Runaway Princess 28*; Underground 28; A Cottage on Dartmoor • Escaped from Dartmoor 29; The Battle of Gallipoli • Tell England 30*; Dance, Pretty Lady 31; The Window Cleaner 32; Leise Flehen Meine Lieder • Lover Divine • The Unfinished Symphony

33*; The Lucky Number 33; Born for Glory • Brown on Resolution • Forever England • Torpedo Raider 35*; I Stand Condemned • Moscow Nights 35; Pygmalion 38*; Blind Dogs • Guide Dogs for the Blind 39; French Without Tears 39; Channel Incident 40; Freedom Radio • A Voice in the Night 40; Quiet Wedding 40; Rush Hour 40; Bombsight Stolen • Cottage to Let 41; Uncensored 42; Adventure for Two • The Demi-Paradise 43; We Dive at Dawn 43; Welcome to Britain 43*; Fanny by Gaslight • Man of Evil 44; The Two Fathers 44; Johnny in the Clouds • The Way to the Stars 45; While the Sun Shines 46; The Winslow Boy 48; The Browning Version 50; Five Angles on Murder • The Woman in Question 50; The Importance of Being Earnest 51; The Final Test 52; The Net • Project M7 52; Carrington V.C. • Court-Martial 54; Chance Meeting • The Young Lovers 54; On Such a Night 55; The Doctor's Dilemma 58; Orders to Kill 58; Libel! 59; The Millionairess '60; Två Levande och En Död • Two Living, One Dead 60; Zero 60; Guns of Darkness 62; An Evening with the Royal Ballet 63*; The V.I.P.s 63; The Yellow Rolls-Royce 64

Assayas, Olivier Désordre • Disorder 86; L'Enfant d'Hiver 89

Asselin, Henry The Oppressed 29

Assonitis, Ovidio Tentacles 77; Desperate Moves 80; Madhouse 81; Piranha II: Flying Killers • Piranha II: The Spawning 81*

Assonitis, Sonia Beyond the Door • Chi Sei? • The Devil Within Her • Who? 74*

Aston, Brian Smedley see Smedley-Aston, Brian

Astruc, Alexandre Aller et Retour • Aller-Retour 48; Ulysse ou Les Mauvaises Rencontres 48; The Crimson Curtain • Le Rideau Cramoisi 52; Les Mauvaises Rencontres 55; End of Desire • A Life • One Life • Una Vita • Une Vie 58; Prey for the Shadows • La Proie pour l'Ombre • Shadow of Adultery 60; L'Éducation Sentimentale 62; The Long March • La Longue Marche 66; Flames Over the Adriatic • Flammes Sur l'Adriatique 68; Sartre par Lui-Même 72*; Louis XI ou La Naissance d'un Roi 77

Atamanov, Lev Adventure in Odessa 54

Atasheva, Pera Czechoslovakia • Liberated Czechoslovakia 46*

Atasoy, İrfan The Seven Bastards • The Seven No-Goods • Yedi Belalılar 70*

Athens, J. D. Cannibal Women in the Avocado Jungle of Death 89

Atıf, Yılmaz see Yılmaz, Atıf

Atkins, Thomas The Silver Streak 34; Hi, Gaucho 35; Mutiny Ahead 35

Atkinson, Jim Can You Keep It Up for a Week? 74

Attenborough, Richard Oh! What a Lovely War 69; Young Winston 71; A Bridge Too Far 77*; Magic 78; Gandhi 82; A Chorus Line 85; Asking for Trouble • Cry Freedom 87

Attias, Daniel Silver Bullet • Stephen King's Silver Bullet 85

Au, Tony Dream Lovers • Mengzhong Ren 86

Aubert, Claude Bernard see Bernard-Aubert, Claude

Aucion, Guillaume Martin Oh! Calcutta! 72

Audiard, Michel Faut Pas Prendre les Enfants du Bon Dieu pour des Canards Sauvages • Operation Leontine 68; Une Veuve en Or 69; Le Cri du Cormoran le Soir Au-Dessus des Jonques 70; Elle Boit Pas, Elle Fume Pas, Elle Drague Pas...Mais Elle Cause! 70; Le Drapeau Noir Flotte sur la Marmite 71; Le Paumé 71; Elle Cause Plus...Elle Flingue 72; Vive la France 73; Bon Baisers à Lundi 74; Comment Réussir dans la Vie Quand On Est Con et Pleurnichard • Comment Réussir Quand On Est Con et Pleurnichard 74

Audley, Michael Accused • Mark of the Hawk 57*

Audry, Jacqueline Les Chevaux du Vercors 43; Les Malheurs de Sophie 45; Gigi 48; Sombre Dimanche 48; L'Ingénue Libertine • Minne • Minne l'Ingénue Libertine 50; Olivia • Pit of Loneliness 50; La Caraque Blonde 53; Huis Clos • No Exit 54; Mitsou 56; C'Est la Faute d'Adam 57; L'École des Cocottes 57; La Garçonne 57; Le Secret du Chevalier d'Eon 60; Cadavres en Vacances 61; Les Petits Matins 61; Fruits Amers • Soledad 66; Le Lis de Mer 70

Auer, John H. Una Vida per Otra 33; The Pervert 34; Rest in Peace 34; Su Última Canción 34; The Crime of Dr. Crespi 35; Frankie and Johnny 35*; Circus Girl 37; A Man Betrayed 37; Rhythm in the Clouds 37; A Desperate Adventure • It Happened in Paris 38; I Stand Accused 38; Invisible Enemy 38; Orphans of the Street 38; Outside of Paradise 38; Calling All Marines 39; Forged Passport 39; S.O.S. Tidal Wave • Tidal Wave 39; Smuggled Cargo 39; Thou Shalt Not Kill 39; Hit Parade of 1941 40; Women in War 40; Citadel of Crime • A Man Betrayed • Wheel of Fortune 41; The Devil Pays Off 41; Johnny Doughboy 42; Moonlight Masquerade 42; Pardon My Stripes 42; Gangway for Tomorrow 43; Tahiti Honey 43; Music in Manhattan 44; Seven Days Ashore 44; Pan-Americana 45; Beat the Band 46; The Flame 47; Angel on the Amazon • Drums Along the Amazon 48; Diary of a Bride • I, Jane Doe 48; The Avengers 50; Hit Parade of 1951 50; Thunderbirds 52; The City That Never Sleeps 53; Hell's Half Acre 54; The Eternal Sea 55; Johnny Trouble 57

Auerbach, Lee The Jupiter Menace 82*

Auerbach, Mikhail see Averbakh, Mikhail

Auguiste, Reece Twilight City 89

August, Bille Honey Moon • Honning Måne 78; Zappa 83; Faith, Hope and Charity • Tro, Håb og Kærlighed • Twist and Shout 84; Buster's World 85; Pelle Erobreren • Pelle the Conqueror 87

August, Edwin Evidence 15; Perils of Divorce 16; The Social Highwayman 16;

The Summer Girl 16; The Yellow Passport 16; The Poison Pen 19

Aured, Carlos El Espanto Surge de la Tumba • Horror Rises from the Tomb 72; The Black Harvest of Countess Dracula • Curse of the Devil • El Retorno de la Walpurgis • The Return of Walpurgis 73; The Blue Eyes of the Broken Doll • House of Doom • The House of Psychotic Women • House of the Psychotic Women • Los Ojos Azules de la Muñeca Rota 73; The Mummy's Revenge • The Mummy's Vengeance • La Venganza de la Momia • The Vengeance of the Mummy 73; Monster Dog 84

Aurel, Jean L'Affaire Manet 50; A Briglia Sciolta • La Bride sur le Cou • Only for Love • Please, Not Now 61*; Over There, 1914-1918 • 14-18 62; All About Loving • De l'Amour 63; La Bataille de France 63; Lamiel 67; Manon 70 68; Les Femmes 69; Êtes-Vous Fiancée à un Marin Grec ou à un Pilote de Ligne? 70; Comme un Pot de Fraises 74

Aurthur, Robert Alan How Many Roads? • The Lost Man 69

Ausino, Carlo Invasione 78; La Villa delle Anime Maledette 83

Aust, Stefan Krieg und Frieden • War and Peace 82*

Auster, Sam Come Again • Screen Test 83

Austin, Albert My Boy 21*; Trouble 22; A Prince of a King 23; Keep Smiling 25*

Austin, Ray It's the Only Way to Go 69; The Sandal 69; Lesbian Twins • Virgin Witch 70; The Perfumed Garden 70; Fun and Games • 1,000 Convicts and a Woman 71; Dr. Maniac • House of the Living Dead 73

Autant-Lara, Claude Fait Divers 23; Construire un Feu 26; Vittel 26; Buster Se Marie 30; Le Fils de Rajah 31; La Pente 31; Le Plombier Amoureux 31; Pur Sang 31; L'Athlète Incomplet 32; Un Client Sérieux 32; Le Gendarme Est Sans Pitié 32; Invite Monsieur à Dîner 32; Monsieur le Duc 32; La Peur des Coups 32; Ciboulette 33; My Partner Master Davis • My Partner Mr. Davis • The Mysterious Mr. Davis 36; L'Affaire du Courrier de Lyon • The Courier of Lyons 37*; Le Ruisseau 37*; Fric-Frac 39*; Le Mariage de Chiffon 41; Lettres d'Amour 42; Douce • Love Story 43; Sylvia and the Ghost • Sylvia and the Phantom • Sylvie and the Phantom • Sylvie et le Fantôme 44; The Devil in the Flesh • Le Diable au Corps 46; Keep an Eye on Amelia • Occupe-Toi d'Amélie • Oh, Amelia! 49; L'Auberge Rouge • The Red Inn 51; Les Sept Péchés Capitaux • I Sette Peccati Capitali • The Seven Deadly Sins 51*; Le Blé en Herbe • The Game of Love • Ripening Seed 53; Le Bon Dieu Sans Confession 53; The Red and the Black • Le Rouge et le Noir • Rouge et Noir • Scarlet and Black 53; Marguérite de la Nuit 55; Four Bags Full • Pig Across Paris • La Traversée de Paris 56; En Cas de Malheur • In Case of Adversity • Love Is My Profession

58; The Gambler • Le Joueur 58; Bedroom Vendetta • La Giumenta Verda • The Green Mare • The Green Mare's Nest • La Jument Verte 59; Les Régates de San Francisco 59; Between Love and Duty • Le Bois des Amants 60; Le Comte de Monte Cristo • Il Conte di Montecristo • The Count of Monte Cristo • The Story of Monte Cristo • The Story of the Count of Monte Cristo 61; Non Uccidere • Thou Shalt Not Kill • Tu Ne Tueras Point 61; Vive Henri IV...Vive l'Amour! 61; Enough Rope • Le Meurtrier • Der Mörder • The Murderer • L'Omicida 62; Le Magot de Joséfa 63; Humour Noir 64*; Le Journal d'une Femme en Blanc • A Woman in White 65; Une Femme en Blanc Se Revolte • Le Nouveau Journal d'une Femme en Blanc • Return of a Woman in White 66; Das Älteste Gewerbe der Welt • L'Amore Attraverso i Secoli • L'Amour à Travers les Âges • The Oldest Profession • Le Plus Vieux Métier du Monde 67*; Le Franciscain de Bourges 67; Les Patates 69; Le Rouge et le Blanc 71; Gloria 77

Auzins, Igor High Rolling • High Rolling in a Hot Corvette 77; The Night Nurse 77; We of the Never Never 82; The Coolangatta Gold 84

Avakian, Aram Lad: A Dog 61*; The End of the Road 70; Cops and Robbers 73; Anything for Love • 11 Harrowhouse • Fast Fortune 74*

Avakyan, G. Melik see *Melik-Avakyan, G.*

Avallone, Marcello Specters • Spettri 87

Avati, Pupi Balsamus • Balsamus l'Uomo di Satana 68; Thomas...Gli Indemoniati 69; La Mazurka del Barone della Santa e del Fico Fiorone 74; Bordella 75; La Casa dalle Finestre Che Ridono 76; Tutti Defunti Tranne i Morti 77; Le Strelle nel Fosso 78; Aiutami a Sognare • Help Me Dream 81; Dancing Paradise 82; Una Gita Scolastica 83; Zeder • Zeder—Voices from the Beyond 83; Employees • Impiegati 84; Noi Tre • We Three 84; Festa di Laurea • Graduation Party 85; Christmas Present • Regalo di Natale 86; The Last Minute • Ultimo Minuto 87; The Story of Boys and Girls 89

Avdeliodis, Demos To Dendro Pou Pligoname • The Tree We Hurt • The Tree We Were Hurting 86

Avdiyenko, Yakiv The Battle for Our Soviet Ukraine • Bitva za Nashu Radyansku Ukrayinu • Bitva za Nashu Sovetskayu Ukrainu • The Fight for Our Soviet Ukraine 43*

Avedis, Hikmet The Stepmother 71; The Seductress • The Teacher 74; Dr. Minx 75; The Specialist 75; Scorchy 76; Texas Detour 78; The Fifth Floor 80; Separate Ways 81; Mortuary 83; They're Playing with Fire 84; Kidnapped 86

Avedis, Howard see *Avedis, Hikmet*

Avellana, Lamberto Cry Freedom 59; Badjao 62

Averbach, Ilya see *Averbakh, Ilya*

Averbach, Mikhail see *Averbakh, Mikhail*

Averback, Hy Chamber of Horrors 66; I Love You Alice B. Toklas • Kiss My Butterfly 68; Where Were You When the Lights Went Out? 68; The Great Bank Robbery 69; Suppose They Gave a War and Nobody Came? • War Games 70; Where the Boys Are • Where the Boys Are '84 84

Averbakh, Ilya Declaration of Love • Obyasnenie v Lubvi 77

Averbakh, Mikhail In the Big City • V Bolshom Gorodye 27*; Life • Zhizn 27*; The Lesson • Man's Value • The Price of Man • Tsena Cheloveka • The Value of Man 28*

Avery, Charles Fatty's New Role 15*; Hogan the Porter 15; Hogan's Mussy Job 15; A Submarine Pirate 15*; A Modern Enoch Arden 16*

Avery, Dwayne Weekend Lover 69; Young and Wild 75

Avery, Fred see *Avery, Tex*

Avery, Tex The Blow-Out 36; Don't Look Now 36; Goldiggers of '49 36; I Love to Singa 36; I'd Love to Take Orders from You 36; Milk and Money 36; Miss Glory • Page Miss Glory 36; Plane Dippy 36; Porky the Rainmaker 36; Porky the Wrestler 36; The Village Smithy 36; Ain't We Got Fun 37; Daffy Duck and Egghead 37; Egghead Rides Again • Egghead Rides On 37; I Only Have Eyes for You 37; I Wanna Be a Sailor 37; Little Red Walking Hood 37; Picador Porky 37; Porky's Duck Hunt 37; Porky's Garden 37; The Sneezing Weasel 37; A Sunbonnet Blue 37; Uncle Tom's Bungalow 37; Cinderella Meets Fella 38; Daffy Duck in Hollywood 38; Daffy's Romance 38; A Feud There Was 38; Hamateur Night 38; The Isle of Pingo Pongo 38; Johnny Smith and Poker Huntas 38; The Mice Will Play 38; The Penguin Parade 38; Believe It or Else 39; Dangerous Dan McFoo 39; A Day at the Zoo 39; Detouring America 39; The Early Worm Gets the Bird 39; Fresh Fish 39; Land of the Midnight Fun 39; Screwball Football 39; Thugs with Dirty Mugs 39*; The Bear's Tale 40; Ceiling Hero 40; Circus Today 40; Cross Country Detours 40; A Gander at Mother Goose 40; Holiday Highlights 40; Of Fox and Hounds 40; Wacky Wild Life 40*; A Wild Hare 40; All This and Rabbit Stew 41; Aloha Hooey 41; Aviation Vacation 41; The Bug Parade 41; The Cagey Canary 41*; The Crackpot Quail 41; Crazy Cruise 41*; The Haunted Mouse 41; The Heckling Hare 41; Hollywood Steps Out 41; Porky's Preview 41; Speaking of Animals Down on the Farm 41; Speaking of Animals in a Pet Shop 41; Speaking of Animals in the Zoo 41; Tortoise Beats Hare 41; The Blitz Wolf 42; Dumb Hounded 42; The Early Bird Dood It 42; One Ham's Family 43; Red Hot Riding Hood 43; What's Buzzin', Buzzard? 43; Who Killed Who? 43; Batty Baseball 44; Big Heel Watha 44; Happy-Go-Nutty 44; Screwball

Squirrel • Screwy Squirrel 44; Jerky Turkey 45; The Screwy Truant 45; The Shooting of Dan McGoo 45; Swing Shift Cinderella 45; Wild and Woolfy 45; Henpecked Hoboes 46; The Hick Chick 46; Lonesome Lenny 46; Northwest Hounded Police 46; Hound Hunters 47; King-Size Canary 47; Little Tinker 47; Red Hot Rangers 47; Slap Happy Lion 47; Uncle Tom's Cabana 47; The Cat That Hated People 48; Half-Pint Pygmy 48; Lucky Ducky 48; What Price Fleadom? 48; Bad Luck Blackie 49; Counterfeit Cat 49; Doggone Tired 49; The House of Tomorrow 49; Little Rural Red Riding Hood • Little Rural Riding Hood 49; Out-Foxed 49; Señor Droopy 49; Wags to Riches 49; The Chump Champ 50; The Cuckoo Clock 50; Garden Gopher 50; The Peachy Cobbler 50; Ventriloquist Cat 50; The Car of Tomorrow 51; Cock-a-Doodle Dog 51; Daredevil Droopy 51; Droopy's Double Trouble 51; Droopy's Good Deed 51; The Magical Maestro 51; Symphony in Slang 51; One Cab's Family 52; Rock-a-Bye Bear 52; Dragalong Droopy 53; Little Johnny Jet 53; T.V. of Tomorrow 53; The Three Little Pups 53; Billy Boy 54; Crazy Mixed-Up Pup 54; Dixieland Droopy 54; Farm of Tomorrow 54; The Flea Circus 54; Homesteader Droopy 54; Cellbound 55*; Chilly Willy in the Legend of Rock-a-Bye Point • The Legend of Rock-a-Bye Point • The Rock-a-Bye Legend 55; Deputy Droopy 55; Field and Scream 55; The First Bad Man 55; I'm Cold • Some Like It Not 55; Sh-h-h-h-h! 55; Cat's Meow 56; Millionaire Droopy 56; Polar Pests 58

Avidan, David Message from the Future 81

Avila, Jac Krik? Krak! Tales of a Nightmare 88*

Avildsen, John G. Smiles 64; Light, Sound, Diffuse 67; Turn On to Love 67; Okay Bill • Sweet Dreams 68; Guess What? • Guess What We Learned in School Today? 69; Cry Uncle! • Super Dick 70; The Gap • Joe 70; Roger the Stoolie • The Stoolie 72*; Save the Tiger 73; Foreplay 74*; W.W. and the Dixie Dance Kings 74; Rocky 76; Slow Dancing in the Big City 78; The Formula 80; Neighbors 81; Traveling Hopefully 82; A Night in Heaven 83; The Karate Kid 84; Happy New Year 85; The Karate Kid Part II 86; For Keeps 88; The Karate Kid Part III 89; Lean on Me 89; Rocky V 90

Avildsen, Thomas K. Things Are Tough All Over 82

Avis, Meiert Far from Home 89

Axel, Gabriel Golden Mountains • Guld og Grønne Skove 58; The Girls Are Willing • Tre Piger i Paris 59; Crazy Paradise • Det Tossede Paradis 65; Hagbard and Signe • Rautha Skikkjan • The Red Mantle • Den Røda Kappan • Den Røde Kappe 67; Det Kære Legetøj 68; Med Kærlig Hilsen 71; Familien Gyldenkål 75; Alt på et Bræt 76; Babette's Feast • Babettes Gæstebud 87; Christian 89

Axel-Branner, Per Pettersson & Bendel

34; Ungdom av i Dag 36; A Cruise in the Albertina • På Kryss med Albertina 40

Axelman, Torbjörn Lejonsommar • Vibration 69

Axelrod, George Lord Love a Duck 66; The Secret Life of an American Wife 68

Ayala, Fernando Nightmare's Passengers • Pasajeros de una Pesadilla 86; Sobredosis 86; El Año del Conejo • The Year of the Rabbit 87

Ayari, Keyanoosh The Monster 86

Ayca, Engin Bez Bebek 88

Ayer, Lewis see Ayres, Lew

Aylott, Dave The Mad Dog 06; The Pirates of Regent's Canal 06; The Giddy Goats 07; Sunday's Dinner 07; Under the Mistletoe 07; Billie's Bugle 08; A Dash for Liberty 08; Dick the Kisser 08; The Dog's Devotion 08; For His Child's Sake 08; The Invisible Button 08; Jessica's First Prayer 08; My Son the Curate 08; The Office Boy's Dream 08; Only a Dart 08; Paddy's Way of Doing It 08; The Pirate Ship 08; Put Me Among the Girls 08; The Skirl of the Pibroch 08; The Tricky Convict, or The Magic Cap 08; Wanted, a Nice Young Man 08; And Then He Woke Up 09; The Boy and the Convict 09; Copping the Coppers 09; A Dash for Help 09; Diver's Diversions • Diver-sions 09; For Her Sake 09; Gingerbread 09; Hypnotic Suggestion 09; Muggins VC 09; Scouts to the Rescue 09; Scratch As Scratch Can 09; Sorry, Can't Stop 09; Squaring the Account 09; Two Naughty Boys 09; The Unwelcome Chaperone 09; The Wanderer's Return, or Many Years After 09; Was It a Serpent's Bite? 09; What the Angler Caught 09; The Young Redskins 09; As Prescribed by the Doctor 10; At the Mercy of the Tide 10; A Bolt from the Blue 10; Bunker's Patent Bellows 10; Comrades, or Two Lads and a Lass 10; The Devoted Ape 10; Erratic Power 10; From Gipsy Hands 10; The Gamekeeper's Daughter 10; The Hindoo's Treachery 10; How Scroggins Found the Comet 10; The Last of the Dandy 10; The Marriage of Muggins VC and a Further Exploit 10; Mistaken Identity 10; Mr. Tubby's Triumph 10; A Modern George Washington 10; Prison Reform 10*; A Race for a Bride 10; A Rare Specimen 10; A Thrilling Story 10; 'Twixt Red Man and White 10; Vice Versa 10; What Happened to Brown 10; The Adventures of Lieutenant Daring RN in a South American Port 11; Auntie's Parrot 11; Bertie's Bid for Bliss 11; Billy's Bible 11; Charley Smiler Competes in a Cycle 11; Charley Smiler Is Robbed • Charley Smiler Loses His Watch 11; Charley Smiler Joins the Boy Scouts 11; Charley Smiler Takes Brain Food 11; Charley Smiler Takes Up Ju-Jitsu 11; Good News for Jones 11; The King's Pardon 11; Lieutenant Daring RN and the Secret Service Agents • Lieutenant Daring RN Saves H.M.S. Medina 11; The Limit Fire Brigade 11; Men Were Deceivers Ever 11; The Pirates of 19... • The Pirates of 1920 11*; The Poison Label 11; Run to Earth by Boy Scouts 11; Scrog-

gins and the Fly Pest 11; Scroggins and the Waltz Dream 11; Scroggins Gets the Socialist Craze 11; Scroggins Takes the Census 11; She Would Talk 11; A Soldier's Sweetheart 11; Spring Cleaning in the House of Scroggins 11; Spy Fever 11; That Terrible Pest 11; The Typist's Revenge 11; Well Done, Scouts 11; Adhesion 12; Bagged 12; Billy Bungler the Silent Burglar 12; Broken Faith 12; Captain Cuff's Neighbours 12; Captain Dandy, Bushranger 12; Caught 12; Charlie Smiler Asks Papa 12; Charlie Smiler at the Picnic 12; Charlie Smiler Catches a Tartar 12; Charlie Smiler's Love Affair 12; Henpeck's Double 12; Honour Among Thieves 12; How Smiler Raised the Wind 12; Lieutenant Daring and the Ship's Mascot 12; Lieutenant Daring Avenges an Insult to the Union Jack 12; The Miner's Mascot 12; Much Ado About... 12; Muggins VC—The Defence of Khuma Hospital, India 12; The Mystic Ring 12; Paul Sleuth, Crime Investigator—The Burglary Syndicate • Paul Sleuth, Investigator and the Burglary Syndicate 12; Private Hector, Gentleman 12; The Rajah's Revenge 12; Sandy's New Kilt 12; A Shock-ing Complaint 12; Sold, A Bear Fact 12; A Son of Mars 12; The Spy Mania 12; Tootles Buys a Gun 12; Uncle's Present 12; What's the Joke? 12; When Father Fetched the Doctor 12; When It Comes Off 12; Woman's Privilege in Leap Year 12; The Wooing of Widow Wilkins 12; Belinda's Elopement 13; Billiken Revolts 13; Billy's Boxing Gloves 13; East Is East • For East Is East • In the Python's Den 13; The Fairy Bottle 13; Furnishing Extraordinary 13; The Gentleman Ranker • Not Guilty • Raised from the Ranks 13; Landladies Beware 13; The Misadventures of Mike Murphy • Murphy and the Magic Cap 13; The Murder of Squire Jeffrey 13; The Mystic Mat 13; The Mystic Moonstone 13; P.C. Platt's Promotion 13; Poor Pa Pays 13; A Present from Uncle • Uncle's Present 13; Professor Hoskins' Patent Hustler 13; A Shocking Job • Shocks and Shorts 13; Two Brown Bags 13; The Warty Wooing 13; Willie's Dream of Mick Squinter 13; Wily William's Washing 13; Biff! Bang!! Wallop!!! 14; A Box of Real Turkish 14; The Daughter of Garcia, Brigand 14; Dreamy Jimmy Dreams Again 14; An Eggs-traordinary Complaint 14; The Enemy Within • To Save the King 14; England's Call 14; Father's Fighting Fever 14; The Fighting Strain of Old England 14; The Gloves of Ptames 14; Held by a Child 14; I Should Say So 14; A Joke in Jerks 14; Jollyboy's Dream 14; Lieutenant Geranium and the Stealed Orders 14; Love and Bullets • Love, Poetry and Paint 14; The Mat That Mattered 14; A Merry Night 14; Mike Joins the Force 14; Mike Murphy As a Picture Actor 14; Mike Murphy, Broker's Man 14; Mike Murphy, Mountaineer 14; Mike Murphy VC 14; Mike Murphy's Dream of Love and Riches • Murphy's Millions 14; Mike Murphy's Dream of the Wild West 14; Mike Wins the Championship 14; The

New Boy 14; Not Likely 14; Panic 14; The Ring That Wasn't 14; The Scout's Motto 14; Shawly Not 14; Shocking Bad Form 14; Some Fish! 14; The Sorrows of Selina 14; The Strength That Failed 14; Telling the Tale 14; Through the Ages 14; Thumbs Up 14; The Tricky Stick 14; Vengeance of the Air 14; War's Grim Reality 14; Awkward Anarchists 15; The Cakes of Khandipore 15; The Charm That Charmed 15; A Chip Off the Old Block 15; The Club of Pharos 15; Conscription 15; Coppers and Cutups 15; The Crimson Triangle 15; The Defective Detective • Jewels and Jimjams 15; Diamond Cut Diamond 15; Fighting Selina 15; Her Fatal Hand 15; His Phantom Burglar 15; The Jade Heart 15; The Kaiser's Present 15; A Kweer Kuss 15; Maloola from Paloona 15; Mike Alone in the Jungle 15; Mike and the Zeppelin Raid 15; Mike Murphy's Marathon 15; Mike's Gold Mine 15; Podgy Porkins' Plot 15; The Second Lieutenant 15; Selina of the Weeklies 15; Selina-ella 15; Slips and Slops 15; Surely You'll Insure 15; When Clubs Were Clubs 15; Yvonne 15; Bob Downe's Schooldays 16; Bobbikins and the Bathing Belles 16; The Gay Deceivers 16; Hitchy-Coo 16; Mike and the Miser 16; Mike Backs the Winner 16; Oh Auntie! 16; The Price He Paid 16; A Shattered Idyll 16; A Soldier and a Man 16; Two Lancashire Lasses in London 16; His Uncle's Heir 17; It's Never Too Late to Mend 17; The Man Who Made Good 17; The Walrus Gang 17; When the Heart Is Young 17; Gamblers All 19; Parkstone Comedies 21; The River of Light 21; More, Please 29; An Old Time Music Hall 29; Popular Pieces 29; Yule 29; The Safe 30

Ayres, Lemuel Ziegfeld Follies 45*

Ayres, Lew Hearts in Bondage 36; Altars of the World 76

Ayrton, Michael Greek Sculpture 59*

Ayrton, Randle Gates of Duty • Tower of Strength 19; The Sands of Time 19; His House in Order 28

Azagarov, Georgy Grekh • Sin 16*

Azarov, Villen Grown-Up Children • Vzroslye Deti 63

Azimzade, Gulbeniz Chkatulka iz Kreposti • A Jewel Box from a Castle 87

Aznar, Tomás Beyond Terror • Further Than Fear • Más Allá del Terror 79

Azzopardi, Mario Deadline 80; State of Survival 86; Fatal Chase • Nowhere to Hide 87

B, Beth The Offenders 80*; The Trap Door 80*; Vortex 82*; Salvation! • Salvation! Have You Said Your Prayers Today? 87; Belladonna 89

B, Scott The Offenders 80*; The Trap Door 80*; Vortex 82*

Baaf, Mohsen Makhmal see Baf, Mohsen Makhmal

Baba, Yasuo Take Me Out to the Snowland • Watashi o Ski ni Tsuretette 87

Babayan, Agasi Rys Vozvrashaetsia 88

Babbitt, Art Giddyap 50; Popcorn Story 50; The Family Circus 51

Babenco, Hector King of the Night 75; Lúcio Flávio 78; Pixote 80; Kiss of the Spider Woman 85; Ironweed 87

Babille, E. J. No Control 27*

Babochkin, Boris Native Fields 43

Babu, D. Rajendra see Rajendra, Babu D.

Babu, Surendra see Surendra, Babu

Babu Rao, Pendharkar Sharashandri 21; Sarkari Prasad 26; Swajara Doran 30; Vishvamitra • Wishwamitra 52

Babych, Iskra Prosti Menya, Alyosha 85

Bachman, Richard see King, Stephen

Backhaus, Helmuth M. River of Evil 64*; Die Banditen von Rio Grande 65

Backner, Arthur Bluff 15; The Taming of the Shrew 15; Memories 25

Bacon, Gerald F. The Silent Witness 17*

Bacon, Lloyd The Host 23; Don't Fail 24; The Wild Goose Chaser 24; Breaking the Ice 25; Good Morning Madam 25; He Who Gets Smacked 25; Merrymakers 25; The Raspberry Romance 25; Take Your Time 25; The Window Dummy 25; Broken Hearts of Hollywood 26; Circus Today 26; Finger Prints 26; Kitty from Killarney 26; Meet My Girl 26; Private Izzy Murphy 26; The Prodigal Bridegroom 26; Two Lips in Holland 26; Wide Open Faces 26; Brass Knuckles 27; The Heart of Maryland 27; A Sailor's Sweetheart 27; Smith's Customer 27; Smith's New Home 27; Smith's Surprise 27; White Flannels 27; The Lion and the Mouse 28; Pay As You Enter 28; The Question of Today 28; The Singing Fool 28; Women They Talk About 28; Honky Tonk 29; No Defense 29; Say It with Songs 29; So Long Letty 29; Stark Mad 29; Moby Dick 30; A Notorious Affair 30; The Office Wife 30; The Other Tomorrow 30; She Couldn't Say No 30; Fifty Million Frenchmen 31; Gold Dust Gertie • Why Change Your Husband? 31; Honor of the Family 31; Kept Husbands 31; Manhattan Parade 31; Sit Tight 31; Alias the Doctor 32*; Crooner 32; The Famous Ferguson Case 32; Fireman Save My Child 32; Miss Pinkerton 32; You Said a Mouthful 32; Footlight Parade 33*; 42nd Street 33; Mary Stevens, M.D. 33; Picture Snatcher 33; Son of a Sailor 33; He Was Her Man 34; Here Comes the Navy • Hey Sailor 34; Six-Day Bike Rider 34; A Very Honorable Guy • A Very Honourable Man 34; Wonder Bar 34; Broadway Gondolier 35; Devil Dogs of the Air 35; Frisco Kid 35; In Caliente 35; The Irish in Us 35; Cain and Mabel 36; Gold Diggers of 1937 36; Sons o' Guns 36; Ever Since Eve 37; Marked Woman 37; San Quentin 37; Submarine D-1 37; Boy Meets Girl 38; Cowboy from Brooklyn • Romance and Rhythm 38; Racket Busters 38; A Slight Case of Murder 38; Wings of the Navy 38; A Child Is Born 39; Devil on Wheels • Indianapolis Speedway 39; Espionage Agent 39; Invisible Stripes 39; The Oklahoma Kid 39; Brother Orchid 40; Knockout • Knute Rockne, All-American • A

Modern Hero 40; Three Cheers for the Irish 40; Affectionately Yours 41; Footsteps in the Dark 41*; Honeymoon for Three 41; Navy Blues 41; Larceny, Inc. 42; Silver Queen 42; Wings for the Eagle 42; Action in the North Atlantic 43; The Fighting Sullivans • The Sullivans 44; Sunday Dinner for a Soldier 44; Captain Eddie 45; Home Sweet Homicide 46; Wake Up and Dream 46; I Wonder Who's Kissing Her Now 47; Don't Trust Your Husband • An Innocent Affair 48; Give My Regards to Broadway 48; Mother Is a Freshman • Mother Knows Best 48; You Were Meant for Me 48; Innocence Is Bliss • Miss Grant Takes Richmond 49; It Happens Every Spring 49; The Affairs of Sally • The Fuller Brush Girl 50; The Good Humor Man 50; Kill the Umpire! 50; Call Me Mister 51; The Frogmen 51; Golden Girl 51; Beautiful But Dangerous • Enough for Happiness • She Couldn't Say No • She Had to Say Yes 52; The I-Don't-Care Girl 52; The French Line 53; The Great Sioux Uprising 53; Walking My Baby Back Home 53

Bacsó, Péter No Problems in Summer 63; Cyclists in Love 65; Summer on the Hill 67; Shot in the Head 68; A Tanú • Without a Trace • The Witness 68; Present Times 72; The Agony of Mr. Boroca 73; Forró Vizet a Kopaszra 77; A Piano in Midair 77; Warning Shot 77; Hány az Óra, Vekker Úr? • What's the Time, Mr. Clock? 85; The Banana Skin Waltz • Banánhéjkeringő 86

Baczynsky, Walter The Proud Rider 71*

Badat, Randall Surf II • Surf II—The End of the Trilogy 83

Badger, Clarence A Duel at Dawn 15; The Danger Girl • Love on Skates 16; A Family Affair 16; Gypsy Joe 16*; Haystacks and Steeples 16; His Wild Oats 16*; A Modern Enoch Arden 16*; A Social Cub 16; Teddy at the Throttle 16; The Nick-of-Time Baby 17; The Pullman Bride 17; The Sultan's Wife 17; Whose Baby? 17; Day Dreams 18; The Floor Below 18; Friend Husband 18; The Kingdom of Youth 18; A Perfect Lady 18; The Venus Model 18; Almost a Husband 19; Daughter of Mine 19; Jubilo 19; Leave It to Susan 19; Sis Hopkins 19; Strictly Confidential 19; Through the Wrong Door 19; Water, Water, Everywhere 19; Cupid, the Cowpuncher 20; Honest Hutch 20; Jes' Call Me Jim 20; The Strange Boarder 20; Boys Will Be Boys 21; Doubling for Romeo 21; Guile of Women 21; A Poor Relation 21; An Unwilling Hero 21; The Dangerous Little Demon 22; Don't Get Personal 22; Quincy Adams Sawyer 22; The Ropin' Fool 22; Dr. Sunshine • Potash and Perlmutter 23; Red Lights 23; Your Friend and Mine 23; One Night in Rome 24; Painted People 24; The Shooting of Dan McGrew 24; Eve's Secret 25; The Golden Princess 25; New Lives for Old 25; Paths to Paradise 25; The Campus Flirt • The College Flirt 26; Hands Up! 26; Miss Brewster's Millions 26; The Rainmaker 26; It 27*; A Kiss in a Taxi 27; Man Power

27; Señorita 27; She's a Sheik 27; Swim, Girl, Swim 27; The Fifty-Fifty Girl 28; Hot News 28; Red Hair 28; Three Week-Ends 28; Paris 29; The Bad Man 30; Murder Will Out 30; No, No, Nanette 30; Sweethearts and Wives 30; The Challenge • Woman Hungry 31; The Hot Heiress 31; Party Husbands 31; When Strangers Marry 33; Rangle River 36; That Certain Something 41

Badham, John The Bingo Long Traveling All-Stars and Motor Kings 76; Saturday Night Fever 77; Dracula 79; Whose Life Is It Anyway? 81; Blue Thunder 82; War-Games 83; American Flyers 85; Short Circuit 86; Stakeout 87; Bird on a Wire 90

Badiyi, Reza Death of a Stranger 72; Trader Horn 73

Badrakhan, Ahmed Mustafa Kamel 53; Allah Maana • God Is on Our Side 54

Badrakhan, Ali El Gooa • Hunger 86

Bae, Chang-ho The Iron Men 82; People in Slum Area 82; Tropical Flower 83; Deep Blue Night 84; Warm It Was That Winter 84; Whale Hunter 84; Whale Hunter II 85; Hwang Jin-i 86; Our Sweet Days of Youth 87

Bae, Yong-kyun Dharmaga Tongjoguro Kan Kkadalgun? • Why Did Bodhi-Djarma Go East? 89

Baer, Max J.J. McCulloch • The McCullochs • The Wild McCullochs 75; Ode to Billy Joe 76; Hometown U.S.A. 79

Baerlin, Anthony The Local Train Mystery 37

Baerwitz, Jerry Daikaijū Baran • The Monster Baran • Varan the Unbelievable 58*; Wild Harvest 62

Baf, Mohsen Makhmal Boycott 86; The Peddler 87; Dustforough 88

Bafaloukos, Theodoros Rockers 78

Baffico, Mario Nobody's Land • Terra di Nessuno 40

Bagby, Milton, Jr. Rebel Love 84

Bagdadi, Maroun L'Homme Voile • The Veiled Man 87

Baggot, King Crime's Triangle 15; Cheated Love 21; Luring Lips 21; Moonlight Follies 21; Nobody's Fool 21; A Dangerous Game 22; Human Hearts 22; The Kentucky Derby 22; Kissed 22; The Lavender Bath Lady 22; Crossed Wires 23; The Darling of New York 23; Gossip 23; The Love Letter 23; The Town Scandal 23; The Gaiety Girl 24; The Tornado 24; The Whispered Name 24; The Home Maker 25; Raffles, the Amateur Cracksman 25; Tumbleweeds 25*; Lovey Mary 26; Down the Stretch 27; The Notorious Lady 27; Perch of the Devil 27; The House of Scandal 28; Romance of a Rogue 28

Bahaduri, Rajesh Hamari Jung 87

Bai, Chen see Chen, Bai

Bai, Ching-zue see Pai, Ching-jui

Bail, Charles see Bail, Chuck

Bail, Chuck Black Samson 74; Cleopatra Jones and the Casino of Gold 75; The Gumball Rally 76; Choke Canyon 86

Bailey, Angus Below the Hill 74

Bailey, David G. G. Passion 66

Bailey, Harry see Bailey, Henry D.

Bailey, Henry D. Are You Married? 20; A Double Life 20; Silly Hoots 20; Black Magic 21; Cabaret Courtesy 21; The Chicken Fancier 21; No Tickee No Shirtee 21; Padding the Bill 21; The Big Game 28; City Slickers 28; A Cross Country Run 28; Flying Hoofs 28; The Wandering Minstrel 28; The War Bride 28; Snapping the Whip 29

Bailey, Norma Martha, Ruth & Edie 88*

Bailey, Oliver D. The Whirl of Life 15; The Blind Love 20

Bailey, Patrick Door to Door 84

Bailey, Rex Fangs of the Arctic 53; Mexican Manhunt 53; Northern Patrol 53

Bailey, Richard The Big Payoff • Just Another Day at the Races • Three for the Money • Win, Place or Steal 75

Bailey, Vernon Howe Vernon Howe Bailey's Sketchbook 15; Vernon Howe Bailey's Sketchbook of Berlin 16; Vernon Howe Bailey's Sketchbook of Boston 16; Vernon Howe Bailey's Sketchbook of Chicago 16; Vernon Howe Bailey's Sketchbook of London 16; Vernon Howe Bailey's Sketchbook of New Orleans 16; Vernon Howe Bailey's Sketchbook of Paris 16; Vernon Howe Bailey's Sketchbook of Petrograd 16; Vernon Howe Bailey's Sketchbook of Philadelphia 16; Vernon Howe Bailey's Sketchbook of Rome 16; Vernon Howe Bailey's Sketchbook of St. Louis 16; Vernon Howe Bailey's Sketchbook of San Francisco 16; Vernon Howe Bailey's Sketchbook of Washington 16

Baillie, Bruce David Lynn's Sculpture 61; The Gymnasts 61; Mr. Hayashi 61; On Sundays 61; Everyman 62; Have You Thought of Talking to the Director? 62; Here I Am 62; News No. 3 62; A Hurrah for Soldiers 63; To Parsifal 63; The Brookfield Recreation Center 64; Mass for the Dakota Sioux 64; Quixote 65; Yellow Horse 65; All My Life 66; Castro Street 66; Port Chicago 66; Show Leader 66; Still Life 66; Termination 66; Tung 66; Valentín de las Sierras 67; Quick Billy 70

Bailly, Raymond My Wife Is a Panther 61

Baim, Harold Playtime for Workers 43; Say Abracadabra 52; Variety Half Hour 54; Invitation to Magic 56

Bain, Bill Romeo and Juliet, 1971—A Gentle Tale of Sex, Violence, Corruption and Murder • What Became of Jack and Jill? 71

Bain, Fred Thundering Through 25; The Ramblin' Galoot 26

Baird, Edward School for Danger 47

Bairstow, David Royal Journey 52

Bajić, Darko Zaboravljeni 88

Bajon, Filip Magnat • The Magnate 87

Bakaba, Sijiri Aduefue • Les Guérisseurs 88

Bakaleinikoff, Constantin Let's Fall in Love 34

Baker, Anthony Beyond Control 71

Baker, David Libido 73*; The Great Macarthy 75

Baker, Fred Events 70; Lenny Bruce Without Tears 72; Murder She Sings 86

Baker, George D. Captain Barnacle's Courtship 11; The New Stenographer 11; The Politician's Dream 11; Bunny All at Sea 12; Chumps 12; The Troublesome Stepdaughters 12; The Autocrat of Flapjack Junction 13; John Tobin's Sweetheart 13; Bunny Buys a Harem 14; Bunny's Birthday 14; Bunny's Mistake 14; Bunny's Scheme 14; Father's Flirtation 14; The Honeymooners 14; Love's Old Dream 14; Pigs Is Pigs 14; Polishing Up 14; The Dust of Egypt 15; A Price for Folly 15; A Night Out 16; The Pretenders 16; The Shop Girl • Winifred the Shop Girl 16; Tarantula 16; The Two-Edged Sword 16; The Wager 16; The Wheel of the Law 16; The Duchess of Doubt 17; The End of the Tour 17; His Father's Son 17; The Lifted Veil 17; Outwitted 17; A Sleeping Memory 17; Sowers and Reapers 17; The White Raven 17; The Demon 18; Her Inspiration 18; The Shell Game 18; Toys of Fate 18; Castles in the Air 19; The Cinema Murder 19; The Lion's Den 19; Peggy Does Her Darndest 19; Heliotrope 20; The Man Who Lost Himself 20; Buried Treasure 21; Garments of Truth 21; The Hunch 21; Proxies 21; Without Limit 21; Don't Write Letters 22; I Can Explain • Stay Home 22; Little Eva Ascends 22; Slave of Desire 23; Revelation 24

Baker, Graham The Final Conflict 81; Impulse 84; Alien Nation 88

Baker, Hugh see Endfield, Cy

Baker, Nancy Dreamland 83*

Baker, R. C. When Destiny Wills 21

Baker, Richard Foster A Bunch of Keys 15

Baker, Robert S. Blackout 50*; 13 East Street 52; The Steel Key 53; Passport to Treason 55; Jack the Ripper • The Return of Jack the Ripper 58*; The Hellfire Club 60*; The Secret of Monte Cristo • The Treasure of Monte Cristo 60*; The Siege of Hell Street • The Siege of Sidney Street 60*

Baker, Roy Ward The October Man 47; The Weaker Sex 48; Morning Departure • Operation Disaster 49; Paper Orchid 49; Highly Dangerous 50; The House in the Square • The House on the Square • I'll Never Forget You 51; Don't Bother to Knock 52; Night Without Sleep 52; Inferno 53; Passage Home 55; Jacqueline 56; Tiger in the Smoke 56; The One That Got Away 57; A Night to Remember 58; The Singer Not the Song 60; L'Affondamento della Valiant • The Valiant 61*; Flame in the Streets 61; Two Left Feet 63; The Anniversary 67; Five Million Years to Earth • The Pit • Quatermass and the Pit 67; The Fiction Makers 68; Journey Into Midnight 68*; Moon Zero Two 69; Scars of Dracula 70; The Vampire Lovers 70; Doctor Jekyll and Sister Hyde 71; Asylum • House of Crazies 72; Further Tales from the Crypt • Tales from the Crypt, Part II • Tales of the Crypt, Part II • Vault of Horror 72; And

Now the Screaming Starts! • Bride of Fen-griffen • Fengriffen • I Have No Mouth But I Must Scream • The Screaming Starts 73; Dracula and the 7 Golden Vampires • The Legend of the Seven Golden Vampires • The Seven Brothers Meet Dracula 73; The Monster Club 80; Mission: Monte Carlo 81; The Masks of Death 84

Bakker, E. G. No Time to Die 84*

Bakshi, Ralph Fritz the Cat 72; Heavy Traffic 73; Coonskin • Street Fight 74; Hey Good Lookin' 75; Wizards 77; The Lord of the Rings 78; American Pop 81; Fire and Ice 82

Baky, Josef von Intermezzo 36; Die Frau am Scheidewege 38; Die Kleine und die Grosse Liebe • Minor Love and the Real Thing 38; Her First Experience • Her First Romance • Ihr Erstes Erlebnis 39; Menschen vom Varieté 39; Der Kleinstadtpoet 40; Annelie 41; The Adventures of Baron Münchhausen • The Amazing Adventures of Baron Münchhausen • Baron Münchhausen • Münchhausen • Münchhausens Abenteuer 43; Via Mala 45; City of Torment • Und Über Uns der Himmel 47; The Last Illusion • Der Ruf 49; Die Seltsame Geschichte des Brandner Kaspar 49; Das Doppelte Lottchen 50; Dreaming Lips • Der Träumende Mund 52; The Diary of a Married Woman • Tagebuch einer Verliebten 53; Dunja 55; Hotel Adlon 55; Führmann Henschel 56; The Girl and the Legend • Robinson Soll Nicht Sterben 57; Confess Dr. Corda! • Gestehen Sie Dr. Corda! 58; Die Frühreifen 58; Stefanie 58; Die Ideale Frau 59; Der Mann Der Sich Verkaufte 59; Marili 59; Sturm im Wasserglas 60; Die Seltsame Gräfin • The Strange Countess 61

Balaban, Bob Parents 88
Balaban, Burt Immediate Disaster • Stranger from Venus • The Venusian 54; Lady of Vengeance 57; High Hell 58; Murder, Inc. 60*; Mad Dog Coll 61; The Gentle Rain 66

Balachander, K. Rudra Veena 88
Balada, Ivan O Zivej Vode 88
Balaguer, Carlos L'Amor Es Estrany 88
Balajan, Roman Dream Flights • Polioty vo Sne Naiavou 83; Khrani Menio Moi Talisman • Protect Me My Talisman 86; Filer 88; Lady Macbeth of the Mtsensk District • Lady Makbet Mitsenskovo Uezda 89

Balajka, Miroslav Nought Out of Ten • Pětka s Hvězdičkov 85; Pravidla Kruhu 88
Balasko, Josiane All Mixed Up • Sac de Nœuds 85; Les Keufs 87

Balayan, Roman see Balajan, Roman
Balázs, Béla Ágyú és Harang 15; Elné mult Harangok 16; Maki Állást Vállal 16; Az Elitélt 17; A Koldusgróf 17; Lotti Ezredes 17; Obsitos 17; A Pál Utcai Fiúk 17; Vengerkák 17; Asszonyfaló 18; Császár Katonai 18; Egyenlőség 18; Halálos Csönd 18; Hivatalnok Urak 18; Rang és Mód 18; Sphynx 18; Udvari Levegő 18; Valós Kérdőjel 18; A Megfagyott Gyermek 21;

Fehér Galambok Fekete Városban 22; Pál Utcai Fiúk • Paul Street Boys 24; Das Blaue Licht • The Blue Light 32*; Édes Mostoha • Kind Stepmother • Sweet Stepmother 35; Havi 200 Fix • Salary, 200 a Month 36; Lady Seeks Room • Úrilány Szobát Keres 37; Tommy 37; Azur Express • Azure Express 38; Sutyi a Szerencsegyerek • Sutyi the Lucky Child 38; Bitter Honeymoon • Keserű Mézeshetek 39; Karosszék 39; Mária Két Éjszakája 40; Vadrózsa • Wild Rose 40; Ne Kérdezd Ki Voltom 41; Ópiumkeringő 43

Balázs, Mária Pókháló 38
Balboni, Silvano The Far Cry 26; The Masked Woman 27
Balbuena, Silvio F. Escrito en la Niebla • It Is Written in the Fog 82
Balcazar, Alfonso El Rancho de los Implacables 64; Die Gejagten der Sierra Nevada 65; The Man from Canyon City • L'Uomo Che Viene da Canyon City 65; Dinamite Jim • Dynamite Jim 66; Quattro Dollari di Vendetta 66; Clint il Solitario 67; Con la Morte alle Spalle 67; L'Uomo della Pistola d'Oro 67; Sartana Non Perdona 68
Balcazar, Jesús Jaime The Man from Oklahoma • Oklahoma John 64*; Sunscorched • Tierra de Fuego • Vergeltung in Cataño 65*; La Lunga Notte di Tombstone 68
Balch, Antony Towers Open Fire 63; The Cut-Ups 67; Bizarre 69; Secrets of Sex 70; Computer Killers • Horror Hospital 73
Balco, Vladimír Pasodoble pre Troch 86; Attitudes • Postoj 89
Baldanello, Gianfranco Thirty Winchesters for El Diablo 65; Kill Johnny Ringo • Uccidete Jonny Ringo 66; Black Jack 68; I Lunghi Giorni dell'Odio 68; Lusty Brawlers • This Man Can't Die 70; The Great Adventure 75
Baldi, Ferdinando David and Goliath • David e Golia 60*; I Tartari • The Tartars 60*; Duel of Champions • Horatio • Orazi e Curiazi 61*; The Tyrant of Castile 64; The Avenger • Texas Addio 66; Little Rita in the West • Little Rita nel West 67; Get a Coffin Ready • Preparati la Bara 68; Odia il Prossimo Tuo 68; Il Pistolero dell'Ave Maria 69; Blindman • Il Cieco 71; Carambola 74; Get Mean 76; My Name Is Trinity 76; Nove Ospiti per un Delitto 76; L'Inquilina del Piano di Sopra 77; The Sicilian Connection 77; La Selvaggia Geometra Prinetti del Vaggiameteosvaldo 78; La Ragazza del Vagone Letto 79; Comin' At Ya! 81; Il Mistero della Quattro Corona • El Tesoro de las Cuatro Coronas • Treasure of the Four Crowns 82
Baldi, Gian Vittorio Il Pianto delle Zitelle 58; Via dei Cessati Spiriti 59; La Vigilia di Mezza Estate 59; La Casa delle Vedove • The Widow's Home 60; Luciano 60; Il Bar di Gigi 61; Le Italiane e l'Amore • Latin Lovers 61*; Il Corrida di Sposa 62; Les Adolescentes • The Adolescents • La Fleur de l'Âge • La Fleur de l'Âge ou Les Adolescentes • That Tender Age 64*;

Ritratto di Pina 66; Fire • Fuoco! 68; ZEN – Zona Espansione Nord 88
Baldi, Marcello Medusa Against the Son of Hercules 63; Night Train to Milan 63; Saul and David • Saul e David • Saúl y David 65; Stunt Man 68
Balducci, Armenia I Love You, I Love You Not • Together? 79
Balducci, Richard Dans la Poussière du Soleil • Lust in the Dust 71; Le Facteur de Saint-Tropez 85; Y'à Pas le Feu 85
Baldwin, Ruth Ann '49-'17 17; A Wife on Trial 17
Baledón, Rafael La Flecha Envenenada • The Poisoned Arrow 57; El Hombre y el Monstruo • The Man and the Monster 58; La Casa Embrujada • The Curse of the Crying Woman • La Maldición de la Llorona 60; The Hell of Frankenstein • El Infierno de Frankenstein • Orlak, El Infierno de Frankenstein • Orlak, The Hell of Frankenstein 60; Bullet for Billy the Kid 63; Los Horrores del Bosque Negro • La Loba • Los Misterios de Bosque Negro • The She-Wolf 64; The Swamp of the Lost Monsters 65; Challenge to Life • Reto a la Vida 87; I Do 'Em In • Las Traigo...Muertas 87
Baletić, Branko Uvek Spremne Žene • Woman's Day 87
Balík, Jaroslav The Death of Tarzan • The Death of the Ape Man • Tarzanova Smrt 68; Experiment Eva 85; An Atomic Cathedral • Atomová Katedrála 86; Óda na Radost • Ode to Happiness 86
Baljinnyam, B. Bi Chamd Khayrtay • I Adore You 86
Balk, Maurice Earle Cheated Vengeance 18
Ball, Alan The Ever-Changing Motorcar 62*
Ball, Murray Footrot Flats 86
Ballard, Carroll The Black Stallion 79; Never Cry Wolf 83; The Nutcracker • Nutcracker: The Motion Picture 86
Ballard, John Friday the Thirteenth... The Orphan • Killer Orphan • The Orphan 79
Ballerini, Piero Lucia di Lammermoor 47
Ballin, Hugo Thaïs 17*; Help Yourself 20; Pagan Love 20; East Lynne 21; Jane Eyre 21; The Journey's End 21; Married People 22; Other Women's Clothes 22; Vanity Fair 23; The Prairie Wife 24; The Shining Adventure 25
Balling, Erik Qivitoq 56; Operation Lovebirds • Slå Først, Frede! 67; One of Those Things 74
Ballman, Herbert A Berlin Love Story • Einmal Ku'damm und Zurück • Girl in a Boot 83
Balogh, Béla see Balázs, Béla
Balraj, Deepak Sheela 87
Balshofer, Fred J. Rosemary 15*; The Silent Voice 15*; The Come-Back 16; A Corner in Cotton 16*; The Masked Rider 16; Pidgin Island 16; Haunted Pajamas 17; Paradise Garden 17; The Square Deceiver 17; Under Handicap 17; Broadway Bill 18;

Lend Me Your Name 18; A Man of Honor 19; The Isle of Love 22; The Three Buckaroos 22

Bamberger, Joseph J. The Apache Dance 13; A Sheffield Blade 18*; Walter Finds a Father 21

Bán, Frigyes Alter Ego 41; The Prophet of the Fields 47; The Soil Under Your Feet • Talpalatnyi Föld • Treasured Earth 48; Liberated Land 51; Baptism by Fire 52; Semmelweis 52; The Lieutenant of Rákóczi • Rákóczi Hadnagya • Rákóczi's Lieutenant 53; Extinguished Flames 56; A Quiet Home 57; Fatia Negra • Szegény Gazdagok 59; The Moneymaker 63; Büdös Víz • The Healing Water 64; Car Crazy 64

Bancroft, Anne Fatso 80

Band, Albert see Antonini, Alfredo

Band, Charles Crash! 77; The Alchemist 81; Parasite 81; Metalstorm: The Destruction of Jared-Syn 83; Future Cop • Trancers 84; The Dungeonmaster 85*; Pulsepounders 88; Kiss of the Beast • Meridian 90

Bandini, Baccio Appointment for Murder 54; Les Dents du Diable • Ombre Bianchi • The Savage Innocents 59*; Le Mercenaire • Il Mercenario • Lo Spadaccino di Siena • The Swordsman of Siena 61*

Banfield, George J. The Burgomaster of Stilemonde 28; The Dance of Death 28*; David Garrick 28*; Lady Godiva 28*; The Man in the Iron Mask 28*; The Princes in the Tower 28*; Sexton Blake, Gambler 28; Spangles 28; The Vanished Hand 28*; Power Over Men 29

Bang, Poul Isen Brydes 47*

Banionis, Raimundas Moya Malenkaya Zhena • My Little Wife 87

Bank, Mirra Enormous Changes at the Last Minute 82*

Banks, Monty Cocktails 28; The Compulsory Husband 28*; Eve's Fall 29; Almost a Honeymoon 30; Amateur Night in London 30; The Black Hand Gang 30; His First Car 30; The Jerry Builders 30; Kiss Me Sergeant 30; The Musical Beauty Shop 30; The New Waiter 30; Not So Quiet on the Western Front 30; Why Sailors Leave Home 30; My Wife's Family • The Wife's Family 31; Old Soldiers Never Die 31; Poor Old Bill 31; What a Night! 31; For the Love of Mike 32; Money for Nothing 32; Tonight's the Night • Tonight's the Night, Pass It On 32; The Charming Deceiver • Heads We Go 33; Leave It to Me 33; You Made Me Love You 33; The Church Mouse 34; Falling in Love • Trouble Ahead 34; Father and Son 34; The Girl in Possession 34; Eighteen Minutes • This Woman Is Mine 35; Hello Sweetheart 35; Man of the Moment 35; No Limit 35; So You Won't Talk? 35; Keep Your Seats Please 36; Queen of Hearts 36; Keep Smiling • Smiling Along 38; We're Going to Be Rich 38; Shipyard Sally 39; Great Guns 41

Bannert, Walter The Inheritors 85

Banno, Yoshimitsu Godzilla vs. Hedora • Godzilla vs. the Smog Monster • Gojira

Tai Hedora 71

Baños, Ricardo de see De Baños, Ricardo

Banos, Richard de see De Baños, Ricardo

Bansbach, Richard Claws • Devil Bear 77*

Bantock, Leedham David Garrick 13; Ivanhoe • Rebecca the Jewess 13; Scrooge 13; Seymour Hicks and Ellaline Terriss 13; Always Tell Your Wife 14; Kismet 14; A Motorcycle Elopement 14; A Patriotic English Girl 14; The Beggar Girl's Wedding 15; A Daughter of England 15; From Flower Girl to Red Cross Nurse 15; The Girl of My Heart 15; The Girl Who Took the Wrong Turning 15; A Prehistoric Love Story 15; The Shopsoiled Girl 15; The Veiled Woman 17

Bao, Fang see Bao, Zhifang

Bao, Zhifang Hua Pi • The Painted Skin 66; Golden Fingernails 90

Bappiah, K. Himmat aur Mehnat 88; Maavuri Magaadu 88

Bapu Kalyana Thambulam 87; Prem Pratigyaa 89

Baqueriza, Guillermo Los Desheredados 36

Baran, Jack March of the Spring Hare • Roommates 69

Baranski, Andrzej Kobieta z Prowincji • The Woman from the Provinces 85; Tabu 88

Baratier, Jacques Désordre 49; Les Filles du Soleil 49; La Cité du Midi • Flying Trapeze 51; La Vie du Vide 52; Métier de Danseur 53; Chevalier de Ménilmontant 54; Histoire du Palais Idéale 54; Paris la Nuit 55*; Goha 57; The Doll • He, She or It • La Poupée 62; Confetti al Pepe • Dragées au Poivre • Sweet and Sour 63; Eves Futures 64; L'Or du Duc 65; Le Désordre A Vingt Ans • Disorder Is Twenty Years Old • Eden Miseria 67; Piège 69; La Décharge 70; Vous Intéressez-Vous à la Chose? 74

Barbaro, Umberto I Cantieri dell'Adriatico 33; The Last Enemy • L'Ultima Nemica 37; Carpaccio 47*; Caravaggio 48*

Barbash, Uri Stigma 83; Beyond the Walls • Me'Achorei Hasoragim 84; Dreamers • Once We Were Dreamers • Unsettled Land 87

Barber, Leslie Count on Me 48

Barber-Fleming, Peter Coming Through 85

Barbera, Joseph Gallopin' Gals 40*; Swing Social 40*; Goose Goes South 41*; The Midnight Snack 41*; The Night Before Christmas 41*; Officer Pooch 41*; The Bowling Alley Cat 42*; Fine Feathered Friend 42*; The Fraidy Cat 42*; Puss 'n' Toots 42*; Baby Puss 43*; Lonesome Mouse 43*; Sufferin' Cats 43*; War Dogs 43*; Yankee Doodle Mouse 43*; Bodyguard 44*; Cat Nipped • Kitty Foiled • Mouse Trouble 44*; Million Dollar Cat 44*; Puttin' on the Dog 44*; Zoot Cat 44*; Flirty Birdy • Love Boids 45*; Manhattan Serenade • Mouse in Manhattan

45*; The Mouse Comes to Dinner • Mouse to Dinner 45*; Quiet Please! 45*; Tee for Two 45*; The Milky Waif 46*; Solid Serenade 46*; Springtime for Thomas 46*; Trap Happy 46*; Cat Fishin' 47*; The Cat's Concerto 47*; Dr. Jekyll and Mr. Mouse 47*; Fair Weather Friend • Part-Time Pal 47*; Invisible Mouse 47*; A Mouse in the House 47*; Salt Water Tabby 47*; Mouse Cleaning 48*; Old Rockin' Chair Tom 48*; Professor Tom 48*; Truce Hurts 48*; The Cat and the Mermouse 49*; Heavenly Puss 49*; Jerry's Diary 49*; Little Orphan 49*; Love That Pup 49*; Polka Dot Puss 49*; Tennis Chumps 49*; Cue Ball Cat 50*; F'r Safety Sake • Safety Second 50*; Framed Cat 50*; Hold That Lion • Jerry and the Lion 50*; Little Quacker 50*; Party Cat • Saturday Evening Puss 50*; Texas Tom 50*; Tom and Jerry in the Hollywood Bowl 50*; Casanova Cat 51*; Cat Napping 51*; City Cousin • Jerry's Cousin • Muscles Mouse 51*; Flying Cat 51*; His Mouse Friday 51*; Jerry and the Goldfish 51*; Nit-Witty Kitty 51*; Sleepy Time Tom 51*; Slicked-Up Pup 51*; Cruise Cat 52*; Dog House 52*; Duck Doctor 52*; Fit to Be Tied 52*; Little Runaway 52*; Push-Button Kitty 52*; Smitten Kitten 52*; Triplet Trouble 52*; The Two Mouseketeers 52*; Jerry and Jumbo 53*; Johann Mouse 53*; Just Ducky 53*; Life with Tom 53*; Posse Cat 53*; Puppy Tale 53*; That's My Pup 53*; Two Little Indians 53*; Baby Butch 54*; Downhearted Duckling 54*; Hick-Cup Pup • Tyke Takes a Nap 54*; Little School Mouse 54*; Mice Follies 54*; Mouse for Sale 54*; Neapolitan Mouse 54*; Pet Peave 54*; Touché Pusse Cat 54*; Barbecue Brawl 55*; Blue Cat Blues 55*; Down Beat Bear 55*; The Egg and Jerry 55*; Flying Sorceress 55*; Happy Go Lucky • One Quack Mind 55*; Make Mine Freedom 55*; Muscle Beach Tom 55*; Tom's Photo Finish 55*; Busy Buddies 56*; Feedin' the Kiddie 56*; Give and Tyke 56*; Mucho Mouse 56*; Robin Hoodwinked 56*; Scat Cats 56*; Tops with Pops 56*; Tot Watchers 56*; The Vanishing Duck 56*; Royal Cat Nap 57*; Little Bo Bopped 59*; Wolf Hounded 59*; Creepy Time Pal 60*; The Do-Good Wolf 60*; Here, Kiddie, Kiddie 60*; Life with Loopy 60*; No Biz Like Shoe Biz 60*; Snoopy Loopy 60*; Tale of a Wolf 60*; Catch Meow 61*; Child Sockology 61*; Count Down Clown 61*; Fee Fie Foes 61*; Happy Go Loopy 61*; Kooky Loopy 61*; Loopy's Hare-Do 61*; This Is My Ducky Day 61*; Two Faced Wolf 61*; Zoo Is Company 61*; Bearly Able 62*; Beef-Fore and After 62*; Bungle Uncle 62*; Bunnies Abundant 62*; Chicken Fraca-See 62*; Common Scents 62*; Rancid Ransom 62*; Slippery Slippers 62*; Swash Buckled 62*; Bear Up! 63*; Chicken Hearted Wolf 63*; Crook Who Cried Wolf 63*; Drum-Sticked 63*; A Fallible Fable 63*; Habit Rabbit 63*; Just a Wolf at Heart 63*; Sheep Stealers

Anonymous 63*; Watcha Watchin'? 63*; Wolf in Sheep Dog's Clothing 63*; Bear Hug 64*; Bear Knuckles 64*; Elephantastic 64*; Habit Troubles 64*; Hey There, It's Yogi Bear 64*; Raggedy Rug 64*; Trouble Bruin 64*; Big Mouse Take 65*; Crow's Fete 65*; Horse Shoo 65*; Pork Chop Phooey 65*; The Man Called Flintstone • That Man Flintstone 66*; Jetsons: The Movie 90*

Barberena, Eduardo La Hora Téxaco • The Texaco Hour 85

Barberis, René Ramuntcho 53

Barboni, Enzo Ciak Mull, l'Uomo della Vendetta • The Unholy Four 69; Lo Chiamavano Trinità • They Call Me Trinity 70; Continuavamo a Chiamarlo Trinità • Trinity Is STILL My Name! 71; ...E Pri lo Chiamavano il Magnifico • A Man from the East • Man of the East 72; Anche gli Angeli Mangiano Fagioli 73; Crime Busters • Deux Super Flics • Two Supercops 76; Renegade: A Very Tough Guy • Renegade: Un Osso Troppo Duro 87

Barbosa, Haroldo Marinho Baixo Gavea • Gavea Girls 87

Barbosa, Otto Lopes Men of Brazil 60*

Barcelloni, Gianni Desideria, la Vita Interiore • Desire, the Interior Life 80

Barclay, Barry Ngati 87

Bardem, Juan Antonio Paseo Sobre una Guerra Antigua 48*; Aeropuerto • Barajas, Aeropuerto Internacional 50; Esa Pareja Feliz • That Happy Couple • That Happy Pair • This Happy Couple 51*; Bridegroom in Sight • Fiancé in Sight • Novio a la Vista 53*; Comedians • Cómicos 53; Felices Pascuas 54; Age of Infidelity • Death of a Cyclist • Muerte de un Ciclista 55; Calle Mayor • Grande Rue • The Lovemaker • Main Street 56; La Muerte de Pío Baroja 57; La Venganza • Vengeance 57; Sonatas 59; A las Cinco de la Tarde • At Five O'Clock in the Afternoon 60; Los Inocentes 62; Nothing Ever Happens • Nunca Pasa Nada 63; Amori di una Calda Estate • Los Pianos Mécanicos • Les Pianos Mécaniques • The Uninhibited 64; The Last Day of the War • El Último Día de la Guerra • L'Ultimo Giorno della Guerra 69; Variétés 71; Behind the Shutters • La Corrupción de Chris Miller • The Corruption of Chris Miller • Sisters of Corruption 72; L'Île Mystérieuse • L'Isola Misteriosa e il Capitano Nemo • The Mysterious Island • The Mysterious Island of Captain Nemo 72*; El Podor del Deseo 75; Foul Play 76; The Dog 77; El Puente 77; Seven Days in January • Siete Días de Enero 79; The Warning 82; Lorca, la Muerte de un Poeta 87

Bare, Richard L. Smart Girls Don't Talk 48; Flaxy Martin 49; The House Across the Street 49; Return of the Frontiersman 50; This Side of the Law 50; Prisoners of the Casbah 53; Border Showdown 56; The Outlanders 56; The Storm Riders 56; Shootout at Medicine Bend 57; The Travellers 57; Born Bad 58; Girl on the Run 58; Lola's Mistake • This Rebel

Breed • Three Shades of Love 60; I Sailed to Tahiti with an All Girl Crew 68; Wicked Wicked 73; Sudden Target 86; The Toolbox Murders II 87

Barea, María Gregorio 85*

Bargir, Raja Gadbad Ghotala 87

Bargy, Charles le see Le Bargy, Charles

Barjol, Jean-Michel Le Cochon • The Pig 70*

Barkas, Geoffrey The Lumberjack 25; The Manitou Trail 25; Prospectin' Around 25; Random Flakes 25; White Water Men 25; Palaver 26; Blockade • Q-Ships 28*; The Infamous Lady 28*; The Third Gun 29*; The Battle of Gallipoli • Tell England 30*; Rhodes • Rhodes of Africa 36*; The Great Barrier • Silent Barriers 37*; King Solomon's Mines 37*

Barker, Bradley Mother's Boy 29*

Barker, Clive Hellraiser 87; Transmutations 88; Nightbreed 89

Barker, Reginald The Bargain 14; The City of Darkness 14; The Typhoon 14*; The Wrath of the Gods • The Wrath of the Gods, or The Destruction of Sakura Jima 14*; The Coward 15*; The Devil 15*; The Golden Claw 15; The Iron Strain 15; The Italian 15; On the Night Stage 15; The Reward 15; Rumpelstiltskin 15*; The Apostle of Vengeance 16; Between Men 16*; The Bugle Call 16; The Captive God 16*; Civilization 16*; The Conqueror 16; The Criminal 16*; Hell's Hinges 16*; Jim Grimsby's Boy 16; The Market of Vain Desire 16; Shell Forty-Three 16; The Stepping Stone 16; The Thoroughbred 16; Back of the Man 17; Golden Rule Kate 17; Happiness 17; The Iced Bullet 17; Madame Who? 17; Paws of the Bear 17; A Strange Transgressor 17; Sweetheart of the Doomed 17; Three of Many 17; Carmen of the Klondike 18; The Hell Cat 18; The One Woman 18; Shackled 18*; The Turn of the Wheel 18; Bonds of Love 19; The Brand 19; The Crimson Gardenia 19; Flame of the Desert 19; The Girl from the Outside 19; Shadows 19; The Stronger Vow 19; The Branding Iron 20; Dangerous Days 20; The Woman and the Puppet 20; Bunty Pulls the Strings 21; Godless Men 21; The Old Nest 21; The Poverty of Riches 21; Snowblind 21; The Storm 22; The Eternal Struggle 23; Hearts Aflame 23; Pleasure Mad 23; Broken Barriers 24; The Dixie Handicap 24; The Great Divide 24; Women Who Give 24; When the Door Opened 25; The White Desert 25; The Flaming Forest 26; Body and Soul 27; The Frontiersman 27; The Toilers 28; The Great Divide 29; The Mississippi Gambler 29; New Orleans 29; The Rainbow 29; Hideout 30; Seven Keys to Baldpate 30; The Moonstone 34; The Healer • Little Pal 35; Women Must Dress 35; Forbidden Heaven 36

Barker, Will The Juvenile Barbers 06; Beckwith's Gun 10; Black and White 10; His Majesty's Guests Steal a Holiday 10; Henry VIII 11; Princess Clementina 11; She 16*

Barkett, Steve The Aftermath 80

Barkhoudian, P. The Power of Evil 29*

Barkov, Yevgeni Ivanov see Ivanov-Barkov, Yevgeni

Barlacchi, Cesare La Favorita 52; La Sonnambula 52

Barlow, Roger The Farmer, Feast or Famine 65*

Barma, Claude Of Beds and Broads • Le Parigine • Les Parisiennes • Tales of Paris 62*

Barnard, Michael Shopping Mall 85; Nights in White Satin 87

Barnes, Arthur W. White Cargo 29*; The Chinese Bungalow 30*

Barnet, Boris Miss Mend 26*; Devuchka s Korobkoi • Devushka s Korobkoi • The Girl with the Hatbox • When Moscow Laughs 27; Moscow in October • Moskva v Octyabr' 27; Dom na Trubnoi • The House on Trubnaya Square 28; The Piano 30; Production of Musical Intruments 30; Anka • Lyodolom • The Thaw 31; Prividenya 31; Borderland • Okraina • Patriots • Patrioty 33; Adin i Dysach • One and Ten 34*; By the Bluest of Seas • U Samova Sinevo Morya • U Samovo Sinyevo Morya 36*; A Night in September • Noch v Sentyabr' 39; The Old Horseman • The Old Jockey • Staryi Nayezhdnik 40; Boevoi Kinosbornik 3 • Courage • Fighting Film Album No. 3 • Manhood • Muzestvo • Muzhestvo 41; Bescennaja Golova • Boevoi Kinosbornik 10 • Fighting Film Album No. 10 • A Priceless Head 42; Men of Novgorod • The Novgorodians • Novgorodnyi 43; Dark Is the Night • Odnazhdi Noch • One Night 45; Exploit of an Intelligence Agent • Podvig Razvedchika • The Scout's Exploit • Secret Agent 47; Pages of Life • Stranitsy Zhizn 48*; Bountiful Summer • Generous Summer • Schedroye Lito 51; Concert of Masters of Ukrainian Art • Kontsert Masterov Ukrainskovo Iskusstva • Kontsert Maystriv Ukrainskogo Mystetstva 52; Liana • Lyana 55; Boryets i Kloun • The Wrestler and the Clown 57*; Poet • The Poet 57; Annushka • Anoushka 59; Alenka • Alionka 61; Polustanok • Whistle Stop 63

Barnett, Charles Betrayed 26; Dead Heat 26; The Gentleman Burglar 26; The Greatest of These 26; The Last Shot 26; Off the Scent 26; Oil on Troubled Waters 26; The Only Way Out 26; Paternal Instinct 26; The Proctor Intervenes 26; Without the Option 26; A Daughter of the Night—Psalm 69 27; Memories—Psalm 46 27; The Parting of the Ways—Psalm 57 27; The Shepherd—Psalm 23 27; The Stranger—Psalm 119 27; The Traitor—Psalm 25 27; Flames of Fear 30; Painted Pictures 30; Thoroughbred 31; A Game of Chance 32; Wedding Eve 35

Barnett, David Faust 10; Il Trovatore 10

Barnett, George Ivan The Fall of the House of Usher 49; Robbery with Violence 58; Meet Mr. Beat 61

Barnett, Ivan see Barnett, George Ivan

Barnett, Ken see Francis, Freddie

Barnett, Laurence The Hot Girls 74*
Barnwell, John Huk! 56; Surrender—Hell! 59
Baron, Allen Blast of Silence 61; Pie in the Sky • Terror in the City • The Truant 64; Outside In • Red, White and Blue • Red, White and Busted 70; Fox Fire Light 81
Baron, David see Pinter, Harold
Baron, Suzanne Les Fils de l'Eau 55*
Baron, William le see Le Baron, William
Baroncelli, Jacques de see De Baroncelli, Jacques
Barouh, Pierre Ça Va, Ça Vient • It Comes, It Goes 70; Le Divorcement 79
Barr-Smith, A. The Hangman Waits 47; Death in the Hand 48
Barralet, Paul I Want to Be an Actress 43; The Tell-Tale Taps 45; Bad Company 46; For Old Times' Sake 48; The Girl from Scotland Yard 48; Irish Melody 50
Barré, Raoul The Animated Grouch Chaser 15; Black's Mysterious Box 15; Cartoons in a Sanitarium 15; Cartoons in a Seminary 15; Cartoons in the Barber Shop 15; Cartoons in the Country 15; Cartoons in the Hotel 15; Cartoons in the Kitchen 15; Cartoons in the Laundry 15; Cartoons in the Parlor 15; Cartoons on a Yacht 15; Cartoons on the Beach 15; Cartoons on Tour 15; Hicks in Nightmareland 15; The Adventures of Tom the Tamer and Kid Kelly 16; Love's Labors Lost 16; The Story of Cook vs. Chef 16; The Bell Hops 17*; The Boarding House 17*; The Chamber of Horrors 17*; The Cheese Tamers 17*; A Chemical Calamity 17*; Cows and Caws 17*; A Day in Camp 17*; A Dog's Life 17*; In the Theatrical Business 17*; The Interpreters 17*; The Janitors 17*; Preparedness 17*; The Prospectors 17*; Revenge Is Sweet 17*; The Submarine Chasers 17*; The Accident Attorney 18*; An Ace and a Joker 18*; Around the World in Nine Minutes 18*; At the Front 18*; Back to the Balkans 18*; Bulling the Bolshevik 18*; The Burglar Alarm 18*; Coal and Cold Feet • Helping McAdoo 18*; The Decoy 18*; The Doughboy 18*; The Draft Board 18*; Efficiency 18*; The Extra Quick Lunch 18*; A Fisherless Cartoon 18*; Freight Investigation 18*; Hitting the High Spots 18*; Hospital Orderlies 18*; Hotel de Mutt 18*; Hunting the U-Boats 18*; Joining the Tanks 18*; The Kaiser's New Dentist 18*; Landing a Spy 18*; The Leak 18*; Life Savers 18*; A Lot of Bull 18*; Meeting Theda Bara 18*; The New Champion 18*; Occultism 18*; On Ice 18*; Our Four Days in Germany 18*; Pot Luck in the Army 18*; The Seventy-Five Mile Gun 18*; The Side Show 18*; Superintendents 18*; The Tale of a Pig 18*; Throwing the Ball 18*; To the Rescue 18*; Tonsorial Artists 18*; All That Glitters Is Not Goldfish 19*; Another Man's Wife 19*; The Bearded Lady 19*; Bound in Spaghetti 19*; The Cave Man's Bride 19*; The Chambermaid's Revenge 19*; Confessions of a Telephone Girl 19*; The Cow's Husband 19*; Cutting Out His Nonsense 19*; Dog-Gone Tough Luck 19*; Downstairs and Up 19*; Everybody's Doing It 19*; Fireman Save My Child 19*; 500 Miles on a Gallon of Gas 19*; For Bitter or for Verse 19*; The Frozen North 19*; Hands Up 19*; Hard Lions 19*; He Ain't Done Right by Our Nell 19*; Here and There 19*; The High Cost of Living 19*; The Honest Book Agent 19*; The Hula Hula Cabaret 19*; In the Money 19*; The Jazz Instructors 19*; Landing an Heiress 19*; Left at the Post 19*; The Lion Tamers 19*; Look Pleasant Please 19*; Mutt and Jeff in Spain 19*; Mutt and Jeff in Switzerland 19*; Mutt the Mutt Trainer 19*; New York Night Life 19*; Oh Teacher 19*; Oil's Well That Ends Well 19*; Out an' In Again 19*; Pets and Pearls 19*; Pigtails and Peaches 19*; The Plumbers 19*; The Pousse Café 19*; A Prize Fight 19*; Seeing Things 19*; The Shell Game 19*; Sir Sidney 19*; Sound Your A 19*; Subbing for Tom Mix 19*; Sweet Papa 19*; A Tropical Eggs-pedition 19*; West Is East 19*; Why Mutt Left the Village 19*; Wild Waves and Angry Women 19*; William Hohenzollern Sausage Maker 19*; The Window Cleaners 19*; All Stuck Up 20*; The Bare Idea 20*; The Beautiful Model 20*; The Berth of a Nation 20*; The Bicycle Race 20*; The Bowling Alley 20*; The Brave Toreador 20*; The Breakfast Food Industry 20*; The Chemists 20*; The Chewing Gum Industry 20*; Cleopatra 20*; The Cowpunchers 20*; Dead Eye Jeff 20*; Departed Spirits 20*; Farm Efficiency 20*; Fisherman's Luck 20*; Fishing 20*; Flapjacks 20*; A Glutton for Punishment 20*; The Great Mystery • The Mystery of the Galvanised Iron Ash Can 20*; The Great Pickle Robbery 20*; Gum Shoe Work 20*; A Hard Luck Santa Claus 20*; His Musical Soup 20*; Home Brew 20*; Home Sweet Home 20*; The Honest Jockey 20*; Hot Dogs 20*; Hula Hula Town 20*; The Hypnotist 20*; I'm Ringing Your Party 20*; In Wrong 20*; The Latest in Underwear 20*; The League of Nations 20*; The Medicine Man 20*; The Merry Cafe 20*; The Mint Spy 20*; Mutt and Jeff in Iceland 20*; Mutt and Jeff's Nooze Weekly 20*; Napoleon 20*; The North Woods 20*; Nothing But Girls 20*; On Strike 20*; On the Hop 20*; One Round Jeff 20*; The Paper Hangers 20*; The Papoose 20*; The Parlor Bolshevist 20*; The Pawnbrokers 20*; The Politicians 20*; Pretzel Farming 20*; The Price of a Good Sneeze 20*; The Private Detectives 20*; Putting on the Dog 20*; A Rose by Any Other Name 20*; The Rum Runners 20*; Shaking the Shimmy 20*; Sherlock Hawkshaw and Co. 20*; The Song Birds 20*; The Soul Violin 20*; The Tailor Shop 20*; The Tango Dancers 20*; Three Rais ins and a Cake of Yeast 20*; A Tightrope Romance 20*; The Toy Makers 20*; A Trip to Mars 20*; The Wrestlers 20*; The Yacht Race 20*; Cold Tea 21*; A Crazy Idea 21*; Crows and Scarecrows 21*; Darkest Africa 21*; Dr. Killjoy 21*; Factory to Consumer 21*; The Far East 21*; The Far North 21*; Fast Freight 21*; Flivvering 21*; Gathering Coconuts 21*; The Glue Factory 21*; The Gusher 21*; A Hard Shell Game 21*; It's a Bear 21*; The Lion Hunters 21*; Mademoiselle Fifi 21*; A Messy Christmas 21*; The Naturalists 21*; Not Wedded But a Wife 21*; The Painter's Frolic 21*; A Rare Bird 21*; Shadowed 21*; A Shocking Idea 21*; The Stampede 21*; The Tong Sandwich 21*; Touring 21*; Training Woodpeckers 21*; The Turkish Bath 21*; The Vacuum Cleaner 21*; The Ventriloquist 21*; The Village Cutups 21*; Watering the Elephants 21*; Any Ice Today 22*; Around the Pyramids 22*; Beside the Cider 22*; Bony Parts 22*; Bumps and Things 22*; The Cashier 22*; Cold Turkey 22*; Court Plastered 22*; The Crystal Gazer 22*; The Fallen Archers 22*; Falls Ahead 22*; Getting Ahead 22*; Getting Even 22*; A Ghostly Wallop 22*; Golfing 22*; Gym Jams 22*; Hither and Thither 22*; The Hole Cheese 22*; Hoot Mon 22*; Hop, Skip and Jump 22*; The Last Laugh 22*; The Last Shot 22*; Long Live the King 22*; Modern Fishing 22*; Nearing the End 22*; The Phoney Focus 22*; Riding the Goat 22*; The Stolen Snooze 22*; Stuck in the Mud 22*; Tin Foiled 22*; Too Much Soap 22*; The Wishing Duck 22*; Down in Dixie 23*
Barrera, Olegario Little Revenge • Pequeña Revancha 86; Un Domingo Feliz • A Happy Sunday 89
Barrera, Víctor Los Invitados • The Invited 87
Barreto, Bruno A Estrela Sobe 74; Dona Flor and Her Two Husbands • Dona Flor e Seus Dois Maridos 76; Amada Amante 79; Amor Bandido 79; Gabriela 83; O Beijo no Asfalto 84; Além da Paixão • Happily Ever After 85; Romance da Empregada • The Story of Fausta 88; A Show of Force 90
Barreto, Fabio King of Rio • Rei do Rio 86; Luzia 88
Barreto, Lima Painel 51; Santuário 52; The Bandit • O Cangaceiro • Cangaceiro—The Story of a Bandit • Cangaceiro—The Story of an Outlaw Bandit 53; Arte Cabocla 54; O Livro 54; O Sertanejo 54; The First Mass • A Primeira Missa 61
Barreto, Victor Lima see Barreto, Lima
Barrett, Lawrence Discipline 35*
Barrett, Lezli-An Business As Usual 87
Barrett, Richard see Piazzoli, Roberto d'Ettore
Barrière, Igor Corps Profond 63*
Barringer, A. B. Vengeance of the Deep 23; Riding to Fame 27
Barringer, Michael Blockade • Q-Ships 28*; The Infamous Lady 28*; Down Channel 29; Murder at Covent Garden 32*
Barrington, A. F. C. Langford Reed's Limericks 35
Barris, Chuck The Gong Show Movie 80
Barrish, Jerry R. Dan's Motel 82

Barron, Arthur Jeremy 73; Brothers 77
Barron, Steve Electric Dreams 84; Teenage Mutant Ninja Turtles 90
Barron, Zelda Secret Places 84; Shag • Shag: The Movie 88; Forbidden Sun 89
Barros, José Leitão de see De Barros, José Leitão
Barros, Wilson Anjos da Noite • Night Angels 87
Barrows, Nicholas Dangerous Holiday 37
Barry, Donald Jesse James' Women 54
Barry, Gerald The Last Waltz 36*
Barry, Ian Chain Reaction 80
Barry, John A. The Fear Woman 19; Passion's Playground 20; The Turning Point 20; Stranger Than Fiction 21; Trust Your Wife 21; The Woman's Side 22
Barry, Jules Karadordе 10
Barry, Michael Stop Press Girl 49
Barry, Michael The Second Coming of Suzanne • Suzanne 74
Barry, Red see Barry, Donald
Barry, Wesley The Steel Fist 52; Trail Blazers 53; The Outlaw's Daughter 54; Racing Blood 54; Creation of the Humanoids 62; The Jolly Genie 64
Barrymore, Dick Last of the Ski Bums 69
Barrymore, Lionel Life's Whirlpool 17; Absinthe • Madame X 29; Breath of Scandal • His Glorious Night 29; Confession 29; The Green Ghost 29; The Rogue Song 29*; The Unholy Night 29; Ten Cents a Dance 31
Barsha, Leon One Man Justice 37; Trapped 37; Two-Fisted Sheriff 37; Two Gun Law 37; Convicted 38; Who Killed Gail Preston? 38; Manhattan Shakedown 39; Murder Is News 39; Special Inspector 39; The Pace That Thrills 52
Barskaya, Margarita Broken Shoes 34
Barsky, Bud The Coast Patrol 25
Barta, Jiří Krysař • The Pied Piper of Hamelin 85
Bartel, Paul Progetti 62; The Secret Cinema 67; Private Parts 72; Death Race 2000 75; Cannonball • Carquake 76; Eating Raoul 82; Lust in the Dust 84; Not for Publication 84; The Longshot 86; Scenes from the Class Struggle in Beverly Hills 89
Bartenev, Sergei Dvadtsat Dva Neschastya • Twenty-Two Misfortunes • Twenty-Two Mishaps 30*
Barth, Moglia Riachuelo 34; El Dancing 35; The Last Meeting • El Último Encuentro 39; Doce Mujeres • Twelve Women 40; Huella • Trail 40
Bartlett, Charles E. The Bruiser 16; The Craving 16; The Thoroughbred 16; The Girl Who Doesn't Know 17; Hell Hath No Fury 17; Headin' North 21; Tangled Trails 21
Bartlett, Hall Unchained 55; Drango 57*; Zero Hour! 57; All the Young Men 60; Borderlines • The Caretakers 63; Changes 69; The Defiant • The Sandpit Generals • The Wild Pack 71; Jonathan Livingston Seagull 73; The Children of Sanchez 78; Comeback 82; Leaving Home

86
Bartlett, Michael Concerto for the Right Hand • Konzert für die Rechte Hand 87
Bartlett, Richard Silent Raiders 54; The Lonesome Trail 55; The Silver Star 55; I've Lived Before 56; Rock, Pretty Baby 56; Two Gun Lady 56; Joe Dakota 57; Slim Carter 57; Money, Women and Guns 58
Bartlett, Richard H. Ruby 71; The Gentle People • The Gentle People and the Quiet Land 72
Bartman, William S. O'Hara's Wife 82
Barton, Charles Caravans West • Wagon Wheels 34; Car 99 35; The Fighting Westerner • Rocky Mountain Mystery 35; The Last Outpost 35*; Nevada 35; And Sudden Death 36; Murder with Pictures 36; O'Riley's Luck • Rose Bowl 36; Timothy's Quest 36; Born to the West • Hell Town 37; The Crime Nobody Saw 37; Forlorn River 37; Thunder Pass • Thunder Trail 37; Behind Prison Gates 39; Crime's End • My Son Is Guilty 39; Five Little Peppers at Home 40; Five Little Peppers in Trouble 40; Island of Doomed Men 40; Nobody's Children 40; Out West with the Peppers 40; The Big Boss 41; Harmon of Michigan 41; Honolulu Lu 41; The Phantom Submarine 41; The Richest Man in Town 41; Sing for Your Supper 41; Two Latins from Manhattan 41; Fighting Spirit • The Spirit of Stanford 42; Hello Annapolis • Personal Honour 42; Laugh Your Blues Away • Let's Have Fun 42; Lucky Legs 42; A Man's World 42; Parachute Nurse 42; Shut My Big Mouth 42; Sweetheart of the Fleet 42; Tramp, Tramp, Tramp 42; Is Everybody Happy? 43; Reveille with Beverly 43; She Has What It Takes 43; What's Buzzin' Cousin? 43; Beautiful But Broke 44; Hey Rookie 44; Jam Session 44; Louisiana Hayride 44; The Beautiful Cheat • What a Woman! 45; Men in Her Diary 45; The Ghost Steps Out • The Time of Their Lives 46; Smooth As Silk 46; The Swindlers • White Tie and Tails 46; Buck Privates Come Home • Rookies Come Home 47; The Wistful Widow • The Wistful Widow of Wagon Gap 47; Abbott and Costello Meet Frankenstein • Abbott and Costello Meet the Ghosts 48; Mexican Hayride 48; The Noose Hangs High 48; Abbott and Costello Meet the Killer, Boris Karloff 49; Africa Screams 49; Free for All 49; Double Crossbones 50; The Milkman 50; Ma and Pa Kettle at the Fair 52; Dance with Me Henry 56; The Shaggy Dog 59; Ten Weeks with a Circus • Toby Tyler • Toby Tyler, or Ten Weeks with a Circus 60; Zorro the Avenger 60; Double Trouble • The Schnook • Swingin' Along 62
Barton, Don Blood Waters of Dr. Z • Zaat 82
Barton, Earl Trip with the Teacher 75
Barton, Otis Titans of the Deep 38
Barua, Jahnu Aparoopa 82; Apeksha 84; Papori 86; Halodhia Choraye Baodhan Khai 88
Barua, Munim Pita Putra 88

Barua, Pramatesh Chandra Devdas 35; Illusion • Maya 36; Liberation • Mukti 37; Adhikar • Authority 38; Zindigi 39; Prija Banhabi 40
Barwood, Hal Warning Sign 85
Bary, Leon The Lady of Lyons 13; In the Grip of the Sultan 15; Married for Money 15; In the Hands of the Spoilers 16
Barzini, Andrea Desiderando Giulia • Desiring Giulia 86
Basaran, Tunc Biro ve Diğerleri 88; Don't Let Them Shoot the Kite • Uçurtmayı Vurmasınlar 89
Basch, Felix Die Geliebte Roswolskys 21; Two Neckties • Zwei Kravatten 30*
Baser, Tevfik Forty Square Meters of Germany • Vierzig M Deutschland 86; Abschied von Fälschen Paradies • Farewell to False Paradise 89
Bashame, E. R. Salvage 19
Bashore, Juliet Kamikaze Hearts 86
Baskin, Richard Sing 89
Basov, Vladimir No Ordinary Summer 56; School of Courage 57; Stillness 64
Bass, Jules The Daydreamer 66; Mad Monster Party 67; The Wacky World of Mother Goose 67; Twas the Night Before Christmas 74; The Last Unicorn 82*
Bass, Saul The Searching Eye 63; From Here to There 64; Why Man Creates 68; Phase IV 73
Bassaligo, Dmitri Fight for the Ultimatum Factory 23; From Sparks, Flames 24
Bassoff, Lawrence Weekend Pass 84; Hunk 87
Bassoli, Carlo Avventura di Giacomo Casanova 38
Bastelli, Cesare Una Domenica Sì • A Good Sunday 86
Bastia, Jean Dynamite Jack 61
Bat-Adam, Michal Each Other • Moments 79; The Thin Line 80; Young Love 83; Hame'ahev • The Lover 86; Thousand and One Wives • The Thousand Wives of Naftali 89
Batalov, Alexei The Cloak • The Overcoat • Shinel 59; Three Fat Men • Tri Tolstyaka 66*
Batapoulos, Takis Youth of Athens 49
Batchelor, Joy Carnival in the Clothes Cupboard 40*; Train Trouble 40*; Dustbin Parade 41*; Filling the Gap 41*; Pocket Cartoon 41*; Digging for Victory 42*; Jungle Warfare 43*; Handling Ships 45*; Modern Guide to Health 46*; Old Wives' Tales 46*; Charley in the New Mines 47*; Charley in the New Schools 47*; Charley in the New Towns 47*; Charley in Your Very Good Health 47*; Charley Junior's Schooldays 47*; Charley's March of Time 47*; Dolly Put the Kettle On 47*; First Line of Defence 47*; Robinson Charley 47*; This Is the Air Force 47*; What's Cooking? 47*; Heave Away My Johnny 48*; Oxo Parade 48*; Fly About the House 49*; The Shoemaker and the Hatter 49*; The Owl and the Pussycat 52*; The Figurehead 53*; Animal Farm 54*; The Candlemaker 56*; Dam the Delta 58*; The First Ninety-Nine 58; All Lit Up 59*;

Winchester Jack 70; Antefatto • L'Ante-fatto—Ecologia del Delitto • Bay of Blood • Before the Fact • Blood Bath • Carnage • Ecologia del Crime • The Ecology of a Crime • Last House on the Left, Part II • Reazione a Catena • Twitch of the Death Nerve 71; Baron Blood • The Blood Baron • Chamber of Tortures • Gli Orrori del Castello di Norimberga • The Thirst of Baron Blood • The Torture Chamber of Baron Blood 72; La Casa dell' Exorcismo • Death and the Devil • The Devil and the Dead • El Diablo Se Lleva a los Muertos • Il Diavolo e i Morti • Il Diavolo e il Morto • The House of Exorcism • Lisa and the Devil • Lisa e il Diavolo • Lise e il Diavolo 72*; Four Times That Night • Quante Volte...Quella Notte 72; Cani Arrabbiati 74; All 33 di Via Orologio Fa Sempre Freddo • Beyond the Door II • Shock • Shock (Transfer Suspense Hypnos) • Suspense 76*; Baby Kong 77; La Venere dell'Ille 79

Baxley, Craig R. Action Jackson 88; Dark Angel • I Come in Peace 90

Baxter, Arnold Cynthia's Sister 75

Baxter, John County Fair • Song of the Plough 33; Doss House 33; Taking Ways 33; Flood Tide 34; Kentucky Minstrels 34; Lest We Forget 34; Music Hall 34; Say It with Flowers 34; Birds of a Feather 35; Jimmy Boy 35; A Real Bloke 35; The Small Man 35; The Crypt • Hearts of Humanity 36; Here and There 36; Men of Yesterday 36; The Academy Decides 37; Song of the Road 37; Talking Feet 37; Stepping Toes 38; Among Human Wolves • Secret Journey 39; What Would You Do Chums? 39; Crook's Tour 40; Laugh It Off 40*; Old Mother Riley in Business 40; Old Mother Riley in Society 40; The Common Touch 41; Love on the Dole 41; Old Mother Riley's Ghosts 41; Let the People Sing 42; We'll Smile Again 42; The Shipbuilders 43; Theatre Royal 43; Dreaming 44; Here Comes the Sun 45; The Grand Escapade 46; Fortune Lane 47; When You Come Home 47; The Last Load 48; Nothing Venture 48; Three Bags Full 48; The Dragon of Pendragon Castle 50; The Second Mate 50; Judgment Deferred 51; Ramsbottom Rides Again 56

Baxter, R. K. Neilson see Neilson-Baxter, R. K.

Baxter, Ronnie For the Love of Ada 72; Never Mind the Quality, Feel the Width 73

Bayer, Rolf Pacific Inferno 77

Bayer, William Mississippi Summer 68

Bayley, Frank G. The Lifeguardsman 16; One Summer's Day 17

Baylis, Peter The Finest Hours 64

Bayly, Stephen Aderyn Papur • And Pigs Might Fly 84; Coming Up Roses • Rhosyn a Rhith 86; Diamond's Edge • Just Ask for Diamond 88

Bazelian, Yakov Andriesh 54*; Dom s Mezoninom • The House with an Attic 64

Bazzoni, Camillo A Long Ride from Hell • Vivo per la Tua Morte 68; Suicide Commando 69

Bazzoni, Luigi La Donna del Lago • The Possessed 65*; Mit Django Kam der Tod 68; Evil Fingers 75

Beaird, David Octavia 84; The Party Animal 84; My Chauffeur 85; Pass the Ammo 87; It Takes Two 88

Beairsto, Ric Close to Home 86

Beal, Frank I'm Glad My Boy Grew to Be a Soldier 15; The Devil, the Servant and the Man 16; The Curse of Eve 17; The Danger Zone 18; Her Moment • Why Blame Me? 18; Mother I Need You 18; Broken Commandments 19; Chasing Rainbows 19; The Devil's Riddle 19; The Divorce Trap 19; Thieves 19; Tin Pan Alley 19; World of Folly 20; Soul and Body 21

Beal, Scott E. Convicts at Large 38*

Beal, Scott R. Just Like a Woman 23*; Straight from the Heart 35

Beale, Lee see Chase, Brandon

Bean, Robert B. Made for Each Other 71

Bear, Archie de see De Bear, Archie

Bear, Liza Force of Circumstance 90

Bearde, Chris Hysterical 83

Beardsley, Nicholas Savage Island 85*

Beattie, Alan Delusion • The House Where Death Lives 80; Stand Alone 85

Beatty, Edgar The Hippie Revolt 67

Beatty, Warren Heaven Can Wait 78*; Reds 81; Dick Tracy 90

Beauchamp, Anthony Fabian of the Yard 54

Beaucler, André Adieu les Beaux Jours 33

Beaudin, Jean J. A. Martin Photographe 76; Cordelia 80; The Alley Cat • Le Matou 86

Beaudine, William Almost a King 15; Beans and Bullets 16; A Crooked Mix-Up 16; In Love with a Fireman 16; The Inspector's Double 16; Jags and Jealousy 16; A Janitor's Vendetta 16; Love in Suspense 16; Mines and Matrimony 16; Musical Madness 16; Scrappily Married 16; A Shadowed Shadow 16; The Tale of a Turk 16; Their Dark Secret 16; Their First Arrest 16; The Tramp Chef 16; When Damon Fell for Pythias 16; Art Aches 17; A Bad Little Good Man 17; Barred from a Bar 17; The Battling Bellboy 17; Behind the Map 17; A Boob for Luck 17; The Boss of the Family 17; Canning the Cannibal King 17; The Careless Cop 17; The Cross-Eyed Submarine 17; The Fountain of Trouble 17; Hawaiian Nuts 17; He Had 'Em Buffaloed 17; His Coming-Out Party 17; His Fatal Beauty 17; The Leak 17; Left in the Soup 17; Love Me, Love My Biscuits 17; The Man with a Package 17; Mule Mates 17; O-My, the Tent Mover 17; Officer, Call a Cop 17; One Damp Day 17; The Onion Hero 17; Out Again, In Again 17; Out for the Dough 17; Passing the Grip 17; Secret Servants 17; 20,000 Legs Under the Sea 17; Uneasy Money 17; Wanta Make a Dollar? 17; What the ----? 17; What'll We Do with Uncle? 17; Who Done It 17; Whose Baby? 17; Why They Left Home 17; Eddie, Get the Mop 18; Mixed Wives 19; Catch My Smoke 22; Heroes of the Street 22; Punch the Clock 22; Strictly Modern 22; Watch Your Step 22; Boy of Mine 23; The Country Kid 23; Her Fatal Millions 23; Lovers' Lane 23*; Penrod and Sam 23; The Printer's Devil 23; Cornered 24; Daring Youth 24; Daughters of Pleasure 24; The Narrow Street 24; A Self-Made Failure 24; Wandering Husbands 24; A Broadway Butterfly 25; How Baxter Butted In 25; Little Annie Rooney 25; The Canadian 26; Hold That Lion 26; Human Sparrows • Sparrows 26; The Social Highwayman 26; That's My Baby 26; Frisco Sally Levy 27; The Irresistible Lover 27; The Life of Riley 27; The Cohens and the Kellys in Paris 28; Do Your Duty 28; Give and Take 28; Heart to Heart 28; Home James 28; Fugitives 29; The Girl from Woolworth's 29; Hard to Get 29; Two Weeks Off 29; Wedding Rings 29; A Hollywood Theme Song 30; Road to Paradise 30; Those Who Dance 30; The College Vamp 31; Father's Son 31; Forgotten Women • The Mad Parade 31; The Great Junction Hotel 31; The Lady Who Dared 31; Men in Her Life 31; Misbehaving Ladies 31; One Yard to Go 31; Penrod and Sam 31; Three Wise Girls 31; Make Me a Star 32; The Crime of the Century 33; Her Bodyguard 33; Dandy Dick 34; Dream Stuff 34; The Old-Fashioned Way 34; See You Tonight 34; Trick Golf 34; Boys Will Be Boys 35; Get Off My Foot 35; Mr. Cohen Takes a Walk 35; Two Hearts in Harmony 35; Educated Evans 36; Good Morning, Boys 36; It's in the Bag 36; Where There's a Will 36; Windbag the Sailor 36; Feather Your Nest 37; Said O'Reilly to McNab • Says O'Reilly to Mc-Nab • Sez O'Reilly to McNab 37; Take It from Me • Transatlantic Trouble 37; Torchy Blane in Chinatown 38; Torchy Gets Her Man 38; Up Jumped the Devil 39; Condemned Men 40; Dummy Trouble • Misbehaving Husbands 40; Lady Luck 40; Mr. Washington Goes to Town 40*; She Done Him Right 40; The Blonde Comet 41; Desperate Cargo 41; Emergency Landing 41; Federal Fugitives 41; The Miracle Kid 41; Mr. Celebrity 41; Prison Girl • The Warden's Daughter 41; Broadway Big Shot 42; Do Not Disturb • No Time for Love • One Thrilling Night 42; Duke of the Navy 42; Foreign Agent 42; Gallant Lady • Prison Girls 42; Lend Me Your Ear • The Living Ghost 42; Men of San Quentin 42; The Panther's Claw 42; The Phantom Killer 42; Professor Creeps 42; The Ape Man • The Gorilla Strikes • Lock Your Doors 43; Clancy Street Boys • Grand Street Boys 43; The East Side Kids Meet Bela Lugosi • Ghosts in the Night • Ghosts on the Loose 43; Her Bachelor Husband • What a Man! 43; Here Comes Kelly 43; The Honor System • Mr. Muggs Steps Out 43; The Mystery of the 13th Guest 43; Spotlight on Scandal • Spotlight Revue • Spotlight Scandals 43; Adventures of Kitty O'Day 44; The Arizona Story 44; Bowery

Champs • Mr. Muggs Meets a Deadline 44; Crazy Knights • Ghost Crazy • Murder in the Family 44; Detective Kitty O'Day 44; East of the Bowery • Follow the Leader 44; A Family Story • Mom and Dad 44; Hot Rhythm 44; Leave It to the Irish 44; Oh, What a Night! 44; Shadow of Suspicion • Shadows of Suspicion 44; The Tiger Man • Voodoo Man 44; Black Market Babies 45; Blonde Ransom 45; Come Out Fighting 45; Fashion Model • The Model Murder 45; Swingin' on a Rainbow 45; Below the Deadline 46; Don't Gamble with Strangers 46; Face of Marble 46; Girl on the Spot 46; Mr. Hex • The Pride of the Bowery 46; One Exciting Week 46; Spook Busters 46; Bowery Buckaroos 47; The Chinese Ring • The Red Hornet 47; Gas House Kids Go West 47; Hard Boiled Mahoney 47; Infamous Crimes • Philo Vance Returns 47; Killer at Large 47; News Hound • News Hounds 47; Too Many Winners 47; Angels' Alley 48; Charlie Chan and the Golden Eye • The Golden Eye • The Mystery of the Golden Eye 48; The Feathered Serpent 48; Incident 48; Jiggs and Maggie in Court 48*; Jinx Money 48; Kidnapped 48; The Shanghai Chest 48; Smugglers' Cove 48; Blonde Dynamite 49; Blue Grass of Kentucky 49; Forgotten Women 49; Jackpot Jitters • Jiggs and Maggie in Jackpot Jitters 49; The Lawton Story 49*; The Prince of Peace 49*; Tough Assignment 49; Trail of the Yukon 49; Tuna Clipper 49; Again—Pioneers! 50; Blues Busters • Bowery Thrush 50; County Fair 50; Ghost Chasers 50; Jiggs and Maggie Out West 50; Lucky Losers 50; Second Chance 50; Bowery Battalion 51; The Congregation 51; Crazy Over Horses • Win, Place and Show 51; Cuban Fireball 51; Havana Rose 51; Let's Go Navy! 51; Rodeo 51; A Wonderful Life 51; Bela Lugosi Meets a Brooklyn Gorilla • The Boys from Brooklyn • The Monster Meets the Gorilla 52; Bowery Leathernecks • Here Come the Marines • Tell It to the Marines 52; Feudin' Fools 52; Hold That Line 52; Jet Job 52; No Holds Barred 52; The Rose Bowl Story 52; Born to the Saddle 53; For Every Child 53; The Hidden Heart 53; Jalopy 53; Murder Without Tears 53; Roar of the Crowd 53; City Story 54; More for Peace 54; Paris Playboys 54; Pride of the Blue Grass • Prince of the Blue Grass 54; Stryker's Progress 54; Yukon Vengeance 54; Bowery Boys • High Society 55; Each According to His Faith 55; Jail Busters 55; Westward Ho the Wagons! 56; In the Money 57; Up in Smoke 57; Moochie of the Little League 59; Ten Who Dared 60; Lassie's Great Adventure • Lassie's Greatest Adventure 63; Beyond the Moon 64*; Billy the Kid vs. Dracula 65; Jesse James Meets Frankenstein's Daughter 66

Beaudry, Jean Jacques and November • Jacques et Novembre 85*

Beaumont, Gabrielle The Godsend 79; Corvini Inheritance 84; He's My Girl • Pulling It Off 87

Beaumont, Harry The Call of the City 15; Her Happiness 15; The Truant Soul • Truant Souls 16; Brown of Harvard 17; Burning the Candle 17; Filling His Own Shoes 17; Skinner's Baby 17; Skinner's Bubble 17; Skinner's Dress Suit 17; Thirty a Week 18; The City of Comrades 19; The Gay Lord Quex 19; Go West, Young Man 19; Heartsease 19; Little Rowdy 19; Lord and Lady Algy 19; A Man and His Money 19; One of the Finest 19; Toby's Bow 19; Wild Goose Chase 19; Dollars and Sense 20; Going Some 20; The Great Accident 20; Officer 666 20; Stop Thief! 20; The Fourteenth Lover 21; Glass Houses 21; The Five Dollar Baby 22; June Madness 22; Lights of the Desert 22; Love in the Dark 22; The Ragged Heiress 22; Seeing's Believing 22; They Like 'Em Rough 22; Very Truly Yours 22; Crinoline and Romance 23; The Gold Diggers 23; Main Street 23; A Noise in Newboro 23; Babbitt 24; Beau Brummel 24; Don't Doubt Your Husband 24; A Lost Lady 24; The Lover of Camille 24; His Majesty Bunker Bean 25; Recompense 25; Rose of the World 25; Sandy 26; Womanpower 26; One Increasing Purpose 27; The Broadway Melody 28; Forbidden Hours 28; Our Dancing Daughters 28; A Single Man 28; Lord Byron of Broadway • What Price Melody? 29*; Speedway 29; Blushing Brides • Our Blushing Brides 30; Children of Pleasure 30; Dance, Fools, Dance 30; The Floradora Girl • The Gay Nineties 30; Those Three French Girls 30; The Great Lover 31; Laughing Sinners 31; West of Broadway 31; Are You Listening? 32; Faithless 32; Unashamed 32; The Girl I Made • Made on Broadway 33; Should Ladies Behave? 33; Truth Is Stranger • When Ladies Meet 33; Murder in the Private Car • Murder on the Runaway Train 34; Enchanted April 35; The Girl on the Front Page 36; When's Your Birthday? 37*; Maisie Goes to Reno • You Can't Do That to Me 44; Twice Blessed 45; Up Goes Maisie • Up She Goes 45; The Show-Off 46; Alias a Gentleman 47; Undercover Girl • Undercover Maisie 47

Beaumont, L. C. The Beauty Doctor 36; Cocktail 36

Beauvais, Peter Ein Fliehendes Pferd • A Runaway Horse 86

Beaver, Chris Dark Circle 82*

Beaver, Lee W. see Lizzani, Carlo

Beban, George Hearts of Men 19; One Man in a Million 21; The Greatest Love of All 24; The Loves of Ricardo 26

Bechard, Gorman Disconnected 84; And Then? 85; Psychos in Love 86; Club Earth • Galactic Gigolo 87; Hack 'Em High 87; Pandevil 88; Teenage Slasher Sluts 88; Twenty Questions 88

Beck, George Behave Yourself! 51

Beck, Martin Any Night 22

Beck, Martin Challenge 74; The Brass Ring 75; The Last Game 83; Manhunter 83

Beck, Reginald Henry V 44*; The Long Dark Hall 51*

Beck, Walter Der Barenhäuter • Bear-Skinned Man 87

Beck-Gaden, Hans Grenzfeuer 36

Becker, Fred G. The Girl from Rocky Point 22

Becker, Harold Interview with Bruce Gordon 64; The Ragman's Daughter 72; The Black Marble 79; The Onion Field 79; Taps 81; Vision Quest 85; The Boost 88; Sea of Love 89

Becker, Israel The Flying Matchmaker • Shnei Kuni Lemel • Two Kouney Lemels 66

Becker, Jacques Le Commissaire Est Bon Enfant • Le Gendarme Est Sans Pitié • The Superintendent Is a Good Sort 34*; Le Bourreau • Tête de Turc • Une Tête Qui Rapporte 35; Communist Party Congress à Arles • Communist Party Congress Documentary at Arles 38; The Gold of Christobal • L'Or du Cristobal 39*; Le Dernier Atout • The Last Trump 42; Goupi-Mains-Rouges • It Happened at the Inn • It Happened in the Inn 43; Falbalas • Paris Frills 45; Antoine and Antoinette • Antoine et Antoinette 46; Rendez-Vous de Juillet • Rendezvous in July 48; Édouard et Caroline • Edward and Caroline 51; Casque d'Or • Golden Helmet • Golden Marie 52; Don't Touch the Loot • Grisbi • Hands Off the Loot • Honour Among Thieves • Touchez Pas au Grisbi 53; Françoise Steps Out • Rue de l'Estrapade 53; Ali Baba • Ali Baba and the Forty Thieves • Ali Baba et les Quarante Voleurs 54; The Adventures of Arsène Lupin • Les Aventures d'Arsène Lupin 56; The Lovers of Montparnasse • Modigliani of Montparnasse • Montparnasse • Montparnasse 19 57; Il Buco • The Hole • The Night Watch • Le Trou 59

Becker, Jean A Man Named Rocca • Un Nommé la Rocca 61; Backfire • Échappement Libre • Escape Libre • Scappamento Aperto 64; Pas de Caviar pour Tante Olga 65; Un Avventuriero a Tahiti • Tender Scoundrel • Tendre Voyou 66; L'Été Meurtrier • One Deadly Summer 83

Becker, Josh Thou Shalt Not Kill...Except 85

Becker, Terry The Blood Cult of Shangri-La • The Thirsty Dead 75

Becker, V. Ich Bin Sebastian Otto 39*

Becker, Vernon The Great Stone Face 68; The Groove Room 74

Becker, Wolfgang Meet Peter Foss 58

Beckett, James ¿Qué Hacer? • What Is to Be Done? 70*

Beckhard, Arthur J. Girl on the Run 61*

Bedford, Terry Slayground 83

Beebe, Ford The Honor of the Range 20*; The Big Payoff • The Pride of the Legion 32; The Last of the Mohicans • Return of the Mohicans 32*; The Shadow of the Eagle 32; Laughing at Life 33; The Adventures of Rex and Rinty 35*; Law Beyond the Range 35; The Man from Guntown 35; Ace Drummond 36*; Stampede 36; Jungle Jim 37*; Radio Patrol 37*; Secret Agent X-9 37*; Tim Tyler's Luck

37; Trouble at Midnight 37; Westbound Limited 37; Wild West Days 37*; The Deadly Ray from Mars • Flash Gordon: Mars Attacks the World • Flash Gordon's Trip to Mars • Mars Attacks the World 38*; Red Barry 38*; Buck Rogers • Destination Saturn 39*; Oklahoma Frontier 39; The Oregon Trail 39*; The Phantom Creeps 39*; Flash Gordon Conquers the Universe • Perils from the Planet Mongo • Purple Death from Outer Space 40*; The Green Hornet 40*; The Green Hornet Strikes Again 40*; Junior G-Men 40*; Son of Roaring Dan 40; Winners of the West 40*; The Masked Rider 41; The Reluctant Dragon 41*; Riders of Death Valley 41*; Sea Raiders 41*; Sky Raiders 41*; Don Winslow of the Navy 42*; Gang Busters 42*; House of Mystery • The Night Monster 42; Overland Mail 42*; Frontier Bad Men 43*; Enter Arsène Lupin 44; The Invisible Man's Revenge 44; Easy to Look At 45; My Dog Shep 46; Six Gun Serenade 47; Courtin' Trouble 48; Shep Comes Home 48; Bomba on Panther Island • Panther Island 49; Bomba, the Jungle Boy 49; The Dalton Gang • Outlaw Gang 49; Red Desert 49; Satan's Cradle 49; Bomba and the Hidden City • The Hidden City 50; Bomba and the Lost Volcano • The Lost Volcano 50; Bomba and the Elephant Stampede • Elephant Stampede 51; Bomba and the Lion Hunters • The Lion Hunters 51; African Treasure • Bomba and the African Treasure 52; Bomba and the Jungle Girl • Jungle Girl 52; Wagons West 52; Bomba and the Safari Drums • Safari Drums 53; The Golden Idol 54; Killer Leopard 54*; Lord of the Jungle 55; Alaska Boy • Frontier Alaska • Joniko • Joniko and the Kush Ta Ka 69; Challenge to Be Free • The Mad Trapper • Mad Trapper of the Yukon 72*

Beech, John Goosey Goosey 73
Beek, Hans van Donna Donna! 87*
Beek, Luc van Donna Donna! 87*
Beeman, Greg License to Drive 88
Begeja, Liria Avril Brise • Broken April 87

Beggs, Lee Folks from Way Down East 24

Beggs, W. G. Fistful of Rawhide 70
Behagan, Miki Ha' Instalator • The Plumber 87

Behat, Gilles Urgence 85; The Long Coats • Les Longs Manteaux 86; Charlie Dingo • Charlie Loco 87

Behi, Ridha La Mémoire Tatouée 86
Behrendt, Hans A Royal Scandal 29; Danton 31; Gloria 32; Ich Geh' Aus und Du Bleibst Da 32; Hochzeit am Wolfgangsee 34; Doña Francisquita 35; Grün Ist die Heide 35

Behrens, Alfred S-Bahn Pictures 82; Walkman Blues 86

Beiersdorf, Dagmar Der Sexte Sinn • The Sexth Sense 86*

Beineix, Jean-Jacques Diva 80; La Lune dans le Caniveau • The Moon in the Gutter 83; Betty Blue • 37.2 Degrés le Matin

• 37°2 le Matin 86; Roselyne and the Lions • Roselyne et les Lions 89

Beizai, Bahram Gharibeh-Va-Meh • The Stranger and the Fog 74; Bashu, the Little Stranger 90

Bek-Nazarov, Amo In the Pillory • U Pozernovo Stolba 24; Honor • Namus 26; Natella 26; Khaz-Push 27; Zare 27; The House on a Volcano 28; Igdenbu 30; Pepo 35; Zanguezour 38; David-Bek 44; Anait 48; The New Residence 55

Bekes, George The Ballad of Dickie Jones 71

Belding, Richard Sloane 86*
Beleta, Rovira see Rovira-Beleta
Beleyev, Vassili see Belyaev, Vasily
Belgard, Arnold The Big Search • East of Kilimanjaro • La Grande Caccia 57*; The Mighty Jungle 64*

Belikov, Mikhail How Young We Were Then • Kak Molody My Byli • When We Were Young 85

Bell, Colin For Your Entertainment 52; The Rescue Squad 63

Bell, J. Ford Dangerous Relations 73
Bell, Jorge El Pulpo Humano 35
Bell, Martin Streetwise 84
Bell, Monta Broadway After Dark 24; How to Educate a Wife 24; Lady of the Night 24; The Snob 24; Ibáñez' Torrent • The Torrent 25*; The King on Main Street 25; Lights of Old Broadway • Merry Wives of Gotham 25; Pretty Ladies 25; The Boy Friend 26; The Mask of Comedy • Upstage 26; After Midnight 27; Man, Woman and Sin 27; The Bellamy Trial 28; East Is West 30; Young Man of Manhattan 30; The Fires of Youth • Up for Murder 31; Personal Maid 31*; Downstairs 32; The Worst Woman in Paris 33; China's Little Devils • Little Devils 45

Bellamy, Earl Seminole Uprising 55; Blackjack Ketchum, Desperado 56; Toughest Gun in Tombstone 58; Stagecoach to Dancer's Rock 62; Fluffy 65; The Faceless Men • Incident at Phantom Hill 66; Gunpoint 66; Munster Go Home 66; Three Guns for Laredo • Three Guns for Texas 67*; Backtrack 69; Joaquin Murrieta 70; Against a Crooked Sky 75; House Without Windows • Seven Alone 75; Part 2, Walking Tall • Walking Tall, Part 2 75; Sidecar Racers 75; Sidewinder One 77; Speedtrap 77; Magnum Thrust 81

Bellamy, George Broken Barrier • Quicksands 17

Bellisario, Donald P. Last Rites 88
Bellmunt, Francesc Crazy Radio • La Radio Folla 86

Bello, John de see De Bello, John
Bellocchio, Marco Abbasso lo Zio 61; La Colpa e la Pena 61; Ginepro Fatto Uomo 62; Between Two Worlds • Fist in His Pocket • Fists in the Pocket • I Pugni in Tasca 65; China Is Near • La Cina È Vicina 66*; Amore e Rabbia • La Contestation • Love and Anger • Vangelo '70 67*; Paola 69*; Viva il Primo Maggio Rosso 69*; In il Nome del Padre • In the Name of the Father • Nel Nome del Padre 71; Beat the

Monster on Page One • Rape on the Front Page • Sbatti il Mostro in Prima Pagina • Strike the Monster on Page One 72; Fit to Be Untied • Matti da Slegare • Nessuno o Tutti, Matti da Slegare 74*; La Marche Triomphale • Marcia Trionfale • Triumphal March • Victory March 75; Il Gabbiano 77; Les Yeux Fertiles 77; La Macchina Cinema 78; Leap Into the Void • Salto nel Vuoto 79; Vacanze in Val Trebbia 80; The Eyes, the Mouth • Gli Occhi, la Bocca • Les Yeux, la Bouche 82; Enrico IV • Henry IV 84; The Devil in the Flesh • Il Diavolo in Corpo 86; La Visione del Sabba 87

Bellon, Yannick Goémons 47; Colette 50; Varsovie Quand Même 53; Un Matin Comme les Autres 54; The Compass • Die Windrose • The Windrose 56*; Le Second Souffle 59; Zaa le Petit Chameau Blanc 60; Le Bureau des Mariages 62; Quelque Part, Quelqu'un 72; La Femme de Jean 73; Jamais Plus Toujours 75; L'Amour Violé • Rape of Love • Violated Love 77; La Triche 84; Les Enfants du Désordre 89

Belmar, Henry Life's Shop Window 14*
Belmont, Charles L'Écume des Jours 68; Rak 71; L'Histoire d'A 74; Pour Clemence 77

Belmont, Joseph Prejudice 22
Belmont, Vera Red Kiss • Rouge Baiser 85

Belmore, Lionel Britton of the Seventh 16; The Supreme Sacrifice 16*; The Wasp 18

Belson, Jerry Jekyll and Hyde…Together Again 82; Surrender 87

Belson, Jordan Phenomena 68
Belyaev, Vasily Black Sea Fighters 43; People's Avengers 44; Russia on Parade 46*; Lenin • Vladimir Ilyich Lenin 48*

Bemberg, María Luisa Momentos 81; Señora de Nadie 82; Camila 84; Miss Mary 86

Ben-Ami, Jacob Green Fields • Greene Felde • Grüner Felder 37*

Ben Ammar, Abdel-Latif Aziza 80
Ben Mabrouk, Nadjia Sama 88
Benacerraf, Margot Araya 58
Benavides, José Tierra de Pasiones 44
Benazeraf, José Paris Erotika • Paris Ooh-La-La • 24 Heures d'un Américain à Paris 63; Le Cri de la Chair • Romance on the Beach • Sin on the Beach 64; Le Concerto de la Peur • Night of Love • Night of Lust • Notte Érotique 65

Bencivenga, Edoardo La DuBarry 14
Bendell, Don The Instructor 83
Bender, Erich Helga 67*
Bender, Joel Gas Pump Girls 79; The Returning 83

Bendick, Robert Cinerama Holiday 55*
Bendit, Daniel Cohn see Cohn-Bendit, Daniel

Benedek, Laslo The Kissing Bandit 48; Port of New York 49; Death of a Salesman 51; Mask of the Himalayas • Storm Over Tibet 51; The Wild One 53; Bengal Brigade • Bengal Rifles 54; Kinder, Mütter und ein General 55; Affair in Havana 57; Malaga • Moment of Danger • The Takers

59; Recours en Grâce 60; Namu, the Killer Whale 66; The Daring Game • The Unkillables 67; The Night Visitor 70; Assault on Agathon 74

Benedetti, A. The Uncle from America • Lo Zio d'America 39

Benedict, Richard Winter à Go-Go 65; Golden Bullet • Impasse 69

Benedict, Tony Santa and the Three Bears 70

Benegal, Shyam Child of the Streets 67; Close to Nature 67; The Flower Path • Poovanam 68; Indian Youth: An Exploration 68; Sinhasta, or The Path to Immortality 68; Horoscope for a Child 69; The Pulsating Giant 71; Raga and the Emotions 71; Sruti and Graces of Indian Music 71; Steel: A Whole New Way of Life 71; Thaal and Rhythm 71; Foundations of Progress 72; Notes on the Green Revolution 72; Power to the People 72; Ankur • The Seedling 74; Quiet Revolution 74; Charandas Chor • Charandas the Thief 75; Learning Modules for Rural Children 75; Night's End • Nishant 75; The Churning • Manthan 76; Epilepsy 76; Tomorrow Begins Today: Industrial Research 76; Anugrahan • The Boon • Kondura • The Sage from the Sea 77; Bhumika • The Role 77; New Horizons in Steel 77; Flight of Pigeons • Junoon • The Obsession • Possessed 78; Hari Hondal Bargadar • Share Cropper 80; Kalyug • The Machine Age 80; Arohan • Ascending Scale • The Ascent 82; Jawaharlal Nehru 82; Satyajit Ray, Film Maker 82; Mandi • The Marketplace 83; The Essence • Susman 86; Past, Present, Future • Trikal 86

Bengell, Norma Eternamente Pagu 88

Benhadj, Mohamed Rachid Louss • Rose of the Desert 89

Benigni, Roberto Tu Mi Turbi 82; Non Ci Resta Che Piangere 84; Il Piccolo Diavolo 88

Benjamin, Richard My Favorite Year 82; City Heat 84; Racing with the Moon 84; The Money Pit 86; Little Nikita 88; My Stepmother Is an Alien 88; Downtown 90; Mermaids 90

Benlyazid, Farida Bab Sama Maftouh 88

Bennati, Giuseppe Fausses Ingénues • Labbra Rosse • Red Lips 64

Benner, Richard London Drag 70; Outrageous! 77; Happy Birthday Gemini 80; Too Outrageous! 87

Bennet, Spencer G. Behold the Man 21*; Plunder 23*; The Green Archer 25; Play Ball 25; The Fighting Marine 26; The House Without a Key 26; Snowed In 26; Hawk of the Hills 27; Melting Millions 27; The Man Without a Face 28; Marked Money 28; The Terrible People 28; The Tiger's Shadow 28; The Yellow Cameo 28; The Black Book 29*; The Fire Detective 29; Queen of the Northwoods 29; Rogue of the Rio Grande 30; Isle of Lost Wranglers • Ninety-Nine Wounds 31; The Mystery of Compartment C 31; Nick Harris 31; The Last Frontier 32*; Midnight Warning 32; Jaws of Justice 33; Justice Takes a Holi-

day 33; Badge of Honor 34; Dangerous Enemy • The Fighting Rookie 34; The Ferocious Pal • His Ferocious Pal 34; Night Alarm 34; The Oil Raider 34; Young Eagles 34; Calling All Cars 35; Get That Man 35; Heir to Trouble 35; Lawless Riders 35; Rescue Squad 35; Western Courage 35; Avenging Waters 36; The Cattle Thief 36; The Fugitive Sheriff • Law and Order 36; Heroes of the Range 36; Ranger Courage 36; Rio Grande Ranger 36; The Unknown Ranger 36; Law of the Ranger 37; The Mysterious Pilot 37; The Rangers Step In 37; The Reckless Ranger 37; Across the Plains • Riders of the Rio Grande 39; Oklahoma Terror 39; Riders of the Frontier 39; Westbound Stage 39; The Cowboy from Sundown 40; Arizona Bound • Rough Riders 41; Arizona Ranch Hands • Ridin' the Cherokee Trail 41; Bad Man from Bodie • The Gunman from Bodie 41; The Secret Code 42; They Raid by Night • They Raid by Night: A Story of the Commandos 42; The Valley of Vanishing Men 42; The Baron's African War • Secret Service in Darkest Africa 43; California Joe 43; Calling Wild Bill Elliott 43; Canyon City 43; The Masked Marvel • Sakima and the Masked Marvel 43; Beneath Western Skies 44; Code of the Prairie 44; Haunted Harbor 44*; Jungle Gold • Perils of the Darkest Jungle • The Tiger Woman 44*; Mojave Firebrand 44; Tucson Raiders 44; Zorro's Black Whip 44*; Captain Mephisto and the Transformation Machine • Manhunt of Mystery Island 45*; D-Day on Mars • The Purple Monster Strikes 45*; FBI 99 • Federal Operator 99 45*; Lone Texas Ranger 45; The Black Widow • Sombra the Spider Woman 46*; Daughter of Don Q 46*; King of the Forest Rangers 46*; The Phantom Rider 46*; Brick Bradford 47; Son of Zorro 47*; Adventures of Sir Galahad 48; Bruce Gentry • Bruce Gentry—Daredevil of the Skies 48*; Congo Bill 48*; Superman 48*; Batman and Robin • The New Adventures of Batman and Robin • The Return of Batman 49; Atom Man vs. Superman 50; Cody of the Pony Express 50; Pirates of the High Seas 50*; Roar of the Iron Horse 50*; Captain Video 51*; Mysterious Island 51; Blackhawk 52*; Brave Warrior 52; King of the Congo 52*; Son of Geronimo 52; Voodoo Tiger 52; Gunfighters of the Northwest 53; Killer Ape 53; The Lost Planet 53; Savage Mutiny 53; Riding with Buffalo Bill 54; Adventures of Captain Africa 55; Devil Goddess 55; Phantom of the Jungle 55; Blazing the Overland Trail 56; Perils of the Wilderness 56; Submarine Seahawk 58; The Atomic Submarine 59; The Bounty Killer 65; Requiem for a Gunfighter 65

Bennett, Bill A Street to Die 85; Backlash 86; Dear Cardholder 87; Jilted 87; Malpractice 89

Bennett, Charles Madness of the Heart 49; City on a Hunt • No Escape 53

Bennett, Chester A Master Stroke 20; The Purple Cipher 20; The Romance Pro-

moters 20; When a Man Loves 20; Diamonds Adrift 21; The Secret of the Hills 21; Three Sevens 21; Belle of Alaska 22; Colleen of the Pines 22; The Snowshoe Trail 22; Thelma 22; Divorce 23; The Lullaby 24; The Painted Lady 24; The Ancient Mariner 25*; The Champion of Lost Causes 25; Honesty—The Best Policy 26

Bennett, Compton Find, Fix and Strike 41; Freedom Must Have Wings 41; Men of Rochdale 44; Julius Caesar 45; The Seventh Veil 45; Daybreak 46; The Years Between 46; My Own True Love 48; The Forsyte Saga • That Forsyte Woman 49; King Solomon's Mines 50*; So Little Time 51; Fanfare for Figleaves • It Started in Paradise 52; The Gift Horse • Glory at Sea 52; Desperate Moment 53; After the Ball 57; City After Midnight • That Woman Opposite 57; The Flying Scot • Mailbag Robbery 57; Beyond the Curtain 60; First Left Past Aden 61; How to Undress in Public Without Undue Embarrassment 65

Bennett, Edward Ascendancy 82

Bennett, Hugh Henry Aldrich for President 41; Henry Aldrich, Editor 42; Henry Aldrich Gets Glamour 42; Henry and Dizzy 42; Henry Aldrich Haunts a House 43; Henry Aldrich Swings It 43; Henry Aldrich, Boy Scout 44; Henry Aldrich Plays Cupid 44; Henry Aldrich's Little Secret 44; National Barn Dance 44

Bennett, Richard Harper Valley P.T.A. 78; A State of Emergency 86

Bennett, Rodney Sense and Sensibility 86

Bennett, Wallace C. George 73

Bennett, Whitman Wife Against Wife 21; Love of Women 24; Two Shall Be Born 24; Virtuous Liars 24; Back to Life 25; Children of the Whirlwind 25; Lena Rivers 25; Scandal Street 25; Share and Share Alike 25

Bennett, William The Iron Man • A Man of Iron 25

Benning, James 11 x 14 77; Landscape Suicide 86

Bennison, Andrew Men Without Women 29*; Born Reckless 30*; This Sporting Age 32*

Benoit, Ben Blood of the Iron Maiden • Is This Trip Really Necessary? • Trip to Terror 69

Benoît, Jacques W. Comment Faire l'Amour avec un Nègre Sans Se Fatiguer • How to Make Love to a Negro Without Getting Tired 89

Benoît, Jean-Louis Les Poings Fermés 85

Benoît-Lévy, Jean Âmes d'Enfants 22; Pasteur 22*; Peau de Pêche 25*; The Holy Veil • Le Voile Sacré 26; The Nest • Le Nid 26; Maternité • Maternity 27*; Âmes d'Enfants • The Souls of Children 28*; Jimmy Bruiteur • Le Petit Jimmy 30*; Le Chant de la Mine et du Feu 31; Le Cœur de Paris 31*; Children of Montmartre • La Maternelle • Nursery School 32*; Itto • Itto d'Afrique 34*; Hélène 36; Altitude 3200 • Youth in Revolt 37*; Ballerina • La Mort du Cygne 37; Le Feu de Paille • Fire in the Straw 39

Benpar, Carlos *see Parra, Carlos Benito*
Benson, Leon Flipper and the Pirates • Flipper's New Adventure 64
Benson, Richard *see Heusch, Paolo*
Benson, Robby Crack in the Mirror • Do It Up • White Hot 87; Modern Love 90
Benson, Roy Joey and Sam 65
Benson, Steven Endgame 84
Benstead, Geoffrey Hints on Horsemanship 24; Naughty Husbands 30; Stepping Stones 31; The Television Follies 33; Cavalcade of the Stars 38; It Happened in Leicester Square 49
Bentley, Bob Recluse 81
Bentley, Christopher *see Amar, Denis*
Bentley, Thomas Leaves from the Books of Charles Dickens 12; The Miracle 12; Oliver Twist 12; David Copperfield 13; The Old Curiosity Shop 13; The Chimes 14; Barnaby Rudge 15; Hard Times 15; A Soul for Sale • The Woman Who Dared 15; Beau Brocade 16; Milestones 16; Les Cloches de Corneville 17; Daddy 17; The Labour Leader 17; The Divine Gift 18; Once Upon a Time 18; The Lackey and the Lady 19; Beyond the Dreams of Avarice 20; General Post 20; The Adventures of Mr. Pickwick 21; The Old Curiosity Shop 21; A Master of Craft 22; The Battle of Love 23; The Courage of Despair 23; The Last Stake 23; Secret Mission 23; Shadow of Death 23; Through Fire and Water 23; The Velvet Woman 23; After Dark 24; The Cavern Spider 24; Chappy, That's All 24; Love and Hate 24; Old Bill Through the Ages 24; Wanted, a Boy 24; Money Isn't Everything 25; A Romance of Mayfair • A Romance of the Mayfair 25; The Man in the Street • Man of Mystery 26; White Heat 26; The Antidote 27; The Silver Lining 27; Not Quite a Lady 28; Acci-dental Treatment 29; The American Prisoner 29; Young Woodley 29; Compromised! • Compromising Daphne 30; Harmony Heaven 30; It's a Deal 30; Young Woodley 30; Hobson's Choice 31; Keepers of Youth 31; After Office Hours 32; The Last Coupon 32; Sleepless Nights 32; Hawleys of High Street 33; The Living Dead • The Scotland Yard Mystery 33; The Love Nest 33; The Great Defender 34; The Old Curiosity Shop 34; Those Were the Days 34; Music Hath Charms 35*; Regal Cavalcade • Royal Cavalcade 35*; She Knew What She Wanted 36; The Angelus • Who Killed Fen Markham? 37; The Last Chance 37; Murder at the Baskervilles • Silver Blaze 37; Marigold 38; A Night Alone 38; Dead Man's Shoes 39; Lucky to Me 39; Me and My Pal 39; The Middle Watch 39; Cavalcade of Variety 40; Three Silent Men 40; Old Mother Riley's Circus 41
Benton, Robert A Texas Romance—1909 64; Bad Company 72; The Late Show 76; Kramer vs. Kramer 79; Still of the Night 82; Places in the Heart 84; Nadine 87
Benveniste, Michael Flesh Gordon 74*
Benvenuti, Alessandro Era una Notte

Buia e Tempestosa 85
Benvenuti, Leonardo Calypso 58*; Goodnight, Ladies and Gentlemen • Signore e Signori, Buonanotte 76*
Benvenuti, Paolo Il Bacio di Giuda 88
Benz, Obie Heavy Petting 88
Benzheng, Yu *see Yu, Benzheng*
Ber, Ryszard Cudzoziemka • The Stranger 87
Beranger, George A. Manhattan Knight 20; Number 17 20; Uncle Sam of Freedom Ridge 20; Burn 'Em Up Barnes 21*; Sinister Street 22; Was She Guilty? 22; Western Luck 24
Béraud, Luc Like a Turtle on Its Back 78; Heat of Desire • Plein Sud 80; La Petite Amie 88
Bercovici, Leonardo Nasilje na Trgu • Square of Violence 61; Storia di una Donna • Story of a Woman 70
Bercovici, Luca Ghoulies 84; Rockula 90
Berdych, Vaclav Bylo To v Máji • May Events 51*
Beremenyi, Géza The Disciples • A Tanítványok 85; Eldorado 88
Beresford, Al Dreamhouse 81; Screamtime 83
Beresford, Bruce The Hunters 60; The Devil to Pay 62; Clement Meadmore 63; It Droppeth As the Gentle Rain 63; Eastern Nigerian Newsreel No. 30 65; Film for Guitar 65; King Size Woman 66; Picasso's Sculpture 67; Barbara Hepworth at the Tate 68; The End 68; Extravaganza 68; Lichtenstein in London 68; Martin Agrippa 69; Arts of Village India 70; The Cinema of Raymond Fark 70; View from the Satellite 71; The Adventures of Barry McKenzie 72; Barry McKenzie Holds His Own 74; Side by Side 75; Don's Party 76; The Getting of Wisdom 77; Money Movers 78; Breaker Morant 79; The Club • Players 80; Fortress 81; Puberty Blues 81; Tender Mercies 82; The Fringe Dwellers 84; King David 85; Crimes of the Heart 86; Aria 87*; Driving Miss Daisy 89; Her Alibi 89
Beresnyef, Nikolai Enemies of Progress 34
Berezantseva, Tatyana The Duel 64*; Lover for Love • Lyubovyu za Lyubov 87
Berezko, G. If War Comes Tomorrow 38*
Berg, Rudolf van den The Alien 80; Bastille 85; Looking for Eileen • Zoeken naar Eileen 87
Bergenstråhle, Johan Made in Sweden 69; A Baltic Tragedy 71; Hello Baby! 75
Bergenstrahle, Marie-Louise de Geer Still Life • Stilleben 85; Fadern, Sonen och den Helige Ande • The Father, the Son and the Holy Ghost 87
Berger, A. Arme Eva • Dear Eva • Frau Eva 14*
Berger, Axel Hanna D. la Fille du Vondel Park • Hanna D. la Ragazza del Vondel Park • Hanna D. the Girl from Vondel Park 85
Berger, Helmut Du Mich Auch • Same to You • So What? 87*
Berger, Henri Diamant *see Diamant-*

Berger, Henri
Berger, Jerome Diamant *see Diamant-Berger, Jerome*
Berger, Ludwig Der Richter von Zalamea 20; Der Roman der Christine von Herre 21; Cinderella • Der Verlorene Schuh 23; Ein Glas Wasser • Das Spiel der Königin 23; A Waltz Dream • Ein Walzertraum 25; Meistersinger • Die Meistersinger von Nürnberg 27; Sins of the Fathers 28; The Woman from Moscow 28; Das Brennende Herz • The Burning Heart 29; If I Were King • The Vagabond King 30; La Petite Café • The Playboy of Paris 30; Ich bei Tag und Du bei Nacht 32; Early to Bed 33; Waltz Time in Vienna • Walzerkrieg • War of the Waltzes 33; The Thief of Bagdad 40*; Ballerina • Dream Ballerina 50
Berger, Martin Echo of a Dream • Verklungene Träume 30; Rasputin • Rasputin the Holy Devil 30
Berger, Pamela The Imported Bridegroom 90
Berger, Rea A Million for Mary 16; The Overcoat 16; Purity 16; Three Pals 16; The Valley of Decision 16; The Voice of Love 16; Danger Within 18; The Magic Eye 18
Berglund, Per Beyond the Line of Duty 71
Bergman, Andrew So Fine 81; The Freshman 90
Bergman, Edward Confessor 73*
Bergman, Ingmar Crisis • Kris 45; Det Regnar på Vår Kärlek • It Rains on Our Love • The Man with an Umbrella 46; Frustration • The Land of Desire • A Ship Bound for India • A Ship to India • Skepp till Indialand 47; Music in Darkness • Music in the Dark • Musik i Mörker • Night Is My Future 47; The Devil's Wanton • Fängelse • Prison 48; Hamnstad • Port of Call 48; Thirst • Three Strange Loves • Törst 49; Till Glädje • To Joy 49; High Tension • Sånt Händer Inte Här • This Can't Happen Here • This Doesn't Happen Here 50; Illicit Interlude • Sommarlek • Summer Interlude • Summerplay 50; Kvinnors Väntan • Secrets of Women • Waiting Women 52; Monika • Sommaren med Monika • Summer with Monika 52; Gycklarnas Afton • The Naked Night • Sawdust and Tinsel • Sunset of a Clown 53; En Lektion i Kärlek • A Lesson in Love 53; Dreams • Journey Into Autumn • Kvinnodröm 54; Smiles of a Summer Night • Sommarnattens Leende 55; The Seventh Seal • Det Sjunde Inseglet 56; Brink of Life • Nära Livet • So Close to Life 57; Smultronstället • Wild Strawberries 57; Ansiktet • The Face • The Magician 58; Jungfrukällan • The Virgin Spring 59; The Devil's Eye • Djävulens Öga 60; Såsom i en Spegel • Through a Glass Darkly 61; The Communicants • Nattsvardsgästerna • Winter Light 62; The Silence • Tystnaden 63; All These Women • För Att Inte Tala Om Alla Dessa Kvinnor • Now About All These Women • Now About These Women... 64; Stimulantia

White Lightning 53; The Bowery Boys
Meet the Monsters 54; Bowery to Bagdad
54; Jungle Gents 54*; Spy Chasers 55;
Calling Homicide 56; Dig That Uranium
56; Mother, Sir! • Navy Wife 56; World
Without End 56; Reform School Girl 57;
The Storm Rider 57; Escape from Red
Rock 58; High School Hellcats • School for
Violence 58; Joy Ride 58; Mutiny in Outer
Space • Spacemaster X-7 58; Quantrill's
Raiders 58; Queen of Outer Space 58;
Alaska Passage 59; The Return of the Fly
59; Valley of the Dragons 61; The Three
Stooges in Orbit 62; The Three Stooges
Meet Hercules 62; Alarm on Eighty-Third
Street 65; Prehistoric Valley 66

Berne, Josef Dawn to Dawn 33; Mirele
Efros 39; They Live in Fear 44; Down
Missouri Way • Missouri Hayride 46; Cat-
skill Honeymoon 50

Berneis, Peter Der Chef Wünscht Keine
Zeugen • The Chief Wants No Survivors •
No Survivors Please 63*

Berner, Dieter Die Verlockung 88

Bernhard, Jack Decoy 46; Sweetheart of
Sigma Chi 46; In Self Defense • Perilous
Waters 47; Violence 47; Appointment with
Murder 48; The Hunted 48; Unknown
Island 48; Alaska Patrol 49; Blonde Ice 49;
Search for Danger 49; The Second Face 50

Bernhardt, Curtis see Bernhardt, Kurt

Bernhardt, Kurt Qualen der Nacht 26;
Die Waise von Lowood 26; Kinderseelen
Klagen An • Kinderseelen Klagen Euch
An 27; Das Letzte Fort 27; Das Mädchen
mit den Fünf Nullen 27; The Prince of
Rogues • Schinderhannes 27; Das Grosse
Los 28; Enigma • Die Frau Nach der Mann
Sich Sehnt • Three Loves 29; L'Homme
Qui Assassina 30; The Last Company • Die
Letzte Kompanie • Thirteen Men and a
Girl 30; The Man Who Murdered • Der
Mann Der den Mord Beging 31; Der
Grosse Rausch 32; Der Rebell 32*; Der
Tunnel • Le Tunnel • The Tunnel 33; The
Beloved Vagabond 34; L'Or dans la Rue
34; Carrefour • Crossroads 38; Nuit de
Décembre 39; The Lady with Red Hair 40;
My Love Came Back 40; Million Dollar
Baby 41; Happy Go Lucky 42; Juke Girl
42; Devotion 43; Conflict 45; My Reputa-
tion 46; A Stolen Life 46; High Wall 47;
Possessed 47; The Doctor and the Girl 49;
The Blue Veil 51; Payment on Demand •
The Story of a Divorce 51; Sirocco 51; The
Merry Widow 52; Miss Sadie Thompson
53; Beau Brummel 54; Interrupted Melody
55; Gaby 56; Stefanie in Rio • Stephanie
in Rio 60; Damon and Pythias • Il Tirano
di Siracusa • The Tyrant of Syracuse 61;
Kisses for My President • Kisses for the
President 64

Bernier, George Miracle of Saint Thérèse
59

Bernstein, Armyan Windy City 84;
American Date • Cross My Heart 87

Bernstein, Walter Little Miss Marker 80

Berri, Claude Les Baisers 63*; La
Chance et l'Amour 64*; Le Poulet 64;
Claude • The Old Man and the Boy • The

Two of Us • Le Vieil Homme et l'Enfant
66; Marry Me! Marry Me! • Mazel Tov ou
Le Mariage 68; The Man with Connec-
tions • Le Pistonnée 70; Le Cinéma du
Papa 71; Sex Shop • Le Sex Shop 72; Le
Male du Siècle • The Male of the Century
75; The First Time • La Première Fois 76;
In a Wild Moment • Un Moment d'Égare-
ment • One Wild Moment • A Summer
Affair 77; Je Vous Aime 80; Le Maître
d'École 81; A Summer Affair 81; Tchao
Pantin 83; Jean de Florette 86; Jean de
Florette II • Manon des Sources • Manon
of the Spring 86; Uranus 90

Berruti, Giulio Killer Nun • Suor Omicidi 78

Berry, Bill Brotherhood of Death 76;
Crazy Legs • Off the Mark 87

Berry, Dale Passion in the Sun • Passion
of the Sun 64

Berry, Denis Last Song 86

Berry, Jack see Berry, John

Berry, John Miss Susie Slagle's 44; Tues-
day in November 45; Cross My Heart 46;
From This Day Forward 46; Casbah 48;
Caught 49; Tension 49; Atoll K • Escap-
ade • Robinson Crusoeland • Utopia 50*;
Dix de Hollywood • The Hollywood Ten
50; He Ran All the Way 51; C'Est Arrivé à
Paris • It Happened in Paris 52*; Ça Va
Barder! • There Goes Barder 54; Give 'Em
Hell 54; El Amor de Don Juan • Don
Juan • Pantaloons 55; Headlines of
Destruction • Je Suis un Sentimental 55;
Tamango 57; Oh! Qué Mambo! 58; Maya
64; À Tout Casser • Breaking It Up 67;
Claudine 74; Thieves 77*; The Bad News
Bears Go to Japan 78; Saturn 3 79*; Le
Voyage à Paimpol 85; Il Y A Maldonne
• Maldonne 87

Berry, Julian see Gastaldi, Ernesto

Berry, Robert House of Dreams 63

Berry, Thomas Something About Love
88; The Amityville Curse 90

Bersenev, N. Golden Honey • Zolotoi
Med 28*

Berthelet, Arthur The Chaperone 16;
The Havoc 16; The Misleading Lady 16;
The Return of Eve 16; Sherlock Holmes 16;
The Golden Idiot 17; Little Shoes 17; Pants
17; The Saint's Adventure 17; Young
Mother Hubbard 17; Men Who Have Made
Love to Me 18; Young America 18; Penny
of Top Hill Trail 21; Enemies of Youth 25

Berthomieu, André Pas Si Bête 28; Ces
Dames aux Chapeaux Verts 29; Le Crime
de Sylvestre Bonnard 30; Rapacité 30; Mon
Ami Victor 31; Barranco 32; Les Ailes
Brisées 33; Mademoiselle Josette Ma
Femme 33; L'Aristo 34; La Femme Idéale
34; La Flamme 36; Le Mort en Fuite 36; Le
Secret de Polichinelle 36; La Chaste Suz-
anne 37; The Girl in the Taxi 37; L'Incon-
nue de Monte-Carlo 38; Les Nouveaux
Riches 38; La Neige sur les Pas 41; La
Croisée des Chemins 42; Dedée de Mont-
martre 42; L'Ange de la Nuit 44; J'Ai 17
Ans • My First Love 45; Peloton d'Exécu-
tion • Resistance 45; Amours, Délices et
Orgues • College Swing 46; Gringalet 46;

Pas Si Bête 47; Blanc Comme Neige 48;
L'Ombre 48; Le Bal des Pompiers 49; Le
Cœur sur la Main 49; La Femme Nue •
The Naked Woman 49; La Petite Chocola-
tière 50; Chacun Son Tour 51; Le Roi des
Camelots 51; Belle Mentalité 53; Le Por-
trait de Son Père 53; Scènes de Ménage 54;
Quatre Jours à Paris 55; La Joyeuse Prison
56; Sacrée Jeunesse 58; Préméditation 60

Berto, Giuseppe Anna 51*

Berto, Juliet Neige • Snow 81*; Cap
Canaille 83; Havre 86

Bertolucci, Bernardo La Commare Secca
• The Grim Reaper 62; Before the Revolu-
tion • Prima della Rivoluzione 64; Il
Canale 66; La Via del Petrolio 66; Amore e
Rabbia • La Contestation • Love and
Anger • Vangelo '70 67*; Partner 68; The
Conformist • Il Conformista 69; The Spi-
der's Strategem • The Spider's Strategy •
La Strategia del Ragno 69; I Poveri Muor-
iono Prima • La Saluta e Malato o I Poveri
Muoriono Prima • La Sante Est Malade ou
Les Pauvres Meurent les Premiers 71; Le
Dernier Tango à Paris • Last Tango in
Paris • Ultimo Tango a Parigi 72; 1900 •
Novecento 76; Luna • La Luna • The
Moon 79; La Tragedia di un Uomo Ridi-
colo • La Tragédie d'un Homme Ridicule •
The Tragedy of a Ridiculous Man 81; The
Last Emperor 87; The Sheltering Sky 90

Bertolucci, Giuseppe Secrets Secrets •
Segreti Segreti 85; I Cammelli 88; Strana
la Vita 88

Bertram, William A Little Patriot 17;
Tears and Smiles 17; The Understudy 17;
Cupid by Proxy 18; Daddy's Girl 18; A
Daughter of the West 18; Dolly Does Her
Bit 18; Dolly's Vacation 18; Milady o' the
Bean Stalk 18; The Voice of Destiny 18;
Winning Grandma 18; The Arizona Cat-
claw 19; The Old Maid's Baby 19; The Saw-
dust Doll 19; Ghost City 21; The Wolverine
21; Alias Phil Kennedy 22; Texas 22; The
Western Musketeer 22; The Smoking Trail
24; Ace of Action 26; Hoodoo Ranch 26;
Tangled Herds 26; Gold from Weepah 27;
The Phantom Buster 27

Bertrand, René Barbe-Bleue 36*

Bertsch, Marguerite The Devil's Prize
16; The Glory of Yolanda 17; The Soul
Master 17

Bertucelli, Jean-Louis Ramparts of Clay
• Remparts d'Argile 70; Paulina 1880 72;
On S'Est Trompé d'Histoire d'Amour 74;
Docteur Françoise Gailland • No Time for
Breakfast 75; L'Imprécateur 77; The Ac-
cuser 78

Berwick, Irvin The Monster of Piedras
Blancas 58; The Seventh Commandment
61; The Street Is My Beat 66; Hitchhike to
Hell 78; Malibu High 79

Berwick, Wayne Microwave Massacre 79

Berz, Michael Snow White 87

Beshears, James Growing Pains •
Homework 79

Besnard, Jacques Le Fou du Labo 4 •
The Madman of Lab 4 67

Besozzi, Angelo Come le Foglie • Like
the Leaves 38

Bessada, Milad A Quiet Day in Belfast 74

Bessie, Dan Hard Traveling 85

Besson, Luc Le Dernier Combat • The Last Battle 83; Subway 85; Kamikaze 86*; The Big Blue • Le Grand Bleu 88; La Femme Nikita • Nikita 90

Betriu, Francesc Requiem for a Spanish Peasant • Requiem por un Campesino Español 86

Bettettini, Gianfranco The Last Mazurka • L'Ultima Mazurka 86

Bettman, Gil Crystal Heart 85; Never Too Young to Die 86

Betuel, Jonathan My Science Project 85

Beute, Chris The Headleys at Home 39

Beverly, Eddie, Jr. Modern Day Houdini 83

Bevilacqua, Alberto La Donna delle Meraviglie • The Woman of Marvels 85; Tango Blu 88

Beville, Richard Radio Parade 33*

Beyer, Frank Nackt Unter Wölfen • Naked Among the Wolves 63; Jacob the Liar • Jakob der Lügner 74

Beyfuss, Alex E. Salomy Jane 14*; Mignon 15

Beymer, Richard The Innerview 74

Beyzai, Bahram see Beizai, Bahram

Bezencenet, Peter Bomb in the High Street 61*; Band of Thieves 62; City of Fear 65; Twenty-Four Hours to Kill 65

Bezhanov, Gerald The Most Charming and Attractive • Samaya Obayatelnaya i Privlekatelnaya 87

Bharathan Nilakurinhi Poothappol 87; Oru Minnaminuginte Nurungu Vettam 88

Bhargava Kurukshetra 88; Shanthinivasa 88; Shubhamilana 88

Bhaskar, Bijay Thili Jhai Heli Bahu 88

Bhatt, Mahesh Thikana 88

Bhatt, Parveen Khoon Baha Ganga Mein 88

Bhattacharya, Basu Panchvati 87

Biagetti, Giuliano L'Età del Malessere • Love Problems 70

Bianchi, Adelchi Lost Souls • Vite Perdute 61*; Buckaroo 68

Bianchi, Andrea Le Notti del Terrore • Zombie Horror • Zombie III 80; Angela's Sweet Skin • Dolce Pelle di Angela 87

Bianchi, Bruno Heathcliff: The Movie 86

Bianchi, Edward The Fan 81

Bianchi, Giorgio The Merry Chase 48; My Gun Is Quick 57*; The Moralist • Il Moralista 59; Destination Fury 61; Island Affair 62; Femmine di Lusso • Love, Italian Style • Love, the Italian Way 64

Bianchi, Mario An Ambiguous Story • Una Storia Ambigua 86

Bianchi, Sergio Romance 88

Bianchini, Paolo Devilman Story • The Devil's Man 67; Our Men in Bagdad 67; Day of Fire • Quel Caldo Maledetto Giorno di Fuoco 68; Dio Li Crea...Io Li Ammazzo 68; The King of the Criminals • Il Re dei Criminali • Superargo • Superargo e i Giganti Senza Volto • Superargo el Gigante • Superargo the Giant 68; Lo

Voglio Morto 68; Ehi Amico, Sei Morto 70

Bianco, Tony lo see Lo Bianco, Tony

Biancoli, Oreste Amicizia • Friendship 40; La Mazurka di Papa 40

Biberman, Abner The Golden Mistress 54; The Looters 55; Running Wild 55; Behind the High Wall 56; The Price of Fear 56; Gun for a Coward 57; The Night Runner 57; Flood Tide 58; Too Many Thieves 66

Biberman, Herbert J. One Way Ticket 35; Meet Nero Wolfe 36; The Master Race 44*; Salt of the Earth 53; Slaves 68

Biebrach, Rudolph False Shame • Fools of Passion 26

Bielek, Pal'o Far Freedom 45; Foxholes • Vlcie Diery 48; The Dam • Priehrada 50; Lazy Sa Pohli • The Mountains Are Stirring 52; Friday the Thirteenth • V Piatok Trinasteho 53; Forty-Four • Štyridsat-Štyri 57; Captain Dabac • Kapitan Dabac 59; Janošík I 62; Janošík II 63; The Hangman • Majster Kat 65; Traja • Trio 69

Bielski, Henryk Chrzesniak • The Godson 86

Bierbichler, Josef Triumph der Gerechten • Triumph of the Just 87

Bierman, Robert The Dumb Waiter 79; The Rocking Horse Winner 83; Vampire's Kiss 88

Biette, Jean-Claude Le Théâtre des Matières 78; Loin de Manhattan 81; Chasse Garde 86; Les Champignon des Carpates 89

Bigelow, Kathryn Breakdown 81; The Loveless 81*; Near Dark 87; Blue Steel 89

Biggar, Helen Hell Unlimited 36*

Bigwood, Joseph Bloodrage 79

Bijay see Vijay

Bilal, Enki Bunker Palace Hotel 89

Bilbal, Robert Amour, Amour 37

Bilcock, David Alvin Rides Again 74*

Bill, Buffalo, Jr. see Wilsey, Jay

Bill, Tony My Bodyguard 80; Six Weeks 82; Five Corners 87; Crazy People 90

Billington, Kevin Interlude 68; The Rise and Rise of Michael Rimmer 70; The Light at the Edge of the World 71; Voices 73; Reflections 84

Billon, Pierre The House on the Dune • La Maison dans la Dune 34; Deuxième Bureau • Second Bureau 35; Courrier Sud 37; The Eternal Husband • L'Homme au Chapeau Rond 46; Ruy Blas 48; Vautrin the Thief 49

Bilson, Bruce Hill's Angels • The North Avenue Irregulars 78; Chattanooga Choo Choo 84

Bilson, Danny Zone Troopers 86; The Wrong Guys 88

Binder, John UFOria 80

Binder, Steve The T.A.M.I. Show 64; Give 'Em Hell, Harry 75

Bing, Mack All the Loving Couples 69; The Class of '74 72*; Gabriella 74

Binger, Maurits Carmen of the North 20

Bini, Carlos Guru das Siete Cidades 72

Binney, Josh Hi-De-Ho 47; Boarding House Blues 48; Killer Diller 48; Merry-Go-Round 48

Binyon, Claude And the Angels Sing 44*; Family Honeymoon 48; The Saxon Charm 48; Mother Didn't Tell Me 50; Stella 50; Aaron Slick from Punkin Crick • Marshmallow Moon 52; Dreamboat 52; Champagne for Everybody • Here Come the Girls 53

Binzer, Rollin Ladies and Gentlemen, the Rolling Stones 75

Birch, Cecil Algy Goes In for Physical Culture 14; Birds of a Feather Plot Together 14; A Game of Bluff 14; How Winky Fought for a Bride 14; How Winky Whacked the Germans 14; Kill That Fly 14; Love and the Boxing Gloves 14; The Muddleton Fire Brigade 14; Papa's Little Weakness 14; Peppering His Own Porridge 14; The Wanderer Returns 14; Who's Which? 14; Winky Accused of an 'Orrible Crime 14; Winky and the Ants 14; Winky and the Cannibal Chief 14; Winky and the Gorgonzola Cheese 14; Winky and the Leopard 14; Winky As a Suffragette 14; Winky at the Front 14; Winky Becomes a Family Man 14; Winky, Bigamist 14; Winky Causes a Smallpox Panic 14; Winky Diddles the Hawker 14; Winky Dons the Petticoats 14; Winky Gets Puffed Up 14; Winky Gets Spotted 14; Winky Goes Camping 14; Winky Goes Spy Catching 14; Winky Learns a Lesson in Honesty 14; Winky, Park Policeman 14; Winky Takes to Farming 14; Winky the Tallyman 14; Winky Tries Chicken Raising 14; Winky Waggles the Wicked Widow 14; Winky Wins 14; Winky's Carving Knife 14; Winky's Cat 14; Winky's Fireworks 14; Winky's Guilty Conscience 14; Winky's Insurance Policy 14; Winky's Invisible Ink 14; Winky's Jealousy 14; Winky's Lifeboat 14; Winky's Mother-in-Law 14; Winky's Next-Door Neighbour 14; Winky's Ruse 14; Winky's Stratagem 14; Winky's Weekend 14; Always Love Your Neighbours 15; Always Tell Your Husband 15; And That's How the Row Began 15; Artful, Not 'Alf 15; A Bachelor's Babies 15; A Bid for Bounty 15; Bumbles' Blunder 15; A Chip Off the Old Block 15; Codfish and Aloes 15; A Comedy of Errors 15; The Counterfeit Cowboy 15; Dr. Violet Dearing 15; Don't Jump to Conclusions 15; Ever Been Had? 15; Foul Play 15; Getting on His Nerves 15; A Good Little Pal 15; The Green-Eyed Monster 15; Have Some More Meat 15; Hilda Routs the Enemy 15; Hilda's Busy Day 15; 'Igh Art 15; Lily, Tomboy 15; Lily's Birthday 15; Love and a Legacy 15; Love and Cameras 15; Mama's D-E-A-R 15; The Man in Possession 15; Miss Madcap May 15; Monty's Monocle 15; Moonstruck 15; Mushroom Stew 15; Never Again 15; Never Despair 15; No Fool Like an Old Fool 15; Oh My! 15; Once Upon a Time 15; One on Ikey 15; A Pair of Dummies 15; A Pair of Stars 15; Papa Scores 15; Paula 15; Peace at Any Price 15; Pin Pricks 15; Putting on the 'Fluence 15; Scottie and the Frogs 15; Scottie Loves Ice Cream 15; Scottie Turns the Handle 15; Scottie's Day

Out 15; Sharps and Flats 15; The Tell-Tale Globe 15; That's Done It 15; There's Hair 15; Tommy's Freezing Spray 15; The Troubles of a Hypochondriac 15; Venus and the Knuts 15; What a Find 15; What a Picnic 15; What Scottie Heard 15; What the? 15; What's in a Name? 15; The White Hand 15; Who Were You With Last Night? 15; A Wife on Loan 15; Winky Is the Long and Short of It 15; Winky's Blue Diamond 15; Won by a Fluke 15; The Better Bet 16; Love and 'Fluence 16; My Wife's Husband 16; The Scarecrow 16; Starve a Fever 16; Stormy Is Misunderstood 16; Telling the Tale 16; Zeppelins of London 16

Birch, Dudley Flight from Singapore 62; The Chimney Sweeps 63

Birch, Frank Ashes 30

Birch, Patricia Grease II 82

Bird, Lance The World of Tomorrow 84*

Bird, Richard The Terror 37; Island Man • Men of Ireland • West of Kerry 38

Bird, Stewart Home Free All 83

Birdwell, Russell Masquerade 29*; Street Corners 29; The Flying Circus • Flying Devils 33; The Come-On 56; The Girl in the Kremlin 57

Birkett, Michael The Soldier's Tale 64

Birkin, Andrew Melody • S.W.A.L.K. 71*; Sredni Vashtar 81; Burning Secret 88

Birkinshaw, Alan Confessions of a Sex Maniac • The Man Who Couldn't Get Enough 75; Killer's Moon 78; Dead End 80; The House of Usher 88; Agatha Christie's Ten Little Indians • Ten Little Indians 89

Birman, Naum Black and White Magic • Magia Chyornaya i Byelaya 87; Voskresniye Papa 88

Birri, Fernando Alfabeto Notturno 51; Selinunte 51; Immagini Populari Siciliane Profane 52; Immagini Populari Siciliane Sacre 52; Tire Die • Toss Me a Dime 54; La Primera Fundación de Buenos Aires 59; Flooded Out • Los Inundados 61; Che, Buenos Aires 62; Org 79*; Un Señor Muy Viejo con Unas Alas Enormes • A Very Old Man with Enormous Wings 88

Birt, Daniel Silt 31; Dai Jones 41; Butterfly Bomb 43; No Room at the Inn 48; The Three Weird Sisters 48; The Interrupted Journey 49; She Shall Have Murder 50; Circumstantial Evidence 51; The Night Won't Talk 52; Background • Edge of Divorce 53; Laughing in the Sunshine 53; Three Steps in the Dark 53; Big Deadly Game • The Deadly Game • Third Party Risk 54; Burnt Evidence 54; Meet Mr. Malcolm 54

Bischoff, Sam The Last Mile 32

Bishara, Khairy The Collar and the Bracelet • Fetters • Al Tauq wal Iswira • El Touk wa el Esswera 86; Yoom Helw. Yoom Mor 88

Bishop, Curtis Cow Country 53*

Bishop, Terry Kill That Rat 41; Down Our Street 42; More Eggs from Your Hens 42; Western Isles 42; Out of the Box 44;

Five Towns 47; Thee and Me 48; Daybreak in Udi 49; The Titfield Thunderbolt 52*; You're Only Young Twice 52; Tim Driscoll's Donkey 55; Light Fingers 57; Model for Murder 58; Cover Girl Killer 59; Life in Danger 59; Danger Tomorrow 60, The Unstoppable Man 60; Bomb in the High Street 61*; Hair of the Dog 61; Hamile 65

Bispo, Louis Flight 60

Bistritzky, A. Romance of a Russian Ballerina 13*

Bito, Antonio Mak π 100 88

Bitsch, Charles Le Dernier Homme • The Last Man 68

Bivens, Loren Trespasses 83*

Bizzarri, Nino The Second Night • La Seconda Notte 86

Björkman, Stig I Love You Love 68; Georgia, Georgia 72; The White Wall 75

Blaché, Alice see Guy-Blaché, Alice

Blaché, Alice Guy see Guy-Blaché, Alice

Blaché, Herbert The Fight for Millions 13; The Star of India 13*; The Temptations of Satan 13; The Burglar and the Lady 14; The Chimes 14*; A Fight for Freedom, or Exiled to Siberia 14; Fighting Death 14; Hook and Hand 14; The Million Dollar Robbery 14; The Mystery of Edwin Drood 14*; Greater Love Hath No Man 15*; Her Own Way 15; The Lady and the Burglar 15; The Shooting of Dan McGrew 15; The Song of the Wage Slave 15; The Girl with the Green Eyes 16*; A Woman's Fight 16; The Auction of Virtue 17; A Man and the Woman 17*; The Peddler 17; Think It Over 17; Loaded Dice 18; A Man's World 18; The Silent Woman 18; The Brat 19; The Divorcee • Lady Frederick 19; Fools and Their Money 19; Jeanne of the Gutter 19; The Man Who Stayed at Home 19; The Parisian Tigress 19; Satan Junior 19; The Uplifters 19; The Hope 20; The New York Idea 20; The Saphead 20; Stronger Than Death 20*; The Walk-Offs 20; The Bashful Suitor 21; The Beggar Maid 21; Out of the Chorus 21; The Young Painter 22; Fools and Riches 23; The Near Lady 23; Nobody's Bride 23; The Two-Souled Woman • The Untameable • The White Cat 23; The Wild Party 23; High Speed 24; The Calgary Stampede 25; Headwinds 25; Secrets of the Night 25; The Mystery Club 26; Burning the Wind 29*

Black, Cathal Pigs 84

Black, George The Penny Pool 37; Calling All Crooks 38

Black, John The Zoo Robbery 73*; Robin Hood Junior 75*; The Unbroken Arrow 76*

Black, Michael Pictures 82

Black, Noel Skaterdater 64; The River Boy 67; Pretty Poison • She Let Him Continue 68; Cover Me Babe • Run, Shadow, Run 70; Jennifer on My Mind 71; Marianne • Mirrors 78; A Man, a Woman and a Bank • A Very Big Withdrawal 79; Private School 83

Black, Preston Back to the Woods 37

Blackburn, Richard Lady Dracula • The Legendary Curse of Lemora • Lemora — A

Child's Tale of the Supernatural • Lemora — Lady Dracula • Lemora, the Lady Dracula 73

Blackton, J. Stuart The Burglar on the Roof 1897; The Battle of Santiago Bay 1898; Tearing Down the Spanish Flag 1898*; Spot Filming of Windsor Hotel Fire in New York 1899; A Visit to the Spiritualist 1899; The Enchanted Drawing 00; Happy Hooligan 00; A Gentleman of France 03; The Adventures of Sherlock Holmes • Sherlock Holmes 05; The Automobile Thieves 05; Monsieur Beaucaire 05; Raffles the Amateur Cracksman 05; And the Villain Still Pursued Her 06; The Haunted Hotel 06; Humorous Phases of Funny Faces 06; Hundred to One Shot 06; The Jail Bird and How He Flew 06; A Modern Oliver Twist 06; The San Francisco Earthquake 06; A Curious Dream 07; The Easterner 07; Francesca da Rimini 07; The Inventor's Galvanic Fluid • Liquid Electricity 07; Lightning Sketches 07; The Magic Fountain Pen 07; The Mechanical Statue and the Ingenious Servant 07; The Mill Girl 07; Work Made Easy 07; The Airship • 100 Years Hence 08; Barbara Frietchie 08; Galvanic Fluid • More Fun with Liquid Electricity 08; Get Me a Step Ladder 08; Macbeth 08; Making Moving Pictures 08; The Merchant of Venice 08; Romeo and Juliet 08; Salome 08; Scenes of True Life 08; The Viking's Daughter 08; An Alpine Echo 09; The Auto Maniac 09; The Diamond Maker • Fortune or Misfortune • A Maker of Diamonds 09; The Life Drama of Napoleon Bonaparte and Empress Josephine of France • Napoleon Bonaparte and Empress Josephine of France • Napoleon, Man of Destiny • Napoleon the Man of Destiny 09; The Life of Moses 09; Little Nemo • Winsor McCay • Winsor McCay and His Animated Comics • Winsor McCay Explains His Moving Cartoons to John Bunny • Winsor McCay Makes His Cartoons Move 09*; Les Misérables 09; Oliver Twist 09; Princess Nicotine, or The Smoke Fairy 09*; The Romance of an Umbrella 09; Saul and David 09; The Way of the Cross 09; A Brother's Devotion 10; Chew-Chew Land 10; Convict 796 10; Elektra 10; Fruits of Vengeance 10; A Modern Cinderella 10; True Life 10; Uncle Tom's Cabin 10; The Derelict Reporter 11; The Mate of the John M 11; The Spirit of the Light 11; The Wooing of Winifred 11; Alma's Champion 12; As You Like It 12*; Cardinal Wolsey 12*; The Diamond Brooch 12; The Lady of the Lake 12; The Light of St. Bernard 12; Lincoln's Gettysburg Address 12*; The Pink Pajama Girl 12; The Two Portraits 12; Beau Brummel 13*; Hamlet 13; The Vengeance of Durand 13; Love, Luck and Gasoline 14; A Million Dollar Bid 14; The Battle Cry of Peace 15*; Country Life • Scenes from Country Life 17; The Glory of a Nation 17; The Judgment House 17; The Message of the Mouse 17; Womanhood 17*; The Common Cause 18; Life's

Greatest Problem • Safe for Democracy 18; Missing 18*; World for Sale 18; Dawn 19; A House Divided 19; The Littlest Scout 19; The Moonshine Trail 19; My Husband's Other Wife 19; The Blood Barrier 20; Forbidden Valley 20; The House of the Tolling Bell 20; Man and His Woman 20; Passers-By 20; Respectable by Proxy 20; The Glorious Adventure 21; A Gipsy Cavalier 22; On the Banks of the Wabash 23; The Virgin Queen 23; Behold This Woman 24; The Beloved Brute 24; Between Friends 24; The Clean Heart 24; Let No Man Put Asunder 24; The Redeeming Sin 24; The Gilded Highway 25; The Happy Warrior 25; Tides of Passion 25; Bride of the Storm 26; Hell-Bent for Heaven 26; The Passionate Quest 26

Blackwell, Carlyle The Good for Nothing 17; His Royal Highness 18; Leap to Fame 18; Bedrock 30; Beyond the Cities 30

Blackwood, Christian Spoleto: Festival of Two Worlds 67; Harlem Theater 68; Summer in the City 68; Eliot Feld: Artistic Director 70; San Domingo 70*; Juilliard 71; Kentucky Kith and Kin 72; Black Harvest 73; Living with Fear 74; Yesterday's Witness: A Tribute to the American Newsreel 74; To Be a Man 77; Roger Corman: Hollywood's Wild Angel 78; Cousins 79; Tapdancin' 80; All by Myself 82; Charles Aznavour: Breaking America 83; Observations Under the Volcano 84; My Life for Zarah Leander 85; Private Conversations 85; Nik and Murray 86; Signed: Lino Brocka 87; Two Hotels in Our Troubled Middle East 88; Motel 89

Blackwood, Maureen The Passion of Remembrance 86

Blackwood, Michael Pablo Picasso, The Legacy of a Genius 82

Blagg, Linda Just Out of Reach 79

Blain, Gérard Les Amis 71; Le Pélican 73; Un Enfant dans la Foule 77; Un Second Souffle • A Second Wind 78; Le Rebelle 80; Pierre et Djemila 87

Blaine, Cullen R.O.T.O.R. 88

Blair, George End of the Road 44; Secrets of Scotland Yard 44; Silent Partner 44; Gangs of the Waterfront 45; Scotland Yard Investigator 45; A Sporting Chance 45; Thoroughbreds 45; The Affairs of Geraldine 46; G.I. War Brides 46; Gay Blades 46; Exposed 47; The Ghost Goes Wild 47; That's My Gal 47; The Trespasser 47; Daredevils of the Clouds 48; Homicide for Three • An Interrupted Honeymoon 48; King of the Gamblers 48; Lightnin' in the Forest 48; Madonna of the Desert 48; Alias the Champ 49; Daughter of the Jungle 49; Duke of Chicago 49; Flaming Fury 49; Post Office Investigator 49; Rose of the Yukon 49; Streets of San Francisco 49; Destination Big House 50; Federal Agent at Large 50; Lonely Heart Bandits • Lonely Hearts Bandits 50; The Missourians 50; Under Mexicali Skies • Under Mexicali Stars 50; Unmasked 50; Woman from Headquarters • Women from Headquarters 50; Insurance Investigator 51;

Secrets of Monte Carlo 51; Silver City Bonanza 51; Thunder in God's Country 51; Desert Pursuit 52; Woman in the Dark 52; Perils of the Jungle 53; The Twinkle in God's Eye 55; Fighting Trouble 56; Jaguar 56; Sabu and the Magic Ring 57; Spook Chasers 57; The Hypnotic Eye 60

Blair, Les Number One 84; Honest, Decent and True 85; Leave to Remain 88

Blair, Milton Surfari 67

Blake, Alan Victims 80

Blake, Alfonso Corona see Corona Blake, Alfonso

Blake, B. K. see Blake, Ben

Blake, Ben The Porcelain Lamp 21; Deliverance 28; Two Sisters 38

Blake, Edmund Flotsam 21

Blake, Gerald The Dance of Death 38

Blake, T. C. see Collector, Robert

Blakeley, John E. Musical Medley 35; Dodging the Dole 36; Somewhere in England 40; Somewhere in Camp 42; Somewhere on Leave 42; Demobbed 44; Home Sweet Home 45; Honeymoon Hotel • Under New Management 46; Cup-Tie Honeymoon 48; Holidays with Pay 48; School for Randle 49; Somewhere in Politics 49; What a Carry On 49; Let's Have a Murder • Stick 'Em Up 50; Over the Garden Wall 50; It's a Grand Life 53

Blakemore, Michael A Personal History of the Australian Surf 82; Privates on Parade 82

Blakley, Ronee I Played It for You 85

Blanc, Jean-Pierre The Old Maid • La Vieille Fille 72

Blancarte, Oscar Let Them Kill Me Once and for All • Que Me Maten de Una Vez 86

Blancato, Ken Stewardess School 86

Blanchar, Pierre Secrets 43; Un Seul Amour 43

Blanche, Francis Tartarin de Tarascon 62

Blancocello, Enrico The Strange Fetishes • The Strange Fetishes of the Go-Go Girls 67

Blangsted, Folmer The Old Wyoming Trail 37; Westbound Mail 37

Blank, Les Dizzy Gillespie 65; The Blues Accordin' to Lightnin' Hopkins 68; God Respects Us When We Work But Loves Us When We Dance 68; Chicken Real 70; Spend It All 71; A Well Spent Life 71; Dry Wood 73; Hot Pepper 73; A Poem Is a Naked Person 74; Chulas Fronteras 76; Always for Pleasure 78; Del Mero Corazón 79; Garlic Is As Good As Ten Mothers 80; Werner Herzog Eats His Shoe 80; Burden of Dreams 82; Sprout Wings and Fly 83; In Heaven There Is No Beer!? 84; Cigarette Blues 85; Huey Lewis and the News: Be-Fore! 86; Gap-Toothed Women 87; Ziveli!: Medicine for the Heart 87; Ry Cooder and the Moula Banda Rhythm Aces 88; I Went to the Dance • J'Ai Été au Bal 89*; Routes of Rhythm, with Harry Belafonte 90*; Yum, Yum, Yum! • Yum, Yum, Yum! A Taste of Cajun & Creole Cooking 90

Blareau, Richard Ballet de France 55

Blasco, Riccardo Autopsy of a Criminal 62; Duello nel Texas • Gringo • Gunfight at Red Sands 63; Swordsmen Three • The Three Swords of Zorro • Las Tres Espadas del Zorro 63; El Zorro Cabalga Otra Vez 64

Blasetti, Alessandro Sole • Sun 28; Nero • Nerone 30; Resurrectio • Resurrection 30; Terra Madre 31; Assisi 32; Palio 32; The Table of the Poor • La Tavola dei Poveri 32; Il Caso Haller 33; Gesuzza la Sposa Garibaldina • I Mille di Garibaldi • 1860 33; L'Impiegata di Papà 33; The Old Guard • Vecchia Guardia 33; Aldebaran 35; La Contessa di Parma • The Countess of Parma 37; Patria, Amore e Dovere 37; Piccolo Eroe 37; Caccia alla Volpe 38; Ettore Fieramosca 38; Abuna Messias 39*; An Adventure of Salvator Rosa • Un'Avventura di Salvator Rosa 39; Dora Nelson 39*; Retroscena 39; La Corona di Ferro • The Iron Crown 40; La Cena delle Beffe • The Joker's Banquet 41; Four Steps in the Clouds • Quattro Passi fra le Nuvole 42; Nessuno Torna Indietro • No One Turns Back 43; Castel Sant'Angelo 45; Sulla Cupola di San Pietro 45; A Day in the Life • A Day of Life • Un Giorno nella Vita 46; Il Duomo di Milano 46; La Gemma Orientale dei Papi 46; Fabiola 47*; Father's Dilemma • First Communion • His Majesty Mr. Jones • Prima Communione 50; Ippodromi all'Alba 50; Quelli Che Soffrono per Noi 51; Altri Tempi • In Olden Days • Infidelity • Times Gone By 52; The Blaze • La Fiammata • Pride, Love and Suspicion 52; Anatomy of Love • Our Times • Slice of Life • Tempi Nostri 53; Miracolo a Firenze 53; Peccato Che Sia una Canaglia • Too Bad She's Bad 54; La Fortuna di Essere Donna • Lucky to Be a Woman 55; Amore e Chiacchiere • Love and Chatter 57; Europa di Notte • European Nights 58; I Love, You Love • Io Amo, Tu Ami • J'Aime, Tu Aimes 60; Las Cuatro Verdades • The Four Truths • Les Quatres Vérités • Le Quattro Verità • Three Fables of Love 62*; Liolà • A Very Handy Man 63; Io, Io, Io...e gli Altri • Me, Me, Me...and the Others 65; The Girl of the Bersagliere • La Ragazza del Bersagliere 66; La Epopeya de Simon Bolivar • Simon Bolivar 68; Venezia, una Mostra per il Cinema 69

Blatt, Edward A. Between Two Worlds 44; Escape in the Desert 44*; Smart Woman 48

Blattner, Louis My Lucky Star 33*

Blatty, William Peter The Ninth Configuration • Twinkle Twinkle Killer Kane 79; The Exorcist III 90

Blazevski, Vladimir Hi-Fi 87

Bleckner, Jeff Rites of Summer • White Water Summer 85

Bletcher, William The Wild Girl 25; The Silent Guardian 26

Blier, Bertrand Hitler...Connais Pas! 62; La Grimace 66; Breakdown • If I Were a Spy • Si J'Étais un Espion 67; Going Places • Making It • Les Valseuses 73;

Calmos • Cool, Calm and Collected • Femmes Fatales 75; Get Out Your Handkerchiefs • Préparez Vos Mouchoirs 77; Buffet Froid • Cold Cuts 79; Beau-Père • Stepfather 81; La Femme de Mon Pôte • My Best Friend's Girl 82; Notre Histoire • Our Story • Separate Rooms 84; Evening Dress • Ménage • Tenue de Soirée 86; Too Beautiful for You • Trop Belle pour Toi 89

Bliokh, Yakov Shanghai Document 28; The Front 31; Sergei Kirov • Sergo Kirov 35; Serge Ordjonikidze • Sergei Ordzhonikidzye • Sergo Ordzhonikidzye 37*

Blistène, Marcel Macadam 46; Étoile Sans Lumière • Star Without Light 47; Back Streets of Paris 48; Fire Under Her Skin 54; Gueule d'Ange • Pleasures and Vices 62

Block, Bruce The Princess Academy 87

Blom, August The Monocle 06; At the Prison Gates • Temptations of a Great City • Ved Fængslets Port 10; Den Dødes Halsbånd • The Necklace of the Dead 10; The Ghost of the Variety • Spøgelset i Gravkælderen 10; Hamlet 10; Den Hvide Slavehandel I • The White Slave 10; Jagten på Gentlemanrøveren 10; Life's Tempest • Livets Storme • Storms of Life 10; The Red Light • Spionen fra Tokio 10; Robinson Crusoe 10; Singaree 10; Adventure While Strolling • Eventyr på Fodrejsen • The Two Convicts • Den Udbrudte Slave 11; The Aeroplane Inventor • En Opfinders Skæbne 11; Annie Bell • Mamie Rose • Det Mørke Punkt 11; Aviatikeren og Journalistens Hustru • The Aviator and the Journalist's Wife • Ens Hustru • Flyveren og Journalisten • En Lektion 11; The Ballet Dancer • A Ballet Dancer's Love • Balletdanserinden 11*; The Bank Book • Vildledt Elskov 11; Den Blå Natviol • The Daughter of the Fortune Teller 11; Det Bødes Der For • Hævnen • Hævnet • Vengeance 11; A Bride of Death • Dødens Brud 11; Convicts No. 10 and No. 13 • Politimesteren • Tugthusfangerne Nr. 10 og 13 11; Damernes Blad • The Ladies' Journal 11; The Dangerous Age • Den Farlige Alder • The Price of Beauty 11; The Daughter of the Railway • Jernbanens Datter • The Little Railroad Queen 11; Desdemona 11; Dødsdrømmen • A Dream of Death 11; Ekspeditricen • In the Prime of Life • Ungdom og Letsind 11; Fader og Søn • Father and Son • Onkel og Nevø • A Poisonous Love 11; A Fatal Lie • Fru Potifar • Den Skæbnesvangre Løgn 11; Det Gamle Købmandshus • Midsommer • Midsummer-Tide • Midsummer-Time 11; Herr Storms Første Monokel • His First Monocle • Hr. Storms Første Monokel • Min Første Monokel 11; Den Hvide Slavehandel II • In the Hands of Imposters 11; Kærlighedens Magt • Kærlighedens Styrke • The Power of Love 11; Lady Mary's Love • Den Nådige Frøken 11; Love in the Tropics • Tropisk Kærlighed 11; Madame Potiphar • Potifars Hustru • The Victim of a Character 11; Mormonens Offer • The Victims of the Mormon 11; The Right of Youth • The Rights of Youth • Ungdom-

mens Ret 11; The Vampire Dancer • Vampyrdanserinden 11; Alt på et Kort • Gold from the Gutter • Guldmønten 12; At the Eleventh Hour • Hvem Var Forbryderen? • Samvittighedsnag 12; Battle of Hearts • A High Stake • Hjerternes Kamp 12; Bedstemoders Vuggevise • Operabranden • The Song Which Grandmother Sang 12; The Birthday Gift • Fødselsdagsgaven • Gaven 12; The Black Chancellor • Den Sorte Kansler 12; Brillantstjernen • For Her Sister's Sake 12; Caught in His Own Trap • Direktørens Datter 12; A Court Intrigue • En Hofintrige 12; Dearly Purchased Friendship • Dyrekøbt Venskab 12; Elskovsmagt • Gøgleren • Man's Great Adversary 12*; Faithful Unto Death • Et Hjerte af Guld • Hjertets Guld 12; Flugten Gennem Skyerne • The Fugitives • Den Sande Kærlighed 12; Det Første Honorar • Hans Første Honorar • His First Patient 12; Den Første Kærlighed • Her First Love Affair 12; The Governor's Daughter • Guvernørens Datter 12; Hans Vanskeligste Rolle • His Most Difficult Part 12; Historien om en Moder • The Life of a Mother • En Moders Kærlighed 12; Kærlighed Gør Blind • Love Is Blind 12; The Secret Treaty • Den Tredie Magt 12; The Three Comrades • De Tre Kammerater 12; Acquitted • Af Elskovs Nåde 13; Artists • Gøglerblod • Troløs 13; Atlantis 13; Et Bankrun • A Harvest of Tears • The Power of the Press • Pressens Magt 13; Bristet Lykke • A Paradise Lost 13; The Chinese Vase • Den Kinesiske Vase • Vasens Hemmelighed 13; A Dash for Liberty • Et Forfejlet Spring • Højt Spil 13; Elskovsleg • Liebelei • Love's Devotee 13*; En Farlig Forbryder • Knivstikkeren • A Modern Jack the Ripper 13; Fem Kopier • Five Copies 13; The Lost Bag • Når Fruen Går på Eventyr • Pompadourtasken 13; The Adventuress • Eventyrersken • Exiled 14; Ægteskab og Pigesjov • Mr. King på Eventyr • A Surprise Packet 14; Arbejdet Adler 14; The Doctor's Legacy • En Ensom Kvinde • Hvem Er Han? 14; Escaped the Law, But... • The Greatest Love • En Moders Kærlighed • Den Største Kærlighed 14; The Evil Genius • Et Skud i Mørket • Truet Lykke 14; Fædrenes Synd • Nemesis 14; En Gæst fra en Anden Verden • The Outcast's Return • Tugthusfange No. 97 14; The Guestless Dinner Party • Den Store Middag 14; Her Son • Sønnen 14; Kærligheds Væddemålet • The Wager 14; Et Læreår • The Reformation 14; Den Lille Chauffør • The Little Chauffeur 14; Pro Patria 14; The Professor 14; A Revolution Marriage • Revolutionsbryllup 14; Blind Fate • Den Blinde Skæbne • Lotteriseddel No. 22152 15; The Cripple Girl • Kærligheds Længsel • Den Pukkelryggede 15; Den, Der Sejrer • Nobody's Daughter • Syndens Datter 15; Du Skal Elske Din Næste • For de Andre • The Samaritan 15; The End of the World • The Flaming Sword • Flammesværdet • Verdens Undergang • The World's End 15; Eremitten • Guilty Love • The Hermit • Syndig

Kærlighed 15; For His Country's Honor • For Sit Lands Ære • Hendes Ære 15; Giftpilen • The Poisonous Arrow 15; Hjertestorme 15; The Robber Spider • Den Røde Enke • Rovedderkoppen • The White Widow 15; Gillekop 16; The Hostage of the Embassy • Legationens Gidsel • The Mysterious Lady's Companion • Den Mystiske Selskabsdame 16; The Countess' Honor • Grevindens Ære • Kniplinger • Lace 18; A Daughter of Brahma • The Favorite Wife of the Maharaja • Maharadjæns Yndlingshustru II • The Maharajah's Favorite 18; Dentelles 18; The Indian Tomb 18; Via Crucis 18; Bonds of Hate • Prometheus 19; Hans Gode Genius • His Guardian Angel • Mod Stjernerne 20; The Land of Fate • Præsten i Vejlby • The Vicar of Vejlby 20; Lights from Circus Life • Side Lights of the Sawdust Ring • Det Store Hjerte 24; Den Store Magt • With All Force 24; Hendes Nåde Dragonen • His Highness the Dragon 25

Blom, Per The Ice Palace • Is-Slottet 87

Blomberg, Erik Valkoinen Peura • The White Reindeer 52; When They Fall in Love 54; Betrothed 55

Błoński, Jan Kidawa see *Kidawa, Janusz*

Bloom, George Jay III Brothers in Arms 89

Bloom, Jeffrey Dogpound Shuffle • Spot 74; Mud • The Stick-Up 77; Blood Beach 80; Flowers in the Attic 87

Bloome, A. J. see *Blume, A. J.*

Bloomfield, George And Jenny Makes Three • Jenny 69; To Kill a Clown 72; Child Under a Leaf 74; Riel 79; Deadly Companion • Double Negative 80; Nothing Personal 80

Blue, James Amal le Voleur 59; L'Avare 60*; La Princesse Muette 60; The Olive Trees of Justice • Les Oliviers de la Justice 62; Letter from Columbia 63; The March • The March to Washington 63; School at Rincón Santo 63; A Few Notes on Our Food Problem 68

Bluemke, Ralph C. Robby 68

Blum, Chris Big Time 88

Blume, A. J. The Greater Sinner 19; The Dream of My People 34

Blumenberg, Hans-Christof Der Sommer des Samurai • Summer of the Samurai 86; Der Madonna Mann 88

Blumenstock, Mort Morals for Women 31

Bluth, Don The Secret of NIMH 82; An American Tail 86; The Land Before Time 88; All Dogs Go to Heaven 89*

Bluwal, Marcel Le Monte-Charge • La Morte Salé in Ascenseur • Paris Pick-Up 63

Blystone, Jack see *Blystone, John G.*

Blystone, Jasper The Reluctant Dragon 41*

Blystone, John G. Friendly Husband 23; Our Hospitality 23*; Soft Boiled 23; Ladies to Board 24; The Last Man on Earth 24; Oh You Tony! 24; Teeth 24; The Best Bad Man 25; Dick Turpin 25; The Everlasting Whisper 25; The Lucky Horseshoe 25; The Family Upstairs 26; Hard Boiled 26; My

Own Pal 26; Wings of the Storm 26; Ankles Preferred 27; Pajamas 27; Slaves of Beauty 27; Mother Knows Best 28*; Sharp Shooters 28; Captain Lash 29; The Sky Hawk 29; Thru Different Eyes 29; The Big Party 30; Men on Call 30; So This Is London 30; Tol'able David 30; Mr. Lemon of Orange 31; Young Sinners 31; Amateur Daddy 32; Charlie Chan's Chance 32; The Painted Woman 32; She Wanted a Millionaire 32; Too Busy to Work 32; Hot Pepper 33; My Lips Betray 33; Shanghai Madness 33; Change of Heart 34; Coming Out Party 34; The County Chairman 34; Hell in the Heavens 34; Bad Boy 35; Gentle Julia 36; Great Guy • Pluck of the Irish 36; Little Miss Nobody 36; The Magnificent Brute 36; Music for Madame 36; 23½ Hours Leave 37; Woman Chases Man 37; Block-Heads 38; Swiss Miss 38*;

Blyth, David Death Warmed Up 84
Blyth, Jeff Cheetah 89
Bo, Armando Positions of Love • Put Out or Shut Up • Put Up or Shut Up • Sabaleros 68; Heat • Y el Demonio Creó a los Hombres 70*
Board, John The Merry Wives of Tobias Rourke 72
Boasberg, Al Laughter in the Air • Myrt and Marge 33
Bobrov, G. U.S.S.R. Today 53*
Bobrovsky, Anatoli Mumu 61*; Litsom k Litsu 88
Bocan, Hynek Laughter Sticks to Your Heels • Smích Se Lepí na Paty 86
Boccacci, Antonio Metempsycose • Tomb of Torture 66
Bocchi, Arrigo Friends vs. Foes 14; Some Little Things Our Tommies Leave Behind Them 14; The Man and the Moment 18; Peace, Perfect Peace 18; The Slave 18; The Top Dog 18; The Wages of Sin 18; Damages for Breach 19; Fettered 19; Not Guilty 19; The Polar Star 19; Splendid Folly 19; When It Was Dark 19; Whosoever Shall Offend 19
Boccia, Tanio Conqueror of the Orient 61; Caesar the Conqueror • Giulio Cesare il Conquistatore delle Gallie 63; Desert Raiders 63; Samson and the Sea Beasts 63; Triumph of the Son of Hercules 63; Atlas Against the Czar • Machiste Against the Czar • Samson vs. the Giant King 64; Hercules of the Desert 64; Terror of the Steppe 64; The Revenge of Ivanhoe 65; La Valle del'Eco Tonante 65; Kill or Be Killed • Uccidi o Muori 66; Dio Non Paga il Sabato 67; La Lunga Cavalcata della Vendetta 72
Bocharov, Eduard Chiisai Tōbōsha • Chiisana Tōbōsha • The Little Runaway • Malenki Beglyets 66*
Bockmayer, Walter Geierwally 88
Bodo, Eugene Królowa Przedmiejscia • Queen of the Market Place 37; For Crimes Not Theirs • Za Winy Niepopelnione 39
Boer, Leo de The Way to Bresson • De Weg naar Bresson 84*
Boese, Carl Nocturno der Liebe 18; Der Geisha und der Samurai 19; Drei Nächte

20; Der Golem • The Golem • The Golem: How He Came Into the World • Der Golem: Wie Er in die Welt Kam 20*; Das Floss der Toten 21; Die Rote Mühle 21; Das Auge der Toten 22; Die Grosse Lüge 22; Das Ungeschriebene Gesetz 22; Graf Cohn 23; Maciste und die Chinesische Truhe 23; Die Frau im Feuer 24; Sklaven der Liebe 24; Die Eiserne Braut 25; Heiratsschwindler 25; Krieg im Frieden 25; Es Blasen die Trompeten 26; Die Letzte Droschke von Berlin 26; Der Mann Ohne Schlaf 26; The Eleven Devils • Die Elf Teufel 27*; Die Indiskrete Frau 27; Die Weisse Spinne 27; Eva in Seide 28; Kinder der Strasse 28; Sir or Madam 28; Alimente 29; Geschminkte Jugend 29; Bockbierfest 30; Der Detektiv des Kaisers 30; Komm Mit zum Rendezvous • Rendez-Vous 30; Dienst Ist Dienst 31; Grock 31; His Majesty King Ballyhoo • Man Braucht Kein Geld • We Need No Money • Wir Brauchen Kein Geld 31; Keine Feier Ohne Meyer 31; Meine Cousine aus Warschau 31; Der Schrecken der Garnison 31; Der Ungetreue Eckehart 31; Annemarie, die Braut der Kompanie 32; Drei von der Kavallerie 32; Die Herrin vom Maxim 32; Paprika 32; Theodor Körner 32; Drei Tage Mittelarrest 33; Eine Frau Wie Du 33; Gruss und Kuss Veronika! 33; Das Lied vom Glück • The Song of Happiness 33; Roman einer Nacht 33; Die Unschuld vom Lande 33; Fräulein Frau 34; Der Frechdachs 34*; Herz Ist Trumpf 34; Im Heidekrug • Der Schrecken vom Heidekrug 34; Wie Man Männer Fesselt 34; Die Fahrt in die Jugend 35; Ein Falscher Fuffziger 35; Der Gefangene des Königs 35; Gretl Zieht das Grosse Los 35; Die Kalte Mamsell 35; Meine Frau die Schützenkönigin 35; Eine Nacht an der Donau • A Night on the Danube 35; Der Schüchterne Felix 35; Drei Blaue Jungs, Ein Blondes Mädel 36; Engel mit Kleinen Fehler 36; Ein Ganzer Kerl 36; Männer Vor der Ehe 36; Abenteuer in Warschau 37; Mädchen für Alles 37; Die Schwebende Jungfrau 37; Dyplomatyczna Żona 38*; Five Millions Seek an Heir • Fünf Millionen Suchen einen Erben 38; The Heart Thief • Die Herzensdieb 38; Der Klapperstorchverband • The Stork Society 38; Die Kleine Sünderin • The Little Sinner • Schwarzfahrt ins Glück 38; Back in the Country • Dahinten in der Heide 39; Hearts in Love • Verliebte Herzen 39; Meine Tante, Deine Tante 39; O Schwarzwald! O Heimat! • Oh Black Forest! Oh Home! 39; The Unrecognized Man of the World • Der Verkannte Lebemann 39; Drei Vater um Anna • Three Fathers for Anna 40; Glück auf dem Lande • Rural Happiness 40; Polterabend 40; Familienanschluss 41; Das Hochzeitshotel 44; Der Posaunist 45; Beate 48; Wenn Männer Schwindeln 50; Der Onkel aus Amerika 52; Vater Macht Karriere 57

Boettger, Fritz see Böttger, Fritz
Boetticher, Budd Behind Closed Doors • One Mysterious Night 44; The Missing

Juror 44; Youth on Trial 44; Escape in the Fog 45; The Fleet That Came to Stay 45; A Guy, a Gal and a Pal 45; Assigned to Danger 48; Behind Locked Doors 48; Black Midnight 49; The Wolf Hunters 49; Killer Shark 50; The Bullfighter and the Lady 51; The Cimarron Kid 51; The Sword of D'Artagnan 51; Bronco Buster 52; Horizons West 52; Red Ball Express 52; Blades of the Musketeers 53; City Beneath the Sea • One Hour to Doom's Day 53; East of Sumatra 53; The Man from the Alamo 53; Seminole 53; Wings of the Hawk 53; The Brave and the Beautiful • The Magnificent Matador 55; The Killer Is Loose 55; Seven Men from Now 56; Decision at Sundown 57; The Tall T 57; Buchanan Rides Alone 58; Westbound 58; Ride Lonesome 59; The Rise and Fall of Legs Diamond 59; Comanche Station 60; Olle 67; Arruza 68; A Time for Dying 69; My Kingdom for… 85
Boetticher, Oscar, Jr. see Boetticher, Budd
Bogart, Paul Little Sister • Marlowe 69; Halls of Anger 70; Skin Game 71*; Cancel My Reservation 72; House Without a Christmas Tree 72; Class of '44 73; Mr. Ricco 74; The Three Sisters 77; Oh, God! You Devil 84; Torch Song Trilogy 88
Bogayevicz, Yurek Anna 87
Bogdanovich, Josef Boxoffice 82
Bogdanovich, Peter Gill Woman • Gill Women of Venus • Voyage to a Prehistoric Planet • Voyage to the Planet of Prehistoric Women • Voyage to the Prehistoric Planet 65*; Targets 67; Directed by John Ford 70; The Last Picture Show 71; What's Up, Doc? 72; Paper Moon 73; Daisy Miller 74; At Long Last Love 75; Nickelodeon 76; Saint Jack 79; They All Laughed 81; Mask 85; Illegally Yours 88; Texasville 90
Boger, Chris Cruel Passion 78
Bogin, Mikhail A Ballad of Love 66
Bogle, Andrew Dark Water 80; The Inside Man 80; Haunters of the Deep 85
Bogle, James Kadaicha 88
Bogner, Willy Benjamin 73; Fire and Ice 87
Bogris, Demetre The Girl Refugee • Prosfygopoula 38
Boguszewska, Helena Ludzie Wisłły • People of the Vistula • The Vistula People 37*
Böhm, Hark Chetan, Indian Boy • Tschetan der Indianerjunge 73; Moritz, Dear Moritz 78; Der Kleine Staatsanwalt • The Little Prosecutor 87; Yasemin 88
Bohr, José ¿Quién Mató a Eva? 34; La Sangre Manda 34; Tu Hijo 34; Así Es la Mujer 36; Sueño de Amor 36; El Traidor 38; By My Pistols • Por Mis Pistolas 39; La Herencia Macabra • The Macabre Legacy 39; El Látigo • The Whip 39
Boisrond, Michel C'Est Arrivé à Aden 56; Cette Sacrée Gamine • Mam'zelle Pigalle • Naughty Girl 56; Lorsque l'Enfant Paraît 56; La Parisienne • Une Parisienne 57; Le Chemin des Écoliers • The Way of Youth 59; Come Dance with

Me! • Voulez-Vous Danser avec Moi? 59;
Faibles Femmes • 3 Murderesses • Women
Are Weak 59; La Française et l'Amour •
Love and the Frenchwoman 60*; Un Soir
sur la Plage • Violent Summer 60; Les
Amours Célèbres 61; Comment Réussir en
Amour 62; Of Beds and Broads • Le Pari-
gine • Les Parisiennes • Tales of Paris 62*;
Comment Trouvez-Vous Ma Souer? 63;
Cherche l'Idole 64; Comment Epouser un
Premier Ministre 64; Atout Cœur à Tokyo
pour OSS 117 66; L'Homme Qui Valait des
Milliards 67; Aux Purs Tout Est Pur 68; La
Leçon Particulière • The Private Lesson •
The Tender Moment 68; Du Soleil Plein
les Yeux 70; On Est Toujours Trop Bon
avec les Femmes 71; Le Petit Poucet • Tom
Thumb 72; Dis-Moi Que Tu M'Aime 74;
Catherine & Co. • Catherine et Cie. 75

Boisset, Yves Coplan Sauve Sa Peau 68;
Un Condé • The Cop 70; Cran d'Arrêt 70;
Le Saut de l'Ange 71; L'Attentat • The
French Conspiracy • Plot 72; R.A.S. 73;
Dupont la Joie • Dupont Lajoie • Rape of
Innocence 75; Une Folle à Tuer 75; Le
Juge Fayard Dit le Sheriff 77; The Purple
Taxi • Un Taxi Mauve 77; La Clé sur la
Porte 78; La Femme Flic 80; Canicule •
Dog Day 83; Le Prix du Danger • The
Prize of Peril 83; Bleu Comme l'Enfer •
Blue Like Hell 85; Radio Corbeau 88; La
Travestie 88

Boissol, Claude Julie la Rousse • Julie
the Redhead 59; Three Etceteras and the
Colonel 60; Napoléon II, L'Aiglon 61

Boivin, Jerome Baxter 89

Bojorquez, Alberto Childstealers •
Robachicos 87

Bokova, Jana Hôtel du Paradis 86

Boland, John I'm Crazy About
You • Te Quiero con Locura 35

Boleslawski, Richard Three Meetings •
Tri Vstrechi 15; Bread • Khleb 18*; Boha-
terstwo Polskiego Skauta 19; Cud nad
Wisła • The Miracle of the Vistula 20; Last
of the Lone Wolf 30; Treasure Girl 30;
The Gay Diplomat 31; Woman Pursued
31; Rasputin • Rasputin and the Empress
• Rasputin—The Mad Monk 32*; Beauty
• Beauty for Sale 33; Fugitive Lovers 33;
Operator 13 • Spy 13 33; Storm at Day-
break 33; Clive of India 34; Hollywood
Party 34*; Men in White 34; The Painted
Veil 34*; Metropolitan 35; Les Misérables
35; O'Shaughnessy's Boy 35; The Garden
of Allah 36; Miracle in the Sand • Three
Godfathers 36; Theodora Goes Wild 36;
The Last of Mrs. Cheyney 37*

Boley, Raymond Peace for a Gunfighter 67

Bolívar, César Beyond Silence • Más
Allá del Silencio 87

Bolkov, B. One Day with Russians 61*

Böll, Heinrich Deutschland im Herbst •
Germany in Autumn 78*; Krieg und
Frieden • War and Peace 82*

Bollain, Juan Sebastián Las Dos Orillas •
The Two Banks 87

Bologna, Joseph It Had to Be You 88*

Bolognini, Mauro Ci Troviamo in Galleria 53; I Cavalieri della Regina 54; Gli

Innamorati • Wild Love 55; La Vena d'Oro
55; Guardia, Guardia Scelta, Brigadiere e
Maresciallo 56; Giovani Mariti • Newly-
weds • Young Husbands 57; Marisa la
Civetta 57; Arrangiatevi 59; Bad Girls
Don't Cry • Les Garçons • Night Heat • La
Notte Brava • On Any Street 59; Il
Bell'Antonio • Handsome Antonio 60; Ça
S'Est Passe à Rome • A Crazy Day • A Day
of Sin • From a Roman Balcony • La Gior-
nata Balorda • Love Is a Day's Work •
Pickup in Rome 60; The Lovemakers • La
Viaccia 60; Careless • Senilità 61; Agostino
62; La Corruzione 63; Bambole! • Le Bam-
bole • The Dolls • Four Kinds of Love
64*; La Donna È una Cosa Meravigliosa
64*; La Mia Signora 64*; Three Faces of a
Woman • I Tre Volti 64*; Le Chevalier de
Maupin • Madamigella di Maupin •
Mademoiselle de Maupin 65; The Fairies •
Le Fate • Les Ogresses • The Queens • Sex
Quartet 66*; Les Sorcières • Le Streghe •
The Witches 66*; Das Alteste Gewerbe der
Welt • L'Amore Attraverso i Secoli •
L'Amour à Travers les Âges • The Oldest
Profession • Le Plus Vieux Métier du
Monde 67*; Arabella 67; Un Bellissimo
Novembre • That Splendid November 68;
Capriccio all'Italiana 68*; L'Assoluto Na-
turale 69*; Metello 69; She and He 69;
Bubú 70; Imputazione di Omicidio per
uno Studente 71; Libera, Amore Mio! 73;
Drama of the Rich • Fatti di Gente Per-
bene • La Grande Bourgeoise • The Murri
Affair 74; Down the Ancient Staircase •
Down the Ancient Stairs • Per le Antiche
Scale 75; L'Eredità Ferramonti • The In-
heritance 76; Black Journal • La Signora
degli Orrori 77; Gran Bollito 77; Dove Vai
in Vacanza? 78*; La Dame aux Camélias •
The Lady of the Camellias • The True
Story of Camille • La Vera Storia della
Signora delle Camelie 80; The Venetian
Woman • La Venexiana 85; Mosca Addio
• Moscow Farewell 86

Bolshintsov, M. Law of the Siberian
Taiga 30

Bolt, Ben Black Island 79; The Arm •
The Big Town 87

Bolt, Robert Lady Caroline Lamb 72

Bolton, Albert C. The Poacher 29

Bolváry, Géza von Die Gefangene von
Shanghai 27*; The Ghost Train 27; Num-
ber Seventeen 28; The Wrecker 28; The
Vagabond Queen 29; Zwei Herzen in
Dreiviertel Takt 30; Die Lustigen Weiber
von Wien 31; Der Raub der Mona Lisa •
The Theft of the Mona Lisa 31; Sein
Liebeslied 31; Liebeskommando 32; Das
Lied Ist Aus 32; Ich Will Nicht Wissen
Wer Du Bist 33; Der Liebling von Wien
33; Pardon Tévedtem • Romance in Buda-
pest • Skandal in Budapest 33*; Das
Schloss im Süden 33; Was Frauen Trau-
men • What Women Dream 33; Pesti
Szerelem 34; I Don't Know You But I
Love You • Ich Kenn' Dich Nicht und
Liebe Dich 35; Winternachtstraum 35; Ein
Lied, ein Kuss, ein Mädel 36; The Irresist-
ible Man • Der Unwiderst Ehliche 37; The

Night of Great Love 37; Das Schloss im
Flandern 37; The Abduction 38; The
Charm of La Bohème 38; Flower of the
Tisza • Tiszavirág 39; Die Julika 39; Gypsy
Ways • Zigeunerweisen 40; Life's Mirror •
Der Spiegel des Lebens 40; Maria Ilona 40;
Opera Ball • Opernball 40; Vienna Tales •
Wiener Geschichten 40; The Bat • Die
Fledermaus 48

Bom, Rim Chang see Rim, Chang Bom

Bomay, Jack Solomon King 74*

Bonanova, Fortunio Don Juan 24

Bonch-Tomashevsky, M. Thief 16

Bond, Jack Separation 68; Anti-Clock
80*; It Couldn't Happen Here 88

Bond, James III Def by Temptation 90

Bond, Timothy Deadly Harvest 72; One
Night Only 83

Bondarchuk, Sergei Destiny of a Man •
Fate of a Man • Sudba Cheloveka 59;
Voina i Mir • War and Peace 67; Waterloo
70; Oni Srajalis za Rodinou • Oni Srazhalis
za Rodinu • They Fought for Their Coun-
try • They Fought for Their Motherland
74; The Peaks of Zelengore • Vrhovi Zel-
engore 76; Step • The Steppe • The Step-
pes 77; Krasnye Kolokola: Meksika v Ogne
• Mexico in Flames • Red Bells: Mexico in
Flames 82; Krasnye Kolokola: Ya Videl
Rozhdenie Novogo Mira • Red Bells: I've
Seen the Birth of a New World 83; Boris
Godunov 86

Bonerz, Peter Nobody's Perfekt 81;
Police Academy VI: City Under Siege 89

Bonfanti, Antoine La Guerre Populaire
au Laos 68*

Bonnard, Mario Passa la Ruina 19; I
Promessi Sposi 19; Pupilla nell'Ombra 19;
La Morte Piagne 20; Il Tacchino 23; Altro
Io 24; Teodoro e Socio 24; Der Kampf
ums Matterhorn 28*; Russia 29; Der Sohn
der Weissen Berge 30; Fra Diavolo 31;
L'Amore Che Cantà • Tre Uomini in Frak
32; Cinque a Zero 32; Pas de Femmes 32;
Il Trattato Scomparso 33; Marcia Nuziale
34; Milizia Territoriale 35; Trenta Secondi
D'Amore 36; Adam's Tree • L'Albero di
Adamo 37; Il Feroce Saladino 37; Il Conte
di Brechard • The Count of Brechard 38;
Io Suo Padre 38; Jeanne Dore 38; Frenesia
• Frenzy 39; Papà per una Notte 39; La
Fanciulla di Portici 40; Marco Visconti 40;
Il Ponte dei Sospiri 40; L'Uomo del
Romanzo 40; The King's Jester • Il Re Si
Diverte 41; Rossini 41; Avanti C'È Posto
42; Campo di Fiori • The Peddler and the
Lady 43; Una Distinta Famiglia 43; Il Ratto
delle Sabine 45; Addio Mia Bella Napoli!
46; La Città Dolente • City of Pain 49;
Disillusion 49; Margaret of Cortona • Mar-
gherita da Cortona 50; Stasera Sciopero 51;
L'Ultima Sentenza 51; Il Voto 51; I Figli
Non Si Vendono 52; Tormento del Passato
52; Frine, Cortigiana D'Oriente 53; Con-
cert of Intrigue • Night of Love 54; Hanno
Rubato um Tram 54; La Ladra 55; Mi
Permette Babbo! 56; Gastone 59; The Last
Days of Pompeii • Gli Ultimi Giorni di
Pompeii 59*; I Masnadieri 61; Aphrodite,
Goddess of Love 62; Rome 1585 63

Bonnardot, Jean-Claude Moranbong 59; Ballade pour un Voyou 63

Bonner, Lee Adventure of the Action Hunters • Two for the Money 82

Bonnicksen, Ted Fast Buck Duck 63*

Bonnière, René Amanita Pestilens 63

Bonns, Miguel Iglesias *see Iglesias Bonns, Miguel*

Bonsels, Waldemar The Adventures of Maya 29

Bonsignori, Umberto Confessions of a Vahine • Maeva • Maeva—Portrait of a Tahitian Girl • Pagan Hellcat • True Diary of a Vahine • True Diary of a Wahine • True Story of a Wahine • Wahine 61

Bontross, Thomas Blood on His Lips • The Hideous Sun Demon • The Sun Demon • Terror from the Sun 59*

Bonucci, Alberto L'Amore Difficile • Erotica • Of Wayward Love 62*

Bonzi, Leonardo Blue Continent • Continente Perduto • The Lost Continent • Sesto Continento • The Sixth Continent 54*

Bookbinder, Lester Dire Straits Presents Making Movies 81

Boorman, John Catch Us If You Can • Having a Wild Weekend 65; The Great Director 66; Point Blank 67; The Enemy • Hell in the Pacific 68; Leo the Last 69; Deliverance 72; Zardoz 73; Exorcist II: The Heretic • The Heretic • The Heretic: Exorcist II 77; Excalibur 81; The Emerald Forest 85; Hope and Glory 87; Where the Heart Is 89

Boos, H. Gordon Red Surf 90

Booth, Harry Blitz on Britain 60; A King's Story 67; River Rivals 67; The Magnificent Six and ½ 68; Bachelor of Arts 69; The Magnificent 6 and ½ 69; On the Buses 71; Double Take • Go for a Take 72; Mutiny on the Buses 72; The Flying Sorcerer 74

Booth, Walter R. The Miser's Doom 1899; Upside Down, or The Human Flies 1899; Britain's Welcome to Her Sons 00; Chinese Magic • Yellow Peril 00; Diving for Treasure 00; The Hairbreadth Escape of Jack Sheppard 00; Hindoo Jugglers 00; Kruger's Dream of Empire 00; The Last Days of Pompeii 00; Plucked from the Burning 00; A Railway Collision 00; 'Arry on the Steamboat 01; Artistic Creation 01; Britain's Tribute to Her Sons 01; The Captain's Birthday 01; The Cheese Mites, or Lilliputians in a London Restaurant • Cheesemites 01; The Devil in the Studio 01; The Drunkard's Conversion • The Horrors of Drink 01; The Famous Illusion of De Kolta 01; The Haunted Curiosity Shop 01; The Magic Sword • The Magic Sword, or A Medieval Mystery 01; Mr. Pickwick's Christmas at Wardle's 01; Ora Pro Nobis • Ora Pro Nobis, or The Poor Orphan's Last Prayer 01; An Over-Incubated Baby 01; Scrooge • Scrooge, or Marley's Ghost 01; Undressing Extraordinary, or The Troubles of a Tired Traveller 01; The Waif and the Wizard • The Waif and the Wizard, or The Home Made Happy 01; The En-

chanted Cup 02; The Extraordinary Waiter • The Mysterious Heads 02; Father Thames' Temperance Cure 02; Soap vs. Blacking 02; The Adventurous Voyage of The Arctic • The Voyage of The Arctic 03; The Dice Player's Last Throw 03; An Extraordinary Cab Accident 03; Pocket Boxers 03; The Haunted Scene Painter 04; The Music Hall Manager's Dilemma 04; Topical Tricks 05; The Conjuror's Pupil 06; Following in Father's Footsteps 06; The Hand of the Artist 06; The Magic Bottle 06; The ? Motorist 06; Puck's Pranks on a Suburbanite 06; The Vacuum Cleaner Nightmare 06; Accidents Will Happen 07; The Apple of Discord 07; The Baffled Burglar 07; Catch Your Own Fish 07; Comedy Cartoons 07; The Curate's Double 07; Diabolo Nightmare 07; Dreamland Adventures 07; Hanky Panky Cards 07; The Haunted Bedroom 07; His Daughter's Voice 07; A Juvenile Scientist 07; The Magical Press 07; A Modern Galatea 07; Sammy's Sucker 07; The Sorcerer's Scissors 07; The Thousand Pound Spook 07; The Waif and the Statue 07; When the Devil Drives 07; Willie Goodchild Visits His Auntie 07; Willie's Magic Wand 07; The Adventures of a Watch 08; The Chauffeur's Dream 08; Following in Mother's Footsteps 08; The Guard's Alarum 08; The Hands of a Wizard 08; The Lightning Postcard Artist 08; Paper Tearing 08; Polka on the Brain 08; The Prehistoric Man 08; A Quick-Change Mesmerist 08; The Star Globe-Trotter 08; The Tramp's Cycling Mania 08; Two Little Motorists 08; Waterproof Willie 08; Your Dog Ate My Lunch Mum 08; An Absorbing Tale 09; The Aerial Torpedo • The Airship Destroyer • The Battle in the Clouds 09; Animated Cotton 09; Apples 09; Bobby Wideawake 09; A Bogus Motor Elopement 09; The Electric Servant 09; From Working House to Mansion 09; How I Cook-ed Peary's Record • Up the Pole 09; The Invisible Dog 09; The Magic Carpet 09; Marie Lloyd's Little Joke 09; Monty Learns to Swim 09; Professor Puddenhead's Patents—The Aerocab and the Vacuum Provider 09; Professor Puddenhead's Patents—The Electric Enlarger 09; The Professor's Dream 09; Saved by a Burglar 09; Sooty Sketches 09; That Awful Pipe 09; The Uncontrollable Motorcycle 09; Why Father Grew a Beard 09; Why Tommy Was Late for School 09; The Wizard's Walking Stick 09; The Aerial Submarine 10; The Bewitched Boxing Gloves 10; The Electric Vitalizer 10; The Freezing Mixture • Potted Plays No. 3 10; The Great Fight at All-Sereno 10; His Mother's Necklace 10; The Hunt for a Collar 10; Juggling on the Brain 10; Seeing London in One Day 10; The Aerial Anarchists 11; An Aerial Elopement 11; Animated Putty 11; The Automatic Motorist 11; The Cap of Invisibility 11*; The Fakir's Fan • The Magic Fan 11; Giles Has His Fortune Told 11; The Hypnotist and the Convict 11*; A Juvenile Hyp-

notist • Juvenile Pranks 11; Kitty in Dreamland 11; Little Lady Lafayette 11*; Mischievous Puck 11*; The Modern Pygmalion and Galatea 11*; Mystic Manipulations 11*; Simpkins' Dream of a Holiday 11*; Uncle's Picnic 11*; The Wizard and the Brigands 11*; Animated Toys 12; Card Manipulations 12; Clever Egg Conjuring 12; The Conjuror As a Good Samaritan 12; An Eccentric Sportsman 12; From Behind the Flag 12; Getting His Own Back • The Joker's Mistake 12; Gollywog's Motor Accident • In Gollywog Land 12*; In Fairyland 12; The Jester's Joke • The Merry Jester 12; Modelling Extraordinary 12; A Modern Mystery 12; Paper Cuttings 12; Santa Claus 12*; And Very Nice Too 13; Artful Athletics 13; Fantasie: Dresden China 13; Good Queen Bess 13; His Father's Voice: Mrs. Kelly 13; Little Micky the Mesmerist 13; Persian Dance: Eightpence a Mile 13; Recitation by James Welch 13; Sailor's Song 13; A Sister to Assist 'Er 13; Trio: Everybody's Doing It 13; Love and Magic 14; Magical Mysteries 14; The Shirker's Nightmare 14; The Tangram 14; Can You Do This? 15; A Devil of a Honeymoon 15; Kineto's Side-Splitters No. 1 15; The Portrait of Dolly Grey 15; The World's Worst Wizard 15; Tank Cartoons • Tanks 16; Too Much Sausage 16; Tommy's Initiation 18

Borau, José Luis En el Río • In the River 61; Brandy, el Sheriff de Losatumba • Brandy, the Sheriff of Losatumba 63; Cavalca e Uccidi • Ride and Kill 63; Crimen de Doble Filo • Double-Edged Murder 64; B Must Die • Hay Que Matar a B 74; Furtivos • Poachers 75; La Sabina • The Sabina 79; On the Line • Río Abajo 83

Borcosque, Carlos Dos Noches 33; Fighting Lady 35; Alas de Mi Patria • My Country's Wings 40

Borden, Lizzie Born in Flames 82; Working Girls 86

Borderie, Bernard Poison Ivy 53; Dishonorable Discharge 58; The Gorilla Greets You • Le Gorille Vous Salue Bien 58; Ladies' Man 60; Women Are Like That 60; Clash of Steel 62; Rocambole 62; À Toi de Faire Mignonne • Your Turn Darling 63; Vengeance of the Three Musketeers 63; Angélique • Angélique, Marquise des Anges 64

Borek, Jaromír An Exceptional Situation • Výjímečná Situace 85; Cena Medu 87

Borg, Reginald le *see LeBorg, Reginald*

Borghesio, Carlo Due Milioni per un Sorriso 39*

Borgnetto, Romano Maciste Alpino 16*

Boris, Robert Oxford Blues 84; Steele Justice 87; Buy & Cell 88

Born, Adolf Mach a Šebestová, k Tabuli! • Mach and Sebestova, Come to the Blackboard Please! 85*

Bornebusch, Arne Skärgårds-Flirt 36; Våran Pojke 36; Sun Over Sweden 38

Borneman, Ernest Betty Slow Drag 53

Boroomand, M. City of Mice 86*

Borowczyk, Walerian Głowa • The Head 53; Atelier de Fernand Léger 54;

Photographies Vivantes 54; Autumn • Jesień 56; Banner of Youth • Sztandar Młodych 57*; Był Sobie Raz • Once Upon a Time 57*; Dni Oświaty 57*; Love Requited • Love Rewarded • Nagrodzone Uczucie 57*; Striptease 57*; Dom • House 58*; L'École • School • Szkoła 58; Les Astronautes 59*; Le Magicien 59; Terra Incognita 59; Le Dernier Voyage de Gulliver 60; Boîte à Musique 61*; Solitude 61*; Concert • Le Concert de Monsieur et Madame Kabal • The Concert of Mr. and Mrs. Kabal 62; Les Bibliothèques 63; Les Écoles 63; L'Écriture 63; L'Encyclopédie de Grand'maman en 13 Volumes • Grandma's Encyclopedia 63; Holy Smoke 63; Renaissance 63; Les Stroboscopes 63; La Fille Sage 64; The Games of the Angels • Les Jeux des Anges 64; Gancia 64; Le Musée 64; Le Dictionnaire de Joachim • Joachim's Dictionary 65; Un Été Torride 65; Le Petit Poucet 65; Rosalie 66; Diptych • Diptyque 67; Gavotte 67; Le Théâtre de Monsieur et Madame Kabal 67; Goto, Island of Love • Goto, l'Île d'Amour 68; Mazepa 68; Le Phonographe 69; Blanche 70; Une Collection Particulière • A Particular Collection 73; Contes Immoraux • Immoral Tales 74; The Beast • La Bête 75; Dzieje Grzechu • Story of a Sin • The Story of Sin 75; La Marge • The Margin • The Streetwalker 76; Behind Convent Walls • Interior of a Convent • L'Interno di un Convento • Interno d'un Convento • Sex Life in a Convent 77; Les Héroïnes du Mal • Heroines of Evil • Three Immoral Women 78; Collections Privées 79*; Lulu 80; The Blood of Dr. Jekyll • Docteur Jekyll et les Femmes • Dr. Jekyll • Dr. Jekyll and Miss Osbourne • Dr. Jekyll and the Women • The Strange Case of Dr. Jekyll and Mrs. Osbourne 81; Ars Amandi • L'Art d'Aimer • The Art of Love 82; Emmanuelle V 87; Cérémonie d'Amour 88

Borremans, Guy Un Homme et Son Boss 70*

Borris, Clay Rose's House 77; Alligator Shoes 81; Quiet Cool 86

Borsody, Eduard von The Green Hell • Die Grüne Hölle 39; Congo Express 40; Liane, Jungle Goddess 56; Corinna Darling 58

Borsos, Phillip The Grey Fox 82; The Mean Season 85; One Magic Christmas 85; Bethune: The Making of a Hero 88

Bortko, Vladimir Yedinozhdy Solgar 88

Borup, C. A Glue-my Affair 13

Borzage, Frank The Pitch o' Chance 15; The Code of Honor 16; The Courtin' of Calliope Clew 16; The Demon of Fear 16; Dollars of Dross 16; Enchantment 16; The Forgotten Prayer 16; Hair Trigger Casey • Immediate Lee 16; Land o' Lizards • Silent Shelby 16; Life's Harmony 16*; Mammy's Rose 16*; Nell Dale's Men Folks 16; Nugget Jim's Pardner 16; The Pride and the Man 16; The Silken Spider 16; That Gal of Burke's • That Girl of Burke's 16; The Curse of Iku 17; Flying Colors 17; The Ghost Flower 17; Until They Get Me 17;

Wee Lady Betty 17*; The Gun Woman 18; An Honest Man 18; Innocent's Progress 18; Shoes That Danced 18; Society for Sale 18; Who Is to Blame? 18; Ashes of Desire 19; Prudence of Broadway 19; Toton 19; Whom the Gods Destroy • Whom the Gods Would Destroy 19; Humoresque 20; The Duke of Chimney Butte 21; Get-Rich-Quick Wallingford 21; Back Pay 22; Billy Jim 22; The Good Provider 22; The Pride of Palomar 22; The Valley of Silent Men 22; The Age of Desire 23; Children of Dust • Children of the Dust 23; The Higher Law • The Nth Commandment 23; Secrets 24; The Circle 25; Daddy's Gone A-Hunting • A Man's World 25; The Lady 25; Lazybones 25; Wages for Wives 25; The Dixie Merchant 26; Early to Wed 26; The First Year 26; Marriage License? • The Pelican 26; Seventh Heaven 27; La Femme au Corbeau • The River 28; Street Angel 28; Lucky Star 29; They Had to See Paris 29; Liliom 30; Song o' My Heart 30; As Young As You Feel • Young As You Feel 31; Bad Girl 31; Doctors' Wives 31; We Humans • Young America 31; After Tomorrow 32; A Farewell to Arms 32; A Man's Castle 33; Secrets 33*; Flirtation Walk 34; Little Man, What Now? 34; Living on Velvet 34; No Greater Glory 34; Shipmates Forever 35; Stranded 35; Desire 36; Hearts Divided 36; The Big City • Skyscraper Wilderness 37; The Green Light 37; History Is Made at Night 37; Mannequin 37; The Shining Hour 38; Three Comrades 38; Disputed Passage 39; I Take This Woman 39*; Flight Command 40; The Mortal Storm 40; Strange Cargo 40; Smilin' Through 41; The Vanishing Virginian 41; Seven Sweethearts 42; His Butler's Sister 43; Stage Door Canteen 43; Till We Meet Again 44; The Spanish Main 45; Concerto • I've Always Loved You 46; Magnificent Doll 46; That's My Man • Will Tomorrow Ever Come? 46; Moonrise 48; China Doll 58; The Big Fisherman 59; Antinea, l'Amante della Città Sepolta • L'Atlantide • L'Atlantide—Antinea, l'Amante della Città Sepolta • Atlantis the Lost Continent • Atlantis the Lost Kingdom • Journey Beneath the Desert • The Lost Kingdom • Queen of Atlantis 61*

Bosch, Juan La Diligencia de los Condenados 70; Lo Credevano uno Stingo di Santo 72; Exorcismo 74

Bose, Debaki Kumar Pansahar 28; Aparadhi • The Culprit 31; Chandidas 32; The Devotee • Puran Bhagat 33; Seeta 33; Inquilbad 37; Vidyapathi 37; Kusha Laila 40; Apna Ghar 41; Ratna Deep 47; Kavi Kewi • The Poet 49

Bose, Nitin Bhagya Chakra • The Wheel of Fate 35

Bosio, Gianfranco de see De Bosio, Gianfranco

Boskovich, John Without You, I'm Nothing 90

Bosnick, Ned How Now Sweet Jesus? • Imago • To Be Free 70

Bossak, Jerzy Maidanek • Majdanek •

Majdanek, Cmentarzysko Europy • Majdanek, Extermination Camp 44*; The Battle of Kolberg • The Battle of Kolobrzeg • Bitwa o Kołobrzeg 45*; Berlin • The Fall of Berlin 45*; The Flood • Powódz • Storm Over Poland 46; Peace Conquers the World • Peace Will Win • Pokój Zwycięży Świat 50*; Our Oath 52; Bicycle Race 54; Warsaw 56 54; Meeting in Warsaw 55*; September 56 56*; Songs of the Vistula 56; Requiem dla 500,000 • Requiem for 500,000 63*; Dokumenty Walki 67; Mr. Dódek 69

Bostan, Elisabeta The Clowns • Saltimancii 85

Bostwick, Elwood A Factory Magdalene 14

Bosustow, Stephen Hell-Bent for Election 44*; Brotherhood of Man 47*; Swab Your Choppers 47

Bosworth, Hobart The Sea Wolf 13; Burning Daylight 14; John Barleycorn 14; An Odyssey of the North 14; The Pursuit of the Phantom 14; The Valley of the Moon 14; Buckshot John 15; Captain Courtesy 15; Fatherhood 15; A Little Brother of the Rich 15*; Pretty Mrs. Smith 15; The Scarlet Sin 15*; The White Scar 15

Boszormenyi, Géza Laura 87

Botcharov, Édouard Three Tales of Chekhov 61*

Botelho, Chico Cidade Oculta • Hidden City 87

Botelho, João Um Adeus Português • A Portuguese Goodbye 85; Hard Times • Tempos Difíceis 88

Böttger, Fritz Body in the Web • Girls of Spider Island • Horrors of Spider Island • Hot in Paradise • It's Hot in Paradise • The Spider's Web • Ein Toter Hing im Netz 59

Bottia, Luis Fernando The Accordionist's Wedding • La Boda del Acordeonista 86

Bottia, Pacho see Bottia, Luis Fernando

Boucharebe, Rachid Baton Rouge 85

Boudrioz, Robert L'Âpre Lutte 17; La Distance 18; Un Soir 19; Zon 20; Tempêtes 22; L'Âtre • Tillers of the Soil 23; L'Épervier 24; In the Spider's Web 24; Les Louves 25; La Chaussée des Géants 26; Trois Jeunes Filles 28; Vivre 28

Boujenah, Paul Yiddish Connection 86

Boulting, John Journey Together 45; Brighton Rock • Young Scarface 47; Seven Days to Noon 50; The Magic Box 51; Crest of the Wave • Seagulls Over Sorrento 53*; Private's Progress 55; Lucky Jim 57; I'm All Right, Jack 59; The Risk • Suspect 60*; Heavens Above! 63; Rotten to the Core • Rotten to the Corps 65

Boulting, Laurence Dawn Breakers 76

Boulting, Roy Consider Your Verdict 37; The Landlady 37; Ripe Earth 38; Seeing Stars 38; Design for Murder • Trunk Crime 39; Inquest 39; Pastor Hall 40; Dawn Guard 41; They Serve Abroad 42; Thunder Rock 42; Desert Victory 43; Tunisian Victory 43*; Minefield! 44; Burma Victory 45; Fame Is the Spur 46; The Guinea Pig • The Outsider 48; Able

Seaman Brown • Brown on Resolution • Sailor of the King • Single-Handed 51; High Treason 51; Crest of the Wave • Seagulls Over Sorrento 53*; Josephine and Men 55; Brothers in Law 56; Run for the Sun 56; Happy Is the Bride! 57; Carleton-Browne of the F.O. • Man in a Cocked Hat 58*; The French Mistress 60; The Risk • Suspect 60*; The Family Way 66; Twisted Nerve 68; There's a Girl in My Soup 70; Cry of the Penguins • Mr. Forbush and the Penguins 71*; Soft Beds and Hard Battles • Soft Beds, Hard Battles • Undercover Hero • Undercovers Hero 73; Danny Travis • The Last Word • The Number 78

Bourdon, Jacques Scheherazade • La Schiava di Bagdad • Shéhérazade 63*

Bourgeois, Gérard Life in the Next Century 09; Les Victimes de l'Alcool 11; Christophe Colomb 19; Les Mystères du Ciel 20; Un Drame Sous Napoléon 21; Faust 22; La Dette de Sang 23

Bourguignon, Serge Le Rhin, Fleuve International 52*; Médecin des Sols 53; Bornéo 54; Démons et Merveilles de Bali 54; Le Langage du Sourire • Sikkim, Terre Secrète 56; Jeune Patriarche 57; Escale 59; L'Étoile de Mer 59; Le Montreur d'Ombres 59; Le Sourire 60; Cybèle • Cybèle ou Les Dimanches de Ville d'Avray • Les Dimanches de Ville d'Avray • Sundays and Cybèle 62; La Chevauchée 64; The Reward 65; À Cœur Joie • Two Weeks in September • With Joyous Heart 67; The Picasso Summer 67; My Kingdom for a Horse 86; The Fascination 87

Bourke, Terry Inn of the Damned 74; Lady Stay Dead 82; Brothers 84

Bourne, Peter Forty-Eight Hours to Live • Man in the Middle 59

Boutel, Maurice Prostitution • La Prostitution 65

Boutet, Richard La Guerre Oubliée 88

Boutron, Pierre Les Années Sandwiches 88

Bouvier, François Jacques and November • Jacques et Novembre 85*; Les Matins Infidèles 89

Bouwmeester, Theo The Anarchist's Sweetheart 08; Poverty and Compassion 08; To the Custody of the Father 08; An Attempt to Smash a Bank 09; The Bailiff and the Dressmakers 09; The Blind Man 09; The Burglar and the Child 09; A Coward's Courage 09; The Curse of Money 09; Farmer Giles in London 09; A Father's Mistake 09; Fellow Clerks 09; The Idiot of the Mountains 09; The Luck of the Cards 09; Mistaken Identity 09; A Narrow Escape from Lynching 09; The New Servant 09; One Good Turn Deserves Another 09; Only a Tramp 09; Robbing the Widowed and Fatherless 09; Salome Mad 09; A Sinner's Repentance 09; The Sleepwalker 09; The Special License 09; Teaching a Husband a Lesson 09; The Treacherous Policeman 09; When Thieves Fall Out 09; Within an Ace 09; A Woman's Vanity 09; The Wrong Coat 09; Almost 10; The

Brothers 10; The Bully 10; By Order of Napoleon • Checkmated 10; The Child and the Fiddler 10; The Coster's Wedding 10; From Factory Girl to Prima Donna 10; From Storm to Sunshine 10; His Only Daughter 10; His Wife's Brother 10; Impersonating the Policeman Lodger 10; In the Hands of the Enemy 10; Jailbird in Borrowed Feathers 10; Jake's Daughter 10; The Little Orphan 10; Lord Blend's Love Story 10; A Mad Infatuation 10; The Moving Picture Rehearsal 10; The Old Soldier 10; The Picture Thieves 10; The Plans of the Fortress 10; A Sailor's Sacrifice 10; The Stricken Home 10; The Suffragettes and the Hobble Skirt 10; True to His Duty 10; The Two Fathers 10; The Wedding That Didn't Come Off 10; A Woman's Folly 10; A Woman's Treachery 10; A Worker's Wife 10; The Adopted Child 11; The Amorous Doctor 11; Boys Will Be Boys 11; Buffalo Bill on the Brain 11; The Burglar As Father Christmas 11; The Cap of Invisibility 11*; Dandy Dick of Bishopsgate 11; An Elizabethan Romance 11; Fate 11; The Fisherman's Daughter 11; Following Mother's Footsteps • In Mother's Footsteps 11; A Gambler's Villainy 11; The General's Only Son 11; Gerald's Butterfly 11; The Highlander 11; His Conscience 11; His Last Burglary 11; The Hypnotist and the Convict 11*; The Inventor's Son 11; Johnson at the Wedding 11; Kinemacolor Songs 11; The King of Indigo 11; Kitty the Dressmaker 11; Lady Beaulay's Necklace 11; The Last Farewell 11; The Little Daughter's Letter 11; Little Lady Lafayette 11*; The Little Wooden Soldier 11; The Lost Ring, or Johnson's Honeymoon 11; Love Conquers 11; Love or Riches 11; A Love Story of Charles II 11; Love's Strategy 11; The Magic Ring 11; Major the Red Cross Dog 11; The Millionaire's Nephew 11; Mischievous Puck 11*; A Modern Hero 11; The Modern Pygmalion and Galatea 11*; Music Hath Charms 11; Mystic Manipulations 11*; Nell Gwynn the Orange Girl 11; A Noble Heart 11; The Old Hat 11; Oliver Cromwell 11; A Seaside Comedy 11; Simpkins' Dream of a Holiday 11*; Through Fire to Fortune 11; The Tide of Fortune 11; A Tragedy of the Olden Times 11; A True Briton 11; The Two Chorus Girls 11; Two Christmas Hampers 11; Uncle's Picnic 11*; The Vicissitudes of a Top Hat 11; The Wizard and the Brigands 11*; The Woodcutter's Romance 11; Light After Darkness 12; The Boatswain's Daughter 13; A Whiff of Onion 13

Bouzid, Nouri L'Homme de Cendres • Man of Ashes • Rih Essed 86

Bove, Hans Dieter Immer Wenn Es Nacht Wird • The Love Feast 66

Bowden, Frank This Oxford 31

Bowen, Edward White Death 36

Bowen, Jenny Street Music 81; Animal Behavior 85*; The Wizard of Loneliness 88

Bower, Dallas The Path of Glory 34; Alice in Wonderland 50; The Second Mrs. Tanqueray 52

Bowers, Charles Cramps 16; The Dog Pound 16; The Hock Shop 16; The Indestructible Hats 16; Jeff's Toothache 16; Mutt and Jeff in the Submarine 16; The Promoters 16; Two for Five 16; Wall Street 16; The Bell Hops 17*; The Boarding House 17*; The Chamber of Horrors 17*; The Cheese Tamers 17*; A Chemical Calamity 17*; Cows and Caws 17*; A Day in Camp 17*; A Dog's Life 17*; In the Theatrical Business 17*; The Interpreters 17*; The Janitors 17*; Preparedness 17*; The Prospectors 17*; Revenge Is Sweet 17*; The Submarine Chasers 17*; The Accident Attorney 18*; An Ace and a Joker 18*; Around the World in Nine Minutes 18*; At the Front 18*; Back to the Balkans 18*; Bulling the Bolshevik 18*; The Burglar Alarm 18*; Coal and Cold Feet • Helping McAdoo 18*; The Decoy 18*; The Doughboy 18*; The Draft Board 18*; Efficiency 18*; The Extra Quick Lunch 18*; A Fisherless Cartoon 18*; Freight Investigation 18*; Hitting the High Spots 18*; Hospital Orderlies 18*; Hotel de Mutt 18*; Hunting the U-Boats 18*; Joining the Tanks 18*; The Kaiser's New Dentist 18*; Landing a Spy 18*; The Leak 18*; Life Savers 18*; A Lot of Bull 18*; Meeting Theda Bara 18*; The New Champion 18*; Occultism 18*; On Ice 18*; Our Four Days in Germany 18*; Pot Luck in the Army 18*; The Seventy-Five Mile Gun 18*; The Side Show 18*; Superintendents 18*; The Tale of a Pig 18*; Throwing the Ball 18*; To the Rescue 18*; Tonsorial Artists 18*; All That Glitters Is Not Goldfish 19*; Another Man's Wife 19*; The Bearded Lady 19*; Bound in Spaghetti 19*; The Cave Man's Bride 19*; The Chambermaid's Revenge 19*; Confessions of a Telephone Girl 19*; The Cow's Husband 19*; Cutting Out His Nonsense 19*; Dog-Gone Tough Luck 19*; Downstairs and Up 19*; Everybody's Doing It 19*; Fireman Save My Child 19*; 500 Miles on a Gallon of Gas 19*; For Bitter or for Verse 19*; The Frozen North 19*; Hands Up 19*; Hard Lions 19*; He Ain't Done Right by Our Nell 19*; Here and There 19*; The High Cost of Living 19*; The Honest Book Agent 19*; The Hula Hula Cabaret 19*; In the Money 19*; The Jazz Instructors 19*; Landing an Heiress 19*; Left at the Post 19*; The Lion Tamers 19*; Look Pleasant Please 19*; Mutt and Jeff in Spain 19*; Mutt and Jeff in Switzerland 19*; Mutt the Mutt Trainer 19*; New York Night Life 19*; Oh Teacher 19*; Oil's Well That Ends Well 19*; Out an' In Again 19*; Pets and Pearls 19*; Pigtails and Peaches 19*; The Plumbers 19*; The Pousse Café 19*; A Prize Fight 19*; Seeing Things 19*; The Shell Game 19*; Sir Sidney 19*; Sound Your A 19*; Subbing for Tom Mix 19*; Sweet Papa 19*; A Tropical Eggs-pedition 19*; West Is East 19*; Why Mutt Left the Village 19*; Wild Waves and Angry Women 19*; William Hohenzollern Sausage Maker 19*; The Window Cleaners 19*; All Stuck Up 20*; The Bare Idea 20*;

The Beautiful Model 20*; The Berth of a Nation 20*; The Bicycle Race 20*; The Bowling Alley 20*; The Brave Toreador 20*; The Breakfast Food Industry 20*; The Chemists 20*; The Chewing Gum Industry 20*; Cleopatra 20*; The Cowpunchers 20*; Dead Eye Jeff 20*; Departed Spirits 20*; Farm Efficiency 20*; Fisherman's Luck 20*; Fishing 20*; Flapjacks 20*; A Glutton for Punishment 20*; The Great Mystery • The Mystery of the Galvanised Iron Ash Can 20*; The Great Pickle Robbery 20*; Gum Shoe Work 20*; A Hard Luck Santa Claus 20*; His Musical Soup 20*; Home Brew 20*; Home Sweet Home 20*; The Honest Jockey 20*; Hot Dogs 20*; Hula Hula Town 20*; The Hypnotist 20*; I'm Ringing Your Party 20*; In Wrong 20*; The Latest in Underwear 20*; The League of Nations 20*; The Medicine Man 20*; The Merry Cafe 20*; The Mint Spy 20*; Mutt and Jeff in Iceland 20*; Mutt and Jeff's Nooze Weekly 20*; Napoleon 20*; The North Woods 20*; Nothing But Girls 20*; On Strike 20*; On the Hop 20*; One Round Jeff 20*; The Paper Hangers 20*; The Papoose 20*; The Parlor Bolshevist 20*; The Pawnbrokers 20*; The Politicians 20*; Pretzel Farming 20*; The Price of a Good Sneeze 20*; The Private Detectives 20*; Putting on the Dog 20*; A Rose by Any Other Name 20*; The Rum Runners 20*; Shaking the Shimmy 20*; Sherlock Hawkshaw and Co. 20*; The Song Birds 20*; The Soul Violin 20*; The Tailor Shop 20*; The Tango Dancers 20*; Three Raisins and a Cake of Yeast 20*; A Tightrope Romance 20*; The Toy Makers 20*; A Trip to Mars 20*; The Wrestlers 20*; The Yacht Race 20*; Cold Tea 21*; A Crazy Idea 21*; Crows and Scarecrows 21*; Darkest Africa 21*; Dr. Killjoy 21*; Factory to Consumer 21*; The Far East 21*; The Far North 21*; Fast Freight 21*; Flivvering 21*; Gathering Coconuts 21*; The Glue Factory 21*; The Gusher 21*; A Hard Shell Game 21*; It's a Bear 21*; The Lion Hunters 21*; Mademoiselle Fifi 21*; A Messy Christmas 21*; The Naturalists 21*; Not Wedded But a Wife 21*; The Painter's Frolic 21*; A Rare Bird 21*; Shadowed 21*; A Shocking Idea 21*; The Stampede 21*; The Tong Sandwich 21*; Touring 21*; Training Woodpeckers 21*; The Turkish Bath 21*; The Vacuum Cleaner 21*; The Ventriloquist 21*; The Village Cutups 21*; Watering the Elephants 21*; Any Ice Today 22*; Around the Pyramids 22*; Beside the Cider 22*; Bony Parts 22*; Bumps and Things 22*; The Cashier 22*; Cold Turkey 22*; Court Plastered 22*; The Crystal Gazer 22*; The Fallen Archers 22*; Falls Ahead 22*; Getting Ahead 22*; Getting Even 22*; A Ghostly Wallop 22*; Golfing 22*; Gym Jams 22*; Hither and Thither 22*; The Hole Cheese 22*; Hoot Mon 22*; Hop, Skip and Jump 22*; The Last Laugh 22*; The Last Shot 22*; Long Live the King 22*; Modern Fishing 22*; Nearing the End 22*; The Phoney Focus 22*; Riding the Goat 22*; The Stolen Snooze 22*; Stuck in the Mud 22*; Tin Foiled 22*; Too Much Soap 22*; The Wishing Duck 22*; Down in Dixie 23*; Accidents Won't Happen 25; All at Sea 25; The Bear Facts 25; Invisible Revenge 25; A Link Missing 25; Mixing in Mexico 25; Oceans of Trouble 25; Soda Clerks 25; Thou Shalt Not Pass 25; Where Am I? 25; Alona of the South Seas 26; The Big Swim 26; Bombs and Boobs • Bombs and Bums 26; Dog Gone 26; The Globe Trotters 26; Mummy o' Mine 26; On Thin Ice 26; Playing with Fire 26; A Roman Scandal 26; Slick Sleuths 26; Ups and Downs 26; Westward Whoa 26; When Hell Froze Over 26

Bowers, Geoffrey G. Danger Zone II: Reaper's Revenge 89

Bowers, George The Hearse 80; Body and Soul 81; My Tutor 82; Private Resort 85

Bowman, Anthony Cappuccino 89

Bowman, William J. Pennington's Choice 15; Rosemary 15*; The Second in Command 15; The Silent Voice 15*; The Bait 16; From Broadway to a Throne 16; The Heart of Tara 16; The Avenging Arrow 21*; Walter's Winning Ways 21

Bowser, Kenneth In a Shallow Grave 88

Box, Muriel The Lost People 49*; The Happy Family • Mr. Lord Says No! 52; Both Sides of the Law • Street Corner 53; A Prince for Cynthia 53; The Beachcomber 54; Cash on Delivery • To Dorothy a Son 54; Simon and Laura 55; Eye Witness • Eyewitness 56; A Novel Affair • The Passionate Stranger 56; Subway in the Sky 58; The Truth About Women 58; This Other Eden 59; Too Young to Love 59; The Piper's Tune 62; Rattle of a Simple Man 64

Boyd, Daniel Chillers 88

Boyd, Don Intimate Reflections 75; East of Elephant Rock 76

Boyd, Joe Jimi Hendrix 73*

Boyd-Anderson, Barbara The Still Point 86

Boyer, Jean Monsieur, Madame et Bibi 32; Un Mauvais Garçon 36; Prends la Route 37; La Chaleur du Sein 38; Ma Sœur de Lai 38; Circonstances Atténuantes • Extenuating Circumstances 39; Noix de Coco 39; Miquette et Sa Mère 40; Schubert's Serenade • Sérénade 40; L'Acrobate 41; Romance de Paris 41; Boléro 42; Le Prince Charmant 42; La Bonne Étoile 43; La Femme Fatale 45; Les Aventures de Casanova • Loves of Casanova 47; Mademoiselle S'Amuse 48; Nous Irons à Paris 49; Tous les Chemins Ménent à Rome 49; Garou-Garou le Passe-Muraille • Mr. Peek-a-Boo • Le Passe-Muraille 50; The Prize • Le Rosier de Madame Husson 50; La Valse Brillante 50; Monte Carlo Baby • Nous Irons à Monte Carlo 51*; An Artist with Ladies • Coiffeur pour Dames • The French Touch 52; Crazy for Love • Le Trou Normand 52; I Had Seven Daughters • I Have Seven Daughters • J'Avais Sept Filles 52; My Seven Little Sins 54; La Madelon 55; Le Couturier de Ces Dames • Fernandel the Dressmaker 56; Le Chômeur de Clochemerle 57; Sénéchal le Magnifique • Senechal the Magnificent 57; Nina 58; Les Vignes du Seigneur 58; Le Confident de Ces Dames 59; The Easiest Profession 60; Coup de Bamboo 62; Relaxe-Toi Chérie 64

Boyette, Pat The Weird Ones 62; Dungeons of Harrow • Dungeons of Horror 64

Boyle, E. G. The Fighting Failure 26

Boyle, Joseph C. Broadway Nights 27; Convoy 27*; The Head of the Family 28; The Mad Hour 28; Through the Breakers 28; The Whip Woman 28; Times Square 29

Boytler, Arcady Arcady 16; Mano a Mano 33; La Mujer del Puerto 33; Celos 36; El Tesoro de Pancho Villa 36; The Adventurous Captain • El Capitán Aventurero 39; Así Es Mi Tierra • Such Is My Country 39

Bozzacchi, Gianni I Love N.Y. 87

Bozzetto, Bruno West and Soda 65; Two Castles 67; Allegro Non Troppo 76; Sotto il Ristorante Cinese • Under the Chinese Restaurant 87

Bozzuffi, Marcel L'Américain • The American 69

Brabant, Charles La P... Respectueuse • La Putain Respectueuse • The Respectful Prostitute 52*; Passionate Summer 57; No Escape 58

Brabin, Charles The Awakening of John Bond 11; A Soldier's Duty 12; The Unsullied Shield 12; The Coastguard's Sister 13; The Daughter of Romany 13; The Floodtide 13; Keepers of the Flock 13; The Man Who Disappeared 13; The Stroke of Phoebus Eight 13; The Antique Brooch 14; The Best Man 14; The Birth of Our Saviour 14; The Foreman's Treachery 14; The King's Move in the City 14; The Letter That Never Came Out 14; The Long Way 14; The Man in the Street 14; The Midnight Ride of Paul Revere 14; The Necklace of Rameses 14; The President's Special 14; The Price of the Necklace 14; A Question of Identity 14; The Stolen Plans 14; The House of the Lost Court 15; An Invitation and an Attack 15; The Raven 15; The Stoning 15; Vanity Fair 15; The Price of Fame 16; The Regeneration of Margaret 16; That Sort • That Sort of Girl 16; The Adopted Son 17; Babette 17; Mary Jane's Pa 17; Persuasive Peggy 17; Red, White and Blue Blood 17; The Secret Kingdom 17*; The Sixteenth Wife 17; La Belle Russe 18; Breakers Ahead 18; Buchanan's Wife 18; His Bonded Wife 18; A Pair of Cupids 18; The Poor Rich Man 18; Social Quicksands 18; Kathleen Mavourneen 19; Thou Shalt Not 19; Blind Wives 20; While New York Sleeps 20; Footfalls 21; The Broadway Peacock 22; The Lights of New York 22; Driven 23; Six Days 23; So Big 24; Stella Maris 25; Mismates 26; Twinkletoes 26; Framed 27; Hard-Boiled Haggerty 27; The Valley of the Giants 27; Burning Daylight 28; The Whip 28; The Bridge of San Luis

Rey 29; The Ship from Shanghai 29; Call of the Flesh • The Singer from Seville 30; The Great Meadow 31; Sporting Blood 31; The Beast of the City • City Sentinel 32; Mad Masquerade • Washington Masquerade 32; The Mask of Fu Manchu 32*; New Morals for Old 32; Rasputin • Rasputin and the Empress • Rasputin—The Mad Monk 32*; Day of Reckoning 33; The Secret of Madame Blanche 33; Stage Mother 33; A Wicked Woman 34

Brach, Gérard Le Bateau sur l'Herbe 71

Bracken, Bertram East Lynne 16; The Eternal Sappho 16; The Shrine of Happiness 16; Sporting Blood 16; The Best Man 17; A Branded Soul 17; Conscience 17; For Liberty 17; The Inspirations of Harry Larrabee 17; The Martinache Marriage 17; The Primitive Call 17; And a Still, Small Voice 18; Moral Law 18; The Boomerang 19; Code of the Yukon 19; In Search of Arcady 19; The Long Arm of Mannister 19; The Confession 20; Harriet and the Piper 20; Kazan 21; The Mask 21; Parted Curtains 21*; Defying the Law 24; Passion's Pathway 24; Heartless Husbands 25; Dame Chance 26; Speeding Through 26; Duty's Reward 27; Fire and Steel 27; Rose of the Bowery 27; The Face on the Barroom Floor 32

Bracknell, David Cup Fever 65; The Chiffy Kids 77; The Chiffy Kids II 78

Bradbury, Basil A Taste of Hell 73*

Bradbury, Robert North The Iron Test 18*; The Faith of the Strong 19; The Last of His People 19; The Death Trap 20; Things Men Do 21; Riders of the Law 22; Desert Rider 23; The Forbidden Trail 23; Gallopin' Through • Galloping Thru 23; The Red Warning 23; What Love Will Do 23; Behind Two Guns 24; The Galloping Ace 24; In High Gear 24; The Man from Wyoming 24; The Phantom Horseman 24; Wanted by the Law 24; Yankee Speed 24; The Battler 25; The Danger Zone 25; Hidden Loot 25; Just Plain Folks 25; Moccasins 25; Riders of Mystery 25; The Speed Demon 25; The Border Sheriff 26; Daniel Boone Thru the Wilderness 26*; Davy Crockett at the Fall of the Alamo • With Davy Crockett at the Fall of the Alamo 26; The Fighting Doctor 26; Looking for Trouble 26; The Mojave Kid 27; Sitting Bull at the Spirit Lake Massacre • With Sitting Bull at the Spirit Lake Massacre 27; The Bantam Cowboy 28*; Headin' for Danger 28; Lightning Speed 28; Dugan of the Badlands 31; Son of the Plains • Vultures of the Law 31; Hidden Valley 32; Law of the West 32; The Man from Hell's Hinges 32; Riders of the Desert 32; Son of Oklahoma 32; Texas Buddies 32; Breed of the Border • Speed Brent Wins 33; The Gallant Fool 33; Galloping Romeo 33; The Ranger's Code 33; Riders of Destiny 33; Blue Steel 34; Happy Landing 34; He Wore a Star • The Star Packer 34; The Lawless Frontier 34; The Lucky Texan 34; The Man from Utah 34; The Trail Beyond 34; West of the Divide 34; Alias John Law 35; Between Men 35; Big Calibre 35; The Courageous Avenger 35; The Dawn Rider 35; Gangster's Enemy No. 1 • Trail of Terror 35; Kid Courageous 35; The Lawless Range 35; No Man's Land • No Man's Range 35; Rainbow Valley 35; The Rider of the Law 35; Smokey Smith 35; Texas Terror 35; Tombstone Terror 35; Western Justice 35; Westward Ho! 35; Brand of the Outlaws 36; Cavalry 36; Headin' for the Rio Grande 36; The Kid Ranger 36; Last of the Warrens 36; The Law Rides 36; Sundown Saunders 36; Valley of the Lawless 36; Danger Valley 37; God's Country and the Man 37; The Gun Ranger 37; Hittin' the Trail 37; Riders of the Dawn 37; Riders of the Rockies 37; Romance of the Rockies 37; Sing, Cowboy, Sing 37; Stars Over Arizona 37; Trouble in Texas 37; The Trusted Outlaw 37; Where Trails Divide 37; Forbidden Trails 41

Bradford, James C. Parted Curtains 21*

Bradford, Peter A Solid Explanation 51; Heights of Danger 53

Bradley, Al see *Brescia, Alfonso*

Bradley, David Oliver Twist 40; Peer Gynt 41; Macbeth 46; Julius Caesar 49; Talk About a Stranger 52; Dragstrip Riot • The Reckless Age 58; 12 to the Moon 60; Madmen of Mandoras • The Return of Mr. H • They Saved Hitler's Brain 63

Bradley, Samuel Dangerous Toys • Don't Leave Your Husband 21; The Supreme Passion 21; Women Men Love 21; False Fronts 22

Bradley, William Moonglow 21; The Tame Cat 21

Bradshaw, John That's My Baby 85*

Brady, Hal see *Miraglia, Emilio*

Bragaglia, Carlo Ludovico Un Cattivo Soggetto 33; Non Son Gelosia 33; O la Borsa! O la Vita! 33; Frutto Acerbo 34; Quella Vecchia Canaglia 34; Amore 36; The Angel's Pit • La Fossa degli Angeli 37; L'Amore Si Fa Così 39; Animali Pazzi 39; Belle o Brutte Si Sposan Tutte 39; Una Famiglia Impossibile 40; Un Mare di Guai 40*; Pazza di Gioia 40; Il Prigioniero di Santa Cruz 40; L'Allegro Fantasma 41*; Allessandro, Sei Grande! 41; Barbablù 41; Due Cuori Sotto Sequestro 41; La Forza Bruta 41; Casanova Farebbe Così 42; La Guardia del Corpo 42; Non Ti Pago! 42; La Scuola dei Timidi 42; Se Io Fossi Onesto 42; Violette nei Capelli 42; Il Fidanzato di Mia Moglie 43; Fuga a Due Voci 43; Non Sono Superstizioso, Ma... 44; Tutta la Vita in Ventiquatt'Ore 44; La Vita È Bella 44; Lo Sbaglio di Essere Vivo 45; Pronto, Chi Parla? 46; Torna a Sorrento 46; Albergo Luna-Camera Trentaquattro 47; L'Altra 47; La Primula Bianca 47; Totò le Mokò 47; Il Falco Rosso 50; Figaro Qua, Figaro La 50; My Widow and I 50; Le Sei Moglie di Barbablù 50; Totò Cerca Moglie 50; The Voice of Love 50; Una Bruna Indiavolata 51; L'Eroe Sono Io • I'm the Hero 51*; 47, Morto Che Parla 51; A Fil di Spada • At Sword's Point 52; The Secret of the Three Sword Points • Il Segreto delle Tre Punte 52; Don Lorenzo 53; La Cortigiana di Babilonia • The Queen of Babylon • Semiramis • The Slave Woman 55; Orient Express 55; Il Falco d'Oro 56; Gerusalemme Liberata • Jerusalem Set Free • The Mighty Crusaders 57; Lazzarella 57; La Camériere 58*; Caporale di Giornata • Soldier on Duty 58; E' Permesso Maresciallo? 58; Io, Mammeta e Tu • Me, Mother and You 58; La Spada e la Croce • The Sword and the Cross 58; Annibale • Hannibal 59*; Amazons of Rome • Le Vergini di Roma • The Virgins of Rome • The Warrior Women 60*; Gli Amori di Ercole • Hercules and the Hydra • The Loves of Hercules 60; Pastasciutta nel Deserto • Spaghetti in the Desert 61; Ursus in the Valley of the Lions • Ursus nella Valle dei Leoni • Valley of the Lions 61; The Four Monks • I Quattro Monaci 62; The Four Musketeers • I Quattro Moschettieri 63

Bragan, A. Attento Gringo...e Tornato Sabata 72; I Bandoleros della Dodicesima Ora 72

Brahm, Hans see *Brahm, John*

Brahm, John Broken Blossoms 36; Counsel for Crime 37; Girls' School 38; Penitentiary 38; Let Us Live 39; Rio 39; Escape to Glory • Submarine Zone 40; Wild Geese Calling 41; The Hammond Mystery • The Undying Monster 42; Tonight We Raid Calais 43; Wintertime 43; A Guest in the House 44*; The Lodger 44; Hangover Square 45; The Locket 46; The Brasher Doubloon • The High Window 47; Singapore 47; Atlantis • Atlantis the Lost Continent • Queen of Atlantis • Siren of Atlantis 48*; Il Ladro di Venezia • The Thief of Venice 50; The Bride Comes to Yellow Sky • Face to Face 52*; Miracle of Fatima • The Miracle of Our Lady of Fatima • Our Lady of Fatima 52; A Star Shall Rise 52; The Diamond Queen 53; The Golden Plague • Die Goldene Pest 54; The Mad Magician 54; Bengazi 55; Special Delivery • Vom Himmel Gefallen 55; 52 Miles to Midnight • 52 Miles to Terror • Hot Rods to Hell 64

Brahms, Helma Sanders see *Sanders-Brahms, Helma*

Brakel, Nouchka van Een Maand Later • One Month Later 87

Brakhage, Stan Interim 51; The Boy and the Sea 53; Desistfilm 53; Unglassed Windows Cast a Terrible Reflection 53; Bolts of Melody • Centuries of June • Portrait of Julie • Tower House 54*; The Extraordinary Child 54*; In Between 54; The Way to Shadow Garden 54; Reflections on Black 55; The Wonder Ring 55*; Flesh of Morning 56; Loving 56; Nightcats 56; Zone Moment 56; Anticipation of the Night 57; Daybreak and Whiteye 57; Martin Missil Quarterly Reports 57; Cat's Cradle 59; Colorado Legend • The Colorado Legend and the Ballad of the Colorado Ute 59; Sirius Remembered 59; Wedlock House: An Intercourse 59; Window Water Baby Moving 59; The Dead 60;

Films by Stan Brakhage: An Avant-Garde Home Movie 61; Prelude 61; Thigh Line Lyre Triangular 61; Blue Moses 62; Mr. Tomkins Inside Himself 62; Silent Sound Sense Stars Subotnik and Sender 62; Mothlight 63; O Life—A Woe Story—The A-Test News 63; The Art of Vision 64; Dog Star Man 64; Black Vision 65; Blood's Tone 65; Blue White 65; Fire of Waters 65; Pasht 65; Two: Creeley/McClure 65; Vein 65; The Horseman, the Woman and the Moth 68; Lovemaking 68; Songs 69; The Weir-Falcon Saga 69; The Act of Seeing with One's Own Eyes 70; The Animals of Eden and After 70; Deus Ex 70; Eyes 70; The Machine of Eden 70; Scenes from Under Childhood 70; Angels' Door 71; Fox Fire Child Watch 71; The Peaceable Kingdom 71; The Trip to the Door 71; Western History 71; Eye Myth 72; Gift 72; The Presence 72; The Process 72; The Riddle of Lumen 72; Sexual Meditations 72; The Shores of Phos: A Fable 72; The Wold-Shadow 72; Sincerity 73; The Women 73; Aquarian 74; Clancy 74; Dominion 74; Flight 74; He Was Born, He Suffered, He Died 74; Hymn to Her 74; Skein 74; Sol 74; Star Garden 74; The Stars Are Beautiful 74; The Text of Light 74; Short Films, 1975 75; Sincerity II 75; Absence 76; Airs 76; Desert 76; The Dream, N.Y.C., the Return, the Flower 76; Gadflies 76; Highs 76; Rembrandt, Etc. and Jane 76; Short Films, 1976 76; Sketches 76; Tragoedia 76; Trio 76; Window 76; The Domain of the Moment 77; The Governor 77; Soldiers and Other Cosmic Objects 77; Bird 78; Burial Path 78; Centre 78; Duplicity 78; Duplicity II 78; Nightmare Series 78; Purity and After 78; Sincerity III 78; Sluice 78; Thot Fal'n 78; 23rd Psalm Branch 78; ⅛ 79; Creation 79; Aftermath 80; Duplicity III 80; Made Manifest 80; Murder Psalm 80; Other 80; Salome 80; Sincerity IV 80; Sincerity V 80; Songs 1-14 80; The Garden of Earthly Delights 81; Nodes 81; R.R. 81; Roman Numeral Series 81; Arabics 82; Unconscious London Strata 82; Hell Spit Flexion 83; Tortured Dust 84; I...Dreaming 88; Marilyn's Window 88

Bramble, A. V. The Boy and the Cheese 14; Hearts That Are Human 15; The Blind Man of Verdun 16; Fatal Fingers 16*; Jimmy 16*; The Laughing Cavalier 17*; Profit and the Loss 17*; When Paris Sleeps 17; Bonnie Mary 18; Heart and Soul • A Nonconformist Parson 19; Her Cross 19; The Single Man 19; A Smart Set 19; Her Benny 20; Mr. Gilfil's Love Story 20; Torn Sails 20; Wuthering Heights 20; The Bachelors' Club 21; The Old Country 21; The Prince and the Beggarmaid 21; The Rotters 21; The Will 21; The Card 22; The Little Mother 22; Shirley 22; Zeebrugge 24*; Bodiam Castle • Bodiam Castle and Eric the Slender 26; Shooting Stars 27*; Chick 28; The Man Who Changed His Name 28; A Lucky Sweep 32; Mrs. Dane's Defence 33; The Veteran of Waterloo 33

Brame, Bill The Cycle Savages 69; Free

Grass • Scream Free 69; Miss Melody Jones 73; Jive Turkey 76

Branagh, Kenneth Henry V 89

Brand, Larry The Drifter 88; Edgar Allan Poe's Masque of the Red Death • Masque of the Red Death 89; Overexposed 90

Brand, Steve Kaddish 84

Brandão, Rodolfo Dede Mamata 88

Brandauer, Karin Blessings of the Earth • Erdsegen 86; Einstweilen Wird Es Mittag 88

Brandauer, Klaus Maria Georg Elser • Seven Minutes 89

Brander, Richard Sizzle Beach, U.S.A. 74

Brandner, Uwe I Love You I Kill You • Ich Liebe Dich Ich Töte Dich 71; 50/50 86

Brando, Marlon One-Eyed Jacks 61

Brandon, Phil The Missing Million 42; We'll Meet Again 42; Happidrome 43; Up with the Lark 43; Tarzan and the Jungle Goddess • Tarzan and the Jungle Queen • Tarzan's Peril 51*

Brandt, Antonio Amore, Piombo e Furore 79

Brandt, Carsten Demoner • Demons 86

Brandt, Edward Harmony Heaven 29*

Brandt, Henry Masters of the Congo Jungle • Les Seigneurs de la Forêt 58*

Brandt, J. Marionetten des Teufels 23*

Brandt, Michael The Missing Note 61

Branner, Per Axel see Axel-Branner, Per

Brannon, Fred C. D-Day on Mars • The Purple Monster Strikes 45*; The Black Widow • Sombra the Spider Woman 46*; The Crimson Ghost • Cyclotrode X 46*; King of the Forest Rangers 46*; The Phantom Rider 46*; Code 645 • G-Men Never Forget 47*; Jesse James Rides Again 47*; Son of Zorro 47*; Adventures of Frank and Jesse James 48*; Dangers of the Canadian Mounted • R.C.M.P. and the Treasure of Genghis Khan 48*; Bandit King of Texas 49; Federal Agents vs. Underworld, Inc. • Golden Hands of Kurigal 49; Frontier Investigator • Frontier Marshal 49; Ghost of Zorro 49; King of the Rocket Men • Lost Planet Airmen 49; Code of the Silver Sage 50; Desperadoes of the West 50; Gunmen of Abilene 50; The Invisible Monster • Slaves of the Invisible Monster 50; The James Brothers of Missouri 50; Radar Patrol vs. Spy King 50; Rustlers on Horseback 50; Salt Lake Raiders 50; Vigilante Hideout 50; Arizona Manhunt 51; Don Daredevil Rides Again 51; Flying Disc Men from Mars • Missile Monsters 51; Government Agents vs. the Phantom Legion 51; Night Riders of Montana 51; Rough Riders of Durango 51; Captive of Billy the Kid 52; Radar Men from the Moon • Retik the Moon Menace 52; Satan's Satellites • Zombies of the Stratosphere 52; Wild Horse Ambush 52; Commando Cody 53*; Jungle Drums of Africa • U-238 and the Witch Doctor 53

Branscombe, Arthur The Foundations of Freedom 18

Branss, Truck Swan Lake 67

Brasch, Thomas Der Passagier • Welcome to Germany 88

Brascia, Dominick Evil Laugh 88

Brasloff, Stanley H. Toys Are Not for Children 72

Brason, John Walk a Crooked Path 69

Brass, Giovanni Tinto see Brass, Tinto

Brass, Tinto Chi Lavora È Perduto • In Capo al Mondo 63; Ça Ira • Ça Ira, il Fiume della Rivolta • Il Fiume della Rivolta 64; Il Disco Volante • The Flying Saucer 64; La Mia Signora 64*; Yankee 66; Col Cuore in Gola 67; Black on White • Nero su Bianco 69; Dropout 70; L'Urlo 70; La Vacanza • The Vacation 71; Salon Kitty 76; Caligula 77; Action 79; La Chiave • The Key 84; Miranda 85; Capriccio • Caprice • Letters from Capri • Remembering Capri 86; Snack Bar Budapest 88

Brasselle, Keefe If You Don't Stop It, You'll Go Blind 77*

Braubach, Mary Ann A Great Bunch of Girls 78*

Brauer, Jürgen Gritta of the Rat Castle • Gritta vom Rattenschloss 86

Brauer, Peter Paul The Girl of Last Night • Das Mädchen von Gestern Nacht 38; Jugend von Heute • Youth of Today 38

Brault, Michel Le Dément du Lac Jean-Jeune 47*; Mouvement Perpétuel 49*; De Gais Lurons en Congrès • Les Raquetteurs • The Snowshoers 58*; The Fight • La Lutte • Wrestling 61*; Les Enfants du Silence 62*; L'Invasion Pacifique • Québec-U.S.A. • Québec-U.S.A. ou L'Invasion Pacifique • Visit to a Foreign Country 62*; The Moontrap • Pour la Suite du Monde 62*; Les Adolescentes • The Adolescents • La Fleur de l'Âge • La Fleur de l'Âge ou Les Adolescentes • That Tender Age 64*; Le Temps Perdue 64; Entre la Mer et l'Eau Douce • Geneviève 66; Les Enfants de Néant 67*; L'Acadie, l'Acadie! 70*; Moncton 70*; The Orders • Les Ordres 74; A Paper Wedding 90

Braun, Alfred Girls Behind Bars 50

Braun, Harald The Alfred Nobel Story • No Greater Love 52; Keepers of the Night 53; As Long As You're Near Me • Solange du da Bist 54; Herrscher Ohne Krone • King in Shadow 56; Der Gläserne Turm • The Glass Tower 57

Braun, L. Maximka 53

Braun, Vladimir Heroes of the Sea 41; The Blue Cliff 43; Malva 57

Braunberger, Pierre Bullfight 51; La Course de Taureaux 51

Braverman, Charles Hit and Run • Revenge Squad 82

Bravman, Jack Zombie Nightmare 87

Braw, Lars Trachoma • Trakom 64*

Bray, John R. Col. Heeza Liar in Africa 13; Col. Heeza Liar, Explorer 14; Col. Heeza Liar, Farmer 14; Col. Heeza Liar in Mexico 14; Col. Heeza Liar in the Wilderness 14; Col. Heeza Liar, Naturalist 14; Col. Heeza Liar Shipwrecked 14; Col. Heeza Liar's African Hunt • Col. Heeza Liar's Big Game Hunt 14; Col. Heeza Liar and the Torpedo 15; Col. Heeza Liar and the Zeppelin 15; Col. Heeza Liar at the Bat 15; Col. Heeza Liar at the Front 15; Col. Heeza Liar, Dog Fancier 15; Col. Heeza Liar Foils the Enemy 15; Col. Heeza Liar, Ghost Breaker 15; Col. Heeza Liar, Ghost Breaker: Second Night • Col. Heeza Liar in the Haunted Castle 15; Col. Heeza Liar in the Trenches 15; Col. Heeza Liar Invents a New Kind of Shell 15; Col. Heeza Liar, Nature Faker 15; Col. Heeza Liar Runs the Blockade 15; Col. Heeza Liar Signs the Pledge 15; Col. Heeza Liar, War Aviator 15; Col. Heeza Liar, War Dog 15; The Bronco Buster 16; Col. Heeza Liar and the Bandits 16; Col. Heeza Liar and the Pirates 16; Col. Heeza Liar at the Vaudeville Show 16; Col. Heeza Liar Captures Villa 16; Col. Heeza Liar Gets Married 16; Col. Heeza Liar, Hobo 16; Col. Heeza Liar on Strike 16; Col. Heeza Liar Plays Hamlet 16; Col. Heeza Liar Wins the Pennant 16; Col. Heeza Liar's Bachelor Quarters 16; Col. Heeza Liar's Courtship 16; Col. Heeza Liar's Waterloo 16; Fisherman's Luck 16; Found a Big Stick 16; The House in Which They Live 16; The Long Arm of Law and Order 16; Miss Nomination 16; O.U. Rooster 16; Our Watch Dog 16; The Struggle 16; Watchful Waiting 16; Why? 16; Col. Heeza Liar, Detective 17; Col. Heeza Liar on the Jump 17; Col. Heeza Liar, Spy Dodger 17; Col. Heeza Liar's Temperance Lecture 17; How Animated Cartoons Are Made 19; The Debut of Thomas Katt 20

Brayne, William Christopher Plummer 64*

Brazybulski, N. Fulfilled Dreams • Spelnione Marzenia 39

Brazzi, Rossano The Christmas That Almost Wasn't • Il Natale Che Quasi Non Fu 66; The Mafia Girls 69; Psychout for Murder • Salvare la Faccia 69

Brdečka, Jiří The Devil of the Springs • The Devil on Springs • Perák a S.S. • Perak Against the S.S. • The Springer and S.S. Men 45*; Love and the Dirigible • Vzducholod' a Láska • The Zeppelin and Love 47; A Comic History of Aviation • How Man Learned to Fly • Jak Se Člověk Naučil Létat • Než Nám Narostla Křídla 58; Look Out! • Pozor! 59; Naše Karkulka • Our Little Red Riding Hood • Our Red Riding Hood 60; Člověk Pod Vodou • Man Under Water 61*; The Television Fan 61; Závada Není na Vašem Přijímači 61; Reason and Emotion • Rozum a Cit 62; Gallina Vogelbirdae • The Grotesque Chicken • The Grotesque Hen • Špatně Namalovaná Slepice 63; The Letter M • Slowce M 63; The Minstrel's Song 63; A Song of Love 64; Blaho Lásky • The Bliss of Love • Felicity of Love 65; The Deserter • Dezertér 65; Forester's Song • On Watch in the Forest 66; Why Do You Smile Mona Lisa? • Why Is the Mona Lisa Smiling? 66; The Hand 68; The Nights of Prague • Prague Nights • Pražské Noci 68*; Pomsta • Revenge 68*; Power of Destiny 68; Aristotele • Aristotle 71*

Breakston, George Urubu 48*; Jungle Stampede 50; Geisha Girl 52*; Golden Ivory • White Huntress 54; The Scarlet Spear 54*; Escape in the Sun 56; Triangle on Safari • The Woman and the Hunter 57; Half Man Half Monster • The Manster • The Manster — Half Man, Half Monster • The Split 62*; Shadow of Treason 63; The Boy Cried Murder • Ein Junge Schrie Mord 66; Blood River 68

Brealey, Gil Annie's Coming Out • A Test of Love 84

Brecher, Irving S. The Life of Riley 48; Somebody Loves Me 52; Sail a Crooked Ship 61

Breebaart, Willy Dorst 88

Breen, Joseph Los Misterios del Rosario • The Redeemer 65

Breen, Richard L. Stopover Tokyo 57

Breer, Robert Form Phases I 52; Form Phases II and III 53; Form Phases IV 54; Image by Images I 54; Un Miracle 54*; Cats 55; Image by Images II and III 55; Image by Images IV 55; Motion Pictures 55; Jamestown Baloos 57; A Man and His Dog Out for Air 57; Par Avion 57; Recreation I 57; Recreation II 57; Cassis Colank 59; Eyewash 59; Trailer 59; Homage to Jean Tinguely's Homage to New York 60; Inner and Outer Space 60; Blazes 61; Kinetic Art Show, Stockholm 61; Horse Over Tea Kettle 62; Pat's Birthday 62*; Breathing 63; Fist Fight 64; 66 66; PBL 68; PBL II 68; 69 68; 70 70; Gulls and Buoys 72; Fuji 74; Etc. 75; Rubber Cement 75; 77 77; LMNO 78; TZ 79; Swiss Army Knife with Rats and Pigeons 81; Trial Balloons 82

Breien, Anja Hustruer • Wives 75; Forfølgelsen • The Witch Hunt 81; Hustruer — Ti År Efter • Hustruer — Ti År Etter • Hustruer II • Wives — Ten Years After 85

Breillat, Catherine Une Vraie Jeune Fille 77; Tapage Nocturne 79; 36 Fillette 88

Bren, Milton Three for Bedroom C 52

Brenon, Herbert All for Her 12; The Clown's Triumph 12; Leah the Forsaken 12; The Long Strike 12; The Nurse 12; Absinthe 13; Across the Atlantic • The Secret of the Air 13; The Anarchist 13; The Angel of Death 13; Dr. Jekyll and Mr. Hyde 13; Ivanhoe 13; Kathleen Mavourneen 13; Time Is Money 13; Life's Shop Window 14*; Neptune's Daughter 14*; The Clemenceau Case 15; The Heart of Maryland 15; The Kreutzer Sonata 15; Sin 15; The Soul of Broadway 15; The Two Orphans 15; The Bigamist 16; Bubbles 16; A Daughter of the Gods 16; The Governor's Decision 16; Joan of Flanders • War Brides 16; Love or an Empire 16; The Marble Heart 16*; The Missing Witness 16; The Ruling Passion 16; The Voice Upstairs 16; Whom the Gods Destroy • Whom the Gods Would Destroy 16; Empty Pockets 17; The Eternal Sin • Lucretia Borgia 17; The Fall of the Romanoffs 17; Kismet 17; The Lone Wolf 17; The Invasion of Britain • Victory and Peace 18; The Passing of the Third Floor Back 18;

The Mysterious Princess • Princess Impudence • La Principessa Misteriosa 19; A Sinless Sinner 19; 12-10 19; Beatrice 20; Chains of Evidence 20; Sister Against Sister • Sorella Contro Sorella 20; The Passion Flower 21; The Sign on the Door 21; The Wonderful Thing 21; Any Wife 22; The Custard Cup 22; Forbidden Paradise 22; Moonshine Valley 22; Shackles of Gold 22; A Stage Romance 22; The Stronger Passion 22; The Rustle of Silk 23; The Spanish Dancer 23; The Woman with Four Faces 23; The Alaskan 24; The Breaking Point 24; Peter Pan 24; Shadows of Paris 24; The Sideshow of Life 24; The Little French Girl 25; The Street of Forgotten Men 25; Beau Geste 26; Dancing Mothers 26; God Gave Me Twenty Cents 26; The Great Gatsby 26; A Kiss for Cinderella 26; The Song and Dance Man 26; Sorrell and Son 27; The Telephone Girl 27; Laugh, Clown, Laugh 28; The Rescue 29; The Case of Sergeant Grischa 30; Lummox 30; Beau Ideal 31; Transgression 31; The Dove • Girl of the Rio 32; Wine, Women and Song 33; Honors Easy 35; Regal Cavalcade • Royal Cavalcade 35*; Living Dangerously 36; Someone at the Door 36; The Dominant Sex 37; The Live Wire 37; Spring Handicap 37; The Housemaster 38; Yellow Sands 38; Black Eyes • False Rapture • Secrets of Sin 39; The Flying Squad • The Flying Squadron 40

Brenton, Guy Thursday's Children 53*

Brescanu, Vasily O Rozvrashchenii Zabyt • Without Return 87

Brescia, Alfonso Conqueror of Atlantis 63; Revolt of the Praetorians 65; Days of Violence • I Giorni della Violenza 67; Killer Calibre 32 • Killer Calibro 32 67; Voltati...Ti Uccido 67; Carogne Si Nasce 68; Battle of the Amazons 73; Three Stooges vs. the Wonder Women 75; Cosmo 2000: Planet Without a Name • Cosmos: War of the Planets • War of the Planets 77; Iron Warrior 87

Breslow, Lou You Never Can Tell • You Never Know 51

Bressan, Arthur, Jr. Abuse 83; Buddies 85

Bressane, Julio Bras Cubas 86

Bresson, Henri Cartier see Cartier-Bresson, Henri

Bresson, Robert Les Affaires Publiques 34; Angels of the Streets • Les Anges du Péché 43; Les Dames du Bois de Boulogne • The Ladies of the Bois de Boulogne • Ladies of the Park 45; Diary of a Country Priest • Journal d'un Curé de Campagne 50; Un Condamné à Mort S'Est Échappé • Un Condamné à Mort S'Est Échappé ou Le Vent Souffle Où Il Vent • A Condemned Man Escapes • A Man Escaped • A Man Escaped, or The Wind Bloweth Where It Listeth • Le Vent Souffle Où Il Vent • The Wind Bloweth Where It Listeth 56; Pickpocket 59; Le Procès de Jeanne d'Arc • The Trial of Joan of Arc 61; Au Hasard, Balthazar • Balthazar • Min Van Balthazar 66; Mouchette 66; Une Femme Douce • A

Gentle Creature 69; Four Nights of a Dreamer • Quatre Nuits d'un Rêveur 71; Le Graal • The Grail • Lancelot • Lancelot du Lac • Lancelot of the Lake 74; The Devil, Probably • Le Diable, Probablement 77; L'Argent • Money 82

Brest, Martin Hot Tomorrows 77; Going in Style 79; Beverly Hills Cop 84; Midnight Run 88

Bretherton, Howard While London Sleeps 26; The Black Diamond Express 27; The Bush Leaguer 27; Hills of Kentucky 27; One-Round Hogan 27; The Silver Slave 27; Across the Atlantic 28; Caught in the Fog 28; The Chorus Kid 28; Turn Back the Hours 28; The Argyle Case 29; From Headquarters 29; The Greyhound Limited 29; The Redeeming Sin 29; The Time, the Place and the Girl 29; Isle of Escape 30; Second Choice 30; The Match King 32*; Ladies They Talk About • Women in Prison 33*; Il Cantante di Napoli • The Singer of Naples 34; The Return of the Terror 34; Bar 20 Rides Again 35; Dinky 35*; The Eagle's Brood 35; Hopalong Cassidy • Hopalong Cassidy Enters 35; Call of the Prairie 36; The Girl from Mandalay 36; Heart of the West 36; King of the Royal Mounted 36; The Leathernecks Have Landed 36; Three on the Trail 36; Wild Brian Kent 36; County Fair 37; Gangster's Bride • Secret Valley 37; It Happened Out West • The Man from the Big City 37; The Mysterious Stranger • Western Gold 37; Amateur Detective • Irish Luck 38; The Fifth Round • Tough Kid 38; Wanted by the Police 38; Boys' Reformatory 39; Danger Flight • Scouts of the Air 39; Navy Secrets 39; Sky Patrol 39; Star Reporter 39; Sweepstake Racketeers • Undercover Agent 39; Chasing Trouble 40; Hidden Enemy 40; Laughing at Danger 40; The Midnight Limited 40; On the Spot 40; The Showdown 40; Up in the Air 40; In Old Colorado 41; Outlaws of the Desert 41; Riders of the Badlands 41; Sign of the Wolf 41; Twilight on the Trail 41; You're Out of Luck 41; Below the Border 42; Dawn of the Great Divide • Dawn on the Great Divide 42; Down Texas Way 42; Ghost Town Law 42; Pirates of the Prairie 42; Rhythm Parade 42*; Riders of the West 42; West of the Law 42; West of Tombstone 42; Beyond the Last Frontier 43; Bordertown Gunfighters 43; Carson City Cyclone 43; Fugitive from Sonora 43; The Man from the Rio Grande 43; Riders of the Rio Grande 43; Santa Fe Scouts 43; Wagon Tracks West 43; Whispering Footsteps 43; The Girl Who Dared 44; Hidden Valley Outlaws 44; Law of the Valley 44; Outlaws of Santa Fe 44; The San Antonio Kid 44; Bank Robbery • Renegades of the Rio Grande 45; The Big Show-Off 45; Gun Smoke 45; The Monster and the Ape 45; The Navajo Trail 45; The Topeka Terror 45; Who's Guilty? 45*; Murder at Malibu Beach • The Trap 46; Ridin' Down the Trail 47; Trail of the Mounties 47; Where the North Begins 47;

Because of Eve 48; The Prince of Thieves 48; The Story of Life 48; Triggerman 48; Whip Law 50; Night Raiders 52

Breton, André Essai de Simulation de Délire Cinématographique 35*

Brett, B. Harold A Factory Girl's Honour 12; The Wager 13; The Chase of Death 14; Her Hour of Retribution 14; The Houseboat Mystery 14; Thelma, or Saved from the Sea 14; Through Stormy Seas 14

Brewster, Eugene V. Love's Redemption 21

Brialy, Jean-Claude Églantine 71; Closed Shutters • Les Volets Clos 72; L'Oiseau Rare 73; Un Amour de Pluie • Loving in the Rain 74; Un Bon Petit Diable 83

Brian, J. First Time 'Round 72

Brice, Monte Casey at the Bat 27; The Golf Specialist 30; Moonlight and Melody • Moonlight and Pretzels 33*; Take a Chance 33*; Sweet Surrender 35

Bricken, Jules Drango 57*; The Blast • Explosion 69; Danny Jones 72

Bricker, Clarence see Brown, Clarence

Brickman, Marshall Simon 80; Lovesick 83; The Manhattan Project • Manhattan Project: The Deadly Game 86

Brickman, Paul Risky Business 83; Men Don't Leave 90

Bridges, Alan Act of Murder 64; Invasion 65; The Lie 70; The Hireling 73; Out of Season • Winter Rates 75; Age of Innocence • Ragtime Summer 77; La Petite Fille en Velours Bleu 78; The Return of the Soldier 81; Very Like a Whale 81; The Shooting Party 84; Apt Pupil 88

Bridges, Beau Devil's Odds • The Wild Pair 87; Seven Hours to Judgment 88

Bridges, James The Baby Maker 70; The Paper Chase 73; 9/30/55 • September 30, 1955 • 24 Hours of the Rebel 77; The China Syndrome 79; Urban Cowboy 80; Mike's Murder 82; Perfect 85; Bright Lights, Big City 88

Bright, Maurice A. see Lucidi, Maurizio

Brignone, Guido Maciste in Hell 26; The Hero of the Circus 28; Rubacuori 32; After a Night of Love • Dopo una Notte d'Amore 35; Lorenzino de Medici 36; Passaporto Rosso 36; Destino di Donna 37; Loyalty of Love 37; Tre Anni Senza Donne 37; La Voce Lontana 37; The Ancestor • L'Antenato 38; The Little School Mistress • La Maestrina 38; To Live • Vivere 38; For Men Only • Per Uomini Soli 39; La Wally 39; Chi È Più Felice Di Me? • Who Is Happier Than I? 40; Broken Love 46; Dishonored • Onore e Sacrificio 50; Buried Alive • La Sepolta Viva 51; A Dead Woman's Kiss 51; Tears of Blood 52; The Count of St. Elmo 53; Genoese Dragnet 54; Ivan, Son of the White Devil 54

Brignone, Guy see Brignone, Guido

Brill, Richard The Tennessee Beat • That Tennessee Beat 66

Brims, Ian Albert Carter, Q.O.S.O. 67; The Green Shoes 68

Brinckerhoff, Burt Dogs • Slaughter 76; Acapulco Gold 78

Brinder, Lloyd Yoicks 32

Bringmann, Peter F. Die Heartbreakers • The Heartbreakers 83; Der Schneemann 85; African Timber 89

Brismée, Jean Forges 53*; Cinéma, Bonjour! 58*; La Planète Fauve 59*; Au Service du Diable • The Devil's Longest Night • The Devil's Nightmare • La Notte Più Lunga del Diavolo • La Plus Longue Nuit du Diable • La Terrificante Notte del Demonio 71

Brisseau, Jean-Claude Sound and Fury 88

Brittain, Donald Memorandum 67*; Volcano 76; Accident 83

Brittain, Frank The Set 70

Britten, Lawrence Feelings 76; Whose Child Am I? 76

Britton, George B. Everyday 76

Briz, José Three Bad Sisters 56; Now It Can Be Told • The Secret Door 61; The Tower 65; A Harvest of Evil 66; Comanche Blanco • White Comanche 67; Ragan 67; Devil May Care 69; Maybe September 70

Brizzi, Gaetan Asterix et la Surprise de César • Asterix the Gaul • Asterix vs. Caesar 85*

Brizzi, Paul Asterix et la Surprise de César • Asterix the Gaul • Asterix vs. Caesar 85*

Broadwell, Robert R. A Law Unto Himself • Vengeance Is Mine! 16

Broca, Philippe de Salon Nautique 54; Opération Gas-Oil 55; Sous un Autre Soleil 55; Les Jeux de l'Amour • The Love Game • Playing at Love 59; Le Farceur • The Joker 60; L'Amant de Cinq Jours • The Five Day Lover • Infidelity • Time Out for Love 61; Cartouche • Swords of Blood 61; Les Sept Péchés Capitaux • I Sette Peccati Capitali • Seven Capital Sins • The Seven Deadly Sins 61*; People in Luck • Les Veinards 62*; L'Homme de Rio • That Man from Rio • L'Uomo di Rio 63; Male Companion • Un Monsieur de Compagnie • Poi Ti Sposero 64; Chinese Adventures in China • Les Tribulations d'un Chinois en Chine • L'Uomo di Hong Kong • Up to His Ears 65; King of Hearts • Le Roi de Cœur • Tutti Pazzi Meno Io 66; Das Alteste Gewerbe der Welt • L'Amore Attraverso i Secoli • L'Amour à Travers les Âges • The Oldest Profession • Le Plus Vieux Métier du Monde 67*; The Devil by the Tail • Le Diable par la Queue • Non Tirate il Diavolo per la Coda 68; Les Caprices de Marie • Les Figurants du Nouveau Monde • Give Her the Moon 69; La Poudre d'Escampette • La Route au Soleil • Touch and Go 70; Chère Louise • Louise 72; Comment Détruire la Réputation du Plus Célèbre Agent Secret du Monde • How to Destroy the Reputation of the Greatest Secret Agent • The Magnificent One • Le Magnifique 73; Incorrigible • L'Incorrigible 75; Dear Detective • Dear Inspector • Tendre Poulet 77; Julie Pot de Colle 77; Le Cavaleur • Practice Makes Perfect 78; Jupiter's Thigh • On A Volé la Cuisse de Jupiter • Somebody's Stolen the Thigh of Jupiter 79; Psy 80;

L'Africain • The African 82; Louisiane 84; Le Crocodile 85; La Gitane • The Gypsy 85; Piranha d'Amour 85; Chouans! 87; Shéhérazade 90

Brock, Deborah Slumber Party Massacre II 87; Andy and the Airwave Rangers • Andy Colby's Incredibly Awesome Adventure 90

Brocka, Lino Santiago 70; Tubog sa Ginto 70; Wanted: Perfect Mother 70; Cadena de Amor 71; Lumuha Pati mga Anghel 71; Now 71; Stardoom 71; Cherry Blossoms 72; Villa Miranda 72; Tatlo, Dalawa, Isa • Three, Two, One 74; Tinimbang Ka Nguni't Kulang • You Are Weighed in the Balance But Are Found Lacking • You Are Weighed in the Balance But Are Found Wanting 74; Dung-Aw 75; Manila, in the Claws of Light • Manila: In the Claws of Neon • Maynila, sa mga Kuko ng Liwanag 75; Insiang 76; Lunes, Martes, Miyerkules... • Lunes, Martes, Miyerkules, Huwebes, Biyernes, Sabado, Linggo • Monday, Tuesday, Wednesday, Thursday, Friday, Saturday, Sunday 76; Inay 77; Lahing Pilipino 77; Tahan na Empoy, Tahan 77; Gumising Ka, Maruja 78; Hayop sa Hayop 78; Init 78; Rubia Servios 78; Ina Ka ng Anak Mo 79; Ina, Kapatid, Anak 79; Jaguar • Maynila: Jaguar 79; Angela Markado 80; Bona 80; Nakaw na Pag-Ibig 80; Binata si Mister, Balaga si Misis 81; Borgis 81; Hello Young Lovers 81; Cain at Abel 82; Caught in the Act 82; In This Corner 82; Kontrobersyal 82; Mother Dear 82; P.X. 82; Palipat-Lipat, Papalit-Palit 82; Experience 83; Strangers in Paradise 83; Bayan Ko • Bayan Ko—Kapit sa Patalim • Bayan Ko: My Own Country • Clutching a Knife in Desperation • Kapit sa Palatim • My Country • My Own Country 84; Hot Property 84; Misquelito 84; Ano Ang Kulay ng Mukha ng Diyos? 85; Hinugot sa Langit 86; Macho Dancer 87; I Carry the World 88; Fight for Us • Les Insoumis • Ora Pro Nobis 89

Brockwell, Robert see Broadwell, Robert R.

Brodax, Al Strawberry Fields 88

Broderick, John Sam's Song • The Swap 69*; Bad Georgia Road 76; The Warrior and the Sorceress 84

Brodie, Kevin Delta Pi • Mugsy's Girls 84

Brodl, Herbert Inseln der Illusion 88

Brodsky, Samuel The House Without Children 19

Brody, Hugh 1919 84

Brodyansky, Boris Krasnaya Derevnya 35*

Bromberger, Hervé Identité Judiciaire 51; Seul dans Paris 52; Les Fruits Sauvages 54; Nagana 55; La Bonne Tisane 58; Asphalte 59; Les Loups dans la Bergerie 60; Las Cuatro Verdades • The Four Truths • Les Quatres Vérités • Le Quattro Verità • Three Fables of Love 62*; Mort, Où Est Ta Victoire? 64; Un Soir à Tibériade 65

Bromfield, Rex Love at First Sight 74;

Tulips 81*; Melanie 82; Home Is Where the Hart Is 87

Bromly, Alan The Angel Who Pawned Her Harp 54; Follow That Horse 60

Bromski, Jacek Kill Me, Cop • Zabij Mnie, Glino 89

Broner, Erwin The Story of the Motorcar Engine 58*

Bronstein, Joseph L. Madame Olga's Pupils 81

Brook, Clive On Approval 43

Brook, Peter The Sentimental Journey 43; The Beggar's Opera 53; Moderato Cantabile • Seven Days, Seven Nights 60; Lord of the Flies 62; Marat/Sade • The Persecution and Assassination of Jean-Paul Marat As Performed by the Inmates of the Asylum of Charenton Under the Direction of the Marquis de Sade • Die Verfolgung und Ermordung Jean Paul Marats Dargestellt Durch die Schauspielgruppe des Hospizes zu Charenton Anleitung des Herrn de Sade 66; The London Scene 67*; Make and Break • Tell Me Lies 67; Red, White and Zero 67*; King Lear 69; Meetings with Remarkable Men 79; La Tragédie de Carmen 83; The Mahabharata 89

Brooke, Hugh Silence 26*

Brooke, Ralph Bloodlust 59

Brooke, Van Dyke The Artist's Revenge 09; The Baker Boy • Conscience 10; A Dixie Mother 10; Her Hero 11; The Adventure of the Italian Model 12; The Adventure of the Retired Army Colonel 12; Billy's Burglar 12; Counsel for the Defense 12; Ida's Christmas 12; The Money Kings 12; O'Hara, Squatter and Philosopher 12; Cupid Through a Keyhole 13; The Doctor's Secret 13; Fanny's Conspiracy 13; Father's Hatband 13; His Silver Bachelorhood 13; The Honorable Algernon 13; Just Show People 13; O'Hara As a Guardian Angel 13; O'Hara Helps Cupid 13; A Soul in Bondage 13; Under the Daisies 13; Wanted, a Stronghand 13; Cupid vs. Money 14; A Daughter of Israel 14; Goodbye Summer 14; The Hidden Letters 14; His Little Page 14; John Rance, Gentleman 14; Memories in Men's Souls 14; Officer John Donovan 14; Old Reliable 14; The Peacemaker 14; Politics and the Press 14; The Right of Way 14; The Salvation of Kathleen 14; Sawdust and Salome 14; Sunshine and Shadows 14; Under False Colors 14; The Barrier of Faith 15; The Criminal 15; A Daughter's Strange Inheritance 15; Elsa's Brother 15; Janet of the Chorus 15; A Pillar of Flame 15; Rags and the Girl 15; The Crown Prince's Double 16; The Lights of New York 16; An Amateur Orphan 17; It Happened to Adele 17

Brookner, Howard Burroughs 84; Bloodhounds of Broadway 89

Brooks, Adam Almost You 84; Little Red Riding Hood • Red Riding Hood 87

Brooks, Albert Real Life 78; Modern Romance 81; Lost in America 85

Brooks, Bob Tattoo 80

Brooks, Dwight Poco...Little Dog Lost 77

Brooks, James L. Terms of Endearment 83; Broadcast News 87

Brooks, Joseph You Light Up My Life 77; If Ever I See You Again 78; Headin' for Broadway 80; Invitation to the Wedding 84

Brooks, Mel The Critic 63*; The Producers 67; The Twelve Chairs 70; Blazing Saddles 73; Young Frankenstein 74; Silent Movie 76; High Anxiety 77; History of the World—Part I 81; Spaceballs 87

Brooks, Richard Crisis 50; The Light Touch 51; Battle Circus 52; Deadline • Deadline U.S.A. 52; The Last Time I Saw Paris 53; Take the High Ground 53; Flame and the Flesh 54; The Blackboard Jungle 55; The Last Hunt 55; The Catered Affair • Wedding Breakfast 56; The Brothers Karamazov 57; Something of Value 57; Cat on a Hot Tin Roof 58; Elmer Gantry 60; Sweet Bird of Youth 61; Lord Jim 64; The Professionals 66; In Cold Blood 67; The Happy Ending 69; $ • Dollars • The Heist 71; Bite the Bullet 75; Looking for Mr. Goodbar 77; The Man with the Deadly Lens • Wrong Is Right 82; Fever Pitch 85

Brooks, Thor Legion of the Doomed 58; Arson for Hire 59

Broom, Barney Knights Electric 81

Broomfield, Nicholas Soldier Girls 81*; Chicken Ranch 83*; Lily Tomlin 86*; Dark Obsession • Diamond Skulls 89

Brosio, Valentino The Spirit and the Flesh 48

Brouett, Albert Who Is the Boss? 21; A Rogue in Love 22; Early Birds 23; Jail Birds 23; Mumming Birds 23

Broughton, James The Potted Psalm 46*; Mother's Day 48; Adventures of Jimmy 50; Four in the Afternoon 51; Loony Tom • Loony Tom, the Happy Lover 51; The Pleasure Garden 52; The Bed 67; Nuptiae 69; The Golden Positions 70; This Is It 71; Dreamwood 72; High Kukus 73; Testament 74; The Water Circle 75; Erogeny 76; Together 76; Song of the Godbody 77; Windmobile 77; Hermes Bird 79; The Gardener of Eden 81; Shaman Psalm 81

Brower, Otto Avalanche 28; Stairs of Sand 29; The Sunset Pass 29; The Border Legion 30*; The Law Rides West • The Santa Fe Trail 30*; The Light of Western Stars 30*; Paramount on Parade 30*; Blazing Arrows • Fighting Caravans 31*; Clearing the Range 31; Hard Hombre 31; The Devil Horse 32*; Fighting for Justice 32; Gold 32; Law of the Sea 32; The Local Bad Man 32; Spirit of the West 32; Crossfire 33; Evidence in Camera • Headline Shooter 33; Pleasure 33; Scarlet River 33; I Can't Escape 34; Mystery Mountain • Radio Ranch 34*; Speed Wings 34; Straightaway 34; Couldn't Possibly Happen • Men with Steel Faces • The Phantom Empire 35*; The Outlaw Deputy 35; Postal Inspector 36; Sins of Man 36*; Under Two Flags 36*; Road Demon 38; Speed to Burn 38; Stop, Look and Love 39; Too Busy to Work 39; Winner Take All 39; The Gay Caballero 40; Girl from

Avenue A 40; On Their Own 40; Youth Will Be Served 40; Little Tokyo U.S.A. 42; Dixie Dugan 43; Behind Green Lights 45; Duel in the Sun 46*

Brown, Alex Dress Rehearsal • Opening Night • Rhythm and Song 35

Brown, Barry The Way We Live Now 70; Cloud Dancer 77

Brown, Bernard Pettin' in the Park 34; Those Were Wonderful Days 34

Brown, Bruce The Endless Summer 66; On Any Sunday 71

Brown, Clarence The County Fair 19*; The Great Redeemer 20*; The Last of the Mohicans 20*; The Foolish Matrons • Is Marriage a Failure? 21*; The Light in the Dark 22; The Acquittal 23; Don't Marry for Money 23; Robin Hood, Jr. 23; Butterfly 24; The Signal Tower 24; Smouldering Fires 24; The Eagle 25; The Goose Woman 25; Flesh and the Devil 26; Kiki 26; The Cossacks 28*; The Trail of '98 28; A Woman of Affairs 28; Navy Blues 29; The Wonder of Women 29; Anna Christie 30; Inspiration 30; Romance 30; Emma 31; A Free Soul 31; The Possessed 31; This Modern Age 31*; Letty Lynton 32; The Son-Daughter 32; Looking Forward • Service 33; Night Flight 33; Chained 34; Sadie McKee 34; Ah, Wilderness! 35; Anna Karenina 35; The Gorgeous Hussy 36; Wife vs. Secretary 36; Conquest • Maria Walewska • Marie Walewska 37; Held for Ransom 38; Idiot's Delight 38; Of Human Hearts 38; The Rains Came 39; Come Live with Me 40; Edison, the Man 40; They Met in Bombay 41; The Human Comedy 43; National Velvet 44; The White Cliffs of Dover 44; The Yearling 46; Song of Love 47; Intruder in the Dust 49; Red Hot Wheels • To Please a Lady 50; The Angels and the Pirates • Angels in the Outfield 51; It's a Big Country 51*; When in Rome 51; Plymouth Adventure 52

Brown, Clifford see Franco, Jesús

Brown, Curtis The Game 90

Brown, Don The Satin Mushroom • A Soft Warm Experience 69

Brown, Edwin Simply Irresistible 83; The Prey 84

Brown, Ewing M. A Whale of a Tale 77

Brown, Gregory Dead Man Walking 87; Street Asylum 90

Brown, Harcourt How I Won the Belt 14; A Startling Announcement 14

Brown, Harry Joe Bashful Buccaneer 25; Broadway Billy 26; Danger Quest 26; The Dangerous Dude 26; Fighting Thoroughbreds 26; The High Flyer 26; Kentucky Handicap 26; Moran of the Mounted 26; The Night Owl 26; One Punch O'Day 26; Racing Romance 26; Rapid Fire Romance 26; The Self Starter 26; Stick to Your Story 26; The Windjammer 26; The Winner 26; Gun Gospel 27; The Land Beyond the Law 27; The Racing Fool 27; Romantic Rogue 27; The Royal American 27; The Scorcher 27; The Wagon Show 27; The Cloud Patrol 28; Code of the Scarlet 28; The Sky Ranger 28; The Skywayman 28; The Air

Derby 29; The Lawless Legion 29; The Royal Rider 29; Señor Americano 29; The Wagon Master 29; The Fighting Legion 30; Kettle Creek • Mountain Justice 30; Lucky Larkin 30; Parade of the West 30; Song of the Caballero 30; Sons of the Saddle 30; The Squealer 30; Registered Woman • A Woman of Experience 31; Billion Dollar Scandal 32; Madison Square Garden 32; I Love That Man 33; Sitting Pretty 33; Knickerbocker Holiday 44

Brown, Jack W. The Shadow 21*

Brown, Jenny The Rugged Island 34

Brown, Jim Wasn't That a Time! • The Weavers: Wasn't That a Time! 82; Musical Passage 84

Brown, Jim Slam Dunk 87

Brown, John Monique 70

Brown, Karl His Dog 27; Stark Love 27; Prince of Diamonds 30*; Fatal Alarm • Fire Alarm • Flames 32; Any Man's Wife 36; In His Steps 36; The White Legion 36; Federal Bullets 37; Michael O'Halloran 37; Barefoot Boy 38; The Circus Comes to Town • Under the Big Top 38; Numbered Woman • Private Nurse 38; The Port of Missing Girls 38

Brown, Larry An Eye for an Eye • Psychopath 73

Brown, Melville Her Big Night 26; Fast and Furious 27; Taxi, Taxi 27; Buck Privates 28; Cream of the Earth • Red Lips 28; 13 Washington Square 28; Dance Hall 29; Geraldine 29; Jazz Heaven 29; The Love Doctor 29; Amos 'n' Andy • Check and Double Check 30; Lovin' the Ladies 30; She's My Weakness 30; Behind Office Doors 31; Fanny Foley Herself • Top of the Bill 31; White Shoulders 31; Lost in the Stratosphere • Murder in the Stratosphere 34; Redhead 34; Champagne for Breakfast 35; Forced Landing 35; The Nut Farm 35; Head Office 36; He Loved an Actress • Mad About Money • Stardust 37

Brown, Mende The Clown and the Kids • The Pied Piper • The Piper • Sviračut 68; Little Jungle Boy • Momman, Little Jungle Boy 69; Strange Holiday 69; On the Run 83

Brown, Phil The Harlem Globetrotters 51*

Brown, Ralph see Polselli, Renato

Brown, Reginald Son of the Renegade 53

Brown, Rowland Quick Millions 31; Hell's Highway 32; Blood Money 33; The Scarlet Pimpernel 34*; Sing As We Go 34*

Brown, Tony The White Girl 87

Brown, William O. One-Way Wahine • One-Way Wahini 65; Legend of Witch Hollow • The Witchmaker 69

Browning, Ricou Island of the Lost 67*; Salty 73

Browning, Tod The Burned Hand 15; The Electric Alarm 15; The Highbinders 15; An Image of the Past 15; Little Marie 15; The Living Death 15; The Lucky Transfer 15; The Slave Girl 15; The Spell of the Poppy 15; The Story of a Story 15; The Woman from Warren's 15; The Deadly

Glass of Beer • The Fatal Glass of Beer 16; Everybody's Doing It 16; Puppets 16; Hands Up! 17*; Jim Bludso 17*; The Jury of Fate 17; A Love Sublime 17*; Peggy, the Will-o'-the-Wisp 17; The Unpainted Woman 17; The Brazen Beauty 18; The Deciding Kiss 18; The Eyes of Mystery 18; The Legion of Death 18; Revenge 18; Set Free 18; Which Woman? 18; Bonnie, Bonnie Lassie 19; The Exquisite Thief 19; A Petal on the Current 19; The Wicked Darling 19; The Virgin of Stamboul 20; No Woman Knows 21; Outside the Law 21; The Man Under Cover 22; Under Two Flags 22; The Wise Kid 22; The Day of Faith 23; Drifting 23; The White Tiger 23; The Dangerous Flirt • A Dangerous Flirtation 24; Silk Stocking Girl • Silk Stocking Sal 24; The Black Bird 25; Dollar Down 25; The Mystic 25; The Unholy Three 25; The Road to Mandalay 26; The Show 26; The Big City 27; The Hypnotist • London After Midnight 27; The Unknown 27; West of Zanzibar 28; The Thirteenth Chair 29; Where East Is East 29; Dracula 30; Outside the Law 30; The Iron Man 31; Forbidden Love • Freaks • The Monster Show • Nature's Mistakes 32; Fast Workers 33; Mark of the Vampire 35; The Devil-Doll 36; Miracles for Sale 39

Brownlow, Kevin The Capture 55; Ascot: A Race Against Time 60; It Happened Here 63*; 9 Dalmuir West 66; Winstanley 75*

Brownrigg, S. F. Don't Look in the Basement 73; Poor White Trash II • Scum of the Earth 76; Keep My Grave Open 80; Thinkin' Big 85

Bruce, George Fury in Paradise 55*

Bruce, James The Suicide Club 87

Bruce, Neville Film Pie 20*; The Film Star's Perfect Day 21; The Fisherman's Perfect Day 21

Bruce, Nicholas Wings of Death 85*

Bruce, Robert C. The Wanderer and the Whozitt 18; The Restless Three 19; The River Gray and the River Green 19; And Women Must Weep 22

Bruck, Jerry, Jr. I. F. Stone's Weekly 73

Bruckberger, R. The Carmelites • Le Dialogue des Carmélites 59*

Bruckman, Clyde The General 26*; The Battle of the Century 27; Call of the Cuckoos 27; Horse Shoes 27; Love 'Em and Feed 'Em 27; A Perfect Gentleman 27*; Putting Pants on Philip 27; The Finishing Touch 28*; Leave 'Em Laughing 28; Welcome Danger 29*; Feet First 30; Everything's Rosie 31; Movie Crazy 32; The Fatal Glass of Beer 33; The Human Fish 33; Too Many Highballs 33; Horses' Collars 34; The Man on the Flying Trapeze • The Memory Expert 35; Spring Tonic 35

Bruckner, Jutta Ein Blick—und die Liebe Bricht Aus • One Look—and Love Begins 86

Bruell, Jed Mr. Washington Goes to Town 40*

Brunchugin, Yevgeni Mother and Daughter 62*; Ukrainian Festival 65*

Brunel, Adrian The Cost of a Kiss 17; Bookworms 20; The Bump 20; Five Pounds Reward 20; Twice Two 20; The Temporary Lady 21; Too Many Crooks 21; Sheer Trickery 22; Lovers in Araby 23; The Man Without Desire 23; Moors and Minarets 23; The Shimmy Sheik 23; Two-Chinned Chow 23; Yes We Have No… 23; The Boy Goes to Biskra 24; Crossing the Great Sagrada 24; The Pathetic Gazette 24; Battling Bruisers 25; The Blunderland of Big Game 25; Cut It Out 25; So This Is Jollygood 25; A Typical Budget 25; Blighty 26; Love, Life and Laughter at Swaythling Court 26; Money for Nothing 26; The Vortex 27; The Constant Nymph 28*; Dolores • A Light Woman 28; The Crooked Billet 29; In a Monastery Garden 29; Elstree Calling 30*; Follow the Lady 33; I'm an Explosive 33; The Laughter of Fools 33; Little Napoleon 33; Taxi to Paradise 33; Two Wives for Henry 33; Badger's Green 34; The City of Beautiful Nonsense 34; Important People 34; Menace • Sabotage • When London Sleeps • While London Sleeps 34; Variety 34; Cross Currents 35; The Invader • An Old Spanish Custom 35; Vanity 35; While Parents Sleep 35; Love at Sea 36; Prison Breaker 36; The Barbarian and the Lady • The Rebel Son • Taras Bulba 38*; The Girl Who Forgot 39; The Lion Has Wings 39*; Food for Thought 40; Salvage with a Smile 40; The Gentle Sex 43*

Brunius, Jacques To the Rescue 52; The Blakes Slept Here • Family Album 54*

Brunius, John W. Mästerkatten i Stövlar • Puss in Boots 18; Ah, i Morgon Kväll • Oh, Tomorrow Night 19; The Fairy of Solbakken • Synnöve Solbakken 19; The Gyurkovics • Gyurkovisarna 20; Thora van Deken 20; A Fortune Hunter • En Lyckoriddare 21; Kvarnen • The Mill 21; En Vild Fågel • A Wild Bird 21; The Eyes of Love • Kärlekens Ögon 22; Hard Wills • Hårda Viljor • Iron Wills 22; The Best of All 23; Johan Ulfstjerna 23; A Maid Among Maids • En Piga Bland Pigor 24; Charles XII • Karl XII 25; Fänrik Stals Sägner • The Tales of Ensign Steel 26; Gustaf Wasa 26; The Doctor's Secret • Doktorns Hemlighet 30; The Two of Us • Vi Två 30; Längtan till Havet • Longing for the Sea 31; False Greta • Falska Greta 34; Havets Melodi • The Melody of the Sea 34*

Brunner, Patrick We've Got to Have Love 35; Happy Event 39

Bruno, Federico Black Tunnel 86

Bruno, John Heavy Metal 81*

Brusati, Franco Il Padrone Sono Me 56; Le Désordre • Disorder • Il Disordine 62; The Girl Who Couldn't Say No • Il Suo Modo di Fari • Tenderly 68; I Tulipani di Harlem 70; Bread and Chocolate • Pane e Cioccolata 74; Dimenticare Venezia • Forget Venice • To Forget Venice 79; The Good Soldier 82; Lo Zio Indegno 89

Brusseau, William E. Three Weeks of Love 65

Brustellin, Alf Deutschland im Herbst •

Germany in Autumn 78*

Bruun, Einar J. Enchantment 20; Judge Not 20; The Corner Man 21; Her Penalty 21; In Full Cry 21; The Penniless Millionaire 21

Bruyere, Christian Shelley 87

Bryant, Baird Celebration at Big Sur 71*

Bryant, Charles Stronger Than Death 20*; A Doll's House 22; Salome 22

Bryant, Gerard All Square Aft 57; Rock Around the World • The Tommy Steele Story 57; Stars of a Summer Night 59; The Dover Road Mystery 60; Ouch! 67

Bryant, James Don't Go in the Woods 80; The Executioner, Part Two 84; Hell Riders 85

Bryant, Peter The Supreme Kid 76

Bryce, Alex Sexton Blake and the Mademoiselle 35; The Big Noise 36; The End of the Road • Song of the Road 36; Servants All 36; Wedding Group • Wrath of Jealousy 36*; Against the Tide 37; The Black Tulip 37; Macushlah 37; The Last Barricade 38; Little Miss Molly • My Irish Molly 38; The Londonderry Air 38; The Owner Comes Aboard 40; Robin Hood • The Story of Robin Hood • The Story of Robin Hood and His Merrie Men 52*; The Cockleshell Heroes 55*

Bryden, Bill Ill Fares the Land 82; Aria 87*

Brynych, Zbyněk …A Pátý Jezdec Je Strach • The Fifth Horseman Is Fear 65; Transport from Paradise • Transport z Ráje 67; Ošetřovna • Sign of the Virgin • Souhvězdí Panny 69; O Happy Day! • Seventeen and Anxious 70; Ants Bring Death • Mravenci Nesou Smrt 85

Bub, Klaus Adrian und die Römer 88*

Buba, Tony Lightning Over Braddock: A Rust Bowl Fantasy 89

Buch, Fritz Peter Königin der Liebe 36; Waldwinter 36; For Freedom and Love • Um Freiheit und Liebe 38; Katzensteg 38

Buchanan, Andrew All Living Things 39; The Backyard Front 40; Hullo Fame 40; The Fine Feathers 41; Surprise Broadcast 41

Buchanan, Beau Sex du Jour 76

Buchanan, Jack That's a Good Girl 33*; Yes, Mr. Brown 33*; The Sky's the Limit 37*

Buchanan, Larry Free, White and Twenty-One 63; The Trial of Lee Harvey Oswald 64; Under Age 64; The Eye Creatures 65; Hell Raiders 65; High Yellow 65; Curse of the Swamp Creature 66; In the Year 2889 • Year 2889 66; Mars Needs Women 66; Zontar, the Thing from Venus 66; Creature of Destruction 67; It's Alive 68; The Other Side of Bonnie and Clyde 68; A Bullet for Pretty Boy 70; Strawberries Need Rain 70; Goodbye Norma Jean 76; Hughes and Harlow: Angels in Hell 78; Mistress of the Apes 81; The Loch Ness Horror 82; Down on Us 84

Buchma, A. The Land 55*

Buchowetzki, Dmitri The Brothers Karamazov • Die Brüder Karamasoff 20*; Das Experiment des Professor Mithrany 20;

Die Letzte Stunde 20; All for a Woman • Danton 21; Der Galiläer 21; Mad Love • Sappho 21; Der Stier von Olivera 21*; Die Gräfin von Paris 22; Othello 22; Peter der Grosse • Peter the Great 22; Das Karussell des Lebens 23; Lily of the Dust 24; Men 24; Graustark 25; The Swan 25; The Crown of Lies 26; The Love Song • Valencia 26; The Midnight Sun 26; Le Réquisitoire 30; Weib im Dschungel 30; Die Nacht der Entscheidung 31; Stamboul 31

Buchs, José Dos Mujeres y Un Don Juan 34

Buchs, Julio E Divenne il Più Spietato Bandito del Sud • A Few Bullets More • El Hombre Que Mató a Billy el Niño • The Man Who Killed Billy the Kid 67; A Bullet for Sandoval • Quei Disperati Che Puzzano di Sudore e di Morte • Vengeance Is Mine 69; Crossroads for a Nun • Encrucijada para una Monja • Nun at the Crossroads • Violenza per una Monaca 70

Buck, Frank Fang and Claw 35; Jungle Cavalcade 41*

Buckalew, Bethel Mag Wheels 78; My Boys Are Good Boys 78

Buckhantz, Allan A. Willy 63; Jim Buck • Portrait of a Hitman 77

Buckingham, Thomas Arizona Express 24; The Cyclone Rider 24; Forbidden Cargo 25; Troubles of a Bride 25; Ladies of Leisure 26; Tony Runs Wild 26; Land of the Lawless 27; The Lure of the Night Club 27; Crashing Through 28; What Price Beauty? 28; Cock of the Air 32

Buckland, Warwick At the Eleventh Hour 12; The Avaricious Monk 12; The Bachelor's Ward 12; A Bold Venture 12; Church and Stage 12; The Codicil 12; The Coming-Back of Kit Denver 12; The Convict's Daughter 12; The Dear Little Teacher 12; A Double Life 12; The Generosity of Mr. Smith 12; The Heart of a Woman 12; Jasmine 12; Jim All-Alone 12; Jimmy Lester, Convict and Gentleman 12; Jo the Wanderer's Boy 12; Lady Angela and the Boy 12; Love Wins in the End 12; The Lure of the Footlights 12; The Miser and the Maid 12; Out of Evil Cometh Good 12; The Passing of the Old Four-Wheeler 12; A Peasant Girl's Revenge 12; Rose o' the River 12; A Woman's Wit 12; Adrift on Life's Tide 13; At the Foot of the Scaffold 13; The Book 13; The Broken Oath 13; The Broken Sixpence 13; A Case for Solomon • Motherhood or Politics 13; The Cat and the Chestnuts 13; The Christmas Strike • For Such Is the Kingdom of Heaven 13; For Love of Him 13; For Marion's Sake 13; For the Honour of the House 13; The Forsaken 13; The Girl at Lancing Mill 13; A Helping Hand 13; Her Crowning Glory 13; In the Hour of His Need 13; The Lesson 13; A Little Knowledge 13; The Man or His Money 13; The Mill Girl 13; A Mist of Errors 13; The Mysterious Philanthropist 13; On the Brink of the Precipice 13; One Fair Daughter 13; Over the Ferry 13; Partners in Crime 13; Paying the Penalty 13; The Promise 13; A

Question of Identity 13; The Red Light 13; Sally in Our Alley 13; The Silence of Richard Wilton 13; A Storm in a Teacup 13; The Touch of a Babe 13; Tried in the Fire 13; Two Little Pals 13; We Are But Little Children Weak 13; The Angel of Deliverance 14; Brief Authority 14; By Whose Hand? • The Mystery of Mr. Marks 14; The Corporal's Kiddies 14; The Curtain 14; Diamond Cut Diamond 14; The Double Event 14; The Girl Who Lived in Straight Street 14; The Girl Who Played the Game 14; Her Suitor's Suit 14; His Great Opportunity 14; The Kleptomaniac 14; A Knight of the Road 14; Little Boy Bountiful 14; The Man Behind the Mask 14; Memory 14; A Noble Deception 14; Only a Flower Girl 14; The Price of a Gift 14; The Price of Fame 14; A Price on His Head 14; The Quality of Mercy 14; The Stress of Circumstance 14; They Say — Let Them Say 14; Thou Shalt Not Steal 14; Wildflower 14; After Dark 15; Her One Redeeming Feature 15; His Brother's Wife 15; The Little Mother 15; The Midnight Mail 15; On the Brink 15; A Park Lane Scandal 15; The Story of a Punch and Judy Show 15; Time and the Hour 15

Buckland, Wilfred The Man on the Box 14*

Buckley, David Saturday Night at the Baths 75

Bucknell, Robert More Deadly Than the Male 59

Buckner, Noel The Good Fight 83*

Bucksey, Colin Blue Money 84; The McGuffin 85; Dealers 89

Bucquet, Harold S. Little People 35; Windy 35; Torture Money 36; Behind the Criminal 37; It May Happen to You 37; Soak the Poor 37; Come Across 38; They're Always Caught 38; What Price Safety? 38; Young Dr. Kildare 38; Calling Dr. Kildare 39; On Borrowed Time 39; The Secret of Dr. Kildare 39; Dr. Kildare Goes Home 40; Dr. Kildare's Crisis 40; Dr. Kildare's Strange Case 40; We Who Are Young 40; Dr. Kildare's Wedding Day • Mary Names the Day 41; Kathleen 41; My Life Is Yours • The People vs. Dr. Kildare 41; The Penalty 41; Calling Dr. Gillespie 42; The War Against Mrs. Hadley 42; Adventures of Tartu 43; Dragon Seed 43*; Without Love 45

Buczkowski, Leonard The Demented 28; Star Squadron 30; Baltic Rhapsody 36; The Testament of Professor Wilczur 39; Łódz 45; Forbidden Songs 47; Skarb • Treasure 49; The First Start 51; Adventure in Warsaw • The Marienstadt Adventure 54; The Case of Pilot Maresz 56; A Rainy July 58; Time Past 61; Teenager 62; The Interrupted Flight 64; Maria and Napoleon 66

Budd, Leighton The Courtship of Miss Vote 16; In Lunyland 16; The Mexican Border 16; Uncle Sam's Christmas 16; Evolution of the Dachshund 17; Oh Girls What Next 17; Sic 'Em Cat 17; Stung 17; Uncle Sam's Dinner Party 17; A German Trick That Failed 18; The Greased Pole 18;

The Kaiser's Surprise Party 18; The Peril of Prussianism 18; Putting Fritz on the Water Wagon 18; The Third Liberty Loan Bomb 18; A Tonsorial Slot Machine 18; Uncle Sam's Coming Problem 18; In 1998 AD: The Automatic Reducing Machine 19; My How Times Have Changed 19

Budkiewicz, Jan Battlefield • Pobojowisko 85

Budsan, Ronald R. Every Sparrow Must Fall 64

Buduris, Vassilis O Paradissos Anigi me Antiklidi • Red Ants 87

Buechler, John The Dungeonmaster 85*; Troll 86; Cellar Dweller 88; Friday the 13th Part VII — The New Blood 88

Buel, Kenean The School for Scandal 14; Blazing Love 16; Daredevil Kate 16; Hypocrisy 16; The Marble Heart 16*; The War Bride's Secret 16; The Bitter Truth 17; The New York Peacock 17; She 17; Trouble Makers 17; Two Little Imps 17; American Buds 18; Doing Their Bit 18; We Should Worry 18; The Woman Who Gave 18; The Fallen Idol 19; My Little Sister 19; Woman, Woman 19; The Place of the Honeymoons 20; The Veiled Marriage 20

Buesst, Nigel Compo 89

Bufa, Peter Ghost Dance 82

Bugajski, Richard see Bugajski, Ryszard

Bugajski, Ryszard The Interrogation • Przesłuchanie 82

Bugiani, Carlo Anything for a Song 47

Bugler, Bror Each Heart Has Its Own Story 53

Bujold, Geneviève Marie-Christine 70*

Bujtor, István Az Elvarázsolt Dollár • The Enchanted Dollars 85

Bukaee, Raphi Avanti Popolo 86

Bukovsky, Anatoly Mother and Daughter 62*; Ukrainian Festival 65*

Bulajić, Veljko Train Without a Timetable • Vlak Bez Voznog Reda 58; Atomic War Bride • Rat • War 60; Boom Town • Uzavreli Granična 61; Hill of Death • Kozara 62; Skopje 1963 64; A Glance at the Pupil of the Sun • Pogled u Zenicu Sunca 66; The Battle of Neretva • Battle of the Neretva • Battle on the River Neretva • Bitva na Neretvi 69; Assassination in Sarajevo • The Day That Shook the World 76; Obećana Zemlja • The Promised Land 86

Buld, Wolfgang Der Formel eins Film 85

Bulgakov, Leo After the Dance 35; I'll Love You Always 35; White Lies 35; Marusia 38

Bullo, Gianfranco Tutta Colpa della Sip 88

Bulow, Vicco von see Loriot

Bunce, Alan Babar: The Movie 89

Bundsmann, Anton see Mann, Anthony

Bunnag, Rom Kan Pi • Kun Pi • Pregnant by a Ghost 75

Buntzman, Mark Exterminator II 84*

Buñuel, Joyce Dirty Dishes 78

Buñuel, Juan At the Meeting with Joyous Death • Au Rendez-Vous de la Mort Joyeuse 72; La Femme aux Bottes Rouges

• The Woman with Red Boots 74; Leonor 75; The Island of Passion 84; La Rebelión de los Colgados 87

Buñuel, Luis An Andalusian Dog • Un Chien Andalou 28*; La Chute de la Maison Usher • The Fall of the House of Usher 28*; L'Âge d'Or • Age of Gold • The Golden Age 30*; Las Hurdes • Las Hurdes, Tierra Sin Pan • Land Without Bread • Terre Sans Pain • Tierra Sin Pan • Unpromised Land 32; ¡Centinela Alerta! • On Alert, Sentinel! 35*; Espagne 37 • ¡España Leal en Armas! • Spain Loyal in Arms • Spain '37 37; En el Viejo Tampico • Gran Casino • Tampico 47; El Gran Calavera • The Great Madcap • The Great Profligate 49; Demonio y Carne • Demonio y Carne, Susana • Devil and Flesh • The Devil and the Flesh • Susana 50; The Forgotten • Los Olvidados • The Young and the Damned 50; Ascent to Heaven • Climbing to the Sky • Mexican Bus Ride • Subida al Cielo 51; Cuando los Hijos Nos Juzgan • Una Mujer Sin Amor • Pierre and Jean • A Woman Without Love 51; Daughter of Deceit • Don Quintín el Amargado • Don Quintin the Bitter • La Hija del Engaño 51; Abismos de Pasión • Cumbres Borrascosas • Wuthering Heights 52; The Adventures of Robinson Crusoe • Las Aventuras de Robinson Crusoe • Robinson Crusoe 52; The Brute • El Bruto • L'Enjôleuse 52; El • El, This Strange Passion • Him • This Strange Passion • Torments 52; Illusion Travels by Streetcar • La Ilusión en Tranvía • La Ilusión Viaja en Tranvía 53; El Río y la Muerte • The River and Death 54; Amanti di Domani • Cela S'Appelle l'Aurore • That's Called the Dawn 55; The Criminal Life of Archibaldo de la Cruz • Ensayo de un Crimen • Rehearsal for a Crime • La Vida Criminal de Archibaldo de la Cruz 55; Death in the Jungle • Death in This Garden • Evil Eden • Gina • La Mort en Ce Jardin • La Muerte en Este Jardín 56; Nazarín 58; Los Ambiciosos • Fever Mounts at El Pao • La Fièvre Monte à El Pao • Republic of Sin 59; Island of Shame • La Jeune Fille • La Joven • The Young One 60; Viridiana 61; El Ángel Exterminador • The Exterminating Angel 62; Il Diario di una Cameriera • The Diary of a Chambermaid • Le Journal d'une Femme de Chambre 63; Simón del Desierto • Simon of the Desert 63; Belle de Jour 66; The Milky Way • La Via Lattea • La Voie Lactée 68; Tristana 70; Le Charme Discret de la Bourgeoisie • The Discreet Charm of the Bourgeoisie 72; Le Fantôme de la Liberté • The Phantom of Liberty • The Spectre of Freedom 74; Cet Obscur Objet du Désir • That Obscure Object of Desire 77

Burbidge, Derek Fish Out of Water 76; Urgh! A Music War 81; Men Without Women 83

Burch, John Gun Law 29

Burch, Noel Correction Please, or How We Got Into Pictures 80

Burckhardt, Jacob It Don't Pay to Be an Honest Citizen 84; Landlord Blues 88

Burel, Léonce-Henri La Floraison 13; L'Industrie du Verre 13; La Pousse des Plantes 13; Les Rapaces Diurnes et Nocturnes 13; La Conquête des Gaules 22*; L'Évadée 29*; La Fada 32

Buren, A. H. van see *Van Buren, A. H.*

Burge, Robert A. Vasectomy: A Delicate Matter 86

Burge, Stuart There Was a Crooked Man 60; Uncle Vanya 63; Othello 65*; The Mikado 67; Julius Caesar 69

Burger, Germain Devil's Rock 38; Sheepdog of the Hills 41; Rose of Tralee 42; My Ain Folk 44

Burger, Hans Seeds of Freedom 43

Burguet, Charles Les Deux Amours 17; Pour Épouser Gaby 17; Son Héros 17; L'Âme de Pierre 18; Au Paradis des Enfants 18; La Sultane de l'Amour 19*; Le Chevalier de Gaby 20; Un Ours 21; Faubourg Montmartre 24; Barocco 25; Martyre 26; Le Meneur de Joies 29

Buria, Lázaro Operación Abril del Caribe • Operation April in the Caribbean 82*

Burke, Edwin Now I'll Tell • When New York Sleeps 34

Burke, Martyn The Clown Murders 75; Operation Overthrow • Power Play 78; The Last Chase 81; Witnesses 88

Burkestone, Graham Meech see *Meech-Burkestone, Graham*

Burks, Alex see *Bazzoni, Camillo*

Burlyayev, Nikolai Lermontov 87

Burman, Tom Meet the Hollowheads 89

Burn, Oscar Castle Sinister 48; Fun on the Farm 52; The Great Day 52; Potter of the Yard 52*; Mr. Beamish Goes South 53*; Too Many Detectives 53*

Burnama, Jopi The Intruder 86; Ferocious Female Freedom Fighters 89

Burness, Pete Bungled Bungalow 50; Trouble Indemnity 50; Bare Faced Flatfoot 51; Grizzly Golfer 51; The Oompahs 51*; Captains Outrageous 52; Dog Snatcher 52; Pink and Blue Blues 52; Sloppy Jalopy 52; Magoo Slept Here 53; Magoo's Masterpiece 53; Safety Spin 53; Destination Magoo 54; Kangaroo Courting 54; Magoo Goes Skiing 54; When Magoo Flew 54; Madcap Magoo 55; Magoo Makes News 55; Magoo's Check Up 55; Magoo's Express 55; Stage Door Magoo 55; Calling Dr. Magoo 56; Magoo Beats the Heat 56; Magoo Goes West 56; Magoo's Caine Mutiny 56; Magoo's Problem Child 56; Magoo's Puddle Jumper 56; Meet Mother Magoo 56; Trailblazer Magoo 56; Magoo Breaks Par 57; Magoo Goes Overboard 57; Magoo Saves the Bank 57; Magoo's Glorious Fourth 57; Matador Magoo 57; Rock Hound Magoo 57; The Explosive Mr. Magoo 58; Magoo's Three-Point Landing 58; Magoo's Young Manhood 58

Burnett, Charles Killer of Sheep 77; My Brother's Wedding 83; To Sleep with Anger 90

Burnford, Paul Dark Shadows 44; Patrolling the Ether 44; Adventures of Rusty 45; Fall Guy 45

Burnley, Fred Neither the Sea Nor the Sand 72

Burns, Allan Just Between Friends 86

Burns, Ken Huey Long 85; The Civil War 90

Burns, Paul What Three Men Wanted 24

Burns, Robert A. Mongrel 82

Burns, Walter Barbara 70

Burnside, R. H. Manhattan 24

Burr, Jeff Divided We Fall 82*; From a Whisper to a Scream • The Offspring 86; The Vault 88; Stepfather II • Stepfather 2: Make Room for Daddy 89; Leatherface: Texas Chainsaw Massacre III 90

Burrill, Robert L. The Milpitas Monster 80

Burroughs, Jackie A Winter Tan 87*

Burrowes, Geoff The Man from Snowy River II • Return to Snowy River 88; Run 90

Burrowes, Michael see *Hartford-Davis, Robert*

Burrows, James Partners 82

Burrud, Bill Curse of the Mayan Temple 77

Burstall, Tim Two Thousand Weeks 69; Stork 71; Alvin Purple 73; Libido 73*; Jock Petersen • Petersen 74; End Play 75; Eliza Fraser 76; The Last of the Knucklemen 79; Attack Force Z 81; Duet for Four • Partners 81; The Naked Country 85; Great Expectations—The Australian Story • Great Expectations—The Untold Story 86; Kangaroo 86

Burt, Keith Erik see *Larsen, Keith*

Burt, William P. The Woman in Chains • The Women in Chains 23

Burton, David The Bishop Murder Case 29*; The Circle • Strictly Unconventional 30; The Spoilers 30*; Blazing Arrows • Fighting Caravans 31*; Confessions of a Co-Ed • Her Dilemma 31*; Dancers in the Dark 32; Brief Moment 33; Let's Fall in Love 33; Lady by Choice 34; The Romantic Age • Sisters Under the Skin 34; The Melody Lingers On 35; Princess O'Hara 35; Make Way for a Lady 36; Jennie 40; The Man Who Wouldn't Talk 40; Manhattan Heartbeat 40; Private Nurse 41

Burton, John Nelson Never Mention Murder 64

Burton, Richard Doctor Faustus 67*

Burton, Tim Pee-wee's Big Adventure 85; Beetlejuice 88; Batman 89; Edward Scissorhands 90

Burzynski, Leszek Cry Wolf 80

Buschmann, Christel Auf Immer und Ewig • Forever and Always 86; Felix 87*; Ballhaus Barmbek 88

Bushell, Anthony The Angel with the Trumpet 49; The Long Dark Hall 51*; Richard III 55*; The Prince and the Showgirl 57*; Terror of the Hatchet Men • The Terror of the Tongs 60; A Woman's Privilege 62

Bushelman, John The Silent Call 61; Sniper's Ridge 61; The Broken Land • Vanishing Frontier 62; Day of the Nightmare • Day of the Nitemare • Don't

Scream, Doris Mays 65; Cruisin' High 75; Cat Murkil and the Silks 76; High Seas Hijack 76

Bushman, Francis X. In the Diplomatic Service 16; Romeo and Juliet 16*

Bushnell, Brooks Favors 90

Bushnell, William, Jr. Prisoners 73; The Four Deuces 74

Buss, Harry Cinderella 13; Sister Susie's Sewing Shirts for Soldiers 15; A.W.S. 16; Bored 16; The Model 16; Rescuing an Heiress 16; Some Fish 16

Bussmann, Tom Whoops Apocalypse 86

Bustamante, Adolfo Fernández see *Fernández Bustamante, Adolfo*

Busteros, Raúl Redondo 86

Bustillo Oro, Juan Dos Monjes • Two Monks 34; Malditas Sean las Mujeres 36; El Misterio del Rostro Pálido 37; Nostradamus 37; El Rosal Bendito 37; Huapango 38; Cada Loco con Su Tema • Every Madman to His Specialty 39; The Girls' Aunt • La Tía de las Muchachas 39; Caballo a Caballo • Horse for Horse 40; El Hombre Sin Rostro • The Man Without a Face 50; Madcap of the House 50

Butcher, Frank E. The Work of the First Aid Nursing Yeomanry Corps 09

Bute, Mary Ellen Allegro 39*; Spook Sport 40*; Finnegans Wake • Passages from Finnegans Wake • Passages from James Joyce's Finnegans Wake 65

Butler, Alex From Istanbul, Orders to Kill 65

Butler, Alexander The Anarchist's Doom • The Tube of Death 13; For Fifty Thousand Pounds 13; The Great Bullion Robbery 13; Greater Love Hath No Man 13; In London's Toils 13; In the Hands of the London Crooks 13; A Little Child Shall Lead Them 13; London by Night 13; O.H.M.S. 13; The Passions of Men 13; A Fair Imposter 16; The Girl Who Loves a Soldier 16; Just a Girl 16; Nursie Nursie 16; A Pair of Spectacles 16; The Valley of Fear 16; In Another Girl's Shoes 17*; Little Women 17*; My Lady's Dress 17; The Sorrows of Satan 17; Jo the Crossing Sweeper 18; On Leave 18*; The Beetle 19; Damaged Goods 19; The Disappearance of the Judge 19; The Lamp of Destiny 19; The Life of a London Actress 19; The Odds Against Her 19; The Thundercloud 19; David and Jonathan 20; Her Story 20; Love in the Wilderness 20; The Night Riders 20; The Ugly Duckling 20; For Her Father's Sake 21; The Knockout 23; Maisie's Marriage • Married Love 23; A Royal Divorce 23; Should a Doctor Tell? 23; Napoleon and Josephine 24; Absence Makes the Heart Grow Fonder 25; All That Glistens Is Not Gold 25; At the Mercy of His Wife 25; Auld Lang Syne 25; The Choice 25; The Death of Agnes 25; Do Unto Others 25; Driven from Home 25; The Eternal Triangle 25; Her Golden Hair Was Hanging Down Her Back 25; Her Great Mistake 25; How It Happened 25; Hung Without Evidence 25; I Do Like to Be Beside the Seaside 25; It Is Never Too Late to Mend 25; Laugh and

35; One Frightened Night 35; Rendezvous at Midnight 35; Storm Over the Andes 35; Criminal Lawyer 36; It's Up to You 36; The Last Outlaw 36; We Who Are About to Die 36; Annapolis Salute • Salute to Romance 37; Don't Tell the Wife 37; The Outcasts of Poker Flat 37; The Westland Case 37; You Can't Beat Love 37; Everybody's Doing It 38; Night Spot 38; Smashing the Spy Ring 38; This Marriage Business 38; Alas Sobre el Chaco • Wings Over the Chaco 39; Danger on Wheels 39; Legion of Lost Flyers 39; The Man from Montreal 39; Mutiny on the Blackhawk 39; Tropic Fury 39; Alias the Deacon 40; Black Diamonds 40; The Devil's Pipeline 40; Hot Steel 40; The Mummy's Hand 40; Scattergood Baines 41; Scattergood Meets Broadway 41; Scattergood Pulls the Strings 41; Cinderella Swings It • Scattergood Swings It 42; Drums of the Congo 42; Scattergood Rides High 42; Scattergood Survives a Murder 42; Timber 42; Top Sergeant 42; Keep 'Em Slugging 43; Dixie Jamboree 44; Club Paradise • Main Street Girl • Party Girl • Sensation Hunters 45; The Man Who Walked Alone 45; Accent on Horror • The Autopsy • Scared to Death 47; King of the Bandits 47; Robin Hood of Monterey 47; Back Trail 48; Silver Trails 48

Cabanne, William Christy see *Cabanne, Christy*

Cabiddu, Gianfranco Disamistade 89

Cabrera, Sergio A Matter of Honor • Técnicas de Duelo 88

Cacoyannis, Michael Kyriakatiko Xyprima • Sunday Awakening • Windfall in Athens 53; Stella 54; The Girl in Black • To Koritsi me ta Mavra 55; The Final Lie • A Matter of Dignity • To Telefteo Psemma 57; Eroica • Our Last Spring 59; Il Relitto • The Wastrel 60*; Electra • Elektra 61; Zorba the Greek 64; The Day the Fish Came Out 67; The Trojan Women 71; Attila 1974—The Rape of Cyprus • Attila '74 75 • The Rape of Cyprus 75; Iphigenia 76; Sweet Country 86

Cadena, Jordi The Lady • La Señora 87

Cadiou, Claude The Platinum Life • Treichville Story • La Vie Platinée 87

Cadman, Frank The Bailiffs 32; The Dreamers 33; Post Haste 33; Tooth Will Out 33; The Mystery of the Snakeskin Belt 50

Cagney, James Short Cut to Hell 57

Cahill, David You Can't See 'Round Corners 69

Cahn, Edward L. Homicide Squad • Lost Men 31*; Afraid to Talk 32; Guns A-Blazing • Law and Order 32; Radio Patrol 32; Emergency Call 33; Laughter in Hell 33; Confidential 35; Death Drives Through 35; Hit and Run Driver 35; A Thrill for Thelma 35; Foolproof 36; Perfect Set Up 36; Bad Guy 37; Redhead 41; Plan for Destruction 43; Main Street After Dark 44; Dangerous Partners 45; Born to Speed 47; Gas House Kids in Hollywood 47; Bungalow 13 48; The Checkered Coat 48; I

Cheated the Law 48; Prejudice 49; Destination Murder 50; Experiment Alcatraz 50; The Great Plane Robbery 50; Beginner's Luck • Two Dollar Bettor 51; Betrayed Women 55; Creature with the Atom Brain 55; Flesh and the Spur 56; Girls in Prison 56; Runaway Daughters 56; Shake, Rattle and Rock 56; The She-Creature 56; The Dead That Walk • Zombies of Mora-Tau 57; Dragstrip Girl 57; The Hell Creatures • Invasion of the Hell Creatures • Invasion of the Saucer Men • Spacemen Saturday Night 57; Motorcycle Gang 57; Voodoo Woman 57; Curse of the Faceless Man 58; Guns, Girls and Gangsters 58; Hong Kong Confidential 58; It! The Terror from Beyond Space • It! The Vampire from Beyond Space 58; Jet Attack • Jet Squad • Through Hell to Glory 58; Suicide Battalion 58; A Dog's Best Friend 59; The Four Skulls of Jonathan Drake 59; Inside the Mafia 59; Invisible Invaders 59; Pier 5, Havana 59; Riot in Juvenile Prison 59; Vice Raid 59; Cage of Evil 60; Gunfighters of Abilene 60; The Music Box Kid 60; Noose for a Gunman 60; Oklahoma Territory 60; The Police Dog Story 60; Three Came to Kill 60; Twelve Hours to Kill 60; The Walking Target 60; The Boy Who Caught a Crook 61; The Clock Strikes Three • When the Clock Strikes • You Can't Run Far 61; The Clown and the Kid 61; Five Guns to Tombstone 61; Frontier Uprising 61; The Gambler Wore a Gun 61; Gun Fight 61; Gun Street 61; Man Missing • You Have to Run Fast 61; Operation Bottleneck 61; Secret of Deep Harbor 61; Beauty and the Beast 62; Incident in an Alley • Line of Duty 62

Cahn, Philip I've Been Around 34

Cai, Chusheng see *Tsai, Tsou-sen*

Cai, Jiquang Grow Up in Anger • Qingchun Nuchao 86

Caiano, Mario Hercules vs. Ulysses • Ulysses Against Hercules • Ulysses Against the Son of Hercules 61; Duel at the Rio Grande • Il Segno di Zorro 62; Goliath the Rebel Slave 63; Il Segno del Coyote 63; Tyrant of Lydia Against the Son of Hercules 63; Las Pistolas No Discuten • Le Pistole Non Discutono • Pistols Don't Say No 64; The Terror of Rome Against the Son of Hercules 64; Two Gladiators 64; Amanti d'Oltretomba • The Faceless Monster • The Faceless Monsters • Lovers Beyond the Tomb • Lovers from Beyond the Tomb • Night of the Doomed • Nightmare Castle • Orgasmo 65; Una Bara per lo Sceriffo 65; Ringo: Il Volto della Vendetta • Ringo: The Face of Revenge 66; Train to Durango • Un Treno per Durango 67; Il Suo Nome Gridava Vendetta 68; Blood • L'Occhio nel Labirinto 71; Il Mio Nome È Shanghai Joe • To Kill or to Die 73

Caig, Arthur Mac The Patriot Game 78

Cain, Christopher Brother, My Song 76; The Buzzard 76; Grand Jury 76; Elmer 77; Sixth and Main 77; The Stone Boy 84; That Was Then…This Is Now 85; Where

the River Runs Black 86; The Principal 87; Young Guns 88

Cain, Errol le see *Le Cain, Errol*

Caird, Laurence The Fairy Doll 12

Cairns, Dallas The Silver Bridge 20; Unrest 20

Calarco, Reno Road Rebels 63

Calcagno, Eduardo I Love You • Te Amo 86

Calder, Joseph Hate 22

Calderón, Alberto Cortés see *Cortés Calderón, Alberto*

Calderone, Gian Luigi Appassionata 85

Caldura, Federico Le Avventure di Topo Gigio • The Italian Mouse • The Magic World of Topo Gigio 61*

Caldwell, Fred Night Life in Hollywood 22; The Lone Horseman 23; Western Justice 23; The Hurricane 26; The Night Watch 26

Caldwell, Henry Giselle 52

Calef, Henri L'Extravagante Mission 45; Jéricho 46; Les Chouans 47; La Maison Sous la Mer 47; Bagarres • The Wench 48; Les Eaux Troubles 49; La Souricière 50; Ombre et Lumière 51; La Passante 51; Les Amours Finissent à l'Aube 53; Le Secret d'Hélène Marimon 54; The Violent Ones • Les Violents 57; L'Heure de la Vérité • Hour of Truth 64; Féminin-Féminin 73

Calenda, Antonio Fury 73; One Russian Summer 73

Calhado, Raul O Macabro Dr. Scivano 71

Callaghan, Mary Tender Hooks 88

Callahan, Jerry Gunners and Guns 35

Callegari, Gian Paolo Killers of the East • Vendetta dei Thugs 54*; Pontius Pilate • Ponzio Pilato 61*

Calles, Guillermo El Héroe de Nacozari 35; El Vuelo de la Muerte 35; La Virgen de la Sierra 39

Calloway, Ray Vendetta per Vendetta 68

Callum, R. H. Santa Claus 12*; The Fish and the Ring 13*; The Tempter 13*

Calmettes, André L'Assassinat du Duc de Guise • The Assassination of the Duke de Guise 08*; Le Retour d'Ulysse 08*; La Tosca 08; L'Arlésienne 09; Macbeth 09; Résurrection 09; La Tour de Nesle 09; L'Avare 10; Camille • La Dame aux Camélias 10; Don Carlos 10; Werther 10; Camille Desmoulins 11; Madame Sans-Gêne 11*; The Three Musketeers • Les Trois Mousquetaires 12*

Calnek, Roy Hearts of the Woods 21; Abie's Imported Bride 25; The Prince of His Race 26

Calogero, Francesco La Gentilezza del Tocco • The Gentle Touch 88

Caltabiano, Alfio Ballata per un Pistolero 67; Rocco—Der Einzelgänger von Alamo 67; Così Sia • Mamma Mia È Arrivato Così Sia 72

Calthrop, John The Gentlemen Go By 48*

Calvert, Charles C. Detective Sharp and the Stolen Miniatures 12; Diddled 12; Grandad's Exile 12; The Great Tiger Ruby 12; The Missing Tiara 12; A Smoky Story

12; The Trials of a Merry Widow 12; William Drake, Thief 12; A Workman's Honour 12; Caught Napping 13; The Cracksman's Daughter 13; Daylight Robbery 13; The Electric Snuff 13; The Foreign Spy 13; Getting His Own Back 13; Good for Evil 13; Got 'Em Again 13; Have You a Match? 13; His Younger Brother 13; In the Dead Man's Room 13; Isaacs As a Broker's Man 13; Larry's Revenge 13; A Life for a Life 13; The Mill on the Heath 13; Miss Austen's Adventure 13; Mother Gets the Wrong Tonic 13; Old Flynn's Fiddle 13; One of the Nuts 13; Paul Sleuth and the Mystic Seven • The Secret Seven 13; Persevering Peter 13; Pistols for Two 13; Proving His Worth 13; Secret Service 13; Smudge the Great Detective 13; Snatched from Death 13; Spud Murphy's Redemption 13; Stop Thief! 13; The Surprise Packet 13; Through the Keyhole 13; A True Scout 13; The Villain Still Pursued Her 13; What a Holiday! 13; Where There's a Swill There's a Spray 13; Willy Would A-Wooing Go 13; The Aviator Spy • His Country's Honour 14; Brother Officers • A Soldier's Honour 14; The Coward 14; The Fiends of Hell • Guarding Britain's Secrets 14; Fitznoodle's Hunt for Wealth 14; Have a Cigar 14; His Second Childhood 14; A London Mystery 14; Saved by the Sun 14; Temptation 14; Unlucky Thirteen 14; The Wrecker of Lives 14; The Avenging Hand • The Wraith of the Tomb 15; The Lure of the World 15; The Winner 15; The Ace of Hearts 16; The Cellar of Death 16; Disraeli 16*; How Love Came 16; The Test 16; Branded 20; The Edge of Youth 20; Walls of Prejudice 20; In His Grip 21; Roses in the Dust 21; The Way of a Man 21; A Prince of Lovers 22; Silent Evidence 22; Bonnie Prince Charlie 23; The Lights o' London • Lights of London 23; The Romance of Postal Telegraphy 23; Children of the Night No. 1 25; Children of the Night No. 2 25; Ashridge Castle—The Monmouth Rebellion 26; The Mistletoe Bough 26; The City of Youth 28; Oxford 28

Calvert, Elisha H. One Wonderful Night 14; Under Royal Patronage 14; The Unplanned Elopement 14; Affinities 15; The Crimson Wing 15; A Daughter of the City 15; The Man Trail 15; The Outer Edge 15; The Reaping 15; The Slim Princess 15; According to the Code 16; Vultures of Society 16

Calvert, John Dark Venture 56

Calzavara, Flavio Little Adventures • Piccoli Avventurieri 40; Carmela 49

Cambenellis, George The Cannon and the Nightingale 69*

Cambenellis, Jacovos The Cannon and the Nightingale 69*

Camerini, Augusto Cento di Questi Giorni 33*

Camerini, Mario Jolly, Clown da Circo 23; La Casa dei Pulcini 24; Maciste Contro lo Sceicco 25; Saetta: Principe per un Giorno 25; Voglio Tradire Mio Marito 25; As You

Please • Desert Lovers • Kiff Tebbi 27; Rails • Rotaie 29; La Riva dei Bruti 30; Figaro e la Sua Gran'Giornata • Figaro's Big Day 31; L'Ultima Avventura 31; I'll Always Love You • T'Amerò Sempre 32; Men Are Such Rascals • Gli Uomini, Che Mascalzoni 32; Cento di Questi Giorni 33*; Giallo • Mystery 33; Il Cappello a Tre Punte • The Three-Cornered Hat 34; Come le Foglie 34; Darò un Milione • I'll Give a Million 35; But It's Nothing Serious • Ma Non È una Cosa Seria 36; Il Grande Appello • The Last Roll Call 36; Der Mann Der Nicht Nein Sagen Kann 37; Max the Gentleman • Mr. Max • Il Signor Max 37; Batticuore • Heartbeat 38; Il Documento • Il Documento Fatale 39; I Grandi Magazzini 39; The Betrothed • I Promessi Sposi • The Spirit and the Flesh 40; Centomila Dollari 40; Una Romantica Avventura 40; Una Storia d'Amore 42; T'Amerò Sempre 43; Due Lettere Anonime • Two Anonymous Letters 45; L'Angelo e il Diavolo 46; The Captain's Daughter • La Figlia del Capitano 47; Molti Sogni per le Strade • Woman Trouble 48; Il Brigante Musolino • The Fugitive • Musolino the Bandit 50; Due Mogli Sono Troppe 50; Honeymoon Deferred 51; Moglie per una Notte • Wife for a Night 51; Gli Eroi della Domenica • Sunday Heroes 52; Ulisse • Ulysses 53; La Bella Mugnaia! • The Miller's Beautiful Wife • The Miller's Wife 55; The Awakening • Last Temptation • Suor Letizia • When Angels Don't Fly 56; Holiday Island • Holiday on Ischia • One Week with Love • Vacanze a Ischia 57; First Love • Prima Amore 58; La Rue des Amours Faciles • Run with the Devil • Via Margretha • Via Margutta 59; ...And Suddenly It's Murder! • Chacun Son Alibi • Crimen • Killing at Monte Carlo • Suddenly It's Murder 60; I Briganti Italiani • Seduction in the South 61; Goddess of Vengeance • Kali Yug, Goddess of Vengeance • Kali Yug—La Dea della Vendetta 63; Il Mistero del Tempio Indiano 63; The Almost Perfect Crime • Delitto Quasi Perfetto • Imperfect Murder 66; Io Non Vedo Tu Non Parli Lui Non Sente 71; Don Camillo e i Giovani d'Oggi 72

Cameron, James Eyewitness, North Vietnam 66

Cameron, James Piranha II: Flying Killers • Piranha II: The Spawning 81*; The Terminator 84; Aliens 86; The Abyss 89

Cameron, Ken Monkey Grip 82; Fast Talking 83; The Good Wife • The Umbrella Woman 86

Cameron, Ray Bloodbath at the House of Death 83

Camiel, Eric Riff '65 66

Camiller, Edgar J. The Definite Object 20

Caminito, Augusto Nosferatu a Venezia • Vampires in Venice 88

Camino, Jaime Dragon Rapide 86; Luces y Sombras 88

Cammage, Maurice Bouquets from Nicholas 39

Cammell, Donald Performance 68*; Demon Seed 76; White of the Eye 86

Cammer, Joseph Professor Wiseguy's Trip to the Moon 15

Cammermans, Paul Het Gezin Van Paemel • The Van Paemel Family 86

Camp, Joe Benji 74; Hawmps! 76; For the Love of Benji 77; The Double McGuffin 79; Oh, Heavenly Dog! 80; Benji the Hunted 87

Campanile, Pasquale Festa I Castrati • The Counter Tenors • Le Sexe des Anges • Undercover Rogue • Le Voci Bianche • White Voices 63*; Un Tentativo Sentimentale 63*; La Costanza della Regione 64; A Maiden for a Prince • A Maiden for the Prince • There's Something Funny Going On • Una Vergine per il Principe • Une Vierge pour le Prince • A Virgin for the Prince 65; Adulterio all'Italiana • Adultery, Italian Style 66; The Girl and the General • La Ragazza e il Generale 66; The Chastity Belt • La Cintura di Castità • On My Way to the Crusades I Met a Girl Who... 67; Drop Dead • Drop Dead My Love • Il Marito È Mio e l'Amazzo Quando Mi Pare 68; The Libertine • La Matriarca 68; Con Quel' Amore, con Quanto Amore 69; Dove Vai Tutta Nuda? 69; Quando le Donne Avevano la Coda • When Women Had Tails 70; Scacco alla Regina 70; Il Merlo Maschio 71; La Calandria 72; Jus Prima Noctis 72; Quando le Donne Perserano la Coda • When Women Lost Their Tails 72; L'Émigrante 73; Rugantino 73; Soldier of Fortune 75; Humunqus Hector 76; Autostop 77; Cara Sposa 77; Parlami d'Amore Maria 77; Corne Perdere una Moglie È Trovare un'Amante 78; Il Ritorno di Casanova 78; Bello Ma Dannato 79; Gege Bellavita 79; Bingo Bongo 83; The Girl from Trieste 83; Il Petomane • The Windbreaker 83

Campbell, Alan A Throw of Dice • A Throw of the Dice 29*

Campbell, Colin Cinderella 11; The Coming of Columbus 12; The Count of Monte Cristo • Monte Cristo 12; The God of Gold 12; Greater Wealth 12; Kings of the Forest 12; The Little Organ Player of San Juan 12; Old Songs and Memories 12; Sammy Orpheus 12; Alas, Poor Yorick 13; Alone in the Jungle 13; In the Long Ago 13; An Old Actor 13; Thor, Lord of the Jungles 13; A Wild Ride 13; A Wise Old Elephant 13; Chip of the Flying U 14; Hearts and Masks 14; Her Sacrifice 14; In Defiance of the Law 14; In the Days of the Thundering Herd 14; The Lily of the Valley 14; The Losing Fight 14; The Salvation of Nancy O'Shaughnessy 14; The Spoilers 14; The Story of the Blood Red Rose 14; The Tragedy of Ambition 14; Vengeance Is Mine 14; The Wilderness Mail 14; The Carpet from Bagdad 15; The Crisis 15; The Rosary 15; The Runt 15; Sweet Alyssum 15; The Vision of the Shepherd 15; The Garden of Allah 16; The Ne'er-Do-Well 16; The Smouldering Flame 16; Thou Shalt Not Covet 16; Unto Those Who Sin 16;

Beware of Strangers 18; City of Purple Dreams 18; A Hoosier Romance 18; The Sea Flower 18; The Still Alarm 18; Tongues of Flame 18; Who Shall Take My Life? 18; The Yellow Dog 18; The Beauty Market 19; The Corsican Brothers 19; Little Orphan Annie • Little Orphant Annie 19; The Railroaders 19; Thunderbolt 19; Big Happiness 20; Moon Madness 20; When Dawn Came 20; Black Roses 21; The First Born 21; The Lure of Jade 21; The Swamp 21; When Lights Are Low • Where Lights Are Low 21; Two Kinds of Women 22; The World's a Stage 22; Bucking the Barrier 23; The Buster 23; The Grail 23; Three Who Paid 23; The Bowery Bishop 24; Pagan Passions 24

Campbell, Doug Season of Fear 89

Campbell, Graeme Into the Fire 87; Blood Relations 88; Murder One 88

Campbell, Ivar Reunion 32; Eyes of Fate 33; The Golden Cage 33; Side Streets 33; Designing Women • House of Cards 34; Big Ben Calling • Radio Pirates 35; Expert's Opinion 35; The Mad Hatters 35; The Belles of St. Clement's 36; Grand Finale 36; Hands in Harmony • Talking Hands 36; Captain's Orders 37; Too Many Husbands 38

Campbell, Martin The Sex Thief 73; Eskimo Nell 75; Three for All 75; Edge of Darkness 86; Criminal Law 88

Campbell, Maurice An Amateur Devil 20; Burglar-Proof 20; Oh Lady, Lady 20; Ducks and Drakes 21; First Love 21; The March Hare 21; One Wild Week 21; She Couldn't Help It 21; The Speed Girl 21; Two Weeks with Pay 21; Midnight 22; Through a Glass Window 22; The Exciters 23; Girls Men Forget 24; Wandering Fires 25; Burnt Fingers 27

Campbell, Norman The Magic Show 83

Campbell, Sterling Bush Pilot 47

Campbell, Webster Moral Fibre 21; The Single Track 21; What's Your Reputation Worth? 21; Divorce Coupons 22; Island Wives 22; A Virgin's Sacrifice • A Woman's Sacrifice 22; Bright Lights of Broadway 23; The Pace That Thrills 25

Campbell, William A Tray Full of Trouble 20; Ingagi 31

Campioli, Michel Carre Blanc 85*

Campion, Jane Peel 82; A Girl's Own Story 83; Passionless Moments 84; Two Friends 86; Sweetie 89; An Angel at My Table 90

Campo, Gianni da see Da Campo, Gianni

Campogalliani, Carlo Quando Si Ama 15; L'Amazzone Macabra 16; Il Marchi Rosso 18; Cortile 30; La Lanterna del Diavolo 31; Medico per Forza 31; Stadio 34; La Grande Luce • The Great Light • Montevergine 38; La Notte delle Beffe 40; Il Bravo di Venezia 41; Cuori nella Tormenta 41; Perdizione 42; Musica Proibita 43; L'Innocente Casimirio 45; La Gondola del Diavolo 47; La Mano della Morta 49; Bellezze in Bicicletta 51; Foglio di Via 54; L'Orfana del Ghetto 54; La Canzone del

Cuore 55; L'Angelo della Alpi 57; Capitan Fuoco • Captain Falcon 58; Goliath and the Barbarians • Il Terrore dei Barbari 59; Fontana di Trevi 60; Le Géant de la Vallée des Rois • Machiste—The Mighty • Maciste nella Valle dei Re • Son of Samson 60; The Mighty Ursus • Ursus 60; Rosmunda e Alboino • Sword of the Conqueror 61

Campus, Michael Z.P.G. • Z.P.G.: Zero Population Growth • Zero Population Growth 71; The Mack 73; The Education of Sonny Carson 74; The Passover Plot 76; Survival 76

Camus, Marcel Renaissance 50; Fugitive in Saigon • Mort en Fraude 56; Black Orpheus • Orfeu Negro 58; Os Bandeirantes 60; Dragon Sky • L'Oiseau de Paradis 62; Le Chant du Monde 65; L'Homme de New York • The Man from New York 67; Vivre la Nuit 68; Un Été Sauvage 70; Le Mur de l'Atlantique 70; Trinità Voit Rouge 75; Bahia • Otália de Bahia • Os Pastores da Noite 77

Camus, Mario Con el Viento Solano 65; Los Pájaros de Baden-Baden 74; La Colmena 82; Guerrilla—Los Desastres de la Guerra 83; The Holy Innocents • Los Santos Inocentes 84; The Old Music • La Vieja Música 85; La Casa de Bernarda Alba • The House of Bernarda Alba 87; La Rusa • The Russian 87

Cancellieri, E. First Opera Film Festival 48

Candeias, Ozualdo Trilogia de Terror • Trilogy of Terror 68*; A Margem • The Margin 69

Candimir, Attila Kirlangic Firtinasi • The Swallow Storm 86

Canevari, Cesare Matalo! 70

Canfield, Kid Kid Canfield the Reform Gambler 22

Canijo, João Três Menos Eu 88

Cann, Bert Hampton Court Palace 26

Cannistraro, Richard Violated 84

Cannon, Dyan Growing Pains: Number One 76; The End of Innocence 90

Cannon, Raymond Let's Make Whoopee • Red Wine 28; Joy Street 29; Why Leave Home? 29; Ladies Must Play 30; Night Life in Reno 31; Swanee River 31; Hotel Variety • The Passing Show 33; Behind Prison Bars • The Outer Gate 37; He Wanted to Marry • Swing It, Sailor 37; Samurai 45

Cannon, Robert Fear 45; Brotherhood of Man 47*; Gerald McBoing Boing 50*; The Miner's Daughter 50; Georgie and the Dragon 51; The Oompahs 51*; Wonder Gloves 51; Madeline 52; Willie the Kid 52; Christopher Crumpet 53; Gerald McBoing Boing's Symphony • Gerald's Symphony 53; The Little Boy with a Big Horn 53; Ballet-Oops 54; Fudget's Budget 54; How Now Boing Boing 54; Christopher Crumpet's Playmate 55; The Jaywalker 55; Gerald McBoing Boing on the Planet Moo 56; Magoo's Moose Hunt 57; Department of the Navy 58; Scoutmaster Magoo 58; Moonbird 59*

Cannon, Roy Man on the Staircase 70

Cannon, William The Square Root of

Zero • This Immoral Age 64

Canto, Jorge Brum do see Do Canto, Jorge Brum

Canutt, Joe The Last Great Treasure • Mother Lode • Search for the Mother Lode • Search for the Mother Lode: The Last Great Treasure 82*

Canutt, Yakima Captain Mephisto and the Transformation Machine • Manhunt of Mystery Island 45*; FBI 99 • Federal Operator 99 45*; Sheriff of Cimarron 45; Code 645 • G-Men Never Forget 47*; Adventures of Frank and Jesse James 48*; Carson City Raiders 48; Dangers of the Canadian Mounted • R.C.M.P. and the Treasure of Genghis Khan 48*; Oklahoma Badlands 48; Sons of Adventure 48; The Lawless Rider 54; Zarak 56*; Khartoum 66*; The Flim Flam Man • One Born Every Minute 67*; Where Eagles Dare 68*

Cao, Zheng Broken Moon • Can Yue 86

Cap, Franz Sand, Love and Salt 56; Am Anfang War Es Sünde • The Beginning Was Sin • Greh 62

Caparros, Ernesto The Red Serpent • La Serpiente Roja 37

Čapek, Ladislav Člověk Pod Vodou • Man Under Water 61*

Capellani, Albert Aladdin • Aladin 06; La Peine du Talion 06; Les Apprentissages de Boireau 07; Cendrillon • Cinderella 07; Don Juan 07; Le Chat Botté • Puss 'n Boots 08; L'Homme au Gants Blancs 08; Jeanne d'Arc • Joan of Arc 08; Peau d'Âne 08; L'Assommoir 09; La Mort du Duc d'Enghien 09; Athalie 10; Les Deux Orphelines • The Two Orphans 10; L'Évadé de Tuileries 10; Le Voile du Bonheur 10; Le Courrier de Lyon 11; The Hunchback of Notre Dame • Notre-Dame de Paris 11; Les Misérables 11; Les Mystères de Paris 11; L'Arlésienne 12; Germinal 13; La Glu 13; Patrie 13; Peau de Chagrin 13; Quatre-vingt-Treize 14; Le Tragique Amour de Mona Lisa 14; Camille 15; Les Épaves de l'Amour 15; The Face in the Moonlight 15; The Flash of an Emerald 15; Le Rêve Interdit 15; La Bohème • La Vie de Bohème 16; The Common Law 16; The Dark Silence 16; The Feast of Life 16; An American Maid 17; Daybreak 17; The Easiest Way 17; The Foolish Virgin 17; Eye for Eye 18; The House of Mirth 18; The Richest Girl 18; Social Hypocrites 18; Oh Boy! 19; Out of the Fog 19; The Red Lantern 19; The Virtuous Model 19; The Fortune Teller 20; The Inside of the Cup 21; The Wild Goose 21; Sisters 22; The Young Diana 22*

Capellani, Roger Avec l'Assurance 35

Capes, Renault Artful Dodgers 49

Capetanos, Leon Summer Run 74

Capitani, Giorgio L'Affondamento della Valiant • The Valiant 61*; Each Man for Himself • Each One for Himself • Every Man for Himself • Das Gold von Sam Cooper • Ognuno per Se • The Ruthless Four • Sam Cooper's Gold 68; I Hate Blondes • Odio le Bionde 81; Heroic Misson • Missione Eroica 87; Arrivederci e Grazie 88

Capitani, Lucio Giorgio see *Capitani, Giorgio*

Capogna, Sergio Diario di un Italiano • Diary of an Italian 72

Capolino, Edoardo The Big Search • East of Kilimanjaro • La Grande Caccia 57*

Capon, Paul Radio Lover 36*

Capra, Frank Fultah Fisher's Boarding House 22; The Strong Man 26; Tramp, Tramp, Tramp 26*; For the Love of Mike 27; Long Pants 27; The Burglar • Smith's Burglar 28; The Matinee Idol 28; The Power of the Press 28; Say It with Sables 28; So This Is Love 28; Submarine 28; The Swim Princess 28; That Certain Thing 28; The Way of the Strong 28; The Donovan Affair 29; Flight 29; The Younger Generation 29; Ladies of Leisure 30; Rain or Shine 30; Dirigible 31; Forbidden 31; The Miracle Woman 31; Platinum Blonde 31; American Madness 32; The Bitter Tea of General Yen 32; Lady for a Day 33; Broadway Bill • Strictly Confidential 34; It Happened One Night 34; Mr. Deeds Goes to Town 36; Lost Horizon 37; You Can't Take It with You 38; Mr. Smith Goes to Washington 39; Arsenic and Old Lace 41; John Doe, Dynamite • Meet John Doe 41; Divide and Conquer 42*; The Nazis Strike 42*; Prelude to War 42*; Battle of Britain 43*; Battle of China 43*; Know Your Ally: Britain 43; Tunisian Victory 43*; The American People • War Comes to America 44*; Battle of Russia 44*; Here Is Germany • Know Your Enemy: Germany 45; Know Your Enemy: Japan 45*; Two Down and One to Go! 45; Your Job in Germany 45; It's a Wonderful Life 46; State of the Union • The World and His Wife 48; Riding High 49; Here Comes the Groom 51; Our Mr. Sun 56; Hemo the Magnificent 57; The Strange Case of the Cosmic Rays 57; The Unchained Goddess 57; A Hole in the Head 59; A Pocketful of Miracles 61; Rendezvous in Space 64

Caprioli, Vittorio Leoni al Sole 61; Parigi o Cara 62; Cuori Infranti 63*; I Maniaci 63; Et Si On Faisant l'Amour • Listen, Let's Make Love • Scusi, Facciamo l'Amore 68; Splendorie e Miserie di Madame Royale 70

Capuano, Luigi Stormbound 51; Flying Squadron 52; What Price Innocence? 53; Revenge of Ursus • Vengeance of Ursus 61; The Masked Conqueror 62; Revenge of the Conquered 62; Revenge of the Gladiators 62; Tiger of the Seven Seas • La Tigre dei Sette Mari • Le Tigre des Sept Mers 62; Il Leone di San Marco • The Lion of St. Mark 63*; Adventurer of Tortuga 64; Das Geheimnis der Lederschlinge • I Misteri della Giungla Nera • The Mystery of Thug Island 64; Sandokan Against the Leopard of Sarawak 64; Sandokan Fights Back 64; Il Magnifico Texano 67; Sangue Chiama Sangue 68

Caputo, Michel L'Exécutrice 86

Caras, Chris Come with Me My Love • Take Time to Smell the Flowers 81

Carax, Leos Boy Meets Girl 84; Bad Blood • Mauvais Sang • The Night Is Young 86; Les Amants du Pont Neuf 88

Carayan, Dacosta see *Carayiannis, Costas*

Carayiannis, Costas The Devil's Men • The Devil's People • Land of the Minotaur • Minotaur 76; The Rape Killer 76

Carbonneaux, Norbert Les Corsaires du Bois de Boulogne 54; Courte Tête 56; Photo Finish 57; Le Temps des Œufs Durs 58; Candide 60; La Gamberge 62

Carco, Francis de see *De Carco, Francis*

Card, Lamar The Clones 73*; Supervan 77; Disco Fever 78

Cárdenas, Hernán Island Claws • Night of the Claw 80

Cardiff, Albert see *Cardone, Alberto*

Cardiff, Jack Intent to Kill 58; Beyond This Place • Web of Evidence 59; Holiday in Spain • Scent of Mystery 60; Sons and Lovers 60; My Geisha 61; The Lion 62; Dugi Brodovi • The Long Ships 63; Young Cassidy 64*; The Liquidator 65; Dark of the Sun • The Mercenaries 67; The Girl on a Motorcycle • La Motocyclette • Naked Under Leather 68; The Freakmaker • The Mutation • The Mutations 73; Penny Gold 73

Cardinal, Roger Malarek: A Street Kid Who Made It 89

Cardona, René Don Juan Tenorio 37; Tierra Brava 38; Alarma 39; Allá en el Rancho Chico • Out on the Little Ranch 39; El Cobarde • The Coward 39; Estrellita • Starlet 39; The Queen of the River • La Reina del Río 40; El As Negro 43; El Espectro de la Novia 43; The Headless Woman • La Mujer Sin Cabeza 43; El Museo del Crimen 44; A New World 56; Pulgarcito • Tom Thumb 58; La Llorona 59; Santa Claus 60; Doctor of Doom • Las Luchadoras Contra el Médico Resino 62; El Asesino Invisible 64; Las Luchadoras Contra la Momia • The Wrestling Women vs. the Aztec Mummy 64; Gomar the Human Gorilla • La Horriplante Bestia Humana • Horror y Sexo • Night of the Bloody Apes 68; Santo and Dracula's Treasure • Santo Contra Drácula • Santo en El Tesoro de Drácula • Santo y el Tesoro de Drácula • El Tesoro de Drácula • El Vampiro y el Sexo 68; El Asesino Loco y el Sexo • Las Luchadoras Contra el Robot Asesino • El Robot Asesino • Sex Monster • Wrestling Women vs. the Murdering Robot 69; Santo Contra los Jinetes del Terror 72

Cardona, René, Jr. Robinson Crusoe and the Tiger 69; Night of a Thousand Cats • The Night of the Thousand Cats • La Noche de los Mil Gatos 72; Survive! 76; Tintorera • Tintorera…Bloody Waters • Tintorera…Tiger Shark 77; Guyana, Crime of the Century • Guyana, Cult of the Damned 80; El Tesoro del Amazonas • The Treasure of the Amazon 83; Fiebre de Amor • Love Fever 85; The Market of the Humble • El Mercado de Humildes 86; Beaks • Birds of Prey 87

Cardone, Alberto Alla Conquista dell' Arkansas • Die Goldsucher von Arkansas •

Massacre at Marble City 64*; I Gringos Non Perdonano 65; Killer's Carnival 65*; Mille Dollari sul Nero 66; Sette Dollari del Rosso 66; Sartana 67; L'Ira di Dio • The Wrath of God 68; Il Lungo Giorno del Massacro 68; Kidnapped 69

Cardone, J. S. Nightmare Island • The Slayer 82; Thunder Alley 85; Shadowzone 90

Cardos, Bud see *Cardos, John*

Cardos, John The Female Bunch • A Time to Run 69*; Men of the Tenth • The Red, White and Black • Soul Soldier • Soul Soldiers 70; Drag Racer 74; Kingdom of the Spiders 77; The Day Time Ended • Time Warp • Vortex 78; The Dark • The Mutilator 79; Other Realms 83; Mutant • Night Shadows 84; Outlaw • Outlaw of Gor 87; Skeleton Coast 87; Act of Piracy 88

Cardoso, Ivan see *Cardozo, Ivan*

Cardoza, Anthony Smokey and the Hotwire Gang 80

Cardozo, Ivan Lago Maldito • O Segredo da Múmia 82; As Sete Vampiras • The Seven Female Vampires 86

Carew, Topper Breakin' and Enterin' 85

Carewe, Edwin Across the Pacific 14; Cora 15; Destiny • The Soul of a Woman 15; The Final Judgment 15; The House of Tears 15; Marse Covington 15; The Dawn of Love 16; God's Half Acre 16; Her Great Price 16; Snowbird 16; The Sunbeam 16; The Upstart 16; The Barricade 17; The Greatest Power 17; Her Fighting Chance 17; Their Compact 17; The Trail of the Shadow 17; The Voice of Conscience 17; The House of Gold 18; Pals First 18; The Splendid Sinner 18; The Trail to Yesterday 18; Easy to Make Money • It's Easy to Make Money 19; False Evidence 19; The Right to Lie 19; Shadows of Suspicion 19; Way of the Strong 19; Isobel • Isobel, or The Trail's End 20; Rio Grande 20; The Web of Deceit 20; Habit 21; Her Mad Bargain 21; The Invisible Fear 21; My Lady's Latchkey 21; Playthings of Destiny 21; I Am the Law 22; A Question of Honor 22; Silver Wings 22*; The Bad Man 23; The Girl of the Golden West 23; Mighty Lak' a Rose 23; Madonna of the Streets 24; A Son of the Sahara 24; Joanna 25; The Lady Who Lied 25; My Son 25; The Sea Women • Why Women Love 25; High Steppers 26; Pals First 26; Prince Dimitri • Resurrection 27; Ramona 28; Revenge 28; Evangeline 29; The Spoilers 30*; Resurrection 31; Are We Civilized? 34

Carey, Harry The Master Cracksman 14; Love's Lariat 16*

Carey, Timothy The World's Greatest Sinner 62

Caringi, Rudolph Warm in the Bud 70

Carle, Gilles La Vie Heureuse de Leopold Z 65; Place à Olivier Guimond 66; Place aux Jerolas 67; Le Viol d'une Jeune Fille Douce 68; Les Mâles 70; Red 70; Les Chevaliers 72; Le Vraie Nature de Bernadette 72; Les Corps Célestes 73; La Mort d'un Bûcheron 73; La Tête de

Normande St. Onge 75; The Angel and the Woman 77; Normande 79; Fantastica 80; The Plouffe Family 81; The Great Chess Movie 82*; Maria Chapdelaine 83; Le Crime d'Ovide Plouffe • The Crime of Ovide Plouffe • Les Plouffe 84*; Scalp 85; La Guêpe • The Wasp 86; Québec, un Ville 88

Carle, Philip In a Moment of Temptation 27

Carleton, Lloyd B. The Ragged Earl 14; Through Fire to Fortune, or The Sunken Village 14; The Girl I Left Behind Me 15; The Idler 15; The Jungle Lovers 15; Barriers of Society 16; Black Friday 16; The Devil's Bondswoman 16; Dr. Neighbor 16; In the Days of the Missions • The Yoke of Gold 16; A Miracle of Love 16; The Morals of Hilda 16; Two Men of Sandy Bar 16; The Unattainable 16; The Way of the World 16; The Yaqui 16; Mountain Madness 20; Beyond the Crossroads 22; The Flying Dutchman 23; Nine and Three-Fifths Seconds 25

Carlile, C. Douglas Sexton Blake 09

Carlino, Lewis John The Sailor Who Fell from Grace with the Sea 75; The Ace • The Great Santini 79; Class 83

Carlisle, Robert Sofi 67

Carlmar, Edith The Wayward Girl 59

Carlo, Andrea de see De Carlo, Andrea

Carlo-Rim Hercule 37*; Simplet 42*; L'Armoire Volante • The Cupboard Was Bare 48; La Maison Bonnadieu 51; Les Sept Péchés Capitaux • I Sette Peccati Capitali • The Seven Deadly Sins 51*; Virgile 53; Escalier de Service 55; Les Truands 56; Ce Joli Monde 57; Le Petit Prof' 58

Carlsen, Esben Høilund Slingrevalsen • Stepping Out 81

Carlsen, Henning I Formerlære • Molder's Apprentice 49; Civil Defense • Civilforsvaret 50; Doll's House • Dukkestuen 50; Post Mortem Technique 51; El-Gørt Er Velgørt • Electricity-Made Is Well Made 52; Haakon VII • King Haakon VII • Konge Haakon VII 52*; Danish Motorboat Story 53; På Vej Mod et Job 53; Havets Husmand 54; Knive • Knives 54; Køleskabe • Refrigerator 54; Mælkehygiejne • Milk Hygiene 54; Money and Economy • Penge og Økonomi 54; Velkommen til Vendsyssel • Welcome to Vendsyssel 54; Floor Treatment • Gulvbehandling 55; The House I Wish to Build • Jeg et Hus Mig Bygge Vil 55; The Cyclist • Cyklisten 57; Forward to the Sky • Ligeud ad Luftvejen 58; Danfoss • Danfoss, Jorden Rundt Døgnet Rundt 59; A Knotty Problem • Et Knudeproblem 59; Souvenirs from Sweden 60; De Gamle • Old People 61; Limfjorden 61; Clean Words About Dirt • Ren Besked Om Snavs 62; Dilemma • A World of Strangers 62; Epilogue • How About Us? • Hvad med Os? 63; The Cats • Kattorna • Kvindedyr 64; Familiebilleder • Family Portraits 64; Ung • Young People 65; Hunger • Sult • Svält 66; Människor Mötas och Ljuv Musik Uppstär i Hjärtat • Mennesker Mødes og Sød Musik Opstår i

Hjertet • People Meet and Sweet Music Fills the Heart 67; Hvor Er Magten Blevet Af? 68; Klabautermanden • We Are All Demons 69; Are You Afraid? • Are You Afraid? Of What? • Er I Bange? • Er I Bange?—Hvad Er I Bange For? 70; Man Sku' Være Noget ved Musikken • Oh to Be on the Bandwagon 72; Un Divorce Heureux • A Happy Divorce • En Lykkelig Skilsmisse 74; Da Svante Forsvandt • When Svante Disappeared 75; Did Somebody Laugh? • Hør, Var Der Ikke En, Som Lo? 78; A Street Under the Snow 78; Pengene eller Livet • Your Money or Your Life 81; Gauguin: Wolf at the Door • Oviri • Oviri: The Wolf at the Door • The Wolf at the Door 86

Carlsen, Jon Bang Ofelia Kommer til Byen 85; Baby Doll 88; Time Out 88

Carlson, Richard Four Guns to the Border 54; Riders to the Stars 54; Appointment with a Shadow • The Big Story 57; The Saga of Hemp Brown 58; Kid Rodelo 66; Island of the Lost 67*

Carlson, Wallace A. Joe Boko Breaking Into the Big League 14; An Alley Romance 15; The Canimated Nooz Pictorial No. 1 15; The Canimated Nooz Pictorial No. 2 15; The Canimated Nooz Pictorial No. 3 15; Dreamy Dud at the Ole Swimmin' Hole 15; Dreamy Dud Cowboy 15; Dreamy Dud Goes Bear Hunting 15; Dreamy Dud in King Koo Koo's Kingdom 15; Dreamy Dud in Love 15; Dreamy Dud in the Swim 15; Dreamy Dud Resolves Not to Smoke 15; Dreamy Dud Sees Charlie Chaplin 15; Dreamy Dud Up in the Air 15; Introducing Charlie Chaplin 15; Joe Boko in a Close Shave 15; Joe Boko in Saved by Gasoline 15; Lost in the Jungle 15; A Visit to the Zoo 15; A Visit to Uncle Dudley's Farm 15; The Canimated Nooz Pictorial No. 4 16; The Canimated Nooz Pictorial No. 5 16; The Canimated Nooz Pictorial No. 6 16; The Canimated Nooz Pictorial No. 7 16; The Canimated Nooz Pictorial No. 8 • Joe Boko in Canimated Nooz Pictorial No. 8 16; The Canimated Nooz Pictorial No. 9 16; The Canimated Nooz Pictorial No. 10 16; The Canimated Nooz Pictorial No. 11 16; The Canimated Nooz Pictorial No. 12 16; The Canimated Nooz Pictorial No. 13 16; The Canimated Nooz Pictorial No. 14 16; The Canimated Nooz Pictorial No. 15 16; The Canimated Nooz Pictorial No. 16 16; The Canimated Nooz Pictorial No. 17 16; The Canimated Nooz Pictorial No. 18 16; The Canimated Nooz Pictorial No. 19 16; The Canimated Nooz Pictorial No. 20 16; The Canimated Nooz Pictorial No. 21 16; Dreamy Dud Has a Laugh on the Boss 16; Dreamy Dud in the African War Zone 16; Dreamy Dud Joyriding with Princess Zlim 16; Dreamy Dud Lost at Sea 16; Joe Boko's Adventures 16; The Canimated Nooz Pictorial No. 22 17; The Canimated Nooz Pictorial No. 23 17; The Canimated Nooz Pictorial No. 24 17; The Canimated Nooz Pictorial No. 25 17; The Canimated Nooz Pictorial No. 26 17;

The Canimated Nooz Pictorial No. 27 17; The Canimated Nooz Pictorial No. 28 17; Goodrich Dirt Among the Beach Nuts • Goodrich Dirt at the Seashore 17; Goodrich Dirt and the $1,000 Reward 17; Goodrich Dirt at the Amateur Show • Goodrich Dirt's Amateur Night 17; Goodrich Dirt at the Training Camp 17; Goodrich Dirt Lunch Detective 17; Otto Luck and Ruby Razmataz • Otto Luck and the Ruby of Razmataz 17; Otto Luck in the Movies 17; Otto Luck to the Rescue 17; Otto Luck's Flivvered Romance 17; Goodrich Dirt and the Duke de Whatanob 18; Goodrich Dirt Bad Man Tamer 18; Goodrich Dirt Coin Collector 18; Goodrich Dirt Cowpuncher 18; Goodrich Dirt in Darkest Africa 18; Goodrich Dirt in Spot Goes Romeoing 18; Goodrich Dirt in the Barber Business 18; Goodrich Dirt King of Spades 18; Goodrich Dirt Mat Artist 18; Goodrich Dirt Millionaire 18; Goodrich Dirt the Cop 18; Goodrich Dirt the Dark and Stormy Knight 18; Goodrich Dirt When Wishes Come True 18; Goodrich Dirt's Bear Facts • Goodrich Dirt's Bear Hunt 18; At the Ol' Swimmin' Hole 19; A Chip Off the Old Block 19; Dud Leaves Home 19; Dud Perkins Gets Mortified 19; Dud the Circus Performer 19; Dud's Geography Lesson 19; Dud's Greatest Cirkus on Earth 19; Dud's Home Run 19; Goodrich Dirt Hypnotist 19; Goodrich Dirt in a Difficult Delivery 19; The Parson 19; Wounded by the Beauty 19; Accidents Will Happen 20; A-Hunting We Will Go 20; Andy and Min at the Theatre 20; Andy at Shady Rest 20; Andy Fights the High Cost of Living 20; Andy on a Diet 20; Andy on Pleasure Bent 20; Andy on Skates 20; Andy on the Beach 20; Andy Plays Golf 20; Andy Plays Hero • Andy the Hero 20; Andy Redecorates His Flat 20; Andy Spends a Quiet Day at Home 20; Andy the Actor 20; Andy the Chicken Farmer 20; Andy the Model 20; Andy Visits His Mamma-in-Law 20; Andy Visits the Osteopath 20; Andy's Dancing Lesson 20; Andy's Inter-Ruben Guest 20; Andy's Mother-in-Law Pays Him a Visit 20; Andy's Night Out 20; Andy's Picnic 20; Andy's Wash Day 20; The Broilers 20; Dud the Lion Tamer 20; Dud's Haircut 20; Equestrian Andy 20; Flat Hunting 20; Flicker Flicker Little Star 20; Get to Work 20; Howdy Partner 20; Ice Box Episodes 20; Militant Min 20; Mixing Business with Pleasure 20; Ship Ahoy 20; There's a Reason 20; The Toreador 20; Up She Goes 20; Westward Ho 20; Wim and Wigor 20; Andy Has a Caller 21; Andy's Cow 21; Andy's Dog Day 21; Andy's Holiday 21; The Best of Luck 21; Chester's Cat 21; The Chicken Thief 21; Il Cuspidore • Le Cuspidorée 21; Fatherly Love 21; Give 'Er the Gas 21; Jilted and Jolted 21; The Masked Ball 21; The Promoters 21; A Quiet Little Game 21; Rolling Around 21; A Terrible Time 21

Carlsson, Janne Business Is Booming • Svindlande Affärer 85*

Carlsten, Rune The Bomb 19; Family Traditions 20; A Modern Robinson 21; The Young Nobleman 24; Dangerous Paradise 31; House of Silence 33; Dr. Glas • Doktor Glas 42; Anna Lans 43; Black Roses 45; The Eternal Bond 47

Carlstrom, Bjorn Wardogs 87*

Carlton, Frank The Blackmailer 19; An Insurance Fraud 19; A Murder in Limehouse 19; A Well Planned West End Jewel Robbery 19

Carlton, Wilfred The Case of a Doped Actress 19

Carmineo, Giuliano Django—Ein Sarg Voll Blut 68; Find a Place to Die • Joe, Cercati un Posto per Morire 68; The Moment to Kill • Il Momento di Uccidere 68; I'm Sartana...I'll Dig Your Grave • Sono Sartana, il Vostro Becchino 69; Arrivano Django e Sartana...e la Fine 70; Buon Funerale Amigos, Paga Sartana 70; C'È Sartana...Vendi la Pistola e Comprati la Bara 70; Gunman in Town • Una Nuvola di Polvere...un Grido di Morte...Arriva Sartana 70; Bullet for a Stranger • Gli Fumavano le Colt...Lo Chiamavano Camposanto 71; ...E Chiamavano Spirito Santo 71; Heads I Kill You—Tails You Die • Testa T'Ammazzo, Croce Sei Morto...Mi Chiamano Alleluja 71; Blazing Guns • Uomo Mezzo Ammazzato...Parola di Spirito Santo 72; They Call Me Hallelujah 72; Il West Ti Va Stretto, Amico...È Arrivato Alleluja 72; Lo Chiamavano Tresette...Giocava Sempre col Morto 73; Di Tresette Ce N'È Uno Tutti gli Altri Son Nessuno 74

Carmody, Don The Surrogate 84

Carné, Marcel Nogent—Eldorado du Dimanche • Nogent, the Sunday Eldorado 29*; Bizarre, Bizarre • Drôle de Drame 36; Jenny 36; Hôtel du Nord 38; Port of Shadows • Quai des Brumes 38; Daybreak • Le Jour Se Lève 39; The Devil's Envoys • Les Visiteurs du Soir 42; Children of Paradise • Les Enfants du Paradis 44; Gates of Night • Gates of the Night • Les Portes de la Nuit 46; La Marie du Port 49; Juliet, or The Key to Dreams • Juliette, or The Key of Dreams • Juliette ou la Clé des Songes 51; The Adulteress • Thérèse Raquin 53; L'Air de Paris • The Song of Paris 54; The Country Whence I Come • Le Pays d'Où Je Viens 56; The Cheaters • The Cheats • Peccatori in Blue Jeans • Les Tricheurs • Youthful Sinners 58; Terrain Vague • Wasteland 60; Du Mouron pour les Petits Oiseaux • Some Chickweed for the Little Birds 62; Three Rooms in Manhattan • Trois Chambres à Manhattan 65; Les Jeunes Loups • The Young Wolves 67; La Force et le Droit • Might and Right 70; Les Assassins de l'Ordre • The Assassins of Order 71; La Merveilleuse Visite • The Wonderful Visit 74; La Bible • The Bible 76; The Immortal Heritage 80

Carney, George Some Waiter 16

Caron, Glenn Gordon Clean and Sober 88

Caron, Pierre Cinderella 37

Caronatto Paz, Miguel Los Apuros de Claudina • Claudina's Troubles 40

Carow, Heiner So Many Dreams • So Viele Träume 87

Carpenter, Freddie Gaiety George • Showtime 45*

Carpenter, Horace B. Riding Fool 24; Desperate Odds 25; Fangs of Fate 25; Flashing Steeds 25; The Sagebrush Lady 25*; The Last Chance 26; The Lovin' Fool • The Loving Fool 26; Lucky Spurs 26; Western Trails 26; Just Travelin' 27; The Arizona Kid 29; False Fathers 29; West of the Rockies 29; The Pecos Dandy 34*

Carpenter, John Firelight 66; The Resurrection of Bronco Billy 70*; Dark Star 74; Assault on Precinct 13 76; Halloween 78; Elvis 79; The Fog 79; Escape from New York 81; The Thing 82; Christine 83; Starman 84; Big Trouble in Little China 86; Prince of Darkness 87; They Live 88

Carpenter, Stephen The Dorm That Dripped Blood • Pranks 82*; The Power 83*; The Kindred 86*

Carpi, Fabio Basileus Quartet 82

Carr, Adrian Now and Forever 83

Carr, Bernard The Fabulous Joe 46*; Curley 47; Curley and His Gang in the Haunted Mansion • Sinister House • Who Killed Doc Robbin? 48

Carr, J. F. Curly's Holiday 17

Carr, John The Savage American • The Talisman 66; Night Train to Terror 85*

Carr, Terry Welcome to 18 86

Carr, Thomas Bandits of the Badlands 45; The Cherokee Flash 45; Oregon Trail 45; Rough Riders of Cheyenne 45; Santa Fe Saddlemates 45; Alias Billy the Kid 46; Days of Buffalo Bill 46; The El Paso Kid 46; Red River Renegades 46; Rio Grande Raiders 46; The Undercover Woman 46; Code of the Saddle 47; Jesse James Rides Again 47*; Song of the Wasteland 47; Bruce Gentry • Bruce Gentry—Daredevil of the Skies 48*; Congo Bill 48*; Superman 48*; Blazing Guns • Marshal of Heldorado 50; Colorado Ranger • Guns of Justice 50; Crooked River • The Last Bullet 50; The Daltons' Women 50; Fast on the Draw • Sudden Death 50; Hostile Country • Outlaw Fury 50; Outlaws of Texas 50; Pirates of the High Seas 50*; Rangeland Empire • West of the Brazos 50; Roar of the Iron Horse 50*; Wanted: Dead or Alive 51; Behind Southern Lines 52; Hired Guns • Wyoming Roundup 52; The Man from Black Hills • Man from the Black Hills 52; The Maverick 52; Trail of the Arrow 52; Captain Scarlett 53; The Fighting Lawman 53; Rebel City 53; The Star of Texas 53; Topeka 53; Bitter Creek 54; The Desperado 54; The Forty-Niners 54; Bobby Ware Is Missing 55; Three for Jamie Dawn 56; Dino • Killer Dino 57; The Tall Stranger 57; Gunsmoke in Tucson 58; Cast a Long Shadow 59; Sullivan's Empire 67*

Carr, Trem Near the Trail's End 31

Carradine, David You and Me 72; Americana 73

Carras, Anthony Operation Bikini • The Seafighters 63

Carrasco Zanini, Eduardo Derrumbe 88

Carre, Bartlett Gunsmoke on the Guadalupe 35; Gun Smoke 36

Carré, Louise A Question of Loving • Qui à Tiré Sur Nos Histoires d'Amour? 86

Carreras, Enrique The Master of Horror • Masterpieces of Horror • Masterworks of Terror • Obras Maestras del Terror • Short Stories of Terror 60

Carreras, Michael Cyril Stapleton and the Show Band 55; Eric Winstone Band Show 55; Eric Winstone's Stagecoach 56; Just for You 56; Parade of the Bands 56; Edmundo Ros Half Hour 57; Steel Bayonet 57; Passport to China • Visa to Canton 60; The Savage Guns • Tierra Brutal 61; Maniac 62; What a Crazy World 63; The Curse of the Mummy's Tomb 64; Prehistoric Women • Slave Girls 66; The Lost Continent 68*; Blood from the Mummy's Tomb 71*; Call Him Mr. Shatter • Shatter • They Call Him Mr. Shatter 74*

Carrick, Allyn B. Her Story 22

Carrier, Rick Strangers in the City 62

Carrière, Jean-Claude The Break • Rupture 61*; Happy Anniversary • Heureux Anniversaire 61*

Carrière, Marcel The Fight • La Lutte • Wrestling 61*

Carrière, Matthieu Fool's Mate • Zugzwang 89

Carrigan, Anna Roses in December 86

Carril, Hugo del see Del Carril, Hugo

Carrol, Frank G. see Baldanello, Gianfranco

Carroll, F. J. For the Freedom of the World 17*

Carroll, Gene The Adventurous Soul 27; The Air Mail Pilot 28

Carroll, J. Larry Ghost Warrior • Swordkill 84

Carroll, Robert Martin Sonny Boy 88

Carruth, Clyde The Cowboy Kid 28

Carruth, Milton Love Letters of a Star 36*; Breezing Home 37; The Lady Fights Back 37; The Man in Blue 37; Reported Missing 37; She's Dangerous 37*; Some Blondes Are Dangerous 37

Carson, L. M. Kit The American Dreamer 71*

Carstairs, John Paddy Paris Plane 33; Holiday's End 36; Alibi Breaker • Double Exposures 37; Incident in Shanghai 37; Missing, Believed Married 37; Night Ride 37; Lassie from Lancashire 38; Maxwell Archer, Detective • Meet Maxwell Archer 39; The Saint in London 39; The Second Mr. Bush 39; All Hands 40; Dangerous Comment 40; Now You're Talking 40; Spare a Copper 40; Telefootlers 40; He Found a Star 41; Dancing with Crime 46; Sleeping Car to Trieste 48; The Amazing Mr. Beecham • The Chiltern Hundreds 49; Fools Rush In 49; Tony Draws a Horse 50; Talk of a Million • You Can't Beat the Irish 51; Made in Heaven 52; Treasure Hunt 52; Top of the Form 53; Trouble in Store 53; One Good Turn 54; Up to His

Neck 54; Jumping for Joy 55; Man of the Moment 55; The Big Money 56; Up in the World 56; Just My Luck 57; The Square Peg 58; Tommy the Toreador 59; Sands of the Desert 60; A Weekend with Lulu 61; The Devil's Agent • Im Namen des Teufels 62

Carter, Donald The Gap 37; Where Love Is, God Is 37; Prince of Peace 39

Carter, Dorothy Elizabeth *see Gish, Lillian*

Carter, John N. Zombie Island Massacre 84

Carter, Peter The Rowdyman 71; The Creeper • Rituals 78; High-Ballin' 78; Highpoint 79; Jack London's Klondike Fever • Klondike Fever 80

Cartier, Henri *see Cartier-Bresson, Henri*

Cartier, Rudolph Passionate Summer • Storm in Jamaica 58

Cartier-Bresson, Henri Return to Life 37*; Le Retour 46

Cartwright, Justin Rosie Dixon, Night Nurse 78

Carvalho, J. P. de *see De Carvalho, J. P.*

Carvalho, Nelson Marcellino de *see De Carvalho, Nelson Marcellino*

Carvana, Hugo Bar Esperanza 83

Carver, H. P. The Silent Enemy 30

Carver, Steve The Arena • Naked Warriors 73; Big Bad Mama 74; Capone 75; Drum 76*; Fast Charlie and the Moonbeam • Fast Charlie the Moonbeam Rider 79; Look Down and Die • Men of Steel • Steel 80; An Eye for an Eye 81; Lone Wolf McQuade 83; Jocks • Road Trip 84; Bulletproof 87; River of Death 89

Casabianca, Camille de *see De Casabianca, Camille*

Casaril, Guy L'Astragale 68; The Legend of Frenchie King • The Oil Girls • The Petroleum Girls • Les Pétroleuses • Le Pistolère 71*; The Beguines • Le Rempart des Béguines 72; Piaf • Piaf—The Early Years • The Sparrow of Pigalle 74

Casati, Ferruccio The Garden of Deception • Il Giardino degli Inganni 86

Casaus, Victor Come la Vida Misma • Like Life Itself 86

Casden, Ron Campus Man 87

Caserini, Mario Garibaldi 07; Otello • Othello 07; Giovanna d'Arco • Joan of Arc 08; Marco Visconti 08; Romeo and Juliet • Romeo e Giulietta 08; Beatrice Cenci 09; La Gerla di Papa Martin 09; L'Innominato 09; Macbeth 09; Amleto • Hamlet 10; Anna Garibaldi 10; Il Cid 10; Federico Barbarossa 10; Giovanni delle Bande Nere 10; Lucrezia Borgia 10; Messalina 10; L'Adultera 11; Antigone 11; Jane Gray 11; La Mala Pianta 11; Santarellina 11; L'Ultimo dei Frontignac 11; I Cavalieri di Rodi 12; Dante e Beatrice 12; Infamia Araba 12; Mater Dolorosa 12; Parsifal 12; La Ribalta 12; Siegfried 12; Florette e Patapon 13; The Last Days of Pompeii • Gli Ultimi Giorni di Pompeii 13; Ma l'Amor 13; Mio Non Muore 13; Nerone e Agrippina 13; Romanticismo 13; Somnambulismo 13; Il Treno

degli Spettri 13; La Gorgona 14; La Pantomima della Morte 15; La Divetta del Regimento 16; Maschera di Misterio 16; Vita e Morte 16; La Vittima dell'Amore 16; Amor Che Uccide 17; Capitan Fracassa 17; Il Dramma di una Notte 17; Resurrection • Resurrezione 17; La Via Più Lunga 17; Il Filo della Vita 18; Madama Arlecchino • La Signora Arlecchino 18; Una Notte a Calcutta 18; Primerose 18; Anima Tormentata 19; L'Imprevisto 19; Il Miracolo 19; Musica Profana 19; Il Romanzo di una Vespa 19; Tragedia Senza Lacrime 19; Fior d'Amore 20; La Modella 20; Sorella 20; La Voce del Cuore 20

Casler, Christopher Teenage Graffiti 77

Casolaro, S. V. Parlami d'Amore Maria 34

Casparius, Hans G. Drums 61

Cass, Henry Lancashire Luck 37; HMS Minelayer 41; Ask the C.A.B. 42; Free House 42; Common Cause 43; Danger Area 43; Catholics in Britain 44; Jigsaw 44; The Facts of Love • 29 Acacia Avenue 45; Famous Scenes from Shakespeare—Julius Caesar 45; Famous Scenes from Shakespeare—Macbeth 45; The Great Game 45; The Glass Mountain 48; No Place for Jennifer 49; Last Holiday 50; Young Wives' Tale 51; Castle in the Air 52; Father's Doing Fine 52; No Smoking 55; The Reluctant Bride • Two Grooms for a Bride 55; Windfall 55; Bond of Fear 56; Breakaway 56; The Crooked Sky 56; The High Terrace 56; Booby Trap 57; Professor Tim 57; Blood of the Vampire 58; Boyd's Shop 59; The Hand 60; The Man Who Couldn't Walk 60; Mr. Brown Comes Down the Hill 66; Give a Dog a Bone 67; Happy Deathday 69

Cassarino, Gianbatista Blood on His Lips • The Hideous Sun Demon • The Sun Demon • Terror from the Sun 59*

Cassavetes, John Shadows 59; Too Late Blues 61; A Child Is Waiting 62; Faces 68; Husbands 70; Minnie and Moskowitz 71; A Woman Under the Influence 74; The Killing of a Chinese Bookie 76; Opening Night 77; Gloria 80; Love Streams 83; Big Trouble 84

Cassenti, Franck Testament d'un Poète Juif Assassine • Testament of a Murdered Jewish Poet 87

Castellani, Leandro Il Coraggio di Parlare • The Courage to Speak 87

Castellani, Renato Un Colpo di Pistola • A Pistol Shot 41; Zaza 42; La Donna della Montagna • The Woman from the Mountain 43; Mio Figlio Professore • My Son the Professor • Professor My Son 46; Sotto il Sole di Roma • Under the Sun of Rome 47; È Primavera • It's Forever Springtime • Springtime in Italy 49; Due Soldi di Speranza • Two Cents Worth of Hope • Two Pennyworth of Hope 51; Giulietta e Romeo • Romeo and Juliet 54; Dreams in a Drawer • I Sogni nel Cassetto 57; And the Wild Wild Women • Caged • Hell in the City • Nella Città l'Inferno • The Wild Wild Women 58; Il Brigante • Italian

Brigands 61; Mare Matto 62; Contro Sesso • Controsesso 64*; Three Nights of Love • Tre Notti d'Amore 64*; Sotto il Cielo Stellato 66; Ghosts, Italian Style • Questi Fantasmi • Three Ghosts 67; Una Breva Stagione • A Brief Season 69; Leonardo da Vinci 71

Castellano, Franco Llegaron los Marcianos • I Marziani Hanno Dodici Mani • Siamo Quattro Marziani • The Twelve-Handed Men of Mars 64*; È Arrivato Mio Fratello • My Brother's Come to Stay 85*; Department Store • Grandi Magazzini 86*; Il Burbero • The Grouch 87*

Castellari, Enzo G. Any Gun Can Play • For a Few Bullets More • I'll Go, I'll Kill Him, and Come Back • Vado...l'Ammazzo e Torno 67; Payment in Blood • Sette Winchester per un Massacro 67; Ammazzali Tutti e Torna Solo • Kill Them All and Come Back Alone • Mátalos y Vuelve 68; Johnny Hamlet • Quella Sporca Storia del West • That Dirty Story of the West 68; I Tre Che Sconvolsero il West 68; Vado, Vedo e Sparo 68; Eagle Over London • Eagles Over London 70; The Con Men • Te Deum 73; High Crime 73; The Loves and Times of Scaramouche • Scaramouche 75; The Anonymous Avenger 76; Cipolla Colt 76; Keoma • The Violent Breed 76; Django's Great Return 77; Counterfeit Commandos • Inglorious Bastards 78; The Day of the Cobra 80; The Great White • The Last Jaws • Shark • L'Ultimo Squalo 81; Bronx Warriors • I Guerrieri del Bronx • 1990: I Guerrieri del Bronx • 1990: The Bronx Warriors 82; 2019: I Nuovi Barbari • The New Barbarians • I Nuovi Barbari • Warriors of the Wasteland 82; The Last House Near the Lake • L'Ultima Casa Vicino al Lago 83; A Colpi di Luce • Colpi di Luce • Lightblast • Rays of Light 85; Escape from the Bronx 85

Castellvi, José Mercedes 35

Castilla, Sergio The Disappeared 79

Castillo, Celso ad *see Ad Castillo, Celso*

Castillo, Nardo The Gunrunner 83

Castillo, Oscar Eulalia 87

Castle, James W. Her Vocation 15; The Test 15

Castle, Nick T.A.G. The Assassination Game • Tag 82; The Last Starfighter 84; The Boy Who Could Fly 86; Tap 89

Castle, William The Chance of a Lifetime 43; Klondike Kate 43; Mr. Smug 43; Betrayed • When Strangers Marry • When Strangers Meet 44; The Mark of the Whistler • The Marked Man 44; She's a Soldier Too 44; The Whistler 44; Crime Doctor's Warning • The Doctor's Warning 45; Voice of the Whistler 45; Crime Doctor's Man Hunt 46; Just Before Dawn 46; Mysterious Intruder 46; The Return of Rusty 46; Crime Doctor's Gamble • The Doctor's Gamble 47; The Gentleman from Nowhere 48; The Girl from Texas • Texas, Brooklyn and Heaven 48; Johnny Stool Pigeon 49; Undertow 49; Hollywood Story 50; It's a Small World 50; Cave of Outlaws

51; The Fat Man 51; Charge of the Lancers 53; Conquest of Cochise 53; Drums of Tahiti 53; Fort Ti 53; Jesse James vs. the Daltons 53; Serpent of the Nile 53; Slaves of Babylon 53; Battle of Rogue River 54; The Iron Glove 54; The Law vs. Billy the Kid 54; Masterson of Kansas 54; New Orleans Uncensored • Riot on Pier 6 54; The Saracen Blade 54; The Americano 55; Duel on the Mississippi 55; The Gun That Won the West 55; The Houston Story 56; Uranium Boom 56; Macabre 57; House on Haunted Hill 58; The Tingler 59; 13 Ghosts 60; Homicidal 61; Mr. Sardonicus • Sardonicus 61; The Old Dark House 62; Zotz! 62; The Candy Web • 13 Frightened Girls 63; Strait-Jacket 63; The Night Walker 64; I Saw What You Did 65; The Busy Body 66; Let's Kill Uncle 66; The Spirit Is Willing 66; Project X 67; Shanks • Shock 74

Castleman, William Allen Bummer 73; Johnny Firecloud 75

Caston, Hoite The Dirt Bike Kid 86

Castri, Marco di *see Di Castri, Marco*

Castro, Eduardo de *see De Castro, Eduardo*

Castro, Emmanuele La Guerre Populaire au Laos 68*

Castro, Guero *see Castro, Víctor Manuel*

Castro, Pedro Jorge de *see De Castro, Pedro Jorge*

Castro, Víctor Manuel All Life Long • Toda la Vida 87; Esta Noche Cena Pancho (Despedida de Soltero) • Tonight Pancho Dines Out (Bachelor Party) 87; The Female Cabbie • La Ruletera 87; El Mofles y los Mecanicos • Muffler and the Mechanics 87; Nos Reímos de la Migra • Poking Fun at the Border Patrol 87; The Race Never Loses—It Smells Like Gas • La Raza Nunca Pierde—Huele a Gas 87

Catching, Bill Les Corrumpus • The Corrupt Ones • Hell to Macao • Die Hölle von Macao • The Peking Medallion • Il Sigillo de Pechino 66*

Catelain, Jaque Le Marchand de Plaisir 23; La Galerie des Monstres 24

Cates, Gilbert Rings Around the World 66; I Never Sang for My Father • Strangers 70; Summer Wishes, Winter Dreams 73; Dragonfly • One Summer Love 76; Face of a Stranger • The Promise 78; The Last Married Couple in America 80; Oh, God! Book Two 80; Backfire 87

Cates, Joseph Girl of the Night 60; The Fat Spy 65; Who Killed Teddy Bear? 65

Catling, Darrell Tom's Ride 44; Trouble at Townsend 46; Dusty Bates 47; Material Evidence 48; Under the Frozen Falls 48; The Magic Marble 51; The Marble Returns 51; The Case of the Old Rope Man 52; The Cat Gang 59

Cato, Don Indian Summer 87

Caton-Jones, Michael Scandal 89; Memphis Belle 90

Caulfield, Michael Fighting Back 82

Cause, Bill Box Car Bill Falls in Luck 17

Cauvin, André Hans Memling 38; Van Eyck 38; Black Shadows 49

Cava, Gregory la *see La Cava, Gregory*

Cavalcanti, Alberto Rien Que les Heures 25; Le Train Sans Yeux 25; En Rade • Sea Fever 27; La Jalousie de Barbouillé 27; La Petite Lili • La P'tite Lili 27*; Yvette 27; Le Capitaine Fracasse 28; À Mi-Chemin du Ciel 29; Little Red Riding Hood • Le Petit Chaperon Rouge 29; Vous Verrez la Semaine Prochaine 29; A Canção do Berço 30; Dans une Île Perdue 30; Toute Sa Vie 30; Les Vacances du Diable 30; Le Tour de Chant 31; En Lisant le Journal 32; Le Garçon Divorcé • Le Mari Garçon 32; Le Jour du Frotteur 32; Nous Ne Ferons Jamais de Cinéma 32; Revue Montmartroise 32; Le Truc du Brésilien 32; Coralie et Cie 33; Plaisirs Défendus 33; New Rates 34; Pett and Pott 34; S.O.S. Radio Service 34; Coal Face 35; The Line to Tcherva Hut • The Line to Tschierva Hut 36; Message from Geneva 36; Four Barriers 37; We Live in Two Worlds 37; Who Writes to Switzerland 37; The Chiltern Country 38; Alice in Switzerland 39; Men of the Alps 39; A Midsummer Day's Work 39; The Warning 39; La Cause Commune • Factory Front 40; The Heel of Italy • Yellow Caesar 40; Mastery of the Sea 41; Young Veterans 41*; Film and Reality 42; 48 Hours • Went the Day Well? 42; Greek Testament 42; Ship Safety • Watertight 43; Champagne Charlie 44; Trois Chansons de la Résistance • Trois Chants pour la France 44; Dead of Night 45*; The Life and Adventures of Nicholas Nickleby • Nicholas Nickleby 46; Affairs of a Rogue • The First Gentleman 47; I Became a Criminal • They Made Me a Criminal • They Made Me a Fugitive 47; For Them That Trespass • Mr. Drew 48; Caiçara 50*; O Canto do Mar • The Song of the Sea 52; Simão o Caolho • Simon the One-Eyed 52; Mulher de Verdade • A Real Woman 54; Herr Puntila and His Servant Matti • Herr Puntila und Sein Knecht Matti 55; The Compass • Die Windrose • The Windrose 56*; Castle in the Carpathians 57; Les Noces Vénitiennes • La Prima Notte 58; The Monster of Highgate Pond 60; Yerma 62; Herzl • The Story of Israel • Thus Spake Theodor Herzl 67

Cavalcanti, Ibere Um Sonho de Vampiros • A Vampire's Dream 69

Cavalheiro, Elyseu Visconti Os Monstros de Babaloo 70; O Lobishomem 74

Cavalier, Alain Le Combat dans l'Île 62; Fire and Ice 63; L'Insoumis 64; Mise à Sac 67; La Chamade • Heartbeat 68; Le Plein de Super 76; Martin et Lea 78; Ce Répondeur Ne Prend Pas de Messages 79; Thérèse 86; Portraits d'Alain Cavalier 88

Cavanaugh, W. H. Evangeline 14*

Cavani, Liliana Francesco d'Assisi 66; Galileo 68; I Cannibali • The Cannibals • The Year of the Cannibals 69; L'Ospite 71; Milarepa 74; The Night Porter • Il Portiere di Notte 74; Al di Là del Bene e del Male • Beyond Evil • Beyond Good and Evil • Oltre il Bene e il Male 77; La Pelle 81; Beyond Obsession • Beyond the Door • Oltre la Porta • The Secret Beyond the

Door 82; The Berlin Affair • Interno Berlinese 85; Francesco • St. Francis of Assisi 89

Cavara, Paolo La Donna del Mondo • Women of the World 62*; Malamondo 64; L'Occhio Selvaggio • The Wild Eye 68; The Ravine 69; The Black-Bellied Tarantula • The Black Belly of the Tarantula • La Tarantola dal Ventre Nero • La Tarentule au Ventre Noir 71; Los Amigos • Deaf Smith and Johnny Ears 72

Caviglia, Orestes Con las Alas Rotas • With Broken Wings 40; El Matrero • The Outlaw 40

Cawley, Bob Treasure of Tayopa 74

Cayatte, André La Fausse Maîtresse 42; Au Bonheur des Dames • Shopgirls of Paris 43; Pierre et Jean 43; Le Dernier Sou 44; Roger-la-Honte 45; Sérénade aux Nuages 45; Le Chanteur Inconnu 46; La Revanche de Roger-la-Honte 46; Les Dessous des Cartes 47; Les Amants de Vérone • The Lovers of Verona 48; Retour à la Vie • Return to Life 49*; Justice Est Faite • Justice Has Been Done • Justice Is Done • Let Justice Be Done 50; Are We All Murderers? • Nous Sommes Tous des Assassins • We Are All Murderers 52; Avant le Déluge • Before the Flood 53; The Black Dossier • Le Dossier Noir 55; An Eye for an Eye • Eyes of the Sahara • Œil pour Œil 56; Le Miroir A Deux Faces • The Mirror Has Two Faces • The Mirror with Two Faces 58; The Crossing of the Rhine • Jenseits des Rheins • Le Passage du Rhin • Il Passaggio del Reno • Tomorrow Is My Turn 60; Le Glaive et la Balance • The Sword and the Balance • Two Are Guilty • Uno Dei Tre 62; Anatomy of a Marriage • Anatomy of a Marriage (My Days with Jean-Marc and My Nights with Françoise) • Anatomy of a Marriage (My Nights with Françoise, My Days with Jean-Marc) • Françoise • Jean-Marc, or Conjugal Life • My Days with Jean-Marc • My Nights with Françoise • Per il Bene e per il Male • La Vie Conjugale • La Vie Conjugale: My Nights with Françoise 63; Piège pour Cendrillon • A Trap for Cinderella 65; Occupational Hazards • Les Risques du Métier 67; Les Chemins de Khatmandou • The Road to Katmandu • The Roads to Katmandu 69; Mourir d'Aimer • To Die of Love 70; Il N'Y A Pas de Fumée Sans Feu • Where There's Smoke 72; Jury of One • Le Testament • La Tigresse et l'Éléphant • Verdict 74; À Chacun Son Enfer • To Each His Hell 76; L'Amour en Question • Love in Question 78; Justices 78; La Raison d'État • Reasons of State 78

Cayrol, Jean On Vous Parle 60*; La Frontière 61*; Madame Se Meurt 61*; De Tout pour Faire un Monde 62*; Le Coup de Grâce 65*; La Déesse 66

Cayton, William Jack Johnson 71

Cazals, Felipe La Manzana de la Discordia 68; Familiaridades 69; Emiliano Zapata 70; El Jardín de la Tía Isabel 71; Aquellos Años 72; Los Que Viven Donde Sopla el Viento Suave 73; El Apando 75; Canoa 75;

Las Poquianchis 76; La Guerra Rodríguez 77; El Año de la Peste 78; Bajo la Metralla 83; Cuentos de la Madrugada 85; Los Motivos de Luz 85; Lo del César • What Is Caesar's 87; El Tres de Copas 87

Cazeneuve, Fabrice The King of the Ragpickers • Le Roi de la Chine 85

Cazeneuve, Paul The Iron Heart 17*; Her Honor the Mayor 20; The Spirit of Good 20; Square Shooter 20; Sunset Sprague 20*

Cecil-Wright, Robin With Love in Mind 70

Ceder, Ralph Wife Savers 28; Roman Scandals 33*; She Had to Choose 34; Captain Bill 35; Here Comes a Policeman • Strictly Illegal 35; Meet the Mayor 38; The Showdown • West of Abilene 40

Cederstrand, Sølve Near Relatives • Tjocka Släkten 35

Cekalski, Eugeniesz Forward, Co-Operation • Na Start 35*

Celano, Guido Giuro...e Li Uccise ad Uno ad Uno • Piluk 68

Celentano, Adriano Robbery, Roman Style 65; Joan Lui: But One Monday I Arrive in Town • Joan Lui: Ma un Giorno nel Paese Arrivo Io di Lunedì 85

Cellan-Jones, James Bequest to the Nation • The Nelson Affair 73

Celles, Pierre de see DeCelles, Pierre

Čenevski, Kiril Jazol • The Knot 86

Cerchio, Fernando The Count of Bragelonne • The Last Musketeer • Le Vicomte de Bragelonne 54; Mistress of the Mountains 54; Los Amantes del Desierto • Gli Amanti del Deserto • The Desert Warrior • La Figlia dello Sceicco 58*; Giudetta e Oloferne • Head of a Tyrant • Judith and Holophernes 58; La Venere di Cheronea 58*; Cleopatra's Daughter • Daughter of Cleopatra • Il Sepolcro dei Re • La Vallée des Pharaons 60*; Col Ferro e Col Fuoco • Daggers of Blood • Invasion 1700 • Par le Fer et par le Feu • With Fire and Sword 61; Nefertite, Regina del Nilo • Queen of the Nile 62; The Red Sheik • Lo Sceicco Rosso 62; Per un Dollaro di Gloria 66

Cerf, Norman A. Jungle Hell 56

Cerio, Ferrucio The Barbarians • The Pagans 57

Cervera, Pascual Aventuras de Quinque y Arturo el Robot • El Rayo Disintegrador 65

Cervi, Tonino The Moment of Truth • El Momento de la Verdad • Il Momento della Verità • Vivir Desviviéndose 64*; Oggi a Me...Domani a Te! • Today It's Me...Tomorrow You! 68; El Cadáver Exquisito • The Cruel Ones • Las Crueles • The Exquisite Cadaver 71; Il Delitto del Diavolo • Queens of Evil • Le Regine • Les Sorcières du Bord du Lac 71; Nest of Vipers • Ritratto di Borghesia in Nero 79

Cetin, Sinan Fourteen Numara • Number Fourteen • Ondört Numara 86; Prenses • Princess 86

Chabot, Jean La Nuit avec Hortense 88

Chabrol, Claude Le Beau Serge • Bitter

Reunion • Handsome Serge 58; Les Cousins • The Cousins 58; A Doppia Mandata • À Double Tour • Leda • Web of Passion 59; Les Bonnes Femmes • The Girls 59; Les Godelureaux 60; L'Œil du Malin • The Third Lover 61; Les Sept Péchés Capitaux • I Sette Peccati Capitali • Seven Capital Sins • The Seven Deadly Sins 61*; Bluebeard • Landru 62; Ophelia • Ophélie 62; The Beautiful Swindlers • Les Plus Belles Escroqueries du Monde • World's Greatest Swindles • The World's Most Beautiful Swindlers 63*; Code Name Tiger • The Tiger Likes Fresh Blood • Le Tigre Aime la Chair Fraîche 64; Paris Vu par... • Six in Paris 64*; The Blue Panther • Marie-Chantal Contre le Docteur Kha 65; An Orchid for the Tiger • Le Tigre Se Parfume à la Dynamite 65; The Champagne Murders • Le Scandale 66; La Ligne de Démarcation 66; Les Biches • The Does • The Girlfriends • The Heterosexuals 67; The Road to Corinth • La Route de Corinthe • Who's Got the Black Box? 67; La Femme Infidèle • The Unfaithful Wife 68; The Beast Must Die • Killer! • Que la Bête Meure • This Man Must Die! • Uccidero un Uomo 69; Le Boucher • The Butcher 69; The Break Up • Le Jour des Parques • La Rupture 70; La Décade Prodigieuse • Ten Days' Wonder 70; Just Before Nightfall • Juste Avant la Nuit 70; Docteur Popaul • Dr. Popaul • High Heels! • Scoundrel in White 72; Le Banc de Désolation • The Bench of Desolation • De Grey—Le Banc de Désolation 73; Blood Wedding • Les Noces Rouges • Red Wedding • Wedding in Blood 73; Nada • The Nada Gang 73; Dirty Hands • Les Innocents aux Mains Sales • Innocents with Dirty Hands 74; Love Match • Une Partie de Plaisir • A Piece of Pleasure • Pleasure Party 74; Initiation à la Mort • Les Magiciens • Profezia di un Delitto 75; Alice, or The Last Escapade • Alice ou La Dernière Fugue 76; Folies Bourgeoises • The Twist 76; Blood Relatives • Les Liens du Sang 77; La Folie des Miens 77; Violette • Violette Nozière 77; Le Cheval d'Orgueil • The Horse of Pride • The Proud Ones 79; Les Menteurs • Splintered 79; Les Fantômes du Chapelier • The Hatmaker • The Hatter's Ghosts 81; The Blood of Others • Le Sang des Autres 83; Cop au Vin • Poulet au Vinaigre 84; Inspecteur Lavardin • Inspector Lavardin 86; Le Cri du Hibou • The Cry of the Owl 87; Masques 87; Une Affaire de Femmes • Story of Women 88; Club Extinction • Docteur M • Dr. M 89; Jours Tranquilles à Clichy • Quiet Days in Clichy 90

Chabukiani, V. Ballet Tales 56*; The Ballet of Othello 64

Chace, Haile Damaged Goods • V.D. 61

Chaffey, Don The Mysterious Poacher 49; The Case of the Missing Scene 51; Bouncer Breaks Up 52; A Good Pull-Up 53; The Mask 53; Skid Kids 53; Strange Journey 53; Watch Out 53; Time Is My

Enemy 54; Dead on Time 55; The Girl in the Picture 56; The Secret Tent 56; The Flesh Is Weak 57; The Case of Mrs. Loring • A Question of Adultery 58; The Man Upstairs 58; Breakout • Danger Within 59; Dentist in the Chair 60; Lies My Father Told Me 60; Greyfriars Bobby 61; A Matter of WHO 61; Middle of Nowhere • The Webster Boy 61; Nearly a Nasty Accident 61; The Prince and the Pauper 62; For He's a Jolly Bad Fellow • A Jolly Bad Fellow • They All Died Laughing 63; The Horse Without a Head 63; Jason and the Argonauts • Jason and the Golden Fleece 63; The Three Lives of Thomasina 63; The Crooked Road • Krivi Put 64; One Million Years B.C. 66; The Viking Queen 66; Twist of Sand 67; Creatures the World Forgot 70; Clinic Xclusive • With These Hands 71; Charley One-Eye 72; The Graveyard • Persecution • Sheba • The Terror of Sheba 73; The Fourth Wish 75; Born to Run • Ride a Wild Pony 76; Harness Fever 76; Pete's Dragon 77; Surf 77; The Magic of Lassie 78; C.H.O.M.P.S. 79

Chagrin, Claude The Concert 74; Christmas Tree 75; The Morning Spider 77

Chahin, Mohamed The Sun on a Hazy Day 86

Chahine, Youssef Baba Amin • Father Amin • Papa Amin 50; The Great Clown • Al Muharraj al Kabir 51; Ibn al Nil • The Nile's Son • The Son of the Nile 51; The Lady in the Train • The Lady of the Train • Lady on the Train • Sayidat al Kitar 51; The Blazing Sky • The Blazing Sun • Seraa fil Wadi • Sira fi'l Wadi • Struggle in the Valley 52; Nessa Bala Rejal • Nisa Bala Rijal • Women Without Men 52; Devil of the Desert • Shaitan el Sahara • Shaytan al Sahara 54; Black Waters • Seraa fil Mina • Sira fi'l Mina • Struggle in the Port • Struggle on the Pier 55; Farewell My Love • Farewell to Your Love • Wada at Hobak • Wada at Hubbak 56; Inta Habibi • You Are My Love 56; Bab el Hadid • Cairo: Central Station • Cairo Station • Gare Centrale • Iron Gate 57; Djamila • Gamila Bohraid • Gamila Buhrayd • Jamila al Gazairia • Jamila the Algerian • Jamila the Algerian Girl 58; Forever Yours • Hub Ilal Abad • Hubbun Ila'l Abad 58; Bayen Idek • Bayn Idayk • Between Your Hands • Take Me in Your Arms 59; Lover's Call • Nedaa el Ochak • Nida al Ushaq 60; The Man in My Life • Rajol fi Hayati • Rajul fi Hayati 61; The Leader Saladin • Al Nasr Salah al Din • El Nasser Salah-el-Dine • Saladin • Saladin and the Great Crusades • Saladin the Victorious 62; Dawn of a New Day • Fajr Yawm Jadid 64; Auliban 65; Baya el Khawatim • Bayya al Khawatim • The Ring Seller 65; Rimal al Dhahab • Rimal Min Zahab • Sands of Gold 66; The Feast of Mayrun • Id al Mayrun 67; El Ard • The Earth • The Land 68; The Choice • Al Ekhtiar • Al Ikhtiyar 70; Men and the Nile • Al Nas fi'l Nil • El Nas wal Nil • People and the Nile • People of the Nile 72; Salwa • Salwa, or The Little Girl Who

Talks to the Cows 72; UNICEF 72; Al Asfour • The Sparrow • Al Usfur 73; Al Intilaq • The Release 74; Awdat al Ibn al Dhal • Return of the Prodigal Son 75; Alexandria...Why? • Iskindariya...Lih? • Iskindirya—Leh? 78; An Egyptian Story • Hadduta Misriya • Hadota Misreya • La Mémoire 82; Adieu Bonaparte • Al Wedaa ya Bonaparte 84; Le Sixième Jour • The Sixth Day • El Yom el Sades 86; Iskindirya Kaman Oue Kaman 90

Chaitin, Norman C. Flaming Desire • The Small Hours 62

Chakraborty, Srinivas Arpan 87

Chakraborty, Uptlendu The Child God • Debshishu 86

Chalbaud, Román Manon 86; The Black Sheep • La Oveja Negra 87

Chalder, Adolpho see Da Costa, Cicero Adolpho Vittorio

Chalonge, Christian de see De Chalonge, Christian

Chamberlain, Win Brand X 70

Chambers, Everett Run Across the River 59; The Lollipop Cover 64

Champavert, Georges Mea Culpa 19; L'Œil de Saint-Yves 19; L'Été de la Saint-Martin 20; Le Remous 20; La Hurle 21; Le Porion 21; L'Évasion 22; La Neuvaine de Colette 25

Champion, Gower My Six Loves 63; Bank Shot 74

Champion, Gregg Short Time 90

Champion, John Mustang Country 76

Champlain, Yves see Allégret, Yves

Champreux, Maurice Lucette 24*; Le Stigmate 24*; Judex 33

Chan, Angie Huajie Shidai • My Name Ain't Suzie 86

Chan, Henry Gui an Yan • Obsessed 83

Chan, Jackie The Fearless Hyena 79; Young Master 80; Dragon Lord 82; Project A 83; Jackie Chan's Police Story • Jingcha Gushi • Police Force • Police Story 85; The Armour of God 86; The Brothers 87; Project A—Part II 87; Police Story—Part II 88

Chan, Louis see Chen, Guoxi

Chan, Philip Tongs—A Chinatown Story 86; Chocolate Inspector 87

Chanas, René Desert Fighters 54; To Catch a Spy 57

Chanderli, Jamal Yasmina 61*; Les Fusils de la Liberté 62*

Chandra, N. Counter-Attack • Pratighaat 87

Chandreshekhar, S. A. Kudrat ka Kanoon • Qudrat ka Qanoon 88

Chaney, Lon The Chimney's Secret 15; For Cash 15; The Oyster Dredger 15; The Stool Pigeon 15; The Trust 15; The Violin Maker 15

Chang, Mei Chung Revenge of the Shogun Women 82

Chang, Sylvia Passion 85; Posterity and Perplexity 89

Chang, Yan Deep at Heart 83

Chang, Yi see Zhang, Yi

Chang-ho, Bae see Bae, Chang-ho

Chang-ho, Lee see Lee, Chang-ho

Chanois, Jean-Paul le see Le Chanois, Jean-Paul

Chao, Lili Hari sa Hari, Lahi sa Lahi 87*

Chaperot, Georges The Little Flower of Jesus 38

Chapin, Harry The Legendary Champions 68

Chapin, James After Dark 24; Hutch of the U.S.A. • Hutch—U.S.A. 24; Poison 24; Surging Seas 24; Turned Up 24; Virtue's Revolt 24

Chaplin, Charles At It Again • Caught in the Rain • Who Got Stung? 14; The Blundering Boob • The New Janitor • The Porter 14; Busted Hearts • The Rival Mashers • Those Love Pangs 14; A Busy Day • Lady Charlie • Militant Suffragette 14; Caught in a Cabaret • Faking with Society • Jazz Waiter • The Waiter 14*; The Caveman • A Dream • His Prehistoric Past • King Charlie 14; Charlie and the Sausages • Hot Dogs • Love and Lunch • Mabel's Busy Day 14*; Charlie at the Races • Gentlemen of Nerve • Some Nerve 14; The Cook • Dough and Dynamite • The Doughnut Designer 14; The Dentist • Down and Out • Laughing Gas • Tuning His Ivories 14; The Face on the Barroom Floor • The Ham Artist 14; A Fair Exchange • Getting Acquainted • Hullo Everybody 14; Family Home • His Trysting Place 14; The Fatal Mallet • Hit Him Again • The Pile Driver • The Rival Suitors 14*; The Female Impersonator • The Masquerader • Putting One Over 14; Getting His Goat • The Property Man • The Roustabout • Vamping Venus 14; The Good-for-Nothing • Helping Himself • His New Profession 14; Her Friend the Bandit • Mabel's Flirtation • A Thief Catcher 14*; His Musical Career • Musical Tramps • The Piano Movers 14; The Love Thief • Oh, What a Night! • Revelry • The Rounders • Two of a Kind 14; Mabel's Married Life • The Squarehead • When You're Married 14*; Recreation • Spring Fever 14; The Bank • Charlie at the Bank 15; Battling Charlie • The Champion • Champion Charlie 15; By the Sea • Charlie's Day Out 15; Carmen • Charlie Chaplin's Burlesque on Carmen 15; Champagne Charlie • A Night Out 15; Charlie and the Perfect Lady • The Perfect Lady • A Woman 15; Charlie at the Show • A Night in the Show 15; Charlie on the Ocean • Charlie the Sailor • Shanghaied 15; Charlie on the Spree • In the Park 15; Charlie the Hobo • The Tramp 15; His New Job 15; A Jitney Elopement • Married in Haste 15; The Paper Hanger • The Plumber • Work 15; Behind the Screen 16; Charlie the Burglar • Police! 16; The Count 16; Easy Street 16; The Essanay-Chaplin Revue of 1916 16; The Fireman 16; The Floorwalker • The Store 16; One A.M. 16; The Pawnshop 16; The Rink 16; The Vagabond 16; The Adventurer 17; The Cure 17; The Immigrant 17; Shoulder Arms 17; The Bond • Charles Chaplin in a Liberty Loan Appeal 18; A Dog's Life 18; Triple Trouble 18; A Day's Pleasure 19; Sunnyside 19; The Kid 20;

The Idle Class 21; Nice and Friendly 22; Pay Day 22; The Pilgrim 23; A Woman of Paris 23; The Gold Rush 25; The Sea Gull • A Woman of the Sea 26*; The Circus 27; City Lights 31; Modern Times 36; The Great Dictator 40; Monsieur Verdoux 47; Limelight 52; A King in New York 57; A Countess from Hong Kong 66

Chaplin, Sydney A Submarine Pirate 15*; King, Queen, Joker 21

Chapman, Christopher Kelly 81

Chapman, Matthew Hussy 79; Strangers Kiss 84; Heart of Midnight 87

Chapman, Michael All the Right Moves 83; The Clan of the Cave Bear 86

Chappell, Robert Java Burn 89

Chappuis, Alain-Patrick Blue Money 75

Charbakshi, Henri The Last Affair 76

Chardeaux, François Douce France • Gentle France 86

Chardynin, Pyotr Accession of the Romanov Dynasty 13*; Chrysanthemums 14; Woman of Tomorrow 14; Flood 15; Love of a State Councillor 15; Natasha Rostova 15; Story of Seven Who Were Hanged 20

Charef, Mehdi Tea in the Harem • Tea in the Harem of Archimedes • Le Thé au Harem d'Archimèdes 85; Miss Mona 87; Camomille 88

Charell, Erik Congress Dances • Der Kongress Tanzt 31; Caravan 34

Chargonin, Alexander In the Whirlwind of Revolution 22

Charlot, André Elstree Calling 30*

Charlot, Martin Memento Mei 63; Apocalypse 3:16 64

Charlton, Robert No Big Deal 83

Charlton, William S. Love's Influence 22*

Charon, Jacques A Flea in Her Ear 68

Charrington, Arthur East Lynne 13; Flying from Justice 13; The Grip of Iron 13; Mercia the Flower Girl 13; Tracking the Baby 13; Wanted, a Husband 13

Chart, Jack The Bully and the Recruit 08; Raised from the Ranks 08; Still Worthy of the Name 08; How They Made a Man of Billy Brown 09

Chase, Brandon Girl in Trouble 63

Chase, Charlie The Anglers 14; Dirty Work in a Laundry 15; Do-Re-Mi-Fa 15; His Father's Footsteps 15*; The Hunt 15*; Only a Messenger Boy 15; A Dash of Courage 16; His Pride and Shame 16*; Chased Into Love 17; Hello Trouble 18; All at Sea 19; Ship Ahoy! 19; Kids Is Kids 20; Live and Learn 20; Why Go Home? 20; Blue Sunday 21; His Best Girl 21; The Hustler 21; Days of Old 22; The Dumb Bell 22; In the Movies 22; The Stone Age 22; The Courtship of Miles Sandwich 23; Jack Frost 23; Sold at Auction 23; The Bargain of the Century 33; The Cracked Ice Man 33*; Luncheon at Twelve 33; Midsummer Mush 33; Sherman Said It 33; Another Wild Idea 34*; The Chases of Pimple Street 34; Fate's Fathead 34; Four Parts 34*; I'll Take Vanilla 34*; It Happened One Day 34*; Something Simple 34*; You Said a Hatful 34; Life Hesitates at Forty 35*; Manhattan Monkey Business 35*; The Count Takes the Count 36*; The Four-Star Boarder 36; Neighborhood House 36*; Nurse to You 36*; Okay Toots 36*; On the Wrong Trek 36*; Poker at Eight 36; Public Ghost No. 1 36*; Southern Exposure 36; Vamp Till Ready 36*; Oh What a Knight! 37; Ankles Away 38; Flat Foot Stooges 38; Half Way to Hollywood 38; Mutts to You 38; A Nag in the Bag 38; The Old Raid Mule 38; Tassels in the Air 38; Violent Is the Word for Curly 38; Boom Goes the Groom 39; Mutiny on the Body 39; Saved by the Belle 39; Static in the Attic 39

Chase, Richard Hell's Angels Forever 83*

Chase, Ronald Lulu 78

Chatiliez, Étienne Life Is a Long Quiet River • La Vie Est un Long Fleuve Tranquille 87

Chatterjee, Nabyendu Chopper 86

Chatterjee, Shakti Lalan Fakir 87

Chaudet, Louis The Edge of the Law 17; Follow the Girl 17; Society's Driftwood 17; The Girl of My Dreams 18; Hoop-la 19; The Long Lane's Turning 19; The Love Call 19; The Blue Bonnet 20; Common Sense 20; The Kingfisher's Roost 22*; Defying Destiny 23; A Man of Nerve 25; A Captain's Courage 26; Eyes Right 26; Fighting Jack 26; Lightning Bill 26; Tentacles of the North 26; Speeding Hoofs 27; Outcast Souls 28

Chaudhri, Amin Q. Vice Girls, Ltd. 64; Once Again 86; Tiger Warsaw 87; An Unremarkable Life 89

Chaumont, Segundo see De Chomón, Segundo

Chaussois, Dominique The Field Agent • Le Moustachu 87

Chautard, Émile La Légende de l'Aigle 11; Le Poison de l'Humanité 11; L'Aiglon 12; Le Mystère de la Chambre Jaune • Rouletabille I — Le Mystère de la Chambre Jaune 13*; L'Appentis 14; The Arrival of Perpetua 15; The Boss 15; Human Driftwood 15*; The Little Dutch Girl 15; All Man 16; Friday the Thirteenth 16; The Heart of a Hero 16; Love's Crucible 16; Sudden Riches 16; Double Crossed 17*; The Eternal Temptress 17; The Family Honor 17; The Fires of Youth 17; Forget-Me-Nots 17; The Heart of Ezra Greer 17; A Hungry Heart 17; Magda 17; The Man Who Forgot 17; Poppy 17*; Sappho 17; Shirley Kaye 17; Under False Colors 17; The Web of Desire 17; A Daughter of the Old South 18; Fedora 18*; Her Final Reckoning 18; The House of Glass 18; The Marionettes 18; The Ordeal of Rosetta 18; Resurrection 18*; The Studio Girl 18*; Under the Greenwood Tree 18; Eyes of the Soul 19; His Parisian Wife 19; The Marriage Price 19; The Mystery of the Yellow Room 19; Out of the Shadow 19; Paid in Full 19; The Black Panther's Cub 21; Forsaking All Others 22; The Glory of Clementina 22; Living Lies 22; Whispering Shadows 22; Youth to Youth 22; Daytime Wives 23; Untamed Youth 24

Chauvel, Charles In the Wake of the Bounty 33; Heritage 35; Uncivilized 37; Forty Thousand Horsemen 40; Fighting Rats of Tobruk • The Rats of Tobruk 45; The Rugged O'Riordans • Sons of Matthew 49; Jedda the Uncivilized 56

Chavarri, Jaime The Golden River • El Río de Oro • The River of Gold 86; I'm the One You're Looking For 88

Chbib, Bachar Memoirs 84; Evixion 86

Chebotarev, Vladimir The Amphibian Man • The Amphibious Man • Chelovek Amfibia 61*

Checchi, Andrea L'Eroe Sono Io • I'm the Hero 51*

Chechik, Jeremiah S. National Lampoon's Christmas Vacation 89

Checiński, Sylwester Historia Żółtej Ciżemki • The Yellow Slippers 61

Chediak, Braz Forgive Me for Your Betrayal • Perdoe Me por Me Traires 86

Cheek, Douglas C.H.U.D. 84

Cheh, Cheng see Cheng, Cheh

Cheik, Kamal el see El Sheik, Kamel

Chelieu, Arman Toast to Love 51

Chelintsev, B. M. Mysterious Island • Tainstvenni Ostrov 41*

Chellappan Adholokam 88

Chen, Bai Under the Bridge 85

Chen, Guoxi Half-Duan Qing • Infatuation 85

Chen, Jialin The Last Empress 87*

Chen, Kaige Huang Tudi • Yellow Earth 84; The Big Parade • Da Yuebing 86; Hai zi Wang • King of Children • King of the Children 87

Chen, Kuo-fu High School Girls 90

Chen, Lo see Lo, Chen

Chen, Yu Carry On Doctors and Nurses 85

Chénal, Pierre Paris-Cinéma 29*; Le Martyre de l'Obèse 33; La Rue Sans Nom 33; Crime and Punishment • Crime et Châtiment 35*; Les Mutinés de l'Elseneur 36; L'Alibi • The Alibi 37; Il Fu Mattia Pascal • L'Homme de Nulle Part • The Late Mathias Pascal 37; L'Affaire Lafarge 38; La Maison du Maltais • Sirocco 38; Le Dernier Tournant • The Last Bend • The Postman Always Rings Twice 39; Todo un Hombre 43; El Muerto Falta a la Cita 44; Se Abre el Abismo 45; The Devil and the Angel • La Foire aux Chimères 46; El Viaje Sin Regreso 46; Clochemerle • The Scandals of Clochemerle 47; El Ídolo 49; Native Son • Sangre Negra 50; Confesional Amanecer 51; Le Fleuve d'Argent 56; Section des Disparus 56; Dangerous Games • Jeux Dangereux 58; Rafles sur la Ville • Sinners of Paris 58; La Bête à l'Affût 59; Giant Monster • The Night They Killed Rasputin • The Nights of Rasputin • Les Nuits de Raspoutine • L'Ultimo Zar 60; L'Assassin Connaît la Musique 63

Cheng, Cheh The New One-Armed Swordsman • Triple Irons 73

Cheng, Kent Heartbeat 100 87*

Cheng, Y. C. Fight to the Last 38

Cheng-han, Liu see Liu, Cheng-han

Chereau, Patrice L'Homme Blesse 83;

Hôtel de France 87

Cherikover, G. Gricher see Gricher-Cherikover, G.

Cherry, John R. III Dr. Otto and the Riddle of the Gloom Beam 83; Ernest Goes to Camp 87; Ernest Saves Christmas 88; Ernest Goes to Jail 90

Cherviakov, Evgeni see Tcherviakov, Yevgeni

Cherviakov, Yevgeni see Tcherviakov, Yevgeni

Chesebro, George Wolf Blood 25

Chester, George Randolph The Son of Wallingford 21

Chetwynd, Lionel Two Solitudes 77; The Hanoi Hilton 87

Cheverton, Roy P. Love Is a Carousel 70

Chiang, David Silent Love • Tingbudaode Shuohua 86

Chiang, John The Wrong Couples 87

Chiantaretto, Alberto Enigma 87*

Chiari, Mario Boschi sul Mare 42; Monte Sant'Angelo 42; I Trulli di Alberobello 43; Fabiola 47*; Amori di Mezzo Secolo 53*

Chiarini, Luigi La Bella Addormentata • Sleeping Beauty 42; Via delle Cinque Lune 42; La Locandiera 43; L'Ultimo Amore 46; Patto Col Diavolo 48

Chiaureli, Mikhail First Cornet Streshnev • Trumpeter Treshney 28*; The Last Hour 29; Saba 29; Khabarda • Out of the Way! 31; The Last Masquerade • Posledni Maskarad 34; Arsen 37; The Great Dawn • They Wanted Peace 38; Georgi Saakadze I 42; Georgi Saakadze II 43; Klyatva • The Vow 46; The Fall of Berlin • Padeniye Berlina 49; Nezabyvayemi 1919 Godu • The Unforgettable Year of 1919 52; Otar's Widow 57; The Story of a Girl 60

Chiba, Yasuke Honkon no Yoru • A Night in Hong Kong 61; Different Sons • Futari no Musuko 62; Honkon no Hoshi • Star of Hong Kong 62; Honolulu-Tokyo-Hong Kong 63; Bankokku no Yoru • Night in Bangkok 66; The Daphne • Jinchōge 67

Chiesa, Aurelio Distant Lights • Luci Iontane 87

Chi-gyoon, Kwak see Kwak, Chi-gyoon

Chi-hung, Kuei see Gui, Zhihong

Chi-hung, Kwei see Gui, Zhihong

Chikly, Scemana Ain el Ghezal • The Girl from Carthage 24

Childs, Clinton Blonde Captive 32*

Chin-chuan, Hu see Hu, King

Ching-chuen, Hoo see Hu, King

Ching-jui, Pai see Pai, Ching-jui

Ching-zue, Bai see Pai, Ching-jui

Chinn, Robert C. Panama Red 76

Chinoy, Firoze Bad aur Badnam 88

Chinquy, Gerry The Dumb Patrol 64; Hawaiian Aye Aye 64

Chiodo, Stephen Killer Klowns • Killer Klowns from Outer Space 88

Chisnell, Frank Jim the Penman 47; It Happened in Soho 48; Rover and Me 49; Slick Tartan 49

Chkeidze, Bidzina Gentlemen Adventurers • Gospoda Avantyuristy 87

Chkeidze, Revaz Dimitri Arakishvili 52*; Our Palace 53*; The Georgian State Dancing Company 54*; Lurdzha Magdany • Magdana's Donkey • Magdan's Donkey 55*; Nash Dvor • Our Courtyard 56; Maya from Tskhneti • Maya iz Tskhneti 60; The Treasure 61; A Sea Route 63; Father of a Soldier • Otets Soldata • A Soldier's Father 65; The Saplings 72

Chmielewski, Tadeusz Eve Wants to Sleep • Ewa Chce Spać 57; The Faithful River • Wierna Rzeka 87

Chobocky, Barbara A. Witch Hunt 87

Chodakowski, Andrzej Workers '80 82*

Choi, Clifford Hong Kong, Hong Kong 85

Choi-su, Park see Park, Choi-su

Chokheli, Goderdzi In Search of the Bride • Velikii Pokhod za Nevestoi 87

Chomette, Henri Jeux des Reflets et de la Vitesse 23; À Quoi Rêvent les Jeunes Filles 25; Cinq Minutes de Cinéma Pur 25; Le Chauffeur de Mademoiselle 27; Le Requin 30; Prenez Garde à la Peinture 33; Donogoo 36; Êtes-Vous Jalouse? 38

Chomón, Segundo de see De Chomón, Segundo

Chomón, Sogon de see De Chomón, Segundo

Chomsky, Marvin Evel Knievel 71; Live a Little, Steal a Lot • Murph the Surf • You Can't Steal Love 74; Mackintosh and T.J. 75; Good Luck, Miss Wyckoff • Secret Yearnings • The Shaming • The Sin 79; Tank 84

Chong see Chong, Thomas

Chong, Song see Song, Chong

Chong, Thomas Cheech & Chong's Next Movie • High Encounters of the Ultimate Kind • The Next Cheech & Chong Movie 80; Cheech & Chong's Nice Dreams • Nice Dreams 81; Cheech & Chong, Still Smokin' • Cheech & Chong's Still Smokin' • Still Smokin' 83; Cheech & Chong's The Corsican Brothers • The Corsican Brothers 84; Far Out Man 90

Chooluck, Leon Three Blondes in His Life 60

Chopra, Joyce A Happy Mother's Day • Happy Mother's Day Mrs. Fisher • Quint City, U.S.A. 63*; Martha Clarke, Light and Dark 81; Smooth Talk 85; The Lemon Sisters 89

Chopra, Vidhu Vinod Parinda 88

Chorlton, Michael Late at Night 46

Chorny, L. Conquest of the Caucasus 13*

Chotin, André E. Clandestine • Les Clandestins 48

Chou, See-loke The Female Prince 66

Chouikh, Mohamed Rupture 82; La Citadelle • El Kalaa 88

Chouinard, Ivan À l'Automne de la Vie 88

Chouraqui, Elie Mon Premier Amour • My First Love 78; Qu'Est-Ce Qui Fait Courir David? • What Makes David Run? 82; Love Songs • Paroles et Musique • Words and Music 84; Man on Fire 87

Choux, Jean Jean de la Lune 32; Mater-nité 37; La Boîte aux Rêves 43*

Chow, Peter Pickles Make Me Cry 88

Chowdhury, Anjan Bidrohi 87

Chowdhury, Pinaki Apan Gharey 87

Chrisander, Nils Olaf Fighting Love 27; The Heart Thief 27

Christenberry, Chris Little Cigars 73

Christensen, Benjamin Det Hemmelig-hedsfulde X • The Mysterious X 13; Blind Justice • Hævnens Nat • The Night of Revenge • Night of Vengeance 15; Häxan • Witchcraft Through the Ages 21; Among Jews • Unter Juden 22; His Mysterious Adventure • Seine Frau die Unbekannte 23; Die Frau mit dem Schlechten Ruf • The Woman Who Did 24; The Devil's Circus 25; The Mysterious Island 26*; Mockery 27; The Haunted House 28; The Hawk's Nest 28; The House of Horror 28; Seven Footprints to Satan 29; Children of Divorce • Skilsmissens Børn 39; Barnet • The Child 40; Come Home with Me • Gå med Mig Hjem • Return with Me 41; Damen med de Lyse Handsker • Damen med de Sorte Handsker • The Lady with the Colored Gloves • The Lady with the Light Gloves 42

Christensen, Bent South of Tana River 64*; The Only Way 70

Christensen, Carlos Hugo Maos Sangrentas Assassinos • The Violent and the Damned 62; Curse of the Stone Hand 65*; Enigma para Demonios 74

Christensen, Nils Reinhardt Line • The Passionate Demons 61

Christian, John Dawn Comes Late • Guerrilla Girl 53

Christian, Roger Black Angel 80; The Dollar Bottom 81; The Sender 82; Lorca and the Outlaws • Starship 85

Christian-Jaque Le Bidon d'Or 31; Achilles' Heel • Le Tendron d'Achille 32; Adhémar Lampiot 32*; Le Bœuf sur la Langue 33; Ça Colle 33; L'Hôtel du Libre-Échange 33*; La Montre 33; Atroce Menace 34; Compartiment des Dames Seules • Compartiment pour Dames Seules • Ladies Only 34; Le Père Lampion 34; Vilaine Histoire 34; La Famille Pont-Biquet 35; Sacré Léonce 35; La Sonnette d'Alarme 35; Sous la Griffe 35; Voyage d'Agrément 35; L'École des Journalistes 36; Francis the First • François Iᵉʳ 36; The House Across the Street • La Maison d'en Face 36; Josette 36; Mr. Nobody • Monsieur Personne 36; On Ne Roule Pas Antoinette 36; Rigolboche 36; Un de la Légion 36; À Venise, Une Nuit 37; Les Dégourdis de la Onzième 37; The Pearls of the Crown • Les Perles de la Couronne 37*; Les Pirates du Rail 37; Boys' School • Les Disparus de Saint-Agil • Runaways of St. Agil 38; C'Était Moi • Ernest le Rebelle 38; Le Grand Élan 38; Raphaël le Tatoué 38; L'Enfer des Anges 39; L'Assassinat du Père Noël • The Killing of Santa Claus • The Murder of Father Christmas • Who Killed Santa Claus? 40; Premier Bal 41; La Symphonie Fantastique 41; Carmen 42; Voyage Sans Espoir 43; The Bellman • The

Sorcerer • Sortilèges 44; Angel and Sinner • Boule de Suif 45; A Lover's Return • Un Revenant 46; La Certosa di Parma • La Chartreuse de Parme 47; D'Homme à Hommes • Man to Men 48; Barrières 49; Gypsy Fury • The Mask and the Sword • The Saga of Singoalla • Singoalla • The Wind Is My Lover 49; Lost Property • Souvenirs Perdus 49; Barbe-Bleue • Blaubart • Bluebeard 51; Fanfan la Tulipe • Fanfan the Tulip • Soldier in Love • Soldier of Love 51; Adorable Creatures • Adorables Créatures • Night Beauties 52; Daughters of Destiny • Destinées • Love, Soldiers and Women 52*; Lucrèce Borgia • Lucretia Borgia • Lucrezia Borgia • Sins of the Borgias 52; La DuBarry • Madame DuBarry 54; Nana 54; If All the Guys in the World... • Race for Life • Si Tous les Gars du Monde... 55; The Foxiest Girl in Paris • Nathalie • Nathalie Agent Secret 56; The Law Is the Law • La Loi...C'Est la Loi 57; Babette Goes to War • Babette S'en Va-t-en Guerre 59; La Française et l'Amour • Love and the Frenchwoman 60*; Madame • Madame Sans-Gêne 61; The Black Tulip • La Tulipe Noire 63; Les Bonnes Causes • Don't Tempt the Devil 63; Donne, Mitra e Diamanti • Le Gentleman de Cocody • Ivory Coast Adventure • Man from Cocody 64; L'Échiquier de Dieu • La Fabuleuse Aventure de Marco Polo • The Fabulous Adventures of Marco Polo • Marco le Magnifique • Marco Polo • Marco the Magnificent • Marko Polo • Le Meravigliose Avventure di Marco Polo 64*; Le Repas des Fauves 64; The Dirty Game • The Dirty War • La Guerra Segreta • La Guerre Secrète • The Secret Agents • The Secret War • Spione Unter Sich 65*; Le Saint • Le Saint Prend l'Affût • The Saint Versus... 66; La Seconde Vérité 66; Dead Run • Deux Billets pour Mexico • Geheimnisse in Golden Nylons • Qui Veut Tuer Carlos? • Segreti Che Scottano • Two Tickets to Mexico 67; Les Amours de Lady Hamilton • Emma Hamilton • Lady Hamilton • Lady Hamilton—Zwischen Schmach und Liebe • The Making of a Lady 68; The Legend of Frenchie King • The Oil Girls • The Petroleum Girls • Les Pétroleuses • Le Pistolère 71*; Docteur Justice • Dr. Justice 75; La Vie Parisienne 77; Carné: L'Homme à la Caméra 80

Christiansen, Benjamin see Christensen, Benjamin

Christianson, Benjamin see Christensen, Benjamin

Christie, Al All Aboard 15; Almost a King 15; Eddie's Little Love Affair 15; Little Egypt Malone 15; Love and a Savage 15; Mrs. Plum's Pudding 15*; Wanted: A Leading Lady 15; When the Mummy Cried for Help 15; Never Lie to Your Wife 16; Seminary Scandal 16; Wanted: A Husband 16; Five Little Widows 17; Who's Looney Now? 17; Out of the Night 20; The Reckless Sex 20; So Long, Letty 20; Wedding Blues 20; Kiss and Make Up 21; See My Lawyer 21; One Stormy Knight 22; That

Baba Bound 40; The Chewin' Bruin 40; Patient Porky 40; Pilgrim Porky 40; Porky's Last Stand 40; Porky's Poor Fish 40; Prehistoric Porky 40; Slap Happy Pappy 40; The Sour Puss 40; The Timid Toreador 40*; Wacky Wild Life 40*; The Cagey Canary 41*; A Coy Decoy 41; Crazy Cruise 41*; Farm Frolics 41; Goofy Groceries 41; The Henpecked Duck 41; Meet John Doughboy 41; Porky's Pooch 41; Porky's Snooze Reel 41*; Wabbit Twouble 41; We, the Animals Squeak 41; Any Bonds Today 42; Bugs Bunny Gets the Boid 42; Coal Black and de Sebben Dwarfs 42; Eatin' on the Cuff 42; The Hep Cat 42; Horton Hatches the Egg 42; Nutty News 42; A Tale of Two Kitties 42; The Wacky Blackout • Wacky Blackouts 42; The Wacky Wabbit 42; A Corny Concerto 43; Falling Hare 43; Fighting Tools 43; An Itch in Time 43; Tin Pan Alley Cats 43; Tortoise Wins by a Hare 43; The Wise Quacking Duck 43; Birdy and the Beast 44; Booby Traps 44; Buckaroo Bugs 44; Hare Ribbin' 44; The Old Grey Hare 44; Russian Rhapsody 44; Slightly Daffy 44; Tick Tock Tuckered 44; What's Cookin' Doc? 44; The Bashful Buzzard 45; Draftee Daffy 45; A Gruesome Twosome 45; Wagon Heels 45; Baby Bottleneck 46; Bacall to Arms 46; The Big Snooze 46; Book Revue 46; The Great Piggy Bank Robbery 46; Kitty Kornered 46; The Goofy Gophers 47*; It's a Grand Old Nag 47; Tweety Pie • Tweety Pie and Sylvester 47*

Clardy, George Boomer Bill's Awakening 17

Clare, Jack The Blind Boy 17*

Clarendon, Hal One Day 16; Alma, Where Do You Live? 17

Clarfield, Stuart Welcome to the Parade 86

Clark, B. D. see Clark, Bruce

Clark, Benjamin see Clark, Bob

Clark, Bob Fixation • The She-Man 67; Children Shouldn't Play with Dead Things 72; Dead of Night • Deathdream • The Night Andy Came Home • The Night Walk • The Veteran 72; Black Christmas • Silent Night, Evil Night • Stranger in the House 74; Breaking Point 76; Murder by Decree • Sherlock Holmes and Saucy Jack • Sherlock Holmes: Murder by Decree 78; Tribute 80; Porky's 81; A Christmas Story 83; Porky's II: The Next Day 83; Rhinestone 84; Turk 182! 85; From the Hip 87; Loose Cannons 89

Clark, Bruce Naked Angels 69; The Ski Bum 71; Hammer 72; Galaxy of Terror • Mindwarp: An Infinity of Terror • Planet of Horrors 81

Clark, Colbert Fighting with Kit Carson 33*; Mystery Squadron 33*; The Three Musketeers 33*; Whispering Shadows 33*; The Wolf Dog 33*; Burn 'Em Up Barnes 34*

Clark, David Rayner Film 79

Clark, Don The Fighting Guide 22*

Clark, Frank C. Beyond the Reef • Sea Killer • Shark Boy of Bora Bora 79

Clark, Frank Howard Wizard of the

Saddle 27; The Texas Tornado 28

Clark, Greydon The American Love Thing • Mothers, Fathers and Lovers • Tom 73; The Bad Bunch 76; Black Shampoo 76; Satan's Cheerleaders 77; The Hi-Riders 78; Angels' Brigade 79; The Alien's Return • The Return 80; It Came Without Warning • Without Warning 80; Wacko 81; Joysticks • Video Madness 82; Final Justice 85; The Uninvited 88; The Forbidden Dance 90; Skinheads—The Second Coming of Hate 90

Clark, James B. Under Fire 57; Sierra Baron 58; Villa! 58; A Dog of Flanders 59; The Sad Horse 59; One Foot in Hell 60; The Big Show 61; Misty 61; Drums of Africa 63; Flipper 63; Island of the Blue Dolphins 64; ...And Now Miguel 66; My Side of the Mountain 69; The Little Ark 72

Clark, Jesse Hell's Playground • Riot at Lauderdale 67

Clark, Jim The Christmas Tree 66; Day of Rest 70; Every Home Should Have One • Think Dirty 70*; Madhouse • The Revenge of Dr. Death 72; Rentadick 72*

Clark, Larry Passing Through 77

Clark, Les Sleeping Beauty 59*

Clark, Louise A Winter Tan 87*

Clark, Matt Da 88

Clark, Richard Dr. Hackenstein 88

Clark, Robin see Clark, Bob

Clark, Ron The Funny Farm 82

Clarke, Alan Scum 79; Billy the Kid and the Green Baize Vampire 85; Rita, Sue and Bob, Too! 86

Clarke, James Kenelm Got It Made • Sweet Virgin 73; Exposé • The House on Straw Hill • Trauma 75; Hardcore 77; Let's Get Laid 77; Funny Money 82; Going Undercover 84; Yellow Pages 85

Clarke, Robert Blood on His Lips • The Hideous Sun Demon • The Sun Demon • Terror from the Sun 59*

Clarke, Shirley A Dance in the Sun 53; In Paris Parks 54; Bullfight 55; A Moment in Love • A Moment of Love 57; Bridges-Go-Round 58; Brussels Film Loops • Brussels Loops • Loops 58*; Skyscraper 58*; The Connection 60; A Scary Time 60; The Cool World 63; Robert Frost: A Love Letter to the World • Robert Frost: A Lover's Quarrel with the World 63; Man in Polar Regions 67; Portrait of Jason 67; Initiation 78; Mysterium 79; Trans 79; Four Journeys Into Mystic Time 80; Savage/Love 81; Tongues 83; Ornette: Made in America 85

Clarkson, Stephen Death Goes to School 53

Clausen, Erik The Dark Side of the Moon • The Man in the Moon • Manden i Månen 86; Rami og Julie 88

Clausen, Richard Reflections from a Brass Bed 76

Clavel, Robert Une Histoire d'Amour • Love Story 51

Clavell, James Five Gates to Hell 59; Walk Like a Dragon 60; The Sweet and the Bitter 62; To Sir, with Love 66; Run, Rebel, Run • Where's Jack? 68; The Last

Valley 70

Claver, Bob Jaws of Satan • King Cobra 79

Claxton, William F. Half Past Midnight 48; Tucson 49; All That I Have 51; Fangs of the Wild • Follow the Hunter • Follow the Leader 54; Stagecoach to Fury 56; God Is My Partner 57; The Quiet Gun 57; Rockabilly Baby 57; Young and Dangerous 57; I'll Give My Life 59; Desire in the Dust 60; Young Jesse James 60; The Day of the Hanging • Invitation to a Hanging • Law of the Lawless 63; Stage to Thunder Rock • Stagecoach to Hell 64; Night of the Lepus 72

Clayton, Jack Naples Is a Battlefield 44; The Bespoke Overcoat 55; Room at the Top 58; The Innocents • Suspense 61; The Pumpkin Eater 64; Our Mother's House 67; The Great Gatsby 74; Something Wicked This Way Comes 82; The Lonely Passion of Judith Hearne 87

Clayton, John Redneck Miller 77; Summerdog 77

Cleese, John Away from It All 79*; The Secret Policeman's Ball 80*

Clegg, Tom Love Is a Splendid Illusion 70; Sweeney 2 78; McVicar 80; G'Ole! 83; The Inside Man 84; Any Man's Death 90

Clein, John Keep Punching 39

Clemens, Brian Captain Kronos, Vampire Hunter • Kronos • Vampire Castle 72

Clemens, William The Case of the Velvet Claws 36; Down the Stretch 36; Here Comes Carter • The Voice of Scandal 36; The Law in Her Hands 36; Man Hunt 36; The Case of the Stuttering Bishop 37; The Footloose Heiress 37; Missing Witness • Missing Witnesses 37; Once a Doctor 37; Studio Romance • Talent Scout 37; Accidents Will Happen 38; Mr. Chump 38; Nancy Drew, Detective 38*; Torchy Blane in Panama • Trouble in Panama 38; Dead End Kids at Military School • Dead End Kids on Dress Parade • Dress Parade • On Dress Parade 39*; Devil's Island 39; Nancy Drew and the Hidden Staircase 39; Nancy Drew—Reporter 39*; Nancy Drew—Troubleshooter 39; Calling Philo Vance 40; King of the Lumberjacks 40; Knockout 41; The Night of January 16th 41; She Couldn't Say No 41; Lady Bodyguard 42; A Night in New Orleans 42; Sweater Girl 42; The Falcon and the Co-Eds 43; The Falcon in Danger 43; Crime by Night 44; The Falcon Out West 44; The 13th Hour 47

Clement, Dick Otley 68; A Severed Head 70; Catch Me a Spy • Les Doigts Croisés • Keep Your Fingers Crossed • To Catch a Spy 71; Doing Time • Porridge 79; To Russia with Elton 79*; Bullshot 83; Water 84

Clément, Magali La Maison de Jeanne 88

Clément, Michel Danger in the Middle East 59

Clément, René César chez les Gaulois 31; Remember Your Left • Soigne Ton Gauche 36; Arabie Inconnue • L'Arabie Interdite • Forbidden Arabia 37; Paris la

Nuit 37; Flèche d'Argent 38; La Grande Chartreuse • The Great Chartreuse 38; La Bièvre • La Bièvre, Fille Perdue • La Bièvre, Lost Girl 39; Énergie Électrique 39; Histoire du Costume 39; The Draught • Le Tirage 40; Ceux du Rail • Those of the Railroad 42; Toulouse 42; Chefs de Demain • Leaders of Tomorrow 43; La Grande Pastorale • The Great Pastorale 43; Mountain 44; La Bataille du Rail • Battle of the Rails 45; Mr. Orchid • Le Père Tranquille • The Tranquil Father 46; The Damned • Les Maudits 47; Au-Delà des Grilles • Beyond the Gates • Le Mura di Malapaga • The Walls of Malapaga 49; Le Château de Verre • The Glass Castle 50; Forbidden Games • Les Jeux Interdits • The Secret Game • Secret Games 51; Knave of Hearts • Lover Boy • Lovers, Happy Lovers! • Monsieur Ripois • Monsieur Ripois et Son Nemesis 54; Gervaise 55; Barrage Contre le Pacifique • La Diga sul Pacifico • The Sea Wall • This Angry Age 57; In Pieno Sole • Lust for Evil • Lust of Evil • Plein Soleil • Purple Noon 59; Che Gioìa Vivere! • Quelle Joie de Vivre! • What Joie de Vivre! 61; The Day and the Hour • Il Giorno e l'Ora • Le Jour et l'Heure • Today We Live • Viviamo Oggi 62; The Cage • Les Félins • Joy House • The Love Cage 63; Is Paris Burning? • Paris Brûle-t-il? 65; Écrit sur le Sable • Written in the Sand 66; Le Passager de la Pluie • Rider on the Rain 69; The Deadly Trap • Death Scream • La Maison Sous les Arbres 71; And Hope to Die • La Course du Lièvre à Travers les Champs 72; La Baby-Sitter • Baby Sitter—Un Maledetto Pasticcio • The Babysitter • Wanted: Babysitter 75

Clements, John Call of the Blood 47*

Clements, Ron Basil the Great Mouse Detective • The Great Mouse Detective 86*; The Little Mermaid 89*

Clements, Roy Crown Jewels 18; When a Woman Strikes 19; King Spruce 20; The Tiger's Coat 20; The Double O 21; A Motion to Adjourn 21; Sparks of Flint 21; A Desert Bridegroom 22; The Desert's Crucible 22; The Marshal of Moneymint 22; Two-Fisted Jefferson 22; Tongues of Scandal 27; Wanted, a Coward 27

Cliff, Laddie The Co-Optimists 29*

Clifford, Bill Birthright 52

Clifford, Graeme Frances 82; Burke & Wills 85; Gleaming the Cube 88

Clifford, William H. The Golden Goose 14*; Love's Sacrifice 14*; Denny from Ireland 18*; The Man Alone 23; The Soul Harvest • Souls in Bondage 23; Missing Daughters 24; The Black Boomerang 25

Clift, Denison The Iron Heart 17*; Demos • Why Men Forget 20; The Last Straw 20*; What Would You Do? 20*; The Diamond Necklace 21; The Old Wives' Tale 21; Sonia 21; A Woman of No Importance 21; Bentley's Conscience 22; A Bill for Divorce 22; Diana of the Crossways 22; The Loves of Mary Queen of Scots 23; Out to Win 23; This Freedom 23; Flames of Desire 24; The Great Diamond Mystery 24; Honor Among Men 24; There's Millions in It 24; Ports of Call 25; Paradise 28; City of Play 29; High Seas 29; Taxi for Two 29*; The Mystery of the Marie Celeste • Mystery of the Mary Celeste • Phantom Ship • Secrets of the Marie Celeste 35

Clifton, Elmer The Artist's Wife 15; The Flame of Youth 17; Flirting with Death 17; Her Official Fathers 17*; The High Sign 17; High Speed 17*; The Man Trap 17; The Midnight Man 17; A Stormy Knight 17; Battling Jane 18; Brace Up 18; The Eagle 18; The Flash of Fate 18; The Guilt of Silence 18; The Hope Chest 18; Kiss or Kill 18; Smashing Through 18; The Two-Soul Woman 18; Winner Takes All 18; Boots 19; I'll Get Him Yet 19; Nobody Home • Out of Luck 19; Nugget Nell 19; Peppy Polly 19; Turning the Tables 19; Mary Ellen Comes to Town 20; Down to the Sea in Ships 22; Six Cylinder Love 23; Daughters of the Night 24; The Warrens of Virginia 24; The Truth About Men 26; Wives at Auction 26; The Wreck of the Hesperus 27; Beautiful But Dumb 28; Let 'Er Go Gallegher 28; Tropical Nights 28; Virgin Lips 28; The Devil's Apple Tree 29; Maid to Order 31; Dark Endeavour 33; Captured in Chinatown 35; Cyclone of the Saddle 35; Fighting Caballero 35; The Mystery of Diamond Island • Rip Roaring Riley 35; Pals of the Range 35; Rough Riding Ranger • The Secret Stranger 35; Skull and Crown 35; Custer's Last Stand 36; Gambling with Souls 36; Wildcat Trooper 36; Assassin of Youth 37; Crime Afloat 37; Crusade Against Rackets 37; Death in the Air • Death in the Sky 37; Mile-a-Minute Love 37; California Frontier 38; Jungle Island • Wolves of the Sea 38; Law of the Texan 38; Main Street Girl • Paroled from the Big House 38; The Secret of Treasure Island 38; The Stranger from Arizona 38; Ten Laps to Go 38; Crashin' Thru • Crashing Thru 39; Isle of Destiny 40; City of Missing Girls 41; Hard Guy • Professional Bride 41; I'll Sell My Life 41; Swamp Lady • Swamp Woman 41; Deep in the Heart of Texas 42; The Old Chisholm Trail 42; The Sundown Kid 42; The Blocked Trail 43; Boss of Rawhide 43; The Days of Old Cheyenne 43; Frontier Law 43; Return of the Rangers 43; Captain America 44*; Dead or Alive 44; Gangsters of the Frontier 44; Guns of the Law 44; The Pinto Bandit 44; Seven Doors to Death 44; Spook Town 44; Swing, Cowboy, Swing 44; The Whispering Skull 44; Marked for Murder 45; Youth Aflame 45; The Gamblers • The Judge 48; Not Wanted • Streets of Sin 49*; Red Rock Outlaw 50; The Silver Bandit 50

Clifton, Peter Popcorn 69; Superstars in Film Concert 71; The London Rock and Roll Show 73; The Song Remains the Same 76*; Sweet Soul Music 77; Rock City • Sound of the City: London 1964-1973 81

Cline, Edward F. Bubbles of Trouble 16; Her First Beau 16; His Bread and Butter 16; His Busted Trust 16; Sunshine 16; The Winning Punch 16; A Bedroom Blunder • Room 23 17; The Dog Catcher's Love 17; Her Nature Dance 17; The Pawnbroker's Heart 17; That Night 17; Villa of the Movies 17; Cupid's Day Off 18; Hide and Seek Detectives 18; His Smothered Love 18*; The Kitchen Lady 18; A Schoolhouse Scandal 18; The Summer Girls 18; Those Athletic Girls 18; Training for Husbands 18; Whose Little Wife Are You? 18; East Lynne with Variations 19; Hearts and Flowers 19; When Love Is Blind 19; Convict 13 20*; The High Sign 20*; Mary's Little Lobster 20; Monkey Business 20; Neighbors 20*; One Week 20*; The Scarecrow 20*; Sheriff Nell's Comeback 20; Ten Nights Without a Barroom 20; The Boat 21*; The Golfer 21*; Hard Luck 21*; The Haunted House 21*; His Meal Ticket 21; The Paleface 21*; The Playhouse 21*; Singer Midget's Scandal 21; Singer Midget's Side Show 21; Whose Who? 21; Cops 22*; Day Dreams 22*; The Electric House 22*; The Frozen North 22*; My Wife's Relations 22*; The Balloonatic • Balloonatics 23*; Circus Days 23; The Love Nest 23*; The Meanest Man in the World 23; Room 23 23; The Three Ages 23*; Along Came Ruth 24; Captain January 24; Galloping Bungalows 24; The Good Bad Boy 24; Little Robinson Crusoe 24; Off His Trolley 24; The Plumber 24; The Rag Man 24; When a Man's a Man 24; Bashful Jim 25; Beloved Bozo 25; Cold Turkey 25; Dangerous Curves Behind 25; Hotsy Totsy 25; Love and Kisses 25; Old Clothes 25; The Soapsuds Lady 25; A Sweet Pickle 25; Tee for Two 25; Alice Be Good 26; A Blonde's Revenge 26; Flirty Four-Flushers 26; The Ghost of Folly 26; Gooseland 26; The Gosh Darn Mortgage • That Gosh Darn Mortgage 26; A Harem Knight 26; A Love Sundae 26; Puppy Lovetime 26; Smith's Baby 26; Smith's Vacation 26; Spanking Breezes 26; When a Man's a Prince 26; The Bull Fighter • The Bullfighters 27; The Girl from Everywhere 27; Hold That Pose 27; The Jolly Jilter 27; Let It Rain 27; Soft Cushions 27; Broadway Fever 28; The Crash 28; The Head Man 28; Ladies' Night • Ladies' Night in a Turkish Bath 28; Love at First Flight • Love at First Sight 28; Vamping Venus 28; The Forward Pass 29; His Lucky Day 29; Conflict • Sweet Mama 30; Don't Bite Your Dentist 30; Hook, Line and Sinker 30; In the Next Room 30; Leathernecking • Present Arms 30; Take Your Medicine 30; The Widow from Chicago 30; Cracked Nuts 31; The Girl Habit 31; In Conference 31; Mlle. Irene the Great 31; The Naughty Flirt 31; No, No, Lady 31; Shove Off 31; The Door Knocker 32; His Week-End 32; Million Dollar Legs 32; The Mysterious Mystery 32; The Rookie 32; Detective Tom Howard of the Suicide Squad 33; Parole Girl 33; So This Is Africa 33; Uncle Jake 33; The Dude Ranch • The Dude Ranger 34;

de Riri 08; Affaires de Cœur • Affairs of the Heart 09; L'Agent de Poche • Pocket Policeman 09; The Ambassador's Despatch • La Bourse • La Valise Diplomatique 09; L'Armée d'Agenor • L'École du Soldat 09; The Automatic Monkey • Les Beaux-Arts de Jocko • Jocko the Artist 09; La Bataille d'Austerlitz • The Battle of Austerlitz 09; Les Chapeaux des Belles Dames 09; Les Chaussures Matrimoniales 09; Un Chirurgien Distrait 09; Clair de Lune Espagnol • The Man in the Moon • The Moon-Struck Matador 09; Un Coup de Jarnac • Jarnac's Treacherous Blow 09; Les Couronnes • Laurels 09; Le Docteur Carnaval 09; Don Quichotte • Don Quixote 09; L'Éventail Animé • Historical Fan • Magic Fan 09; Génération Spontanée • Les Générations Comiques • Magic Cartoons 09; Les Gricheux 09; A Japanese Fantasy • Japanese Magic • Japon de Fantaisie 09; Les Joyeaux Microbes • The Merry Microbes 09; La Lampe Qui File • The Smoking Lamp 09; Le Ligne Turbulent 09*; Les Locataires d'à Côté • Next Door Neighbors 09; La Lune dans Son Tablier • Moon for Your Love 09; Les Lunettes Féeriques • X-Ray Glasses 09; Magic Eggs • L'Omelette Fantastique 09; Moderne École 09*; Monsieur Clown chez les Lilliputiens 09; Porcelaines Tendres • Sevres Porcelain 09; Soyons Doncs Sportifs • A Sportive Puppet 09; Les Transfigurations 09; Le Baron de Crac • Monsieur de Crac • The Wonderful Adventures of Herr Münchhausen 10; The Beautiful Margaret • Le Tout Petit Faust 10; Les Beaux Arts Mystérieux 10; Le Binettoscope • The Comedy-Graph 10; Bonsoirs Russes 10; Brains Required • Le Retapeur de Cervelle 10; Cadres Fleuris • Floral Studies 10; Cafe Waiter's Dream • The Hasher's Delirium • Le Rêve du Garçon de Café • Le Songe d'un Garçon de Café 10; Les Chaînes 10; Le Champion du Jeu à la Mode • Solving the Puzzle 10; Les Chefs d'Œuvres de Bébé 10; Dix Siècles d'Élégance 10; Les Douze Travaux d'Hercule • Hercules and the Big Stick 10; En Route 10; L'Enfance de l'Art 10; The Four Little Tailors • Les Quatres Petits Tailleurs 10; Le Grand Machin et le Petit Chose 10; Headdresses of Different Periods • Histoire de Chapeaux 10; The Jolly Whirl • Singeries Humaines 10; Le Mobilier Fidèle 10; Monsieur Stop 10; La Musicomanie 10; Le Peintre Neo-Impressioniste 10; Le Petit Chanteclair 10; Le Placier Est Tenace 10; Rêves Enfantins 10; Rien N'Est Impossible à l'Homme 10; La Télécouture Sans Fil 10; Toto Devient Anarchiste 10; Les Aventures d'un Bout de Papier 11; Les Bestioles Artistes 11; La Boîte Diabolique 11; Les Fantaisies d'Agenor Maltrace 11; Jobard a Tue Sa Belle-Mère 11; Jobard Amoureux Timide 11; Jobard Change de Bonne 11; Jobard Chauffeur • Jobard Fiancé par Intérim 11; Jobard Est Demande en Mariage 11; Jobard Garçon de Recettes 11; Jobard Ne Peut Pas Rire 11; Jobard Ne Peut Pas Voir les Femmes Travailler 11; Jobard Portefaux par

Amour 11; Les Melons Baladeurs 11; Le Musée des Grotesques 11; Poudre de Vitesse 11; La Vengeance des Esprits 11; Les Allumettes Fantaisies • Les Allumettes Magiques 12; Campbell Soups 12; Cuisine Express 12; Dans la Vallée d'Ossau 12; Les Exploits de Feu-Follet 12; Les Extraordinaires Exercices de la Famille Cœur-de-Bois 12; Fruits et Légumes Vivants 12; L'Homme Sans Tête 12; Jeunes Gens a Marier 12; Les Jouets Animés • Les Joujoux Savants 12; Le Marié a Mal aux Dents 12; La Marseillaise 12; Les Métamorphoses Comiques 12; Moulai Hafid et Alphonse XIII 12; Une Poule Mouillée Qui Se Sèche 12; Poulot N'Est Pas Sage 12; Le Premier Jour de Vacances de Poulot 12; Le Prince de Galles et Fallières 12; Quelle Drôle de Blanchisserie 12; Ramoneur Malgré Lui 12; The Artist 13; The Auto 13; Aventures de Maltracé 13; The Brand of California 13; Bryant and the Speeches 13; Business Must Not Interfere 13; Castro in New York 13; Coal 13; Confidence 13; The Cubists 13; Exhibition of Caricatures 13; Gaynor and the Night Clubs 13; Graft 13; The Hat 13; He Does Not Care to Be Photographed 13; He Likes Things Upside Down 13; He Loves to Be Amused 13; He Loves to Watch the Flight of Time 13; He Poses for His Portrait • Snookums' Portrait 13; He Ruins His Family's Reputation 13; He Slept Well 13; He Wants What He Wants When He Wants It 13; He Was Not Ill, Only Unhappy 13; It Is Hard to Please Him, But It Is Worth It 13; The Masquerade 13; Milk 13; The Mosquito 13; Pickup Is a Sportsman 13; Poker 13; The Police Women 13; The Polo Boat 13; Poor Little Chap He Was Only Dreaming 13; The Red Balloons 13; Rockefeller 13; The Safety Pin 13; The Subway 13; Thaw and the Lasso 13; Thaw and the Spider 13; The Two Presidents 13; The Two Suffragettes 13; Uncle Sam and His Suit 13; Universal Trade Marks 13; War in Turkey 13; When He Wants a Dog He Wants a Dog 13; Wilson and the Broom 13; Wilson and the Hats 13; Wilson and the Tariffs 13; Wilson's Row Row 13; The Anti-Neurasthenic Trumpet • La Trompette Anti-Neurasthénique 14; L'Avenir Dévoile par les Lignes des Pieds • The Future Revealed by the Lines of the Feet 14; La Baignoire • The Bath 14; Bewitched Matches 14; Carte Américaine 14; Clara and Her Mysterious Toys 14; L'Enlèvement de Déjanire Goldebois 14; Exposition de Caricatures • Unforeseen Metamorphosis 14; The Greedy Neighbor • Le Voisin Trop Gourmand 14; He Never Objects to Noise • Il Aime le Bruit 14; He Only Wanted to Play with Dodo • Il Joue avec Dodo 14; His Ancestors • Ses Ancêtres 14; Le Ouistiti de Totò 14; Pick-Me-Up Est un Sportsman 14; Serbia's Card 14; The Social Group 14; Le Terrible Bout de Papier • The Terrible Scrap of Paper 14; A Vegetarian's Dream 14; What They Eat 14; La Blanchisserie Américaine 15; Les Braves Petits Soldats de Plomb 15; Un Drame sur la Planche a

Chaussures 15; Fantaisies Truquées 15; Fruits et Légumes Animés 15; Les Aventures de Clementine 16*; Les Aventures des Pieds-Nickelés 16*; La Campagne de France 16; Croquemitaine et Rosalie 16; Les Évasions de Bob Walter 16; Les Exploits de Farfadet 16; Fantoche Cherche un Logement • La Maison du Fantoche 16; Les Fiançailles de Flambeau 16*; Figures de Cire et Têtes de Bois 16; Flambeau au Pays des Surprises • Flambeau aux Lignes 16*; Flambeau, Chien Perdu • La Journée de Flambeau 16*; Jeux de Cartes 16; La Main Mystérieuse 16; Mariage par Suggestion 16; Pages d'Histoire 16; Pulchérie et Ses Meubles 16; Les Tableaux Futuristes et Incohérents 16; Les Victuailles de Gretchen Se Révoltant 16; L'Oreille 23; La Conquête d'Angleterre 35

Cohn, Bennett Fightin' Odds 25; Dangerous Traffic 26; The Grey Devil 26; Hi-Jacking Rustlers 26; Midnight Faces 26; Midnight Fires 26; A Ridin' Gent 26; Roaring Bill Atwood 26; West of the Rainbow's End 26; Code of the Range 27*; The Laffin' Fool 27; Where the North Holds Sway 27; Laddie Be Good 28; Law of the Rio Grande • Wanted Men 31*

Cohn, Bernard Natalia 88

Cohn, Jack Mussolini Speaks 33

Cohn-Bendit, Daniel East Wind • Le Vent d'Est • Vento dell'Est • Wind from the East 69*

Coiffart, René Black Smoke • Fumée Noir 20*

Coigne, Frank B. The Battle of Ballots 15

Coke, Cyril Pride and Prejudice 85

Cokliss, Harley Chicago Blues 72; The Battle of Billy's Pond 76; The Glitterball 77; That Summer 79; Battletruck • Warlords of the 21st Century 81; Black Moon Rising 86; Malone 87; The Dream Demon 88

Colas, Daniel Man Eaters 88

Colby, Vincent I Should Worry 15; Seven Cutey Pups 17

Colchart, Thomas see Coppola, Francis Ford

Cole, Adam Electric Blue, The Movie 81

Cole, Sidney Behind the Spanish Lines 38*; Spanish A.B.C. 38*; Roads Across Britain 39*; Train of Events 49*

Coleby, A. E. Day Duty 07; Don't Go to the Law 07; A Drink Cure 07; Even a Worm Will Turn 07; Fun in the Studio 07; His Only Pair of Trousers 07; May and December 07; Only a Limerick 07; Saved from the Burning Wreck 07; Serving a Summons 07; Billy Borntired 08; Brave Children, or The Little Thief Catchers 08; The Devil's Bargain 08; Diabolo Mad 08; Father Buys a Picture 08; A Fight for Honour 08; The Flies • Those Flies 08; For Baby's Sake 08; Freddy's Little Love Affair 08; The Freebooters 08; Grandfather's Birthday, or The Last Roll-Call 08; The Guardian of the Bank 08; High Game 08; His Wedding Morn 08; How Jones Got a New Suit 08; How the Artful Dodger

Secured a Meal 08; An Ingenious Revenge 08; An Interrupted Bath 08; Lord Algy's Beauty Show 08; Love's Strategy 08; March Winds 08; The Mission of a Flower 08; Mutiny in the Kitchen 08; The Phantom Ship 08*; Polly's Excursion 08; Professor Bounder's Pills 08; She Would Be Wed, or Leap Year Proposals 08; The Somnambulist's Crime 08; Tommy and the Sticktite 08; A Traitor to His King 08; 'Twixt Love and Duty, or A Woman's Heroism 08; The Village Blacksmith 08; Adopting a Baby 09; Bertie Buys a Bulldog 09; The Biter Bit 09; Boxing Fever 09; The Butcher's Boy and the Penny Dreadful 09; A Cold and Its Consequences 09; The Convict's Dream 09; Dancing Tabloids 09; Father Hold My Wool 09; Getting Father's Consent 09; How Potts Backed the Winner 09; Little Jim 09; A Man Housemaid 09; A Motherless Waif 09; My Word, If I Catch You Smoking 09; Nat's Conversion 09; The Receiver's Doom 09; The Robber's Ruse, or Foiled by Fido 09; Salome Mad 09; Saved by Carlo 09; A Seaside Episode 09; The Secretary's Crime 09; The Unfortunate Canvasser 09; When Jack Comes Home 09; When Jack Got His Pay 09; A Youthful Hero 09; Accompanied on the Tomtom 10; The Airtight Safe 10; Billy's Bulldog 10; Bumpkin's Patent Spyopticon 10; A Clown's Crime 10; Compromised by a Key 10; A Costly Gift 10; The Five Pound Note 10; Married for Love 10; A Modern Paul Pry 10; A Noble Outcast 10; Prison Reform 10*; Professor Piecan's Discovery 10; A Rake's Romance 10; Scroggins Puts Up for Blankshire 10; The Sculptor's Dream 10; Sleepy Sam's Awakening 10; The Squire's Romance 10; The Stolen Heir 10; Temptation and Forgiveness 10; The Terror and the Terrier 10; Too Many Admirers 10; Wanted, a Mummy 10; The Advantages of Hypnotism 11; The Adventures of PC Sharpe 11; Adventures of PC Sharpe—The Stolen Child 11; Aunt Tabitha's Visit 11; A Bag of Monkey Nuts • The Mad Monkey 11; The Brigand's Revenge 11; Brown Bewitched 11; A Case for Sherlock Holmes 11; Charley Smiler Is Stage Struck • Smiler Has Stage Fever 11; Constable Smith's Dream of Promotion 11; The Courtship of Miss Twiggles 11; Dippy's Plight • Mephisto's Plight 11; Dusty Dick's Awakening • Dusty Gets a Shock 11; Fate and the Woman 11; Father's Saturday Afternoon 11; Fool's Fancy • Scroggins Wins the Fiddle-Faddle Prize 11; Have It Out My Boy, Have It Out 11; How Mary Decided • The Result of a Picnic 11; How Puny Peter Became Strong 11; The Hunchback 11; Left in Trust • Saved by a Child 11; Little Red Riding Hood 11; Love and War 11; The Mighty Atom 11; Our Village Heroes 11; A Pair of Antique Vases 11; The Pirates of 19... • The Pirates of 1920 11*; Polly the Girl Scout 11; The Portrait • Zillah, A Gipsy Romance 11; The Resourceful Scout • A Scout's Strategy 11; Royal England—A Story of an Empire's Throne

11*; A Ruined Life 11; Scroggins Goes In for Chemistry and Discovers a Marvellous Powder 11; Scroggins Has His Fortune Told • Scroggins Visits a Palmist 11; Scroggins Plays Golf 11; She Dreamt of Onions 11; Signor Potti's Love Affair 11; Tatters, a Tale of the Slums 11; Topsy's Dream of Toyland 11; A Woman in the Case 11; Battling Kelly 12; Big Ben's Dream of Greatness 12; The Bloomsbury Burglars 12; Bob the Coster's Pony 12; Bobby's Letter 12; A Brute's Revenge 12; Compulsory Insurance 12; Constable Smith in Trouble Again 12; Coster Bill 12; Dr. Russell's Lie 12; From Country to Town 12; Her Sister's Silence 12; His Burglar Brother 12; His Secret Sin 12; His Wife's Brother 12; The Little Mother 12; The Lonely Inn 12; The Mummy 12; The Old Colonel's Gratitude 12; The Orphan 12; Out of His Element 12; A Pair of Trousers 12; Peg Woffington 12; Peggie and the Roundheads 12; Soppy Green Loses a Legacy 12; A Telephone Tangle 12; To Their Mutual Benefit 12; A Vapour Bath 12; What Happened to Mary 12; While the Cook Slept 12; The Widow's Legacy 12; A Case of Arson 13; A Dream of Glory 13; The False Clue 13; The Fate of a King 13; The Grip 13; Mary the Flower Girl 13; A Master of Men 13; The Opal Stealers 13; The Ghurka's Revenge 14; And Then He Woke Up 15; The Blackmailers 15; The Cobbler • The Fighting Cobbler 15; The Lure of Drink 15; The Mysteries of London 15; Satan's Amazon 15; The Under-Secretary's Honour 15; Chains of Bondage 16; Kent the Fighting Man 16; The Stolen Bride 16; The Treasure of Heaven 16; The Wheel of Death 16; For All Eternity 17*; Holy Orders 17*; A Just Deception 17; A Pit-boy's Romance 17*; A Strong Man's Weakness • The Will of the People 17; The Third Witness 17; The Village Blacksmith 17*; The Great Game 18; Matt 18; The Secret Woman 18; Thelma 18*; World Power or Downfall 18; I Hear You Calling Me 19; The Silver Lining 19; The Call of the Road 20; The Hour of Trial 20; The Pride of the North 20; The Way of the World 20; Children of Courage • Froggy's Little Brother 21; The Fifth Form at St. Dominics 21; The Right to Live 21; Long Odds 22; The Peacemaker 22; Aaron's Rod 23; The Call of Siva 23; The Clue of the Pigtail 23; The Cry of the Nighthawk 23; The Fiery Hand 23; The Flying Fifty-Five 23; The Fungi Cellars 23; Harlequinade 23; The Knocking on the Door 23; The Man with the Limp 23; The Miracle 23; The Prodigal Son • The Return of the Prodigal 23; The Queen of Hearts 23; The Rest Cure 23; The Sacred Order 23; The Scented Envelopes 23; The Shrine of the Seven Lamps 23; The Silver Buddha 23; The West Case 23; The Great Prince Shan 24; The Prehistoric Man 24; Sen Yan's Devotion 24; The Clue of the Oak Leaf 26; The Copper Cylinder 26; The Curse of Ravenscroft 26; Fake Spiritualism

Exposed • Spiritualism Exposed 26; The Locked Door 26; The Moon Diamond 26; The River House Mystery 26; Il Trovatore 27; Over the Sticks 29*; Unto Each Other 29

Coleman, C. C., Jr. Voice in the Night 34; Code of the Range 36; Dodge City Trail 36; Legion of Terror 36; The Circus Shadow • The Shadow 37; Criminals of the Air 37; A Fight to the Finish 37; Hard to Handle • Paid to Dance 37; Parole Racket 37; Flight to Fame 38; Highway Patrol 38; Homicide Bureau 38; Squadron of Honor 38; When G-Men Step In 38; Missing Daughters 39; My Son Is a Criminal 39; On Guard • Outpost of the Mounties 39; Spoilers of the Range 39

Coleman, Charles C., Jr. see Coleman, C. C., Jr.

Coleman, Herbert The Battle at Bloody Beach • Battle on the Beach 61; Posse from Hell 61

Coles, John David One for Sorrow, Two for Joy • Signs of Life 89

Coletti, Duilio Pierpin la Figlia Ritrovata 36; The Earth Cries Out • Il Grido della Terra 49; Lure of the Sila • Il Luro della Sila 49; Merchant of Slaves 49; Bullet for Stefano • Il Passatore 50; Heart and Soul 50; Miss Italy 52; La Grande Speranza • The Great Hope 54; Hell Raiders of the Deep 54; The House of Intrigue • Londra Chiama Polo Nord 59; Under Ten Flags 60*

Colgecen, Nesli Züğürt Ağa 86

Colizzi, Giuseppe Blood River • Dio Perdona...Io No! • God Forgives, I Don't • Tú Perdonas...Yo No 67; Ace High • I Quattro dell'Ave Maria • Revenge at El Paso • Revenge in El Paso 68; Boot Hill • La Collina degli Stivali 69; All the Way, Boys 73

Coll, Julio Fuego • Man Without a Face • Pyro • Pyro—Man Without a Face • Pyro—The Thing Without a Face • A Thing Without a Face 64; The Narco Men • Persecución Hasta Valencia • The Persecution of Hasta Valencia • Il Sapore della Vendetta 68

Colla, Richard A. False Witness • Zig-zag 70; Never Give an Inch • Sometimes a Great Notion 71*; Fuzz 72; Battlestar Galactica 78; The Great Balloon Adventure • Olly, Olly, Oxen Free 78

Collachia, Jeanne Odd Birds 85

Colle, Ugo del see Del Colle, Ugo

Collector, Robert Red Heat 84; Nightflyers 87

Colleran, Bill Windjammer 58*; Hamlet 64*

Colli, Ferrán Llagostera i see Llagostera i Colli, Ferrán

Colli, Marco Giovanni Senzapensieri • Thoughtless Giovanni 86

Collier, James F. For Pete's Sake! 66; His Land 67; Two a Penny 67; Catch a Pebble 71; Time to Run 72; The Hiding Place 75; Joni 80; The Prodigal 84; Cry from the Mountain 86; Caught 87

Collier, William Up the River 30*; Pilgrimage 33*

Collin, Fabien Love Play • Playtime • La Récréation 61*

Collings, Esme The Broken Melody 1896

Collins, Alf American Knockabouts 02; Baker and Boy 02; Boudoir Secrets 02; Clown, Pantaloon and Bobby 02; The Dead Cat 02; A Policeman's Dream 02; The Professor and the Butterfly 02; A Resourceful Dentist 02; Serpentine Dancer 02; Trained Dogs 02; The Tramp's Surprise 02; The Christmas Waifs, or High Life Below Stairs 03; Dotheboys Hall • Dotheboys Hall, or Nicholas Nickleby 03; The Double-Bedded Room 03; The Effects of Too Much Scotch 03; The Inspector's Birthday 03; King of Coins 03; Little Nell and Burglar Bill 03; A Lover's Troubles 03; Marriage by Motor • The Runaway Match 03; The Marvellous Syringe 03; Mind the Wet Paint 03; Murphy's Wake 03; The Mysterious Mechanical Toy • Phroso the Mysterious Mechanical Doll 03; Notice to Quit 03; Our New Cook 03; Papa's Bath 03; A Photographic Episode 03; The Pickpocket • The Pickpocket—A Chase Through London 03; A Pleasant Breakfast 03; A Political Discussion 03; Rip Van Winkle 03; The Rivals 03; A Row in a Laundry 03; The Sleepwalker • The Somnambulist 03; The Sportive Navvies 03; A Substantial Ghost 03; Such Is Life, or Mind Your Own Business 03; That Naughty Girl 03; Tommy Atkins' Dream 03; Two Little Vagabonds, or The Pugilistic Parson 03; Welshed, A Derby Day Incident 03; An Affair of Honour 04; All Through the Page Boy 04; The Amorous Militiaman 04; The Apple Woman 04; Artist and Musician 04; Bed and Breakfast Two Shillings 04; Behind the Scenes • Behind the Scenes, or Algy's Mishap 04; Bill Bailey's Return 04; Brown's Pudding • When Father Makes a Pudding 04; Chased by Dogs 04; Cook's Lovers 04; The Coster's Wedding 04; A Day at Brighton 04; Dr. Cut'emup 04; The Electric Shock 04; The Eviction 04; The Fatal Wig 04; Father's Birthday Party 04; Fixing the Swing 04; The Fruits of Matrimony 04; Future Hackenschmidts 04; Hands Up, or Captured by Highwaymen 04; The Haunted Houseboat 04; Jack's Rival 04; The Jealous Wife 04; The Lost Shuttlecock 04; Lovers on the Sands • A Stroll on the Sands 04; The Masher's Dilemma 04; Military Tactics 04; Mr. Mosenstein 04; Mixed Bathing 04; My Mother-in-Law 04; Night Duty 04; No Room for Father 04; The Office Boy's Revenge 04; On Brighton Pier 04; Raid on a Coiner's Den 04; Rejected by Pa 04; Revenge 04; The Silver Tenor, or The Song That Failed 04; A Smart Capture 04; Stewed Missionary 04; The Sweep 04; That Busy Bee 04; The Tramp's Toilet 04; Two Deceived Old Maids 04; The Alien Question 05; An Artful Dodge 05; As Sparrows See Us 05; Auntie's Cycling Lesson 05; The Awkward Horseman 05; The Birthday Umbrella • The Unlucky Umbrella 05; The Blind Man's Child 05; The Bobby's Night-

mare 05; The Burglar • The Burglar, or The Hue and Cry 05; The Burglar Lover 05; The Coster's Christening 05; Darling Puggy 05; A Day with the Fresh Air Fiend 05; The Electric Goose 05; Eyes Right 05; A False Alarm, or The Masher's Ducking 05; Father in the Kitchen 05; Father Makes Love to the Pump 05; The Gardener's Nap 05; The Gentleman Beggar 05; The Gipsy Fortune Teller 05; Grandpa and the Butterfly 05; Greedy Billy 05; The Henpecked Hindoo 05; How Brown Brought Home the Goose 05; How the Poor Help the Poor 05; Jack's Return 05; Keiro's Cat • Pussy's Breakfast 05; A Macaroni Feast 05; Married Bliss 05; The Milkmaid 05; Mixed Bathing at Home 05; The Motor Competition 05; A Motor Masquerade 05; A Motorbike Adventure 05; Mutiny on a Russian Battleship • Potemkin 05; The New Woman 05; Nobbler's Card Party 05; The Peashooter, or A New Weapon for the Army 05; A Raid on a Canteen 05; The Record Sneeze 05; Robbery with Violence 05; Santa Claus' Mistake 05; The Scent Spray 05; Stump Speech 05; The Tale of a Coat 05; The Terror of the House 05; That Awful Baby 05; The Three Tramps 05; Tommy's Experiments in Photography 05; The Ups and Downs of Murphy 05; W. Weary and T. Tired 05; When Extremes Meet 05; Who's That A-Calling? 05; Why the Lodger Left 05; Wig and Buttons 05; The Young Ladies' Dormitory 05; All's Well That Ends Well 06; The Catch of the Season 06; The Convict's Daughter 06; Curfew Shall Not Ring Tonight 06; Dinner Hour 06; Dolly Varden 06; Flypaper 06; The Four Hooligans 06; The Henpecked Husband 06; Her Morning Dip 06; Hot Pie 06; In Our Alley 06; It's a Have 06; Jam Now in Season 06; Jane on the Warpath 06; A Lodging House Comedy 06; Lost, a Leg of Mutton • The Lost Leg of Mutton 06; The Missing Legacy, or The Story of a Brown Hat 06; My Wife's a Teetotaler 06; Nosey Parker 06; Not Detained at the Office 06; The Postman's Christmas Box 06; The Puzzle Maniac 06; Rescued by Lifeboat 06; A Sailor's Courtship 06; Saved by a Pillar Box 06; This Side Up 06; The Two Orphans 06; The Two Tomboys 06; Uncle George's Trip to London 06; The Undergraduates 06; Wanted, a Husband 06; When Cripples Meet 06; Willie and Tim Get a Surprise 06; The Adventures of a Roll of Lino • Father Buys Some Linoleum 07; All for Nothing 07; The Bachelor's Piece of Wedding Cake 07; Catch the Kid 07; Cheap Beer 07; The Drunken Motorcyclist 07; Father Buys a Lawn Roller 07; The Ice Cream Jack 07; Ju-Jitsu 07; Oh That Cat! 07; Remember Remember the Fifth of November 07; A Shilling Short of His Wages 07; Short-Sighted Jane 07; This Little Girl and That Little Girl 07; Tommy the Tinpot Hero 07; Black-Eyed Susan 08; The Burglar's Joke with the Automatic Doll 08; A Christmas Raffle • Father Wins

a Turkey 08; The Convict and the Dove 08; The Dancing Girl 08; The Drunkard's Dream 08; Harry Lauder in a Hurry 08; Honours Even 08; The Mechanical Legs 08; Moving In 08; Napoleon and the English Sailor 08; Only a Penny a Box 08; Put Pa Amongst the Girls 08; A Race for a Rose 08; The Sloshton Quartette 08; A Stitch in Time 08; Sweet Liberty 08; Tommy and the Policeman's Whistle 08; Washing Day 08; The Woman Who Wasn't 08; The Boxing Waiter 09; The Four Tomboys 09; From Servant Girl to Duchess 09; Quicksilver Pudding 09; Algy Goes on the Stage 10; Algy Tries for Physical Culture • Algy Tries Physical Culture 10; The Coster's Phantom Fortune 10; Father Minds the Baby 10; The Sleep Breakers 10; The Traveling Stiltwalkers 10; Wait and See 10; Winning a Widow 10; Algy's Expensive Stick 12; A Maid of the Alps 12

Collins, Arthur Greville A Modern Hero 34*; Personal Maid's Secret 35; The Widow from Monte Carlo 35; Nobody's Fool 36; Thank You, Jeeves • Thank You, Mr. Jeeves 36; Paradise Isle • Siren of the South Seas 37; Saleslady 38; Little Australians 40

Collins, Boon Sally Fieldgood & Co. 75; Abducted 86

Collins, Edward God Bless Dr. Shagetz 77*; Evil Town 87*

Collins, Edwin J. Against the Tide 12; The Bandit's Daughter 12; Blackmail 12; Brown's Day Off 12; Caught in His Own Net 12; Cold Steel 12; Constable Smith and the Magic Baton 12; Constable Smith in Command 12; Constable Smith on the Warpath 12; A Country Lass 12; The Dancing Girl 12; Economical Peter 12; The Farmer's Daughter 12; The Harvest of Sin 12; The Hearts of Men 12; Her Brother's Tutor 12; Jones' Mistake 12; A Man's Shadow 12; The Masked Smuggler 12; Nan in Fairyland 12; Not Such a Fool 12; Oh What a Peach! 12; Out of the Past 12; The Patched Coat 12; Peter's Rival 12; Pursued by Priscilla 12; The Sixth Commandment 12; The Stolen Violin 12; The Thief 12; Turning the Tables 12; The Vengeance of Daniel Whidden 12; What Matter the Price 12; The Adventures of a Bad Shilling 13; Algy and the Pierrette 13; All's Well That Ends Well 13; A Brigand's Wooing 13; A Broken Life 13; Daydreams 13; The Diamond Star 13; Express Delivery 13; A Fishergirl's Love 13; A Fishy Story 13; For Her Mother's Sake • A Typist's Love Affair 13; From the Depths 13; Good for the Gout 13; The Harlequinade • Here We Are Again 13; He Attended the Meeting 13; The Headman's Vengeance 13; The Heart of a Gypsy Maid 13; His Wonderful Lamp 13; Hitchy-Koo 13; How Cecil Played the Game 13; In the Smuggler's Grip 13; An Island Romance 13; The Jailbird 13; Land and Sea 13; Money for Nothing 13; Nabbem Joins the Force 13; A Newsboy's Christmas Dream 13; Oh! My Aunt 13; P.C. Nabbem and the Anarchists

51*; Architecture et Lumière 53*; Barrage du Chatelot 53; Materiaux Nouveaux, Demeures Nouvelles 56; Une Aussi Longue Absence • L'Inverno Ti Fara Tornare • The Long Absence 61; Codine 62; Mona, l'Étoile Sans Nom • Pour une Étoile Sans Nom 66; Beethoven Third Symphony, Eroica • Symphony Nr 3 in Es-Dur, Opus 55: Eroica von Ludwig van Beethoven 67; Heureux Qui Comme Ulysse 69; L'Île Mystérieuse • L'Isola Misteriosa e il Capitano Nemo • The Mysterious Island • The Mysterious Island of Captain Nemo 72*

Colson-Malleville, M. A. Des Rails Sous les Palmiers 51*

Colucci, Mario Something Creeping in the Dark 72

Coluche Vous N'Aurez Pas l'Alsace et la Lorraine 77

Coluche, Michel see Coluche

Columbus, Chris Adventures in Babysitting 87; Heartbreak Hotel 88; Home Alone 90

Colwell, James The Great Alone 22*

Combret, Georges Raspoutine 54; Marie des Îles • Marie of the Isles 60; Frustrations • Hot Frustrations • La Traite des Blanches • La Tratta delle Bianche 67

Comencini, Cristina Zoo 88

Comencini, Francesca La Lumière du Lac 88

Comencini, Luigi La Novelletta 37; Bambini in Città 46; Guaglio • Proibito Rubare 48; Il Museo dei Sogni 48; L'Ospedale del Delitto 48; L'Imperatore di Capri 49; Behind Closed Shutters • Persiane Chiuse 50; Girls Marked Danger • La Tratta delle Bianche • White Slave Trade 52; Heidi • Son Tornata per Te 52; Bread, Love and Dreams • Pane, Amore e Fantasia 53; La Valigia dei Sogni 53; Bread, Love and Jealousy • Frisky • Pane, Amore e Gelosia 54; La Bella di Roma • Roman Signorina 55; La Finestra sul Luna Park 56; Mariti in Città 57; Mogli Pericolose 58; Le Sorprese dell'Amore 59; Und Das am Montagmorgen 59; Everybody Go Home! • La Grande Pagaille • Tutti a Casa 60; A Cavallo della Tigre • Jailbreak • On the Tiger's Back 61; Il Commissario 62; Bebo's Girl • La Ragazza di Bube 63; Bambole! • Le Bambole • The Dolls • Four Kinds of Love 64*; Il Compagno Don Camillo 64; La Mia Signora 64*; Three Nights of Love • Tre Notti d'Amore 64*; La Bugiarda • Le Partage de Catherine, la Bugiarda, la Mentirosa • Six Days a Week 65; Incompreso • Misunderstood • Vita Col Figlio 66; Italian Secret Service 67; Casanova • Infanzia, Vocazione e Prima Esperienze di Giacomo Casanova—Veneziano 69; Senza Sapere Niente di Lei • Senza Sapere Nulla di Lei 69; Le Avventure di Pinocchio 71; Il Frigorifero 71*; The Scientific Cardplayer • Lo Scopone Scientifico 72; Delitto d'Amore 74; Dio Mio, Come Sono Caduta in Basso • How Low Can You Fall? • Till Marriage Do Us Part 74; La Donna della Domenica • The Sunday Woman 75; Basta Che Non Si Sappia in Giro! 76*; La Goduria 76*;

Goodnight, Ladies and Gentlemen • Signore e Signori, Buonanotte 76*; Quelle Strane Occasioni 76*; Il Gatto 77; Tra Moglie e Marito 77; Bottleneck • Le Grand Embouteillage • L'Ingorgo • L'Ingorgo, una Storia Impossibile • Traffic Jam 79; Voltati Eugenio 79; They All Loved Him 80; Cercasi Gesù 82; Il Matrimonio di Caterina 82; Till Marriage Do Us Part 82; Cuore 84; History • La Storia • The Story 86; La Bohème 87; A Boy from Calabria • Un Ragazzo di Calabria 87; Buon Natale, Buon Anno 89

Comerford, Joe Traveller 81; Rough Touch 86; Reefer and the Model 88

Comfort, Lance Sandy Steps Out 38; Judy Buys a Horse 39; The Courageous Mr. Penn • Penn of Pennsylvania 41; Hatter's Castle 41; Those Kids from Town 41; Squadron Leader X 42; When We Are Married 42; Escape to Danger 43*; Old Mother Riley, Detective 43; Hotel Reserve 44*; Great Day 45; Bedelia 46; Temptation Harbour 46; Daughter of Darkness 47; Silent Dust 49; Portrait of Clare 50; The Genie 53*; Girl on the Pier 53; Bang! You're Dead • Game of Danger 54; Eight O'Clock Walk 54; The Last Moment 54; Face in the Night • Menace in the Night 56; The Man in the Road 56; At the Stroke of Nine 57; The Man from Tangier • Thunder Over Tangier 57; Look Before You Laugh • Make Mine a Million 59; The Ugly Duckling 59; The Breaking Point • The Great Armored Car Swindle 60; Murder Can Be Deadly • The Painted Smile 61; Pit of Darkness 61; Rag Doll • Young, Willing and Eager 61; The Break 62; Tomorrow at Ten 62; Touch of Death 62; Blind Corner • Man in the Dark 63; Live It Up • Sing and Swing 63; Devils of Darkness 64; Be My Guest 65

Comin, Jacopo La Rivale dell'Imperatrice 49*

Cominetti, Edino The Gold Route • La Via de Oro 32

Commons, David The Angry Breed 69

Como, Don Unknown Powers 79

Companeez, Jacques Crossroads of Passion 51

Companeez, Nina Faustine and the Beautiful Summer • Faustine et le Bel Été 71; Colinot Trousse Chemise 73; Comme sur des Roulettes 77

Compton, J. C. Buckeye and Blue 88

Compton, Juleen Stranded 65; The Plastic Dome of Norma Jean 66

Compton, Richard Gun Runner • The Gunrunners 69; Angels Die Hard • The Violent Angels 70; Five Days Home • Welcome Home Soldier Boys 72; Macon County Line 74; Return to Macon County 75; Assault on Paradise • Maniac • Ransom • The Town That Cried Terror 77; The Ravagers 79

Compton, Spencer Angels 76

Concari, Attilio 45th Parallel • 45mo Parallelo 86

Concini, Ennio de see De Concini, Ennio

Conde, José Antonio Nieves see Nieves Conde, José Antonio

Condon, William Sister, Sister 87

Confortes, Claude Vive les Femmes! 85; Paulette 86

Coninx, Stijn Hector 87

Conklin, Gary Paul Bowles in Morocco 70

Connell, Barbara A Time for Burning 66*

Connell, Thelma A Tale of Three Women 54*

Connell, W. Merle Trouble at Melody Mesa 49; The Devil's Sleep 51; Untamed Women 52; The Flesh Merchant 56

Connelly, Marc The Green Pastures 36*

Conner, Bruce A Movie 58; Cosmic Ray 61; Leader 64; Report 65; Ten Second Film 65; Vivian 65; Breakaway 66; Liberty Crown 67; Looking for Mushrooms 67; The White Rose 67; Permian Strata 69; Marilyn Times Five 73; Crossroads 76; Take the 5:10 to Dreamland 76; Valse Triste 77; Mongoloid 78; America Is Waiting 81

Connery, Sean The Bowler and the Bonnet 69

Connolly, Bobby The Devil's Saddle Legion 37; Expensive Husbands 37; The Patient in Room 18 38*

Connor, Edward Anne of Little Smoky 21

Connor, Kevin The Creatures • The Creatures from Beyond the Grave • From Beyond the Grave • Tales from Beyond the Grave • Tales from the Beyond • The Undead 73; The Land That Time Forgot 74; At the Earth's Core 76; Choice of Arms • A Choice of Weapons • Dirty Knights' Work • Trial by Combat 76; The People That Time Forgot • Seven Cities to Atlantis • Warlords of Atlantis 78; Arabian Adventure 79; Motel Hell 80; The House Where Evil Dwells 82

Connor, Lee Slick and Tricky • Slinky the Yegg 16

Conrad, Jack Country Blue 75

Conrad, Mikel The Flying Saucer 50

Conrad, Patrick Mascara 87

Conrad, Randall The Dozens 81*

Conrad, Robert The Bandits 67*

Conrad, William The Man from Galveston 63; Two on a Guillotine 64; Brainstorm 65; My Blood Runs Cold 65

Considine, John W., Jr. Disorderly Conduct 32

Constantinescu, Mihai Un Oaspete la Cină 86

Contat, Michel Sartre par Lui-Même 72*

Conte, Richard Operation Cross Eagles • Unakrsna Vatra 69

Conte, Therese Chasing Dreams 81*

Contreras, Miguel Torres see Torres Contreras, Miguel

Contreras Torres, Miguel see Torres Contreras, Miguel

Convy, Bert Weekend Warriors 86

Conway, Gary The Fire in the Stone 83

Conway, Jack The Old Armchair 12; Snowball and His Pal 12; Captain McLean 14; Captain Macklin 15*; The Mystic Jewel

15; The Penitentes 15; The Price of Power 15; The Way of a Mother 15; The Beckoning Trail 16; Bitter Sweet 16; Judgment of the Guilty 16; The Mainspring 16; Mary, Keep Your Feet Still 16; The Measure of a Man 16; The Silent Battle 16; The Social Buccaneer 16; Because of a Woman • Because of the Woman 17; Bond of Fear 17; The Charmer 17; Come Through 17; Her Soul's Inspiration 17; A Jewel in Pawn 17; Little Mary Fix-It 17; The Little Orphan 17; Polly Redhead 17; Desert Law 18; Desert of Wheat • Riders of the Dawn 18; Diplomatic Mission 18; Her Decision 18; Little Red Decides 18; A Long Chance 18; Royal Democrat 18; You Can't Believe Everything 18; Lombardi Ltd. 19; Restless Souls 19*; The Dwelling Place of Light 20; The Lure of the Orient 20; The Money Changers 20; Servant in the House 20; The U.P. Trail 20; A Daughter of the Law 21; The Killer 21*; The Kiss 21; The Millionaire 21; The Rage of Paris 21; The Respondent • The Spenders 21; Across the Deadline 22; Another Man's Shoes 22; Don't Shoot! 22; The Long Chance 22; Step on It! 22; Flaming Passion • Lucretia Lombard 23; The Prisoner 23; Quicksands 23; Sawdust 23; Trimmed in Scarlet 23; What Wives Want 23; The Heart Buster 24; The Roughneck • Thorns of Passion 24; The Trouble Shooter 24; The Hunted Woman 25; The Only Thing 25; Soul Mates 25; Brown of Harvard 26; The Understanding Heart 26; Twelve Miles Out 27; Alias Jimmy Valentine • Jimmy Valentine 28; Bringing Up Father 28; Our Modern Maidens 28; The Smart Set 28; While the City Sleeps 28; They Learned About Women 29*; Untamed 29; New Moon 30; The Unholy Three 30; The Dancing Partner • Just a Gigolo 31; Daughter of Luxury • Five and Ten 31*; The Easiest Way 31; Arsène Lupin 32; But the Flesh Is Weak 32; Red-Headed Woman 32; Accidents Wanted • Ambulance Chaser • The Chaser • Never Give a Sucker a Break • The Nuisance 33; Hell Below 33; The Solitaire Man 33; Born to Be Kissed • Eadie Was a Lady • The Girl from Missouri • 100% Pure 34; The Gay Bride 34; Tarzan and His Mate 34*; Viva Villa! 34*; One New York Night • The Trunk Mystery 35; A Tale of Two Cities 35*; Libeled Lady 36; Saratoga 37; A Yank at Oxford 37; Too Hot to Handle 38; Lady of the Tropics 39; Let Freedom Ring 39; Northwest Passage • Northwest Passage, Book One: Rogers' Rangers • Northwest Passage, Part One: Rogers' Rangers 39*; Boom Town 40; Honky Tonk 41; Love Crazy 41; Crossroads • The Man Who Lost His Way 42; Assignment in Brittany 43; Dragon Seed 43*; Desire Me 47*; High Barbaree 47; The Hucksters 47; Julia Misbehaves 48

Conway, James L. In Search of Noah's Ark 76; The Lincoln Conspiracy 77; Beyond and Back 78; The Fall of the House of Usher 79; Hangar 18 • Invasion Force 80; The Boogens 81; Earthbound 81; The President Must Die 81

Conway, Kevin The Sun and the Moon • The Violins Came with the Americans 86

Conyers, D'Arcy The Secret of the Forest 55; The Devil's Pass 57; Soapbox Derby 58; Make Mine a Double • The Night We Dropped a Clanger 59; The Night We Got the Bird 60; In the Doghouse • Vet in the Doghouse 61; Nothing Barred 61

Coogan, George Escape from Terror 60*
Coogan, Jackie Escape from Terror 60*
Coogan, Rif The Invisible Maniac 90
Cook, Ad Western Grit 24
Cook, Bruce The Census Taker 84; Nightwish 89
Cook, Clyde Strictly in Confidence 33; Trouble in Store 34
Cook, Fielder Patterns • Patterns of Power 56; Home Is the Hero 59; Big Deal at Dodge City • A Big Hand for the Little Lady 66; Band of Gold • How to Save a Marriage…and Ruin Your Life 67; Prudence and the Pill 68*; Eagle in a Cage 70; From the Mixed-Up Files of Mrs. Basil E. Frankweiler • The Hideaways 73; Beauty and the Beast 76; Seize the Day 86
Cook, Philip Beyond the Rising Moon • Space 2074 • Star Quest: Beyond the Rising Moon 88
Cooke, Alan Black Legend 48*; The Starfish 50*; Flat 2 62; The Mind of Mr. Soames 69; Nadia 84
Coolidge, Martha Old Fashioned Woman 74; Not a Pretty Picture 75; The City Girl 83; Valley Girl 83; Joy of Sex 84; Real Genius 85; Plain Clothes 88
Cooney, Ray Not Now Darling 72*; Not Now Comrade 77*; There Goes the Bride 79
Cooper, Arthur The Village Blacksmith 1898; The Amorous Cook • Soldier, Policeman and Cook 1899; Fight Between a Miller and a Sweep 1899; The Fireman's Snapshot 1899; Briton v. Boer 00; Dan Leno's Cricket Match 00; Farmer Giles and His Portrait 00; It's No Use Crying Over Spilt Milk 00; Dolly's Toys 01; Bill Sykes Up to Date 03; Blind Man's Bluff 03; Car Ride 03; Ducks on Sale or Return 04; The Enchanted Toymaker • The Old Toymaker's Dream 04; The Death of the Iron Horse 05; The Ducking Stool 05; Grandfather's Tormentors 05; His Washing Day 05; In the Good Old Times • Poor Old Mr. and Mrs. Brown in the Stocks 05; McNab's Visit to London 05; The Motor Highwayman 05; What Is It Master Likes So Much? 05; Who's to Blame? • Why the Typist Got the Sack 05; A Catching Story 06; The Fairy Godmother 06; The Guinea Entertainer 06; The Happy Man 06; Held to Ransom 06; The Modern Pirates • The Raid of the Armoured Motor 06; The Motor Valet • The New Moto Valet 06; The Policeman's Love Affair 06; Robbing H.M. Mails 06; A Slippery Visitor 06; Target Practice 06; A Visit to a Spiritualist 06; When the Cat's Away 06; Youth Regained 06; The Adventures of a Performing Flea 07; The Animated Pillar Box • Our New Pillar Box 07; The Bad Shilling • The Bad Sixpence 07; Between One and Two A.M. 07; The Boys' Half Holiday • Those Boys Again 07; The 5-30 Collection 07; Her First Attempt • Her First Pancake • Lottie's Pancakes 07; His Sweetheart When a Boy 07; In Quest of Health 07; The Lodger Had the Haddock 07; The Lovers' Charm 07; Luck of Life 07; Oh That Molar! 07; The Poet's Bid for Fame 07; A Sacrifice for Work 07; Seen at the Chiropodist's 07; The Showman's Treasure 07; The Smoker's Joke 07; Soapy Soup 07; The Tricky Twins 07; When the Mistress Took Her Holiday 07; The Wily Fiddler 07; The Woes of a Married Man 07; Animated Matches 08; The Curate's Honeymoon 08; Dreams of Toyland 08; Grandpa's Forty Winks • In the Land of Nod 08; Grandpa's Pension Day 08; Green's Goose 08; Harlequinade 08; The Hypnotist's Joke 08; It's Just My Luck 08; A Little Stranger 08; Oh Those Boys! 08; Tommy on a Visit to His Aunt 08; What Farmer Jones Saw at the Picture Show 08; The Tale of the Ark 09; The Toymaker's Dream 10; The Cats' Cup Final 12; Cinderella 12; Father's Forty Winks 12; Old Mother Hubbard 12; Ten Little Nigger Boys 12; Larks in Toyland 13; An Old Toymaker's Dream 13

Cooper, Bob I Was a Teenage Alien 80
Cooper, Buddy Fall Break • The Mutilator 83

Cooper, George A. The Big Strong Man 22; The Cunninghames Economise 22; Fallen Leaves 22; Geraldine's First Year 22; Her Dancing Partner 22; His Wife's Husband 22; Keeping Man Interested 22; The Letters 22; Pearl for Pearl 22; Poetic License 22; A Question of Principle 22; The Thief 22; The White Rat 22; Constant Hot Water 23; Darkness 23; Finished 23; The Man Who Liked Lemons 23; The Reverse of the Medal 23; Three to One Against 23; Claude Duval 24; The Eleventh Commandment 24; The Happy Ending 25; Settled Out of Court 25; Somebody's Darling 25; If Youth But Knew 26; Julius Caesar 26; Santa Claus 26; His Rest Day 27; Musical Medley No. 5 • Olly Oakley 27; Nan Wild 27; Topsey Turvey 27; Blake the Lawbreaker 28; The Clue of the Second Goblet 28; Master and Man 29; The World, the Flesh and the Devil 32; His Grace Gives Notice 33; Home Sweet Home 33; The Man Outside 33; Mannequin 33; Puppets of Fate • Wolves of the Underworld 33; The Roof 33; The Shadow 33; Anything Might Happen 34; The Black Abbot 34; The Case for the Crown 34; Tangled Evidence 34; Sexton Blake and the Bearded Doctor 35; Royal Eagle 36*; Down Our Alley • Gang Show 39

Cooper, J. Gordon Sin Town 29
Cooper, Jackie Stand Up and Be Counted 71; Go for the Gold 84
Cooper, Merian C. Grass • Grass—A Nation's Battle for Life • Grass—The Epic

of a Lost Tribe 25*; Chang 27*; Gow the Headhunter 28*; The Four Feathers 29*; King Kong 33*

Cooper, Peter H. Ordinary Heroes 86

Cooper, Stuart Little Malcolm • Little Malcolm and His Struggle Against the Eunuchs 74; Overlord 75; The Disappearance 77

Cooper, Thomas G. The Dawn • Dawn Over Ireland 36; Uncle Nick 38

Cooper, Toby A Beautiful Garden of Roses 14; Beer and Pyjamas 14; Bringing It Home to Him 14; A Co'd in His Head 14; Divergent Views, No.s 41 and 42 John Street 14; Following the Trail 14; A Husband's Love 14; Jack Spratt As a Blackleg Waiter 14; Jack Spratt As a Bricklayer 14; Jack Spratt As a Bus Conductor 14; Jack Spratt As a Dude 14; Jack Spratt As a Gardener 14; Jack Spratt As a Policeman 14; Jack Spratt As a Special Constable 14; Jack Spratt As a War Lord 14; Jack Spratt As a Wounded Prussian 14; The Kango Fire Brigade 14; A Knight in Armour 14; The Little Darlings 14; Love Thy Neighbour 14; The Mid-Nightly Wedding 14; The Open Door 14; The Proof of the Pudding 14; Twenty Years After 14; A Warm Reception 14; A Day of Rest 15; Double and Quits 15; Jack Spratt's Parrot 15; Keep It Dark 15; Sentimental Tommy 15; Sh! Not a Word 15; She Didn't Want to Do It 15; The Tiff and What Became of It 15; The Unmentionables 15; A Wild Night 15; Jack Spratt's Parrot As the Artful Dodger 16; Jack Spratt's Parrot Getting His Own Back 16; Jack Spratt's Parrot in Putting the Lid on It 16; Only a Room-er 16; Wanderful Will 16

Copelan, Jodie Ambush at Cimarron Pass 58

Copeland, Jack L. Hell's Five Hours 57

Coplen, Yorke Urubu 48*

Copping, David Outbreak of Hostilities 79

Copping, Robin Alvin Rides Again 74*

Coppola, Christopher Dracula's Widow 87

Coppola, Francis Ford Ayamonn the Terrible 60; The Bellboy and the Playgirls • Mit Eva Fing die Sünde An • The Playgirls and the Bellboy 61*; Come On Out 61; The Peeper 61; Tonight for Sure 61; Dementia 13 • The Haunted and the Hunted 62; Lady of the Shadows • The Terror 62*; The Young Racers 62*; Battle Beyond the Sun 63*; You're a Big Boy Now 66; Finian's Rainbow 68; The Rain People 69; The Godfather 72; The Conversation 74; The Godfather, Part II 74; Apocalypse Now 79; One from the Heart 81; The Outsiders 83; Rumble Fish 83; The Cotton Club 84; Captain Eo 86; Peggy Sue Got Married 86; Gardens of Stone 87; Tucker • Tucker: The Man and His Dream 88; New York Stories 89*; The Godfather, Part III 90

Corarito, Greg The Hard Bunch • Hard on the Trail • Hard Trail 69; Diamond Stud 70; Carnal Madness 75

Corbett, James Meet the Duke 49

Corbett, Stanley see Corbucci, Sergio

Corbiau, Gérard Le Maître de Musique • The Music Teacher 88

Corbucci, Bruno Ringo e Gringo Contro Tutti 66; The Longest Hunt • Spara, Gringo, Spara 68; Isabel, Duchess of the Devils • Isabella, Duchessa dei Diavoli 69; Tutti per Uno, Botte per Tutti 73; Crime at Porta Romana • Delitto a Porta Romana 80; Aladdin • Superfantagenio 87; Rimini Rimini un Anno Dopo 88

Corbucci, Sergio Salvate Mia Figlia 51; The Island Sinner • La Peccatrice dell'Isola 53; I Due Marescialli • Two Colonels 61; Duel of the Titans • Romolo e Remo 61; Goliath and the Island of Vampires • Goliath and the Vampires • Machiste Against the Vampires • Machiste vs. the Vampire • Maciste Contro il Vampiro • The Vampires 61*; Il Figlio di Spartacus • The Slave • Son of Spartacus 62; Castle of Blood • Castle of Terror • Coffin of Terror • La Danse Macabre • La Danza Macabra • Dimensions in Death • Edgar Allan Poe's Castle of Blood • The Long Night of Terror • La Lunga Notte del Terrore • Terrore • Tombs of Horror 63*; Il Giorno Più Corto • Il Più Corto Giorno • The Shortest Day 63; L'Homme du Minnesota • Minnesota Clay 64; Massacre at Grand Canyon • Massacro al Grande Canyon 64*; I Crudeli • Los Despiadados • The Hellbenders 66; Django 66; Un Dollaro a Testa • Joe el Implacable • Navajo Joe 66; Johnny Oro • Ringo and His Golden Pistol 66; The Man Who Laughs • L'Uomo Che Ride 66; Bersaglio Mobile • Moving Target 67; The Big Silence • Il Grande Silenzio 67; Il Mercenario • The Mercenary • A Professional Gun • Salario para Matar 68; Drop Them or I'll Shoot • Le Spécialiste • Gli Specialisti 69; ¡Compañeros! • Lässt Uns Töten, Compañeros • ¡Vamos a Matar, Compañeros! 70; Che C'Entriamo Noi con la Rivoluzione? 72; La Banda J & S — Cronaca Criminale del Far West • J & S — Storia Criminale del Far West • Sonny and Jed 73; Il Bestione 74; Il Bianco, il Giallo, il Nero • White, Yellow, Black 75; Bluff, Storie di Truffe e di Imbraglione 75; Un Genio, Due Compari e un Pollo • The Genius 75*; Di Che Segno Sei? 76; Il Signor Robinson, Monstruosa Storia d'Amore e d'Avventure 76; The Con Artists • The Con Men 77; Ecco Noi per Esempio 77; Tre Tigri Contro Tre Tigri 77*; La Mazzetta 78; Atti Atrocissima de Amore e di Vendetta 79; Giallo Napoletano 79; Pari e Dispari 79; I Don't Understand You Any More 80; Chi Trovo un Amico, Trova un Tesoro 81; I'm Getting Myself a Yacht 81; Super Fuzz • Supersnooper 81; Count Tacchia 82; My Darling, My Dearest 82; Three Wise Kings 82; Questo e Quello 83; Sing Sing 83; A Tu per Tu 84; I Am a Paranormal Phenomenon • Sono un Fenomeno Paranormale 85; Rimini, Rimini • Rimini, Rimini, Etc. 86; For the Rich • Monte-

carlo, Montecarlo • Roba da Ricchi 87; Monstruose Storie d'Amore 87; I Giorni del Commissario Ambrosio • Grazie Commissario 88

Corby, Travers Here He Comes 26

Corda, Sursum see Korda, Alexander

Cordeiro, Margarida Ana 85*

Cordier, Gilbert see Rohmer, Eric

Cordier, Robert Injun Fender 73

Cordova, Frederick de see De Cordova, Frederick

Cordova, Leander de see De Cordova, Leander

Corjos, Nicolae Confessions of Love • Declaratie de Dragoste • Declaration of Love 85; Liceeni • The Teenagers 86

Corkidi, Rafael Ángeles y Querubines 71; Auandar Anapu 74; Pafnucio Santo 76; Deseos 77

Corlish, Frank B. see Corbucci, Bruno

Cormack, Robert Make Mine Music 46*

Corman, Roger Five Guns West 54; Apache Woman 55; Cruel Swamp • Swamp Diamonds • Swamp Woman • Swamp Women 55; The Day the World Ended 55; The Oklahoma Woman 55; Attack of the Crab Monsters 56; The Gunslinger 56; It Conquered the World 56; Naked Paradise • Thunder Over Hawaii 56; Not of This Earth 56; Rock All Night 56; The Undead 56; The Bad One • Confessions of a Sorority Girl • Sorority Girl 57; Carnival Rock 57; The Saga of the Viking Women and Their Voyage to the Waters of the Great Sea Serpent • Viking Women • The Viking Women and the Sea Serpent • Viking Women vs. the Sea Serpent • The Voyage of the Viking Women to the Waters of the Great Sea Serpent 57; Teenage Doll • The Young Rebels 57; War of the Satellites 57; I, Mobster • The Mobster 58; The Last Woman on Earth 58; Machine Gun Kelly 58; Out of the Darkness • Prehistoric World • Teenage Caveman 58; Shark Reef • She Gods of Shark Reef 58; A Bucket of Blood 59; The Wasp Woman 59; Atlas 60; Creature from the Haunted Sea 60; The Fall of the House of Usher • House of Usher 60; The Little Shop of Horrors 60; Ski Troop Attack 60; I Hate Your Guts! • The Intruder • Shame • The Stranger 61; The Pit and the Pendulum 61; Poe's Tales of Terror • Tales of Terror 61; The Premature Burial 61; Lady of the Shadows • The Terror 62*; The Raven 62; Tower of London 62; The Young Racers 62*; The Haunted Palace 63; The Man with X-Ray Eyes • X • X: The Man with the X-Ray Eyes 63; The Secret Invasion 63; The Last Tomb of Ligeia • Ligeia • The Tomb of Ligeia • Tomb of the Cat 64; The Masque of the Red Death 64; The St. Valentine's Day Massacre 66; The Wild Angels 66; The Long Ride Home • A Time for Killing 67*; The Trip 67; How to Make It • Target: Harry • What's in It for Harry? 68; Das Ausschweifende Leben des Marquis de Sade • De Sade 69*; Bloody Mama 69; Gas • Gas! or It Became Necessary to

Destroy the World in Order to Save It • Gas-s-s-s! • Gas-s-s-s, or It Became Necessary to Destroy the World in Order to Save It • Gas-s-s-s, or It May Become Necessary to Destroy the World in Order to Save It 70; The Red Baron • Von Richthofen and Brown 70; Frankenstein Unbound • Roger Corman's Frankenstein Unbound 90

Cornea, George Vulcanul Stins 88

Corneau, Alain France Société Anonyme 74; Police Python 357 76; La Menace 77; The Case Against Ferro 80; Choice of Arms 81; Fort Saganne 84; The Kid • Le Môme 86

Cornelius, Henry Passport to Pimlico 48; The Galloping Major 50; Genevieve 53; I Am a Camera 55; Law and Disorder 56*; Next to No Time 58

Cornell, John Crocodile Dundee II 88; Almost an Angel 90

Cornell, Jonas Hej 65; Hugs and Kisses • Puss och Kram 66; Like Night and Day • Som Natt och Dag 69

Cornell, Joseph Bolts of Melody • Centuries of June • Portrait of Julie • Tower House 54*; The Wonder Ring 55*

Cornfield, Hubert Sudden Danger 55; Lure of the Swamp 57; Plunder Road 57; The Third Voice 59; Angel Baby 61*; Point Blank • Pressure Point 62; The Night of the Following Day 68; Les Grands Moyens 76

Cornsweet, Harold Return to Campus 75

Cornwallis, Donald The Convict's Dream 14; The Newsboy's Debt 14; Papa's Letter 14

Corona, Alfonso see Corona Blake, Alfonso

Corona Blake, Alfonso El Camino de la Vida 56; La Mujer y la Bestia 58; El Mundo de los Vampiros • El Mundo de Vampiros • The World of the Vampires 60; Samson and the Vampire Woman 63; Samson in the Wax Museum • Santo en El Museo de Cera • Santo in the Wax Museum 63; Deathstalker and the Warriors from Hell • Deathstalker III • Deathstalker III: The Warriors from Hell 89

Coronado, Celestino Hamlet 76; A Midsummer Night's Dream • Sueño de Noche de Verano 84

Corr, Eugene Over-Under, Sideways-Down 77*; Desert Bloom 86

Correll, Richard Ski Patrol 90

Corrigan, Lloyd Along Came Youth 30*; Follow Thru 30*; The Beloved Bachelor 31; Daughter of the Dragon 31; The Broken Wing 32; No One Man 32; He Learned About Women 33; By Your Leave 34; La Cucaracha 34; Murder on a Honeymoon 35; The Dancing Pirate 36; Night Key 37; Lady Behave 38

Cort, Harvey Friends and Lovers • The Vixens • The Women 69

Cort, Michael Zeta One 69; Plod 72

Corte, Frédéric see Cortez, Fernando

Cortés Calderón, Alberto Amor a la Vuelta de la Esquina • Love Around the

Corner 86

Cortez, Fernando La Pícara Susanna 44; Creature of the Walking Dead • La Marca del Muerto 60*

Cortez, Ricardo Inside Story 38; Chasing Danger 39; City of Chance 39; The Escape 39; Heaven with a Barbed Wire Fence 39; Free, Blonde and Twenty-One 40; Girl in 313 40

Corti, Axel Der Fall Jägerstätter • The Refusal • Die Verweigerung 72; The Condemned • Totstellen 75; An Uns Glaubt Gott Nicht Mehr • God Does Not Believe in Us Anymore 81; A Woman's Pale Blue Handwriting 84; Santa Fe 85; Welcome in Vienna 86; The King's Whore 90

Cortini, Bruno Giochi d'Estate • Summer Games 85; L'Estate Sta Finito • The Summer Is Nearly Over 87

Cosby, Bill Bill Cosby, Himself 82

Coscarelli, Don Jim — The World's Greatest • Story of a Teenager 76*; Kenny & Co. 76; Phantasm 78; The Beastmaster 82; Big Wilderness • Survival Quest 86; Phantasm II 88

Coscia, Jorge Chorros • Crooks 87*; Feelings: Mirta from Liniers to Istanbul • Sentimientos: Mirta de Liniers a Estambul 87*

Cosini, Nelo The Blue Squadron • El Escuadrón Azul 38

Cosmatos, George Pan The Beloved 71; Massacre in Rome • Rappresaglia 73; The Cassandra Crossing 77; Restless 78; Escape to Athena 79; Of Unknown Origin 82; Rambo: First Blood Part II 85; Cobra 86; Leviathan 89

Cosmatos, Yorgo Pan see Cosmatos, George Pan

Cosper, Wilbert Leroy The Kingdom of Human Hearts 21

Coss, Joachim El Automóvil Gris • The Gray Automobile 19*

Costa, Cicero Adolpho Vittorio da see Da Costa, Cicero Adolpho Vittorio

Costa, José Fonseca e see Fonseca e Costa, José

Costa, Mario La Sua Strada 43; The Barber of Seville • Il Barbiere di Siviglia 46; Elisir d'Amore • This Wine of Love 46; Follie per l'Opera • Mad About Opera 47; Love of a Clown • I Pagliacci 48; Cavalcata d'Eroi 49; Canzone di Primavera 50; La Città Canora 52; Perdonami 52; Pietà per Chi Cade 53; Gli Amori di Manon Lescaut 54; Melody of Love 54; Prigionieri del Male 55; Arrivano i Dollari 56; Addio per Sempre 57; Le Belle dell'Aria 57; Cavalier in Devil's Castle 59; I Reali di Francia 59; Attack of the Moors 60; Queen of the Pirates • La Venere dei Pirati • Venus der Piraten 60*; The Black Buccaneer • Gordon il Pirata Nero • The Rage of the Buccaneers 61; Buffalo Bill • Buffalo Bill, Hero of the Far West • Buffalo Bill, l'Eroe del Far West • Das War Buffalo Bill 62; The Centurion • Conqueror of Corinth • Il Conquistatore di Corinto 62; Gladiator of Rome • Il Gladiatore di Roma 62; Gli Amanti Latini • Latin Lovers 65; La Belva

70

Costa, Morton da see Da Costa, Morton

Costa, Piero Barrier of the Law 50; Los Mercenarios • Revolt of the Mercenaries • La Rivolta dei Mercenari 62

Costa-Gavras Compartiment Tueurs • The Sleeping Car Murder 64; One Man Too Many • Shock Troops • Une Homme de Trop 66; Z 68; L'Aveu • The Confession 69; État de Siège • State of Siege 72; Section Spéciale • Special Section 75; Clair de Femme • Womanlight 79; Missing 81; Hanna • Hanna K • Hannah K 83; Conseil de Famille • Family Business • Family Council 86; Betrayed 88; Music Box 89

Costa-Gavras, Constantin see Costa-Gavras

Costa e Silva, Manuel A Moura Encantada 85

Costantini, Romeo Una Notte di Pioggia • One Rainy Night 86

Costello, Maurice The Chamber of Horrors • Conscience 12; The Ambassador's Disappearance 13; Cupid vs. Women's Rights 13; Extremities 13; Matrimonial Maneuvers 13; The Sale of a Heart 13; The Weapon 13; The Blood Ruby 14; Mr. Barnes of New York 14*; The Moonstone of Fez 14*; The Mysterious Lodger 14*; The Plot 14*; The Man Who Couldn't Beat God 15*

Costner, Kevin Dances with Wolves 90

Coteau, David de see DeCoteau, David

Cotes, Peter The Right Person 55; The Young and the Guilty 58

Cotlow, Lewis Primitive Paradise 61

Cottafavi, Vittorio I Nostri Sogni 43; Lo Sconosciuto di San Marino 46*; La Grande Strada 48*; La Fiamme Che Non Si Spegne 49; Una Donna a Ucciso 51; Il Boia di Lilla • La Vita Avventurosa di Milady 52; Il Cavaliere di Maison Rouge 53; In Amore Si Pecca in Due 53; Traviata '53 53; Avanzi di Galera 54; Una Donna Libera 54; Nel Gorgo del Peccato 54; Fiesta Brava 56; The Revolt of the Gladiators • La Rivolta del Gladiatori • The Warrior and the Slave Girl 58; Le Legioni di Cleopatra • Legions of the Nile 59; Messalina • Messalina, Venere Imperatrice 59; Amazons of Rome • Le Vergini di Roma • The Virgins of Rome • The Warrior Women 60*; Goliath and the Dragon • La Vendetta di Ercole • The Vengeance of Hercules 60; Ercole alla Conquista di Atlantide • Hercule à la Conquête de l'Atlantide • Hercules and the Captive Women • Hercules and the Conquest of Atlantis • Hercules and the Haunted Women • Hercules Conquers Atlantis 61; I Cento Cavalieri • Los Cien Caballeros • The Hundred Horsemen 64

Cotter, John Mountain Family Robinson 79

Cotti, Carlo I'll Marry Simon le Bon • Sposero Simon le Bon 86

Cottrell, William Snow White and the Seven Dwarfs 37*

Coudari, Camille The Great Chess Movie 82*

Couffer, Jack Nikki, Wild Dog of the North 61*; Ring of Bright Water 69; The Darwin Adventure 72; Living Free 72

Coughlan, Ian The Spiral Bureau 74; Alison's Birthday 79

Coulson, Michael Wings of Death 85*

Courcy, Walter de see De Courcy, Walter

Cournot, Michel Les Gauloises Bleues 68

Court, Ulf van see Van Court, Ulf

Courtenay, Syd Darby and Joan 37

Courtice, Michael see Curtiz, Michael

Courtland, Jerome Diamonds on Wheels 72; Run, Cougar, Run 72

Courtois, Miguel Preuve d'Amour 88

Courville, Albert de see De Courville, Albert

Cousteau, Jacques-Yves Par Dix-Huit Mètres de Fond 43; Épaves 45; Paysages du Silence 47; Au Large des Côtes Tunisiennes 49; Autour d'un Récif 49; Dauphins et Cétacés 49; Les Phoques du Rio d'Oro • Les Phoques du Sahara 49; Carnet de Plongée 50; Une Plongée du Rubis • Une Sortie du Rubis 50; La Mer Rouge 52; Un Musée dans la Mer 53; Le Monde du Silence • The Silent World 55*; Le Monde Sans Soleil • Il Mondo Senza Sole • World Without Sun 64; Le Voyage au Bout du Monde • Voyage to the Edge of the World 76*

Cousteau, Philippe Le Voyage au Bout du Monde • Voyage to the Edge of the World 76*

Coutard, Raoul Tu Es Danse et Vertige 67; Hoa-Binh 70; La Légion Saute sur Kolwezi 79; S.A.S. à San Salvador 82

Coutaz, Gérard Frot see Frot-Coutaz, Gérard

Coutsomitis, Costas Klios • The Noose 87

Couturie, Bill Dear America: Letters Home from Vietnam 87

Covacevich, Álvaro New Love • La Revolución de las Flores 68

Cowan, Tom The Office Picnic 74; Journey Among Women 77; Sweet Dreamers 81

Cowan, Will The Big Beat 58; The Thing That Couldn't Die 58

Coward, Noël In Which We Serve 42*

Cowell, Adrian The Tribe That Hides from Man 70

Cowen, Lawrence A Dream of Tomorrow • Wake Up! • Wake Up! or A Dream of Tomorrow 14; The Hidden Hand • It Is for England 16

Cowen, William Half Marriage 29; Ned McCobb's Daughter 29; Kongo 32; Oliver Twist 33; Woman Unafraid 34

Cowl, George The Beloved Adventuress 17; Betsy Ross 17*; The Corner Grocer 17; Her Hour 17; Tides of Fate 17

Cox, Alex Repo Man 84; Sid and Nancy 86; Straight to Hell 86; Walker 87

Cox, George L. The Hellion 19; The Tiger Lily 19; The Blue Moon 20; The Dangerous Talent 20; The Gamesters 20; The House of Toys 20; Life in the Orange Groves 20; A Light Woman 20; Their Mutual Child 20; The Thirtieth Piece of Silver 20; The Week-End 20; A Parisian Scandal 21; Payment Guaranteed 21; Sunset Jones 21

Cox, Nell Old Age: The Wasted Years 66*; Portrait of Van Cliburn 66*; The Roommate 85

Cox, Paul Illuminations 75; Inside, Looking Out 77; Kostas 79; Lonely Hearts 81; Man of Flowers 83; My First Wife 84; Death and Destiny 85; Cactus 86; Vincent • Vincent — The Life and Death of Vincent van Gogh 87; Island 89; The Golden Braid 90

Coy, Christopher Mixed Doubles 79

Coyle, John T. Day of Triumph 54*

Coyne, James Carry It On • Joan, Carry It On 70*

Cozarinsky, Edgardo La Guerre d'un Seul Homme • One Man's War 81

Cozzi, Luigi La Portiera Nuda 75; L'Assassino È Costretto ad Uccidere Ancora 76; Dedicato a una Stella 78; Take All of Me 78; Starcrash • Stella Star 79; Alien Contamination 80; The Adventures of Hercules • Hercules II 83; Hercules 83

Crabtree, Arthur Madonna of the Seven Moons 44; They Were Sisters 45; Caravan 46; Dear Murderer 47; The Calendar 48; The Facts of Life • Quartet 48*; Don't Ever Leave Me 49; Lili Marlene • Lilli Marlene 50; Hindle Wakes • Holiday Week 51; The Wedding of Lilli Marlene 53; Death Over My Shoulder 57; Fiend Without a Face 57; Fighting Wildcats • West of Suez • West of the Suez 57; Morning Call • The Strange Case of Dr. Manning 58; Horrors of the Black Museum 59

Craddock, Malcolm Mister Lewis 65

Craft, William James Love's Battle 20; The White Rider 20; Another Man's Boots 22; False Brands 22; Headin' West 22; Saved by Radio 22; Wolf Pack 22; The Flash 23; The Power Divine 23*; Smilin' On 23; The Way of the Transgressor 23; Battling Mason 24*; Big Timber 24; Pride of Sunshine Alley 24; Reckless Speed 24; South of the Equator 24; The Bloodhound 25; Galloping Vengeance 25; The Range Terror 25; That Man Jack 25; The Galloping Cowboy 26; King of the Saddle 26; The Power of the Weak 26; The Arizona Whirlwind 27; Birds of Prey 27; The Clown 27; A Hero for a Night 27; Painting the Town 27; Poor Girls 27; The Wreck 27; Fresh Every Hour • How to Handle Women • Prince of Peanuts 28; The Gate Crasher 28; Hot Heels 28; The Kid's Clever 28; The Cohens and Kellys in Atlantic City • The Cohens and the Kellys in Atlantic City 29; Skinner Steps Out 29; The Cohens and Kellys in Scotland 30; Czar of Broadway 30; Dames Ahoy 30; Embarrassing Moments 30; The Little Accident 30; One Hysterical Night 30; See America Thirst 30; Honeymoon Lane 31; Lovable and Sweet • The Runaround • Waiting at the Church • Waiting for the Bride 31

Craigie, Jill The Way We Live 46; Blue Scar 49

Crain, William Blacula 72; Dr. Black and Mr. Hyde • Dr. Black, Mr. Hyde • The Watts Monster 76; The Kid from Not-So-Big 78; Standing in the Shadows of Love 84

Cramer, Massey The Legend of Blood Mountain 65   **Cramer, Ross** The Waterloo Bridge Handicap 78

Cranche, Albert see Carné, Marcel

Crandall, Eddie From Nashville with Music 69*

Crandall, R. D. Professor B. Flat 20*

Crane, Barry Conquest of the Earth 80*

Crane, Frank As Ye Sow 14; The Family Cupboard 15; The Man Who Found Himself 15; The Moonstone 15; As in a Looking Glass 16; Fate's Boomerang 16; The Man Who Stood Still 16; Paying the Price 16; Whoso Findeth a Wife • Whoso Taketh a Wife 16; The World Against Him 16; Stranded in Arcady 17; Thaïs 17*; The Life Mask 18; Neighbors 18; Vengeance Is Mine 18; Her Game 19; His Father's Wife 19; Miss Crusoe 19; The Praise Agent 19; The Scar 19; The Unveiling Hand 19; Wanted for Murder 19; The Door That Has No Key 21; The Puppet Man • Puppets of Fate 21; The Grass Orphan 22; The Pauper Millionaire 22; Hutch Stirs 'Em Up 23; Tons of Money 24; Fair Play 25; The Jade Cup 26; The Trunk Mystery 27

Crane, George Hollywood, Ciudad de Ensueño 34

Crane, Kenneth Half Human • Jūjin Yūkiotoko 55*; Monster from Green Hell • The Monster from the Green Hell 57; When Hell Broke Loose 58; Half Man Half Monster • The Manster • The Manster — Half Man, Half Monster • The Split 62*

Crane, Larry Beware the Black Widow 68

Crane, Peter Hunted 72; Assassin 73; Moments 74; Cover Up 84

Craven, Frank The Very Idea 29*; That's Gratitude 34

Craven, Wes Krug and Company • The Last House on the Left • Sex Crime of the Century 72; The Hills Have Eyes 77; Summer of Fear 78; Deadly Blessing 81; Swamp Thing 82; The Hills Have Eyes Part II 83; A Nightmare on Elm Street 84; Deadly Friend 86; The Serpent and the Rainbow 87; Shocker 89

Craveri, Mario Blue Continent • Continente Perduto • The Lost Continent • Sesto Continento • The Sixth Continent 54*; Empire of the Sun • Impero del Sole 55*; Soledad 58; I Sogni Muoiono all'Alba 61*

Crawford, Harold A. The Controllers 20

Crawford, Richard Captain Milkshake 70

Crawley, Constance Thaïs 14*

Crea, G. Se Ti Incontrato T'Ammazzo 71; Il Magnifico West 72

Creelman, James Ashmore High Hat 27

Creighton, Walter One Family 30; The Shaming of the True 30

Crescenzo, Luciano de see De Crescenzo, Luciano

Cresswell, Peter The Gay Duellist • Meet Me at Dawn 46*

Crevenna, Alfredo B. La Rebelión de los Colgados • The Rebellion of the Hanged • Revolt of the Hanged 54*; Circle of Death 55; Cry of the Bewitched • Yambao • Young and Evil 57; H. G. Wells' New Invisible Man • El Hombre Invisible • El Hombre Que Logró Ser Invisible • The Invisible Man • The New Invisible Man 57; Bring Me the Vampire • Échenme al Vampiro 60; La Huella Macabra 62; Aventura al Centro de la Tierra 65; Gigantes Interplanetarios • Gigantes Planetarios 65; El Planeta de las Mujeres Invasoras 65; Santo Contra la Invasión de los Marcianos • Santo vs. the Martian Invasion 66; Camarena Taken Hostage • El Secuestro de Camarena 86; Albures Mexicanos • Mexican Double-Entendres 87; Better Than Bread • Más Buenas Que el Pan 87; Carrasco's Escape • La Fuga de Carrasco 87; Cinco Nacos Asaltan a Las Vegas • Five Nerds Take Las Vegas 87

Crichton, Charles Young Veterans 41*; For Those in Peril 43; Dead of Night 45*; The Girl on the Canal • Painted Boats 45; Hue and Cry 46; Against the Wind 48; Another Shore 48; Train of Events 49*; Dance Hall 50; The Lavender Hill Mob 50; Hunted • The Stranger in Between 51; The Titfield Thunderbolt 52*; The Divided Heart 54; The Love Lottery 54; Decision Against Time • The Man in the Sky 56; Law and Disorder 56*; Floods of Fear 58; The Battle of the Sexes 59; The Boy Who Stole a Million 60; The Third Secret 64; He Who Rides a Tiger 65; Tomorrow's Island 68; London—Through My Eyes 70; Perishing Solicitors 83; A Fish Called Wanda 88

Crichton, Michael Westworld 73; Coma 77; The First Great Train Robbery • The Great Train Robbery 78; Looker 81; Runaway 84; Physical Evidence 88

Crisp, Donald Another Chance 14; The Availing Prayer 14; The Dawn 14; Down the Hill to Creditville 14; Her Father's Silent Partner 14; Her Mother's Necklace 14; The Little Country Mouse 14; The Mysterious Shot 14; The Newer Woman 14; The Niggard 14; Sands of Fate 14; The Tavern of Tragedy 14; Their First Acquaintance 14; The Warning 14; An Old-Fashioned Girl 15; Ramona 16; The Bond Between 17; The Clever Mrs. Carfax • Mrs. Carfax the Clever 17; The Cook of Canyon Camp 17; The Countess Charming 17; The Eyes of the World 17; His Sweetheart 17; Lost in Transit 17; The Marcellini Millions 17; A Roadside Impresario 17; Believe Me Xantippe 18; The Firefly of France 18; The Goat 18; The House of Silence 18; Jules of the Strong Heart 18; Less Than Kin 18; The Pursuit 18; Rimrock Jones 18; The Source 18*; Under the Top 18; The Way of a Man with a Maid 18; It Pays to Advertise 19; Johnny Get Your Gun 19; Love Insurance 19; Poor Boob 19; Putting It Over 19; Something to Do 19; Too Much John-

son 19; Venus in the East 19; A Very Good Young Man 19; Why Smith Left Home 19; The Barbarian 20; Held by the Enemy 20; Miss Hobbs 20; The Six Best Cellars 20; Appearances 21; Beside the Bonnie Brier Bush • The Bonnie Brier Bush 21; The Princess of New York 21; Tell Your Children 22; Ponjola 23; The Navigator 24*; Don Q, Son of Zorro 25; The Black Pirate 26*; Man Bait 26; Sunny Side Up 26; Young April 26; Dress Parade 27; The Fighting Eagle 27; Nobody's Widow 27; Vanity 27; The Cop 28; Stand and Deliver 28; The Runaway Bride 30

Crispino, Armando John il Bastardo • John the Bastard 67; Commandos 68; The Dead Are Alive 72; Autopsy • Macchie Solari 74; Frankenstein all'Italiana • Frankenstein, Italian Style 76

Crist, Harry P. Cactus Trails 27

Cristaldi, Franco China Is Near • La Cina È Vicina 66*

Cristallini, Giorgio I Quattro Pistoleri di Santa Trinità 71; Sei Iellato Amico…Hai Incontrato Sacramento 72

Critchlow, Keith F. The California Reich 77*

Croft, David Not Now Darling 72*

Croise, Hugh From Hen to Hospital 16; Judged by Appearances 16; Four Men in a Van 21; Always Tell Your Wife 22*; The Cowgirl Queen 22; The Affair at the Novelty Theatre 24; The Brighton Mystery 24; The Happy Prisoner 24; The Hocussing of Cigarette 24; The Kensington Mystery 24; The Mystery of Brudenell Court 24; The Mystery of Dogstooth Cliff 24; The Mystery of the Khaki Tunic 24; The Northern Mystery 24; The Regent's Park Mystery 24; The Tragedy of Barnsdale Manor 24; The Tremarne Case 24; The York Mystery 24; The Ball of Fortune 26; Dream Faces 26; The Irish Emigrant 26; The Legend of Tichborne Dole 26; Shipmates 26; Songs My Mother Sang 26; Songs of the West Countree 26; The Veteran 26; The Barrister 28; The Burglar and the Girl 28; Grandfather Smallweed 28; Joining Up 28; Musical Medley No. 1 • The Victoria Girls 28; Musical Medley No. 6 • Victoria Girls Skipping 28; Nap 28; The Orderly Room 28; The Raw Recruit 28; Safety First 28; Scrooge 28; That Brute Simmons 28; The Bride 29; Doing His Duty 29; Josser, K.C. 29; Mrs. Mephistopheles 29; Spirits 29

Crombie, Donald Caddie 76; The Irishman 78; Cathy's Child 79; The Killing of Angel Street 81; Kitty and the Bagman 82; Robbery Under Arms 85*; Playing Beatie Bow 86

Crome, John Nelson's Touch 79; The Naked Cell 88

Cromwell, John Close Harmony 29*; The Dance of Life 29*; Medals • Seven Days' Leave 29*; The Mighty 29; The Big Race • The Texan 30; For the Defense 30; Street of Chance 30; Tom Sawyer 30; The Dark Page • Scandal Sheet 31; Huckleberry Finn 31*; Rich Man's Folly 31; Unfaithful

31; The Vice Squad 31; The World and the Flesh 32; Ann Vickers 33; Double Harness 33; The Silver Cord 33; Sweepings 33; The Fountain 34; Of Human Bondage 34; Spitfire 34; This Man Is Mine 34; I Dream Too Much 35; Jalna 35; Village Tale 35; Banjo on My Knee 36; Little Lord Fauntleroy 36; To Mary—with Love 36; The Prisoner of Zenda 37*; Algiers 38; In Name Only 39; Made for Each Other 39; Abe Lincoln in Illinois • Spirit of the People 40; Victory 40; So Ends Our Night 41; Son of Fury 42; Since You Went Away 44*; The Enchanted Cottage 45; Anna and the King of Siam 46; Dead Reckoning 47; Memory of Love • Night Song 47; Adventure in Baltimore • Bachelor Bait 48*; Caged 50; The Company She Keeps 50; The Racket 51*; The Goddess 58; City of Sin • The Scavengers 59; A Matter of Morals • De Sista Stegen 60

Crone, George Never Say Die 24; Introduce Me 25; The Floating College 28; Blaze o' Glory 29*; The Gentleman Chauffeur • What a Man! 30; Reno 30; Get That Girl 32; Speed Madness 32

Cronenberg, David Stereo 69; Crimes of the Future 70; Frissons • The Parasite Murders • Shivers • They Came from Within 74; Rabid • Rage 76; Fast Company 78; The Brood 79; Scanners 80; Videodrome 82; The Dead Zone 83; The Fly 86; Dead Ringers 88

Crosby, William G. The Enchanted Island 27

Crosfield, Paul H. Manolis 62

Crosland, Alan The Apple-Tree Girl 17; Chris and the Wonderful Lamp 17; Friends, Romans and Leo 17; Kidnapped 17; Knights of the Square Table • Knights of the Square Table, or The Grail 17; Light in Darkness • Light in the Darkness 17; The Little Chevalier 17; The Story That the Keg Told Me 17; The Unbeliever 18; The Whirlpool 18; The Country Cousin 19; Broadway and Home 20; Everybody's Sweetheart 20; The Flapper 20; Greater Than Fame 20; The Point of View 20; Youthful Folly 20; Is Life Worth Living? 21; Room and Board 21; Worlds Apart 21; The Face in the Fog 22; The Prophet's Paradise 22; Shadows of the Sea 22; Slim Shoulders 22; The Snitching Hour 22; Why Announce Your Marriage? 22; The Enemies of Women 23; Under the Red Robe 23; Miami 24; The Romance of a Queen • Three Weeks 24; Sinners in Heaven 24; Unguarded Women 24; Bobbed Hair 25; Compromise 25; Contraband 25; Don Juan 26; His Lady • When a Man Loves 26; The Beloved Rogue 27; The Jazz Singer 27; Old San Francisco 27; Glorious Betsy 28; The Scarlet Lady • The Scarlet Woman 28; General Crack 29; On with the Show 29; Big Boy 30; Captain Thunder 30; The Furies 30; Song of the Flame 30; Viennese Nights 30; Children of Dreams 31; The Silver Lining • Thirty Days 31; Week-Ends Only 32; Massacre 33; The Case of the Howling Dog 34; Midnight

Alibi 34; The Personality Kid 34; The Gay Lady • Lady Tubbs 35; The Great Impersonation 35; It Happened in New York 35; King Solomon of Broadway 35; Mr. Dynamite 35; The White Cockatoo 35

Crosland, Alan, Jr. Fury River 58*; Natchez Trace 60

Cross, J. H. Martin The Lone Scout 29; When Scouting Won 30

Crouch, William Forest Reet, Petite and Gone 47

Crounse, Avery Eyes of Fire 84; The Invisible Kid 88

Crowe, Cameron Say Anything... 89

Crowe, Cristopher Off Limits 88

Crowley, William X. *see Beaudine, William*

Crowther, John Damned River • Devil's Odds 90*

Crump, Owen Cease Fire 53; The River Changes 56; The Couch 62

Cruze, James The Dub 18; Too Many Millions 18; An Adventure in Hearts • Captain Dieppe 19; Alias Mike Moran 19; Hawthorne of the U.S.A. • Hawthorne the Adventurer 19; The Lottery Man 19; The Love Burglar 19; The Roaring Road 19; The Valley of the Giants 19; You're Fired! 19; Always Audacious 20; The Charm School 20; Food for Scandal 20; A Full House 20; Mrs. Temple's Telegram 20; Salvage • Terror Island 20; The Sins of St. Anthony 20; What Happened to Jones 20; Crazy to Marry 21; The Dollar-a-Year Man 21; The Fast Freight • Freight Prepaid • Via Fast Freight 21; Gasoline Gus 21; Leap Year • Skirt Shy 21; The Dictator 22; Is Matrimony a Failure? 22; The Old Homestead 22; One Glorious Day 22; Thirty Days 22; The Covered Wagon 23; Hollywood 23; Ruggles of Red Gap 23; To the Ladies 23; The City That Never Sleeps 24; The Enemy Sex 24; The Fighting Coward 24; The Garden of Weeds 24; Merton of the Movies 24; Beggar on Horseback 25; The Goose Hangs High 25; Marry Me 25; The Pony Express 25; Waking Up the Town 25; Welcome Home 25; Mannequin 26; Old Ironsides • Sons of the Sea 26; The Waiter from the Ritz 26; The City Gone Wild 27; On to Reno 27; We're All Gamblers 27; Excess Baggage 28; The Mating Call 28; The Red Mark 28; The Duke Steps Out 29; The Great Gabbo 29; A Man's Man 29; Got What She Wanted • She Got What She Wanted 30; Once a Gentleman 30; Men Women Love • Salvation Nell 31; If I Had a Million 32*; Invisible Power • Washington Merry-Go-Round 32; Racetrack 32; I Cover the Waterfront 33; Mr. Skitch 33; Sailor Be Good 33; Afterwards • Their Big Moment 34; David Harum 34; Helldorado 34; Two Fisted 35; Sutter's Gold 36; The Wrong Road 37; Come On, Leathernecks! 38; Gangs of New York 38; Prison Nurse 38

Csepcsányi, Béla Macaroni Blues 86*

Csepreghy, Jenő Búsulni Nem Jó • Don't Worry 38; Kis Bence 40

Cuerda, José Luis El Bosque Animado •

The Enchanted Forest 87

Cukor, George Cascarrabias • Grumpy 30*; Cast Iron • The Virtuous Sin 30*; The Royal Family • The Royal Family of Broadway • Theatre Royal 30*; Girls About Town 31; Tarnished Lady • Tarnished Lady: A Story of a New York Lady 31; The Animal Kingdom • The Woman in His House 32*; A Bill of Divorcement 32; One Hour with You 32*; Our Betters 32; Rockabye 32; What Price Hollywood? 32; Dinner at Eight 33; Little Women 33; David Copperfield • The Personal History, Adventures, Experience and Observations of David Copperfield the Younger 34; No More Ladies 35*; Sylvia Scarlett 35; Camille 36; Romeo and Juliet 36; I Met My Love Again 37*; The Prisoner of Zenda 37*; Free to Live • Holiday • Unconventional Linda 38; Zaza 38; The Gay Mrs. Trexel • Susan and God 39; Gone with the Wind 39*; The Women 39; The Philadelphia Story 40; Two-Faced Woman 41*; A Woman's Face 41; Her Cardboard Lover 42; Keeper of the Flame 42; Resistance and Ohm's Law 43; Gaslight • The Murder in Thornton Square 44; I'll Be Seeing You 44*; Winged Victory 44; Desire Me 47*; A Double Life 47; Edward, My Son 48; Adam's Rib 49; Born Yesterday 50; A Life of Her Own 50; The Model and the Marriage Broker 51; The Marrying Kind 52; Pat and Mike 52; The Actress 53; It Should Happen to You 53; A Star Is Born 54; Bhowani Junction 55; Les Girls 57; Wild Is the Wind 57; Hot Spell 58*; Heller in Pink Tights 59; Song Without End 59*; Let's Make Love 60; The Chapman Report 61; My Fair Lady 64; Justine 68*; Travels with My Aunt 72; Love Among the Ruins 75; The Blue Bird 76; Rich and Famous 81

Cullen, Robert Every Mother's Son 26; When That Yiddisher Band Played an Irish Tune 26; The King's Cup 32*

Cullimore, Alan The Clouded Crystal 48; Vengeance Is Mine 48; Let's Go Crazy 51

Cullison, Webster In for Thirty Days 19; The Fighting Stranger 21; God's Gold 21; The Last Chance 21; Battling Bates 23

Culp, Robert Hickey and Boggs 72

Cummings, Eugene The Crime Patrol 36

Cummings, Howard Big Time 89*

Cummings, Irving Broad Daylight • In Broad Daylight 22; Environment 22; Flesh and Blood 22; Hell's River • The Man from Hell's River 22; The Jilt 22; Paid Back 22; Broken Hearts of Broadway 23; The Drug Traffic 23; East Side, West Side 23; Stolen Secrets 23; The Dancing Cheat 24; Fools' Highway 24; In Every Woman's Life 24; Riders Up 24; The Rose of Paris 24; As Man Desires 25; The Desert Flower 25; Infatuation 25; Just a Woman 25; One Year to Live 25; Bertha the Sewing Machine Girl 26; The Country Beyond 26; The Flood • The Johnstown Flood 26; The Midnight Kiss 26; Rustling for Cupid 26;

The Brute 27; The Port of Missing Girls 27; Dressed to Kill 28; In Old Arizona 28*; Romance and Bright Lights • Romance of the Underworld 28; Behind That Curtain 29; Not Quite Decent 29; Cameo Kirby 30; A Devil with Women • On the Make 30; On the Level 30; The Cisco Kid 31; A Holy Terror 31; Attorney for the Defense 32; Man Against Woman 32; The Night Club Lady 32; The Mad Game 33; Man Hunt 33; Tampico • The Woman I Stole 33; Grand Canary 34; I Believed in You 34; The White Parade 34; Curly Top 35; It's a Small World 35; Girls' Dormitory 36; Poor Little Rich Girl 36; White Hunter 36; All This and Glamour Too • Vogues • Vogues of 1938 37; Merry-Go-Round of 1938 37; Just Around the Corner 38; Little Miss Broadway 38; Alexander Graham Bell • The Modern Miracle • The Story of Alexander Graham Bell 39; Everything Happens at Night 39; Hollywood Cavalcade 39*; Down Argentine Way 40; Lillian Russell 40; Belle Starr 41; Louisiana Purchase 41; That Night in Rio 41; My Gal Sal 42; Springtime in the Rockies 42; The Beautiful Cheat • What a Woman! 43; Sweet Rosie O'Grady 43; The Impatient Years 44; The Dolly Sisters 45; Double Dynamite • It's Only Money 48

Cummings, Samuel War Is a Racket 34*

Cummins, Brian Twenty-Nine 69; The Undertakers 69

Cunard, Grace Washington at Valley Forge 14*

Cunha, Cláudio Vítimas do Prazer—Snuff 74

Cunha, Richard Frankenstein's Daughter • She-Monster of the Night 58; Giant from the Unknown 58; Missile to the Moon 58; She-Demons 58; Girl in Room 13 61

Cunningham, Sean S. Together 71; The Case of the Full Moon Murders • The Case of the Smiling Stiffs • Sex on the Groove Tube 73*; Here Come the Tigers • Manny's Orphans 78; Friday the 13th 80; A Stranger Is Watching 82; Spring Break 83; The New Kids 85; DeepStar Six 89

Cunshou, Song *see Song, Cunshou*

Cuny, Louis Belles and Ballets 60

Curi, Giandomenico Ciao Ma 88

Curiel, Federico The Blood of Nostradamus • The Curse of Nostradamus • La Maldición de Nostradamus 59*; Los Autómatas de la Muerte 60; Neutrón Contra el Dr. Caronte 60; Neutrón el Enmascarado Negro 60; Santo Contra el Cerebro Diabólico 62; Arañas Infernales • Cerebros Diabólicos 66; The Empire of Dracula • El Imperio de Drácula • Las Mujeres de Drácula • Sinfonía del Más Allá 66; The Shadow of the Bat • La Sombra del Murciélago 66; Enigma de Muerte 68; Santo en La Venganza de las Mujeres Vampiro • La Venganza de las Mujeres Vampiro • The Vengeance of the Vampire Women 69; Las Vampiras • The Vampire Girls • The Vampires 69

Curik, Jan Wandering 67*

Thin Ice 61; The Phone Rings Every Night 62; Die Fledermaus 64

Czinner, Paul Homo Immanis • Der Unmensch 19; Inferno 20; Husbands or Lovers • Nju 24; Der Geiger von Florenz • Impetuous Youth • The Violinist of Florence 26; Liebe 26; Doña Juana 27; Fräulein Else 29; The Way of Lost Souls • The Woman He Scorned 29; Ariane • Ariane, Russian Maid • The Loves of Ariane 31; Dreaming Lips • Mélo • Der Träumende Mund 32; Catherine the Great • The Rise of Catherine the Great 34*; Escape Me Never 35; As You Like It 36; Dreaming Lips 37*; A Stolen Life 39; Don Giovanni 55*; Kings and Queens 56; Salzburg Pilgrimage 56; The Bolshoi Ballet 57; The Royal Ballet 59; Der Rosenkavalier 61; Romeo and Juliet 65

Da, A *see A, Da*

Daalder, Renee De Blanke Slavin 69; Blackboard Massacre • Massacre at Central High 76; Population: One 86

Daay, Alfred Nem Élhetek Muzsikaszó Nélkül 36

Da Campo, Gianni Sapore del Grano • A Taste of Corn 86

Da Costa, Cicero Adolpho Vittorio Incredible, Fantastic, Extraordinary • Incrivel, Fantastico, Extraordinario 69

Da Costa, Morton Auntie Mame 58; The Music Man 62; Island of Love • Not on Your Life 63

Dad, Seyfollah In the Rain 86

Dada, Jorge M. Tras la Reja 37; Ojos Tapatíos 39*

Dadaras, D. The Shepherd's Daughter 56

Dadmum, Leon E. The Lure of Love 24; The Pearl of Love 25

Dague, Jean-Claude Le Bal des Voyous • Les Femmes • Playmates 69*

Dahl, John Kill Me Again 89

Dahlin, Bob Monster in the Closet 83

Dahlin, Hans Unmarried Mothers 56

Dahme, F. A. Screen Follies No. 1 20*; Screen Follies No. 2 20*

Dahr, Eva Brennende Blomster • Burning Flowers 86*

Dai, Sijie China, My Sorrow • Chine Ma Douleur 89

Daikubara, Akira Magic Boy • Shōnen Sarutobi Sasuke 60*

D'Ailly, Cedric Lydia 64

Dale, Allan Redheads Preferred 26; The Princess from Hoboken 27; The Tired Business Man 27

Dalen, Zale Skip Tracer 77; The Hounds of Notre Dame 80; Hollywood North 87

Daley, Oscar Bourbon Street • Passion Street • Passion Street U.S.A. • Passion Streets 64

Daley, Tom The Lamp • The Outing 87

Dali, Salvador An Andalusian Dog • Un Chien Andalou 28*; L'Âge d'Or • Age of Gold • The Golden Age 30*; Salvador Dali: A Soft Self-Portrait 69

Dalianidis, Yannis Prized As a Mate • Spoiled Rotten 68; Stefania • Stephania 68

DaLie, David The Mighty Jungle 64*

Dall, Christine The Dozens 81*

Dallamano, Massimo Bandidos • Crepo Tue...Che Vivo 67; A Black Veil for Lisa 68; Das Bildnis des Dorian Gray • Il Dio Chiamato a Dorian • Dorian Gray • The Evils of Dorian Gray • The Secret of Dorian Gray 70; Blue Movie Blackmail • Superbitch 73; The Cursed Medallion • Il Medaglione Insanguinato • The Night Child 74; Blue Belle 77; Mafia Junction 77

D'Almedia, Neville Lady on the Bus 78

Dalrymple, Ian Storm in a Teacup 37*; Old Bill and Son 40; Esther Waters 47*

Dalton, Cal Bingo Crosbyana 36*; A-Lad-in Bagdad 38*; Count Me Out 38*; Katnip Kollege 38*; Love and Curses 38*; Porky the Gob 38*; Porky's Hare Hunt 38*; Porky's Phoney Express 38*; Bars and Stripes Forever 39*; Fagin's Freshmen 39*; Gold Rush Daze 39*; Hare-um Scare-um 39*; The Hobo Gadget Band 39*; It's an Ill Wind 39*; Porky and Teabiscuit 39*; Porky the Giant Killer 39*; Sioux Me 39*; Busy Bakers 40*

Dalva, Robert The Black Stallion Returns 83

Daly, Arnold An Affair of Three Nations 15*; The House of Fear 15*

Daly, William Robert Forgiven, or The Jack o' Diamonds 14; Uncle Tom's Cabin 14; At Piney Ridge 16

Damak, Mohamed The Cup • Al Kas 86

D'Amato, Joe *see Massaccesi, Aristide*

Damiani, Amasi Una Forca per un Bastardo 68; The Last Day • L'Ultimo Giorno 86

Damiani, Damiano Jeux Précoces • Lipstick • Red Lips • Il Rossetto 60; Il Sicario 61; Arturo's Island • L'Isola di Arturo 62; The Empty Canvas • L'Ennui et Sa Diversion, l'Érotisme • La Noia 63; The Reunion • La Rimpatriata 63; Le Ho Amate Tutte 65; Aura • The Strange Obsession • La Strega in Amore • The Witch • The Witch in Love 66; A Bullet for the General • ¿Quién Sabe? 66; The Day of the Owl • Il Giorno della Civetta • La Maffia Fait la Loi • Mafia 68; Una Ragazza Piuttosto Complicata 69; Confessione di un Commissario • Confessione di un Commissario di Polizia al Procuratore della Repubblica • Confessions of a Police Captain 70; La Moglie Più Bella 70; L'Istruttoria e Chiusa: Dimentichi! 71; Assassins of Rome • Girolimoni, il Mostro di Roma 72; The Devil Is a Woman • Il Sorriso del Grande Tentatore 72; Perche Si Uccide un Magistrato 74; The Tempter 74; Un Genio, Due Compari e un Pollo • The Genius 75*; I Am Afraid 77; Goodbye and Amen 78; L'Ultimo Nome 79; Un Uomo in Ginocchio 79; Time of the Jackals 80; Amityville II: The Possession 82; Attaco alla Piovra 84; The Pizza Connection • The Sicilian Connection 85; L'Inchiesta • The Inquest • The Inquiry • The Investigation 86; Il Re Ferito 88; Gioco al Massacro • Gioco di Massacro 89; The Dark Sun • Il Sole Buio

90

Damiano, Gerard Deep Throat 72; The Devil in Miss Jones 73; Legacy of Satan 73; Memories Within Miss Aggie 73; The Story of Joanna 75; Let My Puppets Come 77; Odyssey 77; Waterpower 78; For Richer for Poorer 80; Throat — 12 Years After 84

Damic, Charles Bomb at 10:10 66

D'Amico, Luigi Filippo Desert War 62; I Complessi • Complexes 65*; I Nostri Mariti • Our Husbands 66*

Damski, Mel Yellowbeard 83; Mischief 85; Murder by the Book 86; Happy Together 89

Damude, Brian Sudden Fury 75

D'Andrea, Anthony Thrillkill 84*

Dane, Lawrence Heavenly Bodies 85

Danelia, Georgy Seryozha • The Splendid Days • A Summer to Remember 60*; The Way to the Harbour 62; Walking the Streets of Moscow 63; Meet Me in Moscow • Ya Shagayu po Moskve 66; Don't Grieve 69*; Hopelessly Lost 72; Afonya 75; Mimino 77; Autumn Marathon • Osenny Marafon 78; Kin-Dza-Dza 87; Tridtsat Tri 88

Daneliuc, Mircea Jacob 88

Danford, Joe Weekend of Fear 66

D'Angelo, Nino Giuro Che Ti Amo • I Swear I Love You 86

Daniel, Jean-Louis Angel Skin • Peau d'Ange 83

Daniel, Rod Teen Wolf 85; Like Father, Like Son 87; K-9 89

Daniel-Norman, Jacques Ne Le Criez Pas sur les Toits 42; The Red Angel 50

Danielewski, Tad The Big Wave 60; Huis Clos • No Exit • Sinners Go to Hell • Stateless 62; The Guide • Survival 65

Daniels, Harold The Woman from Tangier 48; Daughter of the West 49; The Lawton Story 49*; The Prince of Peace 49*; Roadblock 51; Island of Monte Cristo • Sword of Venus 52; Beast of Paradise Island • Beast of Paradise Isle • Port Sinister 53; Bayou • Poor White Trash 57; My World Dies Screaming • Terror in the Haunted House 58; A Date with Death 59; Blood of the Man Devil • House of the Black Death • Night of the Beast 65*; Annabelle Lee 72

Daniels, Jack Meet Me at the Fair 52*

Daniels, Marc The Big Fun Carnival 57; Squeeze a Flower 69

Danielsson, Tage The Adventures of Picasso 78

Daninos, Jean-Daniel A Martian in Paris • Un Martien à Paris 61

D'Anna, Claude Partenaires 85; Salome 86; Macbeth 87; Équipe de Nuit 88

Danneborn, Bengt Promises • Det Stora Löftet 87

Danniel, Danniel Egg 88

Dansereau, Mireille Deaf to the City • Le Sourd dans la Ville 87

Danska, Herbert Black Love — White Love • It Won't Rub Off, Baby • Sweet Love, Bitter 67; Right On! 70

Dante, Joe Hollywood Boulevard 76*; Piranha 78; The Howling 80; Twilight Zone — The Movie 83*; Gremlins 84;

Explorers 85; Amazon Women on the Moon 86*; Innerspace 87; The 'burbs 89; Gremlins 2: The New Batch 90

Dantine, Helmut Thundering Jets 58

Danton, Ray Crypt of the Dead • Crypt of the Living Dead • Hannah, Queen of the Vampires • La Tumba de la Isla Maldita • Vampire Woman • Vampire Women • Young Hannah, Queen of the Vampires 72*; The Deathmaster 72; Psychic Killer 75

D'Antoni, Philip The Seven-Ups 73

Daquin, Louis Le Joueur 38*; Nous les Gosses • Portrait of Innocence • Us Kids 41; Madame et le Mort 42; Le Voyageur de la Toussaint 42; Premier de Cordée 43; Patrie 45; Nous Continuons la France 46; Les Frères Bouquinquant 47; La Grande Lutte des Mineurs 48; Le Point du Jour 48; La Bataille de la Vie • L'Oiseau Blanc 49; Le Parfum de la Dame en Noir 49; Maître Après Dieu • Skipper Next to God 50; Bel Ami 54; Les Chardons du Baragan • Ciulinii Bărăganului • The Thistles of Baragan 57; Les Arrivistes • La Rabouilleuse • Trübe Wasser 59; Machine Mon Ami 60; Parallèles 62; La Foire aux Cancres 63; Naissance d'une Cité 64

D'Arbo, Sebastián Trip to the Beyond • Viaje al Más Allá 80; El Ser 82

Darcus, Jack The Wolfpen Principle 74; Deserters 83; Overnight 86

Darday, István Film Novel, Three Sisters 78*; The Documentator • A Dokumentátor 89*

Dardenne, Jean-Pierre Falsch 87*

Dardenne, Luc Falsch 87*

Dare, Daniel The Main Event 38

Darellada, Juan Incertidumbre 36*

Darène, Robert Bernadette of Lourdes • Il Suffit d'Aimer 60

Dargay, Attila Saffi 85; The Captain of the Forest • Az Erdő Kapitánya 87

Daring, Jack see Moran, Percy

Dark, Gregory Bitter Cherry 83; The Cure 83; Retribution 83; The Superstitious Man 83

Darling, Joan First Love 77; The Check Is in the Mail 84

Darnborough, Anthony The Astonished Heart 49*; So Long at the Fair 50*

Darnley-Smith, Jan Go Kart Go! 64; Runaway Railway 65; A Ghost of a Chance 68; Up in the Air 69; The Waiters 69; Hoverbug 70; Fern the Red Deer 77; A Hitch in Time 78

Daroy, Jacques Generals Without Buttons 38; Rumors 49

D'Arrast, Harry D'Abbadie A Gentleman of Paris 27; Serenade 27; Service for Ladies 27; Dry Martini 28; The Magnificent Flirt 28; Laughter 30*; Raffles 30*; Topaze 33; It Happened in Spain • El Sombrero de Tres Picos • The Three-Cornered Hat • La Traviesa Molinera 34*; La Meunière Debauchée • Le Tricorne 34

Darroy, Jean Négatifs 32*

Dartonne, Monique High Speed 86*

Das, K. S. R. Satyagraham 88

Das, Sukhen Amar Kantak 87

Dasgupta, Buddhadep Phera 87

Dashiev, Arya The Dawn of the Doomed Gold Mine • Utro Obrachennogo Priiska 87

Dassin, Jules Artur Rubinstein 41; Nazi Agent • Salute to Courage 41; Pablo Casals 41; The Tell-Tale Heart 41; The Affairs of Martha • Once Upon a Thursday 42; Mademoiselle France • Reunion • Reunion in France • Reunion in Paris 42; Young Ideas 43; The Canterville Ghost 44; A Letter for Evie 45; Two Smart People 46; Brute Force 47; The Naked City 48; Thieves' Highway 49; Night and the City 50; Million Dollar Trio • Trio • The Trio: Rubinstein, Heifetz and Piatigorsky 52; Du Rififi chez les Hommes • Rififi 54; Celui Qui Doit Mourir • He Who Must Die 57; The Law • La Legge • La Loi • Where the Hot Wind Blows 58; Never on Sunday • Pote tin Kyriaki • Sonntags...Nie 59; Phaedra 61; The Light of Day • Topkapi 63; 10:30 P.M. Summer 66; Survival 1967 • Survival '67 67; Uptight! 68; La Promesse de l'Aube • Promise at Dawn 70; The Rehearsal 74; A Dream of Passion 77; Circle of Two 79

Dassin, Julius see Dassin, Jules

Datta, Raj Sarja 88

Datta, Salil Jar Je Priya 88

Dattaraj, Chi. Shrutiseridaga 88

Daugherty, Herschel Life with Father 47*; The Light in the Forest 58; The Plainsman • The Raiders 63; Il Magnifico Straniero 65

Daumery, John Rough Waters 30; Blind Spot 32; Help Yourself 32; A Letter of Warning 32; Meet My Sister 32; Postal Orders 32; Call Me Mame 33; Head of the Family 33; Little Miss Nobody 33; Mr. Quincey of Monte Carlo 33; Naughty Cinderella 33; The Thirteenth Candle 33; This Acting Business 33; Over the Garden Wall 34; Without You 34

Davenport, Charles E. The Governor's Boss 15; Broken Barriers 19

Davenport, Dorothy Linda 29; Sucker Money • Victims of the Beyond 33*; The Road to Ruin 34*; Woman Condemned 34

Davenport, Harry The Island of Regeneration 15; The Making Over of Geoffrey Manning 15; For a Woman's Fair Name 16; The Supreme Temptation 16; The False Friend 17; A Man's Law 17; The Millionaire's Double 17; A Son of the Hills 17; Tillie Wakes Up 17; A Woman Alone 17

Davenport, Harry Bromley Whispers of Fear 74; Xtro 82

D'Aversa, Alberto Una Voce nel Tuo Cuore • A Voice in Your Heart 52

Daves, Delmer Destination Tokyo 43; Hollywood Canteen 44; The Very Thought of You 44; Body and Soul • Forever in Love • Pride of the Marines 45; Dark Passage 47; The Red House 47; To the Victor 48; A Kiss in the Dark 49; Task Force 49; Broken Arrow 50; Bird of Paradise 51; Return of the Texan 52; Demetrius and the Gladiators 53; Never Let Me Go 53; Treasure of the Golden

Condor 53; Drum Beat 54; Jubal 56; The Last Wagon 56; 3:10 to Yuma 57; The Badlanders 58; Cowboy 58; Kings Go Forth 58; The Hanging Tree 59; A Summer Place 59; Parrish 60; Susan Slade 61; Lovers Must Learn • Rome Adventure 62; Spencer's Mountain 63; Affair at the Villa Fiorita • The Battle of the Villa Fiorita 64; Youngblood Hawke 64

Davey, Horace The Lion's Breath 16; The Sagebrush Lady 25*

David, Allan The Magic Fountain 61; Twist Craze 61

David, Charles Mam'zelle Nitouche 33; Lady on a Train 45; River Gang 45

David, Constantin J. Berlin After Dark 29; Herzblut 32

David, Graydon F. Six Pack Annie 75

David, Harold Career Girl 59

Davidson, Boaz Azit the Paratrooper Dog 72; Charlie and a Half 73; Lupo Goes to New York 77; The Tzanani Family 78; Seed of Innocence • Teen Mothers 80; Be My Valentine or Else... • Hospital Massacre • Ward 13 • X-Ray 81; Going Steady • Lemon Popsicle II 81; Hot Bubblegum • Lemon Popsicle III 81; Lemon Popsicle 81; The Last American Virgin 82; Lemon Popsicle IV • Private Popsicle 82; Alex Falls in Love • Alex Khole Ahava • Lovesick Alex 86; Dutch Treat 86; Going Bananas • My African Adventure 87; Salsa 88

Davidson, Carson The Wrong Damn Film 75

Davidson, Gordon The Trial of the Catonsville Nine 72

Davidson, Martin The Lords of Flatbush 74*; Almost Summer 78; Hero at Large 80; Eddie and the Cruisers 83; Heart of Dixie 89

Davidson, Robert W. Cry to the Wind 79

Davidson, Tito see Davison, Tito

Davidson, William Now That April's Here 58; Ivy League Killers 62

Davies, Bill Legend of Horror 72

Davies, Gareth Oliver Twist 85

Davies, John Acceptable Levels 83

Davies, Ray Return to Waterloo 85

Davies, Robert Saturday Night at the Palace 87

Davies, Terence Distant Voices, Still Lives 88

Davies, Valentine The Benny Goodman Story 55

Davila, Jacques Qui Trop Embrasse 86

Davis, A. Byron Fools of Fortune 22

Davis, Allan Rogue's March 52; The Clue of the New Pin 60; Clue of the Twisted Candle 60; The Fourth Square 61; The Square Mile Murder 61; Wings of Death 61; Moonshiner's Woman 68

Davis, Andrew My Main Man from Stony Island • Stony Island 78; Bump in the Night • Campsite Massacre • The Final Terror • The Forest Primeval 81; Code of Silence 85; Above the Law 88; The Package 89

Davis, Art Aw, Nurse 34*; The Concert Kid 34*; The Great Experiment 34*; Happy

Butterfly 34*; Holiday Land 34*; Scrappy's
Art Gallery 34*; Scrappy's Dog Show 34*;
Scrappy's Expedition 34*; Scrappy's Relay
Race 34*; Scrappy's Television 34*; Scrap-
py's Theme Song 34*; Scrappy's Toy Shop
34*; The Gloom Chasers 35*; Gold Get-
ters 35*; Graduation Exercises 35*; Let's
Ring Doorbells 35*; The Puppet Murder
Case 35*; Scrappy's Big Moment 35*;
Scrappy's Ghost Story 35*; Scrappy's
Trailer 35*; Dizzy Ducks 36*; Looney
Balloonists 36*; Playing Politics 36*;
Scrappy's Boy Scouts 36*; Scrappy's
Camera Troubles 36*; Scrappy's Pony 36*;
Canine Capers 37*; The Clock Goes
Round and Round 37*; The Fire Plug 37*;
I Want to Be an Actress 37*; Puttin' Out
the Kitten 37*; Scrappy's Band Concert
37*; Scrappy's Music Lesson 37*; Scrappy's
News Flashes 37*; The City Slicker 38*;
The Early Bird 38*; The Foolish Bunny 38;
Happy Birthday 38*; Hollywood Gradua-
tion 38; The New Homestead 38*; Scrap-
py's Playmates 38*; Scrappy's Trip to Mars
38*; The Charm Bracelet 39*; Millionaire
Hobo 39*; Park Your Baby 39*; Scrappy's
Added Attraction 39*; Scrappy's Rodeo
39*; Scrappy's Side Show 39*; A Worm's
Eye View 39*; Man of Tin 40*; Mr. Ele-
phant Goes to Town 40; A Peep in the
Deep 40*; Pooch Parade 40*; Practice
Makes Perfect 40*; Schoolboy Dreams 40*;
The Great Cheeze Mystery 40*; The Little
Theatre 41*; Way of All Pests 41; Who's
Zoo in Hollywood 41; Mouse Menace 46;
Catch As Cats Can 47; Doggone Cats 47;
A Foxy Duckling 47; The Goofy Gophers
47*; Mexican Joyride 47; Bone Sweet Bone
48; Dough Ray Me-ow 48; A Hick, a Slick
and a Chick 48; Nothing But the Tooth
48; Odor of the Day 48; The Pest That
Came to Dinner 48; The Rattled Rooster
48; Riff Raffy Daffy 48; The Stupor Sales-
man 48; Two Gophers from Texas 48;
What Makes Daffy Duck? 48; Bowery Bugs
49; Bye Bye Bluebeard 49; Dough for the
Do-Do 49*; Holiday for Drumsticks 49;
Porky Chops 49; Bugs Bunny's 3rd Movie:
1001 Rabbit Tales 82*
Davis, B. J. White Ghost 88
Davis, Charles The Day Kelly Came
Home • Gangster's Revenge • Get Out of
Town • Get Outta Town 60; Happy As the
Grass Was Green 73; Hazel's People 78
Davis, Dale Golden Breed 68
Davis, Desmond Born for Trouble 55;
The Girl with Green Eyes • Once Upon a
Summer 63; The Uncle 64; I Was Happy
Here • Passage of Love • Time Lost and
Time Remembered 65; Smashing Time 67;
A Nice Girl Like Me 69; Night Flight 79;
Clash of the Titans 81; The Country Girls
83; Sign of Four 83; Agatha Christie's
Ordeal by Innocence • Ordeal by Inno-
cence 84
Davis, Don For Love and Money • For
Love of Money 67; The Golden Box 70
Davis, Eddie Panic in the City 68; Col-
our Me Dead 69; It Takes All Kinds 69;
That Lady from Peking 70

Davis, Glenn Vincent Chiedi Perdono a
Dio Non a Me 68; Quintana 69
Davis, Hassoldt Sorcerers' Village 58
Davis, Herbert see Davis, Redd
Davis, J. Charles The Shadow 21*
Davis, James Trouble Brewing 24*
Davis, Joe Oddo 67
Davis, John Cry Wolf 68; Danger Point
71
Davis, Kate Girltalk 87
Davis, Mannie The Junk Man 27; The
Baby Show 28; A Blaze of Glory 28; High
Seas 28; A Jungle Triangle 28; Monkey
Love 28; Puppy Love 28; Scaling the Alps
28; The Spider's Lair 28; Sunny Italy 28;
Break of Day 29; Wash Day 29
Davis, Ossie Cotton Comes to Harlem
70; Kongi's Harvest 71; Black Girl 72; Gor-
don's War 73; Countdown at Kusini 76
Davis, Peter Hearts and Minds 74; The
White Laager 78; Generations of Resistance
80; The Rise and Fall of the Borscht Belt
86; Winnie/Nelson 86
Davis, Redd The Bells of St. Mary's 28;
Bunkered 29; Here's George 32; The Spare
Room 32; Ask Beccles 33; Excess Baggage
33; The Medicine Man 33; Send 'Em Back
Half Dead 33; The Umbrella 33; Easy
Money 34; The Girl in the Flat 34; Seeing
Is Believing 34; Handle with Care • Look
Out Mr. Haggis 35; Say It with Diamonds
35; Everything Okay • On Top of the
World 36; Excuse My Glove 36; King of
the Castle 36; The Biter Bit • Calling All
Ma's 37; Let the People Laugh • Sing As
You Swing 37; Underneath the Arches 37;
Variety Hour 37; Anything to Declare? 38;
Special Edition 38; Discoveries 39; That's
the Ticket 40; The Balloon Goes Up 42
Davis, Rex Motherland 27*
Davis, Robert Hartford see Hartford-
Davis, Robert
Davis, Robin I Married a Shadow 82;
Hors la Loi 85
Davis, Ronnie Have You Heard of the
San Francisco Mime Troup? 68*
Davis, Roy Surabaya Conspiracy 75
Davis, Ulysses The Iron Hand 16; The
Soul's Cycle 16
Davis, Walt Substitution 70
Davis, Will S. Thou Shalt Not 14; The
Avalanche 15; The Curious Conduct of
Judge Legarde 15; Destruction 15; Dr.
Rameau 15; The Family Stain 15; A Mod-
ern Magdalene 15; The Fool's Revenge 16;
Jealousy 16; Slander 16; The Straight Way
16; A Tortured Heart 16; The Victim 16;
Alias Mrs. Jessop 17; The Brass Check 18;
In Judgment of... 18; No Man's Land 18;
Under Suspicion 18; With Neatness and
Dispatch 18; The Eternal Mother 21; In-
discretion 21
Davis, Wray The Deadly Game 74
Davison, D. E. see Davis, Allan
Davison, Donn Demented Death Farm
Massacre 87*
Davison, Tito The Price of Living • El
Valor de Vivir 54; The Big Cube 69
Davletshin, Fardi The Emir's Secret
Voyage • Taynoe Puteshestvie Emira 87

Davy, Jean-François Érotique • Traque-
nards • Traquenards Érotiques 69
Dawei, Li see Lai, David
Dawkins, David Floodstage 86; Dépêche
Mode • Dépêche Mode 101 88*
Dawley, Herbert M. The Absent Minded
Poet 23; The Classic Centaur 23; The Lob-
ster Nightmare 23; Silliettes 23; Aladdin
and the Wonderful Lamp 24; Beauty and
the Beast 24; Cinderella 24; Jack and the
Beanstalk 24; Pan the Piper 24; Sleeping
Beauty 24; Tattercoats 24; Thumbelina 24;
Jack the Giant Killer 25
Dawley, J. Searle College Chums 07*;
Jack the Kisser 07*; Laughing Gas 07*; A
Little Girl Who Did Not Believe in Santa
Claus 07*; The Midnight Ride of Paul
Revere 07*; The Nine Lives of a Cat 07*;
A Race for Millions 07*; Rescued from an
Eagle's Nest 07*; The Rivals 07*; Stage
Struck 07*; Three American Beauties No.
2 07*; The Trainer's Daughter 07*; Blue-
beard 09*; Faust 09; Hansel and Gretel
09*; The Prince and the Pauper 09; A
Christmas Carol 10; Frankenstein 10;
Michael Strogoff 10; Aida 11*; The Battle
of Bunker Hill 11; The Battle of Trafalgar
11; The Doctor 11; Under the Tropical Sun
11; Van Bibber's Experiment 11; Aladdin
Up-to-Date 12; The Charge of the Light
Brigade 12; Partners for Life 12; Treasure
Island 12; Caprice 13; A Daughter of the
Hills 13; The Diamond Crown 13; A Good
Little Devil 13*; An Hour Before Dawn 13;
In the Bishop's Carriage 13*; A Lady of
Quality 13; Leah Kleschna 13; Mary Stuart
13; The Port of Doom 13; Tess of the
D'Urbervilles 13*; An American Citizen
14; In the Name of the Prince of Peace 14;
Marta of the Lowlands 14; Mrs. Black Is
Back 14; The Oath of a Viking 14; One of
Millions 14; The Pride of Jennico 14;
Salomy Jane 14*; A Woman's Triumph 14;
Always in the Way 15; A Daughter of the
People 15; Four Feathers 15; Helene of the
North 15; Still Waters 15; Little Lady
Eileen 16; Mice and Men 16; Miss George
Washington 16; Molly Make-Believe 16;
Out of the Drifts 16; The Rainbow Princess
16; Silks and Satins 16; Snow White 16;
Bab's Burglar 17; Bab's Diary 17; Bab's
Matinee Idol • Her Shattered Idol 17; The
Mysterious Miss Terry 17; The Seven Swans
17; The Valentine Girl 17; The Death
Dance 18; The Lie 18; Rich Man, Poor Man
18; Uncle Tom's Cabin 18; Everybody's
Business 19; The Phantom Honeymoon 19;
Twilight 19; Harvest Moon 20; Beyond
Price 21; A Virgin Paradise 21; A Little
Child Shall Lead Them • Who Are My
Parents? 22; As a Man Lives 23; Broadway
Broke 23; Has the World Gone Mad? 23
Daw-ming, Lee see Lee, Daw-ming
Dawn, Jack A Desperate Moment 26
Dawn, Norman Lasca 19; The Adorable
Savage 20; A Tokyo Siren 20; White
Youth 20; The Fire Cat 21; Thunder Island
21; Wolves of the North 21; Five Days to
Live 22; The Son of the Wolf 22; The Ver-
milion Pencil 22; Lure of the Yukon 24;

After Marriage 25; Justice of the Far North 25; Typhoon Love 26; Black Cargoes of the South Seas 29; Black Hills 29; The Mighty Tundra • Tundra 36; Orphans of the North 40; Arctic Fury 49*; Two Lost Worlds 50

Dawn, Vincent *see Mattei, Bruno*

Dawson, Anthony *see Margheriti, Antonio*

Dawson, Ralph The Girl in the Glass Cage 29; The Bermondsey Kid 33; The Life of the Party 34

Dawson, Vivienne T. Dan Smith 87*

Day, Ernest Green Ice 81; Waltz Across Texas 82

Day, Robert The Green Man 56; Strangers' Meeting 57; Corridors of Blood • The Doctor from Seven Dials 58; First Man Into Space • Satellite of Blood 58; Grip of the Strangler • The Haunted Strangler 58; Bobbikins 59; Life in Emergency Ward 10 59; Call Me Genius • The Rebel 60; Tarzan the Magnificent 60; Two-Way Stretch 60; Operation Snatch 62; Tarzan's Three Challenges 63; She 65; Tarzan and the Valley of Gold • Tarzan '65 • Tarzan '66 65; I Think We're Being Followed 67; Tarzan and the Great River 67; The Big Game 72; The Man with Bogart's Face • Sam Marlowe, Private Eye 80

Day, Will Whitewashing the Ceiling 14

Dayan, Nissim Light from Darkness 72; The End of Milton Levy 80; Children of Villa Emma 83; On a Narrow Bridge 85

Dayton, Lyman Baker's Hawk 76; Rivals 79; The Avenging 81; Solo 84; The Red Fury 85

De Almeida, Paulo Sérgio Beijo na Boca • The French Kiss 87

De Alva, Alfonso The Narc—Red Duel • El Narco—Duelo Rojo 86

Dean, A. L. The Half-Day Excursion 35

Dean, Basil The Constant Nymph 28*; The Return of Sherlock Holmes 29; Birds of Prey • The Perfect Alibi 30; Escape 30; Looking on the Bright Side 31*; The Impassive Footman • Woman in Bondage • Woman in Chains 32; Nine Till Six 32; The Constant Nymph 33; Loyalties 33; Autumn Crocus 34; Lorna Doone 34; Sing As We Go 34*; Look Up and Laugh 35; Mozart • Whom the Gods Love 36; The First and the Last • 21 Days • 21 Days Together 37; The Show Goes On 37; Penny Paradise 38*

Dean, Ralph The Accomplice 17; Madame Sherry 17; The Rainbow 17; A Song of Sixpence 17

De Anda, Gilberto El Ansia de Matar • The Urge to Kill 87; Fieras en Brama • Savage Creatures in Heat 87; Narcotics Police • Policías de Narcóticos 87

De Anda, Raúl The Country of the Mariachi • La Tierra del Mariachi 38; Wild Stampede 59

De Andrade, Joaquim Pedro Macunaima 70

Deane, Charles The World's a Stage 53; Blonde Blackmailer • Stolen Time 55

De Angelis, Fabrizio Deadly Impact 83; Thunder • Thunder Warrior 83; The Manhunt 84; Cobra Mission • Mission Cobra • The Rainbow Professional 86; Thunder Warrior II 87; Il Ragazzo dal Kimono d'Oro 88*

De Angelis, Nato Crossed Swords • Il Maestro di Don Giovanni 52*

De Angelis, Vertunio The Masked Man Against the Pirates 65

Deans, Marjorie The Girl Is Mine 50

De Antonio, Emile Point of Order 63; Rush to Judgement 66; America Is Hard to See 68; In the Year of the Pig 68; Millhouse: A White Comedy • Millhouse: A White House Comedy 71; Painters Painting 72; Underground 76*; In the King of Prussia 82; Mr. Hoover and I 89

Dear, Frank L. At the Old Crossed Roads 14; The Trail of the Lonesome Pine 14

Dear, William The Northfield Cemetery Massacre • The Northville Cemetery Massacre 76*; The Adventures of Lyle Swann • Timerider • Timerider: The Adventures of Lyle Swann 82; Big Foot and the Hendersons • Harry and the Hendersons 87

Dearden, Basil The Black Sheep of Whitehall 41*; The Goose Steps Out 42*; The Bells Go Down 43; The Halfway House 43; My Learned Friend 43*; They Came to a City 44; Dead of Night 45*; The Captive Heart 46; Frieda 47; Saraband • Saraband for Dead Lovers 48*; The Blue Lamp 49; Train of Events 49*; Cage of Gold 50; Pool of London 50; I Believe in You 51*; The Gentle Gunman 52*; The Square Ring 53*; Out of the Clouds 54*; The Rainbow Jacket 54*; PT Raiders • The Ship That Died of Shame 55*; Who Done It? 55*; Big Time Operators • The Smallest Show on Earth 57; Violent Playground 57; The League of Gentlemen 59; Sapphire 59; Man in the Moon 60; The Secret Partner • The Street Partner 60; All Night Long 61*; Victim 61; Condemned to Life • Life for Ruth • Walk in the Shadow 62; The Mind Benders 63; A Place to Go 63; Woman of Straw 63; Masquerade • Operation Masquerade • The Shabby Tiger 64; Khartoum 66*; Only When I Larf 67; The Assassination Bureau 68; The Man Who Haunted Himself 70

Dearden, James The Contraption 78; Panic 79; Diversion 80; Pascali's Island 88

Dearholt, Ashton At Devil's Gorge 23

De Armiñán, Jaime Mi Querida Señorita • My Dearest Señorita 72; It's Never Too Late 77; The Nest • El Nido 80; La Hora Bruja • The Witching Hour 85; Mi General • My General 87

Deasy, Frank The Courier 88*

De Baños, Ricardo El Mochuelo 05; Secrets of the Confession 06; Don Juan Tenorio 10; La Fuerza del Destino 10; Locura de Amor 11; The Lovers of Teruel 12; Magda 12; Don Juan de Serralonga 13; Juan José 17; The White Gypsy 19; Don Juan Tenorio 21; El Relicario • The Reliquary 33

De Banos, Richard *see De Baños, Ricardo*

De Baroncelli, Jacques La Maison de l'Espoir 15; Le Jugement de Salomon 16; La Nouvelle Antigone 16; Le Roi de la Mer 17; Une Vengeance 17; Le Retour aux Champs 18; Le Scandale 18; Le Siège des Trois 18; Ramuntcho 19; Flipotte 20; L'Héritage 20; La Rafale 20; Le Secret du Lone Star 20; Champi-Tortu 21; Le Père Goriot 21; Le Rêve 21; Le Carillon de Minuit 22; Roger-la-Honte 22; La Femme Inconnue 23; La Légende de Sœur Béatrix 23; Nêne 23; La Flambée de Rêves 24; Gitanes 24; Pêcheurs d'Islande 24; Nitchevo 25; Le Réveil 25; Veille d'Armes 25; Le Passager 26; Le Duel 27; Feu 27; La Femme et le Pantin 29; La Femme Su Voisin 29; La Tentation 29; L'Arlésienne 30; Je Serai Seule Après Minuit 31; Le Rêve Brumes 31; Le Dernier Choc 32; Crainquebille 33; Cease Firing • Cessez le Feu 34; Mystère de Paris 34; Michel Strogoff 36; Nitchevo 36; La Belle Étoile 38; S.O.S. Sahara 38; Fausse Alerte • The French Way 40; Forbidden Love • L'Homme du Niger 40; Le Pavillon Brûle 41; La Duchesse de Langeais • The Wicked Duchess 42; Haut de Vent 42; Les Mystères de Paris 43; Marie la Misère 45; La Rose de la Mer 46; Rocambole 47

De Barros, José Leitão Nazaré 28; Maria do Mar 29; Ala Ariba 42; The Dead Queen 45; Camoens 46

De Bear, Archie Radio Parade 33*

De Bello, John Attack of the Killer Tomatoes 78; Happy Hour • Sour Grapes 85; Return of the Killer Tomatoes! 88

De Bernardi, Piero Goodnight, Ladies and Gentlemen • Signore e Signori, Buonanotte 76*

De Boer, Leo *see Boer, Leo de*

De Bosio, Gianfranco Il Terrorista 63; La Bestia 71; Moses • Moses the Lawgiver 76

De Broca, Philippe *see Broca, Philippe de*

Decaë, Henri Le Carnaval Sacre 51; Faits d'Hiver 51; Le Garde-Chasse 51; Visite au Haras 51

De Carco, Francis Marked Girls 49

De Carlo, Andrea Trena di Panna 88

De Carvalho, J. P. Bonitinha Mas Ordinária • Pretty But Wicked 65

De Carvalho, Nelson Marcellino Men of Brazil 60*

De Casabianca, Camille Pékin Central • Peking Central 86; After the Rain • Après le Pluie 89

De Castro, Eduardo Zamboanga 38

De Castro, Pedro Jorge Tigipio 85

DeCelles, Pierre Pound Puppies and the Legend of Big Paw 88

De Chalonge, Christian O Salto • Le Saut • Voyage of Silence 67; Malevil 81

Dechang, Yang *see Yang, Edward*

De Chomón, Segundo The Electric Hotel • Hotel Eléctrico 05; Los Guapos del Parque 05; Le Chevalier Mystère 07; La

Légende du Fantôme 07; La Maison Hantée 07; Les Ombres Chinoises 07; La Passion de Jésus 07; Voyage à la Planète Jupiter 07; Cuisine Magnétique 08; Fabrique d'Argent 08; Les Jouets Vivants 08; Mars 08; Sleeping Beauty 08; La Table Magique 08; Transformation Élastique 08; A Journey to the Middle of the Earth • Voyage au Centre de la Terre 09; Liquéfaction des Corps Durs 09; Nuevo Viaje a la Luna • Voyage dans la Lune 09; Sculpteur Moderne 09; Adiós de un Artista 10; Amor Gitano 10; La Expiación 10; La Fatalidad 10; Flores y Perlas 10; El Puente de la Muerte 10; Pulgarcito 11

De Chomón, Sogon see De Chomón, Segundo

Decker, Jean-Pierre de see De Decker, Jean-Pierre

Decoin, Henri Les Bleus du Ciel 33; Je Vous Aimerai Toujours 33; Les Requins du Pétrole 33; Toboggan 34; Le Domino Vert 35; Abus de Confiance • Abuse of Confidence • Abused Confidence 37; Mademoiselle Ma Mère 37; Retour à l'Aube • She Returned at Dawn 38; Battements de Cœur 39; Her First Affair • Premier Rendez-Vous 41; Les Inconnus dans la Maison • Strangers in the House 41; Le Bienfaiteur 42; Mariage d'Amour 42; L'Homme de Londres 43; Je Suis avec Toi 43; Devil's Daughter • La Fille du Diable 46; Les Amants du Pont Saint-Jean 47; Les Amoureux Sont Seuls au Monde Monelle • Monelle 47; Non Coupable • Not Guilty 47; Between Eleven and Midnight • Entre Onze Heures et Minuit 48; Au Grand Balcon 49; Paris Incident • Three Telegrams • Trois Télégrammes 50; Clara de Montargis 51; Le Désir et l'Amour 51; The Truth About Our Marriage • La Vérité Sur le Bébé Donge 51; Les Amants de Tolède • The Lovers of Toledo 52; The Bed • Il Letto • Secrets d'Alcôve 53*; Dortoir des Grandes • Girls' Dormitory • Inside a Girls' Dormitory 53; Bonnes à Tuer • One Step to Eternity 54; Chnouf • Razzia • Razziá sur la Chnouf 54; Les Intrigantes 54; L'Affaire des Poissons 55; Le Feu aux Poudres 56; Folies Bergère 56; Anyone Can Kill Me • Tous Peuvent Me Tuer 57; Charmants Garçons 57; Too Many Lovers 57; The Cat • La Chatte • The Face of the Cat 58; Too Late to Love 58; Atomic Agent • Nathalie, Agent Secret 59; The Cat Shows Her Claws • La Chatte Sort Ses Griffes 59; Pourquoi Viens-Tu Si Tard? 59; La Française et l'Amour • Love and the Frenchwoman 60*; Passionate Affair • Tendre et Violente Élisabeth 60; Le Pavé de Paris 60; Maléfices • Where the Truth Lies 61; Le Masque de Fer 62; Casablanca, Nid d'Espions 63; Pariahs of Glory • Parias de la Gloire 63; License to Kill 64; Nick Carter Va Tout Casser 64

De Concini, Ennio Hitler: The Last Ten Days 73

De Cordova, Frederick Too Young to Know 45; Her Kind of Man 46; Always Together 47; Love and Learn 47; That Way

with Women 47; The Countess of Monte Cristo 48; For the Love of Mary 48; Wallflower 48; The Gal Who Took the West 49; Illegal Entry 49; Buccaneer's Girl 50; The Desert Hawk 50; Peggy 50; Bedtime for Bonzo 51; Chicago Masquerade • Little Egypt 51; Finders Keepers 51; Katie Did It 51; Bonzo Goes to College 52; Here Come the Nelsons • Meet the Nelsons 52; Yankee Buccaneer 52; Column South 53; I'll Take Sweden 65; Frankie and Johnny 66

De Cordova, Leander A Scream in the Night 19*; Love, Honor and Obey 20; Polly with a Past 20; She 25; After the Fog 30; Trails of the Golden West 31

DeCoteau, David Creepozoids 87; Dreamaniac 87; I Was a Teenage Sex Mutant 87; The Imp • Sorority Babes in the Slimeball Bowl-O-Rama • Sorority Sisters 87; Lady Avenger 87; Dr. Alien 88

De Courcy, Walter Fighting for Justice 24

De Courville, Albert Wanted Men • Wolves 30; Night Shadows 31; Park Lane • 77 Park Lane 31; The Midshipmaid • Midshipmaid Gob 32; There Goes the Bride 32; This Is the Life 33; Things Are Looking Up 34; Wild Boy 34; The Case of Gabriel Perry 35; Charing Cross Road 35; Doomed Cargo • Seven Sinners 36; Strangers' Honeymoon • Strangers on a Honeymoon 36; Clothes and the Woman 37; Oh Boy! 37; The Barbarian and the Lady • The Rebel Son • Taras Bulba 38*; Crackerjack • The Man with a Hundred Faces 38; Hidden Menace • Star of the Circus 38; An Englishman's Home • Mad Men of Europe 39; The Lambeth Walk 39

Decout, Bob Adieu Blaireau 85

De Crescenzo, Luciano The Bellavista Mystery • Il Mistero di Bellavista 85; 32 Dicembre 88

De Decker, Jean-Pierre Jumping • Springen 86

De Diestro, Alfredo Nobleza Ranchera • Rural Chivalry 39

Deek, Bashir el see El Deek, Bashir
Deem, Miles see Fidani, D.
Deerson, Jacques The Dark Side of Tomorrow 70*

Deesy, Alfréd A Triton • The Triton • A Tryton 17; Léleklátó Sugár • The Mind-Detecting Ray 18

De Falco, Martin Cold Journey 75
De Felice, Domenico The Blade in the Body • The Knife in the Body • La Lama nel Corpo • The Murder Clinic • The Murder Society • The Night of Terrors • Les Nuits de l'Épouvante • Revenge of the Living Dead 66*

De Felice, Lionello The Age of Indiscretion • L'Età dell'Amore 53; Cento Anni d'Amore 54; Constantine and the Cross 60

De Feo, Francesco The Prisoner of the Iron Mask • Vendetta della Maschera di Ferro • La Vengeance du Masque de Fer 60*

Deferre, Pierre Granier see Granier-Deferre, Pierre
De Filippo, Eduardo In Campagna È

Caduta una Stella 40; Ti Conosco Mascherina! 43; Napoli Milionaria • Side Street Story 50; Filumena Marturano 51; Les Sept Péchés Capitaux • I Sette Peccati Capitali • The Seven Deadly Sins 51*; Husband and Wife • Marito e Moglie 52; Ragazze da Marito 52; Napoletani a Milano 53; Questi Fantasmi 54; Fortunella 58; Il Sogno di una Notte di Mezza Sbornia 59; The Blonde Wife • Kiss the Other Sheik • Oggi, Domani e Dopodomani • Paranoia 64*; Shoot Loud, Louder...I Don't Understand • Spara Forte, Più Forte...Non Capisco 66

De Fuentes, Fernando El Anónimo 32; La Calandria 33; El Compadre Mendoza 33; El Prisionero 13 33; El Tigre de Yautepec 33; Cruz Diablo • The Devil's Cross 34; El Fantasma del Convento • The Fantasy of the Monastery • The Phantom of the Convent 34; La Familia Dressel • The Family Dressel 35; Let's Go with Pancho Villa • Vámonos con Pancho Villa • Allá en el Rancho Grande 36; Las Mujeres Mandan 36; Bajo el Cielo de México • Beneath the Mexican Sky • Beneath the Sky of Mexico 37; La Zandunga 37; La Casa del Ogro • The House of the Ogre 38; His Great Adventure • Su Gran Aventura 38; Rancho Grande 38; Papacito Lindo • Sugar Daddy 39; Allá en el Trópico 40; Creo en Dios 40; El Jefe Máximo 40; La Gallina Clueca 41; Así Se Quiere en Jalisco 42; Doña Bárbara 43; La Mujer Sin Alma 43; El Rey Se Divierte 44; Hasta Que Perdió Jalisco 45; La Selva de Fuego 45; La Devoradora 46; Allá en el Rancho Grande 48; Jalisco Canta en Sevilla 48; Hipólito, El de Santa 49; Crimen y Castigo 50; Por la Puerta Falsa 50; Canción de Cuna 52; Los Hijos de María Morales 52; Tres Citas con el Destino 53

DeGaetano, Michael A. U.F.O. Target Earth 74; The Haunted 76; Scoring 80
Degas, André American Autobahn 84
De Gastyne, Marco Inch'Allah 22; L'Aventure 23; À L'Horizon du Sud 24; La Blessure 25; La Châtelaine du Liban 26; Mon Cœur au Ralenti 28; La Merveilleuse Vie de Jeanne d'Arc 29; Rothschild 38
Degelin, Émile Dock 55; Faits Divers 56; Si le Vent Te Fait Peur 59
De Givray, Claude The Army Game • The Sad Sack • Tire-au-Flanc • Tire-au-Flanc 62 61*; Une Grosse Tête 62; Un Mari à Prix Fixe 63; L'Amour à la Chaîne • Chainwork Love • Loose Pleasures • Tight Skirts • Tight Skirts, Loose Pleasures 64

De Goldschmidt, Gilbert L'Étincelle 84
De Grasse, Joseph Alas and Alack 15; All for Peggy 15; Father and the Boys 15; Bobbie of the Ballet 16; The Gilded Spider 16; The Grasp of Greed 16; The Grip of Jealousy 16*; If My Country Should Call 16; The Mark of Cain 16; The Piper's Price 16; The Place Beyond the Winds 16; The Price of Silence 16; Tangled Hearts 16; Undertow 16; Anything Once 17; A Doll's House 17; The Girl in the Checkered Coat

17; Hell Morgan's Girl 17; Pay Me • Vengeance of the West 17; The Scarlet Car 17; Triumph 17; The Winged Mystery 17; After the War 18; Broadway Scandal 18; The Fighting Grin 18; The Rough Lover 18; The Wildcat of Paris 18; L'Apache 19; His Wife's Friend 19; Market of Souls 19; Bonnie May 20*; The Brand of Lopez 20; Forty-Five Minutes from Broadway 20; The Midlanders 20*; Nineteen and Phyllis 20; The Old Swimmin' Hole 21; A Tailor-Made Man 22; The Girl I Loved 23; Thundergate 23; Flowing Gold 24; The Hidden Way 26

De Gregorio, Eduardo Serail 76; Aspern 81

De Grunwald, Anatole The Gay Adventure 53

De Guia, Eric see Tahimik, Kidlat

De Guzman, Ruben Wild Force 87

De Haas, Max Ballad of the Top Hat 36; LO-LKP 48; Men and Microbes 51; Maskerage 52

DeHaven, Carter A Gentleman of Nerve 16; The Wrong Door 16; The Losing Winner 17; What Could Be Sweeter? 20; The Panic's On 22; Say It with Diamonds 23

De Heer, Rolf Tail of a Tiger • Tail of the Tiger 84; Driving Force 88; Incident at Raven's Gate 88

De Heredia, Álvaro Sáenz see Sáenz de Heredia, Álvaro

De Hesselle, Armand Congo Express 86*

Dehlavi, Jamil The Blood of Hussein 81; Born of Fire 87

Deimel, Mark The Perfect Match 87

Dein, Edward Sword of Granada 53*; Shack Out on 101 55; Calypso Joe 57; Seven Guns to Mesa 58; Curse of the Undead • Mark of the West 59; The Leech Woman 60; Das Bett einer Jungfrau • The Psychic Lover • Sweet Smell of Love • Una Vergine per un Bastardo 66

Deitch, Donna Desert Hearts 85

Deitch, Gene Alice of Wonderland in Paris 66

De Jarnatt, Steve Tarzana 79; Cherry 2000 86; Miracle Mile 88

De Jong, Ate see Jong, Ate de

De Kermadec, Liliane Aloïse 75

Dekeukeleire, Charles Combat de Boxe 27; Flamme Blanche 28; Impatience 28; Histoire de Lourdes 32; Terres Brulées 34; Le Mauvais Œil 38; Au Service des Prisonniers 42; Le Fondateur 47; Maisons 48; L'Espace d'une Vie 49

Dekker, Fred Night of the Creeps 86; The Monster Squad 87

De Kuharski, Jean Emerald of the East 28

De Lacey, Robert The Cowboy Musketeer 25; Let's Go Gallagher 25; The Wyoming Wildcat 25; The Arizona Streak 26; Born to Battle 26; The Cowboy Cop 26; The Masquerade Bandit 26; Out of the West 26; Red Hot Hoofs 26; Tom and His Pals 26; Wild to Go 26; The Cherokee Kid 27; Cyclone of the Range 27; The Flying U Ranch 27; Lightning Lariats 27; The

Sonora Kid 27; Splitting the Breeze 27; Tom's Gang 27; King Cowboy 28; Red Riders of Canada 28; Tyrant of Red Gulch 28; When the Law Rides 28; The Drifter 29; Idaho Red 29; The Pride of Pawnee 29; The Trail of the Horse Thieves 29; Pardon My Gun 30

De Lacy, Joseph see Elorrieta, José María

De Lacy, Philippe Cinerama Holiday 55*

De Lacy, Robert see De Lacey, Robert

De la Falaise, Henry Legong 35; Kliou the Killer 37

De la Iglesia, Eloy The Apartment on the Thirteenth Floor • Cannibal Man • La Semana del Asesino 72; El Diputado 77; Otra Vuelta de Tuerca • Turn of the Screw 85; La Estanquera de Vallecas 87

De la Loma, José Antonio Un Mundo para Mí • Soft Skin and Black Lace • Soft Skin on Black Silk • Tentations 64*; ¿Por Qué Seguir Matando? 66; The Boldest Job in the West • El Más Fabuloso Golpe del Far West • Nevada 71; Killing Machine 83; Target Eagle 84; A Man of Passion 89

Delamar, Mickey On Top of the Underworld 38*

De la Maza, Armando Vargas see Vargas de la Maza, Armando

Del Amo, Antonio One Against All • Solo Contro Tutti 65

De la Mothe, Leon The Desert Hawk 24; Northern Code 25; Ridin' Wild 25

De la Muir, Jean Mon Gosse de Père • The Parisian 31

De Lancy, Joseph see Elorrieta, José María

De Lane Lea, Jacques see Lea, Jacques de Lane

Delannoy, Gilles Carre Blanc 85*

Delannoy, Jean Franches Lippées 33; L'École des Détectives 34; Une Vocation Irrésistible 34; Paris-Deauville 35; La Moule 36; Ne Tirez Pas Dolly! • Ne Tuez Pas Dolly! 37; Tamara la Complaisante 37*; Le Paradis de Satan 38*; La Vénus de l'Or 38; Le Diamant Noir 39; Gambling Hell • Macao, l'Enfer du Jeu 39; Fièvres 41; L'Assassin A Peur de la Nuit 42; Pontcarral, Colonel d'Empire 42; The Eternal Return • L'Éternel Retour • Love Eternal 43; Le Bossu 44; Blind Desire • La Part de l'Ombre 45; La Symphonie Pastorale 46; The Chips Are Down • The Die Is Cast • Les Jeux Sont Faits 47; Aux Yeux du Souvenir • Souvenir 48; Dieu A Besoin des Hommes • God Needs Men • Isle of Sinners 49; Le Secret de Mayerling • The Secret of Mayerling 49; Le Garçon Sauvage • Savage Triangle • Wild Boy 51; Daughters of Destiny • Destinées • Love, Soldiers and Women 52*; La Minute de Vérité • The Moment of Truth • L'Ora della Verità 52; The Bed • Il Letto • Secrets d'Alcôve 53*; La Route Napoléon 53; Obsession 54; Chiens Perdus Sans Collier • The Little Rebels 55; Marie Antoinette • Shadow of the Guillotine 55; The Hunchback of Notre Dame • Notre-Dame de Paris 56; Inspector Maigret • Maigret Lays a Trap •

Maigret Sets a Trap • Maigret Tend un Piège • Woman Bait 57; Guinguette 58; Maigret et l'Affaire Saint-Fiacre 58; Le Baron de l'Écluse 59; La Française et l'Amour • Love and the Frenchwoman 60*; La Princesse de Clèves 60; Le Rendez-Vous 61; Imperial Venus • Venere Imperiale • Vénus Impériale 62; Les Amitiés Particulières • This Special Friendship 64; Le Majordôme 64; The Double Bed • Le Lit à Deux Places 65*; Les Sultans 65; Action Man • Leather and Nylon • Il Più Grande Colpo del Secolo • Le Soleil des Voyous 66; La Peau de Torpédo 69; Pas Folle la Guêpe 72; La Messagère 84; Bernadette 88

De la Parelle, L. Stripped for a Million 19

De la Parra, Pim see Parra, Pim de la

De la Patellière, Denys Les Aristocrates • The Aristocrats 55; Le Salaire du Péché 56; Les Œufs de l'Autruche 57; The Ostrich Has Two Eggs 57; Retour de Manivelle • There's Always a Price Tag 57; Les Grandes Familles • The Possessors 58; Thérèse Étienne 58; Rue de Paris • Rue des Prairies • Streets of Paris 59; Les Yeux de l'Amour 60; Taxi for Tobruk • Taxi nach Tobruk • Un Taxi para Tobrouk • Un Taxi pour Tobrouk 61; Le Bateau d'Émile 62; Pourquoi Paris 62; Tempo di Roma 63; L'Échiquier de Dieu • La Fabuleuse Aventure de Marco Polo • The Fabulous Adventures of Marco Polo • Marco le Magnifique • Marco Polo • Marco the Magnificent • Marko Polo • Le Meravigliose Avventure di Marco Polo 64*; God's Thunder • Le Tonnerre de Dieu 65; Black Sun • Dark Sunlight • Soleil Noir 66; Du Rififi à Paname • Rififi in Paris • Rififi Internazionale • The Upper Hand 66; Le Voyage du Père 66; Caroline Chérie 67; Le Tatoué 68; Death of a Jew • Sabra 70

De la Riva, Juan Antonio Obdulia 86

De la Texera, Diego Tesoro 88

De la Torre, Raúl Pobre Mariposa • Poor Butterfly 86; Color Escondido 88

De la Tour, Charles see De Lautour, Charles

De Lautour, Charles The Limping Man 53*; Impulse 54*; Child in the House 56*

Delavena, Jim see Madrid, José Luis

DeLay, Melville The Mystic Hour 34; Law of the Saddle • The Lone Rider in Law of the Saddle 43

D'Elba, Henri Alias Mary Brown 18*; Marked Cards 18

Delbez, Maurice On Foot, on Horse and on Wheels 57

Del Carril, Hugo Historia del 900 49; Sucros de Sangre 50; Las Aguas Bajan Turbias • Dark River • The River of Blood 52; La Quintrala 55; Una Cita con la Vida 58; Culpable 59; Las Tierras Blancas 59; Esta Tierra Es Mía 60; Amorina 61

Del Colle, Ugo Nobody's Children 26

De Leon, Gerardo see De Leon, Gerry

De Leon, Gerry Blood Creature • Terror Is a Man 59*; Amok • Moro Witch Doctor 64*; Intramuros • The Walls of Hell 64*; The Blood Drinkers • Vampire People 66;

Blood Doctor • Mad Doctor of Blood Island • Tomb of the Living Dead 68*; Brides of Blood • Grave Desires • Island of Living Horror • Orgy of Blood • Terror on Blood Island 68*; Creatures of Evil • Curse of the Vampires 70; Women in Cages • Women's Penitentiary III 72*

Delgado, Miguel Romeo and Juliet 44; El Supersabio 48; El Fantasma de la Casa Roja • The Phantom of the Red House 54; La Magia Negra • Misterios de la Magia Negra • Mysteries of Black Magic • Return from the Beyond 57; Chiquito Pero Picoso • El Superflaco • Il Superflaco 67; Por Mis Pistolas 69; The Daughter of Frankenstein • La Hija de Frankenstein • Santo Contra la Hija de Frankenstein • Santo vs. Frankenstein's Daughter • Santo vs. la Hija de Frankenstein 71; Santo y Blue Demon Contra Drácula y el Hombre Lobo 71; A Night on the Town • Noche de Juerga 86; The Devil Lurks Among Bar-Girls • Entre Ficheras Anda el Diablo 87

Delgado, Sean Alexa • Alexa: A Prostitute's Own Story 89

Del Grosso, Remigio The Savage Hordes 61; Tartar Invasion 62

D'Elia, Bill The Feud 89

Delia, Francis Freeway 88

De Liguoro, Eugenio Stop That Cab 51

De Lillo, Antonietta Una Casa in Bilico • A House on the Brink • A Tottering House • Tottering Lives 86*

De Limur, Jean Jealousy 29; The Letter 29; Runaway Ladies • The Slipper Episode 35

Deling, Bert Pure S 76

Dell, Jeffrey The Flemish Farm 43; Don't Take It to Heart 44; It's Hard to Be Good 48; The Dark Man 50; Carleton-Browne of the F.O. • Man in a Cocked Hat 58*

Delluc, Louis L'Américain • L'Américain ou Le Chemin d'Ernoa • Le Chemin d'Ernoa • The Road to Ernoa 20; Black Smoke • Fumée Noir 20*; Evangeline et le Tonnerre • Thunder • Le Tonnerre 20; Silence • Le Silence 20; Fever • Fièvre 21; La Femme de Nulle Part • The Woman from Nowhere 22; The Flood • L'Inondation 23

Delmaine, Barry Here We Come Gathering 45

Delman, Jeffrey S. Deadtime Stories 86

Delmer, Paul Caravan to Russia 59

Del Monte, Peter Fuori Campo 69; La Parole a Venire 70; Irene Irene 75; L'Altra Donna 80; Piso Pisello 81; Invitation au Voyage • Invitation to the Voyage 82; Little Flames • Piccoli Fuochi 85; Giulia e Giulia • Julia and Julia 87; Étoile • Star 89

Del Negro, Daniel Do Outro Lado do Espelho Atlantida 85

Delon, Alain Pour la Peau d'un Flic 81; Le Battant 83

Delon, Nathalie They Call That an Accident 82; Sweet Lies 86

De los Arcos, Luis Operación Dalila • Operation Delilah 66

Delouche, Dominique Twenty-Four Hours in a Woman's Life • Vier und

Zwanzig Stunden im Leben einer Frau • Vingt-Quatre Heures de la Vie d'une Femme 68

Del Río, Ernesto El Amor de Ahora • Love Today 87

Del Río, José L. López *see* López del Río, José L.

Del Ruth, Hampton Skirts 21; The Marriage Chance 22; Blondes by Choice 27; Naughty 27; Strange Adventure • The Wayne Murder Case 32*

Del Ruth, Roy Chase Me 20; Farmyard Follies 20; The Heart Snatcher 20*; His Noisy Still 20; Hungry Lions and Tender Hearts 20*; The Jazz Bandits 20; A Lightweight Lover 20; Should Dummies Wed? 20; Through the Keyhole 20; Be Reasonable 21; Hard Knocks and Love Taps 21; Love and Doughnuts 21; By Heck! 22; The Duck Hunter 22; Gymnasium Jim 22; Ma and Pa 22; Oh Daddy! 22; On Patrol 22; When Summer Comes 22; Asleep at the Switch 23; Flip Flops 23; Nip and Tuck 23; The Cat's Meow 24; A Deep Sea Panic 24; His New Mamma 24; The Hollywood Kid 24; The Masked Marvel 24; A Nip of Scotch 24; Shanghaied Lovers 24; Eve's Lover 25; Head Over Heels 25; Hogan's Alley 25; House of Flickers 25*; The Mysterious Stranger 25; Three Weeks in Paris 25; Across the Pacific 26; Fine Feathers • Footloose Widows 26; The Little Irish Girl 26; The Man Upstairs 26; The First Auto 27; Ham and Eggs • Ham and Eggs at the Front 27; If I Were Single 27; Wolf's Clothing 27; Ambitious Annie • Five and Ten Cent Annie 28; Beware of Bachelors 28; Conquest 28; Powder My Back 28; The Terror 28; The Aviator 29; The Desert Song 29; The Gold Diggers of Broadway 29; The Hottentot 29; Divorce Among Friends 30; Hold Everything 30; The Life of the Party 30; The Second Floor Mystery • The Second Story Murder 30; Three Faces East 30; Blonde Crazy • Larceny Lane 31; Dangerous Female • The Maltese Falcon 31; My Past 31; Side Show 31; Taxi! 31; Beauty and the Boss 32; Blessed Event 32; Winner Take All 32; Bureau of Missing Persons • Missing Persons 33; Captured! 33; Employees' Entrance 33; Lady Killer 33; The Little Giant 33; The Mind Reader 33; Bulldog Drummond Strikes Back 34; Kid Millions 34*; Upperworld 34; Broadway Melody of 1936 35; Folies Bergère • The Man from the Folies Bergère 35; Thanks a Million 35; Born to Dance 36; It Had to Happen 36; Private Number • Secret Interlude 36; Broadway Melody of 1938 37; On the Avenue 37; Happy Landing 38; My Lucky Star 38; Tail Spin 38; He Married His Wife 39; Here I Am a Stranger 39; The Star Maker 39; The Chocolate Soldier 41; Topper Returns 41; Maisie Gets Her Man • She Got Her Man 42; Broadway Rhythm 43; DuBarry Was a Lady 43; Barbary Coast Gent 44; Ziegfeld Follies 45*; It Happened on Fifth Avenue 47; The Babe Ruth Story 48; Always Leave Them Laughing 49; Red Light 49; Fine

and Dandy • The West Point Story 50; On Moonlight Bay 51; Starlift 51; About Face 52; Stop, You're Killing Me 52; Three Sailors and a Girl 53; Phantom of the Rue Morgue 54; The Alligator People 59; Thirteen Steps to Death • Why Must I Die? 60

Delson, Susan Far from Poland 83*

De Luca, Paul Wire Service 42

De Luca, Rudy Transylvania 6-5000 85

De Lucenay, A. Martin A lo Macho • In Rough Style 39

De Lue, Eugene The Thrill Hunter 26

DeLuise, Dom Hot Stuff 79

De Lussanet, Paul Mysteries 78; Dear Boys 81

Delvaux, André Forges 53*; Nous Étions Treize 56; Cinéma, Bonjour! 58*; La Planète Fauve 59*; Two Summer Days 59; Yves Boit du Lait 60; Den Haagschool • Schooldays • Le Temps des Écoliers 62; L'Homme au Crâne Rasé • De Man Die Zijn Haar Kort Liet Knippen • The Man Who Had His Hair Cut Short • The Man with the Shaven Head 65; Les Interprètes • Tolken 68; One Night...a Train • Un Soir...un Train 68; Appointment in Bray • Rendez-Vous à Bray 71; Belle 73; Met Dieric Bouts • With Dieric Bouts 75; Femme Entre Chien et Loup • Een Vrouw Tussen Hond en Wolf • Woman in a Twilight Garden • Women in Twilight 79; To Woody Allen, from Europe with Love 80; Benvenuta 82; Babel Opéra • Babel-Opéra • Babel-Opéra ou La Répétition de Don Juan 85; The Abyss • L'Œuvre au Noir 88

De Manby, Alfred Mephisto 12*

Demare, Lucas Guerra des Gauchos 42; Pampa Bárbara • Savage Pampas 43*; La Zafra 58

De Mareuil, Stephanie Cœurs Croisés 87

De Marguenat, Jean Miche 32; Le Prince Jean 36; The Street Singer 37

De Marsan, Charles Renoncement 17*; La Mascotte des Poilus 18*; La Bourasque 20*; Le Droit de Tuer 20*; Le Lys Rouge 20*; L'Assommoir 21*; Un Aventurier 21*; La Fiancée du Disparu 21*; L'Inconnu 21*; Le Merchant Homme 21*; Près de Crime 21*; Le Talison 21*; Serge Panin 22*; L'Homme du Train 117 23*; Rocambole 23*; Les Amours de Rocambole 24*; Les Premières Armes de Rocambole 24*

De Martino, Alberto Blancheville Monster 63; La Carica del 70 Cavallegeri • The Charge of the Seventh Cavalry 64; Gli Eroi di Fort Worth 64; Hercules and the Ten Avengers 64; Hercules vs. the Giant Warriors • Il Trionfo di Ercole • The Triumph of Hercules 64; Centomila Dollari per Ringo 65; Django Spara per Primo • He Who Shoots First 66; Los Invencibles • Gli Invincibili Sette • The Secret Seven 66; Bandits in Rome • Rome Like Chicago 67; O.K. Connery • Operation Kid Brother • Secret Agent OO 67; Dirty Heroes • Là dalle Ardenne all'Inferno • Und Morgen Fahrt Ihr zur Hölle 69; Crime Boss 72; Scenes from a Murder 72; Ci Risiamo Vero Provvidenza 73; The

Antichrist • L'Anticristo • The Tempter 74; Blazing Magnum • Shadows in an Empty Room • Strange Shadows in an Empty Room 76; The Chosen • Holocaust 2000 77; The Puma Man 80; Formula for a Murder • Formula for Murder 86; Miami Golem 86

Dembo, Richard Dangerous Moves • La Diagonale du Fou 83

Demchuk, Bob Whatever It Takes 86

Deme, Masanobu Station to Heaven 85; Ballad of Genkai Sea • Genkai Tsurezure Bushi 86

De Meideros, Richard The Newcomer • Le Nouveau Venu 79

Demert, V. The Double 16

Demetrakas, Johanna Celebration at Big Sur 71*; Right Out of History: The Making of Judy Chicago's Dinner Party 80

Demicheli, Tulio Carmen, La de Ronda • The Devil Made a Woman • A Girl Against Napoleon 59; Il Figlio del Capitano Blood • El Hijo del Capitán Blood • The Son of Captain Blood 62; Desafío en Río Bravo • Duel at Rio Bravo • Duelo a Río Bravo • Gunmen of the Rio Grande • Jennie Lees Ha una Nuova Pistola • Sfida a Rio Bravo • El Sheriff del O.K. Corral 64; Un Uomo e una Colt 67; Assignment Terror • Dracula Jagt Frankenstein • Dracula vs. Frankenstein • Frankenstein • El Hombre Que Vino de Ummo • The Man Who Came from Ummo • Los Monstruos del Terror 69*; Arriva Sabata 70; The Cauldron of Death 79

DeMille, Cecil B. The Squaw Man • The White Man 13*; Brewster's Millions 14*; The Call of the North 14*; The Ghost Breaker 14*; The Girl of the Golden West 14; The Man from Home 14; The Man on the Box 14*; The Master Mind 14*; The Only Son 14*; Rose of the Rancho 14; The Virginian 14; The Warrens of Virginia 14; What's His Name 14; The Arab 15; The Captive 15; Carmen 15; The Cheat 15; Chimmie Fadden 15; Chimmie Fadden Out West 15; The Golden Chance 15; The Goose Girl 15*; Kindling 15; Maria Rosa 15; Temptation 15; The Trail of the Lonesome Pine 15; The Unafraid 15; The Wild Goose Chase 15; The Dream Girl 16; The Heart of Nora Flynn 16; Joan the Woman 16; The Devil Stone 17; The Little American 17; Nan of Music Mountain 17*; A Romance of the Redwoods 17; The Whispering Chorus 17; The Woman God Forgot 17; Don't Change Your Husband 18; Old Wives for New 18; The Squaw Man • The White Man 18; Till I Come Back to You 18; We Can't Have Everything • You Can't Have Everything 18; The Admirable Crichton • Male and Female 19; For Better, for Worse 19; Why Change Your Wife? 19; The Affairs of Anatol • A Prodigal Knight 20; Forbidden Fruit 20; Something to Think About 20; Don't Tell Everything 21*; Fool's Paradise 21; Saturday Night 21; Adam's Rib 22; Manslaughter 22; The Ten Commandments 23; Feet of Clay 24; The Golden

Bed 24; Triumph 24; The Road to Yesterday 25; The Volga Boatman 25; The King of Kings 26; The Godless Girl 28; Dynamite 29; Madame Satan 30; The Squaw Man • The White Man 31; The Sign of the Cross 32; This Day and Age 32; Four Frightened People 33; Cleopatra 34; The Crusades 35; The Plainsman 36*; The Buccaneer 37; Union Pacific 38; North West Mounted Police 40; Reap the Wild Wind 42; The Story of Dr. Wassell 43*; Unconquered 46; California's Golden Beginning 48; Samson and Delilah 48; The Greatest Show on Earth 51; The Ten Commandments 54

DeMille, William Anton the Terrible 16; The Black List 16; The Clown 16; Common Ground 16; The Heir to the Hoorah 16; The Ragamuffin 16; The Sowers 16; The Ghost House 17; Hashimura Togo 17; The Secret Game 17; The Honor of His House 18; Mirandy Smiles 18; The Mystery Girl 18; One More American 18; The Widow's Might 18; Yellow Tickets 18; Peg o' My Heart 19; Conrad in Quest of His Youth 20; Jack Straw 20; Midsummer Madness 20; Prince Chap 20; The Tree of Knowledge 20; After the Show 21; The Lost Romance 21; Miss Lulu Bett 21; What Every Woman Knows 21; Bought and Paid For 22; Clarence 22; Nice People 22; Don't Call It Love 23; Grumpy 23; The Marriage Maker 23; Only 38 23; The World's Applause 23; The Bedroom Window 24; The Fast Set 24; Icebound 24; Locked Doors 25; Lost: A Wife 25; Men and Women 25; New Brooms 25; The Splendid Crime 25; For Alimony Only 26; The Runaway 26; The Little Adventuress 27; Craig's Wife 28; Tenth Avenue 28; The Doctor's Secret 29; The Idle Rich 29; Passion Flower 30; This Mad World 30; Two Kinds of Women 32; His Double Life 33*

Deming, Norman Mandrake, the Magician 39*; Overland with Kit Carson 39*; Riders of Black River 39; The Taming of the West 39

De Mitri, Leonardo Angelo in the Crowd 52; Verginità 53; A Bride for Frank 56

Demme, Jonathan Gidgette Goes to Hell 72*; Caged Heat • Renegade Girls 74; Crazy Mama 75; Fighting Mad 76; Citizens Band • Handle with Care 77; The Last Embrace 78; Melvin and Howard 80; Swing Shift 83; Stop Making Sense 84; The Perfect Kiss 85; Something Wild 86; Swimming to Cambodia 87; Haiti Dreams of Democracy 88*; Married to the Mob 88

De Morlhon, Camille L'Ambitieuse 12; Sacrifice Surhumain 13; Une Brute Humaine 14; Sous l'Uniforme 14; Fille d'Artiste 16; Maryse 17; Miséricorde 17; L'Orage 17; Expiation 18; Simone 18; Éliane 19; L'Ibis Bleu 19; Fabienne 20; La Fille du Peuple 20; Une Fleur dans les Ronces 21

De Moro, Pierre Devil's Ivy 73; Christmas Mountain 80; Savannah Smiles 82; Hellhole 85

De Mott, Joel Seventeen 84*

Demsky, Isidore *see Douglas, Kirk*

Demy, Jacques Le Sabotier du Val de Loire 55; Le Bel Indifférent 57; Musée Grévin 58*; Ars 59; La Mère et l'Enfant 59*; Donna di Vita • Lola 60; Les Sept Péchés Capitaux • I Sette Peccati Capitali • Seven Capital Sins • The Seven Deadly Sins 61*; La Baie des Anges • Bay of Angels • Bay of the Angels 62; Les Parapluies de Cherbourg • The Umbrellas of Cherbourg 64; Les Demoiselles de Rochefort • The Young Girls of Rochefort 66; Far from Vietnam • Loin du Viêt-nam 66*; The Model Shop 68; Donkey Skin • The Magic Donkey • Peau d'Âne 70; The Pied Piper • The Pied Piper of Hamelin 71; L'Événement le Plus Important Depuis Que l'Homme A Marché sur la Lune • A Slightly Pregnant Man 73; Lady Oscar 78; Une Chambre en Ville • A Room in Town 82; Parking 85; La Table Tournante 87; Trois Places pour le 26 88

DeMyest, E. G. We Lived Through Buchenwald 47

Denbaum, Drew Nickel Mountain 83

Den Berg, Rudolf van *see Berg, Rudolf van den*

Denby, Jerry Whip's Women 68; Pleasure Plantation 70

Denham, Reginald Called Back 33*; The Jewel 33; Borrow a Million 34; Brides to Be 34; Death at a Broadcast • Death at Broadcasting House 34; Lucky Loser 34; The Primrose Path 34; Lieutenant Daring, RN 35; Lucky Days 35; The Price of Wisdom 35; The Silent Passenger 35; The Village Squire 35; Calling the Tune 36; The Crimson Circle 36; Dreams Come True 36; The House of the Spaniard 36; Kate Plus Ten • Queen of Crime 38; Blind Folly 39; Flying Fifty-Five 39; Anna di Brooklyn • Anna of Brooklyn • Fast and Sexy 58*

Den Horst, Herman van *see Horst, Herman van den*

Denis, Armand Goona-Goona 32*; Wild Cargo 34; Dark Rapture 38; Frank Buck's Jungle Cavalcade • Jungle Cavalcade 41*; Below the Sahara 53; Among the Headhunters 55*

Denis, Claire Chocolat 88

Denis, Jean-Pierre The Bird Watch • La Palombière 83; Champ d'Honneur • Field of Honor 87

Denis, Michaela Among the Headhunters 55*

Denison, Jane All Clear, No Need to Take Cover 17

Denney, Craig The Astrologer 75

Dennis, Charles Reno and the Doc 84

Denny, Reginald The Big Bluff • Worthy Deceivers 33

D'Enrico, Corrado All of Life in One Night • Tutta la Vita in Una Notte 40; Star of the Sea • Stella del Mare 40

Densham, Pen The Zoo Gang 85*; The Kiss 88

Denton, Jack The Yule Log 14; The Airman's Children 15; Barnaby 19; The Heart of a Rose 19; A Lass o' the Looms 19;

Ernest Maltravers 20; Lady Audley's Secret 20; The Twelve Pound Look 20; Our Aggie 21; Sybil 21; The Doddington Diamonds 22

Deodato, Ruggero Donne...Botte e Bersaglieri 68; Fenomenal e il Tesori di Tutankamen 68; Gungala la Pantera Nuda 68; I Quattro del Pater Noster 69; Vacanze sulla Costa Smeralda 69; Zenabel 69; Una Ondata di Piacere 75; The Last Cannibal World • The Last Survivor • Ultimo Mondo Cannibale 76; Uomini Si Nasce Poliziotti Si Muore 76; L'Ultimo Sapore dell'Aria 78; Cannibal Holocaust 79; Concorde Affaire '79 79; La Casa nel Parco • La Casa Sperduta nel Parco • The House on the Edge of the Park 80; I Predatori di Atlantide 83; Cut and Run • Hell, Live • Inferno in Diretta 85; The Lone Runner 86; The Barbarians • The Barbarians and Co. 87; Camping del Terrore • Terror Camping Site 87; Casablanca Express 88; Un Delitto Poco Comune 88; Dial: Help 88; Phantom of Death 88

De Oliveira, Manoel Douro, Faina Fluvial • Hard Labor on the River Douro 29; Estátuas de Lisboa 31; A Canção de Lisboa 33; Em Portugal Já Se Fazem Automóveis • Já Se Fabricam Automóveis em Portugal 38; Miramar, Beach of Roses • Miramar, Praia de Rosas 39; Famalicão 40; Aniki-Bobo 42; The Painter and the City • O Pintor e a Cidade 56; O Coração • The Heart 58; Bread • O Pão 59; Ato da Primavera • The Passion of Jesus 60; A Caça • The Hunt 60; My Brother Julio's Paintings • Pictures of My Brother Julio • As Pinturas do Meu Irmão Julio 65; O Passado e o Presente • Past and Present 72; Benilde ou A Virgem Mãe • Benilde, Virgin and Mother 75; Amor de Perdição • Ill-Fated Love 78; Francisca 81; Memórias e Confissões • Memories and Confessions 82; Cultural Lisbon • Lisboa Cultural 83; À Propos de Vigo • Nice à Propos de Jean Vigo 84; O Sapato de Cetim • The Satin Slipper • Le Soulier de Satin 85; O Meu Caso—Repetições 86; Mon Cas • My Case 86; Os Canibais 88

De Orduna, Juan Locura de Amor • The Mad Queen • The Siege 50

De Ossorio, Amando I Tre del Colorado 65; Fangs of the Living Dead • Malenka • Malenka—La Nipote del Vampiro • Malenka—La Sobrina del Vampiro • Malenka the Vampire • The Niece of the Vampire • La Nipote del Vampiro • The Vampire's Niece 68; The Night of the Sorcerers • La Noche de los Brujos 70; The Blind Dead • Crypt of the Blind Dead • Night of the Blind Dead • La Noche de la Muerte Ciega • La Noche del Terror Ciego • Tombs of the Blind Dead 71; Las Garras de Lorelei • The Lorelei's Grasp • When the Screaming Stops 72; El Ataque de los Muertos Sin Ojos • The Return of the Evil Dead 73; El Buque Maldito • The Ghost Galleon • Horror of the Zombies • La Noche del Buque Maldito 74; Demon Witch Child • La Endemoniada • El Poder de las Tinieblas

74; Night of the Seagulls • La Noche de las Gaviotas 75; People Who Own the Dark • Planeta Ciego 75

DePalma, Brian Icarus 60; 660124: The Story of an IBM Card 61; Wotan's Wake 62; Jennifer 64; Mod 64; The Wedding Party 64*; Bridge That Gap 65; The Responsive Eye 65; Show Me a Strong Town and I'll Show You a Strong Bank 66; Murder à la Mod 67; Dionysus in '69 68*; Greetings 68; Blue Manhattan • Confessions of a Peeping John • Hi, Mom! • Son of Greetings 70; Blood Sisters • Sisters 72; Get to Know Your Rabbit 72; Phantom of the Paradise 74; Obsession 75; Carrie 76; The Fury 78; Home Movies 79; Dressed to Kill 80; Blow Out 81; Scarface 83; Body Double 84; Wise Guys 86; The Untouchables 87; Casualties of War 89; Bonfire of the Vanities 90

De Paola, Alessio Chastity 69

Depardieu, Gérard Le Tartuffe 84

Depardon, Raymond Empty Quarter 85

De Paula, Francisco Areias Escaldantes • Burning Sands 87

De Poligny, Serge Acres of Turf • Les As du Turf 35; Claudine 40; Le Baron Fantôme • The Phantom Baron 43; The Thirst of Men 52

Deppe, Hans Ferien Vom Ich 35; Die Heilige und Ihr Narr • The Saint and Her Fool 35; Herr Kobin Geht auf Abenteuer • Mr. Kobin Seeks Adventure 35; The Rider of the White Horse • Der Schimmelreiter 35*; Schloss Hubertus 35; Der Mutige Seefahrer 36; Der Jäger von Fall 37; Pretty Miss Schragg 37; Das Schweigen im Walde • The Silence of the Forest 37; Gewitter im Mai • Storms in May 38; Das Ekel • The Grouch 39; Die Kluge Schwiegermutter • The Wise Mother-in-Law 39; Twice Two in a Four-Post Bed • Zweimal Zwei im Himmelbett 39; Die Drei um Christine • The Three After Christine 40; Eternal Love 60

Deray, Jacques Le Gigolo 60; Rififi à Tokyo • Rififi in Tokyo 61; The Corrupt • The Mystifiers • Sinfonia per un Massacro • Symphonie pour un Massacro • Symphony for a Massacre 63; Par un Beau Matin d'Été 64; Gold Fever • L'Homme de Marrakech • Our Man in Marrakesh • Los Saqueadores del Domingo • That Man George! 65; Avec la Peau des Autres 66; La Piscine • The Sinner • The Swimming Pool 68; Borsalino 70; Doucement les Basses! • Easy Down There! 71; Un Peu de Soleil dans l'Eau Froide 71; Un Homme Est Mort • The Outside Man 72; Borsalino and Co. 74; Flic Story 75; Le Gang 76; A Butterfly on the Shoulder • Un Papillon sur l'Épaule 78; Three Men to Destroy • Trois Hommes à Abattre 80; Le Marginal 83; He Died with His Eyes Open • On Ne Meurt Que Deux Fois 85; Règlements de Comptes 86; The Loner • Le Solitaire 87; Maladie d'Amour • Malady of Love 87*; Les Bois Noirs 89

Derbysheva, L. The World Dances 58

Derek, John No Toys for Christmas • Once Before I Die 65; Childish Things •

Confessions of Tom Harris • Tale of the Cock 66*; A Boy...a Girl • The Sun Is Up 68; And Once Upon a Love • And Once Upon a Time • Fantasies 73; Tarzan, the Ape Man 81; Bolero • Bolero: An Adventure in Ecstasy 84; Ghosts Can't Do It 90

Deren, Eleanora see Deren, Maya

Deren, Maya Meshes of the Afternoon 43*; At Land 44; Choreography for Camera • A Study in Choreography for Camera 45; The Private Life of a Cat 45*; Ritual in Transfigured Time 46; Meditation on Violence 48; The Very Eye of Night 58; The Witch's Cradle 61; Out-Takes from Maya Deren's Study in Choreography for Camera 75

De Renzy, Alex Little Sisters 72

Der Heyde, Nikolai van see Heyde, Nikolai van der

De Ribon, Roberto Man of the Sea 48*

De Rico, Luca Le Avventure di Topo Gigio • The Italian Mouse • The Magic World of Topo Gigio 61*

De Ridder, Hans see Ridder, Hans de

De Rieux, Max La Cousine Bette 28

Der Kloot, William van see Kloot, William van der

Der Meulen, Karst van see Meulen, Karst van der

Der Noss, Rudolf von see Noss, Rudolf von der

De Robertis, Francesco Mine in Vista 40; S.O.S. Submarine • Uomini sul Fondo 41; Alfa Tau 42; Marina Senza Stella 43; Uomini e Cieli 43; La Vite Semplice 45; La Voce di Paganini 47; Fantasmi del Mare 48; Il Murato 49; Gli Amanti di Ravello 50; Angelo 51; Carica Eroica • Heroic Charge 52; Frogman Spy • Mizar 54; Uomini-Ombra 55; La Donna Che Venne dal Mare 56; Ragazzi della Marina 58

De Rochemont, Louis III The First World War 34; The Ramparts We Watch 40; We Are the Marines 42; Windjammer 58*

De Rooy, Felix see Rooy, Felix de

De Roubaix, Paul Villes-Lumière 59*

Dertano, Robert C. Blonde Pickup 55; Journey to Freedom 57

Deruddere, Dominique Crazy Love • Love Is a Dog from Hell 87; Wait Until Spring, Bandini 89

De Sano, Marcel Beautifully Trimmed 20; The Dangerous Moment 21; The Girl Who Wouldn't Work 25; Blarney 26; Peacock Alley 30

De Santis, Giuseppe Days of Glory • Giorni di Gloria 45*; Caccia Tragica • Pursuit • Tragic Hunt • The Tragic Pursuit 47; Bitter Rice • Riso Amaro 48; Blood on Easter Sunday • No Peace Among the Olives • No Peace Under the Olives • Non C'È Pace Tra gli Ulivi • Under the Olive Tree 49; It Happened in Rome • Roma, Ora Undici • Rome, Eleven o'Clock 51; A Husband for Anna • Un Marito per Anna Zaccheo 53; Days of Love • Giorni d'Amore 54; Men and Wolves • Uomini e Lupi 56; Cesta Duga Godinu Dana • The Road a Year Long • La Strada Lunga un

Anno 57; L'Uomo Senza Domenica 57; La Garçonnière 60; Attack and Retreat • Italiani Brava Gente • Oni Shli na Vostok • They Went to Vostok 64; Un Apprezzato Professionista di Sicuro Avvenire 71

De Sanzo, John C. *see De Sanzo, Juan Carlos*

De Sanzo, Juan Carlos En Retirada • In Retirement 84; La Búsqueda • The Search 87

De Sarkar, Rathis *see Sarkar, Rathis De*

Deschamps, Dominique Bernard *see Bernard-Deschamps, Dominique*

Deschanel, Caleb The Escape Artist 81; Crusoe 88

De Seta, Vittorio Isole di Fuoco 54; Lu Tempu di li Pisci Spata 54; Bluefin Fury • Contadini del Mare 55; Easter in Sicily • Pasqua in Sicilia 55; Parabolo d'Oro 55; Sulfatara 55; Fishermen • Pescherecci 57; Un Giorno in Barbagia 58; Pastori di Orgosolo 58; I Dimenticati 59; Banditi a Orgosolo • The Bandits at Orgosolo • Bandits of Orgosolo 61; Almost a Man • Half a Man • Un Uomo a Metà 65; L'Invitata • The Invited • L'Invitée 69; Diary of a Teacher 72

Desfontaines, Henri Les Amours de la Reine Élisabeth • Élisabeth Reine d'Angleterre • Queen Elizabeth 12*; Les Bleus de l'Amour 18; Sa Gosse 19; La Suprême Épopée 19; Autour du Mystère 20; La Marseillaise 20; Chichinette et Clé 21; La Fille des Chiffonniers 22; L'Insigne Mystérieux 22; Château Historique 23; L'Espionne 23; Madame Flirt 23; L'Œillet Blanc 23; Vers Abécher la Mystérieuse 24; L'Espionne aux Yeux Noirs 26

Deshon, Ramiro Lacayo *see Lacayo-Deshon, Ramiro*

De Sica, Vittorio Due Dozzine di Rose Scarlatte • Red Roses • Rose Scarlatte • Rose Scarlatte, Mélodie Éterne 39*; Maddalena, Zero for Conduct • Maddalena, Zero in Condotta 40; Doctor Beware • Teresa Venerdì 41; A Garibaldian in the Convent • Un Garibaldino al Convento 41; I Bambini Ci Guardano • The Children Are Watching Us • The Little Martyr • Il Piccolo Martire 42; The Gate of Heaven • La Porta del Cielo 44; Sciuscià • Shoeshine 46; The Bicycle Thief • Bicycle Thieves • Ladri di Biciclette 48; Miracle in Milan • Miracolo a Milano 50; Umberto D 52; Indiscretion • Indiscretion of an American Wife • Stazione Termini • Terminal Station • Terminal Station Indiscretion • Terminus Station 53; Every Day's a Holiday • The Gold of Naples • L'Oro di Napoli 54; The Roof • Il Tetto 55; La Ciociara • Two Women 60; Il Giudizio Universale • The Last Judgment 61; Boccaccio '70 62*; The Condemned of Altona • I Sequestrati di Altona 62; Il Boom 63; Ieri, Oggi, Domani • Ieri, Oggi e Domani • She Got What She Asked For • Yesterday, Today and Tomorrow 63; Mariage à l'Italienne • Marriage, Italian Style • Matrimonio all'Italiana 64; After the Fox • Caccia alla Volpe 65; Un Monde Jeune • Un Monde

Nouveau • Un Mondo Nuovo • A New World • A Young World 65; Les Sorcières • Le Streghe • The Witches 66*; Sept Fois Femmes • Sette Volte Donna • Woman Times Seven 67; Gli Amanti • A Place for Lovers • Le Temps des Amants 68; Les Fleurs du Soleil • I Girasoli • Sunflower 69; Le Coppie • Les Couples • The Couples 70*; The Garden of the Finzi-Continis • Il Giardino dei Finzi-Contini 70; Lo Chiameremo Andrea • We'll Call Him Andrew 72; Una Breve Vacanza • A Brief Vacation • The Holiday 73; The Journey • The Trip • Il Viaggio • The Voyage 73

DeSimone, Tom Terror in the Jungle 68*; Chatterbox 77; Hell Night 81; The Concrete Jungle 82; Reform School Girls 86; Angel III: The Final Chapter 88

De Sisti, Vittorio Delitti e Profumi 88

Deslaw, Eugene La Marche des Machines 28; Montparnasse 29; La Nuit Électrique 30; Le Monde en Parade 31; Négatifs 32*; La Cité Universitaire de Paris 33

Desmond, James Monterey Pop 67*

DeSoto, Bruno *see Ve Sota, Bruno*

De Souza, Steve Arnold's Wrecking Co. 73

Despins, Joseph Moon Over the Alley 80

De Staak, Frans van *see Staak, Frans van de*

Detiege, David The Man from Button Willow 65; shinbone alley 71*; Bugs Bunny's 3rd Movie: 1001 Rabbit Tales 82*

De Toth, André At 5:40 • Öt Óra 40 38; Hat Hét Boldogság • Six Weeks of Happiness 38; Két Lány az Utcán • Two Girls of the Street 38; Semmelweiss 38; Toprini Nász • Wedding in Toprin 38; Balalaika 39; Jungle Book • Rudyard Kipling's Jungle Book 42*; Passport to Suez 43; Dark Waters 44; A Guest in the House 44*; None Shall Escape 44; Since You Went Away 44*; Mankiller • The Other Love 47; Ramrod 47; Pitfall 48; Slattery's Hurricane 49; Man in the Saddle • The Outcast 51; Carson City 52; The Last of the Comanches • The Sabre and the Arrow 52; Springfield Rifle 52; Thunder Over the Plains 52; The City Is Dark • Crime Wave 53; House of Wax 53; The Stranger Wore a Gun 53; The Bounty Hunter 54; Riding Shotgun 54; Tanganyika 54; The Indian Fighter 55; Hidden Fear 57; Monkey on My Back 57; The Two-Headed Spy 58; Day of the Outlaw 59; Capitaine Morgan • Morgan il Pirata • Morgan the Pirate 60*; Confessions of a Counterspy • Man on a String 60; I Mongoli • Les Mongols • The Mongols 61*; Gold for the Caesars • Or pour les Césars • Oro per i Cesari 62*; Play Dirty • Written on the Sand 68

De Trolignac, M. Gaston *see Griffith, D. W.*

De Trolignac, Marquis *see Griffith, D. W.*

Deubel, Robert Norman Rockwell's World—An American Dream 72; Girls' Night Out • The Scaremaker 84

Deusen, Courtlandt J. van *see Van Deusen, Courtlandt J.*

Deutch, Howard Pretty in Pink 86; Some Kind of Wonderful 87; The Great Outdoors 88

Devaivre, Jean Caprice of Dear Caroline • Dear Caroline 50; Alert in the South • Alerte au Sud 53; The Son of Dear Caroline 55

Deval, Jacques Club de Femmes 37

Deveau, Jack Left-Handed 72

Devenish, Ross Goal! • Goal! World Cup 1966 67*; Boesman and Lena 74; The Guest at Steenkampskraal 77; Marigolds in August 80; The Guest 84; Bleak House 85

Deverell, Roy Mary Millington's World Striptease Extravaganza 82*

Deverich, Nat C. The Invisible Divorce 20*; The Power of Love 22; Forbidden Lover 23

Devers, Claire Black and White • Noir et Blanc 86; Chimère 89

Deville, Michel Une Balle dans le Canon • A Slug in the Heater 58*; Ce Soir ou Jamais • Tonight or Never 60; Adorable Liar • Adorable Menteuse 61; À Cause, à Cause d'une Femme • Because of a Woman 62; L'Appartement des Filles 63; Lucky Jo 64; On A Volé la Joconde 65; Benjamin • Benjamin, or The Diary of an Innocent Young Man • Benjamin ou Les Mémoires d'un Puceau • Benjamin—The Diary of an Innocent Young Boy • The Diary of an Innocent Boy 66; Kiss Me General • Martin Soldat • Soldier Martin 66; Tender Sharks • Tendres Requins 66; Bye Bye Barbara 68; The Bear and the Doll • L'Ours et la Poupée 69; Raphaël ou Le Débauché 70; La Femme en Bleu 72; The French Way • Love at the Top • Le Mouton Enragé 73; L'Apprenti Salaud • The Apprentice Heel 76; Dossier 51 • Le Dossier 51 78; Sentimental Journey • Voyage en Douce 79; Deep Water • Eaux Profondes 81; The Little Bunch • La Petite Bande 83; Les Capricieux • The Capricious Ones 84; Danger in the House • Death in a French Garden • Peril • Péril en la Demeure 84; The Nonentity • Le Paltoquet 86; La Lectrice • The Reader 88; Nuit d'Été en Ville 90

DeVilliers, Dirk The Kingfish Caper • The Kingfisher Caper 75

DeVito, Danny Throw Momma from the Train 87; The War of the Roses 89

De Vito, Ralph Death Collector • Family Enforcer 75

De Vonde, Chester Even As Eve 20*; Voices 20

Dew, Edward The Naked Gun 56; Stump Run 60; Wings of Chance 61

Dewever, Jean Opération La Fontaine 54; L'Agriculture 55; La Crise du Logement 55; Au Bois Piget 56; Tante Esther 56; Des Logis et des Hommes 58; La Vie des Autres 58; Contrastes 59*; Les Honneurs de la Guerre 61; César Grandblaise 70

Dewhurst, George A Great Coup 19; The Home Maker 19; A Dead Certainty

20; The Shadow Between 20; Dollars in Surrey 21*; The Doubles 22; Lonesome Farm 22; A Sister to Assist 'Er 22; The Evil That Men Do • The Little Door Into the World 23; The Uninvited Guest 23; What the Butler Saw 23; Sweeney Todd 26; Bright Young Things 27; Motoring 27; A Sister to Assist 'Er 27; The Rising Generation 28*; A Sister to Assist 'Er 30; A Sister to Assist 'Er 38*; A Sister to Assist 'Er 47

Dewolf, Patrick Moi Vouloir Toi 85

Dewsbury, Ralph The Kitchen Countess 14; Luncheon for Three 14; His Vindication • The King's Outcast 15; The Lion's Cubs 15; The Man in the Attic 15; Whoso Diggeth a Pit 15; The Greater Need 16; His Daughter's Dilemma 16; The Man in Motley 16; Partners at Last 16; Paste 16; Everybody's Business 17; The Golden Dawn 21

Dexter, John Othello 65*; The Virgin Soldiers 69; Pigeons • The Sidelong Glances of a Pigeon Kicker 70; I Want What I Want 71

Dexter, Maury The High-Powered Rifle 60; Walk Tall 60; The Purple Hills 61; Womanhunt 61; Air Patrol 62; The Day Mars Invaded Earth • Spaceship 62; The Firebrand 62; House of the Damned 62; Young Guns of Texas 62; Harbor Lights 63; Police Nurse 63; Surf Party 63; The Young Swingers 63; Raiders from Beneath the Sea 64; Beach House Party • Wild on the Beach 65; The Naked Brigade 65; Maryjane 67; Born Wild • The Young Animals 68; The Mini-Skirt Mob 68; Girl in the Leather Suit • Hell's Belles 69

Deyries, Bernard Here Come the Littles 85; Rainbow Brite and the Star Stealer 85*

De Zarate, Américo Ortiz Another Love Story • Otra Historia de Amor 86

De Zavalia, Alberto A Vida de Carlos Gardel 40

Dhananjaya, N. S. Thayi Karulu 88

Dhawan, David Taaqatwar 89

Dhéry, Robert Branquignol 49; La Patronne 49; Bertrand Cœur de Lion 50; The American Beauty • La Belle Américaine • What a Chassis! 61; Allez France! • The Counterfeit Constable 64; Le Petit Baigneur 68

Dhomme, Sylvaine Les Sept Péchés Capitaux • I Sette Peccati Capitali • Seven Capital Sins • The Seven Deadly Sins 61*

Dia, Lam Ibrahim La 504 et les Foudroyers 74*; Cocorico, Monsieur Poulet 74*

Dial, B. H. Fly Now, Pay Later 69

Diamant-Berger, Henri Le Lord Ouverier 15; Paris Pendant la Guerre 16; Ils y Viennent Tous au Cinéma 17; Les Quatre Cavaliers de l'Apocalypse 17; Le Mauvais Garçon 21; Les Trois Mousquetaires 21; Gonzague 22; Milady • Vingt Ans Après 22; L'Affaire de la Rue de Loureine 23; Jim Bougne Boxeur 23; Le Roi de la Vitesse 23; L'Emprise 24; La Marche du Destin 24; Fifty-Fifty 25; Lover's Island 25; L'Éducation de Prince 26; The Unfair Sex 26; Rue de la Paix 27; Paris la Nuit 30; Sola 30; La Bonne Aventure 32; Clair de Lune 32; Les

Trois Mousquetaires 32; Miquette et Sa Mère 33; La Grande Vie 34; Arsène Lupin, Detective 37; La Vierge Folle 38; Tourbillon de Paris • Whirlwind of Paris 46; La Maternelle 48; The Amazing Monsieur Fabre • Monsieur Fabre 51; Le Chasseur de Chez Maxim's 53; Messieurs les Ronds-de-Cuir 59; Song of the Balalaika 71

Diamant-Berger, Jerome The One and Only • L'Unique 86

Diamond, Frank Nicaragua, September 1978 78

Díaz, Jesús Distance • Lejanía • The Parting of the Ways 86

Díaz, Leody M. The Bionic Boy 77

Díaz Morales, José Loyola the Soldier Saint 52; Atacan las Brujas • Santo Ataca las Brujas • Santo Attacks the Witches • Santo en La Casa de las Brujas 65

Díaz Torres, Daniel Jíbaro • Wild Dog 86

Di Castri, Marco Enigma 87*

Dick, Nigel P.I. Private Investigations • Private Investigations 87; Deadly Intent 88

Dickens, Stafford Please Teacher 37; Skimpy in the Navy 49

Dickinson, Desmond Her Father's Daughter 40; Eating Out with Tommy 41

Dickinson, Lucky Giù le Mani…Carogna 71

Dickinson, Thorold Java Head 34*; The General Goes Too Far • The High Command 36; Behind the Spanish Lines 38*; Spanish A.B.C. 38*; Angel Street • Gaslight 39; The Arsenal Stadium Mystery 39; Westward Ho! 40; Yesterday Is Over Your Shoulder 40; The Prime Minister 41; The Next of Kin 42; Kisenga, Man of Africa • Men of Two Worlds • Witch Doctor 46; The Queen of Spades 48; Secret People 52; Border Incident • Hakarka Ha a Dom • The Red Ground 53; Hagiva • Hill 24 Doesn't Answer 55

Dickson, Paul The Undefeated 50; David 51; The Story of an Achievement 52; Gilbert Harding Speaks of Murder 53; Star of My Night 54; A Tale of Three Women 54*; Satellite in the Sky 56; The Depraved 57; Fun at the Movies 57; Enquiry Into General Practice • Inquiry Into General Practice 59; Stone Into Steel 61

Diege, Samuel Killers of the Prairie • King of the Sierras 38; Ride 'Em Cowgirl 38; The Singing Cowgirl 39; Water Rustlers 39

Diego, Constante El Corazón Sobre la Tierra • The Heart on the Land 86

Dieguês, Carlos Fuga 60*; Cinco Vezes Favela 61*; Domingo 61; Ganga Zumba 63; A 8a. Bienal de São Paulo 65; The Big City • A Grande Cidade 66; Oito Universitários 67; Os Herdeiros • The Inheritors 69; Quando o Carnaval Chegar • When Carnival Comes 72; Jeanne la Française • Joana a Francesa 73; Xica • Xica da Silva 75; Chuvas de Verão • A Summer Rain • Summer Showers 77; Bye Bye Brasil • Bye Bye Brazil 79; Quilombo 84; Subway to the Stars • A Train for the Stars • Um Trem para as Estrelas 87; Dias Melhores

Virão 90

Dieguez, Manuel Zecena Detrás de Esa Puerta • Political Asylum 75

Diehl, William, Jr. Naked River 77

Dienar, Baruch Hem Hayu Asar • They Were Ten 61

Dierker, Hugh The Other Side 22; Cause for Divorce 23; Camille of the Barbary Coast 25; The Wrong Doers 25; Broken Homes 26; False Pride 26; Things Wives Tell 26

Diestro, Alfredo de see De Diestro, Alfredo

Dieterle, Wilhelm see Dieterle, William

Dieterle, William The Man at the Crossroads • The Man by the Roadside • Der Mensch am Wege 23; Die Gesunkenen • The Sunken 25*; Behind the Altar • Das Geheimnis des Abbé X • Der Mann Der Nicht Lieben Darf • The Secret of Abby X 27; Chaînes • Geschlecht in Fesseln • Geschlecht in Fesseln—Die Sexualnot der Gefangenen • Sex in Chains • Sex in Fetters • Les Sexes Enchaînes 28; Die Heilige und Ihr Narr • The Saint and Her Fool • La Sainte et le Fou 28; Eine Stunde Glück • One Hour of Happiness 29; Frühlingsrauschen • Nostalgie • Rêves de Printemps • Tränen Die Ich Dir Geweint 29; Ich Lebe für Dich • Le Triomphe de la Vie • Triumph des Lebens • Triumph of Love 29; Ludwig der Zweite, König von Bayern • Ludwig II, King of Bavaria 29; La Nuit de la Saint-Jean • Das Schweigen im Walde • Le Silence dans la Forêt • The Silence of the Forest 29; The Dance Goes On • Der Tanz Geht Weiter 30; Die Heilige Flamme 30*; Kismet 30; Die Maske Fällt 30; Dämon des Meeres • Moby Dick 31*; Her Majesty, Love 31; The Last Flight 31; The Crash 32; Jewel Robbery 32; Lawyer Man 32; Man Wanted 32; Scarlet Dawn 32; Six Hours to Live 32; Adorable 33; The Devil's in Love 33; Fashion Follies of 1934 • Fashions • Fashions of 1934 33; Female 33*; From Headquarters 33; Grand Slam 33; Concealment • The Secret Bride 34; Dr. Monica 34*; The Firebird 34; Fog Over Frisco 34*; Madame DuBarry 34; Dr. Socrates 35; A Midsummer Night's Dream 35*; The Story of Louis Pasteur 35; Men on Her Mind • Satan Met a Lady 36; The White Angel 36; Another Dawn 37; The Great O'Malley 37; The Life of Emile Zola 37*; Blockade 38; The Hunchback of Notre Dame 39; Juarez 39; All That Money Can Buy • A Certain Mr. Scratch • Daniel and the Devil • The Devil and Daniel Webster • Here Is a Man 40; A Dispatch from Reuters • This Man Reuter 40; Dr. Ehrlich's Magic Bullet • The Magic Bullet • The Story of Dr. Ehrlich's Magic Bullet 40; The Man on America's Conscience • Tennessee Johnson 42; Syncopation 42; Kismet • Oriental Dream 44; I'll Be Seeing You 44*; Love Letters 45; This Love of Ours 45; Duel in the Sun 46*; The Searching Wind 46; The Accused • Strange Deception 48; Bitter Victory • Paid in Full 48; Jennie • Portrait of Jennie •

Tidal Wave 48; Rope of Sand 49; Volcano • Vulcano 49; Dark City 50; Red Mountain 50*; September Affair 50; Boots Malone 51; Peking Express 51; This Is Dynamite! • The Turning Point 52; Elephant Walk 53; Salome 53; Magic Fire 55; The Loves of Omar Khayyam • Omar Khayyam 57; L'Aigle Noir • Dubrowsky • Revolt on the Volga • Révolte sur la Volga • Il Vendicatore 58; Apocalisse sull' Fiume Giallo • Herrin der Welt • Il Mistero dei Tre Continenti • Mistress of the World • Les Mystères d'Angkor 59; Ash Wednesday Confession • Die Fastnachtsbeichte 60; The Confession • Quick! Let's Get Married • Seven Different Ways 63

Dieterlen, Germaine Sigui Année Zéro 66*; Sigui 1968: Les Danseurs de Tyogou 68*; Sigui 1969: La Caverne de Bongo 69*; Sigui 1970: Les Clameurs d'Amani 70*; Sigui 1971: La Dune d'Idyeli 71*; Funérailles à Bongo: Le Vieux Anai • Funérailles du Vieil Anai 72*; Sigui 1972: Les Pagnes de Iame 72*; Ambara Dama 74*

Dieudonné, Albert Son Crime 21; Gloire Rouge 23; Backbiters • Catherine • Une Vie Sans Joie 24

Dikovichni, Ivan Cerni Monakh 88

Di Leo, Fernando Code Name, Red Roses • Red Roses for the Führer 69; Brucia, Ragazzo, Brucia • A Woman on Fire 70; Asylum Erotica • La Bestia Uccide a Sangue Freddo • Slaughter Hotel 71; Wipeout! 72; The Italian Connection • La Mala Ordina • Manhunt 73; Kidnap Syndicate 75; Mr. Scarface 77; The Violent Breed 83

Dillmann, Max see Dallamano, Massimo

Dillon, Eddie see Dillon, Edward

Dillon, Edward The Alarm 14*; A Brand New Hero 14*; Fatty and Minnie He-Haw 14*; Fatty and the Heiress 14*; Fatty's Debut 14*; Fatty's Gift 14*; Fatty's Jonah Day 14*; Fatty's Magic Pants 14*; Fatty's Wine Party 14*; Leading Lizzie Astray 14*; The Rejuvenation of Aunt Mary 14; The Sky Pirate 14*; Fatty and the Broadway Stars 15*; Fatty's Faithful Fido 15*; Fatty's New Role 15*; Mabel and Fatty's Simple Life 15*; Mabel and Fatty's Wash Day 15*; Don Quixote 16; Mr. Goode the Samaritan 16; Sunshine Dad 16; The Antics of Ann 17; A Daughter of the Poor 17; The Heiress at Coffee Dan's 17; Might and the Man 17; The Embarrassment of Riches 18; Our Little Wife 18; Help! Help! Police! 19; Luck and Pluck 19; Never Say Quit 19; Putting One Over 19; The Winning Stroke 19; The Amateur Wife 20; The Frisky Mrs. Johnson 20; Parlor, Bedroom and Bath 20; The Education of Elizabeth 21; A Heart to Let 21; Sheltered Daughters 21; The Beauty Shop 22; Women Men Marry 22; Broadway Gold 23; The Drums of Jeopardy 23; Bred in Old Kentucky 26; The Danger Girl 26; Flame of the Argentine 26; The Dice Woman 27

Dillon, Jack see Dillon, John Francis

Dillon, John Francis Almost a Widow 15; Anita's Butterfly 15; Indiscreet Corinne 17; Beans 18; Betty Takes a Hand 18; The Follies Girl 18; An Heiress for a Day 18; Limousine Life 18; The Love Swindle 18; Nancy Comes Home 18; She Hired a Husband 18; Burglar by Proxy 19; Love's Prisoner 19; The Silk-Lined Burglar 19; Taste of Life 19; Blackbirds 20; The Right of Way 20; Suds 20; Children of the Night 21; The Plaything of Broadway 21; The Roof Tree 21; Calvert's Valley 22; The Cub Reporter 22; Gleam O'Dawn 22; Man Wanted 22; The Yellow Stain 22; The Broken Violin 23; Flaming Youth 23; The Self-Made Wife 23; Flirting with Love 24; Lilies of the Field 24; The Perfect Flapper 24; Chickie 25; The Halfway Girl 25; If I Marry Again 25; One-Way Street 25; We Moderns 25; Don Juan's Three Nights 26; Love's Blindness 26; Midnight Lovers 26; Too Much Money 26; The Crystal Cup 27; Man Crazy 27; The Prince of Headwaiters 27; The Sea Tiger 27; Smile, Brother, Smile 27; The Heart of a Follies Girl 28; The Noose 28; Out of the Ruins 28; Careers 29; Children of the Ritz 29; Fast Life 29; Sally 29; Scarlet Seas 29; Bride of the Regiment • Lady of the Rose 30; The Girl of the Golden West 30; Kismet 30; One Night at Susie's 30; Spring Is Here 30; The Finger Points 31; Millie 31; Pagan Lady 31; The Reckless Hour 31; Your Number's Up 31; Behind the Mask 32; Call Her Savage 32; The Cohens and Kellys in Hollywood 32; Man About Town 32; Humanity 33; The Big Shakedown • Shakedown 34

Dillow, Jean Carmen The Pawn 68

Di Mello, Victori Giselle 82

Dimopoulos, Dinos Horse and Carriage 57; Astero 60; The House on Stournara Street 60; Amok • The Rape 65; Madalena 65

Dimsey, Ross The Final Cut 80

Dindo, Richard El Suizo—Un Amour en Espagne • The Swiss—A Love in Spain 86

Dinenzon, Victor Abierto de 18 a 24 • Open from Six to Midnight 88

Dinesen, Robert De Fire Djævele • The Four Devils 11; The Demon's Daughter 12; Help 12; The Female Demon 13; Midnight Sun 13; Mother 13; Gypsy Blood 14; The Last Night 14; Dr. X 15; The Race with Death 15; The Secret of the Sphynx 15; Between Brothers 16; Opium 16; Paradise Hotel 17; Potiphar's Wife 17; Jephtah's Daughter 19; Tatjana 23; Malva 24; Die Feuertänzerin 25; Im Namen des Kaisers 25; Wenn die Liebe Nicht Wär! 25; Ariadne in Hoppegarten 28; Der Weg Durch die Nacht 29

Dinet, James Music City U.S.A. 66*

Dingwall, John Phobia 88

Dinner, Michael Miss Lonelyhearts 83; Catholic Boys • Heaven Help Us 85; Off Beat 86; Hot to Trot 88

Dino, Abidine Goal! • Goal! World Cup 1966 67*

Dinov, Todor Iconostasis • Ikonostasut 69*

Dionysius, Eric AC/DC: Let There Be Rock 82*

Di Palma, Carlo Teresa la Ladra • Teresa the Thief 73

DiPersio, Vincent Flying Blind 88

Diphusa, Patti see Almodóvar, Pedro

Di Robiland, Alessandro Anche Lei Fumava il Sigaro • She Too Smoked Cigars 86

DiSalle, Mark Kickboxer 89*

Di Silvestro, Rino see Di Silvestro, Salvatore

Di Silvestro, Salvatore Daughter of a Werewolf • Legend of the Wolfwoman • La Lupa Mannera • Werewolf Woman • The Wolf Man 76; Diario Segreto di un Carcere Femminele • Women in Cell Block 7 77

Disney, Walt Cinderella 22; The Four Musicians of Bremen 22; Goldie Locks and the Three Bears • Goldilocks and the Three Bears 22; Jack and the Beanstalk 22; Little Red Riding Hood 22; Puss in Boots 22; Tommy Tucker's Tooth 22; Alice's Wonderland 23*; Martha 23; Alice and the Dog Catcher 24*; Alice and the Three Bears 24*; Alice Cans the Cannibals 24*; Alice Gets in Dutch 24*; Alice Hunting in Africa 24*; Alice Plays the Piper • Alice the Piper 24*; Alice the Peacemaker 24*; Alice the Toreador 24*; Alice's Day at the Sea 24*; Alice's Fishy Story 24*; Alice's Spooky Adventure 24*; Alice's Wild West Show 24; Alice Chops the Suey 25*; Alice Gets Stung 25*; Alice in the Jungle 25*; Alice Is Stage Struck 25*; Alice Loses Out 25*; Alice on the Farm 25*; Alice Picks the Champ 25*; Alice Plays Cupid 25*; Alice Rattled by Rats 25*; Alice Solves the Puzzle 25*; Alice Stage Struck 25; Alice the Jail Bird 25*; Alice Wins the Derby 25*; Alice's Balloon Race 25*; Alice's Eggplant 25*; Alice's Little Parade 25*; Alice's Mysterious Mystery 25*; Alice's Ornery Orphan 25*; Alice's Tin Pony 25*; Alice Charms the Fish 26*; Alice Cuts the Ice 26*; Alice Helps the Romance 26*; Alice in Slumberland 26*; Alice in the Wooly West 26*; Alice the Fire Fighter 26*; Alice the Lumberjack 26*; Alice's Brown Derby 26*; Alice's Monkey Business 26*; Alice's Spanish Guitar 26*; Clara Cleans Her Teeth 26; Alice at the Carnival 27*; Alice at the Rodeo • Alice's Rodeo 27*; Alice Foils the Pirates 27*; Alice in the Alps 27*; Alice in the Big League 27*; Alice in the Klondike 27*; Alice the Beach Nut 27*; Alice the Collegiate 27*; Alice the Golf Bug 27*; Alice the Whaler 27*; Alice's Auto Race 27*; Alice's Channel Swim 27*; Alice's Circus Daze 27*; Alice's Knaughty Knight 27*; Alice's Medicine Show 27*; Alice's Picnic 27*; Alice's Three Bad Eggs 27*; All Wet 27; The Banker's Daughter 27; Empty Socks 27; Great Guns 27; Harem Scarem 27; The Mechanical Cow 27; Neck 'n' Neck 27; The Ocean Hop 27; Oh, Teacher 27; Rickety Gin 27; Trolley Troubles 27; Africa Before Dark

28; The Barn Dance 28*; Bright Lights 28; The Fox Chase 28; The Gallopin' Gaucho 28*; Hot Dog 28; Hungry Hoboes 28; Oh, What a Knight 28; The Ol' Swimmin' 'Ole • The Ole Swimmin' Hole 28; Ozzie of the Mounted 28; Plane Crazy 28*; Poor Papa 28; Ride 'Em Plowboy! 28; Rival Romeos 28; Sagebrush Sadie 28; Sky Scrappers 28; Sleigh Bells 28; Steamboat Willie 28*; Tall Timber 28; The Barnyard Battle 29*; The Cat's Away • When the Cat's Away 29*; El Terrible Toreador 29*; The Haunted House 29*; The Jazz Fool 29*; Jungle Rhythm 29*; The Karnival Kid 29*; The Merry Dwarfs 29; Mickey's Choo Choo 29*; Mickey's Follies 29*; The Opry House 29*; The Plow Boy 29*; The Skeleton Dance 29*; The Barnyard Concert 30; The Cactus Kid 30; Fiddlin' Around • Just Mickey 30; The Golden Touch 35

Dittrich, Scott Freewheelin' 76

Divad, David A Girl's Desire 22; Little Wildcat 22

Dixon, Denver see *Adamson, Victor*

Dixon, Ivan Trouble Man 72; The Spook Who Sat by the Door 73

Dixon, John Anzacs • Anzacs: The War Down Under 85*; Free Enterprise 86; Running from the Guns 87

Dixon, Ken Slave Girls from Beyond Infinity 87

Dixon, Thomas Mark of the Beast 23

Dizdarević, Nenad I To Će Proći • That Too Will Pass 86

Djaparidze, Revas Chuzhie Deti • Somebody Else's Children • Someone Else's Children • Stepchildren 58*

Djarot, Eros Tjoet Nja'Dhien 89

Djordjević, Puriša Jutro • Morning 67; War Trilogy 67; Noon 68; Cross Country Runner 69

Dmitriev, A. Rivals 33

Dmochowski, Borys Zygmunt Kołosowski 47*

Dmytryk, Edward The Hawk • Trail of the Hawk 35; Emergency Squad 39; Golden Gloves 39; Million Dollar Legs 39*; Television Spy 39; Her First Romance • The Right Man 40; Mystery Sea Raider 40; The Blonde from Singapore • Hot Pearls 41; Broadway Ahead • Sweetheart of the Campus 41; Confessions • Confessions of Boston Blackie 41; The Devil Commands • When the Devil Commands 41; Secrets • Secrets of the Lone Wolf 41; Under Age 41; Counter-Espionage 42; Hitler's Children 42; Seven Miles from Alcatraz 42; Behind the Rising Sun 43; Captive Wild Woman 43; The Falcon Strikes Back 43; Tender Comrade 43; Farewell My Lovely • Murder, My Sweet 44; Back to Bataan 45; Cornered 45; Till the End of Time 46; Crossfire 47; So Well Remembered 47; The Hidden Room • Obsession 48; Give Us This Day • Salt and the Devil • Salt to the Devil 49; Eight Iron Men 52; Mutiny 52; The Sniper 52; The Juggler 53; Three Lives 53; Broken Lance 54; The Caine Mutiny 54; The End of the Affair 54; Bing Presents Oreste 55; The

Left Hand of God 55; Soldier of Fortune 55; The Mountain 56; Raintree County 57; The Young Lions 58; The Blue Angel 59; Warlock 59; Cronache di un Convento • Joseph Desa • The Reluctant Saint 61; Walk on the Wild Side 62; The Carpetbaggers 63; Mirage 64; Where Love Has Gone 64; Alvarez Kelly 65; Anzio • The Battle for Anzio • Lo Sbarco di Anzio 67; Shalako 68; Barbe-Bleue • Bluebeard 72; The Human Factor 74; He Is My Brother 76

Dmytryk, Madeleine The Master Race 44*

Dmytryk, Michael Kings of the Hill 76

Dobbs, Frank Q. Disciples of Death 72; Hotwire 80; Uphill All the Way 85

Dobkin, Lawrence The Deadly Silence • Tarzan's Deadly Silence 70*; Like a Crow on a June Bug • Sixteen 72

Dobray, György Love Till First Blood • Szerelem Első Vérig 85*; Szerelem Második Vérig 88

Dobson, Kevin Demolition 77; Image of Death 77; The Mango Tree 77; Squizzy Taylor 82

Do Canto, Jorge Brum The Country Doctor 63

Doerrie, Doris see *Dörrie, Doris*

Doheny, Lawrence Teenage Millionaire 61

Dohler, Donald M. The Alien Factor 78; Fiend 80; Nightbeast 82; Terror from the Unknown 83

Doillon, Jacques La Tentation d'Isabelle 85; La Vie de Famille 85; The Prude • La Puritaine 86; Comédie • Comedy 87; L'Amoureuse 88; The 15-Year-Old Girl • La Fille de Quinze Ans 89

Dolenz, Micky Gateway to the South 81

Dolidze, S. The Dragonfly 55

Dolin, Boris In the Depths of the Sea 38*; The Law of the Great Love • Zakon Velikoi Lyubvi 45; Istoria Odnogo Kolza • The Tale of a Link 48; A New Number Comes to Moscow 59; The Surprising Hunt 60; Blind Bird 62; More Amazing Than a Fairy Tale 64

Dolinin, Dmitri A Sentimental Trip to a Farm • Sentimentalnoe Puteshestvie na Kartoshku 87

Doller, Mikhail The End of St. Petersburg • Konyets Sankt-Pyoterburga 27*; Chiny i Lyudi • An Hour with Chekhov • Ranks and People 29*; Life Is Beautiful • Life Is Good • Life Is Very Good • Ochen Khorosho Zhevyotsa • Prostoi Sluchai • A Simple Case 30*; Mother and Sons • Pobeda • Samyi Schastlivyi • Victory 38*; Minin and Pozharsky • Minin i Pozharsky 39*; General Suvorov • Suvorov 40*; Feast at Zhirmunka • Pir v Zhirmunka 41*

Dolman, Martin see *Martino, Sergio*

Domalik, Andrzej Siegfried • Zygfryd 87; Schodami w Górę, Schodami w Dół 88

Domaradzki, Jerzy The Big Race 81; The Tailor's Planet 83; White Dragon 86

Dombasle, Arielle Les Pyramides Bleues 88

Domeneghini, Anton Gino La Rosa di Bagdad • The Singing Princess 67

Dominguez, Rudy No Blood No Surrender 87

Domnick, Ottomar Jonas 59

Domolky, János Hajnali Háztetők • Roofs at Dawn 86

Donahue, Patrick G. Kill Squad 81

Donahue, R. E. Mr. Ima Jonah's Home Brew 21*; Skipping the Pen 21*; Burr's Novelty Review No. 1 22*; Burr's Novelty Review No. 2 22*; Burr's Novelty Review No. 3 22*; Burr's Novelty Review No. 4 22*; Burr's Novelty Review No. 5 22*; Burr's Novelty Review No. 6 22*

Donaldson, Arthur The Salamander 15

Donaldson, Dick The Good Loser 18

Donaldson, Roger Sleeping Dogs 77; Smash Palace 81; The Bounty 84; Marie 85; No Way Out 86; Cocktail 88; Cadillac Man 90

Donan, Martin see *Donen, Mario*

Donat, Robert The Cure for Love 49

Donati, Dario La Monaca nel Peccato • A Nun in the State of Sin 86

Donatien Une Histoire de Brigands 20; La Sin-Ventura 22; La Chevauchée Blanche 23; L'Île de la Mort 23; Nantas 24; Pierre et Jean 24; Princesse Lulu 24; Un Château de la Mort Lente 25; Mon Curé chez les Pauvres 25; Mon Curé chez les Riches 25; Florine la Fleur du Valois 26; Simone 26; La Martyre de Ste. Maxence 27; Miss Edith, Duchesse 28; L'Arpète 29

Donehue, Vincent J. Lonelyhearts 58; Sunrise at Campobello 60

Donen, Mario Les Espions Meurent à Beyrouth • Killers Are Challenged • Secret Agent Fireball • Le Spie Uccidono a Beirut 65

Donen, Stanley On the Town 49*; Royal Wedding • Wedding Bells 50; The Light Fantastic • Love Is Better Than Ever 51; Singin' in the Rain 51*; Fearless Fagan 52; Give a Girl a Break 53; Deep in My Heart 54; Seven Brides for Seven Brothers 54; It's Always Fair Weather 55*; Kismet 55*; Funny Face 56; Kiss Them for Me 57; The Pajama Game 57*; Damn Yankees • What Lola Wants • Whatever Lola Wants 58*; Indiscreet 58; Once More, with Feeling! 59; The Grass Is Greener 60; Surprise Package 60; Charade 63; Arabesque 66; Two for the Road 66; Bedazzled 67; Staircase 68; The Little Prince 74; Lucky Lady 75; Movie Movie 78; Saturn 3 79*; Blame It on Rio 84

Doner, William The Torrent 24*

Dongtian, Zheng see *Zheng, Dongtian*

Doniger, Walter Duffy of San Quentin • Men Behind Bars 53; The Steel Cage 54; The Steel Jungle 55; Unwed Mother 58; House of Women • Ladies of the Mob 60*; Safe at Home! 62; Mad Bull 77*; Kentucky Woman 83

Doniol-Valcroze, Jacques Bonjour Monsieur la Bruyère 56; L'Œil du Maître 57; Les Surmenés 58; L'Eau à la Bouche • A Game for Six Lovers • The Game of Love • Games for Six Lovers 59; Le Cœur Battant

• The French Game 60; La Dénonciation • The Immoral Moment 62; Jean-Luc Godard 64; La Bien Aimée 66; Övergreppet • A Question of Rape • The Rape • Le Viol • Le Viol ou Un Amour Fou 67; La Maison des Bories 69; L'Homme au Cerveau Greffé • The Man with the Transplanted Brain 72; Anne ou La Mort d'un Pilote 74

Donnelly, Dennis The Toolbox Murders 77

Donnelly, Tom Quicksilver 86

Donner, Clive The Secret Place 56; Heart of a Child 58; Marriage of Convenience 60; The Purple Stream 61; The Sinister Man 61; Weekend in Paris 61; Some People 62; The Caretaker • The Guest 63; Nothing But the Best 63; Quoi de Neuf Pussycat? • What's New, Pussycat? 65; Here We Go 'Round the Mulberry Bush 67; Luv 67; Alfred the Great 68; Fly Me to the Bank 73; Old Drac • Old Dracula • Vampir • Vampira • Vampirella 74; Jenny's Diary 75; The Thief of Bagdad 78; The Nude Bomb • The Return of Maxwell Smart 79; Charlie Chan and the Curse of the Dragon Queen 80; Stealing Heaven 88

Donner, Jörn Aamua Kaupungissa • Morning in the City 54; In These Days • Näinä Päivinä 55; Porkala 56; Vettä • Water 57; En Söndag i September • A Sunday in September 63; Testimonies of Her • Vittnesbörd om Henne 63; Att Älska • To Love 64; Adventure Starts Here • Här Börjar Äventyret 65; Stimulantia 65*; Crossbeam • Rooftree • Tvärbalk 66; Black on White • Mustaa Valkoisella 67; Mondo Teeno • Teenage Rebellion 67*; 69 69; Anna 70; Naisenkuvia • Portraits of Women 70; Fuck Off! — Images of Finland • Perkele! • Perkele! — Kuvia Suomesta 71*; Baksmälla • Hangover • Hellyys • Ömhet • Sexier Than Sex • Tenderness 72; Ingmar Bergmanin Maailma • Three Scenes with Ingmar Bergman • Tre Scener med Ingmar Bergman • The World of Ingmar Bergman 75; The American Dream • Drömmen om Amerika 76; Man Cannot Be Raped • Män Kan Inte Våltas • Manrape • Men Can't Be Raped • Miestä Ei Voi Raiskata 78; Yhdeksan Tapaa Lähestyä Helsinkiä 82; Dirty Story 84; Brev från Sverige 87

Donner, Richard X-15 61; Salt and Pepper 68; Lola • The Statutory Affair • Twinky 69; Birthmark • The Omen 76; Superman • Superman — The Movie 77; Inside Moves 80; Superman II 80*; The Toy 82; The Goonies 85; Ladyhawke 85; Lethal Weapon 87; Scrooged 88; Lethal Weapon 2 89

Donohue, Jack Close-Up 48; The Yellow Cab Man 49; Watch the Birdie 50; Lucky Me 54; Babes in Toyland 61; Marriage on the Rocks 65; Assault on a Queen 66

Donovan, Frank P. Bullin' the Bullsheviki 19; Silas Marner 22; The Mad Marriage 25

Donovan, King Promise Her Anything • Promises! Promises! 63

Donovan, Martin Apartment Zero 88

Donovan, Paul South Pacific 1942 • Torpedoed 80; Self-Defense • Siege 83*; Def-Con 4 84; Caribe 87*; A Switch in Time 87; The Squamish Five 88

Donovan, Terence Yellow Dog 73

Donovan, Tom Lovespell • Tristan and Isolde • Tristan and Isolt 79

Donskoi, Mark In the Big City • V Bolshom Gorodye 27*; Life • Zhizn 27*; The Lesson • Man's Value • The Price of Man • Tsena Cheloveka • The Value of Man 28*; The Fop • The Pigeon • Pizhon 29; Alien Shore • Chuzhoi Bereg • The Other Shore 30; Fire • Ogon 30; Pesnya o Shchastye • Song About Happiness • The Song of Happiness 34*; Childhood of Gorky • The Childhood of Maxim Gorky • Detstvo Gorkovo • Dyetstvo Gorkovo • Gorky's Childhood 38; Among People • In the World • My Apprenticeship • On His Own • Out in the World • V Lyudyakh 39; Moi Universiteti • My Universities • My University • University of Life 40; Beacon • Boevoi Kinosbornik 9 • Fighting Film Album No. 9: Beacon 41; Children of the Soviet Arctic • The Romantics • Romantiki 41; The Diary of a Nazi 42*; Heroes Are Made • How the Steel Was Tempered • Kak Zakalyalas Stal 42; Raduga • The Rainbow 43; Nepokorenniye • Nepokorenniye Semya Tarassa • Semya Tarassa • The Taras Family • Unconquered • The Unvanquished 45; An Emotional Education • Rural Institute • Selskaya Uchitelnitsa • Varvara • The Village School Teacher • Village Teacher 46; Alitet Goes Into the Mountains • Alitet Leaves for the Hills • Alitet Ukhodit v Gory • Zakonye Bolshoi Zemli 48; Nashi Chempiony • Our Champions • Sporting Fame • Sportivnaya Slava 50; Mat • Mother • 1905 55; At a High Cost • At a High Price • At Great Cost • Dorogoi Tsenoi • A High Cost • The Horse That Cried 57; Foma Gordeyev • The Gordeyev Family • Thomas Gordeyev 59; Hello Children • Zdravstvuitye Deti 62; Heart of a Mother • A Mother's Heart • Serdtsye Materi • Serdtze Materi • Sons and Mothers 66; A Mother's Devotion • A Mother's Loyalty • Vernost Materi 66; Chaliapin 69; Nadezhda 73

Doo, John see Tu, Chien Lun

Doob, Nick Sanford Meisner: The Theatre's Best Kept Secret 85

Dooley, John Rover Makes Good 53; The Assistant 69; Strange Tales 69

Doo-yong, Lee see Lee, Doo-yong

Doran, Thomas Spookies 86*

Dore, Mary The Good Fight 83*

Dorfman, Ron Groupies 70*

Dorfman, Stanley Volunteer Jam 76

Dorfmann, Jacques La Palanquin des Larmes 88

Doria, Alejandro Becoming Aware • Darse Cuenta 85; Awaiting the Pallbearers • Esperando la Carroza 86; Sofía • Sophia 87

Dorian, Charles Two-Faced Woman 41*

Dorin, Filip Robar see Robar-Dorin, Filip

Dorman, Veniamin Devichya Vesna • Springtime on the Volga 61*; The End of Operation Resident • Konets Operatsii Rezident 87

Dormand, Frank Cheerio 35; Clap Hands 35

Dormand, S. W. Second Sight 38; Sink or Swim 38

Dorn, Rudi Death Trap • Take Her by Surprise • Taken by Surprise • Violent Love 67

Dornhelm, Robert The Children of Theater Street 77*; She Dances Alone 81; Digital Dreams 83; Echo Park 85; Cold Feet 89; Requiem for Dominic 90

Doronin, Mikhail The Last Insult 32

Dörrie, Doris Der Erste Walzer • The First Waltz 78; Mitten ins Herz • Straight Through the Heart 83; Im Innern des Wals • In the Belly of the Whale 84; Männer • Men... 85; Land of Milk and Honey • Paradies • Paradise • Schlaraffenland 86; Ich und Er • Me and Him 88; Geld 89

Dos Santos, Luiz Paulino Um Dia na Rampa 57*

Dos Santos, Nelson Pereira Atividades Políticas • Atividades Políticas em São Paulo 50; Juventude • Youth 50; Rio, Forty Degrees • Rio, Quarenta Graus 54; Rio, Northern Zone • Rio, Zona Norte • Rio, Zone Nord 57; Soldados do Fogo 58; Cinco Vezes Favela 61*; Mandacaru Vermelho 61; Ballet do Brasil 62; A Boca de Ouro • The Mouth of Gold 62; Barren Lives • Sécheresse • Vidas Secas 63; Um Moço de 74 Anos 63; O Rio de Machado Assis 64; Fala, Brasilia 65; Cruzada ABC 66; O Justiceiro • Le Justicier • El Justiciero 67; Abastecimento, Nova Política 68; Desperate for Love • Fome de Amor • Hunger for Love • Soif d'Amour 68; The Alienist • O Alienista • L'Aliéniste • Um Asilo Muito Louco • The Craziest Asylum 69; Comme Il Est Bon Mon Français • Como Era Gostoso o Meu Francês • How Tasty Was My Little Frenchman • Qu'Il Était Bon Mon Petit Français 71; Pas de Violence Entre Nous • Quem É Beta? • Who Is Beta? 72; The Amulet of Ogum • O Amuleto de Ogum 74; La Boutique des Miracles • Tenda da Milagres • The Tent of Miracles 75; Estrada da Vida • Na Estrada da Vida • On the Highway of Life • Road of Life 80; Memoirs of Prison • Memórias do Cárcere • Memories of Prison 84; Jubiabá 85; Castro Alves 87

Dossick, Philip H. The P.O.W. 73

Dostal, Nikolai Chelovek c Akkordeonom • The Man with the Accordion 87

Dotan, Shimon Repeat Dive 82; 83 83*; Hiuch ha'Gdi • The Smile of the Lamb 86

Doubrava, Jaroslav Mach a Šebestová, k Tabuli! • Mach and Sebestova, Come to the Blackboard Please! 85*

Douchet, Jean Paris Vu par... • Six in Paris 64*

Doueb, Tam-Sir Boulevards d'Afrique 88*

Doughton, Russell, Jr. The Hostage 66; Fever Heat 68

Douglas, Bill My Childhood 72; My Ain Folk 73; My Way Home 78; Comrades 86

Douglas, Gordon The Infernal Triangle 35; Lucky Beginners 35; Bored of Education 36; General Spanky 36*; Glove Taps 36; Pay As You Exit 36; Reunion in Rhythm 36; Spooky Hooky 36; Two Too Young 36; Fishy Tales 37; Framing Youth 37; Hearts Are Thumps 37; Mail and Female 37; Night 'n' Gales 37; Our Gang Follies of 1938 37; The Pigskin Palooka 37; Roamin' Holiday 37; Rushin' Ballet 37; Three Smart Boys 37; Aladdin's Lantern 38; Bear Facts 38; Came the Brawn 38; Canned Fishing 38; Feed 'Em and Weep 38; Hide and Shriek 38; The Little Ranger 38; Elephants Never Forget • Zenobia 39; Saps at Sea 40; The Baby Vanishes • Broadway Limited 41; Niagara Falls 41; Road Show 41*; The Devil with Hitler 42; The Great Gildersleeve 42; Gildersleeve on Broadway 43; Gildersleeve's Bad Day 43; The Falcon in Hollywood 44; Gildersleeve's Ghost 44; Girl Rush 44; A Night of Adventure 44; First Yank Into Tokyo • Mask of Fury 45; Loonies on Broadway • Zombies on Broadway 45; Dick Tracy vs. Cueball 46; San Quentin 46; The Black Arrow • The Black Arrow Strikes 48; If You Knew Susie 48; Walk a Crooked Mile 48; The Doolins of Oklahoma • The Great Manhunt 49; House of Settlement • Mr. Soft Touch 49*; Between Midnight and Dawn 50; Fortunes of Captain Blood 50; The Great Missouri Raid 50; Kiss Tomorrow Goodbye 50; The Man from Nevada • The Nevadan 50; Rogues of Sherwood Forest 50; Come Fill the Cup 51; I Was a Communist for the FBI 51; Only the Valiant 51; The Iron Mistress 52; Mara Maru 52; The Charge at Feather River 53; The Grace Moore Story • So This Is Love 53; She's Back on Broadway 53; Them! 54; Young at Heart 54; The McConnell Story • Tiger in the Sky 55; Sincerely Yours 55; The Gun Runner • Santiago 56; The Big Land • Stampeded! 57; Bombers B-52 • No Sleep Till Dawn 57; Fort Dobbs 57; The Fiend Who Walked the West 58; Up Periscope! 58; Yellowstone Kelly 59; Rachel Cade • The Sins of Rachel Cade 60; Claudelle Inglish • Jilted • Young and Eager 61; Gold of the Seven Saints 61; Follow That Dream • Pioneer Go Home 62; Call Me Bwana 63; Rio Conchos 64; Robbo • Robin and the Seven Hoods 64; Harlow 65; Sylvia 65; Stagecoach 66; Way…Way Out 66; Chuka 67; In Like Flint 67; Tony Rome 67; The Detective 68; Lady in Cement 68; Barquero! 69; Skullduggery 70*; They Call Me MISTER Tibbs! 70*; Skin Game 71*; Slaughter's Big Rip-Off 73; Evel Knievel • Seconds to Live • Viva Knievel! 77

Douglas, John The Vicar of Wakefield 13

Douglas, John Milestones 75*

Douglas, John see *Elorrieta, José María*

Douglas, Kirk Scalawag 73; Posse 75

Douglas, Lamont Rebel Angel 62

Douglas, Peter A Tiger's Tale 87

Douglas, Robert The Final Hour 62; Night Train to Paris 64

Douglas, W. A. Beware of the Law 22

Douglass, James Mammy's Rose 16*

Doukas, Bill Feedback 79

Douy, Max Les Sept Péchés Capitaux • I Sette Peccati Capitali • Seven Capital Sins • The Seven Deadly Sins 61*

Dovgan, Vladimir I Nikto na Svete • No One in the World 87

Dovlatyan, Frunze The Lone Hazel • Odinokaya Oreshina 87

Dovzhenko, Alexander The Fruits of Love • Jean Kolbasink the Hairdresser • The Little Fruits of Love • Love's Berries • Love's Berry • The Marriage Trap • Yagodki Lyubvi • Yahidka Kokhannya 26; Vasya-Reformator • Vasya the Reformer 26*; The Diplomatic Pouch • Sumka Dipkuryera • Teka Dypkuryera 27; Zvenigora • Zvenyhora 27; Arsenal • Arsenal — The January Uprising in Kiev in 1918 29; Earth • Soil • Song of New Life • Zemlya 30; Ivan 32; Aerograd • Air City • Frontier 35; Shchors • Shors 39*; Liberation • Osvobozhdeniye 40*; The Native Country • Strana Rodnaya 42*; Pobeda na Pravoberezhnoi Ukrainye • Pobeda na Pravoberezhnoi Ukrainye i Izgnanie Nemetsikh Zakhvatchikov za Predeli Ukrainskikh Sovetskikh Zemel • Ukraine in Flames • Victory in Right-Bank Ukraine • Victory in Right-Bank Ukraine and the Expulsion of the Germans from the Boundaries of the Ukrainian Soviet Earth • Victory in the Ukraine • Victory in the Ukraine and the Expulsion of the Germans from the Boundaries of the Ukrainian Soviet Earth 45*; Life in Bloom • Life in Blossom • Michurin 47*

Dow, Sergio The Day You Love Me • El Día Que Me Quieras 86

Dowd, Nancy Love 81*

Dowdey, Kathleen A Celtic Trilogy 79; Blue Heaven 84; Ralph McGill and His Times 88

Dowlan, William The College Orphan 15; Drugged Waters 16; The Light 16; The Madcap 16; Rose of the Alley 16*; Youth's Endearing Charm 16; The Outsider 17; Alias Mary Brown 18*; The Atom 18; Daughter Angele 18; Irish Eyes 18; Common Property 19*; Cowardice Court 19; Loot 19; Restless Souls 19*; Under Suspicion 19; A Chorus Girl's Romance 20; Dangerous to Men 20; Locked Lips 20; The Peddler of Lies 20; The Lost World 25*

Downey, Robert Babo 73 63; Chafed Elbows 65; No More Excuses 68; Putney Swope 69; Pound 70; Greaser's Palace 72; Two Tons of Turquoise to Taos • Two Tons of Turquoise to Taos Tonight 76; Jive 79; The Brave Young Men of Weinberg • Mad Magazine Presents Up the Academy • Mad Magazine's Up the Academy • Up the Academy 80; America 82; Rented Lips 88

Doxat-Pratt, B. E. As God Made Her 20; Fate's Plaything 20; John Heriot's Wife 20; The Little Hour of Peter Wells 20; The Skin Game 20; Circus Jim 21; Laughter and Tears 21; The Other Person 21; My Lord the Chauffeur 27

Doxiadis, Apostolos C. Terirem 87

Drach, Michel Le Revenant • Les Soliloques du Pauvre 51; La Mer Sera Haute à 16 Heures 54; Auditorium 57; On N'Enterre Pas le Dimanche 59; Amelia, or The Time for Love • Amelie • Amelie, or The Time to Die 60; Les Belles Conduites • La Bonne Occase 64; Safari Diamants 65; Élise ou La Vraie Vie 70; Les Violons du Bal 74; Parlez Moi d'Amour 75; Le Passé Simple • Replay 77; Run for Your Life Lola • Sauve-Toi Lola 86; Gramps Is a Great Guy • Il Est Génial Papy 87

Dragan, Mircea Oil 77

Dragin, Bert L. The Butterfly Revolution • Summer Camp Nightmare 87; Twice Dead 88

Dragojević, Žarko Kuća Pored Pruge 88

Dragoljub Innocence Unprotected 42

Dragoti, Stan Dirty Little Billy 72; Love at First Bite 79; Mr. Mom • Mr. Mum 83; The Man with One Red Shoe 85; She's Out of Control 89

Drainville, Elaine T. Dan Smith 87*

Drake, James R. Police Academy IV: Citizens on Patrol 87; Speed Zone! 89

Drake, Oliver Texas Tornado 32; Today I Hang 42*; Border Buckaroos 43; Fighting Valley 43; Shootin' Irons • West of Texas 43; Trail of Terror 43; Lonesome Trail 45; Riders of the Dawn 45; Saddle Serenade 45; Springtime in Texas 45; Moon Over Montana 46; Song of the Sierras 46; Trail to Mexico 46; West of the Alamo 46; Ginger 47; Rainbow Over the Rockies 47; Deadline 48; Fighting Mustang 48; Sunset Carson Rides Again 48; Across the Rio Grande 49; Boom Town Badmen • Roaring Westward 49; Brand of Fear 49; Lawless Code 49; Battling Marshal 50; The Kid from Gower Gulch 50; Outlaw Treasure 55; The Parson and the Outlaw 57

Drake, Ronald A Killer Walks 52

Drake, Tom The Keeper 76

Drakulić, Nikola Gods of Bali 52

Drapkin, Z. Red Tanks 42*

Drašković, Boro Horoscope • Horoskop 50

Dream, Rinse Cafe Flesh 82

Drechsel, Sammy An Affair of State 66

Dreifuss, Arthur Frozen Affair 37; Murder in Swingtime 37; Double Deal 39; A Night at the Troc 39; Yankee Doodle Home 39; Mystery in Swing 40; Murder on Lenox Avenue 41; Reg'lar Fellers 41; Sunday Sinners 41; Baby Face Morgan 42; Boss of Big Town 42; The Payoff 42; Campus Rhythm • Fraternity Sweetheart 43; Eadie Was a Lady 43; Melody Parade 43; Nearly Eighteen 43; Sarong Girl 43; The Sultan's Daughter 43; Ever Since Venus 44; Blackie Booked on Suspicion • Booked on Suspicion • Boston Blackie Booked on Suspicion 45; Blackie's Rendezvous • Boston Blackie's Rendezvous 45; The Gay Señorita 45;

Prison Ship 45; Betty Co-Ed • The Melting Pot 46; Freddie Steps Out • Sweet Sixteen 46; High School Hero 46; Junior Prom 46; Follow the Music 47; Glamour Girl • Nightclub Girl 47; Little Miss Broadway 47; Sweet Genevieve 47; Two Blondes and a Redhead 47; Vacation Days 47; All-American Pro 48; I Surrender Dear 48; Manhattan Angel 48; Mary Lou 48; An Old-Fashioned Girl 48; Shamrock Hill 49; There's a Girl in My Heart 49; Assignment Abroad 55; Secret File 55; The Last Blitzkrieg 58; Life Begins at 17 58; Juke Box Rhythm 59; The Quare Fellow 62; The Love-Ins 67; Riot on Sunset Strip 67; For Singles Only 68; A Time to Sing 68; The Young Runaways 68

Dressler, Holm Zärtliche Chaoten 2 88*

Dréville, Jean Autour de l'Argent 28; Pomme d'Amour 32; Un Homme en Or • A Man and His Wife 34; Touche-à-Tout 35; Maman Colibri 37; La Brigade Sauvage • Savage Brigade 38*; The Checker Player • The Chess Player • The Devil Is an Empress • Le Joueur d'Échecs 38; Les Nuits Blanches de Saint-Pétersbourg 38; Les Affaires Sont les Affaires 42; La Cage aux Rossignols • A Cage of Nightingales 45; La Ferme du Pendu • Hanged Man's Farm 46; Tainted • Le Visiteur 46; La Bataille de l'Eau Lourde • Operation Swallow 47*; Confessions of a Rogue • Copie Conforme 47; Les Casse-Pieds • The Spice of Life 48*; Le Grand Rendez-Vous 48; Retour à la Vie • Return to Life 49*; Les Sept Péchés Capitaux • I Sette Peccati Capitali • The Seven Deadly Sins 51*; Horizons Sans Fin 53; La Reine Margot 54; Escale à Orly 55; Les Suspects 57; À Pied à Cheval et en Spoutnik • A Dog, a Mouse and a Sputnik • Sputnik 58; Normandie-Niémen 59; Lafayette • Lafayette (Una Spada per Due Bandiere) 61; Troisième Jeunesse 65; La Sentinelle Endormie 66; La Nuit des Adieux 67

Drew, Di The Right Hand Man 87

Drew, Mrs. Sidney Pay Day 18*; Cousin Kate 21

Drew, Robert Eddie • Eddie Sachs at Indianapolis 60*; Primary 60*; X-15 Pilot • X-Pilot 60*; Football • Mooney vs. Fowle 61*; Jane 62*; Storm Signal 66

Drew, Sidney Rankin A Florida Enchantment 14; Playing Dead 15; Thou Art the Man 15; The Daring of Diana 16; The Hunted Woman 16; The Suspect 16; The Vital Question 16; The Girl Philippa 17; Who's Your Neighbor? 17; Pay Day 18*; The Belle of the Season 19

Dreyer, Carl Theodor Præsidenten • The President 18; Blade af Satans Bog • Leaves from Satan's Book 19; The Fourth Marriage of Dame Margaret • The Parson's Widow • Prästänkan • The Witch Woman 20; Die Gezeichneten • Love One Another • The Stigmatized One 21; Der Var Engang • Once Upon a Time 22; Chained • Michael • Mikaël 24; The Bride of Glomdal • Glomdalsbruden 25; Du Skal Ære Din Hustru • Master of the House • Thou Shalt

Honor Thy Wife 25; Jeanne d'Arc • La Passion de Jeanne d'Arc • The Passion of Joan of Arc 27; Castle of Doom • The Dream of Allan Gray • Not Against the Flesh • The Strange Adventure of Allan Gray • The Strange Adventure of David Gray • The Vampire • Vampyr •Vampyr —Der Traum des David Gray • Vampyr ou L'Étrange Aventure de David Gray 31; Good Mothers • Mødrehjælpen 42; Day of Wrath • Dies Irae • Vredens Dag 43; Två Människor • Two People 45; Vandet på Landet • Water from the Land 46; The Danish Village Church • Landsbykirken 47; Kampen Mod Kræften • The Struggle Against Cancer 47; De Nåede Færgen • They Caught the Ferry 48*; Thorvaldsen 49; The Bridge of Storstrøm • Storstrømsbroen 50; Castle Within a Castle • Krogen og Kronborg • Et Slot i et Slot 54*; Ordet • The Word 54; Gertrud 64

Dreyfus, Lilliane Femmes au Soleil 74

Drha, Vladimír Do Zubu a do Srdíčka 85; Mezek 85; O Je! • Oh Dear! 86; Dotyky 88

Driver, Donald The Naked Ape 73

Driver, Sara Sleepwalk 86

Drobażyński, Romuald Guests Are Coming • Jada Goście Jada 65*

Dromgoole, Patrick Dead Man's Chest 65; The Hidden Face 65

Drove, Antonio El Túnel 88

Drury, David Forever Young 84; Defence of the Realm • Defense of the Realm 85; Split Decisions 88

Drury, William Grass Widowers 21; Levity and Laity 22

Dryden, Wheeler A Little Bit of Fluff • Skirts 28*

Dryhurst, Edward The Dizzy Limit 30; The Woman from China 30; Dangerous Seas 31; Commissionaire 33

Dryhurst, Michael The Hard Way 80

Dschordschadse, Nana Robinsoniad, or My English Grandfather • Robinsoniada anu Chemi Ingliseli Papa 87

Duan, Ji-shun The Go Masters • Mikan no Taikyoku 82*

Duarte, Anselmo Absolutamente Certo 57; The Given Word • O Pagador de Promessas 61; Vereda da Salvação 65; O Impossível Acontece 69*; Quelé do Pajéu 69

Dubin, Charles Mr. Rock and Roll 57; Moving Violation 76

Dubin, Jay Dice Rules 90

Dubois, Albert La Flor del Irupe • Love Hunger 65

Dubois, Bernard Dernier Cri • The Last Word 86

Dubois, Charles Canevas la Ville 85

Dubroux, Danièle Les Amants Terribles 84; La Petite Allumeuse 87

Dubs, Arthur Vanishing Wilderness 73*

Dubson, M. Concert Waltz • Kontsert-Vals 40*

Duceppe, Pierre I Love You • Je T'Aime 74

Ducey, Lillian Enemies of Children 23*

Duchamp, Marcel Anemic Cinema 25; Abstract 27

Duchesne, Louis Sins of Youth 60; Un Mundo para Mí • Soft Skin and Black Lace • Soft Skin on Black Silk • Tentations 64*

Duchowny, Roger Murder Can Hurt You 70

Dudko, Apollinari The Sleeping Beauty • Spyashchaya Krasavitsa 66*

Dudley, Bernard Love in the Welsh Hills 21; Boy Scouts 22; The Conjurors 22; Cutting Out Pictures 22; Football Fun 22; Making Good Resolutions 22; Making Paper Money 22; Paper Hanging 22; Peter the Barber 22; Playing at Doctors 22; Sold and Healed 22; Spring Cleaning 22; The Sweep 22

Dudley, Carl Cinerama—South Seas Adventure • South Seas Adventure 58*

Dudley, Frank Mazeppa 08

Dudley, Terence All Creatures Great and Small 86

Dudow, Slatan Bulles de Savon • Seifenblasen • Soap Bubbles 29; Wie der Berliner Arbeiter Wohnt 30; Kühle Wampe • Kühle Wampe oder Wem Gehört die Welt? • To Whom Does the World Belong? • Whither Germany? 32; Our Daily Bread • Unser Täglich Brot 49; Familie Benthin 50*; Frauenschicksale • A Woman's Destiny 52; Stärker Als die Nacht • Stronger Than the Night 54; The Captain from Cologne • Der Hauptmann von Köln 56; Love's Confusion • Verwirrung der Liebe 58

Dudrumet, Jean-Charles La Corde Raide • Lovers on a Tightrope 60; The Reluctant Spy 63

Duffell, Peter The Grand Junction Case 61; The Never Never Murder 61; Partners in Crime 61; The Silent Weapon 61; Company of Fools 66; Payment in Kind 67; The House That Dripped Blood 70; England Made Me 72; The Golden Heist • Hitler's Gold • Inside Out 75; Experience Preferred...But Not Essential 83; Letters to an Unknown Lover • Les Louves 85; Inspector Morse 87

Dufour, A. P. Voyage dans le Ciel 36*

Dugan, Dennis Problem Child 90

Dugan, Harry The Hills of Ireland 51; The Spell of Ireland 54

Dugan, James The Desert Pirate 28; Her Summer Hero 28; Phantom of the Range 28

Dugan, Michael Super Seal 76; Mausoleum 81

Dugan, Robert Paul Le Père de Mademoiselle 53*

Dugdale, George Slaughter High 86*

Duges, A. The Great Test 28*; The Legion of Honor • The Soul of France 28*

Duggal, Satish Khel Mohabbat Ka 88

Duhamel, Marcel Paris Express • Souvenirs de Paris 28*

Duhour, Clément Les Trois Font la Paire 57*; La Vie à Deux 58

Duigan, John The Firm Man 75; The Trespassers 76; Mouth to Mouth 78; Dimboola 79; The Winter of Our Dreams 81; Far East 82; One Night Stand 84; The Year My Voice Broke 87; Romero 89

Duke, Bill The Killing Floor 84; A Raisin in the Sun 89

Duke, Daryl Payday 72; The Silent Partner 78; Hard Feelings 81; Tai-Pan 86

Dukes, Robert The Lost City 82

Dukinsky, Ivan China Liberated • Liberated China • The New China • Osvobozhdeniye Kitai 50*

Dulac, Germaine Enemy Sisters • Les Sœurs Ennemies 15; Dans l'Ouragan de la Vie • Venus Victrix • Venus Victrix, or In the Whirlwind of Life • Vénus Victrix ou Dans l'Ouragan de la Vie 16; Géo le Mystérieux • Geo the Mysterious 16; Âmes de Fous • Mad Souls 17; Le Bonheur des Autres • The Happiness of Others 18; La Cigarette • The Cigarette 19; La Fête Espagnole • The Spanish Fiesta 19; The Beautiful Lady Without Pity • La Belle Dame Sans Merci 20; Malencontre • Misadventure 20; The Death of the Sun • La Mort du Soleil 21; The Smiling Madame Beudet • La Souriante Madame Beudet 22; Werther 22; Gossette 23; The Devil in the Streets • Le Diable dans la Ville 24; Âme d'Artiste • Soul of an Artist 25; La Folie des Vaillants • The Folly of the Brave 25; Antoinette Sabrier 26; Le Cinéma au Service de l'Histoire • The Cinema in the Service of History 27; La Coquille et le Clergyman • The Seashell and the Clergyman 27; L'Invitation au Voyage • Invitation to the Voyage 27; Oublié • Oublié — La Princesse Mandane • La Princesse Mandane 27; Arabesque • Étude Cinégraphique sur une Arabesque • Film Study of an Arabesque 28; Disc 927 • Disque 927 28; Germination d'un Haricot • Germination of a Bean 28; Themes and Variations • Thèmes et Variations 28

Duletić, Vojko The Doctor • Doktor 86

Dull, Orville The Flying Horseman 26; Black Jack 27; The Broncho Twister 27

Du Luart, Yolande Angela — Portrait of a Revolutionary 71

Duncan, F. Martin Cheese Mites 03

Duncan, Patrick 84 Charlie Mopic 89

Duncan, Victor Second Fiddle to a Steel Guitar 65

Duncan, William The Dynamiters 12; A Rough Ride with Nitroglycerine 12; An Apache's Gratitude 13; Billy's Birthday Present 13; Buck's Romance 13; An Embarrassed Bridegroom 13; The Escape of Jim Dolan 13; Galloping Romeo 13; The Good Indian 13; His Father's Bridegroom 13; Howlin' Jones 13; The Jealousy of Miguel and Isabella 13; Juggling with Fate 13; The Law and the Outlaw 13; Made a Coward 13; A Matrimonial Deluge 13; Rejected Lover's Luck 13; Religion and Gun Practice 13; The Señorita's Repentance 13; The Silver Grindstone 13; The Suffragette 13; The Taming of Texas Pete 13; Marian the Holy Terror 14; Marrying Gretchen 14; Out West 14; Romance of the Forest Reserve 14; The Servant Question 14; The Last Man 16*; Dead-Shot Baker 17; The Fighting Trail 17; Money Magic 17; The Tenderfoot 17; Vengeance and the Woman 17; A Fight for Millions 18; Man of Might 19; Smashing Barriers 19; The Silent Avenger 20; Fighting Fate 21; No Defense 21; Steelheart 21; Where Men Are Men 21; The Fighting Guide 22*; The Silent Vow 22; When Danger Smiles 22; Playing It Wild 23; The Steel Trail 23; The Fast Express 24; Wolves of the North 24

Dungern, Baron A. von Pori 30

Dunlap, Scott R. Be a Little Sport 19; The Lost Princess 19; Love Is Love 19; Vagabond Luck 19; Words and Music • Words and Music by... 19; The Challenge of the Law 20; Forbidden Trails 20; The Hell Ship 20; Her Elephant Man 20; The Iron Rider 20; The Twins of Suffering Creek 20; Would You Forgive? 20; The Cheater Reformed 21; Too Much Married 21; Bells of San Juan 22; Bluebeard Junior 22; Pawn Ticket 210 22; Trooper O'Neill 22*; West of Chicago 22*; Western Speed 22*; Boston Blackie 23; The Footlight Ranger 23; Skid Proof 23; Snowdrift 23; The Fatal Mistake 24; One Glorious Night 24; Traffic in Hearts 24; Beyond the Border 25; Blue Blood 25; Silent Sanderson 25; The Texas Trail 25; Wreckage 25; The Better Man 26; Desert Valley 26; Doubling with Danger 26; Driftin' Thru 26; The Frontier Trail 26; The Seventh Bandit 26; Winning the Futurity 26; Good As Gold 27; Whispering Sage 27; Midnight Life 28; Object — Alimony 28; One Stolen Night 29; Smoke Bellew 29

Dunlop, Frank The Winter's Tale 66

Dunn, Eddie The Cracked Ice Man 33*; Another Wild Idea 34*; Four Parts 34*; I'll Take Vanilla 34*; It Happened One Day 34*

Dunne, Philip Prince of Players 55; Secret Interlude • The View from Pompey's Head 55; Hilda Crane 56; Three Brave Men 56; In Love and War 58; Ten North Frederick 58; Blue Denim • Blue Jeans 59; The Inspector • Lisa 61; Wild in the Country 61; Blindfold 65

Dunning, George Auprès de Ma Blonde 43; Grim Pastures 43; J'Ai Tant Danse 43; Keep Your Mouth Shut 44*; Three Blind Mice 45; Cadet Rousselle 46*; The Adventures of Baron Münchausen 47*; Arbre Généalogique • Family Tree 47*; Up, Right and Wrong 47*; The Story of the Motorcar Engine 58*; The Wardrobe 59; The Apple 61; Mr. Know-How 61; The Ever-Changing Motorcar 62*; The Flying Man 62; Visible Manifestations 63; Discovery, Penicillin 64; The Adventures of Thud and Blunder 65; Canada Is My Piano 66*; The Ladder 67; Yellow Submarine 68; Hands, Knees and Boomps-a-Daisy 70; Moon Rock 70

Dunstall, George The Count of No Account 21; Dutch Courage 22; The Exclusive Model 22

Dupeyron, François Drôle d'Endroit pour une Rencontre 88

Dupont, E. A. Durchlaucht Hyperchonder 17; Es Werde Licht! • Let There Be Light! 17*; Der Ewige Zweifel 17; Das Geheimnis des Amerika-Docks • The Secret of the America-Dock 17; Die Japanerin 17; Das Perlenhalsband 17; Die Schwarze Schachdame 17; Europa-Postlagernd! • Post Office Europe 18; Der Lebende Schatten • Der Schatten 18; The Man from Naples • Der Mann aus Neapel 18; Mitternacht 18; Der Teufel 18; Alkohol 19*; Die Apachen • Paris Underworld 19; Das Derby 19; Das Grand Hotel Babylon 19; Die Maske 19; Die Spione 19; Die Würger der Welt 19; Herztrumpt 20; Mord Ohne Täter • Murder Without Cause 20; Der Weisse Pfau • The White Peacock 20; Whitechapel 20; Der Geierwally • Ein Roman aus den Bergen 20; The Woman Who Killed a Vulture 21; Children of Darkness • Kinder der Finsternis 22; Kämpfende Welten • Worlds in Struggle 22; She and the Three • Sie und die Drei 22; Das Alte Gesetz • The Ancient Law • Baruch 23; Ein Film aus dem Süden • The Green Manuela • Die Grüne Manuela 23; Der Demütige und die Sängerin • The Humble Man and the Singer • La Meurtrière 24; Variété • Varieties • Variety • Vaudeville 25; Implacable Destiny • Love Me and the World Is Mine 27; Affairs of Hannerl 28; Moulin Rouge 28; Piccadilly 28; Atlantic 29; Atlantik 29; Atlantis 30*; Le Cap Perdu 30; Cape Forlorn • The Love Storm 30; Les Deux Mondes 30; Menschen im Käfig 30; Two Worlds 30; Zwei Welten 30; The Circus of Sin • Salto Mortale • Trapeze 31; Peter Voss der Millionendieb • Peter Voss Who Stole Millions 32; The Bishop Misbehaves • The Bishop's Misadventures 33; Ladies Must Love 33; Der Läufer von Marathon • The Marathon Runner 33; Forgotten Faces 36; The Greene Murder Case • Night of Mystery 36; A Son Comes Home 36; Love on Toast 37; On Such a Night 37; Hell's Kitchen 39*; The Dungeon • The Scarf 50; Pictura, an Adventure in Art 51; The Neanderthal Man 53; Problem Girls 53; Secret of the Sahara • The Steel Lady • The Treasure of Kalifa 53; Bandit Island of Karabei • Return to Treasure Island 54; Miss Robin Crusoe 54*

Dupont, Jacques Congolaise 50; Heartbreak Ridge 55; La Passe du Diable 57*; Trapped by Fear 69

Du Pont, Michael The Bloodless Vampire 65; The Secret of the Sacred Forest 70

Dupont-Midi, François The Double Bed • Le Lit à Deux Places 65*

Dupuy-Mazuel, Henri The Chess Player • Le Joueur d'Échecs 30

Duque, Lisandro see *Naranjo, Lisandro Duque*

Durán, Fernando The Aces of Contraband • Los Ases de Contrabando 86; El Extraño Hijo del Sheriff • The Sheriff's Strange Son 86; Herencia de Valientes • Legacy of the Brave 87

Durán, Javier Mofles' Escapades • Las Movidas del Mofles • Muffler's Escapades 87

Duran, Jorge The Color of Destiny • A Cor do Seu Destino 87

Durán, Rafael Rosales *see Rosales Durán, Rafael*

Durand, Claude On Vous Parle 60*; La Frontière 61*; Madame Se Meurt 61*; De Tout pour Faire un Monde 62*; Le Coup de Grâce 65*

Durand, Jean La Prairie en Feu 07; Arizona Bill 09; L'Attaque d'un Train 09; Pendaison à Jefferson City 11; Cent Dollars 12; Mort ou Vif 12; Le Collier Vivant 15; Serpentin au Harem 19; Marie la Gaieté 21; Marie la Bohémienne 22; Face aux Loups 26; Palaces 27; L'Île d'Amour 28; La Femme Revée 29

Durand, Rudy Tilt 78

Durant, Alberto Malabrigo 86

Duras, Marguerite Music • La Musica 66*; Destroy She Said • Détruire Dit-Elle 69; Jaune le Soleil • Yellow the Sun 71; Nathalie Granger 72; La Femme du Gange • La Ragazza di Passaggio • Woman of the Ganges 73; Her Name of Venice in Calcutta Desert • Son Nom de Venise dans Calcutta Désert 75; India Song 75; Baxter, Vera Baxter • Vera Baxter, or The Atlantic Beaches • Vera Baxter ou Les Plages de l'Atlantique 76; Days in the Trees • Des Journées Entières dans les Arbres • Entire Days in the Trees 76; Le Camion • The Truck 77; Le Navire Night 78; Aurelia Steiner 79; Agatha • Agatha et les Lectures Illimitées 81; Il Dialogo di Roma 83; The Children • Les Enfants 84*

Durham, Todd Visions of Sugar-Plums 84; Tales of the Third Dimension 85*; Hyperspace 86

Durkin, James The Incorrigible Dukane 15; The Mummy and the Hummingbird 15; By Whose Hand? 16; The Clarion 16

Durlam, George Arthur Two-Fisted Justice 31; Our Bill of Rights 41; Our Constitution 41; Our Declaration of Independence 41; Our Freedom of the Seas 41; Our Louisiana Purchase 41; Our Monroe Doctrine 41

Durning, Bernard J. Aliens • The Unwritten Code 19; The Devil Within 21; One Man Trail 21; Partners of Fate 21; The Primal Law 21; Straight from the Shoulder 21; To a Finish 21; The Fast Mail 22; Iron to Gold 22; Oathbound 22; Strange Idols 22; While Justice Waits 22; The Yosemite Trail 22; The Eleventh Hour 23

Durrance, Dick Ski Champs 51

Durrant, Fred W. If England Were Invaded • The Raid of 1915 14; Mrs. Cassell's Profession • The Striped Stocking Gang 15; Fate and the Woman 16; The Girl Who Didn't Care 16; The Little Mayoress • The Mill Owner's Daughter 16; The Picture of Dorian Gray 16; The Strange Case of Philip Kent 16; What Every Woman Knows 17; Edge o' Beyond 19; Women Who Win 19*; The Husband Hunter 20; A Temporary Gentleman 20; Number 7 Brick Row 22

Durst, John The Secret Cave 53; One Wish Too Many 56

Durston, David Dry Summer • I Had My Brother's Wife • Susuz Yaz • Waterless Summer 64*; I Drink Your Blood 70; Blue Sextet 72; Stigma 72

Duru, Süreyya The Dawn of Hope • Umutlu Şafaklar 86

Dusen, Bruce van *see* Van Dusen, Bruce

D'Usseau, Leon Fury of the Wild 29; The One Man Dog 29; Girl from Calgary 32*

Dutillieu, José La Flûte à Six Schtroumpfs • The Smurfs and the Magic Flute 84*

Dutt, Raj Pudhche Paol 87

Dutta, J. P. Hathyar 89

Duval, Daniel The Confessions of a Streetwalker • La Dérobade • The Evasion • The Getaway Life • Memoirs of a French Whore 79

Duvall, Earl Buddy's Beer Garden 33; Sittin' on a Backyard Fence 33; Buddy's Garage 34; Honeymoon Hotel 34

Duvall, Robert We're Not the Jet Set 75; Angelo, My Love 82

Duvivier, Julien Haceldama • Haceldama ou Le Prix du Sang • Le Prix du Sang 19; La Réincarnation de Serge Renaudier 20; L'Agonie des Aigles 21*; Le Logis de l'Horreur • Der Unheimliche Gast 22; L'Ouragan sur la Montagne 22; Les Roquevillard 22; Cœurs Farouches 23; Credo • Credo ou La Tragédie de Lourdes • La Tragédie de Lourdes • The Tragedy of Lourdes 23; L'Œuvre Immortelle 23; Le Reflet de Claude Mercœur 23; La Machine à Refaire la Vie • The Machine for Recreating Life 24*; L'Abbé Constantin 25; Carrot-Top • Poil de Carotte • The Redhead 25; L'Agonie de Jérusalem • The Agony in Jerusalem 26; L'Homme à l'Hispano 26; Le Mariage de Mademoiselle Beulemans 26; Le Mystère de la Tour Eiffel • Les Mystères de la Tour Eiffel • Tramel S'en Fiche 27; La Divine Croisière 28; Le Tourbillon de Paris 28; La Vie Miraculeuse de Thérèse Martin 28; Au Bonheur des Dames 29; Maman Colibri 29; David Golder 30; Allô Berlin? Ici Paris! • Hallo! Hallo! Hier Spricht Berlin 31; Les Cinq Gentlemen Maudits • Sous la Lune du Maroc 31; Die Fünf Verfluchten Gentlemen 31; Carrot-Top • Poil de Carotte • The Redhead 32; La Tête d'un Homme 32; La Vénus du Collège 32; La Machine à Refaire la Vie • The Machine for Recreating Life 33; Le Paquebot Tenacity 33; Le Petit Roi 33; La Bandera • Escape from Yesterday 34; Maria Chapdelaine • The Naked Heart 34; La Belle Équipe • The Good Bunch • They Were Five 35; Der Golem • Le Golem • The Golem • The Golem—The Legend of Prague • The Legend of Prague • The Man of Stone 35; Golgotha 35; L'Homme du Jour • The Man of the Day • Man of the Hour 35; Un Carnet de Bal • Christine • A Dance Program • The Dance Programme • Life Dances On 36; Pépé le Moko 36; The End of a Day • The End of the Day • La Fin du Jour 38; The Great Waltz • Toute la Ville Danse 38*; Marie Antoinette 38*; La Charrette Fantôme • The Phantom Carriage • The Phantom Wagon 39; The

Heart of a Nation • Untel Père et Fils 40; Lydia 40; Tales of Manhattan 42; Flesh and Fantasy • Obsession 43; The Imposter • Strange Confession 43; Destiny 44*; Panic • Panique 46; Anna Karenina • Anna Karénine 47; Au Royaume des Cieux • The Sinners • Woman Hunt 49; Black Jack • Captain Black Jack 49; Sous le Ciel de Paris • Sous le Ciel de Paris Coule la Seine • Under the Paris Sky 50; Don Camillo • The Little World of Don Camillo • Le Petit Monde de Don Camillo • Il Piccolo Mondo di Don Camillo 51; La Fête à Henriette • Henriette • Henriette's Holiday • Holiday for Henrietta 52; L'Affaire Maurizius • The Maurizius Case • On Trial! 53; Le Retour de Don Camillo • The Return of Don Camillo • Il Ritorno di Don Camillo 53; Marianne de Ma Jeunesse • Marianne of My Youth 54; Deadlier Than the Male • Murder à la Carte • Le Temps des Assassins • Voici le Temps des Assassins 55; L'Homme à l'Imperméable • The Man in the Raincoat 56; The House of Lovers • Lovers of Paris • Pot Bouille 57; The Female • La Femme et le Pantin • The Woman and the Puppet • A Woman Like Satan 58; Marie Octobre • Secret Meeting 58; La Grande Vie • Das Kunstseidene Mädchen 59; Boulevard 60; Das Brennende Gericht • The Burning Court • La Chambre Ardente • The Curse and the Coffin • The Curse of the Coffin 61; The Devil and the Ten Commandments • Le Diable et les Dix Commandements 62; Chair de Poule • Highway Pickup 63; Diabolically Yours • Diaboliquement Vôtre 67

Dvořák, Ivo Förvandlingen • Metamorphosis 75

Dvoretsky, A. Drunkenness and Its Consequences 13

Dwan, Allan The Actress and the Cowboys 11; The Angel of Paradise Ranch • The Girl of the Ranch 11; Auntie and the Cowboys 11; Battleships 11; The Blotted Brand 11; Bonita of El Cajón 11; The Brand of Fear • Branding a Bad Man 11; The Broncho Buster's Bride 11; Broncho Busting for Flying A Pictures • Bucking Horses 11; The Call of the Open Range 11; Cattle, Gold and Oil 11; The Cattle Rustler's End 11; The Cattle Thief's Brand 11; Caves of La Jolla 11; The Circular Fence 11; The Claim Jumpers • The Range Squatter 11; The Cowboy and the Artist 11; The Cowboy and the Outlaw 11; The Cowboy's Deliverance 11; The Cowboy's Ruse 11; Cupid in Chaps 11; Dams and Waterways 11; A Daughter of Liberty 11; The Diamond Smugglers • The Smuggler and the Girl 11; The Duel of the Candles 11; The Eastern Cowboy 11; The Elopements on Double L Ranch 11; $5,000 Reward, Dead or Alive 11; The Foreman's Fixup • The Ranch Tenor 11; The Gold Lust 11; The Gunman 11; The Hermit's Gold 11; The Horse Thief's Bigamy 11; The House That Jack Built 11; The Land Thieves 11; The Last Notch 11; Law and Order on Bar L

Ranch 11; The Lawful Holdup 11; The Lonely Range 11; The Love of the West 11; Magic Isle of the Pacific 11; Man Hunt 11; The Master of the Vineyard 11; The Mexican 11; A Midwinter Trip to Los Angeles 11; The Miner's Wife 11; The Misadventures of a Claim Agent 11; The Mother of the Ranch 11; The Outlaw's Trail 11; The Parting Trails 11; The Poisoned Flume 11; The Ranch Chicken 11; The Ranch Girl • The Ranch Girl's Rustler 11; The Ranchman's Nerve 11; Rattlesnakes and Gunpowder 11; The Rustler Sheriff 11; The Sagebrush Phrenologist 11; Santa Catalina • Santa Catalina – Magic Isle of the Pacific 11; The School Ma'am of Snake 11; The Sheepman's Daughter 11; The Sheriff's Sisters 11; The Sky Pilot's Intemperance 11; Sloppy Bill of the Rollicking R 11; The Smoke of the 45 11; The Stage Robbers of San Juan 11; The Stronger Man 11; The Test 11; Three Daughters of the West 11; Three Million Dollars 11; The Three Shell Game 11; The Trail of the Eucalyptus 11; The Trained Nurse at Bar Z 11; A Trouper's Heart 11; The Water War 11; The Way of the West 11; The Western Doctor's Peril 11; A Western Dreamer 11; A Western Waif 11; When East Comes West 11; The Witch of the Range 11; The Yiddisher Cowboy 11; After School 12; The Agitator • The Cowboy Socialist 12; The Animal Within 12; Another Man's Wife 12; An Assisted Elopement 12; Auto Race, Lakeside • Fifty Mile Auto Contest 12; A Bad Investment 12; The Bad Man and the Ranger 12; The Bandit of Point Loma 12; The Battleground 12; The Best Man Wins 12*; The Best Policy 12; Blackened Hills 12; The Brand 12; The Broken Ties 12; Calamity Anne's Ward 12; The Canyon Dweller 12; Checkmate 12; The Coward 12; Cupid Through Padlocks 12; Curtiss' School of Aviation 12; The Daughters of Señor Lopez 12; The Dawn of Passion 12; The Distant Relative 12; Driftwood 12; The Eastern Girl • Her Mountain Home 12; The End of the Feud 12; The Evil Inheritance 12; The Fatal Mirror 12; Father's Favorite • The Favored Son 12; The Fear 12; February 29 • The Leap Year Cowboy 12; Fidelity 12; For the Good of Her Men 12; The Foreclosure 12; The Fraud That Failed 12; From the Four Hundred to the Herd 12; The Full Value 12; The Girl and the Gun 12; The Girl Back Home 12; God's Unfortunate 12; The Good Love and the Bad 12; The Greaser and the Weakling 12; The Green-Eyed Monster 12; The Grubstake Mortgage 12; The Haters 12; Her Own Country 12; The Horse Thief 12; Indian Jealousy 12; An Innocent Grafter 12; The Intrusion at Lompoc 12; It Pays to Wait 12; Jack of Diamonds • Queen of Hearts 12; Jack's Word • A Man's Word 12; The Jealous Rage 12; Justice of the Sage 12; The Land Baron of San Tee 12; The Land of Death 12; The Law of God 12; The Liar 12; A Life for a Kiss 12; The Locket 12; The Loneliness of Neglect 12;

The Lost Watch • The Reformation of Sierra Smith 12; Love and Lemons 12; The Maid and the Man 12; Maiden and Men 12; The Man from the East 12; Man's Calling 12; The Marauders 12; The Meddlers 12; The Mormon 12; Mountain Kate 12; Mystical Maid of Jamasha Pass 12; Nell of the Pampas 12; The New Cowpuncher 12; Objections Overruled 12; The Odd Job Man 12; One, Two, Three 12; The Other Wise Man 12; The Outlaw Colony 12; Paid in Full 12; Pals 12; The Pensioners 12; Point Loma – Old Town 12; The Power of Love 12; The Promise 12; Ranch Life on the Range 12; The Ranchman's Marathon 12; The Range Detective 12; The Real Estate Fraud 12; The Recognition 12; The Relentless Outlaw 12; The Reward of Valor 12; San Diego 12; The Simple Love 12; Society and Chaps 12; The Stepmother 12; The Stranger at Coyote 12; The Tell-Tale Shells 12; Their Hero Son 12; The Thief's Wife 12; The Thread of Life 12; The Tramp's Gratitude 12; Under False Pretenses 12; The Vanishing Race • The Vanishing Tribe 12; The Vengeance That Failed 12; The Wanderer 12; The Wandering Gypsy 12; The Weaker Brother 12; The Wedding Dress 12; Where Broadway Meets the Mountains 12; Where There's a Heart 12; White Treachery 12; The Will of James Waldron 12; The Winning of La Mesa 12; Winter Sports and Pastimes of Coronado Beach 12; The Wooers of Mountain Kate 12; The Wordless Message 12; The Would-Be Heir 12; Andrew Jackson 13; Angel of the Canyons 13; The Animal 13; Ashes of Three 13; Back to Life 13; The Battle of Wills 13; Bloodhounds of the North 13; Boobs and Bricks 13; The Brothers 13; Building the Great Los Angeles Aqueduct 13; Calamity Anne, Detective 13; Calamity Anne, Parcel Post 13; Calamity Anne's Beauty 13; Calamity Anne's Inheritance 13; Calamity Anne's Trust 13; Calamity Anne's Vanity 13; The Call to Arms • In Love and War 13; The Chase 13; Criminals 13; Cupid Never Ages 13; Cupid Throws a Brick 13; An Eastern Flower 13; The Echo of a Song 13; The Finer Things 13; The Fugitive 13; The Great Harmony 13; The Greater Love 13; He Called Her In 13; Hearts and Horses 13*; Her Big Story 13; Her Innocent Marriage 13*; High and Low 13; His Old-Fashioned Mother 13; Human Kindness 13; In Another's Nest 13; Jewels of Sacrifice 13; The Jocular Winds 13; The Lie 13; Love Is Blind 13; The Marine Law 13; Matches 13; The Menace 13; Mental Suicide 13; The Mute Witness 13; Oil on Troubled Waters 13; On the Border 13; The Orphan's Mine 13; The Picket Guard 13; The Powder Flash of Death 13; Red Margaret, Moonshiner 13; The Renegade's Heart 13; The Restless Spirit 13; The Reward of Courage 13; The Road to Ruin 13; The Road to Success 13; The Romance 13; A Rose of Old Mexico 13*; The Silver-Plated Gun 13; The Soul of a Thief 13; The Spirit of the Flag 13; Suspended Sentence 13; That Sharp Note 13; Their Masterpiece 13; The Transgression of Manuel 13; The Wall of Money 13; The Ways of Fate 13*; When a Woman Won't 13; When Luck Changes 13; When the Light Fades 13; Where Destiny Guides 13; The Wishing Seat 13; Woman's Honor 13; Women and War 13; Women Left Alone 13; Youth and Jealousy 13; The Conspiracy 14; The County Chairman 14; Discord and Harmony 14; The Embezzler 14; The End of the Feud 14; The Forbidden Room 14; The Great Universal Mystery 14; Honor of the Mounted 14; The Hopes of Blind Alley 14; The Lamb, the Woman, the Wolf 14; The Man on the Case 14; The Menace to Carlotta 14; Remember Mary Magdalene 14; Richelieu 14; The Small Town Girl 14; The Straight Road 14; Tragedy of Whispering Creek 14; The Unlawful Trade 14; The Unwelcome Mrs. Hatch 14; Wildflower 14; The Commanding Officer 15; The Dancing Girl 15; David Harum 15; The Foundling 15; A Girl of Yesterday 15; Jordan Is a Hard Road 15; The Love Route 15; May Blossom 15; The Pretty Sister of José 15; Betty of Greystone 16; The Carquenez Woods • The Half-Breed 16; Fifty-Fifty 16; The Good Bad Man • Passing Through 16; The Habit of Happiness • Laugh and the World Laughs 16; An Innocent Magdalene 16; Manhattan Madness 16; Panthea 16; The Fighting Odds 17; A Modern Musketeer 17; Superstition 17; Bound in Morocco 18; He Comes Up Smiling 18; Mr. Fix-It 18; Cheating Cheaters 19; The Dark Star 19; Getting Mary Married 19; The Luck of the Irish 19; Soldiers of Fortune 19; The Forbidden Thing 20; Heart of a Fool • In the Heart of a Fool 20; The Scoffer 20; A Broken Doll 21; A Perfect Crime 21; The Sin of Martha Queed • Sins of the Parents 21; Douglas Fairbanks in Robin Hood • Robin Hood 22; The Hidden Woman 22; Big Brother 23; The Glimpses of the Moon 23; Lawful Larceny 23; Zaza 23; Argentine Love 24; Her Love Story 24; Manhandled 24; A Society Scandal 24; Wages of Virtue 24; The Coast of Folly 25; Night Life of New York 25; Stage Struck 25; Padlocked 26; Sea Horses 26; Summer Bachelors 26; Tin Gods 26; East Side, West Side 27; French Dressing • Lessons for Wives 27; The Joy Girl 27; The Music Master 27; The Big Noise 28; The Far Call 29; Frozen Justice 29; The Iron Mask 29; South Sea Rose 29; Tide of Empire 29; Man to Man 30; What a Widow! 30; Chances 31; Wicked 31; Her First Affaire 32; While Paris Sleeps 32; Counsel's Opinion 33; I Spy • The Morning After 33; Hollywood Party 34*; Beauty's Daughter • Navy Wife 35; Black Sheep 35; 15 Malden Lane 36; High Tension • Troublemakers 36; Human Cargo 36; The Song and Dance Man 36; Heidi 37; One Mile from Heaven 37; That I May Live 37; Woman-Wise 37; Josette 38; Rebecca of Sunnybrook Farm 38; The Singing Musketeer • The Three Musketeers 38; Suez 38; Frontier Marshal 39; The Gorilla

39; Sailor's Lady 40; Trail of the Vigilantes 40; Young People 40; Look Who's Laughing 41; Rise and Shine 41; Friendly Enemies 42; Here We Go Again 42; Around the World 43; Abroad with Two Yanks 44; Up in Mabel's Room 44; Brewster's Millions 45; Getting Gertie's Garter 45; Calendar Girl 46; Corporal Dolan, A.W.O.L. • Rendezvous with Annie 46; Driftwood 47; End of the Rainbow • Northwest Outpost 47; Angel in Exile 48*; The Inside Story 48; Montana Belle 48; Sands of Iwo Jima 49; Surrender 50; Belle le Grande 51; Bombs Over Japan • Thunder Across the Pacific • The Wild Blue Yonder 51; I Dream of Jeannie 52; Flight Nurse 53; Sweethearts on Parade 53; The Woman They Almost Lynched 53; Cattle Queen of Montana 54; Escape to Burma 54; Passion 54; Silver Lode 54; Pearl of the South Pacific 55; Tennessee's Partner 55; Hold Back the Night 56; Slightly Scarlet 56; The Restless Breed 57; The River's Edge 57; Enchanted Island 58; The Most Dangerous Man Alive 58

Dwoskin, Stephen Hindered 74; Further and Particular 88

Dwyer, John Crimes of a Drifter • The Texas Serial Killings 86

Dyal, H. Kaye Memory of Us 74

Dyall, Franklin Duke's Son • Squandered Lives 20

Dyer, Anson Dollars in Surrey 21*

Dyke, Robert Moontrap 89

Dyke, Thomas L. The Northfield Cemetery Massacre • The Northville Cemetery Massacre 76*

Dyke, W. S. van see Van Dyke, W. S.

Dyke, Willard van see Van Dyke, Willard

Dyke, William S. van II see Van Dyke, W. S.

Dyke, Woody van see Van Dyke, W. S.

Dylan, Bob Renaldo and Clara 78

Dymon, Frankie, Jr. Death May Be Your Santa Claus 69

Dziedzina, Julian Bokser • The Boxer 67

Dzigan, Yefim First Cornet Streshnev • Trumpeter Treshney 28*; The War God 29; Woman's World 32; We Are from Kronstadt • We from Kronstadt 36; If War Comes Tomorrow 38*; Cine-Concert... • Film-Concert Dedicated to the 25th Anniversary of the Red Army • Film-Concert for the Red Army's 25th Anniversary • Kinokontsert k 25-Letiyu Krasnoy Armii • Moscow Music Hall 43*; Jambul 53; Prologue 56

Dziki, Waldemar Cudowne Dziecko • Le Jeune Magicien • The Young Magician 87

Eades, Wilfred You Can't Escape 55

Eadington, Dave T. Dan Smith 87*

Eady, David Lord Mountdrago • Three Cases of Murder 54*; You Killed Elizabeth 55; The Heart Within 57; Zoo Baby 57; In the Wake of a Stranger 58; The Crowning Touch 59; The Man Who Liked Funerals 59; Faces in the Dark 60; The Verdict 64; Operation Third Form 66; Scramble 70;

Hide and Seek 72; Anoop and the Elephant 73; The Laughing Girl Murder 73; Where's Johnny? 74; Crime Casebook • The Hand of Fate 75; The Hostages 75; Echo of the Badlands 77*; Night Ferry 77; Deep Waters 79; Danger on Dartmoor 80

Eagle, Bill Blonde Goddess 82

Eagle, Oscar The Royal Box 14; The Cotton King 15; The Little Mademoiselle 15; Sins of Society 15; The Fruits of Desire 16; Charlotte 17; The Frozen Warning 18

Eagle, Vincent ...E Venne il Tempo di Uccidere 68

Eames, Charles Traveling Boy 50*; Blacktop 51*; Here They Come Down the Street • Parade 51*; Bread 53*; Calligraphy 53*; Communications Primer 53*; Sofa Compact 54*; House 55*; Textiles and Ornamental Arts of India 55*; Two Baroque Churches in Germany 55*; Eames Lounge Chair 56*; Day of the Dead 57*; The Information Machine 57*; Toccata for Toy Trains 57*; The Expanding Airport 58*; Herman Miller at the Brussels Fair 58*; De Gaulle Sketch 59*; Glimpses of U.S.A. 59*; Introduction to Feedback 60*; Jazz Chair 60*; IBM Mathematics Peep Show 61*; Kaleidoscope 61*; Kaleidoscope Shop 61*; Before the Fair 62*; ECS 62*; House of Science 62*; IBM Fair Presentation Film, Part I 62*; IBM Fair Presentation Film, Part II 63*; IBM at the Fair 65*; IBM Puppet Shows 65*; The Smithsonian Institution 65*; The Smithsonian Newsreel 65*; Think • View from the People Wall 65*; Westinghouse ABC 65*; Boeing—The Leading Edge 66*; A Computer Glossary 67*; IBM Museum 67*; National Aquarium Presentation 67*; Schütz Machine 67*; Babbage 68*; Lick Observatory 68*; Powers of 10 68*; Photography and the City 69*; Tops 69*

Eames, Ian see Emes, Ian

Eames, Ray Traveling Boy 50*; Blacktop 51*; Here They Come Down the Street • Parade 51*; Bread 53*; Calligraphy 53*; Communications Primer 53*; Sofa Compact 54*; House 55*; Textiles and Ornamental Arts of India 55*; Two Baroque Churches in Germany 55*; Eames Lounge Chair 56*; Day of the Dead 57*; The Information Machine 57*; Toccata for Toy Trains 57*; The Expanding Airport 58*; Herman Miller at the Brussels Fair 58*; De Gaulle Sketch 59*; Glimpses of U.S.A. 59*; Introduction to Feedback 60*; Jazz Chair 60*; IBM Mathematics Peep Show 61*; Kaleidoscope 61*; Kaleidoscope Shop 61*; Before the Fair 62*; ECS 62*; House of Science 62*; IBM Fair Presentation Film, Part I 62*; IBM Fair Presentation Film, Part II 63*; IBM at the Fair 65*; IBM Puppet Shows 65*; The Smithsonian Institution 65*; The Smithsonian Newsreel 65*; Think • View from the People Wall 65*; Westinghouse ABC 65*; Boeing—The Leading Edge 66*; A Computer Glossary 67*; IBM Museum 67*; National Aquarium Presentation 67*; Schütz Machine 67*; Babbage 68*; Lick Observa-

tory 68*; Powers of 10 68*; Photography and the City 69*; Tops 69*

Earle, Ferdinand P. Ben-Hur • Ben-Hur—A Tale of the Christ 25*; A Lover's Oath 25

Earle, William P. S. The Law Decides 16; The Courage of Silence 17; I Will Repay 17; Who Goes There? 17; Within the Law 17; Womanhood 17*; Blood of the Trevors • Heredity 18; His Own People 18; Little Miss No-Account 18; The Little Runaway 18; T'Other Dear Charmer 18; The Wooing of Princess Pat 18; The Better Wife 19; The Lone Wolf's Daughter 19; The Love Hunger 19; The Broken Melody 20; The Dangerous Paradise; The Road of Ambition 20; Whispers 20; The Woman Game 20; Gilded Lies 21; The Last Door 21; Poor, Dear Margaret Kirby 21; The Way of a Maid 21; Destiny's Isle 22; Love's Masquerade 22; The Dancer of the Nile 23

Eason, B. Reeves After the Storm 15; The Assayer of Lone Gap 15; The Barren Gain 15; The Blot on the Shield 15; The Bluffers 15; A Broken Cloud 15; Competition 15; The Day of Reckoning 15; Drawing the Line 15; The Exile of the Bar K Ranch 15; A Good Business Deal 15; Hearts in Shadow 15; The Honor of the District Attorney 15; In Trust 15; The Little Lady Next Door 15; Mountain Mary 15; The Newer Way 15; The Poet of the Peaks 15; Profit from Loss 15; A Question of Honor 15; She Walketh Alone 15; The Silver Lining 15; The Smuggler's Cave 15; The Solution of the Mystery 15; The Spirit of Adventure 15; The Substitute Minister 15; To Melody a Soul Responds 15; To Rent—Furnished 15; The Wasp 15; Yes or No? 15; The Head of the House 16; Matching Dreams 16; Pay Dirt 16*; A Sanitarium Scandal 16; Shadows 16; Time and Tide 16; Viviana 16; The Fighting Heart 18; The Four-Bit Man 18; Nine-Tenths of the Law 18; The Crow 19; The Fighting Line 19; Jack of Hearts 19; The Kid and the Cowboy 19; The Prospector's Vengeance 19; The Tell Tale Wire 19; Blue Streak McCoy 20; Hair Trigger Stuff 20; Held Up for the Makins 20; Human Stuff 20; The Moon Riders 20; Pink Tights 20; The Rattler's Hiss 20; The Texas Kid 20; Two Kinds of Love 20; The Big Adventure 21; Colorado 21; The Fire Eater 21; Red Courage 21; The Adventures of Robinson Crusoe 22*; False Play • The Lone Hand 22; Pardon My Nerve! 22; Rough Shod 22; When East Comes West 22; Around the World • Around the World in 18 Days 23; His Last Race 23; Tiger Thompson 23; Fighting the Flames 24; Flashing Spurs • Spider's Web 24; Trigger Finger 24; The Turf Sensation • Women First 24; Border Justice 25; A Fight to the Finish 25; Fighting Youth 25; The New Champion 25; The Shadow on the Wall 25; The Texas Bearcat 25; Johnny Get Your Hair Cut 26*; Lone Hand Saunders 26; The Sign of the Claw 26; The Test of Donald Norton

26; The Denver Dude 27; Galloping Fury 27; Painted Ponies 27; The Prairie King 27; Through Thick and Thin 27*; Clearing the Trail 28; The Flyin' Cowboy 28; Riding for Fame 28; A Trick of Hearts 28; The Lariat Kid 29; Troopers Three 29*; The Winged Horseman 29*; Bimi • King of the Wild 30*; Spurs 30; Trigger Tricks 30; The Galloping Ghost 31; The Vanishing Legion 31; Behind Jury Doors 32; Cornered 32; The Heart Punch 32; Honor of the Press • The Scoop 32; The Last of the Mohicans • Return of the Mohicans 32*; The Sunset Trail 32; Alimony Madness 33; Dance Hall Hostess 33; Her Resale Value 33; Mystery at Monte Carlo • Revenge at Monte Carlo 33; Neighbors' Wives 33; The Evil Eye of Kalinor 34; Hollywood Hoodlum • Hollywood Mystery • What Price Fame? 34; The Law of the Wild 34*; Mystery Mountain • Radio Ranch 34*; The Adventures of Rex and Rinty 35*; Couldn't Possibly Happen • Men with Steel Faces • The Phantom Empire 35*; The Fighting Marines 35*; The Miracle Rider 35*; Batmen of Africa • Darkest Africa • Hidden City • King of the Jungleland 36*; Red River Valley 36; Sharad of Atlantis • Undersea Kingdom 36*; Don't Pull Your Punches • The Kid Comes Back 37; Empty Holsters 37; Give Me Liberty 37; Land Beyond the Law 37; Law for Tombstone 37*; Prairie Thunder 37; Sergeant Murphy 37; Army Girl • The Last of the Cavalry 38*; Call of the Yukon 38*; The Daredevil Drivers 38; Blue Montana Skies 39; Mountain Rhythm 39; Wild West Days 39; March On, Marines 40; Meet the Fleet 40; Service with the Colors 40; Sockeroo 40; Take the Air 40; Young America Flies 40; Soldiers in White 41; The Tanks Are Coming 41; Wings of Steel 41; Born for Trouble • Human Sabotage • Murder in the Big House 42; Maybe Darwin Was Right 42; Men of the Sky 42; Spy Ship 42; The Fighting Engineers 43; Mountain Fighters 43; Murder on the Waterfront 43; Oklahoma Outlaws 43; The Phantom 43; Truck Busters 43; Wagon Wheels West 43; The Desert Hawk 44; Duel in the Sun 46*; 'Neath Canadian Skies 46; North of the Border • Ranson of the Mounted 46; Rimfire 49; Kamong Sentosa 52; The Singapore Story 52; Junge Justice 53; Paper Tiger 53

Eason, Breezy see *Eason, B. Reeves*
Eason, Reaves see *Eason, B. Reeves*
Eason, Reeves see *Eason, B. Reeves*
Eason, Walter B. The Sea Hound 47*
Eastman, Allan Snap Shot • A Sweeter Song 76; The War Boy 84; Crazy Moon • Huggers 85
Eastman, Charles The All-American Boy 73
Eastman, David Ambush at Devil's Gap 66; Calamity the Cow 67
Eastman, G. L. Metamorphosis 90
Eastman, Gordon The Savage Wild • Wild Arctic 70
Eastway, John Melvin, Son of Alvin 84

Eastwood, Clint Play Misty for Me 71; High Plains Drifter 72; Breezy 73; The Eiger Sanction 74; The Outlaw Josey Wales 75; The Gauntlet 77; Bronco Billy 80; Firefox 82; Honkytonk Man 82; Sudden Impact 83; Pale Rider 85; Heartbreak Ridge 86; Bird 88; The Rookie 90; White Hunter, Black Heart 90
Eberhardt, Thom Night of the Comet 84; Sole Survivor 84; The Night Before 86; Sherlock and Me • Without a Clue 88; Gross Anatomy 89
Eberson, Drew The Overland Express • The Phantom Stage 38
Écaré, Desiré Faces of Women 83
E Costa, José Fonseca see *Fonseca e Costa, José*
Eddy, Robert Action Galore 25; Galloping Jinx 25; The Handsome Brute 25; Hurricane Horseman 25; Readin"Ritin"Rithmetic 26; Stacked Cards 26
Edel, Uli see *Edel, Ulrich*
Edel, Ulrich Christiane F. • Christiane F. Wir Kinder vom Bahnhof Zoo 81; Last Exit to Brooklyn 89
Edelstein, Robert Sally's Hounds 68
Edenkoben, Richard Schneider see *Schneider-Edenkoben, Richard*
Edgren, Gustaf The Young Lady of Björneborg 22; The Ghost Baron 27; Black Rudolf 28; The Crown's Cavaliers 30; People of Värmland 32; Röda Dagen 32; Tired Teodor • Trötte Teodor 32; Karl-Fredrik Reigns 34; Walpurgis Night 35; Johan Ulfstjerna 36; John Ericsson Victor of Hampton Roads 37; A Big Hug 40; Katrina 43; Little Napoleon 43; His Majesty Will Have to Wait 45; Sunshine Follows Rain 46; A Swedish Tiger 48; Helen of Troy 51
Edmonds, Don Southern Double Cross 73; Ilsa: She-Wolf of the SS 74; Tender Loving Care 74; Bare Knuckles 77; Terror on Tour 80; Striker 85
Edmondson, Adrian More Bad News 87
Edmunds, Robert Television Talent 37
Edvardsson, Egill The House • Husid 82
Edwall, Allan Åke and His World • Åke och Hans Värld 84; Mälarpirater • Pirates of Lake Mälaren 87
Edwards, Blake Bring Your Smile Along 55; He Laughed Last 55; Mister Cory 56; The Perfect Furlough • Strictly for Pleasure 58; This Happy Feeling 58; Operation Petticoat 59; High Time 60; Breakfast at Tiffany's 61; Days of Wine and Roses 62; Experiment in Terror • The Grip of Fear 62; The Pink Panther 63; The Great Race 64; A Shot in the Dark 64; Gunn 66; What Did You Do in the War, Daddy? 66; The Party 68; Darling Lili • Darling Lili, Where Were You the Night I Shot Down Baron Von Richthofen? 69; Wild Rovers 71; The Carey Treatment • Emergency Ward 72; The Return of the Pink Panther 74; The Tamarind Seed 74; The Pink Panther Strikes Again 76; Revenge of the Pink Panther 78; 10 79; S.O.B. 80; Victor/Victoria 81; Trail of the Pink Panther 82; Curse of the Pink Panther 83; The

Man Who Loved Women 83; Micki and Maude • Micki + Maude 84; Blake Edwards' That's Life! • That's Life! 86; A Fine Mess 86; Blind Date 87; Sunset 88; Skin Deep 89
Edwards, Charles The Flaming Teen-Age 56*
Edwards, George The Attic 79
Edwards, H. P. Wild, Free and Hungry 70
Edwards, Harry Boobs in the Woods 25; Plain Clothes 25; Remember When? 25; Saturday Afternoon 26; Tramp, Tramp, Tramp 26*; The Best of Friends 27; Daddy Boy 27; Fiddlesticks 27; The Golf Nut 27; His First Flame 27; A Hollywood Hero 27; The Beach Club 28; The Best Man 28; The Campus Vamp 28; A Dumb Waiter 28; The Girl from Nowhere 28; Clunked on the Corner 29; Matchmaking Mamas 29
Edwards, Henry Doorsteps 15; A Welsh Singer 15; East Is East 16; Broken Threads 17; Dick Carson Wins Through • The Failure 17; Merely Mrs. Stubbs 17; Against the Grain 18; Anna 18; The Hanging Judge 18; Her Savings Saved 18; The Inevitable 18; The Message 18; Old Mother Hubbard 18; The Poet's Windfall 18; The Secret 18; Towards the Light 18; What's the Use of Grumbling? 18; The City of Beautiful Nonsense 19; His Dearest Possession 19; The Kinsman 19; Possession 19; The Amazing Quest of Mr. Ernest Bliss 20; Aylwin 20; John Forrest Finds Himself 20; A Temporary Vagabond 20; The Bargain 21; The Lunatic at Large 21; Simple Simon 22; Tit for Tat 22; Boden's Boy 23; Lily of the Alley 23; The Naked Man 23; Owd Bob 24; The World of Wonderful Reality 24; A Girl of London 25; King of the Castle 25; The Island of Despair 26; One Colombo Night 26; The Girl in the Night 31; Stranglehold 31; The Barton Mystery 32; Brother Alfred 32; The Flag Lieutenant 32; Anne One Hundred 33; Discord 33; General John Regan 33; Lord of the Manor 33; One Precious Year 33; Purse Strings 33; Are You a Mason? 34; The Lash 34; Lord Edgware Dies 34; The Man Who Changed • The Man Who Changed His Name 34; Captain Moonlight • D'Ye Ken John Peel? 35; High Treason • The Rocks of Valpré 35; The Lad 35; The Private Secretary 35; Scrooge 35; Squibs 35; Vintage Wine 35; The Demon Doctor • Juggernaut 36; Eliza Comes to Stay 36; In the Soup 36; Beauty and the Barge 37; Song of the Forge • The Village Backsmith 37; The Vicar of Bray 37
Edwards, Hilton Return to Glennascaul 51
Edwards, J. Gordon Anna Karenina 14; Blindness of Devotion 15; A Celebrated Scandal 15; The Galley Slave 15; Should a Mother Tell? 15; The Song of Hate 15; The Unfaithful Wife 15; A Woman's Resurrection 15; The Green-Eyed Monster 16; Her Double Life 16; Romeo and Juliet 16; The Spider and the Fly 16; Under Two Flags 16; The Vixen 16; A Wife's Sacrifice 16; Camille 17; Cleopatra 17; The Darling of

Paris 17; Heart and Soul 17; Her Greatest Love 17; Madame DuBarry 17; The Rose of Blood 17; Tangled Lives 17; The Tiger Woman 17; The Forbidden Path 18; Salome 18; The She-Devil 18; The Soul of Buddha 18; Under the Yoke 18; When a Woman Sins 18; The Last of the Duanes 19; The Light 19; The Lone Star Ranger 19; The Siren's Song 19; When Men Desire 19; Wings of the Morning 19; Wolves of the Night 19; A Woman There Was 19; The Adventurer 20; Drag Harlan 20; Heart Strings 20; If I Were King 20; The Joyous Troublemakers 20; The Orphan 20; The Scuttlers 20; His Greatest Sacrifice 21; The Queen of Sheba 21; Nero 22; The Net 23; The Shepherd King 23; The Silent Command 23; It Is the Law 24

Edwards, J. Harrison The Fighting Kentuckians 20

Edwards, J. Steven Barcelona 27; Because I Love You 27; Chinese Moon 27; Hi Diddle Diddle 27; The More We Are Together 27; On with the Dance 27*; Abide with Me 28*; Ave Maria 28*; Lead Kindly Light 28*; The Lost Chord 28*; Rock of Ages 28*; The Rosary 28*; A Broken Romance 29; Human Cargo 29; The Pride of Donegal 29; The Second Mate 29; The Fear Ship 33

Edwards, Robert Thunder in the Pines 48

Edwards, Roland G. Daring Love 24

Edwards, Vincent Maneater 73; Mission Galactica: The Cylon Attack 79*

Edwards, Walter The Brink 15; The Man from Oregon 15; The Winged Idol 15; The Beckoning Flame 16; Civilization 16*; The Corner 16; The Deserter 16; The Dividend 16; The Eye of the Night 16; A Gamble in Souls 16*; The Jungle Child 16; Lieut. Danny U.S.A. • Lieutenant Danny U.S.A. 16; The No-Good Guy 16; The Sin Ye Do 16; The Wolf Woman 16*; Ashes of Hope 17; The Bride of Hate • Wanted for Murder, or Bride of Hate 17; The Crab 17; Fuel of Life 17; Idolators 17; The Last of the Ingrahams 17; Love or Justice 17; Master of His Home 17; Time Locks and Diamonds 17; Evidence 18; Goodnight Paul 18; The Gypsy Trail 18; I Love You 18; A Lady's Name 18; The Man from Funeral Range 18; Mrs. Leffingwell's Boots 18; A Pair of Silk Stockings 18; Real Folks 18; Sauce for the Goose 18; Viviette 18; The Final Close-Up 19; The Girl Named Mary 19; Girls 19; Happiness à la Mode 19; Luck in Pawn 19; The Rescuing Angel 19; Romance and Arabella 19; The Veiled Adventure 19; Who Cares? 19; Widow by Proxy 19; All of a Sudden Peggy 20; Easy to Get 20; A Lady in Love 20; Young Mrs. Winthrop 20

Edwards, William Dracula (The Dirty Old Man) 69

Edwin, Walter The Spendthrift 15; A Mute Appeal 17

Edzard, Christine Stories from a Flying Trunk 79; Biddy 83; Little Dorrit 87

Eerhart, Bobby Stronghold • Wildschut 85

Efendiev, I. Arshin Takes a Wife 50

Effendy, Basuki Si Menje 50; Si Melati 54

Effenterre, Bertrand van see Van Effenterre, Bertrand

Egan, Henry L. see Equiluz, Enrique L.

Egea, José Luis Los Desafíos 68*

Egerton, Mark Crosstalk 82

Eggeling, Viking Diagonal Sinfonie • Diagonal Symphony 24; Parallels and Horizontal 24

Egger, Urs Motten im Licht 86

Eggert, Konstantin The Bear's Wedding • The Marriage of the Bear 26*; Aelita • Aelita: The Revolt of the Robots 29; Gobsek 37

Eggleston, Colin Long Weekend 78; The Little Feller 79; Sky Pirates 86; Cassandra 87

Egilmaz, Ertam Arabesk • Arabesque 89

Egleson, Jan Billy in the Lowlands 79; The Dark End of the Street 81; The Little Sister 85; Lemon Sky 87; Big Time 89*; A Shock to the System 90

Egorov, Oleg Osa 85

Egoyan, Atom Next of Kin 84; Family Viewing 87; Speaking Parts 89

Eguino, Antonio Chuquiago 77

Ehmck, Gustav Ein Schweizer Namens Nötzli 88

Ehrenborg, Lennart The Ra Expeditions 71

Eichberg, Richard Monna Vanna 23; Wasted Love 29; The Whirl of Life 29; The Copper • Der Greifer 30; The Flame of Love 30*; Nacht-Bummler • Night Birds 30; Why Cry at Parting? 30; Bridegroom for Two • Let's Love and Laugh 31; The Daredevil • Der Draufgänger 32; Königin der Unterwelt 32; Es Geht um Mein Leben • My Life Is at Stake 38

Eichhorn, Franz Mundo Extraño • Strange World 50; Female • The Violent Years 56; River of Evil 64*

Einarson, Odvar X 86

Einfeld, Richard Ghost Diver 57*

Eisenstein, Sergei Glumov's Film Diary • Kinodnevik Glumova 23; Stachka • Strike 24; The Battleship Potemkin • Bronenosets Potemkin • Bronenosets Potyomkin • Potemkin 25; October • Oktyabar • Oktyabr' • Ten Days That Shook the World 27*; The General Line • Generalnaya Linya • Old and New • The Old and the New • Staroye i Novoye 29*; Kampf des Unabhängigen Gegen den Kommerziellen Film • Sturm Über la Sarraz 29*; Romance Sentimentale 30*; Que Viva Mexico! 32*; Bezhin Lug • Bezhin Meadow 35; Aleksandr Nevskii • Alexander Nevsky 38*; The Ferghana Canal • Mighty Stream 39; Ivan Grozny • Ivan the Terrible, Part One 44; Ivan Grozny II—Boyarskii Zagovor • Ivan the Terrible, Part Two • Ivan the Terrible, Part Two: The Boyars' Plot • The Revolt of the Boyars 46; The Battles of Ivan • Ivan Grozny III • Ivan the Terrible, Part Three 47

Eisimont, Victor The Girl from Leningrad 41; Once There Was a Girl 45; Apartment in Moscow 62

Ejve, Ingemar Den Blödiga Tiden • Mein Kampf 59*

Ekk, Nikolai Putyovka v Zhizn • The Road to Life 30*; Grunya Kornakova • Little Nightingale • Nightingale 36; Sorochinskaya Yamarka • The Sorochinski Fair 39; A Night in May 41

Ekman, Gösta A Perfect Gentleman 27*
Ekman, Gösta Morrhår och Ärtor • Peas and Whiskers 86

Ekman, Hasse Med Dej i Mina Armar • With You in My Arms 40; First Division • Första Divisionen 41; Flames in the Dark • Lågor i Dunklet 42; Luck Arrives • Lyckan Kommer 42; Changing Trains • Ombyte av Tåg • Unexpected Meeting 43; The Sixth Shot • Sjätte Skottet 43; En Dag Skall Gry • A Day Shall Dawn 44; Excellensen • His Excellency 44; Like Most People • Som Folk Är Mest 44; Fram för Lilla Märta • Three Cheers for Little Märta 45; Kungliga Patrasket • The Royal Rabble 45; Vandring med Månen • Wandering with the Moon 45; I Dödens Väntrum • In Death's Waiting Room • In the Waiting Room of Death • Interlude 46; Medan Porten Var Stängd • When the Door Was Closed 46; Möte i Natten • Nightly Encounter 46; En Fluga Gör Ingen Sommar • En Svala Gör Ingen Sommar • One Swallow Doesn't Make a Summer 47; Banketten • The Banquet 48; Each Goes His Own Way • Var Sin Väg 48; Lilla Märta Kommer Tillbaka • Little Märta Returns 48; Flickan från Tredje Raden • The Girl from the Gallery 49; Flicka och Hyacinter • Girl with Hyacinths • The Suicide 50; Hjärter Knekt • Jack of Hearts 50; Den Vita Katten • The White Cat 50; Eldfågeln • The Fire Bird 52; Vi Tre Debutera • We Three Are Making Our Debut 53; Gabrielle 54; Egen Ingång • Private Entrance 56; Ratataa 56; The Seventh Heaven • Sjunde Himlen 56; The Jazz Boy • Jazzgossen 57; Med Glorian på Sned • With the Halo Askew 57; Sommarnöje Söks • A Summer Place Is Wanted 57; The Great Amateur • Den Stora Amatören 58; Fröken Chic • Miss Chic 59; Good Heavens • Himmel och Pannkaka 59; The Decimals of Love • Kärlekens Decimaler 60; On a Bench in a Park • På en Bänk i en Park 60; The Job • Stöten 61; Min Kära Är en Ros • My Love Is a Rose 63; Äktenskapsbrottaren • The Marriage Wrestler 64

Ekman, Mikael The Jönsson Gang Turns Up Again • Jönssonligan Dyker Upp Igen 86

El Cheik, Kamal see El Sheik, Kamel
Elçi, Ümit Hero's Way • Kurşun Ata Ata Biter 86

El Deek, Bashir Sikat Safar • The Travel Path 86

Elder, Clarence The Silver Darlings 47*
Eldridge, E. M. Forbidden Grass 28
Eldridge, John S.O.S. 39; The Story of Michael Flagherty 40; Young Farmers 42; Ashley Green Goes to School 43; New

Towns for Old 43; Fuel for Battle 44; Our Country 44; Tank Patrol 44; A City Reborn 45; Conquest of a Germ 45; Civil Engineering 46*; North East Corner 46; Three Dawns to Sydney 47; Waverly Steps 48; Brandy for the Parson 51; Laxdale Hall • Scotch on the Rocks 52; Conflict of Wings • Fuss Over Feathers 53*

Elek, Judit The Lady from Constantinople • Sziget a Szárazföldön 68

Elfelt, Clifford S. Big Stakes 22; Flaming Hearts 22; Crimson Gold 23; Danger 23; Fifty Thousand Dollar Reward 24; Fighting Courage 25; Under Fire 26

Elfman, Richard Forbidden Zone 80

Elford, Peter Pass of Arms 72

Elfstrom, Robert Johnny Cash: The Man, His World, His Music 69; The Nashville Sound 70*; Pete Seeger—A Song and a Stone 71; The Gospel Road 73; The American Game 79*; Mysteries of the Sea 80*; Moses Pendleton Presents Moses Pendleton 82

Elias, Aguy Ayahku • My Father 89

Elías, Francisco Boliche 35; Mi Madrecita • My Little Mother 40

Elisofon, Eliot Khartoum 66*

Elles, Fred Mrs. Pym of Scotland Yard 39

Elling, Alwin Befehl Ist Befehl 36; Kein Wort von Liebe • Not a Word About Love 38; A Merry Sea Trip • Eine Seefahrt Die Ist Lustig 38; Hummel-Hummel 39; Kleines Bezirksgericht • Little Country Court 39; Der Lustige Witwenball • The Merry Widow's Ball 39

Elliott, B. Ron The Smell of Honey • A Smell of Honey, a Swallow of Brine • A Taste of Honey, a Swallow of Brine 66; The Acid Eaters 68; Brand of Shame 68

Elliott, Clyde E. The Lamp Lighter 22; My Rural Relations 22; Western Ways 22; Bring 'Em Back Alive 32; Devil Tiger 34; Booloo 38; Frank Buck's Jungle Cavalcade • Jungle Cavalcade 41*

Elliott, Lang The Private Eyes 80; Cage 89

Elliott, Michael She Stoops to Conquer 71

Elliott, W. F. The Adventures of Parker 46

Elliott, William J. The Gentleman 25; The Cab 26; The Contrast 26; The Test 26

Elliotts, Paul see *Baldanello, Gianfranco*

Ellis, Arthur Out of Order 83

Ellis, Bob Unfinished Business 85; Warm Nights on a Slow Moving Train 87

Ellis, Carlyle Home-Keeping Hearts 21

Ellis, Deb Doris Eddy 85; Dream/Slap 86; Snap 86

Ellis, Robert The Apaches of Paris 15; The Fringe of Society 18; The Daughter Pays 20; The Figurehead 20; A Fool and His Money 20; The Imp 20; Chivalrous Charley 21; A Divorce of Convenience 21; The Woman Who Fooled Herself 22*

Ellison, Joseph Don't Go in the House 80; Joey 85

El Maanouni, Ahmed El Hal • Trances • Transes 81

El Mihi, Rafaat Broken Images • Lel Hab Kessa Akhira • Lil Hob Kessa Akhira 86; The Gentleman • El Sada el Rigal 86

Elmore, Milton Teddy Laughs Last 21

Elorrieta, Javier Blood and Sand 89

Elorrieta, José María Apache Fury • La Furia degli Apache • Fury of the Apaches 63; Fuerte Perdido • Massacre at Fort Grant • Massacre at Fort Perdition 64; El Tesoro de Makuba • The Treasure of Makuba 66; Una Bruja Sin Escoba • A Witch Without a Broom 67; Flame Over Vietnam 67; The Vengeance of Pancho Villa 67; A Thousand and One Nights 68; Las Amantes del Diablo 71; Aquellarre de Vampiros • The Curse of the Vampyr • La Llamada del Vampiro 71; El Espectro del Terror 72

Else, Jon The Day After Trinity: J. Robert Oppenheimer and the Atomic Bomb 81

Elsey, Michael Citizen Soldier 84

El Sheik, Kamel Hayat ou Maut • Life or Death 55; La Esfinge de Cristal • The Glass Sphinx • La Sfinge d'Oro • Una Sfinge Tutta d'Oro 67*; Conquerors of Time • Kahir Elzaman 86

Elst, Gerrit van Blond Dolly 87

El Tayeb, Atef Al Bari • The Innocent 85

Elter, Marco Alpine Love 36; Measure for Measure 51

Elton, Arthur Shadow on the Mountain 31; Upstream 31; Voice of the World 32; Aero-Engine 33; Housing Problems 35*; Workers and Jobs 35; Men Behind the Meters 40

Elton, Leslie The Whozit Weekly No. 115 19; The Whozit Weekly No. 123 19; The Whozit Weekly No. 124 19; The Whozit Weekly No. 126 19; The Whozit Weekly No. 129 19; The Whozit Weekly No. 131 19; The Whozit Weekly No. 134 19; The Whozit Weekly No. 137 19; The Whozit Weekly No. 143 19; The Whozit Weekly No. 144 19; The Whozit Weekly No. 164 20

Éluard, Paul Essai de Simulation de Délire Cinématographique 35*

Elvey, Maurice Bridegrooms Beware 13; The Cup Final Mystery 13; The Fallen Idol 13; The Great Gold Robbery 13; Inquisitive Ike 13; Maria Marten • Maria Marten—A Murder in the Red Barn • Maria Marten, or The Murder in the Red Barn • A Murder in the Red Barn 13; Popsy Wopsy 13; The Battling British • Black-Eyed Susan • In the Days of Trafalgar 14; Beautiful Jim • The Price of Justice 14; The Bells of Rheims 14; Her Luck in London 14; The Idol of Paris 14; It's a Long Long Way to Tipperary • It's a Long Way to Tipperary 14; Lest We Forget 14; The Loss of the Birkenhead 14; The Sound of Her Voice 14; The Suicide Club 14; There's Good in Everyone 14; The White Feather 14; Charity Ann 15; Fine Feathers 15; Florence Nightingale 15; From Shopgirl to Duchess 15; Gilbert Dying to Die 15; Gilbert Gets Tiger-Itis 15; Grip 15; Her Nameless Child 15; Home 15; A Honeymoon for Three 15;

London's Yellow Peril 15; Love in a Wood 15; Midshipman Easy 15; A Will of Her Own 15; Desperation • Driven 16; Esther 16; The King's Daughter 16; Meg the Lady 16; Money for Nothing 16; Motherlove 16; The Princess of Happy Chance 16; Trouble for Nothing 16; Vice Versa 16; When Knights Were Bold 16; Dombey and Son 17; Flames 17; The Gay Lord Quex 17; Goodbye 17; The Grit of a Jew 17; Justice 17; Mary Girl 17; Smith 17; The Woman Who Was Nothing 17; Adam Bede 18; Bleak House 18; The Greatest Wish in the World 18; Hindle Wakes 18; The Life Story of David Lloyd George 18; Nelson 18; Comrades in Arms • Comradeship 19; The Elusive Pimpernel 19; God's Good Man 19; Keeper of the Door 19; Mr. Wu 19; The Rocks of Valpré 19; The Swindler 19; The Victory Leaders 19; The Amateur Gentleman 20; At the Villa Rose 20; The Hundredth Chance 20; A Question of Trust 20; The Tavern Knight 20; The Beryl Coronet 21; A Case of Identity 21; The Copper Beeches 21; The Devil's Foot 21; The Dying Detective 21; The Empty House 21; The Fruitful Vine 21; A Gentleman of France 21; The Hound of the Baskervilles 21; Innocent 21; Man and His Kingdom 21; The Man with the Twisted Lip 21; The Noble Bachelor 21; The Priory School 21; The Red-Headed League 21; The Resident Patient 21; A Romance of Wastdale 21; A Scandal in Bohemia 21; The Solitary Cyclist 21; The Tiger of San Pedro 21; The Tragedy of a Comic Song 21; Yellow Face 21; A Debt of Honour 22; Dick Turpin's Ride to York 22; The Passionate Friends 22; Running Water 22; Don Quixote 23; Guy Fawkes 23; The Royal Oak 23; Sally Bishop 23; The Sign of Four 23; The Wandering Jew 23; Curlytop 24; The Folly of Vanity 24*; Henry, King of Navarre 24; The Love Story of Aliette Brunton 24; My Husband's Wives 24; Slaves of Destiny 24; Every Man's Wife 25; The Flag Lieutenant 25; She-Wolves 25; Baddesley Manor • Baddesley Manor—The Phantom Gambler 26; Glamis Castle 26; Human Law 26; Kenilworth Castle • Kenilworth Castle and Amy Robsart 26; The Tower of London 26; Windsor Castle 26; The Woman Tempted 26; Fanny Hawthorne • Hindle Wakes 27*; The Flight Commander 27; The Glad Eye 27; Quinneys 27; Roses of Picardy 27; Balaclava • Jaws of Hell 28*; Mademoiselle Parley-Voo 28; Palais de Danse 28; You Know What Sailors Are 28; High Treason 29; The School for Scandal 30; Footsteps in the Night • A Honeymoon Adventure 31; Her Strange Desire • Potiphar's Wife 31; The Lodger • The Phantom Fiend 31; Sally in Our Alley 31; The Water Gipsies • The Water Gypsies 31; Blame the Woman • Diamond Cut Diamond 32*; Frail Women 32; In a Monastery Garden • Monastery Garden 32; The Marriage Bond 32; I Lived with You 33; The Lost Chord 33; Soldiers of the King • The Woman in

Command 33; This Week of Grace 33; The Wandering Jew 33; Bride of the Lake • Lily of Killarney 34; The Clairvoyant • Evil Mind 34; The Escape of Princess Charming • Princess Charming 34; Love, Life and Laughter 34; My Song for You 34; Road House 34; Heat Wave 35; Transatlantic Tunnel • The Tunnel 35; The Man in the Mirror 36; Spy of Napoleon 36; Change for a Sovereign 37; Lost on the Western Front • A Romance in Flanders • Romance on the Western Front 37; Melody and Romance 37; Who Killed John Savage? 37; Lightning Conductor 38; The Return of the Frog 38; Sword of Honour 38; Who Goes Next? 38; Sons of the Sea 39; The Spider 39; For Freedom 40; Goofer Trouble 40; Room for Two 40; Under Your Hat 40; Salute John Citizen 42; The Gentle Sex 43*; The Lamp Still Burns 43; The Gay Intruders • Medal for the General 44; Strawberry Roan 44; Beware of Pity 46; The Late Edwina Black • Obsessed 51; The Third Visitor 51; The Great Game 52; My Wife's Lodger 52; House of Blackmail 53; Is Your Honeymoon Really Necessary? 53; The Gay Dog 54; The Happiness of Three Women 54; The Harassed Hero 54; What Every Woman Wants 54; Wishing Well 54; Fun at St. Fanny's 55; Room in the House 55; You Lucky People 55; Dry Rot 56; Stars in Your Eyes 56; Second Fiddle 57

Elwyn, Robert That Man from Tangier 53

Ember, Judit The Resolution 72*

Emerson, John Geronimo's Last Raid 12; Ghosts 15*; In Old Heidelberg • Old Heidelberg 15; The Americano 16; His Picture in the Papers 16; Less Than the Dust 16; Macbeth 16; The Mystery of the Leaping Fish 16; The Social Secretary 16; Down to Earth 17; In Again, Out Again 17; Reaching for the Moon 17; Wild and Woolly 17; Come On In 18; Goodbye Bill 18; Oh You Women! 19; Polly of the Follies 22

Emery, Robert J. Ghetto Freaks • Love Commune • Sign of Aquarius 70; Scream Bloody Murder 72; Ride in a Pink Car 74; Willie and Scratch 75; My Brother Has Bad Dreams 77

Emes, Ian The Magic Shop 82; Goodie Two Shoes 83; Knights and Emeralds 86; The Yob 88

Emigholz, Heinz Normalsatz 81; Die Basis des Make-Up 84; Die Wiese der Sachen 88

Emlyn, Endaf The Storms of August 88

Emmer, Luciano Giotto • Racconto da una Affresco 40*; Il Paradiso Terrestre 40*; Romanzo di un'Epoca 41*; Il Cantico delle Creature 42*; Guerrieri 42*; Il Conte di Luna 43*; Destino d'Amore 43*; Il Paese del Nascita Mussolini 43*; Bianchi Pascoli 47*; San Gennaro 47*; Sulla Via di Damasco 47*; La Terra del Melodramma 47*; Bosch • Il Paradiso Perduto 48*; Il Dramma di Cristo 48*; Islands on the Lagoon •Isole della Laguna 48*; The Legend of St. Ursula • La Leggenda di Sant'Orsola 48*;

Luoghi Verdiani • Sulle Rome di Verdi 48*; Romantici a Venezia • Romantics in Venice 48*; Allegoria di Primavera • Boticelli • The Story of Spring 49*; La Colonna Traiana 49*; I Fratelli Miracolosi • The Miraculous Brothers 49*; L'Invenzione della Croce • Legend of the True Cross • La Leggenda della Croce 49*; Domenica d'Agosto • Sunday in August 50; Festa di S Isadoro • Goya 50; Matrimonio alla Modo 51; Parigi È Sempre Parigi • Paris Is Always Paris 51; Girls of the Piazza di Spagna • Le Ragazze di Piazza di Spagna • Three Girls from Rome 52; Leonardo da Vinci 52*; High School • Terza Liceo 53; Camilla 54; Picasso 54; The Bigamist • Il Bigamo • A Plea for Passion 56; À Chacun Son Paradis • Paradiso Terrestre • Ritual of Love 57*; Il Momento Più Bello • The Most Wonderful Moment 57; The Girl in the Window • La Ragazza in Vetrina • Woman in the Window 60

Emmerich, Roland The Noah's Ark Principle 84; Joey • Making Contact 85; Hollywood Monster 87; Intruder • Moon 44 89

Emmett, E. V. H. Bothered by a Beard 46

Emmett, Robert see Tansey, Robert E.

Emo, E. W. Der Hampelmann 31; Der Storch Streikt 32; Heute Nacht Eventuell 33; Fräulein Falsch Verbunden! 34; Marion, Das Gehört Sich Night 34; Der Himmel auf Erden 35; Jungfrau Gegen Mönch • Maiden vs. Monk 35; Der Unbekannte Gast • The Unknown Guest 35; The Cabbie's Song • Das Fiakerlied 37; Drei Mäorl um Schubert 37; Endstation 37; Schabernack 37; Familie Schimek 39; Immortal Waltz • Unsterblicher Walzer 39; Anthony the Last • Anton der Letzte 40; Kleine Melodie aus Wien • Little Melody from Vienna 48; Alas! I'm Invisible • Help! I'm Invisible • Hilfe! Ich Bin Unsichtbar 52

Empey, Arthur Guy Into No Man's Land 28*

Emshwiller, Ed Paintings by Ed Emshwiller 58; Dance Chromatic 59; Transformation 59; Lifelines 60; Time of the Heathen 61*; Variable Studies 61; Thanatopsis 62; Scrambles 63; Totem 63*; George Dumpson's Place 64; Dlugoszewski Concert 65; Faces of America 65; Art Scene U.S.A. 66; Relativity 66; Fusion 67*; Project Apollo 68; Image, Flesh and Voice 69; Branches 70; Carol 70; Film with Three Dancers 70; The Chalk Line 71; Choice Chance Woman Dance 71; Inside the Gelatin Factory 71; Wo Oh Ho No 71; Chrysalis 73*; Identities 73; Interrupted Solitude 74

Emyl, Rolf The Businessman's Lunch • Mid-Day Miss • Mid-Day Mistress 68

Endelson, Robert Fight for Your Life 77

Enders, Robert Stevie 78

Endfield, C. Raker see Endfield, Cy

Endfield, Cy Dancing Romeo 44; Nostradamus IV 44*; Radio Bugs 44; Tale of a Dog 44; The Great American Mug 45;

Magic on a Stick 45; Gentleman Joe Palooka 46; Our Old Car 46; Stork Bites Man 47; The Argyle Secrets 48; Joe Palooka in The Big Fight 49; The Sound of Fury • Try and Get Me 50; The Underworld Story • The Whipped 50; Colonel March Investigates 52; Tarzan's Savage Fury 52; The Limping Man 53*; Impulse 54*; The Master Plan 54; The Secret 55; Child in the House 56*; Hell Drivers 57; Sea Fury 58; Jet Storm • Jetstream • The Killing Urge 59; Mysterious Island 60; Hide and Seek 62; Zulu 63; Sands of the Kalahari 65; Das Ausschweifende Leben des Marquis de Sade • De Sade 69*; Universal Soldier 71

Endre, Tóth see De Toth, André

Eng, Esther Golden Gate Girl 41

Engel, Andi Melancholia 89

Engel, Erich Wer Nimmt die Liebe Ernst? • Who Takes Love Seriously? 31; Five of the Jazzband • Fünf von der Jazzband • The Jazzband Five 32; Inge und Die Millionen 33; College • Hohe Schule 34; Pechmarie 34; Wenn Herzen Sich Finden 34; Pygmalion 35; Girlhood of a Queen • Mädchenjahre einer Königin 36; Ein Hochzeitstraum • Thunder, Lightning and Sunshine 36; Kirschen in Nachbars Garten 37; Die Nacht mit dem Kaiser 37; Die Graue Dame • The Gray Lady 38; Der Maulkorb 38; Ein Hoffnungsloser Fall 39; Hotel Sacher 39; Nanette • Peter, Paul und Nanette 39; Unser Fräulein Doktor 40; Sommerliebe 42; Fahrt ins Glück 45; The Affair Blum • Affare Blum • The Blum Affair 48; Der Fröhliche Weinberg • The Grapes Are Ripe 52; Liebe Ohne Illusion 55; Geschwader Fledermaus 59

Engel, Morris The Little Fugitive 53*; Lovers and Lollipops 55*; Weddings and Babies 58

Engelbach, David America 3000 86

Engholm, F. W. The Bogus House Agent 26; The Confidence Trick 26; Dud Cheque Chicanery 26; Employment with Investment and the Masked Fraud 26; Honesty Is the Best Policy 26; Miscreants of the Motor World 26; The Mock Auctioneer 26; Street Corner Frauds 26

England, Paul The Trial of Madame X 48

Engle, Harrison The Indomitable Teddy Roosevelt 83

English, Jack see English, John

English, John His Fighting Blood 35; The Red Blood of Courage 35; Arizona Days 37; Whistling Bullets 37; Zorro Rides Again 37*; Call the Mesquiteers • Outlaws of the West 38; Dick Tracy Returns 38*; Fighting Devil Dogs • The Torpedo of Doom 38*; Hawk of the Wilderness • Lost Island of Kioga 38*; Hi-Yo Silver! • The Lone Ranger 38*; Daredevils of the Red Circle 39*; Dick Tracy's G-Men 39*; The Lone Ranger Rides Again 39*; Zorro's Fighting Legion 39*; Adventures of Red Ryder 40*; Doctor Satan's Robot • Mysterious Dr. Satan 40*; Drums of Fu Manchu 40*; King of the Royal Mounted 40*; Adventures of Captain Marvel 41*; Dick

Tracy vs. Crime, Inc. 41*; Gangs of Sonora 41; Jungle Girl 41*; King of the Texas Rangers 41*; Code of the Outlaw 42; The Phantom Plainsmen 42; Raiders of the Range 42; The Valley of Hunted Men 42; Westward Ho! 42; The Yukon Patrol 42*; Black Hills Express 43; Daredevils of the West 43; Dead Man's Gulch 43; Death Valley Manhunt 43; The Man from Thunder River 43; Overland Mail Robbery 43; Raiders of Sunset Pass 43; Thundering Trails 43; Call of the South Seas 44; Captain America 44*; Faces in the Fog 44; Grissly's Millions 44; The Laramie Trail 44; The Port of Forty Thieves 44; San Fernando Valley 44; Silver City Kid 44; Behind City Lights 45; Don't Fence Me In 45; The Phantom Speaks 45; Utah 45; Midnight Melody • Murder in the Music Hall 46; The Last Round-Up 47; Trail to San Antone 47; Fools Awake • The Strawberry Roan 48; Loaded Pistols 48; The Brat • Sons of New Mexico 49; The Cowboy and the Indians 49; Riders in the Sky 49; Riders of the Whistling Pines 49; Rim of the Canyon 49; Beyond the Purple Hills 50; The Blazing Sun 50; Cow Town 50; Indian Territory 50; Mule Train 50; Gene Autry and the Mounties 51; Hills of Utah 51; Silver Canyon 51; Valley of Fire 51; Whirlwind 51

Englund, George The Ugly American 63; Signpost to Murder 64; Zachariah 70; The Great Ski Caper • The Ski Raiders • Snow Job 72

Englund, Robert 976-EVIL 88

Engstfeld, Axel see Ängstfeld, Axel

Engstrom, Ingemo Flight North • Flucht in den Norden 86

Enrico, Robert Jehanne 56; À Chacun Son Paradis • Paradiso Terrestre • Ritual of Love 57*; Villes-Lumière 59*; Le Métier des Autres 60; Thaumatopoea 60; Chikamauga 61; Incident at Owl Creek • An Occurrence at Owl Creek Bridge • La Rivière du Hibou 61; L'Oiseau Moquerr 61; Au Cœur de la Vie 62; Magic Mountains • Montagnes Magiques 62; La Belle Vie 63; Contrepoint 64; The Big Shots • Les Grandes Gueules • The Wise Guys 65; Aunt Zita • Tante Zita • Zita 67; Les Aventuriers • The Last Adventure • I Tre Avventurieri 67; Ho! • Ho! Criminal Face 68; Boulevard du Rhum • Rum Runner 71; Un Peu, Beaucoup, Passionnément 71; Les Caïds 72; Le Compagnon Indésirable 73; Le Secret • The Secret 74; The Old Gun • Le Vieux Fusil 75; Coup de Foudre 78; Un Neveu Silencieux 78; L'Empreinte des Géants 79; Heads or Tails 80; For Those I Loved 83; Red Zone • Zone Rouge 86; De Guerre Lasse 88; The French Revolution 89*

Enright, Ray His Unlucky Job 21*; Verse and Worse 21; The Girl from Chicago 27; Jaws of Steel 27; Tracked by the Police 27; Domestic Troubles 28; Land of the Silver Fox 28; The Little Wildcat 28; Kid Gloves 29; Skin Deep 29; Stolen Kisses 29; Dancing Sweeties 30; Golden Dawn 30; Scarlet

Pages 30; Song of the West 30; The Tenderfoot 31; Play Girl 32; Blondie Johnson 33; Havana Widows 33; The Silk Express 33; Tomorrow at Seven 33; The Circus Clown 34; Dames 34; I've Got Your Number 34; A Perfect Weekend • The St. Louis Kid 34; Twenty Million Sweethearts 34; Alibi Ike 35; Miss Pacific Fleet 35; The Traveling Saleslady 35; We're in the Money 35; While the Patient Slept 35; China Clipper 36; Come Up Smiling • Sing Me a Love Song 36; Earthworm Tractors • A Natural Born Salesman 36; Snowed Under 36; Back in Circulation 37; The Gay Imposters • Gold Diggers in Paris 37; Ready, Willing and Able 37; The Singing Marine 37; Slim 37; Swing Your Lady 37; Going Places 38; Hard to Get 38; Angels Wash Their Faces 39; Baby Be Good • Brother Rat and a Baby 39; Naughty But Nice 39; On Your Toes 39; An Angel from Texas 40; River's End 40; Teddy, the Rough Rider 40; Throwing a Party 40; Bad Men of Missouri 41; Law of the Tropics 41; Thieves Fall Out 41; The Wagons Roll at Night 41; Wild Bill Hickok Rides 41; Men of Destiny • Men of Texas 42; Sin Town 42; The Spoilers 42; Destroyer 43*; Good Luck, Mr. Yates 43; Gung Ho! 43; The Iron Major 43; The Rear Gunner 43; China Sky 45; Man Alive 45; One Way to Love 45; Albuquerque • Silver City 47; Trail Street 47; Coroner Creek 48; Return of the Badmen 48; Montana 49*; South of St. Louis 49; Kansas Raiders 50; Flaming Feather 51; Avventura ad Algeri • Crime Squad • The Man from Cairo 53

Ensminger, Robert The Midnight Burglar 18; Wanted, a Brother 18; Whatever the Cost 18; Bring Him In 21*; Fortune's Mask 22; Restless Souls 22; You Never Know 22; One Stolen Night 23

Enyedi, Ildikó Az Én XX. Századom • My 20th Century 89

Ephron, Henry Sing, Boy, Sing 58

Eppel, I. J. Irish Destiny • An Irish Mother 25

Epstein, Jean Pasteur 22*; Les Vendanges 22; L'Auberge Rouge • The Red Inn 23; The Beauty from Nivernaise • The Beauty of Nivers • La Belle Nivernaise 23; Cœur Fidèle • The Faithful Heart 23; La Montagne Infidèle 23; L'Affiche • The Poster 24; La Goutte de Sang 24*; Le Lion des Mogols • The Lion of the Moguls 24; Les Aventures de Robert Macaire 25; Le Double Amour • Double Love 25; Photogénies 25; Au Pays de Georges Sand 26; Mauprat 26; La Glace à Trois Faces • The Three-Sided Mirror 27; 6½ x 11 • 6½ x 11: A Kodak • Six et Demi-Onze • Six et Demi-Onze: Un Kodak 27; La Chute de la Maison Usher • The Fall of the House of Usher 28*; Finis Terrae 29; His Head • Sa Tête 29; La Mer des Corbeaux • Mor'Vran • The Sea of Ravens 30; Le Pas de la Mule 30; La Chanson des Peupliers 31; Le Cor 31; Notre-Dame de Paris 31; Les Berceaux 32; Gold from the Sea • L'Or des Mers 32; L'Homme à l'Hispano • The Man in the

Hispano-Suiza • The Man with the Hispano 32; Le Vieux Chaland 32; La Villanelle des Rubans 32; Chanson d'Armor 33; La Châtelaine du Liban 33; La Vie d'un Grand Journal 34; Marius et Olive à Paris 35; La Bourgogne 36; La Bretagne 36; Cœur de Gueux • Cuor di Vagabondo 36; La Femme du Bout du Monde 37; Vive la Vie 37; Les Bâtisseurs 38; Eau-Vive 38; La Relève 38; Artères de France 39*; The Storm • Le Tempestaire 47; Les Feux de la Mer 48

Epstein, Jerome Follow That Man 61; The Adding Machine 68

Epstein, Jerry see Epstein, Jerome

Epstein, Marcelo Body Rock 84

Epstein, Marie Peau de Pêche 25*; Maternité • Maternity 27*; Âmes d'Enfants • The Souls of Children 28*; Jimmy Bruiteur • Le Petit Jimmy 30*; Le Cœur de Paris 31*; Children of Montmartre • La Maternelle • Nursery School 32*; Itto • Itto d'Afrique 34*; Altitude 3200 • Youth in Revolt 37*

Epstein, Robert The Times of Harvey Milk 84; Common Threads: Stories from the Quilt 89*

Equiluz, Enrique L. Frankenstein's Bloody Terror • Hell's Creatures • El Hombre Lobo • La Marca del Hombre Lobo • The Mark of the Wolfman • The Vampire of Dr. Dracula • The Wolfman of Count Dracula 67

Eran, Doron Flash 86

Erdman, Richard Bleep 71; The Brothers O'Toole 73; Teenage Tease 83

Erdöss, Pál Countdown • Visszaszámlálás 85; The Princess 85; Gondoviselés • Tolerance 87

Ergün, Mahinur Mor Defter 64; Öldürmek Hakkimdir 68; Belanın Yedi Türlüsü • Seven Kinds of Trouble 69; Kurşunların Kanunu 69; Captives of a Night Dance • Gece Dansı Tutsakları 89

Erh, Derek see Yee, Tung-shing

Erice, Victor En la Terraza 61; Páginas de un Diario 62; Los Días Perdidos 63; Entre Vías 66; Los Desafíos 68*; El Espíritu de la Colmena • The Spirit of the Beehive 73; The South • El Sur 83

Erichsen, Bente The Feldmann Case • Over Grensen 87; Folk og Røvere i Kardemomme By 88

Erickson, A. F. The Woman from Hell 29; Lone Star Ranger 30; Rough Romance 30; Under Suspicion 30; This Sporting Age 32*

Eriksen, Dan A Midsummer Night's Dream 66

Eriksen, Gordon The Big Dis 90*

Eriksson, Claes Leif 87; Hajen Som Visste För Mycket • The Shark That Knew Too Much 89

Erksan, Metin see Metin, Erkan

Erler, Rainer Operation Ganymed 77; Plutonium 78

Erman, John Making It 71; Ace Eli and Rodger of the Skies 73; Stella 90

Ermler, Friedrich Scarlet Fever • Skarlatina 24; Children of the Storm • Deti Buri 26*; Katka Bumazhnyi Ranyot • Katka the

Apple Girl • Katka's Reinette Apples 26*; Dom v Sugrobakh • The House in the Snowdrifts 28; Parisian Cobbler • Parizhsky Sapozhnik 28; A Chip of the Empire • Fragment of an Empire • Oblomok Imperii 29; The Challenge • Counterplan • Pozor • Shame • Vstrechnyi 32*; Krestyaniye • Peasants 35; The Great Citizen • Velikii Grazhdanin 39; Autumn • Osen 40*; No Greater Love • Ona Zashchishchayet Rodinu • She Defends Her Country 43; The Great Turning Point • The Turning Point • Velikii Perelom 46; The Great Force • Great Power • Great Strength • Velikaya Sila 49; Neokonchennaya Povest • An Unfinished Story 55; Den Pervyi • The First Day • Pervyi Den 58; Dinner Time 62; From New York to Issanaia Poliana 63; Before the Judgment of History • Pered Sudom Istorii • Under the Trial of History 64

Ermolieff, Joseph N. Taras Bulba 27

Ersgard, Joakim Besökarna 88

Erskine, Chester Call It Murder • Midnight 34; Frankie and Johnny 35*; The Egg and I 47; Take One False Step 49; Androcles and the Lion 52*; A Girl in Every Port 52; Irish Whiskey Rebellion 72

Erukker, Sarah see Erulkar, Sarah

Erulkar, Sarah The Hunch 67

Esadze, Rezo Neylonovaya Yolka • A Nylon Christmas Tree 87

Esadze, S. Conquest of the Caucasus 13*

Escamilla Espinosa, Benjamín The Black Side of Blackie • Lo Negro del Negro 87*

Escorel Filho, Lauro Endless Dream • Sonho Sem Fim 86

Escriva, Vicente Dulcinea 62; Montoyas y Tarrantos 89

E Silva, Manuel Costa see Costa e Silva, Manuel

Esper, Dwain Maniac 34; Marihuana • Marijuana — The Devil's Weed 36; How to Undress in Front of Your Husband 37; The Narcotic 37

Espinosa, Benjamín Escamilla see Escamilla Espinosa, Benjamín

Espinosa, Fernando Gregorio 85*; Juliana 88*

Espinosa, Julio García The Charcoal Burner • El Mégano 55*; Cuba Baila 60; One Year of Freedom • Un Año de Libertad 60*

Essex, Harry I, the Jury 53; Mad at the World 55; Octaman • Octoman 71; The Cremators 72

Estabrook, Howard Giving Becky a Chance 17; The Highway of Hope 17; The Wild Girl 17; Heavenly Days 44

Esteba, M. Sei una Carogna…e T'Ammazzo 72

Estevez, Emilio Wisdom 86; Men at Work 90

Esway, Alexander Taxi for Two 29*; Children of Chance 30; Shadows 31; Bad Blood • Mauvaise Graine 33*; It's a Bet 35; Music Hath Charms 35*; Conquest of the Air 36*; Hercule 37*; The Man Who Seeks the Truth 41; The Bargekeeper's

Daughter 45; Steppin' in Society 45; They Are Not Angels 48

Eszterhas, Peter Når Engel Elsker 85

Etaix, Pierre The Break • Rupture 61*; Happy Anniversary • Heureux Anniversaire 61*; Le Soupirant • The Suitor 62; Insomnia • Insomnie 63; Nous N'Irons Plus au Bois 63; As Long As You're Healthy • Tant Qu'On A la Santé 65; Yoyo 65; Le Grand Amour • The Great Love 68; Pays de Cocagne 70; La Polonaise 71; L'Âge de Monsieur Est Avance 88

Etherridge, Frank Jenny Omroyd of Oldham 20

Étiévant, Henri Être Aime pour Soi-Même 20; Nine 20; La Poupée 20; Crépuscule d'Épouvante 21; Cœur de Titi 24; La Neige sur les Pas 24; La Nuit de la Revanche 24; Le Réveil de Maddalone 24; La Fin de Monte 27; La Sirène des Tropiques 28; Fécondité 29; La Symphonie Pathétique 29

Eustache, Jean Bad Company • Les Mauvaises Fréquentations 63; As Distant As My Childhood • Aussi Loin Que Mon Enfance 68*; La Rosière de Pessac • The Virgin of Pessac 68; Le Cochon • The Pig 70*; Number Zero • Numéro Zéro 71; La Maman et la Putain • The Mother and the Whore 73; Mes Petites Amoureuses • My Little Loves 75; A Dirty Story • Une Salé Histoire 77; Job Offer • Offre d'Emploi 79; La Rosière de Pessac 79 • The Virgin of Pessac '79 79; Alix's Photos • Photos d'Alix 80; Avec Passion Bosch ou Le Jardin des Délits de Jérôme Bosch • Bosch with Passion, or The Garden of Delights of Hieronymous Bosch 80; Grand'mères — Odette Robert • Grandmothers 80

Evans, Clifford The Silver Darlings 47*

Evans, Fred Stop the Fight 11; Fifty Years After 12; The Little General 12; A Novel Burglary 12; Pimple As a Ballet Dancer 12*; Pimple As a Cinema Actor 12*; Pimple As a Rent Collector 12*; Pimple Becomes an Acrobat 12*; Pimple Gets a Quid 12*; Pimple Wins a Bet 12*; Pimple's Eggs-traordinary Story 12*; Pimple's Fire Brigade 12*; The Adventures of Pimple — Pimple PC • Pimple Joins the Police Force 13; Adventures of Pimple — The Battle of Waterloo • Pimple's Battle of Waterloo 13*; Adventures of Pimple — The Indian Massacre 13*; A Bathroom Problem 13*; Dicke Turpin's Ride to Yorke 13*; How Pimple Saved Kissing Cup 13*; Lieutenant Pimple on Secret Service 13*; Miss Pimple, Suffragette 13*; Once Upon a Time 13*; Pimple and the Gorilla 13*; Pimple, Detective 13*; Pimple Does the Hat Trick 13*; Pimple Gets the Jumps 13*; Pimple Gets the Sack 13*; Pimple Goes A-Busking 13*; Pimple Goes Fishing 13*; Pimple Joins the Army 13*; Pimple Meets Captain Scuttle 13*; Pimple Takes a Picture 13*; Pimple the Sport 13*; Pimple Writes a Cinema Plot 13; Pimple's Complaint 13*; Pimple's Great Bull Fight 13*; Pimple's Inferno 13*; Pimple's Ivanhoe 13*; Pimple's Midnight Ramble 13*; Pim-

ple's Motor Bike 13*; Pimple's Motor Trap 13*; Pimple's New Job 13*; Pimple's Rest Cure 13*; Pimple's Sporting Chance 13*; Pimple's Wife 13*; Pimple's Wonderful Gramophone 13*; Slippery Pimple 13*; The Story of Hyam Touched 13; A Tragedy in Pimple's Life 13*; Two to One on Pimple 13*; What Happened to Pimple — The Suicide 13*; When Pimple Was Young 13*; The Adventures of Pimple — The Spiritualist 14*; The Adventures of Pimple — Trilby • Trilby by Pimple and Co. 14*; The Battle of Gettysownback 14*; Big Chief Little Pimple 14*; Broncho Pimple 14*; The Clowns of Europe 14*; The House of Distemperley 14*; How Lieutenant Pimple Captured the Kaiser 14*; How Pimple Won the Derby 14*; Inspector Pimple 14*; Lieutenant Pimple and the Stolen Invention 14*; Lieutenant Pimple and the Stolen Submarine 14*; Lieutenant Pimple Goes to Mexico 14*; Lieutenant Pimple, Gunrunner 14*; Lieutenant Pimple, King of the Cannibal Islands 14*; Lieutenant Pimple's Dash to the Pole 14*; Lieutenant Pimple's Sealed Orders 14*; Pimple, Anarchist 14*; Pimple and Galatea 14*; Pimple and the Stolen Plans 14*; Pimple Beats Jack Johnson 14*; Pimple, Counter Jumper 14*; Pimple Elopes 14*; Pimple Enlists 14*; Pimple Goes to Paris 14*; Pimple in Society 14*; Pimple in the Grip of the Law 14*; Pimple, MP 14*; Pimple 'Midst Raging Beasts 14*; Pimple on Football 14*; Pimple Pinched 14*; Pimple, Special Constable 14*; Pimple Turns Honest 14*; Pimple's Advice 14*; Pimple's Burglar Scare 14*; Pimple's Charge of the Light Brigade 14*; Pimple's Escape from Portland 14*; Pimple's Great Fire 14*; Pimple's Humanity 14*; Pimple's Last Resource 14*; Pimple's Leap to Fortune 14*; Pimple's Prison 14*; Pimple's Proposal 14*; Pimple's Trousers 14*; Pimple's Vengeance 14*; What Happened to Pimple — In the Hands of the London Crook 14*; What Happened to Pimple — The Gentleman Burglar 14*; When Pimple Was Young — His First Sweetheart 14*; When Pimple Was Young — Young Pimple's Schooldays 14*; The Whitewashers 14*; Young Pimple and His Little Sister 14*; Young Pimple's Frolics 14*; Aladdin 15*; Driven by Hunger 15; Flash Pimple the Master Crook 15*; Flivver's Art of Mystery • Pimple's Art of Mystery 15*; Flivver's Dilemma • Pimple's Dilemma 15*; Flivver's Good Turn • Pimple's Good Turn 15*; Flivver's Still Alarm • Pimple's Burlesque of The Still Alarm 15*; For Her Brother's Sake 15; Judge Pimple 15*; The Kaiser Captures Pimple 15*; Mademoiselle Pimple 15*; Mrs. Raffles nee Pimple 15*; Pimple Acts 15*; Pimple, Child Stealer 15*; Pimple Copped 15*; Pimple Explains 15*; Pimple Gets the Hump 15*; Pimple Has One 15*; Pimple in the Kilties 15*; Pimple Sees Ghosts 15*; Pimple, the Bad Girl of the Family 15*; Pimple Up the Pole 15*; Pimple Will Treat 15*; Pimple's Artful Dodge 15*;

Pimple's Boy Scout 15*; Pimple's Dream of Victory 15*; Pimple's Holiday 15*; Pimple's Motor Tour 15*; Pimple's Rival 15*; Pimple's Road to Ruin 15*; Pimple's Scrap of Paper 15*; Pimple's Some Burglar 15*; Pimple's Storyette 15*; Pimple's Three 15*; Pimple's Three O'Clock Race 15*; Pimple's Uncle 15*; Pimple's Willit-Wasit-Isit 15*; Ragtime Cowboy Pimple 15*; Sexton Pimple 15*; The Smugglers 15; Some Fun 15*; A Study in Skarlit 15*; Tally Ho! Pimple 15*; Was Pimple (W)right? 15*; The Clutching Hand • Pimple's Clutching Hand 16*; Diamond Cut Diamond 16*; The Merry Wives of Pimple • Pimple's Merry Wives 16*; Pimple As Hamlet 16*; Pimple Ends It 16*; Pimple—Himself and Others 16*; Pimple, Poor But Dishonest 16*; Pimple Splits the Difference 16*; Pimple Strafing the Kaiser 16*; Pimple's A Woman in the Case 16*; Pimple's Arm of the Law 16*; Pimple's Crime 16*; Pimple's Double 16*; Pimple's Great Adventure 16*; Pimple's Midsummer Night's Dream 16*; Pimple's Monkey Business • Some Monkey Business 16*; Pimple's Nautical Story 16*; Pimple's Part 16*; Pimple's Pink Forms 16*; Pimple's Silver Lagoon 16*; Pimple's Tenth Commandment 16*; Pimple's Zeppelin Scare 16*; Oliver Twisted 17*; Pimple—His Voluntary Corps 17*; Pimple's Lady Godiva 17*; Pimple's Motor Tour 17*; Pimple's Mystery of the Closed Door 17*; Pimple's Pitter-Patter 17*; Pimple's Romance 17*; Pimple's Senseless Censoring 17*; Pimple's Tableaux Vivants 17*; Pimple's The Whip 17*; Pimple's The Woman Who Did 17*; Saving Raffles 17*; Some Dancer 17*; Inns and Outs 18*; Pimple's Better 'Ole 18*; Pimple's Topical Gazette 20*; Pimple's Three Musketeers 22*

Evans, Jay Jitney Jack and Gasolena 16
Evans, Joe Pimple As a Ballet Dancer 12*; Pimple As a Cinema Actor 12*; Pimple As a Rent Collector 12*; Pimple Becomes an Acrobat 12*; Pimple Gets a Quid 12*; Pimple Wins a Bet 12*; Pimple's Eggs-traordinary Story 12*; Pimple's Fire Brigade 12*; Adventures of Pimple—The Battle of Waterloo • Pimple's Battle of Waterloo 13*; Adventures of Pimple—The Indian Massacre 13*; A Bathroom Problem 13*; Dicke Turpin's Ride to Yorke 13*; How Pimple Saved Kissing Cup 13*; Lieutenant Pimple on Secret Service 13*; Miss Pimple, Suffragette 13*; Once Upon a Time 13*; Pimple and the Gorilla 13*; Pimple, Detective 13*; Pimple Does the Hat Trick 13*; Pimple Gets the Jumps 13*; Pimple Gets the Sack 13*; Pimple Goes A-Busking 13*; Pimple Goes Fishing 13*; Pimple Joins the Army 13*; Pimple Meets Captain Scuttle 13*; Pimple Takes a Picture 13*; Pimple the Sport 13*; Pimple's Complaint 13*; Pimple's Great Bull Fight 13*; Pimple's Inferno 13*; Pimple's Ivanhoe 13*; Pimple's Midnight Ramble 13*; Pimple's Motor Bike 13*; Pimple's Motor Trap 13*; Pimple's New Job 13*; Pimple's Rest Cure 13*; Pimple's Sporting Chance 13*; Pimple's Wife 13*; Pimple's Wonderful Gramophone 13*; Slippery Pimple 13*; A Tragedy in Pimple's Life 13*; Two to One on Pimple 13*; What Happened to Pimple—The Suicide 13*; When Pimple Was Young 13*; The Adventures of Pimple—The Spiritualist 14*; The Adventures of Pimple—Trilby • Trilby by Pimple and Co. 14*; Archibald in a Tangle 14; Archibald's Egg Diet 14; The Battle of Gettysownback 14*; Big Chief Little Pimple 14*; Broncho Pimple 14*; The Clowns of Europe 14*; The Fiery Deeds of the Terrible Two 14; The House of Distemperley 14*; How Lieutenant Pimple Captured the Kaiser 14*; How Pimple Won the Derby 14*; Inspector Pimple 14*; Lieutenant Pimple and the Stolen Invention 14*; Lieutenant Pimple and the Stolen Submarine 14*; Lieutenant Pimple Goes to Mexico 14*; Lieutenant Pimple, Gunrunner 14*; Lieutenant Pimple, King of the Cannibal Islands 14*; Lieutenant Pimple's Dash for the Pole 14*; Lieutenant Pimple's Sealed Orders 14*; The Passing of Black Pete 14; Pearls of Death 14; Pimple, Anarchist 14*; Pimple and Galatea 14*; Pimple and the Stolen Plans 14*; Pimple Beats Jack Johnson 14*; Pimple, Counter Jumper 14*; Pimple Elopes 14*; Pimple Enlists 14*; Pimple Goes to Paris 14*; Pimple in Society 14*; Pimple in the Grip of the Law 14*; Pimple, MP 14*; Pimple 'Midst Raging Beasts 14*; Pimple on Football 14*; Pimple Pinched 14*; Pimple, Special Constable 14*; Pimple Turns Honest 14*; Pimple's Advice 14*; Pimple's Burglar Scare 14*; Pimple's Charge of the Light Brigade 14*; Pimple's Escape from Portland 14*; Pimple's Great Fire 14*; Pimple's Humanity 14*; Pimple's Last Resource 14*; Pimple's Leap to Fortune 14*; Pimple's Prison 14*; Pimple's Proposal 14*; Pimple's Trousers 14*; Pimple's Vengeance 14*; Stolen Honours 14; The Terrible Two 14; The Terrible Two on the Mash 14; The Terrible Two on the Stage 14; The Terrible Two on the Twist 14; The Terrible Two on the Warpath 14; What Happened to Pimple—In the Hands of the London Crook 14*; What Happened to Pimple—The Gentleman Burglar 14*; When Pimple Was Young—His First Sweetheart 14*; When Pimple Was Young—Young Pimple's Schooldays 14*; The Whitewashers 14*; Who Will Marry Martha? 14; Young Pimple and His Little Sister 14*; Young Pimple's Frolics 14*; Aladdin 15*; Flash Pimple the Master Crook 15*; Flivver's Art of Mystery • Pimple's Art of Mystery 15*; Flivver's Dilemma • Pimple's Dilemma 15*; Flivver's Good Turn • Pimple's Good Turn 15*; Flivver's Still Alarm • Pimple's Burlesque of The Still Alarm 15*; In the Clutches of the Hun 15; Joey's Twenty-First Birthday 15; Judge Pimple 15*; The Kaiser Captures Pimple 15*; The Kidnapped King 15; The Lady Detective 15; Liza on the Stage 15; Liza's Legacy 15; Mademoiselle Pimple 15*; Mr. and Mrs. Piecan—The Giddy Husband 15; Mrs. Raffles nee Pimple 15*; Piecan's Tonic 15; Pimple Acts 15*; Pimple, Child Stealer 15*; Pimple Copped 15*; Pimple Explains 15*; Pimple Gets the Hump 15*; Pimple Has One 15*; Pimple in the Kilties 15*; Pimple Sees Ghosts 15*; Pimple, the Bad Girl of the Family 15*; Pimple Up the Pole 15*; Pimple Will Treat 15*; Pimple's Artful Dodge 15*; Pimple's Boy Scout 15*; Pimple's Dream of Victory 15*; Pimple's Holiday 15*; Pimple's Motor Tour 15*; Pimple's Rival 15*; Pimple's Road to Ruin 15*; Pimple's Scrap of Paper 15*; Pimple's Some Burglar 15*; Pimple's Storyette 15*; Pimple's Three 15*; Pimple's Three O'Clock Race 15*; Pimple's Uncle 15*; Pimple's Willit-Wasit-Isit 15*; Poor Old Piecan 15; Ragtime Cowboy Pimple 15*; Sexton Pimple 15*; Shells, More Shells 15; Some Fun 15*; A Study in Skarlit 15*; Tally Ho! Pimple 15*; Was Pimple (W)right? 15*; When the Germans Came 15; When Women Rule 15; A Boarding House Scandal 16; The Clutching Hand • Pimple's Clutching Hand 16*; Diamond Cut Diamond 16*; Joey the Showman 16; Joey Walks in His Sleep 16; Joey's Apache Mania 16; Joey's Aunt 16; Joey's Automatic Furniture 16; Joey's Black Defeat 16; Joey's Dream 16; Joey's High Jinks 16; Joey's Liar Meter 16; Joey's Night Escapade 16; Joey's Permit 16; Joey's Pluck 16; The Merry Wives of Pimple • Pimple's Merry Wives 16*; Pimple As Hamlet 16*; Pimple Ends It 16*; Pimple—Himself and Others 16*; Pimple, Poor But Dishonest 16*; Pimple Splits the Difference 16*; Pimple Strafing the Kaiser 16*; Pimple's A Woman in the Case 16*; Pimple's Arm of the Law 16*; Pimple's Crime 16*; Pimple's Double 16*; Pimple's Great Adventure 16*; Pimple's Midsummer Night's Dream 16*; Pimple's Monkey Business • Some Monkey Business 16*; Pimple's Nautical Story 16*; Pimple's Part 16*; Pimple's Pink Forms 16*; Pimple's Silver Lagoon 16*; Pimple's Tenth Commandment 16*; Pimple's Zeppelin Scare 16*; Silas at the Seaside 16; Taming Liza 16; West End Pals 16; Oliver Twisted 17*; Pimple—His Voluntary Corps 17*; Pimple's Lady Godiva 17*; Pimple's Motor Tour 17*; Pimple's Mystery of the Closed Door 17*; Pimple's Pitter-Patter 17*; Pimple's Romance 17*; Pimple's Senseless Censoring 17*; Pimple's Tableaux Vivants 17*; Pimple's The Whip 17*; Pimple's The Woman Who Did 17*; Saving Raffles 17*; Some Dancer 17*; Inns and Outs 18*; Pimple's Better 'Ole 18*; Pimple's Topical Gazette 20*; Pimple's Three Musketeers 22*

Evans, John The Black Godfather 74; Blackjack 78
Evans, Mark One Day Last Summer 84*
Evans, Osmond Rise of Duton Lang 55
Eveleigh, Leslie The Dance of Death 28*; David Garrick 28*; Lady Godiva 28*; The Man in the Iron Mask 28*; The

Mystery of the Silent Death 28; The Princes in the Tower 28*; Silken Threads 28; The Vanished Hand 28*; Nemesis 29; The Snare 29

Everett, D. S. *see Shebib, Donald*

Everett, George The Crimson Cross 21

Export, Valie Invisible Adversaries • Unsichtbare Gegner 77

Eyre, Richard Loose Connections 83; The Ploughman's Lunch 83; Laughterhouse • Singleton's Pluck 84; The Insurance Man 85; Past Caring 85

Ezra, Mark Slaughter High 86*

Faber, Christian Bail Jumper 89

Fábri, Zoltán Colony Under Ground • Gyarmat a Föld Alatt • Underground Colony 51; The Storm • Vihar 52; Életjel • Fourteen Lives • Fourteen Lives in Danger • Fourteen Lives Saved • Vierzehn Menschenleben 54; Karussell • Körhinta • Little Fairground Swing • Merry-Go-Round 55; Hannibál Tanár Úr • Professor Hannibal 56; Anna • Édes Anna • Schuldig? 57; April Fools • Bolond Április • Summer Clouds 57; The Beast • The Brute • Dúvad • Das Scheusal 59; Eleven Men • Két Félidő a Pokolban • The Last Goal • Two Halftimes in Hell 61; Darkness in Daytime • Dunkel bei Tageslicht • Nappali Sötétség 63; Húsz Óra • Twenty Hours 64; Late Season • Utószezon 67; The Boys of Paul Street • A Pál Utcai Fiúk • The Paul Street Boys 68; Isten Hozta, Örnagy Úr! • The Tóth Family 69; Ants' Nest • Hangyaboly 71; One Day More, One Day Less • Plusz-Mínusz Egy Nap 73; 141 Perc a Befejezetlen Mondatból • 141 Minutes from the Unfinished Sentence • The Unfinished Sentence 75; The Fifth Seal • Az Ötödik Pecsét 76; The Hungarians • Magyarok 77; Balint Fabian Meets God • Fábián Bálint Találkozása Istennel 79; Requiem 81; Gyertek El a Névnapomra • The Housewarming 83

Fabrizi, Aldo Emigrantes 49; La Famiglia Passaguai 51; Papà Diventa Mamma 52; Of Life and Love • Questa È la Vita 54*; El Maestro • Il Maestro • The Teacher and the Miracle 58*

Faccini, Luigi Deceptions • Inganni 85

Faenza, Roberto Cop Killers • Corrupt • Order of Death 83

Fagerström-Olsson, Agneta Seppan 87

Fago, Amedeo La Donna del Traghetto • The Ferry Woman 87

Fago, Giovanni Per Cento Mille Dollari T'Ammazzo 67; Uno di Più all'Inferno 68; O Cangaceiro • The Magnificent Bandits 69; Mai con le Donne • Never with Women 85

Faiman, Peter Crocodile Dundee 86

Fairbairn, Kenneth That Day of Rest 48; That Golf Game 48; Fake's Progress 50; All at Sea 69; A Horse Called Jester 80

Fairbanks, Douglas Arizona 18*; Around the World in 80 Minutes • Around the World in 80 Minutes with Douglas Fairbanks • Around the World with Douglas Fairbanks 31*

Fairchild, William John and Julie 55;

The Extra Day • One Extra Day • Twelve Desperate Hours 56; The Silent Enemy 58; The Horsemasters 61

Fairfax, Ferdinand Nate and Hayes • Savage Islands 83; The Rescue 88; The Secret Life of Ian Fleming • Spymaker 90

Fairfax, Marion The Lying Truth 22

Fairman, Huck Refuge 81

Faithfull, Geoffrey Death by Design 43; For You Alone 44; I'll Turn to You 46

Faiziyev, Latif Hunting the Dragon • Okhota na Drakona 87

Falaise, Henry de la *see De la Falaise, Henry*

Falardeau, Pierre Elvis Gratton, le King des Kings • Elvis Gratton, the King of Kings 86

Falcão, Celso The Ring of Evil • A Virgem da Colina 77

Falck, Åke Bröllopsbesvär • Swedish Wedding Night • Wedding — Swedish Style 64; Princess • Prinsessan • A Time in the Sun 70

Falco, Martin de *see De Falco, Martin*

Falconer, Alun Missing Persons 53

Falconi, Dino The Loves of Don Juan 48

Falena, Ugo Camille • La Signora delle Camelie 09; Carmen 09; Othello 09; Beatrice Cenci 10; Lucrezia Borgia 10; Rigoletto 10; Il Mercante di Venezia • The Merchant of Venice 11; Francesca da Rimini 13; Marco Visconti 13; Il Re Fantasma 14; Il Figlio della Guerra 15; Ceneri e Vampe 16; Dementiae Caligulae Imperatoris 16; I Promessi Sposi 16; Suor Teresa 16; Cavalleria Rusticana 17; Esmeralda 17; La Vagabonda 17; Adriana Lecouvreur 18; L'Ingenuo 19; La Scala di Giacobbe 20; Natalizio dell Nonna 23

Falk, Feliks Top Dog 78; Bohater Roku • Hero of the Year 87

Falk, Harry High Desert Kill 90

Fanaka, Jamaa Welcome Home Brother Charles 75; Emma Mae 76; Penitentiary 79; Penitentiary II 82; Penitentiary III 87

Fanari, Mohamed Mournir Al Asheke • The Lover 86

Fancey, E. J. London Entertains 51; Into the Unknown 54; The March of the Movies 65

Fancey, O. Negus *see Negus, Olive*

Fanck, Arnold Marvels of Ski • Das Wunder des Schneeschuhs 20*; Im Kampf mit dem Berg 21*; Eine Fuchsjagd auf Skiern Durchs Engadin 22; Pömperlys Kampf mit dem Schneeschuh 22*; Der Berg des Schicksals • Peak of Fate 24; Der Heilige Berg • Peaks of Destiny 26; The Big Jump • Der Grosse Sprung 27; Die Weisse Hölle vom Piz Palü • The White Hell of Pitz Palu 29*; Avalanche • Stürme Über dem Montblanc 30; The Ski Chase • Der Weisse Rausch • The White Ecstasy • The White Frenzy 31; Nordpol-Ahoi! • S.O.S. Eisberg • S.O.S. Iceberg 32*; S.O.S. Iceberg 33*; Balmat 34; Der Ewige Traum • König des Montblanc 34; Die Liebe der Mitsu • Die Tochter des Samurai 37; The New Earth 37*; Ein Robinson • Das Tagebuch eines Matrosen 40

Fang, Bao *see Bao, Zhifang*

Fanning, Frank The Masked Avenger 22

Fansten, Jacques États d'Âme • Moods 86

Fant, Kenne The Shadow 53; Wing Beats in the Night 53; Young Summer 54; Love Chastised 55; Tarps Elin 57; The Clergyman from Uddarbo 58; The Love Game 59; Wedding Day 60; The Wonderful Adventures of Nils 62

Faradine, Oskar Un Bounty Killer a Trinità 72

Faragoh, Francis The Last Man 32*

Faraldo, Claude La Jeune Morte 70; Bof 72; Themroc 72; Tabarnac 75; Les Fleurs du Miel 76; Deux Lions au Soleil • Two Lions in the Sun 80; A Certain Desire • Flagrant Désir • Flagrant Desire 86

Faralla, William D. Two Before Zero 62

Fargo, James The Enforcer 76; Caravans 78; Every Which Way But Loose 78; Game for Vultures 79; Forced Vengeance 82; Voyage of the Rock Aliens 84; When the Rain Begins to Fall 84; Born to Race 87

Faria, Reginaldo Quem Tem Medo de Lobishomem 74

Farias, Luiz Com Licenca, Eu Vou a Luta • Sorry, I'll Make It My Way 86

Farias, Roberto Assalto ao Trem Pagador • Tião Medonho • Train Robbery Confidential 62

Farina, Corrado Hanno Cambiato Faccia • They Have Changed Their Faces • They've Changed Faces 71; Baba Yaga • The Devil Witch 73

Farina, Felice He Looks Dead...But He Just Fainted • He Seems to Be Dead...But He Has Simply Fainted • Sembra Morto... Ma È Solo Svenuto 86; Affetti Speciali 88

Farino, Ernest Steel and Lace 90

Farkas, Michael Prime Risk 84

Farkas, Nicolas The Battle • Hara-Kiri • Thunder in the East 34; I Give My Life 41

Farkas, Zoltán Love of Sport • Sportszerelem 38*

Farmanara, Bahman Saiehaien Bolan de Bad • Tall Shadows of the Wind 78

Farmer, Ernest Women for Sale 75

Farnum, Marshall Wormwood 15; Driftwood 16; The House of Mirrors 16; My Husband's Friend 18*

Farocki, Harun Between Two Wars • Zwischen Zwei Kriegen 77; Betrogen 85

Farrario, Cesare The Monster of Florence • Il Mostro di Firenze 86

Farrell, Jeff The Revenge of the Teenage Vixens from Outer Space 86

Farris, John Dear, Dead Delilah 72

Farrow, John The Spectacle Maker 34; War Lord 34; The Invisible Menace 37; Men in Exile 37; She Loved a Fireman 37; War Lord • The Warlord • West of Shanghai 37; Broadway Musketeers 38; Little Miss Thoroughbred 38; My Bill 38; Five Came Back 39; Full Confession 39; Reno 39; The Saint Strikes Back 39; Sorority House • That Girl from College 39; Women in the Wind 39; A Bill of Divorcement • Never to Love 40; Married and in Love 40; The Commandos Strike at

Dawn 42; Wake Island 42; China 43; The Hitler Gang 44; You Came Along 45; California 46; Two Years Before the Mast 46; Blaze of Noon 47; Calcutta 47; Easy Come, Easy Go 47; Alias Nick Beal • The Contact Man 48; Beyond Glory 48; The Big Clock 48; The Night Has a Thousand Eyes 48; Red, Hot and Blue 49; Copper Canyon 50; Red Mountain 50*; Where Danger Lives 50; His Kind of Woman 51*; Submarine Command 51; Ride, Vaquero! 52; Botany Bay 53; Hondo 53; Plunder of the Sun 53; A Bullet Is Waiting 54; The Sea Chase 55; Back from Eterity 56; The Unholy Wife 57; John Paul Jones 59

Farwagi, André Le Temps de Mourir • Twice Upon a Time 69; Boarding School • The Passion Flower Hotel 77

Fasano, John Black Roses • The Edge of Hell • Rock 'n' Roll Nightmare 87

Fassbinder, Franz see Fassbinder, Rainer Werner

Fassbinder, Rainer Werner The City Tramp • Der Stadtstreicher 65; Das Kleine Chaos • The Little Chaos 66; Gods of the Plague • Götter der Pest 69; Katzelmacher 69; Liebe Ist Kälter Als der Tod • Love Is Colder Than Death 69; Warum Läuft Herr R. Amok? • Why Does Herr R. Run Amok? 69*; The American Soldier • Der Amerikanische Soldat 70; Beware of a Holy Whore • Beware of the Holy Whore • Beware the Holy Whore • Warning of a Holy Whore • Warnung vor einer Heiligen Nutte 70; The Coffee House • Das Kaffeehaus 70; The Nicklehausen Journey • Die Niklashauser Fahrt 70*; Pioneers in Ingolstadt • Pioniere in Ingolstadt 70; Rio das Mortes 70; Whity 70; Der Händler der Vier Jahreszeiten • The Merchant of Four Seasons 71; Acht Stunden Sind Kein Tag • Acht Stunden Sind Kein Tag: Eine Familienserie • Eight Hours Are Not a Day 72; The Bitter Tears of Petra von Kant • Die Bitteren Tränen der Petra von Kant 72; Bremen Coffee • Bremer Freiheit 72; Game Pass • Jail Bait • Wild Game • Wildwechsel 72; Ali • Ali: Fear Eats the Soul • Angst Essen Seele Auf • Fear Eats the Soul 73; Nora Helmer 73; Welt am Draht • World on a Wire 73; Effi Briest • Fontane Effi Briest 74; Faustrecht der Freiheit • Fist-Right of Freedom • Fox • Fox and His Friends • Might Makes Right 74; Like a Bird on a Wire • Wie ein Vogel auf dem Draht 74; Martha 74; Angst vor der Angst • Fear of Fear 75; Mother Kuster Goes to Heaven • Mother Kuster's Journey to Heaven • Mother Kuster's Trip to Heaven • Mutter Küsters Fahrt zum Himmel 75; Chinese Roulette • Chinesisches Roulette 76; I Only Want You to Love Me • Ich Will Doch Nur, Dass Ihr Mich Liebt 76; Satan's Brew • Satansbraten 76; Bolwieser • The Station Master's Wife 77; Despair • Eine Reise ins Licht 77; Frauen in New York • Women in New York 77; Deutschland im Herbst • Germany in Autumn 78*; Die Ehe der Maria Braun • The Marriage of Maria Braun 78; In a Year

of Thirteen Months • In a Year of Thirteen Moons • In a Year with Thirteen Moons • In einem Jahr mit Dreizehn Monden • In the Year of Thirteen Moons 78; Berlin Alexanderplatz 79; Die Dritte Generation • The Third Generation 79; Lili Marleen 80; Lola 81; Die Sehnsucht der Veronika Voss • Veronica Voss • Veronika Voss 81; Querelle • Querelle—A Pact with the Devil • Querelle de Brest • Querelly—Ein Pakt mit dem Teufel 82

Fatigati, Giuseppe Laugh Pagliacci 48
Faulkner, Brendan Spookies 86*
Faurez, Jean Counter Investigation 49
Faust, Martin J. Jane Eyre 14
Faustman, Erik Natt i Hamn • Night in the Harbor 43; Sonja 43; Flickan och Djävulen • The Girl and the Devil 44; Vi Behöver Varann • We Need Each Other 44; Brott och Straff • Crime and Punishment 45; Harald Handfaste 46; När Ängarna Blommar • When Meadows Bloom 46; Krigsmans Erinran • A Soldier's Duties 47; Foreign Harbor • Främmande Hamn 48; Lars Harde 48; Smeder på Luffen • Vagabond Blacksmiths 49; Restaurang Intim 50; Kvinnan Bakom Allt • Woman Behind Everything 51; Hon Kom Som en Vind • She Came Like a Wind 52; U-Boat 39 • Ubåt 39 52; House of Women • Kvinnohuset 53; Cafe Lunchrasten 54; God and the Gypsy • Gud Fader och Tättaren 54; Ingen Så Tokig Som Jag • No One Is Crazier Than I Am 55; Night Journey • Resa i Natten 55

Faustman, Hampe see Faustman, Erik
Fawcett, George Deadline at Eleven 20; Little Miss Rebellion 20; Such a Little Queen 21

Faye, Randall Hyde Park 34; Born That Way 36; If I Were Rich 36; Luck of the Turf 36; Music and Millions • Such Is Life 36; This Green Hell 36; The Vandergilt Diamond Mystery 36; Accidental Spy • Mr. Stringfellow Says No 37; Scruffy 38

Fazil Poovizhi Vasalile 87
Feazell, Jim Psycho from Texas 82
Fechner, Eberhard Tadellöser and Wolff: Right or Wrong, My Country 74
Feder, Sid This Is Russia 57
Federov, V. F. House of Death 32
Feferman, Linda Seven Minutes in Heaven 86

Feher, Friedrich Das Blutgeld 13; Der Unsichtbare Gast 19; Die Rote Hexe 20; Die Tänzerin Marion 20; Tyrannei des Todes 20; Carrière 21; Marionetten des Teufels 23*; Sanin 25; Das Graue Haus 26; Die Geliebte des Gouverneurs 27; Maria Stuart 27; Mata Hari • Mata Hari the Red Dancer 27; Verbotene Liebe 27; Hotelgeheimnisse 28; That Murder in Berlin 29; Ihr Junge • Wenn die Geigen Klingen 31; Gehetzte Menschen • Steckbrief Z 48 32; Le Loup Garou 32; The Robber Symphony 36

Fehér, Imre Bakaruhában • A Sunday Romance 57; A Bird of Heaven • Égi Madár 57; Gyalog a Mennyországba • Walking to Heaven 59; Kard és

Kocka • Sword and Dice 59; Asszony a Telepen • Woman at the Helm 62; Húsz Évre Egymástól • The Truth Cannot Be Hidden 62; Harlekin és Szerelmese • Harlequin and Her Love 66

Fei, Xie see Xie, Fei
Feigelson, Julius D. The Windsplitter 71
Feigenbaum, William Hugo the Hippo 75

Feijoo, Beda Ocampo see Ocampo Feijoo, Beda
Feikel, Bernard White Hell 22
Fei-kwong, Ho see Ho, Fei-kwong
Fein, Rudolf Walther see Walther-Fein, Rudolf
Feinstein, Barry Monterey Pop 67*; You Are What You Eat 68

Feinzimmer, Alexander The Czar Wants to Sleep 34; Men of the Sea 38; Secret Brigade 51*; The Gadfly • The Grasshopper • Poprigunya 55*; The Girl with the Guitar 60

Feist, Felix E. Deluge 33; My Grandfather's Clock 34; Strikes and Spares 34; Football Teamwork 35; Prince, King of Dogs 35; Every Sunday 36; Hollywood Extra! 36; Hollywood—The Second Step 36; How to Be a Detective 36; How to Vote 36; Decathlon Champion—The Story of Glenn Morris 37; Double Diving 37; Give Till It Hurts 37; Golf Mistakes 37; The Romance of Digestion 37; What Do You Think? 37*; Follow the Arrow 38; The Magician's Daughter 38; Culinary Carving 39; Happily Buried 39; Let's Talk Turkey 39; Prophet Without Honor 39; Radio Hams 39; Set 'Em Up 39; Take a Cue 39; Dreams 40; Pound Foolish 40; All by Myself 42; You're a Lucky Fellow, Mr. Smith 43; Pardon My Rhythm 44; Reckless Age 44; This Is the Life 44; George White's Scandals 45; The Devil Thumbs a Ride 47; The Winner's Circle 48; Guilty of Treason • Treason 49; The Threat 49; The Golden Gloves Story 50; The Man Who Cheated Himself 50; The Basketball Fix • The Big Decision 51; Tomorrow Is Another Day 51; Battles of Chief Pontiac 52; The Big Trees 52; The Man Behind the Gun 52; This Woman Is Dangerous 52; Donovan's Brain 53; Pirates of Tripoli 55

Feitshans, Fred R., Jr. Arctic Fury 49*
Fejér, Tamás Az Idő Ablaka • The Windows of Time 69

Fejős, Pál The Crime of Lord Arthur Saville • Hallucination • Lidércnyomás • Lord Arthur Saville's Crime • Nightmare 19; The Black Captain • Fekete Kapitány 20; Jóslat • Prophecy 20; Pán 20; Reincarnation • The Resurrected • Revived • Újraélők 20; Arsén Lupin Utolsó Kalandja • Arsène Lupin's Last Adventure • The Last Adventure of Arsène Lupin 21; Pique Dame • The Queen of Spades • Sensation • Szenzáció 22; Le Dernier Moment • The Last Moment 27; Lonesome • Solitude 28; Broadway 29; Erik the Great • Erik the Great Illusionist • The Last Call • The Last Performance 29; Big House • Révolte dans la Prison 30; Captain of the Guard • La

Marseillaise 30*; King of Jazz 30*; Menschen Hinter Gittern 30; American Love • L' Amour à l'Américaine 31*; Fantômas 31; Une Histoire d'Amour • Marie • Marie—A Hungarian Legend • Marie, Légende Hongroise • Spring Shower • A Story of Love • Tavaszi Zápor 32; Ítél a Balaton • Storm at Balaton • The Verdict of Lake Balaton 32; Flight from the Millions • Flugten fra Millionerne • Les Millions en Fuite • Millions in Flight 33; Frühlingsstimmen • The Voice of Spring • Les Voix du Printemps 33; Gardez le Sourire • The Golden Smile • A Ray of Sunshine • Sonnenstrahl 33; Menschen im Sturm 34; Fange Nr. 1 • Prisoner No. 1 35; Fredlös 35; The Golden Smile • Det Gyldne Smil • Le Sourire d'Or 35; The Bilo 36; Black Horizons • Horizons Noirs • Sværta Horisonter 36; The Age of Bamboo at Mentawei • The Bamboo Age of Mentawei • Bambuåldern på Mentawei 37; Beauty Care in the Jungle • Beauty Salon in the Jungle • Skönhetsvård i Djungeln 37; The Chief's Son Is Dead • Hövdingens Son Är Död 37; Dance Contest in Esira • Danstävlingen i Esira 37; The Dance of the Jungle • Djungeldansen • Jungle Dance 37; The Dragon of Komodo • Draken på Komodo • The Komodo Dragon 37; The Graves of Our Fathers • Tombs of Our Ancestors • Våra Faders Gravar 37; Havets Djävul • Sea Devil 37; The Most Useful Tree in the World • Världens Mest Användbara Träd 37; Stammen Lever An • The Tribe Lives On • The Tribe Still Lives 37; Tambora 37; Att Segla Är Nödvändigt • To Sail Is Neccessary 38*; Byn Vid den Trivsamma Brunnen • The Village Near the Pleasant Fountain 38; A Handful of Rice • En Handfull Ris • Homme et Femme • Jungle of Chang • Man and Woman • Man och Kvinna • Une Poignée de Riz • Saggakh 38*; Yagua 41

Fejos, Paul see Fejös, Pál
Feldberg, Mark Getting Even 81
Feldman, Dennis Real Men 87
Feldman, Gene Danny 79
Feldman, John Alligator Eyes 90
Feldman, Marty The Last Remake of Beau Geste 77; In God We Tru$t • In God We Tru$t, or Gimme That Prime Time Religion 79
Feldman, Simon Memorias y Olvidos 88
Feldshuh, David Just Be There 77
Felice, Domenico de see De Felice, Domenico
Felice, Lionello de see De Felice, Lionello
Félix, Louis Chaleurs d'Éte • Heat of the Summer 61; Heures Chaudes • Hot Hours 63
Felix, Seymour Girls Demand Excitement 31; Stepping Sisters 32
Fellbom, Claes Aida 88
Fellini, Federico Lights of Variety • Luci del Varietà • Variety Lights 50*; Lo Sceicco Bianco • The White Sheik 51; Amore in Città • Love in the City 53*; The Loafers • Spivs • I Vitelloni • The Wastrels • The Young and the Passionate 53; The Road • La Strada 54; Il Bidone • The Swindle • The Swindlers 55; Cabiria • Nights of Cabiria • Le Notti di Cabiria 56; La Dolce Vita • The Sweet Life 59; Boccaccio '70 62*; 8½ • Federico Fellini's 8½ • Otto e Mezzo 62; Giulietta degli Spiriti • Julia und die Geister • Juliet of the Spirits • Juliette des Esprits 65; Histoires Extraordinaires • Spirits of the Dead • Tales of Mystery • Tre Passi nel Delirio 67*; Appunti di Federico Fellini • Block Notes—Appunti di un Regista • Block-Notes di un Regista • A Director's Block Notes • A Director's Notebook • Federico Fellini's Notebooks • Federico Fellini's Scrapbook • Fellini's Scrapbook 68; Fellini Satyricon • Satyricon 69; I Clowns • The Clowns 70; Fellini's Roma • Roma 72; Amarcord • Fellini's Amarcord 73; Casanova • Il Casanova di Federico Fellini • Fellini Casanova • Fellini's Casanova 76; Orchestra Rehearsal • Prova d'Orchestra 78; La Città delle Donne • City of Women 79; And the Ship Sails On... • E la Nave Va... 83; Ginger and Fred • Ginger e Fred 84; Federico Fellini's Intervista • Fellini's Interview • The Interview • Intervista 87; Le Voci della Luna • Voices of the Moon 90

Fels, Hans Four Hands • Quatre Mains 87
Felsenstein, Walter Fidelio 61
Feltham, Kerry Chicago '70 • The Great Chicago Conspiracy Circus 70
Felton, Paul M. Old Tire Man Diamond Cartoon Film 18; Paradental Anesthesia 19; Re-Blazing the '49 Trail in a Motor Car Train 19; Tire Injury 19; A Movie Trip Through Film Land 21; For Any Occasion 22; In Hot Weather 22; The Champion 23; Land of the Unborn Children 23; Some Impressions on the Subject of Thrift 24; Live and Help Live 25; The Carriage Awaits 26; Family Album 26; For Dear Life 26; What Price Noise? 26
Fen, Suzanne La Guerre Populaire au Laos 68*
Fenady, Georg Arnold 73; Terror in the Wax Museum 73
Feng, Huang see Huang, Feng
Feng, Yueh see Yueh, Feng
Fengler, Michael Warum Läuft Herr R. Amok? • Why Does Herr R. Run Amok? 69*
Fengpan, Yao see Yao, Fengpan
Fenic, Fero Dzusovy Roman 88
Fennell, Paul This Changing World—Broken Treaties 41; This Changing World—How War Came 41; This Changing World—The Carpenters 41
Fenton, Leslie Captain Kidd's Treasure 38; A Criminal Is Born 38; The Forgotten Ship 38; Miracle Money 38; Tell No Tales 38; Stronger Than Desire 39; Arouse and Beware • The Man from Dakota 40; The Golden Fleecing 40; The Saint's Vacation 41; There's a Future in It 43; Tomorrow the World 44; Pardon My Past 45; Lulu Belle 48; A Miracle Can Happen • On Our Merry Way 48*; Saigon 48; Whispering Smith 48; Streets of Laredo 49; The Redhead and the Cowboy 50

Feo, Francesco de see De Feo, Francesco
Ferét, René Mystère Alexina • The Mystery of Alexina 85
Ferguson, Al Shackles of Fear 24; The Trail of Vengeance 24; The Fighting Romeo 25; Phantom Shadows 25
Ferguson, Graeme The Seducers 62; The Virgin President 68
Ferguson, Guy see Ferguson, S. G.
Ferguson, Nicholas Pictures at an Exhibition 72
Ferguson, Norman Saludos Amigos 43*; The Three Caballeros 44*
Ferguson, S. G. The Gold Express 55; Supersonic Saucer 56
Ferhati, Jillali Poupées de Roseau • Reed Dolls 81
Ferhout, John see Ferno, John
Fernandel Simplet 42*
Fernández, Emilio La Isla de la Pasión • Passion Island 41; María Candelaria • Portrait of Maria • Xochimilco 42; Soy Puro Mexicano 42; Flor Silvestre 43; Las Abandonadas 44; Bugambilia 44; The Pearl • La Perla 45; Pepita Jiménez 45; Enamorada 46; Hidden River • Río Escondido 47; Maclovia 48; Pueblerina 48; Salón México 48; The Bandit General • Beloved • Del Odio Nació el Amor • The Torch 49; Duelo en las Montañas 49; La Malquerida 49; Un Día de Vida 50; Islas Marías 50; Siempre Tuya 50; Víctimas del Pecado 50; Acapulco 51; La Bien Amada 51; El Mar y Tú • Tú y el Mar 51; Suave Patria 51; Cuando Levanta la Niebla 52; The Net • La Red • Rosanna 53; El Rapto 53; El Reportaje 53; La Rosa Blanca 53; Nosotros Dos 54; La Rebelión de los Colgados • The Rebellion of the Hanged • Revolt of the Hanged 54*; La Tierra del Fuego Se Apaga 55; Una Cita de Amor • The Rebel 56; La Pasionaria 56; El Gesticulador • El Impostor 57; Pueblito • Pueblito o El Amor 61; Paloma Herida 63; Un Dorado de Pancho Villa • A Loyal Solder of Pancho Villa 66; El Crepúscolo de un Dios 68; La Choca 73; Zona Roja 75
Fernández, Raúl Lola's Kidnapping—Lola the Trucker II • El Secuestro de Lola—Lola la Trailera II 86
Fernández Bustamante, Adolfo La Rebelión de los Fantasmas • The Revolt of the Ghosts 46
Fernández Violante, Marcela De Todos Modos Juan Te Llamas 76; Cananea 79; Misterio 81; En el País de los Pies Ligeros 83; Nocturna Amor Que Te Vas • Nocturnal Love That Goes Away 87
Fernando, Manuel San see San Fernando, Manuel
Ferno, John China's 400 Million • The 400 Million 38*; A Child Went Forth 41*
Ferrara, Abel Driller Killer 79; Angel of Vengeance • Ms. 45 • Ms. 45—Angel of Vengeance 80; Fear City 84; China Girl 87; Cat Chaser 89; King of New York 90
Ferrara, Giuseppe Il Caso Moro • The Moro Affair 86

Ferrara, Romano Hands of a Killer • The Man with the Yellow Eyes • The Monster with Green Eyes • I Pianeti Contro di Noi • The Planets Against Us 61

Ferrater-Mora, J. A Hero of Our Time 69

Ferre Serra, Ignasi P. Morbus • Morbus, o Que Aproveche 82

Ferrer, José The Cockleshell Heroes 55*; The Shrike 55; The Great Man 56; I Accuse! 57; The High Cost of Loving 58; Return to Peyton Place 61; State Fair 62

Ferrer, Mel The Girl of the Limberlost 45; The Secret Fury 50; Vendetta 50*; Green Mansions 59; Cabriola • Every Day Is a Holiday 65

Ferrer, Melchor G. *see Ferrer, Mel*

Ferreri, Marco El Pisito 58; The Boys • Los Chicos 59; El Cochecito • The Motorcart • The Wheelchair 59; Caravan pour Zagora • Le Secret des Hommes Bleus • El Secreto de los Hombres Azules 60*; Le Italiane e l'Amore • Latin Lovers 61*; L'Ape Regina • The Conjugal Bed • Queen Bee • Una Storia Moderna • Una Storia Moderna: L'Ape Regina 63; The Ape Woman • La Donna Scimmia • The Monkey Woman 64; The Blonde Wife • Kiss the Other Sheik • Oggi, Domani e Dopodomani • Paranoia 64*; Contro Sesso • Controsesso 64*; Break-Up • The Man with the Balloons • L'Uomo dai Cinque Palloni • L'Uomo dai Palloncini 65; Marcia Nuziale 65; L'Harem 67; Dillinger È Morto • Dillinger Is Dead 68; The Seed of Man • Il Seme dell'Uomo 69; The Audience • L'Udienza 71; La Cagna • Liza 71; Perchè Pagare per Essere Felici! 71; The Big Feast • Blow-Out • La Grande Abbuffata • La Grande Bouffe • The Grande Bouffe • The Great Feed 73; Don't Touch the White Woman • Non Toccate la Donna Bianca • Touchez Pas la Femme Blanche • La Vera Storia del Generale Custer 73; La Dernière Femme • The Last Woman • L'Ultima Donna 76; Bye Bye Monkey • Ciao Maschio • Rêve de Singe 78; Why? Why Not? 78; Chiedo Asilo • My Asylum • No Child's Land • Pipi, Caca, Dodo 79; Storie di Ordinaria Follia • Tales of Ordinary Madness 81; Piera's Story • Storia di Piera • The Story of Piera 82; The Future Is a Woman • The Future Is Woman • Il Futuro È Donna 84; I Love You 86; Oh Come Sono Buoni i Bianchi 87; Y'à Bon les Blancs 87; Le Banquet de Platon 89

Ferrero, G. K.O. Va e Uccidi 66

Ferretti, Robert A. Fear 88

Ferreyra, José A. El Tango de la Muerte 17; Campo Ajuera 19; La Chica de la Calle Florida 21; La Guacha 21; Mientre Buenos Aires Duerme 21; Buenos Aires 22; Ciudad de Ensueño 22; El Arriero de Yacanto 24; Mi Último Canto 24; El Organito de la Tarde 24; Muchachita de Chiclana 26; Perdón Viejita 27; La Canción del Gaucho 30; El Cantar de Mi Ciudad 30; Muñequitas Porteñas 31; Calles de Buenos Aires 34; Puente Alsina 35; Ayúdame a Vivir • Help

Me to Live 36; Besos Brujos • Bewitching Kisses 37; Muchachos de la Ciudad 37; The Law They Forgot • La Ley Que Olvidaron 38; Chimbella 39; El Hijo del Barrio 40; La Mujer y la Selva 41

Ferrin, Frank The Hindu • Sabaka 53

Ferrini, Franco Caramelle da uno Sconosciuto • Sweets from a Stranger 87

Ferris, Costas Rembetiko 84; Oh Babylon! 87

Ferris, Stan *Pseudonym for Rex Bromfield with Mark Warren and Al Waxman*

Ferroni, Giorgio Il Fanciullo del West 43; Tombolo 49; Drops of Blood • The Horrible Mill Women • Horror of the Stone Women • Mill of the Stone Maidens • Mill of the Stone Women • Le Moulin des Supplices • Il Mulino delle Donne di Pietra 60; The Bacchantes 61; La Guerra di Troia • La Guerre de Troie • The Mighty Warrior • The Trojan Horse • The Trojan War 62; Conquest of Mycene • Ercole Contro Molock • Hercule Contre Moloch 63; The Lion of Thebes 64; One Silver Dollar • Un Dollaro Buccato 64; Fort Yuma Gold • Per Pochi Dollari Ancora 66; Höllenjagd auf Heisse Ware • New York Appelle Super Dragon • New York Chiam a Superdrago • Secret Agent Super Dragon • Super Dragon 66; Due Pistole e un Vigliacco • Two Guns and a Coward 67; Battle of El Alamein 68; Wanted 68; Night of the Devils • La Noche de los Diablos • La Notte dei Diavoli 72

Ferry, Isidoro Martínez *see Martínez Ferry, Isidoro*

Fescourt, Henri Le Bonheur Perdu 12; Jeux d'Enfants 13; Peine d'Amour 14; La Menace 15; Mathias Sandorf 20; La Nuit du 13 21; Rouletabille 22; Mandrin 23; Les Grands 24; Le Fils d'Amérique 25; Les Misérables 25; La Glu 27; La Maison du Maltais 27; L'Occident 27; Le Comte de Monte Cristo • Monte Cristo 29; Pour Service de Nuit 31; Serments 31; La Maison de la Flèche 32; L'Occident 37; Bar du Sud 38; Retour de Flamme 42

Fetin, V. The Colt 61

Fettar, Said Ali Rai 86

Feuillade, Louis Le Billet de Banque 06; C'Est Papa Qui Prend la Purge 06; Les Deux Gosses 06; Mireille 06*; N'Te Promène Donc Pas Toute Nue 06; La Porteuse de Pain 06; Un Accident d'Auto 07; La Course des Belles-Mères 07; Un Facteur Trop Ferré 07; L'Homme Aimanté 07; La Légende de la Fileuse 07; Un Pacquet Embarrassant 07; La Sirène 07; Le Thé chez la Concierge 07; Vive le Sabotage 07; Les Agents Tels Qu'On Nous les Présente 08; Une Dame Vraiment Bien 08; La Grève des Apaches 08; Nettoyage par le Vide 08; Une Nuit Agitée 08; Prométhée 08; Le Récit du Colonel 08; Le Roman de Sœur Louise 08; Un Tic 08; L'Aveugle de Jérusalem 09; La Chatte Métamorphosée en Femme 09; La Cigale et la Fourmi 09; Le Collier de la Reine 09; Les Filles du Cantonnier 09; Fra Vincenti 09; Les Heures 09; Histoire de Puce 09; Le Huguenot 09;

Judith et Holopherne 09; La Légende des Phares 09; Mater Dolorosa 09; La Mère du Moine 09; La Mort 09; La Mort de Mozart 09; La Possession de l'Enfant 09; Le Printemps 09; Le Savetier et le Financier 09; Vainqueur de la Course Pédestre 09; L'An 1000 10; Bébé Apache 10; Bébé Fume 10; Bébé Pêcheur 10; Benvenuto Cellini 10; Le Christ en Croix 10; Esther 10; L'Exode 10; Le Festin de Balthazar 10; La Fille de Jephté 10; Maudite Soit la Guerre 10; Mil Huit Cent Quatorze 10; Molière 10*; La Nativité 10; Le Pater 10; Le Roi de Thulé 10; Les Sept Péchés Capitaux 10; Aux Lions les Chrétiens 11; L'Aventurière, Dame de Compagnie 11; Le Bas de Laine • Le Trésor 11; Les Batailles de l'Argent • Le Trust 11; Le Bracelet de la Marquise 11; Charles VI 11; Le Chef-Lieu de Canton 11; Dans la Vie 11; Le Destin des Mères 11; Les Doigts Qui Voient 11; En Grève 11; Fidélité Romaine 11; La Fille du Juge d'Instruction 11; Le Fils de Locuste 11; Le Fils de Sunamite 11; Le Mariage de l'Aînée 11; Les Petites Apprenties 11; Le Poison 11; Quand les Feuilles Tombent 11; Le Roi Lear au Village 11; La Souris Blanche 11; Sous le Joug 11; Tant Que Vous Serez Heureux 11; La Tare 11; Le Trafiquant 11; La Vierge d'Argos 11; Les Vipères 11; L'Accident 12; Amour d'Automne 12; Androclès 12; L'Anneau Fatal 12; L'Attrait du Bouge 12; Au Pays des Lions 12; L'Aventurière 12; Bout-de-Zan Revient du Cirque 12; Les Braves Gens 12; La Cassette de l'Émigrée 12; Le Château de la Peur 12; Les Cloches de Paques 12; Le Cœur et l'Argent 12; La Course aux Millions 12; Dans la Brousse 12; La Demoiselle du Notaire 12; La Fille du Margrave 12; La Hantise 12; Haut les Mains! 12; L'Homme de Proie 12; La Maison des Lions 12; Le Maléfice 12; Le Mort Vivant 12; Le Nain 12; Napoléon 12; Les Noces Siciliennes 12; Le Noël de Francesca 12; L'Oubliette 12; Le Petit Poucet 12; Le Pont sur l'Abîme 12; Préméditation 12; La Prison sur le Gouffre 12; Le Proscrit 12; Le Témoin 12; Le Tourment 12; Tyrtée 12; La Vertu de Lucette 12; La Vie ou la Mort 12; Les Yeux Qui Meurent 12; L'Agonie de Byzance 13; L'Angoisse 13; Au Gré des Flots 13; Les Audaces du Cœur 13; Bébé en Vacances 13; Le Bon Propriétaire 13; Bonne Année 13; Le Browning 13; Les Chasseurs de Lions 13; La Conversion d'Irma 13; Un Drame au Pays Basque 13; L'Écrin du Rajah 13; L'Effroi 13; Erreur Tragique 13; Fantômas 13; Fantômas II • Juve Contre Fantômas 13; Fantômas III • Le Mort Qui Tue 13; La Gardienne du Feu 13; Le Guet-Apens 13; L'Intruse 13; La Marche des Rois 13; Le Mariage de Miss Nelly 13; Le Ménestrel de la Reine Anne 13; Les Millions de la Bonne 13; La Momie 13; La Mort de Lucrèce 13; La Petite Danseuse 13; Le Revenant 13; La Rose Blanche 13; S'Affranchir 13; Un Scandale au Village 13; Le Secret du Forçat 13; La Vengeance du Sergent de la Ville 13; Les Yeux Ouverts 13; Le Calvaire 14; Le Coffret de Tolède 14; Le Diamant du

Sénéchal 14; L'Enfant de la Roulotte 14; L'Épreuve 14; Fantômas Contre Fantômas • Fantômas IV 14; Fantômas V • Le Faux Magistrat 14; Les Fiancés de 1914 14; Les Fiancés de Séville 14; Le Gendarme Est Sans Culotte 14; La Gitanella 14; L'Hôtel de la Gare 14; L'Illustre Machefer 14; La Joconde 14; Les Lettres 14; Manon de Montmartre 14; La Neuvaine 14; Paques Rouges 14; La Petite Andalouse 14; La Rencontre 14; Severo Torelli 14; Les Somnambules 14; Tu N'Épouseras Jamais un Avocat 14; L'Angoisse au Foyer 15; La Bague Qui Tue 15; La Barrière 15; Le Blason 15; Celui Qui Reste 15; Le Collier de Perles 15; Le Colonel Bontemps 15; Le Coup de Fakir 15; La Course à l'Abîme 15; Le Cryptogramme Rouge 15; Deux Françaises 15; L'Escapade de Filoche 15; L'Expiation 15; Le Fer à Cheval 15; Fifi Tambour 15; Le Furoncle 15; Les Noces d'Argent 15; Le Noël de Poilu 15; Le Sosie 15; La Tête Coupée 15; Union Sacrée 15; Les Vampires 15; L'Aventure des Millions 16; Bout-de-Zan et la Torpille 16; C'Est le Printemps 16; Le Double Jeu 16; L'Évasion du Mort 16; Les Fiançailles d'Agénor 16; Les Fourberies de Pingouin 16; L'Homme des Poisons 16; Judex • Le Plus Grand Succès de René Creste 16; Lagourdette, Gentleman Cambrioleur 16; Le Maître de la Foudre 16; Le Malheur Qui Passe 16; Un Mariage de Raison 16; Les Mariés d'un Jour 16; Les Noces Sanglantes 16; Notre Pauvre Cœur 16; La Peine du Talion 16; Le Poète et Sa Folle Amante 16; Le Retour de Manivelle 16; Satanas 16; Si Vous Ne M'Aimez Pas 16; Le Spectre 16; Les Yeux Qui Fascinent 16; L'Autre 17; Le Bandeau sur les Yeux 17; Débrouille-Toi 17; La Déserteuse 17; La Femme Fatale 17; La Fugue de Lily 17; Herr Doktor 17; Mon Oncle 17; La Nouvelle Mission de Judex 17; Le Passé de Monique 17; Aide-Toi 18; L'Homme Sans Visage 18; Les Petites Marionnettes 18; Tih Minh 18; Vendémiaire 18; Barrabas 19; L'Engrenage 19; L'Énigme • Le Mot de l'Énigme 19; Le Nocturne 19; Les Deux Gamines 20; Gustave Est Médium 21; Marjolin ou La Fille Manquée 21; L'Orpheline 21; Parisette 21; Saturnin ou Le Bon Allumeur 21; Séraphin ou Les Jambes Nues 21; Zidore ou Les Métamorphoses 21; Le Fils de Flibustier 22; Gaétan ou Le Commis Audacieux 22; Lahire ou Le Valet de Cœur 22; Le Gamin de Paris 23; La Gosseline 23; L'Orphelin de Paris 23; Vindicta 23; La Fille Bien Gardée 24; Lucette 24*; Pierrot, Pierrette 24; Le Stigmate 24*

Feyder, Jacques Monsieur Pinson, Policier 15*; Abrégeons les Formalités! 16; Le Billard Cassé 16; Le Bluff 16; Un Conseil d'Ami 16; Le Frère de Lait 16; L'Homme au Foulard à Pois 16; L'Homme de Compagnie 16; L'Instinct Est Maître 16; Le Pied Qui Étreint 16; Têtes de Femmes, Femmes de Tête 16; Tiens, Vous Êtes à Poitiers? 16; La Trouvaille de Buchu 16; Le Pardessus de Demi-Saison 17; Le Ravin Sans Fond 17*; Les Vieilles Femmes de l'Hospice 17; La

Faute d'Orthographe 19; L'Atlantide • Lost Atlantis • Missing Husbands • Woman of Atlantis 21; Coster Bill of Paris • Crainquebille • Old Bill of Paris 22; Faces of Children • Visages d'Enfants 23*; Das Bildnis 25; Gribiche 25; L'Image 25; Carmen 26*; Au Pays du Roi Lépreux 27; Du Sollst Nicht Ehebrechen! 28; The New Gentlemen • Les Nouveaux Messieurs 28; Shadows of Fear • Thérèse Raquin • Thou Shalt Not 28; Anna Christie 29; The Kiss 29; Olympia 30; Si l'Empereur Savait Ça 30; Le Spectre Vert 30; Daybreak 31; Son of India 31; Card of Fate • Le Grand Jeu 33; Pension Mimosas 34; Carnival in Flanders • La Kermesse Héroïque 35; Die Klugen Frauen 35; Fahrendes Volk 37; Les Gens du Voyage • The Wanderers 37; Knight Without Armour 37; Une Femme Disparaît • Portrait of a Woman • A Woman Disappeared 39; La Loi du Nord • La Piste du Nord 39

Feyder, Paul L'Éché le Blanche • Secret World 69*

Fidani, D. Ed Ora Raccomanda l'Anima a Dio 68; Straniero Fatti il Segno della Croce 68; E Vennero in Quattro per Uccidere Sartana 69; Inginocchiati Straniero...i Cadaveri Non Fanno Ombra! 70; Quel Maledetto Giorno d'Inferno Django e Sartana all'Ultimo Sangue 70; Doppia Taglia per Minnesota Stinky 71; Era Sam Wallash 71; Per un Bara Piena di Dollari 71

Field, C. C. The Human Orchid 16

Field, Connie The Life and Times of Rosie the Riveter • Rosie the Riveter 80

Field, Mary The Changing Year 32; Strictly Business 32*

Fielding, Romaine Eagle's Nest 15; The Valley of Lost Hope 15; A Western Governor's Humanity 15; The Crimson Dove 17; Moral Courage 17; Youth 17; The Man Worth While 21; The Rich Slave 21

Fielding, Tom Middle Passage 78

Fields, Don The Curse of Bigfoot 72

Fields, Leonard Irish and Proud of It • Kelly of the U.S.A. • King Kelly of the U.S.A. 34; Manhattan Love Song 34; Streamline Express 35

Fifthian, Douglas The Hunted • Touch Me Not 74

Figgis, Mike Stormy Monday 88; Internal Affairs 90

Figman, Max The Truth Wagon 14; Jack Chanty 15

Filan, L'udovít Cena Odvahy 87

Filho, Lauro Escorel see Escorel Filho, Lauro

Filipelli, Rafael Hay Unos Tipos Abajo • There Are Some Guys Downstairs 85*

Filippo, Eduardo de see De Filippo, Eduardo

Filippov, F. Chelkash 64

Finbow, Colin Dark Enemy 84; Mr. Skeeter 85; School for Vandals 86

Finch, Charles Priceless Beauty 87; Love Dream 88

Finch, Nigel The Errand 81

Finch, Peter The Day 60*

Findlay, Andrea The Privilege 83*

Findlay, Michael Mutilated • Shriek of the Mutilated 74; The Slaughter • Snuff 74*

Findlay, Roberta The Slaughter • Snuff 74*; Angel Number 9 77; The Oracle 84; Game of Survival • Tenement 86; Blood Sisters 87; Lurkers 88

Findlay, Seaton Janis 74*

Finegan, John P. Girl School Screamers 86

Fink, Michael Force Four 75

Finkel, R. Fugitive Valley 41*

Finkleman, Ken Airplane II: The Sequel 82; Head Office 86

Finlay, George see Stegani, Giorgio

Finley, George see Stegani, Giorgio

Finn, Arthur Detective Finn and the Foreign Spies • The Foreign Spies 14; For King and Country 14; The Girl Next Door 14; The Great Python Robbery 14; Our Baby 14; Was He a Gentleman? 14; What a Kiss Will Do 14; Your Name Brown? 14; Forty Winks 20

Finn, Michael J. The Black Connection 74

Finn, Oscar Barney Contar Hasta 10 • Count to Ten 86

Finney, Albert Charlie Bubbles 67

Finney, Edward Riot Squad 41; Silver Stallion 41; King of the Stallions 42; Queen of the Amazons 47

Fiore, Robert Dionysus in '69 68*; Pumping Iron 77*

Firestone, Cinda Attica 74

Firstenberg, Sam One More Chance 81; Revenge of the Ninja 83; Breakdance II: Electric Boogaloo • Breakin' II: Electric Boogaloo • Electric Boogaloo: Breakin' II 84; Ninja III — The Domination 84; American Ninja • American Warrior 85; Avenging Force 86; American Ninja II: The Confrontation 87; Riverbend 90

Firth, Michael Off the Edge 77; Heart of the Stag 84; Sylvia 85; The Leading Edge 87

Fischa, Michael Crack House 89

Fischer, David G. Dad's Girl 19; The Law of Nature 19; Where Bonds Are Loosed 19

Fischer, Markus Der Nachbar • The Neighbor 87; Zimmer 36 88

Fischer, Max Mews en Meijn 65; Dreams 70; The Lucky Star 80; Killing 'Em Softly 85

Fischer, O. W. Hanussen 55*; Ich Suche Dich 56

Fischerman, Alfredo The Days of June • Los Días de Junio 85

Fischinger, Oskar Pierrette No. 1 24; Spirals 25; München-Berlin Wanderung 27; R-1 • Regenbogen-1, ein Formspiel 27; Seelische Konstruktionen • Spiritual Constructions 27; Staffs 27; Dein Schicksal • Your Destiny 28; Study No. 1 29; Das Hohelied der Kraft • The Hymn of Energy 30; Study No. 2 30; Study No. 3 30; Study No. 4 30; Study No. 5 30; Study No. 6 30; Liebesspiel • Love Games 31; Study No. 7 31; Study No. 8 31; Study

No. 9 31; Coloratura • Koloraturen 32; Study No. 10 32; Study No. 11 32; Study No. 12 32; Synthetic Sound Experiments 32; Circles • Kreise 33; A Quarter Hour of City Statistics • Eine Viertelstunde Groß-stadtstatistik 33; Study No. 13 33; Study No. 14 33; Cigarette Tests 34; Muratti Greift Ein • Muratti Marches On 34; Muratti Privat 34; A Play in Colors • Ein Spiel in Farben 34; Quadrate • Squares 34; Rivers and Landscapes • Swiss Trip 34; Composition in Blue • Komposition in Blau 35; Lichtkonzert No. 2 35; Allegretto 36; An Optical Poem 37; American March 41; Color Rhythm 42; Radio Dynamics 42; Organic Fragment 45; Motion Painting No. 1 47; Lumigraph Test Reel 51; Muntz TV 53; Oklahoma 54

Fishelson, David City News 83*

Fisher, David Liar's Moon 81; Toy Soldiers 83

Fisher, Jack Torn Apart 89

Fisher, Mary Ann Lords of the Deep 89

Fisher, Michael Tale of a City 48

Fisher, Richard Haunted Palace 49

Fisher, T. R. *see Fisher, Terence*

Fisher, Terence To the Public Danger 47; Colonel Bogey 48; The Girl in the Painting • Portrait from Life 48; A Song for Tomorrow • Song of Tomorrow 48; The Astonished Heart 49*; Marry Me 49; Home to Danger 50; So Long at the Fair 50*; The Stolen Face 51; Dead on Course • Wings of Danger 52; Distant Trumpet 52; The Last Page • Man Bait 52; Blood Orange 53; Four Sided Triangle 53; Man in Hiding • Mantrap • Woman in Hiding 53; Spaceways 53; The Stranger Came Home • The Unholy Four 53; Three's Company 53*; The Black Glove • Face the Music 54; Blackout • Murder by Proxy 54; Children Galore 54; Final Appointment 54; Mask of Dust • Race for Life 54; The Flaw 55; Stolen Assignment 55; Birth of Frankenstein • The Curse of Frankenstein 56; The Dynamiters • The Gelignite Gang 56*; The Last Man to Hang? 56; Kill Me Tomorrow 57; Dracula • Horror of Dracula 58; The Hound of the Baskervilles 58; The Man Who Could Cheat Death 58; The Revenge of Frankenstein 58; The Mummy • Terror of the Mummy 59; The Strangler of Bengal • The Stranglers of Bombay 59; The Brides of Dracula 60; House of Fright • Jekyll's Inferno • The Two Faces of Dr. Jekyll 60; Sword of Sherwood Forest 60; The Curse of the Werewolf • The Wolf-man 61; The Phantom of the Opera 62; Sherlock Holmes • Sherlock Holmes and the Deadly Necklace • Sherlock Holmes und das Halsband des Todes • Valley of Fear 62*; The Gorgon 63; The Horror of It All 63; The Earth Dies Screaming 64; The Bloody • Disciple of Dracula • Dracula—Prince of Darkness • Revenge of Dracula 65; Frankenstein Created Woman • Frankenstein Made Woman 65; The Creepers • Island of Terror • Night of the Silicates • The Night the Creatures Came • The Night the Silicates Came • The Silicates

66; The Devil Rides Out • The Devil's Bride 67; Island of the Burning Damned • Island of the Burning Doomed • Night of the Big Heat 67; Frankenstein Must Be Destroyed! 69; Frankenstein and the Monster from Hell 72

Fishman, Bill Tapeheads 88

Fisk, Jack Raggedy Man 81; Violets Are Blue... 86; Daddy's Dyin'...Who's Got the Will? 90

Fist, Fletcher Wander Love Story • Wanderlove 70

Fitchen, John Crossroads 55

Fitchett, Christopher Fair Game 85

Fitzgerald, Dallas M. The Open Door 19; Blackmail 20; Cinderella's Twin 20; The Price of Redemption 20; Big Game 21; The Infamous Miss Revell 21; Life's Darn Funny 21; The Match-Breaker 21; The Off-Shore Pirate 21; Playing with Fire 21; Puppets of Fate 21; The Guttersnipe 22; Her Accidental Husband 23; After the Ball 24; My Lady of Whims 25; Passionate Youth 25; Tessie 25; Out of the Past 27; The Princess of Broadway 27; The Rose of Kildare 27; Web of Fate 27; Wilful Youth 27; Woman's Law 27; The Girl He Didn't Buy 28; Golden Shackles 28; Jazzland 28; The Look Out Girl 28

Fitzgerald, Ed Blue Movies 88*

Fitzgerald, J. A. Ignorance 16; The Wives of the Prophet 26

Fitzhamon, Lewin Briton vs. Boer 00; His Mother's Portrait, or The Soldier's Vision 00; After the 'Oliday 04; The Bewitched Traveller • The Jonah Man • The Jonah Man, or The Traveller Bewitched 04*; A Cheap Boot Store 04; The Confidence Trick 04; The Coster's Wedding 04; Decoyed 04; A Den of Thieves 04; Don't Interfere with a Coalheaver 04; An Englishman's Trip to Paris from London • A Trip to Paris 04; For the Hand of a Princess 04; The Great Servant Question 04; The Haunted Oak 04; His Superior Officer 04; The Honeymoon: First, Second and Third Class 04; An Interrupted Honeymoon 04; Lady Plumpton's Motor 04; The Lover's Crime • The Lover's Ruse • Poison or Whiskey 04; The Nigger Boy's Revenge 04; The Other Side of the Hedge • Over the Hedge 04; The Parson's Cookery Lesson 04; The Press Illustrated 04; A Race for a Kiss 04; A Rough Time for the Broker 04; The Slavey's Dream 04; The Spoilt Child 04; The Stolen Puppy 04; The Story of Two Christmasses 04; Two Leap Year Proposals 04; When the Sleeper Wakes 04; Won by Strategy 04; The Aliens' Invasion 05; The Amateur Architect 05; The Annual Trip of the Mothers' Meeting 05; The Babes in the Wood 05; Bathers Will Be Prosecuted 05; A Battle of Cauliflowers 05; The Burglar's Boy 05; Charity Covers a Multitude of Sins 05; Children vs. Earthquakes—Earthquakes Preferred 05; The Death of Nelson 05; The Duel 05; False Money 05; Falsely Accused 05; How the Tramps Tricked the Motorist 05; The Inquisitive Boots 05; International

Exchange 05; Lodgings to Let 05; Lost, Stolen or Strayed 05; Only Her Brother 05; Paint and Perfidy 05; Prehistoric Peeps 05; Rehearsing a Play 05; The Reluctant Bridegroom 05; Rescued by Rover 05; The Rival Sportsmen 05; Rover Takes a Call 05; The Stolen Guy 05; Table Turning 05; A Terrible Flirt 05; The Two Imps 05; Two Sentimental Tommies 05; The Villain's Wooing 05; What the Curate Really Did 05; After the Matinee 06; The Best Little Girl in the World 06; Black Beauty 06; The Brigands 06; The Burglar and the Cat 06; The Burglar and the Judge 06; Cupid and the Widow 06; A Cure for Lumbago 06; Dick Turpin's Ride to York 06; The Doll Maker's Daughter 06; An Episode of the Derby 06; The Fatal Leap 06; A Grandchild's Devotion 06; Harlequinade 06; His Daughter and His Gold 06; In the Summer Time 06; The Jerry-Built House 06; Just in Time 06; The Kidnapper and the Child 06; Little Meg and the Wonderful Lamp 06; The Lucky Necklace 06; The Magic Ring 06; Our New Policeman 06; The Peasant Girl's Revenge 06; The Pill Maker's Mistake 06; The Pirate Ship 06; A Poet and His Babies 06; The Rivals 06; The Squatter's Daughter 06; A Tragedy of the Sawmills 06; The Tramp's Dream 06; The Valet Who Stole the Tobbaco 06; The Voter's Guide 06; When Father Eloped with Cook 06; When Jenkins Washed Up 06; The Absent-Minded Man 07; The Artful Lovers 07; The Artist's Model 07; The Boaster 07; Burglars at the Ball 07; The Busy Man 07; Cinderella 07; The Doll's Revenge 07; Drink 07; Dumb Sagacity 07; Dying of Thirst 07; A Father's Vengeance 07; A Feather in His Cap 07; The Fraudulent Solicitor 07; The Ghosts' Holiday 07; The Green Dragon 07; Hair Restorer 07; The Heavenly Twins 07; Her Friend the Enemy 07; Johnny's Gun 07; Kidnapped 07; A Letter in the Sand 07; A Lover's Quarrel 07; The Madman's Bride 07; The Man Who Could Not Commit Suicide 07; The Milkman's Wedding 07; Mischievous Girls 07; A Modern Don Juan 07; Never Complain to Your Laundress 07; The New Dress 07; Not Such a Fool As He Looks 07; The Nun 07; A Painless Extraction 07; Persevering Edwin 07; Pillage by Pillar Box 07; Rebellious Schoolgirls 07; A Sailor's Lass 07; A Seaside Girl 07; Serving the Writ 07; Simpkins' Saturday Off 07; Sister Mary Jane's Top Note 07; A Smart Capture 07; A Soldier's Jealousy 07; The Sticky Bicycle 07; The Stolen Bridle 07; That Fatal Sneeze 07; A Too-Devoted Wife 07; A Tramp's Dream of Wealth 07; The Tramp's Revenge 07; The Viking's Bride 07; Young Scamps 07; The Amorous Nurse 08; The Artful Dodger 08; An Attractive Catch 08; Baby's Playmate 08; The Beauty Competition 08; Bicycles Repaired 08; The Burglar and the Clock 08; Cabby's Sweetheart 08; Catching a Burglar 08; Catching a Tartar 08; A Convict's Dash for Liberty 08; A Country Girl 08; The

Curate's Courtship 08; The Deserter 08; The Detective's Ruse 08; The Devil and the Cornet 08; The Dishonest Barber 08; The Doctor's Dodge 08; The Dog Outwits the Kidnapper 08; The Dog Thief 08; Don Quixote's Dream 08; The Electric Torch 08; An Enemy in the Camp 08; The Fairy's Sword 08; A Faithless Friend 08; A Fascinating Game 08; Father's Lesson 08; The Fickle Husband and the Boy 08; For the Little Lady's Sake 08; Forced to Consent • A Thoughtless Beauty 08; A Free Pardon 08; The Gentleman Gypsy • The Trials of a Gypsy Gentleman 08; The Greedy Girl 08; The Harmless Lunatic's Escape 08; A Heartless Mother 08; Hi! Stop Those Barrels 08; The Hidden Hoard 08; The Hottentot and the Gramophone 08; Jack in the Letterbox 08; John Gilpin's Ride 08; The Love Token 08; The Lucky Pie 08; The Man and His Bottle 08; The Man and the Latchkey 08; The Man Who Learned to Fly 08; Marrying Under Difficulties 08; The Motherly Pram 08; My Little Lady Bountiful 08; The Ne'er-Do-Well and the Baby 08; The Nursemaid's Dream 08; Our Cousin from Abroad 08; The Pets' Tea Party 08; The Photographer's Flirtation 08; The Professor's Antigravitational Fluid 08; The Runaway Kids 08; The Safety Suit for Skaters 08; The Schoolboys' Revolt 08; The Serpent's Tooth 08; Snatched from a Terrible Death 08; The Stubborn Moke 08; The Tell-Tale Kinematograph 08; The Thief at the Casino 08; A Ticket for Two 08; Tomkins Buys a Donkey 08; The Tramps and the Purse 08; The Troubles of a House Agent 08; Unemployed and Unemployable 08; An Unfortunate Bathe 08; The Unlucky Bridegroom 08; The Unlucky Thief 08; Weary Willie Steals a Fish 08; When Women Rule 08; The Wrong Medicine 08; All's Fair in Love and War 09; Baiting the Bobby 09; The Boy and His Kite 09; A Brutal Master 09; The Cabman's Good Fairy 09; The Cat Came Back 09; A Cheap Removal 09; Cupid's Loaf 09; The Curate at the Races 09; The Dentist's Daughter 09; The Dog Came Back 09; A Drunkard's Son 09; The Faithful Clock 09; The Fancy Dress Ball 09; The Fatal Appetiser 09; A Friend in Need 09; A Gamin's Gratitude 09; The Gipsy Child 09; The Girl Who Joined the Bushrangers 09; The Gypsy Lover 09; The Gypsy's Baby 09; His Only Friend 09; In the Service of the King 09; Invisibility 09*; The Jewel Thieves 09; Last Year's Timetable 09; The Lazy Boy 09; The Little Flower Girl's Christmas 09; The Little Milliner and the Thief 09; The Lost Memory 09; A Man and His Bees 09; The Meanest Man on Earth 09; The Miser and the Child 09; Mr. Poorluck Gets Married 09; Mother-in-Law Has All the Luck 09; Necessity Is the Mother of Invention 09; No More Hats Wanted 09; A Pair of Desperadoes 09; A Pair of Truants 09; The Penalty of Beauty 09; A Plucky Little Girl 09; A Present for Her Husband 09; The Race for the Farmer's Cup 09; The Ranch

Owner's Daughter • The Redskin's Offer 09; The Rival Mesmerist 09; The Rivals 09; Saved by the Telegraph 09; Saved from the Sea 09; The Shepherd's Dog 09; The Sorrows of a Chaperone 09; The Spoilt Child 09; The Spy 09; The Story of a Picture 09; A Street Arab 09; That Marvellous Gramophone 09; Too Much Lobster 09; The Villain's Downfall 09; Why Father Learned to Ride 09; The Wrong Cab 09; The Adventures of a Five Pound Note 10; All's Fair in Love 10; Are You John Brown? 10; A Baby's Power 10; Black Beauty 10; The Black Kitten 10; The Burglar and Little Phyllis 10; The Cardsharpers 10; A Chanticler Hat 10; The Conquering Cask 10; Dave Craggs, Detective 10; The Detective in Peril 10; The Detective's Dog 10; A Difficult Courtship 10; Dumb Comrades 10; Extracting a Cheque from Uncle 10; The Fakir's Flute 10; The Farmer's Daughter 10; Father Buys a Screen 10; A Fickle Girl 10; Fits and Misfits 10; He Eloped with Her Father 10; The Heart of a Fishergirl 10; Heart of Oak 10; His New Mama 10; Hot Pickles 10; In Pursuit of Fashion 10; In the Good Old Days 10; Invigorating Electricity 10; Josephine and Her Lovers 10; The Little Blue Cap 10; The Little Housekeeper 10; Love Me, Love My Dog 10; Love's Strategy 10; Married in Haste 10; Mary the Coster 10; The Mechanical Mary Anne 10; The Merry Beggars 10; Mr. Poorluck Buys Some Furniture 10; Mr. Poorluck's Dream 10; Mr. Poorluck's Lucky Horseshoe 10; A Modern Love Potion 10; The Moneylender's Mistake 10; Never Send a Man to Match a Ribbon 10; A New Hat for Nothing 10; The New Reporter 10; A Night in Armour 10; Over the Garden Wall 10; Persuading Papa 10; The Poorlucks' First Tiff 10; The Poorlucks Take Part in a Pageant 10; A Present for His Wife 10; A Sailor's Lass 10; Saved by His Sweetheart 10; The Scaramouches 10; Seven, Seventeen and Seventy 10; The Sharp-Witted Thief 10; The Sheriff's Daughter 10; The Short-Sighted Errand Boy 10; A Spoilt Child of Fortune 10; The Stowaway 10; The Telephone Call 10; Tempered with Mercy 10; Tilly at the Election 10; Tilly the Tomboy Buys Linoleum 10; Tilly the Tomboy Goes Boating 10; Tilly the Tomboy Plays Truant 10; Tilly the Tomboy Visits the Poor 10; Uncle Joe 10; Unlucky Bill 10; Who's Got My Hat? 10; The Widow's Wooers 10; Without Her Father's Consent 10; A Woman Scorned 10; An Absorbing Game 11; All's Right with the World 11; The Amateur Burglar 11; The Bailiff's Little Weakness 11; Children Mustn't Smoke 11; College Chums 11; The Course of True Love 11; The Demon Dog 11; The Detective and the Jewel Trick 11; The Dog's Devotion 11; A Double Deception 11; The Double Elopement 11; The Early Worm 11; Envy, Hatred and Malice 11; Evicted 11; Exceeding His Duty 11; A Fight with Fire 11; The Fireman's Daughter 11; For a Baby's Sake 11; The Gay Lord Ducie 11; Gipsy Nan 11; The Greatest of

These 11; A Halfbreed's Gratitude 11; A Happy Event in the Poorluck Family 11; Harry the Footballer 11; Hawkeye Learns to Punt 11; A Horse and Mrs. Grundy 11; In Jest and Earnest 11; Janet's Flirtation 11; Jim of the Mounted Police 11; The Lawyer's Message 11; The Little Black Pom 11; Love and a Sewing Machine 11; Many a Slip 11; Mr. and Mrs. Poorluck Separate 11; Mr. Poorluck Buys Some China 11; Mother's Boy 11; My Dear Love 11; N Stands for Nelly 11; The New Cook 11; Not Guilty 11; Now I Have to Call Him Father 11; PC Hawkeye Leaves the Force 11; PC Hawkeye Turns Detective 11; PC Hawkeye's Busy Day 11; The Parson's Wife 11; Poorluck's Excursion Tickets 11; Rachel's Sin 11; Rover the Peacemaker 11; A Seaside Introduction 11; The Smuggler's Stepdaughter 11; A Sprained Ankle 11; The Stolen Letters 11; The Subaltern's Joke 11; The Three Lovers 11; Tiger the 'Tec 11; Till Death Do Us Part 11; Tilly and the Fire Engines 11; Tilly and the Mormon Missionary 11; Tilly and the Smugglers 11; Tilly at the Seaside 11; Tilly, Matchmaker 11; Tilly's Party 11; Tilly's Unsympathetic Uncle 11; Toddles, Scout 11; Tracked by Tiger 11; Twin Roses 11; A Very Powerful Voice 11; When Tilly's Uncle Flirted 11; A Wilful Maid 11; The Wisdom of Brother Ambrose 11; Amorous Arthur 12; The Blind Man's Dog 12; The Broken Melody 12; The Burglar's Daughter 12; A Case of Explosives • Munition Workers 12; Children of the Forest 12; The Copper's Revenge 12; A Curate's Love Story 12; A Day in London 12; A Day in the Country 12; The Editor and the Millionaire 12; A Fisherman's Love Story 12; The Flapper and the Curates 12; The Flapper's Elopement 12; Flo the Flapper 12; A Gipsy Girl's Honour 12; Her Only Pal 12; Hubby's Letter 12; An Indian Vendetta 12; Jemima and the Editor 12; The Lost Will 12; The Mermaid 12; A Mother and Sons of 1776 12; Never Again, Never 12; The Pony Who Paid the Rent 12; Repaying the Debt 12; Saving the Royal Mail 12; The Unjust Steward 12; Unlucky Ann 12; A Village Scandal 12; The Wrong Envelopes 12; Algy's Tormentor 13; Beauty and the Boat 13; A Bore of a Boy 13; Daddy's Darlings 13; A Day on Rollers 13; The First Steeplechase 13; The Flappers and the Colonel 13; The Flappers and the Nuts 13; Freddy's Dumb Playmates 13; Gipsy Hate 13; The Girl Next Door 13; He Was So Fond of Animals 13; Her Pony's Love 13; Home for the Holidays • Three Little Vagabonds 13; The Lass of Gloucester 13; Little Willie's Apprenticeships 13; Love in a Boarding House 13; The Picnic on the Island 13; A Race for Love 13; A Terrible Plant 13; When the Hurricanes Visited the Doughnuts 13; While Shepherds Watched 13; A Footballer's Honour 14; A Hateful Bondage 14; Her Faithful Companions 14; The Loosened Plank 14; Men Will Deceive 14; The Scallawag 14; Two Little Angels 14; When the Hurricanes Bought the Lino

14; When the Hurricanes Took Up Farming 14; When the Hurricanes Visited the Sawmills 14; The Whirlwind Kids 14

Fitzmaurice, Aubrey A Successful Operation 16

Fitzmaurice, George The Bomb Boy 14; The Quest of the Sacred Gem 14; At Bay 15; The Commuters 15; The Money Master 15; Stop Thief! 15; The Test 15; Via Wireless 15; Who's Who in Society 15; Arms and the Woman 16; Big Jim Garrity 16; Fifth Avenue 16; New York 16; The Romantic Journey 16; Blind Man's Luck 17; The Hunting of the Hawk 17; The Iron Heart 17; Kick In 17; The Mark of Cain 17; The On-the-Square Girl 17; The Recoil 17; Sylvia of the Secret Service 17; The Cry of the Weak 18; The Hillcrest Mystery 18; Innocence • Innocent 18; The Japanese Nightingale 18; The Narrow Path 18; The Naulahka 18; Our Better Selves 18; The Avalanche 19; Common Clay 19; Counterfeit 19; Profiteer • The Profiteers 19; A Society Exile 19; The Witness for the Defense 19; Idols of Clay 20; On with the Dance 20; The Right to Love 20; Experience 21; Forever • Peter Ibbetson 21; Paying the Piper 21; Kick In 22; The Man from Home 22; Three Live Ghosts 22; To Have and to Hold 22; Bella Donna 23; The Cheat 23; The Eternal City 23; Cytherea 24; Tarnish 24; The Dark Angel 25; His Supreme Moment 25; A Thief in Paradise 25; Son of the Sheik 26; The Love Mart 27; The Night of Love 27; Rose of the Golden West 27; The Tender Hour 27; The Barker 28; Lilac Time • Love Never Dies 28; His Captive Woman 29; The Locked Door 29; The Man and the Moment 29; Tiger Rose 29; The Bad One 30; The Devil to Pay 30; One Heavenly Night 30; One Romantic Night 30*; Raffles 30*; Strangers May Kiss 31; The Unholy Garden 31; As You Desire Me 32; Mata Hari 32; All Men Are Enemies 34; Petticoat Fever 36; Suzy 36; Arsène Lupin Returns 37; The Emperor's Candlesticks 37; The Last of Mrs. Cheyney 37*; Live, Love and Learn 37; Vacation from Love 38; Adventure in Diamonds 40

Fitzpatrick, James A. Songs of England 25; Songs of Ireland 25; Songs of Scotland 25; Songs of the British Isles 25; The Lady of the Lake 28; David Livingstone 36; Auld Lang Syne 37; The Bells of St. Mary's 37; The Last Rose of Summer 37; A Dream of Love 38; George Bizet, Composer of Carmen 38; The Life of Chopin 38; Song of Mexico 45

Fiveson, Robert S. The Clonus Horror • Parts: The Clonus Horror 78

Fiz, Robert It's Your Move • Mad Checkmate 68

Fizzarotti, Ettore M. I'll Sell My Skin Dearly • Vendo Cara la Pelle 68

Flagg, Cash see Steckler, Ray Dennis

Flaherty, David What's Happened to Sugar? 45; Guernica 49*; The Gift of Green • Green Mountain Land 50

Flaherty, Frances Moana • Moana—A Romance of the Golden Age • Moana—The Love Life of a South Sea Siren 25*

Flaherty, Paul 18 Again! 88; Who's Harry Crumb? 89

Flaherty, Robert Nanook of the North 21; Moana • Moana—A Romance of the Golden Age • Moana—The Love Life of a South Sea Siren 25*; The Pottery Maker • Story of a Potter 25; The Twenty-Four Dollar Island 26; White Shadows in the South Seas 28*; Industrial Britain 31*; Tabu 31*; Art of the English Craftsman 33; The English Potter 33; The Glassmakers of England 33; Man of Aran 34; Elephant Boy 36*; The Land 41; Louisiana Story 48; Guernica 49*

Flaven, Arthur J. The Son of Tarzan 20*; The Jungle Trail of the Son of Tarzan 23*

Fleck, Freddie The Magnificent Ambersons 42*

Fleck, Jakob Hoffmanns Erzählungen • Tales of Hoffmann 11*

Fleischer, Dave Experiment No. 1 18; The Clown's Pup 19; Experiment No. 2 19; Experiment No. 3 19; Slides 19; Tantalizing Fly 19; All Aboard for a Trip to the Moon • The First Man to the Moon 20; The Automobile Ride 20; The Boxing Kangaroo • Kangaroo 20; The Card Game • Poker 20; Cartoonland 20; The Chinaman 20; The Circus 20; The Clown's Little Brother 20; Hello Mars 20; If You Could Shrink 20; The Ouija Board 20; Perpetual Motion 20; The Restaurant 20; The Fish • Fishing 21; The Hypnotist 21; Invisible Ink 21; Modeling 21; November 21; Birthday 22; Bubbles 22; The Challenge 22; The Dancing Doll • The Dresden Doll 22; Flies 22; Jumping Beans 22; Mosquito 22; Pay Day 22; Reunion 22; The Show 22; Balloons 23; The Battle 23; Bedtime 23; The Contest 23; False Alarm 23; The Fortune Teller 23; Fun from the Press No. 1 23; Fun from the Press No. 2 23; Fun from the Press No. 3 23; Laundry 23; The Puzzle 23; Shadows 23; Surprise 23; Trapped 23; Clay Town 24; The Cure 24; Echo and Narcissus 24; A Fable of the Future • Fable of the Future: The Proxy Lover • The Proxy Lover • The Proxy Lover: A Fable of the Future 24; Goodbye My Lady Love 24; Ko-Ko in 1999 24; Ko-Ko the Hot Shot 24; League of Nations 24; The Masquerade 24; Mother, Mother, Mother, Pin a Rose on Me 24; Oh, Mabel! 24; The Runaway 24; Sparring Partner 24; A Stitch in Time 24; A Trip to Mars 24; Vacation 24; Vaudeville 24; Big Chief Ko-Ko 25; The Cartoon Factory 25; Come Take a Trip in My Airship 25; Daisy Bell 25; Dixie 25; I Love a Lassie 25; Ko-Ko Celebrates the Fourth 25; Ko-Ko Eats 25; Ko-Ko in Toyland 25; Ko-Ko Nuts 25; Ko-Ko on the Run 25; Ko-Ko Packs 'Em • Ko-Ko Packs Up 25; Ko-Ko Sees Spooks 25; Ko-Ko the Barber 25; Ko-Ko Trains Animals • Ko-Ko Trains 'Em 25; Ko-Ko's Thanksgiving 25; Mother Goose Land 25; My Bonnie • My Bonnie Lies Over the Ocean 25; Nutcracker Suite 25; Old Folks at Home 25; Sailing, Sailing • Sailing, Sailing Over the Bounding Main 25; The Storm 25; Suwanee River 25; Ta-Ra-Ra-Boom-De-A • Ta-Ra-Ra-Boom-Dee-Aye 25; Another Bottle, Doctor 26; Berth Mark 26; By the Light of the Silvery Moon 26; Coming Through the Rye 26; Darling Dolly Gray • Dolly Gray 26; East Side, West Side 26; The Fadeaway • Ko-Ko in The Fade-Away 26; Has Anybody Here Seen Kelly? 26; In the Good Old Summertime 26; It's the Cats 26; Ko-Ko at the Circus 26; Ko-Ko Baffles the Bulls 26; Ko-Ko Gets Egg-cited 26; Ko-Ko Hot After It 26; Ko-Ko Kidnapped 26; Ko-Ko Steps Out 26; Ko-Ko the Convict 26; Ko-Ko's Paradise 26; Ko-Ko's Queen 26; Morning Judge 26; My Old Kentucky Home 26; Oh, You Beautiful Doll 26; Old Black Joe 26; Pack Up Your Troubles 26; Sweet Adeline 26; Take a Trip 26; Toot! Toot! 26; Trail of the Lonesome Pine 26; Tramp, the Boys Are Marching • Tramp Tramp Tramp • Tramp, Tramp, Tramp the Boys Are Marching 26; Jingle Bells 27; Ko-Ko Back Tracks 27; Ko-Ko Chops Suey 27; Ko-Ko Explores 27; Ko-Ko Hops Off 27; Ko-Ko Kicks 27; Ko-Ko Makes 'Em Laugh 27; Ko-Ko Needles the Boss 27; Ko-Ko Plays Pool 27; Ko-Ko the Kavalier 27; Ko-Ko the Kid 27; Ko-Ko the Knight 27; Ko-Ko the Kop 27; Ko-Ko's Kane 27; Ko-Ko's Klock 27; Ko-Ko's Quest 27; That Little Big Fellow 27; Waiting for the Robert E. Lee 27; After the Ball 28; Ko-Ko Cleans Up 28; Ko-Ko Goes Over 28; Ko-Ko Heaves Ho 28; Ko-Ko in the Rough 28; Ko-Ko Lamps Aladdin 28; Ko-Ko on the Track 28; Ko-Ko Smokes 28; Ko-Ko Squeals 28; Ko-Ko's Act 28; Ko-Ko's Bawth 28; Ko-Ko's Big Pull 28; Ko-Ko's Catch 28; Ko-Ko's Chase 28; Ko-Ko's Courtship 28; Ko-Ko's Dog Gone 28; Ko-Ko's Earth Control 28; Ko-Ko's Field Daze 28; Ko-Ko's Germ Jam 28; Ko-Ko's Haunted House 28; Ko-Ko's Hot Dog 28; Ko-Ko's Kink 28; Ko-Ko's Kozy Korner 28; Ko-Ko's Magic 28; Ko-Ko's Parade 28; Ko-Ko's Tattoo 28; Ko-Ko's War Dogs 28; Telefilm 28; Accordion Joe 29; Chemical Ko-Ko 29; Chinatown My Chinatown 29; Daisy Bell 29; Dixie 29; Goodbye My Lady Love 29; I've Got Rings on My Fingers 29; Ko-Ko Beats Time 29; Ko-Ko's Big Sale 29; Ko-Ko's Conquest 29; Ko-Ko's Crib 29; Ko-Ko's Focus 29; Ko-Ko's Harem Scarem 29; Ko-Ko's Hot Ink 29; Ko-Ko's Hypnotism 29; Ko-Ko's Knock-Down 29; Ko-Ko's Reward 29; Ko-Ko's Saxaphonies 29; Ko-Ko's Signals 29; Mother Pin a Rose on Me 29; My Pony Boy 29; No Eyes Today 29; Noah's Lark 29; Noise Annoys Ko-Ko 29; Oh, You Beautiful Doll 29; Old Black Joe 29; Put on Your Old Gray Bonnet 29; The Sidewalks of New York 29; Smiles 29; Yankee Doodle Boy 29; Ye Olde Melodies 29; Barnacle Bill • Barnacle Bill the Sailor 30; Bedelia 30; Come Take a Trip in My Airship 30; Dizzy Dishes 30; Fire Bugs 30; The Glow Worm 30; The

Grand Uproar 30; Hot Dog 30; A Hot Time in the Old Town Tonight 30; I'm Afraid to Come Home in the Dark 30; I'm Forever Blowing Bubbles 30; In the Good Old Summertime 30; In the Shade of the Old Apple Tree 30; La Paloma 30; Mariutch 30; Marriage Wows 30; My Gal Sal 30; Mysterious Mouse 30; On a Sunday Afternoon 30; Prisoner's Song 30; Radio Riot 30; Row, Row, Row 30; Sky Scraping 30; The Stein Song 30; Strike Up the Band 30; Swing, You Sinners 30; Up to Mars 30; Wise Flies 30; Yes! We Have No Bananas 30; The Ace of Spades 31; Alexander's Ragtime Band 31; And the Green Grass Grew All Around 31; Any Little Girl That's a Nice Little Girl 31; Betty Co-Ed 31; Bimbo's Express 31; Bimbo's Initiation 31; The Bum Bandit 31; By the Beautiful Sea 31; The Cow's Husband 31; Dizzy Red Riding Hood 31; Graduation Day in Bugland 31; The Herring Murder Case 31; Hurry, Doctor 31; I Wonder Who's Kissing Her Now 31; I'd Climb the Highest Mountain 31; In My Merry Oldsmobile 31; In the Shade of the Old Apple Sauce 31; Jack and the Beanstalk 31; A Jolt for General Germ 31; Kitty from Kansas City 31; Little Annie Rooney 31; The Male Man 31; Mask-a-Raid 31; Minding the Baby 31; Mr. Gallagher and Mr. Shean 31; My Baby Just Cares for Me 31; My Wife's Gone to the Country 31; Please Go 'Way and Let Me Sleep 31; Russian Lullaby 31; Silly Scandals 31; Somebody Stole My Gal 31; Step on It 31; Suited to a T. 31; Teacher's Pest 31; Texas in 1999 31; That Old Gang of Mine 31; Tree Saps 31; Twenty Legs Under the Sea 31; You're Driving Me Crazy 31; Admission Free 32; A-Hunting We Will Go 32; Any Rags 32; Betty Boop for President 32; The Betty Boop Limited 32; Betty Boop, M.D. 32; Betty Boop's Bamboo Isle 32; Betty Boop's Bizzy Bee 32; Betty Boop's Museum 32; Betty Boop's Ups and Downs 32; Boop-Oop-a-Doop 32; Chess-Nuts 32; Crazy Town 32; The Dancing Fool 32; Down Among the Sugar Cane 32; Hide and Seek 32; I Ain't Got Nobody 32; I'll Be Glad When You're Dead You Rascal You 32; Just a Gigolo 32; Just One More Chance 32; Let Me Call You Sweetheart 32; Minnie the Moocher 32; Oh! How I Hate to Get Up in the Morning 32; The Robot 32; Romantic Melodies 32; Rudy Vallee Melodies 32; School Days 32; Shine On Harvest Moon 32; Show Me the Way to Go Home 32; Sing a Song 32; Sleepy Time Down South • When It's Sleepy Time Down South 32; Stopping the Show 32; Sweet Jenny Lee 32; Swim or Sink 32; Time on My Hands 32; Wait Till the Sun Shines, Nellie 32; When the Red Red Robin Comes Bob Bob Bobbin' Along 32; You Try Somebody Else 32; Ain't She Sweet 33; Aloha Oe 33; Betty Boop's Big Boss 33; Betty Boop's Birthday Party 33; Betty Boop's Crazy Inventions 33; Betty Boop's Hallowe'en Party 33; Betty Boop's Ker-Choo 33; Betty Boop's May Party 33;

Betty Boop's Penthouse 33; Blow Me Down 33; Boilesk 33; Boo, Boo, Theme Song 33; Dinah 33; Down by the Old Mill Stream 33; I Eats My Spinach 33; I Heard 33; I Like Mountain Music 33; I Yam What I Yam 33; Is My Palm Read 33; Morning, Noon and Night 33; Mother Goose Land 33; The Old Man of the Mountain 33; Parade of the Wooden Soldiers 33; The Peanut Vendor 33; Popeye the Sailor 33; Popular Melodies 33; Reaching for the Moon 33; Season's Greetinks 33; Sing, Babies, Sing 33; Sing, Sisters, Sing! 33; Snow White 33; Song Shopping 33; Stoopnocracy 33; When Yuba Plays the Rumba on the Tuba 33; Wild Elephinks 33; Axe Me Another 34; Betty Boop's Lifeguard 34; Betty Boop's Little Pal 34; Betty Boop's Prize Show 34; Betty Boop's Rise to Fame 34; Betty Boop's Trial 34; Betty in Blunderland 34; Can You Take It? 34; The Dance Contest 34; A Dream Walking 34; Ha! Ha! Ha! 34; Keep in Style 34; Keeps Rainin' All the Time 34; Lazy Bones 34; Let's All Sing Like the Birdies Sing 34; Let's You and Him Fight 34; Little Dutch Mill 34; Love Thy Neighbor 34; The Man on the Flying Trapeze 34; Poor Cinderella 34; Red Hot Mama 34; She Reminds Me of You 34; She Wronged Him Right 34; Shiver Me Timbers! 34; Shoein' Hosses 34; Sock-a-Bye Baby 34; Strong to the Finich 34; There's Something About a Soldier 34; This Little Piggie Went to Market 34; Tune Up and Sing 34; The Two-Alarm Fire 34; We Aim to Please 34; When My Ship Comes In 34; Adventures of Popeye 35; Baby Be Good 35; Be Kind to Aminals 35; Betty Boop and Grampy 35; Betty Boop, with Henry, the Funniest Living American 35; Beware of Barnacle Bill 35; Choose Your Weppins 35; Dancing on the Moon 35; Dizzy Divers 35; An Elephant Never Forgets 35; For Better or Worser 35; The Hyp-nut-tist 35; I Wished on the Moon 35; It's Easy to Remember 35; Judge for a Day 35; The Kids in the Shoe 35; King of the Mardi Gras 35; A Language All My Own 35; A Little Soap and Water 35; Making Stars 35; Musical Memories 35; No! No! A Thousand Times No! 35; Pleased to Meet Cha! 35; The Song of the Birds 35; The Spinach Overture 35; Stop That Noise 35; Swat the Fly 35; Taking the Blame 35; Time for Love 35; You Gotta Be a Football Hero 35; Be Human 36; Betty Boop and Little Jimmy 36; Betty Boop and the Little King 36; Bridge Ahoy! 36; Brotherly Love 36; Christmas Comes But Once a Year 36; A Clean Shaven Man 36; The Cobweb Hotel 36; Grampy's Indoor Outing 36; Greedy Humpty Dumpty 36; Happy You and Merry Me 36; Hawaiian Birds 36; The Hills of Old Wyomin' 36; Hold the Wire 36; I Can't Escape from You 36; I Don't Want to Make History 36; I Feel Like a Feather in the Breeze 36; I-Ski Love-Ski You-Ski 36; I Wanna Be a Lifeguard 36; I'm in the Army Now 36;

Let's Get Movin' 36; Little Nobody 36; The Little Stranger 36; Little Swee' Pea 36; Making Friends 36; More Pep 36; Never Kick a Woman 36; No Other One 36; Not Now 36; Play Safe 36; Popeye the Sailor Meets Sinbad the Sailor 36; Somewhere in Dream Land 36; A Song a Day 36; The Spinach Roadster 36; Talking Through My Heart 36; Training Pigeons 36; Vim, Vigor and Vitaliky 36; We Did It 36; What, No Spinach? 36; You're Not Built That Way 36; Bunny-Mooning 37; The Candid Candidate 37; A Car-Tune Portrait 37; Chicken à la King 37; Ding Dong Doggie 37; Educated Fish 37; The Football Toucher Downer 37; Fowl Play 37; The Foxy Hunter 37; Hospitaliky 37; The Hot Air Salesman 37; House Cleaning Blues 37; I Like Babies and Infinks 37; I Never Changes My Altitude 37; The Impractical Joker 37; Little Lamby 37; Lost and Foundry 37; Magic on Broadway 37; Morning, Noon and Nightclub 37; My Artistical Temperature 37; Never Should Have Told You 37; The New Deal Show 37; Organ Grinder's Swing 37; The Paneless Window Washer 37; Peeping Penguins 37; Please Keep Me in Your Dreams 37; Popeye the Sailor Meets Ali Baba's Forty Thieves 37; Proteck the Weakerist 37; Pudgy Picks a Fight 37; Pudgy Takes a Bow-Wow 37; Service with a Smile 37; Twilight on the Trail 37; The Twisker Pitcher 37; Whispers in the Dark 37; Whoops! I'm a Cowboy 37; You Came to My Rescue 37; Zula Hula 37; All's Fair at the Fair 38; Be Up to Date 38; Beside a Moonlit Stream 38; Big Chief Ugh-Amugh-Ugh 38; Bulldozing the Bull 38; Buzzy Boop 38; Buzzy Boop at the Concert 38; Cops Is Always Right 38; A Date to Skate 38; Goonland 38; Hold It! 38; Honest Love and True 38; The House Builder Upper 38; Hunky and Spunky 38; I Yam Love Sick 38; The Jeep 38; Learn Polikeness 38; Let's Celebrake 38; Mutiny Ain't Nice 38; On with the New 38; Out of the Inkwell 38; The Playful Polar Bears 38; Plumbing Is a Pipe 38; Pudgy and the Lost Kitten 38; Pudgy in Thrills and Chills • Thrills and Chills 38; Pudgy the Watchman 38; Riding the Rails 38; Sally Swing 38; Swing School 38; The Tears of an Onion 38; Thanks for the Memory 38; You Leave Me Breathless 38; You Took the Words Right Out of My Heart 38; Aladdin and His Wonderful Lamp 39; Always Kickin' 39; Barnyard Brat 39; Customers Wanted 39; The Fresh Vegetable Mystery 39; Ghosks Is the Bunk 39; Gulliver's Travels 39; Hello, How Am I? 39; It's the Natural Thing to Do 39; Leave Well Enough Alone 39; Musical Mountaineers 39; My Friend the Monkey 39; Never Sock a Baby 39; Rhythm on the Reservation 39; The Scared Crows 39; Small Fry 39; So Does an Automobile 39; Wotta Nitemare 39; Yip, Yip, Yippy 39; Ants in the Plants 40; Bring Himself Back Alive 40; The Constable 40; The Dandy Lion 40; Doing Impossikible Stunts 40;

Eugene the Jeep • Popeye Presents Eugene the Jeep 40; Females Is Fickle 40; Fightin' Pals 40; The Foul Ball Player 40; The Fulla Bluff Man 40; Granite Hotel 40; A Kick in Time 40; King for a Day 40; Little Lambkin 40; Mommy Loves Puppy 40; My Feelin's Is Hurt 40; My Pop, My Pop 40; Nurse Mates 40; Onion Pacific 40; Pedagogical Institution (College to You) 40; Poopdeck Pappy • With Poopdeck Pappy 40; Popeye Meets William Tell 40; Puttin' on the Act 40; Shakespearian Spinach 40; Sneak, Snoop and Snitch 40; Snubbed by a Snob 40; Springtime in the Rock Age 40; Stealin' Ain't Honest 40; The Ugly Dino 40; Way Back When a Nag Was Only a Horse 40; Way Back When a Nightclub Was a Stick 40; Way Back When a Razzberry Was a Fruit 40; Way Back When a Triangle Had Its Points 40; Way Back When Women Had Their Weigh 40; Wedding Belts 40; Wimmin Hadn't Oughta Drive 40; Wimmin Is a Myskery 40; You Can't Shoe a Horsefly 40; All's Well 41; Child Psykolojiky 41; Copy Cat 41; Fire Cheese 41; Flies Ain't Human 41; Gabby Goes Fishing 41; Hoppity Goes to Town • Mr. Bug Goes to Town 41; I'll Never Crow Again 41; It's a Hap-Hap-Happy Day 41; The Mechanical Monsters • Superman in The Mechanical Monsters 41; The Mighty Navy 41; Nix on Hypnotricks 41; Olive's Boithday Presink 41; Olive's Sweepstakes Ticket 41; Pest Pilot 41; Pop and Mom in Wild Oysters 41; Popeye Meets Rip Van Winkle 41; Problem Pappy 41; Quiet! Pleeze 41; Raggedy Ann and Andy • Raggedy Ann and Raggedy Andy 41; Sneak, Snoop and Snitch in Triple Trouble 41; Superman 41; Swing Cleaning 41; Twinkletoes Gets the Bird 41; Twinkletoes in Hat Stuff 41; Twinkletoes—Where He Goes Nobody Knows 41; Two for the Zoo 41; Vitamin Hay 41; The Wizard of Ants 41; Zero, the Hound 41; The Arctic Giant • Superman in The Arctic Giant 42; Baby Wants a Bottleship 42; Billion Dollar Limited • Superman in Billion Dollar Limited 42; Blunder Below 42; The Bulleteers • Superman in The Bulleteers 42; Electric Earthquake • Superman in Electric Earthquake 42; Fleets of Stren'th 42; Kickin' the Conga 'Round 42; The Magnetic Telescope • Superman in The Magnetic Telescope 42; Many Tanks 42; Olive Oyl and Water Don't Mix 42; Pip-Eye, Pup-Eye, Poop-Eye and Peep-Eye 42; The Raven 42; Superman in Terror on the Midway • Terror on the Midway 42; Superman in Volcano • Volcano 42

Fleischer, Max How to Fire a Lewis Gun 18; How to Fire a Stokes Mortar 18; How to Read an Army Map 18; The Einstein Theory of Relativity 23; Darwin's Theory of Evolution • Evolution 25; Finding His Voice 29*; Rudolph, the Red-Nosed Reindeer 48

Fleischer, Richard Flicker Flashbacks 43; This Is America 43; Memo for Joe 44; Child of Divorce 46; Banjo 47; Design for

Death 47; Bodyguard 48; Make Mine Laughs 48*; So This Is New York 48; The Clay Pigeon 49; Follow Me Quietly 49*; Trapped 49; Armored Car Robbery 50; His Kind of Woman 51*; The Narrow Margin 51; The Happy Time 52; Arena 53; 20,000 Leagues Under the Sea 54; Violent Saturday 54; The Girl in the Red Velvet Swing 55; Bandido! 56; Between Heaven and Hell 56; These Thousand Hills 58; The Vikings 58; Compulsion 59; The Big Gamble 60*; Crack in the Mirror 60; Barabba • Barabbas 61; Fantastic Voyage • Microscopia • Strange Journey 66; Doctor Dolittle 67*; Think 20th 67; The Boston Strangler 68; Che! 69; 10 Rillington Place 70; Tora! Tora! Tora! 70*; Blind Terror • See No Evil 71; The Last Run 71*; The New Centurions • Precinct 45—Los Angeles Police 72; Soylent Green 72; Beautiful But Deadly • The Don Is Dead 73; Mr. Majestyk 74; The Spikes Gang 74; Mandingo 75; The Incredible Sarah 76; Crossed Swords • The Prince and the Pauper 77; Ashanti • Ashanti: Land of No Mercy 79; The Jazz Singer 80; Tough Enough 81; Amityville: The Demon • Amityville 3-D • Amityville III: The Demon 83; Conan the Destroyer 84; Red Sonja 85; Million Dollar Mystery 87; Call from Space 89

Fleischmann, Peter Die Hamburger Krankheit 79; Es Ist Nicht Leicht ein Gott zu Sein • Hard to Be a God 89

Fleming, Andrew Bad Dreams 88

Fleming, Caryl S. The Clouded Name 19; The Devil's Partner 23; The Valley of Lost Souls 23

Fleming, Edward Chronic Innocence • Den Kroniske Uskyld 85; Final Curtain • Sidste Akt • Waiting in the Wings 87

Fleming, Paul Operation Atlantis 65

Fleming, Peter Barber see Barber-Fleming, Peter

Fleming, Victor Private Film for the Duke of Sutherland 19; When the Clouds Roll By 19*; The Mollycoddle 20; Mama's Affair • Mamma's Affair 21; Woman's Place 21; Anna Ascends 22; The Lane That Has No Turning 22; Red Hot Romance 22; The Call of the Canyon 23; Dark Secrets 23; The Law of the Lawless 23; To the Last Man 23; The Code of the Sea 24; Empty Hands 24; Adventure 25; The Devil's Cargo 25; Lord Jim 25; A Son of His Father 25; The Blind Goddess 26; Mantrap 26; Hula 27; The Rough Riders • The Trumpet Call 27; The Way of All Flesh 27; Abie's Irish Rose 28; The Awakening 28; The Virginian 29; Wolf Song 29; Common Clay 30; Renegades 30; Around the World in 80 Minutes • Around the World in 80 Minutes with Douglas Fairbanks • Around the World with Douglas Fairbanks 31*; Red Dust 32; The Wet Parade 32; The Blonde Bombshell • Bombshell 33; The White Sister 33; Treasure Island 34; The Farmer Takes a Wife 35; Reckless 35; The Good Earth 36*; Captains Courageous 37; The Great Waltz • Toute la Ville Danse 38*; Test

Pilot 38; The Wizard of Oz 38*; Gone with the Wind 39*; Dr. Jekyll and Mr. Hyde 41; Tortilla Flat 42; A Guy Named Joe 43; Adventure 45; Joan of Arc 48

Flemyng, Gordon Solo for Sparrow 62; Five to One 63; Just for Fun 63; Dr. Who and the Daleks 65; Daleks: Invasion Earth, 2150 A.D. • Invasion Earth, 2150 A.D. 66; Great Catherine 67; The Split 68; Grigsby • The Last Grenade 70

Fleury, Joy Tristesse et Beauté 85

Flicker, Theodore J. The Troublemaker 64; The President's Analyst • T.P.A. 67; Hi in the Cellar • Three in the Cellar • Up in the Cellar 70; Jacob Two-Two Meets the Hooded Fang 77; Soggy Bottom, U.S.A. 81

Flídr, Zdeněk Moře Začíná za Vsí 88; Tichý Společník 89

Flocker, James T. Ground Zero 73; Legend of Cougar Canyon 74; Secret of Navajo Cave 76; Ghosts That Still Walk 77

Flohri Patriotism 15; The Wily Jap 15

Flood, James Times Have Changed 23; When Odds Are Even 23; The Tenth Woman 24; The Man Without a Conscience 25; Satan in Sables 25; The Wife Who Wasn't Wanted 25; The Woman Hater 25; The Honeymoon Express 26; Why Girls Go Back Home 26; The Lady in Ermine 27; Three Hours 27; The Count of Ten 28; Domestic Meddlers 28; Marriage by Contract 28; Midstream 29; Mr. Antonio 29*; Whispering Winds 29; Sisters 30; The Swellhead 30; Mother's Millions • She-Wolf • The She-Wolf of Wall Street 31; The Dawn of Life • Dream of Life • Life Begins 32*; The Mouthpiece 32*; Under-Cover Man 32; All of Me 34; Such Women Are Dangerous 34; Shanghai 35; We're Only Human 35; Wings in the Dark 35; Everybody's Old Man 36; The Lonely Road • Scotland Yard Commands 36; Midnight Madonna 37; Off the Record 39; The Big Fix 47; Stepchild 47

Florea, John Island of the Lost 67*; Pickup on 101 • Where the Eagle Flies 72; The Astral Factor • Invisible Strangler 76; Where's Willie? 78; Hot Child in the City 87

Florey, Robert Heureuse Intervention 19; Isidore à la Déveine 19; Isidore sur le Lac 19; Fifty-Fifty 23; Valentino en Angleterre 23; One Hour of Love 26; That Model from Paris 26*; The Coffin Maker 27; Face Value 27; A Hollywood Extra • Hollywood Rhapsody • The Life and Death of a Hollywood Extra • The Life and Death of 9413, a Hollywood Extra 27*; Johann the Coffin Maker 27; The Loves of Zero 27; The Romantic Age 27; Bonjour New York! 28; A Hole in the Wall 28; Night Club 28; The Pusher-in-the-Face 28; Skyscraper Symphony 28; The Battle of Paris • The Gay Lady 29; The Cocoanuts 29*; Eddie Cantor 29; Lillian Roth and Her Piano Boys 29; The Road Is Fine • La Route Est Belle 29; L'Amour Chante 30*; Le Blanc et le Noir 30*; Komm zu Mir zum Rendezvous 30; El Profesor de Mi

Mujer • El Profesor de Mi Señora 30; The Blue Moon Murder Case 32; Ex-Lady 32; Girl Missing 32; The Man Called Back 32; Murders in the Rue Morgue 32; Those We Love 32; Bedside 33; Hit Me Again • Smarty 33; The House on 56th Street 33; Registered Nurse 33; I Am a Thief 34; I Sell Anything 34; The Woman in Red 34; Casino de Paree • Casino de Paris • Go Into Your Dance 35*; Don't Bet on Blondes 35; The Florentine Dagger 35; Going Highbrow 35; The Pay-Off 35; The Preview Murder Mystery 35; Rose of the Rancho 35*; Ship Cafe 35; Forgotten Faces • Till We Meet Again 36; Hollywood Boulevard 36; Outcast 36; Czar of the Slot Machines • King of Gamblers • The King of the Gamblers 37; Daughter of Shanghai • Daughter of the Orient 37; Disbarred 37; King of Alcatraz • King of the Alcatraz 37; Mountain Music 37; This Way Please 37; Dangerous to Know 38; Hotel Imperial 38; Death of a Champion 39; The Magnificent Fraud 39; Parole Fixer 39; Women Without Names 39; The Face Behind the Mask 40; Meet Boston Blackie 40; Dangerously They Live 41; Lady Gangster 41; Two in a Taxi 41; The Desert Song 42; Bomber's Moon 43*; The Last Gangster • Roger Touhy, Gangster 43; The Man from Frisco 43; Escape in the Desert 44*; God Is My Co-Pilot 44; The Beast with Five Fingers 45; Danger Signal 45; Tarzan and the Mermaids 47; Outpost in Morocco 48; Rogues' Regiment 48; The Crooked Way 49; Johnny One-Eye 49; The Gangster We Made • The Vicious Years 50

Florio, Aldo I Cinque della Vendetta • Five Giants from Texas 66; Anda Muchacho, Spara • Dead Men Ride • Il Sole Sotta Terra 71

Florio, Maria Broken Rainbow 85*

Flothow, Rudolph Lucky Boy 29*

Floyd, Calvin Terror of Frankenstein • Victor Frankenstein 75; L'Auberge du Dragon Volant • The Inn of the Flying Dragon • Ondskans Värdshus • The Sleep of Death 81

Flynn, Emmett J. The Married Virgin 18; A Bachelor's Wife 19; The Bondage of Barbara 19; Eastward Ho! 19; The Lincoln Highwayman 19; Racing Strain 19; Virtuous Sinners 19; Yvonne from Paris 19; Leave It to Me 20; The Man Who Dared 20; Shod with Fire 20; Untamed 20; The Valley of Tomorrow 20; A Connecticut Yankee at King Arthur's Court 21; The Last Trail 21; Shame 21; A Fool There Was 22; Monte Cristo 22; Without Compromise 22; Hell's Hole 23; In the Palace of the King 23; Gerald Cranston's Lady 24; The Man Who Came Back 24; Nellie the Beautiful Cloak Model 24; The Dancers 25; East Lynne 25; Wings of Youth 25; The Palace of Pleasure 26; The Yankee Señor 26; Yellow Fingers 26; Married Alive 27; Early to Bed 28; Hold Your Man 29; The Shannons of Broadway 29; The Veiled Woman 29

Flynn, Errol Cruise of the Zaca 46

Flynn, John The Sergeant 68; The Jerusalem File 71; The Good Guys Always Win • The Outfit 73; Rolling Thunder 77; Defiance 79; Marilyn: The Untold Story 80*; Touched 83; Best Seller 87; Lock Up 89

Flynn, Ray Blood Will Tell 27

Foam, John see Bava, Mario

Foernbacher, Helmut see Förnbacher, Helmut

Fogelman, Yuri Before It's Too Late 57*

Fogwell, Reginald The Warning 28; The Imposter 29; Outlawed 29; Crossroads 30; Guilt 30; Madame Guillotine 31; The Written Law 31; Betrayal 32; The Wonderful Story 32; Murder at the Cabaret 34

Foldes, Joan Animated Genesis 52*

Foldes, Lawrence Don't Go Near the Park 81; The Great Skycopter Rescue 82; Young Warriors 83; Night Fighters • Nightforce 86

Foldes, Peter Animated Genesis 52*

Foleg, Peter The Unseen 80

Foley, James Reckless 84; At Close Range 86; Who's That Girl? 87; After Dark, My Sweet 90

Follett, F. M. Mr. Fuller Pep Breaks for the Beach 16; Mr. Fuller Pep Dabbles in the Pond 16; Mr. Fuller Pep Tries Mesmerism 16; Billy Sunday's Tabernacle 17; Help Wanted 17; The Mexican Crisis 17; Mr. Fuller Pep: An Old Bird Pays Him a Visit • An Old Bird Pays Him a Visit 17; Mr. Fuller Pep Celebrates His Wedding Anniversary 17; Mr. Fuller Pep Does Some Quick Moving 17; Mr. Fuller Pep Goes to the Country 17; Mr. Fuller Pep's Day of Rest 17; Mr. Fuller Pep's Wife Goes for a Rest 17; Quacky Doodles As the Early Bird 17; Quacky Doodles' Food Crisis 17; Quacky Doodles' Picnic 17; Quacky Doodles Signs the Pledge 17; Quacky Doodles Soldiering for Fair 17; Quacky Doodles the Cheater 17

Fomenko, Pyotr Poezdki na Starom Automobile • Rides on an Old Car 87

Fonda, Jane Introduction to the Enemy 74*

Fonda, Peter The Hired Hand 71; Idaho Transfer 73; Wanda Nevada 79

Fondato, Marcello Certain, Very Certain, As a Matter of Fact...Probable 70; ...Altrimenti Ci Arrabbiamo • Watch Out, We're Mad 74; A Mezzanotte Va la Ronda del Piacere • Midnight Pleasures 75; Charleston 78; The Immortal Bachelor 79

Fong, Allen Father and Son • Fuzi Qing 81; Ah Ying 84; Aiqing Qianfeng Xunhao • Just Like the Weather • Meiguo Xin • Tempest 86; Dancing Bull 90

Fong, Yuk-ping see Fong, Allen

Fong, Yu-ping see Fong, Allen

Fons, Jorge Jory 72

Fonseca, José see Fonseca e Costa, José

Fonseca, Lew The Ninth Inning 42

Fonseca e Costa, José A Balada da Praia dos Cães • The Ballad of Dogs' Beach • Dogs' Beach • La Playa de los Perros 86; A Mulher do Próximo • Thy Neighbor's Wife • Your Neighbor's Wife 89

Fontaine, André Notre Paris 61*; Les

Contes Zaghaura 66*

Fontaine, Richard Happy Birthday Davy • I Am Curious Gay 70; The Sins of Rachel 75; I Heard It Through the Grape Vine 82*

Forbes, Bryan Whistle Down the Wind 61; The L-Shaped Room 62; Séance on a Wet Afternoon 63; Of Human Bondage 64*; King Rat 65; The Whisperers 66; The Wrong Box 66; Deadfall 67; The Madwoman of Chaillot 69*; Long Ago Tomorrow • The Raging Moon 70; I Am a Dancer 72*; Juggernaut 74*; The Stepford Wives 74; The Slipper and the Rose • The Slipper and the Rose—The Story of Cinderella • The Story of Cinderella 76; International Velvet 78; Sunday Lovers 80*; Better Late Than Never • Ménage à Trois 82 The Naked Face 83; The Endless Game 89

Force, Lewis J. Night After Night • Night After Night After Night 69

Forcier, Marc-André Kalamazoo 88

Ford, Aleksander At Dawn • Nad Ranem 28; Łódź—The Polish Manchester • Tetno Polskiego Manchesteru 28; The Mascot • Mascotte 30; Narodziny Gazety 31; Legion of the Street • Legion of the Streets • Legion Ulicy • The Street Legion • Ulica 32; Cactus • Chalutzim • Sabra 33; The Awakening • Probuzeni • Przebudzenie 34*; Forward, Co-Operation • Na Start 35*; Grandmother Had No Worries 35*; Children Must Laugh • Droga Młodych • Mir Kumen An • The Road for Youth • Street of the Young • Youth's Journey 36; Społem 36; Ludzie Wisły • People of the Vistula • The Vistula People 37*; Battle of Leningrad • Bitwa pod Leninem • Bitwa pod Lenino 43; Przysiegam u Ziemi Polskiej 43*; Maidanek • Majdanek • Majdanek, Cmentarzysko Europy • Majdanek, Extermination Camp 44*; The Battle of Kolberg • The Battle of Kolobrzeg • Bitwa o Kołobrzeg 45*; Border Street • That Others May Live • Ulica Graniczna 48; Młodość Chopina • Young Chopin • The Youth of Chopin 52; Five Boys from Barska Street • Five Boys of Barska Street • Five from Barska Street • Piatka z Ulicy Barskiej 53; Der Achte Wochentag • The Eighth Day of the Week • Ósmy Dzień Tygodnia 57; Black Cross • Knights of the Black Cross • Knights of the Teutonic Order • Krzyżacy 60; The First Day of Freedom • Pierwszy Dzień Wolności 64; Angeklagt nach Paragraph 218 • Der Arzt Stellt Fest • The Doctor Says • The Doctor Speaks Out • The Right to Be Born 66; Good Morning, Poland 69; The First Circle • Den Første Kreds 72; The Martyr • Der Märtyrer • Sie Sind Frei, Doktor Korczak! 73

Ford, Charles E. Jacaré 42

Ford, Dennis Il Suo Nome Era Pot... Ma...lo Chiamavano Allegria 71

Ford, Derek A Promise of Bed • This, That and the Other 69; Groupie Girl • I Am a Groupie 70; The Swappers • The Wife Swappers 70; Suburban Wives 71;

Secret Rites 72; Commuter Husbands • Sex Games 73; Keep It Up Jack! 74; Diary of a Space Virgin • The Girl from Starship Venus • The Sexplorer 75; Sex Express 75; What's Up Nurse? 77; What's Up Superdoc? 78; Riding High 81

Ford, Francis The Army Surgeon 12; The Invaders 12*; The Favorite Son 13; When Lincoln Paid 13; Wynona's Vengeance 13; Lucille Love, the Girl of Mystery 14; The Mysterious Rose 14; Phantom of the Violin 14; Washington at Valley Forge 14*; And They Called Him Hero 15; The Broken Coin 15; The Campbells Are Coming 15; The Doorway of Destruction 15; The Hidden City 15; Three Bad Men and a Girl 15; The Adventures of Peg o' the Ring 16*; The Bandit's Wager 16; Chicken-Hearted Jim 16; The Lumber Yard Gang 16; In Treason's Grasp 17; John Ermine of Yellowstone 17; The Mystery Ship 17*; The Purple Mask 17; The Trail of Hate 17*; Who Was the Other Man? 17; The Avenging Trail 18; Berlin via America 18; The Craving • Delirium 18*; The Isle of Intrigue 18; The Crimson Shoals 19; The Mystery of Thirteen 19; The Silent Mystery 19; A Man from Nowhere 20; Cyclone Bliss 21; I Am the Woman 21; The Stampede 21; Angel Citizens 22; Cross Roads 22; Gold Grabbers 22; The Heart of Lincoln 22; The Man Getter • Trail's End 22; So This Is Arizona 22; Storm Girl 22; They're Off 22; Thundering Hoofs 22; The Cowboy Prince 24; Cupid's Rustler 24; The Diamond Bandit 24; The Lash of Pinto Pete 24; Lash of the Whip 24; Midnight Shadows 24; Range Blood 24; A Rodeo Mixup 24; Western Feuds 24; Western Yesterdays 24; The Four from Nowhere 25; False Friends 26; The Ghetto Shamrock 26; Her Own Story 26; Melodies 26; Officer 444 26*; The Winking Idol 26; Wolf's Trail 27; Wolves of the Air 7; Call of the Heart 28

Ford, Greg Daffy Duck's Quackbusters 88*

Ford, Hugh The Prisoner of Zenda 13*; The Crucible 14*; Monsieur Beaucaire 14*; Such a Little Queen 14*; Bella Donna 15*; The Eternal City 15*; Gretna Green 15*; Jim the Penman 15; Lydia Gilmore 15*; Poor Schmaltz 15; The Prince and the Pauper 15*; Sold 15*; When We Were Twenty-One 15*; Zaza 15*; The Slave Market 16; A Woman in the Case 16; Sappho 17; Seven Keys to Baldpate 17; Sleeping Fires 17; The Danger Mark 18; Mrs. Dane's Defense 18; In Mizzoura 19; Mrs. Wiggs of the Cabbage Patch 19; Secret Service 19; The Woman Thou Gavest Me 19; The Call of Youth 20; Civilian Clothes 20; The Great Day 20; His House in Order 20; Lady Rose's Daughter 20; The Price of Possession 21

Ford, Jack see Ford, John

Ford, John Bucking Broadway 17; Cheyenne's Pal 17; A Marked Man 17; The Scrapper 17; The Secret Man 17; The Soul Herder 17; Straight Shooting 17; The Tor-

nado 17; The Trail of Hate 17*; The Craving • Delirium 18*; Hell Bent 18; Hill Billy • The Scarlet Drop 18; The Phantom Riders 18; Thieves' Gold 18; Three Mounted Men 18; Wild Women 18; A Woman's Fool 18; The Ace of the Saddle 19; Bare Fists 19; By Indian Post • By Indian Posts 19; A Fight for Love 19; The Fighting Brothers 19; Gun Law 19; The Gun Packer • The Gun Pusher 19; A Gunfightin' Gentleman 19; The Last Outlaw 19; Marked Men 19; The Outcasts of Poker Flat 19; The Rider of the Law 19; Riders of Vengeance 19; Roped 19; The Rustlers 19; The Big Punch 20; The Girl in Number 29 20; Hitchin' Posts 20; Just Pals 20; The Prince of Avenue A 20; Action 21; Desperate Trails 21; The Freeze Out 21; Jackie 21; Sure Fire 21; The Wallop 21; The Face on the Barroom Floor • The Love Image 22; Little Miss Smiles 22; Silver Wings 22*; The Village Blacksmith 22; Cameo Kirby 23; Hoodman Blind 23; North of Hudson Bay • North of the Yukon 23; Three Jumps Ahead 23; Hearts of Oak 24; The Iron Horse 24; The Fighting Heart • Once to Every Man 25; Kentucky Pride 25; Lightnin' 25; Thank You 25; The Blue Eagle 26; The Shamrock Handicap 26; Three Bad Men 26; Footlight Glamour • Upstream 27; Mother Machree 27; Four Sons 28; Hangman's House 28; Napoleon's Barber 28; Riley the Cop 28; The Black Watch • King of the Khyber Rifles 29*; Men Without Women 29*; Salute 29*; Strong Boy 29; Born Reckless 30*; Up the River 30*; Arrowsmith 31; The Brat 31; Flesh 31; The Seas Beneath 31; Air Mail 32; Doctor Bull 33; Pilgrimage 33*; Judge Priest 34; The Lost Patrol 34; Passport to Fame • The Whole Town's Talking 34; The World Moves On 34; The Informer 35; Steamboat 'Round the Bend 35; Mary of Scotland 36; The Plough and the Stars 36; The Prisoner of Shark Island 36; The Hurricane 37*; Wee Willie Winkie 37; The Adventures of Marco Polo 38*; Four Men and a Prayer 38; Submarine Patrol 38; Drums Along the Mohawk 39; Stagecoach 39; Young Mr. Lincoln 39; The Grapes of Wrath 40; The Long Voyage Home 40; How Green Was My Valley 41; Sex Hygiene 41; Tobacco Road 41; The Battle of Midway 42; December 7th • December 7th: The Movie 42*; How to Operate Behind Enemy Lines 42; Torpedo Squadron 42; We Sail at Midnight 43; They Were Expendable 45*; My Darling Clementine 46; The Fugitive 47; Fort Apache 48*; Three Godfathers 48; Pinky 49*; She Wore a Yellow Ribbon 49; Rio Grande 50; Wagonmaster 50; When Willie Comes Marching Home 50; This Is Korea! 51; The Quiet Man 52; What Price Glory? 52; Mogambo 53; The Sun Shines Bright 53; Mister Roberts 54*; The Long Gray Line 55; The Red, White and Blue Line 55; The Searchers 56; The Wings of Eagles 56; The Growler Story 57; The Rising of the Moon 57; Gideon of Scotland Yard •

Gideon's Day 58; The Last Hurrah 58; So Alone 58; The Horse Soldiers 59; Korea 59; Sergeant Rutledge • The Trial of Sergeant Rutledge 60; The Man Who Shot Liberty Valance 61; Two Rode Together 61; How the West Was Won 62*; Donovan's Reef 63; Cheyenne Autumn 64; Young Cassidy 64*; Seven Women 65; Chesty • Chesty—A Tribute to a Legend 70

Ford, Philip The Tiger Woman 45; Crime of the Century 46; The Inner Circle 46; Invisible Informer 46; The Last Crooked Mile 46; The Mysterious Mr. Valentine 46; Valley of the Zombies 46; Bandits of Dark Canyon 47; The Web of Danger 47; The Wild Frontier 47; Angel in Exile 48*; The Bold Frontiersman 48; California Firebrand 48; The Denver Kid 48; Desperadoes of Dodge City 48; Marshal of Amarillo 48; The Timber Trail 48; Train to Alcatraz 48; Hideout 49; Law of the Golden West 49; Outcasts of the Trail 49; Pioneer Marshal 49; Powder River Rustlers 49; Prince of the Plains 49; Ranger of Cherokee Strip • Rangers of Cherokee Strip 49; San Antone Ambush 49; South of Rio 49; The Wyoming Bandit 49; The Old Frontier 50; Prisoners in Petticoats 50; Redwood Forest Trail 50; Trial Without Jury 50; The Vanishing Westerner 50; Buckaroo Sheriff of Texas 51; The Dakota Kid 51; Missing Women 51; Pride of Maryland 51; Rodeo King and the Señorita 51; Utah Wagon Train 51; Wells Fargo Gunmster 51; Bal Tabarin 52; Desperadoes' Outpost 52; Beware of the Dog 64

Ford, Steve The Dungeonmaster 85*

Ford, Terence see Sato, Hajime

Ford, Wesley Her Forgotten Past 33; Secret Sinners 33; Twenty Dollars a Week 35

Forde, Eugene Daredevil's Reward • Five Thousand Dollar Reward 28; Hello Cheyenne 28; Painted Post 28; Son of the Golden West 28; The Big Diamond Robbery 29; Outlawed 29; Smoky 33; Charlie Chan in London 34; Charlie Chan's Courage 34*; The Great Hotel Murder • The Great Hotel Mystery 34; Mystery Woman 34; Your Uncle Dudley 35*; The Country Beyond 36; Thirty-Six Hours to Kill • Thirty-Six Hours to Live 36; Charlie Chan on Broadway 37; The Lady Escapes 37; Midnight Taxi 37; Step Lively Jeeves! 37; Charlie Chan at Monte Carlo 38; International Settlement 38; Meet the Girls 38; One Wild Night 38; The Honeymoon's Over 39; Inspector Hornleigh 39; Charlie Chan's Murder Cruise 40; Charter Pilot 40; Michael Shayne, Private Detective 40; Pier 13 40; Buy Me That Town 41; Dressed to Kill 41; Man at Large 41; Sleepers West 41; Berlin Correspondent 42; Right to the Heart 42; Crime Doctor's Strangest Case • The Strangest Case 43; Shadows in the Night 44; Backlash 47; The Crimson Key 47; TheInvisible Wall 47; Jewels of Brandenburg 47

Forde, Walter The Handy Man 20; Never Say Die 20; Walter Makes a Move

22*; Walter Wants Work 22*; Walter Wins a Wager 22*; Walter's Trying Frolic 22*; Wait and See 28; What Next? 28; The Silent House 29; Would You Believe It! 29; Bed and Breakfast 30; The Last Hour 30; Lord Richard in the Pantry 30; Red Pearls 30; You'd Be Surprised! 30; The Gaunt Stranger • The Ringer 31; The Ghost Train 31; Splinters in the Navy 31; Third Time Lucky 31; Condemned to Death 32; Jack's the Boy • Night and Day 32; Lord Babs 32; Rome Express 32; Orders Is Orders 33; Alias Bulldog Drummond • Bulldog Jack 34; Chu Chin Chow 34; Jack Ahoy! 34; Born for Glory • Brown on Resolution • Forever England • Torpedo Raider 35*; King of the Damned 35; Forbidden Music • Land Without Music 36; The Gaunt Stranger • The Phantom Strikes 38; Kicking the Moon Around • Millionaire Merry-Go-Round • The Playboy 38; Cheer, Boys, Cheer 39; The Four Just Men • The Secret Four 39; Inspector Hornleigh on Holiday 39; Let's Be Famous 39; Charley's Big-Hearted Aunt 40; Gasbags 40*; Inspector Hornleigh Goes To It • Mail Train 40; Neutral Port 40*; Sailors Three • Three Cockeyed Sailors 40; Saloon Bar 40; Atlantic Ferry • Sons of the Sea 41; The Ghost Train 41; Flying Fortress 42; Go to Blazes 42; It's That Man Again 42; The Peterville Diamond 42; One Exciting Night • You Can't Do Without Love 44; Time Flies 44; Master of Bankdam 47; Cardboard Cavalier 49; Ali Baba Nights 53

Forder, Timothy Indian Summer 87
Fordson, J. W. *see Costa, Mario*
Fordson, John W. *see Costa, Mario*
Foreman, Carl The Victors 63
Foreman, Richard Strong Medicine 79
Foriadis, Aris And Two Eggs from Turkey • Ke Dyo Avga Tourkias 87
Forlong, Michael Suicide Mission 56; The Green Helmet 61; Over the Odds 61; Stork Talk 61; Lionheart 68; Raising the Roof 71; Rangi's Catch 73; Hijack 75; High Rise Donkey 80
Forman, Miloš Audition • Competition • Konkurs • Talent Competition 63; Black Peter • Černý Petr • Peter and Pavla 63; If There Was No Music • Kdyby Ty Muziky Nebyly 63; A Blonde in Love • Láska Jedné Plavovlásky • Loves of a Blonde 65; Dobře Placená Procházka • A Well Paid Stroll 65; Fire! Fire! • The Fireman's Ball • Hoří, Má Panenko • Like a House on Fire 67; Taking Off 70; Olympic Visions • Visions of Eight 72*; One Flew Over the Cuckoo's Nest 75; Hair 79; Ragtime 81; Amadeus 83; Valmont 89
Forman, Tom The Ladder of Lies 20; The Sins of Rozanne 20; Cappy Ricks 21; The City of Silent Men 21; The Easy Road 21; A Prince There Was 21; White and Unmarried 21; If You Believe It, It's So 22; Shadows 22; White Shoulders 22; The Woman Conquers 22; April Showers 23; Are You a Failure? 23; The Broken Wing 23; The Girl Who Came Back 23; Money! Money! Money! 23; The Virginian 23; The

Fighting American 24; The Flaming Forties 24*; Roaring Rails 24; The Crimson Runner 25; Flattery 25; The Midnight Flyer 25; Off the Highway 25; The People vs. Nancy Preston 25; Devil's Dice 26; Whispering Canyon 26
Förnbacher, Helmut Beiss Mich, Liebling • Bite Me, Darling 70
Forque, José María Last Romance • Romanza Final 87
Forsberg, Lars Jänken • The Yankee 70
Forsch, Gerd Roman Dann Ist Nichts Mehr Wie Vorher • Then Nothing Was the Same Anymore 87
Forslund, Bengt The Air Cage 72
Forst, Willi Leise Flehen Meine Lieder • Lover Divine • The Unfinished Symphony 33*; Maskerade • Masquerade in Vienna 34; Mazurka 35; Allotria 36; Burgtheater • Vienna Burgtheater 36; Serenade 37; Bel Ami • Der Liebling Schöner Frauen 39; Ich Bin Sebastian Otto 39*; Operetta • Operette 40; Wiener Blut 42; Frauen Sind Keine Engel 43; Wiener Mädeln 45; The Sinner • Die Sünderin 50; Es Geschehen Noch Wunder 51; Im Weissen Rössl • The White Horse Inn 52; Cabaret • Dieses Lied Bleibt bei Dir 54; Kaiserjäger 56 Die Unentschuldigte Stunde 57; Wien, Du Stadt Meiner Träume 57
Forster, Robert Harry's Machine • Hollywood Harry 85
Forsyth, Bill The Odd Man 78; That Sinking Feeling 79; Gregory's Girl 80; Local Hero 83; Comfort and Joy 84; Housekeeping 87; Breaking In 89
Forsyth, Ed I'm Going to Get You...Elliot Boy 71; Superchick 73; Anderson's Angels • Chesty Anderson, USN • Chesty Anderson, US Navy 76; On Any Sunday II 81*
Fortuny, Juan Las Ratas No Duermen de Noche 74; El Pobre Drácula 76
Forzano, Andrea *see Losey, Joseph*
Forzano, Giovacchino Man of Courage 34; One Hundred Days of Napoleon 36; The Father of His Country • Il Padre delle Patria 38
Fosco, Piero *see Pastrone, Giovanni*
Foss, Kenelm A Peep Behind the Scenes 18*; Fancy Dress 19; I Will 19*; A Little Bit of Fluff 19; A Bachelor Husband 20; The Breed of the Treshams 20; The Glad Eye 20; All Roads Lead to Calvary 21; Cherry Ripe 21; The Double Event 21; The Headmaster 21; Number 5 John Street 21; The Street of Adventure 21; The Wonderful Year 21; Dicky Monteith 22; The House of Peril 22; A Romance of Old Bagdad 22
Fosse, Bob Sweet Charity 68; Cabaret 72; Lenny 74; All That Jazz 79; Star 80 83
Foster, Bob Remember Me This Way 74*
Foster, Charlie Ape Man of the Jungle 62
Foster, Giles The Aerodrome 83; Silas Marner 85; Consuming Passions 88; Innocent Victim • The Tree of Hands 90
Foster, Harry Keep It Cool • Let's Rock!

58
Foster, Harve The Fabulous Joe 46*; Song of the South 46*
Foster, John Carnival Week 27; A Day Off 28; Dinner Time 28; The Early Bird 28; Everybody's Flying 28; The Flying Age 28; Jungle Days 28; Sunday on the Farm 28; By Land and Air 29; The Farmer's Goat 29; Fruitful Farm 29; Wooden Money 29
Foster, Lewis R. Double Whoopee 28; Angora Love 29; The Bacon Grabbers 29; Berth Marks 29; Hotter Than Hot 29; Loud Soup 29; Men o' War 29; Movie Night 29; Unaccustomed As We Are 29; Broken Wedding Bells 30; Cash and Marry 30; Dizzy Dates 30; A Fall to Arms 30; Knights Before Xmas 30; The Land of the Sky Blue Daughters 30; Man Without Skirts 30; Pure and Simple 30; The Setting Son 30; The Sleeping Cutie 30; Too Hot to Handle 30; Blondes Prefer Bonds 31; Dumbbells in Derbies 31; Eventually But Not Now 31; The Itching Hour 31; Lime Juice Nights 31; Second Hand Kisses 31; Love Letters of a Star 36*; Armored Car 37; The Man Who Cried Wolf 37; She's Dangerous 37*; The Lucky Stiff 48; Captain China 49; El Paso 49; Manhandled 49; The Eagle and the Hawk • Spread Eagle 50; Bombs Over China • Hong Kong 51; Crosswinds • Jungle Attack 51; High Venture • Passage West 51; The Last Outpost 51; Tropic Zone 52; Jamaica Run 53; Those Redheads from Seattle 53; Crashout 55; Top of the World 55; The Bold and the Brave 56; Dakota Incident 56; A Horse Named Comanche • Tonka 58; The Sign of Zorro 60*
Foster, Norman I Cover Chinatown 36; Fair Warning 37; Think Fast, Mr. Moto 37; Mr. Moto Takes a Chance 38; Mr. Moto Takes a Vacation 38; Mysterious Mr. Moto • Mysterious Mr. Moto of Devil's Island 38; Thank You, Mr. Moto 38; Walking Down Broadway 38; Charlie Chan at Treasure Island 39; Charlie Chan in Reno 39; Mr. Moto's Last Warning 39; Charlie Chan in Panama 40; Viva Cisco Kid 40; Ride, Kelly, Ride 41; Scotland Yard 41; Journey Into Fear 42*; Santa 43; La Fuga 44; Hora de la Verdad 44; El Ahijado de la Muerte 45; El Canto de la Sireno • Song of the Siren 46; Blood on My Hands • Kiss the Blood Off My Hands 48; Rachel and the Stranger 48; Tell It to the Judge 49; Father Is a Bachelor 50*; Woman on the Run 50; Navajo 51; Sky Full of Moon 52; Sombrero 52; Davy Crockett—King of the Wild Frontier 54; Davy Crockett and the River Pirates 55; The Nine Lives of Elfego Baca 59; The Sign of Zorro 60*; Indian Paint 64; Brighty • Brighty of the Grand Canyon 67
Fou, Sen The Light of Thousands of Families 47; Humanity's Hope 48
Fouad, Ahmed Al Kettar • The Train 86
Foucaud, Pierre The Infiltrator 55
Foulsham, Fraser The River House

Mystery 35; The Strange Case of Mr. Todmorden 35*; The Sky Raiders 38

Fournier, Claude Normetal 59*; La France sur un Caillou 60*; The Fight • La Lutte • Wrestling 61*; Alien Thunder • Dan Candy's Law 73; Les Tisserands du Pouvoir 88

Fowler, Gene, Jr. I Was a Teenage Werewolf 57; Gang War 58; I Married a Monster from Outer Space 58; Showdown at Boot Hill 58; Beatsville • The Rebel Set 59; Here Come the Jets 59; The Oregon Trail 59

Fowler, Robert Below the Belt 80

Fowley, Douglas Macumba Love 60

Fox, Finis Man's Law and God's 22; Bag and Baggage 23; The Bishop of the Ozarks 23; The Man Between 23; Tipped Off 23; A Woman Who Sinned 25; Dangerous Friends 26

Fox, Ted Toilers of the Sea 36*

Fox, Wallace The Bandit's Son 27; The Avenging Rider 28; Breed of the Sunsets 28; Driftin' Sands 28; Man in the Rough 28; The Riding Renegade 28; The Trail of Courage 28; The Amazing Vagabond 29; Come and Get It 29; Laughing at Death 29; Partners of the Trail 31; The Cannonball Express 32; Devil on Deck 32; Red Morning 34; Powdersmoke Range 35; Yellow Dust 36; Racing Lady 37; Gun Packer 38; The Mexicali Kid 38; Pride of the Plains 40; Bowery Blitzkrieg • Stand and Deliver 41; Bowery at Midnight 42; Bullets for Bandits 42; The Case of the Missing Brides • The Corpse Vanishes 42; The Devil's Price • The Lone Star Vigilantes 42; Let's Get Tough! • Little MacArthurs 42; 'Neath Brooklyn Bridge 42; Smart Alecks 42; The Ghost Rider 43; The Girl from Monterey 43; Kid Dynamite • Little Mobsters • Queen of Broadway 43; Outlaws of Stampede Pass 43; Block Busters 44; Career Girl 44; The Great Mike 44; Men on Her Mind 44; Mile a Minute • Riders of the Santa Fe 44; Million Dollar Kid 44; Song of the Range 44; Bad Men of the Border 45; Bowery Boys • Docks of New York 45; Brenda Starr, Reporter 45; Code of the Lawless • The Mysterious Stranger 45; Mr. Muggs Rides Again 45; Pillow of Death 45; Trail to Vengeance • Vengeance 45; Gun Town 46; Gunman's Code 46; The Lawless Breed • Lawless Clan 46; Rustler's Hideout • Rustler's Roundup 46; Wild Beauty 46; Jack Armstrong 47; The Vigilante 47; The Valiant Hombre 48; The Daring Caballero 49; The Gay Amigo 49; Western Renegades 49; Arizona Territory 50; Fence Riders 50; Gunslingers 50; Massacre Valley • Outlaw Gold 50; Over the Border 50; Silver Raiders 50; Six Gun Mesa 50; West of Wyoming 50; Blazing Bullets • Gold Bullets 51; Montana Desperado 51; Ramar of the Jungle • The White Goddess 53

Foy, Bryan The Home Towners 28; Lights of New York 28; Queen of the Night Clubs 29; The Royal Box 29; The Gorilla 30; Elysia 33

Fracassi, Clemente Barefoot Savage • Sensualita 52; Aida 53; Andrea Chenier 55

Fraga, Jorge Escambray 61*

Fragoso Montoya, Jesús A Bird in the Hand Is Worth... • Más Vale Pájaro en Mano... 87

Fraker, William A. Monte Walsh 70; Autumn Child • Labyrinth • A Reflection of Fear 71; The Legend of the Lone Ranger 81

Frame, Park The Gray Wolf's Ghost • Maruja 19*; The Man Who Turned White 19; The Mints of Hell 19; The Pagan God 19; Forgotten Woman 21; Looped for Life 24; Drug Store Cowboy 25

Frampton, Hollis Information 66; Manual of Arms 66; Process Red 66; Heterodyne 67; States 67; Maxwell's Demon 68; Snowblind 68; Surface Tension 68; Artificial Light 69; Carrots & Peas 69; Lemon (For Robert Huot) 69; Palindrome 69; Prince Rupert's Drops 69; Works and Days 69; Zorn's Lemma 70; Hapax Legomena I: Nostalgia 71; Hapax Legomena II: Poetic Justice 71; Hapax Legomena III: Critical Mass 71; Hapax Legomena IV: Travelling Matte 71; Hapax Legomena V: Ordinary Matter 72; Hapax Legoena VI: Remote Control 72; Hapax Legomena VII: Special Effects 72

France, Charles H. The Natural Law 17

France, Floyd The Princess' Necklace 17; Putting the Bee in Herbert 17

Franchon, Leonard Cold Steel • The Trail to Red Dog 21; Cotton and Cattle 21; A Cowboy Ace 21; Flowing Gold 21; Out of the Clouds 21; The Range Pirate 21; Rustlers of the Night 21

Franciolini, Gianni Fari nella Nebria • Lighthouse in the Fog 41; Buon Giorno Elefante • Hello Elephant • Pardon My Trunk 52; The Bed • Il Letto • Secrets d'Alcôve 53*; It Happened in the Park 57; Femmes d'un Été • Love on the Riviera • Racconti d'Estate • Summer Tales 64

Franciosa, Massimo I Castrati • The Counter Tenors • Le Sexe des Anges • Undercover Rogue • Le Voci Bianche • White Voices 63*; Un Tentativo Sentimentale 63*

Francis, Coleman The Beast of Yucca Flats • Girl Madness 61; The Skydivers 63; Night Train to Mundo Fine 66

Francis, Freddie A Change of Heart • The Girl Swappers • 2 and 2 Make 6 61; The Brain • Over My Dead Body • Ein Toter Sucht Seiner Mörder • Vengeance 62; The Day of the Triffids 62*; Paranoiac 62; The Evil of Frankenstein 63; Here's the Knife Dear, Now Use It • Nightmare 63; The Blood Suckers • Dr. Terror's House of Horrors 64; Hysteria 64; The Psychopath • Schizoid 64; Traitor's Gate • Das Verrätertor 64; The Skull 65; The Deadly Bees 66; They Came from Beyond Space 66; Torture Garden 67; Dracula Has Risen from the Grave • Dracula's Revenge 68; The Intrepid Mr. Twigg 68; Girly • Mumsy, Nanny, Sonny & Girly 69; Gebissen Wird Nur Nachts • Happening der Vam-

pire • The Happening of the Vampire • The Vampire Happening 70; Trog 70; Tales from the Crypt 71; The Creeping Flesh 72; Craze • The Infernal Idol 73; Tales That Witness Madness 73; Count Downe • Son of Dracula • Young Dracula 74; The Ghoul • The Thing in the Attic 74; Legend of the Werewolf 74; Golden Rendezvous • Nuclear Terror 77*; The Doctor and the Devils 85; Dark Tower 87

Francis, Karl The Mouse and the Woman 81; And Nothing But the Truth • Giro City 82; Yr Alcoholig Lion • The Happy Alcoholic 84; Boy Soldier • Milwr Bychan 86

Francisci, Pietro Escape Into Dreams 50; Anthony of Padua 52; The Queen of Sheba 53; Attila • Attila, Flagello di Dio • Attila the Hun 54; Le Fatiche di Ercole • Hercules 57; Roland the Mighty 58; Ercole e la Regina di Lidia • Hercules and the Queen of Lydia • Hercules Unchained 59; Saffo, Venere di Lesbo • Sapho • The Warrior Empress 60; Archimède • L'Assedio di Siracusa • Le Siège de Syracuse • The Siege of Syracuse 62; Ercole, Sfida e Sansone • Hercules, Samson and Ulysses 64; 2 + 5: Missione Hydra • Star Pilot 66

Franck, Jess see Franco, Jesús

Franco, Jess see Franco, Jesús

Franco, Jesús The Awful Dr. Orloff • Cries in the Night • Gritos en la Noche • L'Horrible Dr. Orloff 61; Brides of Dr. Jekyll • Dr. Jekyll's Mistress • Dr. Orloff's Monster • Mistresses of Dr. Jekyll • The Secret of Dr. Orloff • El Secreto del Dr. Orloff 64; Dans les Griffes du Maniaque • The Diabolical Dr. Z • Miss Death • Miss Death and Dr. Z • Miss Muerte 65; Attack of the Robots • Cartes sur Table 67; Bésame Monstruo • Castle of the Doomed • Kiss Me Monster 67; Black Angel • Paroxismus • Può una Morta Rivivere per Amore? • Venus in Furs • Venuz im Pelz 67; The Case of the Two Beauties • El Caso de las Dos Bellezas • Red Lips • Rote Lippen • Sadiserótica 67; Geträumte Stunden • Necronomicón • Succubus 67; Against All Odds • The Blood of Fu Manchu • Fu Manchu and the Kiss of Death • Fu Manchu y el Beso de la Muerte • Kiss and Kill • Der Todeskuss des Dr. Fu Manchu 68; Assignment Istanbul • Il Castello di Fu Manchu • El Castillo de Fu Manchu • The Castle of Fu Manchu • Die Folterkammer des Dr. Fu Manchu • Fu Manchu's Castle 68; The Bloody Judge • Der Hexentöter von Blackmoor • El Juez Sangriento • Night of the Blood Monster • El Processo de las Brujas • Throne of the Blood Monster • The Trial of the Witches • Il Trono di Fuoco • The Witches' Trial • The Witchkiller of Blackmoor 69; Isle of Lost Women • Ninety-Nine Women 69; Justine • Marquis de Sade: Justine 69; Bram Stoker's Count Dracula • El Conde Drácula • Il Conte Dracula • Count Dracula • Dracula 71 • Nachts Wenn Dracula Erwacht • The Nights of Dracula 70; De Sade 70 • Eugenie—The Story of Her

Journey Into Perversion • Die Jungfrau und die Peitsche • Philosophy in the Boudoir 70; Die Erbin des Dracula • The Heritage of Dracula • Lesbian Vampires • The Sign of the Vampire • El Signo del Vampiro • Las Vampiras • Vampyros Lesbos 70; Future Women • Río 70 • River 70 • The Seven Secrets of Su-Maru • Die Sieben Männer der Su-Maru • Sumuru 70; Mrs. Hyde • Sie Tötete in Extase 70; Os De-mônios • Les Démons • The Demons • Les Démons du Sexe • The Sex Demons 72; Dracula Against Frankenstein • Drácula Contra el Dr. Frankenstein • Drácula Contra Frankenstein • Dracula, Prisonnier de Frankenstein • Dracula vs. Frankenstein • Satana Contra Dr. Exortio 72; Les Expériences Érotiques de Frankenstein • La Maldición de Frankenstein • La Malediction de Frankenstein 72; A Filha de Drácula • La Fille de Dracula 72; Lorna l' Exorciste • Les Possédées du Démon • Les Possédées du Diable 72; Les Avaleuses • La Comtesse aux Seins Nus • La Comtesse Noire • Jacula • The Last Thrill • Sicarius—The Midnight Party • Yacula 73; Beyond the Grave • Inceste • Inside a Dark Mirror • Le Miroir Obscène • El Otro Lado del Espejo • Outre-Tombe • Ultratumba 73; Les Chasses de la Comtesse Zaroff • La Comtesse Perverse • La Comtesse Zaroff • Les Croqueuses • The Evil Countess 73; How to Seduce a Virgin • Les Inassouvies n.2 • Plaisir à Trois 73; La Noche de los Asesinos 74; Frauengefängnis 75; Juliette la Fille au Sexe Brillant 75; Lèvres Rouges et Bottes Noires 75; Das Bildnis des Doriana Gray 76; Der Dirnenmörderer von London • Jack the Ripper 76; Die Liebesbriefe einer Portugiesischen Nonne 76; Frauen im Liebeslager 77; Die Teuflischen Schwestern 77; The Black Masses of Exorcism • L'Éventreur de Notre Dame • Exorcisme • Exorcisme et Messes Noires • The Ripper of Notre Dame • El Sádico de Notre Dame • La Sadique de Notre Dame 79; Mondo Cannibale 79; Il Cacciatore di Uomini • The Man Hunter 80; Gefangene Frauen 80; Sadomania 80; Bloody Moon • Die Säge des Todes 81; El Lago de las Vírgenes 81; Macumba Sexual 81; The Grave of the Living Dead • The Treasure of the Living Dead • Le Trésor des Morts Vivants • La Tumba de los Muertos Vivientes 82; La Mansión de los Muertos Vivientes 82; El Siniestro Dr. Orloff • The Sinister Dr. Orloff 82; The Fall of the House of Usher • El Hundimiento de la Casa Usher 83; El Tesoro de la Diosa Blanca • The Treasure of the White Goddess 83; Faceless • Les Prédateurs de la Nuit 88

Franco, Ricardo Gringo Mojado • In 'n' Out 84; Berlin Blues 88

Francovich, Allan On Company Business 79

Franju, Georges Le Métro 34*; The Blood of Animals • Blood of the Beasts • Le Sang des Bêtes 48; En Passant par la Lorraine • Passing by the Lorraine 50;

Hôtel des Invalides 51; Le Grand Méliès • The Great Méliès 52; Monsieur et Madame Curie 53; Dusts • Les Poussières 54; La Marine Marchande • Merchant Marine • Navigation Marchande 54; À Propos d'une Rivière • About a River • Au Fil d'une Rivière • Le Saumon Atlantique 55; Mon Chien • My Dog 55; The National Popular Theatre • Le T.N.P. • Le Théâtre National Populaire 56; On the Bridge at Avignon • Sur le Pont d'Avignon 56; Notre-Dame, Cathedral of Paris • Notre-Dame, Cathédrale de Paris 57; The First Night • La Première Nuit 58; The Keepers • La Tête Contre les Murs 58; Eyes Without a Face • The Horror Chamber of Dr. Faustus • Occhi Senza Volto • Les Yeux Sans Visage 59; Pleins Feux sur l'Assassin • Spotlight on Murder • Spotlight on the Killer 60; Thérèse • Thérèse Desqueyroux 62; Judex 63; Thomas l'Imposteur • Thomas the Imposter 64; Les Rideaux Blancs 65; The Demise of Father Mouret • La Faute de l'Abbé Mouret • The Sin of Abbé Mouret • The Sin of Father Mouret 70; L'Homme Sans Visage • The Man Without a Face • Nuits Rouges • Red Nights • Shadowman 73; Le Dernier Mélodrame 80

Frank, Astrid Red 76

Frank, Barbara Rising Target 76

Frank, Carol Sorority House Massacre 86

Frank, Charles The Inheritance • Uncle Silas 47; Disobedient • Intimate Relations 53; Johnny the Giant Killer 53*

Frank, Christopher Josepha 82; L'Année des Méduses • The Year of the Jellyfish 84; Femmes de Personne • Nobody's Women 84; Spiral • Spirale 87

Frank, Ernest L. Nagana 33; One Exciting Adventure 34

Frank, Hubert Warm Nights, Hot Pleasures 81

Frank, Jess see Franco, Jesús

Frank, Melvin The Reformer and the Redhead 49*; Callaway Went Thataway • The Star Said No! 51*; Strictly Dishonorable 51*; Above and Beyond 52*; Knock on Wood 54*; The Court Jester 55*; That Certain Feeling 56*; The Jayhawkers 59; Li'l Abner 59; The Facts of Life 60; Strange Bedfellows 64; Buona Sera, Mrs. Campbell 68; A Touch of Class 72; The Prisoner of Second Avenue 74; The Duchess and the Dirtwater Fox 76; Lost and Found 79; Bobo • Walk Like a Man 86

Frank, Robert Pull My Daisy 58*; Sin of Jesus 61; O.K. End Here 63; Me and My Brother 68; Conversations in Vermont 69; Life-Raft Earth 69; About Me: A Musical 71; CS Blues • Cocksucker Blues 72; Keep Busy 75; Energy and How to Get It 80; Life Dances On... 80; This Song for Jack 83; Candy Mountain 87*

Frank, T. C. see Laughlin, Tom

Franke, Anja Du Mich Auch • Same to You • So What? 87*

Frankel, Cyril Eagles of the Fleet 50; Explorers of the Depths 50; Wing to Wing 51; Man of Africa 53; The Nutcracker 53; Devil on Horseback 54; Make Me an Offer!

54; It's Great to Be Young! 55; No Time for Tears 57; Alive and Kicking 58; She Didn't Say No! 58; The Molester • Never Take Candy from a Stranger • Never Take Sweets from a Stranger 60; Scheidungsgrund: Liebe 60; Don't Bother to Knock • Why Bother to Knock? 61; On the Fiddle • Operation Snafu • Operation Warhead • War Head 61; The Very Edge 63; The Devil's Own • The Witches 66; The Trygon Factor 67; Permission to Kill 75; The Saint and the Brave Goose 81

Franken, Mannus Branding • The Breakers 28*; Rain • Regen 29*; Redding 29; De Trekschuit 32; Pareh, Song of the Rice 35; Tanah Sabrang 38; 'T Sal Waarachtig Wel Gaen • 'T Zal Waarachtig Wel Gaan 39

Frankenberg, Pia Brennende Betten 88

Frankenheimer, John The Young Stranger 56; All Fall Down 61; Birdman of Alcatraz 61; A Matter of Conviction • The Young Savages 61; The Manchurian Candidate 62; Seven Days in May 63; Le Train • The Train • Il Treno 64*; Grand Prix 66; Seconds 66; The Extraordinary Seaman 67; The Fixer 68; The Gypsy Moths 69; The Horsemen 70; I Walk the Line 70; The Iceman Cometh 73; Impossible Object • L' Impossible Objet • Story of a Love Story 73; Call Harry Crown • 99 and 44/100% Dead 74; The French Connection II 75; Black Sunday 76; Prophecy 79; The Challenge 81; Pursuit • The Pursuit of D. B. Cooper 81*; The Holcroft Covenant 85; 52 Pick-Up 86; Dead-Bang 88; The Fourth War 90

Franklin, Carl Nowhere to Run 89; Full Fathom Five 90

Franklin, Chester M. The Sheriff 14*; A Ten Cent Adventure 14*; The Ash Can, or Little Dick's First Adventure • Little Dick's First Adventure 15*; The Baby 15*; Dirty Face Dan 15*; The Dollhouse Mystery 15*; Her Filmland Hero 15*; The Kid Magicians 15*; Let Katie Do It 15*; The Little Cupids 15*; Little Dick's First Case 15*; Martha's Vindication • The Silence of Martha 15*; Pirates Bold 15*; The Rivals 15*; The Runaways 15*; The Straw Man 15*; The Children in the House 16*; Going Straight 16*; Gretchen, the Greenhorn 16*; The Little School Ma'am 16*; A Sister of Six 16*; Aladdin and the Wonderful Lamp 17*; Babes in the Woods 17*; Jack and the Beanstalk 17*; Treasure Island 17*; Ali Baba and the Forty Thieves 18*; Fan Fan 18*; The Girl with the Champagne Eyes 18*; You Never Can Tell 20; All Souls' Eve 21; The Case of Becky 21; A Private Scandal 21; The Game Chicken 22; Nancy from Nowhere 22; The Toll of the Sea 22; The Song of Love 23*; Where the North Begins 23; Behind the Curtain 24; The Silent Accuser 24; Wild Justice 25; The Thirteenth Hour 27; Detectives 28; File No. 113 • File 113 32; A Parisian Romance 32; The Stoker 32; Vanity Fair 32; The Iron Master 33; Malibu • Sequoia 34; Tough Guy 36

Franklin, Harry Kildare of Storm 18; The Successful Adventure 18; Sylvia on a Spree 18; The Winning of Beatrice 18; After His Own Heart 19; The Fourflusher 19; Full of Pep 19; In His Brother's Place 19; Johnny-on-the-Spot 19; That's Good 19; Alias Miss Dodd 20; Her Five-Foot Highness 20; Rouge and Riches 20; The Secret Gift 20

Franklin, Harry S. Red Snow 52*

Franklin, Howard Quick Change 90*

Franklin, Irwin R. Harlem Is Heaven 32

Franklin, Richard Belinda 72; Loveland 73; Dick Down Under • The True Story of Eskimo Nell 75; Fantasm 76; Patrick 78; Road Games 81; Psycho II 83; Cloak & Dagger 84; Link 86

Franklin, Sidney The Sheriff 14*; A Ten Cent Adventure 14*; The Ash Can, or Little Dick's First Adventure • Little Dick's First Adventure 15*; The Baby 15*; Dirty Face Dan 15*; The Dollhouse Mystery 15*; Her Filmland Hero 15*; The Kid Magicians 15*; Let Katie Do It 15*; The Little Cupids 15*; Little Dick's First Case 15*; Martha's Vindication • The Silence of Martha 15*; Pirates Bold 15*; The Rivals 15*; The Runaways 15*; The Straw Man 15*; The Children in the House 16*; Going Straight 16*; Gretchen, the Greenhorn 16*; The Little School Ma'am 16*; A Sister of Six 16*; Aladdin and the Wonderful Lamp 17*; Babes in the Woods 17*; Jack and the Beanstalk 17*; Treasure Island 17*; Ali Baba and the Forty Thieves 18*; The Bride of Fear 18; Confession 18; Fan Fan 18*; The Forbidden City 18; The Heart of Wetona 18; Her Only Way 18; The Safety Curtain 18; Six Shooter Andy 18; Heart o' the Hills 19; The Hoodlum • The Ragamuffin 19; The Probation Wife 19; Two Weeks 20; Unseen Forces 20; Courage 21; Not Guilty 21; East Is West 22; The Primitive Lover 22; Smilin' Through 22; Brass 23; Dulcy 23; Tiger Rose 23; Her Night of Romance 24; Her Sister from Paris 25; Learning to Love 25; Beverly of Graustark 26; The Duchess of Buffalo 26; Quality Street 27; The Actress • Trelawney of the Wells 28; Wild Orchids 28; Devil May Care 29; The Last of Mrs. Cheyney 29; The High Road • Lady of Scandal 30; Jenny Lind • A Lady's Morals 30; The Soul Kiss 30; The Guardsman 31; Private Lives 31; Smilin' Through 32; Reunion in Vienna 33; The Barretts of Wimpole Street • The Forbidden Alliance 34; The Dark Angel 35; The Good Earth 36*; Gone with the Wind 39*; Duel in the Sun 46*; The Barretts of Wimpole Street 56

Franklin, Sidney, Jr. Gun Battle at Monterey 57*

Franklin, Wendall James The Bus Is Coming 71

Franz, Joseph Bare-Fisted Gallagher 19; The Blue Bandanna 19; Dangerous Waters 19; The Gray Wolf's Ghost • Maruja 19*; A Sagebrush Hamlet 19; The Broadway Cowboy 20; The Cave Girl 21; Fightin' Mad 21; The Parish Priest 21; The Love

Gambler 22; The New Teacher 22; Smiling Jim 22; Tracks 22; Youth Must Have Love 22; Alias the Night Wind 23; Stepping Fast 23; Horseshoe Luck 24; The Pell Street Mystery 24; Blue Blazes 26; The Desperate Game 26

Fraser, Christopher Coast of Terror • Summer City 76

Fraser, George The Hurricane • Voice of the Hurricane 64

Fraser, Harry Oil and Romance 25; Queen of Spades 25; West of the Mojave 25; The Fighting Gob 26; General Custer at Little Big Horn • With General Custer at Little Big Horn 26; Sheep Trail 26; The Wildcat 26; Little Big Horn 27; Land of Wanted Men 31; The Montana Kid 31; Oklahoma Jim 31; The Blood Brother • Texas Pioneers 32; Broadway to Cheyenne • From Broadway to Cheyenne 32; The Diamond Trail 32; Ghost City 32; Honor of the Mounted 32; Law of the North 32; The Man from Arizona 32; Mason of the Mounted 32; The Reckoning 32; The Savage Girl 32; Vanishing Men 32; The Fighting Parson 33; The Fugitive 33; Rainbow Ranch 33; The Wolf Dog 33*; Fighting Through 34; 'Neath Arizona Skies • 'Neath the Arizona Skies 34; Randy Rides Alone 34; Fighting Pioneers 35; Gunfire 35; The Last of the Clintons 35; The Reckless Buckaroo 35; Rustler's Paradise 35; Saddle Aces 35; The Tonto Kid 35; Wagon Trail 35; Wild Mustang 35; Aces Wild 36; Cavalcade of the West 36; Feud of the West • Vengeance of Gregory 36; Ghost Town 36; Hair-Trigger Casey 36; The Riding Avenger 36; Romance Rides the Range 36; Wildcat Saunders 36; Dark Manhattan 37; Galloping Dynamite 37; Heroes of the Alamo • Remember the Alamo 37; Jungle Menace 37*; Spirit of Youth 37; Fury Below 38; Six-Shootin' Sheriff 38; Songs and Saddles 38; Lure of the Wasteland 39; Lightning Strikes West 40; Phantom Rancher 40; Jungle Man 41; Brand of the Devil 44; Gunsmoke Mesa 44; Outlaw Roundup • Outlaw's Roundup 44; Enemy of the Law 45; Flaming Bullets 45; Frontier Fugitives 45; The Navajo Kid 45; Three in the Saddle 45; Ambush Trail 46; Six Gun for Hire • Six Gun Man 46; Thunder Town 46; White Gorilla 47; Stallion Canyon 49; Chained for Life 50

Frawley, James The Christian Licorice Store 71; Kid Blue 73; Delancey Street—The Crisis Within • The Sinner 75; The Big Bus 76; The Muppet Movie 79; Fraternity Vacation 85

Frazee, Edwin A Favorite Fool 15*; Mrs. Plum's Pudding 15*

Frazer, D. R. Carry On London 37

Frazer-Jones, Peter George and Mildred 80

Frears, Stephen The Burning 67; Gumshoe 71; Bloody Kids 79; Loving Walter 83; Saigon—Year of the Cat 83; The Hit 84; My Beautiful Laundrette 85; Mr. Jolly Lives Next Door 87; Prick Up Your Ears 87; Sammy and Rosie Get Laid 87;

Dangerous Liaisons 88; The Grifters 90

Freck, H. M. Jerry McDub Collects Some Accident Insurance • Zippy's Insurance 16; The Fighting Blood of Jerry McDub 17

Freda, Riccardo Don Cesare di Bazan • La Lama del Giustiziere 42; Non Canto Più 43; Sei per Otto, Quarantotto • Tutta la Città Cantà 45; Aquila Nera • The Black Eagle 46; I Miserabili • Les Misérables 46; Il Cavaliere Misterioso • Le Cento Donne di Casanova • The Mysterious Rider 47; L'Astuto Barone 48; Guarany 48; Tenore per Forza 48; O Caçula do Barulho 49; Il Cavaliere di Ferro • Il Conte Ugolino • Count Ugolin • The Iron Swordsman 49; Double Cross 49; Il Figlio di D'Artagnan • The Gay Swordsman • Son of D'Artagnan 49; Return of the Black Eagle 49; Magia a Prezzi Modici 50; Perfido Ricatto • See Naples and Die • Vedi Napoli e Poi Muori 51; Revenge of the Black Eagle • La Vendetta di Aquila Nera 51; Il Tradimento 51; La Leggenda del Piave 52; Sins of Rome • Spartaco • Spartacus • Spartacus the Gladiator 52; Mosaici di Ravenna 53; Teodora, Imperatrice di Bisanzio • Theodora, Slave Empress 53; The Devil's Commandments • Lust of the Vampire • The Vampires • I Vampiri 54; Beatrice Cenci • I Maledetti 55; Da Qui all'Eredità 55; Agguato a Tangeri • Trapped in Tangiers 57; Agi Murad il Diavolo Bianco • Beli Djavo • The White Warrior 58; Nel Segno di Roma • La Regina del Deserto • Sign of the Gladiator 58*; Caltiki il Monstro Immortale • Caltiki the Immortal Monster • The Immortal Monster 59*; Gli Argonauti • The Giants of Thessaly • I Giganti della Tessaglia 60; Alone Against Rome • The Fall of Rome • Solo Contro Roma • Vengeance of the Gladiators 61*; L'Avventura di un Italiano in Cina • Grand Khan • Marco Polo 61*; Le Avventure di Dox • Caccia all'Uomo • Dox, Caccia all'Uomo 61; Il Dominatore dei Sette Mari • Il Re dei Sette Mari • Seven Seas to Calais 61*; Le Géant à la Cour de Kublai Khan • Goliath and the Golden City • Machiste at the Court of the Great Khan • Maciste alla Corte del Gran Khan • Samson and the Seven Miracles of the World 61; I Mongoli • Les Mongols • The Mongols 61*; Gold for the Caesars • Or pour les Césars • Oro per i Cesari 62*; The Horrible Dr. Hichcock • L'Orribile Segreto del Dottor Hichcock • Raptus • The Secret of Dr. Hichcock • The Terrible Secret of Dr. Hichcock • The Terror of Dr. Hichcock 62; Machiste in Hell • Maciste all'Inferno • The Witch's Curse 62; Le Sette Spade del Vendicatore • Sette Spade per il Re • The Seventh Sword 62; Avenger of Venice 63; The Ghost • The Spectre • Lo Spettro 63; The Magnificent Adventurer • Il Magnifico Avventuriero 63; Los Amantes de Verona • Giulietta e Romeo • Romeo and Juliet 64; The Revenge of Black Eagle 64; Agente Coplan, Missione Spionaggio • Coplan FX 18 Casse Tout • The Exterminators • FX-

Superspy 65; The Two Orphans 65; Roger la Honte • Trap for the Assassin 66; Coplan III 67; La Morte Non Conta i Dollari 67; A Doppia Faccia • Double Face • Puzzle of Horrors 69; Tamar, Wife of Er 69; L'Iguana dalla Lingua di Fuoco 71; Superhuman 79; Deliria • Fear • Murder Obsession • Murder Syndrome • Murderous Obsession • L'Ossessione Che Uccide • Unconscious 80

Freddie, W. Det Definitiv Afslag på Anmodningen om et Kys 49*; Spiste Horisonter 50*

Fredersdorf, Herbert B. Long Is the Road 48*; Rumpelstiltskin • Rumpelstilzchen 65; Der Gestiefelte Kater • Puss 'n Boots 67

Freed, Herb A.W.O.L. 72; Haunts • The Veil 77; Beyond Evil 80; Graduation Day 81; Tomboy 85; Survival Game 87

Freedland, George Moon Wolf • Und Immer Ruft das Herz 59*

Freedman, Jerrold Kansas City Bomber 72; Borderline 80; Native Son 86

Freedman, Joel L. Skezag 70*; Broken Treaty at Battle Mountain 75

Freedman, Laurie Tails You Lose 48

Freedman, Robert Goin' All the Way 82

Freeland, Thornton Three Live Ghosts 29; Be Yourself! 30; Whoopee! 30; The Secret Witness • Terror by Night 31; Six Cylinder Love 31; Love Affair 32; They Call It Sin • The Way of Life 32; Unexpected Father 32; Weekend Lives • Weekend Marriage • Working Wives 32; Flying Down to Rio 33; George White's Scandals • George White's Scandals of 1934 • Scandals 34*; Brewster's Millions 35; Accused 36; The Amateur Gentleman 36; Skylarks 36; Dark Sands • Jericho 37; The Gaiety Girls • Paradise for Two 37; Over the Moon 37*; Hold My Hand 38; The Amazing Mr. Forrest • The Gang's All Here 39; So This Is London 39; Marry the Boss' Daughter 41; Too Many Blondes 41; The Gay Duellist • Meet Me at Dawn 46*; The Brass Monkey • Lucky Mascot 47; Dear Mr. Prohack 49

Freeman, Al, Jr. A Fable • The Slave 71

Freeman, Joan Streetwalkin' 84; The Girls of Summer • Satisfaction 88

Freeman, Robert Nude Heat Wave • The Touchables 68; L'Éché le Blanche • Secret World 69*; The Erotic Adventures of Zorro 72

Freeman, Warwick Demonstrator 71

Freen, Howard Dirty O'Neil 74*

Freer-Hunt, J. L. Karma 33

Freers, Rick Scorching Fury 52

Frees, Paul The Beatniks 58

Fregonese, Hugo Bariloche 39; El Delta 39; Pampa Bárbara • Savage Pampas 43*; Donde Mueren las Palabras • When Words Fail • Where Words Fail 46; Apenas un Delincuente • Hardly a Criminal • Live in Fear 47; De Hombre a Hombre 49; One-Way Street 50; Saddle Tramp 50; Apache Drums 51; Mark of the Renegade 51; Decameron Nights 52; My Six Convicts 52; Untamed Frontier 52; Blowing Wild 53;

Man in the Attic 53*; Black Tuesday 54; The Raid 54; I Girovaghi 56; The Beasts of Marseilles • Seven Thunders 57; La Spada Imbattibile 57; Harry Black • Harry Black and the Tiger 58; Live in Fear 58; L'Avventura di un Italiano in Cina • Grand Khan • Marco Polo 61*; Un Aereo per Baalback 63; Apache's Last Battle • Les Cavaliers Rouges • Old Shatterhand • Shatterhand 64; La Battaglia di Fort Apache 64; Dr. Mabuse's Rays of Death • Die Todesstrahlen des Dr. Mabuse 64; Freddy und das Lied der Prärie • The Sheriff Was a Lady 64; Pampas Salvaje • Savage Pampas 66; Assignment Terror • Dracula Jagt Frankenstein • Dracula vs. Frankenstein • Frankenstein • El Hombre Que Vino de Ummo • The Man Who Came from Ummo • Los Monstruos del Terror 69*; La Mala Vida 73; Más Allá del Sol 75

Freisler, Fritz The Other Self 18

Freleng, Friz Fiery Fireman 28*; Homeless Homer 28*; Ride 'Em Bosko • Ride Him, Bosko 32*; Beau Bosko 33*; Bosko in Dutch 33*; Bosko in Person 33*; Bosko's Picture Show 33*; Beauty and the Beast 34; Buddy and Towser 34; Buddy the Gob 34; Buddy's Trolley Troubles 34; The Girl at the Ironing Board 34; Goin' to Heaven on a Mule 34; How Do I Know It's Sunday? 34; The Miller's Daughter 34; Pop Goes My Heart 34; Shake Your Powder Puff 34; Those Beautiful Dames 34; Why Do I Dream Those Dreams? 34; Along Flirtation Walk 35; Billboard Frolics 35; The Country Boy 35; The Country Mouse 35; Flowers for Madame 35; I Haven't Got a Hat 35; Into Your Dance 35; The Lady in Red 35; Little Dutch Plate 35; A Merrie Old Soul 35; Mr. and Mrs. Is the Name 35; My Green Fedora 35; At Your Service Madame 36; Boulevardier from the Bronx 36; The Cat Came Back 36; The Coocoonut Grove 36; I Wanna Play House (With You) • I Want to Play House 36; I'm a Big Shot Now 36; Let It Be Me 36; Sunday Go to Meetin' Time 36; Toytown Hall 36; When I Yoo-Hoo 36; Clean Pastures 37; Dog Daze 37; The Fella with the Fiddle 37; He Was Her Man 37; The Lyin' Mouse 37; Pigs Is Pigs 37; Plenty of Money and You 37; September in the Rain 37; She Was an Acrobat's Daughter 37; Streamlined Greta Green 37; Sweet Sioux 37; Jungle Jitters 38; My Little Buckaroo 38; Poultry Pirates 38; Pygmy Hunt 38; A Star Is Hatched 38; Calling Dr. Porky 40; Confederate Honey 40; Hardship of Miles Standish 40; Little Blabbermouse 40; Malibu Beach Party 40; Porky's Baseball Broadcast 40; Porky's Hired Hand 40; Shop, Look and Listen 40; You Oughta Be in Pictures 40; The Cat's Tale 41; The Fighting 69th½ 41; Hiawatha's Rabbit Hunt 41; Notes to You 41; Porky's Bear Facts 41; Rhapsody in Rivets 41; The Rookie Revue 41; Sport Chumpions 41; The Trial of Mr. Wolf 41; The Wacky Worm 41*; Ding Dong Daddy 42; Double Chaser 42; Foney Fables 42; Fresh Hare 42;

The Hare Brained Hypnotist 42; Hop, Skip and a Chump 42; Lights Fantastic 42; Porky's Pastry Pirates 42; Saps in Chaps 42; The Sheepish Wolf 42; The Wabbit Who Came to Supper 42; Daffy the Commando 43; The Fifth Column Mouse 43; Greetings Bait! 43; Hiss and Make Up 43; Jack Wabbit and the Beanstalk 43; Pigs in a Polka 43; Yankee Doodle Daffy 43; Bugs Bunny Nips the Nips 44; Duck Soup to Nuts 44; Goldilocks and the Jivin' Bears 44; Hare Force 44; Little Red Riding Rabbit 44; Meatless Flyday 44; Stage Door Cartoon 44; Ain't That Ducky 45; Hare Trigger 45; Herr Meets Hare 45; Life with Feathers 45; Peck Up Your Troubles 45; Baseball Bugs 46; Holiday for Shoestrings 46; Hollywood Daffy 46; Of Thee I Sting 46; Racketeer Rabbit 46; Rhapsody Rabbit 46; Sam the Pirate 46; Along Came Daffy 47; The Gay Anties 47; A Hare Grows in Manhattan 47; Rabbit Transit 47; Slick Hare 47; Tweety Pie • Tweety Pie and Sylvester 47*; Back Alley Oproar 48; Buccaneer Bunny 48; Bugs Bunny Rides Again 48; Hare Splitter 48; I Taw a Puddy Tat 48; Kit for Cat 48; Bad Ol' Puddy Tat 49; Curtain Razor 49; Dough for the Do-Do 49*; Each Dawn I Crow 49; Hare-Do 49; High Diving Hare 49; Knights Must Fall 49; Mouse Mazurka 49; So Much for So Little 49*; Which Is Witch? 49; Wise Quackers 49; All Abi-r-r-rd 50; Big House Bunny 50; Bunker Hill Bunny 50; Canary Row 50; Golden Yeggs 50; His Bitter Half 50; Home Tweet Home 50; The Lion's Busy 50; Mutiny on the Bunny 50; Stooge for a Mouse 50; Ballot Box Bunny 51; A Bone for a Bone 51; Canned Feud 51; Fair-Haired Hare 51; Hare We Go 51; His Hare Raising Tale 51; Puddy Tat Twouble 51; Rabbit Every Monday 51; Room and Bird 51; Tweet, Tweet, Tweety 51; Tweety's S.O.S. 51; Ain't She Tweet 52; Bird in a Guilty Cage 52; Cracked Quack 52; 14 Carrot Rabbit 52; Foxy by Proxy 52; Gift Wrapped 52; Hare Lift 52; Little Red Rodent Hood 52; Tree for Two 52; Ant Pasted 53; Catty Cornered 53; Dog Pounded 53; Fowl Weather 53; Hare Trimmed 53; A Mouse Divided 53; Robot Rabbit 53; Snow Business 53; Southern Fried Rabbit 53; A Street Cat Named Sylvester 53; Tom-Tom Tomcat 53; Bugs and Thugs 54; By Word of Mouse 54; Captain Hareblower 54; Dr. Jerkyl's Hide 54; Goo Goo Goliath 54; I Gopher You 54; Muzzle Tough 54; Satan's Waitin' 54; Yankee Doodle Bugs 54; Hare Brush 55; Heir Conditioned 55; Hyde and Hare 55; A Kiddie's Kitty 55; Lumber Jerks 55; Pappy's Puppy 55; Pests for Guests 55; Pizzicato Pussycat 55; Red Riding Hoodwinked 55; Roman Legion-Hare 55; Sahara Hare 55; Sandy Claws 55; Speedy Gonzales 55; Stork Naked 55; This Is a Life? 55; Tweety's Circus 55; Napoleon Bunny-Part 56; Rabbitson Crusoe 56; A Star Is Bored 56; Tree Cornered Tweety 56; Tugboat Granny 56; Tweet and Sour 56; Two Crows from

Tacos 56; Wideo Wabbit 56; Yankee Dood It 56; Birds Anonymous 57; Bugsy and Mugsy 57; Gonzales' Tamales 57; Greedy for Tweety 57; Mouse-taken Identity 57; Piker's Peak 57; Show Biz Bugs 57; The Three Little Bops 57; Tweet Zoo 57; Tweety and the Beanstalk 57; A Bird in a Bonnet 58; Hare-less Wolf 58; Knighty Knight Bugs 58; A Pizza Tweety Pie 58; Tortilla Flaps 58; A Waggily Tale 58; Apes of Wrath 59; Mexicali Shmoes 59; Trick or Tweet 59; Tweet and Lovely 59; Tweet Dreams 59; Wild and Woolly Hare 59; From Hare to Heir 60; Goldimouse and the Three Cats 60; Horse Hare 60; Hyde and Go Tweet 60; Lighter Than Hare 60; Mouse and Garden 60; Person to Bunny 60; Trip for Tat 60; West of Pesos 60; Cannery Woe 61; D'Fightin' Ones 61; The Last Hungry Cat 61; The Pied Piper of Guadalupe 61*; Prince Varmint • Prince Violent 61; Rebel Without Claws 61; What's My Lion? 61; Crow's Feat 62; Honey's Money 62; The Jet Cage 62; Mexican Boarders 62; Quackodile Tears 62; Shishkabugs 62; Chili Weather 63; Devil's Feud Cake 63; Mexican Cat Dance 63; The Unmentionables 63; Nuts and Volts 64; Pancho's Hideaway 64; The Road to Andalay • Tequila Mockingbird 64; Señorella and the Glass Hurache 64; Cats and Bruises 65; It's Nice to Have a Mouse Around the House 65; Friz Freleng's Looney, Looney, Looney Bugs Bunny Movie • The Looney, Looney, Looney Bugs Bunny Movie 81; Uncensored Cartoons 81*; Daffy Duck's Movie: Fantastic Island 83*; Porky Pig in Hollywood 86*

Freleng, I. see *Freleng, Friz*
Freleng, Isadore see *Freleng, Friz*
Frenais, Ian la see *La Frenais, Ian*
French, Harold The Cavalier of the Streets 37; Dead Men Are Dangerous 38; Castle of Crimes • The House of the Arrow 40; Girl in Distress • Jeannie 41; Major Barbara 41*; The Avengers • The Day Will Dawn 42; Secret Mission 42; Talk About Jacqueline 42; Unpublished Story 42; Dear Octopus • The Randolph Family 43; English Without Tears • Her Man Gilbey 44; Mr. Emmanuel 44; Quiet Weekend 46; The Blind Goddess 47; High Fury • White Cradle Inn 47; My Brother Jonathan 47; The Facts of Life • Quartet 48*; Adam and Evalyn • Adam and Evelyne 49; The Dancing Years 49; Trio 50*; Encore 51*; The Hour of 13 52; Isn't Life Wonderful! 52; The Man Who Watched Trains Go By • Paris Express 52; Rob Roy • Rob Roy the Highland Rogue 53; Forbidden Cargo 54; The Man Who Loved Redheads 54

French, Lloyd That's My Wife 29; Busy Bodies 33; Dirty Work 33; Me and My Pal 33*; Midnight Patrol 33; Oliver the Eighth 33

Frend, Charles The Big Blockade 41; The Foreman Went to France • Somewhere in France 41; San Demetrio London 43; Return of the Vikings 44; Johnny Frenchman 45; The Loves of Joanna Godden 47;

Scott of the Antarctic 48; The Magnet 49; A Run for Your Money 49; The Cruel Sea 52; Lease of Life 54; The Long Arm • The Third Key 56; All at Sea • Barnacle Bill 57; Cone of Silence • Trouble in the Sky 60; Girl on Approval 61; Beta Som • Finchè Dura la Tempesta • Torpedo Bay 62*; The Sky Bike 67

Frenguelli, Albert G. Because • The Laundry Girl 19*; The Cry for Justice 19
Frenguelli, Alfonse Christmas Eve 15; Coster Joe 15; Three Christmasses 15; Burglar Bill 16*; Solomon's Twins 16*; The Awakening 38
Frenguelli, Anthony House of Dreams 33; Dr. Sin Fang 37; Chinatown Nights 38
Frenke, Eugene Two Who Dared • A Woman Alone 36; Life Returns 38; Miss Robin Crusoe 54*
Freshman, William Ants in His Pants 40; Appointment in Persia • Conspiracy in Teheran • The Plot to Kill Roosevelt • Teheran 47*

Freund, Jay The American Game 79*
Freund, Karl A Chinese Moon 28; A Fascinating Vamp 28; In a Japanese Garden 28; The Keys of Heaven 28; Madeleine 28; A Snowman's Romance 28; Toddlin' Along 28; Tune Up the Uke 28; Zulu Love 28; The Mummy 32; The Countess of Monte Cristo 33; Madame Spy 33; Moonlight and Melody • Moonlight and Pretzels 33*; The Gift of Gab 34; I Give My Love 34; Uncertain Lady 34; The Hands of Orlac • Mad Love 35

Frez, Ilya Dimka • Ya Kupil Papu 64; Love and Lies 81; The Case of a Judge • Lichnoye Delo Sudyi Ivanovoy 87

Fric, Mac see *Frič, Martin*

Frič, Martin Father Vojtěch • Páter Vojtěch 28; Chudá Holka • Poor Girl 29; The Organist at St. Vitus • The Organist of St. Vitus • Varhaník u Svatého Víta 29; All for Love • Vše pro Lásku 30; Dobrý Voják Švejk • Good Soldier Schweik 31; Hadimrsku Doesn't Know • To Neznáte Hadimršku • You Should Know Hadimrska 31*; He and His Sister • On a Jeho Sestra 31*; The Informer • Der Zinker 31*; Anton Špelec, Ostrostřelec • Anton Spelec the Thrower 32; Conduct Unsatisfactory • Kantor Ideál • Master Ideal 32; Sestra Angelika • Sister Angelica 32; Accountant • The Inspector • The Inspector General • Revisor 33; Der Adjutant Seiner Hoheit • Adjutant to His Highness • Assistant to His Highness • Pobočník Jeho Výsosti 33; Closed Doors • S Vyloučením Veřejnosti 33; A Dog's Life • Život Je Pes 33; Dvanáct Křesel • The Twelve Chairs 33*; The Emptied-Out Grocer's Shop • The Ransacked Shop • The Ruined Shopkeeper • U Sněděného Krámu 33; Darling • The Effeminate One • Mazlíček 34; Der Doppelbräutigam • The Double Fiance 34; Heave-Ho! • Hej Rup! 34; The Last Man • Poslední Muž 34; Ať Žije Nebožtík • Long Live Kindness • Long Live the Deceased 35; The Eleventh Commandment • Jedenácté Přikázání 35; Hero for a Night •

Hrdina Jedné Noci 35; Jánošík 35; Father Vojtěch • Páter Vojtěch 36; Das Gasschen zum Paradies • Paradise Road • Ulička v Ráji 36; The Seamstress • Švadlenka 36; Advokátka Věra • Vera the Lawyer 37; The Hordubal Brothers • Hordubalové • The Hordubals 37; Lidé na Kře • Lost on the Ice • People on a Glacier 37; Morality Above All • Mravnost Nade Vše 37; Svět Patří Nám • The World Belongs to Them • The World Is Ours 37; Three Eggs in a Glass • Tři Vejce do Skla 37; Krok do Tmy • Madman in the Dark 38; School—The Basis of Life • School—The Beginning of Life • School—Where Life Begins • Škola—Základ Života 38; Cesta do Hlubin Studákovy Duše • Searching the Hearts of Students 39; Christian • Kristián 39; The Escapades of Eva • Eva Plays the Fool • Eva Tropí Hlouposti 39; Fresh Air • Jiny Vzduch 39; Muž z Neznáma • The Reluctant Millionaire 39; Baron Münchhausen • Baron Prášil 40; Catacombs • Katakomby 40; Druhá Směna • Second Lawyer • Second Shift • Second Tour 40; Liduška of the Stage • Musician's Girl • Muzikantská Liduška 40; Adventure Is a Hard Life • Hard Is the Life of an Adventurer • The Hard Life of an Adventurer • Těžký Život Dobrodruha 41; Auntie's Fantasies • Tetička 41; The Hotel Blue Star • Hotel Modrá Hvězda 41; Roztomilý Člověk 41; Barbora Hlavsová 42; Valentin Dobrotivý 42; Experiment 43; The Second Shot • Der Zweite Schuss 43; Počestné Paní Pardubické • The Respectable Ladies of Pardubicke • The Virtuous Dames of Pardubicke 44; Prstýnek • The Ring • The Wedding Ring 44; Beat 13 • 13. Revír 45; Čapkovy Povídky • Tales by Capek • Tales from Capek 47; Reiterate the Warning • Varuj! • Warning! 47; Homecoming • Lost in Prague • Návrat Domů • Return Home 48; A Kiss at the Stadium • Polibek ze Stadionu 48; The Kind Millionaire • The Poacher's God-Daughter • Pytlákova Schovanka 49; Motorcycles • Pětistovka 49; Past • The Trap 50; Steel Town • Tempered Steel • Zocelení 50; Action B • Akce B 51; Bylo To v Máji • May Events 51*; Císařův Pekař a Pekařův Císař • The Emperor and His Baker • The Emperor and the Golem • The Emperor's Baker • The Emperor's Baker and the Baker's Emperor • The Return of the Golem 51; The Mystery of Blood • The Secret of Blood • Tajemství Krve 53; Dog Heads • Psohlavci 54; Leave It to Me • Nechte To na Mně! 55; Master of Winter Sports • Mistr Zimních Sportů 55; Watch the Birdie! • Zaostřit, Prosím 56; Dnes Naposled • Today for the Last Time 58; The Flood • Povodeň 58; Theodor Pištěk 58; The Princess with the Golden Star • Princezna se Zlatou Hvězdou 59; Bílá Spona • The White Slide 60; A Compact with Death • Dařbuján a Pandrhola 60; Růžena Nasková 60; King of Kings • Král Králů 63; The Three Golden Hairs of Old Man Know-All • Tři Zlaté Vlasy Děda Vševěda 63; Hvězda Zvaná

Pelyněk • A Star Called Wormwood • A Star Named Wormwood 64; Lidé na Kolečkách • Lidé z Maringotek • People on Wheels 66; Přísně Tajné Premiéry • Recipe for a Crime • Strictly Secret Previews 67; The Best Girl in My Life • The Best Woman of My Life • Nejlepší Ženská Mého Života 68

Frick, Jonas Strul 88

Fridolinski, Alex They Call Her One-Eye 74

Fridriksson, Fridrik Thor Skyt turnar • White Whales 87

Fried, Y. Twelfth Night 56

Friedberg, David R. Torture Me, Kiss Me 70

Friedberg, Rick K-God • Pray TV 80; Off the Wall 83

Friedel, Frederick R. The Axe • California Axe Massacre • Lisa 77

Friedenberg, Richard The Life and Times of Grizzly Adams 74; The Adventures of Frontier Fremont • Frontier Fremont 76; The Bermuda Triangle 78

Friedgin, Ray Killers of the Sea 37

Friedkin, David Hot Summer Night 56; Handle with Care 58

Friedkin, William Good Times 67; The Birthday Party 68; The Night They Invented Striptease • The Night They Raided Minsky's 68; The Boys in the Band 70; The French Connection 71; The Exorcist 73; Sorcerer • Wages of Fear 77; The Brink's Job 78; Cruising 80; Deal of the Century 83; To Live and Die in L.A. 85; Rampage 87; The Guardian 90

Friedlander, Louis see Landers, Lew

Friedman, David Convicts at Large 38*

Friedman, Ed Mighty Mouse in the Great Space Chase 83*; The Secret of the Sword 85*

Friedman, Jeffrey Common Threads: Stories from the Quilt 89*

Friedman, Ken Death by Invitation 71; Made in U.S.A. 86

Friedman, Max Encounters in Salzburg 64

Friedman, Richard Deathmask • Unknown 83; Doom Asylum 88; Phantom of the Mall: Eric's Revenge 89

Friedman, Serge Double Deception 60

Friedman, Seymour Trapped by Boston Blackie 48; Bodyhold 49; Boston Blackie's Chinese Venture • Chinese Adventure 49; Chinatown at Midnight 49; The Crime Doctor's Diary 49; The Devil's Henchman 49; Prison Warden 49; Rusty Saves a Life 49; Rusty's Birthday 49; Counterspy Meets Scotland Yard 50; Customs Agent 50; Rookie Fireman 50; Criminal Lawyer 51; Girls Never Tell • Her First Romance 51; The Son of Dr. Jekyll 51; Escape Route • I'll Get You 52*; Loan Shark 52; Flame of Calcutta 53; The Saint's Girl Friday • The Saint's Return 53; Khyber Patrol 54; African Manhunt 55; The Secret of Treasure Mountain 56

Friedmann, Anthony Bartleby 70

Friedrich, Günther Operation Violin Case • Unternehmen Geigenkasten 86;

Hasenherz 88

Friend, Chan Happy Bigamist 87

Friend, Robert L. The Deadly Silence • Tarzan's Deadly Silence 70*

Friendly, Fred W. Satchmo the Great 57*

Friese-Greene, Claude The Pride of Nations 15

Frisch, Larry Tel Aviv Taxi 56; The Pillar of Fire 63; Casablan 64

Fritsch, Günther von The Curse of the Cat People 44*; Cigarette Girl 47; Stolen Identity 53

Frizzell, John A Winter Tan 87*

Froehlich, Bill Return to Horror High 87

Froehlich, Carl see Fröhlich, Carl

Froehlich, Gustav see Fröhlich, Gustav

Froemke, Susan Horowitz Plays Mozart 87*

Fröhlich, Carl Zu Spät 11; Richard Wagner 13; The Brothers Karamazov • Die Brüder Karamasoff 20*; Irrende Seelen 22; Josef und Seine Brüder • Joseph and His Brethren 22; Der Taugenichts 22; Die Toteninsel 22; Mutter und Kind 24; Kammermusik 25; Tragödie 25; Rosen aus dem Süden 25; Die Grosse Pause 27; Violantha 27; Lotte 28; Die Nacht Gehört Uns 29; Brand in der Oper • Fire in the Opera House 30; Luise—Königin von Preussen 31; Mitternachtsliebe 31*; Die oder Keine • Her or Nobody 32; Gitta Entdeckt Ihr Herz 32; Der Choral von Leuten 33; Reifende Jugend 33; Frühlingsmärchen 34; Krach um Iolanthe 34; Frauen um den Sonnenkönig • Lisolette von der Pfalz • The Private Life of Louis XIV 35; Ich War Jack Mortimer 35; If We All Were Angels • Wenn Wir Alle Engel Wären 36; Oberwachtmeister Schwenke 36; Traumulus 36; Wenn der Hahn Kräht 36; The Four Companions • Die Vier Gesellen 38; Heimat • Magda 38; Es War eine Rauschende Ballnacht • It Was a Gay Ball Night 39; Das Herz einer Königin 40; Familie uchholz 44; Stips 51

Fröhlich, Gustav Rákóczi Induló • Rákóczi Marsch 33*; Abenteuer eines Jungen Herrn in Polen • Liebe und Trompetenklang 34; Leb' Wohl Christina 45; Wege im Zwielicht 48; Der Bagnosträfling 49; Die Lüge 50; Torreani 51; Seine Tochter Ist der Peter 55

Frohman, Daniel The Day of Days 14

Frohman, Mary Hubert The Fairy and the Waif 15*

Frolov, Andrei The Winner 47

Frost, F. Harvey Something's Rotten 79

Frost, Lee see Frost, R. Lee

Frost, R. L. see Frost, R. Lee

Frost, R. Lee Call Girl 77 • Call Surftide 77 • Surftide 77 • Surftide 777 62; Fiery Spur • Hot Spur • The Longest Spur • The Naked Spur 68; Love Camp Seven 68; The Grabbers • The Scavengers 69; Chrome and Hot Leather 71; Chain Gang Women 72; The Thing with Two Heads 72; Policewoman 74; The Black Gestapo 75; Dixie Dynamite 76

Frost, Robert L. see Frost, R. Lee

Frot-Coutaz, Gérard Beau Temps, Mais Orageux en Fin de Journée • Fine Weather, But Storms Due Towards Evening 86

Fruet, William Wedding in White 72; Death Weekend • The House by the Lake 76; Search and Destroy • Striking Back 79; Cries in the Night • Funeral Home 81; Death Bite • Spasms 81; Baker County U.S.A. • Trapped 82; Bedroom Eyes 84; Killer Party 86; Blue Monkey • Green Monkey 87

Frumin, Boris The Errors of Youth 89

Frumkes, Roy Document of the Dead 80

Fryer, Bertram The Feather Bed 33

Fuehrer, Volker see Führer, Volker

Fuentes, C. México, México • Soy México 67*

Fuentes, Fernando de see De Fuentes, Fernando

Fuerstenberg, Veith von see Fürstenberg, Veith von

Fuest, Robert Just Like a Woman 66; And Soon the Darkness 70; Wuthering Heights 70; The Abominable Dr. Phibes 71; Dr. Phibes Rises Again 72; The Final Programme • The Last Days of Man on Earth 73; The Devil's Rain 75; Aphrodite 82

Fuhr, Charles Pseudonym for Robert Florey with Edward Ludwig and Harold Schuster

Führer, Volker On the Outskirts • Stadtrand 87

Fuka, Otakar Černá Punčocha 88; Piloti • Pilots 89

Fukasaku, Kinji Battle Beyond the Stars • Death and the Green Slime • Gamma Sango Uchū Daisakusen • The Green Slime 68; Black Lizard 68; Black Rose 69; Tora! Tora! Tora! 70*; Ōkami to Buta to Ningen 72; The Yakuza Papers 73; Message from Space • Uchū Kara no Messeji • Uchū no Messeji 78*; Fukkatsu no Hi • Virus 79; The Shogun's Samurai 79; Devil Resuscitation 80; The Fall Guy • Kamata Kōshinkyoku • Kamata March 80; Makai Tensho • Samurai Reincarnation 81; Under the Flag of the Rising Sun 82; Legend of the Dogs of Satomi 84; Shanghai Vance King 84; House on Fire • Kataku no Hito • Man in a Hurry 86; Sure Death IV 87

Fukuda, Jun Densō Ningen • The Secret of the Telegian • The Telegian 60; The Weed of Crime 63; Honkon no Shiroibara • White Rose of Hong Kong 65; Big Duel in the North Sea • Ebirah, Horror of the Deep • Ebirah, Terror of the Deep • Godzilla vs. the Sea Monster • Nankai no Daikettō 66; Dotō Ichiman Kairi • The Mad Atlantic 67; Gojira no Musuko • Son of Godzilla 67; Furesshuman Wakadaishō • Young Guy Graduates 69; Nyūjirando no Wakadaishō • Young Guy on Mt. Cook 69; Godzilla on Monster Island • Godzilla vs. Gigan • Gojira Tai Gaigan • Gojira Tai Gigan • War of the Monsters 72; Godzilla vs. Megalon • Gojira Tai Megalon • Gojira Tai Megaro 73; Godzilla vs. Mechagodzilla • Godzilla vs. the Bionic Monster •

Godzilla vs. the Cosmic Monster • Gojira Tai Meka-Gojira 74; Cosmos: War of the Planets • Nakusei Daisensō • War in Space • War of the Planets 77

Fukushima, Atsuko Robot Carnival 87*

Fulci, Lucio I Ladri 59; I Ragazzi del Juke-Box 59; Urlatori alla Sbarra 60; Colpo Gobbo all'Italiana 62; I Due della Legione 62; Le Massaggiatrici 62; Gli Imbroglioni 63; Uno Strano Tipo 63; Agenti Segretissimi • 002 Agenti Segretissimi • 00-2 Most Secret Agents • Oh! Those Most Secret Agents • Worst Secret Agents 64; I Due Evasi di Sing Sing 64; I Maniaci 64; Come Inguaiammo l'Esercito 65; I Due Pericoli Pubblici 65; The Brute and the Beast • Le Colt Cantarono la Morte È Fu: Tempo di Massacro • Tempo di Massacro 66*; Come Svaligiammo la Banca d'Italia 66; 002 Operazione Luna 66; I Due Para' 66; Come Rubammo la Bomba Atomica 67; Dos Cosmonautas a la Fuerza 67; Il Lungo, il Corto, il Gatto 67; Operation St. Peter's • Operazione San Pietro 68; Beatrice Cenci 69; Una sull'Altra 69; Una Lagartija con Piel de Mujer • A Lizard in a Woman's Skin • Una Lucertola con la Pelle di Donna • Schizoid • Le Venin de la Peur 71; All' Onorevole Piacciono le Donne 72; Don't Torture the Duckling • Non Si Sevizia un Paperino 72; White Fang • Zanna Bianca 72; Il Ritorno di Zanna Bianca 74; Il Cavaliere Constante Nicosia Demoniaco ovvero Dracula in Brianza • Dracula in the Provinces 75; La Pretora 76; I Quattro dell' Apocalisse 76; Dolce Come Morire • The Psychic • Sette Notte in Nero 77; Sella d'Argento 78; Island of the Living Dead • Zombi 2 • Zombie • Zombie Flesh Eaters • Zombie 2 79; L'Aldilà • And You'll Live in Terror: The Beyond • The Beyond • E Tu Vivrai nel Terrore! L'Aldilà • The Seven Doors of Death 80; The Black Cat • Il Gatto di Park Lane • Il Gatto Nero 80; City of the Living Dead • The Fear • Fear in the City of the Living Dead • The Gates of Hell • Paura nella Città dei Morti Viventi • Twilight of the Dead 80; Luca il Contrabbandiere 80; The House by the Cemetery • The House Outside the Cemetery • Quella Villa Accanto al Cimitero 81; The New York Ripper • The Ripper • Lo Squartatore di New York 81; The Eye of the Evil Dead • Manhattan Baby • L'Occhio del Male • The Possessed 82; Conquest 83; I Guerrieri dell'Anno 2072 83; Murderock, Uccide a Passo di Danza 84; The Devil's Honey • Il Miele del Diavolo 86; Ænigma 87; L'Adorazione 88

Fuller, Lester You Can't Ration Love 44; Monte Carlo Baby • Nous Irons à Monte Carlo 51*

Fuller, Louis see Fulci, Lucio

Fuller, Samuel I Shot Jesse James 48; The Baron of Arizona 49; The Steel Helmet 50; Fixed Bayonets! 51; Park Row 52; Pickup on South Street 52; Hell and High Water 53; House of Bamboo 55; Hot Lead • Run of the Arrow 56; China Gate 57; Forty Guns • Woman with a Whip 57;

Verboten! 58; The Crimson Kimono 59; Underworld, U.S.A. 60; The Marauders • Merrill's Marauders 61; The Iron Kiss • The Naked Kiss 63; Long Corridor • Shock Corridor • Straitjacket 63; Un Arma de Dos Filos • Caine • Maneater • Shark! 67; The Meanest Men in the West 67; Dead Pigeon on Beethoven Street • Kressin und die Tote Taube in der Beethovenstrasse 72; The Big Red One 79; Trained to Kill • White Dog 82; Thieves After Dark • Thieves in the Night • Les Voleurs de la Nuit 83; Sans Espoir de Retour 88

Fuller, Tex Stranded 87

Fumagalli, Gianluca A Fior di Pelle • Skin Deep 87

Fung, Raymond For Your Heart Only 85; The Family 86

Funke-Stern, Monika Am Nächsten Morgen Kehrte der Minister Nicht an Seinen Arbeitsplatz Zuruck • On the Next Morning the Minister Didn't Return to His Post 86

Funt, Allen What Do You Say to a Naked Lady? • What Do You Say to a Naked Woman? 70; Money Talks 71

Furdivall, Gwyneth Slag's Place 65*

Furey, Lewis Night Magic 85; Shadow Dancing 88

Furie, Sidney J. A Dangerous Age 57; A Cool Sound from Hell 58; Doctor Blood's Coffin • Face of Evil 60; During One Night • Night of Passion 60; The Snake Woman • The Terror of the Snake Woman 60; The Boys 61; Three on a Spree 61; Wonderful to Be Young • The Young Ones 61; The Leather Boys 63; Swinger's Paradise • Wonderful Life 63; The Ipcress File 65; The Appaloosa • Southwest to Sonora 66; Eye of the Devil • Thirteen 66*; The Naked Runner 67; The Lawyer 68; Little Fauss and Big Halsy 70; Lady Sings the Blues 72; Hit! 73; Sheila Levine Is Dead and Living in New York 74; Gable and Lombard 76; The Boys in Company C 77; The Entity 81; Purple Hearts • Purple Hearts: A Vietnam Love Story 83; Iron Eagle 86; Superman IV: The Quest for Peace 87; Iron Eagle II • Iron Eagle II: The Battle Beyond the Flag 88

Furniss, Harry Mrs. Scrubbs' Discovery 14; Rival Reflections 14

Fürstenberg, Veith von Fire and Sword 82

Furthman, Jules G. The Land of Jazz 20; The Blushing Bride 21; Colorado Pluck 21; Jet Pilot 50*

Furtwängler, Florian Tommaso Blu 86

Furuhata, Yasuo Yasha 85

Furusawa, Kengo Chintao Yōsai Bakugeki Meirei • The Siege of Fort Bismarck 63; Kyomo Ware Ōzorani Ari • Tiger Flight 65; Arupusu no Wakadaishō • It Started in the Alps 66; Daibōken • Don't Call Me a Con Man 66; Buchamukure Daihakken • Computer Free-for-All 69; Duel at Ezo • Ezo Yakata no Kettō 70

Futter, Walter Africa Speaks 30

Fyodorova, Maria Gift for Music 57

Gaál, Béla Csókolj Meg Édes 32; Filléres

Gyönyör 33; A Csúnya Lány 35; The New Relative • Az Új Rokon 35; Budai Cukrászda 36; Címzett Ismeretlen 36; Meseautó 36; Az Új Földesúr 36; Aranyember 37; Hotel Sunrise 37; Az Ember Néha Téved • Man Sometimes Errs 38; Maga Lesz a Férjem • You Will Be My Husband 38; Majd a Zsuzsi 38; Pesti Mese • Tales of Budapest 38; János Vitéz • John the Hero 39; The Wheat Ripens 39

Gaál, István Pályamunkások • Railroaders • Surfacemen 57; Etüd • Étude 61; Cigányok • Gypsies 62; Oda-Vissza • To and Fro 62; Current • Sodrásban • The Stream 63; Tisza—Autumn Sketches • Tisza—Őszi Vázlatok 63; Férfiarckép • Portrait of a Man 64; Green Flood • The Green Years • Zöld Ár 65; Baptism • Christening Party • Keresztelő 67; Chronicle • Krónika 68; Cuba's Ten Years • Tíz Éves Kuba 69; Bartók Béla: Az Éjszaka Zenéje • Béla Bartók: The Night's Music 70; The Falcons • Magasiskola 70; The Dead Country • Dead Landscape • Holt Vidék 71; Képek egy Város Életéből • Pictures from the Life of a Town 75; Örökségünk • Our Heritage 75; Legato • Ties 77; Buffer Zone • Cserepek • Potteries • Shards 81; Orfeusz és Euridiké • Orpheus and Eurydice 85

Gabale, Ram Sher Shivaji 88

Gabay, Gennady Forty-Nine Days • 49 Dney 64

Gabel, Martin The Lost Moment 47

Gábor, Pál Forbidden Ground • Tiltott Terület 68; Horizon • Horizont 71; Journey with Jacob • Utazás Jakabbal 73; Epidemic • Járvány 75; Angi Vera 78; Kettévált Mennyezet • Wasted Lives 82; Brady's Escape • The Long Ride • The Long Run 83; The Bride Was Very Beautiful • La Sposa Era Bellissima 86

Gabourie, Mitchell Buying Time 88

Gabrea, Radu A Man Like Eva • Ein Mann Wie Eva 83

Gabriadze, R. Don't Grieve 69*

Gabriel, Michael The Rescuers Down Under 90*

Gad, Urban The Abyss • Afgrunden 10; Ædel Dåd • The Aviator's Generosity • Flyveren og Journalistens Hustru • Generosity • Den Store Flyver 11; The Ballet Dancer • A Ballet Dancer's Love • Balletdanserinden 11*; Dyrekøbt Glimmer • Hulda Rasmussen • When Passion Blinds Honesty 11; Der Fremde Vogel 11; Gennem Kamp til Sejr • Through Trials to Victory 11; Gypsy Blood • Zigeunerblut 11; Heisses Blut 11; In dem Grossen Augenblick 11; Die Macht des Goldes • The Power of Gold 11; Nachtfalter 11; Sins of the Children 11; Den Sorta Drøm 11; Till Death • Zum Tode Gehetz 11; Die Verräterin 11; The Woman Always Pays 11; Die Arme Jenny 12; Det Berygtete Hus • Den Hvide Slavehandel III • Nina, in the Hands of the Imposters 12; Jugend und Tollheit 12; Die Kinder des Generals 12; Komödianten 12; Das Mädchen Ohne Vaterland 12; Der Totentanz 12; Wenn die Maske Fällt 12;

Engelein 13; Die Filmprimadonna 13; S.I. 13; Die Suffragette 13; Die Sünden der Vater 13; Der Tod in Sevilla 13; Aschenbrödel 14; Cinderella 14; Engeleins Hochzeit 14; Die Ewige Nacht 14; Das Feuer 14; Das Kind Ruft 14; Die Tochter der Landstrasse 14; Vordertreppe und Hintertreppe 14; Weisse Rosen 14; Zapatas Bande 14; Der Rote Streifen 16; Der Breite Weg 17; Die Gespensterstunde 17; Klosterfriede 17; Die Vergangenheit Rächt Sich 17; Die Verschlossene Tür 17; Die Kleptomanin 18; Die Neue Dalila 18; Der Schmuck des Rajah 18; Das Sterbende Modell 18; Vera Panina 18; Das Verhängnisvolle Andenken 18; Mein Mann der Nachtredakteur 19; Das Spiel von Liebe und Tod 19; Der Abgrund der Seelen 20; Der Liebes-Korridor 20; So ein Mädel 20; Weltbrand 20; Christian Wahnschaffe 21; Die Insel der Verschollenen 21; Der Vergiftete Brunnen 21; Hanneles Himmelfahrt 22; The Gay Huskies • Lykkehjulet 26

Gade, Svend Maharadjæns Yndlingshustru 16; Hamlet 20; Herrin von Brinkenhof 22; Fifth Avenue Models 25; Peacock Feathers 25; Siege 25; The Blonde Saint 26; Into Her Kingdom 26; Watch Your Wife 26; Balleten Danser 38

Gaden, Hans Beck see Beck-Gaden, Hans

Gadette, Frédéric This Is Not a Test 62

Gadney, Alan Full Moon • Moonchild 72; West Texas 73

Gaeng, Elfriede Electric Blue 88

Gaetano, Michael A. de see DeGaetano, Michael A.

Gaffney, Robert Duel of the Space Monsters • Frankenstein Meets the Space Monster • Frankenstein Meets the Spacemen • Mars Invades Puerto Rico 65

Gage, George Skateboard 77; Fleshburn 84

Gage, John Hotel Berlin 45*; The Velvet Touch 48

Gagne, Jean La Couleur Encerclée • The Encircling of Color 87*

Gagne, Serge La Couleur Encerclée • The Encircling of Color 87*

Gagnon, Claude La Rose, Pierrot et la Luce 82; Pale Face • Visage Pale 85; The Kid Brother 87

Gahris, Roy Trooper 44 17

Gai, Alexander Ivanov see Ivanov-Gai, Alexander

Gaidai, Leonid The Long Path 56*; A Fiancée from the Other World 58; Barbos the Dog and a Cross-Country Run 61; Bootleggers 61; Business People 63; Operation Y and Shurik's Other Adventures 65; Prisoner of the Caucasus 67; The Diamond Hand 69; The Twelve Chairs 71; Ivan Vassilievich Changes His Profession 73; It Can't Be 75; Sportloto—82 • Sports Lottery—82 87

Gaignaire, Claude Timon Une Touche de Bleue 88

Gaillard, Robert Mr. Barnes of New York 14*; The Moonstone of Fez 14*; The Mysterious Lodger 14*; The Plot 14*; The Man Who Couldn't Beat God 15*

Gaines, Walter Assault with a Deadly Weapon 83

Gainsbourg, Serge Charlotte Forever 86

Gainville, René The Man from Mykonos 67; Le Démoniaque 68; The Young Couple 69; Alise and Chloe 70; Le Complot 75; Un Bon Samaritain 76; The Associate • L'Associé 80

Gaisseau, Pierre-Dominique Des Hommes Qu'On Apelle Sauvages 50; Naloutai 52; Pays Bassari 52; Forêt Sacrée 54; Survivants de la Préhistoire 55; Le Ciel et la Boue • The Sky Above, the Mud Below 61; New York sur Mer • Only One New York 63; Flame and the Fire 65; Round Trip 67

Gaither, David The Forest Ring 30*

Galbreath, Richard Night of Evil 62

Galeen, Heinrich see Galeen, Henryk

Galeen, Henryk Der Golem • The Golem • The Monster of Fate 14*; Die Rollende Kugel 19; Judith Trachtenberg 20; Der Verbotene Weg: Ein Drama mit Glücklichem Ausgang 20; Stadt in Sicht 23; Die Liebesbriefe der Baronin von S...24; The Man Who Cheated Life • The Student of Prague • Der Student von Prag 26; Alraune • A Daughter of Destiny • Mandragore • Mandrake • Unholy Love 27; His Greatest Bluff • Sein Grösster Bluff 27*; After the Verdict 29; Die Falle • Salon Dora Green 33

Galentine, Wheaton Rice 64*; To the Fair! 64*

Galettini, Carlos I May Be Anything, But I Love You • Maybe I'm a Loser, But I Love You • Seré Cualquier Cosa Pero Te Quiero 86

Galfas, Timothy Bogard 75; Black Fist • The Black Streetfighter • Homeboy 76*; Sunnyside 79

Galić, Eduard Horvatov Izbor • Horvat's Choice 86

Galich, Alexander The House on the Front Line • Na Semi Vetrakh 63*

Galindo, Alejandro Rebel Souls 37; Mientras México Duerme • While Mexico Sleeps 38; The Dead Man Died • El Muerto Murió 39; Corazón de Niño • Heart of a Child 40; Campeón Sin Corona 45; Espaldos Nojaldas 53

Galindo, Pedro III Burst of Lead • Rafaga de Plomo 86; The Death of Palomo • El Muerto del Palomo 87; Mi Nombre Es Gatillo • My Name Is Gatillo 87

Galindo, Rubén, Jr. Cementerio del Terror 85; Child of the Palenque • Hijo del Palenque 86; Yako—Cazador de Malditos • Yako—Hunter of the Damned 86; Narco Terror • Narcotics Terror 87

Galkin, Noah Neurasthenia 29

Gallaga, Peque Gold, Silver, Bad Luck • Oro, Plata, Mata 82

Gallagher, Donald Nix on Dames 29; Pleasure Crazed 29*; Temple Tower 30; Let Them Live 37*

Gallagher, John A. Beach House 82; This Is Barbara Barondess: One Life Is Not Enough 85

Galland, Philippe Le Mariage du Siècle 85

Gallego, Leonel The Train of the Pioneers • El Tren de los Pioneros 86

Gallego, Manuel Esteba Horror Story 72; Viciosas al Desnudo 80; Bloodthirsty Sex • Sexo Sangriento 81

Gallo, Mario El Fusillamiento de Dorrego 08; Juan Moreira 09; Muerte Civil 10; Revolución de Mayo 10; Balata de Maipo 11; Tierra Baja 11

Gallone, Carmine Il Bacio di Cirano 13; La Donna Nuda 13; Turbine d'Odio 14; Avatar 15; Fior di Male 15; Marcia Nuziale 15; Maria di Magadala 15; Redenzione 15; Senza Colpa 15; La Falena 16; Fede 16; Malombra 16; La Storia dei Tredici 16; Tra i Gorghi 16; Lo Chiamavano Cosetta 17; Madonna Grazia 17; Storia di un Peccato 17; Maman Poupée 18; Il Destino e il Timoniere 19; La Figlia del Mare 19; Il Mare di Napoli 19; Amleto e il Suo Clown • On with the Motley 20; Il Bacio di Cirano 20; Il Colonello Chabert 20; La Fanciulla, il Poeta e la Laguna 20; La Figlia del Tempesta 20; La Grande Tormenta 20; Marcella 20; La Vie d'une Femme 20; Nemesis 21; L'Ombra di un Trono 21; Le Braccia Aperte 22; La Madre Folle 22; Il Reggimento Royal Cravate 22; Il Segreto della Grotta Azzurra 22; La Vedova Scaltra 22; Amore 23; La Cavalcata Ardente 23; Il Corsaro 23*; Nella Tormenta • Tormenta 23; I Volti dell'Amore 23; La Fiammata 24; Jerry 24; La Signorina Madre di Famiglia 24; The Last Days of Pompeii • Gli Ultimi Giorni di Pompeii 26; Celle Qui Domine 27*; L'Inferno dell'Amore • Inferno di Amore • Liebeshölle • Pawns of Passion 27; Marter der Liebe 27; S.O.S. 27; Die Stadt der Tausend Freuden 27; Bride 68 • Das Land Ohne Frauen • Terra Senza Donne 29; Die Singende Stadt 30; Le Chant du Marin 31; La Città Canora • The City of Song • Farewell to Love 31; Dragnet Night • Un Soir de Rafle 31; Ma Cousine de Varsovie 31; Un Fils d'Amérique 32; Le Roi des Palaces 32; For Love of You 33; Going Gay • Kiss Me Goodbye 33; King of the Ritz 33; Una Notte a Venezia 33; E Lucean le Stelle • Mein Herz Ruft nach Dir • Mon Cœur T'Appelle • My Heart Is Calling 34; Two Hearts in Waltz Time 34*; Al Sole 35; Casta Diva • The Divine Spark 35; Im Sonnenschein • Opernina • Opernring • Thank You Madame 35; Liszt Rhapsody • Wenn die Musik Nicht Wär 35; Blood Bond • Stimme des Blutes 37; Cristoforo Colombo 37; The Defeat of Hannibal • Scipio • Scipio Africanus • Scipio the African • Scipione l'Africano 37; Dir Gehört Mein Herz • Marionette • My Heart Belongs to Thee 38; Un Dramma al Circo • Manège 38; Giuseppe Verdi • The Life and Music of Giuseppe Verdi 38; Only for Thee • Solo per Te 38; Das Abenteuer Geht Weiter • Another Experience • Das Erlebnis Geht Weiter 39; The Dream of Butterfly • Il Sogno di Butterfly 39; Manon Lescaut 39; Amami Alfredo! 40; Eternal Melodies •

Mélodie Éterne 40; Marcella 40; Oltre l'Amore 40; L'Amante Segreta • Troppo Bella 41; Primo Amore 41; La Regina di Navarra 41; Le Due Orfanelle • The Two Orphans 42; Harlem • Knockout 42; Odessa in Fiamme • Odessa in Flames 42; Tristi Amori 43; Il Canto della Vita 45; Before Him All Rome Trembled • Davanti a Lui Tremava Tutta Roma • Tosca 46; Biraghin 46; Rigoletto 46; Addio Mimi • Her Wonderful Lie 47; The Lost One • La Signora delle Camelie • La Traviata 47; Faust and the Devil • La Leggenda di Faust 48; The Force of Destiny • La Forza del Destino 49; The Troubadour • Il Trovatore 49; Bambino • Singing Taxi Driver • Taxi di Notte 50; The Affairs of Messalina • Messalina • Messaline 51; Cavalleria Rusticana • Fatal Desire 52; His Two Loves • Puccini 52; Senza Veli 52; Vissi d'Arte, Vissi d'Amore 52; Casa Ricordi • House of Ricordi 54; Casta Diva 54; Daughter of Mata Hari • La Figlia di Mata Hari • La Fille de Mata Hari • Mata Hari's Daughter 54*; Don Camillo e l'Onorevole Peppone • Don Camillo's Last Round 55; Madama Butterfly • Madame Butterfly 55; Michael Strogoff • Michel Strogoff 56; Revolt of the Tartars 56; Tosca 56; Polijuschka 58; Cartagine in Fiamme • Carthage en Flammes • Carthage in Flames 59; Don Camillo Monsignore Ma Non Troppo 61; Carmen di Trastevere 62; La Monaca di Monza 62

Gallu, Samuel The Blood Fiend • The Female Fiend • Theatre of Death 66; The Man Outside 67; The Limbo Line 68; Arthur, Arthur 69

Gamba, Giuliana Perfume • Profumo 87; The Belt • La Cintura 89

Gamba, Sao Kolormask 87

Gambino, Domenico Battles in the Shadow • Lotte nell'Ombra 39

Ganancia, J. P. Architecture et Lumière 53*

Gance, Abel La Digue • La Digue ou Pour Sauver la Hollande • The Dike • Pour Sauver la Hollande 11; Il Y A des Pieds au Plafond • There Are Feet on the Ceiling 12; The Mask of Horror • Le Masque d'Horreur 12; Le Nègre Blanc • The White Negro 12*; Le Pierre Philosophe 12; Drama at the Château d'Acre • Un Drame au Château d'Acre • Un Drame au Château d'Acre ou Les Morts Reviennent-Ils? • Les Morts Reviennent-Ils? 14; L'Énigme de Dix Heures • The Ten O'Clock Mystery 14; La Folie du Docteur Tube • The Madness of Dr. Tube 14; Ce Que les Flots Racontent • What the Waves Tell 15; Fioritures • Fioritures ou La Source de Beauté • Flourishes • La Source de Beauté 15; La Fleur des Ruines • The Flower of the Ruins 15; Le Fou de la Falaise • The Madman on the Cliff 15; L'Héroïsme de Paddy • Paddy the Hero 15; Le Périscope • The Periscope 15; Strass and Co. • Strass et Cie 15; Barberousse • Red Beard 16; Le Brouillard sur la Ville • The Deadly Gas • Les Gaz Mortels • Les Gaz Mortels ou Le Brouillard sur la Ville 16; The Death Zone • La Zone de la Mort 16; Le Droit à la Vie • The Right to Live 16; La Femme Inconnue 16; The Call of Motherhood • Mater Dolorosa • The Sorrowing Mother 17; La Dixième Symphonie • The Tenth Symphony 17; Ecce Homo 18; I Accuse! • J'Accuse! 18; La Roue • The Wheel 21; Au Secours! • The Haunted House • Help! 23; Napoléon • Napoleon • Napoleon As Seen by Abel Gance • Napoléon Vu par Abel Gance 26; About Napoleon • Autour de Napoléon 27; Cristeaux 28; Danses 28; Galops 28; Marines 28; The End of the World • La Fin du Monde 30; Mater Dolorosa 32; Le Maître de Forges 33; Poliche 33; La Dame aux Camélias 34*; Napoléon Bonaparte 34; Le Serment 34; Jérôme Perreau, Héros des Barricades • The Queen and the Cardinal 35; Lucrèce Borgia • Lucrezia Borgia 35; Le Roman d'un Jeune Homme Pauvre • The Story of a Poor Young Man 35; Abel Gance's Beethoven • Beethoven • Beethoven's Great Love • Un Grand Amour de Beethoven • The Life and Loves of Beethoven • The Life and Times of Beethoven 36; Ladro di Donne • The Robber of Women • Le Voleur de Femmes 36; I Accuse! • J'Accuse! • That They May Live • We Accuse 37; Four Flights to Love • Le Paradis Perdu • Paradise Lost 38; Louise 38; Christophe Colomb 39; Profil de la France 39; Blind Venus • La Vénus Aveugle 40; Une Femme dans la Nuit 41*; Le Capitaine Fracasse 42; Le Quatorze Juillet 53; La Tour de Nesle • The Tower of Lust 54; Magirama 56*; Austerlitz • The Battle of Austerlitz 59*; Cyrano and D'Artagnan • Cyrano et D'Artagnan 62; Bonaparte et la Révolution 71

Gandéra, Félix Les Mystères de Paris 37; Tamara la Complaisante 37*; Le Paradis de Satan 38*; Crime in the Maginot Line • Double Crime in the Maginot Line 39

Ganguly, Ajit Boba Shahnai 88

Ganguly, Anil Pyar ke Kabil 88

Gann, M. J. Girl from Poltava • Natalka Poltavka 36*

Gannaway, Albert C. Daniel Boone, Trail Blazer 56*; Hidden Guns 56; The Badge of Marshal Brennan 57; Raiders of Old California 57; Man Mad • No Place to Land 58; Man or Gun 58; Plunderers of Painted Flats 59; Betrayer • Chivato • Rebellion in Cuba 61; Buffalo Gun 61

Gannon, Wilfred Auntie's Antics 29; Chris's Mrs. 29; Nick's Knickers 29

Gant, Harry A. The Sagebrush League 19; Absent 28; Georgia Rose 30

Gantillon, Bruno L'Intruse 85

Ganzer, Alvin The Girls of Pleasure Island 53*; The Leather Saint 56; Country Music Holiday 58; Girl Crazy • When the Boys Meet the Girls 65; Three Bites of the Apple 66

Garay, Jesús Beyond Passion • Más Allá de la Pasión 86

Garcia, Federico God's Partner • El Socio de Dios 87

Garcia, Jerry The Grateful Dead 77

García, José Luis see García Agraz, José Luis

Garcia, Ron The Toy Box 71; Inside Army 75

García Agraz, José Luis Asignatura Pendiente • Flunking Out 76; Solos en la Madrugada 77; Las Verdes Praderas 79; El Crack 81; To Begin Again • Volver a Empezar 81; El Crack II 83; Nocout 84; Sesión Continua 84; Dreams of Gold • Treasure of the Moon Goddess 85*; The Caliph's Nights • The Nights of the Caliph • Las Noches del Califas 86; Asignatura Aprobada • Course Completed • Passing the Course 87

García Berlanga, Luis Paseo Sobre una Guerra Antigua 48*; El Circo 49; Tres Cantos 49; Esa Pareja Feliz • That Happy Couple • That Happy Pair • This Happy Couple 51*; ¡Bienvenido, Sr. Marshall! • Welcome, Mr. Marshall! 52; Bridegroom in Sight • Fiancé in Sight • Novio a la Vista 53*; Los Gancheros 55; Calabuch • The Rocket from Calabuch 56; Los Jueves Milagro • Thursdays, Miracle 57; Plácido 61; Las Cuatro Verdades • The Four Truths • Les Quatres Vérités • Le Quattro Verità • Three Fables of Love 62*; La Ballata del Boia • The Executioner • Not on Your Life • El Verdugo 63; La Boutique • The Boutique 67; Las Pirañas 67; Long Live the Bride and Groom • Long Live the Newlyweds • ¡Vivan los Novios! 69; Grandeur Nature • Life Size • Love Doll • Tamaño Natural 73*; La Escopeta Nacional • The National Rifle • The National Shotgun • The Spanish Shotgun 78; National Trust • Patrimonio Nacional 80; Nacional III 83; The Heifer • The Little Bull • La Vaquilla 84; Moors and Christians • Moros y Cristianos 87

García Sánchez, José Luis La Corte de Faraón • The Court of the Pharaoh • Pharaoh's Court 85; Divinas Palabras • Divine Words 87; Hay Que Deshacer la Casa • We Must Undo the House 87; Pasodoble 88

Garcin, Laure Métropolitain 58*; Étroits Sont les Vaisseaux 62*

Gardan, Julius Halka 38

Gardin, Vladimir Keys to Happiness • Klyuchi Shchastya 13*; Anna Karenina 14; Days of Our Life 14; The Kreutzer Sonata 14; Ghosts 15; A Nest of Noblemen 15; Petersburg Slums • Petersburgskiye Trushchobi 15*; Voina i Mir • War and Peace 15*; Thought 16*; Our Heart 17; The Iron Heel 19; Golod...Golod...Golod • Hunger...Hunger...Hunger 21*; Serp i Molot • Sickle and Hammer 21*; The Duel 22; Locksmith and Chancellor 23; A Spectre Haunts Europe 23; Cross and Mauser 25; The Bear's Wedding • The Marriage of the Bear 26*; Czar and Poet 27

Gardner, Cyril Cascarrabias • Grumpy 30*; Only Saps Work 30*; The Royal Family • The Royal Family of Broadway • Theatre Royal 30*; Reckless Living 31; The Doomed Battalion 32; Perfect Understanding 33; Big Business 34; Widow's Might 34

Gardner, Frank Jivin' and Jammin' 48

Gardner, Herb The Goodbye People 84

Gardner, Robert Man on a Mission 65; Clarence and Angel 80

Gardos, Péter The Philadelphia Attraction • Uramisten! 85; Szamárköhögés • Whooping Cough 87

Garen, Leo Hex • The Shrieking 73

Garfein, Jack End As a Man • The Strange One 57; Something Wild 61

Garfield, Frank see Giraldi, Franco

Garguilo, Mike It's Your Thing 70

Gariazzo, Mario Passport for a Corpse 62; Dio Perdoni la Mia Pistola 69*; Aquasanta Joe 71; Last Moments 73; La Mano Spietata della Legge 73; The Balloon Vendor • The Last Circus Show 74; Eerie Midnight Horror Show • L'Ossessa • The Sexorcist • The Tormented 74; Incontri Molto Ravvicinati • Very Close Encounters of the Fourth Kind 79; Amazonia—The Catherine Miles Story • Schiave Bianche, Violenza in Amazzonia • White Slave 86

Gariazzo, Piero Antonio After Six Days 22*

Garland, Patrick A Doll's House 73

Garmes, Lee Conquest of the Air 36*; Miss Bracegirdle Does Her Duty 36; Dreaming Lips 37*; The Sky's the Limit 37*; Angels Over Broadway 40*; Actors and Sin 52*; Hannah Lee • Outlaw Territory 53*

Garnett, Tay Celebrity 28; The Flying Fool 28; The Spellbinder • The Spieler 28; No Brakes • Oh, Yeah! 29; Her Man 30; Officer O'Brien 30; Bad Company 31; One Way Passage 31; Okay America! • Penalty of Fame 32; Prestige 32; Destination Unknown 33; S.O.S. Iceberg 33*; China Seas 35; Professional Soldier 35; She Couldn't Take It • Woman Tamer 35; Love Is News 37; Slave Ship 37; Stand-In 37; Joy of Living 38; Trade Winds 38; Eternally Yours 39; Slightly Honorable 39; Cafe of Seven Sinners • Seven Sinners 40; Cheers for Miss Bishop 41; My Favorite Spy 42; Bataan 43; The Cross of Lorraine 43; See Here, Private Hargrove 43*; Mrs. Parkington 44; The Valley of Decision 45; The Postman Always Rings Twice 46; Wild Harvest 47; A Connecticut Yankee • A Connecticut Yankee in King Arthur's Court • A Yankee in King Arthur's Court 48; Cause for Alarm 50; The Fireball 50; Soldiers Three 51; One Minute to Zero 52; Main Street to Broadway 53; The Black Knight 54; Seven Wonders of the World 56*; The Night Fighters • A Terrible Beauty 60; Cattle King • Guns of Wyoming 63; The Delta Factor 70; Challenge to Be Free • The Mad Trapper • Mad Trapper of the Yukon 72*; Timber Tramp 72

Garnett, Tony Prostitute 80; Deep in the Heart • Handgun 82

Garnier, Max Massimino Aristotele • Aristotle 71*

Garrel, Philippe Elle à Passe Tant d'Heures Sous les Sunlights 85

Garrett, Oliver H. P. Careful, Soft Shoulders 42

Garrett, Otis The Black Doll 38; The Case of the Missing Blonde • Corpse in the Morgue • The Lady in the Morgue 38; Danger on the Air 38; The Last Express 38; Personal Secretary 38; Exile Express 39; Mystery of the White Room 39; The Witness Vanishes 39; Margie 40*; Sandy Gets Her Man 40*

Garrett, Roy see Gariazzo, Mario

Garrick, Richard The New Adam and Eve 15; According to Law 16; The Drifter 16; The Idol of the Stage 16; The Quality of Faith 16; A Rank Outsider 20; The Romance of a Movie Star 20; Trent's Last Case 20

Garris, Mick Critters II • Critters II: The Main Course 88

Garrison, Greg Hey, Let's Twist! 61; Two Tickets to Paris 62

Garrone, Sergio If You Want to Live... Shoot • Se Vuoi Vivere...Spara 68; Una Lunga Fila di Croci • No Room to Die • Tre Croci per Non Morire 68; Django de Bastardo • Django il Bastardo • Django the Bastard • The Stranger's Gundown 69; Uccidi Django...Uccidi per Primo 71; Lager SSadis Kastrat Kommandantur 76; Lager SS5—L'Inferno delle Donne 76

Garson, Harry For the Soul of Rafael 20; The Forbidden Woman 20; Midchannel 20; Whispering Devils 20; Charge It 21; Hush 21; Straight from Paris 21; What No Man Knows 21; The Hands of Nara 22; The Sign of the Rose 22; The Worldly Madonna 22; An Old Sweetheart of Mine 23; Thundering Dawn 23; The Breed of the Border 24; The Millionaire Cowboy 24; The No-Gun Man 24; Heads Up 25; High and Handsome 25; O.U. West 25; Smilin' at Trouble 25; Speed Wild 25; The College Boob 26; Glenister of the Mounted 26; Mulhall's Great Catch 26; Sir Lumberjack 26; The Traffic Cop 26; Beast of Borneo 35

Gary, Jerome Stripper 85; Traxx 88

Gary, Romain The Birds Come to Die in Peru • Birds in Peru • Les Oiseaux Vont Mourir au Pérou 68; Kill • Kill! Kill! Kill! 71

Gaskill, Charles L. Cleopatra 13; Princess of Bagdad 13; Sylvia Gray 14

Gasnier, Louis La Première Sortie d'un Collégien 05; Le Pendu 06; La Mort d'un Toréador 07; Tirez S'Il Vous Plaît 08; Max Fait du Ski 10; Detective Swift 14*; The Exploits of Elaine 14*; The Perils of Pauline 14*; The Stolen Birthright 14; The New Exploits of Elaine 15*; Annabel's Romance 16; Hazel Kirke 16; The Shielding Shadow 16; The Mystery of the Double Cross 17; Hands Up! 18*; The Seven Pearls 18; The Tiger's Trail 19; The Butterfly Man 20*; The Corsican Brothers 20; Kismet 20; Good Women 21; Silent Years 21; A Wife's Awakening 21; The Call of Home 22; Rich Men's Wives 22; Thorns and Orange Blossoms 22; Daughters of the Rich 23; The Hero 23; Maytime 23; Mothers-in-Law 23; Poor Men's Wives 23; The Breath of Scandal 24; Poisoned Paradise • Poisoned Paradise—The Forbidden Story of Monte Carlo 24; The Triflers 24; White Man 24; Wine 24; The Boomerang 25; Faint Perfume 25; The Parasite 25; Parisian Love 25; Lost at Sea 26; Out of the Storm 26; Pleasures of the Rich 26; Sin Cargo 26; That Model from Paris 26*; The Beauty Shoppers 27; Streets of Shanghai 27; Fashion Madness 28; Darkened Rooms 29; Cast Iron • The Virtuous Sin 30*; L'Énigmatique Monsieur Parkes 30; The Shadow of the Law 30*; Slightly Scarlet 30*; The Lawyer's Secret 31*; Silence 31*; The Case of Clara Deane • The Strange Case of Clara Deane 32*; Forgotten Commandments 32*; Topaze 32; Espérame 33; Gambling Ship 33*; Iris Perdue et Retrouvée 33; Melodía de Arrabal 33; Cuesta Abajo 34; Fedora 34; El Tango en Broadway 34; The Last Outpost 35*; The Burning Question • Dope Addict • Doped Youth • Love Madness • Reefer Madness • Tell Your Children 36; Bank Alarm 37; The Gold Racket 37; The Sunset Murder Case • The Sunset Strip Case 38; La Inmaculada 39; John the Soldier, or Vengeance • Juan Soldado, o Venganza 39; Murder on the Yukon 40; Adolescence • Stolen Paradise 41; Fight On, Marines! • The Marines Come Through 42

Gaspard-Huit, Pierre Maid in Paris 57; Christine 58; The Girl on the Third Floor • Sophie et le Crime 58; Scheherazade • La Schiava di Bagdad • Shéhérazade 63*

Gasparini, Ludovico Italian Fast Food 86

Gasparov, Samvel Coordinates of Death • Koordinaty Smerti 87*; Kak Doma, Kak Dela? 88

Gassman, Vittorio Kean • Kean, Genius or Scoundrel? 54*; L'Alibi 69; Senza Famiglia Nullatenenti Cercano Affetto • Senza Famiglie 72; Di Padre in Figlio 83

Gast, Leon Salsa 76*; Hell's Angels Forever 83*

Gast, Michael I Spit on Your Grave • J'Irai Cracher sur Vos Tombes 62

Gastaldi, Ernesto Libido 66*

Gastern, Louis van see Van Gastern, Louis

Gastyne, Marco de see De Gastyne, Marco

Gates, Harvey The Marriage Lie 18*; The Wine Girl 18*

Gates, Tudor Intimate Games 76

Gatlif, Tony Les Princes • The Princes 82; Rue de Départ • Street of Departures 86

Gatti, Armand L'Enclos • The Enclosure 60; El Otro Cristóbal 62

Gatti, Attilio Bitter Spears 56

Gaudio, Antonio The Price of Success 25; Sealed Lips 25

Gaudio, Tony see Gaudio, Antonio

Gaudioz, John Layout for Five Models 73

Gaugh, Homer Goliathon • The Mighty Peking Man 79

Gaup, Nils Ofelas • Pathfinder • Veiviseren 87

Gavala, Maria To Aroma tis Violettas • The Scent of Violets 85; To Magiko Viali 88

Gavaldón, Roberto El Conde de Monte Cristo 41; La Barraca 44; El Socio 45; La Otra 46; La Vida Íntima de Marco-Antonio y Cleopatra 46; Adventures of Casanova 48; La Casa Chica 49; Deseada 50; En la Palma de Tu Mano • Kill Him for Me 50; Camelia 53; El Rebozo de Soledad 53; The Littlest Outlaw 55; La Escondida • The Hidden Woman 56; Viva Revolución 56; Beyond All Limits • Flor de Mayo • Spoilers of the Sea 57; Macario 60; La Rosa Blanca 72; El Hombre de los Hongos • The Mushroom Eater 76; La Playa Vacía 79

Gaver, Eleanor Slipping Into Darkness 89

Gaviria, Víctor Rodrigo D: No Future 90

Gavoty, Bernard Yehudi Menuhin—Chemin de la Lumière • Yehudi Menuhin—Road of Light • Yehudi Menuhin Story 70*

Gavras, Constantin Costa see Costa-Gavras

Gavras, Costa see Costa-Gavras

Gavronsky, A. The Circle • Duty and Love • Kpyr • The Ring 27*

Gavronsky, M. Beethoven Concerto 37*

Gaye, Howard Restitution 18; March of the Movies 38

Gaylor, Richard The Alternative Miss World • Gay Confessions 80

Gazcón, Edgardo El Bronco 86

Gazcón, Gilberto Pursuit Across the Desert 60; El Mal • Rage 66

Gazdag, Gyula The Whistling Cobblestone 71; The Resolution 72*; Singing on the Treadmill 74; Swap 77; The Banquet 82; Lost Illusions 82; Package Tour 84; Hol Volt Hol Nem Volt... • A Hungarian Fairy Tale • Once Upon a Time... 87

Gaziadis, Dimitrios The Greek Miracle 21; Prometheus Desmotis 27; Eros ke Kimata 28; To Limani ton Dacrion • The Port of Tears 28; Astero 29; The Storm • I Thiella 29; The Apaches of Athens • I Apachides ton Athinon 30; Kiss Me Marisa • Philise Me Maritsa 31; Be Happy • Exo Ptochia 32; The End of Bad Luck 33

Gazlades, Michael Anna of Rhodes 50*

Gazzara, Ben Beyond the Ocean 90

Gebel, Bruno La Caleta Olvidida • The Forgotten Cove 58

Gebler, Carlo Rating Notman 82

Geddes, Henry Ali and the Camel 60; The Last Rhino 61; Eagle Rock 64

Gedris, Marionas see Giedrys, Marijonas

Gee, Vanyoska Krik? Krak! Tales of a Nightmare 88*

Gehr, Ernie Morning 68; Wait 68; Reverberation 69; Transparency 69; Field 70; History 70; Serene Velocity 70; Still 71; Eureka 74; Shift 74; Table 76; Mirage 81

Geis, Rainer Kleines Zeit und Grosse Liebe • Two in a Sleeping Bag 64

Geisinger, Elliot The Adventures of the Prince and the Pauper • The Prince and the Pauper 69

Geiss, Alec The Bulldog and the Baby 42; Cholly Polly 42; The Gullible Canary 42; Malice in Slumberland 42; Wacky Wigwams 42; Dizzy Newsreel 43; Duty and the Beast 43; Kindly Scram 43; Mass Mouse Meeting 43; Nursery Crimes 43; There's Something About a Soldier 43; Tangled Travels 44

Geissendörfer, Hans W. Jonathan • Jonathan—Vampiren Sterben Nicht 69; Carlos 71; Marie 72; The Wild Duck • Die Wildente 76; The Glass Cell 77; Der Zauberberg 81; Edith's Diary 83; Boomerang Boomerang • Bumerang Bumerang 89

Gelabert, Fructuoso Dorotea 1897

Geldert, Clarence Wasted Lives 23; My Neighbor's Wife 25

Gelenbevi, Baha Dertli Pinar 43; Deniz Kızı 44; Yanık Kaval 46; Çıldıran Kadın 48; Barbaros Hayrettin Paşa 51; Boş Beşik 52; Balıkçı Güzeli 53; Kaldırım Çiçeği 53

Gélin, Daniel Les Dents Longues 52

Geller, Bruce Harry in Your Pocket 73

Gemmiti, Arturo Monte Cassino 48

Genée, Heidi 1 + 1 = 3 79

Geneen, Sascha Express Love 29; Comets 30; Infatuation 30

Gengnagel, Klaus Ätherbräusch 88

Genina, Augusto La Gloria 13; La Moglie di Sua Eccellenza 13; L'Anello di Siva 14; Dopo il Veglione 14; La Fuga degli Amanti 14; La Parole Che Uccide 14; Il Piccolo Cerinaio 14; Il Segreto del Castello di Monroe 14; La Doppia Ferita 15; Gelosia 15; Lulù 15; Mezzanotte 15; Cento HP 16; Conquista dei Diamanti 16; Drama della Corona 16; La Menzogna 16; Il Presagio 16; La Signora Ciclone 16; Il Sogno di un Giorno 16; Il Sopravvissuto 16; L'Ultimo Travestimento 16; Femina • Femmina 17; Lucciola 17; Maschiaccio 17; Il Siluramento dell'Oceania 17; Addio Giovinezza! 18; I Due Crocifissi 18; L'Emigrata 18; Kalidaa • La Storia di una Mummia 18; L'Onestà del Peccato 18; Il Principe dell'Impossibile 18; Il Trono e la Seggiola 18; Le Avventure di Bijou 19; Bel Ami 19; Debito d'Odio 19; La Donna e il Cadavere 19; Lucrezia Borgia 19; La Maschera e il Volto 19; Noris 19; Lo Scaldino 19; L'Avventura di Dio 20; Il Castello della Malinconia 20; I Diabolici 20; La Douloureuse 20; Moglie, Marito e... 20; La Ruota del Vizio 20; Tre Meno Due 20; I Tre Sentimentali 20; Crisi 21; L'Incatenata 21; L'Innamorata 21; Una Donna Passò 22; Lucie de Tréceur 22; La Peccatrice Senza Peccato 22; Un Punto Nero 22; Cirano di Bergerac • Cyrano de Bergerac 23; Il Corsaro 23*; Germaine 23; La Moglie Bella 24; Il Focolare Spento • Il Più Grande Amore 25; L'Ultimo Lord 26; Addio Giovinezza! 27; Die Gefangene von Shanghai 27*; Die Geschichte einer Kleine Pariserin • Sprung ins Glück • Totte et Sa Chance 27; Die Weisse Sklavin 27; Liebeskarnaval 28; Scampolo 28; Un Dramma a 16 Anni 29; Quartier Latin 29; L'Amour Chante 30*; Miss Europe • Prix de Beauté 30; Les Amants de Minuit 31*; La Femme

en Homme 31; Mitternachtsliebe 31*; Paris-Béguin 31; Ne Sois Pas Jalouse 32; Nous Ne Sommes Plus des Enfants 34; Vergiss Mein Nicht 35; Blumen aus Nizza • Flowers from Nice 36; La Gondole aux Chimères 36; Lo Squadrone Bianco • The White Squadron 36; Une Baiser de Feu • The Kiss of Fire • Naples au Baiser de Feu 37; Frauenleid • Frauenliebe 37; Castelli in Aria • Ins Blaue Leben 38; L'Assedio dell'Alcazar 40; Bengasi 42; Cielo sulla Palude • Heaven Over the Marshes 49; Devotion • L'Edera 50; Three Forbidden Stories • Tre Storie Proibite 52; Maddalena 53; Frou Frou 55*

Genock, Edward Cassino to Korea 50

Genoino, Arnaldo Erode il Grande • Herod the Great 59

Genschow, Fritz Dornröschen • Sleeping Beauty 65; Die Gänsemagd • The Goose Girl 67

Gentil, Michel see Rollin, Jean

Gentili, Giorgio Madigan's Millions • El Millón de Madigan • El Testamento de Madigan • Un Dollaro per 7 Vigliacchi 67*

Gentilomo, Giacomo Appointment in Persia • Conspiracy in Teheran • The Plot to Kill Roosevelt • Teheran 47*; Lieutenant Craig, Missing 51; The Young Caruso 53; The Dragon's Blood 59; Le Dernier des Vikings • The Last of the Vikings • L'Ultimo dei Vichinghi 60; Charge of the Black Lancers 61; Goliath and the Island of Vampires • Goliath and the Vampires • Machiste Against the Vampires • Maciste vs. the Vampire • Maciste Contro il Vampiro • The Vampires 61*; Brennus, Enemy of Rome 64; Hercules Against the Moon Men • Maciste Contre les Hommes de Pierre • Maciste Contro gli Uomini della Luna • Maciste e la Regina di Samar 64; Slave Girls of Sheba 64*

Gentner, Willy Schmidt see Schmidt-Gentner, Willy

George, Burton Blade o' Grass 15; Celeste of the Ambulance Corps 16; The Heritage of Hate 16; The Isle of Life 16; The Law of the North 17; Eve in Exile 19; Ginger 19; The Valley of Doubt 20; Conceit 21; Devotion 21; Human Desires 24

George, George W. The James Dean Story 57*

George, Heinrich Schleppzug M-17 33

George, Henry W. The Deputy Drummer 35; Trust the Navy 35; Who's Your Father? 35

George, K. G. Kathakku Pinnil 87

George, Leslie Screw Loose 84

George, Peter Surf Nazis Must Die 87

Georgescu, Jean Î̂n Sat la Noi • Our Village 51*

Georgiades, Vassilis Blood on the Land • To Homa Vaftike Kokkino 65; Kokkina Phanaria • Red Lanterns 65

Georgias, Andrew Big Time 77

Georgiyev, Viktor An Ideal Husband • Idealny Muzh 81

Geraghty, Maurice The Sword of Monte Cristo 51

Geraghty, Tom Love's Boomerang • Perpetua 22*; Spanish Jade 22*

Gérard, Charles Une Balle dans le Canon • A Slug in the Heater 58*; Les Démons de Minuit • Midnight Folly 61*

Gérard, Michel Retenez Moi ou Je Fais un Malheur • To Catch a Cop 84; Blastfighter • Blessure 1985 85

Gerasimov, Sergei Dvadtsat Dva Neschastya • Twenty-Two Misfortunes • Twenty-Two Mishaps 30*; The Forest • The Woods 31; The Heart of Solomon • Serdtsye Solomona • Solomon's Heart 32*; Do I Love You? • If I Love You? • Lyubliyu Li Tebya 34; The Bold Seven • The Brave Seven • Semero Smelykh • Seven Brave Men 36; City of Youth • The Far North • Komsomolsk 38; The New Teacher • The Teacher • Uchitel 39; Boevoi Kinosbornik 1 • Fighting Film Album No. 1: Meeting with Maxim • Meeting with Maxim • Vstrecha s Maksimom • Wstretscha s Maksimom 41; Maskarad • Masquerade 41; The Old Guard 41; The Invincible • Nepobedimye • The Unconquerable 42*; Cine-Concert . . . • Film-Concert Dedicated to the 25th Anniversary of the Red Army • Film-Concert for the Red Army's 25th Anniversary • Kinokontsert k 25-Letiyu Krasnoy Armii • Moscow Music Hall 43*; The Big Land • Bolshaya Zemlya • The Great Earth • Great Land • The Mainland • The Ural Front 44; The Berlin Conference 45*; Molodaya Gvardiya • The Young Guard 47; China Liberated • Liberated China • The New China • Osvobozhdeniye Kitai 50*; The Country Doctor • Selski Vrach • The Village Doctor 51; Nadezhda 55; The Compass • Die Windrose • The Windrose 56*; And Quiet Flows the Don • Quiet Flows the Don • Tikhi Don 57; Sputnik Speaking • The Sputnik Speaks 59*; Lyudi i Zveri • Men and Beasts • Menschen und Tiere 62*; The Journalist • Zhurnalist 66; At the Lake • By the Lake • V Ozera 69; For Love of Man • For the Love of Man • Lyubit Cheloveka • To Love a Man 72; Dochki-Materi • Materi i Docheri • Mothers and Daughters 74; At the Beginning of Glorious Deeds • V Natchale Skavnykh Del 81; The Youth of Peter • Yunost Piotra 81; Leo Tolstoy • Lev Tolstoi 84

Gerasimov, Yevgeni Zabavy Molodykh 88

Gerber, Yvonne Le Père Hugo • Victor Hugo 51*

Gerhards, Christiane Viva Portugal 75*

Gerhardt, Karl Ein Einsam Grab • Die Tat der Gräfin Worms 16*; Das Rätselhafte Inserat 16*

Gerima, Haile Harvest: 3000 Years • Mirt Sost Shi Amit 72; Ashes and Embers 82

Gering, Marion The Hours Between • Le Lieutenant Souriant • Twenty-Four Hours 31; I Take This Woman 31*; Ladies of the Big House 31; The Devil and the Deep 32; Madame Butterfly 32; Jennie Gerhardt 33; Pick-Up 33; Good Dame • Good Girl 34; Ready for Love 34; Thirty Day Princess 34; Rose of the Rancho 35*; Rumba 35; Lady of Secrets 36; Thunder in

the City 37; She Married an Artist 38; Sarumba 50; The Diving Girls' Island • Diving Girls of Japan • Scintillating Sin • Sea Nymphs • Violated Paradise 63

Gerlach, Arthur von Vanina • Vanina oder Die Galgenhochzeit 22; At the Grey House • The Chronicles of the Grey House • Zur Chronik von Grieshuus 23

Germi, Pietro Il Testimone • The Witness 45; Gioventù Perduta • Lost Youth 47; In Nome della Legge • In the Name of the Law • Mafia 48; Il Cammino della Speranza • The Path of Hope • The Road to Hope 50; La Città Si Difende • Four Ways Out • Passport to Hell 51; Il Brigante di Tacca del Lupo 52; The Lady President • Mademoiselle Gobette • La Presidentessa 52; Amori di Mezzo Secolo 53*; Gelosia 53; Il Ferroviere • Man of Iron • The Railroad Man 55; The Facts of Murder • Un Maledetto Imbroglio • A Sordid Affair • An Ugly Mess 57; Man of Straw • The Seducer • L'Uomo di Paglia 57; Divorce—Italian Style • Divorzio all'Italiana 61; Sedotta e Abbandonata • Seduced and Abandoned • Séduite et Abandonnée 63; The Birds, Bees and the Italians • The Birds, the Bees and the Italians • Mesdames et Messieurs • Signore e Signori • Signori e Signore 65; Beaucoup Trop pour un Seul Homme • The Climax • L'Immorale • The Immoralist • Too Much for One Man 66; La Bomba 66; Serafino • Serafino ou L'Amour aux Champs 68*; Le Castagne Sono Buone • Pocketful of Chestnuts • Till Divorce Do You Part 70; Alfredo, Alfredo 71; Amici Miei • My Friends 75*

Geronimi, Clyde How the Camel Got His Hump 25; The Leopard's Spots 25; The Giraffe's Long Neck • How the Giraffe Got His Long Neck 26; The Goat's Whiskers 26; The King of the Beasts 26; The Ostrich's Plumes 26; The Stork Brought It 26; Along Came Fido 27; Bone Dry 27; The Farm Hand 27; The Hyena's Laugh 27*; Pete's Pow-Wow 27; The Three Caballeros 44*; Make Mine Music 46*; Melody Time 48*; The Adventures of Ichabod and Mr. Toad • Ichabod and Mr. Toad 49*; Cinderella 50*; Alice in Wonderland 51*; Peter Pan 53*; Lady and the Tramp 55*; Sleeping Beauty 59*; 101 Dalmations 61*

Gerrard, Douglas Polly Put the Kettle On 16; Eternal Love 17; The Cabaret Girl 18; The Empty Cab 18; $5,000 Reward 18; Madame Spy 18; A Mother's Secret 18; Playthings 18; The Velvet Hand 18; His Divorced Wife 19; The Sealed Envelope 19; The Forged Bride 20; The Phantom Melody 20

Gerrard, Gene Out of the Blue 31*; Let Me Explain, Dear 32*; Lucky Girl 32*; Wake Up Famous 37; It's in the Blood 38

Gerrard, Paul Count of Twelve 55

Gerretsen, Peter Night Friend 88

Gerron, Kurt Meine Frau die Hochstaplerin 32; Rauschgift • Der Weisse Dämon • The White Demon 32; Es Wird Schon Wieder Besser 34; Ein Toller Einfall 34

Gershuny, Theodore Death House • Night of the Dark Full Moon • Silent Night, Bloody Night 72; Love, Death 73; Sugar Cookies 77; Deathouse 81

Gerstad, Harry 13 Fighting Men 60

Gerstein, Cassandra Tales 70

Gertler, Victor All Men Are Crazy • A Férfi Mind Örült 37; Mária Növér 37; Marika 38; Changed Man • Elé Sérelt Ember 39; Leányvári Boszorkány • Witch of Leányvár 39

Gervitz, Roberto Feliz Ano Velho 88

Gessner, Nicolas Le Blonde de Pekin • The Blonde from Peking • Peking Blonde • Professional Blonde 67; Thirteen • The Thirteen Chairs • 12 + 1 70; Quelqu'un Derrière la Porte • Someone Behind the Door • Two Minds for Murder 71; The Little Girl Who Lives Down the Lane 76; It Rained All Night the Day I Left 81; Quicker Than the Eye 88

Gessner, Peter Over-Under, Sideways-Down 77*

Getino, Octavio La Hora de los Hornos • The Hour of the Furnaces 66*; Actualización Política y Doctrinaria para la Toma del Poder • Perón: Actualización Política y Doctrinaria para la Toma del Poder 71*; Perón: La Revolución Justicialista • La Revolución Justicialista 71*; El Familiar 73; La Familia Pichilín 78

Gevorkyan, Karen Znaju Tolko Ia 88

Ghaffary, Farrokh Jonube Shahr • Southern Teheran 59; Arous Kodume? • Who Is the Bride? 60; Shabe Quzi 63

Ghai, Subhash Ram Lakhan 89

Gharizadeh, Majid The Grandfather 86

Ghatak, Ritwik The Citizen • Nagarik 52; Oraon 55; Ajantrik • The Mechanical Man • Pathetic Fallacy 58; Bari Theke Paliye • Bari Thekey Pauye • The Runaway • The Vagrants 59; The Cloud-Capped Star • The Hidden Star • Meghe Dhaka Tara • Meghey Dhaaka Taara • The Red Star Hidden by the Moon 60; E Flat • Komal Gandhar • The Soft Ga of the Sargam 61; Scissors 62; Subarnarekha 62; Ustad Alauddin Khan 63; Fear 65; Scientists of Tomorrow 68; Amar Lenin 70; Chhou Dances of Purulia 70; Communal Harmony • The Question • Why • Yeh Kyon 70; Durbargati Padma • Where the Padma Flows 71; A River Called Titash • Titash Ekti Nadir Naam 73; Jukti, Takko ar Gappo • Reason, Debate and a Tale 74

Ghazal, Aziz Before and After 85

Ghedevanshvili, S. Keto and Kote 54*

Gherman, Alexei Sedmoi Sputnik 68*; Proverka na Dorogakh • Trial on the Road 71; Dvadtsat Dnei Bez Voini • Twenty Days Without War 76; Moi Drug Ivan Lapshin • My Friend Ivan Lapshin 86

Gherzo, Paul Fatal Journey 54; The Mysterious Bullet 55; The Stateless Man 55

Ghione, Emilio La Cricca Dorata 13; Idolo Infranto 13; L'Amazzone Mascherata 14; Danzatrice della Taverna Nera 14; Ultimo Dovere 14; Za la Mort 14; Anime Buie 15; La Banda delle Cifre 15; Cicernacchio 15; Guglielmo Oberdan il Martire di

Trieste 15; Il Naufragatore 15; La Sposa della Morte 15; Tresa 15; Don Pietro Caruso 16; Un Dramma Ignorato 16; La Grande Vergogna 16; La Rosa di Granada 16; Tormento Gentile 16; Il Numero 121 17; Il Triangolo Giallo 17; L'Ultima Impressa 17; Il Gorgo • Nel Gorgo 18; I Topi Grigi 18; Dollari e Fraks 19; Il Quadrante d'Oro 20; I Quattro Tramonti 20; L'Ultima Livrea 20; Za la Mort Contro Za la Mort 21; Ultimissime della Notte 22; Il Sogno di Za la Vie 23; Za la Mort e Za la Vie 24; La Nostra Patria 25

Ghose, Gautam Antarjali Yatra 88

Ghosh, P. P. Tere Bina Kya Jina 89

Giacalone, A. Solo per Danne 39; Legittima Difesa • Self Defense 40

Giacobetti, Francis Emmanuelle — The Joys of a Woman 76

Giagni, Gianfranco Il Nido del Ragno • The Spider's Nest 89

Giannarelli, Ansano Remake 88

Giannetti, Alfredo Amori Pericolosi 64*; Engagement Italiano • La Ragazza in Prestito 66

Giannini, Ettore Carosello Napoletano • Neapolitan Carousel 61

Giannini, Giancarlo Jackpot • Nini Terno-Secco • Nini the Gambler • Ternosecco 86

Giannone, Joe Madman 82

Giannopoulou, E. Take Me Away My Love 62

Gibbins, Duncan Fire with Fire 86

Gibbons, Cedric Tarzan and His Mate 34*

Gibbons, Pamela Belinda 87

Gibbs, B. C. Gold and the Dross 16

Giblyn, Charles The Battle of Gettysburg 13*; Civilization's Child 16; Honor Thy Name 16; Not My Sister 16; Peggy 16; The Phantom 16; Somewhere in France 16; The Sorrows of Love 16; The Vagabond Prince 16; The Honeymoon 17; The Lesson 17; The Price She Paid 17; Scandal 17; Just for Tonight 18; Let's Get a Divorce 18; Peck's Bad Girl 18; A Perfect 36 18; The Studio Girl 18*; Sunshine Nan 18; The Spite Bride 19; Upstairs and Down 19; Black Is White 20; The Dark Mirror 20; The Thief 20; The Tiger's Cub 20; Know Your Man • Know Your Men 21; The Mountain Woman 21; Singing River 21; A Woman's Woman 22; The Hypocrites 23; The Leavenworth Case 23; Loyal Lives 23; The Price of a Party 24; The Adventurous Sex 25; Ladies Beware 27

Gibson, Alan Journey Into Midnight 68*; Crescendo 69; Goodbye Gemini 70; Dracula, A.D. 1972 • Dracula Chases the Mini Girls • Dracula Chelsea 72 • Dracula Today 72; Count Dracula and His Vampire Bride • Dracula Is Alive and Well and Living in London • Dracula Is Dead... and Well and Living in London • The Satanic Rites of Dracula 73; Checkered Flag or Crash 77; The Two Faces of Evil 81*; Martin's Day 84

Gibson, Brian Breaking Glass 79; Poltergeist II • Poltergeist II: The Other Side 86

Gibson, Sarah Landslides 87*

Gibson, Stephen Black Lolita 75

Gibson, Tom The Web of the Law 23; A Game Fighter 24; Paying the Limit 24; Three Days to Live 24; Waterfront Wolves 24; The Mystery of the Lost Ranch 25*; Range Buzzards 25; Reckless Courage 25; Stampede Thunder 25; Triple Action 25; West of Arizona 25; Tex 26; The Singing Buckaroo 37

Gic, Jean Ze American Girl 20; A Continuous Line of Thought 20; Stories in Lines 20; A Tragedy in One Line 21

Gicca, Enzo Giorni di Sangue 68; The Price of Death • Il Vendicatore di Morte 71

Giddings, Al Mysteries of the Sea 80*; Visions of the Deep 83

Gideon, Ralph see Reynolds, Sheldon

Giedrys, Marijonas Bludnyy Syn • The Prodigal Son • Sunus Palaidunas 86

Gielgud, John Hamlet 64*

Gies, Hajo Schimanski — Zahn um Zahn • Zahn um Zahn 85; Zabou 87

Giesler, Rodney The Insomniac 72

Gietinger, Klaus Daheim Sterben die Leut' 85*; The Good Old Days • Schön War die Zeit 89*

Giffard, Ellen Christo's Valley Curtain 72*

Giger, Bernhard The Informer • Der Pendler 86

Gil, Margarida Relação Fiel e Verdadeira • A True and Accurate Story 87

Gil, Rafael Don Quixote 49; The Nail 49; I Was a Parish Priest 52; The Song of Sister Maria 52; The Blackmailers 63

Gilbert, Arthur Dreamy Eyes 05; Animal Imitations 06; Ave Maria 06; Captain of the Pinafore 06; Chorus, Gentlemen 06; Excelsior 06; The Fireman's Song 06; The Flowers That Bloom in the Spring 06; Goodbye Sweet Marie 06; The Heart Bowed Down 06; Here's a How-D'Ye-Do 06; Home to Our Mountains 06; In Montezuma from The Belle of Mayfair 06; Lakmé: Les Stances 06; Little Nell 06; The Lord High Executioner 06; The Love Song 06; Miserère 06; Onward Christian Soldiers 06; Serenade from Faust 06; Strolling Home with Angelina 06; Swing Song from Véronique 06; There Is a Green Hill Far Away 06; They Can't Diddle Me 06; Three Little Maids from School 06; Tit Willow 06; The Waltz Must Change to a March 06; We All Walked Into the Shop 06; Wert Thou Not to Koko Plighted 06; You'll Remember Me 06; Are You Sincere? 07; The Bedouin's Love Song 07; The Blind Violinist 07; The Broken Melody 07; Carmen 07; Christians Awake! 07; Cupid 07; Curfew Shall Not Ring Tonight 07; Every Little Bit Helps 07; Faust 07; The Fireman 07; Glow, Little Glow Worm, Glow 07; Harrigan 07; Home Again My Cherry Blossom 07; I Love a Lassie 07; Inverary 07; The Laughing Nigger 07; March of the Light Cavalry 07; My Indian Anna 07; Navaho 07; Nelson's Victory 07; Please Conductor, Don't Put Me Off the Train 07; Regiment of Frocks and Frills 07; The

Royal Standard 07; She Is My Daisy 07; Stop Your Tickling, Jock 07; Tala — Indian Love Song 07; Twin Brothers from The French Maid 07; Wait Till the Work Comes 'Round 07; We Parted on the Shore 07; The Wedding of Sandy McNab 07; Will Evans: On the Doorstep — Novelette — The Jockey 07; Won't You Throw Me a Kiss? 07; All Coons Look Alike to Me 08; Come My Lad and Be a Soldier 08; D'Ye Ken John Peel? 08; Following in Father's Footsteps 08; Goodbye Little Sister 08; Hello Little Girl Hello 08; I Get Dizzy When I Do That Twostep Dance 08; The Keys of Heaven 08; Many Is the Time 08; Montezuma 08; Redwing 08; She's Proud and She's Beautiful 08; Waltz Me Around Again Willie 08; We Close at Two on Thursday 08; Zuyder Zee 08; Convict 99 09; A Gaiety Duet 09; The Mystery of Edwin Drood 09

Gilbert, Brad Touch of a Stranger 90

Gilbert, Brian French Lesson • The Frog Prince 84; Sharma and Beyond 84; Vice Versa 88

Gilbert, C. Allen The Chess Queen 16; Haunts for Rent 16; In the Shadows 16; Inbad the Sailor 16; Inbad the Sailor Gets Into Deep Water 16; The Toyland Paper Chase 16

Gilbert, Jack The Bait 20*; Love's Penalty 21

Gilbert, James Sunstruck 72

Gilbert, Lewis Burglar Bill 16*; Solomon's Twins 16*; The Web of Fate 16

Gilbert, Lewis Sailors Do Care 44; The Ten Year Plan 45; Arctic Harvest 46; Under One Roof 46; Fishing Grounds of the World 47; The Little Ballerina 47; Once a Sinner 50; Scarlet Thread 50; There Is Another Sun • Wall of Death 51; Cosh Boy • The Slasher • Tough Guy 52; Emergency! • Emergency Call • The Hundred Hour Hunt 52; Johnny on the Run 52*; Nothing to Lose • Time Gentlemen, Please! 52; Albert, R.N. • Break to Freedom • Spare Man 53; The Good Die Young 54; The Sea Shall Not Have Them 54; Cast a Dark Shadow 55; Reach for the Sky 56; The Admirable Crichton • Paradise Lagoon 57; Carve Her Name with Pride 58; A Cry from the Streets 58; Ferry to Hong Kong 59; Light Up the Sky! • Skywatch 60; Sink the Bismarck! 60; Damn the Defiant! • H.M.S. Defiant • The Mutineers 61; The Greengage Summer • Loss of Innocence 61; The 7th Dawn • The Third Road 63; Alfie 66; You Only Live Twice 67*; The Adventurers 69; Friends 71; Paul and Michelle • Paul et Michele 74; Operation Daybreak • The Price of Freedom • Seven Men at Daybreak 75; Seven Nights in Japan 76; The Spy Who Loved Me 77; Moonraker 79; The World of Gilbert & George 81; Educating Rita 83; Not Quite Jerusalem • Not Quite Paradise 84; Shirley Valentine 89

Gilbert, Philip Blood and Lace 70

Gilbert, Rod Le Sette Magnifiche Pistole 66

Glackens, L. M. Another Fallen Idol 15; Greenland's Icy Mountains 16; Haddem Baad's Elopement 16; How Dizzy Joe Got to Heaven 16; Independent Poland 16; Jack the Giant Killer 16; The Pen Is Mightier Than the Sword 16; The Stone Age Roost Robber 16; What Happened to Willie 16; What Next? 16; The First Flyer 18; Me und Gott 18; Von Loon's Non-Capturable Aeroplane 18; Von Loon's 25,000 Mile Gun 18; The Biography of Madame Fashion 19; Private Bass Has Pass 19; Tying the Nuptial Knot 19; Yes Times Have Changed 20

Gladstone, John Discipline 35*

Gladwell, David Requiem for a Village 77; Memoirs of a Survivor 81

Gladwish, Hugh The Ghost Goes Gear 66

Glagolev, Gennady Razmakh Kryliev • Wingspan 87

Glagolin, Boris The Coward 14*; Kira Kiralina 27

Glaister, Gerard Clue of the Silver Key 61; The Share Out 62; The Partner 63; The Set-Up 63

Glaser, Paul Michael Band of the Hand 86; The Running Man 87

Glasser, Bernard The Sergeant Was a Lady 61; Diamond Country • Diamond Hunters • Robo de Diamantes • Run Like a Thief 67

Glavany, Guarino G. Downstream 29; Hours of Loneliness • An Obvious Situation 30

Glazer, Benjamin Strange Cargo 29*; Song of My Heart 47

Gleason, James Hot Tip 35*

Gleason, Joseph The Beloved Imposter 18; Fortune's Child 19; Miss Dulcie from Dixie 19

Gleason, Michie Broken English 81; Summer Heat 87

Gleize, Maurice La Main Qui à Tue 24; La Nuit Rouge 24; La Justicière 25; La Faute de Monique 28; La Madone des Sleepings • The Madonna of the Sleeping Cars 28; Tu M'Appartiens 29

Glen, John Gold 74*; Shout at the Devil 76*; For Your Eyes Only 81; Octopussy 83; A View to a Kill 85; The Living Daylights 87; Licence to Kill 89

Glendon, Frank see Glendon, J. Frank

Glendon, J. Frank Circle of Death 35

Glenister, John Miss Julie 72*

Glenn, Jack Cry Murder 36

Glenn, Pierre-William Les Enragés 85; End of the Line • Terminus 86

Glennon, Bert The Air Legion 28; Gang War 28; The Perfect Crime 28; Stepping High 28; Syncopation 29; Around the Corner 30; Girl of the Port 30; Paradise Island 30; In Line of Duty • In the Line of Duty 31; South of Santa Fe 32

Glenville, Peter The Prisoner 55; Me and the Colonel 58; Summer and Smoke 61; Term of Trial 62; Becket 63; Hotel Paradiso 66; The Comedians 67

Glickenhaus, James The Astrologer 79; The Exterminator 80; Codename: The Soldier • The Soldier 82; The Protector 85;

Shakedown 88

Glicker, Paul The Cheerleaders 73; Running Scared 80

Gliddon, John The Night Hawk 21; Pins and Needles 21; Señorita 21

Gliese, Rochus Der Yoghi • The Yogi 16*; Der Golem und die Tänzerin 17*; The Pied Piper of Hamelin • The Ratcatcher • Der Rattenfänger von Hameln 17*; The Lost Shadow • Der Verlorene Schatten 21*; La Chasse à la Fortune • La Chasse au Bonheur • Die Jagd nach dem Glück 30*

Glinski, Robert Labedzi Spiew 88

Glom, Lasse Dream of Northern Lights • Havlandet 86; Sweetwater 88

Gloor, Kurt Die Plötzliche Einsamkeit des Konrad Steiner 75; Der Erfinder 80; Mann Ohne Gedächtnis 84

Glowna, Vadim Desperado City 81; The Devil's Paradise 87

Glück, Wolfgang Five Sinners • Das Nachtlokal zum Silbermond • The Sinners 61; Mädchen für die Mambobar • $100 a Night 68; '38 86

Glyn, Elinor Knowing Men 30; The Price of Things 30

Gniazdowski, Tom Tin Star Void 88

Gobbett, T. J. A Modern Grace Darling 08; Anarchy in England 09; A Bad Day for Levinsky 09; Father Buys the Fireworks 09; Jaggers Breaks All Records 09; The Price of Bread 09; A Tragedy of the Truth 09; When Mama's Out 09; A Child's Message to Heaven 10; The Emigrant 10; The New Recruit 10

Gobbi, Sergio Temps des Loups • Time of the Wolves 70; The Heist 79

Gobjitti, Chart Ban • House 87*

Gobjitti, Egalag Ban • House 87*

Gochis, Constantine S. The Redeemer • The Redeemer...Son of Satan 76

Godal, Edward Adventurous Youth 28; Chips 38

Godard, Jean-Luc Opération Béton 54; Une Femme Coquette 55; All Boys Are Called Patrick • Charlotte et Véronique • Charlotte et Véronique ou Tous les Garçons S'Appellent Patrick • Tous les Garçons S'Appellent Patrick 57; Charlotte et Son Jules 58; Une Histoire d'Eau • A Story of Water 58*; À Bout de Souffle • Breathless 59; La Donna È Donna • Une Femme Est une Femme • A Woman Is a Woman 60; The Little Soldier • Le Petit Soldat 60; Les Sept Péchés Capitaux • I Sette Peccati Capitali • Seven Capital Sins • The Seven Deadly Sins 61*; It's My Life • My Life to Live • Vivre Sa Vie • Vivre Sa Vie: Film en Douze Tableaux 62; RoGoPaG 62*; The Beautiful Swindlers • Les Plus Belles Escroqueries du Monde • World's Greatest Swindles • The World's Most Beautiful Swindlers 63*; Les Carabiniers • The Riflemen • The Soldiers 63; Contempt • Il Disprezzo • A Ghost at Noon • Le Mépris 63; Band of Outsiders • Bande à Part • The Outsiders 64; La Femme Mariée • Une Femme Mariée • A Married Woman • The Married Woman 64; Paris Vu par... • Six

in Paris 64*; Reportage sur Orly 64; Alphaville • Alphaville—A Strange Case of Lemmy Caution • Alphaville—Une Étrange Aventure de Lemmy Caution • Une Étrange Aventure de Lemmy Caution • Tarzan vs. IBM 65; Crazy Pete • Peter the Crazy • Pierrot le Fou 65; Deux ou Trois Choses Que Je Sais d'Elle • Two or Three Things I Know About Her 66; Far from Vietnam • Loin du Viêt-nam 66*; Made in U.S.A. 66; Masculin-Féminin • Masculin-Féminin—15 Faits Precis • Masculine Feminine • Maskulinum-Femininum 66; Das Alteste Gewerbe der Welt • L'Amore Attraverso i Secoli • L'Amour à Travers les Âges • The Oldest Profession • Le Plus Vieux Métier du Monde 67*; Amore e Rabbia • La Contestation • Love and Anger • Vangelo '70 67*; The Chinese Girl • La Chinoise • La Chinoise ou Plutôt à la Chinoise: Un Film en Train de Se Faire • Plutôt à la Chinoise 67; Le Gai Savoir • Happy Knowledge • The Joy of Learning • The Joyful Wisdom • Merry Wisdom 67; Weekend • Le Week-End 67; British Sounds • See You at Mao • Sons Anglais 68*; Ciné-Tracts 68; Un Film Comme les Autres • A Film Like All the Others • A Film Like Any Other 68*; One Plus One • Sympathy for the Devil 68; East Wind • Le Vent d'Est • Vento dell'Est • Wind from the East 69*; Lotte in Italia • Luttes en Italie • Struggle in Italy 69*; Pravda 69*; Jusqu'à la Victoire • Till Victory 70*; Vladimir and Rosa • Vladimir et Rosa 70*; Just Great • Tout Va Bien 71*; Letter to Jane • Letter to Jane: Investigation of a Still • Lettre à Jane 72*; Moi Je 73; Ici et Ailleurs 74*; Comment Ça Va 75*; Number Two • Numéro Deux 75; Every Man for Himself • Every Man for Himself (Slow Motion) • Sauve Qui Peut (La Vie) • Slow Motion 79; Godard's Passion • Passion 81; First Name: Carmen • Prénom Carmen 82; Lettre à Freddy Buache 82; Hail, Mary • Je Vous Salue, Marie 83; Détective 84; Grandeur and Decadence of a Small-Time Film Company • Grandeur et Décadence d'un Petit Commerce de Cinéma 86; Aria 87*; Keep Your Right Up • Soigné Ta Droite 87; King Lear 87; New Wave • Nouvelle Vague 90

Godbout, J. Rose et Landry 62*

Goddard, Frederick Through Stormy Waters 20

Goddard, Gary Masters of the Universe 87

Goddard, Jim Parker 84; Hitler's SS: Portrait in Evil 85; Shanghai Surprise 86

Goddard, Keith The Princess and the Pea 79

Gödel, Peter The Hothouse • Das Treibhaus 87

Godfrey, Bob The Battle of New Orleans 60; The Plain Man's Guide to Advertising 62; One Man Band 65; Art for Art's Sake • L'Art pour l'Art 66; Great: Isambard Kingdom Brunel 75

Godfrey, Peter Thread o' Scarlet 30;

Down River 31; The Lone Wolf Spy Hunt • The Lone Wolf's Daughter 39; Unexpected Uncle 41; Highways by Night 42; Make Your Own Bed 44; Christmas in Connecticut • Indiscretion 45; Hotel Berlin 45*; One More Tomorrow 46; Cry Wolf 47; Escape Me Never 47; That Hagen Girl 47; The Two Mrs. Carrolls 47; The Decision of Christopher Blake 48; The Woman in White 48; The Girl from Jones Beach 49; One Last Fling 49; Barricade 50; The Great Jewel Robber 50; He's a Cockeyed Wonder 50; One Big Affair 52; Please Murder Me! 56

Godley, Kevin The Cooler 82*; The Police, Synchronicity Concert 84*

Godmilow, Jill Antonia: A Portrait of the Woman 74*; Far from Poland 83*; On the Trail of the Lonesome Pine • Waiting for the Moon 87

Godoy, Armando Robles see Robles Godoy, Armando

Godwin, Frank Electric Eskimo 79; The Boy Who Never Was 80; Break Out 84; Terry on the Fence 85

Goebel, O. E. The Eternal Light 19*; The Blasphemer 21

Goedel, Peter see Gödel, Peter

Goel, Jyotin Inaam Das Hazaar 87

Goetz, Ben The Inevitable 17

Goetz, John Uncle Vanya 58*

Goetz, Siggi see Götz, Siggi

Gogh, Theo van Charley 86; Return to Oestgeest • Terug naar Oestgeest 87

Gogoberidze, Lana Interviews on Personal Problems • Neskolko Intervyu po Lichnyam Voprosam • Several Interviews on Personal Matters 79; Krugovorot • Turnover 87

Gogoberidze, Nutsa Ikh Tsartsvo • 18-28 28*

Goitein, Alex E. Cherry Hill High 77; Cheerleaders Beach Party 78

Golan, Menahem El Dorado 63; Einer Spielt Falsch • Mivtza Kahir • Trunk to Cairo 66; The Girl from the Dead Sea 67; Love in Jerusalem • Margo • My Margo 67; Tevye and His Seven Daughters 68; Fortuna 69; What's Good for the Gander • What's Good for the Goose 69; Lupo 70; Malkat Hakvish • Queen of the Road 70; Katz and Karasso 71; 999 — Aliza the Policeman 71; Escape to the Sun • Habricha el Hashemesh 72; The Great Telephone Robbery 72; Kazablan 73; Eagles Attack at Dawn 74; Diamonds 75; Lepke 75; The Ambassador 76; Entebbe: Operation Thunderbolt • Operation Thunderbolt 77; Agenten Kennen Keine Tränen • The Uranium Conspiracy 78; The Magician of Lublin 79; The Apple • Star-Rock 80; Enter the Ninja 81; My Darling Shiksa • Over the Brooklyn Bridge 83; The Delta Force 86; Over the Top 87; Hanna's War 88; Mack the Knife • The Threepenny Opera 89

Golaszewski, Włodzimierz Dłużnicy Śmierci 85

Gold, Jack Happy As Can Be 58; The Visit 59; Living Jazz 60; The Snowdon

Aviary 66; The Bofors Gun 68; The Reckoning 69; The Man in the Steel Mask • Man Without a Face • Prisoner of the Skull • Robo Man • Who? 73; The National Health • The National Health, or Nurse Norton's Affairs 73; Man Friday 75; Aces High 76; The Medusa Touch 78; The Naked Civil Servant 78; The Sailor's Return 78; Little Lord Fauntleroy 80; Praying Mantis 82; Good and Bad at Games 83; Red Monarch 83; The Chain 84; Ball-Trap on the Côte Sauvage 89

Gold, Joel Joe and Maxi 80*

Gold, Myron J. La Rabia • The Rage • The Rage Within 63; Frankenstein's Great-Aunt Tillie 85

Goldbeck, Willis Dr. Gillespie's New Assistant 42; Crazy to Kill • Dr. Gillespie's Criminal Case 43; Rationing 43; Between Two Women 44; Three Men in White 44; She Went to the Races 45; Love Laughs at Andy Hardy 46; Cynthia's Secret • Dark Delusion 47; Johnny Holiday 49; Ten Tall Men 51

Goldberg, Dan The MUSE Concert: No Nukes • No Nukes 80*; Feds 88

Goldberg, Gary David Dad 89

Goldberg, Maurice The Feeling of Inferiority 48

Goldblatt, M. Gypsies 36*

Goldblatt, Mark The Punisher 87; Dead Heat 88

Golden, John Fat Guy Goes Nutzoid • Zeisters 83; The Boiler Room 87

Golden, Joseph A. The Count of Monte Cristo 13*; The Exploits of Elaine 14*; The Better Woman 15; Divorced 15; The New Exploits of Elaine 15*; Not Guilty 15; The Price 15; The Romance of Elaine 15*; The Senator 15; The Libertine 16*; Love's Cross Roads 16; The Prima Donna's Husband 16*; The Law of Compensation 17*; Redemption 17*; Fangs of the Wolf 24*

Golden, Robert Honeymoon 28

Goldfarb, Lawrence G. Stuckey's Last Stand 80

Goldin, Sidney The Last of the Maffia 15; The Gates of Doom 19; The Bird Fancier 20; The Woman Hater 20; East Side Sadie 29; His Wife's Lover 31; Shulamis 31; Uncle Moses 32*

Golding, Paul Pulse 88

Goldman, F. Lyle The Ear 20; Wireless Telephony 20

Goldman, Gary All Dogs Go to Heaven 89*

Goldman, Martin The Legend of Nigger Charley 72; Dark August 75

Goldman, Mical The Divided Trail 80*

Goldman, Peter Echoes of Silence 66; Wheel of Ashes 70

Goldman, Stuart Senior Week 88

Goldschmidt, Didier A Foreign City • Ville Étrangère 88

Goldschmidt, Gilbert de see De Goldschmidt, Gilbert

Goldschmidt, John Crime of Honor 85; She'll Be Wearing Pink Pajamas • She'll Be Wearing Pink Pyjamas 85; Maschenka 87

Goldstein, Allan The Outside Chance of

Maximilian Glick 88

Goldstein, Marek Long Is the Road 48*

Goldstein, Scott Flanagan • Walls of Glass 85

Goldstone, James Jigsaw 68; A Man Called Gannon 68; Winning 69; Brother John 70; Red Sky at Morning 70; The Gang That Couldn't Shoot Straight 71; They Only Kill Their Masters 72; The Scarlet Buccaneer • Swashbuckler 76; Rollercoaster 77; The Day the World Ended • Earth's Final Fury • When Time Ran Out... 79

Goldstone, Phil Montana Bill 21; Backstage 27; The Girl from Gay Paree 27; Once and Forever 27; Snowbound 27; Wild Geese 27; The Sin of Nora Moran • Voice from the Grave 33; Damaged Goods • Marriage Forbidden 37

Goldstone, Richard Cinerama — South Seas Adventure • South Seas Adventure 58*; Island Escape • No Man Is an Island 62*

Goldvani, M. The Power of Evil 29*

Goldwasser, Yankul Abba Ganuv 88

Goldwyn, Samuel, Jr. Chance Meeting • The Young Lovers 64

Golestan, Ebrahim Fire 61; Darya 64; Wave, Coral and Rock 64

Gollings, Franklin Connecting Rooms 69

Golubović, Predrag Dobrovoljci • Volunteers 86

Gomer, Steve Sweet Lorraine 86

Gomes, Flora Mortu Nega 88

Gómez, Fernando Fernán Mambrú Se Fué a la Guerra • Mambru Went to War 86; Viaje a Ninguna Parte • Voyage to Nowhere 86

Gómez, Guillermo Hernández see Hernández Gómez, Guillermo

Gómez, Manuel Octavio Cooperativas Agrícolas: El Agua 60; Historia de una Batalla • History of a Battle 62; Cuentos del Alhamnara: Guancanayabo 63; El Encuentro: La Salación 65; Tulipa 67; Nuevitas 68; First Charge of the Machete • La Primera Carga al Machete 69; Days of Water 72; Now It's Up to You • Ustedes Tienen la Palabra 74; La Tierra y el Cielo 77; Una Mujer, un Hombre, una Ciudad • A Woman, a Man, a City 78; Patakin 85

Gómez, Sara Iré a Santiago 64; Excursión a Vueltabajo 65; Y Tenemos Sabor 67; En la Otra Isla 68; Isla del Tesoro 69; Poder Local, Poder Popular 70; Un Documental a Propósito del Tránsito 71; Año Uno 72; Atención Prenatal 72; Sobre Horas Extras y Trabajo Voluntaria 73; De Cierta Manera • One Way or Another 74

Gómez Muriel, Emilio Pescados • Redes • The Wave 34*; 800 Leagues Over the Amazon 58; The Empty Star • La Estrella Vacía 62; Shipwreck Island 62

Goncalves, Vitor Uma Rapáriga no Verão 86

Goncharov, Vasili M. Conquest of Siberia 08; The Death of Ivan the Terrible 09*; Mazeppa 09; Moscow Drama 09; Song of the Merchant Kalashnikov 09*;

The Life and Death of Pushkin 10; Napoleon in Russia 10; Peter the Great 10*; Crime and Punishment 11; The Defense of Sevastopol 11*; Eugene Onegin • Yevgeni Onegin 11; Life for the Czar 11; 1812 12*; Accession of the Romanov Dynasty 13*; Volga and Siberia 14

González, Cristián Thanatos 86

González, Julián El Rayo 35

González, Rogelio A. La Nave de los Monstruos 59; Clavillazo en la Luna • El Conquistador de la Luna 60

González, Rogelio A., Jr. El Hombre Desnudo • The Naked Man 87

González, Servando Yanco 60; Los Mediocres 62; The Fool Killer • Violent Journey 65; Viento Negro 65; El Último Túnel 87

González Sinde, José María A la Pálida Luz de la Luna • By the Pale Light of the Moon 86

Good, T. Kid il Monello del West 73

Goode, Frederic The Flood 63; Stopover Forever 64; Valley of the Kings 64; Death Is a Woman • Love Is a Woman • Sex Is a Woman 65; Go Go Mania • Pop Gear 65; The Beast of Morocco • The Hand of Night 66; Davey Jones' Locker 66; Son of the Sahara 67; The Great Pony Raid 68; The Syndicate 68; Avalanche 75

Goodell, Gregory Beyond the Gate • Human Experiments 79

Goodell, John Jackpot 82

Goodkind, Saul Buck Rogers • Destination Saturn 39*; The Oregon Trail 39*; The Phantom Creeps 39*

Goodman, Daniel Carson Thoughtless Women 20

Goodman, Edward Man of the World 31*; Women Love Once 31

Goodman, Philip We Shall Return 63

Goodrich, William B. see Arbuckle, Roscoe

Goodwin, Robert L. Black Chariot 71

Goodwins, Fred The Artistic Temperament • Her Greater Gift 19; The Chinese Puzzle 19; Build Thy House 20; Colonel Newcome the Perfect Gentleman 20; The Department Store 20; The Ever-Open Door 20; The Impossible Man 20; The Noble Art 20; The Scarlet Kiss 20; Blood Money 21

Goodwins, Leslie Heave Two 33; Shakespeare—With Tin Ears 33; Thrown Out of Joint 33*; Camp Meetin' 36; Deep South 36; Dummy Ache 36; Framing Father 36; Grandma's Buoys 36; High Beer Pressure 36; One Live Ghost 36; Radiobarred 36; Swing It! 36; Vocalising 36; A Wedtime Story 36; Who's Looney Now? 36; With Love and Kisses 36; Anything for a Thrill 37; Bad Housekeeping 37; Dumb's the Word 37; Edgar and Goliath 37; Harris in the Spring 37; Headline Crasher 37; Hillbilly Goat 37; Lochs and Bonds 37; Mississippi Moods 37; Morning, Judge 37; Should Wives Work? 37; That Man Samson 37; Tramp Trouble 37; Wrong Romanie 37; Young Dynamite 37; Almost a Gentleman • Magnificent Outcast 38;

Crime Ring 38; Ears of Experience 38; False Roomers 38; Fool Coverage 38; Fugitives for a Night 38; His Pest Friend 38; The Jitters 38; Kennedy's Castle 38; Mr. Doodle Kicks Off 38; Romancing Along 38; Tarnished Angel 38; Twenty Girls and a Band 38; A Western Welcome 38; The Day the Bookies Wept 39; The Girl from Mexico 39; Mexican Spitfire 39; Sued for Libel 39; Glamour Boy • Millionaire Playboy 40; Let's Make Music 40; Men Against the Sky 40; Mexican Spitfire Out West 40; Pop Always Pays 40; Mexican Spitfire at Sea 41; Mexican Spitfire's Baby 41; Parachute Battalion 41; They Met in Argentina 41*; Mexican Spitfire Sees a Ghost 42; Mexican Spitfire's Elephant 42; Silver Skates 42; The Adventures of a Rookie 43; Gals, Inc. 43; Ladies' Day 43; Mexican Spitfire's Blessed Event 43; Rookies in Burma 43; Casanova in Burlesque 44; Goin' to Town 44; Hi Beautiful! • Pass to Romance 44; The Mummy's Curse 44; Murder in the Blue Room 44; The Singing Sheriff 44; An Angel Comes to Brooklyn 45; I'll Tell the World 45; Radio Stars on Parade 45; What a Blonde! 45; Genius at Work 46; Riverboat Rhythm 46; Vacation in Reno 46; The Dragnet 47; The Lone Wolf in London 47; Bachelor Blues 48; Pal's Return 48; Put Some Money in the Pot 49; Brooklyn Buckaroos 50; Photo Phonies 50; From Rogues to Riches 51; Lord Epping Returns 51; Punchy Pancho 51; Tinhorn Troubadors 51; Gold Fever 52; Fireman Save My Child 54; Fresh from Paris • Paris Follies of 1956 • Showtime 55; A Comedy Tale of Fanny Hill 65; Tammy and the Millionaire 67*

Goosens, Ray Pinocchio dans le Space • Pinocchio in Outer Space • Pinocchio's Adventure in Outer Space 64

Gopal, B. Raktha Tilakam 88

Gopalakrishnan, Adoor Elippathayam • Rat-Trap 81; Anantaram • The Rest of the Story 86; Face to Face • Mukhamukham 86

Gopinath, V. R. Oru Maymasappulariyil 88

Gopo, Ion Popescu see Popescu-Gopo, Ion

Gora, Claudio The Sky Is Red 52; Il Nero—Hass War Sein Gebet 69

Gordeladze, Leila Five Brides, Then a Sweetheart • Pyat Nevest do Lyubimoy 87

Gordon, Alexander The Ransom • Vykup 87

Gordon, Bert I. Serpent Island 54; King Dinosaur 55; The Amazing Colossal Man 57; Attack of the Puppet People • Six Inches Tall 57; Beginning of the End 57; Cyclops 57; Earth vs. the Spider • The Spider 58; The Terror Strikes • War of the Colossal Beast 58; The Boy and the Pirates 60; Tormented 60; The Magic Sword • St. George and the Seven Curses 62; Village of the Giants 65; Picture Mommy Dead 66; How to Succeed with Sex 70; Detective Geronimo • The Police Connection • Police Connection: Detective Geronimo 72; Necromancy • The Witching 72; The

Mad Bomber 73; The Food of the Gods 76; Empire of the Ants 77; The Coming 81; Doing It 84; The Big Bet 86

Gordon, Bette Variety 83; Seven Women, Seven Sins 87*

Gordon, Edward R. The Case of a Packing Case 21; Fight in a Thieves' Kitchen 21; The Girl Who Came Back 21; The Lady in Black 21; Lost, Stolen or Strayed 21; Mother's Darling 21; The Notorious Mrs. Fagin 21; The Prodigal Son 21; Something in the City 21; The Stolen Jewels 21; Love's Influence 22*; Repentance 22; Lieutenant Daring RN and the Water Rats 24*; Gun-Hand Garrison 27; Ridin' Luck 27; Wild Born 27

Gordon, Gerald So Long Blue Boy 73

Gordon, James Hoodman Blind 13

Gordon, John J. This Is Your Army 54

Gordon, Jonathan King, Murray 69*

Gordon, Keith The Chocolate War 88

Gordon, Leslie Howard The House of Unrest 31; Account Rendered 32; The Double Event 34

Gordon, Lewis H. see Lewis, Herschell Gordon

Gordon, Michael Blackie Goes Hollywood • Blackie Goes to Hollywood • Boston Blackie Goes Hollywood 42; One Dangerous Night 42; Underground Agent 42; Crime Doctor 43; The Web 47; An Act of Murder • Live Today for Tomorrow 48; Another Part of the Forest 48; The Lady Gambles 49; Woman in Hiding 49; Cyrano de Bergerac 50; I Can Get It for You Wholesale • Only the Best • This Is My Affair 51; The Secret of Convict Lake 51; Wherever She Goes 51; All Hallowe'en 53; Pillow Talk 59; Portrait in Black 60; Boys' Night Out 62; For Love or Money 63; Move Over, Darling 63; A Very Special Favor 65; Texas Across the River 66; The Impossible Years 68; How Do I Love Thee? 70

Gordon, Robert Blind Spot 47; Heart Royal • Sport of Kings 47; Black Eagle 48; The Joe Louis Story 53; It Came from Beneath the Sea 55; Damn Citizen 58; The Rawhide Trail 58; Black Zoo • Horrors of the Black Zoo 63; Tarzan and the Jungle Boy • Tarzan No. 22 68; The Gatling Gun • King Gun 71

Gordon, Steve Arthur 81

Gordon, Stuart H. P. Lovecraft's Re-Animator • Re-Animator 85; Dolls 86; From Beyond 86; Robojox • Robot Jox 87

Gordon, Warren Woman's Man 20

Gordy, Berry Mahogany 75

Gore, Arthur Holmes see Holmes-Gore, Arthur

Goren, Rowby Cracking Up 77*

Gören, Şerif Osman the Infantryman • Osman the Wanderer • Piyade Osman 70*; The Example • İbret 71*; Anxiety • Endişe 74*; The Trek of Life • The Way • Yol 81; Derman • Remedy 84; The Frogs • Kurbağalar 86; Revenge of the Serpents • Yılanların Öcü 86; Sen Türkülerini Söyle • Sing Your Songs 86; The Street of Hope • Umut Sokağı 86

Goretta, Claude Nice Time 57*; Le Fou • The Madman 70; L'Invitation • The Invitation 73; Not As Bad As That • Not As Wicked As That • Pas Si Méchant Que Ça... • This Wonderful Crook • The Wonderful Crook 74; La Dentellière • The Lacemaker 77; The Epistemology of Jean Piaget • Jean Piaget 77; Les Chemins de l'Exil ou Les Dernières Années de Jean-Jacques Rousseau • The Roads of Exile 78; Bonheur Toi-Même 80; A Girl from Lorraine • La Provinciale 80; The Death of Mario Ricci • La Mort de Mario Ricci 83; Orfeo 85; If the Sun Never Returns • Si le Soleil Ne Revenait Pas 87; Les Ennemis de la Mafia 88

Gorikker, Vladimir Iolanta • Yolanta 64; The Tsar's Bride • Tsarskaya Nevesta 66

Gorin, Jean-Pierre British Sounds • See You at Mao • Sons Anglais 68*; Un Film Comme les Autres • A Film Like All the Others • A Film Like Any Other 68*; East Wind • Le Vent d'Est • Vento dell'Est • Wind from the East 69*; Lotte in Italia • Luttes en Italie • Struggle in Italy 69*; Pravda 69*; Jusqu'à la Victoire • Till Victory 70*; Vladimir and Rosa • Vladimir et Rosa 70*; Just Great • Tout Va Bien 71*; Letter to Jane • Letter to Jane: Investigation of a Still • Lettre à Jane 72*; Poto and Cabengo 82; Ordinary Pleasures 85

Gorkovenko, Yuri Geroy Yeyo Romana • The Hero of Her Dreams 87

Görling, Lars Guilt • Tillsammans med Gunilla • Tillsammans med Gunilla Måndag Kväll och Tisdag • With Gunilla Monday Evening and Tuesday 67

Gorman, Jack see Gorman, John

Gorman, John Little Orphan 15; The Soul of a Child 16; Corruption 17; The Butterfly Girl 21; Why Women Remarry 23; The Painted Flapper 24; Wasted Lives 25; The Prince of Broadway 26; Black Tears 27

Gormezano, Gerardo El Vent de l'Illa 88

Gormley, Charles The Gospel According to Vic • Heavenly Pursuits • Just Another Miracle 85

Gornick, Michael Creepshow II 87

Gorpenko, Vladimir Tvoyo Mirnoe Nebo • Your Peaceful Sky 87*

Gorris, Marleen A Question of Silence • De Stilte Rond Christine M. 82; Broken Mirrors • Gebroken Spiegels 84

Gorski, Peter Faust 63

Goscinny, René Lucky Luke 71

Gosha, Hideo Goyōkin 69; Hitokiri • Tenchū 70; Hunter in the Dark 70; The Wolves 72; Bandits vs. Samurai Squadron 80; Onimasa 82; Yokiro 84; Cracked 85; Fireflies of the North 85; The Paddle 85; Face Powder • Usugeshō 86; Tokyo Bordello • Yoshiwara Enjo 86; Death Shadows • Jittemai 87; Fire Over the Women's Castle 87; A Woman Who Wouldn't Marry 87; The Four Days of Snow and Blood 88; The Gates of Flesh • Nikutai no Mon 88

Gosho, Heinosuke A Casket for Living

• Contemporary Jewelry Box • Tosei Tamatebako 25; First Love • Hatsukoi 25; Man's Heart • Otoko Gokoro 25; Nanto no Haru • Spring in Southern Islands • Spring of Southern Island 25; No Clouds in the Sky • The Sky Is Clear • The Sky Shines • Sora wa Haretari 25; Seishun • Youth 25; Bamboo Leaf Flute of No Return • Kaeranu Sasabue • No Return 26; A Daughter • Musume 26; The Girl Friend • Kanojo • She 26; Haha yo Koishi • Mother I Miss You • Mothers' Love 26; Honryū • A Rapid Stream • A Torrent 26; Itoshii no Wagako • My Beloved Child • My Loving Child 26; Machi no Hitobito • People in the Town • Town People 26; Death of a Maiden • Death of a Virgin • Shojo no Shi 27; Fake Girl • Karakuri Musume • Tricky Girl 27; Hazukashii Yume • Intimate Dream • Shameful Dream 27; Lonely Hoodlum • The Lonely Roughneck • Sabishiki Ranbōmono 27; Moon-Faced • Ōkame • A Plain Woman 27; Mura no Hanayome • The Village Bride 27; Because I Love • If You Like It • Suki Nareba Koso 28; Cat of the Night • Yoru no Meneko • Yoru no Mesuneko 28; Debauchery Is Wrong • Dōraku Goshinan • Guidance to the Indulgent 28; Gaitō no Kishi • Kaidō no Kishi • Knight of the Street 28; Haha yo Kimi no Na o Kegasu Nakare • Mother Do Not Shame Your Name 28; Hito no Yo Sugata • Man's Worldly Appearance • The Situation of the Human World 28; Kami e no Michi • The Road to God • The Way to the God 28; A New Kind of Woman • New Woman's Guidance • Shin Josei no Kagami • Shin Joseikan 28; The Bath Harem • Bath of the Transitory World • Ukiyo-Buro 29; Father and His Child • Father and His Son • Oyaji to Sono Ko 29; Jōnetsu no Ichiya • Netsujō no Ichiya • A Night of Passion • One Night of Passion 29; Aiyoku no Yoru • Desire of Night • Record of Love and Desire 30; Bachelors Beware • Dokushinsha Goyōjin 30; Big Forest • Dai Shinrin 30; A Corner of Great Tokyo • Dai-Tōkyō no Ikkaku 30; Hohoemu Jinsei • A Smiling Character • A Smiling Life 30; Jokyū Aishi • Sad Story of a Barmaid 30; Kinuyo Monogatari • The Kinuyo Story • Story of Kinuyo 30; Onna yo Kimi no Na o Kegasu Nakare • Woman Don't Make Your Name Dirty • Women Do Not Shame Your Names 30; Shojo Nyūyō • Virgin Wanted • We Need Virgins 30; Blooming at Night • Open at Night • Yoru Hiraku 31; Excitement of a Young Day • Memories of Young Days • Wakaki Hi no Kangeki 31; Gutai Kenkai • Silly Younger Brother and Clever Elder Brother • Stupid Young Brother and Wise Old Brother 31; Island of Naked Scandal • Naked Murder Case of the Island • Shima no Ratai Jiken 31; Madame and Wife • Madamu to Nyōbo • The Neighbor's Wife and Mine • Next Door Madame and My Wife 31; A Cuckoo • Hototogisu 32; Ginza no Yanagi • A Willow Tree in the Ginza • Willows of

Ginza 32; Heaven Linked with Love • Tengoku ni Musube Koi 32; Koi no Tōkyō • Love in Tokyo 32; My Brother • My Stupid Brother • Niisan no Baka • You Are Stupid 32; Romance at the Studio: Guidance to Love • Satsueijō Romansu: Ren-Ai Annai • A Studio Romance 32; Aibu • L'Amour • Caress • Ramūra 33; The Bride Talks in Her Sleep • Hanayome no Negoto • Sleeping Words of the Bride 33; Dancer of Izu • Dancing Girl from Izu • Dancing Girls of Izu • Izu no Odoriko 33; Goodbye My Girl • Shojo Yō Sayōnara • Virgin, Goodbye 33; Jūku no Haru • Jūku-Sai no Haru • The Nineteenth Spring • Spring of a Nineteen-Year-Old 33; The Bridegroom Talks in His Sleep • Hanamuko no Negoto • Sleeping Words of the Bridegroom 34; Cherry Blossom Chorus • Sakura Dance • Sakura Ondō 34; Everything That Lives • Ikitoshi Ikerumono • The Living 34; Now That I Was Born a Woman • Onna to Umareta Karanya 34; Akogare • Longing • Yearning 35; Blow, Love Wind • Breezes of Love • Fukuyō Koikaze 35; Burden of Life • Jinsei no Onimotsu 35; Good Financial Situation • Hidari Uchiwa • Left-Handed Fan • A Life of Luxury 35; A Married Lady Borrows Money • Okusama Shakuyōshō 36; The New Road • New Way • Shindo 36; Oboro yo no Onna • A Woman of a Misty Moonlight • Woman of a Pale Night • Woman of Pale Night • Woman of the Mist 36; Hanakago no Uta • Song of a Flower Basket • Song of the Flower Basket 37; Nameless People 37; Mokuseki • Wood and Stone • Wooden Head 40; New Snow • Shinsetsu 42; Ikite Iru Sugoroku • The Living Sugoroku 43; The Five-Storied Pagoda • Gojū no Tō • The Pagoda 44; The Girls of Izu • Izu no Musumetachi 45; Ima Hitotabi no • Once More • One More Time 47; Image • Omokage • A Vestige 48; Dispersing Clouds • Drifting Clouds • Spreading Cloud • Wakare-Gumo 51; Asa no Hamon • Morning Conflicts • Trouble in the Morning 52; Entotsu no Mieru Basho • Four Chimneys • Where Chimneys Are Seen 53; Ai to Shi no Tanima • The Valley Between Love and Death 54; The Cock Crows Again • The Cock Crows Twice • A Hen Will Squawk Again • Niwatori wa Futatabi Naku 54; Hotel at Osaka • An Inn at Osaka • Inn of Osaka • Ōsaka no Yado 54; Adolescence • Comparison of Heights • Daughters of Yoshiwara • Growing Up • Growing Up Twice • Hibari no Takekurabe • Skylark Growing Up • Takekurabe 55; Again One Night • Aru yo Futatabi • Twice on a Certain Night 56; Banka • Dirge • An Elegy • Elegy of the North 57; Behold Thy Son • Kiiroi Karasu • Yellow Crow 57; Ari no Machi no Maria • Maria of the Ant Village • Maria of the Street of Ants • Village Wife 58; Avarice • Desire • Yoku 58; The Fireflies • Firefly Light • Hotarubi 58; Journal of the Orange Flower • Karatachi Nikki • The Trifoliate Orange Diary 59; My Love • Waga Ai • When a

Woman Loves 59; Shiroi Kiba • White Fangs 60; Aijō no Keifu • Love's Family Tree • Record of Love 61; As the Clouds Scatter • Kumo ga Chigieru Toki 61; Hunting Rifle • Ryōjū 61; Get Married, Mother • Kāchan Kekkon Shiroyo • Mother, Get Married • You Must Marry 62; Hyakuman-Nin no Musumetachi • A Million Daughters • A Million Girls 63; An Innocent Witch • Osorezan no Onna • A Woman of the Osore Mountains 64; Kāchan to Jūichi-Nin no Kodomo • Mother and Eleven Children • Our Wonderful Years 66; Feast • Rebellion in Japan • Utage 67; A Girl of the Meiji Era • A Girl of the Meiji Period • Meiji Haru Aki • Seasons of Meiji • Seasons of the Meiji Period 68; Onna to Misoshiru • Woman and Bean Soup • Women and Miso Soup 68

Goskind, S. I Have Sinned • Al Khet 37

Goslar, Jürgen Neunzig Minuten Nach Mitternacht • Terror After Midnight 62; Amuck • Maniac • Maniac Mansion • Replica of a Crime 72; Slavers 77; Night of the Askari • Whispering Death 78; Albino 80

Gosov, Marran Bengelchen Hat's Wirklich Schwer • Bengelchen Liebt Kreuz und Quer • Crunch • Twenty-Four Hour Lover 70

Gothár, Péter A Priceless Day 79; Megáll az Idő • Time Stands Still 81; Idő Van • The Time 85; Just Like America • Pure America • Tiszta Amerika 87

Goto, Koichi Pirates ni Yoroshiku • Regards to Pirates 88

Goto, Toshio Forest of Little Bear • Itazu 87

Gottlieb, Carl Caveman 81; Amazon Women on the Moon 86*

Gottlieb, David Neil Game Show Models 77

Gottlieb, Franz-Josef The Black Abbot 63; The Curse of the Yellow Snake 63; The Secret of the Black Widow 63; The Curse of the Hidden Vault 64; The Phantom of Soho • Das Phantom von Soho 67; Lady Dracula 77; Death Stone 87; Without You • Zärtliche Chaoten 87

Gottlieb, Lisa Just One of the Guys 85

Gottlieb, Michael Mannequin • Perfect Timing 87; The Shrimp on the Barbie 90

Gottschalk, Robert Dangerous Charter 62

Gottschalk, Thomas Zärtliche Chaoten 2 88*

Götz, Siggi Sex on the Rocks 81; Die Einsteiger 85

Gould, Charles S. The Great Adventures of Captain Kidd 53*; Jungle Moon Men 55

Gould, Dave Rhythm Parade 42*

Gould, Manny Aero Nuts 27*; Bee Cause 27*; For Crime's Sake 27*; Grid Ironed 27*; Loco Motifs • Rail Rode 27*; Milk Made 27*; Pie Curs 27*; School Daze 27*; Sealing Whacks 27*; Skinny 27*; Stork Exchange 27*; Tired Wheels 27*; Topsy Turvy 27*; Web Feet 27*; Baby

Feud 28*; Beaches and Scream 28*; A Bum Steer 28*; Come Easy, Go Slow 28*; A Companionate Mirage 28*; Gold Bricks 28*; A Hunger Stroke 28*; Ice Boxed 28*; Liar Bird 28*; The Long Count 28*; Love Sunk 28*; News Reeling 28*; Nicked Nags 28*; Night Howls 28*; The Patent Medicine Kid 28*; The Phantom Trail 28*; Pig Styles 28*; The Rain Dropper 28*; Sea Sword 28*; Shadow Theory 28*; The Show Vote 28*; Stage Coached 28*; Still Waters 28*; Tong Tied 28*; Wired and Fired 28*; Auto Suggestion 29*; Canned Music 29*; Cow Belles 29*; Farm Relief 29*; Flying Yeast 29*; A Fur Peace 29*; Golf Socks 29*; Hat Aches 29*; Hospitalities 29*; A Joint Affair 29*; The Lone Shark 29*; Petting Larceny 29*; Port Whines 29*; Ratskin 29*; Reduced Weights 29*; Sheep Skinned 29*; Sleepy Holler 29*; Sole Mates 29*; Vanishing Screams 29*; Alaskan Knights 30*; The Apache Kid 30*; The Band Master 30*; The Cat's Meow 30*; Cinderella 30*; Desert Sunk 30*; Honolulu Wiles 30*; Jazz Rhythm 30*; Lambs Will Gamble 30*; The Little Trail 30*; An Old Flame 30*; Slow Beau 30*; Spook Easy 30*; Bars and Stripes 31*; Disarmament Conference 31*; Hash House Blues 31*; The Restless Sax 31*; Rodeo Dough 31*; Soda Poppa 31*; The Stork Market 31*; Svengarlic 31*; Swiss Movements 31*; Taken for a Ride 31*; The Weenie Roast 31*; Birth of Jazz 32*; The Crystal Gazebo 32*; Hic-Cups the Champ 32*; Hollywood Goes Krazy 32*; Lighthouse Keeping 32*; Love Krazy 32*; The Medicine Show 32*; The Minstrel Show 32*; Piano Mover 32*; Prosperity Blues 32*; Ritzy Hotel 32*; Seeing Stars 32*; Show Time 32*; Soldier Old Man 32*; What a Knight 32*; Antique Antics 33*; The Bill Poster 33*; The Broadway Malady 33*; Bunnies and Bonnets 33*; The Curio Shop 33*; House Cleaning 33*; Krazy Spooks 33*; Out of the Ether 33*; Russian Dressing 33*; Stage Krazy 33*; Wedding Bells 33*; Whacks Museum 33*; Wooden Shoes 33*; The Autograph Hunter 34*; Bowery Daze 34*; Busy Bus 34*; Cinder Alley 34*; Goofy Gondolas 34*; Katnips of 1940 34*; Krazy's Waterloo 34*; The Masquerade Party 34*; Southern Exposure 34*; Tom Thumb 34*; The Trapeze Artist 34*; The Bird Man 35*; Garden Gaieties 35*; A Happy Family 35*; Hotcha Melody 35*; Kannibal Kapers 35*; The King's Jester 35*; The Peace Conference 35*; Bird Stuffer 36*; Highway Snobbery 36*; Krazy's Newsreel 36*; Li'l Anjil 36*; Merry Cafe 36*; Krazy's Race of Time 37*; The Lyin' Hunter 37*; The Masque Raid 37*; Railroad Rhythm 37*; The Auto Clinic 38*; Gym Jams 38*; Hot Dogs on Ice 38*; Krazy Magic 38*; Krazy's Travel Squawks 38*; Little Buckaroo 38*; The Lone Mountie 38*; Sad Little Guinea Pigs 38*; Golf Chumps 39*; Krazy's Bear Tales 39*; Krazy's Shoe Shop 39*; Mother Goose in Swingtime 39; Mountain Ears 39

Gould, Merle S. The Body Is a Shell 57

Gould, Terry Love Variations 70; Love and Marriage • Sex, Love and Marriage 71

Goulder, Stanley The Silent Playground 63; The Man with Two Lives • Troubled Waters 64; Exorcism at Midnight • Naked Evil 66

Goulding, Alfred Excuse Me 24; Don't! 25; All at Sea 28; Everything Is Rhythm 36; Honeymoon Merry-Go-Round • Olympic Honeymoon 36; One Good Turn 36; The Gang • The Gang Show 37; It's Sam Small Again • Sam Small Leaves Town 37; Splinters in the Air 37; A Chump at Oxford 40; The Dark Road 48; Dick Barton, Special Agent 48; The Adventures of Jane 49; The Devil's Jest 54

Goulding, Edmund Sally, Irene and Mary 25; Sun-Up 25; Paris • Shadows of Paris 26; Anna Karenina • Love 27; Women Love Diamonds 27; The Trespasser 29; The Devil's Holiday 30; Paramount on Parade 30*; The Night Angel 31; Reaching for the Moon 31; Blondie of the Follies 32; Grand Hotel 32; Hollywood Party 34*; Riptide 34; The Flame Within 35; That Certain Woman 37; The Dawn Patrol 38; White Banners 38; Dark Victory 39; The Old Maid 39; We Are Not Alone 39; 'Til We Meet Again 40; The Great Lie 41; Claudia 43; The Constant Nymph 43; Forever and a Day 43*; Of Human Bondage 46; The Razor's Edge 46; Nightmare Alley 47; Everybody Does It 49; Mister 880 50; Down Among the Sheltering Palms 52; We're Not Married 52; Teenage Rebel 56; Mardi Gras 58

Goulian, Ludmilla Sergeant X of the Foreign Legion 60

Goupillières, Roger Dr. Knock • Knock 33*

Gout, Alberto St. Francis of Assisi 47; Adam and Eve • Adam y Eva 56; The Mating of the Sabine Women • The Rape of the Sabines • El Rapto de las Sabinas • The Shame of the Sabine Women 62

Govar, René Nights of the Werewolf • Las Noches del Hombre Lobo 68

Govar, Yvan Agent of Doom 63; La Croix des Vivants • Cross of the Living 63

Gover, Victor M. Rainbow Round the Corner 44; The Curse of the Wraydons 46; Dancing Thru 46; A Ghost for Sale 52; King of the Underworld 52; Murder at Scotland Yard 52; Murder at the Grange 52; Bunty Wins a Pup 53; All Living Things 58

Governor, Richard Ghost Town 88

Gow, Ronald The Man Who Changed His Mind 28*; The Glittering Sword 29

Gowing, David The Mine and the Minotaur 80

Graef, Roger The Secret Policeman's Ball 80*; The Secret Policeman's Other Ball 81*

Graeff, Tom The Gargon Terror • Teenagers from Outer Space 59

Graeme, Kenneth The Great Hunger Duel 22; The Hypnotic Portrait 22; The War at Wallaroo Mansions 22

Graewert, Gunter *see Gräwert, Günther*

Graf, Dominik The Second Face • Second Sight • Das Zweite Gesicht 82; Drei Gegen Drei 85; Die Kätze 88

Graf, Roland Das Haus am Fluss • The House by the River • The House on the River • The House on the Riverside 86

Graham, Bob The End of August 81

Graham, David C. The Undertaker and His Pals 66

Graham, Frank Challenge of the Wild • Challenge the Wild 54

Graham, Jo Always in My Heart 42; You Can't Escape Forever 42; The Good Fellows 43

Graham, S. Edwin Devil Monster 46

Graham, William A. The Doomsday Flight 66; Submarine X-1 67; Waterhole No. 3 • Waterhole 3 67; Change of Habit 68; Then Came Bronson 69; Honky 71; The Last Generation 71; Apache Massacre • Count Your Bullets • Cry for Me, Billy • Face to the Wind • The Long Tomorrow • Naked Revenge 72; Birds of Prey 73; Police Story • The Stake Out 73; Where the Lilies Bloom 73; Together Brothers 74; Part Two, Sounder • Sounder, Part Two 76; Shark Kill 76; 21 Hours at Munich 76; Harry Tracy • Harry Tracy—Desperado 80

Grall, Sebastien La Femme Secrète • The Secret Wife 86

Gramlich, Charles When Quackel Did Hyde 20

Grammatikov, Vladimir Mio, Moy Mio • Mio, My Mio 87

Granatman, V. Pesn o Metallye • A Song of Steel 28*

Grand, Richard The Commitment 76*; Fyre 79

Grandl, Peter AIDS—Die Schleichende Gefahr 85

Grandon, Francis J. The Fifth Man 14; Cross Currents 16; The Danger Path • The Narrow Path 16; The Lure of Heart's Desire 16; Playing with Fire 16; The Soul Market 16; The Dummy 17; Glory 17*; Heart's Desire 17; The Little Boy Scout 17; Conquered Hearts 18; The Daredevil 18; Love's Law 18; The Lamb and the Lion 19; Modern Husbands 19; Wild Honey 19; Miss Nobody 20; Nobody's Girl 20; Lotus Blossom 21; Barb Wire • Barbed Wire 22; Scarlet and Gold 25

Grandon, Frank *see Grandon, Francis J.*

Grangier, Gilles Adémaï Bandit d'Honneur 42; Le Cavalier Noir 44; L'Aventure de Cabassou 45; Leçon de Conduite 46; Danger de Mort 47; Rendez-Vous à Paris 47; Jo la Romance 49; Amour et Compagnie 50; Les Femmes Sont Folles 50; L'Amant de Paille 51; L'Amour, Madame 51; Jupiter 52; Faites-Moi Confiance 53; Jeunes Mariés 53; La Vierge du Rhin 53; Poisson d'Avril 54; Le Printemps, l'Automne et l'Amour 54; Gas-Oil • Hijack Highway 55; Reproduction Interdite 56; Le Rouge Est Mis • Speaking of Murder 56; Le Sang à la Tête • The Schemer 56; Trois Jours à Vivre 56; Échec au Porteur 57; Archimède le Clochard • Archimède the

Tramp • Le Clochard • The Magnificent Tramp 58; Le Désordre et la Nuit • Night Affair 58; 125 Rue Montmartre 59; Les Vieux de la Vieille 60; Le Cave Se Rebiffe • The Counterfeiters • The Counterfeiters of Paris • Money Money Money • Il Re dei Faisari 61; Le Gentleman d'Epsom 62; Le Voyage à Biarritz 62; Cucina al Burro • La Cuisine au Beurre • My Wife's Husband 63; Maigret Voit Rouge 63; L'Âge Ingrat 64; Les Bons Vivants • How to Keep the Red Lamp Burning 65*; Train d'Enfer 65; L'Homme à la Buick 66; Fin de Journée 68; Sous le Signe du Taureau 69; Un Cave 72; Gross Paris 74; Banlieu Sud Est 78

Granier-Deferre, Pierre Mensonges 58; Le Petit Garçon de l'Ascenseur 61; Les Aventures de Salavin • La Confession de Minuit 63; Cloportes • La Métamorphose des Cloportes • Sotto il Tallone 65; Paris au Mois d'Août • Paris in August • Paris in the Month of August 65; Le Grand Dadais 67; La Horse 69; The Cat • Le Chat 71; La Veuve Couderc • The Widow Couderc 71; Le Fils 73; Le Train 73; Creezy 74; Adieu Poulet • The French Detective 75; La Cage 75; Une Femme à Sa Fenêtre • A Woman at Her Window 76; La Bourgeoise 79; Harmonie 79; L'Étoile du Nord • The North Star • The Northern Star 82; L'Homme aux Yeux d'Argent 85; Cours Privé • Private Classes 86; No Drowning • Noyade Interdite • Widow's Walk 87; Blanc de Chine 88; La Couleur du Vent 88

Granowsky, Alexis Jewish Luck 25; Das Lied vom Leben • The Song of Life 31; Bauen und Heiraten • Die Koffer des Herrn O.F. • The Trunks of Mr. O.F. 32; The Barbarian and the Lady • The Rebel Son • Taras Bulba 38*; Moscow Nights 38

Grant, David Escape to Entebbe 76*; The Office Party 76; End of Term 77; Sensations 77; Under the Bed 77; Marcia 78; You're Driving Me Crazy 78

Grant, Frances E. The Sword of Fate 21

Grant, James Edward Angel and the Badman 46; Ring of Fear 54*

Grant, Lee The Stronger 76; Tell Me a Riddle 80; The Wilmar 8 80; Staying the Same • Staying Together 89

Grant, Michael Fatal Attraction • Head On 80

Granville, Fred LeRoy At the Mercy of Tiberius • The Price of Silence 20; The Honeypot 20; The Fighting Lover 21; Love Maggy 21; The Shark Master 21; The Smart Sex 21; Shifting Sands 22; The Beloved Vagabond 23; The Sins Ye Do 24; A Dear Liar 25; Forbidden Cargoes 25

Granville, Harry A Lively Day 21

Gras, Enrico Giotto • Racconto da una Affresco 40*; Il Paradiso Terrestre 40*; Romanzo di un'Epoca 41*; Il Cantico delle Creature 42*; Guerrieri 42*; Il Conte di Luna 43*; Destino d'Amore 43*; Il Paese del Nascita Mussolini 43*; Bianchi Pascoli 47*; San Gennaro 47*; Sulla Via di Damasco 47*; La Terra del Melodramma 47*; Bosch • Il Paradiso Perduto 48*; Il Dramma di Cristo 48*; Islands on the

Lagoon • Isole della Laguna 48*; The Legend of St. Ursula • La Leggenda di Sant' Orsola 48*; Luoghi Verdiani • Sulle Rome di Verdi 48*; Romantici a Venezia • Romantics in Venice 48*; Allegoria di Primavera • Boticelli • The Story of Spring 49*; La Colonna Traiana 49*; I Fratelli Miracolosi • The Miraculous Brothers 49*; L'Invenzione della Croce • Legend of the True Cross • La Leggenda della Croce 49*; Blue Continent • Continente Perduto • The Lost Continent • Sesto Continento • The Sixth Continent 54*; Empire of the Sun • Impero del Sole 55*

Gras, Marcel Heritage 40

Grasse, Joseph de *see De Grasse, Joseph*

Grasshoff, Alexander The Jailbreakers 60; Young Americans 67; Pepper and His Wacky Taxi 72; Crackle of Death 74*; Journey to the Outer Limits 74; J.D. and the Salt Flat Kid 78; Smokey and the Goodtime Outlaws 78; Wacky Taxi 82; A Billion for Boris 85

Grassia, Nini Il Cantante e il Campione • The Singer and the Champ 85; Summer Holidays • Vacanze d'Estate 85; A Tender Folly • Una Tenera Follia 86; Il Fascino Sottile del Peccato • The Subtle Fascination of Sin 87

Grassick, Richard T. Dan Smith 87*

Grassjan, Dolores 1 = 2? 75

Grattan, Alejandro *see Grattan, Alexander*

Grattan, Alexander No Return Address 61; Terror in the Jungle 68*; Only Once in a Lifetime 79

Grau, Jordi El Estrangero de la Calle Cruz del Sur • The Stranger from Cruz del Sur Street 86

Grau, Jorge El Don del Mar 57; Costa Brava '59 59; Medio Siglo en un Pincel 60; Sobre Madrid 60; Barcelona, Vieja Amiga 61; Laredo, Costa de Esmeralda 61; Niños 61; Ocharcoaga 61; Noche de Verano 62; El Espontáneo 63; Acteón 64; Una Historia de Amor 67; Historia de una Chica Sola 69; Cantico 70; Blood Ceremony • Bloody Ceremony • Ceremonia Sangrienta • Countess Dracula • The Female Butcher • Lady Dracula • The Legend of Blood Castle • Le Vergini Cavalcano la Morte 72; Pena de Muerte 73; Breakfast at the Manchester Morgue • Don't Open the Window • Fin de Semana para los Muertos • The Living Dead at the Manchester Morgue • No Profanar el Sueño de los Muertos • Non Si Deve Profanare il Sonno dei Morti 74; La Trastienda 75; Cartas de Amor de una Monja 78

Grauding, Tatiana Giotto • Racconto da una Affresco 40*; Il Paradiso Terrestre 40*; Romanzo di un'Epoca 41*; Il Cantico delle Creature 42*; Guerrieri 42*; Il Conte di Luna 43*; Destino d'Amore 43*; Il Paese del Nascita Mussolini 43*

Grauman, Walter Manhunt in Space 54; The Disembodied 57; Lady in a Cage 64; 633 Squadron • Squadron 633 64; A Rage to Live 65; I Deal in Danger 66; The Last Escape 70

Graver, Gary The Embracers • The Great Dream • Now 66; The Kill 68; The Hard Road 70; Texas Lightning 81; Trick or Treats 82; Party Camp 86; Moon in Scorpio 87

Graves, Ralph Counted Out • The Swell-Head 27; The Kid Sister 27; A Reno Divorce 27; Rich Men's Sons 27

Graves, Rex Lost Over London 34

Gräwert, Günther Whiskey and Sofa 63

Gray, Bob Denny from Ireland 18*

Gray, George The Fighting Parson 12*; The Road to Ruin 13*

Gray, John Billy Galvin 86

Gray, Mike Wavelength 83

Gray, Ray Down on the Farm 19*

Grayson, Godfrey The Adventures of PC 49 • The Adventures of PC 49—The Case of the Guardian Angel 49; Dick Barton Strikes Back 49; Dr. Morelle • Dr. Morelle —The Case of the Missing Heiress 49; Meet Simon Cherry 49; Room to Let 49; Dick Barton at Bay 50; What the Butler Saw 50; To Have and to Hold 51; The Fake 53; The Black Ice 57; Date at Midnight 59; High Jump 59; An Honourable Murder 59; Innocent Meeting 59; A Woman's Temptation 59; Escort for Hire 60; The Spider's Web 60; The Pursuers 61; So Evil, So Young 61; The Battleaxe 62; Design for Loving 62; The Durant Affair 62; The Lamp in Assassin Mews 62; She Always Gets Their Man 62

Grazer, Brian Kindergarten Cop 90*

Greber, Ulf Gategutter • Gods of the Street • Guttersnipes 49*

Greco, Emidio Ehrengard 86

Grede, Kjell Hugo and Josefin • Hugo and Josephine • Hugo och Josefin 67; Harry Munter 69; Claire Lust 72; A Simple Melody 74; A Madman's Defense 76; Hip, Hip, Hooray! • Hip, Hip, Hurrah! 87

Greek, Janet The Ladies' Club 84; Spellbinder 88

Green, A. Lo Sceriffo di Rockspring 71

Green, Alfred E. The Temptation of Adam 16; For Reward of Service 17; The Lad and the Lion 17; Little Lost Sister 17; Lost and Found 17; The Princess of Patches 17; The Friendship of Beaupère 18; Trials and Tribulations 18; In Old Kentucky 19*; Love, Honor and Obey 19; Right After Brown 19; The Web of Chance 19; A Double-Dyed Deceiver 20; Just Out of College 20; The Man Who Had Everything 20; Silk Husbands and Calico Wives 20; Little Lord Fauntleroy 21*; Through the Back Door 21*; The Bachelor Daddy 22; Back Home and Broke 22; Come On Over • Darlin' 22; The Ghost Breaker 22; The Man Who Saw Tomorrow 22; Our Leading Citizen 22; The Ne'er-Do-Well 23; Woman-Proof 23; The Good Bad Girl • Inez from Hollywood 24; In Hollywood with Potash and Perlmutter • So This Is Hollywood 24; Pied Piper Malone 24; The Man Who Found Himself 25; Sally 25; The Talker 25; Ella Cinders 26; The Girl from Montmartre 26; Irene 26; It Must Be Love 26; Ladies at Play 26; The Auctioneer 27; Come to My House 27; Is Zat So? 27; Two Girls Wanted 27; Honor Bound 28; Disraeli 29; The Five O'Clock Girl 29; Making the Grade 29; The Green Goddess 30; The Man from Blankley's 30; Old English 30; Sweet Kitty Bellairs 30; Men of the Sky 31; Road to Singapore 31; Smart Money 31; The Dark Horse 32; Gentleman for a Day • Union Depot 32; It's Tough to Be Famous 32; The Parachute Jumper 32; The Rich Are Always With Us 32; Silver Dollar 32; Baby Face 33; I Loved a Woman 33; The Narrow Corner 33; As the Earth Turns 34; Courageous • A Lost Lady 34; Dark Hazard 34; Gentlemen Are Born 34; The Happy Family • The Merry Frinks 34; Housewife 34; Side Streets • A Woman in Her Thirties 34; Sweet Music 34; Dangerous 35; The Girl from 10th Avenue • Men on Her Mind 35; The Goose and the Gander 35; Here's to Romance 35; Colleen 36; The Golden Arrow 36; More Than a Secretary 36; They Met in a Taxi 36; Two in a Crowd 36; The League of Frightened Men 37; Let's Get Married 37; Mr. Dodd Takes the Air 37; Thoroughbreds Don't Cry 37; The Duke of West Point 38; Escape from Yesterday • Ride a Crooked Mile 38; The Gracie Allen Murder Case 39; King of the Turf 39; 20,000 Men a Year 39; East of the River 40; Flowing Gold 40; Shooting High 40; South of Pago-Pago 40; Adventure in Washington • Female Correspondent 41; Badlands of Dakota 41; The Mayor of 44th Street 42; Meet the Stewarts 42; Appointment in Berlin 43; There's Something About a Soldier 43; Arms and the Woman • Mr. Winkle Goes to War 44; Strange Affair 44; Tars and Spars 45; A Thousand and One Nights 45; The Jolson Story 46*; Copacabana 47; The Fabulous Dorseys 47; Four Faces West • They Passed This Way 48; The Girl from Manhattan 48; Cover-Up 49; The Jackie Robinson Story 50; Sierra 50; Two Gals and a Guy 51; Invasion, U.S.A. 52; The Eddie Cantor Story 53; Paris Model 53; Top Banana 54

Green, Austin The Princess and the Magic Frog 65

Green, Bert Animated Crosswords No. 1 25; Around the World in 28 Days 26

Green, Charles W. The Super Secret Service 53

Green, David Car Trouble 85; Buster 88; Firebirds • Wings of the Apache 90

Green, Frank Piccadilly Playtime 36

Green, George The Children and the Lions 00; An Incident in the Boer War 00

Green, Guy River Beat 54; Lost • Tears for Simon 55; Portrait of Alison • Postmark for Danger 55; House of Secrets • Triple Deception 56; The Snorkel 57; Desert Patrol • Sea of Sand 58; The Angry Silence 59; S.O.S. Pacific 59; The Mark 60; Light in the Piazza 61; Diamond Head 62; A Patch of Blue 65; A Matter of Innocence • Pretty Polly 67; The God Game • The Magus 68; A Walk in the Spring Rain 69; Luther 73; Jacqueline Susann's Once Is Not Enough • Once Is Not Enough 74; L'Avvocato del Diavolo • Des Teufels Advokat • The Devil's Advocate 77

Green, Joseph Yiddle with His Fiddle • Yidl Mitn Fidl 36*; Der Purimspieler 37*; Little Mothers • Mamele 38*; A Brivele der Mamen • A Little Letter to Mother 39

Green, Joseph see Vari, Giuseppe

Green, Tom The Advent of the Mother-in-Law 05; The Adventures of an Insurance Man 05; Attempted Nobbling of the Derby Favourite 05; Beware of the Raffled Turkey 05; Carving the Christmas Turkey 05; The Coster Burglar and His Dog 05; A Difficult Shave 05; The Disappointed Suitor's Strategy and Reward 05; Drink and Repentance 05; The Horse Stealer, or A Casual Acquaintance 05; Inquisitive Visitors at the Dye Works 05; Jovial Expressions 05; Mistaken for a Burglar in His Own House 05; Natural Laws Reversed 05; The Old Homestead, or Saved from the Workhouse 05; Peeping Tom 05; A Quarter Day Episode 05; Reversing a Shave 05; The Same Old Tale 05; Shamus O'Brien, or Saved from the Scaffold 05; The Animated Dress Stand 06; The Attack on the Agent 06; A Bather's Difficulties 06; A Comic Duel 06; Down by the Old Bull and Bush 06; Father and the Bookmaker • Father's Derby Tip 06; Foiled by a Woman, or Falsely Accused 06; The Humours of a River Picnic 06; The Master's Razor 06; The New Apprentice, or Fun in a Bakehouse 06; Night Duty, or A Policeman's Experiences 06; Poor Pa, or Mother's Day Out 06; Portraits for Nothing 06; Punch and Judy 06; The Return of the Missus 06; Seaside Views 06; Slippery Jim the Burglar 06; Sweet Suffragettes 06; The Tell-Tale Telephone 06; A Woman's Sacrifice 06; Bertie's Love Letter 07; Schoolboys' Pranks 07; Their First Cigar 07; The Wrong Chimney 07

Green, Walon Here's Las Vegas • Las Vegas by Night • Spree! 63*; The Hellstrom Chronicle 71; The Secret Life of Plants 78

Greenaway, Peter Train 66; Tree 66; Five Postcards from Capital Cities 67; Revolution 67; Intervals 69; Erosion 71; Water 75; Water Wrackets 75; Windows 75; Goole by Numbers 76; Dear Phone 77; 1-100 78; Vertical Features Remake 78; A Walk Through H 78; The Falls 80; Act of God 81; Zandra Rhodes 81; The Draughtsman's Contract 82; Making a Splash 84; Inside Rooms—The Bathroom 85; A Zed and Two Noughts 85; The Belly of an Architect 87; Drowning by Numbers 87; The Cook, the Thief, His Wife and Her Lover 89; Death in the Seine 89

Greenbaum, Mutz see Greene, Max

Greenberg, Alan Land of Look Behind 82

Greenberg, Richard Little Monsters 89

Greene, Claude Friese see Friese-Greene, Claude

Greene, Clay M. The Ogre and the Girl 15; Her Wayward Sister 16

Greene, Danford B. The Secret Diary of Sigmund Freud 84

Greene, David Blood Island • The Shuttered Room 66; Mr. Sebastian • Sebastian 67; The Strange Affair 68; I Start Counting 69; The People Next Door 70; Madame Sin 71; Godspell 73; The Count of Monte Cristo 74; Gray Lady Down 77; Hard Country 81

Greene, David Allen Come Back Baby 68

Greene, Felix Inside North Vietnam 67; One Man's China 72

Greene, Herbert Outlaw Queen 57; The Cosmic Man 59

Greene, Max Escape to Danger 43*; Hotel Reserve 44*; The Man from Morocco 44

Greene, Sergio Olhovich Angel River 86

Greene, Sparky The Oasis • A Savage Hunger 84

Greengrass, Paul Resurrected 89

Greenidge, John Silence 26*; Next Gentleman Please 27*

Greening, H. C. Percy Brains He Has Nix 16

Greening, L. Stuart The Shoeblack of Piccadilly 20

Greens, Gregory The Sea Serpent 84

Greenspan, Bud 16 Days of Glory 85

Greenwald, Maggie Home Remedy • Xero 88; The Kill-Off 90

Greenwald, Robert Xanadu 80; Sweet Heart's Dance 88

Greenwalt, David Secret Admirer 85; Rude Awakening 89*

Greenwood, Edwin An Affair of Honour 22; Mary, Queen of Scots 22; The Queen's Secret 22; Seadogs of Good Queen Bess 22; The Threefold Tragedy 22; The Unwanted Bride 22; The Audacious Mr. Squire 23; The Bells 23; The Dream of Eugene Aram 23; Empress Josephine, or Wife of a Demigod 23; The Fair Maid of Perth 23; Falstaff the Tavern Knight 23; Heartstrings 23; Henrietta Maria, or The Queen of Sorrow 23; Lady Jane Grey, or The Court of Intrigue 23; Love in an Attic 23; Lucrezia Borgia, or Plaything of Power 23; Madame Récamier, or The Price of Virtue 23; The School for Scandal 23; Scrooge 23; She Stoops to Conquer 23; Simone Evrard, or Deathless Devotion 23; The Sins of a Father 23; The Test 23; Caught in the Web • The Lady in Lace 25*; Hearts Trump Diamonds • The Lady in Jewels 25*; Heel Taps • The Lady in High Heels 25*; The Lady in Furs • Sables of Death 25*; The Lady in Silk Stockings • The Weakness of Men 25*; The Painted Lady • Red Lips 25*; Back to the Trees 26; The Escape 26; Miss Bracegirdle Does Her Duty 26; Fangs of Death • Fear 27; Tesha • A Woman in Pawn • A Woman in the Night 27*; Whispering Gables 27; What Money Can Buy 28; The Co-Optimists 29*; To What Red Hell 29; Leap of Faith 31; The Black Skull 34; The Man Downstairs 34; Three Women 34

Greepy, Anthony see Zeglio, Primo

Grefé, William The Checkered Flag 63; Racing Fever 64; Death Curse of Tartu 66; The Devil's Sisters 66; Sting of Death 66; The Wild Rebels 67; The Hooked Generation • The Pushers 68; The Grove • The Hallucinators • The Naked Lovers • The Naked Zoo 70; Stanley 72; Impulse • Want a Ride Little Girl? 74; The Jaws of Death • Mako: The Jaws of Death 76; Whiskey Mountain 77

Gregg, Colin Begging the Ring 79; Remembrance 81; Lamb 85; We Think the World of You 88

Gregor, Arthur The Count of Luxembourg 26; Women's Wares 27; The Scarlet Dove 28; Strange Cargo 29*; What Price Decency? 33

Gregoretti, Ugo The New Angels • I Nuovi Angeli 61; RoGoPaG 62*; The Beautiful Swindlers • Les Plus Belles Escroqueries du Monde • World's Greatest Swindles • The World's Most Beautiful Swindlers 63*; Omicron 63; Le Belle Famiglie 64

Gregorio, Eduardo de see De Gregorio, Eduardo

Gregory, Carl Louis Love's Flame 20

Gregory, Frank see Momplet, Anthony

Gregory, Sebastian Come One, Come All 70

Grémillon, Jean Le Cathédrale de Chartres • Chartres 23; Le Revêtement des Routes 23; La Bière 24; Du Fil à l'Aiguille 24; L'Étirage des Ampoules Électriques 24; La Fabrication du Ciment Artificiel 24; La Fabrication du Fil 24; Les Parfums 24; La Photogénie Mécanique 24; Le Roulement à Bille 24; Les Aciéries de la Marine et d'Homecourt 25; L'Auvergne 25; L'Éducation Professionelle des Conducteurs de Tramway 25; L'Électrification de la Ligne Paris-Vierzon 25; La Naissance des Cigognes 25; La Croisière de l'Atalante 26; Un Tour au Large 26; La Vie des Travailleurs Italiens en France 26; Gratuités 27; Maldonne 27; Bobs 28; Gardiens de Phare • Lighthouse Keepers 29; The Little Lise • La Petite Lise 30; Daïnah la Métisse 31; Pour un Sou d'Amour 31; Le Petit Babouin 32; L'Accordeur • Gonzague • Gonzague ou L'Accordeur 33; La Dolorosa 34; ¡Centinela Alerta! • On Alert, Sentinel! 35*; La Valse Royale 35; Pattes de Mouche • A Scrap of Paper 36; Gueule d'Amour 37; L'Étrange Monsieur Victor • The Strange Mr. Victor 38; Remorques • Stormy Waters 41; The Light of Summer • Lumière d'Été • Summer Light 42; Le Ciel Est à Vous • The Sky Is Yours • The Woman Who Dared 43; Journal de la Résistance 45; Le Six Juin à l'Aube • The Sixth of June at Dawn 45; Pattes Blanches • White Paws 48; Le Printemps de la Liberté 48; L'Apocalypse de Saint-Sévres 49; Les Charmes de l'Existence 49*; L'Étrange Madame X • The Strange Mrs. X 50; Astrologie • Astrologie ou Le Miroir de la Vie • Le Miroir de la Vie 51; Les Désastres de la Guerre • Goya • Goya ou Les Désastres de la Guerre 51*; L'Encyclopédie Filmée • L'Encyclopédie Filmée—Alchimie, Azur, Absence 51*; L'Amour d'une Femme • A Woman's Love 53; Au Cœur de l'Île-de-France 53; La Maison aux Images 55; Haute Lisse 56; André Masson and the Four Elements • André Masson et les Quatre Éléments 58

Gremm, Wolf Fabian 80; Kamikaze • Kamikaze '89 • Kamikaze 1989 82

Grenville-Taylor, H. Potter's Clay 22*

Gres, Victor Novyi Priklyucheniya Yanki Pri Dvore Korolya Artura 88

Greshler, Abner J. Yesterday and Today 53

Greville, Arthur see Collins, Arthur Greville

Gréville, Edmond T. Elle Est Bicimidine 27; Un Grand Journal Illustré 27; 24 Heures de la Vie d'un Faux-Col 28; Més-Estimations 29; Le Mystère de la Villa Rose 29; La Naissance des Heures 30; La Belle Madame Moyse 31; Un Crime Passionel 31; La Guerre aux Sauterelles 31; Le Mariage de Sarah 31; Marius, Amateur de Cidre 31; Moyse et Cohen, Businessmen 31; Moyse, Marchand d'Habits 31; Le Tapis de Moyse 31; Le Testament de Moyse 31; Le Train des Suicidés 31; Berlingot 32; Je Suis un Homme Perdu 32; Maître chez Soi 32; Plaisirs de Paris 32; Le Rayon des Amours 32; Le Triangle de Feu 32*; Remous • Whirlpool 33; Vacances Conjugales 33; La Croix des Cimes 34; Marchand d'Amour 35; Princess Tam-Tam • Princesse Tam-Tam 35; Gypsy Melody 36; Brief Ecstasy 37; I Married a Spy • Secret Lives 37; Mademoiselle Docteur • Under Secret Orders 37; What a Man! 37; Dangerous Secrets 38; Forty Years • Veertig Jaren 38; Cinq Jours d'Angoisse • Ménaces 39; L'Île du Péché 39; Une Femme dans la Nuit 41*; Dorothée Cherche l'Amour 45; Passionelle • Pour Une Nuit d'Amour 46; Le Diable Souffle 47; But Not in Vain 48; Naughty Arlette • The Romantic Age 48; Niet Tevergeefs 48; Noose • The Silk Noose 48; Der Bildschnitzer vom Walsertal 50; Im Banne der Madonna 50; L'Envers du Paradis 53; The House on the Waterfront • Le Port du Désir • Sauveur d'Épaves 54; Tant Qu'Il Y Aura des Femmes 55; Guilty? • Je Plaide Non Coupable 56; Quand Sonnera Midi 57; L'Île du Bout du Monde • Temptation • Temptation Island 58; Beat Girl • Wild for Kicks 59; Hands of a Strangler • The Hands of Orlac • Hands of the Strangler • Les Mains d'Orlac 59; The Liars • Les Menteurs • Twisted Lives 61; L'Accident • The Accident 62

Grey, John Wesley Wide Open 27

Grey, Richard Eyes That Kill 47; A Gunman Has Escaped 48; The Man with the Twisted Lip 51

Greyson, John Urinal 88

Griaule, Marcel Les Magiciens de Wanzerbé • Les Magiciens Noirs • Ouanzerbé, Capitale de la Magie • Wanzerbé, Capitale de la Magie 48*

Gribble, Harry Wagstaff Madame Racketeer • The Sporting Widow 32*

Grice, Malcolm le *see Le Grice, Malcolm*
Gricher-Cherikover, G. Wandering Stars 27; Laughter Through the Tears 33

Grieco, Sergio The Violent Patriot 57; La Camèrière 58*; Il Pirata dello Sparviero Nero • Le Pirate de l'Épervier Noir • Pirate of the Black Hawk 58; The Huns • La Regina dei Tartari • La Reine des Barbares 60; The Nights of Lucretia Borgia • Nights of Temptation • Le Notti di Lucrezia Borgia 60; The Loves of Salammbo • Salambo • Salammbô 62; Sword of the Empire 63; The Fuller Report 66; Rififi in Amsterdam 66; Tiffany Memorandum 66; Agent 077—Missione Bloody Mary • Agente 077—Mision Bloody Mary • Mission Bloody Mary • La Muerte Espera en Atenas • Operación Loto Azul • Operation Lotus Bleu 67; Man of Legend 71; Tutti Fratelli nel West...per Parti di Padre 72

Grierson, John Drifters 29; Conquest 30*; Scottish Poultry 30; Australian Wine 31*; Burma Teak 31; The Country Comes to Town 31*; Empire Timber 31; Home Plums 31; Industrial Britain 31*; National Mark Eggs 31; Scottish Tomatoes 31; The Fishing Banks of Skye 33; Granton Trawler 33*; So This Is London 34*

Gries, Tom Hell's Horizon 55; The Last Stop 56; The Girl in the Woods 58; Will Penny 67; 100 Rifles 68; Number One • The Pro 69; Fools 70; The Hawaiians • Master of the Islands 70; Earth II 71; The Glass House 72; Journey Through Rosebud 72; Lady Ice 73; The Migrants 74; Breakheart Pass 75; Breakout 75; Helter Skelter 76; The Greatest 77

Grieve, Andrew On the Black Hill 87
Griffi, Giuseppe Patroni Il Mare • The Sea 62; The Love Circle • Metti una Sera a Cena 69; Addio Fratello Crudele • 'Tis a Pity She's a Whore 73; The Driver's Seat • Identikit 73; Divine Creature • Divine Nymph 79; The Cage • La Gabbia 85

Griffin, David Pledge to Bataan 43; Orders from Tokyo 45

Griffin, Frank Where Love Leads 16; Robart's Adventure in the Great War 20; Conductor 1492 23*

Griffith, Charles B. Forbidden Island 59; Eat My Dust! 76; Up from the Depths 79; Dr. Heckyl and Mr. Hype 80; Smokey Bites the Dust 81

Griffith, D. W. The Adventures of Dollie 08; After Many Years 08; The Awful Moment 08; Balked at the Altar 08; The Bandit's Waterloo 08; The Barbarian Ingomar 08; Behind the Scenes • Behind the Scenes: Where All Is Not Gold That Glitters 08; Betrayed by a Hand Print • Betrayed by Hand Prints 08; The Black Viper 08; A Calamitous Elopement 08; The Call of the Wild 08; The Christmas Burglars 08; The Clubman and the Tramp 08; Concealing a Burglar 08; Coney Island Police Court • Monday Morning in a Coney Island Police Court 08; The Criminal Hypnotist 08; The Curtain Pole 08; The Devil 08; The Fatal Hour 08; Father Gets in the Game 08; The Feud and the Turkey 08;

The Fight for Freedom 08; For a Wife's Honor 08; For Love of Gold • For Love of Gold: A Story of the Underworld 08; The Girl and the Outlaw 08; The Girls and a Daddy • The Girls and Daddy 08; The Greaser's Gauntlet 08; The Guerrilla 08; Heart of O Yama • The Heart of Oyama 08; The Helping Hand 08; The Hindoo Dagger 08; The Honor of Thieves 08; The Ingrate 08; Jones at the Ball • Mr. Jones at the Ball 08; Jones Entertains • Mrs. Jones Entertains 08; Love Finds a Way 08; The Man and the Woman 08; The Maniac Cook 08; Mr. Jones Has a Card Party 08; Money Mad 08; One Touch of Nature 08; The Pirate's Gold 08; The Planter's Wife 08; The Reckoning 08; The Red Girl 08; The Redman and the Child 08; The Romance of a Jewess 08; A Rural Elopement 08; A Smoked Husband 08; The Song of the Shirt 08; The Stolen Jewels 08; The Taming of the Shrew 08; The Tavern Keeper's Daughter 08; The Test of Friendship 08; The Valet's Wife 08; The Vaquero's Vow 08; A Welcome Burglar 08; Where Breakers Roar • Where the Breakers Roar 08; A Woman's Way 08; A Wreath in Time 08; The Zulu's Heart 08; And a Little Child Shall Lead Them 09; At the Altar 09; The Awakening 09; A Baby's Shoe 09; The Better Way 09; The Brahma Diamond 09; The Broken Locket 09; A Burglar's Mistake 09; The Call 09; The Cardinal's Conspiracy • Richelieu • Richelieu, or The Cardinal's Conspiracy 09*; A Change of Heart 09; The Children's Friend 09; Choosing a Husband 09; The Cloister's Touch 09; Comata, the Sioux 09; Confidence 09; A Convict's Sacrifice 09; The Cord of Life 09; A Corner in Wheat 09; The Country Doctor 09; The Course of True Love 09; The Cricket on the Hearth 09; The Day After 09; The Death Disc 09; The Deception 09; Drive for a Life • The Drive for Life 09; A Drunkard's Reformation 09; The Duke's Plan 09; The Eavesdropper 09; Edgar Allan Poe 09; Eloping with Aunty 09; Eradicating Aunty 09; The Expiation 09; The Faded Lilies 09; A Fair Exchange 09; The Fascinating Mrs. Francis 09; Fools of Fate 09; A Fool's Revenge 09; The French Duel 09; The Friend of the Family 09; Getting Even 09; The Gibson Goddess 09; Golden Louis 09; Her First Biscuits 09; Her Terrible Ordeal 09; The Hessian Renegades • 1776 • 1776, or The Hessian Renegades 09; His Duty 09*; His Lost Love 09; His Ward's Love 09; His Wife's Mother 09; His Wife's Visitor 09; The Honor of His Family 09; I Did It, Mama 09; I Want My Hat! • Mrs. Jones' Lover • Mrs. Jones' Lover, or I Want My Hat! 09; In a Hempen Bag 09; In Little Italy 09; In Old Kentucky • In Old Kentucky: A Stirring Episode of the Civil War 09; In the Watches of the Night 09; In the Window Recess 09; The Indian Runner's Romance 09; Jealousy and the Man 09; The Jilt 09; Jones and His New Neighbors 09; Jones and the Lady Book Agent 09;

Jones' Burglar • Mr. Jones' Burglar 09; The Joneses Have Amateur Theatricals 09; Lady Helen's Escapade 09; The Last Deal 09; Leather Stocking 09; The Light That Came 09; Lines of White on a Sullen Sea 09; The Little Darling 09; The Little Teacher 09; The Lonely Villa 09; Lucky Jim 09; The Lure of the Gown 09; The Medicine Bottle 09; The Mended Lute 09; The Message 09; Mexican Sweethearts 09; A Midnight Adventure 09; The Mills of the Gods 09; The Mountaineer's Honor • The Mountaineer's Honor: A Story of the Kentucky Hills 09; The Necklace 09; A New Trick 09; The Note in the Shoe 09; Nursing a Viper 09; Oh, Uncle! 09; On the Reef 09; One Busy Hour 09; One Night and Then . . . 09; The Open Gate 09; The Peachbasket Hat 09; Pippa Passes • The Song of Conscience 09; The Politician's Love Story 09; Pranks 09; The Prussian Spy 09; The Redman's View 09; The Renunciation 09; The Restoration 09; Resurrection 09; The Road to the Heart 09; The Rocky Road 09; The Roué's Heart 09; A Rude Hostess 09; The Sacrifice 09; The Salvation Army Lass 09; Schneider's Anti-Noise Crusade 09; The Sealed Room 09; The Seventh Day 09; The Slave 09; The Son's Return 09; A Sound Sleeper 09; A Strange Meeting 09; The Suicide Club 09; Sweet and Twenty 09; Sweet Revenge 09; Tender Hearts 09; The Test 09; They Would Elope 09; Those Awful Hats 09; Those Boys! 09; Through the Breakers 09; 'Tis an Ill Wind That Blows No Good 09; To Save Her Soul 09; Tragic Love 09; A Trap for Santa Claus 09; The Trick That Failed 09; A Troublesome Satchel 09; Trying to Get Arrested 09; Twin Brothers 09; Two Memories 09; Two Women and a Man 09; The Violin Maker of Cremona 09; The Voice of the Violin 09; Wanted: A Child 09; Was Justice Served? 09; The Way of Man 09; What Drink Did 09; What's Your Hurry? 09; The Winning Coat 09; With Her Card 09; The Woman from Mellon's 09; The Wooden Leg 09; The Affair of an Egg 10; An Affair of Hearts 10; An Arcadian Maid 10; As It Is in Life 10; As the Bells Rang Out! 10; The Banker's Daughters 10; The Broken Doll 10; The Call to Arms 10; A Child of the Ghetto 10; A Child's Faith 10; A Child's Impulse 10; A Child's Stratagem 10; The Chink at Golden Gulch • That Chink at Golden Gulch 10; The Converts 10; The Dancing Girl of Butte 10; A Decree of Destiny 10; The Diamond Star 10; Effecting a Cure 10; The Englishman and the Girl 10; Examination Day at School 10; The Face at the Window 10; Faithful 10; Fate's Turning 10; The Final Settlement 10; A Flash of Light 10; The Fugitive 10; Gold Is Not All 10; A Gold Necklace 10; The Gold Seekers 10; The Golden Supper 10; Heart Beats of Long Ago 10; Her Father's Pride 10; His Last Burglary 10; His Last Dollar 10; His New Lid 10; His Sister-in-Law 10*; His Trust 10; His Trust Fulfilled 10; The House with

Closed Shutters • The House with the Closed Shutters 10; The Iconoclast 10; The Impalement 10; In Life's Cycle 10; In Old California 10; In the Border States 10; In the Season of Buds • In the Season of the Buds 10; The Italian Barber 10; A Knot in the Plot 10; The Lesson 10; The Lily of the Tenements • The Lily of the Tenements: A Story of the East Side of New York 10; Little Angels of Luck 10; Love Among the Roses 10; The Man 10; The Marked Time-Table 10; May and December 10; The Message of the Violin 10; A Midnight Cupid 10; The Modern Prodigal 10; A Mohawk's Way 10; Muggsy Becomes a Hero 10*; Muggsy's First Sweetheart 10; Never Again 10; The Newlyweds 10; Not So Bad As He Seemed 10; The Oath and the Man • The Oath and the Man: A Story of the French Revolution 10; Over Silent Paths 10; A Plain Song 10; The Purgation 10; Ramona 10; A Rich Revenge 10; A Romance of the Western Hills 10; Rose o' Salem Town • Rose o' Salem Town: A Story of Puritan Witchcraft 10; A Salutary Lesson 10; Serious Sixteen 10; Simple Charity 10; The Smoker 10; The Song of the Wildwood Flute 10; The Sorrows of the Unfaithful 10; A Summer Idyll 10; A Summer Tragedy 10*; Sunshine Sue 10; Taming a Husband 10; The Tenderfoot's Triumph 10; Thou Shalt Not 10; The Thread of Destiny 10; Three Sisters 10; The Twisted Trail 10; The Two Brothers 10; Two Little Waifs • Two Little Waifs: A Modern Fairy Tale 10; The Two Paths 10; The Unchanging Sea 10; Unexpected Help 10; Up a Tree 10; The Usurer • The Usurer: What Doth It Profit? An Old Story with a New Ending 10; A Victim of Jealousy 10; Waiter No. 5 • Waiter No. 5: A Story of Russian Despotism 10; The Way of the World 10; What Shall We Do with Our Old? 10; What the Daisy Said 10; When a Man Loves 10; When We Were in Our Teens 10; White Roses 10; Wilful Peggy 10; Winning Back His Love 10; A Wreath of Orange Blossoms 10; The Adventures of Billy 11; As in a Looking Glass 11; The Baby and the Stork 11; The Battle 11; Billy's Stratagem 11; The Blind Princess and the Poet 11; A Blot in the 'Scutcheon 11; Bobby the Coward 11; The Broken Cross 11; A Change of Spirit 11; The Chief's Daughter 11; Conscience 11; A Country Cupid 11; The Crooked Road 11; Crossing the American Prairies in the Early Fifties 11; Dan, the Dandy 11; Enoch Arden, Part I 11; Enoch Arden, Part II 11; The Eternal Mother 11; The Failure 11; Fighting Blood 11; Fisher Folks 11; For His Son 11; The Heart of a Savage 11; Heaven Avenges 11; Her Awakening • Her Awakening: The Punishment of Pride 11; Her Sacrifice 11; His Daughter 11; His Mother's Scarf 11; Homefolks 11; How She Triumphed 11; In the Days of '49 11; The Indian Brothers 11; An Indian Summer 11; The Inner Circle 11; Italian Blood 11; The Jealous Husband 11*; A Knight of the

Road 11; The Last Drop of Water • The Last Drop of Water: A Story of the Great American Desert 11; Lena and the Geese 11; The Lonedale Operator 11; The Long Road 11; Love in the Hills 11; Madame Rex 11; The Making of a Man 11; Man's Genesis 11; Man's Lust for Gold 11; The Miser's Heart 11; The Narrow Road 11; The New Dress 11; The Old Bookkeeper 11; The Old Confectioner's Mistake 11; Out from the Shadow 11; An Outcast Among Outcasts 11; Paradise Lost 11; The Poor Sick Men 11; The Primal Call 11; The Revenue Man and the Girl 11; A Romany Tragedy 11; The Root of Evil 11; The Rose of Kentucky 11; The Ruling Passion 11; The Sands of Dee 11; Saved from Himself 11; The School Teacher and the Waif 11; A Sister's Love 11; A Smile of a Child 11; The Sorrowful Example 11; The Spanish Gypsy 11; The Spirit Awakened 11; The Squaw's Love 11; A String of Pearls 11; The Stuff Heroes Are Made Of 11; The Sunbeam 11; Sunshine Through the Dark 11; Swords and Hearts 11; A Tale of the Wilderness 11; Teaching Dad to Like Her 11; A Temporary Truce 11; A Terrible Discovery 11; The Thief and the Girl 11; Through Darkened Vales 11; The Trail of Books • The Trail of the Books 11; The Transformation of Mike 11; The Two Sides 11; The Unveiling 11; The Voice of the Child 11; Was He a Coward? 11; The White Rose of the Wilds 11; A Woman Scorned 11; An Adventure in the Autumn Woods 12*; A Beast at Bay 12; The Black Sheep 12; Blind Love 12; Brothers 12; Brutality 12; The Burglar's Dilemma 12; A Chance Deception 12*; The Chief's Blanket 12; A Child's Remorse 12; A Cry for Help 12; Drink's Lure 12*; Fate 12*; Fate's Interception 12; The Female of the Species 12; A Feud in the Kentucky Hills 12; Friends 12; The Girl and Her Trust 12; The God Within 12; The Goddess of Sagebrush Gulch 12; Gold and Glitter 12; Heredity 12; His Lesson 12; In the Aisles of the Wild 12; In the North Woods 12; The Informer 12; Iola's Promise 12; Just Like a Woman 12; The Lesser Evil 12; A Lodging for the Knight • A Lodging for the Night 12; Love in an Apartment Hotel 12; The Massacre 12; The Mender of Nets 12; A Misappropriated Turkey 12; The Musketeers of Pig Alley 12; My Baby 12; My Hero 12; The New York Hat 12; Oil and Water 12; The Old Actor 12; One Is Business, the Other Crime 12; The One She Loved 12; The Painted Lady 12; Pirate Gold 12; A Pueblo Legend 12; The Punishment 12; The Ranchero's Revenge 12*; A Siren of Impulse 12; So Near, Yet So Far 12; The Telephone Girl and the Lady 12; The Tender-Hearted Boy 12; Three Friends 12; Two Daughters of Eve 12; Under Burning Skies • Under Burning Skies: A Tale of the American Desert 12; An Unseen Enemy 12; The Unwelcome Guest 12; When Kings Were the Law 12; With the Enemy's Help 12; The Battle at Elderbush Gulch 13; Broken Ways 13; Brute Force •

In Prehistoric Days • Primitive Man • Wars of the Primal Tribes 13; The Coming of Angelo 13; Death's Marathon 13; During the Round Up 13; A Girl's Stratagem 13; Her Mother's Oath 13; The Hero of Little Italy 13; His Mother's Son 13; The House of Darkness 13; The Indian's Loyalty 13; Judith of Bethulia 13; Just Gold 13; The Lady and the Mouse 13; The Left-Handed Man 13; The Little Tease 13; The Madonna of the Storm 13; The Mistake 13; A Misunderstood Boy 13; A Modest Hero 13; The Mothering Heart 13; Near to Earth 13; Olaf, an Atom 13; The Perfidy of Mary 13; The Reformers, or The Lost Art of Minding One's Business 13; The Sheriff's Baby 13; The Sorrowful Shore 13*; A Timely Interception 13; Two Men of the Desert 13; The Wanderer 13; A Welcome Intruder 13; A Woman in the Ultimate 13; The Yaqui Cur 13; The Avenging Conscience • The Avenging Conscience, or Thou Shalt Not Kill • Thou Shalt Not Kill 14; The Battle of the Sexes • The Single Standard 14; The Escape 14; Home, Sweet Home 14; The Birth of a Nation • The Clansman 15; A Day with Governor Whitman 16; A Day with Mary Pickford 16; Hoodoo Ann 16*; Intolerance 16; Pillars of Society 16*; The Great Love 17; The Greatest Thing in Life 17; Hearts of the World 17; Her Condoned Sin 17; Buy Liberty Bonds 18; A Romance of Happy Valley 18; Broken Blossoms 19; The Fall of Babylon 19; The Girl Who Stayed at Home 19; The Greatest Question 19; The Mother and the Law 19; Scarlet Days 19; True Heart Susie 19; The World of Columbus 19; The Idol Dancer 20; The Love Flower 20; Way Down East 20; Dream Street 21; The Evolution of the Motion Picture 21; Orphans of the Storm 21; One Exciting Night 22; The White Rose 23; America • Love and Sacrifice 24; Isn't Life Wonderful! 24; D. W. Griffith's That Royle Girl • That Royle Girl 25; Sally of the Sawdust 25; The Sorrows of Satan 26; The Battle of the Sexes 27; Drums of Love 27; Topsy and Eva 27*; Lady of the Night • Lady of the Pavements 29; Abraham Lincoln 30; The Struggle 31; San Francisco 36*; The Cave Dwellers • Cave Man • Man and His Mate • One Million B.C. 40*

Griffith, E. H. see *Griffith, Edward H.*

Griffith, Edward H. The Awakening of Ruth 17; Billy and the Big Stick 17; The Boy Who Cried Wolf 17; In Love's Laboratory 17; One Touch of Nature 17; The Star-Spangled Banner 17; Your Obedient Servant 17; Fit to Fight 18; The End of the Road 19; Fit to Win 19; Bab's Candidate 20; The Garter Girl 20; A Philistine in Bohemia 20; Thimble Thimble 20; The Vice of Fools 20; Dawn of the East 21; If Women Only Knew 21; The Land of Hope 21; Scrambled Wives 21; Free Air 22; Sea Raiders 22; The Go-Getter 23; Unseeing Eyes 23; Another Scandal 24; Week-End Husbands 24; Bad Company 25; Headlines 25; Atta Boy! 26; White Mice 26; Afraid to Love 27; Alias the Lone Wolf 27; At

Flying 38; The False Step • Der Schritt vom Wege 39; Zwei Welten 40

Grüne, Karl Der Mädchenhirt 19; Menschen in Ketten 19*; Die Jagd nach der Wahrheit 20; Nacht Ohne Morgen 20; Nachtbesuch 20; Mann Über Bord 21; Frauenopfer 22; Der Graf von Charolais 22; Der Stärkste Trieb 22; Schlagende Wetter 23; Die Strasse • The Street 23; Arabella 24; Komödianten 24; Eifersucht • Jealousy 25; Die Brüder Schellenberg 26; Am Rande der Welt • At the Edge of the World • On the Edge of the World 27; Königin Luise 27; Marquis d'Eon, der Spion der Pompadour • Spy of Madame Pompadour 28; Waterloo 28; Katherine Knie 29; Das Gelbe Haus des King-Fu 31; La Maison Jaune 32; Abdul the Damned 35; A Clown Must Laugh • Pagliacci 36; The Marriage of Corbal • Prisoner of Corbal 36

Grunebaum, Marc The Adoption 78
Grunewald, Allan see Caiano, Mario
Grunwald, Anatole de see De Grunwald, Anatole
Grunwalsky, Ferenc Egy Teljes Nap 88
Grusch, Werner White Elephant 84
Gruyaert, Jan The Flaxfield • De Vlasaard 84
Gruza, Jerzy Pierścien i Róża • The Rose and the Ring 87
Gryaznof, E. Born Anew 33
Grzimek, Bernhard Serengeti • They Shall Not Die 59*
Grzimek, Michael Serengeti • They Shall Not Die 59*
Guan, Jinpeng see Kwan, Stanley
Guareschi, Giovanni The Frenzy • La Rabbia 63*
Guazzoni, Enrico Un Invito a Pranzo 07; Messalina 09; La Nuova Mammina 09; Il Sacco di Roma 09; Adriana di Berteaux 10; Agrippina 10; Andreuccio da Perugia 10; Bruto • Brutus 10; I Maccabei 10; La Gerusalemme Liberata 11; Gradenico e Tiepolo ovvero Amori e Congiure a Venezia 11; Pinocchio 11; San Francesco, il Poverello d'Assisi 11; Quo Vadis? 12; Il Lettino Vuoto 13; Marcantonio e Cleopatra 13; Scuola d'Eroi 13; Caius Giulio Cesare 14; Immolazione 14; L'Istruttoria 14; Alma Mater 15; L'Amica 15; Ivan il Terribile 15; Madame Tallien 16; Marcantonio e Cleopatra 16; Fabiola 17; La Gerusalemme Liberata 17; Lady Macbeth 18; Il Sacco di Roma e Clemento VII 20; Messalina 23; Miriam • Myriam 28; La Sperduta di Allah 28; Il Domo del Mattino 32; Signora Paradiso 34; Il Re Burlone 35; I Due Sergenti 36; Ho Perduto Mio Marito • I Have Lost My Husband 36; Money King • Re di Denari 36; Il Dottor Antonio 37; Il Suo Destino 38; Ho Visto Brillare le Stelle 39; Antonio Meucci 40; La Figlia del Corsaro Verde 40; Oro Nero 40; I Pirati della Malesia 41; La Fornarina 42

Gubbles, Luk Congo Express 86*
Gubenko, Nikolai Away from It All 81; Zapretnaya Zona 88
Guðmundsson, Ágúst Land and Sons •

Land og Synir 80; Outlaw: The Saga of Gisli • Útlaginn: Gísla Saga Súrssonar 82
Guedes, Ann Rocinante 86*
Guedes, Eduardo Rocinante 86*
Guediguian, Robert Rouge Midi 85
Guenette, Robert The Tree 69; Bigfoot—The Mysterious Monsters • The Mysterious Monsters 75; The Amazing World of Psychic Phenomena 76; The Man Who Saw Tomorrow 81
Guerassimov, Evgueni see Gerasimov, Yevgeni
Guercio, James William Electra Glide in Blue 73
Guerin, M. The Best 79
Guerlais, Pierre Pêcheurs d'Islande 35
Guerman, Alexei see Gherman, Alexei
Guerra, Ruy Os Cafajestes • La Plage du Désir • The Unscrupulous Ones 62; Les Fusils • Os Fuzis • The Guns 63; Far from Vietnam • Loin du Viêt-nam 66*; Sweet Hunters • Tendres Chasseurs 69; Os Deuses e os Mortos • Les Dieux et les Morts • The Gods and the Dead 70; La Chute • The Fall • A Queda 78*; Mueda—Memória e Massacre • Mueda—Memory and Massacre 79; Erendira 82; Malandro • Ópera do Malandro 86; Fable of the Beautiful Pigeon Fancier • Fábula da Bela Palomera • Fabula de la Bella Palomera 87; Kuarup 89
Guerra, Tonino Il Caso Mattei • The Mattei Affair 72*
Guerraz, Sergio After Darkness 85*
Guerrero, Francisco Tragic Earthquake in Mexico • Trágico Terremoto en México 87
Guerrieri, Romolo 10,000 Dollari per un Massacro • 10,000 Dollars Blood Money 66; Johnny Yuma 66; L'Adorable Corps de Deborah • Il Dolce Corpo di Deborah • The Soft Body of Deborah • The Sweet Body • The Sweet Body of Deborah 67; Un Détective • Detective Belli 70; Covert Action 78; The Final Executioner • The Last Warrior 83
Guerrini, Mino Contro Sesso • Controsesso 64*; L'Idea Fissa • Love and Marriage 64*; Amore in Quattro Dimensioni • L' Amour en Quatre Dimensions • Love in Four Dimensions 65*; The Mines of Kilimanjaro • Le Minière del Kilimangiaro 86
Guest, Christopher The Big Picture 89
Guest, Cliff The Disturbance 90
Guest, Val The Nose Has It 42; Bees in Paradise 43; Miss London, Ltd. 43; Give Us the Moon 44; I'll Be Your Sweetheart 45; Just William's Luck 47; William at the Circus • William Comes to Town 48; Miss Pilgrim's Progress 49; Murder at the Burlesque • Murder at the Windmill • Mystery at the Burlesque 49; The Body Said No! 50; Mr. Drake's Duck 50; Penny Princess 51; Family Affair • Life with the Lyons 53; Dance Little Lady 54; Men of Sherwood Forest 54; The Runaway Bus 54; Break in the Circle 55; The Creeping Unknown • The Quatermass Experiment • The Quatermass Xperiment 55; The Lyons in Paris 55; They Can't Hang Me! 55; It's a Wonderful

World 56; The Weapon 56; The Abominable Snowman • The Abominable Snowman of the Himalayas 57; Carry On Admiral • The Ship Was Loaded 57; Enemy from Space • Quatermass II 57; The Camp on Blood Island 58; Further Up the Creek! 58; Life Is a Circus 58; Up the Creek 58; Expresso Bongo 59; Hell Is a City 59; Yesterday's Enemy 59; The Day the Earth Caught Fire 61; The Full Treatment • Stop Me Before I Kill! • The Treatment 61; Jigsaw 62; 80,000 Suspects 63; The Beauty Jungle • Contest Girl 64; Passport to Oblivion • Where the Spies Are 65; Assignment K 67; Casino Royale 67*; When Dinosaurs Ruled the Earth 69; Toomorrow 70; The Persuaders 71; Au Pair Girls 72; Confessions of a Window Cleaner 73; The Diamond Mercenaries • Killer Force 75; And the Band Played On • The Shillingbury Blowers 80; Dangerous Davies, the Last Detective 80; The Boys in Blue 83; Child's Play 84
Guggenheim, Charles The Great St. Louis Bank Robbery 59*
Guglielmi, Massimo Rebus 89
Guha, Sujit Amar Sangi 87; Dolonchapa 88
Gui, Zhihong Hex • Xie 80; Bewitched • Gu 81; Corpse Mania • Shi Yao 81; The Boxer's Omen • Mo 83
Guia, Eric de see Tahimik, Kidlat
Guibourg, Edmundo Bloody Wedding • Bodas de Sangre 39
Guidice, King Timberesque 37
Guiguet, Jean-Claude Faubourg Saint-Martin 86
Guilfoyle, Paul Tess of the Storm Country 60
Guillemot, Claude La Trêve • The Truce 68; La Brute • The Brute 87
Guillermin, John High Jinks in Society 49*; Paper Gallows • Torment 49; Four Days 51; School for Brides • Two on the Tiles 51; Smart Alec 51; Bachelor in Paris • Song of Paris 52; Miss Robin Hood 52; Operation Diplomat 53; The Strange Mr. Bartleby • Strange Stories 53; Adventure in the Hopfields 54; The Crowded Day 54; Dust and Gold 55; Thunderstorm 55; Town on Trial! 56; The Whole Truth 57; Hell, Heaven and Hoboken • Hell, Heaven or Hoboken • I Was Monty's Double 58; Tarzan's Greatest Adventure 59; The Day They Robbed the Bank of England 60; Moment of Truth • Never Let Go 60; The Amorous General • Waltz of the Toreadors 62; Tarzan Goes to India 62; Guns at Batasi 64; Rapture 65; The Blue Max 66*; New Face in Hell • P.J. 67; House of Cards 68; The Bridge at Remagen 69; El Condor 70; Sky Terror • Skyjacked 72; Shaft in Africa 73; The Towering Inferno 74*; King Kong 76; Death on the Nile 78; Mr. Patman 80; Sheena • Sheena, Queen of the Jungle 84; King Kong Lives 86
Guiol, Fred The Battling Orioles 24*; What's Your Racket? 34; The Rainmakers 35; Mummy's Boys 36; Silly Billies 36; Miss Polly 41; Tanks a Million 41; Hayfoot

42; Here Comes Trouble 48; As You Were! 51; Mr. Walkie Talkie 52

Guissart, René Artist with the Ladies • Coiffeur pour Dames 32; La Chance 32; Tu Seras Duchesse 32; Mon Cœur Balance 33; Sweet Devil 37

Guitry, Sacha Ceux de chez Nous 14; Une Petite Main Qui Se Place 22; Bonne Chance 35; Pasteur 35; The Cheat • Le Roman d'un Tricheur • The Story of a Cheat 36; Faisons un Rêve 36; Mon Père Avait Raison 36; Le Mot de Cambronne 36; Le Nouveau Testament 36*; Désiré 37; The Pearls of the Crown • Les Perles de la Couronne 37*; Quadrille 37; Champs-Elysées • Remontons les Champs-Elysées 38; Ils Étaient Neuf Célibataires • Nine Bachelors 39; Indiscretions 39; Le Destin Fabuleux de Désirée Clary • Mademoiselle Désirée • Mlle. Désirée 41; Donnez-Moi Tes Yeux 42; La Loi du 21 Juin 1907 42; La Malibran 42; La Nuit du Cinéma 42; Le Comédien • En Scène • The Private Life of an Actor 47; Le Diable Boiteux 48; Aux Deux Colombes 49; Toâ 49; Le Trésor de Cantenac 49; Deburau 50; Tu M'As Sauvé la Vie 50; Le Poison 51; Je l'Ai Été Trois Fois 52; La Vie d'un Honnête Homme • The Virtuous Scoundrel 52; Affairs in Versailles • Royal Affairs in Versailles • Si Versailles M'Était Conté • Versailles 53; Napoléon 54; If Paris Were Told to Us • Si Paris Nous Était Conté 55; Assassins et Voleurs • Lovers and Thieves 56; Les Trois Font la Paire 57*

Guldbrandsen, Peer Der Kom en Soldat • Scandal in Denmark 70

Gullan, Campbell Caste 30; Wedding Group • Wrath of Jealousy 36*

Gulliver, Clifford Love Up the Pole 36; Museum Mystery 37

Guming, Xu see Xu, Guming

Gumm, Detlef Zivile Knete 85*

Gunay, Enis Vatanyolu—Die Heimreise • Vatanyolu—The Journey Home 89*

Gundrey, V. Gareth The Devil's Maze 29; Just for a Song 30; Symphony in Two Flats 30; The Hound of the Baskervilles 31; The Stronger Sex 31

Güney, Yılmaz At Avret Silah • The Horse, the Woman and the Gun 66; Bana Kurşun İşlemez • Bullets Cannot Pierce Me • The Bullets Cannot Touch Me 67; Benim Adım Kerim • My Name Is Kerim 67; Bride of the Earth • Seyyit Han, Toprağın Gelini • Seyyit Khan, Bride of the Earth 68; Nuri the Flea • Pire Nuri 68*; Aç Kurtlar • The Hungry Wolves 69; Bir Çirkin Adam • An Ugly Man 69; Hope • Umut 70; Osman the Infantryman • Osman the Wanderer • Piyade Osman 70*; The Seven Bastards • The Seven No-Goods • Yedi Belalılar 70*; Acı • Pain 71; Ağıt • Elegy 71; Baba • The Father 71; The Criminals • Vurguncular • The Wrongdoers 71; The Desperate Ones • The Hopeless Ones • Umutsuzlar 71; The Example • İbret 71*; The Fugitives • Kaçaklar 71; Tomorrow Is the Final Day • Tomorrow Is the Last Day • Yarın Son Gündür 71;

Anxiety • Endişe 74*; Arkadaş • The Friend 74; The Poor Ones • The Suffering Ones • Zavallılar 75*; Duvar • Güney's The Wall • Le Mur • The Wall 82

Gunn, Bill STOP 70; Blood Couple • Double Possession • Ganja and Hess 73

Gunn, Gilbert The Owner Goes Aloft 42; The Elstree Story 52; The Good Beginning 53; Men Are Children Twice • Valley of Song 53; My Wife's Family 56; Accused • Mark of the Hawk 57*; The Cosmic Monster • Cosmic Monsters • The Crawling Terror • The Strange World • The Strange World of Planet X 57; Girls at Sea 58; Girls in Arms • Operation Bullshine 59; What a Whopper! 61; Wings of Mystery 62; The Young Detectives 63

Gunnlaugsson, Hrafn Father's Estate 80; Hrafninn Flýgur • When the Raven Flies 85; Í Skugga Hrafnsins • The Shadow of the Raven 88

Gunter, George The Young Man's Bride 68

Guoxi, Chen see Chen, Guoxi

Gupta, Mridul Sutrapat 88

Gurney, Robert, Jr. Cage of Doom • The Girl from 5000 A.D. • Terror from 5000 A.D. • Terror from the Year 5000 58; Edge of Fury 58*

Gurov, S. Circus Daredevils • Daring Circus Youth 53*; U.S.S.R. Today 53*; Spring Voices • Voices of Spring 55*

Gurrin, Geoffrey The Boy and the Pelican 64

Gurrola, Alfredo The Death Game • El Juego de la Muerte 86; Death Squad • Escuadrón de la Muerte 86; Gavilán o Paloma • Hawk or Dove 86; Once Again • Va de Nuez 87

Gustafsson, Lennart Rattis • Ratty 86

Gustavsen, Erik Blackout 85

Guter, Johannes Leap Into Life 24; Der Falsche Ehemann 32; Fräulein Liselott 35

Guthrie, Tyrone King Oedipus • Oedipus Rex 57

Gutiérrez Alea, Tomás A Common Confusion • Una Confusión Cotidiana 50*; El Sueño de Juan Bassín 53; The Charcoal Burner • El Mégano 55*; Havana 1762 58; Asamblea General • General Assembly 59; Esta Tierra Nuestra • This Land of Ours 59; Historias de la Revolución • Stories of the Revolution 60; Death to the Invader • Muerte al Invasor 61*; Las Doce Sillas • The Twelve Chairs 62; Cumbite 64; Death of a Bureaucrat • La Muerte de un Burocrata 66; Memorias del Subdesarrollo • Memories of Underdevelopment 68; A Cuban Fight Against the Demons • A Cuban Struggle Against the Demons • Una Pelea Cubana Contra los Demonios 71; The Art of the Cigar • El Arte del Tabaco 74; The Last Supper • La Última Cena 76; Los Sobrevivientes • The Survivors 79; Hasta Cierto Punto • Hasta un Cierto Punto • Up to a Certain Point • Up to a Point 83; Cartas del Parque • Letters from the Park 88

Gutiérrez Aragón, Manuel Habla Mudita 73; Black Brood • Camada Negra

77; Sonámbulos 77; El Corazón del Bosque 78; Demonios en el Jardín • Demons in the Garden 82; Feroz 83; La Noche Más Hermosa 84; Half of Heaven • La Mitad del Cielo 86; Malaventura 88

Gutman, D. Captain Grant's Children 39*

Gutman, Nathaniel Deadline • War Zone 87

Gutman, Walter The March on Paris, 1914, of Generaloberst Alexander von Klück and His Memory of Jessee Holladay 77

Guttfreund, André Breach of Contract 84

Guttman, Amos Drifting • Nagooa 84; Bar 51 • Bar 51—Sister of Love • Sister of Love 86; Hemo, King of Jerusalem • Himmo, King of Jerusalem • Himmo Melech Yerushalaim 87

Guy, Alice see Guy-Blaché, Alice

Guy, Jack That Girl Is a Tramp 74

Guy-Blaché, Alice The Cabbage Fairy • La Fée aux Choux • Sage-Femme de Première Classe 1896; Les Dangers de l'Alcoolisme 1896; L'Aveugle 1897; Baignade dans le Torrent 1897; Ballet Libella 1897; Coucher d'Yvette 1897; Danse Fleur de Lotus 1897; Idylle 1897; Leçon de Danse 1897; Une Nuit Agitée 1897; Le Pêcheur dans le Torrent 1897; Le Planton du Colonel 1897; L'Arroseur Arrosé 1898; Au Réfectoire 1898; Les Cambrioleurs 1898; Chez le Magnétiseur 1898; Le Cocher de Fiacre Endormi 1898; Déménagement à la Cloche de Bois 1898; En Classe 1898; Les Farces de Jocko 1898; Idylle Interrompue 1898; Je Vous y Prends • Je Vous y Prrrrends! 1898; Les Mésaventures d'une Tête de Veau 1898; Scène d'Escamotage 1898; Leçons de Boxe 1899; La Vie du Christ 1899; L'Angélus 00; Au Bal de Flore 00; Au Cabaret 00; Avenue de l'Opera 00; L'Aveugle 00; Ballet Japonais 00; Bataille de Boules de Neige 00; Bataille d'Oreillers 00; La Bonne Absinthe 00; Chez le Maréchal-Ferrant 00; Chez le Photographe 00; Le Chiffonnier 00; Chirurgie Fin de Siècle 00; La Concierge 00; Coucher d'une Parisienne 00; Courte Échelle 00; Dans les Coulisses 00; Danse de l'Ivresse 00; La Danse des Saisons 00; Danse du Papillon 00; Danse du Pas des Foulards par des Almées 00; Danses 00; Le Déjeuner des Enfants 00; Erreur Judiciaire 00; Les Fredaines de Pierrette 00; Leçon de Danse 00; Un Lunch 00; Le Marchand de Coco 00; Marché à la Volaille 00; La Mauvaise Soupe 00; Mésaventure d'un Charbonnier 00; Monnaie de Lapin 00; La Petite Magicienne 00; Une Rage de Dents 00; Retour des Champs 00; Saut Humidifié de M. Plick 00; Sidney's Joujoux 00; La Source 00; La Tarantelle 00; Le Tondeur de Chiens 00; Le Tonnelier 00; Transformations 00; Vénus et Adonis 00; Charmant FrouFrou 01; Danse Basque 01; La Danse du Ventre 01; Folies Masquées 01; Frivolité 01; Hussards et Grisettes 01; Lavatory Moderne 01; Lecture Quotidienne 01; Tel

Est Pris Qui Croyait Prendre 01; Les Vagues 01; Les Chiens Savants 02; Les Clowns 02; La Cour des Miracles 02; Danse Mauresque 02; La Dent Récalcitrante 02; En Faction 02; L'Équilibriste 02; Farces de Cuisinière 02; La Fiole Enchantée 02; Fruits de Saison 02; La Gavotte 02; Le Lion Savant 02; Le Marchand de Ballons 02; Miss Lina Esbrard Danseuse Cosmopolite et Serpentine 02; Le Pommier 02; Pour Secourer la Salade 02; La Première Gamelle 02; Quadrille Réaliste 02; Une Scène en Cabinet Particulier Vue à Travers le Trou de la Serrure 02; Trompé Mais Content 02; Les Apaches Pas Veinards 03; Les Aventures d'un Voyageur Trop Pressé 03; Les Braconniers 03; Cake-Walk de la Pendule 03; Comment Monsieur Prend Son Bain 03; Compagnons de Voyage Encombrants 03; Enlèvement en Automobile et Mariage Précipité 03; Faust et Méphistophélès 03; Le Fiancé Ensorcelé 03; Illusioniste Renversant 03; Jocko Musicien 03; La Liqueur du Couvent 03; Lutteurs Américains 03; La Main du Professeur Hamilton ou Le Roi des Dollars 03; Modelage Express 03; Ne Bougeons Plus 03; Potage Indigeste 03; La Poule Fantaisiste 03; Répétition dans un Cirque 03; Service Précipité 03; La Valise Enchantée 03; Le Voleur Sacrilège 03; L'Assassinat de la Rue du Temple • Le Crime de la Rue du Temple 04; L'Assassinat du Courrier de Lyon • Le Courrier de Lyon 04; L'Attaque d'un Diligence 04; La Baptème de la Poupée 04; Les Bienfaits du Cinématographe 04; Cambrioleur et Agent 04; Les Cambrioleurs de Paris 04; La Chasse au Cambrioleur 04; Cible Humaine 04; Clown en Sac 04; Comme On Fait Son Lit On Se Couche 04; Comment On Disperse les Foules 04; Concours de Bébés 04; Culture Intensive ou Le Vieux Mari 04; Départ pour les Vacances 04; Les Deux Rivaux 04; Duel Tragique 04; Electrocutée 04; Les Enfants du Miracle 04; Erreur de Poivrot 04; La Faim...L'Occasion...L' Herbe Tendre 04; Gage d'Amour 04; Le Jour du Terme 04; Magie Noire 04; Mauvais Cœur Puni 04; Militaire et Nourrice 04; Le Monolutteur 04; La Mouche 04; Nos Bons Étudiants 04; Paris la Nuit • Paris la Nuit ou Exploits d'Apaches à Montmartre 04; Pâtissier et Ramoneur 04; Les Petits Coupeurs de Bois Vert 04; Les Petits Peintres 04; Pierrot Assassin 04; Le Pompon Malencontreux 04; La Première Cigarette 04; Rafle de Chiens 04; Rapt d'Enfant par les Romanichels • Volée par les Bohémiens 04; Le Rêve du Chasseur 04; Le Réveil du Jardinier 04; Robert Macaire et Bertrand 04; Scènes Directoire 04; Secours aux Naufragés 04; Les Secrets de la Prestidigitation Dévoilés 04; Les Surprises de l'Affichage 04; Tentative d'Assassinat en Chemin de Fer 04; Le Testament de Pierrot 04; Transformations 04; Triste Fin d'un Vieux Savant 04; Vieilles Estampes 04; Au Poulailler! 05; Le Bébé Embarrassant 05; La Charité du Prestidigitateur 05; Chien Jouant à la Balle 05; Comment On Dort à

Paris! 05; Douaniers et Contrebandiers • La Guérité 05; La Esmeralda 05; La Fantassin Guignard 05; Le Képi 05; Le Lorgnon Accusateur 05; Les Maçons 05; Mort de Robert Macaire et Bertrand 05; Un Noce au Lac Saint-Fargeau 05; On Est Poivrot, Mais On a du Cœur 05; Le Pantalon Coupé 05; Le Pavé 05; Peintre et Ivrogne 05; Le Plateau 05; Réhabilitation 05; Roméo Pris au Piège 05; La Statue 05; Villa Dévalisée 05; À la Recherche d'un Appartement 06; La Chaussette 06; Conscience de Prêtre 06; Course de Taureaux à Nîmes 06; La Crinoline 06; Les Druides 06; La Fée au Printemps 06; Le Fils du Garde-Chasse 06; L'Honneur du Corse 06; J'Ai un Hanneton dans Mon Pantalon 06; Lèvres Closes • Sealed Lips 06; La Marâtre 06; Le Matelas Alcoolique 06; La Messe de Minuit 06; Mireille 06*; Pauvre Pompier 06; La Pègre de Paris 06; Le Régiment Moderne 06; La Vie du Christ 06*; La Vie du Marin 06; La Voiture Cellulaire 06; Voyage en Espagne 06; Ballet de Singe • La Vérité Sur l'Homme-Singe 07; Déménagement à la Cloche de Bois 07; L'Enfant de la Barricade • Sur la Barricade 07; Fanfan la Tulipe 07; Les Gendarmes 07; A Child's Sacrifice • The Doll 10; Across the Mexican Line 11; The Altered Message 11; A Daughter of the Navajos 11; Eclipse 11; An Enlisted Man's Honor 11; The Girl and the Bronco Buster 11; His Better Self 11; His Sister's Sweetheart 11; The Hold-Up 11; The Mascot of Troop C 11; A Revolutionary Romance 11; Rose of the Circus 11; The Silent Signal 11; The Stampede 11; The Violin Maker of Nuremberg 11; Algie the Miner 12; At the Phone 12; The Blood Stain 12; Canned Harmony 12; The Child of Fate • Mignon • Mignon or The Child of Fate 12; Dick Whittington and His Cat 12; The Equine Spy 12; The Face at the Window 12; Falling Leaves 12; Flesh and Blood 12; Fra Diavolo 12; His Lordship's White Feather 12; Hotel Honeymoon 12; In the Year 2000 12; Mickey's Pal 12; The Paralytic 12; Phantom Paradise 12; Playing Trumps 12; The Sewer 12; A Terrible Lesson 12; A Terrible Night 12; Two Little Rangers 12; The Beasts of the Jungle 13; Ben Bolt 13; Beneath the Czar 13; Blood and Water 13; The Eyes That Could Not Close 13; The Fortune Hunters 13; The Girl in the Armchair 13; A House Divided 13; Kelly of the Emerald Isle 13; The Little Hunchback 13; Matrimony's Speed Limit 13; The Pit and the Pendulum 13; Rogues of Paris 13; The Shadows of the Moulin Rouge 13; The Star of India 13*; Western Love 13; The Courier to the Czar • Michael Strogoff 14; The Cricket on the Hearth 14; The Dream Woman 14; The Lure 14; The Monster and the Girl 14; The Prisoner of the Harem 14; The Tigress 14; The Woman of Mystery 14; The Yellow Traffic 14; Barbara Frietchie 15*; Greater Love Hath No Man 15*; The Heart of a Painted Woman 15; My Madonna 15; The Vampire 15; What Will People Say? 15; The Girl

with the Green Eyes 16*; House of Cards 16; The Ocean Waif 16; The Adventurer 17; Behind the Mask 17; The Empress 17; A Man and the Woman 17*; When You and I Were Young 17; The Great Adventure 18; A Soul Adrift • Tarnished Reputations 18*; Vampire 20

Guylder, Van The Ramrodder • Ramrodders 69

Guzmán, Claudio Antonio 73; Linda Lovelace for President 75

Guzmán, Patricio Cien Metros con Charlot • A Hundred Meters with Chaplin 67; Escuela de Sordomudos • School for Deafmutes 67; Imposibrante 68; La Tortura • Torture 68; Opus Seis • Opus Six 69; Orthopedic Paradise • El Paraíso Ortopédico 69; Elecciones Municipales • Municipal Elections 70; The First Year • El Primer Año 70; Comandos Comunales • Communal Organization 72; The Response in October • La Respuesta de Octubre 72; La Insurrección de la Burguesía • Insurrection of the Bourgeoisie 74; La Batalla de Chile • The Battle of Chile 76; Coup d'État • El Golpe de Estado 76; El Poder Popular • The Popular Power 79; La Rosa de los Vientos • Rose of the Winds 81

Guzman, Ruben de see De Guzman, Ruben

Gwisdek, Michael Rendezvous in Travers • Treffen in Travers 89

Gyarmathy, Livia Blind Endeavor • Vakvilágban 86

Gyllenhaal, Stephen Certain Fury 85

Gyöngyössy, Imre Jób Lázadása • The Revolt of Job 83*

György, István Nagymama 35; A Királyné Huszárja 36; Zivatar a Pusztán 37; The Eternal Secret • Az Örök Titok 40; A Szovjet Mezőgazdasági Küldöttségek Tanításai • The Teachings of a Soviet Agricultural Delegation 51*

Gyu, Yun Ryong Talmae and Pomdari • Talmae wa Pomdari 87

Haanstra, Bert The Muider Circle Lives AgainThe Muider Group Revived • De Muiderkring Herleeft 48; Mirror of HollandSpiegel van Holland 50; All Things Flow • Panta Rhei 51; Medieval Dutch Sculpture • Nederlandse Beeldhouwkunst Tijdens de Late Middeleeuwen 51; Dijkbouw • Dike Builders 52; Aardolie • De Opsporing van Aardolie • The Search for Oil 53; The Changing Earth • Ont Staan en Vergaan 53; The Oilfield • Het Olieveld 53; De Verkenningsboring • The Wildcat 53; The Rival World • Strijd Zonder Einden 54; And There Was No More Sea • En de Zee Was Niet Meer 55; God Shiva 55; Rembrandt, Painter of Man • Rembrandt, Schilder van de Mens 56; Over Glas Gesproken • Speaking About Glass • Speaking of Glass 57; Fanfare 58; Glas • Glass 58; Paleontologie • Schakel met het Verleden • Story in the Rocks 59; The M.P. Case • De Zaak M.P. 60; Delta Phase One 62; Zoo 62; Alleman • The Human Dutch • Twelve Millions 63; De Stem van het Water • The Voice of the

Dear Father 62; Barnaby—Overdue Dues Blues 62; Automania 2000 63; The Axe and the Lamp 63; Is There Intelligent Life on Earth? 63*; Birds, Bees and Storks 64; The Maestro 64*; The Music Academy 64*; The Palm Court Orchestra 64; Professor Ya-Ya's Memoirs 64*; Les Aventures de la Famille Carre 65*; The Carters of Greenwood 65; Do Do 65; Martian in Moscow 65; Dying for a Smoke 66; ICOGRADA Congress 66; Lone Ranger 67*; The Question 67; To Our Children's Children 69; Flurina 70; Short Tall Story 70; Tomfoolery 70; Children and Cars 71; Contact 73*; The Glorious Musketeers 73; Christmas Feast 74; How Not to Succeed in Business 75; Skyrider 76; Making It Move 77; Max and Moritz 78; Autobahn 79; Ten for Survival 79; Heavy Metal 81*

Haldane, Bert All Is Not Gold That Glitters 10; Behind the Scenes 10; Cast Thy Bread Upon the Waters 10; A Chum's Treachery 10; Circumstantial Evidence 10; Coals of Fire 10; Dora 10; The Farmer's Two Sons 10; A Flowergirl's Romance 10; Her Debt of Honour 10; Hunger's Curse 10; Lust for Gold 10; The Miser's Lesson 10; A Plucky Kiddie 10; The Queen of the May 10; The Thieves' Decoy 10; Tried and Found True 10; A Village Love Story 10; Woman vs. Woman 10; An' Good in the Worst of Us 11; The Baby and the Bomb 11; A Bid for Fortune 11; The Broad Arrow 11; A Burglar for a Night 11; The Convict's Sister 11; Elsie the Gamekeeper's Daughter 11; The Faith Healer 11; A Fool and His Money 11; For Better or Worse 11; The Foreign Spy 11; A Girl's Love-Letter 11; Hilda's Lovers 11; His Son 11; The Impediment 11; Jack's Sister 11; Kiddie 11; Lottery Ticket No. 66 11; The Man Who Kept Silent 11; A Nephew's Artifice 11; Our Wealthy Nephew John • Wealthy Brother John 11; Proud Clarissa 11; The Reclamation of Snarky 11; Right Is Might 11; The Road to Ruin 11; The Silver Lining 11; A Struggling Author 11; The Torn Letter 11; A Touch of Nature 11; The Trail of Sand 11; Bill's Reformation 12; Bill's Temptation 12; The Birthday That Mattered 12; The Blind Heroine 12; A Brother's Sacrifice 12; The Child Detective 12; The Deception 12; The Disinherited Nephew 12; The Draughtsman's Revenge 12; A Dumb Matchmaker 12; The Eccentric Uncle's Will 12; Ethel's Danger 12; A Fight for Life 12; The Fighting Parson 12*; For Baby's Sake 12; A Girl Alone 12; The Girl at the Lodge 12; Her Better Self 12; Her Sacrifice 12; His Actress Daughter 12; His Honour at Stake 12; How Molly and Polly Got Pa's Consent 12; How Vandyck Won His Wife 12; The Irony of Fate 12; Jeff's Downfall 12; The Lieutenant's Bride 12; The Little Poacher 12; Muriel's Double 12; Neighbours 12; A Night of Peril 12; Only an Outcast 12; Our Bessie 12; Peter Pickles' Wedding 12; Phoebe of the Inn 12; Pippin Up to His Pranks 12; The Poachers' Fight for Liberty 12; The Poacher's Reform 12; The Prodigal

Wife 12; The Reward of Perseverance 12; Robert's Lost Supper 12; The Stab of Disgrace 12; The Tell-Tale Umbrella 12; The Trail of the Fatal Ruby 12; Was He Justified? 12; When Gold Is Dross 12; Won by a Snapshot 12; Alfred Harding's Wooing 13; Allan Field's Warning 13; Binks' Wife's Uncle 13; The Debt of Gambling 13; A Double Life 13; East Lynne 13; Fisherman's Luck 13; Humanity, or Only a Jew 13*; In the Shadow of Darkness 13; In the Toils of the Blackmailer 13; The Interrupted Honeymoon 13; Just Like a Mother 13; Little Elsie 13; A Lucky Escape for Dad 13; Luggage in Advance 13; Mary of Briarwood Dell 13; Molly's Burglar 13; Never Forget the Ring 13; Now She Lets Him Go Out 13; Peter Pens Poetry 13; Peter Tries Suicide 13; Polly the Girl Scout and Grandpa's Medals 13; Polly the Girl Scout and the Jewel Thieves 13; Polly the Girl Scout's Timely Aid 13; The Price of Deception 13; The Road to Ruin 13*; Sixty Years a Queen 13; Suspicious Mr. Brown 13; The Test 13; That Awful Pipe 13; Uncle As Cupid 13; A Village Scandal 13; Was He a Coward? 13; When Paths Diverge 13; Younita • Younita, from Gutter to Footlights 13; Zaza the Dancer 13; As a Man Sows • As a Man Sows, or An Angel of the Slums 14; A Brother's Atonement 14; By His Father's Orders 14; The German Spy Peril 14; His Sister's Honour 14; Jim the Fireman 14; The Last Encampment 14; The Last Round 14; The Lights o' London 14; The Lure of London 14; Their Only Son 14; Your Country Needs You 14; The Barnstormers 15; Beneath the Mask 15; Brigadier Gerard 15; By the Shortest of Heads 15; Cowboy Clem 15; Darkest London • Darkest London, or The Dancer's Romance 15; Do Unto Others 15; Five Nights 15; Jack Tar 15; Jane Shore • The Strife Eternal 15*; The Knut and the Kernel 15; Poor Clem 15; The Rogues of London 15; Tommy Atkins 15; The Lady Slavey • The Slavey's Legacy 16; Some Detectives 16; Truth and Justice 16; A Birmingham Girl's Last Hope 17; A Boy Scout's Dream, or How Billie Captured the Kaiser 17; The Child and the Fiddler 17; Men Were Deceivers Ever 17; On Leave 18*; The Ticket-of-Leave Man 18; The Romance of Lady Hamilton 19; The Grip of Iron 20; Mary Latimer, Nun 20; The Winding Road 20*; The Woman and Officer 26 20*; The Affected Detective 22; Auntie's Wedding Present 22; Eliza's Romeo 22; Gipsy Blood 22

Haldane, Don Nikki, Wild Dog of the North 61*; Drylanders 63; The Reincarnate 71

Hale, Alan Braveheart 25; The Scarlet Honeymoon 25; The Wedding Song 25; Forbidden Waters 26; Risky Business 26; The Sporting Lover 26; Rubber Tires 27; Neighborhood House 36*

Hale, Albert Percy Pimpernickel, Soubrette 14

Hale, Billy see *Hale, William*

Hale, Rex Racing Blood 38

Hale, Sonnie Gangway 37; Head Over Heels • Head Over Heels in Love 37; Sailing Along 38

Hale, Walter The Lightning Conductor 14

Hale, William Lonnie 63; Gunfight at Abilene • Gunfight in Abilene 67; Journey to Shiloh 68

Hales, Gordon Evidence in Concrete 60; Return to Sender 63; The Undesirable Neighbour 63

Haley, Earl King of the Wild • The King of the Wild Horses • King of Wild Horses 33; The Gentleman from Arizona 39

Haley, Jack, Jr. Norwood 70; The Love Machine 71; That's Entertainment! 74; That's Entertainment, Part 2 • That's Entertainment, Too! 75*; That's Dancing! 85

Halicki, H. B. Gone in 60 Seconds 74; Junkman 82; Deadline Auto Theft 83

Halimi, André Corps Z'à Corps 88

Hall, Alexander Jazz Babies 32; Madame Racketeer • The Sporting Widow 32*; Sinners in the Sun 32; Broadway Singer • Torch Singer 33*; The Girl in 419 33*; Kidnapped • Miss Fane's Baby • Miss Fane's Baby Is Stolen 33; Midnight Club 33*; East End Chant • Limehouse Blues 34; The Girl in Pawn • Little Miss Marker 34; The Pursuit of Happiness 34; Annapolis Farewell • Gentlemen of the Navy 35; Goin' to Town 35; Give Us This Night 36; Yours for the Asking 36; Exclusive 37; I Am the Law 38; There's Always a Woman 38; There's That Woman Again • What a Woman! 38; The Amazing Mr. Williams 39; Good Girls Go to Paris 39; The Lady's from Kentucky 39; The Doctor Takes a Wife 40; He Stayed for Breakfast 40; Married—But Single • This Thing Called Love 40; Bedtime Story 41; Here Comes Mr. Jordan 41; My Sister Eileen 42; They All Kissed the Bride 42; The Heavenly Body 43; Once Upon a Time 44; She Wouldn't Say Yes 45; Down to Earth 47; The Great Lover 49; Louisa 50; Love That Brute 50; Up Front 51; Because You're Mine 52; Let's Do It Again 53; Forever, Darling 55

Hall, Arch, Sr. Eegah! 62

Hall, Bert The Border Scouts 22

Hall, George Edwardes Nobody's Child 19; Desire • The Magic Skin 20; The Temptress 20; Judge Her Not 21; The Prairie Mystery 22

Hall, Ivan Funeral for an Assassin 77; Kill or Be Killed 80; Kill and Kill Again 81

Hall, Jon The Beach Girls and the Monster • Monster from the Surf • Surf Terror 65

Hall, Ken On Our Little Place • On Our Selection 30; Squatter's Daughter 33; The Silence of Dean Maitland 34; Grandad Rudd 35; Thoroughbred 36; It Isn't Done 37; Orphan of the Wilderness 37; Tall Timbers 37; Wild Innocence 37; Broken Melody 38; Dad and Dave Come to Town

38; Let George Do It 38; Lovers and Luggers 38; Gone to the Dogs 39; Mr. Chedworth Steps Out 39; Timberland Terror 40; Vengeance of the Deep 40; Pacific Adventure • Smithy 45

Hall, Kenneth J. Alive by Night • Deadly Sting • Evil Spawn 87

Hall, Peter Work Is a Four Letter Word 67; A Midsummer Night's Dream 68; Three Into Two Won't Go 69; Perfect Friday 70; The Homecoming 73; Akenfield 74

Hall, Sheridan The Steadfast Heart 23

Hall, Walter Richard Hate 17

Hallam, Paul Nighthawks 78*

Halldoff, Jan Myten • The Myth 66; Life's Just Great • Livet Är Stenkul 67; Ola and Julia • Ola och Julia 67; The Corridor • Korridoren 68; A Dream of Freedom • En Dröm om Frihet 69; Dog Days • Rötmånad 71; The Office Party 72; The Last Adventure 75; Buddies 76

Hallenbeck, E. Darrell One of Our Spies Is Missing 66

Haller, Daniel Die, Monster, Die! • The House at the End of the World • Monster of Terror 65; Devil's Angels 67; The Wild Racers 68; The Dunwich Horror 69; Goodbye to the Hill • Paddy 69; Pieces of Dreams • The Wine and the Music 70; My Sweet Lady • Sunshine Part II 75; Buck Rogers in the Twenty-Fifth Century 79; Follow That Car 81

Halligan, George Thorobred 22

Halloway, George see *Capitani, Giorgio*

Halloway, Jack The Man from Manhattan 16; Overalls 16

Hallowell, Todd Love or Money 88

Hallström, Lasse A Lover and His Lass 75; Abba—The Movie 77; Father to Be 79; The Rooster 81; Happy We • Två Killar och en Tjej 83; Mitt Liv Som Hund • My Life As a Dog 85; Alla Vi Barn i Bullerbyn • The Children of Bullerby Village 86; Mer Om Oss Barn i Bullerbyn • More About the Children of Bullerby Village 87

Hällström, Roland af see *Af Hällström, Roland*

Halperin, Victor Greater Than Marriage 24; When a Girl Loves 24; School for Wives 25; The Unknown Lover 25; In Borrowed Plumes 26; Dance Magic 27; Ex-Flame 30; Party Girl 30; White Zombie 32; Supernatural 33; I Conquer the Sea 36; Revolt of the Zombies 36; Nation Aflame 37; Buried Alive 39; Torture Ship 39; Girls Town 42

Hama, Boubou Babatou ou Les Trois Conseils • Babatu 76*

Hamblin, Maurice Just One More Time • The Over-Amorous Artist 74

Hambly, Glenda Fran 85

Hamer, Robert Dead of Night 45*; Pink String and Sealing Wax 45; It Always Rains on Sunday 47; Kind Hearts and Coronets 49; The Spider and the Fly 49; His Excellency 51; The Long Memory 52; The Detective • Father Brown • Father Brown, Detective 54; To Paris with Love 54; The Scapegoat 58; School for Scoundrels •

School for Scoundrels, or How to Win Without Actually Cheating 59

Hamilton, David Bilitis 76; Laura • Laura—Les Ombres de l'Été 79; Cousins in Love • Tender Cousins • Tendre Cousines 80; Un Été à Saint-Tropez 83; Premiers Désirs 83; Tatiana 84

Hamilton, Gilbert P. The Lust of the Red Man 14; Samson 14*; Aloha Oe 15; Inherited Passions 16; The Maternal Spark 17; Captain of His Soul 18; Everywoman's Husband 18; False Ambition 18; The Golden Fleece 18; High Tide 18; The Last Rebel 18; A Soul in Trust 18; The Vortex 18; Coax Me 19; Open Your Eyes 19; Woman of Lies 19

Hamilton, Guy The Ringer 52; The Intruder 53; The Colditz Story 54; An Inspector Calls 54; Charley Moon 56; Manuela • Stowaway Girl 57; The Devil's Disciple 58*; A Touch of Larceny 59; The Best of Enemies • I Due Nemici • Two Enemies 61; The Party's Over 62; The Man in the Middle • The Winston Affair 63; Goldfinger 64; Funeral in Berlin 66*; The Battle of Britain 68; Diamonds Are Forever 71; Live and Let Die 73; The Man with the Golden Gun 74; Force 10 from Navarone 78; The Mirror Crack'd 80; Evil Under the Sun 81; Remo: Unarmed and Dangerous • Remo Williams: The Adventure Begins... 85; Sauf Votre Respect 89

Hamilton, Michael see *Scardamaglia, Elio*

Hamilton, Rollin Farmyard Follies 28*; High Up 28*; A Horse Tale 28*

Hamilton, Strathford Blueberry Hill 88

Hamilton, William Freckles 35*; Seven Keys to Baldpate 35*; Bunker Bean • His Majesty Bunker Bean 36*; Murder on a Bridle Path 36*; Call Out the Marines 42*

Hamina, Mohammed Lakhdar see *Lakhdar-Hamina, Mohammed*

Hamlin, Jerome Invasion of the Love Drones 75

Hamman, Joe Le Gardien 21; L'Étrange Aventure 22; L'Enfant Roi 23; La Fille de Pachas 26*; La Grande Épreuve 27*; Le Brigand Gentilhomme 42

Hammer, Robert Don't Answer the Phone • The Hollywood Strangler 80

Hammer, Will Musical Merrytone No. 1 36; Polly's Two Fathers 36

Hammid, Alexander Aimless Walk • Bezúčelná Procházka 30; Na Pražském Hradě • Prague Castle 32; City of Live Water • Město Živé Vody 34; Jáchymov 34; Karlovy Vary 34; The Highway Sings • Silnice Zpívá 37; The Last Summer • Poslední Léto 37; Come with Us • Pojd'te s Námi 38; Historie Fíkového Listu • History of the Fig Leaf 38; Dvakrát Kaučuk • Rubber Twice 40; Harbor in the Heart of Europe • Přístav v Srdci Evropy 40; Meshes of the Afternoon 43*; Hymn of the Nations • Toscanini, Hymn of the Nations 44; Valley of the Tennessee 44; A Better Tomorrow 45; Library of Congress 45; The Private Life of a Cat 45*; Princeton 48; Marriage for Moderns 49; Angry Boy 50; Of Men

and Music 50*; The Gentleman in Room 6 • Gentlemen in Room 8 51; Il Medium • The Medium 51*; Shrimp Fisherman 53; Conversation with Arnold Toynbee 54; Workshop for Peace 54; Operation Hourglass 55; Kid Brother 56; Israel, an Adventure 57*; Power Among Men 58*; Night Journey 60; Pablo Casals Master Class 60; Collage 61; Family Centered Maternity Care 61; River Music 61; Jascha Heifetz Master Class 62*; To Be Alive 62*; To the Fair! 64*; We Are Young 67*; US 68*; City Out of Wilderness 73; American Years 76; To Fly 76; The Living Earth 78

Hammond, Peter Spring and Port Wine 70; The Phantom Kid 83; The Death of the Heart 86

Hammond, William C. Jean's Plan 46; The Secret Tunnel 47; The Fool and the Princess 48; The Lone Climber 50; Looking for Trouble 51; Juno Helps Out • Juno Home Help 53; The Flying Eye 55; The Carringford School Mystery 58; Rockets in the Dunes 60

Hamos, Gusztav Der Unbesiegbare 85

Hampton, Benjamin B. Mysterious Rider 21; Golden Dreams 22; Heart's Haven 22

Hampton, Jesse D. The Drifters 19; The End of the Game 19; What Every Woman Wants 19

Hampton, Robert see *Freda, Riccardo*

Hampton, William J. Metamorphosis 51

Hanák, Dušan Silent Joy • Tichá Radost 85

Hanbury, Terence see *Losey, Joseph*

Hanbury, Victor see *Losey, Joseph*

Hancock, Herbert The Leech 21

Hancock, John Let's Scare Jessica to Death 71; Bang the Drum Slowly 73; Baby Blue Marine 75; California Dreaming 79; Weeds 87; Prancer 89

Hand, David The Tail of the Monkey • The Tale of the Monk 26*; Snow White and the Seven Dwarfs 37*; Bambi 42; Victory Through Air Power 43*; Animaland 47; Musical Paintbox 47; Bound for the Rio Grande 48; The Cuckoo 48; The House Cat 48; The Lion 48; The Thames 48; Canterbury Road 49; Cornwall 49; A Fantasy on Ireland 49; Ginger Nutt's Bee Bother 49; Ginger Nutt's Christmas Circus 49; It's a Lovely Day 49; The Ostrich 49; The Platypus 49; Sketches from Scotland • Sketches of Scotland 49; Somerset 49; Wales 49; A Yorkshire Ditty 49; Devon Whey 50; A Fantasy on London Life 50; Ginger Nutt's Forest Dragon 50

Hand, Slim Penny and the Pownall Case 48

Handel, Leo The Case of Patty Smith • The Shame of Patty Smith 62

Handke, Peter The Left-Handed Woman • Die Linkshändige Frau 77; Das Mal des Todes 85

Handler, Ken A Place Without Parents 74; Truckin' 75; Delivery Boys 84

Handley, Jim The Reluctant Dragon 41*

Handworth, Harry Toll of Mamon 14; When Fate Leads Trump 14; In the

Shadow 15; Artie the Millionaire Kid 16; The Question 16

Haneff, René le see Le Haneff, René

Haneke, Michael The Seventh Continent • Der 7. Kontinent 89

Han-hsiang, Li see Li, Han-hsiang

Hani, Susumu Seikatsu to Mizu • Water • Water in Our Life 52*; Snow Festival • Yuki Matsuri 52; Machi to Gesui • The Town and Its Drains 53; Anata no Bīru • Your Beer 54; Children in the Classroom • Kyōshitsu no Kodomotachi 54; Children Who Draw • Eo Kaku Kodomotachi 55; Dōbutsuen Nikki • Zoo Diary • Zoo Story 56; Group Instruction • Group no Shidō 56; Soseiji Gakkyū • Twin Sisters 56; Dances in Japan • Nihon no Buyō 58; Horyū-Ji • Horyu Temple 58; The Living Sea • Umi wa Ikiteiru 58; Shiga Naoya 58; Tokyo 1958 58*; Bad Boys • Furyō Shōnen 60; Children Hand in Hand • Te o Tsunagu Kora 62; A Full Life • Mitasareta Seikatsu 62; Kanojo to Kare • She and He 63; Bwana Toshi • Bwana Tōshi no Uta • The Song of Bwana Toshi 65; Andes no Hanayome • Bride of the Andes 66; Hatsukoi Jigokuhen • Inferno of First Love • Nanami, Inferno of First Love 68; Aido • Aido, Slave of Love 69; Mio 70; Gozenchū no Jikanwari • Morning Schedule • Timetable 72; Afurika Monogatari • The Green Horizon • A Tale of Africa 81*

Hanin, Roger Le Protecteur 74; Le Faux-Cul 75; La Rumba 87

Hankey, Anthony Dangerous to Live • Too Dangerous to Live 39*

Hankinson, Michael Chick 36; House Broken 36; The Scarab Murder Case 36; Ticket of Leave 36

Hanmer, Charles Black Diamonds 32

Hanna, William Blue Monday 38; What a Lion 38; Gallopin' Gals 40*; Swing Social 40*; Goose Goes South 41*; The Midnight Snack 41*; The Night Before Christmas 41*; Officer Pooch 41*; The Bowling Alley Cat 42*; Fine Feathered Friend 42*; The Fraidy Cat 42*; Puss 'n' Toots 42*; Baby Puss 43*; Lonesome Mouse 43*; Sufferin' Cats 43*; War Dogs 43*; Yankee Doodle Mouse 43*; Bodyguard 44*; Cat Nipped • Kitty Foiled • Mouse Trouble 44*; Million Dollar Cat 44*; Puttin' on the Dog 44*; Zoot Cat 44*; Flirty Birdy • Love Boids 45*; Manhattan Serenade • Mouse in Manhattan 45*; The Mouse Comes to Dinner • Mouse to Dinner 45*; Quiet Please! 45*; Tee for Two 45*; The Milky Waif 46*; Solid Serenade 46*; Springtime for Thomas 46*; Trap Happy 46*; Cat Fishin' 47*; The Cat's Concerto 47*; Dr. Jekyll and Mr. Mouse 47*; Fair Weather Friend • Part-Time Pal 47*; Invisible Mouse 47*; A Mouse in the House 47*; Salt Water Tabby 47*; Mouse Cleaning 48*; Old Rockin' Chair Tom 48*; Professor Tom 48*; Truce Hurts 48*; The Cat and the Mermouse 49*; Heavenly Puss 49*; Jerry's Diary 49*; Little Orphan 49*; Love That Pup 49*; Polka Dot Puss 49*; Tennis Chumps 49*; Cue Ball Cat 50*; F'r Safety Sake • Safety Second 50*; Framed Cat 50*; Hold That Lion • Jerry and the Lion 50*; Little Quacker 50*; Party Cat • Saturday Evening Puss 50*; Texas Tom 50*; Tom and Jerry in the Hollywood Bowl 50*; Casanova Cat 51*; Cat Napping 51*; City Cousin • Jerry's Cousin • Muscles Mouse 51*; Flying Cat 51*; His Mouse Friday 51*; Jerry and the Goldfish 51*; Nit-Witty Kitty 51*; Sleepy Time Tom 51*; Slicked-Up Pup 51*; Cruise Cat 52*; Dog House 52*; Duck Doctor 52*; Fit to Be Tied 52*; Little Runaway 52*; Push-Button Kitty 52*; Smitten Kitten 52*; Triplet Trouble 52*; The Two Mouseketeers 52*; Jerry and Jumbo 53*; Johann Mouse 53*; Just Ducky 53*; Life with Tom 53*; Posse Cat 53*; Puppy Tale 53*; That's My Pup 53*; Two Little Indians 53*; Baby Butch 54*; Downhearted Duckling 54*; Hick-Cup Pup • Tyke Takes a Nap 54*; Little School Mouse 54*; Mice Follies 54*; Mouse for Sale 54*; Neapolitan Mouse 54*; Pet Peave 54*; Touché Pusse Cat 54*; Barbecue Brawl 55*; Blue Cat Blues 55*; Down Beat Bear 55*; The Egg and Jerry 55*; Flying Sorceress 55*; Happy Go Lucky • One Quack Mind 55*; Make Mine Freedom 55*; Muscle Beach Tom 55*; Tom's Photo Finish 55*; Busy Buddies 56*; Feedin' the Kiddie 56*; Give and Tyke 56*; Mucho Mouse 56*; Robin Hoodwinked 56*; Scat Cats 56*; Tops with Pops 56*; Tot Watchers 56*; The Vanishing Duck 56*; Royal Cat Nap 57*; Little Bo Bopped 59*; Wolf Hounded 59*; Creepy Time Pal 60*; The Do-Good Wolf 60*; Here, Kiddie, Kiddie 60*; Life with Loopy 60*; No Biz Like Shoe Biz 60*; Snoopy Loopy 60*; Tale of a Wolf 60*; Catch Meow 61*; Child Sockology 61*; Count Down Clown 61*; Fee Fie Foes 61*; Happy Go Loopy 61*; Kooky Loopy 61*; Loopy's Hare-Do 61*; This Is My Ducky Day 61*; Two Faced Wolf 61*; Zoo Is Company 61*; Bearly Able 62*; Beef-Fore and After 62*; Bungle Uncle 62*; Bunnies Abundant 62*; Chicken Fraca-See 62*; Common Scents 62*; Rancid Ransom 62*; Slippery Slippers 62*; Swash Buckled 62*; Bear Up! 63*; Chicken Hearted Wolf 63*; Crook Who Cried Wolf 63*; Drum-Sticked 63*; A Fallible Fable 63*; Habit Rabbit 63*; Just a Wolf at Heart 63*; Sheep Stealers Anonymous 63*; Watcha Watchin'? 63*; Wolf in Sheep Dog's Clothing 63*; Bear Hug 64*; Bear Knuckles 64*; Elephantastic 64*; Habit Troubles 64*; Hey There, It's Yogi Bear 64*; Raggedy Rug 64*; Trouble Bruin 64*; Big Mouse Take 65*; Crow's Fete 65*; Horse Shoo 65*; Pork Chop Phooey 65*; The Man Called Flintstone • That Man Flintstone 66*; Jetsons: The Movie 90*

Hannah, Jack No Sail 45; Double Dribble 46; Rugged Bear 53

Hannam, Ken Sunday Too Far Away 75; Break of Day 77; Summerfield 77; Dawn 79; Robbery Under Arms 85*

Hannant, Brian Three to Go 69*; Flashpoint 72; The Time Guardian 87

Hanooka, Izhak Red Nights 87

Hanoun, Marcel Une Simple Histoire 58; Le Huitième Jour 59; Octobre à Madrid 65; L'Authentique Procès de Carl Emmanuel Jung 67; Le Printemps 68; L'Hiver 69

Hansel, Howell Road o' Strife 15*; Tillie's Tomato Surprise 15; The Deemster 17; The Long Trail 17

Hansel, Marion Dust 85; The Barbarous Wedding • The Cruel Embrace • Les Noces Barbares 87

Hansen, Kai Peter the Great 10*; 1812 12*

Hansen, Mark see Lewis, Herschell Gordon

Hansen, Rolf The Affairs of Dr. Holl • Angelika • Dr. Holl • Doktor Holl 51; Desires 54; Devil in Silk • Teufel in Seide 68

Hanson, Curtis The Arousers • A Kiss from Eddie • Sweet Kill 70; The Little Dragons 80; Losin' It 83; The Bedroom Window 86; Bad Influence 90

Hanson, John Northern Lights 78*; Wildrose 84; Smart Money 88

Hanwright, Joseph Uncle Joe Shannon 78

Hanxiang, Li see Li, Han-hsiang

Haowei, Wang see Wang, Haowei

Hara, Takahita Bakayaroo! (Watakushi Okotteimasu) 88*

Harada, Masato Goodbye Flickmania 79; The Heartbreak Yakuza • Saraba Itoshiki Hito Yo 87

Harbaugh, Carl The Iron Woman 16; All for a Husband 17; The Broadway Sport 17; The Derelict 17; A Rich Man's Plaything 17; The Scarlet Letter 17; When False Tongues Speak 17; Brave and Bold 18; Jack Spurlock, Prodigal 18; Marriages Are Made 18; Other Men's Daughters 18; The Other Man's Wife 19; The North Wind's Malice 20*; The Poppy Trail 20; Big Town Ideas 21; Bucking the Line 21; Hickville to Broadway 21; Little Miss Hawkshaw 21; The Tomboy 21

Harbinger, Richard The Pay-Off • T-Bird Gang 59

Harbou, Thea von Elisabeth und der Narr 33; Hanneles Himmelfahrt 34

Harbutt, Sandy Stone 74

Hardaway, Ben Buddy of the Apes 34; Buddy in Africa 35; Buddy of the Legion 35; Buddy the Dentist 35; Buddy's Adventures 35; Buddy's Pony Express 35; Buddy's Theatre 35; Rhythm in the Bow 35; Count Me Out 38*; Katnip Kollege 38*; Love and Curses 38*; Porky the Gob 38*; Porky's Hare Hunt 38*; Bars and Stripes Forever 39*; Fagin's Freshmen 39*; Gold Rush Daze 39*; Hare-um Scare-um 39*; The Hobo Gadget Band 39*; It's an Ill Wind 39*; Porky and Teabiscuit 39*; Porky the Giant Killer 39*; Sioux Me 39*; Busy Bakers 40*

Harder, Emil William Tell 25

Hardwicke, Cedric Forever and a Day 43*

Hardy, Jonathan Backstage 86
Hardy, Joseph Great Expectations 74
Hardy, Robin The Wicker Man 73; The Fantasist 86
Hardy, Rod Thirst 79
Hare, Bill Finney 69
Hare, David Licking Hitler 77; Wetherby 85; Paris by Night 88; Strapless 89
Hare, Ellin T. Dan Smith 87*
Hare, Lumsden The Black Watch • King of the Khyber Rifles 29*; Masquerade 29*
Harel, David Raoul Wallenberg: Buried Alive 84
Hargrove, Dean The Manchu Eagle Murder Caper Mystery 73
Hariharan Amritamgamaya 87; Anjaam 87; Five Fires • Panchagni 87; Aranyakam 88
Hark, Tsui see Tsui, Hark
Harker, Ed Dream On 81
Harkrider, John Glorifying the American Girl 29*
Harlan, Richard Odio 35; Bachelor Father • Papá Soltero 39; Mercy Plane • Wonder Plane 39
Harlan, Veidt Krach im Hinterhaus • Trouble Back Stairs 35; Die Pompadour 35*; Alles für Veronika 36; Katerlampe 36; Maria die Magd 36; Der Müde Theodor 36; Der Herrscher • The Ruler 37; The Kreutzer Sonata • Die Kreutzersonate 37; Mein Sohn der Herr Minister 37; Covered Tracks • Verwehte Spuren 38; Jugend • Youth 38; The Immortal Heart • Das Unsterbliche Herz 39; Die Reise nach Tilsit • The Trip to Tilsit 39; Jew Suss • Jud Süss 40; Pedro Soll Hängen 41; Die Goldene Stadt 42; Der Grosse König 42; Immensee 43; Opfergang 44; Burning Hearts • Kolberg 45; Unsterbliche Geliebte 50; Hanna Amon 51; Die Blaue Stunde 52; Die Gefangene des Maharadscha 53; Sterne Über Colombo 53; Verrat an Deutschland 54; Anders Als Du und Ich • Das Dritte Geschlecht • The Third Sex 57; Ich Werde Dich auf Händen Tragen 58; Liebe Kann Wie Gift Sein 58; Die Blonde Frau des Maharadscha 62
Harley, Pat I Heard It Through the Grape Vine 82*
Harlin, Renny Arctic Heat • Born American 86; A Nightmare on Elm Street 4: The Dream Master 88; Prison 88; The Adventures of Ford Fairlane • Ford Fairlane 90; Die Hard 2 • Die Hard 2—Die Harder 90
Harling, Donn Fallguy 62
Harlow, John Phototone Reels 28*; My Lucky Star 33*; Song Birds 33; Bagged 34; Master and Man 34; Passing Clouds • The Spell of Amy Nugent • Spellbound 40; So This Was Paris • This Was Paris 41; Headline 42; The Dark Tower 43; One Company 43; The Agitator 44; Candles at Nine 44; Meet Sexton Blake 44; Appointment with Crime 45; The Echo Murders 45; Green Fingers 46; Dream of Olwen • While I Live 47; Mother Riley's New Venture • Old Mother Riley • Old Mother

Riley's New Venture 49; Old Mother Riley, Headmistress 50; Those People Next Door 52; The Blue Parrot 53; Dangerous Cargo 54; Delayed Action 54
Harman, Bobby The Big Show 29; House Warmers 29; Jackie and the Beanstalk 29; Jackie's Nightmare 29; Kollege Kapers 29; A Runaway Holiday 29
Harman, Hugh Panicky Pancakes 28*; Rocks and Socks 28; The South Pole Flight 28*; Sinkin' in the Bathtub 30*; Ride 'Em Bosko • Ride Him, Bosko 32*; Beau Bosko 33*; Bosko in Dutch 33*; Bosko in Person 33*; Bosko the Drawback 33*; Bosko the Musketeer 33; Bosko the Sheep Herder 33; Bosko the Speed King 33; Bosko's Dizzy Date 33; Bosko's Knightmare 33; Bosko's Mechanical Man 33; Bosko's Picture Show 33*; Bosko's Woodland Daze 33; The Mad Maestro 39; Peace on Earth 39
Harmon, Robert The Hitcher 86
Harnack, Falk The Plot to Assassinate Hitler 55; Tempestuous Love 57; All Night Through • Restless Night • Unruhige Nacht 58; Arzt Ohne Gewissen • Doctor Without Scruples • Das Letzte Geheimnis • Privatklinik Prof. Lund 59
Harrington, Curtis The Fall of the House of Usher 42; Crescendo 43; Renaissance 44; Fragment of Seeking • Symbol of Decadence 46; Picnic 48; On the Edge 49; Dangerous Houses 52; The Assignation 53; The Wormwood Star 55; Night Tide 61; Images of Productivity 64; The Four Elements 66; Planet of Blood • Queen of Blood 66*; Games 67; Gingerbread House • Who Slew Auntie Roo? • Whoever Slew Auntie Roo? 71; What's the Matter with Helen? 71; The Killing Kind 73; Ruby 77*; Mata Hari 85
Harris, Buddy Chinese Cabaret 36; International Revue 36
Harris, Clarence J. Barbara Frietchie 15*
Harris, Claude Sanctuary 16
Harris, Damian The Rachel Papers 89
Harris, Denny Silent Scream 80
Harris, Doug Remembering Mel 85
Harris, Elmer Name the Woman 28*
Harris, Frank Killpoint 84; Low Blow 86; The Patriot 86; Aftershock 90
Harris, Harry B. Risky Business 20; Desperate Youth 21; The Man Tamer 21; Rich Girl, Poor Girl 21; Short Skirts 21; The Trouper 22
Harris, Harry Thurston The Surgeon's Child 12
Harris, Jack Called Back 33*
Harris, Jack H. Mother Goose à Go-Go • The Unkissed Bride 66
Harris, James B. The Bedford Incident 65; Some Call It Loving 73; Fast-Walking 81; Blood on the Moon • Cop 87
Harris, Ken Hare-abian Knights 59
Harris, Lawson Law or Loyalty 26
Harris, Lionel The Guilty Party 62; The Double 63; Position of Trust 63
Harris, Maxine Signal Through the Flames 84*
Harris, Richard Bloomfield • The Hero 69

Harris, Vernon Johnny on the Run 52*
Harrison, Ben Aero Nuts 27*; Bee Cause 27*; For Crime's Sake 27*; Grid Ironed 27*; Loco Motifs • Rail Rode 27*; Milk Made 27*; Pie Curs 27*; School Daze 27*; Sealing Whacks 27*; Skinny 27*; Stork Exchange 27*; Tired Wheels 27*; Topsy Turvy 27*; Web Feet 27*; Baby Feud 28*; Beaches and Scream 28*; A Bum Steer 28*; Come Easy, Go Slow 28*; A Companionate Mirage 28*; Gold Bricks 28*; A Hunger Stroke 28*; Ice Boxed 28*; Liar Bird 28*; The Long Count 28*; Love Sunk 28*; News Reeling 28*; Nicked Nags 28*; Night Howls 28*; The Patent Medicine Kid 28*; The Phantom Trail 28*; Pig Styles 28*; The Rain Dropper 28*; Sea Sword 28*; Shadow Theory 28*; The Show Vote 28*; Stage Coached 28*; Still Waters 28*; Tong Tied 28*; Wired and Fired 28*; Auto Suggestion 29*; Canned Music 29*; Cow Belles 29*; Farm Relief 29*; Flying Yeast 29*; A Fur Peace 29*; Golf Socks 29*; Hat Aches 29*; Hospitalities 29*; A Joint Affair 29*; The Lone Shark 29*; Petting Larceny 29*; Port Whines 29*; Ratskin 29*; Reduced Weights 29*; Sheep Skinned 29*; Sleepy Holler 29*; Sole Mates 29*; Vanishing Screams 29*; Alaskan Knights 30*; The Apache Kid 30*; The Band Master 30*; The Cat's Meow 30*; Cinderella 30*; Desert Sunk 30*; Honolulu Wiles 30*; Jazz Rhythm 30*; Lambs Will Gamble 30*; The Little Trail 30*; An Old Flame 30*; Slow Beau 30*; Spook Easy 30*; Bars and Stripes 31*; Disarmament Conference 31*; Hash House Blues 31*; The Restless Sax 31*; Rodeo Dough 31*; Soda Poppa 31*; The Stork Market 31*; Svengarlic 31*; Swiss Movements 31*; Taken for a Ride 31*; The Weenie Roast 31*; Birth of Jazz 32*; The Crystal Gazebo 32*; Hic-Cups the Champ 32*; Hollywood Goes Krazy 32*; Lighthouse Keeping 32*; Love Krazy 32*; The Medicine Show 32*; The Minstrel Show 32*; Piano Mover 32*; Prosperity Blues 32*; Ritzy Hotel 32*; Seeing Stars 32*; Show Time 32*; Soldier Old Man 32*; What a Knight 32*; Antique Antics 33*; The Bill Poster 33*; The Broadway Malady 33*; Bunnies and Bonnets 33*; The Curio Shop 33*; House Cleaning 33*; Krazy Spooks 33*; Out of the Ether 33*; Russian Dressing 33*; Stage Krazy 33*; Wedding Bells 33*; Whacks Museum 33*; Wooden Shoes 33*; The Autograph Hunter 34*; Bowery Daze 34*; Busy Bus 34*; Cinder Alley 34*; Goofy Gondolas 34*; Katnips of 1940 34*; Krazy's Waterloo 34*; The Masquerade Party 34*; Southern Exposure 34*; Tom Thumb 34*; The Trapeze Artist 34*; The Bird Man 35*; Garden Gaieties 35*; A Happy Family 35*; Hotcha Melody 35*; Kannibal Kapers 35*; The King's Jester 35*; The Peace Conference 35*; Bird Stuffer 36*; Highway Snobbery 36*; Krazy's Newsreel 36*; Li'l Anjil 36*; Merry Cafe 36*; Krazy's Race of Time 37*; The Lyin' Hunter 37*; The Masque Raid 37*;

Railroad Rhythm 37*; Animal Cracker Circus 38; The Auto Clinic 38*; Gym Jams 38*; Hot Dogs on Ice 38*; The Kangaroo Kid 38; Krazy Magic 38*; Krazy's Travel Squawks 38*; Little Buckaroo 38*; The Lone Mountie 38*; Poor Little Butterfly 38; Sad Little Guinea Pigs 38*; Golf Chumps 39*; Happy Tots 39; Hollywood Sweepstakes 39; Krazy's Bear Tales 39*; Krazy's Shoe Shop 39*; Lucky Pigs 39; A Boy, a Gun and Birds 40; The Happy Tots' Expedition 40; Paunch 'n' Judy 40; The Timid Pup 40

Harrison, Bertram The $5,000,000 Counterfeiting Plot 14

Harrison, Ed N. Song of the Land 53*

Harrison, Eric Many a Slip 20; The Worldlings 20

Harrison, Jack Dimples and Tears 29; The Fighting Fool 29; Mr. Smith Wakes Up 29; Holiday Lovers 32

Harrison, John Tales from the Darkside: The Movie 90

Harrison, Jules Exterminators of the Year 3000 85

Harrison, Ken 1918 84; On Valentine's Day 86

Harrison, Marcus Woman, Wake Up! 21*

Harrison, Marguerite Grass • Grass—A Nation's Battle for Life • Grass—The Epic of a Lost Tribe 25*

Harrison, Norman Locker 69 62; Calculated Risk 63; Incident at Midnight 63; The Invisible Asset 63

Harrison, Paul The House of Seven Corpses 72

Harrison, Saul The Customary Two Weeks 17; Salt of the Earth 17

Harrivirta, Holger Sampo 58*; The Day the Earth Froze 59*

Harry, Lee Silent Night, Deadly Night Part II 87

Hars, Mihály Lutra 87

Hart, Ben R. Frozen Fate 29*; Birds of a Feather 31; Crime Reporter 47; River Patrol 48; Dangerous Assignment 50

Hart, Christopher Eat and Run 86

Hart, David The Other People 68

Hart, Derek Backstage at the Kirov 83

Hart, Harvey Bus Riley's Back in Town 65; Dark Intruder 65; Sullivan's Empire 67*; The Sweet Ride 68; Fortune and Men's Eyes 71; The Hooker Cult Murders • The Pyx 72; Shoot 76; The First Hello • The High Country 80; Getting Even • Utilities 81

Hart, Neal When the Desert Smiles 19; Hell's Oasis 20; Butterfly Ranch • Butterfly Range 22; Lure of Gold 22; Rangeland 22; South of Northern Lights 22; West of the Pecos 22; Below the Rio Grande 23; The Devil's Bowl • In the Devil's Bowl 23; The Fighting Strain 23; The Forbidden Range 23; Salty Saunders 23; The Secret of the Pueblo 23; Branded a Thief 24; Lawless Men 24; The Left Hand Brand 24; Trucker's Top Hand 24; The Valley of Vanishing Men 24; The Verdict of the Desert 25

Hart, Walter Easy Life 44; The Last Installment 45; The Goldbergs • Molly 50

Hart, William S. The Passing of Two-Gun Hicks 14; The Bad Buck of Santa Ynez 15; The Conversion of Frosty Blake 15*; The Darkening Trail 15*; The Disciple 15*; The Grudge 15; Keno Bates—Liar 15*; Mr. Silent Haskins 15*; Pinto Ben 15; The Roughneck 15*; The Ruse 15*; Scourge of the Desert 15*; The Taking of Luke McVane 15*; The Aryan 16*; Between Men 16*; The Dawn Maker 16; The Devil's Double 16; Hell's Hinges 16*; The Patriot 16; The Primal Lure 16; The Return of Draw Egan 16; The Cold Deck 17; The Desert Man 17; The Gunfighter 17; The Narrow Trail 17*; The Silent Man 17*; The Square Deal Man 17; Truthful Tulliver 17; Wolf Lowry 17; Blue Blazes Rawden 18; The Border Wireless 18; Branding Broadway 18*; Riddle Gawne 18*; Selfish Yates 18; Shark Monroe 18; The Tiger Man 18; Wolves of the Rail 18; The Breed of Men 19*; The Money Corral 19*; Poppy Girl • The Poppy Girl's Husband 19*; Square Deal Sanderson 19*; Wild Bill Hickok 23*; Pinto Ben 24; Tumbleweeds 25*

Hartford, David M. Civilization 16*; Inside the Lines 18; The Man of Bronze 18; Back to God's Country 19; It Happened in Paris 19; Nomads of the North 20; The Golden Snare 21; Jack o' Hearts • Jack of Hearts 26; The Man in the Shadow 26; Then Came the Woman 26; God's Great Wilderness 27

Hartford, Ken The Lucifer Complex 78*; Hell Squad 83

Hartford-Davis, Robert City of Contrast 52; Dollars for Sale 53*; The Man on the Cliff 55; A Christmas Carol 60; Crosstrap 61; Gutter Girls • Thrill Seekers • The Yellow Golliwog • The Yellow Teddybears 63; Saturday Night Out 63; The Black Torment 64; Gonks Go Beat 65; The Sandwich Man 66; Carnage • Corruption 67; House of Unclaimed Women • School for Unclaimed Girls • The Smashing Bird I Used to Know 68; Bloodsuckers • Doctors Wear Scarlet • Incense for the Damned 70; Beware My Brethren • Beware of the Brethren • Beware the Brethren • The Fiend 71; Nobody Ordered Love 71; Black Gunn 72; The Take 74; Hell House Girls 75

Hartl, Karl Berge in Flammen • The Doomed Battalion 31*; Ein Burschenlied aus Heidelberg 31; F.P. 1 • F.P. 1 Antwortet Nicht • F.P. 1 Doesn't Answer • Secrets of F.P. 1 32; Ihre Durchlacht, die Verkäuferin 33; Gold • L'Or 34; Zigeunerbaron 35; The Man Who Was Sherlock Holmes • Der Mann Der Sherlock Holmes War 37; Ritt in die Freiheit 37; Two Merry Adventures • Zwei Lustige Abenteuer 38; The Mozart Story 48*; The Beethoven Story • Eroica 51*; Entführung ins Glück • Wonder Boy • Wonder Child • The Wonder Kid 51; Haus des Lebens • House of Life 53; Give Me Your Hand My Love • The Life and Loves of Mozart • Mozart •

Reich Mir die Hand Mein Lieben 56

Hartley, Hal Trust 90; The Unbelievable Truth 90

Hartman, Don It Had to Be You 47*; Every Girl Should Be Married 48; Holiday Affair 49; It's a Big Country 51*; Mr. Imperium • You Belong to My Heart 51

Hartman, Ferris G. A Phantom Husband 17; Framing Framers 18*; The Forest King 22

Hartman, Philip No Picnic 88

Hartman, Rivka Bachelor Girl 87

Hartmann, Siegfried Das Feuerzeug • The Tinder Box 68

Hartzell, Päivi Lumikuningatar • The Snow Queen 86

Harvard, Emile A. Fugitive Killer 75

Harvel, John The Beggar Student 31*; Captivation 31

Harvey, Anthony Dutchman 66; The Lion in Winter 68; They Might Be Giants 71; The Abdication 74; Eagle's Wing 78; Players 79; Richard's Things 80; Grace Quigley • The Ultimate Solution of Grace Quigley 83

Harvey, Harry The Twin Triangle 16; Brand's Daughter 17; The Clean Gun 17; The Devil's Bait 17; Feet of Clay 17; The Mystery Ship 17*; The Phantom Shotgun 17; The Stolen Play 17; The Yellow Bullet 17

Harvey, Herk Carnival of Souls 62

Harvey, John The Wolf of Debt 15; The Lords of High Decision 16; The Kaiser's Finish 18*; The Night of the Pub 20; The Woman Who Believed 22; The Right Man 25; Keep Going 26; The Baby Mother • No Babies Wanted 28

Harvey, Laurence La Ceremonia • The Ceremony 63; A Dandy in Aspic 67*; Tender Flesh • Welcome to Arrow Beach 73

Harvey, Russ No Man's Land 64

Harwitz, Joseph A Pesky Pup • That Pesky Pup 17

Has, Wojciech Harmonia 48; Moje Miasto 48; Puchar Tatr 48; Parowóz PF-47 49; Ulica Brzozowa 49*; Pierwszy Plon 50; Jeden Dzień w Polsce 51; Mechanizacja Robót Ziemnych 51; Scentralizowana Kontrola Przebiegu Produkcji 51; Harcerze na Złocie 52; Przeglad Kulturalny 2/53 52; Zielarze z Kamiennej Doliny 52; Karmnik Jankowy • Nasz Zespół 55; The Noose • Petla 57; Farewells • Lydia Ate the Apple • Partings • Pożegnania 58; One-Room Tenants • Shared Room • Wspólny Pokój 60; Goodbye to the Past • Parting • Rozstanie 61; Gold • Gold Dreams • Golden Dreams • Złoto 62; How to Be Loved • Jak Być Kochana 62; Adventures of a Nobleman • Manuscript Found in Saragossa • Rekopis Znaleziony w Saragossie • The Saragossa Manuscript 64; The Code • Szyfry 66; The Doll • Lalka 68; The Hourglass Sanatorium • Sanatorium pod Klepsydra • The Sandglass 73; Pismak 85; The Memoirs of a Sinner • Osobisty Pamietnik Grzesznika Przez Niego Samego Spisany 86; Niezwyłka Podróż Baltazara Kobera 88

Hase, Kazuo Cruel Ghost Legend • Curse of the Blood • Kaidan Zankoku Monogatari **68**

Hasegawa, Kazuhiko The Man Who Stole the Sun • Taiyō o Nusunda Otoko **80**

Hashimoto, Koji Godzilla 1985 • Godzilla—The Legend Is Reborn **85***

Haskin, Byron The Broadway Kid • Ginsberg the Great 27; Irish Hearts 27; Matinee Ladies 27; The Siren 27; Canaries Sometimes Sing **30***; One Embarrassing Night • Rookery Nook **30***; Plunder **30***; I Walk Alone 47; Man-Eater of Kumaon 48; Killer Bait • Too Late for Tears 49; Treasure Island 50; High Vermilion • Silver City 51; Tarzan and the Jungle Goddess • Tarzan and the Jungle Queen • Tarzan's Peril **51***; Warpath 51; The Denver and Rio Grande 52; War of the Worlds 52; His Majesty O'Keefe 53; The Naked Jungle 53; Conquest of Space 54; Long John Silver • Long John Silver Returns to Treasure Island 54; The Boss 56; The First Texan 56; From the Earth to the Moon 58; Jet Over the Atlantic 59; The Little Savage 59; September Storm 60; Armored Command 61; Captain Sinbad 63; Robinson Crusoe on Mars 64; The Power **67***

Hass, Hans Under the Red Sea 52

Hassan, Mamoun The Meeting 64

Hasse, Charles Shrine of Victory 43

Hasselbach, Hagen Denmark Grows Up **47***

Hastrup, Jannik Strit og Stumme • Subway to Paradise 87

Hata, Masanori The Adventures of Chatran • The Adventures of Milo and Otis • Koneko Monogatari 86

Hathaway, Henry Heritage of the Desert 32; Wild Horse Mesa 32; In the Days of the Thundering Herd • The Thundering Herd 33; Man of the Forest 33; Sunset Pass 33; To the Last Man 33; Under the Tonto Rim 33; Come On Marines! 34; The Last Round-Up 34; The Lives of a Bengal Lancer 34; Now and Forever 34; The Witching Hour 34; Peter Ibbetson 35; Go West, Young Man 36; The Trail of the Lonesome Pine 36; Lest We Forget 37; Souls at Sea 37; Spawn of the North 38; The Real Glory 39; Brigham Young • Brigham Young—Frontiersman 40; Johnny Apollo 40; Sundown 40; Shepherd of the Hills 41; China Girl 42; Ten Gentlemen from West Point 42; The Cowboy and the Girl • A Lady Takes a Chance **43***; Home in Indiana 44; Wing and a Prayer 44; The House on 92nd Street 45; Nob Hill 45; The Dark Corner 46; 13 Rue Madeleine 46; Kiss of Death 47; Call Northside 777 • Calling Northside 777 48; The Black Rose 49; Down to the Sea in Ships 49; Desperate Siege • Rawhide 50; U.S.S. Teakettle • You're in the Navy Now 50; The Desert Fox • Rommel—Desert Fox • The Story of Rommel 51; Fourteen Hours 51; Diplomatic Courier 52; Full House • O. Henry's Full House **52***; Red Skies of Montana • Smoke Jumpers **52***; The Coronation Parade 53; Niagara 53; White Witch

Doctor 53; Garden of Evil 54; Prince Valiant 54; The Racers • Such Men Are Dangerous 54; Beyond the River • The Bottom of the Bottle 56; 23 Paces to Baker Street 56; Legend of the Lost 57; The Wayward Bus **57***; From Hell to Texas • Manhunt 58; Seven Thieves 59; Woman Obsessed 59; North to Alaska 60; How the West Was Won **62***; Jungle Rampage • Rampage! **62***; Circus World • The Magnificent Showman 64; Of Human Bondage **64***; The Sons of Katie Elder 65; Nevada Smith 66; The Last Safari 67; Five Card Stud 68; Airport **69***; True Grit 69; Raid on Rommel **70***; Shootout 71; Hangup • Superdude 73

Hathaway, Terence see Grieco, Sergio

Hathcock, Bob DuckTales: The Movie—Treasure of the Lost Lamp **90**

Hatot, Georges The Magnetic Squirt **09**

Hatton, Maurice Scene Nun, Take One 64; Praise Marx and Pass the Ammunition 68; Long Shot 78; Nelly's Version 83; The Rewards of Virtue 83; American Roulette • Latin Roulette 88

Hatton, Richard The Seventh Sheriff 23; The Sting of the Scorpion 23; Unblazed Trail 23; Sagebrush Gospel 24; Two-Fisted Justice 24; The Whirlwind Ranger 24; A He-Man's Country 26; Temporary Sheriff 26

Hatwig, Hans Green Men from Outer Space • Gröna Gubbar från Y.R. 86

Hauff, Reinhard Ausweg Los 69; Die Revolte 69; Untermann, Obermann 69; Offener Hass Gegen Unbekannt 70; Mathias Kneissl 71; Haus am Meer 72; Desaster 73; Die Verrohrung des Franz Blums 74; Zündschnüre 74; Paule Pauländer 75; Der Hauptdarsteller • The Main Actor 77; Knife in the Head • Messer im Kopf 78; Endstation Freiheit • Slow Attack 80; Der Mann auf der Mauer 82; Stammheim 86; Linie 1 88

Haugh, Dietrich Agatha—Lass das Morden Sein • Agatha—Stop the Murders 60; Heldinnen 62

Haugse, William Breakfast in Bed 78

Havelock-Allan, Anthony From the Four Corners 41; An Evening with the Royal Ballet **63***

Haven, Carter de see DeHaven, Carter

Hawes, Stanley Monkey Into Man **41***

Hawkes, Steven Stevie, Samson and Delilah 75

Hawkins, William see Caiano, Mario

Hawks, Howard Fig Leaves 26; The Road to Glory 26; The Cradle Snatchers 27; Fazil 27; Paid to Love 27; The Air Circus **28***; A Girl in Every Port 28; Trent's Last Case 29; The Criminal Code 30; The Dawn Patrol • Flight Commander 30; Hell's Angels **30***; The Crowd Roars 32; Scarface • Scarface, Shame of a Nation • Scarface, the Shame of a Nation • The Shame of a Nation 32; Tiger Shark 32; Today We Live 33; Twentieth Century 34; Viva Villa! **34***; Barbary Coast • Port of Wickedness 35; Ceiling Zero 35; Come and Get It • Roaring Timber **36***; The

Road to Glory • Wooden Crosses • Zero Hour 36; Bringing Up Baby 38; His Girl Friday 39; Only Angels Have Wings 39; The Outlaw **40***; Ball of Fire • The Professor and the Burlesque Queen 41; Sergeant York 41; Air Force 43; Corvette K-225 • The Nelson Touch **43***; To Have and Have Not 44; The Big Sleep 46; Red River 47; A Song Is Born 47; I Was a Male War Bride • You Can't Sleep Here 49; The Thing • The Thing (From Another World) • The Thing That Came from Another World **51***; The Big Sky 52; Darling I Am Growing Younger • Monkey Business 52; Full House • O. Henry's Full House **52***; Gentlemen Prefer Blondes 53; Land of the Pharaohs 55; Rio Bravo 58; The African Story • Hatari! 62; Man's Favorite Sport? 63; Red Line 7000 65; El Dorado 66; Rio Lobo 70

Hawks, Kenneth Masked Emotions **27***; Big Time 29; Such Men Are Dangerous 30

Hawtrey, Charles Dumb Dora Discovers Tobacco • Fag End 45; What Do We Do Now? 45

Hay, Rod Breaking Loose 88

Hay, Will The Black Sheep of Whitehall **41***; The Goose Steps Out **42***; My Learned Friend **43***

Hayashi, Kaizo To Sleep So As to Dream • Yume Miruyoni Nemuritai 86

Hayden, Jeffrey The Vintage 57

Hayden, Russell When the Girls Take Over 62

Hayden, Tom Introduction to the Enemy **74***

Haydn, Richard Miss Tatlock's Millions 48; Dear Wife 49; Mr. Music 50

Haydon, J. Charles The Alster Case 15; The Phantom Buccaneer 16; The Sting of Victory 16; The Night Workers 17; Satan's Private Door 17; Hearts of Love 18

Hayers, Sidney Echo of Barbara 58; Violent Moment 58; Circus of Horrors 59; The White Trap 59; The Malpas Mystery 60; Burn, Witch, Burn • Night of the Eagle 61; I Promised to Pay • Payroll 61; This Is My Street 63; Three Hats for Lisa 63; L'Aventure Sauvage • The Trap 66; Finders Keepers 66; L'Étoile du Sud • The Southern Star 69; Mister Jericho 69; Assault • The Creepers • In the Devil's Garden • Tower of Terror 70; The Firechasers 70; After Jenny Died • Inn of the Frightened People • Revenge • Terror from Under the House 71; All Coppers Are... 71; The Bananas Boat • What Changed Charley Farthing 74; Deadly Strangers 74; Diagnosis: Murder 74; One Away 75; A Bridge Too Far **77***; Conquest of the Earth **80***

Hayes, John The Grass Eater 61; Walk the Angry Beach 61; Five Minutes to Love • It Only Takes Five Minutes • The Rotten Apple • The Wrecking Yard 63; Shell Shock 64; Farm Girl • The Farmer's Other Daughter 65; The Hang-Up 69; All the Lovin' Kinfolk • The Closest of Kin • Kinfolk 70; Fandango 70; Sweet Trash 70; Garden of the Dead 72; Grave of the

Vampire • Seed of Terror 72; Tomb of the Undead 72; Mama's Dirty Girls 74; End of the World 77

Hayes, John J. The Fatal 30 21

Hayes, Michael The Promise 69

Hayes, Ward Come On Cowboys! 24; Horse Sense 24; Sell 'Em Cowboy 24; The Cactus Cure 25; My Pal 25; Range Justice 25; Ridin' Easy 25; The Rip Snorter 25; The Secret of Black Canyon 25; The Strange Rider 25; Where Romance Rides 25; Wolves of the Road 25

Haynes, H. Manning Monty Works the Wires 21*; The Head of the Family 22; Sam's Boy 22; The Skipper's Wooing 22; A Will and a Way 22; The Constable's Move 23; The Convert 23; The Monkey's Paw 23; An Odd Freak 23; The Boatswain's Mate 24; Dixon's Return 24; Lawyer Quince 24; London Love 26; Passion Island 27; The Ware Case 28; Those Who Love 29; Should a Doctor Tell? 30; The Officer's Mess 31; The Old Man 31; To Oblige a Lady 31; Love's Old Sweet Song • The Missing Witness 33; The Perfect Flaw 34; Smith's Wives 35; Highland Fling 36; Tomorrow We Live 36; East of Ludgate Hill 37; Pearls Bring Tears 37; The Claydon Treasure Mystery 38; Coming of Age 38

Haynes, Manning see Haynes, H. Manning

Haynes, Stanley Carnival 46; Carnation Frank 61

Haynes, Tom Lyndon see Lyndon-Haynes, Tom

Hays, Bill Time After Time 85

Hayward, Frederick Lend Me Your Husband 35; The Elder Brother 37

Hayward, Rudall C. The Goodwin Sands 48

Hazan, Jack A Bigger Splash 74; Rude Boy 80*

Head, John Jimi Hendrix 73*

Heale, Patrick K. Hanging Rain 35; Just for Tonight 35; Murder at Ten 35; Our Husband 35

Heard, Howard Shadows Run Black 81

Heard, Paul F. Hong Kong Affair 58

Hearn, J. Van The Calico Queen • The Hanging of Jake Ellis 69

Heath, Arch Melody of Love 28; Modern Love 29

Heath, Harold The Mystery of the £500,000 Pearl Necklace • $1,000,000 Pearl Mystery 13; Nobody's Child 13; £1000 Reward 13

Heath, Simon Bullamakanka 84; Charly's Web 86

Heavener, David Outlaw Force 88; Twisted Justice 90

Hébert, Pierre Histoire d'une Pépite 62; Histoire Grise 62; Opus 1 64; Op Hop 65; Explosion de la Population 67; Opus 3 67; Une Souris la Semaine Prochaine 67

Hecht, Ben Crime Without Passion 34*; Once in a Blue Moon 34*; The Scoundrel 35*; Soak the Rich 36*; Angels Over Broadway 40*; Until I Die 40*; Specter of the Rose • Spectre of the Rose 46; Actors

and Sin 52*

Heckerling, Amy Fast Times • Fast Times at Ridgemont High 82; Johnny Dangerously 84; National Lampoon's European Vacation 85; Look Who's Talking 89; Look Who's Talking Too 90

Hečko, Kvetoslav Iba Den • Just One Day 89*

Hedden, Rob Friday the 13th Part VIII: Jason Takes Manhattan 89

Hedqvist, Ivan The Downy Girl 19; Carolina Rediviva 20; Pilgrimage to Kevlaar 21; Life in the Country 24

Heer, Rolf de see De Heer, Rolf

Heerman, Victor Don't Ever Marry 20*; The Poor Simp 20; The Chicken in the Case 21; My Boy 21*; John Smith 22; Love Is an Awful Thing 22; The Dangerous Maid 23; Modern Matrimony 23; Rupert of Hentzau 23; The Confidence Man 24; Irish Luck 25; Old Home Week 25; For Wives Only 26; Ladies Must Dress 27; Rubber Heels 27; Love Hungry 28; Animal Crackers 30; Paramount on Parade 30*; Personality 30; Sea Legs 30

Heffner, Avram But Where Is Daniel Vax? 72

Heffron, Richard T. Fillmore 72; Newman's Law 74; Futureworld 76; Trackdown 76; Outlaw Blues 77; Foolin' Around 78; I, the Jury 81; The French Revolution 89*

Heffron, Thomas Aristocracy 14; The Man from Mexico 14; One of Our Girls 14; The Only Son 14*; The Scales of Justice 14; Are You a Mason? 15; A Black Sheep 15; Gretna Green 15*; The House of a Thousand Candles 15; Into the Primitive 16; Lonesome Town 16; Peck o' Pickles 16; The Valiants of Virginia 16; Mountain Dew 17; The Planter 17*; The Stainless Barrier 17; The Sudden Gentleman 17; Deuce Duncan 18; The Hopper 18; The Lonely Woman 18; Madame Sphinx 18; The Mask • Mask of Riches 18; Old Hartwell's Cub 18; The Painted Lily 18; The Price of Applause 18; The Sea Panther 18; Tony America 18; Who Killed Walton? 18; The Best Man 19; Life's a Funny Proposition 19; The Prodigal Liar 19; The City of Masks 20; Firebrand Trevision 20; Sunset Sprague 20*; Thou Art the Man 20; Her Face Value 21; Her Sturdy Oak 21; A Kiss in Time 21; The Little Clown 21; The Love Charm 21; Sham 21; The Truant Husband 21; Bobbed Hair 22; Too Much Wife 22; The Truthful Liar 22; A Wife's Romance 23

Hegedus, Chris Town Bloody Hall 79*; Dance Black America 85*; Rocky X 86*; Dépêche Mode • Dépêche Mode 101 88*

Heifits, Josef Pesn o Metallye • A Song of Steel 28*; Against the Wind • Facing the Wind • Veter v Litso • Wind in the Face 29*; Midday • Noon • Poldien 31*; Moi Rodina • My Country • My Fatherland • My Homeland • My Motherland 32*; Goryachie Deneki • Hectic Days • Red Army Days • Those Were the Days 35*; Baltic Deputy • Deputat Baltiki 36*; Chlen Pravitelstva • The Great Begin-

ning • Member of the Government 37*; His Name Is Sukhe-Bator • Yevo Zovut Sukhe-Bator 42*; The Last Hill • The Malakhov Burial Mound • Malakhov Kirgan • Malakov Hill 44*; The Defeat of Japan 45*; For the Living • In the Name of Life • Vo Imya Zhizni 46*; Dragotsennye Zerna • Precious Grain • Precious Seeds 48*; Fires of Baku • Flames Over Baku • The Lights of Baku • Ogni Baku 50*; Soviet Mordovia 51; Spring in Moscow • Vesna v Moskve 53*; The Big Family • Bolchaia Semia • Bolshaya Semya • The Great Family 54; Delo Rumiantseva • The Rumiantsev Case 55; The Cause We Serve • Dorogoi Moi Chelovek • My Beloved • My Dear Fellow • My Dear Man 58; Dama s Sobachkoi • The Lady with a Dog • The Lady with a Little Dog • The Lady with the Dog • The Lady with the Little Dog 59; Gorizont • The Horizon 61; A Day of Happiness • Den Schastya 63; In the Town of S • V Gorodye S 66; Saliut Marya • Salute Maria 70; The Bad Good Man • The Bad Goody • Plohoy Horoshii Chelovek 73; Edinstvennaya • The One and Only • The Only One 75; Asya • Love Should Be Guarded 77; First Marriage • V Pervyi Zamushem 80; The Accused • Podsudimye 87

Heilig, Morton Once 74

Heilner, Van Campen The Angry God 48

Heinrich, André Le Mystère de l'Atelier Quinze 57*

Heinz, Ray Blazing Guns 35; Border Vengeance 35; Just My Luck 36

Heinz, Russell Ray see Heinz, Ray

Heisler, Stuart Poppy 36*; Straight from the Shoulder 36; The Hurricane 37*; Melody of Love • Melody of Youth • Ragged Angels • They Shall Have Music 39*; The Biscuit Eater • God Gave Him a Dog 40; Among the Living 41; The Monster and the Girl 41; The Glass Key 42; The Remarkable Andrew 42; The Negro Soldier 44; Along Came Jones 45; Blue Skies 46*; Smash-Up, the Story of a Woman • A Woman Destroyed 47; Tokyo Joe 49; Tulsa 49; Chain Lightning 50; Dallas 50; Storm Warning 50; Vendetta 50*; Journey Into Light 51; Island of Desire • Saturday Island 52; The Star 52; Beachhead 54; This Is My Love 54; I Died a Thousand Times 55; The Lone Ranger 55; The Burning Hills 56; Hitler • Women of Nazi Germany 61

Helbig, Heinz Die Pompadour 35*; His Daughter Is Peter • Seine Tochter Ist der Peter 38

Helfer, Daniel The Record 88

Helge, Mats Ninja Mission 84

Hellberg, Thomas Råttornas Vinter 88

Hellbom, Olle Pippi in the South Seas • Pippi Långstrump på de Sju Haven 74; Pippi on the Run 77

Hellman, Jerome Promises in the Dark 79

Hellman, Monte The Beast from Haunted Cave • Beast from the Haunted Cave 59; Lady of the Shadows • The Terror

62*; Back Door to Hell 64; Cordillera • Flight to Fury 65; Ride in the Whirlwind • Ride the Whirlwind 65; The Shooting 66; Two-Lane Blacktop 71; Born to Kill • Cockfighter • Gamblin' Man • Wild Drifter 74; Call Him Mr. Shatter • Shatter • They Call Him Mr. Shatter 74*; China 9, Liberty 37 • Clayton and Catherine • Gunfighters 77; Avalanche Express 78*; Iguana 88; Silent Night, Deadly Night III: Better Watch Out! 89

Hellman, Oliver *see Assonitis, Sonia*

Hellström, Gunnar Just Once More • Just One More 63; The Female Trap • Lovers in Limbo • The Name of the Game Is Kill 68; Raskenstam 83

Helman, Henri Le Cœur Froid 77; Where Is Parsifal? 84

Helmick, Paul Teenage Thunder 57; Thunder in Carolina 60

Helpern, David, Jr. I'm a Stranger Here Myself 74; Hollywood on Trial 76; Something Short of Paradise 79

Helpmann, Robert Don Quixote 73*

Helu, Antonio The Obligation to Assassinate 37; Alma Jarocha 38; El Hotel de los Chiflados 39; La India Bonita • The Pretty Indian Girl 39

Hemert, Ruud van Schatjes 84; Mama Is Boos! • Mama Is Mad! 86; Honeybunch 88

Hemmer, Edward L. Orphan Sally 22; Sunshine Harbor 22

Hemmings, David Running Scared 72; The 14 73; Just a Gigolo • Schöner Gigolo—Armer Gigolo 78; The Survivor 80; Race for the Yankee Zephyr • Race to the Yankee Zephyr • Treasure of the Yankee Zephyr 81

Henabery, Joseph E. Children of the Feud 16; Her Official Fathers 17*; The Man from Painted Post 17; Say, Young Fellow 18; His Majesty the American 19; The Fourteenth Man • The Man from Blankley's 20; The Inferior Sex 20; The Life of the Party 20; Love Madness 20; Brewster's Millions 21; The Call of the North • The Conjurer's House 21; Don't Call Me Little Girl 21; Her Winning Way 21; Moonlight and Honeysuckle 21; The Traveling Salesman 21; Her Own Money 22; Making a Man 22; The Man Unconquerable 22; Missing Millions 22; North of the Rio Grande 22; While Satan Sleeps 22; A Gentleman of Leisure 23; Sixty Cents an Hour 23; Stephen Steps Out 23; The Tiger's Claw 23; The Guilty One 24; A Sainted Devil 24; The Stranger 24; Tongues of Flame 24; Cobra 25; The Pinch Hitter 25; The Broadway Boob 26; Meet the Prince 26; Shipwrecked 26; Lonesome Ladies 27; Play Safe 27; See You in Jail 27; Hellship Bronson 28; The River Woman 28; Sailors' Wives 28; United States Smith 28; Clear the Decks 29; Light Fingers 29; The Quitter 29; Red Hot Speed 29; Island of Desire • The Love Trader 30; The Leather Burners 43

Henabery, Ralph Speed Devils 35

Hendel, Günther Ein Langer Ritt nach Eden 72

Henderson, Clark Highriders 87; Saigon Commandos 87; Primary Target 90

Henderson, Del Ambrose's First Falsehood 14; Among the Mourners 14; As It Might Have Been 14; The Genius 14; Liberty Belles 14; Divorcons 15; A Favorite Fool 15*; A Janitor's Wife's Temptation 15; That Springtime Feeling 15; Because He Loved Her 16; A Coney Island Princess 16; The Great Pearl Tangle 16; Kennedy Square 16; The Kiss 16; Perils of the Park 16; Rolling Stones 16; The Beautiful Adventure 17; A Girl Like That • The Turning Point 17; The Outcast 17; Please Help Emily 17; The Runaway 17; The Beloved Blackmailer 18; By Hook or Crook 18; The Golden Wall 18; Her Second Husband 18; Hitting the Trail 18; The Imposter 18; My Wife 18; The Road to France 18; Who Loved Him Best? 18; Allies • Love in a Hurry 19; Courage for Two 19; The Dead Line 19; Hit or Miss 19; The Social Pirate 19; Three Green Eyes 19; The Plunger 20; The Servant Question 20; The Shark 20; Dead or Alive 21; Dynamite Allen 21; The Girl from Porcupine 21; The Broken Silence 22; Sure Fire Flint 22; Blazing Barriers • Jacqueline, or Blazing Barriers 23; Battling Brewster 24; Gambling Wives 24; The Love Bandit 24; One Law for the Woman 24; Accused 25; The Bad Lands 25; Defend Yourself 25; Pursued 25; Quick Change 25; Rough Stuff 25; The Pay-Off 26; The Rambling Ranger 27

Henderson, Dell *see Henderson, Del*

Henderson, Don The Babysitter • Weekend Babysitter • Weekend with the Babysitter 69; Curse of Melissa • Night of the Demon • The Touch of Melissa • The Touch of Satan 71

Henderson, Lucius Dr. Jekyll and Mr. Hyde 12; Under Southern Skies 15; The Huntress of Men 16; The Strength of the Weak 16; Thrown to the Lions 16

Hendrickson, Robert Close Shave 81

Henenlotter, Frank Basket Case 81; Brain Damage 87; Basket Case 2 90; Frankenhooker 90

Hengstler, Willi Purgatory 88

Henkel, Peter Three Bullets for a Long Gun 73; Scotty & Co. 79

Henley, Hobart A Child of Mystery 16; The Double Room Mystery 17; All Woman 18; The Face in the Dark 18; The Glorious Adventure 18; Laughing Bill Hyde 18; Money Mad 18; Mrs. Slacker 18; Parentage 18; Too Fat to Fight 18; The Gay Old Dog 19; One Week of Life 19; The Peace of Roaring River 19*; The Woman of the Index 19; The Miracle of Money 20; The Sin That Was His 20; Cheated Hearts 21; Society Snobs 21; Star Dust 21; The Flirt 22; Her Night of Nights 22; The Scrapper 22; The Abysmal Brute 23; The Flame of Life 23; A Lady of Quality 24; Sinners in Silk 24; So This Is Marriage 24; The Tornado • The Turmoil 24; The Auction Block 25; The Denial 25; An Exchange of Wives 25; His Secretary 25; A Slave of Fashion 25; A Certain Young Man 26;

Tillie the Toiler 27; Wickedness Preferred 27; His Tiger Lady 28; A Lady of Chance 28*; The Lady Lies 29; The Big Pond 30; Free Love 30; Mothers Cry 30; Roadhouse Nights 30; Bad Sister 31; Captain Applejack 31; Expensive Women 31; Night World 32; The Man Who Pawned His Soul • Unknown Blonde 34

Hennig, William K. The Wicked Die Slow 68

Henning-Jensen, Astrid S.O.S. Kindtand • S.O.S. Molars 43*; Det Danske Politi i Sverige 45; Flyktningar Finner en Hamn • Fugitives Find Shelter 45*; Folketingsvalg 45*; Denmark Grows Up 47*; De Pokkers Unger • Those Blasted Kids 47*; Stemning i April 47*; Kristinus Bergman 48*; Palle Alene i Verden • Palle Alone in the World 49; Boys from the West Coast • Vesterhavsdrenge 50*; Krane's Bakery Shop • Kranes Konditori 50; Ukjent Mann • Unknown Man 52; Solstik 53*; Ballet Girl • Ballettens Børn 54; Tivoli Garden Games • Tivoligarden Spiller 54*; Kærlighed på Kredit • Love on Credit 55; Nye Venner 56; Boy of Two Worlds • The Lure of the Jungle • Paw • Paw—Boy of Two Worlds 59*; Hest på Sommerferie 59; En Blandt Mange 61*; De Blå Undulater 65; Unfaithful • Utro 66; Min Bedstefar Er en Stok 67; Kald Mig Miriam 68; Me and You • Mej och Dej • Mig og Dig 68; Nille 68; Vinterbørn • Winter Children 78; The Moment • Øjeblikket 80; Barndommens Gade • Street of My Childhood 86

Henning-Jensen, Bjarne Cykledrengene i Tørvegraven 40; Arbejdet Kalder 41; Brunkul • Carbon 41; Chr. IV Som Bygherre • Christian IV: Master Builder 41; Hesten på Kongens Nytorv 41; Sugar • Sukker 42; Corn • Korn 43; Føllet 43; Hesten • Horses 43; Når Man Kun Er Ung • To Be Young 43; Paper • Papir 43; S.O.S. Kindtand • S.O.S. Molars 43*; Danish Island • De Danske Sydhavsøer 44; Brigaden i Sverige • Danish Brigade in Sweden 45; Flyktningar Finner en Hamn • Fugitives Find Shelter 45*; Folketingsvalg 45*; Freedom Committee • Frihedsfonden 45; Child of Man • Ditte: Child of Man • Ditte Menneskebarn 46; De Pokkers Unger • Those Blasted Kids 47*; Stemning i April 47*; Kristinus Bergman 48*; Boys from the West Coast • Vesterhavsdrenge 50*; Solstik 53*; Tivoli Garden Games • Tivoligarden Spiller 54*; Hvor Bjergene Sejler • Where Mountains Float 55; En Sælfangst i Nordgrønland 55; Boy of Two Worlds • The Lure of the Jungle • Paw • Paw—Boy of Two Worlds 59*; En Blandt Mange 61*; Kort Är Sommaren • Short Is the Summer 62; Skipper & Co. 74; The Ship and the Stars 75

Hennion, Robert Sextette 53

Henreid, Paul For Men Only • The Tall Lie 51; Battle Shock • War Shock • A Woman's Devotion 56; Girls on the Loose 58; Live Fast, Die Young 58; Ballad in Blue • Blues for Lovers 64; Dead Image • Dead Ringer 64

Henrikson, Anders The Girl from the Department Store 33*; It Pays to Advertise 36; 65, 66 och Jag • 65, 66 and Me 37; The Great Love 38; Valfångare • Whalers 39; A Crime 40; Life Goes On 41; Only a Woman 41; Dangerous Roads 42; Blood and Fire 45; The Key and the Ring 47; The Girl from the Mountain Village 48; Giftas • Married Life • Of Love and Lust 51

Henry, Buck Heaven Can Wait 78*; First Family 80

Henryson, Robert The Queen Steps Out 51; Melodies from Grand Hotel 52; Blue Tunes 60; Dill Jones and His All-Stars 60; Eric Delaney and His New Band 60; Free and Easy 60; Making Music 60; Ray Ellington and His Quartet 60; Sixteen Flying Fingers 60; Cuban Melody 61; Cuban Rhythm 61; Listen to My Music 61; Ted Heath and His Music 61; The Tony Kinsey Quartet 61; Modern Rhythm 63

Henson, Jim The Great Muppet Caper 81; The Dark Crystal 82*; Labyrinth 86; Hey, You're As Funny As Fozzie Bear! 88; Mother Goose Stories 88; Neat Stuff...to Know and to Do 88; Peek-a-Boo 88; Sing-Along, Dance-Along, Do-Along 88; Wow You're a Cartoonist! 88

Henson, Laurence Songs of Scotland 66*; Flash the Sheepdog 67; The Big Catch 68; The Duna Bull 72; Mauro the Gypsy 73

Henson, Leslie Broken Bottles 20
Henszelman, Stefan Friends Forever • Venner for Altid 87
Henzell, Perry The Harder They Come 73

Hepworth, Cecil M. Exchange Is No Robbery 1898; The Immature Punter 1898; An Interrupted Picnic 1898; The Oxford and Cambridge Boat Race 1898; The Quarrelsome Anglers • The Stolen Drink 1898; Two Cockneys in a Canoe • Two Fools in a Canoe 1898; The Conjuror and the Boer 1899; Express Train in a Railway Cutting 1899; The Punter's Mishap 1899; Wiping Something Off the Slate 1899; The Bathers 00; The Beggar's Deceit 00; The Burning Stable 00; Clown and Policeman 00; The Delights of Automobiling • The Explosion of a Motor Car 00; The Eccentric Dancer 00; The Egg Laying Man 00; The Electricity Cure 00; The Gunpowder Plot 00; How It Feels to Be Run Over 00; The Kiss 00; Leapfrog As Seen by the Frog 00; The Sluggard's Surprise 00; Topsy Turvy Villa 00; The Comic Grimacer 01; The Coronation of King Edward VII 01; The Funeral of Queen Victoria 01; How the Burglar Tricked the Bobby 01; The Indian Chief and the Seidlitz Powder 01; Interior of a Railway Carriage—Bank Holiday 01; The Call to Arms 02; Peace with Honour 02*; The Absent-Minded Bootblack 03; Alice in Wonderland 03*; Firemen to the Rescue 03; Saturday Shopping • Saturday's Shopping 03; The Bewitched Traveller • The Jonah Man • The Jonah Man, or The Traveller Bewitched 04*; Invisibility 09*;

Tilly the Tomboy 09; Embroidery Extraordinary 10; Faust 11; The Basilisk 14; Blind Fate 14; The Call • His Country's Bidding 14; The Hills Are Calling 14; Morphia, the Death Drug 14; Oh My Aunt! 14; The Quarry Mystery 14; Time, the Great Healer 14; Unfit, or The Strength of the Weak 14; The Baby on the Barge 15; The Battle • The Bottle 15; Be Sure Your Sins • The Canker of Jealousy 15; Courtmartialled • The Traitor 15; The Deadly Drug 15; The Golden Pavement 15; Iris 15; The Man Who Stayed at Home 15; A Moment of Darkness 15; The Outrage 15; The Passing of a Soul 15; Sweet Lavender 15; Annie Laurie 16; The Cobweb 16; Comin' Thro' the Rye 16; A Fallen Star 16; Love in a Mist 16; The Marriage of William Ashe 16; Molly Bawn 16; Sowing the Wind 16; Trelawney of the Wells 16; The American Heiress 17; Nearer My God to Thee 17; Boundary House 18; Broken in the Wars 18; The Leopard's Spots 18; A New Version 18; The Refugee 18; Tares 18; The Touch of a Child 18; The W.L.A. Girl 18; The Forest on the Hill 19; The Nature of the Beast 19; Sheba 19; Sunken Rocks 19; Alf's Button 20; Anna the Adventuress 20; Helen of Four Gates 20; Mrs. Erricker's Reputation 20; The Narrow Valley 21; Tansy 21; The Tinted Venus 21; Wild Heather 21; Comin' Thro' the Rye 22; Mist in the Valley 22; The Pipes of Pan 22; Strangling Threads 22; Film Favourites 24; The House of Marney 26; Royal Remembrances 29

Herbert, Andrew Song of the Loon 70
Herbert, Bill Warlock Moon 73
Herbert, F. Hugh There You Are 26; He Knew Women 30; Scudda Hoo! Scudda Hay! • Summer Lightning 48; The Girls of Pleasure Island 53*
Herbert, Henry Malachi's Cove • The Seaweed Children 73; Emily 76
Herbert, Hugh see Herbert, F. Hugh
Herbert, Martin see De Martino, Alberto
Herbert, Norman Mondo Teeno • Teenage Rebellion 67*
Herbst, I. Six Days to Eternity 68
Heredia, Álvaro Sáenz de see Sáenz de Heredia, Álvaro
Herek, Stephen Critters 85; Bill and Ted's Excellent Adventure 88
Herkomer, Hubert von His Choice 13; Love in a Teashop 13; The Old Wood Carver 13; The White Witch 13; The Grit of a Dandy 14
Herkomer, Siegfried von A Highwayman's Honour 14
Herman, Albert Beyond the Trail 26; Sporting Chance 31; Exposed • Strange Roads 32; The Big Chance 33; Whispering Shadows 33*; Big Boy Rides Again 35; The Cowboy and the Bandit 35; Danger Ahead 35; Gun Play • The Invisible Message • Lucky Boots 35; Hot Off the Press 35; Trail's End 35; Twisted Rails 35; Western Frontier 35; What Price Crime? 35; Bars of Hate 36; The Black Coin 36; Blaz-

ing Justice 36; The Clutching Hand 36; Outlaws of the Range 36; Renfrew of the Royal Mounted 37; Valley of Terror 37; Little Tenderfoot • Song of the Buckaroo 38; The Man from Texas 38; On the Great White Trail • Renfrew of the Royal Mounted on the Great White Trail • Renfrew on the Great White Trail 38; Rollin' Plains 38; Starlight Over Texas 38; Utah Trail 38; Where the Buffalo Roam 38; Down the Wyoming Trail • The Wild Herd 39; Roll, Wagons, Roll 39; Rollin' Westward 39; Sundown on the Prairie 39; Arizona Frontier 40; The Colorado Trail • Pals of the Silver Sage 40; The Golden Trail 40; Oklahoma Bound • Take Me Back to Oklahoma 40; Rainbow Over the Range 40; Rhythm of the Rio Grande 40; Rollin' Home to Texas 40; Speed Limited 40; Gentleman from Dixie • Li'l Louisiana Belle 41; The Pioneers 41; The Dawn Express • Nazi Spy Ring 42; Intrigue in Paris • Miss V from Moscow 42; The Rangers Take Over 42; A Yank in Libya 42; Bad Men of Thunder Gap • Thundergap Outlaws 43; Delinquent Daughters 44; Rogues' Gallery 44; Shake Hands with Murder 44; The Missing Corpse • Stranger in the Family 45; The Phantom of 42nd Street 45

Herman, Jean Le Dimanche de la Vie • The Sunday of Life 65; Adieu l'Ami • Farewell Friend • Honor Among Thieves 68; The Butterfly Affair • Popsy Pop 70
Herman, Norman Tokyo After Dark 59
Hermann, Villi Innocence • Innocenza 86
Hermansson, Bo På Stigande Kurs • Rising Stock 87
Hermeantier, R. L'Avare 60*
Hermosillo, Jaime Humberto La Verdadera Vocación de Magdalena 71; El Señor de Osanto 72; El Cumpleaños del Perro 74; La Pasión Según Berenice 77; Matinée 78; Naufragio 78; El Amor Libre 79; Las Apariencias Engañan 82; María de Mi Corazón 83; Confidencias 84; Doña Herlinda and Her Son • Doña Herlinda and Her Two Sons • Doña Herlinda y Su Hijo 85; Clandestinos Destinos 87; El Eterno Esplendor 87; The Summer of Miss Forbes • El Verano de la Señorita Forbes 88

Hernández Gómez, Guillermo La Adelita 38

Hernandi, Tibor Felix the Cat 88
Héroux, Denis Seul ou avec d'Autres 62*; Jacques Brel Is Alive and Well and Living in Paris 75; The Uncanny 77
Herraldo, Gonzalo Jetlag 81; Laura 88
Herrera, Manuel Capablanca 86
Herrick, F. Herrick Obeah 35; Norway Replies 44
Herrick, Hubert All the Sad World Needs 18; I Will 19*
Herrington, Ramsey Compelled 60; For Members Only • The Nudist Story 60
Herrington, Rowdy Jack's Back 88; Road House 89
Herschensohn, Bruce John F. Kennedy: Years of Lightning, Day of Drums 64

Hersholt, Jean The Deceiver 20*; The Golden Trail 20*; The Gray Dawn 22*

Herskó, János Under the City 53; The Iron Flower 57; A Houseful of Happiness 60; Dialogue • Párbeszéd 63; Hello Vera 67; Requiem in the Hungarian Manner 70

Herts, Kenneth Daughter of the Sun God 62

Hertz, Aleksander Antek Cwaniak 10; Meir Ezofewicz 11; The Married Ones 13; The Beast • Bestia 15; Arabella 16; The Mysteries of Warsaw 16; Students 16; The Daughter of Madame X 17; I Want a Husband 19; The Czar's Favorite 20; The Promised Land 27

Hertz, Jan Elvis Hansen—En Samfundshjælper 88

Hertz, Nathan see Juran, Nathan

Hervil, René Suzanne 16*; Mères Françaises 17*; Midinette 17*; Oh! Ce Baiser 17*; La P'tite du Sixième 17*; Le Tablier Blanc 17*; Bouclette 18*; Un Roman d'Amour et d'Aventures 18*; Le Torrent 18*; Simplette 19; Son Aventure 19; L'Ami Fritz 20; Blanchette 21; Le Crime de Lord Arthur Saville 22; Aux Jardins de Murcie 23*; Sarati-le-Terrible 23*; Le Secret de Polichinelle 23; Paris 24; La Flamme 25; Knock 26; La Petite Chocolatière 27; Minuit…Place Pigalle 28; Le Prince Jean 28; La Meilleure Maîtresse 29; Le Mystère de la Villa Rose 30*; Azaïs 31; La Douceur d'Aimer 31

Herz, Juraj The Cremator 68; The Ninth Heart 80; I Was Caught in the Night • Zastihla Ma Noc 85; Galoše Štastia • Overshoes of Happiness 86; Sladke Starosti • Sweet Worries 86; Straka v Hrsti 88

Herz, Michael Squeeze Play 80*; Soup to Nuts • Waitress! 82*; Stuck on You 83*; The First Turn-On 84*; The Toxic Avenger 84*; Troma's War • War 87*; The Toxic Avenger, Part II 89*; The Toxic Avenger Part III—The Last Temptation of Toxie 89*

Herzfeld, John Two of a Kind 83

Herzog, Werner Herakles • Hercules 62; Game in the Sand • Spiel im Sand 64; Die Beispiellose Verteidigung der Festung Deutschkreuz • The Unparalleled Defense of the Fortress of Deutschkreuz • The Unprecedented Defense of Fortress Deutschkreutz • The Unprecedented Defense of the Fortress Deutschkreutz 66; Feuerzeichen • Lebenszeichen • Signs of Life 67; Last Words • Letzte Worte 67; Auch Zwerge Haben Klein Angefangen • Even Dwarfs Started Small 68; Die Fliegenden Ärzte von Ostafrika • The Flying Doctors of East Africa 68; Fata Morgana 69; Massnahmen Gegen Fanatiker • Measures Against Fanatics • Precautions Against Fanatics 69; Behinderte Zukunft • Frustrated Future • Handicapped Future 70; Land des Schweigens und der Dunkelheit • Land of Silence and Darkness 71; Aguirre, der Zorn Gottes • Aguirre, the Wrath of God • Aguirre, Wrath of God 72; The Enigma of Kaspar Hauser • Every

Man for Himself and God Against All • Jeder für Sich und Gott Gegen Alle • The Mystery of Kaspar Hauser 74; The Great Ecstasy of the Sculptor Steiner • The Great Ecstasy of Woodcarver Steiner • Die Grosse Ekstase des Bildschnitzers Steiner 74; Heart of Glass • Herz aus Glas 76; How Much Wood Would a Woodchuck Chuck 76; Mit Mir Will Keiner Spielen • No One Will Play with Me 76; La Soufrière 76; Stroszek 77; Nosferatu, Phantom der Nacht • Nosferatu the Vampire • Nosferatu the Vampyre 78; Woyseck • Woyzeck • Wozzeck 78; Glaube und Wahrung 80; God's Angry Man 80; Huie's Predigt 80; Fitzcarraldo 82; Ballad of the Little Soldier • Ballade vom Kleinen Soldaten 84; The Dark Glow of the Mountains • The Green Glow of the Mountains 84; Where the Green Ants Dream • Wo die Grünen Ameisen Träumen 84; Gasherbrum—Der Leuchtende Berg 85; Cobra Verde • Green Cobra • Slave Coast 87; Herdsmen of the Sun 88; Echos aus einem Düsteren Reich 90

Hesera, Simon A Day at the Beach 70; Ben-Gurion Remembers 72

Hess, David To All a Goodnight 80

Hess, Joachim Fidelio 70; Der Freischutz 70; Die Hochzeit des Figaro • The Marriage of Figaro 70

Hess, Jon Watchers 88

Hesselle, Armand de see De Hesselle, Armand

Hessens, Robert Guernica 50*

Hesser, Edwin Bower The Triumph of Venus 18

Hessler, Gordon Catacombs • The Woman Who Wouldn't Die 64; The Last Shot You Hear 68; Das Ausschweifende Leben des Marquis de Sade • De Sade 69*; Edgar Allen Poe's The Oblong Box • The Oblong Box 69*; Scream and Scream Again • Screamer 69; Cry of the Banshee 70; Murders in the Rue Morgue 71; Embassy 72; The Golden Voyage of Sinbad 73; Medusa 73; Call Him Mr. Shatter • Shatter • They Call Him Mr. Shatter 74*; Tracco di Veleno in una Coppa di Champagne 75; Escape from El Diablo 83; Pray for Death 85; Rage of Honor 86; The Misfit Brigade • Wheels of Terror 87; The Girl in a Swing 89

Heston, Charlton Antony and Cleopatra 70; The Last Great Treasure • Mother Lode • Search for the Mother Lode • Search for the Mother Lode: The Last Great Treasure 82*

Heuberger, Edmund The Asian Sun 21; Das Verlorene Tal 36

Heusch, Paolo Le Danger Vient de l' Espace • The Day the Sky Exploded • Death from Outer Space • La Morte Viene della Spazio 58; Bei Vollmond Mord • Ghoul in a Girl's Dormitory • The Ghoul in School • I Married a Werewolf • Lycanthropus • Monster Among the Girls • Werewolf in a Girl's Dormitory 61; Una Vita Violenta 62*

Heuze, André La Course des Sergents de Ville 05; Le Voleur de Bicyclette 05; À

Biribi 06; L'Ange du Cœur 06; Le Déserteur 06; Les Meurt-de-Faim 06

Hewett, Graham Hearts of Oak 33*

Hewitt, David L. Wizard of Mars 64; The Girls from Thunder Strip 66; The Blood Suckers • Dr. Terror's Gallery of Horrors • Gallery of Horrors • Return from the Past 67; Journey to the Center of Time 67; Hell's Chosen Few 68; The Mighty Gorga 69; The Lucifer Complex 78*

Hewitt, G. Fletcher Comic Golf • Golfing 13; Was It He? 14; A Pottery Girl's Romance 18

Hewitt, Jean Blood of Dracula's Castle • Dracula's Castle 67*

Hewitt, Rod Verne Miller 87

Heyde, Nikolai van der Nitwits 87

Heyerdahl, Thor Kon-Tiki 51

Heyes, Douglas Kitten with a Whip 64; Beau Geste 66

Heymann, Claude American Love • L' Amour à l'Américaine 31*

Heynemann, Laurent La Question • The Question 77; Birgit Haas Must Be Killed 81; April Is a Deadly Month • Les Mois d'Avril Sont Meurtriers 87

Hiatt, Albert Combat 27

Hiatt, Frederick Montmartre Rose 29*

Hibbs, Jesse The All-American • The Winning Way 52; The World's Most Beautiful Girls 53; Black Horse Canyon 54; Rails Into Laramie 54; Ride Clear of Diablo 54; The Yellow Mountain 54; The Spoilers 55; To Hell and Back 55; Walk the Proud Land 56; World in My Corner 56; Joe Butterfly 57; Ride a Crooked Mile • Ride a Crooked Trail 58

Hibler, Winston Charlie the Lonesome Cougar 67

Hickey, Bruce Necropolis 86

Hickey, Kieran Criminal Conversation 80

Hickman, Howard The Heart of Rachael 18; Two Gun Betty 18; All of a Sudden Norma 19; Hearts Asleep 19; Her Purchase Price 19; Josselyn's Wife 19; Kitty Kelly, M.D. 19; A Trick of Fate 19; Beckoning Roads 20; Just a Wife 20; A Certain Rich Man 21; The Killer 21*; The Lure of Egypt 21; Nobody's Kid 21

Hickox, Anthony Waxwork 88

Hickox, Douglas Behemoth the Sea Monster • The Giant Behemoth 59*; Four Hits and a Mister 62; Disk-o-Tek Holiday • Just for You 63; It's All Over Town 63; Take Six 63; Les Bicyclettes de Belsize 68; Entertaining Mr. Sloane 69; Sitting Target 71; Much Ado About Murder • Theatre of Blood 73; Brannigan 74; Sky Riders 76; Zulu Dawn 79; The Hound of the Baskervilles 83

Hicks, Scott Sebastian and the Sparrow 88

Hicks, Seymour Always Tell Your Wife 22*; Sleeping Partners 30; Glamour 31*

Hidaka, Shigeaki Dai Sanji Sekai Taisen • Dai Sanji Sekai Taisen—Yonjū Ichi Jikan no Kyōfu • The Final War • Jikan no Kyōfu • The Last War • World War III Breaks Out • Yonjū Ichi Jikan no Kyōfu • 41 Jikan no Kyōfu 60

Hidari, Sachiko The Far Road 77
Hiemer, Leo Daheim Sterben die Leut'
85*; The Good Old Days • Schön War die
Zeit 89*
Higashi, Yoichi Love Letter 87
Higgin, Howard Rent Free 22; In the
Name of Love 25; The New Command-
ment 25; The Great Deception 26; The
Wilderness Woman 26; The Wreckless
Lady 26; The Perfect Sap 27; Power 28;
Skyscraper 28; High Voltage • Wanted 29;
The Leatherneck 29; The Racketeer 29; Sal
of Singapore 29; The Painted Desert 31;
Determination 32; The Final Edition 32;
Hell's House 32; The Last Man 32*; Car-
nival Lady 33; Marriage on Approval •
Married in Haste 33; Battle of Greed 34;
Identity Parade • The Line-Up 34
Higgins, Colin Foul Play 78; 9 to 5 80;
The Best Little Whorehouse in Texas 82
Higson, Patrick Big Banana Feet 77*
Hiken, Nat The Love God? 69
Hilbard, John Yes, Det Er Far! • Yes,
It's Your Dad! 86
Hildebrand, Staffan Ingen Kan Älska
Som Vi 88
Hildebrand, Weyler Söderkåkar 36;
Nothing But the Truth • Rena Rama San-
ningen 39
Hill, Claudio Guerín Los Desafíos 68*;
A Bell from Hell • The Bell of Hell • La
Campana del Infierno 73
Hill, George Roy Period of Adjustment
62; Toys in the Attic 63; The World of
Henry Orient 64; Hawaii 66; Thoroughly
Modern Millie 67; Butch Cassidy and the
Sundance Kid 69; Slaughterhouse Five 71;
The Sting 73; The Great Waldo Pepper
75; Slap Shot 77; A Little Romance 79;
The World According to Garp 82; The Lit-
tle Drummer Girl 84; Funny Farm 88
Hill, George W. Get Your Man! 21*;
While the Devil Laughs 21; The Foolish
Virgin 24; The Hill Billy 24; The Midnight
Express 24; Through the Dark 24; The
Limited Mail 25; Zander the Great 25; The
Barrier 26; Tell It to the Marines 26; But-
tons 27; The Callahans and the Murphys
27; The Cossacks 28*; The Flying Fleet 28;
The Big House 30; Min and Bill 30; Hell
Divers 31; The Secret Six 31; Clear All
Wires 33; The Good Earth 36*
Hill, Howard Tembo 52
Hill, Jack Lady of the Shadows • The
Terror 62*; Cannibal Orgy • Cannibal
Orgy, or The Maddest Story Ever Told •
The Liver Eaters • The Maddest Story Ever
Told • Spider Baby • Spider Baby, or The
Maddest Story Ever Told 64; Portrait in
Terror 65; Blood Bath • Track of the Vam-
pire 66*; La Cámara del Terror • The Fear
Chamber 68*; House of Evil • Serenata
Macabra 68*; La Isla de los Muertos • Is-
land of the Snake People • The Isle of the
Dead • Isle of the Snake People • The Liv-
ing Death • La Muerte Viviente • The
Snake People 68*; Pit Stop • The Winner
69; The Big Doll House • Women's Peni-
tentiary I 71; The Incredible Invasion • La
Invasión Siniestra • Sinister Invasion 71*;

The Big Bird Cage • Women's Penitentiary
II 72; Coffy 73; Foxy Brown 74; The
Swinging Cheerleaders 74; The Jezebelles •
The Jezebels • Playgirl Gang • Switchblade
Sisters 75
Hill, James Science Joins an Industry 46;
Journey for Jeremy 47; Friend of the Fam-
ily 49; Britain's Comet 52; The Clue of the
Missing Ape • Gibraltar Adventure 52;
The Stolen Plans 52; Peril for the Guy 56;
Cold Comfort 57; Mystery in the Mine 59;
Giuseppina 60; David and Golightly 61;
The Kitchen 61; The Dock Brief • Trial
and Error 62; Lunch Hour 62; Every Day's
a Holiday • Seaside Swingers 64; The
Home-Made Car 64; Born Free • Frei
Geboren 65; Fog • Sherlock Holmes Grös-
ster Fall • A Study in Terror 65; Les Cor-
rumpus • The Corrupt Ones • Hell to
Macao • Die Hölle von Macao • The Pek-
ing Medallion • Il Sigillo de Pechino 66*;
The Specialist 66; Journey Into Darkness
68*; Captain Nemo and the Underwater
City 69; An Elephant Called Slowly 70;
Man From O.R.G.Y. • The Real Gone
Girls 70; Black Beauty 71; Christian the
Lion • The Lion at World's End 71*; The
Belstone Fox • Free Spirit 73; The Man
from Nowhere 76
Hill, Jerome Grandma Moses 50; Albert
Schweitzer 57; The Sand Castle 60; Open
the Door and See All the People • Peacock
Feathers 64
Hill, Robert F. Temptation and the
Man 16; The Great Radium Mystery 19*;
The Flaming Disc 20; The Adventures of
Tarzan 21; The Adventures of Robinson
Crusoe 22*; The Radio King 22; Crooked
Alley 23; His Mystery Girl 23; The Phan-
tom Fortune 23; Shadows of the North 23;
The Social Buccaneer 23; The Breathless
Moment 24; The Dangerous Blonde 24;
Dark Stairways 24; Excitement 24; Jack o'
Clubs 24; Young Ideas 24; Idaho 25; The
Wild West 25; The Bar-C Mystery 26;
Blake of Scotland Yard 27; Haunted Island
28; Life's Mockery • Reform 28; A Million
for Love 28; Melody Lane 29; Silks and
Saddles • Thoroughbreds 29; Spell of the
Circus 31; Sundown Trail 31; Come On
Danger! 32; Love Bound • Souls for Sables
32; The Cheyenne Kid 33; Tarzan the
Fearless 33; Cowboy Holiday 34; A Demon
for Trouble 34; Frontier Days 34; Inside
Information 34; Outlaws' Highway 34; The
Cyclone Ranger 35; Danger Trails 35;
Queen of the Jungle 35; Six Gun Justice
35; The Texas Rambler 35; The Vanishing
Riders 35; A Face in the Fog 36; Idaho
Kid 36; Kelly of the Secret Service 36; Law
and Lead 36; Men of the Plains 36; The
Phantom of the Range 36; Prison Shadows
36; Put on the Spot 36; Rio Grande Romance 36; Rip Roarin' Buckaroo 36; The
Rogues' Tavern 36; Shadow of Chinatown
36; Too Much Beef 36; West of Nevada
36; Cheyenne Rides Again 37; The Feud
of the Trail 37; Fighting Playboy 37; Madcap • Taming the Wild 37; Million Dollar
Racket 37; Mystery Range 37; The Roam-

ing Cowboy 37; Two Minutes to Play 37;
The Deadly Ray from Mars • Flash Gor-
don: Mars Attacks the World • Flash Gor-
don's Trip to Mars • Mars Attacks the
World 38*; The Flying Fists 38; Man's
Country 38; The Painted Trail 38; Silks
and Saddles 38; Whirlwind Horseman 38;
Wild Horse Canyon 38; Blake of Scotland
Yard 39; Drifting Westward 39; Overland
Mail 39; East Side Kids 40; Wanderers of
the West 41
Hill, Robert Jordan Melody in the Dark
48; Bless 'Em All 49; High Jinks in Society
49*; The Nitwits on Parade 49; The Kilties
Are Coming • Lads and Lasses on Parade
51
Hill, Sinclair The Tidal Wave 20; The
Mystery of Mr. Bernard Brown 21; One
Week to Live 21; The Place of Honour 21;
The Experiment 22; Expiation 22; Half a
Truth 22; The Lonely Lady of Grosvenor
Square 22; The Nonentity 22; Open Coun-
try 22; The Truants 22; The Indian Love
Lyrics 23; One Arabian Night • Widow
Twan-Kee 23; The Acid Test 24; The
Barnes Murder Case • The Conspirators 24;
The Drum 24; Holloway's Treasure 24;
The Honourable Member for Outside Left
24; The Port of Lost Souls • White Slip-
pers 24; Beyond the Veil • The Secret
Kingdom 25; The Presumption of Stanley
Hay, MP 25; The Qualified Adventurer 25;
A Romance of Riches • The Squire of Long
Hadley 25; Boadicea 26; The Chinese
Bungalow 26; Sahara Love 26; The Guns
of Loos 27; The King's Highway 27; A
Woman Redeemed 27; The Price of Di-
vorce 28; The Crimson Circle 29*; Dark
Red Roses 29; Peace and Quiet 29; The
Unwritten Law 29; Greek Street • Latin
Love 30; Such Is the Law 30; A Gentleman
of Paris 31; The Great Gay Road 31; Other
People's Sins 31; The First Mrs. Fraser 32;
The Man from Toronto 32; Britannia of
Billingsgate 33; My Old Dutch 34; Hyde
Park Corner 35; The Cardinal 36; The Gay
Adventure 36; Bombs Over London • Mid-
night Menace 37; Command Performance
37; Take a Chance 37; Follow Your Star 38
Hill, Walter Hard Times • The Street-
fighter 75; The Driver 78; The Warriors
79; The Long Riders 80; Southern Comfort
81; 48 HRS. 82; Streets of Fire 83; Brew-
ster's Millions 85; Crossroads 86; Extreme
Prejudice 87; Red Heat 88; Johnny Hand-
some 89; Another 48 HRS. 90
Hillcoat, John Ghosts of the Civil Dead
88
Hille, Heinz Der Frechdachs 34*; Und
Es Leuchtet die Puszta 34; Szerelmi
Álmodik 37
Hiller, Arthur The Careless Years 57;
The Flight of the White Stallions • The
Miracle of the White Stallions 62; This
Rugged Land 62; Separate Beds • The
Wheeler Dealers 63; The Americanization
of Emily • Emily 64; Promise Her Any-
thing 65; Eye of the Devil • Thirteen 66*;
Penelope 66; Tobruk 66; The Tiger Makes
Out 67; The Out-of-Towners 69; Popi 69;

Confrontation 70; Love Story 70; Plaza Suite 70; Raid on Rommel 70*; The Hospital 71; Man of La Mancha • L'Uomo della Mancha 72; The Crazy World of Julius Vrooder • Vrooder's Hooch 74; The Man in the Glass Booth 74; Silver Streak 76; W.C. Fields and Me 76; The In-Laws 79; Nightwing 79; Making Love 81; Author! Author! 82; Romantic Comedy 83; The Lonely Guy 84; Teachers 84; Outrageous Fortune 86; See No Evil, Hear No Evil 89; Filofax • Taking Care of Business 90

Hilliard, Richard Psychomania • Violent Midnight 63; Wild Is My Love 63; The Playground 65

Hillman, William Byron Betta Betta 71; The Trail Ride 73; The Photographer 74; The Man from Clover Grove 77; Thetus 79; Double Exposure 82; The Master 84; Loner 87

Hills, David Ator • Ator the Invincible • The Blade Master 83; Ator, the Fighting Eagle 83

Hills, Mike Russell see Russell-Hills, Mike

Hillyer, Lambert An Even Break 17; The Narrow Trail 17*; The Silent Man 17*; Branding Broadway 18*; Riddle Gawne 18*; The Breed of Men 19*; John Petticoats 19; The Money Corral 19*; Poppy Girl • The Poppy Girl's Husband 19*; Sand 19; Square Deal Sanderson 19*; Wagon Tracks 19; The Cradle of Courage 20; O'Malley of the Mounted 20; The Testing Block 20; The Toll Gate 20; Three Word Brand 21; Travelin' On 21; The Whistle 21; White Oak 21; The Altar Stairs 22; Caught Bluffing 22; Skin Deep 22; The Super-Sex 22; White Hands 22; Eyes of the Forest 23; The Lone Star Ranger 23; Mile-a-Minute Romeo 23; Scars of Jealousy 23; The Shock 23; The Spoilers 23; Temporary Marriage 23; Barbara Frietchie 24; Idle Tongues 24; Those Who Dance 24; I Want My Man 25; The Knockout 25; The Making of O'Malley 25; The Unguarded Hour 25; Her Second Chance 26; Miss Nobody 26; 30 Below Zero 26*; Chain Lightning 27; Hills of Peril 27; The War Horse 27; The Branded Sombrero 28; Fleetwing 28; Beau Bandit 30; The Deadline 31; One Man Law 31; The Fighting Fool 32; The Forbidden Trail 32; Hello, Trouble 32; South of the Rio Grande 32; White Eagle 32; Before Midnight 33; The California Trail 33; Dangerous Crossroads 33; The Fighting Code 33; Master of Men 33; Police Car 17 33; The Sundown Rider 33; Unknown Valley 33; Against the Law • Urgent Call 34; The Defense Rests 34; Hidden Evidence 34; The Man Trailer 34; Men of the Night 34; The Most Precious Thing • The Most Precious Thing in Life 34; Once to Every Woman 34; One Is Guilty 34; One Way Out 34; The Professor Gives a Lesson 34; The Awakening of Jim Burke • Iron Fist 35; Behind the Evidence 35; Guard That Girl! 35; In Spite of Danger 35; The Invisible Ray 35; Men of the

Hour 35; Superspeed 35; Dangerous Waters 36; Dracula's Daughter 36; All American Sweetheart 37; Fielder's Field • Girls Can Play 37; Speed to Spare 37; Women in Prison 37; Extortion! 38; Gang Bullets 38; My Old Kentucky Home 38; Convict's Code 39; Girl from Nowhere • Should a Girl Marry? 39; The Girl from Rio 39; All Square • The Pinto Kid 40; Beyond the Sacramento • Power of Justice 40; The Durango Kid • The Masked Stranger 40; North from Lone Star • North from the Lone Star 40; Promise Fulfilled • The Wildcat of Tucson 40; Blue Clay • The Son of Davy Crockett 41; Doctor's Alibi • The Medico of Painted Springs 41; Giants A'Fire • The Royal Mounted Patrol 41; Hands Across the Rockies 41; King of Dodge City 41; The Marked Bullet • Prairie Stranger 41; The Mayor's Nest • The Return of Daniel Boone 41; Roaring Frontiers 41; Thunder Over the Prairie 41; The Black Shadow • Vengeance of the West 42; The Devil's Trail • Rogues' Gallery 42; False Clues • North of the Rockies 42; Fighting Frontier 42; Prairie Gunsmoke 42; Batman • An Evening with Batman and Robin 43; Gem Jams 43; Radio Runaround 43; Six Gun Gospel 43; Smart Guy • You Can't Beat the Law 43; The Stranger from Pecos 43; The Texas Kid 43; Beyond the Pecos • Beyond the Seven Seas 44; Ghost Guns 44; Land of the Outlaws 44; Law Men 44; Partners of the Trail 44; Range Law 44; West of the Rio Grande 44; Border Bandits 45; Flame of the West • Flaming Frontier 45; Frontier Feud 45; The Lost Trail 45; South of the Rio Grande 45; Stranger from Santa Fe 45; The Fighting Texan • The Gentleman from Texas 46; Raiders of the South 46; Shadows on the Range 46; Silver Range 46; Trigger Fingers 46; Under Arizona Skies 46; Backfire • The Law Comes to Gunsight 47; The Case of the Baby Sitter 47; Flashing Guns 47; Gun Talk 47; The Hat Box Mystery 47; Land of the Lawless 47; Prairie Express 47; Song of the Drifter 47; Trailing Danger 47; Valley of Fear 47; Arizona Sunset • Range Renegades 48; Crossed Trails 48; The Fighting Ranger 48; Frontier Agent 48; Oklahoma Blues 48; Outlaw Brand 48; Overland Trails 48; Partners of the Sunset 48; The Sheriff of Medicine Bow 48; Sundown Riders 48; Gun Law Justice 49; Gun Runner 49; Haunted Trails 49; Range Land 49; Riders from the Dusk • Riders of the Dusk 49; Trail's End 49

Hilpert, Heinz Drei Tage Liebe • Three Days of Love 31; Liebe, Tod und Teufel 35*

Hilton, Arthur The Return of Jesse James • Return of the James Boys 50; Cat Women of the Moon • Rocket to the Moon 53; The Big Chase 54

Hiltzik, Robert Sleepaway Camp 83
Hilyard, Dene Vengeance 64
Hin, Kees De Laastste Reis 88
Hines, Charles Conductor 1492 23*; Little Johnny Jones 23*; The Speed Spook

24; The Crackerjack 25; The Early Bird 25; The Live Wire 25; The Brown Derby 26; Rainbow Riley 26; Stepping Along 26; All Aboard 27; Home Made 27; White Pants Willie 27; Chinatown Charlie 28; The Wright Idea 28

Hines, Gordon Trail Dust 24
Hines, Johnny Burn 'Em Up Barnes 21*
Hinkle, Robert Ole Rex 61; Country Music 72; Guns of a Stranger 73

Hinrich, Hans Between the Parents • Zwischen den Eltern 38; Dreikland • Triad 38

Hinter, Cornelius Az Ösember • The Prehistoric Man 17

Hinzman, Bill The Majorettes 88
Hird, Robert Mr. Horatio Knibbles 71
Hirokawa, Kazuyuki Lensman 84*
Hirsch, Bettina Munchies 87
Hirsch, Hy Ah Nurture 48*
Hirschenson, Bernie Pick-Up 75
Hirszman, Leon A Falecida 65; São Bernardo 70; Eles Não Usam Black Tie • They Don't Wear Black Tie 81; Imágens do Inconsciente 88

Hisamatsu, Seiji Women in Prison 57; Angry Island 60; Robō no Ishi • The Wayside Pebble 60; Minami no Shima ni Yuki ga Fura • Snow in the South Seas 63

Hiscott, Leslie Billets 25; Cats 25; A Fowl Proceeding 25; A Friend of Cupid 25; Raising the Wind 25; Spots 25; This Marriage Business 27; The Passing of Mr. Quin 28; S.O.S. 28; The Feather 29; Ringing the Changes 29; At the Villa Rose • Mystery at the Villa Rose • The Mystery of the Pink Villa 30; The Call of the Sea 30; The House of the Arrow 30; Alibi 31; Black Coffee 31; Brown Sugar 31; A Night in Montmartre 31; Sherlock Holmes' Fatal Hour • The Sleeping Cardinal 31; The Crooked Lady 32; Double Dealing 32; The Face at the Window 32; The Iron Stair 32; The Missing Rembrandt • Sherlock Holmes and the Missing Rembrandt 32; Murder at Covent Garden 32*; Once Bitten 32; A Safe Proposition 32; A Tight Corner 32; When London Sleeps 32; Cleaning Up 33; Flat No. 3 33; Great Stuff 33; I'll Stick to You 33; Marooned 33; The Melody Maker 33; Out of the Past 33; The Stickpin 33; The Stolen Necklace 33; Strike It Rich 33; That's My Wife 33; Yes, Madam 33; The Big Splash 34; Crazy People 34; Gay Love 34; Keep It Quiet 34; The Man I Want 34; Passing Shadows 34; Annie, Leave the Room! 35; Bargain Basement • Department Store 35; Death on the Set • Murder on the Set 35; A Fire Has Been Arranged 35; Inside the Room 35; She Shall Have Music 35; Three Witnesses 35; The Triumph of Sherlock Holmes 35; Fame 36; The Interrupted Honeymoon 36; Millions 36; Fine Feathers 37; Ship's Concert 37; Take Cover 38; Tilly of Bloomsbury 39; The Seventh Survivor 41; The Lady from Lisbon 42; Sabotage at Sea 42; The Butler's Dilemma 43; Welcome Mr. Washington 44; The Time of His Life 55; Tons of Trouble 55

Hitchcock, Alfred Always Tell Your Wife 22*; Irrgarten der Leidenschaft • The Pleasure Garden 25; Der Bergadler • Fear o' God • The Mountain Eagle 26; The Case of Jonathan Drew • The Lodger • The Lodger — A Story of the London Fog • A Story of the London Fog 26; Downhill • When Boys Leave Home 27; Easy Virtue 27; The Ring 27; Champagne 28; The Farmer's Wife 28; Blackmail 29; Harmony Heaven 29*; The Manxman 29; An Elastic Affair 30; Elstree Calling 30*; Juno and the Paycock • The Shame of Mary Boyle 30; Mary • Sir John Greift Ein 30; Murder! 30; The Skin Game 31; East of Shanghai • Rich and Strange 32; Number Seventeen 32; The Great Waltz • Strauss' Great Waltz • Waltzes from Vienna 33; The Man Who Knew Too Much 34; The Thirty-Nine Steps 35; Sabotage • A Woman Alone 36; Secret Agent 36; The Girl Was Young • Young and Innocent 37; The Lady Vanishes 38; Jamaica Inn 39; Foreign Correspondent 40; Rebecca 40; Mr. and Mrs. Smith 41; Suspicion 41; Saboteur 42; Lifeboat 43; Shadow of a Doubt 43; Aventure Malgache • The Malgache Adventure 44; Bon Voyage 44; Spellbound 45*; Notorious 46; The Paradine Case 47; Rope 48; Under Capricorn 49; Stage Fright 50; Strangers on a Train 51; I Confess 52; Dial M for Murder 54; Rear Window 54; To Catch a Thief 55; The Trouble with Harry 55; The Man Who Knew Too Much 56; The Wrong Man 56; Vertigo 58; North by Northwest 59; Psycho 60; The Birds 63; Marnie 64; Torn Curtain 66; Topaz 69; Frenzy 72; Family Plot 76

Hittleman, Carl K. Kentucky Rifle 56; The Buckskin Lady 57; Gun Battle at Monterey 57*; Big Daddy • Paradise Road 69

Hitzig, Rupert Backstreet Dreams 90; Never Cry Devil • Night Visitor 90

Hively, Jack Panama Lady 39; The Spellbinder 39; They Made Her a Spy 39; Three Sons 39; Two Thoroughbreds 39; Anne of Windy Poplars • Anne of Windy Willows 40; Laddie 40; The Saint Takes Over 40; The Saint's Double Trouble 40; Father Takes a Wife 41; Four Jacks and a Jill 41; The Saint in Palm Springs 41; They Met in Argentina 41*; Street of Chance 42; Appointment in Tokyo 45; Are You With It? 48; Lassie the Voyager 66*; Starbird and Sweet William 75; Adventures of Starbird 78

Hjulström, Lennart Berget på Månens Baksida • A Hill on the Dark Side of the Moon 83

Hladnik, Boštjan Dance in the Rain 61; Sandcastle 62; Erotikon 63

Hledik, Peter The Third Dragon • Třetí Sarkan 85

Ho, Cheng Chang Tianxia Diyi Quan 72; Five Fingers of Death • Hand of Death 73

Ho, Fei-kwong Maid of Formosa 49

Ho, Godfrey Ninja Thunderbolt 87

Ho, Meng-hau The Flying Guillotine 75

Ho, Yim see Yim, Ho

Hobbs, Christopher Jubilee 78*

Hobbs, Frederic Troika 69*; Alabama's Ghost 72

Hobbs, Hayford An Irish Medley 38; London 38; The Old Sailor's Tale 38

Hobbs, Lyndall Steppin' Out 79; Dead on Time 83; Back to the Beach 87

Hobl, Pavel The Lost Face • Ztracená Tvář 65; Do You Keep a Lion at Home? • Máte Doma Lva? 66

Hochbaum, Werner The Eternal Mask • Die Ewige Maske 35; Leichte Kavallerie 36; Wir Sind vom K und K Infanterie-Regiment 38; Drei Unteroffiziere • Three Non-Coms 39; Schatten der Vergangenheit • Shadows of the Past 40

Hockman, Ned Hate Within • Stark Fear 63

Hodges, Michael Get Carter 70; Pulp 72; The Terminal Man 74; Flash Gordon 80; Squaring the Circle 83; Buried Alive 84; Morons from Outer Space 85; A Prayer for the Dying 87; Black Rainbow 89

Hodi, Jeno Deadly Obsession 89

Hodson, Christopher The Best Pair of Legs in the Business 73

Hoellering, George Glasgow Orpheus Choir 51; Murder in the Cathedral 51

Hoenack, Jeremy Killer's Delight 78

Hoerl, Arthur Big Town 32; Before Morning 33; Shadow Laughs 33; Drums o' Voodoo • She-Devil 34

Hoey, Michael The Navy vs. the Night Monsters • The Night Crawlers 65

Hofbauer, Ernst Black Eagle of Santa Fe • Die Schwarzen Adler von Santa Fe 64; A-009 Missione Hong Kong • Das Geheimnis der Drei Dschunken • Mission to Hong Kong • Red Dragon 65; The Fountain of Love • Die Liebesquelle 68; Office Girls 74

Hoffman, David King, Murray 69*; The Nashville Sound 70*; Sing Sing Thanksgiving 74*

Hoffman, Dustin Straight Time 78*

Hoffman, Harold The Black Cat 66

Hoffman, Herman The Bar Sinister • It's a Dog's Life 55; The Great American Pastime 56; The Invisible Boy 57

Hoffman, Jerzy Are You Among Them? 54; Attention Hooligans 55; A Souvenir from Calvary 58; The Rail 59; Two Faces of God 60; Patria o Muerte 61; They Met in Havana 61; Gangsters and Philanthropists 62; Visit Zakopane 63; The Law and the Fist 64; Three Steps on Earth 65; Market of Miracles 66; Colonel Wolodyjowski 69; The Deluge 74; Leper 76

Hoffman, John The Crimson Canary 45; Strange Confession 45; The Wreck of the Hesperus 48; The Lone Wolf and His Lady 49; I Killed Geronimo 50

Hoffman, Julian The Bloody Brood 59

Hoffman, Michael Privileged 82; Restless Natives 85; Promised Land • Young Hearts 87; Some Girls 88

Hoffman, Otto The Secret of Black Mountain 17

Hoffman, Peter Valentino Returns 86

Hoffman, Renaud The Legend of Hollywood 24; Not One to Spare • Which Shall It Be? 24; His Master's Voice 25; On the Threshold 25; Private Affairs 25; The Unknown Soldier 26; A Harp in Hock 27; Stool Pigeon 28; Blaze o' Glory 29*; The Climax 30

Hoffmann, Karl Der Geheimnisvolle Spiegel • The Mystic Mirror 27*; Die Lustigen Weiber 34; Viktoria 34; Das Einmaleins der Liebe 37; Ab Mitternacht 38

Hoffmann, Kurt Bachelors' Paradise • Paradies der Junggesellen 40; Hurra! Ich Bin Papa • Hurrah! I'm a Papa 40; Secrets of a Soul 50; The Confessions of Felix Krull 57; Aren't We Wonderful? • Wir Wunderkinder 58; The Flying Classroom 58; The Haunted Castle • The Spook Castle of Spessart • Das Spukschloss im Spessart 60; The Spessart Inn • Das Wirtshaus im Spessart 61

Hoffmann, Nico Der Polenweiher • The Polish War Worker 86*; Land der Vater, Land der Söhne 88

Hoffs, Tamar Simon The Allnighter • Cutting Loose 86

Hofler, Franz Drei Kaiserjäger 35*

Hofsiss, Jack I'm Dancing As Fast As I Can 82

Hogan, James P. The Daredevil • The Skywayman 20; The Little Grey Mouse 20; Bare Knuckles 21; Where Is My Wandering Boy Tonight? 22*; Black Lightning 24; Capital Punishment 24; Unmarried Wives 24; Women and Gold 24; The Bandit's Baby 25; Jimmie's Millions 25; The Mansion of Aching Hearts 25; My Lady's Lips 25; S.O.S. Perils of the Sea 25; Steel Preferred 25; Flaming Fury 26; The Isle of Retribution 26; The King of the Turf 26; The Final Extra 27; Finnegan's Ball 27; Mountains of Manhattan 27; The Silent Avenger 27; The Border Patrol 28; The Broken Mask 28; Burning Bridges 28; Code of the Air 28; Hearts of Men 28; Top Sergeant Mulligan 28; The Sheriff's Secret 31; Life Returns 35; The Accusing Finger 36; Arizona Mahoney 36; The Arizona Raiders 36; Desert Gold 36; Bulldog Drummond Escapes 37; Ebb Tide 37; The Last Train from Madrid 37; Scandal Street 37; Bulldog Drummond's Peril 38; Sons of the Legion 38; The Texans 38; Arrest Bulldog Drummond! 39; Bulldog Drummond's Bride 39; Bulldog Drummond's Secret Police 39; Grand Jury Secrets 39; $1,000 a Touchdown 39; The Farmer's Daughter 40; Queen of the Mob 40; The Texas Rangers Ride Again 40; Ellery Queen and the Murder Ring • The Murder Ring 41; Ellery Queen and the Perfect Crime • The Perfect Crime 41; Ellery Queen's Penthouse Mystery 41; Power Dive 41; A Close Call • A Close Call for Ellery Queen 42; A Desperate Chance • A Desperate Chance for Ellery Queen 42; Enemy Agents Meet Ellery Queen • The Lido Mystery 42; The Mad Ghoul 43; No Place for a Lady 43; The Strange Death of Adolf Hitler 43

Hogan, Paul The Humpty Dumpty Man 89

Hogg, Michael Lindsay *see Lindsay-Hogg, Michael*

Höglund, Gunnar Kungsleden • Obsession • The Royal Track 68

Holbrook, J. K. The Profiteer 19

Holcomb, Rod Stitches 85

Holcomb, Theodore Russia 72

Hold, John *see Bava, Mario*

Holden, Anton Aroused 68

Holden, Lansing She 35*

Holder, Erich Frischer Wind aus Kanada 35

Hole, William, Jr. Hell Bound 57; Devil's Doll • The Devil's Hand • Live to Love • The Naked Goddess • Witchcraft 59; Four Fast Guns 59; The Ghost of Dragstrip Hollow 59; Speed Crazy 59; The Continental Twist • Twist All Night • The Young and the Cool 61; The Man from the First Century • The Man from the Past • Man in Outer Space • Muž z Prvního Století 61*

Holger-Madsen, Forest Elskovsmagt • Gøgleren • Man's Great Adversary 12*; Guldet og Vort Hjerte • The Heart's Voice • Et Vanskeligt Valg 12; Kun en Tigger 12; The Adventures of a Millionaire's Son • Millionærdrengen • Ned med Millionærdrengen 13; Ballettens Datter • Danserinden • Unjustly Accused 13; During the Plague • Lægens Hustru • Mens Pesten Raser • Under Pesten 13; Elskovsleg • Liebelei • Love's Devotee 13*; Fra Fyrste til Knejpevært • The Gambler's Wife 13; Den Gamle Bænk • Left Alone • Under Mindernes Træ 13; Den Hvide Dame • The White Ghost • The White Woman 13; In the Bonds of Passion • Skæbnes Veje • Under Kærlighedens Åg • Under Skæbnens Hjul 13; Lykken Dræber 13; The Mechanical Saw • Under Savklingens Tænder • The Usurer's Son 13; Det Mørke Punkt • Stålkongens Vilje • The Steel King's Last Wish 13; The Princess' Dilemma • Prinsesse Elena 13; An Adventure in a Harem • Et Haremseventyr 14; En Æresoprejsning • Misunderstood • Alone at Last • Endelig Alene 14; Ansigtet • The Missing Admiralty Plans • Det Stjælne Ansigt 14; Bajaderens Hævn • The Bayadere's Revenge • Tempeldanserindens Elskov 14; Barnet • Barnets Magt • The Child 14; Børnevennerne • A Marriage of Convenience 14; The Candle and the Moth • Evangeliemandens Liv • The Evangelist Preacher • The Life of the Lay Preacher 14; A Deal with the Devil • Den Mystike Fremmede 14; Den Dødes Røst • Nancy Keith • Testamentets Hemmelighed • The Voice of the Dead 14; Enough of It • Et Huskors • Lysten Styret 14; De Forviste • Uden Fædreland • Without a Country 14; Genopstandelsen • En Opstandelse • A Resurrection 14; Husassistenten • Når Fruen Skifter Pige • The New Cook 14; Kærlighedens Triumf • The Romance of a Will • Testamentet • The Triumph of Charity 14; Krig og Kærlighed • Love and War 14; Lay Down Your Arms

• Ned med Våbnene • Våbnene 14; Min Ven Levy • My Friend Levy 14; Opium Dreams • The Opium Smoker's Dream • Opiumsdrømmen 14; The Somnambulist • Søvngængersken 14; Spiritisten • The Spirits • The Spiritualist • A Voice from the Past 14; The Taming of the Shrew • Trold Kan Tæmmes 14; Acostates Første Offer • Krigens Fjende • The Munition Conspiracy 15; The Beggar Princess • Grevinde Hjerteløs 15; The Buried Secret • Det Unge Blod 15; Cigaretpigen • The Cigarette Maker 15; Circus Arrives • The Dancer's Revenge • Danserindens Hævn 15; The Clay Heart • Guldets Gift • Lerhjertet • The Poison of Gold • The Tempting of Mrs. Chestney 15; The Condemned • A Dancer's Strange Dream • Danserindens Kærlighedsdrøm • Den Dødsdrømte 15; The Crossroads of Life • I Livets Brænding 15; The Devil's Protégé • Djævelens Protégé • Den Hvide Djævel • The White Devil 15; Den Dødes Sjæl • En Kunstners Gennembrud • The Sound of the Violin 15; The Earth's Revenge • Jordens Hævn • Den Omstridte Jord 15; Faklen • Hvo Som Elsker Sin Fader • Who So Loveth His Father's Honor 15; The Foundling of Fate • Hittebarnet 15; Den Frelsende Film • The Woman Tempted Me 15; His Innocent Dupe • Sjælens Ven • Sjæletyven • The Unwilling Sinner 15; Hvem Er Gentlemantyven? • Strakoff the Adventurer 15; Hvor Sorgerne Glemmes • Sister Cecilia • Søster Cecilies Offer 15; En Ildprøve • A Terrible Ordeal 15; Kornspekulantens Datter 15; The Man Without a Future • Manden Uden Fremtid 15; Notitsen i Morgenbladet 15; Temptation of the Big Cities 15; Den Æreløse • The Infamous • The Prison Taint 16; The Beggar Man of Paris • Fars Sorg • Father Sorrow • Smil 16; Børnenes Synd • The Sins of the Children 16; Convict No. 113 • Fange Nr. 113 • Prisoner No. 113 16; Dødens Kontrakt • Hendes Moders Løfte • A Super Shylock 16; Edison Maes Dagbog • Nattevandreren • Out of the Underworld 16; Eternal Peace • Pax Æterna 16; False Evidence • For Sin Faders Skyld • The Veiled Lady 16; Guiding Conscience • Lykken • The Road to Happiness 16; Hans Rigtige Kone • His Real Wife • Which Is Which? 16; An Impossible Marriage • Livets Gøglespil 16; Kamæleonen • Måneprinsessen • The May-Fly • The Mysterious Lady 16; Klubvennen • Nattens Mysterium • Who Killed Barno O'Neal? 16; Lydia • The Music Hall Star 16; Manden Uden Smil 16; The Pastor's Daughter • Præstens Datter 16; The Airship • 400 Million Miles from the Earth • Himmelskibet • The Sky Ship • A Trip to Mars 17; Disarmament 17; Hendes Helt • Vogt Dig for Dine Venner 17; Justice Victorious • Retten Sejrer 17; Skovens Børn 17; Chariots of the Sky 18; Fighting Instinct • The Man Who Tamed the Victors • Manden Der Sejrede 18; Folkets Ven • A Friend of the People 18; Mod Lyset • Towards the Light 18; Beyond the

Barricade • Can We Escape? • The Flight from Life • Flugten fra Livet • Har Jeg Ret til At Tage Mit Eget Liv? 19; Digterkongen • Gudernes Yndling • The Penalty of Fame • Trials of Celebrity 19; The Greatest in the World • Janes Gode Ven • The Love That Lives • Det Største i Verden 19; Am Webstuhl der Zeit 21; Thomas Bundschuh • Tobias Buntschuh 21; Pömperlys Kampf mit dem Schneeschuh 22*; Darskab, Dyd og Driveri 23; Das Evangelium 23; Zaida —Die Tragödie eines Modells 23; Der Mann um Mitternacht • Midnatsgæsten • Midnight Hosts 24; Ole Opfinders Offer 24; Der Evangelimann 25; Die Heilige Lüge • Hellige Løgne • The Sacred Lie 25; Ein Lebenskünstler 25; Kniplinger 26; Die Seltsame Nacht 26; Skæbnenatten 26; Spitzen 26; Die Sporck'schen Jäger 26; Kunsten At Leve Livet 27; Midnatsjægernen 27; Vester Vov Vov 27; Freiwild 28; Die Seltsame Nacht der Helga Wansen 28; Was Ist Los mit Nanette? 28; Længslernes Nat 29; Nein, Nein, Nanette 30; Vask, Videnskab og Velvære 33; København-Kalundborg • København, Kalundborg og... 34*; Sol Over Danmark • Sun Over Denmark 36; Alens Livsmysterium 40

Holl, Fritz Nanu Sie Kennen Korff Noch Nicht? • So You Don't Know Korff Yet? 39

Holland, Agnieszka Screen Tests • Zdjecia Próbne 77; Aktorzy Prowincjonalni • Provincial Actors 79; Fever • Goraczka 80; Kobieta Samotna • Woman on Her Own 81; Angry Harvest • Bittere Ernte 85; Le Complot • To Kill a Priest 88; Popiełusko 88; Europa, Europa 90

Holland, Rodney The Detour 79

Holland, Savage Steve Better Off Dead 85; One Crazy Summer 86; How I Got Into College 89

Holland, Todd The Wizard 89

Holland, Tom Fright Night 85; Fatal Beauty 87; Child's Play 88

Hollander, Eli Out 82

Holländer, Friedrich The Empress and I • Ich und die Kaiserin 33; Heart Song • The Only Girl 33

Hollander, Judith Min Pappa Är Tarzan • My Dad Is Tarzan 86

Holleb, Allan Candy Stripe Nurses 74; School Spirit 85

Hollmann, Frank *see Franco, Jesús*

Holloway, George *see Capitani, Giorgio*

Holloway, John Across the Divide • Across the Great Divide 21

Holly, Martin ...Nebo Byť Zabit • ...Or Be Killed 85

Hollywood, Edwin L. One Hour 17*; Polly of the Circus 17*; The Challenge Accepted 18; The Birth of a Soul 20; The Flaming Clue 20; The Gauntlet 20; The Sea Rider 20; French Heels 22; No Trespassing 22; Columbus 23; Jamestown 23

Holmes, Andrew Mr. Shepard and Mr. Milne 75

Holmes, Ben Lightning Strikes Twice 34; The Farmer in the Dell 36; The Plot Thickens • The Swinging Pearl Mystery 36;

There Goes My Girl 37; Too Many Wives 37; We're on the Jury 37; I'm from the City 38; Little Orphan Annie 38; Maid's Night Out 38; The Saint in New York 38; Petticoat Larceny 43

Holmes, Cecil Three in One 56
Holmes, Fenwicke L. The Offenders 24
Holmes, Fred Dakota 87
Holmes, J. B. Ordinary People 42*; Coastal Command 43
Holmes-Gore, Arthur His Reformation 14; Nan Good-for-Nothing 14; Turtle Doves 14
Holmsen, Egil The Time of Desire 57
Holst, Per Last of the Nomads 58; Walter & Carlo: Op på Fars Hat 85
Holt, George The White Masks 21; In the West 23; Trouble Trail 24; Western Fate 24
Holt, Joel Karate • Karate, the Hand of Death 61
Holt, Seth Nowhere to Go 58; Scream of Fear • Taste of Fear 60; Endstation 13—Sahara • Station Six—Sahara 62; Wildlife in Danger 64; The Nanny 65; Danger Route • The Eliminator • Escape Route 67; Blood from the Mummy's Tomb 71*; Call Him Mr. Shatter • Shatter • They Call Him Mr. Shatter 74*
Holubar, Allen Fear Not 17; The Field of Honor 17; Heartstrings 17; The Reed Case 17; Sirens of the Sea 17; Treason 17; The Heart of Humanity 18; The Mortgaged Wife 18; A Soul for Sale 18; The Talk of the Town 18; The Girl Who Dared • Paid in Advance 19; The Right to Happiness 19; Once to Every Woman 20; Man, Woman, Marriage 21; Broken Chains 22; Hurricane's Gal 22; Slander the Woman 23
Holzberg, Roger Midnight Crossing 88
Holzman, Allan Forbidden World • Mutant 81; Grunt! The Wrestling Movie 85; Out of Control 85; Programmed to Kill • Retaliator 86*
Hom, Jesper Take It Easy 86
Honarmand, Mohammad-Reza The Telephone Calls 86
Honda, Inoshiro Godzilla • Godzilla, King of the Monsters • Gojira 54*; Half Human • Jūjin Yūkiotoko 55*; Radan • Radon • Radon the Flying Monster • Rodan 56; Chikyū Bōeigun • Earth Defense Force • The Mysterians 57; Beautiful Women and the Hydrogen Man • Bijō to Ekitai Ningen • The H-Man • Uomini H 58; Daikaijū Baran • The Monster Baran • Varan the Unbelievable 58*; Battle in Outer Space • Uchū Daisensō • The World of Space 59; Gasu Ningen Daiichigo • The Human Vapor 60; Mosura • Mothra 61*; Gorath • Yōsei Gorasu • Yōsei Gorath 62; Ataragon • Atoragon • Atragon • Atragon the Flying Supersub • The Flying Supersub • Kaitei Gunkan 63; Attack of the Mushroom People • Curse of the Mushroom People • Fungus of Terror • Matango • Matango Fungus of Terror 63; King Kong Tai Godzilla • King Kong Tai Gojira • King Kong vs. Godzilla 63*; Dagora • Dagora the Space Monster • Space Monster

Dogora • Uchūdai Dogora 64; Frankenstein and the Giant Lizard • Frankenstein Conquers the World • Frankenstein vs. the Giant Devilfish • Furankenshutain Tai Baragon 64; Godzilla Fights the Giant Moth • Godzilla Tai Mothra • Godzilla vs. Mothra • Godzilla vs. the Giant Moth • Godzilla vs. the Thing • Gojira Tai Mosura • Mosura Tai Gojira • Mothra vs. Godzilla 64; Battle of the Astros • Godzilla vs. Monster Zero • Invasion of Planet X • Invasion of the Astro-Monsters • Invasion of the Astros • Kaijū Daisensō • Monster Zero 65; The Biggest Battle on Earth • The Biggest Fight on Earth • Chikyū Saidai no Kessen • Ghidora the Three-Headed Monster • Ghidorah Sandai Kaijū Chikyū Saidai no Kessen • Ghidrah • Ghidrah the Three-Headed Monster • The Greatest Battle on Earth • Monster of Monsters • Sandai Kaijū Chikyū Saidai no Kessen 65; Duel of the Gargantuas • Furankenshutain no Kaijū—Sanda Tai Gailah • Sanda Tai Gailah • The War of the Gargantuas 66; King Kong Escapes • King Kong no Gyakushū • King Kong's Counterattack • The Revenge of King Kong 67*; Destroy All Monsters! • Kaijū Sōshingeki • The March of the Monsters • Operation Monsterland 68; Godzilla's Revenge • Oru Kaijū Daishingeki 69; Ido Zero Daisakusen • Latitude Zero 69; Kessen Nankai no Daikaijū • Nankai no Daikaijū • The Space Amoeba • Yog—Monster from Space 70; The Escape of Megagodzilla • Mekagojira no Gyakushū • Monsters from the Unknown Planet • Terror of Godzilla • Terror of Mechagodzilla 75
Honda, Ishiro see Honda, Inoshiro
Hondo, Med Oh, Sun • Soleil Ô 70; West Indies 79; Sarraounia 86
Honey, John Manganinnie 80
Hong, Elliot Kill the Golden Goose 79; Hot and Deadly • The Retrievers 81; A Fistful of Chopsticks • They Call Me Bruce? 82
Hong, James The Girls Next Door 79; The Vineyard 88*
Hong, Jinbao see Hung, Samo
Honigmann, Heddy De Deur van het Huis 85*; Hersenschimmen • Mind Shadows 88
Honkasalo, Pirjo Flame Top • Tulipää 80*; Da Capo 85*
Honquan, Liu see Liu, Honquan
Honri, Baynham Bank Holiday Luck 47
Honthaner, Ron The House on Skull Mountain 73
Hoo, Ching-chuen see Hu, King
Hood, George F. Stark Raving Mad 83
Hood, Randall The Two Little Bears 61; Die, Sister, Die 78
Hook, Harry Sins of the Fathers 82; The Kitchen Toto 87; Lord of the Flies 90
Hooker, Ted The Crucible of Terror 71
Hool, Lance Missing in Action 2—The Beginning 84; Steel Dawn 87
Hooper, Tobe The Heiress 65; Down Friday Street 66; A Way of Learning 67; Eggshells 69; The Heisters 70; The Texas

Chainsaw Massacre 74; Death Trap • Eaten Alive • Horror Hotel • Horror Hotel Massacre • Legend of the Bayou • Starlight Slaughter 76; Salem's Lot: The Movie 79; The Funhouse 80; Poltergeist 82; Lifeforce 85; Invaders from Mars 86; The Texas Chainsaw Massacre 2 86; Spontaneous Combustion 89
Hope, Harry The Doomsday Machine 67*
Hopkins, Albert Faust 36; Railroad Rhythm 36
Hopkins, Alec Film Fare 37
Hopkins, Arthur The Eternal Magdalene 19; His Double Life 33*
Hopkins, John Torment 86*
Hopkins, Omar see Zeglio, Primo
Hopkins, Stephen Dangerous Game 88; A Nightmare on Elm Street 5: The Dream Child 89; Predator 2 90
Hopper, Dennis Easy Rider 69; Chinchero • The Last Movie 71; Out of the Blue 80; Colors 88; Backtrack 89; The Hot Spot 90
Hopper, E. Mason Mr. Wise, Investigator 11; Alkali Ike in Jayville 13; The Labyrinth 15; The Birth of Character 16; Gloriana 16; The Right Direction 16; The Selfish Woman 16; As Men Love 17; Firefly of Tough Luck 17; The Hidden Spring 17; The Prison Without Walls 17; The Red Woman 17; The Regenerates 17; The Spirit of Romance 17; Tar Heel Warrior 17; The Wax Model 17; Without Honor 17; The Answer 18; Boston Blackie's Little Pal 18; Her American Husband 18; The Love Brokers 18; Love's Pay Day 18; Mystic Faces 18; Unexpected Places 18; Wife or Country 18; As the Sun Went Down 19; Come Again Smith 19; Edgar and the Teacher's Pet 20; Edgar's Hamlet 20; It's a Great Life 20; All Is Fair in Love • All's Fair in Love 21; Dangerous Curve Ahead 21; From the Ground Up 21; Hold Your Horses 21; Brothers Under the Skin 22; The Glorious Fool 22; Hungry Hearts 22; Daddy 23; The Love Piker 23; The Beautiful Rebel • Janice Meredith 24; The Great White Way 24; The Crowded Hour 25; Almost a Lady 26; Paris at Midnight 26; Up in Mabel's Room 26; Getting Gertie's Garter 27; My Friend from India 27; The Night Bride 27; The Rush Hour 27; The Wise Wife 27; A Blonde for a Night 28; The Carnation Kid 29; Kempy • Wise Girls 29; Square Shoulders 29; Their Own Desire 29; So Like a Woman • Temptation 30; Alias Mary Smith 32; Her Mad Night 32; Midnight Morals 32; No Living Witness 32; Shop Angel 32; Malay Nights • Shadows of Singapore 33; One Year Later 33; Sister to Judas 33; Backstage Mystery • Curtain at Eight 34; Hong Kong Nights 35
Hopper, Jerry The Atomic City 52; Hurricane Smith 52; Pony Express 53; Alaska Seas 54; Naked Alibi 54; The Secret of the Incas 54; Never Say Goodbye 55*; One Desire 55; The Private War of Major Benson 55; Smoke Signal 55; The Square Jungle 55; Everything But the Truth 56;

The Sharkfighters 56; Toy Tiger 56; The Missouri Traveler 58; Blueprint for Robbery 61; Madron 70; The Bull of the West 71*

Hoppin, Hector Joie de Vivre 34*; Foxhunt 37*; Indian Fantasy 38*

Hopton, Russell Song of the Trail 36

Hopwood, R. A. Bottle Party 36; Digging for Gold 36; Full Steam 36; Concert Party 37; Footlights 37; Song in Soho 37; Uptown Revue 37; West End Frolics 37; Windmill Revels 37; Behind the Tabs 38; The Interrupted Rehearsal 38; Revue Parade 38; Spotlight 38; Swing 38; Two Men in a Box 38

Horan, Charles T. Tables Turned 15; The Blindness of Love 16; The Quitter 16; Rose of the Alley 16*; The Upheaval 16; Polly of the Circus 17*; Man's Plaything 20; Love, Hate and a Woman 21; You Find It Everywhere 21; The Splendid Lie 22; Does It Pay? 23; No Mother to Guide Her 23

Horian, Richard Student Confidential 87

Horikawa, Hiromichi Eternity of Love • Wakarete Ikiru Toki Mo 61; Pressure of Guilt • Shiro to Kuro 61; The Beautiful Swindlers • Les Plus Belles Escroqueries du Monde • World's Greatest Swindles • The World's Most Beautiful Swindlers 63*; Hadaka no Taishō • The Naked General 64; Onna Goroshi Abura Jigoku • The Prodigal Son 64; The Blue Beast 65; Goodbye Moscow • Saraba Mosukuwa Gūrentai 68; Sogeki • Sun Above, Death Below 69; Master Hand • Ōshō 73; Mutchan no Uta • Song of Mutsuko 86

Horkheimer, H. D. The Power of Evil 16*; Spellbound 16*

Horkheimer, H. M. The Power of Evil 16*; Spellbound 16*

Horn, Andrew The Big Blue 89

Horn, Buddy van see Van Horn, Buddy

Horn, Leonard Rogues' Gallery 68; The Magic Garden of Stanley Sweetheart 70; Corky • Lookin' Good 71

Hornby, Fred The Call of the Hills 23

Horne, James W. The Accomplice 15; The Barnstormers 15; The Pitfall 15; Mystery of the Grand Hotel 16; Social Pirates 16; Stingaree 16; Bull's Eye 18; Hands Up! 18*; The Midnight Man 19; Occasionally Yours 20; The Third Eye 20; The Bronze Bell 21; Dangerous Pastime 21; Don't Doubt Your Wife 22; The Forgotten Law 22; The Hottentot 22; Blow Your Own Horn 23; Can a Woman Love Twice? 23; Itching Palms 23; A Man of Action 23; The Sunshine Trail 23; Alimony 24; American Manners 24; Hail the Hero 24; In Fast Company 24; Laughing at Danger 24; Stepping Lively 24; Thicker Than Water 24; The Yankee Consul 24; Youth and Adventure 25; The Cruise of the Jasper B 26; Kosher Kitty Kelly 26; College 27; The Big Hop 28; Black Butterflies 28; Big Business 29; Beau Chumps • Beau Hunks 31; Chickens Come Home 31; Come Clean 31; Laughing Gravy 31; One Good Turn 31; Our Wife 31; Any Old Port 32; Love Pains

32; The Bohemian Girl 35*; Bonnie Scotland 35; Way Out West 36; All Over Town 37; The Spider's Web 38*; Flying G-Men 39*; Deadwood Dick 40; The Green Archer 40; The Shadow 40; Terry and the Pirates 40; Holt of the Secret Service 41; The Iron Claw 41; The Spider Returns 41; White Eagle 41; Captain Midnight 42; Perils of the Royal Mounted 42

Horne, Nigel One Day Last Summer 84*

Horner, Harry Beware, My Lovely 52; Red Planet Mars 52; Vicki 53; New Faces • New Faces of 1954 54; A Life in the Balance 55; Man from Del Rio 56; The Wild Party 56

Horner, Robert J. Defying the Law 22; Virginian Outcast 24; Cowboy Courage 25; His Greatest Battle 25; The Millionaire Orphan 26; Pony Express Rider 26; Twin Six O'Brien 26; Walloping Kid 26; Across the Plains 28; Arizona Speed 28; Cheyenne Trails 28; Forbidden Trails 28; Mystery Rider 28; Ranger's Oath 28; Riders of Vengeance 28; Rip Roaring Logan 28; Secrets of the Range 28; Texas Flash 28; The Thrill Chaser 28; Throwing Lead 28; Trails of Treachery 28; Two Gun O'Brien 28; Where the West Begins 28; Far Western Trails 29; Midnight on the Barbary Coast 29; The White Outlaw 29; The Apache Kid's Escape 30; The Kid from Arizona 31; Wild West Whoopee 31; Defying the Law 35; The Phantom Cowboy 35; Western Racketeers 35; The Whirlwind Rider 35

Hornisher, Christina Hollywood 90028 73

Horst, Hartmut Aufbruche 88

Horst, Herman van den Metamorphose 45; Het Bijstere Land van Veluwen • Rape of a Country 48; Der Zee Ontrukt • Wrested from the Sea 49; Het Schot Is te Board • Shoot the Nets 52; Houwen Zo • Steady Now 53; Lekko • Vieren Maar 54; Praise the Sea • Prijs de Maar 58; Faja Lobbi • Fiery Love • Symphony of the Tropics 60; Pan 61; Amsterdam 65; Toccata 67

Horton, Peter Amazon Women on the Moon 86*

Horváth, Péter Love Till First Blood • Szerelem Első Vérig 85*

Horwitz, James Suspended Forth 69

Hosch, Karl Ryder, P.I. 86*

Hoskins, Bob The Raggedy Rawney • The Rawney 88

Hossein, Robert Les Salauds Vont en Enfer • The Wicked Go to Hell 55; Pardonnez-Nous Nos Offenses 56; Blonde in a White Car • Nude in a White Car • Toi le Venin 58; The Double Agents • Night Encounter • La Notte delle Spie • La Nuit des Espions 59; Les Scélérats 59; Le Goût de la Violence 60; The Game of Truth • Le Jeu de la Vérité 61; Haut für Haut 61; La Mort d'un Tueur 63; Le Vampire de Düsseldorf 64; Les Yeux Cernés 64; I Killed Rasputin • J'Ai Tué Raspoutine 67; Une Corde, un Colt 68; Point de

Chute 70; Les Misérables 82; Le Caviar Rouge 85

Hotaling, Arthur A Gentleman Preferred 28

Hou, Hsiao-hsien Green, Green Grass of Home 82; Growing Up 82; All the Youthful Days • The Boys from Fengkuei • The Boys of Fengkuei • Feng-Kuei-Lai-Tejen 83; The Sandwich Man 83; Dongdong de Jiaqui • A Summer at Grandpa's • Tung-Tung-Te-Chia-Ch'i 84; A Time to Live and a Time to Die • The Time to Live and the Time to Die • Tong Nien Wang Shi • Tongnian Wangshi • Tung-Nien Wang-Shih 85; Daughter of the Nile • Ni-Lo-Ho Nu-Erh • Nilouhe, Nuer 87; Dust in the Wind • Lien Lien Fung Chen 87; City of Sadness 89

Hou, Xiaoxian see Hou, Hsiao-hsien

Houck, Joy, Jr. Night of Bloody Horror 69; His Wife's Habit • Women and Bloody Terror • Women of Bloody Terror 70; The Brain Machine 72; The Creature from Black Lake 75; Night of the Strangler 75

Houdini, Harry Haldane of the Secret Service 23

Hough, Harold Attack on a Russian Outpost 04; The Bombardment of Port Arthur 04; Garrotting a Motor Car 04; Man the Lifeboat 04; The Story of a Colliery Disaster 04; The Amorous Policeman 06; Attack in the Rear 06; Bertie at the Gymnasium • Inquisitive Bertie 06; The Chaser Chased 06; The Dentist's Revenge 06; The Dog Detective 06; A Great Temptation 06; How Isaacs Won the Cup 06; A Naval Engagement 06; Slavery Days—The New Master 06; Turning the Tables 06; The Bet That Didn't Come Off 07; The Child Accuser 07; The Gamekeeper's Dog 07; Getting His Change 07; A Husband and How to Train It 07; Husbands Beware 07; Jones' Birthday 07; Rent Day 07; Tommy's Box of Tools 07; The Unlucky Horseshoe 07

Hough, John Wolfshead—The Legend of Robin Hood 69; Eyewitness • Sudden Terror 70; The Gemini Twins • Twins of Dracula • Twins of Evil • Virgin Vampires 71; The Practice 71; La Isla del Tesoro • Treasure Island 72; The Legend of Hell House 73; Dirty Mary, Crazy Larry 74; Escape to Witch Mountain 74; Brass Target 78; Return from Witch Mountain 78; Incubus 80; The Watcher in the Woods 80*; Triumphs of a Man Called Horse 82; Black Carrion 84; Czech Mate 84; Biggles • Biggles: Adventures in Time 86; American Gothic 87; Howling IV: The Original Nightmare 88

Hough, R. Lee Girl-Shy Cowboy 28; Wild West Romance 28; The Silent Witness 32*

Houry, Henri The Clutch of Circumstance 18; Love Watches 18; Miss Ambition 18; Daring Hearts 19

Houston, Clyde Fox Style 73

Houston, Norman Exposure 32

Houston, Robert Shogun Assassin 80; Bad Manners • Growing Pains 84; Trust Me 88

Houston, Tony Outlaw Riders 71

Hovde, Ellen Gray Gardens 75*; Enormous Changes at the Last Minute 82*

Hoven, Adrian Castle of Bloody Lust • Castle of Lust • The Castle of Unholy Desires • Im Schloss der Bluten Begierde • In the Castle of Bloody Lust 67; Hexen Geschandet und zu Tode Gequält • Mark of the Devil, Part Two • Witches: Violated and Tortured to Death 72

Howard, Cal A-Lad-in Bagdad 38*; Porky's Phoney Express 38*

Howard, Cy Lovers and Other Strangers 70; Every Little Crook and Nanny 72

Howard, David The Golden West 32; The Killer • Mystery Ranch 32; The Rainbow Trail 32; Cuando el Amor Ríe • When Love Laughs 33; Mystery Squadron 33*; Smoke Lightning 33; Crimson Romance 34; In Old Santa Fe 34; The Lost Jungle 34*; Hard Rock Harrigan 35; The Marines Are Coming 35; Thunder Mountain 35; Whispering Smith Speaks 35; The Abysmal Brute • Conflict 36; The Border Patrolman 36; Daniel Boone 36; The Mine with the Iron Door 36; O'Malley of the Mounted 36; Millionaire Playboy • Park Avenue Logger 37; Border G-Man 38; Gun Law 38; Hollywood Stadium Mystery • The Stadium Murders 38; Lawless Valley 38; Painted Desert 38; The Renegade Ranger 38; Arizona Legion 39; The Fighting Gringo 39; The Marshal of Mesa City 39; The Rookie Cop • Swift Vengeance 39; Timber Stampede 39; Trouble in Sundown 39; Bullet Code 40; The Legion of the Lawless 40; Prairie Law 40; Triple Justice 40; Dude Cowboy 41; Six-Gun Gold 41

Howard, Leslie Pygmalion 38*; The Fighting Pimpernel • Mister V • Pimpernel Smith 41; The First of the Few • Spitfire 42; The Gentle Sex 43*

Howard, Nick see Nostro, Nick

Howard, Noel 55 Days at Peking 63*; L'Échiquier de Dieu • La Fabuleuse Aventure de Marco Polo • The Fabulous Adventures of Marco Polo • Marco le Magnifique • Marco Polo • Marco the Magnificent • Marko Polo • Le Meravigliose Avventure di Marco Polo 64*; Don't You Hear the Dogs Bark? • Entends-Tu les Chiens Aboyer? • ¿No Oyes Ladrar los Perros? 74*

Howard, Ron Grand Theft Auto 77; Night Shift 82; Splash! 84; Cocoon 85; Gung Ho 86; Willow 88; Parenthood 89

Howard, Sandy Tarzan and the Trappers 58*; Diary of a Bachelor 64; Caccia ai Violenti • King of Africa • One Step to Hell • Rey de Africa 67

Howard, William K. Get Your Man! 21*; Play Square 21; What Love Will Do 21; Captain Fly-by-Night 22; The Crusader 22*; Deserted at the Altar 22*; Extra! Extra! 22; Lucky Dan 22; Trooper O'Neill 22*; Danger Ahead 23; The Fourth Musketeer 23; Let's Go! 23; The Border Legion 24; East of Broadway 24; Code of the West 25; The Light of Western Stars 25; The Thundering Herd 25; Bachelor Brides • Bachelor's Brides 26; Gigolo 26; Red Dice 26; Volcano 26; The Main Event 27; White Gold 27; His Country • A Ship Comes In 28; The River Pirate 28; Christina 29; Love, Live and Laugh 29; The Valiant 29; Detective Clive, Bart • Scotland Yard 30; Good Intentions 30; Don't Bet on Women • More Than a Kiss 31; Surrender 31; Transatlantic 31; The First Year 32; Sherlock Holmes 32; The Trial of Vivienne Ware 32; The Cat and the Fiddle 33; Power and Glory • The Power and the Glory 33; This Side of Heaven 33; Evelyn Prentice 34; Mary Burns—Fugitive 35; The Rendezvous 35; Vanessa • Vanessa: Her Love Story 35; Fire Over England 36; The Princess Comes Across 36; Four Dark Hours • The Green Cockatoo • Race Gang 37*; Murder on Diamond Row • The Squeaker 37; Over the Moon 37*; Back Door to Heaven 39; Money and the Woman 40; Bullets for O'Hara 41; Klondike Fury • Klondike Victory 42; Johnny Come Lately • Johnny Vagabond 43; When the Lights Go On Again 44; A Guy Could Change 45

Howe, Eliot With Hoops of Steel 18; The Silver Girl 19*; Todd of the Times 19; The Gray Dawn 22*; When Romance Rides 22

Howe, J. A. The Kid Brother 27*

Howe, James Wong Go, Man, Go! 54; Dong Kingman 55; Bourbon Street Shadows • Invisible Avenger 58*

Howe, John Why Rock the Boat? 74

Howell, Charles E. Dr. Zippy Opens a Sanatorium • Zippy in a Sanatorium 16; Henry W. Zippy Buys a Motor Boat 16; Henry W. Zippy Buys a Pet Pup • Zippy Buys a Pet Pup 16; When Does a Hen Lay? 17

Howes, Oliver Three to Go 69*; Let the Balloon Go 77

Howley, John Happily Ever After 90

Hoyland, Margaret Little Paper People 35

Hoyt, Arthur High Stakes 18; Station Content 18

Hoyt, Harry Broadway Saint 19; The Forest Rivals 19; The Hand Invisible 19; Through the Toils 19; The Rider of the King Log 21; The Curse of Drink 22; That Woman 22; Fangs of the Wolf 24*; The Fatal Plunge 24; The Law Demands 24; The Radio Flyer 24; Sundown 24*; The Woman on the Jury 24; The Lost World 25*; The Primrose Path 25; The Unnamed Woman 25; When Love Grows Cold 25; The Belle of Broadway 26; Bitter Apples 27; The Return of Boston Blackie 27; The Passion Song 28; Dark Skies • Darkened Skies 30*; Jungle Bride 33*

Hoyt, Robert Racketeer Round-Up 34

Hristov, Hristo Iconostasis • Ikonostasut 69*

Hryhorovych, Yavheniya Alexander Dovzhenko 64

Hsiao-hsien, Hou see Hou, Hsiao-hsien

Hsing, Li see Li, Han-hsiang

Hsu, An-hua see Hui, Ann

Hu, Chin-chuan see Hu, King

Hu, Jingqin The Mantis Stalks the Cicada 88; Cock-Fighting 89; Pursuing Mice 89; The Stronger Get Hooked 89

Hu, King The Story of Sue San 62; Eternal Love • Liang Shan-Po and Chu Ying-T'ai • Liang Shan-Po yu Chu Ying-T'ai • The Love Eterne 63*; Sons and Daughters of the Good Earth • Sons of Good Earth • Sons of the Good Earth • Ta-Ti Erh-Nu • Ta-Ti Nu-Erh 64; Come Drink with Me • Ta Tsui Hsia 65; Dragon Gate Inn • Dragon Inn • Lung Men K'o-Chan 66; Hsia Nu • A Touch of Zen 68; Four Moods • Hsi Nu Ai Le 70*; The Fate of Lee Khan • Ying-Ch'un ko Chih Feng-Po 72; Chung Lieh T'u • The Valiant Ones 74; K'ung Shan Ling Yu • Raining in the Mountains • Raining on the Mountain 77; Legend in the Mountains • Legend of the Mountain • Shan Chung Ch'uan-Ch'i 78; Chung-Shen Ta-Shih • The Juvenizer • The Rejuvenator 81; All the King's Men • T'ien-Hsia Ti-Yi • The World's Best Men 83; Ta Luan-Hui • The Wheel of Life 83*; The Boiling Sea • Chang-Yu Chu-Hai 85

Hu, King-chuan see Hu, King

Hu, Mei Far from War 87; Yuan Ni Zan Zeng De Nian Dai 88

Hu, Sang Pai Mao Nu • The White-Haired Girl 70

Hua-Shan Infra-Man • The Infra Superman • The Super Inframan 75

Huang, Feng Deadly China Doll 73; Deep Thrust—The Hand of Death 73

Huang, Jianxin The Black Cannon Incident • Hei Pao Shi Jian 85; A Girl of Good Family • Liang Jia Funu 86; Cuo Wei • The Stand-In 87; Yi Ge Si Zhe Dul Sheng Zhe De Fang Wen 88; Zhen Nu 88

Huang, Jianzhong see Huang, Jianxin

Huang, Ming-chuan Man from Island West 90

Huang, Shuquin Woman Demon Human 90

Huangjian, Zhong see Huang, Jianxin

Hubbard, Lucien The Mysterious Island 26*; Rose Marie 27

Hubenbecker, Daniel Wardogs 87*

Hubert, Jean-Loup L'Année Prochaine Si Tout Va Bien 81; La Smala 84; The Big Road • Le Grand Chemin • The Grand Highway 87; After the War • Après le Guerre 89

Hubert, Roger Le Retour à la Vie 23

Hübler-Kahla, J. A. Tanzmusik 36; Frühling im Wien 37; Der Geheimnisvolle Mister X • The Mysterious Mr. X 39; Das Veilchen vom Potsdamer Platz • The Violet of Potsdam Square 39

Hubley, Faith The Adventures of * • Adventures of an Asterisk 56*; Harlem Wednesday 57*; Tender Game 58*; Moonbird 59*; Of Stars and Men 61*; The Hat 64*; Herb Alpert and the Tijuana Brass Double Feature 66*; Windy Day 67*; Of Men and Demons 69*; Cockaboody 73*; The Cosmic Eye 85

Hubley, John The Dumb Conscious Mind 42*; King Midas, Junior 42*; Old Blackout Joe 42*; He Can't Make It Stick

43*; Professor Small and Mister Tall 43*; The Vitamin G-Man 43*; Operation of the K-13 Gunsight 44; Position Firing 44; Flat Hatting 46; The Magic Fluke 48; Robin Hoodlum 48; Mr. Magoo 49; Punchy de Leon 49; The Ragtime Bear 49; Gerald McBoing Boing 50*; Spellbound Hound 50; Fuddy Duddy Buddy 51; Rooty Toot Toot 51; The Adventures of * • Adventures of an Asterisk 56*; Harlem Wednesday 57*; A Date with Dizzy 58; Tender Game 58*; Moonbird 59*; Seven Lively Arts 59; Children of the Sun 60; Of Stars and Men 61*; The Hole 62; Horses and Their Ancestors 62; Man and His Tools 62; The Hat 64*; Herb Alpert and the Tijuana Brass Double Feature 66*; . . .Urbanissimo 66; The Cruise 67; Windy Day 67*; Zuckerkandl! 68; Of Men and Demons 69*; Eggs 70; Cockaboody 73*; Upkeep 73; Voyage to Next 74; People People People 75

Huckabee, Tom Taking Tiger Mountain • Trechi Mynydd y Teigr 83*

Huckert, John W. Orange Sunshine: The Reincarnation of Ludwig van Beethoven 72; Ernie and Rose 82; The Passing 83

Hudlin, Reginald House Party 90

Hudson, Arch Male Service 66

Hudson, Gary Thunder Run 85

Hudson, Hugh Fangio 77; 12 Squadron Buccaneers 78; Chariots of Fire 81; Greystoke: The Legend of Tarzan • Greystoke: The Legend of Tarzan, Lord of the Apes • Greystoke: The Legend of Tarzan of the Apes 84; Revolution 85; Lost Angels 89

Huebler-Kahla, J. A. see *Hübler-Kahla, J. A.*

Hueh, Shih The Window of America 52*

Huemer, Dick The Dog Snatcher 31; The Little Pest 31; Minding the Baby 31; Showing Off 31; Sunday Clothes 31; Yelp Wanted 31; The Bad Genius 32; Battle of the Barn 32; Black Sheep 32; Camping Out 32; Chinatown Mystery 32; Fare-Play 32; Flop House 32; The Great Bird Mystery 32; The Pet Shop 32; Railroad Wretch 32; Stepping Stones 32; Treasure Hunt 32; The Wolf at the Door 32; Auto Show 33; The Beer Parade 33; The False Alarm 33; Hollywood Babies 33; The Match Kid 33; Movie Struck 33; Sandman Tales 33; Sassy Cats 33; Scrappy's Party 33; Technoracket 33; The World's Affair 33

Huemer, Peter Ily Kiss Daddy Good Night 87

Huestis, Marc Men in Love 90

Huettner, Ralf see *Hüttner, Ralf*

Huggins, Roy Hangman's Knot 52

Hugh, R. John Yellowneck 55; Naked in the Sun 57; The Touch of Flesh 60; A Crowd for Lisette • Fall Girl • Lisette 61; Deadly Encounter • The Meal 75

Hugham, Oxley The Queen's Royal Tour 54

Hughes, David Emmanuelle in Soho 81

Hughes, Harry Adam's Film Review 24; Unnatural Life Studies 24; A Wet Night

26; A Daughter in Revolt 27; The Hellcat 28; Troublesome Wives 28; Virginia's Husband 28; Little Miss London 29; Star Impersonations 30; We Take Off Our Hats 30; The Gables Mystery • The Man at Six 31; Glamour 31*; Bachelor's Baby 32; His Wife's Mother 32; Facing the Music 33; A Southern Maid 33; Their Night Out 33; The Broken Rosary 34; Song at Eventide 34; Womanhood 34; Barnacle Bill 35; Joy Ride 35; Play Up the Band 35; The Improper Duchess 36; Tropical Trouble 36; The Gables Mystery 38; Mountains o' Mourne 38; The Voyage of Peter Joe 46; Stage Frights 47

Hughes, Howard Hell's Angels 30*; The Outlaw 40*; Vendetta 50*

Hughes, John Sixteen Candles 84; The Breakfast Club 85; Weird Science 85; Ferris Bueller's Day Off 86; Planes, Trains and Automobiles 87; She's Having a Baby 87; Uncle Buck 89

Hughes, Ken Soho 44; The Burning Question 45; Beach Recovery 46; Those Nuisances 46; If the Cap Fits 47; The Man on the Flying Trapeze 47; The Mystery of the White Handkerchief 47; Wide Boy 52; The Atomic Man • Timeslip 53; Black 13 53; The Brain Machine • The Great Brain Machine 53; The Candlelight Murder 53; The Case of the Red Monkey • Little Red Monkey 53; Confession • The Deadliest Sin 53; The Dark Stairway 53; The Drayton Case 53; The Missing Man 53; The Blazing Caravan 54; Heat Wave • The House Across the Lake 54; Passenger to Tokyo 54; The Strange Case of Blondie 54; Joe Macbeth 55; Murder Anonymous 55; Night Plane to Amsterdam 55; Portrait in Smoke • Wicked As They Come 56; The Long Haul 57; The Green Carnation • The Man with the Green Carnation • The Trials of Oscar Wilde 60; In the Nick 60; Jazz Boat • Jazzboat 60; Play It Cooler 61; The Small World of Sammy Lee 62; Of Human Bondage 64*; Arrivederci, Baby! • Drop Dead, Darling • My Last Duchess • You Just Kill Me • You're Dead Right 66; Casino Royale 67*; Chitty Chitty Bang Bang 68; Cromwell 70; The Internecine Project 74; Alfie Darling • Oh! Alfie 75; Sextette 77; Night School • Terror Eyes 80

Hughes, Robert Hunter's Blood 86; Down the Drain 90

Hughes, Roy M. Fightin' Thru 24

Hughes, Rupert Remembrance 22; The Wall Flower 22; Gimme • Gimmie 23; Look Your Best 23; Reno 23; Souls for Sale 23; True As Steel 24

Hughes, Terry Monty Python Live at the Hollywood Bowl 82

Hugon, André Beauté Fatale 16; Chignon d'Or 16; L'Empreinte 16; Fleur de Paris 16; Sous la Menace 16; Angoisse 17; Mariage d'Amour 17; Mystère d'une Vie 17; Requins 17; Le Vertige 17; Chacals 18; La Fugitif 18; Johannes, Fils de Johannes 18; Un Crime à Été Commis 19; Jacques Landauze 19; Les Chères Images 20; Fille de Rien 21; La Preuve 21; Le Roi de

Camargue 21; Diamant Noir 22; Notre Dame d'Amour 22; Le Petit Chose 23; La Rue du Pavé d'Amour 23; L'Arriviste 24; Gitanella 24; L'Homme des Baleares 25; La Princesse aux Clowns 25; Yasmina 26; À l'Ombre des Tombeaux 27; La Vestale du Gange 27; La Grande Passion 28; La Marche Nuptiale 29; La Famille Lefrançois • Heroes of the Marne 39; Dawn Over France 45

Hugon, M. The Polo Champion 15

Huhn, Austin O. A Clouded Mind • A Clouded Name 23

Hui, Ann The Secret 79; The Spooky Bunch 80; Hu-Yueh-Te Ku-Shih • The Story of Woo Viet 81; Boat People • T'ou-Pen Hu-Hai 82; Love in a Fallen City 84; The Book and the Sword • The Romance of Book and Sword • Shue Gim Yan Shau Luk 87; Jinye Xingguang Canlan • Starry Is the Night 89; Ke Tu Chiu Hen • The Swordsman 90*; Song of the Exile 90

Hui, Michael Happy Din Don • Huanle Dingdang 86

Huillet, Danièle Die Augen Wollen Sich Nicht zu Jeder Zeit Schliessen, oder Vielleicht eines Tages Wird Rom Sich Erlauben Seinerseits zu Wählen • Eyes Cannot Forever Remain Closed, or Perhaps Rome Will One Day Allow Itself to Choose in Its Turn • Eyes Do Not Want to Close at All Times, or Perhaps One Day Rome Will Permit Herself to Choose in Her Turn • Othon • Les Yeux Ne Peuvent Pas en Tout Temps Se Fermer ou Peut-Être Qu'un Jour Rome Se Permettra de Choisir à Son Tour • Les Yeux Ne Veulent Pas en Tout Temps Se Fermer ou Peut-Être Qu'un Jour Rome Se Permettra de Choisir à Son Tour 69*; Einleitung zu Arnold Schönbergs Begleitmusik zu einer Lichtspielszene • Introduction to Arnold Schönberg's Accompaniment to a Cinematic Scene 72*; Geschichtsunterricht • History Lessons 72*; Moses and Aaron • Moses und Äron 74*; I Cani del Sinai • Fortini/Cani 76*; Every Revolution Is a Throw of the Dice • Toute Révolution Est un Coup de Dés 77*; Della Nube alla Resistenza • From the Cloud to the Resistance 79*; Too Early, Too Late • Trop Tôt, Trop Tard 81*; Class Relations • Klassenverhältnisse 84*; The Death of Empedocles • Der Tod des Empedokles 86*; Schwarze Sünde 89*

Huit, Pierre Gaspard see *Gaspard-Huit, Pierre*

Hulbert, Jack Elstree Calling 30*; Falling for You 33*; Jack of All Trades • The Two of Us 35*

Hulcup, Jack The Gift • Kissing Cup 13

Hulette, Don Breaker Breaker 77; Great Ride 78; Tennessee Stallion 82; The Eagle • You're It 86

Hulten, Pontus Un Miracle 54*

Humaloja, Timo Valkoinen Kääpiö • The White Dwarf 86

Humberstone, Bruce see *Humberstone, H. Bruce*

Humberstone, H. Bruce The Crooked Circle 32; If I Had a Million 32*; Strangers of the Evening 32; Goodbye Love 33; King of the Jungle 33*; The Dragon Murder Case 34; The Merry Wives of Reno 34; Ladies Love Danger 35; Silk Hat Kid 35; Three Live Ghosts 35; Charlie Chan at the Opera 36; Charlie Chan at the Race Track 36; Charlie Chan at the Olympics 37; Checkers 37; In Old Chicago 37*; Charlie Chan in Honolulu 38; Rascals 38; Time Out for Murder 38; While New York Sleeps 38; Pack Up Your Troubles • We're in the Army Now 39; Pardon Our Nerve 39; Lucky Cisco Kid 40; The Quarterback 40; Hot Spot • I Wake Up Screaming 41; Sun Valley Serenade 41; Tall, Dark and Handsome 41; Iceland • Katina 42; To the Shores of Tripoli 42; Hello, Frisco, Hello 43; Pin Up Girl 44; Within These Walls 45; Wonder Man 45; Three Little Girls in Blue 46; The Homestretch 47; Fury at Furnace Creek 48; East of Java • South Sea Sinner 49; Happy Go Lovely 51; She's Working Her Way Through College 52; The Desert Song 53; Ten Wanted Men 54; The Purple Mask 55; Tarzan and the Lost Safari 56*; Tarzan's Fight for Life 58; Madison Avenue 61

Humberstone, Lucky see *Humberstone, H. Bruce*

Humbert, Humphrey see *Lenzi, Umberto*

Hume, Kenneth Cheer the Brave 51; Hot Ice 52; Bullet from the Past 57; Sail Into Danger 57; Go Go Big Beat • Mods and Rockers 64; I've Gotta Horse • Wonderful Day 65

Humfress, Paul Sebastiane 76*

Humphrey, William A Tale of Two Cities 11; The Snare of Fate 13; An Affair for the Police 14; On Her Wedding Night 15; The Return of Maurice Donnelly 15; Fathers of Men 16; The Footlights of Fate 16; Babbling Tongues 17; Two Men and a Woman 17; Joan of Plattsburg 18*; The Unchastened Woman 18; Atonement 20; The Black Spider 20; The Midnight Bride 20; Tangled Hearts • The Wife Whom God Forgot 20; Foolish Monte Carlo 22

Humphreys, Anderson The Cayman Triangle 77

Humphreys, William see *Humphrey, William*

Humphries, William see *Humphrey, William*

Humphris, Eric Shooting Stars 37; Starlight Parade 37; Take Off That Hat 38

Hundt, Charles Mona Kent • The Sin of Mona Kent • The Sins of Mona Kent 61

Hunebelle, André Métier de Fous 48; Mission à Tanger 49; Méfiez-Vous des Blondes 50; Millionnaires d'un Jour • A Simple Case of Money 50; Ma Femme Est Formidable 51; Massacre en Dentelles 52; Monsieur Taxi 52; Mon Mari Est Merveilleux 53; The Three Musketeers • Les Trois Mousquetaires 53; Cadet Rousselle 54; L'Impossible Monsieur Pipelet 55; Mannequins de Paris 56; Treize à Table 56; Casino de Paris 57; Les Collégiennes • The Twilight Girls 57; Ami Ami 58; Les Fem-

mes Sont Marrantes 58; Taxi Roulotte et Corrida 58; Arrêtez le Massacre 59; Le Bossu 59; Le Capitaine • Captain Blood 60; Blood on His Sword 61; Le Miracle des Loups 61; Les Mystères de Paris 62; Méfiez-Vous Mesdames 63; Banco à Bangkok • Banco à Bangkok pour O.S.S. 117 • O.S.S. 117 Minaccia Bangkok • Shadow of Evil 64; Fantômas 64; Fantômas Se Déchaîne • Fantômas Strikes Back 65; Furia à Bahia pour O.S.S. 117 • O.S.S. 117 Furia à Bahia • O.S.S. 117, Mission for a Killer 65; Fantômas • Fantômas Against Scotland Yard • Fantômas Contre Scotland Yard 66; No Roses for O.S.S. 117 • O.S.S. 117, Double Agent • Pas de Roses pour O.S.S. 117 67; Sous le Signe de Monte-Cristo 69; Les Quatre Charlots Mousquetaires 74

Hung, Kam-bo see *Hung, Samo*

Hung, Samo Encounter of the Spooky Kind • Ghost Against Ghost • Gui Da Gui • Spooky Encounters 80; Prodigal Son 83; Winners and Sinners 83; Wheels on Meals 84; Heart of the Dragon 85; Twinkle Twinkle Lucky Stars 85; The Millionaire's Express 86; Eastern Condors 87

Hung-wei, Yeh see *Yeh, Hung-wei*

Hunsicker, Jackson The Frog Prince 87

Hunt, Austin Dark Moves 74

Hunt, Charles J. The Dixie Flyer 26; The Smoke Eaters 26; The Warning Signal 26; A Boy of the Streets 27; Casey Jones 27; The Midnight Watch 27; Million Dollar Mystery 27; Modern Daughters 27; On the Stroke of Twelve 27; The Show Girl 27; Obey Your Husband 28; Queen of the Chorus 28; Thundergod 28; You Can't Beat the Law 28

Hunt, Ed Alien Encounter • Starship Invasions • War of the Aliens • Winged Serpent 77; The Gemini Strain • M3: The Gemini Strain • Plague • Plague M3 78; Bloody Birthday • Creeps 80; Alien Warrior • King of the Streets 86; The Brain 88

Hunt, J. L. Freer see *Freer-Hunt, J. L.*

Hunt, Jay The Black Sheep of the Family 16; Civilization 16*; What Love Can Do 16; The Promise 17

Hunt, John White Ensign 34; Full Speed Ahead 39

Hunt, Leigh Don't Make Waves 67*

Hunt, Paul Desert Odyssey • The Harem Bunch, or War and Peace • The Harem Bunch, or War and Piece • War and Piece 69; 40 Graves for 40 Guns • Machismo—40 Graves for 40 Guns 70; The Clones 73*; Savage Red—Outlaw White 74; Woman in the Rain 76; The Great Gundown 77; Twisted Nightmare 88

Hunt, Peter H. 1776 72; Bully 78; Mysterious Stranger 82; The Adventures of Huckleberry Finn 85

Hunt, Peter R. On Her Majesty's Secret Service 69; Gold 74*; Gulliver's Travels 76; Shout at the Devil 76*; Death Hunt 80; Wild Geese II 85; Assassination 86; Hyper Sapien • Hyper Sapien: People from Another Star 86

Hunter, A. C. Deception 18; The Golden Pippin Girl • Why Men Leave

Home 20; The Holiday Husband 20; Marzipan of the Shapes 20

Hunter, Happy see *Hunter, T. Hayes*

Hunter, Max see *Pupillo, Massimo*

Hunter, Robert Western Blood 23

Hunter, T. Hayes The Vampire 13*; Fire and Sword 14; The Seats of the Mighty 14; The Vampire's Trail 14*; Comrade John 15; Judy Forgot 15; The Crimson Stain Mystery 16; The Border Legion 18; Desert Gold 19; Once to Every Man 19; Cup of Fury 20; Earthbound 20; The Light in the Clearing 21; Damaged Hearts 24; The Recoil 24; Trouping with Ellen 24; The Sky Raider 25; Wildfire 25; One of the Best 27; The Scarlet Daredevil • The Triumph of the Scarlet Pimpernel 28; A South Sea Bubble 28; The Silver King 29; Bachelor's Folly • The Calendar 31*; The Man They Couldn't Arrest 31; Criminal at Large • The Frightened Lady 32; Sally Bishop 32; White Face 32; The Ghoul 33; The Green Pack 34; Josser on the Farm 34; Warn London! 34

Hunter, Tim Tex 82; Sylvester 85; River's Edge 86; Paint It Black 89

Huntington, Lawrence After Many Years 29; Night Club Murder • Romance in Rhythm 34; Bad Boy • Branded 36; The Bank Messenger Mystery 36; Cafe Mascot 36; Full Speed Ahead 36; Strange Cargo 36; Two on a Doorstep 36; Passage to London • Passenger to London 37; Screen Struck 37; Twin Faces 37; Dial 999 • The Revenge of Scotland Yard 38; Flickers 40; The Patient Vanishes • This Man Is Dangerous 41; The Tower of Terror 41; Suspected Person 42; Women Aren't Angels 42; Warn That Man 43; Night Boat to Dublin 45; A Voice in the Night • Wanted for Murder 46; The Upturned Glass 47; When the Bough Breaks 47; Mr. Perrin and Mr. Traill 48; Man on the Run 49; The Franchise Affair 50; There Was a Young Lady 52; The Accused 53*; The Genie 53*; The Red Dress 54*; Contraband Spain 55; Deadly Record 59; The Fur Collar 62; Stranglehold 62; Death Drums Along the River • Sanders 63; Manutara • The Vulture 66

Huntington, G. P. G. P. As Basil the Brainless 15; Little Pippin 15

Huppert, Caroline Signé Charlotte • Sincerely Charlotte 86

Huppertz, Toni Soldaten-Kameraden 36

Hurd, Earl Bobby Bumps' Adventures 15; Bobby Bumps Gets Pa's Goat 15; Ski-Hi the Cartoon Chinaman 15; The Troubles of Mr. Munk 15; Bobby Bumps and His Goatmobile 16; Bobby Bumps and His Pointer Pup 16; Bobby Bumps and the Detective Story • Bobby Bumps' Detective Story 16; Bobby Bumps and the Fly Swatter • Bobby Bumps' Fly Swatter 16; Bobby Bumps and the Stork 16; Bobby Bumps at the Circus 16; Bobby Bumps Gets a Substitute 16; Bobby Bumps Goes Fishing 16; Bobby Bumps Helps Out a Book Agent 16; Bobby Bumps Loses His Pup 16; Bobby Bumps Queers the Choir 16; Bobby Bumps

Starts a Lodge 16; Teddy and the Angel Cake 16; Bobby Bumps Adopts a Turtle 17; Bobby Bumps' Amusement Park 17; Bobby Bumps and Fido's Birthday Party 17; Bobby Bumps, Baseball Champion • Bobby Bumps' World Serious 17; Bobby Bumps, Chef 17; Bobby Bumps, Daylight Camper 17; Bobby Bumps, Early Shopper • Bobby Bumps Goes Shopping 17; Bobby Bumps' Fourth 17; Bobby Bumps in The Great Divide 17; Bobby Bumps, Office Boy 17; Bobby Bumps Outwits the Dogcatcher 17; Bobby Bumps Starts for School 17; Bobby Bumps, Submarine Chaser 17; Bobby Bumps, Surf Rider 17; Bobby Bumps' Tank 17; Bobby Bumps Volunteers 17; Bobby Bumps and the Speckled Death 18; Bobby Bumps at the Dentist 18; Bobby Bumps Becomes an Ace • Bobby Bumps, Sharpshooter 18; Bobby Bumps Caught in the Jamb 18; Bobby Bumps' Disappearing Gun 18; Bobby Bumps' Fight 18; Bobby Bumps Films a Fire 18; Bobby Bumps in Before and After 18; Bobby Bumps' Incubator 18; Bobby Bumps on the Doughnut Trail 18; Bobby Bumps on the Road 18; Bobby Bumps Out West 18; Bobby Bumps Puts a Beanery on the Bum 18; Bobby Bumps and the Hypnotic Eye 19; Bobby Bumps and the Sand Lizard 19; Bobby Bumps' Eel-ectric Launch 19; Bobby Bumps' Last Smoke 19; Bobby Bumps' Lucky Day 19; Bobby Bumps' Night Out with Some Night Owls 19; Bobby Bumps' Pup Gets the Flea-enza 19; Bobby Bumps Throwing the Ball 19; Bobby Bumps 20; Bobby Bumps' Orchestra 20; Bobby Bumps the Cave Man 20; Bobby Bumps Checkmated 21; Bobby Bumps in Hunting and Fishing 21; Bobby Bumps in Shadow Boxing 21; Bobby Bumps Working on an Idea 21; Hootch and Mootch in A Steak at Stake 21; Shootin' Fish 21; Bobby Bumps at School 22; Fresh Fish 22; One Ol' Cat 22; Railroading 22; Chicken Dressing 23; The Message of Émile Coué 23; The Movie Daredevil 23; Their Love Growed Cold 23; The Artist's Model 24; Boneyard Blues 24; Broadcasting 24; The Hoboken Nightingale 24; The Sawmill Four 24; Bobby Bumps and Co. 25; He Who Gets Socked 25; The Mellow Quartette 25; Monkey Business 25; Props and the Spirits 25; Props' Dash for Cash 25; Two Cats and a Bird 25; Two Poor Fish 25

Hurley, Frank The Jungle Woman 26; Pearl of the South Seas 27

Hurley, Maury It Ain't Easy 72

Hurn, Philip Framing Framers 18*

Hurst, Brian Desmond Bucket of Blood • The Tell-Tale Heart 34; Irish Hearts • Norah O'Neale 34; Riders to the Sea 35; Ourselves Alone • River of Unrest 36*; Sensation 36; The Tenth Man 36; Glamorous Night 37; Prison Without Bars 38*; The Fugitive • On the Night of the Fire 39; The Lion Has Wings 39*; A Call for Arms 40; Miss Grant Goes to the Door 40; Aquella Noche de Varsovia • Dangerous Moonlight • Suicide Squadron 41;

Alibi 42; A Letter from Ulster 42; The Hundred Pound Window 43; Caesar and Cleopatra 44*; Men of Arnhem 44*; Theirs Is the Glory 45; Hungry Hill 46; The Mark of Cain 47; Gay Lady • Trottie True 49; A Christmas Carol • Scrooge 51; Malta Story 53; Simba 54; The Black Tent 56; Dangerous Exile 57; Behind the Mask 58; His and Hers 60; The Playboy of the Western World 62

Hurst, Paul Lass of the Lumberlands 16*; The Iron Test 18*; Black Sheep 21; Shadows of the West 21; The Crow's Nest 22; The Heart of a Texan 22; The Kingfisher's Roost 22*; Table Top Ranch 22; Golden Silence 23; Branded a Bandit 24; The Courageous Coward 24; The Passing of Wolf MacLean 24; Battling Bunyon 25; The Demon Rider 25; The Fighting Cub 25; The Gold Hunters 25; The Rattler 25; The Son of Sontag 25; A Western Engagement 25; Battling Kid 26; Blue Streak O'Neil 26; Fighting Ranger 26; The Haunted Ranch • The Haunted Range 26; The Law of the Snow Country 26; The Midnight Message 26; Roaring Road 26; Shadows of Chinatown 26; Son of a Gun 26; The Range Raiders 27; Rider of the Law 27

Hurtz, William Hotsy Footsy 52; A Unicorn in the Garden 53; Bringing Up Mother 54

Hurwitz, Harry The Projectionist 70; The Comeback Trail 71; Chaplinesque, My Life and Hard Times 72; Richard 72*; Fairy Tales 78; Nocturna • Nocturna, Granddaughter of Dracula 78; Rally • Safari 3000 • Two in the Bush 82; The Big Lobby • The Rosebud Beach Hotel 84; That's Adequate 86

Hurwitz, Leo T. Hunger 32; Scottsboro 34; Pay Day 38*; Native Land 42*; Strange Victory 48; The Museum and the Fury 56; Here at the Water's Edge 60; Verdict for Tomorrow 61

Husberg, Rolf The Children 49; Laila • Laila—Liebe Unter der Mitternachtssonne • Lila • Lila—Love Under the Midnight Sun • Make Way for Lila 62

Husni, Kameran Said Effendi 59

Hussein, Waris Thank You All Very Much • A Touch of Love 69; Fun Loving • Quackser Fortune Has a Cousin in the Bronx 70; Melody • S.W.A.L.K. 71*; The Possession of Joel Delaney 71; Henry VIII and His Six Wives 72

Huster, Francis Charlie Spencer's Been Robbed • On A Volé Charlie Spencer 86

Huston, Danny Mr. North 88

Huston, Jimmy Death Driver 77; Buckstone County Prison • Seabo 78; Dark Sunday 78; Final Exam 81; The Sleuth Slayer 84; My Best Friend Is a Vampire 88

Huston, John The Maltese Falcon 41; Across the Pacific 42*; In This Our Life 42; Report from the Aleutians 43; The Battle of San Pietro • San Pietro 44; Let There Be Light 45; Key Largo 48; A Miracle Can Happen • On Our Merry Way 48*; The Treasure of the Sierra Madre 48; We Were

Strangers 49; The Asphalt Jungle 50; The African Queen 51; The Red Badge of Courage 51; Moulin Rouge 52; Beat the Devil 53; Moby Dick 56; Heaven Knows, Mr. Allison 57; The Barbarian and the Geisha 58; The Roots of Heaven 58; The Unforgiven 59; The Misfits 60; Freud • Freud—The Secret Passion • The Secret Passion 62; The List of Adrian Messenger 63; Night of the Iguana 64; La Bibbia • The Bible • The Bible...In the Beginning 65; Casino Royale 67*; Reflections in a Golden Eye 67; Sinful Davey 68; The Kremlin Letter 69; The Madwoman of Chaillot 69*; A Walk with Love and Death 69; Fat City 71; The Last Run 71*; The Life and Times of Judge Roy Bean 72; The Mackintosh Man 73*; The Man Who Would Be King 75; Independence 76; Wise Blood 79; Phobia 80; Escape to Victory • Victory 81; Annie 82; Under the Volcano 84; Prizzi's Honor 85; The Dead 87

Huszárik, Zoltán Sinbad • Sindbad • Szindbád 71

Hutchinson, Charles Hurricane Hutch in Many Adventures 24; On Probation 24; The Hidden Menace 25; Was It Bigamy? 25; Flying High 26; The Winning Wallop 26; Catch As Catch Can 27; The Down Grade 27; The Little Firebrand 27; When Danger Calls 27; Bitter Sweets 28; Out with the Tide 28; Women Men Marry 31; Gangsters of the Sea • Out of Singapore 32; A Private Scandal 32; Bachelor Mother 33; Found Alive 34; House of Danger 34; Circus Shadows 35; The Judgment Book 35; On Probation 35; Desert Guns 36; Night Cargo 36; Phantom Patrol 36; Riddle Ranch 36; Born to Fight 38; Topa Topa 38*; Children of the Wild • Killers of the Wild 40*

Hutchinson, James C. Red Blood and Blue 25

Hutchison, Charles *see Hutchinson, Charles*

Huth, Harold Dangerous Cargo • Hell's Cargo 39; Bulldog Sees It Through 40; East of Piccadilly • The Strangler 40; Adventure in Blackmail • Breach of Promise • Manhattan Madness 41*; Night Beat 47; Look Before You Love 48; My Sister and I 48; The Hostage 56

Hüttner, Ralf The Cripples Go Christmas • Das Mädchen mit den Feuerzeugen 88

Hutton, Brian G. Daffy • Fargo • The Rebellious One • The Wild Seed 64; The Pad (And How to Use It) 66; The Heroin Gang • Sol Madrid 67; Where Eagles Dare 68*; Kelly's Heroes • The Warriors 70; X, Y & Zee • Zee & Co. 71; Night Watch 73; The First Deadly Sin 80; High Road to China 82

Hutton, Clayton Her Cardboard Lover 29; Heavily Married 37; Intimate Relations 37

Hutton, Robert The Slime People 63

Huyck, Willard Dead People • Messiah of Evil • Return of the Living Dead •

Revenge of the Screaming Dead • The Second Coming 72; French Postcards 79; Best Defense 84; Howard, a New Breed of Hero • Howard the Duck 86

Hyams, Nessa Leader of the Band 87
Hyams, Peter Busting 73; Death of Her Innocence • Our Time 74; Fat Chance • Peeper 75; Capricorn One 77; Hanover Street 79; Outland 81; The Star Chamber 83; 2010 84; Running Scared 86; The Presidio 88; Narrow Margin 90
Hyeong-myeong, Kim see Kim, Hyeong-myeong
Hyland, Peggy With Father's Help 22
Hylkema, Hans Julius Geheim • Juliet's Secret 87
Hyman, Bernard Morals for Men 25
Hyslop, Andrew Maxwell World Without Walls: Beryl Markham's African Memoir 85
Hyuk-jin, Kwon see Kwon, Hyuk-jin
Ibáñez, John pseudonym for Jack Hill with Juan Ibáñez
Ibáñez, Juan La Cámara del Terror • The Fear Chamber 68*; House of Evil • Serenata Macabra 68*; La Isla de los Muertos • Island of the Snake People • The Isle of the Dead • Isle of the Snake People • The Living Death • La Muerte Viviente • The Snake People 68*; The Incredible Invasion • La Invasión Siniestra • Sinister Invasion 71*
Ibáñez Serrador, Narciso The Boarding School • The House That Screamed • La Residencia 69; Death Is Child's Play • Island of Death • Island of the Damned • ¿Quién Puede Matar a un Niño? • Who Can Kill a Child? • Who Would Kill a Child? • Would You Kill a Child? 75
Ichac, Marcel Karakoram 36; Missions de France 39; À l'Assaut des Aiguilles du Diable 42; Sondeurs d'Abîme 43; Tempête sur les Alpes 45; Skis de France 47; Padirac, Rivière de la Nuit 48; Himalaya 50; Groenland • Groenland, Terre des Glaces 51*; Annapurna • Victoire sur l'Annapurna 53; Nouveaux Horizons 53; Vie Pôle Nord 54; L'Aluminium 55; Tour du Monde Express 55; Les Étoiles de Midi 59; Le Conquérant de l'Inutile 67; Trente Ans de la Vie d'un Skieur 72
Ichaso, León El Super 79*; Crossover Dreams 85
Ichikawa, Jun Bu-Su 88
Ichikawa, Kon A Girl at Dojo Temple • Musume Dōjōji 46; 1001 Nights with Toho • A Thousand and One Nights • Tōhō Senichiya 47*; A Flower Blooms • Hana Hiraku 48; Sanbyaku-Rokujūgo Ya • 365 Nights 48; Design of a Human Being • Human Patterns • Ningen Moyō 49; Endless Passion • Hateshinaki Jōnetsu • Passion Without End • The Passion Without Limit 49; Akatsuki no Tsuiseki • Pursuit at Dawn 50; Ginza Sanshiro • Sanshiro at Ginza • Sanshiro of Ginza 50; Heat and Mud • The Hot Marshland • Netsudeichi 50; Bungawan Solo • River Solo Flows 51; Deadly Nightshade • Ieraishan • Nightshade Flower 51; Kekkon

Kōshinkyoku • Wedding March 51; Koibito • The Lover • The Sweetheart 51; Man Without a Country • The Man Without a Nationality • Mukōkūseki Mono • Mukōkūseki-Sha 51; Nusumareta Koi • Stolen Love 51; Ano Te Kono Te • This Way, That Way 52; Ashi ni Sawatta Onna • The Woman Who Touched Legs • The Woman Who Touched the Legs 52; Lucky-San • Mr. Lucky • Rakkii-San 52; Wakai Hito • The Young Generation • Young People 52; Aijin • The Lover • The Lovers • Two Lovers 53; Aoiro Kakumei • The Blue Revolution 53; Mr. Poo • Pū-San 53; Seishun Zenigata Heiji • The Youth of Heiji Zenigata 53; All of Myself • Watashi no Subete o 54; A Billionaire • Okuman Chōja 54; The Heart • Kokoro 54; Josei ni Kansuru Jūnishō • Twelve Chapters About Women • Twelve Chapters on Women • Twelve Stories About Women 54; Ghost Story of Youth • Seishun Kaidan • The Youth's Ghost Story 55; Biruma no Tategoto • The Burmese Harp • Harp of Burma 56; Bridge of Japan • Nihonbashi 56; Punishment Room • Shokei no Heya 56; Ana • The Hole • The Lady Has No Alibi • The Pit 57; The Crowded Streetcar • The Crowded Train • A Full-Up Train • Manin Densha 57; The Man in the North • Man of the North • The Men of Tohoku • Tōhoku no Zunmutachi 57; Conflagration • Enjō • Flame of Torment 58; Gennama to Bijo to San-Akunin • Money and Three Bad Men 58; Code of Women • Jokei • Jokyō • A Woman's Testament 59*; Earthly Rituals • Kankon Sōsai 59; Fires on the Plain • Nobi 59; Goodbye and Good Day • Goodbye, Good Day • Goodbye, Hello • Sayōnara, Konnichiwa 59; Kagi • The Key • Odd Obsession 59; Keisatsukan to Boroyuku-Dan • Police and Small Gangsters 59; Bonchi 60; Ginza no Mosa • A Ginza Veteran 60; Her Brother • Otōto • Younger Brother 60; The Apostasy • The Broken Commandment • Hakai • The Outcast • The Sin 61; Kuroi Jūnin no Onna • Ten Black Women • Ten Dark Women 61; Being Two Isn't Easy • I Am Two • Watashi wa Nisai 62; An Actor's Revenge • The Revenge of Ukeno-Jo • The Revenge of Yukinojo • Yūkinojō Henge 63; Alone on the Pacific • The Enemy the Sea • My Enemy the Sea • Taiheiyō Hitoribōchi 63; Dōkonji Monogatari • The Money Dance • Money Talks • Zeni no Odori 64; Tokyo Olympiad • Tōkyō Ōrimpikku 65; Topo Gigio e i Sei Ladri • Topo Gigio e la Guerra del Missile • Toppo Gigio and the Missile War • Toppo Jijo no Botan Sensō 67; Kyōtō • Seishun • Tournament • Youth 68; Japan and the Japanese • Nihon to Nihonjin 70; Ai Futatabi • Pourquoi • To Love Again 71; Olympic Visions • Visions of Eight 72*; Matatabi • The Wanderers 73; I Am a Cat • Wagahai wa Neko de Aru 75; Between Wife and Lady • Between Women and Wives • Tsuma to Onna no Aida 76*; The Inugami Family • Inugami-Ke no

Ichizoku • The Inugamis 76; Akuma no Temari-Uta • The Devil's Bouncing Ball Song • The Devil's Song of Ball • A Rhyme of Vengeance 77; The Devil's Island • Gokumonto • Hell's Gate Island • Island of Hell • Island of Horrors 77; Firebird • Hi no Tori • The Phoenix 78; Jōō Bachi • Queen Bee 78; Byōin-Zaka no Kubikukuri no Ie • House of Hanging • The House of the Hanging on Hospital Hill 79; Ancient City • Kōto • The Old Capitol • The Old City 80; Happiness • Kōfuku • Lonely Hearts 81; Fine Snow • The Makioka Sisters • Sasameyuki 83; Ōhan 84; Biruma no Tategoto • The Burmese Harp • The Harp of Burma 85; The Hall of the Crying Deer • Rokumeikan • Rokumeikan, High Society of Meiji 86; Actress • Eiga Joyū • Film Actress • Movie Actress 87; Princess from the Moon • Taketori Monogatari 87
Ichikawa, Yoshihiro The Ghost of Otamage-Ike • Kaibyō Otamage-Ike 60
Ichimura, Hirokazu Eikō e no Kurōhyō • Fight for the Glory 70; Hotsprings Holiday • Kigeki Dai Shōgeki • Onsen Gerira Dai Shōgeki 70
Icho, Arvo see Ikho, Arvo
I Colli, Ferrán Llagostera see Llagostera i Colli, Ferrán
Ida, Tan Tiger of the Sea 64; The House of Strange Loves • Onna Ukiyoburō 69
Idrizović, Mirza Azra 88
Iglesia, Eloy de la see De la Iglesia, Eloy
Iglesias, Antonio La Segua 85
Iglesias, Miguel see Iglesias Bonns, Miguel
Iglesias Bonns, Miguel Las Hijas del Cid • La Spada del Cid • The Sword of El Cid 62; Occhio per Occhio 67; Klima, Reina de las Amazonas 75; La Maldición de la Bestia • Night of the Howling Beast • The Werewolf and the Yeti 75
Ihnat, Steve Do Not Throw Cushions Into the Ring 70; The Honkers 71
Ikehiro, Kazuo Broken Swords • Hiken Yaburi 69; Make Up 85
Ikho, Arvo Keep Smiling, Baby • Naerata Ometi 86*; Games for Schoolchildren • Igry Dlja Detej Sko'nogo Vozrasta 87*; Nablyudatel 88
Ildari, Hassan Face of the Enemy 90
Iliu, Victor În Sat la Noi • Our Village 51*; Mitrea Cocor 52; The Mill of Luck and Plenty • Moara cu Noroc 56
Illes, Eugen Alraune 18
Ilyenko, Mikhail Every Hunter Wants to Know • Kazhdyy Okhotnik Zhelaet Znat 87
Ilyenko, Yuri A Fountain for the Thirsty • Rodnik dlia Zhazhdushchikh • A Spring for the Thirsty 65; Ivan Kupala's Eve 68; Byelaya Ptitsa s Tchornem Piatnom • The White Bird Marked with Black • A White Bird with Black Marking 70; To Dream and to Live 74; The Baked Potato Festival 77; Solomennie Kolokoka 88
Im, Kwon-taek Goodbye! Duman River 61; The Great Long For Husband 63; War

and Woman Teacher 66; Testimony 73; Weeds 73; Wangsibri Street 76; War! Nakdong River 76; The Family Tree Book 78; The Hidden Hero 79; Mandala 81; Angemaeul • Village in the Mist 82; Gilsodom 85; Surrogate Woman 86; Ticket 86; Adada 88; Come, Come, Come Upward 89; The General's Son 90

Image, Jean Johnny the Giant Killer 53*

Imai, Tadashi Numazu Heigakkō • The Numazu Military Academy 39; Our Instructor • Our Teacher • Waga Kyōkan • Warera ga Kyōkan 39; The General • Kakka • Your Highness 40; Kekkon no Seitai • Married Life • The Situation of Marriage 40; Onna no Machi • Women's Street • Women's Town 40; Tajinko Mura • Tajinko Village • The Village of Tajinko 40; Bōrō no Kesshitai • The Death Command of the Tower • The Suicide Troops of the Watch Tower 42; The Angry Sea • Cruel Sea • Ikari no Umi 44; Ai to Chikai • Love and Pledge 45; An Enemy of the People • Minshū no Teki • The People's Enemy 46; Jinsei Tombogaeri • Life Is Like a Somersault • Somersault of Life 46; Aoi Sammyaku • Blue Mountains 47; Chikagai Nijūyojikan • Twenty-Four Hours of a Secret Life • Twenty-Four Hours of the Underground Street 47*; Onna no Kao • A Woman's Face 49; Mata Au Hi Made • Until the Day We Meet Again • Until We Meet Again 50; And Yet We Live • Dōkkoi Ikiteru • Still We Live • We Are Living 51; Genbaku no Zu • Pictures of the Atom Bomb 51; Echo School • School of Echoes • Yamabiko Gakkō 52; The Girls of Okinawa • Himeyuri Lily Tower • Himeyuri no Tō • The Tower of Lilies • The Young Girls of Okinawa 53; Muddy Waters • Nigorie • Troubled Waters 53; Aisureba Kōsō • Because I Love • If You Love Me 54*; Here Is a Fountain • Here Is a Spring • Koko ni Izumi Ari 54; Yukikō 55; Darkness at Noon • Mahiru no Ankoku • Shadows in Sunlight 56; Junai Monogatari • Story of Pure Love 57; Kome • Men of the Rice Fields • Rice 57; The Adulteress • Night Drum • Yoru no Tsuzumi 58; Kiku and Isamu • Kiku to Isamu 58; The Cliff • Shiroi Gake • White Cliff 60; Are ga Minato no Hi Da • Pan Chopali • That Is the Port Light 61; Japanese Grandmothers • Nippon no Obāsan • The Old Women of Japan 62; Bushido • Bushido, Samurai Saga • Bushidō Zankoku Monogatari • Cruel Story of the Samurai's Way • The Oath of Obedience 63; Adauchi • Revenge 64; Death in the Snow • Echigo Tsutsuishi Oyashirazu • Oyashirazu in the Echigo Regime • A Story for Echigo 64; Satōgashi ga Kowareru Toki • When Sugar Cookies Are Broken • When the Cookie Crumbles 67; Fushin no Toki • Time of Losing Faith • The Time of Reckoning • When You Can't Believe Anyone 68; Bridge Across No River • Hashi no Nai Kawa • River Without a Bridge 69; En to Iu Onna • A Woman Named En 71; Aa Koe Naki

Tomo • Ah! My Friends Without Voice 72; Kaigun Tokubetsu Shōnen Hei • Special Boy-Soldiers of the Navy 72; Kobayashi Takiji • The Life of a Communist Writer • Takiji Kobayashi 74; Ani Imōto • His Younger Sister • Mon and Ino • Older Brother and Younger Sister 76; The Old Woman Ghost • Yoba 76; Himeyuri Lily Tower • Himeyuri no Tō 82

Imamura, Shohei Endless Desire • Hateshinaki Yokubō 58; Lights of Night • Nishi Ginza Ekimae • Nishi Ginza Station • Streets of Night 58; Nusumareta Yokubō • Stolen Desire 58; The Diary of Sueko • My Second Brother • Nianchan 59; Buta to Gunkan • The Dirty Girls • The Flesh Is Hot • Hogs and Warships • Pigs and Battleships • Pigs and Warships 61; The Insect • The Insect Woman • Nippon Konchūki 63; Akai Satsui • Intentions of Murder • Unholy Desire 64; The Amorists • Jinruigaku Nyūmon • The Pornographer • The Pornographers • The Pornographers: Introduction to Anthropology 66; A Man Vanishes • Ningen Jōhatsu 67; Deep Desire of Gods • Kamigami no Fukaki Yokubō • Kuragejima: Legends from a Southern Island • Kuragejima: Tales from a Southern Island • The Profound Desire of the Gods • A Profound Longing for the Gods 68; History of Postwar Japan As Told by a Bar Hostess • Nippon Sengoshi: Madamu Omboro no Seikatsu • Postwar Japanese History 70; Karayuki-San • Karayuki-San: The Making of a Prostitute 73; Fukushū Suruwa Wareni Ari • Vengeance Is Mine 79; Eijanaika • Why Not? 80; The Ballad of Narayama • Narayama Bushikō 83; Lord of the Brothels • The Pimp • Zegen 87; Black Rain • Kuroi Ame 88

Imberman, Shmuel I Don't Give a Damn • Lo Sam Zayin 87; Tel Aviv—Los Angeles 88

Imeson, A. B. Discipline 35*; The Strange Case of Mr. Todmorden 35*

Imhoof, Markus Fluchtgefahr 74; Tauwetter 78; Isewixer 79; The Boat Is Full • Das Boot Ist Voll 80; The Journey • Die Reise 86

Ina, Seichi Asahi wa Kagayaku • The Morning Sun Shines • The Rising Sun Is Shining • The Rising Sun Shines 29*

Inagaki, Hiroshi Peace on Earth • Tenka Taiheiki 28; The Wandering Gambler 28; Elegy of Hell 29; A Samurai's Career 29; The Image of a Mother 31; Ippon-Gatana Dohyōiri • A Sword and the Sumo Ring 31; Travels Under the Blue Sky 32; Yataro-Gasa • Yataro's Sedge Hat 32; Chuji Kunisada 33; Bad Luck 34; The White Hood 35; White Snows of Fuji 35; Journey of a Thousand and One Nights 36; Spirit of the Wilderness 37; A Great World Power Rising 38; Shadows of Darkness 38; Mazo 39; Miyamoto Musashi • Musashi Miyamoto • Samurai 40; Edo Saigo no Hi • The Last Days of Edo 41; Festival Across the Sea • Umi o Wataru Sairei 41; One-Eyed Dragon 42; The Life of Matsu the Untamed • Muhō Matsu no Isshō 43;

Signal Fires of Shanghai 44; The Last Abdication 45; Children Hand in Hand • Te o Tsunagu Kora 48; Forgotten Children • Wasurerareta Kora 49; Kojiro • Kojiro Sasaki • Sasaki Kojiro 51; Pirates 51; Sword for Hire 52; The Legend of Musashi • Master Swordsman • Miyamoto Musashi • Musashi Miyamoto • Samurai • Samurai I 54; Samurai II 54; The Lone Journey 55; Samurai III 55; Arashi • The Storm 56; A Geisha in the Old City 57; Secret Scrolls (Part One) • Yagyu Bugeichō • Yagyu Secret Scrolls 57; Muhō Matsu no Isshō • The Rickshaw Man 58; Ninjutsu • Secret Scrolls (Part Two) • Sōryū Hiken 58; Samurai Saga 59; The Country Doctor • Fundoshi Isha • Life of a Country Doctor • Life of the Country Doctor 60; Bandits on the Wind • Yatō Kaze no Naka o Hashiru 61; Daredevil in the Castle • Devil in the Castle • Ōsaka-Jō Monogatari • Ōsaka Monogatari • The Story of the Castle of Osaka 61; Gen to Fudōmyōō • The Youth and His Amulet 61; Chūshingura • Forty-Seven Samurai • The Loyal 47 Ronin 62; Doburōku no Tatsu • Tatsu 62; Hiken • Young Swordsman 63; Daitatsu-Maki • Whirlwind 64; Furin Kazan • Samurai Banners • Under the Banner of Samurai 64; Garakuta • The Rabble 64; Abare Goemon • Rise Against the Sword 66; Duel at Ganryu Island • Kettō Ganryū Jima • Samurai, Part Three 67; Ichijoji no Kettō • Samurai, Part Two • Zoku Miyamoto Musashi 67; Kojiro • Kojiro Sasaki • Sasaki Kojiro 67; The Ambush • Machibuse 70

Ince, John The Price of Victory 13; The Battle of Shiloh 14; A Cruel Revenge 14; The House of Fear 14; The Puritan 14; Road o' Strife 15*; Sealed Lips 15; The Urchin 15; The Crucial Test 16*; Her Maternal Right 16*; The Struggle 16; The Planter 17*; Secret Strings 18; Blackie's Redemption 19; Blind Man's Eyes 19; A Favor to a Friend 19; One-Thing-at-a-Time O'Day 19; Please Get Married 19; Should a Woman Tell? 19; Held in Trust 20; Old Lady 31 20; Someone in the House 20; Passion Fruit 21; The Love Trap 23; Cheap Kisses 24; The Girl of Gold 25; The Great Jewel Robbery 25; If Marriage Fails 25; Her Big Adventure 26; The Hour of Reckoning 27; Wages of Conscience 27; Black Feather 28

Ince, Ralph The Godmother 12; Mr. Fixer • Mr. Fixit 12; Bingle's Nightmare 13; The Call 13; Diana's Dress Reform 13; Fatty on the Job 13; Fatty's Affair of Honor 13; His Last Fight 13; His Second Wife 13; The Lost Millionaire 13; The Lucky Elopement 13; A Million Bid 13; Peggy's Burglar 13; A Prince of Evil 13; A Regiment of Two 13; The Right and the Wrong of It 13; The Treasure of Desert Isle 13; Why Am I Here? 13; The Wreck 13; Back to Broadway 14; Fatty's Sweetheart 14; The Girl from Prosperity 14; The Goddess 14; He Danced Himself to Death 14; He Never Knew 14; Lincoln the Lover 14; Midst Woodland

Shadows 14; The Painted World 14; Shadows of the Past 14; Two Women 14; Uncle Bill 14; Wife Wanted 14; The Awakening 15; Count 'Em 15; From Headquarters 15; His Phantom Sweetheart 15; The Juggernaut 15; The Ninety and Nine 15; The Sins of the Mothers 15; Some White Hope 15; The Sort-of-Girl Who Came from Heaven 15; The Combat 16; Conflict 16; The Destroyers 16; His Wife's Good Name 16; My Lady's Slipper 16; The Thorn and the Rose 16; The Argyle Case 17; The Co-Respondent 17; Today 17; The Battle Cry • Her Man 18; The Eleventh Commandment 18; Fields of Honor 18; Five Thousand an Hour 18; Our Mrs. McChesney 18; The Panther Woman 18; Tempered Steel 18; The Woman Eternal 18; From Headquarters 19; The Naked Truth • The Perfect Lover 19; Out Yonder 19; The Painted World 19; Sealed Hearts 19; Shadows of the Past 19; A Stitch in Time 19; Too Many Crooks 19; Two Women 19; Virtuous Men 19; The Wreck 19; His Wife's Money 20; The Land of Opportunity 20; The Law Bringers 20; Out of the Snows 20; Red Foam 20; After Midnight 21; The Highest Law 21; A Man's Home • A Man's House 21; Remorseless Love 21; Tropical Love 21; Wet Gold 21; Channing of the Northwest 22; Reckless Youth 22; The Referee 22; A Wide Open Town 22; Counterfeit Love 23*; Homeward Bound 23; The Moral Sinner 23; Success 23; The Chorus Lady 24; Dynamite Smith 24; The House of Youth 24; The Uninvited Guest 24; Alias Mary Flynn 25; Lady Robinhood 25; Playing with Souls 25; The Sea Wolf 25; Smooth As Satin 25; The Better Way 26; Bigger Than Barnum's 26; Breed of the Sea 26; The Lone Wolf Returns • The Return of the Lone Wolf 26; Home Struck 27; Moulders of Men 27; Not for Publication 27; Shanghaied 27; South Sea Love 27; Wandering Girls 27; Chicago After Midnight 28; Coney Island 28; Danger Street 28; Hit of the Show 28; The Singapore Mutiny • The Wreck of the Singapore 28; Hardboiled • A Real Girl 29; Hurricane 29; The Great Decision • Men of America 32; Lucky Devils 32; Flaming Gold 33; A Glimpse of Paradise 34; Murder at Monte Carlo 34; No Escape 34; What's in a Name? 34; Black Mask 35; Blue Smoke 35; Crime Unlimited 35; Gaol Break • Jail Break 35; Mr. What's-His-Name 35; Rolling Home 35; Fair Exchange 36; Hail and Farewell 36; It's You I Want 36; Jury's Evidence 36; Twelve Good Men 36; The Vulture 36; It's Not Cricket 37; The Man Who Made Diamonds 37; The Perfect Crime 37; Side Street Angel 37

Ince, T. H. *see* Ince, *Thomas*

Ince, Thomas Little Nell's Tobacco 10; The Aggressor 11*; Artful Kate 11; Behind the Stockade 11*; A Dog's Tale 11; The Dream 11*; The Fisher Maid 11; For Her Brother's Sake 11; Her Darkest Hour 11; The Hidden Trail 11; His Message 11; In Old Madrid 11; In the Sultan's Garden 11;

A Manly Man 11; The Message in the Bottle 11; The New Cook 11; The Prospector's Daughter 11; The Silver Dollar 11; Sisters 11; Sweet Memories 11; Their First Misunderstanding 11*; Across the Plains • War on the Plains 12; The Battle of the Red Men 12; Blazing the Trail 12; The Clod 12; The Colonel's Peril 12; The Colonel's Son 12; The Colonel's Ward 12; The Crisis 12; Custer's Last Fight • The Lieutenant's Last Fight 12; Custer's Last Raid 12; The Deserter 12; A Double Reward 12; For Freedom of Cuba 12; His Nemesis 12; The Indian Massacre 12; The Invaders 12*; The Law of the West 12; A Mexican Tragedy 12; The Mosaic Law 12; On the Firing Line 12; Renegade 12; Shadow of the Past 12; A Tale of the Foothills 12; When Lee Surrenders 12; The Winning of Wonega 12; With Lee in Virginia 12; The Ambassador's Envoy 13; The Battle of Gettysburg 13*; The Boomerang 13; Bread Cast Upon the Waters 13; Days of '49 13; The Drummer of the 8th 13; For the Cause 13; The Hateful God 13; The Paymaster's Son 13; The Pride of the South 13; A Romance of the Sea 13; The Seal of Silence 13; The Soldier's Honor 13; The Yellow Flame 13; The Golden Goose 14*; The Hour of Reckoning 14; The Last of the Line 14; Love's Sacrifice 14*; One of the Discard 14*; A Relic of Old Japan 14; The Typhoon 14*; The Wrath of the Gods • The Wrath of the Gods, or The Destruction of Sakura Jima 14*; The Alien 15; The Coward 15*; The Despoiler 15; The Devil 15*; The Sign of the Rose 15; Civilization 16*

Indovina, Franco Das Älteste Gewerbe der Welt • L'Amore Attraverso i Secoli • L'Amour à Travers les Âges • The Oldest Profession • Le Plus Vieux Métier du Monde 67*; Catch As Catch Can • Lo Scatenato • Tutti Frutti 67

Infascelli, Fiorella La Maschera • The Mask 88

Inghram, Frank L. Biff Bang Buddy 24

Ingleton, E. Magnus The Birth of Patriotism 17

Ingraham, Harrish Blood of His Fathers 17; The Eye of Envy 17; Child of M'sieu 19

Ingraham, Lloyd The Fox Woman 15; The Missing Links 15; The Sable Lorcha 15; American Aristocracy 16; Casey at the Bat 16; A Child of Paris • A Child of the Paris Streets 16; The Children Pay 16; Hoodoo Ann 16*; The Little Liar 16; Stranded 16; Charity Castle 17; Her Country's Call 17; Miss Jackie of the Army 17; Nina the Flower Girl 17; An Old-Fashioned Young Man 17; Peggy Leads the Way 17; Ann's Finish 18; The Eyes of Julia Deep 18; Impossible Susan 18; Jilted Janet 18; Molly Go Get 'Em 18; The Primitive Woman 18; Rosemary Climbs the Heights 18; A Square Deal 18; Wives and Other Wives 18; The Amazing Imposter 19; The House of Intrigue 19; The Intrusion of Isabel 19; Man's Desire 19; What's Your Husband Doing? 19; The Jailbird 20; Let's Be Fashionable 20; Mary's Ankle 20; Old Dad 20; Twin

Beds 20; The Girl in the Taxi 21; Keeping Up with Lizzie 21; Lavender and Old Lace 21; Marry the Poor Girl 21; My Lady Friends 21; At the Sign of Jack O'Lantern 22; The Danger Point 22; Second-Hand Rose 22; The Veiled Woman 22; Going Up 23; The Beauty Prize 24; The Lightning Rider 24; No More Women 24; The Wise Virgin 24; Midnight Molly 25; Soft Shoes 25; Hearts and Fists 26; The Nutcracker 26; Oh! What a Night 26; Arizona Nights 27; Don Mike 27; Jesse James 27; Silver Comes Through • Silver Comes Thru • Silver King Comes Thru 27; Kit Carson 28*; The Pioneer Scout 28*; The Sunset Legion 28*; Take the Heir 30

Ingram, Rex Black Orchids • The Fatal Orchids 16; Broken Fetters • A Human Pawn 16; Chalice of Sorrow • The Fatal Promise 16; The Great Problem • Truth 16; The Flower of Doom 17; The Little Terror 17; The Pulse of Life 17; The Reward of the Faithless • The Ruling Passion 17; His Robe of Honor 18; Humdrum Brown 18; The Day She Paid 19; The Beach Comber • Under Crimson Skies 20; Hearts Are Trumps 20; Shore Acres 20; The Conquering Power • Eugenia Grandet 21; The Four Horsemen of the Apocalypse 21; Turn to the Right 21; The Prisoner of Zenda 22; Trifling Women 22; Where the Pavement Ends 22; Scaramouche 23; The Arab • L'Arabe 24; Mare Nostrum • Our Sea 25; The Magician 26; The Garden of Allah 27; The Three Passions • Les Trois Passions 28; Baroud • Les Hommes Bleus • Love in Morocco • Passion in the Desert 31*

Ingrams, Jonathan Headline Hunters 68; The Boy with Two Heads 74; The Firefighters 75

Ingrams, Michael Palaces of a Queen 67

Ingria, Robert Michael One Minute to Midnight 88

Ingster, Boris Stranger on the Third Floor 40; Indian Summer • The Judge Steps Out 49; Southside 1-1000 50

Ingvordsen, J. Christian Firehouse 87; Mob War 89

Inkpen, Ron Remember Me This Way 74*

Innemann, S. Song of the Lark 37; Erste Liebe • First Love • Die Sextänerin 38

Inoue, Akira Hiroku Onna-Rō • Onna Niko • Women's Prison 67

Inoue, Umeji Higashikara Kita Otoko • The Man from the East 61; Hana to Namida to Honō • The Performers 70

Intrator, Jerald Pattern of Evil • Satan in High Heels 62

Ioganson, Edward A Son of the Land 31

Ionesco, Eugene Les Sept Péchés Capitaux • I Sette Peccati Capitali • Seven Capital Sins • The Seven Deadly Sins 61*

Ioseliani, Otar The Song About Flowers 59; April • Stories About Things 61; Cast-Iron 64; Falling Leaves • Listopad • When Leaves Fall 66; There Lived a Thrush • There Was a Singing Blackbird • Žil Zpívající Drozd 72; Pastoral • The Summer in the Country 76; Les Favoris de la Lune • Favourites of the Moon 84

Ippolito, Ciro Birds of Italy • Uccelli d'Italia 85

Ipsen, Bodil Afsporet 42*; En Herre i Kjole og Hvidt 42; Basættelse 44; The Red Earth • Red Meadows • De Røde Enge 45*; Café Paradis 50*; Det Sande Ansigt 51*

Iquino, Ignacio F. Juventud a la Intemperie • The Unsatisfied 61; Cinque Pistole del Texas 65; Oeste Nevada Joe 65; La Sfida degli Implacabili 65; Cinque Dollari per Ringo 66; Prima Ti Perdono...Poi T'Ammazzo 70; I Corni, Ti Scaveranno la Fossa 71; Sei Già Cadavere Amigo...Ti Cera Garringo 71; Dio in Cielo...Arizona in Terra 72; Domani Passo a Salutare la Tua Vedova...Parola di Epidemia 72

Ireland, John Hannah Lee • Outlaw Territory 53*; The Fast and the Furious 54*

Ireland, O'Dale Date Bait 60; High School Caesar 60

Iribe, Paul Changing Husbands 24*; Forty Winks 25*; The Night Club 25*

Irvin, John Gala Day 63; The Malakeen 64; Carousella 65; Pedro Cays 65; Bedtime 67; Mafia No! 67; The Dogs of War 80; Ghost Story 81; Champions 83; Turtle Diary 85; Raw Deal 86; Hamburger Hill 87; Next of Kin 89

Irving, David Goodbye Cruel World 82; Rumpelstiltskin 86; Sleeping Beauty 86; The Emperor's New Clothes 87; C.H.U.D. II – Bud the C.H.U.D. 89; Night of Cyclone 90

Irving, George The Fairy and the Waif 15*; Jaffery 15; John Glayde's Honor 15; The Ballet Girl 16; Then I'll Come Back to You 16; What Happened at 22 16; The Witching Hour 16; The Woman in 47 16; Daughter of Destiny 17; God's Man 17; Raffles the Amateur Cracksman 17; Back to the Woods 18; Her Boy 18; Hidden Fires 18; The Landloper 18; To Hell with the Kaiser 18; As a Man Thinks 19; Glorious Lady 19; The Silver King 19; The Volcano 19; The Blue Pearl 20; The Capitol 20; Children of Destiny 20; The Misleading Lady 20; Just Outside the Door 21; The Wakefield Case 21; Her Majesty 22; Lost in a Big City 23; Floodgates 24

Irving, Henry George see *Irving, George*

Irving, I. W. Sky's the Limit 25

Irving, Judy Dark Circle 82*

Irving, Stanley Forever Yours • Forget Me Not 34*

Irwin, Jack Lightnin' Smith Returns 31; White Renegade 31

Irwin, John A Piece of Cake 48; Badger's Green 49; Five O'Clock Finish 54; Black in the Face 55; Playground Express 55; That's an Order 55

Isaac, Alberto En Este Pueblo No Hay Ladrones 65; La Olimpiada en México • The Olympics in Mexico 68; Los Días de Amor 71; Las Visitaciones del Diablo 71; El Rincón de las Vírgines 72; Tivoli 74; Cuartelazo 76; Las Noches de Paloma 78; Tiempo de Lobos 82; Las Batallas en el

Desierto • Mariana, Mariana 87; Un Hogar Muy Decente 87

Isaac, James The Horror Show 89

Isaksen, Eva Brennende Blomster • Burning Flowers 86*

Isamendi, Antonio The Adventures of Scaramouche • Scaramouche 64; Colpo Grosso a Galata Bridge • Estamboul '65 • L'Homme d'Istambul • That Man in Istanbul 66; An einem Freitag in Las Vegas • Les Hommes de Las Vegas • Las Vegas 500 Millones • Las Vegas 500 Millions • Radiografia d'un Colpo d'Oro • They Came to Rob Las Vegas 68; Summertime Killer 73; El Aire de un Crimen 88

Isasi, Antonio see *Isamendi, Antonio*

Isasi-Isasmendi, Antonio see *Isamendi, Antonio*

Isasi-Isasmendi, J. Antonio see *Isamendi, Antonio*

Isasmendi, Antonio Isasi see *Isamendi, Antonio*

Isasmendi, J. Antonio Isasi see *Isamendi, Antonio*

Ishara, B. R. Sila 88

Ishihara, Shintaro Amore a Vent'Anni • L'Amour à Vingt Ans • Hatachi no Koi • Liebe mit Zwanzig • Love at Twenty • Miłość Dwudziestolatków 62*

Ishii, Chris Terror Faces Magoo 59

Ishii, Sogo Panic in High School 78; Crazy Thunder Road 80; Shuffle 81; Burst City 82; Revenge of Asia 83; The Black-Jet Family • The Crazy Family • Gyakufunsha Kazoku 84; Half-Man 86

Ishii, Teruo The Appearance of Supergiant • Supergiant 56; The Atomic Rulers of the World • Attack of the Flying Saucers • Supergiant II 57*; Attack from Space • Invaders from Space • Supergiant Against the Satellites 58; Gonin no Hanzaisha 59; Jōtai Sambashi • Red Piers 59; Criminal Women • The Joys of Torture • Tokugawa Onna Keibatsushi 68; Horror of a Deformed Man • The Horror of Malformed Men • Kyōfu Kikei Ningen 69; The Blind Woman's Curse • The Haunted Life of a Dragon-Tattooed Lass • Kaidan Noboriryū • Tattooed Swordswoman 70; The Friendly Killer • Noboriryū Tekkahada 70

Ishmukhamedov, Elior Rendezvous 63; Tenderness 66; In Love 69; Meetings and Partings 74; The Birds of Our Hopes 77; Farewell Green Summer • Proshal Zelen Leta 87

Ising, Rudolf Fiery Fireman 28*; High Up 28*; Homeless Homer 28*; Sinkin' in the Bathtub 30*; The Dish Ran Away with the Spoon 33; A Great Big Bunch of You 33; I Like Mountain Music 33; I Love a Parade 33; I Wish I Had Wings 33; One Step Ahead of My Shadow 33; The Organ Grinder 33; The Shanty Where Santy Claus Lives 33; Shuffle Off to Buffalo 33; Three's a Crowd 33; Wake Up the Gypsy in Me 33; We're in the Money 33; Young and Healthy 33; You're Too Careless with Your Kisses 33; The Bear That Couldn't Sleep 39; The Milky Way 40; Puss Gets

the Boot 40; The Bear and the Beavers 42

Isle, Evans Last Stop on the Night Train 76; The New House on the Left • Second House from the Left 78

Ismai, Osman Embun 56

Isomi, Tadahiko East China Sea • Higashi Shinakai 69

Israel, Neal Tunnelvision 76*; Americathon 79; Bachelor Party 84; Moving Violations 85

Israelson, Peter Side Out 90

Issar, Sudesh Bhai ka Dushman Bhai 88

Issermann, Aline L'Amant Magnifique • The Magnificent Lover 86

Itami, Ichizu see *Itami, Juzo*

Itami, Juzo The Funeral • Ōsōshiki 84; Dandelion • Tampopo 86; Marusa no Onna • A Taxing Woman 87; Marusa no Onna II • A Taxing Woman Returns • A Taxing Woman II • A Taxing Woman's Return 88; A-Ge-Man 90

Itami, Mansaku Kakita Akanishi 36; The New Earth 37*

Ito, Daisuke The Diary of a Drunkard • Shōchū Nikki 24; Jōgashima 24; Smoke 25; The First Shrine 26; Evil Spirit 27; Gerō • The Servant 27; Chuji Tabinikki • A Diary of Chuji's Travels 28; Ōka Seidan • Ooka's Trial 28; Man-Slashing Horse-Piercing Sword • Zanjin Zamba Ken 29; The Rise and Fall of Shinsengumi 30; Samurai Nippon 31; The First Year of the Meiji Era 32; Tange Sazen 33; The Loyal 47 Ronin 34; The Forty-Eighth Comrade 36; The Swordsman 38; The Eagle's Tail 41; Duel at Hannya-Zaka 43; International Smugglers 44; King of Chess 48; Les Misérables 50; Five Men of Edo 51; Lion's Dance 53; Samurai's Love 54; The Story of Shunkin 54; Gerō no Kubi • The Servant's Neck 55; The Life of a Woman in the Meiji Era 55; Flowers of Hell 57; The Gay Masquerade 58; The Woman and the Pirates 59; The Conspirator • Hangyakusha 61; Tokugawa Ieyasu 65; The Ambitious 70

Ito, Takashi see *Wakamatsu, Koji*

Ito, Toshiya Hana Ichimomme • Life with Senility 86

Itoh, Chisho Gondola 87

Itygilov, Alexander Obvinyaetsya Svadba • A Wedding Party Is Accused 87

Itzkovitch, Sam Monte Carlo or Bust! • Quei Temerari sulle Loro Pazze, Scatenate, Scalcinate Carriole • Those Daring Young Men in Their Jaunty Jalopies 68*

Ivaldi, Mauro Emmanuell's Silver Tongue 81*

Ivanov, Alexander Moon on the Left • The Moon on Your Left 28; The Fiery Transport • Transport of Fire 29; Three Soldiers 32; The Wedding of Ian Knuck 35; Soviet Border 38; The Passage 40; Submarine T-9 43; The Road Home • The Sons 46; The Star 53; Four Soldiers from Stalingrad 57; If a Comrade Calls 63

Ivanov, Boris The Law of Life 40*; A Fellow from Our Town • A Lad from Our Town 42*; Wait for Me! 43*; Song and Dance Over the Vistula 56*

Ivanov, Victor Chasing Two Hares • A

Kiev Comedy • Za Dvunmya Zaytsami
63

Ivanov-Barkov, Yevgeni The Deluge
25*; Flood • Mabul 27; Judas 30; Under
Sunny Skies 50

Ivanov-Gai, Alexander Tsar Ivan Vasilyevich Grozny 15; He Who Gets Slapped
16*

Ivanov-Vano, Ivan Senka the African
27; The Czar Durandai 34; The Three
Musketeers 38; The Little Humpbacked
Horse • The Magic Horse 47; The Snow
Maiden 52; The Brave Hare 55; The Left
Hander 64; The Mechanical Flea 64; Go to
Nowhere 66; Legend of a Cruel Giant 68;
Seasons 70; Battle Under the Walls of Ker-
chenetz 71; The Humpbacked Horse •
Magic Pony 76

Ivanovsky, Alexander I Shall Not Yield
18; Three Portraits 19; Khveska 20; The
Actress 23; Palace and Fortress 24; Stepan
Khalturin 25; Decembrists 27; Asia 28;
Caucasian Prisoner 30; Dom Zhdanosti •
House of Greed 34; Dubrovsky 36; The
Enemies 38; A Musical Story 40*; Spring
Song 42; Sylva 45; Russian Ballerina 47;
Concert of Stars • Song and Dance Concert
52*; Tiger Girl 55*

Ivchenko, Viktor Nazar Stodolya 54*;
Lesnaya Pesnya • Song of the Forest 63

Iveberg, Hans Enkel Resa 88

Ivens, Joris De Brandende Straal • Flam-
ing Arrow • The Shining Ray • De Wig-
wam • The Wigwam 11; Filmstudy, Zeedijk
• Zeedijk Film Study • Zeedijk-Filmstudie
27; Arm Drenthe • Poor Drenthe 28; La
Bar de Juffrouw Heyens 28; Branding •
The Breakers 28*; The Bridge • De Brug
28; Caissounbouw Rotterdam 28; Études
de Mouvements • Studies in Movement 28;
Heien 28; Nieuwe Architectuur 28; Zuid
Limburg 28; Congres der Vakvereinigingen
• NVV Congres 29; 1-Film • 1K-Film 29;
Rain • Regen 29*; Schaatsenrijden • Skat-
ers • Skating 29; We Are Building • Wij
Bouwen 29; Day of Youth • Jeugddag 30;
Demonstratie van Proletarische Solidariteit
• Demonstration of Proletarian Solidarity
30; Filmnotities uit de Sovjet-Unie • News
from the Soviet Union 30; Timber In-
dustry • Timmerfabriek 30; The Tribune
Film: Break and Build • De Tribune Film:
Breken en Bouwen 30; Zuiderzee • Zuy-
derzee 30; Creosoot • Creosote 31; Indus-
trial Symphony • Philips-Radio • Sym-
phonie Industrielle • Symphonie van den
Arbeid 31; Komsomol • Pesn o Gero-
jach • Pesn o Geroyazh • Song of Heroes
• Youth Speaks 32; Borinage • Misère au
Borinage 33*; New Earth • Nieuwe Gronden 33; The Spanish Earth 37; China's 400
Million • The 400 Million 38*; New Fron-
tiers 40; The Power and the Land 40; Bip
Goes to Town 41; Notre Front Russe • Our
Russian Front 41*; Worst of Farm Disasters
41; Action Stations! • Alarme! • Branle-Bas
de Combat • Corvette Port Arthur 42;
Alone 42; Oil for Aladdin's Lamp 42;
Know Your Enemy: Japan 45*; Indonesia
Calling 46; The First Years • Pierwsze Lata

47; Peace Conquers the World • Peace
Will Win • Pokój Zwycieży Świat 50*;
Freundschaft Siegt • Friendship Triumphs
• My za Mir • Naprzód Młodziezy Świata •
We Are All for Peace • We Are for Peace •
World Festival of Song and Dance 51*;
Friedensfahrt 1952 • Friendship Tour 1952
• Peace Tour 1952 • Wyścig Pokoju Wars-
zawa-Berlina-Praga 52; Lied der Ströme •
Song of the Rivers 54; Die Abenteuer des
Till Eulenspiegel • The Adventures of Till
Eulenspiegel • Les Aventures de Till L'Es-
piègle • The Bold Adventure • Till Eulen-
spiegel 56*; Before Spring • Early Spring •
Letters from China • Lettres de Chine 57;
La Seine à Rencontre Paris • The Seine
Meets Paris 57; L'Italia Non È un Paese
Povere • Italy Is Not a Poor Country 58;
Six Cents Million Avec Vous • 600 Million
People Are With You • 600 Million With
You • The War of 600 Million People 58;
Carnet de Viaje • Travel Notebook 60; De-
main à Nanguila • Nanguila Tomorrow 60;
An Armed Nation • An Armed People •
Cuba, Pueblo Armado • Pueblo Armado •
Pueblo en Armas 61; A Valparaíso • Val-
paraíso 62; El Circo Más Pequeño del
Mundo • The Little Circus • Le Petit
Chapiteau 62; Le Train de la Victoire • El
Tren de la Victoria • The Victory Train 64;
Le Ciel, la Terre • The Sky, the Earth 65;
Le Mistral • Pour le Mistral 65; The
Threatening Sky 65; Viêt-nam! 65; Far
from Vietnam • Loin du Viêt-nam 66*;
The Flying Dutchman • Rotterdam-
Europoort 66; Aggrippés à la Terre 68*;
Déterminés à Vaincre 68*; Le Dix-
Septième Parallèle • Le Dix-Septième
Parallèle: Le Viêt-nam en Guerre • The
Seventeenth Parallel • Seventeenth Paral-
lel: Vietnam in War 68*; La Guerre Popu-
laire au Laos 68*; Meeting with President
Ho Chi Minh • Rencontre avec le Président
Ho Chi Minh 68*; The People and Their
Guns • Le Peuple et Ses Fusils 68*; L'Ar-
mée Populaire Arme le Peuple 69*; Le
Peuple Est Invincible 69*; Le Peuple Ne
Peut Rien Sans Ses Fusils 69*; Le Peuple
Peut Tout 69*; Qui Commande aux Fusils
69*; Comment Yukong Déplaça les Mon-
tagnes • How Yukong Moved the Moun-
tains 76*; Les Kazaks—Minorité Nationale
—Sinkiang 77*; Les Ouigours—Minorité
Nationale—Sinkiang 77*; Une Histoire de
Vent 88*

Ivers, Julia The Majesty of the Law 15;
A Son of Erin 16; The White Flower 23

Ivonin, A. Tsar Nikolai II 17*

Ivory, James Four in the Morning 53;
Venice: Theme and Variations 57; The
Sword and the Flute 59; Gharbar • The
Householder 63; The Delhi Way 64;
Shakespeare Wallah 65; The Guru 68;
Bombay Talkie 70; Adventures of a Brown
Man in Search of Civilization 71; Mahatma
and the Mad Boy 72*; Savages 72; Helen
—Queen of the Nautch Girls 73; The
Wild Party 74; Autobiography of a Prin-
cess 75; Sweet Sounds 76; Roseland 77;
Hullabaloo Over Georgie and Bonnie's Pic-

tures 78; The Europeans 79; Jane Austen
in Manhattan 80; Quartet 81; The Courtesans of Bombay 82*; Heat and Dust 82;
The Bostonians 84; A Room with a View
85; Maurice 87; Slaves of New York 89;
Mr. & Mrs. Bridge 90

Iwauchi, Katsumi Let's Go, Wakadaisho! • Let's Go, Young Guy! 67; The
Night of the Seagull • Suna no Kaori 70

Iwerks, Ubbe Alice's Wonderland 23*;
Alice and the Dog Catcher 24*; Alice and
the Three Bears 24*; Alice Cans the Can-
nibals 24*; Alice Gets in Dutch 24*; Alice
Hunting in Africa 24*; Alice Plays the
Piper • Alice the Piper 24*; Alice the
Peacemaker 24*; Alice the Toreador 24*;
Alice's Day at the Sea 24*; Alice's Fishy
Story 24*; Alice's Spooky Adventure 24*;
Alice Chops the Suey 25*; Alice Gets
Stung 25*; Alice in the Jungle 25*; Alice
Is Stage Struck 25*; Alice Loses Out 25*;
Alice on the Farm 25*; Alice Picks the
Champ 25*; Alice Plays Cupid 25*; Alice
Rattled by Rats 25*; Alice Solves the Puz-
zle 25*; Alice the Jail Bird 25*; Alice
Wins the Derby 25*; Alice's Balloon Race
25*; Alice's Eggplant 25*; Alice's Little
Parade 25*; Alice's Mysterious Mystery
25*; Alice's Ornery Orphan 25*; Alice's
Tin Pony 25*; Alice Charms the Fish 26*;
Alice Cuts the Ice 26*; Alice Helps the
Romance 26*; Alice in Slumberland 26*;
Alice in the Wooly West 26*; Alice the
Fire Fighter 26*; Alice the Lumberjack
26*; Alice's Brown Derby 26*; Alice's
Monkey Business 26*; Alice's Spanish
Guitar 26*; Alice at the Carnival 27*;
Alice at the Rodeo • Alice's Rodeo 27*;
Alice Foils the Pirates 27*; Alice in the
Alps 27*; Alice in the Big League 27*;
Alice in the Klondike 27*; Alice the Beach
Nut 27*; Alice the Collegiate 27*; Alice
the Golf Bug 27*; Alice the Whaler 27*;
Alice's Auto Race 27*; Alice's Channel
Swim 27*; Alice's Circus Daze 27*; Alice's
Knaughty Knight 27*; Alice's Medicine
Show 27*; Alice's Picnic 27*; Alice's Three
Bad Eggs 27*; The Barn Dance 28*; The
Gallopin' Gaucho 28*; Plane Crazy 28*;
Steamboat Willie 28*; Autumn 29; The
Barnyard Battle 29*; The Cat's Away •
When the Cat's Away 29*; El Terrible
Toreador 29*; The Haunted House 29*;
Hell's Bells 29; The Jazz Fool 29*; Jungle
Rhythm 29*; The Karnival Kid 29*;
Mickey's Choo Choo 29*; Mickey's Follies
29*; The Opry House 29*; The Plow Boy
29*; The Skeleton Dance 29*; Springtime
29; Summer 29; Arctic Antics 30; The
Cuckoo Murder Case 30; Fiddlesticks 30;
Flying Fists 30; Little Orphan 30; Puddle
Pranks 30; The Village Barber 30; Africa
Squeaks 31; Jail Birds 31; Laughing Gas 31;
Movie Mad 31; The New Car 31; Ragtime
Romeo 31; The Soup Song 31; Spooks 31;
The Village Smithie 31; The Village Spe-
cialist 31; Bully 32; Circus 32; Fire! Fire!
32; Funny Face 32; Goal Rush 32; The
Milkman 32; The Music Lesson 32; Nurse
Maid 32; The Office Boy 32; Phoney

Express 32; Puppy Love 32; Room Runners 32; School Days 32; Stormy Seas 32; What a Life! 32; Bulloney 33; Chinaman's Chance 33; Cuckoo the Magician 33; Davy Jones 33; Flip's Lunch Room 33; Jack and the Beanstalk 33; Pale-Face 33; Play Ball 33; Soda Squirt 33; Spite Fright 33; Stratos-Fear 33; Techno-Cracked 33; Aladdin and the Wonderful Lamp 34; The Brave Tin Soldier 34; Cave Man 34; Don Quixote 34; Good Scout 34; The Headless Horseman 34; Hell's Fire 34; Insultin' the Sultan 34; Jack Frost 34; Jungle Jitters 34; The Little Red Hen 34; Puss 'n Boots 34; The Queen of Hearts 34; Rasslin' Round 34; Reducing Creme 34; Robin Hood, Jr. 34; The Valiant Tailor 34; Viva Willie 34; Balloon Land 35; Bremen Town Musicians 35; Humpty Dumpty 35; Little Black Sambo 35; Mary's Little Lamb 35; Old Mother Hubbard 35; Simple Simon 35; Sinbad the Sailor 35; Summertime 35; The Three Bears 35; Ali Baba 36; Dick Whittington's Cat 36; Happy Days 36; Little Boy Blue 36; Tom Thumb 36; The Foxy Pup 37; Merry Mannequins 37; Porky and Gabby 37; Porky's Super Service 37; Skeleton Frolics 37; The Frog Pond 38; Horses on the Merry-Go-Round 38; Midnight Frolics 38; Showtime 38; Crop Chasers 39; The Gorilla Hunt 39; Nell's Yells 39; Blackboard Revue 40; The Egg Hunt 40; Wise Owl 40; Ye Olde Swap Shop 40

Izmailov, Rasim I Loved You More Than Life • Ya Lyubil Vac Bolshe Zhizni 87

Izzard, Bryan Holiday on the Buses 73

Jabbour, Soubeil Feel My Love • Two Faces of Love 78

Jabor, Arnaldo All Nudity Shall Be Punished • Toda Nudez Será Castigada 73; I Love You 81; Eu Sei Que Vou Te Amar • Love Me Forever or Never 86

Jaccard, Jacques The Diamond from the Sky 15*; The Adventures of Peg o' the Ring 16*; A Knight of the Range 16; The Great Air Robbery 19; Desert Love 20; Honor Bound 20; The Terror 20; Under Northern Lights 20; 'If Only' Jim 21; Riding with Death 21; The Great Alone 22*; California in '49 24; His Majesty the Outlaw 24; Ridin' Mad 24; Unseen Hands 24; Sand Blind 25; Vic Dyson Pays 25; Desert Greed 26; The Cheyenne Kid 30; Señor Jim 36; Phantom of Santa Fe 37

Jack, Del A Session with the Committee 68

Jackman, Fred White Eagle 21*; The Call of the Wild 23; The King of the Wild Horses 24; Black Cyclone 25; The Devil Horse 26; No Man's Land • No Man's Law 27

Jacks, Robert L. Man in the Attic 53*

Jackson, Brian Yesterday 74

Jackson, David E. Mystery Mansion 84

Jackson, Donald G. The Demon Lover 76*; I Like to Hunt People 85; Rollerblade 85; Hell Comes to Frogtown 87*; Rollerblade Warriors 88

Jackson, Douglas Whispers 90

Jackson, Frederick The Perfect Lady 31*

Jackson, Harry York State Folks 15

Jackson, Horace Tough 74; Joey 77

Jackson, Larry Cottonpickin' Chickenpickers 67; The Road Hustlers 68; Bugs Bunny, Superstar 75

Jackson, Lewis Christmas Evil • Terror in Toyland • You Better Watch Out 80

Jackson, Mick Threads 84; Chattahoochee 90

Jackson, Mike see Olsson, Mats

Jackson, Pat Book Bargain 35*; Big Money 36*; Men in Danger 37; Happy in the Morning 38*; A City Prepares • The First Days 39*; Health in War 40; Welfare of the Workers 40*; Ferry Pilot 41; Builders 42; The Raider • Western Approaches 44; Patent Ductus Arteriosus 47; Shadow on the Wall 49; Encore 51*; White Corridors 51; Something Money Can't Buy 52; The Feminine Touch • The Gentle Touch 56; The Birthday Present 57; Our Virgin Island • Virgin Island 58; Snowball 60; No Place Like Homicide! • What a Carve Up! 61; Don't Talk to Strange Men 62; Seven Keys 62; Dead End Creek 64; Seventy Deadly Pills 64; On the Run 69

Jackson, Peter Bad Taste 88

Jackson, Richard Our Man in Jamaica 65; The Big Bust-Out 73

Jackson, Travis The Mountain 35

Jackson, Wilfred Midnight in a Toy Shop • Midnite in a Toy Shop 30; The Busy Beavers 31; The Castaway 31; The Cat's Nightmare • The Cat's Out 31; The China Plate 31; The Clock Store • In a Clock Store 31; Egyptian Melodies 31; The Fox Hunt 31; The Spider and the Fly 31; The Ugly Duckling 31; Barnyard Olympics 32; The Bird Store 32; The Grocery Boy 32; Mickey in Arabia 32; Mickey's Revue 32; Musical Farmer 32; Snow White and the Seven Dwarfs 37*; Saludos Amigos 43*; Song of the South 46*; Melody Time 48*; Cinderella 50*; Alice in Wonderland 51*; Peter Pan 53*; Lady and the Tramp 55*

Jacob, Dennis Lady of the Shadows • The Terror 62*

Jacobovici, Simcha Falasha: Exile of the Black Jews 83

Jacobs, Irving see Amendola, Mario

Jacobs, Jim AKA Cassius Clay 70

Jacobs, Raymond The Minx 69

Jacobs, Werner Guitars of Love 54; The Beggar Student 58; Heidi 65

Jacobsen, Johan Mens Sagføreren Sover • While the Attorney Is Asleep 45; The Invisible Army 50; En Fremmed Banker på • A Stranger Knocks 63

Jacobsen, Søren Kragh see Kragh-Jacobsen, Søren

Jacobson, Arthur Home on the Range 35

Jacobson, Steven Teammates 78

Jacoby, Georg Romance of a Russian Ballerina 13*; The Last Payment 21; Vendetta 21; The Little Napoleon 23; The Fake 27; The Physician 28; Geld auf der Strasse • Money on the Street 30; Die Blumenfrau von Lindenau • The Flower Woman of Lindenau • Storm in a Water Glass • Sturm im Wasserglas 31; Die Lindenwirtin vom Rhein 31; Mother Love 31; Hurra! Ein Junge! 32; Pension Schöller 32; Kadetten 33; Ja, Treu Ist die Soldatenliebe 34; The Last Waltz • Der Letzte Walzer 34; Liebe in Uniform 34; Melodie der Liebe 34; Csárdásfürstin 35; Ehestreik 35; Geschichten aus dem Wienerwald • Tales from the Vienna Woods 35; The Beggar Student • Der Bettelstudent 36; Heisses Blut 36; Ist Mein Mann Nicht Fabelhaft? 36; Madonna, Wo Bist Du? 36; Besuch am Abend 37; The Big Bluff • Der Grosse Bluff 37; Drama on the Threshing Floor 37; Zwei im Sonnenschein 37; A Devil of a Fellow • Ein Teufelskerl 38; Gasparone 38; Husaren Heraus 38; Eine Nacht im Mai • A Night in May 38; Fall Maneuvers • Herbst-Manöver 39; Marika 53

Jacoby, Irving The Lonely Night 54; Skyscraper 58*; Snow Treasure 68

Jacoby, Joseph Shame, Shame, Everybody Knows Her Name 69; Hurry Up or I'll Be 30 73; The Great Bank Hoax • The Great Georgia Bank Hoax • Shenanigans 77

Jacopetti, Gualtiero A Dog's Life • Mondo Cane 61; La Donna del Mondo • Women of the World 62*; Crazy World • Insane World • Mondo Cane n.2 • Mondo Insanity • Mondo Pazzo 63*; Africa Addio • Africa, Blood and Guts 65*; Farewell, Uncle Tom • Zio Tom 72*

Jacot, Michael The Last Act of Martin Weston 70

Jacoves, Felix Embraceable You 48; Homicide 49

Jacques, André Noah's Ark 50

Jacques, Christian see Christian-Jaque

Jacques, Henri Adorables Canailles • Michelle • Sexy Gang 67

Jacquot, Benoît Corps et Biens • Lost with All Hands 86; The Beggars • Les Mendiants 87

Jaeckin, Just Emmanuelle 74; The Story of O 75; Collections Privées 79*; The French Woman • Madame Claude 79; Girls 80; The Last Romantic Lover 80; Lady Chatterley's Lover 81; Gwendoline • The Perils of Gwendoline • The Perils of Gwendoline in the Land of the Yik Yak 84

Jaenzon, Julius Opium Den 11; Two Swedish Immigrants in America 11; Agaton and Fina 12; Condemned by Society 12; The Vagabond's Galoshes 12*; The Downey Girl 20*; Ulla My Ulla 30

Jaerrel, Stig see Järrel, Stig

Jafelice, Raymond The Care Bears Adventure in Wonderland! 87

Jaffe, Patricia Lewis Who Does She Think She Is? 74*

Jaffe, Stanley Without a Trace 83

Jaffe, Steven Charles Scarab 82

Jaglom, Henry A Safe Place 71; Tracks 76; Sitting Ducks 79; National Lampoon Goes to the Movies • National Lampoon's Movie Madness 81*; Can She Bake a Cherry Pie? 83; Always 85; Is It You? •

Someone to Love 86; New Year's Day 88; Eating 90

Jahn, Hartmut Transit Dreams • Transitträume 86*

Jaibi, Fadhel A'rab 88*

Jakubisko, Juraj The Deserter and the Nomads • Il Desertore e i Nomadi • Zbehovia a Poutníci 68; Frau Hölle 85; Perinbaba 85; Teta—Behavy Max a Strašidla 88

Jakubisko, Juro *see Jakubisko, Juraj*

Jakubowska, Wanda The Awakening • Probuzeni • Przebudzenie 34*; Forward, Co-Operation • Na Start 35*; Nad Niemnem • On the Banks of the Niemen • On the Niemen River 39*; Budujemy Nowe Wsie 46; The Last Stage • The Last Stop • Ostatni Etap 47; Soldier of Victory • Żolnierz Zwyciestwa 53; An Atlantic Story • Opowieść Atlantycka 54; Farewell to the Devil • Pożegnanie z Diabłem 56; King Matthew I • Król Maciuś Pierwszy • Król Maciuś I 57; A Contemporary Story • Historia Współczesna • It Happened Yesterday 60; Encounters in the Dark • Spotkanie w Mroku 60; The End of Our World • Koniec Naszego Czasu • Koniec Naszego Świata 64; Goraca Linia • The Hot Line 65; 150 na Godzine 71; Biały Mazur 73; Ludwik Waryński 78

Jallaud, Pierre Le Temps d'un Instant 85

Jamain, Patrick Honeymoon • Lune de Miel 85

Jamal, Ahmed A. Majdhar 84

James, Alan *see Neitz, Alvin J.*

James, Henry C. Swiss Honeymoon 47*

James, J. Frank The Sweet Creek County War 79

James, Rian Best of Enemies 33

James, Wharton The Call from the Wild 21

Jameson, Jerry Brute Corps 71; The Dirt Gang 72; Bat People • It Lives by Night 74; Airport '77 77; Raise the Titanic! 80; Starflight One 82

Jan, Tomáš *see Forman, Miloš*

Janakiram Antima Ghatta 88

Jancsó, Miklós Kezünkbe Vettük a Béke Ügyét • We Took Over the Cause of Peace 50*; A Szovjet Mezőgazdasági Küldöttségek Tanításai • The Teachings of a Soviet Agricultural Delegation 51*; The Eighth Free Mayday • Ezerkilencszázötvenkettő • 1952 Május 1 a 8 • Május 1 • A Nyolcadik Szabad Május 1 • A 8. Szabad Május 1 52; Arat az Oroshází Dózsa • Harvest at the Oroshaza Collective Dózsa 53; Before Election • Választás Előtt 53; Collective Ways • Közös Úton • On a Common Path • Ordinary Ways 53*; Along the Galga River • At the River Galga • Galga Mentén 54; Autumn in Badacsony • Ősz Badacsonyban 54; Comrades! Don't Put Up with It! • Emberek! Ne Engedjétek! 54*; Éltető Tisza-Víz • The Health-Giving Waters of Tisza • Life-Bringing Water 54; Egy Kiállítás Képei • Pictures at an Exhibition 54; An Afternoon in the Village • Egy Délután Koppánymonostorban • One Afternoon in Koppánymonostor 55; Angyalföldi Fiatalok • Children of Angyalföld • The Youth of

The Land of Angels 55; Emlékezz, Ifjúság! • Young People, Remember! 55; Varsói Világifjúsági Találkozó I-III • A Varsói Vit • Warsaw World Youth Meeting I-III • World Youth Festival in Warsaw 55; Móricz Zsigmond • Zsigmond Móricz 1879-1942 56; Colorful China • Colors of China • Színfoltok Kínából 57; Dél Kína Tájain • In the South China Countryside • The Landscapes of Southern China 57; In the Outskirts of the City • On the Outskirts of Town • A Város Peremén 57; Kína Vendégei Voltunk • Our Visit to China • We Have Been the Guests of China 57; Palaces of Peking • Peking Palotái 57; The Bells Have Gone to Rome • A Harangok Rómába Mentek 58; Derkovitz Gyula 1894-1934 58; Halhatatlanság • Immortality 59; Isotopes in Medical Science • Izotópok a Gyógyászatban 59; The Art of Revival • The Art of Salesmanship • Az Eladás Művészete 60*; Construction Design • Szerkezettervezés 60; Három Csillag • Three Stars 60*; Az Idő Kereke • The Wheels of Time 60; Alkonyok és Hajnalok • Dusks and Dawns • Twilights and Dawns 61; Indian Adventure • Indian Story • Indiántörténet 61; Cantata • Oldás és Kötés 62; Hej, Te Eleven Fa... • Living Tree... • An Old Folk Song • An Old Labor Song 63; Így Jöttem • My Way Home 64; The Hopeless Ones • Nehézéletüek • Poor Outlaws • The Round-Up • Szegénylegények • Szegénylegények Nehézéletüek 65; Jelenlét • Presence 65; Close-Up: The Blood • Közelről: A Vér 66; Csend és Kiáltás • Silence and Cry 67; Csillagosok, Katonák • The Red and the White • Zvyozdy i Soldaty 67; The Confrontation • Fényes Szelek • Sparkling Winds 68; Red May • Vörös Május 68; Sirocco d'Hiver • Sirokkó • Téli Sirokkó • Téli Sirokkó Lék • Winter Sirocco • Winter Wind 69; Agnus Dei • Égi Bárány 70; Füst • Smoke 70; The Pacifist • La Pacifista 70; Il Giovane Attila 71; La Tecnica e il Rito 71; Még Kér a Nép • The People Still Ask • Red Psalm • Red Song 72; Roma Rivuole Cesare • Rome Wants Another Caesar 73; Electra • Electra, My Love • Elektreia • Szerelmem, Elektra 74; Private Vices and Public Virtues • Private Vices, Public Virtue • Vices and Pleasures • Vizi Privati, Pubbliche Virtù 76; Masterwork 77; Életünket és Vérünket • Életünket és Vérünket, Magyar Rapszódia 1 • Hungarian Rhapsody 78; Allegro Barbaro • Allegro Barbaro, Magyar Rapszódia 2 79; Boccaccio in Hungary • Il Cuore del Tiranno • Heart of a Tyrant • The Tyrant's Heart • The Tyrant's Heart, or Boccaccio in Hungary • A Zsarnok Szíve avagy Boccaccio Magyarszágon 81; Omega, Omega 82; Muzsika 84; Budapest 85; L'Aube • The Dawn 86; Season of Monsters • Szörnyek Évadja 87; Jézus Krisztus Horoszkópja 89

Jang, Yeong-il Waebulleo 86

Janigro, Angilola De Deur van het Huis 85*

Janis, Nikolas Resting Rough 79

Jankel, Annabel D.O.A. 88*

Jankovic, Stole Hell River 77

Janneau, Daniel Le Débutant 86

Janos, Victor The Fun House • Last House on Dead End Street 77

Jansen, Viktor The Love Commandment 28; Thou Shalt Not Steal 29; Hungarian Nights 30; Der Bettelstudent 33; Die Frau von Der Man Spricht 33; Holzapfel Weiss Alles 33; Das Blaue vom Himmel 34; Es War Einmal ein Walzer 34; Lügen auf Rügen 34; Die Grosse Chance 35; Der Page vom Dalmasse-Hotel 35; Eine Frau Die Weiss Was Sie Will 36; Die Stimme der Liebe 36; Hilde Petersen, Postlagernd 37; Rendezvous in Wien 38; She and the Three • Sie und die Drei 38; Die Blonde Carmen 39; Über Alles die Treue 39

Janssen, Walter Rosen aus dem Süden • Roses from the South 35; Alle Tage Ist Kein Sonntag 36; Schön Ist Es Verliebt zu Sein 36; Leidenschaft • Passion 40; Hansel and Gretel • Hansel und Gretel 65

Jansz, Hereward Farewell to Childhood 50*

Janzack, Andy Terror in the Jungle 68*

Japrisot, Sebastien Juillet en Septembre 88

Jaque, Christian *see Christian-Jaque*

Jarabek, Julius Žaby a Ine Ryby 86

Jarman, Derek Broken English 72; Sebastiane 76*; Jubilee 78*; The Tempest 79; In the Shadow of the Sun 81; T.G.—Psychic Rally in Heaven 81; The Dream Machine 82; Waiting for Waiting for Godot 82; Imagining October 84; The Angelic Conversation • Angelic Conversations 85; Caravaggio 86; Aria 87*; The Last of England 87; War Requiem 88; The Garden 90

Jarmusch, Jim Permanent Vacation 82; Stranger Than Paradise 84; Coffee and Cigarettes 86; Down by Law 86; Coffee and Cigarettes Part Two 88; Mystery Train 89

Jarnatt, Steve de *see De Jarnatt, Steve*

Järrel, Stig Evil Eyes 47; The Sixth Commandment 47

Jarrott, Charles Time to Remember 62; Anne of the Thousand Days 69; Mary, Queen of Scots 71; Lost Horizon 72; The Dove 74; Escape from the Dark • The Littlest Horse Thieves 76; The Other Side of Midnight 77; The Last Flight of Noah's Ark 80; Condorman 81; The Amateur 82; The Boy in Blue 85

Jarva, Risto Night and Day • Night or Day • Yö vai Päivä 62*; Baron X • X-Paroni 64*; Game of Luck • Onnenpeli 65; Työmiehen Päiväkirja • A Worker's Diary 67; Ruusujen Aika • Time of Roses 69*; Bensaa Suonissa • Rally 71

Jarvik, Laurence Who Shall Live and Who Shall Die? 81

Jarvis, Richard Sins of the Fathers 48*; Forbidden Journey 50*

Jasný, Vojtěch The Clouds Will Roll Away • It's Not Always Cloudy • Není Stále Zamračeno 50*; They Knew How to Help Themselves • They Know What to

Do • Věděli Si Rady **50***; For a Joyful Life • A Happy Life • Za Život Radostný **51***; Extraordinary Years • Neobyčejná Léta • Strange Years • Unusual Years **52***; Věda Jde s Lidem • Wisdom Is of the People **52***; Lidé Jednoho Srdce • People of One Heart **53***; The Classical Chinese Opera • Old Chinese Opera • Stará Čínská Opera **54***; Dnes Večer Všechno Skončí • Everything Ends Tonight **54***; The Frightened Marksman • Váhavý Střelec **54***; From a Chinese Journal • From a Chinese Notebook • Z Čínského Zápisníku **54***; Pozdrav z Velké Země • Salute to a Great Nation **54***; Bez Obav • Fearless **55**; September Nights • Zářijové Noci **57**; Desire • Touha **58**; I Survived Certain Death • I Survived My Death • Přežil Jsem Svou Smrt **60**; Pilgrimage to the Virgin • Pilgrimage to the Virgin Mary • Procesí k Panence **60**; Až Přijde Kocour • The Cassandra Cat • The Cat • One Day a Cat • That Cat • When the Cat Comes **63**; Dýmky • Pipes **65**; All Good Citizens • All My Good Countrymen • Moravian Chronicle • Our Countrymen • Všichni Dobří Rodáci **68**; Česká Rapsódie • Czech Rhapsody **69**; Ansichten eines Clowns • The Clown • A Clown's Opinions **75**; Ernst Fuchs **76**; Escape Attempt • Fluchtversuch **76**; Metamorphoses **77**; The Return • Die Rücehr **78**; Sebevrah • The Suicide **84**; The Great Land of Small • Tales for All (Part 5) **86**
Jason, Leigh The Price of Fear **28**; The Stool Pigeon • The Tip-Off • Underworld Love **28**; The Body Punch **29**; Eyes of the Underworld **29***; Wolves of the City **29**; Apples to You **32**; Bubbling Over **32**; The Big Thrill • High Gear **33**; A Preferred List **33**; Everybody Likes Music **34**; If This Isn't Love **34**; The Knife of the Party **34**; Nifty Nurses **34**; Roamin' Vandals **34**; Super Stupid **34**; Hail Brother! **35**; Metropolitan Nocturne **35**; A Returned Engagement **35**; The Spirit of 1776 **35**; The Bride Walks Out **36**; The Girl from Paris • That Girl from Paris **36**; Love on a Bet **36**; New Faces of 1937 **37**; Wise Girl **37**; The Mad Miss Manton **38**; Career **39**; The Flying Irishman **39**; Model Wife **41**; Three Girls About Town **41**; Lady for a Night **42**; Dangerous Blondes **43**; Carolina Blues **44**; Nine Girls **44**; Meet Me on Broadway **46**; Lost Honeymoon **47**; The Man from Texas **47**; Out of the Blue **47**; Okinawa **52**; The Choppers **61**
Jason, Will The Soul of a Monster **44**; Dancing Ladies • Ten Cents a Dance **45**; Eve Knew Her Apples **45**; Tahiti Nights **45**; Blonde Alibi **46**; The Dark Horse **46**; Idea Girl **46**; Slightly Scandalous **46**; Sarge Goes to College **47**; Campus Sleuth **48**; Music Man **48**; The Old Gray Mayor • Smart Politics **48**; Rusty Leads the Way **48**; Kazan **49**; Everybody's Dancin' **50**; Chain of Circumstance **51**; Disc Jockey **51**; The Harlem Globetrotters **51***; The Thief of Damascus **52**
Jassan, Ernest Forgive Me • Prosti **87**
Jasset, Victorin Nick Carter **06**; Rêve d'un Fumeur d'Opium **06**; Âme Corse **08**; Meskal le Contrebandier **08**; Rifle Bill • Rifle Bill—Le Roi de la Prairie **08**; Les Dragonnades Sous Louis XIV **09**; Morgan le Pirate **09**; Nouveaux Exploits de Nick Carter **09**; Le Vautour de la Sierra **09**; Herodiade **10**; Zigomar • Zigomar, Roi des Voleurs **10**; La Fin de Don Juan **11**; Nick Carter Contre Paulin Broquet **11**; La Passante **11**; Rédemption **11**; Les Batailles de la Vie **12**; Zigomar Contre Nick Carter **12**; Zigomar Peau d'Anguille **12**; Balaoo • Balaoo ou Des Pas au Plafond • Balaoo the Demon Baboon **13**; Protea **13**
Jawad, Ahmed Abdel Kasset Gharam • Story of Love **46***
Jayagopal, R. N. Hrudaya Pallavi **88**
Jayanthi Vijay **88**
Jayaram, K. V. Olavine Aasare **88**
Jayatilaka, Amarnath Arunata Pera • Before the Dawn **86**
Jaziri, Fadhel A'rab **88***
Jeanson, Henri Lady Paname **51**
Jeapes, Harold The Army Cap **05**; Incidents in the Life of Lord Nelson **05**; Jack and Jill **05**; Photographic Expressions Illustrated **05**; Racing Sayings Illustrated **05**; The Tale of a Shirt **05**; The Adventures of Maud • A Little Bit of Sugar for the Birds **06**; Early Birds **06**; The End of the Trouble **06**; He Wasn't Engaged at the Office **06**; Oh That Hat! **06**; Quit Ye Like Men **06**; Some of Our Relations **06**; Stolen Fruit **06**; Woman Supreme **06**; The Ride of the Valkyries **07**; Who Winked at the Soldier? **07**; A Woodland Tragedy **07**
Jefferson, L. V. Partners of the Tide **21**
Jeffrey, R. E. Alpine Melodies **29**; An Arabian Knight **29**; Black and White **29**; Chelsea Nights **29**; In an Old World Garden **29**; Jazz Time **29**; Memories of the Great Sacrifice **29**; Musical Medley **29**; Musical Moments **29**; Notes and Notions **29**; Odd Numbers **29**; A Song or Two **29**; Song-copation **29**; Up the Poll **29**; Choral Cameos **30**; Claude Deputises **30**; A Feast of Harmony **30**; Goodbye to All That **30**; Heard This One **30**; The Jolly Farmers **30**; Tam o' Shanter **30**; Tell Tales **30**; Double Bluff **33**; Flashbacks **38**
Jeffrey, Tom The Removalists **75**; Weekend of Shadows **78**; The Odd Angry Shot **79**
Jeffreys, Arthur Demented **80**
Jeffries, Lionel The Railway Children **70**; The Amazing Mr. Blunden **72**; Baxter **72**; Wombling Free **77**; Slip Slide Adventures • The Water Babies **78**
Jeffries, Richard Blood Tide • The Red Tide **80**
Jekan, Ali The Mare **86**
Jellinghaus, Beate Mainka see Mainka-Jellinghaus, Beate
Jen, Wan see Wan, Jen
Jenkins, C. Paper People Land **39**
Jenkins, Michael Rebel **85**; Emerald City **89**; Sweet Talker **90**
Jenkins, Patrick The Gambler and the Lady **52***
Jennings, F. H. see Jennings, Humphrey
Jennings, Humphrey Locomotives **34**; Post-Haste **34**; The Story of the Wheel **35**; Birth of a Robot • The Birth of the Robot **36***; Cargoes • Her Last Trip • S.S. Ionian **38**; Design for Spring **38**; English Harvest **38**; Penny Journey **38**; Speaking from America **38**; A City Prepares • The First Days **39***; Spare Time **39**; Britain Can Take It! • London Can Take It! **40***; Spring Offensive • An Unrecorded Victory **40**; Welfare of the Workers **40***; The Heart of Britain • This Is England **41**; Listen to Britain **41***; Words for Battle **41***; Fires Were Started • I Was a Fireman **43**; The Silent Village **43**; The Eighty Days **44**; The True Story of Lilli Marlene **44**; V1 **44**; A Defeated People **45**; A Diary for Timothy **45**; Myra Hess **45**; The Cumberland Story **47**; The Dim Little Island **49**; Family Portrait **50**
Jensen, Astrid Henning see Henning-Jensen, Astrid
Jensen, Bjarne Henning see Henning-Jensen, Bjarne
Jensen, Frederick S. Her Secret **19**
Jensen, Peter Hilary's Blues **83**
Jepson, Selwyn Toilers of the Sea **36***
Jerger, Burr General Massacre **73**
Jersey, William A Time for Burning **66***
Jeske, George Flaming Signal **33***
Jessner, Leopold Backstairs • Hintertreppe **21***; Children of the Fog **35***
Jessop, Clytie Emma's War **86**
Jessua, Alain Léo la Lune • Leo the Moon **57***; Inside Out • Life Upside Down • La Vie à l'Envers **64**; All Weekend Lovers • Comic Strip Hero • Jeu de Massacre • The Killing Game **67**; Les Panthères Blanches **71**; Shock • Shock Treatment • Traitement de Choc **72**; Armageddon • Armaguedon **77**; Les Chiens • The Dogs **78**; Paradis pour Tous **82**; Frankenstein 90 **84**; En Toute Innocence **88**
Jevne, Jack The Ghost Rider **35**
Jewell, Austen Jungle Gents **54***; Hold That Hypnotist! **57**; Looking for Danger **57**
Jewison, Norman 40 Pounds of Trouble **62**; The Thrill of It All **63**; Send Me No Flowers **64**; The Art of Love **65**; The Cincinnati Kid **65**; The Russians Are Coming! The Russians Are Coming! **66**; In the Heat of the Night **67**; The Crown Caper • The Thomas Crown Affair • Thomas Crown and Company **68**; Chicago, Chicago • Gaily, Gaily **69**; Fiddler on the Roof **71**; Jesus Christ Superstar **73**; Rollerball **75**; F.I.S.T. **78**; ...And Justice for All **79**; Best Friends **82**; A Soldier's Story **84**; Agnes of God **85**; Moonstruck **87**; In Country **89**
Jézéquel, Sidney Bâtir à Notre Âge **56***; En Plein Midi **57***; La Traversée de la France **61***; Douze Mois en France **70***
Jha, Prakash Anaadi Anant • End Without End **86**; Parinati **88**
Jhabvala, Ruth Prawer The Courtesans of Bombay **82***
Jialiang, Liu see Liu, Jialiang
Jialin, Chen see Chen, Jialin
Jiang, Zhai see Zhai, Jiang
Jianming, Lu see Lu, Jianming

Jianxin, Huang *see Huang, Jianxin*
Jianzhong, Huang *see Huang, Jianxin*
Jiayi, Wang *see Wang, Jiayi*
Jiguang, Cai *see Cai, Jiquang*
Jiménez, Mary Half of Love • La Moitié de l'Amour 86; L'Air de Rien • Easy in Mind 89
Jiménez-Leal, Orlando El Super 79*; Improper Conduct • Mauvaise Conduite 84*; The Other Cuba 85
Jin, Weng Elephant Wife • The Leech Girl • Zhi Mo Nu 68*
Jin, Xie *see Xie, Jin*
Jin, Young Y. A Place in the Sun 88
Jinbao, Hong *see Hung, Samo*
Jingqin, Hu *see Hu, Jingqin*
Jinpeng, Guan *see Kwan, Stanley*
Jin-woo, Chung *see Chung, Jin-woo*
Jiquang, Cai *see Cai, Jiquang*
Jiras, Robert I Am the Cheese 83
Jireš, Jaromil Fever • Horečka 58; Strejda • Uncle 59; Footprints • Stopy 60; The Hall of Lost Steps • Sál Ztracených Kroků 60; Polyecran for the Brno Industrial Fair • Polyekrán pro BVV 60*; Polyecran for International Exposition of Labor Turin • Polyekrán pro Mezinárodní Výstavu Práce Turin 61*; Houslový Koncert • The Violin Concert 62*; The Cry • Křik 63; Pearls at the Bottom • Pearls of the Deep • Perličky na Dně 64*; The Log Cabin • Srub 65; Citizen Karel Havlíček • Občan Karel Havlíček 66; Hra na Krále • The King Game 67; Dědáček • Grandpa 68; Don Juan 68 68; The Joke • Žert 68; Cesta do Prahy Vincence Mošteka a Simona Pešla z Vlčnova, L.P. 1969 • The Journey of Vincenc Moštek and Simon Pešl of Vlčnov to Prague, 1969 A.D. 69; Valerie a Týden Divů • Valerie and a Week of Wonders • Valerie and Her Week of Wonders 70; A Pozdravuji Vlaštovky • Greetings to the Swallows • My Love to the Swallows 72; Kasař • The Safecracker 73; Lidé z Metra • People from the Metro • People in the Subway 74; Il Divino Boemo 75; The Island of Silver Herons • Ostrov Stříbrných Volavek 76; Flying Saucers Coming! • Flying Saucers Over Our Town • Talíře Nad Velkým Malíkovem 77; Mladý Muž a Bílá Velryba • The Young Man and Moby Dick • The Young Man and the White Whale 78; Causa Králík • The Rabbit Case 79; Escapes Home • Útěky Domů 80; Svět Alfonse Muchy • The World of Alphonse Mucha 80; Opera in the Vineyard • Opera ve Vinici 81; Kouzelná Praha Rudolfa II • The Magic Prague of Rudolph II 82; Neúplné Zatmění • Partial Eclipse 82; Lev s Bílou Hřívou 86
Ji-shun, Duan *see Duan, Ji-shun*
Jittlov, Mike The Wizard of Speed and Time 88
Joannides, Evangelos Aphrousa 71
Joannon, Léo Adieu les Copains 30; Suzanne 32*; Six Cents Mille Francs par Mois 33; Bibi la Purée 34; Quelle Drôle de Gosse 35; Train de Plaisir 35; Le Chanteur de Minuit 36; Mais N'Te Promène Donc Pas Toute Nue 36; Quand Minuit Sonnera

36; Le Traverseur d'Atlantique 36; Vous N'Avez Rien à Déclarer? 36*; Alerte en Méditerranée • Hell's Cargo • S.O.S. Mediterranean 37; L'Homme Sans Cœur 37; L'Émigrante 38*; Documents Secrets 40; Caprices 41; Confessions of a Newly-wed 41; Le Camion Blanc 42; Le Carrefour des Enfants Perdus • Children of Chaos 43; Lucrèce 43; Le Quatrevingt-Quatre Prend des Vacances 49; Atoll K • Escapade • Robinson Crusoeland • Utopia 50*; Drôle de Noce 51; Le Défroqué • The Renegade Priest 53; Le Secret de Sœur Angèle • Sister Angela's Secret 55; L'Homme aux Clefs d'Or • The Man with the Golden Keys 56; Le Désert de Pigalle 58; Tant d'Amour Perdu 58; L'Assassin Est dans l'Annuaire 61; Fort du Fou 62; Outpost in Indochina 64; Trois Enfants dans le Désordre 66; Les Arnaud • The Arnauds 67
Joanou, Phil Three O'Clock High 87; U2: Rattle and Hum 88; State of Grace 90
Jobin, Victor Potpourri 63*
Jobson, Dickie Countryman 81
Jodoin, René Chalk River Ballet 50*
Jodorowsky, Alejandro Fando and Lis 70; The Mole • El Topo 71; The Holy Mountain 73; Tusk 80; Santa Sangre 89
Jodrell, Steve Shame 88
Joens, Michael My Little Pony • My Little Pony—The Movie 86
Joffé, Alex Six Heures à Perdre 46; Lettre Ouverte à un Mari 53; Les Hussards 55; Les Assassins du Dimanche • Every Minute Counts • Every Second Counts 56; Je Reviendrai à Kandara 56; A Bomb for a Dictator • The Fanatics • Les Fanatiques 57; Du Rififi chez les Femmes • Riff Raff Girls • Rififi for Girls • Rififi fra le Donne 59; Fortunat 60; Le Tracassin ou Les Plaisirs de la Ville 61; Les Culottes Rouges • The Red Culottes 62; Impossible on Saturday • Pas Question le Samedi • Raq lo B'Shabbat 65; La Grosse Caisse 66; Les Cracks 68
Joffe, Arthur Harem 85
Joffe, Mark Grievous Bodily Harm 88
Joffé, Roland The Killing Fields 84; The Mission 86; Fat Man and Little Boy 89
Johansen, Eduard Children of the Storm • Deti Buri 26*; Katka Bumazhnyi Ranyot • Katka the Apple Girl • Katka's Reinette Apples 26*
Johansen, Ernst You Are Not Alone 78*
Johansen, Svend Rødtotterne og Tyrannos 88
Johansson, Ivar Hälsningar 34; Bränningar • Ocean Breakers • The Surf 35; Sången till Henne • The Song to Her 35; Fröken Blir Piga 37
Johnsen, Sande Teenage Gang Debs 66
Johnson, Alan To Be or Not to Be 83; Solarbabies 86
Johnson, Bobby Living Between Two Worlds 63
Johnson, Emory In the Name of the Law 22; The Third Alarm 22; The Mailman 23; The Westbound Limited 23; Life's Greatest Game 24; The Spirit of the U.S.A. 24; The Last Edition 25; The Non-

Stop Flight 26; The Fourth Commandment 27; The Lone Eagle 27; The Shield of Honor 27; The Third Alarm 30; The Phantom Express 32
Johnson, Fred Eden Cried • In the Fall of '55; Eden Cried 67
Johnson, J. P. *see Franco, Jesús*
Johnson, James *see Franco, Jesús*
Johnson, Jed Andy Warhol's Bad 71
Johnson, Kenneth The Incredible Hulk 78*; Short Circuit 2 88
Johnson, Lamont Thin Ice 61; A Covenant with Death 66; Kona Coast 67; A Gunfight 70; The McKenzie Break • Wolfpack 70; My Sweet Charlie 70; The Groundstar Conspiracy 72; You'll Like My Mother 72; Hard Driver • The Last American Hero 73; Visit to a Chief's Son 74; Lipstick 76; One on One 77; Somebody Killed Her Husband 78; Cattle Annie and Little Britches 80; Road Gangs: Adventures in the Creep Zone • Spacehunter: Adventures in the Forbidden Zone 82
Johnson, Martin E. Cannibals of the South Seas • Head Hunters of Malekula 12; Jack London's Adventures in the South Seas 12; Among the Cannibal Isles of the South Pacific 18; Jungle Adventures 21; Head Hunters of the South Seas 22; Hunting African Animals • Trailing African Wild Animals • Trailing Big Game in Africa 23; East of Suez 25; Simba the King of Beasts 27; Across the World with Mr. and Mrs. Johnson 30; Wonders of the Congo 31; Congorilla 32; Baboona 35; Borneo 37
Johnson, Nunnally Black Widow 54; Night People 54; How to Be Very, Very Popular 55; The Man in the Gray Flannel Suit 55; Oh, Men! Oh, Women! 56; The Three Faces of Eve 57; The Man Who Understood Women 59; The Angel Wore Red • La Sposa Bella 60
Johnson, Patrick Read Spaced Invaders 90
Johnson, Raymond K. North of Nome 25; Call of the Rockies 31; Kentucky Blue Streak 35; Skybound 35; I'll Name the Murderer 36; Special Agent K-7 37; Code of the Fearless 39; Daughter of the Tong 39; In Old Montana 39; The Lone Troubador • Two Gun Troubador 39; The Cheyenne Kid 40; Covered Wagon Trails 40; The Kid from Santa Fe 40; Land of Six Guns • Land of the Six Guns 40; Pinto Canyon 40; Rider from Nowhere • Riders from Nowhere 40; Ridin' the Trail 40; Wild Horse Range 40; Law of the Wild • Law of the Wolf 41
Johnson, Robert Colorado Charlie 65
Johnson, Rule Royce Recess 67
Johnson, S. H. Charleston Dance 27; Love's Old Sweet Song 27
Johnson, Tefft C.O.D. 15; The Turn of the Road 15; Who Killed Joe Merrion? 15; She Left Without Her Trunks 16; The Writing on the Wall 16; Love's Law 17; The Love Net 18; Home Wanted 19; Love and the Woman 19; The Love Defender 19
Johnson, Tom The World of Tomorrow 84*

Johnson, William R. Country Western Hoedown 67

Johnston, Denis Guests of the Nation 35

Johnston, Joe Honey, I Shrunk the Kids 89

Johnston, Lorimer The Envoy Extraordinary 14; Samson 14*; Life's Harmony 16*; Breezy Jim 19; Devil McCare 19; The Cricket on the Hearth 23

Johnston, Tucker Blood Salvage 90

Jolivet, Pierre Le Complexe du Kangourou • The Kangaroo Complex 86; Force Majeure • Uncontrollable Circumstances 89

Jolivet, René The Adventures of Gil Blas 55

Jones, Amy Slumber Party Massacre 82*; Love Letters • My Love Letters 83; Maid to Order 87

Jones, Andy The Adventure of Faustus Bidgood 86*

Jones, Arthur A. Mission to Hell • Savage 62

Jones, Bryan Ocean Drive Weekend 84; The Rejuvenator 88

Jones, Buck For the Service 36; Black Aces 37*; Law for Tombstone 37*

Jones, Charles see Jones, Buck

Jones, Charles M. see Jones, Chuck

Jones, Chuck Dog Gone Modern 38; The Night Watchman 38; The Curious Puppy 39; Daffy Duck and the Dinosaur 39; The Good Egg 39; Little Brother Rat 39; The Little Lion Hunter 39; Naughty But Mice 39; Old Glory 39; Presto Change-O 39; Robin Hood Makes Good 39; Sniffles the Bookworm 39; Snow Man's Land 39; Bedtime for Sniffles 40; The Egg Collector 40; Elmer's Candid Camera 40; Ghost Wanted 40; Good Night Elmer 40; The Mighty Hunters 40; Sniffles Bells the Cat 40; Sniffles Takes a Trip 40; Stage Fright 40; Tom Thumb in Trouble 40; The Bird Came C.O.D. 41; The Brave Little Bat 41; Conrad the Sailor 41; Dog Tired 41; The Draft Horse 41; Elmer's Pet Rabbit 41; Hold the Lion, Please 41; Inki and the Lion 41; Joe Glow, the Firefly 41; Porky's Ant 41; Porky's Midnight Matinee 41; Porky's Prize Pony 41; Saddle Silly 41; Snow Time for Comedy 41; Toy Trouble 41; The Wacky Worm 41*; Case of the Missing Hare 42; The Dover Boys • The Dover Boys (At Pimento University) 42; Fox Pop 42; My Favorite Duck 42; Porky's Cafe 42; The Squawkin' Hawk 42; To Duck or Not to Duck 42; The Aristo-Cat 43; Fin 'n' Catty 43; Flop Goes the Weasel 43; Inki and the Mynah Bird 43; Super Rabbit 43; The Unbearable Bear 43; Wackiki Wabbit 43; Angel Puss 44; Bugs Bunny and the Three Bears 44; From Hand to Mouse 44; Hell-Bent for Election 44*; Lost and Foundling 44; The Odorable Kitty 44; Tom Turk and Daffy 44; The Weakly Reporter 44; The Eager Beaver 45; Fresh Airedale 45; Hair Raising Hare 45; Hare Conditioned 45; Hare Tonic 45; Hush My Mouse 45; Quentin Quail 45; Trap Happy Porky 45; Fair and Wormer 46; Roughly Squeaking 46; Scent-imental

Over You 46; Haredevil Hare 47; House Hunting Mice 47; Inki at the Circus 47; Little Orphan Airedale 47; A Pest in the House 47; Rabbit Punch 47; What's Brewin' Bruin? 47; The Awful Orphan 48; The Bee-Deviled Bruin 48; Daffy Dilly 48; A Feather in His Hare 48; Long-Haired Hare 48; Mississippi Hare 48; Mouse Wreckers 48; My Bunny Lies Over the Sea 48; Scaredy Cat 48; You Were Never Duckier 48; Bear Feat 49; Fast and Furry-ous 49; For Scent-imental Reasons 49; Frigid Hare 49; Homeless Hare 49; Often an Orphan 49; Rabbit Hood 49; So Much for So Little 49*; Caveman Inki 50; Dog Gone South 50; The Ducksters 50; 8 Ball Bunny 50; The Hypochondri-Cat 50; The Rabbit of Seville 50; The Scarlet Pumpernickel 50; Two's a Crowd 50; A Bear for Punishment 51; Bunny Hugged 51; Cheese Chasers 51; Chow Hound 51; Dripalong Daffy 51; A Hound for Trouble 51; Rabbit Fire 51; Scent-imental Romeo 51; The Wearing of the Grin • Wearing the Grin 51; Beep Beep 52; Don't Give Up the Sheep 52; Feed the Kitty 52; Going! Going! Gosh! 52; The Hasty Hare 52; Kiss Me Cat 52; Little Beau Pepe 52; Mouse Warming 52; Operation: Rabbit 52; Rabbit Seasoning 52; Terrier Stricken 52; Water, Water Every Hare 52; Bully for Bugs 53; Duck Amuck 53; Duck Dodgers in the 24th½ Century 53; Duck! Rabbit! • Duck, Rabbit, Duck 53; Feline Frame-Up 53; Forward March Hare 53; Much Ado About Nutting 53; Punch Trunk 53; Wild Over You 53; Zipping Along 53; Baby Buggy Bunny 54; Bewitched Bunny 54; The Cat's Bah 54; Claws for Alarm 54; From A to Z-Z-Z-Z 54; Lumber Jack Rabbit 54; My Little Duckaroo 54; No Barking 54; Sheep Ahoy 54; Stop, Look and Hasten! 54; Beanstalk Bunny 55; Double or Mutton 55; Guided Muscle 55; Jumpin' Jupiter 55; Knight-Mare Hare 55; One Froggy Evening 55; Past Perfumance 55; Rabbit Rampage 55; Ready, Set, Zoom! 55; Two Scents' Worth 55; Barbary Coast Bunny 56; Broomstick Bunny 56; Bugs Bonnets 56; Deduce You Say 56; Gee Whiz-z-z-z 56; Heaven Scent 56; Rocket Bye Baby 56; Rocket Squad 56; There They Go-Go-Go! 56; To Hare Is Human 56; Ali Baba Bunny 57; Boyhood Daze 57; Go Fly a Kite 57; Scrambled Aches 57; Steal Wool 57; Touché and Go 57; What's Opera, Doc? 57; Zoom and Bored 57; Cat Feud 58; Hare-Way to the Stars 58; Hip, Hip — Hurry! 58; Hook, Line and Stinker 58; Robin Hood Daffy 58; To Itch His Own 58; Whoa, Be Gone! 58; Baton Bunny 59; Hot Rod and Reel 59; Really Scent 59*; Wild About Hurry 59; The Fastest with the Mostest 60; The High Note 60; Hopalong Casualty 60; Rabbit's Feat 60; Ready Woolen and Able 60; Who Scent You? 60; The Abominable Snow Rabbit 61; The Adventures of the Road-runner 61; Beep Prepared 61; Compressed Hare 61; Lickety Split 61; The Mouse on

57th Street 61; Nelly's Folly 61; A Scent of the Matterhorn 61; Zip 'n' Snort 61; Louvre Come Back to Me 62; Martian Thru Georgia 62; A Sheep in the Deep 62; Zoom at the Top 62; Hare-Breadth Hurry 63; I Was a Teenage Thumb 63; Mad As a Mars Hare 63; Now Hear This 63; Penthouse Mouse 63; To Beep or Not to Beep 63; Transylvania 6-5000 63; Woolen Under Where 63; The Cat Above and the Mouse Below 64; Is There a Doctor in the Mouse? 64; Much Ado About Mousing 64; Snowbody Loves Me 64; The Unshrinkable Jerry Mouse 64; War and Pieces 64; Ah Sweet Mouse-Story of Life 65; Bad Day at Cat Rock 65; Brothers Carry Mouse Off 65; Cat's Me-Ouch 65; The Dot and the Line 65; Haunted Mouse 65; I'm Just Wild About Jerry 65; Of Feline Bondage 65; Tom-ic Energy 65; Year of the Mouse 65; Duel Personality 66; Jerry Jerry Quite Contrary 66; Love Me, Love My Mouse 66*; The Bear That Wasn't 67; Cat and Duplicat • The Cat Duplicat 67; The Phantom Tollbooth 69*; The Bugs Bunny/Road Runner Movie • The Great American Bugs Bunny/Road Runner Chase • The Great American Chase 79*; Uncensored Cartoons 81*; Daffy Duck's Movie: Fantastic Island 83*; Porky Pig in Hollywood 86*; Daffy Duck's Quackbusters 88*

Jones, David Betrayal 83; 84 Charing Cross Road 86; Jacknife 89

Jones, Dick see Jones, F. Richard

Jones, Don The Love Butcher 75*; Sweater Girls 78; The Forest • Terror in the Forest 83; Murder Lust 85

Jones, Edgar Nothing to Be Done 14; Courage and the Man 15; An Enemy to Society 15; On Bitter Creek 15; The Woman Pays 15; Dimples 16; The Half Million Bribe 16; Lovely Mary 16; The Turmoil 16; The Girl Angle 17; The Lady in the Library 17; Mentioned in Confidence 17; Zollenstein 17; The Girl Who Wouldn't Quit 18; A Rich Man's Daughter 18; Lonesome Corners 22

Jones, Eugene S. A Face of War 68; Two Men of Karamoja • The Wild and the Brave 74

Jones, F. Richard A Game Old Knight 15; The Great Vacuum Robbery 15; Her Painted Hero 15; His Hereafter 16; A Love Riot 16; The Battle Royal 18; His Smothered Love 18*; It Pays to Exercise 18; Mickey 18; Saucy Madeline 18; Sleuths 18; The Dentist 19; The Foolish Age 19; Love's False Faces 19; Never Too Old 19; The Speakeasy 19; Yankee Doodle in Berlin 19; Flying Pat 20; Gee Whiz! 20; Love, Honor and Behave 20*; The Ghost in the Garret 21; Molly O 21; Oh, Jo! 21; The Country Flapper 22; The Crossroads of New York 22; Suzanna 22; The Extra Girl 23; The Shriek of Araby 23; The First 100 Years 24; Little Robinson Corkscrew 24; The Gaucho 27; The Big Killing 28; Someone to Love 28; The Water Hole 28; Bulldog Drummond 29

Jones, Grover The Unknown 21; Putting It Over 22; Taking Chances 22; Slow As

Lightning 23; Speed King 23; A Gentleman Roughneck 25; Heir-Loons 25; Thrilling Youth 26; Unknown Dangers 26; God of Mankind 28; Cap'n Jericho • Hell and High Water 33*

Jones, Harmon As Young As You Feel 51; Bloodhounds of Broadway 52; The Pride of St. Louis 52; City of Bad Men 53; The Kid from Left Field 53; The Silver Whip 53; Gorilla at Large 54; Princess of the Nile 54; Target Zero 55; Canyon River 56; A Day of Fury 56; The Beast of Budapest 58; Bullwhip! 58; Wolf Larsen 58; Don't Worry, We'll Think of a Title 66

Jones, Harry O. see Fraser, Harry

Jones, James Cellan see Cellan-Jones, James

Jones, Kentucky The Manson Massacre 76

Jones, L. Q. The Devil's Bedroom 64; A Boy and His Dog 75

Jones, Michael The Adventure of Faustus Bidgood 86*

Jones, Michael Caton see Caton-Jones, Michael

Jones, Peter Frazer see Frazer-Jones, Peter

Jones, Robert Carry It On • Joan, Carry It On 70*; Mission Hill 82

Jones, Terry Monty Python and the Holy Grail 75*; Life of Brian • Monty Python's Life of Brian 79; Monty Python's The Meaning of Life 83; Personal Services 86; Erik the Viking 89

Jones, Winston UFO • UFOs: Unidentified Flying Objects • Unidentified Flying Objects 56; Wink of an Eye 58

Jong, Ate de A Flight of Rainbirds 81; In de Schaduw van de Overwinning • Shadow of Victory 85

Jordan, Glenn It Hurts Only When I Laugh • Neil Simon's Only When I Laugh • Only When I Laugh 81; The Buddy System 84; Mass Appeal 84; Something in Common 86

Jordan, Larry The Extraordinary Child 54*; Hildur and the Magician 69

Jordan, Neil Angel • Danny Boy 82; The Company of Wolves 84; Mona Lisa 86; High Spirits 88; We're No Angels 89

Jordan, Robert Stone Sector 13 82

Jorge, Jean-Louis The Serpents of the Pirate Moon 73

Jorjani, Fereidun G. The Fox Affair 78

José, Edward The Corsair 14; The Beloved Vagabond 15; The Closing Net 15; Nedra 15; Simon the Jester 15; The Iron Claw 16*; The Light That Failed 16; Pearl of the Army 16*; Her Silent Sacrifice 17; May Blossom 17; The Moth 17; Poppy 17*; The Doctor and the Bricklayer 18; Fedora 18*; Love's Conquest 18; My Cousin 18; Private Peat 18; Resurrection 18*; The Splendid Romance 18; La Tosca 18; Woman and Wife 18; A Woman of Impulse 18; Fires of Faith 19; The Isle of Conquest 19; Two Brides 19; The Fighting Shepherdess 20; Mothers of Men 20*; The Riddle, Woman 20; The Yellow Taifun • Yellow Typhoon 20; Her Lord and Master

21; The Inner Chamber 21; The Matrimonial Web 21; Rainbow 21; The Scarab Ring 21; What Woman Will Do • What Women Will Do 21; The Girl in His Room 22; The Man from Downing Street 22; The Prodigal Judge 22; God's Prodigal 23*; Perils of Paris • Terreur 24; A Daughter of Israel • Le Puits de Jacob 26

Joseliani, Otar see Ioseliani, Otar

Joseph, Eugenie Spookies 86*

Joseph, George Creatures of the Prehistoric Planet • Creatures of the Red Planet • The Flesh Creatures • Flesh Creatures of the Red Planet • Horror Creatures of the Prehistoric Planet • Horror Creatures of the Red Planet • Horror of the Blood Monsters • Space Mission of the Lost Planet • Vampire Men of the Lost Planet 70*

Joseph, Peter Richthofen • Richthofen, The Red Knight of the Air 29*

Josephson, Erland En och En • One and One • One Plus One 78*; The Marmalade Revolution • Marmeladupproret 79*

Joshi Dinarathrangal 88

Joshi, Chandrakant January Ororma 87; Sutradhar 87

Joshi, Madan Pati Parmeshwar 89

Josipovici, Jean Flesh and Desire 55; Delitto allo Specchio • Sex Party 63*

Joslyn, Don Mother • The Toy Grabbers • Up Your Teddy Bear 68

Jost, Jon Speaking Directly • Speaking Directly: Some American Notes 73; Angel City 77; Last Chants for a Slow Dance 77; Chameleon 78; Stage Fright 81; Slow Moves 83; Bell Diamond 86; Uncommon Senses 87; Laughing Rembrandt • Rembrandt Laughing 88; All the Vermeers in New York 90; Sure Fire 90

Joulout, Jean Le Nègre Blanc • The White Negro 12*

Jourdan, Erven The Half Pint 60; Money in My Pocket 62

Jourdan, Pierre I Am a Dancer 72*

Jouvet, Louis Dr. Knock • Knock 33*

Joy, Ron The Animals • Five Savage Men 70

Joyce, Paul The Engagement 70

Jozani, Massoud Jafari Djadde Haye Sard • Frosty Roads 86; Sheere Sanggy • Stony Lion 87

Judels, Charles Mother Knows Best 28*

Judge, Joel see Biberman, Abner

Juegert, Rudolf see Jügert, Rudolf

Juergens, Curd see Jürgens, Curd

Jügert, Rudolf Film Ohne Titel • Film Without a Name • Film Without a Title • Film Without Title 47; Jonny Rettet Nebrador 53; A Day Will Come • Es Kommt ein Tag 60; The Scarlet Baroness 62

Jugnot, Gérard Scout Toujours 85; Sans Peur et Sans Reproche 88

Jugo, William J. Ballad of Gavilan • Gavilan 68

Julian, Paul Baby Boogie 55

Julian, Rupert The Underworld 15; The Water Clue 15; Bettina Loved a Soldier 16; The Blackmailer 16; The Bugler of Algiers 16; A Christmas Carol • The Right to Be

Happy 16; The Evil Women Do 16; John Pellet's Dream 16; Little Boy Blue 16; The Marriage of Arthur 16; Naked Hearts 16; The Turn of the Wheel 16; We French 16; The Circus of Life 17; Desire of the Moth 17; The Door Between 17; The Gift Girl 17; A Kentucky Cinderella 17; Mother o' Mine 17; The Mysterious Mr. Tiller 17; The Savage 17; Fires of Youth 18; Hands Down 18; Hungry Eyes 18; The Kaiser • The Kaiser—The Beast of Berlin 18; Midnight Madness 18; Creaking Stairs 19; The Fire Flingers 19; The Millionaire Pirate 19; The Sleeping Lion 19; The Honey Bee 20; The Girl Who Ran Wild 22; Merry-Go-Round 23*; Hell's Highroad 24; Love and Glory 24; The Phantom of the Opera 25*; Silence 26; Three Faces East 26; The Country Doctor 27; The Yankee Clipper 27; The Leopard Lady 28; Walking Back 28; The Cat Creeps 30; Love Comes Along 30

July, Serge Viva Portugal 75*

Juncker, Michael Wann—Wenn Nicht Jetzt? 88

Juneja, Tony Abhimanyu 89

Jung-Alsen, Kurt Betrogen Bis zum Jüngsten Tag • Duped Till Doomsday 57; Private Pooley • The Story of Private Pooley 62

Junghans, Karl Such Is Life 29

Júnior, Francisco Ramalho see Ramalho Júnior, Francisco

Júnior, Walter Lima see Lima Júnior, Walter

Junker, Gottfried Secret Love • Versteckte Liebe 87

Junli, Zheng see Zheng, Junli

Juráček, Pavel Joseph Kilián • Postava k Podpírání 63*

Juran, Nathan The Black Castle 52; Gunsmoke! 52; The Golden Blade 53; Law and Order 53; Tumbleweed 53; Drums Across the River 54; Highway Dragnet 54; The Crooked Web 55; The Deadly Mantis • The Incredible Praying Mantis • The Incredible Preying Mantis • Third Party Risk 56; Hellcats of the Navy 57; Le Imprese di una Spada Leggendaria 57*; 20 Million Miles to Earth 57; Attack of the Fifty Foot Woman 58; The Brain from Planet Arous 58; Good Day for a Hanging 58; The 7th Voyage of Sinbad 58; Flight of the Lost Balloon 60; The Giant Killer • Jack the Giant Killer 61; The Siege of the Saxons 63; East of Sudan 64; First Men in the Moon 64; Day of the Landgrabbers • Land Raiders 68; The Boy Who Cried Werewolf 73

Jürgens, Curd Prämien auf den Tod 50; Gangsterpremiere 51; Ohne Dich Wird Es Nacht 56; Bankraub in der Rue Latour 61

Jurgens, Curt see Jürgens, Curd

Jury, Dan Chillysmith Farm 82*

Jury, Mark Chillysmith Farm 82*

Jusid, Juan José Made in Argentina 87

Justice, Martin Blind Man's Holiday 17; The Indian Summer of Dry Valley Johnson 17; The Skylight Room 17; The Soap Girl 18; They Shall Pay 21

Justiniano, Gonzalo Children of the

Cold War • Los Hijos de la Guerra Fría **85**; Sussi **88**

Justman, Paul Gimme an F **84**

Jutra, Claude Le Dément du Lac Jean-Jeune **47***; Mouvement Perpétuel **49***; Pierrot des Bois **54**; Les Jeunesses Musicales **56**; A Chairy Tale • Il Était une Chaise **57***; Les Mains Nettes **58**; Anna la Bonne **59**; Félix Leclerc, Troubadour **59**; Fred Barry, Comédien **59**; Le Niger—Jeune République • Niger 60 **60**; The Fight • La Lutte • Wrestling **61***; Les Enfants du Silence **62***; L'Invasion Pacifique • Québec-U.S.A. • Québec-U.S.A. ou L'Invasion Pacifique • Visit to a Foreign Country **62***; À Tout Prendre • Take It All **63**; Petit Discours de la Méthode **63***; Comment Savoir • Knowing to Learn **66**; The Devil's Toy • Rouli-Roulant **66**; Au Cœur de la Ville • In the Heart of the City **69**; Le Québec Vu par Cartier-Bresson **69**; Wow! **69**; Marie-Christine **70***; Mon Oncle Antoine • My Uncle Antoine **70**; Kamouraska **72**; For Better or for Worse • Pour le Meilleur et pour le Pire **75**; Arts Cuba **77**; The Patriarch #1 and #2 **77**; Seer Was Here **78**; Surfacing **78**; The Wordsmith **78**; By Design **80**; La Dame en Couleurs • Our Lady of the Paints **85**

Jutzi, Phil *see Jutzi, Piel*

Jutzi, Piel Das Blinkende Fenster **19**; Der Maskierte Schrecken **19**; Die Rache des Banditen **19**; Das Licht Scheuen... **20**; Red Bull der Letzte Apache **20**; Klass und Datsch die Pechvögel **26**; Kindertragödie **27**; Die Machnower Schleusen **27**; Hunger in Waldenburg • Our Daily Bread • Unser Tägliches Brot **28**; Berlin-Alexanderplatz **29**; Mother Krause's Journey to Happiness • Mutter Krausens Fahrt ins Glück **29**; Der Kosak und die Nachtigall **35**; Lockspitzel Asew **35**

Kabay, Barna Jób Lázadása • The Revolt of Job **83***

Kabierske, Henry Argonauts of California **16**; The Daughter of the Don **17**

Kaboré, Gaston J. M. The Gift of God • Wend Kuuni **82**; Zan Boko **88**

Kachivas, Lou Mighty Mouse in the Great Space Chase **83***; The Secret of the Sword **85***

Kachlík, Antonín Conjurer's Return • Kouzelníkův Návrat **86**; O Princezně Julince **88**

Kachyňa, Karel The Clouds Will Roll Away • It's Not Always Cloudy • Není Stále Zamračeno **50***; They Knew How to Help Themselves • They Know What to Do • Věděli Si Rady **50***; For a Joyful Life • A Happy Life • Za Život Radostný **51***; Extraordinary Years • Neobyčejná Léta • Strange Years • Unusual Years **52***; Věda Jde s Lidem • Wisdom Is of the People **52***; Lidé Jednoho Srdce • People of One Heart **53***; The Classical Chinese Opera • Old Chinese Opera • Stará Čínská Opera **54***; Dnes Večer Všechno Skončí • Everything Ends Tonight **54***; The Frightened Marksman • Váhavý Střelec **54***; From a Chinese Journal • From a Chinese Note-book • Z Čínského Zápisníku **54***; Pozdrav z Velké Země • Salute to a Great Nation **54***; Crooked Mirror • Křivé Zrcadlo **56**; The Lost Track • The Lost Trail • Ztracená Stopa **56**; Mistrovství Světa Leteckých Modelářů • World Championship of Air Models **57**; Pokušení • Temptation **57**; The City Has Your Face • Město Má Svou Tvář **58**; Čtyřikrát o Bulharsku • Four Times About Bulgaria **58**; Tenkrát o Vánocích • That Christmas **58**; The King of the Sumava • Král Šumavy • Smugglers of Death **59**; Práče • The Slinger **60**; The Country Doctor • Fetters • Pouta **61**; Lenka and Prim • Piebald • The Proud Stallion • Stress of Youth • Trápení • Trials of Youth **61**; Vertigo • Závrať **62**; Hope • Naděje **63**; The High Wall • Vysoká Zed' **64**; Ať Žije Republika! • Long Live the Republic! **65**; Carriage to Vienna • Coach to Vienna • Kočár do Vídně **66**; The Night of the Bride • Noc Nevěsty **67**; Christmas with Elizabeth • Vánoce s Alžbětou **68**; Funny Old Man • Our Foolish Family • Směšný Pán **69**; I'm Jumping Over Puddles Again • Jumping Over Puddles Again • Jumping the Puddles Again • Už Zase Skáču Přes Kaluže **70**; Horká Zima • Hot Winter **72**; Láska • Love **72**; Train to Heaven • Vlak do Stanice Nebe **72**; Pavlínka **74**; Robinson Girl • Robinsonka **74**; The Death of the Fly • Smrt Mouchy **75**; Škaredá Dědina • The Ugly Village **75**; The Little Mermaid • The Little Sea Nymph • Malá Mořská Víla **76**; Meeting in July • Setkání v Červenci **77**; Čekání na Déšť • Waiting for the Rain **78**; Láska Mezi Kapkami Deště • Love Between the Raindrops **79**; Cukrová Bouda • The Little Sugar House • Sugar Cottage **80**; Doctor's Round • Vizita **81**; Fandy Ó Fandy **82**; Nursing Sisters • Sestřičky **83**; Amateur Photographer • Dobré Světlo **86**; The Death of a Beautiful Dream • Smrt Krásných Srnců **86**; Kam Pánové, Kam Jdete? **88**; Oznamuje Se Láskám Vašim **88**

Kaczender, George Don't Let the Angels Fall **68**; The Girl in Blue • U-Turn **73**; In Praise of Older Women **78**; Your Ticket Is No Longer Valid **79**; Agency **80**; Chanel Solitaire **81**; Prettykill • Tomorrow's a Killer **87**

Kadár, Ján Life Is Rising from the Ruins **45**; Cathy • Katka • Katya • Kitty **50**; The Hijack • The Hijacking • Kidnap • Kidnapped • Únos **52***; Hudba z Marsu • Music from Mars **53***; Young Days **55***; At the Terminal Station • The House at the Terminus • Tam na Konečné **56***; The Third Wish • Three Wishes • Třetí Přání • Tři Přání **57***; Magic Lantern II **59***; Polyecran for the Brno Industrial Fair • Polyekrán pro BVV **60***; Spartakiáda **60***; Because We Do Not Forget • Death Is Called Engelchen • For We Too Do Not Forgive • Smrt Si Říká Engelchen **62***; The Accused • The Defendant • Obžalovaný **63***; Obchod na Korze • Shop in the High Street • The Shop on High Street • The Shop on Main Street • A Shop on the High Street **64***; Adrift • Hrst Plná Vody • Something Is Adrift in the Water • Something Is Drifting on the Water • Touha Zvaná Anada • Zmítaná **69***; The Angel Levine **70**; Lies My Father Told Me **73**; Freedom Road **79**

Kadison, Ellis Git! **65**; The Cat **66**; You've Got to Be Smart **67**

Kadokawa, Haruki Cabaret • Left Alone **86**; Heaven and Earth **90**

Kaeriyama, Norimasa The Glow of Life **18**; The Lasciviousness of the Viper **20**

Kagan, Jeremy Paul Heroes **77**; Scott Joplin **77**; The Big Fix **78**; The Chosen **81**; The Sting II **83**; The Journey of Natty Gann **85**

Kahane, Peter Ete und Ali **85**

Kahane, Roger The Love Mates • Madly **70**

Kahla, J. A. Hübler *see Hübler-Kahla, J. A.*

Kahn, Jeff Astonished **88***

Kahn, Richard Secret Menace **31**; A Dangerous Man • Un Hombre Peligroso **35**; Two-Gun Man from Harlem **38**; The Bronze Buckaroo **39**; Harlem Rides the Range **39**; Buzzy Rides the Range **40**; Son of Ingagi **40**; Buzzy and the Phantom Pinto **41**

Kai, Johannes Flitterwochen in der Hölle • Isle of Sin **60**

Kaidanovski, Aleksandr Gost **88**

Kaige, Chen *see Chen, Kaige*

Kairs, Hugh *see Shepherd, Horace*

Kaiserman, Constance My Little Girl **85**

Kajima, Koichi Firefly • Hotaru **89**

Kalatozov, Mikhail Ikh Tsartsvo • 18-28 **28***; Blind • Slepaya **30**; Djim Chuante • Salt for Svanetia • The Salt of Svanetia • Sol dlya Svanetia **30**; Gvozd v Sapogye • A Nail in the Boot **32**; Courage • Manhood • Mut **39**; The Red Flyer • Valeri Chkalov • Wings of Victory **41**; The Invincible • Nepobedimye • The Unconquerable **42***; Cine-Concert... • Film-Concert Dedicated to the 25th Anniversary of the Red Army • Film-Concert for the Red Army's 25th Anniversary • Kinokontsert k 25-Letiyu Krasnoy Armii • Moscow Music Hall **43***; Conspiracy of the Doomed • Zagavor Obrechyonnikh **50**; Close Friends • Firm Friends • True Friends • Verniye Druzya **54**; The First Echelon • Pervyi Eshelon **55**; The Hostile Wind • Vikhri Vrazhdebnye **56**; The Woman from Warsaw **56**; The Cranes Are Flying • Letyat Zhuravli **57**; Felix Dzerzhinsky **57**; The Letter That Was Never Sent • The Letter That Wasn't Sent • Neotpravlennoye Pismo • The Unsent Letter **60**; Here Is Cuba • I Am Cuba • Soy-Kuba • Ya Cuba • Ya-Kuba **62**; Krasnaya Palatka • The Red Tent • La Tenda Rossa **69**

Kalik, Mikhail Kolybelnaya • The Lullaby **61**; Chelovek Idyot za Solntsem • Man Following the Sun • Sandu Follows the Sun **65**

Kalik, Mosei *see Kalik, Mikhail*

Kalim, S. K. Basanti Apa **88**

Kalmanowicz, Max The Children **80**

Kalmár, László The Sun Shines • Süt a Nap **39**

Kalmus, Herbert T. The Gulf Between **17**

Kalptaru Ghar ka Sukh **88**

Kam, Kwok-leung Wonder Women **87**

Kam, Lam Chi Kung Fu Halloween **81***

Kamal Kakothikavile Appuppan Thadigal **88**

Kamarof, A. The Road North **32**

Kam-bo, Hung see Hung, Samo

Kamecke, Theo Moonwalk One **72**

Kamei, Fumio Nanking **38**; Peking **38**; Shanghai **38**; Soldiers at War • Tatakai Heitai **40**; Shinano Fudok **41**; A Japanese Tragedy • Nihon no Higeki **45**; Sensō to Heiwa • War and Peace **45***; Onna no Isshō • A Woman's Life **49**; Onna Hitori Daichi o Iku • A Woman Walks the Earth Alone **53**; To Be a Mother, to Be a Wife **53**; It Is Better to Live • Living Is Better **56**

Kamen, Jay Transformations **88**

Kamin, Bebe Chechechela—Una Chica del Barrio • Hey, Hey, Chela **86**

Kaminka, Didier As Long As There Are Women • Tant Qu'Il y Aura des Femmes **87**

Kaminsky, Avrom Yitskhok The Forgotten **12**; The Cantor's Daughter **13**; Fatalna Klatwa **13**; His Wife's Husband **13**; The Slaughter **13**; The Stepmother **14**

Kamler, Piotr Chronopolis **82**

Kam-pang, Kwan see Kwan, Stanley

Kampers, Fritz Ich Sing Mich in Dein Herz Hinein **35**; Konjunkturritter **35**

Kampmann, Steven Stealing Home **88***

Kanakis, Nikos To Kollie • The Necklace **85**

Kane, Dennis French Quarter **77**

Kane, Joseph The Fighting Marines **35***; Melody Trail **35**; The Sagebrush Troubador **35**; Tumbling Tumbleweeds **35**; Batmen of Africa • Darkest Africa • Hidden City • King of the Jungleland **36***; Ghost Town Gold **36**; Guns and Guitars **36**; King of the Pecos **36**; The Lawless Nineties **36**; The Lonely Trail **36**; Oh, Susanna! **36**; The Old Corral • Texas Serenade **36**; Ride, Ranger, Ride **36**; Sharad of Atlantis • Undersea Kingdom **36***; Boots and Saddles **37**; Come On, Cowboys! **37**; Git Along, Little Dogies • Serenade of the West **37**; Gunsmoke Ranch **37**; Heart of the Rockies **37**; The Hero of Pine Ridge • Yodelin' Kid from Pine Ridge **37**; Paradise Express **37**; Public Cowboy No. 1 **37**; Round-Up Time in Texas **37**; Springtime in the Rockies **37**; Arson Gang Busters • Arson Racket Squad • Fire Fighters **38**; Billy the Kid Returns **38**; Born to Be Wild **38**; Come On, Rangers! **38**; Gold Mine in the Sky **38**; Man from Music Mountain **38**; The Old Barn Dance **38**; Shine On, Harvest Moon **38**; Under Western Stars **38**; The Arizona Kid **39**; Days of Jesse James **39**; Frontier Pony Express **39**; In Old Caliente **39**; In Old Monterey **39**; Rough Riders' Round-Up **39**; Saga of Death Valley **39**; Southward Ho! **39**; Wall Street Cowboy **39**; The Border Legion • West of the Badlands **40**; The Carson City Kid **40**; Colorado **40**; The Ranger and the Lady **40**; Young Bill

Hickok **40**; Young Buffalo Bill **40**; Badman of Deadwood **41**; The Great Train Robbery **41**; In Old Cheyenne **41**; Jesse James at Bay **41**; Nevada City **41**; Rags to Riches **41**; Red River Valley **41**; Robin Hood of the Pecos **41**; Sheriff of Tombstone **41**; Heart of the Golden West **42**; Man from Cheyenne **42**; Ridin' Down the Canyon **42**; Romance of the Range • Romance on the Range **42**; Sons of the Pioneers **42**; South of Santa Fe **42**; Sunset on the Desert **42**; Sunset Serenade **42**; Hands Across the Border **43**; Idaho **43**; King of the Cowboys **43**; The Man from Music Mountain **43**; Silver Spurs **43**; Song of Texas **43**; The Cowboy and the Señorita **44**; Song of Nevada **44**; The Yellow Rose of Texas **44**; The Castaway • The Cheaters **45**; Dakota **45**; Flame of the Barbary Coast **45**; Flame of Sacramento • In Old Sacramento **46**; The Plainsman and the Lady **46**; Wyoming **47**; The Gallant Legion **48**; In Old Los Angeles • Old Los Angeles **48**; The Plunderers **48**; Brimstone **49**; The Last Bandit **49**; California Passage **50**; Rock Island Trail • Transcontinent Express **50**; The Savage Horde **50**; Fighting Coast Guard **51**; Hoodlum Empire **51**; Oh, Susanna! **51**; The Sea Hornet **51**; Ride the Man Down **52**; Woman of the North Country • Women of the North Country **52**; Fair Wind to Java **53**; San Antone **53**; Sea of Lost Ships **53**; Hell's Outpost **54**; Jubilee Trail **54**; The Road to Denver **55**; Timberjack **55**; The Vanishing American **55**; Accused of Murder **56**; The Maverick Queen **56**; Thunder Over Arizona **56**; The Crooked Circle **57**; Duel at Apache Wells **57**; Gunfire at Indian Gap **57**; Last Stagecoach West **57**; The Lawless Eighties **57**; Spoilers of the Forest **57**; The Man Who Died Twice **58**; The Notorious Mr. Monks **58**; Country Boy • Here Comes That Nashville Sound **66**; Search for the Evil One **67**; Track of Thunder **67**; Smoke in the Wind **71**

Kaneko, Shusuke 1999—Nen no Natsu Yasumi • Summer Vacation: 1999 **89**

Kanevski, Vitaly Freeze—Die—Come to Life • Zamri Oumi Voskresni **90**

Kanew, Jeff Black Rodeo **72**; Natural Enemies **79**; Eddie Macon's Run **83**; Revenge of the Nerds **84**; Gotcha! **85**; Tough Guys **86**; Troop Beverly Hills **89**

Kanievska, Marek Another Country **84**; Less Than Zero **87**

Kanin, Garson A Man to Remember **38**; Next Time I Marry **38**; Bachelor Mother **39**; The Great Man Votes **39**; My Favorite Wife **40***; They Knew What They Wanted **40**; Night Shift **41**; Tom, Dick and Harry **41**; Fellow Americans **42**; Ring of Steel **42**; German Manpower **43***; Night Stripes **43**; Battle Stations **44**; Salut à France • Salut à la France • Salute to France **44***; The True Glory **45***; The One with the Fuzz • Some Kind of a Nut **69**; Where It's At **69**

Kanin, Michael When I Grow Up **51**

Kanizsay, József Pillanatnyi Pénzzavar • Temporarily Broke **39**

Kanner, Alexis Kings and Desperate Men **81**

K'an-p'ing, Yu see Yu, K'an-p'ing

Kanter, Hal I Married a Woman **56**; Loving You **57**; Hot Horse • Once Upon a Horse **58**

Kanter, Richard Angels for Kicks • Wild Riders **71**; The Affairs of Robin Hood **81**

Kantor, Ron Emerson, Lake and Palmer in Concert **81**

Kanturek, Otto Student Romance • The Student's Romance **35**

Kao, Li see Li, Kao

Kaplan, Henry The Girl on the Boat **61**

Kaplan, Jonathan Street Scenes **70***; Night Call Nurses **72**; The Slams **73**; The Student Teachers **73**; Truck Turner **74**; White Line Fever **75**; Mr. Billion **76**; Over the Edge **79**; Heart Like a Wheel **82**; Project X **87**; The Accused **88**; Immediate Family **89**

Kaplan, Nelly Magirama **56***; Gustave Moreau **61**; Rodolphe Bresdin 1825-1885 **61**; Abel Gance, Hier et Demain **63**; À la Source, la Femme Aimée **66**; Les Années 25 **66**; Dessins et Merveilles **66**; La Nouvelle Orangerie **66**; Le Regard Picasso **66**; Dirty Mary • La Fiancée du Pirate • Pirate's Fiancée • A Very Curious Girl • A Very Private Affair **69**; Papa les Petits Bateaux **71**; Néa • Néa—A Young Emmanuelle • A Young Emmanuelle **76**; Le Satellite de Vénus **77**; Au Bonheur des Dames **79**; Charles and Lucie • Charles et Lucie **79**; Abel Gance et Son Napoléon **83**

Kaplan, Richard The Eleanor Roosevelt Story **65**

Kaplan, Robert J. Scarecrow in a Garden of Cucumbers **72**; Gums **76**

Kaplunovsky, V. The Mexican **57**; The Captain's Daughter **59**

Kapoor, Raj Aag **48**; Fire **48**; Barsaat **49**; Awara • The Vagabond **51**; Mister 420 • Shri Char Saw Bees • Shri 420 **55**; Jagte Raho **57**; Jis Desh Men Ganga Behti • Where the Ganges Flows **61**; Sangam **64**; Mera Naam Joker • My Name Is Joker **70**; Bobby **74**; Satyam Shivam Sundaram **78**; Prem Rog **82**

Kapoor, Shekhar see Kapur, Shekhar

Kapps, Walter Détournement de Mineures • The Price of Flesh **62**

Kapsakis, D. You Came Too Late **62**

Kapsakis, Sokrates Lisa, the Greek Tosca • Lisa, Tosca of Athens **61**; The Hot Month of August • O Zestos Menas Augoustos **69**

Kaptur, Michel High Speed **86***

Kapur, Shekhar Mr. India **87**

Kara, Yuri Tomorrow There Came War • Zavtra Bila Voina **87**; Kings of Crime • Vory v Zakone **88**

Karabasz, Kazimierz People from the Empty Area **57***; A Day Without Sun **59***; Musicians **60**; People on the Road **61**; Railway Junction **61**; Where Do You Go? **61**; The First Steps **62**; Jubilee **62**; The Birds **63**; In the Club **63**; Born 1944 **64**; A Year in Frank's Life **67***; Cień Już Niedaleko • A Looming Shadow **85**

Karakorpi, Titta Ruusujen Aika • Time of Roses 69*

Karanović, Srđan The Fragrance of Wild Flowers • Miris Poljskog Cveća 77; Za Sada Bez Dobrog Naslova 88

Karanovich, Anatoly Banya • Bath • The Bath House 62*; Mayakovsky Laughs • Mayakovsky Smeyotsia 75*

Karasik, Yuli Shestoe Iulya • The Sixth of July 68; Chaika • The Seagull 71; Bez Solntsa 88

Karayannis see Carayiannis, Costas

Karayannis, Kostas see Carayiannis, Costas

Kardar, Ajay No Greater Glory • Qasam Us Waqt ki 69

Kardish, Larry Slow Run 68

Kardos, László see Kardos, Leslie

Kardos, Leslie 120 Kilometers an Hour 37; Love of Sport • Sportszerelem 38*; Dark Streets of Cairo 40; The Strip 51; Small Town Girl 52; The Man Who Turned to Stone 57; The Tijuana Story 57

Karel, Russ Almonds and Raisins 83

Karelov, Y. The Last Game • Tretyi Taym 64

Kares, Peter The Night They Robbed Big Bertha's 75

Karevsky, B. Private Ivan 57

Karger, Maxwell The Hole in the Wall 21; The Idle Rich 21; The Man Who 21; A Message from Mars 21; A Trip to Paradise 21; The Golden Gift 22; Kisses 22

Karin, Vladimir Uprising 18*

Karina, Anna Vivre Ensemble 73

Karipidis, Giorgos Sti Skia tou Fovou 88

Karis, Helle Dikie Lebedi 88

Kar-leung, Lau see Lau, Kar-leung

Karlson, Phil G.I. Honeymoon 44; There Goes Kelly 44; A Wave, a WAC and a Marine 44; Live Wires 45; The Shanghai Cobra 45; Behind the Mask • The Shadow Behind the Mask 46; Bowery Bombshell 46; Charlie Chan in Alcatraz • Dark Alibi • Fatal Fingertips 46; The Missing Lady • The Shadow and the Missing Lady 46; Shadow of Blackmail • Wife Wanted 46; Swing Parade of 1946 46; Above All Laws • Adventures in Silverado 47; Black Gold 47; Kilroy Was Here 47; Louisiana 47; Fury • Thunderhoof 48; Ladies of the Chorus 48; Rocky 48; The Big Cat 49; Down Memory Lane 49; The Iroquois Trail • The Tomahawk Trail 50; The Dark Page • Scandal Sheet 51; Lorna Doone 51; Mask of the Avenger 51; The Texas Rangers 51; The Brigand 52; Kansas City Confidential • The Secret Four 52; 99 River Street 53; Hell's Island • Love Is a Weapon • The Ruby Virgin • South Seas Fury 54; They Rode West 54; Five Against the House 55; The Phenix City Story 55; Tight Spot 55; The Brothers Rico 57; Gunman's Walk 58; The Scarface Mob • Tueur de Chicago • The Untouchables 59; Hell to Eternity 60; Key Witness 60; No Deadly Machine • The Young Doctors 61; The Secret Ways 61*; Jungle Rampage • Rampage! 62*; Kid Galahad 62; The Silencers 65; The Long Ride Home • A Time for

Killing 67*; Alexander the Great 68; House of Seven Joys • The Wrecking Crew 68; Hornet's Nest 70; Ben 72; Walking Tall 73; Framed 74

Karlstein, Phil see Karlson, Phil

Karlstein, Philip N. see Karlson, Phil

Karman, Janice The Chipmunk Adventure 86

Karmazinski, N. If War Comes Tomorrow 38*

Karmen, Roman Moscow • Moskva 32; Moscow, Kara Kum, Moscow 33; Parade in Red Square, Moscow 33; At Home 34; Salute to the Spanish Pioneers 36; Ispaniya • Spain 37*; China Defends Herself 38; A Day in the New World • Den Novogo Mira 40; Sedovchy • The Sedovites • Sedov's Expedition 40; In China • V Kitai 41; Days and Nights of Leningrad • The Defense of Leningrad • Leningrad in Combat • Leningrad v Borbye 42*; Albania 45; Judgment of the People • Nuremburg 47; Soviet Turkmenistan 50; Soviet Georgia 51; Caspian Oil Workers • Caspian Story • Povest o Neftyanikakh Kaspiya • Story of the Caspian Oil Men 53; Vietnam 54; Dawn of India • India Morning • Utro India • Visit to India 56; Great Is My Country • How Broad Is Our Country 58; Conquered Seas • Pokoriteli Morya 59; Cuba, Island in Flames • Cuba Segodnya • Cuba Today • Island of Flame 60; Our Indonesian Friend 60; September Sixteenth 60; One Day with Russians 61*; Gost o Ostrova Svobody • A Guest from the Island of Freedom • Guest on Freedom Island 63; The Great Patriotic War • Velikaya Otechestvennaya 65; Death of a Commissar 66; Granada, My Granada 67

Karmitz, Marin Nuit Noire, Calcutta 64; Sept Jours Ailleurs 67; Camarades • Comrades 70; Blow for Blow • Coup pour Coup 72

Karn, Bill Gang Busters 55; Ma Barker's Killer Brood 60; Door-to-Door Maniac • Five Minutes to Live 61

Karnad, Girish The Forest • Kaadu 73

Karr, Tom see Clark, Bob

Karson, Eric Dirt 79*; The Octagon 80; Hellcamp • Opposing Force 86; Black Eagle 88; Angel Town 90

Kar-wai, Wong see Wong, Kar-wai

Kar-wing, Lau see Lau, Kar-wing

Karya, Teguh Bitter Coffee • Secangkir Kopi Pahit 86; Doea Tanda Mata • Mementos 86; Ibunda • Mother 87

Karyukov, Mikhail The Heavens Call • Nebo Zovyot • Nebo Zowet • Niebo Zowiet • The Sky Calls 59*; Battle Beyond the Sun 63*; A Dream Come True • Meshte Nastreshu 63*; Planet of Blood • Queen of Blood 66*

Kasancki, Y. see Kazansky, Gennady

Kasaravalli, Girish The Story of Tabarana • Tabarana Kathe 86

Kasdan, Lawrence Body Heat 81; The Big Chill 83; Silverado 85; The Accidental Tourist 88; I Love You to Death 90

Kasheverova, Nadezhda Christmas Slippers 45*

Kashyap, Ajay Do Qaidi 89

Kasi, Zmarai Ghame Afghan • The Tragedy of the Afghan 86*

Kaspar, Stefan Gregorio 85*

Kass, Peter Time of the Heathen 61*

Kassila, Matti Elokuu 56; Farewell to the President • Jäähyväiset Presidentille 87; The Glory and Misery of Human Life • Ihmiselon Ihanuus ja Kurjuus 89

Kassila, Taavi Petos 88

Kast, Pierre Les Charmes de l'Existence 49*; Les Désastres de la Guerre • Goya • Goya ou Les Désastres de la Guerre 51*; L'Encyclopédie Filmée • L'Encyclopédie Filmée — Alchimie, Azur, Absence 51*; Les Femmes du Louvre 51; La Guerre en Dentelles • Jacques Callot, Correspondant du Guerre 52; Je Sème à Tout Vent 52; À Nous Deux, Paris! 53; La Chasse à l'Homme 53; L'Architecte Maudit, Claude-Nicolas Ledoux • Claude-Nicolas Ledoux, Architecte Maudit 54; Monsieur Robida, Prophète et Explorateur de Temps 54; Nos Ancêtres les Explorateurs 55; Le Corbusier, l'Architecte du Bonheur 55; Un Amour de Poche • Girl in His Pocket • Nude in His Pocket 57; Des Ruines et des Hommes 58*; Images pour Baudelaire 58; Le Bel Âge • Love Is When You Make It 59; Japon, d'Hiver et d'Aujourd'hui 59*; Promenade Quotidienne aux Indes 59; Une Question d'Assurance 59; Regards sur le Pakistan 59; Les Liaisons Amoureuses • La Morte-Saison des Amours • The Season for Love 60; Merci, Natercia 60; Les Sourires de la Destinée • Vacances Portugaises 63; La Brûlure de Mille Soleils • The Fire of a Thousand Suns • The Radiance of a Thousand Suns 64; Circular Triangle • Le Grain de Sable • Le Triangle Circulaire 64; Drôle de Jeu • The Most Dangerous Game 68; Candomblé et Macumba • Le Drapeau Blanc d'Oxala • Macumba 69; Les Soleils de l'Île de Pâques 72

Kastle, Leonard Dear Martha • The Honeymoon Killers • The Lonely Hearts Killer • The Lonely Hearts Killers 69

Kastner, Elliott Likewise 88*

Kasyanov, Vladimir Death of the Gods 17

Kaszubowski, Jerzy The Road Home 88

Katakouzinos, George see Katakouzinos, Yorgos

Katakouzinos, Yorgos Angel • Angelos 82; Absences • Apousies 87

Katcher, Aram Right Hand of the Devil 63

Kathner, Rupe The Glenrowan Affair 51

Kato, Tai see Tai, Kato

Katscher, Rudolf Teilnehmer Antwortet Nicht 32*; Invisible Opponent • Unsichtbare Gegner 33

Katselas, Milton Butterflies Are Free 72; 40 Carats 73; Operation Undercover • Report to the Commissioner 74; When You Comin' Back Red Ryder? 79

Katsouridis, Dinos A Leftist Night's Dream • Oniro Aristeris Nichtas 87

Katz, James C. The Anatomy of a

Pinup 72; The Rise and Fall of Ivor Dickie 78*

Katz, Max Jim the Man 67

Katzin, Lee H. Hondo and the Apaches 67; Heaven with a Gun 68; What Ever Happened to Aunt Alice? 69; Le Mans 70; The Phynx 70; The Salzburg Connection 72; World Gone Wild 87

Katzman, Leonard First Woman Into Space • Space Monster • Voyage Beyond the Sun 65

Katzman, Mosche see Stiller, Mauritz

Katzman, Sam Amateur Crook 37; Brothers of the West 37; Lost Ranch 37; Orphan of the Pecos 37

Kaufer, Jonathan Soup for One 82

Kaufman, Andy My Breakfast with Blassie 83*

Kaufman, Charles The Secret Dreams of Mona Q 77; Mother's Day 80; When Nature Calls 85; Jakarta 88

Kaufman, George S. Mr. Ashton Was Indiscreet • The Senator Was Indiscreet 47

Kaufman, Jack The Rise and Fall of the Third Reich 65

Kaufman, Joseph Heartaches 15; Ashes of Embers 16; Dollars and the Woman 16; Nanette of the Wilds 16; Sorrows of Happiness 16; The Traveling Salesman 16; The World's Great Snare 16; The Amazons 17; Arms and the Girl 17; Broadway Jones 17; Great Expectations 17*; The Land of Promise 17; The Song of Songs 18

Kaufman, Lloyd The Battle of Love's Return 71; Squeeze Play 80*; Soup to Nuts • Waitress! 82*; Stuck on You 83*; The First Turn-On 84*; The Toxic Avenger 84*; Class of Nuke 'Em High • Nuke 'Em High 85*; Troma's War • War 87*; The Toxic Avenger, Part II 89*; The Toxic Avenger Part III — The Last Temptation of Toxie 89*

Kaufman, Mikhail Moscow • Moskva 26*; Spring • Vesnoy 29; The Great Victory 33; Air March 36; Folk Dances of the USSR 39; Our Moscow 39; The Tretyakov Gallery 56

Kaufman, Millard Convicts Four • Reprieve 62

Kaufman, Philip Goldstein 64*; Fearless Frank • Frank's Greatest Adventure 67; The Great Northfield Minnesota Raid 71; The White Dawn 74; Invasion of the Body Snatchers 78; Up Your Ladder 79; The Wanderers 79; The Right Stuff 83; The Unbearable Lightness of Being 87; Henry & June 90

Kaufmann, Wilhelm von Gretel and Liesel • Kohlhiesel's Daughters • Kohlhiesels Töchter 31

Kaul, Mani The Traveler • Yatrik 66; A Day's Bread • Uski Roti 70; Ashad ka Ek Din • A Monsoon Day 71; Duvidha • In Two Minds 73; The Nomad Puppeteers 74; Ghashiram Kotwol • Ghashiram the Police Chief 76; Chitrakkathi 77; Arrival 80; Rising from the Surface • Satah se Uthata Aadmi 80; Dhrupad 83

Kaurismäki, Aki Saimaa-Ilmiö 82; Crime and Punishment • Rikos ja Rangais-

tus 83; Calamari Union 85; Rocky VI 86; Shadows in Paradise • Varjoja Paratiisissa 86; Hamlet • Hamlet Goes Business • Hamlet Liikemaailmassa 87; Ariel 88; Leningrad Cowboys Go America 89; I Hired a Contract Killer 90; The Match Factory Girl • Tulitikkutehtaan Tyttö 90

Kaurismäki, Mika Arvottomat • The Worthless 82; The Clan • Klaani — Tarina Sammakoiden Suvusta 84; Rosso 85; Helsinki-Napoli: All Night Long 87; Cha-Cha-Cha 89

Käutner, Helmut Die Acht Entfesselten 39; Kitty and the World Conference • Kitty und die Weltkonferenz 39; Clothes Make the Man • Kleider Machen Leute 40; Frau Nach Mass 40; Auf Wiedersehen, Franziska 41; Anuschka 42; Wir Machen Musik 42; Romance in a Minor Key • Romanze in Moll 43; Grosse Freiheit Nr 7 • La Paloma • Port of Freedom 44; Under the Bridges • Unter den Brücken 45; In Former Days • In Jenen Tagen • Seven Journeys 47; Der Apfel Ist Ab • The Apple Fell • The Apple Is Picked • The Fallen Apple • The Original Sin 48; Königskinder 49; Epilog • Epilogue 50; Weisse Schatten 51; Käpt'n Bay-Bay 52; The Last Bridge • Die Letzte Brücke 53; Bildnis einer Unbekannten • Portrait of an Unknown Woman 54; Ludwig II 54; Des Teufels General • The Devil's General 55; The Girl from Flanders • Ein Mädchen aus Flandern 55; Griff nach den Sternen 55; Himmel Ohne Sterne • Sky Without Stars 55; Auf Wiedersehen, Franziska Monpti • Love from Paris • Monpti 56; The Captain from Koepenick • The Captain of Koepenick • Der Hauptmann von Köpenick 56; Engagement in Zurich • Die Zürcher Verlobung 56; The Affairs of Julie 57; Duel in the Forest 58; The Reckless Years • The Restless Years • The Wonderful Years 58; Der Schinderhannes 58; A Stranger in My Arms 58; Die Gans von Sedan • Sans Tambour ni Trompette 59; The Rest Is Silence • Der Rest Ist Schweigen 59; Black Gravel • Schwarzer Kies 60; Das Glas Wasser • A Glass of Water 60; Der Traum von Lieschen Müller 61; The Redhead • Die Rote 62; Das Haus in Montevideo 63; Lausbubengeschichten 64; Die Feuerzangenbowle 70

Kavaleridze, E. Mass Struggle 34; Girl from Poltava • Natalka Poltavka 36*

Kavanagh, Brian Double Deal 81; Departure 86

Kavanagh, Denis On Top of the Underworld 38*; The Banjo Fool 40; Camp Concert 40; Fiddlers All 40; Music Box 40; Swing Tease 40; Twinkling Fingers 40; Starlight Serenade 44; The Ghost of Rashmon Hall • Night Comes Too Soon 48; Dollars for Sale 53*; Flight from Vienna 56; They Never Learn 56; Fighting Mad 57; Rock You Sinners 57

Kavur, Ömer Amansız Yol • The Desperate Road 86; Anayurt Öteli • Motherland Hotel 87; Gece Yolculuğu 88

Kawadri, Anwar Confessions of the

Naughty Nymphos • Sex with the Stars 80; Nutcracker 82

Kawajiri, Yoshiaki Lensman 84*

Kawalerowicz, Jerzy Commune • The Community • Gromada • Rural Community • The Village Mill 50*; Cellulose • Celuloza • A Night of Remembrance • Pamiatka z Celuloza 54; Pod Gwiazda Frygijska • Under the Phrygian Sky 54; Cień • The Shadow 56; Prawdziwy Koniec Wielkiej Wojny • The Real End of the Great War 57; Baltic Express • Night Train • Pociag 59; The Devil and the Nun • Joan of the Angels • Matka Joanna od Aniołów • Mother Joan of the Angels 60; Faraon • Pharaoh 65; The Game • Gra • Play 68; Magdalena 70; Death of the President • The President's Death • Śmierć Prezydenta 77; Chance Meeting on the Atlantic • Chance Meeting on the Ocean • Meeting on the Atlantic • Spotkanie na Atlantyku 79; Austeria 82

Kawashima, Yuzo Evening Stream • Flowing Night • The Lovelorn Geisha • Yoru no Nagare 60*; The Dangerous Kiss 61; Aobe Ka Monogatari • This Madding Crowd 64

Kay, Gilbert see Briz, José

Kay, James H. III The Gardener • Seeds of Evil 72

Kay, Jonathon Walking After Midnight 88

Kay, Roger The Cabinet of Caligari • The Cabinet of Dr. Caligari 62; The Rawhide Halo • Shoot Out at Big Sag 62

Kay, Wong Wah Sapporo Story 87

Kaye, Richard Black Fist • The Black Streetfighter • Homeboy 76*

Kaye, Stanton Georg 64; Brandy in the Wilderness 69

Kaygun, Sahin Dolunay 88

Kayko, Sixto Private Show 85

Kaylor, Robert Derby 70; Carny 80; Nobody's Perfect 89

Kazan, Elia Pie in the Sky 34*; The People of the Cumberland 37*; It's Up to You 41; A Tree Grows in Brooklyn 45; The Sea of Grass 46; Boomerang 47; Gentleman's Agreement 47; Pinky 49*; Panic in the Streets 50; A Streetcar Named Desire 51; Viva Zapata! 52; Man on a Tightrope 53*; On the Waterfront 54; East of Eden 55; Baby Doll 56; A Face in the Crowd 57; Wild River 60; Splendor in the Grass 61; America, America • The Anatolian Smile 63; The Arrangement 69; The Visitors 71; The Last Tycoon 75

Kazan, Gadge see Kazan, Elia

Kazansky, Gennady The Flying Carpet 60; The Amphibian Man • The Amphibious Man • Chelovek Amfibia 61*

Kazui, Fran Rubel Tokyo Pop 87

Ke, Xu see Shu, Kei

Keach, James False Identity 90

Keach, Stacy The Repeater 72

Keady, Gary L. Sons of Steel 88

Kean, Richard see Civirani, Osvaldo

Keane, James Money 15; The Spreading Evil 19; Whispering Women 21

Keane, Laurence Samuel Lount 86

Kearton, Cherry A Primitive Man's Career to Civilization 11

Keatering, Michael Eves on Skis 63

Keating, Kevin Hell's Angels Forever 83*

Keaton, Buster Convict 13 20*; The High Sign 20*; Neighbors 20*; One Week 20*; The Scarecrow 20*; The Blacksmith 21*; The Boat 21*; The Goat 21*; Hard Luck 21*; The Haunted House 21*; The Paleface 21*; The Playhouse 21*; Cops 22*; Day Dreams 22*; The Electric House 22*; The Frozen North 22*; My Wife's Relations 22*; The Balloonatic • Balloonatics 23*; The Love Nest 23*; Our Hospitality 23*; The Three Ages 23*; The Navigator 24*; Sherlock, Jr. 24; Go West 25; Seven Chances 25; Battling Butler 26; The General 26*; Hollywood Handicap 38; Life in Sometown, U.S.A. 38; Streamlined Swing 38

Keaton, Diane Heaven 87

Keays, Vernon Strictly in the Groove 42; Arizona Trail 43; Marshal of Gunsmoke 44; Trail to Gunsight 44; Trigger Law 44; The Utah Kid 44; Blazing the Western Trail • Who Killed Waring? 45; Dangerous Intruder 45; Fortune Hunter • Sing Me a Song of Texas 45; Honest John • Rhythm Round-Up 45; Lawless Empire • Power of Possession 45; Partners in Fortune • Rockin' in the Rockies 45; The Claw Strikes • Landrush 46; The Mysterious Mr. M 46*; State Police • Whirlwind Raiders 48

Kedzielawska, Grażyna Another Island • Inna Wyspa 87

Keenan, Frank Brothers Divided 19; The Silver Girl 19*; Dollar for Dollar 20; Smouldering Embers 20

Keenan, Haydn Pandemonium 88

Keeslar, Don Bog 78

Keeter, Worth Wolfman 79; Lady Grey 80; Living Legend 80; Dogs of Hell • Rotweiler: Dogs of Hell 84; Order of the Black Eagle 85; Tales of the Third Dimension 85*; L.A. Bounty 89

Keglevic, Peter Bella Donna 83; Der Bulle und das Mädchen 85; Magic Sticks 87

Kei, Shu see Shu, Kei

Keifer, Warren Il Castello dei Morti Vivi • Castle of the Living Dead • Le Château des Morts Vivants • Crypt of Horror 64*

Keighley, William The Match King 32*; Easy to Love 33; Footlight Parade 33*; Ladies They Talk About • Women in Prison 33*; Babbitt 34; Big-Hearted Herbert 34; Dr. Monica 34*; Journal of a Crime 34; Kansas City Princess 34; G-Men 35; Mary Jane's Pa • Wanderlust 35; The Right to Live • The Sacred Flame 35; Special Agent 35; Stars Over Broadway 35; Bullets or Ballots 36; God's Country and the Woman 36; The Green Pastures 36*; The Singing Kid 36; The Prince and the Pauper 37; Varsity Show 37; The Adventures of Robin Hood • Robin Hood 38*; Brother Rat 38; Secrets of an Actress 38;

Valley of the Giants 38; Each Dawn I Die 39; Yes, My Darling Daughter 39; The Fighting 69th 40; Guy with a Grin • No Time for Comedy 40; Torrid Zone 40; The Bride Came C.O.D. 41; Four Mothers 41; The Man Who Came to Dinner 41; George Washington Slept Here 42; Target for Today 44; Honeymoon • Two Men and a Girl 47; The Street with No Name 48; Rocky Mountain 50; Close to My Heart 51; The Master of Ballantrae 53

Keith, Anthony The Island of Wisdom 20

Keith, David The Curse • The Farm 87; The Further Adventures of Tennessee Buck • Sacrifice 88

Keith, Harvey Jezebel's Kiss 90

Keleti, Márton Viki 37; Keep On Smoking, Ladányi • Te Csak Pipálj Ladányi 38; Torockoi Bride • Torockói Menyasszony 38; Barbara in America • Borcsa Amerikában 39; Biting Husband • Harapós Férj 39; Fehérvári Huszárok • Hussars of Fehérvári 39; Mickey Magnate 49; Singing Makes Life Beautiful 50; Tegnap • Yesterday 59

Keller, Frederick King Tuck Everlasting 80; The Eyes of the Amaryllis 82; Vamping 84; My Dark Lady 87

Keller, Harry The Blonde Bandit 49; Tarnished 50; Desert of Lost Men 51; Fort Dodge Stampede 51; Black Hills Ambush 52; Leadville Gunslinger 52; Rose of Cimarron 52; Thundering Caravans 52; Bandits of the West 53; Commando Cody 53*; El Paso Stampede 53; Marshal of Cedar Rock 53; Red River Shore 53; Savage Frontier 53; The Phantom Stallion 54; The Unguarded Moment 56; Man Afraid 57; Quantez 57; Touch of Evil 57*; Day of the Bad Man 58; The Female Animal 58; The Silent Stranger • Step Down to Terror 58; Texas John Slaughter 58; The Voice in the Mirror 58; Seven Ways from Sundown 60; Gunfight at Sandoval 61; Tammy Tell Me True 61; Geronimo's Revenge 62*; Six Black Horses 62; Tammy and the Doctor 63; The Brass Bottle 64; In Enemy Country 67

Keller, Lew Sailing and Village Sand 58; Spring and Saganaki 58; Trees and Jamaica Daddy 58; Picnics Are Fun and Dino's Serenade 59

Kellett, Bob Futtock's End 69; Girl Stroke Boy 71; Up Pompeii 71; Up the Chastity Belt 71; The Alf Garnett Saga 72; Our Miss Fred 72; Up the Front 72; Don't Just Lie There, Say Something! 73; All I Want Is You and You and You 75; Spanish Fly 75; Are You Being Served? 77; Tightrope to Terror 77; The Waiting Room 77

Kelley, Albert Home Stuff 21; Deserted at the Altar 22*; Dancing Days 26; His New York Wife 26; Shameful Behavior? 26; Stage Kisses 27; The Charge of the Gauchos 28; Confessions of a Wife 28; Campus Knights 29; Lights and Shadows • The Woman Racket 29*; Jungle Bride 33*; Double Cross • Motorcycle Squad 41; Submarine Base 43; Slippy McGee 48; Street

Corner 48

Kelley, J. Winthrop The Submarine Eye 17; Girl of the Sea 20

Kelley, Winthrop see Kelley, J. Winthrop

Kellino, Roy Atlantic Episode • Catch As Catch Can 37; Concerning Mr. Martin 37; Down to the Sea in Ships • The Last Adventurers 37; Father o' Nine 38; I Met a Murderer 39; Guilt Is My Shadow 50; Charade 52; Lady Possessed 52*; The Silken Affair 56

Kellino, Will P. The Coster's Honeymoon 12; Grand Harlequinade 12; Pimple and the Snake 12; Pimple Does the Turkey Trot 12; The Taming of Big Ben 12; The Whistling Bet 12; Yiddle on My Fiddle 12; Baby's Photograph 13; Bumbles and the Bass 13; Bumbles Becomes a Crook 13; Bumbles' Diminisher 13; Bumbles' Electric Belt 13; Bumbles' Goose 13; Bumbles' Holiday 13; Bumbles, Photographer 13; Bumbles' Radium Minstrels 13; Bumbles' Walk to Brighton 13; The Dustmen's Holiday 13; Everybody's Doing It 13; The Flight of Wealth 13; The Happy Dustmen 13; He Did It for the Best 13; How Willy Joined Barnum Bill 13; The Jovial Fluid 13; Juggling Mad 13; A Knife to Grind 13; Money-Making Coats 13; Mrs. Letare Lets Apartments 13; Nobby and the Pearl Mystery 13; Nobby the New Waiter 13; Nosey Parker 13; Oh That Woollen Undervest! 13; On the Hop 13; Parcels or the Baby 13; The Rival Musicians 13; Stoggles' Christmas Dinner 13; After the Ball Was Over 14; Bertie's Baby 14; Betty's Birthday 14; Bumbles' Appetite 14; Bumbles Goes Butterflying 14; Chums 14; Conspicuous Bravery 14; Dip 'Em and Do 'Em, Ltd. 14; Dr. Dosem's Deputy 14; The Domestic Game Hunt 14; Fidgett's Superstitions 14; Ginger Seeks a Situation 14; Grand Christmas Harlequinade 14; The Gypsy's Curse 14; The Happy Dustmen Play Golf 14; The Happy Dustmen's Christmas 14; How Spotted Duff Saved the Squire 14; Love and a Tub 14; The Mystery of the Landlady's Cat 14; Nobby the Knut 14; Nobby Wins the Cup 14; Nobby's Ju-Jitsu Experiments 14; Nobby's Stud 14; Nobby's Tango Teas 14; The Pet Hen 14; Picture Palace Piecans 14; A Pointed Joke 14; The Postman's Dilemma 14; Potted Pantomimes 14; Snooks As a Fireman 14; Spy Catchers 14; The Students' Night Out 14; The Tromboner's Strong Note 14; The White Stocking 14; Who Was to Blame? 14; You're Wanted on the Phone, Sir 14; Bill's Monicker 15; Billy's Spanish Love Spasm 15; Caught in a Kilt 15; The Dustman's Nightmare 15; Eggs 15; Extravagant Molly 15; A Fight for Life 15; Fighting Billy 15; Hamlet 15; He Would Act 15; His Father's Sin 15; Inventing Trouble 15; The Man in Possession 15; None But the Brave 15; Oh That Face! 15; The Only Man 15; The Order of the Bath 15; Paying Him Out 15; Playing the Deuce 15; Pote's Poem 15; Romeo and Juliet 15;

Some Actors 15; Spoof 15; What a
Bounder 15; Who Kissed Her? 15; The
Wrong House 15; Billy's Stormy Courtship
16; The Dummy 16; The Dustman's Wed-
ding 16; The Dustmen's Outing 16; Park-
er's Weekend 16; Patriotic Mrs. Brown 16;
The Perils of Pork Pie 16; Screen Struck 16;
The Tale of a Shirt 16; The Terrible 'Tec
16; A Wife in a Hurry 16; Billy Strikes Oil
17; Billy the Truthful 17; Economy 17;
How's Your Poor Wife? 17; Hullo! Who's
Your Lady Friend? 17; The Missing Link
17; Splash Me Nicely 17; The Exploits of
Parker 18; Angel Esquire 19; The Green
Terror 19; A Broken Contract 20; Cousin
Ebenezer 20; Cupid's Carnival 20; The Fall
of a Saint 20; The Fordington Twins 20;
The Lightning Liver Cure 20; On the
Reserve 20; Run! Run! 20; Saved from the
Sea 20; Souvenirs 20; Sweep 20; The Au-
tumn of Pride 21; Class and No Class 21;
The Fortune of Christina McNab 21; Rob
Roy 22; A Soul's Awakening 22; Young
Lochinvar 23; The Colleen Bawn • The
Loves of Colleen Bawn 24; His Grace Gives
Notice 24; The Mating of Marcus 24; Not
for Sale 24; Caught in the Web • The
Lady in Lace 25*; Confessions 25; The
Gold Cure 25; Hearts Trump Diamonds •
The Lady in Jewels 25*; Heel Taps • The
Lady in High Heels 25*; The Lady in Furs
• Sables of Death 25*; The Lady in Silk
Stockings • The Weakness of Men 25*;
The Painted Lady • Red Lips 25*; We
Women 25; Further Adventures of the
Flag Lieutenant 27; Sailors Don't Care 28;
Smashing Through 28; Alf's Carpet 29;
Alf's Button 30; Aroma of the South Seas
30; Bull Rushes 30; Hot Heir 30; Who
Killed Doc Robin? 30; My Old China 31;
The Poisoned Diamond 34; Sometimes
Good 34; Wishes 34; Lend Me Your Wife
35; Regal Cavalcade • Royal Cavalcade
35*; Hot News 36; Paybox Adventure 36

Kelljan, Robert Count Yorga, Vampire
70; The Return of Count Yorga 71;
Scream, Blacula, Scream! 73; Act of Vengeance • Rape Squad 74; Black Oak Conspiracy 77

Kellman, Barnet Key Exchange 85

Kellogg, Ray The Giant Gila Monster
59; The Killer Shrews 59; My Dog, Buddy
60; The Green Berets 68*; Tora! Tora!
Tora! 70*

Kelly, Albert see Kelley, Albert

Kelly, Duke My Name Is Legend 75

Kelly, Gene On the Town 49*; Singin'
in the Rain 51*; It's Always Fair Weather
55*; Circus • Invitation to the Dance 56;
The Happy Road 56; The Tunnel of Love
58; Gigot 62; A Guide for the Married
Man 67; Hello, Dolly! 69; The Cheyenne
Social Club 70; That's Entertainment, Part
2 • That's Entertainment, Too! 75*

Kelly, James Are You Dying Young
Man? • The Beast in the Cellar • Young
Man I Think You're Dying 70; Child of
the Night • Night Hair Child • What the
Peeper Saw 71

Kelly, Patrick Beer • The Selling of

America 85

Kelly, Robert The Ranger and the Law
21; Blue Blazes 22*

Kelly, Ron Waiting for Caroline 67;
King of the Grizzlies 70

Kelly Ramírez, Luis Calacan 86

Kelsey, Fred A. The Almost Good Man
17; The Fighting Gringo • Red Saunders
Plays Cupid 17; The One-Way Trail 20

Kelson, George The Tenth Case 17; The
Purple Lily 18; Stolen Orders 18*; The
Strong Way 18; The Way Out 18

Kememy, Adalbert São Paulo: Sinfonía
de una Metrópoli 29

Kemm, Jean Les Deux Marquises 16; Le
Dédale 17; Honneur d'Artiste 17; André
Cornélis 18; Le Délai 18; L'Obstacle 18;
L'Énigme 19; Le Destin Est Maître 20;
Micheline 20; Miss Rovel 20; L'Absolution
22; Le Ferme du Choquart 22; Hantise 22;
Ce Pauvre Chéri 23; André Cornélis 27;
L'Amour Maître des Choses 31; Le Barbier
de Séville 36; Le Juif Polonais 37

Kemp, Jack Miracle in Harlem 47

Kemplen, Ralph The Spaniard's Curse
58

Kendal-Savegar, Brian Inheritor 90

Kendall, David Luggage of the Gods!
83

Kendall, Preston Heads Win 19

Kenepp, Errett LeRoy The Man Nobody
Knows 25

Kenjiro, Komuri Mother on the Quay
76

Kennedy, Aubrey M. Liquid Gold 19;
Sky-Eye 20

Kennedy, Burt The Canadians 61; Mail
Order Bride • West of Montana 63; The
Rounders 64; The Money Trap 65; Killer
on a Horse • Welcome to Hard Times 66;
Return of the Magnificent Seven • Return
of the Seven 66; The War Wagon 67; Sup-
port Your Local Sheriff! 68; Who Rides
with Kane • Young Billy Young 68; The
Good Guys and the Bad Guys 69; The
Deserter • Ride to Glory • La Spina Dor-
sale del Diavolo 70; Dirty Dingus Magee
70; Support Your Local Gunfighter 70;
Hannie Caulder 71; The Train Robbers 73;
The Killer Inside Me 75; Drum 76*; The
Honor Guard • Wolf Lake 78; The Trouble with Spies 84; Big Bad John 90

Kennedy, Edgar From Soup to Nuts 28;
You're Darn Tootin' 29

Kennedy, Ken The Silent Witness 62;
Iron Angel 64; The Velvet Trap 66; Kino,
the Padre on Horseback 77

Kennedy, Lem F. The Power Within 21;
Down Upon the Suwannee River 25

Kennedy, Michael Caribe 87*; Erik 89

Kennedy, Tom Time Walker 82

Kenner, Elly The Black Room 82*

Kent, Charles Anthony and Cleopatra •
Antony and Cleopatra 08; A Midsummer
Night's Dream 09; Twelfth Night 10; Bar-
naby Rudge 11; A Christmas Carol 11;
Vanity Fair 11; Fortunes of a Composer 12;
The Tables Turned 12

Kent, Gary The Devil Wolf of Shadow
Mountain 64; Rainy Day Friends 85

Kent, Laurence L. Caressed • Sweet
Substitute 64; When Tomorrow Dies 66;
High • In 68; Yesterday 80; High Stakes
87

Kent, Leon D. The Red Virgin 15

Kent, Willis Mad Youth 40

Kenton, Erle C. Among Those Present
19*; Down on the Farm 19*; A Lady's
Tailor 19*; No Mother to Guide Him 19*;
Salome vs. Shenandoah 19*; Dabbling in
Art 20; Fickle Fancy 20; Love, Honor and
Behave 20*; Married Life 20; Movie Fans
20; Business Is Business 21; A Perfect Vil-
lain 21; She Sighed by the Seaside 21; A
Small Town Idol 21; False Alarm 22; The
Haunted House 22; The Landlord 22;
Laughing Gas 22; The Piper 22; A Poor
Fish 22; Splitting Hairs 22; Dance or Die
23; Hello Pardners 23; The Income Tax
Collector 23; The Roaring Lion 23; Tea
with a Kick 23; The Three Gun Man 23;
The Wise Cracker 23; The Danger Signal
24; Fight and Win 24; A Fool and His
Money 24; Red Hot Tires 25; The Love
Toy 26; Other Women's Husbands 26; The
Palm Beach Girl 26; The Sap 26; The Girl
in the Pullman • The Girl on the Train
27; The Rejuvenation of Aunt Mary 27;
Wedding Bill$ 27; Bare Knees • Short
Skirts 28; The Companionate Marriage •
The Jazz Bride 28; Golf Widows 28; Name
the Woman 28*; Nothing to Wear 28;
The Sideshow 28; The Sporting Age • The
Stronger Love 28; The Street of Illusion
28; Father and Son 29; The Girl from
Mexico • Mexicali Rose 29; The Song of
Love 29; Trial Marriage 29; A Royal
Romance 30; Broken Links • Leftover
Ladies 31; The Last Parade 31; Lover Come
Back 31; X Marks the Spot 31; Guilty As
Charged • Guilty As Hell 32; Island of
Lost Souls 32; Stranger in Town 32; Big
Executive 33; Disgraced! 33; From Hell to
Heaven 33; The Best Man Wins 34; The
Search for Beauty 34; You're Telling Me
34; Grand Exit 35; Party Wire 35; The
Public Menace 35; Counterfeit 36; Devil's
Squadron 36; End of the Trail • Revenge!
36; Devil's Playground 37; Racketeers in
Exile 37; She Asked for It 37; The Lady
Objects 38; Little Tough Guys in Society
38; Escape to Paradise 39; Everything's on
Ice 39; Petticoat Politics 40; Remedy for
Riches 40; Flying Cadets 41; The Ghost of
Frankenstein 41; Melody for Three 41;
Naval Academy 41; They Meet Again 41;
Frisco Lil 42; North to the Klondike 42;
Pardon My Sarong 42; Who Done It? 42;
Always a Bridesmaid 43; Hit the Ice • Oh
Doctor! 43*; How's About It? 43; It Ain't
Hay • Money for Jam 43; Chamber of Hor-
rors • House of Frankenstein 44; She Gets
Her Man 44; House of Dracula 45;
Salome, Where She Danced 45*; Baxter's
Millions • Little Miss Big 46; The Cat
Creeps 46; Bob and Sally • Should Parents
Tell? • The Story of Bob and Sally 48;
Killer with a Label • One Too Many 50

Kenward, Allen For the Common
Defense 42

Kenworthy, N. Paul, Jr. Perri 57*

Kerbosch, Roland Any Day Now • Vandaag af Morgen 76

Kermadec, Liliane de see De Kermadec, Liliane

Kern, George The Unfoldment 22

Kern, James V. The Doughgirls 44; Never Say Goodbye 46; Stallion Road 47*; April Showers 48; Ellen • Here Lies Love • The Second Woman • Twelve Miles Out 50; Two Tickets to Broadway 51; Lum and Abner Abroad 56

Kern, Peter Crazy Boys 87

Kern, Russell S. Spittin' Image 83

Kernochan, Sarah Marjoe 72*

Kerr, Barry R. Forbidden Under the Censorship of the King 73

Kerr, Frank True Blood 89

Kerr, Robert T. 30 Below Zero 26*; A Trip to Chinatown 26

Kerrigan, Joseph M. The Flood of Love 16; The Miser's Gift 16; O'Neil of the Glen 16; A Romance of Puck Fair 16; An Unfair Love Affair 16; Widow Malone 16; Woman's Wit 16

Kershner, Glenn Island Captives 37

Kershner, Irvin Stakeout on Dope Street 58; The Young Captives 58; The Hoodlum Priest 61; A Face in the Rain 63; The Luck of Ginger Coffey 64; A Fine Madness 66; The Flim Flam Man • One Born Every Minute 67*; Loving 70; Up the Sandbox 72; S*P*Y*S 74; Raid on Entebbe 76; The Return of a Man Called Horse 76; Eyes of Laura Mars 78; The Empire Strikes Back 80; Never Say Never Again 83; Robocop 2 90

Kertes, Michael see Curtiz, Michael

Kertesz, Michael see Curtiz, Michael

Kertész, Mihály see Curtiz, Michael

Kervyn, Emmanuel Rabid Grannies 89

Kerwin, Harry My Third Wife, by George • My Third Wife George 68; God's Bloody Acre 75; Cheering Section 77; Tomcats 77; Barracuda • The Lucifer Project 78

Kesler, Henry S. She Who Dares • Three Russian Girls 43*; Song of the Land 53*; Five Steps to Danger 56

Kessler, Bruce Angels from Hell 68; Killers Three 68; The Gay Deceivers 69; Simon, King of Witches 71

Keusch, Erwin Baker's Bread • Das Brot des Bäckers 76; Der Flieger • The Flyer 87

Keyes, Vernon see Keays, Vernon

Kezdi, Zsolt see Kézdi-Kovács, Zsolt

Kézdi-Kovács, Zsolt Ha Megjön József • When Joseph Returns... 75; Forbidden Relations • Visszaesők 83; The Absentee • A Rejtőzködő 85; Kiáltás és Kiáltás 88

Khamrayev, Ali I Remember You • Ya Tebya Pomnyu 85; Sad Zhlani 88

Khamrayev, Iskander Krasnaya Strela • The Red Arrow 87*

Khan, Mohamed Awdat Mowatin • Return of a Citizen 86; Meshwar Omar • Omar's Journey 86; Wife of an Important Man • Wife of an Important Person • Zawgat Ragol Mohim 87; Ahlam Hind wa Camelia 88

Khan, Ramjankhan Mehboob see Mehboobkhan, Ramjankhan

Khanna, Prabhat Uttar Dakshin 88

Khanna, Rajbans Gautama the Buddha 55*

Khanzhonkov, Alexander The Defense of Sevastopol 11*

Khemir, Nacer Les Baliseurs du Désert 85

Kheyfits, Iosef see Heifits, Josef

Khilkevich, Georgy Ungwald see Ungwald-Khilkevich, Georgy

Khleifi, Michel La Mémoire Fertile 80; Noce en Galilée • A Wedding in Galilee 87

Khodjikov, Sultan That's Us • Znay Nashikh 87

Khokhlova, Alexandra Klyatva Timura • The Oath of Timur • Timur's Oath 42*

Khotinenko, Vladimir Shooting in the Back-Country • V Strelyayushchey Glushi 87; Zerkalo dlya Geroya 88

Khouri, Walter Hugo Daughters of Fire • As Filhas do Fogo 78; Love, Strange Love • Eu • I 87

Khudonazarov, Davlat Ringing Streams in Thawing Snow • V Talom Snege Zvon Ruchia 87

Khukhunashvili, M. Dzhoi and His Friends • Dzhoi i Druzhok 28*

Khutsiev, Marlen Spring on Zarechnaya Street 56*; Two Fyodors 58; I Am Twenty Years Old 65; July Rain 67; In the Month of May 70

Kiasashvili, Ivan Poputchik 88

Kibbee, Roland The Midnight Man 74*

Kidawa, Janusz Trzy Stopy Nad Ziemia 85; Komedianci z Wczorajszej Ulicy • Pretenders from Yesterday's Street 87; Mr. Fancy Car and the Eerie Manor • Pan Samochodzik i Niesamowity Dwór 87

Kidawa-Błoński, Jan see Kidawa, Janusz

Kidd, Michael Merry Andrew 58

Kidron, Beeban Vroom 88

Kiduck, Kim see Kim, Kiduck

Kiegel, Leonard Les Déchaînes 50; André Malraux 58; La Paysanne Pervertie 60; The Footbridge • Léviathan 61; La Dame de Pique • The Queen of Spades 65; Qui? 70

Kier, H. W. Border Fence 51*

Kiersch, Fritz Children of the Corn 84; Tuff Turf 85; Supercross • Winners Take All 86; Gor 87; Under the Boardwalk 89

Kieślowski, Krzysztof From the City of Lodz 69; Personel 75; Spokój 76; Amator • Camera Buff 79; Blind Chance • Przypadek 81; Długi Dzień Pracy 81; Bez Końca • No End 84; Dekalog 1 • I Am the Lord Thy God 88; Dekalog 2 • Thou Shalt Not Take the Name of the Lord Thy God in Vain 88; Dekalog 3 • Honor the Sabbath Day 88; Dekalog 4 • Honor Thy Father and Thy Mother 88; Dekalog 5 • Krótki Film o Zabijaniu • A Short Film About Killing • Thou Shalt Not Kill 88; Dekalog 6 • Krótki Film o Miłości • A Short Film About Love • Thou Shalt Not Commit Adultery 88; Dekalog 7 • Thou Shalt Not Steal 88; Dekalog 8 • Thou Shalt Not Bear False Witness 88; Dekalog 9 • Thou Shalt Not Covet Thy Neighbor's Wife 88; Dekalog 10 • Thou Shalt Not Covet Thy Neighbor's Goods 88; City Life 90*

Kijowski, Janusz Maskarada • The Masquerade 87

Kikoine, Gérard Le Feu Sous la Peau 85; Edge of Sanity 89; Buried Alive 90

Kilgore, Al Hansu Kurishitan Anderusan no Sekai • The World of Hans Christian Anderson 68*

Killy, Edward Freckles 35*; Seven Keys to Baldpate 35*; Bunker Bean • His Majesty Bunker Bean 36*; Murder on a Bridle Path 36*; Second Wife 36; Wanted: Jane Turner 36; The Big Shot 37; China Passage 37; Quick Money 37; Saturday's Heroes 37; The Fargo Kid 40; Stage to Chino 40; Wagon Train 40; Along the Rio Grande 41; The Bandit Trail 41; Cyclone on Horseback 41; Land of the Open Range 41; Robbers of the Range 41; Come On Danger 42; Riding the Wind 42; Nevada 44; Wanderer of the Wasteland 45*; West of the Pecos 45

Kim, Hyeong-myeong Agada • Agatha 85; Female Rebellion • Yeojaui Banran 86

Kim, In Soo Grudge of the Moon Lady • Wolnyoui Han 80; Huphyokwi Yanyo • The Vengeful Vampire Girl 81

Kim, Kiduck Daikaijū Yongkari • Great Monster Yongkari • Monster Yongkari • Yongkari—Monster from the Deep 67

Kim, Si-hyun Samwonnyo • The Valley of Ghosts 81; The White Rose 81

Kim, Soo-gil Have You Seen the Barefoot God? • Kimi wa Hadashi no Kami o Mitaka 86

Kim, U Son The Town of Yun • Yun no Machi 89

Kim, Young-hyo Capriciousness • Yo 80

Kimball, Ward The Mickey Mouse Anniversary Show 68*; Bedknobs and Broomsticks 71*

Kimbrough, Clinton Nightingales • The Young Nurses 73

Kimiavi, Parviz Baghe Sangui • Garden of Stones 76

Kimmel, Bruce The First Nudie Musical 76*; The Creature Wasn't Nice • Spaceship 81

Kimmins, Anthony Bypass to Happiness 34; The Diplomatic Lover • How's Chances? 34; All at Sea 35; His Majesty and Co. 35; Once in a New Moon 35; Keep Fit 37; George Takes the Air • It's in the Air 38; I See Ice 38; Come On George 39; Trouble Brewing 39; Mine Own Executioner 47; Bonnie Prince Charlie 48*; Flesh and Blood 49; Mr. Denning Drives North 51; The Passionate Sentry • Who Goes There? 52; The Captain's Paradise 53; Aunt Clara 54; Smiley 56; Smiley Gets a Gun 58; The Amorous Mr. Prawn • The Amorous Prawn • The Playgirl and the War Minister 62

Kimura, Keigo Utamaro, Painter of Women 64

Kin, Lo see Lo, Kin

Kincade, John Terminal Entry 87; Back to Back 90

Kincaid, Tim The Female Response 72; Escape from Bad Girls' Dormitory 85; Breeders 86; Matt Riker: Mutant Hunt • Mutant Hunt 86; Robot Holocaust 87; Maximum Thrust 88; She's Back 88

Kinder, Stuart Alas, Poor Bunny 11; The Bargee's Daughter 11; Caught in Her Own Trap 11; The Dejected Lover 11; A Merry Christmas to All Our Friends 11; The Parson Puts His Foot in It • With the Best Intentions 11; Sloper's New Hat 11; A Canine Sherlock Holmes 12; The Chaperone 12; A Country Holiday 12; The Dancer's Dream 12; A Day with Poachers 12; The Flying Despatch 12; Jack and the Fairies 12; Japanese Magic 12; Mirth and Mystery 12; Mischievous Margery 12; The Palace of Mystery 12; The Regimental Pet • The Stolen Airship Plans 12; Spot As Cupid 12; Belinda's Dream 13; Black and White 13; Buttercup PC 13; Buttercup PC, Detective 13; Crime at the Mill 13; Dan Backs a Winner 13; Five Pounds Reward 13; Only a Wedding 13; Ponky's Burglar 13; Ponky's Houseboat 13; The Regeneration of Dan • The Rejuvenation of Dan 13; A Riverside Romance 13; The Adventures of a Football 14; Better Late Than Never 14; By the Sad Sea Waves 14; Captured by Consent 14; Forgotten 14; The Kiss of Clay 14; Marjory's Goldfish 14; The Nation's Peril 14; The Opium Cigarettes 14; Poppies 14; Rip Van Winkle 14; Sports in Toyland 14; The Third God 14; Britons Awake! 15; Mizpah, or Love's Sacrifice 15; If... 16

King, Allan Skid Row 56; The Yukoners 56; Gyppo Loggers 57; Pemberton Valley 57; Portrait of a Harbor 57; Morocco 58; Where Will They Go? 58; Bull Fight 59; Josef Drenters 60; Rickshaw 60; Dreams 61; A Matter of Pride 61; Three Yugoslavian Portraits 61; Joshua, a Nigerian Portrait 62; The Pursuit of Happiness 62; The Field Day 63; The Peacemakers 63; Bjorn's Inferno 64; Christopher Plummer 64*; Coming of Age in Ibiza • Running Away Backwards 64; Lynn Seymour 64; The Most Unlikely Millionaire 65; Warrendale 66; The New Woman 68; A Married Couple 69; Come On Children 72; Who Has Seen the Wind 77; One Night Stand 78; Silence of the North 81

King, Burton L. The Black Butterfly 16; The Devil at His Elbow 16; The Eternal Question 16; Extravagance 16; The Flower of Faith 16; Man and His Angel 16; The Reapers 16; The Spell of the Yukon 16; Glory 17*; More Truth Than Poetry 17; Public Defender 17; The Silence Sellers 17; The Soul of Magdalene 17; To the Death 17; The Waiting Soul 17; Her Husband's Honor 18; The Master Mystery 18; Treason 18; The Lost Battalion 19; A Scream in the Night 19*; A Common Level 20; The Common Sin • For Your Daughter's Sake 20; The Discarded Woman 20; Love or Money 20; Neglected Wives 20; Wit Wins

20; Everyman's Price 21; The Man from Beyond 22; The Road to Arcady 22; The Streets of New York 22; The Empty Cradle 23; The Fair Cheat 23; None So Blind 23; The Man Without a Heart 24; The Masked Dancer 24; Playthings of Desire 24; Those Who Judge 24; The Truth About Women 24; Counsel for the Defense 25; Ermine and Rhinestones 25; A Little Girl in a Big City 25; Mad Dancer 25; The Police Patrol 25; Bowery Cinderella 27; Broadway Madness 27; The Adorable Cheat 28; Broken Barriers 28; Manhattan Knights 28; Satan and the Woman 28; Women Who Dare 28; Daughters of Desire 29; The Dream Melody 29; In Old California 29; One Splendid Hour 29

King, Carlton S. A Child in Judgement 15; The Way Back 15; Tempest and Sunshine 16; Just a Song at Twilight 22

King, Fred Gunsmoke 47

King, George Leave It to Me 30; Too Many Crooks 30; Deadlock! 31; Midnight 31; Number, Please 31; The Professional Guest 31; Two Way Street 31; Men of Steel 32; Self-Made Lady 32; To Brighton with Gladys 32; Beware of Women 33; Enemy of the Police 33; Her Imaginary Lover 33; High Finance 33; I Adore You 33; Matinee Idol 33; Mayfair Girl • Society Girl 33; Smithy 33; Too Many Wives 33; Adventure Limited 34; The Blue Squadron 34; Get Your Man 34; Guest of Honour 34; Little Stranger 34; Murder at the Inn 34; Nine Forty-Five 34; The Office Wife 34; Oh No Doctor! 34; The Silver Spoon 34; To Be a Lady 34; The Demon Barber of Fleet Street • Sweeney Todd • Sweeney Todd, the Demon Barber of Fleet Street 35; Full Circle 35; Gay Old Dog 35; The Man Without a Face 35; Maria Marten, or The Murder in the Red Barn 35; Windfall 35; The Crimes of Stephen Hawke • Strangler's Morgue 36*; Reasonable Doubt 36; Merry Comes to Stay • Merry Comes to Town 37; Silver Top 37; The Ticket of Leave Man 37; Under a Cloud 37; Wanted 37; John Halifax, Gentleman 38; Sexton Blake and the Hooded Terror 38; The Chinese Bungalow • Chinese Den 39; Crimes at the Dark House 39; The Face at the Window 39; The Case of the Frightened Lady • Frightened Lady 40; George and Margaret 40; Two for Danger 40; At Dawn We Die • Tomorrow We Live 42; Candlelight in Algeria 43; Gaiety George • Showtime 45*; The Code of Scotland Yard • The Shop at Sly Corner 46; Forbidden 48

King, Henry The Brand of Man 15; Should a Woman Forgive? 15; Who Pays? 15; Faith's Reward 16; Joy and the Dragon 16; Little Mary Sunshine 16; The Oath of Hate 16; Pay Dirt 16*; The Sand Lark 16; Shadows and Sunshine 16; The Strained Pearl 16; The Bride's Silence 17; The Climber 17; A Game of Wits 17; The Mate of the Sally Ann • Peggy Rebels 17; Souls in Pawn 17; Southern Pride 17; The Spectre of Suspicion 17; Sunshine and Gold 17; Told at Twilight 17; Twin Kiddies 17; The

Unafraid 17; Vengeance of the Dead 17; All the World to Nothing 18; Beauty and the Rogue 18; Hearts or Diamonds 18; Hobbs in a Hurry 18; King Social Briars 18; The Locked Heart 18; Mademoiselle Tiptoes • Mlle. Tiptoes 18; Powers That Prey 18; Up Romance Road 18; When a Man Rides Alone 18; Brass Buttons 19; A Fugitive from Matrimony 19; Haunting Shadows 19; Six Feet Four 19; Some Liar 19; A Sporting Chance 19; This Hero Stuff 19; 23½ Hours Leave • 23½ Hours on Leave 19; Where the West Begins 19; Dice of Destiny 20; Help Wanted—Male 20; A Live Wire Hick 20; One Hour Before Dawn 20; Uncharted Channels 20; When We Were Twenty-One 20; The White Dove 20; The Mistress of Shenstone 21; Salvage 21; The Sting of the Lash 21; Tol'able David 21; The Bond Boy 22; Fury 22; The Seventh Day 22; Sonny 22; The White Sister 23; Romola 24; Any Woman 25; Sackcloth and Scarlet 25; Stella Dallas 25; Partners Again 26; The Winning of Barbara Worth 26; The Magic Flame 27; The Woman Disputed 28*; Hell Harbor 29; She Goes to War 29; The Eyes of the World 30; Lightnin' 30; Merely Mary Ann 31; Over the Hill 31; The Woman in Room 13 32; I Loved You Wednesday 33*; State Fair 33; Carolina • House of Connelly 34; Marie Galante 34; One More Spring 35; Way Down East 35; The Country Doctor 36; Lloyds of London 36; Ramona 36; In Old Chicago 37*; Seventh Heaven 37; Alexander's Ragtime Band 38; Jesse James 38; Stanley and Livingstone 39; Chad Hanna 40; Little Old New York 40; Maryland 40; Remember the Day 41; A Yank in the R.A.F. 41; The Black Swan 42; The Song of Bernadette 43; Wilson 44; A Bell for Adano 45; Margie 46; Captain from Castile 47; Deep Waters 48; The Prince of Foxes 49; Twelve O'Clock High 49; The Gunfighter 50; David and Bathsheba 51; I'd Climb the Highest Mountain 51; Full House • O. Henry's Full House 52*; The Snows of Kilimanjaro 52; Wait 'Til the Sun Shines, Nellie 52; King of the Khyber Rifles 53; Love Is a Many Splendored Thing 55; Untamed 55; Carousel 56; The Sun Also Rises 57; The Bravados 58; The Old Man and the Sea 58*; Beloved Infidel 59; This Earth Is Mine 59; Tender Is the Night 61

King, Hu see Hu, King

King, Jack Kiss Me 20; Why Change Your Husband? 20; Too Much Pep 21; Buddy's Day Out 33; Buddy's Show Boat 33; Buddy the Detective 34; Buddy the Woodsman 34; Buddy's Bearcats 34; Buddy's Circus 34; Viva Buddy 34; Buddy Steps Out 35; Buddy the Gee Man 35; Buddy's Bug Hunt 35; Buddy's Lost World 35; A Cartoonist's Nightmare 35; Hollywood Capers 35; Alpine Antics 36; Boom Boom 36; The Fire Alarm 36; Fish Tales 36; The Phantom Ship 36; Porky's Moving Day 36; Porky's Pet 36; Shanghaied Shipmates 36; Westward Whoa! 36

King, Joe Her Bitter Cup 16*
King, Lewis *see Capuano, Luigi*
King, Louis Peaceful Peters 22; The Devil's Dooryard 23; The Law Hustlers • The Law Rustlers 23; Sun Dog Trails 23; The Boy Rider 27; Is Your Daughter Safe? 27*; The Slingshot Kid 27; The Bantam Cowboy 28*; The Fightin' Redhead 28; The Little Buckaroo 28; Orphan of the Sage 28; The Pinto Kid 28; Rough Ridin' Red 28; Terror • Terror Mountain • Tom's Vacation 28; Young Whirlwind 28; The Freckled Rascal 29; The Little Savage 29; Pals of the Prairie 29; The Vagabond Cub 29; The Lone Rider 30; Men Without Law 30; Shadow Ranch 30; Border Law 31; The Deceiver 31; Desert Vengeance 31; The Fighting Sheriff 31; Arm of the Law 32; The County Fair 32; Crooked Road 32; Drifting Souls 32; Fame Street • Police Court • Son of Mine 32; Life in the Raw 33; Robbers' Roost 33; Bachelor of Arts 34; Cardboard City • La Ciudad de Cartón 34; Murder in Trinidad 34; Pursued 34; Angelita • Little Angel 35; Charlie Chan in Egypt 35; Juliet Buys a Baby • Julieta Compra un Hijo 35; The Bengal Tiger 36; The Cave-In • Draegerman Courage 36; Injustice • Road Gang 36; Shadow Ranch 36; Song of the Saddle 36; Special Investigator 36; Bulldog Drummond Comes Back 37; Bulldog Drummond's Revenge 37; Melody for Two 37; That Man's Here Again 37; Wild Money 37; Wine, Women and Horses 37; Bulldog Drummond in Africa 38; Crime Gives Orders • Hunted Men 38; Illegal Traffic 38; Persons in Hiding 38; Prison Farm 38; Tip-Off Girls 38; Tom Sawyer—Detective 38; Undercover Doctor 39; Moon Over Burma 40; Seventeen 40; Typhoon 40; The Way of All Flesh 40; Chetniks • Chetniks—The Fighting Guerrillas • Underground Guerrillas 42; We Humans • Young America 42; Ladies in Washington • Ladies of Washington 44; Thunderhead—Son of Flicka 45; Smoky 46; Bob, Son of Battle • Thunder in the Valley 47; Green Grass of Wyoming 48; Mrs. Mike 49; Sand • Will James' Sand 49; Frenchie 50; The Lion and the Horse 52; Powder River 53; Sabre Jet 53; Dangerous Mission 54; Massacre 56
King, Michael Powerforce 83
King, Rich Off the Wall 77
King, Rick Hard Choices 84; Hotshot 86; The Killing Time 87; Forced March 89
King, Stephen Maximum Overdrive 86
King, Tim Echo of the Badlands 77*
King, Woodie, Jr. The Long Night 76
King, Zalman Wildfire 87; Two Moon Junction 88; Wild Orchid 90
King-chuan, Hu *see Hu, King*
Kingsley, Pierce After the Ball 14; Silver Threads Among the Gold 15
Kinney, Jack Bone Trouble 40; Der Führer's Face 43; Saludos Amigos 43*; The Three Caballeros 44*; Make Mine Music 46*; Fun and Fancy Free 47*; Melody Time 48*; The Adventures of Ichabod and

Mr. Toad • Ichabod and Mr. Toad 49*; How to Play Football 49; The Brave Engineer 50; Motormania 51; Pigs Is Pigs 54; 1000 Arabian Knights • 1001 Arabian Nights 59
Kinnoch, Ronald The Secret Man 58
Kino, Kitty Die Nachtmeerfahrt • The Nocturnal Voyage • Voyage by Night 86
Kinoshita, Keisuke The Blossoming Port • Hanasaku Minato • Port of Flowers 43; Ikite Iru Magoroku • The Living Magoroku • Magoroku Is Still Alive 43; The Army • Rikugun 44; Cheering Town • Jubilation Street • Kanko no Machi 44; The Girl I Loved • The Girl That I Love • Waga Koiseshi Otome 46; Morning for the Osone Family • A Morning with the Osone Family • Osone-Ke no Asa 46; Fushichō • Phoenix 47; Kekkon • Marriage 47; Apostasy • Hakai 48; Onna • Woman 48; Portrait • Shōzō 48; The Broken Drum • Yabure Daiko • Yabure Taiko 49; The Ghost of Yotsuya—New Version • Illusion of Blood • New Version of the Ghost of Yotsuya • Shinshaku Yotsuya Kaidan • The Yotsuya Ghost Story • Yotsuya Kaidan 49; Here's to the Girls • Ojōsan Kampai • A Toast to the Young Miss 49; Engagement Ring • Kon-Yaku Yubiwa 50; The Good Fairy • Zemma 50; A Record of Youth • Shōnen Ki • Youth 50; Carmen Comes Home • Karumen Kokyō ni Kaeru 51; Fireworks Over the Sea • Sea of Fireworks • Umi no Hanabi 51; Carmen's Pure Love • Karumen Junjōsu 52; A Japanese Tragedy • Nihon no Higeki 53; The Eternal Generation • The Garden of Women • Onna no Sono 54; Nijūshi no Hitomi • Twenty-Four Eyes 54; Distant Clouds • Tōi Kumo 55; My First Love Affair • Nogiku no Gotoki Kimi Nariki • She Was Like a Daisy • She Was Like a Wild Chrysanthemum • You Were Like a Wild Chrysanthemum 55; Clouds at Twilight • Farewell to Dreams • Yūyake-Gumo 56; The Rose on His Arm • Sun and Rose • Taiyō to Bara 56; A Candle in the Wind • Danger Stalks Near • Fūzen no Tomoshibi 57; The Lighthouse • Times of Joy and Sorrow • Yorokobi mo Kanashimi mo Ikutoshitsuki 57; The Ballad of Narayama • Ballad of the Narayama • Narayama Bushikō 58; The Eternal Rainbow • Kono Ten no Niji • The Rainbow of This Sky 58; The Bird Missing Spring • The Bird of Springs Past • Sekishun-Chō 59; Kazahana • Snow Flurry 59; Kyō mo Mata Kakute Arinan • Thus Another Day 59; Fuefuki-Gawa • The River Fuefuki 60; Haru no Yume • Spring Dreams 60; The Bitter Spirit • Eien no Hito • Eternal Love • Immortal Love 61; Ballad of a Workman • Ballad of a Young Workman • Futari de Aruita Ikuharuaki • Futari de Aruita Ikushunjū • The Seasons We Walked Together 62; Kotoshi no Koi • New Year's Love • This Year's Love 62; Legend of a Duel to the Death • A Legend, or Was It? • Shito no Densetsu 63; Sing, Young People • Utae Wakodotachi 63;

Kōge • The Scent of Incense 64; Eyes, the Sea and a Ball • Lovely Flute and Drum • Natsukashiki Fueya Taiko 67; Love and Separation in Sri Lanka • Sri Lanka no Ai to Wakare • Suri Lanka no Ai to Wakare 76; The Impulse Murder of My Son • My Son • Shōdō Satsujin, Musukoyo 79; Chichi yo Haha yo • Parents, Awake 80; Children of Nagasaki • Konoko o Nokoshite • Leaving These Children Behind • Leaving This Child 83; Big Joys, Small Sorrows • The Lighthouse Keeper's Family • Shin Yorokobi mo Kanashimi mo Ikutoshitsuki 86
Kinoshita, Ryo Nikutai no Gakkō • School for Sex • School of Love 66
Kinsella, E. P. George Robey's Day Off 18*
Kinugasa, Teinosuke The Death of My Sister • Imōto no Shi 21; Hibana • Spark 22; Niwa no Kotori • Two Little Birds 22; Beyond Decay • Chōraku no Kanata 23; The Golden Demon • Konjiki Yasha 23; Hanasake Jijii • Happy Old Man 23; Jinsei o Mitsumete • Ways of Life 23; Lady, Be Not Wronged • Onna yo Ayamaru Nakare 23; Ma no Ike • The Spirit of the Pond 23; Dance Training • Kyōren no Butō 24; Detective Yuri • Kishin Yuri Keiji 24; Fog and Rain • Kiri no Ame • Love, Fog and Rain • The Polownia Rains 24; The Foot • Shōhin—Shūsoku • Shūsoku 24; Jashūmon no Onna • A Woman's Heresy 24; Kanojo to Unmei • She Has Lived Her Destiny 24; Koi • Love 24; Koi To wa Narinu • Thus It Turned Love 24; Lonely Village • Sabishiki Mura 24; Secret of a Wife • Tsuma no Himitsu 24; Shōhin—Shūto 24; Shūto • The Theft 24; Chuji's Early Days • Wakaki Hi no Chuji 25; Double Suicide • Shinju Yoimachigusa 25; Hanpeita, Master Swordsman • Tsukigata Hanpeita 25; Koi to Bushi • Love and a Warrior • Love and the Warrior 25; Nichirin • The Sun 25; Akatsuki no Yūshi • A Brave Soldier at Dawn 26; Cassowary • Hikuidori 26; A Crazy Page • Kurutta Ippeiji • A Page of Madness 26; Dōchū Sugoroku Bune • The Ship 26; Dōchū Sugoroku Kago • The Palanquin 26; Epoch of Loyalty • Kinnō Jidai 26; Gekka no Kyōjin • Moonlight Madness 26; The Government Vessel • Goyosen 26; The Horse Thistle • Oni Azami 26; Kirinji 26; Meoto Boshi • Star of Married Couples 26; Ōjo Kichiza 26; Shining Sun Becomes Clouded • Teru hi Kumoru hi 26; Tenichibo and Iganosuke • Tenichibo to Iganosuke 26; Benten Kozō • The Gay Masquerade 28; Chōken Yasha • Female Demon 28; Crossroads • Crossways • Jūjiro • The Shadows of the Yoshiwara • The Shadows of Yoshiwara • Shadows Over Yoshiwara 28; Kaikokuki • Tales from a Country by the Sea 28; Keiraku Hichō • The Secret Documents 28; Slums of Tokyo 28; Before Dawn • Reimei Izen 31; Okichi the Mistress • Tojin Okichi 31; Chūshingura • Genroku Chūshingura • The Loyal 47 Ronin • The Vengeance of the Forty-Seven Ronin 32; Ikinokata Shinsengumi • The

Surviving Shinsengumi 32; Futatsu Doro • Two Stone Lanterns 33; Ginpei from Koina • Koina no Ginpei 33; Tenichibo and Iganosuke • Tenichibo to Iganosuke 33; The Beaten Kochiyama • Nagurareta Kochiyama 34; The Double Suicide in Winter • Fuyuki Shinju 34; Ippon-Gatana Dohyōiri • The Sword and the Sumo Ring 34; Kutsukake Tokijiro 34; Kurayami no Ushimatsu • Ushimatsu in the Darkness 35; The Revenge of Yukinojo • Yūkinojō Henge • Yukinojo's Disguise • Yukinojo's Revenge 35; Hito Hada Kannon • The Sacred Protector 37; Ōsaka Natsu no Jin • The Summer Battle of Osaka 37; Hebi Himesama • Miss Snake Princess • The Serpent Princess • The Snake Princess 38; Kuroda Seichūroku • Loyalism at Kuroda 38; The Battle of Kawanakajima • Kawanakajima Kassen 41; Forward, Flag of Independence • Susume Dokuritsuki 43; Rose of the Sea • Umi no Bara 45; Aru yo no Tonosama • Lord for a Night 46; Actress • Joyū 47; Four Love Stories • The Story of Four Loves • Yottsu no Koi no Monogatari 47*; The Face of a Murderer • Satsujinsha no Kao 49; Kobanzame 49*; Koga Mansion • Koga Yashiki 49; Nichirin • The Sun 50; Beni Kōmori • The Scarlet Bat 51; Lantern Under a Full Moon • Mei-getsu Sōmatō 51; Migratory Birds Under the Moon • Tsuki no Wataridōri 51; The Castle of Carnage • Shurajō Hibun 52; Daibutsu Kaigen • The Dedication of the Great Buddha • Saga of the Great Buddha 52; Gate of Hell • Jigokumon 53; Duel of a Snowy Night • Yuki no Yo no Kettō 54; End of a Prolonged Journey • Hana no Nagadosū 54; The Great Administrator • Tekka Bugyō 54; Shinkin Stones 54; Bara Ikutabi • A Girl Isn't Allowed to Love 55; It Happened in Tokyo • Kawa no Aru Shitamachi no Hanashi • The Story of a River Downtown 55; The Romance of Yushima • White Sea of Yushima • Yushima no Shiraume • Yushima no Shiraume—Onna Keizu 55; Hibana • Spark 56; Three Women Around Yoshinaka • Yoshinaka o Meguru Sannin no Onna 56; Tsukigata Hanpeita 56; A Fantastic Tale of Naruto • Naruto Fantasy • Naruto Hichō 57; Floating Vessel • Ukifune 57; Shirasagi • The Snowy Heron • The White Heron 57; Haru Koro no Hana no En • A Spring Banquet • Symphony of Love 58; Ōsaka no Onna • A Woman of Osaka 58; The Red Cloak 58; The Affair • Jōen • Tormented Flame • Tormented Love 59; Kagerō Ezu • Stop the Old Fox 59; The Lantern • The Old Lantern • Uta Andon 60; Blind Devotion • Dishevelled Hair • Midaregami 61; Okoto and Sasuke • Okoto to Sasuke 61; Lies • Uso • When Women Lie 63*; Priest and Empress • The Sorcerer • Yoso 63; Chiisai Tōbōsha • Chiisana Tōbōsha • The Little Runaway • Malenki Beglyets 66*

Kiral, Erden Dilan 87; Av Zamanı 88
Kiralfy, A. The Arab's Curse 15
Kirchhoff, Fritz Wenn Frauen Schwei-

gen • When Women Keep Silent 37; Meine Freundin Barbara • My Friend Barbara 38
Kirk, Robert Destroyer 88
Kirkland, David The Crippled Hand 15*; A Temperamental Wife 19; A Virtuous Vamp 19; In Search of a Sinner 20; The Love Expert 20; Nothing But the Truth 20; The Perfect Woman 20; The Rowdy 21; The Barefoot Boy 23; For Another Woman 24; The Tomboy 24; Who Cares? 24; All Around Frying Pan 25; Hands Across the Border 26; A Regular Scout 26; The Tough Guy 26; The Two Gun Man 26; The Gingham Girl 27; Uneasy Payments 27; Yours to Command 27; The Candy Kid 28; Riders of the Cactus 31; Soul of Mexico 32; Pecados de Amor 34; El Impostor 37
Kirkland, John Curse of the Headless Horseman 72
Kirkwood, James Prince Charming 12*; The House of Discord 13; Ashes of the Past 14; Behind the Scenes 14; Cinderella 14; Classmates 14; The Eagle's Mate 14; The Floor Above 14; Lord Chumley 14; Men and Women 14; The Mountain Rat 14; The Soul of Honor 14; Strongheart 14; Dawn of a Tomorrow 15; Esmeralda 15; Fanchon the Cricket 15; The Heart of Jennifer 15; Little Pal 15; The Masqueraders 15; Mistress Nell 15; Rags 15; A Dream or Two Ago 16; Dulcie's Adventure 16; Faith • The Virtuous Outcast 16; The Lost Bridegroom 16; The Old Homestead 16; Saints and Sinners 16; Susie Snowflake 16; Annie-for-Spite • Sally Shows the Way 17; Environment 17; The Gentle Intruder 17; The Innocence of Lizette 17; Melissa of the Hills 17; Over There 17; Periwinkle 17; Eve's Daughter 18; I Want to Forget 18; Out of the Night 18; A Romance of the Underworld 18; The Struggle Everlasting 18; Bill Apperson's Boy • Bill Apperson's Son 19; In Wrong 19
Kirman, Leonard Carnival of Blood 71
Kirsanoff, Dimitri see Kirsanov, Dmitri
Kirsanov, Dmitri L'Ironie du Destin • The Irony of Fate 23; Ménilmontant 24; Destin • Destins • Sylvie Destin 26; Sables 27; Brumes d'Automne 28; Die Nächte von Port Said • Les Nuits de Port Said 31*; The Mystic Mountain • Rapt • La Séparation des Races 33; Les Berceaux 35; La Fontaine d'Aréthuse 36; La Jeune Fille au Jardin 36; Visages de France 36; Franco de Port 37; L'Avion de Minuit 38; La Plus Belle Fille du Monde 38; Quartier Sans Soleil 39; Deux Amis 46; Faits Divers à Paris 49; Arrière Saison 50; Une Chasse à Courre • Une Chasse à Courre à Villiers-Cotterets • La Mort du Cerf 51; Le Témoin de Minuit 52; Le Craneur • La Vallée du Paradis 55; Ce Soir les Jupons Volent • Tonight the Skirts Fly 56; Miss Catastrophe 56
Kis, József see Kiss, József
Kish, Joseph see Kiss, József
Kishon, Ephraim Sallah • Sallah Shabati 63; The Big Dig 69; The Policeman 71; Er-

vinka 74; Fox in the Chicken Coop 78
Kishore, Raj Thaviya Aase 88
Kiss, József World Youth Festival 50; A Sánta Dervis 87*
Kitakubo, Hiroyuki Robot Carnival 87*
Kitazume, Kiroyuki Robot Carnival 87*
Kitiparaporn, Lek Angkor-Cambodia Express 81
Kiysk, Kalie Cherez Sto Let v Mae • May, Hundred Years After 87
Kizer, R. J. Godzilla 1985 • Godzilla—The Legend Is Reborn 85*; Hell Comes to Frogtown 87*
Kjærulff-Schmidt, Palle Bundfald • Dregs 57; De Sjove År 59; Weekend 62; To • Two People 64; Sommerkrig • Summer War 65; Der Var Engang en Krig • Once There Was a War • Once Upon a War 66; Historien om Barbara • Story of Barbara 67; I den Grønne Skov • In the Green of the Woods 68; Tænk på et Tal • Think of a Number 68; Peter von Scholten 87
Kjellgren, Lars-Eric Private Bom 48
Kjellin, Alf Flickan i Regnet • Girl in the Rain 55; Encounters at Dusk • Möten i Skymningen 57; Seventeen Years Old • Sjutton År 57; Det Svänger på Slottet • Swinging at the Castle 59; Bara en Kypare • Only a Waiter 60; Lustgården • Pleasure Garden 61; Siska 62; The Blood Crowd • The McMasters • The McMasters... Tougher Than the West Itself 69; Midas Run • A Run on Gold 69
Klahn, Thees Ossegg oder Die Wahrheit Über Hansel und Gretel 88
Klane, Robert Thank God It's Friday 78
Klaren, Georg C. Ruf aus dem Äther 53; Wozzeck 62
Klass, Ric Elliot Fauman, Ph.D. 90
Klauss, Jürgen Treffpunkt Leipzig 85
Klein, Bonnie Sherr Not a Love Story 81
Klein, Charles Blindfold 28; Pleasure Crazed 29*; Sin Sister 29; Wenn am Sonntagabend die Dorfmusik Spielt 35; Zigeunerblut 35
Klein, Dennis One More Saturday Night 86
Klein, Dušan Kdo Se Bojí Utíká 86; Dobří Holubi Se Vracejí 88; Jak Básníkům Voní Život? 88
Klein, James Seeing Red—Stories of American Communists 83*
Klein, Larry The Adversary 70
Klein, William Far from Vietnam • Loin du Viêt-nam 66*; Qui Êtes-Vous Polly Maggoo? • Who Are You Polly Maggoo? 66; Mr. Freedom 68; Festival Panafricain 69; Float Like a Butterfly, Sting Like a Bee 69; Eldridge Cleaver • Eldridge Cleaver, Black Panther 70; Le Couple Témoin 77; The French 81; Mode in France 85
Kleine, George Julius Caesar 14; Naidra the Dream Woman 14; The Danger Signal 15; DuBarry 15; Keep Moving 15
Kleinschmidt, Frank E. Primitive Love 27
Kleiser, Randal Grease 78; The Blue Lagoon 80; Summer Lovers 82; Grandview, U.S.A. 84; Flight of the Navigator 86; Big Top Pee-wee 88; Getting It Right 89

Kleven, Max The Loner • Ruckus 81; The Night Stalker 85

Klick, Roland Jimmy Orpheus 66; Deadlock 70

Klim, Leon *see Klimovsky, Leon*

Klimov, Elem Welcome, or No Entry for Unauthorized Persons 64; Adventures of a Dentist 65; Sport, Sport, Sport 70; And Nonetheless I Believe 74*; Agonia • Agoniya • Agony 75; Rasputin 77; Larissa 80; The Farewell • Farewell to Majorca • Farewell to Matyora • Proshchanie 81; Come and See • Go and See • Idi i Smotri 85

Klimov, Ilya Dobra Pozhalovat ili Postoronnim Vkhod Vospreshchen • Dobro Pozhalovat • Postoronnim Vkhod Vospreshchen • Welcome Kostya! 65

Klimovsky, Leon Los Amantes del Desierto • Gli Amanti del Deserto • The Desert Warrior • La Figlia dello Sceicco 58*; Edge of Fear • Night of Fear 64; Dos Mil Dolares per Coyote 66; A Few Dollars for Django • Pochi Dollari per Django 66; A Ghentar Si Muore Facile 67; Un Hombre Vino a Matar • Rattler Kid 68; Challenge of the Mackennas • La Sfida dei Mackenna 69; The Black Harvest of Countess Dracula • Nacht der Vampire • La Noche de Walpurgis • Shadow of the Werewolf • The Werewolf vs. the Vampire Woman • The Werewolf's Shadow 70; Reverendo Colt 70; Dr. Jeckill y el Hombre Lobo • Dr. Jekyll and the Werewolf • Dr. Jekyll and the Wolfman • Dr. Jekyll y el Hombre Lobo 71; Su le Mani...Cadaverei Sei in Arresto 71; Dracula's Saga • La Saga de los Drácula • The Saga of Dracula • The Saga of the Draculas 72; La Rebelión de las Muertas • The Rebellion of the Dead Women • Revolt of the Dead Ones • La Vendetta dei Morti Viventi • Vengeance of the Zombies 72; La Orgía Nocturna de los Vampiros • The Vampire's Night Orgy 73; El Extraño Amor de los Vampiros • La Noche de los Vampiros • Los Vampiros También Duermen 75; I Hate My Body • Odio Mi Cuerpo 75

Kline, Benjamin The Lightning Warrior 31*; Cowboy in the Clouds 43; Cowboy from Lonesome River • Signed Judgment 44; Cyclone Prairie Rangers 44; The Poisoner • Saddle Leather Law 44; Sundown Valley 44; Sagebrush Heroes 45

Kline, Herbert Return to Life 37*; Crisis • Crisis—A Film of the Nazi Way 38; Lights Out in Europe 39; The Forgotten Village 40; A Boy, a Girl and a Dog • Lucky 46; My Father's House 46; The Kid from Cleveland 49; The Fighter • The First Time 51; Walls of Fire 74; The Challenge • The Challenge—A Tribute to Modern Art • The Challenge of Greatness 75; Acting—Lee Strasberg and the Actors Studio 81; Great Theatres of the World 87

Klinger, Tony The Butterfly Ball 77

Klingler, Werner Standschütze Bruggler 37; Razzia 48; Lebensborn • Ordered to Love 60; The Terror of Dr. Mabuse • The Terror of the Mad Doctor • Das Testament des Dr. Mabuse • The Testament of Dr. Mabuse 60; The Secret of the Black Trunk 62; The Dirty Game • The Dirty War • La Guerra Segreta • La Guerre Secrète • The Secret Agents • The Secret War • Spione Unter Sich 65*

Klockner, Beate Mein Lieber Schatz 85

Kloot, William van der Mace • The Sofia Conspiracy 87; Dead Aim 90

Klopčić, Matjaz Moj Tata, Socialistički Kulak 88

Klopfenstein, Clemens Macao 88

Klos, Elmar Chudý Lidé • Poor People 39; Řeka Života a Smrti • The River of Life and Death 40; Souvenir of Paradise • Vzpomínka na Ráj 40; The Hijack • The Hijacking • Kidnap • Kidnapped • Únos 52*; Hudba z Marsu • Music from Mars 53*; Young Days 55*; At the Terminal Station • The House at the Terminus • Tam na Konečné 56*; The Third Wish • Three Wishes • Třetí Přání • Tři Přání 57*; Magic Lantern II 59*; Spartakiáda 60*; Because We Do Not Forget • Death Is Called Engelchen • For We Too Do Not Forgive • Smrt Si Říká Engelchen 62*; The Accused • The Defendant • Obžalovaný 63*; Obchod na Korze • Shop in the High Street • The Shop on High Street • The Shop on Main Street • A Shop on the High Street 64*; Adrift • Hrst Plná Vody • Something Is Adrift in the Water • Something Is Drifting on the Water • Touha Zvaná Anada • Zmítaná 69*

Klotz, Nicolas The Bengali Night 88

Klotzel, André Marvada Carne • Strong Meat 86

Kloves, Steve The Fabulous Baker Boys 89

Kluba, Henryk Gwiazda Piołun 88

Kluge, Alexander Brutalität in Stein • Brutality in Stone • Die Ewigkeit von Gestern • Yesterday Goes On Forever 60*; Racing • Rennen 61*; Rennfahrer 61; Thema Amore 61; Lehrer im Wandel • Teachers in Transformation 63*; Portrait of a Conservator • Portrait of One Who Proved His Mettle • Porträt einer Bewährung 63; Abschied von Gestern • Anita G. • Yesterday Girl 66; Pokerspiel 66; Die Artisten in der Zirkuskuppel: Ratlos • Artistes at the Top of the Big Top: Disoriented • Artists at the Top of the Big Top: Disorientated • Artists Under the Big Top: Perplexed 67; Frau Blackburn, Born 5 Jan. 1872, Is Filmed • Frau Blackburn, Geb. 5 Jan. 1872, Wird Gefilmt • Frau Blackburn Wird Gefilmt 67; Feuerlöscher E. A. Winterstein • Fireman E. A. Winterstein 68; Ein Arzt aus Halberstadt • A Doctor from Halberstadt 69; The Indomitable Leni Peickert • Die Unbezähmbare Leni Peickert 69; The Big Dust-Up • The Big Mess • Der Grosse Verhau 70; Willi Tobler and the Decline of the 6th Fleet • Willi Tobler und der Untergang der 6. Flotte • Willy Tobler and the Wreck of the 6th Fleet • Willy Tobler und der Untergang der 6. Flotte 70; Der Angriffsschlachter • The Destroyer • We'll Blow 3 x 27 Billion Dollars on a Destroyer • Wir Verbauen 3 x 27 Milliarden Dollar in einen Angriffsschlachter 71; Das Krankheitsbild des Schlachtener—Problem Unteroffiziers in der Endsehlacht 71*; Besitzbürgerin, Jahrgang 1908 • A Woman from the Property-Owning Middle Class, Born 1908 72; Gelegenheitsarbeit einer Sklavin • Occasional Work of a Female Slave • Part-Time Work of a Domestic Slave 73; Blind Alley • In Danger and Great Need the Middle Road Leads to Death • In Gefahr und Grösster Not Bringt der Mittelweg den Tod • The Middle of the Road Is a Very Dead End 74*; Augen aus einem Anderen Land 75; Der Starke Ferdinand • Strongman Ferdinand 75; In Such Trepidation I Creep Off Tonight to the Evil Battle • Zu Böser Schlacht Schleich' Ich Heut' Nacht so Bang 77; Die Menschen Die das Stauferjahr Vorbereiten • Die Menschen Die die Staufer-Ausstellung Vorbereiten • The People Who Are Preparing the Year of the Hohenstaufens 77*; Nachrichten von der Staufern 77; Deutschland im Herbst • Germany in Autumn 78*; The Patriot • Die Patriotin 79; The Candidate • Der Kandidat 80*; Krieg und Frieden • War and Peace 82*; Auf der Suche nach einer Praktisch-Realistischen Haltung 83; Die Macht der Gefühle • The Power of Emotion 83; Der Angriff der Gegenwart auf die Übrige Zeit • The Assault of the Present Upon the Rest of Time • The Blind Director 85; Odds and Ends • Vermischte Nachrichten 86*

Kluge, Karen Lehrer im Wandel • Teachers in Transformation 63*

Klushantsev, Pavel Road to the Stars 58; Cosmonauts on Venus • Planet of Storms • Planeta Burg • Storm Planet 62; Gill Woman • Gill Women of Venus • Voyage to a Prehistoric Planet • Voyage to the Planet of Prehistoric Women • Voyage to the Prehistoric Planet 65*

Kneeland, Ted Dr. Coppelius • El Fantástico Mundo del Dr. Coppelius 66; The Mysterious House of Dr. C. 76

Knight, Arthur My Bare Lady 62

Knight, C. Pattinson Escape to Justice 42

Knight, Castleton Prelude 27; The Flying Scotsman 29; Goodwin Sands • The Lady from the Sea 29; The Plaything 29; All Riot on the Western Front • The Cockney Spirit in the War No. 1 30; The Cockney Spirit in the War No. 2 30; The Cockney Spirit in the War No. 3 30; Kissing Cup's Race 30; The Olympic Games of 1948 48

Knight, Christopher Carry It On • Joan, Carry It On 70*

Knight, John The Mail Van Murder 57; Moment of Decision 62; The Main Chance 64

Knight, Peter Panther Squad 85

Knights, Robert The Dawning 88

Knilli, Maria Follow Me 89

Knobler, Albert Un Mur à Jérusalem • A Wall in Jerusalem 68*

Knoles, Harley The Antique Dealer 15; The Greater Will 15; Bought and Paid For 16; The Devil's Toy 16; The Gilded Cage 16; His Brother's Wife 16; Miss Petticoats 16; The Supreme Sacrifice 16*; The Adventures of Carol 17; The Burglar 17; The Little Duchess 17; The Page Mystery 17; The Price of Pride 17; The Social Leper 17; Souls Adrift 17; A Square Deal 17; The Stolen Paradise 17; The Cabaret 18; Gates of Gladness 18; Little Women 18; The Oldest Law 18; Stolen Orders 18*; The Volunteer 18; Wanted—A Mother 18; Bolshevism on Trial 19; The Cost 20; The Great Shadow 20; Guilty of Love 20; Half an Hour 20; A Romantic Adventuress 20; Carnival 21; The Bohemian Girl 22; Lew Tyler's Wives 26; Oh Baby! 26; Land of Hope and Glory 27; The Rising Generation 28*; The White Sheik 28

Knopf, Edwin H. Fast Company 29*; The Border Legion 30*; The Law Rides West • The Santa Fe Trail 30*; The Light of Western Stars 30*; Only Saps Work 30*; Paramount on Parade 30*; Slightly Scarlet 30*; Nice Women 31; The Rebel 32*; The Law and the Lady 51

Knott, James The Tahitian 56

Knowles, Bernard A Place of One's Own 45; The Magic Bow 46; Bad Sister • The White Unicorn 47; Jassy 47; The Man Within • The Smugglers 47; Easy Money 48; The Lost People 49*; The Perfect Woman 49; The Reluctant Widow 50; Norman Conquest • Park Plaza 605 53; The Death of Michael Turbin 54; Forever My Heart 54*; Barbados Quest • Murder on Approval 55; Handcuffs, London 55; Hell Is Empty 63*; Der Fall X701 • Frozen Alive 64; Spaceflight IC-1 65

Knox, Ian The Privilege 83*; Shoot for the Sun 86

Knox, Werner Scalps 86

Ko, Clifton Chicken and Duck Talk 89

Kobayashi, Masaki Musuko no Seishun • My Son's Youth 52; Kabe Atsuki Heya • Room with Thick Walls • The Thick-Walled Room 53; Magokoro • Sincere Heart • Sincerity 53; Kono Hiroi Sora no Dokokani • Somewhere Beneath the Wide Sky • Somewhere Under the Broad Sky 54; Mittsu no Ai • Three Loves 54; Beautiful Days • The Beautiful Years • Uruwashiki Saigetsu 55; Anata Kaimasu • I'll Buy You 56; The Fountainhead • Izumi • The Spring 56; Black River • Kuroi Kawa 57; The Human Condition • The Human Condition, Part One • The Human Condition, Part One: No Greater Love • Ningen no Jōken I-II • No Greater Love 59; The Human Condition II • The Human Condition II: Road to Eternity • Ningen no Jōken III-IV • The Road to Eternity • Zoku Ningen no Jōken 59; The Human Condition III • The Human Condition III: A Soldier's Prayer • Ningen no Jōken V-VI • A Soldier's Prayer 61; The Entanglement • The Inheritance • Karami-Ai 62; Harakiri • Seppuku 62; Ghost Stories • Kaidan • Kwaidan • Weird Tales 64; Jōi-

Uchi • Rebellion • Samurai Rebellion 67; Diary of a Tired Man • Hymn to a Tired Man • Journal of an Exhausted Man • Nihon no Seishun • Nippon no Seishun • The Youth of Japan 68; At the Risk of My Life • Inn of Evil • Inochi Bōnifuro 70; Fossil • Fossils • Kaseki 74; Fiery Autumn • Glowing Autumn • Moeru Aki 78; The Far East Martial Court • International Military Tribunal for the Far East • Tōkyō Saiban • The Tokyo Trial • The Tokyo Trials 83; The Empty Table • Fate of a Family • Shokutaku no Nai Ie 85

Kobayashi, Tsuneo Gekkō Kamen • The Man in the Moonlight Mask • The Moonbeam Man 58; Curse of the One-Eyed Corpse • Ghost of the One-Eyed Man • Kaidan Katame no Otoko 65

Kober, Drich Lilith and Ly • Lilith und Ly 19

Koberidze, Otar A Dream Come True • Meshte Nastreshu 63*

Kobler, Erich Schneeweisschen und Rosenrot • Snow White and Rose Red 55; Schneewittchen und die Sieben Zwerge • Snow White 56; Heinzelmännchen • The Shoemaker and the Elves 67

Kobzev, Viktor The Golden Woman • Zolotaya Baba 87

Koch, Carlo Una Signora dell'Ovest 42

Koch, Howard W. Shield for Murder 54*; Big House, U.S.A. 55; Bop Girl • Bop Girl Goes Calypso 57; The Girl in Black Stockings 57; Jungle Heat 57; Untamed Youth 57; Andy Hardy Comes Home 58; Fort Bowie 58; Frankenstein 1970 58; Hell's Highway • The Violent Road 58; Born Reckless 59; The Last Mile 59; Badge 373 73

Koch, Karl La Chasse à la Fortune • La Chasse au Bonheur • Die Jagd nach dem Glück 30*; The Story of Tosca • La Tosca 40*

Koch, Philip Pink Nights 85

Kocking, Leonardo La Estación del Regreso • The Season of Our Return 87

Koenig, Hans Rape on the Moor 57

Koenig, Wolf The Romance of Transportation in Canada 52*; City of Gold 57*; It's a Crime 57*; Glenn Gould—Off the Record 60*; Glenn Gould—On the Record 60*; Festival in Puerto Rico 61*; Lonely Boy 62*; The Canadian Businessman 63*; Stravinsky 65*

Koeppe, Sigrun see *Köppe, Sigrun*

Koerfer, Thomas see *Körfer, Thomas*

Koerpel, Jacques War Is a Racket 34*

Koff, David Blacks Britannica 78

Kofman, Teo Dogs of the Night • Perros de la Noche 86

Kogan, Márcio Fogo e Paixão 88*

Kohanyi, Julius Summer's Children 79

Kohler, Manfred A Coffin from Hong Kong 64; Agent 505 • Agent 505—Todesfalle Beirut 65; A Target for Killing 66

Kohler, Will So Lovely, So Deadly 57

Kohlert, Lutz Lyudi i Zveri • Men and Beasts • Menschen und Tiere 62*

Kohlhaase, Wolfgang Solo Sunny 79*

Kohli, Raj Kumar Insaniyat ke

Dushman 87

Kohlmar, Lee High Heels 21

Kohner, Pancho The Bridge in the Jungle 70; Mr. Sycamore 74

Kok, Marja In for Treatment • Opname 79*

Kokkonen, Ere Liian Iso Keikka • Too Big Gig 87; Little Boys • Pikkupojat 87; Numbskull Emptybrook Back in the Country • Uuno Turhapuro Muuttaa Maalle 87

Kolar, Boris Return to the Land of Oz 71

Kolditz, Gottfried Spur des Falken • Track of the Falcon 68; Signale—Ein Weltraumabenteuer • Signals—An Adventure in Space 70

Kolker, Henry A Man's Country 19; The Woman Michael Married 19; Bright Skies 20; The Greatest Love 20; The Heart of Twenty 20; The Palace of the Darkened Windows 20; The Third Generation 20; Bucking the Tiger 21; Disraeli 21; The Fighter 21; Who Am I? 21; I Will Repay • Swords and the Woman 23; The Leopardess 23; The Purple Highway 23; The Snow Bride 23; The Great Well • Neglected Women 24

Kollek, Amos Worlds Apart 80*; Goodbye, New York 85; Forever, Lulu 86; High Stakes • Melanie Rose 89

Koller, Xavier The Black Tanner • Der Schwarze Tanner 86; Journey of Hope 90

Kolm, Anton Hoffmanns Erzählungen • Tales of Hoffmann 11*

Kolm, Luise Hoffmanns Erzählungen • Tales of Hoffmann 11*

Kolm-Veltee, H. W. see *Kolm-Veltee, Walter*

Kolm-Veltee, Walter Csárdás—Ihre Tollste Nacht 37; The Beethoven Story • Eroica 51*; Don Juan 56

Kolstad, Morten Noe Helt Annet • Something Entirely Different 86

Kolstø, Egil Bibbi, Elin and Christina 86; Fengslende Dager for Christina Berg 88

Koltunov, Grigori Iskushenie Don Zhuana • The Temptation of Don Juan 87*

Komack, James Porky's Revenge 85

Komarov, Sergei The Kiss of Mary Pickford • Mary Pickford's Kiss • Potselui Meri Pikford 27; The Doll with Millions • Kukla s Millionami 28

Komatsu, Takashi Bus 87

Komatsubara, Kazuo Warriors of the Wind 84

Komisarjevsky, James The Way of the World 47; The Enchanted Mirror 59*

Komisarjevsky, Theodor Yellow Stockings 28

Konchalovsky, Andrei see *Mikhalkov-Konchalovsky, Andrei*

Konchalovsky, Andrei Mikhalkov see *Mikhalkov-Konchalovsky, Andrei*

Konermann, Lutz Black and Without Sugar • Schwarz und Ohne Zucker 86

Kong, Jackie The Being • Easter Sunday 80; Night Patrol 84; Blood Diner 87; The Underachievers 87

Konrad, Kazimierz Stanislaw and Anna • Stanisław i Anna 87*

Konstantarakos, Stavros En Plo • On Course 85

Konttinen, Sirkka-Liisa T. Dan Smith 87*

Konwicki, Tadeusz The Last Day of Summer • Ostatni Dzień Lata 58*; Halloween • Zaduszki 61; Augenblick des Friedens • A Moment of Peace 65*; Salto 65; How Far and Yet How Near 72; Lava • Lawa 89

Konyar, Rasmin Vatanyolu—Die Heimreise • Vatanyolu—The Journey Home 89*

Koo, Kang Bum Koesi • Strange Dead Bodies 81

Kopalin, Ilya Moscow • Moskva 26*; Soviet Frontiers on the Danube 41*; Defeat of the German Armies Near Moscow 42*; The Berlin Conference 45*; Czechoslovakia • Liberated Czechoslovakia 46*; August 14 • August 14—One Day in the U.S.S.R. • The Day of the Victorious Country • One Day in the U.S.S.R. 47*; Transformation of the Land 50; The Glorious Road 51*; Albania 52*; The Unforgettable Years 57; City of Great Destiny 60; First Trip to the Stars 61; Inside the U.S.S.R. 61*; Pages of Immortality 65

Kopjitti, Chart see Gobjitti, Chart

Köppe, Sigrun November Cats • Novemberkatzen 86

Kopple, Barbara Harlan County, U.S.A. 76; Keeping On 81; American Dream 89

Kopřiva, Antonín An Accident • Havárie 85; Až do Konce • Till the Very End 86

Koprowicz, Jacek Déjà Vu • Medium 85

Korainik, Pierre Cannabis 70

Korber, Serge À Notre Regrettable Époux 88

Korda, Alexander A Becsapott Újságíró • The Duped Journalist 14*; Örház a Kárpátokban • Watch-Tower in the Carpathians 14*; Tutyu and Totyo • Tutyu és Totyó 14*; Lea Lyon • Lyon Lea 15*; The Officer's Swordknot • A Tiszti Kardbojt 15; Ciklámen • Cyclamen 16; Az Egymillió Fontos Bankó • The Million Pound Note • The One Million Pound Note 16; Fedora • Fehér Éjszakák • White Nights 16; Fighting Hearts • Struggling Hearts • Vergődő Szívek 16; The Grandmother • A Nagymama 16; A Kétszínű Férfi • The Man with Two Hearts 16; The Laughing Saskia • A Nevető Szászkia 16; Mágnás Miska • Miska the Great • Miska the Magnate 16; Mesék az Írógépről • Tales of the Typewriter • Typewriter Tales 16; Faun 17; A Gólyakalifa • The Stork Caliph 17; Harrison and Barrison • Harrison és Barrison 17; Mágia • Magic 17; St. Peter's Umbrella • Szent Péter Esernyője 17; Az Aranyember • The Man with the Golden Touch 18; Mary Ann 18; Neither In, Nor Out • Not In, or Out • Se Ki, Se Be 18; Ave Caesar! 19; A 111-es • Number 111 19; Fehér Rózsa • White Rose 19; Yamata 19; The Prince and the Pauper • Prinz und Bettelknabe • Seine Majestät das Bettelkind 20; Herren der Meere • Masters of the Sea 21; Samson and Delilah • Samson und Dalila 22; Die

Tragödie eines Verschollenen Fürstensohnes • A Vanished World • Eine Versunkene Welt 22; Das Unbekannte Morgen • The Unknown Tomorrow 23; Das Drama von Mayerling • Mayerling • Der Prinz der Legende • Tragedy in the House of Hapsburg • Tragödie im Hause Hapsburg 24; Everybody's Woman • Jedermanns Frau • Jedermanns Weib 24; Dancing Mad • Der Tänzer Meiner Frau 25; Eine DuBarry von Heute • A Modern DuBarry 26; Madame Wants No Children • Madame Wünscht Keine Kinder 26; Helen of Troy • The Private Life of Helen of Troy 27; The Stolen Bride 27; The Night Watch 28; The Yellow Lily 28; Her Private Life 29; Lilies of the Field 29; Love and the Devil 29; The Squall 29; Laughter 30*; The Princess and the Plumber 30*; Women Everywhere 30; Die Männer um Lucie • Rive Gauche 31; Marius 31; Reserved for Ladies • Service for Ladies 31; Zum Goldener Anker 31; Henry VIII • The Private Life of Henry VIII 32; Wedding Rehearsal 32; La Dame de Chez Maxim 33; The Girl from Maxim's 33; Catherine the Great • The Rise of Catherine the Great 34*; Don Juan • The Private Life of Don Juan 34; The Scarlet Pimpernel 34*; Rembrandt 36; The Lion Has Wings 39*; The Thief of Bagdad 40*; Lady Hamilton • That Hamilton Woman 41; Perfect Strangers • Vacation from Marriage 45; An Ideal Husband 47; Bonnie Prince Charlie 48*

Korda, Sándor see Korda, Alexander

Korda, Zoltán Károly-Bakák 18*; A Csodagyerek 24; The Eleven Devils • Die Elf Teufel 27*; Cash • For Love or Money • If I Were Rich 32; Men of Tomorrow 32*; Forever Yours • Forget Me Not 34*; Bosambo • Coast of Skeletons • Sanders of the River 35; Conquest of the Air 36*; Elephant Boy 36*; Revolt in the Jungle 37; The Drum • Drums 38; The Four Feathers 39; The Thief of Bagdad 40*; Jungle Book • Rudyard Kipling's Jungle Book 42*; Sahara 43; Counter-Attack • One Against Seven 45; The Macomber Affair 47; A Woman's Vengeance 47; African Fury • Cry, the Beloved Country 51; Storm Over the Nile 55*

Kordium, A. The Black Sea Mutiny 31

Kordon, Arkady Nabat na Rassvete • The Tocsin 87

Korenev, Alexei Akseleratka 88

Körfer, Thomas Concert for Alice • Konzert für Alice 86

Kornacki, J. Ludzie Wisły • People of the Vistula • The Vistula People 37*

Korolevitch, Vladimir Killing to Live 31

Koromoitsev, Paul Sunny Youth 35

Korras, Giorgos The Cronos Children • Ta Paidia tou Kronou 85; Lipotakis 88*

Korsh-Sablin, Vladimir Krasnaya Derevnya 35*; A Greater Promise 36; Secret Brigade 51*

Kortesz, D. Richthofen • Richthofen, The Red Knight of the Air 29*

Kortner, Fritz Gregor Marold 18; Else von Erlenhof 19; Der Brave Sünder • The

Upright Sinner 31; So ein Mädel Vergisst Man Nicht 32; City of Secrets • Secrets of the City • Die Stadt Ist Voller Geheimnisse 55; Sarajevo 55

Kortwich, Werner Friesennot 36*

Korty, John Language of Faces 63; Crazy Quilt 65; Funnyman 67; Riverrun 68; Breaking the Habit 69; Imogen Cunningham—Photographer 70; The Autobiography of Miss Jane Pittman 74; Crazy Jack and the Boy • Silence 74; Alex and the Gypsy • Love and Other Crimes 76; Who Are the De Bolts? . . . And Where Did They Get 19 Kids? 77; Oliver's Story 78; Twice Upon a Time 83*; Caravan of Courage • The Ewok Adventure 84

Korzeniowsky, Waldemar The Chair • Hot Seat 87

Kósa, Ferenc The Ten Thousand Suns • Tízezer Nap 67; Snowfall 74; A Másik Ember • The Other Man 88

Kosek, Otakar Sedme Nebe 88

Kosheverova, N. Spring in Moscow • Vesna v Moskve 53*; Tiger Girl 55*

Kosovac, Milutin Ada 86

Koster, Dieter What to Do with Willfried? • Wohin mit Willfried? 86

Koster, Henry Das Abenteuer der Thea Roland • Das Abenteuer einer Schönen Frau • Thea Roland 32; Das Hässliche Mädchen 33; Peter 33; Der Storch Hat Uns Getraut 33; Kleine Mutti • Little Mother 34; Catherine the Last • Katharina die Letzte 35; Kribbe Bejter 35; Die Privatsekretärin Heiratet 35; Affairs of Maupassant • Maria Baschkirtzeff 36; Il Diario di una Amata 36; Marie Baschkirtzeff 36; Das Tagebuch der Geliebten 36; Three Smart Girls 36; One Hundred Men and a Girl 37; The Rage of Paris 38; First Love 39; Three Smart Girls Grow Up 39; Spring Parade 40; It Started with Eve 41; Between Us Girls 42; Music for Millions 44; Two Sisters from Boston 46; The Bishop's Wife 47; The Unfinished Dance 47; The Luck of the Irish 48; Come to the Stable 49; Happy Times • The Inspector General 49; Harvey 50; My Blue Heaven 50; Wabash Avenue 50; Elopement 51; Mr. Belvedere Rings the Bell 51; No Highway • No Highway in the Sky 51; Full House • O. Henry's Full House 52*; Marching Along • Stars and Stripes Forever 52; My Cousin Rachel 52; The Robe 53; Desirée 54; A Man Called Peter 54; Good Morning, Miss Dove 55; The Virgin Queen 55; D-Day: The Sixth of June • The Sixth of June 56; The Power and the Prize 56; My Man Godfrey 57; Fräulein 58; La Maja Desnuda • The Naked Maja 59*; The Story of Ruth 60; Flower Drum Song 61; Mr. Hobbs Takes a Vacation 62; Take Her, She's Mine 63; Dear Brigitte • Erasmus with Freckles 65; The Singing Nun 65

Kosterlitz, Hermann see Koster, Henry

Kotani, Tom The Bloody Bushido Blade • The Bushido Blade 78

Kotcheff, Ted Tiara Tahiti 62; Life at the Top 65; Two Gentlemen Sharing 68; Outback • Wake in Fright 70; Billy Two

Hats • The Lady and the Outlaw 72; The Apprenticeship of Duddy Kravitz 74; Fun with Dick and Jane 76; Someone Is Killing the Great Chefs of Europe • Too Many Chefs • Who Is Killing the Great Chefs of Europe? 78; North Dallas Forty 79; Captured! • Split Image 81; First Blood 82; Ain't No Heroes • Uncommon Valor 83; Joshua Then and Now 85; Switching Channels 88; Winter People 88; Hot and Cold • Weekend at Bernie's 89

Kotcheff, William T. *see Kotcheff, Ted*

Koterski, Marek Madhouse 84; Inner Life • Życie Wewnetrzne 87

Kothari, Mahesh De Danadan 88

Kotkowski, Andrzej In an Old Manor House • W Starym Dworku 87

Kotler, Oded Roman Behemshechim 85

Kotto, Yaphet The Limit • Speed Limit 65 • Time Limit 72; Nightmares of the Devil 88

Kotulla, Theodor Aus einem Deutschen Leben • Death Is My Trade 77

Kouf, Jim Miracles 84; Disorganized Crime • Waiting for Salazar 89

Koundouros, Nikos Magic City • I Maijiki Poli 54; O Dracos • The Ogre of Athens 56; The Hunted • The Lawless • The Outlaws • I Paranomi 58; To Potami • The River 60; Mikres Afrodites • Young Aphrodites 62; The Flowers 64; Face of the Medusa • To Prosopo tes Medousas 67; Bordello 85

Kovács, András A Summer Rain • Zápor 60; On the Roofs of Budapest • Pesti Háztetők • Rooftops of Budapest 61; Autumn Star • God's Autumn Star • Isten Őszi Csillaga 62; Difficult People • Nehéz Emberek 64; Két Arckép • Two Portraits 65; Ma vagy Holnap • Today or Tomorrow 65; Cold Days • Hideg Napok 66; Falak • Walls 68; Heirs • Örökösök 70; Relay Race • Staféta 70; Fallow Land • A Magyar Ugaron 72; Bekötött Szemmel • Blindfold 74; Kié a Müvészet? • People and Art 75; Labirintus • Labyrinth 76; The Chief of the Horse Farm • A Ménesgazda • The Stud Farm 78; Októberi Vasárnap • A Sunday in October 79; Ideiglenes Paradicsom • Temporary Paradise 81; An Afternoon Affair • Szeretök 83; Közelkap 83; The Red Countess • Vörös Grófnö 85; Két Választás Magyarországon • Rear-Guard • Valahol Magyarországon 87

Kovacs, Steven '68 88

Kovács, Zsolt Kézdi *see Kézdi-Kovács, Zsolt*

Kovácsi, János Megfelelő Ember Kényes Feladatra • The Right Man for a Delicate Job 85

Koval, Oto Hry pro Mírně Pokročilé 86

Koval, Paul Blue Movies 88*

Kovalyov, Mark The Star Inspector • Zvyozdnyi Inspector 80*

Kowalski, Bernard Hot Car Girl 58; Night of the Blood Beast 58; Attack of the Giant Leeches • Demons of the Swamp • The Giant Leeches 59; Blood and Steel 59; Krakatoa, East of Java • Volcano 69; Stiletto 69; Macho Callahan 70; SSSSnake! •

SSSSSSSS 73

Kowalski, Lech D.O.A. 81; Gringo 85

Koyama, Seijiro Ballad of Pony • Harukoma no Uta 86

Kozintsev, Grigori The Adventures of an Octoberite • The Adventures of Oktyabrina • Pokhozdeniya Oktyabrini 24*; The Bears Versus Yudenich • Mishka Against Yudenich • Mishka Versus Yudenich • Mishki Protiv Yudenicha 25*; Bratishka • Buddy • Little Brother 26*; Chyortovo Koleso • The Devil's Wheel • Moyak s Aurora • The Sailor from the Aurora 26*; The Cloak • The Overcoat • Shinel 26*; Bleeding Snows • The Club of the Big Deed • The Club of the Great Deed • S.V.D. • Soyuz Velikovo Dela 27*; The New Babylon • Novyi Vavilon 29*; Alone • Odna 31*; The Youth of Maxim • Yunost Maksima 35*; The Return of Maxim • Vozvrashcheniye Maksima 37*; Maxim at Vyborg • New Horizons • The Vyborg Side • Vyborgskaya Storona 38*; Boevoi Kinosbornik 2 • Fighting Film Album No. 2 • Incident at the Telegraph Office • Slutshai na Telegrafe 41; Ordinary People • Plain People • Prostiye Lyudi • Simple People 45*; Pirogov 47; Belinsky 53; Don-Kikhot • Don Quixote 57; Gamlet • Hamlet 63; King Lear • Korol Lir 70

Kozma, Ludwig Salome 22*

Kozole, Damjan The Fatal Telephone • Usodni Telefon 87

Kozyr, Alexander The Heavens Call • Nebo Zovyot • Nebo Zowet • Niebo Zowiet • The Sky Calls 59*; Battle Beyond the Sun 63*; Planet of Blood • Queen of Blood 66*

Kraemer, F. W. *see Krämer, F. W.*

Krafft, Jens W. Die Kaukasierin 18*

Kragh-Jacobsen, Søren Emma's Shadow • Skyggen af Emma 88; Guldregn 88

Králová, Drahomíra Kam Doskáče Ranní Ptáče 86

Králová, Drahuše Vyhrávat Potichu • Winning Discreetly 86

Kramarsky, David The Beast with a Million Eyes 55

Krämer, F. W. Dreyfus • The Dreyfus Case 31*; The Flying Squad 32; Tin Gods 32; Daughters of Today 33

Kramer, Frank *see Parolini, Gianfranco*

Kramer, Jerry Modern Girls 86

Kramer, Remi High Velocity 77

Kramer, Robert FALN 65; In the Country 66; The Edge 68; People's War 69*; Ice 70; Milestones 75*; Scenes from the Portuguese Class Struggle 77*; Guns 80; À Toute Allure 81; Birth • Naissance 81; Unser Nazi 84; Diesel 85; Across the Heart • Doc's Kingdom 87

Kramer, Stanley Not As a Stranger 55; The Pride and the Passion 56; The Defiant Ones 58; On the Beach 59; Inherit the Wind 60; Judgment at Nuremberg 61; It's a Mad, Mad, Mad, Mad World 63; Ship of Fools 65; Guess Who's Coming to Dinner 67; The Secret of Santa Vittoria 69; R.P.M. • Revolutions Per Minute 70; Bless the Beasts and Children 71; Oklahoma

Crude 73; The Domino Killings • The Domino Principle 76; The Runner Stumbles 79

Kramreither, Anthony Thrillkill 84*

Krancer, Bert The Lift 65

Krasilovsky, Alexis End of the Art World 71; Blood 75; Created and Consumed by Light 76; Childbirth Dream 78; Exile 84

Krasna, Norman Princess O'Rourke 43; The Big Hangover 50; The Ambassador's Daughter 56

Krasny, Paul Christina 74; Joe Panther 76

Krauss, Henry Papa Hulin 16; Le Chemineau 17; Marion de Lorme 18; Fromont Jeunné et Risler Aîné 21; Les Trois Masques 21; La Calvaire de Dona Pisa 25

Krawczyk, Gérard I Hate Actors • Je Hais les Acteurs 86; L'Été en Pente Douce • Summer on a Soft Slope 87

Krawicz, Mieczysław Każdemu Wolno Kochać 33*; Love in the Army • Śluby Ułańskie 35; Jego Wielka Miłość 36*; Miłość Wszystko Zwycieża 36; Good for Nothing • Niedorajda 37; Dyplomatyczna Żona 38*

Kreines, Jeff Seventeen 84*

Krejčík, Jiří Božská Ema • The Divine Emma 79

Kremnev, Valery Confrontation • Ochnaya Stavka 87

Krenkler, Ulrich Zoning 86

Kresel, Lee The Prisoner of the Iron Mask • Vendetta della Maschera di Ferro • La Vengeance du Masque de Fer 60*; Guns of the Black Witch • La Terreur des Mers • Il Terrore dei Mare 61*; Mosura • Mothra 61*; Serafino • Serafino ou L'Amour aux Champs 68*; Lovers and Liars • Travels with Anita • A Trip with Anita • Viaggio con Anita 78*

Kresoja, Dragan The End of the War • Kraj Rata 86; Oktoberfest 87

Kress, Harold F. Wardcare of Psychotic Patients 41; Purity Squad 45; No Questions Asked 51; The Painted Hills 51; Apache War Smoke 52

Kressin, M. The Heart of Solomon • Serdtsye Solomona • Solomon's Heart 32*

Krieger, Martin Theo Zischke 87

Krievs, Arvid Fotografia s Zhenshchinoi i Dikim Kabanom 88

Krims, Milton Crossed Swords • Il Maestro di Don Giovanni 52*

Krish, John Companions in Crime 54; The Salvage Gang 58; Let My People Go 60; Unearthly Stranger 63; The Wild Affair 63; Decline and Fall • Decline and Fall of a Bird Watcher 68; The Man Who Had Power Over Women 70; Jesus 79*; Friend or Foe 82; Out of the Darkness 85

Krishen, Pradip Massey Sahib 86

Krishna Kaliyuga Krishnu 88

Krishtofovich, Vyacheslav A Lonely Woman Is Looking for a Life Companion • Lonely Woman Seeks Life Companion • Lonely Woman Seeks Lifetime Companion • Odinokaya Zhenchina Zhelaet Poznakomitaya 87

Křístek, Václav Přátelé Bermudského Trojúhelníku 87*

Kristy, L. The Enchanted Mirror 59*; Circus Stars 60*

Kristye, Anthony *see Boccacci, Antonio*

Kroeker, Allan Tramp at the Door 86

Kroitor, Roman Paul Tomkowitz, Railway Switchman 54; Farm Calendar 55; The Great Plains 57; Glenn Gould—Off the Record 60*; Glenn Gould—On the Record 60*; Universe 60*; Festival in Puerto Rico 61*; The Living Machine 61; Lonely Boy 62*; The Canadian Businessman 63*; Stravinsky 65*; Above the Horizon 66*

Królikiewicz, Grzegorz Zabicie Ciotki 85

Kroll, Georg Das Spiel mit dem Feuer 21*

Kroll, Nathan The Guns of August 64

Kromarov, Grigori The Dead Mountaineer Hotel • Otel 'u Pogibshchego Alpinista 79

Kronsberg, Jeremy Joe Going Ape! 81

Krška, Václav Bohemian Rapture 48; Dívka s Třemi Velbloudy • The Girl with Three Camels 68

Krueger, Michael Mind Killer 87; Night Vision 88

Krumgold, Joseph Dream No More 50

Kruntorad, Paul Racing • Rennen 61*

Kruse, John October Moth 59

Krzystek, Waldemar Suspended • W Zawieszeniu 87

Kubasek, Vaclav Thunder in the Hills 47

Kubelka, Peter Mosaic in Confidence • Mosaik im Vertrauen 55; Adebar 57; Schwechater 58; Arnulf Rainer 60; Unsere Afrikareise 66

Kubrick, Stanley Day of the Fight 49; Flying Padre 51; The Seafarers 52; Fear and Desire 53; Killer's Kiss 55; The Killing 56; Paths of Glory 57; Spartacus 59*; Lolita 61; Dr. Strangelove, or How I Learned to Stop Worrying and Love the Bomb 63; 2001: A Space Odyssey 68; A Clockwork Orange 71; Barry Lyndon 75; The Shining 79; Full Metal Jacket 87

Kuchar, George Corruption of the Damned 65; Unstrap Me 68; Knocturne 72*

Kuchar, Mike Sins of the Fleshapoids 65; Knocturne 72*

Kuckelmann, Norbert Man Under Suspicion 84

Kuehl, Kliff Murder Rap 88

Kuehn, Andrew J. Flush 81; Terror in the Aisles 84; Rolling in the Aisles 87

Kuehn, Siegfried *see Kühn, Siegfried*

Kuei, Chi-hung *see Gui, Zhihong*

Kuemel, Harry *see Kümel, Harry*

Kuenster, Dan All Dogs Go to Heaven 89*

Kuharski, Jean de *see De Kuharski, Jean*

Kühn, Siegfried I Dreamed of My Elk • Der Traum vom Elch 87; Die Schauspielerin 88

Kul, Raghuvir Mohre 88

Kuleshov, Leo *see Kuleshov, Lev*

Kuleshov, Lev After Happiness • Toward Happiness • Za Schastem 17*;

Engineer Prite's Project • Proekt Inzhenera Praita • The Project of Engineer Prite • Proyekt Inzhenera Praita 18; Pesn Lyubvi Nedopetaya • Pesn'Liubvi Nedopetaia • The Unfinished Love Song 18*; Na Krasnom Frontye • On the Red Front 20; The Extraordinary Adventures of Mr. West in the Land of the Bolsheviks • Neobychainiye Prikluchenyiya Mistera Vesta v Stranye Bolshevikov 24; The Death Ray • Luch Smerti 25*; By the Law • Dura Lex • Po Zakonu 26; Locomotive No. 10006 • Parovoz No. 10006 26; The Girl Journalist • Journalist • Vasha Znakomaya • Your Acquaintance • Zhurnalista 27; Dva, Bouldej, Dva • Dva-Buldi-Dva • The Great Buldis • Two-Buldi-Two 29*; The Gay Canary • Veselaia Kanaraika • Veselaya Kanareika 29; Electrification 30; Forty Hearts • Sorok Serdets 31; Gorizont • Horizon • Horizon—The Wandering Jew 32; The Great Consoler • Velikii Uteshitel 33; Dohunda 34; The Siberians • Sibiraki • Sibiryaki 40; Incident in a Volcano • Incident on a Volcano • Sluchai v Vulkanye 41*; Klyatva Timura • The Oath of Timur • Timur's Oath 42*; The Young Partisans • Yunye Partizany 42; Boevoi Kinosbornik 13 • Fighting Film Album No. 13 43; My s Urala • We Are from the Urals • We from the Urals • We of the Urals 44*

Kulidzhanov, Lev Damy • Ladies 54*; Eto Nachinados Tak • It Started Like This • This Is How It Began 54*; Dom v Kotorom Ya Zhivu • The House I Live In • The House Where I Live 57*; A Home for Tanya • Otchi Dom • Our Father's House • The Paternal Home 59; The Lost Photograph • Poteryannaya Fotografiya 60; Kogda Derevya Byli Bolshimi • When the Trees Were Big • When the Trees Were Tall 61; The Blue Notebook • Sinaya Tetrad 63; Crime and Punishment • Prestupleniye i Nakazaniye 69; The Moment in the Stars 75

Kuliev, Eldar The Legend of Silver Lake • Legenda Serebryanogo Ozera 87

Kulijanov, Lev *see Kulidzhanov, Lev*

Kulik, Buzz The Explosive Generation 61; The Case Against Paul Ryker • The Court Martial of Sergeant Ryker • Sergeant Ryker • Torn Between Two Values 63; Evil Come, Evil Go • The Yellow Canary 63; Warning Shot 66; Riot 68; Villa Rides! 68; The Boy Next Door • Sex and the Teenager • To Find a Man 71; Brian's Song 72; Shamus 72; The Hunter 80; Pursuit • The Pursuit of D. B. Cooper 81*

Kull, Edward The Pointing Finger 19*; The Vanishing Dagger 20*; The Diamond Queen 21; The Man Trackers 21; Barriers of Folly 22; Bulldog Courage 22; Man's Best Friend 35; The New Adventures of Tarzan • Tarzan and the Green Goddess • Tarzan's New Adventure 35*

Kulle, Jarl Bokhandlaren Som Slutade Bada • The Bookseller Who Gave Up Bathing 68

Kumai, Kei Kurobe no Taiyō • Tunnel to the Sun 68; Sandakan-8 • Sandakan

Hachiban Shōkan: Bōkyo 75; The Sea and Poison • Umi to Dokuyaku 87

Kumar, Ashok Abhinandana 88

Kumar, Jatin Hum Farishte Nahin 88

Kumar, Kranti Sharadama 88

Kumar, Mehul Jungbaaz 89; Na-Insaafi 89; Nafrat ki Aandhi 89

Kumar, Rakesh Kaun Jeeta? Kaun Hara? 88

Kumar, Shiv Mati Balidan ki 88

Kumar, Swaroop Param Dharam 88

Kumar, Vimal Jaisi Karni Waisi Bharani 89

Kumashiro, Tatsumi Inferno • Jigoku 81; Koibumi • Love Letter 86; Kamu Onna 88

Kümel, Harry Monsieur Hawarden 68; Blut an den Lippen • Daughters of Darkness • Erszebet • Erzebeth • The Promise of Red Lips • The Red Lips • Le Rouge aux Lèvres 70; The Legend of Doom House • Malpertuis • Malpertuis: Histoire d'une Maison Maudite 71

Kunert, Joachim Die Abenteuer des Werner Holt • The Adventures of Werner Holt 63

Kuo, Joseph Return of Eighteen Bronzemen 84

Kuo-fu, Chen *see Chen, Kuo-fu*

Kuplerski, Edward A. Curse of Kilimanjaro 78

Kurahara, Koreyoshi Kyōnetsu no Kisetsu • The Weird Love-Makers • Wild Love-Makers 63; Ai no Kawaki • Longing for Love • The Thirst for Love 66; The Glacier Fox 78; Antarctica 84; Haru no Kane • Spring Ball 86

Kurcenli, Yusuf Eternal Tree • Ölmez Ağacı 86

Kurganov, S. The Soldiers of Freedom 76*

Kuri, Rafael Villaseñor *see Villaseñor Kuri, Rafael*

Kuri, Yoji Kitte no Gensō • Stamp Fantasia 59; Nihiki no Sama 59; Fashion • Fasshon 60; People • Warai no Ningen 60; Clap Vocalism • Human Zoo • Ningen Dōbutsuen 61; Ai • Love 62; Atchi wa Kotchi • Here and There 62; The Chair • Isu 62; Botan • The Button 63; The Discovery of Zero • Zero no Hakken 63; The Face • Kao 63; Kiseki • Locus 63; Aos • Chiisana Kūkan • Small Space 64; Man, Woman and Dog • Otoko to Onna to Inu 64; Ring-Ring Bōi • Ring Ring Boy 64; Mado • The Window 65; The Man Next Door • Tonari no Yarō 65; Samurai 65; Au Fou! • Satsujinkyō Shidai 66; Chiisana Sasayaki • Little Murmurs 66; The Eggs • Sado no Tamago 66; Anata wa Nani o Kangaete Iru Ka? • What Do You Think? 67; The Flower • Hana 67; Heya • The Room 67; Concerto in X Minor 68; Crazy World 68; Futatsu no Yakizakana • Two Grilled Fish 68; Imagination 69; Little Island 69; The Bathroom 70; Fantasy for Piano 72

Kuriyama, Tomio Congratulatory Speech • Shukuji 86; I Go to Tokyo • Ora Tōkyō Sā Yukuda 86

Quinine 17*; Robbers and Thieves 17*; Roses and Thorns 17*; Sharks Is Sharks 17; The Tale of a Fish 17; The Tale of a Monkey 17; A Tankless Job 17*; The Tanks 17; Three Strikes You're Out 17; Throwing the Bull 17*; 20,000 Legs Under the Sea 17; The White Hope 17; All for the Ladies 18; The Best Man Loses 18; The Black Fist • Der Black Mitt 18; A Bold Bad Man 18; Burglars 18; Crabs Are Crabs • Crabs Iss Crabs 18; Der Captain's Birthday • Der Kaptain's Birthday 18; Doing His Bit 18; Fisherman's Luck 18; Hash and Hypnotism 18; Hearts and Horses 18; A Heathen Benefit 18; His Dark Past 18; His Day Off • Judge Rummy's Off Day 18; His Last Will 18; The Latest in Underwear 18; Mopping Up a Million 18; Pep 18; A Picnic for Two 18; Policy and Pie 18; Rheumatics 18; Rub-a-Dud-Dud 18; Spirits 18; Swat the Fly 18; Too Many Cooks 18; Tramp Tramp Tramp 18; Twinkle Twinkle 18; The Two Twins 18; Up in the Air 18; Vanity and Vengeance 18; War Gardens 18; Where Are the Papers? 18; After the Ball 19; The Breath of a Nation 19; Business Is Business 19; Der Wash on der Line 19; Good Night Nurse 19; The Great Handicap 19; How Could William Tell? 19; Judge Rummy's Miscue 19; Jungle Jumble 19; Knocking the "H" Out of Heinie 19; Pigs in Clover 19; Rubbing It In 19; The Sawdust Trail 19; A Smash-Up in China 19; Snappy Cheese 19; A Sweet Pickle 19; The Tale of a Shirt 19; That Reminds Me 19; Transatlantic Flight 19; A Wee Bit o' Scotch 19; Where Has My Little Coal Bin? 19; All for the Love of a Girl 20; Apollo 20; Bear Facts • Judge Rummy in Bear Facts 20; The Chinese Honeymoon 20*; A Close Shave 20; Cupid's Advice 20; Dr. Jekyll and Mr. Zip 20; Doctors Should Have Patience 20; A Family Affair 20*; A Fish Story 20; A Fitting Gift 20; The Fly Guy 20; The Great Cheese Robber 20*; The Great Umbrella Mystery 20; Happy Hooldini 20; My Country Cousin 20; His Last Legs 20; The Hooch Ball 20; The Last Rose of Summer 20; Luring Eyes • The Mysterious Vamp 20; The Prize Dance 20; Roll Your Own 20; A Romance of '76 20; Shedding the Profiteer 20; Shimmie Shivers 20; Smokey Smokes 20; The Sponge Man 20; Spring Fever 20; Swinging His Vacation 20; The Tale of a Wag 20*; Turn to the Right Leg 20; A Very Busy Day 20; A Warm Reception 20*; The Wrong Track 20*; The Awful Spook 21*; His Nibs 21; The Skating Fool 21; Faint Heart 22; A Social Error 22; Beware of the Dog 23; The Busybody 23; The Fiddling Fool 23; The Four Orphans 23; Helpful Hogan 23; The Life of Reilly 23; The Pill Pounder 23; So This Is Hamlet? 23; Wild and Wicked 23; The New School Teacher 24; Restless Wives 24; Womanhandled 25; Let's Get Married 26; Paradise for Two 26; Say It Again 26; So's Your Old Man 26; The Gay Defender 27; Running Wild 27; Tell It to Sweeney 27; Feel My Pulse 28; Half a Bride 28; Big

News 29; His First Command 29; Saturday's Children 29; Laugh and Get Rich 31; Smart Woman 31; The Age of Consent • Are These Our Children? 32; The Half Naked Truth 32; Melody of Life • Symphony of Six Million 32; Bed of Roses 33; Gabriel Over the White House 33; Gallant Lady 33; Affairs of Cellini 34; What Every Woman Knows 34; Private Worlds 35; She Married Her Boss 35; My Man Godfrey 36; Stage Door 37; Fifth Avenue Girl 39; The Primrose Path 40; Unfinished Business 41; Lady in a Jam 42; Living in a Big Way 47; One Touch of Venus 48*

Lacayo-Deshon, Ramiro El Espectro de la Guerra • The Spectre of War 88

Lacerda, Luiz Carlos Leila Diniz 87

Lacerte, Jacques Love Me Deadly 72

Lacey, Robert de see De Lacey, Robert

Lachman, Harry The Compulsory Husband 28*; Weekend Wives 28; The Greenwood Tree • Under the Greenwood Tree 29; Song of Soho 30; The Yellow Mask 30; The Love Habit 31; The Outsider 31; Aren't We All? 32*; La Belle Marinière 32; La Couturière de Luneville 32; Down Our Street 32; Face in the Sky 32; Insult 32; Mistigri 32; Paddy the Next Best Thing 33; Baby Take a Bow 34; George White's Scandals • George White's Scandals of 1934 • Scandals 34*; I Like It That Way 34; Nada Más Que una Mujer • Only a Woman 34; Dante's Inferno 35; Dressed to Thrill 35; Charlie Chan at the Circus 36; The Man Who Lived Twice 36; Our Relations 36; The Devil Is Driving 37; It Happened in Hollywood • Once a Hero 37; No Time to Marry 38; They Came by Night 39; Murder Over New York 40; Charlie Chan in Rio 41; Dead Men Tell 41; Castle in the Desert 42; Dr. Renault's Secret 42; The Loves of Edgar Allan Poe 42

Lackey, W. T. Roaring Fires 27

Lacombe, Georges La Zone 27; Boule de Gomme 31; Un Coup de Téléphone 32; La Femme Invisible 33; Jeunesse 34; La Route Heureuse 36; Café de Paris 38*; Derrière la Façade • 32 Rue de Montmartre 39*; Elles Étaient Douze Femmes 40; Les Musiciens du Ciel 40; Le Dernier des Six 41; Montmartre-sur-Seine 41; Le Journal Tombe à Cinq Heures 42; Midnight in Paris • Monsieur la Souris 42; L'Escalier Sans Fin 43; Martin Roumagnac 46; The Room Upstairs 46; Le Pays Sans Étoiles 46; Les Condamnés 47; Prélude à la Gloire 50; The Night Is My Kingdom • La Nuit Est Mon Royaume 51; Les Sept Péchés Capitaux • I Sette Peccati Capitali • The Seven Deadly Sins 51*; Leur Dernière Nuit • Their Last Night 53; Female and the Flesh • The Light Across the Street • La Lumière d'en Face 55; La Cargaison Blanche • Illegal Cargo 57; Mon Coquin de Père 58

Lacroix, Georges Dans la Rafale 16; L'Heure Tragique 16; Beauté Qui Meurt 17; Les Écrits Restant 17; Haine 18; Son Destin 19; La Vengeance de Mallet 20; Passionnément 21

Lacy, Joe see Elorrieta, José María

Lacy, Joseph de see Elorrieta, José María

Lacy, Philippe de see De Lacy, Philippe

Lacy, Robert de see De Lacey, Robert

Lado, Aldo La Corta Notte delle Bambole di Vetro • Malastrana 72; Scirocco 88

Ladoire, Oscar Es Cosa con Plumas 88

Ladowicz, B. Jews in Poland 57

Laemmle, Edward The Top o' the Morning 22; The Victor 23; The Man in Blue 25; Spook Ranch 25; A Woman's Faith 25; The Still Alarm 26; The Whole Town's Talking 26; Cheating Cheaters 27; Held by the Law 27; The Thirteenth Juror 27; The Drake Case 29; Fallen Angels • Man, Woman and Wife 29; Lasca of the Rio Grande 31; The Texas Bad Man 32; Embarrassing Moments 34; A Notorious Gentleman 35

Laemmle, Ernst The Phantom of the Opera 25*; Prowlers of the Night 26; The Broncho Buster 27; Hands Off 27; A One Man Game 27; Range Courage 27; Red Clay 27; The Grip of the Yukon 28; Phyllis of the Follies 28; What Men Want 30

La Falaise, Henry de see De la Falaise, Henry

Lafia, John The Blue Iguana 88; Child's Play 2 90

La Frenais, Ian To Russia with Elton 79*

Laguionie, Jean-François De l'Autre Côté de l'Image • The Other Side of the Image 85

Lah, Michael Cellbound 55*

Lahiff, Craig Coda 87; Fever 88; Deadly Possession 89

Lahlou, Latif La Compromission 87

Lahola, Leopold Until Hell Is Frozen 60; Duell vor Sonnenuntergang 65

Lai, David Lonely 15 82; Possessed 83; Sworn Brothers 87

Lai-choi, Nam see Nam, Lai-choi

La Iglesia, Eloy de see De la Iglesia, Eloy

Laiming, Wan see Wan, Laiming

Laine, Edvard Akaton Mies 84; Akallinen Mies • The Farmer Has a Wife 87

Laine, Edvin Tuntematon Sotilas • The Unknown Soldier 55

Laing, John Beyond Reasonable Doubt 80; The Lost Tribe 83; Other Halves 85; Dangerous Orphans 86

Laird, Marlena Friendship, Secrets and Lies 79*

Laius, Leida see Lajus, Lejda

Lajus, Lejda Keep Smiling, Baby • Naerata Ometi 86*; Games for Schoolchildren • Igry Dlja Detej Sko'nogo Vozrasta 87*

Lakhdar-Hamina, Mohammed Hassan Terro • Hassan, Terrorist 68; Ahdat Sanawouach el-Djamr • Chronicle of the Burning Years • Chronicle of the Years of Embers • Chronicle of the Years of the Brazier 75; Le Dernière Image • The Last Image 86

Lakso, Edward J. Head On 71; Boots Turner 73; 43 — The Petty Story • Smash-Up Alley 73

LaLoggia, Frank Fear No Evil • Mark of the Beast 80; Lady in White 87

La Loma, José Antonio de *see De la Loma, José Antonio*

Lalou, Étienne Corps Profond 63*

Laloux, René Fantastic Planet • La Planète Sauvage 73; Les Maîtres du Temps 82; Gandahar • Light Years 87*

Lam, Ringo Aces Go Places IV • Mad Mission IV 86; City on Fire 87; Prison on Fire 87

Lamač, Karel Akord Smrti 19; The Crystal Princess 25; Lucerna 25; The Good Soldier Schweik 26; Schweik at the Front 26; Dcery Eviny 28; Suzy Saxophone 29; Die vom Rummelplatz 30; Der Falsche Feldmarschall 30; Eine Freundin So Goldig Wie Du 30; Das Mädel aus U.S.A. 30; Versuchen Sie Meine Schwester 30; Die Fledermaus 31; Hadimrsku Doesn't Know • To Neznáte Hadimršku • You Should Know Hadimrska 31*; He and His Sister • On a Jeho Sestra 31*; The Informer • Der Zinker 31*; Mamsell Nitouche 31; Baby 32; Die Grausame Freundin 32; Der Hexer 32; Kiki 32; Eine Nacht im Paradies 32; Die Tochter des Regiments 33; Frasquita 34; Karneval und Liebe 34; Klein Dorrit 34; Polenblut • Polish Blood 34; Ich Liebe Alle Frauen 35; J'Aime Toutes les Femmes 35; Der Junge Graf 35; Knock-Out 35*; Ein Mädel vom Ballett 36; Der Postillon von Lonjumeau 36; Der Schüchterne Casanova 36; Peter im Schnee 37; General Housecleaning • Gross Reinemachen 38; The Hoboes • Die Landstreicher 38; Immer Wenn Ich Glücklich Bin • Waltz Melodies • Walzerlange 38; Place de la Concorde 39; It Happened One Sunday 43; It Started at Midnight • Schweik's New Adventures 43; They Met in the Dark 43*; La Colère des Dieux 47; Une Nuit à Tabarin 47

La Maie, Elsier The Unfortunate Sex 20

Lamas, Fernando The Magic Fountain 61; Touch White, Touch Black • The Violent Ones 67

La Maza, Armando Vargas de *see Vargas de la Maza, Armando*

Lamb, Ande The Texan Meets Calamity Jane 50

Lamb, Dana Quest for the Lost City 55*

Lamb, Ginger Quest for the Lost City 55*

Lamb, John The Aqua Sex • The Mermaids of Tiburon • The Virgin Aqua Sex 62

Lambart, Harry The Tangle 14; The Heights of Hazards 15; The Silent Witness 17*; The Crucible of Life 18; Romance and Reality 21; Down Under Donovan 22

Lamberson, Gregory Slime City 88

Lambert, Evelyn Arbre Généalogique • Family Tree 47*; Begone Dull Care 49*; Around Is Around 50*; Rhythmetic 56*; Le Merle 58*; Short and Suite 59*; Lignes Verticales • Lines Vertical 60*; Lignes Horizontales • Lines Horizontal 62*

Lambert, Gavin Another Sky 60

Lambert, Glen Heartbound 25

Lambert, Lothar The Desert of Love • Die Liebeswüste 86; Der Sexte Sinn • The Sexth Sense 86*

Lambert, Mary Siesta 87; Pet Sematary 89

Lambert, Susan Landslides 87*

Lambrinos, Fotos Doxobus 87

Lamdo, Mao Robot Carnival 87*

Lamond, John Breakfast in Paris 82

Lamont, Charles Hollywood Bound 23; Almost a Husband 24; Big Game 24; Built on a Bluff 24; Clear the Way 24; A Diving Fool 24; Make It Snappy 24; The Midnight Watch 24; Raising Cain 24; Sailing Along 24; Tin Can Alley 24; Tourists de Luxe 24; Accidents Can Happen 25; Al's Troubles 25; Baby Be Good 25; Cupid's Victory 25; Dog Daze 25; Educating Buster 25; Helpful Al 25; In Deep 25; Love Sick 25; Maid in Morocco 25; Married Neighbors 25; Paging a Wife 25; Piping Hot 25; Puzzled by Crosswords 25; A Rough Party 25; A Winning Pair 25; Bachelor Babies 26; Bear Cats 26; Close Shaves 26; Excess Baggage 26; Going Crazy 26; Her Ambition 26; Jane's Honeymoons 26; My Kid 26; Open House 26; Open Spaces 26; Sea Scamps 26; Thanks for the Boat Ride 26; Why, George! 26; A Yankee Doodle Duke 26; Atta Baby 27; Brunettes Prefer Gentlemen 27; Funny Face 27; Grandpa's Boy 27; A Half-Pint Hero 27; Kid Tricks 27; Live News 27; Monty of the Mounties 27; Naughty Boy 27; Scared Silly 27; Shamrock Alley 27; She's a Boy 27; Wedding Yells 27; Who's Afraid? 27; Angel Eyes 28; Chilly Days 28; Circus Blues 28; Come to Papa 28; Companionate Service 28; Follow Teacher 28; Girlies Behave 28; The Gloom Chaser 28; Hot Luck 28; Kid Hayseed 28; Ladies Preferred 28; Making Whoopee 28; Misplaced Husbands 28; Navy Beans 28; No Fare 28; The Quiet Worker 28; Wildcat Valley 28; Auntie's Mistake 29; The Crazy Nut 29; Fire Proof 29; The Fixer 29; Ginger Snaps 29; Helter Skelter 29; Joy Tonic 29; Only Her Husband 29; Sole Support 29; Top Speed 29; All Excited 31; Divorce à la Carte 31; Fast and Furious 31; The Gossipy Plumber 31; Hollywood Half Backs 31; Hot and Bothered 31; Models and Wives 31; One Hundred Dollars 31; Out-Stepping 31; Foiled Again 32; The Hollywood Handicap 32; Hollywood Kids 32; Hollywood Runaround 32; The Marriage War 32; The Pie-Covered Wagon 32; Running Hollywood 32; War Babies 32; The Big Squeal 33; Blue Blackbirds 33; Git Along, Little Wifie 33; Glad Rags to Riches 33; Keyhole Katie 33; Kid 'n Hollywood 33; The Kids' Last Fight 33; Merrily Yours 33; A Pair of Socks 33; Polly-Tix in Washington 33; Techno-Crazy 33; Trimmed in Furs 33; Two Black Crows in Africa 33; Allez Oop 34; The Curtain Falls 34; Educating Papa 34; The Gold Ghost 34; Half-Baked Relations 34; Hello, Prosperity 34; Managed Money 34; No Sleep on the Deep 34; Palooka from Paducah 34; Pardon My Pups 34; Plumbing for Gold 34; Tomorrow's Youth 34; Alimony Aches 35; The Captain Hits the Ceiling 35; Choose Your Partners 35; Circumstantial Evidence 35; The E Flat Man 35; False Pretenses 35; Gigolette • Night Club 35; The Girl Who Came Back 35; Happiness C.O.D. 35; Hayseed Romance 35; His Last Fling 35; Knockout Drops 35; The Lady in Scarlet 35; One Run Elmer 35; Restless Knights 35; A Shot in the Dark 35; Sons of Steel 35; Tars and Stripes 35; Tramp Tramp Tramp 35; The World Accuses 35; August Week-End • Weekend Madness 36; Below the Deadline 36; Bulldog Edition • Lady Reporter 36; The Dark Hour 36; Grand Slam Opera 36; Knee Action 36; Lady Luck 36; Little Red Schoolhouse • Schoolboy Penitentiary 36; Lucky Corrigan 36; Oh, Duchess! 36; Ring Around the Moon 36; Three on a Limb 36; Calling All Doctors 37; Community Sing 37; Ditto 37; Fiddling Around 37; He Done His Duty 37; Jail Bait 37; Love Nest on Wheels 37; My Little Feller 37; New News 37; Playing the Ponies 37; Sailor Maid 37; Wallaby Jim of the Islands 37; The Wrong Miss Right 37; Cipher Bureau 38; A Doggone Mix-Up 38; International Crime 38; The Long Shot 38; Shadows Over Shanghai 38; Slander House 38; Inside Information 39; Little Accident 39; Panama Patrol 39; Pride of the Navy 39; Sandy Takes a Bow • Unexpected Father 39; The Tragic Festival • La Verbena Trágica 39; Give Us Wings 40; Love, Honor and Oh Baby! 40; Oh, Johnny, How You Can Love! 40; Sandy Is a Lady 40; Don't Get Personal 41; Melody Lane 41; Moonlight in Hawaii 41; Road Agent • Texas Road Agent 41; San Antonio Rose 41; Sing Another Chorus 41; Almost Married 42; A Date with an Angel • Get Hep to Love 42; Hi, Neighbor! 42; It Comes Up Love • She's My Lovely 42; When Johnny Comes Marching Home 42; You're Telling Me 42; Fired Wife 43; Hit the Ice • Oh Doctor! 43*; Man of the Family • Top Man 43; Mr. Big 43; Bowery to Broadway 44; Chip Off the Old Block 44; Her Primitive Man 44; The Merry Monahans 44; The Bride Wasn't Willing • Frontier Gal 45; Salome, Where She Danced 45*; That's the Spirit 45; The Runaround 46; She Wrote the Book 46; Slave Girl 47; Ma and Pa Kettle 48; The Untamed Breed 48; Bagdad 49; Curtain Call at Cactus Creek • Take the Stage 49; Going to Town • Ma and Pa Kettle Go to Town 49; I Was a Shoplifter 49; Abbott and Costello in the Foreign Legion 50; Abbott and Costello Meet the Invisible Man 51; Comin' Round the Mountain 51; Flame of Araby 51; Abbott and Costello Meet Captain Kidd 52; Ma and Pa Kettle Go to Paris • Ma and Pa Kettle on Vacation 52; Abbott and Costello Go to Mars • On to Mars 53; Abbott and Costello Meet Dr. Jekyll and Mr. Hyde 53; Ma and Pa Kettle at Home 54; Ricochet Romance 54; Untamed Heiress 54; Abbott and Costello Meet the Keystone Kops 55; Abbott and Costello Meet the Mummy 55; Carolina Cannonball 55; Lay That Rifle Down 55; Francis in the Haunted

House 56; The Kettles in the Ozarks 56

Lamore, Marsh Mighty Mouse in the Great Space Chase 83*; The Secret of the Sword 85*

Lamorisse, Albert Djerba 47; Bim • Bim, le Petit Âne 49; Crin Blanc • Crin Blanc le Cheval Sauvage • White Mane • Wild Stallion 52; Le Ballon Rouge • The Red Balloon 55; Stowaway in the Sky • Le Voyage en Ballon • Voyage in a Balloon 60; Fifi la Plume 64; Versailles 66; Paris Jamais Vu • Paris Rediscovered 68; Islande de Flammes et d'Eaux 69; The Lovers' Wind • Le Vent des Amoureux 70

Lamothe, Arthur Bûcherons de la Manouane 62; De Montréal à Manicouagan 63; La Neige à Fondu sur la Manicouagan 65; Poussière sur la Ville 65; Le Train de Labrador 67; Actualités Québecoises 68*; Au-Delà des Murs 68; Ce Soir-Là, Gilles Vigneault 68; Pour une Éducation de Qualité 69; Un Homme et Son Boss 70*; Le Mépris N'Aura Qu'un Temps 70; Révolution Industrielle 70; Techniques Minières 70; Équinoxe 86

La Mothe, Leon de see De la Mothe, Leon

Lamoureux, Robert La Brune Que Voilà 60; Ravissante 61; On à Retrouvé la 7e Compagnie 75

Lampin, Georges L'Idiot • The Idiot 46; Éternel Conflit 48; The Honorable Catherine 48; Le Paradis des Pilotes Perdus 49; Retour à la Vie • Return to Life 49*; Les Anciens de Saint-Loup 50; Passion 51; La Maison dans la Dune 52; Suivez Cet Homme! 53; Crime and Punishment • Crime et Châtiment • The Most Dangerous Sin 56; Rencontre à Paris 56; King on Horseback 57; Killer Spy 58; La Tour Prends Garde! 58; Mathias Sandorf 62

Lamprecht, Gerhard Der Friedhof der Lebenden 21; Fliehende Schatten 22; Die Buddenbrooks 23; Das Haus Ohne Lachen 23; Die Andere 24; Hanseaten 25; Slums of Berlin • Die Verrufenen 25; Children of No Importance • Die Unehelichen 26; Schwester Veronika 26; Der Alte Fritz 27; Der Katzensteg 27; Unter der Laterne 28; Zweierlei Moral 30; Emil and the Detectives • Emil und die Detektive 31; Zwischen Nacht und Morgen 31; Der Schwarze Husar 32; Herthas Erwachen 33; Spione am Werk 33; Einmal eine Grosse Dame Sein 34; Ein Gewisser Herr Gran 34; Prinzessin Turandot 34; Barcarole 35; Einer zu Viel an Bord 35; Der Höhere Befehl 36; Ein Seltsamer Gast 36; Die Gelbe Flagge 37; Madame Bovary 37; Le Joueur 38*; Der Spieler 38; Frau im Strom 39; Die Geliebte 39; Clarissa 41; Diesel 42; Kamerad Hedwig 45; Irgendwo in Berlin • Somewhere in Berlin 46; Madonna in Ketten 49; Meines Vaters Pferde 54; Oberwachtmeister Borck 55; Menschen im Werk 58

Lampson, Mary Underground 76*

Lamsweerde, Pino van Heavy Metal 81*; Asterix chez les Bretons • Asterix in Britain

86

La Muir, Jean de see De la Muir, Jean

Lamy, Benoît Life Is Rosy • La Vie Est Belle 87*

Lan, Niao see Niao, Lan

Lan, U see Niao, Lan

Lancaster, Burt The Kentuckian 55; The Midnight Man 74*

Lancer, George The Teasers 77

Lanctot, Micheline The Handyman 80

Land, Owen see Landow, George

Land, Robert The Art of Love • Princess Olala 28; Dame Care 28; Primanerliebe 28; I Kiss Your Hand, Madame 32; Weekend im Paradies 32; Drei Kaiserjäger 35*

Landau, Gerald Five on a Treasure Island 57

Landau, Saul Fidel 70; ¿Qué Hacer? • What Is to Be Done? 70*; Brazil: A Report on Torture 71*

Landers, Lew The Red Rider 34; Tailspin Tommy 34; The Vanishing Shadow 34; The Call of the Savage 35; The Raven 35; Rustlers of Red Dog 35; Stormy 35; Night Waitress 36; Parole! 36; Without Orders 36; Border Cafe 37; Crashing Hollywood 37; Danger Patrol 37; Flight from Glory 37; Living on Love 37; The Man Who Found Himself 37; They Wanted to Marry 37; You Can't Buy Luck 37; Annabel Takes a Tour 38; Blind Alibi 38; Condemned Women 38; Double Danger 38; Law of the Underworld 38; Pacific Liner 38; Sky Giant 38; Smashing the Rackets 38; Bad Lands 39; Conspiracy 39; Double Daring • Fixer Dugan 39; The Girl and the Gambler 39; Twelve Crowded Hours 39; Enemy Agent • Secret Enemy 40; Girl from Havana 40; Honeymoon Deferred 40; La Conga Nights 40; Melody Girl • Sing, Dance, Plenty Hot 40; Ski Patrol 40; Slightly Tempted 40; Wagons Westward 40; Back in the Saddle 41; Harvard, Here I Come • Here I Come 41; I Was a Prisoner on Devil's Island 41; Lucky Devils 41; Mystery Ship 41; Ridin' on a Rainbow 41; The Singing Hill • The Singing Hills 41; The Stork Pays Off 41; Alias Boston Blackie 42; Atlantic Convoy 42; The Boogie Man Will Get You 42; Cadets on Parade 42; Canal Zone 42; Junior Army 42; The Man Who Returned to Life 42; Not a Ladies' Man 42; Sabotage Squad 42; Smith of Minnesota 42; Stand by All Networks 42; Submarine Raider 42; After Midnight • After Midnight with Boston Blackie 43; Deerslayer 43; Doughboys in Ireland 43; The Ghost That Walks Alone 43; Murder in Times Square 43; Power of the Press 43; Redhead from Manhattan 43; The Return of the Vampire 43*; Black Arrow 44; The Black Parachute 44; Close Harmony • Cowboy Canteen 44; Dangerous Mists 44; U-Boat Prisoner 44; I'm from Arkansas 44; Stars in Uniform 44; Stars on Parade 44; Swing and Sway • Swing in the Saddle 44; Two-Man Submarine 44; Arson Squad 45; Checkmate • Shadow of Terror

45; Crime, Inc. 45; The Enchanted Forest 45; Follow That Woman 45; Here Comes Trouble • Trouble Chasers 45; The Power of the Whistler 45; Tokyo Rose 45; A Close Call for Boston Blackie • Lady of Mystery 46; Death Valley 46; Hot Cargo 46; The Lie Detector • The Truth About Murder 46; The Mask of Diijon 46; Secret of Linda Hamilton • Secrets of a Sorority Girl 46; Danger Street 47; Devil Ship 47; Seven Keys to Baldpate 47; The Son of Rusty 47; Thunder Mountain 47; Under the Tonto Rim 47; Adventures of Gallant Bess 48; Inner Sanctum 48; My Dog Rusty 48; Air Hostess 49; Barbary Pirate 49; Davy Crockett, Indian Scout • Indian Scout 49; I Found a Dog 49; Law of the Barbary Coast 49; Stagecoach Kid 49; Beauty on Parade 50; Chain Gang 50; Dangerous Inheritance • Girls' School 50; Dynamite Pass 50; Last of the Buccaneers 50; Revenue Agent 50; State Penitentiary 50; Tyrant of the Sea 50; The Big Gusher 51; Blue Blood 51; Hurricane Island 51; Jungle Manhunt 51; Letter from Korea • A Yank in Korea 51; The Magic Carpet 51; When the Redskins Rode 51; Aladdin and His Lamp 52; Arctic Flight 52; California Conquest 52; Jungle Jim in the Forbidden Land 52; Burning Arrows • Captain John Smith and Pocahontas 53; Man in the Dark 53; Run for the Hills 53; Tangier Incident 53; Torpedo Alley 53; Captain Kidd and the Slave Girl • The Slave Girl 54; The Cruel Tower 56; Fury Unleashed • Hot Rod Gang 58; Terrified! 62

Landi, Mario Patrick Is Still Alive • Patrick Still Lives • Patrick Vive Ancora 80

Landis, James The Magic Voyage of Sinbad • Sadko 53*; Airborne 62; Stakeout 62; Profile of Terror • The Sadist 63; The Nasty Rabbit • Spies à Go-Go 64; Deadwood '76 65; My Soul Runs Naked • Rat Fink • The Swinging Fink • Wild and Willing 65; Jennie, Wife/Child 68*

Landis, John The Banana Monster • Schlock 71; The Kentucky Fried Movie 77; Animal House • National Lampoon's Animal House 78; The Blues Brothers 80; An American Werewolf in London 81; Making Michael Jackson's Thriller 83; Thriller 83; Trading Places 83; Twilight Zone—The Movie 83*; Into the Night 85; Spies Like Us 85; Amazon Women on the Moon 86*; ¡Three Amigos! 86; Coming to America 88

Lando, George see Landow, George

Landon, Michael Sam's Son 84

Landow, George Faulty Pronoun Reference, Comparison, and Punctuation of the Restrictive or Non-Restrictive Element 61; A Stringent Prediction at the Early Hermaphroditic Stage 61; Two Pieces for the Precarious Life 61; Fleming Faloon 63; Film in Which There Appear Sprocket Holes, Edge Lettering, Dirt Particles, Etc. 65; Studies and Sketches 65; Diploteratology or Bardo Folly 67; The Film That Rises to the Surface of Clarified Butter 68; Institutional Quality 69; Remedial Reading

Comprehension 70; What's Wrong with This Picture? 72; Thank You Jesus for the Eternal Present: 1 73; Thank You Jesus for the Eternal Present: 2 — A Film of Their 1973 Spring Tour Commissioned by Christian World Liberation Front of Berkeley, California 74; In the Environment of Liquids and Nasals a Parasitic Vowel Sometimes Develops 75; New Improved Institutional Quality 75; "No Sir" Orison 75; Wide Angle Saxon 75; On the Marriage Broker Joke As Cited by Sigmund Freud in Wit and Its Relation to the Unconscious, or Can the Avant-Garde Artist Be Wholed 79

Landres, Paul Grand Canyon 49; Square Dance Jubilee 49; Frigid Wife • A Modern Marriage 50; Hollywood Varieties 50; Navy Bound 51; Rhythm Inn 51; Army Bound 52; Destination Danger • Eyes of the Jungle 53; Chain of Evidence 57; Hell Canyon Outlaws • The Tall Trouble 57; Last of the Badmen 57; Mark of the Vampire • The Vampire 57; New Day at Sundown 57; Oregon Passage 57; The Curse of Dracula • The Fantastic Disappearing Man • The Return of Dracula 58; The Flame Barrier • It Fell from the Flame Barrier 58; Frontier Gun 58; Go, Johnny, Go! 58; Johnny Rocco 58; Man from God's Country 58; Lone Texan 59; Miracle of the Hills 59; El Hijo del Pistolero • Son of a Gunfighter 64

Landron, Franck Sandra 89
Landy, Ruth Dark Circle 82*
Lane, Andrew Jake Speed 86
Lane, Charles Sidewalk Stories 89
Lane, David Thunderbirds Are Go 66; Thunderbird 6 68
Lane, Lupino Love Lies 31; The Love Race 31*; Never Trouble Trouble 31; No Lady 31; The Innocents of Chicago • Why Saps Leave Home 32; The Maid of the Mountains 32; Old Spanish Customers 32; Letting in the Sunshine 33; My Old Duchess • Oh What a Duchess! 33
Lane, Michael J. The Spare Tyres 67
Lane Lea, Jacques de *see Lea, Jacques de Lane*
Lanfield, Sidney Eight Cylinder Bull 26*; El Barbero de Napoleon 30; Cheer Up and Smile 30; Dance Team 31; Hush Money 31; Three Girls Lost 31; Embassy Girl • Hat Check Girl 32; Society Girl 32; Broadway Bad • Her Reputation 33; The Last Gentleman 34; Moulin Rouge 34; Arms and the Girl • Her Enlisted Man • Red Salute • Runaway Daughter 35; Hold 'Em Yale • Uniform Lovers 35; King of Burlesque 35; Half Angel 36; One in a Million 36; Sing, Baby, Sing 36; Love and Hisses 37; Lovely to Look At • Thin Ice 37; Wake Up and Live 37; Always Goodbye 38; The Hound of the Baskervilles 39; Second Fiddle 39; Swanee River 39; You'll Never Get Rich 41; The Lady Has Plans 42; My Favorite Blonde 42; Let's Face It 43; The Meanest Man in the World 43; Standing Room Only 44; Bring On the Girls 45; The Trouble with Women 45;

The Well Groomed Bride 46; Where There's Life 47; Station West 48; Sorrowful Jones 49; The Lemon Drop Kid 50*; Follow the Sun 51; Skirts Ahoy! 52

Lanfranchi, Mario La Traviata 66; Death Sentence • Sentenza di Morte 67

Lang, Fritz Die Abenteuer des Kay Hoog • The Golden Lake • The Golden Sea • Der Goldene See • The Spiders — Part I: Der Goldene See • Die Spinnen 19; Halbblut • Half Breed • Half Caste 19; Hara-Kiri • Madame Butterfly 19; Der Herr der Liebe • The Master of Love 19; Das Brillantenschiff • The Diamond Ship • The Spiders, Part Two • Die Spinnen Part II: Das Brillantenschiff 20; Four Around the Woman • Kämpfende Herzen • Struggling Hearts • Vier um die Frau 20; The Moving Image • The Wandering Image • Das Wandernde Bild 20; Above All Law • The Hindu Tomb • The Indian Tomb • Das Indische Grabmal • Mysteries of India 21*; Between Two Worlds • Beyond the Wall • Destiny • The Light Within • Der Müde Tod • Der Müde Tod — Ein Deutsches Volkslied in Sechs Versen • The Three Lights • Tired Death • Weary Death 21; Ein Bild der Zeit • Dr. Mabuse, Part One • Doctor Mabuse, the Gambler • Dr. Mabuse, the Gambler — Part One: Ein Bild der Zeit • Doktor Mabuse, der Spieler • The Fatal Passions, Part One • The Great Gambler • Der Grosse Spieler • A Picture of the Time • Spieler aus Leidenschaft 22; Dr. Mabuse, King of Crime • Dr. Mabuse, Part Two • Dr. Mabuse the Gambler, Part Two • Dr. Mabuse der Spieler — Part II: Inferno • The Fatal Passions, Part Two • Inferno • Inferno — A Play About People of Our Time • Inferno des Verbrechens • Inferno — Ein Spiel von Menschen Unserer Zeit • Inferno — Men of the Time • Inferno — Menschen der Zeit • Inferno — People of the Time 22; Death of Siegfried • Die Nibelungen — Part I: Siegfrieds Tod • The Nibelungs, Part One • Siegfried • Siegfried's Death • Siegfrieds Tod 23; Kriemhilds Rache • Kriemhild's Revenge • Die Nibelungen II • The Nibelungs — Part II:Kriemhilds Rache 24; Metropolis 26; Spies • Spione • The Spy 27; By Rocket to the Moon • Die Frau im Mond • The Girl in the Moon • The Girl on the Moon • The Woman in the Moon • The Woman on the Moon 28; M • Mörder Unter Uns • Murderer Among Us 31; The Crimes of Dr. Mabuse • The Last Will of Dr. Mabuse • Das Testament des Dr. Mabuse • Le Testament du Dr. Mabuse • The Testament of Dr. Mabuse 32; Liliom 33; Fury 36; You Only Live Once 37; You and Me 38; The Return of Frank James 40; Confirm or Deny 41*; Man Hunt 41; Western Union 41; Hangmen Also Die • Lest We Forget 42; Moontide 42*; Ministry of Fear 43; The Woman in the Window 44; Scarlet Street 45; Cloak and Dagger 46; The Secret Beyond the Door 48; The House by the River 49; An American Guerrilla in the Phillipines • I Shall Return 50; Clash by

Night 51; Rancho Notorious 51; The Blue Gardenia 52; The Big Heat 53; Human Desire 54; Moonfleet 54; While the City Sleeps 55; Beyond a Reasonable Doubt 56; The Hindu Tomb • The Indian Tomb • Das Indische Grabmal 58; Journey to the Lost City 58; Tiger of Bengal • The Tiger of Eschnapur • Der Tiger von Eschnapur 58; The Diabolical Dr. Mabuse • El Diabólico Dr. Mabuse • Le Diabolique Docteur Mabuse • Eye of Evil • The Secret of Dr. Mabuse • The Shadow vs. the Thousand Eyes of Dr. Mabuse • Die Tausend Augen des Dr. Mabuse • The Thousand Eyes of Dr. Mabuse 60

Lang, Hsiao Hari sa Hari, Lahi sa Lahi 87*

Lang, Michel À Nous les Petites Anglaises! 76; L'Hôtel de le Plage 77; The Gift 82; À Nous les Garçons 85; Club de Rencontres • Lonelyhearts Club 87

Lang, Otto Search for Paradise 57; Fury River 58*

Lang, Perry Little Vegas 90
Lang, Richard The Mountain Men 79; A Change of Seasons 80
Lang, Rocky All's Fair 89; American Built • Race for Glory 89
Lang, W. It's a Bare, Bare World 64
Lang, Walter Red Kimono 25; The Earth Woman 26; The Golden Web 26; Money to Burn 26; By Whose Hand? 27; The College Hero 27; The Ladybird 27; Sally in Our Alley 27; The Satin Woman 27; Alice Through a Looking Glass 28; The Desert Bride 28; The Night Flyer 28; Shadows of the Past 28; Blood Brothers • Brothers • Two Sons 29; The Spirit of Youth 29; The Big Fight 30; Cock o' the Walk 30*; The Costello Case • The Costello Murder Case 30; Hello Sister 30; Command Performance 31; Hell Bound 31; Women Go On Forever 31; No More Orchids 32; Meet the Baron 33; The Warrior's Husband 33; Carnival • Carnival Nights 34; The Mighty Barnum 34; The Party's Over 34; Whom the Gods Destroy 34; Hooray for Love 35; Love Before Breakfast 36; Second Honeymoon 37; Wife, Doctor and Nurse 37; The Baroness and the Butler 38; I'll Give a Million 38; The Little Princess 39; The Blue Bird 40; The Great Profile 40; Star Dust 40; Tin Pan Alley 40; Moon Over Miami 41; Week-End in Havana 41; The Magnificent Dope 42; Song of the Islands 42; Coney Island 43; Greenwich Village 44; It Happened One Summer • State Fair 45; Claudia and David 46; Sentimental Journey 46; Mother Wore Tights 47; Sitting Pretty 47; When My Baby Smiles at Me 48; You're My Everything 49; Cheaper by the Dozen 50; The Jackpot 50; On the Riviera 51; With a Song in My Heart 52; Call Me Madam 53; There's No Business Like Show Business 54; The King and I 56; The Desk Set • His Other Woman 57; But Not for Me 59; Can-Can 60; The Marriage-Go-Round 60; Snow White and the Three Clowns • Snow White and the Three Stooges 61

Langan, John Nancy Drew, Detective 38*; Nancy Drew—Reporter 39*

Langdon, Harry Three's a Crowd 27; The Chaser 28; Heart Trouble 28; Wise Guys 37

Langer, Carole Radium City 87

Langley, Noel The Pickwick Papers 52; The Adventures of Sadie • Our Girl Friday 53; Svengali 54; The Search for Bridey Murphy 56

Langlois, Henri Le Métro 34*; Marc Chagall 62; From Lumière to Langlois 70

Langlois, Olivier Jaune Revolver 88

Langman, Chris Moving Targets 87

Langton, Simon The Whistle Blower 86

Languepin, Jean-Jacques Groenland • Groenland, Terre des Glaces 51*; Des Hommes et des Montagnes 53; Neiges 55; La Route des Cimes 57; Saint-Exupéry 57; Des Hommes dans le Ciel 59; La Vitesse Est à Vous 61

Lanoë, Annick Les Nanas 85

Lanoë, Henri Comme Mars en Carême • Don't Play with Martians • Ne Jouez Pas avec les Martiens 67

Lanru, Yang see Yang, Lanru

Lansburgh, Larry Mystery Lake 53; Run, Appaloosa, Run 66; The Horse in the Gray Flannel Suit • Year of the Horse 68*; Hang Your Hat on the Wind 69

Lantz, Walter Tad's Indoor Sports 18*; Col. Heeza Liar's Forbidden Fruit 23; Col. Heeza Liar's Vacation 23; African Jungle 24; Aladdin's Lamp • The Magic Lamp 24; Col. Heeza Liar's Ancestors 24; Col. Heeza Liar's Knighthood 24; The Giant Killer • Jack and the Beanstalk 24; Horse Play 24; The Pied Piper 24; Sky Pilot 24; The Babes in the Woods 25; Captain Kid • The Captain's Kid 25; Cinderella 25; Dinky Doodle and the Bad Man 25; Dinky Doodle in the Circus 25; Dinky Doodle in the Hunt 25; Dinky Doodle in the Restaurant 25; The House That Dinky Built 25; How the Bear Got His Short Tail 25; How the Elephant Got His Trunk 25; Just Spooks 25; Little Red Riding Hood 25; Lyin' Tamer 25; The Magic Carpet • The Magic Rug 25; Peter Pan Handled 25; Robinson Crusoe 25; The Three Bears 25; Bedtime Stories • Dinky Doodle's Bedtime Story 26; The Cat's Whiskers 26; Dinky Doodle and the Little Orphan 26; Dinky Doodle in Egypt 26; Dinky Doodle in Lost and Found 26; Dinky Doodle in the Arctic 26; Dinky Doodle in the Army 26; Dinky Doodle in the Wild West 26; Dinky Doodle in Uncle Tom's Cabin 26; For the Love o' Pete 26; The Magician 26; The Mule's Disposition 26; The Pelican's Bill 26; Pete's Haunted House 26; Pete's Party 26; The Pig's Curly Tail 26; The Tail of the Monkey • The Tale of the Monk 26*; The Cat's Nine Lives 27; Dog Gone It 27; The Hyena's Laugh 27*; Jingle Bells 27; Lunch Hound 27; Petering Out 27; The Puppy Express 27; S'Matter, Pete? 27; Bull-oney 28*; Farmyard Follies 28*; Mississippi Mud 28; Yanky Clippers 28*; Amature Nite 29; Cold Turkey 29; Hurdy Gurdy 29; Ice

Man's Luck 29; Jungle Jingles 29; Nuts and Jolts 29; Nutty Notes 29; Oil's Well 29; Ozzie of the Circus 29; Permanent Wave 29; Race Riot 29; Saucy Sausages 29; Stage Stunt 29; Stripes and Stars 29; Weary Willies 29; Wicked West 29; Africa 30; Alaska 30; Bowery Bimboes • Bowling Bimboes 30; Broadway Folly 30; Chile Con Carmen 30; Cold Feet 30; The Detective 30; The Fowl Ball 30; The Hash House • The Hash Shop 30; Hell's Heels 30; Hen Fruit • Henpecked 30; Hollywood • Hot for Hollywood 30; Kisses and Kurses 30; Mars 30; Mexico 30; My Pal Paul 30; The Navy 30; Not So Quiet 30; The Prison Panic 30; The Singing Sap 30; Snappy Salesman 30; Spooks 30; Tramping Tramps 30; The Band Master 31; China 31; The Clown 31; College 31; The Country School 31; The Farmer 31; The Fireman 31; The Fisherman 31; The Hare Mail 31; Horse Race • Kentucky Bells 31; Hot Feet 31; The Hunter 31; North Woods 31; Radio Rhythm 31; Shipwrecked 31; The Stone Age 31; Sunny South 31; Wonderland 31; The Athlete 32; Beau and Arrows 32; The Busy Barber 32; The Butcher Boy 32; Carnival Capers 32; Cat Nipped 32; Cats and Dogs 32; The Crowd Snores 32; Day Nurse 32; Foiled • Let's Eat 32; Grandma's Pet 32; A Jungle Jumble 32; Making Good 32; Mechanical Man 32; The Teacher's Pests 32; To the Rescue 32; The Underdog 32; A Wet Knight 32; Wild and Woolly 32; The Winged Horse 32; Wins Out 32; Beau Beste 33; Confidence 33; Five and Dime 33; Going to Blazes 33; Ham and Eggs 33; Hot and Cold 33; King Klunk 33; The Lumber Chumps 33; Merry Dog 33; The Merry Old Soul 33; Nature's Workshop 33; Parking Space 33; Pin Feathers 33; The Plumber 33; She Done Him Right 33; The Shriek 33; The Terrible Troubador 33; The Zoo 33; Annie Moved Away 34; The Candy House 34; Chicken Reel 34; Chris Columbus, Jr. 34; The Country Fair 34; The Dizzy Dwarf 34; The Ginger Bread Boy 34; Goldielocks and the Three Bears 34; Jolly Little Elves 34; The Sky Larks 34; Spring in the Park 34; The Toy Shoppe 34; Toyland Premiere 34; The Wax Works 34; William Tell 34; Wolf! Wolf! 34; Ye Happy Pilgrims 34; Amateur Broadcast 35; At Your Service 35; Bronco Buster 35; Candy Land 35; The Case of the Lost Sheep 35; Do a Good Deed 35; Doctor Oswald 35; Elmer, the Great Dane 35; The Fox and the Rabbit 35; Hill Billies • The Hillbilly 35; Monkey Wretches 35; The Quail Hunt 35; Robinson Crusoe Isle 35; Springtime Serenade 35; Three Lazy Mice 35; Towne Hall Follies 35; Two Little Lambs 35; Alaska Sweepstakes 36; Barnyard Five 36; Battle Royal 36; Beach Combers 36; Beauty Shoppe 36; Farming Fools 36; Fun House 36; Gopher Trouble 36; Kiddie Review 36; Knights for a Day 36; Music Hath Charms 36; Night Life of the Bugs 36; The Puppet Show 36; Slumberland Express 36; Soft Ball Game 36; Turkey Dinner 36; Unpop-

ular Mechanic 36; Air Express 37; The Big Race 37; The Birthday Party 37; Country Store 37; Duck Hunt 37; The Dumb Cluck 37; Everybody Sings 37; Fireman's Picnic 37; Football Fever 37; The Golfers 37; House of Magic 37; The Keeper of the Lions 37; Lovesick 37; Lumber Camp 37; The Mechanical Handy Man 37; The Mysterious Jug 37; Ostrich Feathers 37; The Playful Pup 37; Rest Resort 37; Steel Workers 37; The Stevedores 37; Trailer Thrills 37; The Wily Weasel 37; Yokel Boy Makes Good 38; Crazy House 40; Knock, Knock 40; Syncopated Sioux 40; The Boogie Woogie Bugle Boy of Company B 41; The Cracked Nut • Woody Woodpecker 41; Dizzy Kitty 41; Fair Today 41; Hysterical High Spots in American History 41; Man's Best Friend 41; Pantry Panic • What's Cookin'? 41; Salt Water Daffy 41; The Screwdriver 41; Scrub Me Mama with a Boogie Beat 41; $21.00 a Day Once a Month 41; Goodbye Mr. Moth 42; The Hams That Couldn't Be Cured 42; Hollywood Matador 42; Mother Goose on the Loose 42; Destination Meatball 51; Redwood Sap 51; Slingshot 6⅞ 51; Wicket Wacky 51; Woody Woodpecker Polka 51; Born to Peck 52; The Great Who Dood It 52; Scalp Treatment 52; Stage Hoax 52; Woodpecker in the Rough 52

Lanuza, Rafael Superzan and the Space Boy • Superzan y el Niño del Espacio 72

Lanyi, András The New Landlord • Az Új Földesúr 89

Lanza, Anthony M. The Glory Stompers 67; The Incredible Two-Headed Transplant 70

Lanzmann, Claude Israel Why? • Pourquoi Israel? 73; Shoah 85

La Parelle, L. de see De la Parelle, L.

La Parra, Pim de see Parra, Pim de la

La Patellière, Denys de see De la Patellière, Denys

Laperrousaz, Jerome Hu-Man 75

Lapine, James Impromptu 90

Lapoknysh, Vasil A Cossack Beyond the Danube 54; Lileia 60*

Lapshin, Yaropolk The Iron Field • Zheleznoe Pole 87

Lara, Claude Autant see Autant-Lara, Claude

Larin, Nikolai Tercentenary of the Romanov Dynasty's Accession to the Throne 13*; Rasputin 29

La Riva, Juan Antonio de see De la Riva, Juan Antonio

Larkin, Christopher A Very Natural Thing 74

Larkin, John Quiet Please, Murder 42; Circumstantial Evidence 45

Larraz, José Ramón Whirlpool 69; The House That Vanished • Psycho Sex Fiend • Scream and Die 73; The Blood Virgin • Symptoms 74; Daughters of Dracula • The Vampyre Orgy • Vampyres • Vampyres—Daughters of Darkness • Vampyres—Daughters of Dracula 74; The Golden Lady 79; Estigma • Stigma 81; La Momia

Nacional • The National Mummy 81; Los Ritos Sexuales del Diablo 81

Larraz, Joseph see Larraz, José Ramón

Larriva, Rudy Magoo's Masquerade 57; Magoo's Private War 57; Magoo's Cruise 58; Magoo's Lodge Brother 59; Merry Minstrel Magoo 59; Boulder Wham 65; Chaser on the Rocks 65; Harried and Hurried 65; Highway Runnery 65; Just Plane Beep 65; Run Run Sweet Roadrunner 65; Tired and Feathered 65; Clippetty Clobbered 66; Out and Out Rout 66; Shot and Bothered 66; The Solid Tin Coyote 66; Music Mice-tro 67; Quacker Tracker 67; Spy Swatter 67

Larry, Sheldon Terminal Choice 85

Larsen, Keith Mission Batangas 68; Night of the Witches • Night of Witches 70; Trap on Cougar Mountain 72

Larsen, Robert W. The Dreaded Persuasion • The Narcotics Story 58

Larsen, Viggo The Black Mask 06; Revenge 06; Camille 07; Doktor Nikola 09; Den Grå Dame • The Grey Dame • The Grey Lady 09; Dr. Jekyll and Mr. Hyde • Jekyll and Hyde • Den Skæbnesvanger Opfindelse 10; Die Sumpfblume 12; Der Graue Herr 15

Larson, Eric Sleeping Beauty 59*

Larson, Larry Deadly Passion 85

Larsson, Stig Angel 89

Lasbats, Chantal Les Interdits du Monde 85

Lascelle, Ward Rip Van Winkle 21; Affinities 22; Mind Over Motor 23

Laskos, Orestes Daphnis and Chloe 30; Girl of the Mountains • Golfo • Golfo, Girl of the Mountains 58; Madame X 60

Laskowski, Jan The Last Day of Summer • Ostatni Dzień Lata 58*

Lasky, Leo Das Nachtigall Mädel 33

Lasseby, Stig Pelle Svanslös i Amerikatt • Peter-No-Tail in Americat 85*

Lasticati, Carlo Anna di Brooklyn • Anna of Brooklyn • Fast and Sexy 58*

La Texera, Diego de see De la Texera, Diego

Lathan, Stan Save the Children 73; Amazing Grace 74; Beat Street 84; Go Tell It on the Mountain 84

Latif, Latif Abdul Migrating Birds • Perlyotniye Ptit 87

La Torre, Raúl de see De la Torre, Raúl

La Tour, Charles de see De Lautour, Charles

Latsis, Eric Oboroten Tom • Werewolf Tom 87

Lattuada, Alberto Giacomo l'Idealista 42; The Arrow • La Freccia • La Freccia nel Fianco 43; La Nostra Guerra • Our War 43; The Bandit • Il Bandito 46; Il Delitto di Giovanni Episcopo • Flesh Will Surrender • Giovanni Episcopo 47; Senza Pietà • Without Pity 47; The Mill on the Po • The Mill on the River • Il Mulino del Po 49; Lights of Variety • Luci del Varietà • Variety Lights 50*; Anna 51*; Il Cappotto • The Overcoat 51; Amore in Città • Love in the City 53*; The Beach • La Spiaggia 53; La Lupa • The She-Wolf •

The Vixen 53; Elementary School • Scuola Elementare 54; Guendalina 55; Tempest • La Tempesta 58*; I Dolci Inganni 60; Lettere di una Novizia • Letters from a Novice • La Novice • Rita 60; L'Imprevisto • L'Imprévu • The Unexpected 61; La Steppa • La Steppe • The Steppe 61; The Mafia • Il Mafioso 62; The Love Root • La Mandragola • Mandragola—The Love Root • The Mandrake 65; Matchless 66; Don Giovanni in Sicilia 67; The Betrayal • Fräulein Doktor • Gospođica Doktor—Špijunka Bez Imena • Nameless 68; L'Amica 69; Come Have Coffee with Us • The Man Who Came for Coffee • Venga a Prendere il Caffè...da Noi 70; Bianco, Rosso e... • The Sin • White Sister 71; I Did It • Sono Stato Io 72; Bambina • Le Faro da Padre 74; Cuore di Cane • Heart of a Dog 75; Bruciati da Cocente Passione • Oh, Serafina! 76; Così Come Sei • The Daughter • Stay As You Are 78; La Cicala 79; Nudo di Donna 81*; Cristofero Columbus 83; Una Spina nel Cuore • A Thorn in the Heart 85; Amori 89*

Lau, Kar-leung Martial Arts of Shaolin 86

Lau, Kar-wing Till Death Do We Scare • Till Death Us Do Scare • Xiaosheng Papa 82

Lau, Kun Wai Mr. Vampire 86

Lau, Shing-hon see Liu, Cheng-han

Laudadio, Francesco Fatto su Misura • Made to Measure 85; The Nuke Trap • Topo Galileo 88

Laughlin, Frank see Laughlin, Tom

Laughlin, Michael Dead Kids • Strange Behavior 81; Strange Invaders 83; Mesmerized 85

Laughlin, Tom The Proper Time 59; Among the Thorns • Like Father Like Son • The Young Sinner 61; Born Losers 67; Billy Jack 71; The Trial of Billy Jack 74; The Master Gunfighter 75; Billy Jack Goes to Washington 77; The Return of Billy Jack 86

Laughton, Charles The Night of the Hunter 55

Launder, Bill Waters of Time 50*

Launder, Frank Partners in Crime 42*; Millions Like Us 43*; Two Thousand Women 43; The Adventuress • I See a Dark Stranger 46; Captain Boycott 47; The Blue Lagoon 48; The Happiest Days of Your Life 50; Lady Godiva Rides Again 51; Folly to Be Wise 52; The Belles of St. Trinian's 54; Geordie • Wee Geordie 55; Blue Murder at St. Trinian's 57; The Bridal Path 58; Left, Right and Centre 58*; The Pure Hell of St. Trinian's 60; Joey Boy 65; The Great St. Trinian's Train Robbery 66*; The Wildcats of St. Trinian's 80

Laurance, Lister Mr. Smith Carries On 37

Laurence, Ken Howzer 73

Laurent, Christine Vertiges 85; Eden Miseria 88

Laurenti, Fabrizio Witchery 89

Laurenti, Mariano Il Segno di Zorro 75; Carabinieri Are Born • Carabinieri Si

Nasce 85; Pop Corn and Chips • Pop Corn and Potato Chips • Pop Corn e Patatine 85; Fotoromanzo • Picture Story 86

Lauris, George Buffalo Rider 78

Lauritzen, Lau, Jr. Julia Jubilerar 38*; Västkustens Hjältar 40*; Afsporet 42*; The Red Earth • Red Meadows • De Røde Enge 45*; Jag Älskar Dig, Karlsson 47*; Café Paradis 50*; Det Sande Ansigt 51*; Dangerous Youth 53; We Want a Child 54*; The Richest Girl in the World 60

Lautner, Georges La Môme aux Boutons 58; Marche ou Crève 59; Arrêtez les Tambours • Women and War • Women in War 61; The Black Monocle • Le Monocle Noir 61; En Plain Cirage 61; The Eye of the Monocle • L'Œil du Monocle 62; Le Septième Juré • The Seventh Juror 62; Monsieur Gangster 63; Operation Gold Ingot 63; Les Tontons Flingueurs 63; Les Barbouzes • The Great Spy Chase 64; Des Pissenlits par la Racine 64; The Monocle • Le Monocle Rit Jaune 64; Les Bons Vivants • How to Keep the Red Lamp Burning 65*; Galia • I and My Love • I and My Lovers 65; Ne Nous Fachons Pas 65; Femmina • La Grande Sauterelle • Ein Mädchen Wie das Meer • Sauterelle 66; Fleur d'Oseille 67; Le Pacha 67; Michel Strogoff 68; Laisse Aller—C'Est une Valse 70; Quando il Sola Scotta • The Road to Salina • La Route de Salina • Sur la Route de Salina 70; Il Était un Fois un Flic 72; The Girl in the Trunk • La Valise 73; Quelque Messieurs Trop Tranquilles 73; Icy Breasts • Les Seins de Glace 74; On Aura Tout Vu 76; Mort d'un Pourri 77; Il Sont Fous Ces Sorciers 78; The Bottom Line 82; Attention! Une Femme Peut en Cacher une Autre • My Other "Husband" 83; La Cage aux Folles III: The Wedding 85; Le Cowboy 85; The Debauched Life of Gerard Floque • La Vie Dissolue de Gérard Floque 87; La Maison Assassinée 88

Lautour, Charles de see De Lautour, Charles

Lautrec, Linda My Breakfast with Blassie 83*

Laux, Michael Richy Guitar 85

Lauzier, Gérard Tu Empêches Tout le Monde de Dormir 82; Petit Con • P'tit Con 84; La Tête dans le Sac 84

Lauzon, Jean-Claude Night Zoo • Un Zoo la Nuit 87

Lavanić, Zlatko The Magpie's Strategy • Strategija Svrake 87

Laven, Arnold The Story Without a Name • Without Warning 52; The Girl in Room 17 • Vice Squad 53; Down Three Dark Streets 54; The Rack 56; The Monster That Challenged the World 57; Slaughter on Tenth Avenue 57; Anna Lucasta 58; Geronimo 62; The Glory Guys 65; Rough Night in Jericho 67; Sam Whiskey 69

Lavia, Gabriele Scandalosa Gilda 85; Evil Senses • Sensi 86

Lavorel, Henri A Trip to America • Le Voyage en Amérique • Voyage to America 51; C'Est Arrivé à Paris • It Happened in Paris 52*

Le Chanois, Jean-Paul People of France • La Vie Est à Nous 36*; Le Temps des Cerises 38; La Vie d'un Homme 38; Une Idée à l'Eau • L'Irrésistible Rebelle 39; Messieurs Ludovic 46; Au Cœur de l'Orage 47; L'École Buissonière • I Have a New Master • Passion for Life 48; La Belle Que Voilà 50; Sans Laisser d'Adresse 50; Agence Matrimoniale 52; Le Village Magique 53; Les Évadés 54; Mama, Papa, the Maid and I • Papa, Mama, the Maid and I • Papa, Maman, la Bonne et Moi 54; Papa, Maman, Ma Femme et Moi 55; Le Cas du Docteur Laurent • The Case of Dr. Laurent 56; Les Misérables 57; Pardessus le Mur 59; La Française et l'Amour • Love and the Frenchwoman 60*; Mandrin • Mandrin, Bandit Gentilhomme 62; Monsieur 64; Blüten, Gauner und Die Nacht von Nizza • Le Jardinier d'Argenteuil 66

Leconte, Patrice Les Spécialistes 85; Duo • Tandem 87; M. Hire • Monsieur Hire 89

Leder, Herbert J. Pretty Boy Floyd 60; Nine Miles to Noon 63; Anger of the Golem • The Curse of the Golem • It! 66; The Frozen Dead 66; The Candy Man 69

Leder, Max Miss Mischief 19

Leder, Paul Marigold Man 70; I Dismember Mama • Poor Albert and Little Annie 72; A*P*E 76; I'm Going to Be Famous 81; My Friends Need Killing 84; Vultures in Paradise 84; Body Count 88; Murder by Numbers 90

Lederer, Carl Francis Bunny in Bunnyland 15; Ping Pong Woo 15; Wandering Bill 15; When They Were 21 15

Lederer, Charles Fingers at the Window 42; On the Loose 51; Never Steal Anything Small 58

Lederer, George W. The Fight 15; The Decoy 16; Runaway Romany 17

Lederer, Otto The Struggle 21

Lederman, D. Ross A Dog of the Regiment 27; A Race for Life 28; Rinty of the Desert 28; Shadows of the Night 28; The Million Dollar Collar 29; The Man Hunter 30; Branded 31; The Fighting Marshal 31; The Phantom of the West 31; Range Feud 31; The Texas Ranger 31; Daring Danger 32; The End of the Trail 32; High Speed 32; McKenna of the Mounted 32; Ridin' for Justice 32; The Riding Tornado 32; Speed Demon 32; Texas Cyclone 32; Two-Fisted Law 32; Mark It Paid 33; Rusty Rides Alone 33; Silent Men 33; Soldiers of the Storm 33; State Trooper 33; The Whirlwind 33; Beyond the Law 34; The Crime of Helen Stanley 34; Girl in Danger 34; Hell Bent for Love 34; A Man's Game 34; Murder in the Clouds 34; The Case of the Missing Man 35; Dinky 35*; Moonlight on the Prairie 35; Racing Luck • Red Hot Tires 35; Too Tough to Kill 35; Alibi for Murder 36; Come Closer, Folks 36; The Final Hour 36; Hell Ship Morgan 36; Panic on the Air 36; Pride of the Marines 36; Counterfeit Lady 37; A Dangerous Adventure 37; The Frame-Up 37; The Game That Kills 37; I Promise to Pay 37; Motor Madness 37; Adventure in Sahara 38;

Juvenile Court 38; The Little Adventuress 38; Tarzan's Revenge 38; North of Shanghai 39; Racketeers of the Range 39; Glamour for Sale 40; Military Academy 40; Thundering Frontier 40; Across the Sierras • Welcome Stranger 41; The Body Disappears 41; Father's Son 41; Passage from Hong Kong 41; Shadows on the Stairs 41; Strange Alibi 41; Bullet Scars 42; Busses Roar 42; Escape from Crime 42; The Gorilla Man 42; I Was Framed 42; Adventure in Iraq • Adventures in Iraq 43; Find the Blackmailer 43; Cooking Up Trouble • Three of a Kind 44; The Last Ride 44; The Racket Man 44; Out of the Depths 45; Blackie and the Law • Boston Blackie and the Law 46; Dangerous Business 46; The Notorious Lone Wolf 46; The Phantom Thief 46; Sing While You Dance 46; Key Witness 47; The Lone Wolf in Mexico 47; Return of the Whistler 48; Military Academy • Military Academy with That 10th Avenue Gang • Sentence Suspended 50; The Tanks Are Coming 51*

Leduc, Jacques Ordinary Tenderness 73

Leduc, Jean Incident in Saigon 60

Leduc, Paul Reed: Insurgent Mexico • Reed: México Insurgente 70; Estudios para un Retrato 78; Etnocidio: Notas Sobre el Mezquital 78; Francis Bacon 78; Monjas Coronadas 78; Historias Prohibidas de Pulgarcito 79; Complot Petrolero: La Cabeza de la Hidra 81; Frida • Frida: Naturaleza Vida 84; ¿Hambre Cómo Ves? 86; Baroque • Barroco • Concierto Barocco 89

Lee, Alan S. The Desert Raven • Fly, Raven, Fly 65

Lee, Bruce Return of the Dragon 73

Lee, Chang-ho The Rain Yesterday 74; Stars' Home 74; Deep Love 75; Fine Windy Days 80; Come Unto Dawn 81; The Sons of Darkness 81; Dance of the Widow 83; Declaration of Fools 83; Between Knee and Knee 84; The Entertainer • The Entertainer Er Woo-Dong • Er Woo-Dong 86; Lee Chang-ho's Alien Baseball Team 86; The Man with Three Coffins 87

Lee, Damian Last Man Standing 88; Food of the Gods II • Gnaw: Food of the Gods II 89

Lee, Daw-ming The Suona Player 86

Lee, Doo-yong Lost Wedding Veil 70; Your Daddy Like This? 71; The General in Red Robe 73; Chobun 77; Police Story 78; Muldori Village 79; Pimak 80; Moul Le Ya, Moul Le Ya • Spinning Wheel • The Wheel 83; First Son 84; Bbong • The Mulberry Tree • Pong • Ppong 85; Jangnam 85; Eunuchs • Nae-Shi 86; Karma 88; Silent Assassins 88*

Lee, Evan Hollywood Meatcleaver Massacre • Meatcleaver Massacre • Revenge of the Dead 75

Lee, Hyoung Pyo Dracula Rises from the Coffin 82

Lee, Hyuk Soo Reversed Enemy 82

Lee, Jack The Pilot Is Safe 41; Ordinary People 42*; Close Quarters • Undersea Raider 43; By Sea and Land 44; The Eighth Plague 45; Children on Trial 46;

The Woman in the Hall 47; Maniacs on Wheels • Once a Jolly Swagman 48*; The Wooden Horse 50; The Golden Mask • South of Algiers 52; Turn the Key Softly 53; The Rape of Malaya • A Town Like Alice 56; Robbery Under Arms 57; The Captain's Table 58; Circle of Deception • Destruction Test 60

Lee, Joseph Girl on the Run 61*; The Courier 88*

Lee, Leon Is Your Daughter Safe? 27*

Lee, Manli Marine Battleground 66*

Lee, Norman Lure of the Atlantic 28; The Streets of London 28; City of Shadows • The Night Patrol 29; Dr. Josser KC 31; Josser in the Army 32; Josser Joins the Navy 32; Josser on the River 32; Money Talks 32; The Strangler 32; Strip, Strip, Hooray! 32; A Political Party 33; The Pride of the Force 33; Doctor's Orders 34; The Outcast 34; Spring in the Air 34*; Forgotten Men 35; Happy Days Are Here Again • Happy Days Revue • Variety Follies 35; Regal Cavalcade • Royal Cavalcade 35*; Don't Rush Me 36; No Escape • No Escape, No Exit 36; Bulldog Drummond at Bay 37; Dangerous Fingers • Wanted by Scotland Yard 37; French Leave 37; The Girl from Ireland • Kathleen • Kathleen Mavourneen 37; Knights for a Day 37*; Saturday Night Revue 37; Almost a Honeymoon 38; Luck of the Navy • North Sea Patrol 38; Mr. Reeder in Room 13 • Mystery of Room 13 38; Murder in Soho • Murder in the Night 38; Save a Little Sunshine 38; Yes Madam? 38; Chamber of Horrors • The Door with Seven Locks 40; The Farmer's Wife 40*; Mein Kampf—My Crimes 40; The Monkey's Paw 48; The Case of Charles Peace 49; The Girl Who Couldn't Quite 49

Lee, Rowland V. The Cup of Life 20; A Thousand to One 20; Blind Hearts 21; Cupid's Brand 21; The Dust Flower 21; The Sea Lion 21; Alice Adams 22; His Back Against the Wall 22; The Men of Zanzibar 22; Mixed Faces 22; Money to Burn 22; A Self Made Man 22; Shirley of the Circus 22; Whims of the Gods 22; Desire 23; Gentle Julia 23; You Can't Get Away with It 23; In Love with Love 24; As No Man Has Loved • The Man Without a Country 25; Havoc 25; The Outsider 26; The Silver Treasure 26; Barbed Wire 27*; The Whirlwind of Youth 27; Doomsday 28; The First Kiss 28; Loves of an Actress 28; The Secret Hour 28; Three Sinners 28; A Dangerous Woman 29; The Insidious Dr. Fu Manchu • The Mysterious Dr. Fu Manchu 29; The Wolf of Wall Street 29; Derelict 30; Ladies Love Brutes 30; A Man from Wyoming 30; The New Adventures of Dr. Fu Manchu • The Return of Dr. Fu Manchu 30; Paramount on Parade 30*; The Guilty Generation 31; The Ruling Voice • Upper Underworld 31; Overnight • That Night in London 32; The Sign of Four 32*; I Am Suzanne! 33; Zoo in Budapest 33; The Count of Monte Cristo 34; Gambling 34; Cardinal Richelieu

• Richelieu 35; The Three Musketeers 35; Love from a Stranger 36; One Rainy Afternoon 36; The Toast of New York 37; Mother Carey's Chickens 38; Service de Luxe 38; Son of Frankenstein 39; The Sun Never Sets 39; Tower of London 39; The Son of Monte Cristo 40; Powder Town 42; The Bridge of San Luis Rey 44; Captain Kidd 45

Lee, Sam The Last Wish 49

Lee, Sammy Soak the Old 40

Lee, Sheng see Lee, Shing

Lee, Shing Execution in August 85; Heroic Pioneers 87

Lee, Spike Joe's Bed-Stuy Barbershop: We Cut Heads 82; She's Gotta Have It 86; School Daze 87; Do the Right Thing 89; Mo' Better Blues 90

Lee, Tse Nam see Nam, Lee Tse

Lee, William The Fall of Black Hawk 12

Lee, Yoo Sub Hannyo • Revenge of the Ghost 81

Lee-Thompson, J. Murder Without Crime 50; The Yellow Balloon 52; The Weak and the Wicked • Young and Willing 53; Cocktails in the Kitchen • For Better, for Worse 54; An Alligator Named Daisy 55; As Long As They're Happy 55; Blonde Sinner • Yield to the Night 56; The Good Companions 56; Woman in a Dressing Gown 57; Desert Attack • Ice Cold in Alex 58; No Tree in the Street • No Trees in the Street 58; Flame Over India • North West Frontier 59; Tiger Bay 59; I Aim at the Stars 60; Cape Fear 61; The Guns of Navarone 61; Taras Bulba 62; Kings of the Sun 63; John Goldfarb, Please Come Home 64; What a Way to Go! 64; Return from the Ashes 65; Eye of the Devil • Thirteen 66*; Before Winter Comes 68; MacKenna's Gold 68; Brotherly Love • Country Dance 69; The Chairman • The Most Dangerous Man in the World 69; Conquest of the Planet of the Apes 72; Battle for the Planet of the Apes 73; Huckleberry Finn 74; The Reincarnation of Peter Proud 74; St. Ives 76; Hunt to Kill • The White Buffalo 77; The Greek Tycoon 78; The Passage 78; Caboblanco 79; Happy Birthday to Me 80; 10 to Midnight 82; The Evil That Men Do 83; The Ambassador • Peacemaker 84; King Solomon's Mines 85; Firewalker 86; Murphy's Law 86; Death Wish 4: The Crackdown 87; Messenger of Death 88; Kinjite • Kinjite: Forbidden Subjects 89

Leeds, David Shoot the Sun Down 76

Leeds, Herbert I. Arizona Wildcat 38; Danger Island • Mr. Moto in Danger Island • Mr. Moto on Danger Island 38; Five of a Kind 38; Island in the Sky 38; Keep Smiling • Miss Fix-It 38; Love on a Budget 38; Charlie Chan in City in Darkness • Charlie Chan in the City of Darkness • City of Darkness 39; Chicken Wagon Family 39; The Cisco Kid and the Lady 39; The Return of the Cisco Kid 39; Yesterday's Heroes 40; Blue, White and Perfect 41; Ride On Vaquero 41; Romance of the Rio Grande 41; Just Off Broadway 42; The Man Who Wouldn't Die 42; Manila Call-

ing 42; Time to Kill 42; It Shouldn't Happen to a Dog 46; Let's Live Again 48; Bunco Squad 50; Father's Wild Game 50

Leeman, Dicky A Date with a Dream 48

Leenhardt, Roger En Crête Sans les Dieux 34*; L'Orient Qui Vient 34*; Le Pain de Barbarie 34; Le Père Hugo 34; Le Rezzou 34*; Le Vrai Jeu 34; Le Tapis Moquette 35; RN 37 37; La Course au Pétrole 38; Pavage Moderne 38; Revêtements Routiers 38; Fêtes de France 39*; À la Poursuite du Vent 43; Le Chant des Ondes 43; Le Chantier en Ruines 45; Lettre de Paris 45; Le Barrage de l'Aigle 46; Départs pour l'Allemagne 46; Naissance du Cinéma 46; Les Dernières Vacances • The Last Holidays • The Last Vacation 47; La Côte d' Azur 48; Entrez dans la Danse 48; Le Pain de Barbarie 48; La Fugue de Mahmoud 50; L'Héritage du Croissant 50; Les Hommes du Champagne 50; Métro 50; Le Père Hugo • Victor Hugo 51*; Du Charbon et des Hommes 52; La France Est un Jardin • France Is a Garden 53; François Mauriac 54; Louis Capet • Louis XVI 54*; Le Bruit 55; La Conquête de l'Angleterre 55; Notre Sang 55; Les Transmissions Hydrauliques 55; Bâtir à Notre Âge 56*; En Plein Midi 57*; Jean-Jacques • Jean-Jacques Rousseau 57*; Paris Est le Désert Français 57; Daumier 58; Paul Valéry 59; Entre Seine et Mer 60; Le Maître de Montpelier 60; Midnight Meeting • Rendezvous at Midnight • Le Rendez-Vous de Minuit 61; La Traversée de la France 61*; Le Cœur de la France 62; L'Homme à la Pipe 62; Des Femmes et des Fleurs 63; George 63; 1989 63; Monsieur de Voltaire 63; Daguerre ou La Naissance de la Photographie • La Naissance de la Photographie 64; Demain Paris 64; Europe 64; Corot 65; Le Beatnik et le Minet 66; Monsieur Ingres 67; Douze Mois en France 70*; Abraham Bosse 72; Pissarro 75; La Languedocienne 76; Var-Matin 76; Anjou 77; Du Plaisir à la Joie 78; Manet ou le Novateur Malgré Lui 80

Leeson, Bill Waveband 83

Leewood, Jack 20,000 Eyes 61; Thunder Island 63

Lefebvre, Geneviève Le Jupon Rouge • Manuela's Loves • The Red Skirt 87

Lefèbvre, Jean-Pierre L'Homoman 64; The Revolutionary • Le Révolutionnaire 65; Patricia et Jean-Baptiste 66; Don't Let It Kill You • Il Ne Faut Pas Mourir Pour Ça • No Good to Die for That 67; Mon Amie Pierrette 67; Jusqu'au Cœur • Straight to the Heart 68; La Chambre Blanche • The House of Light • Quand Je Vis 69; Q-bec My Love • Struggle for Love • Un Succès Commercial 70; L'Eau de Vie et de Mort • Les Maudits Sauvages • Those Damned Savages 71; Mon Œil 71; Ultimatum 71; Backyard Theatre 72; Les Dernières Fiançailles • The Last Betrothal 73; On N'Engraisse Pas les Cochons à l'Eau Claire • Pigs Are Seldom Clean 73; L' Amour Blessé • L'Amour Blessé: Confidences de la Nuit • Confessions of the

Night 75; Le Gars des Vues 75; The Old Country Where Rimbaud Died • Le Vieux Pays Où Rimbaud Est Mort 77; Avoir Seize Ans • To Be Sixteen 78; Les Fleurs Sauvages • Wild Flowers 81; Au Rythme de Mon Cœur • To the Rhythm of My Heart 83; Le Jour "S"... • "S" As in... 84; La Boîte à Soleil

Lefèbvre, Philippe Le Transfuge 85

Lefèvre, René Opéra Musette 42*

Lefranc, Guy Dr. Knock • Knock 55; Keep Talking, Baby 61; La Moucharde • Woman of Sin 61; Le Caporal Épinglé • The Elusive Corporal • The Vanishing Corporal 62*

Leftwich, Ed Squad Car 60

Legaspi, Alejandro Gregorio 85*; Juliana 88*

Legend, Johnny see Kaufman, Andy

Léger, Fernand Le Ballet Mécanique 24

Legg, Stuart Aunt Matilda's Nephew 29; Varsity 30; The New Generation 32; The New Operator 32; The Coming of the Dial 33; Telephone Ship 33; Telephone Workers 33; BBC—The Voice of Britain 34; Powered Flight 53

Legoshin, Vladimir Pesnya o Shchastye • Song About Happiness • The Song of Happiness 34*; Byelyet Parus Odinoky • The Lone White Sail • Lonely White Sail 37; Military Secret 45

Legrand, François see Antel, Franz

Legrand, Michel Cinq Jours en Juin • Five Days in June 89

Le Grice, Malcolm Castle One 66; China Tea 66; Blind White Duration 67; Little Dog for Roger 67; Talla 67; Yes, No, Maybe, Maybenot 67; Castle Two 68; Grass 68; Wharf 68; Berlin Horse 70; Horror Film One 70; Lucky Pigs 70; Reign of the Vampire 70; Spot the Microdot 70; Your Lips One 70; Love Story One 71; Love Story Two 71; 1919—A Russian Funeral 71; Your Lips Three 71; Blue Field Duration 72; Duration • Whitchurch Down 72; Horror Film Two 72; Love Story Three 72; Newport 72; Threshold 72; White Field Duration 72; After Leonardo 73; After Leslie Wheeler 73; Don't Say 73; FRPS 73; Four Wall Duration 73; Gross Fog 73; MBKS 73; Matrix and Joseph's Coat 73; Pre-Production 73; Principles of Cinematography 73; After Lumière, L'Arroseur Arrosé 74; Screen—Entrance Exit 74; After Manet, After Giorgione, Le Déjeuner sur l'Herbe 75; Art Works One: Academic Still Life • Cézanne 77; Art Works Two: Time and Motion Study 77; Blackbird Descending • Blackbird Descending: Tense Alignment • Tense Alignment 77; Emily • Third Party Speculation 79; Finnegan's Chin 83

Le Haneff, René Colonel Chabert 47; Hoboes in Paradise 50

Lehman, Ernest Portnoy's Complaint 72

Lehman, Louis South of Hell Mountain 71*; The Pit 84

Lehmann, Maurice L'Affaire du Courrier de Lyon • The Courier of Lyons 37*; Le Ruisseau 37*; Fric-Frac 39*

Canary 27; The Chinese Parrot 27; The Man Who Laughs 27; The Last Warning 28; Puzzles 29

Lenica, Jan Banner of Youth • Sztandar Młodych 57*; Był Sobie Raz • Once Upon a Time 57*; Dni Oświaty 57*; Love Requited • Love Rewarded • Nagrodzone Uczucie 57*; Striptease 57*; Dom • House 58*; Le Langage des Fleurs 59; Mr. Head • Monsieur Tête 59*; Janko the Musician • New Janko the Musician • Nowy Janko Muzykant 60; Boîte à Musique 61*; Italia 61 • Italy 61 61*; Solitude 61*; Labirynt • Labyrinth 62; Die Nashörner • The Rhinoceros 63; A 64; La Féminin Fleur • La Femme Fleur • The Flower Woman • Woman Is a Flower • Woman the Flower 65; Quadratonia • Quadratonien 67; Adam II 68; Still Life • Stilleben 69; The Automobile 70; Nature Morte 70; Hell 71; Fantorro le Dernier Justicier • Fantorro the Last Just Man 72; Landscape 74; King Ubu • Ubu Roi 76; Ubu and the Great Gidouille • Ubu et la Grande Gidouille 79

Lennon, John Number 5 69*; Rape 69*; Two Virgins 69*; Apotheosis 70*; Legs • Up Your Legs Forever 70*; The Fly 71*; Imagine 73*

Lennon, Terry Daffy Duck's Quackbusters 88*

Lennox, Gerald B. Porno Erotico Western 68

Lent, Dean Border Radio 87*

Lentz, Sebastian Lock 17 • Schleuse 17 86

Lenzer, Don Have You Heard of the San Francisco Mime Troup? 68*

Lenzi, Bert see Lenzi, Umberto

Lenzi, Giovanna Crimes • Delitti 87

Lenzi, Umberto Terror of the Black Mask 60; Queen of the Seas 61; Catherine of Russia 62; Duel of Fire 62; Samson and the Slave Queen • Zorro Against Machiste • Zorro Contro Maciste 63; Temple of the White Elephants 63; I Pirati della Malesia • Sandokan • Sandokan la Tigre di Mompracem • Sandokan le Tigre de Borneo • Sandokan the Great • Sandokan the Tiger of Mompracem 64; Messalina Against the Son of Hercules 65; All Out • Tutto per Tutto 68; Orgasmo • Paranoia 68; Battle of the Commandos • Legion of the Damned 69; Paranoia • A Quiet Place to Kill 69; Deep River Savages • Mondo Cannibale • Il Paese del Sesso Selvaggio 72; Das Rätsel des Silbernen Halbmonds 72; Almost Human • The Kidnap of Mary Lou 74; Spasmo 76; Battle Force • The Battle of Mareth • The Biggest Battle • The Great Battle • The Greatest Battle 78; Brutal Justice 78; Eyeball • Gatto Rossi in un Labirinto do Vetro 78; From Hell to Victory 79; City of the Walking Dead • Incubo sulla Città Contaminata • Invasion by the Atomic Zombies • La Invasión de los Zombies Atómicos • Nightmare • Nightmare City 80; Doomed to Die • Eaten Alive • Eaten Alive by the Cannibals • Mangiati Vivi • Mangiati Vivi dai Cannibali 80; Cannibal Ferox • Make Them

Die Slowly 81; Ironmaster 82; Squadra Selvaggia • Wild Team 86; Ghosthouse 89

Leo, Fernando di see Di Leo, Fernando

Leo, Malcolm This Is Elvis 81*; It Came from Hollywood 82*; The Beach Boys: An American Band 85

Leon, Gerardo de see De Leon, Gerry

Leon, Gerry de see De Leon, Gerry

Léon, Jean Aimez-Vous les Femmes? • Do You Like Women? • A Taste for Women 64

Leonard, Arthur The Devil's Daughter • Pocomania • Poncomania 39; Straight to Heaven 39; Boy! What a Girl! 46; Sepia Cinderella 47

Leonard, Brett Dead Pit 90

Leonard, Harry D. One Hundred Per Cent Proof 20; The Transatlantic Night Express 20; In Old Madrid 21; School Days 21; The Sheriff 21; Some Sayings of Benjamin Franklin 21; Spaghetti for Two 21

Leonard, Herbert The Perils of Pauline 67*; Going Home 71

Leonard, Leon Omoo-Omoo • Omoo-Omoo, the Shark God • The Shark God 49

Leonard, Marian The Treasure 51

Leonard, Robert Z. The Master Key 14; A Boob's Romance 15; The Crippled Hand 15*; Heritage 15; Idols of Clay 15; Judge Not • Judge Not, or The Woman of Mona Diggins • The Woman of Mona Diggins 15; Little Blonde in Black 15; Shattered Memories 15; The Silent Command 15; The Boob's Victory 16; The Eagle's Wings 16; The Evidence 16; Little Eva Egerton 16; The Love Girl 16; The Plow Girl 16; Secret Love 16; The Silent Man of Timber Gulch 16; The Silent Member 16; The Winning of Miss Construe 16; The Woman Who Followed Me 16; At First Sight 17; Christmas Memories 17; Face Value 17; Life's Pendulum 17; A Mormon Maid 17; On Record 17; The Primrose Ring 17; Princess Virtue 17; The Bride's Awakening 18; Danger, Go Slow 18; Her Body in Bond 18; Modern Love 18; April Folly 19; The Big Little Person 19; The Delicious Little Devil 19; Miracle of Love 19; The Scarlet Shadow 19; The Way of a Woman 19; What Am I Bid? 19; The Restless Sex 20; The Gilded Lily 21; Heedless Moths 21; Peacock Alley 21; Broadway Rose 22; Fascination 22; Fashion Row 23; The French Doll 23; Jazzmania 23; Cheaper to Marry 24; Circe the Enchantress 24; Love's Wilderness 24; Mademoiselle Midnight 24; Bright Lights 25; Dance Madness 25; Time, the Comedian 25; The Demi-Bride 26; A Little Journey 26; Mademoiselle Modiste 26; The Waning Sex 26; Adam and Evil 27; Baby Mine 27; Tea for Three 27; The Cardboard Lover 28; A Lady of Chance 28*; Marianne 29; The Bachelor Father 30; The Divorcee 30; In Gay Madrid 30; Let Us Be Gay 30; Daughter of Luxury • Five and Ten 31*; It's a Wise Child 31; The Rise of Helga • Rising to Fame • Susan Lenox • Susan Lenox (Her Fall and Rise) 31; Lovers Courageous 32;

Strange Interlude • Strange Interval 32; Dancing Lady 33; Peg o' My Heart 33; Outcast Lady • A Woman of the World 34; After Office Hours 35; Escapade 35; The Great Ziegfeld 36; Piccadilly Jim 36; The Firefly 37; Maytime 37*; The Girl of the Golden West 38; Broadway Serenade • Serenade 39; New Moon 40; Pride and Prejudice 40; Third Finger, Left Hand 40; Strange Skirts • When Ladies Meet 41; We Were Dancing 41; Ziegfeld Girl 41; Cargo of Innocents • Stand by for Action! 42; The Man from Down Under 43; Marriage Is a Private Affair 44; Week-End at the Waldorf 45; The Secret Heart 46; B.F.'s Daughter • Polly Fulton 47; Cynthia • The Rich, Full Life 47; The Bribe 48; In the Good Old Summertime 49; Nancy Goes to Rio 49; Duchess of Idaho 50; Grounds for Marriage 50; Too Young to Kiss 51; The Clown 52; Everything I Have Is Yours 52; The Great Diamond Robbery 53; Her Twelve Men 54; Beautiful But Dangerous • La Belle des Belles • La Donna Più Bella del Mondo • The Most Beautiful Woman in the World 55; The King's Thief 55; Kelly and Me 56

Leonard, Terry Death Before Dishonor 86

Leonardi, Francesca Romana La Rosa Blanca 88

Leondopoulos, Jordan Pseudonym for John Broderick with John Shade

Leone, Alfred La Casa dell'Exorcismo • Death and the Devil • The Devil and the Dead • El Diablo Se Lleva a los Muertos • Il Diavolo e i Morti • Il Diavolo e il Morto • The House of Exorcism • Lisa and the Devil • Lisa e il Diavolo • Lise e il Diavolo 72*

Leone, John The Great Smokey Roadblock • The Last of the Cowboys 76

Leone, Sergio Taxi...Signore? 57; The Last Days of Pompeii • Gli Ultimi Giorni di Pompeii 59*; El Coloso de Rodas • Il Colosso di Rodi • The Colossus of Rhodes 60; The Last Days of Sodom and Gomorrah • Sodom and Gomorrah • Sodoma e Gomorra • Sodome et Gomorrhe 61*; A Fistful of Dollars • For a Fistful of Dollars • Per un Pugno di Dollari • Por un Puñado de Dólares 64; For a Few Dollars More • Per Qualche Dollari in Più 64; Le Bon, la Brute et le Truand • El Bueno, el Feo y el Malo • Il Buono, il Brutto, il Cattivo • The Good, the Bad and the Ugly • Zwei Glorreiche Halunken 66; C'Era una Volta il West • Once Upon a Time in the West 68; Duck, You Sucker! • A Fistful of Dynamite • Giù la Testa • Il Était une Fois la Révolution 71; Un Genio, Due Compari e un Pollo • The Genius 75*; Once Upon a Time in America 83; Too Strong • Troppo Forte 85*

Leong, Po-chih Jumping Ash 76; Foxbat 77; Itchy Fingers 77; No Big Deal 79; Super Fool 81; He Lives by Night 82; Ye Jinghum 82; Banana Cop 84; Hong Kong 1941 85; The Island • The Island (Life and Death) 85; Ping Pong 85; Time Traveler 85

Leoni, Guido Emmanuell's Silver Tongue 81*

Leonidov, Leonid Wings of a Serf 26*

Leoniv, A. Chekhov 54

Leonviola, Antonio Angel in a Taxi 59; Atlas Against the Cyclops • Maciste nella Terra dei Ciclopi 61; Machiste, Strongest Man in the World • Mole Men Against the Son of Hercules 61; Taur the Mighty 63; Thor and the Amazon Woman 63

Lepage, Henri La Machine à Refaire la Vie • The Machine for Recreating Life 24*; Sins of Paris 54

Lepard, Ernest Dodging the Landlord 13; Inkey and Co. 13; Inkey and Co. — Glad Eye 13; Inkey and Co. in Business 13; The Temperance Lecture 13

LePéron, Serge Laissé Béton 84

Lepeuve, Monique Dunoyer de Segonzac 65*

Leprince, René La Comtesse Noire 12*; Le Roi de l'Air 13*; Zyte 16; La Vie d'une Reine 17; Le Noël d'un Vagabond 18; Le Calvaire d'une Reine 19; Les Larmes du Pardon 19; Face a l'Océan 20; Force de la Vie 20; La Lutte pour la Vie 20; Être ou Ne Pas Être 22; Jean d'Agrève 22; Un Bon Petit Diable 23; La Folie du Doute 23; Mon Oncle Benjamin 23; Pax Domine 23; Vent Debout 23; Le Jardin sur l'Oronte 25; Princesse Masha 27; La Revanche du Maudit 29

Lerner, Carl Black Like Me • No Man Walks Alone 64

Lerner, Irving Muscle Beach 48*; Suicide Attack 51; Man Crazy 53; Edge of Fury 58*; Murder by Contract 58; City of Fear 59; Studs Lonigan 60; Cry of Battle • To Be a Man 63; Custer of the West • A Good Day for Fighting 66*; The Royal Hunt of the Sun 68

Lerner, Joseph Olympic Cavalcade 48; C-Man 49; Guilty Bystander 50; Mr. Universe 51

Lerner, Murray Secrets of the Reef 56*; Festival 67; From Mao to Mozart • From Mao to Mozart: Isaac Stern in China 80*

Lerner, Richard Revenge of the Cheerleaders 76

Leroy, Francis Emmanuelle IV 83*

LeRoy, Mervyn Her Primitive Mate • No Place to Go 27; Flying Romeos 28; Harold Teen 28; Naughty Baby • Reckless Rosie 28; Oh, Kay! 28; Broadway Babies • Broadway Daddies 29; Hot Stuff 29; Little Johnny Jones 29; Playing Around 29; Broken Dishes • Too Young to Marry 30; A Gentleman's Fate 30; Little Caesar 30; Numbered Men 30; Showgirl in Hollywood 30; Top Speed 30; Broad-Minded 31; Five Star Final • One Fatal Hour 31; I Am a Fugitive • I Am a Fugitive from a Chain Gang • I Am a Fugitive from the Chain Gang 31; Local Boy Makes Good 31; Tonight or Never 31; A Bad Boy • Hard to Handle • The Inside 32; Big City Blues 32; Elmer the Great 32; The Heart of New York 32; High Pressure 32; Three on a Match 32; Two Seconds 32; The World Changes 32; Gold Diggers of 1933 33;

Tugboat Annie 33; Happiness Ahead 34; Heat Lightning 34; Hi, Nellie! 34; Sweet Adeline 34; I Found Stella Parish • Stella Parish 35; Oil for the Lamps of China 35; Page Miss Glory 35; Anthony Adverse 36; Three Men on a Horse 36; The King and the Chorus Girl • Romance Is Sacred 37; They Won't Forget 37; Fools for Scandal 38; Escape • When the Door Opened 40; Waterloo Bridge 40; Blossoms in the Dust 41; Johnny Eager 41; Unholy Partners 41; Random Harvest 42; Madame Curie 43; Thirty Seconds Over Tokyo 44; The House I Live In 45; Without Reservations 46; Desire Me 47*; Homecoming 48; Little Women 48; Any Number Can Play 49; East Side, West Side 49; Lovely to Look At 51*; Quo Vadis? 51*; Latin Lovers 52; Million Dollar Mermaid • The One Piece Bathing Suit 52; Rose Marie 53; Mister Roberts 54*; Strange Lady in Town 54; The Bad Seed 55; Brink of Hell • Toward the Unknown 56; No Time for Sergeants 57; Home Before Dark 58; The F.B.I. Story 59; Wake Me When It's Over 60; The Devil at 4 O'Clock 61; A Majority of One 61; Gypsy 62; Mary, Mary 63; Moment to Moment 65; The Green Berets 68*

Leroy, Serge Les Passagers • Shattered 76; Attention! The Kids Are Watching 78; Le 4ème Pouvoir 85; Contrainte par Corps 88

LeSaint, Edward J. The Circular Staircase 15; The Long Chance 15; The Supreme Test 15; The Honorable Friend 16; The Soul of Kura San 16; The Three Godfathers 16; The Victoria Cross 16; Each to His Kind • The Rajah's Amulet 17; Fighting Mad 17; The Golden Fetter 17; The Heir of the Ages 17; The Lonesome Chap 17; The Squaw Man's Son 17; The Wolf and His Mate 17; The Bird of Prey 18; Cupid's Roundup 18; The Devil's Wheel 18; Her One Mistake 18; Kultur 18; Nobody's Wife 18; Painted Lips 18; The Scarlet Road 18; The Strange Woman 18; Call of the Soul 19; The Daredevil 19; The Feud 19; Fighting for Gold 19; Hell Roarin' Reform 19; The Sneak 19; The Speed Maniac 19; The Wilderness Trail 19; Flames of the Flesh 20; Girl of My Heart 20; Merely Mary Ann 20; The Mother of His Children 20; Rose of Nome 20; A Sister to Salome 20; Two Moons 20; White Lies 20; More to Be Pitied Than Scorned 22; Only a Shop Girl 22; The Sleep Walker 22; Innocence 23; The Marriage Market 23; Temptation 23; Yesterday's Wife 23; Discontented Husbands 24; Pal o' Mine 24; The Love Gamble 25; Speed 25; Three Keys 25; The Unwritten Law 25; Brooding Eyes 26; The Millionaire Policeman 26

Lesiewicz, Witold Gwiazdy Musza Płonać • The Stars Must Shine 54*; Pasażerka • La Passagère • Die Passagierin • The Passenger 63*

Leslie, Alfred Pull My Daisy 58*

Leslie, Bill Nail Gun Massacre 87*

Leslie, Desmond Stranger at My Door 50*; The Missing Princess 54*

Le Somptier, René La Sultane de l' Amour 19*; La Croisade 20; La Montée Vers l'Acropole 20; La Bête Traquée 23; La Porteuse de Pain 23; La Forêt Qui Tue 24; Les Terres d'Or 25

Lessey, George A. The Suburban 15; The Purple Lady 16

Lessing, Bruno The Scarlet Road 16*

Lester, Mark L. Twilight of the Mayas 71; Tricia's Wedding 72; Steel Arena 73; Truck Stop Women 74; White House Madness 75; Bobbie Jo and the Outlaw 76; Stunts • Who Is Killing the Stuntmen? 77; Roller Boogie 79; Class of '84 • Class of 1984 81; Firestarter 84; Commando 85; Armed and Dangerous 86; Class of 1999 90

Lester, Richard The Running, Jumping and Standing Still Film 59; It's a Trad, Dad! • It's Trad, Dad! • Ring-a-Ding Rhythm! 61; The Mouse on the Moon 63; A Hard Day's Night 64; Eight Arms to Hold You • Help! 65; The Knack • The Knack...and How to Get It 65; A Funny Thing Happened on the Way to the Forum 66; How I Won the War 67; Mondo Teeno • Teenage Rebellion 67*; The Bed Sitting Room 68; Petulia 68; The Four Musketeers • The Four Musketeers: The Revenge of Milady • The Revenge of Milady 73; The Queen's Diamonds • The Three Musketeers • The Three Musketeers: The Queen's Diamonds 73; Juggernaut 74*; Royal Flash 75; The Ritz 76; Robin and Marian 76; Butch and Sundance • Butch and Sundance: The Early Days 79; Cuba 79; Superman II 80*; Superman III 83; Finders Keepers 84; The Return of the Musketeers 89

L'Estrange, Dick Teen Age 44

Le Strange, Norman The Amorous Adventures of Bux 26

Le Strange, Richard The Hidden Code 20

Lestringuez, Pierre Monseigneur 50*

Leszczyłowski, Michał Directed by Andrei Tarkovsky 88

Leszczyński, Witold Axiliad • Siekierezada 87

Letans, Iris Emmanuelle IV 83*

Leterrier, François Les Mauvais Coups • Naked Autumn 61; Un Roi Sans Divertissement 63; La Chasse Royale 68; Projection Privée 73; Milady 75; Goodbye Emmanuelle 78; Va Voir Maman...Papa Travaille 78; Your Turn, My Turn 78; Tranches de Vie 85

Leto, Marco Black Holiday 73; La Donna Spezzata 88

Lettich, Sheldon A.W.O.L. • Lionheart • Wrong Bet 90

Letts, Don The Punk Rock Movie 78

Levanios, Michael, Jr. Uncle Scam 81*

Levchuk, Timofei My Obvinyaem • We Accuse 87

Leventhal, J. D. An Engineering Problem 16; The Aeroplane Machine Gun 17; Fiske Torpedo Plane 17; Freak Patents: The Balloon R.R. 17; The Gasoline Engine 17;

Mechanical Operation of British Tanks 17; Putting Volcanoes to Work 17; A Submarine Destroyer 17; The Submarine Mine-Layer 17; Traveling Forts 17; The Panama Canal 18; The Rudiments of Flying 18; The Torpedo, Hornet of the Sea 18; Behind the Signs on Broadway 20; Breathing 20; Here's Your Eyesight 20; How You See 20; If We Went to the Moon 20; Lightning 20; Professor B. Flat 20*; The Automatic Riveter 21

Levering, Joseph Little Miss Fortune 17; The Little Samaritan 17; The Road Between 17; The Victim 17; The Transgressor 18; His Temporary Wife 20; Husbands and Wives 20; Luring Shadows 20; Determination 22; Flesh and Spirit 22; Finger Prints 23; The Tie That Binds 23; Who's Cheating? 24; Lilies of the Streets 25; Unrestrained Youth 25; Defenders of the Law 31; Sea Devils 31; Cheating Blondes 33; In Early Arizona 38; Phantom Gold 38; Pioneer Trail 38; Rolling Caravans 38; Stagecoach Days 38; Frontiers of '49 39; The Law Comes to Texas 39; Lone Star Pioneers • Unwelcome Visitors 39

Leversuch, Ted Tangier Assignment 54; Adulterous Affair • The Love Blackmailer • Room for a Stranger 66

Levesque, Michel Werewolves on Wheels 71; Chaingang Girls • Sweet Sugar 72

Levey, Jay UHF 89

Levey, William A. Black Frankenstein • Blackenstein 73; To Be a Rose 74; Wam Bam Thank You Spaceman 75; The Happy Hooker Goes to Washington 77; Slumber Party • Slumber Party '57 77; Skatetown, U.S.A. 79; Lightning, the White Stallion 86

Levi, Alan J. Blood Song 82

Levie, Pierre Merci Monsieur Robertson • Thank You Mr. Robertson 86

Levigard, Josef Born to the Saddle 29; Grit Wins 29; Slim Fingers 29; The Smiling Terror 29

Levigard, Joseph see Levigard, Josef

Levin, Henry Cry of the Werewolf 44; Dancing in Manhattan 44; The Fighting Guardsman 44; Sergeant Mike 44; I Love a Mystery 45; The Bandit of Sherwood Forest 46*; The Devil's Mask 46; Monte Cristo's Revenge • The Return of Monte Cristo 46; Night Editor • The Trespasser 46; The Unknown 46; The Corpse Came C.O.D. 47; The Guilt of Janet Ames 47; The Gallant Blade 48; The Man from Colorado 48; The Mating of Millie 48; And Baby Makes Three 49; House of Settlement • Mr. Soft Touch 49*; Jolson Sings Again 49; Convicted • One Way Out 50; The Flying Missile 50; Girl of the Year • The Petty Girl 50; The Family Secret 51; Two of a Kind 51; Belles on Their Toes 52; The Farmer Takes a Wife 53; Mister Scoutmaster 53; The President's Lady 53; The Gambler from Natchez 54; Three Young Texans 54; The Dark Avenger • The Warriors 55; Let's Be Happy 56; April Love 57; Bernardine 57; The Lonely Man 57; How

to Rob a Bank • A Nice Little Bank That Should Be Robbed 58; Holiday for Lovers 59; Journey to the Center of the Earth 59; The Remarkable Mr. Pennypacker 59; Where the Boys Are 60; Le Meraviglie di Aladino • Les Mille et Une Nuits • The Wonders of Aladdin 61*; If a Man Answers 62; The Wonderful World of the Brothers Grimm 62*; Come Fly with Me • The Friendliest Girls in the World 63; His and His • Honeymoon Hotel 64; Dschingis Khan • Dzingis-Kan • Genghis Khan • Ghengis Khan 65; Kiss the Girls and Make Them Die • Operazione Paradiso • Si Tutte le Donne del Mondo… 66*; Murderers' Row 66; The Ambushers 67; The Desperados 68; Jamaica Gold 71; That Man Bolt • Thunderbolt • To Kill a Dragon 72*; Run for the Roses • Thoroughbred • The Thoroughbreds • Treasure Seekers 77

Levin, Meyer The Illegals 48

Levin, Moissei Poet and Tsar 38; Amangeldy 39

Levin, Sidney Let the Good Times Roll 73*; The Great Brain 78

Levin, Vasily Iskushenie Don Zhuana • The Temptation of Don Juan 87*

Levine, Jack see Jevne, Jack

Levinson, Barry Diner 82; The Natural 84; Young Sherlock Holmes • Young Sherlock Holmes and the Pyramid of Fear 85; Good Morning, Vietnam 87; Tin Men 87; Rain Man 88; Avalon 90

Levinson, Fred Hail • Hail to the Chief • Washington, B.C. 73

Levitan, Nadav Stalin's Kids • Yaldei Stalin 87

Levitin, Jacqueline Eva: Guerrillera 87

Levitow, Abe Really Scent 59*; Unnatural History 59; A Witch's Tangled Hare 59; Gay Purr-ee 62; The Phantom Tollbooth 69*; Mr. Magoo's Holiday Festival 70

Levkoyer, G. Pupils of the Seventh Class • Pupils of the Seventh Grade • Sedmiklassniki • Seventh Grade 38*

Levring, Kristian A Shot from the Heart • Et Skud fra Hjertet 86

Levy, Benn W. Lord Camber's Ladies 32

Levy, Bob If You Don't Stop It, You'll Go Blind 77*

Levy, Dani Du Mich Auch • Same to You • So What? 87*

Levy, Don Herostratus 67; The Belt and Suspenders Man 70

Levy, Gary Raw Tunes 86*

Levy, Gerry Where Has Poor Mickey Gone? 64; The Body Stealers • Invasion of the Body Stealers • Out of Thin Air • Thin Air 69

Levy, I. Robert Can I Do It…'Til I Need Glasses? 77

Lévy, Jean Benoît see Benoît-Lévy, Jean

Levy, Ralph Bedtime Story • King of the Mountain 64; Do Not Disturb 65

Lévy, Raoul Da New York • Da New York Maffia Uccide • Hail, Mafia • Je Vous Salue, Mafia • Mafia Uccide 65; The Defector • L'Espion • Lautlose Waffen 66

Levy, Shuki Perfect Victim 88

Lewald, Eric Incoming Freshmen 79*

Lewicki, Stephen Jon A Certain Sacrifice 81

Lewin, Albert The Moon and Sixpence 42; The Picture of Dorian Gray 44; The Private Affairs of Bel Ami 47; Pandora and the Flying Dutchman 50; Saadia 53; The Living Idol 56

Lewin, Ben Georgia 88

Lewin, Robert Third of a Man 62

Lewin, Sam The Dunera Boys 85

Lewis, Al Our Miss Brooks 55

Lewis, Cecil How He Lied to Her Husband 30; Carmen • Gipsy Blood 31; Arms and the Man 32; Indiscretions of Eve 32

Lewis, Christopher Revenge 86

Lewis, Cullen see Collins, Lewis D.

Lewis, David Dangerous Curves 88

Lewis, Edgar Captain Swift 14; Northern Lights 14; A Gilded Fool 15; The Nigger 15; The Plunderer 15; Samson 15; The Thief 15; The Bondman 16; The Flames of Johannis 16; The Great Divide 16; The Light at Dusk 16; Souls in Bondage 16; Those Who Toil 16; The Bar Sinister 17; The Sign Invisible 18; Calibre 38 19; Love and the Law • The Troop Train 19; A Beggar in Purple 20; Lahoma 20; Other Men's Shoes 20; Sherry 20; The Sage Hen 21; Strength of the Pines 22; You Are Guilty 23; The Right of the Strongest 24; Red Love 25; One Glorious Scrap 27; Arizona Cyclone 28; The Fearless Rider 28; The Gun Runner 28; Life's Crossroads 28; A Made-to-Order Hero 28; Put 'Em Up 28; Stormy Waters 28; Unmasked 29; Ladies in Love 30; Love at First Sight 30

Lewis, George B. The Humanoid • L' Umanoide 79

Lewis, Herschell Gordon Living Venus 60; The Prime Time 60; The Adventures of Lucky Pierre 61; Daughter of the Sun 62; Nature's Playmates 62; Bell, Bare and Beautiful 63; Blood Feast 63; Boin-n-g 63; The Devil's Camera • Scum of the Earth 63; Goldilocks and the Three Bares • Goldilocks' Three Chicks 63; Color Me Blood Red 64; Moonshine Mountain • White Trash on Moonshine Mountain 64; 2,000 Maniacs 64; Monster à Go-Go • Terror at Halfday 65; Sin, Suffer and Repent 65*; Alley Tramp 66; The Eerie World of Dr. Jordan • Something Weird 66; An Eye for an Eye 66; The Gruesome Twosome 66; Jimmy the Boy Wonder 66; Blast-Off Girls 67; The Girl, the Body and the Pill • The Pill 67; How to Make a Doll 67; Santa Claus Visits the Land of Mother Goose • (Santa Visits) The Magic Land of Mother Goose 67; The Secret of Dr. Alucard • A Taste of Blood 67; Suburban Roulette 67; Just for the Hell of It 68; The Psychic 68; She-Devils on Wheels 68; The Wizard of Gore 68; The Ecstasies of Women 69; Linda and Abilene 69; Miss Nymphet's Zap-In 70; Blood Orgy • The Gore-Gore Girls 71; This Stuff'll Kill Ya! 71; Year of the Yahoo! 71; Black Love 72

Lewis, J. E. Bringing It Home 40

Lewis, J. P. Heartland Reggae 80

Lewis, Jay A Man's Affair 49; The Baby and the Battleship 56; Invasion Quartet 61; Live Now, Pay Later 62; A Home of Your Own 64

Lewis, Jerry Come Back, Little Shicksa 49; Fairfax Avenue 49; I Should Have Stood in Bedlam 49; Melvin's Revenge 49; The Re-Inforcer 49; Son of Lifeboat 49; Son of Spellbound 49; A Spot in the Shade 49; Watch on the Lime 49; The Whistler 49; The Bellboy 60; The Errand Boy 61; The Ladies' Man 61; The Nutty Professor 63; The Patsy 64; The Family Jewels 65; Three on a Couch 66; The Big Mouth 67; One More Time 69; Ja, Ja, Mein General, But Which Way to the Front? • Which Way to the Front? 70; The Day the Clown Cried 72; Hardly Working 79; Cracking Up • Smorgasbord 82

Lewis, Jonathan Before Hindsight 77; Towers of Babel 81

Lewis, Joseph H. Courage of the West 37; Navy Spy 37*; The Singing Outlaw 37; Border Wolves 38; International Spy • The Spy Ring 38; The Last Stand 38; Forestalled • Two-Fisted Rangers 39; Blazing Six Shooters • Stolen Wealth 40; Boys of the City • The Ghost Creeps 40; False Evidence • The Return of Wild Bill 40; The Man from Tumbleweeds 40; Texas Stagecoach • Two Roads 40; That Gang of Mine 40; Arizona Cyclone 41; Criminals Within 41; Here We Go Again • Pride of the Bowery 41; The Invisible Ghost • Murder by the Stars • The Phantom Killer 41; The Mad Doctor of Market Street 41; Bombs Over Burma 42; Boss of Hangtown Mesa 42; Secret Witness • Secrets of a Co-Ed • Silent Witness 42; The Silver Bullet 42; Minstrel Man 44; The Falcon in San Francisco 45; My Name Is Julia Ross 45; The Jolson Story 46*; So Dark the Night 46; The Swordsman 47; A Date with Destiny • The Return of October 48; Deadly Is the Female • Gun Crazy 49; The Undercover Man 49; A Lady Without Passport 50; Desperate Search 52; Retreat Hell! 52; Cry of the Hunted 53; The Big Combo 54; A Lawless Street 55; 7th Cavalry 56; The Halliday Brand 57; Terror in a Texas Town 58

Lewis, Milo Egghead's Robot 70; The Troublesome Double 71

Lewis, Morton M. Blueprint for Danger • The Wallet 52; Naughty Girls on the Loose 76; Secrets of a Superstud 76

Lewis, Robert Ziegfeld Follies 45*; Anything Goes 56

Lewis, Robert Michael No Room to Run 78

Lewis, Vance see Vanzi, Luigi

Lewiston, Denis Hot Target 85

Lewk, Dan Raw Tunes 86*

Leytes, Josef Młody Las • The Young Forest 34; The Day of the Great Adventure 36; Love or a Kingdom 37; Dziewczęta z Nowolipku • Girls of Nowolipek 38; Kościuszko 38; Faithful City 52; Stranded • Valley of Mystery 67; The Counterfeit

Killer • Crackshot • The Faceless Man 68*

Lezama, Luis El Cemeterio de las Áquilas • The Eagles' Cemetery 39; An Old Love • Un Viejo Amor 40

L'Herbier, Marcel Phantasmes 18; Rose-France 18; Le Bercail 19; Le Carnaval des Vérités 19; L'Homme du Large • Man of the Open Seas 20; Villa Destin 20; El Dorado 21; Prométhée...Banquier 21; Don Juan et Faust 22; Futurismo • L'Inhumaine • The New Enchantment 23; Resurrection 23; Feu Mathias Pascal • The Late Mathias Pascal • The Late Matthew Pascal • The Living Dead Man 24; Le Vertige 26; L'Argent • Geld, Geld, Geld • Money 27; Le Diable au Cœur • L'Ex-Voto 27; Nuits de Prince 28; L'Enfant de l'Amour 29; La Donna d'Una Notte • La Femme d'Une Nuit 30; Le Mystère de la Chambre Jaune • The Mystery of the Yellow Room 30; Le Parfum de la Dame en Noir • The Perfume of the Lady in Black 30; Les Amoureux • Bird of Prey • L'Épervier 33; L'Aventurier 34; Le Bonheur 34; Le Scandale 34; Children's Corner 35; Door to the Open Sea • The Great Temptation • La Porte du Large 35; Les Hommes Nouveaux 35; La Route Impériale 35; Sacrifice d'Honneur • Sacrifice of Honor • Veille d'Armes • The Vigil 35; Le Coin des Enfants 36; The Living Corpse • Nuits de Feu 36; The Cheat • Forfaiture 37; The Citadel of Silence • La Citadelle du Silence 37; Adrienne Lecouvreur 38; La Brigade Sauvage • Savage Brigade 38*; Entente Cordiale 38; La Mode Rêvée 38; Rasputin • La Tragédie Impériale 38; Terre de Feu 38; La Comédie du Bonheur • The Comedy of Happiness 39; Foolish Husbands • Histoire de Rire • Just for Fun 41; La Vie de Bohème 41; The Fantastic Night • La Nuit Fantastique 42; L'Honorable Catherine 42; Au Petit Bonheur 45; L'Affaire du Collier de la Reine • The Queen's Necklace 46; La Révoltée • Stolen Affections 47; Les Derniers Jours de Pompéï • The Last Days of Pompeii • Gli Ultimi Giorni di Pompei 48; Le Père de Mademoiselle 53*; Hommage à Debussy 63; Le Cinéma du Diable 67; Le Féerie des Fantasmes 78

Li, Dawei see Lai, David

Li, Han-hsiang Ch'ien-Nu Yu-Hin • Enchanted Shadow • Soul of a Beautiful Girl 59; Eternal Love • Liang Shan-Po and Chu Ying-T'ai • Liang Shan-Po yu Chu Ying-T'ai • The Love Eterne 63*; The Magnificent Concubine • Yang Kwei Fei 64; Chin Nu Yu Hun • The Enchanting Shadow 65; Empress Wu • Wu-Hou 65; Four Moods • Hsi Nu Ai Le 70*; Reign Behind the Curtain 83; Ta Luan-Hui • The Wheel of Life 83*; The Last Emperor 86; Snuff Bottle 88

Li, Hanxiang see Li, Han-hsiang

Li, Hsing see Li, Han-hsiang

Li, Kao The Mermaid 60

Li, Sheng see Lee, Shing

Li, Shing see Lee, Shing

Li, Tie Vampire Woman • Xi Xuefu 62

Li, Ting The Ideological Problem 50*

Li, Ya-lin Bei Aiqing Yiwangde Jiaoluo

• A Love-Forsaken Corner 86*; Jin 88

Li, Zhao Kung Fu from Beyond the Grave • Yin Ji 82

Liabel, Audre L'Appassionata 29*

Liappa, Frieda Enas Isichos Thanatos • A Quiet Death 86

Liberatore, Ugo Il Sesso degli Angeli • The Sex of Angels 68; May Morning 70

Libosit, Juraj Zakázané Uvolnenie 86

Lichtenfeld, Ted Personal Foul 87

Lichtner, Marvin Some Kind of Hero 72

Liconti, Carlo Concrete Angels 87

Liddle, Ralph Spirit of the Wind 79

Liddle, Robert Attila 81

Lie, David da see DaLie, David

Liebeneiner, Wolfgang Promise Me Nothing 37; The Model Husband • Der Mustergatte 38; Der Florentiner Hut • The Leghorn Hat 39; Goal in the Clouds • Ziel den Wolken 39; Bismarck 40; Ich Klage An 41; April 1st, 2000 • April 1, 2000 • 1. April 2000 52; Die Trapp-Familie • The Trapp Family 56; The Dancing Heart • Das Tanzende Herz 58; Taiga 59

Lieberman, Art Up Your Alley 75; The Melon Affair 79

Lieberman, Jeff Blue Sunshine 76; Squirm 76; Just Before Dawn 80; Remote Control 87

Lieberman, Robert Table for Five 82

Lieberman, Robert H. Hong Kong and Onward 67; Faces in a Famine 86

Liebman, Max Ten from Your Show of Shows 73

Liechti, Hans Dunki-Schott 86*

Lieropl, Robert van see Van Lieropl, Robert

Liguoro, Eugenio de see De Liguoro, Eugenio

Lilason, Prinya 1 2 3 Duan Mahaphai • 1 2 3 Monster Express 77*

Lili, Chao see Chao, Lili

Lilienthal, Peter La Victoria 73; Er Herrscht Ruhe im Land 76; David 79; Der Aufstand • The Uprising 80; Dear Mr. Wonderful 82; The Autograph 84; The Poet's Silence • Das Schweigen des Dichters 86

Lilley, Edward Allergic to Love 43; Honeymoon Lodge 43; Larceny with Music 43; Lucky Days • Sing a Jingle 43; Moonlight in Vermont 43; Never a Dull Moment 43; Babes on Swing Street 44; Hi, Good Lookin' 44; My Gal Loves Music 44; Her Lucky Night 45; Swing Out, Sister 45

Lillo, Antonietta de see De Lillo, Antonietta

Lilly, Lou Playing the Pied Piper 41

Lim, Kwon-taek see Im, Kwon-taek

Lima Júnior, Walter Brasil Ano 2.000 68; Chico Rei • King Chico 86; The Dolphin • Ele o Boto • He the Dolphin 87

Limosin, Jean-Pierre Gardien de la Nuit • Night Guardian 86; L'Autre Nuit 88

Limur, Jean de see De Limur, Jean

Lin, He Yong R E D Spells Red 83

Lin, Yi The Heroes of the Liulang Mountains 50*

Lin, Yixiu Elephant Wife • The Leech Girl • Zhi Mo Nu 68*

Heaven Too 40; Castle on the Hudson • Years Without Days 40; City for Conquest 40; Blues in the Night 41; Out of the Fog 41; Divide and Conquer 42*; The Nazis Strike 42*; Prelude to War 42*; This Above All 42; Battle of China 43*; Operation Titanic 43; The American People • War Comes to America 44*; Battle of Russia 44*; The Long Night 47; The Snake Pit 48; Sorry, Wrong Number 48; Decision Before Dawn 51; Act of Love • Un Acte d'Amour 53; The Deep Blue Sea 55; Anastasia 56; The Journey • Some of Us May Die 58; Aimez-Vous Brahms? • Goodbye Again 61; Le Couteau dans la Plaie • Five Miles to Midnight 62; The Night of the Generals • La Nuit des Généraux 66; La Dame dans l'Auto avec des Lunettes et un Fusil • The Lady in the Car with Glasses and a Gun 69

Liu, Cheng-han House of the Lute • Yuhuo Fen Qin 79

Liu, Honquan Devil Foetus • Mo Tai 83

Liu, Jialiang Spiritual Boxer, Part Two 79

Liu, Pan Li Oke 25; Tche Sen 25; The Heroes of the Liulang Mountains 50*; New Heroes and Heroines 50*; Gate No. 6 52; Heroic Railway Engineers 54; When the New Director Arrives at His Post 56

Liu, San Kung Fu Halloween 81*

Livaneli, Ömer Zülfü Iron Earth, Copper Sky • Yer Demir, Gök Bakır 87; Mist • Sis 89

Livingstone, Leonard Pitfalls of Passion 27

Lizzani, Carlo Via Emilia Km 147 49; Viaggio al Sud 49; Modena, Città del Emilia Rossa 50; Nel Mezzogiorno Qualcosa È Cambiato 50; Achtung! Banditi! 51; Ai Margini della Metropoli 52; Amore in Città • Love in the City 53*; Chronicle of Poor Lovers • Cronache di Poveri Amanti 54; Lo Svitato 56; Behind the Great Wall • Il Fiume Giallo • La Muraglia Cinese 58; Esterina • L'Herbe Folle 59; Il Gobbo • The Hunchback of Rome 60; Il Carabiniere a Cavallo 61; L'Oro di Roma 61; Il Processo di Verona • The Verona Trial 62; Amori Pericolosi 64*; La Celestina • La Celestina P . . . R . . . 64; La Vita Agra 64; The Dirty Game • The Dirty War • La Guerra Segreta • La Guerre Secrète • The Secret Agents • The Secret War • Spione Unter Sich 65*; Thrilling 65*; Un Fiume di Dollari • The Hills Run Red • A River of Dollars 66; Lutring • Lutring . . . Réveille-Toi et Meurs • Réveille-Toi et Meurs • Svegliati e Uccidi • Too Soon to Die • Wake Up and Die • Wake Up and Kill 66; I Sette Fratelli 66; Amore e Rabbia • La Contestation • Love and Anger • Vangelo '70 67*; Banditi a Milano • The Violent Four 67; Let Them Rest • Mögen Sie in Frieden Ruhen? • Requiescant 67; L'Amante di Gramigna • The Bandit 68; Assassinio a Sarajevo 68; Barbagia 69; Roma Bene 71; Torino Nera 72; Crazy Joe 74; Last Days of Mussolini • The Last Four Days • Mussolini—Ultimo Atto 74; Un

Delitto Gratuito 76; San Babila Oro 20: Un Delitto Inutile 76; Uomini Merce 76; Kleinhoff Hotel 77; Fontamara 80; Casa del Tappeto Giallo 83; Rome—The Image of a City 83; Nucleo Zero 84; Mamma Ebe 85; Caro Gorbaciov 88; Selina 89

Llagostera i Colli, Ferrán Bar-cel-ona 87

Llaneza, Julio Ruiz Ese Loco Loco Hospital • That Mad Mad Hospital 86; It Hurts But It Feels Good • Se Sufre Pero Se Goza 86

Llerendi, Antonio Profundo 88

Llewellyn, Richard The Barber's Shop 39; Eye Witness 39; Oh Dear Uncle! 39

Llosa, Luis Hour of the Assassin 87; Crime Zone 88

Lloyd, Frank As the Wind Blows 14; Billie's Baby 14; The Chorus Girl's Thanksgiving 14; For His Superior's Honor 14; The Link That Binds 14; A Page from Life 14; A Prince of Bavaria 14; Traffic in Babes 14; The Vagabond 14; According to Value 15; An Arrangement with Fate 15; The Bay of Seven Islands • The Bay of Seven Isles 15; The Call of the Cumberlands 15; Dr. Mason's Temptation 15; A Double Deal in Pork 15; Eleven to One 15; Fate's Alibi 15; From the Shadows 15; The Gentleman from Indiana 15; His Captive 15; His Last Serenade 15; His Last Trick 15; His Superior's Honor 15; In the Grasp of the Law • In the Grip of the Law 15; Jane 15; Life's Furrow 15; The Little Girl of the Attic 15; Little Mr. Fixer 15; Martin Lowe, Financier 15; Martin Lowe, Fixer 15; Nature's Triumph 15; Paternal Love 15; Pawns of Fate 15; The Pinch 15; Prophet of the Hills 15; The Reform Candidate 15; The Source of Happiness 15; The Temptation of Edwin Swayne 15; 10,000 Dollars 15; Their Golden Wedding 15; To Redeem a Value 15; To Redeem an Oath 15; The Toll of the Youth • The Toll of Youth 15; Trickery 15; When the Spider Tore Loose 15; Wolves of Society 15; The Code of Marcia Gray 16; David Garrick 16; An International Marriage 16; The Intrigue 16; Madame la Presidente • Madame President 16; The Making of Maddalena 16; Sin of the Parent • Sins of Her Parents 16; The Stronger Love 16; The Tongues of Men 16; American Methods 17; The Heart of a Lion 17; The Kingdom of Love 17; The Price of Silence 17; A Tale of Two Cities 17; When a Man Sees Red 17; The Blindness of Divorce 18; For Freedom 18; Les Misérables 18; The Rainbow Trail 18; The Riders of the Purple Sage 18; True Blue 18; The Loves of Letty 19; The Man Hunter 19; Pitfalls of a Big City 19; The World and Its Woman 19; The Great Lover 20; Madame X 20; The Silver Horde 20; A Voice in the Dark 20; The Woman in Room 13 20; The Grim Comedian 21; The Invisible Power 21; The Man from Lost River 21; Roads of Destiny 21; The Sin Flood 21; A Tale of Two Worlds 21; The Eternal Flame 22; Oliver Twist 22; Ashes of Vengeance 23; Black Oxen 23; The Voice from the Minaret 23; Within the Law 23; The Sea Hawk

24; The Silent Watcher 24; Her Husband's Secret 25; The Splendid Road 25; Winds of Chance 25; The Eagle of the Sea 26; The Wise Guy 26; Children of Divorce 27*; Adoration 28; Dark Streets 29; The Divine Lady 29; Drag • Parasites 29; Weary River 29; Young Nowheres 29; Adiós • The Lash 30; East Lynne 30; Sin Flood • The Way of All Men 30; Son of the Gods 30; The Age for Love 31; The Right of Way 31; Burnt Offering • A Passport to Hell 32; Cavalcade 32; Berkeley Square 33; Hoopla 33; Servants' Entrance 34; Mutiny on the Bounty 35; The Big Noise • Modern Madness 36; Under Two Flags 36*; Maid of Salem 37; Wells Fargo 37; If I Were King 38; Rulers of the Sea 39; The Howards of Virginia • The Tree of Liberty 40; The Lady from Cheyenne 41; This Woman Is Mine 41; Forever and a Day 43*; Air-Pattern Pacific 44; Blood on the Sun 45; The Last Bomb 46; The Shanghai Story 54; The Last Command 55

Lloyd, George A Letter from Wales 53

Lloyd, Ian The Face of Darkness 76

Lloyd, Sam Picto Puzzles No. 1 17; Picto Puzzles No. 2 17; Picto Puzzles No. 3 17; Picto Puzzles No. 4 17; Picto Puzzles No. 5 17; Picto Puzzles No. 6 17; Picto Puzzles No. 7 17

Lo, Chen Shan-Ko Lien • The Shepherd Girl 65; Vermilion Door 69

Lo, Gio The Black Dragon 87

Lo, Kin The Final Test 87; Heartbeat 100 87*

Lo, Mar Bruce Lee and I 76

Lo, Ming-yau Song of China 36

Lo, Wei The Big Boss • Fists of Fury 72; The Chinese Connection 73

Lo, Wong Tai Rich and Famous 87

Loach, Kenneth Poor Cow 67; Kes 69; After a Lifetime 71; Family Life • Wednesday's Child 71; Black Jack 79; The Gamekeeper 80; Looks and Smiles 81; Fatherland • Singing the Blues in Red 86; Hidden Agenda 90

Loader, Jayne The Atomic Cafe 82*

Loan, Philip van see Van Loan, Philip

Lobato, Ebar Four-Cornered Triangle • The Passion Pit • Scream of the Butterfly 65

Lobet, Marc Home Murders • Meurtres à Domicile 82

Lo Bianco, Tony Too Scared to Scream 82

Locke, Peter You've Got to Walk It Like You Talk It or You'll Lose That Beat 68; Kitty Can't Help It 75; Carhops 80

Locke, Sondra Ratboy 86; Impulse 90

Locker, Kenneth Pleasantville 76*

Lockwood, Roy The Mutiny of the Elsinore 37; You're the Doctor 38; Disc Jockey Jamboree • Jamboree 57

Loden, Barbara Wanda 71

Lods, Jean Vingt-Quatre Heures en Trente Minutes 27; Champs-Elysées 28; La Vie d'une Fleuve 31; Ladoumègue • Le Mile avec Jules Ladoumègue 32; Histoire d'Odessa 35; Aristide Maillol, Sculpteur • Maillol 42; Aubusson • Aubusson et Jean

Lurçat 46; Hommage à Albert Einstein 55; Mallarmé 60

Loewenbein, Richard Tenderness 30

Lofton, Terry Nail Gun Massacre 87*

Lofven, Chris Twentieth Century Oz 77

Logan, Bob Up Your Alley 89; Repossessed 90

Logan, Bruce Vendetta 86

Logan, Jacqueline Strictly Business 32*

Logan, Joshua I Met My Love Again 37*; Picnic 55; Bus Stop • The Wrong Kind of Girl 56; Sayonara 57; South Pacific 57; Tall Story 59; Fanny 61; Ensign Pulver • Mr. Pulver and the Captain 64; Camelot 67; Paint Your Wagon 69

Logan, Stanley First Lady 37; Love, Honor and Behave 38; Women Are Like That 38; The Falcon's Brother 42

Logereau, Édouard Paris Secret 65

Loggia, Frank la *see LaLoggia, Frank*

Logothetis, Dimitri Pretty Smart 87; Slaughterhouse Rock 88; Champions Forever 89; The Closer 90

Logue, Charles Man and Woman 20; The Woman Who Fooled Herself 22*; The Tents of Allah 23

Lokatinsky, Faust Vasya-Reformator • Vasya the Reformer 26*; False Uniforms 32

Løkkeberg, Vibeke The Betrayal • Kamilla • Løperjenten • The Story of Kamilla 81; Hud • Skin 86

Loma, Anthony *see De la Loma, José Antonio*

Loma, J. Anthony *see De la Loma, José Antonio*

Loma, José Antonio de la *see De la Loma, José Antonio*

Lombard, Vincent Lucky Ravi 87

Lombardi, Francisco José The City and the Dogs • La Ciudad y los Perros 85; La Boca del Lobo • In the Mouth of the Wolf 88

Lombardo, Lou Russian Roulette 75; P.K. and the Kid 82

Lommel, Ulli Haytabo 70; Tenderness of the Wolves • The Tenderness of Wolves • Zärtlichkeit der Wölfe 73; Sgt. Rahn 74; Second Spring 75; Adolf and Marlene • Der Mann von Oberzalzberg — Adolf und Marlene 76; Monkey Business 77; Blank Generation 79; Cocaine Cowboys 79; The Bogey Man • The Boogeyman 80; Boogeyman II • Revenge of the Boogeyman 82*; Brainwaves 82; The Devonsville Terror 83; Double Jeopardy • Olivia • A Taste of Sin 83; Strangers in Paradise 84; Revenge of the Stolen Stars 85; Defense Play • IFO 86; Overkill 87; Cold Heat 88; The Big Sweat 89; War Birds 89; Natural Instinct 90; A Smile in the Dark 90

Łomnicki, Jan Ziemia Czeka 54; Master Nikifor • Mistrz Nikifor 56; Dom Starych Kobiet • The End of the Road 58; The Birth of a Town • Narodziny Miasta 59; Huta 59 59; Stal • Steel 59; Koncert Wawelski • Wawel Concert 60; Narodziny Statku • A Ship Is Born 61; Polish Suite • Suita Polska 62; The Dowry • Wiano 63; Ab Urbe Condita 65; Meetings with Warsaw • Spotkania z Warszawa 65; Contribu-

tion • Kontrybucja 66; The Slip-Up 72; Awards and Decorations 74; Save the City 77

Loncraine, Richard Radio Wonderful 72; Rentadick 72*; Flame 74; Full Circle • The Haunting of Julia 76; The Missionary 81; Brimstone and Treacle 82; Bellman and True 87

London, James Due Fratelli in un Posto Chiamato Trinita • Jesse and Lester — Two Brothers in a Place Called Trinity • Trinity 72

London, Jerry Shogun 81; Rent-a-Cop 87

Long, Dwight Tanga Tika 53

Long, Richard Make Like a Thief • Run Like a Thief 64*

Long, Stanley Bread 71; Naughty 71; Sex and the Other Woman 73; On the Game 74; Adventures of a Taxi Driver 76; Intimate Teenage Secrets • It Could Happen to You 76; Adventures of a Private Eye 77; Adventures of a Plumber's Mate 78; That's the Way to Do It 82

Longan, Humphrey *see Lenzi, Umberto*

Longden, John Come Into My Parlour 32

Longford, Raymond The Blue Mountain Mystery 22

Longhi, R. Carpaccio 47*; Caravaggio 48*

Longo, Francesco The Ballad of Eva • La Ballata di Eva 86

Lonskoy, Valery Mozjukhin's Field Guard • Polevaya Gvardia Mozzhukhina 87

López, Diego Crónica de Familia • A Family Chronicle 86

Lopez, John S. Sins of the Children 18; The Devil's Confession 21; Why Not Marry? 22

López del Río, José L. Casas Viejas 85

López Moctezuma, Juan Dr. Tarr's Torture Dungeon • House of Madness • La Mansión de la Locura • The Mansion of Madness • The System of Dr. Tarr and Professor Feather 72; Mary, Mary, Bloody Mary 74; Alucarda 75; To Kill a Stranger 85; Welcome Maria 87

López-Portillo, Jorge Five Bold Women 59

Lopushansky, Konstantin Letters from a Dead Man • Pisma Mertvogo Cheloveka • Pisma Myortvovo Chelovyeka 86

Lorca, Cristián Nemesio 86

Lord, Alfred A British Bulldog Conquers • The Scales of Justice 14

Lord, Del Lost at the Front 27; Topsy and Eva 27*; Barnum Was Right 29; Caught by Television • Trapped by Television 36; Vengeance • What Price Vengeance? 37; Kansas City Kitty 44; She's a Sweetheart 44; The Blonde from Brooklyn 45; Hit the Hay 45; I Love a Bandleader • Memory for Two 45; Let's Go Steady 45; Men of the Deep • Rough, Tough and Ready 45; Give and Take • Singin' in the Corn 46; High Gear • In Fast Company 46; It's Great to Be Young 46

Lord, Jean-Claude Délivrez-Nous du Mal 65; Les Colombes 72; Bingo 74;

Parlez-Nous d'Amour 77; Éclair au Chocolat • Panique 78; The Fright • Get Well Soon • Visiting Hours 81; Covergirl • Dreamworld 84; Frankenstein '88 • The Vindicator 85; Toby McTeague 85; Tadpole and the Whale 88; Eddie and the Cruisers II: Eddie Lives! 89; Mind Field 90

Lorentz, Pare The Plow That Broke the Plains 36; The River 37; The Fight for Life 40; Name, Age, Occupation 42; Nuremburg Trials • Nürnberg 46

Lorenze, Anton Back Page 34

Lorenzi, Stellio Climats 62; The Rosenbergs Must Not Die 81

Loridan, Marceline Le Dix-Septième Parallèle • Le Dix-Septième Parallèle: Le Viêt-nam en Guerre • The Seventeenth Parallel • Seventeenth Parallel: Vietnam in War 68*; La Guerre Populaire au Laos 68*; Meeting with President Ho Chi Minh • Rencontre avec le Président Ho Chi Minh 68*; The People and Their Guns • Le Peuple et Ses Fusils 68*; Comment Yukong Déplaça les Montagnes • How Yukong Moved the Mountains 76*; Les Kazaks — Minorité Nationale — Sinkiang 77*; Les Ouigours — Minorité Nationale — Sinkiang 77*; Une Histoire de Vent 88*

Loring, Thomas Z. Through Different Eyes • Thru Different Eyes 42; Who Is Hope Schuyler? 42; He Hired the Boss 43

Loriot Odipussi 88

Lorraine, Harry London's Underworld 14; Wireless 15; Big Money 18; The Further Exploits of Sexton Blake • The Further Exploits of Sexton Blake — The Mystery of the S.S. Olympic 19; The Lads of the Village 19; The Woman and Officer 26 20*

Lorre, Peter The Lost One • Der Verlorene 51

Losansky, Rolf Blumen für den Mann im Mond • Flowers for the Man in the Moon 75

Los Arcos, Luis de *see De los Arcos, Luis*

Losego, Giorgio Castighi • Punishment 86*

Losey, Joseph The Beggar Student 31*; Where Is This Girl? • Where Is This Lady? 32*; Dick Turpin 33*; No Funny Business 33*; Scandals of Paris • There Goes Susie 34*; Spring in the Air 34*; Admirals All 35; The Crouching Beast 35; The Avenging Hand 36; Ball at Savoy 36; Beloved Imposter 36; Second Bureau 36; The Face Behind the Scar • Return of a Stranger 37; Pete Roleum and His Cousins 39; A Child Went Forth 41*; Youth Gets a Break 41; Escape to Danger 43*; Hotel Reserve 44*; A Gun in His Hand 45; The Boy with Green Hair 48; The Dividing Line • The Lawless 49; M 50; The Prowler 50; The Big Night 51; Encounter • Un Homme à Détruire • Imbarco a Mezzanotte • Stranger on the Prowl 51; Pellegrini d'Amore 54; The Sleeping Tiger 54; Finger of Guilt • The Intimate Stranger 55; A Man on the Beach 55; Time Without Pity 56; X the Unknown 56*; The Gypsy and the Gentleman 57; Blind Date • Chance Meeting 59; The Concrete Jungle • The

Criminal 60; First on the Road 60; The Damned • On the Brink • These Are the Damned 61; The Devil's Woman • Eva • Eva the Devil's Woman • Eve 62; The Servant 63; Hamp • King and Country 64; Modesty Blaise 66; Accident 67; Boom! • Goforth 68; Secret Ceremony 68; Figures in a Landscape 70; The Go-Between 70; The Assassination of Trotsky • L'Assassinio di Trotsky 72; A Doll's House 73; Galileo 73; The Romantic Englishwoman 75; Mr. Klein 76; The Roads of the South • The Roads to the South • Les Routes du Sud 78; Don Giovanni 79; The Trout • La Truite 82; Steaming 84

Lotar, Eli Aubervilliers 46
Loteanu, Emil *see Lotyanu, Emil*
Lotianou, Emil *see Lotyanu, Emil*
Lotinga, R. W. The Unholy Quest 34; The Dream Doctor 36
Lotyanu, Emil The Great Hora 58; There Lived a Boy 59; Stone, Time, Song 60; Wait for Us at Dawn 63; Red Meadows 66; Frescos on the White 68; This Instant 69; Lautary 72; My White City 73; Into the Sunset 76; The Shooting Party 78; Anna Pavlova — A Woman for All Time • Pavlova — A Woman for All Time 85
Loubert, Patrick 125 Rooms of Comfort 74
Loubignac, Jean Barber of Seville 49; Ah! Les Belles Bacchantes • Femmes de Paris • Peek-a-Boo 53
Loucka, Andreas O. The Thin Line 87
Lounguine, Pavel Taxi Blues 90
Lounsbery, John The Rescuers 77*
Lourié, Eugène The Beast from 20,000 Fathoms 53; The Colossus of New York 58; Behemoth the Sea Monster • The Giant Behemoth 59*; Gorgo 59
Loventhal, Charles The First Time 83; My Demon Lover 87
Lover, Anthony The Dove 68*; Distance 75
Lovering, Otho Wanderer of the Wasteland 35; Border Flight 36; Drift Fence • Texas Desperadoes 36; The Sky Parade 36
Lovitt, Bert Prince Jack 84
Lovy, Alex Life Begins for Andy Panda 39; Wacky Quacky 47; Flora 48; Lo, the Poor Buffal 48; Short Snorts on Sports 48; Grape Nutty 49; Chilly Willy 53; Cool Cat 67; Fiesta Fiasco 67; Go Away Stowaway 67; Merlin the Magic Mouse 67; Rodent to Stardom 67; Speedy Ghost to Town 67; Big Game Hunt 68; Chimp and Zee 68; Feud with a Dude 68; Flying Circus 68; Hippydrome Tiger 68; Hocus Pocus Powwow 68; Norman Normal 68; See You Later Gladiator 68; Sky Scraper Caper 68; Three Wing Wing Ding 68
Lovy, Steven Circuitry Man 90
Low, Colin Cadet Rousselle 46*; The Adventures of Baron Münchausen 47*; Time and Terrain 47; Up, Right and Wrong 47*; Science Against Cancer 48; The Age of the Beaver 51; The Romance of Transportation in Canada 52*; Corral 54; Gold 55; Jolifou Inn 55; City of Gold 57*; It's a Crime 57*; City Out of Time 59;

Circle of the Sun 60; Universe 60*; Days of Whisky Gap 61; The Hutterites 63; Potpourri 63*; The Winds of Fogo 70
Lowe, William Slaughter in San Francisco 73
Lowell, Ogden How to Score with Girls 80
Lowenstein, Richard Strikebound 83; Dogs in Space 86; Australian Made 87
Lowenthal, John The Trials of Alger Hiss 80
Lowry, Dick Smokey and the Bandit 3 83
Lowry, Ira M. For the Freedom of the World 17*; For the Freedom of the East 18; High Pockets 19; A Misfit Earl 19; Oh, Johnny 19; The Road Called Straight 19; Sandy Burke of the U-Bar-U 19; Speedy Meade 19
Loy, Nanni Il Marito 55*; Parola di Ladro 56*; Audace Colpo dei Soliti Ignoti • Fiasco in Milan • Hold-Up à la Milanaise 59; Un Giorno da Leoni 61; La Battaglia di Napoli • The Four Days of Naples • Le Quattro Giornate di Napoli 62; À l'Italienne • Made in Italy 65; The Head of the Family • Jeux d'Adultes • Il Padre di Famiglia 67; L'Inferno del Deserto 69; Operation Snafu • Situation Normal All Fouled Up 70; Rosolino Paterno — Soldato 70; Detenuto in Attesa di Giudizio • Why? 71; Sistemo l'America È Torno 73; Basta Che Non Si Sappia in Giro! 76*; La Goduria 76*; Goodnight, Ladies and Gentlemen • Signore e Signori, Buonanotte 76*; Il Caffè È un Piacere... Se Non È Buono Che Piacere È? 78; Insieme 79; Cafe Express 80; Testa or Croce 82; Mi Manda Picone • Where's Picone? 84; Amici Miei, Atto III • Amici Miei III • My Dear Friends, Act III 85; Gioco di Società 88
Loza, Pepe Juana la Cantinera • Juana the Saloon Keeper 87
Lozano, José Luis Among the Shadows • En Penumbra 86
Lu, Jianming Cuodian Yuanyang • Love with the Perfect Stranger • Zuodian Yuanyang 86
Lu, Shing Four Moods • Hsi Nu Ai Le 70*
Luanxin, Zhang *see Zhang, Luanxin*
Luart, Yolande du *see Du Luart, Yolande*
Lubin, Arthur A Successful Failure 34; Frisco Waterfront • When We Look Back 35; Great God Gold 35; Honeymoon Limited 35; Two Black Sheep • Two Sinners 35; The House of a Thousand Candles 36; Mickey the Kid 36; Mysterious Crossing 36; Yellowstone 36; Adventure's End 37; California Straight Ahead 37; I Cover the War 37; Idol of the Crowd 37; The Beloved Brat • A Dangerous Age 38; Midnight Intruder 38; Prison Break 38; Secrets of a Nurse 38; The Big Guy 39; Big Town Czar 39; Call a Messenger 39; Risky Business 39; Black Friday 40; Buck Privates • Rookies 40; Gangs of Chicago 40; I'm Nobody's Sweetheart Now 40; Meet the Wild-

cat 40; San Francisco Docks 40; Who Killed Aunt Maggie? 40; Abbott and Costello in the Navy • In the Navy 41; Hold That Ghost • Oh, Charlie 41; Keep 'Em Flying 41; Where Did You Get That Girl? 41; Eagle Squadron 42; Ride 'Em Cowboy 42; Ali Baba and the 40 Thieves 43; Phantom of the Opera 43; White Captive • White Savage 43; Delightfully Dangerous 45; A Night in Paradise 46; The Spider Woman Strikes Back 46; New Orleans 47; Francis 49; Impact 49; Francis Goes to the Races 51; Horsie • Queen for a Day 51; Rhubarb 51; Francis Goes to West Point 52; It Grows on Trees 52; Francis Covers the Big Town 53; Pearl of the South Pacific • South Sea Woman 53; Star of India 53; Francis Joins the WACs 54; Footsteps in the Fog 55; Francis in the Navy 55; Lady Godiva • Lady Godiva of Coventry 55; The First Traveling Saleslady 56; Escapade in Japan 57; Il Ladro di Bagdad • The Thief of Bagdad • Le Voleur de Bagdad 60; Henry Limpet • The Incredible Mr. Limpet • Mr. Limpet 63; Hold On! • There's No Place by Space 65; The Sword of Ali Baba 65*; Rain for a Dusty Summer 71
Lubinsky, I. Chuk and Gek 53
Lubitsch, Ernst Auf Eis Geführt • A Trip on the Ice 14; Blind Man's Buff • Blinde Kuh 14; Fräulein Seifenschaum • Miss Soapsuds 14; Meyer Als Soldat 14; Der Erste Patient • Sein Einziger Patient 15; Der Kraftmeier 15; Der Letzte Anzug 15; Leutnant auf Befehl • Lieutenant by Command 15; Sugar and Spice • Zucker und Zimt 15*; Als Ich Tot War • When I Was Dead 16; Black Moritz • Schwarze Moritz 16; Der G.m.b.H. Tenor • Tenor, Inc. 16; Der Gemischte Frauenchor • The Mixed Ladies Chorus 16; Käsekönig Holländer 16; Die Neue Nase • Seine Neue Nase 16; Das Schönste Geschenk 16; Schuh-Salon Pinkus • Schuhpalast Pinkus • Shoe Salon Pinkus • Shoestore Pinkus 16; Where Is My Treasure? • Wo Ist Mein Schatz? 16; The Blouse King • Der Blusenkönig 17; Ein Fideles Gefängnis • A Merry Jail 17; Ossi's Diary • Ossis Tagebuch 17; Prinz Sami 17; Wenn Vier Dasselbe Machen • Wenn Vier Dasselbe Tun • When Four Do the Same 17; Die Augen der Mumie Mâ • The Eyes of the Mummy • The Eyes of the Mummy Ma 18; The Ballet Girl • Das Mädel vom Ballett 18; Carmen • Gypsy Blood 18; Der Fall Rosentopf • The Rosentopf Case 18; Führmann Henschel 18; I Don't Want to Be a Man • Ich Möchte Kein Mann Sein 18; Marionetten 18; Meier aus Berlin • Meyer from Berlin 18; Meine Frau, die Filmschauspielerin • My Wife, the Film Star 18; Der Rodelkavalier • The Toboggan Cavalier 18; Vendetta 18; Die Austernprinzessin • The Oyster Princess 19; The Doll • Die Puppe 19; The Girl from Swabia • The Schwab Maiden • Das Schwabenmädel 19; Intoxication • Rausch 19; Der Lustige Ehemann • The Merry Husband 19; Madame DuBarry • Passion

19; Anna Boleyn • Anne Boleyn • Deception 20; His Two Daughters • Kohlhiesel's Daughters • Kohlhiesels Töchter 20; One Arabian Night • Sumurun 20; Romeo and Juliet in the Snow • Romeo und Julia im Schnee • Romeo und Juliet im Schnee 20; Die Bergkatze • The Mountain Cat • The Wildcat 21; The Loves of Pharaoh • Das Weib des Pharao • The Wife of Pharaoh • The Wife of the Pharaoh 21; Die Flamme • Montmartre 22; Rosita 23; Forbidden Paradise 24; The Marriage Circle 24; Three Women 24; Kiss Me Again 25; Lady Windermere's Fan 25; So This Is Paris 26; In Old Heidelberg • Old Heidelberg • The Student Prince • The Student Prince in Old Heidelberg 27; The Patriot 28; Eternal Love 29; The Love Parade • Parade d' Amour 29; Monte Carlo 30; Paramount on Parade 30*; Broken Lullaby • The Man I Killed 31; The Smiling Lieutenant 31; If I Had a Million 32*; One Hour with You 32*; Trouble in Paradise 32; Design for Living 33; The Lady Dances • The Merry Widow 34; Angel 37; Bluebeard's Eighth Wife 38; Ninotchka 39; The Shop Around the Corner 39; That Uncertain Feeling 41; To Be or Not to Be 42; Heaven Can Wait 43; Czarina • A Royal Scandal 45*; Cluny Brown 46; That Lady in Ermine 48*

Luby, S. Roy Arizona Badman 35; Lightning Triggers 35; Outlaw Rule 35; Range Warfare 35; The Crooked Trail • Lead Law 36; Desert Phantom 36; Rogue of the Range 36; Border Phantom 37; The Red Rope 37; Tough to Handle 37; The Range Busters 40; Trailin' Double Trouble • Trailing Double Trouble 40; Triple Threat • West of Pinto Basin 40; Bullets and Bullion • Underground Rustlers 41; Fugitive Valley 41*; The Kid's Last Ride 41; Saddle Mountain Roundup 41; Tonto Basin Outlaws 41; Trail of the Silver Spurs 41; Tumbledown Ranch in Arizona 41; Wrangler's Roost 41; Arizona Stagecoach 42; Boot Hill Bandits 42; Pride of the Army • Unsung Heroes • War Dogs 42; Rock River Renegades 42; Texas Trouble Shooters 42; Thunder River Feud 42; Black Market Rustlers • Land and the Law 43; Cowboy Commandos 43; Land of Hunted Men 43

Luca, Paul de see De Luca, Paul
Luca, Rudy de see De Luca, Rudy
Lucas, F. R. The Woodpigeon Patrol 30*
Lucas, George Electronic Labyrinth: THX-1138: 4 EB • THX-1138: 4 EB 65; Freiheit 65; Look at Life 65; Herbie Anyone Lived in a Pretty Hometown 66; 1:42:08: A Man and His Car 66; The Emperor 67; 6-18-67 67; Filmmaker 68; THX-1138 70; American Graffiti 73; Star Wars 77

Lucas, Hans see Godard, Jean-Luc
Lucas, Wilfred A Sailor's Heart 12; The Horse Thief 13; The Rogues' Gallery 13; The Desert's Sting 14; A Glimpse of Los Angeles 14; Trey of Hearts 14*; The Spanish Jade 15; Hands Up! 17*; Jim Bludso

17*; A Love Sublime 17*; Morgan's Raiders 18*; The Red Red Heart 18; The Return of Mary 18; Romance of Tarzan 18; The Testing of Mildred Vane 18; The Girl from Nowhere 19*; The Better Man 21; The Fighting Breed 21; The Shadow of Lightning Ridge 21; Her Sacrifice 26

Lucenay, A. Martin de see De Lucenay, A. Martin
Lucente, Francesco The Virgin Queen of St. Francis High 87
Luchetti, Daniele Domani Accadra 88
Lucia, Luis King of the Vikings 60
Lucidi, Maurizio Due Once di Piombo 66; Mio Nome È Pecos • My Name Is Pecos 66; The Greatest Kidnapping in the West • La Più Grande Rapina del West 67; Pecos Cleans Up • Pecos e Qui: Prega e Muori 67; The Big and the Bad • It Can Be Done, Amigo • Si Può Fare…Amigo 71; Last Chance for a Born Loser • Stateline Motel 75; Street People 76; Il Lupo di Mare • The Sea Dog 87
Lucio, Paco Teo el Pelirrojo • Teo the Redhead 86
Lucoque, H. Lisle Fairyland 16; She 16*; Tatterly 16; Dawn 17; Castles in Spain 20; Lorna Doone 20; Where the Rainbow Ends 21
Lucot, M. Melbourne Rendezvous 57
Lucot, René Artères de France 39*
Luddy, Edward I. The Man Who Waited 22; Jake the Plumber 27; So It's Sunday 32
Ludman, Larry see De Angelis, Fabrizio
Ludwig, Edward Steady Company 32; They Just Had to Get Married 33; The Friends of Mr. Sweeney 34; Let's Be Ritzy • Millionaire for a Day 34; The Man Who Reclaimed His Head 34; A Woman's Man 34; Age of Indiscretion 35; The Baxter Millions • Three Kids and a Queen 35; Old Man Rhythm 35; Adventure in Manhattan • Manhattan Madness 36; Fatal Lady 36; Her Husband Lies 37; The Last Gangster 37; That Certain Age 38; Coast Guard 39; Swiss Family Robinson 40; Born to Sing 41; The Man Who Lost Himself 41; Bomber's Moon 43*; They Came to Blow Up America 43; The Fighting Seabees 44*; Three Is a Family 44; The Fabulous Texan 47; Wake of the Red Witch 48; The Big Wheel 49; Smuggler's Island 51; Big Jim McLain 52; The Blazing Forest 52; Caribbean • Caribbean Gold 52; Jivaro • Lost Treasure of the Amazon 53; Sangaree 53; The Vanquished 53; Flame of the Islands 55; The Black Scorpion 57; The Gun Hawk 63
Lue, Eugene de see De Lue, Eugene
Luetzelburg, Helmer von see Lützelburg, Helmer von
Luise, Dom de see DeLuise, Dom
Luitz-Morat Les Cinq Gentlemen Maudits 19; Monsieur Lebureau 20; Petit Ange 20; La Terre du Diable 21; Au Seuil du Harem 22; La Cité Foudroyée 22; Le Sang d'Allah 22; Petit Ange et Son Pantin 23; La Course au Flambeau 25; Le Juif Errant 26; La Ronde Infernale 27; La Vierge Folle

29
Lukashevich, Tatiana Bride with a Dowry 54*; Problem Child 55; Slepoy Muzikant • The Sound of Life 62
Łukaszewicz, Jerzy The Friend of a Jolly Devil • Przyjaciel Wesołego Diabła 87
Lukov, Leonid The October Drive 31; Convoy 33; Youth 35; I Love • Ya Lyublyu 36; Bolshaya Zhizn I • A Great Life, Part One 40; Alexander Parkhomenko 42; Two Soldiers 43; It Happened in Donbas 45; A Great Life, Part Two 46; Miners of the Don 51; The Mistress • Vassa Zheleznova 53; It Mustn't Be Forgotten • Lest We Forget 54; Toward New Shores 55; Oleko Dundich 58; Two Lives 61
Lumet, Sidney 12 Angry Men 56; Stage Struck 58; The Fugitive Kind 59; That Kind of Woman 59; A View from the Bridge • Vu du Pont 61; Long Day's Journey Into Night 62; Fail Safe 63; The Pawnbroker 64; The Group 65; The Hill 65; The Deadly Affair 66; Bye Bye Braverman 67; The Sea Gull 68; The Appointment 69; Blood Kin • Last of the Mobile Hot-Shots 69; King: A Filmed Record, Montgomery to Memphis 69*; The Anderson Tapes 71; Child's Play 72; Lovin' Molly • The Wild and the Sweet 73; The Offence • The Offense • Something Like the Truth 73; Serpico 73; Murder on the Orient Express 74; Dog Day Afternoon 75; Network 76; Equus 77; The Wiz 78; Just Tell Me What You Want 79; Prince of the City 81; Deathtrap 82; The Verdict 82; Daniel 83; Garbo Talks 84; The Morning After 86; Power 86; Running on Empty 88; Family Business 89; Q&A 90
Lumière, Auguste Charcuterie Mécanique • The Mechanical Butcher 1895*
Lumière, Louis Aquarium 1895; Arrival of a Train at La Ciotat • Arrivée d'un Train à La Ciotat • Arrivée d'un Train en Gare de La Ciotat 1895; L'Arroseur Arrosé • The Gardener • Le Jardinier • The Sprinkled • Watering the Gardner 1895; Assiettes Tournantes • Spinning Plates 1895; Ateliers de La Ciotat • Workshops at La Ciotat 1895; Backgammon Game • Partie de Tric-Trac 1895; Baignade en Mer • Bathing in the Sea 1895; Barque Sortant du Port • Boat Leaving the Harbor • La Sortie du Port 1895; Blacksmiths • Forgerons 1895; The Blanket Game • Brimade dans une Caserne • Hazing in the Barracks • Saut à la Couverture 1895; Bocal aux Poissons Rouges • Goldfish Bowl 1895; The Card Party • Partie d'Écarté 1895; The Cat's Lunch • Le Déjeuner du Chat 1895; Chapeaux à Transformations • Transformations with Hats • Trewey: Under the Hat 1895; Charcuterie Mécanique • The Mechanical Butcher 1895*; Children's Games • Enfants aux Jouets 1895; Children's Quarrel • Querelle Enfantine 1895; Conversation Between M. Janssen and M. Lagrange • Discussion de M. Janssen et de M. Lagrange 1895; Course en Sac • Sack Race 1895; Débarquement des Congressistes à Neuville-sur-Saône • Landing of

Passion 34*; Once in a Blue Moon 34*; The Scoundrel 35*; Soak the Rich 36*; Until I Die 40*

MacBean, L. C. The Angels of Mons 15*; Answer the Call 15; Deadwood Dick and the Mormons 15*; Deadwood Dick Spoils Brigham Young 15*; Deadwood Dick's Detective Pard 15*; Deadwood Dick's Red Ally 15*; Deadwood Dick's Vengeance 15*; The Dop Doctor • The Love Trail 15*; The Face at the Telephone 15*; How Richard Harris Became Known As Deadwood Dick 15*; Infelice 15*; The Ways of the World 15; Eve's Daughter • Love 16; The Real Thing at Last 16; Trapped by the London Sharks 16; Bladys of the Stewpony 19; Forgive Us Our Trespasses 19; The Dawn of Truth 20

McBrearty, Don American Nightmare 81

McBride, Jim David Holzman's Diary 67; My Girlfriend's Wedding 68; Glen and Randa 71; A Hard Day for Archie • Hot Times • My Erotic Fantasies 73; Breathless 83; The Big Easy 86; Great Balls of Fire! 89

Macc, Jerzy Heisser Sand auf Sylt • Just to Be Loved • The New Life Style 70*

McCabe, Gene Follow Me 69

McCabe, Norm The Timid Toreador 40*; Porky's Snooze Reel 41*; Robinson Crusoe, Jr. 41; Confusions of a Nutsy Spy 42; The Daffy Duckaroo 42; Daffy's Southern Exposure 42; The Ducktators 42; Gopher Goofy 42; Hobby Horse Laffs 42; The Impatient Patient 42; Who's Who in the Zoo 42; Hop and Go 43; Tokyo Jokio 43

McCahon, Robert Running Wild 73; Deliver Us from Evil 75

Mac Caig, Arthur see Caig, Arthur Mac

McCallum, John The Nickel Queen 71

McCann, Charles Hansu Kurishitan Anderusan no Sekai • The World of Hans Christian Anderson 68*

McCarey, Leo Society Secrets 21; Accidental Accidents 24; All Wet 24; Bungalow Boobs 24; Jeffries, Jr. 24; Outdoor Pajamas 24; The Poor Fish 24; Publicity Pays 24; The Royal Razz 24; Seeing Nellie Home 24; Sittin' Pretty 24; Stolen Goods 24; Sweet Daddy 24; A Ten Minutes Egg 24; Too Many Mamas 24; Why Husbands Go Mad 24; Why Men Work 24; Young Oldfield 24; Bad Boy 25; Big Red Riding Hood 25; The Caretaker's Daughter 25; The Family Entrance 25; Fighting Fluid 25; Hard Boiled 25; Hello Baby 25; His Wooden Wedding 25; Innocent Husbands 25; Is Marriage the Bunk? 25; Isn't Life Terrible? 25; Looking for Sally 25; No Father to Guide Him 25; Plain and Fancy Girls 25; Should Husbands Be Watched? 25; The Uneasy Three 25; What Price Goofy? 25; Be Your Age 26; Bromo and Juliet 26; Charley My Boy 26; Crazy Like a Fox 26; Dog Shy 26; Long Live the King 26; Mama Behave 26; Mighty Like a Moose 26; Mum's the Word 26; Tell 'Em Nothing 26; Eve's Love Letters 27; We Faw Down • We Slip Up 27; Blow by Blow 28*; The Boy Friend 28; Came the Dawn 28; Do

Gentlemen Snore? 28; Dumb Daddies 28; The Family Group 28*; The Fight Pest 28*; The Finishing Touch 28*; Going Ga-Ga 28; Limousine Love 28*; A Pair of Tights 28; Pass the Gravy 28; Should Married Men Go Home? 28*; Should Women Drive? 28; Tell It to the Judge 28; That Night 28; Two Tars 28*; Dad's Day 29; Freed 'Em and Weep 29; Hurdy Gurdy 29; Liberty 29; Madame Q 29; Red Hot Rhythm 29; Sky Boy 29; The Sophomore 29; The Unkissed Man 29; When Money Comes 29; Why Is Plumber 29; Wrong Again 29; Let's Go Native 30; Part Time Wife • The Shepper-Newfounder 30; Wild Company 30; Indiscreet 31; The Kid from Spain 32; Duck Soup 33; Belle of the Nineties • It Ain't No Sin 34; Ruggles of Red Gap 34; Six of a Kind 34; The Milky Way 35; The Awful Truth 37; Make Way for Tomorrow • When the Wind Blows • The Years Are So Long 37; Love Affair 38; My Favorite Wife 40*; Once Upon a Honeymoon 42; Going My Way 44; The Bells of St. Mary's 45; Good Sam 47; My Son John 51; You Can Change the World 51; An Affair to Remember 56; Rally 'Round the Flag, Boys! 58; China Story • The Devil Never Sleeps • Flight from Terror • Satan Never Sleeps 61

McCarey, Ray Pack Up Your Troubles 32*; Scram! 32; Girl o' My Dreams • Love Race 34; Hot Tip 35*; Millions in the Air 35; The Mystery Man 35; Sunset Range 35; Three Cheers for Love 36; Let's Make a Million 37; Life Begins with Love 37; Love in a Bungalow 37; Oh Doctor! 37; The Devil's Party 38; Goodbye Broadway 38; Outside These Walls 39; Torchy Blane Runs for Mayor • Torchy Runs for Mayor 39; Little Orvie 40; Millionaires in Prison 40; You Can't Fool Your Wife 40; Accent on Love 41; Cadet Girl 41; The Cowboy and the Blonde 41; Murder Among Friends 41; The Perfect Snob 41; A Gentleman at Heart 42; It Happened in Flatbush 42; That Other Woman 42; So This Is Washington 43; Atlantic City 44; Passport to Adventure • Passport to Destiny 44; The Falcon's Alibi 46; Strange Alibi • Strange Triangle 46; The Gay Intruders 48

Maccari, Ruggero Goodnight, Ladies and Gentlemen • Signore e Signori, Buonanotte 76*

McCarthy, Henry Blazing Arrows 22; Silver Spurs 22; Trapped in the Air 22; The Night Ship 25; The Part-Time Wife 25; Shattered Lives 25; Silent Pal 25; Flashing Fangs 26; The Lodge in the Wilderness 26; The Phantom of the Forest 26

McCarthy, John K. Handle with Care 64; Pardon My Brush 64

McCarthy, John P. Out of the Dust 20; Shadows of Conscience 21; Brand of Cowardice 25; Pals 25; The Border Whirlwind 26; Vanishing Hoofs 26; Becky 27; The Devil's Masterpiece 27; His Foreign Wife 27; The Lovelorn 27; Diamond Handcuffs 28; The Eternal Woman 29; Headin'

North 30; The Land of Missing Men • Land of the Missing Men 30; Oklahoma Cyclone 30; At the Ridge 31; Cavalier of the West 31; God's Country • God's Country and the Man • Rose of the Rio Grande 31; The Greater Love • Rider of the Plains 31; Mother and Son 31; The Nevada Buckaroo 31; The Ridin' Fool 31; Ships of Hate 31; Sunrise Trail 31; The Fighting Champ 32; The Forty-Niners 32; Lucky Larrigan 32; The Man from New Mexico 32; The Western Code 32; Crashing Broadway 33; The Return of Casey Jones • Train 2419 33; Trailin' North • Trailing North 33; Border Patrol • Lawless Border 35; Law of the 45s 35; The Lion Man 36; The Old Corral • Song of the Gringo 36; Marked Trails 44; Raiders of the Border 44; The Cisco Kid Comes Through • The Cisco Kid Returns 45

McCarthy, Matt The Zoo Robbery 73*; Robin Hood Junior 75*; The Unbroken Arrow 76*

McCarthy, Michael Assassin for Hire 51; Mystery Junction 51; Crow Hollow 52; John of the Fair 52; Shadow of a Man 55; It's Never Too Late 56; The Accursed • The Traitor 57; Operation Amsterdam 59

McCarthy, Pat T. Dan Smith 87*

McCarthy, Peter Space Rage • Trackers 85*

McCarty, Henry see McCarthy, Henry

McCarty, Robert The Light Fantastic 62; I Could Never Have Sex with Any Man Who Has So Little Respect for My Husband 73; Foreplay 74*

McCauley, John Rattlers 76

McCay, Robert The Flying House • Watch Your House 20*

McCay, Winsor Little Nemo • Winsor McCay • Winsor McCay and His Animated Comics • Winsor McCay Explains His Moving Cartoons to John Bunny • Winsor McCay Makes His Cartoons Move 09*; How a Mosquito Operates • The Hungry Mosquito • The Story of a Mosquito • Winsor McCay and His Jersey Skeeters 12; Gertie • Gertie the Dinosaur • Gertie the Dinosaurus • Gertie the Trained Dinosaur 14; Bug Vaudeville 16; The Last Word • The Pet 16; Gertie on Tour 17; The Sinking of the Lusitania 18; The Flying House • Watch Your House 20*; The Centaurs 21; Flip's Circus 21

Macchi, Giulio see Sherman, Vincent

McClatchy, Gregory Vampire at Midnight 88

McClintic, Guthrie On Your Back 30; Once a Lady 31; Once a Sinner 31

McClory, Kevin The Boy and the Bridge 59

McCloskey, Justin H. Flapper Wives 24*; Anything Once 25

McClung, Hugh Just Like a Woman 23*

McConnell, Edward Songs of Scotland 66*

McConnell, Guy W. The Penny Philanthropist 17

McCord, Vera The Good-Bad Wife 21

McCormick, F. J. Fun at a Finglas Fair 16

McCormick, Merrill *see McCormick, William Merrill*

McCormick, William Merrill Good Men and Bad 23; A Son of the Desert 28

McCowan, George Affair with a Killer 65; Frogs 72; The Magnificent Seven Ride! 72; Winter Comes Early 72; The Inbreaker 74; Shadow of the Hawk 76; H. G. Wells' The Shape of Things to Come • The Shape of Things to Come 79

McCowen, Tom The Case of the 44's 64

McCoy, Denys The Last Rebel 71

McCoy, Steve The Bloody Sect • Secta Siniestra 82

McCracken, Harold Heart of Alaska 24

McCrann, Chuck Bloodeaters • Forest of Fear • Toxic Zombies 79

McCreadie, Tom Always Another Dawn 48; Into the Straight 50

McCullough, Jim The Charge of the Model T's 79; The Aurora Encounter 85; Mountaintop Motel Massacre 85

McCullough, Philo Maid of the West 21*

McCune, Hank Wetbacks 56

McCutcheon, John L. Man and Wife 23; The Law and the Lady 24

McCutcheon, Wallace The X-Ray Mirror 1899; The Lost Child 04; The Moonshiner 04; Personal 04; The Widow and the Only Man 04; Looking for John Smith • Si Jones Looking for John Smith 06; Dr. Skinum 07; The Love Microbe 07; At the French Ball 08; Bobby's Kodak 08; The Boy Detective 08; Caught by Wireless 08; Classmates 08; Energizer 08; Her First Adventure 08; The Invisible Fluid 08; The Snowman 08; The Stage Rustler 08; When Knights Were Bold 08

McDermott, John Dinty 20*; Patsy 21; Mary of the Movies 23; The Spider and the Rose 23; Her Temporary Husband 24; Manhattan Madness 25; Where the Worst Begins 25; The Love Thief 26

McDonagh, John Blarney 17; The Byeways of Fate 17; The Irish Girl 17; The Upstart 17; A Girl of Glenbeigh 18; Willy Reilly and His Colleen Bawn 18; Paying the Rent 20; Casey's Millions 22; Cruiskeen Lawn 22

MacDonagh, Paulette Two Minutes' Silence 34

MacDonald, Alexander The Unsleeping Eye 28*; The Kingdom of Twilight 29

MacDonald, David Double Alibi 36; Death Croons the Blues 37; It's Never Too Late to Mend 37; The Last Curtain 37; Remember When • Riding High 37; When the Poppies Bloom Again 37; Dead Men Tell No Tales 38; Make It Three 38; Meet Mr. Penny 38; A Spot of Bother 38; This Man Is News 38; The Midas Touch 39; Shadows of the Underworld • This Man in Paris 39; Spies in the Air • Spies of the Air 39; Law and Disorder 40; Lofoten 40; Men of the Lightship 40; Our Heritage • This England 40; The Brothers 47; Good Time Girl 48; Snowbound 48; The Bad Lord Byron 49; Christopher Colombus 49; Diamond City 49; The Adventurers • Fortune

in Diamonds • The Great Adventure 50; Cairo Road 50; The Big Frame • The Lost Hours 52; Tread Softly 52; Operation Malaya 53; Devil Girl from Mars 54; Three-Cornered Fate 54; The Yellow Robe 54; Alias John Preston 55; The Final Column 55; One Just Man 55; Small Hotel 57; A Lady Mislaid 58; The Moonraker 58; Petticoat Pirates 61; The Golden Rabbit 62

MacDonald, Donald The Abandonment 16; April 16; True Nobility 16; The White Rosette 16

McDonald, Frank Broadway Hostess 35; The Murder of Dr. Harrigan 35; All One Night • Love Begins at Twenty 36; Boulder Dam 36; Isle of Fury • Three in Eden 36; Murder by an Aristocrat 36; Smart Blonde 36; Treachery Rides the Range 36; The Adventures of Torchy Blane • Fly-Away Baby 37; The Adventurous Blonde • Torchy Blane the Adventurous Blonde 37; Dance, Charlie, Dance 37; Her Husband's Secretary 37; Midnight Court 37; Blondes at Work 38; Flirting with Fate 38; Freshman Year 38; Over the Wall 38; Reckless Living 38; Death Goes North 39; First Offenders 39; Jeepers Creepers • Money Isn't Everything 39; They Asked for It 39; Barnyard Follies 40; Carolina Moon 40; Gaucho Serenade 40; Grand Ole Opry 40; In Old Missouri 40; Rancho Grande 40; Ride, Tenderfoot, Ride 40; Village Barn Dance 40; Arkansas Judge 41; Country Fair 41; Flying Blind 41; The Gang Made Good • Tuxedo Junction 41; No Hands on the Clock 41; Under Fiesta Stars 41; Mountain Rhythm 42; The Old Homestead 42; Shepherd of the Ozarks • Susanna 42; The Traitor Within 42; Wildcat 42; Wrecking Crew 42; Alaska Highway 43; High Explosive 43; Hoosier Holiday 43; O My Darling Clementine • Oh My Darling Clementine 43; Submarine Alert 43; Swing Your Partner 43; Timber Queen 43; Gambler's Choice 44; Lights of Old Santa Fe 44; One Body Too Many 44; Sing, Neighbor, Sing 44; Take It Big 44; Along the Navajo Trail 45; Bells of Rosarita 45; The Chicago Kid 45; The Man from Oklahoma 45; Scared Stiff • Treasure of Fear 45; Sunset in El Dorado 45; Tell It to a Star 45; My Pal Trigger 46; Rainbow Over Texas 46; Sioux City Sue 46; Song of Arizona 46; Under Nevada Skies 46; Bulldog Drummond Strikes Back 47; Hit Parade of 1947 47; Linda Be Good 47; Twilight on the Rio Grande 47; When a Girl's Beautiful 47; French Leave • Kilroy on Deck 48; Gun Smugglers 48; Mr. Reckless 48; Thirteen Lead Soldiers 48; Apache Chief 49; The Big Sombrero 49; Ringside 49; Call of the Klondike 50; Snow Dog 50; Father Takes the Air 51; Northwest Territory 51; Sierra Passage 51; Texans Never Cry 51; Yellow Fin 51; Yukon Manhunt 51; The Ghost of Crossbones Canyon 52; Sea Tiger 52; The Yellow-Haired Kid 52; Yukon Gold 52; Secret of Outlaw Flats 53; Six-Gun Decision 53; Son of Belle Starr 53; Marshals in Disguise 54;

Outlaw's Son 54; Thunder Pass 54; Trouble on the Trail 54; The Big Tip Off 55; Treasure of Ruby Hills 55; The Purple Gang 60; Raymie 60; The Underwater City 62; The Great Gunfighter • Gunfight at Comanche Creek 63; Mara of the Wilderness • Valley of the White Wolves 65

MacDonald, J. Farrell And She Never Knew 14; His Majesty the Scarecrow of Oz • The New Wizard of Oz 14; The Patchwork Girl of Oz 14; The Tides of Sorrow 14; Droppington's Family Tree 15; Hash House Mashers 15; Lonesome Luke 15; Lorna Doone 15

McDonald, J. K. Flaming Love 25

MacDonald, Jack Do the Dead Talk? 20

MacDonald, Norman The Great Gay Road 20; Christie Johnstone 21

MacDonald, Peter Rambo: First Blood, Part Three • Rambo III 88

MacDonald, Sherwood Bab the Fixer 17; Betty Be Good 17; A Bit of Kindling • Sticks 17; The Checkmate 17; Sold at Auction 17; Sunny Jane 17; The Wildcat 17; Little Miss Grown-Up 18; Miss Mischief Maker 18; No Children Wanted 18

McDonald, Tom Love Comes to Magoo 58; Bwana Magoo 59

MacDonald, Wallace Girl from the West 23; Free Lips 28; Gunmen from Laredo 59

McDonnell, Fergus Hideout • The Small Voice 48; Prelude to Fame 50; Private Information 52

McDonough, Joseph A. Pirates of the Skies 39

McDougall, Donald Hot Cars 56

MacDougall, Kenneth The Bulldogs of the Trail 15

MacDougall, Ranald Queen Bee 55; Man on Fire 57; The World, the Flesh and the Devil 58; Go Naked in the World 60; The Subterraneans 60

McDowall, Roddy The Ballad of Tam-Lin • The Devil's Widow • The Devil's Woman • Tam-Lin 70

McDowell, J. B. A Breach of Promise Case 08; The Cheekiest Man on Earth 08; Baby's Revenge 09; Domestic Rivals 09; The Life of Shakespeare • Loves and Adventures in the Life of Shakespeare 14*

Mace, Fred Without Hope 14

Mace, Nicole The Guardians 78

McElwee, Ross Sherman's March 86

McEndree, Maurice Self-Portrait 73*

McEveety, Bernard The Broken Sabre 65; Night of the Tiger • Ride Beyond Vengeance 66; The Brotherhood of Satan 70; Napoleon and Samantha 72; One Little Indian 73; The Bears and I 74

McEveety, Bernard F. Back to Liberty 27; The Broadway Drifter 27; His Rise to Fame 27; The Winning Oar 27; Inspiration 28; The Stronger Will 28; The Clean-Up 29; Montmartre Rose 29*

McEveety, Vincent Firecreek 68; The Road West • This Savage Land 68; $1,000,000 Duck 71; The Biscuit Eater 72; Charley and the Angel 72; Menace on the Mountain 72; Superdad 72; The Castaway

Cowboy 74; The Strongest Man in the World 75; Gus 76; Herbie Goes to Monte Carlo 76; Treasure of Matecumbe 76; The Apple Dumpling Gang Rides Again 79; Herbie Goes Bananas 80; The Watcher in the Woods 80*; Amy 81

McEvoy, Charles The Man in the Shadows 15

McEvoy, Earl Cargo to Capetown 50; Frightened City • The Killer That Stalked New York 50; The Barefoot Mailman 51

MacFadden, Bernard Zongar 18

MacFadden, Hamilton Are You There? • Exit Laughing 30; Crazy That Way 30*; Harmony at Home • She Steps Out 30; Oh for a Man! 30; The Black Camel 31; Charlie Chan Carries On 31; Riders of the Purple Sage 31; Their Mad Moment 31*; Cheaters at Play 32; The Fourth Horseman 32; As Husbands Go 33; Charlie Chan's Greatest Case 33; The Illegal Divorce • Second Hand Wife 33; The Man Who Dared 33; Trick for Trick 33; Elinor Norton 34; Hold That Girl 34; She Was a Lady 34; Stand Up and Cheer 34; Fighting Youth 35; Three Crazy Legionnaires • Three Legionnaires 36; Escape by Night 37; It Can't Last Forever 37; The Legion of Missing Men 37; Sea Racketeers 37; Inside the Law 42

MacFarland, Mike Goodbye Franklin High 78; Motel • Pink Motel 83

McGaha, William Speed Lovers 68; J.C. 72

McGann, William On the Border 30; I Like Your Nerve 31; Her Night Out 32; Illegal 32; Impromptu 32; Little Fella 32; Murder on the Second Floor 32; On the Air 32; The Silver Greyhound 32; A Voice Said Goodnight 32; Long Live the King 33; La Buenaventura 34; Man of Iron 35; Maybe It's Love 35; A Night at the Ritz 35; Brides Are Like That 36; The Case of Mrs. Pembrook • One Fatal Hour • Two Against the World 36; The Case of the Black Cat 36; Fish 36; Freshman Love • Rhythm on the River 36; His Best Man • Times Square Playboy 36; Hot Money 36*; Polo Joe 36; Alcatraz Island 37; Marry the Girl 37; Penrod and Sam 37; Sh! The Octopus 37; Girls on Probation 38*; Penrod and His Twin Brother 38; When Were You Born? 38; Blackwell's Island 39; Everybody's Hobby 39; Pride of the Blue Grass 39; Sweepstakes Winner 39; Dr. Christian Meets the Women 40; Wolf of New York 40; Highway West 41; The Parson of Panamint 41; The Shot in the Dark 41; We Go Fast 41; American Empire • My Son Alone 42; In Old California 42; Tombstone • Tombstone (The Town Too Tough to Die) 42; Frontier Bad Men 43*

McGaugh, Wilbur F. Whistling Jim 25; Oıcer Jim 26; Three Pals 26; The New Adventures of Tarzan • Tarzan and the Green Goddess • Tarzan's New Adventure 35*

McGavin, Darren Happy Mother's Day …Love George • Run, Stranger, Run 73

McGee, Mark Thomas Equinox 69*

McGill, Lawrence Arizona 13; The Greyhound 14; How Molly Made Good • How Molly Malone Made Good 15; The Sealed Valley 15; The Woman's Law 16; The Angel Factory 17; Crime and Punishment 17; The First Law 18; The Girl from Bohemia 18

McGillivray, Maxine Montreal Main 74*

MacGillivray, William D. Life Classes 87

McGlynn, Don Art Pepper: Notes from a Jazz Survivor 82; Jazz Profiles: Joe Williams 85; The Mills Brothers Story 86; The Soundies 86; The Spike Jones Story 88; TV's First Music Videos 88

McGlynn, Frank Faith and Fortune 15; The Truth About Helen 15

McGoohan, Al Don't Open Till Christmas 83*

McGoohan, Patrick Catch My Soul • Santa Fe Satan • To Catch a Spy 74

McGowan, Dorrell The Showdown 50*; Tokyo File 212 51*; Snowfire 58*; The Bashful Elephant 62*

McGowan, John P. The Operator at Black Rock 14; The Hazards of Helen 15*; The Diamond Runners 16; The Girl and the Game 16; Judith of the Cumberlands 16; Lass of the Lumberlands 16*; The Man from Medicine Hat • The Manager of the B & A 16; Medicine Bend 16; Whispering Smith 16; The Lost Express 17; The Railroad Raiders 17; Lure of the Circus 18; The Red Glove 19; Elmo the Fearless 20; King of the Circus 20; The Vanishing Dagger 20*; Below the Dead Line 21; Discontented Wives 21; Do or Die 21; The Moonshine Menace 21; The Ruse of the Rattler 21; Tiger True 21; Captain Kidd 22; Hills of Missing Men 22; Reckless Chances 22; One Million in Jewels 23; Stormy Seas 23; Baßed 24; Calibre 45 24; Courage 24; Crossed Trails 24; A Desperate Adventure 24; A Two Fisted Tenderfoot 24; Western Vengeance 24; The Whipping Boss 24; Barriers of the Law 25; Blood and Steel 25; Border Intrigue 25; Cold Nerve 25; Duped 25; The Fighting Sheriff 25; The Gambling Fool 25; Outwitted 25; Peggy of the Secret Service 25; The Train Wreckers 25; Webs of Steel 25; The Ace of Clubs 26; Buried Gold 26; Crossed Signals 26; Cyclone Bob 26; Desperate Chance 26; Fighting Luck 26; Iron Fist 26; The Lost Express 26; The Lost Trail 26; Mistaken Orders 26; The Open Switch 26; Peril of the Rail 26; Red Blood 26; Riding for Life 26; Riding Romance 26; Road Agent 26; Silver Fingers 26; Tarzan and the Golden Lion 26; Unseen Enemies 26; Aflame in the Sky 27; The Lost Limited 27; The Outlaw Dog 27; Red Signals 27; Thunderbolt's Tracks 27; When a Dog Loves 27; Arizona Days 28; The Chinatown Mystery 28; Devil's Tower 28; Law of the Mounted 28; Lightnin' Shot 28; Manhattan Cowboy 28; Mystery Valley 28; On the Divide 28; Painted Trail 28; Silent Trail 28; Texas Tommy 28; Trail Riders 28; Trailin' Back 28; West of Santa Fe 28; Bad Man's Money • Bad Men's Money 29; Below the Deadline 29; Captain Cowboy 29; Code of the West 29;

The Cowboy and the Outlaw 29; The Fighting Terror 29; Headin' Westward 29; The Invaders 29; The Last Round-Up 29; The Lone Horseman 29; The Man from Nevada 29; 'Neath Western Skies 29; The Oklahoma Kid 29; The Phantom Rider 29; Pioneers of the West 29; Riders of the Rio Grande 29; Riders of the Storm 29; Beyond the Law 30; Breezy Bill 30; Call of the Desert 30; Canyon Hawks 30; The Canyon of Missing Men 30; Code of Honor 30; Covered Wagon Trails 30; Hunted Men 30; The Man from Nowhere • Western Honor 30; Near the Rainbow's End 30; The Oklahoma Sheriff 30; O'Malley Rides Alone 30; Parting of the Trails 30; Under Texas Skies 30; The Cyclone Kid 31; Headin' for Trouble 31; Quick Trigger Lee 31; Riders of the North 31; Shotgun Pass 31; Human Targets 32; The Hurricane Express 32*; Lawless Valley 32; Mark of the Spur 32; The Scarlet Brand 32; Tangled Fortunes 32; Deadwood Pass 33; Drum Taps 33; War of the Range 33; When a Man Rides Alone 33; The Lone Bandit 34; The Outlaw Tamer 34; Roaring Six Guns 37; Rough Ridin' Rhythm • Rough Riding Rhythm 37; Where the West Begins 38

McGowan, Robert Frontier Justice 36; Too Many Parents 36; The Haunted House 40; The Old Swimmin' Hole • When Youth Conspires 40; Tomboy 40

McGowan, Stuart The Showdown 50*; Tokyo File 212 51*; Snowfire 58*; The Bashful Elephant 62*; Cold Blood • The Ice House • Love in Cold Blood • The Passion Pits 69; The Billion Dollar Hobo 77; They Went That-a-Way and That-a-Way 78*

McGowan, Tom The Amazon Trader 56; Manhunt in the Jungle 58; The Hound That Thought He Was a Racoon 60; Cataclysm 80*; Night Train to Terror 85*

McGrath, John Blood Red Roses 86

McGrath, Joseph Casino Royale 67*; 30 Is a Dangerous Age, Cynthia 67; The Bliss of Mrs. Blossom 68; The Magic Christian 69; Ner Ist Wer? 70; Digby—The Biggest Dog in the World 73; The Great McGonagall 74; Girls Come First 75; Escape to Entebbe 76*; I'm Not Feeling Myself Tonight 76; Rising Damp 79

McGreeney, P. S. The Germ 23

McGregor, Edgar J. Good News 30*

MacGregor, Norval Colorado 15; The Target 16; Children of Banishment 19; Jacques of the Silver North 19; Impulse 22

McGregor, Sean Camper John 73; Devil Times Five • The Horrible House on the Hill • People Toys • Peopletoys 74; Nightmare County 77

McGuane, Thomas 92° in the Shade 75

McGuire, Dennis Shoot It: Black, Shoot It: Blue 74

McGuire, Don Johnny Concho 56; The Delicate Delinquent 57; Hear Me Good 57

Mach, Josef Die Söhne der Grossen Bärin • The Sons of Great Bear 65

Machard, Alfred Les Petits 36*

Macharet, Alexander Men and Jobs 33;

Peter Vinogradof 35; Call to Arms 37; Concentration Camp 39; Pages of Life • Stranitsy Zhizn 48*

Machatý, Gustav Teddy By Kovril • Teddy Wants to Smoke 19; The Kreutzer Sonata • Kreutzerova Sonáta • Sonáta Kreutzerova 26; Schweik As a Civilian • Švejk v Civilu 27; Erotikon • Seduction 29; From Saturday to Sunday • Ze Soboty na Neděli 31; Načeradec, Král Kibiců 31; Ecstasy • Ekstase • Extase • Symphony of Love 32; Nocturno 34; Ballerine 36; The Good Earth 36*; The Wrong Way Out 38; Within the Law 39; Jealousy 45; Suchkind 312 55

Machin, Alfred Chasse à l'Hippopotame sur le Nil Bleu 08; Chasse à la Panthère 09; Babylas à Hérité d'une Panthère 11; Babylas Explorateur 11; Le Cinéma en Afrique 11; Le Dévouement d'un Gosse 11; La Nuit de Noël 11; L'Âme des Moulins • Les Moulins Chantent et Pleurent 12; The Escape of Hugo van Groot 12; La Fleur Sanglante 12; Histoire de Minna Claessens 12; L'Histoire d'un P'tit Gars 12; The Interloper 12; Het Lijden van der Scheepsjongen 12; Little Moritz Soldat d'Afrique 12; De Molens die Juichen en Weenen 12; L'Or Qui Brûle 12; La Révolte des Gueux 12; De Strijd der Geuzen 12; L'Agent Rijolo et Son Chien Policier 13; Au Ravissement des Dames 13; Le Baiser de l'Empereur 13; Le Diamant Noir 13; De Droppel Bloed 13; Un Épisode à Waterloo • Un Épisode de Waterloo 13; Maudite Soit la Guerre • Le Moulin Maudit 13; La Ronde Infernale 13; Saïda a Enlevé Manneken-Pis 13; Supreme Sacrifice 13; La Fille de Delft 14; Napoléon: Du Sacre à Sainte-Hélène 14; La Tulipe d'Or 14; La Bataille de la Somme 16; La Bataille de Verdun 17; Moi Aussi, J'Accuse 20*; Une Nuit Agitée 20; On Attend Polochon 20; Serpentin à Engagé Bouboule 20; Pervenche 21*; Bêtes...Comme les Hommes 23*; Le Cabinet de l'Homme Noir 24*; L'Énigme du Mont Agel 24*; Les Héritiers de l'Oncle James • Les Millions de l'Oncle James 24*; Le Cœur des Gueux 25*; L'Homme Noir • Le Manoir de la Peur 27*; Le Retour 28; Black and White • Robinson Junior 29; De la Jungle à l'Écran 29

Machulski, Juliusz Seksmisja • Sex Mission 84; Kingsajz 88

McIndoe, George The Roller-Skating Groupie 71; Hyde Park Pop 73*

McIntyre, J. Border Shootout 90

McIntyre, Thom Tales of the Third Dimension 85*

Mack, Brice Jennifer • Jennifer (The Snake Goddess) 78; Half a House 79; Swap Meet 79

Mack, Charles W. Blue Blazes 22*

Mack, Earle The Children of Theater Street 77*

Mack, Max Der Andere • The Other 12; Ein Seltsamer Fall 14; Nur am Rhein 31; Tausend für Eine Nacht 34; Be Careful, Mr. Smith • His Night Out • Singing Through 35

Mack, Roy Enemy Round-Up • Hillbilly Blitzkrieg 42

Mack, Russell Big Money 30; Night Work 30; Second Wife 30; Heaven on Earth • Mississippi 31; Lonely Wives 31; The Spirit of Notre Dame • Vigour of Youth 31; The All-American • Sport of a Nation 32; Once in a Lifetime 32; Scandal for Sale 32; Private Jones 33; The Band Plays On 34; The Meanest Gal in Town 34

Mack, Wayne Bubbles 20; No Man's Woman 21*; Nine Points of the Law 22

Mack, Willard Voice of the City 29; Broadway to Hollywood • Ring Up the Curtain 33; Shall the Children Pay? • What Price Innocence? 33; Together We Live 35

MacKane, David Swinging the Lead 34; Men of the Mines 45; Othello 46; The Gorbals Story 50

McKay, James Midnight Gambols • A Sinless Sinner 19; Queen's Evidence 19; Souls for Sables 25; Fools of Fashion 26; The Broken Gate 27; Lightning 27

Mackay, Yvonne The Silent One 84

McKee, L. S. Lone Hand Wilson 20*

Mackendrick, Alexander Tight Little Island • Whisky Galore! 48; The Man in the White Suit 51; Crash of Silence • Mandy • The Story of Mandy 52; High and Dry • The Maggie 53; The Ladykillers 55; Sweet Smell of Success 57; The Devil's Disciple 58*; A Boy Ten Feet Tall • Sammy Going South 62; A High Wind in Jamaica 65; Oh Dad, Poor Dad, Mama's Hung You in the Closet and I'm Feeling So Sad • Oh Dad, Poor Dad, Mamma's Hung You in the Closet and I'm Feelin' So Sad 66*; Don't Make Waves 67*

MacKenna, Kenneth Always Goodbye 31*; Good Sport 31; The Spider 31*; Careless Lady 32; Walls of Gold 33; Sleepers East 34

McKenzie, Brian With Love to the Person Next to Me 87

Mackenzie, Donald Detective Craig's Coup 14; Detective Swift 14*; The Hand of Destiny 14; Leaves of Memory 14; The Perils of Pauline 14*; The Galloper 15; Mary's Lamb 15; The Spender, or The Fortunes of Peter 15; The Challenge 16; The Precious Packet 16; The Shielding Shadow 16*; The Carter Case 19

Mackenzie, John One Brief Summer 69; Unman, Wittering and Zigo 71; Made 72; The Long Good Friday 80; Beyond the Limit • The Honorary Consul 83; The Innocent 84; A Sense of Freedom 85; The Fourth Protocol 86; Blue Heat • The Last of the Finest • Street Legal 89

Mackenzie, Kent The Exiles 66; Saturday Morning 71

McKenzie, Robert A Knight of the West 21; Fightin' Devil 22; A Western Demon 22

Mackenzie, Will Worth Winning 89

McKeown, Douglas The Deadly Spawn 83*

McKeown, Jack Her Father Said No 27

Mackey, Clarke The Only Thing You

Know 71

Mackey, Edward The Coming Power 14; The Span of Life 14

McKimmie, Jackie Australian Dream 86

McKimson, Robert Acrobatty Bunny 46; Daffy Doodles 46; Hollywood Canine Canteen 46; The Mouse-merized Cat 46; Walky Talky Hawky 46; The Birth of a Notion 47; Crowing Pains 47; Easter Yeggs 47; Hobo Bobo 47; One Meat Brawl 47; The Upstanding Sitter 47; Daffy Duck Slept Here 48; The Foghorn Leghorn 48; Gorilla My Dreams 48; Hop, Look and Listen 48; A Horsefly Fleas 48; Hot Cross Bunny 48; A Lad in His Lamp 48; The Shell Shocked Egg 48; Daffy Duck Hunt 49; The Grey Hounded Hare 49; A Ham in a Role 49; Hen House Henery 49; Hippety Hopper 49; Rebel Rabbit 49; Swallow the Leader 49; The Windblown Hare 49; Boobs in the Woods 50; Bushy Hare 50; An Egg Scramble 50; A Fractured Leghorn 50; Hillbilly Hare 50; Hurdy Gurdy Hare 50; It's Hummertime 50; The Leghorn Blows at Midnight 50; Pop 'Im Pop 50; Strife with Father 50; What's Up Doc? 50; Big Top Bunny 51; Corn Plastered 51; Dog Collared 51; Early to Bet 51; A Fox in a Fix 51; The French Rarebit 51; Leghorn Swoggled 51; Lovelorn Leghorn 51; The Prize Pest 51; Sleepy Time Possum 51; Fool Coverage 52; Hoppy Go Lucky 52; Kiddin' the Kitten 52; The Oily Hare 52; Rabbit's Kin 52; Sock-a-Doodle Doo 52; The Super Snooper 52; Thumb Fun 52; The Turn Tale Wolf 52; Who's Kitten Who? 52; Cat-Tails for Two 53; Cat's A-Weigh 53; Easy Peckins 53; Muscle Tussle 53; Of Rice and Hen 53; A Peck o' Trouble 53; Plop Goes the Weasel 53; There Auto Be a Law 53; Upswept Hare 53; Bell Hoppy 54; Design for Leaving 54; Devil May Hare 54; Gone Batty 54; Little Boy Boo 54; No Parking Hare 54; The Oily American 54; Quack Shot 54; Wild Wife 54; All Fowled Up 55; Dime to Retire 55; Feather Duster 55; The Hole Idea 55; Lighthouse Mouse 55; Half Fare Hare 56; The High and the Flighty 56; The Honeymousers 56; Mixed Master 56; Raw! Raw! Rooster 56; Slap-Hoppy Mouse 56; Stupor Duck 56; Too Hop to Handle 56; The Unexpected Pest 56; Weasel Stop 56; Bedevilled Rabbit 57; Boston Quackie 57; Cheese It, the Cat 57; Ducking the Devil 57; Fox Terror 57; Rabbit Romeo 57; Tabasco Road 57; Dog Tales 58; Don't Axe Me 58; Feather Bluster 58; Gopher Broke 58; Now Hare This 58; Pre-Hysterical Hare 58; Weasel While You Work 58; Backwoods Bunny 59; Bonanza Bunny 59; A Broken Leghorn 59; The Cat's Paw 59; China Jones 59; Here Today, Gone Tamale 59; Mouse Place Kitten 59; The Mouse That Jack Built 59; A Mutt in a Rutt 59; People Are Bunny 59; Crockette Doodle-Doo 60; The Dixie Fryer 60; Doggone People 60; Mice Follies 60; Wild Wild World 60; Birds of a Father 61; Daffy's Inn Trouble 61; Hoppy Daze 61; Strangled Eggs 61; Bill of Hare 62; Fish and Slips 62; Good Noose 62; Mother Was a Rooster 62; The Slick Chick 62; Wet Hare 62; Aqua-Duck 63; Banty-Raids 63; Claws in the Lease 63; Fast Buck Duck 63*; Million-Hare 63; Bartholomew Versus the Wheel 64; Doctor Devil and Mister Hare 64; False Hare 64; Freudy Cat 64; A Message to Gracias 64; Assault and Peppered 65; Chili Corn Corny 65; Go Go Amigo 65; Moby Duck 65; Rushing Roulette 65; Suppressed Duck 65; Tease for Two 65; Well Worn Daffy 65; A-Haunting We Will Go 66; Astro-Duck 66; Daffy Rents 66; Feather Finger 66; Mexican Mouse-Piece 66; Muchos Locos 66; Snow Excuse 66; A Squeek in the Deep 66; Sugar and Spies 66; Swing Ding Amigo 66; A Taste of Catnip 66; Daffy's Diner 67; Bunny and Claude 68; Bugged By a Bee 69; The Fistic Mystic 69; The Great Carrot Train Robbery 69; Injun Trouble 69; Rabbit Stew and Rabbits Too 69; Sham Rock 'n' Roll 69

Macklin, A. N. C. Dangerous Companions 34

McLachlan, Duncan Scavengers 88

McLaglen, Andrew V. Man in the Vault 55; Arizona Mission • Gun the Man Down 56; The Abductors 57; Freckles 60; The Little Shepherd of Kingdom Come 61; McLintock! 63; Fields of Honor • Shenandoah 65; The Rare Breed 65; Monkeys, Go Home! 66; The Ballad of Josie • Meanwhile, Back at the Ranch 67; The Way West 67; Bandolero! 68; The Devil's Brigade 68; Hellfighters 68; The Undefeated 69; Chisum 70; Dynamite Man from Glory Jail • Fools' Parade 71; One More Train to Rob • The Train Robbers 71; something big 71; Cahill • Cahill—U.S. Marshal • Cahill—United States Marshal 73; Mitchell 75; The Last Hard Men 76; Breakthrough • Sergeant Steiner • Steiner—Das Eiserne Kreuz 2. Teil 78; The Wild Geese 78; Assault Force • ffolkes • North Sea Hijack 79; The Sea Wolves 80; Sahara 83; Return to the River Kwai 89

MacLaine, Shirley The Other Half of the Sky—A China Memoir 74*

McLaren, Norman Seven Till Five 33; Hand-Painted Abstraction 34; Book Bargain 35*; Camera Makes Whoopee 35; Colour Cocktail 35; Hell Unlimited 36*; Defense of Madrid 37; Love on the Wing 37; Money a Pickle 37; News for the Navy 37; Allegro 39*; The Obedient Flame 39; Rumba 39; Scherzo 39; Stars and Stripes 39; Boogie Doodle 40; Dots 40; Loops 40; Spook Sport 40*; Mail Early 41; V for Victory 41; Five for Four 42; Hen Hop 42; Dollar Dance 43; Alouette 44; C'Est l' Aviron 44; Keep Your Mouth Shut 44*; La Haut sur Ces Montagnes 45; Hoppity Pop 46; A Little Fantasy on a Nineteenth Century Painting • A Little Phantasy 46; Fiddle-De-Dee 47; Poulette Grise 47; A Phantasy 48; Begone Dull Care 49*; Around Is Around 50*; Chalk River Ballet 50*; Pen Point Percussion 50; Now Is the Time 51; Neighbors • Les Voisins 52; Twirl-

igig 52; Two Bagatelles 52; Blinkity Blank 54; Rhythmetic 56*; A Chairy Tale • Il Était une Chaise 57*; Le Merle 58*; Mail Early for Christmas 59; Serenal 59; Short and Suite 59*; Discours de Bienvenue de McLaren • Opening Speech 60; Lignes Verticales • Lines Vertical 60*; New York Light Record • New York Lightboard 60; Lignes Horizontales • Lines Horizontal 62*; Dance Squared 63; Canon 64*; Mosaic • Mosaïque 65; Pas de Deux 67; Sphères • Spheres 69; Striations 70; Synchromy 71; Ballet Adagio 72; L'Écran d'Épingles 73*; Le Mouvement Image par Image 78; Narcissus 83

McLaren, W. N. see *McLaren, Norman*

McLaughlin, J. W. Beyond the Shadows 18; Closin' In 18; Hell's End 18; The Man Who Woke Up 18

McLaughlin, Sheila Committed 85*; She Must Be Seeing Things 87

McLean, Barrie Angus Golden Apples of the Sun 71

MacLean, Stephen Around the World in Eighty Ways 86

McLennan, Don Hard Knocks 80; Slate, Wyn & Me 87; Mullaway 88

McLeod, Norman Z. Taking a Chance 28; Along Came Youth 30*; Finn and Hattie 30*; The Miracle Man 31; Monkey Business 31; Playing the Game • Touchdown 31; Horse Feathers 32; If I Had a Million 32*; Alice in Wonderland 33; A Lady's Profession 33; Mama Loves Papa 33; It's a Gift 34; Many Happy Returns 34; Melody in Spring 34; Coronado 35; Here Comes Cookie • The Plot Thickens 35; Redheads on Parade 35; Early to Bed 36; Mind Your Own Business 36; Pennies from Heaven 36; Topper 37; Merrily We Live 38; There Goes My Heart 38; Topper Takes a Trip 38; Remember? 39; Little Men 40; The Trial of Mary Dugan 40; Jackass Mail 41; Lady Be Good 41; Hello! Beautiful • The Powers Girl 42; Panama Hattie 42*; The Girl in Overalls • Swing Shift Maisie 43; The Kid from Brooklyn 46; Road to Rio 47; The Secret Life of Walter Mitty 47; Isn't It Romantic? 48; The Paleface 48; Let's Dance 50; My Favorite Spy 51; Never Wave at a WAC • The Newest Profession • The Private Wore Skirts 52; Casanova's Big Night 53; Public Pigeon No. 1 57; Alias Jesse James 59

McLoughlin, Tom One Dark Night 82; Friday the 13th Part VI: Jason Lives 86; Date with an Angel 87

McLuhan, Teri The Third Walker 78

McMahon, E. M. The Fifth Horseman 24

McMahon, Louis A. Captain Celluloid vs. the Film Pirates 74

McManus, J. J. Mr. Ima Jonah's Home Brew 21*; Skipping the Pen 21*; Burr's Novelty Review No. 1 22*; Burr's Novelty Review No. 2 22*; Burr's Novelty Review No. 3 22*; Burr's Novelty Review No. 4 22*; Burr's Novelty Review No. 5 22*; Burr's Novelty Review No. 6 22*

MacMillan, Keith Bob Marley and the

Wailers Live • Exodus Bob Marley Live 78

MacMullen, Hugh Footsteps in the Dark 41*

McMullen, Ken Resistance 76; Ghost Dance 83; Being and Doing 84; Zina 85; Partition 88; 1871 89

McMurray, Mary The Assam Garden 85

McNamara, Richard Atom Age Vampire • Seddok—L'Erede di Satana • Seddok—Son of Satan 60*; Cleopatra's Daughter • Daughter of Cleopatra • Il Sepolcro dei Re • La Vallée des Pharaons 60*; Queen of the Pirates • La Venere dei Pirati • Venus der Piraten 60*; Castle of Terror • Castle of the Living Dead • Horror Castle • Terror Castle • La Vergine di Norimberga • The Virgin of Nuremberg • Where the Blood Flows 63*; Il Leone di San Marco • The Lion of St. Mark 63*

MacNamara, Walter P. The Heart of New York 16; The Supreme Test 23

McNaught, Bob Grand National Night • Wicked Wife 53; Sea Wife • Sea Wyf and Biscuit 57; A Story of David 60

MacNaughton, Ian And Now for Something Completely Different 71

McNaughton, John Henry: Portrait of a Serial Killer 86

McNaughton, R. Q. Maniacs on Wheels • Once a Jolly Swagman 48*

McNutt, William Slavens Cap'n Jericho • Hell and High Water 33*

Macourek, Miloš Císařův Slavík • The Emperor and the Nightingale • The Emperor's Nightingale 48*; The Nights of Prague • Prague Nights • Pražské Noci 68*; Což Takhle Dát Si Špenát • A Nice Plate of Spinach • What Would You Say to Some Spinach? 76*; Mach a Šebestová, k Tabuli! • Mach and Sebestova, Come to the Blackboard Please! 85*

MacQuarrie, Murdock In the Web of the Grafters 16; Nancy's Birthright 16; The Sign of the Spade 16; The Stain in the Blood 16

McQueen, Justice see *Jones, L. Q.*

Macrae, Duncan June Friday 15; Through Turbulent Waters 15; The Usurper 19; The Auction Mart 20; Burnt In 20; Money 21; Love and a Whirlwind 22*

MacRae, Henry The Werewolf 13; Trey of Hearts 14*; Coral 15; The Mysterious Contragrav 15; Behind the Lines 16; The Bronze Bride 17; Man and Beast 17; Money Madness 17; God's Crucible 21; The Critical Age 23; The Man from Glengarry 23; The Fearless Lover 24; A Fight for Honor 24; The Price She Paid 24; Racing for Life 24; Tainted Money 24; The Scarlet Streak 26; Wild Beauty 27; The Danger Rider 28; Guardians of the Wild 28; The Two Outlaws 28; Burning the Wind 29*; The Harvest of Hate 29; Hoofbeats of Vengeance 29; King of the Rodeo 29; Plunging Hoofs 29; Smilin' Guns 29; Tarzan the Tiger 29; Wild Blood 29; The Indians Are Coming 30; The Lightning Express 30; Terry of the Times 30; Detective Lloyd • The Green Spot Mystery • Lloyd of the C.I.D. 31; The

Lost Special 32; Rustlers' Roundup 33

McRoots, George Una Donna Chiamata Apache 77

MacTaggart, James All the Way Up 70

McTiernan, John Nomads 85; Predator 87; Die Hard 88; The Hunt for Red October 90

Madden, Lee Hell's Angels '69 69; Angel Unchained • Unchained 70; The Night God Screamed • Scream 73; The Manhandlers 75; Fear • Night Creature • Out of the Darkness 78; Ghost Fever 85

Maddin, Guy Tales from the Gimli Hospital 88

Maddow, Ben The Bridge 42*; The Steps of Age 51; The Stairs 53; The Savage Eye 59*; An Affair of the Skin 63; Storm of Strangers 69

Mäder, Fritz Swiss Made 68*

Madhu, K. Oohakachavadam 88; Oru Chi Diary Kurippu 88

Madigan, Sylvain Rotten Fate • Salé Destin 87

Madison, Cleo Her Bitter Cup 16*; A Soul Enslaved 16

Madrid, José Luis 5000 Dollar für den Kopf von Johnny R • Wer Kennt Johnny R? 65; Gringo's Pitiless Colt • La Spietate Colt del Gringo 66; The Horrible Sexy Vampire • The Vampire of the Highway • El Vampiro de la Autopista 70; Jack el Destripador de Londres • Jack the Mangler of London • Jack the Ripper 71

Madrid, Miguel El Descuartizador de Binbrook • Graveyard of Horror • Necrophagus 71; El Asesino de Muñecas 74

Madsen, Forest Holger see Holger-Madsen, Forest

Madsen, Holger see Holger-Madsen, Forest

Madsen, Peter Valhalla 86

Maeder, Fritz see Mäder, Fritz

Maesso, José Order to Kill 74

Maetzig, Kurt see Mätzig, Kurt

Maffei, Mario La Grande Notte di Ringo • The Night of the Desperado • La Notte del Desperado 65

Magar, Guy Retribution 87

Magatani, Morihei Ama no Bakemono Yashiki • Girl Divers from Spook Mansion • The Haunted Cave 59; The Blood Sword of the 99th Virgin • Kyūjū-Kyūhonme no Kimusume 59

Maggi, Luigi Galileo Galilei 08; The Last Days of Pompeii • Gli Ultimi Giorni di Pompei 08; Luigi XI, Re di Francia 09; Spergiura 09; Il Garantiere Rolland 10; La Fiaccola Sotto il Moggio 11; La Gioconda 11; La Nave 11; Nozze d'Oro 11; La Lampada della Nonna 12; Il Ponte dei Fantasmi 12; Satana 12; The Barber of Seville • Il Barbiere di Siviglia 13; The Marriage of Figaro • Il Matrimonio di Figaro 13; Notturno di Chopin 13; Il Fornaretto di Venezia 14; Per un'Ora d'Amore 14; Maciste Alpino 16*; Il Mistero dei Bauli Neri 18; I Conquistatori 20; La Danza delle Ore 20; Teodora 27

Magill, Mark Far from Poland 83*

Magliulo, Giorgio Una Casa in Bilico • A House on the Brink • A Tottering House • Tottering Lives 86*

Magni, Luigi Basta Che Non Si Sappia in Giro! 76*; Goodnight, Ladies and Gentlemen • Signore e Signori, Buonanotte 76*; In the Name of the Pope King 77; Secondo Ponzio Pilato 88

Magnoli, Albert Purple Rain 84; American Anthem 86

Magnusson, Charles Memories from the Boston Club 09; The Pirate 09; Orpheus in the Underworld 10; The Talisman 11; The Green Necklace 12; The Vagabond's Galoshes 12*

Magwood, Paul Chandler 71

Maher, Brendan The Bit Part 87

Mahmudov, Mukadas Jackal Trap • Kapkan dlya Shakalov 87

Mahomo, Nana End of the Dialogue 70; Last Grave at Dimbaza 75

Mahon, Barry White Slave Racket 53; Assault of the Rebel Girls • Attack of the Rebel Girls • Cuban Rebel Girls 57; Rocket Attack, U.S.A. 59; Girls, Inc. 60; Housewives, Inc. 60; Juke Box Racket 60; Smorgasbord 60; Violent Women 60; The Dead One 61; Pagan Island 61; Prostitutes' Protective Society 61; The Beast That Killed Women 62; 1,000 Female Shapes • 1,000 Shapes of a Female 63; Fanny Hill Meets Dr. Erotico 67; Fanny Hill Meets Lady Chatterley 67; Fanny Hill Meets the Red Baron 67; Girl Smugglers 67; The Land of Oz • The Wonderful Land of Oz 68; Santa's Christmas Elf 69; Jack and the Beanstalk 70; Thumbelina 70

Mahon, Joe The Best Man 86

Mahoney, Bob The Last of Linda Cleer 82

Mai, O. Das Krankheitsbild des Schlachtener—Problem Unteroffiziers in der Endsehlacht 71*

Maiden, Cecil Forbidden Journey 50*

Maie, Elsier la see La Maie, Elsier

Maigne, Charles Her Great Chance 18; The Hollow of Her Hand • In the Hollow of Her Hand 18; The Firing Line 19; The Indestructible Wife 19; The Invisible Bond 19; Redhead 19; The World to Live In 19; The Copperhead 20; A Cumberland Romance 20; The Fighting Chance 20; The Fighting Schoolmaster • The Kentuckians 21; Frontier of the Stars 21; Hush Money 21; The Cowboy and the Lady 22; Received Payment 22; Drums of Fate 23; The Silent Partner 23; The Trail of the Lonesome 23

Mailer, Norman Beyond the Law 68; Wild 90 68; Maidstone 70; Tough Guys Don't Dance 87

Maillard, Pierre Poisons 87

Maiman, R. Red Tanks 42*

Mainka, Maximiliane Die Menschen Die das Stauferjahr Vorbereiten • Die Menschen Die die Staufer-Ausstellung Vorbereiten • The People Who Are Preparing the Year of the Hohenstaufens 77*; Deutschland im Herbst • Germany in Autumn 78*

Mainka-Jellinghaus, Beate Deutschland

im Herbst • Germany in Autumn 78*

Mainwaring, Bernerd O.K. Chief 30; Realities 30; Cupboard Love 31; The Lame Duck 31; The New Hotel 32; The Crimson Candle 34; The Public Life of Henry the Ninth 34; Line Engaged 35; Old Roses 35; Show Flat 36; Cross My Heart • Loaded Dice 37; Jenifer Hale 37; Member of the Jury 37; The Villiers Diamond 38

Maisch, Herbert Königswalzer • The Royal Waltz 35; Boccaccio 36; Andalusische Nächte • Nights in Andalusia 38; Frau Sylvelin 39; D III 88—Die Neue Deutsche Luftwaffe Greift An • D III 88—The New German Air Force Attacks 40

Maitland, George Invasion Earth: The Aliens Are Here! 87

Maiuri, Dino Kiss the Girls and Make Them Die • Operazione Paradiso • Si Tutte le Donne del Mondo... 66*

Majano, Anton Giulio Eternal Chains 56; Atom Age Vampire • Seddok—L'Erede di Satana • Seddok—Son of Satan 60*; The Corsican Brothers 61

Majewski, Janusz The Bear • Lokis 70; C.K. Dezerterzy • The Deserters 87

Majewski, Lech The Flight of the Spruce Goose 86; Prisoner of Rio 87

Majo, Fred see May, Joe

Major, Anthony Super Spook 75

Majumdar, Tarun Contract Mother • Sibaji 87

Mak, Johnny Long Arm of the Law 84; Red Guards in Hong Kong 87

Mak, Michael Isle of Fantasy 86

Mak, Peter The Loser, the Hero 85

Maka, Karl The Thirty Million Rush 87

Makavejev, Dušan Jatagan Mala 53; Pečat • The Seal 55; Anthony's Broken Mirror • Antonijevo Razbijeno Ogledalo 57; Beekeeper's Scrapbook • Slikovnica Pčelara 58; Boje Sanjaju • Colors Are Dreaming 58; Damned Holiday • Prokleti Praznik 58; Don't Believe in Monuments • Spomenica Ne Treba Verovati 58; Što Je Radnički Savjet? 59; Eci, Peci, Pec • One Potato, Two Potato... 61; Educational Fairy Tale • Pedagoška Bajka 61; Osmjeh 61 • Smile 61 61; Dole Plotovi • Down with the Fences 62; Film About the Book • Film o Knjizi A.B.C. 62; Ljepotica 62 • Miss Yugoslavia 62 62; Parada • Parade 62; New Domestic Animal • Nova Domaća Zivotinja 64; New Toy • Nova Igračka 64; Čovek Nije Tica • Man Is Not a Bird 65; An Affair of the Heart • The Case of the Missing Switchboard Operator • Ljubavni Slučaj • Ljubavni Slučaj ili Tragedija Službenice P.T.T. • Ljubavni Slučaj, Tragedija Službenice P.T.T. • Love Affair • Love Affair, or The Case of the Missing Switchboard Operator • Love Dossier, or The Tragedy of a Switchboard Operator • The Switchboard Operator • Tragedija Službenice P.T.T. • The Tragedy of a Switchboard Operator 66; Innocence Unprotected • Nevinost Bez Zaštite 68; WR: Misterije Organizma • WR: Mysteries of the Organism 71; I Miss Sonia Henie 72; Sweet Movie 74; Wet Dreams 74; Montenegro • Montenegro, or Pigs and Pearls • Pigs and Pearls 80; The Coca-Cola Kid 85; For a Night of Love • Manifesto 88

Makdissy, Issam B. Liar's Dice 80

Mäkelä, Ville Lain Ulkopuolella • Outside the Law 87

Makelim, Hal Man of Conflict 53

Makharam, Ababacar Samb Jom • Jom: Ou, L'Histoire d'un Peuple 82

Makhmalbaf, Mohsen see Baf, Mohsen Makhmal

Mäkinen, Visa Pekka As a Policeman • Pekka Puupää Poliisina 87

Makk, Károly A Harag Napja 53; Liliomfi 54; Simon Menyhért Születése 54; 9-es Kórterem • Ward No. 9 55; Mese a Tizenkét Találatról • Tale on the Twelve Points 56; Ház a Sziklák Alatt • The House Under the Rocks 58; Brigade No. 39 • A 39-es Dandár 59; Don't Keep Off the Grass • Füre Lépni Szabad 60; The Fanatics • Megszállottak 61; Elveszett Paradicsom • The Lost Paradise 62; The Last But One • Az Utolsó Előtti Ember 63; His Majesty's Dates • Mit Csinált Felséged 3-tól 5-ig 64; Bolondos Vakáció • A Cloudless Vacation 67; Before God and Man • Isten és Ember Előtt 68; Love • Szerelem 71; Cats' Play • Macskajáték 74; Egy Erkölcsös Éjszaka • A Very Moral Night 77; Két Történet a Félmúltból 79; Another Way • Egymásra Nézve • Ölelkező Tekintetek 82; Játszani Kell • Lily in Love • Playing for Keeps 85; The Last Manuscript • Az Utolsó Kézirat 86

Makourek, Miloš see Macourek, Miloš

Makovek, Milos see Macourek, Miloš

Makris, Dimitris I Kekarmeni • Shaved Heads 87

Maksakov, Vyacheslav I Promise • Obeshchayu Byt 87

Malaparte, Curzio Il Cristo Proibito • The Forbidden Christ • Strange Deception 50

Malasomma, Nunzio Der Kampf ums Matterhorn 28*; La Cieca di Sorrento 36; I Tre Innamorati 37; Eravamo Sette Sorelle • We Were Seven Sisters 39; Il Diavolo Bianco • The White Devil 48; La Rebelión de los Esclavos • The Revolt of the Slaves • La Rivolta degli Schiavi • Die Sklaven Roms 61; Fifteen Scaffolds for a Killer • Quindici Forche per un Assassino 68

Malatesta, Guido Colossus and the Headhunters 60; Goliat Contra los Gigantes • Goliath Against the Giants • Goliath and the Giants • Goliath Contro i Giganti 61; La Furia dei Barbari • Fury of the Pagans 62

Malayil, Siby Ezhuthapurangal 88; Vicharana 88

Malcon, Boris La Isla Maldita 35; Infidelidad 39; Novillero 39; Ojos Tapatíos 39*

Malden, Karl Time Limit 57

Maldonado, Rosangela A Deusa de Mármore—Escrava do Diabo 78

Malenotti, Roberto Le Schiave Esistono Ancora • Slave Trade in the World Today 63*

Maley, Jean X-Ray of a Killer 63

Malhotra, Harmesh Dharam Shatru 88

Malick, Terrence Lanton Mills 72; Badlands 73; Days of Heaven 78

Malik, Pervaiz The Chain • Zangir 86

Malikoff, Nikolai Apaches of Paris 28

Maline, Alain Ni Avec Toi, Ni Sans Toi 85; Cayenne-Palace 87

Malins, Geoffrey H. Abide with Me 15; The Castaways 15; Hearts of Gold 15; On the Banks of Allan Water 15; The Battle of the Somme 16; With the French Army in Vosges 16; The Girl from Downing Street 18; A Peep Behind the Scenes 18*; Everybody's Doing It 19; The Greater Love 19; Patricia Brent, Spinster 19; The Rainbow Chasers 19; All the Winners 20; Film Pie 20*; The Golden Web 20; Our Girls and Their Physique 20; Settled in Full 20; Watch Your Step 20; Ally Sloper Goes Bathing 21; Ally Sloper Goes Yachting 21; Ally Sloper Runs a Revue 21; Ally Sloper's Haunted House 21; Ally Sloper's Loan Office 21; Ally Sloper's Teetotal Island 21; Bluff 21; Watching Eyes 21; Fortune's Fool • The Scourge 22; The Recoil 22; The Way of a Woman • The Wonderful Wooing 25; The Fighting Gladiator 26*; Find the Woman 26*; For a Woman's Eyes 26*; For My Lady's Happiness 26; Gypsy Courage 26*; The Phantom Foe 26*; When Giants Fought 26*; East of Singapore 27; The Bravo 28; The Changeling 28; Double Dealing 28; In Borrowed Plumes 28; Two of a Trade 28; London Melody 30*

Malle, Louis Fontaine de Vaucluse 53; Station 307 54; Le Monde du Silence • The Silent World 55*; Ascenseur pour l'Échafaud • Elevator to the Gallows • Frantic • Lift to the Scaffold 57; Les Amants • The Lovers 58; Zazie • Zazie dans le Métro • Zazie in the Subway • Zazie in the Underground 60; Private Life • A Very Private Affair • La Vie Privée • Vita Privata 61; Vive le Tour! 61; Le Feu Follet • The Fire Within • Fuoco Fatuo • A Time to Live and a Time to Die • Will o' the Wisp 63; Touriste Encore 63; Bons Baisers de Bangkok 64; Viva Maria! 65; Far from Vietnam • Loin du Viêt-nam 66*; The Thief • The Thief of Paris • Le Voleur 66; Histoires Extraordinaires • Spirits of the Dead • Tales of Mystery • Tre Passi nel Delirio 67*; Calcutta 69; L'Inde Fantôme • L'Inde 68 • Louis Malle's India • Phantom India 69; Dearest Love • Murmur of the Heart • Le Souffle au Cœur 71; Humain, Trop Humain • A Human Condition • Human, Too Human 72; Lacombe, Lucien 73; Place de la République 73; Black Moon 75; La Petite 78; Pretty Baby 78; Close Up 79; Atlantic City • Atlantic City, U.S.A. 80; My Dinner with André 81; Crackers 83; Alamo Bay 84; And the Pursuit of Happiness • God's Country 85; Au Revoir les Enfants • Goodbye, Children 87; May Fools • Milou en Mai 90

Mallett, David Queen—The Works E.P. 84*

Malleville, M. A. Colson see Colson-Malleville, M. A.

Mallinson, Matthew Fist of Fear, Touch of Death 80

Mallon, James Blood Hook 87

Malmros, Nils The Beauty and the Beast • Skønheden og Udyret 83; Århus by Night 89

Malmuth, Bruce Foreplay 74*; Nighthawks 81; The Man Who Wasn't There 83; Where Are the Children? 86; Hard to Kill 90

Malone, William Scared to Death • The Terror Factor 80; Creature • Titan Find 85

Maloney, Leo D. The Honor of the Range 20*; No Man's Woman 21*; King's Creek Law 23*; Headin' Through 24; Huntin' Trouble 24; Not Built for Runnin' 24; Payable on Demand 24; Ridin' Double • Riding Double 24; Across the Deadline 25; Flash O'Lightning 25; Luck and Sand 25; The Shield of Silence 25; The Trouble Buster 25; Win, Lose or Draw 25; Blind Trail 26; The High Hand 26; The Outlaw Express 26; Without Orders 26; Border Blackbirds 27; The Devil's Twin 27; Don Desperado 27; The Long Loop • The Long Loop on the Pecos 27; The Man from Hardpan 27; Two-Gun of the Tumbleweed 27; The Apache Raider 28; The Black Ace 28; The Boss of Rustler's Roost 28; The Bronc Buster • The Bronc Stomper 28; Yellow Contraband 28; 45 Calibre War 29; Overland Bound 29

Malouf, Yusuf The Broken Wings 64

Malraux, André Days of Hope • L'Espoir • Man's Hope • Sierra de Teruel 39

Malyan, Genrikh Poshchyochina • A Slap in the Face 80

Mamet, David House of Games 87; Things Change 88

Mamilov, Sulambek Day of Wrath • Den' Gneva 86

Mamoulian, Rouben Applause 29; City Streets 31; Dr. Jekyll and Mr. Hyde 31; Aimez-Moi Ce Soir • Love Me Tonight 32; Queen Christina 33; Song of Songs 33; We Live Again 34; Becky Sharp 35; The Gay Desperado 36; High, Wide and Handsome 37; Golden Boy 39; The Mark of Zorro 40; Blood and Sand 41; Rings on Her Fingers 42; Summer Holiday 46; Gone to Earth • Gypsy Blood • The Wild Heart 50*; Silk Stockings 57

Man, Chung Chi see Chung, David

Man, Paul Headquarters State Secret 62

Managadze, Nodar Amagleba 77; Hey Maestro! 88

Managadze, S. Ballet Tales 56*

Manan, Has No Time to Die 84*

Manaryan, Armen Land and Gold • Zemlya i Zoloto 87*

Manassarova, Aida Oglyanis 88

Manaster, Benjamin Goldstein 64*

Manatis, Janine I, Maureen 78

Manby, Alfred de see De Manby, Alfred

Mancini, Mario Frankenstein • Frankenstein 1980 • Mosaico 73

Mancuso, Kevin 2020 Texas Gladiators 85

Mandel, Joseph see May, Joe

Mandel, Robert Nights at O'Rear's 80; Follow Your Dreams • Independence Day 82; F/X • F/X—Murder by Illusion • Murder by Illusion 85; Touch and Go 86; Big Shots 87

Mander, Kay Mardi and the Monkey 53; The Kid from Canada 57

Mander, Miles The Fair Maid of Perth 26; Knee Deep in Daisies 26; The Sheik of Araby 26; The Whistler 26; As We Lie • Lost One Wife 27; False Colours 27; His Great Moment • The Sentence of Death 27; Packing Up 27; The First Born 28; Fascination 31; The Woman Between • The Woman Decides 31; Youthful Folly 34; The Morals of Marcus 35; The Flying Doctor 36

Mandić, Miroslav A Worker's Life • Život Radnika 87

Mandoki, Luis Motel 83; Gaby—A True Story 87; White Palace 90

Manduke, Joseph Jump 71; Cornbread, Earl and Me 75; Kid Vengeance 77; Beatlemania • Beatlemania—The Movie 81; Omega Syndrome 86; The Detective Kid • The Gumshoe Kid 90

Manera, Franco see Franco, Jesús

Manfredi, Nino Hercules' Pills • Le Pillole di Ercole 60*; L'Amore Difficile • Erotica • Of Wayward Love 62*; Per Grazia Ricevuta 71; Nudo di Donna 81*

Mangine, Joseph Neon Maniacs 86

Mangini, L. Bastardo...Vamos a Matar 71

Manglamele, Giorgio Clay 64

Mangolte, Babette What Maisie Knew 76

Maniatis, Sakis Megara 75*

Manivarnan Chinnathambi Periyathambi 87

Manker, Paulus Schmutz 86

Mankiewic, Joseph see Mankiewicz, Joseph L.

Mankiewicz, Francis Le Temps d'une Chasse 73; Les Bons Débarras! • Good Riddance! 78; Les Beaux Souvenirs • Fond Memories 82; Les Portes Tournantes • The Revolving Doors 87

Mankiewicz, Joseph L. Dragonwyck 46; The Late George Apley 46; Somewhere in the Night 46; The Ghost and Mrs. Muir 47; Escape 48; A Letter to Three Wives 48; House of Strangers 49; All About Eve 50; No Way Out 50; People Will Talk 51; Five Fingers • Operation Cicero 52; Julius Caesar 53; The Barefoot Contessa 54; Guys and Dolls 55; The Quiet American 57; Suddenly, Last Summer 59; Cleopatra 63; Anyone for Venice? • The Honey Pot • It Comes Up Murder • Mr. Fox of Venice 66; King: A Filmed Record, Montgomery to Memphis 69*; There Was a Crooked Man 69; Sleuth 72

Mankiewicz, Tom Dragnet 87

Manli, Lee see Lee, Manli

Mann, Anthony Dr. Broadway 42; Moonlight in Havana 42; My Best Gal 43;
Nobody's Darling 43; Strangers in the Night 44; The Great Flamarion 45; Sing Your Way Home 45; Strange Impersonation 45; Two O'Clock Courage 45; The Bamboo Blonde 46; Desperate 47; Railroaded! 47; T-Men 47; He Walked by Night 48*; Raw Deal 48; The Black Book • Reign of Terror 49; Border Incident 49; Follow Me Quietly 49*; Side Street 49; Devil's Doorway 50; The Furies 50; Winchester '73 50; It's a Big Country 51*; Quo Vadis? 51*; The Tall Target 51; Bend of the River • Where the River Bends 52; The Glenn Miller Story 53; The Naked Spur 53; Thunder Bay 53; The Far Country 54; The Last Frontier • Savage Wilderness 55; The Man from Laramie 55; Serenade 55; Strategic Air Command 55; Men in War 56; God's Little Acre 57; Night Passage 57*; The Tin Star 57; Man of the West 58; Spartacus 59*; Cimarron 60; El Cid 61; The Fall of the Roman Empire 63; The Heroes of Telemark • The Unknown Battle 65*; A Dandy in Aspic 67*

Mann, Anton see Mann, Anthony

Mann, Daniel The Counterfeiters 48*; Come Back, Little Sheba 52; About Mrs. Leslie 54; I'll Cry Tomorrow 55; The Rose Tattoo 55; The Teahouse of the August Moon 56; Hot Spell 58*; The Last Angry Man 59; Butterfield 8 60; The Mountain Road 60; Ada 61; Five Finger Exercise 62; Who's Got the Action? 62; Who's Been Sleeping in My Bed? 63; Conflict • Judith 65; Our Man Flint 65; For Love of Ivy 68; A Dream of Kings 69; Willard 70; The Revengers 72; Big Mo • Maurie 73; Interval 73; Lost in the Stars 74; Burn Out • Journey Into Fear 75; Matilda 78; The Incredible Mr. Chadwick 80

Mann, Delbert Marty 55; The Bachelor Party 57; Desire Under the Elms 57; Separate Tables 58; Middle of the Night 59; The Dark at the Top of the Stairs 60; Lover Come Back 61; The Outsider • The Sixth Man 61; That Touch of Mink 62; A Gathering of Eagles 63; Dear Heart • The Out-of-Towners 64; Quick, Before It Melts 64; Mister Buddwing • Woman Without a Face 65; Fitzwilly • Fitzwilly Strikes Back 67; The Pink Jungle 68; David Copperfield 70; Kidnapped 71; Birch Interval 75; Torn Between Two Lovers 79; Night Crossing 81; Brontë 83

Mann, Edward see Alcocer, Santos

Mann, Michael Thief • Violent Streets 81; The Keep 83; Manhunter • Red Dragon 86

Mann, Milton Marine Battleground 66*

Mann, Ron Imagine the Sound 81; Poetry in Motion 83; Listen to the City 84; Comic Book Confidential 88

Mannering, Cecil Giddy Golightly 17; The Bitten Biter 20; A Complete Change 20; Home Influence 20; Horatio's Deception 20; A Little Bet 20; Oh! Jemimah! 20; The Other Dog's Day 20; A Pair of Gloves 20

Manning, Bruce The Amazing Mrs. Holliday 43*
Manning, Michelle Blue City 86

Manoogian, Peter The Dungeonmaster 85*; Eliminators 86; Enemy Territory 87; Arena 88

Manoussakis, Costas The Fear • O Fovos 67

Manoussakis, Manoussos The Enchantress • I Skiachtra 85

Mansfield, Duncan Girl Loves Boy 37; Sweetheart of the Navy 37

Mansfield, Mike Elton John in Central Park 81

Mansfield, Scott Deadly Games • Who Fell Asleep? 80

Manshi, Yonfan Rose 86

Mantilla, Fernando Castillos de Castilla 33*; Galicia y Compostela 33*; Terraco Augusta 33*; Almadrabas 34*; La Ciudad y el Campo 35*; Felipe II y el Escorial 35*; Infinitos 35*

Mänttäri, Anssi The King Goes Forth to France • Kuningas Lähtee Ranskaan 86; Morena 86; Farewell, Goodbye • Näkemiin, Hyvästi 87; King Lear • Kuningas Lear 87

Manuel, Jacques Une Grande Fille Toute Simple • Just a Big, Simple Girl 49

Manuelli, Massimo Una Notte, un Sogno 88

Manupelli, George Cry, Dr. Chicago 71

Manzor, René Le Passage • The Passage 86

Mao, Lamdo see Lamdo, Mao

Maple, John E. Before the White Man Came 20

Mar, Lo see Lo, Mar

Mărăscu, Tudor Miracolul 88

Marbœuf, Jean Vaudeville 85; Grand Guignol 87; Corentin ou Les Infortunes Conjugales 88

Marcel, Terence Why Not Stay for Breakfast? 79; Hawk the Slayer 80; Prisoners of the Lost Universe 83; Jane and the Lost City 87

Marcellini, Romolo Fünf Mädchen und Ein Mann • Geschichte von Fünf Städten • A Tale of Five Cities • A Tale of Five Women 51*; Rommel's Treasure • Il Tesoro di Rommel 58; The Grand Olympics 64; Taboos of the World 65; Macabro 67

Marcellini, Siro Il Colpo Segreto di D'Artagnan • Le Secret de D'Artagnan • The Secret Mark of D'Artagnan 62; The Beast of Babylon Against the Son of Hercules • Hero of Babylon 63; Lola Colt 67

March, Alex Paper Lion 68*; The Big Bounce 69; Mastermind 76; The Amazing Captain Nemo 78

Marchal, Juan Xiol Sette Pistole per El Gringo • Seven Guns for Gringo 67

Marchant, Jay The Fighting Smile 25; The Great Sensation 25; Speed Mad 25

Marcharet, A. see Macharet, Alexander

Marchent, Joaquín Luis Romero see Romero Marchent, Joaquín Luis

Marchent, Joaquín Romero see Romero Marchent, Joaquín Luis

Marchent, Rafael Romero see Romero Marchent, Rafael

Marcin, Max The Shadow of the Law 30*; The Lawyer's Secret 31*; Silence 31*; The Case of Clara Deane • The Strange Case of Clara Deane 32*; Gambling Ship 33*; King of the Jungle 33*; The Love Captive 34

Marcus, Sid Aw, Nurse 34*; The Concert Kid 34*; The Great Experiment 34*; Happy Butterfly 34*; Holiday Land 34*; Scrappy's Art Gallery 34*; Scrappy's Dog Show 34*; Scrappy's Expedition 34*; Scrappy's Relay Race 34*; Scrappy's Television 34*; Scrappy's Theme Song 34*; Scrappy's Toy Shop 34*; The Gloom Chasers 35*; Gold Getters 35*; Graduation Exercises 35*; Let's Ring Doorbells 35*; The Puppet Murder Case 35*; Scrappy's Big Moment 35*; Scrappy's Ghost Story 35*; Scrappy's Trailer 35*; Dizzy Ducks 36*; Looney Balloonists 36*; Playing Politics 36*; Scrappy's Boy Scouts 36*; Scrappy's Camera Troubles 36*; Scrappy's Pony 36*; Canine Capers 37*; The Clock Goes Round and Round 37*; The Fire Plug 37*; I Want to Be an Actress 37*; Puttin' Out the Kitten 37*; Scrappy's Band Concert 37*; Scrappy's Music Lesson 37*; Scrappy's News Flashes 37*; The City Slicker 38*; The Early Bird 38*; Happy Birthday 38*; Little Moth's Big Flame 38; The New Homestead 38*; Poor Elmer 38; Scrappy's Playmates 38*; Scrappy's Trip to Mars 38*; Window Shopping 38; The Charm Bracelet 39*; Dreams on Ice 39; The House That Jack Built 39; Jitterbug Knights 39; Millionaire Hobo 39*; Park Your Baby 39*; Peaceful Neighbors 39; Scrappy's Added Attraction 39*; Scrappy's Rodeo 39*; Scrappy's Side Show 39*; A Worm's Eye View 39*; Barnyard Babies 40; The Mad Hatter 40; Man of Tin 40*; A Peep in the Deep 40*; Pooch Parade 40*; Practice Makes Perfect 40*; Schoolboy Dreams 40*; Tangled Television 40; The Cuckoo I.Q. 41; A Helping Paw 41; The Land of Fun 41; The Little Theatre 41*; Red Riding Hood Rides Again 41; The Streamlined Donkey 41; Tom Thumb's Brother 41; Amoozin' But Confoozin' 44; A Peekoolyr Sitcheeayshun 44; Goofy News Views 45; Boston Beany 47; Kitty Caddy 47; Swiss Tease 47; Up 'n' Atom 47; Topsy Turkey 48; Cat-tastrophy 49; Coo-Coo Bird Dog 49

Marczewski, Wojciech Creeps • Dreszcze • Shivers 80

Mardanov, S. By the Bluest of Seas • U Samova Sinevo Morya • U Samovo Sinyevo Morya 36*

Marek, Andrzej The Harsh Father 11; Mirele Efros 12

Mareuil, Stephanie de see De Mareuil, Stephanie

Margheriti, Antonio Assignment Outer Space • Space-Men 60; Battle of the Worlds • Guerre Planetari • Il Pianeta degli Uomini Spenti • Planet of the Lifeless Men 61; The Outsider 61; Il Crollo di Roma • The Fall of Rome 62; La Freccia d'Oro • The Golden Arrow 62; Castle of Blood • Castle of Terror • Coffin of Terror • La Danse Macabre • La Danza Macabra • Dimensions in Death • Edgar Allan Poe's Castle of Blood • The Long Night of Terror • La Lunga Notte del Terrore • Terrore • Tombs of Horror 63*; Castle of Terror • Castle of the Living Dead • Horror Castle • Terror Castle • La Vergine di Norimberga • The Virgin of Nuremburg • Where the Blood Flows 63*; Anthar l'Invincibile 64; I Giganti di Roma 64; Hercules, Prisoner of Evil 64; The Long Hair of Death • I Lunghi Capelli della Morte 64; Il Pelo nel Mondo 64*; Ursus il Terrore dei Kirghisi 64; I Criminali della Galassia • The Criminals of the Galaxy • Wild, Wild Planet 65; The Devil Men from Space • The Devils from Space • I Diavoli della Spazio • Snow Demons • Snow Devils • Snow Man • Space Devils 65; Devil of the Desert Against the Son of Hercules 65; I Diafanoidi Portano la Morte • I Diafanoidi Vengono da Morte • War of the Planets 65; Lightning Bolt • Operación Goldman • Operazione Goldman 65; Missione Pianeta Errante • Il Pianeta Errante • Planet on the Prowl • War Between the Planets 65; Dinamite Joe • Dynamite Joe • Joe l'Implacabile 66; A 077 Sfida ai Killers 67; Io Ti Amo 68; Joko Invoca Dio ...e Muori • Vengeance 68; Nude...Si Muore • Sette Vergini per il Diavolo • The Young, the Evil and the Savage 68; And God Said to Cain... • Dio Disse a Caino ... • E Dio Disse a Caino... 69; Contronatura • The Innaturals • Schreie in der Nacht • The Unnaturals 69; And Comes the Dawn...But Colored Red • Dracula im Schloss des Schreckens • Dracula in the Castle of Blood • E Venne l'Alba...Ma Tinto di Rosse • Edgar Poe chez les Morts Vivants • In the Grip of the Spider • Nella Stretta Morsa del Ragno • Prisonnier de l'Araignée • Web of the Spider 70; L'Inafferabile Invincibile Mr. Invisibile • El Invencible Hombre Invisible • Mr. Invisible • Mister Superinvisible 70; Finalmente... Le Mille e Una Notte 72; Novele Galeotte d'Amore 72; Andy Warhol's Dracula • Andy Warhol's Young Dracula • Blood for Dracula • Dracula • Dracula Cerca Sangue di Vergine e...Mori di Sete • Dracula Vuole Vivere: Cerca Sangue di Vergine! • Young Dracula 73*; Andy Warhol's Frankenstein • Carne per Frankenstein • The Devil and Dr. Frankenstein • Flesh for Frankenstein • Frankenstein • The Frankenstein Experiment • Il Mostro È in Tavola ...Barone Frankenstein • Up Frankenstein • Warhol's Frankenstein 73*; Corringa • La Morte negli Occhi del Gatto • Seven Dead in the Cat's Eyes 73; Decameron 3 73; Ming, Ragazzi 73; Blood Money • The Stranger and the Gunfighter 74; Les Diablesses 74; Hercules vs. Kung Fu • Mr. Hercules Against Karate • Sciaffoni e Karati 74; Manone il Ladrone 74; La Parola di un Fuorilegge e Legge • Take a Hard Ride 74; Whisky e Fantasmi 74; La Dove No Batte il Sole 75; Con la Rabbia agli Occhi • Death Rage 76; The Rip-Off • The Squeeze 76; House of a Thousand Pleasures 77; Deadly Treasure of the Piranha • Killer Fish • Treasure of the Piranha 78*; Death Race 78; Apocalipse Cannibal • Apocalisse Domani • Apocalypse Domani • Caníbal Apocalipsis • Cannibal Apocalypse • The Cannibals Are in the Streets • Cannibals in the City • Cannibals in the Streets • Hunter of the Apocalypse • Invasion of the Flesh Hunters • The Last Hunter • Savage Apocalypse • The Slaughterers • Virus 80; Car Crash 81; Cacciatori del Cobra d'Oro • The Hunters of the Golden Cobra • The Raiders of the Golden Cobra 82; Fuga dall'Arcipelago Maladetto 82; The Ark of the Sun God 83; Il Mondo di Yor • The World of Yor • Yor • Yor—The Hunter from the Future 83; Tornado 83; Captain Yankee • Jungle Raiders • La Leggenda del Rubino Malese 84; Codename: Wildgeese • Geheimcode Wildganse 84; I Sopravvissuti della Città Morta 84; The Commander • Commando Leopard • Kommando Leopard 85; Indio 88; Le Ore Contate 88

Mărgineanu, Nicolae The Maiden of the Woods • Pădureanca 87; Flăcări pe Comori 88

Margolin, Stuart The Glitter Dome 84; Paramedics 88

Margolis, Jeff Richard Pryor Is Back Live in Concert 79; Richard Pryor Live in Concert 79

Marguenat, Jean de see De Marguenat, Jean

Mari, Febo Il Critico 12; Il Fauno 16; La Gloria 16; Attila il Flagello di Dio 17; Ercole 17; L'Eroica 19; Tormento 19

Marian, David In the Far East 37

Máriássy, Félix Ann Szabó • Anna Szabó • Szabó Anna • Szabóné 49; Catherine's Marriage • Kis Katalin Házassága 49; Full Steam Ahead • Teljes Gőzzel 51; Relatives • Rokonok 54; Budapest • Spring in Budapest • Springtime in Budapest 55; A Glass of Beer • Egy Pikoló Világos 55; A Legend of the Suburbs 57; Csempészek • Smugglers 58; Álmatlan Évek • The Sleepless Years 59; Fapados Szerelem • A Simple Love • Third-Class Love 59; Hosszú az Út Hazáig • It's a Long Way Home 60; Próbaút • Test Trip 60; Every Day Sunday • Pirosbetűs Hétköznapok 62; Goliath • Karambol 64; Figleaf • Fügefalevél 66; Bondage • Kötelék 68

Mariaud, Maurice Le Crépuscule de Cœur 16; Larmes de Crocodile 16; La Marche Triomphale 16; La Calomnie 17; Les Dames de Croix-Mort 17; La Danseuse Voilée 17; L'Épave 17; Le Nocturne 17; Les Mouettes 19; L'Étau 20; L'Idole Brisée 20; L'Homme et la Poupée 21; L'Aventurier 24; La Goutte de Sang 24*; Mon Oncle 25; Le Secret de Cargo 29

Marier, Captain Victor see Griffith, D. W.

Marin, Cheech Born in East L.A. 87

Marin, Edwin L. The Death Kiss 32; A Study in Scarlet 32; The Avenger 33;

Bombay Mail 33; Girl of My Dreams • The Sweetheart of Sigma Chi 33; Affairs of a Gentleman 34; The Crosby Case • The Crosby Murder Case 34; Paris Interlude 34; The Casino Murder Case 35; Pursuit 35; The All American Chump • The Country Bumpkin 36; The Garden Murder Case 36; I'd Give My Life 36; Moonlight Murder 36; Speed 36; Sworn Enemy 36; Everybody Sing 37; Man of the People 37; Married Before Breakfast 37; The Chaser 38; A Christmas Carol 38; Hold That Kiss 38; Listen, Darling 38; Fast and Loose 39; Henry Goes Arizona • Spats to Spurs 39; Maisie 39; Society Lawyer 39; Florian 40; Gold Rush Maisie 40; Hullabaloo 40; Maisie Was a Lady 40; Cash and Carry • Ringside Maisie 41; Paris Calling 41; A Gentleman After Dark 42; Invisible Agent 42; Miss Annie Rooney 42; Two Tickets to London 43; Show Business 44; Tall in the Saddle 44; Abilene Town 45; Johnny Angel 45; Lady Luck 46; Mr. Ace 46; Nocturne 46; Young Widow 46; Christmas Eve • Sinners' Holiday 47; Intrigue 47; Race Street 48; Canadian Pacific 49; Fighting Man of the Plains 49; The Younger Brothers 49; Canyon Pass • Raton Pass 50; Cariboo Trail • The Caribou Trail 50; Colt .45 • Thundercloud 50; Fort Worth 51; Sugarfoot • Swirl of Glory 51

Marin, Richard see Marin, Cheech
Marinego, I. E Così Divennero i Tre Supermen del West 73
Marinos, Lex An Indecent Obsession 85; Boundaries of the Heart 88
Marins, José Mojica Esta Noite Encarnarei No Teu Cadáver • Tonight I Will Make Your Corpse Turn Red • Tonight I Will Paint in Flesh Color 66; A Meia Noite Levarei a Sua Alma 66; O Estranho Mundo de Zé do Caixão • The Strange World of Zé do Caixão 68; Trilogia de Terror • Trilogy of Terror 68*; Finis Hominis 70; O Ritual dos Sádicos 70; Quando os Deuses Adormecem 71; O Exorcismo Negro 74; Delírios de um Amoral 78; O Estupro 78; Mundo Mercado do Sexo 78; Perversão 78; Encarnação de Demônio 81
Marion, Frances Just Around the Corner 21; The Love Light 21; The Song of Love 23*
Marion, George F. Madame X 16; Robinson Crusoe 16
Maris, Peter Delirium 79; Land of Doom 84; Terror Squad 88; Ministry of Vengeance 89
Mariscal, Alberto The Blood of Nostradamus • The Curse of Nostradamus • La Maldición de Nostradamus 59*; El Sabor de la Venganza • The Taste of the Savage 70; Los Marcados • They Call Him Marcados 72; Forajidos en la Mira • Outlaws in the Viewfinder 87
Marischka, Ernst St. Matthew Passion 52; Du Bist die Welt für Mich • The Richard Tauber Story • You Are the World for Me 53; Forever My Love • Sissi • Sissi—Die Junge Kaiserin • Sissi—Schicksalsjahre einer Kaiserin 55; The Story of Vickie 58;

Embezzled Heaven • Der Veruntreute Himmel 59; Das Dreimäderlhaus • The House of the Three Girls • The House of Three Girls 61
Marischka, Georg Hanussen 55*; Viva Gringo 66
Marischka, Hubert Liebe im Dreiviertel Takt • Love in Waltz Time 38; Fasching in Wien 39
Mark, David Superbug, the Wild One 77
Mark, Robert see Zehetgruber, Rudolf
Markaryan, Henry Land and Gold • Zemlya i Zoloto 87*
Marker, Chris Olympia 52 52; Les Statues Meurent Aussi 53*; Dimanche à Pékin • Sunday in Peking 55; Les Hommes de la Baleine 56*; Letter from Siberia • Lettre de Sibérie 57; Le Mystère de l'Atelier Quinze 57*; Les Astronautes 59*; Description d'un Combat • Description of a Struggle 60; ¡Cuba Sí! • Cuba Yes! 61; Liberté 61*; La Jetée • The Jetty • The Pier 62; Le Joli Mai 63; The Koumiko Mystery • Le Mystère Koumiko 65; Far from Vietnam • Loin du Viêt-nam 66*; If I Had Four Dromedaries • Si J'Avais Quatre Dromadaires 66; Les Mots Ont un Sens 67; À Bientôt J'Espère 68*; La Sixième Face du Pentagone • The Sixth Side of the Pentagon 68*; The Day of the Shoot—Costa-Gavras' "L'Aveu" • Jour de Tournage 69; Le Deuxième Procès d'Artur London • The Second Trial of Arthur London 69; On Vous Parle de Brésil • They Tell You About Brazil 69; Rhoudiacéta 69; La Bataille des Dix Millions • The Battle of the Ten Millions • Cuba: Battle of the 10,000,000 70*; Classe de Luttes 70*; Le Train en Marche • The Train Rolls On 71; La Solitude du Chanteur de Fond 74; Carlos Marighela 75; La Spirale 75*; Le Fond de l'Air Est Rouge 77; Quand le Siècle A Pris Formes • When the Century Had Shapes 78; Junkopia 81; Sans Soleil • Sunless 82; 2084 • 2084: Vidéo Clip pour une Réflexion Syndicale et pour le Plaisir 84*; A.K. 85; Mémoire de Simone • Memory of Simone 86; L'Héritage de la Chouette 89
Marker, Russ The Demon from Devil's Lake 64
Marketaki, Tonia The Price of Love • I Timi tis Agapis 84
Markey, Alexander Hei Tiki 35
Markham, Kyra The Forest Ring 30*
Markham, Mansfield The Return of Raffles 32; Maid Happy 33
Markham, Monte Defense Play 87
Markle, Fletcher Gun Moll • Jigsaw 49; The Man with a Cloak 51; Night Into Morning 51; The Incredible Journey 63
Markle, Peter The Personals 81; Hot Dog…The Movie 84; Youngblood 86; Bat 21 88
Markopoulos, Gregory A Christmas Carol 40; Du Sang de la Volupté et de la Mort 47; The Dead Ones 48; Flowers of Asphalt 49; Swain 50; Arbres aux Champignons 51; Eldora 52; Serenity 61; Twice a

Man 63; The Death of Hemingway 65; Galaxie 66; Mark Turbyfill 66; Ming Green 66; Through a Lens Brightly 66; Bliss 67; The Divine Damnation 67; Eros, o Basileas 67; Gammelion 67; Himself As Herself 67; The Iliac Passion • The Markopoulos Passion 67; Mysteries 68; Index Hans Richter 69; Political Portraits 69; Sorrows Moment 69; Alph 70; Genius 70; The Olympian 70; Doldertal 7 71; Hagiographia 71; 35 Boulevard General Koenig 71
Markos, Miklós Kismaszat és a Gézengúzok • Little Smite and the Scamps 86
Marković, Goran Déjà Vu • Već Viđeno 87
Markowitz, Murray Recommendation for Mercy 75; I Miss You, Hugs and Kisses 78
Markowitz, Robert Voices 79
Marks, Arthur Togetherness 70; The Class of '74 72*; Bonnie's Kids 73; Detroit 9000 73; The Roommates 73; Bucktown 75; Friday Foster 75; A Woman for All Men 75; J.D.'s Revenge 76; The Monkey Hustle 76
Marks, George Harrison Naked As Nature Intended 61; The Dream World of Harrison Marks • The Naked World of Harrison Marks 67; The Nine Ages of Nakedness 69; Come Play with Me 77
Marks, Harrison see Marks, George Harrison
Marks, Harry Unlucky Jim 36; Shadow of Death 39
Markson, Morley Off Your Rocker 80*
Markson, S. Quei Dannati Giorni dell' Odio e dell'Inferno 71
Marmont, Percy The Captain's Table 36
Marner, Eugene Beauty and the Beast 87; Puss in Boots 87
Marnham, Christian The Orchard End Murder 81
Marno, Erwin All Bad • Indecent • Schwarze Nylons—Heisse Nächte • Waylaid Women 58
Marodon, Pierre Le Diamant Vert 17; Qui à Tué 19; La Fée des Neiges 20; La Femme aux Deux Visages 20; Les Femmes des Autres 20; Les Morts Qui Parlent 20; Le Tocsin 20; Les Trois Gants de la Dames en Noir 20; Buridan—Le Héros de la Tour de Nesle 24; Salammbô 25; Les Dieux Ont Soif 26; Les Voleurs de Gloire 26
Maros, Basil The Aegean Tragedy 65
Marquand, Christian Il Baro • Les Grands Chemins • Of Flesh and Blood 62; Candy 68
Marquand, Richard Do Yourself Some Good 75; The Legacy • The Legacy of Maggie Walsh 78; Birth of the Beatles 79; Eye of the Needle 81; Return of the Jedi 83; Until September 84; Jagged Edge 85; Hearts of Fire 87
Marquette, Jacques Meteor Monster • Teenage Monster 57
Marquis, Don Blood Test 23
Marquis, Eric Shamus 59
Marr, Leon Dancing in the Dark 86
Marsan, Charles de see De Marsan, Charles
Marsden, Ralph Lawrence The Sabbat of

the Black Cat 71; Boys and Girls Together 80

Marsh, David The Lords of Magick 90

Marsh, Julian The Touch of Her Flesh • The Touch of Her Life • Way Out Love 67

Marsh, Ray The Last Porno Flick • The Mad, Mad Movie Makers 74; Lord Shango 75

Marshak, Philip Dracula Sucks 79; Cataclysm 80*; Night Train to Terror 85*

Marshall, Anthony Bullets and Saddles 43

Marshall, Don Cycles South 71

Marshall, Frank Feet of Clay 60; Identity Unknown 60; Gang War 62; The Gentle Terror 62; A Guy Called Caesar 62

Marshall, Frank Arachnophobia 90

Marshall, Fred Popdown 68

Marshall, Garry Young Doctors in Love 82; The Flamingo Kid • Mr. Hot Shot • Sweet Ginger Brown 84; Nothing in Common 86; Overboard 87; Beaches 88; Pretty Woman 90

Marshall, Gene Two Catch Two 79*

Marshall, George The Devil's Own 16; Love's Lariat 16*; A Woman's Eyes 16*; Bill Brennan's Claim 17; Border Wolves 17; Casey's Border Raid 17; The Comeback 17; The Desert Ghost 17; Double Suspicion 17; The Honor of Men 17; The Man from Montana 17; Meet My Wife 17; The Raid 17; Right-of-Way Casey 17; Roped In 17; They Were Four 17; Won by Grit 17; The Fast Mail 18; Husband Hater 18; The Adventures of Ruth 19; Prairie Trails 19; Ruth of the Rockies 19; Hands Off 20; A Ridin' Romeo 20; After Your Own Heart 21; The Jolt 21; The Lady from Longacre 21; Why Trust Your Husband? 21; The Committee on Credentials 22; Smiles Are Trumps 22; West Is West 22; Don Quickshot of the Rio Grande 23; Haunted Valley 23; Men in the Raw 23; Where Is This West? 23; The Burglar 24; The Fight 24; The Hunt 24; Paul Jones, Jr. 24; The Big Game Hunter 25; A Parisian Knight 25; The Sky Jumper 25; A Spanish Romeo 25; It's a Pipe 26; Gentlemen Prefer Scotch 27; He Loved Her Not 30; Hey Diddle Diddle 30; Practice Shots 31; Alum and Eve 32; Big Dame Hunting 32; A Firehouse Honeymoon 32; Just a Pain in the Parlor 32; The Old Bull 32; Pack Up Your Troubles 32*; The Soilers 32; Strictly Unreliable 32; Their First Mistake 32; Towed in a Hole 32; The Big Fibber 33; Caliente Love 33; Down Swing 33; Easy on the Eye 33; Fine Points 33; Hip Action 33; Husbands' Reunion 33; Impact 33; Knockout Kisses 33; Position and Back Swing 33; Sweet Cookie 33; Ever Since Eve 34; She Learned About Sailors 34; 365 Nights in Hollywood 34; Wild Gold 34; In Old Kentucky 35; Life Begins at Forty 35; Mr. Faintheart • Ten Dollar Raise 35; Music Is Magic 35; Show Them No Mercy! • Tainted Money 35; Can This Be Dixie? 36; The Crime of Dr. Forbes 36; A Message to Garcia 36; Love Under Fire 37; Nancy Steele Is Missing 37; Battle of Broadway 38; The Goldwyn Fol-

lies 38*; Hold That Co-Ed • Hold That Girl 38; You Can't Cheat an Honest Man 38*; Destry Rides Again 39; The Ghost Breakers 40; When the Daltons Rode 40; The Golden Hour • Pot o' Gold 41; Texas 41; The Forest Rangers 42; Star Spangled Rhythm 42; Valley of the Sun 42; Melody Inn • Riding High 43; True to Life 43; And the Angels Sing 44*; Hold That Blonde 45; Incendiary Blonde 45; Murder, He Says 45; The Blue Dahlia 46; Monsieur Beaucaire 46; The Perils of Pauline 47; Variety Girl 47; Hazard 48; Tap Roots 48; Lust for Gold 49*; My Friend Irma 49; Fancy Pants 50; Never a Dull Moment 50; A Millionaire for Christy 51; Military Policemen • Off Limits 52; The Savage 52; Scared Stiff 52; Duel in the Jungle 53; Houdini 53; Money from Home 53; Destry 54; Red Garters 54; The Second Greatest Sex 55; Beyond Mombasa 56; Pillars of the Sky • The Tomahawk and the Cross 56; The Guns of Fort Petticoat 57; The Sad Sack 57; Imitation General 58; The Mating Game 58; The Sheepman 58; The Gazebo 59; It Started with a Kiss 59; Cry for Happy 61; The Happy Thieves 61; The Oldest Confession • Once a Thief 61; How the West Was Won 62*; Advance to the Rear • Company of Cowards? 63; Dark Purpose • L'Intrigo 63*; Papa's Delicate Condition 63; Boy, Did I Get a Wrong Number! 66; Eight on the Lam • Eight on the Run 66; Hook, Line and Sinker 68; The Wicked Dreams of Paula Schultz 68

Marshall, Herbert Tinker 49; Method and Madness • Mr. Pastry Does the Laundry 50

Marshall, Maurice The Wife's Relations 28

Marshall, Noel Roar 81

Marshall, Penny Jumpin' Jack Flash 86; Big 88; Awakenings 90

Marshall, Stuart Desire 89

Marshall, William Adventures of Captain Fabian 51; Hello God 51; The Phantom Planet 61

Marston, Lawrence The Star of Bethlehem 12; The Fatal Wedding 13*; The Woman in Black 14; Dora Thorne 15; The Millionaire Baby 15; The Primrose Path 15; The Marriage Bond 16; A Wall Street Tragedy 16

Marston, Theodore Robin Hood 13; The Caveman 15; Mortmain 15; Pawns of Mars 15; Wheels of Justice 15; The Dawn of Freedom 16*; The Surprises of an Empty Hotel 16; The Girl by the Roadside 17; Greed 17; The Raggedy Queen 17; The Secret Kingdom 17*; The Seventh Sin 17; Sloth 17; Wrath 17; Beyond the Law 18; The Black Gate 19

Mart, Paul Beauty and the Body 63

Martel, Alphonse Gigolettes of Paris 33

Martel, Gene The Black Forest 54; Diplomatic Passport 54

Marten, Alexander Without a Home 39

Martin, Charles No Leave, No Love 46; My Dear Secretary 48; Death of a Scoundrel • The Loves and Death of a Scoundrel

56; If He Hollers Let Him Go • Night Hunt 68; How to Seduce a Woman 74; One Man Jury 78

Martin, D'Urville Dolemite 75; Disco 9000 77

Martin, E. A. The War O'Dreams 15; The Heart of Texas Ryan • Single Shot Parker 17

Martin, Ernst Heimatland • Homeland 39

Martin, Eugenio Conqueror of Maracaibo 61; Hipnosis • Hypnosis • Ipnosi • Nur Tote Zeugen Schweigen 62; Golden Goddess of Rio Beni 64; The Bounty Killers • El Precio de un Hombre • The Ugly Ones 66; A Candle for the Devil • It Happened at Nightmare Inn • Nightmare Hotel • Una Vela para el Diablo 70; Bad Man's River • E Continuano a Fregarsi il Milione di Dollari • Y Seguían Robándose el Milión de Dólares 71; Pancho Villa 71; Horror Express • Panic in the Trans-Siberian Train • Panic on the Trans-Siberian Express • Pánico en el Transiberiano 72; Aquella Casa en las Afueras • That House in the Outskirts • That House on the Outskirts 80; Sobrenatural • Supernatural 80

Martin, Francis Tillie and Gus 33

Martin, Frank see Girolami, Marino

Martin, Gene see Martin, Eugenio

Martin, George Under Western Skies 21; The Winding Trail 21

Martin, George see Martin, Jorge

Martin, Herbert see De Martino, Alberto

Martin, J. H. The Adventures of a £100 Bank Note 05; A Christmas Card, or The Story of Three Homes 05; The Conjuring Clown • The Pierrot and the Devil's Dice 05; The Dancer's Dream 05; The Fatal Necklace 05; The Freak Barber 05; He Learned Ju-Jitsu—So Did the Missus 05; The King of Clubs 05; The Misguided Bobby 05; A Race for Bed 05; A Shave by Instalments on the Uneasy System 05; Short-Sighted Sammy 05; The Tramp and the Typewriter 05; Trouble Below Stairs 05; The Visions of an Opium Smoker 05; When the Wife's Away 05; While the Household Sleeps 05; Brown's Fishing Excursion 06; The Curate's Dilemma 06; The Doctored Beer 06; The Fakir and the Footpads 06; He Cannot Get a Word in Edgeways 06; Home Without Mother 06; House to Let 06; How to Make Time Fly 06; Introductions Extraordinary 06; Jim the Signalman 06; Just a Little Piece of Cloth 06; A Lively Quarter Day 06; The Lover's Predicament 06; The Madman's Fate 06; The Medium Exposed 06; Mistaken Identity 06; Oh That Doctor's Boy! 06; The Old Lie and the New 06; Seaside Lodgings 06; Spooning 06; Various Popular Liquors Illustrated 06; Woman Supreme 06; The World's Wizard 06; Adventures of a Broker's Man 07; The Amateur Paper Hanger 07; The Bookmaker 07; The Bothered Bathers 07; The Burglar's Surprise 07; The Cheaters Cheated 07; The Chef's Revenge

07; The Cook's Dream 07; The Fatal Hand 07; The Fidgety Fly 07; His First Top Hat 07; How a Burglar Feels 07; An Inhuman Father 07; A Knight Errant 07; A Mother's Sin 07; My Lady's Revenge 07; Pity the Poor Blind 07; The Sailor's Return • Saved by a Sailor 07; The Tale of a Mouse 07; A Tragedy of the Ice 07; The Phantom Ship 08*

Martin, Jorge Diabolical Shudder • Escalofrío Diabólico 71

Martin, Karl Heinz La Paloma 36; Der Abenteurer von Paris 37; Punks Kommt aus Amerika 37; Die Glücklichste Ehe von Wien • The Happiest Married Couple in Vienna 38; Konzert in Tirol 39; Du Bist Mein Glück • Thou Art My Joy 40

Martin, L. Llegaron los Marcianos • I Marziani Hanno Dodici Mani • Siamo Quattro Marziani • The Twelve-Handed Men of Mars 64*

Martin, Murray T. Dan Smith 87*

Martin, Paul A Blonde Dream • Ein Blonder Traum 32; Liebe Ist Liebe • Love Is Love 32; Orient Express 34; Black Roses • Did I Betray? 35; Glückskinder 37; Seven Slaps • Sieben Ohrfeigen 38; Desert Song • Das Lied der Wüste 40; Alla Conquista dell'Arkansas • Die Goldsucher von Arkansas • Massacre at Marble City 64*; Graf Bobby, der Schrecken des Wilden Westens 65

Martin, Richard Infamous Conduct 66; King Monster 77

Martin, Sobey see Fregonese, Hugo

Martin, William Jacktown 62

Martinek, H. Oceano Drowsy Dick's Dream 09; The Exploits of Three-Fingered Kate 09; Her Lover's Honour 09; The Professor's Twirly-Whirly Cigarettes 09; Shipmates 09; Three-Fingered Kate—Her Second Victim, the Art Dealer 09; The Artist's Hoax • The Artist's Ruse 10; The Baby, the Boy and the Teddy-Bear 10; The Butler's Revenge 10; A Cheap Removal 10; A Deal in Broken China 10; Drowsy Dick Dreams He's a Burglar 10; His Master's Voice 10; The Kid's Kite 10; Lost, a Monkey 10; Marie's Joke with the Flypapers 10; Only Two Little Shoes 10; Playing Truant 10; A Plucky Lad 10; The Tables Turned 10; Three-Fingered Kate—Her Victim the Banker 10; Three-Fingered Kate—The Episode of the Sacred Elephants 10; Trust Those You Love 10; Wanted, a Bath Chair Attendant 10; What Happened to the Dog's Medicine 10; When Women Join the Force 10; Accidents Will Happen 11; Billy's Book on Boxing 11; A Comrade's Treachery 11; Giles' First Visit to London 11; Her Father's Photograph 11; The King's Peril 11; The Misadventures of Bill the Plumber 11; A Noble Revenge 11; The Plum Pudding Stakes 11; The Prehistoric Man 11; The Puritan Maid 11; Quits 11; The Sacred (?) Elephant 11; A Soldier's Honour 11; A Tangle of Fates 11; Wanted, Field Marshals for the Gorgonzola Army 11; The Wild, Wild Westers 11; Autumn Roses 12; The Battalion Shot 12; The

Bliggs Family at the Zoo 12; A Child, a Wand and a Wish 12; A Deal in Crockery 12; Don Q and the Artist 12; Don Q—How He Outwitted Don Luis 12; Don Q—How He Treated the Parole of Gevil Hay 12; Dora 12; The First Chronicles of Don Q—The Dark Brothers of the Civil Guard 12; The Gentleman Ranker 12; Her Bachelor Guardian 12; The International Spies • Lieutenant Daring and the Plans of the Minefields 12; Lieutenant Daring and the Photographing Pigeon 12; Lily of Letchworth Lock 12*; The Old Gardener 12; Three-Fingered Kate—The Case of the Chemical Fumes 12; Three-Fingered Kate—The Pseudo-Quartette 12; Two Bachelor Girls 12; Yiddle and His Fiddle 12; The Antique Vase 13; The Chaplet of Pearls 13; The Coastguard's Haul • Reub's Little Girl 13; His Maiden Aunt 13; In the Grip of Death 13; Jobson's Luck 13; The Nest on the Black Cliff 13; Sagacity vs. Crime 13; The Sanctimonious Spinsters' Society 13; Signals in the Night 13; Stock Is As Good As Money 13; With Human Instinct 13; Black Roderick the Poacher 14; The Corner House Burglary 14; A Desperate Stratagem 14; The False Wireless 14; The Friend in Blue 14; The Hidden Witness 14; In the Grip of Spies 14; The Mystery of the Old Mill 14; The Power to Kill 14; The Rajah's Tiara 14; The Stolen Masterpiece 14; A Warm Reception 14; At the Torrent's Mercy 15; The Clue of the Cigar Band 15; The Deadly Model 15; Harry the Swell 15; The Ingrate 15; Jim the Scorpion 15; The Octopus Gang 15; That Silly Ass 15; Glastonbury Past and Present 22

Martinelli, Franco see Girolami, Marino

Martinenghi, Italo Three Supermen in Santo Domingo • Tre Supermen a Santo Domingo 86

Martínez, Arturo All Because of a Wedding Dress • Por un Vestido de Novia 86

Martinez, Chuck Nice Girls Don't Explode 87

Martínez, René, Jr. The Guy from Harlem 77; Road of Death 77

Martínez Ferry, Isidoro La Cara del Terror • Face of Fear • Face of Terror 62

Martínez-Lazaro, Emilio Lulu by Night • Lulu de Noche 86; El Juego Más Divertido 88

Martínez Ortega, Gonzalo Es Mi Vida—El Noa Noa 2 • It's My Life—El Noa Noa 2 86

Martínez Solares, Gilberto The Mayor • El Señor Alcalde 39; Three-and-a-Half Musketeers 57; La Casa del Terror • La Casa del Vampiro • The Face of the Screaming Werewolf • House of Terror 59*; Santo and the Blue Demon vs. the Monsters • Santo Contra los Monstruos de Frankenstein • Santo y Blue Demon Contra los Monstruos 68; Bricklayer's Day II • El Día de los Albaniles II 86; The Neighborhood—Oh Those Hot Mexicans • El Vecindario—Los Mexicanos Calientes 86

Martini, Richard You Can't Hurry Love

88; Limit Up 89

Martino, Alberto de see De Martino, Alberto

Martino, Sergio Arizona Colt Si Scateno e Li Fece 70; Next • The Next Victim • Lo Strano Vizio della Signora Ward 71; Excite Me • Il Tuo Vizio È una Stanza Chiusa e Solo Io Ne Ho la Chiave • Your Vice Is a Closed Room and Only I Have the Key 72; Una Strana Orchidea con Cinque Goccie di Sangue • They're Coming to Get You • Todos los Colores de la Oscuridad • Tutti i Colori del Buio 72; The Bodies Bear Traces of Carnal Violence • I Corpi Presentano Tracce di Violenza Carnale • Torso 73; The Violent Professionals 73; Sex with a Smile 76; The Island of the Fishmen • L'Isola degli Uomini Pesce • Screamers • Something Waits in the Dark 78*; Mannaja 78; La Montagna del Dio Cannibale • Il Montagna di Dio Cannibale • Mountain of Cannibal Gods • Prisoner of the Cannibal God • Slave of the Cannibal God 78; Alligators • Il Fiume del Grande Caimano • The Great Alligator • Great Alligator River 79; After the Fall of New York • Due Mille Dicianuove • 2019: Dopo la Caduta di New York 84; Half Right, Half Left • Mezzo Destro, Mezzo Sinistro 85; Hands of Steel 86; The Opponent 90

Martinson, Leslie The Atomic Kid 54; Hot Car Girl • Hot Rod Girl 56; Hot Rod Rumble 57; Lad: A Dog 61*; Black Gold 63; PT 109 63*; FBI Code 98 64; For Those Who Think Young 64; Batman 66; Fathom 67; The Challengers 68; Charlie Chan: Happiness Is a Warm Clue 71; Mrs. Pollifax—Spy 71; And Millions Will Die 73; Escape from Angola 76; Cruise Missile 78

Martiny, Didier Jusqu'à la Nuit 85

Martoglio, Nino Il Romanzo 13; Capitan Bianco 14; Lost in the Dark • Sperduti nel Buio 14; Teresa Raquin 15

Marton, Andrew The Hour of Fear • Two O'Clock in the Morning 29; Hirsekorn 31; Die Nacht Ohne Pause 31*; Nordpol-Ahoi! • S.O.S. Eisberg • S.O.S. Iceberg 32*; Beast of the Himalayas • Der Dämon der Berge • Demon of the Himalayas 34; Elnök Kisasszony • Miss President 35; The Secret of Stamboul • The Spy in White 36; Wolf's Clothing 36; School for Husbands 37; A Little Bit of Heaven 40; Two-Faced Woman 41*; Gentle Annie 44; Gallant Bess 46; King Solomon's Mines 50*; The Big North • The Wild North 51; Mask of the Himalayas • Storm Over Tibet 51*; The Devil Makes Three 52; Gypsy Colt 53; Green Fire 54; Men of the Fighting Lady 54; Prisoner of War 54; Seven Wonders of the World 56*; Underwater Warrior 58; It Happened in Athens 61; The Longest Day 62*; The Sword of Islam 62; 55 Days at Peking 63*; The Thin Red Line 64; Birds Do It 65; Clarence the Cross-Eyed Lion 65; Crack in the World 65; El Valle de los Caídos 65; Around the World Under the Sea 66; Africa—Texas Style! • Cowboy in Africa 67

Marton, Endre see Marton, Andrew

Martonffy, Emil Vasember 35; Az Okos Mama 36; Eb Ura Fakó 40

Martov, M. Slave of Passion, Slave of Vice 14

Marvin, Joseph Kitosch, l'Uomo Che Venna dal Nord 67

Marvin, Mike Hamburger • Hamburger . . . The Motion Picture 86; The Wraith 86

Marzano, Joseph Man Outside 65

Masa, Antonin Wandering 67*

Masadi, Krishna Avasthe 88

Mascelli, Joseph The Atomic Brain • Monstrosity 64

Mascolo, Jean The Children • Les Enfants 84*

Maselli, Francesco Bagnaia Paese Italico 49; Tibet Proibito 49; Finestre 50; Bambini 51; Sport Minore 51; Stracciaroli 51; Zona Pericolosa 51; I Fiori 52; Ombrellai 52; Amore in Città • Love in the City 53*; Città Che Dorme 53; Festa dei Morti in Sicilia 53; Uno Spettacolo di Pupi 53; Cantamaggio a Cervarezza 54; Gli Sbandati 55; Bambini al Cinema 56; The Doll That Took the Town • La Donna del Giorno 56; Adolescenza 59; I Delfini 60; La Suola Romana 60; Le Italiane e l'Amore • Latin Lovers 61*; Les Deux Rivales • Gli Indifferenti • Time of Indifference 63; Una Coppia Tranquilla • A Fine Pair • Ruba al Prossimo Tuo 68; Fai in Fretta ad Uccidermi. . .Ho Freddo! • Kill Me Quick, I'm Cold 68; Lettera Aperta a un Giornale della Sera 70; Il Sospetto 75; Storia d' Amore • A Story of Love 86; Codice Privato • Private Access 88

Masheret, A. V. see Macharet, Alexander

Masini, Giuseppe Antinea, l'Amante della Città Sepolta • L'Atlantide • L'Atlantide — Antinea, l'Amante della Città Sepolta • Atlantis the Lost Continent • Atlantis the Lost Kingdom • Journey Beneath the Desert • The Lost Kingdom • Queen of Atlantis 61*; Guilt Is Not Mine • L'Ingiusta Condanna • Quelli Che Non Muoiono 68

Maskalyk, Antonín see Moskalyk, Antonín

Maslansky, Paul Sugar Hill • Voodoo Girl • The Zombies of Sugar Hill 74

Maslyukov, A. Children of the Revolution 36; The Road to Life 56*

Mason, Bill Cry of the Wild 72

Mason, Christopher Fish and Milligan 66

Mason, Herbert Bad Blood • First Offence 36; East Meets West 36; His Lordship • Man of Affairs 36; Take My Tip 37; Strange Boarders 38; Continental Express • The Silent Battle 39; Dr. O'Dowd 39; Lady in Distress • A Window in London 39; The Briggs Family 40; Fingers 40; Mr. Proudfoot Shows a Light 41; Once a Crook 41; Back Room Boy 42; The Night Invader 42; It's in the Bag 43; Flight from Folly 44

Mason, Noel see Smith, Noel Mason

Mason, Walt Bunked and Paid For 17; The Dipper 17; Hash 17; True Love and Fake Money 17

Massaccesi, Aristide Death Smiles on a Murder 74; Eva Nera 76; Emanuelle e gli Ultimi Cannibali • Trap Them and Kill Them 77; Emanuelle in America 77; Beyond the Darkness • Blue Holocaust • Buio Omega 79; The Anthropophagous Beast • Anthropophagus • The Grim Reaper • Man Eater 80; Absurd • Absurd — Anthropophagous II • Anthropophagus II 81; Buried Alive 84; L'Alcova 85; The Pleasure 85; The Desire to Watch • Voglia di Guardare 86; Lussuri • Lust 86; Delight • Delizia 87; Eleven Days, Eleven Nights • Ugiorni, Unotti • Undici Giorni, Undici Notte 87; Top Model 88

Massaro, Francesco Private Affairs • Ti Presento un'Amica 88

Massetti, Ivana Domino 88

Massey, Jane Problems of Sleep 48

Massi, Stevio Blood, Sweat and Fear 75

Massingham, Richard Tell Me If It Hurts 34; And So to Work 36; The Daily Round 37*; Fear and Peter Brown 40; The Greedy Boy's Dream 49; The Cure 50*; The Blakes Slept Here • Family Album 54*

Masson, Jean Musée Grévin 58*; La Mère et l'Enfant 59*

Massot, Joe Wonderwall 68; The Song Remains the Same 76*; Dance Craze 81; Eddy Grant Live at Notting Hill Carnival 82; Space Riders 84

Masten, Werner Die Falsche • The False One • The Tramp 86

Masters, Quentin Thumb Tripping 72; The Stud 78; The Psi Factor 80; The Burning Man • A Dangerous Summer 81; Midnite Spares 83

Masterson, Peter The Trip to Bountiful 85; Blood Red 88; Full Moon in Blue Water 88; Night Game 89

Mastorakis, Nico Death Has Blue Eyes 74; Island of Death 75; The Next One 82; Blind Date 84; Skyhigh 85; The Zero Boys 85; The Wind 86; Double Exposure 87; Glitch • Nico Mastorakis' Glitch 87; Nightmare at Noon 87

Mastrocinque, Camillo The Cuckoo Clock • L'Orologio a Cucu 38; Un Matrimonio Ideale 39; Fedora 46; When Love Calls 48; Lost in the Dark 49; The Fighting Men • Gli Inesorabili 50; The Life of Donizetti 51; Duel Without Honor 53; The Man with the Grey Glove 53; Tarantella Napoletana 54; Totò all'Inferno • Totò in Hell 54; Dites 35 • Lady Doctor • Mi Mujer Es Doctor • Totò, Vittorio e la Dottoressa 56; Beach Party, Italian Style • Diciottenni al Sole • Eighteen in the Sun 63; Carmilla • La Cripta e l'Incubo • The Crypt and the Nightmare • Crypt of Horror • The Crypt of the Vampire • The Curse of the Karnsteins • Karnstein • The Karnstein Curse • La Maldición de los Karnstein • La Maledizione dei Karnstein • Terror in the Crypt • The Vampire's Crypt 63; Full Hearts and Empty Pockets 64; An Angel for Satan • Un Angelo per Satana 66

Mastroianni, Armand He Knows You're Alone 80; The Clairvoyant • The Killing Hour 82; The Supernaturals 85; Cameron's Closet 87; Distortions 87

Masucci, Jerry Salsa 76*

Masuda, Toshio Daikanbu • The Gangster VIP 68; Tora! Tora! Tora! 70*; Catastrophe 1999 • The Last Days of Planet Earth • Nostradamus no Daiyogen • Prophecies of Nostradamus • Prophecies of Nostradamus: Catastrophe 1999 74; An Angel with One Wing • Katayoku Dake no Tenshi 86; Shūtō Shōshitsu • Tokyo Blackout 87

Masumura, Yasuzo Kisses 57; The Buildup 58; Disobedience 58; Across Darkness 59; The Cast-Off 59; Code of Women • Jokei • Jokyō • A Woman's Testament 59*; Afraid to Die 60; The False Student 60; All for Love 61; Love and Life 61; Wife's Confession 61; Life of a Woman 62; Stolen Pleasure 62; Black Report 63; Delinquents of Pure Heart 63; Love and Greed 64; Manji • Passion 64; The Hoodlum Soldier 65; The Wife of Seisaku 65; The Red Angel 66; School for Spies 66; Spider Girl 66; An Idiot in Love 67; Two Wives 67; The Wife of Seishu Hanaoka 67; Evil Trio 68; The House of Wooden Blocks 68; One Day at Summer's End 68; The Sex Check 68; The Blind Beast • Mōjū 69; Jotai • Vixen 69; Sembazuru • A Thousand Cranes 69; Denki Kurage • Play It Cool 70; Warehouse 73; Sword of Justice, Part Two 75; Double Suicide of Sonezaki 78

Masur, Richard Love Struck 87

Matalon, Eddy Cathy's Curse • Cauchemars 76; Blackout 78

Matanski, Larry The Naked Flame 70

Matarazzo, Raffaello Lacrime e Sorrisi 36; Il Serpente a Sonagli 36; It Was I • Sono Stato Io 40; Giuseppe Verdi • The Life and Music of Giuseppe Verdi 53; Paolo and Francesca 53; Tormento 53; La Fille de la Rizière • Rice Girl • La Risaia 63; La Nave delle Donne Maledette • The Ship of Condemned Women 63

Matcheret, A. see Macharet, Alexander

Maté, Rudolph Le Costaud des P.T.T. 31; Aren't We All? 32*; It Had to Be You 47*; The Dark Past 48; D.O.A. 49; Branded 50; No Sad Songs for Me 50; The Prince Who Was a Thief 50; Union Station 50; The Green Glove 51; When Worlds Collide 51; Paula • The Silent Voice 52; Sally and Saint Anne 52; Forbidden 53; The Mississippi Gambler 53; Second Chance 53; The Black Shield of Falworth 54; Rough Company • The Violent Men 54; The Siege at Red River • The Siege of Red River 54; The Far Horizons • The Untamed West 55; Miracle in the Rain 56; Port Afrique 56; The Rawhide Years 56; Three Violent People 56; The Deep Six 57; Come Prima • For the First Time • Serenade einer Grossen Liebe 58; The Barbarians • Revak — Lo Schiavo di Cartagine • Revak the Rebel • Rivak the Barbarian 59; The Immaculate Road 60; Il Dominatore dei Sette Mari • Il Re dei Sette Mari • Seven Seas to Calais 61*; Lion of Sparta • The 300 Spartans 62; Aliki • Aliki My Love 63

Matêjka, Václav Můj Hříšný Muž 86; Closed Circuit • Uzavřený Okruh 89

Mather, Ted Body Beat 86

Matheson, Katherine Comedienne 84

Mathews, Harry C. Welcome, Children 21

Mathot, Léon L'Appassionata 29*; L'Instinct 30; Embrassez-Moi 32; Le Révolté 38; Rappel Immédiat • Thunder Over Paris 39; Nuits d'Alerte 45; La Dernière Chevauchée 46; La Danseuse de Marrakech 49; Mon Gosse de Père 52

Matji, Manolo La Guerra de los Locos • The War of the Madmen 87

Matray, F. Sugar and Spice • Zucker und Zimt 15*

Matsubayashi, Shue I Bombed Pearl Harbor • The Storm Over the Pacific • Taiheiyō no Arashi 60; The Final War • The Last War • Sekai Daisensō 62; Attack Squadron 63

Matsubayashi, Shukei Yamashita Shōnen Monogatari 86

Matsuda, Sadatsugu Traitors 57

Matsumoto, Toshio Pandemonium • Shura 70; Dogura Magura 88

Matsuno, Hiroshi Kyūketsu Dokurosen • Living Skeleton 68

Matsuyama, Zenzo Happiness of Us Alone • Namonaku Mazushiku Utsukushiku 62; Burari Burabura Monogatari • My Hobo 63; Could I But Live 65; Senjō ni Nagareru Uta • We Will Remember 66; Chichi to Ko • Our Silent Love 69

Mattei, Bruno Apocalipsis Caníbal • Cannibal Virus • Hell of the Living Dead • Hell of the Living Death • Inferno dei Morti-Viventi • Night of the Zombies • Virus Cannibale • Virus—L'Inferno dei Morti Viventi • Zombie Creeping Flesh 81; Caged Women • Women's Penitentiary IV 84; L'Apache Bianco • White Apache 86; Strike Commando 87

Matter, Alex The Drifter 66; Scratch Harry 69

Matthau, Charles Doin' Time on Planet Earth 87

Matthau, Walter Gangster Story 59

Matthews, Jessie Victory Wedding 44

Mattinson, Burny Mickey's Christmas Carol 83; Basil the Great Mouse Detective • The Great Mouse Detective 86*

Mattison, Frank S. The Better Man Wins 22*; Shell Shocked Sammy 23; Circus Lure 24; The Last White Man 24; The Lone Wagon 24; Mile a Minute Morgan 24; North of Alaska 24; Ragged Robin 24; Flying Fool 25; Kit Carson Over the Great Divide • With Kit Carson Over the Great Divide 25; Slow Dynamite 25; Buffalo Bill on the U.P. Trail 26; Code of the Northwest 26; Daniel Boone Thru the Wilderness 26*; Better Days 27; King of the Herd 27; The Little Wild Girl 28; Must We Marry? 28; Old Age Handicap 28; Broken Hearted 29; Bye-Bye Buddy 29;

China Slaver 29; Girls Who Dare 29

Mattòli, Mario Amo Te Sola 36; Musica in Piazza 36; Tempo Massimo 36; L'Uomo Che Sorr'de 37; Il Destino • Destiny 38; Love's Triumph • Il Trionfo dell'Amore 38; Al Vostri Ordini Signora • At Your Orders, Madame 40; La Dama Bianca • The Lady in White 40; Eravamo Sette Vedove • We Were Seven Widows 40; Lezione di Chimica • Schoolgirl Diary 47; Life Begins Anew • La Vita Ricomincia 47; The Lady Is Fickle 48; Scarred 51; I Cadetti di Guascogna 52; Due Notti con Cleopatra • Two Nights with Cleopatra 53; The Lucky Five 53; My Heart Sings 54; Poverty and Nobility 54; Hercules in the Vale of Woe • Maciste Against Hercules in the Vale of Woe 62; For a Few Dollars Less • Per Qualche Dollaro in Meno 66

Matton, Charles La Pomme 68; Spermula 76

Mattray, Ernest Adventure in Music 43*

Mattsson, Arne And All These Women • Och Alla Dessa Kvinnor 44; I Som Här Inträdden • You Who Are About to Enter 45; Maria på Kvarngården • Marie in the Windmill 45; Susie • Sussie 45; Bad Eggs • Incorrigible • Rötägg 46; Peggy on a Spree • Peggy på Vift 46; Det Kom en Gäst • A Guest Came 47; Father Wanted • Pappa Sökes 47; Railroad Workers • The Railway Workers • Rallare 47; Dangerous Spring • Farlig Vår 48; Kvinna i Vitt • Woman in White 49; Kastrull Resan • Saucepan Journey 50; The Kiss on the Cruise • Kyssen på Kryssen 50; När Kärleken Kom till Byn • When Love Comes to the Village 50; Bärande Hav • Rolling Sea 51; Hon Dansade En Sommar • One Summer of Happiness 51; Because of My Hot Youth • För Min Heta Ungdoms Skull 52; Dull Clang • Hård Klang 52; The Bread of Love • Kärlekens Bröd 53; Enchanted Walk • Förtrollad Vandring 54; Salka Valka 54; Storm Över Tjurö 54; Hemsöborna • The People of Hemsö 55; Männen i Mörker • Men in Darkness 55; Flickan i Frack • Girl in a Dresscoat 56; Litet Bo • A Little Place of One's Own 56; Ingen Morgondag • No Tomorrow 57; Livets Vår • Spring of Life 57; Damen i Svart • The Lady in Black • Woman in Black 58; Det Kom Två Män • There Came Two Men 58; Körkarlen • The Phantom Carriage • The Phantom Chariot 58; Mannekäng i Rött • Mannequin in Red 58; Får Jag Låna Din Fru? • May I Borrow Your Wife? 59; Rider in Blue • Ryttare i Blått 59; När Mörket Faller • When Darkness Falls 60; Sommar och Syndare • Summer and Sinners 60; Ljuvlig Är Sommarnatten • The Summer Night Is Sweet 61; Biljett till Paradiset • Ticket to Paradise 62; The Doll • Vaxdockan 62; Lady in White • Vita Frun 62; Det Är hos Mig Han Har Varit • Yes, He's Been with Me 63; Den Gula Bilen • The Yellow Car 63; Blåjackor • Blue Boys • Boys in Blue 64; Här Kommer Bärsärkarna • Two Vikings 65; I, the Body • Morianerna • Morianna

65; Nattmara • Nightmare 66; Woman of Darkness • Yngsjömordet 66; En Helt Vanlig Person • Mördaren • The Murderer • An Ordinary Person 67; Bamse • My Father's Mistress • The Teddy Bear 68; Anna och Eva • Anne and Eve 69; The Truck 76; Black Sun 78; The Girl 87; Sleep Well, My Love 87

Matula, Julius The Man on the Line • The Man on the Phone • Muž na Drátě 85; Bloudění Orientačního Běžce • Going Astray in an Orientation Course 86; Stupně Poražených 88

Matulavich, Peter The Jupiter Menace 82*

Mätzig, Kurt Ehe im Schatten • Marriage in the Shadows 47; Die Buntkarierten 49; Council of the Gods 50; Familie Benthin 50*; Roman einer Ehe • Roman einer Jungen Ehe 51; Ernst Thalmann 55; Schlosser und Katen 57; Das Lied der Matrosen 58*; The Astronauts • First Spaceship on Venus • Milczaca Gwiazda • Raumschiff Venus Antwortet Nicht • Der Schweigende Stern • Silent Star • Spaceship to Venus 60; Septemberliebe 61; Preludio 11 64; Das Mädchen auf dem Brett 67

Mauch, Thomas Adrian und die Römer 88*; Maria von den Sternen • Mary of the Stars 89

Maude, Arthur Thaïs 14*; The Courtesan 16; Embers 16; Lord Loveland Discovers America 16; Powder 16; Revelations 16; Poppies of Flanders 27; The Ringer 28; Toni 28; The Clue of the New Pin 29; The Flying Squad 29; The Lyons Mail 31; Watch Beverly 32; The Lure 33; She Was Only a Village Maiden 33; The Wishbone 33; Boomerang 34; Borrowed Clothes 34; Live Again 36; One Good Turn 51

Maudru, Charles Renoncement 17*; La Mascotte des Poilus 18*; La Bourasque 20*; Le Droit de Tuer 20*; Le Lys Rouge 20*; L'Assommoir 21*; Un Aventurier 21*; La Fiancée du Disparu 21*; L'Inconnu 21*; Le Merchant Homme 21*; Près de Crime 21*; Le Talison 21*; Serge Panin 22*; L'Homme du Train 117 23*; Rocambole 23*; Les Amours de Rocambole 24*; Les Premières Armes de Rocambole 24*

Maurer, Norman The Three Stooges Go Around the World in a Daze 63; The Outlaws Is Coming • The Three Stooges Meet the Gunslinger 65

Mauri, Roberto The Saracens 60; Curse of the Blood Ghouls • Curses of the Ghouls • Slaughter of the Vampires 61; Lost Souls • Vite Perdute 61*; Zorikan the Barbarian 64; The Invincible Brothers Machiste 65; La Vendetta È il Mio Perdono 68; Sartana nella Valle degli Avvoltoi 70; Wanted Sabata 70; Bada alla Tua Pelle Spirito Santo 72; Semino Morte...lo Chiamavano Castigo di Dio 72

Mauro, Humberto Valadão o Cratera • Valadão the Disaster 25; In the Springtime of Life • Na Primavera da Vida 26; Lost Treasure • Tesouro Perdido 27; Blood of Minas • Minas Blood • Sangue Mineiro 28; Brasa Dormida • Dead Embers • Extinguished Cinders • Sleeping Embers 28; Cataguases 29; Lábios Sem Beijos • Lips Without Kisses 30; O Descobrimento do Brasil • The Discovery of Brazil 32; Ganga Bruta • Rough Diamond 32; Mulher 32; The Voice of Carnival • A Voz do Carnaval 33; Cidade Mulher • City Woman 34; Favela dos Meus Amores • Favela of My Loves 34; Um Apólogo 39; Argila • Clay 40*; Os Bandeirantes 40; O Despertar da Redentora 42; The Secret of Wings • O Segredo das Asas 44; Lição de Taxiderma 50; O Canto da Saudade • The Song of Sadness • The Song of Yearning 52; João de Barro 55; I Am Eight • Meus Oito Anos 56; A Velha a Fiar 64

Mavrogordato, Anthony Born of the Sea 48

Mavroidis, Dinos Scenario 85

Mawra, Joseph P. Olga's Girls 64; All Men Are Apes 65; Murder in Mississippi • Murder Mississippi 65

Maxwell, John The Man I Love 46*

Maxwell, Joseph Frivolous Wives 20

Maxwell, Paul see *Bianchini, Paolo*

Maxwell, Peter Blind Spot 58; The Desperate Man 59; The Ghost Train Murder 59; The Long Shadow 61; Dilemma • The Man with Two Faces 62; Serena 62; Impact 63; The Switch 63; Country Town 71; Plunge Into Darkness 77; Touch and Go 80; The Highest Honour • The Highest Honour—A True Story • Southern Cross 82

Maxwell, Ronald F. Little Darlings 80; The Night the Lights Went Out in Georgia 81; Kidco 82

May, Alan le see *LeMay, Alan*

May, Elaine A New Leaf 71; The Heartbreak Kid 72; Mikey and Nicky 76; Ishtar 87

May, Joe In der Tiefe des Schachts 12; Vorgluten des Balkanbrandes 12; Ein Ausgestossener • Ein Ausgestossener 1. Teil: Der Junge Chef 13; Entsagungen 13; Die Geheimnisse Villa • Die Geheimnisvolle Villa 13; Heimat und Fremde 13; Die Unheilbringende Perle 13; Verschleierte Bild von Gross Kleindorf 13; Der Mann im Keller 14; Die Pagode 14; Das Panzergewölbe 14; Der Spuk im Hause des Professors 14; Charly der Wunderaffe 15; Der Geheimskretär 15; Das Gesetz der Mine 15; Der Schuss im Traum 15; Sein Schwierigster Fall 15; Ein Blatt Papier 16; Ein Einsam Grab • Die Tat der Gräfin Worms 16*; Die Gespensteruhr 16; Hilde Warren and Death • Hilde Warren und der Tod 16; Nebel und Sonne 16; Das Rätselhafte Inserat 16*; Die Sünde der Helga Arndt 16; Wie Ich Detektiv Wurde 16; Des Vaters Letzter Wille 17; Das Geheimnis der Leeren Wasserflasche 17; Die Hochzeit im Exzentric-Club 17; Das Klima von Vancourt 17; Krähen Fliegen um den Turm 17; Ein Lichtstrahl im Dunkel 17; Die Liebe der Hetty Raymond 17; Der Onyxknopf 17; Der Schwarze Chauffeur 17; Die Silhouette des Teufels 17; Die Bettelgräfin 18*; Ihr Grosses Geheimnis 18; Die Kaukasierin

18*; Opfer 18; Sein Bester Freund 18; Veritas Vincit 18; Wogen des Schicksals 18; Fräulein Zahnarzt 19; Die Gräfin von Monte Cristo 19; Die Wahre Liebe 19; Die Heilige Simplizia • Legende von der Heiligen Simplizia 20; Die Herrin der Welt • Mistress of the World 20; Die Schuld der Lavinia Morland 20; Sodom und Gomorrah 20; Above All Law • The Hindu Tomb • The Indian Tomb • Das Indische Grabmal • Mysteries of India 21*; The Dragon's Claw 22; The Greatest Truth 22; Tragedy of Love • Tragödie der Liebe 23; Der Farmer aus Texas 25; Dagfin 26; Heimkehr • Homecoming 28; Asphalt 29; Ihre Majestät die Liebe 30; That's All That Matters • Und Das Ist die Hauptsache 31; Zwei in einem Auto 31; Le Chemin de Bonheur 32; Into the Blue • On Demande un Compagnon • Paris-Meditérránee 32; Le Dactylo Se Marié 33; Eine Liebesnacht 33; Ein Lied für Dich 33; Tout pour l'Amour 33; Voyages des Noces 33; Music in the Air 34; Two Hearts in Waltz Time 34*; Confession 37; The House of Fear 39; Society Smugglers 39; The House of Seven Gables • The House of the Seven Gables 40; The Invisible Man Returns 40; You're Not So Tough 40; Hit the Road 41; And So They Were Married • Johnny Doesn't Live Here Any More 44

May, Paul see *Ostermayer, Paul*

May, Wilfred The Substitute Wife 25

Mayberry, Russ The Jesus Trip 71; The Spaceman and King Arthur • A Spaceman in King Arthur's Court • UFO • Unidentified Flying Oddball 79

Mayer, Gerald Dial 1119 • The Violent Hour 50; Inside Straight 51; The Sellout 51; Holiday for Sinners 52; Bright Road 53; The Marauders 55; Diamond Safari 58

Mayer, Harold The Inheritance 64

Mayer, Henry see *Mayer, Hy*

Mayer, Hy The Adventures of Mr. Phiffles 13; Antics in Ink by Hy Mayer 13; Filmograph Cartoons 13; Fun in Film by Hy Mayer • The Magnetic Maid 13; Funny Fancies by Hy Mayer 13; Hilarities by Hy Mayer 13; Humors of Summer 13; Hy Mayer: His Merry Pen 13; Hy Mayer's Cartoons 13; In Cartoonland with Hy Mayer 13; In Laughland with Hy Mayer 13; Jolly Jottings by Hy Mayer 13; Just for Luck 13; Leaves from Hy Mayer's Sketchbook 13; Lightning Sketches by Hy Mayer 13; The Magic Hand 13; Pen Talk • Pen Talks by Hy Mayer 13; Sketches from Life by Hy Mayer 13; A Study in Crayon 13; Summer Caricatures 13; Whimsicalities by Hy Mayer 13; Pen Laughs 14; Topical Topics 14; Topical War Cartoons 14; Topical War Cartoons No. 2 14; War Cartoons by Hy Mayer 14; To Frisco by the Cartoon Route 15; Globe Trotting with Hy Mayer 16; High Life on a Farm 16; Pen and Inklings Around Jerusalem • Pen and Inklings in and Around Jerusalem 16; A Pen Trip to Palestine 16; Such Is Life in Alaska 16; Such Is Life in China 16; China Awakened 17; Seeing Ceylon • Seeing Ceylon with Hy

Mayer 17; Seeing New York • Seeing York with Hy Mayer 17; Such Is Life in Algeria • Such Is Life in South Algeria 17; New York by Heck 18; Universal Screen Magazine No. 77 18; Universal Screen Magazine No. 81 18; Universal Screen Magazine No. 82 18; Universal Screen Magazine No. 90 18; Universal Screen Magazine No. 92 18; Universal Screen Magazine No. 93 18; Universal Screen Magazine No. 94 18; Universal Screen Magazine No. 105 19; Baseball 20; Coney Island • Such Is Life at Coney Island 20; East Side New York • Such Is Life in East Side New York 20; Greenwich Village • Such Is Life in Greenwich Village 20; Such Is Life Among the Dogs 20; Such Is Life at the Zoo • The Zoo 20; Such Is Life in Midwinter 20; Such Is Sporting Life 20; Winter Sports 20; All Aboard 21; All the Merry Bow-Wows 21; Behind the Scenes of the Circus 21; The Circus 21; The County Fair 21; Day Dreams 21; The Door That Has No Lock 21; Down to the Fair 21; In the Silly Summertime 21; The Little City of Dreams 21; New York • Such Is Life in New York 21; Puppies 21; The Race Track • Such Is Life at the Race Track 21; A Ramble Through Provincetown 21; Scenes in the Zoo • Such Is Life at the Zoo 21; Spring Hats 21; Such Is Life at a County Fair 21; Such Is Life in Ramblerville 21; Such Is Life in Summer 21; Such Is Life in the Land of Fancy 21; Summer Scenes 21; Travelaugh 21; Water Stuff 21; How It Feels 22; In the Dear Old Summertime 22; Sporting Scenes 22; Such Is Life 22; Such Is Life Among the Children of France 22; Such Is Life Among the Idlers of Paris 22; Such Is Life Among the Paris Shoppers 22; Such Is Life at a Dutch County Fair 22; Such Is Life in Amsterdam and Alkmaar 22; Such Is Life in Busy London 22; Such Is Life in Italy 22; Such Is Life in London's West End 22; Such Is Life in Mon Petit Paris 22; Such Is Life in Monte Carlo 22; Such Is Life in Montmartre 22; Such Is Life in Munich 22; Such Is Life in Vollendam 22; Such Is Life Near London 22; Such Is Life on the Riviera 22; Faces 23; A Movie Fantasy 23; The Makin's of an Artist 24; The Making of a Man 25; The Family Album 26; Nurenberg the Toy City 26; A Pup's Tale 26; Tripping the Rhine 26

Mayersberg, Paul Captive • Heroine 86; Nightfall 88

Mayevsky, A. The Road to Life 56*

Mayflower, Z. Ada—To Nie Wypada 37

Maylam, Tony Genesis—A Band in Concert 77; White Rock 77; The Riddle of the Sands 79; The Burning 80; Sins of Dorian Gray 82

Maynard, Ken Fiddlin' Buckaroo 33

Mayo, Archie Double Dukes 17*; Kid Snatchers 17; The Nurse of an Aching Heart 17; Beaches and Peaches 18; Don't Play Hookey 23; Mama's Baby Boy 23; A Man of Position 23; Spring Fever 23; High Gear 24; Husbands Wanted 24; Short Change 24; Good Spirits 25; The Imperfect

Lover 25; Off His Beat 25; Oh Bridget 25; A Rarin' Romeo 25; Tender Feet 25; Why Hesitate? 25; Christine of the Big Tops 26; Johnny Get Your Hair Cut 26*; Money Talks 26; Unknown Treasures 26; Weak But Willing 26; The College Widow 27; Dearie 27; Quarantined Rivals 27; Slightly Used 27; Beware of Married Men 28; Charles Rogers in The Movie Man 28; The Crimson City 28; The Foreigner 28; The Girl from State Street • State Street Sadie 28; Henry B. Walthall in Retribution 28; My Man 28; On Trial 28; Is Everybody Happy? 29; The Sacred Flame 29; The Sap 29; Sonny Boy 29; Courage 30; Doorway to Hell • A Handful of Clouds 30; Oh! Sailor, Behave! 30; Vengeance 30; Wide Open 30; Bought 31; Illicit 31; Svengali 31; The Expert 32; Night After Night 32; Street of Women 32; Two Against the World 32; Under Eighteen 32; Convention City 33; Ever in My Heart 33; The Kid's Last Fight • The Life of Jimmy Dolan 33; The Mayor of Hell 33; Bordertown 34; Desirable 34; Gambling Lady 34; The Man with Two Faces 34; The Case of the Lucky Legs 35; Casino de Paree • Casino de Paris 35 • Go Into Your Dance 35*; The Petrified Forest 35; Black Legion 36; Give Me Your Heart • I Give My Heart • Sweet Aloes 36; I Married a Doctor • Main Street 36; Call It a Day 37; Gentlemen After Midnight • It's Love I'm After 37; The Adventures of Marco Polo 38*; Youth Takes a Fling 38; Melody of Love • Melody of Youth • Ragged Angels • They Shall Have Music 39*; Four Sons 40; The House Across the Bay 40; Charley's American Aunt • Charley's Aunt 41; Confirm or Deny 41*; The Great American Broadcast 41; Moontide 42*; Orchestra Wives 42; Crash Dive 43; Sweet and Low Down 44; Angel on My Shoulder 46; A Night in Casablanca 46

Mayolo, Carlos Carne de Tu Carne • Flesh of Your Flesh 84; The Araucaima Mansion • La Mansión de Araucaima 86

Mayoux, Valérie La Bataille des Dix Millions • The Battle of the Ten Millions • Cuba: Battle of the 10,000,000 70*

Mayring, Philipp L. Die Schlacht von Bademunde 31

Maysles, Albert Psychiatry in Russia 55; Youth in Poland • Youth of Poland 57*; Primary 60*; Kenya, Africa • Kenya 61 • Kenya, South Africa 61*; Safari ya Gari 61*; Showman 62*; The Beatles in New York • What's Happening • What's Happening! New York Meets the Beatles • What's Happening! The Beatles in the U.S.A. • Yeah! Yeah! Yeah! • Yeah! Yeah! Yeah! New York Meets the Beatles 64*; Meet Marlon Brando 65*; Truman Capote • With Love from Truman • With Love from Truman: A Visit with Truman Capote 66*; Monterey Pop 67*; Salesman 68*; Gimme Shelter 70*; Christo's Valley Curtain 72*; La Pupa del Gangster 74*; Grey Gardens 75*; Running Fence 77*; Ozawa 84*; Vladimir Horowitz: The Last

Romantic 85*; Islands 86*; Horowitz Plays Mozart 87*

Maysles, David Youth in Poland • Youth of Poland 57*; Kenya, Africa • Kenya 61 • Kenya, South Africa 61*; Safari ya Gari 61*; Showman 62*; The Beatles in New York • What's Happening • What's Happening! New York Meets the Beatles • What's Happening! The Beatles in the U.S.A. • Yeah! Yeah! Yeah! • Yeah! Yeah! Yeah! New York Meets the Beatles 64*; Meet Marlon Brando 65*; Truman Capote • With Love from Truman • With Love from Truman: A Visit with Truman Capote 66*; Salesman 68*; Gimme Shelter 70*; Christo's Valley Curtain 72*; La Pupa del Gangster 74*; Grey Gardens 75*; Running Fence 77*; Ozawa 84*; Vladimir Horowitz: The Last Romantic 85*; Islands 86*

Maza, Armando Vargas de la see *Vargas de la Maza, Armando*

Mazuel, Henri Dupuy see *Dupuy-Mazuel, Henri*

Mazursky, Paul Bob & Carol & Ted & Alice 69; Alex in Wonderland 70; Blume in Love 73; Harry and Tonto 74; Next Stop, Greenwich Village 75; An Unmarried Woman 78; Willie and Phil 79; Tempest 82; Moscow on the Hudson 84; Down and Out in Beverly Hills 86; Moon Over Parador 88; Enemies, A Love Story 89

Mazzacurati, Carlo Italian Night • Notte Italiana 87

Mazzetti, Lorenza Together 55; Le Italiane e l'Amore • Latin Lovers 61*

Mazzola, Frank Thirteen O'Clock 88*

Mazzuca, Joseph Sisters of Death 76

Mazzucco, Massimo Summertime 85; Romance 86

Meador, Joshua Make Mine Music 46*

Meagher, John Fantasy Man 84

Meals, A. R. The Unknown Rider 29

Meaney, John W. Jung on Film 57

Medak, Peter Funeral in Berlin 66*; Negatives 68; A Day in the Death of Joe Egg 70; The Ruling Class 72; Ghost in the Noonday Sun 73; The Odd Job 78; The Changeling 79; Zorro, the Gay Blade 81; The Men's Club 86; The Krays 90

Medeiros, Marcos História do Brasil • History of Brazil 74*

Medeolti, J. Gottes Mühlen Mahlen Langsam • The Mills of the Gods 39

Medford, Don To Trap a Spy • The Vulcan Affair 65; The Hunting Party 70; The Organization 71; Juggernaut 74*; The November Plan 76

Medoway, Cary The Heavenly Kid 85; Paradise Motel 85

Medved, Joseph Sedmi Kontinent • The Seventh Continent • Siedma Pevnina 66*

Medvedkin, Alexander Happiness • Schaste • Snatchers 34; My Zhdom Vas s Pobedoi • We Expect Victory There 41*

Mee, Captain The Man Who Changed His Mind 28*

Meech-Burkestone, Graham Burnout 79

Meehan, James Leo Michael O'Halloran

23; A Girl of the Limberlost 24; The Keeper of the Bees 25; Laddie 26; The Harvester 27; Judgment of the Hills 27; Little Mickey Grogan 27; The Magic Garden 27; Mother 27; Naughty Nanette 27; The Devil's Trademark 28; Freckles 28; The Little Yellow House 28; Wallflowers 28

Meehan, Leo see *Meehan, James Leo*

Meerapfel, Jeanine Malou 80; Die Kümmeltürkin Geht 85; Days to Remember • Die Verliebten 87; La Amiga 88

Megahy, Francis Just One More Time 63; Freelance 70; Only Takes Two 78; The Great Riviera Bank Robbery 79; Sewers of Gold 81; Real Life 83; Taffin 88

Mehboob see *Mehboobkhan, Ramjankhan*

Mehboobkhan, Ramjankhan Al Hilal 32; Bread • Roti 36; Watan 36; Aurat • Woman 39; We Three 39; Manmohan 40; Ek Hi Rasta • The Only Life 41; Andaz 42; Jagirdar 42; Fate • Taqdeer 43; Huma Gun Anmogaldi 46; Amar 48; Aan • Savage Princess 52; Bharat Mata • Mother India 57; A Handful of Grain 58; Son of India 60

Meher, Sadhu Babula 87

Mehra, Umesh Guru 89

Mehrjui, Dariush Almast 33 • Diamond 33 66; The Cow • Gav 68; Aghaye Hallou • Mr. Gullible • Mr. Naive 70; The Mailman • Postchi • The Postman 70; Ajor 71; Ghanat 71; Alamut 74; The Cycle • Dayereh Mina 74; Isar 76; Bakhshesh 77; Enfagh 77; Peyvast Kolieh 78; The Backyard • Hayate Poshti 80; Voyage au Pays de Rimbaud 83; Lodgers 87

Mehta, Kartik Kharidar 88

Mehta, Ketan Bhavni Bhavai • A Folk Tale 80; Holi 84; Mirch Masala • Spices • A Touch of Spice 86

Mehta, Pervez Kamyabi 88

Mehta, Vijaya Rao Saheb 86; Pestonjee 88

Mehta, Vivakar Kesudano Rang 88

Mei, Hu see *Hu, Mei*

Meideros, Richard de see *De Meideros, Richard*

Meineche, Annelise Eric Soya's Seventeen • Seventeen • Sytten 65; Den Røde Rubin • Sangen om den Røde Rubin • The Song of the Red Ruby 70

Meinert, Rudolf The Hound of the Baskervilles • Der Hund von Baskerville 14; Eleven Who Were Loyal 29; Marie Antoinette 29; The Strange Case of District Attorney M. 30

Meins, Gus Babes in Toyland • Laurel and Hardy in Toyland • March of the Toys • March of the Wooden Soldiers • Revenge Is Sweet • Wooden Soldiers 34*; Kelly the Second 36; The Californian • The Gentleman from California 37; The Hit Parade 37; Nobody's Baby 37; Roll Along, Cowboy 37; The Higgins Family 38; His Exciting Night 38; Ladies in Distress 38; Romance on the Run 38; The Covered Trailer 39; My Wife's Relatives 39; The Mysterious Miss X 39; Should Husbands

Work? 39; Earl of Puddlestone • Jolly Old Higgins 40; Grandpa Goes to Town 40; Money to Burn 40; Scatterbrain 40

Meisel, Kurt Madeleine 58; Court-Martial • Kriegsgericht 59; The Red Hand 60

Meisel, Norbert The Adulteress 73; I Remember Love 81; Walking the Edge 85

Mekas, Adolfas Hallelujah the Hills 63; The Brig 64*; Double-Barrelled Detective Story 65; Story of a Draft Dodger • Windflowers • Windflowers: The Story of a Draft Dodger 67; Victory Lane 68; Compañeras and Compañeros 70*

Mekas, Jonas Grand Street 53; Silent Journey 55; Guns of the Trees 61; The Secret Passions of Salvador Dali 61; Film Magazine of the Arts 63; Moires 63; Award Presentation to Andy Warhol 64; The Brig 64*; Cassis 66; Hare Krishna 66; The Millbrook Report • Report from Millbrook 66; Notes on the Circus 66; Diaries, Notes and Sketches • Walden 68; Time & Fortune Vietnam Newsreel 69; Reminiscences of a Journey to Lithuania 72; Diaries, Notes and Sketches—Volume I, Reels 1-6: Lost Lost Lost • Lost Lost Lost 75; In Between 78; Paradise Not Yet Lost, or Oona's Fifth Year 80; Notes for Jerome 81

Melançon, André The Dog Who Stopped the War 84; Bach and Broccoli • Bach et Bottine 87

Melani, M. Leggenda Sinfonica 47*

Melchior, Ib The Angry Red Planet • Invasion of Mars 59; Time Trap • The Time Travelers 64

Melendez, Agliberto A One-Way Ticket 88

Melendez, Bill A Boy Named Charlie Brown 68; Snoopy Come Home 72; Dick Deadeye • Dick Deadeye, or Duty Done 75; Race for Your Life, Charlie Brown 77*; Bon Voyage, Charlie Brown • Bon Voyage, Charlie Brown (And Don't Come Back!) 80

Meléndez, Jerónimo Mitchell see Mitchell Meléndez, Jerónimo

Melford, Austin Car of Dreams 35*; Oh Daddy! 35*; Radio Lover 36*

Melford, George Arizona Bill 11*; Daughter of the Confederacy 13*; The Perils of the Sea 13*; The Struggle 13; The Boer War 14; A Celebrated Case 14; The Invisible Power 14; Shannon of the Sixth 14; Armstrong's Wife 15; The Fighting Hope 15; The Immigrant 15; The Marriage of Kitty 15; The Puppet Crown 15; Stolen Goods 15; The Unknown 15; The Woman 15; Young Romance 15; Each Pearl a Tear 16; The Evil Eye 16; The Gutter Magdalene 16; The House of the Golden Windows 16; The Race 16; Tennessee's Pardner 16; To Have and to Hold 16; The Victory of Conscience 16*; The Years of the Locust 16; The Yellow Pawn 16; The Call of the East 17; The Cost of Hatred 17; The Crystal Gazer 17; Her Strange Wedding 17; Nan of Music Mountain 17*; On the Level 17; Sandy 17; A School for Husbands 17; The Sunset Trail 17; The Winning of Sally Temple 17; The Bravest Way 18; The City

of Dim Faces 18; The Cruise of the Make-believe 18; The Hidden Pearls 18; Jane Goes A'Wooing 18; The Source 18*; Such a Little Pirate 18; Wild Youth 18; Everywoman 19; Good Gracious Annabelle 19; Men, Women and Money 19; Pettigrew's Girl 19; A Sporting Chance 19; Told in the Hills 19; Behold My Wife 20; The Jucklins 20; The Round-Up 20; The Sea Wolf 20; The Faith Healer 21; The Great Impersonation 21; The Money Master • A Wise Fool 21; The Sheik 21; Burning Sands 22; Ebb Tide 22; Moran of the Lady Letty 22; The Woman Who Walked Alone 22; Java Head 23; The Light That Failed 23; Salomy Jane 23; You Can't Fool Your Wife 23; The Dawn of a Tomorrow 24; Flaming Barriers 24; Tiger Love 24; Friendly Enemies 25; Simon the Jester 25; The Top of the World 25; Without Mercy 25; The Flame of the Yukon 26; Going Crooked 26; Rocking Moon 26; Whispering Smith 26; A Man's Past 27; Freedom of the Press 28; Lingerie 28; Sinners in Love 28; The Charlatan 29; Love in the Desert 29; Sea Fury 29; The Woman I Love 29; Oriente y Occidente 30; The Poor Millionaire 30; La Voluntad del Muerto 30; Don Juan Diplomático 31; Drácula 31; East of Borneo 31; Homicide Squad • Lost Men 31*; The Viking 31; The Boiling Point 32; Cowboy Counsellor 32; A Scarlet Weekend 32; The Dude Bandit 33; The Eleventh Commandment 33; Man of Action 33; Officer 13 33; The Penal Code 33; Hired Wife • Marriage of Convenience 34; East of Java • Java Seas 35; Jungle Menace 37*

Melford, Jakidawdra The Inn on the Heath 14

Melford, Mark The Courtier Caught 12; A Day's Sport 12; Gretna Green 12; The Herncrake Witch 12; His First Sovereign 12; The Land of the Nursery Rhymes 12; Bottled Courage 13; Pat's Idea 13

Méliès, Georges Academy for Young Ladies • Un Lycée de Jeunes Filles 1896; Arrival of a Train at Vincennes Station • Arrivée d'un Train Gare de Vincennes 1896; Arrival of a Train—Joinville Station • Arrivée d'un Train—Gare de Joinville 1896; L'Arroseur • Watering the Flowers 1896; Automobiles Starting on a Race • Départ des Automobiles 1896; Baby and Young Girls • Bébé et Fillettes 1896; A Badly Managed Hotel • L'Hôtel Empoisonné 1896; Baignade en Mer • Sea Bathing 1896; Barque Sortant du Port de Trouville • Boat Leaving the Harbor of Trouville 1896; Bateau-Mouche sur la Seine • Steamboats on River Seine 1896; Batteuse à Vapeur • Steam Threshing-Machines 1896; Beach and Pier at Trouville, Part One • Jetée et Plage de Trouville, 1ère Partie 1896; Beach and Pier at Trouville, Part Two • Jetée et Plage de Trouville, 2ème Partie 1896; The Beach at Villiers in a Gale • Plage de Villiers par Gros Temps 1896; Le Bivouac • The Bivouac 1896; Blacksmith in His Workshop • Les Forgerons 1896; Les Blanchisseuses •

The Washerwomen 1896; Bois de Boulogne • Bois de Boulogne—Porte de Madrid • Touring Club 1896; Un Bon Petit Diable • A Little Devil • Un Petit Diable 1896; Une Bonne Farce • Le Chiffonnier • A Good Joke • The Rag-Picker 1896; Boulevard des Italiens 1896; Breaking Up of the Territorial Army—France • Libération des Territoriaux 1896; Campement de Bohémiens • Gipsies at Home 1896; Le Château Hanté • The Devil's Castle • The Devil's Manor • The Haunted Castle • Le Manoir du Diable • The Manor of the Devil 1896; Les Chevaux de Bois • A Merry-Go-Round 1896; Children Playing on the Beach • Enfants Jouant sur la Plage 1896; Closing Hours at Vibert's Perfume Factory • Sortie des Ateliers Vibert 1896; Conjuring • Séance de Prestidigitation 1896; Conjuror Making Ten Hats in Sixty Seconds • Dix Chapeaux en 60 Secondes 1896; Coronation of a Village Maiden • Couronnement de la Rosière 1896; Cortège de Tzar Allant à Versailles • The Czar and His Cortege Going to Versailles 1896; Cortège de Tzar au Bois de Boulogne • The Czar's Cortege in the Bois de Boulogne 1896; Danse Serpentine • A Serpentine Dance 1896; Déchargement de Bateaux—Le Havre • Unloading the Boat—Havre 1896; Défense d'Afficher • Post No Bills 1896; Départ des Officiers • Officers of the French Army Leaving Service 1896; Dessinateur: Chamberlain • A Lightning Sketch: Chamberlain 1896; Dessinateur Express: M. Thiers • A Lightning Sketch: Mr. Thiers 1896; Dessinateur: Reine Victoria • A Lightning Sketch: H.M. Queen Victoria 1896; The Docks at Marseille • Les Quais à Marseille 1896; Effet de Mer sur les Rochers • Sea Breaking on the Rocks 1896; English Jig • Miss De Vère 1896; Escamotage d'une Dame chez Robert-Houdin • The Vanishing Lady 1896; The Fakir—A Hindoo Mystery • Le Fakir—Mystère Indien 1896; French Officers' Meeting • Réunion d'Officiers 1896; French Regiment Going to the Parade • Le Régiment 1896; Gardener Burning Weeds • Jardinier Brûlant des Herbes 1896; La Gare Saint-Lazare • St. Lazare Railroad Station 1896; Grandes Manœuvres • Maneuvers of the French Army 1896; Les Haleurs de Bateaux • Towing a Boat on the River 1896; A Janitor in Trouble • Tribulations d'un Concierge 1896; Jour de Marché à Trouville • Market Day—Trouville 1896; Marée Montante sur Brise-Lames • Tide Rising Over the Breakwater 1896; The Mysterious Paper • Le Papier Proté 1896; A Naval Review at Cherbourg • Revue Navale à Cherbourg 1896; Une Nuit Terrible • A Terrible Night 1896; Panorama du Havre Pris d'un Bateau • Panorama of Havre Taken from a Boat 1896; Une Partie de Cartes • Playing Cards 1896; The Pier at Tréport During a Storm • Tempête sur la Jetée du Tréport 1896; Place de la Bastille 1896; Place de la Concorde 1896; Place de l'Opéra, 1st View • Place de l'Opéra, 1er Aspect 1896;

Place de l'Opéra, 2nd View • Place de l'Opéra, 2ème Aspect 1896; Place du Théâtre Français 1896; Place Saint-Augustin 1896; Plus Fort Que le Maître • Smarter Than the Teacher 1896; The Potter's Cart • La Voiture du Potier 1896; Retour au Cantonnement • Return to the Barracks 1896; Sac au Dos • Sacks Up! 1896; Salut Malencontreux d'un Déserteur • A Soldier's Unlucky Salutation 1896; Sauvetage en Rivière 1896; After the Ball • Après le Bal • Le Bain de la Parisienne 1897; Les Apprentis Militaires • Military Apprentices 1897; Arlequin et Charbonnier • The Charcoal Man's Reception 1897; Ascension d'un Ballon • A Balloon Ascension 1897; Attack on an English Blockhouse • Attaque d'un Poste Anglais 1897; L'Auberge Ensorcelée • The Bewitched Inn 1897; Auguste and Bibb • Auguste et Bibb 1897; The Barber and the Farmer • Figaro et l'Auvergnant 1897; Bataille de Confettis • Battle with Confetti 1897; Behind the Scenes • Dans les Coulisses 1897; Between Calais and Dover • Entre Calais et Douvres 1897; Black Art • Devilish Magic • Magie Diabolique 1897; Boxing Match • Match de Boxe—École de Joinville 1897; Le Cabinet de Mephistophélès • Laboratory of Mephistopheles 1897; Le Cauchemar • A Nightmare 1897; Chicot, Dentiste Américain • An Up-to-Date Dentist 1897; Chirurgien Américain • A Twentieth-Century Surgeon 1897; La Cigale et la Fourmi • The Grasshopper and the Ant 1897; The Clown and the Automaton • Gugusse and the Automaton • Gugusse et l'Automate 1897; Combat dans une Rue aux Indes • Fighting in the Streets in India 1897; Combat Naval en Grèce • Sea Fighting in Greece 1897; Comedian Paulus Singing "Coquin de Printemps" • Paulus Chantant "Coquin de Printemps" 1897; Comedian Paulus Singing "Derrière l'Omnibus" • Paulus Chantant "Derrière l'Omnibus" 1897; Comedian Paulus Singing "Duelliste Marseillais" • Paulus Chantant "Duelliste Marseillais" 1897; Cortège de la Mi-Carême • Mid-Lent Procession in Paris 1897; Cortège du Bœuf Gras Boulevard des Italiens 1897; Cortège du Bœuf Gras Passant Place de la Concorde 1897; Une Cour de Ferme • A Farm Yard 1897; D. Devant, Conjuror • D. Devant, Prestidigitateur 1897; Dancing Girls, Jardin de Paris • Danseuses au Jardin de Paris 1897; Dancing in a Harem • Danse au Sérail 1897; A Dangerous Pass, Mont Blanc • Passage Dangereux, Mont Blanc 1897; Défilé des Pompiers • Firemen on Parade 1897; Les Dernières Cartouches • The Last Cartridges 1897; Dessinateur: Von Bismark • A Lightning Sketch: Von Bismark 1897; The Drunkards • Les Ivrognes 1897; A Drunkard's Dream • Vision d'Ivrogne 1897; L'École des Gendres • The School for Sons-in-Law 1897; En Cabinet Particulier • A Private Dinner 1897; Épisodes de Guerre • War Episodes 1897; Exécution d'un Espion • Execution of a Spy 1897; Faust and

Marguerite • Faust et Marguerite 1897; A Funny Mahometan • Le Musulman Rigolo 1897; An Hallucinated Alchemist • L'Hallucination de l'Alchimiste 1897; A Hypnotist at Work • Le Magnétiseur • While Under a Hypnotist's Influence 1897; An Imaginary Patient • Le Malade Imaginaire 1897; L'Indiscret aux Bains de Mer • Peeping Tom at the Seaside 1897; Les Indiscrets • The Peeping Toms 1897; An Irritable Model • Le Modèle Irascible 1897; Massacre in Crete • Massacres en Crète 1897; A Novice at X-Rays • Les Rayons Röntgen • Les Rayons X 1897; On the Roofs • Sur les Toits 1897; Paulus Chantant "En Revenant d'la Revue" 1897; Paulus Chantant "Père la Victoire" 1897; A Potterymaker • Tourneur en Poterie 1897; La Prise de Tournavos • The Surrender of Tournavos 1897; Slave Trading in a Harem • Vente d'Esclaves au Harem 1897; Tom Old Boot • Tom Old Boot, a Grotesque Dwarf 1897; Adventures of William Tell • Guillaume Tell et le Clown • William Tell and the Clown 1898; The Artist's Dream • Rêve d'Artiste 1898; Assaut d'Escrime—École de Joinville • Fencing at the Joinville School 1898; The Astronomer's Dream • L'Homme dans la Lune • La Lune à un Mètre • The Man in the Moon • A Trip to the Moon 1898; Atelier d'Artiste, Farce de Modèles • The Painter's Studio 1898; Battleship Maine • A View of the Wreck of the Maine • Visite de l'Épave du Maine 1898; Black Magic • The Magician • Le Magicien 1898; The Blowing Up of the Maine in Havana Harbour • Quais de la Havane 1898; Carrefour de l'Opéra • Place de l'Opéra, 3rd View 1898; The Cave of the Demons • La Caverne Maudite • The Haunted Cavern 1898; A Clumsy Mason • Le Maçon Maladroit 1898; Collision and Shipwreck at Sea • Collision et Naufrage en Mer 1898; Combat Naval Devant Manille • Defending the Fort at Manila 1898; Corvée de Quartier Accidenté • A Soldier's Tedious Duty 1898; Créations Spontanées • Fantastical Illusions • Illusions Fantastiques 1898; La Damnation du Faust • The Damnation of Faust 1898; Dédoublement Cabalistique • The Triple Lady 1898; A Dinner Under Difficulties • Salle à Manger Fantastique 1898; Divers at Work on a Wreck Under the Sea • Divers at Work on the Wreck of the Maine • Visite Sous-Marin du Maine 1898; The Famous Box Trick • Illusions Fantasmagoriques 1898; The Four Troublesome Heads • Un Homme de Tête • The Man with Four Heads 1898; Fresh Paint • Prenez Garde à la Peinture 1898; La Main Cuirassée 1898; Montagnes Russes Nautiques • Shooting the Chutes 1898; Panorama from Top of a Moving Train • Panorama Pris d'un Train en Marche 1898; Pygmalion and Galatea • Pygmalion et Galathée 1898; A Soldier's French Leave • Sortie Sans Permission 1898; The Temptation of St. Anthony • La Tentation de Saint-Antoine 1898; Absent-Minded Lecturer • Le Conférencier Distrait 1899; Ad-

dition and Subtraction • Tom Whisky ou L'Illusioniste Toqué 1899; L'Affaire Dreyfus • The Dreyfus Affair • The Dreyfus Case • Dreyfus Court Martial 1899; Automobilisme et Autorité • The Clown and Automobile • The Clown and Motor Car 1899; The Beggar's Dream • Rêve du Pauvre 1899; Bird's-Eye View of St. Helier, Jersey • Panorama du Port de Saint-Hélier 1899; Un Bon Lit • A Midnight Episode 1899; The Bridegroom's Dilemma • Le Coucher de la Mariée ou Triste Nuit de Noce 1899; Cagliostro's Mirror • Le Miroir de Cagliostro 1899; Cendrillon • Cinderella 1899; The Chameleon Man • L'Homme Protée • The Lightning Change Artist 1899; Charmant Voyages de Noces • The Interrupted Honeymoon 1899; Le Chevalier Mystère • The Mysterious Knight 1899; Le Christ Marchant sur les Eaux • Le Christ Marchant sur les Eaux ou Le Miracle des Flots • Le Christ Marchant sur les Flots • Christ Walking on the Water 1899; Cleopatra • Cléopâtre • Robbing Cleopatra's Tomb • Un Vol dans la Tombe de Cléopâtre 1899; Combat de Coqs • Lively Cockfight 1899; La Crémation • The Spanish Inquisition 1899; La Danse du Feu • Haggard's "She"—The Pillar of Fire 1899; Débarquement de Voyageurs, Port de Granville • Passengers Landing at Harbour of Granville 1899; The Devil in a Convent • Le Diable au Couvent • The Sign of the Cross 1899; A Drop Too Much • Pick-Pocket et Policeman 1899; Duel Politique • A Political Duel 1899; Entrée d'un Paquebot, Port de Jersey • Steamer Entering the Harbour of Jersey 1899; Évocation Spirite • Summoning the Spirits 1899; An Extraordinary Wrestling Match • Luttes Extravagantes 1899; Force Doit Rester à la Loi • The Slippery Burglar 1899; Funérailles de Félix Faure • Funeral of Felix Faure 1899; The Human Pyramid • La Pyramide de Triboulet 1899; L'Île du Diable 1899; Illusioniste Fin de Siècle • L'Impressioniste Fin de Siècle • An Up-to-Date Conjurer 1899; Les Miracles du Brahmane • The Miracles of Brahmin 1899; Murder Will Out • Le Spectre 1899; A Mysterious Portrait • Le Portrait Mystérieux 1899; Neptune and Amphitrite • Neptune et Amphitrite 1899; L'Ours et la Sentinelle • The Sentry's Stratagem 1899; The Philosopher's Stone • La Pierre Philosophale 1899; Richesse et Misère ou La Cigale et la Fourmi • The Wandering Minstrel 1899; The Snow Man • La Statue de Neige 1899; The Artist and the Mannequin • L'Artiste et le Mannequin 00; The Balloonist's Mishap • Mésaventures d'un Aéronaute 00; The Bewitched Dungeon • La Tour Maudite 00; Bouquet d'Illusions • The Triple-Headed Lady 00; The Christmas Dream • Le Rêve de Noël 00; The Conjuror with a Hundred Tricks • L'Homme aux Cent Trucs 00; The Cook's Revenge • La Vengeance du Gâte-Sauce 00; Coppelia • Coppelia ou La Poupée Animée • Coppelia the Animated Doll 00; Crying and Laughing • Gens Qui Pleurent et Gens Qui Rient 00; The Danaids' Barrel • Eight Girls in a Barrel • Le Tonneau des Naïades 00; The Dangerous Lunatic • Le Fou Assassin 00; Le Déshabillage Impossible • Going to Bed Under Difficulties • An Increasing Wardrobe 00; Les Deux Aveugles • The Two Blind Men 00; Don't Move! • Ne Bougeons Plus! 00; L'Exposition de 1900 • Paris Exposition, 1900 00; A Fantastical Meal • Le Repas Fantastique 00; Farce de Marmitons • Scullion's Joke on the Chef 00; Fat and Lean Wrestling Match • Nouvelles Luttes Extravagantes • The Wrestling Sextette 00; Fatale Méprise • The Railroad Pickpocket • The Railway Pickpocket 00; The Gouty Patient • L' Homme Qui A des Roues dans la Tête • Le Malade Hydrophobe • Le Malade Hydrophobe ou L'Homme Qui A des Roues dans la Tête • The Man with Wheels in His Head 00; L'Homme-Orchestre • The One Man Band 00; L'Illusioniste Double et la Tête Vivante • The Triple Conjuror and the Living Head 00; Les Infortunes d'un Explorateur • The Misfortunes of an Explorer 00; An Intruder Behind the Scenes • Un Intrus dans une Loge de Figurantes 00; Jeanne d'Arc • Joan of Arc 00; Le Livre Magique • The Magic Book 00; La Maison Tranquille • What Is Home Without the Boarder? 00; The Miser, or The Gold Country • The Miser's Dream of Gold • Le Songe d'Or de l'Avare 00; Panorama de la Seine • Panorama of River Seine 00; Le Prisonnier Récalcitrant • The Tricky Prisoner 00; The Rajah's Dream, or The Bewitched Wood • Le Rêve du Rajah ou La Forêt Enchantée 00; Remerciement au Public • Thanking the Audience • Vue de Remerciements au Public 00; Les Sept Péchés Capitaux • The Seven Capital Sins • The Seven Deadly Sins 00; The Sorcerer, the Prince and the Good Fairy • Le Sorcier, le Prince et le Bon Génie • The Wizard, the Prince and the Good Fairy 00; Spiritisme Abracadabrant • Up-to-Date Spiritualism 00; The Three Bacchants • Les Trois Bacchantes 00; L'Antre des Esprits • The House of Mystery • The Magician's Cavern 01; The Bachelor's Paradise • Chez la Sorcière 01; Barbe-Bleue • Bluebeard 01; Le Bataillon Élastique • The Elastic Batallion 01; Le Brahmane et le Papillon • The Brahmin and the Butterfly • Le Chrysalide et le Papillon d'Or 01; Le Chapeau à Surprises • The Hat with Many Surprises 01; Le Charlatan • Painless Dentistry 01; Le Chevalier Démontable et le Géneral Boum • The Fierce Charger and the Knight • A Good Trick 01; Le Chimiste Repopulateur • A Maiden's Paradise 01; China Versus Allied Powers • Congrès des Nations en Chine 01; La Chirurgie de l'Avenir • Twentieth Century Surgery 01; The Clown Versus Satan • Gugusse et Belzebuth 01; Contempt of Court • Fun in Court • Une Noce au Village 01; The Dancing Midget • La Danseuse Microscopique 01; The Devil and

the Statue • Le Diable Géant ou Le Miracle de la Madone • The Gigantic Devil 01; Dislocation Extraordinary • Dislocation Mystérieuse • Dislocations Mystérieuses • Extraordinary Illusions 01; The Doctor and the Monkey • Le Savant et le Chimpanzé 01; The Dragon-Fly • La Libellule 01; The Dream of a Hindu Beggar • Le Rêve du Paria 01; Échappés de Charenton • Off to Bedlam • Off to Bloomingdale Asylum • L'Omnibus des Toqués • L'Omnibus des Toqués ou Les Échappés de Charenton 01; L'École Infernale • The Trials of a Schoolmaster 01; The Egg in Black Art • Marvellous Egg Producing with Surprising Developments • L'Œuf du Sorcier • L'Œuf Magique Prolifique • Prolific Magical Egg 01; Excelsior! • The Prince of Magicians 01; La Fontaine Sacrée ou La Vengeance de Boudha • The Sacred Fountain • La Vengeance de Boudha ou La Fontaine Sacrée 01; L'Homme à la Tête de Caoutchouc • The Man with the Rubber Head • A Swelled Head 01; How He Missed His Train • Le Réveil d'un Monsieur Pressé 01; Little Red Riding Hood • Le Petit Chaperon Rouge 01; Une Mauvaise Plaisanterie • Practical Joke in a Bar Room 01; A Phrenological Burlesque • Le Phrénologique Burlesque • The Phrenologist and the Lively Skull 01; Le Temple de la Magie • The Temple of the Sun 01; The Adventures of Robinson Crusoe • Les Aventures de Robinson Crusoe • Robinson Crusoe • Robinson Crusoe en Vingt-Cinq Tableaux 02; L'Armoire des Frères Davenport • The Cabinet Trick of the Davenport Brothers • The Mysterious Cabinet 02; The Burglars in the Wine Cellar • Les Piqueurs de Fûts • Wine Cellar Burglars 02; Catastrophe du Ballon "Le Pax" • The Catastrophe of the Balloon "Le Pax" 02; Chirurgie Fin de Siècle • Une Indigestion • Sure Cure for Indigestion • Up-to-Date Surgery 02; La Clownesse Fantôme • The Shadow-Girl • Twentieth Century Conjuring 02; The Colonel's Shower Bath • Douche du Colonel • The Painter's Mishap in the Barracks 02; The Coronation of Edward VII • The Coronation of Their Majesties King Edward VII and Queen Alexandra • Reproduction, Coronation Ceremonies—King Edward VII • Le Sacre d'Édouard VII 02*; The Devil's Money Bags • The Treasures of Satan • Les Trésors de Satan 02; Drunkard and Inventor • Le Pochard et l'Inventeur • What Befell the Inventor's Visitor 02; The Dwarf and the Giant • The Long and Short of It • Nain et Géant 02; L'Équilibre Impossible • An Impossible Balancing Feat 02; L'Éruption du Mont Pelé • The Eruption of Mount Pelee • Éruption Volcanique à la Martinique • The Terrible Eruption of Mount Pelee and Destruction of St. Pierre, Martinique 02; La Femme Volante • Marvellous Suspension and Evolution 02; Gulliver's Travels • Gulliver's Travels Among the Lilliputians and the Giants • Le Voyage de Gulliver à Lilliput et chez les Géants • Voyages de Gulliver 02; L'

Homme-Mouche • The Human Fly 02; A Trip to Mars • A Trip to the Moon • Le Voyage dans la Lune 02; Accidents Never Happen Singly • Un Malheur N'Arrive Jamais Seul • Misfortune Never Comes Alone 03; Alcofrisbas the Master Magician • The Enchanter • L'Enchanteur Alcofrisbas 03; The Apparition • The Apparition, or Mr. Jones' Comical Experiences with a Ghost • The Ghost and the Candle • Le Revenant 03; L'Auberge du Bon Repos • The Inn of Good Rest • The Inn Where No Man Rests 03; The Ballet Master's Dream • The Dream of the Ballet Master • Le Rêve du Maître de Ballet 03; Beelzebub's Daughters • Les Filles du Diable • The Women of Fire 03; Bob Kick, l'Enfant Terrible • Bob Kick, the Mischievous Kid 03; La Boîte à Malice • The Mysterious Box • The Shallow Box Trick 03; Le Cake-Walk Infernal • The Infernal Cakewalk 03; Le Chaudron Infernal • The Infernal Caldron • The Infernal Cauldron • The Infernal Cauldron and the Phantasmal Vapours 03; Comical Conjuring • Jack and Jim • Jack et Jim 03; The Condemnation of Faust • La Damnation du Faust • The Damnation of Faust • Faust aux Enfers • Faust aux Enfers ou La Damnation du Faust 03; La Corbeille Enchantée • The Enchanted Basket 03; Dix Femmes dans un Parapluie • The Girls in One Umbrella • La Parapluie Fantastique • La Parapluie Fantastique ou Dix Femmes Sous Une Ombrelle • Ten Ladies in an Umbrella • Ten Ladies in One Umbrella • Ten Ladies Under One Umbrella 03; The Drawing Lesson, or The Living Statue • La Statue Animée 03; The Enchanted Well • Le Puits Fantastique 03; Extraordinary Illusions • Illusions Fantasmagoriques • Illusions Funambulesques • The Twentieth Century Illustrationist 03; Fairyland, or The Kingdom of the Fairies • The Kingdom of the Fairies • Le Royaume des Fées • Wonders of the Deep 03; La Flamme Merveilleuse • The Mystical Flame 03; La Guirlande Merveilleuse • The Marvellous Hoop • The Marvellous Wreath 03; Jack Jaggs and Dum Dum • The Rival Music Hall Artistes • Tom Tight et Dum Dum 03; Jupiter's Thunderbolts • Jupiter's Thunderbolts, or The Home of the Muses • Le Tonnerre de Jupiter 03; La Lanterne Magique • The Magic Lantern 03; Le Mélomane • The Melomaniac 03; The Monster • Le Monstre 03; Les Mousquetaires de la Reine • The Musketeers of the Queen • The Queen's Musketeers 03; L' Oracle de Delphes • The Oracle of Delphi 03; Le Portrait Spirituel • A Spiritualist Photographer • A Spiritualistic Photographer 03; The Sorcerer's Revenge • Le Sorcier • The Witch's Revenge 03; An Adventurous Automobile Trip • Le Raid Paris-Monte Carlo en Deux Heures 04; The Animated Costumes • Les Costumes Animés 04; Les Apaches • A Burlesque Highway Robbery in Gay Paree 04; Les Apparitions Fugitives • Fugitive

Apparitions 04; The Astonishing Frame • Le Cadre aux Surprises 04; Au Clair de la Lune • Au Clair de la Lune ou Pierrot Malheureux • A Moonlight Serenade, or The Miser Punished • Pierrot Malheureux 04; The Barber of Seville, or The Useless Precaution • Le Barbier de Seville 04; Benvenuto Cellini • Benvenuto Cellini, or A Curious Evasion • Benvenuto Cellini ou Une Curieuse Évasion • Curieuse Évasion 04; The Bewitched Trunk • Le Coffre Enchanté 04; Une Bonne Farce avec Ma Tête • Un Prêté pour un Rendu • Un Prêté pour un Rendu ou Une Bonne Farce avec Ma Tête • Tit for Tat, or A Good Joke with My Head 04; Une Bonne Surprise • Les Invités de M. Latourte • Simple Simon's Surprise Party 04; Le Bourreau Turc • Le Terrible Bourreau Turc • The Terrible Turkish Executioner • The Terrible Turkish Executioner, or It Served Him Right 04; La Cascade de Feu • The Firefall 04; The Clockmaker's Dream • Rêve de l'Horloger • Le Rêve d'Horloger 04; The Cook in Trouble • Sorcellerie Culinaire 04; La Dame Fantôme • The Shadow Lady 04; La Damnation du Docteur Faust • Faust • Faust and Marguerite • Faust et Marguerite 04; The Devilish Plank • La Planche du Diable 04; Le Dîner Impossible • The Impossible Dinner 04; Every Man His Own Cigar Lighter • Un Peu de Feu S.V.P. 04; The Fake Russian Prophet • Le Joyeux Prophète Russe 04; La Fête au Père Mathieu • Uncle Rube's Birthday 04; The Imperceptible Transformations • The Imperceptible Transmutations • Les Transmutations Imperceptibles 04; An Impossible Voyage • Voyage • Le Voyage à Travers l'Impossible • Voyage Across the Impossible • Whirling the Worlds 04; The Invisible Silvia • Siva l'Invisible 04; Le Juif Errant • The Wandering Jew 04; Mariage par Correspondence • A Wedding by Correspondence 04; Match de Prestidigitation • A Wager Between Two Magicians, or Jealous of Myself 04; The Mermaid • La Sirène 04; Le Merveilleux Éventail Vivant • The Wonderful Living Fan 04; Les Mésaventures de M. Boit-Sans-Soif • The Mischances of a Drunkard 04; Un Miracle Sous l'Inquisition • A Miracle Under the Inquisition 04; La Providence de Notre-Dame des Flots • The Providence of the Waves, or The Dream of a Poor Fisherman 04; Le Roi du Maquillage • The Untamable Whiskers • Untameable Whiskers 04; Le Rosier Miraculeux • The Wonderful Rose Tree 04; Tchin-Chao the Chinese Conjurer • Le Thaumaturge Chinois 04; À President-Elect Roosevelt 05; L'Ange de Noël • The Beggar Maiden • The Christmas Angel • Détresse et Charité 05; The Angler's Nightmare, or A Policeman's Troubles • Le Cauchemar du Pêcheur ou L'Escarpolette Fantastique 05; Le Baquet de Mesmer • A Mesmerian Experiment 05; The Black Imp • Le Diable Noir 05; Les Cartes Vivantes • The Living Playing Cards 05; La Chaise à Porteurs Enchantée • The

Enchanted Sedan Chair 05; Les Chevaliers du Chloroforme • The Chloroform Fiends 05; La Compositeur Toqué • A Crazy Composer 05; The Crystal Casket • Le Phénix • Le Phénix ou Le Coffret de Cristal 05; Les Dernières Moments d'Anne de Boleyn • La Tour de Londres • La Tour de Londres et les Dernières Moments d'Anne de Boleyn • The Tower of London 05; Un Feu d'Artifice Improvisé • Unexpected Fireworks 05; La Grotte aux Surprises • The Grotto of Surprises 05; L'Île de Calypso: Ulysse et le Géant Polyphème • L'Île de Calypso: Ulysse et Polyphème • The Mysterious Island 05; The King of Sharpshooters • Le Roi des Tireurs 05; La Légende de Rip Van Winkle • Rip Van Winkle • Rip's Dream 05; Life-Saving Up-to-Date • Le Système du Docteur Sonflamort 05; The Lilliputian Minuet • Le Menuet Lilliputien 05; Une Mésaventure de Shylock • Le Miroir de Venise • Le Miroir de Venise ou Les Mésaventures de Shylock • The Venetian Looking-Glass 05; Mr. Dauber and the Whimsical Picture • Le Peintre Barbouillard et le Tableau Diabolique • Tableau Diabolique 05; The Palace of the Arabian Nights • Le Palais des Mille et Une Nuits • A Thousand and One Nights 05; The Scheming Gamblers' Paradise • Le Tripot Clandestin 05; Les Affiches en Goguette • The Hilarious Posters 06; L'Alchimiste Parafaragamus • L'Alchimiste Parafaragamus ou La Cornue Infernale • La Cornue Infernale • The Mysterious Retort 06; L'Anarchie chez Guignol • Punch and Judy 06; Les Bulles de Savon Animées • Soap Bubbles 06; La Cardeuse de Matelas • The Tramp and the Mattress Makers 06; The Chimney Sweep • Jack le Ramoneur 06; Une Chute de Cinq Étages • A Mix-Up in the Gallery 06; A Desperate Crime • L'Histoire d'un Crime • Les Incendiaires 06; Le Dirigeable Fantastique • Le Dirigeable Fantastique ou Le Cauchemar d'un Inventeur • The Fantastical Airship • The Inventor Crazybrains and His Wonderful Airship 06; Le Fantôme d'Alger • A Spiritualistic Meeting 06; La Fée Carabosse • La Fée Carabosse ou Le Poignard Fatal • The Witch 06; L'Honneur Est Satisfait • Who Looks, Pays! 06; L'Hôtel des Voyageurs de Commerce • A Roadside Inn 06; Le Maestro Do-mi-sol-do • Professor Do-mi-sol-do 06; Magic Through the Ages • La Magie à Travers les Âges • Old and New Style Conjurors 06; The Merry Frolics of Satan • Les Quatre Cent Farces du Diable 06; Le Rastaquouère Rodriquez y Papanaguaz • A Seaside Flirtation 06; Ali Barbouyou et Ali Bouf à l'Huile • Delirium in a Studio 07; An Angelic Servant • La Perle des Savants 07; Bakers in Trouble • La Boulangerie Modèle 07; Bernard le Bucheron ou Le Miracle de Saint Hubert • A Forester Made King 07; The Bewildering Cabinet • Le Placard Infernal 07; Le Carton Fantastique • A Mischievous Sketch 07; Chopin's Funeral March • Chopin's Funeral March Bur-

lesqued • La Marche Funèbre de Chopin 07; Le Civilisation à Travers les Âges • Civilization Through the Ages • Humanity Through the Ages 07; La Colle Universelle • Good Glue Sticks 07; La Cuisine de l'Ogre • In the Bogie Man's Cave 07; The Death of Julius Caesar • La Mort de Jules César • Shakespeare Écrivant "Jules César" • Shakespeare: La Mort de Jules César • Shakespeare Writing "Julius Caesar" 07; Le Délirium Tremens • Le Délirium Tremens ou La Fin d'un Alcoolique • Drink! A Great Temperance Story • La Fin d'un Alcoolique 07; Deux Cent Mille Lieues Sous les Mers ou Le Cauchemar d'un Pêcheur • 20,000 Leagues Under the Sea • Under the Seas • Vingt Mille Lieues Sous les Mers 07; La Douche d'Eau Bouillante • Rogue's Tricks 07; The Dream of an Opium Fiend • Le Rêve d'un Fumeur d'Opium 07; The Eclipse • L'Éclipse du Soleil en Plein Lune • The Eclipse, or The Courtship of the Sun and the Moon 07; François Ier et Triboulet • The King and the Jester 07; Les Fromages Automobiles • The Skipping Cheeses 07; Le Génie du Feu • The Genie of Fire 07; The Good Luck of a Souse • Il Y A un Dieu pour les Ivrognes 07; Hamlet • Hamlet, Prince de Danemark • Hamlet, Prince of Denmark 07; How Bridget's Lover Escaped • Le Mariage de Victoire • Le Mariage de Victorine 07; In the Barber Shop • Salon de Coiffure 07; Justinian's Human Torches • Torches Humaines • Les Torches Humains de Justinien 07; The Knight of Black Art • Le Tambourin Fantastique 07; Long Distance Wireless Photography • La Photographie Électrique à Distance 07; A New Death Penalty • La Nouvelle Peine de Mort 07; A Night with Masqueraders in Paris • Nuit de Carnaval 07; Pauvre John ou Les Aventures d'un Buveur de Whiskey • Sight-Seeing Through Whiskey 07; The Prophetess of Thebes • La Prophétesse de Thèbes 07; Robert Macaire and Bertrand • Robert Macaire et Bertrand 07; Satan en Prison • Satan in Prison 07; Seek and Thou Shalt Find 07; Le Tunnel Sous la Manche • Le Tunnel Sous la Manche ou Le Cauchemar Franco-Anglais • Tunneling the English Channel 07; Why That Actor Was Late • Why the Actor Was Late 07; Anaie ou Le Balafré • L'Ascension de la Rosière 08; At the Hotel Mix-Up 08; Au Pays des Jouets • Conte de la Grand-Mère et Rêve de l'Enfant • Grandmother's Story • Toyland 08; L'Avare • The Miser 08; Aventures de Don Quichotte • Incident from Don Quixote 08; La Bonne Bergère et la Méchante Princesse • The Good Shepherdess and the Evil Princess 08; The Broken Violin • Lulli ou Le Violon Brisé 08; Buncoed Stage Johnnie 08; Le Conseil de Pipelet • Up-to-Date Clothes Cleaning 08; Le Crime de la Rue de Cherche-Midi à Quatorze Heures • La Curiosité Punie • Curiosity Punished 08; The Duke's Good Joke 08; Le Fabricant de Diamants • A Fake-Diamond Swindler • L'Habit Ne Fait

Pas le Moine **08**; Le Fakir de Singapoure •
The Indian Sorcerer **08**; La Fée Libellule •
Le Lac Enchanté **08**; La Fête du Son-
neur • Le Génie des Cloches **08**; La Fon-
taine Merveilleuse **08**; The Forester's
Remedy • Le Jugement du Garde-
Champêtre **08**; French Cops Learning
English • French Interpreter Policeman **08**;
Fun with the Bridal Party • Le Mariage de
Thomas Poirot **08**; Hallucinations Phar-
maceutiques • Pharmaceutical Hallucina-
tions • Le Truc du Potard **08**; Helping
Hand • La Main Secourable **08**; High Life
Taylor • Sideshow Wrestlers **08**; His First
Job **08**; Honeymoon in a Balloon • Voyage
de Noces en Ballon **08**; Hunting the Teddy
Bear • Tartarin de Tarascon • Tartarin de
Tarascon ou Une Chasse à l'Ours **08**; The
Little Peacemaker • Le Trait d'Union **08**;
Love and Molasses **08**; A Lover's Hazing •
Mariage de Raison et Mariage d'Amour **08**;
Magic of Catchy Songs **08**; The Mischances
of a Photographer **08**; Mishaps of the
N.Y.-Paris Race • Le Raid Paris-New York
en Automobile **08**; A Mistaken Identity •
Quiproquo **08**; Moitié de Polka **08**; Mys-
tery of the Garrison **08**; The New Lord of
the Village • Le Nouveau Seigneur du
Village **08**; No Trifling with Love • On Ne
Badine Pas avec l'Amour **08**; Not Guilty
08; Old Footlight Favourite • Trop Vieux!
08; Oriental Black Art **08**; Pochardiana •
Pochardiana ou Le Rêveur Éveillé **08**; La
Poupée Vivante **08**; Pour les P'tiots **08**;
Pour l'Étoile S.V.P. **08**; Pranks with a Fake
Python • Le Serpent de la Rue de la Lune
08; Rivalité d'Amour • A Tragedy in Spain
08; Rude Awakening **08**; La Toile d'
Araignée Merveilleuse **08**; A Tricky
Painter's Fate **08**; Two Crazy Bugs **08**; Two
Talented Vagabonds **08**; The Woes of
Roller Skates **08**; Wonderful Charm **08**;
Cinderella Up-to-Date **09**; Count's Wooing
09; The Diabolic Tenant • Le Locataire
Diabolique **09**; The Doctor's Secret •
Hydrothérapie Fantastique • Le Secret du
Médécin **09**; For Sale: A Baby **09**; For the
Cause of Suffrage **09**; Fortune Favours the
Brave **09**; La Gigue Merveilleuse **09**; Hyp-
notist's Revenge **09**; Les Illusions Fan-
taisistes • Whimsical Illusions **09**; Mrs. and
Mr. Duff **09**; Le Papillon Fantastique **09**;
Seein' Things **09**; A Tumultuous Elope-
ment **09**; À la Conquête du Pôle • The
Conquest of the Pole **10**; Apparitions Fan-
tômatiques • Le Roi des Médiums **10**; Les
Aventures du Baron de Münchausen •
Baron Münchausen's Dream • Les Halluci-
nations du Baron de Münchausen **10**; Cen-
drillon • Cendrillon ou La Pantoufle Mys-
térieuse • Cinderella • Cinderella, or The
Glass Slipper **10**; Le Chevalier des
Neiges • The Knight of the Snows **10**; Le
Conte du Vieux Talute **10**; Fin de Réveil-
lon **10**; Galatée **10**; Guérison de l'Obésité
en 5 Minutes • Le Traitement 706 **10**;
L'Homme aux Mille Inventions **10**; Un
Homme Comme Il Faut **10**; If I Were
King • Si J'Étais le Roi • Si J'Étais Roi **10**;
Le Mousquetaire de la Reine **10**; Les Sept

Barres d'Or **10**; Le Vitrail Diabolique **10**;
Le Voyage de la Famille Bourrichon **10**

Melik-Avakyan, G. The Heart Sings **58**

Mello, Victori di see Di Mello, Victori

Mellor, Edith Because • The Laundry
Girl **19***

Melnikov, Vitaly To Marry the Captain
• Vyiti Zamuzh za Kapitana **86**; Pervaya
Vstrecha, Poslednaya Vstrecha **88**

Melo, Jorge Silva Agosto **88**

Melson, Søren Denmark Grows Up **47***

Melville, Jean-Pierre Vingt-Quatre
Heures de la Vie d'un Clown **45**; Le
Silence de la Mer **47**; Les Enfants Ter-
ribles • The Strange Ones **49**; Quand Tu
Liras Cette Lettre **52**; Bob le Flambeur •
Bob, the Gambler • Fever Heat **55**;
L'A.F.P. Nous Communiqué **58**; Deux
Hommes dans Manhattan **58**; The Forgiven
Sinner • Léon Morin Prêtre • Léon Morin,
Priest **61**; Le Doulos • Doulos—The Finger
Man • The Finger Man • The Stoolie **62**;
L'Aîné des Ferchaux • Un Jeune Homme •
Magnet of Doom **63**; Le Deuxième Souffle
• Second Breath • Second Wind **65**; The
Godson • Le Samourai • The Samurai **67**;
L'Armée des Ombres • The Army in the
Shadows • The Army of Shadows • The
Shadow Army **68**; Le Cercle Rouge • The
Red Circle **70**; A Cop • Dirty Money • Un
Flic **72**

Melville, Wilbert Saved from the Harem
15; The Terrible One **15**; Soldier's Sons **16**

Menaker, I. Autumn • Osen **40***; Kino-
Concert 1941 • Leningrad Music Hall **41***

Menaker, Leonid The Last Road • Poslednaya Doroga **87**

Menchen, Joseph The Miracle **12**

Mendeluk, George Stone Cold Dead **79**;
The Kidnapping of the President **80**; Doin'
Time **84**; Meatballs III • Meatballs III:
Summer Job **86**

Mendes, Lothar Das Abenteuer • Der
Abenteurer **21**; Die Scheide des Todes **21**;
Deportiert **22**; S.O.S.—Die Insel der
Tränen **23**; Liebė Macht Blind • Love
Blinds Us • Love Makes Us Blind **25**; Die
Drei Kuckucksuhren **26**; The Prince of
Tempters **26**; Convoy **27***; Adventure Mad
28; Interference **28***; A Night of Mystery
28; Dangerous Curves **29**; The Four
Feathers **29***; Illusion **29**; The Marriage
Playground **29**; Paramount on Parade **30***;
Ladies' Man **31**; Personal Maid **31***; If I
Had a Million **32***; Payment Deferred **32**;
Strangers in Love **32**; Luxury Liner **33**; Jew
Suss • Power **34**; The Man Who Could
Work Miracles **36**; The Charmer • Moon-
light Sonata **37**; International Squadron
41; Flight for Freedom **43**; Tampico **44**;
The Walls Came Tumbling Down **46**

Méndez, Fernando The Legend of a
Bandit • La Leyenda de Bandido **45**; El
Ladrón de Cadáveres **56**; El Ataúd del
Muerto • El Ataúd del Vampiro • El Re-
torno del Vampiro • The Vampire's Coffin
57*; The Vampire • El Vampiro **57***; The
Black Pit • The Black Pit of Dr. M • Dr.
M • Misterios del Ultratumba • Mysteries
from Beyond the Grave **58**; Los Diablos

del Terror • Night Riders **58**; El Grito de
la Muerte • The Living Coffin **58**

Mendoza, Joe Mystery at Monstein **54**;
Five Clues to Fortune **57**

Menegoz, Robert Contrastes **59***

Menell, Jo Haiti Dreams of Democracy
88*

Menéndez, Ramón Stand and Deliver
87

Menges, Chris East 103rd Street **83**; A
World Apart **87**

Meng-hau, Ho see Ho, Meng-hau

Menkes, Nina Magdalena Viraga **87**

Menon, Balachandra Vilambaram **87**

Menotti, Gian Carlo Il Medium • The
Medium **51***

Menoud, Jean-Bernard Day and Night •
Jour et Nuit **86**

Menshov, Vladimir Moscow Distrusts
Tears • Moscow Does Not Believe in Tears
• Moskva Slezam Ne Verit **79**

Menzel, Jiří Pearls at the Bottom •
Pearls of the Deep • Perličky na Dně **64***;
Crime at a Girls' School • Crime in a Girls'
School • Zločin v Dívčí Škole **65***; Closely
Observed Trains • Closely Watched Trains
• A Difficult Love • Ostře Sledované Vlaky
66; Capricious Summer • Indian Summer •
Rozmarné Léto **68**; Crime at the Nightclub
• Crime in a Nightclub • Crime in the
Nightclub • Zločin v Šantánu **68**; Larks on
a String • Larks on a Thread • Skřivánci na
Nítích • Skylarks on a String **69**; Kdo
Hledá Zlaté Dno • Who Looks for Gold •
Who Seeks a Handful of Gold • Who
Seeks the Gold Bottom • Whoever Looks
for Gold **74**; A Cottage Near the Woods •
Na Samotě u Lesa • Seclusion Near a
Forest **76**; Báječní Muži s Klikou • Magi-
cians of the Silver Screen • Those Wonder-
ful Men with a Crank • Those Wonderful
Movie Cranks **78**; Une Blonde Émoustil-
lante • A High-Spirited Blonde **80**; Cut-
ting It Short • Postřižiny • Short Cut •
Short Cuts **80**; Slavnosti Sněženek • Snow-
drop Feast • Snowdrop Festival **82**; My
Sweet Little Village • Vesničko Má Středisková **85**; Prague **85***; The End of the
Good Old Days • Konec Starých Časů **89**

Menzies, William Cameron Always
Goodbye **31***; The Spider **31***; Almost
Married **32***; Chandu the Magician **32***; I
Loved You Wednesday **33***; Wharf Angel
34*; Conquest of the Air **36***; Things to
Come • La Vida Futura **36**; Four Dark
Hours • The Green Cockatoo • Race Gang
37*; Gone with the Wind **39***; The Thief
of Bagdad **40***; Address Unknown **44**;
Spellbound **45***; Duel in the Sun **46***;
Drums in the Deep South **51**; The Man He
Found • The Whip Hand **51**; Invaders
from Mars **53**; The Maze **53**; Autumn in
Rome **54**; Star Studded Ride **54**

Mercanti, Pino The Black Duke **61**;
Gentlemen of the Night **63**

Mercanton, Louis Les Amours de la
Reine Élisabeth • Élisabeth Reine
d'Angleterre • Queen Elizabeth **12***;
Adrienne Lecouvreur **13***; Jeanne Doré **15**;
Le Lotus d'Or **16***; Suzanne **16***; Mères

Eine Liebe 37; Gilgi, Eine von Uns 37; Die Kleine Schwindlerin 37; Discretion with Honor • Diskretion-Ehrensache 39; Fridericus 39; Her Greatest Success • Ihr Grösster Erfolg 39; Hangmen, Women and Soldiers • Henker, Frauen und Soldaten 40

Meyer, Marc Blu Gang • E Vissero per Sempre Felici e Ammazzati 73

Meyer, Muffie Gray Gardens 75*

Meyer, Nicholas Time After Time 79; Star Trek II: The Wrath of Khan 82; Volunteers 85; The Deceivers 88

Meyer, Otto Insel der Amazonen • Seven Daring Girls 60

Meyer, Paul Klinkart 57; Déjà S'Envole la Fleur Maigre 60

Meyer, Russ The French Peep Show 50; The Immoral Mr. Teas 59; This Is My Body 59; Eve and the Handyman 60; Naked Camera 60; Erotica • Eroticon 61; The Immoral West and How It Was Lost • Naked Gals of the Golden West 62; Europe in the Raw 63; Heavenly Bodies 63; Steam Heat 63; Dr. Breedlove • Kiss Me Quick! 64; Fanny Hill • Fanny Hill: Memoirs of a Woman of Pleasure 64; Lorna 64; Faster Pussycat! Kill! Kill! 65; Motor Psycho • Rio Vengeance 65; Mudhoney • Rope • Rope of Flesh 65; Mondo Topless 66; Common Law Cabin 67; Good Morning . . . and Goodbye! • The Lust Seekers 67; How Much Loving Does a Normal Couple Need? 67; Finders Keepers, Lovers Weepers! 68; Russ Meyer's Vixen! • Vixen! 68; Cherry, Harry and Raquel! 69; Beyond the Valley of the Dolls 70; The Seven Minutes 71; Blacksnake • Slaves • Sweet Suzy! 73; Supervixens 74; Russ Meyer's Up! • Up! 76; Beneath the Valley of the Ultravixens 79; The Breast of Russ Meyer 83

Meyerhold, Vsevolod The Picture of Dorian Gray 15; The Strong Man 17

Meyers, Byron Sword of Heaven 85

Meyers, Ross The Swinging Coeds 76

Meyers, Sidney White Flood 40*; The History and Romance of Transportation 41*; The Quiet One 49; The Savage Eye 59*

Meynard, Serge A Black Eye • L'Œil au Beurre Noir 87

Miakar, Andrzej Christophorus 86

Michael, George White Hunter 65

Michaels, Mike The World of Travel: Bangkok 82; The World of Travel: Las Vegas 84; The World of Travel: Osaka 87

Michaels, Richard How Come Nobody's on Our Side? 75; Death Is Not the End 76; Blue Skies Again 83

Michalakias, John Elias I Was a Teenage Zombie 87

Micheaux, Oscar Circumstantial Evidence 19; The Homesteader 19; Within Our Gates 20; The Brute 21; Deceit 21; The Gunsaulus Mystery 21; The Hypocrite 21; The Shadow 21; Symbol of the Unconquered 21; The Wages of Sin 21; The Dungeon 22; The Ghost of Tolston's Manor 22; Uncle Jasper's Will 22; The House Behind the Cedars 23; Birthright 24; Body and Soul 24; Son of Satan 24;

Marcus Garland 25; The Conjure Woman 26; The Devil's Disciple 26; The Broken Violin 27; The Girl from Chicago 27; The Millionaire 27; The Spider's Web 27; Easy Street 28; Thirty Years Later 28; When Men Betray 28; A Daughter of the Congo 30; The Exile 31; Ten Minutes to Live 32; Veiled Aristocrats 32; Harlem After Midnight 34; The Brand of Cain • Lem Hawkins' Confession 35; Swing • Swing: The Story of Mandy 36; Temptation 36; Underworld 36; God's Stepchildren 37; Miracle in Harlem 37; Birthright 39; Lying Lips 39; The Notorious Elinor Lee 40; The Betrayal 48

Michel, André Dix Minutes sur le FFI 44; The Rose and the Mignonette • La Rose et le Réséda 45; Sport et Parapluie 47; Combat Sans Haine 48; Edgar et Sa Bonne 49; Maroc d'Aujourd'hui 49; Trois Femmes • Trois Femmes, Trois Âmes 51; Aventures au Radio-Circus 53; Gestāndnis Unter Vier Angen 54; The Sorceress • La Sorcière 55; The Adventures of Rémi • Sans Famille 58; Comme un Poisson dans l'Eau 61; Ton Ombre Est la Mienne • Your Shadow Is Mine 61; Tous les Enfants du Monde 64

Michel, Bernard T. see Toublanc-Michel, Bernard

Michel, Bernard Toublanc see Toublanc-Michel, Bernard

Michel, Thierry Issue de Secours 88

Michenaud, Gerald Means and Ends 85

Michener, Dave Basil the Great Mouse Detective • The Great Mouse Detective 86*

Mida, Massimo Amore in Quattro Dimensioni • L'Amour en Quatre Dimensions • Love in Four Dimensions 65*; Bianco, Rosso, Giallo, Rosa • Love Factory • White, Red, Yellow and Pink • White, Red, Yellow, Pink 66

Middleton, Edwin Wildfire 15; The Haunted Manor 16; The Isle of Love 16

Middleton, George E. The Woman Who Dared 16; Heart of Juanita 19; Just Squaw 19; The Flame of Hellgate 20; Double Cross Roads 30*

Midi, François Dupont see Dupont-Midi, François

Miehe, Ulf The Invisible Man • Der Unsichtbare 87

Miéville, Anne-Marie Mon Cher Sujet 88

Mifune, Toshiro Gojūman-Nin no Isan • The Legacy of the Five Hundred Thousand 64

Mihalka, George My Bloody Valentine 81; Pick-Up Summer • Pinball Pick-Up • Pinball Summer 81; Scandale 82; The Blue Man • Eternal Evil 85; Hostile Takeover • Office Party 88

Mihály, Kertész see Curtiz, Michael

Mihálfy, Sándor Gyermekrablás a Palánk Utcában • Palisade Street Kidnapping 85

Mihi, Rafaat el see El Mihi, Rafaat

Mikaelyan, Sergei Flight 222 • Reis 222 86

Mikels, Ted V. The Doctors 63; Strike Me Deadly 63; One Shocking Moment • Suburban Affair 64*; The Black Klansman • I Crossed the Color Line • I Crossed the Line 66; Astro-Zombies 67; The Girl in Gold Boots 68; The Corpse Grinders 71; Blood Orgy of the She-Devils 72; The Doll Squad • Hustler Squad • Seduce and Destroy 73; The Worm Eaters 75*; Alex Joseph and His Wives • The Rebel Breed 78; Devil's Gambit 82; Operation Overkill 82; Ten Violent Women 82; Space Angels 85; Angel of Vengeance • Naked Vengeance 86

Mikesch, Elfi Seduction: The Cruel Woman 85*

Mikhailovsky, Valery Secret Walk • Taynaya Progulka 87

Mikhalkov, Nikita A Quiet Day at the End of the War • Spokoinyi Den v Kontse Voiny 70; At Home Among Strangers • At Home Among Strangers, a Stranger at Home • Svoi Sredi Chuzhikh, Chuzhoi Sredi Svoikh 74; Neokonchennaya Pyesa dlya Mekhanicheskovo Pianina • An Unfinished Piece for Mechanical Piano • An Unfinished Piece for Player Piano 76; Raba Lubvi • A Slave of Love 76; Five Evenings • Pyat' Vecherov 78; A Few Days in the Life of I. I. Oblomov • Neskolko Dnei iz Zhizni I. I. Oblomova • Oblomov • Several Days in the Life of I. I. Oblomov 79; Family Relations • Kinfolk • Rodnya 81; Bez Svidetelei • A Private Conversation • Without Witnesses 83; Black Eyes • Dark Eyes • Oci Ciornie • Otchi Tchiornie 87

Mikhalkov-Konchalovsky, Andrei A Boy and a Pigeon • The Boy and the Pigeon • Malchik i Golub 60; The First Teacher • Pervyi Uchitel 65; Asya's Happiness • The Happiness of Asya • Happy Asya • Istoria Asi Klyachinoi, Kotoraya Lyubila, Da Nie Vshla Zamuzh • Istoria Asi Klyachinoy, Kotoraya Lyubila, Da Nye Vyshla Zamuzh • The Story of Asya Klyachina, Who Loved But Did Not Marry 66; Dvoryanskoye Gnezdo • A Nest of Gentlefolk • A Nest of Gentry 69; Dyadya Vanya • Uncle Vanya 70; A Lover's Romance • Romance for Lovers • The Romance of Lovers • Romans o Vljublennych 74; The Siberiad • Siberiada • Siberiade 78; Maria's Lovers 84; Runaway Train 85; Duet for One 86; Shy People 87; Homer & Eddie 89; Tango & Cash 89

Mikhin, Boris Tsar Nikolai II 17*; The Eagle of the Caucasus 32

Mikkelsen, Jarl Friis The Fight for the Red Cow • Kampen om den Røde Ko 87*

Mikkelsen, Laila Liten Ida • Little Ida 81; Children of God's Earth 83

Mikuni, Rentaro Shinran: Path to Purity • Shinran: Shiro Michi 87

Milan, Wilfred Ultimax Force 87

Milani, Kathy B-Movie 88

Miler, Zdenek The Man Who Stole the Sun 48; The Red Stain 63

Miles, Bernard Tawny Pipit 44*; Chance of a Lifetime 50*

Miles, Christopher À Vol d'Oiseau 62;

The Six-Sided Triangle 63; Rhythm 'n' Greens 64; Up Jumped a Swagman 65; The Rue Lepic Slow Race 68; The Virgin and the Gypsy 70; Paris Was Made for Lovers • Time for Loving 71; The Maids 74; That Lucky Touch 75; Priest of Love 80

Miles, Wynn Miami Rendezvous • Passion Holiday 63

Milestone, Hank see Lenzi, Umberto

Milestone, Lewis The Caveman 25; Seven Sinners 25; The New Klondike 26; The Kid Brother 27*; Two Arabian Knights 27; The Garden of Eden 28; The Racket 28; Betrayal 29; New York Nights 29; All Quiet on the Western Front 30; Hell's Angels 30*; The Front Page 31; Rain 32; Hallelujah, I'm a Bum • Hallelujah, I'm a Tramp • Happy Go Lucky • The Heart of New York • Lazybones • New York • The Optimist 33; The Captain Hates the Sea 34; Paris in Spring • Paris Love Song 35; Anything Goes • Tops Is the Limit 36; The General Died at Dawn 36; The Night of Nights 39; Of Mice and Men 39; Lucky Partners 40; The Westerner 40*; My Life with Caroline 41; Notre Front Russe • Our Russian Front 41*; Armored Attack • The North Star 43; Edge of Darkness 43; A Guest in the House 44*; The Purple Heart 44; Salerno Beachhead • A Walk in the Sun 45; The Strange Love of Martha Ivers 46; Arch of Triumph 48; No Minor Vices 48; The Red Pony 49; The Halls of Montezuma 50; Kangaroo 52; Les Misérables 52; Melba 53; They Who Dare 53; La Vedova • La Vedova X • The Widow 55; Pork Chop Hill 59; Ocean's Eleven 60; Mutiny on the Bounty 62*; PT 109 63*

Milford, Gene The Pusher 60

Milius, John Marcello, I'm So Bored 67; Dillinger 73; The Wind and the Lion 75; Big Wednesday • Summer of Innocence 78; Conan the Barbarian 81; Red Dawn 84; Farewell to the King 88

Milkina, Sofia The Kreutzer Sonata • Kreutzerova Sonata 87*

Millais, Warren Her Secret 33

Milland, Ray A Man Alone 55; Lisbon 56; The Safecracker 57; End of the World • Panic in the Year Zero • Panic in Year Zero • Survival 62; Hostile Witness 67

Millar, Adelqui Pages of Life 22; The Apache 25; Life 28; The Inseparables 29*; Toda una Vida 33; Luci Sommerse 36

Millar, Gavin Secrets 83; The Weather in the Streets 83; Dreamchild 85

Millar, Stuart Paper Lion 68*; When the Legends Die 72; Rooster Cogburn 75

Millarde, Harry The Lotus Woman 16; Every Girl's Dream 17; Little Miss Nobody 17; Miss U.S.A. 17; Unknown 274 17; Blue-Eyed Mary 18; Bonnie Annie Laurie 18; The Camouflage Kiss 18; Caught in the Act 18; The Heart of Romance 18; Miss Innocence 18; Gambling in Souls 19; The Girl with No Regrets 19; The Love That Dares 19; Rose of the West 19; Sacred Silence 19; When Fate Decides 19; Over the Hill • Over the Hill to the Poorhouse

20; White Moll 20; Perjury 21; My Friend the Devil 22; The Town That God Forgot 22; The Governor's Lady 23; If Winter Comes 23; The Fool 25; The Taxi Dancer 26; On ze Boulevard 27

Mille, Cecil B. de see DeMille, Cecil B.

Mille, William de see DeMille, William

Miller, Allan From Mao to Mozart • From Mao to Mozart: Isaac Stern in China 80*; High Fidelity • High Fidelity: The Adventures of the Guarneri String Quartet 88

Miller, Arnold Louis Nudes of the World 61; Kil 1 • The Skin Game • Skin Games 62; Take Off Your Clothes and Live 63; Our Love Is Slipping Away 65; Secrets of a Windmill Girl 66; Under the Table You Must Go 69; A Touch of the Other 70; Top of the Bill 71; Showcase 72; Sex Farm 74

Miller, Ashley The Foundling 12; A Letter to the Princess 12; A Suffragette in Spite of Himself 12; Fog 13; How They Got the Vote 13; The Lady Clare 13; The New Squire 13; An Old Appointment 13; An Affair of Three Nations 15*; The House of Fear 15*; The Menace of the Mute 15; Out of the Ruins 15; With Bridges Burned 15; The Working of a Miracle 15; Did Sherman Say Law or War? 16; Fifty-Fifty 16; The High Cost of Living 16; The King's Game 16*; The Law of Gravitation 16; Priscilla and the Pesky Fly 16; The Quest of Life 16; Why the Sphinx Laughed 16; Infidelity 17; The Marriage Speculation 17; The Moral Code 17; The Princess of Park Row 17

Miller, Charles Bawbs o' Blue Ridge 16; A Corner in Colleens 16*; Home 16; Plain Jane 16; The Dark Road 17; The Flame of the Yukon 17*; Hater of Men 17; The Little Brother 17; Persnickety Polly Ann • Polly Ann 17; A Princess of the Dark 17*; The Sawdust Ring 17*; The Secret of the Storm Country 17; Wee Lady Betty 17*; Wild Winship's Widow 17; At the Mercy of Men 18; By Right of Purchase 18; The Fair Pretender 18; Ghosts of Yesterday 18; The Great Victory—Wilson or the Kaiser? • Wilson or the Kaiser? 18; The Service Star 18; A Dangerous Affair 19; Love, Honor and ? 19; Why Germany Must Pay 19; High Speed 20; The Law of the Yukon 20; The Man She Brought Back 22; Ship of Souls 25

Miller, Clarkson The Scarlet Road 16*

Miller, Claude The Best Way • The Best Way to Walk • La Meilleure Façon de Marcher 76; Dites-Lui Que Je l'Aime • This Sweet Sickness 77; Garde à Vue • The Inquisitor 81; Charlotte and Lulu • L'Effrontée • An Impudent Girl 85; The Little Thief 89

Miller, Dan T. The Island of the Fishmen • L'Isola degli Uomini Pesce • Screamers • Something Waits in the Dark 78*

Miller, David Let's Dance 35; Trained Hoofs 35; Aquatic Artistry 36; Crew Racing 36; Dare-Deviltry 36; Dexterity 36;

Hurling 36; Racing Canines 36; Table Tennis 36; Equestrian Acrobatics 37; Gilding the Lily 37; Penny Wisdom 37; Tennis Tactics 37; Fisticuffs 38; The Great Heart 38; It's in the Stars 38; Modeling for Money 38; Nostradamus 38; Penny's Party 38; La Savate 38; Drunk Driving 39; Ice Antics 39; The Flag Speaks 40; The Happiest Man on Earth 40; Billy the Kid 41; More About Nostradamus 41; Flying Tigers 42; Further Prophecies of Nostradamus 42; Sunday Punch 42; Top o' the Morning 48; Kleptomaniacs • Love Happy 49; Our Very Own 50; Idols in the Dust • Saturday's Hero 51; Sudden Fear 52; The Beautiful Stranger • Twist of Fate 54; Diane 55; The Opposite Sex 56; Golden Virgin • The Story of Esther Costello 57; Happy Anniversary 59; Midnight Lace 60; Back Street 61; The Last Hero • Lonely Are the Brave 62; Captain Newman M.D. 63; Hammerhead 68; Hail Hero! 69; Executive Action 73; Bittersweet Love 76

Miller, Frank A Marked Man 16; Odd Charges 16; The Persecution of Bob Pretty 16; The Skipper of the Osprey 16; Arcadia Revisited 19; The Auction 19; The Dream That Came True 19; Eena Deena Dinah Do 19; Kiffer's High Finance 19; The Lodger Who Wasn't Exactly a Paying Guest 19; The March Hare 19; The Coal Shortage 20; Control 20; The Golden Ballot 20; Housing 20; The Joyous Adventures of Aristide Pujol 20; Strike Fever 20; Treasure Trove 22; Goose and Stuffing 26; The Happy Rascals 26; The Little Shop in Fore Street 26; Mined and Counter-Mined 26; Regaining the Wind 26; Mr. Nobody 27; Bad Sir Brian Botany 28; Houp-la • The Lion Tamer 28; In the Dark 28; The King's Breakfast 28; Knights and Ladies 28; The Market Square 28; Nursery Chairs 28; Cupid in Clover 29; Let Me Explain, Dear 32*; Lucky Girl 32*; Verdict of the Sea 32*

Miller, George Violence in the Cinema, Part One 71; Devil in Evening Dress 73; Mad Max 79; Mad Max II • The Road Warrior 81; Twilight Zone—The Movie 83*; Anzacs • Anzacs: The War Down Under 85*; Mad Max Beyond Thunderdome 85*; The Witches of Eastwick 87

Miller, George (Trumbull) The Man from Snowy River 82; The Aviator 85; Cool Change 85; Bushfire Moon 87; Les Patterson Saves the World 87; NeverEnding Story II • NeverEnding Story II: The Next Chapter 90

Miller, Gilbert The Lady Is Willing 33

Miller, Harvey Bad Medicine 85

Miller, Ira Coming Attractions • Loose Shoes 80

Miller, J. C. No Dead Heroes 87

Miller, Jason That Championship Season 82

Miller, Jonathan Take a Girl Like You 69

Miller, Michael Street Girls 75; Jackson County Jail 76; Outside Chance 78; National Lampoon's Class Reunion 82; Silent Rage 82

Miller, Robert Ellis Any Wednesday •
Bachelor Girl Apartment 66; Sweet
November 67; The Heart Is a Lonely
Hunter 68; The Buttercup Chain 70; Big
Truck and Poor Clare 72; The Girl from
Petrovka 74; The Baltimore Bullet 80;
Reuben, Reuben 82; Brenda Starr 86;
Hawks 88

Miller, Sharron Alien Zone 78

Miller, Sidney Lou Costello and His 30
Foot Bride • The 30 Foot Bride of Candy
Rock 59; Get Yourself a College Girl •
Go-Go Set • The Swingin' Set • Swinging
Set • Watusi à Go-Go 64; Tammy and the
Millionaire 67*

Miller, Thomas see *Mastrocinque,
Camillo*

Miller, Warren Ski on the Wild Side 67

Milligan, Andy The Naked Temptress •
The Naked Witch 61; Blood Rites • The
Ghastly Ones 68; Bloodthirsty Butchers 70;
The Body Beneath 70; Torture Dungeon
70; Garu the Mad Monk • Guru the Mad
Monk 71; Curse of the Full Moon • The
Rats Are Coming • The Rats Are Coming,
the Werewolves Are Here • The Were-
wolves Are Here 72; Dr. Jekyll and Mr.
Blood • The Man with Two Heads 72;
Blood 74; Girls of 42nd Street 74; Blood
Legacy • Legacy of Blood • Legacy of Hor-
ror 78; Carnage • Hell House 83

Millin, David Ride the High Wind 65;
Seven Against the Sun 68

Milling, Bill Caged Fury 90

Millioni, Enzo Tenerezza 87

Mills, Barney Platts see *Platts-Mills,
Barney*

Mills, John Gypsy Girl • Sky West and
Crooked 65

Mills, Peter Journey Ahead 47

Mills, Reginald Peter Rabbit and Tales
of Beatrix Potter • Tales of Beatrix Potter
71

Mills, Thomas R. The Defeat of the
City 17; The Duplicity of Hargraves 17; A
Night in New Arabia 17; The Renaissance
at Charleroi 17; An American Live Wire
18; The Girl in His House 18; A Mother's
Sin 18; The Seal of Silence 18; A Girl at
Bay 19; The Girl Woman 19; Thin Ice 19;
The Unknown Quantity 19; Duds 20; The
Invisible Divorce 20*

Milman, R. M. The Return of Nathan
Becker 33*

Milne, Peter Name the Woman 28*

Milner, Dan The Last Assignment 36;
The Phantom from 10,000 Leagues 56;
From Hell It Came 57

Milonako, Ilia Love, Lust and Ecstasy 81

Milroy, Vivian Don't Say Die • Never
Say Die 50

Milton, Jack Please Stand By 72*

Milton, Joanna Please Stand By 72*

Milton, Meyrick Auld Robin Gray 17;
The Profligate 17; My Sweetheart 18; Red
Pottage 18; The Impossible Woman 19; La
Poupée 20; The Adventures of Captain
Kettle 22

Milton, Robert Charming Sinners • The
Constant Wife 29*; The Dummy 29;

Behind the Makeup 30*; Outward Bound
30; The Bargain 31; Devotion 31; Husband's Holiday 31; Strange Evidence 32;
Westward Passage 32; Belladonna 34; The
Luck of a Sailor 34

Mimet, François La Jeune Fille et les
Leçons de l'Enfer 85

Mimica, Vatroslav In the Storm • U
Oluji 52; Jubilej G. Ikla • Mr. Ikla's
Jubilee 55; At the Photographer's • Kod
Fotografa 59; The Egg • Jaje 59; The In-
spector Returns Home • Inspektor Se Vraća
Kući 59; Solimano il Conquistare • Soli-
mano il Conquistatore • Suleiman the
Conqueror 61*; Everyday Chronicle • Mala
Hronika 62; Tifusari • Typhoid 63; Prom-
etej sa Otoka Viševice • Prometheus from
the Island of Visevice • Prometheus from
Visevica Island 65; Monday or Tuesday •
Ponedeljak ili Utorak 66; Kaja, Ubit Ću
Te • Kaya • Kaya, I'll Kill You 67; Dog-
adaj • An Event 69; Hranjenik 70

Mimura, Haruhiko Amagi Goe • Amagi
Pass 85; The Street of Desires 85

Minaev, Igor Kholodni Mart 88

Mindlin, Michael, Jr. A Journey to
Jerusalem 68

Minello, Gianni A Boy Like the Others
• Un Ragazzo Come Tanti 86

Miner, Allen H. The Black Pirates 54;
Naked Sea 55; Ghost Town 56; Black
Patch 57; The Ride Back 57; Chubasco 68

Miner, Michael Deadly Weapon 87

Miner, Steve Friday the 13th Part 2 81;
Friday the 13th Part 3 82; House 86; Soul
Man 86

Miner, Worthington Hat, Coat and
Glove 34; Let's Try Again • Marriage Symphony 34

Ming, Luk Kim My Will, I Will 87

Mingay, David Rude Boy 80*

Ming-chuan, Huang see *Huang,
Ming-chuan*

Mingozzi, Gianfranco Festa a Pamplona
59; Gli Uomini e i Tori 59; Le Italiane e
l'Amore • Latin Lovers 61*; Via dei Piop-
poni 61; Il Finestre 62; La Taranta 62; Il
Mali Mestieri 63; Il Putto 63; Notte su una
Minoranza 64; Al Nostro Sonno Inquieto
65; Michelangelo Antonioni • Michelangelo
Antonioni—Storia di un Autore 65; Con il
Cuore Fermo Sicilia 66; Trio 67; Ransom
in Sardinia • Sardinia: Ransom • Sequestro
di Persona 68; La Sensitiva 70; Flavia la
Monaca Musulmana • Flavia la Nonne
Musulmane • Flavia, Priestess of Violence •
The Rebel Nun 74; Bellissimo: Images of
the Italian Cinema 87; Les Exploits d'un
Jeune Don Juan • The Exploits of a Young
Don Juan 87; Il Frullo del Passero • The
Sparrow's Fluttering 89

Ming-yau, Lo see *Lo, Ming-yau*

Minh, Ho Quang Karma 86

Minion, Joseph Daddy's Boys 88

Minkin, Adolph Conquerors of the
Night 33*; Professor Mamlock 38*; Kino-
Concert 1941 • Leningrad Music Hall 41*

Minks, Wilfried The Birth of the Witch
• Geburt der Hexe 81

Minnelli, Vincente Cabin in the Sky 42;

Panama Hattie 42*; By Hook or by Crook
• I Dood It! 43; Thousands Cheer 43*;
Meet Me in St. Louis 44; The Clock •
Under the Clock 45; Yolanda and the
Thief 45; Ziegfeld Follies 45*; Till the
Clouds Roll By 46*; Undercurrent 46; The
Pirate 47; Madame Bovary 49; Father of
the Bride 50; Father's Little Dividend 50;
An American in Paris 51; Lovely to Look
At 51*; The Bad and the Beautiful 52;
The Band Wagon 53; Historia de Tres
Amores • The Story of Three Loves • War
Es die Grosse Liebe? 53*; The Long, Long
Trailer 53; Brigadoon 54; The Cobweb 55;
Kismet 55*; Lust for Life 56; Tea and
Sympathy 56; Designing Woman 57; The
Seventh Sin 57*; Gigi 58; The Reluctant
Debutante 58; Some Came Running 58;
Bells Are Ringing 60; Home from the Hill
60; The Four Horsemen of the Apocalypse
61; Two Weeks in Another Town 62; The
Courtship of Eddie's Father 63; Goodbye,
Charlie 64; The Flight of the Sandpiper •
The Sandpiper 65; On a Clear Day You
Can See Forever 69; A Matter of Time 76

Minoui, Mehrzad Manuscripts 87

Mintz, Charles Bon Bon Parade 35;
Monkey Love 35; Birds in Love 36; A Boy
and His Dog 36; Doctor Bluebird 36;
Mother Hen's Holiday 37; The Big Birdcast
38; Bluebird's Baby 38

Mintz, Murray Cardiac Arrest 80

Minzenty, Gustave A Yell of a Night
32; A Royal Demand 33

Mira, Carlos Daniya, Jardín del Harem 88

Miragala, E. see *Miraglia, Emilio*

Miragala, Emil see *Miraglia, Emilio*

Miraglia, Emilio The Vatican Affair 69;
The Night Evelyn Came Out of the Grave
• The Night She Arose from the Tomb •
The Night That Evelyn Left the Tomb • La
Notte Che Evelyn Usci dalla Tomba 71; La
Dama Rossa Uccide Sette Volte • The Red
Queen Kills Seven Times 72; Spara Joe...
e Così Sia 72; Blood Feast • Feast of Flesh
76

Miranda, Thomas N. Hearts of Youth
20*

Mirande, Yves Café de Paris 38*; Derrière la Façade • 32 Rue de Montmartre
39*; Moulin Rouge 44

Miri, Sa'id Haji see *Haji-Miri, Sa'id*

Miró, Pilar The Crime of Cuenca • El
Crimen de Cuenca 80; Werther 86

Miró, Sergio La Canción del Regreso •
Homecoming Song 40

Mironer, F. Spring on Zarechnaya Street
56*

Mirza, Saeed Akhtar Mohan Joshi
Haazir Ho • Summons for Mohan Joshi 84

Mirzayev, Mukhtar Aga see *Aga-Mirzayev, Mukhtar*

Mischwitzki, Holger see *Praunheim,
Rosa von*

Mishiku, Richard At the Havana 40

Mishkin, Lew Pelvis 77

Mishra, Sudhir This Is Not Our Destination 87

Mishurin, Alexei Age of Youth • Gody
Molodiye • The Train Goes to Kiev 61

Missiaen, Jean-Claude La Baston 85
Mistler, Eric AC/DC: Let There Be Rock 82*

Misumi, Kenji Buddha 65; Daimajin Ikaru • Return of Giant Majin • The Return of Majin • The Return of the Giant Majin 66*; Showdown for Zatoichi • Zatōichi Jigokutabi 68; Devil's Temple • Oni no Sumu Yakata 69; The Magoichi Saga • Shirikurae Magoichi 70; Zatoichi Challenged • Zatōichi Chikemuri Kaidō 70; Baby Cart at the River Styx • Kosure Ookami—Sanzu no Kawa no Ubaguruma • Kosure Ookami II • Shogun Assassin 72; Kosure Ookami • Kosure Ookami—Kō wo Kashi Ude Kashi Tsukamatsuru • Lightning Swords of Death • Sword of Vengeance 72; Kosure Ookami—Shinikaze no Mukau Ubaguruma • Kosure Ookami III 72; Kosure Ookami IV • Kosure Ookami—Meifu 73

Misuraca, Pasquale Angelus Novus 87
Mita, Merata Patu 83; Mauri 87
Mitchell, Bruce The Stranger of the Hills 22; The Air Hawk 24; Another Man's Wife 24; Dynamite Dan 24; The Hellion 24; Love's Whirlpool 24; The Cloud Rider 25; Flyin' Thru 25; Savages of the Sea 25; Speed Madness 25; Tricks 25; Cupid's Knockout 26; The Hollywood Reporter 26; Sky High Saunders 27; Three Miles Up 27; The Air Patrol 28; The Cloud Dodger 28; Last Lap 28; The Phantom Flyer • The Phantom Ranger 28; The Speed Classic 28; Won in the Clouds 28; The Sky Skidder 29; The Lonesome Trail 30; Trapped 31; Forty-Five Calibre Echo 32; The Rawhide Terror 34

Mitchell, Claude H. Seeing It Through 20

Mitchell, Craig Jim—The World's Greatest • Story of a Teenager 76*

Mitchell, Edmund The Lone Star Rush 15

Mitchell, Eric Underground U.S.A. 80; The Way It Is 86

Mitchell, Howard Betrayed 16; The Traffic Cop 16; Petticoats and Politics 18; A Girl in Bohemia 19; The Law That Divides 19; Snares of Paris 19; The Splendid Sin 19; Beware of the Bride 20; Black Shadows 20; Faith 20; Flame of Youth 20; The Husband Hunter 20; The Little Wanderer 20; Love's Harvest 20; Molly and I 20; The Tattlers 20; Cinderella of the Hills 21; Ever Since Eve 21; The Lamplighter 21; Lovetime 21; The Mother Heart 21; Queenie 21; Wing Toy 21; Winning with Wits 21; The Crusader 22*; The Great Night 22; Forgive and Forget 23; A Man's Size 23; The Lone Chance 24; Romance Ranch 24; The Jazz Girl 26; The Road to Broadway 26; Breed of Courage 27; Hidden Aces 27

Mitchell, Oswald Danny Boy 34*; Cock o' the North 35*; Stars on Parade 35*; King of Hearts • Little Gel 36*; Shipmates o' Mine 36; Variety Parade 36; Old Mother Riley • The Original Old Mother Riley • The Return of Old Mother Riley 37; Rose of Tralee 37; Almost a Gentleman 38; Lily of Laguna 38; Little Dolly Daydream 38; Night Journey 38; Old Mother Riley Catches a Quisling • Old Mother Riley in Paris 38; Jailbirds 39; Music Hall Parade 39; Old Mother Riley MP 39; Pack Up Your Troubles 40; Sailors Don't Care 40; Asking for Trouble 41; Bob's Your Uncle 41; Danny Boy 41; The Dummy Talks 43; Old Mother Riley Overseas 43; Old Mother Riley at Home 45; Loyal Heart 46; Black Memory 47; The Mysterious Mr. Nicholson 47; The Greed of William Hart • Horror Maniacs 48; House of Darkness 48; The Man from Yesterday 49; The Temptress 49

Mitchell, Sollace Call Me 88
Mitchell Meléndez, Jerónimo Heroin • Heroína 65
Mitra, Raja Ekti Jiban • Portrait of a Life 88
Mitrani, Michel Black Thursday • The Gates of the Louvre • Les Guichets du Louvre 74; Monsieur de Pourceaugnac 85
Mitri, Leonardo de *see* De Mitri, Leonardo
Mitrotti, Roberto Little Girl, Big Tease 77
Mitrović, Zita Witness Out of Hell • Zeugin Aus der Hölle 67
Mitrović, Živka Bitter Grass 65; The Knife 66; Operation Belgrade 68
Mitrović, Živorad Vendetta 62
Mitry, Jean Paris-Cinéma 29*; Pacific 231 49; Liberté • Le Paquebot "Liberté" 50; En Bateau 51; Images pour Debussy 51; Rêverie pour Claude Debussy 51; Au Pays des Grandes Causses 52; Le Fleuve 52; Hauteterre 52; Symphonie Mécanique 55; Écoles de Pilotage 56; La Machine et l'Homme 56; Le Miracle des Ailes 56; Chopin 57; Écrire en Images 57; Énigme aux Folies-Bergère 59; The Big Fair • La Grande Foire 60; Rencontres 60
Mitsuwa, Akira The Atomic Rulers of the World • Attack of the Flying Saucers • Supergiant II 57*
Mitta, Alexander My Friend Kolka 61*; Without Fear or Reproach 63; Someone's Buzzing, Open the Door 65; The Girl and the Bugler • Zvonyat Otkroyte Dver 67; Shine Bright My Star 69; Make a Funny Face 72; Moscow My Love 74*; The Story of How Tsar Peter Married Off His Moor • The Tale of How Tsar Peter Married Off His Moor 76; Shag 88
Mittler, Leo In der Heimat Da Gibt's ein Wiedersehen! 26*; Honeymoon for Three 35; Cheer Up! 36; The Last Waltz 36*
Miwa, Akira The Brain from Outer Space 59*
Mix, Tom Cactus Jake, Heartbreaker 14; The Moving Picture Cowboy 14; The Ranger's Romance 14; A Child of the Prairie 15; On the Eagle Trail 15; The Range Girl and the Cowboy 15; The Daredevil 20
Miyazaki, Hayao Laputa: The Castle in the Sky • Tenkū no Shiro Laputa 87
Mizener, Don von Mulefeathers • The West Is Still Wild 77
Mizoguchi, Kenji The Adventures of Arsène Lupin • 813 • 813: The Adventures of Arsène Lupin • Rupimono 22; Ai ni Yomigaeru Hi • The Day When Love Returns • Resurrection of Love 22; Blood and Soul • Chi to Rei 22; City of Desire • Jōen no Chimata • Town of Fire 22; The Dream Path of Youth • Dreams of Youth • Seishun no Yumeji 22; Failure's Song Is Sad • Haizan no Uta wa Kanashi • Sad Song of the Defeated • The Song of Failure 22; Furusato • Home Town • Kokyō • Native Country 22; Among the Ruins • Haikyo no Naka • In the Ruins 23; Anna Christie • Foggy Harbor • Harbor in the Fog • Kiri no Minato 23; Kantō 23; The Night • Yoru 23; The Song of the Mountain Pass • Tōge no Uta 23; Akatsuki no Shi • Death at Dawn 24; A Chronicle of May Rain • Chronicle of the May Rain • May Rain and Silk Paper • Samidare Zōshi 24; Gendai no Joō • The Queen of Modern Times 24; Jinkyō • This Dusty World • The World Down Here 24; Josei wa Tsuyoshi • Strong Is the Female • Women Are Strong 24; Kanashiki Hakuchi • The Sad Idiot 24; Kanraku no Onna • Woman of Pleasure 24; Kyokubadan no Joō • Queen of the Circus 24; Musen Fusen • No Fight Without Money • No Money, No Fight 24; Shichimenchō no Yukue • The Trace of a Turkey • Turkeys in a Row • Turkeys, Whereabouts Unknown 24; Aa Tokumukan Kantō • Ah the Special Service Vessel 25*; After Years of Study • Gakusō o Idete • Out of College 25; Akai Yūhi ni Terasarete • In the Red Rays of the Sleeping Sun • Shining in the Red Sunset • Under the Crimson Sunset 25*; Daichi wa Hohoemu • The Earth Smiles • Smile of Our Earth • The Smiling Earth 25; Furusato no Uta • Hometown Song • The Song of Home • Song of the Native Country 25; Gaijo no Sukechi • A Sketch on the Road • Street Scenes • Street Sketches 25*; General Nogi and Kuma-San • Nogi Shōgun to Kuma-San • Nogi Taishō to Kuma-San 25; The Human Being • Humanity • The Man • Ningen 25; Lament of a White Lily • Shirayuri wa Nageku • The White Lily Laments 25; The Boy from the Navy • The Boy of the Sea • The Boys from the Sea • Children of the Sea • Kaikoku Danji 26; The Copper Coin King • The Copper King • Dōka Ō • King of a Penny 26; Gold • Kane • Kin • Money 26; It's My Fault • My Fault • My Fault, Continued • My Fault, New Version • Shin Ōno Ga Tsumi 26; Kaminingyō Haru no Sasayaki • A Paper Doll's Whisper of Spring 26; Kyōren no Onna Shishō • The Love-Mad Teacher • The Passion of a Woman Teacher 26; The Bird of Mercy • The Cuckoo • Jihi Shincho • Like the Changing Heart of a Bird 27; Gratitude to the Emperor • The Imperial Grace • Kōon 27; Hito no Isshō • The Life of a Man • A Man's Life 27; Musume Kawaiya • My Lovely Daughter • My Loving Daughter 28; Asahi wa Kagayaku • The Morning Sun Shines • The Rising Sun

Is Shining • The Rising Sun Shines 29*; City Symphony • Metropolitan Symphony • Symphony of the Metropolis • Tokai Kōkyōgaku 29; The Nihon Bridge • Nihonbashi 29; Tōkyō Kōshinkyoku • Tokyo March 29; Furusato • Home Town • Hometown 30; Mistress of a Foreigner • Okichi, Mistress of a Foreigner • Okichi the Stranger • Tojin Okichi 30; And Yet They Go On • Nevertheless They Go On • Shikamo Karera wa Yuku 31; Dawn in Manchuria • The Dawn of Manchukuo and Mongolia • The Dawn of Manchuria and Mongolia • The Dawn of Mongolia • The Dawn of the Founding of Manchukuo and Mongolia • Mam-Mō Kenkoku no Reimei 32; The Man of the Moment • The Man of the Right Moment • Timely Mediator • Toki no Ujigami 32; Gion Festival • Gion Matsuri 33; Group Kamikaze • Group Shimpu • The Jinpu Group • Jinpu-Ren • The Kamikaze Group • Kamikaze-Ren • The Shimpu Group • Shimpu-Ren 33; Taki no Shiraito • The Water Magician • White Threads of the Cascades • The White Threads of the Waterfall 33; Aizō Tōge • The Gorge Between Love and Hate • The Mountain Pass of Love and Hate • The Passing of Love and Hate 34; The Downfall • The Downfall of Osen • Orizuru Osen • Osen of the Paper Cranes • Paper Cranes from Osen 34; The Field Poppy • Gubijinsō • The Poppies • Poppy 35; Maria no Oyuki • Oyuki the Madonna • Oyuki the Virgin • The Virgin from Oyuki 35; Gion no Shimai • Sisters of Gion • Sisters of the Gion 36; Naniwa Elegy • Naniwa Ereji • Naniwa Hika • Ōsaka Elegy 36; Aienkyō • The Gorge Between Love and Hate • The Straits of Love and Hate 37; Aa Furusato • Aa Kokyō • Ah, My Home Town 38; Roei no Uta • The Song of the Camp 38*; The Story of the Last Chrysanthemums • The Story of the Late Chrysanthemums • Zangiku Monogatari 39; Geido Ichidai Otoko • The Life of an Actor • The Life of an Artist 40; Naniwa Onna • Woman of Naniwa • Woman of Osaka 40; The 47 Ronin • Genroku Chūshingura • The Loyal 47 • The Loyal 47 of the Genroku Era • The Loyal 47 Ronin • The Loyal 47 Ronin of the Genroku Era 42; Miyamoto Musashi • Musashi Miyamoto • The Swordsman 42; Danjuro Sandai • Three Danjuros • Three Generations of Danjuro • Three Generations of the Danjuro Family 44; Bijomaru Sword • Bijomaru the Noted Sword • The Famous Sword Bijomaru • Meitō Bijomaru • The Noted Sword • The Sword 45; Hisshōka • Song of Victory • Victory Song 45*; Five Women Around Utamaro • Utamaro and His Five Women • Utamaro o Meguru Gonin no Onna 46; Josei no Shōri • The Victory of Women • Women's Victory 46; Joyū Sumako no Koi • The Love of Actress Sumako • The Love of Sumako the Actress 47; Women of the Night • Yoru no Onnatachi 48; Flame of My Love • My Love Burns • My Love Has

Been Burning • Waga Koi wa Moeru 49; Picture of Madame Yuki • Portrait of Madame Yuki • Sketch of Madame Yuki • Yuki Fujin Ezu 50; The Lady from Musashino • Lady Musashino • Madame Musashino • Musashino Fujin • Woman of Musashino 51; Miss Oyu • Oyu-Sama 51; Diary of Oharu • Kōshoku Ichidai Onna • The Life of a Woman by Saikaku • The Life of Oharu • Oharu • Saikaku Ichidai Onna 52; A Geisha • Gion Bayashi • Gion Festival Music • Gion Music • Gion Music Festival 53; Tales After the Rain • Tales of the Pale and Silvery Moon After the Rain • Ugetsu • Ugetsu Monogatari 53; The Bailiff • Sansho Dayu • Sansho the Bailiff • The Superintendent Sansho 54; Chikamatsu Monogatari • The Crucified Lovers • A Story from Chikamatsu 54; The Crucified Woman • Uwasa no Onna • The Woman in the Rumor • A Woman of Rumour • The Woman of the Rumor 54; Empress Yang Kwei Fei • Princess Yang Kwei Fei • Yang Kwei Fei • Yokihi 55; New Tales of the Taira Clan • The Sacrilegious Hero • Saga of the Taira Clan • Shin Heike Monogatari • The Taira Clan • Tales of the Taira Clan 55; Akasen Chitai • Red Light District • Street of Shame 56; Ōsaka Monogatari • An Osaka Story 56*

Mizrahi, Moshe Sophie's Ways • Les Stances à Sophie 70; Ani Ohev Otach Rosa • I Love You, Rosa 71; The House on Chelouche Street 73; Rachel's Man 74; Daughters, Daughters 75; Madame Rosa • La Vie Devant Soi 77; Chère Inconnue • I Sent a Letter to My Love 80; Life Goes On • La Vie Continue 82; Youth 83; War and Love 85; Every Time We Say Goodbye • Love Is Ever Young 86; Mangeclous 88

Mizrahi, Toga Dr. Epameinondas 38; Otan o Syzygos Taxeideyei • When the Husband Travels 39

Mkrtchyan, Albert Marriage of Convenience • Zakonny Brak 86; Pesn Proshedshikh Dney • Song of Bygone Days 87

Mnouchkine, Ariane Molière 75

Moberly, Luke Little Laura and Big John 73*

Mobley, James Self-Portrait 73*

Moccia, Giuseppe Llegaron los Marcianos • I Marziani Hanno Dodici Mani • Siamo Quattro Marziani • The Twelve-Handed Men of Mars 64*; È Arrivato Mio Fratello • My Brother's Come to Stay 85*; Department Store • Grandi Magazzini 86*; Il Burbero • The Grouch 87*

Mocky, Jean-Pierre The Chasers • Les Dragueurs • The Young Have No Morals 59; Un Couple • The Love Trap 60; Snobs! • Les Snobs 61; Les Vierges 62; Deo Gratias • Un Drôle de Paroissien • The Funny Parishioner • Heaven Sent • Thank Heaven for Small Favors 63; The Big Scare • La Grande Frousse 64; La Bourse et la Vie • Your Money or Your Life 65; Les Compagnons de la Marguerite • Order of the Daisy 66; The Big Wash! • La Grande Lessive 68; L'Étalon • The Stud 69; Solo 69; L'Albatros • The Albatross • Love Hate

70; Pavane pour un Crétin Défunt 71; Chut! 72; L'Ombre d'une Chance 73; Un Linceul N'A Pas de Poches 74; L'Ibis Rouge 75; Le Roi des Bricoleurs 77; Le Témoin 78; Le Piège à Cons 79; Y'A-t-Il un Français dans la Salle? 82; À Mort l'Arbitre 83; La Machine à Découdre • The Unsewing Machine 85; Le Pactole 85; Le Miracle • The Miracle Healing 86; Agent Trouble 87; Les Saisons du Plaisir 87; Une Nuit à l'Assemblée Nationale 88; Divine Enfant 89; Il Gèle en Enfer 90

Moctezuma, Juan López see *López Moctezuma, Juan*

Moder, Dick Lassie the Voyager 66*

Modi, Sohrab M. The Tiger and the Flame 55

Moeller, Philip The Age of Innocence 34; Break of Hearts 35

Moffa, Paolo The Island Princess 55; All'Ultimo Sangue • Bury Them Deep 68

Moffat, Ivan Citizen's Army • Home Guard 41

Moffatt, Graham Till the Bells Ring 33

Moffitt, Jefferson Nurse to You 36*

Moffitt, John Burnin' Love • Love at Stake 87

Mogherini, Flavio Lunatics and Lovers 75; The Lilac Girl • La Ragazza dei Lilla 86; Come È Dura l'Avventura 88

Moguy, Léonide Prison Sans Barreaux • Prison Without Bars 33; Forty Little Mothers • Le Mioche 36; The Affair Lafont • Conflict • Conflit 38; Le Déserteur • Je T'Attendrai • Three Hours 39; L'Empreinte du Dieu • Two Women 40; The Night Is Ending • Paris After Dark 43; Action in Arabia 44; Whistle Stop 45; Bethsabée 46; Domani È Troppo Tardi • Tomorrow Is Too Late 49; Domani È un Altro Giorno 49; Les Enfants de l'Amour 53; Diary of a Bad Girl • Le Long des Trottoirs 56; Donnez-Moi Ma Chance • Give Me My Chance 57; Les Hommes Veulent Vivre • Gli Uomini Vogliono Vivere 62

Mohammad, Oussama Noujoum A'Nahar 88

Mohan Thirtham 87; Sruthi 88

Mohan, Surendra Pathar Dil 88

Mohanan, K. R. Purushartham 88

Mohr, Hal The Big Idea 18; When Love Is Young 37

Mohr, Hanro Colt—Flight 802 • Hostage 87

Molander, Gustaf Bodakungen • King of Boda 20; En Ungdomsäventyr 21; The Amateur Film • Amatör Filmen • Pärlorna 22; Thomas Graals Myndling • Thomas Graal's Ward 22; Mälarpirater • Pirates on Lake Mälar 23; Constable Paulus' Easter Bomb • Polis Paulus Påskasmäll 24; 33.333 24; The Ingmar Inheritance • Ingmarsarvet 25; Till Österland • To the Orient 25; Discord • Hans Engelska Fru • His English Wife 26; Hon, den Enda • She, the Only One • She's the Only One 26; The Doctor's Women • Parisiskor • Women of Paris 27; Förseglade Läppar • Sealed Lips 27; Sin • Synd 28; Hjärtats Triumf • Triumph

My Friends 2 82; Bertoldo, Bertoldino e...Cacasenno 84; Le Due Vite di Mattia Pascal • The Two Lives of Mattia Pascal 85; Let's Hope It's a Girl • Pourvu Que Ce Soit une Fille • Speriamo Che Sia Femmina 85; I Picari • The Picaros • The Rogues 87; Il Male Oscuro • The Obscure Illness 90

Monk, Meredith Book of Days 88

Monkman, Noel Typhoon Treasure 39; King of the Coral Sea 56*

Monks, John, Jr. Island Escape • No Man Is an Island 62*

Monnet, Jacques Promis, Juré! 88

Monroe, Phil The Iceman Ducketh 64; The Bugs Bunny/Road Runner Movie • The Great American Bugs Bunny/Road Runner Chase • The Great American Chase 79*

Monson, Carl Blood Legacy • Legacy of Blood 71; GLUMP • Hungry Pets • Please Don't Eat My Mother! • Please, Not My Mother • Please Release My Mother 72

Montagne, Edward Crime Lab 48; Project X 49; The Tattooed Stranger 50; The Man with My Face 51; McHale's Navy 64; McHale's Navy Joins the Air Force 65; The Reluctant Astronaut 67; They Went That-a-Way and That-a-Way 78*

Montagu, Ivor Bluebottles 28; Day Dreams 28; The Tonic 28; Kampf des Unabhängigen Gegen den Kommerziellen Film • Sturm Über la Sarraz 29*; Peace and Plenty 39

Montaldo, Giuliano Tiro al Piccione 61; Una Bella Grinta 65; Extraconiugale 65*; Ad Ogni Costo • Diamantes à Go-Go • Grand Slam • Top Job 68; Gli Intoccabili • Machine Gun McCain 68; Gott Mit Uns 69; Sacco and Vanzetti • Sacco e Vanzetti 71; The Fifth Day of Peace 72; Giordano Bruno 73; L'Agnese un a Morire 76; Circuito Chiuso 78; Il Giocattolo 78; The Day Before • Il Giorno Prima 87; The Gold-Rimmed Glasses • The Gold Spectacles • Gli Occhiali d'Oro 87; Shortcut 89

Montanari, Lidia Castighi • Punishment 86*

Montaya, Romeo Hill 171 87

Montazel, Pierre Young Girls of Good Families 63

Monte, Peter del see Del Monte, Peter

Monteiro, João Cesar A Flor do Mar 86

Monter, José As If It Were Raining 63

Montero, Robert see Montero, Roberto Bianchi

Montero, Roberto Bianchi The Cliff of Sin 52; Monster of the Island • Il Mostro dell'Isola 53; Colossus and the Huns 62; Agent Z55—Desperate Mission 64; I Due Facce del Dollaro 67; Arriva Durango, Paga o Muori 71; I Senzo Dio 71; Bad Girls • The Slasher 75

Montesano, Enrico A Me Mi Piace • I Like Her 85

Montesi, Jorge Birds of Prey 86

Montgomery, George The Steel Claw 61; Samar 62; From Hell to Borneo 64; Guerrillas in Pink Lace 64; Satan's Harvest 70; Ride the Tiger 71

Montgomery, Michael Swinging Teacher

74

Montgomery, Monty The Loveless 81*

Montgomery, Patrick The Man You Love to Hate 79; The Compleat Beatles 82

Montgomery, Robert They Were Expendable 45*; Lady in the Lake 46; Ride the Pink Horse 47; Once More, My Darling 49; Eye Witness • Your Witness 50; The Gallant Hours 60

Montgomery, Thomas King Kong Tai Godzilla • King Kong Tai Gojira • King Kong vs. Godzilla 63*

Monton, Vincent Windrider 86

Montoro, Edward The Losers 68*

Montoya, Jesús Fragoso see Fragoso Montoya, Jesús

Montresor, Beni Pilgrimage 72

Moody, Harry G. Lone Hand Wilson 20*; Crashing Courage 23; Flames of Passion 23; The Frame Up 23; The Power Divine 23*; The Range Patrol 23; Scars of Hate 23; The Vow of Vengeance 23; Beaten 24

Moody, Titus Outlaw Motorcycles 67; The Last of the American Hoboes 74

Moomaw, Lewis H. The Deceiver 20*; The Golden Trail 20*; The Chechahcos 24; Under the Rouge 25; Flames 26

Moore, Charles Philip Demon Wind 90

Moore, Emmett Sweet Inniscarra 34

Moore, Eugene see Moore, W. Eugene

Moore, James The Secret Seven 40

Moore, Matt Her Invisible Husband 16

Moore, Michael An Eye for an Eye • Talion 66; Paradise, Hawaiian Style 66; The Fastest Guitar Alive 67; Kill a Dragon 67; Buckskin • The Frontiersman 68

Moore, Michael Roger and Me 89

Moore, Richard Circle of Iron • The Silent Flute 78

Moore, Robert Murder by Death 76; The Cheap Detective 78; Chapter Two 79

Moore, Ronald W. Future-Kill 85

Moore, Rowland Billie "Bow-Wow" 15

Moore, Tara Hawkins Fire in Eden • Tusks 86

Moore, Thomas see Castellari, Enzo G.

Moore, Tom The Secret Room 15

Moore, Tom Mark of the Witch 70; Return to Boggy Creek 77; 'Night Mother 86

Moore, Vin The Cohens and Kellys in Africa 30; Ex-Bad Boy 31; Many a Slip 31; Virtuous Husband • What Wives Don't Want 31; Racing Youth 32; Dames and Dynamite • Flirting with Danger • Reckless Romeos 34; Cheers of the Crowd 35; Topa Topa 38*; Children of the Wild • Killers of the Wild 40*

Moore, W. Eugene Joseph in the Land of Egypt 14; The Mill on the Floss 15; Her Father's Gold 16; The Oval Diamond 16; The Woman in Politics 16; The World and the Woman 16; The Candy Girl 17; Captain Kiddo 17; The Girl Who Won Out 17; His Enemy's Daughter • A Modern Monte Cristo 17; The Image Maker 17; Pots and Pans Peggie 17; When Baby Forgot 17; Sue of the South 19

Moorse, George Inside Out 64; London Pop 64; Zero in the Universe 65; Der

Findling • The Foundling • The Orphan 67; Kuckucksjahre 67; Der Griller 68; Liebe und So Weiter 68; Robinson 68; Lenz 71; Inki 73

Mora, Anghel Rezerva la Start 88

Mora, J. Ferrater see Ferrater-Mora, J.

Mora, Miguel Bitter Taste in the Morning • Mañana de Cobre 86

Mora, Philippe Trouble in Molopolis 72; Swastika 74; Brother, Can You Spare a Dime? 75; Mad Dog • Mad Dog Morgan 76; The Beast Within 81; Legend in Leotards • The Return of Captain Invincible 82; A Breed Apart 83; Howling II: Your Sister Is a Werewolf 85; Death of a Soldier • The Leonski Incident 86; Howling III • The Marsupials: The Howling III 87; Communion 89

Morahan, Christopher All Neat in Black Stockings 68; Diamonds for Breakfast 68; The Jewel in the Crown 84*; In the Secret State 85; Clockwise 86; Troubles 88; Paper Mask 90

Morais, José Alvaro O Bobo • The Jester 87

Morales, José Díaz see Díaz Morales, José

Moran, Lee Everything But the Truth 20*; Fixed by George 20*; La La Lucille 20*; Once a Plumber 20*; A Shocking Night 21*

Moran, Percy Lily of Letchworth Lock 12*; OHMS—Our Helpless Millions Saved 14; Britain's Naval Secret 15; How Men Love Women 15; London Nighthawks 15; Nurse and Martyr 15; Parted by the Sword 15; Slavers of the Thames 15; London's Enemies 16; The Redemption of His Name 18; Jack, Sam and Pete 19; The Field of Honour 22; Lieutenant Daring RN and the Water Rats 24*

Moranis, Rick Strange Brew 83*

Morante, Milburn Hearts o' the Range 21; The Recoil 21; Blind Circumstances 22; Diamond Carlisle 22; For Love of Service 22; The Hate Trail 22; Bucking the Truth 26; Chasing Trouble 26; The Escape 26

Morassi, Mauro The Success • Il Successo 63*

Morat, Luitz see Luitz-Morat

Morayta, Miguel La Invasión de los Muertos • La Invasión de los Vampiros • The Invasion of the Vampires 61; The Bloody Vampire 63

Mordente, Tony Just Tell Me You Love Me 79

Morder, Joseph Mémoires d'un Juif Tropical • Memories of a Tropical Jew 86

Mordillat, Gérard Billy ze Kick 85; F...ing Fernand 87

More O'Ferrall, George Her Panelled Door • The Woman with No Name 50*; Angels One Five 52; The Holly and the Ivy 52; The Heart of the Matter 53; The Green Scarf 54; Lord Mountdrago • Three Cases of Murder 54*; The Woman for Joe 55; The March Hare 56

Moreau, Jeanne Light • Lumière 76; The Adolescent • An Adolescent Girl • L'Adolescente 78; Lillian Gish 84

Moreno, Antonio Santa 32

Moreno Alba, Rafael Exorcism's Daughter • House of Insane Women • Las Melancólicas • Women of Doom 71; Long Strider • Pasos Largos: El Último Bandido Andaluz 87

Morera, Eduardo Ídolos de la Radio 35; Por Buen Camino 36

Moretti, Nanni Io Sono un Autarchico 76; Ecce Bombo 78; Sogni d'Oro 81; Bianca 84; The Mass Is Ended • La Messa È Finita 85; Palombella Rossa 89

Moreuil, François Love Play • Playtime • La Récréation 61*

Morey, Edward, Jr. Killer Leopard 54*

Morey, Larry Snow White and the Seven Dwarfs 37*

Morgan, Glenn Incoming Freshmen 79*

Morgan, Horace George Robey's Day Off 18*

Morgan, Sidney The Brass Bottle 14; Dr. Paxton's Last Crime 14; The Great Spy Raid 14; Huns of the North Sea 14; Esther Redeemed 15; Iron Justice 15; Light 15; The Lord Gave • The World's Desire 15; Our Boys 15; The Charlatan 16; Frailty • Temptation's Hour 16; The Stolen Sacrifice 16; What's Bred...Comes Out in the Flesh 16; Auld Lang Syne 17; A Bid for Fortune 17; Derelicts 17; Drink 17; Because 18; Democracy 18; After Many Days 19; All Men Are Liars 19; Sweet and Twenty 19; The Black Sheep 20; By Berwin Banks 20; The Children of Gibeon 20; Lady Noggs • Lady Noggs, Peeress 20; Little Dorrit 20; A Man's Shadow 20; The Scarlet Wooing 20; Two Little Wooden Shoes 20; The Woman of the Iron Bracelets 20; A Lowland Cinderella 21; The Mayor of Casterbridge 21; Moth and Rust 21; Fires of Innocence 22; The Lilac Sunbonnet 22; The Woman Who Obeyed 23; Miriam Rozella 24; The Shadow of Egypt 24; Bulldog Drummond's Third Round 25; The Thoroughbred 28; A Window in Piccadilly 28; Contraband Love 31; Her Reputation 31; Chelsea Life 33; Mixed Doubles 33; Faces 34; The Minstrel Boy 37

Morgan, W. T. The Unheard Music 85

Morgan, William Bowery Boy 40; The Gay Vagabond 41; Mercy Island 41; Mr. District Attorney 41; Sierra Sue 41; Sunset in Wyoming 41; Bells of Capistrano 42; Cowboy Serenade • Serenade of the West 42; Heart of the Rio Grande 42; Home in Wyomin' 42; Stardust on the Sage 42; Headin' for God's Country 43; Secrets of the Underground 43; Fun and Fancy Free 47*

Morgan, William M. see Eichhorn, Franz

Morgenstern, Janusz Do Widzenia Do Jutra • See You Tomorrow 60; Jovita • Jowita 70

Mori, Issei Daimajin Gyakushū • Majin Strikes Again • The Return of Majin 66; The Curse of the Ghosts • Yotsuya Kaidan—Ōiwa no Bōrei 69

Morikawa, Tokihisa Live Your Own Way • Wakamono Tachi 70; Glittering

You • Kimi ga Kagayaku Toki 86

Morimoto, Kouji Robot Carnival 87*

Morin, Edgar Chronicle of a Summer • Chronique d'un Été 60*

Morishita, Kozo The Transformers—The Movie 86*

Morita, Yoshimitsu The Family Game • Kazoku Geimu 83; And Then • Sorekara 86; Deaths in Tokimeki • Tokimeki ni Shisu 86; All for Business' Sake • The Mercenaries • Sorobanzuku 87

Moritani, Shiro Japan Sinks • Nippon Chinbotsu • The Submersion of Japan • Tidal Wave 73*

Morland, John Church Parade from "The Catch of the Season" 07; The Criminal Cried 07; Down by the Old Bull and Bush 07; The Flowers That Bloom in the Spring 07; Fly Ann 07; Four Jolly Sailor Boys from "The Princess of Kensington" 07; Great Finale to Act 1 of "The Yeoman of the Guard" 07; Here's a Fine How-D'Ye-Do 07; Hereupon We're Both Agreed 07; I Would Like to Marry You 07; If You Want to Know Who We Are 07; It's a Different Girl Again 07; The Lord High Executioner 07; Miya Sama 07; A More Human Mikado 07; The Old Folks at Home 07; Our Great Mikado 07; Riding on Top of a Car 07; They Can't Diddle Me 07; Three Little Maids 07; Tit Willow 07; Waiting for Him Tonight 07; A Wandering Minstrel 07; We All Walked Into the Shop 07; Were I Thy Bride 07; Were You Not to Koko Plighted? 07; What D'Yer Want to Talk About It For? 07; Where Oh Where Has My Little Dog Gone? 07; Zuyder Zee 07

Morley, Royston Attempt to Kill 61

Morlhon, Camille de see De Morlhon, Camille

Moro, Pierre de see De Moro, Pierre

Moroni, M. Il Mio Nome È Mallory: "M" Come Morte 71

Morosco, Walter Silken Shackles 26

Morrice, Norman Swan Lake 80

Morris, David Burton Loose Ends 75; Purple Haze 82; Patti Rocks 87

Morris, Ernest Operation Murder 57; Son of a Stranger 57; Three Sundays to Live 57; A Woman of Mystery 57; The Betrayal 58; On the Run 58; Three Crooked Men • Three Wanted Men 58; Night Train for Inverness 59; The Hidden Room of 1,000 Horrors • Panic • The Tell-Tale Heart 60; Highway to Battle 60; The Court Martial of Major Keller 61; Strip Tease Murder 61; Tarnished Heroes 61; Transatlantic 61; Masters of Venus 62; Night Cargoes 62; Operation Stogie 62; The Spanish Sword 62; Three Spare Wives 62; What Every Woman Wants 62; Echo of Diana 63; Shadow of Fear 63; Five Have a Mystery to Solve 64; The Sicilians 64; Mr. Moto and the Persian Oil Case • The Return of Mr. Moto 65

Morris, Errol Gates of Heaven 78; Vernon, Florida 81; The Thin Blue Line 87

Morris, Howard Who's Minding the Mint? 67; A Man in Mommy's Bed • With

Six You Get Eggroll 68; Don't Drink the Water 69; Goin' Coconuts 78

Morris, Reginald When Winter Went 25

Morris, Robert King of Kong Island • Kong Island 78

Morris, W. C. The Dove of Peace 15; The Pilot of Peace 15; Some Presidential Possibilities 15; Wilson Surrenders 15; The Black List 16; Responsibility for the War 16

Morrison, Bruce Constance 84; Shaker Run 85; Queen City Rockers • Tearaway 86

Morrison, Don Towards the Morning 81

Morrison, Duke see Wayne, John

Morrison, Ian 69 Minutes 77

Morrison, Jane The Two Worlds of Angelita 82

Morrison, Lee Miles Against Minutes 24; Peacetime Spies 24; Speeding Into Trouble 24

Morrissey, Edward The House Built Upon Sand 17; Stage Struck 17; The Pointing Finger 19*

Morrissey, Paul Taylor Mead Dances 63; Civilization and Its Discontents 64; Blue Movie • Fuck 68*; Flesh 68; Trash 70; Andy Warhol's Women 71; Heat 71; Women in Revolt 71*; L'Amour 72*; Andy Warhol's Dracula • Andy Warhol's Young Dracula • Blood for Dracula • Dracula • Dracula Cerca Sangue di Vergine e...Mori di Sete • Dracula Vuole Vivere: Cerca Sangue di Vergine! • Young Dracula 73*; Andy Warhol's Frankenstein • Carne per Frankenstein • The Devil and Dr. Frankenstein • Flesh for Frankenstein • Frankenstein • The Frankenstein Experiment • Il Mostro È in Tavola...Barone Frankenstein • Up Frankenstein • Warhol's Frankenstein 73*; The Hound of the Baskervilles 77; Forty-Deuce 81; Madame Wang's 81; Mixed Blood 84; Beethoven's Nephew • Le Neveu de Beethoven 85; Spike of Bensonhurst 88

Morrow, Frank Let Him Buck 24; Reckless Riding Bill 24

Morrow, Vic Deathwatch 66; A Man Called Sledge • Sledge 70; The Evictors 79*

Morse, Hollingsworth Beyond the Moon 64*; H.R. Pufnstuf • Pufnstuf 70; Daughters of Satan 72

Morse, Terry The Adventures of Jane Arden 39; No Place to Go 39; On Trial 39; Smashing the Money Ring 39; Waterfront 39; British Intelligence • Enemy Agent 40; A Fugitive from Justice 40; Tear Gas Squad 40; Fog Island 45; Charlie Chan in Dangerous Money • Dangerous Money 46; Danny Boy 46; Don Ricardo Returns 46; The Mandarin Secret • Shadows Over Chinatown 46; The Bells of San Fernando 47; Night Without Stars • Unknown World 51; Godzilla • Godzilla, King of the Monsters • Gojira 54*; Taffy and the Jungle Hunter 65; Young Dillinger 65

Morsi, Ahmad Kamel El Amel • The Worker 43; El Naeb el Am • The Public Prosecutor 45

Mortelliti, Rocco Adelmo 87

Mortimer, Edmund The Road Through the Dark 18; The Savage Woman 18; The County Fair 19*; Alias Jimmy Valentine 20; The Hushed Hour 20; The Misfit Wife 20; The Broad Road 23; The Exiles 23; Railroaded 23; Against All Odds 24; The Desert Outlaw 24; Just Off Broadway 24; A Man's Mate 24; That French Lady 24; The Wolf Man 24; Arizona Romeo 25; Gold and the Girl 25; The Man from Red Gulch 25; The Prairie Pirate 25; Scandal Proof 25; Stardust Trail 25; Satan Town 26; A Woman's Way 28

Mortola, Rodolfo El Dueño del Sol • The Owner of the Sun 87

Morton, Cavendish The Broken Melody 16

Morton, Derek Wild Horses 84

Morton, Pat The Love Race 31*

Morton, Rocky D.O.A. 88*

Morton, Walter The Chocolate Soldier 15

Moser, Frank Kid Casey the Champion 16; Parcel Post Pete: Not All His Troubles Are Little Ones 16; Bud and Susie Join the Tecs 20; Bud and Tommy Take a Day Off 20; Bud Takes the Cake 20; Down the Mississippi 20; Fifty-Fifty 20; The Great Clean Up 20; Handy Mandy's Goat 20; The Kids Find Candy's Catching 20; Mice and Money 20; The New Cook's Debut 20; The North Pole 20; Play Ball 20; Romance and Rheumatism 20; Bud and Susie 21; By the Sea 21; Circumstantial Evidence 21; Clean Your Feet 21; Dashing North 21; Getting Theirs 21; Kitchen, Bedroom and Bath 21; Ma's Wipe Your Feet Campaign 21; $10,000 Under a Pillow 21; The Wars of Mice and Men 21; Alaska or Bust 28; Barnyard Lodge Number One 28; Coast to Coast 28; The Good Ship Nellie 28; Grid Iron Demons 28; The Huntsman 28; Land o' Cotton 28; On the Ice 28; Our Little Nell 28; Cabaret 29; The Enchanted Flute 29; Sweet Adeline 29

Moser, Giorgio Blue Continent • Continente Perduto • The Lost Continent • Sesto Continento • The Sixth Continent 54*

Moses, Gilbert Willie Dynamite 73; The Fish That Saved Pittsburgh 79

Mosjoukine, Ivan see Mozhukhin, Ivan

Mosjukine, Ivan see Mozhukhin, Ivan

Moskalyk, Antonín A Cuckoo in a Dark Wood • Kukačka v Temném Lese 86

Moskin, Andrei Katka Bumazhnyi Ranyot • Katka the Apple Girl • Katka's Reinette Apples 26*

Moskine, Ivan see Mozhukhin, Ivan

Moskov, George I Married Too Young • Married Too Young 62

Moskvin, Ivan see Mozhukhin, Ivan

Mosquera, Gustavo Lo Que Vendrá • Times to Come 88

Moss, Carlton The House on Cedar Hill 26

Moss, Howard S. The Dream Doll 17

Moss, Hugh Jewels and Fine Clothes 12; Sexton Blake vs. Baron Kettler 12

Moss, Jack Snafu • Welcome Home 45

Moss, Stewart B. Kiddies on Parade 35

Motevasselani, Mohammad Mirza Nowrouz' Shoes 86

Mothe, Leon de la see De la Mothe, Leon

Mott, Joel de see De Mott, Joel

Motta, Marcelo A Estranha Hospedaria dos Prazeres • The Strange Inn of Pleasures 76

Mottershaw, Frank A Coach Holdup in Dick Turpin's Days • Jack Sheppard • Robbery of the Mail Coach 03; The Convict's Escape from Prison 03; A Daring Daylight Burglary 03; Attack on a Japanese Convoy 04; Bertie's Courtship 04; The Bobby's Downfall 04; Boys Will Be Boys 04; The Coiners 04; A Cycle Teacher's Experiences 04; A Dash with the Despatches 04; Fly Catchers 04; Late for Work 04; The Market Woman's Mishap 04; A Picnic Disturbed 04; A Soldier's Romance 04; That Dreadful Donkey 04; The Tramps and the Washerwoman 04; The Tramp's Duck Hunt 04; A Trip to the Pyramids 04; The Demon Motorist 05; An Eccentric Burglary 05; A Fireman's Story 05; Lazy Workmen 05; The Life of Charles Peace 05; A Man Although a Thief 05; The Masher and the Nursemaid 05; Mixed Babies 05; The Shoplifter 05; Two Young Scamps 05; When Father Laid the Carpet on the Stairs 05; After the Club 06; The Eccentric Thief 06; His First Silk Hat 06; The Impossible Lovers 06; Lost in the Snow 06; The Lucky Horseshoe 06; Our Boyhood Days 06; Our Seaside Holiday 06; That Terrible Dog 06; The Troubles of the Twins 06; The Blackmailer 07; The Dodgers Dodged 07; His Cheap Watch 07; Johnny's Rim 07; My Word, If You're Not Off 07; Oh That Limerick! 07; The Romany's Revenge 07; Sold Again 07; Willie's Dream 07; The Artful Tramps 08; Banana Skins 08; Father's First Baby 08; The Fighting Curate • The Little Flower Girl 08; An Indian's Romance 08; The Stolen Duck 08; That Nasty Sticky Stuff 08; What Willie Did 08; When Boys Are Forbidden to Smoke 08; The Mad Musician 09

Motyl, V. The White Sun of the Desert 72

Motylev, Ilya The Cantor's Son 37

Mou-che, Yen see Yen, Mou-che

Moul, Alfred The Soldier's Courtship 1896

Mouli see Movli

Moullet, Luc Les Contrebandières • The Smugglers 69; La Comédie du Travail 88

Mouradian, Sarky Tears of Happiness 74; Forty Days of Musa Dagh 87

Mouris, Caroline Ahlfors Beginner's Luck 83*

Mouris, Frank Beginner's Luck 83*

Mourlan, Albert Gulliver in Lilliput 23*

Mous, T. F. Black Sun 731 • Hei Tai Yang 731 • Men Behind the Sun 89

Moussy, Marcel Saint-Tropez Blues 60; Les Grandes Pelouses • The Great Fields 61

Movli Rowdy Police 87; Chandamama Raave 88

Mowbray, Malcolm A Private Function 84; Out Cold 88; The Boyfriend School • Don't Tell Her It's Me 90

Moxey, John see Moxey, John Llewellyn

Moxey, John Llewellyn The City of the Dead • Horror Hotel 60; Foxhole in Cairo 60; Death Trap 62; The £20,000 Kiss 62; Downfall 63; Ricochet 63; Face of a Stranger 64; Strangler's Web 65; Circus of Fear • Psycho-Circus 66; The Tormentor 67

Moyer, Larry The Moving Finger 63

Moyle, Allan Montreal Main 74*; The Rubber Gun 77; Times Square 80; Pump Up the Volume 90

Mozart, George Coney As Peacemaker 13; Coney Gets the Glad Eye 13; Coney, Ragtimer 13

Mozhukhin, Ivan L'Enfant du Carnaval 18; Le Brasier Ardent 23*; The Station Master 28*

Muchna, Milan Green Years • Zelena Letá 85; Devet Kruhú Pekla • Nine Circles of Hell 89

Mudd, Victoria Broken Rainbow 85*

Mueller, Dieter see Müller, Dieter

Mueller, Gordon Troika 69*

Mueller, Hanns Christian see Müller, Hanns Christian

Mueller, Manfred see Müller, Manfred

Mueller, Titus Vibé see Vibé-Müller, Titus

Muellerschon, Nikolai see Müllerschon, Nikolai

Mugge, Robert Sun Ra: A Joyful Noise 80

Muhsin, Ertuğrul Ankara Postası • The Courier of Angora 29

Muir, Jean de la see De la Muir, Jean

Mujica, Francisco Así Es la Vida • Such Is Life 40

Mujica, René Demon in the Blood • El Demonio en la Sangre 64

Mukdasnit, Euthana Butterflies and Flowers • Peesua lae Dokmai 85

Mukherjee, Anjan Chhannachchara 88

Mukherjee, Hrishikesh Jhoothi 87

Mukherjee, Pinaki Rudrabeena 87

Mukherjee, Shyamal Jaidev 87

Mukiljan, Miroslav Crveni i Crni • Red and Black 86

Mulargia, Eduardo Vaya con Dios, Gringo 66; Cjamango 67; Non Aspettare Django Spara 67; La Taglia È Tua e l'Ammazzo Io 69; Shangoo la Pistola Infallibile 70; W. Django 71; Escape • Escape from Hell • Orinoco — Prison of Sex 79; Savage Island 85*

Mulargia, K. Rimase uno Solo e Fu la Morte per Tutti 71

Mulcahy, Russell Derek and Clive Get the Horn 80; Razorback 84; Highlander 86

Mullen, Eugene The Road to London 21

Mullen, Steve White Rat 72

Müller, Dieter Die Grosse Treibjagd • The Last Mercenary • El Mercenario • El Último Mercenario • L'Ultimo Mercenario 69

Muller, Edward G. see Mulargia, Eduardo

Muller, Geoffrey The Unseeing Eye 59; The Witness 59; The Last Train 60

Müller, Hanns Christian Man Spricht Deutsch 88

Müller, Manfred Der Werwolf von W. 88

Müller, Titus Vibé *see Vibé-Müller, Titus*

Müllerschon, Nikolai Orchideen des Wahnsinns 85

Mulligan, Robert Fear Strikes Out 56; The Great Imposter 60; The Rat Race 60; Come September 61; The Spiral Road 62; To Kill a Mockingbird 62; Love with the Proper Stranger 63; Baby, the Rain Must Fall • Traveling Lady 64; Inside Daisy Clover 65; Up the Down Staircase 66; The Stalking Moon 68; The Pursuit of Happiness 70; Summer of '42 71; The Other 72; The Nickel Ride 74; Bloodbrothers • A Father's Love 78; Same Time, Next Year 78; Kiss Me Goodbye 82; Clara's Heart 88

Mulligan, Ted *see Mollica, A.*

Mulot, Claude The Blood Rose • La Rose Escorchée 69

Munchkin, Richard Dance or Die 88

Munden, Maxwell The House in the Woods 57; The Bank Raiders 58

Mundhra, Jag Mohan Suraag 82; Kamla 85; Death Mask 87; Open House 87; Hidden Vision • Night Eyes 90; Last Call 90

Mundie, Ken The Door 68

Mune, Ian Came a Hot Friday 84; Bridge to Nowhere 85

Munger, Chris Kiss of the Tarantula • Shudder 72; Black Starlet 74

Munk, Andrzej Art of the Young • Art of Youth • Sztuka Młodych 49; Kongres Kombatantów 49*; It Began in Spain • It Started in Spain • Zaczeło Sie w Hiszpanii 50; Closer to Life • Nauka Bliżej Życia • Science Closer to Life 51; Direction—Nowa Huta • Kierunek Nowa Huta 51; Bajka • Bajka w Ursusie • Poemat Symfoniczny "Bajka" Stanisława Moniuszki • The Tale of Ursus • Ursus 52; Diaries of the Peasants • Pamietniki Chłopów • Peasant Memoirs 52; Kolejarskie Słowo • A Railroad Man's Word • A Railwayman's Word 53; Gwiazdy Musza Płonać • The Stars Must Shine 54*; Błekitny Krzyż • Blue Cross • Les Hommes de la Croix Bleue • Die Männer vom Blauen Kreuz • Men of the Blue Cross 55; Un Dimanche Matin • Niedzielny Poranek • On a Sunday Morning • One Sunday Morning • Ein Sonntagmorgen in Warschau • Sunday Morning 55; Człowiek na Torze • Un Homme sur la Voie • Man on the Tracks • Der Mann auf den Schienen 56; Eroica • Eroica—Polen 44 • Heroism 57; Spacerek Staromiejski • A Walk in the Old City of Warsaw • A Walk in the Old Town 58; Bad Luck • Cross-Eyed Fortune • Crosseyed Luck • De la Veine à Revendre • Das Schielende Glück • Squinting Luck • Zezowate Szczeście 59; Jubilee Story • Kronika Jubileuszowa • Polska Kronika Filmowa Nr 52 A-B 59; Pasażerka • La Passagère • Die Passagierin • The Passenger 63*

Muñoz, Susan Las Madres de Plaza de Mayo 85

Muñoz Suay, Ricardo Los Amantes del Desierto • Gli Amanti del Deserto • The Desert Warrior • La Figlia dello Sceicco 58*

Munro, Grant It's a Crime 57*; Canon 64*

Munro, Ian Custody 87

Munroe, Cynthia The Wedding Party 64*

Murakami, Jimmy T. Battle Beyond the Stars 79; Heavy Metal 81*; When the Wind Blows 86

Murakami, Ryu Almost Transparent Blue 80; All Right, My Friend 83

Murakawa, Tooru No More God, No More Love 85

Murata, Minoru Souls on the Road 21*; Seisaku's Wife 24; The Street Juggler 25

Muratova, Alex The She-Wolf • U Krutogo Yara 63*

Muratova, Kira The She-Wolf • U Krutogo Yara 63*; Brief Encounters • Korotkie Vstrechi • Short Encounters • Short Meetings 67; Dolghyie Provod • The Long Goodbye 71; Sredi Sreyrk Kamney 83

Murayama, Mitsuo Aa Kaigun • Gateway to Glory 70; The Falcon Fighters • Rikugun Hayabusa Sentōtai 70

Murayama, Shinji Iro • Spoils of the Night 69

Murch, Walter Return to Oz 85

Murdmaa, Helle Caroline's Silver Yarn • Serebryanaya Pryazha Karoliny 87

Murer, Fredi M. Swiss Made 68*; Alpine Fire • Höhenfeuer 85

Murfin, Jane Flapper Wives 24*

Muriel, Emilio Gómez *see Gómez Muriel, Emilio*

Murnau, F. W. The Blue Boy • The Boy in Blue • The Child in Blue • Emerald of Death • Der Knabe in Blau • Der Todessmaragd 19; Satanas 19; Abend...Nacht...Morgen • Evening...Night...Morning 20; Bajazzo • Longing • Sehnsucht 20; Der Bucklige und die Tänzerin • The Hunchback and the Dancer 20; Dr. Jekyll and Mr. Hyde • The Head of Janus • Janus-Faced • The Janus Head • Der Januskopf • Love's Mockery • Schrecken 20; Der Gang in die Nacht • Journey Into the Night • The Walk in the Night 20; Castle Vogelöd • The Haunted Castle • Schloss Vogelöd • Vogelöd Castle 21; Dracula • Eine Nacht des Grauens • Nosferatu • Nosferatu—A Symphony of Horror • Nosferatu—A Symphony of Terror • Nosferatu—Eine Symphonie des Grauens • Nosferatu the Vampire • Terror of Dracula • The Twelfth Hour • The Twelfth Hour—A Night of Horror • Die Zwölfte Stunde • Die Zwölfte Stunde—Eine Nacht des Grauens 21; Marizza, Called the Smugglers' Madonna • Marizza, Gennant die Schmugglermadonna • Der Brennende Acker • The Burning Acre • The Burning Earth • The Burning Path • Burning Soil 22; Phantom 22; Die Austreibung • Die Austreibung—Die Macht der Zweiten Frau • Driven from Home • Expulsion 23; The Finances of the Grand Duke • Die Finanzen des Grossherzogs • The Grand Duke's Finances 23; The Last Laugh • The Last Man • Der Letzte

Mann 24; Tartüff • Tartuffe 25; Faust 26; Song of Two Human Beings • A Song of Two Humans • Sunrise • Sunrise: A Song of Two Humans • Sunrise: A Story of Two Humans 27; Four Devils 28; City Girl • Our Daily Bread 29; Tabu 31*

Muro, Jim Street Trash 87

Murolo, Giuseppe Silhouettes 82

Murphy, Dudley High Speed Lee 23; Alex the Great 28; Stocks and Blondes 28; Confessions of a Co-Ed • Her Dilemma 31*; The Sport Parade 32; The Emperor Jones 33; The Night Is Young 34; Don't Gamble with Love 36; Main Street Lawyer • Small Town Lawyer 39; One Third of a Nation 39; Yolanda 42*; Alma del Bronce 44

Murphy, Eddie Harlem Nights 89

Murphy, Edward Raw Force • Shogun Island 82; Heated Vengeance 85

Murphy, Geoff Goodbye Pork Pie 80; Utu 83; The Quiet Earth 85; Never Say Die 88; Young Guns II 90

Murphy, Maurice Fatty Finn 80; Doctors and Nurses 83

Murphy, Pat Anne Devlin 84

Murphy, Patrick J. Riding Tall • Squares 71

Murphy, Ralph The Big Shot • The Optimist 31; Looking for Trouble • The Tip-Off 31*; Panama Flo 32; 70,000 Witnesses 32; Girl Without a Room 33; Golden Harvest 33; Song of the Eagle 33; Strictly Personal 33; The Great Flirtation 34; Menace 34; The Notorious Sophie Lang • Sophie Lang 34; One Hour Late 34; Private Scandal 34; She Made Her Bed 34; The Charm School • Collegiate 35; McFadden's Flats 35; Men Without Names 35; Florida Special 36; The Man I Marry 36; Night Club Scandal 37; Partners in Crime 37; Top of the Town 37; Our Neighbors, the Carters 39; The Gay City • Las Vegas Nights 40; Glamour Boy • Hearts in Springtime 40; I Want a Divorce 40; Midnight Angel • Pacific Blackout 41; You're the One 41; Mrs. Wiggs of the Cabbage Patch 42; Night Plane from Chungking 42; Salute for Three 43; The Man in Half Moon Street 44; Rainbow Island 44; The Town Went Wild 44; Belle of the Bowery • Sunbonnet Sue 45; How Do You Do? • How Doooo You Do? 45; The Spirit of West Point 47; Mickey 48; Red Stallion in the Rockies 49; Lost Stage Valley • Stage to Tucson 50; Dick Turpin's Ride • The Lady and the Bandit 51; Never Trust a Gambler 51; Captain Blood, Fugitive • Captain Pirate 52; Lady in the Iron Mask 52; Killers of the East • Vendetta dei Thugs 54*; The Black Devils of Kali • Mystery of the Black Jungle 55

Murphy, Richard The Gentle Sergeant • Three Stripes in the Sun 55; The Wackiest Ship in the Army 60

Murphy, Roger Monterey Pop 67*

Murray, Bill Quick Change 90*

Murray, Don The Cross and the Switchblade 70; Damien • Damien's Island 76

Murray, John B. Libido 73*

Murray, Paul Elstree Calling **30***
Murray, Scott Devil in the Flesh **86**
Murray, William Hellfire **86**; Primal Scream **88**
Murrow, Edward R. Satchmo the Great **57***
Murton, Walter Through Solid Walls **16**
Murua, Lautaro Alias Big Shot **62**
Musca, Carmelo Zombie Brigade **88***
Music, Al California Girls **81***
Musidora La Flamme Cache **18***; Vicenta **18**; Pour Don Carlos **21***; La Terre des Taureaux • La Terre des Toros **25**
Musk, Cecil Circus Boy **47**; Trapped by the Terror **49**; Blow Your Own Trumpet **58**
Musker, John Basil the Great Mouse Detective • The Great Mouse Detective **86***; The Little Mermaid **89***
Musser, Charles Before the Nickelodeon **82**
Mussetta, Piero *see Vorhaus, Bernard*
Musso, Jeff Le Puritain • The Puritan **37**; Last Desire **39**
Mustafa, Niazi Antar wa Abla **45**; Rahba **45**
Mustafayev, Vaghif Merzavets **88**
Muste, Pedro Costa Redondela **87**
Muto, Anthony Holy Year 1950 **50**
Mutrux, Floyd Dusty and Sweets McGee **71**; aloha, bobby and rose **75**; American Hot Wax **78**; The Hollywood Knights **80**
Mutteraman, S. P. Samsaram Oka Chadarangam **87**
Muzhi, Yuan *see Yuan, Muzhi*
Muzikant, R. Ski Battalion **38***
Muzikant, Y. Ski Battalion **38***
Mweze, Ngangura Life Is Rosy • La Vie Est Belle **87***
Mycroft, Walter C. Spring Meeting • Three Wise Brides **40**; Banana Ridge **41**; My Wife's Family **41**; Comin' Thro' the Rye **47**
Myers, Frank Lost, Lonely and Vicious **58**
Myers, Gordon Hands Across the Ocean **46**
Myers, Harry C. The Accusation **14**; The Artist and the Vengeful One **15**; Baby **15**; The Earl of Pawtucket **15**; Love's Pilgrimage to America **15**; The Man of Shame **15**; The Queen of the Band **15**
Myers, Richard Floor Show **78**
Myers, Zion The Sidewalks of New York **31***; Lucky Dog **33**
Myerson, Alan The Final Crash • Steelyard Blues **73**; Philly • Private Lessons **81**; Police Academy V: Assignment Miami Beach **88**
Myest, E. G. de *see DeMyest, E. G.*
Myhers, John Saturday Night Bath in Apple Valley • Saturday Night in Apple Valley **65**
Myles, Bruce Ground Zero **87***
Myles, Norbert The Daughter of Dawn **20**; Faithful Wives **26**
Myton, Frank The Terror **17***
Nabili, Marva The Sealed Soil **78**; Nightsongs **84**
Nadasdy, Kálmán Gül Baba **40**; The

Goose Boy **51**
Nadejdine, Serge Le Chiffonnier de Paris **24**; L'Heureux Mort **24**; La Cible **25**; Naples au Baiser de Feu **25**; Le Nègre Blanc **25**
Nadel, Arthur H. Clambake **67**; Underground **70**
Naden, David Slag's Place **65***
Nader, George Walk by the Sea **63**
Naderi, Amir Dawandeh • The Race • The Runner **85**
Nadjafi, Mohammed Ali Gozaresh-e Yek Ghatl • Report on a Murder **87**
Nagabharana, T. S. Aasphota **88**
Nagao, Keiji Time and Tide 2 **85**
Nagel, Conrad Love Takes Flight **37**
Nagle, Paul El Ataúd del Muerto • El Ataúd del Vampiro • El Retorno del Vampiro • The Vampire's Coffin **57***; The Vampire • El Vampiro **57***; Curse of the Doll People • Devil Doll Men • Muñecos Infernales **60***
Nagy, István Homoki *see Nagy, Ivan*
Nagy, Ivan A Kingdom on the Waters **52**; From Blossom Time to Autumn Leaves **54**; Bad Charleston Charlie **73**; Five Minutes of Freedom **73**; Money, Marbles and Chalk **73**; Deadly Hero **76**
Nahay, Michael The Thursday Morning Murders **76**
Nahum, Jacques Dance of Death **59**
Nair, Mira Jama Masjid Street Journal **79**; So Far from India **82**; India Cabaret **85**; Children of a Desired Sex **87**; Chull Bumbai Chull • Salaam Bombay! **88**
Nakagawa, Nobuo The Depths • The Ghost of Kasane • Ghost Story—The Kasane Swamp • Kaidan Kasanegafuchi **57**; Bōrei Kaibyō Yashiki **58**; The Ghost of Yotsuya • Ghost Story of Yotsuya in Tokaido • Tokaido Yotsuya Kaidan **59**; The Male Vampire • Onna Kyūketsuki • Vampire Man • The Woman Vampire **59**; Hell • Jigoku • The Sinners to Hell **60**
Nakahira, Ko Crazed Fruit **56**; Summer Storm **56**; The Flesh Is Weak **57**; Temptation **57**; Crimson Wings **58**; The Four Seasons of Love **58**; A Secret Rendezvous **59**; Storm Over Arabia **61**; These Young People **62**; Bright Sea **63**; A Hunter's Diary **64**; Onna no Uzu to Fuchi to Nagare • Whirlpool of Flesh • Whirlpool of Women **64**; Modern Hooligans **65**; The Devil's Left Hand **66**; Taro's Youth **67**; Spiders à Go-Go **68**; Chimimorya • A Soul to Devils **71**
Nakajima, Takehiro Kyoshu **88**
Nakajima, Tetsuya Bakayaroo! (Watakushi Okotteimasu) **88***
Nakamura, Noboru Kōtō • The Old Capitol • Twin Sisters of Kyoto **63**; Chieko-Shō • Portrait of Chieko **67**; Hi mo Tsuki mo • Through Days and Months **69**; The Song from My Heart • Waga Koi Waga Uta **70**
Nakamura, Takashi Robot Carnival **87***
Nakamura, Takeo Nutcracker Fantasy **79**
Nakasako, Spencer Life Is Cheap . . . But Toilet Paper Is Expensive **89***
Nakhapetov, Rodion Umbrella for the

Newlyweds • Zontik dlya Novobrachnykh **87**; Na Iskhode Nochi **88**
Nakhimoff, Edward Hiking with Mademoiselle **33**
Nam, Lai-choi Killer's Nocturne **87**
Nam, Lee Tse Exit the Dragon, Enter the Tiger **77**
Name, Hernando Death Crossed the Rio Bravo • La Muerte Cruzó el Río Bravo **86**; El Placer de la Venganza • The Pleasure of Vengeance **87**; Rosa de la Frontera • Rose of the Border **87**
Names, Arthur A. Fangs **74**
Nanda, Prashanta Lal Paan Bibi **88**
Nandakumar Nalla Thrachu **88**
Nankin, Michael Midnight Madness **80***
Nanovich, Volslav The Magic Sword **52**
Naon, Sebastián Gaucho Chivalry • Nobleza Gaucha **38**
Napier, Henry J. The Faithless Sex **22**
Napoleon, Art Man on the Prowl **57**; Too Much, Too Soon **58**; Ride the Wild Surf **64***; The Activist **69**
Napolitano, Gian Gaspare Green Magic **55**; Native Drums **55**
Naranjo, Lisandro Duque Visa U.S.A. **86**; Milagro en Roma • Miracle in Rome **88**
Narbey, Leon Illustrious Energy **87**
Nardo, Don Stuff Stephanie in the Incinerator **90**
Narizzano, Silvio Under Ten Flags **60***; Die! Die! My Darling • Fanatic **64**; Georgy Girl **66**; Blue **68**; Loot **70**; Redneck • Senza Ragione **72**; The Sky Is Falling **75**; Why Shoot the Teacher? **76**; The Class of Miss MacMichael **78**; Choices **81**; The Body in the Library **87**
Narliev, Khodzhakuli My Brothers and I **64**; The Daughter-in-Law **72**; Man Overboard **72**; When a Woman Saddles a Horse **74**; Dare to Say No **76**
Naroditsky, Arcady Young Pushkin **37**
Narokov, M. Daredevil **19***
Naruse, Mikio Chambara Fūfu • Mr. and Mrs. Swordplay **29**; Junjō • Pure Love **29**; Ai wa Chikara da • Love Is Strength • Strength of Love **30**; Depression Period • Fukeiki Jidai • Hard Times **30**; Oshikiri Shinkonki • Record of Newlyweds • A Record of Shameless Newlyweds • Shinkonki **30**; Aozora ni Naku • Crying to the Blue Sky • Weeping Blue Sky **31**; Beard of Strength • Hige no Chikara • The Strength of a Mustache **31**; Fickleness Gets on the Train • Uwaki wa Kisha ni Notte **31**; Flunky, Work Hard • Hardworking Clerk • Koshiben Gambare **31**; Ne Kōfun Shicha Iyayo • Now Don't Get Excited **31**; Nikai no Himei • Screams from the Second Floor **31**; Tonari no Yane no Shita • Under the Neighbors' Roof **31**; Apart from You • Kimi to Wakarete **32**; Be Great! • Eraku Nare • Erroneous Practice **32**; Chocolate Girl • Chokoreito Garu **32**; Ladies Be Careful of Your Sleeves • Onna wa Tamoto o Goyōjin **32**; Lost Spring • Motheaten Spring • Mushibameru Haru **32**; Nasanu Naka • Not Blood Relations • Stepchild **32**; Boku no Marumage • A Man with a Married Woman's Hairdo **33**;

Hill 47; Law of the Canyon • The Price of Crime 47; No Escape • Over the Santa Fe Trail 47; Rose of Santa Rosa 47; The Sea Wall • West of Dodge City 47; The Arkansas Swing • Wrong Number 48; Blazing Across the Pecos • Under Arrest 48; Condemned in Error • Quick on the Trigger 48; Desperate Men • El Dorado Pass 48; Phantom Valley 48; Sign of the Dagger • Trail to Laredo 48; Singing Spurs 48; Six Gun Law 48; Smoky Mountain Melody 48; Song of Idaho 48; West of Sonora 48; Bandits of El Dorado • Tricked 49; The Blazing Trail • The Forged Will 49; Challenge of the Range • Moonlight Raid 49; The Fort • Renegades of the Sage 49; Frontier Outpost 49; Harmony Inn • Home in San Antone 49; Laramie 49; River of Poison • South of Death Valley 49; The Clue • Outcast of Black Mesa 50; David Harding, Counterspy 50; Hills of the Brave • The Palomino 50; Hoedown 50; Lost River • Trail of the Rustlers 50; Streets of Ghost Town 50; Suspected • Texas Dynamo 50; The Tougher They Come 50; Al Jennings of Oklahoma 51; China Corsair 51; Cyclone Fury 51; Flame of Stamboul 51; Fort Savage Raiders 51; Indian Uprising 51; The Kid from Amarillo • Silver Chains 51; War Cry 51; Cripple Creek 52; Junction City 52; Laramie Mountains • Mountain Desperadoes 52; Montana Territory 52; The Rough, Tough West 52; The Bandits of Corsica • The Return of the Corsican Brothers 53; Gun Belt 53; Kansas Pacific 53; The Black Dakotas 54; Camels West • Southwest Passage 54; The Lone Gun 54; Top Gun 55; The White Squaw 56; The Domino Kid 57; The Hired Gun 57; The Phantom Stagecoach 57; Return to Warbow 57; Apache Territory 58; Dog Eat Dog • Einer Frisst den Anderen • La Morte Vestita di Dollari • When Strangers Meet 64*; Arrivederci, Cowboy 67

Neal, Peter Glastonbury Fayre 73; Yessongs 73; Ain't Misbehavin' 75*

Neall, Frank 'Round Rainbow Corner 50

Neame, Elwin Dream Paintings 12; The Lady of Shallot 12; The Legend of King Cophetua 12; Pygmalion and Galatea 12; The Sleeping Beauty 12; La Cigale 13; Mifanwy — A Tragedy 13; Ghosts 14; The Girl from the Sky 14; The Hon. William's Donah 14; Ivy's Elopement 14; The Terrible Twins 14; Two Elderly Cupids 14; The Haunting of Silas P. Gould 15

Neame, Ronald Take My Life 47; The Golden Salamander 49; The Card • The Promoter 51; Man with a Million • The Million Pound Note 53; The Man Who Never Was 55; The Seventh Sin 57*; Windom's Way 57; The Horse's Mouth 58; Tunes of Glory 60; Escape from Zahrain 61; I Could Go On Singing • The Lonely Stage 62; The Chalk Garden 63; Mister Moses 64; Gambit 66; A Man Could Get Killed • Welcome, Mr. Beddoes 66*; The Prime of Miss Jean Brodie 68; Prudence and the Pill 68*; Scrooge 70; The Poseidon

Adventure 72*; The Odessa File 74; Meteor 78; Hopscotch 80; First Monday in October 81; Foreign Body 86

Neatrour, Jane T. Dan Smith 87*

Nebbia, Michael Life Study 73

Needham, Hal Smokey and the Bandit 77; Hooper 78; Cactus Jack • The Villain 79; The Cannonball Run 80; Smokey and the Bandit Ride Again • Smokey and the Bandit II 80; Megaforce 82; The Cannonball Run II • Cannonball II 83; Stroker Ace 83; Body Slam 86; Rad 86

Ne'eman, Yehuda Elsa, Elsa 85

Negishi, Kichitaro Hotohira no Yuki • A Snowdrop 86; The Hours of Wedlock • Uhoho Tankentai 87

Negrin, Alberto Il Segreto del Sahara 88

Negro, Daniel del see Del Negro, Daniel

Negroni, Baldassare La Gloria 12; Idillio Tragico 12; Histoire d'un Pierrot • Storia di un Pierrot 13; L'Ultima Carta 13; L'Ereditiera 14; L'Ostacolo 14; La Signora delle Camelie 15; La Morsa 16; La Principessa di Bagdad 16; La Donna Abandonata 17; Madame Flirt 18; Vertigine 19; Bimbi Lontani 20; Madame Sans-Gêne 21; Il Figlio di Madame Sans-Gêne • The Little Corporal 22; Beatrice Cenci 26; Gli Ultimi Zar 26; Giuditta e Oloferne 29; Due Cuori Felici 32; L'Ambasciatore 36

Negulesco, Jean Three and a Day 39; Alice in Movieland 40; A Dog in the Orchard 40; The Flag of Humanity 40; Henry Busse and His Orchestra 40; Joe Reichmann and His Orchestra 40; At the Stroke of Twelve 41; Carioca Serenaders 41; Cliff Edwards and His Buckaroos 41; Freddy Martin and His Orchestra 41; Hal Kemp and His Orchestra 41; Jan Garber and His Orchestra 41; Marie Green and Her Merrie Men 41; Singapore Woman 41; Skinny Ennis and His Orchestra 41; Those Good Old Days 41; The U.S.C. Band and Glee Club 41; The Army Air Force Band 42; Borrah Minnevitch and His Harmonica School • Californian Junior Symphony 42; Capriccio Espagnol • Spanish Fiesta 42; Carl Hoff and His Band 42; The Daughter of Rosie O'Grady 42; The Don Cossack Chorus 42; Emil Coleman and His Orchestra 42; Gaieté Parisienne • The Gay Parisian 42; Glen Gray and His Casa Loma Band 42; Leo Reishmann and His Orchestra 42; Playgirls 42; Richard Himber and His Orchestra 42; A Ship Is Born 42; Six Hits and a Miss 42; The Spirit of Annapolis 42; The Spirit of West Point 42; The U.S. Marine Band 42; The All American Band 43; Army Show 43; Cavalcade of the Dance 43; Childhood Days 43; The Hit Parade of the Gay Nineties 43; Over the Wall 43; Ozzie Nelson and His Orchestra 43; Sweetheart Serenade 43; The U.S. Army Band 43; The U.S. Navy Band 43; U.S. Service Bands 43; The Voice That Thrilled the World 43; Women at War 43*; All Star Melody Masters 44; The Conspirators 44; Grandfather's Follies 44; Listen to the Bands 44; The Mask of Dimitrios 44; Roar-

ing Guns 44; South American Sway • South American Swing 44; The Serenaders 45; Humoresque 46; Nobody Lives Forever 46; Three Strangers 46; Deep Valley 47; Johnny Belinda 48; Road House 48; Affairs of Adelaide • Britannia Mews • Forbidden Street 49; The Mudlark 50; Three Came Home 50; Under My Skin 50; Take Care of My Little Girl 51; Full House • O. Henry's Full House 52*; Lure of the Wilderness 52; Lydia Bailey 52; Phone Call from a Stranger 52; Scandal at Scourie 52; How to Marry a Millionaire 53; Titanic 53; Three Coins in the Fountain 54; Woman's World 54; Daddy Long Legs 55; The Rains of Ranchipur 55; Boy on a Dolphin 57; A Certain Smile 58; The Gift of Love 58; The Best of Everything 59; Count Your Blessings 59; Jessica 61*; The Pleasure Seekers 64; The Heroes • The Invincible Six 68; Hello-Goodbye 70

Negus, Olive Children's Cabaret 54; Faithful to the Rescue 56; Fun on a Weekend 56; The Magic Ring 56; Was It a Dream? 56; Jack Trent Investigates 57; 'Round the Bend 66

Neilan, Marshall The American Princess 13; Ham the Lineman 14; Ham the Piano Mover 14; The Chronicles of Bloom Center 15; The Come Back of Percy 15; Spooks 15; The Country God Forgot • The Country That God Forgot 16; The Cycle of Fate 16; The Prince Chap 16; The Bottle Imp 17; Freckles 17; The Girl at Home 17; The Jaguar's Claws 17; The Little Princess 17; Rebecca of Sunnybrook Farm 17; The Silent Partner 17; Those Without Sin 17; The Tides of Barnegat 17; Amarilly of Clothes-Line Alley 18; Heart of the Wilds 18; Hit-the-Trail Holliday 18; M'liss 18; Out of a Clear Sky 18; Stella Maris 18; Daddy Long Legs 19; Her Kingdom of Dreams 19; In Old Kentucky 19*; Three Men and a Girl 19; The Unpardonable Sin 19; Dinty 20*; Don't Ever Marry 20*; Go and Get It 20*; The River's End 20; Bits of Life 21; Bob Hampton of Placer 21; The Lotus Eater 21; Fools First 22; Minnie 22*; Penrod 22*; The Stranger's Banquet 22; The Eternal Three 23*; The Rendezvous 23; Dorothy Vernon of Haddon Hall 24*; Tess of the D'Urbervilles 24; The Great Love 25; Sporting Venus 25; Diplomacy 26; Everybody's Acting 26; Mike 26; The Skyrocket 26; Wild Oats Lane 26; Her Wild Oat 27; Venus of Venice 27; His Last Haul • Pious Crooks 28; Take Me Home 28; Taxi 13 28; Three-Ring Marriage 28; The Awful Truth 29; Black Waters 29; Tanned Legs 29; The Vagabond Lover 29; Hell's Angels 30*; Sweethearts on Parade 30; Catch As Catch Can 31; Ex-Sweeties 31; War Mamas 31; Secrets 33*; Chloe • Chloe, Love Is Calling You 34; The Lemon Drop Kid 34; Social Register 34; This Is the Life 35; Sing While You're Able 36; Partly Confidential • Thanks for Listening 37; Swing It, Buddy • Swing It, Professor 37

Neilan, Mickey see Neilan, Marshall

Neill, Harry see *Corman, Roger*
Neill, Henry see *Corman, Roger*
Neill, James Where the Trail Divides 14; The Clue 15
Neill, Roy William A Corner in Colleens 16*; The Criminal 16*; A Gamble in Souls 16*; The Flame of the Yukon 17*; The Girl Glory 17; Love Letters 17; The Mother Instinct 17; The Price Mark 17; They're Off 17; Flare-Up Sal 18; Green Eyes 18; The Kaiser's Shadow 18; Love Me 18; The Mating of Marcella 18; Tyrant Fear 18; Vive la France! 18; The Bandbox 19; The Career of Catherine Bush 19; Charge It to Me 19; Puppy Love 19; Trixie from Broadway 19; Dangerous Business 20; Good References 20; The Inner Voice 20; Something Different 20; The Woman Gives 20; Yes or No 20; The Conquest of Canaan 21; The Idol of the North 21; The Iron Trail 21; What's Wrong with the Women? 22; M.A.R.S. • The Man from Mars • Mars Calling • Radio-Mania 23; Toilers of the Sea 23; Broken Laws 24; By Divine Right • The Way Men Love 24; Vanity's Price 24; Greater Than a Crown 25; The Kiss Barrier 25; Marriage in Transit 25; Mother's Boy • Percy 25; Black Paradise 26; The City 26; The Cowboy and the Countess 26; The Fighting Buckaroo 26; A Man Four-Square 26; The Arizona Wildcat 27; Marriage 27; The All-American • The Olympic Hero 28; Cleopatra 28; The Czarina's Secret 28; Divorce • The Fruit of Divorce • San Francisco Nights 28; The Heart of General Robert E. Lee 28; The Lady of Victories 28; Lady Raffles 28; Madame DuBarry 28; The Viking 28; The Virgin Queen 28; Behind Closed Doors 29; Wall Street 29; Cock o' the Walk 30*; Just Like Heaven 30; Melody Man 30; The Avenger 31; Fifty Fathoms Deep 31; The Good Bad Girl 31; The Menace 32; That's My Boy 32; Above the Clouds • Winged Devils 33; As the Devil Commands 33*; The Circus Queen Murder 33; Fury of the Jungle • Jury of the Jungle 33; Black Moon 34; Blind Date • Her Sacrifice 34; I'll Fix It 34; Jealousy 34; Mills of the Gods 34; The Ninth Guest 34; Whirlpool 34; The Black Room • The Black Room Mystery 35; Eight Bells 35; The Lone Wolf Returns 35; Gypsy 36; Dr. Syn 37; Double or Quits 38; Everything Happens to Me 38; Many Tanks Mr. Atkins 38; Quiet Please 38; Simply Terrific 38; Thank Evans 38; The Viper 38; Anything to Declare? 39; A Gentleman's Gentleman 39; The Good Old Days 39; His Brother's Keeper 39; Hoots Mon 39; Murder Will Out 39; Eyes of the Underworld 42; Madame Spy 42; The Secret Weapon • Sherlock Holmes and the Secret Weapon 42; Frankenstein Meets the Wolf Man 43; Rhythm of the Islands 43; Sherlock Holmes and the Spider Woman • The Spider Woman 43; Sherlock Holmes Faces Death 43; Sherlock Holmes in Washington 43; Gypsy Wildcat 44; The Pearl of Death 44; The Scarlet Claw • Sherlock Holmes and the Scarlet Claw 44; The House of

Fear 45; Pursuit to Algiers 45; Sherlock Holmes and the Woman in Green • The Woman in Green 45; The Black Angel 46; Dressed to Kill • Sherlock Holmes and the Secret Code 46; Terror by Night 46
Neilson, James The Country Husband 55; The Blackwell Story 57; Night Passage 57*; A Holster Full of Law 61; Moon Pilot 61; Bon Voyage! 62; Dr. Syn • Dr. Syn Alias the Scarecrow 62; Geronimo's Revenge 62*; Summer Magic 62; Johnny Shiloh 63; The Moon-Spinners 63; The Adventures of Bullwhip Griffin 65; The Legend of Young Dick Turpin 65; Return of the Gunfighter 66; Gentle Giant 67; Where Angels Go...Trouble Follows! 67; The Beginners • The Beginners Three • The First Time • They Don't Wear Pajamas at Rosie's • You Don't Need Pajamas at Rosie's • You Don't Need Pyjamas at Rosie's 68; Flareup 69
Neilson-Baxter, R. K. The House of Silence 37
Neiman, L. E. Morgen Grauen • Morning Terror • Time Troopers 84*
Neitz, Alvin J. Outlawed 21; Back Fire 22; The Firebrand 22; Gun Shy 22; Dangerous Trails 23; Wolves of the Border 23; Border Women 24; Call of the Mate 24; The Cowboy and the Flapper • The Sheriff's Lone Hand 24; Crashin' Through 24; Cyclone Buddy 24; Down by the Rio Grande 24; Fighter's Paradise 24; The Man from God's Country 24; That Wild West 24; The Virgin 24; The White Panther 24; Girl of the West 25; Lure of the West 25; The Reckless Sex 25; Warrior Gap 25; Bad Man's Bluff 26; Beyond All Odds 26; Thundering Speed 26; Born to Battle 27; Hazardous Valley 27; The Cheer Leader 28; The Sky Rider 28; Silent Sentinel 29; Breed of the West 30; Firebrand Johnson • Firebrand Jordan 30; Trails of Danger • Trails of Peril 30; Flying Lariats 31; Hell's Valley 31; Lariats and Sixshooters 31; Pueblo Terror 31; Red Fork Range 31; Come On, Tarzan 32; Tex Takes a Holiday 32; Tombstone Canyon 32; Fargo Express 33; Gun Justice 33; King of the Arena 33; The Lone Avenger 33; The Phantom Thunderbolt 33; Strawberry Roan 33; Trail Drive 33; Honor of the Range 34; Smoking Guns 34; Wheels of Destiny 34; When a Man Sees Red 34; Arizona Trails 35; Desert Mesa 35; Men of Action 35; Swifty 35; Valley of Wanted Men 35; Lucky Terror 36; Dick Tracy 37*; The Painted Stallion 37*; S.O.S. Coast Guard 37*; Wild Horse Round-Up 37; Call of the Rockies 38; Flaming Frontiers 38*; Land of Fighting Men 38; Red Barry 38*; Two Gun Justice 38; West of Rainbow's End 38; Scouts to the Rescue 39*; Trigger Smith 39; The Law Rides Again 43; Wild Horse Stampede 43
Nelli, Piero Cavatori di Marmo 50; Patto d'Amicizia 51; Salviamo, la Montagna Muore 52; Crepuscolo di un Mondo 53; La Pattuglia Perduto 54; Le Italiane e l'Amore • Latin Lovers 61*

Nelson, Art J. see *Sherwood, John*
Nelson, Barrie Heavy Metal 81*
Nelson, David Childish Things • Confessions of Tom Harris • Tale of the Cock 66*; Death Screams 81; A Rare Breed 81; Last Plane Out 83
Nelson, Dusty Effects • The Manipulator 79; Sakura Killers 87*; White Phantom 87; Necromancer 89
Nelson, Gary Molly and Lawless John 72; Santee 72; Freaky Friday 76; The Black Hole 79; Jimmy the Kid 82; Allan Quatermain and the Lost City of Gold 85*
Nelson, Gene Five Fingers of Death • Hand of Death 62; Hootenanny Hoot 62; The Hank Williams Story • Your Cheatin' Heart 64; Kissin' Cousins 64; Harem Holiday • Harum Scarum 65; The Cool Ones 67
Nelson, Jack Chickens 21; The Home Stretch 21; I Am Guilty 21; One a Minute 21; The Rookie's Return 21; Watch Him Step 22; Thru the Flames 23; After a Million 24; Battling Mason 24*; The Covered Trail 24; A Fighting Heart 24; Midnight Secrets 24; He Who Laughs Last 25; The Isle of Hope 25; The Mysterious Stranger 25; The Prince of Pep 25; The Wall Street Whiz 25; Beyond the Rockies 26; The Call of the Wilderness 26; The Dead Line 26; The Devil's Gulch 26; The Dude Cowboy 26; The Fighting Boob 26; Hair Trigger Baxter 26; The Mile-a-Minute Man 26; Modern Youth 26; Sunshine of Paradise Alley 26; The Valley of Bravery 26; Bulldog Pluck 27; The Fighting Hombre 27; Say It with Diamonds 27; The Shamrock and the Rose 27; Through Thick and Thin 27*; Tarzan the Mighty 28*; The Diamond Master 29; Two Gun Caballero 31; Border Guns 34; The Border Menace 34
Nelson, Mervyn The Bar • Some of My Best Friends Are... 71; Fun and Games 73
Nelson, Ozzie Love and Kisses 65
Nelson, Ralph Blood Money • Requiem for a Heavyweight 62; Lilies of the Field 63; Soldier in the Rain 63; Fate Is the Hunter 64; Father Goose • Grand Méchant Loup Appelle 64; Once a Thief 65; Duel at Diablo 66; Counterpoint 67; Charly • The Two Worlds of Charly Gordon 68; ...tick...tick...tick... 69; Soldier Blue 70; Flight of the Doves 71; The Wrath of God 72; The Wilby Conspiracy 74; Created to Kill • Embryo 76; A Hero Ain't Nothin' But a Sandwich 77
Nelson, Sam Outlaws of the Prairie 37; Cattle Raiders 38; The Colorado Trail 38; The Great Adventures of Wild Bill Hickok 38*; Law of the Plains 38; Rio Grande • Rio Grande Stampede 38; South of Arizona 38; West of Cheyenne 38; West of Santa Fe 38; Konga • Konga, the Wild Stallion 39; The Man from Sundown • A Woman's Revenge • A Woman's Vengeance 39; Mandrake, the Magician 39*; North of the Yukon 39; Overland with Kit Carson 39*; Parents on Trial 39; The Stranger • The Stranger from Texas 39;

Texas Stampede 39; The Thundering West 39; Western Caravans 39; The Anchor • Pioneers of the Frontier 40; Bullets for Rustlers • On Special Duty • Special Duty 40; Prairie Schooners • Through the Storm 40; Faro Jack • Outlaws of the Panhandle 41; The Avenging Rider 43; Sagebrush Law 43

Němec, Jan A Bite to Eat • The Loaf • Loaf of Bread • The Morsel • A Piece of Bread • Sousto 59; The Memory of Our Day 63; Démanty Noci • Diamonds of the Night 64; Pearls at the Bottom • Pearls of the Deep • Perličky na Dně 64*; Life After Ninety Minutes 65*; Martyrs of Love • Mučedníci Lásky 66; O Slavnosti a Hostech • The Party and the Guests • A Report on the Party and the Guests • Summer Carnival 66; Mother and Son 67; Oratorio for Prague • Oratorium for Prague 68; Between Three and Five Minutes 72; The Czech Connection 75; Le Décolleté dans le Dos • The Low-Cut Back 75; Metamorphosis 75; Friends 88

Nepomuceno, Luis Igorota • Igorota, the Legend of the Tree of Life • The Legend of the Tree of Life 70

Neroni, Nicola Fausto Il Miracolo di Sant'Antonio 32

Nesbitt, Derren The Amorous Milkman 75

Nesbitt, Frank Walk a Tightrope 63; Do You Know This Voice? 64; Dulcima 70

Nesher, Avi Halahaka • The Troupe 78; Dizengoff 99 79; She 82; Breaking 85; Rage and Glory 85; Heavy Armor 88

Nestor, John see *Almendros, Nestor*

Nethercott, Geoffrey Accidental Death 63; Who Was Maddox? 64; The Material Witness 65; Personal and Confidential 65

Neufeld, Max Hoffmanns Erzählungen • Tales of Hoffmann 23; K und K Ballettmädel • The Royal Ballet Girl 28; Prince and the Dancer 29; Rasputin • Rasputin the Holy Sinner 29; Opera Ball • Der Opern-Ball • Opernredoute 31; Drunter und Drüber 32; Purpur und Waschblau 32; Geld Regiert die Welt 34; Temptation 34; La Canzone del Sole 36; An Orphan Boy of Vienna 37; Una Moglie in Pericolo • A Wife in Danger 40; Revenge 47

Neufeld, Samuel see *Newfield, Sam*

Neufeld, Sigmund, Jr. The Incredible Hulk 78*; Conquest of the Earth 80*

Neuland, Olav Requiem 87; Vo Vremena Volchyika Zakonov • When Man Was Wolf to Man 87

Neumann, Hans A Midsummer Night's Dream 28

Neumann, József see *Korda, Alexander*

Neumann, Kurt House of Mystery 31; Sealed Lips 31; Trapped 31; Fast Companions • Information Kid 32; My Pal the King 32; The Red Shadow 32; The Big Cage 33; King for a Night 33; The Secret of the Blue Room 33; Half a Sinner 34; Let's Talk It Over 34; Wake Up and Dream 34; The Affair of Susan 35; Alias Mary Dow 35; Let's Sing Again 36; Rainbow on the River 36; Violets in Spring 36;

Espionage 37; Hold 'Em Navy • That Navy Spirit 37; Make a Wish 37; Ambush 38; Generals of Tomorrow • Touchdown, Army 38; Wide Open Faces 38; All Women Have Secrets 39; Island of Lost Men 39; Night Club Hostess • Unmarried 39; Ellery Queen—Master Detective 40; A Night at Earl Carroll's 40; About Face 42; Brooklyn Orchid 42; The McGuerins from Brooklyn 42; Fall In 43; I Was a Criminal • The Unknown Guest 43; The Return of the Vampire 43*; Taxi Mister! 43; Yanks Ahoy! 43; Tarzan and the Amazons 45; Tarzan and the Leopard Woman 46; Tarzan and the Huntress 47; Bad Men of Tombstone 48; The Dude Goes West 48; Bad Boy 49; The Kid from Texas • Texas Kid—Outlaw 49; Two Knights in Brooklyn • Two Mugs from Brooklyn 49; Expedition Moon • Rocketship Expedition Moon • Rocketship X-M 50; Cattle Drive 51; Reunion in Reno 51; Hiawatha 52; The Ring 52; Son of Ali Baba 52; Tarzan and the She-Devil 53; Carnival Story 54; Circus of Love • Rummelplatz der Liebe 54; Adventure in Rio • They Were So Young • They Were So Young and So in Danger 55; The Desperadoes Are in Town 56; Mohawk 56; The Deerslayer 57; Kronos 57; She-Devil 57; The Fly 58; Machete 58; Counterplot 59; Watusi 59

Neumeier, John Die Kameliendame • Lady of the Camellias 87

Nevard, Peter Groupies 70*

Neves, David Muito Prazer 79; Fulaninha 86; The Garden of Allah • Jardim de Allah 89

Neville, Edgar La Torre de los Siete Jorobados • The Tower of the Seven Hunchbacks 44; Flamenco 54

Nevin, Robyn The More Things Change 86

Nevzorov, V. The Long Path 56*

New, Michael Cubagua 87

Newall, Guy Testimony 20; The Bigamist 21; Beauty and the Beast 22; Boy Woodburn 22; Fox Farm 22; A Maid of the Silver Sea 22; The Persistent Lovers 22; The Starlit Garden 23; Boat from Shanghai • Chin Chin Chinaman 31; The Other Mrs. Phipps 31; Rodney Steps In 31; The Rosary 31; The Chinese Puzzle 32; The Admiral's Secret 34

Newbrook, Peter The Asphyx • The Horror of Death • Spirit of the Dead 72

Newell, Mike The Awakening 80; Bad Blood 81; Dance with a Stranger 85; The Good Father 86; Amazing Grace and Chuck 87; Soursweet 88

Newfield, Sam Jane's Engagement Party 26; Jane's Predicament 26; Please Excuse Me 26; What's Your Hurry? 26; Which Is Which? 26; Ask Dad 27; Auntie's Ante 27; Big Game George 27; A Disorderly Orderly 27; George's School Daze 27; A Gym Dandy 27; High Flyin' George 27; Jane's Sleuth 27; Man of Letters 27; My Mistake 27; On Deck 27; On Furlough 27; Rushing Business 27; Watch, George! 27; What an Excuse 27; When George Hops

27; Buster Minds the Baby 28; Buster Trains Up 28; Busting Buster 28; George's False Alarm 28; Good Scout Buster 28; Half Back Buster 28; Newlyweds' Visit 28; Out at Home 28; Sailor George 28; She's My Girl! 28; Watch the Birdie 28; Buster's Spooks 29; Chaperons 29; Night Owls 29; This Way Please 29; Too Many Women 29; All Wet 30; The Beauty Parade 30; Fellow Students 30; French Leave 30; Her Bashful Beau 30; Peek-a-Boo 30; She's a He 30; Sid's Long Count 30; Big Time or Bust • Heaven Bound 33; Important Witness 33; Reform Girl 33; Under Secret Orders 33; African Incident 34; Beggar's Holiday 34; Marrying Widows 34; Arrest at Sundown • Trails of the Wild 35; Branded a Coward 35; Bulldog Courage 35; Code of the Mounted 35; Northern Frontier 35; Racing Luck 35; Timber War 35; Undercover Men 35; You Can Be Had 35; Aces and Eights 36; Border Caballero 36; Burning Gold 36; Federal Agent 36; Ghost Patrol 36; Go-Get-'Em Haines 36; Lightnin' Bill Carson 36; The Lion's Den 36; Roarin' Guns 36; Roarin' Lead 36*; Stormy Trails 36; The Traitor 36; Arizona Gunfighter 37; Bad Man of Harlem • Harlem on the Prairie 37; Bar Z Bad Men 37; Boothill Brigade 37; The Colorado Kid 37; Doomed at Sundown 37; The Fighting Deputy 37; The Gambling Terror 37; Gun Lords of Stirrup Basin 37; Guns in the Dark 37; A Lawman Is Born 37; Lightnin' Crandall 37; Melody of the Plains 37; Moonlight on the Range 37; Ridin' the Lone Trail 37; Trail of Vengeance 37; Code of the Rangers 38; Crashin' Thru Danger 38; Desert Patrol 38; Durango Valley Raiders 38; The Feud Maker 38; Frontier Scout 38; Gunsmoke Trail 38; Knight of the Plains 38; Lightnin' Carson Rides Again 38; Paroled to Die 38; The Phantom Ranger 38; The Ranger's Roundup 38; Six-Gun Trail 38; Songs and Bullets 38; The Terror of Tiny Town 38; Thunder in the Desert 38; Beasts of Berlin • Goose Step • Hell's Devils • Hitler—Beast of Berlin 39; Code of the Cactus 39; Fighting Mad 39; The Fighting Renegade 39; Flaming Lead 39; The Invisible Killer • Wanted for Murder 39; Outlaws' Paradise 39; Six-Gun Rhythm 39; Straight Shooter 39; Texas Wildcats 39; Trigger Fingers 39; Trigger Pals 39; Am I Guilty? 40; Arizona Gangbusters 40; Billy the Kid in Texas 40; Billy the Kid Outlawed 40; Billy the Kid's Gun Justice 40; Death Rides the Range 40; Frontier Crusader 40; Gun Code 40; Hold That Woman! 40; I Take This Oath • Sons of the Finest 40; Marked Men 40; Riders of Black Mountain 40; The Sagebrush Family Trails West 40; Secrets of a Model 40; Swift Justice • Texas Renegades 40; Billy the Kid in Santa Fe 41; Billy the Kid Trails West • Billy the Kid's Fighting Pals • Trigger Pals 41; Billy the Kid Wanted 41; Billy the Kid's Range War 41; Billy the Kid's Roundup 41; Frontier Fury • The Lone Rider in Frontier Fury 41; The Lone Rider

Ambushed 41; The Lone Rider Crosses the Rio 41; The Lone Rider Fights Back 41; The Lone Rider in Ghost Town 41; The Lone Rider Rides On 41; Outlaws of the Rio Grande 41; The Texas Marshal 41; Along the Sundown Trail 42; Billy the Kid in Law and Order • The Double Alibi • Law and Order 42; Billy the Kid in The Mysterious Rider • The Mysterious Rider • Panhandle Trail 42; Billy the Kid, Sheriff of Sage Valley • Sheriff of Sage Valley 42; Billy the Kid Trapped 42; Billy the Kid's Smoking Guns • Smoking Guns 42; Border Roundup • The Lone Rider in Border Roundup 42; Frontier Marshal in Prairie Pals • Prairie Pals 42; Jungle Siren 42; The Lone Rider and the Bandit 42; The Lone Rider in Cheyenne 42; The Lone Rider in Outlaws of Boulder Pass • Outlaws of Boulder Pass 42; The Lone Rider in Overland Stagecoach • Overland Stagecoach 42; The Lone Rider in Texas Justice • Texas Justice 42; The Mad Monster 42; Raiders of the West 42; Rolling Down the Great Divide 42; Texas Man Hunt 42; Tumbleweed Trail 42; Billy the Kid in Blazing Frontier • Blazing Frontier 43; Billy the Kid in Cattle Stampede • Cattle Stampede 43; Billy the Kid in Fugitive of the Plains • Fugitive of the Plains • Raiders of Red Rock 43; Billy the Kid in The Renegade • Code of the Plains • The Renegade 43; Billy the Kid in Western Cyclone • Frontier Fighters • Western Cyclone 43; Billy the Kid Rides Again • The Kid Rides Again 43; The Black Raven 43; Creature of the Devil • Dead Men Walk 43; Danger! Women at Work 43; Death Rides the Plains • The Lone Rider in Death Rides the Plains 43; Devil Riders 43; Harvest Melody 43; The Lone Rider in Wild Horse Rustlers • Wild Horse Rustlers 43; Queen of Broadway 43; Raiders of Red Gap 43; Tiger Fangs 43; Wolves of the Range 43; The Contender 44; The Drifter 44; Frontier Outlaws 44; Fuzzy Settles Down 44; The Girl and the Gorilla • Gorilla • The Jungle Woman • Nabonga 44; I Accuse My Parents 44; The Monster Maker 44; Oath of Vengeance 44; Outlaws of the Plains 44; Rustlers' Hideout 44; Swing Hostess 44; Thundering Gun Slingers 44; Valley of Vengeance • Vengeance 44; Wild Horse Phantom 44; Adventure Unlimited • Congo Pongo • White Pongo 45; Apology for Murder 45; Barber of Red Gap • Shadows of Death 45; Border Badmen 45; Fighting Bill Carson 45; The Flying Serpent 45; Gangster's Den 45; His Brother's Ghost 45; The Kid Sister 45; The Lady Confesses 45; Lightning Raiders 45; Prairie Rustlers 45; Stagecoach Outlaws 45; Blonde for a Day 46; East Side Rascals • Gas House Kids 46; Gentlemen with Guns 46; Ghost of Hidden Valley 46; Ladies of the Chorus • Queen of Burlesque 46; Lady Chaser 46; Larceny in Her Heart 46; Mantan Messes Up 46; Murder Is My Business 46; Outlaw of the Plains 46; Overland Riders 46; Prairie Badmen 46; Terrors on

Horseback 46; Adventure Island 47; Jungle Flight 47; Three on a Ticket 47; Assignment in China • State Department—File 649 48; The Counterfeiters 48*; Lady at Midnight 48; Miraculous Journey 48; Money Madness 48; The Strange Mrs. Crane 48; Devil's Weed • She Should'a Said No • Wild Weed 49; Highway Patrol • Motor Patrol 50; Hi-Jacked 50; Radar Patrol • Radar Secret Service 50; Western Pacific Agent 50; Fingerprints Don't Lie 51; Leave It to the Marines 51; The Lost Continent 51; Mask of the Dragon 51; Skipalong Rosenbloom • The Square Shooter 51; Sky High 51; Three Desperate Men 51; The Gambler and the Lady 52*; Lady in the Fog • Scotland Yard Inspector 52; Outlaw Women 52*; Last of the Desperadoes 55; Thunder Over Sangoland 55; Frontier Gambler 56; The Long Rifle and the Tomahawk 56*; The Three Outlaws 56; The Wild Dakotas 56; Flaming Frontier 58; Wolf Dog 58

Newland, John That Night 57; The Violators 57; The Double Affair • The Spy with My Face 65; Don't You Cry • Hush-a-Bye Murder • My Lover, My Son 70; The Legend of Hillbilly John • My Name Is John • Who Fears the Devil 72

Newley, Anthony Can Hieronymus Merkin Ever Forget Mercy Humppe and Find True Happiness? 69; Summertree 71*

Newlin, Martin see *Laurenti, Fabrizio*

Newman, Frank The Fakir's Spell 14; The Great German North Sea Tunnel 14

Newman, Joan Widgey The Gentlemen Go By 48*

Newman, Joseph M. Man's Greatest Friend 38; Money to Loan 39; The Story of Alfred Nobel 39; The Story That Couldn't Be Printed 39; Buyer Beware 40; Cat College 40; Know Your Money 40; Maintain the Right 40; Women in Hiding 40; Coffins on Wheels 41; Respect the Law 41; Triumphs Without Drums 41; Don't Talk! 42; Northwest Rangers 42; Vendetta 42; Diary of a Sergeant 45; The Amazing Mr. Nordill 47; The Luckiest Guy in the World 47; Jungle Patrol 48; Abandoned • Abandoned Woman 49; The Great Dan Patch • Ride a Reckless Mile 49; I'll Get You for This • Lucky Nick Cain 50; 711 Ocean Drive 50; The Guy Who Came Back 51; Love Nest 51; MacDonald of the Canadian Mounties • Pony Soldier 51; The Outcasts of Poker Flat 52; Red Skies of Montana • Smoke Jumpers 52*; Dangerous Crossing 53; The Human Jungle 54; Kiss of Fire 55; This Island Earth 55*; Flight to Hong Kong 56; Death in Small Doses 57; Fort Massacre 58; The Big Circus 59; The Gunfight at Dodge City 59; Tarzan the Ape Man 59; The Lawbreakers 60; The Big Bankroll • King of the Roaring Twenties • King of the Roaring Twenties—The Story of Arnold Rothstein • The Story of Arnold Rothstein 61; The George Raft Story • Spin of a Coin 61; It Started in Tokyo • Twenty Plus Two 61; A Thunder of Drums 61

Newman, Paul A Jest of God • Now I

Lay Me Down • Rachel, Rachel 68; Never Give an Inch • Sometimes a Great Notion 71*; The Effect of Gamma Rays on Man-in-the-Moon Marigolds 72; Harry and Son 84; The Glass Menagerie 87

Newman, Widgey R. Broadcasting • The Romance of Broadcasting 25*; Camera Cocktales • Nervo and Knox 26; Home Construction 26*; How I Began 26*; Listening In 26*; The Loud Speaker 26*; Oscillation 26*; Dilly and Dally 27; Dora 27; Dot and Carrie 27; Edith Sitwell 27; John Citizen 27; The Merchant of Venice 27; Pop 27; Saint Joan 27; De Forest Phonofilms 28; The Man in the Saddle • A Reckless Gamble 28; Castle Sinister 32; Danse Macabre 32; Funeral March of a Marionette 32; Heroes of the Mine 32; Liebestraum 32; Little Waitress 32; Melody in F 32; The Merry Men of Sherwood 32; The Moonlight Sonata 32; Rachmaninov's Prelude 32; Lucky Blaze 33; Oh for a Plumber! 33; His Apologies 35; Immortal Gentleman 35; What the Parrot Saw 35; Apron Fools 36; Pal o' Mine 36; What the Puppy Said 36; The Inspector 37; Songs of the Organ 37; Ghost Tales Retold 38; Horse Sense 38; On Velvet 38; A Sister to Assist 'Er 38*; Men Without Honour 39; Pandamonium 39; Henry Steps Out 40; Two Smart Men 40; Strange to Relate 43

Newmeyer, Fred Among Those Present 21*; Grandma's Boy 21; I Do 21*; Never Weaken 21*; Now or Never 21*; A Sailor-Made Man 21; Doctor Jack 22; Safety Last 23*; Why Worry? 23*; Foolish Men and Smart Women 24; Girl Shy 24*; Hot Water 24*; The Freshman 25*; The Perfect Clown 25; Seven Keys to Baldpate 25; The Lunatic at Large 26; The Quarterback 26; The Savage 26; On Your Toes 27; The Potters 27; That's My Daddy 27; Too Many Crooks 27; The Night Bird 28; Warming Up 28; It Can Be Done 29; Morgan's Marauders 29; The Rainbow Man 29; Sailors' Holiday 29; Fast and Loose 30; The Grand Parade 30*; Queen High 30; Subway Express 31; Discarded Lovers 32; The Fighting Gentleman 32; The Gambling Sex 32; They Never Come Back 32; The Big Race • Raising the Wind 33; Easy Millions 33; Bonds of Honour • No Ransom 34; Lost in the Legion 34; The Moth • Seeing It Through 34; Secrets of Chinatown 35; General Spanky 36*; Rodeo Rhythm 41; Murder in Morocco • Scream in the Night 43

Newton, Joel Jennifer 53

Newton, Peter see *Massaccesi, Aristide*

Ngakane, Lionel Jemima and Johnny 66

Niao, Lan Girl from Hunan • Hunan Girl Xiaoxiao • Xiangnu Xiaoxiao 86*

Niblo, Fred Get-Rich-Quick Wallingford 15; A Princess of the Dark 17*; A Desert Wooing 18; Fuss and Feathers 18; Happy Though Married 18; The Marriage Ring 18; When Do We Eat? 18; Dangerous Hours 19; Greater Than Love 19*; The Haunted Bedroom 19; The Law of Men 19; Partners Three 19; Stepping Out 19; The

Virtuous Thief 19; What Every Woman Learns 19; The Woman in the Suitcase 19; The False Road 20; Hairpins 20; Her Husband's Friend 20; The Mark of Zorro 20; Sex 20; Silk Hosiery 20; Mother o' Mine 21; The Three Musketeers 21; Blood and Sand 22; Rose o' the Sea 22; The Woman He Married 22; The Famous Mrs. Fair 23; The Red Lily 23; Strangers of the Night 23; Thy Name Is Woman 24; Ben-Hur • Ben-Hur—A Tale of the Christ 25*; The Temptress 26*; Camille 27; The Devil Dancer 27*; The Enemy 27; Dream of Love 28; The Mysterious Lady 28; Two Lovers 28; Redemption 30; Way Out West 30; The Big Gamble 31; Donovan's Kid • Young Donovan's Kid 31; Blame the Woman • Diamond Cut Diamond 32*; Two White Arms • Wives Beware 32; The Good Earth 36*

Niblo, Fred, Jr. The Devil Dancer 27*

Nicart, Eddie Commander Lamin 87

Nichetti, Maurizio Ratataplan 79; The Bi and the Ba • Il Bi e il Ba 86; The Icicle Thief • Ladri di Saponette 89

Nichev, Ivan Boomerang 79; Black Swans • Cernite Lebedi 84

Nicholas, Paul Bad Blood • Julie Darling 82*; Chained Heat 83; The Naked Cage 86

Nicholls, Allan Dead Ringer 82

Nicholls, George In the Clutches of the Gang 14*; Ghosts 15*; A Man's Prerogative 15

Nicholls, George, Jr. Anne of Green Gables 34; Finishing School 34*; Chasing Yesterday 35; Chatterbox 35; The Return of Peter Grimm 35; The Big Game 36; M'liss 36; The Witness Chair 36; Adventures of Michael Strogoff • Michael Strogoff • The Soldier and the Lady 37; Portia on Trial • The Trial of Portia Merriman 37; Army Girl • The Last of the Cavalry 38*; Man of Conquest 39; High School 40; The Marines Fly High 40*

Nichols, Charles A. Charlotte's Web 72*

Nichols, Dudley Government Girl 43; Sister Kenny 46; Mourning Becomes Electra 47

Nichols, Mike Who's Afraid of Virginia Woolf? 66; The Graduate 67; Catch-22 70; Carnal Knowledge 71; The Day of the Dolphin 73; The Fortune 74; Gilda Live 80; Chain Reaction • Silkwood 83; Heartburn 86; Biloxi Blues 88; Working Girl 88; Postcards from the Edge 90

Nicholson, Arch Buddies 83; Dark Age 86

Nicholson, Jack Lady of the Shadows • The Terror 62*; Drive, He Said 71; Goin' South 78; The Two Jakes 90

Nicol, Alex The Screaming Skull 58; Then There Were Three 61; Point of Terror 71

Nicolae, Christiana Hanul dintre Dealuri 88

Nicolaescu, Sergiu The Last Assault • Noi Cei din Linia Intîi 86

Nicolaou, Ted The Dungeonmaster 85*;

Terrorvision 86

Nicolas, Paul see Nicholas, Paul

Nicolayssen, Hans Otto Andersen's Run • The Magic Bag • The Plastic Bag • Plastikkposen • Plastposen 86

Nicolle, Douglas C. Ladies of the Lotus 87*

Niddam, Igaal We Are Arab Jews in Israel 79

Niebuhr, Walter The Money Habit 24; Venetian Lovers 25*; City of Temptation 29

Niehoff, Sidney Raw Weekend 64

Nielsen, Lasse You Are Not Alone 78*

Nierenberg, George T. The Hollow 75; No Maps on My Taps 78; Say Amen, Somebody • Say Amen, Someone 82; That Rhythm, Those Blues 89

Niermans, Édouard Anthracite 80; Angel Dust • Poussière d'Ange 87

Nieto Ramírez, José Murieron a Mitad del Río • They Died in the Middle of the River 87

Nieves Conde, José Antonio Senda Ignorada 46; Angustia 47; Llegada de Noche 48; Balarasa 50; Surcos 51; Rebeldía 52; Los Peces Rojos 54; Todos Somos Necesarios 56; El Inquilino 57; Prohibido Enamorarse 61; The Prehistoric Sound • El Sonido de la Muerte • El Sonido Prehistórico • Sound from a Million Years Ago • The Sound of Horror 64

Nifontov, Gleb Hunting in Siberia • Zverolovy 62

Nigh, William Emmy of Stork's Nest • The Stork's Nest 15; A Royal Family 15; A Yellow Streak 15; The Child of Destiny 16; A Debt of Honor • Her Debt of Honor 16; His Great Triumph • The Notorious Gallagher 16; The Kiss of Hate 16; Life's Shadows 16*; The Blue Streak 17; The Slave 17; Thou Shalt Not Steal 17; Wife Number Two 17; My Four Years in Germany 18; Beware 19; The Fighting Roosevelts 19; Our Teddy 19; Democracy • Democracy—The Vision Restored 20; School Days 21; Skinning Skinners 21; The Soul of a Man • The Soul of Man 21; Why Girls Leave Home 21; Your Best Friend 21; Notoriety 22; Marriage Morals 23; Born Rich 24; Fear-Bound 25; Casey of the Coast Guard 26; Fire • The Fire Brigade 26; Free Kisses 26; The Little Giant 26; The Law of the Range 27; Mr. Wu 27; The Nest 27; Across to Singapore 28; Four Walls 28; Desert Nights • Thirst 29; Lord Byron of Broadway • What Price Melody? 29*; Thunder 29; California in 1878 • Fightin' Thru • Fighting Through 30; Today 30; The Lightning Flyer 31; The Sea Ghost 31; The Single Sin 31; Border Devils 32; Men Are Such Fools 32; The Night Rider 32; Without Honors 32; Born Tough • He Couldn't Take It • One of the Many • The Process Server 33; The Ape • The House of Mystery 34; City Limits 34; The Ghost of John Holling • Mystery Liner 34; Monte Carlo Nights • Numbers of Monte Carlo 34; Once to Every Bachelor 34; Two Heads on a Pillow 34; Dizzy Dames 35; The

Headline Woman • The Woman in the Case 35; His Night Out 35; The Mysterious Mr. Wong 35; The Old Homestead 35; School for Girls 35; She Gets Her Man 35; Sweepstake Annie 35; Crash Donovan 36; Don't Get Personal 36; North of Nome 36; Penthouse Party • Without Children 36; Atlantic Flight 37; Bill Cracks Down • Men of Steel 37; Boy of the Streets 37; A Bride for Henry 37; Forgotten Hero • The Hoosier Schoolboy • Yesterday's Hero 37; The Law Commands 37; The Thirteenth Man 37; Female Fugitive 38; Gangster's Boy 38; I Am a Criminal 38; Mr. Wong, Detective 38; Romance of the Limberlost 38; Rose of the Rio Grande 38; The Abe Lincoln of Ninth Avenue • Streets of New York 39; Mr. Wong in Chinatown 39; Mutiny in the Big House 39; The Mystery of Mr. Wong 39; The Ape 40; Doomed to Die • The Mystery of the Wentworth Castle 40; The Fatal Hour • Mr. Wong at Headquarters 40; Son of the Navy • The Young Recruit 40; The Underdog 40; The Kid from Kansas 41; Mob Town 41; No Greater Sin • Social Enemy No. 1 41; Secret Evidence 41; Zis Boom Bah 41; Black Dragons • Yellow Menace 42; City of Silent Men 42; College Sweethearts 42; Escape from Hong Kong 42; Lady from Chungking 42; Mr. Wise Guy 42; The Strange Case of Dr. Rx 42; Tough As They Come 42; Corregidor 43; The Ghost and the Guest 43; Where Are Your Children? 43; Are These Our Parents? • They Are Guilty 44; Trocadero 44; Allotment Wives • Allotment Wives, Inc. • Woman in the Case 45; Divorce 45; Forever Yours • The Right to Live • They Shall Have Faith 45; Beauty and the Bandit • Cisco and the Angel 46; The Gay Cavalier 46; Partners in Time 46; South of Monterey 46; Riding the California Trail 47; I Wouldn't Be in Your Shoes 48; Stage Struck 48

Nihalani, Dayal Disciples' Offerings to the Priest • Guru Dakshina 86

Nihalani, Govind Ardh Satya • Half-Truth 83; Aghaat • Blood of Brothers 86; Tamas 87

Nihalsingha, D. B. Maldeniye Simion • Simion of Maldeniye 87

Nihonmatsu, Kazui Girara • Guilala • Guirara • Uchū Daikaijū Guilala • The X from Outer Space 64

Nikola, Louis Magic Squares 14

Nikolaidis, Nikos Morning Patrol • Proini Peripolos 87

Nikolais, Alwin Totem 63*; Fusion 67*; Chrysalis 73*

Nikolić, Živko The Beauty of Vice • Lepota Poroka 86; In the Name of the People • U Ime Naroda 87

Nikolov, Miaden Romantic Story • Romantichna-Istorija 86

Nikonenko, Sergei Korabl Prisheltsev • The Ship of Aliens 87

Nikosa, V. Indonesia Today 55

Nilsson, Leopoldo Torre see Torre-Nilsson, Leopoldo

Nilsson, Rob Northern Lights 78*;

Signal 7 **83**; On the Edge **85**; Heat and Sunlight **86**

Nimoy, Leonard Star Trek III: The Search for Spock **84**; Star Trek IV: The Voyage Home • The Voyage Home: Star Trek IV **86**; 3 Men and a Baby **87**; The Good Mother **88**; Funny About Love **90**

Nioun, Mahoun Tien The Ratanapoum House **56**

Nisbet, Charles The Girl with the Fabulous Box **69**

Nishimura, Kiyoshi The Creature Called Man • Jaga wa Hashitta **70**

Nishiyama, Masateru Judo Showdown • Yawara Sempū Dotō no Taiketsu **66**

Nishizaki, Yoshinobu Space Cruiser • Space Cruiser Yamato • Uchūsenkan Yamato **77**

Nishizawa, Nobutaka The Adventures of the American Rabbit **86***

Niskanen, Mikko Käpy Selän Alla • Skin Skin **67**

Niskanen, Tuija-Maija The Farewell • Jäähyväiset **82**; The Grand Illusion • Suuri Illusioni **86**

Nissimoff, Riki Shelach The Last Winter **83**; Mercenary Fighters **88**

Nitchev, Ivan see Nichev, Ivan

Nizet, Charles The Ravager **70**; Three-Way Split **70**; Voodoo Heartbeat **72**; Help Me…I'm Possessed **76**

Noa, Manfred The Lady from Paris **27**; The Wrath of the Seas **29**; Survival **30**; Der Walzerkönig **32**

Noble, Barbara Worlds Apart **80***

Noble, Jack see Noble, John W.

Noble, John W. The Better Man • The Bigger Man **15**; Black Fear **15**; Fighting Bob **15**; The High Road **15**; One Million Dollars **15**; The Right of Way **15**; Satan Sanderson **15**; The Three of Us **15**; The Awakening of Helena Richie **16**; The Brand of Cowardice **16**; Man and His Soul **16**; A Million a Minute **16**; Romeo and Juliet **16***; The Wall Between **16**; The Beautiful Lie **17**; The Call of Her People **17**; A Magdalene of the Hills **17**; The Power of Decision **17**; Sunshine Alley **17**; My Own United States **18**; Shame **18**; Birth of a Race **19**; The Golden Shower **19**; The Gray Towers Mystery **19**; Footlights and Shadows **20**; The Song of the Soul **20**; Cardigan **22**; His Darker Self **24**; Lightning Reporter **26**; Burning Gold **27**

Noble, Nigel Voices of Sarafina! **88**

Noe, Yvan Meet Miss Mozart **37**

Noël, Jean-Guy Ti-Cul Tougas **77**

Noël-Noël Les Casse-Pieds • The Spice of Life **48***; La Vie Chantée **51**

Noelte, Rudolf The Castle • Das Schloss **68**

Noever, Hans AIDS—A Danger for Love • AIDS—Gefahr für die Liebe **85**

Nofal, Emil Kimberley Jim **65**; Wild Season • Wilde Seison **68**; My Way • The Winner **74***; The Super-Jocks **80***

Noguchi, Haruyasu Daikaijū Gappa • Gappa the Trifibian Monster • Monster from a Prehistoric Planet **67**

Nogueira, Helen Quest for Love **88**

Noice, Harold Red Majesty **29**; Explorers of the World **31**

Nolan, Jamie see Böttger, Fritz

Nolan, William C. Tad's Indoor Sports **18***; Tad's Little Daffydills **18**; A Doity Deed **20**; Happy Hooligan in Oil **20**; Fatherly Love **21**; Bokays and Brickbatz **25**; The Flight That Failed **25**; Hair Raiser **25**; Hot Dogs **25**; James and Gems **25**; Monkey Business **25**; The New Champ **25**; The Smoke Eater **25**; A Uke-Calamity **25**; Back to Backing **26**; Battling for Barleycorn **26**; Cheese It **26**; The Chicken Chaser **26**; Cops Suey **26**; Dots and Dashes **26**; Double Crossed **26**; East Is Best **26**; Feather Pushers **26**; The Ghost Fakir **26**; Gold Struck **26**; A Picked Romance **26**; Scents and Nonsense **26**; Shore Enough **26**; Sucker Game **26**; Watery Gravey **26**; The Wrong Queue **26**; Best Wishes **27**; Black and White **27**; Burnt Up **27**; Busy Birds **27**; Don Go On **27**; A Fool's Errand **27**; Hire a Hall **27**; Horse Play **27**; Kiss Crossed **27**; Newslaffs No. 1 **27**; Newslaffs No. 2 **27**; Newslaffs No. 3 **27**; Newslaffs No. 4 **27**; Newslaffs No. 5 **27**; Newslaffs No. 6 **27**; Newslaffs No. 7 **27**; Newslaffs No. 8 **27**; Newslaffs No. 9 **27**; Night Owl **27**; On the Trail **27**; Passing the Hat **27**; The Rug Fiend **27**; Sharps and Flats **27**; Stomach Trouble **27**; Wild Rivals **27**; Newslaffs No. 10 **28**; Newslaffs No. 11 **28**; Newslaffs No. 12 **28**; Newslaffs No. 13 **28**; Newslaffs No. 14 **28**; Newslaffs No. 15 **28**; Newslaffs No. 16 **28**; Newslaffs No. 17 **28**; Newslaffs No. 18 **28**; Newslaffs No. 19 **28**; Newslaffs No. 20 **28**; Newslaffs No. 21 **28**; Newslaffs No. 22 **28**; Newslaffs No. 23 **28**; Newslaffs No. 24 **28**

Nolbandov, Sergei Ships with Wings **41**; Chetnik • Undercover • Underground Guerrillas **43**

Nolte, William The Duke Is Tops **38**

Nomura, Yoshitaro Goben no Tsubaki • The Scarlet Camellia **65**

Nonguet, Lucien The Life and Passion of Christ • La Passion • La Vie et la Passion de Jésus Christ **02***

Noonan, Tommy Three Nuts in Search of a Bolt **64**

Nordeen, Arthur Johan **20***

Noriega, Manuel Madrid en el Año 2000 • Madrid in the Year 2000 **25**

Norland, Tom Misha The Commuter **67**

Norling, J. A. The Mystery Box **22**; The Sky Splitter **22**; Black Sunlight **23**; Gambling with the Gulf Stream **23**; The Immortal Voice **23**; The Romance of Life **23**

Norman, Jacques Daniel see Daniel-Norman, Jacques

Norman, Leslie Dangerous to Live • Too Dangerous to Live **39***; The Night My Number Came Up **55**; X the Unknown **56***; The Shiralee **57**; Dunkirk **58**; Season of Passion • Summer of the Seventeenth Doll **59**; Jungle Fighters • The Long and the Short and the Tall • The Long, the Short and the Tall **60**; Mix Me a Person **61**; Spare the Rod **61**; The Lost Continent **68***

Norman, Roger von Play in the Summer Breezes • Spiel in Sommerwind **39**

Norman, Ron A Death **79**; VT **80**; Rennie **82**; Horizons **83**

Norman, Zack see Zuker, Howard

Normand, Mabel Foiling Fickle Father **13***; Caught in a Cabaret • Faking with Society • Jazz Waiter • The Waiter **14***; Charlie and the Sausages • Hot Dogs • Love and Lunch • Mabel's Busy Day **14***; Her Friend the Bandit • Mabel's Flirtation • A Thief Catcher **14***; Mabel at the Wheel **14***; Mabel's Married Life • The Squarehead • When You're Married **14***; Mabel's Nerve **14**; Mabel's New Job **14**; Won in a Closet **14**; Fatty and Mabel Viewing the World's Fair at San Francisco • Mabel and Fatty Viewing the World's Fair at San Francisco **15***; Fatty and Mabel's Simple Life • Mabel and Fatty's Simple Life **15***; Mabel and Fatty's Wash Day **15***

Norris, Aaron Braddock: Missing in Action III **88**; Platoon Leader **88**; Delta Force 2 **90**

North, Wilfred When Women Go on the Warpath **13***; The Battle Cry of Peace **15***; Hearts and the Highway **15**; The Blue Envelope Mystery **16**; The Dollar and the Law **16**; Green Stockings **16**; Hesper of the Mountains **16**; The Kid **16**; The Ordeal of Elizabeth **16**; Salvation Joan **16**; Clover's Rebellion **17**; Indiscretion **17**; Kitty MacKay **17**; Sally in a Hurry **17**; Over the Top **18**; The Human Desire **19**; The Mind-the-Paint Girl **19**; The Undercurrent **19**; His Brother's Keeper **21**; Lucky Carson **21**; A Millionaire for a Day **21**; Mrs. Dane's Danger **22**

Northcote, Sidney The Belle of Bettws-y-Coed • The Belle of North Wales **12**; A Cornish Romance **12**; The Fishergirl of Cornwall **12**; The Pedlar of Penmaenmawr **12**; Saved by Fire **12**; The Smuggler's Daughter of Anglesea **12**; Through Death's Valley **12**; A Tragedy of the Cornish Coast **12**; The Witch of the Welsh Mountains **12**; Detective Daring and the Thames Coiners **14**; The King of Crime **14**; Mary the Fishergirl **14**; The Troubles of an Heiress **14**; The Monkey's Paw **15**; Verdict of the Sea **32***

Norton, B. W. L. Cisco Pike **71**; More American Graffiti **79**; Baby • Baby…Secret of the Lost Legend • Dinosaur…Secret of the Lost Legend **85**; Three for the Road **87**

Norton, Bill L. see Norton, B. W. L.

Norton, C. Goodwin Good Night **1898**; The Bill Poster **1899**; The Butcher and the Tramp **1899**; Dancing Niggers **1899**; The Distracted Bather **1899**; Expressions **1899**; A Game of Snowballing **1899**; The Postman and the Nursemaid **1899**; A Reminiscence of the War **1899**

Nosler, Lloyd Galloping Thru **31**; The Man from Death Valley **31**; Single-Handed Sanders **32**; Son of the Border **33**

Noss, Rudolf von der Aufforderung zum Tanz • Invitation to the Dance **35**

Nosseck, Martin see Nosseck, Max

Nosseck, Max Um die Welt Ohne Geld

27; Der Tanz ins Glück 30; Der Schlemiel 31; Einmal Möcht'Ich Keine Sorgen Haben 32; Gado Bravo 33; Alegre Voy! 34; One Week of Happiness • Una Semana de Felicidad 34; Ponderoso Caballero 34; Le Roi des Champs Elysées 34; Girls Under 21 40; Overture to Glory 40; Gambling Daughters 41; The Brighton Strangler 45; Dillinger • John Dillinger, Killer 45; Black Beauty 46; The Return of Rin Tin Tin 47; Kill or Be Killed 50; The Hoodlum 51; Korea Patrol 51; Body Beautiful 53; The Garden of Eden 54; Der Hauptmann und Sein Held 55; Singing in the Dark 56; Moon Wolf • Und Immer Ruft das Herz 59*; Geschminkte Jugend 60

Nosseck, Noel Best Friends 73; Las Vegas Lady 76; Youngblood 78; Dreamer 79; King of the Mountain 81

Nostro, Nick Blood and Defiance 62; Triumph of the Ten Gladiators 64; Spartacus and the Ten Gladiators 65; Superargo Contra Diabolicado: Superargo el Hombre Enmascarado • Superargo Contro Diabolikus • Superargo el Hombre Enmascarado • Superargo vs. Diabolicus 66; Tre Notti Violente • Tres Noches Violentas • Web of Violence 66; A Dollar of Fire • Un Dollaro di Fuoco 67; Uno Dopo l'Altro 68

Notz, Thierry The Terror Within 88; Watchers 2 90

Novak, Blaine Good to Go • Short Fuse 86

Novák, Ivo Operace Mé Dcery 86

Novelli, Enrico A Marriage in the Moon • Un Matrimonio Interplanetario 10

Novikov, F. H. see Gunn, Bill

Nowak, Amram Isaac in America • Isaac in America: A Journey with Isaac Bashevis Singer 86

Nowina-Przybylski, Jan Maryjka 34; Manewry Miłosne 36; Yiddle with His Fiddle • Yidl Mitn Fidl 36*; Der Purimspieler 37*

Nowland, Eugene A Bird of Prey 16; The Flight of the Duchess 16; Miss Deception 17; Peg o' the Sea 17; Threads of Fate 17

Noxon, Nicholas Birds Do It, Bees Do It 74

Noy, Wilfred Daddy's Little Didums Did It 10; Dr. Brian Pellie, Thief and Coiner 10; Father and Son 10; The Jealous Cavalier 10; Parted to Meet Again 10; A Woman's Folly 10; The Coward 11; Daddy's Didums and the Tale of the Tailor 11; Daddy's Didums and the Umbrella 11; Daddy's Little Didums and the New Baby 11; Didums and the Bathing Machine 11; Didums and the Christmas Pudding 11; Didums and the Haddock 11; Dr. Brian Pellie and the Bank Robbery 11; Dr. Brian Pellie and the Baronet's Bride 11; A False Friend 11; The Finger of Fate 11; Her Guardian 11; In Castle or Cottage • In Cottage and Castle 11; Lady Lucy Runs Away 11; The Lure of London 11; Maud 11; A Miraculous Recovery 11; A Sailor's Bride 11; The Sergeant's Daughter 11; The Sisters

11; A Soldier and a Man 11; A Sporting Offer 11; The Strike Leader 11; The Two Brothers 11; An Adventuress Outwitted 12; An Afrikander Girl 12; At the Hour of Three 12; Business Is Business 12; A Christmas Adventure 12; Didums and a Policeman 12; Didums and the Monkey 12; Didums As an Artist 12; Didums at School 12; Didums on His Holidays 12; Dr. Brian Pellie and the Secret Despatch 12; Dr. Brian Pellie and the Spanish Grandees 12; Dr. Brian Pellie Escapes from Prison 12; The Eye of the Idol 12; The Flooded Mine 12; Foiled by a Girl 12; For Her Mother's Sake 12; The Forced Confession 12; The Gamekeeper's Revenge 12; Lorna Doone 12; The Lost Love Letter 12; The New Housekeeper • Wanted, a Housekeeper 12; Nina's Evening Prayer 12; Norah's Debt of Honour 12; Partners 12; A Rough Diamond 12; Sharp Practice 12; An Ape's Devotion 13; Behind the Scenes 13; Coming Home 13; The Convent Gate 13; Daddy's Didums and the Box Trick 13; Dagobert the Jester 13; Dr. Brian Pellie and the Wedding Gifts 13; The Dramatic Story of the Vote 13; Face to Face 13; Freda's Photo 13; The Gardener's Daughter 13; The Hand of a Child 13; Here She Goes and There She Goes 13; The House of Mystery 13; Kind Hearts Are More Than Coronets 13; King Charles 13; The Little Vulgar Boy 13; Mr. Pickwick in a Double Bedded Room 13; Mrs. Corney Makes Tea 13; Phil Blood's Leap 13; Pickwick vs. Bardell 13; The Pride of Battery B 13; A Strong Man's Love 13; The Enemy in Our Midst 14; The Family Solicitor 14; The Heroine of Mons 14; In Peace and War 14; The Love of an Actress 14; Old St. Paul's • When London Burned 14; The Passions of Men 14; A Secret Life 14; Southern Blood 14; Wreck and Ruin 14; The Great Bank Sensation 15; The Great Motor Bus Outrage 15; The Guest of the Regiment 15; In Search of a Husband 15; In the Blood 15; The Ivory Hand 15; The Locket 15; The Master of Merripit 15; Night and Morning 15; The Outpost 15; A Princess of the Blood 15; The Queen Mother 15; The Seventh Word 15; Under the German Yoke 15; Under the Red Robe 15; The Verdict of the Heart 15; When East Meets West 15; When Passions Rise 15; All Through Betty 16; Betty's Night Out 16; The Five Wishes 16; Honour Among Thieves 16; The Interrupted Honeymoon 16; It's Always the Woman 16; The Little Breadwinner 16; The Little Damozel 16; The Lost Chord 16; More to Him Than Life 16; The New Girl 16; On the Banks of Allan Water 16; Asthore 17; Home Sweet Home 17; A Master of Men 17; Sister Susie's Sewing Shirts for Soldiers 17; Ave Maria 18; Spinner o' Dreams 18; What Would a Gentleman Do? 18; As He Was Born 19; Castle of Dreams 19; The Lady Clare 19; The Face at the Window 20; Inheritance 20; The Marriage Lines 21; Little Miss Nobody 23; Rogues of the Turf 23;

The Temptation of Carlton Earle 23; The Midnight Girl 25; Eager Lips 27; Spider Webs 27; The Devil's Cage 28; Circumstantial Evidence 29; Father O'Flynn 35*; Melody of My Heart 36; Well Done, Henry 36

Noyce, Phillip Backroads 77; Newsfront 78; Heatwave 81; Echoes in Paradise • Echoes of Paradise • Promises to Keep • Shadows of the Peacock 86; Dead Calm 88; Blind Fury 89

Nuchtern, Simon Girl Grabbers 68; To Hex with Sex 69; The Cowards 70; The Broad Coalition 72; What Do I Tell the Boys at the Station? 72; The Bodyguard 76; New York Nights 81; Nightkillers 83; Savage Dawn 84; Silent Madness 84

Nuefeld, Massimiliano Ball at the Castle • Ballo al Castello 39

Nugent, Elliott The Dawn of Life • Dream of Life • Life Begins 32*; The Mouthpiece 32*; Scared! • Whistling in the Dark 32; Behold We Live • If I Were Free 33; Three-Cornered Moon 33; Enter Madame 34; She Loves Me Not 34; Strictly Dynamite 34; Two Alone 34; The Clock Strikes Eight • College Scandal 35; Love in Bloom 35; Splendor 35; And So They Were Married 36; Wives Never Know 36; It's All Yours 37; Give Me a Sailor 38; Professor Beware 38; The Cat and the Canary 39; Never Say Die 39; Nothing But the Truth 41; The Male Animal 42; The Crystal Ball 43; Up in Arms 44; My Favorite Brunette 47; Welcome Stranger 47; My Girl Tisa 48; The Great Gatsby 49; Mr. Belvedere Goes to College 49; The Skipper Surprised His Wife 50; My Brother the Outlaw • My Outlaw Brother 51; Just for You 52

Nugmanov, Rashid The Needle 89

Nuñez, Victor Gal Young 'Un 79; A Flash of Green 84

Nunn, Trevor Hedda 75; Lady Jane 85

Nureyev, Rudolf Don Quixote 73*

Nuse, Deland The Chilling 89*

Nussbaum, Raphael Blazing Sand 60; The Invisible Man • The Invisible Terror • Der Unsichtbare 63; Kommando Sinai • Ha' Matarah Tiran • Schatten Über Tiran —Kommando Sinai • Der Sechs Tage Krieg • Sinai Commandos • Sinai Commandos: The Story of the Six Day War 68; Pets 74; The Amorous Adventures of Don Quixote and Sancho Panza 76; WAR • WAR: Women Against Rape 86; Private Road (No Trespassing) 87

Nussgruber, Rudolph Mediterranean Holiday 64*

Nuti, Francesco All the Fault of Paradise • Blame It on Paradise • Tutta Colpa del Paradiso 85; Casablanca Casablanca 85; Bewitched • Stregati 87

Nutley, Colin Company 9 • Nionde Kompaniet 87

Nutter, David Cease Fire 85

Nuytten, Bruno Camille Claudel 88

Nyberg, Börje I, a Lover 68

Nyby, Christian The Thing • The Thing (From Another World) • The Thing That

Came from Another World 51*; Hell on Devil's Island 57; Last Message from Saigon • Operation C.I.A. 65; Young Fury 65; First to Fight 67

Nyby, Christian II Mission Galactica: The Cylon Attack 79*

Nydrle, Peter Eugene Among Us 81

Nykvist, Carl-Gustaf Kvinnorna på Taket • The Women on the Roof 89

Nykvist, Sven Under the Southern Cross 52*; Gorilla 56*; Lianbron • The Vine Bridge 64; Kallelsen • The Vocation 74; En och En • One and One • One Plus One 78*; The Marmalade Revolution • Marmeladupproret 79*

Nyswaner, Ron The Prince of Pennsylvania 88

Nyznik, Bruce The Man Who Skied Down Everest 75

Oaks, Joe Deadly Twins 88

Oba, Hideo Snow Country • Yukiguni 65; Farewell My Beloved • Wakare 69

Obal, Max Reserve Hat Ruh 32; Die Lustigen Musikanten 33; Zwei Gute Kameraden 33; Die vom Niederrhein • Lower Rhine Folks 35; Annette in Paradise 36; Die Fahrt ins Grüne 36; Der Klosterjäger 36; Schloss Vogelöd 36; Slalom 36; Jede Frau Hat ein Geheimnis 37

O'Bannon, Dan The Return of the Living Dead 85

Obayashi, Nobuhiko House • Ie 77; Tenkosai 85; Beijing Watermelon • Pekin Teki Suika 89; The Discarnates • Ijintachi Tono Natsu 89

Obenhaus, Mark Nomadic Lives 77

Ober, Robert Lights and Shadows • The Woman Racket 29*

O'Bielek, Pal see Bielek, Pal'o

Obimori, Michihiko Kokosei Banchō • Way Out, Way In 70

Oblowitz, Michael King Blank 83

Oblowsky, Stefan Guardian of Hell 80

Oboler, Arch Bewitched 45; The Day After Tomorrow • Strange Holiday 45; The Arnelo Affair 47; Five 51; Bwana Devil 52; The Twonky 53; 1+1 • 1+1: Exploring the Kinsey Report 61; The Bubble • Fantastic Invasion of Planet Earth 66; Dōmo Arigatō 72

Obón, Ramón Cien Gritos de Terror • One Hundred Cries of Terror 64

O'Brien, Edmond Shield for Murder 54*; Deadlock • Man in Hiding • Man-Trap • Restless 61

O'Brien, Jack see O'Brien, John B.

O'Brien, Jim The Jewel in the Crown 84*; The Dressmaker 88

O'Brien, John The Big Dis 90*

O'Brien, John B. Captain Macklin 15*; Her Shattered Idol 15; The Outcast 15; Souls Triumphant 15; The Big Sister 16; Destiny's Toy 16; The Eternal Grind 16; The Flying Torpedo 16*; The Foundling 16; Hulda from Holland 16; A Daughter of Maryland 17; Her Sister 17; Mary Lawson's Secret 17; Maternity 17; Queen X 17; Reputation 17; The Unforeseen 17; Vanity 17; The Girl and the Judge 18; The Street of Seven Stars 18; The Bishop's Emeralds 19;

Impossible Catherine 19; The Family Closet 21; Father Tom 21; Lonely Heart 21; Those Who Dare 24; Daring Days 25; The Outlaw's Daughter 25

O'Brien, Patrick see Brunner, Patrick

Obrow, Jeffrey The Dorm That Dripped Blood • Pranks 82*; The Power 83*; The Kindred 86*

Ocampo Feijoo, Beda Debajo del Mundo • Under the World 86*

Ochs, Jackie The Secret Agent 84

O'Connell, Jack Birthplace of the Hootenanny • Greenwich Village Story • They Love As They Please 63; Revolution 68; Christa • Swedish Fly Girls 71

O'Connell, Maura Self-Defense • Siege 83*

O'Connolly, James The Hi-Jackers 63; Smokescreen 64; The Little Ones 65; Berserk! • Circus of Blood • Circus of Terror 67; Vendetta for the Saint 68; Crooks and Coronets • Sophie's Place 69; The Valley of Gwangi 69; Beyond the Fog • Horror on Snape Island • Tower of Evil 72; Mistress Pamela 73

O'Connor, Frank Everything for Sale 21; A Virginia Courtship 21; A Homespun Vamp 22; Penrod 22*; Free to Love 25; Go Straight 25; Lawful Cheaters 25; One of the Bravest 25; The Block Signal 26; Devil's Island 26; Exclusive Rights 26; The False Alarm 26; Hearts and Spangles 26; The Silent Power 26; Spangles 26; The Speed Limit 26; Colleen 27; Heroes of the Night 27; Sinews of Steel 27; Your Wife and Mine 27; Masked Angel 28; Just Off Broadway 29; Call of the Circus 30; Mystic Circle Murders • Religious Racketeers 39

O'Connor, Hugh Above the Horizon 66*

O'Connor, John Prisoner in the Middle 74; Warhead 74

O'Connor, Pat Cal 84; A Month in the Country 86; The January Man 88; Stars and Bars 88; Fools of Fortune 90

O'Connor, William A. Playthings of Hollywood 31; Ten Nights in a Barroom 31; The Drifter 32; Her Splendid Folly 33; Cheyenne Tornado 35; The Cocaine Fiends • The Pace That Kills 36

Oddsson, Hilmar As the Beast Dieth • Eins og Skepnan Deyr 86

Ode, Eric Schlager-Parade 53

Odell, David Martians Go Home! 90

Odets, Clifford None But the Lonely Heart 44; The Story on Page One 59

Odo, Motoyoshi Counterattack of the Monster • The Fire Monster • Gigantis • Gigantis the Fire Monster • Godzilla Raids Again • Godzilla's Counterattack • Gojira no Gyakushū • The Return of Godzilla • The Volcano Monster 59*

Ödön, Fritz Alraune 18*

O'Donoghue, Michael Mr. Mike's Mondo Video 79

O'Donovan, Fred The Eleventh Hour 18; Knocknagow 18; Rafferty's Rise 18; When Love Came to Gavin Burke 18

O'Donovan, Harry Blarney • Ireland's Border Line 38

Odorisio, Luciano Dear Maestro 83; La Monaca di Monza • The Nun of Monza 87

Odzhagov, Rasim Drugaya Zhizn 88

Oedon, Fritz see Ödön, Fritz

Oekten, Zeki see Ökten, Zeki

Oertel, Curt see Örtel, Kurt

Oertel, Kurt see Örtel, Kurt

O'Feeney, Sean see Ford, John

O'Ferrall, George More see More O'Ferrall, George

O'Fredericks, Alice Julia Jubilerar 38*; Västkustens Hjältar 40*; We Want a Child 54*

Ofugi, Naburo The Whale 27; The Whale 52

Oganisyan, Bagrat Khoziain • The Master 86

Oganisyan, Genrikh Damy • Ladies 54*; Devichya Vesna • Springtime on the Volga 61*

Oganisyan, Nerses Chuzhie Igry 88

Ogawa, Shinsuke The Peasants of the Second Fortress 71; Magino—Mura Monogatari • Tales from the Magino Village 87

Ogilvie, George Mad Max Beyond Thunderdome 85*; Short Changed 85; The Bee-Eater • The Place at the Coast 86

Ogorodnikov, Valery Burglar • Vzlomshchik 87

Oguri, Kohei Doro no Kawa • Muddy River 81; For Kayako 86

Oğuz, Orhan Herşeye Rağman 88; The Third Eye • Üçüncü Göz 89

O'Hanlon, George The Rookie 59

O'Hara, Gerry Game for Three Losers 63; Models, Inc. • Teenage Tramp • That Kind of Girl 63; The Pleasure Girls 65; Maroc 7 66; Amsterdam Affair 68; All the Right Noises 69; Fidelia 70; The Chairman's Wife 72; The Spy's Wife 72; Paganini Strikes Again 74; Professor Popper's Problems 75; The Brute 76; Blind Man's Bluff 77; Leopard in the Snow 78; The Bitch 79; Fanny Hill 83; Strictly for Cash 84

Öhberg, Åke Romance 40; Scanian Guerilla 42; Elvira Madigan 43; Snowstorm 44; Girls in the Harbor 45; Brita in the Wholesaler's House 46; Dynamite 47; People of Simlangen Valley 48; Where the Winds Lead 48; Destination Rio 49; Young and in Love 50; Where the Summer Wind Blows 53

O'Herlihy, Michael The Fighting Prince of Donegal 66; Mosby's Marauders 66; The One and Only Genuine, Original Family Band 67; Smith! 69

Ohlsson, Terry Scobie Malone 75

Ohmori, Hidetoshi Robot Carnival 87*

O'Horgan, Tom Futz 69; Rhinoceros 74

Ojeda, Manuel R. Judas 37; El Circo Trágico • The Tragic Circus 39

Okabe, Kazuhiko Hakuja Den • Panda and the Magic Serpent 61*

Okamoto, Kihachi The Last Gunfight 59; Dokuritsu Gurentai Nishie • Westward Desperado 61; Dobunezumi Sakusen • Operation X 63; Sengoku Yaro • Warring Clans 63; Samurai • Samurai Assassin 64; Chi to Suna • Fort Graveyard 66;

Daibōsatsu Tōge • The Sword of Doom 66; The Emperor and a General • The Emperor and the General • The Longest Day in Japan • Nihon no Ichiban Nagai Hi • Nippon no Ichiban Nagai Hi 67; The Human Bullet 68; Kill • Kiru 68; Akage • Red Lion 69; Zatoichi Meets Yojimbo • Zatōichi to Yōjimbō 70; Battle Cry • Tokkan 75; Dixieland Daimyō 86

Okan, Bay Drôle de Samedi 85

Okazaki, Steven Unfinished Business 85; Living on Tokyo Time 86

O'Keefe, Dennis The Diamond • The Diamond Wizard 54*; Angela 55

Okey, Jack Outlaws of the Sea 23

Okeyev, Tolomush Horses 65; Niebo Nashevo Detstva • The Sky of Our Childhood 67; The Inheritance 70; Pay Tribute to the Fire 72; The Fierce One 73; The Red Apple 75; Uhlan 77; The Descendant of the Snow Leopard • Potomok Belogo Barssa 85; Mirages of Love • Mirazhi Lyubri 87

Okhlopkov, Nikolai Pavlovich Mitya 27; Prodannyi Appetit • The Sold Appetite 28; Put Entuziastov • Way of the Enthusiast 30

Ökten, Zeki The Flock • The Herd • Sürü 78; Duşman • The Enemy 79; Ses • The Voice 86

Olcott, Sidney Ben-Hur • The Chariot Race 07*; The Scarlet Letter 07; The Sleigh Bells 07; Dr. Jekyll and Mr. Hyde 08; Florida Crackers • A Florida Feud 08; Washington at Valley Forge 08; The Wooing of Miles Standish 08; A Brother's Wrong 09; The Cardboard Baby 09; The Cattle Thieves 09; The Conspirators 09; Dora 09; Escape from Andersonville 09; The Factory Girl 09; The Geisha Who Saved Japan 09; The Girl Scout 09; The Governor's Daughter 09; The Hand Organ Man 09; Her Indian Hero 09; Hiram's Bride 09; The Lad from Old Ireland 09; The Law of the Mountains 09; The Man and the Girl 09; The Mystery of the Sleeper Trunk 09; Out of Work 09; The Pay Car 09; The Queen of the Quarry 09; The Rally 'Round the Flag 09; The Tomboy 09; The Winning Boat 09; The Aigrette Hunter • The Egret Hunt 10; The Bravest Girl in the South 10; The Canadian Moonshiners 10; The Deacon's Daughter 10; The Feud 10; For a Woman's Honor 10; The Forager 10; Further Adventures of the Girl Spy 10; The Girl Spy Before Vicksburg 10; Hannah Dusten 10; Her Soldier Sweetheart 10; The Indian Mother 10; An Indian Scout's Vengeance 10; The Little Spreewald Maiden 10; The Love Romance of the Girl Spy 10; The Miser's Child 10; The Priest of Wilderness 10; A Romance of Old Erin 10; The Sacred Turquoise of the Zuni 10; The Seminole Halfbreed 10; Seth's Temptation 10; The Stranger 10; Up the Thames to Westminster 10; Arrah-na-Pogue 11; The Carnival 11; The Colleen Bawn 11; The Fiddle's Requiem 11; The Fisherman of Bally David 11; Grandmother's War Story 11; Her Chum's Brother 11; Hunted Through the Everglades 11; In Blossom Time 11; In Old Florida 11; The Irish Honeymoon 11; Little Sister 11; The Little Soldier of '64 11; Rory O'Moore 11; Sailor Jack's Reformation 11; The Seminole's Vengeance 11; The Sister 11; Tangled Lives 11; To the Aid of Stonewall Jackson 11; When the Dead Return 11; You Remember Ellen? 11; Along the River Nile 12; Ancient Temples of Egypt 12; An Arabian Tragedy 12; Captured by Bedouins 12; Conway the Kerry Dancer 12; A Day in Jerusalem 12; Driving Home the Cows 12; Easter Celebration at Jerusalem 12; Egypt 12; Egypt the Mysterious 12; Egyptian Sports 12; The Fighting Dervishes 12; From Jerusalem to the Dead Sea 12; From the Manger to the Cross 12; His Mother 12; Ireland the Oppressed 12; An Irish Girl's Love 12; The Kalemites Visit Gibraltar 12; The Kerry Gow 12; The Major from Ireland 12; Making Photoplays in Egypt 12; Missionaries in Darkest Africa 12; The O'Kalems' Visit to Killarney 12; Palestine 12; The Poacher's Pardon 12; A Prisoner of the Harem 12; The Shaughraun 12; Tragedy of the Desert 12; The Vagabonds 12; Winning a Widow 12; Daughter of the Confederacy 13*; In the Clutches of the Ku Klux Klan • In the Power of the Ku Klux Klan 13; Lady Peggy's Escape 13; The Little Rebel 13; The Mystery of Pine Tree Camp 13; The Octoroon 13; The Perils of the Sea 13*; The Vampire 13*; The Wives of Jamestown 13; The Brute 14; Come Back to Erin 14; The Eye of the Government 14; The Moth and the Flame 14; A Mother of Men 14; A Passover Miracle 14; Tricking the Government 14; When Men Would Kill 14; Wolfe, or The Conquest of Quebec 14; All for Ireland • All for Old Ireland 15; Bold Emmett, Ireland's Martyr 15; Famous Men of Today 15; Famous Rulers of the World 15; The Ghost of the Twisted Oaks 15; Great Americans Past and Present 15; The Irish in America 15; Madame Butterfly 15; The Melting Pot 15; Nan o' the Backwoods 15; New York and Its People 15; The Sentimental Lady 15; The Seven Sisters 15; The Taint 15; The Daughter of MacGregor 16; Diplomacy 16; The Innocent Lie 16; Jean o' the Heather 16; My Lady Incog • My Lady Incognito 16; Poor Little Peppina 16; The Smugglers 16; The Belgian 17; Marriage for Convenience 19; Mothers of Men 20*; Scratch My Back 20; God's Country and the Law 21; Making Good • The Right Way • Within Prison Walls 21; Pardon My French 21; Timothy's Quest 22; The Green Goddess 23; Little Old New York 23; The Humming Bird 24; Monsieur Beaucaire 24; The Only Woman 24; The Best People 25; The Charmer 25; Not So Long Ago 25; Salome of the Tenements 25; The Amateur Gentleman 26; Ranson's Folly 26; The White Black Sheep 26; The Claw 27

Old, John see Bava, Mario

Old, John, Jr. see Bava, Lamberto

Olden, John Die Glücklichen Jahre der Thorwalds 62*; Die Gentlemen Bitten zur Kasse • The Great British Train Robbery • Der Postzug-Überfall 65*

Oldenburg, Claes Pat's Birthday 62*

Oldoini, Enrico He Is Worse Than Me • Lui È Peggio di Me 85; Bellifreschi • Lovely and Fresh 87; Una Botta di Vita 88; Bye Bye Baby 88

Olea, Pedro The Ancines Woods • El Bosque de Ancines • El Bosque del Lobo • The Wolf Forest • The Wolfman of Galicia • The Wolf's Forest 68; Anguish 74; Bandera Negra • Black Flag 86

Olgac, Bilge Gülsusan 86; Three Rings Twenty-Five • Üç Halka Yirmibeş 86; Gömlek • The Shirt 89

Olguín, Carlos A Dos Aguas • The Entire Life 87

Olhovich, Sergio La Muñeca Reina 71

Oliansky, Joel The Competition 80; The Silence at Bethany 88

Olin, Stig The Journey to You 53; The Yellow Squadron 54; Murder, My Little Friend 55; Swing It Miss! 56; A Guest in One's Own Home 57; You Are My Adventure 58

Oliphant, Peer Viva Portugal 75*

Oliveira, José María Las Flores del Miedo 72; The Dead, the Devil and the Flesh • The Dead, the Flesh and the Devil • Los Muertos, la Carne y el Diablo 73

Oliveira, Manoel de see De Oliveira, Manoel

Oliver, David Cavegirl 85

Oliver, Robert H. Il Castello della Paura • Il Castello delle Donne Maledette • El Castello dell'Orrore • Frankenstein's Castle of Freaks • The House of Freaks • The Monsters of Dr. Frankenstein • Terror • Terror Castle 73

Olivera, Héctor Psexoanálisis 67; Las Venganzas de Beto Sánchez 72; La Patagonia Rebelde • Rebellion in Patagonia 74; El Muerto 75; La Nona 78; Los Viernes de la Eternidad 81; Buenos Aires Rock '82 82; A Funny, Dirty Little War • No Habrá Más Penas ni Olvido 83; Barbarian Queen 85; Wizards of the Lost Kingdom 85; Cocaine Wars 86; The Night of the Pencils • La Noche de los Lapices 86; Two to Tango 89

Olivier, Laurence Henry V 44*; Hamlet 48; Richard III 55*; The Prince and the Showgirl 57*; Three Sisters 70*

Olivo, Pablo El Hombre de la Deuda Externa • The Man of the Foreign Debt 87

Ollendorff, Julian Eve's Leaves 21; Jiggin' on the Old Sod 21; Just for Fun 21; Play Ball 21; Seeing Greenwich Village 21; What's the Limit? 21; Animals and Humans 22; Athletics and Women 22; Champions 22; The Coastguard 22; Famous Men 22; Mackerel Fishing 22; Family Album 23; Beauty and the Beach 26; The Big Show 26; Everybody Rides 26; Fair Weather 26; Revolution of the Sexes 26; Tin Pan Alley 26; Watch Your Step 26

Ollstein, Marty Dangerous Love 88

Olmer, Vít Druhý Tah Pěsce 85; Jako Jed • Like Poison 85; Bony a Klid 88

Padres 37; El Derecho y el Deber 38; Eterna Mártir 38

Oross, Emmerich Again 69; Kodály's Methods 70; Last Call 85

Orr, James Breaking All the Rules 85; They Still Call Me Bruce 86*; Mr. Destiny 90

Orsini, Valentino San Miniato, July '44 • San Miniato, Luglio '44 54*; Voltera, Comune Medievale 55*; A Man for Burning • Un Uomo da Bruciare 62*; I Fuorilegge del Matrimonio • The Matrimonial Criminals 63*; I Dannati della Terra 68; Corbari 70; Figlio Mio Infinitamente Caro • My Infinitely Dear Son 85

Ortega, Gonzalo Martínez see *Martínez Ortega, Gonzalo*

Örtel, Kurt The Rider of the White Horse • Der Schimmelreiter 35*

Orth, Marion Crazy That Way 30*

Ortion, Bernard La Guerre Populaire au Laos 68*

Orton, Harold Wreck Raisers 72; Chimpmates 76; Chimpmates II 77; Chimpmates III 78; 4D Special Agents 81

Orton, John The Celestial City 29; The Windjammer 30; Bill and Coo 31; Creeping Shadows • The Limping Man 31; Out of the Blue 31*; The Bad Companions 32

Orton, Wallace Sunshine Ahead 36; Overcoat Sam 37; Laugh It Off 40*

Orzechowski, Witold Death Sentence • Wyrok Śmierci 81

Osanai, Kaoru Souls on the Road 21*

Osbiston, Alan Chance of a Lifetime 50*

Osborne, Kent The Blood Seekers • Cain's Cutthroats • Cain's Way • Justice Cain 69; Wild Wheels 69; Ballad of Billie Blue 72; Five Angry Women 75

Osepyan, Mark see *Ossepijan, Mark*

O'Shaughnessy, John The Sound of Laughter 63

Oshima, Nagisa Ai to Kibō no Machi • A Street of Love and Hope • A Town of Love and Hope 59; Asu no Taiyō 59; Cruel Story of Youth • Naked Youth • Naked Youth: A Story of Cruelty • Seishun Monogatari • Seishun Zankoku Monogatari • A Story of the Cruelties of Youth 60; Night and Fog in Japan • Nihon no Yoru to Kiri 60; The Sun's Burial • Taiyō no Hakaba 60; The Catch • Shiiku 61; Amakusa Shiro Tokisada • The Rebel • The Revolutionary • Shiro Amakusa from Tokisada • Shiro Amakusa the Christian Rebel 62; Chiisana Bōken Ryokō • A Child's First Adventure • Small Adventure • A Small Child's First Adventure 64; I'm Here, Bellett • It's Me Here, Bellett • Watashi wa Bellett 64; The Diary of Yunbogi • Diary of Yunbogi Boy • Yunbogi no Nikki • Yunbogi's Diary 65; Etsuraku • The Pleasures of the Flesh 65; Hakuchū no Tōrima • Violence at High Noon • Violence at Noon 66; Band of Ninja • Ninja Bugeichō • Tales of the Ninja 67; Japanese Summer: Double Suicide • Muri Shinjū Nihon no Natsu • Night of the Killer 67; Nihon Shunka-Kō • Sing a Song of Sex •

A Treatise on Japanese Bawdy Song 67; Daitōa Sensō • The Pacific War 68; Death by Hanging • Kōshukei 68; Diary of a Shinjuku Burglar • Diary of a Shinjuku Thief • Shinjuku Dorobō Nikki 68; Kaette Kita Yopparai • A Sinner in Paradise • Three Resurrected Drunkards 68; Boy • Shōnen 69; Mō Taku-To to Bunkadaika-Kumei 69; He Died After the War • The Man Who Left His Will on Film • Tōkyō Sensō Sengo Hiwa 70; The Ceremony • Gishiki 71; Dear Summer Sister • Natsu no Imōto • Summer Sister 72; Ai no Corrida • Corrida of Love • L'Empire des Sens • Empire of the Passions • Empire of the Senses • In the Realm of the Senses • The Realm of the Senses 76; Ai no Bōrei • L' Empire de la Passion • The Empire of Passion • In the Realm of Passion • Phantom Love • The Phantom of Love 78; Merry Christmas, Mr. Lawrence • Senjō no Merii Kurisumasu 82; A Better Man • Itoshi no Max • Max, Mon Amour • Max, My Love 86; Yunbogi no Nikki 86

Osiecki, Stefan No Way Back 49

Oskarsson, Lars The Frozen Leopard • Den Frusna Leoparden 86

Osmond, Cliff The Penitent 86

Osone, Tatsuo The Imposter 55

Ospina, Luis Pura Sangre • Pure Blood 83

Ossang, François-Jacques L'Affaire des Divisions Morituri 85

Ossepijan, Mark Three Days of Viktor Tschernikoff 68; Ivanov Kater 88

Ossorio, Amando de see *De Ossorio, Amando*

Ostashenko, Yevgeni An Elephant Got Lost • Poteryalsya Slon 86

O'Steen, Sam Sparkle 76

Osten, Franz Light of Asia 25; Shiraz 28*; A Throw of Dice • A Throw of the Dice 29*; Der Judas von Tirol 35; At the Strassburg • Zu Strassburg auf der Schanz 36; Fürst Sepp'l 37

Osten, Suzanne Bröderna Mozart • The Mozart Brothers 86; Livsfarlig Film 88

Ostermayer, Paul Beyond Sing the Woods • Duel with Death • Duell mit dem Tod 49; 08/15 54; 08/15, II Teil 55; 08/15 in der Heimat 55; Dr. Mabuse vs. Scotland Yard • Scotland Yard Hunts Dr. Mabuse • Scotland Yard Jägt Dr. Mabuse 63

Ostermayr, Peter Youth Astray 28; Der Edelweisskönig 39

Ostrovski, Grisha The Detour • Otklonenie 68*

Oswald, Gerd Man on a Tightrope 53; The Ox-Bow Incident 55; The Brass Legend 56; A Kiss Before Dying 56; Crime of Passion 57; Fury at Showdown 57; Valerie 57; Paris Holiday 58; Screaming Mimi 58; Am Tag Als der Regen Kam • The Day It Rained • The Day the Rains Came 59; Brainwashed • The Royal Game • Schachnovelle • Three Moves to Freedom 60; The Longest Day 62*; The Scarlet Eye • Storm Over Ceylon • Tempesta Su Ceylon 63*; Agent for H.A.R.M. • The H.A.R.M.

Machine 65; 80 Steps to Jonah 69; Bunny O'Hare 70; Bis zur Bitteren Neige • To the Bitter End 75

Oswald, Richard Das Eiserne Kreuz • The Iron Cross 14; Die Geschichte der Stillen Mühle 14; Iwan Koschula 14; Lache, Bajazzo • Laugh, Bajazzo 14; And You Will Wander Restless... • The Beautiful Sinner • Die Schöne Sünderin • Und Wandern Sollst Du Ruhelos... 15; Dämon und Mensch 15; Der Fund im Neubau 15; Hampels Abenteuer 15; Hoffmanns Erzählungen • Tales of Hoffmann 15; The Hound of the Baskervilles • Der Hund von Baskerville • Der Hund von Baskerville III 15; Das Laster 15; Ein Lebensbild • Schlemihl 15; Die Sage vom Hund von Baskerville 15; Die Silberne Kugel 15; The Uncanny Room • Das Unheimliche Haus 15; Die Verschleierte Dame 15; Der Chinesischen Götze • Das Unheimliche Haus III 16; Rennfieber 16; Seine Letzte Maske 16; Das Unheimliche Haus II: Freitag der 13 16; Zirkusblut 16; Das Bildnis des Dorian Gray • The Picture of Dorian Gray 17; Des Goldes Fluch 17; Es Werde Licht! • Let There Be Light! 17*; Königliche Bettler 17; Die Rache der Toten 17; Schatten der Vergangenheit 17; Der Schlossherr von Hohenstein 17; Die Seeschlacht 17; Die Sintflut 17; Die Zweite Frau 17; Dida Ibsens Geschichte 18; Das Dreimäderlhaus 18; Henriette Jacoby 18; Jettchen Gebert 18; Der Lebende Leichnam • The Living Corpse • The Living Dead 18; Peer Gynt 18*; Die Seltsame Geschichte des Barons Torelli 18; Das Tagebuch einer Verlorenen 18; Der Weg ins Freie 18; Anders Als die Anderen 19; Die Arche 19; Die Arche II • Die Letzten Menschen 19; Around the World in 80 Days • Die Reise Um die Erde in 80 Tagen • Die Reise Um die Welt 19; Die Sich Verkaufen 19; Five Sinister Stories • Tales of Horror • Tales of the Uncanny • Unheimliche Geschichten 19; Das Kainszeichen 19; Die Prostitution 19; Die Schwarze Katze 19; Sündige Eltern 19; Der Tod des Andern 19; Antisemiten 20; Eleagabl Kuperus • Nachtgestalten 20; Fürst Lahory, der König der Diebe • Manolescus Memoiren 20; Die Geheimnisse von London • Das Siebente Gebot • Die Tragödie eines Kindes 20; Der Grosse Krach 20; Ein Höllenspuk in Sechs Akten • Kurfürstendamm 20; Der Reigen • Ein Werdegang 20; Der Selbstmörderklub • The Suicide Club 20; Die Spielerin 20; Das Vierte Gebot 20; Engelchen 21; Das Haus in der Dragonergasse 21; Lady Hamilton 21; Das Leben des Menschen 21; Die Liebschaften des Hektor Dalmore 21; Macbeth 21; Sündige Mütter 21; Lucrezia Borgia • Lukrezia Borgia 22; Carlos und Elisabeth • Don Carlos und Elisabeth 24; Lumpen und Seide 24; Die Frau von Vierzig Jahren 25; Halbseide 25; Vorderhaus und Hinterhaus 25*; Als Ich Wiederkam 26; Dürfen Wir Schweigen? 26; Im Weissen Rössl 26; Eine Tolle Nacht 26; Wir Sind vom K. und K. Infanterie-Regiment

26; Doktor Bessels Verwandlung 27; Feme 27; Funkzauber 27; Gehetzte Frauen • Lebende Ware 27; Lützows Wilde Verwegene Jagd 27; Cagliostro 28; Die Rothausgasse 28; Villa Falconieri 28; The Awakening of Spring • Frühlingserwachen 29; Ehe in Not • Ehen zu Dritt 29; Die Herrin und Ihr Knecht 29; The Hound of the Baskervilles • Der Hund von Baskerville 29; Alraune • Daughter of Evil 30; City of Songs • Vienna—City of Songs • Wien—Du Stadt der Lieder 30; Dreyfus 30; Die Zärtlichen Verwandten 30; Arm Wie eine Kirchenmaus 31; Asylum of Horror • Extraordinary Tales • The Living Dead • Tales of the Uncanny • Unheimliche Geschichten 31; Captain from Koepenick • The Captain of Koepenick • Der Hauptmann von Köpenick 31; 1914, die Letzten Tage Vor dem Weltbrand • 1914, the Last Days Before the War 31; Schuberts Frühlingstraum 31; Viktoria und Ihr Husar 31; Gräfin Mariza 32; Die Blume von Hawaii 33; Ganovenehre 33; The Joseph Schmidt Story • Ein Lied Geht Um die Welt 33; My Song Goes 'Round the World 34; Heute Ist der Schönste Tag in Meinem Leben 36; Tempête sur l'Asie 38; Dreyfus • The Dreyfus Case 40; The Living Dead 40; The Captain of Koepenick • I Was a Criminal 41; Isle of Fury • Isle of Missing Men • Isle of Terror 42; The Lovable Cheat 49

Osyka, Leonid Bow Your Head • Poklonis Do Zemli 87

Ota, Koji Invasion of the Neptune Men 61

Othénin-Girard, Dominique After Darkness 85*; Halloween 5 • Halloween 5: The Revenge of Michael Myers 89; Night Angel 90

Oti, Manuel Mur Fedra the Devil's Daughter 57

Otmezguine, Jacques Prunelle Blues 86

Otomo, Katsuhiro Robot Carnival 87*; Akira 88

Otsep, Fyodor see Ozep, Fedor

Otsep, Theodore see Ozep, Fedor

Ottaviano, Matteo see Cimber, Matt

Ottinger, Ulrike Chine: Die Künste, der Alltag 85; Johanna d'Arc of Mongolia 89

Otto, Hans The Life of Beethoven 29

Otto, Henry Big Tremaine 16; Half a Rogue 16; The Man from Nowhere 16; Mr. 44 16; The River of Romance 16; Undine 16; The Butterfly Girl 17; Lorelei of the Sea • A Modern Lorelei 17; Angel Child 18; Wild Life 18; The Amateur Adventuress 19; Fair and Warmer 19; The Great Romance 19; The Island of Intrigue 19; The Microbe 19; Some Bride 19; The Cheater 20; A Slave of Vanity 20; The Willow Tree 20; Lovebound 23; The Temple of Venus 23; Dante's Inferno 24; The Folly of Vanity 24*; The Ancient Mariner 25*

Otto, Paul Tradition 21

Otto, Philip The Day Santa Claus Cried 80

Ottoni, Filippo Questo Si' Che E'Amore 77; Asilo di Polizia • Detective School Dropouts • Dumb Dicks 86; Stray Days 87

Ottosen, Carl Præriens Skrappe Drenge 70

Ottoson, Lars Henrik Gorilla 56*

Ouedraogo, Idrissa The Choice • Yam Daabo 87; Grandmother • Yaaba 89

Ouellette, Jean-Paul The Unnameable 88

Oulfsak, Lembit Radosti Srednego Vozrasta 88

Oumansky, Alexander Al Fresco 30; Black and White 30; Classic vs. Jazz 30; Dusky Melodies 30; Gypsy Land 30; Toyland 30

Oury, Gérard La Main Chaude 59; La Menace • The Menace 60; Crime Does Not Pay • Le Crime Ne Paie Pas • The Gentle Art of Murder 62; Colpo Grosso Ma Non Troppo • Le Corniaud • The Sucker • The Sucker...or How to Be Glad When You've Been Had 65; Don't Look Now • Don't Look Now...We're Being Shot At! • La Grande Vadrouille 66; The Brain • Le Cerveau 69; Delusions of Grandeur • La Folie des Grandeurs 71; The Adventures of Rabbi Jacob • Les Aventures de Rabbi Jacob • The Mad Adventures of Rabbi Jacob 73; La Carapate 78; Le Coup de Parapluie 80; Ace of Aces • L'As des As 82; La Vengeance du Serpent à Plumes 84; Lévi et Goliath • Levy and Goliath • Lévy et Goliath 86; Vanille Fraise 89

Ousseini Médecines et Médecins 76*; Le Griot Badye 77*

Ovanessian, Arby Le Tablier Brode de Ma Mère S'Étale dans Ma Vie 85

Ovcharov, Sergei Impossible Things • Nebyvalshina 86; Left-Hander • Levsha 87

Ove, Horace Pressure 76; Stretch Hunter 80; Playing Away 86

Owen, Cliff The Devil Inside • Offbeat 60; A Prize of Arms 61; The Wrong Arm of the Law 62; A Man Could Get Killed • Welcome, Mr. Beddoes 66*; That Riviera Touch 66; The Magnificent Two • What Happened at Campo Grande? 67; The Return of She • The Vengeance of She 67; Get Charlie Tully • Ooh...You Are Awful 72; Steptoe and Son 72; No Sex Please—We're British 73; The Adventures of Tom Jones • The Bawdy Adventures of Tom Jones 75

Owen, Don The Runner 62; Nobody Waved Goodbye 64; High Steel 66; Notes for a Film About Donna and Gail 66; The Ernie Game 67; Partners 67; Unfinished Business 84; Turnabout 86

Owen, Ruth Bryan Once Upon a Time 22

Owens, Richard Un Killer per Sua Maestà • Le Tueur Aime les Bonbons 68*; All'Ovest di Sacramento 71

Owensby, Earl Chain Gang 85

Oz, Frank The Dark Crystal 82*; The Muppets Take Manhattan 84; Little Shop of Horrors 86; Dirty Rotten Scoundrels 88

Ozep, Fedor Miss Mend 26*; Earth in Chains • The Yellow Pass • The Yellow Ticket • Zemlya v Plenu 28; Der Lebende Leichnam • The Living Corpse • Zhivoi Trup 28; The Brothers Karamazov • Karamazov • Der Mörder Dimitri Karamasoff • Murder of Karamazov • The Murderer Dmitri Karamazov 31; Mirages de Paris 33; Amok 34; Betrayal • Tarakanova 37; La Dame de Pique • The Queen of Spades 37; Gibraltar • It Happened in Gibraltar 38; The Music Master • Le Père Chopin 43; She Who Dares • Three Russian Girls 43*; La Forteresse • Whispering City 47

Ozer, Muammar Bir Avuç Cennet • A Handful of Paradise 86; Cloud in Love • Kara Sevdeli Bulut 89

Ozerov, Yuri In the Nikitsky Botanical Garden 52; Circus Daredevils • Daring Circus Youth 53*; Holiday Night 54; The Son 55; Kochubei 58; Fortuna 59; The Big Road 63; The Breakthrough • Liberation, Part Two 68; The Bulge of Fire • Liberation, Part One 68; The Direction of Main Strike • Liberation, Part Three 70; Battle for Berlin • Liberation, Part Four 71; The Last Assault • Liberation, Part Five 71; Olympic Visions • Visions of Eight 72*; The Great Battle 74; The Soldiers of Freedom 76*; Boj om Moskva • The Struggle for Moscow 85

Özgentürk, Ali At • The Horse • Horse, My Horse 82; Bekçi • The Guard 85; Su Da Yanar • Water Also Burns 87

Ozores, Mariano El Liguero Mágico 80; Brujas Mágicas 81

Ozu, Yasujiro Sword of Penitence • Zange no Yaiba 27; Body Beautiful • Nikutai Bi 28; A Couple on the Move • Hikkoshi Fūfu 28; Dreams of Youth • Wakodo no Yume 28; Kabocha • Pumpkin 28; Nyōbo Funshitsu • Wife Lost 28; Daigaku wa Deta Keredo • I Graduated, But... 29; Days of Youth • Wakaki Hi 29; Fighting Friends • Fighting Friends, Japanese Style • Wasei Kenka Tomodachi 29; Kaisha-In Seikatsu • The Life of an Office Worker 29; A Straightforward Boy • Tokkan Kozō 29; Takara no Yama • Treasure Mountain 29; Ashi ni Sawatta Kōun • Lost Luck • Luck Touched My Legs 30; Erogami no Onryō • The Revengeful Spirit of Eros 30; Hogaraka ni Ayume • Walk Cheerfully 30; I Failed, But... • I Flunked, But... • Rakudai wa Shita Keredo 30; Introduction to Marriage • Kekkon-Gaku Nyūmon 30; The Lady and Her Favorites • The Lady and the Beard • Shukujo to Hige 30; Ojōsan • Young Miss 30; Sono Yo no Tsuma • That Night's Wife 30; Beauty's Sorrows • Bijin Aishū 31; The Chorus of Tokyo • Tokyo Chorus • Tōkyō no Gasshō 31; Haru wa Gofujin Kara • Spring Comes from the Ladies • Spring Comes with the Ladies 32; I Was Born, But... • Umarete wa Mita Keredo 32; Mata Au Hi Made • Until the Day We Meet Again 32; Seishun no Yume Ima Izuko • Where Are the Dreams of Youth? • Where Now Are the Dreams of Youth? 32; Dekigokoro • Passing Fancy 33; Dragnet Girl • Hijōsen no Onna • Women on the Firing Line 33; Tōkyō no Onna • A Tokyo Woman • Woman of

Tokyo 33; Haha o Kōwazu-Ya • A Mother Ought to Be Loved • A Mother Should Be Loved 34; Hakoiri Musume • An Innocent Maid • The Young Virgin 34; Story of Floating Weeds • Ukigusa Monogatari 34; An Inn in Tokyo • Tōkyō no Yado 35; Tōkyō Yoi Toko • Tokyo's a Nice Place 35; College Is a Nice Place • Daigaku Yoi Toko 36; Hitori Musuko • The Only Son 36; Shukujo wa Nani o Wasuretaka • What Did the Lady Forget? 37; The Brothers and Sisters of the Toda Family • The Toda Brothers and Sisters • Toda-Ke no Kyōdai 41; Chichi Ariki • There Was a Father 42; Nagaya no Shinshi Roku • The Record of a Tenement Gentleman 47; A Hen in the Wind • Kaze no Naka no Mendori 48; Banshūn • Late Spring 49; Bakushū • Early Summer 50; Munekata Shimai • The Munekata Sisters 50; The Flavor of Green Tea Over Rice • Ochazuke no Aji • Tea and Rice 52; Their First Trip to Tokyo • Tōkyō Monogatari • Tokyo Story 53; Early Spring • Sōshun 56; Tōkyō Boshoku • Tokyo Twilight • Twilight in Tokyo 57; Equinox Flower • Higanbana 58; Drifting Weeds • The Duckweed Story • Floating Weeds • Tales of the Floating Weeds • Ukigusa 59; Good Morning • Ohayō • Too Much Talk 59; Akibiyori • Late Autumn 60; The Autumn of the Kohayagawa Family • Early Autumn • The End of Summer • Kohayagawa-Ke no Aki • The Last of Summer 61; An Autumn Afternoon • Samma no Aji • Sanma no Aji • The Taste of Mackerel • The Widower 62

Pabst, G. W. Der Schatz • The Treasure 23; Countess Donelli • Gräfin Donelli 24; Die Freudlose Gasse • The Joyless Street • The Street of Sorrow 25; Geheimnisse einer Seele • Secrets of a Soul 25; Don't Play with Love • Man Spielt Nicht mit der Liebe • One Does Not Play with Love 26; Die Liebe der Jeanne Ney • The Love of Jeanne Ney • Lusts of the Flesh 27; Abwege • Begierde • Crisis • Desire 28; Die Büchse der Pandora • Lulu • Pandora's Box 28; The Diary of a Lost Girl • Das Tagebuch einer Verlorenen 29; Die Weisse Hölle vom Piz Palü • The White Hell of Pitz Palu 29*; Comrades of 1918 • Four from the Infantry • Vier von der Infanterie • The Western Front, 1918 • Westfront 1918 30; Scandalous Eva • Skandal um Eva 30; The Beggar's Opera • Die Dreigroschenoper • The Threepenny Opera 31; Comradeship • Kameradschaft • La Tragédie de la Mine 31; L'Opéra de Quat'Sous 31; Adventures of Don Quixote • Don Quichotte • Don Quixote 32; L'Atlantide • Die Herrin von Atlantis • Lost Atlantis • The Mistress of Atlantis • Queen of Atlantis 32; Du Haut en Bas • From Top to Bottom • High and Low 33; A Modern Hero 34*; Mademoiselle Docteur • Salonique Nid d'Espions • Spies from Salonika • Street of Shadows 36; Le Drame de Shanghai • The Shanghai Drama 37; Jeunes Filles en Détresse 39;

The Actors • Comedians • Komödianten • The Players 41; Paracelsus 43; In Name der Menschlichkeit • Der Prozess • The Trial 47; Geheimnisvolle Tiefen • Mysterious Shadows 49; La Voce del Silenzio • The Voice of Silence 52; Cose da Pazzi • Droll Stories 53; Afraid to Live • Afraid to Love • Das Bekenntnis der Ina Kahr • The Confession of Ina Kahr 54; Es Geschah am 20. Juli • Jackboot Mutiny 55; The Last Ten Days • The Last Ten Days of Adolf Hitler • Der Letzte Akt • Ten Days to Die 55; Ballerina • Licht in der Finsternis • Rosen für Bettina 56; Durch die Wälder, Durch die Auen 56

Padget, Calvin Jackson see *Ferroni, Giorgio*

Padrón, Juan Vampires in Havana • Vampiros en la Habana 85

Page, Anthony Inadmissible Evidence 68; Alpha Beta 73; I Never Promised You a Rose Garden 77; Absolution • Murder by Confession 78; The Lady Vanishes 79; Forbidden 85

Page, Will The Course of True Love 16; The Gentle Art of Fishing 16; Sandy at Home 16; Sandy's Suspicion 16; A String of Pearls 16; When Flirting Didn't Pay 16

Pages, Jean The Story of the Vatican 41

Paget, Robert Drummer of Vengeance 74

Pagliero, Marcello Desiderio • Woman 43*; 07 Taxi 43; Roma, Città Libera 46; Un Homme Marche dans la Ville 49; Les Amants de Bras-Mort 50; L'Encyclopédie Filmée • L'Encyclopédie Filmée—Alchimie, Azur, Absence 51*; La Rose Rouge 51; Daughters of Destiny • Destinées • Love, Soldiers and Women 52*; La P… Respectueuse • La Putain Respectueuse • The Respectful Prostitute 52*; Vergine Modrna 54; Vestire gli Ignudi 54; Chéri-Bibi 55; L'Odyssée du Capitaine Steve • La Vallée du Paradis • Walk Into Paradise 56; Twenty Thousand Leagues Across the Land • Vingt Mille Lieues Sur la Terre 60

Pagnol, Marcel Direct au Cœur 33*; Le Gendre de Monsieur Poirier 33; Jofroi • Ways of Love 33; Léopold le Bien-Aimé 33; Angel • Angèle 34; L'Article 330 34; Le Voyage de Monsieur Perrichon 34; César 35; Cigalon 35; Merlusse 35; Topaze 36; Harvest • Regain 37; The Baker's Wife • La Femme du Boulanger 38; Heartbeat • Le Schpountz 38; La Fille du Puisatier • The Well-Digger's Daughter 40; Nais 45; L'Amore • Love • Ways of Love • Woman 48*; La Belle Meunière 48*; Topaze 50; Manon des Sources • Manon of the Springs 52; Letters from My Windmill • Les Lettres de Mon Moulin 54

Pai, Ching-jui Four Moods • Hsi Nu Ai Le 70*; Ta Luan-Hui • The Wheel of Life 83*

Paige, Alain Taxi Boy 86

Painlevé, Jean Évolution de l'Œuf d'Épinoche (Gastroteus Aculeatus) de la Fécondation à l'Éclosion • Œuf d'Épinoche 22; La Daphnie 25; Le Sérum du Docteur Hormet 25; La Pieuvre 26; Bernard l'Er-

mite 27; L'Inconnue des Six Jours 27; Les Oursins 28; Les Crabes 29; Les Crevettes 29; Le Hyas • Hyas et Sténorinque 29; Mouvements Intraprotoplasmiques de l'Élodéa Canadensis • Mouvements Protoplasmiques dans les Cellules d'Élodéa Canadensis en Milieux Isotoniques, Hypertoniques, Hypotoniques 29; Reviviscence d'un Chien 29; Caprelles et Pantopèdes 30; Ruptures de Fibres 31; Électrolyse du Nitrate d'Argent • Électrophorèse du Nitrate d'Argent 32; Évolution d'un Grain d'Argent dans une Émulsion Photographique 33; L'Hippocampe 33; Corethre 35; Culture des Tissus • La Culture des Tissus et Formation de Macrocytes 35; Barbe-Bleue 36*; Microscopie à Bord d'un Bateau de Pêche 36; Voyage dans le Ciel 36*; Images Mathémathiques de la Quatrième Dimension 37; L'Évolution Géologique de la Chaîne des Alpes 38; Images Mathémathiques de la Lutte pour la Vie 38; Similitudes de Longueurs et des Vitesses 38; La Chirurgie Correctrice et Réparatrice 39; Solutions Françaises 39; Le Vampire 45; Jeux d'Enfants 46; Assassins d'Eau Douce 47; Notre Planète la Terre 47; L'Œuvre Scientifique de Pasteur • Pasteur 47*; Écriture de la Danse • Écriture du Mouvement 48; Solutions Françaises 48; Les Oursins 53; Albinisme 55; Réactions Nutritives d'Haliotis: Réactions d'Haliotis de Clamys et de Différents Échinodermes à la Présence de Certains Stellérides 56; Influence de la Lumière sur les Mouvements de l'Œuf de Truite 57; L'Astérie 58; Éleutheria en Culture 58; Embrogynèse d'Orizias Latipes 59; Comment Naissent les Méduses 60; Les Danseuses da la Mer 60; Destructeurs Marins des Bois 64; Histoire des Crevettes 64; Arénicole 65; Méthode de Gymnastique Penchante 65; Les Amours de la Pieuvre 67; Dynamique de l'Évolution de l'Œuf de Pieuvre 67

Pakdivijit, Chalong S.T.A.B. 76

Pakkasvirta, Jaakko Night and Day • Night or Day • Yö vai Päivä 62*; Baron X • X-Paroni 64*; The Castle • Linna 86

Pakula, Alan J. Pookie • The Sterile Cuckoo 69; Klute 71; Liebe, Schmerz und das Ganze Verdammte Zeug • Love and Pain and the Whole Damn Thing • Love and Pain and the Whole Darn Thing • The Widower 72; The Parallax View 74; All the President's Men 76; Comes a Horseman 78; Starting Over 79; Rollover 81; Sophie's Choice 82; Dream Lover 86; Orphans 87; See You in the Morning 89; Presumed Innocent 90

Pal, George On Parade 36; Love on the Range 37; She Bumps 37; Sky Pirates 37; What Ho! 37; The Ship of the Ether 38; South Sea Sweetheart 38; Dipsy Gipsy 41; The Gay Knighties 41; Hoola Boola 41; Rhythm in the Ranks 41; Western Daze 41; Jasper and the Choo Choo 42; Jasper and the Haunted House • Jasper's Haunted House 42; Jasper and the Watermelons 42; The Little Broadcast 42; Mr. Strauss Takes a Walk 42; The Sky Princess 42; Tulips

Paolucci, Giovanni Shamed 49; Il Relitto • The Wastrel 60*

Papadopoulos, John Matchless 74

Papas, Michael The Private Right 67; The Lifetaker 75; Avrianos Polemistis • Tomorrow's Warrior 81

Papastathis, Lakis Letters from America 72; Ton Kero tou Ellinon • When the Greeks Ruled 81; Theofilos 87

Papatakis, Nico see Papatakis, Nikos

Papatakis, Nikos Les Abysses 62; Les Pâtres du Désordre • The Shepherds of Confusion • Thanos and Despina 67; Gloria Mundi 75; The Photograph • I Photographia 86

Papayannidis, Takis Birthday Town • Yenethlia Poli 87

Papić, Krsto Handcuffs • Lisice 70; Izbavitelj • The Rat Saviour • The Redeemer 77; The Secret of Nikola Tesla • Tajna Nikole Tesle • Tesla 80; My Uncle's Legacy • Život Sa Stricem 88

Papoušek, Jaroslav The Best Age • The Most Beautiful Age • Nejkrásnější Věk 68

Pappas, Robert Kane Now I Know 88

Parachuri Prajaswamyam 88

Paradise, Michael J. see Paradisi, Giulio

Paradisi, Giulio Il Visitatore • The Visitor 79

Paradjanian, Sergei see Paradzhanov, Sergei

Paradjanov, Sergei see Paradzhanov, Sergei

Paradzhanov, Sergei Moldavian Fairy Tale • Moldavskaia Skazka 51; Andriesh 54*; Ataliva Uzhvii 57; The Ballad • Dumka 57; Golden Hands 57; The First Lad • Pervyi Paren 58; Ukrainian Rhapsody • Ukrainskaia Rapsodiia • Ukrainskaja Rapsodija 61; Flower on the Stone • Tsvetok na Kamne • Zwetok na Kamne 62; Shadows of Forgotten Ancestors • Shadows of Our Ancestors • Shadows of Our Forgotten Ancestors • Teni Zabytykh Predkov 64; The Color of Pomegranates • Nran Gouyne • Red Pomegranate • Sayat Nova • Tsvet Granata 68; Achraroumès • Retour à la Vie • Return to Life 78; The Legend of Suram Fortress • The Legend of the Suram Fortress • Legenda Suramskoi Kreposti 84*; Arabeski na Temu Pirosmani • Arabesques on the Pirosmani Theme 85*; Ashik Kerib • Traveling Artists 88*

Parashar, Punkaj Jalwa 87

Parco, Paul S. Pucker Up and Bark Like a Dog 90

Pardo, Rafael Fuster In der Wüste • In the Wilderness 87

Parelle, L. de la see De la Parelle, L.

Parenti, Neri The Fireman • I Pompieri 85; Fracchia Contro Dracula • Fracchia vs. Dracula 85; School for Thieves • Scuola di Ladri 86; School for Thieves II • Scuola di Ladri II 87; Superfantozzi 87; Casa Mia, Casa Mia 88

Pareto, Willy see Freda, Riccardo

Parfitt, Eric The New Frontiersmen 37

Parikka, Pekka Pohjanmaa 88; Talvisota • The Winter War 89

Paris, Domonic Dracula's Last Rites •

Last Rites 80; Splitz 84

Paris, Henry see Metzger, Radley

Paris, Jerry Don't Raise the Bridge, Lower the River 68; How Sweet It Is! 68; Never a Dull Moment 68; Viva Max! 69; The Grasshopper • The Passing of Evil 70; Star Spangled Girl 71; Leo and Loree 80; Police Academy II: Their First Assignment 85; Police Academy III: Back in Training 86

Parish, Richard C. The Magic Christmas Tree 64

Park, Choi-su The Rain Only When at Night 79; The Painful Maturity 80; The Wild Dog 82; The Bell of Nirvana 83; Mother 85; The Pillar of Mist 86

Park, Ida May The Grip of Jealousy 16*; Bondage 17; Broadway Love 17; Fires of Rebellion 17; The Flashlight 17; The Rescue 17; Bread 18; The Grand Passion 18; Her Fling 18; Model's Confession 18; The Risky Road 18; The Vanity Pool 18; The Amazing Wife 19; Bonnie May 20*; The Butterfly Man 20*; The Midlanders 20*

Park, John The Private Life of Mussolini 38

Park, Lester Sidewalks of New York 23

Park, Richard L.A. Streetfighters • Ninja Turf 86

Park, Yoon Kyo The Ghost • Myonuriui Han 71; Bloody Smile • Mangryongui Kok 80; Mangryongui Wechingturesu • Wedding Dress of the Ghost 81; Two Women from the Netherworld 82

Parke, William Great Men Among Us 15; Other People's Money 16; Prudence the Pirate 16; The Shine Girl 16; The Cigarette Girl 17; A Crooked Romance 17; The Last of the Carnabys 17; Miss Nobody 17; Over the Hill 17; The Streets of Illusion 17; Convict 993 18; The Key to Power 18; The Yellow Ticket 18; Out of the Storm • Tower of Ivory 20; The Paliser Case 20; A Woman Who Understood 20; Beach of Dreams 21; The Clean Up 23; Legally Dead 23; A Million to Burn 23

Parker, Alan Footsteps 73; Our Cissy 73; Evacuees 75; Bugsy Malone 76; Midnight Express 78; Fame 80; Shoot the Moon 81; Pink Floyd — The Wall • The Wall 82; Birdy 84; A Turnip Head's Guide to the British Cinema 87; Angel Heart 87; Mississippi Burning 88; Come See the Paradise 90

Parker, Albert The Food Gamblers 17; For Valour 17; The Haunted House 17; Her Excellency the Governor 17; The Man Hater 17; Annexing Bill 18; Arizona 18*; From Two to Six 18; The Other Woman 18; The Secret Code 18; Shifting Sands 18; Waifs 18; Eyes of Youth 19; The Knickerbocker Buckaroo 19; The Branded Woman 20; Love's Redemption 21; Moriarty • Sherlock Holmes 22; The Rejected Woman 24; Second Youth 24; The Black Pirate 26*; The Love of Sunya 27; After Dark 32; The Right to Live 33; Rolling in Money 34; The Third Clue 34; Late Extra 35; The Riverside Murder 35; White Lilac 35; Blind Man's Bluff 36; Troubled Waters 36; The

£5 Man 37; Strange Experiment 37; There Was a Young Man 37; The Crime of Peter Frame • Second Thoughts 38; Murder in the Family 38

Parker, Ben George Washington Carver 40; Bourbon Street Shadows • Invisible Avenger 58*; Frigid Wife • A Modern Marriage 62; The Shepherd of the Hills • Thunder Mountain 64

Parker, Bonnie Bass Bus II 83*

Parker, Cary The Girl in the Picture 85

Parker, Claire Night on a Bare Mountain • Night on Bald Mountain • Une Nuit sur le Mont Chauve 33*; La Belle au Bois Dormant 35*; Lingner Werke 35*; Opta Empfangt 35*; L'Orchestre Automatique 35*; Parade des Chapeaux 36*; Le Trône de France 36*; La Crème Simon 37*; L'Eau d'Évian 37*; Franck Aroma 37*; Grands Feux 37*; Huilor 37*; Les Vêtements Sigrand 37*; Balatum 38*; Les Cigarettes Bastos 38*; Les Fonderies Martin 38*; Les Oranges de Jaffa 38*; Cenpa 39*; Les Gaines Roussel 39*; Gulf Stream 39*; En Passant 43*; Fumées 51*; Masques 52*; Esso 54*; Nocturne 54*; Pure Beauté 54*; Rimes 54*; Le Buisson Ardent 55*; The Earth's Cap • La Sève de la Terre 55*; Bain d'X • Bendix 56*; Osram 56*; Quatre Temps 56*; Cent pour Cent 57*; Constance 57*; Anonyme 58*; Automation 58*; La Dauphine Java 60*; Divertissement 60*; À Propos de Jivago 62*; Le Nez • The Nose 63*; L'Eau 66*; Pictures at an Exhibition • Tableaux d'une Exposition 72*; L'Écran d'Épingles 73*; Three Themes • Trois Thèmes 79*

Parker, David, Jr. Il Ragazzo dal Kimono d'Oro 88*

Parker, Francine F.T.A. 72

Parker, Frank Tally Ho! 01

Parker, Joe Eighteen and Anxious • No Greater Sin 57; The Hot Angel 58

Parker, John Daughter of Horror • Dementia 55

Parker, Morrie The Wackiest Wagon Train in the West 76

Parker, Morten The Stratford Adventure 54

Parker, Norton The Pace That Kills 28; The Road to Ruin 28

Parker, Percy G. see Hoven, Adrian

Parker, Tom Amazing Love Secret 75

Parkes, Walter F. The California Reich 77*

Park-huen, Kwan see Kwan, Park-huen

Parkhurst, Michael Moonfire 70

Parkinson, H. B. The Law Divine 20*; After the Ball 21; Belle of the Gambling Den 21; Home Sweet Home 21; The Man Who Came Back 21; Bleak House 22; Crushing the Drug Traffic 22; Fagin 22; In the Signal Box 22; Macbeth 22; Married to a Mormon 22; The Mormon Peril • Trapped by the Mormons 22; Nancy 22; The Old Actor's Story 22; Rowing to Win 22; The Leading Man • The Only Man 25; Bindle at the Party 26; Bindle in Charge 26; Bindle Introduced 26; Bindle, Matchmaker 26; Bindle, Millionaire 26; Bindle's

Cocktail 26; The Fighting Gladiator 26*; Find the Woman 26*; For a Woman's Eyes 26*; Fun at the Fair 26; The Game Chicken 26; Gypsy Courage 26*; The Life Story of Charles Chaplin 26; The Phantom Foe 26*; The Simple Life 26; When Giants Fought 26*; The Bohemian Girl 27; Carmen 27; Daughter of the Regiment 27; Faust 27; Lily of Killarney 27; Maritana 27; Martha 27; On with the Dance 27*; Rigoletto 27; The Ring 27; Samson and Delilah 27; La Traviata 27; Abide with Me 28*; Ave Maria 28*; Laughter and Tears 28; Lead Kindly Light 28*; The Lost Chord 28*; Rock of Ages 28*; The Rosary 28*; Romantic England 29

Parkinson, Tom Disciple of Death 72

Parks, Gordon Learn, Baby, Learn • The Learning Tree 69; Shaft 71; Shaft's Big Score! 72; The Super Cops 73; Leadbelly 76; Moments Without Proper Names 86

Parks, Gordon, Jr. Superfly 72; Thomasine and Bushrod 74; Three the Hard Way 74; Aaron Loves Angela 75

Parks, Michael The Return of Josey Wales 86*

Parmelee, E. Dean Aerial Warfare 18; Animated Technical Drawing 18; The Depth Bomb 18; Theory of the Hand Grenade 19; Theory of the Long Range Shell 19

Parmelee, Ted Pete Hothead 52; The Emperor's New Clothes 53; The Man on the Flying Trapeze 54; The Tell-Tale Heart 54; Four Wheels and No Brake 55

Parmentel, Noel Campaign Manager • Republicans—The New Breed 64*; Chiefs 69*

Parnicky, Stanislav The Cart Full of Pain • Kára Plná Bolesti 85; Južná Pošta 88

Parolini, Gianfranco La Furia di Ercole • The Fury of Hercules 60; The Fury of Samson • Samson • Sansone 60; The Old Testament 63; 79 A.D. 63; Gli Invincibili Tre • The Three Avengers 64; Mission to Hell with Secret Agent FX15 64; The Ten Gladiators 64; Johnny West il Mancino 65; The Fantastic Three • I Fantastici Tre Supermen 67; Se Incontri, Sartana Prega per la Tua Morte 68; Ehi, Amico...C'È Sabata, Hai Chiuso • Sabata 69; Sartana—Bete um Deinen Tod 69; Adiós, Sabata • The Bounty Hunters • Indio Black • Indio Black, Sai Che Ti Dico: Sei un Gran Figlio di... 70; E' Tornato Sabata...Hai Chiuso un'Altro Volto • The Return of Sabata 71; Sotto a Chi Tocca 72; God's Gun 76; Yeti 77

Parolini, Marilu As Distant As My Childhood • Aussi Loin Que Mon Enfance 68*

Parr, Larry A Soldier's Tale 88

Parra, Carlos Benito El Jovencito Drácula 75

Parra, Pim de la Paul Chevrolet and the Ultimate Hallucination • Paul Chevrolet en de Ultieme Hallucinatie 85; Als in een Roes • Intoxicated 87; Love Odyssey • Odyssée d'Amour 87

Parravicini, Florencio Melgarejo 37

Parriott, James D. Misfits of Science 85; Heart Condition 90

Parrish, David P. The Pledgemasters 71

Parrish, Robert German Manpower 43*; Cry Danger 51; The Mob • Remember That Face 51; Assignment in Paris • Assignment—Paris! 52*; The Lusty Men 52*; My Pal Gus 52; The San Francisco Story 52; Rough Shoot • Shoot First 53; The Purple Plain 54; Lucy Gallant • Oil Town 55; Fire Down Below 57; Saddle the Wind 58; The Wonderful Country 59; À la Française • In the French Style 62; The Day After • Up from the Beach 65; The Bobo 67; Casino Royale 67*; Duffy 68; Doppelgänger • The Far Side of the Sun • Journey to the Far Side of the Sun 69; A Town Called Bastard • A Town Called Hell 71; The Destructors • The Marseille Contract 74; Mississippi Blues • Pays d'Octobre 83*

Parrott, Charles see Chase, Charlie

Parrott, James The Lighter That Failed 27; Never the Dames Shall Meet 27; The Way of All Pants 27; All for Nothing 27; Blow by Blow 28*; Habeas Corpus 28; Ruby Lips 28; Should Married Men Go Home? 28*; Their Purple Moment 28; Two Tars 28*; Furnace Trouble 29; Happy Birthday 29; The Hoosegow 29; Lesson Number 1 29; The Perfect Day 29; Stewed, Fried and Boiled 29; The Sting of Stings 29; They Go Boom 29; Aerial Antics • Hog Wild 30; Another Fine Mess 30; Be Big 30; Below Zero 30; Blotto 30; Brats 30; The Laurel and Hardy Murder Case 30; Night Owls 30; Helpmates 31; Jailbirds • Pardon Us 31; One of the Smiths 31; The Panic Is On 31; The Pip from Pittsburgh 31; Rough Seas 31; Skip the Maloo! 31; What a Bozo! 31; The Chimp 32; County Hospital 32; Girl Grief 32; Mr. Bride 32; The Music Box 32; Young Ironsides 32; Now We'll Tell One 33; Twice Two 33; Twin Screws 33; A Duke for a Day 34; Mixed Nuts 34; Opened by Mistake 34; Penny from Panama 34; Washee Ironee 34; The Misses Stooge 35; Sing, Sister, Sing 35; The Tin Man 35; Treasure Blues 35

Parry, Gordon Bond Street 47; Third Time Lucky 48; The Gay Adventure • Golden Arrow • Three Men and a Girl 49; Now Barabbas... • Now Barabbas Was a Robber 49; Midnight Episode 50; Tom Brown's Schooldays 51; Another Chance • Twilight Women • Women of Twilight 52; Front Page Story 53; Innocents in Paris 53; Fast and Loose 54; A Yank in Ermine 55; Panic in the Parlor • Sailor Beware! 56; A Touch of the Sun 56; The Surgeon's Knife 57; Tread Softly Stranger 58; Friends and Neighbours 59; The Navy Lark 59

Parry, Hugh Governor Bradford • Governor William Bradford 38

Parry, Robert see Selander, Lesley

Parsons, Herbert R. The Romance of Dancing 38

Parsons, John Watched! 72

Parys, Armand see Lewis, Herschell Gordon

Pasasen, Spede Baron X • X-Paroni 64*

Pascal, Christine Zanzibar 89

Pascal, Gabriel Major Barbara 41*; Caesar and Cleopatra 44*; Caesar Against the Pirates 60

Pasinetti, Francesco Il Canale degli Angeli 34

Paskaljević, Goran The Beach Guard in Winter 76; The Dog That Liked Trains 78; The Days Are Passing 80; Poseban Tretman • Special Treatment 80; Twilight Time 83; The Illusory Summer of '68 84; Anđeo Čuvar • Guardian Angel 87

Pasolini, Pier Paolo Accattone! 61; Mamma Roma 62; RoGoPaG 62*; The Frenzy • La Rabbia 63*; On Location in Palestine • Sopraluoghi in Palestina 63; Assembly of Love • Comizi d'Amore • Love Meetings 64; L'Évangile Selon Saint-Matthieu • The Gospel According to St. Matthew • Il Vangelo Secondo Matteo 64; Hawks and Sparrows • The Hawks and the Sparrows • Uccellacci e Uccellini 66; Les Sorcières • Le Streghe • The Witches 66*; Amore e Rabbia • La Contestation • Love and Anger • Vangelo '70 67*; Edipo Re • Oedipus Rex 67; Appunti per un'Film Indiano • Appunti per un'Film sull'India 68; Capriccio all'Italiana 68*; Teorema • Theorem 68; Appunti per un'Orestiade Africana • Notes for an African Oresteia 69; Medea 69; Pig Pen • Pigsty • Il Porcile 69; Appunti per un Romanzo dell'Immondeza • Notes for a Lewd Novel 70; The Decameron • Il Decamerone 70; Le Mura di Sana • I Muri di Sana • The Walls of Sana 70; The Canterbury Tales • I Racconti di Canterbury 71; December 12, 1972 • Dodici Dicembre • Dodici Dicembre 1972 • 12 Dicembre 72*; The Arabian Nights • Il Fiore delle Mille e Una Notte • The Flower of the Arabian Nights • A Thousand and One Nights 74; Salò o Le Centoventi Giornate di Sodoma • Salo, or The 120 Days of Sodom • Salo—The 120 Days of Sodom 75

Pasquali, Ernesto Maria I Due Sergenti 08; Capitan Fracassa 09; Cirano di Bergerac 09; Ettore Fieramosca 09; Teodora, Imperatrice di Bisanzio 09; Zaza 09; Isabella d'Aragon 10; Il Carabiniere 11; Spartaco 11; La Porta Aperta 13; I Promessi Sposi 13; Passione Tzigane 16

Passendorfer, Jerzy Answer to Violence • Zamach 58

Passer, Ivan A Boring Afternoon • Fádní Odpoledne 65; Intimate Lighting • Intimní Osvětlení 65; The Legend of Beautiful Julia • Legenda o Krásné Julice 68; Addict • Born to Lose • Born to Win 71; Law and Disorder 74; An Ace Up My Sleeve • Crime and Passion 75; Silver Bears 77; Cutter and Bone • Cutter's Way 81; Creator 85; Haunted Summer 88

Pastina, Giorgio Streets of Sorrow 52; Journey to Love 53; Of Life and Love • Questa È la Vita 54*

Pastor, Susana Gregorio 85*

Pastore, Sergio Crisantemi per un Branco di Carogne • A Wreath for the Bandits 68; The Crimes of the Black Cat • Sette Scialli di Seta Gialla 72; I Mercenari Raccontano • The Mercenaries 85; Amore Inquieto di Maria • Maria's Restless Love 86; Crimes • Delitti 86

Pastrone, Giovanni Giordano Bruno • Giordano Bruno, Eroe di Valmy 08; La Maschera di Ferro 09; Agnese Visconti 10; La Caduta di Troia • The Fall of Troy 10; Lucia di Lammermoor 10; Manon Lescaut 10; Padre 12*; Tigris 13; Cabiria 14; Il Fuoco 15*; Maciste 15; Maciste Alpino 16*; Tigre Reale 16; The Hand of the Hun 17; Outwitting the Hun 18; Hedda Gabler 19; Maciste Atleta 19; Povere Bimbe 23

Pásztor, Béla Sárga Csikó • Yellow Boy 36; Evil Village • A Falu Rossza • The Village Rogue 37; Piros Bugyelláris • Red Purse 38

Pásztory, Miklós Lea Lyon • Lyon Lea 15*; Károly-Bakák 18*

Pataki, Michael Mansion of the Doomed • The Terror of Dr. Chaney 75

Pate, Michael Tim 79

Patel, Raju In the Shadow of Kilimanjaro 84

Patel, Sharad Amin—The Rise and Fall • The Rise and Fall of Idi Amin 81

Patellière, Denys de la see De la Patellière, Denys

Patil, Dinkar Bhatak Bhawani 88

Patino, Basilio Martín The Lost Paradise • Los Paraísos Perdidos 86; Madrid 87

Paton, Stuart Conscience 15; Court-Martialed 15; The White Terror 15; Elusive Isabel 16; 20,000 Leagues Under the Sea 16; Beloved Jim 17; Like Wildfire 17; The Border Raiders 18; The Girl in the Dark 18; The Marriage Lie 18*; The Wine Girl 18*; The Devil's Trail 19; The Little Diplomat 19; Wanted at Headquarters 20; The Conflict 21; Reputation 21; The Torrent 21; The Black Bag 22; Man to Man 22; The Man Who Married His Own Wife 22; The Married Flapper 22; One Wonderful Night 22; Wolf Law 22; Bavu 23; Burning Words 23; The Love Brand 23; The Scarlet Car 23; The Night Hawk 24; Baited Trap 26; Forest Havoc 26; Frenzied Flames 26; The Lady from Hell 26; The Wolf Hunters 26; Fangs of Destiny 27; The Bullet Mark 28; The Four-Footed Ranger 28; The Hound of Silver Creek 28; Air Police 31; Chinatown After Dark 31; First Aid • In Strange Company 31; The Guest House • In Old Cheyenne 31; Hell Bent for 'Frisco 31; Is There Justice? 31; Mounted Fury 31; The Mystery Trooper 31; The Silent Code 35; Thunderbolt 35; Clipped Wings 38

Patrick, Diana The Man Who Shot Christmas 85

Patrick, Nigel How to Murder a Rich Uncle 57*; Johnny Nobody 61

Patrick, Robert Swamp Country 66; Road to Nashville 67; From Nashville with Music 69*

Patris, S. Gerard Artur Rubinstein—L'Amour de la Vie • Artur Rubinstein—

The Love of Life • Love of Life 68*

Patrizi, Massimo Musketeers of the Sea 60

Patry, Pierre Petit Discours de la Méthode 63*; Trouble-Fête 64

Patterson, Garry How Willingly You Sing 75

Patterson, John D. The Legend of Earl Durand 74

Patterson, Pat The Electric Chair 77

Patterson, Ray Gobots: Battle of the Rock Lords 86

Patterson, Richard The Gentleman Tramp 75; The Day the Earth Got Stoned 78; J-Men Forever! 79

Pattinson, Michael Moving Out 82; Ground Zero 87*

Pattison, Barrie Zombie Brigade 88*

Patton, Phil The Snow Queen 59

Pattrea, Purnendu Letter from the Wife • Stir Patra 74

Patwardhan, Anand Bombay Our City • Hamara Shaher 85

Patzak, Peter Slaughterday 81; The Uppercrust 82; Der Joker • Lethal Obsession 88; Midnight Cop 89

Paul, Byron Lt. Robin Crusoe, U.S.N. 66

Paul, Fred The Angels of Mons 15*; Deadwood Dick and the Mormons 15*; Deadwood Dick Spoils Brigham Young 15*; Deadwood Dick's Detective Pard 15*; Deadwood Dick's Red Ally 15*; Deadwood Dick's Vengeance 15*; The Dop Doctor • The Love Trail 15*; The Face at the Telephone 15*; How Richard Harris Became Known As Deadwood Dick 15*; Infelice 15*; Dr. Wake's Patient 16; Her Greatest Performance 16; Lady Windermere's Fan 16; The Lyons Mail 16; The New Clown 16; The Second Mrs. Tanqueray 16; Still Waters Run Deep 16; The Vicar of Wakefield 16; Whoso Is Without Sin 16; Masks and Faces 17; The Duchess of Seven Dials 19; The House on the Marsh 19; The English Rose 20; Lady Tetley's Decree 20; The Lights of Home 20; The Little Welsh Girl 20; The Money Moon 20; Uncle Dick's Darling 20; Barbara Elopes 21*; A Bit of Black Stuff 21; The Curse of Westacott 21*; Delilah 21; The Flat 21; The Flirtations of Phyllis 21*; A Game for Two 21*; The Gentle Doctor 21; The Guardian of Honour 21; The Happy Pair 21; Her Romance 21; The Jest 21; The Joke That Failed 21*; The Last Appeal 21; Letters of Credit 21; Mary's Work 21*; The Nurse 21; The Oath 21; Polly 21; The Return 21; The Secret of the Safe 21; Six and Half a Dozen 21; The Sting of Death 21; That Love Might Last 21; The Upper Hand 21*; A Voice from the Dead 21; A Woman Misunderstood 21*; The Woman Upstairs 21; Brown Sugar 22; Castles in the Air • Let's Pretend 22; The Faithful Heart 22; If Four Walls Told 22; The Hotel Mouse 23; The Right to Strike 23; The Café l'Égypte 24; The Coughing Horror 24; Cragmire Tower 24; The Golden Pomegranates 24; The Green Mist 24; Greywater Park 24;

Karamaneh 24; The Midnight Summons 24; The Last Witness 25; A Madonna of the Cells 25; Ragan in Ruins 25; Guy of Warwick 26; Safety First 26; Thou Fool 26; The Luck of the Navy 27; The Light on the Wall 28; The Living Death 28; The Scarred Face 28; The Torture Cage 28; Under the Tide 28; The Zone of Death 28; The Broken Melody 29; In a Lotus Garden 31; Morita 31; Romany Love 31; Under the Palms 31

Paul, Heinz U-Boat 9 29; Student Sein 31; Zirkus Leben 32; Namensheirat 33; Tannenberg 34; Trenck 34; The Four Musketeers • Die Vier Musketiere 35; The Legend of William Tell 35; Immortal Melodies • Unsterbliche Melodien 38; Comrades at Sea • Kameraden auf See 39

Paul, John Hansel and Gretel 54

Paul, Stefan Reggae Sunsplash 79

Paul, Steven Falling in Love Again • In Love 80; Slapstick • Slapstick (Of Another Kind) 82

Paul, Stuart Emanon 86

Paul, Val Hearts Up! 20; Sundown Slim 20; West Is West 20; Good Men and True 22; The Kick Back 22; Canyon of the Fools 23; Crashin' Thru 23; Desert Driven 23; The Miracle Baby 23

Paula, Francisco de see De Paula, Francisco

Paulin, Jean-Paul La Femme Nue 33

Pauls, Cristián Sinfin, Death Is No Solution • Sinfin, la Muerta No Es Ninguna Solución 87

Paulsen, David The Killer Behind the Mask • Savage Weekend • The Upstate Murders 76; Murder by Mail • Schizoid 80

Paulus, Wolfram Heidenlöcher • Hideouts 86; Nachsaison 88

Pauly, Marco Black Mic-Mac 2 88

Paviot, Paul Pantalaskas 59; Portrait-Robot 60

Pavithran Uppu 87

Pavlou, George Underworld 85; Rawhead Rex 86

Pavlović, Sveta Orchestra of Youth • Orkestar Jedne Mladosti 86

Pavlović, Živojin The Enemy 65; The Return 66; The Rats Wake Up 67; When I'm Dead and White 68; Na Putu za Katangu • On the Road to Katanga 87

Paylow, Clark Ring of Terror 62

Payne, Douglas Potter's Clay 22*

Payne, J. H. With the Aid of a Rogue 27

Payne, John They Ran for Their Lives 68

Payne, John M. The Antagonists 16; Doing Her Bit 16; The Economists 16; The Sacrament of Confirmation 24

Paz, Miguel Caronatto see Caronatto Paz, Miguel

Pazzaglia, Riccardo Separated at Home • Separati in Casa 86

Peacock, Leslie T. The Midnight Flower 23

Pead, Greg see Serious, Yahoo

Peak, Barry The Big Hurt 86; As Time Goes By 87

Peake, Bladon You're Telling Me! 41

Pearce, A. Leslie *see Pearce, Leslie*

Pearce, Leslie The Delightful Rogue 29*; The Fall Guy • Trust Your Wife 30; Meet the Wife 31; The Dentist 32; Can You Hear Me Mother? 35; Shovel Up a Bit More Coal • The Stoker 35; You Must Get Married 36

Pearce, Michael James Joyce's Women 85; Initiation 87

Pearce, Perce Snow White and the Seven Dwarfs 37*; Victory Through Air Power 43*

Pearce, Richard Heartland 79; Threshold 81; Country 84; No Mercy 86; The Long Walk Home 90

Pearse, John Moviemakers 70

Pearson, George In Dickens' Land 12; Fair Sussex 13; A Fishergirl's Folly 13; The Fool 13; The Great Mine Disaster • Heroes of the Mine 13; Kentish Industries 13; A Lighter Burden 13; Lynmouth 13; Mr. Henpeck's Dilemma 13; Rambles Through Hopland 13; The Sentence of Death 13; Where History Has Been Written 13; Buttons 14; The Cause of the Great European War 14; Christmas Day in the Workhouse 14; Incidents of the Great European War 14; The Life of Lord Roberts VC 14; The Live Wire 14; A Son of France 14; A Study in Scarlet 14; Wonderful Nights with Peter Kinema 14; A Cinema Girl's Romance 15; John Halifax, Gentleman 15; The True Story of the Lyons Mail 15; Ultus 1: The Townsend Mystery • Ultus—The Man from the Dead • Ultus 2: The Ambassador's Diamond 15; For the Empire 16; Sally Bishop 16; Ultus and the Grey Lady • Ultus 3: The Grey Lady • Ultus 4: The Traitor's Fate 16; Ultus and the Secret of the Night • Ultus 5: The Secret of the Night 16; Canadian Officers in the Making 17; The Man Who Made the Army 17; Ultus and the Three Button Mystery • Ultus 6: The Three Button Mystery • Ultus 7 17; The Better 'Ole • The Better 'Ole, or The Romance of Old Bill • Carry On 18; The Kiddies in the Ruins 18; Ultus and the Phantom of Pengate 18; Hughie at the Victory Derby 19; Garryowen 20; Nothing Else Matters 20; Mary Find-the-Gold 21; Me and My Girl • Mord Em'ly 21; Squibs 21; Squibs Wins the Calcutta Sweep 22; The Wee MacGregor's Sweetheart 22; Love, Life and Laughter 23; Squibs' Honeymoon 23; Squibs MP 23; Reveille 24; Mr. Preedy and the Countess 25; Satan's Sister 25; Blinkeyes 26; The Little People 26; Huntingtower 27; Love's Option 28; Auld Lang Syne 29; East Lynne on the Western Front 31; I Love a Lassie 31; I Love to Be a Sailor 31; Nanny 31; Roaming in the Gloaming 31; The Saftest of the Family 31; She Is Ma Daisy • She Is My Daisy 31; Somebody's Waiting for Me 31; Tobermory 31; Wee Hoose Amang the Heather 31; The Third String 32; The Pointing Finger 33; The River Wolves 33; A Shot in the Dark 33; Four Masked Men 34; Open All Night 34; Whispering Tongues 34; The Ace of Spades 35; Checkmate

35; Gentleman's Agreement 35; Jubilee Window 35; Once a Thief 35; That's My Uncle 35; Midnight at Madame Tussaud's • Midnight at the Wax Museum 36; Murder by Rope 36; The Secret Voice 36; Wednesday's Luck 36; The Fatal Hour 37; Mother of Men 38; Old Soldiers 38; Souvenirs 38; British Made 39; A British Family in Peace and War 40; Land of Water 40; Rural School 40; Take Cover 40; An African in London 41; British Youth 41

Pearson, Peter Paperback Hero 73; Only God Knows 74

Pearson, W. B. Hell's Crater 18

Pecas, Max Daniella by Night • De Quoi Tu Te Mêles, Daniéla! • Zarte Haut in Schwarzer Seide 62; Douce Violence • Sweet Ecstasy • Sweet Violence 62; Cinq Filles en Furie • Five Wild Girls • Five Wild Kids 66; Espions a l'Affût • Heat at Midnight • Heat of Midnight 66; I Am Frigid . . . Why? 73; Brigade des Mœurs 85

Pech, Antonín Faust 12

Peck, Raoul Haitian Corner 88

Peck, Ron Nighthawks 78*; Empire State 87

Peckinpah, Sam The Deadly Companions • Trigger Happy 61; Guns in the Afternoon • Ride the High Country 61; Major Dundee 65; The Wild Bunch 69; The Ballad of Cable Hogue 70; Straw Dogs 71; The Getaway 72; Junior Bonner 72; Pat Garrett and Billy the Kid 73; Bring Me the Head of Alfredo Garcia 74; The Killer Elite 75; Cross of Iron 77; Convoy 78; The Osterman Weekend 83

Peclet, Georges Pirate Submarine 52

Pedelty, Donovan Flame in the Heather 35; The Luck of the Irish 35; School for Stars 35; The Early Bird 36; Irish and Proud of It 36; Behind Your Back 37; False Evidence 37; First Night 37; Landslide 37; Bedtime Story 38; Murder Tomorrow 38

Pedersen, John Tuesday Wednesday 87

Peebles, Melvin van *see Van Peebles, Melvin*

Peebles, Mort The Fly Cop 20*

Peerce, Larry One Potato, Two Potato 64; The Big T.N.T. Show 66; The Incident 67; Goodbye, Columbus 69; The Sporting Club 71; A Separate Peace 72; Ash Wednesday 73; The Other Side of the Mountain • A Window to the Sky 74; Two Minute Warning 76; The Other Side of the Mountain Part 2 77; The Bell Jar 79; Why Would I Lie? 80; Love Child 82; Hard to Hold 83; Wired 89

Peers, Victor Carry On 27*; Shiraz 28*; Sacrifice 29

Peeters, Barbara The Dark Side of Tomorrow 70*; Bury Me an Angel 71; Just the Two of Us 75; Summer School Teachers 75; Starhops 78; Humanoids from the Deep • Humanoids of the Deep • Monster 80

Pehrsson, Emil A. Baldvins Bröllop • Baldwin's Wedding 38*; Skanör-Falsterbo 39; Kalle på Spången 40

Pei, Vivian Iron Bread 70

Peixoto, Mario Limite 30

Pekalski, Aleksander Cabman No. 13 37

Peláez, Antonio Crystalstone 88

Pelayo Rangel, Alejandro Días Difíciles • Difficult Days 88

Pelc, Stanley The Reluctant Nudist 63

Pelissie, Jean-Marie The Bride • The House That Cried Murder 73

Pelissier, Anthony The History of Mr. Polly 49; The Rocking Horse Winner 49; Encore 51*; Night Without Stars 51; Meet Me Tonight • Tonight at 8:30 52; Meet Mr. Lucifer 52; Personal Affair 53

Peloe, Mark Samson and Delilah 85

Pelt, Ernest van Avenging Fangs 27

Pember, Clifford Wanted Men 36

Pembroke, Scott For Ladies Only 27*; Galloping Thunder 27; The Light in the Window 27; Polly of the Movies 27; Ragtime 27; The Terror of Bar X 27; The Black Pearl 28; Branded Man 28; Divine Sinner 28; Gypsy of the North 28; Law and the Man 28; My Home Town 28; Sisters of Eve 28; Sweet Sixteen 28; Brothers 29; Shanghai Rose 29; Should a Girl Marry? 29; Two Sisters 29; Jazz Cinderella • Love Is Like That 30; The Last Dance 30*; The Medicine Man 30; The Oregon Trail 36; Telephone Operator 37

Pena, Nettie Home Sweet Home 81

Penard, Serge Le Gaffeur 85

Penczner, Marius I Was a Zombie for the FBI 82

Pene, Julian, Jr. Skateboard Madness 80

Penn, Arthur The Left-Handed Gun 58; The Miracle Worker 62; Mickey One 64; Le Train • The Train • Il Treno 64*; The Chase 65; Bonnie and Clyde 67; Alice's Restaurant 69; Little Big Man 70; Olympic Visions • Visions of Eight 72*; Night Moves 75; The Missouri Breaks 76; Four Friends • Georgia's Friends 81; Target 85; Dead of Winter 86; Penn & Teller Get Killed 89

Penn, Leo A Man Called Adam 66; Escape to Freedom • Judgment in Berlin 86

Pennebaker, D. A. Daybreak Express 53; Brussels Film Loops • Brussels Loops • Loops 58*; Opening in Moscow 59; Balloon 60*; Breaking It Up at the Museum 60; On the Pole 60*; Primary 60*; David 61*; The Chair 62*; On the Road to Button Bay 62*; Susan Starr 62*; Crisis • Crisis: Behind a Presidential Commitment 63*; Casals at 88 64; Elizabeth and Mary 64; Lambert & Co. 64; Timothy Leary's Wedding • Timothy Leary's Wedding Day • You're Nobody Till Somebody Loves You 64; Don't Look Back 67; Monterey Pop 67*; Goin' to San Francisco 68; Godard on Godard • Two American Audiences 69*; Moscow—Ten Years After 69; Company • Original Cast Album: "Company" 70*; Keep On Rockin' • Sweet Toronto 70; 1 A.M. • One American Movie 70; Ziggy Stardust and the Spiders from Mars 73; Town Bloody Hall 79*; Elliott Carter 80; Dance Black America 85*; Jimi • Jimi Plays Monterey 86; Rocky X 86*; Shake (Otis Redding) 86; Dépêche Mode • Dépêche Mode 101 88*

Pennell, Eagle The Whole Shootin' Match 78; Last Night at the Alamo 83; City Life 88

Pennington-Richards, C. M. The Horse's Mouth • The Oracle 52; Hour of Decision 57; Black Tide • Stormy Crossing 58; Double Bunk 60; Inn for Trouble 60; Carry On TV • Dentist on the Job • Get On with It 61; Decoy • Mystery Submarine 62; Ladies Who Do 63; Danny the Dragon 66; A Challenge for Robin Hood • The Legend of Robin Hood 67; Sky Pirates 77

Penrose, Anthony Strange Behaviour 80; Cut Down 82

Pentti, Pauli Pimeys Odottaa • Waiting for Darkness 86

Penzlin, E. A. Mysterious Island • Tainstvenni Ostrov 41*

Peón, Ramón La Virgen de la Caridad 30; The Crying Woman • The Ghost • La Llorona 33; Oro y Plata 34; Sagrario 34; Sobre las Olas 34; Tiburón 34; Tierra, Amor y Dolor 35; Más Allá de la Muerta 36; Mujeres de Hoy 36; Mujeres Sin Alma 36; ¿Qué Hago con la Criatura? 36; Sor Juana Inés de la Cruz 36; Todo un Hombre 36; Forgive Me, Son 37; La Liaga • The Torment 37; The Newspaper Boys 37; Silencio Sublime 37; The Devil's Godmother • La Madrina del Diablo 38; The Mexican Woman • La Mujer Mexicana 38; Motherhood Is Not Enough • No Basta Ser Madre 38; El Romance del Palmar 39; Una Aventura Peligrosa • The Dangerous Adventure 40

Peoples, David The Blood of Heroes • Salute of the Jugger 90

Peploe, Clare Couples and Robbers 81; High Season 87

Peppard, George Five Days from Home 77

Perakis, Nicos Living Dangerously • Vios ke Politia 87

Perala Athiratha Maharath 88; Kankana Bhagya 88

Percy, David The Anna Contract 78

Pereda, Ramón Las Cuatro Milpas • The Four Corn Patches 37; México Lindo 39; El Gavilán • The Hawk 40; Los Olvidados de Dios • Those Forgotten by God 40

Peregini, Frank The Scar of Shame 27

Pereira, Miguel The Debt • La Deuda Interna • Verónico Cruz 88

Perelli, Luigi Lo Chiamavano Verità 72

Perelman, Pablo Imagen Latente • Latent Image 88

Perestiani, Ivan Eva 18; Love, Hate, Death 18; The Murder of General Gryaznov 21; Red Imps 23; Scandal? 29; Anush 32

Perez, Bill Bugs Bunny's 3rd Movie: 1001 Rabbit Tales 82*

Perez, Elwood Silip 85

Pérez, Fernando Living Dangerously 88

Perez, Marcel The Way Women Love 20; Luxury 21; The Better Man Wins 22*; Duty First 22; Unconquered Woman 22; West Is East • West vs. East 22; The Vulgar Yachtsmen 26

Pérez Tabernero, Julio Sexy Cat 72;

Terror Caníbal 81

Pergament, André Adventure in Indochina 57; The River of Three Junks 57

Peri see Perry, Peter

Peri, Enzo Three Golden Boys • Tre Pistole Contro Cesare • Tre Ragazzi d'Oro 66

Périer, Étienne Bobosse 59; Meurtre en 45 Tours • Murder at 45 R.P.M. 60; Bridge to the Sun 61; Le Mercenaire • Il Mercenario • Lo Spadaccino di Siena • The Swordsman of Siena 61*; Dis-Moi Qui Tuer 65; The Day the Hot Line Got Hot • Hot Line • Le Rouble à Deux Faces • Rublo de las Caras • El Rublo de las Dos Caras 68; Des Garçons et des Filles 68; When Eight Bells Toll 71*; Zeppelin 71; Un Meurtre Est un Meurtre • A Murder Is a Murder...Is a Murder 72; La Main à Couper 74; The Investigation • Un Si Joli Village 78; La Part du Feu 78; Rosso Veneziano 89

Peries, Lester James Soliloquy 49; Farewell to Childhood 50*; A Sinhalese Dance 50; Conquest in the Dry Zone • Conquest of the Dry Zone 54; Be Safe or Be Sorry 55; The Line of Destiny • The Line of Life • Rekava 56; The Message • Sandesaya 60; Too Many Too Soon 61; Home from the Sea 62; Changes in the Village • The Changing Countryside • Gamperaliya 64; Forward Into the Future 64; Between Two Worlds • Delovak Athara 66; Golden Shawl • Ran Salu • The Yellow Robe 67; Golu Hadawatha • Silence of the Heart 68; Akkara Paha • Five Acres of Land 69; Steel 69; A Dream of Kings 70; Forty Leagues from Paradise 70; Nidhanaya • The Treasure 70; Kandy Perahera • The Procession of Kandy 71; Desa Nisa • The Eyes 72; The God King 75; Enchanted Island • Madol Duwa 76; Ahasin Polawatha • White Flowers for the Dead 78; Pinhamy 79; Rebellion • Veera Puran Appu 79; Baddegama • Village in the Jungle 80; Kaliyugaya • The Time of Kali 82; End of an Era • Yuganthayo 83

Peries, Sumitra Gehenu Lamai • The Girls 77

Perincioli, Cristina Die Macht der Männer Ist die Geduld der Frauen • The Power of Men Is the Patience of Women 78

Perisic, Zoran Gun Bus • Sky Bandits 86

Perkins, Anthony Psycho III 86; Lucky Stiff • Mr. Christmas Dinner 88

Perkins, Mike see Caiano, Mario

Perlini, Meme Cartoline Italiane • Italian Postcards 87

Perlov, David Ben-Gurion • 42:6 69

Perojo, Benito Mamá 33; El Hombre Que Se Reía del Amor 35; Se Ha Fugado un Preso 35; Susana Tiene un Secreto 35; Crisis Mundial • World Crisis 37; La Verbena de la Paloma 38; Bound for Cairo • Rumbo al Cairo 40; Goyescas 44; La Copla de la Dolores • Dolores • Song of Dolores 49

Perold, Jan The Rider in the Night • Ruiter in die Nag 68

Péron, Serge le see LePéron, Serge

Perraudin, René Z.B. Otto Spalt 88

Perrault, Pierre The Moontrap • Pour la Suite du Monde 62*; Le Règne du Jour 66; Le Beau Plaisir 69; Les Voitures d'Eau 69; L'Acadie, l'Acadie! 70*; Moncton 70*; Un Pays Sans Bon Sens 70; Le Goût de la Farine 76; Le Retour à la Terre 76; Un Royaume Vous Attend 76; C'Était un Québécois en Bretagne, Madame! 77; Gens d'Abitibi 79; Le Pays de la Terre Sans Arbre 79; La Bête Lumineuse 82; Les Voiles Bas et en Travers 83

Perret, Léonce Noël d'Artistes 08; Le Petit Soldat 08; Le Voile des Nymphes 08; André Chénier 09; Daphné 09; Pauvres Gosses 09; Le Portrait de Mireille 09; Le Crime de Grand-Père 10; Mimosa 10; Molière 10*; L'Âme de Violon 11; L'Amour et l'Argent 11; Le Chrysanthème Rouge 11; La Dette d'Honneur 12; Main de Fer 12; L'Ange de la Maison 13; L'Enfant de Paris 13; Molière 13; Par l'Amour 13; L'Heure de Rêve 14; Les Mystères de l'Ombre 14; Le Roi de la Montagne 14; Aimer Pleurer Mourir 15; Le Dernier Amour 15; Françaises Veillez 15; France et Angleterre Forever 15; Les Héros de l'Yser 15; Mort au Champ d'Honneur 15; Les Poilus de la Revanche 15; La Voix de la Patrie 15; La Belle aux Cheveux d'Or 16; La Fiancée du Diable 16; L'Imprévu 16; The Lash of Jealousy • The Mad Lover • A Modern Othello • The Shadow of Night 17; The Silent Master 17; The Accidental Honeymoon 18; Lafayette, We Come! 18; Lest We Forget 18; The Million Dollar Dollies 18; A Soul Adrift • Tarnished Reputations 18*; The ABC of Love 19; Lifting Shadows 19; A Modern Salome 19; The Thirteenth Chair 19; The Twin Pawns 19; Unknown Love 19; L'Empire du Diament • The Empire of Diamonds 20; The Money Maniac 21; L'Écuyère 22; Königsmark 23; Après l'Amour 24; Madame Sans-Gêne 25; La Femme Nue 26; Printemps d'Amour 27; La Danseuse Orchidée 28; The Model from Montmartre 28; Morgane la Sirène • Morgane the Enchantress 28; La Possession 29; Quand Nous Étions Deux 29; Après l' Amour 31; Arthur • Le Culte de Beauté 31; Enlevez-Moi 32; Il Était une Fois 33; Sappho 34; Les Précieuses Ridicules 35

Perrin, Francis Çà N'Arrive Qu'à Moi 85

Perrin, Laurent Passage Secret 85; Buisson Ardent • Burning Bush 87

Perrin, Nat The Great Morgan 46

Perry, Anthony Emma 65

Perry, Frank David and Lisa 62; Ladybug, Ladybug 63; The Swimmer 67*; Last Summer 69; Trilogy • Truman Capote's Trilogy 69; Diary of a Mad Housewife 70; Doc 71; Play It As It Lays 72; Man on a Swing 74; Rancho Deluxe 74; Mommie Dearest 81; Monsignor 82; Compromising Positions 85; Hello Again 87

Perry, Peter Ecstasy of Lovers • Ecstasy on Lovers Island • Honeymoon of Terror 61; The Young Cycle Girls 79

Perry, Simon Eclipse 77

Persio, Vincent di see DiPersio, Vincent

Persky, Bill Serial 80

Person, Luiz Sérgio Trilogia de Terror • Trilogy of Terror 68*

Pertwee, Roland Adventure in Blackmail • Breach of Promise • Manhattan Madness 41*

Perzanowska, S. Jego Wielka Miłość 36*

Pesić, Slobodan D. Slučaj Harms 88

Pessis, Claude Mannequin 76

Petelska, Ewa Kim Jest Ten Człowiek • Who Is That Man? 85*

Petelski, Czesław Kim Jest Ten Człowiek • Who Is That Man? 85*

Petelski, Ewa see Petelska, Ewa

Peters, Barbara see Peeters, Barbara

Peters, Brooke L. The World Dances 54; The Unearthly 57; Anatomy of a Psycho 61

Petersen, Mark Stop 68

Petersen, Wolfgang For Your Love Only 76; The Consequence • Die Konsequenz 77; Black and White Like Day and Night • Schwarz und Weiss Wie Tage und Nächte 78; Einer von Uns Beiden 78; The Boat • Das Boot 81; Reifezeugnis 82; The Never-Ending Story • Die Unendliche Geschichte 84; Enemy Mine 85

Peterson, Kristine Deadly Dreams 88; Body Chemistry 90

Peterson, Sidney The Potted Psalm 46*; The Cage 47; Clinic of Stumble 47; Horror Dream 47; Ah Nurture 48*; Mr. Frenhofer and the Minotaur 48*; The Petrified Dog 48; Adagio for Election Day 49; The Lead Shoes 49; The White Rocker 49; Blunden Harbor 52; Chocolate Factory 52; Doll Hospital 52; Vein Stripping 52; Architectural Millinery 54; Manhole Covers 54; Japanese House 55

Petit, Christopher Radio On 79; An Unsuitable Job for a Woman 81; Flying Fish Over Hollywood 83; Chinese Boxes 84; Flight to Berlin 84

Petko, Alex see Petković, Aleksandar

Petković, Aleksandar The Wild Wind 86; Dirty Rebel 87

Petraglia, Sandro Fit to Be Untied • Matti da Slegare • Nessuno o Tutti, Matti da Slegare 74*

Petrashevich, Victor Death on Credit 76

Petri, Elio Nasce un Campione 54; I Sette Contadini 57; The Assassin • L'Assassino • The Ladykiller from Rome • The Ladykiller of Rome 60; Days Are Numbered • I Giorni Contati 61; Il Maestro di Vigevano 63; Alta Infedeltà • Haute Infidélité • High Infidelity • Sex in the Afternoon 64*; La Decima Vittima • La Dixième Victime • The Tenth Victim 65; A Ciascuno il Suo • To Each His Own • We Still Kill the Old Way • Zwei Särge auf Bestellung 66; Un Coin Tranquille à la Campagne • A Quiet Place in the Country • Un Tranquillo Posto di Campagna 68; Indagine su un Cittadino al di Sopra di Ogni Sospetto • Investigation of a Citizen Above Suspicion • Story of a Citizen Above All Suspicion • Story of a Citizen Above Suspicion 70; Ipotesi 70*; La Classe Operaia Va in Paradiso • Lulu the Tool • The Working Class Go to Heaven • The Working Class Goes to Heaven • The Working Class Goes to Paradise 71; Il Premio della Bonta' 71; Property Theft Is No Longer a Crime • La Proprietà Non È Più un Furto 73; One Way or Another • Todo Modo 76; Le Buone Notizie • Good News 79

Petrie, Ann Mother Teresa 85*

Petrie, Daniel The Bramble Bush 59; A Raisin in the Sun 61; The Main Attraction 62; Stolen Hours • Summer Flight 63; The Idol 66; The Spy with a Cold Nose 66; The Neptune Disaster • The Neptune Factor • An Undersea Odyssey • An Underwater Odyssey 73; Buster and Billie 74; Cat and Mouse • Mousey 74; Lifeguard 76; Sybil 76; The Betsy • Harold Robbins' The Betsy 78; Resurrection 79; Fort Apache, the Bronx 81; Six Pack 82; The Bay Boy 84; Half a Lifetime 86; Home Is Where the Heart Is • Square Dance 86; Cocoon: The Return 88; Rocket Gibraltar 88

Petrie, Donald Mystic Pizza 88; Opportunity Knocks 90

Petrie, Jeanette Mother Teresa 85*

Petrocchi, Roberto Illuminations • Illuminazioni 87

Petroff, Boris Hats Off 36; Red Snow 52*; Outcasts of the City 58; The Shotgun Wedding 63

Petroff, Hamil California 63; Runaway Girl 66

Petroni, Giulio Da Uomo a Uomo • Death Rides a Horse 67; E per Tetto un Cielo di Stelle 68; The Night of the Snakes • La Notte del Serpenti 69; Providenza: Mauserfalle für Zwei Schräge Vögel 72; La Vita, a Volte, e Molto Dura, Vero "Providenza" 72; Blood and Guns 79

Petropoulakis, J. The Girl from Corfu 57

Petrov, Vladimir Dzhoi and His Friends • Dzhoi i Druzhok 28*; Golden Honey • Zolotoi Med 28*; Address by Lenin • Adres Lenina • Lenin's Address 29; Children of the New Day 30; The Cold Feast • Ledyanaya Sudba 30; Fritz Bauer 30; Beglets • The Fugitive 32; The Carpenter • Plotina 32; Groza • Thunderstorm 34; Peter the First, Part One • Peter the Great, Part One • Pyotr Pervyi I 37; The Conquests of Peter the Great • Peter the First, Part Two • Peter the Great, Part Two • Pyotr Pervyi II 39; Chapayev Is with Us • Chapayev s Nami 41; The Elusive Jan • Neulovimyi Yan 42*; Jubilee • Yubilei 44; Kutuzov • 1812 44; Bez Viny Vinovatye • Guilty Though Guiltless • Guilty Though Innocent 45; Battle of Stalingrad, Part One • The First Front • Stalingradskaya Bitva I 49; Battle of Stalingrad, Part Two • Stalingradskaya Bitva II • The Victors and the Vanquished 50; Sporting Honor • Sportivnaya Chest 51; The Inspector General • Revizor 52; 300 Years Ago • Trista Let Tomu 56; The Duel • Poedinok 57; First Lesson • The Old Lady • Parvi Urok 59*; On the Eve 59; The Russian Forest 63

Petrov-Bytov, P. Cain and Artem 30; Miracles 34; Pugachev 38

Petrova, Roumyana Prizemyavane • Return to Earth 87

Petrović, Aleksandar Two • Where Love Has Gone 61; The Days 63; Three • Tri 65; Happy Gypsies • I Even Knew Happy Gypsies • I Even Met Happy Gypsies • I Even Met Some Happy Gypsies • Skupljači Perja • Sreo Sam Čak i Srećne Cigane 67; It Rains in My Village 69; Il Maestro e Margherita • The Master and Margarita 72; Gruppenbild mit Dame 77

Petrucci, Luigi It Happened in Canada 62

Petrushansky, Yevsie Girl Fever 61*

Pettinari, Daniele Cagliostro 75

Petty, Cecil The Peregrine Hunters 78

Pevney, Joseph Shakedown 50; Undercover Girl 50; Air Cadet • Jet Men of the Air 51; Flesh and Fury 51; Iron Man 51; The Lady from Texas 51; Meet Danny Wilson 51; The Strange Door 51; Because of You 52; Just Across the Street 52; Back to God's Country 53; Desert Legion 53; It Happens Every Thursday 53; Jerrico the Wonder Clown • Three Ring Circus 54; Playgirl 54; Yankee Pasha 54; Female on the Beach 55; Foxfire 55; Six Bridges to Cross 55; Away All Boats! 56; Congo Crossing 56; Istanbul 56; Appointment with a Shadow • The Midnight Story 57; Man of a Thousand Faces 57; Tammy • Tammy and the Bachelor 57; Torpedo Run 58; Twilight for the Gods 58; Cash McCall 59; The Crowded Sky 60; The Plunderers 60; Portrait of a Mobster 61; The Night of the Grizzly 66; Prisoners of the Sea 85

Peyser, John Undersea Girl 57; The Murder Men 61; Alcatraz Express 62; The Young Warriors 67; Massacre Harbor 68; Four Rode Out 69; Kashmiri Run 69; The Centerfold Girls 74

Pfandler, Helmut The Devil's Bed • The She-Wolf of Devil's Moor • Tod im November • Die Wölfin von Teufelsmoor 78

Pfleghar, Michael The Corpse of Beverly Hills • That Girl from Beverly Hills • Die Tote von Beverly Hills 65; Bel Ami 2000 oder Wie Verführt Man einen Playboy? • 100 Ragazze per un Playboy • How to Seduce a Playboy 66; Serenade for Two Spies • Serenade für Zwei Spione • Sinfonia per Due Spie 66; Das Alteste Gewerbe der Welt • L'Amore Attraverso i Secoli • L'Amour à Travers les Âges • The Oldest Profession • Le Plus Vieux Métier du Monde 67*; Sinatra: A Man and His Music 67; Olympic Visions • Visions of Eight 72*

Phalke, D. G. Harishandra • Rajah Harishandra 12; Bhasamur Mohini • The Legend of Bhasamur • The Legend of Mohini 13; Savitri 14; The Birth of Krishna • Krishna Janma • The Life of Krishna 18; The Burning of Lanka • Lanka Dahan 18; Kaliya Maradan • The Slaying of the Serpent 19; Sati Manahanda 23; Bridge Across the Sea • Bridge Over the Ocean • Setu Bandhan 27; The Desert of Ganga • Ganga Vataren 32

Phelan, Raymond A. Rebels Die Young • Too Young, Too Immoral 62

Phelps, William North Shore 87

Philipe, Gérard Die Abenteuer des Till Eulenspiegel • The Adventures of Till Eulenspiegel • Les Aventures de Till L' Espiègle • The Bold Adventure • Till Eulenspiegel 56*

Philipp, Harald Punishment Battalion 60; Bimbo the Great • Rivalen der Manège 61; Kralj Petroleja • Der Ölprinz • Rampage at Apache Wells 65; Winnetou und das Halbblut Apanatschi 66

Philippou, John Anna of Rhodes 50*

Philips, Lee On the Right Track 81

Phillips, Alex Hoy Comienza la Vida 36

Phillips, Arthur Life's a Stage 29; Three Men in a Cart 29

Phillips, Bertram White Star 15; The Chance of a Lifetime 16; Frills 16; Something in the Wind 16; Won by Losing 16; A Man the Army Made 17; Ye Wooing of Peggy 17; It's Happiness That Counts 18; Meg o' the Woods 18; Rock of Ages 18; A Little Child Shall Lead Them 19; Trousers 20; Dickens Up to Date 23; Faust 23; Juliet and Her Romeo 23; One Excited Orphan 23; The School for Scandal 23; Stung by a Woman 23; Tut-Tut and His Terrible Tomb 23; The Alley of Golden Hearts 24; The Gayest of the Gay • Her Redemption 24; Straws in the Wind 24; Arthur Roberts 27; De Forest Phonofilms 27; The Tale-Teller Phone 28; Ag and Bert 29

Phillips, Maurice The American Way • Riders of the Storm 86; Enid Is Sleeping 90

Phillips, Robin Miss Julie 72*

Phipps, John R. Smugglers' Harvest 38

Physioc, Wray The Shadow of Doubt 16; The Gulf Between 18; The Blonde Vampire 22; The Love Nest 22; The Madness of Love 22

Pialat, Maurice L'Amour Existe 60; Jardins d'Arabie 63; Byzance 64; Istanbul 64; Pehlivan 64; L'Enfance Nue • Me • Naked Childhood 67; Villages d'Enfants 69; Break-Up • Nous Ne Vieillirons Pas Ensemble • We Will Not Grow Old Together • We Won't Grow Old Together 72; La Gueule Ouverte • The Mouth Agape 73; Do Your Exams First • Get Your Diploma First • Graduate First • Pass Your Exam First • Passe Ton Bac d'Abord • Passe Tous Bac 76; Loulou 79; À Nos Amours • To Our Loves 83; Police 84; Sous le Soleil de Satan • Under Satan's Sun • Under the Sun of Satan 87

Piana, Dario Sotto il Vestito Niente II 88

Pianciola, Daniele Enigma 87*

Piazzoli, Roberto d'Ettore Beyond the Door • Chi Sei? • The Devil Within Her • Who? 74*

Picault, Chantal Accroche-Cœur • Lovelock 87

Picazo, Miguel Habitación de Alquilar 60; La Tria Tula 64; Dark Dreams of August • Oscuros Sueños de Agosto 67; Homenaje para Adriana 68; La Tierra de los Alvargonzález 69; Extramuros 85

Piccioni, Giuseppe Il Grande Blek 87

Picha see Picha, Jean-Marc

Picha, Jean-Marc Shame of the Jungle • Tarzoon—Shame of the Jungle 75*; Le Big Bang • The Big Bang 87

Pichel, Irving The Hounds of Zaroff • The Most Dangerous Game 32*; Before Dawn 33; She 35*; Beware of Ladies 36; The Gentleman from Louisiana 36; The Call of the Ring • The Duke Comes Back 37; Larceny on the Air 37; The Sheik Steps Out 37; The Great Commandment 39; Earthbound 40; Hudson's Bay 40; I Married a Nazi • The Man I Married 40; Dance Hall 41; Life Begins at Eight-Thirty • The Light of Heart 42; The Moon Is Down 42; The Pied Piper 42; Secret Agent of Japan 42; Happy Land 43; And Now Tomorrow 44; Colonel Effingham's Raid • Man of the Hour 45; A Medal for Benny 45; Tomorrow Is Forever 45; The Bride Wore Boots 46; O.S.S. 46; Temptation 46; Something in the Wind 47; They Won't Believe Me 47; The Miracle of the Bells 48; Mr. Peabody and the Mermaid 48; Twilight • Without Honor 49; Destination Moon 50; The Great Rupert 50; Quicksand 50; Santa Fe 51; Martin Luther 53; Day of Triumph 54*

Pichul, Vasily Little Vera • Malenkaya Vera 88

Pick, Lupu Die Liebe des Van Royk 18; Die Rothenburger 18; Die Tolle Heirat von Laló 18; Der Weltspiegel 18; Herr Über Leben und Tod 19; Kitsch 19; Marionetten der Leidenschaft 19; Mein Wille Ist Gesetz 19; Misericordia • Tötet Nicht Mehr! 19; Der Seelenverkäufer 19; Der Dummkopf • The Idiot 20; Das Lachende Grauen 20; Niemand Weiss Es 20; Oliver Twist 20; Aus den Erinnerungen eines Frauenarztes II 21; Grausige Nächte 21; Scherben • Shattered 21; Zum Paradies der Damen 22; New Year's Eve • Sylvester 23; Der Verbotene Weg 23; La Péniche Tragique 24; Arme Kleine Hedwig • Das Haus der Lüge 25; Armored Vault • Das Panzergewölbe 25; A Knight in London • Eine Nacht in London • A Night in London 27; Napoléon à Sainte-Hélène • Napoleon auf Sankt Helena 29; Gassenhauer 31; Les Quatres Vagabonds 31

Pickett, Rex From Hollywood to Deadwood 89

Pickford, Jack Little Lord Fauntleroy 21*; Through the Back Door 21*

Pickford, Mary Dorothy Vernon of Haddon Hall 24*

Pico, Marco Savannah (La Ballade) 88

Piehl, Vern Evidence of Power 79

Piel, Harry The Great Bet • Die Grosse Wette 15; Zigano der Brigant vom Monte Diavolo 25; His Greatest Bluff • Sein Grösster Bluff 27*; Schatten der Unterwelt 31; Johnny Steals Europe • Jonny Stiehlt Europa 32; Der Herr der Welt • An Invisible Man Goes Through the City • Master of the World • Mein Ist die Welt • Ruler of the World • Ein Unsichtbarer Geht

Durch die Stadt • The World Is Mine 33; Die Welt Ohne Maske • The World Without a Mask 34; Der Dschungel Ruft 37; His Best Friend • Sein Bester Freund 38

Pierce, Arthur C. Country Music, U.S.A. • Las Vegas Hillbillys 66; Prehistoric Planet Women • Women of the Prehistoric Planet 66

Pierce, Charles B. The Legend of Boggy Creek 72; Bootleggers • Bootleggers' Angel 74; Winterhawk 75; The Winds of Autumn 76; Grayeagle • Greyeagle 77; The Town That Dreaded Sundown 77; The Norseman 78; The Evictors 79*; Sacred Ground 83; The Barbaric Beast of Boggy Creek, Part Two • Boggy Creek II 85; Hawken • Hawken's Breed 86

Pierce, Douglas Love in Waiting 48; The Delavine Affair • Murder Is News 54

Pierotti, Piero Hercules Against Rome 60; Terror of the Red Mask 60; L'Avventura di un Italiano in Cina • Grand Khan • Marco Polo 61*; Hercules and the Treasure of the Incas • Lost Treasure of the Aztecs 61; The Pirate and the Slave Girl • La Scimitarra del Saraceno • La Vengeance du Sarrasin 61; A Queen for Caesar • Una Regina per Cesare 62*; Hercules and the Masked Rider 63; Giant of the Evil Island 64; Samson und der Schatz der Inkas 65; Heads or Tails • Testa o Croce 69

Pierson, Arthur Dangerous Years 47; The Fighting O'Flynn • The O'Flynn 49; Home Town Story 51

Pierson, Carl The New Frontier 35; Paradise Canyon 35; The Singing Vagabond 35

Pierson, Claude Ils Sont Nus • We Are All Naked 70

Pierson, Frank The Looking Glass War 69; A Star Is Born 76; King of the Gypsies 78

Pierson, Robert E. Claws • Devil Bear 77*

Piesis, Gunars A Fairy Tale About Tiny • Malchik s Palchik • Pohádka o Malíčkovi • Skazka o Malchik s Palchik 85

Piestrak, Marek Doznaniye Pilota Pirksa • The Test of Pilot Pirx • Test Pilot Pirx 78; Zaklyatie Doliny Zmei 88

Pieters, Guido The Good Hope • Op Hoop van Zegen 86

Pietrangeli, Antonio Amori di Mezzo Secolo 53*; Celestina • Il Sole negli Occhi 53; Alberto il Conquistatore • Lo Scapolo 55; It Happened in Rome • It Happens in Rome • Souvenir d'Italie 57; Nata di Marzo 57; Adua and Her Companions • Adua and Her Friends • Adua e le Compagne • Hungry for Love • Love à la Carte 60; Fantasmi a Roma • Ghosts in Rome • Ghosts of Rome • Phantom Lovers 61; La Parmigiana 62; The Visit • La Visita 63; Le Cocu Magnifique • The Magnificent Cuckold • Il Magnifico Cornuto 64; I Knew Her Well • Io La Conoscevo Bene 65; The Fairies • Le Fate • Les Ogresses • The Queens • Sex Quartet 66*; Come, Quando e con Chi 68; L'Assoluto Naturale 69*

Pike, James A. Feelin' Good 66

Pileggi, Tom Uncle Scam 81*

Pilgrim, Ronnie Operation Diamond 48

Pillsbury, Sam The Scarecrow 81; Starlight Hotel 87

Pincus, David These Thirty Years 34

Pine, Phillip The Cat Ate the Parakeet 72; Posse from Heaven 75; Pot, Parents, Police 75

Pine, William Aerial Gunner 43; Swamp Fire 46; Seven Were Saved 47; Disaster 48; Dynamite 48

Ping, Wang see Wang, Ping

Ping, Yuen Wo see Yuen, Wo Ping

Pinheiro, José Les Mots pour le Dire 83; Cop's Honour • Parole de Flic 85; Mon Bel Amour, Ma Déchirure • My True Love, My Wound 87; Let Sleeping Cops Lie • Ne Réveillez Pas un Flic Qui Dort 88

Pinion, Efren C. see Piñon, Efren C.

Pinisetty, Raviraja Donga Pelli 88; Krishna Leela 88

Pink, Sidney see Zehetgruber, Rudolf

Pinkava, Josef Automat na Přání • Wishing Machine 67; Pohlad' Kočce Uši • Stroke the Cat's Ears 85; Cizím Vstup Povolen 87

Piñon, Efren C. Blind Rage 78; The Killing of Satan 86; Raging Vendetta 86

Pinoteau, Claude Escape to Nowhere • Le Silencieux • The Silent One 73; The Angry Man • L'Homme en Colère 79; La Boum • The Party 81; La Boum II 82; L'Étudiante 88

Pinoteau, Jack Monsieur Robinson Crusoe 59

Pinsent, Gordon John and the Missus 87

Pinter, Harold Butley 74

Pinto, Joaquim Uma Pedra no Bolso 88

Pintoff, Ernest Aquarium 56; Blues Pattern 56; Fight On for Old 56; Good Ole Country Music 56; The Martians Come Back 56; Performing Painter 56; The Wounded Bird 56; Flebus 57; The Haunted Night 57; The Violinist 60; The Interview 61; The Shoes 61; The Old Man and the Flower 62; The Critic 63*; Harvey Middleman, Fireman 64; Death of a Hooker • Who Killed Mary What's'ername? 71; Dynamite Chicken 71; Blade 73; Jaguar Lives! 79; Come and Get It • Lunch Wagon • Lunch Wagon Girls 80; St. Helens 81

Pinzauti, M. Vamos a Matar Sartana 71

Pinzón, Leopoldo Pisingana 86

Piperno, J. Henry Ambush in Leopard Street 59; Breath of Life 62

Pipolo see Moccia, Giuseppe

Pipolo, G. see Moccia, Giuseppe

Piquer, Juan see Simon, Juan Piquer

Pirès, Gérard Erotissimo 68; Act of Aggression • L'Agression 75

Piriev, Ivan see Pyriev, Ivan

Piriev, K. see Pyriev, K.

Pirosh, Robert Go for Broke! 51; Target for Scandal • Washington Story 52; Valley of the Kings 54; The Girl Rush 55; Spring Reunion 57

Pirri, Massimo Better Kiss a Cobra • Meglio Baciare un Cobra 86

Pirro, Mark Deathrow Gameshow 87

Pirro, Ugo Goodnight, Ladies and Gentlemen • Signore e Signori, Buonanotte 76*

Pisanti, Achille Anemia 86*

Piscator, Erwin The Revolt of the Fishermen • Vostaniye Rybakov 34

Piscicelli, Salvatore Blues Metropolitano 85; Regina 87

Pisier, Marie-France Le Bal du Gouverneur 90

Piskov, Hristo A Lesson in History 57*

Piţa, Dan Nunta de Piatră • Stone Wedding 73*; Chained Justice • Dreptate în Lanţuri 83; Paso Doble 86

Pitchul, Vassili see Pichul, Vasily

Pither, Kevin The Kiss 77

Pitre, Glen Belizaire the Cajun 86

Pitt, Arthur Sundance Cassidy and Butch the Kid 75; Convoy Buddies 77

Pittman, Bruce The Mark of Cain 85; Confidential 86; The Haunting of Hamilton High • Hello Mary Lou: Prom Night II 87

Pittman, Ken Finding Mary March 88

Pivnick, Anita Prism 71

Pivoňková, Magdalena Když v Ráji Pršelo 88

Piwowarski, Radysław My Mother's Lovers 86; Pociag do Hollywood • Train to Hollywood 87

Piwowski, Marek Foul Play 78

Place, Lou Daddy-O • Out on Probation 59

Plack, Tom van see Van Plack, Tom

Plaissetty, René The Yellow Claw 20; The Broken Road 21; The Four Feathers 21; The Knave of Diamonds 21; The Woman with the Fan 21

Planchon, Roger Dandin 88

Platt, George Foster His Wife 15; The Five Faults of Flo 16; The Net 16; Deliverance 19

Platts-Mills, Barney Bronco Bullfrog 70; Private Road 71; Hero 82

Plesch, Honoria The Yellow Hat 66

Plicka, Karel The Earth Sings 33

Plimpton, George Hickory Hill 68*

Plimpton, H. G. see Plympton, Horace G.

Plívová, Věra Šimková see Plívová-Šimková, Věra

Plívová-Šimková, Věra Hledám Dům Holubů • I Look for a House of Pigeons 85; Nefňukej, Veverko 88

Ploquin, Raoul Avocat d'Amour • Counsel for Romance 38

Ploug, Claus Elise 87; Opbrud 88

Plumb, Hay The Apache 12; The Bishop's Bathe 12; The Burglar Helped 12; Curfew Must Not Ring Tonight 12; The Emperor's Messenger 12; For Love and Life 12; Ghosts 12; A Harlequinade Let Loose 12; Hawkeye, Coastguard 12; Hawkeye, Showman 12; Her Awakening 12; Her "Mail" Parent 12; Her Only Son 12; King Robert of Sicily 12; The Last of the Black Hand Gang 12; Lieutenant Lilly and the Plans of the Divided Skirt 12; The Luck of the Red Lion 12; A Man and a Serving Maid 12; Mary Has Her Way 12; Mr. Poorluck's River Suit 12; Oh for a Smoke! 12; PC Hawkeye Falls in Love 12; PC Hawkeye Goes Fishing 12; PC Hawkeye, Sportsman 12; Pamela's Party 12; Plot and Pash 12; Poorluck's Picnic 12; She Asked for Trouble 12; Tilly in a Boarding House 12; Town Mouse and Country Mouse 12; The Traitress of Parton's Court 12; The Transit of Venus 12; Two Brothers and a Spy 12; The Unmasking of Maud 12; Was He a German Spy? 12; Welcome Home 12; Whist! 12; Here Comes the Picture Man 12; All's Fair 13; As the Sparks Fly Upward 13; Blood and Bosh 13; Bounding Bertie's Bungalow 13; The Burglar at the Ball 13; Captain Jack VC 13; The Cloister and the Hearth 13; The Curate's Bride 13; A Damp Deed • Look Before You Leap 13; David Garrick 13; Deceivers Both 13; The Defective Detective 13; Drake's Love Story • The Love Romance of Admiral Sir Francis Drake 13; An Eggs-traordinary Affair 13; The Fairies' Revenge 13; George Barnwell the London Apprentice • In the Toils of the Temptress 13; Hamlet 13; Haunted by Hawkeye 13; Hawkeye Has to Hurry 13; Hawkeye Meets His Match 13; Hawkeye Rides in a Point-to-Point 13; Highwayman Hal 13; Lieutenant Lilly and the Splodge of Opium 13; Lieutenant Pie's Love Story 13; Love and a Burglar 13; The Lover Who Took the Cake 13; Many Happy Returns 13; The Of-Course-I-Can Brothers 13; The Old Nuisance 13; Peter's Little Picnic 13; Petticoat Perfidy 13; A Policy of Pinpricks 13; A Precious Cargo 13; The Princes in the Tower 13; Props' Angel 13; Ragtime Mad 13; The Real Thing 13; The Tailor's Revenge 13; Aladdin, or A Lad Out 14; Algy's Little Error 14; All in a Day's Work 14; The Also-Rans 14; A Bother About a Bomb 14; Caught Bending 14; The Chick That Was Not Eggs-tinct 14; Cinder-Elfred 14; The Dead Heart 14; An Engagement of Convenience 14; Entertaining Uncle 14; Follow Your Leader 14; Getting His Own Back 14; A Ghostly Affair 14; Hawkeye, Hall Porter 14; How Things Do Develop 14; Judged by Appearances 14; The Magic Glass 14; The Maid and the Money 14; A Misleading Miss 14; Mr. Meek's Missus 14; Mr. Meek's Nightmare 14; Oh What a Day! 14; On a False Scent 14; Once Aboard the Lugger 14; Out of the Frying Pan 14; Outlined and Outwitted 14; Over the Garden Wall 14; Rhubarb and Rascals 14; Simpkins' Little Swindle 14; Simpkins, Special Constable 14; Simpkins' Sunday Dinner 14; The "Simple Life" Cure 14; The Sneeze 14; Tango Mad 14; The Terrible Two 14; The Terrible Two Join the Police Force 14; That Mysterious Fez 14; Tilly at the Football Match 14; Topper Triumphant 14; Two of a Kind 14; We Don't Think 14; What a Sell! 14; Cock o' the Walk 15; Hawkeye, King of the Castle 15; Jill and the Old Fiddle 15; A Losing Game 15; The Man Who Wasn't 15; Things We Want to Know 15; What'll the Weather Be? 15; A Son of David 19

Plummer, Albert Darkness and Daylight 23

Plummer, Christian Assassino al Cimitero Etrusco • Crime au Cimetière Étrusque • Murder in the Etruscan Cemetery 82

Plummer, Peter Junket 89 70

Plympton, Horace G. The Stream of Life 19; Ashamed of Parents 21; Should a Wife Work? 22; Through the Storm 22

Plyta, Mary Moment of Passion 60

Po-chih, Leong see Leong, Po-chih

Podmanitzky, Felix von The Executioners • Hitler's Executioners 58

Podniek, Yuri Is It Easy to Be Young? 82

Podskalský, Zdeněk Never Strike a Woman — Even with a Flower • Ženu Ani Květinou Neuhodíš 66; The Great Movie Robbery • Velká Filmová Loupež 86*

Poe, Amos The Foreigner 78; Subway Riders 81; Alphabet City 84

Poe, Rudiger Monster High 90

Pogačić, Vladimir Priča o Fabrika • Story of a Factory 48; The Last Day • Poslednji Dan 51; Equinox • Nevjera 53; Anikina Vremena • Legends About Anika • Legends of Anika 54; Big and Small • Veliki i Mali 56; Nikola Tesla 56; Saturday Evening • Subotom Uveče 57; Alone • Sam 59; Heaven with No Love • Pukotina Raja 61; Čovek sa Fotografije • The Man from the Photography Department 63

Pogačnik, Jože Naš Čovek • Our Man 86

Pogany, Willy Kid Millions 34*

Poggioli, Ferdinando Maria Impressioni Siciliani 31; Paestum 32; Il Presepi 32; Arma Bianca 36; Ricchezza Senza Domani 39; Addio Giovinezza! 40; L'Amore Cantà 41; L'Amico delle Donne 42; La Bisbetica Domata 42; Gelosia 42; La Morte Civile 42; Sissignora 42; Il Capello da Prete 43; Le Sorelle Materassi 43

Pogostin, S. Lee Hard Contract 69

Poh, Richard Sable Cicada 39

Pohland, William Old Explorers 90

Poire, Jean-Marie Les Hommes Préfèrent les Grosses • Men Prefer Fat Girls 81; Twist Again à Moscou • Twist Again in Moscow 86

Poirier, Anne Claire Mourir à Tue-Tête • Primal Fear • A Scream from Silence 79; Beyond Forty • Over Forty 82

Poirier, Léon Cadette 13; Monsieur Charlemagne 13; L'Amour Passe 14; Le Jugement des Pierres 14; Le Nid 14; Âmes d'Orient 19; Le Penseur 19; Narayana 20; Le Coffret de Jade • The Jade Casket 21; L'Ombre Déchirée 21; Jocelyn 22; L'Affaire du Courrier de Lyon 23; Geneviève 23; La Brière 24; La Croisière Noire 26; Amours Exotiques 27; Verdun — Visions d'Histoire 28; Caïn 30; Madagascar 30; Chouchou Poids Plume 32; La Folle Nuit 32; La Voie Sans Disque 33; L'Appel du Silence • The Call 36; Sœurs d'Armes 37; Brazza 40; Jeannou 43; La Route Inconnue 47

Poitier, Sidney They Call Me MISTER Tibbs! 70*; Buck and the Preacher 71; A Warm December 72; Uptown Saturday

Night 74; Let's Do It Again 75; A Piece of the Action 77; Stir Crazy 80; Hanky Panky 82; Fast Forward 85; Ghost Dad 90

Poitrenaud, Jacques Of Beds and Broads • Le Parigine • Les Parisiennes • Tales of Paris 62*; Stranger from Hong Kong 64; Strip-Tease • Sweet Skin 65; Ce Sacre Grand-Père • The Marriage Came Tumbling Down 68

Pojar, Břetislav Gingerbread Hut • Perníková Chaloupka 51; Joseph Mánes 52; O Skleničku Víc • One Glass Too Many 53; An Adventure in the Bay of Gold • Bay of Gold • The Big Fish • Dobrodružství na Zlaté Zátoce 55; Spejbl na Stopě • Spejbl on the Train 55; The Brolly • Paraplíčko 57; Bombomania • Bombomanie 59; The Midnight Event • Půlnoční Příhoda 60

Pol, Jacques van It Was in April • 'T Was Een April 35*

Pola, Eddie The Vanishing Dagger 20*; Harmony Heaven 29*

Polaco, Jorge Diapason 86; En el Nombre del Hijo • In the Name of the Son 87

Polák, Jindřich Clown Ferdinand and the Rocket • Klaun Ferdinand a Raketa • Rocket to Nowhere 62; Icarus XB-1 • Ikaria XB-1 • Ikarie XB-1 • Voyage to the End of the Universe 63; Tomorrow I'll Wake Up and Scald Myself with Tea • Zítra Vstanu a Opařím Se Čajem 77; The Octopuses Wish You a Merry Christmas • Veselé Vánoce Přejí Chobotnice 86; Chobotnice z II. Patra 87; Mr. Tau 88

Polakoff, James Sunburst 75; Love and the Midnight Auto Supply • Midnight Auto Supply 78; Swim Team 79; Dark Eyes • Demon Rage • Fury of the Succubus • Satan's Mistress 80; Balboa 82; The Vals 83

Polanski, Roman Breaking Up the Dance • Breaking Up the Party • Rozbijemy Zabawe 57; The Crime • Morderstwo 57; Dwaj Ludzie z Szafa • Two Men and a Wardrobe 58; The Lamp • Lampa 58; Anioły Spadaja • Gdy Spadaja Anioły • When Angels Fall 59; The Fat and the Lean • Le Gros et le Maigre 60; Knife in the Water • The Long Sunday • Nóż w Wodzie • The Young Lover 61; Mammals • Ssaki 62; The Beautiful Swindlers • Les Plus Belles Escroqueries du Monde • World's Greatest Swindles • The World's Most Beautiful Swindlers 63*; Repulsion 65; Cul-de-Sac 66; Dance of the Vampires • The Fearless Vampire Killers • The Fearless Vampire Killers, or Pardon Me But Your Teeth Are in My Neck • Pardon Me But Your Teeth Are in My Neck • Your Teeth Are in My Neck 67; Rosemary's Baby 68; Cinéma Différent 3 70*; Macbeth 71; Che? • Diary of Forbidden Dreams • What? 73; Chinatown 74; Le Locataire • The Tenant 76; Tess 79; Pirates 86; Frantic 88

Poledňáková, Marie Zkrocení Zlého Muže 86

Poliakoff, Stephen Hidden City 87

Polidoro, Gian Luigi Amore in Stockholm • The Devil • Il Diavolo • To Bed...

or Not to Bed 63; An American Wife • Mes Femmes Américaines • Una Moglie Americana • Run for Your Wife 65; Thrilling 65*; Rent Control 81; Claretta and Ben • Permette Signora Che Ami Vostra Figlia 83; Below Zero • Sottozero 87

Poligny, Serge de see De Poligny, Serge

Polin, Vladimir The Star Inspector • Zvyozdnyi Inspector 80*

Pollack, Barry Cool Breeze 72; This Is a Hijack 73

Pollack, Jack see Polák, Jindřich

Pollack, Sydney The Slender Thread 65; This Property Is Condemned 66; The Swimmer 67*; Castle Keep 68; The Scalphunters 68; They Shoot Horses, Don't They? 69; Jeremiah Johnson 72; The Way We Were 73; Brotherhood of the Yakuza • The Yakuza 74; Three Days of the Condor 75; Bobby Deerfield 77; The Electric Horseman 79; Absence of Malice 81; Tootsie 82; Sanford Meisner — The Theater's Best-Kept Secret 84; Out of Africa 85; Havana 90

Pollak, Kay Elvis, Elvis 77; Älska Mig! • Love Me! 86

Pollard, Bud The Danger Man 30; Alice in Wonderland 31; Black King 32; Victims of Persecution 33; The Dead March 37; It Happened in Harlem 45; Beware 46; Tall, Tan and Terrific 46; Big Timers 47; Look Out Sister 48; Love Island 52

Pollard, Harry A. Motherhood 14; The Peacock Feather Fan 14; The Girl from His Town 15; The Miracle of Life 15; The Quest 15; The Dragon 16; Miss Jackie of the Navy 16; The Pearl of Paradise 16; The Devil's Assistant 17; The Girl Who Couldn't Grow Up 17; The Danger Game 18; The Reckoning Day 18; The Invisible Ray 20; Confidence 22; The Loaded Door 22; Trimmed 22; Trifling with Honor 23; K — The Unknown • The Unknown 24; Oh Doctor! 24; The Reckless Age 24; Sporting Youth 24; California Straight Ahead 25; I'll Show You the Town 25; The Cohens and Kellys • The Cohens and the Kellys 26; Poker Faces 26; Uncle Tom's Cabin 27; Show Boat 29; Tonight at Twelve 29; Undertow 30; The Prodigal • The Southerner 31; Shipmates 31; Fast Life 32; Feller Needs a Friend • When a Feller Needs a Friend • When a Fellow Needs a Friend 32

Pollet, Jean-Daniel Pourvu Qu'On Ait l'Ivresse 57; Gala 61; Méditerranée 63; Basae • Bassae 64; Paris Vu par... • Six in Paris 64*; Une Balle au Cœur • Devil at My Heels • A Shot in the Heart 65; Le Horla 67; Oniros 67; L'Amour C'Est Gai, l'Amour C'Est Triste 68; Le Maître du Temps 69

Pollexfen, Jack Dragon's Gold 53*; The Indestructible Man 56

Pollock, George Stranger in Town 56; Rooney 57; And the Same to You 58; The Poacher's Daughter • Sally's Irish Rogue 58; A Broth of a Boy 59; Don't Panic Chaps! 59; Meet Miss Marple • Murder, She Said 61; Village of Daughters 61; Kill or Cure 62; Murder at the Gallop 63;

Murder Ahoy! 64; Murder Most Foul 64; And Then There Were None • Ten Little Indians 65

Poloka, Gennady Intervention • Interventsia 68

Polon, Vicki Pleasantville 76*

Polonsky, Abraham Force of Evil 48*; Tell Them Willie Boy Is Here 69; Romance of a Horse Thief 71

Polonsky, Vitold Pesn Lyubvi Nedopetaya • Pesn'Liubvi Nedopetaia • The Unfinished Love Song 18*

Polop, Francisco Lara La Mansión de la Niebla • The Murder Mansion • Quando Marta Urlo nella Tomba 70; Cebo para una Adolescente 73; Perversión 74; Virilidad a la Española 75

Polselli, Renato L'Amante del Vampiro • The Dancer and the Vampire • The Vampire and the Ballerina • The Vampire's Lover 59; The Monster of the Opera • Il Mostro dell'Opera • The Vampire of the Opera • Il Vampiro dell'Opera 64; Black Magic Rites—Reincarnations • The Ghastly Orgies of Count Dracula • The Horrible Orgies of Count Dracula • The Reincarnation of Isabel • Riti Magie Nere e Segrete Orge del Trecento 73

Polverini, Attilio Bairoletto 86

Poma, Marco Mefisto Funk 87

Pomeroy, John Dublin Nightmare 58

Pomeroy, Roy Interference 28*; Inside the Lines 30; Shock 34

Pomes, Leopold Andrea 79

Pomilia, Stefano Fiori di Zucca 88

Pommer, Erich The Beachcomber • Vessel of Wrath 38

Pond, Elmer S. see Clifton, Elmer

Pons, Ventura The Blonde at the Bar • La Rossa del Bar • La Rubia del Bar 86

Pont, Michael du see Du Pont, Michael

Pontecorvo, Gillo Missione Timiriazev • The Timiriazev Mission 53; Cani Dietro le Sbarre • Dogs Behind Bars 54; Porta Portese • The Portese Gate 54; Festa a Castelluccio • Festival at Castelluccio 55; Men of Marble • Uomini del Marmo 55; Bread and Sulfur • Pane e Zolfo 56; The Compass • Die Windrose • The Windrose 56*; La Grande Strada Azzurra • The Long Blue Road • La Lunga Strada Azzurra • The Rift • Squarcia • The Wide Blue Road 56; Kapò 59; La Battaglia di Algeri • The Battle of Algiers • Maarakat Alger • Maarakat Madinat al Jazaer 65; Burn! • Queimada! 68; Ogro • Operación Ogro • Operation Ogre • Operation Ogro • Operazione Ogro • Il Tunnel • The Tunnel 79

Ponting, Dudley The Flat Charleston 26

Ponting, Herbert G. 90 Degrees South • The Undying Story of Captain Scott 13

Ponty, Pierre Au Pays des Mages Noirs 47*

Ponzi, Maurizio I Visionari 69; Equinozio 71; Il Caso Raoul 75; Madonna Che Silenzio C'E' Stasera 82; La Chiara e lo Scuro • The Pool Hustlers 83; Son Contento 83; Aurora • Qualcosa di Biondo 85; The Lieutenant of the Carabinieri • Il Tenente dei Carabinieri 86; Noi Uomini

Duri • Uomini Duri • Us Real Men 87; Il Volpone 88

Pool, Léa Anne Trister 86; À Corps Perdu • Straight to the Heart 88

Poole, Wakefield Bijou 72; Take One 77

Pooley, Olaf The Johnstown Monster 71

Poomin, Narong 1 2 3 Duan Mahaphai • 1 2 3 Monster Express 77*

Poomin, Vinai 1 2 3 Duan Mahaphai • 1 2 3 Monster Express 77*

Pope, Tim Queen—The Works E.P. 84*

Popescu, Horea Cuibul de Viespi • The Wasp's Nest 88

Popescu, Petru Death of an Angel 85

Popescu-Gopo, Ion Fetiţa Mincinoasă • The Little Liar 53; A Fly with Money • O Muscă cu Bani 54; A Bomb Was Stolen • S-a Furat o Bombă 61; Paşi spre Lună • Steps to the Moon 63; De-Aş Fi Harap Alb • White Moor 65; Faust XX • Faustus XX 66; My City • Oraşul Meu 67; Sancta Simplicitas 68; Comedia Fantastică • A Fantastic Comedy 75

Popkin, Harry M. Take My Life 42

Popkin, Leo C. One Dark Night 39; Reform School 39; Gang War 40; The Well 51*

Popkov, Vladimir Gruz Bez Markirovki • Unmarked Cargo 85

Poplavskaya, Irina Three Tales of Chekhov 61*; Jamilya 70

Popov, Alexei Three Friends and an Invention 28

Popov, Štole Happy New Year '49 • Srećna Nova '49 86

Popović, Mihailo-Mika With Faith in God 34

Poppe, Nils The Balloon 46; Money 46; Stupid Bom 53

Porchet, Arturo Hogueras en la Noche 37

Poreba, Bohdan The Train of Gold • Złoty Pociąg 87

Porta, Elvio Se lo Scopre Gargiulo 88

Portas, R. Bohemios 35; Adiós, Nicanor 38; Suprema Ley • Supreme Law 38; Un Domingo en la Tarde • On a Sunday Afternoon 39

Porter, Edwin S. The America's Cup Race • "Columbia" Winning the Cup 1899; Animated Luncheon 00; An Artist's Dream 00; Ching Lin Foo Outdone 00; The Clown and the Alchemist 00; Faust and Marguerite 00; The Mystic Swing 00; Why Mrs. Jones Got a Divorce 00; A Wringing Good Joke 00; Another Job for the Undertaker 01; Aunt Sallie's Wonderful Bustle 01; The Automatic Weather Prophet 01; Building Made Easy, or How Mechanics Work in the Twentieth Century 01; Carrie Nation and Her Hatchet Brigade • Kansas Saloon Smashers 01; Catching an Early Train • Trying to Catch an Early Train 01; Circular Panorama of the Electric Tower 01; "Columbia" and "Shamrock II" 01; A Day at the Circus 01; The Donkey Party 01; Execution of Czolgosz with Panorama of Auburn State Prison 01; The Farmer and the Bad Boys 01; Faust Family

of Acrobats 01; The Finish of Bridget McKeen 01; The Finish of Michael Casey, or Blasting Rocks in Harlem 01; Follow the Leader 01; Fun in a Butcher Shop 01; Gordon Sisters Boxing 01; Happy Hooligan April-Fooled 01; Happy Hooligan Surprised 01; How the Dutch Beat the Irish 01; The Jeffreys and Ruhlin Sparring Contest at San Francisco 01; Joke on Grandma 01; Laura Comstock's Bag Punching Dog 01; Life Rescue at Atlantic City • Life Rescue at Long Branch 01; Little Willie's Last Celebration 01; Love by the Light of the Moon 01; Love in a Hammock 01; The Lovers, Coal Box and Fireplace 01; Lukens, Novel Gymnast 01; Martyred Presidents 01; The Musical Ride 01; The Mysterious Cafe 01; The Old Maid Having Her Picture Taken 01; The Old Maid in the Drawing Room 01; The Old Maid in the Horse Carriage 01; Pan-American Exposition by Night 01; Panorama of the Esplanade by Night 01; A Phenomenal Contortionist 01; The Photographer's Mishap 01; Photographing a Country Couple 01; Pie, Tramp and the Bulldog 01; President McKinley and Escort Going to the Capitol 01; President McKinley's Funeral Cortege at Buffalo, NY 01; President McKinley's Funeral Cortege at Washington, DC 01; The Reversible Divers 01; Rubes in the Theatre 01; Sampson-Schley Controversy 01; Soubrette's Troubles on a Fifth Avenue Stage 01; Stage Coach Hold-Up in the Days of '49 01; Terrible Teddy the Grizzly King 01; The Tramp and the Nursing Bottle 01; The Tramp's Dream 01; The Tramp's Miraculous Escape 01; Tramp's Strategy That Failed 01; The Tramp's Unexpected Skate 01; Trapeze Disrobing Act 01; A Trip Around the Pan-American Exhibition • A Trip Through the Columbia Exposition 01; Weary Willie and the Gardener 01; What Demoralized the Barber Shop 01; What Happened on Twenty-Third Street, New York City 01; Why Brigit Stopped Drinking 01; Why Mrs. Nation Wants a Divorce 01; Appointment by Telephone 02; The Bull and the Picnickers 02; Burlesque Suicide 02; The Burning of Durland's Riding Academy 02; Burning of St. Pierre 02; Capture of the Biddle Brothers 02; Charleston Chain Gang 02; Facial Expression • Female Facial Expressions 02; Fun in a Bakery Shop 02; Happy Hooligan and His Airship • The Twentieth Century Tramp • The Twentieth Century Tramp, or Happy Hooligan and His Airship 02; Happy Hooligan Turns Burglar 02; How They Do Things on the Bowery 02; The Interrupted Bathers 02; The Interrupted Picnic 02; Jack and the Beanstalk 02; The Life of an American Fireman 02; The Messenger Boy's Mistake 02; Mt. Pelee in Eruption and Destruction of St. Pierre 02; Mt. Pelee Smoking Before Eruption 02; New York City in a Blizzard 02; Prince Henry at Lincoln Monument, Chicago, Ill. German and American Tableau 02; Rock of Ages 02; Uncle Josh at the Motion

Picture Show • Uncle Josh at the Moving Picture Show 02; Africander Winning the Suburban Handicap 03; The Animated Poster 03; Arabian Jewish Dance 03; The Baby Review 03; Buster's Joke on Papa 03; Casey and His Neighbor's Goat 03; Down Where the Wurzburger Flows 03; East River Novelty 03; East Side Urchins Bathing in a Fountain 03; Electrocuting an Elephant 03; The Extra Turn 03; The Gay Shoe Clerk 03; Goo Goo Eyes 03; The Great Train Robbery 03; Happy Hooligan in a Trap 03; Happy Hooligan's Interrupted Lunch 03; Heavenly Twins at Lunch 03; Heavenly Twins at Odds 03; How Old Is Ann? 03; Lehigh Valley Black Diamond Express 03; Little Lillian, Toe Danseuse 03; Miss Jessie Cameron, Champion Child Sword Dancer 03; Miss Jessie Dogherty, Champion Female Highland Fling Dancer 03; New York Caledonian Club's Parade 03; New York City Police Parade 03; New York City Public Bath 03; New York Harbor Police Boat Patrol Capturing Pirates 03; The Office Boy's Revenge 03; Old Fashioned Scottish Reel 03; Panorama of Blackwell Island 03; Panorama of Riker's Island, New York 03; Panorama Water Front and Brooklyn Bridge from the East River 03; Razzle Dazzle 03; A Romance of the Rail 03; Rube and Mandy at Coney Island 03; Scenes in an Infant Orphan Asylum • Scenes in an Orphans' Asylum 03; Seashore Frolics 03; 69th Regiment N.G.N.Y. 03; Sorting Refuse at Incinerating Plant, New York City 03; Steam Scow "Cinderella" and Ferryboat "Cincinnati" 03; The Still Alarm 03; Street Car Chivalry 03; Subub Surprises the Burglar 03; Throwing the Sixteen Pound Hammer 03; Two Chappies in a Box 03; The Unappreciated Joke 03; Uncle Tom's Cabin 03; Under the Mistletoe 03; What Happened in the Tunnel 03; Animated Painting 04; Annual Parade, New York Fire Department 04; Babe and Puppies 04; Bad Boys' Joke on the Nurse 04; Battle of Chemulpo Bay 04; Buster Brown and His Dog Tige 04; Canoeing on the Charles River, Boston, Mass. 04; Capture of Yegg Bank Burglars 04; Casey's Frightful Dream 04; Circular Panorama of the Horse Shoe Falls in Winter 04; City Hall to Harlem in Fifteen Seconds Via the Subway Route 04; Cohen's Advertising Scheme 04; The Cop Fools the Sergeant 04; Crossing Ice Bridge at Niagara Falls 04; Dog Factory • Edison's Dog Factory 04; Elephants Shooting the Chutes at Luna Park 04; European Rest Cure 04; The Ex-Convict 04; Fire and Flames at Luna Park 04; From Rector's Bank to Claremont 04; Halloween Night at the Seminary 04; Hold-Up in a Country Store 04; How a French Nobleman Got a Wife Through the New York "Herald" Personal Columns 04; Ice Boating on the North Shrewsbury, Red Bank, N.J. 04; Ice Skating in Central Park, N.Y. 04; Inter-Collegiate Athletic Association Championships, 1904 04; Inter-Collegiate Regatta,

Poughkeepsie, N.Y. 04; Japanese Acrobats 04; Little German Band 04; Maniac Chase 04; Midnight Intruder 04; Miss Lillian Shaffer and Her Dancing Horse 04; Nervy Nat Kisses the Bride 04; Old Maid and Fortune Teller 04; Opening Ceremonies, New York Subway, Oct. 27, 1904 04; Parsifal 04; Railway Smash-Up 04; A Rube Couple at the County Fair 04; Scarecrow Pump 04; Skirmish Between Russian and Japanese Advance Guards 04; Sleighing in Central Park, New York 04; Sliding Down Ice Mound at Niagara Falls 04; The Strenuous Life, or Anti-race Suicide 04; Treloar and Miss Marshall, Prize Winners at the Physical Culture Show in Madison Square Garden 04; Weary Willie Kidnaps the Child 04*; The White Caps 04; White Star S.S. "Baltic" Leaving Pier on First Eastern Voyage 04; Wifey's Mistake 04; Boarding School Girls 05; The Burglar's Slide for Life 05; Coney Island at Night 05; Down on the Farm 05; The Electric Mule 05; Empire State Express, the Second, Taking Water on the Fly 05; Everybody Works But Father 05; A Five Cent Trolley Ride 05; Hanging Stockings on a Christmas Tree • The Night Before Christmas 05; Hippodrome Races, Dreamland, Coney Island 05; How Jones Lost His Roll 05; June's Birthday Party 05; The Kleptomaniac 05; The Life of an American Policeman 05; The Little Train Robbery 05; The Miller's Daughter 05; Mystic Shriner's Day 05; Opening of Belmont Park Race Course 05; Phoebe Snow 05; Poor Algy 05; President Roosevelt's Inauguration 05; Raffles the Dog 05; Scenes and Incidents, Russo-Japanese Peace Conference, Portsmouth, New Hampshire 05; Seven Ages 05; Start of Ocean Race for Kaiser's Cup 05; Stolen by Gypsies 05; The Train Wreckers 05; The Watermelon Patch 05; The Whole Dam Family and the Dam Dog 05; The Dream of a Rarebit Fiend 06; Getting Evidence 06; The Honeymoon at Niagara Falls 06; How the Office Boy Saw the Ball Game 06; Kathleen Mavourneen 06; The Life of a Cowboy 06; Minstrel Mishaps 06; A Tale of the Sea 06; The Terrible Kids 06; Three American Beauties 06; Waiting at the Church 06; A Winter Straw Ride 06; Cohen's Fire Sale 07; College Chums 07*; Colonial Virginia—Historical Scenes and Incidents Connected with the Founding of Jamestown, Va. 07; Daniel Boone 07; Jack the Kisser 07*; Laughing Gas 07*; A Little Girl Who Did Not Believe in Santa Claus 07; Lost in the Alps 07; The Midnight Ride of Paul Revere 07*; The Nine Lives of a Cat 07*; A Race for Millions 07*; Rescued from an Eagle's Nest 07*; The Rivals 07*; Stage Struck 07*; The Teddy Bears 07; Three American Beauties No. 2 07*; The Trainer's Daughter 07*; Vesta Victoria Singing "Poor John" 07; Vesta Victoria Singing "Waiting at the Church" 07; The Angel Child 08; Animated Snowballs 08; The Army of Two—An Incident During the American Revolu-

tion 08; The Blue and the Gray, or The Days of '61 08; The Boston Tea Party 08; Bridal Couple Dodging Cameras 08; Buying a Title 08; Cocoa Industry 08; A Comedy in Black and White 08; A Country Girl's Seminary Life and Experiences 08; The Cowboy and the Schoolmarm 08; Curious Mr. Curio 08; The Devil 08; Ex-Convict #900 08; The Face on the Barroom Floor 08; Fireside Reminiscences 08; Fly Paper 08; The Gentleman Burglar 08; Heard Over the Phone 08; Honesty Is the Best Policy 08; The King's Pardon 08; The Little Coxswain of the Varsity Eight 08; Lord Feathertop 08; Love Will Find a Way 08; The Merry Widow Craze • The Merry Widow Waltz Craze 08; Miss Sherlock Holmes 08; Nellie the Pretty Typewriter—A Romance Among the Skyscrapers 08; Nero and the Burning of Rome 08; The New Stenographer 08; Old Maids' Temperance Club 08; The Painter's Revenge 08; Pioneers Crossing the Plains in '49 08; Pocahontas—A Child of the Forest 08*; Romance of a War Nurse 08; Sandy McPherson's Quiet Fishing Trip 08; Saved by Love 08; A Sculptor's Welsh Rabbit Dream 08; She 08; Skinny's Finish 08; Stage Memories of an Old Theatrical Trunk 08; A Suburbanite's Ingenious Alarm 08; Tale the Autumn Leaves Told 08; Tales the Searchlight Told 08; Ten Pickaninnies 08; Trinidad, British West Indies 08*; An Unexpected Santa Claus 08; A Voice from the Dead 08; When Ruben Comes to Town 08; Wife's Strategy 08; A Yankee Man-o-Warman's Fight for Love—An Incident During the Pacific Cruise of the American Fleet 08; The Adventures of an Old Flirt 09; Bear Hunt in Rockies 09; A Burglar Cupid 09; Capital Versus Labor 09; A Cry from the Wilderness 09; The Doctored Dinner Pail 09; Fuss and Feathers 09; Hansel and Gretel 09*; Hard to Beat 09; The Iconoclast 09; Love Is Blind 09; A Midnight Supper 09; A Modest Young Man 09; On the Western Frontier 09; A Persistent Suitor 09; Pony Express 09; A Road to Love, or Romance of a Yankee Engineer in Central America 09; The Strike 09; Toys of Fate 09; Alice's Adventures in Wonderland 10; All on Account of a Laundry Mark 10; Almost a Hero 10; An Attempted Elopement 10; A Bridegroom's Mishaps 10; The Cattle Thief's Revenge 10; A Clause in the Will 10; Cohen's Generosity 10; Cowboy's Courtships 10; The Education of Mary Jane 10; Forgiven 10; A Game for Life 10; The Girl Strike Leader • The Girl Who Dared 10; Great Marshall Jewel Case 10; Hazing a New Scholar 10; Indian Squaw's Sacrifice 10; The Last Straw 10; Married in Haste 10; Repaid with Interest 10; Retribution 10; Russia—The Land of Oppression 10; Saved from Himself 10; A Schoolmarm's Ride for Life 10; Shanghaied 10; The Tale the Camera Told 10; That Letter from Teddy 10; Too Many Girls 10; The Toymaker, the Doll and the Devil 10; Wanted: An Athletic Instructor 10; Wild Bill's Defeat 10;

Matrimaniac 16; The Microscope Mystery 16; The Rummy 16; Susan Rocks the Boat 16; A Wild Girl of the Sierras 16; The Wood Nymph 16; Betsy's Burglar 17; Cheerful Givers 17*; The Girl of the Timber Claims 17; The Sawdust Ring 17*; All Night 18; The Kid Is Clever 18; A Society Sensation 18; The Blinding Trail 19; Common Property 19*; The Little White Savage 19; The Man in the Moonlight 19; The Weaker Vessel 19; Who Will Marry Me? 19; Crooked Streets 20; The Eyes of the Heart 20; Pollyanna 20; Sweet Lavender 20; Dangerous Lies 21; The Mystery Road 21; Borderland 22; The Cradle 22; The Crimson Challenge 22; A Daughter of Luxury 22; For the Defense 22; The Ordeal 22; The Fog 23; Racing Hearts 23; The Awful Truth 25; The Dotted Line • Let Women Alone • On the Dotted Line • On the Shelf 25; Her Market Value 25; North Star 25; The Prince of Pilsen 26; Death Valley 27; Jewels of Desire 27

Powell, Peter The American Game 79*
Power, John The Picture Show Man 77
Powers, Francis The Little Gray Lady 14; The Ring and the Man 14
Powers, William Rosaleen Dhu 20
Poznanski, Dimitri Her Way of Love 29*

Prabhakar Shakti 88
Prabhakar-Umesh Avale Nanna Hendthi 88
Prachenko, Andrei Captain of "The Pilgrim" • Kapitan "Piligrima" 87
Pradeaux, Maurizio Ramón il Messicano • Ramón the Mexican 66
Prado, Guilherme de Almeida A Dama do Cine Shanghai 88
Prager, Stanley see Lelli, L.
Pratap, S. R. Bijilee aur Toofan 88
Pratt, B. E. Doxat see Doxat-Pratt, B. E.
Pratt, Enrico The Message 56
Pratt, Gilbert Keep Smiling 25*; Elmer and Elsie 34; Boys Will Be Girls 37
Pratt, Hawley The Pied Piper of Guadalupe 61*; The Wild Chase 65
Pratt, Jack see Pratt, John H.
Pratt, John H. Shore Acres 14; The Man's Making 15; The Rights of Man 15; The Gods of Fate 16; Her Bleeding Heart 16; Love's Toll 16; Loyalty 18; The Heart of a Woman 20; The Woman Untamed 20; Yankee Doodle, Jr. 22; The Rip-Tide 23
Praunheim, Rosa von Von Rosa von Praunheim 67; Berliner Bettwurst 73; Ich Bin ein Antistar... 76; Underground and Emigrants 76; Armee der Liebenden oder Aufstand der Perversen 78; Tally Brown, N.Y. 79; Stadt der Verlorenen Seelen 83; A Virus Has No Morals • Ein Virus Kennt Keine Moral • A Virus Knows No Morals 86; Anita—Dances of Vice • Anita—Tänze des Lasters 87; Dolly, Lotte und Maria 88; Positiv 89; Silence = Death 90; Surviving in New York • Überleben in New York 90
Pravov, I. Grain 35*; Lust for Gold 57
Preece, Michael The Prizefighter 79

Prégent, Johanne La Peau et les Os 88
Preis, Hassa Die Liebe und die Erste Eisenbahn • Love and the First Railroad 35
Prelić, Svetislav Bata Debeli i Mršavi • Fat and Thin 86
Preloran, Jorge My Aunt Nora 89
Preminger, Otto The Great Love • Die Grosse Liebe 31; Danger—Love at Work 36; Under Your Spell 36; Kidnapped 38*; Margin for Error 43; In the Meantime, Darling 44; Laura 44; Czarina • A Royal Scandal 45*; Fallen Angel 45; Centennial Summer 46; Daisy Kenyon 47; Forever Amber 47; That Lady in Ermine 48*; The Fan • Lady Windermere's Fan 49; Whirlpool 49; The Thirteenth Letter 50; Where the Sidewalk Ends 50; Angel Face 52; Die Jungfrau auf dem Dach 53; The Moon Is Blue 53; Carmen Jones 54; River of No Return 54; The Court Martial of Billy Mitchell • One Man Mutiny 55; The Man with the Golden Arm 55; Bonjour Tristesse 57*; Saint Joan 57; Anatomy of a Murder 58; Porgy and Bess 59; Exodus 60; Advise and Consent 62; The Cardinal 63; In Harm's Way 64; Bunny Lake Is Missing 65; Hurry Sundown 66; Skidoo! 68; Tell Me That You Love Me, Junie Moon 69; Such Good Friends 71; Rosebud 75; The Human Factor 79
Prentiss, Chris Goin' Home 76
Preobrazhenskaya, Olga Miss Peasant 16; Tale of Priest Pankrati 18*; Kashtanka 25; The Village of Sin • Women of Ryazan 27; Luminous City 28; The Last Attraction 29; Cossacks of the Don • The Quiet Don 31; Grain 35*; Stepan Razin 39; Prairie Station 41
Prescott, John The Torch Bearer 16*
Presnell, Robert Attack! The Battle of New Britain 44
Pressburger, Emeric Blackout • Contraband 40*; One of Our Aircraft Is Missing 41*; Colonel Blimp • The Life and Death of Colonel Blimp 43*; The Volunteer 43*; A Canterbury Tale 44*; I Know Where I'm Going! 45*; Black Narcissus 46*; A Matter of Life and Death • Stairway to Heaven 46*; Hour of Glory • The Small Back Room 48*; The Red Shoes 48*; The Elusive Pimpernel • The Fighting Pimpernel 50*; Gone to Earth • Gypsy Blood • The Wild Heart 50*; The Tales of Hoffman 51*; Twice Upon a Time 53; Fledermaus '55 • Oh Rosalinda! 55*; Battle of the River Plate • Pursuit of the Graf Spee 56*; Ill Met by Moonlight • Intelligence Service • Night Ambush 56*
Pressburger, Fred Crowded Paradise 56
Pressman, Michael Dynamite Women • The Great Texas Dynamite Chase 76; The Bad News Bears in Breaking Training 77; Boulevard Nights 79; Those Lips, Those Eyes 80; Some Kind of Hero 82; Doctor Detroit 83
Preston, Gaylene Dark of the Night • Mr. Wrong 85
Preston, Travis Astonished 88*
Prévert, Pierre Paris Express • Souvenirs de Paris 28*; L'Affaire Est dans le Sac • It's

in the Bag 32; Monsieur Cordon 33; Le Commissaire Est Bon Enfant • Le Gendarme Est Sans Pitié • The Superintendent Is a Good Sort 34*; Adieu Léonard 43; Voyage Surprise 46; Paris Mange Son Pain 58; Paris la Belle 59
Previn, Steve Almost Angels • Born to Sing 62; Escapade in Florence 62; The Waltz King 63
Price, B. Lawrence, Jr. see Price, Bamlet L., Jr.
Price, Bamlet L., Jr. Teenage Devil Dolls 52; One Way Ticket to Hell 55
Price, Elwood Mau Mau 55
Price, Paul Are Children to Blame? • Are the Children to Blame? 22
Price, Sherman Girl Fever 61*; The "Imp"probable Mr. Wee Gee 66; Judy's Little No-No • Let's Do It 69
Price, Tony Night Shift 79
Price, Will Strange Bargain 49; First Marines • Tripoli 50; Rock, Rock, Rock! 56
Priego, Alfonso Rosas see Rosas Priego, Alfonso
Priete, José see Prieto, Joseph
Prieto, Joseph Shanty Tramp 67; Big Enough and Old Enough • Savages from Hell 68; Fireball Jungle • Jungle Terror 68; Miss Leslie's Dolls 72
Prince Under the Cherry Moon 86; Sign o' the Times 87; Graffiti Bridge 90
Prince, Harold Black Flowers for the Bride • The Rook • Something for Everyone 70; A Little Night Music 77
Pringle, Ian The Plains of Heaven 82; Wrong World 86
Prinz, LeRoy All-American Co-Ed 41; Fiesta 41; A Boy and His Dog 46
Prior, David A. Kill Zone 85; Aerobicide • Killer Workout 87; Chase • Death Chase 87; Deadly Prey 87; Mankillers 87; Nightwars 87; Battle Ground 88
Prior, Jorge The Navel of the Moon • El Ombligo de la Luna 86
Privitera, Vincent J. Witchfire 86
Priyadarshan Cheppu 88; Mukunthetta, Sumitra Vilikkunnu 88; Oru Muthassi Katha 88
Prochkin, Alexander Cold Summer of 1953 • Kholodnoe Leto Piatdesiat Tretiego 88
Proferes, Nick Monterey Pop 67*
Proietti, Biaggio Storia Senza Parole • Story Without Words 81
Prokhorov, Victor Old Primer • Staraya Azbuka 88
Prokop, Jan Přátelé Bermudského Trojúhelníku 87*
Prola, Gianni Ecco 65
Pronin, Vassili M. Son of the Regiment 48; Journey Beyond Three Seas • Khazdeni za Tri Morya • Pardesi • The Traveller 57*
Prosperi, Franco La Donna del Mondo • Women of the World 62*; Crazy World • Insane World • Mondo Cane n.2 • Mondo Insanity • Mondo Pazzo 63*; Africa Addio • Africa, Blood and Guts 65*; Every Man Is My Enemy 67; The Hired Killer • Technique d'un Meurtre • Tecnica di un Omicidio 67; The Boxer • Ripped Off • Un

Uomo dalla Pelle Dura 71; Farewell, Uncle Tom • Zio Tom 72*; Savage Beasts • Wild Beasts 82*; The Throne of Fire 86

Protazanov, Jacob *see Protazanov, Yakov*

Protazanov, Yakov The Death of Ivan the Terrible 09*; The Fountains of Bakhisarai 09; A Night in May 10; Pesnya Katorzhanina • The Prisoner's Song 11; Anfisa 12; Departure of a Grand Old Man • The Life of Tolstoy • Ukhod Velikovo Startza 12*; The Broken Vase • Razbitaya Vaza • The Shattered Vase 13; A Chopin Nocturne 13; Honoring the Russian Flag 13; How Fine, How Fresh the Roses Were • Kak Khoroshi, Kak Svezhi Byli Rozi 13; How the Baby's Soul Sobs • Kak Rydala Dusha Rebenka 13; Keys to Happiness • Klyuchi Shchastya 13*; Dance of the Vampire 14; The Devil • The Lady Knows a Little of It, from the Devil • Zhenshchina Zakhochet, Chorta Obmorochit 14; Drama by Telephone 14; Gnev Dionisa • The Wrath of Dionysus 14; Guardian of Virtue 14; In the Presence of Life • Mimo Zhizni 14; Love 14; Nikolai Stavrogin 15; Petersburg Slums • Petersburgskiye Trushchobi 15*; Plebei • Plebeian 15; Voina i Mir • War and Peace 15*; Dance of Death • House of Death • Plyaska Smerti 16; Grekh • Sin 16*; Pikovaya Dama • The Queen of Spades 16; Woman with a Dagger • Zhenshchina s Kinzhalom 16; Andrei Kozhukhov 17; Blood Need Not Be Spilled • Ne Nado Krovi 17; Cursed Millions • Damned Millions • Prokliatiye Millyoni 17; Prokuror • Public Prosecutor 17; Satan Triumphant • Satana Likuyushchii 17; Father Sergius • Otets Sergii 18; Parasites of Life 18; The Black Horde 19; The Queen's Secret • Taina Korolevy 19; L'Angoissante Aventure 20; Member of Parliament 20; Justice d'Abord 21; Pour Une Nuit • Pour Une Nuit d'Amour 21; L'Ombre du Péché 22; Le Sens de la Mort 22; Liebes Pilgerfahrt 23; Aelita • Aelita: Queen of Mars • Aelita: The Revolt of the Robots • Revolt of the Robots 24; Broken Chains • His Call • Yevo Prizyv 25; Tailor from Torzhka • The Tailor from Torzhok • Zakroishchik iz Torzhka 25; The Case of the Three Million • Protsess o Troyokh Millyonakh • The Three Million Case • Three Thieves • The Trial of the Three Millions 26; The Forty-First • The Isle of Death • Sorok Pervyi 26; Chelovek iz Restorana • The Man from the Restaurant • The Restaurant Waiter 27; Don Diego and Pelageya • Don Diego i Pelageya 27; Byelyi Orel • The Lash of the Czar • The White Eagle 28; Chiny i Lyudi • An Hour with Chekhov • Ranks and People 29*; The Feast of St. Jorgen • Holiday of St. Jorgen • Prazdnik Svyatovo Yorgena 30; Siberian Patrol • Sibirsky Patrul • Tommi • Tommy 31; Marionetki • Marionettes • Puppets 34; Bespridannitsa • Without Dowry 36; Pupils of the Seventh Class • Pupils of the Seventh Grade • Sedmiklassniki • Seventh Grade 38*; Salavat Yulayev 41; Adventures in

Bukhara • Nasreddin in Bukhara • Nasreddin v Bukharye 43

Proud, Peter Esther Waters 47*

Prowse, Andrew J. Demonstone • Heartstone 90

Proyas, Alexander Spirits of the Air 86

Prunas, Pasquale Blood on the Balcony 64

Pryor, Richard Richard Pryor Here and Now 83; Jo Jo Dancer, Your Life Is Calling 86

Przybylski, Jan Nowina *see Nowina-Przybylski, Jan*

Psarras, Tassos Caravan Sarai 86

Ptashuk, Mikhail Ill Omen • Sign of Disaster • Znak Bedy 86

Ptoushko, Alexander *see Ptushko, Alexander*

Ptushko, Alexander Chto Delat' 28; Shifrovanny Dokument 28; Kniga v Derevne 29; Sluchai na Stadione 29; Stet Priklyuchenni 29; Kino v Derevne 30; Krepi Oboronu 30; Begstvo Puankare 32; Vlasteli Byta 32; The New Gulliver • Novyi Gulliver 33*; Skazka o Rybake i Rybke 37; Vesyolye Musikanty 37; The Golden Key • Zolotoi Klyuchik 39; Kamenny Tsvetok • The Stone Flower 46; Three Encounters • Three Meetings • Tri Vstrechi 48*; The Magic Voyage of Sinbad • Sadko 53*; Ilya Murometz • The Sword and the Dragon 56; Sampo 58*; The Day the Earth Froze 59*; Alye Parusa • Crimson Sails 61; Tale of Lost Time 64; The Tale of Czar Saltan • The Tale of the Tsar Sultan 66

Puccini, Gianni Il Marito 55*; Parola di Ladro 56*; Contro Sesso • Controsesso 64*; L'Idea Fissa • Love and Marriage 64*; Amore in Quattro Dimensioni • L'Amour en Quatre Dimensions • Love in Four Dimensions 65*; The Double Bed • Le Lit à Deux Places 65*; Dove Si Spara di Più 67; My Wife's Enemy • Il Nemico di Mia Moglie 67

Puchinyan, Stepan C.I.D. Chief's Experience • Iz Zhizni Nachalnika Ugolovnogo Rozyska 87; The Mystery of the Pirate Queen • Tayny Madam Vong 87

Pudovkin, Vsevolod I. Golod…Golod …Golod • Hunger…Hunger…Hunger 21*; Serp i Molot • Sickle and Hammer 21*; Chess Fever • Shakhmatnaya Goryachka 25*; The Death Ray • Luch Smerti 25*; Mat • Mother • Mother, 1905 26; Mechanics of the Brain • Mekhanika Golovnovo Mozga 26; The End of St. Petersburg • Konyets Sankt-Pyoterburga 27*; The Heir of Genghis Khan • The Heir to Genghis Khan • The Heir to Jenghiz Khan • Potomok Chingis-Khana • Storm Over Asia • Storm Over Asia, or The Heir of Genghis Khan 28; Life Is Beautiful • Life Is Good • Life Is Very Good • Ochen Khorosho Zhevyotsa • Prostoi Sluchai • A Simple Case 30*; The Deserter • Dezertir 33; Mother and Sons Pobeda • Samyi Schastlivyi • Victory 38*; Minin and Pozharsky • Minin i Pozharsky 39*; General Suvorov • Suvorov 40*;

Kinoza Dvadtsat Let • Twenty Years of Cinema • Twenty Years of Film • Twenty Years of Soviet Cinema 40*; Feast at Zhirmunka • Pir v Zhirmunka 41*; Murderers Are at Large • The Murderers Are Coming • Murderers Are on Their Way • Ubitzi Vykhodyat na Dorogu 42*; In the Name of the Fatherland • In the Name of the Homeland • Vo Imya Rodini 43*; Admiral Nakhimov • Amiral Nakhimov 46*; Three Encounters • Three Meetings • Tri Vstrechi 48*; Joukovsky • Yukovsky • Zhukovsky 50*; The Harvest • The Return of Vassily Bortnikov • Vassily's Return • Vozvrashchenie Vasiliya Bortnikova • Vozvrashcheniye Vasilya Bortnikova 53

Puenzo, Luis Lights of My Shoes 73; La Historia Oficial • The Official History • The Official Story • The Official Version 85; Old Gringo 88

Puffin *see Asquith, Anthony*

Punter, Gordon Betrayal 81; Vampyr 81

Pupillo, Massimo Bloody Pit of Horror • Il Boia Scarlatto • Il Castello di Artena • The Crimson Executioner • The Red Hangman • The Scarlet Hangman 65; Cinque Tombe per un Medium • Coffin of Terror • Five Graves for a Medium • Terror Creatures from the Grave • The Tombs of Horror 66; Bill il Taciturno 67

Purcell, Evelyn Nobody's Fool 86; The Land of Little Rain 88

Purcell, Harold Albert's Savings 40

Purcell, Joseph The Delos Adventure 85

Purdell, Reginald Don't Get Me Wrong 37*; Patricia Gets Her Man 37

Purdom, Edmund Don't Open Till Christmas 83*

Purdy, Jim Destiny to Order 89

Purzer, Manfred The Devil's Elixir • Die Elixiere des Teufels • The Elixirs of the Devil 76

Putra, Sisworo Gautama Nyi Blorong Putri nyi Loro Kidul 82; Pengabdi Setan • Satan's Slave 82

Pütün, Yılmaz *see Güney, Yılmaz*

Puzo, Dorothy Ann Cold Steel 87

Pyhälä, Jaakko Ursula 87

Pyke, Rex Eric Clapton and His Rolling Hotel 81

Pyo, Lee Hyoung *see Lee, Hyoung Pyo*

Pyriev, Ivan The Deluge 25*; Strange Woman 29; The Functionary • State Official 30; Conveyor of Death 33; Anna 36; The Party Card 36; Bogataya Nevesta • Country Bride • The Rich Bride 38; Tractor Drivers • Trakoristi 39; The Loved One 40; Svinyarka i Pastukh • Swineherd and Shepherd • They Met in Moscow 41; Secretary of the District Committee • Sekretar Raikon • We Will Come Back 42; At 6 P.M. After the War • Six P.M. • V Shest Chasov Vechera Posle Voiny 44; Skazaniye o Zemlye Sibirskoi • Songs of Siberia • Symphony of Life • Tales of the Siberian Land 47; Cossacks of the Kuban • Kuban Cossacks • Kubanskie Kazaki 49; Freundschaft Siegt • Friendship Triumphs • My za Mir • Naprzód Młodziezy Świata • We Are All for Peace • We Are for Peace • World

Festival of Song and Dance 51*; Ispystanie Vernosti • Test of Fidelity 54; The Idiot • Nastasia Filipovna 57; Beliye Nochi • Byelyi Nochi • White Nights 59; Nash Obschii Drug • Our Mutual Friend 61; Light of a Distant Star • Svev Dalekoi Zvesdy 65; Bratya Karamazovy • The Brothers Karamazov • The Murder of Dmitri Karamazov 68*

Pyriev, K. Devotion 55
Pytka, Joe Let It Ride 89
Pyun, Albert The Sword and the Sorcerer 82; Dangerously Close 86; Pleasure Planet • Vicious Lips 86; Radioactive Dreams 86; Alien from L.A. 87; Down Twisted • Downtwisted 87; Cyborg 88
Qi, Zhang see Zhang, Qi
Qimin, Wang see Wang, Qimin
Qingguo, Sun see Sun, Qingguo
Qosja, Isa Proka 86; Čuvari Magle • Rojet e Mjegulles 88
Quandour, Mohy The Spectre of Edgar Allan Poe 73
Que, Wen Chilly Nights • Han Ye 85
Queeny, Edgar M. Wakamba 55
Quested, John Here Are Ladies 71; Philadelphia Here I Come 75; Loophole 80
Questi, Giulio Amori Pericolosi 64*; Django Kill • Sei Sei Vivo, Spara! 67; La Mort A Pondu un Œuf • La Morte Ha Fatto l'Uovo • Plucked 69
Queysanne, Bernard L'Amant de Poche • Lover Boy 77
Quifeng, Yuan see Yuan, Quifeng
Quigley, George P. Murder with Music 41
Quigley, Robert Luces de Barriada • Neighborhood Lights 40
Quilici, Folco U-Bu 51; Pinne e Arpioni 52; Blue Continent • Continente Perduto • The Lost Continent • Sesto Continento • The Sixth Continent 54*; Brazza 54; Storia di un Elefante 54; Trofei d'Africa 54; The Last Paradise • L'Ultimo Paradiso 56; Paul Gauguin 57; Dagli Appennini alle Ande 58; Ti-Koyo e il Suo Pescecane • Ti-Koyo et Son Requin • Tiko and the Shark • Tikoyo and His Shark 62; Le Schiave Esistono Ancora • Slave Trade in the World Today 63*; Oceano 71; Killer Whale • Orca • Orca...Killer Whale • Orca the Killer Whale 76*

Quillen, Thomas Pursuit 75
Quin, John Children of the Fog 35*
Quine, Richard Leather Gloves • Loser Take All 48*; The Awful Sleuth 51; No Time for Tears • Purple Heart Diary 51; Sunny Side of the Street 51; Woo Woo Blues 51; Castle in the Air • Rainbow 'Round My Shoulder 52; Sound Off 52; All Ashore 53; Cruisin' Down the River 53; Siren of Bagdad 53; Drive a Crooked Road 54; Extra Dollars 54; Pushover 54; So This Is Paris 54; My Sister Eileen 55; Full of Life • The Lady Is Waiting 56; The Solid Gold Cadillac 56; Operation Mad Ball 57; Bell, Book and Candle 58; It Happened to Jane • That Jane from Maine • Twinkle and Shine 59; Strangers When We Meet 59; The World of Suzie Wong

60; The Notorious Landlady 62; Paris When It Sizzles • Together in Paris 63; How to Murder Your Wife 64; Sex and the Single Girl 64; Get Off My Back • Synanon 65; Oh Dad, Poor Dad, Mama's Hung You in the Closet and I'm Feeling So Sad • Oh Dad, Poor Dad, Mamma's Hung You in the Closet and I'm Feelin' So Sad 66*; Hotel 67; Gun Crazy • A Talent for Loving 68; The Moonshine War 70; Columbo: Dagger of the Mind 72; I Want Her Dead • W 74; The Prisoner of Zenda 78

Quinn, Anthony The Buccaneer 58
Quinn, Bob Poitin 79; Budawanny 87
Quinn, John Bloody Pom Poms • Cheerleader Camp 88
Quinnell, Ken The City's Edge 83
Quintanilla, Luis see Quintanilla Rico, Luis
Quintanilla Rico, Luis The Chicano Connection • Contacto Chicano 86; Land of the Brave • Tierra de Valientes 87
Quintano, Gene For Better or for Worse • Honeymoon Academy 90; Why Me? 90
Quintero, José The Roman Spring of Mrs. Stone • The Widow and the Gigolo 61
Quiribet, Gaston Great Snakes 20*; Once Aboard the Lugger 20*; Mr. Justice Raffles 21*; Do You Remember? 22; If Matches Struck 22; One Too-Exciting Night 22; Peeps Into Puzzle Land 22; The China Peril 24; The Coveted Coat 24; The Death Ray 24; The Fugitive Futurist 24; If a Picture Tells a Story 24; Let's Paint 24; Lizzie's Last Lap 24; The Night of the Knight 24; Plots and Blots 24; Which Switch? 24; The Quaint Q's 25
Quiricadze, Irakli see Kvirikadze, Irakli
Quirk, Billy see Bertram, William
Quisenberry, Byron Scream 81
Rabal, Benito The Bastard Brother of God • El Hermano Bastardo de Dios 86
Rabenalt, Arthur Maria A Child, a Dog, a Vagabond • Ein Kind, ein Hund, ein Vagabond 34; Was Bin Ich Ohne Dich? 35; Die Liebe des Maharadscha • The Maharajah's Love 36; Pappi 36; Das Frauenparadies • Woman's Paradise 39; Männer Müssen So Sein • Men Are That Way 39; Alle Stehen Kopf • General Confusion 40; Johannes Feuer • St. John's Fire 40; Liebespremier • Love's Premier 43; The Renz Circus • Zirkus Renz 43; Chemie und Liebe • Chemistry and Love 48; Christina 51; Alraune • Mandragore • Unnatural • Vengeance 52; The Gypsy Baron • Der Zigeunerbaron 54; Between Time and Eternity • Zwischen Zeit und Ewigkeit 56; Call Girls • Für Zwei Groschen Zärtlichkeit 57; The Last Waltz 58; Der Held Meiner Träume • The Hero of My Dreams 60; Geliebte Bestie • Hippodrome • Das Mädchen im Tigerfell • Männer Müssen So Sein 61
Rabier, Benjamin Les Aventures des Pieds-Nickelés 16*
Rabinowicz, Maurice Le Nosférat ou Les

Eaux Glacées du Calcul Égoïste 74
Raboch, Alfred Obey the Law 26; The Coward 27; The Albany Night Boat 28; Green Grass Widows 28; Their Hour 28; Rocky Rhodes 34; The Crimson Trail 35
Raccioppi, Antonio Conspiracy of the Borgias 58
Rachedi, Ahmed Mr. Fabre's Mill • Tahounet al Sayed Fabre 86
Rademakers, Fons Doctor in the Village • Dorp aan de Rivier • Village on the River 58; The Joyous Eve • Makkers Staakt Uw Wild Geraas • That Joyous Eve 60; The Knife • Het Mes 60; Als Twee Druppels Water • The Dark Room of Damocles • Like Two Drops of Water • The Spitting Image 63; The Dance of the Heron • De Dans van de Reiger 66; Mira 70; Because of the Cats • Niet voor de Poesen • The Rape 73; Max Havelaar 76; The Judge's Friend • Mijn Vriend • My Friend 79; De Aanslag • The Assault 86; The Rose Garden 89
Rademakers, Lili Minuet 82; Dagboek van een Oude Dwaas • Diary of a Mad Old Man 87
Rader, Peter Grandmother's House 89
Radev, Vulo Kradetsut na Praskovi • Kradezat na Praskovi • The Peach Thief 64
Radford, Michael Van Morrison in Ireland 81; Another Time, Another Place 83; 1984 84; White Mischief 87
Radivojević, Miloš Blackbird • Čavka 88
Radler, Bob Best of the Best 89
Radok, Alfred Daleká Cesta • Distant Journey • Ghetto Terezín 49; Divotvorný Klobouk • The Magic Hat 52; Dědeček Automobil • Old Man Motorcar 56
Radunsky, Alexander The Little Humpbacked Horse • Skazka o Konke-Gorbunke 62
Radványi, Géza see Radványi, Géza von
Radványi, Géza von Inferno Giallo 42; Irgendwo in Europa • It Happened in Europe • Somewhere in Europe • Valahol Európában 47; Donne Senza Nome • Women Without Names • L'Étrange Désir de Monsieur Bard 53; Ingrid—Die Geschichte eines Fotomodells 55; Mädchen Ohne Grenzen 55; Der Arzt von Stalingrad 58; Children in Uniform • Girls in Uniform • Jeunes Filles en Uniforme • Mädchen in Uniform 58; Douze Heures d'Horloge 58; Das Schloss in Tirol 58; Angel on Earth • Ein Engel auf Erden 59; Operation Caviar 59; Das Riesenrad 61; La Case de l'Oncle Tom • Cento Dollari d'Odio • Čiča Tomina Koliba • Onkel Toms Hutte • Uncle Tom's Cabin 65; Wiener Kongress 66
Radwanski, Staesch, Jr. Daisy and Simon 88
Rae, Michael Laserblast 78
Raeburn, Michael The Grass Is Singing • Killing Heat 81; Soweto 87
Rafelson, Bob Head 68; Five Easy Pieces 70; The King of Marvin Gardens 72; Stay Hungry 75; The Postman Always Rings Twice 81; Black Widow 86; Mountains of the Moon 90

Rafferty, Kevin The Atomic Cafe 82*
Rafferty, Pierce The Atomic Cafe 82*
Raffill, Stewart The Tender Warrior 71; When the North Wind Blows 74; The Adventures of the Wilderness Family 75; Across the Great Divide 76; The Sea Gypsies • Shipwreck 78; High Risk 81; The Ice Pirates 83; The Philadelphia Experiment 84; Mac and Me 88
Rafkin, Alan Ski Party 65; The Ghost and Mr. Chicken • Running Scared 66; The Ride to Hangman's Tree 67; The Shakiest Gun in the West 67; Nobody's Perfect • Winning Position 68; Angel in My Pocket 69; How to Frame a Figg 70
Ragaky, Mohammed Little Miss Devil 51
Raghav Rakshasa Samharam 88
Raghu, A. T. Aapathbandhava 88
Ragneborn, Arne The Vicious Breed 58
Ragona, Ubaldo The Last Man on Earth • L'Ultimo Uomo della Terra 64*
Ragozzini, Ed Sasquatch • Sasquatch—The Legend of Bigfoot 78
Rahardjo, Slamet Ponirah • Ponirah Terpidana 83
Rahn, Bruno Small Town Sinners 28
Rahnema, Ferydoun Khun-e Siaavash • Siavash in Persepolis 66
Raich, Ken Hollywood Hot Tubs II: Educating Crystal 90
Raimi, Sam The Evil Dead 80; Broken Hearts and Noses • Crimewave • The XYZ Murders 85; Evil Dead 2 • Evil Dead 2: Dead by Dawn 87; Darkman 90
Rainer, Yvonne Foot Film • Volleyball 67; Hand Movie 68; Rhode Island Red 68; Trio Film 68; Line 69; Lives of Performers 72; Film About a Woman Who... 74; Kristina Talking Pictures 76; Journey from Berlin 1971 • Working Title: Journeys from Berlin/1971 80; The Man Who Envied Women 85; Privilege 90
Rains, Fred Absent-Minded Jones 10; The Artful Burglar 10; The Boy and the Physic 10; The Burglar's Misfortune 10; Caught Napping 10; The Harlequinade 10; The Jealous Husband 10; Jones Buys China 10; Jones Dresses for the Pageant 10; Jones Junior, or Money for Nothing 10; Jones' Lottery Prize—A Husband 10; The Kidnapped Servant 10; Looking for Lodgings at the Seaside 10; The Navvy's Fortune 10; The New Park-Keeper 10; One Who Remembered 10; Susan's Revenge 10; Up-to-Date Pickpockets 10; A Yuletide Reformation 10; Jimson Joins the Anarchists 11; Jimson Joins the Piecans 11; Johnson's Strong Ale 11; Jones' Nightmare 11; The Suffragettes' Downfall, or Who Said "Rats? 11; A Village Scandal 11; Aladdin in Pearlies 12; Back at Three 12; Dan Nolan's Cross 12; Duped by Determination 12; His Duty 12; Little Miss Demure 12; Love at Arms 12; Love Conquers Crime 12; Married in Haste 12; The Mexican's Love Affair 12; My Wife's Pet 12; The New Owner of the Business 12; Sammy's Revenge 12; The Stolen Necklace 12; The Wolf and the Waif 12; Daphne and the Dean 13; How a Housekeeper Lost Her Character 13; The

Blunders of Mr. Butterbun: Trips and Tribunals 18; The Blunders of Mr. Butterbun: Unexpected Treasure 18; A Case of Comfort 18; Diamonds and Dimples 18; The Haunted Hotel 18; His Busy Day 18; His Salad Days 18; Love and Lobster 18; Paint and Passion 18; Bamboozled 19; Land of My Fathers 21; Odd Tricks 24
Raisman, Yuli see *Raizman, Yuli*
Raisman, Yuri see *Raizman, Yuli*
Raizman, Yuli The Circle • Duty and Love • Kpyr • The Ring 27*; Convict Labor • Forced Labor • Katorga • Penal Servitude 28; The Earth Thirsts • Zemlya Zhazhdyot 30; Rasskaz ob Umare Hapsoko • A Story About Omar Khaptsoko • The Story of Omar Hapsoko • The Tale of Umar Khaptsoko 32; The Aviators • Flyers • Lyotchiki • Men on Wings • The Pilots 35; The Last Night • Poslednaya Noch 36*; Podnyataya Tzelina • Virgin Soil Upturned 39; Mashenka 42*; À Propos of the Truce with Finland • Towards an Armistice with Finland • Za Pneremirie c Finlandia 44; Moscow Nights • Moscow Sky • Nebo Moskvy 44; Berlin • The Fall of Berlin 45*; Poezd Idet na Vostok • The Train Goes East 47; Rainis 49; Cavalier of the Golden Star • Dream of a Cossack • Kavaler Zolotoi Zvezdy • The Knight of the Gold Star 50; Conflict • A Lesson in Life • Lesson of Life • Urok Zhizni 55; The Communist • Kommunist 57; A Esli Eto Lyubov • Can This Be Love? • If This Be Love • What If It Is Love? 61; Tvoi Sovremennik • Your Contemporary 67; A Courtesy Call • Visit Vezhlivosti 73; A Strange Woman • Strannaya Zhenshchina 77; Chastnaya Zhizn • Private Life 82; A Tale of Wishes • Time of Desire • Vremya Zhelanii 84
Raizman, Yuri see *Raizman, Yuli*
Raja, Bharati Vedam Puthitu 88
Rajaonarivelo, Raymond Tabataba 88
Rajendra, Babu D. Pyar Karke Dekho 87; Prajaprabhutva 88
Raju, K. V. Bandhamukta 88; Sangrama 88
Raker, C. see *Endfield, Cy*
Raker, Hugh see *Endfield, Cy*
Rakoff, Alvin Hot Money Girl • Long Distance • Rhapsodie in Blei • Treasure of San Teresa; Passport to Shame • Room 43 59; An einem Freitag um Halb Zwölf • Il Mondo nella Mia Tasca • On Friday at Eleven • Pas de Mentalité • Vendredi 13 Heures • The World in My Pocket 60; The Comedy Man 63; Crossplot 69; Hoffman 70; Say Hello to Yesterday 70; King Solomon's Treasure 77; City on Fire 79; Death Ship 80; Dirty Tricks 80
Rakonjac, Kokan Raindrops 62; The Traitor 63; The Restless Ones 67; Wild Shadows 68
Raley, Alice Movie House Massacre 86
Ralph, Louis The Raider Emden 28; Cruiser Emden • Kreuzer Emden 31
Ramachandrappa, Baraguru Surya 88
Ramakrishna, Kodi Dongoduchhadu 87; Donga Kapuram 88; Manavidu Osthannadu 88; Srinivasa Kalyanam 88

Ramalho Júnior, Francisco Besame Mucho • Kiss Me Much 87
Ramampy, Benoit Dahalo Dahalo • Once Upon a Time in the Midwest 86
Ramati, Alexander Mordei ha'Or • Rebels Against the Light • Sands of Beersheba 64; The Desperate Ones • Más Allá de las Montañas 68; The Assisi Underground 85; And the Violins Stopped Playing 87
Rambaldi, Vittoria Primal Rage 90
Rameau, Willy Lien de Parente • Next of Kin • Parental Claim 86
Ramesh, Nandamuri Allari Krishnaya 87
Ramírez, José Nieto see *Nieto Ramírez, José*
Ramírez, Luis Kelly see *Kelly Ramírez, Luis*
Ramis, Harold Caddyshack 80; National Lampoon's Vacation 83; Club Paradise 86
Ramnoth, K. Ezai Padam Padu 50
Rampelli, Fabrizio Black Nightmare • Cattivi Pierrot 86; The Transgression • La Trasgressione 87
Ramsay, R. Tulsi Ek Nanhi Munni Ladki Thi 70*; Crime Does Not Pay • Do Gaz Zameen ke Neeche 72*; Andhera 75*; Darwaza 78*; Purani Haveli 89*
Ramsay, Shyam Ek Nanhi Munni Ladki Thi 70*; Crime Does Not Pay • Do Gaz Zameen ke Neeche 72*; Andhera 75*; Darwaza 78*; Purani Haveli 89*
Ramsay, Tulsi see *Ramsay, R. Tulsi*
Randall, John Deadly Reef 78; J.J. Garcia 84
Randel, Tony Hellbound: Hellraiser II 88
Randive, Satish Chal Re Lakshya Mumbaila 88
Randol, George Midnight Shadow 39
Randolf, Rolf O Alte Burschenherrlichkeit 32; Tod Über Schanghai 33; Die Sporck'schen Jäger 37
Randone, B. L. Man of the Sea 48*
Ranfl, Rajko Ljubazan 86
Rangel, Alejandro Pelayo see *Pelayo Rangel, Alejandro*
Rankin, Arthur, Jr. Willy McBean and His Magic Machine 65; King Kong Escapes • King Kong no Gyakushū • King Kong's Counterattack • The Revenge of King Kong 67*; Frosty the Snowman 73; The Last Unicorn 82*
Ranódy, László Csillagosok • Stars 50; The Rising Sea 53*; Hintónjáró Szerelem • Love Travels by Coach 54; Abyss • Discord • Szakadék 55; Dance Macabre • A Tettes Ismeretlen 57; Akikért a Pacsirta Elkísér • For Whom the Larks Sing 59; Be Good Until Death • Légy Jó Mindhalálig 60; Pacsirta • Skylark 64; Aranysárkány • The Golden Kite 66; Árvácska • No Man's Daughter 76
Rao, B. Bhaskara Ummadi Mogudu 87
Rao, Dasari Narayan Majnu 87; Atma Bandhulu 88; Kanchana Seetha 88
Rao, G. Ram Mohan Dongagaru Swagatham 88
Rao, K. Raghavendra Donga Ramudu 88; Manchi Donga 88
Rao, Pendharkar Babu see *Babu Rao, Pendharkar*

Rao, Relangi Narasimah Bhale Mogudu 88; Bhama Kalapam 88; Samsaram 88

Rao, Singeetham Srinivas America Abbai 87; Pushpak 88

Rao, T. Rama Insaf ki Pukar 88

Rao, V. Madhusudan Samrat 88

Raphael, David Song of the Sephardi 80

Rapos, Dušan Fontána pre Zuzanu • A Fountain for Susan 85; Falošný Princ • A False Prince 86; Utekajme, Už Ide! 86

Rapp, Joel High School Big Shot 59; Battle of Blood Island 60

Rapp, Paul The Curious Female 69

Rappaport, Gerbert see *Rappaport, Herbert*

Rappaport, Herbert Professor Mamlock 38*; A Musical Story 40*; A Hundred for One 41; Kino-Concert 1941 • Leningrad Music Hall 41*; Vanka 42; Air-Chauffeur • Taxi to Heaven 43; Life in the Citadel 47; Alexander Popov 49; Concert of Stars • Song and Dance Concert 52*; Stars of the Russian Ballet 54; Rain or Shine 60; Cheryomushki • Song Over Moscow • Wild Cherry Trees 63

Rappaport, Mark Local Color 78; The Scenic Route 78; Imposters 79; Chain Letters 85

Rappeneau, Elisabeth Fréquence Meurtre 88

Rappeneau, Jean-Paul Chronique Provincial 58; Château Life • Life at Home • A Matter of Resistance • La Vie de Château 65; Les Mariés de l'An Deux • The Scoundrel 71; Lovers Like Us • Le Sauvage • The Savage 75; Cyrano de Bergerac 90

Rapper, Irving The Life of Emile Zola 37*; One Foot in Heaven 41; Shining Victory 41; The Gay Sisters 42; Now, Voyager 42; The Adventures of Mark Twain 44; The Corn Is Green 45; Rhapsody in Blue 45; Deception 46; One for the Book • The Voice of the Turtle 47; Anna Lucasta 49; The Glass Menagerie 50; Another Man's Poison 51; Bad for Each Other 53; Forever Female 53; The Brave One 56; Strange Intruder 56; Marjorie Morningstar 58; The Miracle 59; Giuseppe Venduto dai Fratelli • Joseph and His Brethren • Joseph Sold by His Brothers • Sold Into Egypt • The Story of Joseph and His Brethren 60*; Pontius Pilate • Ponzio Pilato 61*; The Christine Jorgensen Story 70; Born Again 78

Rash, Steve The Buddy Holly Story 78; Under the Rainbow 81; Boy Rents Girl • Can't Buy Me Love 87

Rashevskaya, Natalia Fathers and Sons 60*

Raskin, Jay I Married a Vampire 83

Raskov, Daniel Wedding Band 90

Rasky, Harry Upon This Rock 71; Homage to Chagall: The Colors of Love 75; Arthur Miller on Home Ground 79; To Mend the World 87

Rasmussen, Kiehl see *Rasmussen, Kjehl*

Rasmussen, Kjehl Animal Behavior 85*

Rastawiecki, Andrzej Trzos see *Trzos-Rastawiecki, Andrzej*

Rasumny, Alexander The Life and Death of Lieutenant Schmidt 17*; Last Encounter 18; Uprising 18*; Comrade Abram 19; White and Black 19; Mother 20; Beauty and the Bolshevik • Kombrig Ivanov 23; The Gribushin Family 23; Father Knish's Gang 24; Valley of Tears 24; Years of Trial 25; Superfluous People • Überflüssige Menschen 26; Prince or Clown 27; Island in Flight 30; A Personal Affair 40; The Battle of Sokol 42; The Adventures of Corporal Kochekov 55; Homecoming 57

Rathborne, Bettina Phoebe • Zelly and Me 88

Rathborne, Tina see *Rathborne, Bettina*

Rathnam, Mani Nayakan 88

Rathod, David West Is West 88

Ráthonyi, Ákos von Fizessen Nagyság 37; Tisztelet a Kivételnek 37; Gyimesi Vadvirág • Wildflower of Gyimes 39; Don't Blame the Stork 54; Frau Warrens Gewerbe • Mrs. Warren's Profession 60; Daffodil Killer • The Devil's Daffodil • Das Geheimnis der Gelden Narzizzen 61; The Phony American • Toller Hecht auf Krümmer Tour 62; Cave of the Living Dead • The Curse of the Green Eyes • Der Fluch der Grünen Augen • Night of the Vampires 64

Ráthonyi, August see *Ráthonyi, Ákos von*

Ratoff, Gregory Sins of Man 36*; The Lancer Spy 37; Wife, Husband and Friend 38; Barricade 39; Day-Time Wife 39; Elsa Maxwell's Hotel for Women • Hotel for Women 39; Escape to Happiness • Intermezzo • Intermezzo—A Love Story 39; Rose of Washington Square 39; I Was an Adventuress 40; Public Deb No. 1 40; Adam Had Four Sons 41; The Corsican Brothers 41; The Men in Her Life 41; Footlight Serenade 42; Two Yanks in Trinidad 42; The Heat's On • Tropicana 43; Something to Shout About 43; Song of Russia 43; Irish Eyes Are Smiling 44; Madame Pimpernel • Paris Underground 45; Where Do We Go from Here? 45; Do You Love Me? • Kitten on the Keys 46; Carnival in Costa Rica 47; Moss Rose 47; Black Magic 49*; If This Be Sin • That Dangerous Age 49; My Daughter Joy • Operation X 50; Taxi 53; Abdullah the Great • Abdullah's Harem 54; Oscar Wilde 60

Ratti, F. M. see *Ratti, Filippo Walter Maria*

Ratti, Filippo Walter Maria Lost Happiness 48; Dieci Italiani per un Tedesca 62; Night of the Damned • La Notte dei Dannati 71; Eleonora Duse 74

Ratton, Helvécio A Dança dos Bonecos • Dance of the Dolls 87

Rauch, Malte Viva Portugal 75*

Ravel, Gaston Monsieur Pinson, Policier 15*; Document Secret 16; Du Rire aux Larmes 17; L'Homme Qui Revient de Lion 17; Une Femme Inconnue 18; La Maison d'Argile 18; L'Envolée 21; Le Geôle 21; À l'Ombre de Vatican 22; Ferragus 23; Le Gardin du Feu 24; On Ne Badine Pas avec l'Amour 24; Amours, Délices et Orgues 25; L'Avocat 25; Chouchou Poids Plume 25; La Fauteuil 47 26; Mademoiselle Josette Ma Femme 26; Le Bonheur du Jour 27; Jocaste 27; Le Roman d'un Jeune Homme Pauvre 27; Madame Récamier 28; Figaro 29

Ravel, J. Monsieur Albert, Prophète 62*

Ravenskikh, B. Bride with a Dowry 54*

Ravichandran Randheera 88

Ravindranath Thayikotta Thali 88

Ravishankar, K. Dariya Dil 88

Ravn, Jens The Man Who Thought Life • Manden Der Tankte Ting 69

Rawail, Rahul Dacait 87

Rawail, S. S. Banno 88

Rawi, Abdul Hadi al see *Al Rawi, Abdul Hadi*

Rawi, Ousama The Housekeeper • A Judgment in Stone 86

Rawlins, John High Society 32; Lucky Ladies 32; Going Straight 33; Sign Please 33; They're Off! 33; Air Devils 38; The Missing Guest 38; State Police 38; Young Fugitives 38; The Green Hornet Strikes Again 40*; Junior G-Men 40*; The Leather Pushers 40; Bombay Clipper 41; A Dangerous Game 41; Men of the Timberland 41; Mr. Dynamite 41; Mutiny in the Arctic 41; Raiders of the Desert 41; Sea Raiders 41*; Six Lessons from Madame La Zonga 41; Arabian Nights 42; Danger on the River • Mississippi Gambler 42; The Great Impersonation 42; Half Way to Shanghai 42; Overland Mail 42*; Sherlock Holmes and the Voice of Terror • The Voice of Terror 42; Torpedo Boat 42; Unseen Enemy 42; Fighting Command • Texas to Tokyo • We've Never Been Licked 43; Ladies Courageous 44; Sudan 45; Her Adventurous Night 46; Strange Conquest 46; Dick Tracy Meets Gruesome • Dick Tracy Meets Karloff • Dick Tracy's Amazing Adventure 47; Dick Tracy's Dilemma • Mark of the Claw 47; The Arizona Ranger • Arizona Rangers 48; Michael O'Halloran 48; Massacre River 49; Blaze of Glory • Boy from Indiana 50; Rogue River 50; Fort Defiance 51; Shark River 53; Lost Lagoon 58

Raxlen, Rick Horses in Winter 88*

Ray, A. For Mother's Sake 14

Ray, Albert More Pay, Less Work 26; Whispering Wires 26; Love Makes 'Em Wild 27; Publicity Madness 27; Rich But Honest 27; None But the Brave 28; Thief in the Dark 28; Woman Wise 28; Molly and Me 29; Call of the West 30; Kathleen Mavourneen 30; Guilty or Not Guilty 32; The Intruder 32; Lady Beware • The Thirteenth Guest 32; Unholy Love 32; Her Unborn Child 33; A Shriek in the Night 33; West of Singapore 33; Dancing Man 34; The Marriage Bargain 35; St. Louis Woman 35; Everyman's Law 36; Undercover Man 36; Lawless Land 37; Desperate Trails 39

Ray, B. B. see *Ray, Bernard B.*

Ray, Bernard B. Girl Trouble 33; Arizona Nights 34; Loser's End 34; Mystery Ranch 34; Potluck Pards 34; Rawhide Mail

34; West on Parade 34; Coyote Trails 35; The Midnight Phantom 35; Never Too Late 35; Now or Never 35; Rio Rattler 35; Silent Valley 35; The Silver Bullet 35; Texas Jack 35; Ambush Valley 36; Caryl of the Mountains • Get That Girl 36; El Crimen de Medianoche 36; The Last Date • La Última Cita 36; Millionaire Kid 36; Ridin' On 36; Roamin' Wild 36; Speed Reporter 36; Vengeance of Rannah 36; Santa Fe Rides 37; The Silver Trail 37; It's All in Your Mind 38; Smoky Trails 39; Broken Strings 40; Dangerous Lady 41; Fools of Desire 41; Law of the Timber 41; Girl Trouble • Too Many Women 42; Gun Shy • House of Errors 42; Buffalo Bill Rides Again 47; Hollywood Barn Dance 47; Timber Fury 50; Buffalo Bill in Tomahawk Territory 52; Hollywood Stunt Man • Hollywood Thrill-Makers • Movie Stuntmen 53; Spring Affair 60

Ray, Charles A Midnight Bell 21; R.S.V.P. 21; Scrap Iron 21; Two Minutes to Go 21; Alias Julius Caesar 22; The Barnstormer 22; The Deuce of Spades 22; Gas, Oil and Water 22; Smudge 22

Ray, Fred Olen Alien Dead • It Fell from the Sky 80; Scalps 83; Bio-Hazard 84; The Tomb 85; Armed Response 86; Commando Squad 86; Prison Ship: The Adventures of Taura, Part One • Star Slammer 86; Chainsaw Hookers • Hollywood Chainsaw Hookers 87; Cyclone 87; Deep Space 87; Demented Death Farm Massacre 87*; Phantom Empire 87; Star Slammer: The Escape 88; Alienator 89; Beverly Hills Vamp 89

Ray, Gdeh Wajan 38*

Ray, Man Le Retour à la Raison 23; Emak Bakia 26; L'Étoile de Mer 28; Les Mystères du Château du Dé • The Mystery of the Château of the Dice 29; Essai de Simulation de Délire Cinématographique 35*; Dreams That Money Can Buy 46*

Ray, Marc B. Wild Gypsies 69; Scream Bloody Murder 73

Ray, Nicholas They Live by Night • The Twisted Road • Your Red Wagon 47; Knock on Any Door 48; A Woman's Secret 48; Roseanna McCoy 49*; Born to Be Bad 50; In a Lonely Place 50; On Dangerous Ground 50*; Flying Leathernecks 51; The Racket 51*; Androcles and the Lion 52*; The Lusty Men 52*; Macao 52*; Johnny Guitar 54; Run for Cover 54; Hot Blood 55; Rebel Without a Cause 55; Bigger Than Life 56; The James Brothers • The True Story of Jesse James 56; Amère Victoire • Bitter Victory 57; Party Girl 58; Wind Across the Everglades 58; Les Dents du Diable • Ombre Bianchi • The Savage Innocents 59*; King of Kings 61; 55 Days at Peking 63*; We Can't Go Home Again • You Can't Go Home Again 73; Dreams of Thirteen 74*; Lightning Over Water • Nick's Film • Nick's Movie 80*

Ray, Robert Dugan of the Dugouts 28; Riley of the Rainbow Division 28

Ray, Sandip Phatikchand 83

Ray, Satyajit The Lament of the Path •

Pather Panchali • The Saga of the Road • Song of the Little Road • Song of the Road 55; Aparajito • The Unvanquished 56; Paras Pathar • The Philosopher's Stone 57; Apu Sansar • Apur Sansar • The World of Apu 58; Jalsaghar • The Music Room 58; Devi • The Goddess 60; Rabindranath Tagore 60; Portrait of a City 61; Teen Kanya • Three Daughters • Two Daughters 61; Abhijan • The Expedition 62; Kanchanjangha • Kanchenjungha 62; The Big City • The Great City • Mahanagar 63; Charulata • The Lonely Wife 64; The Coward and the Holy Man • The Coward and the Saint • Kapurush-o-Mahapurush 65; Two 65; The Hero • Nayak 66; Chiriakhana • The Menagerie • The Zoo 67; The Adventures of Goopi and Bagha • Goopi and Bagha • Goopi Gyne Bagha Byne 68; Aranyer Din Ratri • Days and Nights in the Forest 69; The Adversary • Pratidwandi • The Rival • Siddhartha and the City 70; Company • Company Limited • Seemabaddha • Simabaddha 71; Sikkim, 1971 71; The Inner Eye 72; Asani Sanket • Ashani Sanket • Distant Thunder 73; The Golden Fortress • Sonar Killa 74; Dahana-Aranja • Jana-Aranya • The Middleman 75; Bala 76; The Chess Players • Shatranj ke Khilari 77; Baba Felunath, Joi • The Elephant God • Joi Baba Felunath 78; Hirok Rajar Deshe • The Kingdom of Diamonds 79; Deliverance • Sadgati 81; Pikoo • Pikoo's Day 81; Ghare-Baire • The Home and the World 82; An Enemy of the People • Ganashatru 89

Raymaker, Herman Racing Luck 24; Below the Line 25; The Love Hour 25; Tracked in the Snow Country 25; Hero of the Big Snows 26; His Jazz Bride 26; Millionaires 26; The Night Cry 26; Flying Luck 27; The Gay Old Bird 27; Simple Sis 27; Under the Tonto Rim 28; Trailing the Killer 32; Adventure Girl 34

Raymond, Alan The Police Tapes 77*

Raymond, Charles Exceeding His Legal Speed 04; A Joke on the Motorist 04; The Kidnapped Child 04; Love's Labour Lost 04; The Serenade 04; The Smugglers 04; Vengeance Is Mine 04; Catching a Tartar 05; How Jones Saw the Derby 05; The Jailbird, or The Bishop and the Convict 05; The Terror of the Neighbourhood 05; Algy's New Suit 06; Anything for Peace and Quietness 06; The Cabby's Dream 06; Dick Turpin's Last Ride to York 06; The Fake Blind Man 06; The Gambler's Nightmare 06; A Life for a Life 06; A Lucky Pig 06; Me and My Two Pals 06; Mr. Henpeck's Quiet Bank Holiday 06; A Pair of Desperate Swindlers 06; Ticket Mania 06; Why Jones Signed the Pledge 06; A Wife's Forgiveness 06; A Brave Lad's Reward 07; Her Rival's Necklace 07; I Never Forget the Wife 07; Love Will Find a Way 07; My Mother-in-Law's Visit 07; Sons of Martha 07; True Till Death 07; Uncle's Present Returned with Thanks 07; A Bird of Freedom 08; The Cracksmen and the Black Diamonds 08; The Diamond

Thieves 08; The Fireman's Daughter 08; A Grateful Dog 08; A Jilted Woman's Revenge 08; Lazy Jim's Luck 08; The Love of a Gypsy 08; A Night Alarm 08; Our Village Club Holds a Marathon Race 08; Uncle's Rejected Present 08; When Other Lips 08; Baby's Chum 09; How the Bulldog Paid the Rent 09; The Immortal Goose 09; The Royalist's Wife 09; They Would Be Acrobats 09; The Clerk's Downfall 10; Every Wrong Shall Be Righted 10; The Fireman's Wedding 10; Nan, a Coster Girl's Romance 11; A Ride for a Bride 11; The Adventures of Dick Turpin—A Deadly Foe, a Pack of Hounds and Some Merry Monks 12; The Adventures of Dick Turpin—The Gunpowder Plot 12; The Adventures of Dick Turpin—The King of Highwaymen 12; The Adventures of Dick Turpin—200 Guineas Reward, Dead or Alive 12; A Father's Sacrifice 12; From Cowardice to Honour 12; The Great Anarchist Mystery 12; Hamlet 12; Her Teddy Bear 12; How 'Arry Sold His Seeds 12; Lieutenant Daring Defeats the Middleweight Champion 12; Lieutenant Daring Quells a Rebellion 12; The Mountaineer's Romance 12; Robin Hood Outlawed 12; Three-Fingered Kate—The Wedding Presents 12; The Undergraduate's Visitor 12; The Winsome Widow 12; Bliggs on the Briny 13; A Creole's Love Story 13; Dick Turpin's Ride to York 13; The Favourite for the Jamaica Cup 13; A Flash of Lightning 13; A Flirtation at Sea 13; Fraudulent Spiritualism Exposed • The Seer of Bond Street • Spiritualism Exposed 13; Ju-Jitsu to the Rescue • Self Defence 13; Lieutenant Daring and the Dancing Girl 13; Lieutenant Daring and the Labour Riots 13; The Old College Badge 13; The Planter's Daughter 13; Tom Cringle in Jamaica 13; Britain's Secret Treaty 14; The Finger of Destiny 14; The Kaiser's Spies 14; The Life of a London Shopgirl 14; The Mystery of the Diamond Belt 14; Queenie of the Circus 14; Those Who Dwell in Darkness 14; The Counterfeiters 15; The Great Cheque Fraud 15; The Stolen Heirlooms 15; The Thornton Jewel Mystery 15; Traffic 15; Betta the Gypsy 18; Checkmated 20; The Daylight Gold Robbery 20; East and West 20; Echoes of the Past 20; The Fraudulent Spiritualistic Seance 20; The Great London Mystery 20; Her Fortune at Stake 20; The House of Mystery 20; The Rogue Unmasked 20; The Sacred Snake Worshippers 20; The Search for the Will 20; The Vengeance of Ching Fu 20

Raymond, Gene Million Dollar Weekend 48

Raymond, Jack Barbara Elopes 21*; The Curse of Westacott 21*; The Flirtations of Phyllis 21*; A Game for Two 21*; The Joke That Failed 21*; Mary's Work 21*; The Upper Hand 21*; A Woman Misunderstood 21*; The Greater War 26; Second to None 26; Somehow Good 27; Zero 28; A Peep Behind the Scenes 29; Splinters 29; French Leave 30; The Great Game 30;

Almost a Divorce 31*; Mischief 31; The Speckled Band 31; Tilly of Bloomsbury 31; Up for the Cup 31; It's a King 32; Life Goes On • Sorry You've Been Troubled 32; Say It with Music 32; Just My Luck 33; Night of the Garter 33; Sorrell and Son 33; Up to the Neck 33; Girls Please 34; The King of Paris 34; Come Out of the Pantry 35; The Hope of His Side • Where's George? 35; When Knights Were Bold 36; The Frog 37; The Rat 37; Blondes for Danger 38; No Parking 38; A Royal Divorce 38; The Mind of Mr. Reeder • The Mysterious Mr. Reeder 39; Missing People 39; You Will Remember 40; Up for the Cup 50; Reluctant Heroes 51; Take Me to Paris 51; Worm's Eye View 51; Little Big Shot 52

Raymond, Susan The Police Tapes 77*

Raynal, Jackie Hotel New York 85

Razumni, Alexander *see Rasumny, Alexander*

Razumovsky, Andrei Takaya Zhestokaya Igra—Khokkey • This Tough Game—Hockey 87

Razzakov, Tynchylyk Volnyi Umirayut na Beregu • Waves Die on the Shore 87

Rea, David C. She'll Follow You Anywhere 71

Reachi, Manuel Yolanda 42*

Read, J. Parker Civilization 16*; His Own Law 20; The Last Moment 23

Read, James The Terrible Two in Luck 14; The Terrible Two, Kidnappers 14; The Terrible Two on the Wait 14; The Terrible Two on the Wangle 14; Arabella and the Soft Soap • Arabella Sells Soft Soap 15; Arabella in Society 15; Arabella Meets Raffles 15; Arabella Out of a Job 15; Arabella Spies Spies • Patriotic Arabella 15; Arabella the Lady Slavey 15; Arabella vs. Lynxeye 15; Arabella's Frightfulness 15; Arabella's Motor 15; Lynxeye on the Prowl 15; Lynxeye Trapped 15; Lynxeye's Night Out 15; MacDougal's Aeroplane 15; Pugilistic Potts 15; Sergeant Lightning and the Gorgonzola Gang 15; The Terrible Two—A.B.S. 15; The Terrible Two Abroad 15; The Terrible Two Had 15; The Tramp's Paradise 15; A Watery Romance 15; Ye Olde Waxworks by the Terrible Two 15

Read, Melanie Trial Run 84; Send a Gorilla 88

Reali, Stefano Laggiu nella Giungla 88

Reardon, James Kiss Me 18; What a Life! 18; Where's the Key? 18; So Like Him 19; To Let 19; Let's Pretend 20; Seeing Double 20; Shadow of Evil 21

Reaton, Eric Wedding Bells 27

Rebane, Bill The Giant Spider Invasion 75; The Alpha Incident 76; Invasion from Inner Earth 77; The Capture of Bigfoot 79; The Demons of Ludlow 83

Rebibo, Rafael Makom Le'Yad Hayam 88

Rebollo, Javier Golfo de Vizcaya 85

Record, Don Summertree 71*

Red, Eric Cohen and Tate 88

Reddy, A. Kothandarami Bhargava Ramudu 87; Jebu Donga 88; Kirai Dada

88; Marana Homann 88

Reddy, N. T. Jayarama Asase 88

Reddy, Prabhakara Mandaladheesudu 87

Reddy, Prasad Nallam Dhoorapu Kondalu 88

Reddy, R. Chandrasekhar Rakhee 88

Reddy, Vijay Jawab Hum Denge 87; Main Tera Dushman 89

Redfern, Jasper The Monkey and the Ice Cream 04; A Funny Story 05; Kick Me, I'm Bill Bailey 05; Uncle Podger's Mishaps 05

Redford, Robert Ordinary People 80; The Milagro Beanfield War 87

Redford, William *see Squitieri, Pasquale*

Redhead, Norman Out of the Bandbox 53

Reed, A. D. Are We Prepared for the International Trade Hunt? 16; The Wild and Woolly West 16

Reed, Bill The Secret of the Sword 85*

Reed, Carol Men of the Sea • Midshipman Easy 33; It Happened in Paris 35*; Laburnum Grove 36; Talk of the Devil 36; Bank Holiday • Three on a Week-End 37; Who's Your Lady Friend? 37; Climbing High 38; Penny Paradise 38*; A Girl Must Live 39; The Stars Look Down 39; Gestapo • Night Train • Night Train to Munich 40; The Girl in the News 40; Kipps • The Remarkable Mr. Kipps 41; A Letter from Home 41; The Young Mr. Pitt 41; The New Lot 42; The Immortal Battalion • The Way Ahead 44; The True Glory 45*; Gang War • Odd Man Out 46; The Fallen Idol • The Lost Illusion 48; The Third Man 49; National Playing Fields 50; Outcast of the Islands 51; The Man Between 53; A Kid for Two Farthings 54; Trapeze 56; The Key 58; Our Man in Havana 59; Mutiny on the Bounty 62*; The Running Man 63; The Agony and the Ecstasy 65; Oliver! 68; Flap • The Last Warrior • Nobody Loves a Drunken Indian • Nobody Loves a Flapping Eagle 70; Follow Me! • The Public Eye 71

Reed, Daniel Fog Over Frisco 34*

Reed, J. T. *see Reed, Theodore*

Reed, Jerry What Comes Around 86

Reed, Joel M. Dragon Lady • The G.I. Executioner • Wit's End 71; Career Bed 72; Blood Bath 76; Bloodsucking Freaks • The Incredible Torture Show 76; Gamma 693 • Night of the Wehrmacht Zombies • Night of the Zombies 81

Reed, Langford The Catch of the Season 14; The Cleansing of a Dirty Dog 14; The Little God 14; The Rival Anarchists 14; The Temptation of Joseph 14; Chase Me Charlie 17

Reed, Luther The Ace of Cads 26; Evening Clothes 27; Honeymoon Hate 27; New York 27; Shanghai Bound 27; The World at Her Feet 27; The Sawdust Paradise 28; Rio Rita 29; Dixiana 30; Hell's Angels 30*; Hit the Deck 30; Convention Girl 35

Reed, Roland In Paris, A.W.O.L. 36; House of Secrets 37; Red Lights Ahead 37

Reed, Theodore When the Clouds Roll

By 19*; The Nut 21; Lady Be Careful 36; Double or Nothing 37; Tropic Holiday 38; I'm from Missouri 39; What a Life! 39; At Good Old Siwash • Good Old Schooldays • Good Old Siwash • Those Were the Days 40; Her First Beau 41; Life with Henry 41

Reel, Frederick, Jr. The Border Rider 24; The Desert Secret 24; The Last Man 24; Eyes of the Desert 26; Gasoline Cowboy 26

Rees, Clive The Blockhouse 73; When the Whales Came 89

Rees, Jerry The Brave Little Toaster 87

Reese, Bea Onno 23 88

Reeve, Geoffrey Puppet on a Chain 70*; Caravan to Vaccares 74; Souvenir 88

Reeve, John The Young Jacobites 59; Along the Way 73*

Reeve, Leonard The Black Swan 52; No Haunt for a Gentleman 52; Stable Rivals 53; Souls in Conflict 55*; The Adventures of Rex 59

Reeves, Michael Il Castello dei Morti Vivi • Castle of the Living Dead • Le Château des Morts Vivants • Crypt of Horror 64*; Il Lago di Satana • The Revenge of the Blood Beast • Satan's Sister • The She-Beast • La Sorella di Satana 65; The Sorcerers 67; The Conqueror Worm • Edgar Allan Poe's Conqueror Worm • Witchfinder General 68; Edgar Allen Poe's The Oblong Box • The Oblong Box 69*

Refik, Halit My Aunt • Teyzem 86

Regamey, Maurice Crazy in the Noodle 57; Cigarettes, Whiskey and Wild Women 58

Regan, Patrick Kiss Daddy Goodbye 81

Regan, W. S. *see Garrone, Sergio*

Regan, Willy S. *see Garrone, Sergio*

Reggio, Godfrey Koyaanisqatsi 82; Powaqqatsi 88; Songlines 89

Regis, Jack Deep Thoughts 81

Regnoli, Piero Curse of the Vampire • Daughters of the Vampire • Desires of the Vampire • The Last Prey of the Vampire • The Last Victim of the Vampire • The Playgirls and the Vampire • L'Ultima Preda del Vampiro • The Vampire's Last Victim 60; I'll See You in Hell 60; Caribbean Hawk 63

Rego, Luis Chicken and Fries • Poule et Frites 87

Regueiro, Francisco Our Father • Padre Nuestro 85; Diario de Invierno 88

Rehfeld, Curt The Greater Glory 26

Reiber, Willy Johannesnacht 35; Die Sonne Geht Auf 35

Reichenbach, Carlos Filme Demência • The Last Faust 86; Anjos do Arrabalde • Suburban Angels 87

Reichenbach, François Impressions de New York 55; New York Ballade 55; Visages de Paris 55; Le Grand Sud 56; Houston Texas 56; Novembre à Paris 56; L'Américain Se Détend 57; Au Pays de Porgy and Bess 57; Carnaval à la Nouvell-Orléans 57; L'Été Indien 57; Les Marines 57; America Through the Keyhole • L' Amérique Insolite • L'Amérique Vu par un Français 60; Un Cœur Gros Comme Ça •

The Winner 61; À la Mémoire du Rock 62; L'Amérique Lunaire 62; Les Amoureux du "France" 62*; Un Bol d'Air à Loué • La Douceur du Village 62; Jeu 1 • Jeux 62*; Le Paris des Mannequins 62; Le Paris des Photographes 62; Le Petit Café • Scènes de la Vie de Café 62; Retour à New York 62; Weekend en Mer 62; Artifices 63; Histoire d'un Petit Garçon Devenu Grand 63; Illuminations 63*; Anges Gardiens 64*; Les Cheveaux d'Hollywood 64; México Nuevo 64; Tout Reste à Découvrir 64; Le Cinqième Soleil 65*; Dunoyer de Segonzac 65*; East African Safari 65; Lapicque 65; Lomelin • Portrait d'un Novillero 65; Aurora 66; El Cordobés 66; Impressions de Paris 66; Manitas de Plata 66; Le Professeur de Piano 66; Reportage sur "Paris Brûle-T-Il?" 66; Voyage de Brigitte Bardot aux U.S.A 66; Concerto Brandenbourgeois 67; Gromaire 67; México, México • Soy México 67*; Artur Rubinstein—L'Amour de la Vie • Artur Rubinstein—The Love of Life • Love of Life 68*; Challenge in the Snow • Grenoble • Thirteen Days in France • Treize Jours en France 68*; Musique en Méditerranée 68; La Sixième Face du Pentagone • The Sixth Side of the Pentagon 68*; À Fleur d'Eau • Vichy 1969 69; Christian Dior 69; Festival dans le Désert 69; France sur Mer 69; L'Indiscrète 69; Israël • Les Moisson de l'Espoir 69; Kill Patrice, un Shérif Pas Comme les Autres 69; Les Mains du Futur 69; Le Massacre 69; Parfums Revillon 69; Prisons à l'Américaine • Violence sur Houston 69; La Caravane d'Amour • The Great Medicine Ball Caravan • Medicine Ball Caravan • We Have Come for Your Daughters 70; La Fête des Morts 70; L'Opéra de Quatre Pesos 70; Yehudi Menuhin—Chemin de la Lumière • Yehudi Menuhin—Road of Light • Yehudi Menuhin Story 70*; Le Chasseur 71; Éliette ou Instants de la Vie d'une Femme 71; Le Hold-Up au Crayon 71; J'Ai Tout Donné • Johnny Hallyday • Johnny's Days 71; Partir 71; Rêver ou Envol 71; Monte-Carlo 72; La Raison du Plus Fou • La Raison du Plus Fou Est Toujours le Meilleure 72*; F for Fake • Fake? • Nothing But the Truth • Vérités et Mensonges 73*; La Passion Selon les Coras 73; Carlos Monzón 74; Don't You Hear the Dogs Bark? • Entends-Tu les Chiens Aboyer? • ¿No Oyes Ladrar los Perros? 74*; Another Way to Love 76; Club Méditerranée 76; Pele • Le Roi Pele 76; Sex O'Clock U.S.A. 76; V.G.E. • Valérie Giscard d'Estaing au Mexique 79; Houston Texas 80; Jacques-Henri Lartigue 80; François Reichenbach's Japan • Le Japon Insolite 81

Reicher, Frank The Case of Becky 15; The Chorus Lady 15; Mr. Grex of Monte Carlo 15; The Secret Orchard 15; The Secret Sin 15; Alien Souls 16; The Black Wolf 16; The Dupe 16; For the Defense 16; The Love Mask 16; Public Opinion 16; Puddin' Head Wilson • Pudd'nhead Wilson 16; The Storm 16; The Victory of Conscience 16*; Witchcraft 16; An American

Widow 17; Betty to the Rescue 17; Castles for Two 17; The Eternal Mother 17; The Inner Shrine 17; Lost and Won 17; Sacrifice 17; The Trouble Buster 17; Unconquered 17; The Claim 18; The Only Road 18; The Prodigal Wife 18; The Sea Waif 18; Suspense 18; The Trap 18; Treasure 18; The Treasure of the Sea 18; The American Way 19; The Battler 19; The Black Circle 19; Empty Arms 20; Behind Masks • Jeanne of the Marshes 21; Idle Hands 21; Out of the Depths 21; Wise Husbands 21; Mr. Antonio 29*; The Grand Parade 30*

Reichert, Julia Seeing Red—Stories of American Communists 83*

Reichert, Mark Union City 80

Reichman, Rachel The Riverbed 85

Reichman, Thomas Mingus 68

Reichmann, Max Manège 28; The Strange Case of Captain Ramper 28; The Alluring Goal • Das Lockende Ziel 30; Die Grosse Attraktion 33; Ich Glaub' Nie Mehr an eine Frau 33

Reid, Alastair Baby Love 68; The Night Digger • The Road Builder 71; Shattered • Something to Hide 71

Reid, Dorothy see Davenport, Dorothy

Reid, Hal see Reid, James Hallek

Reid, James Hallek At Cripple Creek 12; Curfew Shall Not Ring Tonight 12; Illumination 12; Kaintuck 12; A Man's Duty 12; Rip Van Winkle 12; The Seventh Son 12; The Victoria Cross 12; The Deerslayer 13*; Thou Shalt Not Kill 13; Time Lock No. 776 15

Reid, John Middle Age Spread 79; Carry Me Back 82; Leave All Fair 85

Reid, Max Wild Thing 87

Reid, Mrs. Wallace see Davenport, Dorothy

Reid, Wallace Cross Purposes 13*; Dead Man's Shoes 13; Fires of Fate 13*; The Foreign Spy 13; The Gratitude of Wanda 13; The Harvest of Flame 13; The Heart of a Cracksman 13*; Hearts and Horses 13*; Her Innocent Marriage 13*; A Hopi Legend 13; The Kiss 13; The Lightning Bolt 13; Love and the Law 13; The Modern Snare 13; The Mystery of the Yellow Aster Mine 13; Pride of Lonesome 13; Retribution 13*; A Rose of Old Mexico 13*; The Tattooed Arm 13; Via Cabaret 13; The Ways of Fate 13*; When Jim Returned 13; Breed o' the Mountains 14; Children of Fate • Love's Western Flight 14; Cupid Incognito 14; The Den of Thieves 14; Fires of Conscience 14; A Flash in the Dark 14; The Fruit of Evil 14; The Greater Devotion 14; A Gypsy Romance 14; The Heart of the Hills 14; The Intruder 14; The Man Within 14; The Mountaineer 14; Passing of the Beast 14; The Quack 14; Regeneration 14; The Siren 14; The Skeleton 14; The Test 14; The Voice of Viola 14; The Way of a Woman 14; The Wheel of Life 14; Women and Roses 14

Reiner, Carl Enter Laughing 66; The Comic 69; Going Ape • Where's Poppa? 70; Oh, God! 77; The One and Only 78; The Jerk 79; Dead Men Don't Wear Plaid

82; The Man with Two Brains 83; All of Me 84; Summer Rental 85; Summer School 87; Bert Rigby, You're a Fool 89; Sibling Rivalry 90

Reiner, Rob Spinal Tap • This Is Spinal Tap 84; The Sure Thing 85; Stand by Me 86; The Princess Bride 87; When Harry Met Sally 89; Misery 90

Reinert, Al For All Mankind 89

Reinert, Emil E. Not Wanted on Voyage • Treachery on the High Seas 36; L'Affaire 50; Fünf Mädchen und Ein Mann • Geschichte von Fünf Städten • A Tale of Five Cities • A Tale of Five Women 51*; Vienna Waltzes • Wien Tanzt 51; Danger Is a Woman • Quai de Grenelle 52; The Strollers 52; Naughty Martine 53

Reinhard, Pierre B. Dressage 85

Reinhardt, Gottfried Invitation 51; Equilibrium 53; Historia de Tres Amores • The Story of Three Loves • War Es die Grosse Liebe? 53*; Betrayed 54; Vor Sonnenenuntergang 56; Abschied der Götter • Abschied von den Wolken • Rebel Flight to Cuba 59; Menschen im Hotel 59; Shocker • Stadt Ohne Mitleid • Town Without Pity • Ville Sans Pitié 60; Sweetheart of the Gods 60; Elf Jahre und ein Tag 63; Situation Hopeless But Not Serious 65

Reinhardt, John I...Thou...and... She • Yo...Tu...y...Ella 33; Dos Más Uno Dos • Two and One Two 34; Granaderos del Amor • Grenadiers of Love 34; The Day You Love Me • El Día Que Me Quieras 35; Tango-Bar 35; Captain Calamity • Captain Hurricane 36; For You I Die 47; The Guilty 47; High Tide 47; Open Secret 48; Sofia 48; Chicago Calling 51

Reinhardt, Max Sumurun 08; Das Mirakel 12; Insel der Seligen 13; Eine Venezianische Nacht 13; A Midsummer Night's Dream 35*

Reiniger, Lotte Das Ornament des Verliebten Herzens • The Ornament of the Loving Heart 19; Amor und das Standhafte Ehepaar • Amor und das Standhafte Liebespaar 20; Der Fliegende Koffer 21; Der Stern von Bethlehem 21; Aschenputtel • Cinderella 22; Dornröschen 22; Die Abenteuer des Prinzen Achmed • The Adventures of Prince Achmed • Die Geschichte des Prinzen Achmed • Wak-Wak, ein Märchenzauber 26; Die Abenteuer des Doktor Dolittle • The Adventures of Dr. Dolittle • Dr. Dolittle • Doktor Dolittle und Seine Tiere 28; Der Scheintote Chinese 28; Zehn Minuten Mozart 30; Harlekin 31; Sissi 32; Carmen 33; Das Gestohlene Herz • The Stolen Heart 34; Der Graf von Carabas • Puss in Boots 34; Das Rollende Rad 34; Galathea 35; Der Kleine Schornsteinfeger • The Little Chimney Sweep 35; Papageno 35; The King's Breakfast 36; Tochter 37; L'Elisir d'Amore 39; The Daughter 49; Mary's Birthday 49; The Frog Prince 50; Aladdin 53; The Magic Horse 53; Puss in Boots 53; Snow White and Rose Red 53; Caliph Storch • Caliph Stork 54; The Gallant Little Tailor 54; The Grasshopper and the Ant 54; The Sleeping Beauty 54; The Three Wishes 54; Hansel and Gretel 55; Jack and the Beanstalk • Jack the Giant Killer 55; Thumbelina 55; The Star of Bethlehem 56; La Belle Hélène • Helen la Belle 57; The Seraglio 58; The Pied Piper of Hamelin 60; The Frog Prince 61; Wee Sandy 62; Cinderella 63; The Lost Son 74; Aucassin et Nicolette 76; The Rose and the Ring 79

Reinl, Harald The Unholy Intruders 52; Kapitanleutnant Prien—Der Stier von Scapa Flow • U-47 Kapitanleutnant Prien • U-47 Lt. Commander Prien 58; Face of the Frog • Fellowship of the Frog 59; Hand of the Gallows • The Terrible People 60; F.B.I. Contro Dr. Mabuse • Im Stahlnetz des Dr. Mabuse • Phantom Fiend • Le Retour du Docteur Mabuse • The Return of Dr. Mabuse 61; Forger of London 61; The Invisible Dr. Mabuse • The Invisible Horror • Die Unsichtbaren Krallen des Dr. Mabuse 61; Blago u Srebrnom Jezeru • Der Schatz im Silbersee • The Treasure of Silver Lake • Le Trésor du Lac d'Argent 62; The Carpet of Horror 62; Apache Gold • La Révolte des Indiens Apaches • La Valle dei Lunghi Coltelli • Vinetu • Winnetou • Winnetou—I. Teil • Winnetou the Warrior 63; The Strangler of Blackmoor Castle 63; The White Spider 63; Giorni di Fuoco • Last of the Renegades • Le Trésor des Montagnes Bleues • Vinetu II • Winnetou II • Winnetou—II. Teil 64; The Man from Oklahoma • Oklahoma John 64*; Room 13 64; The Desperado Trail • Vinetu III • Winnetou—III. Teil • Winnetou, Part Three • Winnetou III 65; The Last Tomahawk • Der Letzte Mohikaner 65; La Valle delle Ombre Rosse 65; Die Nibelungen • Whom the Gods Wish to Destroy 66; The Blood Demon • Castle of the Walking Dead • Die Schlangengrube und das Pendel • The Snake Pit • The Snake Pit and the Pendulum • The Torture Chamber of Dr. Sadism • The Torture Room 67; Winnetou und Old Shatterhand im Tal der Toten 68; Chariots of the Gods? • Erinnerungen an die Zukunft 69; L'Uomo dal Lungo Facice 69; Der Schrei der Schwarzen Wölfe 72; Die Blutigen Geier von Alaska 73

Reis, Antonio Ana 85*
Reis, Irving The Business of Love 25*; Trout Fishing 32; I'm Still Alive 40; One Crowded Night 40; A Date with the Falcon 41; Footlight Fever 41; The Gay Falcon 41; Week-End for Three 41; The Big Street 42; The Falcon Takes Over 42; Crack-Up 46; The Bachelor and the Bobby-Soxer • Bachelor Knight 47; All My Sons 48; Enchantment 48; Dancing in the Dark 49; Roseanna McCoy 49*; A Letter to Three Husbands • Three Husbands 50; Of Men and Music 50*; New Mexico 51; The Four-Poster 52

Reisch, Walter Pratermizzi 27*; Episode 35; Men Are Not Gods 36; Song of Scheherazade 47; Die Mücke 54; Der Cornet 55
Reisman, Yuli see Raizman, Yuli

Reisman, Yuri see Raizman, Yuli
Reisner, Allen All Mine to Give • The Day They Gave Babies Away 57; St. Louis Blues 58
Reisner, Charles Dog Days 19; A Blue Ribbon Mutt 20; The Champion Loser 20; Dog-Gone Clever 20; Happy Daze 20; The Laundry 20; A Lyin' Tamer 20; His Puppy Love 21; Milk and Yeggs 21; Stuffed Lions 21; Won: One Flivver 21; The Man on the Box 25; The Better 'Ole 26; Oh! What a Nurse! 26; The Fortune Hunter 27; The Missing Link 27; What Every Girl Should Know 27; Brotherly Love 28; Fools for Luck 28; Steamboat Bill, Jr. 28; Chasing Rainbows • Road Show 29; China Bound 29; The Hollywood Revue of 1929 29; Noisy Neighbors 29; Caught Short 30; Love in the Rough 30; Reducing 30; The Christmas Party • Jackie Cooper's Christmas 31; Flying High • Happy Landing 31; Politics 31; Stepping Out 31; Divorce in the Family 32; The Chief • My Old Man's a Fireman 33; The Show-Off 34; Student Tour 34; The Winning Ticket 34; You Can't Buy Everything 34; It's in the Air 35; Everybody Dance 36; Manhattan Merry-Go-Round • Manhattan Music Box 37; Murder Goes to College 37; Sophie Lang Goes West 37; Winter Carnival 39; The Big Store 41; This Time for Keeps 41; Harrigan's Kid 43; Lost in a Harem 44; Meet the People 44; The Cobra Strikes 48; In This Corner 48; The Traveling Saleswoman 50; L'Ultima Cena 50
Reisz, Karel Stars Who Made the Cinema 52; Momma Don't Allow 55*; We Are the Lambeth Boys 58; March to Aldermaston 59*; Saturday Night and Sunday Morning 60; Night Must Fall 63; Morgan! • Morgan—A Suitable Case for Treatment 65; Isadora • The Loves of Isadora 67; The Gambler 74; Dog Soldiers • Who'll Stop the Rain? 78; The French Lieutenant's Woman 81; Sweet Dreams 85; Everybody Wins 90
Reitherman, Wolfgang Sleeping Beauty 59*; 101 Dalmations 61*; The Sword in the Stone 63; The Jungle Book 67; The Aristocats 70; Robin Hood 73; The Rescuers 77*
Reitman, Ivan Cannibal Girls 71; Foxy Lady 71; Meatballs 79; Stripes 81; Ghostbusters 84; Legal Eagles 86; Twins 88; Ghostbusters II 89; Kindergarten Cop 90*
Reitz, Edgar Fate of an Opera • Schicksal einer Oper 58; Baumwolle • Cotton 59; Cancer Research • Krebsforschung 59; Yucatán 60; Ärztekongress • Medical Congress 61; Communication • Kommunikation 61; Mail and Technology • Post und Technik 61; Moltopren I-IV 61; Cinema I—Speed • Kino I—Geschwindigkeit 62; DB-Vision 65; The Children • Die Kinder 66; Footnotes • Fussnoten 67; Lust for Love • Mahlzeiten • Mealtimes 67; Film Hour • Filmstunde 68; Uxmal 68; Cardillac 69; Geschichten vom Kübelkind • Tales of the Trashcan Kid 70*; Cinema Two • Kino Zwei 71; The Golden Fleece • The Golden Stuff • Das Goldene Ding 71*;

Die Reise nach Wien • The Trip to Vienna 73; Blind Alley • In Danger and Great Need the Middle Road Leads to Death • In Gefahr und Grösster Not Bringt der Mittelweg den Tod • The Middle of the Road Is a Very Dead End 74*; Bethanien 75; Picnic 75; We're Going to Play House • Wir Gehen Wohnen 75; Stunde Null • Zero Hour 76; Deutschland im Herbst • Germany in Autumn 78*; Der Schneider von Ulm • The Tailor from Ulm 78; Susan Dances • Susanne Tanzt 79; Geschichten aus den Hunsrückdorfern 81; Heimat • Homeland 83

Rekhviashvili, Alexander The Way Home 81; Sapirhurin • The Step 86; The Stage • Stupen 87
Relph, Michael Saraband • Saraband for Dead Lovers 48*; I Believe in You 51*; The Gentle Gunman 52*; The Square Ring 53*; Out of the Clouds 54*; The Rainbow Jacket 54*; PT Raiders • The Ship That Died of Shame 55*; Who Done It? 55*; Davy 57; Mad Little Island • Rockets Galore! 57; Desert Mice 59; All Night Long 61*
Remo, Andrew King Tut-Ankh-Amen's Eighth Wife • The Mystery of Tut-Ankh-Amen's Eighth Wife 23
Remy, Constant Les Petits 36*
Renán, Sergio Tacos Altos 85
Renan, Sheldon The Killing of America 82
Rénard, Jacques Blanche et Marie 85
René, Norman Longtime Companion 90
Rennie, Barbara Sacred Hearts 84; Echoes 88
Renoir, Claude Opéra Musette 42*
Renoir, Jean La Fille de l'Eau • The Water Girl • The Whirlpool of Fate 24; Charleston • Charleston-Parade • Parade sur un Air de Charleston • Sur un Air de Charleston 26; Nana 26; Marquitta 27; La Petite Lili • La P'tite Lili 27*; The Little Match Girl • The Little Match-Seller • La Petite Marchande d'Allumettes 28*; Tire-au-Flanc 28; Le Tournoi • Le Tournoi dans la Cité 28; Le Bled 29; The Bitch • La Chienne • Isn't Life a Bitch? 31; On Purge Bébé 31; Boudu Sauvé des Eaux • Boudu Saved from Drowning 32; Night at the Crossroads • La Nuit du Carrefour 32; Chotard et Cie 33; Les Amours de Toni • Toni 34; Madame Bovary 34; Crime and Punishment • Crime et Châtiment 35*; Le Crime de Monsieur Lange • The Crime of Monsieur Lange 35; Les Bas-Fonds • The Lower Depths • Underworld 36; Country Excursion • A Day in the Country • Une Partie de Campagne 36; People of France • La Vie Est à Nous 36*; Grand Illusion • La Grande Illusion 37; La Marseillaise • The Marseillaise 37; La Bête Humaine • The Human Beast • Judas Was a Woman 38; La Règle du Jeu • The Rules of the Game 39; The Story of Tosca • La Tosca 40*; The Man Who Came Back • Swamp Water 41; The Amazing Mrs. Holliday 43*; This Land Is Mine 43; Salut à France • Salut à la France • Salute to France 44*; Hold

Autumn in Your Hand • The Southerner 45; Diary of a Chambermaid 46; The Woman on the Beach 46; L'Amore • Love • Ways of Love • Woman 48*; The River 50; Le Carrosse d'Or • La Carrozza d'Oro • The Golden Coach 52; French Cancan • Only the French Can 54; L'Album de Famille de Jean Renoir 56; Elena and Her Men • Éléna et les Hommes • The Night Does Strange Things • Paris Does Strange Things 56; Le Déjeuner sur l'Herbe • Lunch on the Grass • Picnic on the Grass 59; The Doctor's Horrible Experiment • Experiment in Evil • Le Testament du Dr. Cordelier • The Testament of Dr. Cordelier 59; Le Caporal Épinglé • The Elusive Corporal • The Vanishing Corporal 62*; La Direction d'Acteur par Jean Renoir 68; The Little Theater of Jean Renoir • Le Petit Théâtre de Jean Renoir 69

Renoir, Louis Terror on Tiptoe 36
Rens, Peter Jan Maria 86
Renzy, Alex de see De Renzy, Alex
Resnais, Alain L'Aventure de Guy 36; Fantômas 36; Ouvert pour Cause d'Inventaire 46; Schéma d'une Identification 46; L'Alcool Tue 47; La Bague 47; Journée Naturelle • Visite à Max Ernst 47; Le Lait Nestlé 47; Portrait d'Henri Goetz 47; Transfo Transforme l'Énergie du Pyrium 47; Visite à César Domela 47; Visite à Félix Labisse 47; Visite à Hans Hartung 47; Visite à Lucien Coutaud 47; Visite à Oscar Dominguez 47; Châteaux de France 48; Les Jardins de Paris 48; Malfray 48*; Van Gogh 48; Gauguin 50; Guernica 50*; Les Statues Meurent Aussi 53*; Night and Fog • Nuit et Brouillard 55; Toute la Mémoire du Monde 56*; Le Mystère de l'Atelier Quinze 57*; Le Chant du Styrène • The Styrene Song 58; Hiroshima, Mon Amour 59; L'Année Dernière à Marienbad • L'Anno Scorso a Marienbad • Last Year at Marienbad 61; Muriel • Muriel, il Tempo di un Ritorno • Muriel, or The Time of Return • Muriel ou Le Temps d'un Retour • The Time of Return 63; Far from Vietnam • Loin du Viêt-nam 66*; La Guerre Est Finie • Kriget Är Slut • The War Is Over 66; Je T'Aime, Je T'Aime 67; L'Empire d'Alexandre • Stavisky 73; Providence 77; Mon Oncle Américain • Mon Oncle d'Amérique • My American Uncle • My Uncle from America • Les Somnambules 78; Life Is a Bed of Roses • La Vie Est un Roman 83; L'Amour à Mort • Love Unto Death 84; Mélo 86; I Want to Go Home • Je Veux Rentrer à la Maison 89

Resnikoff, Robert The First Power 90
Retes, Gabriel Mujeres Salvajes • Savage Women 87
Retes, Ignacio Trip to Paradise • Viaje al Paraíso 87
Reticker, Hugh Right Off the Bat 15
Reusser, Francis Derborence 85
Revah, Zeev Bouba 87
Révész, György Kétszer Kettő Néha Öt • Two Times Two Are Sometimes Five 54; Gala Dinner • Ünnepi Vacsora 56; At Midnight • Éjfélkor 57; Micsoda

Éjszaka • What a Night! 58; A Megfelelő Ember • The Right Man 59; Danger on the Danube • Four Children in the Flood • Négyen az Árban 61; Angyalok Földje • The Land of Angels 62; Fagyosszentek • Hail Days 62; Hogy Állunk, Fiatalember? • Well, Young Man? 63; Igen • Yes 64; Nem • No 65; All Beginnings Are Hard • Minden Kezdet Nehéz 66; Egy Szerelem Három Éjszakája • Three Nights of Love 67; Isle of the Lion • Az Oroszlán Ugrani Készül 69; Journey Round My Skull • Utazás a Koponyám Körül 70; Akli Miklós 86

Revier, Harry The Weakness of Strength 16; The Lust of the Ages 17; A Grain of Dust 18; The Challenge of Chance 19; A Romance of the Air 19; What Shall We Do with Him? 19; The Return of Tarzan • The Revenge of Tarzan 20; Sailors of the Seven Seas 20; The Son of Tarzan 20*; The Heart of the North 21; Life's Greatest Question 21; The Broadway Madonna 22; The Jungle Trail of the Son of Tarzan 23*; Dangerous Pleasure 25; The Slaver 27; The Thrill Seekers 27; What Price Love? 27; The Mysterious Airman 28; The Convict's Code 30; Bill's Legacy 31; The Lost City 35; Lash of the Penitentes • The Penitente Murder Case 36; Child Bride 37

Rey, Florian La Aldea Maldita 29; La Hermana San Sulpicio 37; Morena Clara 38; Nobleza Baturra • Rustic Chivalry 38; Carmen 49; Manolete 50
Reynaud, Émile Guillaume 1896; Le Premier Cigare 1896
Reynolds, Burt Gator 76; The End 78; Sharky's Machine 81; Stick 85
Reynolds, Christopher Offerings 89
Reynolds, Don see Savino, Renato
Reynolds, Kevin Fandango 85; The Beast 88
Reynolds, Lynn The End of the Rainbow 16; The Girl of Lost Lake 16; God's Crucible 16; It Happened in Honolulu 16; A Romance of Billy Goat Hill 16; Secret of the Swamp 16; Broadway Arizona 17; The Greater Law 17; Mr. Opp 17; Mutiny 17; The Show-Down 17; Southern Justice 17; Up or Down 17; Ace High 18; Fame and Fortune 18; Fast Company 18; The Gown of Destiny 18; Mr. Logan, U.S.A. 18; Western Blood 18; The Brute Breaker 19; The Coming of the Law 19; The Forbidden Room 19; A Little Brother of the Rich 19; Miss Adventure 19; The Rebellious Bride 19; Treat 'Em Rough 19; Bullet-Proof 20; Overland Red 20; The Red Lane 20; The Texan 20; Big Town Roundup 21; The Night Horseman 21; The Road Demon 21; Trailin' 21; Arabia 22; For Big Stakes 22; Just Tony 22; Sky High 22; Up and Going 22; Brass Commandments 23; The Gunfighter 23; The Huntress 23; The Deadwood Coach 24; Last of the Duanes 24; Durand of the Bad Lands 25; The Rainbow Trail 25; Riders of the Purple Sage 25; The Buckaroo Kid 26; Chip of the Flying U 26; The Combat 26; The Man in the Saddle 26*; Prisoners of the Storm 26; The Texas

Streak 26; Hey! Hey! Cowboy 27; The Silent Rider 27
Reynolds, Quentin Death of a Dream 50; Justice and Caryl Chessman 60*
Reynolds, Red see Reynolds, William
Reynolds, S. E. The Great Conway 40
Reynolds, Sheldon Foreign Intrigue 56; Die Hölle von Manitoba • Un Lugar Llamado Glory • A Place Called Glory 64; Killer's Carnival 65*; Assignment to Kill 68
Reynolds, William Chartroose Caboose 60
Rezaie, Rahman Closed Circuit 86
Rezende, Sérgio O Homem da Capa Preta • The Man with the Black Coat 86
Rezyka, Mark South of Reno 87
Rhone, Trevor Smile Orange 76
Riazanov, Eldar see Ryazanov, Eldar
Ribero, Mario El Embajador de la India 88
Ribes, Jean-Michel La Galette du Roi • The King's Cake 86
Ribon, Roberto de see De Ribon, Roberto
Ricci, Luciano Giuseppe Venduto dai Fratelli • Joseph and His Brethren • Joseph Sold by His Brothers • Sold Into Egypt • The Story of Joseph and His Brethren 60*; Alone Against Rome • The Fall of Rome • Solo Contro Roma • Vengeance of the Gladiators 61*; To Have and to Hold 63; Il Castello dei Morti Vivi • Castle of the Living Dead • Le Château des Morts Vivants • Crypt of Horror 64*; The Lovers 72
Ricci, T. see Ricci, Tonino
Ricci, Teodoro see Ricci, Tonino
Ricci, Tonino Monta in Sella Figlio di… 72; Bermuda: La Cueva de los Tiburónes • Bermuda: La Fossa Maledetta • The Cave of Sharks 78; Rush 84; Days of Hell • I Giorni dell'Inferno 86; Rage 86; Night of the Sharks 90
Rice, Bill The Vineyard 88*
Rice, Ron The Flower Thief 60; Senseless 62; The Queen of Sheba Meets the Atom Man 63; Chumlum 64
Rich, David Lowell No Time to Be Young • Teenage Delinquents 57; Senior Prom 58; Have Rocket, Will Travel 59; Hey Boy! Hey Girl! 59; See How They Run 64; Madame X 65; The Plainsman 66; Rosie! 67; Three Guns for Laredo • Three Guns for Texas 67*; A Lovely Way to Die • A Lovely Way to Go 68; Eye of the Cat • Wylie 69; Northeast of Seoul • Northeast to Seoul 72; That Man Bolt • Thunderbolt • To Kill a Dragon 72*; Runaway! • The Runaway Train 73; The Sex Symbol 74; Airport '79 • Airport '79: Concorde • Airport '80: The Concorde • The Concorde: Airport '79 79; Chu Chu and the Philly Flash 81
Rich, John First Wife • Wives and Lovers 63; The New Interns 64; Roustabout 64; Boeing Boeing 65; Easy Come, Easy Go 67
Rich, Richard The Fox and the Hound 81*; The Black Cauldron 85*

Rich, Roy It's Not Cricket 48*; My Brother's Keeper 48*

Richard, Jacques Ave Maria 84; Cent Francs l'Amour 85

Richard, Jean-Louis Bonne Chance Charlie 62; Mata Hari • Mata Hari, Agent H21 • Mata Hari, Agente Segreto H21 64; Diane's Body 69; Le Déclic 85

Richard, Jef see Schellerup, Henning

Richard, Jefferson see Schellerup, Henning

Richard, Pierre Absent-Minded • The Daydreamer • Le Distrait 75

Richards, C. M. Pennington see Pennington-Richards, C. M.

Richards, Dick The Culpepper Cattle Company 72; Farewell, My Lovely 75; Rafferty and the Gold Dust Twins • Rafferty and the Highway Hustlers 75; March or Die 77; Death Valley 82; Man, Woman and Child 82; Heat 87

Richards, James Joey Knows a Villain 60; Joey Leads the Way 60; Joey's No Ass 60

Richards, Lloyd Partners Please 32

Richards, R. M. see Richards, Dick

Richardson, Frank In the Night 20; The Black Tulip 21; Candytuft, I Mean Veronica 21; Kitty Tailleur 21; Sheer Bluff 21; The White Hen 21; King of the Pack 26; Racing Blood 26; Peace and Quiet 31; We Dine at Seven 31; Above Rubies 32; Don't Be a Dummy 32; Flat No. 9 32; The River House Ghost 32; Double Wedding 33; Money Mad 34; Oh, What a Night! 35; The Howard Case 36; Cabaret 45; Sweethearts Forever 45; Amateur Night 46; I Was a Dancer 49; Bait 50

Richardson, John Dusty 82

Richardson, Ken None But the Brave 63

Richardson, Peter The Supergrass 85; Eat the Rich 87

Richardson, Ralph Home at Seven • Murder on Monday 51

Richardson, Richard A. A Man, a Woman and a Killer 75*

Richardson, Tony Momma Don't Allow 55*; Look Back in Anger 58; The Entertainer 60; Sanctuary 60; A Taste of Honey 61; The Loneliness of the Long Distance Runner • Rebel with a Cause 62; Tom Jones 63; The Loved One 64; Mademoiselle • Summer Fires 65; The Sailor from Gibraltar 66; Red and Blue 67; The Charge of the Light Brigade 68; La Chambre Obscure • Laughter in the Dark 69; Hamlet 69; Ned Kelly • Ned Kelly, Outlaw 70; Dead Cert 73; A Delicate Balance 73; Joseph Andrews 77; The Border 81; The Hotel New Hampshire 84

Richebé, Roger L'Agonie des Aigles 34; Monseigneur 50*; Austerlitz • The Battle of Austerlitz 59*

Richert, William First Position 73; Winter Kills 78; American Success • The American Success Company • Success 79; Jimmy Reardon • A Night in the Life of Jimmy Reardon 87

Richmond, Anthony Déjà Vu 85

Richmond, Anthony see Ricci, Tonino

Richmond, J. A. The Barker 17

Richter, Hans Film Is Rhythm • Film Ist Rhythmus • Rhythm 21 • Rhythmus 21 21; Rhythmus 23 23; Film Study • Filmstudie 25 25; Rhythmus 25 25; Inflation 27; Ghosts Before Breakfast • Ghosts Before Noon • Vormittagsspuk 28; Alles Dreht Sich, Alles Bewegt Sich! • Everything Revolves, Everything Moves! 29; Everyday 29; Kampf des Unabhängigen Gegen den Kommerziellen Film • Sturm Über la Sarraz 29*; Nachmittag zu den Wettrennen 29; Race Symphony • Rennsymphonie 29; Twopence Magic • Twopenny Magic • Zweigroschenzauber 29; Neues Leben • New Life 30; Europa Radio 31; Hallo Everybody! 33; From Lightning to Television • Vom Blitz zum Fernsehbild 36; Conquest of the Skies • Die Eroberung des Himmels 38; Die Enstehung der Farbe 38; Hans im Glück 38; Eine Kleine Welt im Dunkelen • A Small World in the Dark 38; Die Börse • The Stock Exchange 39; The Movies Take a Holiday 44*; Dreams That Money Can Buy 46*; Thirty Years of Experiments 51*; Minotaur 54; Acht Mal Acht • 8 x 8 56*; Dadascope I 56; Chesscetera • Passionate Pastime 57; Dadascope II 57; From Dada to Surrealism: Forty Years of Experiment 61*; Alexander Calder: From the Circus to the Moon 63

Richter, Robert Vietnam—An American Journey 78

Richter, W. D. The Adventures of Buckaroo Banzai: Across the Eighth Dimension • Buckaroo Banzai 84

Ricker, Bruce The Last of the Blue Devils 79

Ricketson, James Kiss the Night 88

Ricketts, Thomas The Buzzard's Shadow 15; Damaged Goods 15; The End of the Road 15; The Lure of the Mask 15; The Secretary of Frivolous Affairs 15; Life's Blind Alley 16; The Other Side of the Door 16; The Single Code 17; Crime of the Hour 18; Broth for Supper 19

Rickman, Tom River Rat 84

Ricks, Archie In Broncho Land 26

Rico, Antonio Gimenez see Gimenez-Rico, Antonio

Rico, Luca de see De Rico, Luca

Rico, Luis Quintanilla see Quintanilla Rico, Luis

Riddell, James Discipline 35*; The Obvious Thing 35

Ridder, Hans de The Failure • De Mislukking 86

Riddiford, Richard Arriving Tuesday 86

Ridgely, Richard The Great Physician 13; The Green Eye of the Yellow God 13; The Destroying Angel 15; Eugene Aram 15; The Magic Skin 15; Ranson's Folly 15; Shadows from the Past 15; The Tragedies of the Crystal Globe 15; The Wrong Woman 15; The Heart of the Hills 16; The Martyrdom of Phillip Strong 16; A Message to Garcia 16; Envy 17; The Ghost of Old Morro 17; God of Little Children 17; The Great Bradley Mystery 17; The Master Passion 17; The Mystic Hour 17; Passion 17;

Pride 17

Ridgwell, George The Mystery of Room 13 15; The Match-Makers 16; Somewhere in Georgia 16; Fruits of Passion 19; The Root of Evil 19; The Water Lily 19; A Gamble in Lives 20; The Sword of Damocles 20; The Amazing Partnership 21; The Four Just Men 21; Greatheart 21; The Abbey Grange 22; Black Peter 22; The Boscombe Valley Mystery 22; The Bruce Partington Plans 22; Charles Augustus Milverton 22; The Crimson Circle 22; The Eleventh Hour 22; The Flight of the King 22; The Further Adventures of Sherlock Holmes 22; The Golden Pince-Nez 22; The Great Terror 22; The Greek Interpreter 22; The Knight Errant 22; The Last Crusade 22; The Last King of Wales 22; A Lost Leader 22; The Missioner 22; The Musgrave Ritual 22; The Naval Treaty 22; The Norwood Builder 22; Petticoat Loose 22; The Pointing Finger 22; The Red Circle 22; The Reigate Squires 22; The Second Stain 22; The Six Napoleons 22; The Stockbroker's Clerk 22; The Story of Amy Robsart 22; A Story of Nell Gwynne 22; Becket 23; The Blue Carbuncle 23; The Cardboard Box 23; The Crooked Man 23; The Disappearance of Lady Frances Carfax 23; The Engineer's Thumb 23; The Final Problem 23; The Gloria Scott 23; His Last Bow 23; The Last Adventures of Sherlock Holmes 23; The Missing Three Quarter 23; The Mystery of the Dancing Men 23; The Mystery of Thor Bridge 23; One Colombo Night 23; Silver Blaze 23; The Speckled Band 23; The Stone of Mazarin 23; The Three Students 23; The Notorious Mrs. Carrick 24; Lily of Killarney 29

Ridley, Arnold Royal Eagle 36*

Ridley, Philip The Reflecting Skin 90

Riead, William Scorpion 86

Riefenstahl, Leni Das Blaue Licht • The Blue Light 32*; Sieg des Glaubens • Victory of the Faith 33; Triumph des Willens • Triumph of the Will 34; Day of Freedom • Tag der Freiheit—Unsere Wehrmacht 35; Berlin Olympiad • Olympia • Olympiad • The Olympic Games • Olympische Spiele • Olympische Spiele 1936 38; Lowland • Tiefland 54; Nuba 77

Rieger, Manfred Die Letzten Zwei vom Rio Bravo 65

Riemann, Johannes Ich Sehne Mich nach Dir 36; Ave Maria 37; Dr. Engel, Child Specialist 37; Eva das Fabriksmädel 38

Riesel, Oscar Discomania 80

Riesner, Charles see Reisner, Charles

Riesner, Dean Bill and Coo 47

Riethof, Carol El Maestro • Il Maestro • The Teacher and the Miracle 58*

Riethof, Peter El Maestro • Il Maestro • The Teacher and the Miracle 58*

Rieux, Max de see De Rieux, Max

Rif, Vladimir Very Close Quarters 83

Rifkin, Adam Never on Tuesday 88

Rigby, Clarence Miss Nanny Goat Becomes an Aviator 16; Miss Nanny Goat on the Rampage 16; Miss Nanny Goat at the Circus 17

Righelli, Gennaro Al Buio Insieme 37; La Armata Azzurra • The Blue Fleet 37; Una Commedia Fra i Pazzi 37; Lady Luck • Signora Fortuna 37; L'Aria del Continente • Continental Atmosphere 39; Lo Smemorato 40; Da Bancarella a Bancarotta • Peddlin' in Society 49

Riley, H. Anne *pseudonym for Jenny Bowen with Kjehl Rasmussen*

Rilla, Walter Behold the Man • The Westminster Passion Play—Behold the Man 51

Rilla, Wolf Glad Tidings 53; The Large Rope 53; Marilyn • Roadhouse Girl 53; Noose for a Lady 53; The Black Rider 54; The End of the Road 54; The Blue Peter • Navy Heroes 55; Stock Car 55; Pacific Destiny 56; The Scamp • Strange Affection 57; Bachelor of Hearts • The Freshman • Light Blue 58; Witness in the Dark 59; Piccadilly Third Stop 60; Village of the Damned 60; Die Zornigen Jungen Männer 60; Jessy 61; Watch It, Sailor! 61; Cairo 62; Pussycat Alley • The World Ten Times Over 63; Naughty Wives • Secrets of a Door-to-Door Salesman 73; Bedtime with Rosie 74

Rim, Carlo *see Carlo-Rim*

Rim, Chang Bom Pomnalui Nunsogi • Thaw 86*

Rim, Ko Hak Pomnalui Nunsogi • Thaw 86*

Rin, Taro Galaxy Express 82

Rinaldi, Carlos Male and Female • Male and Female Since Adam and Eve • Souls of Sin 61

Rincón, El Indio *see Rincón, Miguel Ángel*

Rincón, Miguel Ángel Kapax del Amazonas • Kapax of the Amazon 86

Ringoold, Fred La Morte sull'Alta Coclina 69

Río, Ernesto del *see Del Río, Ernesto*

Río, José L. López del *see López del Río, José L.*

Ríos, Humberto The Cry of the People • El Grito de Este Pueblo 72

Ríos, Leopoldo Torres *see Torres Ríos, Leopoldo*

Ripeau, Marie-Geneviève Adieu Voyages Lents 78

Ripley, Arthur The Barber Shop 33; The Pharmacist 33; Counsel on de Fence 34; In the Dog House 34; The Leather Necker 34; Shivers 34; Edgar's Hamlet 35; Gasoloons 35; In Love at 40 35; South Sea Sickness 35; Happy Tho' Married 36; How to Behave 36; How to Train a Dog 36; Will Power 36; I Met My Love Again 37*; Scrappily Married 40; Twincuplets 40; The Last Command • Prisoner of Japan 42*; A Voice in the Wind 44; The Chase 46; Atlantis • Atlantis the Lost Continent • Queen of Atlantis • Siren of Atlantis 48*; Thunder Road 58

Rippert, Otto Homunculus 16; Dance of Death • Totentanz 19; Die Pest in Florenz • The Plague in Florence 19

Ripploh, Frank Taxi zum Klo 81; Taxi nach Kairo • Taxi to Cairo 87

Ripps, Mike All the Young Wives 75

Ripstein, Arturo Tiempo de Morir 65; H.O. 66; Jogo Perigoso • Juego Peligroso 66*; Los Recuerdos del Porvenir 68; La Hora de los Niños 69; El Castillo de la Pureza • Castle of Purity 72; El Santo Oficio 74; Foxtrot • The Other Side of Paradise 75; Lecumberri 76; El Lugar Sin Límites 77; Cadena Perpetua 78; La Tía Alexandra 80; Rastro de la Muerte 83; La Seducción 83; El Otro 84; El Imperio de la Fortuna • The Realm of Fortune 86; Mentiras Piadosas 89

Risan, Leidulv After Rubicon • Etter Rubicon • Rubicon 87

Risi, Dino I Bersaglieri della Signora 45; Barboni 46; Pescatorella 46; Strade di Napoli 46; Verso la Vita 46; Cortili 47; Cuore Rivelatore 47; Trigullio Minore 47; Costumi e Bellezze d'Italia 48; La Fabbrica del Duomo 48; Il Grido della Città 48; 1848 48; Sergantini il Pittore della Montagna 48; Buio in Sala 49; Caccia in Brughiera 49; La Città dei Traffici 49; La Montagna di Luce 49; Seduta Spiritica 49; Il Siero della Verità 49; Terra Ladina 49; Vince il Sistema 49; Fuga in Città 50; L'Isola Bianca 50; Anna 51*; Vacanze col Gangster • Vacation with a Gangster 52; Amore in Città • Love in the City 53*; Hope Avenue • Il Viale della Speranza 53; Bread, Love and... • Pane, Amore e... • Scandal in Sorrento 55; Il Segno di Venere • The Sign of Venus 55; Girl in a Bikini • Poor But Beautiful • Poor But Handsome • Poveri Ma Belli 56; Beautiful But Poor • Belle Ma Povere • Irresistible 57; Grandmother Sabella • La Nonna Sabella • Oh Sabella! 57; I Due Gondolieri • Venezia, la Luna e Tu • Venice, the Moon and You 58; Poor Millionaires • Poveri Milionari 58; Love and Larceny • Il Mattatore • Il Mattatore: L'Homme aux Cent Visages 59; Il Vedovo • The Widower 59; A Porte Chiuse • Behind Closed Doors 60; Un Amore a Roma • L'Inassouvie • Love in Rome 60; A Difficult Life • Una Vita Difficile 61; The Easy Life • The Overtaking • Il Sorpasso 62; Il Giovedi • Thursday 62; The March to Rome • La Marcia su Roma 62; Fifteen from Rome • The Monsters • Les Monstres • I Mostri • Opiate '67 63; The Success • Il Successo 63*; Bambole! • Le Bambole • The Dolls • Four Kinds of Love 64*; Il Gaucho • The Gaucho 64; I Complessi • Complexes 65*; L'Ombrellone • El Parasol • The Parasol • Weekend, Italian Style • Weekend Wives 65; Operation San Gennaro • Operazione San Gennaro • The Treasure of San Gennaro • Unser Boss Ist eine Dame 65; I Nostri Mariti • Our Husbands 66*; Mr. Kinky • Il Profeta • The Prophet 67; The Tiger and the Pussycat • Il Tigre 67; Straziami Ma di Baci Saziami • Tear Me But Satiate Me with Your Kisses • Torture Me But Kill Me with Kisses 68; Il Giovane Normale • The Normal Young Man 69; I See Everybody Naked • Vedo Nudo 69; La Moglie del

Prete • The Priest's Wife 70; In Nome del Popolo Italiano • In the Name of the Italian People 71; Noi Donne Siamo Fatte Così • Women: So We Are Made 71; Bite and Run • Mordi e Fuggi 72; How Funny Can Sex Be? • Mad Sex • Sesso Matto 73; Profumo di Donna • Scent of a Woman • That Female Scent 74; The Career of a Chambermaid • Telefoni Bianchi • White Telephones 75; Duck à l'Orange 75; Âmes Perdues • Anima Persa • The Forbidden Room • Lost Soul 76; The Bishop's Room • La Stanza del Vescovo 77; The New Monsters • I Nuovi Mostri • Viva Italia • Vive l'Italie 77*; First Love • Primo Amore 78; Caro Papa • Dear Father 79; I Am Photogenic • Sono Fotogenico 80; Sunday Lovers 80*; Fantasma d'Amore • Ghost of Love 81; Sesso e Volentieri • Sex and Violence 82; Le Bon Roi Dagobert • The Good King Dagobert 84; Le Fou de Guerre • Madman at War • Scemo di Guerra • War Jester 85; Il Commissario lo Gatto • Commissioner Lo Gatto 86; Teresa 87

Risi, Marco Colpo di Fulmine • Love at First Sight 85; Soldati: 365 Giorni all'Alba • Soldiers: 365 Days Till Dawn 87

Risi, Nelo Dead of Summer • Ondata di Calore 70; Diario di una Schizofrenica • Diary of a Schizophrenic Girl • Why Anna? 70

Rising, Will Pocahontas—A Child of the Forest 08*

Riskin, Robert For You Alone • When You're in Love 37

Risquez, Diego Amerika, Terra Incognita 88

Rissi, Mark M. The Black Spider • Die Schwarze Spinne 83; Ghame Afghan • The Tragedy of the Afghan 86*; Lisi and the General • Lisi und der General 86

Rissient, Pierre One Night Stand 76

Ritchie, Michael Downhill Racer 69; The Candidate 72; Prime Cut 72; Smile 74; The Bad News Bears 76; Semi-Tough 77; An Almost Perfect Affair 79; Divine Madness 80; The Island 80; The Survivors 83; Fletch 84; The Golden Child 86; Wildcats 86; The Couch Trip 87; Fletch Lives 89

Ritelis, Viktors The Corpse • Crucible of Horror • The Velvet House 69

Ritt, Martin Edge of the City • A Man Is Ten Feet Tall 56; The Long, Hot Summer 57; No Down Payment 57; The Black Orchid 58; The Sound and the Fury 58; Five Branded Women • Jovanka e l'Altri 59; Paris Blues 61; Adventures of a Young Man • Ernest Hemingway's Adventures of a Young Man • Hemingway's Adventures of a Young Man 62; Hud 62; Judgment in the Sun • The Outrage 63; The Spy Who Came in from the Cold 65; Hombre 66; The Brotherhood 68; The Molly Maguires 68; The Great White Hope 70; Sounder 71; Pete 'n' Tillie 72; Conrack 73; The Front 76; Casey's Shadow 77; Norma Rae 78; Back Roads 80; Cross Creek 83; Murphy's Romance 85; Nuts 87; Stanley and Iris 90

Rittau, Günther Brand im Ozean 39; U-Boote Westwärts 41; Der Strom 42; Der Ewige Klang • Der Geiger 43; Die Jahre Vergehen • Der Senator 44; Meine Vier Jungen 44; Eine Alltägliche Geschichte 45; Der Scheiterhaufen 45; Die Fünf vom Titan • Vor Uns Liegt das Leben 48

Ritter, Joe Beach Balls 88

Ritter, Karl Weiberregiment 36; Patriots 37; Verräter 37; Furlough on Word of Honor • Urlaub auf Ehrenwort 38; The Private's Job • Unternehmen Michael 38; Die Hochzeitsreise • The Honeymoon • The Wedding Journey 39; Pour le Mérite 39

Ritter, Lloyd Secrets of the Reef 56*

Ritz, Lan Brooks Annie Mae, Brave-Hearted Woman 79

Ritzenberg, Frederick Gospel 82*

Riva, Juan Antonio de la see De la Riva, Juan Antonio

Rivalta, Giorgio I Cosacchi • The Cossacks 59*; La Donna dei Faraoini • The Pharaoh's Woman 60*; The Avenger • The Last Glory of Troy • La Leggenda di Enea 62

Rivera, Ángel Cabos Blancos 54*

Rivera, Roberto G. The Promised Land • La Tierra Prometida 86

Rivero, Fernando El Beso Mortal • The Fatal Kiss 39; Juntos Pero No Revueltos • United But Not Mixed 39; Silk, Blood and Sun 43; Los Miserables 44

Rivers, Fernand La Dame aux Camélias 34*; Le Chemineau • The Open Road 40; Dirty Hands • Les Mains Sales 51

Rivers, Joan Rabbit Test 78

Rivette, Jacques Aux Quatre Coins 49; Le Quadrille 50; Le Divertissement 52; Le Coup du Berger 56; Paris Belongs to Us • Paris Is Ours • Paris Nous Appartient 60; The Nun • La Religieuse • Suzanne Simonin, la Religieuse de Denis Diderot • Suzanne Simonin, la Religieuse de Diderot 65; Jean Renoir, le Patron 66; L'Amour Fou 68; Out 1: Noli Me Tangere 71; Out 1 Out 2 • Out 1: Spectre 72; Céline and Julie Go Boating • Céline et Julie Vont en Bateau 73; Essai sur l'Agression 74; Naissance et Mont de Prométhée 74; Duelle • Les Filles de Feu • Twhylight • Twilight 75; Noroît • Northwest • Northwest Wind • Nor'west 76; La Vengeresse 76; Merry-Go-Round 78; Paris Goes Away • Paris S'en Va 80; North Bridge • The Northern Bridge • Le Pont du Nord 81; L'Amour par Terre • Love on the Ground 84; Hurlevent • Wuthering Heights 85; La Bande des Quatre • The Gang of Four 89

Rivière, Marc Le Crime d'Antoine 89

Rizvi, Sibte Hasan Joshilaay 89

Roach, Bert The Little Widow 19*

Roach, Frank Frozen Scream 80

Roach, Hal Just Nuts 15; Lonesome Luke's Movie Muddle 16; All Aboard 17; The Flirt 17; Lonesome Luke on Tin Can Alley 17; Fireman Save My Child 18; Pipe the Whiskers 18; Bumping Into Broadway 19; Captain Kidd's Kids 19; From Hand to Mouth 19; His Royal Slyness 19; Hoot Mon

19; An Eastern Westerner 20; Get Out and Get Under 20; Haunted Spooks 20; High and Dizzy 20; Number, Please 20; Now or Never 21*; The White Sheep 24; Flying Elephants 27*; The Rogue Song 29*; Men of the North 30; On the Loose 31; Bogus Bandits • The Devil's Brother • Fra Diavolo • The Virtuous Tramps 33*; Swiss Miss 38*; Captain Fury 39; The House-keeper's Daughter 39; The Cave Dwellers • Cave Man • Man and His Mate • One Million B.C. 40*; Turnabout 40; Road Show 41*

Roach, Hal, Jr. The Cave Dwellers • Cave Man • Man and His Mate • One Million B.C. 40*; Road Show 41*; Dudes Are Pretty People 42; Calaboose 43; Prairie Chickens 43

Road, Michael The True and the False 55

Roadwell, Robert The Great Radium Mystery 19*

Roarke, Adam Trespasses 83*

Robar-Dorin, Filip Ovni i Mamuti • Rams and Mammoths 86

Robards, Willis Cross Purposes 13*; Fires of Fate 13*; The Heart of a Cracksman 13*; Retribution 13*; Mothers of Men 17; Every Woman's Problem 21

Robbe-Grillet, Alain L'Immortale • L'Immortelle 62; Trans-Europ-Express 66; L'Homme Qui Ment • The Man Who Lies • Muž Který Lže • Shock Troops 67; L'Éden et Après 69; Les Gommes 72; Glissements Progressifs du Plaisir 73; Giocare col Fuoco • Le Jeu avec le Feu 74; Tender Dracula, or Confessions of a Blood Drinker 74; Piège à Fourrure 77; The Beautiful Prisoner • La Belle Captive 82

Robbie, Seymour C.C. and Company 70; Marco 73

Robbins, Derek The Sex Victims 73; Sextet 76

Robbins, Jerome West Side Story 61*

Robbins, Jess A Front Page Story 22; The Ladder Jinx 22; Too Much Business 22; The Law Forbids 24; The Business of Love 25*; A Little Bit of Fluff • Skirts 28*

Robbins, Matthew Corvette Summer • The Hot One 78; Dragonslayer 81; The Legend of Billie Jean 85; *batteries not included 87

Roberson, James The Legend of Alfred Packer 79; Superstition • The Witch 85

Robert, Genevieve Casual Sex? 88

Robert, Jacques La Vivante Épingle 21; La Bouquetière des Innocents 21; Cousin Pons 24; Le Comte Kostia 25; La Chèvre aux Pieds d'Or 26; En Plongée 27

Robert, Yves Les Bonnes Manières 51; Les Hommes Ne Pensent Qu'à Ça 54; Ni Vu Ni Connu 58; Signé Arsène Lupin • Signed Arsène Lupin 59; La Famille Fenouillard 61; La Guerre des Boutons • The War of the Buttons 62; Bébert and the Train • Bébert et l'Omnibus • The Holy Terror 63; Les Copains 64; Monnaie de Singe 65; Alexander • Alexandre • Alexandre le Bienheureux • Happy Alexander • Very Happy Alexander • Very

Happy Alexandre 67; Clérambard 69; Le Grand Blond avec Une Chaussure Noire • The Tall Blond Man with One Black Shoe 72; Salue l'Artiste • Salut l'Artiste 73; Le Retour du Grand Blond • The Return of the Tall Blond Man with One Black Shoe 74; Un Éléphant Ça Trompe Énormément • Pardon Mon Affaire 76; Nous Irons Tous au Paradis • Pardon Mon Affaire, Too • We Will All Meet in Paradise 77; Courage Fuyons • Courage — Let's Run 78; Le Jumeau 84; My Father's Glory 90; My Mother's Castle 90

Roberti, Charles Hell's Long Road 63

Robertis, Francesco de see De Robertis, Francesco

Roberts, Alan The Zodiac Couples 70*; Panorama Blue 74; Young Lady Chatterley 77; The Happy Hooker Goes Hollywood 80; Flashdance Fever 83; Private Property 85

Roberts, Bill Saludos Amigos 43*; The Three Caballeros 44*; Fun and Fancy Free 47*

Roberts, Bob Sweet Savior 71

Roberts, C. E. see Roberts, Charles E.

Roberts, C. Edward see Roberts, Charles E.

Roberts, Charles E. Corruption 33; Flaming Signal 33*; Adventurous Knights 35; Hurry, Charlie, Hurry 41

Roberts, Darryl The Perfect Model 89

Roberts, Deborah Frankenstein General Hospital 88

Roberts, Edward D. Fatty's Overtime 22; Hims Ancient and Modern 22; The Cause of All the Trouble 23

Roberts, Florian see Florey, Robert

Roberts, Frances Song of the Land 53*

Roberts, Harry A Sheffield Blade 18*; The Barton Mystery 20

Roberts, Peter T. Dan Smith 87*

Roberts, Ralph A. Spiel mit dem Feuer 34

Roberts, Stephen Somebody Lied 23*; Cheer Up 24; Poor Butterfly 24; Fair Warning 25; Fares Please 25*; Fire Away 25; Waiting 25; Wild Waves 25; Flaming Romance 26; Framed 26; Hanging Fire 26; High Sea Blues 26; Hold 'Er Sheriff 26; Hold Your Hat 26; The Jelly Fish 26*; Kiss Papa 26; Light Housekeeping 26; Live Cowards 26; Much Mystery 26; Pink Elephants 26; The Radio Bug 26; Sky Bound 26; Solid Gold 26; The Tin Ghost 26; Who Hit Me? 26; Who's My Wife? 26; Ain't Nature Grand? 27; Batter Up 27; Brain Storm 27; Fox Tales 27; High Spots 27; Hot Lightning 27; Jungle Heat 27; No Cheating 27; Nothing Flat 27; Queens Wild 27; Red Hot Bullets 27; Seeing Stars 27; Sure Cure 27; Call Your Shots 28; Hot or Cold 28; Just Dandy 28; Kitchen Talent 28; The Last Laugh 28; Leaping Luck 28; Polar Perils 28; Racing Mad 28; Social Prestige 28; Stage Fright 28; Who's Lyin'? 28; Wives Won't Weaken 28; Beauties Beware 29; Cold Shivers 29; Going Places 29; Honeymooniacs 29; Hot Times 29; Hunting the Hunter 29; Look Out Below

29; The Madhouse 29; Parlor Pests 29; Smart Steppers 29; Studio Pests 29; The Talkies 29; Those Two Boys 29; Ticklish Business 29; What a Day 29; Whoopee Boys 29; Wise Wimmin 29; The Big Jewel Case 30; Dad Knows Best 30; French Kisses 30; Hail, the Princess 30; His Error 30; Hot—and How! 30; How's My Baby? 30; The Laugh Back 30; Love à la Mode 30; My Harem 30; Oh Darling 30; Romance de Luxe 30; Their Wives' Vacation 30; Western Knights 30; Arabian Knights 31; Here's Luck 31; Let's Play 31; Parisian Gaieties 31; The Royal Bluff 31; Sky Bride 31; If I Had a Million 32*; Lady and Gent 32; The Night of June 13th 32; One Sunday Afternoon 33; The Story of Temple Drake • Temple Drake 33; Romance in Manhattan 34; The Trumpet Blows 34; The Man Who Broke the Bank at Monte Carlo 35; Star of Midnight 35; The Ex-Mrs. Bradford 36; The Lady Consents 36

Roberts, Steve Sir Henry at Rawlinson End 80

Roberts, W. O. see Roberts, Bill
Robertson, Arthur Black Hooker 74
Robertson, Cliff J. W. Coop 71; The Pilot 79
Robertson, D. M. Mania 86*
Robertson, David Firebird 2015 A.D. 81
Robertson, Hugh Melinda 72; Bim 76
Robertson, John S. Baby Mine 17; The Bottom of the Well 17; Intrigue 17; The Money Mill 17; The Better Half 18; Girl of Today 18; The Golden Bird • Little Miss Hoover 18; The Make-Believe Wife 18; The Menace 18; Billeted • The Misleading Widow 19; Come Out of the Kitchen 19; Erstwhile Susan 19; Here Comes the Bride 19; Let's Elope • The Naughty Wife 19; Sadie Love 19; The Test of Honor 19; Away Goes Prudence 20; A Dark Lantern 20; Dr. Jekyll and Mr. Hyde 20; 39 East 20; Footlights 21; The Magic Cup 21; Sentimental Tommy 21; Love's Boomerang • Perpetua 22*; Spanish Jade 22*; Tess of the Storm Country 22; The Bright Shawl 23; The Fighting Blade 23; Twenty-One 23; Classmates 24; The Enchanted Cottage 24; New Toys 25; Shore Leave 25; Soul Fire 25; Annie Laurie 27; Captain Salvation 27; The Road to Romance 27; The Girl from China • Shanghai Lady 29; The Single Standard 29; Captain of the Guard • La Marseillaise 30*; Madonna of the Streets 30; Night Ride 30; Beyond Victory 31*; The Phantom of Paris 31; Little Orphan Annie 32; One Man's Journey 33; The Crime Doctor 34; His Greatest Gamble 34; Wednesday's Child 34; Captain Hurricane 35; Grand Old Girl 35; Our Little Girl 35

Robertson, Michael Going Sane 86
Robiland, Alessandro di see Di Robiland, Alessandro
Robin, Georges Heads I Win 63; Zabaglione 66; Mini Weekend • The Tomcat 67
Robin, Teddy The Legend of Wisely 87
Robins, Herb The Worm Eaters 75*

Robins, John That's Your Funeral 72; Love Thy Neighbour 73; Nearest and Dearest 73; The Best of Benny Hill 74; Man About the House 74; Hot Resort 85
Robinson, Bruce Withnail & I 87; How to Get Ahead in Advertising 88
Robinson, Casey Renegades of the West 32
Robinson, Chris Sunshine Run 79
Robinson, Dave Take It or Leave It 81
Robinson, Lee The Phantom Stockman 53; King of the Coral Sea 56*; Walk Into Hell 57
Robinson, Mark Roadhouse 66 84; Kid 88
Robinson, Peter Asylum 72
Robinson, Phil Alden In the Mood • The Woo Woo Kid 87; Field of Dreams 89
Robinson, R. D. The World Is Just a "B" Movie 71*
Robinson, Richard Brother of the Wind 72; To Hell You Preach • Vengeance of a Gunfighter 72; Poor Pretty Eddie • Red Neck County 75
Robinson, Ted Those Dear Departed 87
Robison, Arthur Nächte des Grauens 16; Die Nacht der Erkenntnis • Schatten • Warning Shadows 22; Zwischen Abends und Morgens 23; Peter the Pirate • Pietro der Korsar 24; Manon Lescaut 26; The Last Waltz • Der Letzte Walzer 27; Looping the Loop 28; Frauenschicksal 29; The Informer 29; Jenny Lind 30; Mordprozess Mary Dugan 31; Quand On Est Belle 31; Des Jungen Dessauers Grosse Liebe • Eines Prinzen Junge Liebe 33; Époux Célibataires 33; Monsieur le Marquis 33; Tambour Battant • Fürst Woronzeff 34; Le Secret de Woronzeff 34; Mach' Mich Glücklich 35; The Student of Prague • Der Student von Prag 35
Robles Godoy, Armando The Green Wall • La Muralla Verde 69; Mirage 72
Roboh, Caroline Clementine Tango 84
Robsahm, Margrete Begynnelsen på en Historie 88
Robson, Mark The Ghost Ship 43; The Seventh Victim 43; Youth Runs Wild 44; Isle of the Dead 45; Bedlam 46; Roughshod 48; Champion 49; Home of the Brave 49; My Foolish Heart 49; Bright Victory • Lights Out 50; Edge of Doom • Stronger Than Fear 50*; I Want You 51; Return to Paradise 53; The Bridges at Toko-Ri 54; Hell Below Zero 54; Phffft! • Phffft 54; Prize of Gold 55; Trial 55; The Harder They Fall 56; The Little Hut 56; Peyton Place 57; The Inn of the Sixth Happiness 58; From the Terrace 59; Nine Hours to Live • Nine Hours to Rama 62; The Prize 63; Von Ryan's Express 65; The Centurions • The Lost Command • Not for Honor and Glory 66; Valley of the Dolls 67; Daddy's Gone A-Hunting 69; Happy Birthday, Wanda June 71; Chained to Yesterday • Limbo • Women in Limbo 72; Earthquake 74; Avalanche Express 78*
Roccardi, Giovanni The Scarlet Eye • Storm Over Ceylon • Tempesta Su Ceylon 63*

Rocco, Gian Andrea Garter Colt • Giarrettiera Colt 67
Rocco, Marc Scenes from the Goldmine 86; Dream a Little Dream 89
Rocco, Pat Someone 68; Drifter • Two-Way Drifter 75
Rocha, Glauber Um Dia na Rampa 57*; A Cross in the Plaza • A Cruz na Praça 58; O Pátio • The Patio 58; Barravento • Storm • The Turning Wind 61; The Black God and the Blond Devil • The Black God and the White Devil • Black God, White Devil • Deus e o Diabo na Terra do Sol 64; Amazonas • Amazonas Amazonas • The Amazons 65; Earth Entranced • Land in Anguish • Land in Trance • Terra em Transe 66; Maranhão • Maranhão 66 66; O Cancer 68; Antonio das Mortes • O Dragão da Maldade Contra o Santo Guerreiro • The Dragon of Evil Against the Holy Warrior • O Santo Guerreiro Contra o Dragão da Maldade 69; Cabeças Cortadas • Severed Heads 70; Der Leone Have Sept Cabeças • The Lion Has Seven Heads 70; História do Brasil • History of Brazil 74*; Claro! • Clear! 75; Di 77; Jorge Amado no Cinema • Jorjamado no Cinema 79; L'Âge de la Terre • The Age of Earth • The Age of the Earth • A Idade da Terra 80
Rocha, Paulo O Desejado—Les Montagnes de la Lune • Mountains of the Moon 87
Rochant, Eric Too Much 87; Love Without Pity • A World Without Pity 89; The 5th Monkey 90
Roche, Sean Chasing Dreams 81*
Rochemont, Louis de III see De Rochemont, Louis III
Rochlin, Sheldon Vali 67; Paradise Now 70; Signal Through the Flames 84*
Rock, Joe The Great Power 29
Roddam, Franc Quadrophenia 79; The Lords of Discipline 82; The Bride 85; Aria 87*; War Party 88
Rodé, Alfred The Maiden • La Môme Pigalle 61; La Fille de Feu • Fire in the Flesh 64
Rodgers, Gaby Who Does She Think She Is? 74*
Rödl, Josef Albert—Warum? • Albert—Why? 78; The Wild Clown • Der Wilde Clown 86
Rodriguez, A. Endre Crow on the Tower • Varjú a Toronyban 39
Rodríguez, Francisco Testigo Azul 88
Rodríguez, Ismael Qué Lindo Es Michoacán 44; The Beast of Hollow Mountain • El Monstruo de la Montaña Hueca 56*; Daniel Boone, Trail Blazer 56*; The Bandit • La Cucaracha • The Soldiers of Pancho Villa 59; Ánimas Trujano • The Important Man • El Mayordomo 61; The Mighty Jungle 64*
Rodríguez, Ismael, Jr. Bloody Weed • Yerba Sangrienta 87; Corrupción • Corruption 87; Olor a Muerte • Scent of Death 87
Rodríguez, Joselito Ay Jalisco No Te Rajes 43
Rodríguez, Roberto I Shall Live Again •

Viviré Otra Vez 40; Little Angel • La Son-risa de la Vírgen 61*; La Caperucita Roja • Little Red Riding Hood 63; Los Espa-dachines de la Reina • The Queen's Swordsmen 63; Caperucita y Sus Tres Amigos • Little Red Riding Hood and Her Friends • Little Red Riding Hood and Her Three Friends 64; Caperucita y Pulgarcito Contra los Monstruos • Little Red Riding Hood and the Monsters 65*

Rodríguez Soltero, José Lupe 65

Rodríguez Vázquez, Ángel The Black Side of Blackie • Lo Negro del Negro 87*

Roe, Willy The Playbirds 78; Confes-sions from the David Galaxy Affair • Star Sex 79; Queen of the Blues 79

Roedl, Josef see *Rödl, Josef*

Roeg, Nicolas Performance 68*; Walk-about 70; The Glastonbury Fair 71; Don't Look Now 73; The Man Who Fell to Earth 76; Bad Timing • Bad Timing/A Sensual Obsession 79; Eureka 81; Insignificance 85; Castaway 86; Aria 87*; Track 29 87; The Witches 90

Roemer, Michael A Touch of the Times 49; Cortile Cascino • Cortile Cascino, Italy • The Inferno 62*; Nothing But a Man 64*; Faces of Israel 67; The Plot Against Harry 69; Pilgrim, Farewell 80; Haunted 83

Roessler, Rick Slaughterhouse 88

Roffman, Julian Eyes of Hell • The Mask • The Spooky Movie Show 61

Rogell, Albert S. The Greatest Menace 23; The Dangerous Coward 24; The Fight-ing Sap 24; Galloping Gallagher 24; Geared to Go 24; Lightning Romance 24; The Mask of Lopez 24; North of Nevada 24; The Silent Stranger 24; Thundering Hoofs 24; The Circus Cyclone 25; Crack o' Dawn 25; Cyclone Cavalier 25; Easy Money 25; The Fear Fighter 25; Fighting Fate 25; Goat Getter 25; The Knockout Kid 25; The Snob Buster 25; Super Speed 25; Youth's Gamble 25; The Man of the West 26; Men of the Night 26; The Patent Leather Pug 26; Red Hot Leather 26; Señor Daredevil 26; The Unknown Cavalier 26; The Wild Horse Stampede 26; The Devil's Saddle 27; The Fighting Three 27; Grin-ning Guns 27; Men of Daring 27; The Overland Stage 27; The Red Raiders 27; Rough and Ready 27; Somewhere in Sonora 27; The Sunset Derby 27; The Western Rover 27; The Western Whirl-wind 27; The Canyon of Adventure 28; The Glorious Trail 28; The Lone Wolf's Daughter 28; The Phantom City 28; The Shepherd of the Hills 28; The Upland Rider 28; The California Mail 29; Cheyenne 29; The Flying Marine 29; Painted Faces 29; Mamba 30; Aloha • No Greater Love 31; Looking for Trouble • The Tip-Off 31*; Suicide Fleet 31; Sweep-stakes 31; Air Hostess 32; Carnival Boat 32; Rider of Death Valley • Riders of Death Valley 32; Below the Sea • Hell's Cargo 33; East of Fifth Avenue • Two in a Million 33; Fog 33; The Wrecker 33; Among the Missing 34; Fugitive Lady 34;

The Hell Cat 34; Name the Woman 34; No More Women 34; Air Hawks 35; Atlantic Adventure 35; Escape from Devil's Island • Song of the Damned 35; Un-known Woman 35; Calling All G-Men • Panic on the Air • Trapped by Wireless • You May Be Next! 36; Grand Jury 36; Roaming Lady 36; Murder in Greenwich Village 37; Start Cheering 37; City Streets 38; The Last Warning 38; The Lone Wolf in Paris 38; For Love or Money • Tomor-row at Midnight 39; Hawaiian Nights 39; Lady Be Gay • Laugh It Off 39; Argentine Nights 40; I Can't Give You Anything But Love, Baby 40; Li'l Abner • Trouble Chaser 40; Private Affairs 40; The Black Cat 41; Public Enemies 41; Sailors on Leave 41; Tight Shoes 41; Butch Minds the Baby 42; Jail House Blues 42; Priorities on Par-ade 42; Sleepytime Gal 42; True to the Army 42; Youth on Parade 42; Change of Heart • Hit Parade of 1943 43; In Old Oklahoma • War of the Wildcats 43; Love, Honor and Goodbye 45; Earl Carroll Sketchbook • Hats Off to Rhythm 46; The Magnificent Rogue 46; Heaven Only Knows • Montana Mike 47; Northwest Stampede 48; Song of India 49; The Ad-miral Was a Lady 50; Before I Wake • Shadow of Fear 54

Roger, Jean-Henri Neige • Snow 81*

Rogers, Charles Bogus Bandits • The Devil's Brother • Fra Diavolo • The Vir-tuous Tramps 33*; Me and My Pal 33*; Babes in Toyland • Laurel and Hardy in Toyland • March of the Toys • March of the Wooden Soldiers • Revenge Is Sweet • Wooden Soldiers 34*; Going Bye-Bye 34; The Live Ghost 34; Them Thar Hills 34; Tit for Tat 34; The Bohemian Girl 35*; The Fixer-Uppers 35

Rogers, Edgar Elsie's Nightmare • The Nightmare of the Glad-Eye 13; Love and War in Toyland 13*; The Little Picture Producer 14*

Rogers, Maclean The Third Eye 28; The Mayor's Nest 32; The Crime at Blossoms 33; Summer Lightning 33; Trouble 33; Up for the Derby 33; The Feathered Serpent 34; It's a Cop 34; The Scoop 34; Virginia's Husband 34; A Little Bit of Bluff 35; Marry the Girl 35; Old Faithful 35; The Right Age to Marry 35; The Shadow of Mike Emerald 35; A Wife or Two 35; All That Glitters 36; Busman's Holiday 36; The Happy Family 36; The Heirloom Mystery 36; Not So Dusty 36; Nothing Like Publicity 36; To Catch a Thief 36; A Touch of the Moon 36; Twice Branded 36; Farewell to Cinderella 37; Father Steps Out 37; Fifty-Shilling Boxer 37; Racing Ro-mance 37; The Strange Adventures of Mr. Smith 37; When the Devil Was Well 37; Why Pick on Me? 37; Darts Are Trumps 38; Easy Riches 38; His Lordship Goes to Press 38; His Lordship Regrets 38; If I Were Boss 38; Merely Mr. Hawkins 38; Miracles Do Happen 38; Paid in Error 38; Romance à la Carte 38; Weddings Are Wonderful 38; Old Mother Riley Joins Up

39; Shadowed Eyes 39; Garrison Follies 40; Facing the Music 41; Gert and Daisy's Weekend 41; The Saving Song 41; Front Line Kids 42; Gert and Daisy Clean Up 42; Variety Jubilee 42; Heaven Is Round the Corner 43; I'll Walk Beside You 43; Somewhere in Civvies 43; Give Me the Stars 44; Don Chicago 45; Murder in the Footlights • The Trojan Brothers 46; Woman to Woman 46; Calling Paul Tem-ple 48; The Story of Shirley Yorke 48; Dark Secret 49; Paul Temple's Triumph 50; Something in the City 50; Madame Louise 51; Old Mother Riley's Jungle Treasure 51; Brighthaven Express • Salute the Toff 52; Down Among the Z Men • Some Kind of a Nut • Stand Easy 52; Hammer the Toff 52; Paul Temple Returns 52; Alf's Baby 53; Behind the Headlines 53; Flannelfoot 53; Forces' Sweetheart 53; Calling All Cars 54; Johnny on the Spot 54; Song of Norway 55; Assignment Red-head • Million Dollar Manhunt • Under-cover Girl 56; Mark of the Phoenix 56; Not So Dusty 56; You Pay Your Money 56; Not Wanted on Voyage 57; A Clean Sweep 58; Noddy in Toyland 58; Just Joe 59; Not a Hope in Hell 60

Rogers, Nate Tanya 76

Rogosin, Lionel On the Bowery 54; Come Back Africa 58; Oysters Are in Season 63; Good Times, Wonderful Times 65; How Do You Like Them Bananas? 66; Black Roots 70; Black Fantasy 72; Wood-cutters of the Deep South 73; Arab-Israeli Dialogue 74

Rogozhkin, S. Miss Millionersha 88

Rohmer, Eric Journal d'un Scélérat 50; Charlotte and Her Steak • Charlotte et Son Steak • Présentation • Présentation ou Charlotte et Son Steak 51; Bérénice 54; The Kreutzer Sonata • La Sonate à Kreut-zer 56; The Sign of Leo • Sign of the Lion • Le Signe du Lion 56; Véronique et Son Cancre 58; La Boulangère de Monceau • La Boulangère de Monceau: Six Contes Mor-aux: 1 62; La Carrière de Suzanne • La Carrière de Suzanne: Six Contes Moraux: 2 • Suzanne's Profession 63; Nadja à Paris 64; Paris Vu par . . . • Six in Paris 64*; La Collectionneuse • La Collectionneuse: Six Contes Moraux: 3 • The Collector 66; Une Étudiante d'Aujourd'hui 66; Fermière à Montfauçon 67; Ma Nuit chez Maud • Ma Nuit chez Maud: Six Contes Moraux: 4 • My Night at Maud's • My Night with Maud 68; Claire's Knee • Le Genou de Claire • Le Genou de Claire: Six Contes Moraux: 5 70; L'Amour l'Après-Midi • L' Amour l'Après-Midi: Six Contes Moraux: 6 • Chloë in the Afternoon • Love in the Afternoon 72; La Marquise d'O . . . • The Marquise of O . . . • Die Marquise von O . . . 76; Perceval • Perceval le Gallois 78; The Aviator's Wife • La Femme de l'Avia-teur • La Femme de l'Aviateur: Comédies et Proverbes: 1 80; Le Beau Mariage • A Good Marriage • The Perfect Marriage • The Well Made Marriage 81; Loup Y Es-Tu? • Wolf, Are You There? 83; Pauline à la Plage • Pauline at the Beach 83; Full Moon in Paris • Nights of the Full Moon • Les Nuits de la Pleine Lune 84; The Green Ray • Le Rayon Vert • Summer 85; The Adventures of Reinette and Mirabelle • Les Aventures de Reinette et Mirabelle • Four Adventures of Reinette and Mirabelle • Quatre Aventures de Reinette et Mirabelle 86; L'Ami de Mon Amie • Boyfriends and Girlfriends • Girlfriends and Boyfriends • My Girlfriend's Boyfriend 86; Conte de Printemps • A Tale of Springtime 89

Roig, Josefina Molina see Molina Roig, Josefina

Rojas, Orlando Una Novia para David 85

Rokos, Jim The Resurrection of Bronco Billy 70*

Roland, Bernard see Bernard-Roland

Roland, George Joseph in the Land of Egypt 32; Abraham Our Patriarch 33; Jewish Daughter 33; The Wandering Jew 33; Love and Sacrifice 36; I Want to Be a Mother 37; A Vilna Legend 49

Roland, Joseph The Green Tree 65

Roland, Jürgen The Red Circle 60; Destination Death 61; The Green Archer 61; Hong Kong Hot Harbor 62; Black Panther of Ratana 63; Die Flusspiraten des Mississippi • The Pirates of the Mississippi 63; A Lotus for Miss Kwen 67

Rolands, George The Lure of New York 13

Roley, Sutton How to Steal the World 66; The Loners 72; Chosen Survivors 74

Rolfe, B. A. Even As Eve 20*; Love Without Question 20; Madonnas and Men 20; A Woman's Business 20; Amazing Lovers 21

Rolfe, David W. The Silent Witness 78

Rollin, Jean Les Femmes Vampires • Queen of the Vampires • The Rape of the Vampire • La Reine des Vampires • Vampire Women • Le Viol du Vampire 67; The Naked Vampire • La Vampire Nue 69; Le Frisson des Vampires • Sex and the Vampire • The Terror of the Vampires • Vampire Thrills 70; Caged Virgins • The Crazed Vampire • Requiem for a Vampire • Requiem pour un Vampire • Sex Vampires • Vierges et Vampires • The Virgins and the Vampires • Virgins and Vampires 71; La Nuit de Cimetière • La Rose de Fer 72; Demoniacs • Les Démoniaques • Deux Vierges pour Satan • Les Diablesses • Perverse • Tins la Naufrageuse 73; Jeunes Filles Impudiques 73; Douces Pénétrations 75; Lèvres de Sang 75; Once Upon a Virgin • Phantasmes • Phantasmes Pornographiques 75; Vibrations Sensuelles 76; Lèvres Entrouvertes 77; Saute Moi Dessus 77; Pesticide • Les Raisins de la Mort 78; Fascination 79; Pénétrations Vicieuses 79; Petites Pensionnaires Impudiques 79; Filles Traquées • La Nuit des Traquées 80; Le Lac des Morts Vivants • El Lago de los Muertos Vivientes • The Lake of the Living Dead 80; Les Échappés 81; The Living Dead Girl • La Morte Vivante 82; Les Meurtrières 83; Ne Prends Pas les

Poulets pour des Pigeons 85

Rollins, Bernie Getting Over 81

Rolos, Don Love Now...Pay Later • Nudes on Credit • Sin Now...Pay Later 66

Romain, Jacques Contro Sesso • Controsesso 64*; Amore in Quattro Dimensioni • L'Amour en Quatre Dimensions • Love in Four Dimensions 65*

Roman, Antonio Nebraska il Pistolero • Nebraska Jim • Ringo del Nebraska • Savage Gringo 65

Roman, Barbro The Flamboyant Sex 63

Roman, Don The Herring Murder Mystery 43

Roman, Phil Race for Your Life, Charlie Brown 77*

Roman, Tony Breakin' New York Style 86

Romanek, Mark Static 85

Romeo, Rosario Amore e Morte • Love and Death 32

Romero, Eddie The Day of the Trumpet 57; Blood Creature • Terror Is a Man 59*; Lost Battalion 61; Cavalleria Commandos • Cavalry Command 63; The Raiders of Leyte Gulf 63; Amok • Moro Witch Doctor 64*; Intramuros • The Walls of Hell 64*; The Kidnappers • Man on the Run 64; The Ravagers 65; Manila, Open City 67; Blood Doctor • Mad Doctor of Blood Island • Tomb of the Living Dead 68*; Brides of Blood • Grave Desires • Island of Living Horror • Orgy of Blood • Terror on Blood Island 68*; The Passionate Strangers 68; Beast of Blood • Beast of the Dead • Return to the Horrors of Blood Island 70; Beast of the Yellow Night 70; Beasts • Twilight People 72; Black Mama, White Mama 72; The Highest Bidder • Woman Hunt 72; Beyond Atlantis 73; Savage Sisters 74; Ganito Kami Noon, Paano Kayo Ngayon? 76; Sino'ng Kapiling, Sino'ng Kasiping? 77; Sudden Death 77; Aguila 80; Desire 83; Hari sa Hari, Lahi sa Lahi 87*; White Fire 88

Romero, George The Man from the Meteor 54; Gorilla 55; Earthbottom 56; Curly 58; Slant 58; Expostulations 62; Feast of Flesh • Night of Anubis • Night of the Flesh Eaters • Night of the Living Dead 68; The Affair • There's Always Vanilla 71; Code Name: Trixie • The Crazies 72; Hungry Wives • Jack's Wife • Season of the Witch 72; Martin 76; Dawn of the Dead • Zombies • Zombies—Dawn of the Dead 77; Knightriders 79; Creepshow 82; Day of the Dead 83; Monkey Shines • Monkey Shines: An Experiment in Fear 88; Due Occhi Diabolici • Two Evil Eyes 90*

Romero, Manuel El Caballo del Pueblo 35; Radio Bar 37; Qué Tiempos Aquellos • Those Were the Days 38; Gente Bien 39; Life Is a Tango • La Vida Es un Tango 39; Divorcio en Montevideo 40; Fuera de la Ley • Outside the Law 40; Mujeres Que Trabajan • Women Who Work 40

Romero Marchent, Joaquín Luis La Espada del Zorro • Zorro 61; L'Ombra di

Zorro • The Shadow of Zorro • Zorro the Avenger 62; Gun Fight at High Noon • El Sabor de la Venganza • I Tre Spietati 63; The Magnificent Three • I Tre Implacabili • Tres Hombres Buenos 63; Adventuras del Oeste • Sette Ore di Fuoco • Seven Hours of Gunfire • Seven Hours Under Fire 64; Camino del Sur • Seven from Texas 64; Die Letzte Kugel Traf den Besten 65; Centomila Dollari per Lassiter 66; Gringo Getta il Fucile 66

Romero Marchent, Rafael Hands of a Gunman • Mani di Pistolero 65; Una Donna per Ringo 66; Due Croci a Danger Pass 67; Ad Uno ad Uno...Spietatomente 68; Io Non Perdono...Uccido 68; I Morti Non Si Contano 68; Ringo, el Caballero Solitario 68; Garringo 69; Lo Irritarono...e Sartana Fece Piazza Pulita 70; Un Par de Asesinos 70; La Preda e l'Avvoltoio 71; E Continuavano a Chiamarlo Figlio di... 72; Santo Contra el Doctor Muerte 73; The Student Connection 75

Romine, Charles Any Body...Any Way 68; Behind Locked Doors 76

Romitelli, Giancarlo Triumph of Robin Hood 62; Si Muore Solo una Volta 67

Romm, Mikhail A Ball of Suet • Boule de Suif • Puishka • Pushka • Pyshka 34; Lenin in October • Lenin v Octyabre • Lenin v Oktiabrye 37*; The Thirteen • Trinadtsat 37; Lenin in 1918 • Lenin v 1918 • Lenin v 1918 Godu 38; Dream • Mechta • Metshta 43; Chelovek No. 217 • Girl No. 217 44; The Russian Question • Russkii Vopros 47; Lenin • Vladimir Ilyich Lenin 48*; Zhivoi Lenin 48*; Secret Mission • Sekretnaya Missiya 49; Admiral Ushakov, Part One • Amiral Tempête • Segel im Sturm 53; Admiral Ushakov, Part Two • Attack from the Sea • Korabli Shturmuyut Bastiony • The Ships Attack the Fortifications • Ships Attacking Forts • The Ships Storm the Bastions 53; Murder on Dante Street • Murder on the Rue Dante • Ubiistvo na Ulitsye Dante • Ubiystvo na Ulitse Dante 56; Devyat Dnei Odnogo Goda • Nine Days of One Year 61; Obyknovennyi Fashizm • Obyknovennyi Fazhism • Ordinary Fascism • Triumph Over Violence 64; Lost Letters 66; A Night of Thought 66

Rona, Yosif Vasya-Reformator • Vasya the Reformer 26*

Rondeau, Charles R. The Devil's Partner 58; The Littlest Hobo 58; The Girl in Lover's Lane 60; The Threat 60; Night Train • Train Ride to Hollywood 75

Rondell, Ronnie No Safe Haven 86

Rondi, Brunello Una Vita Violenta 62*; Il Demonio 63; Domani Non Siamo Più Qui 66; Shocking • Le Tue Mani sul Mio Corpo 70

Rondinella, Thomas R. Blades 90

Ronisz, Wincenty Droga do Nieba • Tramwaj do Nieba • The Way to the Skies 58*

Rood, Jurrien The Way to Bresson • De Weg naar Bresson 84*; Orion Nebula • De Orionnevel 87

Ruscello di Ripasottile 40; La Nave Bianca • The White Ship 41; The Man of the Cross • L'Uomo della Croce 42; A Pilot Returns • Un Pilota Ritorna 42; Desiderio • Woman 43*; Città Aperta • Open City • Roma, Città Aperta • Rome, Open City 45; Ordinary People • Paisà • Paisan 46; Evil Street • Germania, Anno Zero • Germany, Year Zero 47; L'Amore • Love • Ways of Love • Woman 48*; The Infernal Machine • La Macchina Ammazzacattivi • The Machine That Kills Bad People 48; Flowers of St. Francis • Francesco, Giullare di Dio • Francis, God's Jester 49; Stromboli • Stromboli, Terra di Dio 49; Europa '51 • Europe '51 • The Greatest Love 51; Les Sept Péchés Capitaux • I Sette Peccati Capitali • The Seven Deadly Sins 51*; Dov'È la Libertà? 52; Amori di Mezzo Secolo 53*; Journey to Italy • The Lonely Lady • The Lonely Woman • Strangers • A Trip to Italy • Viaggio in Italia • Voyage in Italy • Voyage to Italy 53; Siamo Donne • We Are the Women • We the Women 53*; Die Angst • Fear • Non Credo Più all' Amore • La Paura 54; Giovanna d'Arco al Rogo • Jean au Bucher • Joan at the Stake • Joan of Arc at the Stake 54; Le Psychodrame 56; India 58; L'India Vista da Rossellini 58; General Della Rovere • Il Generale Della Rovere 59; Era Notte a Roma • Escape by Night • It Was Night in Rome • Once Upon a Night in Rome • Wait for the Dawn 60; Garibaldi • Viva l'Italia 60; The Betrayer • Vanina Vanini 61; Torino nei Cent'Anni 61; Anima Nera 62; RoGoPaG 62*; La Prise de Pouvoir par Louis XIV • The Rise of Louis XIV • The Rise to Power of Louis XIV 66; Idea di un' Isola • Idea di un'Isola: La Sicilia 67; Acts of the Apostles • Atti degli Apostoli 68; Socrate • Socrates 70; The Age of Cosimo de'Medici • The Age of the Medici • L'Età di Cosimo de'Medici 72; Agostino di Ippona • Augustine of Hippo 72; Blaise Pascal 72; Cartesius • Descartes 73; Intervista con Salvador Allende 73; Anno Uno • Italy: Year One • Year One 74; Il Messia • The Messiah 75; Le Centre Georges Pompidou 77; Concerto per Michelangelo 77

Rossen, Robert An Affair of the Heart • Body and Soul 47; Johnny O'Clock 47; All the King's Men 49; The Brave Bulls 50; Mambo 54; Alexander the Great 56; Island in the Sun 57; They Came to Cordura 59; The Hustler 61; Lilith 63

Rossetti, Franco El Desperado • The Dirty Outlaws 67; Al Limite, Cioe, Non Glielo Dico • I Don't Think I'll Tell Them 85

Rossi, Al My Therapist 82

Rossi, Franco I Falsari 50; Anita Garibaldi • Camicie Rosse • Red Shirts 51*; Solo per Te, Lucia 52; The Counterfeiters 53; Il Seduttorc 54; Amici per la Pelle • Friends for Life • The Woman in the Painting 55; Amore a Prima Vista • Buenos Días Amor 57; Calypso 58*; Death of a Friend • Morte di un Amico 59; Diary of

a Voyage in the South Pacific • Love — Tahiti Style • Nude Odyssey • Odissea Nuda • L'Odyssée Nue 61; Smog 62; Alta Infedeltà • Haute Infidélité • High Infidelity • Sex in the Afternoon 64*; Bambole! • Le Bambole • The Dolls • Four Kinds of Love 64*; Contro Sesso • Controsesso 64*; Three Nights of Love • Tre Notti d'Amore 64*; I Complessi • Complexes 65*; Every Man's Woman • Everyman's Woman • Una Rosa per Tutti • A Rose for Everyone 65; Don't Make War, Make Love • Make Love Not War • Non Faccio la Guerra, Faccio l'Amore 66; Les Sorcières • Le Streghe • The Witches 66*; The Adventures of Ulysses • Le Avventure di Ulisse 69; Giovinezza, Giovinezza 69; Come una Rosa al Naso 76; Virginità • Virginity 76; L'Altra Meta del Cielo 77

Rossi, John Gambling Hell • Mask of Korea 50

Rossi, Raffaele O Homem Lobo • O Lobishomem • The Werewolf 71; Seduzidas pelo Demônio 75

Rossif, Frédéric Une Histoire d'Éléphants 58; Vel' d'Hiv' 59; Le Monde Instantané 60; Imprévisibles Nouveautés • Unforeseeable Novelties 61; Le Temps du Ghetto • The Witnesses 61; De Notre Temps 62; Mourir à Madrid • To Die in Madrid 62; The Animals • Les Animaux 63; Encore Paris 63; Pour l'Espagne 63; The October Revolution • La Révolution d'Octobre 67; Un Mur à Jérusalem • A Wall in Jerusalem 68*; Pourquoi l'Amérique? 69; Aussi Loin Que l'Amour 71; La Fête Sauvage 75; Brel 82; Picasso, Pablo 82; Sauvage et Beau 84; Le Cœur Musicien 87

Rossman, Earl Kivalina of the Ice Lands 25

Rosso, Franco Babylon 80; The Nature of the Beast 88

Rosso, Salvatore Uno Straniero a Paso Bravo 68

Rosson, Arthur America, That's All • American, That's All 17; A Case at Law 17; Cassidy 17; Grafters 17; The Man Who Made Good 17; A Successful Failure 17; Headin' South 18; Forbidden Fire 19; Married in Haste 19; Rough Riding Romance 19; Sahara 19; Polly of the Storm Country 20; A Splendid Hazard 20; Desert Blossoms 21; For Those We Love 21; Prisoners of Love 21; Always the Woman 22; The Fighting Streak 22; The Fire Bride 22; Condemned 23; Garrison's Finish 23; Little Johnny Jones 23*; The Satin Girl 23; Blasted Hopes 24; The Measure of a Man 24; The Burning Trail 25; The Fighting Demon 25; The Meddler 25; Ridin' Pretty 25; Ridin' Through • Straight Through 25; The Taming of the West 25; Tearing Through 25; Stranded in Paris 26; Wet Paint 26; You'd Be Surprised 26; The Last Outlaw 27; Set Free 27; Silk Legs 27; The Farmer's Daughter 28*; Play Girl 28; The Long, Long Trail 29; Points West 29; The Winged Horseman 29*; The Concentratin' Kid 30; The Mounted Stranger 30; Roaring

Ranch 30; Trailin' Trouble • Trailing Trouble 30; Ebb Tide 32; Flaming Guns • Rough Riding Romeo 32; Hidden Gold 32; Women Who Play 32; The Plainsman 36*; Boots of Destiny 37; Trailin' Trouble • Trailing Trouble 37; The Story of Dr. Wassell 43*

Rosson, Richard Fine Manners 26; Blonde or Brunette 27; Ritzy 27; Rolled Stockings 27; Shootin' Irons 27; The Wizard 27; Dead Man's Curve 28; The Escape 28; Road House 28; The Very Idea 29*; West Point of the Air 35; Come and Get It • Roaring Timber 36*; Behind the Headlines 37; Hideaway 37; Corvette K-225 • The Nelson Touch 43*

Rostand, Jean Aux Frontières de l'Homme • The Border of Life 53*

Rostotsky, Stanislav Land and People 54; It Happened in Penkovo 57; The Stars in May 59; Seven Winds 62; The House on the Front Line • Na Semi Vetrakh 63*; A Hero of Our Time 67; We'll Get by Till Monday 68; The Dawns Are Quiet Here 72; White Bim the Black Ear 77

Rostrup, Kaspar Memories of a Marriage 89

Roter, Ted The Closet Casanova 79; One Page of Love 79

Roth, Bobby Independence Day 76; The Boss' Son 78; Brainwash • Circle of Power • Mystique • The Naked Weekend 81; Heartbreakers 84; Baja Oklahoma 88; The Man Inside 90

Roth, Cy Combat Squad 53; Air Strike 55; Fire Maidens from Outer Space • Fire Maidens of Outer Space 55

Roth, Joe Streets of Gold 86; Revenge of the Nerds II • Revenge of the Nerds II: Nerds in Paradise 87; Coupe de Ville 90

Roth, Murray Don't Bet on Love 33; The Dancing Fool • Harold Teen 34; Million Dollar Ransom 34; Chinatown Squad 35; Flying Hostess 36

Roth, Patrick The Killers 81

Rotha, Paul Australian Wine 31*; Contact 32; Great Cargoes • The Rising Tide 33; Shipyard 33; The Face of Britain 34; Death on the Road 35; Steel 35; The Future's in the Air 36; Peace Film 36; Peace of Britain 36; Statue Parade 37; New Worlds for Old 38; The Fourth Estate 39; Roads Across Britain 39*; Island People 40*; Mr. Borland Thinks Again 40; World of Plenty 43; Soviet Village 44; Land of Promise 45; Total War in Britain 45; A City Speaks 47; The World Is Rich 47; No Resting Place 50; Je Suis un Homme • World Without End 52*; Cat and Mouse • The Desperate Men 57; Cradle of Genius 59; Das Leben von Adolf Hitler • The Life of Adolf Hitler 60; De Overval • The Silent Raid 62

Rothemund, Sigi Big Mac 85

Rothman, Benjamin The Last Chapter 66*

Rothman, Joseph Dynamite Delaney 38

Rothman, Lawrence The Last Chapter 66*

Rothman, Stephanie Blood Bath • Track

of the Vampire 66*; It's a Bikini World 67; The Student Nurses 70; Cemetery Girls • Through the Looking Glass • The Velvet Vampire • The Waking Hour 71; Group Marriage 72; Terminal Island 73; The Working Girls 73; Ruby 77*

Rotoeta, Felix El Placer de Matar 88

Rotov, V. Spartakiada 29*

Rotsler, William Lila • Mantis in Lace 68

Rotsten, Herman The Unwritten Code 44

Rou, Alexander May Night 53; Stars of the Ukraine 53; The Magic Weaver • Maria the Wonderful Weaver • Marya-Iskusnitsa 60; Cinderella 61*; A Night Before Christmas • Vechera na Khutore Bliz Dikanki 63; Jack Frost • Morozko 66

Roubaix, Paul de see De Roubaix, Paul

Roubert, William L. The Waif 15; Heritage 20; For You My Boy 23

Rouch, Jean Au Pays des Mages Noirs 47*; Les Magiciens de Wanzerbé • Les Magiciens Noirs • Ouanzerbé, Capitale de la Magie • Wanzerbé, Capitale de la Magie 48*; La Circoncision 49; Hombori 49; Initiation à la Danse des Possédés 49; Bataille sur le Grand Fleuve 51*; La Chasse à l'Hippopotame 51*; Cimetière dans la Falaise 51*; La Culture du Mil • Les Gens du Mil 51*; Les Faiseurs de Pluie • Les Hommes Qui Font la Pluie • Rainmakers • Yenendi • Yenendi: Les Hommes Qui Font la Pluie 51*; Mammy Water • Mamy Water • Pêche et le Culte de la Mer 53; Les Fils de l'Eau 55*; Les Maîtres Fous 55; I, a Negro • Moi, un Noir • Treichville 56; Baby Ghana 57; Moro Naba 57; La Royale Goumbé 58; Sakpata 58*; Chronicle of a Summer • Chronique d'un Été 60*; Hampi 60; La Punition 60; La Pyramide Humaine 60; Abidjan, Port de Pêche 62; Les Ballets de Niger 62; Le Cocotier • Les Cocotiers 62; Fêtes de l'Indépendance de Niger 62; Le Mil 62; Monsieur Albert, Prophète 62*; Le Palmier à l'Huile 62; Les Pêcheurs de Niger 62; Rose et Landry 62*; Urbanisme Africain 62; Les Adolescents • The Adolescents • La Fleur de l'Âge • La Fleur de l'Âge ou Les Adolescentes • That Tender Age 64*; L'Afrique et la Recherche Scientifique 64; Paris Vu par... • Six in Paris 64*; Les Veuves de Quinze Ans 64; Alpha Noir 65; La Chasse au Lion à l'Arc • The Lion Hunters 65; Festival de Dakar 65; La Goumbé des Jeunes Noceurs 65; Jackville 65; Musique et Danse des Chasseurs Gow 65; Batteries Dogon: Éléments pour une Étude des Rythmes • Les Éléments pour une Étude de Rhythme • Le Tambour des Dogons • Tambours de Pierre 66*; Dongo Horendi 66; Dongo Yenendi 66; Fêtes de Novembre à Bregbo 66; Koli Koli 66; Sigui Année Zéro 66*; Dauda Sorko 67; Jaguar 67; Sigui: L'Enclume de Yougo 67; Tourou et Bitti 67; Un Lion Nommé l'Américain 68; Pierres Chantantes d'Ayorou 68; Sigui 1968: Les Danseurs de Tyogou 68*; Wanzerbé 68; Yenendi de Ganghel 68; Petit à Petit 69; Sigui 1969: La Caverne

de Bongo 69*; Mya: La Mère 70; Sigui 1970: Les Clameurs d'Amani 70*; Yenendi de Yantalla 70; Architects Ayorou 71; Porto Novo: La Danse des Reines 71*; Sigui 1971: La Dune d'Idyeli 71*; Yenendi de Simiri 71; Funérailles à Bongo: Le Vieux Anai • Funérailles du Vieil Anai 72*; Horendi 72; Sigui 1972: Les Pagnes de Iame 72*; Tanda Singui 72; Yenendi de Boukoki 72; Boukoki 73; Dongo Hori 73; L'Enterrement du Hogon 73; Hommage à Marcel Mauss: Taro Okamoto 73; Sécheresse à Simiri 73; Sigui 1973: L'Auvent de la Circoncision 73; VW-Voyou 73; Ambara Dama 74*; La 504 et les Foudroyers 74*; Cocorico, Monsieur Poulet 74*; Lapin, Petit Lapin • Toboy Tobaye 74; Pam Kuso Kar 74; Initiation 75; La Nostalgie de Souna • Souna Kouma 75; Babatou ou Les Trois Conseils • Babatu 76*; Médecines et Médecins 76*; Rythme de Travail 76; Ciné-Portrait of Margaret Mead 77; Fête des Gandyi Bi à Simiri 77; Le Griot Badye 77*; Hommage à Marcel Mauss: Germaine Dieterlen 77; Hommage à Marcel Mauss: Marcel Levy 77; Isphahan 77; Makwayela 77; Simiri Siddo Kuma 78; Dionysus 84; Brise-Glace 87*; Enigma 87*; Boulevards d'Afrique 88*; Folie Ordinaire d'une Fille de Cham 88; Cantate pour Deux Généraux 90

Roudes, Gaston Marthe 19; Au-Delà des Lois Humaines 20; La Dette 20; Les Deux Baisers 20; Maître Évora 21; Prisca 21; La Voix de la Mer 21; La Guitare et la Jazz Band 22; Le Lac d'Argent 22; Le Crime des Hommes 23; Le Petit Moineau de Paris 23; L'Éveil 24; Féliana l'Espionne 24; L'Ombre du Bonheur 24; Les Rantzau 24; La Douleur 25; Les Élus de la Mer 25; La Maternelle 25; Oiseaux de Passage 25; Les Petits 25; Pulcinella 25; Prince Zilah 26; Cousine de France 27; Le Dédale 27; L'Âme de Pierre 28; La Maison du Soleil 29

Rouffio, Jacques Violette et François 77; La Passante 82; L'État de Grâce • State of Grace 86; Mon Beau-Frère A Tué Ma Sœur • My Brother-in-Law Has Killed My Sister 86

Rouget, Gilbert Sakpata 58*; Batteries Dogon: Éléments pour une Étude des Rythmes • Les Éléments pour une Étude de Rhythme • Le Tambour des Dogons • Tambours de Pierre 66*; Porto Novo: La Danse des Reines 71*

Rouleau, Raymond Suzanne 32*; Une Vie Perdue 33; Rose 36; Le Messager 37; Trois-Six-Neuf 37; Le Couple Idéal 46*; The Crucible • Les Sorcières de Salem • The Witches of Salem 57; Les Amants de Teruel • The Lovers of Teruel 61

Rouquier, Georges Vendanges 29; Le Tonnelier 42; Le Charron 43; L'Économie des Métaux 43; La Part de l'Enfant 43; Farrebique • The Four Seasons • Les Quatre Saisons 46; L'Œuvre Scientifique de Pasteur • Pasteur 47*; Le Chaudronnier 49; Les Galeries de Malgovert • Malgovert 50; Le Sel de la Terre 50; Un Jour Comme les Autres 52; Le Lycée sur la Colline 52;

Beauty and the Bullfighter • Love in a Hot Climate • Sang et Lumière 53; Lourdes et Ses Miracles 54; Arthur Honegger 55; La Bête Noire 56; S.O.S. Noronha 57; Une Belle Peur 58; Le Bouclier 60; Sire le Roy N'A Plus Rien Dit 64; Biquefarre 83

Rouse, Russell The Well 51*; The Thief 52; Wicked Woman 53; New York Confidential 55; The Fastest Gun Alive 56; House of Numbers 57; Thunder in the Sun 58; A House Is Not a Home 64; The Caper of the Golden Bulls • Carnival of Thieves 65; The Oscar 65

Rouse, Virginia To Market, to Market 87

Roussel, Gilbert Women's Prison Massacre 86

Roussel, Henri Un Homme Passe 17; L'Âme du Bronze 18; La Faute d'Odette Maréchal 20; The Sheik's Wife • Visages Voiles...Âmes Closes 21; La Vérité 22; Les Opprimes 23; Violettes Impériales 24; La Terre Promise 25; Destinée 26; L'Île Enchantée 27; La Valse de l'Adieu 28; Paris Girls 29; The Night Is Ours • La Nuit • La Nuit Est à Nous 30

Rouve, Pierre Cop-Out • Stranger in the House 67

Rovenský, Josef Ecstasy of Young Love • Řeka • The River • Young Love 33

Rovira-Beleta Los Tarantos 63

Row, Alexander see Rou, Alexander

Rowden, Walter C. The Children's Home 21; Corinthian Jack • Fighting Jack 21; Daniel Deronda 21; Eileen Alannah 21; Sally in Our Alley 21; Silver Threads Among the Gold 21; A Tale of Two Cities 22; Vanity Fair 22

Rowe, George Fortress in the Sun 78

Rowe, Peter The Neon Palace 70; Lost 85; Architects of Fear 86; Take Two 87

Rowe, Victor W. Football Daft 21

Rowland, E. G. see Castellari, Enzo G.

Rowland, Roy Hollywood Party 34*; Sunkist Stars at Palm Springs 36; Cinema Circus 37; Hollywood Party in Technicolor 37; How to Start the Day 37; A Night at the Movies 37; Song of Revolt 37; The Courtship of the Newt 38; An Evening Alone 38; An Hour for Lunch 38; How to Figure Income Tax 38; How to Raise a Baby 38; How to Read 38; How to Sub-Let 38; How to Watch Football 38; Mental Poise 38; Music Made Simple 38; Opening Day 38; Dark Magic 39; Home Early 39; How to Eat 39; Think First 39; Jack Pot 40; Please Answer 40; You the People 40; Changed Identity 41; Sucker List 41; Lost Angel 43; A Stranger in Town 43; Our Vines Have Tender Grapes 45; Boys' Ranch 46; Killer McCoy 47; The Romance of Rosy Ridge 47; Tenth Avenue Angel 48; Scene of the Crime 49; The Outriders 50; Two Weeks with Love 50; Bugles in the Afternoon 51; Excuse My Dust 51; The 5,000 Fingers of Dr. T 52; Affair with a Stranger 53; The Moonlighter 53; Many Rivers to Cross 54; Rogue Cop 54; Witness to Murder 54; Hit the Deck 55; Meet Me in Las Vegas • Viva Las Vegas! 55; Slander 56;

These Wilder Years 56; Gun Glory 57; The Seven Hills of Rome 57; The Chasers • The Girl Hunters 60; The Gunfighters of Casa Grande • Los Pistoleros de Casa Grande 64; La Ley del Forastero • The Man Called Gringo • Sie Nannten Ihn Gringo 64; The Sea Pirate • Surcouf—Le Dernier Corsaire • Surcouf—Le Tigre des Sept Mers • Surcouf—L'Eroe dei Sette Mari • El Tigre de los Siete Mares 67*

Rowland, William Hate • Odio 40; Perfidia • Perfidy 40; Follies Girl 43; A Song for Miss Julie 45; Flight to Nowhere 46; When Men Are Beasts • Woman in the Night • Women in the Night 48; Tobo the Happy Clown 65; The Wild Scene 70

Rowles, Kenneth Take an Easy Ride 77
Rowley, Chris Black Trash 78
Rowson, Leslie The Scat Burglars 37
Roy, Ashok Daku Hasina 87

Roy, Bimal Udahir Pathe 42; Batarcherjee 43; Bengal Famine 43; Humrahi 45; Anjangarh 48; Pehla Admi 48; Mantra-Mugdha 49; Tathapil 50; Baap Beti 51; Maa 51; Calcutta, Cruel City • Do Bigha Zamin • Two Acres of Land 52; Parineeta 52; Biraj Bahu 54; Naukari 54; Amanat 55*; Devdas 55; Gautama the Buddha 55*; Pariwar 56*; Aparadhi Kaun 58; Madhumati 58; Yahudi 58; Sujata 59; Parakh 60; Kabuliwala 61; Prem Patra 62; Bandini 63

Roy, Jean-Louis L'Inconnu de Shandigor • The Unknown Man of Shandigor 67
Roy, Mervyn le see LeRoy, Mervyn
Rozema, Patricia Passion: A Letter in 16mm 86; I've Heard the Mermaids Singing 87; The White Room 90

Różewicz, Stanisław Ulica Brzozowa 49*; Echo 64

Rozier, Jacques Langage de l'Écran 47; Une Épine au Pied 54; La Rentrée des Classes 55; Blue Jeans 58; Adieu Philippine • So Long Philippine 61; Dans le Vent 63; Paparazzi 63; Du Côté d'Orouët 71; Nono Nénesse 75*; Les Naufrages de l'Île de la Tortue 76; Maine-Océan • Maine-Océan Express 86

Rozier, Willy The Girl in the Bikini • The Lighthouse Keeper's Daughter • Manina • Manina la Fille Sans Voile 52; Prisoner of the Jungle 59; Les Chiens dans la Nuit • The Girl Can't Stop 66

Rozkopal, Z. Mr. Prokouk the Acrobat • Pan Prokouk Akrobatem 59

Rózsa, János Sunday Daughters • Vasárnapi Szülők 79; Csók, Anyu • Love, Mother 87

Rubbo, Michael Solzhenitsyn's Children ...Are Making a Lot of Noise in Paris 79; The Peanut Butter Solution 85; Tommy Tricker and the Stamp Traveler 88

Ruben, J. Walter The Public Defender 31; Secret Service 31; The Phantom of Crestwood 32; Roadhouse Murder 32; Ace of Aces 33; The Great Jasper 33; Man of Two Worlds 33; No Marriage Ties 33; No Other Woman 33; The Dover Road • Where Sinners Meet 34; Java Head 34*; Success at Any Price 34; Public Hero No. 1

35; Riffraff 35; Old Hutch 36; The Suicide Club • Trouble for Two 36; The Bad Man of Brimstone 37; The Good Old Soak 37

Ruben, Joseph The Sister-in-Law 74; The Pom-Pom Girls 76; Joyride 77; Our Winning Season 78; G.O.R.P. • Gorp 80; Dreamscape 84; The Stepfather 86; True Believer 89

Ruben, Katt Shea Stripped to Kill 87; Dance of the Damned 88; Stripped to Kill II: Live Girls 89; Streets 90

Rubens, Percival The Foster Gang 64; Three Days of Fire 67; Strangers at Sunrise 69; Mr. Kingstreet's War 70; Saboteurs 74; The Midnight Caller 80; Survival Zone 81; Raw Terror 85; Wild Country 88

Rubie, Howard The Scalp Merchant 77
Rubin, Bruce Dionysus in '69 68*
Rubin, J. Centerbeam 78*
Rubin, Rick Tougher Than Leather 88
Rubinchik, Valery Otstupnik 88
Rubinstein, Amnon Nadia 86
Ruder, Ken Lips of Blood 72
Rudnik, Lev The Duel 64*

Rudolph, Alan Premonition 72; Barn of the Naked Dead • Terror Circus 73; Welcome to L.A. • Welcome to L.A. the City of One Night Stands 76; Remember My Name 78; Roadie 80; Endangered Species 82; Return Engagement 83; Choose Me 84; Songwriter 84; Trouble in Mind 85; Made in Heaven 87; The Moderns 88; Love at Large 90

Rudolph, Oscar The Rocket Man 54; Twist Around the Clock 61; Don't Knock the Twist 62; The Wild Westerners 62

Rudolph, Verena Francesca 86
Ruehmann, Heinz see Rühmann, Heinz
Ruffin, John Crown Trial 38

Ruggles, Wesley Bobby, Movie Director 17; Bobby, Philanthropist 17; Bobby, the Pacifist 17; Bobby's Bravery 17; For France 17; The Blind Adventure 18; The Winchester Woman 19; The Desperate Hero 20; The Leopard Woman 20; Love 20; Piccadilly Jim 20; Sooner or Later 20; The Greater Claim 21; Over the Wire 21; Uncharted Seas 21; If I Were Queen 22; Slippery McGee • Slippy McGee 22; Wild Honey 22; The Heart Raider 23; Mr. Billings Spends His Dime 23; The Remittance Woman 23; The Age of Innocence 24; Broadway Lady 25; The Covered Flagon 25; Don Coo-Coo 25; The Fast Male 25; The Great Decide 25; He Who Gets Rapped 25; Madam Sans Gin 25; Merton of the Goofies 25; Miss Me Again 25; The Plastic Age 25; Three Bases East 25; Welcome Granger 25; What Price Gloria? 25; The Kick-Off 26; A Man of Quality 26; Beware of Widows 27; Silk Stockings 27; Finders Keepers 28; The Fourflusher 28; Condemned • Condemned to Devil's Island 29; Girl Overboard • Port o' Dreams 29; The Haunted Lady 29; High Society • Scandal 29; Street Girl 29; Cimarron 30; Honey 30; The Sea Bat 30; Are These Our Children? 31; No Man of Her Own 32; Roar of the Dragon 32; College Humor 33; I'm No Angel 33; The Monkey's Paw 33*;

Bolero 34; Shoot the Works • Thank Your Stars 34; Accent on Youth 35; The Bride Comes Home 35; The Gilded Lily 35; Valiant Is the Word for Carrie 36; I Met Him in Paris 37; True Confession 37; Sing, You Sinners 38; Invitation to Happiness 39; Arizona 40; My Two Husbands • Too Many Husbands 40; Good Morning, Doctor • You Belong to Me 41; Somewhere I'll Find You 42; See Here, Private Hargrove 43*; Slightly Dangerous 43; London Town • My Heart Goes Crazy 46

Rühmann, Heinz Lauter Lügen 38; Lauter Liebe 40; Sophienlund 43; Der Engel mit dem Saitenspiel 44; Die Kupferne Hochzeit 48; Briefträger Müller 53*

Ruiz, Raúl Three Sad Tigers • Tres Tristes Tigres 68; La Catanaria 69; Militarism and Torture • Militarismo y Tortura 69; La Colonia Penal • The Penal Colony 70; ¿Qué Hacer? • What Is to Be Done? 70*; Ahora Te Vamos a Llamar Hermano • Now We'll Call You Brother 71; La Expropriación • The Expropriation 71; Nadie Dijo Nada • Nobody Said Anything • Nobody Said Nothing 71; The Minutemen • Los Minuteros 72*; Poesía Popular, la Teoría y la Práctica • Popular Poetry, Theory and Practice 72; Abastecimiento • Provisions 73; Brave Little Dove • Palomita Brava 73; Little White Dove • Palomita Blanca • White Little Dove 73; New Chilean Song • Nueva Canción Chilena 73; El Realismo Socialista • Socialist Realism 73; Diálogo de Exiliados • Dialogue d'Exilés • Dialogue of Exiles 74; El Cuerpo Repartido y el Mundo al Revés • Mensch Verstreut und Welt Verkehrt • The Scattered Body and the World Upside Down • Utopia 75; Sotelo 76; Colloque de Chiens • Dogs' Dialog 77; The Suspended Vocation • La Vocation Suspendue 77; Des Grands Événements et des Gens Ordinaires • Of Great Events and Ordinary People 78; Les Divisions de la Nature • The Divisions of Nature 78; L'Hypothèse du Tableau Volé • The Hypothesis of a Stolen Painting • The Hypothesis of the Stolen Painting 78; Le Jeu de l'Oie • Snakes and Ladders 79; Le Borgne • The One-Eyed Man 80; Grey Gold • L'Or Gris 80; The New City • La Ville Nouvelle 80; Teletests 80; Het Dak van de Walvis • On Top of the Whale • The Roof of the Whale • Techo de la Ballena • Le Toit de la Baleine • The Top of the Whale • The Whale's Roof 81; Images de Sable • Images of Sand 81; Le Territoire • The Territory 81; Chinese Shadows • Ombres Chinoises 82; Classification of Plants • Classifications des Plantes 82; The Little Theatre • Le Petit Théâtre 82; Querelle de Jardins • The War of the Gardens 82; The Sailor's Three Crowns • Three Crowns of the Sailor • Les Trois Couronnes Danois de Matelots • Les Trois Couronnes du Matelot 82; Bérenice 83; City of Pirates • La Ville des Pirates 83; L'Éveillé du Pont d'Alma • L'Éveillé du Pont de l'Alma • The Sleepwalkers of the Pont de l'Alma 83; A Journey by Way of the Hand •

• Flügel und Fesseln • The Future of Emily 84; Laputa 86; Felix 87*; Divided Love • Geteilte Liebe 88

Sanderson, Challis The Law Divine 20*; Three Men in a Boat 20; Monty Works the Wires 21*; The Scallywag 21; Billie's Rose 22; The Bride of Lammermoor 22; Fallen by the Way 22; Faust 22; Fra Diavolo 22; The Last Hundred Yards 22; The Lily of Killarney 22; The Making of Gordon's 22; The Masked Rider 22; The Merchant of Venice 22; A Race for a Bride 22; The Road to Heaven 22; The Scarlet Letter 22; Sir Rupert's Wife 22; La Traviata 22; Wheels of Fate 22; Broadcasting • The Romance of Broadcasting 25*; Home Construction 26*; How I Began 26*; Listening In 26*; The Loud Speaker 26*; Oscillation 26*; Scrags 30; Danny Boy 34*; The King of Whales 34; Cock o' the North 35*; Stars on Parade 35*

Sandgren, Åke Johannes Hemmelighed 85

Sandground, Maurice As in Days of Yore 17; Cast Adrift 17; The Girls of the Village 17; The Base Deceivers 18; How Could You, Uncle? 18; Kilties Three 18; Living by Their Wits 18; The Magistrate's Daughter 18; Griff Swims the Channel 19; Griff's Lost Love 19; The Ne'er-Do-Well 19; Pussyfoot Comedy 19; Russia, Land of Tomorrow 19; The Slocum Harriers 19; The Boy Messenger 20; The Hydro 20; In Borrowed Plumes 20; The Lambs of Dove Court 20; The Little Poacher 20; Truants 20; Immortals of Bonnie Scotland • The Life of Robert Burns 26; The Life of Sir Walter Scott 26; The Tallyman 28

Sandø, Toralf Boer Boersen, Jr. • Bør Børsen, Jr. 39

Sándor, Pál Herkulesfürdöi Emlék • Improperly Dressed • Strange Masquerade 77; Daniel Takes a Train • Szerencsés Dániel 83; Csak egy Mozi • Just a Movie 85; Miss Arizona 88

Sándor, Sára Tüske a Korom Alatt 88

Sandoz, Jaques Gemini: The Twin Stars 88

Sandrich, Jay Neil Simon's Seems Like Old Times • Seems Like Old Times 80

Sandrich, Mark Jerry the Giant 26*; Napoleon Junior 26*; Brave Cowards 27; Careless Hubby 27; First Prize 27; Hello Sailor 27; Hold Fast 27; Hold That Bear 27; Hot Soup 27; A Midsummer Night's Steam 27; The Movie Hound 27; Night Owls 27; Shooting Wild 27; Some Scout 27; Bear Knees 28; A Cow's Husband 28; High Strung 28; A Lady Lion 28; Love Is Blonde 28*; Runaway Girls 28; Sword Points 28; The Talk of Hollywood 29; Two-Gun Ginsburg 29; Aunt's in the Pants 30; Barnum Was Wrong 30; General Ginsburg 30; Gunboat Ginsburg 30; Hot Bridge 30; Moonlight and Monkey Business 30; Off to Peoria 30; Razored in Old Kentucky 30; Society Goes Spaghetti 30; Talking Turkey 30; Trader Ginsburg 30; The County Seat 31; Cowslips 31; False Roomers 31; The Gay Nighties 31; Many a

Sip 31; A Melon-Drama 31; Scratch As Catch Can 31; The Strife of the Party 31; The Way of All Fish 31; The Wife o' Riley 31; Ex-Rooster 32; A Hurry Call 32; The Iceman's Ball 32; Jitters, the Butler 32; The Millionaire Cat 32; A Slip at the Switch 32; So This Is Harris 32; When Summons Comes 32; Aggie Appleby, Maker of Men • Cupid in the Rough 33; The Druggist's Dilemma 33; Hokus Focus 33; Melody Cruise 33; Private Wives 33; Thru Thin and Thicket, or Who's Zoo in Africa 33; Cockeyed Cavaliers 34; The Gay Divorce • The Gay Divorcee 34; Hips Hips Hooray 34; Top Hat 35; Follow the Fleet 36; A Woman Rebels 36; Shall We Dance? 37; Carefree 38; Man About Town 39; Buck Benny Rides Again 40; Love Thy Neighbor 40; Skylark 41; Holiday Inn 42; So Proudly We Hail! 43; Here Come the Waves 44; I Love a Soldier 44; Blue Skies 46*

Sands, Sompote Crocodile 79

San Fernando, Manuel El Gato con Botas • Puss 'n Boots 64; Caperucita y Pulgarcito Contra los Monstruos • Little Red Riding Hood and the Monsters 65*

Sanforth, Clifford The Houghland Murder Case • Murder by Television 35; High Hat 37; I Demand Payment 38

Sang, Hu see Hu, Sang

Sanger, Jonathan Code Name: Emerald 85

Sang-ok, Shin see Shin, Sang-ok

Sangster, Jimmy The Horror of Frankenstein 70; Lust for a Vampire • To Love a Vampire 70; Fear in the Night 72

Saniewski, Wiesław Nadzór 81; Dotknięci 88

Sanin, Alexander Polikushka 19

Sanishvila, N. The Scrapper 59

Sanjinés, Jorge Cobre • Copper 58; La Guitarrita • The Little Guitar 58; The Little Magician • El Maguito 59; Dreams and Realities • Sueños y Realidades 62; One Day, Paulino • Un Día, Paulino 62; Revolución • Revolution 63; Bolivia Advances • Bolivia Avanza 64; Aysa! • Landslide! 65; That's It • Ukamau 66; Blood of the Condor • Yawar Mallku 69; El Coraje del Pueblo • The Courage of the People • The Night of San Juan 71; El Enemigo Principal • Jatun Auka • The Principal Enemy 73; ¡Fuera de Aquí! • Llucsi Caimanta • Out of Here! 77; Las Banderas del Amanecer • The Flags of Dawn 84; La Nación Clandestina 89

Sano, Marcel de see De Sano, Marcel

Sant, Gus van, Jr. see Van Sant, Gus, Jr.

Santamaria, Erick Decoy for Terror • The Playgirl Killer 70

Santean, Antonio Bed of Fire • Den of Doom • Don't Touch My Sister • The Glass Cage 63

Santell, Alfred My Valet 15*; Beloved Rogues 17; The Magic Jazzbo 17; Out of the Bag 17; At Swords' Points 18; Home James 18; Main 1-2-3 18; O Susie Behave! 18; Some Job 18; The Stolen Keyhole 18;

Vamping the Vamp 18; As You Were 19; Seeing Things 19; Stop, Cease, Hesitate! 19; Two Tired 19; Pills for Papa 20; Rings and Things 20; A Wild Night 20; It Might Happen to You 21; But a Butler 22; Rented Trouble 22; Wildcat Jordan 22; Lights Out 23; Empty Hearts 24; Fools in the Dark 24; The Man Who Played Square 24; Parisian Nights 24; Bluebeard's Seven Wives 25; Classified 25; The Marriage Whirl 25; The Dancer of Paris 26; Just Another Blonde 26; Subway Sadie 26; Sweet Daddies 26; The Gorilla 27; Orchids and Ermine 27; The Patent Leather Kid 27; Kentucky Courage • The Little Shepherd of Kingdom Come 28; Show Girl 28; Wheel of Chance 28; Romance of Rio Grande • Romance of the Rio Grande 29; This Is Heaven 29; Twin Beds 29; The Arizona Kid 30; The Sea Wolf 30; The Blonde Reporter • Sob Sister 31; Body and Soul 31; Daddy Long Legs 31; Polly of the Circus 32; Rebecca of Sunnybrook Farm 32; Tess of the Storm Country 32; Bondage 33; A Feather in Her Hat 33; The Right to Romance 33; The Life of Vergie Winters 34; The Dictator • For Love of a Queen • The Love Affair of the Dictator • The Loves of a Dictator 35*; People Will Talk 35; Winterset 36; Breakfast for Two 37; Internes Can't Take Money • You Can't Take Money 37; The Arkansas Traveler 38; Cocoanut Grove 38; Having Wonderful Time 38*; Our Leading Citizen 39; Aloma of the South Seas 41; Beyond the Blue Horizon 42; The Adventures of Jack London • Jack London • The Life of Jack London 43; The Hairy Ape 44; Mexicana 45; That Brennan Girl 46

Santer, Carl von The City Without Jews 28

Santi, Giancarlo Drei Vaterunser für Vier Halunken • The Grand Duel • Il Grande Duello 72

Santi, Jacques Flag 88

Santiago, Cirio Women in Cages • Women's Penitentiary III 72*; Fly Me • Fly Me, Savage! 73; Bamboo Gods and Iron Men 74; T.N.T. Jackson 74; Cover Girl Models 75; The Muthers 76; Ebony, Ivory and Jade 77; Fighting Mad 77; Cemetery Girls • Sensuous Vampires • Vampire Hookers 78; Death Force 78; Firecracker 81; Stryker 83; Caged Fury 84; Desert Warrior • Vindicator • Wheels of Fire 85; The Destroyers • The Devastator • King's Ransom 85; Eye of the Eagle 86; Final Mission 86; Naked Vengeance • Satin Vengeance 86; Silk 86; Demon of Paradise 87; Equalizer 2000 87; Fast Gun 87; Killer Instinct 87; The Spear 87; The Sisterhood 88

Santiago, Hugo Écoute Voir... • See Here My Love 78; Les Trottoirs de Saturne 85

Santiago, Pablo Operation: Get Victor Corpus the Rebel Soldier 87

Santiago, Ric Zimatar 87*

Santis, Giuseppe de see De Santis, Giuseppe

Santiso, José Bad Company • Malayunta 86

Santley, Joseph All Americans 29; The Cocoanuts 29*; The Harmony Boys 29; High Hat 29; Hold Up 29; Just One Word 29; Radio Rhythm 29; Raising the Roof 29; Rudy Vallee and His Connecticut Yankees 29; Ruth Etting 29; That Party in Person 29; Tito Schipa 29; Tito Schipa Concert No. 2 29; Swing High 30; Ladies Not Allowed 32; Lambs' All-Star Gambler No. 3 32; $50 Million Can't Be Wrong 33; Hear 'Em and Weep 33; Peeping Tom 33; The Poor Fish 33; The Loudspeaker • The Radio Star 34; Million Dollar Baby 34; Young and Beautiful 34; Harmony Lane 35; Waterfront Lady 35; Dancing Feet 36; The Harvester 36; Her Master's Voice 36; Laughing Irish Eyes 36; The Old School Tie • We Went to College 36; Smartest Girl in Town 36; Walking on Air 36; Meet the Missus 37; She's Got Everything 37; There Goes the Groom 37; Always in Trouble 38; Blonde Cheat 38; Swing, Sister, Swing 38; The Family Next Door 39; Man's Heritage • Spirit of Culver 39; Music in My Heart 39; Two Bright Boys 39; Behind the News 40; Dancing on a Dime 40; Melody and Moonlight 40; Melody Ranch 40; Down Mexico Way 41; Ice-Capades 41; Jamboree • Rookies on Parade 41; Judy Goes to Town • Puddin' Head 41; Sis Hopkins 41; Call of the Canyon 42; Hitting the Headlines • Yokel Boy 42; Joan of Ozark • The Queen of Spies 42; Remember Pearl Harbor 42; A Tragedy at Midnight 42; Chatterbox 43; Here Comes Elmer 43; Shantytown 43; Sleepy Lagoon 43; Thumbs Up 43; Brazil 44; Goodnight Sweetheart 44; In Rosie's Room • Rosie the Riveter 44; Three Little Sisters 44; Earl Carroll Vanities 45; Hitchhike to Happiness 45; Shadow of a Woman 46; Make Believe Ballroom 49; When You're Smiling 50

Santoni, Joel Les Yeux Fermes 72; La Course en Tête • Eddy Merckx 73; Thomas 74; Les Œufs Brouilles 76; Ils Sont Grands Ces Petits 79; Si Je Suis Comme Ça C'Est la Faute à Papa 79; Died on a Rainy Sunday • Mort un Dimanche de Pluie 86

Santos, Briccio Damortis 84

Santos, Carmen Argila • Clay 40*

Santos, Luiz Paulino dos see Dos Santos, Luiz Paulino

Santos, Nelson Pereira dos see Dos Santos, Nelson Pereira

Santry Faces in the Fire • Pictures in the Fire 18; A Watched Pot 18

Santschi, Tom Caryl of the Mountains 14; The Blood Seedling 15; The Heart of Paro 15; His Fighting Blood 15; The Octopus 15; A Sultana of the Desert 15

Sanvoisin, Michel Nogent—Eldorado du Dimanche • Nogent, the Sunday Eldorado 29*

Sanzo, John C. de see De Sanzo, Juan Carlos

Sanzo, Juan Carlos de see De Sanzo, Juan Carlos

Sao-bin, Sui see Sui, Sao-bin

Saparov, Usman Manly Education •

Muzskoe Vospitanie 86; Adventures on Little Islands • Priklyuchenia na Malenkikh Ostrovekh 87

Saperstein, David A Killing Affair 85; My Sister's Keeper • Personal Choice 86

Saponaro, Michele Paul's Awakening • Il Risveglio di Paul 85

Sára, Sándor see Sándor, Sára

Saraceni, Paulo Cesar Natal da Portela 88

Sarafian, Deran Alien Predator • The Falling 84; Interzone 86; To Die For 89; Death Warrant 90

Sarafian, Richard C. Terror at Black Falls 62; Andy 65; Philip • Run Wild, Run Free 69; Fragment of Fear 70; Man in the Wilderness 71; Vanishing Point 71; The Lolly Madonna War • Lolly Madonna XXX 72; The Man Who Loved Cat Dancing 73; The Arab Conspiracy • Double Hit • The Next Man 76; Sunburn 79; The Bear 84; Eye of the Tiger 86; Street Justice 88

Sarecky, Louis The Cuckoos 30*

Sargent, George L. The Gentleman from Mississippi 14; The Call of the Dance 15; Midnight at Maxim's 15; Philip Holden, Waster 16; The Sable Blessing 16; A Gilded Youth 17; High Speed 17*; The Broadway Bubble 20; The Prey 20; The Whisper Market 20; The Charming Deceiver 21; It Isn't Being Done This Season 21

Sargent, Joseph One Spy Too Many 65; The Spy in the Green Hat 66; The Hell with Heroes • Run, Hero, Run • A Time for Heroes 67; Colossus 1980 • Colossus: The Forbin Project • The Day the World Changed Hands • The Forbin Project 69; The Soldier Who Declared Peace • Tribes 70; The Man 72; McKlusky • White Lightning 73; Sunshine 73; The Taking of Pelham 1-2-3 74; MacArthur • MacArthur: The Rebel General 77; Goldengirl 79; Coast to Coast 80; Nightmares 83; Jaws: The Revenge 87

Sargent, P. D. Battling King 22

Sargent, Roy My Way • The Winner 74*

Sargent, W. J. That Lass of Chandler's 29

Sarkar, Rathis De Pratipaksha 88

Sarkar, Suven Kalankini Nayika 88

Särkkä, Toivo The Milkmaid 59; Kuu On Vaarallinen • Prelude to Ecstasy 63

Sarmiento, Valeria The Minutemen • Los Minuteros 72*

Sarne, Michael Road to St. Tropez • La Route de Saint-Tropez 66; Joanna 68; Myra Breckinridge 70; Intimidade • Vera Verão 72; The Rise and Fall of Ivor Dickie 78*; Trouble with a Battery 86

Sarno, Hector V. Sonia 28

Sarno, Joe Lash of Lust 62; Nude in Charcoal 62; Sin in the Suburbs 62; Pandora's Box 63; Sin You Sinners 63; The Lace Rope 64; Moonlighting Wives 64; The Naked Fog 64; Warm Nights and Hot Pleasures 64; Flesh and Lace 65; Step Out of Your Mind 65; The Swap and How They Made It 65; Another Woman,

Another Day • The Love Merchant • Love Merchants 66; Anything for Money 66; The Bed and How They Made It 66; Bed of Violence 66; Come Ride the Wild Pink Horse 66; Deep Inside 66; The Love Rebellion 66; The Magic Touch 66; Red Roses of Passion 66; Scarf of Mist, Thigh of Satin 66; The Sex Cycle 66; Skin Deep in Love 66; All the Sins of Sodom 67; The Beach House 67; Inga 67; My Body Hungers 67; Passion in Hot Hollows 67; Vibrations 67; Wall of Flesh 67; Desire Under the Palms 68; Karla 68; The Layout 68; Marcey 68; The Odd Triangle 68; Daddy Darling 69; Indelicate Balance 69; Inga II 69; The Young Erotic Fanny Hill 70; Any Afternoon 71; Young Playthings 72; Bibi 73; Confessions of a Young American Housewife 73; Deep Throat II 73; The Revenge of the Black Sisters • Veil of Blood 73; Abagail Leslie Is Back in Town 74; Butterflies 74; Oversexed 74; The Switch 74; Laura's Toys 75; Misty 75; Kärleks Ön 77; Fabod Janteix 78; Wolf Cubs 83

Sarno, Jonathan The Kirlian Witness • The Plants Are Watching 78

Sasdy, Peter Journey Into Darkness 68*; Taste the Blood of Dracula 69; Countess Dracula 70; Hands of the Ripper 71; The Devil's Undead • Nothing But the Night • The Resurrection Syndicate 72; Doomwatch 72; The Baby • The Devil Within Her • I Don't Want to Be Born • The Monster • Sharon's Baby 75; Welcome to Blood City 77; The Two Faces of Evil 81*; The Lonely Lady 82

Saslavsky, Luis Crimen a las Tres 35; Escala en la Ciudad 36; La Fuga 37; Nace un Amor 38; Closed Door • Puerta Cerrada 39; The Crazy Musician • El Loco Serenata 39; La Casa del Recuerdo 40; Historia de una Noche 41; Cenizas al Viento 42; Eclipse del Sol 43; Los Ojos Más Lindos del Mundo 43; La Dama Duende • La Donna Duende 45; Camino del Infierno 46; Cinco Besos 46; Historia de una Mala Mujer 48; Vidalita 49; The Black Crown • La Corona Negra 50; La Neige Était Sale • The Snow Was Black 52; Démoniaque • Les Louves • The She-Wolves 57; Ce Corps Tant Désiré • Way of the Wicked 58; Man to Man Talk • Premier Mai • Premier May 58; El Balcón de la Luna 61; Las Ratas 63; Las Mujeres los Prefieren Tantos 66

Sassebo, Fred Macaroni Blues 86*

Sassy, J. P. see Sassy, Jean-Paul

Sassy, Jean-Paul The Mazur File • La Peau et les Os 60*; Colère Froide • Thunder in the Blood • The Warm Body 62*

Sathyu, M. S. Garm Hava • Hot Winds 73; Kahan Kahan se Guzar Gaya • The Many Phases of Life 86

Satlof, Ron Spider-Man Strikes Back 78

Sato, Hajime The Ghost of the Hunchback • House of Terrors • Kaidan Semushi Otoko 65; Kaitei Daisensō • Terror Beneath the Sea • Water Cyborgs 66; Goke, Bodysnatcher from Hell • Goke the Vampire • Kyūketsuki Gokemidoro 68

Sato, Junya The Go Masters • Mikan no Taikyoku 82*; The Shape of the Land 84; Dun-Huang • Lost in the Wilderness • Uemura Naomi Monogatari 86

Sato, Tosuke Banana Shoot 89

Sattar, J. H. Kasturi 88

Sauer, Fred Dangers of the Engagement Period 29; Der Stolz der 3 Kompagnie 32; Der Tanzhusar 33; Heimat am Rhein 34; Die Beiden Seehunde 35; Pantoffelhelden 35; Alles Weg'n dem Hund 36; Alte Kameraden 36; Mädchenrauber 36; Gordian der Tyrann 37; Der Lachdoktor • The Laugh Doctor 38

Saum, Clifford P. The Kaiser's Finish 18*

Saunders, Charles No Exit 30; Tawny Pipit 44*; Fly Away Peter 48; Trouble in the Air 48; Dark Interval 50; Chelsea Story 51; One Wild Oat 51; Black Orchid 52; Blind Man's Bluff 52; Come Back Peter 52; Death of an Angel 52; The Accused 53*; Love in Pawn 53; Three's Company 53*; The Golden Link 54; Meet Mr. Callaghan 54; The Red Dress 54*; The Scarlet Web 54; The Hornet's Nest 55; The Narrowing Circle 55; One Jump Ahead 55; A Time to Kill 55; Behind the Headlines 56; Find the Lady 56; Date with Disaster 57; The End of the Line 57; Kill Her Gently 57; The Man Without a Body 57*; Murder Reported 57; There's Always a Thursday 57; The Woman Eater • Womaneater 57; Naked Fury • Pleasure Lover • The Pleasure Lovers 59; Nudist Paradise 59; Strictly Confidential 59; The Gentle Trap 60; Operation Cupid 60; Dangerous Afternoon 61; Jungle Street • Jungle Street Girls 61; Danger by My Side 62

Saunders, John Monk Conquest of the Air 36*

Saunders, Peter Eight Cylinder Love 34; Bindle • Bindle (One of Them Days) • One of Them Days 68

Saura, Carlos Antonio Saura 55; Sunday Afternoon • Una Tarde de Domingo • La Tarde del Domingo 57; Cuenca 58; Los Golfos • The Hooligans • Riff-Raff • The Urchins 59; Lament for a Bandit • Llanto por un Bandido • Weeping for a Bandit 64; La Caza • The Chase • The Hunt 65; Peppermint Frappé 67; Stress Es Tres, Tres • Stress Is Three, Three 68; The Den • The Honeycomb • La Madriguera 69; The Garden of Earthly Delights • The Garden of Earthly Delights • El Jardín de las Delicias 70; Ana and the Wolves • Ana y los Lobos • Anna and the Wolves 72; Cousin Angelica • La Prima Angélica 73; ¡Cría! • Cría Cuervos • Raise Ravens • Rear Ravens 75; Elisa, My Life • Elisa, My Love • Elisa, Vida Mía 77; Blindfolded • Los Ojos Vendados 78; Mamá Cumple Cien Años • Mama Turns 100 79; Deprisa, Deprisa • Fast, Fast • Hurry, Hurry 80; Antonieta 81; Blood Wedding • Bodas de Sangre 81; Dulces Horas • Sweet Hours 81; Carmen 83; Stilts • Los Zancos 84; El Amor Brujo • A Love Bewitched • Love the Magician 85; El Dorado 87; La Noche Oscura 89; ¡Ay,

Carmela! 90

Saura, Guillermo Chorros • Crooks 87*; Feelings: Mirta from Liniers to Istanbul • Sentimientos: Mirta de Liniers a Estambul 87*

Saurel, Jacques Joy and Joan 85

Saurel, Maurice Devil's Daughter • La Fille du Diable 49

Sauriol, Brigitte Laura Laur 89

Sautell, Al see *Santell, Alfred*

Sautet, Claude Nous N'Irons Plus au Bois 51; Bonjour Sourire • Sourire aux Lèvres 55; The Big Risk • Classe Tous Risques 59; L'Arme à Gauche • The Dictator's Guns • Guns for the Dictator 65; La Tête la Première 65; L'Amante • Les Choses de la Vie • These Things Happen • The Things of Life 69; Max • Max et les Ferrailleurs 70; César and Rosalie • César et Rosalie 72; Vincent, François, Paul...and the Others • Vincent, François, Paul...et les Autres 74; Mado 76; Une Histoire Simple • A Simple Story 78; A Bad Son • Un Mauvais Fils 80; Garçon! 83; A Few Days with Me • Quelques Jours avec Moi 88

Sauvage, André The Yellow Cruise 36

Sauvajon, Marc-Gilbert Just Me • Ma Pomme • My Apple 50; The King • Le Roi • A Royal Affair 50

Sauvy, Jean Au Pays des Mages Noirs 47*

Savage, Henry W. Excuse Me 16

Savage, Peter Heisser Sand auf Sylt • Just to Be Loved • The New Life Style 70*

Savalas, Telly Beyond Reason 77

Savchenko, Igor Nikita Ivanovich and Socialism 31; People Without Hands 33; Accordion • Garmon 34; Chance Meeting • Unexpected Meeting 36; The Ballad of Cossack Gloota • The Song of the Cossack Gloota 37; Guerrilla Brigade • Riders • Vsadniki 39; Bogdan Khmelnitsky 41; Years of Youth • Youthful Years 41; The Diary of a Nazi 42*; Partisans in the Plains of Ukraine • Partisans in the Ukrainian Steppes 42; Ivan Nikulin, Russian Sailor 43; Love's Polka • The Lucky Bride 46; The Third Blow 48; Taras Shevchenko 51*

Savegar, Brian Kendal see *Kendal-Savegar, Brian*

Saver, Frem Blinde Passagier • Stowaways 37

Saville, Alec Inasmuch 34

Saville, Philip Stop the World—I Want to Get Off 66; Oedipus the King 67; The Best House in London 69; Secrets 71; Those Glory, Glory Days 83; Shadey 85; The Fruit Machine • Wonderland 88; Fellow Traveler 89

Saville, Victor Conquest of Oil • The Story of Oil 19; Liquid Sunshine 19; The Arcadians • Land of Heart's Desire 27; Fanny Hawthorne • Hindle Wakes 27*; Tesha • A Woman in Pawn • A Woman in the Night 27*; Kitty 28; Armistice 29; Me and the Boys 29; Woman to Woman 29; The Sport of Kings 30; The W Plan 30; A Warm Corner 30; Bachelor's Folly • The Calendar 31*; Hindle Wakes 31; Michael

and Mary 31; The Office Girl • Sunshine Susie 31; The Faithful Heart • Faithful Hearts 32; The Good Companions 32; Love on Wheels 32; Friday the Thirteenth 33; I Was a Spy 33; Evensong 34; Evergreen 34; The Iron Duke 34; The Dictator • For Love of a Queen • The Love Affair of the Dictator • The Loves of a Dictator 35*; First a Girl 35; Me and Marlborough 35; It's Love Again 36; Action for Slander 37*; Anxious Years • Dark Journey 37; South Riding 37; Storm in a Teacup 37*; Forever and a Day 43*; Tonight and Every Night 44; The Green Years 46; Green Dolphin Street 47; If Winter Comes 47; Conspirator 49; Kim 50; Calling Bulldog Drummond 51; Affair in Monte Carlo • Twenty-Four Hours of a Woman's Life 52; The Long Wait 54; The Silver Chalice 54

Savini, Tom Night of the Living Dead 90

Savino, Renato L'Oro dei Bravados 70; Lo Chiamavano King • My Name Is King 71

Savoca, Nancy True Love 89

Savona, Leopoldo I Mongoli • Les Mongols • The Mongols 61*; La Dernière Attaque • La Guerra Continua • La Guerre Continue • Warriors Five 62; Fra Diavolo • The Last Charge 62; Chamaco • The Killer Kid 67; Dio Perdoni la Mia Pistola 69*; Un Uomo Chiamata Apocalisse Joe 70

Sawai, Shinichiro Love Story • Wa Kimi Ni 88

Sawajima, Tadashi Band of Assassins • Shinsengumi 70

Sawyer, Arthur H. Sandra 24

Sawyer, David Other Voices 69

Saxon, Charles Duke Dolittle's Jungle Fizzle 17

Saxon, John Death House 88

Sayadian, Stephen Dr. Caligari 90

Sayers, Eric Common Law Wife 63; The Garbage Man • The Garbage Man Cometh 63

Sayles, John Return of the Secaucus Seven 79; Lianna 82; Baby, It's You 83; The Brother from Another Planet 84; Matewan 87; Eight Men Out 88

Sayyad, Parviz Bonbast • Dead End 77; Ferestadeh • The Mission 83; Checkpoint 87

Sbardellati, James Under the Gun 89

Scandariato, Romano Quel Ragazzo della Curva "B" • That Boy from the "B" End 87; The Girl on the Underground • La Ragazza del Metro 89

Scandelari, Jacques Vice Squad 78

Scanlan, Joseph L. Spring Fever 83; Calhoun • Nightstick 87

Scardamaglia, Elio The Blade in the Body • The Knife in the Body • La Lama nel Corpo • The Murder Clinic • The Murder Society • The Night of Terrors • Les Nuits de l'Épouvante • Revenge of the Living Dead 66*

Scardino, Jean Paul Naughty School Girls 77

Scardon, Paul The Alibi 16; The Dawn of Freedom 16*; The Enemy 16; The Hero of Submarine D-2 16; The Island of Surprise 16; The Phantom Fortunes 16; A Prince in a Pawnshop 16; The Redemption of Dave Darcey 16; Rose of the South 16; Apartment 29 17; Arsène Lupin 17; The Grell Mystery 17; The Hawk 17; Her Right to Live 17; In the Balance 17; The Love Doctor 17; The Maelstrom 17; Soldiers of Chance 17; The Stolen Treaty 17; Transgression 17; All Man 18; A Bachelor's Children 18; The Desired Woman 18; A Game with Fate 18; The Golden Goal 18; The Green God 18; Hoarded Assets 18; The King of Diamonds 18; The Other Man 18; Tangled Lives 18; Beating the Odds 19; Beauty Proof 19; Fighting Destiny 19; The Gamblers 19; In Honor's Web 19; The Man Who Won 19; Silent Strength 19; The Broken Gate 20; Children Not Wanted 20; The Darkest Hour 20; Her Unwilling Husband 20; Milestones 20; Partners of the Night 20; The Breaking Point 21; False Kisses 21; The Golden Gallows 22; Shattered Dreams 22; When the Devil Drives 22; A Wonderful Wife 22; Her Own Free Will 24

Scarpelli, Umberto The Secret Conclave 53; The Giant of Metropolis • Il Gigante di Metropolis 62

Scattini, Luigi L'Amore Primitivo • Primitive Love 66; Due Marines e un Generale • War, Italian Style 67; La Esfinge de Cristal • The Glass Sphinx • La Sfinge d'Oro • Una Sfinge Tutta d'Oro 67*

Scavolini, Romano Nightmare • Nightmares in a Damaged Brain 81; Dog Tags 90

Scemana, Chikly see Chikly, Scemana
Schaaf, Allen Dracula's Disciple 84
Schaaf, Johannes City of Dreams • Dream Town • Traumstadt 73; Momo 86
Schaefer, Armand Hurricane Horseman • The Mexican 31; The Lightning Warrior 31*; Battling Buckaroo • His Last Adventure 32; The Cheyenne Cyclone • Smashing Through 32; The Hurricane Express 32*; Law and Lawless 32; Outlaw Justice 32; The Reckless Rider 32; Sinister Hands 32; Wyoming Whirlwind 32; The Fighting Texans • Randy Strikes Oil 33; Fighting with Kit Carson 33*; The Sagebrush Trail 33; Terror Trail 33; The Three Musketeers 33*; Burn 'Em Up Barnes 34*; The Law of the Wild 34*; The Lost Jungle 34*; 16 Fathoms Deep 34; The Miracle Rider 35*
Schaefer, George Macbeth 60; Generation • A Time for Giving 69; Pendulum 69; Doctors' Wives 71; Once Upon a Scoundrel 73; An Enemy of the People 77; Deadly Games 82

Schaefer, Jo Cemil 87
Schaeffer, Francis Wired to Kill 86; Headhunter 90
Schaeffer, Franky see Schaeffer, Francis
Schafer, Jerry Not My Daughter 75; Fists of Steel 89
Schaffner, Franklin J. The Stripper • A Woman in July • Woman of Summer 62; The Best Man 64; The War Lord 65; The Double Man • Legacy of a Spy 67; Planet

of the Apes 68; Il Generale d'Acciaio • Lust for Glory • Patton • Patton: A Salute to a Rebel • Patton il Generale d'Acciaio • Patton: Lust for Glory • Salute to a Rebel 69; Nicholas and Alexandra 71; Papillon 73; Islands in the Stream 76; The Boys from Brazil 78; Sphinx 80; Yes, Giorgio 82; Lionheart 87; Welcome Home 89

Schain, Don Ginger 71; The Abductors 72; A Place Called Today 72; Girls Are for Loving 73; Too Hot to Handle 76

Schamoni, Peter Brutalität in Stein • Brutality in Stone • Die Ewigkeit von Gestern • Yesterday Goes On Forever 60*; Potato Fritz 76; Frühlingssinfonie • Spring Symphony 83; Caspar David Friedrich 87; Die Letzte Geschichte von Schloss Königswald • Schloss Königswald 88

Schapiro, Mikhail see Shapiro, Mikhail
Schary, Dore Act One 63
Schatzberg, Jerry Puzzle of a Downfall Child 70; The Panic in Needle Park 71; Scarecrow 73; Dandy, the All-American Girl • Sweet Revenge 76; The Seduction of Joe Tynan • The Senator 79; Honeysuckle Rose • On the Road Again 80; Misunderstood 82; No Small Affair 84; Street Smart 87; Reunion 89

Scheepsmaker, Hans Field of Honor 86
Scheerer, Robert Adam at 6 A.M. 70; The World's Greatest Athlete 73; How to Beat the High Co$t of Living 80
Scheffer, Leo Demon of the Steppes 30
Schell, Maximilian Erste Liebe • First Love 70; Der Fussgänger • The Pedestrian 74; End of the Game • Getting Away with Murder • Murder on the Bridge • Der Richter und Sein Henker 75; Geschichten aus dem Wienerwald • Tales from the Vienna Woods 78; Marlene 83
Schell, Ruth Maya 82*
Schellerup, Henning The Black Bunch 73; Sweet Jesus, Preacher Man 73; The Black Alleycats 74; Beyond Death's Door 79; In Search of Historic Jesus 79; The Legend of Sleepy Hollow 79; Campfire Girls 84; Berserker 87
Schenck, George Superbeasts 72
Schenck, Harry Beyond Bengal 34
Schenkel, Carl Abwärts • Out of Order 84; The Mighty Quinn 89
Schenkkan, Ine Bygones • Vroeger Is Dood • What's Past Is Dead 87
Schepisi, Fred Libido 73*; The Devil's Playground 76; The Chant of Jimmie Blacksmith 78; Barbarosa 82; Iceman 84; Plenty 85; Roxanne 87; A Cry in the Dark 88; The Russia House 90
Schertzinger, Victor The Clodhopper 17; His Mother's Boy 17; The Millionaire Vagrant 17; The Pinch Hitter 17; The Son of His Father 17; Sudden Jim 17; The Claws of the Hun 18; Coals of Fire 18; The Family Skeleton 18; The Hired Man 18; His Own Home Town 18; A Nine O'Clock Town 18; Playing the Game 18; Quicksands 18; String Beans 18; Extravagance 19; Hard Boiled 19; The Homebreaker 19; The Jinx 19; The Lady of Red Butte 19; Other Men's Wives 19; The Peace of Roaring

River 19*; Pinto 19; The Sheriff's Son 19; Upstairs 19; When Doctors Disagree 19; The Blooming Angel 20; The Slim Princess 20; What Happened to Rosa? 20; Beating the Game 21; The Concert 21; Made in Heaven 21; The Bootlegger's Daughter 22; Head Over Heels 22*; The Kingdom Within 22; Mr. Barnes of New York 22; Scandalous Tongues 22; Chastity 23; Dollar Devils 23; The Lonely Road 23; Long Live the King 23; The Man Life Passed By 23; The Man Next Door 23; Refuge 23; The Scarlet Lily 23; A Boy of Flanders 24; Bread 24; Frivolous Sal 25; The Golden Strain 25; Man and Maid 25; Thunder Mountain 25; The Wheel 25; The Lily 26; The Return of Peter Grimm 26; Siberia 26; The Heart of Salome 27; The Secret Studio 27; Stage Madness 27; Forgotten Faces 28; The Showdown 28; Fashions in Love 29; The Laughing Lady 29; Nothing But the Truth 29; Redskin 29; The Wheel of Life 29; Heads Up 30; Paramount on Parade 30*; Safety in Numbers 30; Friends and Lovers 31; Madame Julie • The Woman Between 31; Strange Justice 32; Uptown New York 32; Auction in Souls • The Constant Woman 33; Beloved 33; Cocktail Hour 33; My Woman 33; One Night of Love 34; Let's Live Tonight 35; Love Me Forever • On Wings of Song 35; The Music Goes 'Round 36; Battling Hoofer • Something to Sing About 37; The Mikado 39; Rhythm on the River 40; Road to Singapore 40; Birth of the Blues 41; Kiss the Boys Goodbye 41; Road to Zanzibar 41; The Fleet's In 42*

Scheuer, Tom Alice Goodbody 74; Gosh 74

Schibli, Paul The Nutcracker Prince 90
Schidor, Dieter Cold in Columbia • Kalt in Kolumbien 85
Schiffman, Suzanne La Moine et la Sorcière • The Monk and the Sorceress • Sorceress 87; La Femme de Paille • Femme de Papier • Front Woman • Paperback Woman 89
Schikele, David Bushman 72
Schildt, Peter Business Is Booming • Svindlande Affärer 85*
Schiller, Greta Before Stonewall 84*
Schiller, Lawrence J. The American Dreamer 71*; The Lexington Experience 71; Marilyn: The Untold Story 80*; The Executioner's Song 82
Schiller, Tom Nothing Lasts Forever 84
Schilling, Niklas Nachtschatten • Nightshade 72; Expulsion from Paradise 76; Dormire 85
Schiraldi, Vittorio Family Killer 75
Schirk, Heinz The Wannsee Conference • Wannseekonferenz 84
Schirmbeck, Samuel Viva Portugal 75*
Schito, Giuseppe The Boy from Ebalus • Il Ragazzo di Ebalus 87
Schivazappa, Piero The Lady of the Night • La Signora della Notte 86
Schlamme, Thomas Miss Firecracker 88
Schlank, Morris R. Code of the Range 27*; Drifting 32

Schlatter, George Norman...Is That You? 76

Schleif, Wolfgang Freddy Unter Fremden Sternen 62; Voyage to Danger 62

Schleipper, Carl Curse of the Stone Hand 65*

Schlesinger, John Black Legend 48*; The Starfish 50*; Sunday in the Park 56*; The Class • Monitor: The Class 57; The Innocent Eye 58; Terminus 60; A Kind of Loving 62; Billy Liar! 63; Darling 65; Far from the Madding Crowd 67; Midnight Cowboy 69; Sunday, Bloody Sunday 70; Olympic Visions • Visions of Eight 72*; The Day of the Locust 75; Marathon Man 76; Yanks 79; Honky Tonk Freeway 81; An Englishman Abroad 83; The Falcon and the Snowman 85; The Believers 87; Madame Sousatzka 88; Pacific Heights 90

Schlöndorff, Volker Wen Kümmert's... • Who Cares... 60; Les Désarrois de l'Élève Törless • Der Junge Törless • Young Törless 66; A Degree of Murder • Mord und Totschlag 67; An Uneasy Moment • Ein Unheimlicher Moment 67; Baal 69; Michael Kohlhaas • Michael Kohlhaas—Der Rebell • Michael Kohlhaas—The Rebel 69; Der Plötzliche Reichtum der Armen Leute von Kombach • The Sudden Fortune of the Poor People of Kombach • The Sudden Wealth of the Poor People of Kombach 70; Die Ehegattin • A Free Woman • Strawfire • Strohfeuer • Summer Lightning 71; Die Moral der Ruth Halbfass • The Moral of Ruth Halbfass • The Morals of Ruth Halbfass • Ruth Halbfass 71; The Lost Honor of Katharina Blum • Die Verlorene Ehre der Katharina Blum 75*; Coup de Grâce • Der Fangschuss 76; For Fun, for Play • Just for Fun, Just for Play • Kaleidoskop • Kaleidoskop: Valeska Gert, Nur zum Spass—Nur zum Spiel • Nur zum Spass—Nur zum Spiel: Kaleidoskop Valeska Gert • Only for Fun—Only for Play: Kaleidoscope Valeska Gert 77; The Second Awakening of Christa Klages • Das Zweite Erwachen der Christa Klages 77*; Deutschland im Herbst • Germany in Autumn 78*; Die Blechtrommel • The Tin Drum 79; The Candidate • Der Kandidat 80*; Circle of Deceit • Die Fälschung • False Witness • The Forgery 81; Krieg und Frieden • War and Peace 82*; Un Amour de Swann • Swann in Love 83; Odds and Ends • Vermischte Nachrichten 86*; The Handmaid's Tale 90

Schlossberg, Julian The MUSE Concert: No Nukes • No Nukes 80*; Going Hollywood—The 30's 84; Going Hollywood—The War Years 88

Schmid, Daniel La Paloma 74; Jenatsch 87

Schmid-Wildy, Ludwig Stosstrupp 1917 35*

Schmidt, Eckhart Alphacity—Abgerechnet Wird Nachts 85; Die Küken Kommen 85; Löft 85; Das Wunder 85

Schmidt, I. He Who Gets Slapped 16*

Schmidt, Jan Joseph Kilián • Postava k Podpírání 63*; Life After Ninety Minutes 65*; The End of August at the Hotel Ozone • Konec Srpna v Hotelu Ozon 66; Trilogie z Pravěku 77

Schmidt, Jean Les Clowns de Dieu • The Clowns of God 86

Schmidt, Palle Kjærulff see Kjærulff-Schmidt, Palle

Schmidt, Richard R. A Man, a Woman and a Killer 75*; 1988: The Remake 78; Morgan's Cake 88

Schmidt, Thomas J. Hot Summer Week 73

Schmidt, Wolf The Ideal Lodger • Der Ideale Untermieter 56

Schmidt-Gentner, Willy Die Pompadour 35*; Präter, Wiener • Wiener Präter 38

Schmidthof, V. Beethoven Concerto 37*

Schmitz, Oliver Mapantsula 88

Schmoeller, David Tourist Trap 78; The Seduction 81; Crawlspace 86; Catacombs 88

Schnedler-Sørensen, Edward The Fire of Life • Livets Bål 11; A Dangerous Play • Et Farligt Spil 12

Schneevoigt, George The Pastor of Vejlby 31; En Saga 38

Schneider, Eugene Gypsies 36*; In the Rear of the Enemy 42

Schneider, Ira Lost in Cuddihy 66

Schneider, Paul I Was a Teenage Boy • Something Special • Willy/Milly 85

Schneider-Edenkoben, Richard Die Törichte Jungfrau 35; Inkognito 37

Schneiderhof, Vladimir Al-Yemen 31; Golden Taiga 35

Schnitzer, Robert Allen No Place to Hide 75; The Premonition 75; Kandyland 87

Schnyder, Franz Heidi and Peter • Heidi und Peter 54

Schoedsack, Ernest B. Golden Prince • The Lost Empire 24; Grass • Grass—A Nation's Battle for Life • Grass—The Epic of a Lost Tribe 25*; Chang 27*; Gow the Headhunter 28*; The Four Feathers 29*; Rango 31; The Hounds of Zaroff • The Most Dangerous Game 32*; Blind Adventure 33; King Kong 33*; The Monkey's Paw 33*; Son of Kong 33; Long Lost Father 34; The Last Days of Pompeii 35; Outlaws of the Orient 37; Trouble in Morocco 37; Dr. Cyclops 40; Mighty Joe Young 49; This Is Cinerama 52*

Schoenberg, Mark Parallels 80

Schoendoerffer, Pierre see Schöndörffer, Pierre

Schoenfelder, Erich see Schönfelder, Erich

Scholes, Roger The Tale of Ruby Rose 87

Scholl, Jack Holiday Rhythm 50

Scholz, Günther Ab Heute Erwachsen • Grown Up Today 86; Interrogation of the Witness • Vernehmung der Zeugen 87

Schomer, Abraham S. The Sacred Flame 19; The Chamber of Mystery 20; Hidden Light 20

Schöndörffer, Pierre La Passe du Diable 57*; Thau le Pêcheur 57; Ramuntcho 58; Pêcheur d'Islande 59; Attention! Hélicoptères 62; The 317th Platoon • La 317ème Section 65; The Anderson Platoon • Section Anderson 66; Objectif 500 Million • Objectif 500 Millions • Objective 500 Million 66; Le Crabe Tambour 77

Schonfeld, Victor The Animals Film 81

Schönfelder, Erich Der Stier von Olivera 21*; It's Easy to Become a Father 29; Ein Ausgekochter Junge 32; Schön Ist die Manöverzeit 32; In Wien Hab' Ich Einmal ein Mädel Geliebt 34; Zu Befehl Herr Unteroffizier 34

Schoolnik, Skip Hide and Go Shriek 87

Schorm, Evald Block 15 • Blok 15 59; Kdo Své Nebe Neunese • Too Much to Carry 59; Jan Konstantin 61; The Tourist • Turista 61; The Country of Countries • Country to Country • The Land • Země Zemi 62; Helsinki 62 • Helsinky 62 62; Stromy a Lidé • Trees and People 62; His Life to Live • Living One's Life • To Live One's Life • Žít Svůj Život 63; Railwaymen • Železničáři 63; Courage for Every Day • Everyday Courage • Každý Den Odvahu • Odvahu pro Všední Den 64; Pearls at the Bottom • Pearls of the Deep • Perličky na Dně 64*; Proč? • Why? 64; Heritage • The Legacy • Odkaz 65; Reflections • Zrcadlení 65; Five Girls Equals a Millstone Round One's Neck • Five Girls Like a Millstone Round One's Neck • Five Girls to Cope With • Pět Holek na Krku • Saddled with Five Girls 66; Návrat Ztraceného Syna • Return of the Lost Son • The Return of the Prodigal Son 66; The Psalm • Žalm 66; Carmen Nejen Podle Bizeta • Carmen Not According to Bizet • Carmen Not Only by Bizet 67; The End of a Priest • Farářův Konec • Konec Faráře • Pastor's End • The Priest's End 68; The Nights of Prague • Prague Nights • Pražské Noci 68*; Pomsta • Revenge 68*; Den Sedmý, Osmá Noc • Sedmý Den, Osmá Noc • Seventh Day, Eighth Night • The Seventh Day, the Eighth Night 69; Dogs and People • Psi a Lidé 70; Láska v Barvách Karnevalu • Love in Mardi Gras Colors 74*; An Essay on Rehearsing • Etuda o Zkoušce 76; Kouzelný Cirkus • The Magic Circus 77*; Sněhová Královna • The Snow Queen 78; The Night Rehearsal • Noční Zkouška 80; Killing with Kindness • Vlastně Se Nic Nestalo 88

Schorr, Renen Blues Lahofesh Hagodol • Late Summer Blues 87

Schorr, William Forgotten Commandments 32*

Schott, Dale Care Bears Movie II: A New Generation 86

Schotten, Wayne A. Friday on My Mind 70

Schrader, Paul Blue Collar 78; Hardcore • The Hardcore Life 79; American Gigolo 80; Cat People 82; Mishima • Mishima: A Life in Four Chapters 85; Light of Day 87; Patty Hearst 88; The Comfort of Strangers 90

Schrader, Uwe Sierra Leone 87

Schreiber, Bruno Paul Myrte and the Demons 48

Hollywood Cowboy • Wings Over Wyoming 37; Hollywood Roundup 37; Windjammer 37; Man Hunters of the Caribbean 38*; Untamed Fury 47; Harpoon 48; Arctic Manhunt 49; Red Snow 52*

Scott, George C. Rage 72; The Savage Is Loose 74

Scott, James A Shocking Accident 83; Every Picture Tells a Story 84; Loser Take All • Strike It Rich 88

Scott, Kevin A Story of Tutankhamun 75

Scott, Lewis Three Way Love 77

Scott, Oz Bustin' Loose 81; Dreamland 83*

Scott, Peter Graham Panic at Madame Tussaud's 48; Escape Route • I'll Get You 52*; Sing Along with Me 52; The Hideout 56; Account Rendered 57; The Big Chance 57; Breakout 58; The Headless Ghost 58; Devil's Bait 59; The Big Day 60; Let's Get Married 60; Captain Clegg • Dr. Syn • Night Creatures 61; Bitter Harvest 62; The Pot Carriers 62; The Cracksman 63; Father Came Too • We Want to Live Alone 63; Mister Ten Percent 67; Subterfuge 68; The Magnificent Six and a Half 71

Scott, Rey Kukan—The Battle Cry of China 41

Scott, Ridley The Duellists 77; Alien 79; Blade Runner 82; Legend 85; Someone to Watch Over Me 87; Black Rain 89

Scott, Robert The Video Dead 87

Scott, Sherman see Newfield, Sam

Scott, Tony The Hunger 83; Top Gun 86; Beverly Hills Cop II 87; Days of Thunder 90; Revenge 90

Scott, Will Kids Together 19

Scottenberg, Michael Caracas 89

Scotti, Raimondo L'Atleta Fantasma 19

Scotto, Aubrey H. Uncle Moses 32*; I Hate Women 34; Hitch-Hike Lady 35; $1,000 a Minute 35; Smart Girl 35; Follow Your Heart 36; Happy Go Lucky 36; Palm Springs • Palm Springs Affair 36; Ticket to Paradise 36; Blazing Barriers 37; Little Miss Roughneck 38; Gambling Ship 39; I Was a Convict 39

Scovelle, Phil In the Stretch 14

Scribner, George Oliver and Company 88

Scully, Denis Journey Into Nowhere • Murder by Agreement 63

Scully, William J. Annabel Lee 21

Seabourne, Peter Countdown to Danger 67; Escape from the Sea 68

Seacat, Sandra In the Spirit 90

Sealey, John The Ups and Downs of a Handyman 75

Searl, Leon Mile-a-Minute Monty 15; Monty the Missionary 15

Searle, Francis Ace Cinemagazine 36; A Cornish Idyll 36; War Without End 36; English Oil Wells 39; Sam Pepys Joins the Navy 41; They Keep the Wheels Turning 42; First Day on the Spot 43; Student Nurse 44; A Girl in a Million 46; Things Happen at Night 48; Celia 49; The Man in Black 49; A Case for P.C. 49 50; The Lady Craved Excitement 50; The Rossiter Case

50; Someone at the Door 50; Cloudburst 51; Whispering Smith Hits London • Whispering Smith vs. Scotland Yard 51; The Caretaker's Daughter • Love's a Luxury 52; Never Look Back 52; Murder at 3 A.M. 53; Road House Girl • Wheel of Fate 53; Profile 54; One Way Out 55; The Dynamiters • The Gelignite Gang 56*; Day of Grace 57; Undercover Girl 58; Murder at Site Three 59; Music with Max Jaffa 59; In Trouble with Eve • In Walked Eve • Trouble with Eve 60; Ticket to Paradise 60; Freedom to Die 61; Dead Man's Evidence 62; Emergency 62; Gaolbreak 62; Night of the Prowler 62; The Marked One 63; Miss Mactaggart Won't Lie Down 66; Talk of the Devil 67; Gold Is Where You Find It 68; It All Goes to Show 69; A Hole Lot of Trouble 70

Sears, Fred F. Desert Vigilante 49; Horsemen of the Sierras • Remember Me 49; Across the Badlands • The Challenge 50; Circle of Fear • Raiders of Tomahawk Creek 50; Lightning Guns • Taking Sides 50; Prairie Roundup 50; Bonanza Town • Two-Fisted Agent 51; Pecos River • Without Risk 51; Ridin' the Outlaw Trail 51; Smoky Canyon 51; Snake River Desperadoes 51; Blackhawk 52*; The Hawk of Wild River 52; The Kid from Broken Gun 52; Last Train from Bombay 52; Target—Hong Kong 52; Ambush at Tomahawk Gap 53; Desert Patrol • El Alamein 53; Eyes of the Skies • Mission over Korea 53; The 49th Man 53; The Nebraskan 53; Sky Commando 53; Massacre Canyon 54; The Miami Story 54; The Outlaw Stallion • The White Stallion 54; Overland Pacific 54; Apache Ambush 55; Cell 2455—Death Row 55; Chicago Syndicate 55; Inside Detroit 55; Teen-Age Crime Wave 55; Wyoming Renegades 55; Cha-Cha-Cha Boom! 56; Don't Knock the Rock 56; Earth vs. the Flying Saucers • Invasion of the Flying Saucers 56; Fury at Gunsight Pass 56; Miami Exposé 56; Rock Around the Clock 56; Rumble on the Docks 56; The Werewolf 56; Calypso Heat Wave 57; Crash Landing 57; Escape from San Quentin 57; The Giant Claw 57; The Night the World Exploded 57; Utah Blaine 57; Badman's Country 58; Ghost of the China Sea 58; Going Steady 58; The World Was His Jury 58

Seastrom, Victor see Sjöström, Victor

Seaton, George Billy Rose's Diamond Horseshoe • Diamond Horseshoe 45; Junior Miss 45; The Shocking Miss Pilgrim 46; The Big Heart • Miracle on 34th Street 47; Apartment for Peggy 48; Chicken Every Sunday 49; The Big Lift 50; For Heaven's Sake 50; Anything Can Happen 52; Little Boy Lost 53; The Country Girl 54; The Proud and the Profane 56; Williamsburg: The Story of a Patriot 57; Teacher's Pet 58; The Pleasure of His Company 61; The Counterfeit Traitor 62; The Hook 63; 36 Hours 64; What's So Bad About Feeling Good? 68; Airport 69*; Showdown 72

Seay, Charles M. Fantasma 14; A Daughter of the Sea 15; A Circus Romance 16; Jan of the Big Snows 22

Seban, Paul Music • La Musica 66*

Sebastian, Beverly The Hitchhikers 72*; The Single Girls 73*; Flash and the Firecat 75*; Gator Bait 76*; Delta Fox 77*; Captain Midnight • On the Air Live with Captain Midnight 79*; Gator Bait II: Cajun Justice 88*

Sebastian, Ferd The Hitchhikers 72*; The Single Girls 73*; Flash and the Firecat 75*; Gator Bait 76*; Delta Fox 77*; Captain Midnight • On the Air Live with Captain Midnight 79*; Gator Bait II: Cajun Justice 88*

Sebastian, John see Harrington, Curtis

Sebelious, Gregg The Day the Earth Froze 59*

Secchi, Toni E alla Fine lo Chiamarono Jerusalemme l'Implacabile 72; Padella Calibro 38 • Panhandle Calibre 38 72

Séchan, Edmond Niok • Niok le Petit Éléphant 57; L'Histoire d'un Poisson Rouge • Le Poisson Rouge 58; The Bear • L'Ours • The Talking Bear 60; Le Haricot 62; Pour un Amour Lointain 67

Secter, David The Offering 66; Winter Kept Us Warm 68; Getting Together 76; Feelin' Up 83

Seder, Rufus Butler Screamplay 86

Sedgwick, Edward Bar Nothin' 21; Fantomas 21; Live Wires 21; The Rough Diamond 21; The Bearcat 22; Boomerang Justice 22; Chasing the Moon 22; Do and Dare 22; The Flaming Hour 22; Blinky 23; Dead Game 23; The First Degree 23; The Gentleman from America 23; Out of Luck 23; The Ramblin' Kid 23; Romance Land 23; Shootin' for Love 23; Single Handed 23; The Thrill Chaser 23; Broadway or Bust 24; Forty-Horse Hawkins 24; Hit and Run 24; Hook and Ladder 24; The Hurricane Kid 24; Ride for Your Life 24; The Ridin' Kid from Powder River 24; The Sawdust Trail 24; Let 'Er Buck 25; Lorraine of the Lions 25; The Phantom of the Opera 25*; The Saddle Hawk 25; Two-Fisted Jones 25; The Flaming Frontier 26; The Runaway Express 26; Tin Hats 26; Under Western Skies 26; The Bugle Call 27; Eternal Youth • West Point 27; Slide, Kelly, Slide 27; Spring Fever 27; The Cameraman 28; Circus Rookies 28; Spite Marriage 29; Doughboys • Forward March 30; Easy Go • Free and Easy 30; Remote Control 30*; A Dangerous Affair 31; Maker of Men 31; Parlor, Bedroom and Bath • Romeo in Pyjamas 31; The Passionate Plumber 32; Speak Easily 32; Horse Play 33; Saturday's Millions 33; What! No Beer? 33; Death on the Diamond 34; Here Comes the Groom 34; I'll Tell the World 34; The Poor Rich 34; Father Brown—Detective 35; Murder in the Fleet 35; The Virginia Judge 35; Mister Cinderella 36; Fit for a King 37; Movie Struck • Pick a Star 37; Riding on Air 37; The Gladiator 38; Beware—Spooks! 39; Burn 'Em Up O'Connor 39; So You Won't Talk? 40; Air

Raid Wardens 43; My Hero • A Southern Yankee 48; Ma and Pa Kettle Back on the Farm 51

Sedley, Gerri Teenage Hitchhikers 75

Seel, Luis Screen Follies No. 1 20*; Screen Follies No. 2 20*; Finding the Lost World 26; The Flying Carpet 26; Motoring 26; Pirates Bold 26; Rushing the Gold Rush 26; Safety Not Last 26

Seeley, S. K. *see* Sekely, Steve

Seeling, Charles R. The Jack Rider 21; The Vengeance Trail 21; Western Firebrands 21; Across the Border 22; The Cowboy King 22; Rounding Up the Law 22; The Apache Dancer 23; Cyclone Jones 23; End of the Rope 23; Mysterious Goods 23; $1,000 Reward 23; Purple Dawn 23; Tango Cavalier 23; The Avenger 24; Deeds of Daring 24; The Eagle's Claw 24; Stop at Nothing 24; Yankee Madness 24

See-loke, Chou *see* Chou, See-loke

Sefrioui, Najib Chams 86

Segal, Alex Ransom 55; All the Way Home 63; Harlow 65; Joy in the Morning 65

Segall, Stuart Drive-In Massacre 76; C.B. Hustlers 78

Segawa, Shoji Gyakuten Ryokō • Topsy-Turvy Journey 70; Yosakoi Journey • Yosakoi Ryokō 70

Segel, Yakov Damy • Ladies 54*; Eto Nachinados Tak • It Started Like This • This Is How It Began 54*; Hullabaloo 55*; Dom v Kotorom Ya Zhivu • The House I Live In • The House Where I Live 57*; Farewell Doves • Proshchayte 60; The Day the War Ended • The First Day of Peace • Pervyi Den Mira 61

Seidelman, Arthur Allan Hercules • Hercules Goes Bananas • Hercules in New York • Hercules—The Movie 70; Children of Rage 75; Echoes 83; The Caller 87

Seidelman, Susan Smithereens 82; Desperately Seeking Susan 85; Making Mr. Right 87; Cookie 88; She-Devil 89

Seiden, Joseph Kol Nidre 39; The Living Orphan 39; My Son 39; Paradise in Harlem 39; Eli, Eli 40; The Greater Advisor 40; Her Second Mother 40; The Jewish Melody 40; Motel, the Operator 40; Mazel Tov, Jews 41; God, Man and Devil 49; Three Daughters 49

Seif, Salah Abou *see* Abu Saif, Salah

Seigman, George *see* Siegmann, George

Seiler, Lewis Circus Pals 23*; Jungle Pals 23*; The Monkey Farm 23*; A Monkey Mix-Up 23*; Monks à la Mode 23*; School Pals 23*; The Cowboys 24*; Darwin Was Right 24; Etiquette 24*; He's My Pal 24; Up on the Farm 24; Westward Whoa 24; The Butterfly Man 25; A Cloudy Romance 25; A High Jinx 25; On the Go 25; The Sleepwalker 25; Strong for Love 25; The Great K & A Train Robbery 26; No Man's Gold 26; Rah! Rah! Heidelberg! 26; The Reporter 26; The Last Trail 27; Outlaws of Red River 27; Tumbling River 27; Wolf Fangs • The Wolf's Fangs 27; The Air Circus 28*; Square Crooks 28; The Ghost Talks 29; Girls Gone Wild 29; Song of

Kentucky 29; The Circus Show-Up 32; Deception 32; Divine Love • No Greater Love 32; Frontier Marshal 33; Asegure a Su Mujer • Insure Your Wife 34; Charlie Chan in Paris 35; Ginger 35; Paddy O'Day 35; Career Woman 36; The First Baby 36; Here Comes Trouble 36; Star for a Night 36; He Couldn't Say No 37; Turn Off the Moon 37; Crime School 38; Heart of the North 38; King of the Underworld 38; Penrod's Double Trouble 38; Dust Be My Destiny 39; Hell's Kitchen 39*; The Kid from Kokomo • Orphan of the Ring 39; You Can't Get Away with Murder 39; Flight Angels 40; It All Came True 40; Murder in the Air 40; South of Suez 40; Tugboat Annie Sails Again 40; Kisses for Breakfast 41; The Smiling Ghost 41; You're in the Army Now 41; Beyond the Time of Duty 42; The Big Shot 42; Pittsburgh 42; Guadalcanal Diary 43; Something for the Boys 44; Come Back to Me • Doll Face 45; Molly and Me 45; If I'm Lucky 46; Whiplash 48; Breakthrough 50; The Tanks Are Coming 51*; Operation Secret 52; The Winning Team 52; The System 53; The Bamboo Prison 54; Women's Prison 55; Battle Stations 56; Over-Exposed 56; The Story of Lynn Stuart • The True Story of Lynn Stuart 58

Seilmann, Heinz Masters of the Congo Jungle • Les Seigneurs de la Forêt 58*; Vanishing Wilderness 73*

Seip, Mattijn The Fall of Patricia Haggersmith • De Val van Patricia Haggersmith 86

Seiro, Erkki Fuck Off!—Images of Finland • Perkele! • Perkele!—Kuvia Suomesta 71*

Seiter, William A. Ain't It So? 18; All Fur Her 18; The Fatal Flower 18; The Fly Ball 18; Tangled Threads 19; The Kentucky Colonel 20; The Little Dears 20; The Sure Cure 20; Boy Crazy 21; Eden and Return 21; The Foolish Age 21; Hearts and Masks 21; Passing Through • Passing Thru 21; The Beautiful and the Damned 22; Gay and Devilish 22; The Understudy 22; Up and At 'Em 22; When Love Comes 22; Bell Boy 13 23; The Little Church Around the Corner 23; Daddies 24; The Family Secret 24; The Fast Worker 24; Helen's Babies 24; His Forgotten Wife 24; Listen, Lester 24; The White Sin 24; Dangerous Innocence 25; The Mad Whirl 25; The Teaser 25; Where Was I? 25; Rolling Home 26; Skinner's Dress Suit 26; Take It from Me 26; What Happened to Jones 26; The Cheerful Fraud 27; Out All Night 27; The Small Bachelor 27; Thanks for the Buggy Ride 27; Good Morning Judge 28; Happiness Ahead 28; Outcast 28; Waterfront 28; Footlights and Fools 29; The Love Racket 29; Prisoners 29; Smiling Irish Eyes 29; Synthetic Wife 29; Why Be Good? 29; Back Pay 30; The Flirting Widow 30; Going Wild 30; Kiss Me Again • The Toast of the Legion 30; Strictly Modern 30; Sunny 30; The Truth About Youth 30; Big Business Girl 31; Caught

Plastered 31; Full of Notions 31; Old Greatheart • Other People's Business • Way Back Home 31; Peach O'Reno 31; Too Many Crooks 31; Girl Crazy 32; Hello Everybody! 32; Hot Saturday 32; If I Had a Million 32*; Is My Face Red? 32; Love Starved • Young Bride 32; Chance at Heaven 33; Convention City • Fraternally Yours • Sons of the Desert • Sons of the Legion 33; Diplomaniacs 33; Imaginary Sweetheart • Professional Sweetheart 33; Rafter Romance 33; Love Birds 34; The Richest Girl in the World 34; Sing and Like It 34; We're Rich Again 34; The Daring Young Man 35; If You Could Only Cook 35; In Person 35; Orchids to You 35; Roberta 35; The Case Against Mrs. Ames 36; Dimples 36; The Moon's Our Home 36; Stowaway 36; His Affair • This Is My Affair 37; The Joy Parade • Life Begins at College • Life Begins in College 37; The Life of the Party 37; Room Service 38; Sally, Irene and Mary 38; Thanks for Everything 38; Three Blind Mice 38; Allegheny Frontier • Allegheny Uprising • The First Rebel 39; Hired Wife 40; It's a Date 40; Appointment for Love 41; Nice Girl? 41; Broadway 42; You Were Never Lovelier 42; The Cowboy and the Girl • A Lady Takes a Chance 43*; Destroyer 43*; Belle of the Yukon 44; Four Jills in a Jeep 44; The Affairs of Susan 45; It's a Pleasure! 45; That Night with You 45; Little Giant • On the Carpet 46; Lover Come Back • When Lovers Meet 46; I'll Be Yours 47; One Touch of Venus 48*; Up in Central Park 48; Borderline 50; Dear Brat 51; The Lady Wants Mink 52; Champ for a Day 53; Make Haste to Live 54

Seitz, Franz Bei der Blonden Katherin 34; Die Blonde Christl 34; Der Meisterdetektiv 34; Mit Dir Durch Dick und Dünn 34; Die Mutter der Kompagnie 34; SA Mann Brand 34; Die Frauen vom Tannhof 36; Die Grosse Adele 37; 1A in Oberbayern • 1A in Upper Bavaria 39; The Fight with the Dragon • Der Kampf mit dem Drachen 39; Disorder and Early Torment • Unordnung und Frühes Leid 77

Seitz, George B. The Exploits of Elaine 14*; The Romance of Elaine 15*; The Iron Claw 16*; The King's Game 16*; Pearl of the Army 16*; The Fatal Ring 17; Getaway Kate 18; The Honest Thief 18; The House of Hate 18; The Lightning Raider 18; The Black Secret 19; Bound and Gagged 19; Pirate Gold 20; Rogues and Romance 20; Velvet Fingers 20; Hurricane Hutch 21; The Sky Ranger 21; Go Get 'Em Hutch 22; Speed 22; Plunder 23*; The 40th Door 24; Galloping Hoofs 24; Into the Net 24; Leatherstocking 24; Way of a Man 24; Sunken Silver 25; The Vanishing American • The Vanishing Race 25; Wild Horse Mesa 25; Desert Gold 26; The Ice Flood 26; The Last Frontier 26; Pals in Paradise 26; The Blood Ship 27; Forgotten Women • Isle of Forgotten Women 27; The Great Mail Robbery 27; Jim the Conqueror 27;

The Tigress 27; The Warning 27; After the Storm 28; Beware of Blondes 28; Blockade 28; The Circus Kid 28; Court-Martial 28; Hey Rube! • High Stakes 28; Ransom 28; Black Magic 29; Murder on the Roof 29; Danger Lights 30; Guilty? 30; Midnight Mystery 30; Arizona • Men Are Like That • The Virtuous Wife 31; Drums of Jeopardy • Mark of Terror 31; The Lion and the Lamb 31; Night Beat 31; Shanghaied Love 31; Docks of San Francisco 32; Passport to Paradise 32; Sally of the Subway 32; Sin's Pay Day 32; The Widow in Scarlet 32; The Thrill Hunter 33; Treason 33; The Women in His Life 33; After Eight Hours • Only Eight Hours • Society Doctor 34; The Fighting Ranger 34; Lazy River 34; Alibi Racket 35; Buried Loot 35; Calm Yourself! 35; Desert Death 35; Exclusive Story 35; House of Menace • Kind Lady 35; Shadow of a Doubt • Shadow of Doubt 35; Times Square Lady 35; Woman Wanted 35; Absolute Quiet 36; The Last of the Mohicans 36; Mad Holiday 36; The Thirteenth Chair 36; The Three Wise Guys 36; Under Cover of Night 36; Between Two Women • Surrounded by Women 37; A Family Affair 37; Mama Steps Out 37; My Dear Miss Aldrich 37; Judge Hardy's Children 38; Love Finds Andy Hardy 38; Out West with the Hardys 38; Yellow Jack 38; You're Only Young Once 38; The Hardys Ride High 39; Judge Hardy and Son 39; Six Thousand Enemies 39; Thunder Afloat 39; Andy Hardy Meets Debutante 40; Andy Hardy's Private Secretary 40; Gallant Sons 40; Kit Carson 40; Sky Murder 40; China Caravan • A Yank on the Burma Road 41; The Courtship of Andy Hardy 41; Life Begins for Andy Hardy 41; Andy Hardy's Double Life 42; Pierre of the Plains 42; Andy Hardy's Blonde Trouble 44

Seitzer, Leo Jacqueline Kennedy's Asian Journey 62

Sekely, Steve Rhapsodie der Liebe 29; The Great Yearning • Die Grosse Sehnsucht 30; Seitensprünge 30; Er und Sein Diener 31; Hippolyt the Lackey • Hyppolit a Lakáj 32; Piri Mindent Tud 32; Ein Steinreicher Mann 32; Pardon Tévedtem • Romance in Budapest • Skandal in Budapest 33*; Rákóczi Induló • Rákóczi Marsch 33*; Ball im Savoy 34; Emmy 34; Ida Regénye 34; Lila Akác 34; My Wife the Miss 34; Búzavirág 35; Huszárszerelem 35; An Affair of Honor 36; Café Moszkva 36; Csak Egy Éjszakára 36; Légy Jó Mindhalálig 36; Szenzáció 36*; Beauty of the Pusta • Pusztai Szél 37; Duna-Parti Randevú 37; Help! I'm an Heiress • Segítség Örököltem 37; I Married for Love • Szerelemből Nősültem 37; Két Fogoly • Two Prisoners 37; Nászút Féláron 37; 111-es Szobában • In Room 111 38; Heart to Heart • Szívet Szívért 38; Noszty Fiú Esete Tóth Marival 38; A Miracle on Main Street 39; Behind Prison Walls • Youth Takes a Hand 43; The Corpse Vanished • Revenge of the Zombies 43; Hitler's Women • Women in Bondage

43; The Executioner • Her Last Mile • Lady in the Death House 44; Lake Placid Serenade 44; My Buddy 44; Waterfront 44; The Fabulous Suzanne 46; Blonde Savage 47; Hollow Triumph • The Scar 48; Amazon Quest 49; Furia Roja 51; Stronghold 51; Le Avventure di Cartouche • Cartouche 54*; Desert Desperadoes • The Sinner 59; The Day of the Triffids 62*; Kenner • Year of the Cricket 68; The Girl Who Liked Purple Flowers 73

Sekers, Alan The Arp Statue 72

Sekigawa, Hideo Asu o Tsukuru Hitobito • Those Who Make Tomorrow 46*; Chikagai Nijūyojikan • Twenty-Four Hours of a Secret Life • Twenty-Four Hours of the Underground Street 47*; A Second Life 48; Listen to the Roar of the Ocean 50; Hiroshima 53; Orgy 54; Sound of Youth 57; Horrible Midnight 58; Mother and Gun 58; A Dead Drifter 59; The Silent Murder 59; Devil's Banknotes 60; My Life Is Like Fire 61; The Mysterious Detective Morgan 61; The Dupe 65; The Procurer 65; Devil in My Flesh 68; The Tattooed Temptress 68; Sky Scraper • The Skyscraper Story 69

Selander, Lesley Jerry the Giant 26*; Napoleon Junior 26*; The Boss of Gun Creek • The Boss Rider of Gun Creek 36; Cowboy Roundup • Ride 'Em Cowboy 36; Empty Saddles 36; Sandflow 36; The Barrier 37; Black Aces 37*; Hopalong Rides Again 37; Left-Handed Law 37; Partners of the Plains 37; Smoke Tree Range 37; Bar 20 Justice 38; Cassidy of Bar 20 38; The Frontiersman 38; Heart of Arizona 38; Mark of the Avenger • The Mysterious Rider 38; Pride of the West 38; Sunset Trail 38; Heritage of the Desert 39; Range War 39; Renegade Trail 39; Silver on the Sage 39; Cherokee Strip • Fighting Marshal 40; Hidden Gold 40; Knights of the Range 40; The Light of Western Stars 40; Santa Fe Marshal 40; Stagecoach War 40; Three Men from Texas 40; Doomed Caravan 41; Pirates on Horseback 41; Riders of the Timberline 41; The Roundup 41; Stick to Your Guns 41; Thundering Hoofs 41; Wide Open Town 41; Bandit Ranger 42; Lost Canyon 42; Red River Robin Hood 42; Undercover Man 42; Bar 20 43; Border Patrol 43; Buckskin Frontier • The Iron Road 43; Colt Comrades 43; Riders of the Deadline 43; Bordertown Trail 44; Call of the Rockies 44; Cheyenne Wildcat 44; Firebrands of Arizona 44; Forty Thieves 44; Lumberjack 44; Sheriff of Las Vegas 44; Sheriff of Sundown 44; Stagecoach to Monterey 44; The Fatal Witness 45; The Great Stagecoach Robbery 45; Jungle Raiders 45; Phantom of the Plains 45; Three's a Crowd 45; Trail of Kit Carson 45; The Vampire's Ghost 45; The Catman of Paris 46; Night Train to Memphis 46; Out California Way 46; Passkey to Danger 46; Traffic in Crime 46; Belle Starr's Daughter 47; Blackmail 47; The Last Frontier • The Last Frontier Uprising 47; Panhandle 47; The Pilgrim Lady 47; The Red

Stallion 47; Robin Hood of Texas 47; Saddle Pals 47; Guns of Hate • Guns of Wrath 48; Indian Agent 48; Strike It Rich 48; Brothers in the Saddle 48; Masked Raiders 49; Murder in the Air • The Sky Dragon 49; The Mysterious Desperado 49; Riders of the Range 49; Rustlers 49; Stampede 49; Dakota Lil 50; The Kangaroo Kid 50; Law of the Badlands 50; Rider from Tucson 50; Rio Grande Patrol 50; Short Grass 50; Storm Over Wyoming 50; Cavalry Scout 51; Flight to Mars 51; Gunplay 51; The Highwayman 51; I Was an American Spy 51; Overland Telegraph 51; Pistol Harvest 51; Saddle Legion 51; Battle Zone 52; Desert Passage 52; Eagles of the Fleet • Flat Top 52; Fort Osage 52; The Raiders • Riders of Vengeance 52; Road Agent 52; Trail Guide 52; Arrow in the Dust 53; Cow Country 53*; Fighter Attack 53; Fort Algiers 53; Fort Vengeance 53; The Royal African Rifles • Storm Over Africa 53; War Paint 53; Dragonfly Squadron 54; Return from the Sea 54; The Yellow Tomahawk 54; Desert Sands 55; Fort Yuma 55; Shotgun 55; Tall Man Riding 55; The Broken Star 56; Frontier Scout • Quincannon, Frontier Scout 56; Mark of the Apache • Tomahawk Trail 56; Outlaw's Son 57; Revolt at Fort Laramie 57; Taming Sutton's Gal 57; The Wayward Girl 57; The Lone Ranger and the Lost City of Gold 58; War Party 64; Convict Stage 65; Fort Courageous 65; Town Tamer 65; El Tejano • The Texas Kid • The Texican 66; Arizona Bushwhackers 67; Fort Utah 67

Seldon-Truss, Leslie Fetters of Fear 15; Lochinvar 15; Sir James Mortimer's Wager 16

Selfe, Ray White Cargo 74; Can I Come Too? 79

Selignac, Arnaud Dream One • Nemo 84

Se-ling, Tsou see Chu, Shih-ling

Sell, Jack M. The Psychotronic Man 80; Outtakes 85; Spy Games 87

Sellar, Ian Venus Peter 89

Sellers, Oliver L. When Bearcat Went Dry 19; The Gift Supreme 20; Seeds of Vengeance 20; Diane of Star Hollow 21; The New Disciple 21; The Hoosier Schoolmaster 24

Sellers, Peter I Like Money • Mr. Topaze 61

Sellier, Charles E. In Search of a Golden Sky 83; Silent Night, Deadly Night 84; Smooth Moves • Snow Balling 84; The Annihilators 85

Sellner, Gustav R. Der Junge Lord • The Young Lord 70

Selman, David Remember 26; Paying the Price 27; The Fighting Westerner • The Westerner 34; The Prescott Kid 34; Fighting Shadows 35; Gallant Defender 35; Justice of the Range 35; The Revenge Rider 35; Riding Wild 35; Square Shooter 35; The Cowboy Star 36; Dangerous Intrigue 36; Killer at Large 36; The Mysterious Avenger 36; Secret Patrol 36; Shakedown 36; Tugboat Princess 36; Find the Witness 37; Texas Trail 37; The Accusing Past • El Pasado Acusa 38; Woman Against the World 38

Selpin, Herbert The Love Contract 32; Die Reiter von Deutsch-Ostafrika 35; Der Traum vom Rhein 35; Between Two Hearts • Zwischen Zwei Herzen 36; Ein Idealer Gatte 37; Sergeant Berry 38; Wasser für Canitoga • Water for Canitoga 39

Seltzer, David Lucas 86; Punchline 88

Seltzer, Frank N. Breaking Home Ties 22

Selwyn, Edgar The Girl in the Show 29; War Nurse 30; The Lullaby • The Sin of Madelon Claudet 31; Men Call It Love 31; Skyscraper Souls 32; Men Must Fight 33; Turn Back the Clock 33; The Mystery of Mr. X 34

Selznick, Arna The Care Bears Movie 85

Selznick, David Duel in the Sun 46*

Sembène, Ousmane Borom Sarret 63; L'Empire Sonhrai • The Songhay Empire • Songhays 63; Niaye 64; Black Girl • The Black Girl from... • La Noire de... 65; Mandabi • Le Mandat • The Money Order 68; The Eldest Son • Tauw 70; Emitai 71; The Curse • Impotence • Xala 74; Ceddo • The Common People • The People • The Resisters 76; The Camp at Thiaroye • Camp de Thiaroye 88*

Semedo, Artur O Barão de Altamira 85

Semon, Larry Love and Loot 16; The Man from Egypt 16; A Villainous Villain 16; Boasts and Boldness 17; Footlights and Fakers 17; Plagues and Puppy Love 17; Rough Toughs and Roof Tops 17; Spooks and Spasms 17; Babes and Boobs 18; Bears and Bad Men 18; Spies and Spills 18; Between the Acts 19; Passing the Buck 19; The Simple Life 19; The Fly Cop 20*; The Sportsman 20*; The Stage Hand 20*; The Suitor 20*; The Bell Hop 21*; The Fall Guy 21*; The Hick 21*; The Sawmill 21*; The Show 22*; The Sleuth 22*; The Barnyard 23; The Gown Shop 23; Midnight Cabaret 23; No Wedding Bells 23; The Girl in the Limousine 24; Kid Speed 24*; Trouble Brewing 24*; The Wizard of Oz 25; Stop, Look and Listen 26; Spuds 27

Semschová, Jana Jemné Umění Obrany 88

Sen, Aparna 36 Chowringhee Lane 82

Sen, Arabind Amanat 55*

Sen, Asit Pariwar 56*

Sen, Fou see Fou, Sen

Sen, Mrinal The Dawn • Night's End • Raat Bhore 56; Neel Akasher Neechey • Under Blue Skies • Under the Blue Sky 59; Baishey Sravana • The Wedding Day 60; Over Again • Punascha 61; Abasheshey • And at Last 62; Pratinidhi • The Representative • Two Plus One 64; Akash Kusum • The Daydream • Up in the Clouds 65; Matira Manisha • Two Brothers 67; Moving Perspectives 67; Bhuvan Shome • Mr. Shome 69; Ichhapuran • The Wish-Fulfillment 70; Ek Adhuri Kahani • An Unfinished Story 71; Interview 71; Calcutta '71 72; The Guerrilla • The Guerrilla Fighter

• Padatik 73; Chorus 74; Mrigaya • The Royal Hunt 76; Oka Oorie Katha • The Outsiders • The Story of a Village 77; The Man with the Axe • Parashuram • Parasuram 78; And Quiet Rolls the Dawn • Ek Din Prati Din 79; Aakaler Sandhane • In Search of Famine 80; Chaalchitra • The Kaleidoscope 81; The Case Is Closed • Kharij 82; Khandar • The Ruins 83; Tasveer Apni 84; Genesis 86; Ek Din Achanak • Suddenly, One Day 88; City Life 90*

Sen, Om Ghil Seconds Make a Hero • Sekunda na Podvig 87*

Senft, Haro Jakob Hinter der Blauen Tür 88

Sennett, Mack The Lucky Toothache 10; The Masher 10; Abe Gets Even with Father 11; The Baron 11; Bearded Youth 11; The Beautiful Voice 11; Caught with the Goods 11; Comrades 11; A Convenient Burglar 11; The Country Lovers 11; Cupid's Joke 11; Cured 11; Curiosity 11; Dave's Love Affair 11; The Delayed Proposal 11; The Diving Girl 11; Dooley's Scheme 11; A Dutch Gold Mine 11; $500,000 Reward 11; The Ghost 11; Her Mother Interferes 11; Her Pet 11; An Interrupted Elopement 11; An Interrupted Game 11; The Inventor's Secret 11; The Jealous Husband 11*; Jinks Joins the Temperance Club 11; Josh's Suicide 11; The Lucky Horseshoe 11; The Manicure Lady 11; Misplaced Jealousy 11; Mr. Bragg, a Fugitive 11; Mr. Grouch at the Seashore 11; Mr. Peck Goes Calling 11; A Mix-Up in Raincoats 11; Priscilla and the Umbrella 11; Priscilla's April Fool Joke 11; Resourceful Lovers 11; Stubbs' New Servants 11; Taking His Medicine 11; That Dare Devil 11; Their Fates Sealed 11; Their First Divorce • Their First Divorce Case 11; Through Dumb Luck 11; Through His Wife's Picture 11; Too Many Burglars 11; The Tourists 11; The Tragedy of a Dress Suit 11; Trailing the Counterfeit 11; A Victim of Circumstances 11; The Village Hero 11; The Villain Foiled 11; What the Doctor Ordered 11; When Wifey Holds the Purse Strings 11; Why He Gave Up 11; Won Through a Medium 11; The Wonderful Eye 11; Algy the Watchman 12*; The Ambitious Butler 12; At Coney Island 12; At It Again 12; A Bear Escape 12; The Beating He Needed 12; Brave and Bold 12; The Brave Hunter 12; Brown's Seance 12; A Close Call 12; Cohen at Coney Island • Cohen Collects a Debt 12; A Dash Through the Clouds 12; The Deacon's Troubles 12; A Desperate Lover 12; Did Mother Get Her Wish? 12; The Drummer's Vacation 12; The Duel 12; The Engagement Ring 12; A Family Mixup 12; The Fatal Chocolate 12; The Fickle Spaniard 12; The Flirting Husband 12; The Furs 12; Got a Match? 12; The Grocery Clerk's Romance 12; Helen's Marriage 12; Help! Help! 12; His Own Fault 12; Hoffmeyer's Legacy 12; Hot Stuff 12; The Joke on the Joker 12; Katchem Kate 12; The Leading Man 12; Lily's Lovers 12; Mabel's Adventures 12; Mabel's Lovers 12; Mabel's Strata-

gem 12; A Message from the Moon 12; A Midnight Elopement 12; A Near-Tragedy 12; Neighbors 12; The New Baby 12*; The New Neighbor 12; Oh Those Eyes! 12; One-Round O'Brien 12; Pants and Pansies 12; Pat's Day Off 12; Pedro's Dilemma 12; Priscilla's Capture 12; Riley and Schultz 12; The Rivals 12; A Spanish Dilemma 12; The Speed Demon 12; Stolen Glory 12; A Temperamental Husband 12; Their First Kidnapping Case 12; Those Hicksville Boys 12; Tomboy Bessie 12; Trying to Fool Uncle 12; Useful Sheep 12; A Voice from the Deep 12; The Water Nymph 12; When the Fire Bells Rang 12; Who Got the Reward? 12; Willie Becomes an Artist 12; With a Kodak 12; Won by a Fish 12; The Would-Be Shriner 12; Algy on the Force 13; At Twelve O'Clock 13; Baby Day 13; A Bandit 13; The Bangville Police 13; Barney Oldfield's Race for a Life 13; The Battle of Who Run 13; The Bowling Match 13; The Chief's Predicament 13; Cohen Saves the Flag 13; Cohen's Outing 13; Cupid in the Dental Parlor 13; The Cure That Failed 13; The Darktown Belle 13; The Deacon Outwitted 13; A Deaf Burglar 13; A Doctored Affair 13; A Dollar Did It 13; A Double Wedding 13; The Elite Ball 13; Father's Choice 13; The Firebugs 13; A Fishy Affair 13; Foiling Fickle Father 13*; For Lizzie's Sake 13; Forced Bravery 13; The Foreman of the Jury 13; A Game of Poker 13; The Gangster 13; The Gypsy Queen 13; The Hansom Driver 13; A Healthy Neighborhood 13; Heinze's Resurrection 13; Her Birthday Present 13; Her New Beau 13; Hide and Seek 13; His Chum the Baron 13; His Crooked Career 13; His Ups and Downs 13; How Hiram Won Out 13; The Jealous Waiter 13; Jenny's Pearls 13; Just Brown's Luck 13; The Land Salesman 13; A Landlord's Troubles 13; A Life in the Balance 13; A Little Hero 13; Love and Courage 13; Love and Pain 13; Love Sickness at Sea 13; Mabel's Awful Mistake 13; Mabel's Dramatic Career 13; Mabel's Heroes 13; Mabel's New Hero 13; The Man Next Door 13; The Mistaken Masher 13; Mother's Boy 13; A Muddy Romance 13; Murphy's IOU 13; The New Conductor 13; A Noise from the Deep 13; On His Wedding Day 13; Out and In 13; Peeping Pete 13; Professor Bean's Removal 13; The Professor's Daughter 13; A Red Hot Romance 13; The Riot 13; The Rube and the Baron 13; A Rural Third Degree 13; Safe in Jail 13; Saving Mabel's Dad 13; Sir Thomas Lipton Out West 13; The Sleuths at the Floral Parade 13; The Sleuth's Last Stand 13; The Speed Kings 13; The Speed Queen 13; The Stolen Purse 13; A Strong Revenge 13; The Tale of a Black Eye 13; A Tangled Affair 13; The Telltale Light 13; That Ragtime Band 13; Those Good Old Days 13; The Two Widows 13; The Waiter's Picnic 13; When Dreams Come True 13; A Wife Wanted 13; Willie Minds the Dog 13; Zuzu the Band Leader 13; The Fatal Mallet • Hit Him Again • The Pile Driver • The Rival

Shanin, Ron E. African Safari 69

Shankar, Dilip Kaalchakra 88

Shankar, Uday Imagination • Kalpana 48

Shanklin, Lina Summerspell 83

Shanks, Ann Zane Friendship, Secrets and Lies 79*

Shanley, John Patrick Joe Versus the Volcano 90

Shannon, Frank see Prosperi, Franco

Shantaram, Rajaram Vanakudre Nethaji Palkar 26; Adomi 29; Amar 29; Bhopali 30; Parchain 30; Ayodhyecha Raja • The King of Ayodhya 32; Amar Jyoti • Eternal Light 36; Duniya Na Mane • The Unaccepted • The Unexpected 37; Sant Tukaram 37; Admi • Life Is for Living 39; Neighbors • Pardesi 41; Shakuntala 43; The Journey of Dr. Kotnis 46; Jangle, Jangle Sound the Bells • Jhanak, Jhanak Payal Baje 55; Stree • Woman 62

Shantaram, Shri V. Two Eyes, Twelve Hands 58

Shantaram, V. Jhanjhaar 87

Shapiro, Josef Three Fat Men • Tri Tolstyaka 66*

Shapiro, Ken The Groove Tube 74; Modern Problems 81

Shapiro, Mel Sammy Stops the World • Stop the World, I Want to Get Off 78

Shapiro, Mikhail Pesn o Metallye • A Song of Steel 28*; Goryachie Deneki • Hectic Days • Red Army Days • Those Were the Days 35*; Kino-Concert 1941 • Leningrad Music Hall 41*; Christmas Slippers 45*; Katerina Ismailova • Katerina Izmailova • Lady Macbeth of Mtsensk 66

Shapiro, Paul Hockey Night 84

Sharff, Stefan Across the River 65

Sharma, Chander Ghulami ki Zanjeer 87

Sharma, Eranki Agni Pushpam 88

Sharma, Kamal Dav Pech 89

Sharma, Ramesh New Delhi Times 86

Sharma, Renuka Daivashakti 88

Sharman, Jim Shirley Thompson vs. the Aliens 68; The Rocky Horror Picture Show 75; Summer of Secrets 76; The Night of the Prowler 78; Shock Treatment 81

Sharon, Yoel Betzilo Shel Halem Krav • Shell Shock 88

Sharp, Alan Little Treasure 85

Sharp, Don Ha'penny Breeze 49*; Conflict of Wings • Fuss Over Feathers 53*; The Stolen Airliner 55; The Adventures of Hal 5 57; The Changing Years 58; The Golden Disc • The In-Between Age 58; Linda 60; The Professionals 60; Kiss of Evil • Kiss of the Vampire 62; The Dream Maker • It's All Happening 63; The Devil-Ship Pirates 64; Witch and Warlock • Witchcraft 64; The Curse of the Fly 65; The Face of Fu Manchu • The Mask of Fu Manchu 65; I Killed Rasputin • The Mad Monk • Rasputin—The Mad Monk 65; Those Magnificent Men in Their Flying Machines • Those Magnificent Men in Their Flying Machines, or How I Flew from London to Paris in 25 Hours and 11 Minutes 65*; Bang Bang! • Bang, Bang,

You're Dead! • I Spy, You Spy • Marrakesh • Our Man in Marrakesh 66; The Brides of Fu Manchu • Die Dreizehn Sklavinnen des Dr. Fu Manchu 66; Blast Off • Jules Verne's Rocket to the Moon • Those Fantastic Flying Fools 67; Taste of Excitement • Why Would Anyone Want to Kill a Nice Girl Like You? 68; The Violent Enemy 69; Puppet on a Chain 70*; The Death Wheelers • Psychomania 71; Dark Places 72; Callan • The Neutralizer 74; Hennessy 75; The Four Feathers 78; The Thirty-Nine Steps 78; Bear Island 79; What Waits Below 83

Sharp, Ian The Music Machine 78; The Final Option • Who Dares Wins 82

Sharp, Martin Darling, Do You Love Me? 69*

Sharp, Peter Dead Man's Float 80

Sharpsteen, Ben The Village Blacksmith 20; Snow White and the Seven Dwarfs 37*; Fantasia 40*; Pinocchio 40*; Dumbo 41; Fun and Fancy Free 47*; Melody Time 48*; The Adventures of Ichabod and Mr. Toad • Ichabod and Mr. Toad 49*; Cinderella 50*; Alice in Wonderland 51*

Shatalow, Peter Blue City Slammers 88

Shatner, William Star Trek V: The Final Frontier 89

Shaughnessy, Alfred Suspected Alibi • Suspended Alibi 56; Cat Girl • The Cat Woman 57; Calling All Cats • 6.5 Special 58; The Impersonator 61

Shavelson, Melville The Seven Little Foys 55; Beau James 57; Houseboat 58; The Five Pennies 59; It Started in Naples 60; On the Double 61; The Pigeon That Took Rome 62; A New Kind of Love • Samantha 63; Cast a Giant Shadow 65; His, Hers and Theirs • Yours, Mine and Ours 68; The War Between Men and Women 72; Mixed Company 74

Shaw, Alexander Conquest of the Air 36*; Soldier, Sailor 44

Shaw, Harold M. The House of Temperley 13; Beauty and the Bargee 14; Bootle's Baby 14; The Bosun's Mate 14; Branscombe's Pal 14; Child o' My Heart 14; A Christmas Carol 14; Clancarty 14; Duty 14; England's Menace 14; For Home and Country • For the Empire 14; Her Children 14; The Incomparable Bellairs • The Incomparable Mistress Bellairs 14; The King's Minister 14; Lawyer Quince 14; Liberty Hall 14; Lil o' London 14; The Ring and the Rajah 14; Trilby 14; The Two Columbines 14; Two Little Britons 14; V.C. • The Victoria Cross 14; The Ashes of Revenge 15; Brother Officers 15; The Derby Winner 15; The Firm of Girdlestone 15; A Garret in Bohemia 15; The Heart of a Child 15; The Heart of Sister Anne 15; Mr. Lyndon at Liberty 15; The Third Generation 15; The Two Roads 15; The Last Challenge 16; Me and Me Moke • Me and M'Pal 16; You 16; The Land of Mystery 20; London Pride 20; Love and the Whirlwind 20; The Pursuit of Pamela 20; True Tilda 20; A Dear Fool 21; General John Regan 21; Kipps 21; The Woman of His Dream 21; False Evi-

dence 22; Love and a Whirlwind 22*; The Wheels of Chance 22; Held to Answer 23; Rouged Lips 23; A Fool's Awakening 24; Winning a Continent 24

Shaw, Jimmy Return of the Tiger 79

Shaw, Walter Meg 26

Shawzin, Barry The Day the Sky Fell In 61

Shaye, Robert Book of Love 90

Shayne, Linda Purple People Eater 88

Shea, Jack Dayton's Devils 68; The Monitors 68

Shea, James K. Planet of Dinosaurs 78

Shea, William Girl of the Ozarks 36

Shear, Barry Swingin' in the Groove 60; The Karate Killers 67; Wild in the Streets 68; A Dangerous Friend • Skipper • The Todd Killings 71; Across 110th Street 72; The Deadly Trackers 73

Shebib, Donald Goin' Down the Road 70; Rip-Off 71; Between Friends 73; Get Back 73; Second Wind 76; Fish Hawk 80; Heartaches 81; Running Brave 83; The Climb 86

Sheehan, Perley Poore The Night Message 24

Sheffer, L. Predatel • Predatel Krasnaya Presnya • Red Presnya • Traitor 26*

Sheik, Kamel el see El Sheik, Kamel

Shelach, Riki see Nissimoff, Riki Shelach

Sheldon, David Lovely But Deadly 83

Sheldon, Forrest K. Black Gold 24; Rainbow Rangers 24; Always Ridin' to Win 25; Don X 25; Makers of Men 25; Never Too Late 25; Stampedin' Trouble 25; Who's Your Friend? 25; Ahead of the Law 26; The Grey Vulture 26; Lawless Trails 26; The Man from Oklahoma 26*; The Haunted Ship 27; Law of the Rio Grande • Wanted Men 31*; The Sign of the Wolf 31*; Between Fighting Men 32; Dynamite Ranch 32; Hell Fire Austin 32; The Lone Trail 32*; Wilderness Mail 35

Sheldon, James The Devil's Children 62

Sheldon, Norman Rio Grande 49; Border Fence 51*

Sheldon, Roy The Bootleggers 22; Is a Mother to Blame? 22; Counterfeit Love 23*

Sheldon, Sidney Dream Wife 53; The Buster Keaton Story 57

Shelenkov, Alexander Bolshoi Ballet 67 66*

Shelley, Joshua The Perils of Pauline 67*

Shelton, Ron Bull Durham 88; Blaze 89

Sheng, Lee see Lee, Shing

Sheng, Li see Lee, Shing

Shengelaya, Eldar Legend of an Icy Heart • Legend of the Ice Heart • Legenda o Ledyanom 57*; Snezhnaya Skazka • Snow Fairy Tale • A Snowy Fairy Tale 59*; Byelyi Karavan • The White Caravan 64*; Mikela 65; He Did Not Want to Kill • On Ubivat Ne Khotel 67; An Extraordinary Exhibition • An Unusual Exhibition 68; The Eccentrics 74; Samanishvili's Stepmother 74; Blue Mountains • Golubye Gory Ely Nepravdopodobnaya Istoria 83

Shengelaya, Georgy Alaverdoba 66; Pirosmani 69; Melodies of the Veri Suburb 73; Our Daily Water 76; Achalgazrda Kompozitoris Mogzauroba • Journey of a Young Composer • A Young Composer's Odyssey 86; Khareba i Gogi 88

Shengelaya, Nikolai Giulli 27*; Caucasian Love • Eliso 28; Dvadtsat Shest Komissarov • Twenty-Six Commissars 33; Golden Valley 37; In the Black Mountains 41

Shenson, Walter Welcome to the Club 70

Shepard, Gerald Heroes Die Young 60

Shepard, Sam Far North 88

Shepherd, Antonio Chorus Call 79

Shepherd, Horace A Tale of Tails 33; A Garland of Song 34; Alfredo Campoli and His Orchestra 36; Cedric Sharpe and His Sextette 36; Eugene Pini and His Tango Orchestra 36; Leslie Jeffries and His Orchestra 36; Mario de Pietro and His Estudiantina 36; The Music Maker 36; Reginald King and His Orchestra 36; Melodies of the Moment 38; Eddie Carroll and His Boys 39; Radio Nights 39; Tunes of the Times 39; Dangerous Acquaintance 41; A Musical Cocktail 41; Once Upon a Time 41; Harry Parry and His Radio Rhythm Club Septet 43; King of the Keyboard 43; Swingonometry 43; Musical Masquerade 46; Making the Grade 47; Musical Romance 47; Blonde for Danger • The Flamingo Affair 48; Eugene Pini and His Orchestra 48; Movie Memories 48; Stephane Grappelli and His Quintet 48; A Touch of Shamrock 49; A Ray of Sunshine 50; Death Is a Number 51; Mirth and Melody 51; Winston Lee and His Orchestra 54

Shepitko, Larissa Heat • Znoi 63; Krylya • Wings 66; Ty i Ya • You and I 71; The Ascent • Voskhozhdenie 76

Sheppard, Gordon Eliza's Horoscope 75

Sheppard, John Mania 86*; Higher Education 87

Sheppard, W. H. Love on the Riviera 24

Sher, Jack Four Girls in Town 56; Kathy O 58; The 3 Worlds of Gulliver • The Worlds of Gulliver 59; The Wild and the Innocent 59; Love in a Goldfish Bowl 61

Shergood, Adrian Christabel 88

Sheridan, Jim My Left Foot 89; The Field 90

Sheridan, Oscar M. Big Business 30

Sheriden, Jay Nashville Rebel 66

Sherin, Edwin Valdez Is Coming 70; Glory Boy • My Old Man's Place • The Old Man's Place 71

Sherman, Arthur Likewise 88*

Sherman, Gary Deathline • Raw Meat 72; Dead and Buried 81; Vice Squad 82; Wanted: Dead or Alive 86; Poltergeist III 88; Lisa 90

Sherman, George Wild Horse Rodeo 37; Heroes of the Hills 38; Outlaws of Sonora 38; Overland Stage Raiders 38; Pals of the Saddle 38; The Purple Riders • The Purple Vigilantes 38; Red River Range 38; Rhythm of the Saddle 38; Riders of Black Hills • Riders of the Black Hills 38; Santa Fe Stampede 38; Colorado Sunset 39; Cowboys from Texas 39; Danger Rides the Range • Three Texas Steers 39; Frontier Horizon • Frontier Uprising • New Frontier 39; The Kansas Terrors 39; Mexicali Rose 39; The Night Riders 39; Rovin' Tumbleweeds • Washington Cowboy 39; South of the Border 39; Wyoming Outlaw 39; Covered Wagon Days 40; Ghost Valley Raiders 40; Lone Star Raiders 40; One Man's Law 40; Rocky Mountain Rangers 40; Texas Terrors 40; The Trail Blazers 40; The Tulsa Kid 40; Under Texas Skies 40; The Apache Kid 41; Citadel of Crime • Outside the Law 41; Death Valley Outlaws 41; Desert Bandit 41; Kansas Cyclone 41; A Missouri Outlaw 41; The Phantom Cowboy 41; Two-Gun Sheriff 41; Wyoming Wildcat 41; Arizona Terrors 42; The Cyclone Kid 42; Jesse James, Jr. 42; The London Blackout Murders • Secret Motive 42; The Sombrero Kid 42; Stagecoach Express 42; X Marks the Spot 42; False Faces 43; The Mantrap 43; Mystery Broadcast 43; The Purple V 43; A Scream in the Dark 43; The West Side Kid 43; The Lady and the Doctor • The Lady and the Monster 44; Storm Over Lisbon 44; The Crime Doctor's Courage • The Doctor's Courage 45; The Bandit of Sherwood Forest 46*; Duchess of Broadway • Talk About a Lady 46; The Gentleman Misbehaves 46; Personality Kid 46; Renegades 46; The Secret of the Whistler 46; Last of the Redmen • Last of the Redskins 47; Black Bart • Black Bart, Highwayman 48; Feudin', Fussin' and A-Fightin' 48; Larceny 48; Relentless 48; River Lady 48; Calamity Jane and Sam Bass 49; Red Canyon 49; Sword in the Desert 49; Yes Sir, That's My Baby 49; Battle of Powder River • Tomahawk 50; Comanche Territory 50; Panther's Moon • Spy Hunt 50; The Sleeping City 50; The Battle at Apache Pass 51; The Golden Horde • The Golden Horde of Genghis Khan 51; The Raging Tide 51; Target Unknown 51; Against All Flags 52; Back at the Front • Willie and Joe Back at the Front • Willie and Joe in Tokyo 52; Steel Town 52; The Lone Hand 53; Veils of Bagdad 53; War Arrow 53; Border River 54; Dawn at Socorro 54; Johnny Dark 54; Chief Crazy Horse • Valley of Fury 55; Count Three and Pray 55; The Treasure of Pancho Villa 55; Comanche 56; Reprisal! 56; The Hard Man 57; The Last of the Fast Guns 58; Son of Robin Hood 58; Ten Days to Tulara 58; The Flying Fontaines 59; The Enemy General 60; For the Love of Mike • None But the Brave 60; Hell Bent for Leather 60; The Wizard of Bagdad 60; The Fiercest Heart 61; Panic Button 63; Joaquin Murrieta • Murrieta • Vendetta 64; Daniel Boone—Frontier Trail Rider 66; Smoky 66; Big Jake 71

Sherman, Lowell Lawful Larceny 30; The Losing Game • The Pay-Off 30; The Queen's Husband • The Royal Bed 30; Bachelor Apartment 31; High Stakes 31; False Faces • What Price Beauty? 32; The Greeks Had a Word for Them • Three Broadway Girls 32; Ladies of the Jury 32; Broadway Through a Keyhole • Broadway Thru a Keyhole 33; Morning Glory 33; She Done Him Wrong 33; Born to Be Bad 34; Night Life of the Gods 35

Sherman, Michael California Girls 81*

Sherman, Vincent The Return of Dr. X 39; The Man Who Talked Too Much 40; Saturday's Children 40; All Through the Night 41; Flight from Destiny 41; Underground 41; Across the Pacific 42*; The Hard Way 42; Old Acquaintance 43; In Our Time 44; Mr. Skeffington 44; Pillow to Post 45; Janie Gets Married 46; Nora Prentiss 47; The Unfaithful 47; Adventures of Don Juan • The New Adventures of Don Juan 48; The Hasty Heart 49; Backfire 50; The Damned Don't Cry 50; Harriet Craig 50; Goodbye My Fancy 51; Lone Star 51; Affair in Trinidad 52; Assignment in Paris • Assignment—Paris! 52*; Defend My Love • Difendo il Mio Amore 55; The Garment Center • The Garment Jungle 57*; The Naked Earth 58; The City Jungle • The Young Philadelphians 59; Ice Palace 60; A Fever in the Blood 61; Mother Ought to Marry • The Second Time Around • Star in the West 61; Les Aventures Extraordinaires de Cervantes • Le Aventure e gli Amori di Miguel Cervantes • Cervantes • Young Rebel 67

Sherrin, Ned The Cobblers of Umbrage 72*

Sherry, Gordon Ysani the Priestess 34

Sherstobitov, Yevgeny The Andromeda Nebula • Andromeda the Mysterious • The Cloud of Andromeda • Tumannost Andromedy 68

Shervan, Amir Hollywood Cop 88

Sherwood, Bill Parting Glances 86

Sherwood, John The Creature Walks Among Us 56; Raw Edge 56; The Monolith Monsters 57; The Crawling Monster • The Creeping Terror • Dangerous Charter 64

Sherwood, Skip Didn't You Hear? 83

Sheshukov, Igor Krasnaya Strela • The Red Arrow 87*

Shevchenko, Vladimir Counter-Strike • Kontrudar 87

Shibuya, Minoru Madame Shall Not Know 37; The Fox 39; Mother and Child 39; South Wind 39; Cherry Country 41; A Family 42; The Angry Ghost 43; Passion Fire 47; The Face of a Flower 49; Crazy Uproar 50; First Love 50; The Moderns 52; No Consultation Today 52; Topsy-Turvy 53; Medals 54; Christ in Bronze 55; A Case of Honor 57; Days of Evil Women 58; Bananas 60; The Shrikes 61; Rat Among the Cats 63; Daikon to Ninjin • Mr. Radish and Mr. Carrot • Radishes and Carrots • Twilight Path 64; Ode to an Old Teacher 66

Shields, Frank Hostage • Hostage: The Christine Maresch Story • Savage Attraction 83; The Surfer 87

Shields, Hugh In Verdun Forests 16;

High Stakes 27; Rats in His Garret 27; Barnyard Artists 28; Barnyard Politics 28; The Flight That Failed 28; Kill or Cure 28; Outnumbered 28; A White Elephant 28; The Queen Bee 29

Shields, Pat Frasier the Sensuous Lion 73

Shiffen, Arlo Franchette: Les Intrigues 69

Shiga, Takashi Abnormal • Hentai 66
Shih, Hueh see Hueh, Shih
Shih-ling, Chu see Chu, Shih-ling
Shillingford, Peter Today Mexico, Tomorrow the World 70; Naughty Girls 75; The English Girl Abroad 79

Shilovsky, Vsevolod A Million in the Wedding Basket • Million v Brachnoy Korzine 87

Shima, Koji Golden Demon • Konjiki Yasha 53; The Cosmic Man Appears in Tokyo • The Mysterious Satellite • Space Men Appear in Tokyo • Uchūjin Tōkyō ni Arawaru • Unknown Satellite Over Tokyo • Warning from Space 56; The Phantom Horse 56

Shimazu, Yasujiro Father 22; The Crossing Watchman of the Mountains 23; Market of Human Flesh 23; Sunday 24; Stinker 25; A Village Teacher 25; ABC Lifeline 31; First Steps Ashore 32; Maiden in the Storm 33; Our Neighbor 34; The Woman That Night 34; Ani to Sono Imōto • A Brother and His Younger Sister 39; The Daily Battle 44

Shimizu, Hiroshi Arigatōsan 37; Children in the Wind 37; Children in Torment 38; Four Seasons of Children 39; Sayon's Bell 43; Children of the Beehive 48; Children and the Statue of Buddha 52; Jiro Monogatari 55

Shin, Nelson The Transformers—The Movie 86*

Shin, Sang-ok Prince Yang San 89

Shin, Stephen Brotherhood 87; Heart Into Hearts 90

Shindo, Kaneto Aisai Monogatari • The Story of a Beloved Wife • Story of My Loving Wife 51; Avalanche • Nadare 52; Children of Hiroshima • Children of the Atomic Bomb • Genbaku no Ko 52; Epitome • Geisha Girl Ginko • Ginko the Geisha • Shukuzu 53; A Life of a Woman • Onna no Isshō • A Woman's Life 53; Dobu • Gutter 54; A Geisha's Suicide • Gin-Shinju • Shirogane Shinju • Silver Double Suicide 55; Ōkami • Wolves 55; An Actress • Joyū 56; Bank of Departure • The Boat • The Fishing Boat • Ryūri no Kishi 56; Guys of the Sea • Harbor Rats • Umi no Yarodomo 57; Kanashimi wa Onna Dake Ni • Only Women Have Trouble • Only Women Know Sorrow • Sorrow Is Only for Women 58; The Bride from Japan • Hanayome-San wa Sekai Ichi • The World's Best Bride 59; Daigo Fukuryō Maru • The Lucky Dragon No. 5 59; Graffiti Blackboard • Rakugaki Kokuban 59; Hadaka no Shima • The Island • Naked Island 60; Human Being • The Man • Ningen 61; Haha • Mother 62; The

Demon • Devil Woman • The Hole • Onibaba • Onibaba—The Hole 64; Akutō • Conquest • A Scoundrel 65; Four Seasons of Tateshina • Tateshina no Shiki 66; Honnō • Impotence • Instinct • Lost Sex 66; Monument of Totsuseki • Totsuseki Iseki 66; Black Cat • A Black Cat in the Bush • Kuroneko • Yabu no Naka no Kuroneko 67; Libido • The Origin of Libido • The Origin of Sex • Sei no Kigen 67; Heat Haze • Heat Wave Island • Kagerō 68; Operation Negligee • Strong Woman and Weak Man • Tsuyomushi Onna to Yowamushi Otoko 68; Odd Affinity • Shokkaku • Strange Affinity • Tentacles 69; Hadaka no Jūkyū-Sai • Live Today—Die Tomorrow • Naked Nineteen-Year-Old • Nineteen-Year-Old Misfit 70; Iron Ring • Kanawa 72; A Paean • Sanka 72; Heart • Kokoro 73; My Way • Waga Michi 74; Aru Eiga Kantoku no Shōgai: Mizoguchi Kenji • Aru Eiga Kantoku no Shōgai: Mizoguchi Kenji no Kiroku • The Life of a Film Director • Life of a Film Director: Record of Kenji Mizoguchi 75; Chikuzan • Chikuzan Hitori Tabi • Chikuzan Travels Alone • The Life of Chikuzan 77; Hokusai Manga • Hokusai, Ukiyoe Master 82; Chiheisen • The Horizon 84; A Deciduous Tree 87

Shing, Lee see Lee, Shing
Shing, Li see Lee, Shing
Shing, Lu see Lu, Shing
Shing-hon, Lau see Liu, Cheng-han

Shinoda, Masahiro Dry Lake • Kawaita Mizuumi • Youth in Fury 60; Koi no Katamichi Kippu • One-Way Ticket for Love • One-Way Ticket to Love 60; Epitaph to My Love • Waga Koi no Tabiji 61; Killers on Parade • My Face, Red in the Sunset • Yūhi ni Akai Ore no Kao 61; Love, Old and New • Shamisen and Motorcycle • Shamisen to Ōtobai 61; Glory on the Summit • Glory on the Summit: Burning Youth • Yama no Sanka: Moyuru Wakamono-Tachi 62; Namida o Shishi no Tategami Ni • Tears on the Lion's Mane 62; Our Marriage • Watakushi-Tachi no Kekkon 62; Kawaita Hana • Pale Flower 63; Ansatsu • The Assassin • Assassination 64; Ibun Sarutobi Sasuke • Samurai Spy • Samurai Spy Sarutobi • Sarutobi 65; Utsukushisa to Kanashimi To • With Beauty and Sorrow 65; Captive's Island • Punishment Island • Shokei no Shima 66; Akanegumo • Clouds at Sunset 67; Double Suicide • Shinjō Ten no Amijima 69; Buraikan • Outlaws • The Scandalous Adventures of Buraikan 70; Chinmoku • Silence 71; Sapporo Orimpikku • Sapporo Winter Olympic Games • Sapporo Winter Olympics 72; Kaseki no Mori • The Petrified Forest 73; Sasuke Against the Wind 73; Himiko 74; Sakura no Mori no Mankai no Shita • Under the Cherry Blossoms • Under the Fall of the Cherry Blossoms 75; Nihon-Maru • Nihon-Maru Ship 76; Sado no Kuni Ondeko-Za • Sado's Ondeko-Za 76; The Ballad of Orin • Banished • Banished Orin • Hanare Goze Orin • Melody

in Gray • Orin, a Blind Woman • Orin the Abandoned Girl 77; Demon Pond • Yashaga Ike 79; Akuma-To • Devil's Island • Island of Evil Spirits 80; MacArthur's Children • Setouchi Shōnen Yakyūdan 84; Gonza the Spearman • Yari no Gonza 85; The Dancer 89

Shipman, Nell The Girl from God's Country 21; The Golden Yukon 27

Shirley, Arthur Woman and Wine 15

Shirvanzada, A. Honor 29

Shivdesani, Deepak Dadagiri 87

Shmaruk, Isaac Tvoyo Mirnoe Nebo • Your Peaceful Sky 87*

Shoemaker, Don On Any Sunday II 81*

Sholder, Jack Alone in the Dark 82; A Nightmare on Elm Street 2: Freddy's Revenge 85; The Hidden 87; Renegades 89

Sholem, Lee Tarzan's Magic Fountain 49; Tarzan and the Jungle Queen • Tarzan and the Slave Girl 50; Superman and the Mole Men • Superman and the Strange People 51; The Redhead from Wyoming 52; The Stand at Apache River 53; Cannibal Attack 54; Jungle Man-Eaters 54; Tobor the Great 54; Ma and Pa Kettle at Waikiki 55; Crime Against Joe 56; Emergency Hospital 56; Hell Ship Mutiny 57*; Pharaoh's Curse 57; Sierra Stranger 57; Louisiana Hussy 60; The Catalina Caper • Never Steal Anything Wet 67; The Doomsday Machine 67*

Shonteff, Lindsay The Devil's Spawn • Hired Gun • The Last Gunfighter 61; The Devil Doll 63; Curse of Simba • Curse of the Voodoo • Lion Man • Voodoo Blood Death 64; Licensed to Kill • The Second Best Secret Agent in the Whole Wide World 65; Run with the Wind 66; The 1,000,000 Eyes of Sumuru • Sumuru 67; Clegg 69; Permissive 70; The Fast Kill 72; The Yes Girls 72; Big Zapper • The Sex Life of a Female Private Eye 73; Spy Story 76; The Swordsman 76; Number 1 of the Secret Service 78; Licensed to Love and Kill 79

Shore, Sig Shining Star • That's the Way of the World 75; The Act • Bless 'Em All 84; Sudden Death 85; The Survivalist 86; The Return of Superfly 90

Shores, Lynn Sally of the Scandals 28; Sally's Shoulders 28; Skinner's Big Idea 28; Stolen Love 28; The Delightful Rogue 29*; The Jazz Age 29; The Voice of the Storm 29; The Sin Ship 31*; Glorious Sacrifice • The Glory Trail 36; Rebellion 36; Here's Flash Casey 37; A Million to One 37; The Shadow • The Shadow Strikes • Womantrap 37; Woman in Distress 37; Charlie Chan at the Wax Museum 40; Golden Hoofs 41

Shorr, Richard Witches' Brew 80*

Short, Anthony The Inn Way Out 67

Short, Robert Programmed to Kill • Retaliator 86*; Goblins 87

Shourds, Sherry The Big Punch 48

Shpias, B. V. The Return of Nathan Becker 33*

Shpikovsky, Nikolai Chess Fever • Shakhmatnaya Goryachka 25*

Shu, Kei Laoniang Gou Sao • Soul 86; Sunless Days 88

Shu, Shuen *see Shuen, Cecile Tang Shu*

Shub, Esther The Fall of the Romanov Dynasty • Padeniye Dinasti Romanovikh 27; The Great Road • Velikii Put 27; Lev Tolstoi and the Russia of Nikolai II • Rossiya Nikolaya II i Lev Tolstoy • The Russia of Nicholas II and Leo Tolstoy 28; Segodnya • Today 30; K.S.E. • K.Sh.E. • Komsomol — Leader of Electrification • Komsomol — Patron of Electrification • Komsomol — The Guide to Electrification 32; The Metro by Night • Moscow Builds the Metro • Moscow Builds the Subway • Moskva Stroyit Metro 34; The Country of the Soviets • Land of the Soviets • Strana Sovietov 37; Ispaniya • Spain 37*; Kino za Dvadtsat Let • Twenty Years of Cinema • Twenty Years of Film • Twenty Years of Soviet Cinema 40*; The Face of the Enemy • Fascism Will Be Destroyed • Fashizm Budet Razbit 41; The Native Country • Strana Rodnaya 42*; Across the Arax • On the Banks of the Arax • On the Other Side of the Arax • Potu Storonu Araksa 46; Sud v Smolenske • The Trial in Smolensk 46

Shuen, Cecile Tang Shu The Green Wall 85

Shuen, Shu *see Shuen, Cecile Tang Shu*

Shuker, Gregory The Chair 62*; The Living Camera • Nehru 62*

Shuksin, Vasili How a Young Man Lives • There Was a Lad • Zhivyot Takoi Paren 64; Vash Syn i Brat • Your Son and Brother 66; Odd Folk • Strange People • Strannye Lyudi 70; Pechki Lavochki • That's How It Is 72; Kalina Krasnaya • Red Berry • The Red Snowball Tree 74

Shumlin, Herman Watch on the Rhine 43; Confidential Agent 45

Shuquin, Huang *see Huang, Shuquin*

Shurey, Dinah Carry On 27*; The Last Post 29

Shuster, Solomon Lights • Ogni 87

Shutko, Nina Agadzhanova *see Agadzhanova-Shutko, Nina*

Shvachko, A. The Land 55*

Shveytser, Mikhail Resurrection • Voskresniye 63; The Kreutzer Sonata • Kreutzerova Sonata 87*

Shyer, Charles Irreconcilable Differences 84; Baby Boom 87

Shyer, Melville Sucker Money • Victims of the Beyond 33*; Murder in the Museum 34; The Road to Ruin 34*

Shyman, James Slash Dance 89

Si, Tung *see Tung, Si*

Siano, Silvio Alone in the Streets 56

Sibal, José F. Zimatar 87*

Sica, Vittorio de *see De Sica, Vittorio*

Šicha, Petr Přátelé Bermudského Trojúhelníku 87*

Sichel, John Three Sisters 70*

Siciliano, Mario Alleluja e Sartana, Figli di…Dio • 100 Fäuste und ein Vaterunser 72; Trinità e Sartana Figli di… 72

Sickinger, Robert Love in a Taxi 80

Sidaris, Andy The Racing Scene 70; Stacey • Stacey and Her Gangbusters 73;

Seven 79; Malibu Express 84; Hard Ticket to Hawaii 87; Picasso Trigger 87; Savage Beach 90

Siddalingaiah Sambhavami Yuge Yuge 88

Siddik, Khalid Bas ya Bahar • The Cruel Sea 71

Siddon, J. David Their Only Chance 78

Sidelov, Sergei Aleko 53*

Sidney, George Polo 36; Pacific Paradise 37; Sunday Night at the Trocadero 37; Alfalfa's Aunt 38; Billy Rose's Casa Mañana Review 38; Football Romeo 38; Men in Fright 38; Party Fever 38; Practical Jokers 38; Clown Princes 39; Cousin Wilbur 39; Dog Daze 39; A Door Will Open 39; Duel Personalities 39; Hollywood Hobbies 39; Love on Tap 39; Tiny Troubles 39; No. 2 40; Quicker'n a Wink 40; Third Dimensional Murder 40; What's Your I.Q.? 40; Flicker Memories 41; Free and Easy 41; Of Pups and Puzzles 41; Willie and the Mouse 41; Pacific Rendezvous 42; Pilot No. 5 42; Thousands Cheer 43*; Bathing Beauty 44; Anchors Aweigh 45; The Harvey Girls 45; Ziegfeld Follies 45*; Holiday in Mexico 46; Cass Timberlane 47; The Three Musketeers 48; Key to the City 49; The Red Danube 49; Annie Get Your Gun 50; Show Boat 51; Scaramouche 52; Kiss Me Kate 53; Young Bess 53; Jupiter's Darling 54; The Eddy Duchin Story 56; Jeanne Eagels 57; Pal Joey 57; Who Was That Lady? 59; Pepe 60; Bye Bye Birdie 63; Moon Walk • A Ticklish Affair 63; Love in Las Vegas • Viva Las Vegas! 64; The Swinger 66; Half a Sixpence 67

Sidney, Scott The Mating 15; Matrimony 15; The Painted Soul 15; The Toast of Death 15; Bullets and Brown Eyes 16; The Green Swamp 16; The Road to Love 16; The Waifs 16; Her Own People 17; Tarzan of the Apes 18; "813" 20; Hold Your Breath 24; Reckless Romance 24; Al Christie's Madame Behave • Madame Behave 25; Charley's Aunt 25; The Million Dollar Handicap 25; Seven Days 25; Stop Flirting 25; The Nervous Wreck 26; No Control 27*; The Wrong Mr. Wright 27

Sidorov, Ivan *see Muratova, Kira*

Siegel, Don Hitler Lives? 45; Star in the Night 45; The Verdict 46; Night Unto Night 47; The Big Steal 49; Duel at Silver Creek 52; No Time for Flowers 52; China Venture 53; Count the Hours • Every Minute Counts 53; Private Hell 36 54; Riot in Cell Block 11 54; An Annapolis Story • The Blue and the Gold 55; Crime in the Streets 56; Invasion of the Body Snatchers 56; Baby Face Nelson 57; Spanish Affair 57; The Gun Runners 58; The Lineup 58; Edge of Eternity 59; The Hound Dog Man 59; Flaming Star 60; Hell Is for Heroes! 62; Ernest Hemingway's The Killers • Johnny North • The Killers 64; The Hanged Man 64; Death of a Gunfighter • The Last Gunfighter • Patch 67*; Madigan 67; Coogan's Bluff 68; Two Mules for Sister Sara 69; The Beguiled 70; Dirty Harry 71; Charley Varrick 73; The Black Windmill

• Drabble 74; The Shootist 76; Telefon 77; Escape from Alcatraz 79; Rough Cut 80; Hot Streak • Jinxed! • Stryke and Hyde 82

Siegel, Robert Break Loose • Parades 72; The Line 80

Siegmann, George A Yankee from the West 15; Atta Boy's Last Race • The Best Bet 16; The Little Yank 17; Mother Love and the Law 17; My Unmarried Wife 17; Should She Obey? 17; The Spirit of '76 17; The Spitfire of Seville 19; The Trembling Hour 19; The Woman Under Cover 19

Sierck, Detlef *see Sirk, Douglas*

Sievel, Bernard Dawn of Revenge 22

Signorelli, James Easy Money 83; Elvira: Mistress of the Dark 88

Si-hyun, Kim *see Kim, Si-hyun*

Šijan, Slobodan Ko To Tamo Peva • Who's Singing Over There? • Who's That Singing Over There? 80; How I Was Systematically Destroyed by an Idiot 84; The Marathon Family 84; Strangler vs. Strangler 86; Secret Ingredient 88

Sijie, Dai *see Dai, Sijie*

Sik, Im Won Cu'un Sae Han Nyo • The Revengeful Ghost 72

Sikiewicz, Bazyli Tajemnica Oskarżonej 37

Sikorsky, Jan Swiss Honeymoon 47*

Silano, George Roger the Stoolie • The Stoolie 72*

Silberg, Joel Mishpachat Simchon • The Simchon Family 69; Kuni Lemel in Tel Aviv • The Rabbi and the Shikse 76; Millionaire in Trouble 78; Marriage, Tel Aviv Style 79; My Mother the General 81; Breakdance • Breakdancin' • Breakin' 84; Rappin' 85; Bad Guys 86; Catch the Heat • Feel the Heat 87; Lambada 90

Sillman, Frank Kahuna 81

Sills, Sam The Good Fight 83*

Silva, Manuel Costa e *see Costa e Silva, Manuel*

Silver, Andrew Return 85

Silver, Joan Micklin The Fur Coat Club 73; The Case of the Elevator Duck 74; The Immigrant Experience: The Long Long Journey 74; Hester Street 75; Between the Lines 77; Chilly Scenes of Winter • Head Over Heels 79; Crossing Delancey 88; Loverboy 89

Silver, Marcel Fox Movietone Follies • Fox Movietone Follies of 1929 • Movietone Follies of 1929 • William Fox Movietone Follies of 1929 29*; Married in Hollywood 29; One Mad Kiss 30*; El Precio de un Beso • The Price of a Kiss 33

Silver, Marisa Old Enough 84; Permanent Record 88; Vital Signs 90

Silver, Raphael D. On the Yard 78; A Walk on the Moon 85

Silvera, Charlotte Prisonnières 88

Silverman, Louis *see Wishman, Doris*

Silverman, Marc Le Film Noir 83; Rumsey Statues 86

Silverstein, Elliot Belle Sommers 62; Cat Ballou 65; The Happening • It's What's Happening • Mr. Innocent 67; A Man Called Horse 70; Deadly Honeymoon • Nightmare Honeymoon 73; The Car 77

Silvestro, Rino di *see Di Silvestro, Salvatore*

Silvestro, Salvatore di *see Di Silvestro, Salvatore*

Simandl, Lloyd A. Ladies of the Lotus 87*

Simenon, Marc By the Blood of Others • Par le Sang des Autres 73

Šimková, Věra Plívová *see Plívová-Šimková, Věra*

Šimková-Plívová, Věra *see Plívová-Šimková, Věra*

Simm, Peeter Ideaalmaastik • Ideal Landscape 86

Simmons, Anthony Sunday by the Sea 53; Bow Bells 54; The Gentle Corsican 56; Your Money or Your Wife 59; Four in the Morning 65; The Optimists • The Optimists of Nine Elms 73; Black Joy 77; Little Sweetheart 88

Simmons, Bob You Only Live Twice 67*

Simmons, Robert Wynne *see Wynne-Simmons, Robert*

Simms, J. M. The Lure of a Woman 21

Simon, Adam Brain Dead 90

Simon, Barney City Lovers 82

Simon, Francis The Chicken Chronicles 77

Simon, Frank The Queen 68

Simon, Jean-Daniel Adélaïde • Fino a Farti Male 69

Simon, Juan Piquer Viaje al Centro de la Tierra • Where Time Began 76; Supersonic Man 79; Misterio en la Isla de los Monstruos • Monster Island • Mystery on Monster Island 80; Mil Gritos Tiene la Noche • Pieces • A Thousand Cries Has the Night 81; Slugs 88

Simon, M. Reward of Faith 29

Simon, Piquer *see Simon, Juan Piquer*

Simon, Rainer Jadup und Böl 81

Simon, Roger My Man Adam 85

Simon, S. Sylvan A Girl with Ideas 37; Hollywood Screen Test 37; Prescription for Romance 37; The Crime of Dr. Hallet 38; Four Girls in White 38; Nurse from Brooklyn 38; Road to Reno 38; Spring Madness 38; Dancing Co-Ed • Every Other Inch a Lady 39; The Kid from Texas 39; These Glamour Girls 39; Choose Your Partner • Two Girls on Broadway 40; Dulcy 40; Keeping Company 40; Sporting Blood 40; The Bugle Sounds 41; Washington Melodrama 41; Whistling in the Dark 41; Grand Central Murder 42; Rio Rita 42; Tish 42; Whistling in Dixie 42; Salute to the Marines 43; Whistling in Brooklyn 43; Song of the Open Road 44; Abbott and Costello in Hollywood • Bud Abbott and Lou Costello in Hollywood 45; Bad Bascomb 45; Son of Lassie 45; The Cockeyed Miracle • Mr. Griggs Returns 46; The Thrill of Brazil 46; Her Husband's Affairs 47; I Love Trouble 47; The Fuller Brush Man • That Mad Mr. Jones • That Man Mr. Jones 48; Lust for Gold 49*

Simon, Sándor Farewell to You • Isten Veletek, Barátaim 87

Simone, Charles Il Trovatore 14

Simone, Tom de *see DeSimone, Tom*

Simoneau, Yves Les Célébrations 79; Les Yeux Rouges ou Les Vérités Accidentelles 82; Pourquoi l'Étrange Monsieur Zolock S'Intéressait-Il Tant à la Bande Dessinée? 83; Intimate Power • Pouvoir Intime 86; Les Fous de Bassan • In the Shadow of the Wind 87; Dans le Ventre du Dragon • In the Belly of the Dragon 88; Perfectly Normal 90

Simonelli, Giorgio C. Bertoldo, Bertoldino, Cacasenno 37; Canzone Appasionata 53; Robin Hood and the Pirates 61; The Land of Fire • Son of Hercules in the Land of Fire • Ursus in the Land of Fire 63; Due Mafiosi nel Far West 64; The Amazing Dr. G 65; I Due Sergenti del Generale Custer 65; I Due Figli di Ringo 66

Simonov, Alexei Burys • Otryad 85

Simpson, Gregory The Rogue 76

Simpson, Harold The Derelict 37; The Little Boy That Santa Claus Forgot 38; A Prodigal Son 39

Simpson, Michael A. Impure Thoughts 85; Funland 86; Sleepaway Camp 2: Unhappy Campers 88; Fast Food 89; Sleepaway Camp 3: Teenage Wasteland 89

Sims, George R. Lady Letmere's Jewellery 08; The Martyrdom of Adolf Beck 09

Sinatra, Frank None But the Brave • Yūsha-Nomi 64

Sinclair, Andrew The Breaking of Bumbo 71; Under Milk Wood 72; Blue Blood 73

Sinclair, Irene *see Griffith, D. W.*

Sinclair, Robert B. Dramatic School 38; Woman Against Woman 38; Joe and Ethel Turp Call on the President 39; And One Was Beautiful 40; The Captain Is a Lady 40; Down in San Diego 41; I'll Wait for You 41; Mr. and Mrs. North 41; The Wild Man of Borneo 41; Mr. District Attorney 46; That Wonderful Urge 48

Sinclair, Roy *see Griffith, D. W.*

Sinclair, Vincent L. Women of Desire 68

Sinde, José María González *see González Sinde, José María*

Sindell, Gerald Seth Double-Stop 67; Teenager 74; H.O.T.S. 79

Sinding, Leif Syv Dager før Elisabeth 27

Sindoni, Vittorio The Burning Years 79

Sing, Yee Tung *see Yee, Tung-shing*

Sing, Yinnan Dr. Sun Yatsen 87

Singelow, Alexander Nomadie 31

Singer, Alexander A Cold Wind in August 61; Psyche 59 63; Love Has Many Faces 65; Glass Houses 70; Captain Apache 71

Singer, Stanford Amateur Hour • I Was a Teenage TV Terrorist 85

Singleton, Ralph S. Graveyard Shift • Stephen King's Graveyard Shift 90

Sinha, Tapan Atithi • The Runaway 66; Aaj ka Robin Hood 87

Sinise, Gary Farm of the Year • Miles from Home 88

Sinkel, Bernhard Lina Braake 75; Deutschland im Herbst • Germany in Autumn 78*

Siodmak, Curt Bride of the Gorilla 51; The Magnetic Monster 53; Curucu, Beast of the Amazon 56; Love Slaves of the Amazon 57; Liebesspiele • Liebesspiele im Schnee • Ski Fever 67

Siodmak, Robert Menschen am Sonntag • People on Sunday 29*; Abschied • Farewell • So Sind die Menschen 30; Looking for His Murderer • The Man Who Seeks His Own Murderer • Der Mann Der Seinen Mörder Sucht 30*; Inquest • Preliminary Investigation • Voruntersuchung 31; Storm of Passion • Stürme der Leidenschaft • Tempest 31; Quick • Quick, der Sieger • Quick—König der Clowns • The Victor 32; Le Sexe Faible 32; Brennendes Geheimnis • The Burning Secret 33; La Crise Est Finie • Finie la Crise • The Slump Is Over 34; La Vie Parisienne 35; Compliments of Mr. Flow • Mister Flow 36; Capitaine Mollenard • Hatred • Mollenard 37; Cargaison Blanche • Le Chemin de Rio • French White Cargo • Traffic in Souls • Woman Racket 37; Ultimatum 38*; Personal Column • Pièges • Snares 39; West Point Widow 41; Fly by Night • Secrets of G32 42; My Heart Belongs to Daddy 42; The Night Before the Divorce 42; Cobra Woman 43; Someone to Remember 43; Son of Dracula 43; Christmas Holiday 44; Phantom Lady 44; The Suspect 44; The Spiral Staircase 45; The Strange Affair of Uncle Harry • Uncle Harry • The Zero Murder Case 45; Dark Mirror 46; The Killers • A Man Alone 46; Symphonie d'Amour 46; Time Out of Mind 47; Criss Cross 48; Cry of the City 48; The File on Thelma Jordan • Thelma Jordan 49; The Great Sinner 49; Deported 50; Richer Than the Earth • The Whistle at Eaton Falls 51; The Crimson Pirate 52; The Big Game • Card of Fate • Flesh and the Woman • Flesh and Woman • Le Grand Jeu 53; The Rats • Die Ratten 55; Mein Vater, der Schauspieler 56; The Devil Strikes at Night • Nachts, Wenn der Teufel Kam • Nazi Terror at Night • Nights When the Devil Came 57; Dorothea Angermann 58; Bitter Sweet 59; Une Jeune Fille un Seul Amour • Katia • Katya • Magnificent Sinner • Magnifi-Sinner 59; Portrait of a Sinner • The Rough and the Smooth 59; Mein Schulfreund • Der Schulfreund 60; L'Affaire Nina B • The Nina B Affair 61; Escape from East Berlin • Tunnel 28 62; Una Carabina per Schut • Der Schut • The Shoot 64; Der Schatz der Azteken 64; Die Pyramide des Sonnengottes 65; Custer of the West • A Good Day for Fighting 66*; I Violenti di Rio Bravo 67; The Fight for Rome • Der Kampf um Rom • The Last Roman 69

Siple, J. Law The Unbeatable Game 25

Sippy, Raj Loha 87

Sirk, Douglas April, April 35; The Girl from the Marsh Croft • Das Mädchen vom Moorhof 35; It Was in April • 'T Was Een April 35*; Pillars of Society • Stützen der Gesellschaft 35; La Chanson du Souvenir

• Song of Remembrance 36; The Court Concert • Das Hofkonzert 36; Final Accord • The Final Chord • Ninth Symphony • Schlussakkord 36; Bagne de Femmes • Life Begins Anew • Paramatta • To New Shores • Zu Neuen Ufern 37; La Habañera 37; Die Heimat Ruft • Home Is Calling 37; Liebling der Matrosen 37; Boefje • Wilton's Zoo 39; Hitler's Hangman • Hitler's Madman 42; Summer Storm 44; Scandal in Paris • Thieves' Holiday 46; Lured • Personal Column 47; Atlantis • Atlantis the Lost Continent • Queen of Atlantis • Siren of Atlantis 48*; Sleep, My Love 48; Shockproof 49; Slightly French 49; The First Legion 50; Mystery Submarine 50; Bonaventure • Thunder on the Hill 51; The Lady Pays Off 51; Weekend with Father 51; Has Anybody Seen My Gal? 52; Meet Me at the Fair 52*; No Room for the Groom 52; All I Desire 53; Take Me to Town 53; Captain Lightfoot 54; Magnificent Obsession 54; Sign of the Pagan 54; Taza, Son of Cochise 54; All That Heaven Allows 55; Never Say Goodbye 55*; Battle Hymn 56; There's Always Tomorrow 56; Written on the Wind 56; Interlude 57; Pylon • The Tarnished Angels 57; A Time to Love and a Time to Die 58; Imitation of Life 59

Sirko, Marion I Vigliacchi Non Pregano 68

Sirovy, Zdenek Outsider 86

Sís, Vladimír A Night's Dream • Sen Noci... 85; Jonáš, Dejme Tomu ve Středu • Jonas, Say, for Instance, on Wednesday 86; Jonas 39.5 C 89

Sisé, Solimano see Cissé, Souleymane

Siso, Freddy Diles Que No Me Maten 85

Siso, Roberto El Compromiso 88

Sissel, Sandi Chicken Ranch 83*

Sissoko, Cheik Omar The Garbage Boys • Nyamanton 86

Sisti, Vittorio de see De Sisti, Vittorio

Sittenham, Fred Clothes 20; Fine Feathers 21

Siu-ming, Tsui see Tsui, Siu-ming

Sjöberg, Alf Den Starkaste • The Strongest • The Strongest One 29*; Den Blomstertid • Blossom Time • Flowering Time 39; Med Livet Som Insats • They Staked Their Lives 39; Hem från Babylon • Home from Babylon 41; Himlaspelet • The Road to Heaven 42; Kungajakt • The Royal Hunt 43; Frenzy • Hets • Torment 44; Journey Out • Resan Bort 45; Iris • Iris and the Lieutenant • Iris och Löjtnantshjärta 46; Bara en Mor • Only a Mother 49; Fröken Julie • Miss Julie 50; Barabba • Barabbas 52; Karin, Daughter of Man • Karin Mansdotter 53; Vildfåglar • Wild Birds 54; Last Couple Out • Last Pair Out • Sista Paret Ut 55; Domaren • The Judge 60; The Island • Ön 64; Fadern • The Father 69

Sjöberg, Tore Den Blödiga Tiden • Mein Kampf 59*; Secrets of the Nazi Criminals 62; The Face of War 63

Sjöman, Vilgot Älskarinnan • The Mistress • The Swedish Mistress 62; 491 63; The Dress • Klänningen 64; Stimulantia 65*; My Sister, My Love • Syskonbädd 1782 66; I Am Curious (Yellow) • Jag Är Nyfiken – Gul 67; I Am Curious (Blue) • Jag Är Nyfiken – Blå 68; Journey with Father • Resa med Far 68; Ni Ljuger • You're Lying 69; Blushing Charlie • Lyckliga Skitar 70; Till Sex Do Us Part • Troll 71; Bröderna Karlsson • The Karlsson Brothers 72; A Handful of Love • En Handfull Kärlek 74; Kulisser i Hollywood 74; The Garage • Garaget 75; Siesta Samba 76; Taboo • Tabu 76; Linus • Linus and the Mysterious Red Brick House • Linus eller Tegelhusets Hemlighet 79; I Am Blushing • Jag Rodnar 81; Malacca 86; Fallgropen 89

Sjöström, Victor Äktenskapsbyrån • Här Ni Något att Förtulla • The Marriage Agency • The Marriage Bureau • På Detta Numera Vanliga Sätt 12; Bekännelsen på Dödsbädden • Ett Hemligt Giftermål • En Moder • A Secret Marriage 12; Blodets Röst • The Voice of Blood • The Voice of Passion • Voice of the Blood 12; Dragers Juveler • Laughter and Tears • Löjen och Tårar • Ridicule and Tears • Smiles and Tears 12; Falskt Alarm • The Gardener • Trädgårdsmästaren • Världens Grymhet 12; Lady Marion • Lady Marions Sommarflirt • Lady Marion's Summer Flirtation 12; En Sommarsaga • A Summer Tale 12; Arbetaren • Strejken • Strike! 13; The Clergyman • The Parson • Prästen • The Priest 13; Conflicts of Life • Life's Conflicts • Livets Konflikter 13*; Det Var i Maj • It Was in May 13; Give Us This Day • Ingeborg Holm • Margaret Day 13; Half Breed • Halvblod 13; Kärlek Starkare Än Hat • Love Stronger Than Hate • The Poacher • Skogsdotterns Hemlighet • Tjuvskyttan 13; The Miracle • Miraklet • Underverket 13; On the Fateful Roads of Life • On the Roads of Fate • På Livets Ödesvägar • The Smugglers 13*; Bra Flicka Reder Sig Själv • A Clever Girl Takes Care of Herself • A Good Girl Keeps Herself in Order • A Good Girl Should Solve Her Own Problems 14; Chaufören • Hearts That Meet • Hjärtan Som Möts • Meeting Hearts 14; Children of the Streets • Gatans Barn 14; Daughter of the High Mountain • Daughter of the Mountain • Daughter of the Peaks • Högfjällets Dotter • Lappflickan 14; Do Not Judge • Dömen Icke • Judge Not 14; En av de Många • One of the Many • One Out of Many 14; Expiated Guilt • Guilt Redeemed • Sonad Oskuld 14; At the Moment of Trial • Hour of Trial • I Prövningens Stund • In the Hour of Trial 15; Cobbler Stay at Your Bench • Cobbler Stick to Your Last • Keep to Your Trade • Skomakare Bliv vid Din Läst • Stick to Your Last, Shoemaker 15; Dödens Besegrare • Hon Segrade • She Conquered • She Triumphs • She Was Victorious 15; The Governor's Daughters • Landshövdingens Döttrar • Tvillingsystrarna 15; Havsgamarna • Havsgammar • Predators of the Sea • The Rose of Thistle Island • Rosen på Tistelön • Sea Eagle • Sea Vulture • Smugglarens Dotter 15; Judas Money • Judaspengar • Judaspengene • The Price of Betrayal • Traitor's Reward 15; Meeting Ships • Ships That Meet • Skepp Som Mötas 15; Dödskyssen • The Kiss of Death 16; A Man There Was • Terje Vigen 16; Thérèse 16; Berg-Ejvind och Hans Hustru • Love, the Only Law • The Outlaw and His Wife • You and I 17; The Girl from Stormycroft • Girl from the Marsh Croft • Girl from the Stormy Croft • Lass from the Stormy Croft • Tösen från Stormyrtorpet • The Woman He Chose 17; Ingmarsönerna I & II • The Ingmarssons • The Sons of Ingmar 18; God's Way • Karin, Daughter of Ingmar • Karin, Ingmar's Daughter • Karin Ingmarsdotter 19; Hans Nåds Testamente • His Grace's Last Testament • His Grace's Will • His Lordship's Last Will • The Will of His Grace 19; Klostret i Sendomir • The Monastery of Sendomir • The Secret of the Monastery 19; Clay • Körkarlen • The Phantom Carriage • The Phantom Chariot • The Stroke of Midnight • Thy Soul Shall Bear Witness 20; The Executioner • En Farlig Pant • Master Samuel • Mästerman 20; Love's Crucible • Mortal Clay • Vem Dömer? 20; Eld Ombord • Fire on Board • The Hell Ship • The Tragic Ship 22; Det Omringade Huset • The Surrounded House • This House Surrounded 22; Name the Man 23; Confessions of a Queen 24; He Who Gets Slapped 24; The Tower of Lies 25; The Scarlet Letter 26; The Divine Woman 27; The Wind 27; Masks of the Devil 28; A Lady to Love 29; Father and Son • Fathers and Sons • Markurells i Wadköping • The Markurells of Wadköping • Väter und Söhne 30; Charles XII 33; Under the Red Robe 36

Skagen, Sølve Hard Asfalt • Hard Asphalt 86

Skaife, Michael see Madrid, Miguel

Skalenakis, Georges Apollo Goes on Holiday 68; Dama Spathi • Love Cycles • Queen of Clubs 69

Skinner, Peter A Child Is a Wild Thing 76

Skoglund, Gunnar A Handful of Rice • En Handfull Ris • Homme et Femme • Jungle of Chang • Man and Woman • Man och Kvinna • Une Poignée de Riz • Saggakh 38*

Skogsberg, Ingvar The City of My Dreams 77

Skolimowski, Jerzy L'Érotique • Erotyk 60; Hamles • Le Petit Hamlet 60; L'Œil Torve • Oko Wykół 60; Akt 61; Boks • Boxing 61; La Bourse ou la Vie • Pieniądze Albo Życie 61; Identification Marks: None • Rysopis 64; Walkover • Walkower 65; Bariera • Barrier 66; Le Départ • Setting Out 66; Hands Up! • Ręce do Góry 67; Dialog • Dialogue • Dialogue 20-40-60 68*; The Adventures of Gerard 69; Deep End 70; Herzbube • King, Queen and Knave • King, Queen, Knave 71; The

Shout 78; Moonlighting 82; Success Is the Best Revenge 84; The Lightship 85; Torrents of Spring 89

Skolimowski, Yurek see Skolimowski, Jerzy

Skouen, Arne Gategutter • Gods of the Street • Guttersnipes 49*; Bad Luck • Nödlanding 52; Circus Fandango • Sirkus Fandango 54; Det Brenner i Natt! 54; Barn av Solen 55; Ni Liv • Nine Lives • We Die Alone 57; A God and His Servants • Herren och Hans Tjenere • The Master and His Servants 59; Omringat • Surrounded 60; An-Magritt 69

Skurski, Grzegorz The Rutting Ground • Rykowisko 87

Skuybin, Nikolai Iz Zhizni Potapova • Potapov's Life 87

Slabnevich, Igor Po Zakonu Voennogo Vremeni • Under Wartime Law 87

Slak, Franci Bumpstone • Butnskala 86; Hudodelci 88

Slate, Lane Clay Pigeon 71*

Slater, Guy A Pocketful of Rye 87

Slatter, Chris The Project 81

Slatzer, Robert F. The Hellcats 68; Big Foot 73

Slavenska, Mia Zhivoi Lenin 48*; The Great Battle of the Volga 63

Slavinsky, A. The Essential Spark of Jewishness 12

Slavinsky, M. China Liberated • Liberated China • The New China • Osvobozhdeniye Kitai 50*

Sledge, John Bourbon Street Shadows • Invisible Avenger 58*; New Orleans After Dark 58; Four for the Morgue 62

Slesin, Aviva Directed by William Wyler 86; The Ten Year Lunch: The Wit and Legend of the Algonquin Round Table 87

Slijepčević, Vladan The Protégé 66

Slipyj, Rodion Stranger in Hollywood 68

Sloan, James B. Walter Tells the Tale 26; Walter the Prodigal 26; Walter the Sleuth 26; Walter's Day Out 26; Walter's Paying Policy 26; Walter's Worries 26; Phototone Reels 28*

Sloane, P. H. see Sloane, Paul

Sloane, Paul The Coming of Amos 25; A Man Must Live 25; The Shock Punch 25; Too Many Kisses 25; The Clinging Vine 26; Corporal Kate 26; Eve's Leaves 26; Made for Love 26; Turkish Delight 27; The Blue Danube 28; Hearts in Dixie 29*; The Cuckoos 30*; Half Shot at Sunrise 30; The Three Sisters 30; Consolation Marriage • Married in Haste 31; Traveling Husbands 31; Soldiers of Fortune • War Correspondent 32; Terror Aboard 33; Woman Accused 33; Down to Their Last Yacht • Hawaiian Nights 34; The Lone Cowboy 34; Straight Is the Way 34; Here Comes the Band 35; Geronimo! 39; The Sun Sets at Dawn 50

Sloane, Rick Vice Academy 89

Slobodova, Katarina Citlivá Místa 88

Sloman, Anthony Sweet and Sexy 70; Not Tonight, Darling 71

Sloman, Edward The Convict King 15;

The Bond Within 16; Dust 16; The Embodied Thought 16; The Inner Struggle 16; Lone Star 16; Lying Lips 16; The Reclamation 16; Sequel to The Diamond from the Sky 16; The Twinkler 16; A Woman's Daring 16; Fate and the Child 17; The Fighting Gentleman 17; The Frame-Up • High Gear Jeffrey 17; The Gypsy's Trust 17; High Play 17; The Masked Heart 17; My Fighting Gentleman 17; New York Luck 17; Pride and the Man 17; Sands of Sacrifice 17; The Sea Master 17; Shackles of Truth 17; Slam Bang Jim • Snap Judgment 17; A Bit of Jade 18; Fair Enough 18; The Ghost of Rosy Taylor 18; In Bad 18; Mantle of Charity 18; The Midnight Trail 18; Money Isn't Everything 18; Social Briars 18; Molly of the Follies 19; Put Up Your Hands! 19; The Westerners 19; Blind Youth 20; Burning Daylight 20; The Luck of Geraldine Laird 20; The Mutiny of the Elsinore 20; The Sagebrusher 20; The Star Rover 20; The Marriage of William Ashe 21; The Other Woman 21; Pilgrims of the Night 21; Quick Action 21; The Ten Dollar Raise 21; Shattered Idols 22; The Woman He Loved 22; Backbone 23; The Eagle's Feather 23; The Last Hour 23; His People • Proud Heart 25; The Price of Pleasure 25; The Storm Breaker 25; Up the Ladder 25; The Beautiful Cheat 26; Butterflies in the Rain 26; The Old Soak 26; Alias the Deacon 27; Surrender 27; The Foreign Legion 28; We Americans 28; The Busybody • The Kibitzer 29; The Girl on the Barge 29; The Lost Zeppelin 29; Hell's Island 30; Puttin' on the Ritz 30; Soldiers and Women 30; Caught! 31; The Conquering Horde 31; Gun Smoke 31; His Woman 31; Murder by the Clock 31; Wayward 32; Always Tomorrow • There's Always Tomorrow 34; A Dog of Flanders 35; The Jury's Secret 37

Sloman, Ted see Sloman, Edward

Sluizer, George Red Desert Penitentiary 87; Spoorloos • The Vanishing 88

Slutsky, Mikhail One Day in Soviet Russia 41; Day After Day 43; Poet Iv Montan • Yves Montand Sings 56*; Festival in Moscow 59

Smagghe, André One, Two, Three 61*

Small, Edward Clancy in Wall Street 30*

Smallcombe, John An African Dream 88

Smalley, Phillips Bella's Beau 12; The Chorus Girl 12; The Mind Cure 12; Accident Insurance 13; The Broken Spell 13; The Girl Reporter 13; Heroic Harold 13; The Jew's Christmas 13*; Pearl's Admirers 13; That Other Girl 13; Where Charity Begins 13; Willie's Great Scheme 13; Behind the Veil 14*; The Country Mouse 14; False Colors 14*; Lizzie and the Iceman 14; The Merchant of Venice 14*; The Ring 14; Shadowed 14; The Spider and Her Web 14; Willie's Disguise 14; A Cigarette—That's All 15; Jewel 15*; Madcap Betty 15; Scandal 15*; Sunshine Molly 15*; The Yankee Girl 15; The Dumb Girl of

Portici 16*; The Eye of God 16*; The Flirt 16*; Hop—The Devil's Brew 16*; Idle Wives 16*; John Needham's Double 16*; Saving the Family Name 16*; Wanted—A Home 16*; Where Are My Children? 16*; The Double Standard 17; For Husbands Only 17*; The Hand That Rocks the Cradle 17*; The Price of a Good Time 17*; Borrowed Clothes 18*; The Doctor and the Woman 18*; The Forbidden Box 18*; Scandal Mongers 18*; When a Girl Loves 18*; Forbidden 19*; The Blot 21*

Smallwood, Ray C. The Best of Luck 20; Billions 20; The Heart of a Child 20; Madame Peacock 20; Camille 21; My Old Kentucky Home 22; Queen of the Moulin Rouge 22; When the Desert Calls 22

Smart, Ralph The Woodpigeon Patrol 30*; Bush Christmas 46; A Boy, a Girl and a Bike 47; The Facts of Life • Quartet 48*; Bitter Springs 50; Never Take No for an Answer • The Small Miracle 51*; Curtain Up 52; Always a Bride 53

Smawley, Robert J. American Eagle 90

Smedley-Aston, Brian Paul Raymond's Erotica 81

Smetana, Zdeněk Fairy Tales Under Snow • Pohádky Pod Sněhem 85

Smight, Jack I'd Rather Be Rich 64; In Darkness Waiting • Strategy of Terror 64; The Third Day 65; The Bank Breaker • Kaleidoscope 66; Harper • The Moving Target 66; Harry Frigg • Meanwhile, Far from the Front • The Secret War of Harry Frigg 67; No Way to Treat a Lady 67; The Illustrated Man 68; Rabbit, Run 70; The Traveling Executioner 70; Dr. Frankenstein • Frankenstein: The True Story 73; Airport 1975 74; Damnation Alley • Survival Run 74; The Battle of Midway • Midway 76; Fast Break 79; Loving Couples 80; Number One with a Bullet 87

Smiley, Joseph Over the Hills 11*; The Rose's Story 11*; Threads of Destiny 14; Life Without Soul 15; The Love of Women 15; The Path to the Rainbow 15; Rated at $10,000,000 15; Voices from the Past 15; Whom the Gods Would Destroy 15

Smirnov, Andrei Autumn 74

Smit, Branko Sokol Ga Nije Volio 88

Smith, A. Barr see Barr-Smith, A.

Smith, Albert The Girl Alaska 19

Smith, Albert E. Tearing Down the Spanish Flag 1898*

Smith, Beaumont Splendid Fellows 34

Smith, Brian Trenchard see Trenchard-Smith, Brian

Smith, Bud Johnny Be Good 88

Smith, Charles Martin Trick or Treat 86

Smith, Clifford The Conversion of Frosty Blake 15*; The Darkening Trail 15*; The Disciple 15*; Keno Bates—Liar 15*; Mr. Silent Haskins 15*; The Roughneck 15*; The Ruse 15*; Scourge of the Desert 15*; The Taking of Luke McVane 15*; The Aryan 16*; Hell's Hinges 16*; The Devil Dodger 17; The Learnin' of Jim Benton 17; The Medicine Man 17; One Shot Ross 17; The Boss of the Lazy Y 18; By Proxy 18; Cactus Crandall 18; Faith and Endurin' 18;

The Fly God 18; Keith of the Border 18; The Law's Outlaw 18; Paying His Debt 18; The Pretender 18; A Red-Haired Cupid 18; Silent Rider 18; Untamed 18; Wolves of the Border 18; The She-Wolf 19; The Cyclone 20; The Girl Who Dared 20; The Lone Hand 20; Three Gold Coins 20; Crossing Trails 21; The Stranger in Canyon Valley 21; Western Hearts 21; Daring Danger 22; My Dad 22; Scarred Hands 23; Wild Bill Hickok 23*; The Back Trail 24; Daring Chances 24; Fighting Fury 24; Ridgeway of Montana 24; Singer Jim McKee 24; The Western Wallop 24; Bustin' Thru 25; The Call of Courage 25; Don Dare Devil 25; Flying Hoofs 25; The Open Trail • The Red Rider 25; Ridin' Pretty 25; Ridin' Thunder • Riding Thunder 25; A Roaring Adventure 25; The Sign of the Cactus 25; The White Outlaw 25; The Arizona Sweepstakes 26; The Demon 26; The Desert's Toll • The Devil's Toll 26; The Fighting Peacemaker 26; The Man in the Saddle 26*; The Phantom Bullet 26; The Ridin' Rascal 26; Rustlers' Ranch 26; The Scrappin' Kid 26; The Set Up 26; A Six Shootin' Romance 26; Sky High Corral 26; The Terror 26; The Valley of Hell 26; Loco Luck 27; Open Range 27; Spurs and Saddles 27; The Three Outcasts 29; Riders of the Golden Gulch 32; The Texan 32; Devil's Canyon 35; Five Bad Men 35; Ace Drummond 36*; The Adventures of Frank Merriwell 36; Jungle Jim 37*; Radio Patrol 37*; Secret Agent X-9 37*; Wild West Days 37*

Smith, Clive A. Rock 'n' Rule 83; Ring of Power 84

Smith, David Baree, Son of Kazan 18; By the World Forgot 18; The Changing Woman 18; The Dawn of Understanding 18; A Gentleman's Agreement 18; Cupid Forecloses 19; The Enchanted Barn 19; A Fighting Colleen 19; The Little Boss 19; Over the Garden Wall 19; The Wishing Ring Man 19; A Yankee Princess 19; The Courage of Marge O'Doone 20; Pegeen 20; Black Beauty 21; Flower of the North 21; A Guilty Conscience 21; It Can Be Done 21; The Silver Car 21; The Angel of Crooked Street 22; The Little Minister 22; My Wild Irish Rose 22; The Ninety and Nine 22; The Man from Brodney's 23; Masters of Men 23; The Midnight Alarm 23; Pioneer Trails 23; Borrowed Husbands 24; Captain Blood 24; Code of the Wilderness 24; My Man 24; Baree, Son of Kazan 25; Pampered Youth 25; Steele of the Royal Mounted 25

Smith, Digby Escape Dangerous 47
Smith, Dominic Elmo Get the Terrorists 87; Hostage Syndrome 87; Tough Cop 87
Smith, Doug The Great British Striptease 80
Smith, Earl E. Shadow of Chikara • Wishbone Cutter 78
Smith, Eric l'Épine Down on the Farm 22
Smith, Erle O. Terrors 30
Smith, F. Percy Chemical Portraiture

09; Dissolving the Government 09; The Dissolved Government 10; Bewildering Transformations 12; Transformations 14

Smith, George Albert The Awkward Sign Writer • The Sign Writer 1897; Children Paddling at the Seaside 1897; Comic Barber • Comic Shaving 1897; Comic Face • Man Drinking 1897; The Corsican Brothers 1897; The End of All Things • Making Sausages 1897; Gymnastics, Indian Club Performer 1897; Hanging Out the Clothes • Master, Mistress and Maid 1897; The Haunted Castle 1897; The Maid in the Garden 1897; The Miller and the Sweep 1897; Nursing the Baby 1897; Tipsy-Topsy-Turvy 1897; Weary Willie 1897; The X-Ray Fiend • X-Rays 1897; Ally Sloper 1898; Animated Clown Portrait 1898; The Baker and the Sweep 1898; Cinderella • Cinderella and the Fairy Godmother 1898; Faust and Mephistopheles 1898; A Joke on the Gardener • A Practical Joke 1898; The Lady Barber • Woman Barber 1898; The Mesmerist 1898; Photographing a Ghost 1898; The Policeman, the Cook and the Copper 1898; The Runaway Knock 1898; Santa Claus • The Visit of Santa Claus 1898; Waves and Spray 1898; Aladdin and the Wonderful Lamp 1899; Dick Whittington 1899; The Gambler's Wife 1899; A Game of Chess and Kisses 1899; A Good Joke 1899; Good Stories 1899; The Haunted Picture Gallery 1899; The Hungry Countryman • The Sandwiches 1899; The Inexhaustible Cab 1899; The Kiss in the Tunnel 1899; The Legacy 1899; As Seen Through a Telescope 00; A Bad Cigar 00; The Conjurer 00; The Dull Razor 00; Grandma Threading Her Needle 00; Grandma's Reading Glass 00; The House That Jack Built 00; An Incident on Brighton Pier 00; A Jolly Old Couple 00; Let Me Dream Again 00; Miss Ellen Terry at Home 00; The Old Maid's Valentine • The Valentine 00; A Quick Shave and Brush Up 00; Scandal Over the Teacups 00; Snapshotting an Audience 00; They Are Jolly Good Fellows • Two Jolly Old Fellows 00; Two Grinning Yokels 00; Two Old Boys at the Music Hall • The Two Old Sports at the Music Hall 00; The Two Old Sports 00; The Two Old Sports' Game of Nap • The Winning Hand 00; The Two Old Sports' Political Discussion 00; The Village Choir 00; Where Did You Get It? 00; The Adrian Troupe of Cyclists 01; The Bill Poster's Revenge 01; A Good Story 01; The Kitten Nursery 01; The Last Bottle at the Club • The Last Glass of the Two Old Sports 01; The Little Doctor • The Little Doctor and the Sick Kitten • The Sick Kitten 01; Little Willie and the Mouse • The Mouse in the Art School • Tommy and the Mouse in the Art School 01; Mary Jane's Mishap • Mary Jane's Mishap, or Don't Fool with the Paraffin 01; The Monocle—Me and Joe Chamberlain 01; Photograph from an Area Window • A Study in Feet 01; Whiskey vs. Bullets 01; After Dark • After Dark, or The Policeman

and His Lantern 02; The Amazons' March and Evolutions • The March of the Amazons 02; At Last! That Awful Tooth • Oh! That Awful Tooth 02; The Cakewalk 02; The Comedian and the Flypaper 02; The Coronation of Edward VII • The Coronation of Their Majesties King Edward VII and Queen Alexandra • Reproduction, Coronation Ceremonies—King Edward VII • Le Sacre d'Édouard VII 02*; The Donkey and the Serpentine Dancer 02; Dorothy's Dream 02; Episodes in the Life of a Lodger 02; Hilarity on Board Ship 02; His First Cigar, Probably His Last 02; The Irishman and the Button • Oh That Collar Button! 02; The Monk in the Monastery Wine Cellars 02; The Monk's Macaroni Feast 02; The Monk's Ruse for Lunch 02; Mother Goose Nursery Rhymes • Nursery Rhymes 02; Pantomime Girls Having a Lark 02; Pa's Comments on the Morning News 02; Tambourine Dancing Quartette 02; That Awful Cigar 02; Tommy Atkins and His Harriet on a Bank Holiday 02; Too Much of a Good Thing 02; Topsy-Turvy Dance by Three Quaker Maidens 02; The Baby and the Ape 03; The Free Trade Branch 03; John Bull's Fireside • John Bull's Hearth 03; Lettie Limelight in Her Lair 03; The Little Witness 05; A Visit to the Seaside 08; Choosing the Wallpaper 09; Kinemacolor Puzzle 09; Natural Colour Portraiture 09

Smith, Hagen The Legend of Frank Woods 77
Smith, Hamilton The Inner Man 22; Isle of Doubt 22
Smith, Harry No. 1 39; No. 2 42; No. 3 47; Circular Tensions • No. 5 50; No. 4 50; No. 6 51; No. 7 51; No. 8 54; No. 9 54; Mirror Animations • No. 11 56; No. 10 56; Heaven and Earth Magic • The Magic Feature • No. 12 58; No. 13 62; Late Superimpositions • No. 14 65; No. 15 66; No. 16 • The Tin Woodman's Dream 67
Smith, Harry W. Louisiana Territory 53
Smith, Herbert Musical Film Revues 33; On the Air 34; In Town Tonight 35; Night Mail 35; British Lion Varieties 36; Soft Lights and Sweet Music 36; They Didn't Know 36; Calling All Stars 37; It's a Grand Old World 37; Leave It to Me 37; Around the Town 38; I've Got a Horse 38; All at Sea 39; Home from Home 39
Smith, Howard Marjoe 72*; Gizmo 77
Smith, Jack Fisherman's Luck 00; A Funny Story 00; Living Statues 00; A Morning Wash 00; Scenes Between Two Well Known Comedians 00; Curing a Jealous Wife 07; Mind Your Own Business 07; The Page Boy and the Baby 07; They Would Play Cards 07; Truthful Telegrams 07; Why Jenkins Wears the Blue Ribbon 07; Daddy As of Old 08; The Lady Luna(tic)'s Hat 08; The Magic Box 08; The Robber and the Jew 08; The Tramp 08; The Burning Home 09; The Duped Othello • The Theatrical Chimney Sweep 09; The Escapades of Teddy Bear 09; Love vs. Science 09; My Dolly 09; The Polite

Parson 09; Suspected, or The Mysterious Lodger 09; What Happened to Brown 09

Smith, Jack A Film for Maria 62

Smith, Jan Darnley see Darnley-Smith, Jan

Smith, John The Masculine Mystique 85*; Sitting in Limbo 86; Train of Dreams 87

Smith, Ken Little Angel • La Sonrisa de la Vírgen 61*

Smith, Kent Forever and a Day 43*; Taking Tiger Mountain • Trechi Mynydd y Teigr 83*

Smith, Marshall Judas City • Satan's Bed 65

Smith, Maura Fun Girls • Towing • Who Stole My Wheels? 78

Smith, Maurice Bad Blood • Julie Darling 82*

Smith, Mel The Tall Guy 89

Smith, Noel Mason Kid Speed 24*; Clash of the Wolves 25; The Blue Streak 26; The Broadway Gallant 26; Fangs of Justice 26; The Flying Mail 26; The Merry Cavalier 26; The Night Patrol 26; Cross Breed 27; One Chance in a Million 27; The Snarl of Hate 27; Where Trails Begin 27; Danger Trail 28; Fangs of Fate 28; The Law's Lash 28; Marlie the Killer 28; The Bachelor's Club 29; Back from Shanghai 29; The Heroic Lover 29; Dancing Dynamite 31; Daredevil Dick • Yankee Don 31; Scareheads • The Speed Reporter 31; Fighting Pilot 35; The California Mail 36; King of Hockey • King of the Ice Rink 36; On Secret Service • Trailin' West 36; Blazing Sixes 37; The Cherokee Strip • Strange Laws 37; Guns of the Pecos 37; Over the Goal 37; Mystery House 38; Code of the Secret Service 39; The Cowboy Quarterback 39; Dead End Kids at Military School • Dead End Kids on Dress Parade • Dress Parade • On Dress Parade 39*; Private Detective 39; Secret Service of the Air 39; Torchy Plays with Dynamite 39; Always a Bride 40; Calling All Husbands 40; Father Is a Prince 40; Hometowners • Ladies Must Live 40; Burma Convoy 41; The Case of the Black Parrot 41; Here Comes Happiness 41; The Nurse's Secret 41; Gang Busters 42*; Cattle Town 52

Smith, Paul Margie 40*; Sandy Gets Her Man 40*

Smith, Peter The Trouble with 2B 72; What Next? • What's Next? 74; A Private Enterprise 75

Smith, Peter K. No Surrender 85

Smith, R. L. see Lewis, Herschell Gordon

Smith, Robert The Lovechild 87

Smith, Sidney Old Doc Yak 13; Old Doc Yak and the Artist's Dream 13; Old Doc Yak's Christmas 13; Doc Yak and Santa Claus 14; Doc Yak and the Limited Train 14; Doc Yak Bowling 14; Doc Yak, Cartoonist 14; Doc Yak, Moving Picture Artist 14; Doc Yak Plays Golf 14; Doc Yak, the Marksman 14; Doc Yak, the Poultryman 14; Doc Yak's Bottle 14; Doc Yak's Cats 14; Doc Yak's Temperance Lec-

ture 14; Doc Yak's Wishes 14; Doc Yak's Zoo 14; Over the Fence and Out 14

Smith, Sidney Hello London • London Calling 58

[Smithee, Alan (Allen)] [pseudonym] Death of a Gunfighter • The Last Gunfighter • Patch [Don Siegel, Robert Totten] 67; Fade-In [Jud Taylor] 68; Ghost Fever [Lee Madden] 85; Home Front • Morgan Stewart's Coming Home [Paul Aaron, Terry Winsor] 85; Let's Get Harry [Stuart Rosenberg] 85; Stitches [Rod Holcomb] 85; I Love N.Y. [Gianni Bozzacchi] 87; The Shrimp on the Barbie [Michael Gottlieb] 90]

Smolan, Sandy Rachel River 87

Smoljak, Ladislav Nejistá Sezóna 88

Smyczek, Karel Krajina s Nábytkem 86; Proč? 87; Sedm Hladových 88

Smythe, Ernest Monkey Love 17

Sneller, Sherry Robinson Crusoe 87

Snoad, Harold Not Now Comrade 77*

Snodgrass, Richard Legacy 63

Snody, Robert Kiss Me • The Love Kiss 30; Di Que Me Quieres • Say That You Love Me 39; The Middleton Family at the N.Y. World's Fair 39

Snow, H. A. The Great White North • Lost in the Arctic 28*

Snow, Michael A to Z 56; New York Eye and Ear Control • A Walking Woman Work 64; Short Shave 65; Standard Time 67; Wavelength 67; Back and Forth 69; Dripping Water 69*; One Second in Montreal 69; Side Seat Paintings Slides Sound Film 70; La Région Centrale 71; Breakfast • Table Top Dolly 72; Rameau's Nephew by Diderot (Thanx to Dennis Young) by Wilma Schoen 74; Two Sides to Every Story 74; Presents 81; So Is This 82; Seated Figures 88

Snow, Sidney The Great White North • Lost in the Arctic 28*

Snyder, Mike Caged in Paradiso 90

Snyder, Robert Blood Brothers 53

Soavi, Michele Deliria 87; La Chiesa • The Church 89

Sobel, Mark S. Access Code 84; Sweet Revenge 86

Sociar, Tridro Incertidumbre 36*

Socias, I. Las Cinco Advertencias de Satanás • Satan's Five Warnings 39

Soderbergh, Steven sex, lies, and videotape 89

Soet, John Steven Fire in the Night 86

Soffici, Mario North Wind • Viento Norte 37; Cadetes de San Martín 39; Prisioneros de la Tierra 39; El Alma del Bandoneón • The Soul of the Accordion 40; Héroes Sin Fama 40; The Old Doctor • El Viejo Doctor 40; El Extraño Caso del Hombre y la Bestia • El Hombre y la Bestia • The Man and the Beast • El Sensacional y Extraño Caso del Hombre y la Bestia • The Strange Case of the Man and the Beast 51

Soffin, Alan Confessor 73*

Sohnlein, Rainer Marianne and Sofie 84

Soifer, Josef The Beilis Case 17; Don't Build Your Happiness on Your Wife and

Child 17; Leah's Suffering 17; Bruised by the Storms of Life 18

Soinio, Olli Kuutamosonaatti 88

Sokal, Henri They Met on Skis 40

Sokdowska, Anna The Great Big World and Little Children • Wielka, Większa, Największa 62; ESD 87

Sokurov, Alexander Man's Solitary Voice • Odinokij Golos Celoveka 78; Heartless Grief • Skorbnoe Beschuvstvie 87; Day of Darkness • Dni Satmenyia 89

Solan, Peter Boxer a Smrt • The Boxer and Death 62; O Slave a Trave • On Glory and Grass 86

Solanas, Fernando La Hora de los Hornos • The Hour of the Furnaces 66*; Actualización Política y Doctrinaria para la Toma del Poder • Perón: Actualización Política y Doctrinaria para la Toma del Poder 71*; Perón: La Revolución Justicialista • La Revolución Justicialista 71*; Los Hijos de Fierro 76; Tangos • Tangos—L'Exil de Gardel • Tangos—The Exile of Gardel 85; South • Sur 87

Solares, Gilberto Martínez see Martínez Solares, Gilberto

Solás, Humberto Casablanca 61; Minerva Traduce el Mar 62*; El Retrato 63; Variaciones 63; El Acoso 64; La Acusación 65; Manuela 65; Lucía 68; Un Día de Noviembre 72; Simparele 74; Cantata de Chile 75; Nacer en Leningrado 77; Wilfredo Lam 78; Cecilia Valdés 82; Un Hombre de Éxito • A Successful Man 86

Soldati, Giovanni Attention • L'Attenzione 85; The American Bride • La Sposa Americana 86

Soldati, Mario La Principessa Tarakanova 37; La Signora di Montecarlo 38; Dora Nelson 39*; Due Milioni per un Sorriso 39*; Tutto per la Donna 40; Little Old-Fashioned World • Little Old World • Old-Fashioned World • Piccolo Mondo Antico 41; Tragica Notte 41; Malombra 42; High Places • Quartieri Alti 43; His Young Wife • Le Miserie del Signor Travet 45; Eugenia Grandet 46; Daniele Cortis 47; Chi È Dio? 48; Flight Into France • Fuga in Francia 48; Quel Bandito Sono Io! 49; Botta e Risposta 50; Donne e Briganti • Of Love and Bandits 50; Her Favourite Husband • The Taming of Dorothy 50; È l'Amor Che Mi Rovina 51; O.K. Nero • O.K. Nerone 51; Il Segno di Zorro 51; The Adventures of Mandrin • The Affair of Madame Pompadour • Le Avventure di Mandrin • Captain Adventure • Don Juan's Night of Love • Mountain Brigand 52; Jolanda—La Figlia del Corsaro Nero • Yolanda—The Daughter of the Black Pirate 52; La Provinciale • The Wayward Wife 52; The Three Pirates • I Tre Corsari 52; La Mano dello Straniero • The Stranger's Hand 53; La Donna del Fiume • Woman of the River 54; Of Life and Love • Questa È la Vita 54*; Guerra e Pace • War and Peace 55*; Era di Venerdi 17 • The Virtuous Bigamist 57; Italia Piccola 57; Policarpo • Policarpo de Tappetti, Ufficiale di Scrittura • Policarpo, Master

Writer • Policarpo, Ufficiale di Scrittura **59**

Sole, Alfred Alice, Sweet Alice • Communion • Holy Terror 76; Tanya's Island 80; Pandemonium • Thursday the Twelfth 82

Soler, Julián Los Platillos Voladores • Los Platos Voladores 55; El Castillo de los Monstruos • Castle of the Monsters • Noche de Terror 57; Santo Contra Blue Demon en la Atlántida 68

Solito, Giacinto La Gioconda 58

Sollima, Sergio L'Amore Difficile • Erotica • Of Wayward Love 62*; Agent 3S3—Passport to Hell 65; Requiem for a Secret Agent 65; The Big Gundown • El Halcón y la Presa • La Resa dei Conti 66; Faccia a Faccia • Face to Face 67; Corri, Uomo, Corri • Run, Man, Run 68; Città Violenta • The Family • The Final Shot • Violent City 70; Blood in the Streets • The Revolver 75

Solntseva, Yulia Shchors • Shors 39*; Bucovina-Ukrainian Land • Bukovyna-Zemlya Ukrayinska 40; Liberation • Osvobozhdeniye 40*; The Battle for Our Soviet Ukraine • Bitva za Nashu Radyansku Ukrayinu • Bitva za Nashu Sovetskayu Ukrainu • The Fight for Our Soviet Ukraine 43*; Pobeda na Pravoberezhnoi Ukrainye • Pobeda na Pravoberezhnoi Ukrainye i Izgnanie Nemetsikh Zakhvatchikov za Predeli Ukrainskikh Sovetskikh Zemel • Ukraine in Flames • Victory in Right-Bank Ukraine • Victory in Right-Bank Ukraine and the Expulsion of the Germans from the Boundaries of the Ukrainian Soviet Earth • Victory in the Ukraine • Victory in the Ukraine and the Expulsion of the Germans from the Boundaries of the Ukrainian Soviet Earth 45*; Life in Bloom • Life in Blossom • Michurin 47*; Igor Bulichov 53; The Reluctant Inspectors 55; Poem of a Sea • Poem of an Inland Sea • Poem of the Sea • Poema o Morye 58*; Chronicle of Flaming Years • The Flaming Years • History of the Burning Years • Povest' Plammennykh Let • Story of the Flaming Years • Story of the Turbulent Years • The Turbulent Years 61; The Enchanted Desna • Zacharovannaya Desna 64; Nezabyvayemi • Ukraine in Flames • The Unforgettable 68; The Golden Gate • Zolotye Vorota 69; Such High Mountains 74

Soloman, David Kentucky Days 23; South Sea Love 23; Love Letters 24

Solomon, David see Soloman, David

Solondz, Todd Fear, Anxiety and Depression 89

Soloviev, Alexander Clown George 32

Soloviev, Sergei Chuzhaja, Belaja i Rjaboj • The White Dove 86; Assa 88

Solt, Andrew This Is Elvis 81*; It Came from Hollywood 82*; Imagine: John Lennon 88

Solter, Harry The Lash of Power 17; The Spotted Lily 17; The Wife He Bought 18

Soltero, José Rodríguez see Rodríguez Soltero, José

Solum, Ola Orion's Belt • Orions Belte

85; Deadly Illusion • Turnaround 86

Solvay, P. see Batzella, Luigi

Solvay, Paolo see Batzella, Luigi

Solvay, Paul see Batzella, Luigi

Solway, Clifford Mr. Kennedy, Mr. Reagan and the Big, Beautiful, Beleaguered American Dream 67

Sólyom, András Doktor Minorka Vidor Nagy Napja • Professor Vidor Minorka's Great Day 87

Somai, Shinji Typhoon Club 84; Shonben Raidaa 85; The Catch • Cyoei no Mure 86; Hikaru Onna • Luminous Woman 87

Somers, Dalton Eggs Is Eggs 14; The Girl and the Gold Mine 14; In Pawn 14; A Modern Don Juan 14; A Modern Highwayman 14; The People of the Rocks 14; The Sentence Is Death 14; The Tramp and the Lady 14

Somers, Gerald The Romance of Annie Laurie 20

Somersaulter, J. P. Donna Rosebud 86

Somich, James The Losers 68*

Sommer, Paul The Dumb Conscious Mind 42*; King Midas, Junior 42*; Old Blackout Joe 42*; Black and Blue Market • The Cocky Bantam 43; The Fly in the Ointment 43; He Can't Make It Stick 43*; The Playful Pest 43; Professor Small and Mister Tall 43*; The Rocky Road to Ruin 43; The Vitamin G-Man 43*; Lionel Lion 44; Mutt 'n' Bones 44; River Ribber 45; Simple Siren 45

Sommerfeldt, Gunnar Growth of the Soil 29

Somnes, George Broadway Singer • Torch Singer 33*; The Girl in 419 33*; Midnight Club 33*; Wharf Angel 34*

Somogyi, Julius Der Dorfsgolem • The Golem's Last Adventure • Der Golems Letzte Abenteuer 21

Somptier, René le see Le Somptier, René

Son, Nguyen Xuan Fairytale for 17-Year-Olds 88

Sone, John Love in a Four Letter World 70

Song, Chong The Happy Bachelors 85

Song, Cunshou Ghost in the Mirror • Gu Jing You Hun 74

Sonik, Subhash Ghar Mein Ram Gali Mein Shyam 88

Sontag, Susan Duet for Cannibals 69; Brother Carl 72; Promised Lands 74

Soo-gil, Kim see Kim, Soo-gil

Soós, Mária Tandem • Városbújócska 85

Sopi, Agim Man of Earth • Njeriu Prej Dheu 86

Sorak, Dejan Officer with a Rose • Oficir s Ružom 87

Sordi, Alberto Fumo di Londra 65; Scusi, Lei È Favorevole o Contrario? 66; Un Italiano in America 67; Amore Mio Aiutami 69; Le Coppie • Les Couples • The Couples 70*; Polvere di Stelle 73; Finchè C'È Guerra C'È Speranza 74; Il Commune Senso del Pudore 76; Dove Vai in Vacanza? 78*; Io e Caterina 80; In Viaggio con Papà 82; Io So Che Tu Sai Che Io So

82; Il Tassinaro 82; Tutti Dentro 84; Un Tassinaro a New York • A Taxi Driver in New York 87

Sørensen, Edward Schnedler see Schnedler-Sørensen, Edward

Sørensen, Sune Lund see Lund-Sørensen, Sune

Soria, Gabriel Chucho el Roto 35; The Dead Speak • Los Muertos Hablan 35; Martín Garatuza 35; Mater Nostra 36; Come On, Ponciano • Ora Ponciano 37; The Virgin of Guadalupe 43; La Dama de las Camelias 44

Soriano, Ricardo It Happened in Spain • El Sombrero de Tres Picos • The Three-Cornered Hat • La Traviesa Molinera 34*

Sorin, Carlos A King and His Movie • La Película del Rey 86; Eversmile, New Jersey 89

Sorkin, Marc Teilnehmer Antwortet Nicht 32*; The Pasha's Wives 42

Sorokhtin, Igor Conquerors of the Night 33*

Sos, Mária see Soós, Mária

Sota, Bruno Ve see Ve Sota, Bruno

Soth, Sándor A Szárnyas Ügynök 88

Sotirakis, Dimitri see Sotos, Jim

Soto, Bruno de see Ve Sota, Bruno

Sotos, Jim Forced Entry • The Last Victim 75; Sweet 16 81; Hot Moves 84; Beverly Hills Brats 89

Sotra, Zdravko Držanje za Vazduh • Hanging on to Thin Air 86; Braća Po Materi 88

Souda, Said Ali La Vengeance du Protecteur 87

Soukup, Jaroslav Pěsti ve Tmě 86; Discopříběh 87; Kamarád do Deště 88

Soulanes, Louis Les Filles Sement le Vent • The Fruit Is Ripe 61; Le Bal des Voyous • Les Femmes • Playmates 69*

Southwell, Gilbert A Child's Dream of Christmas 12; Detective Ferris 12; Father's Coat to the Rescue 12; French vs. English 12; Frustrated 12; The Heart of a Man 12; Jack the Handy Man 12; The Misunderstanding 12; The Submarine Plans 12

Soutter, Michel Faces of Love 78; Signé Renart 85

Souza, Steve de see De Souza, Steve

Sow, Thierno Faty The Camp at Thiaroye • Camp de Thiaroye 88*

Spaak, Charles Le Mystère Barton 49

Spafford, Robert Heaven on Earth 60; The Christine Keeler Affair • The Keeler Affair • Scandal '64 64

Spangler, Larry A Knife for the Ladies 73; The Soul of Nigger Charley 73; The Life and Times of Xaviera Hollander 74; The Black Rider • Joshua 76; Silent Sentence 83

Sparey, John Starchaser: The Legend of Orin 85*

Sparks, Teresa Over the Summer 84

Sparr, Robert A Swingin' Summer 65; More Dead Than Alive 68; Once You Kiss a Stranger • The Perfect Set-Up • You Can't Win 'Em All 69

Spassov, Krassimir Forget That Case • Zabravote Tozi Slochai 86

Goose 19; Sufficiency 19; Beaten by a Hare 20; The Best Mouse Loses 20; The Bomb Idea 20; The Chinese Honeymoon 20*; The Chinese Question 20; Dots and Dashes 20; A Family Affair 20*; The Great Cheese Robber 20*; Jerry and the Five Fifteen Train • The Return of the Five Fifteen 20; Kats Is Kats 20; Love's Labor Lost 20; A Punk Piper 20; A Quick Change 20; The Rhyme That Went Wrong 20; The Tale of a Wag 20*; A Tax from the Rear 20; A Thrilling Drill 20; A Tough Pull 20; The Train Robber 20; The Trained Horse 20; A Warm Reception 20*; Water Water Everywhere 20; Without Coal 20; The Wrong Track 20*; The Awful Spook 21*; The Hinges on the Bar Room Door 21; How I Became Krazy 21; Scrambled Eagles 21; The Wireless Wire-Walkers 21; Col. Heeza Liar's Treasure Island 22; Col. Heeza Liar and the Ghost 23; Col. Heeza Liar, Detective 23; Col. Heeza Liar in the African Jungles 23; Col. Heeza Liar in Uncle Tom's Cabin 23; Col. Heeza Liar, Strikebreaker 23; Col. Heeza Liar's Burglar 23; Col. Heeza Liar, Bull Thrower 24; Col. Heeza Liar, Cave Man 24; Col. Heeza Liar, Daredevil 24; Col. Heeza Liar, Nature Faker 24; Col. Heeza Liar, Sky Pilot 24; Col. Heeza Liar the Lyin' Tamer 24; Col. Heeza Liar's Horseplay 24; Col. Heeza Liar's Mysterious Case 24; Col. Heeza Liar's Romance 24

Stallone, Sylvester Paradise Alley 78; Rocky II 79; Rocky III 82; Staying Alive 83; Rocky IV 85

Stambler, Robert Strange Lovers • Stranger Than Love 63

Stambula, Nikolai Karusel na Bazarnoy Ploshchadi • Merry-Go-Round in a Market Square 87

Stamper, Dave Mother Knows Best 28*

Stan, Nicu Cale Liberă 88

Stanchina, Peter Die Gläserne Kugel • The Glass Ball 39

Stanlaws, Penrhyn At the End of the World 21; The House That Jazz Built 21; The Little Minister 21; The Law and the Woman 22; Over the Border 22; Pink Gods 22; Singed Wings 22

Stanley, B. F. The Other Woman's Story 25

Stanley, John Nightmare in Blood 76

Stanley, Paul Cry Tough 59; Three Guns for Laredo • Three Guns for Texas 67*; The Bull of the West 71*; Cotter 72

Stanley, Richard Hardware 90

Stannard, Eliot The Courage of a Coward 14; Fatal Fingers 16*; Jimmy 16*; The Laughing Cavalier 17*; Profit and the Loss 17*

Stanner, C. The Magic Snowman • A Winter Tale 87

Stanojevic, Stanislav Illustres Inconnus 85

Stanton, Richard The Beast 16; The Love Thief 16; Durand of the Bad Lands 17; Her Temptation 17; North of 53 17*; One Touch of Sin 17; The Scarlet Pimpernel 17; The Spy 17; The Yankee Way 17;

The Caillaux Case 18; Cheating the Public 18; Rough and Ready 18; Stolen Honor 18; Why America Will Win 18; Why I Should Not Marry • Why I Would Not Marry 18; Checkers 19; Jungle Trail 19; Face at Your Window 20; Thunderclap 21; McGuire of the Mounted 23; American Pluck 25

Stanton, W. Dane The Life of Lord Kitchener 17*

Stapleford, George Mountain Charlie 82

Stapp, Philip Symmetry 67

Starczewski, Jerzy Heather • Wrzos 38

Starevitch, Ladislas see Starewicz, Władysław

Starewicz, Władysław Christmas Eve 13; Strashnaya Mest • A Terrible Revenge 13; Ruslan i Ludmila 14; The Snow Maiden 14; Inhabitant of a Desert Isle • Zhitel Nyeobitayemovo Ostrova 15; Na Varshavskom Trakte • On the Warsaw Highroad • On the Warsaw Highway 16; Jola 20; Fétiche 33; Le Roman de Renard 39; Fleur de Fougère 50

Stark, Curt A. Im Schatten des Meeres • In the Shadow of the Sea • Der Schatten des Meeres • The Sea's Shadow 12

Stark, Graham Simon, Simon 70; The Magnificent Seven Deadly Sins 71

Stark, W. E. A Barnyard Hamlet 17; Cleopatra and Her Easy Mark 23; Columbus Discovers a New Whirl 23; How Troy Was Collared 23; The Jones Boys' Sister 23; Kidding Captain Kidd 23; Napoleon Not So Great 23; Rip Without a Wink 23; Robinson Crusoe Returns on Friday 23; A Whale of a Story 23; What Did William Tell? 23; Why Sitting Bull Stood Up 23

Starkey, Richard see Starr, Ringo

Starr, Bruce Boogeyman II • Revenge of the Boogeyman 82*

Starr, Ringo Born to Boogie 72

Starrett, Jack Run, Angel, Run 69; Cry Blood, Apache 70; The Losers • Nam Angels 70; Slaughter 72; The Strange Vengeance of Rosalie 72; Cleopatra Jones 73; The Dion Brothers • The Gravy Train 74; Race with the Devil 75; The Hollywood Man 76; A Small Town in Texas 76; Final Chapter, Walking Tall 77; Kiss My Grits • Summer Heat • A Texas Legend 82

Stather, Frank The Fatal Formula 15; The Golden Chance 15; The Sunshine and Clouds of Paradise Alley 15

Staub, Ralph Country Gentlemen 36; The Mandarin Mystery 36; Sitting on the Moon 36; Affairs of Cappy Ricks 37; Join the Marines 37; Meet the Boy Friend 37; Navy Blues 37; Mama Runs Wild 38; Prairie Moon 38; Western Jamboree 38; Chip of the Flying U 39; Danger Ahead 40; The Sky Bandits 40; Yukon Flight 40

Staudte, Wolfgang Akrobat Schö-ö-ön 43; Ich Hab' von Dir Geträumt 44; Frau Über Bord • Kabine 27 45; Der Mann Dem Man den Namen Stahl 45; Die Mörder Sind Unter Uns • Murderers Among Us • The Murderers Are Among Us • The Murderers Are Amongst Us 46; Die Seltsamen Abenteuer des Herrn Fridolin B 48; The Kaiser's Lackey • The

Submissive • The Underdog • Der Untertan 49; Rotation 49; Schicksal aus Zweiter Hand 49; Fünf Mädchen und Ein Mann • Geschichte von Fünf Städten • A Tale of Five Cities • A Tale of Five Women 51*; Die Geschichte des Kleinen Muck • Little Mook • The Story of Little Mook 53; Leuchtfeuer 54; Ciske • Ciske — A Child Wants Love • Ciske de Rat • Ciske — Ein Kind Braucht Liebe 55; Mutter Courage und Ihr Kinder 55; Rose Bernd • The Sins of Rose Bernd 56; Escape from Sahara 57; Madeleine und der Legionär 57; Always Victorious • Il Capitano • Kanonen-Serenade 58; Der Maulkorb • The Muzzle 58; Rosen für den Staatsanwalt • Roses for the Prosecutor 59; Fairground • Kirmes 60; The Last Witness • Der Letzte Zeuge 60; Die Glücklichen Jahre der Thorwalds 62*; Die Rebellion 62; Die Dreigroschenoper • The Threepenny Opera 63; Herrenpartie • Men's Outing • Stag Party 64; The Lamb • Das Lamm 64; Crooks' Honor • Ganovenehre • Hoodlums' Honor 66; Heimlichkeiten • Secrets 68; Die Herren mit der Weissen Weste • The Robbers • Those Gentlemen Who Have a Clean Sheet 70; Fluchtweg St. Pauli • Fluchtweg St. Pauli — Grossalarm für die Davidswache • Heisse Spur St. Pauli 71; Uhrwerk Orange 72; The Sea Wolf 73; Memories • Yesterday's Tomorrow • Zwischengleis 78

Stawiński, Jerzy Stefan No More Divorces • Rozwodów Nie Będzie 63; The Penguin • Pingwin 64; Christmas Eve • Przedświąteczny Wieczór 66*

Stebbins, Robert see Meyers, Sidney

Steckery, Alan The World Is Just a "B" Movie 71*

Steckler, Len Mad Bull 77*

Steckler, Ray Dennis Drivers in Hell • Drivers to Hell • Wild Ones on Wheels 61; The Incredibly Strange Creatures • The Incredibly Strange Creatures Who Stopped Living and Became Crazy Mixed-Up Zombies • The Incredibly Strange Creatures Who Stopped Living and Became Mixed-Up Zombies • The Teenage Psycho Meets Bloody Mary 62; Wild Guitar 62; The Maniacs Are Loose • The Monsters Are Loose • The Thrill Killers 64; Rat Pfink and Boo-Boo 64; The Lemon Grove Kids Meet the Monsters 66; Sinthia the Devil's Doll 68; Body Fever • The Last Original B-Movie • Super Cool 69; Blood Monster • Blood Shack • The Chopper 71; Bloody Jack the Ripper 72; The Hollywood Strangler Meets the Skid Row Slasher 79

Steensland, David Escapes 85

Stefaniak, Piotr Stanislaw and Anna • Stanisław i Anna 87*

Stefankovičova, Eva Salty Sweets • Slané Cukríky 85; Nemožná 88

Stegani, Giorgio Adiós, Gringo 65; Al di Là della Legge • Beyond the Law • Die Letzte Rechnung Zählst Du Selbst 67; Gentleman Joe...Uccidi 67

Steger, Julius The Libertine 16*; The Prima Donna's Husband 16*; The Law of Compensation 17*; Redemption 17*; The

Burden of Proof 18; Cecilia of the Pink Roses 18; Her Mistake 18; The Belle of New York 19; The Hidden Truth 19

Stein, Bob The Zodiac Couples 70*

Stein, Jeff The Kids Are Alright 79

Stein, Paul Der Teufel der Liebe 19; Arme Violetta • The Red Peacock 20; Die Geschlossene Kette 20; Das Martyrium 20; Der Ewige Kampf 21; Das Opfer der Helen 21; The Devil's Pawn 22; Ein Traum vom Glück 24; Ich Liebe Dich 25; Die Insel der Träume 25; Liebesfeuer 25; My Official Wife 26; The Climbers 27; Don't Tell the Wife 27; The Forbidden Woman 27; Manmade Woman • Manmade Women 28; Show Folks 28; Her Private Affair 29; The Office Scandal 29; This Thing Called Love 29; The Lottery Bride 30; One Romantic Night 30*; Sin Takes a Holiday 30; Born to Love 31; The Common Law 31; Lily Christine 32; A Woman Commands 32; Red Wagon 33; The Song You Gave Me 33; April Blossoms • April Romance • Blossom Time 34; Heart's Desire 35; Mimi 35; Cafe Colette • Danger in Paris 36; Faithful 36; Black Limelight 38; Jane Steps Out 38; Just Like a Woman 38; The Outsider 39; Poison Pen 39; Gentleman of Venture • It Happened to One Man 40; The Saint Meets the Tiger 41; Breach of Promise 42; Kiss the Bride Goodbye 44; Twilight Hour 44; Waltz Time 45; The Laughing Lady 46; Lisbon Story 46; Counterblast • Devil's Plot 48; Murder on the Air • The Twenty Questions Murder Mystery 49

Stein, Peter Class Enemy 84

Steinberg, David Paternity 81; Going Berserk 83

Steinberg, David Max Severance 88

Steinberg, Ziggy The Boss' Wife 86

Steinbicker, Reinhardt Liebe, Tod und Teufel 35*

Steiner, Ralph H2O 29; Mechanical Principle 31; Surf and Seaweed 31; Pie in the Sky 34*; People of the Cumberlands 37*; The City 39*

Steinhoff, Hans Bräutigam auf Kredit 21; Der Bettelstudent 22; Birbi 22; Der Falsche Dimitri 22; Kleider Machen Leute 22; Inge Larsen 23; Mensch Gegen Mensch 24; Gräfin Mariza 25; Der Herr des Todes 26; Die Tragödie eines Verlorenen 26; Wien-Berlin 26; Das Frauenhaus von Rio 27; The Alley Cat 29; Nachtgestalten 29; The Three Kings 29; Rosenmontag 30; Mein Leopold 31; Die Pranke 31; Der Wahre Jakob 31; Ein Mädel der Strasse • Scampolo—Ein Kind der Strasse 32; Hitlerjunge Quex 33; Madame Wünscht Keine Kinder 33; Mutter und Kind 33; Freut Euch des Lebens 34; Die Insel 34; Liebe Muss Verstanden Sein 34; Lockvogel 34; Unsere Fahne Flattert Uns Voran 34; Der Alte und der Junge König 35; Eine Frau Ohne Bedeutung 36; Keine Angst vor Liebe 36; Ein Volksfeind 37; Tanz auf dem Vulkan 38; Robert Koch • Robert Koch der Bekämpfer des Todes 39; Die Geierwally 40; Ohm Krüger 41; Rembrandt 42;

Gabriele Dambrone 43; Shiva und die Galgenblume 45

Steinmann, Danny Savage Streets 84; Friday the 13th Part V: A New Beginning 85; Subterraneans 88

Steinmetz, Dennis Record City 77

Steklý, Karel Siréna • The Strike 47; Actor Jesenius' Strange Friendships • Podivná Přátelství Herce Jesenia 85

Stell, Aaron The Gallant One 64

Stelli, Jean The Gold of Christobal • L'Or du Cristobal 39*; The Blue Veil • Le Voile Bleu 42; Operation Abduction 57

Stelling, Jos The Illusionist 85; The Pointsman • De Wisselwachter 86

Stellman, Martin For Queen and Country 88

Stelzer, Manfred The Chinese Are Coming • Die Chinesen Kommen 87

Stember, John 7254 71

Stemmle, Robert A. Glückspilze 36; Ein Mädel mit Tempo 37; Der Raub der Sabinerinnen 37; Gleisdreieck 38; A People Wants to Live • Ein Volk Will Leben 39; The Ballad of Berlin • The Berliner • Berliner Ballade 48; Toxi 52; Emil and the Detectives 54

Stengel, Christian Dreams of Love 54

Stenholm, Katherine Macbeth 50; Red Runs the River 63

Steno Al Diavolo la Celebrità • A Night of Fame • One Night of Fame 48*; Totò Cerca Casa • Totò Looks for a House • Totò Wants a Home 49*; È Arrivato il Cavaliere 50*; It's a Dog's Life • Vita da Cani 50*; Cops and Robbers • Guardie e Ladri 51*; Totò e i Re di Roma 51*; Le Infedeli • The Unfaithfuls 52*; Totò a Colori 52*; Totò e le Donne 52*; Cinema d'Altri Tempi 53; A Day in Court • Un Giorno in Pretura 53; Man, Beast and Virtue • L'Uomo, la Bestia e la Virtù 53; An American in Rome • Un Americano a Roma 54; Le Avventure di Giacomo Casanova • Sins of Casanova 54; Piccola Posta 55; Mio Figlio Nerone • My Son Nero • Nero's Big Weekend • Nero's Mistress • Nero's Weekend 56; Female Times Three • Femmine Tre Volte • Three Times a Woman 57; Susanna Tutta Panna 57; Totò in the Moon • Totò nella Luna 57; Guardia, Ladro e Cameriera 58; Mia Nonna Polizzioto 58; Hard Times for Dracula • Hard Times for Vampires • My Uncle the Vampire • Tempi Duri per i Vampiri • Uncle Was a Vampire 59; The Overtaxed • I Tartassati 59; Totò, Eva e il Pennello Proibito 59; A Noi Piace Freddo! • Some Like It Cold 60; Letto a Tre Piazze 60; Un Militare e Mezzo 60; Psycossissimo 61; La Ragazza di Mille Mesi 61; Copacabana Palace • Girl Game • The Saga of the Flying Hostesses 62; I Due Colonelli • The Two Colonels 62; I Moschettieri del Mare 62; Totò Diabolicus 62; Gli Eroi del West • I Gemelli del Texas 63; Totò Contro i Quattro 63; Amore all'Italiana • I Superdiabolici 65; Letti Sbagliati 65; Rose Rosse per Angelica 66; Arriva Dorellik 67; Capriccio all'Italiana 68*; La Feldmarescialla • The

Girl Field Marshal 68; Il Trapianto 69; Cose di Cosa Nostra 71; Il Vichingo Venuto dal Sud 71; Execution Squad • La Polizia Ringrazia 72; Il Terrore con gli Occhi Storti 72; L'Uccello Migratore 72; Flatfoot • The Knockout Cop 74; Febbre da Cavallo 77; Tre Tigri Contro Tre Tigri 77*; Amori Miei 78; Doppio Delitto 78; Flatfoot on the Nile 78; Dr. and Mrs. Jekyll • Dr. Jekyll, Jr. • Dottor Jekyll e Gentile Signora • Il Dottore Jekyll, Jr. • Jekyll, Jr. 79; Mi Faccia Causa • Sue Me 85

Steno, Stefano see Steno

Stepanova, Lidia Inside the U.S.S.R. 61*

Stephani, Frederick Atomic Rocketship • Flash Gordon • Rocket Ship • Space Soldiers • Spaceship to the Unknown 36; Flash Gordon • Perils from the Planet Mongo 36

Stephen, A. C. Orgy of the Dead 65; Lady Godiva Rides 69; The Cocktail Hostesses 76; Beach Bunnies 77

Stephen, Mary Shades of Silk 79

Stephens, Jack Blinker's Spy Spotter 71

Stephens, Peter Mustang 59

Stephens, Russel Regeneration 88

Stephensen, Ole The Fight for the Red Cow • Kampen om den Røde Ko 87*

Sterling, Ford His Father's Footsteps 15*; The Hunt 15*; His Lying Heart 16; His Pride and Shame 16*; His Wild Oats 16*; The Manicurist 16; Stars and Bars 17; Oh Mabel, Behave 21*

Sterling, Joseph The Case of the Mukkinese Battlehorn 56; Cloak Without Dagger • Operation Conspiracy 56

Sterling, William Alice's Adventures in Wonderland 72

Stern, Anthony Ain't Misbehavin' 75*

Stern, Bert Jazz on a Summer's Day 59

Stern, Leonard Just You and Me, Kid 79

Stern, Monika Funke see Funke-Stern, Monika

Stern, Sándor Pin 88

Stern, Steven Hilliard B.S. I Love You 71; Neither by Day Nor by Night 72; Harrad Summer 74; I Wonder Who's Killing Her Now 75; Running 79; The Devil and Max Devlin 81; Mazes and Monsters • Rona Jaffe's Mazes and Monsters 82; Rolling Vengeance 87

Stern, Tom Clay Pigeon 71*

Sternbeck, Hans Ach! Jodel Mir Noch Einen—Stosstrupp Venus Bläst zum Angriff • Sex Charge • 2069: A Space Odyssey 73

Sternberg, Josef von The Masked Bride 25*; The Salvation Hunters 25; The Exquisite Sinner 26*; The Sea Gull • A Woman of the Sea 26*; Children of Divorce 27*; It 27*; Paying the Penalty • Underworld 27; The Docks of New York 28; The Drag Net 28; The Last Command 28; The Street of Sin 28*; The Case of Lena Smith 29; Thunderbolt 29; Der Blaue Engel • The Blue Angel 30; Morocco 30; An American Tragedy 31; Dishonored 31; Blonde Venus 32; Shanghai Express 32; The Scarlet Empress 34; Crime and

Punishment 35; The Devil Is a Woman 35; The King Steps Out 36; The Great Waltz 38*; I Take This Woman 39*; Sergeant Madden 39; The Shanghai Gesture 41; The Town 43; Duel in the Sun 46*; Jet Pilot 50*; Ana-Ta-Han • Anatahan • The Devil's Pitchfork • The Saga of Anatahan 52; Macao 52*; The Epic That Never Was (I, Claudius) 65

Sternberg, Raoul *see Schmidt, Eckhart*

Sterne, Elaine The Path of Happiness 16

Steven, Geoff Skin Deep 78

Stévenin, Jean-François Passe Montagne 79; Double Gentlemen • Double Messieurs 86

Stevens, Alex Curse of Dark Shadows • Night of Dark Shadows 71*

Stevens, Art The Rescuers 77*; The Fox and the Hound 81*

Stevens, Carter Rollerbabies 76

Stevens, David Roses Bloom Twice 77; The Clinic 82; Undercover 83; Kansas 88

Stevens, Edwin The Honor of Mary Blake 16; The Boy Girl 17; Susan's Gentleman 17

Stevens, George Blood and Thunder 30; Ladies Last 30; Air Tight 31; Call a Cop! 31; High Gear 31; The Kick-Off! 31; Mama Loves Papa 31; Boys Will Be Boys 32; Family Troubles 32; The Finishing Touch 32; Who, Me? 32; The Cohens and Kellys in Trouble 33; A Divorce Courtship 33; Flirting in the Park 33; Grin and Bear It 33; Hunting Trouble 33; Quiet Please 33; Rock-a-Bye Cowboy 33; Room Mates 33; Should Crooners Marry? 33; Walking Back Home 33; What Fur? 33; Bachelor Bait 34; Bridal Bail 34; Cracked Shots 34; Hollywood Party 34*; Kentucky Kernels • Triple Trouble 34; Ocean Swells 34; Rough Necking 34; Strictly Fresh Yeggs 34; The Undie-World 34; Alice Adams 35; Annie Oakley 35; Laddie 35; The Nitwits 35; Swing Time 36; A Damsel in Distress 37; Quality Street 37; Having Wonderful Time 38*; Vivacious Lady 38; Gunga Din 39; Vigil in the Night 40; Penny Serenade 41; Woman of the Year 41; The Talk of the Town 42; The More the Merrier 43; I Remember Mama 47; A Miracle Can Happen • On Our Merry Way 48*; A Place in the Sun 51; Something to Live For 52; Shane 53; Giant 56; The Diary of Anne Frank 59; The Greatest Story Ever Told 65; The Only Game in Town 68

Stevens, George, Jr. America at the Movies 76; George Stevens: A Filmmaker's Journey • George Stevens: A Filmmaker's Odyssey • A Tribute to George Stevens 84

Stevens, Gösta I Am With You 49

Stevens, Leslie Private Property 60; Incubus 61; Hero's Island • The Land We Love 62; Della 64; Fanfare for a Death Scene 67; Fireworks • Three Kinds of Heat 87

Stevens, Mark Cry Vengeance 54; Timetable 56; Gun Fever 58; Escape from Hell Island • The Man in the Water 63; Sunscorched • Tierra de Fuego • Vergeltung in Cataño 65*

Stevens, Norman L. Johnny Ring and the Captain's Sword 21

Stevens, Robert The Big Caper 57; Never Love a Stranger 58; I Thank a Fool 62; In the Cool of the Day 63; Change of Mind 69

Stevens, Stella The American Heroine 79

Stevenson, Robert Happy Ever After 32; Falling for You 33*; Jack of All Trades • The Two of Us 35*; The Brainsnatchers • Dr. Maniac • The Man Who Changed His Mind • The Man Who Lived Again 36; Lady Jane Grey • Nine Days a Queen • Tudor Rose 36; King Solomon's Mines 37*; Non-Stop New York 37; Owd Bob • To the Victor 38; The Ware Case 38; Return to Yesterday 39; Young Man's Fancy 39; Adventures at Rugby • Tom Brown's School Days 40; Back Street 41; Joan of Paris 42; Forever and a Day 43*; Jane Eyre • La Porta Proibita 44; The American Creed 46; Dishonored Lady 47; Bonnie Prince Charlie 48*; To the Ends of the Earth 48; I Married a Communist • The Woman on Pier 13 49; Walk Softly, Stranger 50; My Forbidden Past 51; The Las Vegas Story 52; Johnny Tremain 57; Old Yeller 57; Darby O'Gill and the Little People 58; The Absent-Minded Professor 60; Kidnapped 60; The Castaways • In Search of the Castaways 62; The Misadventures of Merlin Jones 63; Son of Flubber 63; Mary Poppins 64; The Monkey's Uncle 64; That Darn Cat! 65; The Gnome-Mobile 66; Blackbeard's Ghost 67; The Love Bug 68; The Mickey Mouse Anniversary Show 68*; My Dog, the Thief 69; Bedknobs and Broomsticks 71*; Herbie Rides Again 73; The Island at the Top of the World 74; One of Our Dinosaurs Is Missing 75*; The Shaggy D.A. 76

Stevenson, Rosalind A. Deux Voix • Two Voices 66

Stewart, Alan L. Ghettoblaster 89

Stewart, Douglas Day Thief of Hearts 84; Listen to Me 89

Stewart, Larry The Initiation 83

Stewart, Peter *see Newfield, Sam*

Stewart, William G. Father, Dear Father 73

Sti, René La Porteuse de Pain 36

Štiglić, France Na Svojoj Zemlji • On His Own Ground 48; People of Kozarju • Svet na Kozarju 52; Living Nightmare • Volca Noč 55; Dolina Mira • Mr. Jim—American, Soldier and Gentleman • Peace Valley • Sergeant Jim • The Valley of Peace 56; The False Passport • Viza na Zloto 58; Deveti Krug • The Ninth Circle 60; Balada o Trubi i Oblaku • The Ballad of the Trumpet and the Cloud 61; That Fine Day • Tistega Lepega Dne 63; Don't Cry, Peter • Ne Plači Petre 64; Amandus 66

Stiller, Mauritz Barnet • The Child 12; The Black Masks • De Svarta Maskerna 12; The Despotic Fiancé • The Tyrannical Fiancé • Den Tyranniske Fästmannen 12; En Kvinnas Slav • The Vampire • Vampy-

ren 12; Mor och Dotter • Mother and Daughter 12; När Kärleken Dödar • When Love Kills 12; När Larmklockan Ljuder • When the Alarm Bell Rings • When the Tocsin Calls 12; När Svärmor Regerar • När Svärmor Regerar eller Så Tuktas Äkta Män • When Mother-in-Law Dictates • When the Mother-in-Law Reigns 12; Because of Her Love • Because of Love • För Sin Kärleks Skull • The Stockbroker 13; The Border Feud • Frontier People • Gränsfolken • People of the Border 13; Bröderna • Brothers 13; The Chamberlain • Gentleman of the Room • Kammarjunkaren 13; Conflicts of Life • Life's Conflicts • Livets Konflikter 13*; The Fashion Model • Mannekängen • The Model 13; Lily den Suffragetten • The Modern Suffragette • Den Moderna Suffragetten • The Suffragette • Den Suffragetten 13; Den Okända • The Unknown Woman 13; On the Fateful Roads of Life • On the Roads of Fate • På Livets Ödesvägar • The Smugglers 13*; Lekkamraterna • The Playmates 14; The Master • The Red Tower • Det Röda Tornet 14; Mme. Thora Fleming • När Konstnärer Älskar • When Artists Love 14; The Shot • Skottet 14; Storm Bird • Stormfågeln • Stormy Petrel 14; Ace of Thieves • The Master Thief • Mästertjuven • The Son of Fate 15; The Adventure • Äventyret • Hans Bröllopsnatt • His Wedding Night 15; The Avenger • Hämnaren • The Revenger 15; The Dagger • Dolken 15; Hans Hustrus Förflutna • His Wife's Past 15; The Lucky Brooch • The Lucky Pin • Lyckonålen • The Motorcar Apaches 15; Madame de Thèbes 15; The Mine Pilot • Minlotsen 15; Anjuta the Dancer • Balettprimadonnan • The Ballerina • The Ballet Primadonna • Wolo Czarwienko • Wolo, Wolo 16; The Fight for His Heart • Kampen om Hans Hjärta • The Struggle for His Heart 16; Kärlek och Journalistik • Love and Journalism • Love and the Journalist 16; Vingarna • The Wings 16; Alexander den Store • Alexander the Great 17; Thomas Graals Bästa Film • Thomas Graal's Best Film • Thomas Graal's Best Picture • Wanted: A Film Actress • Wanted: An Actress 17; Dans les Remous • The Flame of Life • Sången om den Eldröda Blomman • Song of the Scarlet Flower 18; Thomas Graals Bästa Barn • Thomas Graal's Best Child • Thomas Graal's First Child 18; The Fishing Village • Fiskebyn • The Vengeance of Jakob Vindas 19; Herr Arnes Pengar • Sir Arne's Treasure • Snows of Destiny • The Three Who Were Doomed • The Treasure of Arne 19; Bonds That Chafe • Erotikon 20; Johan 20*; The Emigrants • The Exiles • In Self Defence • De Landsflyktige 21; Gunnar Hedes Saga • The Judgment • The Old Mansion 22; The Atonement of Gösta Berling • Gösta Berlings Saga • The Legend of Gösta Berling • The Saga of Gösta Berling • The Story of Gösta Berling 23; The Blizzard 24; Ibáñez' Torrent • The Torrent 25*; Hotel Imperial 26; The

Temptress 26*; Barbed Wire 27*; The Woman on Trial 27; The Street of Sin 28*

Stiller, Mosche see *Stiller, Mauritz*

Stiller, Mowscha see *Stiller, Mauritz*

Stillman, Whit Metropolitan 90

Stitt, Alexander Grendel Grendel Grendel 80

Stix, John The Great St. Louis Bank Robbery 59*

Stobart, Thomas The Conquest of Everest 53; The Great Monkey Rip-Off 79

Stöckel, Joe Dell Etappenhase 38; Musketier Meier III 38; Wenn Du eine Schwiegermutter Hast • When You Have a Mother-in-Law 38; Der Arme Millionär • The Poor Millionär 39; Stärker Als die Liebe • Stronger Than Love 39; Das Recht auf Liebe • The Right to Love 40

Stocker, Walter Till Death 78

Stocki, Chester The Proud Rider 71*

Stöckl, Ula Geschichten vom Kübelkind • Tales of the Trashcan Kid 70*

Stockwell, Dean Human Highway 82*

Stockwell, John Under Cover 87

Stoeckel, Joe see *Stöckel, Joe*

Stoeckl, Ula see *Stöckl, Ula*

Stoermer, William The Tidal Wave 18

Stoger, Alfred Lysistrata 48

Stokes, Jack Heavy Metal 81*

Stoll, Frederic F. Determination 20

Stoll, Lincoln Me and Myself 30

Stoloff, Ben Circus Pals 23*; Jungle Pals 23*; The Monkey Farm 23*; A Monkey Mix-Up 23*; Monks à la Mode 23*; School Pals 23*; The Canyon of Light 26; The Circus Ace 27; The Gay Retreat 27; Silver Valley 27; A Horseman of the Plains 28; Plastered in Paris 28; The Girl from Havana 29; Protection 29; Speakeasy 29; Fox Movietone Follies of 1930 • Movietone Follies of 1930 • The New Movietone Follies of 1930 30; Happy Days 30; Soup to Nuts 30; Goldie 31; Not Exactly Gentlemen • Three Rogues 31; By Whose Hand? 32; Destry Rides Again • Justice Rides Again 32; The Devil Is Driving 32; The Night Mayor 32; East of Fifth Avenue • Obey the Law 33; He Lived to Kill • Night of Terror 33; The Great Schnozzle • Joe Palooka • Palooka 34; Transatlantic Merry-Go-Round 34; Swell-Head 35; To Beat the Band 35; Don't Turn 'Em Loose 36; Two in the Dark 36; Fight for Your Lady 37; Sea Devils 37; Super Sleuth 37; The Affairs of Annabel 38; Radio City Revels 38; The Lady and the Mob 39; The Marines Fly High 40*; The Great Mr. Nobody 41; Three Sons o' Guns 41; The Hidden Hand 42; Secret Enemies 42; The Mysterious Doctor 43; Bermuda Mystery 44; Take It or Leave It 44; Johnny Comes Flying Home 46; It's a Joke, Son 47

Stoloff, Victor Egypt by Three 53; Tarzan and the Lost Safari 56*; The Deceivers • Intimacy 66; The 300 Year Weekend 71; The Washington Affair 77

Stolper, Alexander A Simple Story 30; The Four Visits of Samuel Vulf 34; The Law of Life 40*; A Fellow from Our Town • A Lad from Our Town 42*; Wait for

Me! 43*; Days and Nights • Dni i Nochi 44; Our Heart 46; The Story of a Real Man 48; Far from Moscow 50; The Road 55; Unforgettable Spring 57; Hard Won Happiness 58; The Living and the Dead 63; Soldiers Aren't Born 68; Vengeance 69; The Fourth 73

Stone, Andrew L. Applejoy's Ghost • Fantasy 27; The Elegy 27; Adoration 28; Dreary House 28; Frenzy 28; Liebenstraum • Two O'Clock in the Morning: Liebenstraum 28; Shadows of Glory • Sombras de Gloria 29; Hell's Headquarters 32; The Girl Said No 36; Stolen Heaven 37; Say It in French 38; The Great Victor Herbert 39; The Hard-Boiled Canary • Magic in Music • There's Magic in Music 41; Diamonds and Crime • Hi Diddle Diddle • Try and Find It 43; Stormy Weather 43; Sensations • Sensations of 1945 44; Bedside Manner • Her Favorite Patient 45; Bachelor Girls • The Bachelor's Daughters 46; Fun on a Weekend 47; Highway 301 50; Confidence Girl 51; The Steel Trap 52; A Blueprint for Murder 53; The Night Holds Terror 55; Julie 56; Cry Terror! 58; The Decks Ran Red 58; The Last Voyage 59; Ring of Fire 61; The Password Is Courage 62; Never Put It in Writing 63; The Secret of My Success 65; Song of Norway 70; The Great Waltz 72

Stone, Barbara Compañeras and Compañeros 70*

Stone, David Compañeras and Compañeros 70*

Stone, Douglas K. see *Montgomery, George*

Stone, Ezra Tammy and the Millionaire 67*

Stone, Marshall Come Spy with Me • Red Over Red 67

Stone, Norman C. S. Lewis: Through the Shadowlands • Shadowlands 85

Stone, Oliver Street Scenes 70*; Seizure 73; The Hand 81; Platoon 86; Salvador 86; Wall Street 87; Talk Radio 88; Born on the Fourth of July 89

Stone, Phil see *Goldstone, Phil*

Stone, Robert Radio Bikini 87

Stone, Virginia Evil in the Deep • The Treasure of Jamaica Reef 74

Stootsberry, A. P. The Notorious Cleopatra 70

Stoppard, Tom Rosencrantz and Guildenstern Are Dead 90

Stora, Bernard Le Jeune Marie 83

Storch, Arthur Death Play 76

Storch, Wolfgang The Two Faces of January • Die Zwei Gesichter des Januar 86

Storck, Henri Les Fêtes du Centenaire 30; Images d'Ostende 30; La Mort de Vénus 30; Ostende, Reine des Plages 30; Une Pêche au Hareng 30; Pour Vos Beaux Yeux 30; Le Service de Sauvetage sur la Côte Belge 30; Suzanne au Bain 30; Tentative de Films Abstraits 30; Trains de Plaisir 30; Une Idylle à la Plage 31; Histoire du Soldat Inconnu 32; Sur les Bords de la Caméra 32; Travaux du Tunnel Sous l'Escaut 32; Borinage • Misère au

Borinage 33*; Trois Vies Une Corde 33; Création d'Ulcères Artificiels chez le Chien 34; La Production Sélective du Réseau à 70 34; Cap du Sud 35; Le Coton 35; Électrification de la Ligne Bruxelles-Anvers 35; L'Île de Pâques 35; L'Industrie de la Tapisserie et du Meuble Sculpté 35; Le Trois-Mâts 35; Les Carillons 36; Les Jeux de l'Été et de la Mer 36; Regards sur la Belgique Ancienne 36; Sur les Routes de l'Été 36; La Belgique Nouvelle 37; Un Ennemi Public 37; Les Maisons de la Misère 37; Comme une Lettre à la Poste 38; Le Patron Est Mort 38; La Roue de la Fortune 38; Terre de Flandre 38; Vacances 38; Voor Recht en Vrijheid te Kortrijk 39; La Foire Internationale de Bruxelles 40; Le Monde de Paul Delvaux • The World of Paul Delvaux 44; Symphonie Paysanne 44*; La Joie de Revivre 47*; Rubens 47*; Au Carrefour de la Vie 49; Carnavals 50; Le Banquet des Fraudeurs 51; La Fenêtre Ouverte 52; Herman Teirlinck 53; Les Belges et la Mer 54; Les Portes de la Maison 54; Le Tour du Monde en Bateau-Stop 54; Le Trésor d'Ostende 55; Décembre—Mois des Enfants 56; Couleur de Feu 57; Masters of the Congo Jungle • Les Seigneurs de la Forêt 58*; Les Gestes du Silence 60; Les Dieux du Feu 61; L'Énergie et Vous 61; Le Bonheur d'Être Aimée 62; Les Malheurs de la Guerre 62; Variation sur le Geste 62; Plastiques 63; Matières Nouvelles 64; Le Musée Vivant 65; Jeudi On Chantera Comme Dimanche 66; Forêt Secrète d'Afrique 68; Paul Delvaux, or The Forbidden Woman • Paul Delvaux ou Les Femmes Défendues 70; Fêtes de Belgiques 72*; Fifres et Tambours d'Entre-Sambre-et-Meuse 74; Les Joyeux Tromblons 75; Les Marcheurs de Sainte Rolende 75

Storey, Thomas The Black Book 29*; The Last Frontier 32*

Storff, Victor see *Salerno, Vittorio*

Storm, Esben 27A 74; In Search of Anna 78

Storm, Howard Once Bitten 85

Storm, Jerome The Biggest Show on Earth 18; The Keys of the Righteous 18; Naughty, Naughty! 18; The Vamp 18; Bill Henry 19; The Busher 19; Crooked Straight 19; The Egg Crate Wallop 19; The Knock-Out Blow 19; The Girl Dodger 19; Greased Lightning 19; Hay Foot, Straw Foot 19; Red Hot Dollars 19; Alarm Clock Andy 20; Homer Comes Home 20; An Old Fashioned Boy 20; Paris Green 20; Peaceful Valley 20; Village Sleuth 20; Her Social Value 21; Arabian Love 22; A California Romance 22; Honor First 22; The Rosary 22; Children of Jazz 23; Goodbye Girls 23; Madness of Youth 23; St. Elmo 23; Truxton King 23; The Brass Bowl 24; The Goldfish 24; The Siren of Seville 24*; Some Pun'kins 25; Sweet Adeline 26; Ladies at Ease 27; Ranger of the North 27; The Swift Shadow 27; Captain Careless 28; Dog Justice 28; Dog Law 28; Fangs of the Wild 28; Law of Fear 28; Tracked 28; Courtin' Wildcats 29; The Yellowback 29; The Racing Strain 33

Stormont, Leo England Invaded 09; Royal England—A Story of an Empire's Throne 11*

Storrie, Kelly The Busker's Revenge 14; Come Back to Hearing 14; Hubby's Beano 14; Mermaids of the Thames 14; Shirts 14; Hello Exchange 16; Home Comforts 16; Matrimonial Bliss 16; When a Man's Single 16; An Episode of Life in Greater London 21

Story, Mark Odd Jobs 84

Stouffer, Larry N. Horror High • Twisted Brain 73

Stouffer, Mark Man Outside 86

Stoumen, Louis Clyde The Naked Eye 57; Girls in Action • Operation Dames 59; The Black Fox 62; Image of Love 65

Stow, Percy The Glutton's Nightmare 01; The Coster and His Donkey 02; The Countryman and the Flute 02; The Frustrated Elopement 02; How to Stop a Motor Car 02; Peace with Honour 02*; The Quarrelsome Couple 02; That Eternal Ping-Pong 02; When Daddy Comes Home 02; The Adventures of a Bill Poster 03; Alice in Wonderland 03*; A Free Ride 03; Fun at the Barber's 03; Getting Up Made Easy 03; How the Old Woman Caught the Omnibus • Stop That Bus! 03; The Knocker and the Naughty Boys 03; The Lady Thief and the Baffled Bobbies 03; The Neglected Lover and the Stile 03; Only a Face at the Window 03; The Revolving Table 03; The Suburban-Bunkum • The Unclean World • The Unclean World: The Suburban-Bunkum Microbe-Guyoscope 03; The Tragical Tale of a Belated Letter 03; The Unexpected Bath 03; The Adventures of Sandy MacGregor 04; Attempted Murder in a Railway Train 04; The Broken Broom • A Kiss and a Tumble 04; The Burglar and the Girls 04; The Convict and the Curate • The Convict's Escape 04; Father's Hat, or Guy Fawkes' Day 04; Fighting Washerwomen 04; The Joke That Failed 04; The Mistletoe Bough 04; Off for the Holidays 04; Once Too Often 04; The Stolen Pig 04; An Up-to-Date Studio 04; Above and Below Stairs 05; Beauty and the Beast 05; Blind Man's Buff 05; Dangerous Golfers 05; Father's Birthday Cheese 05; Fine Feathers Make Fine Birds • Fine Feathers Make Fine Friends • Willie and Tim in the Motor Car 05; The Gamblers 05; Jimmy and Joe and the Water Spout 05; The Love Letters 05; Mr. Brown's Bathing Tent 05; The Sailor's Wedding 05; Saturday's Wages 05; The Stolen Purse 05; An Unlucky Day 05; The Village Blacksmith 05; When Father Laid the Carpet on the Stairs 05; The Artful Dodger 06; Beer Twopence a Glass 06; Caught by the Tide 06; The Coster's Revenge 06; A Double Life 06; The Horse That Ate the Baby 06; How Baby Caught Cold 06; How Father Killed the Cat 06; Rescued in Mid-Air 06; The Runaway Van 06; Saved by a Lie 06; The Stolen Bride 06; Those Boys Again 06; The Truants' Capture 06; When Father Got a Holiday 06; When Mother Fell Ill at Christmas 06; Who Stole the Beer? 06; The Absent-Minded Professor 07; Adventures of a Bath Chair 07; An Anxious Day for Mother 07; An Awkward Situation 07; Curing the Blind 07; Disturbing His Rest 07; An Overdose of Love Potion 07; Paying Off Old Scores 07; The Pied Piper 07; A Soldier's Wedding 07; The Story of a Modern Mother 07; The Sunday School Treat 07; That's Not Right—Watch Me 07; The Water Babies, or The Little Chimney Sweep 07; A Wet Day 07; The Wreck of the Mary Jane 07; Algy's Yachting Party 08; Beware of the Bull • Three Maiden Ladies and a Bull 08; The Captain's Wives 08; The Cavalier's Wife 08; The Downfall of the Burglars' Trust 08; Follow Your Leader and the Master Follows Last 08; Got a Penny Stamp? 08; Ib and Little Christina 08; If Women Were Policemen 08; John Gilpin 08; The Little Waif and the Captain's Daughter 08; The Martyrdom of Thomas a Becket 08; The Memory of His Mother 08; The Missionary's Daughter 08; Mr. Jones Has a Tile Loose 08; A Modern Cinderella 08; Nancy, or The Burglar's Daughter 08; The Old Composer and the Prima Donna 08; The Old Favourite and the Ugly Golliwog 08; Poor Aunt Matilda 08; The Puritan Maid and the Royalist Refugee 08; Robin Hood and His Merry Men 08; Saved by the Telegraph Code 08; The Scandalous Boys and the Fire Chute 08; The Tempest 08; Three Suburban Sportsmen and a Hat 08; When the Man in the Moon Seeks a Wife 08; A Wild Goose Chase 08; An Aerial Elopement 09; Bobby the Boy Scout, or The Boy Detective 09; The Crafty Usurper and the Young King 09; The Dear Old Dog 09; Electric Transformations 09; Father's Baby Boy 09; A Glass of Goat's Milk 09; Hard Times 09; His Work or His Wife 09; In Love with a Picture Girl 09; An Ingenious Safe Deposit 09; The Invaders 09; The Jealous Doll, or The Frustrated Elopement 09; Juggins' Motor Skates 09; A Lesson in Electricity 09; The Love of a Nautch Girl 09; The Morganatic Marriage 09; Never Late, or The Conscientious Clerk 09; Pater's Patent Painter 09; The Professor's Strength Tablets 09; Put a Penny in the Slot 09; The Stolen Favourite 09; Three Sailormen and a Girl 09; Under the Mistletoe Bough 09; When Father Wears Stays 09; The Burglar Expected 10; A Child's Prayer 10; Cock-a-Doodle-Doo 10; The Curate's New Year Gifts 10; Frightened Freddy—How Freddy Won a Hundred Pounds 10; Frightened Freddy the Fearful Policeman 10; A Hero in Spite of Himself 10; His Little Son Was with Him All the Time 10; His Week's Pay 10; Lieutenant Rose and the Chinese Pirates 10; Lieutenant Rose and the Foreign Spy 10; Lieutenant Rose and the Gun-Runners 10; Lieutenant Rose and the Robbers of Fingall's Creek 10; Lieutenant Rose and the Stolen Submarine 10; The Light That Failed 10; Magic of Love 10; The Man Who Couldn't Laugh 10; Mary Had a Lovely Voice 10; Mary Was a Housemaid 10; Miss Simpkins' Boarders 10; Mr. Breakneck's Invention 10; The Nervous Curate 10; Off for the Holidays 10; Only One Girl, or A Boom in Sausages 10; That Skating Carnival 10; Tommy's Locomotive 10; The Truth Will Out 10; Wait Till I Catch You 10; What a Pretty Girl Can Do 10; What the Parrot Saw 10; When Father Buys the Beer 10; When We Called the Plumber In 10; A Window to Let 10; The Actor's Artifice 11; Baden-Powell Junior 11; Clever Illusions and How to Do Them 11; The Doctor's Dilemma • What Could the Doctor Do? 11; The Doll's Revenge 11; Dolly's Birthday Present 11; First Aid Flirtations 11; Frightened Freddy and the Desperate Alien 11; Frightened Freddy and the Murderous Marauder 11; Getting Dad's Consent 11; Great Scot on Wheels 11; I'm So Sleepy 11; Lieutenant Rose and the Boxers 11; Lieutenant Rose and the Royal Visit 11; Lieutenant Rose and the Stolen Code 11; The Little Boys Next Door 11; Little Tom's Letter 11; Oh, It's You! 11; Our Intrepid Correspondent 11; A Pair of New Boots 11; Sarah's Hero 11; Servants Superceded 11; Silly Sammy 11; Speedy the Telegraph Boy 11; The Stage-Struck Carpenter 11; A Test of Affection 11; A Ticket for the Theater 11; All's Fair in Love 12; A Bald Story 12; A Breach in Breeches 12; Don't Touch It 12; The Electric Leg 12; Electrical House-Building 12; Grandma's Sleeping Draught 12; He Would Speak 12; Her Relations 12; Lieutenant Rose and the Hidden Treasure 12; Lieutenant Rose and the Moorish Raiders 12; Lieutenant Rose and the Patent Aeroplane 12; Lieutenant Rose and the Stolen Ship 12; Lieutenant Rose and the Train Wreckers 12; Lieutenant Rose in China Seas 12; Links of Love • A Pair of Handcuffs 12; A Matrimonial Muddle 12; Midnight Marauders 12; Mind the Paint 12; Mr. Diddlem's Will 12; Molly Learns to Mote 12; Mother's Day Out 12; A Peppery Affair 12; Percy's Persistent Pursuit 12; She Must Have Swallowed It 12; Sheepskin Trousers, or Not in These 12; The Suit That Didn't Suit 12; A Tale of Tails 12; A Tame Cat 12; When Jack Comes Home 12; Where's Baby? 12; Which of the Two 12; The Widow's Might 12; Auntie's Secret Sorrow 13; Be Sure and Insure 13; Bill Bumper's Boy 13; Business As Usual During Alterations • Open During Alterations 13; Coming to the Point 13; Coster Joe • The Coster's Wedding 13; The Crowd Outside, or Waiting for You 13; A Cunning Canine • A Little Doggerel 13; Dad Caught Napping 13; Gigantic Marionettes 13; Hay Ho! 13; He Who Takes What Isn't His'n 13; The Home Beautiful 13; A Horse! A Horse! 13; Incompatibility of Temper 13; It's Best to Be Natural 13; It's Love That Makes the World Go Round 13; Kindly Remove Your Hat, or She Didn't Mind 13; Lieutenant Rose and the Stolen

Bullion 13; Love and the Varsity 13; Love vs. Pride 13; Maudie's Adventure 13; Milling the Militants 13; The Misfits • A Surprising Encounter 13; Miss Gladeye Slip's Vacation 13; A Modern Dick Whittington 13; Mrs. Rabbit's Husband Takes the Shilling 13; The New Hat 13; The New Letter Box 13; Not Wanted 13; A Present from Father 13; The Rent in A-Rear 13; Ringing the Changes 13; Sold! 13; Suffragettes in the Bud 13; Sweep! Sweep! 13; There Are Girls Wanted Here 13; Two Flats and a Sharp 13; Unskilled Labour 13; A Violent Fancy 13; What Could the Poor Man Do? 13; What Happened to Lizzie 13; When Mother Is Ill 13; Aunt Susan's Way 14; George's Joy Ride 14; Grandpa's Will 14; The Kinema Girl 14; Lieutenant Rose and the Sealed Orders 14; The Puddleton Police 14; That's Torn It! 14; When Every Man's a Soldier 14; How Lieutenant Rose RN Spiked the Enemy's Guns 15; The Black Triangles 16; Leaves from a Mother's Album 16; Only One Pair 16; A Question of Hairs 16

Stowers, Frederick Old Shoes 27

Stoyanov, Todor The Detour • Otklonenie 68*

Strachwitz, Chris I Went to the Dance • J'Ai Été au Bal 89*

Strand, Paul Manhatta 21*; Pay Day 38*; Native Land 42*

Strange, Norman le see Le Strange, Norman

Strange, Richard le see Le Strange, Richard

Strangeway, Stan Peter Studies Form 64; 1812 65

Strate, Walter The Dance of Life 51; Violated 53

Straub, Jean-Marie Machorka-Muff • Majorka-Muff 63; Es Hilft Nicht Wo Gewalt Herrscht • Nicht Versöhnt oder Es Hilft Nur Gewalt Wo Gewalt Herrscht • Not Reconciled • Not Reconciled, or Only Violence Helps Where It Rules • Not Reconciled, or Only Violence Helps Where Violence Rules • Unreconciled 65; Chronicle of Anna Magdalena Bach • Chronik der Anna Magdalena Bach 67; Der Bräutigam, die Komödiantin und der Zuhälter • The Bridegroom, the Actress and the Pimp • The Bridegroom, the Comedienne and the Pimp 68; Die Augen Wollen Sich Nicht zu Jeder Zeit Schliessen, oder Vielleicht eines Tages Wird Rom Sich Erlauben Seinerseits zu Wählen • Eyes Cannot Forever Remain Closed, or Perhaps Rome Will One Day Allow Itself to Choose in Its Turn • Eyes Do Not Want to Close at All Times, or Perhaps One Day Rome Will Permit Herself to Choose in Her Turn • Othon • Les Yeux Ne Peuvent Pas en Tout Temps Se Fermer ou Peut-Être Qu'un Jour Rome Se Permettra de Choisir à Son Tour • Les Yeux Ne Veulent Pas en Tout Temps Se Fermer ou Peut-Être Qu'un Jour Rome Se Permettra de Choisir à Son Tour 69*; Einleitung zu Arnold Schönbergs Begleitmusik zu einer Lichtspielszene • Introduc-

tion to Arnold Schönberg's Accompaniment to a Cinematic Scene 72*; Geschichtsunterricht • History Lessons 72*; Moses and Aaron • Moses und Äron 74*; I Cani del Sinai • Fortini/Cani 76*; Every Revolution Is a Throw of the Dice • Toute Révolution Est un Coup de Dés 77*; Della Nube alla Resistenza • From the Cloud to the Resistance 79*; Too Early, Too Late • Trop Tôt, Trop Tard 81*; Class Relations • Klassenverhältnisse 84*; The Death of Empedocles • Der Tod des Empedokles 86*; Schwarze Sünde 89*

Strauss, Malcolm Malcolm Strauss' Salome • Salome • Strauss' Salome 23

Strayer, Frank R. An Enemy of Men 25; The Fate of a Flirt 25; The Lure of the Wild 25; Steppin' Out 25; Sweet Rosie O'Grady 26; When the Wife's Away 26; The Bachelor's Baby 27; Now We're in the Air 27; Pleasure Before Business 27; Rough House Rosie 27; Just Married 28; Moran of the Marines 28; Partners in Crime 28; Acquitted 29; The Fall of Eve 29; Let's Go Places • Mirth and Melody 29; Borrowed Wives 30; Anybody's Blonde • When Blonde Meets Blonde 31; Caught Cheating 31; Murder at Midnight 31; The Samaritan • Soul of the Slums 31; Behind Stone Walls 32; The Crusader 32; Dragnet Patrol • Love Redeemed 32; Dynamite Denny 32; Gorilla Ship 32; Love in High Gear 32; Manhattan Tower 32; The Monster Walked • The Monster Walks 32; Tangled Destinies 32; The Vampire Bat 32; By Appointment Only 33; Dance, Girl, Dance 33; Don't Leave the Door Open • No Dejes la Puerta Abierta 33; Forbidden Melody • La Melodía Prohibida 33; The King of the Gypsies • El Rey de los Gitanos 33; The Cross and the Sword • La Cruz y la Espada 34; Cross Streets 34; Fifteen Wives • The Man with the Electric Voice 34; Las Fronteras del Amor • Love's Frontiers 34; Fugitive Road 34; The Ghost Walks 34; In Love with Life • Reunion 34; In the Money 34; One in a Million 34; Twin Husbands 34; Condemned to Live 35; Port of Lost Dreams 35; Public Opinion 35; Society Fever 35; Symphony of Living 35; Death from a Distance 36; Hitchhike to Heaven 36; Murder at Glen Athol 36; Sea Spoilers 36; Big Business 37; Big Town Girl 37; Borrowing Trouble 37; Hot Water 37; Laughing at Trouble 37; Off to the Races 37; Blondie 38; Blondie Brings Up Baby 39; Blondie Meets the Boss 39; Blondie Takes a Vacation 39; Blondie Has Servant Trouble 40; Blondie on a Budget 40; Blondie Plays Cupid 40; Go West, Young Lady 40; Blondie Goes Latin • Conga Swing 41; Blondie in Society • Henpecked 41; Blondie for Victory • Troubles Through Billets 42; Blondie Goes to College • The Boss Said "No" 42; Blondie's Blessed Event • A Bundle of Trouble 42; Brownie • The Daring Young Man 42; Footlight Glamour 43; It's a Great Life 43; I Ring Doorbells 45; Mama Loves Papa 45; Señorita from the West 45; Messenger of Peace 50; The

Sickle or the Cross 51; Seeds of Destruction 52

Streich, Ian see Streitch, Ianas

Streisand, Barbra Yentl 83

Streitch, Ianas Other People's Passions • Svesas Kaislibas 86; The Date in the Milky Way • Svidanie na Mlechnom Puti 87

Stric, Vladimir Iba Den • Just One Day 89*

Strichewsky, Vladimir The Volga Boatman 38

Strick, Joseph Muscle Beach 48*; Jour de Fête 49; The Big Break 53; The Savage Eye 59*; The Balcony 63; Ulysses 67; Justine 68*; Tropic of Cancer 69; Interviews with My Lai Veterans 70; Janice • Road Movie 73; A Portrait of the Artist As a Young Man 77; The Space Works 81

Striker, Jonathan see Ciupka, Richard

Stringer, Robert W. The Daredevil 71

Strittmater, Thomas Der Polenweiher • The Polish War Worker 86*

Strizhak, Alexander Her Way of Love 29*

Strnad, Stanislav The Roundup • Zátah 85; Není Sirotek Jako Sirotek 86

Strock, Herbert L. Mask of the Himalayas • Storm Over Tibet 51*; Gog 54; Battle Taxi 55; Blood Is My Heritage • Blood of Dracula • Blood of the Demon 57; I Was a Teenage Frankenstein • Teenage Frankenstein 57; How to Make a Monster 58; The Devil's Messenger • No. 13 Demon Street 61; Rider on a Dead Horse 62; The Crawling Hand • Strike Me Deadly 63; Brother on the Run 73; Monster 79; Witches' Brew 80*

Stroheim, Erich Oswald Hans Carl Maria see Stroheim, Erich von

Stroheim, Erich von Blind Husbands • The Pinnacle 19; The Devil's Pass Key 20; Foolish Wives 22; Merry-Go-Round 23*; Greed 24; The Merry Widow 25; The Wedding March 27; Queen Kelly 28; Hello, Sister! • Walking Down Broadway 33*

Strom, Gregory Broken Victory 88

Stromberg, Hunt Breaking Into Society 23; The Fire Patrol 24; The Siren of Seville 24*; Paint and Powder 25

Stromberg, William R. The Crater Lake Monster 77

Strömholm, Christer Ansikten i Skugga • Faces in the Shadows 56*

Stross, Raymond The Show's the Thing 36; The Reverse Be My Lot 38

Stroyeva, Vera The Right of Fathers 31; The Man Without a Case 32; Petersburg Nights • Petersburgskaya Nochi 34*; A Generation of Conquerors • Pokoleniye Pobediteli • Revolutionists 36; In Search of Happiness 40*; Marite 47; Bolshoi Koncert • The Grand Concert • Great Concert 51; Variety Stars 54; Boris Godunov 55; Plains, My Plains 57; Khovanschina 59

Stryker, Jonathan see Ciupka, Richard

Stuart, Allen Unashamed 38

Stuart, Brian Sorceress 82

Stuart, Donald London Melody 30*

Stuart, Mark Please Sir 71

Stuart, Mel Four Days in November 64; If It's Tuesday This Must Be Belgium 69; I Love My Wife 70; Willy Wonka and the Chocolate Factory 71; One Is a Lonely Number • Two Is a Happy Number 72; Wattstax 73; Mean Dog Blues 78; The White Lions 79

Stubbs, Ray T. Dan Smith 87*

Stumar, John S. The King's People 37

Sturgeon, Rollin Captain Alvarez 14; The Little Angel of Canyon Creek 14; The Chalice of Courage 15; God's Country and the Woman 16; Through the Wall 16; The American Consul 17; Betty and the Buccaneers 17; The Calendar Girl 17; The Rainbow Girl 17; The Serpent's Tooth 17; The Upper Crust 17; Whose Wife? 17; Her Country First 18; Hugon the Mighty 18; A Petticoat Pilot 18; The Shuttle 18; Unclaimed Goods 18; Destiny 19; Pretty Smooth 19; The Sundown Trail 19; The Breath of the Gods 20; The Gilded Dream 20; The Girl in the Rain 20; In Folly's Trail 20; All Dolled Up 21; Danger Ahead 21; The Mad Marriage 21; West of the Water Tower 23; Daughters of Today • What's Your Daughter Doing? 24

Sturges, John Thunderbolt 45*; Alias Mr. Twilight 46; The Man Who Dared 46; Shadowed 46; For the Love of Rusty 47; Keeper of the Bees 47; The Best Man Wins 48; The Sign of the Ram 48; The Walking Hills 49; The Capture 50; The Magnificent Yankee • The Man with Thirty Sons 50; Mystery Street 50; Right Cross 50; It's a Big Country 51*; Kind Lady 51; The People Against O'Hara 51; The Girl in White • So Bright the Flame 52; Jeopardy 52; Escape from Fort Bravo 53; Fast Company 53; Bad Day at Black Rock 54; The Scarlet Coat 55; Underwater! 55; Backlash 56; Gunfight at the O.K. Corral 57; The Law and Jake Wade 58; The Old Man and the Sea 58*; Last Train from Gun Hill 59; Never So Few 59; The Magnificent Seven 60; By Love Possessed 61; A Girl Named Tamiko 62; Sergeants 3 • Soldiers Three 62; The Great Escape 63; The Satan Bug 64; The Hallelujah Trail 65; Hour of the Gun • The Law and Tombstone 67; Ice Station Zebra 68; Marooned 69; Joe Kidd 72; Chino • The Valdez Horses • Valdez il Mezzosangue • Valdez the Halfbreed • Wild Horses 73; McQ 74; The Eagle Has Landed 76

Sturges, Preston Christmas in July 40; Down Went McGinty • The Great McGinty 40; The Lady Eve 41; New York Town 41*; Sullivan's Travels 41; The Palm Beach Story 42; The Great Moment 43; Hail the Conquering Hero 44; The Miracle of Morgan's Creek 44; Mad Wednesday • The Sin of Harold Diddlebock 46; Unfaithfully Yours 48; The Beautiful Blonde from Bashful Bend 49; Vendetta 50*; Les Carnets du Major Thompson • The Diary of Major Thompson • The French Are a Funny Race • The French They Are a Funny Race • Notebooks of Major Thompson 55

Sturridge, Charles Runners 83; Aria 87*; A Handful of Dust 88

Styles, Richard Shallow Grave 87

Suarez, Bobby A. Dynamite Johnson • The New Adventures of the Bionic Boy • The 12 Million Dollar Boy 78; One Armed Executioner 80; American Commandos • Hitman 85; Searchers of the Voodoo Mountain • Time Raiders • Warriors of the Apocalypse 87

Suárez, Carlos El Jardín Secreto • The Secret Garden 85

Suárez, Gonzalo Ditirambo 67; El Extraño Caso del Dr. Fausto 69; Aoom 70; Morbidness • Morbo 72; Rowing with the Wind 88

Suay, Ricardo Muñoz see Muñoz Suay, Ricardo

Sub, Esfir see Shub, Esther

Sub, Lee Yoo see Lee, Yoo Sub

Subbiah, M. Inspector Pratap 88

Subiela, Eliseo The Conquest of Paradise • La Conquista del Paraíso 81; Hombre Mirando al Sudeste • Man Facing Southeast • Man Looking Southeast 81; Últimas Imágenes del Naufragio 89

Sucksdorff, Arne An August Rhapsody • Augustirapsodi 39; Din Tillvaros Land • This Land Is Full of Life • Your Own Land 40; En Sommarsaga • A Summer Tale • A Summer's Tale 41; Reindeer Time • Sarvtid 42; Vinden från Väster • West Wind • The Wind from the West 42; Cliff Face • Gull! • Trut! 44; Dawn • Gryning 44; Shadows on the Snow • Shadows Over the Snow • Skuggor Över Snön 45; Dream Valley • Den Drömda Dalen • Soria-Moria • Tale of the Fjords 47; Människor i Stad • People of the City • Rhythm of a City • Symphony of a City 47; A Divided World • En Kluven Värld 48; Moving On • The Open Road • Uppbrott 48; Going Ashore • Strandhugg • Summer Interlude 49; Ett Hörn i Norr • The Living Stream 50; Indian Village • Indisk By 51; Vinden och Floden • The Wind and the River 51; The Great Adventure • Det Stora Äventyret 53; En Djungelsaga • The Flute and the Arrow 57; The Boy in a Tree • The Boy in the Tree • Pojken i Trädet 60; Mitt Hem Är Copacabana • My Home Is Copacabana 65; Cry of the Penguins • Mr. Forbush and the Penguins 71*

Sudarsky, Peter see Skinner, Peter

Sugawa, Eizo Ai to Honoho To • Challenge to Live 64; Hotarugawa • River of Fireflies 87

Sugden, Leonard S. Lure of Alaska 19; Way Up Yonder 20

Sugerman, Andrew Basic Training 83

Sugie, Toshio Oneichan Makari Toru • Three Dolls from Hong Kong • Three Dolls Go to Hong Kong 59; Aru Sōnan • Death on the Mountain 61; Saga of the Vagabonds • Sengoku Gunto-Den 64

Sugii, Gisaburo Jack and the Beanstalk 74; Ginga-Tetsudō no Yoru • The Night Train for the Milky Way 86

Sugiyama, Suguru Hi no Tori 2772 • Phoenix 2772 • Space Firebird 2772 79*

Sui, Sao-bin China Liberated • Liberated China • The New China • Osvobozhdeniye Kitai 50*

Suissa, Danièle J. The Morning Man 87; Martha, Ruth & Edie 88*

Sukardi, Kotot Si Pitjang 52

Sulistrowski, Zygmunt Marizinia • Marizinia, the Witch Beneath the Sea • The Witch Beneath the Sea 62; Africa Erotica • Happening in Africa • Karen, the Lovemaker 70

Sullivan, C. Gardner One of the Discard 14*

Sullivan, David Mary Millington's World Striptease Extravaganza 82*

Sullivan, E. P. Evangeline 14*

Sullivan, Fred G. Cold River 78; The Beer Drinker's Guide to Fitness and Filmmaking • Sullivan's Pavilion 87

Sullivan, Frederick Divorce and the Daughter 16; The Fugitive 16; Master Shakespeare, Strolling Player 16; The Pillory 16; Saint, Devil and Woman 16; Her Life and His 17; When Love Was Blind 17; Cove of Missing Men 18; The Solitary Sin 19; The Courtship of Miles Standish 23

Sullivan, James R. Venus of the South Seas 24

Sullivan, Neil Why Russians Are Revolting 70

Sullivan, Pat Motor Mat and His Fliv 16; Sammie Johnsin and His Wonderful Lamp 16; Sammie Johnsin at the Seaside 16; Sammie Johnsin Gets a Job 16; Sammie Johnsin, Hunter 16; Sammie Johnsin in Mexico 16; Sammie Johnsin, Magician 16; Sammie Johnsin Minds the Baby 16; Sammie Johnsin Slumbers Not 16; Sammie Johnsin, Strong Man 16; Sammie Johnsin's Love Affair 16; The Trials of a Movie Cartoonist 16; How Charlie Captured the Kaiser • A Modern Bill Adams 18; Just a Few Lines • Over the Rhine with Charlie 18; Knocking the "I" Out of Kaiser 18; The Whine of the Rhine 18; The Adventures of Hardrock Dome • Hardrock Dome Episode No. 1 19; The Adventures of Hardrock Dome No. 2 • Hardrock Dome Episode No. 2 19; Charlie in Turkey • Turkish Delight 19; Charlie Treats 'Em Rough • Treating 'Em Rough 19; The Further Adventures of Hardrock Dome • Hardrock Dome Episode No. 3 19; Getting a Story, or The Origins of the Shimmie 19; Feline Follies 20; Felix the Cat 20; Felix the Landlord 20; My Hero 20; Felix Goes on Strike 21; Felix in The Love Punch 21; Felix Left at Home 21; Felix Out of Luck 21; Felix the Cat: Free Lunch • Free Lunch 21; Felix the Gay Dog 21; Felix the Hypnotist • The Hypnotist 21; Felix All at Sea 22; Felix at the Fair 22; Felix Fifty-Fifty 22; Felix in Love 22; Felix in The Swim 22; Felix Makes Good 22; Felix Saves the Day 22; Felix Wakes Up 22; Felix Calms His Conscience 23; Felix Fills a Shortage 23; Felix Gets Broadcasted 23; Felix Goes A-Hunting 23; Felix in Fairyland 23; Felix in Hollywood 23; Felix in The Bone Age

Edgara 64; The Coffin House • Rakvič-kárna 66; Byt • The Flat 68; Garden • Zahrada 68; Historia Naturae 68; Don Sanche 69; A Quiet Week in the House • Tichý Týden v Domě 69; Kostnice • The Ossuary 70; Jabberwocky 71; Dimensions of Dialogue • Možnosti Dialogu 82; Do Pivnice • Down to the Cellar 83; Kyvaldo, Jáma a Naděje • The Pit, the Pendulum and Hope 83; Alice 88; Leonardo's Diary • Leonardův Deník 88; Animated Self-Portraits 89; The Male Game • Mužné Hry 89

Svetlanov, G. Songs Over the Dnieper 58

Svetlov, Alexander Chegemskiy Detektiv • Cheghem Detective Story 87

Svetlov, B. In the Kingdom of Oil and Millions 16

Svetozarov, Dmitri Breakthrough • Proryv 87

Svilovoi, Elena China Liberated • Liberated China • The New China • Osvobozhdeniye Kitai 50*

Svoboda, Jiří Scalpel, Please! • Skalpel, Prosím! 85; Papilio 86

Swackhamer, E. W. Man and Boy 72; Spiderman 77; Longshot 81

Swaim, Bob La Nuit de Saint-Germain des Près 77; La Balance • The Nark 81; Escort Girl • Half Moon Street 86; Masquerade 88

Swanson, Donald The Magic Garden • Pennywhistle Blues 52

Swaroop, Kamal Om Dar-B-Dar 88

Swenson, Charles Dirty Duck 77; The Mouse and His Child 77*; Twice Upon a Time 83*

Swerdloff, Arthur The Roadracers 59

Swickard, Charles City of the Dead • The Forbidden Adventure 15; The Beggar of Cawnpore 16; The Captive God 16*; D'Artagnan 16; Hell's Hinges 16*; Mixed Blood 16; The Raiders 16; The Sign of the Poppy 16; The Gates of Doom 17; The Lair of the Wolf 17; The Phantom's Secret 17; The Plow Woman 17; The Scarlet Crystal 17; Hitting the High Spots 18; The Light of Western Stars 18; Almost Married 19; Faith 19; The Spender 19; An Arabian Knight 20; Body and Soul 20; The Devil's Claim 20; The Last Straw 20*; The Third Woman 20

Swift, David Pollyanna 60; The Parent Trap • Petticoats and Bluejeans 61; All This and Money Too • The Grand Duke and Mr. Pimm • Love Is a Ball 62; The Interns 62; Under the Yum Yum Tree 63; Good Neighbor Sam 64; How to Succeed in Business Without Really Trying 67

Swift, Howard As the Fly Flies 44; Disillusioned Bluebird 44; Giddy Yapping 44; Kickapoo Juice 44; Mr. Fore by Fore 44; Polly Wants a Doctor 44; Booby Socks 45*; Carnival Courage 45; The Dog, Cat and Canary 45; Hot Foot Lights 45; Treasure Jest 45; Cagey Bird 46; Catnipped 46; Kongo-Roo 46; Polar Playmates 46; The Schooner the Better 46; Unsure Runts 46; Big House Blues 47; Fowl Brawl 47;

Leave Us Chase It 47; Loco Lobo 47; Tooth or Consequences 47; Pickled Puss 48

Swimmer, Saul Force of Impulse 61; Without Each Other 62; Mrs. Brown You've Got a Lovely Daughter 68; Cometogether 71; Concert for Bangladesh 72; The Black Pearl 77; We Will Rock You 83

Swirnoff, Brad Tunnelvision 76*; American Raspberry 80

Syberberg, Hans-Jürgen Act Five, Scene Seven: Fritz Kortner Rehearses Kabale und Liebe • Fünfter Akt, Siebte Szene: Fritz Kortner Probt Kabale und Liebe 65; Romy: Anatomie eines Gesichts • Romy: Anatomy of a Face 65; Fritz Kortner Recites Monologues for a Record • Fritz Kortner Spricht Monologe für eine Schallplatte 66; The Counts of Pocci—Some Chapters Towards the History of a Family • Die Grafen Pocci • Die Grafen Pocci—Einige Kapitel zur Geschichte einer Familie 67; Scarabea • Scarabea: How Much Land Does a Man Need? • Scarabea: Wieviel Erde Braucht der Mensch? 68; Sex-Business: Made in Passing 69; After My Last Move • Nach Meinem Letzten Umzug 70; San Domingo 70*; Ludwig: Requiem for a Virgin King • Ludwig: Requiem für einen Jungfräulichen König • Ludwig II: Requiem für einen Jungfräulichen König 72; Ludwig's Cook • Theodor Hierneis oder Wie Man Ehem. Hofkoch Wird 72; Karl May 74; The Confessions of Winifred Wagner • Winifred Wagner • Winifred Wagner und die Geschichte des Hauses Wahnfried von 1914-1975 75; Hitler: A Film from Germany • Hitler: Ein Film aus Deutschland • Our Hitler • Our Hitler: A Film from Germany 77; Parsifal 81; Die Nacht • The Night 85

Sydney, Basil They Met in the Dark 43*

Sydow, Max von Katinka 87

Sykes, Eric The Plank 67; Rhubarb 69

Sykes, Peter The Committee • Session with the Committee 68; Blood Will Have Blood • Demons of the Mind 71; The Legend of Spider Forest • Venom 71; Crazy House • The House in Nightmare Park • Night of the Laughing Dead • Nightmare Park 73; Steptoe and Son Ride Again 73; Die Braut des Satans • Child of Satan • To the Devil—A Daughter 76; Jesus 79*; The Blues Band 81

Sylbert, Paul The Steagle 71

Symonds, Henry Go and Get It 20*

Synek, Emil Jana—Das Mädchen aus dem Böhmerwald 36

Syson, Michael Conquista 72

Szabó, Ildikó Damn Real • Hötreal 87

Szabó, István Concert • Konzert 61; Variációk egy Témára • Variations Upon a Theme 61; Te • You 63; The Age of Daydreaming • Age of Illusions • Álmodozások Kora 64; Apa • Diary of One Week • Father 66; Kegyelet • Piety 67; A Film About Love • Love Film • Szerelmesfilm • Your Presence 70; Tüzoltó Utca 25 • 25 Fireman's Street 70; Alkony • Twilight 71; Budapest, Amiért Szeretem • Budapest: Why I Love It 71*; The Danube—Fishes—

Birds • Duna—Halak—Madarak 71; Dawn • Hajnal 71; Leányportré • A Portrait of a Girl 71; A Mirror • Egy Tükör 71; A Square • Tér 71; Ősbemutató • Première 74; Budapest Tales • Budapesti Mesék • Tales of Budapest 76; City Map • Várostérkép 77; Bizalom • Confidence 79; The Green Bird • Der Grüne Vogel 79; Mephisto 80; Colonel Redl • Oberst Redl • Redl Ezredes 84; Hanussen 87

Szabó, László Zig-Zag 75; Sortűz egy Fekete Bivalyért • Volley for a Black Buffalo 85

Szalai, György Film Novel, Three Sisters 78*; The Documentator • A Dokumentátor 89*

Szalkai, Sándor Kojak Budapesten • Kojak in Budapest 80

Szántó, Erika Elysium 86

Szarka, William Revenge of the Innocents • The Runaways • South Bronx Heroes 85

Szaro, Henryk Ułan i Dziewczyna 33; Pan Twardowski 37; The Vow 38; The Anticipated Day • Dzień Upragniony 39

Szász, Péter On the Sidelines 76

Székely, István see Sekely, Steve

Székely, Stefan see Sekely, Steve

Székely, Stephan see Sekely, Steve

Szelubski, Jerzy Peace Conquers the World • Peace Will Win • Pokój Zwycięży Świat 50*

Sziatinay, Sándor Once a Week 37

Szinetár, Miklós Az Erőd • The Fortress 79

Szirtes, András Lenz 87

Szlingerbaum, Samy Le 15/18 73*; Brussels-Transit • Bruxelles-Transit 80

Szdowski, Karol Nad Niemnem • On the Banks of the Niemen • On the Niemen River 39*

Szomjas, György Falfúró • The Wall Driller 85; Mr. Universe 88

Szomogyi, Julius see Somogyi, Julius

Sztwiertnia, Jerzy Komediantka • The Pretender 87

Szuchopa, Julian Heavy Metal 81*

Szulkin, Piotr Golem • The Golem 79; The War of the Worlds—Next Century • Wojna Światów—Następne Stulecie 81; The End of Civilization • O-Bi, O-Ba—Koniec Cywilizacji 85

Szulzinger, Boris Shame of the Jungle • Tarzoon—Shame of the Jungle 75*; Mama Dracula 79

Szurdi, András Képvadászok • The Picture Hunters 85*

Szurdi, Miklós Képvadászok • The Picture Hunters 85*

Szwarc, Jeannot Extreme Close-Up • Sex Through a Window 72; Bug 75; Jaws 2 77; Somewhere in Time 80; Enigma 82; Supergirl 83; Santa Claus • Santa Claus: The Movie 85

Szwebgo, Stanisław Książątko • The Lottery Prince 37*

Tabernero, Julio Pérez see *Pérez Tabernero, Julio*

Tabio, Juan Carlos For Exchange • Se Permuta 85; ¡Plaff! 88

Tabliashvili, V. Keto and Kote 54*

Tacchella, Jean-Charles Les Derniers Hivers • The Last Winters 71; Une Belle Journée 72; Voyage en Grande Tartarie • Voyage to Grand Tartarie 73; Cousin, Cousine 75; Blue Country • Le Pays Bleu 77; Il Y A Longtemps Que Je T'Aime • It's a Long Time That I've Loved You • Soupçon 79; Croque la Vie 81; Escalier C 85; Dolly In • Travelling Avant 87; Dames Galantes 90

Tadej, Vladimir Anticasanova 86

Tadić, Radovan Erreur de Jeunesse • Youthful Indiscretion 89

Tadić, Zoran The Dream of a Rose • San o Ruži 86

Taft, Gene Blame It on the Night 84

Taggart, Errol The Longest Night 36; The Public Pays 36; Sinner Take All 36; Women Are Trouble 36; Song of the City 37; The Women Men Marry 37; Strange Faces 38

Taghvai, Nasser Captain Khorshid 87

Taguchi, Tetsu Araumi no Oja 59

Tahimik, Kidlat The Perfumed Nightmare 77; Turumba 83

Tai, Kato King of the Mongols 64

Tai, Luo Bus Number Three • Xiaozi Bei 80*

Tai, Robert Ninja vs. Mafia 85

Taicher, Robert Inside Out 86

Tairov, Alexander The Dead Man 14

Takabayashi, Yoichi Honjin Satsujin Jiken 75

Takacs, Tibor Metal Messiah 77; Prisoner 984 • The Tomorrow Man 79; The Gate 87; Hardcover 88; I, Madman 89

Takahashi, Banmei Door 88

Takamoto, Iwao Charlotte's Web 72*

Takashi Metamorphoses • Winds of Change 78

Takhmasib, R. Fires of Baku • Flames Over Baku • The Lights of Baku • Ogni Baku 50*

Takita, Yojiro Comic Magazine • Komikku Zasshi Nanka Iranai 86; Yen Family 88

Takizawa, Eisuke Byakuya no Yōjo • The Temptress • The Temptress and the Monk 63

Talan, Len Hansel and Gretel 87

Talankin, Igor Kuzmich 59; Seryozha • The Splendid Days • A Summer to Remember 60*; The Entry • Introduction 62; Day Stars • Stars by Day 66; Tchaikovsky • Tschaikovsky 70*; The Choice of a Goal 74; Father Serge 78; Weekend 87

Talaskivi, Jaakko Fuck Off! — Images of Finland • Perkele! • Perkele! — Kuvia Suomesta 71*

Talbot, Brad The Case of the Full Moon Murders • The Case of the Smiling Stiffs • Sex on the Groove Tube 73*

Talbot, Mike The Reunion 77

Talebi, Ali City of Mice 86*; The End 86

Tallas, Gregg Atlantis • Atlantis the Lost Continent • Queen of Atlantis • Siren of Atlantis 48*; Prehistoric Women 50; Barefoot Battalion 54; Bed of Grass 57;

Bikini Paradise 67; Cataclysm 80*; Night Train to Terror 85*

Talmadge, Richard The Devil Horse 32*; Border Outlaws • The Phantom Horseman 50; Project Moonbase 53; I Killed Wild Bill Hickok 56; Casino Royale 67*

Talwar, Vinod Raat ke Andhere Mein 88

Tam, Patrick Burning Snow 88

Tamburella, Paolo W. Ring Around the Clock 53; I Sette Nani alla Riscossa • The Seven Dwarfs to the Rescue 65

Tampa, Harry see Hurwitz, Harry

Tan, Fred Storm of Youth 80; Lovers 84; Dark Night 86; Split of the Spirit 87; Rouge of the North • Yuan Nu 89

Tan, Louis see Chen, Guoxi

Tana, Paul Caffè Italia 85

Tanaka, Hideo Sukeban Deka — Kazama Sanshimai no Gyakushū 88

Tanaka, Kinuyo Love Letter 53; The Moon Rises 55; Love Under the Crucifix • Ō-Gin Sama 60

Tanaka, Shigeo The Great Wall • Shin no Shikōtei 65; Gambara vs. Barugon • Gamera Tai Barugon • Gamera vs. Barugon • War of the Monsters 66

Tanaka, Tokuzo Zatoichi Enters Again 63; Ghost of the Snow Girl • Kaidan Yuki Onna 68; The Haunted Castle • Hiroku Kaibyōden 69; Secrets of a Woman's Temple 69

Tandon, Ravi Nazrana 87

Taniguchi, Senkichi Man Against Man • Otoko Tai Otoko 61; Daitōzoku • The Lost World of Sinbad • Samurai Pirate 64; Kagi no Kag • Key of Keys 64; Dokuritsu Kikanjūtai Imada Shagekichu • Outpost of Hell 66; The Gambling Samurai • Kunisada Chuji 66; What's Up Tiger Lily? 66*; Arashi no Naka no Otoko • The Man in the Storm 69

Tanko, J. B. Asfalto Selvagem • Forbidden Love Affair • Lollipop 66

Tannebring, Bill Voyeur 84

Tannen, Terrell Young Giants 83; Shadows in the Storm 88

Tannen, William Flashpoint 84; Deadly Illusion • Love You to Death 87*; Hero and the Terror 88

Tanner, Alain Nice Time 57*; Ramuz, Passage d'un Poète 61; L'École 62; Les Apprentis 64; A City at Chandigarh • Une Ville à Chandigarh 66; Charles, Dead or Alive • Charles, Mort ou Vif 69; The Salamander • La Salamandre 71; Le Retour d'Afrique • Return from Africa 72; The Middle of the World • Le Milieu du Monde 74; Jonah Who Will Be 25 in the Year 2000 • Jonas Qui Aura 25 Ans en l'An 2000 75; Messidor 77; Les Années Lumières • Light Years Away 80; Dans la Ville Blanche • In the White City 82; No Man's Land 87; A Flame in My Heart • Une Flamme dans Mon Cœur 87; The Ghost Valley • La Vallée Fantôme 87; La Femme de Rose Hill 89

Tansey, Robert E. Riders of Rio • Riders of the Rio 31; The Galloping Kid 32;

Arizona Cyclone 34; The Lone Rider 34; The Sundown Trail 34; The Way of the West 34; Courage of the North 35; Morton of the Mounted • Timber Terrors 35; The Driftin' Kid 41; Dynamite Canyon 41; Lone Star Law • Lone Star Law Men 41; Riding the Sunset Trail 41; Arizona Roundup 42; The Long, Long Trail • Texas to Bataan 42; Overland Trail • Trail Riders 42; Western Mail 42; Where Trails End 42; Blazing Guns 43; Death Valley Rangers 43; The Haunted Ranch 43; Two-Fisted Justice 43; Arizona Whirlwind 44; Harmony Trail • White Stallion 44; Outlaw Trail 44; Sonora Stagecoach 44; Westward Bound 44; In Old Wyoming • Song of Old Wyoming 45; Wildfire • Wildfire: The Story of a Horse 45; The Caravan Trail 46; Colorado Serenade 46; Driftin' River 46; God's Country 46; Melody Roundup • Prairie Outlaws • Wild West 46; Romance of the West 46; Stars Over Texas 46; Tumbleweed Trail 46; The Enchanted Valley 48; Shaggy 48; Federal Man 50; The Fighting Stallion 50; Forbidden Jungle 50; Badman's Gold 51; Cattle Queen • Queen of the West 51

Tapak, Martin The Hothouse Venus • Skleníková Venuša 85; Jan Petru's Return • Návrat Jana Petru 86; Kohut Nezaspieva 86; Nedaleko do Neba 88

Tapiovaara, Nyrki Juha 35

Taradash, Daniel Storm Center 56

Tarafder, Rajen Ganga • The River 61

Tarantini, Michele Massacre in Dinosaur Valley 85; Italiani a Rio • Italians in Rio 87

Tarasov, Sergei The Black Arrow • Chyornaya Strela 87; Perekhvat 88

Tarich, Yuri Wings of a Serf 26*; Czar Ivan the Terrible 28; Flames on the Volga 29; Murderers Are at Large • The Murderers Are Coming • Murderers Are on Their Way • Ubitzi Vykhodyat na Dorogu 42*

Tarkovsky, Andrei Segodnya Otpuska Nye Budyet • There Will Be No Leave Today • There Will Be No Leave Tonight 59; Katok i Skripka • The Roller and the Violin • The Skating Rink and the Violin • The Steamroller and the Violin • Violin and Roller • The Violin and the Roller 60; Childhood of Ivan • Ivanovo Detstvo • Ivan's Childhood • My Name Is Ivan • The Youngest Spy 62; Andrei Roublev • Andrei Rublev • Andrei Rublyov • Rublyov 65; Solaris • Solyaris 71; The Mirror • A White White Boy • Zerkalo 74; Stalker 79; Nostalghia • Nostalgia 83; Offret • Sacrificatio • The Sacrifice 86

Tarnas, Kazimierz The Golden Mahmudia • Złoty Mahmudia 87; Pražské Tajemství 88

Tarr, Béla Damnation • Kárhozat 88

Tasaka, Tomotaka Rise and Fall of Love 26; Chikyū wa Mawaru • Spinning Earth 28*; Street of Love 28; Behold This Mother 30; Spring Wind 30; Spring and a Girl 32; The Life of a Woman in the Meiji Era 35; Five Scouts 38; A Pebble by the

Wayside 38; Mud and Soldiers 39; You and I 41; Mother-and-Child Grass 42; Navy 43; The Maid's Kid 55; The Baby Carriage 56; The Stream of Youth 59; Carpenter and Children 62; Lake of Tears 66; A House of Shame 67; Scrap Collectors 68

Tashlin, Frank Little Beau Porky 36; Porky of the Northwoods 36; Porky's Poultry Plant 36; The Case of the Stuttering Pig 37; Porky's Building 37; Porky's Double Trouble 37; Porky's Railroad 37; Porky's Road Race 37; Porky's Romance 37; Speaking of the Weather 37; The Woods Are Full of Cuckoos 37; Cracked Ice 38; Have You Got Any Castles? 38; Little Pancho Vanilla 38; The Major Lied Till Dawn 38; Now That Summer Is Gone 38; Porky at the Crocadero 38; Porky the Fireman 38; Porky's Spring Planting 38; Wholly Smoke 38; You're an Education 38; The Fox and the Grapes 41; The Tangled Angler 41; A Battle for a Bottle 42; Cinderella Goes to a Party 42; Concerto in B-Flat Minor 42; Dog Meets Dog 42; A Hollywood Detour 42; Wolf Chases Pig 42; Porky Pig's Feat 43; Puss 'n' Booty 43; Scrap Happy Daffy 43; Booby Hatched 44; Brother Brat 44; I Got Plenty of Mutton 44; Plane Daffy 44; The Stupid Cupid 44; The Swooner Crooner 44; Behind the Meatball 45; Nasty Quacks 45; A Tale of Two Mice 45; The Unruly Hare 45; Hare Remover 46; The Lemon Drop Kid 50*; The First Time 51; Son of Paleface 52; Marry Me Again 53; Susan Slept Here 54; Artists and Models 55; The Lieutenant Wore Skirts 55; The Girl Can't Help It 56; Hollywood or Bust 56; Oh! For a Man! • Will Success Spoil Rock Hunter? 57; The Geisha Boy 58; Rock-a-Bye Baby 58; Say One for Me 59; Cinderfella 60; Bachelor Flat 61; It's Only Money 62; The Man from the Diner's Club 63; Who's Minding the Store? 63; The Disorderly Orderly 64; The ABC Murders • The Alphabet Murders 65; The Glass Bottom Boat 66; Caprice 67; The Private Navy of Sergeant O'Farrell 68

Tass, Nadia Malcolm 86; Rikky and Pete 88

Tassin, G. M. Nazar Stodolya 37
Tassin, George Jimmie Higgins 33
Tassios, Pavlos Paraguelia 80; Knock-Out 86

Tataranowicz, Tom Bravestarr 88
Tate, Cullen Try and Get It 24; The Carnival Girl 26

Tati, Jacques Oscar, Champion de Tennis • Oscar, Tennis Champion 32; Gai Dimanche 35; Retour à la Terre • Return to the Land 38; The Big Day • Holiday • Jour de Fête 47; L'École des Facteurs • The School for Postmen 47; Mr. Hulot's Holiday • Monsieur Hulot's Holiday • Les Vacances de Monsieur Hulot 53; Mon Oncle • My Uncle • My Uncle, Mr. Hulot 58; Playtime 67; Traffic • Trafic 70*; Parade 73
Tatischeff, Jacques *see* Tati, Jacques
Tatos, Alexandru Secvenţe • Sequences 86

Tau, Avraham Make a Face 71*
Taurog, Norman The Fly Cop 20*; School Days 20*; The Sportsman 20*; The Stage Hand 20*; The Suitor 20*; The Bakery 21*; The Bell Hop 21*; The Fall Guy 21*; The Hick 21*; The Rent Collector 21*; The Sawmill 21*; A Pair of Kings 22*; The Show 22*; The Sleuth 22*; The Four Flusher 23; The Mummy 23; Fast and Furious 24; Pain As You Enter 24; Rough and Ready 24; What a Night 24; Below Zero 25; Cheap Skates 25; Going Great 25; Hello Goodbye 25; Hello Hollywood 25; Motor Mad 25; Pleasure Bound 25; Spot Light 25; Step Lightly 25; Careful Please 26; Creeps 26; Here Comes Charlie 26; Honest Injun 26; The Humdinger 26; Jolly Tars 26; Mr. Cinderella 26; Move Along 26; Movieland 26; Nobody's Business 26; Nothing Matters 26; On Edge 26; Teacher Teacher 26; At Ease 27; Breezing Along 27; Drama de Luxe 27; The Drawback 27; Goose Flesh 27; Her Husky Hero 27; His Better Half 27; Howdy Duke 27; Kilties 27; The Little Rube 27; New Wrinkles 27; Papa's Boy 27; Plumb Dumb 27; Somebody's Fault 27; Up in Arms 27; Always a Gentleman 28; At It Again 28; Blazing Away 28; Blondes Beware 28; Cutie 28; The Farmer's Daughter 28*; The Ghetto 28; A Home Made Man 28; Listen Children 28; Rah! Rah! Rah! 28; Slippery Road 28; All Steamed Up 29; Detectives Wanted 29; The Diplomats 29; Hired and Fired 29; In Holland 29; Knights Out 29; Lucky Boy 29*; The Medicine Men 29; Troopers Three 29*; The Fatal Card 30; Finn and Hattie 30*; Follow the Leader 30; Hot Curves 30; Just a Pal 30; Meet the Boyfriend 30; Oh, Teddy 30; The Patient 30; Sing, You Dancers 30; Song Service 30; Sunny Skies 30; Cab Waiting 31; Forbidden Adventure • Newly Rich 31; The Great Pants Mystery 31; Huckleberry Finn 31*; Simply Killing 31; Skippy 31; Sooky 31; Hold 'Em Jail! 32; If I Had a Million 32*; The Phantom President 32; A Bedtime Story 33; The Way to Love 33; College Rhythm 34; Mrs. Wiggs of the Cabbage Patch 34; We're Not Dressing 34; The Big Broadcast of 1936 35; Strike Me Pink 35*; Hearts in Reunion • Reunion 36; Rhythm on the Range 36; Fifty Roads to Town 37; You Can't Have Everything 37; The Adventures of Tom Sawyer • Tom Sawyer 38; Boys Town 38; The Girl Downstairs 38; Mad About Music 38; Lucky Night 39; Young Tom Edison 39; Broadway Melody of 1940 40; Little Nellie Kelly 40; Design for Scandal 41; Men of Boys Town 41; Are Husbands Necessary? 42; A Yank at Eton 42; Girl Crazy • When the Girls Meet the Boys 43; Presenting Lily Mars 43; The Hoodlum Saint 45; The Beginning or the End? 46; Big City 48; The Bride Goes Wild 48; Words and Music 48; That Midnight Kiss 49; Mrs. O'Malley and Mr. Malone 50; Please Believe Me 50; The Toast of New Orleans 50; The Easy Way • Room for One More

51; Rich, Young and Pretty 51; Jumping Jacks 52; The Stooge 52; The Caddy 53; The Stars Are Singing 53; Living It Up 54; You're Never Too Young 55; The Birds and the Bees 56; Bundle of Joy 56; Pardners 56; The Fuzzy Pink Nightgown 57; Onionhead 58; Don't Give Up the Ship 59; G.I. Blues 60; Visit to a Small Planet 60; All Hands on Deck 61; Blue Hawaii • Hawaii Beach Boy 61; Girls! Girls! Girls! • Gumbo Ya-Ya 62; It Happened at the World's Fair • Take Me to the Fair 63; Palm Springs Weekend 63; Dr. G. and the Bikini Machine • Dr. Goldfoot and the Bikini Machine 65; Sergeant Deadhead • Sergeant Deadhead the Astronaut • Sergeant Deadhead the Astronut 65; Tickle Me 65; California Holiday • Spinout 66; Double Trouble 67; Live a Little, Love a Little 68; Speedway 68

Tavella, Dino The Embalmer • The Monster of Venice • Il Mostro di Venezia 65

Tavernier, Bertrand Les Baisers 63*; La Chance et l'Amour 64*; The Clockmaker • The Clockmaker of St. Paul • L'Horloger de Saint-Paul • The Watchmaker of St. Paul 73; Let Joy Reign Supreme • Que la Fête Commence... 74; The Judge and the Assassin • Le Juge et l'Assassin 75; Des Enfants Gâtés • Les Enfants Gâtés • Spoiled Children 77; Death in Full View • Death Watch • La Mort en Direct 79; Femmes Fatales 79; Une Semaine de Vacances • A Week's Holiday • A Week's Vacation 80; Clean Slate • Coup de Torchon 81; Un Dimanche à la Campagne • A Sunday in the Country 83; Mississippi Blues • Pays d'Octobre 83*; Autour de Minuit • Round Midnight 86; Béatrice • La Passion Béatrice • The Passion of Beatrice 86; Life and Nothing But • La Vie et Rien d'Autre 89; Daddy Nostalgia • Daddy Nostalgie 90

Taviani, Franco Masoch 80
Taviani, Paolo San Miniato, July '44 • San Miniato, Luglio '44 54*; Voltera, Comune Medievale 55*; A Man for Burning • Un Uomo da Bruciare 62*; I Fuorilegge del Matrimonio • The Matrimonial Criminals 63*; I Sovversivi • The Subversives 67*; Sotto il Segno dello Scorpione • Under the Sign of Scorpio 68*; St. Michael Had a Rooster • San Michele Aveva un Gallo 71*; Allonsanfan 74*; Father and Master • Father, Master • My Father, My Master • Padre Padrone 77*; The Field • The Meadow • Il Prato 79*; The Night of San Lorenzo • Night of the Shooting Stars • La Notte di San Lorenzo 81*; Chaos • Kaos 84*; Good Morning, Babilonia • Good Morning, Babylon 86*; Night Sun • Il Sole Anche di Notte 90*

Taviani, Vittorio San Miniato, July '44 • San Miniato, Luglio '44 54*; Voltera, Comune Medievale 55*; A Man for Burning • Un Uomo da Bruciare 62*; I Fuorilegge del Matrimonio • The Matrimonial Criminals 63*; I Sovversivi • The Subversives 67*; Sotto il Segno dello Scorpione • Under the Sign of Scorpio 68*; St. Michael

Had a Rooster • San Michele Aveva un Gallo 71*; Allonsanfan 74*; Father and Master • Father, Master • My Father, My Master • Padre Padrone 77*; The Field • The Meadow • Il Prato 79*; The Night of San Lorenzo • Night of the Shooting Stars • La Notte di San Lorenzo 81*; Chaos • Kaos 84*; Good Morning, Babilonia • Good Morning, Babylon 86*; Night Sun • Il Sole Anche di Notte 90*

Taxis, Alexis Thurn see *Thurn-Taxis, Alexis*

Tayeb, Atef el see *El Tayeb, Atef*

Taylor, Charles Thru the Eyes of Men 20; The Half Breed 22

Taylor, Clare Away from It All 79*

Taylor, Don Everything's Ducky 61; Ride the Wild Surf 64*; Jack of Diamonds 67; Un Esercito di 5 Uomini • The Five Man Army 69; Escape from the Planet of the Apes 71; Tom Sawyer 73; Echoes of a Summer • The Last Castle 75; The Great Scout and Cathouse Thursday • Wildcat 76; The Island of Dr. Moreau 77; Damien: Omen II 78; The Final Countdown 79

Taylor, Donald Conquest of the Air 36*; Night Watch 41; Battle for Music 43; Browned Off 44; Barabbas the Robber • Which Will You Have? 49; What a Husband! 52; The Straw Man 53; The Night of the Full Moon 54; The Dawn Killer 59

Taylor, Edward C. The Hand of the Law 15

Taylor, Gilbert W. Dr. Frankenstein on Campus • Flick 67

Taylor, H. Grenville see *Grenville-Taylor, H.*

Taylor, Henry Cockraft Jack Sheppard 23

Taylor, Horace A Romance of Toyland 16; A Toyland Mystery 16; A Toyland Robbery 16; The Toyland Villain 16

Taylor, John Malcolm X: Struggle for Freedom • Now Cinema! 68

Taylor, John H. 21 Today 36

Taylor, Jud Fade-In 68

Taylor, R. O. The Return of Josey Wales 86*

Taylor, Ray Fighting with Buffalo Bill 26; Whispering Smith Rides 27; The Avenging Shadow 28; Beauty and Bullets 28; The Clean-Up Man 28; The Crimson Canyon 28; Greased Lightning 28; Quick Triggers 28; Tarzan the Mighty 28*; The Vanishing Rider 28; The Ace of Scotland Yard 29; The Border Wildcat 29; Come Across 29; Eyes of the Underworld 29*; The Ridin' Demon • Riding Demon 29; The Jade Box 30; Battling with Buffalo Bill 31; Danger Island 31; Fingerprints 31; The One Way Trail 31; The Airmail Mystery 32; Heroes of the West 32; The Jungle Mystery 32; Clancy of the Mounted 33; Gordon of Ghost City • Gordon of Ghost Town 33; The Fighting Trooper • The Trooper 34; The Perils of Pauline 34; Pirate Treasure 34; The Return of Chandu 34; The Ivory-Handled Gun 35; Outlawed Guns 35; The Roaring West 35; Sunset of Power 35; Tailspin Tommy in the Great

Air Mystery 35; The Throwback 35; The Cowboy and the Kid 36; The Phantom Rider 36; Robinson Crusoe of Clipper Island • Robinson Crusoe of Mystery Island 36*; Silver Spurs 36; The Three Mesquiteers 36; The Vigilantes Are Coming 36*; Boss of Lonely Valley 37; Dick Tracy 37*; Drums of Destiny 37; Hawaiian Buckaroo 37; The Mystery of the Hooded Horsemen 37; The Painted Stallion 37*; Raw Timber 37; Sudden Bill Dorn 37; Tex Rides with the Boy Scouts 37; Flaming Frontiers 38*; Frontier Town 38; Panamint's Bad Man 38; Rawhide 38; The Spider's Web 38*; Flying G-Men 39*; Scouts to the Rescue 39*; Bad Man from Red Butte 40; Flash Gordon Conquers the Universe • Perils from the Planet Mongo • Purple Death from Outer Space 40*; The Green Hornet 40*; The Law • Law and Order • Lucky Ralston 40; Pony Post 40; Ragtime Cowboy Joe 40; Riders of Pasco Basin • Riders of the Pasco Basin 40; West of Carson City 40; Winners of the West 40*; Boss of Bullion City 41; Bury Me Not on the Lone Prairie 41; Fighting Bill Fargo 41; Law of the Range 41; Man from Montana • Montana Justice 41; Rawhide Rangers 41; Riders of Death Valley 41*; Sky Raiders 41*; Destination Unknown 42; Don Winslow of the Navy 42*; Gang Busters 42*; Junior G-Men of the Air 42*; Stagecoach Buckaroo 42; Treat 'Em Rough 42; Adventures of Smilin' Jack 43*; Adventures of the Flying Cadets 43*; Cheyenne Roundup 43; The Lone Star Trail 43; Mug Town 43; Boss of Boomtown 44; The Great Alaskan Mystery 44*; Mystery of the Riverboat 44*; Raiders of Ghost City 44*; The Daltons Ride Again 45; Jungle Queen 45*; The Master Key 45*; The Royal Mounted Rides Again 45*; Secret Agent X-9 45*; Lost City of the Jungle 46*; The Scarlet Horseman 46*; Black Hills 47; Border Feud 47; Cheyenne Takes Over 47; The Fighting Vigilantes 47; Ghost Town Renegades 47; Law of the Lash 47; The Michigan Kid 47; Pioneer Justice 47; Range Beyond the Blue 47; Return of the Lash 47; The Return of the Vigilantes • The Vigilantes Return 47; Shadow Valley 47; Stage to Mesa City 47; West to Glory 47; Wild Country 47; The Black Stallion • The Return of Wildfire 48; Check Your Guns 48; Dead Man's Gold 48; Frontier Revenge 48; Gunning for Justice 48; The Hawk of Powder River 48; Hidden Danger 48; Mark of the Lash 48; Range Justice 48; The Tioga Kid 48; Tornado Range 48; The Westward Trail 48; Crashing Thru 49; Law of the West 49; Outlaw Country 49; Shadows of the West 49; Son of a Bad Man 49; Son of Billy the Kid 49; West of Eldorado 49

Taylor, Renée It Had to Be You 88*

Taylor, Richard William Webb Ellis Are You Mad? 71; Pianorama 74; Stingray 78

Taylor, Robert The Nine Lives of Fritz the Cat 74; Heidi's Song 82

Taylor, Sam Among Those Present 21*;

I Do 21*; Never Weaken 21*; Now or Never 21*; Safety Last 23*; Why Worry? 23*; Girl Shy 24*; Hot Water 24*; The Freshman 25*; Exit Smiling 26; For Heaven's Sake 26; My Best Girl 27; Tempest 28*; The Woman Disputed 28*; Coquette • The Virgin Cocotte 29; The Taming of the Shrew 29; DuBarry, Woman of Passion 30; Ambassador Bill 31; Kiki 31; Skyline 31; Devil's Lottery 32; Out All Night 33; The Cat's Paw 34; Vagabond Lady 35; Nothing But Trouble 44

Taylor, Samuel The Monte Carlo Story 56

Taylor, Stanner E. V. A Sight Unseen 14; The Vow 15; Her Great Hour 16; Passers-By 16; The Rise of Susan 16; Public Be Damned 17; The Mohican's Daughter 22; The Lone Wolf 24; Roulette 24; The Miracle of Life 26

Taylor, William Desmond The Beggar Child 14; Billy's Rival 14; When the Road Parts 14; The Caprices of Kitty 15; The Diamond from the Sky 15*; An Eye for an Eye 15; The High Hand 15; The Last Chapter 15; Lonesome Heart 15; Nearly a Lady 15; The American Beauty 16; Ben Blair 16; Davy Crockett 16; The Happiness of Three Women 16; He Fell in Love with His Wife 16; Her Father's Son 16; The House of Lies 16; The Parson of Panamint 16; Pasquale 16; Redeeming Love 16; Big Timber 17; Jack and Jill 17; North of 53 17*; Out of the Wreck 17; The Spirit of '17 17; Tom Sawyer 17; The Varmint 17; The World Apart 17; Captain Kidd, Jr. 18; His Majesty, Bunker Bean 18; How Could You, Jean? 18; Huck and Tom 18; Johanna Enlists 18; Mile-a-Minute Kendall 18; Up the Road with Sallie 18; Anne of Green Gables 19; The Furnace 20; Huckleberry Finn 20; Jenny Be Good 20; Judy of Rogues' Harbor 20; Nurse Marjorie 20; The Soul of Youth 20; Beyond 21; Morals 21; Sacred and Profane Love 21; Wealth 21; The Witching Hour 21; The Green Temptation 22; The Top of New York 22

Tazhbayev, Amangheldy Kmo Ty, Vsadnik? 88

Tazhbayev, Rustem Skazka o Prekrasnoy Aysulu • The Tale of Beautiful Aisulu 87*

Tazi, Mohamed Abbes 87

Tazieff, Haroun Grêle de Feu 52; Eaux Souterraines 57; Les Rendezvous du Diable • Volcano 58; L'Exploration du Lac de Lave du Niragongo 59; Forbidden Volcano • Le Volcan Interdit 65

Tchernia, Pierre Bonjour l'Angoisse 88

Tcherviakov, Yevgeni Cities and Years 31; Prisoners 37

Te, Wei The Cowherd's Flute 64

Teague, Lewis Dirty O'Neil 74*; Guns, Sin and Bathtub Gin • The Lady in Red 79; Alligator 80; Death Vengeance • Fighting Back 82; Cujo 83; Cat's Eye • Stephen King's Cat's Eye 85; The Jewel of the Nile 85; Collision Course 88; Navy SEALS 90

Te-ch'ang, Yang see *Yang, Edward*

Téchiné, André Paulina S'en Va 69; French Provincial • Souvenirs d'en France

74; Barocco 76; The Brontë Sisters • Les Sœurs Brontë 78; Hôtel des Amériques 82; Rendez-Vous 85; Le Lieu du Crime • Scene of the Crime 86; The Innocent • Les Innocents 87; Maladie d'Amour • Malady of Love 87*

Tedesco, Jean The Little Match Girl • The Little Match-Seller • La Petite Marchande d'Allumettes 28*

Tej, Govind Tunda Baida 87

Telford, Frank The Bamboo Saucer • Collision Course • Operation Blue Book 68

Tell, Terry van see Van Tell, Terry

Tellegen, Lou What Money Can't Buy 17; The Things We Love 18; No Other Woman 28

Temple, Julien The Great Rock 'n' Roll Swindle 79; Punk Can Take It 79; Where Is Your Love? 79; The Secret Policeman's Other Ball 81*; The Comic Strip 83; Undercover 83; Jazzin' for Blue Jean 84; Mantrap 84; Running Out of Luck 85; Absolute Beginners 86; Aria 87*; Earth Girls Are Easy 88

Templeman, Conny Nanou 86

Templeman, Harcourt The Impatient Patient 25; An Inconvenient Infant 25; A Medical Mystery 25; A Mercenary Motive 25; There's Many a Slip 25; The White Lie 25; The Bells 31*; Money Means Nothing 32*

Templeton, George The Sundowners • Thunder in the Dust 50; Quebec 51; A Gift for Heidi 58

Teng, Wenji Qiwang 88

Tenney, Del The Curse of the Living Corpse 63; The Horror of Party Beach • Invasion of the Zombies 64; I Eat Your Skin • Voodoo Blood Bath • Zombie • Zombies 64

Tenney, Kevin S. Witchboard 85; Night of the Demons 87; Peacemaker 90

Tennyson, Pen There Ain't No Justice 39; Convoy 40; The Proud Valley 40

Tennyson, Walter Alibi Inn 35; Father O'Flynn 35*; The Ghost Walks 35; When the Cat's Away 35; Annie Laurie 36; King of Hearts • Little Gel 36*; Little Miss Somebody 39; The Body Vanishes 39; Mistaken Identity 39; Trouble for Two 39; Two Days to Live 39

Teno, Jean Marie Bikutsi Water Blues 88

Tenorio, John Grad Night 80

Tenvik, Inge The Prince of Fogo • Prinsen fra Fogo 87

Tenzer, Bert 2000 Years Later 69

Teo, Stephen Bejalai • To Go on a Journey 87

Teptsov, Oleg Gospodin Oformitel 88

Terayama, Shuji Boxer • The Boxer 77; Collections Privées 79*; Les Fruits de la Passion • The Fruits of Passion • Shina Ningyō 81

Terhune, William Okay Toots 36*

Ternovszky, Béla Cat City • Macskafogó 87

Terriss, Tom The Chimes 14*; The Mystery of Edwin Drood 14*; The Flame of Passion 15; The Pearl of Antilles 15; My

Country First 16; Society Wolves 16; The Fettered Woman 17; The Business of Life 18; Everybody's Girl 18; Find the Woman 18; The Song of the Soul 18; To the Highest Bidder 18; The Triumph of the Weak 18; The Woman Between Friends 18; The Bramble Bush 19; The Cambric Mask 19; Cap'n Abe's Niece • The Captain's Captain 19; The Climbers 19; The Lion and the Mouse 19; The Spark Divine 19; The Third Degree 19; The Vengeance of Durand 19; Captain Swift 20; Dead Men Tell No Tales 20; The Fortune Hunter 20; The Tower of Jewels 20; Trumpet Island 20; The Heart of Maryland 21; Boomerang Bill 22; The Challenge 22; Find the Woman 22; Fires of Fate 23; The Harbour Lights 23; The Bandolero 24; The Desert Sheik 24; His Buddy's Wife 25; The Romance of a Million Dollars 26; The Girl from Rio 27; Temptations of a Shop Girl 27; Beyond London Lights 28; Clothes Make the Woman 28; The Naughty Duchess 28

Terry, Alice Baroud • Les Hommes Bleus • Love in Morocco • Passion in the Desert 31*

Terry, John Colman Hands Across the Sea 16; Misadventures of the Bull Moose 16; Now You See It Now You Don't 16; Our Merchant Marine 16; Somewhere in America 16; When Noah's Ark Embarked 17; Ideal Crossword Puzzles No. 1 • Judge's Crossword Puzzles No. 1 25; Ideal Crossword Puzzles No. 2 • Judge's Crossword Puzzles No. 2 25; Ideal Crossword Puzzles No. 3 • Judge's Crossword Puzzles No. 3 25; Ideal Crossword Puzzles No. 4 • Judge's Crossword Puzzles No. 4 25; Ideal Crossword Puzzles No. 5 • Judge's Crossword Puzzles No. 5 25; Ideal Crossword Puzzles No. 6 • Judge's Crossword Puzzles No. 6 25; Ideal Crossword Puzzles No. 7 • Judge's Crossword Puzzles No. 7 25; Ideal Crossword Puzzles No. 8 • Judge's Crossword Puzzles No. 8 25; Ideal Crossword Puzzles No. 9 • Judge's Crossword Puzzles No. 9 25; Ideal Crossword Puzzles No. 10 • Judge's Crossword Puzzles No. 10 25

Terry, Paul Down on the Phoney Farm 15; Little Herman 15; Farmer Al Falfa Invents a New Kite 16; Farmer Al Falfa Sees New York 16; Farmer Al Falfa's Blind Pig 16; Farmer Al Falfa's Catastrophe 16; Farmer Al Falfa's Egg-citement 16; Farmer Al Falfa's Prune Plantation 16; Farmer Al Falfa's Revenge 16; Farmer Al Falfa's Scientific Diary 16; Farmer Al Falfa's Tentless Circus 16; Farmer Al Falfa's Watermelon Patch 16; Farmer Al Falfa's Wolfhound 16; Character As Revealed by the Ear 17; Character As Revealed by the Eye 17; Character As Revealed by the Mouth 17; Character As Revealed by the Nose 17; Farmer Al Falfa and His Wayward Pup 17; Golden Spoon Mary 17; His Trail 17; Some Barrier 17; 20,000 Feats Under the Sea 17; The Bone of Contention 20; Farmer Al Falfa's Bride 23; Farmer Al Falfa's Pet Cat 23

Terwilliger, George Daughters of Men 14; The Cipher Key 15; Destiny's Skein 15; The Nation's Peril 15; The Regenerating Love 15; The Ringtailed Rhinoceros 15; The City of Failing Light 16; The Lash of Destiny 16; Race Suicide 16; The Price Woman Pays 19; Dollars and the Woman 20; The Fatal Hour 20; Slaves of Pride 20; The Sporting Duchess 20; Little Italy 21; The Bride's Play 22; What Fools Men Are 22; Wife in Name Only 23; Daughters Who Pay 25; The Big Show 26; The Highbinders 26; Married? 26; Crime of Voodoo • Drums of the Jungle • Ouanga 35

Teschenbruck, Mano Ziffer see Ziffer-Teschenbruck, Mano

Teschner, Prof. Der Geheimnisvolle Spiegel • The Mystic Mirror 27*

Teshigahara, Hiroshi Hokusai 53; Sofu Teshigahara 57; Tokyo 1958 58*; José Torres 59; A Cheap Sweet and a Kid • Otoshiana • The Pitfall 61; Suna no Onna • Woman in the Dunes • Woman of the Dunes 63; Les Adolescentes • The Adolescents • La Fleur de l'Âge • La Fleur de l'Âge ou Les Adolescentes • That Tender Age 64*; The Face of Another • Tanin no Kao 65; José Torres II 65; Bakusō • Explosion Course 67; The Man Without a Map • Moetsukita Chizu 68; Ichinichi 240 Jikan • One Day, 240 Hours 70; Summer Soldiers 71; Out of Work for Years 75; Rikyu 89

Tessari, Duccio Arrivano i Titani • My Son, the Hero • Sons of Thunder • I Titani • Les Titans 61; Il Fornaretto di Venezia 63; The Scapegoat 63; Secret of the Sphinx • La Sfinge È Sorride Prima di Morire, Stop — Londra 64; A Pistol for Ringo • Una Pistola para Ringo • Una Pistola per Ringo 65; The Return of Ringo • Il Ritorno di Ringo 65; Una Voglio da Morire 65; Kiss Kiss...Bang Bang 66; For Love...for Magic • Per Amore...per Magia 67; I Bastardi • The Cats • Sons of Satan 68; Better a Widow • Meglio Vedova 68; Alive...or Preferably Dead • Vivi o Preferibilmente Morti 69; Matchball 69; Quella Piccola Differenza • That Little Difference 69; Death Occurred Last Night • Death Took Place Last Night • La Morte Risale a Ieri Sera 70; Forza G • Winged Devils 70; Don't Turn the Other Cheek • Long Live Your Death • Viva la Muerte...Tua! 71; Big Guns • No Way Out • Tony Arzenta 72; Gli Eroi • The Heroes 72; Three Tough Guys 74; Zorro 75; Tex e il Signore degli Abissi • Tex Willer and the Lord of the Deep 85

Testa, Dante Padre 12*

Testa, Eugenio Frankenstein's Monster • The Monster of Frankenstein • Il Mostro di Frankenstein 20

Teterin, Yevgeni Mumu 61*

Tetzlaff, Ted World Premiere 41; Riffraff 47; Fighting Father Dunne 48; A Dangerous Profession 49; Hounded • Johnny Allegro 49; The Window 49; Gambling House 50; Under the Gun 50; The White Tower 50; The Treasure of Lost

Canyon 51; Terror on a Train • Time Bomb 53; Nights in a Harem • Son of Sinbad 55; Seven Wonders of the World 56*; The Young Land 57

Teuber, Monica Die Kurve Kriegen 85; Silent Night 88; Magdalene 90

Teveth, Akiva Atalia 85

Tevos, Herbert Lost Women • Lost Women of Zarpa • The Mesa of Lost Women 49*

Tewkesbury, Joan Old Boyfriends 78

Tewksbury, Peter Sunday in New York 63; Emil and the Detectives 64; Doctor, You've Got to Be Kidding 67; Stay Away, Joe 68; The Chautauqua • The Trouble with Girls • The Trouble with Girls (And How to Get Into It) 69

Texera, Diego de la see De la Texera, Diego

Tezuku, Osamu Hi no Tori 2772 • Phoenix 2772 • Space Firebird 2772 79*

Thakkar, Mohan Panetar 88

Thakur, R. Jungal ki Beti 88

Thanh, Huy Loi Re Trai Tren Duong Mon • Return to the Right Path 86

Thayer, Otis B. The Awakening of Bess Morton 16; The Mystery of No. 47 17; Miss Arizona 19; The Desert Scorpion 20; Wolves of the Street 20; Finders Keepers 21; Out of the Depths 21*; Riders of the Range 23; Tracy the Outlaw 23

Theiss, Herbert V. Deadly Treasure of the Piranha • Killer Fish • Treasure of the Piranha 78*

Theos, Dimos Chapetan Meitanos: I Ikona enas Mythikou Prosopou • Ikona enas Mythikou Prosopou • Image of a Mythical Personage 87

Theumer, Ernst R. von Code of Silence • Killers' Cage 60; In der Hölle Ist Noch Platz • Sex Agent • Still Room in Hell • There Is Still Room in Hell 63; Bloodsuckers • Death Island • Das Geheimnis der Todeninsel • La Isla de la Muerte • Island of the Dead • The Island of the Doomed • Man-Eater of Hydra • The Maneaters of Hydra 66; The Daughter of Frankenstein • La Figlia di Frankenstein • Lady Frankenstein • Madame Frankenstein 71; Joy Ride to Nowhere 78; Baby Dolls 82; Jungle Warriors 84; Hell Hunters 88

Thevenet, Virginie La Nuit Porte Jarretelles 85; Games of Artifice • Jeux d'Artifices 87

Thiago, Paulo Jorge, a Brazilian • Jorge um Brasileiro 89

Thiele, Eugen Der Hellseher 33; Der Feldherrnhügel 34

Thiele, Rolf Primanerinnen 51; Der Tag Vor der Hochzeit 52; Geliebtes Leben 53; Sie 54; Die Barrings 55; Friederike von Barring 56; Skandal in Ischl 57; The Girl Rosemarie • Das Mädchen Rosemarie • Rosemarie • Rosemary 58; Labyrinth • Labyrinth der Leidenschaft 59; Der Liebe Augustin 60; Lulu • No Orchids for Lulu 62; Moral '63 63; DM-Killer 64; Tonio Kröger 64; Das Liebeskarussell 65; The Liar and the Nun • Der Lügner und die Nonne

67*; The Duck Rings at Half Past Seven • Die Ente Klingelt um Halb Sieben 69; Ohrfeigen 69; Gelöbt Sei Was Hart Macht 72; Slap in the Face 75; Ondine 76

Thiele, Wilhelm Franz Lehar 23*; Märchen aus Alt-Wien 23; His Late Excellency • Die Selige Exzellenz 27; Orientexpress 27; Die Dame mit der Maske 28; Hurra! Ich Lebe! • Hurrah! I'm Alive! 28; Adieu Mascotte 29; Le Chemin du Paradis 30; Die Drei von der Tankstelle • From the Gas Station • Three from the Gas Station • Three Men and Lilian 30; Liebeswalzer • The Love Waltz 30*; L'Amoureuse Aventure 31; Le Bal 31; Der Ball 31; Madame Hat Ausgang 31; La Fille et le Garçon • The Girl and the Boy 32; Marry Me 32; Zwei Herzen und ein Schlag 32; Grossfürstin Alexandra 33; Waltz Time 33; Lottery Lover 35; The Jungle Princess 36; Beg, Borrow or Steal 37; London by Night 37; Bad Little Angel 39; Bridal Suite • Maiden Voyage 39; The Ghost Comes Home 40; Tarzan Triumphs 43; Tarzan's Desert Mystery 43; The Madonna's Secret 46; Der Letzte Fussgänger 60; Sabine und die 100 Männer 60

Thiele, William see Thiele, Wilhelm

Thiery, Fritz Prinzessin Sissy 39

Thom, Robert Angel, Angel, Down We Go • Cult of the Damned 69

Thomas, Anna The Haunting of M 79

Thomas, Antony Thy Kingdom Come … Thy Will Be Done 88

Thomas, Augustus The Jungle 14; The Nightingale 14; Paid in Full 14; Soldiers of Fortune 14; The Garden of Lies 15

Thomas, Dave Strange Brew 83*; The Experts 87

Thomas, Derek see Bogdanovich, Peter

Thomas, Gerald Circus Friends 56; The Circle • The Vicious Circle 57; Time Lock 57; Carry On Sergeant 58; Chain of Events 58; The Duke Wore Jeans 58; The Solitary Child 58; Carry On Nurse 59; Carry On Teacher 59; Please Turn Over 59; Beware of Children • No Kidding 60; Carry On Constable 60; Watch Your Stern 60; Carry On Regardless 61; Raising the Wind • Roommates 61; Carry On Cruising 62; The Iron Maiden • The Swingin' Maiden 62; Twice Round the Daffodils 62; Call Me a Cab • Carry On Cabbie • Carry On Cabby 63; Carry On Jack • Carry On Venus 63; Nurse on Wheels 63; Carry On Cleo 64; Carry On Spying 64; The Big Job 65; Carry On Cowboy 65; Carry On Screaming • Carry On Vampire 66; Don't Lose Your Head 66; Carry On, Follow That Camel • Follow That Camel 67; Carry On Doctor 68; Carry On…Up the Khyber 68; Carry On Again, Doctor 69; Carry On Camping 69; Carry On Henry • Carry On Henry VIII 70; Carry On Loving 70; Carry On Up the Jungle 70; Carry On at Your Convenience 71; Bless This House 72; Carry On Abroad 72; Carry On Matron 72; Carry On Girls 73; Carry On Dick 74; Carry On Behind 75; Carry On England 76; That's Carry On! 77; Carry On Em-

mannuelle 78; The Second Victory 86

Thomas, Jack W. We'll Bury You 62

Thomas, John G. Tin Man 83; Banzai Runner 87; Arizona Heat 88

Thomas, Michael The Young Seducers 74

Thomas, Pascal Les Zozos 72; Don't Cry with Your Mouth Full • Pleure Pas la Bouche Pleine • Spring Into Summer 73; Le Chaud Lapin 74; Nono Nénesse 75*; La Surprise du Chef 76; Un Oursin dans la Poche 77; Confidences pour Confidences • Heart to Heart 78; Les Maris, les Femmes, les Amants 88

Thomas, Ralph Once Upon a Dream 48; Helter Skelter 49; Traveller's Joy 49; The Clouded Yellow 50; Appointment with Venus • Island Rescue 51; The Assassin • Venetian Bird 52; A Day to Remember 53; Doctor in the House 53; The Dog and the Diamonds 53; Mad About Men 54; Above Us the Waves 55; Doctor at Sea 55; Checkpoint 56; The Iron Petticoat 56; Campbell's Kingdom 57; Doctor at Large 57; A Tale of Two Cities 58; The Wind Cannot Read 58; The 39 Steps 59; Upstairs and Downstairs 59; Conspiracy of Hearts 60; Doctor in Love 60; No Love for Johnnie 61; No, My Darling Daughter 61; A Pair of Briefs 62; The Wild and the Willing • The Young and the Willing • Young and Willing 62; Agent 8¾ • Hot Enough for June 63; Doctor in Distress 63; A Date with Death • The High, Bright Sun • McGuire, Go Home! 64; Carnaby, M.D. • Doctor in Clover 65; Deadlier Than the Male 66; The High Commissioner • Nobody Runs Forever 68; Some Girls Do 68; Doctor in Trouble 70; Percy 70; Quest for Love 71; It's a 2'6" Above the Ground World • The Love Ban 72; It's Not the Size That Counts • Percy's Progress 74; A Nightingale Sang in Berkeley Square 79

Thomas, Ralph L. Ticket to Heaven 81; Apprentice to Murder 87; The First Season 89

Thomas, Ramzi Appointment with Fear 85

Thomas, Richard The Love Pirate • The Silent Accuser 23; Phantom Justice 24; The Truthful Sex 26; The Woman Who Was Forgotten 30

Thomas, Robert La Bonne Soupe • Careless Love • The Good Soup 63; Friend of the Family • Patate 65

Thomas, Scott Silent Assassins 88*

Thomas, Vincent see Gicca, Enzo

Thomas, William C. Midnight Manhunt • One Exciting Night 45; They Made Me a Killer 46; Big Town • Guilty Assignment 47; Big Town After Dark • Underworld After Dark 47; I Cover Big Town • I Cover the Underworld 47; Big Town Scandal • Underworld Scandal 48; Special Agent 49

Thomashefsky, Harry Jewish King Lear 35

Thomason, Harry Encounter with the Unknown 73; So Sad About Gloria 73; The Great Lester Boggs 75; The Day It Came to Earth 79

Thome, Rudolph Tarot 86; Das Mikroscop 88; Forms of Love • Seven Women • Sieben Frauen 89

Thomopoulos, Andreas Asymvivastos • Easy Road 79

Thompson, Brett Not Since Casanova 88

Thompson, David Life's Shadows 16*; The Stolen Triumph 16

Thompson, Ernest 1969 88

Thompson, Francis Jascha Heifetz Master Class 62*; To Be Alive 62*; To the Fair! 64*; We Are Young 67*; US 68*

Thompson, Frederick The Christian 14; After Dark 15; The Country Boy 15; The Goose Girl 15*; Her Mother's Secret 15; The Wonderful Adventure 15; The Chattel 16; An Enemy to the King 16; The Feud Girl • The Trust 16; Nearly a King 16; A Parisian Romance 16; The Saleslady 16; The Danger Trail 17; The Man of Mystery 17; How Could You, Caroline? 18; The Mating 18; A Nymph of the Foothills • A Nymph of the Woods 18; Wild Primrose 18; The Marriage Pit 20; The Heart Line 21

Thompson, Harlan The Past of Mary Holmes 33*; Kiss and Make Up 34

Thompson, Harry The Passage 87

Thompson, J. Lee see Lee-Thompson, J.

Thompson, Keane As the Devil Commands 33*

Thompson, Marshall A Yank in Vietnam • Year of the Tiger 64

Thompson, Palmer Make Like a Thief • Run Like a Thief 64*

Thompson, Tony Swift Water 52

Thompson, Walter Seven Wonders of the World 56*; Cinerama—South Seas Adventure • South Seas Adventure 58*

Thompson, William L. The Irish Gringo 35

Thoms, Albie Palm Beach 79

Thomsen, Christian Braad Dear Irene • Kære Irene 71; Koks i Kulissen • Ladies on the Rocks 83

Thomsen, Knud Leif Gift • Poison • Venom 66

Thomson, Chris The Empty Beach 85

Thomson, Margaret Child's Play 54

Thornburg, Lee Lone Star Country 83*; Hollywood High, Part Two 84*

Thornby, Robert The Almighty Dollar 16; Broken Chains 16; The Crucial Test 16*; Her Maternal Right 16*; A Woman's Power 16; The Fair Barbarian 17; Forbidden Paths 17; The Hostage 17; A Kiss for Susie 17; Little Miss Optimist 17; Molly Entangled 17; On Dangerous Ground 17; Fallen Angel 18; Lawless Love 18; A Little Sister of Everybody 18; Are You Legally Married? 19; Carolyn of the Corners 19; Fighting Cressy 19; The Prince and Betty 19; Rose o' the River • Rose of the River 19; When My Ship Comes In 19; The Deadlier Sex 20; Felix O'Day 20; The Girl in the Web 20; Half a Chance 20; Simple Souls 20; The Blazing Trail 21; The Fox 21; The Magnificent Brute 21; That Girl Montana 21; Lorna Doone 22*; The Sagebrush Trail 22; The Trap 22; The Drivin' Fool 23; Gold Madness 23; Stormswept 23;

The Speeding Venus 26; West of Broadway 26; Young Hollywood 27

Thorndike, Andrew Aus Unseren Tage 49*; Der Dreizehn Oktober 49; Der Weg nach Oben 50; Wilhelm Pieck—Das Leben Unseres Präsidenten 51; Die Entführung 52; Der Prüfung 52*; Sieben vom Rhein 54*; Du und Mancher Kameraden • The German Story 56*; General Speidel 57*; Holiday on Sylt • Urlaub auf Sylt 57*; Unternehmen Teutonenschwert 58*; The Russian Miracle • Das Russische Wunder 63*; Tito in Deutschland 65*; Du Bist Mein—Ein Deutsches Tagebuch • A German Diary 69*

Thorndike, Annelie Der Prüfung 52*; Sieben vom Rhein 54*; Du und Mancher Kameraden • The German Story 56*; General Speidel 57*; Holiday on Sylt • Urlaub auf Sylt 57*; Unternehmen Teutonenschwert 58*; The Russian Miracle • Das Russische Wunder 63*; Tito in Deutschland 65*; Du Bist Mein—Ein Deutsches Tagebuch • A German Diary 69*

Thornhill, Michael The F.J. Holden 77; The Everlasting Secret Family 88

Thornton, F. Martin Algy, Did He Deserve It? 12; Ambitious Children • Children's Thoughts for the Future 12; For Love and the King • The Romance of a Royalist Maid 12; Gollywog's Motor Accident • In Gollywog Land 12*; Illustrated Proverbs 12; An Indian's Recompense 12; The Knockout Blow 12; Making a Man of Him 12; Mephisto 12*; An Outlaw Yet a Man 12; Potted Plays No. 1 • The Society Playwright 12; Santa Claus 12*; Tit for Tat 12; Where There's a Will There's a Way 12; A White Man's Way 12; The Baby • Potted Plays No. 2 13; The Child of a Suffragette 13; The Fish and the Ring 13*; The Fishmonger's Apprentice 13; In the Days of Robin Hood 13; Love and War in Toyland 13*; The Tempter 13*; The World, the Flesh and the Devil 13; Bravo Kilties! 14; By the Kaiser's Orders 14; Carat 14; Chained to the Enemy 14; A Daughter of Belgium 14; Dead Men Tell No Tales 14; The Dead Past Recalled 14; Little Lord Fauntleroy 14; The Little Picture Producer 14*; The Looters of Liege 14; The Lost Collar Stud 14; The Second Penalty 14; Young Briton Foils the Enemy 14; The Call of the Motherland 15; The Faith of a Child 15; A Hero of the Trenches 15; Jane Shore • The Strife Eternal 15*; New Adventures of Baron Münchhausen 15; The Vengeance of Allah 15; Diana and Destiny 16; The Man Who Bought London 16; The Happy Warrior 17; If Thou Wert Blind 17; Love's Old Sweet Song 17; The Great Imposter 18; Nature's Gentleman 18; Rilka • Rilka, or The Gypsy Queen • A Romany Lass 18; The Splendid Coward 18; Where's Watling? 18; The Knave of Hearts 19; The Man Who Forgot 19; The Power of Right 19; The Warrior Strain 19; Bars of Iron 20; The Branded Soul • The Iron Stair 20; The Flame 20; Frailty 21; Gwyneth of the

Welsh Hills 21; My Lord Conceit 21; The Prey of the Dragon 21; The River of Stars 21; Belonging 22; Lamp in the Desert 22; Little Brother of God 22; Melody of Death 22; A Sailor Tramp 22; The Romany 23; Mutiny 24; Women and Diamonds 24

Thorpe, Jerry The Venetian Affair 66; Day of the Evil Gun • Evil Gun 68; Company of Killers • The Protectors 70

Thorpe, Richard That's That 23; Battling Buddy 24; Bringin' Home the Bacon 24; Fast and Fearless 24; Gold and Grit 24; Hard Hittin' Hamilton 24; Rarin' to Go 24; Rip Roarin' Roberts 24; Rough Ridin' 24; Thundering Romance 24; Walloping Wallace 24; The Desert Demon 25; Double Action Daniels 25; Fast Fightin' 25; Full Speed 25; Galloping On 25; On the Go 25; Quicker'n Lightnin' 25; The Saddle Cyclone 25; A Streak of Luck 25; Tearin' Loose 25; The Bandit Buster 26; The Bonanza Buckaroo 26; College Days 26; Coming an' Going 26; The Cyclone Cowboy 26; The Dangerous Dub 26; Deuce High 26; Double Daring 26; Easy Going 26; The Fighting Cheat 26; Josselyn's Wife 26; The Last Card 26; Rawhide 26; Riding Rivals 26; Roarin' Broncs 26; The Roaring Rider 26; A Soda Water Cowboy 26; Speedy Spurs 26; Trumpin' Trouble 26; Twin Triggers 26; Twisted Triggers 26; Between Dangers 27; The Desert of the Lost 27; The First Night 27; The Galloping Gobs 27; The Interferin' Gent 27; The Meddlin' Stranger 27; The Obligin' Buckaroo 27; Pals in Peril 27; Ride 'Em High 27; The Ridin' Rowdy 27; Skedaddle Gold 27; Tearin' Into Trouble 27; White Pebbles 27; The Ballyhoo Buster 28; The Cowboy Cavalier 28; Desperate Courage 28; The Flyin' Buckaroo • The Flying Buckaroo 28; Saddle Mates 28; The Valley of Hunted Men 28; The Vanishing West 28; Vultures of the Sea 28; The Bachelor Girl 29; The Fatal Warning 29; King of the Kongo 29; Bimi • King of the Wild 30*; Border Romance 30; The Dude Wrangler • Feminine Touch 30; The Lone Defender 30; Riding to Win • The Thoroughbred 30; Under Montana Skies 30; The Utah Kid 30; Wings of Adventure 30; The Devil Plays 31; Forgotten Women 31; Grief Street • Stage Whispers 31; The Lady from Nowhere 31; The Lawless Woman 31; Neck and Neck 31; Silver Devil • Wild Horse 31*; The Sky Spider 31; The Beauty Parlor 32; Cross Examination 32; Dangerous Ground • Escapade 32; The Death Ray • Murder at Dawn 32; Dream Mother • The Midnight Lady 32; Forbidden Company 32; The King Murder 32; Probation • Second Chances 32; The Secrets of Wu Sin 32; Slightly Married 32; The Thrill of Youth 32; Women Won't Tell 32; Forgotten 33; I Have Lived 33; Love Is Dangerous • Women Are Dangerous 33; Love Is Like That 33; A Man of Sentiment 33; Notorious But Nice 33; Rainbow Over Broadway 33; Strange People 33; At the Stroke of Nine • Murder on the Campus •

On the Stroke of Nine 34; Cheating Cheaters 34; City Park 34; Green Eyes 34; The Quitter • The Quitters 34; Secret of the Château 34; Stolen Sweets 34; Last of the Pagans 35; Strange Wives 35; Dangerous Number 36; Tarzan Escapes! 36*; The Voice of Bugle Ann 36; Double Wedding 37; Love Is a Headache 37; Man-Proof 37; Night Must Fall 37; The Crowd Roars 38; The First Hundred Years 38; Frou Frou • The Toy Wife 38; Three Loves Has Nancy 38; The Adventures of Huckleberry Finn • Huckleberry Finn 39; The Earl of Chicago 39; Tarzan Finds a Son! 39; The Bad Man • Two-Gun Cupid 40; Bad Man of Wyoming • Wyoming 40; Twenty Mule Team 40; Barnacle Bill 41; Highway to Freedom • Joe Smith, American 41; Tarzan's Secret Treasure 41; Apache Trail 42; Tarzan's New York Adventure 42; Three Hearts for Julia 42; White Cargo 42; Above Suspicion 43; Cry Havoc! 43; The Thin Man Goes Home 44; Two Girls and a Sailor 44; Her Highness and the Bellboy 45; Thrill of a Romance 45; What Next, Corporal Hargrove? 45; Fiesta 47; This Time for Keeps 47; Big Jack 48; A Date with Judy 48; On an Island with You 48; The Sun Comes Up 48; Black Hand 49; Challenge to Lassie 49; East of the Rising Sun • Malaya 49; Three Little Words 50; Vengeance Valley 50; The Great Caruso 51; It's a Big Country 51*; The Unknown Man 51; Carbine Williams 52; Ivanhoe 52; The Prisoner of Zenda 52; All the Brothers Were Valiant 53; The Girl Who Had Everything 53; Knights of the Round Table 53; Athena 54; The Student Prince 54; The Adventures of Quentin Durward • Quentin Durward 55; Bedevilled 55*; The Prodigal 55; Ten Thousand Bedrooms 56; Jailhouse Rock 57; Time for Action • Tip on a Dead Jockey 57; Adamson of Africa • Killers from Kilimanjaro • Killers of Kilimanjaro 59; The House of the Seven Hawks 59; I Tartari • The Tartars 60*; The Honeymoon Machine 61; The Horizontal Lieutenant 62; How the West Was Won 62*; Follow the Boys 63; Fun in Acapulco 63; The Golden Head 64; Miss Jude • The Truth About Spring 64; That Funny Feeling 65; The Scorpio Letters 66; The Last Challenge • Pistolero • The Pistolero of Red River 67

Thorstenson, Espen Grandma and the Eight Children 77

Thring, F. W. His Royal Highness 32; Harmony Row 33

Thulin, Ingrid En och En • One and One • One Plus One 78*; Broken Sky • Bruten Himmel 82

Thurn-Taxis, Alexis A Night for Crime 42; The Yanks Are Coming 42; Man of Courage 43; Daisy Goes to Hollywood • Hollywood and Vine 45

Tian, Zhuangzhuang Daoma Zei • Horse Thief 85

Tianming, Wu see Wu, Tianming

Tie, Li see Li, Tie

Tikhomirov, Roman Eugene Onegin 59; Pikovaya Dama • Queen of Spades 60;

Cholpon—Utrennyaya Zvezda • Morning Star 62

Tikhonov, Nikolai Revolt in the Desert 32

Tilghman, William The Passing of the Oklahoma Outlaws 15

Till, Eric A Great Big Thing 67; Hot Millions 68; The Walking Stick 70; A Fan's Notes 72; All Things Bright and Beautiful • It Shouldn't Happen to a Vet 76; Bethune 77; Wild Horse Hank 79; Improper Channels 81; If You Could See What I Hear 82; Turning to Stone 85

Tilley, Frank Venetian Lovers 25*; Curfew Shall Not Ring Tonight 26; The Pied Piper of Hamelin 26; The Pipes of Lucknow 26; The Wreck of the Hesperus 26

Tillman, Lynne Committed 85*

Tilton, Roger Jazz Dance 54; Spiker 86

Tímár, Péter Egészséges Erotika • Healthy Eroticism • Sound Eroticism 85

Timm, Peter Meier 86; Fifty-Fifty 89

Timoshenko, Semen Sniper 32; Island of Doom 33; Goal Keeper 37; Kino-Concert 1941 • Leningrad Music Hall 41*; The Boys from Leningrad 55

Timreck, Theodore W. A Good Dissonance Like a Man 77

Tinayre, Daniel The Cicada Is Not an Insect • La Cigarra No Es un Bicho • The Games Men Play • The Hotel 68

Ting, Li see Li, Ting

Ting, Shan-hsi Blood Reincarnation • Yin-Yang Chieh 74; The Story of Dr. Sun Yat-Sen 87

Tinling, James Very Confidential 27; Don't Marry 28; Soft Living 28; The Exalted Flapper 29; True Heaven 29; Words and Music 29; For the Love o' Lil • For the Love of Lil 30; One Mad Kiss 30*; The Flood 31; Arizona to Broadway 33; Jimmy and Sally 33; The Last Trail 33; El Último Varón Sobre la Tierra 33; Call It Luck 34; Love Time 34; Three on a Honeymoon 34; Charlie Chan in Shanghai 35; A Married Woman Needs a Husband • Señora Casada Necesita Marido 35; Under the Pampas Moon 35; Welcome Home 35; Your Uncle Dudley 35*; Back to Nature 36; Champagne Charlie 36; Educating Father 36; Every Saturday Night 36; The Holy Terror 36; Pepper 36; Angel's Holiday 37; Change of Heart 37; 45 Fathers 37; The Great Hospital Mystery 37; Sing and Be Happy 37; Mr. Moto's Gamble 38; Passport Husband 38; Sharpshooters 38; Boy Friend 39; Last of the Duanes 41; Riders of the Purple Sage 41; The Lone Star Ranger 42; Sundown Jim 42; Cosmo Jones—Crime Smasher • Cosmo Jones in The Crime Smasher • Crime Smasher 43; Dangerous Millions • The House of Tao Ling 46; Deadline for Murder 46; Rendezvous 24 46; Strange Journey 46; Roses Are Red 47; Second Chance 47; Night Wind 48; Trouble Preferred 48; Tales of Robin Hood 51

Tintner, Hans Cyankali 30; Kaiserliebchen 31; Goethes Jugendgeliebte 32

Tiomkin, Dmitri Tchaikovsky • Tschai-

kovsky 70*

Tirl, Jiří Pistols 74

Tissé, Edward Soviet Russia Today 35; Bessmertnyi Garnizon • The Immortal Garrison 56*

Tissi, Felix Noah und der Cowboy 86

To, Johnny Seven Years Itch 87

Toback, James Fingers 77; Love and Money 80; Exposed 83; The Pick-Up Artist 87; The Big Bang 89

Tobalina, Carlos Double Initiation 70; The Last Tango in Acapulco 75

Tobias, Marice Pulsebeat 86

Tobin, Thomas J. Fraternity Row • Oh Brotherhood 77

Toboada, Carlos Enrique Poison for Fairies • Veneno para las Hadas 86

Tobolowsky, Stephen Two Idiots in Hollywood 88

Todd, Ann Thunder of the Gods 66; Thunder of the Kings 67

Todd, Holbrook Secrets of Hollywood 33*

Todd, J. Hunter The Gold Guitar 66

Todini, Amanzio Big Deal on Madonna Street . . . Twenty Years Later • I Soliti Ignoti Vent'Anni Dopo 85

Todorovsky, Pyotr Voenno-Polevoi Roman • Wartime Romance 85; Downtown with a Band • Po Glavnoy Ulitse s Orkestrom 87

Tognazzi, Ugo Il Mantenuto 61; Il Fischio al Naso 67; Sissignore 68; I Viaggiatori della Sera 79

Tokar, Norman Big Red 62; Sammy the Way-Out Seal 62; Savage Sam 63; A Tiger Walks 63; Those Calloways 64; The Ugly Dachshund 65; Follow Me, Boys! 66; The Happiest Millionaire 67; The Horse in the Gray Flannel Suit • Year of the Horse 68*; Rascal 69; The Boatniks 70; Snowball Express 72; The Apple Dumpling Gang 74; Where the Red Fern Grows 74; Double Trouble • No Deposit, No Return 76; Candleshoe 77; The Cat from Outer Space 78

Tokarev, Boris Insurrection Square • Ploshchad Vosstania 87; Nochnoi Ekipazh 88

Tokatli, Erdoğan Bridge to the Sun • Güneşe Köprü 86

Toland, Gregg December 7th • December 7th: The Movie 42*

Toledano, Philippe Far from Dallas 72

Toledo, Sérgio Vera 87

Tolmár, Tamás The Fall • Zuhanás Közben 87

Tom, Konrad Książątko • The Lottery Prince 37*; Little Mothers • Mamele 38*

Tomashevsky, M. Bonch see Bonch-Tomashevsky, M.

Tomašić, Anton Cormorant • Kormoran 86

Tomić, Živorad King of Endings • Kraljeva Završnica 87

Tomlinson, Judith T. Dan Smith 87*

Tomlinson, Lionel Death in High Heels 47; My Hands Are Clay 48; Who Killed Van Loon? 48*; Take a Powder 53*

Tomson, Randolph Chorus Girl 48

Tone, Franchot Uncle Vanya 58*

Tong, Terry Hong Kong Graffiti 85

Tontichkin, A. Free Wind • Volnyi Veter 61*

Topper, Burt Hell Squad 58; Diary of a High School Bride 59; Tank Commando • Tank Commandos 59; War Hero • War Is Hell • War Madness 63; The Strangler 64; The Devil's Eight 68; The Hard Ride 71; The Day the Lord Got Busted 76

Törhönen, Lauri Burning Angel • Palava Enkeli 84; Riisuminen • The Undressing 86; Jään Kääntöpiiri • Tropic of Ice 87

Torn, Rip The Telephone 88

Tornatore, Giuseppe Zebra Force 77; Il Camorrista • The Professor 86; Code Name Zebra 87; Cinema Paradiso • Nuovo Cinema Paradiso 88; Grotesque 88; Everybody's Fine • Stanno Tutti Bene 90

Tornatore, Joe see *Tornatore, Giuseppe*

Tornes, Stavros Danilo Treles, o Fimismenos Andalousianos Mousikos • Danilo Treles, the Famous Andalusian Musician 86; Enas Erodios via tin Germania 88

Torrado, Ramón La Carga de la Policía Montada • Cavalry Charge 65

Torrance, Robert Mutant on the Bounty 89

Torre, Hans Franz Lehar 23*

Torre, Raúl de la see *De la Torre, Raúl*

Torre-Nilsson, Leopoldo El Muro • The Wall 47; El Crimen de Oribe • Oribe's Crime 49*; El Hijo del Crack • Son of the Star 53*; La Tigra • The Tigress 53; Days of Hate • Days of Hatred • Días de Odio 54; Para Vestir Santos • The Spinsters • To Clothe the Saints 54; Graciela 56; El Protégé • El Protegido 56; Los Árboles de Buenos-Aires 57; La Casa del Ángel • End of Innocence • The House of Angel • The House of the Angel 57; Precursores de la Pintura Argentina 57; La Caída • The Fall 58; The Kidnapper • El Secuestrador 58; The Blood Feast • Fin de Fiesta • The Party Is Over 59; Un Guapo del 1900 • Tough Guy of 1900 60; The Hand in the Trap • La Mano en la Trampa 61; Piel de Verano • Summer Skin 61; The Female • Setenta Veces Siete • Seventy Times Seven 62; Four Women for One Hero • Homage at Siesta Time • Homage to the Siesta • Homenaje a la Hora de la Siesta 62; The Roof Garden • The Terrace • La Terraza 62; The Eavesdropper • El Ojo de la Cerradura 64; Cavar un Foso • To Dig a Pit 66; La Chica del Lunes • Monday's Child 66; Los Traidores de San Ángel • Traitors of San Angel 66; Martín Fierro 68; The Knight of the Sword • El Santo de la Espada 69; Güemes—La Tierra en Armas 70; La Maffia • The Mafia 71; The Seven Madmen • Los Siete Locos 73; Boquitas Pintadas • Painted Lips 74; El Pibe Cabeza 74; Diario de la Guerra del Cerdo • Diary of the Pig War • La Guerra del Cerdo 75; Hide and Seek • Piedra Libre 76

Torres, Daniel Díaz see *Díaz Torres, Daniel*

Torres, Fina Oriane 85

Torres, Miguel see *Torres Contreras, Miguel*

Torres, Miguel Contreras see *Torres Contreras, Miguel*

Torres Contreras, Miguel El Caporal 21*; El Hombre Sin Patria 22; Almas Tropicales 23; Oro Sangre y Sol 25; El Relicario 26; The Shadow of Pancho Villa • La Sombra de Pancho Villa 32; Hombre o Demonio • Juárez and Maximillian • Juárez y Maximiliano • The Mad Empress 33; The Night of Sin • La Noche del Pecado 33; Tribu 34; Don't Fool Thyself, Heart • No Te Engañes Corazón 36; La Paloma 37; Dreamers of Glory • Soñadores de la Gloria 38; La Golondrina • The Swallow 38; The Life of Simon Bolivar • Simón Bolívar 41; Carabelleria del Imperio 42; El Padre Morelos 42; La Vida Inútil de Tito Pérez 43; Bamba 48; Pancho Villa Returns • Vuelva Pancho Villa 49; Amor a la Vida 50; Joaquín Murrieta 58; ¡Viva la Soldera! 58; The Last Rebel • El Último Rebelde 61

Torres Ríos, Leopoldo El Crimen de Oribe • Oribe's Crime 49*; El Hijo del Crack • Son of the Star 53*

Torrini, Cinzia H. Giocare d'Azzardo 82; Hotel Colonial 87

Tors, Ivan Rhino! 64; Zebra in the Kitchen 65

Torstad, Tor M. Nattseilere • Night Voyage 86

Tosso, Raúl Gerónima 86

Tota, Mario Solimano il Conquistare • Solimano il Conquistatore • Suleiman the Conqueror 61*

Toth, André de see *De Toth, André*

Toth, Andreas see *De Toth, André*

Tóth, Endre see *De Toth, André*

Totten, Joseph Byron The Blindness of Virtue 15; The Call of the Sea 15; The Village Homestead 15

Totten, Robert The Quick and the Dead 63; Death of a Gunfighter • The Last Gunfighter • Patch 67*; Ride a Northbound Horse 69; The Newcomers • The Wild Country 70; Pony Express Rider 76; Dark Before Dawn 88

Toublanc-Michel, Bernard Adolphe, or The Awkward Age • Adolphe ou L'Âge Tendre • The Tender Age 68; Cinq Gars pour Singapour • Cinque Marines per Singapore • Five Ashore in Singapore • Singapore, Singapore 68

Tour, Charles de la see *De Lautour, Charles*

Tourane, Jean Une Fée Pas Comme les Autres • Il Paese di Paperino • The Secret of Magic Island • Secret of Outer Space Island 64

Tourjansky, Viacheslav see *Tourjansky, Victor*

Tourjansky, Viatcheslaw see *Tourjansky, Victor*

Tourjansky, Victor Symphony of Love and Death 14; The Brothers Karamazov 15; The Great Magaraz 15; Wanderer Beyond the Grave 15; Isle of Oblivion 17; Paradise Without Adam 18; Les Contes des Mille et Une Nuits • Tales of 1001 Nights 21; L'Or-

donnance 21; Une Aventure 22; La Nuit du Carnaval 22; Le 15ème Prélude de Chopin 22; La Riposte 22; Calvaire d'Amour 23; Le Chant de l'Amour Triomphant 23; Ce Cochon de Morin 24; La Dame Masquée 24; Le Prince Charmant 25; Michael Strogoff • Michel Strogoff 26; The Adventurer • The Gallant Gringo 27*; Tempest 28*; Volga-Volga • Wolga-Wolga 28; Manolescu 29; L'Aiglon 31; Le Chanteur Inconnu 31; Der Herzog von Reichstadt 31; Hôtel des Étudiants 32; The Orderly • L'Ordonnance 33; Volga en Flammes 34; Dark Eyes • Otchi Tchiornie • Les Yeux Noirs 35; Die Ganze Welt Dreht Sich Um Liebe • The World's in Love 35; Stadt Anatol 36; Vertige d'un Soir 36; The Lie of Nina Petrovna • Le Mensonge de Nina Petrovna 37; Nostalgie • The Postmaster's Daughter 37; Der Blaufuchs • The Blue Fox 38; Dead Melody • Verklungene Melodie 38; Eine Frau Wie Du 39; Der Gouverneur 39; Feinde 40; Illusion 41; Liebesgeschichten 43; Tonelli 43; Orientexpress 44; Dreimal Komödie 45; Der Blaue Strohut 49; Vom Teufel Gejagt 50; Ehe für Eine Nacht 52; Salto Mortale 53; Morgengrauen 54; Königswalzer 55; Die Toteninsel 55; Herz Ohne Gnade 58; La Venere di Cheronea 58*; I Battellieri del Volga • Prisoner of the Volga 59; I Cosacchi • The Cossacks 59*; La Donna dei Faraoini • The Pharaoh's Woman 60*; Goddess of Love 60; Le Triomphe de Michel Strogoff • The Triumph of Michael Strogoff 61; A Queen for Caesar • Una Regina per Cesare 62*

Tourjansky, Victor von see *Tourjansky, Victor*

Tourjansky, Wenceslav see *Tourjansky, Victor*

Tourneur, Jacques None of That's Worth Love • Tout Ça Ne Vaut Pas l'Amour 31; Un Vieux Garçon 31; Totò 32; La Fusée 33; Pour Être Aimée • To Be Loved 33; The Concierge's Daughters • Les Filles de la Concierge 34; Harnessed Rhythm 36; The Jonker Diamond 36; Killer-Dog 36; Master Will Shakespeare 36; The Boss Didn't Say Good Morning 37; The Grand Bounce 37; The King Without a Crown 37; The Man in the Barn 37; The Rainbow Pass 37; Romance of Radium 37; What Do You Think? 37*; The Face Behind the Mask 38; The Ship That Died 38; Strange Glory 38; Think It Over 38; Nick Carter—Master Detective 39; They All Come Out 39; Yankee Doodle Goes to Town 39; Phantom Raiders 40; Doctors Don't Tell 41; Cat People 42; The Incredible Stranger 42; The Magic Alphabet 42; Days of Glory 43; I Walked with a Zombie 43; The Leopard Man 43; Experiment Perilous 44; Canyon Passage 46; Build My Gallows High • Out of the Past 47; Berlin Express 48; Easy Living 49; Stars in My Crown 49; The Flame and the Arrow 50; Anne of the Indies 51; Circle of Danger 51; Way of a Gaucho 52; Appointment in Honduras 53; Stranger on Horseback 54; Great Day in the Morning • L'Or et l'Amour 55; Wichita 55; Nightfall 56; Curse of the Demon • The Haunted • Night of the Demon 57; The Fearmakers 58; Fury River 58*; Timbuktu 58; La Battaglia di Maratona • The Battle of Marathon • The Giant of Marathon 59*; Frontier Rangers 59; Mission of Danger 59*; The Comedy of Terrors • The Graveside Story 63; The City Under the Sea • War Gods of the Deep • Warlords of the Deep 65

Tourneur, Maurice La Dame de Montsoreau 12; Figures de Cire 12; Le Friquet 12; Jean la Poudre 12; The Lunatics • The System of Doctor Tarr and Professor Fether • Le Système du Docteur Goudron et du Professeur Plume 12; Le Camée 13; Le Corso Rouge 13; Le Dernier Pardon 13; Les Gaietés de l'Escadron 13; Mademoiselle Cents Millions 13; Le Mystère de la Chambre Jaune • Rouletabille I—Le Mystère de la Chambre Jaune 13*; Le Puits Mitoyen 13; Sœurette • The Sparrow 13; La Dernière Incarnation de Larsan • Rouletabille II: La Dernière Incarnation de Larsan 14; The Man of the Hour 14; Monsieur Lecocq 14; Mother 14; The Pit 14; The Wishing Ring 14; Alias Jimmy Valentine 15; A Butterfly on the Wheel 15; The Cub 15; Human Driftwood 15*; The Ivory Snuff Box 15; Trilby 15; The Closed Road 16; The Hand of Peril 16; The Pawn of Fate 16; The Rail Rider 16; The Velvet Paw 16*; Barbary Sheep 17; Exile 17; A Girl's Folly 17; The Law of the Land 17; The Poor Little Rich Girl 17; The Pride of the Clan 17; The Rise of Jenny Cushing 17; The Undying Flame 17; The Whip 17; The Blue Bird 18; A Doll's House 18; Lady Love • Sporting Life 18; Prunella 18; Rose of the World 18; Woman 18; The Broken Butterfly 19; The County Fair 19*; The Life Line • Romany Rye 19; My Lady's Garter 19; Victory 19; The White Heather 19; The Bait 20*; Deep Waters 20; The Glory of Love • While Paris Sleeps 20; The Great Redeemer 20*; The Last of the Mohicans 20*; Treasure Island 20; The White Circle 20; The Foolish Matrons • Is Marriage a Failure? 21*; Lorna Doone 22*; The Brass Bottle 23; The Christian 23; The Isle of Lost Ships 23; Jealous Husbands 23; Torment 24; The White Moth 24; Clothes Make the Pirate 25*; Never the Twain Shall Meet 25; Sporting Life 25; Aloma of the South Seas 26; The Mysterious Island 26*; Old Loves and New 26; The Crew • L'Équipage • The Last Flight 27; Le Navire des Hommes Perdus • Das Schiff der Verlorene Menschen • The Ship of Lost Men 27; Accused, Stand Up! • Accusée, Levez-Vous! 30; Maison de Danses 30; Partir! 31; Au Nom de la Loi 32; Les Gaietés de l'Escadron 32; Lidoire 32; Les Deux Orphelines • La Frochard et les Deux Orphelines 33; L'Homme Mystérieux • Obsession 33; Le Voleur 33; Crimson Dynasty 34; Justin de Marseille 34; Königsmark 34; Avec le Sourire • With a Smile 36; Samson 36; The Mad Emperor • The Patriot • Le

Patriote 37; Katia 38; Volpone 39; Mam'zelle Bonaparte 41; Péchés de Jeunesse • Sins of Youth 41; Carnival of Sinners • The Devil's Hand • La Main du Diable 42; Cécile Est Morte 43; Le Val d'Enfer 43; Après l'Amour 47; L'Impasse des Deux Anges 48

Towne, Robert Personal Best 82; Tequila Sunrise 88

Townley, Jack The Last Dance 30*; Guilty Parents 34; Home on the Prairie 39; The Pittsburgh Kid 41

Townley, Robert H. Honeymoon Ranch 20; West of the Rio Grande 21; Partners of the Sunset 22; Welcome to Our City 22

Townsend, Bud Crimes in the Wax Museum • Monster of the Wax Museum • Nightmare in Wax 69; Club Dead • The Folks at Red Wolf Inn • The Folks at the Red Wolf Inn • Terror at Red Wolf Inn • Terror House 72; Alice in Wonderland 76; Coach 78; Love Scenes 84

Townsend, Pat The Beach Girls 82

Townsend, Ray Snake Bite 78

Townsend, Robert Eddie Murphy Raw 87; Hollywood Shuffle 87

Toye, Wendy The Stranger Left No Card 52; Lord Mountdrago • Three Cases of Murder 54*; The Teckman Mystery 54; All for Mary 55; Raising a Riot 55; On the Twelfth Day 56; True As a Turtle 56; We Are in the Navy Now • We Joined the Navy 62; The King's Breakfast 63

Toyoda, Shiro Painted Lips 29; Three Women 35; Young People 37; Nightingale 38; Spring on Lepers' Island 40; Young Figure 43; The Four Seasons of Woman 50; Whisper of Spring 52; The Mistress • Wild Geese 53; Grass Whistle 55; Marital Relations 55; Madame White Snake 56; Evening Calm 57; Snow Country 57; Pilgrimage at Night 59; Bokutō Kaidan • The Twilight Story 60; The Diplomat's Mansion • Tōkyō Yawa 61; Ashita Aru Kagiri • Asu Aru Kagiri • Till Tomorrow Comes 62; Madame Aki • Yūshū Heiya 63; Sweet Sweat 64; The Ghost of Yotsuya • Illusion of Blood • Yotsuya Kaidan 65; Tale of a Carpenter 65; Chikumagawa Zesshō • River of Forever 67; The Hell Screen • Jigokuhen • Portrait of Hell • A Story of Hell 69; Between Wife and Lady • Between Women and Wives • Tsuma to Onna no Aida 76*

Tracy, Bert Boots, Boots 34; Love, Mirth, Melody 34

Trader, Joseph Tre Dollari di Piombo 64

Trafford, Steve T. Dan Smith 87*

Tramont, Jean-Claude Le Point de Mire 77; All Night Long 81

Trancik, Dušan Iná Láska 85

Trapani, Enzo Brief Rapture 52

Traube, Shepard Street of Memories 40; The Bride Wore Crutches 41; For Beauty's Sake 41; Once Upon a Coffee House 65

Trauberg, Ilya Leningrad Segodnya • Leningrad Today 27; The Blue Express • China Express • Goluboi Ekspress 29; Kites • Letun 31; We Work for You 32; Chastnyi Sluchai • An Unusual Case 34;

Son of Mongolia • Syn Mongolyi 36*; God Devyatnadtsatyi • The Year 1919 38; Concert Waltz • Kontsert-Vals 40*; My Zhdom Vas s Pobedoi • We Expect Victory There 41*; Pauki • The Spider 42*

Trauberg, Leonid The Adventures of an Octoberite • The Adventures of Oktyabrina • Pokhozdeniya Oktyabrini 24*; The Bears Versus Yudenich • Mishka Against Yudenich • Mishka Versus Yudenich • Mishki Protiv Yudenicha 25*; Bratishka • Buddy • Little Brother 26*; Chyortovo Koleso • The Devil's Wheel • Moyak s Aurora • The Sailor from the Aurora 26*; The Cloak • The Overcoat • Shinel 26*; Bleeding Snows • The Club of the Big Deed • The Club of the Great Deed • S.V.D. • Soyuz Velikovo Dela 27*; The New Babylon • Novyi Vavilon 29*; Alone • Odna 31*; The Youth of Maxim • Yunost Maksima 35*; The Return of Maxim • Vozvrashcheniye Maksima 37*; Maxim at Vyborg • New Horizons • The Vyborg Side • Vyborgskaya Storona 38*; The Actress • Aktrisa 43; Ordinary People • Plain People • Prostiye Lyudi • Simple People 45*; Shli Soldati • The Soldiers March • The Soldiers Marched On • Soldiers Were Marching 57; Dead Souls • Mertvye Dushi • Myortvye Dushi 60; Free Wind • Volnyi Veter 61*

Trautman, Tereza Best Wishes • Sonhos de Menina Moça 88

Travers, Alfred Meet the Navy 46; Dual Alibi 47; The Strangers Came • You Can't Fool an Irishman 49; Solution by Phone 54; Don Giovanni 55*; Alive on Saturday 57; Men of Tomorrow 59; Girls of Latin Quarter 60; The Primitives 62

Travers, Bill Christian the Lion • The Lion at World's End 71*

Traxler, Ernest Caleb Piper's Girl 19; Go Get 'Em Garringer 19

Traxler, Stephen Slithis • Spawn of the Slithis 78

Traynor, Peter S. Death Game • The Seducers 74; God Bless Dr. Shagetz 77*; Evil Town 87*

Trbovich, Tom Free Ride 86

Treatt, Major C. Court Stampede 30

Tregenza, Rob Talking to Strangers 88

Tregubovich, Viktor This Is My Neck of the Woods • Vot Moya Derevnya 87; Bashnya 88

Treilhou, Marie-Claude L'Âne Qui à Bu la Lune • The Donkey That Drank the Moon 88

Tremper, Will The Captives • Escape to Berlin • Flucht nach Berlin 62; The Endless Night • Die Endlose Nacht 63; Berlin Ist eine Sünde Welt•Playgirl•That Woman 68

Trenchard-Smith, Brian The Dragon Flies • The Man from Hong Kong 75; The Love Epidemic 75; Deathcheaters 76; Stunt Rock 78; The Day of the Assassin 81; Escape 2000 • Turkey Shoot 81; BMX Bandits 83; Jenny Kissed Me 85; Dead End Drive-In 86; Frog Dreaming 86; The Quest 86; The Day of the Panther 87; Out of the Body 88

Trenker, Luis Berge in Flammen • The Doomed Battalion 31*; The Rebel 32*; Der Rebell 32*; The Lost Son • The Prodigal Son • Der Verlorene Sohn 34; The Emperor of California • Der Kaiser von Kalifornien 36; Der Berg Ruft 37; The Challenge 37*; Condottiere • Giovanni de Medici—The Leader 37; Liebesbriefe aus dem Engadin • Love Letters from the Engadine 38; Der Feuerteufel 40; Monte Miracolo 43; Germanin im Banne des Monte Miracolo • Im Banne des Monte Miracolo 45; Duell in den Bergen 49; Flucht in die Dolomiten • Il Prigioniero della Montagna 55; Von der Liebe Besiegt 56; Wetterleuchten Um Maria 57; Sein Bester Freund • Wall of Fury 62

Trent, Barbara Coverup: Behind the Iran-Contra Affair 88

Trent, John The Bushbaby 70; Homer 70; The Only Way Out Is Dead 70; It Seemed Like a Good Idea at the Time 75; Sunday in the Country 75; Call the Cops! • Find the Lady 76; Middle Age Crazy 80

Tresgot, Annie Les Enfants de Néant 67*

Tressler, Georg Die Halbstarken • Teenage Wolf Pack • The Wicked Ones • Wolfpack 56; Endstation Liebe • Terminus Love 57; Noch Minderjährig • Unter Achtzehn 57; Ein Wunderbarer Sommer 58; Lange Hosen, Kurze Haare 59; Das Totenschiff 59; Geständnis einer Sechzehnjährigen 60; The Magnificent Rebel 60; Die Lustigen Weiber von Windsor • The Merry Wives of Windsor 65; A Devil of a Woman • Der Weibsteufel 66

Treut, Monika Seduction: The Cruel Woman 85*

Treves, Giorgio Le Mal d'Aimer • The Malady of Love 86; La Coda del Diavolo • The Devil's Tail 87

Treville, Georges The Beryl Coronet 12; The Copper Beeches 12; The Musgrave Ritual 12; The Mystery of Boscombe Vale 12; The Reigate Squires 12; Silver Blaze 12; The Speckled Band 12; The Stolen Papers 12; All Sorts and Conditions of Men 21; Married Life 21

Trevillion, Dale Las Vegas Weekend 85; One Man Force 89

Treviño, Jesús Raíces de Sangre 77

Trevor, Simon The African Elephant • King Elephant 72

Triana, Jorge Ali Tiempo de Morir • A Time to Die 85

Trier, Lars von The Element of Crime • Forbrydelsens Element 84; Epidemic 87

Trieschmann, Charles Captive • Two 75

Trikonis, Gus Five the Hard Way • The Sidehackers 69; Eager Beavers • The Swinging Barmaids 75; Supercock 75; Country Music Daughter • Nashville Girl • New Girl in Town 76; The Student Body 76; Moonshine County Express 77; Cry Demon • The Evil • The Force Beyond 78; To Elvis, with Love • Touched by Love 80; Take This Job and Shove It 81; Dance of the Dwarfs • Jungle Heat 83

Trimble, Lawrence Saved by the Flag 10; The Battle Hymn of the Republic 11; Bunny at the Derby 12; Cardinal Wolsey 12*; The French Spy 12; Michael McShane, Matchmaker 12; The Adventure of the Shooting Party 13; The Adventure of Westgate Seminary 13; Bunny Blarneyed, or The Blarney Stone 13; Checkmated 13; The Deerslayer 13*; The Harper Mystery 13; The Honourable Event 13; Jean's Evidence 13; The Lucky Stone 13; The Pickwick Papers 13; Rose of Surrey 13; Sisters All 13; There's Music in the Hair 13; Under the Make-Up 13; The Younger Sister 13; The Awakening of Norah 14; Creatures of Habit 14; Daisy Doodad's Dial 14; Film Favourites • Florence Turner Impersonates Film Favorites 14; Flotilla the Flirt 14; For Her People 14; The Murdock Trial 14; One Thing After Another 14; Polly's Progress 14; Shepherd Lassie of Argyle 14; Shopgirls • Shopgirls, or The Great Question 14; Snobs 14; Through the Valley of Shadows 14; Alone in London 15; As Ye Repent • Redeemed 15; Caste 15; Far from the Madding Crowd 15; The Great Adventure 15; Lost and Won • Odds Against 15; My Old Dutch 15; Grim Justice 16; A Place in the Sun 16; Sally in Our Alley 16; The Auction Block 17; Castle 17; Mine of Missing Men 17; The Spreading Dawn 17; The Light Within 18; Fool's Gold 19; Spotlight Sadie 19; Darling Mine 20; The Woman God Sent 20; The Silent Call 21; Brawn of the North 22; The Love Master 24; Sundown 24*; White Fang 25; My Old Dutch 26

Tringham, David The Last Chapter 74

Trintignant, Jean-Louis A Full Day's Work • Une Journée Bien Remplié • A Well-Filled Day 73; Le Maître-Nageur 79

Trintignant, Nadine Fragilité—Ton Nom Est Femme 65; Mon Amour, Mon Amour 67; Le Voleur de Crimes 69; Ça N'Arrive Qu'aux Autres • It Only Happens to Others 71; Défense de Savoir 73; Jalousie 1976 • Le Voyage de Noces 76; Premier Voyage 79; L'Éte Prochain • Next Summer 84; La Maison de Jade 88

Trivas, Victor Aufruhr des Blutes 29; Hell on Earth • Niemandsland • No Man's Land 31; Dans les Rues • Song of the Street 33; The Head • A Head for the Devil • Die Nackte und der Satan • The Screaming Head 59

Trnka, Jiří The Devil of the Springs • The Devil on Springs • Perák a S.S. • Perak Against the S.S. • The Springer and S.S. Men 45*; Grandpa Planted a Beet • Zasadil Dědek Řepu 45; The Animals and the Brigands • Zvířátka a Petrovští 46; Dárek • The Gift 46; The Czech Year • Špalíček 47; Císařův Slavík • The Emperor and the Nightingale • The Emperor's Nightingale 48*; Arie Prerie • Song of the Prairie 49; Novel with a Contrabass • Román s Basou • The Story of a Double Bass • The Story of the Bass-Cello 49; Bajaja • Bayaya • Prince Bayaya 50; Čertův Mlýn • The Devil's Mill 50; Circus • The Happy Circus • The Merry Circus • Veselý Cirkus 50; The Golden Fish • O Zlaté Rybce • Rybář a Zlatá Rybka 51; How Grandpa Changed Till Nothing Was Left • Jak Stařeček Měnil Až Vyměnil 52; How Kutasek and Kutilka Got Up in the Morning • Kutásek a Kutilka Jak Ráno Vstávali • Kutasek and Kutilka 52; Old Czech Legends • Staré Pověsti České 53; Dobrý Voják Švejk • The Good Soldier Schweik • Osudy Dobrého Vojáka Švejka 54; Dva Mrazíci • Two Frosts 54; Cirkus Hurvínek • The Hurvinek Circus 55; Proč UNESCO? • Why UNESCO? 58; A Midsummer Night's Dream • Sen Noci Svatojánské 59*; Obsession • Passion • Vášeň 60; Cybernetic Grandma • Kybernetická Babička 62; Archanděl Gabriel a Paní Husa • The Archangel Gabriel and Mother Goose • The Archangel Gabriel and Mrs. Goose 64; The Hand • Ruka 64; Maxplatte, Maxplatten 65

Troell, Jan Stad 58; Sommartåg • A Summer Day • Summer Train 60; Båten • The Boat • The Ship 61; A Boy and His Kite • The Boy and the Kite • Pojken och Draken 61*; New Year's Eve in Skåne • New Year's Eve on the Plains of Scania • Nyår i Skåne • Nyårsafton på Skånska Slätten 61; De Kom Tillbaka • The Return • They Came Back 62; Den Gamla Kvarnen • The Old Mill 62; Spring in the Meadows of Dalby • Spring in the Pastures of Dalby • Vår i Dalby Hage 62; Johan Ekberg 64; Trachoma • Trakom 64*; Four by Four • 4 x 4 65*; Portrait of Åsa • Porträtt av Åsa 65; Här Har Du Ditt Liv • Here Is Your Life • Here's Your Life 66; Eeny Meeny Miny Moe • Ole Dole Doff • Who Saw Him Die? 67; The Emigrants • Utvandrarna 70; The New Land • Nybyggarna • The Settlers • Unto a Good Land 71; For Better, for Worse • Zandy's Bride 74; Bang! 76; The Flight of the Eagle • Ingenjör Andrees Luftfärd 78; Forbidden Paradise • Hurricane 79; Sagolandet 86

Troiani, Marcello Massimamente Folle • Totally Crazy 85

Troisi, Massimo Le Vie del Signore Sono Finite • The Ways of the Lord Are Finite 87

Trolignac, M. Gaston de see Griffith, D. W.

Trolignac, Marquis de see Griffith, D. W.

Tronson, Robert Man at the Carlton Tower 61; Man Detained 61; Never Back Losers 61; Number Six 62; The Traitors 62; Farewell Performance 63; On the Run 63; Ring of Spies • Ring of Treason 63; All in Good Time 64

Trop, Jack Dunn A Briglia Sciolta • La Bride sur le Cou • Only for Love • Please, Not Now 61*

Trope, Tzipi Tell Me That You Love Me 83; Tel Aviv—Berlin 87

Tropia, Marc C. Friars Road 86; Miami Beach Bug Police 86*

Tropia, Tano Miami Beach Bug Police 86*

Troska, Zdeněk Slunce, Seno a Pár Facek • Sun, Hay and a Slap 89

Trotignon, Jean-Luc Le Bonheur A Encore Frappé • Happiness Strikes Again 86

Trotta, Margarethe von The Lost Honor of Katharina Blum • Die Verlorene Ehre der Katharina Blum 75*; The Second Awakening of Christa Klages • Das Zweite Erwachen der Christa Klages 77*; Schwestern oder Die Balance des Glücks • Sisters, or The Balance of Happiness 79; Die Bleierne Zeit • The German Sisters • Leaden Times • Marianne and Julianne 81; Friends and Husbands • Heller Wahn • A Labour of Love • Sheer Madness 82; Rosa Luxembourg • Rosa Luxembourg 85; Felix 87*; Amore e Paura • Love and Fear • Paura e Amore • Three Sisters 88; The African Woman • L'Africana 90

Trotz, Adolf Elisabeth of Austria • Elisabeth von Österreich 31; Rasputin 32; Tatras Zauber 33

Troy, Gary Computer Beach Party 85

Trueba, Fernando Opera Prima 80; Chicho o Mientras el Cuerpo Aguante 82; Sal Gorda 83; Se Infiel y No Mires con Quien 85; El Año de las Luces • The Year of Awakening 86; The Mad Monkey 89; Twisted Obsession 90

Trueblood, Guerdon The Candy Snatchers 74

Truesdell, Howard A Corner in Cotton 16*

Truffaut, François A Visit • Une Visite 54; The Mischief Makers • Les Mistons • The Troublemakers 57; The 400 Blows • Les Quatre Cents Coups 58; Une Histoire d'Eau • A Story of Water 58*; Shoot the Pianist • Shoot the Piano Player • Tirez sur le Pianiste 60; The Army Game • The Sad Sack • Tire-au-Flanc • Tire-au-Flanc 62 61*; Jules and Jim • Jules et Jim 61; Amore a Vent'Anni • L'Amour à Vingt Ans • Hatachi no Koi • Liebe mit Zwanzig • Love at Twenty • Miłość Dwudziestolatków 62*; La Peau Douce • Silken Skin • The Soft Skin 62; Fahrenheit 451 66; The Bride Wore Black • La Mariée Était en Noir 67; Baisers Volés • Stolen Kisses 68; La Mia Droga Si Chiama Julie • The Mississippi Mermaid • La Sirène du Mississippi 68; L'Enfant Sauvage • The Wild Child 69; Bed and Board • Domicile Conjugal 70; Anne and Muriel • Les Deux Anglaises et le Continent • Two English Girls 71; Une Belle Fille Comme Moi • A Gorgeous Bird Like Me • Such a Gorgeous Kid Like Me 72; Day for Night • La Nuit Américaine 73; L'Argent de Poche • Pocket Money • Small Change • Spending Money 75; L'Histoire d'Adèle H. • The Story of Adele H. 75; L'Homme Qui Aimait les Femmes • The Man Who Loved Women 77; La Chambre Verte • The Green Room 78; L'Amour en Fuite • Love on the Run 79; Le Dernier Métro • The Last Metro 80; La Femme d'à Côté • The Woman Next Door 81; Confidentially Yours • Finally Sunday! • Vivement Dimanche! 82

Trujillo, Valentín Un Hombre Violente • A Violent Man 86; City Rats • Ratas de la Ciudad 87; I the Executioner • Yo el

Ejecutor 87

Truman, Michael The Light Touch • Touch and Go 55; Go to Blazes 61; Girl in the Headlines • The Model Murder Case 63; Daylight Robbery 64

Trumbo, Dalton Johnny Got His Gun 71

Trumbull, Douglas Silent Running 71; Brainstorm 83

Truss, Leslie Seldon see Seldon-Truss, Leslie

Tryggvason, Jón Foxtrot 88

Tryon, Glenn Gridiron Flash • The Luck of the Game 34; Easy to Take 36; Two in Revolt 36; Small Town Boy • The Thousand Dollar Bill 37; The Law West of Tombstone 38; Beauty for the Asking 39; Double Date 41; Nazty Nuisance • That Nazty Nuisance 43; Meet Miss Bobby Socks 44; Miss Mink of 1949 49

Trystan, Leon Apartment Above • Piętro Wyżej 38

Trzos-Rastawiecki, Andrzej Objection 85

Tsafos, Manolis Rip Off 77

Tsai, Tsou-sen Southern Spring 32; Morning in the Town 33; Song of the Fisherman 34; A New Woman • New Women 35; Stray Lamb 36; Wang Lao Wou 38; Diabolical Paradise 39; The Great Experience 40; The River Flows East in the Spring • Spring River Flows East • Yijiang Chunshui Xiang Dong Liu 47*

Tsai, Yang-ming Brotherhood 90

Tsanusdi Trader Hornee 70

Tsekhanovsky, M. Kino-Concert 1941 • Leningrad Music Hall 41*

Tselinsky, Gunar Fear • Strakh 87

Tsemberopoulos, Yorgos Megara 75*

Tsiforos, M. O Anemos tou Missous • Wind of Hate 58

Tsiolis, Stavros Mia Toso Makrini Apoussia • Such a Long Absence 85; In Relation with Vassilis • Schetika me ton Vassili 86; Akatanikitoi Erastes·88

Tso-lin, Wang see Wang, Tso-lin

Tsou, Se-ling see Chu, Shih-ling

Tsou-sen, Tsai see Tsai, Tsou-sen

Tsuboshima, Takashi Kureizi Ōgon Sakusen • Las Vegas Free-for-All 68

Tsui, Hark The Butterfly Murders 79; Die Bian 79; Dangerous Encounter — First Kind 80; Diyu Wu Men • Hell Has No Gates • No Door to Hell • We Are Going to Eat You • We're Going to Eat You 80; All the Wrong Clues 81; Guima Zhiduo Zing 81; Zu • Zu: Warriors from the Magic Mountain 82; Shushan 83; Aces Go Places III: Our Man from Bond Street 84; Shanghai Blues 84; A Chinese Ghost Story • Qian Nu Youhun 85*; Working Class 85; Dao Ma Dan • Peking Opera Blues 86; A Chinese Ghost Story II • Sinnui Yauman II 87; A Chinese Ghost Story III 90; Ke Tu Chiu Hen • The Swordsman 90*; Kei Wong • King of Chess 90

Tsui, Siu-ming Mirage 87

Tsukerman, Slava Liquid Sky 82

Tsutsumi, Yukihiko Bakayaroo! (Watakushi Okotteimasu) 88*

Tu, Chien Lun Ninfas Diabólicas 78

Tual, Denise Days of Our Years 51*

Tual, Roland Days of Our Years 51*

Tuber, Joel The Great Wall of China 70

Tuček, Petr Copak Je To Za Vojáka? 88

Tuchner, Michael Villain 71; Fear Is the Key 72; Mister Quilp • The Old Curiosity Shop 75; Bar Mitzvah Boy 76; The Likely Lads 76; Trenchcoat 83; The Misadventures of Mr. Wilt • Wilt 89

Tuchock, Wanda Finishing School 34*

Tucker, David Ciao 67

Tucker, Dean Valley of Blood 73

Tucker, George Loane The Aggressor 11*; Behind the Stockade 11*; The Dream 11*; Over the Hills 11*; The Rose's Story 11*; Their First Misunderstanding 11*; Prince Charming 12*; Traffic in Souls 13; A Bachelor's Love Story 14; The Black Spot 14; The Cage 14; Called Back 14; The Difficult Way 14; England Expects 14; The Fringe of War 14; On His Majesty's Secret Service • On His Majesty's Service • 0-18, or A Message from the Sky 14; The Revenge of Mr. Thomas Atkins 14; She Stoops to Conquer 14; The Third String 14; The Christian 15; Her Uncle 15; His Lordship 15; Jelf's • A Man of His Word 15; The Middleman 15; 1914 15; The Prisoner of Zenda • Rupert of Hentzau 15; The Shulamite 15; The Sons of Satan 15; Arsène Lupin 16; The Folly of Desire • The Folly of Desire, or The Shulamite 16; The Game of Liberty 16; Under Suspicion 16; The Hypocrites • The Morals of Weybury 16; I Believe • The Man Without a Soul 16; The Manxman 16; Mixed Relations 16; The Mother of Dartmoor 16; A Mother's Influence 16; An Odd Freak 16; The Cinderella Man 17; Dodging a Million 18; Joan of Plattsburg 18*; Virtuous Wives 18; The Miracle Man 19; Ladies Must Live 21

Tucker, Phil Dance Hall Racket 53; Monsters from the Moon • Robot Monster 53; Cape Canaveral Monsters 60

Tudor, F. C. S. Island Jess 14; The Cripple of Ypres 15; The Devil's Profession 15

Tuggle, Richard Tightrope 84; Out of Bounds 86

Tuhus, Oddvar Bull Blücher 88

Tully, May The Old Oaken Bucket 21; That Old Gang of Mine 25

Tully, Montgomery From Acorn to Oak 37; Behind the Guns 40; Salute to the Farmers 41; Murder in Reverse 45; Query 45; Spring Song • Springtime 46; Mrs. Fitzherbert 47; Boys in Brown 49; Fünf Mädchen und Ein Mann • Geschichte von Fünf Städten • A Tale of Five Cities • A Tale of Five Women 51*; Girdle of Gold 52; Small Town Story 53; Terror Street • 36 Hours 53; Devil's Harbor • Devil's Point 54; The Diamond • The Diamond Wizard 54*; Five Days • Paid to Kill 54; The Key Man • A Life at Stake 54; Late Night Final 54; The Silent Witness 54; Dial 999 • The Way Out 55; The Glass Cage • The Glass Tomb 55; The Case of the River Morgue 56; The Counterfeit Plan 56; Destination Death 56; Inside Information 56; The

Bloody Spear on Mount Fuji • Chiyari Fuji 55; Each Within His Shell • Jibun no Ana no Nakade 55; Tasogare Sakaba • Twilight Beer Hall 55; Disorder by the Kuroda Clan • Kuroda Sōdō 56; Abarenbō Kaidō 57; Daibōsatsu Tōge I • The Great Bodhisattva Pass • Moonlit Swords 57; Dotanba • The Eleventh Hour • They Are Buried Alive 57; Daibōsatsu Tōge II 58; Mori to Mizuumi no Matsuri • Outsiders 58; Senryo Jishin • The Thief Is Shogun's Kin 58; Daibōsatsu Tōge III 59; Naniwa no Koi no Monogatari • Their Own World 59; Hana no Yoshiwara Hyakuningiri • Murder in Yoshiwara 60; Sake to Onna to Yari • Saki, Woman and a Lance 60; Koiya Koi Nasuna Koi • Love Not Again 61; Miyamoto Musashi I • Untamed Fury 61; Duel Without End • Miyamoto Musashi II 62; Miyamoto Musashi III • The Worthless Duel 63; The Duel at Ichijoji Temple • Miyamoto Musashi IV 64; Fugitive from the Past • Hunger Straits • Kiga Kaikyō 64; The Last Duel • Miyamoto Musashi V 65; Jinsei Gekijō—Hishakaku to Kiratsune • Kaku and Tsune 68; Real Sword Fight • Shinken Shōbei • Swords of Death 69

Uchikawa, Seiichiro Dōjō Yaburi • Kempō Samurai • Samurai from Nowhere 64; Judo Saga • Sugata Sanshiro 65

Uchitel, Edvard Panorama of Russia 64

Ucicky, Gustav Café Electric 27; Hocuspocus 30; Murder for Sale • The Temporary Widow 30; Das Flötenkonzert von Sanssouci 31; The Immortal Vagabond • Der Unsterbliche Lump 31; Menschen Ohne Namen 32; Yorck 32; Morgenrot 33; La Voce del Sangue 33; Flüchtlinge 34; Das Mädchen Johanna 35; The Broken Jug • Der Zerbrochene Krug 38; Die Macht der Berge • The Power of the Mountains 38; Aufruhr in Damaskus • Tumult in Damascus 39; Mother Love • Mutterliebe 40; Singing Angels 52; The Girl of the Moors • Das Mädchen vom Moorhof 61

Uğur, Ömer The Last Man of Urfa • Son Urfalı 87

Uher, Stefan Šiesta Veta • The Sixth Sentence 86; Správca Skanzenu 88

U'Kset, Umban Ntturudu 86

Úleha, Vladimír Mizící Svět • Vanishing World 35

Ulla, Jorge Nadie Escuchaba • Nobody Listened 88*

Ullman, Daniel B. Dial Red O 55; Badlands of Montana 57

Ullmann, Liv Love 81*

Ulloque, José María El Gran Serafín • The Great Seraph 87

Ullrich, Hans-Georg Zivile Knete 85*

Ulmer, Edgar G. Menschen am Sonntag • People on Sunday 29*; Damaged Lives 33; Mr. Broadway 33; The Black Cat • House of Doom • The Vanishing Body 34; Thunder Over Texas 34; From Nine to Nine 35; Girl from Poltava • Natalka Poltavka 36*; Green Fields • Greene Felde • Grüner Felder 37*; The Singing

Blacksmith • Yankel dem Schmidt 38; American Matchmaker • Americaner Schädchen • The Marriage Broker 39; The Cossacks Across the Danube • Cossacks in Exile • Zaporosch sa Dunayem • Zaporozh za Dunayem • Zaporozhetz za Dunayem 39; The Dobbin 39; Fischke der Drume • Fischke the Cripple • Fischke the Lame • Fischke the Lame One • Fishe da Krin • Die Klatsche • The Light Ahead 39; Let My People Live 39; Moon Over Harlem 39; Cloud in the Sky 40; Another to Conquer 41; The Last Command • Prisoner of Japan 42*; The Man with a Conscience • Tomorrow We Live 42; Girls in Chains 43; Isle of Forgotten Sins • Monsoon 43; Jive Junction • Swing High 43; My Son, the Hero 43; Bluebeard 44; Club Havana 45; Detour 45; Out of the Night • Strange Illusion 45; Her Sister's Secret 46; Monte Cristo, Masked Avenger • The Wife of Monte Cristo 46; The Strange Woman 46; Carnegie Hall 47; Ruthless 48; Captain Sirocco • The Masked Pirate • The Pirates of Capri • I Pirati di Capri 49; Escape If You Can • St. Benny the Dip 51; The Man from Planet X 51; Babes in Bagdad 52; L'Amante di Paride • Eterna Femmina • Eternal Woman • The Face That Launched a Thousand Ships • Femmina • Helen of Troy • Love of Three Queens • Loves of Three Queens 53*; Dynamite Anchorage • Murder Is My Beat 54; The Naked Dawn 55; Daughter of Dr. Jekyll 57; The Perjurer 57; The Amazing Transparent Man 59; Annibale • Hannibal 59*; Beyond the Time Barrier 59; Antinea, l'Amante della Città Sepolta • L'Atlantide • L'Atlantide—Antinea, l'Amante della Città Sepolta • Atlantis the Lost Continent • Atlantis the Lost Kingdom • Journey Beneath the Desert • The Lost Kingdom • Queen of Atlantis 61*; The Cavern • Helden—Himmel und Hölle • Neunzig Nächte und ein Tag • Sette Contro la Morte 64

Ulmke, Heidi Lock & Seal • Schloss & Siegel 87

Ulyanov, Mikhail Bratya Karamazovy • The Brothers Karamazov • The Murder of Dmitri Karamazov 68*

Uman, Chaerul The Narrow Bridge • Titan Serambut Dibelah Tujuh 86

Umesh, Prabhakar see Prabhakar-Umesh

Umetsu, Yasuomi Robot Carnival 87*

Umezu, Meijiro Harbor Light Yokohama • Kiri ni Musebu Yoru 70

Umgelter, Fritz The Bellboy and the Playgirls • Mit Eva Fing die Sünde An • The Playgirls and the Bellboy 61*

Underwood, Lawrence That Something 21*

Underwood, Ron Tremors 90

Ungaro, Nestore The Secret of Seagull Island 81

Ungern, R. The Coward 14*

Ungwald-Khilkevich, Georgy Dvoe Pod Odnim Zontom • Two Under One Umbrella 87; Season of Miracles • Sezon Chudes 87

Uno, Michael Toshiyuki The Wash 88

Unterberg, Hannelore The Boy with the Big Black Dog • Der Junge mit dem Grossen Schwarzen Hund 87

Uong, Weiquan see Yung, Peter

Uralsky, A. 1812 12*; Tercentenary of the Romanov Dynasty's Accession to the Throne 13*; Yekaterina Ivanovna 15

Urayama, Kiriro The Girl I Abandoned • Watashi Ga Suteta Onna 70; Yumechiyo Nitsuki • Yumechiyo's Diary 85

Urazbayev, Eldor Seconds Make a Hero • Sekunda na Podvig 87*

Urbahn, K. The Daily Round 37*

Urban, Charles The Coronation of Edward VII • The Coronation of Their Majesties King Edward VII and Queen Alexandra • Reproduction, Coronation Ceremonies—King Edward VII • Le Sacre d'Édouard VII 02*; Ancient Customs of Egypt 21; From Egg to Chick 21; Rare Animals 21; Science of the Soap Bubbles 21; The Tortoise and the Hare 21

Urban, Max The Bartered Bride 13

Urban, Radovan Horká Kaše 88; Náhodou Je Prima! 88

Uribe, Imanol Escape from Segovia 84

Urinov, J. I. Diary of a Revolutionist 32

Urquieta, José Luis La Alacrana • The Scorpion 86; The Bridge • El Puente 86; Matanza en Matamoros • Slaughter in Matamoros 86; Operación Marijuana • Operation Marijuana 87

Urson, Frank Exit the Vamp 21; The Gold Dredgers • The Hell Diggers 21; The Love Special 21; Too Much Speed 21; The Heart Specialist 22; Minnie 22*; South of Suva 22; Tillie • Tillie, a Mennonite Maid 22; The Eternal Three 23*; Changing Husbands 24*; Forty Winks 25*; The Night Club 25*; Her Man o' War 26; Almost Human 27; Chicago 27

Urueta, Chano Enemigos 34; El Escándalo 34; Profanación 34; Jalisco Never Loses • Jalisco Nunca Pierde 37; Canción del Alma • Song of the Soul 38; Hombres de Mar • Men of the Sea 38; Mi Candidato • My Candidate 38; Supreme Sacrifice • Supremo Sacrificio 38; María 39; Night of the Mayas • Noche de los Mayas 39; Los de Abajo 40; El Conde de Monte Cristo 43; Guadalajara 43; Dr. Crimen • El Monstruo Resucitado 53; La Bruja • The Witch 54; The Headless Rider • El Jinete Sin Cabeza 56; Cuentos de Brujas • El Espejo de la Bruja • The Witch's Mirror 60; El Barón del Terror • The Brainiac 61; La Cabeza Viviente • The Living Head • El Ojo de la Muerte 61; Blue Demon Contra Cerebros Infernales • Blue Demon vs. El Crimen • Blue Demon vs. the Infernal Brain • Blue Demon vs. the Infernal Brains • Cerebro Infernal • Cerebros Infernales 66

Urusevsky, Sergei The Ambler's Race • Prashnai Gulsara 69

Ustinov, Peter School for Secrets • Secret Flight 46; Vice Versa 47; Private Angelo 49*; Dig That Juliet • Romanoff and Juliet 61; Billy Budd 62; Lady L 65; Hammersmith Is Out 72; Memed My Hawk 83

Uys, Jamie Dingaka 65; After You, Comrade 66; Lost in the Desert 71; Animals Are Beautiful People • Beautiful People 74; The Gods Must Be Crazy 79; Beautiful People II 83; The Gods Must Be Crazy II 88

Vaala, Valentin Niskavuoren Naiset • Women of Niskavuori 38

Vacek, Jack Double Nickels 77

Vadim, Roger And God Created Woman • And Woman…Was Created • Et Dieu…Créa la Femme 56; Les Bijoutiers du Clair de Lune • Heaven Fell That Night • The Night Heaven Fell 57; No Sun in Venice • Sait-On Jamais? • When the Devil Drives 57; Dangerous Liaisons • Dangerous Liaisons 1960 • Dangerous Love Affairs • Les Liaisons Dangereuses • Les Liaisons Dangereuses 1960 • Relazioni Pericolose 59; Blood and Roses • …Et Mourir de Plaisir 60; A Briglia Sciolta • La Bride sur le Cou • Only for Love • Please, Not Now 61*; Les Sept Péchés Capitaux • I Sette Peccati Capitali • Seven Capital Sins • The Seven Deadly Sins 61*; Love on a Pillow • Le Repos du Guerrier • Il Riposo del Guerriero • Warrior's Rest 62; Vice and Virtue • Le Vice et la Vertu • Il Vizio e la Virtù 62; Il Castello in Svezia • Castle in Sweden • Château en Suède • Château in Sweden • Nutty, Naughty Château 63; Circle of Love • La Ronde 64; La Curée • The Game Is Over • The Quarry 66; Barbarella • Barbarella, Queen of the Galaxy 67; Histoires Extraordinaires • Spirits of the Dead • Tales of Mystery • Tre Passi nel Delirio 67*; Peryl 70; Hellé 71; Pretty Maids All in a Row 71; Don Juan Était une Femme • Don Juan 1973 ou Si Don Juan Était une Femme • Don Juan 1973 • Don Juan 1973, or If Don Juan Were a Woman • If Don Juan Were a Woman • Ms. Don Juan • Si Don Juan Ètait une Femme 73; Charlotte • Charlotte: A Girl Murdered • La Jeune Fille Assassine 74; A Faithful Woman • Une Femme Fidèle • When a Woman Is in Love 76; Night Games 79; The Hot Touch 80; Come Back 82; Surprise Party 82; And God Created Woman 87

Vafeas, Vassilis 120 Decibels 87

Vagnino, Steven A Pleasure Doing Business 79

Vaidya, N. S. Khatyal Sasu Nathal Soon 88

Vailati, Bruno La Battaglia di Maratona • The Battle of Marathon • The Giant of Marathon 59*; Beta Som • Finch Dura la Tempesta • Torpedo Bay 62*

Vainorius, Rimas Yours, Faithfully 77

Vainstok, Vladimir Armed and Dangerous • Wooruzhyon i Ochen Opasen 77

Vajda, Ladislao see Vajda, Ladislas

Vajda, Ladislas Where Is This Girl? • Where Is This Lady? 32*; Love on Skis 33; Halló Budapest! • Hello Budapest! 35; Ember a Híd Alatt • The Man Under the Bridge 36; Három Sárkány • The Three Spinsters 36; Szenzáció 36*; Wings Over Africa 36; The Borrowed Castle • A Kölcsönkért Kastély 37; Az Én Lányom Nem Olyan • My Daughter Is Different 37; The Revenge of General Ling • The Wife of General Ling 37; The Crucial Moment • Döntö Pillanat 38; Fekete Gyémántok 38; Friday Rose • Péntek Rézi 38; Magda Is Expelled • Magdát Kicsapják 38; Rosemary • Rozmaring 38; Giuliano de' Medici 40; La Zia Smemorata 41; Dolce Lunas de Miel 43; Se Vende un Palacio 43; Te Quiero para Mí 44; El Testamento del Virrey 44; Cinco Lobitos 45; Barrio 47; Call of the Blood 47*; Tres Espejos 47; Sin Uniforme 48; The Golden Madonna 49; Her Panelled Door • The Woman with No Name 50*; Séptima Página 50; Ronda Española 51; Doña Francisquita 52; Carne de Horca 53; Aventuras del Barbero de Sevilla 54; Marcelino • Marcelino, Pan y Vino • The Miracle of Marcelino 55; Tarde de Toros 55; Mi Tío Jacinto 56; Un Ángel Pasó por Brooklyn • An Angel Passed Over Brooklyn • Un Angelo È Sceso a Brooklyn • The Man Who Wagged His Tail 57; Pepote 57; Assault in Broad Daylight • Es Geschah am Hellichten Tag • It Happened in Broad Daylight 58; A Man Goes Through the Wall • The Man Who Could Walk Through Walls • The Man Who Walked Through the Wall • Ein Mann Geht Durch die Wand 59; María, Matrícula de Bilbao 60; Defiant Daughters • Girls in the Shadows • Die Schatten Werden Länger • The Shadows Grow Longer 61; Der Lügner 61; Das Feuerschiff 63

Vajda, László see Vajda, Ladislas

Vajda, Marijan Bloodlust • Mosquito der Schänder 76

Valcroze, Jacques Doniol see Doniol-Valcroze, Jacques

Valdez, Julio Sánchez see Sánchez Valdez, Julio

Valdez, Luis Zoot Suit 81; La Bamba 87

Vale, Travers Woman Against Woman 14; What Happened to Jones 15; The Madness of Helen 16; The Men She Married 16; Sally in Our Alley 16; The Scarlet Oath 16*; Tangled Fates 16; Betsy Ross 17*; The Bondage of Fear 17; The Dancer's Peril 17; Darkest Russia 17; The Divorce Game 17; The Dormant Power 17; Easy Money 17; Man's Woman 17; Self Made Widow 17; The Woman Beneath 17; Joan of the Woods 18; Journey's End 18; Just Sylvia 18; The Man Hunt 18; A Soul Without Windows 18; The Spurs of Sybil 18; Stolen Hours 18; Vengeance 18; The Whims of Society 18; The Witch Woman 18; A Woman of Redemption 18; The Zero Hour 18; The Bluffer 19; Heart of Gold 19; The Moral Deadline 19; The Quickening Flame 19; Life 20; A Pasteboard Crown 22; The Street of Tears 24; Western Pluck 26

Valentin, Albert Amphitryon • Aus den Wolken Kommt das Glück • Luck Comes from the Clouds 35*

Valentine, Val Pyjamas Preferred 32

Valère, Jean Paris la Nuit 55*; Jours de Fête à Moscou 57; La Sentence 59; Les Grandes Personnes • Time Out for Love 60; Riffraff 61; Le Gros Coup 64; La Femme Écarlate • The Scarlet Woman 69; Mont-Dragon 71

Valerii, Tonino Per il Gusto di Uccidere • A Taste for Killing 66; Day of Anger • I Giorni dell'Ira • Der Tod Ritt Dienstags 67; Il Prezzo del Potere • The Price of Power 69; Massacre at Fort Holman • Una Ragione per Vivere e Una per Morire • A Reason to Live, a Reason to Die 72; Il Mio Nome È Nessuno • My Name Is Nobody 73; Senza Scrupoli • Without Scruples 86

Valetti, Bruno Amore Che Non Torna • Love That Doesn't Return 38

Valladares, Edmund Bottled Sun • El Sol en Botellitas 86

Vallejo, Gerardo Cruel Fate • Hardships of Destiny • El Rigor del Destino 86

Vallely, Patrick Horses in Winter 88*

Valler, Jorge see Weller, Yohanan

Valletta, Al Alley Cat 83*

Vallois, Philippe Nous Étions un Seul Homme • We Were One Man 78

Valray, Louis Thirteen Days of Love 42

Valtee, Claudius Hoffmanns Erzhlungen • Tales of Hoffmann 11*

Vamsi Lawyer Suhasini 87; Maharshi 88

Van, Wally The Man Behind the Door 14; False Gods 19; Rough Going 25

Van Ackeren, Robert Die Flambierte Frau • A Woman Flambée • A Woman in Flames 82; Die Venusfalle 88

Van Beek, Hans see Beek, Hans van

Van Beek, Luc see Beek, Luc van

Van Brakel, Nouchka see Brakel, Nouchka van

Van Buren, A. H. Hearts in Dixie 29*; Prince of Diamonds 30*

Vance, Daniel J. Entrenados para Matar • The No Mercy Man • Trained to Kill 73

Vance, Stan see Vancini, Florestano

Vance, William The Hearts of Age 34*

Vancini, Florestano The Long Night of '43 • La Lunga Notte del '43 60; Le Italiane e l'Amore • Latin Lovers 61*; La Banda Casaroli 62; La Calda Vita 64; I Lunghi Giorni della Vendetta 65; Seasons of Our Love • Le Stagioni del Nostro Amore 66; L'Isola 68

Van Court, Ulf Sing a Song for Heaven's Sake 60

Vandal, Marcel Graziella 26; Fleur d'Amour 27; Le Sous-Marin de Cristal 28

Vandenberg, Leonard J. Wild Men of Africa 20

Van den Berg, Rudolf see Berg, Rudolf van den

Van den Horst, Herman see Horst, Herman van den

Vanderbeek, Stan Astral Man 57; Mankinda 57; What Who How 57; Ala Mode 58; Visioniii 58; Wheeeeels No. 1 58; Achoo Mr. Keroochev 59; Dance of the Looney Spoons 59; Science Friction 59; Wheeeeels No. 2 59; Blacks and Whites in Days and Nights 60; Skullduggery 60; Snapshots of the City 61; Misc. Happenings 62; Summit 62; Breathdeath 64; Phenomenon No. 1 64; Feedback 65; The Human Face Is a Monument 65; Super-

Imposition 65; Variations No. 5 65; Poem Field No. 1 66; Poem Field No. 2 66; Free Fall 67; The History of Motion in Motion 67; Man and His World 67; Panels for the Walls of the World 67; Poem Field No. 5 67; Poem Field No. 7 67; See Saw Seems 67; Spherical Space No. 1 67; T.V. Interview 67; Newsreel of Dreams No. 1 68; Oh 68; Vanderbeekiana 68; Will 68; Newsreel of Dreams No. 2 69; Film Form No. 1 70; Film Form No. 2 70; Found Film No. 1 70; Transforms 70; Symmetricks 72; Videospace 72; Who Ho Ray No. 1 72; You Do, I Do, We Do 72; Computer Generation 73; Color Fields 77; Euclidean Illusions 78; Dreaming 80; Mirrored Reason 80; Plato's Cave Inn 80; After Laughter 81

Vanderbes, Romano The Sex O'Clock News 86

Vanderbosch, Alfred The Lonely Road 21

Van der Heyde, Nikolai see Heyde, Nikolai van der

Van der Kloot, William see Kloot, William van der

Vanderlyn, S. The Biter Bit 20; A Watery Romance 20

Van der Meulen, Karst see Meulen, Karst van der

Van de Staak, Frans see Staak, Frans van de

Van Deusen, Courtlandt J. The Man Behind the Curtain 16

Van Dusen, Bruce Cold Feet 84

Van Dyke, W. S. Clouds 17; Gift o' Gab 17; Her Good Name 17; The Land of Long Shadows 17; Men of the Desert 17; Mother's Ordeal 17; Open Places 17; Our Little Nell 17; The Range Boss 17; Sadie Goes to Heaven 17; Lady of the Dugout 18; Daredevil Jack 19; Double Adventure 20; The Hawk's Trail 20; The Avenging Arrow 21*; White Eagle 21*; According to Hoyle 22; The Boss of Camp 4 22; Forget-Me-Not 22; The Milky Way 22; Ruth of the Range 22*; The Destroying Angel 23; The Girl Next Door • The Little Girl Next Door • You Are in Danger 23; Half-a-Dollar Bill 23; The Miracle Makers 23; Barriers Burned Away • The Chicago Fire 24; The Battling Fool 24; The Beautiful Sinner 24; Gold Heels 24; Loving Lies 24; Winner Take All 24; The Desert's Price 25; The Gentle Cyclone 25; Hearts and Spurs 25; Ranger of the Big Pines 25; Timber Wolf 25; The Trail Rider 25; Eyes of the Totem 26; The Heart of the Yukon 26; Rider of the Plains • War Paint 26; Winners of the Wilderness 26; The Adventurer • The Gallant Gringo 27*; California 27; Foreign Devils 27; Spoilers of the West 27; The Rock of Friendship • Wyoming 28; Under the Black Eagle 28; White Shadows in the South Seas 28*; The Pagan 29; Trader Horn 30; Cuban Love Song • Rumba 31; Guilty Hands 31; Never the Twain Shall Meet 31; Tarzan, the Ape Man 31; Justice for Sale • Night Court 32; Crooks in Clover • Penthouse 33; Eskimo • Mala the

Magnificent 33; Every Woman's Man • The Prizefighter and the Lady 33; Forsaking All Others 34; Hide-Out 34; Laughing Boy 34; Manhattan Melodrama 34; The Painted Veil 34*; The Thin Man 34; I Live My Life 35; Naughty Marietta 35; A Tale of Two Cities 35*; After the Thin Man • Nick, Gentleman Detective 36; The Devil Is a Sissy • The Devil Takes the Count 36; The Good Earth 36*; His Brother's Wife • Lady of the Tropics 36; Indian Love Call • Rose Marie 36; Love on the Run 36; San Francisco 36*; The Man in Possession • Personal Property 37; The Prisoner of Zenda 37*; Rosalie 37; They Gave Him a Gun 37; Marie Antoinette 38*; Stand Up and Fight 38; Sweethearts 38; Andy Hardy Gets Spring Fever 39; Another Thin Man 39; I Take This Woman 39*; It's a Wonderful World 39; Bitter Sweet 40; I Love You Again 40; The Doctor and the Debutante • Dr. Kildare's Victory 41; The Feminine Touch 41; I Married an Angel 41; Rage in Heaven 41; Shadow of the Thin Man 41; Cairo 42; Journey for Margaret 42; Dragon Seed 43*

Van Dyke, Willard The City 39*; The Children Must Learn 40; Sarah Lawrence 40; To Hear Your Banjo Play 40; Valley Town 40; Tall Tales 41; The Bridge 42*; Oswego 43; Steel Town • Steeltown 43; Northwest U.S.A. • Pacific Northwest 44; San Francisco 45; Journey Into Medicine 46; The Photographer 47; Osmosis 48; Terribly Talented 48; Mount Vernon 49; This Charming Couple 49; New Frontier 50; Years of Change 50; New York University 52; American Frontier 53; There Is a Season 53; Working and Playing to Health 53; Cabos Blancos 54*; Excursion House 54; Recollections of Boyhood • Recollections of Boyhood—An Interview with Joseph Welch 54; Toby and the Tall Corn 54*; Life of the Molds 57; Mountains of the Moon 58; Skyscraper 58*; Tiger Hunt in Assam 58; Land of White Alice 59; The Procession 59; Ireland—The Tear and the Smile 60; Sweden 60; Search Into Darkness 61; Harvest 62; So That Men Are Free 62; Depressed Area U.S.A. 63; Frontiers of News 64; Rice 64*; The Farmer, Feast or Famine 65*; Frontline Cameras, 1935-1965 65; Pop Buell, Hoosier Farmer in Laos 65; Taming the Mekong 65; Shape of Films to Come • Shape of Things to Come 68

Van Dyke, William S. II see Van Dyke, W. S.

Van Dyke, Woody see Van Dyke, W. S.

Vane, Norman Thaddeus Conscience Bay 60; Fledglings 65; The Black Room 82*; Frightmare • The Horror Star 83; Club Life • King of the City 86; Midnight 89

Van Effenterre, Bertrand Mais O et Donc Ornicar 79

Vanel, Charles Dans la Nuit 29; Le Coup de Minuit 35

Van Elst, Gerrit see Elst, Gerrit van

Van Gastern, Louis The House 62; Do

You Get It Now, Why I'm Crying? 70; There's No Plane for Zagreb 71

Van Gogh, Theo see Gogh, Theo van

Van Hemert, Ruud see Hemert, Ruud van

Van Horn, Buddy Any Which Way You Can 80; The Dead Pool 88; Pink Cadillac 89

Vanitchkin, A. The New Gulliver • Novyi Gulliver 33*

Van Lamsweerde, Pino see Lamsweerde, Pino van

Van Lieropl, Robert Luta Continua • The Struggle Continues 71

Van Loan, Philip Forbidden Love • Women Who Wait 21

Vannan, Mani Hum Bhi Insaan Hain 89

Vano, Ivan Ivanov see Ivanov-Vano, Ivan

Van Oostrum, Kees see Oostrum, Kees van

Van Peebles, Melvin Sunlight 58; Three Pickup Men for Herrick 58; La Permission • The Story of a Three Day Pass 67; The Night the Sun Came Out • Watermelon Man 70; Sweet Sweetback's Baadasssss Song 71; Don't Play Us Cheap 73; Identity Crisis 89

Van Pelt, Ernest see Pelt, Ernest van

Van Plack, Tom The Golden Rosary 17

Van Pol, Jacques see Pol, Jacques van

Van Sant, Gus, Jr. Bad Night • Mala Noche 85; Five Ways to Kill Yourself 87; Ken Death Gets Out of Jail 87; My New Friends 87; Junior 88; Drugstore Cowboy 89

Van Tell, Terry The Brute and the Beast • Le Colt Cantarono la Morte È Fu: Tempo di Massacro • Tempo di Massacro 66*; Helga 67*

Van Tuyle, Bert see Tuyle, Bert van

Van Veen, Herman see Veen, Herman van

Van Warmerdam, Alex see Warmerdam, Alex van

Van Winkle, Joseph The Woman Inside 81

Vanzi, Luigi The World by Night 61; Un Dollaro tra i Denti • For a Dollar in the Teeth • The Silent Stranger • A Stranger in Town 66; Ride Bene Chi Spara Ultimo • Shoot First, Laugh Last • The Stranger Returns • Un Uomo, un Cavallo, una Pistola 67

Vanzina, Carlo Luna di Miele in Tre 76; Arrivano i Gatti 79; Figlio delle Stelle 79; I Fichissimi 81; Eccezionale Veramente 82; Sapore di Mare 82; Violentemente...Mia 82; Mystère 83; Il Ras del Quartiere 83; Vacanze di Natale 83; Amarsi un Po 84; Vacanze in America 84; Sotto il Vestito Niente • Under the Dress, Nothing 85; Yuppies—I Giovani di Successo • Yuppies—Youngsters Who Succeed 86; I Miei Primi Quarant'Anni • My First Forty Years 87; Montecarlo Gran Casino 87; Via Montenapoleone 87; The Match • La Partita 88

Vanzina, Stefano see Steno

Van Zuylen, Eric see Zuylen, Eric van

Varda, Agnès La Pointe Courte 54;

Toute la Mémoire du Monde 56*; Castles Through the Ages • Ô Saisons, Ô Châteaux 57; Du Côté de la Côte • The Riviera: Today's Eden 58; L'Opéra-Mouffe 58; La Cocotte d'Azur 59; Cléo de 5 à 7 • Cleo from 5 to 7 61; Les Fiancés du Pont Macdonald 61; Hello Cubans • Salut les Cubains 63; Le Bonheur • Happiness 64; Christmas Carol 65; Les Créatures • The Creatures • Varelserna 66; Elsa • Elsa la Rose 66; Far from Vietnam • Loin du Viêt-nam 66*; Black Panthers • Huey • Les Panthères Noires 68; Uncle Janco • Uncle Yanko 68; Lion's Love 69; Nausicaa 70; Daguerréotypes 75; Réponses de Femmes 75; One Sings, the Other Doesn't • L'Une Chante, l'Autre Pas 76; Mur Murs • Mural Murals • Wall Walls 80; Documenteur • Documenteur: An Emotion Picture 81; Ulysse 82; Une Minute pour Une Image 83; Les Dites-Cariatides • The So-Called Cariatids 84; 7 p., cuis., s. de b. • 7 rms, kitch, bath 84; Sans Toit Ni Loi • Vagabond • Vagabonde 85; Kung Fu Master! • Le Petit Amour 87; Jane B. by Agnès V. • Jane B. par Agnès V. 88

Vardy, Mike Man at the Top 73

Vargas de la Maza, Armando El Indio 39

Vari, Giuseppe The Brain That Wouldn't Die • The Head That Wouldn't Die 59; Revenge of the Barbarians 61; Night Star, Goddess of Electra • Roma Contra Roma • War of the Zombies 63; Duguejo 66; Con Lui Cavalca la Morte 67; The Last Killer • L'Ultimo Killer 67; Un Poker di Pistole • Poker with Pistols 67; Un Buco in Fronte 68; Prega il Morto e Ammazza il Vivo 71; Larsen, Wolf of the Seven Seas • Legend of the Sea Wolf • Wolf Larsen 74; The Perils of P.K. 86

Várkonyi, Zoltán Három Csillag • Three Stars 60*; The Bitter Truth • Keserű Igazság 86

Varley, John Enlighten Thy Daughter 34

Varmalov, Leonid Komsomoliya 29; Pilots 38; Arctic Journey 40; Defeat of the German Armies Near Moscow 42*; Stalingrad 43; Caucasus 44; Victory in the South 44; Yugoslavia 46; Poland 48; Battle for China • Victory of the Chinese People 50; Circus Arena 51; Through India 52; The Romanian People's Republic 53; A Hundred Days in Burma 57; Conflict in the Congo 60; Meeting in America 60; Our "Pravda" 62; Port Said 62; The Suez Canal 62

Varnel, Marcel Almost Married 32*; Chandu the Magician 32*; The Silent Witness 32*; Infernal Machine 33; Freedom of the Seas 34; Girls Will Be Boys 34; Dance Band 35; Give Me Your Heart • I Give My Heart • The Loves of Madame DuBarry 35; No Monkey Business 35; Regal Cavalcade • Royal Cavalcade 35*; All In 36; Public Nuisance No. 1 36; Good Morning, Boys • Where There's a Will 37; Oh! Mr. Porter 37; Okay for Sound 37; Alf's Button Afloat 38; Ask a Policeman

38; Convict 99 38; Hey! Hey! U.S.A. 38; Old Bones of the River 38; Band Waggon 39; The Frozen Limits 39; Where's That Fire? 39; Gasbags 40*; Let George Do It 40; Neutral Port 40*; The Ghost of St. Michael's 41; Hi! Gang 41; I Thank You 41; It's Turned Out Nice Again • Turned Out Nice Again 41; South American George 41; Get Cracking 42; King Arthur Was a Gentleman 42; Much Too Shy 42; Bell-Bottom George 43; He Snoops to Conquer 44; I Didn't Do It 45; George in Civvy Street 46; This Man Is Mine 46

Varnel, Max How to Murder a Rich Uncle 57*; Links of Justice 58; Moment of Indiscretion 58; A Woman Possessed 58; The Child and the Killer 59; Crash Drive 59; The Great Van Robbery 59; No Safety Ahead 59; Top Floor Girl 59; Web of Suspicion 59; Sentenced for Life 60; A Taste of Money 60; Enter Inspector Duval 61; Fate Takes a Hand 61; Murder in Eden 61; Part-Time Wife 61; A Question of Suspense 61; Return of a Stranger 61; Mrs. Gibbons' Boys 62; The Silent Invasion 62; The Rivals 63

Varney, Arthur see Varney-Serrao, Arthur

Varney-Serrao, Arthur Winds of the Pampas 27; Enter the Queen 30; The Road to Fortune 30; Almost a Divorce 31*; The Eternal Feminine 31; Immediate Possession 31; The Wrong Mr. Perkins 31

Vásáry, János see Vaszary, János

Vasconcelos, Antonio-Pedro O Lugar do Morto 85

Vasiliev, Dmitri The Last Night • Poslednaya Noch 36*; Lenin in October • Lenin v Octyabre • Lenin v Oktiabrye 37*; Aleksandr Nevskii • Alexander Nevsky 38*; Mashenka 42*; In the Name of the Fatherland • In the Name of the Homeland • Vo Imya Rodini 43*; Admiral Nakhimov • Amiral Nakhimov 46*; Joukovsky • Yukovsky • Zhukovsky 50*

Vasiliev, Gennady Ancient Russia • Rus Iznachalna 87

Vasiliev, Georgy An Exploit on the Ice • The Ice-Breaker Krassnin • Podvig vo Idach 28*; La Belle au Bois Dormant • Sleeping Beauty • Spyashchaya Krasavitsa • The Woman of the Sleeping Forest 29*; Une Affaire Personnelle • Lichnoye Delo • A Personal Affair • A Personal Matter 31*; Unlikely But True 32; Chapayev 34*; The Days of Volochayev • The Defense of Volochayev • Far East • Intervention in the Far East • Les Jours de Volotchaiev • Volochayevsk Days • Volochayevskiye Dni 37*; La Défense de Tsaritsyne • The Defense of Tsaritsyn • Oborona Tsaritsina 42*; The Front 43*

Vasiliev, Sergei An Exploit on the Ice • The Ice-Breaker Krassnin • Podvig vo Idach 28*; La Belle au Bois Dormant • Sleeping Beauty • Spyashchaya Krasavitsa • The Woman of the Sleeping Forest 29*; Une Affaire Personnelle • Lichnoye Delo • A Personal Affair • A Personal Matter 31*; Chapayev 34*; The Days of Volochayev •

The Defense of Volochayev • Far East • Intervention in the Far East • Les Jours de Volotchaiev • Volochayevsk Days • Volochayevskiye Dni 37*; La Défense de Tsaritsyne • The Defense of Tsaritsyn • Oborona Tsaritsina 42*; The Front 43*; Geroi Shipki • Geroite na Shipka • The Heroes of Shipka • Les Héros de Chipka 54; The Days of October • In the October Days • Les Jours d'Octobre • October Days • Oktyabr' Dni • V Dni Oktyabrya 58

Vasiliev, Vladimir Fouette 86*

Vasquez, Joseph B. Street Story 88

Vassilevsky, Radomir Chto u Senjki Bylo • Shto u Seniki Bylo • The Unjust Stork 86

Vasudhara, Sunh The King of the White Elephant 41

Vaszary, János Édes a Bosszú • Sweet Revenge 38; Mami 38; Tokaji Rapszódia 38; 3:1 a Szerelem Javára • 3 to 1 for Love 39; I Entrust My Wife to You • Rád Bízom a Feleségem 39

Vatteone, Augusto Cesar El Amor Manda • Love Commands 40

Vautier, René Afrique 50 50; Algérie en Flammes 58; Les Anneaux d'Or de Mahdia 60

Vávra, Otakar Light Penetrates Darkness • Světlo Proniká Tmou 31; We Live in Prague • Žijeme v Praze 34; Listopad • November 35; Velbloud Uchem Jehly 36; Filosofská Historie • A Philosophical Story 37; Gaudeamus Igitur 37; Panenství • Virginity 37; Cech Panen Kutnohorských • Guild of the Kutna Hora Virgins • The Guild of the Virgins of Kutna Hora • The Merry Wives 38; Dívka v Modrím 39; The Enchanted House • Kouzelný Dům 39; Humoreska • Humoresque 39; A Fable of May • May Fairy Tales • Pohádka Máje • Romance 40; The Masked Lover • Maskovaná Milenka 40; Pacientka Doktora Hegla 40; Podvod s Runensem 40; Turbina • The Turbine 41; I Shan't Be Long • Přijdu Hned 42; Okouzlen 42; Happy Journey • Šťastnou Cestu 43; Rosina the Foundling • Rozina Sebranec 45; Vlast Vítá 45; Cesta k Barikádám 46; The Mischievous Tutor • Nezbedný Bakalář 46; Předtucha • Presentiment 47; Krakatit 48; Němá Barikáda • The Silent Barricade 49; Fall In • Nástup 52; Hussite Trilogy, Part One • Jan Hus 54; Hussite Trilogy, Part Two • The Hussite Warrior • Jan Žižka • Jan Žižka z Trocnova 54; Against All • All Our Enemies • Hussite Trilogy, Part Three • Proti Všem 57; Citizen Brych • Občan Brych 58; The First Rescue Party • První Parta 59; The Closing Hour • Policejní Hodina • Time Gentlemen, Please 60; Srpnová Neděle • A Sunday in August 60; Night Guest • Noční Host 61; The Ardent Heart • The Burning Heart • Horoucí Srdce • The Passionate Heart 62; The Golden Rennet • Zlatá Reneta 65; Romance for Trumpet • Romance pro Křídlovku 66; The Thirteenth Chamber • The Thirteenth Room • Třináctá Komnata 68; A Hammer Against Witches •

Kladivo na Čarodějnice • Witchhammer 69; Days of Treason 73; Liberation of Prague 77; The Black Sun • Černé Slunce 79; Veronika 85; Oldřich a Božena • Oldřich and Bozena 86

Vay, Armando After Six Days 22*

Vázquez, Ángel Rodríguez see *Rodríguez Vázquez, Ángel*

Veber, Francis Le Jouet • The Toy 76; La Chèvre • The Goat 81; Les Compères 83; Les Fugitifs • The Fugitives 86; Three Fugitives 89

Vecchiali, Paul Rosa la Rose, Fille Publique 85; Encore (Once More) 88

Vedey, Julien Take a Powder 53*

Védrès, Nicole Paris 1900 47; Life Begins Tomorrow • La Vie Commence Demain 49; Amazone 51; Aux Frontières de l'Homme • The Border of Life 53*

Vedyshev, Mikhail The Deal • Sdelka 87

Veen, Herman van Splitting Up • Uit Elkaar 81

Vega, Felipe Mientras Haya Luz • While There Is Light 87

Vega, Isela Las Amantes del Señor de la Noche • The Lovers of the Lord of the Night 83

Vega, Pastor Portrait of Teresa • Retrato de Teresa 79; Amor en Campo Minado • Love in a Minefield 87; En el Aire 88

Veggezi, Giuseppe Sfida al Diavolo 65

Veidt, Conrad Madness • Wahnsinn 19; Die Nacht auf Goldenhall 19; Lord Byron 22

Veiller, Anthony Battle of Britain 43*

Veiller, Bayard Alias Ladyfingers • Ladyfingers 21; The Last Card 21; Sherlock Brown 21; There Are No Villains 21; The Face Between 22; The Right That Failed 22; The Trial of Mary Dugan 29

Vejar, Carlos Sword of Granada 53*

Vejar, Sergio Delincuente • Delinquent 87; One More Saturday • Un Sábado Más 87

Vekroff, Perry N. Hearts of Men 15; Three Weeks 15; When It Strikes Home 15; Bridges Burned 17; Her Secret 17; The More Excellent Way 17; The Question 17; Richard the Brazen 17; The Secret of Eve 17; A Woman's Experience 18; Dust of Desire 19; What Love Forgives 19; Cynthia-of-the-Minute 20

Velazco, Arturo La Banda de los Panchitos • The Panchito Gang 86

Velazco, María Elena From Neither Here Nor There • Ni de Aquí, Ni de Allá 87

Velimirović, Zdravko O Tempo dos Leopardos 85

Velle, Gaston L'Amant de la Lune 05; Around a Star • Voyage Autour d'une Étoile 06; Le Petit Jules Verne 07

Velo, Carlos Castillos de Castilla 33*; Galicia y Compostela 33*; Terraco Augusta 33*; Almadrabas 34*; La Ciudad y el Campo 35*; Felipe II y el Escorial 35*; Infinitos 35*; En un Lugar de Castilla 36; Romancero Marroquín 36; Saudade 36; Pintura Mural Mexicana 53; Tierra Caliente 54; ¡Torero! 55; México Mío 59; Pedro Paramo 67

Veloso, Caetano Cinema Falado • Talking Pictures 86

Veltee, H. W. Kolm see *Kolm-Veltee, Walter*

Veltee, Walter Kolm see *Kolm-Veltee, Walter*

Vengerov, Vladimir Obryv • The Precipice 87

Venne, Stephane Seul ou avec d'Autres 62*

Vennerød, Petter Adjø Solidaritet • Farewell Illusion 84*; The Dream Castle • Drømmeslottet 86*; Jord 87*

Ventura, Michael "I'm Almost Not Crazy..." John Cassavetes: The Man and His Work 84

Venturi, Lauro Leonardo da Vinci 52*

Venturini, Edward D. The Headless Horseman 22; The Old Fool 23; Gente Alegre 33; El Príncipe Gondolero 33; In Old Mexico 38; The Llano Kid 39

Venzher, Ivan Molodost Nashi Stranyi • Our Country's Youth • Young Years of Our Country • The Youth of Our Country 45*; Russia on Parade 46*

Veo, Carlo Sword Without a Country 61

Vera, Luis R. An Accomplished Fact • Hechos Consumados 85; Consuelo • Consuelo—An Illusion 88

Vera, Marilda On the Green Path • Por los Caminos Verdes 87

Verbong, Ben The Girl with the Red Hair • Het Meisje met het Rode Haar 81; The Scorpion 85

Verbrugge, Casper The P-P-Performer 86

Verdaguer, Antoni L'Escot 87

Verdone, Carlo Un Sacco Bello 80; Bianco, Rosso e Verdone 81; Borotalco 81; Acqua and Sapone • Acqua e Sapone 83; I Due Carabinieri 84; Too Strong • Troppo Forte 85*; Io e Mia Sorella • Me and My Sister 87; Compagni di Scuola 88

Verdone, Luca Sette Chili in Sette Giorni • Seven Kilos in Seven Days 86

Vergano, Aldo Pietro Micca 37; Quelli della Montagna 42; Outcry • Il Sole Sorge Ancora • The Sun Always Rises • The Sun Rises Again 46; Czarny Zlep • The Devil's Power 49*; I Fuorilegge 50; La Grande Rinuncia 51; Santa Lucia Luntana 51; Amore Rosso 53; Schicksal am Lenkard 53

Vergez, Gérard Les Cavaliers de l'Orage 84; Bras de Fer 85; Deux Minutes de Soleil en Plus 88

Vergitsis, Nicos Archangelos tou Pathous • Potlatch 87

Vergne, Jean-Pierre Le Téléphone Sonne Toujours Deux Fois 85

Verhage, Gerrard Afzien • Second Wind 86

Verhoeff, Pieter The Dream • De Droom 85; Count Your Blessings • Van Geluk Gesproken 87

Verhoeven, Michael The White Rose 82; Killing Cars 86; The Nasty Girl 90

Verhoeven, Paul The Day After the Divorce • Der Tag Nach der Scheidung 40; Palace Scandal 49; Eternal Waltz • Ewiger Walzer 59; The Judge and the Sinner •

Der Jugendrichter 64

Verhoeven, Paul Business Is Business • Wat Zien Ik 71; Turkish Delight • Turks Fruit 73; Cathy Tippel • Katie's Passion • Keetje Tippel 75; Soldier of Orange 77; Spetters 80; The Fourth Man • Die Vierde Man 82; Flesh + Blood 85; Robocop 87; Total Recall 90

Verity, Erwin The Reluctant Dragon 41*

Verma, Vinod K. Gentleman 89

Vermorel, Claude Les Conquérants Solitaires 52; La Plus Belle des Vies 56

Vernay, Robert Véronique 49; Comte de Monte Cristo • The Count of Monte Cristo 54

Verneuil, Henri La Table aux Crèves • The Village Feud 51; Le Boulanger de Valorgue • The Wild Oat 52; Brelan d'As 52; Forbidden Fruit • Le Fruit Défendu 52; Carnaval • Carnival 53; L'Ennemi Public No. 1 • The Most Wanted Man • The Most Wanted Man in the World • Il Nemico Pubblico n.1 • Public Enemy No. 1 53; Les Amants du Tage • Lovers' Net • The Lovers of Lisbon • Port of Shame 54; Le Mouton A Cinq Pattes • The Sheep Has Five Legs 54; Des Gens Sans Importance 55; Paris Hotel • Paris-Palace-Hôtel 56; The Evil That Is Eve • Une Manche et la Belle • What Price Murder? 57; The Big Chief • Gangster Boss • Le Grand Chef 58; The Cow and I • La Vacca e il Prigioniero • La Vache et le Prisonnier 58; Maxime 58; L'Affaire d'Une Nuit • It Happened All Night 59; La Française et l'Amour • Love and the Frenchwoman 60*; Le Président 60; The Lions Are Loose • Les Lions Sont Lâchés 61; Any Number Can Win • The Big Grab • The Big Snatch • Mélodie en Sous-Sol 62; It's Hot in Hell • A Monkey in Winter • Un Singe en Hiver 62; Cent Mille Dollars au Soleil • Centomila Dollari al Sole • Greed in the Sun 63; Week-End à Zuydcoote • Weekend at Dunkirk 64; The 25th Hour • La Venticinquesima Ora • La Vingt-Cinquième Heure 66; La Bataille de San Sebastian • I Cannoni di San Sebastian • Los Cañónes de San Sebastian • Guns for San Sebastian • The Guns of San Sebastian • Miracle of San Sebastian • Wall for San Sebastian 67; Le Clan des Siciliens • The Sicilian Clan 68; The Burglars • Le Casse 71; Night Flight from Moscow • Le Serpent • The Serpent 72; Night Caller • Peur sur la Ville 74; Le Corps de Mon Ennemi 76; I...Comme Icare 79; Mille Milliards de Dollars 81; Les Morfalous 83

Vernon, Charles Bernardo's Confession 14; Grimaldi 14; The Seven Ages of Man 14; The Street Watchman's Story 14; From Scotland 15

Vernon, Henry The Danger Zone 87

Vernon, Richard Shadow Man • Street of Shadows 53

Vernot, Henry J. The Dead Alive 16; Feathertop 16; The Sport of the Gods 21

Vernuccio, Gianni Le Avventure di Cartouche • Cartouche 54*; Los Amantes del Desierto • Gli Amanti del Deserto • The

Vito, Danny de *see DeVito, Danny*
Vito, Ralph de *see De Vito, Ralph*
Vitti, Monica Scandalo Segreto • Secret Scandal 89
Vivanco, Jorge Tequiman 87
Vivarelli, Piero Satanic 68; Il Dio Serpente • The God Snake • The Serpent God • The Snake God 70
Vivet, Jean-Pierre Louis Capet • Louis XVI 54*; Jean-Jacques • Jean-Jacques Rousseau 57*
Vivian, Arthur Rob Roy 11
Vláčil, František Ďáblova Past • The Devil's Trap 64; Markéta Lazarová 66; The Shadow of a Fern • Stín Kapradiny 85; Magus 88
Vlamos, John Fugitive Valley 41*
Vocoret, Michel Nous Maigrirons Ensemble • We'll Grow Thin Together 79
Vogel, Jesse The Adventures of Pinocchio 78
Vogel, Virgil The Mole People 56; The Kettles on Old MacDonald's Farm 57; The Land Unknown 57; Horror in the Midnight Sun • Invasion of the Animal People • Rymdinvasion i Lappland • Space Invasion from Lapland • Space Invasion of Lapland • Terror in the Midnight Sun 60*; The Sword of Ali Baba 65*
Vogeler, Volker Verflucht Dies Amerika 73; Das Tal der Tanzenden Witwen • Valley of the Widows 74
Vohrer, Alfred Imperfect Angel 58; The Dark Eyes of London • Dead Eyes of London • Geheimnisse von London • Die Toten Augen von London 61; The Door with Seven Locks 62; The Inn on the River 62; Verbrechen nach Schulschluss • The Young Go Wild 62; The Indian Scarf 63; An Alibi for Death 64; Among Vultures • Frontier Hellcat • Među Jastrebovima • Parmi les Vautours • Unter Geiern 64; Der Hexer • The Mysterious Magician • The Squeaker • The Wizard 64; Flaming Frontier • Lavirint Smrti • Old Surehand • Old Surehand, Part One 65; Old Firehand • Thunder at the Border • Winnetou and His Friend Old Firehand • Winnetou und Sein Freund • Winnetou und Sein Freund Old Firehand 66; Ape Creature 68; Creature with the Blue Hand 70
Voinov, Konstantin Solntse Svetit Vsem • The Sun Shines for All • The Sun Shines for Everybody 61; The Marriage of Balzaminov • Zhenitba Balzaminova 66
Vokhotko, Anatoly Aliens Are Forbidden • Chuzhie Zdes Ne Khodyat 87*
Volev, Nikolai Gospodin za Edin Den • King for a Day 85; All for Love • Da Ebichash na Inat 86
Volkov, Alexander The Green Spider 16; Le Brasier Ardent 23*; Edmund Kean, Prince Among Lovers • Kean • Kean—The Madness of Genius 24; Les Ombres Qui Passant 24; Casanova • The Loves of Casanova 27; The White Devil 31; Secrets of the Orient 32
Von Alten, Jürgen *see Alten, Jürgen von*
Von Ambesser, Axel *see Ambesser, Axel*

Von Baky, Josef *see Baky, Josef von*
Von Bolváry, Géza *see Bolváry, Géza von*
Von Borsody, Eduard *see Borsody, Eduard von*
Von Bulow, Vicco *see Loriot*
Von Cziffra, Géza *see Cziffra, Géza von*
Vonde, Chester de *see De Vonde, Chester*
Von der Noss, Rudolf *see Noss, Rudolf von der*
Von Dungern, Baron A. *see Dungern, Baron A. von*
Von Fritsch, Günther *see Fritsch, Günther von*
Von Fürstenberg, Veith *see Fürstenberg, Veith von*
Von Gerlach, Arthur *see Gerlach, Arthur von*
Von Grote, Alexandra *see Grote, Alexandra von*
Von Harbou, Thea *see Harbou, Thea von*
Von Herkomer, Hubert *see Herkomer, Hubert von*
Von Herkomer, Siegfried *see Herkomer, Siegfried von*
Von Kaufmann, Wilhelm *see Kaufmann, Wilhelm von*
Von Lützelburg, Helmer *see Lützelburg, Helmer von*
Von Mizener, Don *see Mizener, Don von*
Von Norman, Roger *see Norman, Roger von*
Von Podmanitzky, Felix *see Podmanitzky, Felix von*
Von Praunheim, Rosa *see Praunheim, Rosa von*
Von Radványi, Géza *see Radványi, Géza von*
Von Ráthonyi, Ákos *see Ráthonyi, Ákos von*
Von Santer, Carl *see Santer, Carl von*
Von Seyffertitz, Gustav *see Seyffertitz, Gustav von*
Von Sternberg, Josef *see Sternberg, Josef von*
Von Stroheim, Erich *see Stroheim, Erich von*
Von Sydow, Max *see Sydow, Max von*
Von Theumer, Ernst R. *see Theumer, Ernst R. von*
Von Tourjansky, Victor *see Tourjansky, Victor*
Von Trier, Lars *see Trier, Lars von*
Von Trotta, Margarethe *see Trotta, Margarethe von*
Von Wymetal, William *see Wymetal, William von*
Vorhaus, Bernard Camera Cocktales 32; Crime on the Hill 33; The Ghost Camera 33; Money for Speed 33; On Thin Ice 33; Blind Justice 34; The Broken Melody • Vagabond Violinist 34; Night Club Queen 34; Dark World 35; The Last Journey 35; Street Song 35; Ten Minute Alibi 35; Daredevils of Earth 36; Dusty Ermine • Hideout in the Alps • Rendezvous in the

Alps 36; Cotton Queen • Crying Out Loud 37; King of the Newsboys 38; Tenth Avenue Kid 38; Fisherman's Wharf 39; Meet Dr. Christian 39; Way Down South 39; The Courageous Dr. Christian 40; The Refugee • Three Faces West 40; Angels with Broken Wings 41; The Carter Case • Mr. District Attorney in the Carter Case 41; Hurricane Smith 41; Lady from Louisiana 41; The Affairs of Jimmy Valentine • Unforgotten Crime 42; Ice-Capades Revue • Rhythm Hits the Ice 42; Bury Me Dead 47; Winter Wonderland 47; The Amazing Dr. X • The Amazing Mr. X • The Spiritualist 48; So Young, So Bad 50; The Lady from Boston • Pardon My French 51; Fanciulle di Lusso • Finishing School • Luxury Girls 52
Vorkapich, Slavko A Hollywood Extra • Hollywood Rhapsody • The Life and Death of a Hollywood Extra • The Life and Death of 9413, a Hollywood Extra 27*; I Take This Woman 31*; The Past of Mary Holmes 33*; Fingal's Cave 46; Forest Murmurs 47; Hanka 55
Vorlíček, Václav Kdo Chce Zabít Jessu? • Who Killed Jessie? • Who Wants to Kill Jessie? • Who Would Kill Jessie? 65; Mister, You Are a Widower • Pane, Vy Jste Vdova • Sir, You Are a Widower 71; Což Takhle Dát Si Špenát • A Nice Plate of Spinach • What Would You Say to Some Spinach? 76*; I Am Not Me • Já Nejsem Já 85; Mladé Víno • Young Wine 86
Voroner, Murray The Super Fight 69
Voshell, John M. Enemies of Children 23*
Voskanian, Robert The Child • Kill and Go Hide • Zombie Child 77
Voss, Kurt Border Radio 87*
Voulgaris, Pantelis The Matchmaking of Anna • To Proxenio tis Annas 72; Happy Day 76; Petrina Chronia • Stone Years 85; I Fanella me to Ennia 88
Voupouras, Christos Lipotakis 88*
Vrdoljak, Anton Od Petka do Petka • One Friday to the Next 86; Glembajevi 88
Vrettakos, Costas The Children of the Swallow • Ta Paidia tis Chelidonas 87
Vronsky, I. Crime and Punishment 13
Vronsky, Vakhtang Lileia 60*
Vukobratović, Mihailo Men Only Mean Trouble • Nije Lako s Mučkarcima 86
Vukotić, Dušan The Enchanted Castle in Dudinci • Začarani Dvorac u Dudincima 51; How Kico Was Born • Kićo 51; The Disobedient Robot • Nestašni Robot • The Playful Robot 56; Abracadabra • Abrakadabra 57; Čarobni Zvuci • Charming Sounds 57; Cowboy Jimmy 57; Great Fear • Veliki Strah 58; Osvetnik • The Revenger 58; Concerto for Submachine Gun • Koncert za Mašinsku Pušku 59; The Cow on the Moon • Krava na Mjesecu 59; My Tail Is My Ticket • Rep Je Ulaznica 59; Piccolo 60; Ersatz • The Substitute • Surogat 61; 1001 Crtež • 1001 Drawings 61; Igra • The Play 62; Astromati • Astromuts 63; The Way to the Neighbor • Weg zum Nachbarn 63; Sedmi Kontinent • The

Seventh Continent • Siedma Pevnina 66*; Mrlja na Savjesti • A Stain on His Conscience 68; Opera Cordis 68; Ars Gratia Artis 69; Operation Stadium 77; Gosti iz Galaksije • Visitors from the Galaxy 81

Vulcev, Nikola Ivailo the Great 64

Vulchanov, Rangel Na Malkia Ostrov • On the Little Island 58; First Lesson • The Old Lady • Parvi Urok 59*; Slantseto i Syankata • Sun and Shadow 62; The Inspector and the Night • Inspectorat i Noshta 63; The She-Wolf • Valchitsata 65; Between Two Worlds 68; Aesop • Esop 69; S Lyubov i Nezhnost • With Love and Tenderness 78; Where Are You Going? • Za Kude Putovate 86; A Sega Nakude • Where Do We Go from Here? • Whither Now? 88

Vyas, Kishore Janetana Sogand 88

Waalkes, Otto Otto—Der Film 85*; Otto—Der Neue Film • Otto—The New Film 87*

Wachsberg, Orin Starlight 86

Wachsmann, Daniel Transit 79; Eastern Wind • Hamsin • Hot Wind 82

Wacks, Jonathan Crossroads South Africa 80; Powwow Highway 88

Wadleigh, Michael Woodstock 70; Wolfen 81

Waggner, George Western Trails 37; Black Bandit 38; Ghost Town Riders 38; Guilty Trails 38; Outlaw Express 38; Prairie Justice 38; Honor of the West 39; Mystery Plane • Sky Pilot 39; The Phantom Stage 39; Stunt Pilot • Wolf Call 39; Drums of the Desert 40; Horror Island 40; Atomic Monster • The Electric Man • Man Made Monster 41; Sealed Lips 41; South of Tahiti • White Savage 41; The Wolf Man 41; The Climax 44; Frisco Sal 45; Shady Lady 45; Tangier 46; The Assassin • Gunfighters 47; The Fighting Kentuckian 49; Operation Pacific 51; Destination 60,000 57; Pale Arrow • Pawnee 57; Fury River 58*; Mission of Danger 59*; Gold, Glory and Custer 63

Wagner, Christian Wallers Last Trip • Wallers Letzter Gang 89

Wagner, Fernando Virgin Sacrifice 59

Wagner, Jane Moment by Moment 78

Wagner, Maria Theresa Die Nacht des Marders 88

Wagner, Robert Fair Week 24; Two Wagons, Both Covered 24

Wahby, Youssef Jawhara 42; Berlanti 43; The Ambassador of Hell • Safir Gehannam 44; Gharam wa Intikam • Passion and the Revenge 44; Banat el Rif • The Country Girls 45; Awlad el Shareh • Children of the Streets 51; Bint el Hawa • Daughter of Love 53

Wahlberg, Gideon The Old Gods Still Live 37; Söder om Landsvägen 37; Baldvins Bröllop • Baldwin's Wedding 38*; Send Home No. 7 • Skicka Hem Nr. 7 39

Wahlgren, Anders Moa 86

Wai, Lau Kun see Lau, Kun Wai

Waimon, Seto The Statue of Liberty 35; The Players at the Gate of Love 37; Yellow Flowers Through a Rainy Day 37; The Bat-

tle of Pao Shan 38; The Song of the Partisans 38; The Nation's Appeal 40

Waite, Glenn The Sacred Ruby 20

Waite, Ralph On the Nickel 79

Wajda, Andrzej The Bad Boy • Evil Boy • Zły Chłopiec 50; Kiedy Ty Śpisz • While You Sleep • While You're Asleep 50; Ceramika Ilzecka • Ilza Ceramics • Pottery at Ilza • The Pottery of Ilza 51; A Generation • Light in the Darkness • Pokolenie 54; I Go Toward the Sun • I Walk to the Sun • Idę do Słońca • Idę ku Słońcu • Je Vais Vers le Soleil • March Towards the Sun 55; Kanał • They Love Life • They Loved Life 56; Ashes and Diamonds • Popiół i Diament 58; Lotna 59; Innocent Sorcerers • Niewinni Czarodzieje 60; Fury Is a Woman • Lady Macbeth of Mtsensk • Lady Macbeth of Siberia • Siberian Lady Macbeth • Sibirska Ledi Magbet 61; Samson 61; Amore a Vent' Anni • L'Amour à Vingt Ans • Hatachi no Koi • Liebe mit Zwanzig • Love at Twenty • Miłość Dwudziestolatków 62*; Ashes The Lost Army • Popioły 65; Bramy Raju • The Gates of Heaven • Gates to Paradise • The Holy Apes • Vrata Raja 67; Everything for Sale • Wszystko na Sprzedaż 67; Przekładaniec 68; Hunting Flies • Polowanie na Muchy 69; The Birch Wood • Brzezina 70; Krajobraz Po Bitwie • Landscape After Battle • Landscape After the Battle 70; Człowiek z Marmuru • Man of Marble 72; Pilatus und Andere 72; The Wedding • Wesele 72; Land of Promise • Promised Land • Ziemia Obiecana 74; Bez Znieczulenia • Rough Treatment • Without Anesthesia • Without Anesthetic • Without Anesthetics 78; Les Demoiselles de Vilko • The Girls from Wilko • Maidens from Wilko • Panny z Wilka • The Young Girls of Wilko • The Young Ladies of Wilko 78; Invitation to the Inside • Invitation to the Interior • Zaproszenie do Wnętrza 78; The Conductor • Dyrygent • The Orchestra Conductor 79; Noc Listopadowa • November Night 79; Człowiek z Żelaza • Man of Iron 80; L'Affaire Danton • Danton 82; Un Amour en Allemagne • Eine Liebe in Deutschland • A Love in Germany 83; Chronicle of a Love Affair • A Chronicle of Amorous Accidents • A Chronicle of Love Affairs • Kronika Wypadków Miłosnych 85; Les Possédés • The Possessed 87; Dr. Korczak • Korczak 90

Wakabayashi, Eijiro Invaders from Space • Invaders from the Spaceship • The Prince of Space • The Star Prince • Yūsei Ōji 59

Wakamatsu, Koji Kabe no Naka no Himegoto 63; The Love Robots 65; Taiji ga Mitsuryō Suru Toki 66; Okasaretu Byūakui • Violated Angels • Violated Women 67; Riyū Naki Bōkō-Gendai Seihanzua Zekkyōhen 69; Gōmon Hyakunenshi 75

Walas, Chris The Fly II 89

Waldron, Gy The Moonrunners 74

Walerstein, Mauricio Macho y Hembra 85; De Mujer a Mujer • Woman to

Woman 87

Waletzky, Josh Partisans of Vilna 86

Walker, Chuck Ryder, P.I. 86*

Walker, Dorian The Last American Preppie • Making the Grade • Preppies 84; Teen Witch 89

Walker, Giles Descent 75; Twice Upon a Time 79; The Masculine Mystique 85*; 90 Days 85; The Last Straw 87

Walker, Hal The Fleet's In 42*; Road to Utopia 44; Duffy's Tavern 45; Out of This World 45; The Stork Club 45; At War with the Army 50; My Friend Irma Goes West 50; Sailor Beware 51; That's My Boy 51; Road to Bali 52

Walker, Ian Nat Gonella and His Georgians • Pity the Poor Rich 35

Walker, John A Winter Tan 87*

Walker, Johnny Bachelor Apartments 20

Walker, Martin Hide and Seek 22

Walker, Nancy Can't Stop the Music 80

Walker, Norman Oxford Bags 26; Tommy Atkins 28; Widecombe Fair 28; The Hate Ship 29; A Romance of Seville 29; Loose Ends 30; The Middle Watch 30; Flirting Wives • Uneasy Virtue 31; The Shadow Between 31; Fires of Fate 32; The Man Who Won • Mr. Bill the Conqueror 32; The Flaw 33; Forging Ahead 33; The Fortunate Fool 33; The House of Trent 33; Skipper of the Osprey 33; Dangerous Ground 34; Lilies of the Field 34; The Way of Youth 34; Key to Harmony 35; Turn of the Tide 35; Debt of Honour 36; Our Fighting Navy • Torpedoed! 37; Suicide Legion • Sunset in Vienna 37; Beyond Our Horizon 39; The Silence • Two Minutes 39; The Man at the Gate • Men of the Sea 40; Hard Steel • What Shall It Profit? 41; The Great Mr. Handel 42; They Knew Mr. Knight 45; The Promise 52; John Wesley 54; The Shield of Faith 56; God Speaks Today • The Supreme Secret 57; The Crowning Gift 67

Walker, Peter Girls for Men Only • Hot Girls for Men Only • I Like Birds 66; The Big Switch • Strip Poker 68; School for Sex 68; Die, Beautiful Maryanne • Die Screaming, Marianne 69; Cool It, Carol! 70; Man of Violence • The Sex Racketeers 70; Asylum of the Insane • The Flesh and Blood Show 72; The Four Dimensions of Greta • Three Dimensions of Greta 72; The Dirtiest Girl I Ever Met 73; Tiffany Jones 73; Frightmare 74; House of Whipcord 74; The Confessional • House of Mortal Sin 75; Amok • Blood of the Undead • Schizo 76; The Comeback • The Day the Screaming Stopped 77; Home Before Midnight 79; The House of Long Shadows • House of the Long Shadows 82; Blind Shot 88

Walker, Robert The Challenge of Rin-Tin-Tin 58; Street of Darkness 58

Walker, Sandy Bingo Crosbyana 36*

Walker, Stuart The False Idol • The False Madonna 31; The Secret Call 31; Evenings for Sale 32; The Misleading Lady 32; Tonight Is Ours 32*; The Eagle and the Hawk 33*; White Woman 33; Great

Expectations 34; Romance in the Rain 34; Manhattan Moon • Sing Me a Love Song 35; The Mystery of Edwin Drood 35; The Werewolf of London 35

Walkow, Gary The Trouble with Dick 87

Wall, John Potter of the Yard 52*; Mr. Beamish Goes South 53*; Too Many Detectives 53*

Wall, Marcel see Ophüls, Marcel

Wallace, C. R. Maid of the West 21*; Whatever She Wants 21; Elope If You Must 22; Trooper O'Neill 22*; West of Chicago 22*; Western Speed 22*

Wallace, Charles Late Flowering Love 81

Wallace, Edgar Red Aces 29; The Squeaker 30

Wallace, Richard Honeymoon Hotel 25; Jiminy Crickets 25; So This Is Paris 26; Syncopating Sue 26; American Beauty • The Beautiful Fraud 27; McFadden's Flats 27; The Poor Nut 27; A Texas Steer 27; Actress and Angel • The Butter and Egg Man 28; Lady Be Good 28; Shopworn Angel 28; Innocents of Paris 29; Medals • Seven Days' Leave 29*; River of Romance 29; Anybody's War 30; The Right to Love 30; Kick In 31; Man of the World 31*; The Road to Reno 31; Thunder Below 32; Tomorrow and Tomorrow 32; The Masquerader 33; Eight Girls in a Boat 34; The Little Minister 34; Wedding Present 36; Blossoms on Broadway 37; John Meade's Woman 37; The Young in Heart 38; The Under-Pup 39; Captain Caution 40; A Girl, a Guy and a Gob • The Navy Steps Out 41; Obliging Young Lady 41; She Knew All the Answers 41; A Night to Remember 42; The Wife Takes a Flyer • A Yank in Dutch 42; Bombardier 43; The Fallen Sparrow 43; My Kingdom for a Cook 43; Bride by Mistake 44; The Fifth Chair • It's in the Bag 45; Kiss and Tell 45; Because of Him 46; Framed • Paula 47; Sinbad the Sailor 47; Tycoon 47; Adventure in Baltimore • Bachelor Bait 48*; Let's Live a Little 48; Almost a Bride • A Kiss for Corliss 49

Wallace, Stephen Loveletters from Teralba Road 77; Stir 80; The Boy Who Had Everything 84; For Love Alone 86

Wallace, Tommy Lee Halloween III: Season of the Witch 82; Aloha Summer • Hanauma Bay • Made in Hawaii 85; Fright Night—Part II 88

Wallace, William Western Speed 22*

Wallen, Sigurd The Count of the Monk's Bridge • The Count of the Old Town • Munkbrogreven 34*; Adolf Armstrong 37; Samvetsömma Adolf 37; The Anderson Family • Familjen Andersson 39; Med Folket för Fosterlandet 39; Johansson Gets Scolded • Vår Herr Luggar Johansson 45

Waller, J. Wallett A Fisherman's Infatuation 12; Hidden Wealth 12; A Message from Mars 13; Dandy Donovan the Gentleman Cracksman 14; The Smugglers' Cave 14; The Call of the Sea 15; A Fisherman's Infatuation 15; A Vagabond's Revenge 15

Wallington, Michael Ice Break 81; Arcade Attack 82

Walls, Tom Canaries Sometimes Sing 30*; On Approval 30; One Embarrassing Night • Rookery Nook 30*; Plunder 30*; Tons of Money 30; Leap Year 32; A Night Like This 32; Thark 32; The Blarney Kiss • The Blarney Stone 33; A Cuckoo in the Nest 33; Just Smith • Leave It to Smith 33; Turkey Time 33; A Cup of Kindness 34; Dirty Work 34; Lady in Danger 34; Fighting Stock 35; Foreign Affaires 35; Stormy Weather 35; Dishonour Bright 36; Pot Luck 36; For Valour 37; Second Best Bed 37; Old Iron 38

Walsch, Franz see Fassbinder, Rainer Werner

Walsh, George Seventh Person 19

Walsh, Raoul The Life of General Villa • The Life of Villa 12*; Outlaw's Revenge 12; The Double Knot 13; The Gunman 13; The Hindu Image • The Mystery of the Hindu Image 13; The Bowery 14; The Final Verdict 14; Sierra Jim's Reformation 14; A Bad Man and Others 15; The Buried Hand 15; Carmen 15; The Celestial Code 15; The Death Dice 15; Eleven-Thirty • 11:30 P.M. 15; The Fatal Black Bean 15; The Fencing Master 15; The Greaser 15; His Return 15; Home from the Sea 15; The Lone Cowboy 15; A Man for All That 15; The Regeneration 15; Blue Blood and Red 16; The Honor System 16; Pillars of Society 16*; The Serpent 16; Betrayed 17; The Conqueror 17; The Innocent Sinner 17; The Pride of New York 17; The Silent Lie 17; This Is the Life 17; Every Mother's Son 18; I'll Say So 18; On the Jump 18; The Prussian Cur 18; The Woman and the Law 18; Evangeline 19; Should a Husband Forgive? 19; The Strongest 19; The Deep Purple 20; From Now On 20; The Oath 21; Serenade 21; Kindred of the Dust 22; Lost and Found • Lost and Found on a South Sea Island • Passions of the Sea 23; The Thief of Bagdad 24; East of Suez 25; The Spaniard • Spanish Love 25; The Wanderer 25; The Lady of the Harem 26; The Lucky Lady 26; What Price Glory? 26; The Loves of Carmen 27; The Monkey Talks 27; In Old Arizona 28*; Me, Gangster 28; Rain • Sadie Thompson 28; The Red Dance • The Red Dancer of Moscow 28; The Cock-Eyed World 29; Hot for Paris 29; The Big Trail 30; The Man Who Came Back 31; Women of All Nations 31; The Yellow Passport • The Yellow Ticket 31; For Me and My Gal • Me and My Gal • Me and My Girl • Pier 13 32; Salomy Jane • Wild Girl 32; The Bowery 33; Going Hollywood 33; Hello, Sister! • Walking Down Broadway 33*; Sailor's Luck 33; Under Pressure 34; Baby Face • Baby Face Harrington 35; Every Night at Eight 35; Big Brown Eyes 36; Klondike Annie 36; O.H.M.S. • You're in the Army Now 36; Spendthrift 36; Artists and Models 37; Hitting a New High 37; Jump for Glory • When Thief Meets Thief 37; Best of the Blues • St. Louis Blues 38; College Swing • Swing, Teacher, Swing 38;

The Roaring Twenties 39*; Dark Command 40; Manpower 40; The Road to Frisco • They Drive by Night 40; High Sierra 41; The Strawberry Blonde 41; They Died with Their Boots On 41; Desperate Journey 42; Gentleman Jim 42; Background to Danger 43; Northern Pursuit 43; San Antonio 44*; Uncertain Glory 44; The Horn Blows at Midnight 45; Objective, Burma! 45; Salty O'Rourke 45; The Man I Love 46*; Cheyenne • The Wyoming Kid 47; Pursued 47; Stallion Road 47*; Fighter Squadron 48; One Sunday Afternoon 48; Silver River 48; Colorado Territory 49; Montana 49*; White Heat 49; The Enforcer • Murder, Inc. 50*; Along the Great Divide 51; Captain Horatio Hornblower • Captain Horatio Hornblower, RN 51; Distant Drums 51; Blackbeard the Pirate 52; Glory Alley 52; The Lawless Breed 52; The World in His Arms 52; Gun Fury 53; A Lion Is in the Streets 53; Sea Devils 53; Battle Cry 54; O'Rourke of the Royal Mounted • Saskatchewan 54; The Revolt of Mamie Stover 55; The Tall Men 55; The King and Four Queens 56; Band of Angels 57; The Naked and the Dead 58; The Sheriff of Fractured Jaw 58; A Private's Affair 59; Esther and the King • Esther e il Re 60; Marines, Let's Go! 61; A Distant Trumpet 64

Walsh, Thomas B. Shams of Society 21

Walters, Charles Spreadin' the Jam 45; Ziegfeld Follies 45*; Good News 47; Easter Parade 48; The Barkleys of Broadway 49; If You Feel Like Singing • Summer Stock 50; Three Guys Named Mike 50; The Belle of New York 51; Texas Carnival 51; Lili 52; Dangerous When Wet 53; Easy to Love 53; Torch Song 53; The Glass Slipper 54; The Tender Trap 55; High Society 56; Don't Go Near the Water 57; Ask Any Girl 59; Please Don't Eat the Daisies 60; I'll Save My Love • The Spinster • Two Loves 61; Billy Rose's Jumbo • Jumbo 62; The Unsinkable Molly Brown 64; Walk, Don't Run 66

Walters, Michael Have a Nice Weekend 75

Walters, R. Martin Marie-Ann 78

Walther-Fein, Rudolf Because I Loved You • Dich Hab Ich Geliebt 30; Der Korvettenkapitän 33; Das Schicksal der Renate Langen 33

Walton, Fred When a Stranger Calls 79; Hadley's Rebellion 84; April Fool's Day 86; The Rosary Murders 87

Walton, Joseph see Losey, Joseph

Waltyre, Edward Then You'll Remember Me 18

Wam, Svend Adjø Solidaritet • Farewell Illusion 84*; The Dream Castle • Drømmeslottet 86*; Jord 87*

Wan, Jen Super Citizen 85; Farewell to the Channel 88; Ah Fei 89

Wan, Laiming Uproar in Heaven 64

Wanamaker, Sam The File of the Golden Goose 68; The Executioner 70; Catlow 71; Sinbad and the Eye of the Tiger 77

Wang, Haowei O! Sweet Snow 90

Wang, Jiayi Bus Number Three • Xiaozi Bei 80*

Wang, Peter Old Treasures from New China 77; A Great Wall • The Great Wall Is a Great Wall 85; The Laserman 88; First Date 89

Wang, Ping The Dream of the Red Chamber • Hing Lou Meng 66

Wang, Qimin At Middle Age 85*

Wang, Tso-lin Hairdresser No. 3 47; The Lower Depths 48; The Watch 49; Corruption 50; The Ideological Problem 50*; The Window of America 52*

Wang, Tung Banana Paradise 89

Wang, Wayne A Man, a Woman and a Killer 75*; Chan Is Missing 81; Dim Sum • Dim Sum: A Little Bit of Heart 84; Slamdance 87; Eat a Bowl of Tea 89; Life Is Cheap...But Toilet Paper Is Expensive 89*

Wang, Yan Report on Pollution at the Women's Kingdom 88*

Wangenheim, Gustav Der Kampf 36

Wanstall, Norman The Rise and Fall of Ivor Dickie 78*

Wanting, Zhang see Zhang, Wanting

Wanzer, Orville The Devil's Mistress 68

Ward, Albert The Female Swindler 16; The Girl Who Wrecked His Home 16; The Phantom Picture 16; The Pleydell Mystery 16; Queen of the Wicked 16; When Woman Hates 16; Queen of My Heart 17; Linked by Fate 19; A Member of Tattersall's • A Member of the Tattersall's 19; Aunt Rachel 20; The Last Rose of Summer 20; Nance 20; The Pride of the Fancy 20; Mr. Pim Passes By 21; Broken Shadows 22; Stable Companions 22

Ward, Bill Ballad of a Gunfighter 63

Ward, David S. Cannery Row 81; Major League 89

Ward, Gil The First Notch 77

Ward, James Somebody's Stolen Our Russian Spy 67

Ward, Richard Sakura Killers 87*

Ward, Vincent A State of Siege 77; In Spring One Plants Alone 81; Vigil 83; The Navigator • The Navigator: A Medieval Odyssey • The Navigator: An Odyssey Across Time 88

Warde, Ernest C. The Hidden Valley 16; King Lear 16; Silas Marner 16; Her Beloved Enemy 17; Hinton's Double 17; The Man Without a Country 17; The Vicar of Wakefield 17; War and the Woman 17; The Woman and the Beast 17; The Woman in White 17; The Bells 18; More Trouble 18; Prisoner of the Pines 18; Ruler of the Road 18; Three X Gordon 18; The False Code 19; Gates of Brass 19; The Joyous Liar 19; The Lord Loves the Irish 19; A Man in the Open 19; The Master Man 19; The Midnight Stage 19; The World Aflame 19; The Coast of Opportunity 20; The Devil to Pay 20; The Dream Cheater 20; The Green Flame 20; The House of Whispers 20; Live Sparks 20; No. 99 20; $30,000 20; Ruth of the Range 22*; The Trail of the Axe 22

Warde, Frederick Richard III 13

Wardenburg, Fred Have You Heard of the San Francisco Mime Troup? 68*

Ware, Clyde No Drums, No Bugles 71; When the Line Gets Through 85; Bad Jim 90

Ware, Derek Privilege 66*

Warfield, Chris Little Miss Innocence 73; Boss Lady 82

Wargnier, Régis La Femme de Ma Vie • The Woman of My Life 86

Warhol, Andy Andy Warhol Films Jack Smith Filming "Normal Love" 63; Blow Job 63; Dance Movie • Roller Skate 63; Eat 63; Haircut 63; Kiss 63; Salome and Delilah 63; Sleep 63; Tarzan and Jane Regained...Sort Of 63*; Batman Dracula 64; Couch 64; Empire 64; The End of Dawn 64; Harlot 64; Henry Geldzahler 64; The Lester Persky Story • Soap Opera 64*; Mario Banana 64; Naomi and Rufus Kiss 64; Shoulder 64; Taylor Mead's Ass 64; The Thirteen Most Beautiful Women 64; Afternoon 65; Beauty #2 65; Bitch 65; Camp 65; The Closet 65; Drunk 65; Face 65; Fifty Fantastics and Fifty Personalities 65; The 14 Year Old Girl • Hedy • Hedy the Shoplifter • The Most Beautiful Woman in the World • The Shoplifter 65; Horse 65; Inner and Outer Space 65; Ivy and John 65; Kitchen 65; Lana Turner • More Milk, Evette • More Milk Yvette 65; The Life of Juanita Castro 65; My Hustler 65; Outer and Inner Space 65; Paul Swan 65; Poor Little Rich Girl 65; Prison 65; Restaurant 65; Screen Test #1 65; Screen Test #2 65; Space 65; Suicide 65; The Thirteen Most Beautiful Boys 65; Vinyl 65; Blow Job #2 • Eating Too Fast 66; Bufferin • Gerard Malanga Reads Poetry 66; The Chelsea Girls • Hanoi Hanna—Queen of China • The Pope Ondine Story • The Trip 66; The Velvet Underground and Nico 66; Bike Boy 67; Four Stars • **** • 24-Hour Movie 67; I, a Man 67; Imitation of Christ 67; The Loves of Ondine 67; Nude Restaurant 67; Blue Movie • Fuck 68*; Lonesome Cowboys 68; Surfing Movie 68; Women in Revolt 71*; L'Amour 72*

Warin, Francis The Easy Life • La Vie Facile 71

Warmerdam, Alex van Abel 85

Warnecki, J. Każdemu Wolno Kochać 33*; Noc Listopadowa 33

Warneke, Lothar Einer Trage des Anderen Last 88

Warner, Jack A Dangerous Adventure 20*

Warner, Jack, Jr. Brushfire! 61

Warner, John see Ulmer, Edgar G.

Warner, Sam A Dangerous Adventure 20*

Warnick, Ed Manchurian Avenger 85

Warren, Charles Marquis The Fighting 7th • Little Big Horn 51; Hellgate 52; Arrowhead 53; Flight to Tangier 53; Seven Angry Men 55; The Black Whip 56; Tension at Table Rock 56; Back from the Dead 57; Copper Sky 57; Ride a Violent Mile 57; Trooper Hook 57; The Unknown Ter-

ror 57; Blood Arrow 58; Cattle Empire 58; Desert Hell 58; Charro! 69

Warren, Deryn Bloodspell 88

Warren, Edward Love and Ambition 17; The Warfare of the Flesh 17; Weavers of Life 17; Thunderbolts of Fate 19

Warren, Frank All Girl • All Woman • Schizo 67

Warren, Giles Your Girl and Mine 14; A Texas Steer 15

Warren, Hal P. Manos—The Hands of Fate 66

Warren, Jerry Man Beast 55; Teenage Zombies 57; The Incredible Petrified World 58; La Casa del Terror • La Casa del Vampiro • The Face of the Screaming Werewolf • House of Terror 59*; Creature of the Walking Dead • La Marca del Muerto 60*; Horror in the Midnight Sun • Invasion of the Animal People • Rymdinvasion i Lappland • Space Invasion from Lapland • Space Invasion of Lapland • Terror in the Midnight Sun 60*; Terror of the Bloodhunters 62; Attack of the Mayan Mummy 63; Curse of the Stone Hand 65*; She Was a Hippy Vampire • The Wild World of Batwoman 66; Frankenstein Island • Frankenstein's Island 81

Warren, Joseph see Vari, Giuseppe

Warren, Mark Come Back, Charleston Blue 72; Crunch! • The Kinky Coaches and the Pom-Pom Pussycats 81; Tulips 81*

Warren, Norman J. Her Private Hell 68; Loving Feeling 69; Satan's Slave 76; Prey 77; Terror 78; Outer Touch • Spaced Out 79; Horror Planet • Inseminoid 80; Bloody New Year • Time Warp Terror 87; Gunpowder 87

Warren, Richard The Bosun's Mate 53

Warrenton, Lule The Birds' Christmas Carol • A Bit o' Heaven 17

Warrington, John It's a Great Day 56

Warshofsky, Fred The Outer Space Connection 75

Waschneck, Erich Sajenko the Soviet 29; Docks of Hamburg 30; Das Alte Lied 31; Zwei Menschen 31; Acht Mädels im Boot • Eight Girls in a Boat 32; Abel mit der Mundharmonika 34; Mein Leben für Maria Isabell • My Life for Maria Isabell 35; Liebesleute 36; The Divine Jetta 37; For Her Country's Sake 37; Streit Um den Knaben Jo • Strife Over the Boy Jo 38; Winter Storms • Winter Stürme 38

Washam, Ben Love Me, Love My Mouse 66*

Washer, Frederick H. Some Picnic 20

Wassermann, H. Fremd im Sudetenland • Strange to the Sudeten Country 38

Wasson, Jim Night of the Demon 80

Waszyński, Michael Kocha, Lubi, Szanuje 34; Parada Rezerwistow 34; Prokurator 34; Grandmother Had No Worries 35*; Dudek na Froncie 36; Będzie Lepiej 37; Dybbuk • The Dybbuk 37; The Miracle Man • Znachor 38; Rena 39; Lo Sconosciuto di San Marino 46*; La Grande Strada 48*

Watanabe, Eriko Bakayaroo! (Watakushi Okotteimasu) 88*

Waters, John Born to the West 26; Forlorn River 26; Man of the Forest 26; Arizona Bound 27; Drums of the Desert 27; The Mysterious Rider 27; Nevada 27; Two Flaming Youths 27; Beau Sabreur 28; The Vanishing Pioneer 28; The Overland Telegraph 29; Sioux Blood 29; The Mighty McGurk 46

Waters, John Mondo Trasho 69; Multiple Maniacs 69; Pink Flamingos 72; Female Trouble 74; Desperate Living 77; Polyester 81; Hairspray 88; Cry-Baby 90

Watkins, Peter The Web 56; The Field of Red 58; Diary of an Unknown Soldier 59; The Forgotten Faces 61; Culloden 64; The War Game 65; Privilege 66*; Gladiatorerna • Gladiators • The Peace Game 68; Punishment Park 71; Edvard Munch 74; Fällan • The Trap 75; The Seventies People • 70-Talets Människor 75; Aftenlandet • Aftonlandet • Evening Land 76; The Journey 86

Watson, John El Cazador de la Muerte • Deathstalker 83

Watson, John K. The Zoo Gang 85*

Watson, William Rip and Stitch Tailors 19*; Up in Mary's Attick 20; Heroes in Blue 39; And Now Tomorrow 52

Watt, Harry 6.30 Collection 33*; BBC: Droitwich 34*; Sorting Office 35; Big Money 36*; Men of the Alps 36; Night Mail • Nightmail 36*; The Saving of Bill Blewitt 37; Health in Industry 38; North Sea 38; A City Prepares • The First Days 39*; Flying Elephants • Squadron 992 39; Britain at Bay 40; Britain Can Take It! • London Can Take It! 40*; Dover: Front Line • The Front Line 40; The Story of an Air Communiqué 40; Christmas Under Fire 41; Target for Tonight 41; Dover Revisited 42; Nine Men 42; 21 Miles 42; Fiddlers Three • While Nero Fiddled 44; The Overlanders 46; Eureka Stockade • Massacre Hill 48; Ivory Hunter • The Ivory Hunters • Where No Vultures Fly 51; West of Zanzibar 53; People Like Maria 58; Four Desperate Men • The Siege of Pinchgut 59

Watt, Nate The Galloping Devil • Galloping Devils • Galloping Dude 20; What Women Love 20; The Hunger of the Blood 21; The Raiders 21; Hopalong Cassidy Returns 36; Navy Born 36; Trail Dust 36; Borderland 37; Carnival Queen 37; Hills of Old Wyoming 37; North of the Rio Grande 37; Rustlers' Valley 37; Frontier Vengeance 39; Law of the Pampas 39; Oklahoma Renegades 40; Fiend of Dope Island 61

Watts, Fred Pathétone Parade 34; Pathétone Parade of 1936 36; Pictorial Revue 36; Pathétone Parade of 1938 37; Pathétone Parade of 1939 39; Pathétone Parade of 1940 39; Pathétone Parade of 1941 41; Pathétone Parade of 1942 42; Pictorial Revue of 1943 43; Pathé Radio Music Hall 45

Watts, Roy Hambone and Hillie 83

Watts, Sal Solomon King 74*

Watts, Tom The Angel of the Ward 15; From the Depths of Despair 15; His Little

Lordship 15; The Little Home in the West 15; Somewhere in France 15; Abide with Me 16; The Call of the Pipes 17; Hear the Pipers Calling 18; The Master of Gray 18; The Autocrat 19; Father O'Flynn 19; The Toilers 19; Ye Banks and Braes 19; A Cigarette Maker's Romance 20

Wax, Steve Over-Under, Sideways-Down 77*

Waxman, Al The Crowd Inside 71; My Pleasure Is My Business 74; Tulips 81*

Way, Ron Frenchman's Farm 87

Wayans, Keenan Ivory I'm Gonna Git You Sucka 88

Wayne, John The Alamo • La Battaglia di Alamo 59; The Green Berets 68*

Webb, Harry S. Coyote Fangs 24; Ridin' West 24; Border Vengeance 25; Cactus Trails 25; Canyon Rustlers 25; Desert Madness 25; Double Fisted 25; The Empty Saddle 25; The Mystery of the Lost Ranch 25*; Santa Fe Pete 25; Silent Sheldon 25; Starlight the Untamed 25; The Man from Oklahoma 26*; Starlight's Revenge 26; Phantom of the North 29; Untamed Justice 29; Bar L Ranch 30; Beyond the Rio Grande 30; Dark Skies • Darkened Skies 30*; Phantom of the Desert 30; Ridin' Law 30; The Sign of the Wolf 31*; West of Cheyenne 31; Westward Bound 31; The Lone Trail 32*; Riot Squad 33; The Cactus Kid 34; Fighting Hero 34; Terror of the Plains 34; Born to Battle 35; The Laramie Kid 35; North of Arizona 35; Ridin' Thru 35; Tracy Rides 35; Trigger Tom 35; Unconquered Bandit 35; Wolf Riders 35; Fast Bullets • Law and Order 36; Pinto Rustlers 36; Santa Fe Bound 36; Riding On 37; Feud of the Range 39; Mesquite Buckaroo 39; The Pal from Texas 39; Port of Hate 39; Riders of the Sage 39; Pioneer Days 40

Webb, Ira El Diablo Rides 39; Wild Horse Valley 40

Webb, Jack Dragnet 54; Pete Kelly's Blues 55; The D.I. 57; Deadline Midnight • -30- 59; The Last Time I Saw Archie 61; Purple Is the Color 64

Webb, Kenneth The Adventure Shop 18; One Thousand Dollars 18; The Girl Problem 19; His Bridal Night 19; Marie, Ltd. 19; Will You Be Staying for Supper? 19; The Devil's Garden 20; The Fear Market 20; The Master Mind 20; Sinners 20; Stolen Kiss 20; The Truth About Husbands 20; The Great Adventure 21; Jim the Penman 21; Salvation Nell 21; Fair Lady 22; His Wife's Husband 22; How Women Love 22; The Secrets of Paris 22; Without Fear 22; The Daring Years 23; Three O'Clock in the Morning 23; The Beautiful City 25; Just Suppose 26; Lucky in Love 29

Webb, Millard Hearts of Youth 20*; Oliver Twist, Jr. 21; Where Is My Wandering Boy Tonight? 22*; The Black Swan • The Dark Swan 24; Her Marriage Vow 24; The Golden Cocoon 25; My Wife and I 25; The Sea Beast 26; An Affair of the Follies 27; The Drop Kick 27; The Love Thrill 27; Naughty But Nice 27; Honey-

moon Flats 28; Gentlemen of the Press 29; Glorifying the American Girl 29*; The Painted Angel 29; The Golden Calf 30; The Happy Ending 31

Webb, Peter Butch Minds the Baby 79; Give My Regards to Broad Street 84

Webb, Robert D. In Old Chicago 37*; The Caribbean Mystery 45; The Spider 45; Beneath the 12 Mile Reef 53; The Glory Brigade 53; Seven Cities of Gold 55; White Feather 55; Love Me Tender 56; On the Threshold of Space 56; The Proud Ones 56; The Way to the Gold 57; Guns of the Timberland • Stampede 60; Pirates of Tortuga 61; Seven Women from Hell 61; The Cape Town Affair 67; The Jackals 67; A Little of What You Fancy 68; The Nutcracker Suite 70

Webb, William Double Exposure 77; California Girls 81*; Sunset Strip 85; Dirty Laundry 86; Discovery Bay 87; Party Line 88; The Banker 89

Webber, Bickford Otis Runaway • Runaway, Runaway 71

Weber, Angelika Marie Ward—Zwischen Galgen und Glorie 85

Weber, Bruce Broken Noses 87; Let's Get Lost 88

Weber, Lois The Troubadour's Triumph 12; The Eyes of God 13; The Female of the Species 13; The Jew's Christmas 13*; Behind the Veil 14*; False Colors 14*; A Fool and His Money 14; Hypocrites 14; It's No Laughing Matter 14; Like Most Wives 14; The Merchant of Venice 14*; Traitor 14; Jewel 15*; Scandal 15*; Sunshine Molly 15*; Alone in the World 16; Discontent 16; The Dumb Girl of Portici 16*; The Eye of God 16*; The Flirt 16*; The French Downstairs 16*; Hop—The Devil's Brew 16*; Idle Wives 16*; John Needham's Double 16*; The People vs. John Doe 16; The Rock of Riches 16; Saving the Family Name 16*; Shoes 16; Wanted—A Home 16*; Where Are My Children? 16*; Even As You and I 17; For Husbands Only 17*; The Hand That Rocks the Cradle 17*; The Man Who Dared God 17; The Mysterious Mrs. M • The Mysterious Mrs. Musslewhite 17; The Price of a Good Time 17*; There's No Place Like Home 17; Borrowed Clothes 18*; The Doctor and the Woman 18*; The Forbidden Box 18*; Scandal Mongers 18*; When a Girl Loves 18*; Forbidden 19*; Home 19; Mary Regan 19; A Midnight Romance 19; To Please One Woman 20; The Blot 21*; Too Wise Wives 21; What Do Men Want? 21; What's Worthwhile? 21; A Chapter in Her Life 23; The Marriage Clause 26; The Angel of Broadway 27; Sensation Seekers 27; White Heat 34

Webster, D. J. Dark Side of the Moon 90

Webster, Harry McRae The Victory of Virtue 15; The Devil's Playground 18; Reclaimed 18; The Heart of a Gipsy 19

Webster, Martyn The Broken Horseshoe 52

Webster, Nicholas Dead to the World 61; Gone Are the Days • The Man from

C.O.T.T.O.N. • Purlie Victorious 63; Santa Claus Conquers the Martians 64; Mission Mars 68; No Longer Alone 78

Webster, Paul Meteor Madness 81

Wechsberg, Peter Deafula 75

Wechter, David Midnight Madness 80*; The Bikini Shop • The Malibu Bikini Shop 85

Wedderburn, Hugh The Lark Still Sings 54

Weeks, Stephen I, Monster 70; 1917 70; Gawain and the Green Knight • Sir Gawain and the Green Knight 72; Asylum of Blood • Ghost Story • Madhouse Mansion 74; Sword of the Valiant 82; Clash of the Swords 84

Weel, Arne Life on the Hegn Farm • Livet på Hegnsgård 39

Weems, Walter Something Simple 34*

Wegener, Paul Die Augen des Ole Brandis 14*; Evintrude—Die Geschichte eines Abenteurers 14*; Der Golem • The Golem • The Monster of Fate 14*; Rübezahls Hochzeit 16*; Der Yoghi • The Yogi 16*; Der Golem und die Tänzerin 17*; Hans Trutz im Schlaraffenland 17; The Pied Piper of Hamelin • The Ratcatcher • Der Rattenfänger von Hameln 17*; Der Fremde Fürst 18*; Welt Ohne Waffen 18; Der Golem • The Golem • The Golem: How He Came Into the World • Der Golem: Wie Er in die Welt Kam 20*; The Lost Shadow • Der Verlorene Schatten 21*; Herzog Ferrantes Ende 22*; Lebende Buddhas • Lebende Buddhas Götter des Tibet 24; Die Freundin eines Grossen Mannes 34; Ein Mann Will nach Deutschland 34; August der Starke 35; Moscow-Shanghai • Moskau-Shanghai • Der Weg nach Shanghai 36; Die Stunde der Versuchung 36; Krach und Glück Um Künnemann • Row and Joy About Künnemann 37; Unter Ausschluss der Öffentlichkeit 37

Wehling, Bob Magic Spectacles • Magical Spectacles • Tickled Pink 61; The Fall Guy • A Fourth for Marriage • What's Up Front 64

Wei, Lo see Lo, Wei

Wei, Te see Te, Wei

Weichert, Richard Two Neckties • Zwei Kravatten 30*

Weidenmann, Alfred Canaris • Canaris, Master Spy • Deadly Decision 54; Buddenbrooks 59; Scampolo 59; Boomerang • Bumerang • Cry Doublecross 60; Adorable Julia • Julia, Du Bist Zauberhaft • The Seduction of Julia 62; Ich Bin Nur eine Frau • Only a Woman 62; And So to Bed • Das Grosse Liebesspiel 63; I Too Am Only a Woman • Ich Bin Auch Nur eine Frau 63; Enter Inspector Maigret 66

Weight, F. Harmon The Man Who Played God • The Silent Voice 22; The Ruling Passion 22; The Ragged Edge 23; On the Stroke of Three 24; Ramshackle House 24; $20 a Week 24; Drusilla with a Million 25; Flaming Waters 25; Three Wise Crooks 25; Forever After 26; A Poor Girl's Romance 26; Hook and Ladder No. 9 27; Jazz Mad • The Symphony 28; Mid-

night Madness 28; Frozen River 29; Hard Boiled Rose 29

Weil, Samuel see Kaufman, Lloyd

Weiland, Paul Leonard Part 6 87

Weill, Claudia The Other Half of the Sky—A China Memoir 74*; Girlfriends 78; It's My Turn 80

Wein, Chuck Rainbow Bridge 72

Weinberg, Herman The Movies Take a Holiday 44*

Weiner, Hal The Imagemaker 86

Weinfeld, Isay Fogo e Paixão 88*

Weinrib, Lennie Beach Ball 65; Out of Sight 66; Wild, Wild Winter 66

Weinstein, Bob Playing for Keeps 86*

Weinstein, Harvey Playing for Keeps 86*; Gandahar • Light Years 87*

Weinstein, Marvin Running Target 56

Weinstock, Vladimir Rubicon 31; Captain Grant's Children 39*

Weinthal, Eric Timing 86

Weintraub, Sandra The Women's Club 87

Weiquan, Uong see Yung, Peter

Weir, Peter Count Vim's Last Exercise 67; The Life and Flight of the Reverend Buckshotte • The Life and Times of the Rev. Buck Shotte 68; Three to Go 69*; Stirring the Pool 70; Homesdale 71; Incredible Floridas 72; Three Directions in Australian Pop Music 72; Whatever Happened to Green Valley? 73; The Cars That Ate Paris • The Cars That Eat People 74; Picnic at Hanging Rock 75; The Last Wave 77; The Plumber 78; Gallipoli 81; The Year of Living Dangerously 82; Witness 85; The Mosquito Coast 86; Dead Poets Society 89; Green Card 90

Weis, Bob Wills and Burke 85

Weis, Don Force of Evil 48*; Bannerline 51; It's a Big Country 51*; Just This Once 51; I Love Melvin 52; You for Me 52; The Affairs of Dobie Gillis 53; Half a Hero 53; Remains to Be Seen 53; A Slight Case of Larceny 53; The Adventures of Hajji Baba 54; Ride the High Iron 56; Deadlock 57; Drum Crazy • The Gene Krupa Story 59; Mr. Pharaoh and His Cleopatra 59; Critic's Choice 63; Looking for Love 64; The Maid and the Martian • Pajama Party 64; Billie 65; The Ghost in the Invisible Bikini • The Girl in the Invisible Bikini • Pajama Party in the Haunted House • Slumber Party in a Haunted House • Slumber Party in Horror House 66; The King's Pirate 67; Did You Hear the One About the Traveling Saleslady? 68; Crackle of Death 74*; Repo • Zero to Sixty 78

Weis, Gary Jimi Hendrix 73*; 80 Blocks from Tiffany's 80; Wholly Moses! 80; Young Lust 82; Marley 85

Weis, Jack Quadroon 72; Storyville 74; Crypt of Dark Secrets • Mardi Gras Massacre 78

Weisenborn, Gordon see Lewis, Herschell Gordon

Weisman, David Ciao! Manhattan • Edie in Ciao! Manhattan 72*

Weisman, Straw Dead Mate 89

Weiss, Adrian The Bride and the

Beast • Queen of the Gorillas 58

Weiss, David Loeb No Vietnamese Ever Called Me Nigger 68

Weiss, Fred Movie-Go-Round 49

Weiss, Helmut Tromba • Tromba, the Tiger Man 52; Affair at Ischia 61

Weiss, Jiří People in the Sun 35; Give Us Wings 36; Song of a Sad Country 37; Journey from the Shadows 38; The Rape of Czechoslovakia • Secret Allies 39; John Smith Wakes Up 40; Eternal Prague 41; 100,000,000 Women 42; Before the Raid 43; Interim Balance • Věrni Zůstaneme 45; The Stolen Frontier • Uloupená Hranice 47; Beasts of Prey • Dravci • Wild Beasts 48; Ves v Pohraničí • The Village on the Frontier 48; High Flies the Hawk • Píseň o Sletu 49; Song of the Meet 49; The Last Shot • Poslední Výstřel 50; New Heroes Will Arise • New Warriors Shall Arise • New Warriors Will Arise • Vstanou Noví Bojovníci 50; Můj Přítel Fabián • My Friend Fabian • My Friend the Gypsy 53; Doggy and the Four • Punt'a a Čtyřlístek • Punta and the Four-Leaf Clover 54; Hra o Život • Life at Stake • Life Was at Stake • Life Was the Stake 56; Vlčí Jáma • Wolf Trap 57; Appassionata • Takova Láska • That Kind of Love 59; Romeo, Julie a Tma • Romeo, Juliet and Darkness • Sweet Light in a Dark Room • Sweet Light in the Dark Window 59; The Coward • Zbabělec 61; Golden Bracken • The Golden Fern • Zlaté Kapradí 63; 90 Degrees in the Shade • Ninety in the Shade • Třicet Jedna ve Stínu 64; Murder, Czech Style • Murder, Our Style • Vražda po Česku • Vražda po Našem 66

Weiss, Peter Hallucinationer • Hallucinations • Studie II 52; Studie I 52; Studie III 53; Frigörelse • Studie IV 54; Studie V • Växelspel 55; Ansikten i Skugga • Faces in the Shadows 56*; Ateljé Interiör • The Studio of Dr. Faustus 56; According to the Law • Enligt Lag 57; Ingenting Ovanligt • Nothing Unusual 57; Vad Ska Vi Göra Nu Då? • What Shall We Do Now? 58; Hägringen • The Mirage 59; Bag de Ens Facader • Behind Uniform Facades 61

Weiss, Robert K. Amazon Women on the Moon 86*

Weissbrod, Ellen Listen Up: The Lives of Quincy Jones 90

Weissman, Aerlyn A Winter Tan 87*

Weisz, Franz Havinck 87

Wei-yen, Yu see Yu, Wei-yen

Welby, Robert Daytona Beach Weekend 65

Welebit, Walter Children's Games 69

Welford, Walter D. Repairing a Puncture 1897; The Writing on the Wall 1897

Weller, Jorge see Weller, Yohanan

Weller, Yohanan All My Loving • Kol Ahavotai 86

Welles, Mel see Theumer, Ernst R. von

Welles, Orson The Hearts of Age 34*; Too Much Johnson 38; Citizen Kane 41; It's All True 42; Journey Into Fear 42*; The Magnificent Ambersons 42*; The Lady from Shanghai 46; The Stranger 46; Macbeth 48*; Black Magic 49*; Othello 51; Confidential Report • Mr. Arkadin 55; Touch of Evil 57*; Le Procès • Il Processo • Der Prozess • The Trial 62; Campanadas a Medianoche • Chimes at Midnight • Falstaff 65; Une Histoire Immortelle • The Immortal Story 68; The Other Side of the Wind 72; F for Fake • Fake? • Nothing But the Truth • Vérités et Mensonges 73*; The Filming of Othello • Filming Othello 77

Wellesley, Gordon The Silver Fleet 42*; Rhythm Serenade 43; Trouble with Junia 66

Wellington, David The Carpenter 88

Wellman, William A. The Twins from Suffering Creek 20; Big Dan 23; Cupid's Fireman 23; The Man Who Won 23; Second Hand Love 23; The Circus Cowboy 24; Not a Drum Was Heard 24; The Vagabond Trail 24; When Husbands Flirt 25; The Boob • The Yokel 26; The Cat's Pajamas 26; You Never Know Women 26; Wings 27; Beggars of Life 28; Ladies of the Mob 28; The Legion of the Condemned 28; Chinatown Nights 29; The Man I Love 29; Woman Trap 29; Dangerous Paradise 30; Maybe It's Love 30; Young Eagles 30; Enemies of the Public • Enemy of the Republic • The Public Enemy 31; The Lost Lady • Safe in Hell 31; Night Nurse 31; Other Men's Women • The Steel Highway 31; Star Witness 31; The Common Ground • Frisco Jenny 32; The Conquerors • Pioneer Builders 32; The Hatchet Man • The Honourable Mr. Wong 32; Love Is a Racket • Such Things Happen 32; The Purchase Price 32; So Big 32; Central Airport 33; College Coach • Football Coach 33; Dangerous Age • Dangerous Days • Wild Boys of the Road 33; Heroes for Sale 33; Lady of the Night • Midnight Mary 33; Lilly Turner 33; Looking for Trouble 33; The President Vanishes • The Strange Conspiracy 34; Stingaree 34; The Call of the Wild 35; One Horse Town • Small Town Girl 36; Robin Hood of El Dorado 36; Tarzan Escapes! 36*; Nothing Sacred 37; A Star Is Born 37; Men with Wings 38; Beau Geste 39; The Light That Failed 39; The Great Man's Lady 41; Reaching for the Sun 41; The Ox-Bow Incident • Strange Incident 42; Roxie Hart 42; Soldiers of the Air • Thunder Birds 42; Lady of Burlesque • Striptease Lady 43; Buffalo Bill 44; This Man's Navy 44; G.I. Joe • The Story of G.I. Joe • War Correspondent 45; Gallant Journey 46; Magic Town 47; Behind the Iron Curtain • The Iron Curtain 48; Yellow Sky 48; Battleground 49; The Happy Years 50; The Next Voice You Hear 50; Across the Wide Missouri 51; It's a Big Country 51*; Westward the Women 51; My Man and I 52; Island in the Sky 53; The High and the Mighty 54; Ring of Fear 54*; Track of the Cat 54; Blood Alley 55; Goodbye, My Lady 56; Darby's Rangers • The Young Invaders 57; Hell Bent for Glory • Lafayette Escadrille 57

Wells, Alex Curfew Breakers 57
Wells, John K. Queen o' Turf 22
Wells, Raymond Fighting for Love 16; Kinkaid, Gambler 16; The Saintly Sinner 16; Fanatics 17; Fighting Back 17; Hero of the Hour 17; Love Aflame 17; Mr. Dolan of New York 17; The Terror 17*; The Flames of Chance 18; The Hand at the Window 18; The Hard Rock Breed 18; His Enemy the Law 18; The Law of the Great Northwest 18; Mademoiselle Paulette 18; Man Above the Law 18; Old Loves for New 18; Fagasa 28; Souls Aflame 28

Wen, Que see Que, Wen
Wencel, H. Mr. Editor Is Crazy • Pan Redaktor Szaleje 38
Wendel, Linda Ballerup Boulevard • Pinky's Gang 86
Wenders, Wim Locations • Schauplätze 67; Same Player Shoots Again 67; Police Film • Polizeifilm 68; Silver City 68; Victor I 68; Alabama—2000 Light Years 69; Drei Amerikanische LPs • Three American LPs 69; Summer in the City • Summer in the City (Dedicated to the Kinks) 70; Die Angst des Tormanns beim Elfmeter • The Anxiety of the Goalie at the Penalty Kick • The Goalie's Anxiety at the Penalty Kick • The Goalkeeper's Fear of the Penalty Kick 71; The Scarlet Letter • Der Scharlachrote Buchstabe 72; Alice in den Städten • Alice in the Cities 73; Falsche Bewegung • The Wrong Move • Wrong Movement 74; Im Lauf der Zeit • In the Course of Time • Kings of the Road 75; The American Friend • Der Amerikanische Freund • Ripley's Game 77; Lightning Over Water • Nick's Film • Nick's Movie 80*; Hammett 81; Chambre 666 • Room 666 82; Reverse Angle 82; Der Stand der Dinge • The State of Things 82; Aus der Familie der Panzereschen 84; Paris, Texas 84; Tokyo-Ga 84; Der Himmel Über Berlin • Wings of Desire 87; Aufzeichnungen zu Kleidern und Städten • A Notebook on Clothes and Cities 89

Wendhausen, Frederick Princess Priscilla's Fortnight • Priscillas Fahrt ins Glück • The Runaway Princess 28*
Wendhausen, Fritz The Stone Rider 23; Familienparade 37; Peer Gynt 39
Wendkos, Paul Dark Interlude 55; The Burglar 56; The Case Against Brooklyn 58; Tarawa Beachhead 58; Battle of the Coral Sea 59; Face of a Fugitive 59; Gidget 59; Because They're Young 60; Angel Baby 61*; Gidget Goes Hawaiian 61; Temple of the Swinging Doll 61; Recoil 62; Gidget Goes to Rome 63; Johnny Tiger 66; Attack on the Iron Coast 67; Guns of the Magnificent Seven 68; Hell Boats 69; Cannon for Cordoba • Dragon Master 70; The Mephisto Waltz 70; Honor Thy Father 73; Special Delivery 76

Weng, Jin see Jin, Weng
Wenji, Teng see Teng, Wenji
Wenk, Richard Vamp 86
Wensierski, Peter Transit Dreams • Transitträume 86*
Wenzler, Franz Die Nacht Ohne Pause

31*; Causa Kaiser • The Kaiser Case 32; Das Ekel 32*; Wenn die Liebe Mode Macht 33; Der Gipfelstürmer 37; Horst Wessel 39

Werckmeister, Hans Algol 20
Werker, Alfred L. Ridin' the Wind 25*; Kit Carson 28*; The Pioneer Scout 28*; The Sunset Legion 28*; Blue Skies 29; Chasing Through Europe 29*; Double Cross Roads 30*; Fair Warning 30; Last of the Duanes 30; Annabelle's Affairs 31; Bachelor's Affairs 31; Heartbreak 31; The Gay Caballero 32; Rackety Rax 32; Advice to the Forlorn • Advice to the Lovelorn 33; Hello, Sister! • Walking Down Broadway 33*; It's Great to Be Alive 33; House of Rothschild 34; You Belong to Me 34; Stolen Harmony 35; Love in Exile 36; City Girl 37; We Have Our Moments 37; Wild and Woolly 37; Gateway 38; Kidnapped 38*; Up the River 38; The Adventures of Sherlock Holmes • Sherlock Holmes 39; It Could Happen to You 39; News Is Made at Night 39; Moon Over Her Shoulder 41; The Reluctant Dragon 41*; A-Haunting We Will Go 42; The Mad Martindales 42; Whispering Ghosts 42; My Pal Wolf 44; Shock 46; Pirates of Monterey 47; Repeat Performance 47; He Walked by Night 48*; Lost Boundaries 49; Sealed Cargo 51; The Crime of the Century • Walk East on Beacon 52; Devil's Canyon 53; The Last Posse 53; Three Hours to Kill 54; At Gunpoint • Gunpoint! 55; Canyon Crossroads 55; Rebel in Town 56; The Young Don't Cry 57

Werkmeister, Hans see Werckmeister, Hans

Werndorff, Oscar M. The Bells 31*
Werner, Gösta Midwinter Sacrifice 46; Loffe the Vagabond 48; Miss Sunbeam 48; The Train 48; Gatan • The Street 49; Backyard 50; Meeting Life 52; Matrimonial Announcement 55
Werner, Jeff Cheerleaders' Wild Weekend 79; Die Laughing 80
Werner, M. Prisoners of the Sea 29
Werner, Peter Findhord 76; Don't Cry, It's Only Thunder 81; Prisoners 84; No Man's Land 87

Wertmuller, Lina I Basilischi • The Lizards 63; Let's Talk About Men • Now Let's Talk About Men • Questa Volta Parliamo di Uomini • This Time Let's Talk About Men 65; Don't Tease the Mosquito • Non Stuzzicate la Zanzara 67; Mimì Metallurgico Ferito nell'Onore • Mimi the Metalworker, Wounded in Honour • The Seduction of Mimi 72; All in Order, Nothing in Place • All in Place • All Screwed Up • Everything's in Order But Nothing Works • Everything's Ready, Nothing Works • Nothing in Order • Tutto a Posto • Tutto a Posto e Niente in Ordine 73; Film d'Amore e d'Anarchia • Film d' Amore e d'Anarchia, ovvero Stamattina alle 10 in Via dei Fiori nella Nota Casa di Toleranza • Film of Love and Anarchy, or This Morning at 10 in the Via dei Fiori at the Well Known House of Tolerance •

Love and Anarchy • Story of Love and Anarchy 73; Swept Away • Swept Away... by a Strange Destiny in a Blue August Sea • Swept Away...by a Strange Destiny on an Azure August Sea • Swept Away... by an Unusual Destiny in the Blue Sea of August • Travolti da un Insolito Destino nell'Azzurro Mare d'Agosto 74; Pasqualino Settebellezze • Seven Beauties 75; The End of the World in Our Usual Bed in a Night Full of Rain • A Night Full of Rain 78; Shimmy Lagano Tarantelle e Vino 78; Blood Feud • Fatto di Sangue Fra Due Uomini per Causa di una Vedova (Si Sospettano Moventi Politici) • Revenge 79; A Joke of Destiny • A Joke of Destiny Lying in Wait Around the Corner Like a Robber • A Joke of Destiny Lying in Wait Around the Corner Like a Street Bandit • Scherzo del Destino in Agguato Dietro l'Angolo Come un Brigante • Scherzo del Destino in Agguato Dietro l'Angolo Come un Brigante di Strada 83; Softly...Softly • Sotto...Sotto 84; Camorra • Camorra: The Naples Connection • A Complex Plot About Women, Alleys and Crimes • A Complicated Intrigue of Women, Alleyways and Crimes • Un Complicato Intrigo di Donne, Vicoli e Delitti 85; Notte d'Estate con Profilo Greco, Occhi a Mandorla e Odore di Basilico • Summer Night with a Grecian Profile, Almond Eyes and the Scent of Basil • Summer Night with Greek Profile, Almond Eyes and Scent of Basil 86; Il Decimo Clandestino • The Tenth One in Hiding • To Save Nine 89; In una Notte di Chiaro di Luna, o di Cristallo o ol Genere, ol Fuoco o di Vento, Purche Sia Amore • Of Crystal or Cinders, Fire or Wind, As Long As It's Love 89; Sabato, Domenica e Lunedi • Saturday, Sunday and Monday 90

Wertz, Jay The Last Reunion 80
Wesley, William Scarecrows 88
Wesnigk, C. Cay Vergessen Sie's 88
Wessel, Kai Martha Jellneck 88
West, Anthony The Pretty Things 66*
West, James Polk County Pot Plane 77; Hot Pursuit 81
West, Langdon Friend Wilson's Daughter 15; The Girl of the Gypsy Camp 15; Her Proper Place 15; The Ring of the Borgias 15; Sally Castleton, Southerner 15
West, R. Harley Her Life in London 15; The Vultures of London 15; Crime and the Penalty 16; On the Steps of the Altar 16
West, Raymond B. The Altar of Death 12; The Witch of Salem 13; The Cup of Life 15; The Edge of the Abyss 15; Rumpelstiltskin 15*; Civilization 16*; The Female of the Species 16; The Honorable Algy 16; Honor's Altar 16; The Moral Fabric 16; The Payment 16; The Wolf Woman 16*; Borrowed Plumage 17; Chicken Casey 17; Madcap Madge 17; Paddy O'Hara 17; Redemption 17; The Snarl 17; Ten of Diamonds 17; The Weaker Sex 17; Whither Thou Goest 17; Wooden Shoes 17; Blindfolded 18; Those Who Pay 18; Within the Cup 18; All Wrong 19*

West, Reginald Afraid of Love 25
West, Robert D. The Wednesday Children 73
West, Roland Lost Souls • A Woman's Honor 16; The Siren 17; De Luxe Annie 18; Nobody 21; The Silver Lining 21; The Unknown Purple 23; The Monster 25; The Bat 26; The Dove 27; Alibi • Nightstick • The Perfect Alibi 29; The Bat Whispers 30; Corsair 31
West, Walter Full Up 14; The Thick and Thin of It 14; A Bold Adventuress 15; By a Brother's Hand • By the Hand of a Brother 15; A London Flat Mystery • The Mystery of a London Flat 15; The Woman Who Did 15; The Answer 16; Burnt Wings 16; The Hard Way 16; The Merchant of Venice 16; The Knockout Blow 17; Missing the Tide 17; The Ware Case 17; A Fortune at Stake 18; Not Negotiable 18; Sisters in Arms 18; A Daughter of Eve 19; The Gentleman Rider • Hearts and Saddles 19; Snow in the Desert 19; Under Suspicion 19; The Case of Lady Camber 20; Her Son 20; Kissing Cup's Race 20; The Imperfect Lover 21; The Loudwater Mystery 21; A Sportsman's Wife 21; Vi of Smith's Alley 21; The Scarlet Lady 22; Son of Kissing Cup 22; Was She Justified? 22; When Greek Meets Greek 22; Beautiful Kitty 23; Hornet's Nest 23; In the Blood 23; The Lady Owner 23; What Price Loving Cup? 23; The Great Turf Mystery 24; The Stirrup Cup Sensation 24; A Daughter of Love 25; Trainer and Temptress 25; Beating the Book 26; The Brotherhood 26; The Golden Spurs 26; Riding for a King 26; The Stolen Favourite 26; Woodcroft Castle 26; Maria Marten 28; Sweeney Todd 28; Warned Off 28; Aura No. 1 30; Aura No. 2 30; Hundred to One 33; Bed and Breakfast 36; We Do Believe in Ghosts 47
West, William The Last Alarm 40; Air Devils • Flying Wild 41; Double Trouble 41
Westman, Jim The Wrestler 74
Weston, Armand The Nesting • Phobia 80; Dawn of the Mummy 81*
Weston, Charles H. The Battle of Waterloo 13; Bess the Detective's Daughter • To Save Her Dad 13; The Broken Chisel • Escape from Broadmoor 13; In Fate's Grip 13; Just a Girl • Only a Girl 13; Lieutenant Daring and the International Jewel Thieves • Lieutenant Daring and the Mystery of Room 41 13; The Little Snow Waif 13; The Master Crook 13; Outwitting Mama 13; The Ragged Prince 13; Riches and Rogues 13; A Son of Japan 13; Through the Clouds 13; A Tragedy in the Alps 13; And Very Nice Too 14; Battling Brown of Birmingham 14; The Bishop's Silence 14; The Bugle Boy of Lancashire 14; Called to the Front 14; The Clever One 14; Detective Finn • Detective Finn, or In the Heart of London • Society Detective 14; The Doctor's Crime 14; Facing the Enemy 14; Get In and Get Out 14; Just a Nut 14; The King of Seven Dials 14; Married Life, the Second Year 14; The Master

Spy 14; A Mother in Exile 14; My Son 14; None But the Brave 14; On the Russian Frontier 14; The Road to Calais 14; Saving the Colours 14; Self-Accused 14; The Seventh Day 14; Through the Firing Line 14; The War Baby 14; What a Night! 14; What a Woman Will Do 14; What Men Will Do 14; Wife of a Thief 14; Bad Boy Billy 15; The Dungeon of Death 15; Flivver's Famous Cheese Hound • Pimple's Million Dollar Mystery 15; Flivver's Terrible Past • Pimple's Past 15; The Hand at the Window 15; The Life of an Actress 15; Pimple's Peril 15; Pimple's Royal Divorce 15; Pimple's The Case of Johnny Walker 15; Pimple's Three Weeks • Pimple's Three Weeks, Without the Option 15; The Port of Missing Women 15; The Underworld of London 15; The Vengeance of Nana 15; Vice and Virtue • Vice and Virtue, or The Tempters of London 15; The Woman Without a Soul 15
Weston, Eric They Went That-a-Way and That-a-Way 78*; Evilspeak 81; Like Father and Son • Marvin and Tige 83; Dreams of Gold • Treasure of the Moon Goddess 85*; The Iron Triangle 89
Weston, Harold The Call of the Drum 14; Admiral's Orders 15; Another Man's Wife 15; The Climax • Motherhood 15; The Mystery of a Hansom Cab 15; Shadows 15; Society Crooks • Strategy 15; The War Cloud 15; Wild Oats 15; The Black Night 16; Cynthia in the Wilderness 16; The Green Orchard 16; Honour in Pawn 16; All the World's a Stage 17
Wetherell, M. A. Livingstone • Stanley 25; Robinson Crusoe 27; The Somme 27; Victory 28; Hearts of Oak 33*; A Moorland Tragedy 33
Wetzl, Fulvio Rorret 88
Wetzler, Gwen Mighty Mouse in the Great Space Chase 83*; The Secret of the Sword 85*
Wexler, Haskell The Bus 65; Nowsreel 68; Medium Cool 69; Brazil: A Report on Torture 71*; Introduction to the Enemy 74*; Underground 76*; The MUSE Concert: No Nukes • No Nukes 80*; Bus II 83*; Latino 85
Whale, James Hell's Angels 30*; Journey's End 30; Frankenstein 31; Waterloo Bridge 31; The Impatient Maiden 32; The Old Dark House 32*; By Candlelight 33; The Invisible Man 33; The Kiss Before the Mirror 33; One More River • Over the River 34; The Bride of Frankenstein 35; Remember Last Night? 35; Show Boat 36; The Great Garrick 37; Return of the Hero • The Road Back 37; Sinners in Paradise 37; Port of Seven Seas 38; Wives Under Suspicion 38; The Man in the Iron Mask 39; Green Hell 40; They Dare Not Love 40; Hello Out There 49
Whale, Peter Change of Heart 51
Wharton, Leopold The Pawn of Fortune 14; A Prince of India 14; The Romance of Elaine 15*; Hazel Kirke 16*; The Great White Trail 17; Squire Phin 21; Mr. Bingle 22; Mr. Potter of Texas 22

Wharton, Theodore The Romance of Elaine 15*; The City 16; Hazel Kirke 16*

Whatham, Claude All Creatures Great and Small 74; Swallows and Amazons 74; That'll Be the Day 74; Sweet William 80; Hoodwink 81

Wheat, Jim Lies 83*; After Midnight 89*

Wheat, Ken Lies 83*; After Midnight 89*

Wheatley, David The Magic Toyshop 86

Wheeler, Anne A War Story 81; Loyalties 86; Cowboys Don't Cry 88; Bye Bye Blues 89

Wheeler, Clifford The Love Wager 27; A Bit of Heaven • Little Bit of Heaven 28; Comrades 28; Into No Man's Land 28*; Making the Varsity 28; The Prince of Hearts 29

Wheeler, Leonard Four Hearts 22

Wheeler, René Premières Armes • The Winner's Circle 50; Castles in Spain • Châteaux en Espagne 54; Vers l'Extase 60

Whelan, Tim Adam's Apple • Honeymoon Ahead 27; When Knights Were Bold 29; Along Came Sally • Aunt Sally 33; It's a Boy 33; The Camels Are Coming 34; The Imperfect Lady • The Perfect Gentleman 35; The Murder Man 35; Larceny Street • Smash and Grab 36; Two's Company 36; Action for Slander 37*; Clouds Over Europe • Q Planes 37*; Farewell Again • Troopship 37; The Mill on the Floss 37; The Divorce of Lady X 38; St. Martin's Lane • Sidewalks of London 38; Missing Ten Days • Spy in the Pantry • Ten Days in Paris 39; A Date with Destiny • The Mad Doctor 40; The Thief of Bagdad 40*; International Lady 41; Nightmare 42; Seven Days' Leave 42; Twin Beds 42; Higher and Higher 43; Swing Fever 43; Step Lively 44; Badman's Territory 46; This Was a Woman 48; Rage at Dawn • Seven Bad Men 55; Texas Lady 55

Whelan, Tim, Jr. Out of the Tiger's Mouth 62

Whitaker, Harold Heavy Metal 81*

Whitby, Cynthia A Letter from East Anglia 53

White, A. N. Street Fighter 59

White, Billy The Love Box 72*; The Stud 75

White, Bob The Wife Hunters 22

White, E. W. Movie Mixture • Wot, No Gangsters? 46

White, George George White's Scandals • George White's Scandals of 1934 • Scandals 34*; George White's 1935 Scandals 35

White, George A. see Bianchi, Giorgio

White, James Love and War 1899; Trinidad, British West Indies 08*

White, Jules The Sidewalks of New York 31*

White, Lennie Little see Little-White, Lennie

White, Merrill G. Ghost Diver 57*

White, Nathan J. The Carrier 88

White, Paul The Crimes of Stephen Hawke • Strangler's Morgue 36*

White, Robert M. Il Ranch degli Spietati • Ranch of the Rustlers 65

White, Sam The Officer and the Lady 41; I Live on Danger 42; People Are Funny 45

White, Teddy The Love Box 72*

White, Tom Who's Crazy 65*

White, William Brother, Cry for Me 70

Whitehead, Peter Benefit of the Doubt • Us 67

Whitelaw, Alexander Lifespan 75

Whiteman, Albert Sigma III 66

Whiting, Edward G. The Adventures of Jane 49*

Whiting, Rowland A Dead Cert 19

Whitman, Phil The Fourth Alarm 30; Mystery Train 31; Air Eagles 32; Girl from Calgary 32*; The Stowaway 32; Strange Adventure • The Wayne Murder Case 32*; His Private Secretary 33; Police Call • Wanted 33

Whitman, Vincent Another Tale 14; The Bottom of the Sea 14; A Hunting Absurdity 14; An Interrupted Nap 14; A Strenuous Ride 14; A Trip to the Moon 14; The Troublesome Cat 14; An African Hunt 15; A Barnyard Mixup 15; Curses Jack Dalton 15; His Pipe Dreams 15; A Hot Time in Punkville 15; A One Reel Feature 15; Relentless Dalton 15; Studies in Clay 15; The Victorious Jockey 15

Whitmore, John Here Comes Every Body 73

Whitney, James Abstract Film Exercise No. 1 43*; Abstract Film Exercise No. 4 and 5 44*; Hot House 49*; Mozart Rondo 49*

Whitney, John Abstract Film Exercise No. 1 43*; Abstract Film Exercise No. 4 and 5 44*; Hot House 49*; Mozart Rondo 49*; Celery Stalks at Midnight 58; Glimpses of U.S.A. 59*; Catalogue 61; Permutations 68; 1-2-3 70; Matrix 71

Whittaker, Bob Darling, Do You Love Me? 69*

Whitten, Norman In the Days of Saint Patrick 20; Wicklow Gold 22

Whorf, Richard Blonde Fever 44; The Hidden Eye 45; The Sailor Takes a Wife 45; Till the Clouds Roll By 46*; It Happened in Brooklyn 47; Love from a Stranger • A Stranger Walked In 47; Luxury Liner 48; Champagne for Caesar 50; The Groom Wore Spurs 51

Wiard, William Tom Horn 79

Wich, Nathan Il Mio Corpo per un Poker 68

Wickersham, Bob Song of Victory 42; Tito's Guitar 42; Toll Bridge Troubles 42; Under the Shedding Chestnut Tree 42; Woodman Spare That Tree 42; A-Hunting We Won't Go 43; Imagination 43; Plenty Below Zero 43; Room and Bored 43; Slay It with Flowers 43; Tree for Two 43; Way Down Yonder in the Corn 43; Willoughby's Magic Hat 43; Be Patient, Patient 44; The Dream Kids 44; The Egg Yegg 44; Magic Strength 44; Mr. Moocher 44; Porkuliar Piggy 44; Sadie Hawkins Day 44; Booby Socks 45; Fiesta Time 45; Ku-Kunuts 45; Phoney Baloney 45; Rippling

Romance 45; Foxey Flatfoots 46; Mysto Fox 46; Picnic Panic 46; Silent Tweetment 46; Snap Happy Traps 46; Cockatoos for Two 47; Mother Hubba-Hubba Hubbard 47; Uncultured Vulture 47

Wickes, David The Moods of Love 72; Sweeney! 76; Silver Dream Racer 80

Wicki, Bernhard Warum Sind Sie Gegen Uns? 58; The Bridge • Die Brücke 59; Frau im Besten Mannesalter 59; Malachias • The Miracle of Father Malachias • The Miracle of Malachias • Das Wunder des Malachias 61; The Longest Day 62*; Der Besuch • La Rancune • La Vendetta della Signora • The Visit 64; Morituri • The Saboteur • The Saboteur—Code Name Morituri 65; Transit 66; Quadriga 67*; Das Falsche Gewicht • The False Weight • The Wanting Weight 71; Die Eroberung der Zitadelle 77; Die Grünstein-Variante 84; The Spider's Web • Das Spinnennetz 87

Wicki, Bernhardt see Wicki, Bernhard

Widerberg, Bo A Boy and His Kite • The Boy and the Kite • Pojken och Draken 61*; The Baby Carriage • Barnvagnen • The Pram 62; Kvarteret Korpen • Raven's End 62; Heja, Roland! • Thirty Times Your Money 65; Kärlek 65 • Love 65 65; Elvira Madigan 67; The Ådalen Riots • Ådalen '31 68; Den Vita Sporten • The White Game 68*; The Ballad of Joe Hill • Joe Hill 71; Fimpen • Stubby 73; The Man on the Roof • Mannen på Taket 76; Victoria 79; Grusfesten 83; The Man from Majorca • Mannen från Mallorca 84; Ormens Väg på Hälleberget • The Serpent's Way • The Serpent's Way Up the Naked Rock • Up the Naked Rock 86

Widmark, Richard The Secret Ways 61*

Wiederhorn, Ken Almost Human • Death Corps • Shock Waves 70; King Frat 79; Eyes of a Stranger 80; Meatballs Part II 84; Return of the Living Dead Part II 88

Wiedermann, Károly Három Csillag • Three Stars 60*

Wieland, Joyce Tea in the Garden 58*; Assault in the Park 59*; Larry's Recent Behaviour 63; Patriotism 64; Peggy's Blue Skylight 64; Barbara's Blindness 65*; Watersark 65; 1933 67; Sailboat 67; Catfood 68; Hand-Tinting 68; Rat Life and Diet in North America 68; Dripping Water 69*; La Raison Avant la Passion • Reason Over Passion 69; Birds at Sunrise 72; Pierre Vallières 72; Solidarity 73; The Far Shore 76

Wieland, Ute Im Jahr der Schildkröte • The Year of the Turtle 89

Wielopolska, Brita Hodja fra Pjort 85

Wiemer, Robert Anna to the Infinite Power 83; Somewhere Tomorrow 83

Wiene, Conrad Am Tor des Lebens • Am Tor des Todes 18; Die Macht der Finsternis 23; Strauss the Waltz King • Der Walzerkönig 29; Ein Prinz Verliebt Sich 32; Ein Walzer vom Strauss 32; Madame Blaubart 33; Wiener Blut 33

Wiene, Robert Arme Eva • Dear Eva • Frau Eva 14*; Er Rechts, Sie Links 15; Die

Konservenbraut 15; The Empress' Love Letter • Die Liebesbrief der Königin 16; Der Mann im Spiegel 16; Die Räuberbraut 16; Der Sekretär der Königin 16; Das Wandernde Licht 16; Das Leben—Ein Traum 17; Der Standhafte Benjamin 17; The Cabinet of Dr. Caligari • Das Kabinett des Dr. Caligari 19; Ein Gefährliches Spiel 19; Die Verführte Heilige 19; Die Drei Tänze der Mary Wilford 20; Genuine • Genuine die Tragödie eines Seltsamen Hauses 20; Die Nacht der Königin Isabeau 20; Die Rache einer Frau 20; Höllische Nacht 21; Das Spiel mit dem Feuer 21*; Salome 22; Tragikomödie 22; Crime and Punishment • Raskolnikoff • Raskolnikov • Raskolnikow • Schuld und Sühne 23; Crown of Thorns • Ein Film der Menschlichkeit • I.N.R.I. 23; Der Puppenmacher von Kiang-Ning 23; The Hands of Orlac • Orlacs Hände 24; Pension Groonen 24; Der Gardeoffizier • The Guardsman • Der Leibgardist 25; Die Königin vom Moulin-Rouge 25; Der Rosenkavalier 25; The Beloved • Die Geliebte 27; Die Berühmte Frau • The Dancer of Barcelona 27; Power of Darkness 27; Le Tombeau Sous l'Arc de Triomphe 27; Die Frau auf der Folter • A Scandal in Paris 28; Die Grosse Abenteurerin 28; Leontines Ehemänner 28; Unfug der Liebe 28; Der Andere • The Other 30; Acht Tage Glück • Der Liebesexpress 31; Panic in Chicago • Panik in Chicago 31; Der Fall Tokeramo • Polizeiakte 909 33; Eine Nacht in Venedig 34; Ultimatum 38*

Wierendorf, Hans Paris After Dark 23

Wiesen, Bernard Fear No More 61

Wiezycki, Joe Satan's Children 75

Wiggins, William H., Jr. In the Rapture 76

Wiland, Harry Sing Sing Thanksgiving 74*

Wilbor, Robert Mark Twain, American 76

Wilbur, Crane The Love Liar 16; The Painted Lie 17; Tomorrow's Children 34; High School Girl 35; The People's Enemy 35; Devil on Horseback 36; Rest Cure • We're in the Legion Now 36; Yellow Cargo 36; Navy Spy 37*; The Patient in Room 18 38*; I Am Not Afraid • The Man Who Dared 39; The Devil on Wheels 47; Canon City 48; The Story of Molly X 49; Outside the Wall 50; Inside the Walls of Folsom Prison 51; The Bat 58; House of Women • Ladies of the Mob 60*

Wilcox, Fred M. Lassie Come Home 43; Blue Sierra • The Courage of Lassie 45; The Birds and the Bees • Three Daring Daughters 47; Hills of Home • Master of Lassie 48; The Secret Garden 49; Shadow in the Sky 51; Code Two 53; Tennessee Champ 54; Forbidden Planet 56; I Passed for White 60

Wilcox, Herbert Chu Chin Chow 23; Decameron Nights 24; Dekameron Nächte 24; Southern Love • A Woman's Secret 24; The Only Way 25; Limehouse • London 26; Nell Gwyn • Nell Gwynne 26; Madame Pompadour 27; Mumsie 27; Tiptoes 27; The Bondman 28; Dawn 28; The Scarlet Pimpernel 28; The Woman in White 29; The Loves of Robert Burns 30; Mountains of Mourne 30; The Blue Danube 31; Carnival • Venetian Nights 31; Chance of a Night Time 31*; Goodnight Vienna • Magic Night 32; The King's Cup 32*; The Little Damozel 32; Money Means Nothing 32*; Bitter Sweet 33; That's a Good Girl 33*; Yes, Mr. Brown 33*; Nell Gwyn • Nell Gwynne 34; The Queen's Affair • Runaway Queen 34; Backstage • Limelight 35; Peg of Old Drury 35; The Show Goes On • The Three Maxims 36; This'll Make You Whistle 36; Girls in the Street • London Melody • Look Out for Love 37; Victoria the Great 37; Queen of Destiny • Queen Victoria • Sixty Glorious Years 38; Nurse Edith Cavell 39; Irene 40; No, No, Nanette 40; Sunny 41; They Flew Alone • Wings and the Woman 42; Forever and a Day 43*; The Yellow Canary 43; I Live in Grosvenor Square • A Yank in London 45; Piccadilly Incident • They Met at Midnight 46; The Courtney Affair • The Courtneys of Curzon Street • Kathy's Love Affair 47; Spring in Park Lane 47; Elizabeth of Ladymead 48; Maytime in Mayfair 49; Into the Blue • The Man in the Dinghy 50; Odette 50; Derby Day • Four Against Fate 51; The Lady with a Lamp • The Lady with the Lamp 51; Trent's Last Case 52; Laughing Anne 53; Trouble in the Glen 53; Let's Make Up • Lilacs in the Spring 54; King's Rhapsody 55; Bad Girl • My Teenage Daughter • Teenage Bad Girl 56; Dangerous Youth • These Dangerous Years 57; The Man Who Wouldn't Talk 58; Wonderful Things! 58; The Heart of a Man 59; The Lady Is a Square 59

Wild, Ernst The Barber of Seville 73

Wild, Franz Josef The End of Mrs. Cheney • Frau Cheneys Ende 63

Wilde, Cornel Storm Fear 55; The Devil's Hairpin 57; Maracaibo 58; Lancelot and Guinevere • Sword of Lancelot 62; The Naked Prey 66; Beach Red 67; No Blade of Grass 70; Shark's Treasure • The Treasure 74

Wilde, Ted The Battling Orioles 24*; Babe Comes Home 27; The Kid Brother 27*; Speedy 28; Clancy in Wall Street 30*; Loose Ankles 30

Wilder, Billy Bad Blood • Mauvaise Graine 33*; The Major and the Minor 42; Five Graves to Cairo 43; Double Indemnity 44; The Lost Weekend 45; The Emperor Waltz 47; A Foreign Affair 48; Sunset Blvd. • Sunset Boulevard 50; Ace in the Hole • The Big Carnival • The Human Interest Story 51; Stalag 17 53; Sabrina • Sabrina Fair 54; The Seven Year Itch 55; Love in the Afternoon 57; The Spirit of St. Louis 57; Witness for the Prosecution 57; Some Like It Hot 59; The Apartment 60; One, Two, Three 61*; Irma la Douce 63; Kiss Me, Stupid 64; The Fortune Cookie • Meet Whiplash Willie 66; The Private Life of Sherlock Holmes 70; Avanti! 72; The Front Page 74; Fedora 78; Buddy Buddy 81

Wilder, Gene The Adventures of Sherlock Holmes' Smarter Brother 75; The World's Greatest Lover 77; Sunday Lovers 80*; The Woman in Red 84; Haunted Honeymoon 86

Wilder, Glenn R. Masterblaster 87

Wilder, W. Lee The Glass Alibi 46; The Pretender 47; Yankee Fakir 47; The Circle • The Vicious Circle • The Woman in Brown 48; Once a Thief 50; Three Steps North 51; Phantom from Space 53; Killers from Space 54; The Snow Creature 54; The Big Bluff 55; Calypso • Manfish 56; Fright • Spell of the Hypnotist 56; The Man Without a Body 57*; Spy in the Sky 58; Bluebeard's Ten Honeymoons 60; The Omegans 68

Wildhagen, Georg Marriage of Figaro 50; The Merry Wives of Windsor 52

Wildy, Ludwig Schmid see Schmid-Wildy, Ludwig

Wiles, Gordon Charlie Chan's Secret 35; Rosa de Francia • Rose of France 35; The Blackmailer 36; Lady from Nowhere 36; Two-Fisted Gentleman 36; Venus Makes Trouble 37; Women of Glamour 37; Face the Facts • Mr. Boggs Buys a Barrel • Mr. Boggs Steps Out 38; People's Enemy • Prison Train 38; Forced Landing 41; The Gangster 47; Ginger in the Morning 73

Wiley, Ethan House II: The Second Story 87

Wileys, Anthony see Sequi, Mario

Wilhelm, Charles At It Again 16

Wilkinson, Charles My Kind of Town 84; Quarantine 89

Willat, Irvin The Wolf Woman 16*; In Slumberland 17; The Zeppelin's Last Raid 17; The Guilty Man 18; The Law of the North 18; The Midnight Patrol 18; Behind the Door 19; Daughter of the Wolf 19; The False Faces 19; The Grim Game 19; Rustling a Bride 19; Below the Surface 20; Down Home 20; Face of the World 21; Fifty Candles 21; On the High Seas 22; Pawned 22; The Siren Call 22; Yellow Men and Gold 22; All the Brothers Were Valiant 23; Fog Bound 23; The Heritage of the Desert 24; North of 36 24; The Story Without a Name • Without Warning 24; Three Miles Out 24; The Wanderer of the Wasteland 24; The Air Mail 25; The Ancient Highway 25; Rugged Water 25; The Enchanted Hill 26; Paradise 26; Back to God's Country 27; The Cavalier 28; The Michigan Kid 28; The Isle of Lost Ships 29; Damaged Love 31; Louisiana Gal • Old Louisiana • Treason 37; The Luck of Roaring Camp 37; Under Strange Flags 37

William, Leonard The Anatomist 61

Williams, Bert The Nest of the Cuckoo Birds 65

Williams, Bill Creatures of Darkness 69

Williams, Brock The Root of All Evil 46; I'm a Stranger 52

Williams, C. Jay Crooky 15; What Happened to Father 15; Wild Oats 19

Williams, D. J. The Shuttle of Life 20

Williams, Derek Hunted in Holland 61;

Treasure in Malta 63; The Taking Mood 69

Williams, Earle Bring Him In 21*

Williams, Elmo The Tall Texan 52; The Cowboy 54; Blonde Bait • Women Without Men 56; Apache Warrior 57; Hell Ship Mutiny 57*; The Big Gamble 60*

Williams, Emlyn Dolwyn • The Last Days of Dolwyn • Woman of Dolwyn 49

Williams, Eric England's Warrior King 15

Williams, J. B. White Cargo 29*; The Chinese Bungalow 30*; The Tell-Tale Heart 53

Williams, Lester see Berke, William

Williams, Oscar The Final Comedown 72; Five on the Black Hand Side 73; Hot Potato 76; Death Drug 78

Williams, Paul Out of It 69; The Revolutionary 70; Dealing, or The Berkeley-to-Boston Forty-Brick Lost-Bag Blues 72; Nunzio 78; Miss Right 81; The Black Planet 82; A Light in the Afternoon 86

Williams, Richard The Little Island 58; The Story of the Motorcar Engine 58*; A Lecture on Man 61; Love Me, Love Me, Love Me 62; Circus Drawings 64; The Dermis Probe 65; Diary of a Madman 65; Pubs and Beaches 66; I. Vor Pittfalks 67; The Sailor and the Devil 67*; Every Home Should Have One • Think Dirty 70*; Nasrudin 70; A Christmas Carol 71; Raggedy Ann and Andy 77; Who Framed Roger Rabbit? 87*

Williams, Spencer Blood of Jesus 41; Go Down Death 44; Beale Street Mama 46; Dirty Gerty from Harlem, U.S.A. 46; Juke Joint 47

Williams, Tony Solo 78; Next of Kin 82

Williamson, Bob King's Creek Law 23*

Williamson, Cecil H. Beyond Price 47; Held in Trust 49; The Clown 50; Hangman's Wharf 50; Soho Conspiracy 50; Action Stations • Hi-Jack 57

Williamson, Fred Adiós Amigo 75; Death Journey 76; Mean Johnny Barrows 76; No Way Back 76; Destinazione Roma • Mr. Mean 77; One Down, Two to Go 82; The Big Score 83; The Last Fight 83; Foxtrap 86; The Messenger 87

Williamson, J. Ernest Wonders of the Sea 22; With Williamson Beneath the Sea 32

Williamson, James A. The Clown Barber 1898; The Forbidden Lover 1898; The Fraudulent Beggar 1898; The Jealous Painter 1898; Norah Mayer the Quick-Change Dancer 1898; Sloper's Visit to Brighton 1898; Two Naughty Boys Sprinkling the Spoons • Two Naughty Boys Upsetting the Spoons 1898; Two Naughty Boys Teasing the Cobbler 1898; Washing the Sweep 1898; Winning the Gloves 1898; Courtship Under Difficulties 1899; The Jovial Monks No. 1 1899; The Jovial Monks No. 2 — Tit for Tat 1899; The Sleeping Lovers 1899; Attack on a China Mission Station • Attack on a Chinese Mission — Bluejackets to the Rescue 00; Clever and Comic Cycle Act 00; The Disabled Motor

00; Are You There? 01; The Big Swallow 01; Cyclist Scouts in Action 01; The Elixir of Life 01; Fire! 01; Harlequinade — What They Found in the Laundry Basket 01; The Magic Extinguisher 01; The Marvellous Hair Restorer 01; Over the Garden Wall 01; The Puzzled Bather and His Animated Clothes 01; Stop Thief! 01; Teasing Grandpa 01; Tomorrow Will Be Friday 01; The Acrobatic Tramps 02; An Amateur Bill Sykes 02; Burlesque of Popular Composers 02; Close Quarters, with a Notion of the Motion of the Ocean 02; A Day in Camp with the Volunteers 02; An Extra Turn • The Extrey Turn 02; Fighting His Battles Over Again 02; A Lady's First Lesson on the Bicycle 02; The Little Match Seller 02; Ping-Pong 02; A Reservist Before and After the War 02; Sambo 02; The Soldier's Return 02; Those Troublesome Boys 02; A Workman's Paradise 02; Boys Will Be Boys • The Dear Boys Home for the Holidays 03; The Deserter 03; An Evil-Doer's Sad End 03; Juggins' Motor 03; No Bathing Allowed 03; Quarrelsome Neighbours 03; Remorse 03; Spring Cleaning 03; A Trip to Southend or Blackpool 03; Wait Till Jack Comes Home • When Our Sailor Son Comes Home 03; The Wrong Chimney 03; The Wrong Poison 03; An Affair of Honour 04; All's Well That Ends Well 04; The Clown's Telegram 04; Gabriel Grub • Gabriel Grub the Surly Sexton 04; The Great Sea Serpent 04; An Interesting Story 04; Oh! What a Surprise! 04; The Old Chorister 04; The Stowaway 04; The Student and the Housemaid 04; They Forgot the Gamekeeper 04; The Tramp's Revenge 04; Two Brave Little Japs 04; Brown's Half Holiday 05; An Eclipse of the Moon • Moonbeams 05; In the Good Old Times 05; Our New Errand Boy 05; The Polite Lunatic 05; The Prodigal Son, or Ruined at the Races 05; Rival Barbers 05; Sausages 05; Two Little Waifs 05; The Angler's Dream 06; A Day on His Own 06; Her First Cake 06; The Miner's Daughter 06; Mrs. Brown Goes Home to Her Mother 06; The Sham Sword Swallower 06; Where There's a Will There's a Way 06; A Wicked Bounder 06; After the Fancy Dress Ball 07; Bobby's Birthday 07; The Brigand's Daughter 07; Cheating the Sweep 07; Getting Rid of His Dog 07; Just in Time 07; Moving Day 07; Orange Peel 07; The Orphans 07; Pa Takes Up Physical Culture • Poor Pa's Folly 07; The Village Fire Brigade 07; Why the Wedding Was Put Off 07; The Ayah's Revenge 08; A Countryman's Day in Town 08; A Day's Holiday 08; The Great Bargain Sale 08; The Little Mother 08; My Wife's Dog 08; £100 Reward 08; The Professor's Great Discovery 08; The Reconciliation 08; The Rent Collector 08; The Rival Cyclists 08; She Would Be a Suffragette 08; Sunshine After Storm 08; Uncle's Picnic 08; 'Arry and 'Arriet's Evening Out 09; The Letter Box Thief 09; Saved by a Dream 09; The Tower of London 09

Williamson, Robin E. The Feud Woman 26; Prince of the Plains 27; Wanderer of the West 27*

Willis, Gordon Windows 79

Willis, Stanley The Haunted Man 66

Willis, Walter A Pair of Hellions 24

Willoughby, Lewis Only a Mill Girl 19; The Secret of the Moor 19; Wisp o' the Woods 19; Fantee 20

Wills, J. Elder M'Blimey 31; Tiger Bay 33; Everything in Life 36; Song of Freedom 36; Sporting Love 36; Big Fella 37

Wilmer, Geoffrey His Last Defence 19

Wilner, Max Live and Laugh 33

Wilsey, Jay Riding Speed 34; Trails of Adventure 35

Wilson, Andrew P. Chester Forgets Himself 24; The Clicking of Cuthbert 24; Fighting Snub Reilly 24; The Long Hole • The Moving Hazard 24; The Magic Plus Fours 24; Ordeal by Golf 24; Rodney Fails to Qualify 24

Wilson, Ben F. The Broken Spur 21; The Innocent Cheat 21; The Man from Texas 21; The Sheriff of Hope Eternal 21; Back to Yellow Jacket 22; Chain Lightning 22; One Eighth Apache 22; The Price of Youth 22; The Sheriff of Sun-Dog 22; Mine to Keep 23; Other Men's Daughters 23; Spawn of the Desert 23; A Daughter of the Sioux 25; The Fugitive 25; The Human Tornado 25; The Man from Lone Mountain 25; The Power God 25; Renegade Holmes, M.D. 25; Ridin' Comet 25; Romance and Rustlers 25; Scar Hanan 25; Tonio, Son of the Sierras 25; A Two-Fisted Sheriff 25; White Thunder 25; The Fighting Stallion 26; Fort Frayne 26; Officer 444 26*; Sheriff's Girl 26; West of the Law 26; Wolves of the Desert 26; The Mystery Brand 27; The Range Riders 27; Riders of the West 27; Saddle Jumpers 27; Western Courage 27; A Yellow Streak 27; The Old Code 28; The Saddle King 29; Thundering Thompson 29; Voice from the Sky 30

Wilson, Bruce Doubles 78; Bombs Away 85

Wilson, Charles C. Lucky Boy 29*

Wilson, Donald B. Warning to Wantons 48

Wilson, Elsie Jane The Cricket 17; The Little Pirate 17; My Little Boy 17; The Silent Lady 17; Beauty in Chains 18; The City of Tears 18; The Dream Lady 18; The Lure of Luxury 18; New Love for Old 18; The Game's Up 19

Wilson, Frank The Pneumatic Policeman 08; The Boys and the Purse 09; The Dog and the Bone 09; An Inexperienced Angler 09; Mary Jane's Loves 09; The Stolen Clothes 09; Two Bad Boys 09; Cocksure's Clever Ruse • Too Clever for Once 10; Cupid's Message Goes Astray 10; The Dog Chaperone 10; A Funny Story 10; A Good Kick-Off 10; Jones Tests His Wife's Courage 10; The Laundryman's Mistake 10; Let Sleeping Dogs Lie 10; A Lunatic Expected 10; The Man Who Thought He Was Poisoned 10; Mr. Mugwump and the Baby 10; Mr. Mugwump

• Snapshot 79; Dark Forces • Harlequin • The Minister's Magician 80; Phar Lap • Phar Lap—Heart of a Nation 83; D.A.R.Y.L. 85; The Lighthorsemen 87; Quigley Down Under 90

Windermere, Fred Soiled 24; Romance Road 25; Three in Exile 25; The Verdict 25; With This Ring 25; Morganson's Finish 26; The Taxi Mystery 26; Broadway After Midnight 27; She's My Baby 27; Broadway Daddies 28; Devil Dogs 28

Windom, Lawrence C. The Discard 16; Efficiency Edgar's Courtship 17; Fools for Luck 17; The Small Town Guy 17; Two-Bits Seats 17; Appearance of Evil 18; The Grey Parasol 18; A Pair of Sixes 18; The Power and the Glory 18; Ruggles of Red Gap 18; Uneasy Money 18; It's a Bear 19; Taxi 19; Upside Down 19; Wanted—A Husband 19; The Girl with a Jazz Heart • The Girl with the Jazz Heart 20; Headin' Home 20; Human Collateral 20; Nothing But Lies 20; The Truth 20; The Very Idea 20; Solomon in Society 22; Modern Marriage 23; Sinner or Saint 23; The Truth About Wives 23; Faithless Lover • The Pasteboard Lover 28; Enemies of the Law 31

Windsor, Chris Big Meat Eater 82

Windust, Bretaigne June Bride 48; Winter Meeting 48; The Enforcer • Murder, Inc. 50*; Perfect Strangers • Too Dangerous to Love 50; Pretty Baby 50; The Bride Comes to Yellow Sky • Face to Face 52*; The Pied Piper of Hamelin 57

Winer, Harry SpaceCamp 86

Winer, Lucy The Silent Pioneers 84

Wing, Ward Samarang 33; Hate in Paradise • Tea Leaves in the Wind 38; The Shark Woman 41

Winick, Gary Curfew 89

Winkelmann, Adolf Bang! You're Dead! • Peng! Du Bist Tot! 87; The Microchip Killer 88

Winkle, Joseph van see *Van Winkle, Joseph*

Winkler, Charles You Talkin' to Me? 87

Winkler, Henry Memories of Me 88

Winkless, Terence H. The Nest 88; Bloodfist 89; Corporate Affairs 90

Winner, Michael The Clock Strikes Eight 58; Climb Up the Wall 60; Shoot to Kill 60; Haunted England 61; Murder on the Campus • Out of the Shadow 61; Old Mac 61; Some Like It Cool 61; Behave Yourself 62; Play It Cool 62; The Cool Mikado 63; West 11 63; The Girl-Getters • The System 64; You Must Be Joking! 65; The Jokers 66; I'll Never Forget What's 'Is Name 67; Hannibal Brooks 68; The Games 69; Lawman 70; Chato's Land 71; The Nightcomers 71; Killer of Killers • The Mechanic 72; Scorpio 72; The Stone Killer 73; Death Wish 74; Won Ton Ton, the Dog Who Saved Hollywood 75; The Sentinel 76; The Big Sleep 77; Firepower 79; Death Wish II 81; The Wicked Lady 82; Scream for Help 84; Death Wish 3 85; Appointment with Death 88; A Chorus of Disapproval 88; Bullseye! 90

Winning, David Storm 83

Winograd, Peter Flicks • Hollyweird • Loose Joints 81

Winslow, Dicky The Corsican Brothers 02; East Lynne 02; Fight with Sledgehammers 02; Little Jim, or The Cottage Was a Thatched One 02; Maria Martin, or The Murder at the Red Barn 02; The Assassination of the King and Queen of Servia • The Servian Tragedy 03; The Octaroon 03

Winslow, Susan All This and World War II 76

Winsor, Terry Party Party 83; Home Front • Morgan Stewart's Coming Home 85*

Winston, Carl Liebeswalzer • The Love Waltz 30*; Looking for His Murderer • The Man Who Seeks His Own Murderer • Der Mann Der Seinen Mörder Sucht 30*

Winston, Ron Ambush Bay 66; Banning 67; Don't Just Stand There 68; The Gamblers 69

Winston, S. K. Adventure in Music 43*

Winston, Stan Pumpkinhead 87

Winter, Donovan The Awakening Hour 57; The Great Expedition 59; The Trunk 60; World Without Shame 62; A Penny for Your Thoughts, or Birds, Dolls and Scratch—English Style 66; Promenade 67; Come Back Peter • Some Like It Sexy 69; Escort Girls 73; The Deadly Females 76; Give Us Tomorrow 78

Winter, Percy The Other Girl 16

Wintergate, John Boarding House 84

Winters, David Dr. Jekyll and Mr. Hyde 73; Welcome to My Nightmare 76; Racquet 79; Fanatic • The Last Horror Film 81; Jayne Mansfield—An American Tragedy 81; Mission Kill 85; Thrashin' 86; Codename Vengeance 88; Mutiny in Space 88; Rage to Kill 88

Winters, Paul The Freeway Maniac 89

Winterstein, Frank Sherlock Holmes • Sherlock Holmes and the Deadly Necklace • Sherlock Holmes und das Halsband des Todes • Valley of Fear 62*

Wionczek, Roman Dignity • Godność 85; Czas Nadziei • Time of Hope 87

Wirth, Franz Peter Arms and the Man • Helden 58; Menschen im Netz • Unwilling Agent 59; Bis zum Ende Aller Tage • The Girl from Hong Kong 61; Hamlet 62

Wisbar, Frank Im Banne des Eulenspiegels 32; Anna und Elisabeth 33; Rivalen der Luft 34; Hermin und die Sieben Aufrechten 35; Die Werft zum Grauen Hecht 35; Death and the Maiden • Fährmann Maria • Ferryboat Woman Maria • Ferryman Maria 36; Die Unbekannte 36; Ball im Metropol 37; Petermann Ist Dagegen 37; Strangler of the Swamp 45; Devil Bat's Daughter 46; Lighthouse 46; The Prairie 47; The Mozart Story 48*; Haie und Kleine Fische • U-Boat 55 57; Nasser Asphalt • Wet Asphalt 58; Battle Inferno • Dogs, Do You Want to Live Forever? • Hunde, Wollt Ihr Ewig Leben? 59; Fabrik der Offiziere 60; Nacht Fiel Über Gotenhaten 60; Barbara 61; Commando • Héros Sans Retour • Marcha o Muere • Marcia o

Crepa • Marschier oder Kreiper 62

Wisberg, Aubrey Dragon's Gold 53*

Wise, Herbert see *Ricci, Luciano*

Wise, Pamela Isabella Stewart Gardner 77*

Wise, Robert The Magnificent Ambersons 42*; The Curse of the Cat People 44*; Mademoiselle Fifi 44; The Body Snatcher 45; A Game of Death 45; Criminal Court 46; Born to Kill 46; Lady of Deceit 47; Blood on the Moon 48; Mystery in Mexico 48; The Set-Up 49; Three Secrets 50; Two Flags West 50; The Day the Earth Stood Still 51; The House on Telegraph Hill 51; The Captive City 52; Destination Gobi 52; Something for the Birds 52; The Desert Rats 53; So Big 53; Executive Suite 54; Helen of Troy 55; Tribute to a Bad Man 55; Somebody Up There Likes Me 56; This Could Be the Night 57; Until They Sail 57; I Want to Live! 58; Run Silent, Run Deep 58; Odds Against Tomorrow 59; West Side Story 61*; Two for the Seesaw 62; The Haunting 63; The Sound of Music 64; The Sand Pebbles 66; Star! • Those Were the Happy Times 68; The Andromeda Strain 70; Two People 73; The Hindenburg 75; Audrey Rose 77; Star Trek—The Motion Picture 79; Rooftops 89

Wiseman, Frederick Titicut Follies 67; High School 68; Law and Order 69; Hospital 70; Basic Training 71; Essene 72; Juvenile Court 73; Primate 74; Welfare 75; Meat 76; Canal Zone 77; Sinai Field Mission 77; Maneuver • Manoeuvre 79; Model 80; Seraphita's Diary 82; The Store 83; Racetrack 85; Adjustment and Work 86; Blind 86; Deaf 86; Multi-Handicapped 86; Missile 87; Near Death 89

Wishman, Doris Bad Girls Go to Hell 65; A Taste of Flesh 67; The Amazing Transplant 70; Deadly Weapons 74; Double Agent 73 74; A Night to Dismember 83

Wiström, Mikael Mitt Hjärta Har Två Tungor • My Heart Has Two Voices 87

Withey, Chester The Devil's Needle 16; The Old Folks at Home 16; The Wharf Rat 16; An Alabaster Box 17; Bad Boys 17; Nearly Married 17; A Woman's Awakening 17; The Hun Within • The Peril Within 18; In Pursuit of Polly • Pursuit of Polly 18; On the Quiet 18; Little Comrade 19; Maggie Pepper 19; The New Moon 19; The Teeth of the Tiger 19; Romance 20; She Loves and Lies 20; Coincidence 21; Lessons in Love 21; Wedding Bells 21; Arctic Adventure 22; Domestic Relations 22; Heroes and Husbands 22; Outcast 22; Richard, the Lion-Hearted 23; A Cafe in Cairo 24; The Pleasure Buyers 25; Going the Limit 26; Her Honor the Governor 26; The Imposter 26; Queen o' Diamonds 26; Secret Orders 26; The Bushranger 28

Withey, Chet see *Withey, Chester*

Withington, Paul C. Blonde Captive 32*

Withrow, Stephen Crazy Horse • Friends, Lovers & Lunatics • She Drives Me Crazy 89

Witney, William The Painted Stallion 37*; S.O.S. Coast Guard 37*; The Trigger Trio 37; Zorro Rides Again 37*; Dick Tracy Returns 38*; Fighting Devil Dogs • The Torpedo of Doom 38*; Hawk of the Wilderness • Lost Island of Kioga 38*; Hi-Yo Silver! • The Lone Ranger 38*; Daredevils of the Red Circle 39*; Dick Tracy's G-Men 39*; The Lone Ranger Rides Again 39*; Zorro's Fighting Legion 39*; Adventures of Red Ryder 40*; Doctor Satan's Robot • Mysterious Dr. Satan 40*; Drums of Fu Manchu 40*; Heroes of the Saddle 40; King of the Royal Mounted 40*; Adventures of Captain Marvel 41*; Dick Tracy vs. Crime, Inc. 41*; Jungle Girl 41*; King of the Texas Rangers 41*; King of the Mounties 42; Nyoka and the Lost Secrets of Hippocrates • Nyoka and the Tigermen • Perils of Nyoka 42; Outlaws of Pine Ridge 42; Spy Smasher • Spy Smasher Returns 42; The Yukon Patrol 42*; Black Dragon of Manzanar • G-Men vs. the Black Dragon 43; The Crimson Ghost • Cyclotrode "X" 46*; Heldorado • Helldorado 46; Home in Oklahoma 46; Roll On Texas Moon 46; Apache Rose 47; Bells of San Angelo 47; On the Old Spanish Trail • On the Spanish Trail 47; Song of the Sierras • Springtime in the Sierras 47; Eyes of Texas 48; The Far Frontier 48; The Gay Ranchero 48; Grand Canyon Trail 48; Night Time in Nevada 48; Under California Skies • Under California Stars 48; Down Dakota Way 49; The Golden Stallion 49; Susanna Pass 49; Bells of Coronado 50; North of the Great Divide 50; Sunset in the West 50; Trail of Robin Hood 50; Trigger, Jr. 50; Twilight in the Sierras 50; Colorado Sundown 51; Heart of the Rockies 51; In Old Amarillo 51; Pals of the Golden West 51; South of Caliente 51; Spoilers of the Plains 51; Army Capers • The WAC from Walla Walla 52; Border Saddlemates 52; The Last Musketeer 52; Old Oklahoma Plains 52; South Pacific Trail 52; Down Laredo Way 53; Iron Mountain Trail 53; Old Overland Trail 53; Shadows of Tombstone 53; The Fortune Hunter • The Outcast 54; City of Shadows 55; The Fighting Chance 55; Headline Hunters 55; Santa Fe Passage 55; A Strange Adventure 56; Stranger at My Door 56; Panama Sal 57; The Bonnie Parker Story 58; The Cool and the Crazy 58; Juvenile Jungle 58; Young and Wild 58; Paratroop Command 59; The Secret of the Purple Reef 60; Valley of the Redwoods 60; The Large Rope • The Long Rope 61; Master of the World 61; The Cat Burglar 62; Apache Rifles 64; Arizona Raiders 65; The Girls on the Beach • Summer of '64 65; 40 Guns to Apache Pass 66; Ride the Wind 66; Tarzan's Jungle Rebellion 70; I Escaped from Devil's Island 73; Darktown Strutters • Get Down and Boogie 75

Witt, Claus Peter Die Gentlemen Bitten zur Kasse • The Great British Train Robbery • Der Postzug-Überfall 65*

Wittliff, William D. Red-Headed Stranger 84

Wittman, Peter Play Dead 81; Ellie 84

Wiziarde, Frank Santa's Christmas Circus 66

Wohl, Ira Best Boy 79

Wohlmuth, Robert Das Kabinett des Dr. Larifari 31

Wójcik, Wojciech Alone Among His Own • Sam Pośród Swoich 85; Private Investigation • Prywatne Śledztwo 87

Wojtyszko, Maciej Lśnisty Anioł 85

Wolbert, William The Last Man 16*; Aladdin from Broadway 17; By Right of Possession 17; The Captain of the Gray Horse Troop 17; The Divorcee 17; The Flaming Omen 17; The Magnificent Meddler 17; Sunlight's Last Raid 17; Cavanaugh of the Forest Rangers 18; The Girl from Beyond 18; The Home Trail 18; That Devil Bateese 18; When Men Are Tempted 18; The Wild Strain 18; Light of Victory 19

Wolcott, James L. Wild Women of Wongo 59

Wolf, David The American Game 79*

Wolf, Fred The Mouse and His Child 77*; The Adventures of the American Rabbit 86*

Wolf, Konrad Einmal Ist Keinmal 55; Genesung 55; Lissy 57; Étoiles • Stars • Sterne 58; Die Sonnensucher 58; Leute mit Flügeln 60; Professor Mamlock 61; Le Ciel Partagé • Der Geteilte Himmel 64; I Was 19 • Ich War 19 67; Goya, oder Der Arge Weg zur Erkenntnis 70; Mama Ich Lebe 77; Der Nackte Mann auf dem Sportplatz • The Naked Man on the Athletic Field 77; Solo Sunny 79*

Wolff, Carl Heinz see Wolff, Karl Heinz

Wolff, David see Maddow, Ben

Wolff, Hans Die Drei von der Tankstelle 55

Wolff, Karl Heinz The Earthquake Motor 17; Kyritz-Pyritz 32; Frau Lehmanns Töchter 33; Heideschulmeister Uwe Karsten 34; Tante Gusti Kommandiert 34; Der Wackere Schustermeister 36

Wolff, Willi Heads Up, Charlie 26; The Imaginary Baron 27; The Carnival Crime • Carnival of Crime 29; Case Van Geldern 32; Theaternächte von Berlin 32; Manulescu 33; Ein Liebesroman im Hause Hapsburg 36; Die Marquise von Pompadour 36

Wolfson, P. J. Boy Slaves 38

Wolheim, Louis The Sin Ship 31*

Wolk, Larry Eternal Summer 61

Wolkoff, Alexander see Volkov, Alexander

Woll, Susan Lulu in Berlin 84*

Wollen, Peter Riddles of the Sphinx 76; Amy! 80; Crystal Gazing 82; Friendship's Death 87

Wolman, Dan The Morning Before Sleep 69; The Dreamer • Ha' Timhoni 70; Floch • Flock 72; My Michael 75; Hide and Seek 80; Nana 80; Baby Love • Lemon Popsicle V 83; Soldier of the Night 83; Anchors Aweigh • Lemon Popsicle VI • Up Your Anchor 85; Choze Ahava • Contract

for Love • The Love Contract 86

Wong, Kar-wai As Tears Go By 88; Days of Being Wild 90

Wong, Kirk True Colors 87

Woo, John A Better Tomorrow • Ying-xiong Bense 85; A Better Tomorrow II 88; The Killer 89

Wood, Duncan The Bargee 64; Cuckoo Patrol 65; Some Will, Some Won't 69

Wood, Edward D., Jr. Bride of the Atom • Bride of the Monster 53; Glen or Glenda? • He or She? • I Changed My Sex • I Led Two Lives • The Transvestite 53; Hidden Face • Jail Bait 54; Grave Robbers from Outer Space • Plan 9 from Outer Space 56; Night of the Ghouls • Revenge of the Dead 59; Hellborn • The Sinister Urge • The Young and Immoral • The Young and the Immoral 61

Wood, James Dr. Jekyll's Dungeon of Death 78

Wood, John see Iquino, Ignacio F.

Wood, Peter Alla Ricerca di Gregory • In Search of Gregory 69

Wood, Richard C. Helen Keller in Her Story • The Unconquered 54

Wood, Sam Double Speed 19; A City Sparrow 20; The Dancin' Fool 20; Excuse My Dust 20; Her Beloved Villain 20; Her First Elopement 20; Sick Abed 20; The Snob 20; What's Your Hurry? 20; Don't Tell Everything 21*; The Great Moment 21; Peck's Bad Boy 21; Under the Lash 21; Beyond the Rocks 22; Her Gilded Cage 22; Her Husband's Trademark 22; The Impossible Mrs. Bellew 22; My American Wife 22; Bluebeard's Eighth Wife 23; His Children's Children 23; Prodigal Daughters 23; Bluff 24; The Female 24; The Mine with the Iron Door 24; The Next Corner 24; The Re-Creation of Brian Kent 25; Fascinating Youth 26; One Minute to Play 26; The Fair Co-Ed • The Varsity Girl 27; A Racing Romeo 27; Rookies 27; The Latest from Paris 28; Telling the World 28; It's a Great Life 29; So This Is College 29; They Learned About Women 29*; Father's Day • The Richest Man in the World • Sins of the Children 30; The Girl Said No 30; Paid • Within the Law 30; Way for a Sailor 30; Get-Rich-Quick Wallingford • The New Adventures of Get-Rich-Quick Wallingford • Wallingford 31; The Man in Possession 31; A Tailor Made Man 31; Huddle • The Impossible Lover 32; Prosperity 32; The Barbarian • A Night in Cairo 33; Christopher Bean • Her Sweetheart • The Late Christopher Bean 33; Hold Your Man 33; Hollywood Party 34*; Stamboul Quest 34; False Faces • Let 'Em Have It 35; A Night at the Opera 35; Whipsaw 35; The Unguarded Hour 36; A Day at the Races 37; Madame X 37; Navy Blue and Gold 37; The Boy from Barnardo's • Lord Jeff 38; Stablemates 38; Gone with the Wind 39*; Goodbye, Mr. Chips 39; Raffles 39*; Kitty Foyle 40; Our Town 40; Rangers of Fortune 40; The Devil and Miss Jones 41; King's Row 41; The Pride of the Yankees 42; For Whom the Bell Tolls

43; The Land Is Bright 43; Saratoga Trunk 43; Casanova Brown 44; Guest Wife 45; Heartbeat 46; Ivy 47; Command Decision 48; Ambush 49; The Stratton Story 49

Woodard, Horace The Adventures of Chico 38*

Woodard, Stacy The Adventures of Chico 38*

Woodberry, Billy Bless Their Little Hearts 84

Woodburn, Bob Little Laura and Big John 73*

Woodcock, Mark Godard on Godard • Two American Audiences 69*

Woode, Hal E. A Lustful Lady 78

Woodhouse, Barbara Juno Makes Friends 57; Trouble for Juno 57

Woodruff, Frank Cross Country Romance 40; Curtain Call 40; Play Girl 40; Wildcat Bus 40; Lady Scarface 41; Repent at Leisure 41; Cowboy in Manhattan 43; Lady, Let's Dance 43; Pistol Packin' Mama 43; Two Señoritas • Two Señoritas from Chicago 43

Woods, Arthur Bedtime at the Zoo 29*; Stark Nature 30; On Secret Service • Secret Agent • Spy 77 33; Timbuctoo 33*; Give Her a Ring 34; Radio Follies • Radio Parade of 1935 34; Drake of England • Drake the Pirate • Elizabeth of England 35; Music Hath Charms 35*; Irish for Luck 36; Once in a Million • Weekend Millionaire 36; Rhythm in the Air 36; Where's Sally? 36; Clouds Over Europe • Q Planes 37*; The Compulsory Wife 37; Don't Get Me Wrong 37*; Mayfair Melody 37; The Windmill 37; You Live and Learn 37; Dangerous Medicine 38; The Dark Stairway 38; Glamour Girl 38; Mr. Satan 38; The Return of Carol Deane 38; The Singing Cop 38; Thistledown 38; Confidential Lady 39; The Nursemaid Who Disappeared 39; They Drive by Night 39; Busman's Honeymoon • Haunted Honeymoon 40

Woods, Frank E. The Absentee 15*

Woods, Jack Equinox 69*

Woody, Swifty see Van Dyke, W. S.

Woolery, Gerry Jokes My Folks Never Told Me 79

Woolf, Julia Camera Reflections 45

Woolfe, H. Bruce The Battle of Jutland 21; Armageddon 23; Zeebrugge 24*; Sons of the Sea 25

Woolley, Richard Brothers and Sisters 80

Workman, Carl see Workman, Chuck

Workman, Chuck The Money 75; Assignment: Kill Castro • Cuba Crossing • Kill Castro • The Mercenaries • Sweet Dirty Tony • Sweet Violent Tony 80; Stoogemania 85

Works, J. C. see Erskine, Chester

Wormald, S. The Lady or the Lions 08; The Next of Kin 08; There's Life in the Old Dog Yet 08; Two Tough Kids 08; All Scotch 09; The Belle Who Talks 09; A Father's Love 09; The Misadventures of a Cycle Thief 09; The Peril of the Fleet 09; Simple Simon at the Races 09; White to

Black 09; Lady Candale's Diamonds 10; A Lively Skeleton 10; A Mechanical Husband 10

Worne, Duke The Branded Four 20; The Screaming Shadow 20; Dangerous Paths 21; Nan of the North 21; The Star Reporter 21; A Yankee Go-Getter 21; Do It Now 24; Marry in Haste 24; The Martyr Sex 24; The Other Kind of Love 24; The Sword of Valor 24; The Canvas Kisser 25; Easy Going Gordon 25; Going the Limit 25; Once in a Lifetime 25; The Pride of the Force 25; Ten Days 25; Too Much Youth 25; The Boaster 26; The Gallant Fool 26; The Heart of a Coward 26; In Search of a Hero 26; Speed Cop 26; Speed Crazed 26; The Cruise of the Hellion 27; Daring Deeds 27; Heroes in Blue 27; The Silent Hero 27; Smiling Billy 27; Speedy Smith 27; The Wheel of Destiny 27; City of Purple Dreams 28; Danger Patrol 28; The Heart of Broadway 28; Into the Night 28; Isle of Lost Men 28; Man from Headquarters 28; The Midnight Adventure 28; Phantom of the Turf 28; Ships of the Night 28; Anne Against the World 29; Bride of the Desert 29; Devil's Chaplain 29; Handcuffed 29; Some Mother's Boy 29; When Dreams Come True 29; Midnight Special 31; The Last Ride 32

Worsley, Wallace An Alien Enemy 18; The Goddess of Lost Lake 18; Honor's Cross 18; Shackled 18*; Social Ambition 18; Wedlock 18; Adele 19; Diane of the Green Van 19; A Woman of Pleasure 19; The Little Shepherd of Kingdom Come 20; The Penalty 20; The Street Called Straight 20; The Ace of Hearts 21; The Beautiful Liar 21; Don't Neglect Your Wife 21; From Rags to Riches • Rags to Riches 21; The Highest Bidder 21; The Night Rose 21; A Blind Bargain 22; Enter Madame 22; Grand Larceny 22; When Husbands Deceive 22; The Hunchback of Notre Dame 23; Is Divorce a Failure? 23; Nobody's Money 23; The Man Who Fights Alone 24; The Shadow of the Law 26; The Power of Silence 28

Worswick, Clark Family Honor 73; Agent on Ice 86

Worth, Cedric Naked Africa 57

Worth, David Hollywood Knight 79; Soldier's Revenge 84; Warrior of the Lost World 85; Kickboxer 89*

Worth, Frank Ha'penny Breeze 49*

Worth, Jan Doll's Eye 82

Worthington, William Love Never Dies 16; A Stranger from Somewhere 16; Bringing Home Father 17; The Car of Chance 17; The Clean-Up 17; The Clock 17; The Devil's Payday 17; The Man Who Took a Chance 17; The Beloved Traitor 18; The Ghost of the Rancho 18; His Birthright 18; Twenty-One 18; All Wrong 19*; Bonds of Honor 19; The Courageous Coward 19; The Debt • His Debt 19; The Dragon Painter 19; The Gray Horizon 19; A Heart in Pawn 19; The Illustrious Prince 19; The Man Beneath 19; The Tong Man 19; The Beggar Prince 20; The Silent Barrier 20;

The Beautiful Gambler 21; Dr. Jim 21; Go Straight 21; The Greater Profit 21; Opened Shutters 21; The Unknown Wife 21; Afraid to Fight 22; Out of the Silent North 22; Tracked to Earth 22; The Bolted Door 23; Fashionable Fakers 23; Kindled Courage 23; The Girl on the Stairs 24; Beauty and the Bad Man 25

Woxholt, Gil The Heroes of Telemark • The Unknown Battle 65*

Wragge, Martin Coastwatcher • The Last Warrior 89

Wrangell, Basil Keep 'Em Sailing 42; Heartaches 47; Philo Vance's Gamble 47; Cinerama—South Seas Adventure • South Seas Adventure 58*

Wray, John Griffith Home Spun Folks 20; Beau Revel 21; Hail the Woman 21; Lying Lips 21; The Marriage Cheat 21; Anna Christie 23; Her Reputation 23; Human Wreckage 23; Soul of the Beast 23; What a Wife Learned 23; The Winding Stair 25; The Gilded Butterfly 26; Hell's 400 26; Singed 27; The Gateway of the Moon 28; The Careless Age 29; A Most Immoral Lady 29

Wray, Maxwell Prison Without Bars 38*

Wrede, Caspar The Barber of Stamford Hill 62; Private Potter 62; One Day in the Life of Ivan Denisovich 71; Ransom • The Terrorists 75

Wren, Trevor Adam and Nicole • Erotic Inferno 75

Wrestler, Philip Frédéric Chopin 61; Johan Sebastian Bach 61

Wright, Basil Conquest 30*; Windmill in Barbados 30; The Country Comes to Town 31*; Lumber 31; O'er Hill and Dale 31; Gibraltar 32; Cargo from Jamaica 33; Liner Cruising South 33; Song of Ceylon 34; Children at School 36; Night Mail • Nightmail 36*; The Face of Scotland 38; Evacuation 39; Harvest Help 40; The Battle for Freedom 42; Southern Rhodesia 45; This Was Japan 45; The Story of Omolo 46; Bernard Miles on Gun Dogs 48; Waters of Time 50*; Je Suis un Homme • World Without End 52*; The Stained Glass at Fairford 55; The Immortal Land 58; Greek Sculpture 59*; A Place for Gold 60

Wright, Fred E. Graustark 15; In the Palace of the King 15; The White Sister 15; The Breaker 16; Captain Jinks of the Horse Marines 16; The Little Shepherd of Bargain Row 16; The Prince of Graustark 16; The Fibbers 17; The Kill-Joy 17; The Man Who Was Afraid 17; The Trufflers 17; For Sale 18; The Mysterious Client 18

Wright, George The Catspaw 16; Typical Mexican Aspects 19

Wright, Harold Bell The Shepherd of the Hills 20

Wright, Humberston Creation 22; The Island of Romance 22

Wright, John The Visitor 73

Wright, Kay Mighty Mouse in the Great Space Chase 83*

Wright, Kenneth We Visit Moscow 54

Wright, Mack V. Haunted Gold 32;

The Man from Monterey 33; Somewhere in Sonora 33; Cappy Ricks Returns 35; The Big Show • Home in Oklahoma 36; Comin' Round the Mountain 36; Roarin' Lead 36*; Robinson Crusoe of Clipper Island • Robinson Crusoe of Mystery Island 36*; The Singing Cowboy 36; The Vigilantes Are Coming 36*; Winds of the Wasteland 36; The Golden Trail • Riders of the Whistling Skull 37; Hit the Saddle 37; Range Defenders 37; Rhythm on the Ranch • Rootin' Tootin' Rhythm 37; The Great Adventures of Wild Bill Hickok 38*; The Sea Hound 47*

Wright, Patrick Hollywood High 76
Wright, Ralph Perri 57*
Wright, Robin Cecil see Cecil-Wright, Robin
Wright, Tenny The Fightin' Comeback 27; Hoof Marks 27; The Big Stampede 32; The Telegraph Trail 33
Wright, Thomas J. Torchlight 84; No Holds Barred 89
Wrye, Donald The Entertainer 75; Ice Castles 78; H.O.G. • The House of God 79
Wu, Ma The Dead and the Deadly 83
Wu, Tianming Life • Rensheng 85; Lao Jing • The Old Well 87
Wu, Yonggang Goddess 34
Wu, Ziniu Evening Bell • Wan Zhong 89; Huanle Yingziong • The Joyous Heroes 89; Realm Between the Living and the Dead • Yingyang Jie 89
Wuhlschleger, Henri Moi Aussi, J'Accuse 20*; Pervenche 21*; Bêtes. . .Comme les Hommes 23*; Le Cabinet de l'Homme Noir 24*; L'Énigme du Mont Agel 24*; Les Héritiers de l'Oncle James • Les Millions de l'Oncle James 24*; Le Cœur des Gueux 25*; L'Homme Noir • Le Manoir de la Peur 27*
Wulicher, Richard House of Shadows 77
Wullner, Robert The Wife Trap 22
Wurlitzer, Rudolph Candy Mountain 87*
Wyckoff, Alvin The Peasant's Wedding 39
Wyler, Robert It Happened in Paris 35*
Wyler, William Crook Buster 25; Don't Shoot 26; Fire Barrier 26; The Gunless Bad Man 26; The Horse Trader 26; Lazy Lightning 26; Martin of the Mounted 26; The Pinnacle Rider 26; Ridin' for Love 26; The Stolen Ranch 26; The Two Fister 26; Blazing Days 27; The Border Cavalier 27; Daze of the West 27; Desert Dust 27; Galloping Justice 27; Gun Justice 27; Hard Fists 27; The Haunted Homestead 27; The Home Trail 27; Kelcy Gets His Man 27; The Lone Star 27; The Ore Raiders 27; Phantom Outlaw 27; Range Riders • Shooting Straight • Straight Shootin' 27; The Silent Partner 27; Square Shooter 27; Tenderfoot Courage 27; Thunder Riders 27; Anybody Here Seen Kelly? • Has Anybody Here Seen Kelly? 28; The Shakedown 28; Hell's Heroes 29; The Love Trap 29; The Storm 30; A House Divided 31; Papa Sans le Savoir 31; The Old Dark House 32*; Tom

Brown of Culver 32; Counsellor at Law 33; Her First Mate 33; Glamour 34; The Gay Deception 35; The Good Fairy 35; Come and Get It • Roaring Timber 36*; Dodsworth 36; These Three 36; Cradle of Crime • Dead End 37; Jezebel 38; Raffles 39*; Wuthering Heights 39; The Letter 40; The Westerner 40*; The Little Foxes 41; Mrs. Miniver 42; The Fighting Lady • The Memphis Belle 43; Thunderbolt 45*; The Best Years of Our Lives • Glory for Me 46; The Heiress 49; Detective Story 51; Carrie 52; Roman Holiday 53; The Desperate Hours 55; Friendly Persuasion 56; The Big Country 58; Ben-Hur • Ben-Hur: A Tale of the Christ 59; The Children's Hour • Infamous • The Loudest Whisper 61; The Collector 64; How to Steal a Million 66; Funny Girl 68; The Liberation of L. B. Jones 69

Wymetal, William von Maytime 37*
Wynn, George Comrades 21; Queen of the Earth 21; Carmen 22; The Extra Knot 22; A Football Favourite 22; It's Never Too Late to Mend 22; The Magic Wand 22; Maritana 22; Martha 22; Playing the Game 22; Rigoletto 22; Scrooge 22; The Sheik 22; The Street Tumblers 22
Wynn, Robert The Resurrection of Zachary Wheeler 71
Wynne, Bert The Manchester Man 20; The Town of Crooked Ways 20; Belphegor the Mountebank 21; Dick's Fairy 21; Handy Andy 21; Jessica's First Prayer 21; Little Meg's Children 21; Stormflower 21; The Call of the East • His Supreme Sacrifice 22; God's Prodigal 23*; Remembrance 27; A Safe Affair 31; A Night of Magic 44
Wynne, Herbert see Wynne, Bert
Wynne-Simmons, Robert The Outcasts 82
Wynorski, Jim The Lost Empire 84; Chopping Mall • Killbots • R.O.B.O.T. 86; Deathstalker II • Deathstalker II: Duel of the Titans 86; Big Bad Mama II 87; Not of This Earth 88; The Return of Swamp Thing 89; The Haunting of Morella 90
Wysbar, Frank see Wisbar, Frank
Wyss, Tobias Dunki-Schott 86*
Xanthopoulos, Lefteris Happy Homecoming, Comrade • Kali Patritha, Syntrofe 86
Xantus, János Hülyeség Nem Akadály • Idiots May Apply 85
Xavier, Nelson La Chute • The Fall • A Queda 78*
Xiaowen, Zhou see Zhou, Xiaowen
Xiaoxian, Hou see Hou, Hsiao-hsien
Xie, Fei Girl from Hunan • Hunan Girl Xiaoxiao • Xiangnu Xiaoxiao 86*; Black Snow 90
Xie, Jin A Crisis 54; Rendezvous at Orchard Bridge 54; A Wave of Unrest 54; Woman Basketball Player No. 5 57; The Red Detachment of Women 60; Big Li, Young Li and Old Li 62; Two Stage Sisters • Wutai Jiemei 64; Youth 77; Ah, Cradle 80; The Legend of Tianyuan Mountain 81; The Herdsman 82; Qui Jin 83; Reeds at the Foot of the Mountain 84; Hibiscus

Town 86; Furong Zhen 88; The Last Aristocrats 89
Xu, Anhua see Hui, Ann
Xu, Guming Neighbors 85*
Xu, Ke see Shu, Kei
Xueshu, Yan see Yan, Xueshu
Yabuki, Kimio Hansu Kurishitan Anderusan no Sekai • The World of Hans Christian Anderson 68*; Rainbow Brite and the Star Stealer 85*
Yabushita, Taiji Alakazam the Great • Saiyu-Ki 60; Hakuja Den • Panda and the Magic Serpent 61*
Yaconelli, Frank I'll Be There 27
Yagi, Shinichi The Fox with Nine Tails • Kyūbi no Kitsune to Tobimaru 69
Yahraus, Bill ¿Qué Hacer? • What Is to Be Done? 70*; Homeboys 78
Yajim, Nobuo Message from Space • Uchū Kara no Messeji • Uchū no Messeji 78*
Yakir, Leonard The Mourning Suit 75
Ya-lin, Li see Li, Ya-lin
Yamada, Yoji The Strangers Upstairs 61; The Sunshine Girl 63; The Donkey Comes on a Tank 64; Honest Fool 64; Honest Fool—Sequel 64; The Trap 65; Gambler's Luck 66; The Lovable Tramp 66; The Greatest Challenge of All 67; Let's Have a Dream 67; Song of Love 67; The Million Dollar Pursuit 68; The Shy Deceiver 68; Am I Trying, Part Two • Tora-San, Part Two • Tora-San's Cherished Mother • Zoku Otoko wa Tsuraiyō 69; Otoko wa Tsuraiyō • Tora-San's Forbidden Love • Torajiro Shinjitsu Ichiro 69; Tora-San, Our Lovable Tramp 69; Vagabond Schemer 69; Tora-San's Runaway 70; Where Spring Comes Late 70; Tora-San: The Good Samaritan 71; Tora-San's Love Call 71; Tora-San's Shattered Romance 71; Home from the Sea 72; Tora-San's Dear Old Home 72; Tora-San's Dream Come True 72; Tora-San Loves an Artist 73; Tora-San's Forget-Me-Not 73; Tora-San's Lovesick 74; Tora-San's Lullaby 74; Tora-San Meets the Songstress Again 75; Tora-San, the Intellectual 75; The Village 75; Tora-San's Heart of Gold 76; Tora-San's Sunrise, Sunset 76; Tora-San Meets His Lordship 77; Tora-San Plays Cupid 77; The Yellow Handkerchief 77; Stage-Struck Tora-San 78; Talk-of-the-Town Tora-San 78; Tora-San, the Matchmaker 79; Tora-San's Dream of Spring 79; A Distant Cry from Spring 80; Tora-San's Tropical Fever 80; Foster Daddy Tora-San 81; Tora-San's Many-Splintered Love 81; Tora-San's Promise 81; Hearts and Flowers for Tora-San 82; Tora-San, the Expert 82; Tora-San Goes Religious? 83; Tora-San's Song of Love 83; Marriage Counselor Tora-San 84; Tora-San, the Go-Between 85; Tora-San's Island Encounter 85; Final Take • Final Take: The Golden Age of Movies • Final Take: The Golden Days of Movies • Kinema no Tenchi 86; Otoko wa Tsuraiyō: Shiawaseno Aoi Tori • Tora-San's Bluebird Fantasy 86; Otoko wa Tsuraiyō, Shibamata yori Ai o Komete • Tora-San, from Shibamata, with

Love 86; Tora-San Goes North 87; Tora-San Plays Daddy 87; Hope and Pain 88; Otoko wa Tsuraiyō Tōraijiro Kokoro no Tabiji • Tora-San Goes to Vienna 89

Yamaguchi, Kazuhiko Champion of Death 76; Der Lindenbaum 89

Yamaguchi, Tetsuya Froggo and Droggo • Grand Duel in Magic • Kairyū Daikessen • The Magic Serpent 66

Yamakawa, Naoto New Kid 21 • The New Morning of Billy the Kid 86

Yamamoto, Kajiro Danun 24; Bomb Hour 25; Ordeal 32; Love Crisis 33; I Am a Cat 36; A Husband's Chastity 37; The Loves of a Kabuki Actor 38; Easy Alley 39; The Loyal 47 Ronin 39; Horse • Uma 41; The Hope of Youth 42; Misfortunes of Love 45; Asu o Tsukuru Hitobito • Those Who Make Tomorrow 46*; Spring Flirtation 49; Wind of Honor 49; Elegy 51; Girls Among the Flowers 53; Mr. Valiant 54; Saturday Angel 54; The History of Love 55; A Man Among Men 55; The Underworld 56; An Elephant 57; Holiday in Tokyo 58; The Rise and Fall of a Jazz Girl 58; Ginza Tomboy 60; Samurai Joker 65; Thief on the Run 65; Swindler Meets Swindler 67

Yamamoto, Masashi Carnival of the Night 82; Robinson no Niwa • Robinson's Garden 87

Yamamoto, Michio Chi o Suu Ningyō • The Night of the Vampire • Yūreiyashiki no Kyōfu-Chi wa Suu Ningyō 70; Bloodthirsty Eyes • Chi o Suu Me • Dracula's Lust for Blood • Japula • Lake of Death • Lake of Dracula • Noroi no Yakata-Chi wa Suu 71; Chi o Suu Bara • The Evil of Dracula 75

Yamamoto, Sanae Magic Boy • Shōnen Sarutobi Sasuke 60*

Yamamoto, Satsuo Haha no Kyoku 37; Young Miss 37; Denen Kōkyōgaku • La Symphonie Pastorale 38; Family Diary 38; The Street 39; End of Engagement 40; Tsubasa no Gaika 42; Hot Wind • Neppu 43; Sensō to Heiwa • War and Peace 45*; Bōryoku no Machi • The Street of Violence 50; Hakone Fūunroke • Storm Clouds Over Mount Hakone 51; Shinku Chitai • Vacuum Zone 52; The Street Without Sun • The Sunless Street • Taiyō no Nai Machi 53; Hi no Hate • To the End of the Sun 54; Duckweed Story • Ukigusa Nikki 55; Avalanche 56; Taifū Sōdōki • Typhoon • Typhoon No. 13 56; Akai Jinbaori • His Scarlet Cloak 58; The Human Wall 59; The Song of the Cart 59; Battle Without Arms • Buki Naki Tatakai 60; A Band of Assassins I • Shinobi no Mono I 62; Chibusa o Daku Musumetachi 62; A Band of Assassins II • Shinobi no Mono II 63; Red Water 63; Kizu Darake no Sanga • A Public Benefactor • Tycoon 64; Shōnin no Isu • The Witness Seat 64; The Burglar Story 65; The Spy 65; Freezing Point • Hyōten 66; The Great White Tower 66; The Blind Swordsman's Rescue • Zatōichi Rō-Yaburi 67; Botan Dōru • The Bride from Hades • The Bride from Hell • Ghost

Beauty • A Ghost Story of Peonies and Stone Lanterns • Kaidan Botan Doru • My Bride Is a Ghost • A Tale of Peonies and Lanterns 68; The Family 74; Annular Eclipse 75; The Story of Yugaku Ohara 76; The Barren Ground 77; August Without the Emperor 78; Ah! Nōmugi Tōge 80

Yamamura, So The Crab-Canning Ship • Kanikōsen 53; Black Tide • Kuroi Ushio 54; Haha Ko Gusa • A Mother and Her Children 59; Kashimanada no Onna • The Maidens of Kashima Sea 59; Fūryū Fukagawa • The Song of Fukagawa 60

Yamanaka, Sadao Bangoku no Isshō • The Life of Bangoku 32; Dakine no Nagadosū • Sleeping with a Long Sword 32; The Elegant Swordsman • Fūryū Katsujinken 34; Chuji Kunisada • Kunisada Chuji 35; Machi no Irezumi Mono • The Village Tattooed Man 35; Humanity and Paper Balloons • Ninjō Kami-Fūsen 37; Ishimatsu of the Forest • Mori no Ishimatsu 37

Yamanouchi, Tetsuya The Day the Sun Rose • Gion Matsuri 69

Yamashita, Kosaku The Man Who Assassinated Ryoma • Ryoma o Kitta Otoko 87

Yan, Chang see Chang, Yan
Yan, Wang see Wang, Yan
Yan, Xueshu In the Wild Mountains • Ye Shan 86

Yanagimachi, Mitsuo God Speed You, Black Emperor 76; A 19-Year-Old's Plan 79; Farewell to the Land 82; Fire Festival • Himatsuri 85

Yang, Chuan Twisted Passion 85
Yang, Dechang see Yang, Edward
Yang, Edward In Our Time • Kuang-Yin-Te Kushih 82*; Hai-T'an-Shang-Te Yi T'ien • That Day, at the Beach • That Day on the Beach 83; Taipei Story 85; Konbu Finze • K'ung-Pu Fen-Tzu • Terrorizer • The Terrorizers 86

Yang, Lanru Report on Pollution at the Women's Kingdom 88*
Yang, Te-ch'ang see Yang, Edward
Yang, Yanjing Nu Shi Zhang De Si Ren Sheng Hua 88
Yang-ming, Tsai see Tsai, Yang-ming
Yanjing, Yang see Yang, Yanjing
Yanne, Jean Moi Y en A Avoir des Sous • Moi Y'en A Vouloir des Sous 72; Tout le Monde Il Est Beau — Tout le Monde Il Est Gentil 72; Les Chinois à Paris 73; Chobizenesse 75; I've Got You, You've Got Me by the Chin Hairs • Je Te Tiens, Tu Me Tiens par la Barbichette 79; Deux Heures Moins le Quart Avant Jésus Christ 82; Liberté, Égalité, Choucroute • Liberty, Equality, Sauerkraut 85

Yanushkevich, R. Putyovka v Zhizn • The Road to Life 30*
Yao, Fengpan All in a Dim Cold Night • Qiu Deng Ye Yu 74
Yarbrough, Jean All Business 36; And So to Wed 36; Bad Medicine 36; Dog Blight 36; Don't Be Like That 36; Fight Is Right 36; Lalapaloosa 36; So and Sew 36; Horse Play 37; Inlawful 37; A Rented Riot

37; Rhythm on the Rampage 37; Singing in the Air 37; Swing Fever 37; Trailing Along 37; Wife Insurance 37; Berth Quakes 38; A Buckaroo Broadcast 38; The Dummy Owner 38; Hectic Honeymoon 38; Music Will Tell 38; The Photographer 38; Picketing for Love 38; Rebellious Daughters 38; Russian Dressing 38; Crime Rave 39; Plumb Crazy 39; Start the Music 39; Swing Vacation 39; The Devil Bat • Killer Bats 40; Molly Cures a Cowboy 40; Caught in the Act • You Betcha My Life 41; City Limits • Father Steps Out 41; Farewell to Fame • Let's Go Collegiate 41; The Gang's All Here • In the Night 41; King of the Zombies 41; South of Panama 41; Top Sergeant Mulligan 41; Attorney for the Defense • Silent Witness 42; Aunt Emma Paints the Town • Meet the Mob • So's Your Aunt Emma! 42; Crime Reporter • Criminal Investigator 42; Freckles Comes Home 42; Law of the Jungle 42; Lure of the Islands 42; Man from Headquarters 42; Police Bullets 42; She's in the Army 42; Follow the Band • Trombone from Heaven 43; Get Going 43; Good Morning, Judge 43; Hi'Ya, Sailor 43; So's Your Uncle! 43; Abbott and Costello in Society • In Society 44; Moon Over Las Vegas 44; South of Dixie 44; Twilight on the Prairie 44; Weekend Pass 44; Here Come the Co-Eds 45; The Naughty Nineties 45; On Stage, Everybody 45; Under Western Skies 45; The Brute Man 46; Cuban Pete • Down Cuban Way 46; The Curse of the Allenbys • She-Wolf of London 46; House of Horrors • Joan Medford Is Missing 46; Inside Job 46; The Challenge 48; The Creeper 48; Henry, the Rainmaker 48; Shed No Tears 48; Triple Threat 48; Angels in Disguise 49; Holiday in Havana 49; Leave It to Henry 49; Master Minds 49; The Mutineers • Pirate Ship 49; Big Timber • Tall Timber 50; Father Makes Good 50; Honeymoon for Five • Joe Palooka Meets Humphrey 50; Humphrey Takes a Chance • Joe Palooka in Humphrey Takes a Chance 50; Sideshow 50; Square Dance Katy 50; Triple Trouble 50; According to Mrs. Hoyle 51; Casa Mañana 51; Abbott and Costello Lost in Alaska • Lost in Alaska 52; Jack and the Beanstalk 52; Night Freight 55; Crashing Las Vegas 56; Hot Shots 56; The Women of Pitcairn Island 56; Yaqui Drums 56; Footsteps in the Night 57; Saintly Sinners 62; Hillbillys in a Haunted House 67

Yarema, Neil A Taste of Hell 73*
Yasan, Earnest A Dream Comes True, or The Valise • Son v Ruku, ili Chemodon 87; Dublyor Nachinaet Deystvovat • The Standby Moves In 87
Yashin, Boris Aeroport so Sluzebnogo Vhoda 88
Yasin, Al The Last Moment 66
Yasuda, Kimiyoshi Daimajin • The Devil Got Angry • Majin • Majin the Hideous Idol • Majin the Monster of Terror • The Vengeance of the Monster 66; The Hundred Ghost Stories • The Hundred

Monsters • Yōkai Hyaku Monogatari 68; Zatoichi • Zatoichi and the Scoundrels • Zatōichi Kenkatabi • Zatoichi on the Road 68; Horror of an Ugly Woman • Kaidan Kasanegafuchi • The Masseur's Curse 70; Zatoichi's Conspiracy 74

Yates, Frank Danvers Apache Dance 09; Land of Hope and Glory 09; Sneezing 09; The Taximeter Cab 09

Yates, Hal Make Mine Laughs 48*; Variety Time 48; Footlight Varieties 51

Yates, Peter Summer Holiday 62*; One Way Pendulum 64; Robbery 67; Bullitt 68; John and Mary 69; Murphy's War 70; The Hot Rock • How to Steal a Diamond in Four Uneasy Lessons 72; The Friends of Eddie Coyle 73; For Pete's Sake • July Pork Bellies 74; Mother, Jugs and Speed 76; The Deep 77; Breaking Away 79; Eyewitness • The Janitor 80; Krull 82; The Dresser 83; Eleni 85; The House on Carroll Street • The House on Sullivan Street 87; Suspect 87; An Innocent Man 89

Yates, Rebecca Milk & Honey 88*

Yeaworth, Irvin S., Jr. The Flaming Teen-Age 56*; The Blob 58; The Evil Force • 4D Man • Master of Horror • The Master of Terror 59; Dinosaurus! 60; Way Out 66

Yee, Tung Sing see Yee, Tung-shing

Yee, Tung-shing The Lunatics 86; People's Hero 87

Yegorov, Vladimir The Frigid Sea 55

Yeh, Hung-wei Curses of the Knife 90; Five Girls and a Rope 90

Yellen, Linda Come Out, Come Out 69; Looking Up 77

Yen, Chun The Grand Substitution 65

Yen, Mou-che Angels of the Street 36; At the Crossroads 37; A Higher Patriotism 37; Yenan and the Eighth Army on the Road 39

Yeong-il, Jang see Jang, Yeong-il

Yerby, Lorees Richard 72*

Yermolayev, Boris Fouette 86*

Yerofeyev, Vladimir Afganistan 29

Yershov, Mikhail Ishchu Druga Zhizni 88

Yershov, Roman Aliens Are Forbidden • Chuzhie Zdes Ne Khodyat 87*

Yersin, Yves Swiss Made 68*

Yeshurun, Itzhak Noa at Seventeen 85; Malkat Hakita • Prom Queen 86

Yeshurun, Zeppel see Yeshurun, Itzhak

Yeung, Ka On Midnight 87

Yevtushenko, Yevgeny Kindergarten 72

Yglesias, Antonio see Iglesias, Antonio

Yi, Chang see Zhang, Yi

Yi, Lin see Lin, Yi

Yi, Zhang see Zhang, Yi

Yılmaz, Atıf Alageyik • The Hind 58; Bu Vatanın Çocukları • The Children of This Country 58; Karacaoğlanin Kara Sevdası • Karacaoğlan's Mad Love 59; Ölüm Perdesi • The Screen of Death 60; Dolandırıcılar • The King of Thieves 61; If I Lose You • Seni Kaybederesem 61; Kızıl Vazo • The Red Vase 61; The Poor Ones • The Suffering Ones • Zavallılar 75*; Bir Udum Sevgi 85; Aah...Belinda 86; Adı Vasfiye •

Her Name Is Vasfiye 86; Sarıpinar 1914 • Şey Sarsılıyor 86; Değirmen • The Mill 87; Hayallerim, Aşkim ve Sen 88

Yim, Ho The Extras 78; The Happenings 79; Wedding Bells, Wedding Belles 80; Homecoming 84; Buddha's Lock 87; Red Dust 90

Yimou, Zhang see Zhang, Yimou

Yinnan, Sing see Sing, Yinnan

Yixiu, Lin see Lin, Yixiu

Yolles, Edie That's My Baby 85*

Yonfan, Manshi see Manshi, Yonfan

Yonggang, Wu see Wu, Yonggang

Yong-kyun, Bae see Bae, Yong-kyun

Yorkin, Bud Come Blow Your Horn 63; Never Too Late 65; Divorce American Style 67; Inspector Clouseau 68; Louie, There's a Crowd Downstairs • Start the Revolution Without Me • Two Times Two 69; The Thief Who Came to Dinner 72; Twice in a Lifetime 85; Arthur 2: On the Rocks 88; Love Hurts 90

Yosha, Yaky Shalom 73; Rockinghorse 78; The Vulture 81; Dead End Street 82; Sunstroke 84

Yoshida, Hiroaki Gōkiburi • Twilight of the Cockroaches 90

Yoshida, Kenji Koto no Taiyō • No Greater Love Than This 69; Moscow My Love 74*

Yoshida, Kiju Arashi Ga Oka 88

Yoshida, Yoshishige Dry Earth • Good-for-Nothing 60; An Affair at Akitsu 62; Nippon Escape 64; Forbidden Love 65; The Lake • Onna no Mizuumi • Woman of the Lake 66; The Affair 67; Impasse 67; Farewell to Summer Light 68; Ningen no Yakusoku • The Promise 86

Yoshimura, Kimisaburo see Yoshimura, Kozaburo

Yoshimura, Kozaburo Nukiashi Sashiashi • Sneaking 34; Ashita no Odoriko • Dancers of Tomorrow • Tomorrow's Dancers 39; Cheerful Alley • Gay Back Alley • Lively Alley • Yōki no Uramachi 39; Danryū • Warm Current 39; Five Brothers and Sisters • Gonin no Kyōdai 39; Onna Kōsō Ie o Mamore • Women Defend the Home! • Women Should Stay at Home 39; Nishizumi Senshacho-Den • The Story of Tank Commander Nishizumi 40; Blossom • Flower • Hana 41; Kanchō Imada Shisezu • The Spy Has Not Yet Died • The Spy Isn't Dead Yet • Yet Spies Haven't Died 42; Minami no Kaze • South Wind 42; South Wind, Sequel • Zoku Minami no Kaze 42; An Attack of the Enemy Planes • Enemy Air Attack • Tekki Kūshu 43; Kaisen no Zenya • The Night Before the War • On the Eve of War 43; Decisive Battle • Kessen 44*; Anjo-Ke no Butōkai • A Ball at the Anjo House • The Ball of the Anjo Family 47; The Fellows Who Ate the Elephant • Zō o Kutta Renchū 47; The Bright Day of My Life • The Day Our Lives Shine • Waga Shōgai no Kagayakeru Hi 48; Seduction • emption • Yūwaku 48; Ishimatsu of Mori • Ishimatsu of the Forest • Mori no Ishimatsu 49; Jealousy • Shitto 49; Mahiru

no Enbukyōku • Waltz at Noon 49; About Twenty Years Old • Nijū-Sai Zengo 50; The End of Battle Fire • End of War Disters • The Height of Battle • Senka no Hate 50; Shunsetsu • Spring Snow 50; Clothes of Deception • Deceiving Costume • Itsuwareru Seisō • Under Silk Garments 51; Free School • Jiyū Gakkyū • The School of Freedom 51; Genji Monogatari • A Tale of Genji 51; Bōryoku • Violence 52; Nishijin no Shimai • The Sisters of Nishijin 52; Before Dawn • Before the Dawn • Yoake Mae 53; Desires • Yokubō 53; Senbazuru • A Thousand Cranes 53; Aisureba Kōsō • Because I Love • If You Love Me 54*; Ashizuri Misaki • Cape Ashizuri 54; People of Young Character • Wakai Hitotachi • Young People 54; Beauty and the Dragon • Bijō to Kairyū 55; Ginza no Onna • Women of the Ginza 55; Date for Marriage • Day of Marriage • The Day to Wed • Totsugu Hi 56; 48-Year-Old Rebel • Protest at 48 Years Old • Yonjūhassai no Teikō 56; Night River • Undercurrent • Yoru no Kawa 56; Ōsaka Monogatari • An Osaka Story 56*; Butterfly of Night • Night Butterflies • Yoru no Chō 57; Chijō • On This Earth 57; A Grain of Wheat • Hitotsubu no Mugi • One Grain of Barley 58; The Ladder of Success • The Naked Face of Night • Yoru no Sugao 58; Aristocrat's Stairs • Kizoku no Kaidan 59; Code of Women • Jokei • Jokyō • A Woman's Testament 59*; Denwa wa Yūgata ni Naru • A Telephone Rings in the Evening 59; Design for Dying • Onna no Kunshō • Woman's Decoration 60; Onna no Saka • Woman's Descent • Women of Kyoto 60; Konki • Marriage Time • Marriageable Age 61; Hiroshima Heartache • I Won't Forget That Night • A Night to Remember • Sono Yo wa Wasurenai 62; Katei no Jijō • Their Legacy 62; The Bamboo Doll • Bamboo Doll of Echizen • Echizen Takeningyō 63*; Lies • Uso • When Women Lie 63*; The Heart of the Mountains • Kokoro no Sammyaku 66; A Corrupted Woman • Daraku Suru Onna • A Fallen Woman 67; Atsui Yoru • A Hot Night 68; The House of the Sleeping Virgins • Nemureri Bijō • Sleeping Beauty 68; Amai Himitsu • Sweet Secret 71; Hamagure no Komoriuta • Lullaby of Hamagure 73; Konketsuji Rika • Rika the Mixed-Blood Girl 73; A Ragged Flag • Ranru no Hata 74

Young, Anthony Penny Points to Paradise 51; My Death Is a Mockery 52; Hands of Destiny 54; Port of Escape 55; Them Nice Americans 58; Hidden Homicide 59; The Runaway 64

Young, Burton The House of Shame 28

Young, Freddie Arthur's Hallowed Ground 83

Young, Gary Alexander End of August 74

Young, Harold Leave It to Blanche 34; The Scarlet Pimpernel 34*; Too Many Millions 34; Without Regret 35; My American Wife 36; Woman Trap 36; 52nd

Street 37; Let Them Live 37*; Little Tough Guy 38; Newsboys' Home 38; The Storm 38; Code of the Streets 39; The Forgotten Woman 39; Hero for a Day 39; Sabotage • Spies at Work 39; Dreaming Out Loud 40; Bachelor Daddy 41; Radio Revels of 1942 • Swing It Soldier 41; Juke Box Jenny 42; The Mummy's Tomb 42; Rubber Racketeers 42; There's One Born Every Minute 42; Everything Happens to Us • Hi'Ya, Chum 43; Hi, Buddy 43; I Escaped from the Gestapo • No Escape 43; Spy Train • Time Bomb 43; Machine Gun Mama • Mexican Fiesta • Tropical Fury 44; The Three Caballeros 44*; The Frozen Ghost 45; I'll Remember April 45; Jungle Captive • Wild Jungle Captive 45; Phantoms, Inc. 45; Song of the Sarong 45; Citizen Saint 47; The Kid Colossus • Roogie's Bump 54; Carib Gold 55

Young, James As You Like It 12*; Lincoln's Gettysburg Address 12*; And His Wife Came Back 13; Beau Brummel 13*; Beauty Unadorned 13*; Delayed Proposals 13; The Dog House Builders 13; The Little Minister 13; When Mary Grew Up 13; When Women Go on the Warpath 13*; Goodness Gracious, or Movies As They Shouldn't Be 14; Happy-Go-Lucky 14; Lola • Without a Soul 14; A Model Young Man 14; My Official Wife 14; The Violin of M'sieur 14; The Win(k)some Widow 14; Deep Purple 15; The Heart of Blue Ridge • The Heart of the Blue Ridge 15; Hearts in Exile 15; The Little Miss Brown 15; Marrying Money 15; Over Night 15; The Lash 16; Oliver Twist 16; Sweet Kitty Bellairs 16; The Thousand Dollar Husband 16; Unprotected 16; On Trial 17; The Man Who Wouldn't Tell 18; Missing 18*; Rose o' Paradise 18; Temple of Dusk 18; White Man's Law 18; Gentleman of Quality 19; The Highest Trump 19; Hornet's Nest 19; A Regular Girl 19; A Rogue's Romance 19; The Usurper 19; The Wolf 19; Curtain 20; Daughter of Two Worlds 20; The Notorious Miss Lisle 20; The Devil 21; Without Benefit of Clergy 21; The Infidel 22; The Masquerader 22; Omar the Tentmaker 22; Trilby 23; Wandering Daughters 23; Welcome Stranger 24; The Unchastened Woman 25; The Bells 26; Driven from Home 27; Midnight Rose 28

Young, Jeffrey Been Down So Long It Looks Like Up to Me 71

Young, Neil Journey Through the Past 72; Rust Never Sleeps 79; Human Highway 82*

Young, Robert M. Secrets of the Reef 56*; Cortile Cascino • Cortile Cascino, Italy • The Inferno 62*; Trauma 62; Nothing But a Man 64*; Romance with a Double Bass 75; Keep It Up Downstairs 76; Alambrista! 77; Deal 77; Short Eyes • Slammer 77; Rich Kids 79; One-Trick Pony 80; The Ballad of Gregorio Cortez • Gregorio Cortez 82; Extremities 86; Saving Grace 86; Dominick and Eugene 88; Triumph of the Spirit 89

Young, Robert William Vampire Circus

71; The World Is Full of Married Men 79

Young, Roger Lassiter 84; Gulag 85; Skip Tracer • The Squeeze 86

Young, Terence Men of Arnhem 44*; Corridor of Mirrors 48; One Night with You 48; Woman Hater 48; They Were Not Divided 50; Valley of Eagles • Valley of the Eagles 51; The Frightened Bride • Tall Headlines 52; Paratrooper • The Red Beret 53; That Lady 54; Storm Over the Nile 55*; Safari 56; Zarak 56*; Action of the Tiger 57; No Time to Die! • Tank Force 57; Immoral Charge • Serious Charge • A Touch of Hell 59; Black Tights • Les Collants Noirs • Un, Deux, Trois, Quatre! 60; Playgirl After Dark • Too Hot to Handle 60; Duel of Champions • Horatio • Orazi e Curiazi 61*; Dr. No 62; From Russia with Love 63; The Amorous Adventures of Moll Flanders 65; The Dirty Game • The Dirty War • La Guerra Segreta • La Guerre Secrète • The Secret Agents • The Secret War • Spione Unter Sich 65*; Thunderball 65; Danger Grows Wild • The Opium Connection • Poppies Are Also Flowers • The Poppy Is Also a Flower 66; Triple Cross 66; The Adventurer • L'Avventuriero • The Rover 67; Wait Until Dark 67; Mayerling 68; L'Arbre de Noël • The Christmas Tree • When Wolves Cry 69; Cold Sweat • De la Part des Copains • The Man with Two Shadows • L'Uomo dalle Due Ombre 70; Red Sun • Soleil Rouge 71; Joe Valachi: I Segreti di Cosa Nostra • The Valachi Papers 72; The Amazons • Le Guerriere del Sno Nuda • War Goddess 73; The Burning Cross • The Klansman 74; Jackpot 75; Bloodline • Sidney Sheldon's Bloodline 79; Inchon! 80; The Jigsaw Man 83

Young, Tony see Young, Anthony

Young, W. W. Alice in Wonderland 16

Youngdeer, James The Belle of Crystal Palace 14; The Black Cross Gang 14; Queen of the Counterfeiters • Queen of the London Counterfeiters 14; The Water Rats of London 14; The World at War 14; Who Laughs Last 20; Lieutenant Daring RN and the Water Rats 24*

Younger, A. P. The Torrent 24*

Younger, Tom Med Mord i Bagaget • No Time to Kill 61

Young-hyo, Kim see Kim, Young-hyo

Younkins, Jerry The Demon Lover 76*

Yu, Albert Devil Woman 76*

Yu, Benzheng Piaobo Qiyu • Strange Encounters 82; Rezhou • Sunrise 86

Yu, Chen see Chen, Yu

Yu, Dennis The Imp • Xiong Bang 81; Bun Mooi 82; City Hero 85

Yu, K'an-p'ing The Outsiders 87

Yu, Ronnie Pao Dan Fei Che • The Trail 83; Legacy of Rage 87

Yu, Sun see Sun, Yu

Yu, Wei-yen Gang of Three Forever 89

Yu, Yunkang see Yu, Dennis

Yuan, Chu see Chu, Yuan

Yuan, Muzhi Malu Tianshi • Street Angel 37

Yuan, Quifeng Midnightmare • Ye

Bang Ge Sheng 61

Yuasa, Noriyaki Daikaijū Gamera • Gamera • Gamera the Invincible • Gammera • Gammera the Invincible 66; Boyichi and the Supermonster • Daikaijū Kūchūsen • Gamera Tai Gaos • Gamera vs. Gaos • Gamera vs. Gyaos • Return of the Giant Monsters 67; Destroy All Planets • Gamera Tai Uchūkaijū Bairasu • Gamera Tai Viras • Gamera vs. Outer Space Monster Viras • Gamera vs. Viras 68; Attack of the Monsters • Gamera Tai Guiron • Gamera vs. Guiron 69; Gamera Tai Daimaju Jaiga • Gamera vs. Jiger • Gamera vs. Monster X • Monsters Invade Expo '70 70; Gamera Tai Shinkai Kaijū Jigura • Gamera vs. the Deep Sea Monster Zigra • Gamera vs. Zigra 71

Yudin, Konstantin Antosha Rybkin 43; Four Hearts 46; Twins 47; The Bold Ones 50; The Horsemen 51; Boryets i Kloun • The Wrestler and the Clown 57*

Yueh, Feng Madame White Snake • Pai-She Chuan 63; The Last Woman of Shang • Ta Chi 64; Hua Mu-Lan • The Lady General 65

Yuen, Chor Last Song in Paris 86

Yuen, Corey No Retreat, No Surrender 86; No Retreat, No Surrender II 89

Yuen, Ng See Bruce Lee—True Story 76; The Unwritten Law 61

Yuen, Wo Ping Shaolin Drunkard 85

Yuk-ping, Fong see Fong, Allen

Yune, Johnny They Still Call Me Bruce 86*

Yung, Peter Life After Life 81; The System 81

Yunkang, Yu see Yu, Dennis

Yu-ping, Fong see Fong, Allen

Yust, Larry The Double Con • Trick Baby 73; Homebodies 74; Say Yes 86

Yutkevich, Sergei Daesh Radio! • Dayoch Radio! • Give Us Radio! • Radio Now! 24*; Bed and Sofa • Third Meshchanskaya • Tretia Mecht Chanskaya • Tretya Meshchanskaya • 3 Meshchanskaya Street 26*; The Black Sail • Chyorni Parus 28; Kruzheva • Lace 28; Golden Mountains • Mountains of Gold • Zlatye Gori 31; The Challenge • Counterplan • Pozor • Shame • Vstrechnyi 32*; Ankara, Heart of Turkey • Ankara, Serdtsye Turkiye • The Soviets Greet New Turkey 34*; Chakhtiery • Miners • Shakhtery 34; How the Elector Will Vote • Kak Boudet Golosovat Izbiratel 37; Chelovek s Ruzhyom • The Man with a Gun • The Man with a Rifle • The Man with the Gun 38; Yakov Sverdlov 40; Novyi Rasskazy Bravogo Soldata Shveika • Schweik in the Concentration Camp 41; The White Raven 41; The New Adventures of Schweik • Novyi Pokhozdeniya Shveika 43; Dmitri Donskoi 44; France Liberated • Liberated France • Osvobozhdeniye Frantsye • Osvobozhdennaya Frantsiya 44; Greetings Moscow! • Hello Moscow! • Hullo Moscow! • Zdravstvui Moskva! 45; Molodost Nashi Stranyi • Our Country's Youth • Young Years of Our Country • The Youth of Our Country

Zebba, Sam Fincho 65

Zecca, Ferdinand Le Muet Mélomane 1899; Comment Fabien Devient Architecte 00; Drame au Fond de la Mer 00; La Loupe de Grand-Mère • La Loupe de Gran' maman 00; Le Mégère Récalcitrante 00; À la Conquête de l'Air • La Conquête de l'Air • The Flying Machine 01; L'Agent Plongeur 01; Ali Baba et les 40 Voleurs 01; L'Assassinat du McKinley 01; La Baignade Impossible 01; Chagrin d'Amour 01*; Le Coucher de la Mariée 01; Une Demande en Mariage Mal Engagée 01*; Discussion Politique 01; L'Enfant Prodigue 01; Histoire d'un Crime 01; Idylle Sous un Tunnel 01; L'Illusioniste Mondain 01; Par le Trou de la Serrure 01; Quo Vadis? 01; Rêve et Réalité 01; Le Salut de Dranem 01*; Les Sept Châteaux du Diable 01; Le Supplice de Tantale 01; Tempête dans une Chambre à Coucher 01; L'Amour à Tous les Étages 02; La Belle au Bois Dormant 02; Catastrophe de la Martinique 02; Ce Que Je Vois dans Mon Télescope 02; The Life and Passion of Christ • La Passion • La Vie et la Passion de Jésus Christ 02*; La Poule Merveilleuse 02; Les Victimes de l'Alcoolisme 02*; Le Chat Botté • Puss 'n Boots 03; Don Quichotte 03; Samson et Delilah 03; Trente Ans ou La Vie d'un Joueur 03; Au Pays Noir 04; La Grève 04; Ce Qu'On Voit de la Bastille 05; Dix Femmes pour un Mari 05; L'Incendiaire 05; Les Petits Vagabonds 05; Pour l'Honneur d'un Père 05; Rêve à la Lune • Le Rêve dans la Lune 05; Roman d'Amour 05; Toto Gâte-Sauce 05; Vendetta 05; Un Drame à Venise 07*; La Légende de Polichinelle 07; Métempsychose 07; L'Affaire Dreyfus 08; L'Homme Invisible • An Invisible Thief 09; Messaline 10*; La Comtesse Noire 12*; Le Roi de l'Air 13*

Zedd, Nick The Freak from Suckweasel Mountain • Geek Maggot Bingo 83

Zeffirelli, Franco Camping 57; La Bohème 65; Florence—Days of Destruction 65; La Bisbetica Domata • The Taming of the Shrew 66; Romeo and Juliet 68; Brother Sun, Sister Moon • Fratello Sole, Sorella Luna 72; Gesù di Nazareth • Jesus of Nazareth 76; The Champ 79; Endless Love 81; La Traviata 82; Otello 86; Il Giovane Toscanini • Young Toscanini 88; Hamlet 90

Zeglio, Primo Revenge of the Pirates 51; Nero and the Burning of Rome 53; Capitaine Morgan • Morgan il Pirata • Morgan the Pirate 60*; Il Figlio del Corsaro Rosso • Son of the Red Corsair 60; Il Dominatore dei Sette Mari • Il Re dei Sette Mari • Seven Seas to Calais 61*; Slave Queen of Babylon 62; Los Rurales de Texas • Two Gunmen 64; L'Uomo della Valle Maledetta 64; The Magnificent Four • I Quattro Inesorabili • The Relentless Four 65; Alarm im Weltall • Muerto 4-3-2-1-0 • Perry Rhodan—S.O.S. aus dem Weltall • Quattro Tre Due Uno Morte 67; The Seven Revenges 67; Killer, Adiós 68; Mission Stardust • Orbito Mortal 68

Zehetgruber, Rudolf Journey to the Seventh Planet 61; Reptilicus 62; The Nylon Noose 63; The Black Cobra 64; The Inn on Dartmoor 64; El Dedo en el Gatillo • Finger on the Trigger 65; The Secret of the Chinese Carnation 65; Donne alla Frontiera • Frauen Die Durch die Hölle Gehen • Las Siete Magníficas • The Tall Women 66; The Christmas Kid • Joe Navidad 67; The Girl of the Nile 67; Ein Käfer Geht aufs Ganze 71; A Beetle Goes Flat Out • Ein Käfer Gibt Vollgas 72; A Beetle in Overdrive • Ein Käfer auf Extratour 73; The Maddest Car in the World • Das Verrückteste Auto der Welt 74; Superbug, Super Agent 76; Nessie—Das Verrückteste Monster der Welt 85

Zehn, Willy The Dark Castle • The Hound of the Baskervilles: The Dark Castle • Der Hund von Baskerville: Das Dunkle Schloss 15; Dr. MacDonald's Sanatorium 20; The Hound of the Baskervilles • Der Hund von Baskerville 20

Zeiden, Josef *see* Seiden, Joseph

Zeisler, Alfred D-Zug 13 Hat Verspätung 31; Sein Scheidungsgrund 32; Ein Tür Geht Auf 33; Der Hochtourist 34; Schuss im Morgengrauen • A Shot at Dawn 34; Der Stern von Valencia 34; Strich Durch die Rechnung 34; The Amazing Adventure • The Amazing Quest • The Amazing Quest of Ernest Bliss • Riches and Romance • Romance and Riches 36; Crime Over London 36; Make-Up 37; Dr. Paul Joseph Goebbels • Enemy of Women • Mad Lover • The Private Life of Dr. Paul Joseph Goebbels • The Private Life of Paul Joseph Goebbels 44; Fear 46; Parole, Inc. 48; Alimony 49

Zeitoun, Ariel Saxo 88

Zelenka, Zdeněk Čarovné Dědictví • A Magic Heritage 85; Jsi Falešný Hráč 86

Zeliff, Seymour The Mysterious Witness 23

Zelinsky, Gunar *see* Tselinsky, Gunar

Zelnik, Fred Menschen in Ketten 19*; Bohemian Dancer 29; The Crimson Circle 29*; Dancing Vienna 29; The Weavers 29; Barberina • Barberina die Tänzerin von Sans-Souci 32; Die Galavorstellung 33; Walzerparadies 33; Happy 34; Kaiserwalzer 34; Mister Cinders 34; Southern Roses 36; The Lilac Domino 37; I Killed the Count • Who Is Guilty? 39

Zelnik, Friedrich *see* Zelnik, Fred

Zeman, Bořivoj Byl Jednou Jeden Král • Once Upon a Time There Was a King 54

Zeman, Karel The Christmas Dream • Vánoční Sen 45*; The Hamster • Křeček 46; A Horseshoe for Luck • Podkova pro Štěstí 46; Brigády • Mr. Prokouk Leaves for Volunteer Work • Mr. Prokouk on a Brigade • Pan Prokouk Jede na Brigádu 47; Mr. Prokouk and the Red Tape • Mr. Prokouk in the Office • Pan Prokouk Úřaduje 47; Mr. Prokouk in Temptation • Pan Prokouk v Pokušení • The Temptation of Mr. Prokouk 47; Mr. Prokouk Is Filming • Mr. Prokouk Makes a Film • Pan Prokouk Filmuje 48; Mr. Prokouk the Inventor • Pan Prokouk Vynálezcem 48; Inspirace • Inspiration 49; King Lavra • Král Lávra 50; Poklad Ptačího Ostrova • The Treasure of Bird Island 52; Cesta do Pravěku • A Journey Into Prehistory • A Journey Into Primeval Times • A Journey to Primeval Times • Journey to the Beginning of Time • Voyage to Prehistory 54; Mr. Prokouk the Animal Fancier • Mr. Prokouk the Animal Lover • Pan Prokouk, Přítel Zvířátek 55; The Deadly Invention • The Diabolical Invention • The Fabulous World of Jules Verne • The Fantastic Invention • An Invention for Destruction • Invention of Destruction • Vynález Zkázy • Weapons of Destruction 57; Baron Münchhausen • Baron Prášil • The Fabulous Baron Münchhausen • The Original Fabulous Adventures of Baron Münchausen 61; Bláznova Kronika • Dva Mušketýři • The Jester's Tale 64; The Stolen Airship • The Stolen Dirigible • Two Years Holiday • Ukradená Vzducholod' 66; Archa Pana Servadaca • Hector Servadac's Ark • Mr. Zervadac's Ark • Na Kometě • On a Comet • On the Comet 68; Pohádky Tisíce a Jedné Noci • A Thousand and One Nights 74; Čarodějův Učeň • Krabat 77; Pohádka o Honzíkovi a Mařence • The Tale of John and Mary 80

Zemann, E. Das Krankheitsbild des Schlachtener—Problem Unteroffiziers in der Endsehlacht 71*

Zemeckis, Robert I Wanna Hold Your Hand 77; Used Cars 80; Romancing the Stone 84; Back to the Future 85; Who Framed Roger Rabbit? 87*; Back to the Future Part II 89; Back to the Future Part III 90

Zemgano, I. Pauki • The Spider 42*

Zeming, Zhang *see* Zhang, Zeming

Zens, Will Capture That Capsule 61; Spy Squad 61; The Starfighters 64; To the Shores of Hell 66; Hell on Wheels 67; Hot Summer in Barefoot County 74; Truckin' Man 75; The Agitators • The Fix 85

Zenyakin, A. Inside the U.S.S.R. 61*

Zerlett, Hans Knock-Out 35*; Die Selige Exzellenz 37; Truxa 37; Es Leuchten die Sterne • The Stars Shine 38

Zervos, Nikos Dracula ton Exarchia 83

Zetterling, Mai The War Game 61; Älskande Par • Loving Couples 64; Längtan • Nattlek • Night Games 65; Dr. Glas • Doktor Glas 67; Flickorna • The Girls 68; Olympic Visions • Visions of Eight 72*; Vi Har Många Namn • We Have Many Faces • We Have Many Names 75; Of Seals and Man 78; Love 81*; Scrubbers 82; Amorosa 86

Zguridi, Alexander In the Depths of the Sea 38*; The Power of Life 40; In the Sands of Central Asia 43; White Fang 46; Real Life in the Forest 50; In the Icy Ocean 52; Life in the Arctic 53; The Story of a Forest Giant 56; In the Pacific 57; Jungle Track 59; In the Steps of Our Ancestors 61; Magnificent Islands 65; Forest Symphony 67

Zhai, Jiang Daughters of China • Zhonghua Nuer 49*

Zhakov, Oleg Invasion • Nashestviye 45*

Zhalakyavichus, Vitautas see *Zalakevicius, Vytautas*

Zhandov, Zahari Alarm • Tregova 49; The September Heroes • Septembrists • Septemvriisti 52; Earth • The Land • Zemlya 57; Beyond the Horizon • Otvad Horizonta 60; The Black River • Chernata Reka 64; Shibil 68

Zhang, Jun Zhao Huguan • The Shining Arc 89

Zhang, Luanxin Qingchun Ji • Sacrifice of Youth 86

Zhang, Qi Bei Aiqing Yiwangde Jiaoluo • A Love-Forsaken Corner 86*

Zhang, Wanting Feifa Yimin • The Illegal Immigrant 86

Zhang, Yi Hang-Sheng, My Son • Wo Erh Han-Sheng 86; Jade Love • Yu Qing Sao 86; Kuei-Mei • Kuei-Mei—A Woman • Wo Che-Yang Kuo-Le Yi-Sheng 86; Wo-Te Ai 88

Zhang, Yimou Hong Gaoliang • Red Sorghum 87; Ju Dou • Judou 89

Zhang, Zeming Jue Xiang • Swan Song 86

Zhao, Li see *Li, Zhao*

Zhao, Zhang Jun see *Zhang, Jun Zhao*

Zhelyabuzhsky, Yuri Children, Flowers of Life 19; Domestic-Agitator 20; Cigarette Girl from Mosselprom • The Cigarette Girl of Mosselprom 24; Father Frost 24; The Station Master 28*; Red and White 32

Zheng, Cao see *Cao, Zheng*

Zheng, Dongtian Neighbors 85*

Zheng, Junli The River Flows East in the Spring • Spring River Flows East • Yijiang Chunshui Xiang Dong Liu 47*; Crows and Sparrows • Wuya yu Maque 49

Zhifang, Bao see *Bao, Zhifang*

Zhifeng, Ling see *Ling, Zhifeng*

Zhihong, Gui see *Gui, Zhihong*

Zhilin, Victor My Daughter 60

Zhong, Huangjian see *Huang, Jianxin*

Zhong, Sun see *Chung, Sun*

Zhou, Xiaowen Desperation: The Last Frenzy • Obsession • Zui Hou De Feng Kuang 89

Zhuangzhuang, Tian see *Tian, Zhuangzhuang*

Zhuravlev, Vasili The Cosmic Voyage • Kosmitchesky Reis • The Space Ship 35

Zi, Ling see *Ling, Zi*

Zichy, Theodore Death Was a Passenger 58; Mingaloo 58; Portrait of a Matador 58; Night Without Pity 62; Doomsday at Eleven 63

Zidi, Claude Les Bidasses en Folie 72; Les Fous du Stade 72; Le Grand Bazar 73; Les Bidasses S'en Vont en Guerre 74; Lucky Pierre • La Moutarde Me Monte au Nez 74; La Course à l'Échalotte • The Wild Goose Chase 75; L'Aile ou la Cuisse 76; L'Animal 77; La Zizanie 78; Dumb But Disciplined 79; Banzai 83; Le Cop • My New Partner • Les Ripoux 84; Les Rois du Gag 85; L'Association des Malfaiteurs • The Association of Wrongdoers 87; Deux 89

Zieff, Howard Slither 73; Hearts of the West • Hollywood Cowboy 75; House Calls 78; The Main Event 79; Private Benjamin 80; Unfaithfully Yours 83; The Dream Team 89

Ziehm, Howard Flesh Gordon 74*

Zielinski, Rafal Hey Babe! 80; Screwballs 83; Loose Screws 85; Recruits 86; Valet Girls 86; Spellcaster 87; State Park 87; Screwball Hotel 88

Ziener, Bruno Die Bettelgräfin 18*

Ziewer, Christian Der Tod des Weissen Pferdes 85

Zifeng, Ling see *Ling, Zhifeng*

Ziffer-Teschenbruck, Mano Parema, Creature from the Starworld 22

Zika, Damouré La 504 et les Foudroyers 74*; Cocorico, Monsieur Poulet 74*

Zikra, Samir What Happened Next Year 86

Zilahy, Gyula A Becsapott Újságíró • The Duped Journalist 14*; Tutyu and Totyo • Tutyu és Totyó 14*

Zilberg, Yoel see *Silberg, Joel*

Žilnik, Želimir Early Works • Rani Radovi 69; Beautiful Women Walking Around Town • Lijepe Žene Prolaze Kroz Grad 86

Zimmerman, Vernon Lemon Hearts 62; Deadhead Miles 71; Leader of the Pack • Unholy Rollers 72; Fade to Black 80

Zimmermann, Gisela Tot oder Lebendig 88

Zincone, Bruno Emmanuelle 6 88

Zingg, Gérard Ada dans la Jungle 88

Ziniu, Wu see *Wu, Ziniu*

Zinman, Zoe City News 83*

Zinnemann, Fred Menschen am Sonntag • People on Sunday 29*; Pescados • Redes • The Wave 34*; A Friend Indeed 37; The Story of Dr. Carver 38; That Mothers Might Live 38; They Live Again 38; Tracking the Sleeping Death 38; Weather Wizards 38; The Ash Can Fleet 39; Forgotten Victory 39; Help Wanted! 39; One Against the World 39; While America Sleeps 39; The Great Meddler 40; The Old South 40; Stuffie 40; A Way in the Wilderness 40; Forbidden Passage 41; The Lady or the Tiger? 41; Your Last Act 41; Eyes in the Night 42; Kid Glove Killer 42; The Seventh Cross 44; Army Brat • Little Mr. Jim 45; My Brother Talks to Horses 46; Die Gezeichneten • The Search 47; Act of Violence 48; Battle Stripe • The Men 50; Teresa 50; Benjy 51; High Noon 52; The Member of the Wedding 52; From Here to Eternity 53; Oklahoma! 55; A Hatful of Rain 57; The Nun's Story 58; The Old Man and the Sea 58*; The Sundowners 60; Behold a Pale Horse 63; A Man for All Seasons 66; The Day of the Jackal 73; Julia 77; Five Days One Summer 82

Zinner, Peter The Salamander 81

Ziolkowski, Fabrice L.A.X. 80

Zion, Allan Who's Crazy 65*

Zirinis, Costas The Last Wager • Telefteo Stichima 87

Zito, Joseph Abduction 75; The Grad-

uation • The Prowler • Rosemary's Killer 81; Friday the 13th—The Final Chapter 84; Missing in Action 84; Invasion U.S.A. 85; Red Scorpion 88

Živanović, Jovan Ostrva • Seduction by the Sea • Verführung am Meer 63

Zivelli, Joseph E. Wanderer of the West 27*

Zoch, Georg Schwarzwaldmädel 35; Der Vetter aus Dingsda 36; Ein Walzer für Dich 36; Der Lachende Dritte 38

Zoeberlein, Hans Stosstrupp 1917 35*

Zohar, Uri Not Mine to Love • Shlosha Yamin ve' Yeled • Three Days and a Child 67; Every Bastard a King • Every Man a King • Kol Mamzer Melech 68

Zolnay, Pál Embriók • Embryos 85

Zorrilla, José A. El Arreglo 83; A los Cuatro Vientos • Lauaxeta 87

Zschoche, Hermann Die Alleinseglerin 88

Zschokke, Matthias Der Wilde Mann 88

Zsoldos, Andor Father Knows Best • Jó az Öreg a Háznál 35*

Zsolnay, Pál see *Zolnay, Pál*

Zsombolyai, János Duty Free Marriage • Tullivapaa Avioliitto • Vámmentes Házasság 80

Zsurzs, Éva Abigail • Abigél 85

Zuber, René En Crête Sans les Dieux 34*; L'Orient Qui Vient 34*; Le Rezzou 34*; Fêtes de France 39*

Zucca, Pierre Rouge Gorge 85; Alouette, Je Te Plumerai 88

Zucker, David Airplane! 80*; Top Secret! 84*; Ruthless People 86*; The Naked Gun • The Naked Gun: From the Files of Police Squad! 88

Zucker, Jerry Airplane! 80*, Top Secret! 84*; Ruthless People 86*; Ghost 90

Zucker, Ralph see *Pupillo, Massimo*

Zuckerman, Michael Black Rainbow 66

Zugsmith, Albert Beauty and the Brain • The Beauty and the Robot • Sex Kittens Go to College 60; College Confidential! 60; The Private Lives of Adam and Eve 60*; Dondi 61; Confessions of an Opium Eater • Evils of Chinatown • Secrets of a Soul • Souls for Sale 62; Dog Eat Dog • Einer Frisst den Anderen • La Morte Vestita di Dollari • When Strangers Meet 64*; The Incredible Sex Revolution 65; The Chinese Room • Il Cuarto Chino 66; LSD—I Hate You! • Movie Star American Style, or LSD—I Hate You! 66; On Her Bed of Roses 66; Two Roses and a Golden Rod 69; The Very Friendly Neighbors 69

Zuker, Howard Chief Zabu 88*

Zukor, Lou Mighty Mouse in the Great Space Chase 83*

Żuławski, Andrzej L'Important C'Est d' Aimer • The Main Thing Is to Love 75; Possession 81; L'Amour Braque 85; Maladie d'Amour • Malady of Love 87*; Na Srebrnym Globie 88

Zuniga, Frank Further Adventures of the Wilderness Family • Further Adventures of the Wilderness Family, Part 2 • Wilderness Family, Part 2 78; The Golden Seal 83; Heartbreaker 83; What Color Is the Wind? 84; Fist Fighter 89

Zurinaga, Marcos Step Away 79; La Gran Fiesta 86; Tango Bar 88

Zurli, Guido Slave Girls of Sheba 64*; Thompson 1880 66; The Mad Butcher • The Mad Butcher of Vienna • Meat Is Meat • The Strangler of Vienna • Il Strangolatore di Vienna • The Vienna Strangler • Der Würger Kommt auf Leisen Socken 71

Zurlini, Valerio Favola del Cappello 49; Racconto del Quartiere • Storia di un Quartiere 49; Sorrida Prego 49; Miniature 50; Pugilatori 50; I Blues della Domenica 51; Il Mercato delle Facce 52; Serenata da un Soldo 52; Soldati in Città 52; La Stazione 52; Ventotte Tonnellate 53; Le Ragazze di San Frediano 54; Estate Violenta • Été Violent • Violent Summer • The Widow Is Willing 59; La Fille à la Valise • The Girl with a Suitcase • Pleasure Girl • La Ragazza con la Valigia 60; Cronaca Familiare • Family Diary 62; The Camp Followers • Le Soldatesse 64; Black Jesus • Out of Darkness • Seated at His Right • Seduto alla Sua Destra 67; La Prima Notte di Quiete 72; Le Désert des Tartares • The Desert of the Tartars • Il Deserto dei Tartari 76

Zuta, Daniel Boran—Time to Aim • Boran—Zeit zum Zielen 87

Zuylen, Eric van In for Treatment • Opname 79*; Beetle • Zjoek 87

Zweiback, Martin Cactus in the Snow • You Can't Have Everything 70

Zwerin, Charlotte The Beatles in New York • What's Happening • What's Happening! New York Meets the Beatles • What's Happening! The Beatles in the U.S.A. • Yeah! Yeah! Yeah! • Yeah! Yeah! Yeah! New York Meets the Beatles 64*; Salesman 68*; Gimme Shelter 70*; Running Fence 77*; Arshile Gorky 82; Dekooning on Dekooning 83; Islands 86*; Horowitz Plays Mozart 87*; Thelonious Monk: Straight, No Chaser 88

Zwick, Edward About Last Night... 86; Glory 89

Zwick, Joel Second Sight 89

Zwicky, Karl Contagion 88; Vicious 88

Zwoboda, André People of France • La Vie Est à Nous 36*; Croisières Sidérales 41; Daughter of the Sands • Desert Wedding • Noces de Sable 48; François Villon 50; Le Rhin, Fleuve International 52*

Żygaldo, Tomasz Childhood Scenes of Provincial Life • Sceny Dziecięce z Życia Prowincji 86

II. Films, Showing Director

@ 79 Stan Brakhage
$ 71 Richard Brooks
**** 67 Andy Warhol
"?" Motorist, The 06 Walter R. Booth
A 64 Jan Lenica
ABC Lifeline 31 Yasujiro Shimazu
ABC Murders, The 65 Frank Tashlin
ABC of Love, The 19 Léonce Perret
À Bientôt J'Espère 68 Chris Marker*
À Biribi 06 André Heuze
À Bout de Souffle 59 Jean-Luc Godard
A Briglia Sciolta 61 Jean Aurel, Jack Dunn Trop, Roger Vadim
AC/DC: Let There Be Rock 82 Eric Dionysius, Eric Mistler
À Cause, à Cause d'une Femme 62 Michel Deville
A Cavallo della Tigre 61 Luigi Comencini
À Chacun Son Enfer 76 André Cayatte
À Chacun Son Paradis 57 Luciano Emmer, Robert Enrico
A Ciascuno il Suo 66 Elio Petri
À Cœur Joie 67 Serge Bourguignon
A Colpi di Luce 85 Enzo G. Castellari
À Corps Perdu 88 Léa Pool
A Doppia Faccia 69 Riccardo Freda
A Doppia Mandata 59 Claude Chabrol
A Dos Aguas 87 Carlos Olguín
A-009 Missione Hong Kong 65 Ernst Hofbauer
À Double Tour 59 Claude Chabrol
A Esli Eto Lyubov 61 Yuli Raizman
A.F.P. Nous Communiqué, L' 58 Jean-Pierre Melville
A Fil di Spada 52 Carlo Ludovico Bragaglia
A Fior di Pelle 87 Gianluca Fumagalli
À Fleur de Peau 61 Claude Bernard-Aubert
À Fleur d'Eau 69 François Reichenbach
A Galope Sobre la Historia 82 Santiago Álvarez
À Gauche en Sortant de l'Ascenseur 88 Édouard Molinaro
A-Ge-Man 90 Juzo Itami
A Ghentar Si Muore Facile 67 Leon Klimovsky
AIDS—A Danger for Love 85 Hans Noever
AIDS—Die Schleichende Gefahr 85 Peter Grandl
AIDS—Gefahr für die Liebe 85 Hans Noever
A.K. 85 Chris Marker
AKA Cassius Clay 70 Jim Jacobs
À la Conquête de l'Air 01 Ferdinand Zecca
À la Conquête du Pôle 10 Georges Méliès
À la Française 62 Robert Parrish
À la Gare 25 Robert Saidreau
À la Mémoire du Rock 62 François Reichenbach
A la Orilla de un Palmar 38 Raphael J. Sevilla
A la Pálida Luz de la Luna 86 José María González Sinde
À la Poursuite du Vent 43 Roger Leenhardt
À la Recherche d'un Appartement 06 Alice Guy-Blaché

À la Salida Nos Vemos 86 Carlos Palau
À la Source, la Femme Aimée 66 Nelly Kaplan
A las Cinco de la Tarde 60 Juan Antonio Bardem
À l'Assaut des Aiguilles du Diable 42 Marcel Ichac
À l'Aube du Troisième Jour 62 Claude Bernard-Aubert
À l'Automne de la Vie 88 Ivan Chouinard
À l'Horizon du Sud 24 Marco De Gastyne
À l'Italienne 65 Nanni Loy
A lo Macho 39 A. Martin De Lucenay
À l'Ombre de Vatican 22 Gaston Ravel
À l'Ombre des Tombeaux 27 André Hugon
A los Cuatro Vientos 87 José A. Zorrilla
A Me Mi Piace 85 Enrico Montesano
A Mezzanotte Va la Ronda del Piacere 75 Marcello Fondato
À Mi-Chemin du Ciel 29 Alberto Cavalcanti
À Mort l'Arbitre 83 Jean-Pierre Mocky
A Noi Piace Freddo! 60 Steno
À Nos Amours 83 Maurice Pialat
À Notre Regrettable Époux 88 Serge Korber
À Nous Deux 79 Claude Lelouch
À Nous Deux, Paris! 53 Pierre Kast
À Nous la Liberté! 31 René Clair
À Nous les Garçons 85 Michel Lang
À Nous les Petites Anglaises! 76 Michel Lang
A*P*E 76 Paul Leder
…A Pátý Jezdec Je Strach 65 Zbyněk Brynych
À Pied à Cheval et en Spoutnik 58 Jean Dréville
A Porte Chiuse 60 Dino Risi
À Pozdravuji Vlaštovky 72 Jaromil Jireš
À President-Elect Roosevelt 05 Georges Méliès
À Propos de Jivago 62 Alexander Alexeïeff, Claire Parker
À Propos de Nice 29 Jean Vigo
À Propos de Nice, Point de Vue Documentée 29 Jean Vigo
À Propos de Vigo 84 Manoel De Oliveira
À Propos d'une Rivière 55 Georges Franju
À Propos of the Truce with Finland 44 Yuli Raizman
A Proposito Luciano 73 Francesco Rosi
A Proposito Lucky Luciano 73 Francesco Rosi
À Quelques Jours Près… 68 Yves Ciampi
À Quoi Rêvent les Jeunes Filles 25 Henri Chomette
A Sega Nakude 88 Rangel Vulchanov
A to Z 56 Michael Snow
À Toi de Faire Mignonne 63 Bernard Borderie
À Tout Casser 67 John Berry
À Tout Prendre 63 Claude Jutra
À Toute Allure 81 Robert Kramer
A Tu per Tu 84 Sergio Corbucci
A Valparaíso 62 Joris Ivens
À Venise, Une Nuit 37 Christian-Jaque
À Vol d'Oiseau 62 Christopher Miles
A.W.O.L. 72 Herb Freed
A.W.O.L. 90 Sheldon Lettich

A.W.S. 16 Harry Buss
A-009 Missione Hong Kong 65 Ernst Hofbauer
A 077 Sfida ai Killers 67 Antonio Margheriti
Aa Furusato 38 Kenji Mizoguchi
Aa Kaigun 70 Mitsuo Murayama
Aa Koe Naki Tomo 72 Tadashi Imai
Aa Kokyō 38 Kenji Mizoguchi
Aa Tokumukan Kantō 25 Kenji Mizoguchi*
Aag 48 Raj Kapoor
Aah…Belinda 86 Atıf Yılmaz
Aaj ka Robin Hood 87 Tapan Sinha
Aakaler Sandhane 80 Mrinal Sen
Aakhri Nischay 88 K. C. Aggarwal
Aamua Kaupungissa 54 Jörn Donner
Aan 52 Ramjankhan Mehboobkhan
Aanslag, De 86 Fons Rademakers
Aapathbandhava 88 A. T. Raghu
Aardolie 53 Bert Haanstra
Aaron Loves Angela 75 Gordon Parks, Jr.
Aaron Slick from Punkin Crick 52 Claude Binyon
Aaron's Rod 23 A. E. Coleby
Aasphota 88 T. S. Nagabharana
Ab Heute Erwachsen 86 Günther Scholz
Ab Mitternacht 38 Karl Hoffmann
Ab Urbe Condita 65 Jan Łomnicki
Abaeté—A Seed of Vengeance 86 Zelito Viana
Abaeté—A Semente da Vinganca 86 Zelito Viana
Abagail Leslie Is Back in Town 74 Joe Sarno
Abandon Ship! 57 Richard Sale
Abandonadas, Las 44 Emilio Fernández
Abandoned 49 Joseph M. Newman
Abandoned Woman 49 Joseph M. Newman
Abandonment, The 16 Donald Mac-Donald
Abare Goemon 66 Hiroshi Inagaki
Abarenbō Kaidō 57 Tomu Uchida
Abasheshey 62 Mrinal Sen
Abastecimento, Nova Política 68 Nelson Pereira Dos Santos
Abastecimiento 73 Raúl Ruiz
Abba Ganuv 88 Yankul Goldwasser
Abba—The Movie 77 Lasse Hallström
Abbasso lo Zio 61 Marco Bellocchio
Abbé Constantin, L' 25 Julien Duvivier
Abbes 87 Mohamed Tazi
Abbey Grange, The 22 George Ridgwell
Abbott and Costello Go to Mars 53 Charles Lamont
Abbott and Costello in Hollywood 45 S. Sylvan Simon
Abbott and Costello in Society 44 Jean Yarbrough
Abbott and Costello in the Foreign Legion 50 Charles Lamont
Abbott and Costello in the Navy 41 Arthur Lubin
Abbott and Costello Lost in Alaska 52 Jean Yarbrough
Abbott and Costello Meet Captain Kidd 52 Charles Lamont
Abbott and Costello Meet Dr. Jekyll and Mr. Hyde 53 Charles Lamont

Abbott and Costello Meet Frankenstein *48*
Charles Barton
Abbott and Costello Meet the Ghosts *48*
Charles Barton
Abbott and Costello Meet the Invisible
Man *51* Charles Lamont
Abbott and Costello Meet the Keystone
Kops *55* Charles Lamont
Abbott and Costello Meet the Killer, Boris
Karloff *49* Charles Barton
Abbott and Costello Meet the Mummy *55*
Charles Lamont
Abby *74* William Girdler
Abdication, The *74* Anthony Harvey
Abducted *86* Boon Collins
Abduction, The *38* Géza von Bolváry
Abduction *75* Joseph Zito
Abductors, The *57* Andrew V. McLaglen
Abductors, The *72* Don Schain
Abdul the Damned *35* Karl Grüne
Abdullah the Great *54* Gregory Ratoff
Abdullah's Harem *54* Gregory Ratoff
Abe Gets Even with Father *11* Mack Sennett
Abe Lincoln in Illinois *40* John Cromwell
Abe Lincoln of Ninth Avenue, The *39*
William Nigh
Abel *85* Alex van Warmerdam
Abel Gance et Son Napoléon *83* Nelly
Kaplan
Abel Gance, Hier et Demain *63* Nelly
Kaplan
Abel Gance's Beethoven *36* Abel Gance
Abel mit der Mundharmonika *34* Erich
Waschneck
Abend...Nacht...Morgen *20* F. W.
Murnau
Abenteuer, Das *21* Lothar Mendes
Abenteuer der Thea Roland, Das *32*
Henry Koster
Abenteuer des Doktor Dolittle, Die *28*
Lotte Reiniger
Abenteuer des Kay Hoog, Die *19* Fritz
Lang
Abenteuer des Prinzen Achmed, Die *26*
Lotte Reiniger
Abenteuer des Till Eulenspiegel, Die *56*
Joris Ivens, Gérard Philipe
Abenteuer des Werner Holt, Die *63*
Joachim Kunert
Abenteuer einer Schönen Frau, Das *32*
Henry Koster
Abenteuer eines Jungen Herrn in Polen *34*
Gustav Fröhlich
Abenteuer eines Zehnmarkscheines, Die
26 Berthold Viertel
Abenteuer Geht Weiter, Das *39* Carmine
Gallone
Abenteuer in Warschau *37* Carl Boese
Abenteurer, Der *21* Lothar Mendes
Abenteurer von Paris, Der *37* Karl Heinz
Martin
Aberglaube *40* Walter Ruttmann
Abgrund der Seelen, Der *20* Urban Gad
Abhijan *62* Satyajit Ray
Abhimanyu *89* Tony Juneja
Abhinandana *88* Ashok Kumar
Abide with Me *15* Geoffrey H. Malins
Abide with Me *16* Tom Watts
Abide with Me *28* J. Steven Edwards, H.

B. Parkinson
Abidjan, Port de Pêche *62* Jean Rouch
Abie Kabibble Outwitting His Rival *17*
Gregory La Cava
Abierto de 18 a 24 *88* Victor Dinenzon
Abie's Imported Bride *25* Roy Calnek
Abie's Irish Rose *28* Victor Fleming
Abie's Irish Rose *46* A. Edward Sutherland
Abigail *85* Éva Zsurzs
Abigél *85* Éva Zsurzs
Abilene Town *45* Edwin L. Marin
Abilene Trail *51* Lewis D. Collins
Abismos de Pasión *52* Luis Buñuel
Abito Nero da Sposa, L' *43* Luigi Zampa
Able Seaman Brown *51* Roy Boulting
Abnormal *66* Takashi Shiga
Abominable Dr. Phibes, The *71* Robert
Fuest
Abominable Homme des Douanes, L' *63*
Marc Allégret
Abominable Snow Rabbit, The *61* Chuck
Jones
Abominable Snowman, The *57* Val Guest
Abominable Snowman of the Himalayas,
The *57* Val Guest
Abortion *24* Grigori Lemberg
About a River *55* Georges Franju
About Argentina *86* Werner Schroeter
About Face *42* Kurt Neumann
About Face *52* Roy Del Ruth
About Last Night... *86* Edward Zwick
About Love *87* Mats Arehn
About Me: A Musical *71* Robert Frank
About Mrs. Leslie *54* Daniel Mann
About Napoleon *27* Abel Gance
About Something Else *63* Věra Chytilová
About Trial Marriage *28* William Hughes
Curran
About Twenty Years Old *50* Kozaburo
Yoshimura
Above All Law *21* Fritz Lang, Joe May
Above All Laws *47* Phil Karlson
Above and Below Stairs *05* Percy Stow
Above and Beyond *52* Melvin Frank, Norman Panama
Above Rubies *32* Frank Richardson
Above Suspicion *43* Richard Thorpe
Above the Clouds *33* Roy William Neill
Above the Horizon *66* Roman Kroitor,
Hugh O'Connor
Above the Law *88* Andrew Davis
Above Us the Waves *55* Ralph Thomas
Abracadabra *57* Dušan Vukotić
Abraham and the Opossum *16* Harry S.
Palmer
Abraham Bosse *72* Roger Leenhardt
Abraham Lincoln *24* Phil Rosen
Abraham Lincoln *30* D. W. Griffith
Abraham Our Patriarch *33* George Roland
Abrakadabra *57* Dušan Vukotić
Abrégeons les Formalités! *16* Jacques Feyder
Abril de Girón *66* Santiago Álvarez
Abril de Vietnam en el Año del Gato *75*
Santiago Álvarez
Abroad with Two Yanks *44* Allan Dwan
Absalon *12* Henri Andréani
Abschied *30* Robert Siodmak
Abschied der Götter *59* Gottfried
Reinhardt

Abschied von den Wolken *59* Gottfried
Reinhardt
Abschied von Fälschen Paradies *89* Tevfik
Baser
Abschied von Gestern *66* Alexander Kluge
Absence *76* Stan Brakhage
Absence Makes the Heart Grow Fonder *25*
Alexander Butler
Absence of Malice *81* Sydney Pollack
Absences *87* Yorgos Katakouzinos
Absent *28* Harry A. Gant
Absent-Minded *75* Pierre Richard
Absent-Minded Bootblack, The *03* Cecil
M. Hepworth
Absent-Minded Jones *10* Fred Rains
Absent-Minded Lecturer *1899* Georges
Méliès
Absent-Minded Man, The *07* Lewin Fitzhamon
Absent Minded Poet, The *23* Herbert M.
Dawley
Absent-Minded Professor, The *07* Percy
Stow
Absent-Minded Professor, The *60* Robert
Stevenson
Absent Minded Willie *17* Harry S. Palmer
Absentee, The *15* Christy Cabanne, Frank
E. Woods
Absentee, The *85* Zsolt Kézdi-Kovács
Absinthe *13* Herbert Brenon
Absinthe *29* Lionel Barrymore
Absolutamente Certo *57* Anselmo Duarte
Absolute Beginners *86* Julien Temple
Absolute Quiet *36* George B. Seitz
Absolution, L' *22* Jean Kemm
Absolution *78* Anthony Page
Absorbing Game, An *11* Lewin Fitzhamon
Absorbing Tale, An *09* Walter R. Booth
Abstract *27* Marcel Duchamp
Abstract Film Exercise No. 1 *43* James
Whitney, John Whitney
Abstract Film Exercise No. 4 and 5 *44*
James Whitney, John Whitney
Absurd *81* Aristide Massaccesi
Absurd—Anthropophagous II *81* Aristide
Massaccesi
Abuna Messias *39* Goffredo Alessandrini,
Alessandro Blasetti
Abus de Confiance *37* Henri Decoin
Abuse *83* Arthur Bressan, Jr.
Abuse of Confidence *37* Henri Decoin
Abused Confidence *37* Henri Decoin
Abwärts *84* Carl Schenkel
Abwege *28* G. W. Pabst
Abysmal Brute, The *23* Hobart Henley
Abysmal Brute, The *36* David Howard
Abyss, The *10* Urban Gad
Abyss *55* László Ranódy
Abyss, The *88* André Delvaux
Abyss, The *89* James Cameron
Abysses, Les *62* Nikos Papatakis
Aç Kurtlar *69* Yılmaz Güney
Academician Ivan Pavlov *49* Grigori
Roshal
Academy Decides, The *37* John Baxter
Academy for Young Ladies *1896* Georges
Méliès
Academy Newsreel *61* Věra Chytilová
Acadie, l'Acadie!, L' *70* Michel Brault,
Pierre Perrault

Acapulco *51* Emilio Fernández
Acapulco Gold *78* Burt Brinckerhoff
Accattone! *61* Pier Paolo Pasolini
Accent on Horror *47* Christy Cabanne
Accent on Love *41* Ray McCarey
Accent on Youth *35* Wesley Ruggles
Acceptable Levels *83* John Davies
Access Code *84* Mark S. Sobel
Accession of the Romanov Dynasty *13* Pyotr Chardynin, Vasili M. Goncharov
Accessories *87* Ina Tumanyan
Accetta per la Luna di Miele, Un' *69* Mario Bava.
Acciaio *32* Walter Ruttmann
Accident, L' *12* Louis Feuillade
Accident *28* Ernö Metzner
Accident, L' *62* Edmond T. Gréville
Accident, The *62* Edmond T. Gréville
Accident *67* Joseph Losey
Accident *83* Donald Brittain
Accident, An *85* Antonín Kopřiva
Accident Attorney, The *18* Raoul Barré, Charles Bowers
Accident d'Auto, Un *07* Louis Feuillade
Accident Insurance *13* Phillips Smalley
Accidental Accidents *24* Leo McCarey
Accidental Death *63* Geoffrey Nethercott
Accidental Honeymoon, The *18* Léonce Perret
Accidental Spy *37* Randall Faye
Accidental Tourist, The *88* Lawrence Kasdan
Accidental Treatment *29* Thomas Bentley
Accidents Can Happen *25* Charles Lamont
Accidents Never Happen Singly *03* Georges Méliès
Accidents Wanted *33* Jack Conway
Accidents Will Happen *07* Walter R. Booth
Accidents Will Happen *11* H. Oceano Martinek
Accidents Will Happen *20* Wallace A. Carlson
Accidents Will Happen *38* William Clemens
Accidents Won't Happen *25* Charles Bowers
Accompanied on the Tomtom *10* A. E. Coleby
Accomplice, The *15* James W. Horne
Accomplice, The *17* Ralph Dean
Accomplice *46* Walter Colmes
Accomplices, The *59* Gianni Vernuccio
Accomplished Fact, An *85* Luis R. Vera
Accordeur, L' *33* Jean Grémillon
According to Hoyle *22* W. S. Van Dyke
According to Law *16* Richard Garrick
According to Mrs. Hoyle *51* Jean Yarbrough
According to the Code *16* Elisha H. Calvert
According to the Law *57* Peter Weiss
According to Value *15* Frank Lloyd
Accordion *34* Igor Savchenko
Accordion Joe *29* Dave Fleischer
Accordionist's Wedding, The *86* Luis Fernando Bottia
Account Rendered *32* Leslie Howard Gordon
Account Rendered *57* Peter Graham Scott
Accountant *33* Martin Frič

Accroche-Cœur *87* Chantal Picault
Accursed, The *57* Michael McCarthy
Accusateur, L' *20* Édouard E. Violet
Accusation, The *14* Harry C. Myers
Accused *25* Del Henderson
Accused *36* Thornton Freeland
Accused, The *48* William Dieterle
Accused, The *53* Lawrence Huntington, Charles Saunders
Accused *57* Michael Audley, Gilbert Gunn
Accused, The *63* Ján Kadár, Elmar Klos
Accused, The *87* Josef Heifits
Accused, The *88* Jonathan Kaplan
Accused of Murder *56* Joseph Kane
Accused, Stand Up! *30* Maurice Tourneur
Accusée, Levez-Vous! *30* Maurice Tourneur
Accuser, The *78* Jean-Louis Bertucelli
Accusing Finger, The *36* James P. Hogan
Accusing Past, The *38* David Selman
Ace, The *79* Lewis John Carlino
Ace and a Joker, An *18* Raoul Barré, Charles Bowers
Ace Cinemagazine *36* Francis Searle
Ace Drummond *36* Ford Beebe, Clifford Smith
Ace Eli and Rodger of the Skies *73* John Erman
Ace High *18* Lynn Reynolds
Ace High *68* Giuseppe Colizzi
Ace in the Hole *51* Billy Wilder
Ace Lucky *52* Edward Bernds
Ace of Aces *33* J. Walter Ruben
Ace of Aces *82* Gérard Oury
Ace of Action *26* William Bertram
Ace of Cactus Range *24* Victor Adamson, Malon Andrus
Ace of Cads, The *26* Luther Reed
Ace of Clubs, The *26* John P. McGowan
Ace of Hearts, The *16* Charles C. Calvert
Ace of Hearts, The *21* Wallace Worsley
Ace of Scotland Yard, The *29* Ray Taylor
Ace of Spades, The *31* Dave Fleischer
Ace of Spades, The *35* George Pearson
Ace of the Saddle, The *19* John Ford
Ace of Thieves *15* Mauritz Stiller
Ace of Trouble, The *34* George B. Samuelson
Ace Up My Sleeve, An *75* Ivan Passer
Aces and Eights *36* Sam Newfield
Aces Go Places III: Our Man from Bond Street *84* Hark Tsui
Aces Go Places IV *86* Ringo Lam
Aces High *76* Jack Gold
Aces of Contraband, The *86* Fernando Durán
Aces Wild *36* Harry Fraser
Ach! Jodel Mir Noch Einen — Stosstrupp Venus Bläst zum Angriff *73* Hans Sternbeck
Achalgazrda Kompozitoris Mogzauroba *86* Georgy Shengelaya
Achilles' Heel *32* Christian-Jaque
Achoo Mr. Keroochev *59* Stan Vanderbeek
Achraroumès *78* Sergei Paradzhanov
Acht Entfesselten, Die *39* Helmut Käutner
08/15 *54* Paul Ostermayer
08/15 in der Heimat *55* Paul Ostermayer

08/15, II Teil *55* Paul Ostermayer
Acht Mädels im Boot *32* Erich Waschneck
Acht Mal Acht *56* Jean Cocteau, Hans Richter
8 x 8 *56* Jean Cocteau, Hans Richter
Acht Stunden Sind Kein Tag *72* Rainer Werner Fassbinder
Acht Stunden Sind Kein Tag: Eine Familienserie *72* Rainer Werner Fassbinder
Acht Tage Glück *31* Robert Wiene
Achte Wochentag, Der *57* Aleksander Ford
48 Stunden bis Acapulco *68* Klaus Lemke
Achtung! Banditi! *51* Carlo Lizzani
Acı *71* Yılmaz Güney
Acid Eaters, The *68* B. Ron Elliott
Acid Test, The *24* Sinclair Hill
Aciéries de la Marine et d'Homecourt, Les *25* Jean Grémillon
Acoso, El *64* Humberto Solás
Acostates Første Offer *15* Forest Holger-Madsen
Acqua and Sapone *83* Carlo Verdone
Acqua e Sapone *83* Carlo Verdone
Acquittal, The *23* Clarence Brown
Acquitted *13* August Blom
Acquitted *16* Paul Powell
Acquitted *29* Frank R. Strayer
Acres of Turf *35* Serge De Poligny
Acrobate, L' *41* Jean Boyer
Acrobatic Toys *08* Émile Cohl
Acrobatic Tramps, The *02* James A. Williamson
Acrobatty Bunny *46* Robert McKimson
Across Darkness *59* Yasuzo Masumura
Across 110th Street *72* Barry Shear
Across the Arax *46* Esther Shub
Across the Atlantic *13* Herbert Brenon
Across the Atlantic *28* Howard Bretherton
Across the Badlands *50* Fred F. Sears
Across the Border *22* Charles R. Seeling
Across the Bridge *57* Ken Annakin
Across the Continent *22* Phil Rosen
Across the Deadline *22* Jack Conway
Across the Deadline *25* Leo D. Maloney
Across the Divide *21* John Holloway
Across the Great Divide *21* John Holloway
Across the Great Divide *76* Stewart Raffill
Across the Heart *87* Robert Kramer
Across the Mexican Line *11* Alice Guy-Blaché
Across the Pacific *14* Edwin Carewe
Across the Pacific *26* Roy Del Ruth
Across the Pacific *42* John Huston, Vincent Sherman
Across the Plains *11* Gilbert M. Anderson
Across the Plains *12* Thomas Ince
Across the Plains *28* Robert J. Horner
Across the Plains *39* Spencer G. Bennet
Across the Rio Grande *49* Oliver Drake
Across the River *65* Stefan Sharff
Across the Sahara *33* Walter Summers
Across the Sierras *41* D. Ross Lederman
Across the Stream and Fire *68* Gleb Panfilov
Across the Wide Missouri *51* William A. Wellman
Across the Wires *15* Ernest G. Batley
Across the World with Mr. and Mrs. Johnson *30* Martin E. Johnson

Across to Singapore *28* William Nigh
Act, The *84* Sig Shore
Act Five, Scene Seven: Fritz Kortner Rehearses Kabale und Liebe *65* Hans-Jürgen Syberberg
Act of Aggression *75* Gérard Pirès
Act of God *81* Peter Greenaway
Act of Love *53* Anatole Litvak
Act of Murder, An *48* Michael Gordon
Act of Murder *64* Alan Bridges
Act of Piracy *88* John Cardos
Act of Seeing with One's Own Eyes, The *70* Stan Brakhage
Act of the Heart *70* Paul Almond
Act of Vengeance *74* Robert Kelljan
Act of Violence *48* Fred Zinnemann
Act One *63* Dore Schary
Acta General de Chile *86* Miguel Littin
Actas de Marusia *75* Miguel Littin
Acte d'Amour, Un *53* Anatole Litvak
Acteón *64* Jorge Grau
Acting — Lee Strasberg and the Actors Studio *81* Herbert Kline
Action *21* John Ford
Action *79* Tinto Brass
Action *87* Vladimir Shamshurin
Action at Mironov, The *19* Dziga Vertov
Action B *51* Martin Frič
Action Craver, The *27* Victor Potel
Action for Slander *37* Victor Saville, Tim Whelan
Action Galore *25* Robert Eddy
Action in Arabia *44* Léonide Moguy
Action in the North Atlantic *43* Lloyd Bacon
Action Jackson *88* Craig R. Baxley
Action Man *66* Jean Delannoy
Action of the Tiger *57* Terence Young
Action Stations! *42* Joris Ivens
Action Stations *57* Cecil H. Williamson
Action: The October Crisis of 1970 *74* Robin Spry
Activist, The *69* Art Napoleon
Actor Jesenius' Strange Friendships *85* Karel Steklý
Actors, The *41* G. W. Pabst
Actors and Sin *52* Lee Garmes, Ben Hecht
Actor's Artifice, The *11* Percy Stow
Actor's Revenge, An *63* Kon Ichikawa
Actress, The *23* Alexander Ivanovsky
Actress, The *28* Sidney Franklin
Actress, The *43* Leonid Trauberg
Actress *47* Teinosuke Kinugasa
Actress, The *53* George Cukor
Actress, An *56* Kaneto Shindo
Actress *87* Kon Ichikawa
Actress and Angel *28* Richard Wallace
Actress and the Cowboys, The *11* Allan Dwan
Actress and the Poet, The *35* Mikio Naruse
Acts of the Apostles *68* Roberto Rossellini
Actualités Québecoises *68* Arthur Lamothe*
Actualización Política y Doctrinaria para la Toma del Poder *71* Octavio Getino, Fernando Solanas
Acusación, La *65* Humberto Solás
Ad Ogni Costo *68* Giuliano Montaldo
Ad Uno ad

Uno . . . Spietatomente *68* Rafael Romero Marchent
Ada *61* Daniel Mann
Ada *86* Milutin Kosovac
Ada dans la Jungle *88* Gérard Zingg
Ada — To Nie Wypada *37* Z. Mayflower
Adada *88* Kwon-taek Im
Adagio for Election Day *49* Sidney Peterson
Ådalen Riots, The *68* Bo Widerberg
Ådalen '31 *68* Bo Widerberg
Adam and Eva *23* Robert Vignola
Adam and Evalyn *49* Harold French
Adam and Eve *56* Alberto Gout
Adam and Evelyne *49* Harold French
Adam and Evil *27* Robert Z. Leonard
Adam and Nicole *75* Trevor Wren
Adam As a Special Constable *18* J. L. V. Leigh
Adam at 6 A.M. *70* Robert Scheerer
Adam Bede *18* Maurice Elvey
Adam Had Four Sons *41* Gregory Ratoff
Adam II *68* Jan Lenica
Adam und Eva *28* Reinhold Schünzel
Adam Wants to Be a Man *59* Vytautas Zalakevicius
Adam y Eva *56* Alberto Gout
Adam's Apple *27* Tim Whelan
Adam's Film Review *24* Harry Hughes
Adam's Rib *22* Cecil B. DeMille
Adam's Rib *49* George Cukor
Adam's Tree *37* Mario Bonnard
Adam's Woman *69* Philip Leacock
Adamson of Africa *59* Richard Thorpe
Adauchi *64* Tadashi Imai
Adauchi Senshō *31* Tomu Uchida
Addict *71* Ivan Passer
Adding Machine, The *68* Jerome Epstein
Addio Fratello Crudele *73* Giuseppe Patroni Griffi
Addio Giovinezza! *18* Augusto Genina
Addio Giovinezza! *27* Augusto Genina
Addio Giovinezza! *40* Ferdinando Maria Poggioli
Addio Mia Bella Napoli! *46* Mario Bonnard
Addio Mimi *47* Carmine Gallone
Addio per Sempre *57* Mario Costa
Addition, L' *83* Denis Amar
Addition and Subtraction *1899* Georges Méliès
Address by Lenin *29* Vladimir Petrov
Address Unknown *44* William Cameron Menzies
Adebar *57* Peter Kubelka
Adéla Ještě Nevečeřela *78* Oldřich Lipský
Adélaïde *69* Jean-Daniel Simon
Adele *19* Wallace Worsley
Adele Hasn't Had Her Supper Yet *78* Oldřich Lipský
Adelita, La *38* Guillermo Hernández Gómez
Adelmo *87* Rocco Mortelliti
Adémaï Bandit d'Honneur *42* Gilles Grangier
Aderyn Papur *84* Stephen Bayly
Adeus Português, Um *85* João Botelho
Adhémar Lampiot *32* Christian-Jaque, Paul Mesnier
Adhesion *12* Dave Aylott

Adhikar *38* Pramatesh Chandra Barua
Adholokam *88* Chellappan
Adhuri Kahani, Ek *71* Mrinal Sen
Adı Vasfiye *86* Atıf Yılmaz
Adieu Blaireau *85* Bob Decout
Adieu Bonaparte *84* Youssef Chahine
Adieu Chérie *46* Raymond Bernard
Adieu l'Ami *68* Jean Herman
Adieu Léonard *43* Pierre Prévert
Adieu les Beaux Jours *33* André Beaucler
Adieu les Copains *30* Léo Joannon
Adieu Mascotte *29* Wilhelm Thiele
Adieu Philippine *61* Jacques Rozier
Adieu Poulet *75* Pierre Granier-Deferre
Adieu Voyages Lents *78* Marie-Geneviève Ripeau
Adin i Dysach *34* Boris Barnet*
Adiós *30* Frank Lloyd
Adiós Amigo *75* Fred Williamson
Adiós de un Artista *10* Segundo De Chomón
Adiós, Gringo *65* Giorgio Stegani
Adiós, Nicanor *38* R. Portas
Adiós, Sabata *70* Gianfranco Parolini
Adjø Solidaritet *84* Petter Vennerød, Svend Wam
Adjustment and Work *86* Frederick Wiseman
Adjutant Seiner Hoheit, Der *33* Martin Frič
Adjutant to His Highness *33* Martin Frič
Adman, The *80* Michael Alexander
Admi *39* Rajaram Vanakudre Shantaram
Admirable Crichton, The *18* George B. Samuelson
Admirable Crichton, The *19* Cecil B. DeMille
Admirable Crichton, The *57* Lewis Gilbert
Admiral Nakhimov *46* Vsevolod I. Pudovkin, Dmitri Vasiliev
Admiral Ushakov, Part One *53* Mikhail Romm
Admiral Ushakov, Part Two *53* Mikhail Romm
Admiral Was a Lady, The *50* Albert S. Rogell
Admirals All *35* Joseph Losey
Admiral's Orders *15* Harold Weston
Admiral's Secret, The *34* Guy Newall
Admission Free *32* Dave Fleischer
Adolescence *41* Louis Gasnier
Adolescence *55* Heinosuke Gosho
Adolescent, The *78* Jeanne Moreau
Adolescent Girl, An *78* Jeanne Moreau
Adolescente, L' *78* Jeanne Moreau
Adolescentes, Les *64* Gian Vittorio Baldi, Michel Brault, Jean Rouch, Hiroshi Teshigahara
Adolescents, The *64* Gian Vittorio Baldi, Michel Brault, Jean Rouch, Hiroshi Teshigahara
Adolescenza *59* Francesco Maselli
Adolf and Marlene *76* Ulli Lommel
Adolf Armstrong *37* Sigurd Wallen
Adolf Hitler, My Part in His Downfall *72* Norman Cohen
Adolphe, or The Awkward Age *68* Bernard Toublanc-Michel
Adolphe ou L'Âge Tendre *68* Bernard Toublanc-Michel

Adomi *29* Rajaram Vanakudre Shantaram
Adopted Brother, The *12* Christy Cabanne
Adopted Child, The *11* Theo Bouwmeester
Adopted Father, The *33* John G. Adolfi
Adopted Son, The *17* Charles Brabin
Adopting a Baby *09* A. E. Coleby
Adoption *75* Márta Mészáros
Adoption, The *78* Marc Grunebaum
Adorable *33* William Dieterle
Adorable Cheat, The *28* Burton L. King
Adorable Corps de Deborah, L' *67* Romolo Guerrieri
Adorable Creatures *52* Christian-Jaque
Adorable Deceiver, The *26* Phil Rosen
Adorable Démons *56* Maurice Cloche
Adorable Idiot *63* Édouard Molinaro
Adorable Julia *62* Alfred Weidenmann
Adorable Liar *61* Michel Deville
Adorable Menteuse *61* Michel Deville
Adorable Savage, The *20* Norman Dawn
Adorables Canailles *67* Henri Jacques
Adorables Créatures *52* Christian-Jaque
Adoration *28* Frank Lloyd
Adoration *28* Andrew L. Stone
Adorazione, L' *88* Lucio Fulci
Adres Lenina *29* Vladimir Petrov
Adrian Troupe of Cyclists, The *01* George Albert Smith
Adrian und die Römer *88* Klaus Bub, Thomas Mauch
Adriana di Berteaux *10* Enrico Guazzoni
Adriana Lecouvreur *18* Ugo Falena
Adrienne Lecouvreur *13* Louis Mercanton*
Adrienne Lecouvreur *38* Marcel L'Herbier
Adrift *69* Ján Kadár, Elmar Klos
Adrift on Life's Tide *13* Warwick Buckland
Adua and Her Companions *60* Antonio Pietrangeli
Adua and Her Friends *60* Antonio Pietrangeli
Adua e le Compagne *60* Antonio Pietrangeli
Aduefue *88* Sijiri Bakaba
Adult Education *87* Bob Giraldi
Adultera, L' *11* Mario Caserini
Adulteress, The *53* Marcel Carné
Adulteress, The *58* Tadashi Imai
Adulteress, The *73* Norbert Meisel
Adulterio all'Italiana *66* Pasquale Festa Campanile
Adulterous Affair *66* Ted Leversuch
Adultery, Italian Style *66* Pasquale Festa Campanile
Advance to the Rear *63* George Marshall
Advantages of Hypnotism, The *11* A. E. Coleby
Advent of the Mother-in-Law, The *05* Tom Green
Adventuras del Oeste *64* Joaquín Luis Romero Marchent
Adventure, The *15* Mauritz Stiller
Adventure *25* Victor Fleming
Adventure *45* Victor Fleming
Adventure, The *59* Michelangelo Antonioni
Adventure for Two *43* Anthony Asquith
Adventure for Two, An *79* Claude Lelouch

Adventure Girl *34* Herman Raymaker
Adventure in a Harem, An *14* Forest Holger-Madsen
Adventure in Baltimore *48* John Cromwell, Richard Wallace
Adventure in Blackmail *41* Harold Huth, Roland Pertwee
Adventure in Diamonds *40* George Fitzmaurice
Adventure in Hearts, An *19* James Cruze
Adventure in Indochina *57* André Pergament
Adventure in Iraq *43* D. Ross Lederman
Adventure in Manhattan *36* Edward Ludwig
Adventure in Music *43* Reginald LeBorg, Ernest Mattray, S. K. Winston
Adventure in Odessa *54* Lev Atamanov
Adventure in Rio *55* Kurt Neumann
Adventure in Sahara *38* D. Ross Lederman
Adventure in the Autumn Woods, An *12* Christy Cabanne, D. W. Griffith
Adventure in the Bay of Gold, An *55* Břetislav Pojar
Adventure in the Hopfields *54* John Guillermin
Adventure in Warsaw *54* Leonard Buczkowski
Adventure in Washington *41* Alfred E. Green
Adventure Is a Hard Life *41* Martin Frič
Adventure Island *47* Sam Newfield
Adventure Limited *34* George King
Adventure Mad *28* Lothar Mendes
Adventure of Faustus Bidgood, The *86* Andy Jones, Michael Jones
Adventure of Salvator Rosa, An *39* Alessandro Blasetti
Adventure of the Action Hunters *82* Lee Bonner
Adventure of the Italian Model, The *12* Van Dyke Brooke
Adventure of the Retired Army Colonel, The *12* Van Dyke Brooke
Adventure of the Shooting Party, The *13* Lawrence Trimble
Adventure of Westgate Seminary, The *13* Lawrence Trimble
Adventure Shop, The *18* Kenneth Webb
Adventure Starts Here *65* Jörn Donner
Adventure Unlimited *45* Sam Newfield
Adventure While Strolling *11* August Blom
Adventurer, The *17* Charles Chaplin
Adventurer, The *17* Alice Guy-Blaché
Adventurer, The *20* J. Gordon Edwards
Adventurer, The *27* Victor Tourjansky, W. S. Van Dyke
Adventurer, The *67* Terence Young
Adventurer of Tortuga *64* Luigi Capuano
Adventurers, The *50* David MacDonald
Adventurers, The *69* Lewis Gilbert
Adventures at Rugby *40* Robert Stevenson
Adventure's End *37* Arthur Lubin
Adventures in Babysitting *87* Chris Columbus
Adventures in Bukhara *43* Yakov Protazanov
Adventures in Iraq *43* D. Ross Lederman
Adventures in Silverado *47* Phil Karlson

Adventures of ', The *56* Faith Hubley, John Hubley
Adventures of a Bad Shilling, The *13* Edwin J. Collins
Adventures of a Bath Chair *07* Percy Stow
Adventures of a Bill Poster, The *03* Percy Stow
Adventures of a Broker's Man *07* J. H. Martin
Adventures of a Brown Man in Search of Civilization *71* James Ivory
Adventures of a Dentist *65* Elem Klimov
Adventures of a Five Pound Note, The *10* Lewin Fitzhamon
Adventures of a Football, The *14* Stuart Kinder
Adventures of a Millionaire's Son, The *13* Forest Holger-Madsen
Adventures of a Nobleman *64* Wojciech Has
Adventures of a £100 Bank Note, The *05* J. H. Martin
Adventures of a Performing Flea, The *07* Arthur Cooper
Adventures of a Plumber's Mate *78* Stanley Long
Adventures of a Private Eye *77* Stanley Long
Adventures of a Roll of Lino, The *07* Alf Collins
Adventures of a Rookie, The *43* Leslie Goodwins
Adventures of a Taxi Driver *76* Stanley Long
Adventures of a Watch, The *08* Walter R. Booth
Adventures of a Young Man *62* Martin Ritt
Adventures of an Asterisk *56* Faith Hubley, John Hubley
Adventures of an Insurance Man, The *05* Tom Green
Adventures of an Octoberite, The *24* Grigori Kozintsev, Leonid Trauberg
Adventures of an Old Flirt, The *09* Edwin S. Porter
Adventures of Antar and Abla, The *48* Salah Abu Saif
Adventures of Arsène Lupin, The *22* Kenji Mizoguchi
Adventures of Arsène Lupin, The *56* Jacques Becker
Adventures of ', The *56* Faith Hubley, John Hubley
Adventures of Baron Münchausen, The *47* George Dunning, Colin Low
Adventures of Baron Münchausen, The *88* Terry Gilliam
Adventures of Baron Münchhausen, The *43* Josef von Baky
Adventures of Barry McKenzie, The *72* Bruce Beresford
Adventures of Billy, The *11* D. W. Griffith
Adventures of Buckaroo Banzai: Across the Eighth Dimension, The *84* W. D. Richter
Adventures of Bullwhip Griffin, The *65* James Neilson
Adventures of Captain Africa *55* Spencer G. Bennet

Adventures of Captain Fabian *51* William Marshall

Adventures of Captain Kettle, The *22* Meyrick Milton

Adventures of Captain Marvel *41* John English, William Witney

Adventures of Carol, The *17* Harley Knoles

Adventures of Casanova *48* Roberto Gavaldón

Adventures of Chatran, The *86* Masanori Hata

Adventures of Chico, The *38* Horace Woodard, Stacy Woodard

Adventures of Corporal Kochekov, The *55* Alexander Rasumny

Adventures of Dick Dolan, The *17* Frank Wilson

Adventures of Dick Turpin—A Deadly Foe, a Pack of Hounds and Some Merry Monks, The *12* Charles Raymond

Adventures of Dick Turpin—The Gunpowder Plot, The *12* Charles Raymond

Adventures of Dick Turpin—The King of Highwaymen, The *12* Charles Raymond

Adventures of Dick Turpin—200 Guineas Reward, Dead or Alive, The *12* Charles Raymond

Adventures of Dr. Dolittle, The *28* Lotte Reiniger

Adventures of Dollie, The *08* D. W. Griffith

Adventures of Don Coyote, The *47* Reginald LeBorg

Adventures of Don Juan *48* Vincent Sherman

Adventures of Don Quixote *32* G. W. Pabst

Adventures of Ford Fairlane, The *90* Renny Harlin

Adventures of Frank and Jesse James *48* Fred C. Brannon, Yakima Canutt

Adventures of Frank Merriwell, The *36* Clifford Smith

Adventures of Frontier Fremont, The *76* Richard Friedenberg

Adventures of Gallant Bess *48* Lew Landers

Adventures of Gerard, The *69* Jerzy Skolimowski

Adventures of Gil Blas, The *55* René Jolivet

Adventures of Goopi and Bagha, The *68* Satyajit Ray

Adventures of Hajji Baba, The *54* Don Weis

Adventures of Hal 5, The *57* Don Sharp

Adventures of Hardrock Dome, The *19* Pat Sullivan

Adventures of Hardrock Dome No. 2, The *19* Pat Sullivan

Adventures of Hercules, The *83* Luigi Cozzi

Adventures of Huckleberry Finn, The *39* Richard Thorpe

Adventures of Huckleberry Finn, The *60* Michael Curtiz

Adventures of Huckleberry Finn, The *85* Peter H. Hunt

Adventures of Ichabod and Mr. Toad, The *49* James Algar, Clyde Geronimi, Jack Kinney, Ben Sharpsteen

Adventures of Jack London, The *43* Alfred Santell

Adventures of Jane, The *49* Alfred Goulding, Edward G. Whiting

Adventures of Jane Arden, The *39* Terry Morse

Adventures of Jimmy *50* James Broughton

Adventures of Kitty O'Day *44* William Beaudine

Adventures of Lieutenant Daring RN in a South American Port, The *11* Dave Aylott

Adventures of Lucky Pierre, The *61* Herschell Gordon Lewis

Adventures of Lyle Swann, The *82* William Dear

Adventures of Mandrin, The *52* Mario Soldati

Adventures of Marco Polo, The *38* John Ford, Archie Mayo

Adventures of Mark Twain, The *44* Irving Rapper

Adventures of Mark Twain, The *85* Will Vinton

Adventures of Martin Eden, The *42* Sidney Salkow

Adventures of Maud, The *06* Harold Jeapes

Adventures of Maya, The *29* Waldemar Bonsels

Adventures of Michael Strogoff *37* George Nicholls, Jr.

Adventures of Milo and Otis, The *86* Masanori Hata

Adventures of Mr. Phiffles, The *13* Hy Mayer

Adventures of Mr. Pickwick, The *21* Thomas Bentley

Adventures of Mr. Wonderbird *52* Paul Grimault

Adventures of Oktyabrina, The *24* Grigori Kozintsev, Leonid Trauberg

Adventures of PC 49, The *49* Godfrey Grayson

Adventures of PC 49—The Case of the Guardian Angel, The *49* Godfrey Grayson

Adventures of PC Sharpe, The *11* A. E. Coleby

Adventures of PC Sharpe—The Stolen Child *11* A. E. Coleby

Adventures of Parker, The *46* W. F. Elliott

Adventures of Peg o' the Ring, The *16* Francis Ford, Jacques Jaccard

Adventures of Picasso, The *78* Tage Danielsson

Adventures of Pimple—Pimple PC, The *13* Fred Evans

Adventures of Pimple—The Battle of Waterloo *13* Fred Evans, Joe Evans

Adventures of Pimple—The Indian Massacre *13* Fred Evans, Joe Evans

Adventures of Pimple—The Spiritualist, The *14* Fred Evans, Joe Evans

Adventures of Pimple—Trilby, The *14* Fred Evans, Joe Evans

Adventures of Pinocchio, The *78* Jesse Vogel

Adventures of Popeye *35* Dave Fleischer

Adventures of Prince Achmed, The *26* Lotte Reiniger

Adventures of Quentin Durward, The *55* Richard Thorpe

Adventures of Rabbi Jacob, The *73* Gérard Oury

Adventures of Red Ryder *40* John English, William Witney

Adventures of Reinette and Mirabelle, The *86* Eric Rohmer

Adventures of Rémi, The *58* André Michel

Adventures of Rex, The *59* Leonard Reeve

Adventures of Rex and Rinty, The *35* Ford Beebe, B. Reeves Eason

Adventures of Robin Hood, The *38* Michael Curtiz, William Keighley

Adventures of Robinson Crusoe, The *02* Georges Méliès

Adventures of Robinson Crusoe, The *22* B. Reeves Eason, Robert F. Hill

Adventures of Robinson Crusoe, The *52* Luis Buñuel

Adventures of Rusty *45* Paul Burnford

Adventures of Ruth, The *19* George Marshall

Adventures of Sadie, The *53* Noel Langley

Adventures of Sandy MacGregor, The *04* Percy Stow

Adventures of Scaramouche, The *64* Antonio Isamendi

Adventures of Sherlock Holmes, The *05* J. Stuart Blackton

Adventures of Sherlock Holmes, The *39* Alfred L. Werker

Adventures of Sherlock Holmes' Smarter Brother, The *75* Gene Wilder

Adventures of Sir Galahad *48* Spencer G. Bennet

Adventures of Smilin' Jack *43* Lewis D. Collins, Ray Taylor

Adventures of Starbird *78* Jack Hively

Adventures of Tartu *43* Harold S. Bucquet

Adventures of Tarzan, The *21* Robert F. Hill

Adventures of the American Rabbit, The *86* Nobutaka Nishizawa, Fred Wolf

Adventures of the Flying Cadets *43* Lewis D. Collins, Ray Taylor

Adventures of the Masked Phantom, The *39* Charles Abbott

Adventures of the Prince and the Pauper, The *69* Elliot Geisinger

Adventures of the Roadrunner, The *61* Chuck Jones

Adventures of the Wilderness Family, The *75* Stewart Raffill

Adventures of Thud and Blunder, The *65* George Dunning

Adventures of Till Eulenspiegel, The *56* Joris Ivens, Gérard Philipe

Adventures of Tom Jones, The *75* Cliff Owen

Adventures of Tom Sawyer, The *38* Norman Taurog

Adventures of Tom the Tamer and Kid Kelly, The *16* Raoul Barré

Africa Before Dark 28 Walt Disney
Africa, Blood and Guts 65 Gualtiero Jacopetti, Franco Prosperi
Africa Erotica 70 Zygmunt Sulistrowski
Africa Screams 49 Charles Barton
Africa Speaks 30 Walter Futter
Africa Squeaks 31 Ubbe Iwerks
Africa Squeaks 40 Robert Clampett
Africa — Texas Style! 67 Andrew Marton
Africain, L' 82 Philippe de Broca
African, The 82 Philippe de Broca
African Dream, An 88 John Smallcombe
African Elephant, The 72 Simon Trevor
African Fury 51 Zoltán Korda
African Hunt, An 15 Vincent Whitman
African in London, An 41 George Pearson
African Incident 34 Sam Newfield
African Jungle 24 Walter Lantz
African Lion, The 55 James Algar
African Manhunt 55 Seymour Friedman
African Queen, The 51 John Huston
African Rage 76 Peter Collinson
African Safari 69 Ron E. Shanin
African Story, The 62 Howard Hawks
African Timber 89 Peter F. Bringmann
African Treasure 52 Ford Beebe
African Woman, The 90 Margarethe von Trotta
Africana, L' 90 Margarethe von Trotta
Africander Winning the Suburban Handicap 03 Edwin S. Porter
Afrikander Girl, An 12 Wilfred Noy
Afrique et la Recherche Scientifique, L' 64 Jean Rouch
Afrique 50 50 René Vautier
Afsporet 42 Bodil Ipsen, Lau Lauritzen, Jr.
Aftenlandet 76 Peter Watkins
After a Lifetime 71 Kenneth Loach
After a Million 24 Jack Nelson
After a Night of Love 35 Guido Brignone
After Business Hours 24 Malcolm St. Clair
After Dark 02 George Albert Smith
After Dark 15 Warwick Buckland
After Dark 15 Frederick Thompson
After Dark 24 Thomas Bentley
After Dark 24 James Chapin
After Dark 32 Albert Parker
After Dark, My Sweet 90 James Foley
After Dark, or The Policeman and His Lantern 02 George Albert Smith
After Darkness 85 Sergio Guerraz, Dominique Othénin-Girard
After Eight Hours 34 George B. Seitz
After Five 15 Oscar Apfel
After Happiness 17 Yevgeni Bauer, Lev Kuleshov
After Her Millions 15 Henry Lehrman
After His Own Heart 19 Harry Franklin
After Hours 85 Martin Scorsese
After Jenny Died 71 Sidney Hayers
After Laughter 81 Stan Vanderbeek
After Leonardo 73 Malcolm Le Grice
After Leslie Wheeler 73 Malcolm Le Grice
After Lumière, L'Arroseur Arrosé 74 Malcolm Le Grice
After Manet, After Giorgione, Le Déjeuner sur l'Herbe 75 Malcolm Le Grice
After Many Days 19 Sidney Morgan
After Many Years 08 D. W. Griffith

After Many Years 29 Lawrence Huntington
After Marriage 25 Norman Dawn
After Midnight 21 Ralph Ince
After Midnight 27 Monta Bell
After Midnight 43 Lew Landers
After Midnight 49 Mitchell Leisen
After Midnight 89 Jim Wheat, Ken Wheat
After Midnight with Boston Blackie 43 Lew Landers
After My Last Move 70 Hans-Jürgen Syberberg
After Office Hours 32 Thomas Bentley
After Office Hours 35 Robert Z. Leonard
After Rubicon 87 Leidulv Risan
After School 12 Allan Dwan
After School 88 William Olsen
After Six Days 22 Piero Antonio Gariazzo, Armando Vay
After the Ball 1897 Georges Méliès
After the Ball 14 Pierce Kingsley
After the Ball 19 Gregory La Cava
After the Ball 21 H. B. Parkinson
After the Ball 24 Dallas M. Fitzgerald
After the Ball 28 Dave Fleischer
After the Ball 32 Milton Rosmer
After the Ball 57 Compton Bennett
After the Ball Was Over 14 Will P. Kellino
After the Club 06 Frank Mottershaw
After the Dance 35 Leo Bulgakov
After the Fall of New York 84 Sergio Martino
After the Fancy Dress Ball 07 James A. Williamson
After the Fog 30 Leander De Cordova
After the Fox 65 Vittorio De Sica
After the Matinee 06 Lewin Fitzhamon
After the 'Oliday 04 Lewin Fitzhamon
After the Rain 89 Camille De Casabianca
After the Rehearsal 83 Ingmar Bergman
After the Show 21 William DeMille
After the Storm 15 B. Reeves Eason
After the Storm 28 George B. Seitz
After the Thin Man 36 W. S. Van Dyke
After the Verdict 29 Henryk Galeen
After the War 18 Joseph De Grasse
After the War 89 Jean-Loup Hubert
After Tomorrow 32 Frank Borzage
After Tonight 33 George Archainbaud
After Years of Study 25 Kenji Mizoguchi
After You, Comrade 66 Jamie Uys
After Your Own Heart 21 George Marshall
Afterglow 23 George B. Samuelson, Walter Summers
Aftermath 80 Stan Brakhage
Aftermath, The 80 Steve Barkett
Afternoon 65 Andy Warhol
Afternoon Affair, An 83 András Kovács
Afternoon in the Village, An 55 Miklós Jancsó
Afternoon with Motorcycles, An 72 Claude Lelouch
Aftershock 90 Frank Harris
Afterwards 28 W. Lawson Butt
Afterwards 34 James Cruze
Aftonlandet 76 Peter Watkins
Afurika Monogatari 81 Susumu Hani*

Afzien 86 Gerrard Verhage
Ag and Bert 29 Bertram Phillips
Aga Khan, The 62 Richard Leacock
Agada 85 Hyeong-myeong Kim
Again 69 Emmerich Oross
Again a Love Story 69 Claude Lelouch
Again One Night 56 Heinosuke Gosho
Again — Pioneers! 50 William Beaudine
Against a Crooked Sky 75 Earl Bellamy
Against All 57 Otakar Vávra
Against All Flags 52 George Sherman
Against All Odds 24 Edmund Mortimer
Against All Odds 68 Jesús Franco
Against All Odds 83 Taylor Hackford
Against the Grain 18 Henry Edwards
Against the Law 34 Lambert Hillyer
Against the Tide 12 Edwin J. Collins
Against the Tide 37 Alex Bryce
Against the Wind 29 Josef Heifits, Alexander Zarkhi
Against the Wind 48 Charles Crichton
Agatha 78 Michael Apted
Agatha 81 Marguerite Duras
Agatha 85 Hyeong-myeong Kim
Agatha Christie's Endless Night 71 Sidney Gilliat
Agatha Christie's Ordeal by Innocence 84 Desmond Davis
Agatha Christie's Ten Little Indians 89 Alan Birkinshaw
Agatha et les Lectures Illimitées 81 Marguerite Duras
Agatha — Lass das Morden Sein 60 Dietrich Haugh
Agatha — Stop the Murders 60 Dietrich Haugh
Agaton and Fina 12 Julius Jaenzon
Âge de la Terre, L' 80 Glauber Rocha
Âge de Monsieur Est Avance, L' 88 Pierre Etaix
Âge d'Or, L' 30 Luis Buñuel, Salvador Dali
Age for Love, The 31 Frank Lloyd
Âge Ingrat, L' 64 Gilles Grangier
Age of Bamboo at Mentawei, The 37 Pál Fejős
Age of Consent, The 32 Gregory La Cava
Age of Consent, The 68 Michael Powell
Age of Cosimo de'Medici, The 72 Roberto Rossellini
Age of Daydreaming, The 64 István Szabó
Age of Desire, The 23 Frank Borzage
Age of Earth, The 80 Glauber Rocha
Age of Gold 30 Luis Buñuel, Salvador Dali
Age of Illusions 64 István Szabó
Age of Indiscretion 35 Edward Ludwig
Age of Indiscretion, The 53 Lionello De Felice
Age of Infidelity 55 Juan Antonio Bardem
Age of Innocence, The 24 Wesley Ruggles
Age of Innocence, The 34 Philip Moeller
Age of Innocence 77 Alan Bridges
Age of the Beaver, The 51 Colin Low
Age of the Earth, The 80 Glauber Rocha
Age of the Medici, The 72 Roberto Rossellini
Age of Youth 61 Alexei Mishurin
Agence Matrimoniale 52 Jean-Paul Le Chanois

Agency *80* George Kaczender

Agent de Poche, L' *09* Émile Cohl

Agent 8¾ *63* Ralph Thomas

Agent et le Violoniste, L' *08* Émile Cohl

Agent 505 *65* Manfred Kohler

Agent for H.A.R.M. *65* Gerd Oswald

Agent 505 — Todesfalle Beirut *65* Manfred Kohler

Agent of Doom *63* Yvan Govar

Agent on Ice *86* Clark Worswick

Agent Plongeur, L' *01* Ferdinand Zecca

Agent Rijolo et Son Chien Policier, L' *13* Alfred Machin

Agent 38-24-36 *63* Édouard Molinaro

Agent 3S3 — Passport to Hell *65* Sergio Sollima

Agent Trouble *87* Jean-Pierre Mocky

Agent Z55 — Desperate Mission *64* Roberto Bianchi Montero

Agent 077 — Missione Bloody Mary *67* Sergio Grieco

Agente Coplan, Missione Spionaggio *65* Riccardo Freda

Agente 077 — Mision Bloody Mary *67* Sergio Grieco

Agenten Kennen Keine Tränen *78* Menahem Golan

Agenti Segretissimi *64* Lucio Fulci

Agents Tels Qu'On Nous les Présente, Les *08* Louis Feuillade

Aggie Appleby, Maker of Men *33* Mark Sandrich

Aggressor, The *11* Thomas Ince, George Loane Tucker

Aggrippés à la Terre *68* Joris Ivens*

Agguato a Tangeri *57* Riccardo Freda

Aghaat *86* Govind Nihalani

Aghaye Hallou *70* Dariush Mehrjui

Agi Murad il Diavolo Bianco *58* Riccardo Freda

Ağıt *71* Yılmaz Güney

Agit-Train *20* Dziga Vertov

Agit-Train of the Central Committee *20* Dziga Vertov

Agitator, The *12* Allan Dwan

Agitator, The *44* John Harlow

Agitators, The *85* Will Zens

Agitpoezd VTsIK *20* Dziga Vertov

Agnes of God *85* Norman Jewison

Agnes of the Port *52* George Tzavellas

Agnese un a Morire, L' *76* Giuliano Montaldo

Agnese Visconti *10* Giovanni Pastrone

Agni Pushpam *88* Eranki Sharma

Agni tou Limaniou *52* George Tzavellas

Agnus Dei *70* Miklós Jancsó

Agonia *75* Elem Klimov

Agonie de Byzance, L' *13* Louis Feuillade

Agonie de Jérusalem, L' *26* Julien Duvivier

Agonie des Aigles, L' *21* Dominique Bernard-Deschamps, Julien Duvivier

Agonie des Aigles, L' *34* Roger Richebé

Agoniya *75* Elem Klimov

Agony *75* Elem Klimov

Agony and the Ecstasy, The *65* Carol Reed

Agony in Jerusalem, The *26* Julien Duvivier

Agony of Love *59* Salah Abu Saif

Agony of Mr. Boroca, The *73* Péter Bacsó

Agostino *62* Mauro Bolognini

Agostino di Ippona *72* Roberto Rossellini

Agosto *88* Jorge Silva Melo

Agression, L' *75* Gérard Pirès

Agriculture, L' *55* Jean Dewever

Agrippina *10* Enrico Guazzoni

Agua en el Suelo, El *35* Eusebio Ardavin

Aguas Bajan Turbias, Las *52* Hugo Del Carril

Aguila *80* Eddie Romero

Aguirre, der Zorn Gottes *72* Werner Herzog

Aguirre, the Wrath of God *72* Werner Herzog

Aguirre, Wrath of God *72* Werner Herzog

Ágyú és Harang *15* Béla Balázs

Ah! Ahh!! Tishoo!!! *14* Edwin J. Collins

Ah, Cradle *80* Jin Xie

Ah Fei *89* Jen Wan

Ah, i Morgon Kväll *19* John W. Brunius

Ah! Les Belles Bacchantes *53* Jean Loubignac

Ah! My Friends Without Voice *72* Tadashi Imai

Ah, My Home Town *38* Kenji Mizoguchi

Ah! Nōmugi Tōge *80* Satsuo Yamamoto

Ah Nurture *48* Hy Hirsch, Sidney Peterson

Ah Sweet Mouse-Story of Life *65* Chuck Jones

Ah the Special Service Vessel *25* Kenji Mizoguchi*

Ah, Wilderness! *35* Clarence Brown

Ah Ying *84* Allen Fong

Ahasin Polawatha *78* Lester James Peries

A-Haunting We Will Go *42* Alfred L. Werker

A-Haunting We Will Go *66* Robert McKimson

Ahdat Sanawouach el-Djamr *75* Mohammed Lakhdar-Hamina

Ahead of the Law *26* Forrest K. Sheldon

Ahijado de la Muerte, El *45* Norman Foster

Ahlam el Chabab *43* Kamel Salim

Ahlam Hind wa Camelia *88* Mohamed Khan

Ahora Seremos Felices *40* William Molte

Ahora Te Vamos a Llamar Hermano *71* Raúl Ruiz

A-Hunting We Will Go *20* Wallace A. Carlson

A-Hunting We Will Go *32* Dave Fleischer

A-Hunting We Won't Go *43* Bob Wickersham

Ai *62* Yoji Kuri

Ai Futatabi *71* Kon Ichikawa

Ai Margini della Metropoli *52* Carlo Lizzani

Ai ni Yomigaeru Hi *22* Kenji Mizoguchi

Ai no Bōrei *78* Nagisa Oshima

Ai no Corrida *76* Nagisa Oshima

Ai no Kawaki *66* Koreyoshi Kurahara

Ai to Chikai *45* Tadashi Imai

Ai to Honoho To *64* Eizo Sugawa

Ai to Kibō no Machi *59* Nagisa Oshima

Ai to Shi no Tanima *54* Heinosuke Gosho

Ai wa Chikara da *30* Mikio Naruse

Ai wa Doko Mademo *32* Tomu Uchida

Aibu *33* Heinosuke Gosho

Aida *11* Oscar Apfel, J. Searle Dawley

Aida *53* Clemente Fracassi

Aida *88* Claes Fellbom

Aide-Toi *18* Louis Feuillade

Aido *69* Susumu Hani

Aido, Slave of Love *69* Susumu Hani

AIDS — A Danger for Love *85* Hans Noever

AIDS — Die Schleichende Gefahr *85* Peter Grandl

AIDS — Gefahr für die Liebe *85* Hans Noever

Aienkyō *37* Kenji Mizoguchi

Aigle à Deux Têtes, L' *47* Jean Cocteau

Aigle et la Colombe, L' *77* Claude Bernard-Aubert

Aigle Noir, L' *58* William Dieterle

Aiglon, L' *12* Émile Chautard

Aiglon, L' *31* Victor Tourjansky

Aigrette Hunter, The *10* Sidney Olcott

Aijin *53* Kon Ichikawa

Aijō no Keifu *61* Heinosuke Gosho

Aika Hyvä Ihmiseksi *77* Rauni Mollberg

Aile ou la Cuisse, L' *76* Claude Zidi

Ailes Brisées, Les *33* André Berthomieu

Aimer Pleurer Mourir *15* Léonce Perret

Aimez-Moi Ce Soir *32* Rouben Mamoulian

Aimez-Vous Brahms? *61* Anatole Litvak

Aimez-Vous les Femmes? *64* Jean Léon

Aimless Walk *30* Alexander Hammid

Ain el Ghezal *24* Scemana Chikly

Aîné des Ferchaux, L' *63* Jean-Pierre Melville

Ain't It So? *18* William A. Seiter

Ain't Love Funny? *27* Del Andrews

Ain't Misbehavin' *55* Edward Buzzell

Ain't Misbehavin' *75* Peter Neal, Anthony Stern

Ain't Nature Grand? *27* Stephen Roberts

Ain't No Heroes *83* Ted Kotcheff

Ain't She Sweet *33* Dave Fleischer

Ain't She Tweet *52* Friz Freleng

Ain't That Ducky *45* Friz Freleng

Ain't We Got Fun *37* Tex Avery

Aiqing Qianfeng Xunhao *86* Allen Fong

Air America *90* Roger Spottiswoode

Air Cadet *51* Joseph Pevney

Air Cage, The *72* Bengt Forslund

Air-Chauffeur *43* Herbert Rappaport

Air Circus, The *28* Howard Hawks, Lewis Seiler

Air City *35* Alexander Dovzhenko

Air de Paris, L' *54* Marcel Carné

Air de Rien, L' *89* Mary Jiménez

Air Derby, The *29* Harry Joe Brown

Air Devils *38* John Rawlins

Air Devils *41* William West

Air Eagles *32* Phil Whitman

Air Express *37* Walter Lantz

Air Force *43* Howard Hawks

Air Hawk, The *24* Bruce Mitchell

Air Hawks *35* Albert S. Rogell

Air Hostess *32* Albert S. Rogell

Air Hostess *49* Lew Landers

Air Legion, The *28* Bert Glennon

Air Mail, The *25* Irvin Willat

Air Mail *32* John Ford

Air Mail Pilot, The *28* Gene Carroll

Air March 36 Mikhail Kaufman
Air Patrol, The 28 Bruce Mitchell
Air Patrol 62 Maury Dexter
Air-Pattern Pacific 44 Frank Lloyd
Air Police 31 Stuart Paton
Air Raid Wardens 43 Edward Sedgwick
Air Strike 55 Cy Roth
Air Tight 31 George Stevens
Air Transport Support 45 Graham Cutts
Airborne 62 James Landis
Aire de un Crimen, El 88 Antonio
  Isamendi
Airmail Mystery, The 32 Ray Taylor
Airman's Children, The 15 Jack Denton
Airman's Letter to His Mother, An 41
  Michael Powell
Airplane! 80 Jim Abrahams, David
  Zucker, Jerry Zucker
Airplane II: The Sequel 82 Ken Finkle-
  man
Airport 69 Henry Hathaway, George
  Seaton
Airport 1975 74 Jack Smight
Airport '77 77 Jerry Jameson
Airport '79 79 David Lowell Rich
Airport '79: Concorde 79 David Lowell
  Rich
Airport '80: The Concorde 79 David
  Lowell Rich
Airs 76 Stan Brakhage
Airship, The 08 J. Stuart Blackton
Airship, The 17 Forest Holger-Madsen
Airship Destroyer, The 09 Walter R.
  Booth
Airtight Safe, The 10 A. E. Coleby
Aisai Monogatari 51 Kaneto Shindo
Aisureba Kōsō 54 Tadashi Imai, Kozaburo
  Yoshimura
Aiutami a Sognare 81 Pupi Avati
Aiyoku no Yoru 30 Heinosuke Gosho
Aizō Tōge 34 Kenji Mizoguchi
Ajantrik 58 Ritwik Ghatak
Ajor 71 Dariush Mehrjui
Ak Altın 57 Lütfü Akat
Akademik Ivan Pavlov 49 Grigori Roshal
Akage 69 Kihachi Okamoto
Akahige 65 Akira Kurosawa
Akai Jinbaori 58 Satsuo Yamamoto
Akai Satsui 64 Shohei Imamura
Akai Yūhi ni Terasarete 25 Kenji
  Mizoguchi*
Akallinen Mies 87 Edvard Laine
Akanegumo 67 Masahiro Shinoda
Akasen Chitai 56 Kenji Mizoguchi
Akash Kusum 65 Mrinal Sen
Akatanikitoi Erastes 88 Stavros Tsiolis
Akaton Mies 84 Edvard Laine
Akatsuki no Shi 24 Kenji Mizoguchi
Akatsuki no Tsuiseki 50 Kon Ichikawa
Akatsuki no Yūshi 26 Teinosuke Kinugasa
Akce B 51 Martin Frič
Åke and His World 84 Allan Edwall
Åke och Hans Värld 84 Allan Edwall
Akenfield 74 Peter Hall
Aki Tachinu 60 Mikio Naruse
Akibiyori 60 Yasujiro Ozu
Akikért a Pacsirta Elkísér 59 László
  Ranódy
Akira 88 Katsuhiro Otomo
Akira Kurosawa's Dreams 90 Akira
  Kurosawa

Akit Ketten Szeretnek 15 Michael Curtiz
Akkara Paha 69 Lester James Peries
Akli Miklós 86 György Révész
Akogare 35 Heinosuke Gosho
Akogare 68 Hideo Onchi
Akord Smrti 19 Karel Lamač
Akrobat Schö-ö-ön 43 Wolfgang Staudte
Akseleratka 88 Alexei Korenev
Akt 61 Jerzy Skolimowski
Äktenskapsbrottaren 64 Hasse Ekman
Äktenskapsbyrån 12 Victor Sjöström
Aktorzy Prowincjonalni 79 Agnieszka
  Holland
Aktrisa 43 Leonid Trauberg
Aktsia 87 Vladimir Shamshurin
Akuma no Temari-Uta 77 Kon Ichikawa
Akuma-To 80 Masahiro Shinoda
Akutō 65 Kaneto Shindo
Al Buio Insieme 37 Gennaro Righelli
Al Capone 59 Richard Wilson
Al Christie's Madame Behave 25 Scott
  Sidney
Al di Là del Bene e del Male 77 Liliana
  Cavani
Al di Là della Legge 67 Giorgio Stegani
Al Diavolo la Celebrità 48 Mario Moni-
  celli, Steno
Al Fresco 30 Alexander Oumansky
Al Jennings of Oklahoma 51 Ray Nazarro
Al Limite, Cioe, Non Glielo Dico 85 Fran-
  co Rossetti
Al Nostro Sonno Inquieto 65 Gianfranco
  Mingozzi
Al Sole 35 Carmine Gallone
Al Vostri Ordini Signora 40 Mario Mattòli
Al-Yemen 31 Vladimir Schneiderhof
Ala Ariba 42 José Leitão De Barros
Älä Itke Iines 87 Janne Kuusi
Ala Mode 58 Stan Vanderbeek
Alabama—2000 Light Years 69 Wim
  Wenders
Alabama's Ghost 72 Frederic Hobbs
Alabaster Box, An 17 Chester Withey
Alacrana, La 86 José Luis Urquieta
Aladdin 06 Albert Capellani
Aladdin 15 Fred Evans, Joe Evans
Aladdin 53 Lotte Reiniger
Aladdin 87 Bruno Corbucci
Aladdin and His Lamp 52 Lew Landers
Aladdin and His Wonderful Lamp 39
  Dave Fleischer
Aladdin and the Wonderful Lamp 1899
  George Albert Smith
Aladdin and the Wonderful Lamp 17
  Chester M. Franklin, Sidney Franklin
Aladdin and the Wonderful Lamp 24
  Herbert M. Dawley
Aladdin and the Wonderful Lamp 34
  Ubbe Iwerks
Aladdin from Broadway 17 William
  Wolbert
Aladdin in Pearlies 12 Fred Rains
Aladdin, or A Lad Out 14 Hay Plumb
Aladdin Up-to-Date 12 J. Searle Dawley
Aladdin's Lamp 24 Walter Lantz
Aladdin's Lantern 38 Gordon Douglas
Aladdin's Other Lamp 17 John H. Collins
Aladin 06 Albert Capellani
A-Lad-in Bagdad 38 Cal Dalton, Cal
  Howard

Alageyik 58 Atıf Yılmaz
Alakazam the Great 60 Taiji Yabushita
Alambrista! 77 Robert M. Young
Alamo, The 59 John Wayne
Alamo Bay 84 Louis Malle
Alamut 74 Dariush Mehrjui
Alarm, The 14 Roscoe Arbuckle, Edward
  Dillon
Alarm, The 17 Yevgeni Bauer
Alarm 49 Zahari Zhandov
Alarm Clock Andy 20 Jerome Storm
Alarm im Weltall 67 Primo Zeglio
Alarm on Eighty-Third Street 65 Edward
  Bernds
Alarma 39 René Cardona
Alarme! 42 Joris Ivens
Alas and Alack 15 Joseph De Grasse
Alas de Mi Patria 40 Carlos Borcosque
Alas! I'm Invisible 52 E. W. Emo
Alas, Poor Bunny 11 Stuart Kinder
Alas, Poor Yorick 13 Colin Campbell
Alas Sobre el Chaco 39 Christy Cabanne
Alaska 30 Walter Lantz
Alaska 44 George Archainbaud
Alaska Boy 69 Ford Beebe
Alaska Highway 43 Frank McDonald
Alaska or Bust 28 Frank Moser
Alaska Passage 59 Edward Bernds
Alaska Patrol 49 Jack Bernhard
Alaska Seas 54 Jerry Hopper
Alaska Sweepstakes 36 Walter Lantz
Alaskan, The 24 Herbert Brenon
Alaskan Knights 30 Manny Gould, Ben
  Harrison
Alaverdoba 66 Georgy Shengelaya
Albania 45 Roman Karmen
Albania 52 Ilya Kopalin*
Albany Bunch, The 31 Mack Sennett
Albany Night Boat, The 28 Alfred
  Raboch
Albatros, L' 70 Jean-Pierre Mocky
Albatross, The 70 Jean-Pierre Mocky
Albéniz 47 Luis César Amadori
Albergo Luna-Camera Trentaquattro 47
  Carlo Ludovico Bragaglia
Albero degli Zoccoli, L' 78 Ermanno Olmi
Albero di Adamo, L' 37 Mario Bonnard
Albert Carter, Q.O.S.O. 67 Ian Brims
Albert, R.N. 53 Lewis Gilbert
Albert Schweitzer 57 Jerome Hill
Albert—Warum? 78 Josef Rödl
Albert—Why? 78 Josef Rödl
Albertfalvai Történet 55 Márta Mészáros
Alberto il Conquistatore 55 Antonio
  Pietrangeli
Albert's Savings 40 Harold Purcell
Albinisme 55 Jean Painlevé
Albino 80 Jürgen Goslar
Album de Famille de Jean Renoir, L' 56
  Jean Renoir
Albuquerque 47 Ray Enright
Albures Mexicanos 87 Alfredo B. Cre-
  venna
Alcatraz Express 62 John Peyser
Alcatraz Island 37 William McGann
Alcestes 86 Tony Lycouressis
Alchemist, The 81 Charles Band
Alchimiste Parafaragamus, L' 06 Georges
  Méliès

Alchimiste Parafaragamus ou La Cornue Infernale, L' *06* Georges Méliès

Alcofrisbas the Master Magician *03* Georges Méliès

Alcoholig Lion, Yr *84* Karl Francis

Alcool Tue, L' *47* Alain Resnais

Alcova, L' *85* Aristide Massaccesi

Aldea Maldita, La *29* Florian Rey

Aldebaran *35* Alessandro Blasetti

Aldilà, L' *80* Lucio Fulci

Alegre Voy! *34* Max Nosseck

Aleko *53* Grigori Roshal, Sergei Sidelov

Aleksandr Nevskii *38* Sergei Eisenstein, Dmitri Vasiliev

Além da Paixão *85* Bruno Barreto

Alenka *61* Boris Barnet

Alens Livsmysterium *40* Forest Holger-Madsen

Alert in the South *53* Jean Devaivre

Alerte au Sud *53* Jean Devaivre

Alerte en Méditerranée *37* Léo Joannon

Alex and the Gypsy *76* John Korty

Alex Falls in Love *86* Boaz Davidson

Alex in Wonderland *70* Paul Mazursky

Alex Joseph and His Wives *78* Ted V. Mikels

Alex Khole Ahava *86* Boaz Davidson

Alex the Great *28* Dudley Murphy

Alexa *89* Sean Delgado

Alexa: A Prostitute's Own Story *89* Sean Delgado

Alexander *67* Yves Robert

Alexander Calder: From the Circus to the Moon *63* Hans Richter

Alexander den Store *17* Mauritz Stiller

Alexander Dovzhenko *64* Yavheniya Hryhorovych

Alexander Graham Bell *39* Irving Cummings

Alexander Hamilton *31* John G. Adolfi

Alexander Nevsky *38* Sergei Eisenstein, Dmitri Vasiliev

Alexander Parkhomenko *42* Leonid Lukov

Alexander Popov *49* Herbert Rappaport

Alexander the Great *17* Mauritz Stiller

Alexander the Great *56* Robert Rossen

Alexander the Great *68* Phil Karlson

Alexander the Great *80* Theodoros Angelopoulos

Alexander's Ragtime Band *31* Dave Fleischer

Alexander's Ragtime Band *38* Henry King

Alexandre *67* Yves Robert

Alexandre le Bienheureux *67* Yves Robert

Alexandria...Why? *78* Youssef Chahine

Alf Garnett Saga, The *72* Bob Kellett

Alf 'n' Family *68* Norman Cohen

Alfa Tau *42* Francesco De Robertis

Alfabeto Notturno *51* Fernando Birri

Alfalfa's Aunt *38* George Sidney

Alfie *66* Lewis Gilbert

Alfie Darling *75* Ken Hughes

Alfred Harding's Wooing *13* Bert Haldane

Alfred Nobel Story, The *52* Harald Braun

Alfred the Great *68* Clive Donner

Alfredo, Alfredo *71* Pietro Germi

Alfredo Campoli and His Orchestra *36* Horace Shepherd

Alf's Baby *53* Maclean Rogers

Alf's Button *20* Cecil M. Hepworth

Alf's Button *30* Will P. Kellino

Alf's Button Afloat *38* Marcel Varnel

Alf's Carpet *29* Will P. Kellino

Algérie en Flammes *58* René Vautier

Algernon Blackwood Stories *49* Anthony Gilkison

Algie the Miner *12* Alice Guy-Blaché

Algiers *38* John Cromwell

Algol *20* Hans Werckmeister

Algy and the Pierrette *13* Edwin J. Collins

Algy, Did He Deserve It? *12* F. Martin Thornton

Algy Goes In for Physical Culture *14* Cecil Birch

Algy Goes on the Stage *10* Alf Collins

Algy on the Force *13* Mack Sennett

Algy the Watchman *12* Henry Lehrman, Mack Sennett

Algy Tries for Physical Culture *10* Alf Collins

Algy Tries Physical Culture *10* Alf Collins

Algy's Expensive Stick *12* Alf Collins

Algy's Little Error *14* Hay Plumb

Algy's New Suit *06* Charles Raymond

Algy's Tormentor *13* Lewin Fitzhamon

Algy's Yachting Party *08* Percy Stow

Ali *73* Rainer Werner Fassbinder

Ali and the Camel *60* Henry Geddes

Ali Baba *36* Ubbe Iwerks

Ali Baba *54* Jacques Becker

Ali Baba and the Forty Thieves *18* Chester M. Franklin, Sidney Franklin

Ali Baba and the 40 Thieves *43* Arthur Lubin

Ali Baba and the Forty Thieves *54* Jacques Becker

Ali Baba and the Sacred Crown *60* Emimmo Salvi

Ali Baba and the Seven Saracens *64* Emimmo Salvi

Ali Baba Bound *40* Robert Clampett

Ali Baba Bunny *57* Chuck Jones

Ali Baba et les 40 Voleurs *01* Ferdinand Zecca

Ali Baba et les Quarante Voleurs *54* Jacques Becker

Ali Baba Goes to Town *37* David Butler

Ali Baba Nights *53* Walter Forde

Ali Barbouyou et Ali Bouf à l'Huile *07* Georges Méliès

Ali: Fear Eats the Soul *73* Rainer Werner Fassbinder

Alias a Gentleman *47* Harry Beaumont

Alias Big Shot *62* Lautaro Murua

Alias Billy the Kid *46* Thomas Carr

Alias Boston Blackie *42* Lew Landers

Alias Bulldog Drummond *34* Walter Forde

Alias French Gertie *30* George Archainbaud

Alias Jesse James *59* Norman Z. McLeod

Alias Jimmy Valentine *15* Maurice Tourneur

Alias Jimmy Valentine *20* Edmund Mortimer

Alias Jimmy Valentine *28* Jack Conway

Alias John Law *35* Robert North Bradbury

Alias John Preston *55* David MacDonald

Alias Julius Caesar *22* Charles Ray

Alias Ladyfingers *21* Bayard Veiller

Alias Mary Brown *18* Henri D'Elba, William Dowlan

Alias Mary Dow *35* Kurt Neumann

Alias Mary Flynn *25* Ralph Ince

Alias Mary Smith *32* E. Mason Hopper

Alias Mike Moran *19* James Cruze

Alias Miss Dodd *20* Harry Franklin

Alias Mr. Twilight *46* John Sturges

Alias Mrs. Jessop *17* Will S. Davis

Alias Nick Beal *48* John Farrow

Alias Phil Kennedy *22* William Bertram

Alias the Bad Man *31* Phil Rosen

Alias the Champ *49* George Blair

Alias the Deacon *27* Edward Sloman

Alias the Deacon *40* Christy Cabanne

Alias the Doctor *32* Lloyd Bacon, Michael Curtiz

Alias the Lone Wolf *27* Edward H. Griffith

Alias the Night Wind *23* Joseph Franz

Alibi, L' *14* Henri Pouctal

Alibi, The *16* Paul Scardon

Alibi *29* Roland West

Alibi *31* Leslie Hiscott

Alibi, L' *37* Pierre Chénal

Alibi, The *37* Pierre Chénal

Alibi *42* Brian Desmond Hurst

Alibi, L' *69* Vittorio Gassman

Alibi Breaker *37* John Paddy Carstairs

Alibi for Death, An *64* Alfred Vohrer

Alibi for Murder *36* D. Ross Lederman

Alibi Ike *35* Ray Enright

Alibi Inn *35* Walter Tennyson

Alibi Racket *35* George B. Seitz

Alice *88* Jan Švankmajer

Alice *90* Woody Allen

Alice Adams *22* Rowland V. Lee

Alice Adams *35* George Stevens

Alice and the Dog Catcher *24* Walt Disney, Ubbe Iwerks

Alice and the Three Bears *24* Walt Disney, Ubbe Iwerks

Alice at the Carnival *27* Walt Disney, Ubbe Iwerks

Alice at the Rodeo *27* Walt Disney, Ubbe Iwerks

Alice Be Good *26* Edward F. Cline

Alice Cans the Cannibals *24* Walt Disney, Ubbe Iwerks

Alice Charms the Fish *26* Walt Disney, Ubbe Iwerks

Alice Chops the Suey *25* Walt Disney, Ubbe Iwerks

Alice Cuts the Ice *26* Walt Disney, Ubbe Iwerks

Alice Doesn't Live Here Anymore *74* Martin Scorsese

Alice Foils the Pirates *27* Walt Disney, Ubbe Iwerks

Alice Gets in Dutch *24* Walt Disney, Ubbe Iwerks

Alice Gets Stung *25* Walt Disney, Ubbe Iwerks

Alice Goodbody *74* Tom Scheuer

Alice Helps the Romance *26* Walt Disney, Ubbe Iwerks

Alice Hunting in Africa *24* Walt Disney, Ubbe Iwerks

Alice in den Städten *73* Wim Wenders

Alice in Movieland *40* Jean Negulesco

Alice in Slumberland *26* Walt Disney, Ubbe Iwerks

Alice in Switzerland *39* Alberto Cavalcanti

Alice in the Alps *27* Walt Disney, Ubbe Iwerks

Alice in the Big League *27* Walt Disney, Ubbe Iwerks

Alice in the Cities *73* Wim Wenders

Alice in the Jungle *25* Walt Disney, Ubbe Iwerks

Alice in the Klondike *27* Walt Disney, Ubbe Iwerks

Alice in the Navy *65* Alekos Sakelarios

Alice in the Wooly West *26* Walt Disney, Ubbe Iwerks

Alice in Wonderland *03* Cecil M. Hepworth, Percy Stow

Alice in Wonderland *16* W. W. Young

Alice in Wonderland *31* Bud Pollard

Alice in Wonderland *33* Norman Z. McLeod

Alice in Wonderland *50* Dallas Bower

Alice in Wonderland *51* Clyde Geronimi, Wilfred Jackson, Hamilton Luske, Ben Sharpsteen

Alice in Wonderland *76* Bud Townsend

Alice Is Stage Struck *25* Walt Disney, Ubbe Iwerks

Alice Loses Out *25* Walt Disney, Ubbe Iwerks

Alice of Wonderland in Paris *66* Gene Deitch

Alice on the Farm *25* Walt Disney, Ubbe Iwerks

Alice, or The Last Escapade *76* Claude Chabrol

Alice ou La Dernière Fugue *76* Claude Chabrol

Alice Picks the Champ *25* Walt Disney, Ubbe Iwerks

Alice Plays Cupid *25* Walt Disney, Ubbe Iwerks

Alice Plays the Piper *24* Walt Disney, Ubbe Iwerks

Alice Rattled by Rats *25* Walt Disney, Ubbe Iwerks

Alice Solves the Puzzle *25* Walt Disney, Ubbe Iwerks

Alice Stage Struck *25* Walt Disney

Alice, Sweet Alice *76* Alfred Sole

Alice the Beach Nut *27* Walt Disney, Ubbe Iwerks

Alice the Collegiate *27* Walt Disney, Ubbe Iwerks

Alice the Fire Fighter *26* Walt Disney, Ubbe Iwerks

Alice the Golf Bug *27* Walt Disney, Ubbe Iwerks

Alice the Jail Bird *25* Walt Disney, Ubbe Iwerks

Alice the Lumberjack *26* Walt Disney, Ubbe Iwerks

Alice the Peacemaker *24* Walt Disney, Ubbe Iwerks

Alice the Piper *24* Walt Disney, Ubbe Iwerks

Alice the Toreador *24* Walt Disney, Ubbe Iwerks

Alice the Whaler *27* Walt Disney, Ubbe Iwerks

Alice Through a Looking Glass *28* Walter Lang

Alice Wins the Derby *25* Walt Disney, Ubbe Iwerks

Alice's Adventures in Wonderland *10* Edwin S. Porter

Alice's Adventures in Wonderland *72* William Sterling

Alice's Auto Race *27* Walt Disney, Ubbe Iwerks

Alice's Balloon Race *25* Walt Disney, Ubbe Iwerks

Alice's Brown Derby *26* Walt Disney, Ubbe Iwerks

Alice's Channel Swim *27* Walt Disney, Ubbe Iwerks

Alice's Circus Daze *27* Walt Disney, Ubbe Iwerks

Alice's Day at the Sea *24* Walt Disney, Ubbe Iwerks

Alice's Eggplant *25* Walt Disney, Ubbe Iwerks

Alice's Fishy Story *24* Walt Disney, Ubbe Iwerks

Alice's Knaughty Knight *27* Walt Disney, Ubbe Iwerks

Alice's Little Parade *25* Walt Disney, Ubbe Iwerks

Alice's Medicine Show *27* Walt Disney, Ubbe Iwerks

Alice's Monkey Business *26* Walt Disney, Ubbe Iwerks

Alice's Mysterious Mystery *25* Walt Disney, Ubbe Iwerks

Alice's Ornery Orphan *25* Walt Disney, Ubbe Iwerks

Alice's Picnic *27* Walt Disney, Ubbe Iwerks

Alice's Restaurant *69* Arthur Penn

Alice's Rodeo *27* Walt Disney, Ubbe Iwerks

Alice's Spanish Guitar *26* Walt Disney, Ubbe Iwerks

Alice's Spooky Adventure *24* Walt Disney, Ubbe Iwerks

Alice's Three Bad Eggs *27* Walt Disney, Ubbe Iwerks

Alice's Tin Pony *25* Walt Disney, Ubbe Iwerks

Alice's Wild West Show *24* Walt Disney

Alice's Wonderland *23* Walt Disney, Ubbe Iwerks

Alicia of the Orphans *16* John G. Adolfi

Alien, The *15* Thomas Ince

Alien *79* Ridley Scott

Alien, The *80* Rudolf van den Berg

Alien Contamination *80* Luigi Cozzi

Alien Dead *80* Fred Olen Ray

Alien Encounter *77* Ed Hunt

Alien Enemy, An *18* Wallace Worsley

Alien Factor, The *78* Donald M. Dohler

Alien from L.A. *87* Albert Pyun

Alien Nation *88* Graham Baker

Alien Predator *84* Deran Sarafian

Alien Question, The *05* Alf Collins

Alien Sabotage *40* Lewis D. Collins

Alien Shore *30* Mark Donskoi

Alien Souls *16* Frank Reicher

Alien Thunder *73* Claude Fournier

Alien Warrior *86* Ed Hunt

Alien Zone *78* Sharron Miller

Alienator *89* Fred Olen Ray

Alienist, The *69* Nelson Pereira Dos Santos

Alienista, O *69* Nelson Pereira Dos Santos

Aliéniste, L' *69* Nelson Pereira Dos Santos

Aliens *19* Bernard J. Durning

Aliens *86* James Cameron

Aliens Are Forbidden *87* Anatoly Vokhotko, Roman Yershov

Aliens' Invasion, The *05* Lewin Fitzhamon

Alien's Return, The *80* Greydon Clark

Aliki *63* Rudolph Maté

Aliki My Love *63* Rudolph Maté

Alimente *29* Carl Boese

Alimony *24* James W. Horne

Alimony *49* Alfred Zeisler

Alimony Aches *35* Charles Lamont

Alimony Madness *33* B. Reeves Eason

Alionka *61* Boris Barnet

Alise and Chloe *70* René Gainville

Alison's Birthday *79* Ian Coughlan

Alitet Goes Into the Mountains *48* Mark Donskoi

Alitet Leaves for the Hills *48* Mark Donskoi

Alitet Ukhodit v Gory *48* Mark Donskoi

Alive and Kicking *58* Cyril Frankel

Alive by Night *87* Kenneth J. Hall

Alive on Saturday *57* Alfred Travers

Alive...or Preferably Dead *69* Duccio Tessari

Alix's Photos *80* Jean Eustache

Alkali Bests Bronco Billy *12* Gilbert M. Anderson

Alkali Ike in Jayville *13* E. Mason Hopper

Alkali Ike's Boarding House *12* Gilbert M. Anderson

Alkali Ike's Misfortunes *13* Gilbert M. Anderson

Alkohol *19* E. A. Dupont*

Alkony *71* István Szabó

Alkonyok és Hajnalok *61* Miklós Jancsó

All Abi-r-r-rd *50* Friz Freleng

All Aboard *15* Al Christie

All Aboard *17* Hal Roach

All Aboard *21* Hy Mayer

All Aboard *27* Charles Hines

All Aboard for a Trip to the Moon *20* Dave Fleischer

All About Eve *50* Joseph L. Mankiewicz

All About Loving *63* Jean Aurel

All-American, The *28* Roy William Neill

All-American, The *32* Russell Mack

All-American, The *52* Jesse Hibbs

All American Band, The *43* Jean Negulesco

All-American Boy, The *73* Charles Eastman

All American Chump, The *36* Edwin L. Marin

All-American Co-Ed *41* LeRoy Prinz

All-American Pro *48* Arthur Dreifuss

All American Sweetheart *37* Lambert Hillyer

All Americans *29* Joseph Santley

All Around Frying Pan *25* David Kirkland

All-Around Reduced Personality—Outtakes, The *78* Helke Sander

All Ashore *53* Richard Quine

All at Sea *19* Charlie Chase
All at Sea *25* Charles Bowers
All at Sea *28* Alfred Goulding
All at Sea *35* Anthony Kimmins
All at Sea *39* Herbert Smith
All at Sea *57* Charles Frend
All at Sea *69* Kenneth Fairbairn
All Bad *58* Erwin Marno
All Because of a Wedding Dress *86* Arturo Martínez
All Beginnings Are Hard *66* György Révész
All Boys Are Called Patrick *57* Jean-Luc Godard
All Business *36* Jean Yarbrough
All by Myself *42* Felix E. Feist
All by Myself *82* Christian Blackwood
All Clear, No Need to Take Cover *17* Jane Denison
All Coons Look Alike to Me *08* Arthur Gilbert
All Coppers Are... *71* Sidney Hayers
All Creatures Great and Small *74* Claude Whatham
All Creatures Great and Small *86* Terence Dudley
All Dogs Go to Heaven *89* Don Bluth, Gary Goldman, Dan Kuenster
All Dolled Up *21* Rollin Sturgeon
All Excited *31* Charles Lamont
All Fall Down *61* John Frankenheimer
All for a Girl *15* Roy Applegate
All for a Husband *17* Carl Harbaugh
All for a Woman *21* Dmitri Buchowetzki
All for Business' Sake *87* Yoshimitsu Morita
All for Her *12* Herbert Brenon
All for Ireland *15* Sidney Olcott
All for Love *30* Martin Frič
All for Love *61* Yasuzo Masumura
All for Love *86* Nikolai Volev
All for Mary *55* Wendy Toye
All for Nothing *07* Alf Collins
All for Nothing *28* James Parrott
All for Old Ireland *15* Sidney Olcott
All for Peggy *15* Joseph De Grasse
All for the Ladies *18* Gregory La Cava
All for the Love of a Girl *20* Gregory La Cava
All Fowled Up *55* Robert McKimson
All Fur Her *18* William A. Seiter
All Girl *67* Frank Warren
All Good Citizens *68* Vojtěch Jasný
All Hallowe'en *53* Michael Gordon
All Hands *40* John Paddy Carstairs
All Hands on Deck *61* Norman Taurog
All I Desire *53* Douglas Sirk
All I Want Is You and You and You *75* Bob Kellett
All In *36* Marcel Varnel
All in a Day's Work *14* Hay Plumb
All in a Dim Cold Night *74* Fengpan Yao
All in a Night's Work *61* Joseph Anthony
All in Good Fun *56* James M. Anderson
All in Good Time *64* Robert Tronson
All in Order *80* Sohrab Shahid Saless
All in Order, Nothing in Place *73* Lina Wertmuller
All in Place *73* Lina Wertmuller
All Is Fair in Love *21* E. Mason Hopper

All Is Not Gold That Glitters *10* Bert Haldane
All Is Not Gold That Glitters *17* Gregory La Cava, Vernon Stallings
All Life Long *87* Víctor Manuel Castro
All Lit Up *59* Joy Batchelor, John Halas
All Living Things *39* Andrew Buchanan
All Living Things *55* Victor M. Gover
All Man *16* Émile Chautard
All Man *18* Paul Scardon
All Men Are Apes *65* Joseph P. Mawra
All Men Are Crazy *37* Victor Gertler
All Men Are Enemies *34* George Fitzmaurice
All Men Are Liars *19* Sidney Morgan
All Mine to Give *57* Allen Reisner
All Mixed Up *85* Josiane Balasko
All My Good Countrymen *68* Vojtěch Jasný
All My Life *66* Bruce Baillie
All My Loving *86* Yohanan Weller
All My Sons *48* Irving Reis
All Neat in Black Stockings *68* Christopher Morahan
All Night *18* Paul Powell
All Night Long *61* Basil Dearden, Michael Relph
All Night Long *81* Jean-Claude Tramont
All Night Long *82* Chantal Akerman
All Night Through *58* Falk Harnack
All Nudity Shall Be Punished *73* Arnaldo Jabor
All of a Sudden Norma *19* Howard Hickman
All of a Sudden Peggy *20* Walter Edwards
All of Life in One Night *40* Corrado D'Enrico
All of Me *34* James Flood
All of Me *84* Carl Reiner
All of Myself *54* Kon Ichikawa
All on Account of a Laundry Mark *10* Edwin S. Porter
All on Account of the Milk *09* Frank Powell
All One Night *36* Frank McDonald
All Our Enemies *57* Otakar Vávra
All Out *68* Umberto Lenzi
All Over the Town *49* Derek Twist
All Over Town *37* James W. Horne
All Quiet on the Western Front *30* Lewis Milestone
All Right, My Friend *83* Ryu Murakami
All Riot on the Western Front *30* Castleton Knight
All Roads Lead to Calvary *21* Kenelm Foss
All Russian Elder Kalinin *20* Dziga Vertov
All Scotch *09* S. Wormald
All Screwed Up *73* Lina Wertmuller
All Sorts and Conditions of Men *21* Georges Treville
All Souls' Eve *21* Chester M. Franklin
All Square *40* Lambert Hillyer
All Square Aft *57* Gerard Bryant
All Star Melody Masters *44* Jean Negulesco
All Stars *16* Edwin J. Collins
All Steamed Up *29* Norman Taurog
All Stuck Up *20* Raoul Barré, Charles Bowers
All That Glistens Is Not Gold *25*

Alexander Butler
All That Glitters *36* Maclean Rogers
All That Glitters Is Not Goldfish *19* Raoul Barré, Charles Bowers
All That Heaven Allows *55* Douglas Sirk
All That I Have *51* William F. Claxton
All That Jazz *79* Bob Fosse
All That Money Can Buy *40* William Dieterle
All the Brothers Were Valiant *23* Irvin Willat
All the Brothers Were Valiant *53* Richard Thorpe
All the Fault of Paradise *85* Francesco Nuti
All the Fine Young Cannibals *60* Michael Anderson
All the Gold in the World *61* René Clair
All the King's Horses *34* Frank Tuttle
All the King's Men *49* Robert Rossen
All the King's Men *83* King Hu
All the Lovin' Kinfolk *70* John Hayes
All the Loving Couples *69* Mack Bing
...All the Marbles *81* Robert Aldrich
All the Merry Bow-Wows *21* Hy Mayer
All the Other Girls Do *66* Silvio Amadio
All the President's Men *76* Alan J. Pakula
All the Right Moves *83* Michael Chapman
All the Right Noises *69* Gerry O'Hara
All the Sad World Needs *18* Hubert Herrick
All the Sins of Sodom *67* Joe Sarno
All the Vermeers in New York *90* Jon Jost
All the Way *57* Charles Vidor
All the Way, Boys *73* Giuseppe Colizzi
All the Way Home *63* Alex Segal
All the Way Up *70* James MacTaggart
All the Winners *20* Geoffrey H. Malins
All the World to Nothing *18* Henry King
All the World's a Stage *15* Frank Wilson
All the World's a Stage *17* Harold Weston
All the Wrong Clues *81* Hark Tsui
All the Young Men *60* Hall Bartlett
All the Young Wives *75* Mike Ripps
All the Youthful Days *83* Hsiao-hsien Hou
All These Women *64* Ingmar Bergman
All Things Bright and Beautiful *76* Eric Till
All Things Flow *51* Bert Haanstra
All 33 di Via Orologio Fa Sempre Freddo *76* Lamberto Bava, Mario Bava
All This and Glamour Too *37* Irving Cummings
All This and Heaven Too *40* Anatole Litvak
All This and Money Too *62* David Swift
All This and Rabbit Stew *41* Tex Avery
All This and World War II *76* Susan Winslow
All Through Betty *16* Wilfred Noy
All Through the Night *41* Vincent Sherman
All Through the Page Boy *04* Alf Collins
All 33 di Via Orologio Fa Sempre Freddo *76* Lamberto Bava, Mario Bava
All Weekend Lovers *67* Alain Jessua
All Wet *24* Leo McCarey
All Wet *27* Walt Disney
All Wet *30* Sam Newfield

All Woman *18* Hobart Henley
All Woman *67* Frank Warren
All Women Have Secrets *39* Kurt Neumann
All Wrong *19* Raymond B. West, William Worthington
Alla Conquista dell'Arkansas *64* Alberto Cardone, Paul Martin
Allá en el Rancho Chico *39* René Cardona
Allá en el Rancho Grande *36* Fernando De Fuentes
Allá en el Rancho Grande *48* Fernando De Fuentes
Allá en el Trópico *40* Fernando De Fuentes
Alla Ricerca di Gregory *69* Peter Wood
Alla Ricerca di Tadzio *70* Luchino Visconti
Alla Vi Barn i Bullerbyn *86* Lasse Hallström
Allah Maana *54* Ahmed Badrakhan
Allan Field's Warning *13* Bert Haldane
Allan Quatermain and the Lost City of Gold *85* Newton Arnold, Gary Nelson
Allari Krishnaya *87* Nandamuri Ramesh
Alle Stehen Kopf *40* Arthur Maria Rabenalt
Alle Tage Ist Kein Sonntag *36* Walter Janssen
Allegheny Frontier *39* William A. Seiter
Allegheny Uprising *39* William A. Seiter
Allegoria di Primavera *49* Luciano Emmer, Enrico Gras
Allegory *86* Costas Sfikas
Allegretto *36* Oskar Fischinger
Allegro *39* Mary Ellen Bute, Norman McLaren
Allegro Barbaro *79* Miklós Jancsó
Allegro Barbaro, Magyar Rapszódia 2 *79* Miklós Jancsó
Allegro Fantasma, L' *41* Carlo Ludovico Bragaglia, Amleto Palermi
Allegro Non Troppo *76* Bruno Bozzetto
Alleinseglerin, Die *88* Hermann Zschoche
Alleluja e Sartana, Figli di...Dio *72* Mario Siciliano
Alleman *63* Bert Haanstra
Aller et Retour *48* Alexandre Astruc
Aller-Retour *48* Alexandre Astruc
Aller Simple, Un *70* José Giovanni
Allergic to Love *43* Edward Lilley
Alles Dreht Sich, Alles Bewegt Sich! *29* Hans Richter
Alles für Geld *23* Reinhold Schünzel
Alles für Veronika *36* Veidt Harlan
Alles um eine Frau *35* Alfred Abel
Alles Weg'n dem Hund *36* Fred Sauer
Allessandro, Sei Grande! *41* Carlo Ludovico Bragaglia
Alley Cat, The *29* Hans Steinhoff
Alley Cat *83* Victor Ordonez, Eduardo Palmos, Al Valletta
Alley Cat, The *86* Jean Beaudin
Alley Cats, The *66* Radley Metzger
Alley of Golden Hearts, The *24* Bertram Phillips
Alley of Nightmares *66* Byron Mabe
Alley Romance, An *15* Wallace A. Carlson
Alley Tramp *66* Herschell Gordon Lewis
Allez France! *64* Robert Dhéry
Allez Oop *34* Charles Lamont

Allez-Vous Perdre d'Ailleurs *73* Édouard Molinaro
Allies *19* Del Henderson
Alligator *80* Lewis Teague
Alligator Eyes *90* John Feldman
Alligator Named Daisy, An *55* J. Lee-Thompson
Alligator People, The *59* Roy Del Ruth
Alligator Shoes *81* Clay Borris
Alligators *79* Sergio Martino
Alligoria *86* Costas Sfikas
Allnighter, The *86* Tamar Simon Hoffs
Allô Berlin? Ici Paris! *31* Julien Duvivier
All'Ombra di una Colt *65* Giovanni Grimaldi
All'Onorevole Piacciono le Donne *72* Lucio Fulci
Allonsanfan *74* Paolo Taviani, Vittorio Taviani
Allotment Wives *45* William Nigh
Allotment Wives, Inc. *45* William Nigh
Allotria *36* Willi Forst
All'Ovest di Sacramento *71* Richard Owens
All's Fair *13* Hay Plumb
All's Fair *89* Rocky Lang
All's Fair at the Fair *38* Dave Fleischer
All's Fair in Love *10* Lewin Fitzhamon
All's Fair in Love *12* Percy Stow
All's Fair in Love *21* E. Mason Hopper
All's Fair in Love and War *09* Lewin Fitzhamon
All's Right with the World *11* Lewin Fitzhamon
All's Well *41* Dave Fleischer
All's Well That Ends Well *04* James A. Williamson
All's Well That Ends Well *06* Alf Collins
All's Well That Ends Well *13* Edwin J. Collins
Alltägliche Geschichte, Eine *45* Günther Rittau
All'Ultimo Sangue *68* Paolo Moffa
Allumettes Animées, Les *08* Émile Cohl
Allumettes Fantaisies, Les *12* Émile Cohl
Allumettes Magiques, Les *12* Émile Cohl
Alluring Goal, The *30* Max Reichmann
Ally Sloper *1898* George Albert Smith
Ally Sloper Goes Bathing *21* Geoffrey H. Malins
Ally Sloper Goes Yachting *21* Geoffrey H. Malins
Ally Sloper Runs a Revue *21* Geoffrey H. Malins
Ally Sloper's Haunted House *21* Geoffrey H. Malins
Ally Sloper's Loan Office *21* Geoffrey H. Malins
Ally Sloper's Teetotal Island *21* Geoffrey H. Malins
Alma del Bandoneón, El *40* Mario Soffici
Alma del Bronce *44* Dudley Murphy
Alma Jarocha *38* Antonio Helu
Alma Mater *15* Enrico Guazzoni
Alma, Where Do You Live? *17* Hal Clarendon
Almacita di Desolato *86* Felix de Rooy
Almadrabas *34* Fernando Mantilla, Carlos Velo
Alma's Champion *12* J. Stuart Blackton
Almas Encontradas *33* Raphael J. Sevilla

Almas Tropicales *23* Miguel Torres Contreras
Almast *33* *66* Dariush Mehrjui
Álmatlan Évek *59* Félix Máriássy
Almighty Dollar, The *16* Robert Thornby
Álmodozások Kora *64* István Szabó
Almonds and Raisins *83* Russ Karel
Almost *10* Theo Bouwmeester
Almost a Bride *49* Richard Wallace
Almost a Divorce *31* Jack Raymond, Arthur Varney-Serrao
Almost a Gentleman *38* Leslie Goodwins
Almost a Gentleman *38* Oswald Mitchell
Almost a Hero *10* Edwin S. Porter
Almost a Honeymoon *30* Monty Banks
Almost a Honeymoon *38* Norman Lee
Almost a Husband *19* Clarence Badger
Almost a Husband *24* Charles Lamont
Almost a King *15* William Beaudine
Almost a King *15* Al Christie
Almost a Lady *26* E. Mason Hopper
Almost a Man *65* Vittorio De Seta
Almost a Widow *15* John Francis Dillon
Almost an Angel *90* John Cornell
Almost Angels *62* Steve Previn
Almost Good Man, The *17* Fred A. Kelsey
Almost Human *14* Percy Nash
Almost Human *27* Frank Urson
Almost Human *70* Ken Wiederhorn
Almost Human *74* Umberto Lenzi
Almost Married *19* Charles Swickard
Almost Married *32* William Cameron Menzies, Marcel Varnel
Almost Married *42* Charles Lamont
Almost Perfect Affair, An *79* Michael Ritchie
Almost Perfect Crime, The *66* Mario Camerini
Almost Summer *78* Martin Davidson
Almost Transparent Blue *80* Ryu Murakami
Almost You *84* Adam Brooks
Aloa—Praznik Kurvi *88* Lordan Zafranović
Aloha *31* Albert S. Rogell
aloha, bobby and rose *75* Floyd Mutrux
Aloha Hooey *41* Tex Avery
Aloha Oe *15* Gilbert P. Hamilton
Aloha Oe *33* Dave Fleischer
Aloha Summer *85* Tommy Lee Wallace
Aloïse *75* Liliane De Kermadec
Aloma of the South Seas *26* Maurice Tourneur
Aloma of the South Seas *41* Alfred Santell
Alona of the South Seas *26* Charles Bowers
Alone *31* Grigori Kozintsev, Leonid Trauberg
Alone *42* Joris Ivens
Alone *59* Vladimir Pogačić
Alone Against Rome *61* Riccardo Freda, Luciano Ricci, Marco Vicario
Alone Among His Own *85* Wojciech Wójcik
Alone at Last *14* Forest Holger-Madsen
Alone in London *15* Lawrence Trimble
Alone in the Dark *82* Jack Sholder
Alone in the Jungle *13* Colin Campbell
Alone in the Streets *56* Silvio Siano
Alone in the World *16* Lois Weber
Alone on the Pacific *63* Kon Ichikawa

Along Came Daffy 47 Friz Freleng
Along Came Fido 27 Clyde Geronimi
Along Came Jones 45 Stuart Heisler
Along Came Love 36 Bert Lytell
Along Came Ruth 24 Edward F. Cline
Along Came Sally 33 Tim Whelan
Along Came Youth 30 Lloyd Corrigan, Norman Z. McLeod
Along Flirtation Walk 35 Friz Freleng
Along the Galga River 54 Miklós Jancsó
Along the Great Divide 51 Raoul Walsh
Along the Navajo Trail 45 Frank McDonald
Along the Oregon Trail 47 R. G. Springsteen
Along the Rio Grande 41 Edward Killy
Along the River Nile 12 Sidney Olcott
Along the Sundown Trail 42 Sam Newfield
Along the Way 73 Tom Lyndon-Haynes, John Reeve
Alouette 44 Norman McLaren
Alouette et la Mésange, L' 22 André Antoine
Alouette, Je Te Plumerai 88 Pierre Zucca
Alph 70 Gregory Markopoulos
Alpha Beta 73 Anthony Page
Alpha Incident, The 76 Bill Rebane
Alpha Noir 65 Jean Rouch
Alphabet, The 68 David Lynch
Alphabet City 84 Amos Poe
Alphabet Murders, The 65 Frank Tashlin
Alphabet of Fear 61 Fadil Hadžić
Alphacity — Abgerechnet Wird Nachts 85 Eckhart Schmidt
Alphaville 65 Jean-Luc Godard
Alphaville — A Strange Case of Lemmy Caution 65 Jean-Luc Godard
Alphaville — Une Étrange Aventure de Lemmy Caution 65 Jean-Luc Godard
Alpine Antics 36 Jack King
Alpine Echo, An 09 J. Stuart Blackton
Alpine Fire 85 Fredi M. Murer
Alpine Love 36 Marco Elter
Alpine Melodies 29 R. E. Jeffrey
Alraune 18 Michael Curtiz, Fritz Ödön
Alraune 18 Eugen Illes
Alraune 27 Henryk Galeen
Alraune 30 Richard Oswald
Alraune 52 Arthur Maria Rabenalt
Als Ich Tot War 16 Ernst Lubitsch
Als Ich Wiederkam 26 Richard Oswald
Als in een Roes 87 Pim de la Parra
Al's Troubles 25 Charles Lamont
Als Twee Druppels Water 63 Fons Rademakers
Alsace 15 Henri Pouctal
Alshazhia 87 Mohamed Ali Alfarjani
Alsino and the Condor 82 Miguel Littin
Alsino y el Cóndor 82 Miguel Littin
Älska Mig! 86 Kay Pollak
Älskande Par 64 Mai Zetterling
Älskarinnan 62 Vilgot Sjöman
Älskling, Jag Ger Mig 43 Gustaf Molander
Also-Rans, The 14 Hay Plumb
Alster Case, The 15 J. Charles Haydon
Alt på et Bræt 76 Gabriel Axel
Alt på et Kort 12 August Blom
Alta Infedeltà 64 Mario Monicelli, Elio Petri, Franco Rossi, Luciano Salce

Altar Chains 16 Bannister Merwin
Altar of Death, The 12 Raymond B. West
Altar Stairs, The 22 Lambert Hillyer
Altars of Desire 26 Christy Cabanne
Altars of the World 76 Lew Ayres
Alte Fritz, Der 27 Gerhard Lamprecht
Alte Gesetz, Das 23 E. A. Dupont
Alte Kameraden 36 Fred Sauer
Alte Lied, Das 31 Erich Waschneck
Alte und der Junge König, Der 35 Hans Steinhoff
Altémer le Cynique 24 Georges Monca
Alter Ego 41 Frigyes Bán
Altered Message, The 11 Alice Guy-Blaché
Altered States 79 Ken Russell
Alternative Miss World, The 80 Richard Gaylor
Alteste Gewerbe der Welt, Das 67 Claude Autant-Lara, Mauro Bolognini, Philippe de Broca, Jean-Luc Godard, Franco Indovina, Michael Pfleghar
Altgermanische Bauernkultur 34 Walter Ruttmann
Altitude 3200 37 Jean Benoît-Lévy, Marie Epstein
Alto Chiese 59 Ermanno Olmi
Altra, L' 47 Carlo Ludovico Bragaglia
Altra Donna, L' 80 Peter Del Monte
Altra Meta del Cielo, L' 77 Franco Rossi
Altri Tempi 52 Alessandro Blasetti
. . .Altrimenti Ci Arrabbiamo 74 Marcello Fondato
Altro Io 24 Mario Bonnard
Alucarda 75 Juan López Moctezuma
Alum and Eve 32 George Marshall
Aluminium, L' 55 Marcel Ichac
Alvarez Kelly 65 Edward Dmytryk
Alvin Purple 73 Tim Burstall
Alvin Rides Again 74 David Bilcock, Robin Copping
Always 85 Henry Jaglom
Always 89 Steven Spielberg
Always a Bride 40 Noel Mason Smith
Always a Bride 53 Ralph Smart
Always a Bridesmaid 43 Erle C. Kenton
Always a Gentleman 28 Norman Taurog
Always Another Dawn 48 Tom McCreadie
Always Audacious 20 James Cruze
Always for Pleasure 78 Les Blank
Always Further On 64 Luis Alcoriza
Always Gay 13 Frank Wilson
Always Goodbye 31 Kenneth MacKenna, William Cameron Menzies
Always Goodbye 38 Sidney Lanfield
Always in My Heart 42 Jo Graham
Always in My Heart 47 Salah Abu Saif
Always in the Way 15 J. Searle Dawley
Always in Trouble 38 Joseph Santley
Always Kickin' 39 Dave Fleischer
Always Leave Them Laughing 49 Roy Del Ruth
Always Love Your Neighbours 15 Cecil Birch
Always Ridin' to Win 25 Forrest K. Sheldon
Always Tell Your Husband 15 Cecil Birch
Always Tell Your Wife 14 Leedham Bantock
Always Tell Your Wife 22 Hugh Croise, Seymour Hicks, Alfred Hitchcock

Always the Woman 22 Arthur Rosson
Always Together 47 Frederick De Cordova
Always Tomorrow 34 Edward Sloman
Always Until Victory 67 Santiago Álvarez
Always Victorious 58 Wolfgang Staudte
Alye Parusa 61 Alexander Ptushko
Am Anfang War Es Sünde 62 Franz Cap
Am I Guilty? 40 Sam Newfield
Am I Trying, Part Two 69 Yoji Yamada
Am Nächsten Morgen Kehrte der Minister Nicht an Seinen Arbeitsplatz Zuruck 86 Monika Funke-Stern
Am Rande der Welt 27 Karl Grüne
Am Tag Als der Regen Kam 59 Gerd Oswald
Am Tor des Lebens 18 Conrad Wiene
Am Tor des Todes 18 Conrad Wiene
Am Webstuhl der Zeit 21 Forest Holger-Madsen
Ama no Bakemono Yashiki 59 Morihei Magatani
Amada Amante 79 Bruno Barreto
Amadeus 83 Miloš Forman
Amagi Goe 85 Haruhiko Mimura
Amagi Pass 85 Haruhiko Mimura
Amagleba 77 Nodar Managadze
Amai Himitsu 71 Kozaburo Yoshimura
Amakusa Shiro Tokisada 62 Nagisa Oshima
Amal le Voleur 59 James Blue
Amami Alfredo! 40 Carmine Gallone
Amanat 55 Bimal Roy, Arabind Sen
Amandus 66 France Štiglić
Amangeldy 39 Moissei Levin
Amanita Pestilens 63 René Bonnière
Amansız Yol 86 Ömer Kavur
Amant avec des Si . . . , L' 62 Claude Lelouch
Amant de Cinq Jours, L' 61 Philippe de Broca
Amant de la Lune, L' 05 Gaston Velle
Amant de Lady Chatterley, L' 55 Marc Allégret
Amant de Paille, L' 51 Gilles Grangier
Amant de Poche, L' 77 Bernard Queysanne
Amant Magnifique, L' 86 Aline Issermann
Amante, L' 69 Claude Sautet
Amante del Vampiro, L' 59 Renato Polselli
Amante di Gramigna, L' 68 Carlo Lizzani
Amante di Paride, L' 53 Marc Allégret, Edgar G. Ulmer
Amante Segreta, L' 41 Carmine Gallone
Amantes, Los 56 Benito Alazraki
Amantes de Verona, Los 64 Riccardo Freda
Amantes del Desierto, Los 58 Goffredo Alessandrini, Fernando Cerchio, Leon Klimovsky, Ricardo Muñoz Suay, Gianni Vernuccio
Amantes del Diablo, Las 71 José María Elorrieta
Amantes del Señor de la Noche, Las 83 Isela Vega
Amanti, Gli 68 Vittorio De Sica
Amanti del Deserto, Gli 58 Goffredo Alessandrini, Fernando Cerchio, Leon Klimovsky, Ricardo Muñoz Suay, Gianni Vernuccio

Amanti di Domani *55* Luis Buñuel
Amanti di Ravello, Gli *50* Francesco De Robertis
Amanti d'Oltretomba *65* Mario Caiano
Amanti Latini, Gli *65* Mario Costa
Amants, Les *58* Louis Malle
Amants de Bras-Mort, Les *50* Marcello Pagliero
Amants de Minuit, Les *31* Marc Allégret, Augusto Genina
Amants de Teruel, Les *61* Raymond Rouleau
Amants de Tolède, Les *52* Henri Decoin
Amants de Vérone, Les *48* André Cayatte
Amants du Pont Neuf, Les *88* Leos Carax
Amants du Pont Saint-Jean, Les *47* Henri Decoin
Amants du Tage, Les *54* Henri Verneuil
Amants et Voleurs *35* Raymond Bernard
Amants Terribles, Les *36* Marc Allégret
Amants Terribles, Les *84* Danièle Dubroux
Amar *29* Rajaram Vanakudre Shantaram
Amar *48* Ramjankhan Mehboobkhan
Amar Bandhan *87* Tapan Saha
Amar Jyoti *36* Rajaram Vanakudre Shantaram
Amar Kantak *87* Sukhen Das
Amar Lenin *70* Ritwik Ghatak
Amar Sangi *87* Sujit Guha
Amarcord *73* Federico Fellini
Amarilly of Clothes-Line Alley *18* Marshall Neilan
Amarrando el Cordón *68* Santiago Álvarez
Amarsi un Po *84* Carlo Vanzina
Amateur, The *82* Charles Jarrott
Amateur Adventuress, The *19* Henry Otto
Amateur Architect, The *05* Lewin Fitzhamon
Amateur Bill Sykes, An *02* James A. Williamson
Amateur Broadcast *35* Walter Lantz
Amateur Burglar, The *11* Lewin Fitzhamon
Amateur Crook *37* Sam Katzman
Amateur Daddy *32* John G. Blystone
Amateur Detective *38* Howard Bretherton
Amateur Devil, An *20* Maurice Campbell
Amateur Film, The *22* Gustaf Molander
Amateur Gentleman, The *20* Maurice Elvey
Amateur Gentleman, The *26* Sidney Olcott
Amateur Gentleman, The *36* Thornton Freeland
Amateur Hour *85* Stanford Singer
Amateur Night *46* Frank Richardson
Amateur Night in London *30* Monty Banks
Amateur Orphan, An *17* Van Dyke Brooke
Amateur Paper Hanger, The *07* J. H. Martin
Amateur Photographer *86* Karel Kachyňa
Amateur Widow, An *19* Oscar Apfel
Amateur Wife, The *20* Edward Dillon
Amator *79* Krzysztof Kieślowski
Amatör Filmen *22* Gustaf Molander
Amature Nite *29* Walter Lantz
Amazing Adventure, The *36* Alfred Zeisler

Amazing Adventures of Baron Münchhausen, The *43* Josef von Baky
Amazing Adventures of Italians in Russia, The *73* Eldar Ryazanov
Amazing Captain Nemo, The *78* Alex March
Amazing Colossal Man, The *57* Bert I. Gordon
Amazing Dobermans, The *76* Byron Chudnow, David Chudnow
Amazing Dr. Clitterhouse, The *38* Anatole Litvak
Amazing Dr. G, The *65* Giorgio C. Simonelli
Amazing Dr. X, The *48* Bernard Vorhaus
Amazing Grace *74* Stan Lathan
Amazing Grace and Chuck *87* Mike Newell
Amazing Imposter, The *19* Lloyd Ingraham
Amazing Love Secret *75* Tom Parker
Amazing Lovers *21* B. A. Rolfe
Amazing Mr. Beecham, The *49* John Paddy Carstairs
Amazing Mr. Blunden, The *72* Lionel Jeffries
Amazing Mr. Forrest, The *39* Thornton Freeland
Amazing Mr. Nordill, The *47* Joseph M. Newman
Amazing Mr. Williams, The *39* Alexander Hall
Amazing Mr. X, The *48* Bernard Vorhaus
Amazing Monsieur Fabre, The *51* Henri Diamant-Berger
Amazing Mrs. Holliday, The *43* Bruce Manning, Jean Renoir
Amazing Partnership, The *21* George Ridgwell
Amazing Quest, The *36* Alfred Zeisler
Amazing Quest of Ernest Bliss, The *36* Alfred Zeisler
Amazing Quest of Mr. Ernest Bliss, The *20* Henry Edwards
Amazing Transparent Man, The *59* Edgar G. Ulmer
Amazing Transplant, The *70* Doris Wishman
Amazing Vagabond, The *29* Wallace Fox
Amazing Wife, The *19* Ida May Park
Amazing World of Psychic Phenomena, The *76* Robert Guenette
Amazon Quest *49* Steve Sekely
Amazon Trader, The *56* Tom McGowan
Amazon Women on the Moon *86* Joe Dante, Carl Gottlieb, Peter Horton, John Landis, Robert K. Weiss
Amazonas *65* Glauber Rocha
Amazonas Amazonas *65* Glauber Rocha
Amazone *51* Nicole Védrès
Amazonia — The Catherine Miles Story *86* Mario Gariazzo
Amazons, The *17* Joseph Kaufman
Amazons, The *65* Glauber Rocha
Amazons, The *73* Terence Young
Amazons *86* Alex Sessa
Amazons' March and Evolutions, The *02* George Albert Smith
Amazons of Rome *60* Carlo Ludovico

Bragaglia, Vittorio Cottafavi
Amazzone Macabra, L' *16* Carlo Campogalliani
Amazzone Mascherata, L' *14* Emilio Ghione
Ambara Dama *74* Germaine Dieterlen, Jean Rouch
Ambasciatore, L' *36* Baldassare Negroni
Ambassador, The *76* Menahem Golan
Ambassador, The *84* J. Lee-Thompson
Ambassador Bill *31* Sam Taylor
Ambassador of Hell, The *44* Youssef Wahby
Ambassador's Daughter, The *56* Norman Krasna
Ambassador's Despatch, The *09* Émile Cohl
Ambassador's Disappearance, The *13* Maurice Costello
Ambassador's Envoy, The *13* Thomas Ince
Ambiciosos, Los *59* Luis Buñuel
Ambiguous Story, An *86* Mario Bianchi
Ambitieuse, L' *12* Camille De Morlhon
Ambitieuse, L' *58* Yves Allégret
Ambition *16* James Vincent
Ambitious, The *70* Daisuke Ito
Ambitious Annie *28* Roy Del Ruth
Ambitious Butler, The *12* Mack Sennett
Ambitious Children *12* F. Martin Thornton
Ambitious People *31* Nick Grindé
Ambler's Race, The *69* Sergei Urusevsky
Amblin' *69* Steven Spielberg
Ambrose's First Falsehood *14* Del Henderson
Ambulance, The *90* Larry Cohen
Ambulance Chaser *33* Jack Conway
Ambush *38* Kurt Neumann
Ambush *49* Sam Wood
Ambush, The *70* Hiroshi Inagaki
Ambush at Cimarron Pass *58* Jodie Copelan
Ambush at Devil's Gap *66* David Eastman
Ambush at Tomahawk Gap *53* Fred F. Sears
Ambush Bay *66* Ron Winston
Ambush in Leopard Street *59* J. Henry Piperno
Ambush Trail *46* Harry Fraser
Ambush Valley *36* Bernard B. Ray
Ambushed *42* William Berke
Ambushers, The *67* Henry Levin
Âme Corse *08* Victorin Jasset
Âme d'Artiste *25* Germaine Dulac
Âme de Pierre, L' *18* Charles Burguet
Âme de Pierre, L' *28* Gaston Roudes
Âme de Violon, L' *11* Léonce Perret
Âme des Moulins, L' *12* Alfred Machin
Âme du Bronze, L' *18* Henri Roussel
Âme du Moteur: Le Carburateur, L' *26* Pierre Colombier
Amel, El *43* Ahmad Kamel Morsi
Amelia and the Angel *57* Ken Russell
Amelia, or The Time for Love *60* Michel Drach
Amelie *60* Michel Drach
Amelie, or The Time to Love *60* Michel Drach
Amélie ou Le Temps d'Aimer *60* Michel Drach

Amère Victoire *57* Nicholas Ray
America *24* D. W. Griffith
America *82* Robert Downey
America Abbai *87* Singeetham Srinivas Rao
America, America *63* Elia Kazan
America at the Movies *76* George Stevens, Jr.
America Is Hard to See *68* Emile De Antonio
America Is Waiting *81* Bruce Conner
America Revisited *71* Marcel Ophüls
America, That's All *17* Arthur Rosson
America 3000 *86* David Engelbach
America Through the Keyhole *60* François Reichenbach
Américain, L' *20* Louis Delluc
Américain, L' *69* Marcel Bozzuffi
Américain ou Le Chemin d'Ernoa, L' *20* Louis Delluc
Américain Se Détend, L' *57* François Reichenbach
American, The *69* Marcel Bozzuffi
American Anthem *86* Albert Magnoli
American Aristocracy *16* Lloyd Ingraham
American Autobahn *84* André Degas
American Beauty, The *16* William Desmond Taylor
American Beauty *27* Richard Wallace
American Beauty, The *61* Robert Dhéry
American Boy *77* Martin Scorsese
American Boy: A Profile of Steven Prince *77* Martin Scorsese
American Boyfriends *90* Sandy Wilson
American Bride, The *86* Giovanni Soldati
American Buds *18* Kenean Buel
American Built *89* Rocky Lang
American Citizen, An *14* J. Searle Dawley
American Commandos *85* Bobby A. Suarez
American Consul, The *17* Rollin Sturgeon
American Creed, The *46* Robert Stevenson
American Date *87* Armyan Bernstein
American Dream, An *66* Robert Gist
American Dream, The *76* Jörn Donner
American Dream *89* Barbara Kopple
American Dreamer, The *71* L. M. Kit Carson, Lawrence J. Schiller
American Dreamer *84* Richard Rosenthal
American Drive-In *85* Krishna Shah
American Eagle *90* Robert J. Smawley
American Empire *42* William McGann
American Farmers Visit Russia *55* Z. Tuzova
American Flyers *85* John Badham
American Friend, The *77* Wim Wenders
American Frontier *53* Willard Van Dyke
American Game, The *79* Robert Elfstrom, Jay Freund, Peter Powell, David Wolf
American Gigolo *80* Paul Schrader
American Girl, Ze *20* Jean Gic
American Gothic *87* John Hough
American Graffiti *73* George Lucas
American Guerrilla in the Phillipines, An *50* Fritz Lang
American Heiress, The *17* Cecil M. Hepworth
American Hero *86* Steven Lustgarden
American Heroine, The *79* Stella Stevens
American Hot Wax *78* Floyd Mutrux

American in Paris, An *51* Vincente Minnelli
American in Rome, An *54* Steno
American Junkyard *83* Meir Zarchi
American Justice *86* Gary Grillo
American Knockabouts *02* Alf Collins
American Live Wire, An *18* Thomas R. Mills
American Love *31* Pál Fejős, Claude Heymann
American Love Thing, The *73* Greydon Clark
American Madness *32* Frank Capra
American Maid, An *17* Albert Capellani
American Manners *24* James W. Horne
American March *41* Oskar Fischinger
American Matchmaker *39* Edgar G. Ulmer
American Methods *17* Frank Lloyd
American Nightmare *81* Don McBrearty
American Nightmares *86* Buddy Giovinazzo
American Ninja *85* Sam Firstenberg
American Ninja II: The Confrontation *87* Sam Firstenberg
American Ninja 3: Blood Hunt *89* Cedric Sundström
American People, The *44* Frank Capra, Anatole Litvak
American Pluck *25* Richard Stanton
American Pop *81* Ralph Bakshi
American Princess, The *13* Marshall Neilan
American Prisoner, The *29* Thomas Bentley
American Raspberry *80* Brad Swirnoff
American Romance, An *44* King Vidor
American Roulette *88* Maurice Hatton
American Soldier, The *70* Rainer Werner Fassbinder
American Stories *88* Chantal Akerman
American Success *79* William Richert
American Success Company, The *79* William Richert
American Taboo *83* Steven Lustgarden
American Tail, An *86* Don Bluth
American, That's All *17* Arthur Rosson
American Tickler *76* Chuck Vincent
American Tragedy, An *31* Josef von Sternberg
American Venus, The *26* Frank Tuttle
American Warrior *85* Sam Firstenberg
American Way, The *19* Frank Reicher
American Way, The *86* Maurice Phillips
American Werewolf in London, An *81* John Landis
American Widow, An *17* Frank Reicher
American Wife, An *65* Gian Luigi Polidoro
American Years *76* Alexander Hammid
Americana *73* David Carradine
Americaner Schädchen *39* Edgar G. Ulmer
Americanization of Emily, The *64* Arthur Hiller
Americano, The *16* John Emerson
Americano, The *55* William Castle
Americano a Roma, Un *54* Steno
Americano in Vacanza, Un *45* Luigi Zampa
America's Cup Race, The *1899* Edwin S. Porter

Americathon *79* Neal Israel
Amerika, Terra Incognita *88* Diego Risquez
Amerikanische Freund, Der *77* Wim Wenders
Amerikanische Soldat, Der *70* Rainer Werner Fassbinder
Amérique Insolite, L' *60* François Reichenbach
Amérique Lunaire, L' *62* François Reichenbach
Amérique Vu par un Français, L' *60* François Reichenbach
Âmes de Fous *17* Germaine Dulac
Âmes d'Enfants *22* Jean Benoît-Lévy
Âmes d'Enfants *28* Jean Benoît-Lévy, Marie Epstein
Âmes d'Orient *19* Léon Poirier
Âmes Mortes, Les *60* René Allio
Âmes Perdues *76* Dino Risi
Ami Ami *58* André Hunebelle
Ami de Mon Amie, L' *86* Eric Rohmer
Ami Fritz, L' *20* René Hervil
Ami Viendra Ce Soir, Un *46* Raymond Bernard
Amica, L' *15* Enrico Guazzoni
Amica, L' *69* Alberto Lattuada
Amiche, Le *55* Michelangelo Antonioni
Amici Miei *75* Pietro Germi, Mario Monicelli
Amici Miei Atto II *82* Mario Monicelli
Amici Miei, Atto III *85* Nanni Loy
Amici Miei III *85* Nanni Loy
Amici per la Pelle *55* Franco Rossi
Amicizia *40* Oreste Biancoli
Amico delle Donne, L' *42* Ferdinando Maria Poggioli
Amico, Stammi Lontano Almeno un Palmo *72* Michele Lupo
Amiga, La *88* Jeanine Meerapfel
Amigos, Los *72* Paolo Cavara
Amigos *86* Ivan Acosta
Amin—The Rise and Fall *81* Sharad Patel
Amiral Nakhimov *46* Vsevolod I. Pudovkin, Dmitri Vasiliev
Amiral Tempête *53* Mikhail Romm
Amis, Les *71* Gérard Blain
Amitiés Particulières, Les *64* Jean Delannoy
Amityville Curse, The *90* Thomas Berry
Amityville Horror, The *79* Stuart Rosenberg
Amityville II: The Possession *82* Damiano Damiani
Amityville 3-D *83* Richard Fleischer
Amityville III: The Demon *83* Richard Fleischer
Amityville: The Demon *83* Richard Fleischer
Amleto *10* Mario Caserini
Amleto e il Suo Clown *20* Carmine Gallone
Amma Ariyan *86* John Abraham
Ammazzali Tutti e Torna Solo *68* Enzo G. Castellari
Ammutinamento, L' *62* Silvio Amadio
Ammutinamento nello Spazio *65* Hugo Grimaldi
Amo Te Sola *36* Mario Mattòli
Amok *34* Fedor Ozep

Amok *64* Gerry De Leon, Eddie Romero
Amok *65* Dinos Dimopoulos
Amok *76* Peter Walker
Among Human Wolves *39* John Baxter
Among Jews *22* Benjamin Christensen
Among People *39* Mark Donskoi
Among the Cannibal Isles of the South Pacific *18* Martin E. Johnson
Among the Cinders *83* Rolf Haedrich
Among the Headhunters *55* Armand Denis, Michaela Denis
Among the Living *41* Stuart Heisler
Among the Missing *34* Albert S. Rogell
Among the Mourners *14* Del Henderson
Among the Ruins *23* Kenji Mizoguchi
Among the Shadows *86* José Luis Lozano
Among the Thorns *61* Tom Laughlin
Among Those Present *19* Erle C. Kenton*
Among Those Present *21* Fred Newmeyer, Sam Taylor
Among Vultures *64* Alfred Vohrer
Amongst the Thieves *46* Ray Nazarro
Amoozin' But Confoozin' *44* Sid Marcus
Amor a la Vida *50* Miguel Torres Contreras
Amor a la Vuelta de la Esquina *86* Alberto Cortés Calderón
Amor Bandido *79* Bruno Barreto
Amor Brujo, El *85* Carlos Saura
Amor Che Uccide *17* Mario Caserini
Amor con Amor Se Paga *40* Carlos Navarro
Amor de Ahora, El *87* Ernesto Del Río
Amor de Don Juan, El *55* John Berry
Amor de Perdição *78* Manoel De Oliveira
Amor en Campo Minado *87* Pastor Vega
Amor Es Estrany, L' *88* Carlos Balaguer
Amor Es una Mujer Gorda, El *87* Alejandro Agresti
Amor Gitano *10* Segundo De Chomón
Amor Libre, El *79* Jaime Humberto Hermosillo
Amor Manda, El *40* Augusto Cesar Vatteone
Amor und das Standhafte Ehepaar *20* Lotte Reiniger
Amor und das Standhafte Liebespaar *20* Lotte Reiniger
Amore *23* Carmine Gallone
Amore *36* Carlo Ludovico Bragaglia
Amore, L' *48* Marcel Pagnol, Jean Renoir, Roberto Rossellini
Amore a Prima Vista *57* Franco Rossi
Amore a Roma, Un *60* Dino Risi
Amore a Vent'Anni *62* Shintaro Ishihara, Marcel Ophüls, Renzo Rossellini, François Truffaut, Andrzej Wajda
Amore all'Italiana *65* Steno
Amore Attraverso i Secoli, L' *67* Claude Autant-Lara, Mauro Bolognini, Philippe de Broca, Jean-Luc Godard, Franco Indovina, Michael Pfleghar
Amore Cantà, L' *41* Ferdinando Maria Poggioli
Amore Che Cantà, L' *32* Mario Bonnard
Amore Che Non Torna *38* Bruno Valetti
Amore Difficile, L' *62* Alberto Bonucci, Nino Manfredi, Sergio Sollima
Amore e Chiacchiere *57* Alessandro Blasetti

Amore e Morte *32* Rosario Romeo
Amore e Paura *88* Margarethe von Trotta
Amore e Rabbia *67* Marco Bellocchio, Bernardo Bertolucci, Jean-Luc Godard, Carlo Lizzani, Pier Paolo Pasolini
Amore in Città *53* Michelangelo Antonioni, Federico Fellini, Alberto Lattuada, Carlo Lizzani, Francesco Maselli, Dino Risi, Cesare Zavattini
Amore in Quarantena *38* Amleto Palermi
Amore in Quattro Dimensioni *65* Mino Guerrini, Massimo Mida, Gianni Puccini, Jacques Romain
Amore in Stockholm *63* Gian Luigi Polidoro
Amore Inquieto di Maria *86* Sergio Pastore
Amore Mio Aiutami *69* Alberto Sordi
Amore nell'Arte, L' *50* Mario Bava
Amore, Piombo e Furore *79* Antonio Brandt
Amore Primitivo, L' *66* Luigi Scattini
Amore Rosso *53* Aldo Vergano
Amore Si Fa Così, L' *39* Carlo Ludovico Bragaglia
Amori *89* Alberto Lattuada*
Amori di Ercole, Gli *60* Carlo Ludovico Bragaglia
Amori di Manon Lescaut, Gli *54* Mario Costa
Amori di Mezzo Secolo *53* Mario Chiari, Pietro Germi, Antonio Pietrangeli, Roberto Rossellini
Amori di una Calda Estate *64* Juan Antonio Bardem
Amori Miei *78* Steno
Amori Pericolosi *64* Alfredo Giannetti, Carlo Lizzani, Giulio Questi
Amorina *61* Hugo Del Carril
Amorists, The *66* Shohei Imamura
Amorosa *86* Mai Zetterling
Amorosa Menzogna, L' *49* Michelangelo Antonioni
Amorous Adventures of Bux, The *26* Norman Le Strange
Amorous Adventures of Don Quixote and Sancho Panza, The *76* Raphael Nussbaum
Amorous Adventures of Moll Flanders, The *65* Terence Young
Amorous Adventures of Uncle Benjamin, The *69* Édouard Molinaro
Amorous Arthur *12* Lewin Fitzhamon
Amorous Cook, The *1899* Arthur Cooper
Amorous Doctor, The *11* Theo Bouwmeester
Amorous General, The *62* John Guillermin
Amorous Militiaman, The *04* Alf Collins
Amorous Milkman, The *75* Derren Nesbitt
Amorous Mr. Prawn, The *62* Anthony Kimmins
Amorous Nurse, The *08* Lewin Fitzhamon
Amorous Policeman, The *06* Harold Hough
Amorous Prawn, The *62* Anthony Kimmins
Amorous Sex, The *59* Ronnie Albert
Amos 'n' Andy *30* Melville Brown

Amour, L' *14* Henri Pouctal
Amour, L' *33* Heinosuke Gosho
Amour, L' *72* Paul Morrissey, Andy Warhol
Amour à la Chaîne, L' *64* Claude De Givray
Amour à l'Américaine, L' *31* Pál Fejős, Claude Heymann
Amour à Mort, L' *84* Alain Resnais
Amour à Paris, Un *87* Merzak Allouache
Amour à Tous les Étages, L' *02* Ferdinand Zecca
Amour à Travers les Âges, L' *67* Claude Autant-Lara, Mauro Bolognini, Philippe de Broca, Jean-Luc Godard, Franco Indovina, Michael Pfleghar
Amour à Vingt Ans, L' *62* Shintaro Ishihara, Marcel Ophüls, Renzo Rossellini, François Truffaut, Andrzej Wajda
Amour, Amour *37* Robert Bilbal
Amour au Féminin, L' *68* Jean-Gabriel Albicocco*
Amour avec des Si..., L' *62* Claude Lelouch
Amour Blessé, L' *75* Jean-Pierre Lefèbvre
Amour Blessé: Confidences de la Nuit, L' *75* Jean-Pierre Lefèbvre
Amour Braque, L' *85* Andrzej Żuławski
Amour C'Est Gai, l'Amour C'Est Triste, L' *68* Jean-Daniel Pollet
Amour Chante, L' *30* Robert Florey, Augusto Genina
Amour d'Automne *12* Louis Feuillade
Amour de Pluie, Un *74* Jean-Claude Brialy
Amour de Poche, Un *57* Pierre Kast
Amour de Swann, Un *83* Volker Schlöndorff
Amour d'une Femme, L' *53* Jean Grémillon
Amour en Allemagne, Un *83* Andrzej Wajda
Amour en Douce, L' *84* Édouard Molinaro
Amour en Fuite, L' *79* François Truffaut
Amour en Quatre Dimensions, L' *65* Mino Guerrini, Massimo Mida, Gianni Puccini, Jacques Romain
Amour en Question, L' *78* André Cayatte
Amour Est un Jeu, L' *57* Marc Allégret
Amour et Compagnie *50* Gilles Grangier
Amour et l'Argent, L' *11* Léonce Perret
Amour Existe, L' *60* Maurice Pialat
Amour Fou, L' *68* Jacques Rivette
Amour l'Après-Midi, L' *72* Eric Rohmer
Amour l'Après-Midi: Six Contes Moraux: 6, L' *72* Eric Rohmer
Amour, Madame, L' *51* Gilles Grangier
Amour Maître des Choses, L' *31* Jean Kemm
Amour par Terre, L' *84* Jacques Rivette
Amour Passe, L' *14* Léon Poirier
Amour Propre...Ne le Reste Jamais Tres Longtemps, L' *85* Martin Veyron
Amour Tenace *12* Max Linder
Amour Violé, L' *77* Yannick Bellon
Amoureuse, L' *88* Jacques Doillon
Amoureuse Aventure, L' *31* Wilhelm Thiele
Amoureux, Les *33* Marcel L'Herbier
Amoureux du "France," Les *62* Pierre Grimblat, François Reichenbach

And There Came a Man *64* Ermanno Olmi

And There Was No More Sea *55* Bert Haanstra

And They Called Him Hero *15* Francis Ford

And to Think That I Saw It on Mulberry Street *44* George Pal

And Two Eggs from Turkey *87* Aris Foriadis

And Very Nice Too *13* Walter R. Booth

And Very Nice Too *14* Charles H. Weston

And Woman...Was Created *56* Roger Vadim

And Women Must Weep *22* Robert C. Bruce

And Women Shall Weep *60* John Lemont

And Yet They Go On *31* Kenji Mizoguchi

And Yet We Live *51* Tadashi Imai

And You Will Wander Restless... *15* Richard Oswald

And You'll Live in Terror: The Beyond *80* Lucio Fulci

Anda Muchacho, Spara *71* Aldo Florio

Andalusian Dog, An *28* Luis Buñuel, Salvador Dali

Andalusische Nächte *38* Herbert Maisch

Andaz *42* Ramjankhan Mehboobkhan

Anđeo Čuvar *87* Goran Paskaljević

Andere, Der *12* Max Mack

Andere, Die *24* Gerhard Lamprecht

Andere, Der *30* Robert Wiene

Anders Als die Anderen *19* Richard Oswald

Anders Als Du und Ich *57* Veidt Harlan

Andersen hos Fotografen *75* Jørgen Roos

Andersens Hemmelighed *71* Jørgen Roos

Andersen's Run *86* Hans Otto Nicolayssen

Anderson Family, The *39* Sigurd Wallen

Anderson Platoon, The *66* Pierre Schöndörffer

Anderson Tapes, The *71* Sidney Lumet

Anderson's Angels *76* Ed Forsyth

Andes no Hanayome *66* Susumu Hani

Andhera *75* R. Tulsi Ramsay, Shyam Ramsay

André Chénier *09* Léonce Perret

André Cornélis *18* Jean Kemm

André Cornélis *27* Jean Kemm

André Gide *51* Marc Allégret

André Malraux *58* Leonard Kiegel

André Masson and the Four Elements *58* Jean Grémillon

André Masson et les Quatre Éléments *58* Jean Grémillon

Andrea *79* Leopold Pomes

Andrea Chenier *55* Clemente Fracassi

Andrei Kozhukhov *17* Yakov Protazanov

Andrei Roublev *65* Andrei Tarkovsky

Andrei Rublev *65* Andrei Tarkovsky

Andrei Rublyov *65* Andrei Tarkovsky

Andreuccio da Perugia *10* Enrico Guazzoni

Andrew Jackson *13* Allan Dwan

Andrews' Raiders *56* Francis D. Lyon

Andriesh *54* Yakov Bazelian, Sergei Paradzhanov

Androclès *12* Louis Feuillade

Androcles and the Lion *52* Chester Erskine, Nicholas Ray

Android *82* Aaron Lipstadt

Andromeda Nebula, The *68* Yevgeny Sherstobitov

Andromeda Strain, The *70* Robert Wise

Andromeda the Mysterious *68* Yevgeny Sherstobitov

Andy *65* Richard C. Sarafian

Andy and Min at the Theatre *20* Wallace A. Carlson

Andy and the Airwave Rangers *90* Deborah Brock

Andy at Shady Rest *20* Wallace A. Carlson

Andy Colby's Incredibly Awesome Adventure *90* Deborah Brock

Andy Fights the High Cost of Living *20* Wallace A. Carlson

Andy Hardy Comes Home *58* Howard W. Koch

Andy Hardy Gets Spring Fever *39* W. S. Van Dyke

Andy Hardy Meets Debutante *40* George B. Seitz

Andy Hardy's Blonde Trouble *44* George B. Seitz

Andy Hardy's Double Life *42* George B. Seitz

Andy Hardy's Private Secretary *40* George B. Seitz

Andy Has a Caller *21* Wallace A. Carlson

Andy of the Royal Mounted *15* Gilbert M. Anderson

Andy on a Diet *20* Wallace A. Carlson

Andy on Pleasure Bent *20* Wallace A. Carlson

Andy on Skates *20* Wallace A. Carlson

Andy on the Beach *20* Wallace A. Carlson

Andy Plays Golf *20* Wallace A. Carlson

Andy Plays Hero *20* Wallace A. Carlson

Andy Redecorates His Flat *20* Wallace A. Carlson

Andy Spends a Quiet Day at Home *20* Wallace A. Carlson

Andy the Actor *20* Wallace A. Carlson

Andy the Chicken Farmer *20* Wallace A. Carlson

Andy the Hero *20* Wallace A. Carlson

Andy the Model *20* Wallace A. Carlson

Andy Visits His Mamma-in-Law *20* Wallace A. Carlson

Andy Visits the Osteopath *20* Wallace A. Carlson

Andy Warhol Films Jack Smith Filming "Normal Love" *63* Andy Warhol

Andy Warhol's Bad *71* Jed Johnson

Andy Warhol's Dracula *73* Antonio Margheriti, Paul Morrissey

Andy Warhol's Frankenstein *73* Antonio Margheriti, Paul Morrissey

Andy Warhol's Women *71* Paul Morrissey

Andy Warhol's Young Dracula *73* Antonio Margheriti, Paul Morrissey

Andy's Cow *21* Wallace A. Carlson

Andy's Dancing Lesson *20* Wallace A. Carlson

Andy's Dog Day *21* Wallace A. Carlson

Andy's Holiday *21* Wallace A. Carlson

Andy's Inter-Ruben Guest *20* Wallace A. Carlson

Andy's Mother-in-Law Pays Him a Visit *20*
Wallace A. Carlson

Andy's Night Out *20* Wallace A. Carlson

Andy's Picnic *20* Wallace A. Carlson

Andy's Wash Day *20* Wallace A. Carlson

Âne Qui à Bu la Lune, L' *88* Marie-Claude Treilhou

Anello di Siva, L' *14* Augusto Genina

Anemia *86* Alberto Abruzzese, Achille Pisanti

Anemic Cinema *25* Marcel Duchamp

Anemos tou Missous, O *58* M. Tsiforos

Anfisa *12* Yakov Protazanov

Anfiteatro Flavio *47* Mario Bava

Ange de la Maison, L' *13* Léonce Perret

Ange de la Nuit, L' *44* André Berthomieu

Ange de Noël, L' *05* Georges Méliès

Ange du Cœur, L' *06* André Heuze

Angeklagt nach Paragraph 218 *66* Aleksander Ford

Angel *34* Marcel Pagnol

Angel *37* Ernst Lubitsch

Angel *82* Neil Jordan

Angel *82* Yorgos Katakouzinos

Angel *83* Robert Vincent O'Neil

Angel *89* Stig Larsson

Angel and Sinner *45* Christian-Jaque

Angel and the Badman *46* James Edward Grant

Angel and the Woman, The *77* Gilles Carle

Angel, Angel, Down We Go *69* Robert Thom

Angel at My Table, An *90* Jane Campion

Angel Baby *61* Hubert Cornfield, Paul Wendkos

Angel Child, The *08* Edwin S. Porter

Angel Child *18* Henry Otto

Angel Citizens *22* Francis Ford

Angel City *77* Jon Jost

Angel Comes to Brooklyn, An *45* Leslie Goodwins

Angel Dust *87* Édouard Niermans

Angel Esquire *19* Will P. Kellino

Ángel Exterminador, El *62* Luis Buñuel

Angel Eyes *28* Charles Lamont

Angel Face *52* Otto Preminger

Angel Factory, The *17* Lawrence McGill

Angel for Satan, An *66* Camillo Mastrocinque

Angel from Texas, An *40* Ray Enright

Angel Heart *87* Alan Parker

Angel in a Taxi *59* Antonio Leonviola

Angel in Exile *48* Allan Dwan, Philip Ford

Angel in My Pocket *69* Alan Rafkin

Angel Levine, The *70* Ján Kadár

Angel Number 9 *77* Roberta Findlay

Angel of Broadway, The *27* Lois Weber

Angel of Crooked Street, The *22* David Smith

Angel of Death, The *13* Herbert Brenon

Angel of Deliverance, The *14* Warwick Buckland

Angel of H.E.A.T. *81* Myrl Schreibman

Angel of Paradise Ranch, The *11* Allan Dwan

Angel of the Canyons *13* Allan Dwan

Angel of the Ward, The *15* Tom Watts

Angel of Vengeance *80* Abel Ferrara

Angel of Vengeance *86* Ted V. Mikels

Angel on Earth 59 Géza von Radványi

Angel on My Shoulder 46 Archie Mayo

Angel on the Amazon 48 John H. Auer

Ángel Pasó por Brooklyn, Un 57 Ladislas Vajda

Angel Passed Over Brooklyn, An 57 Ladislas Vajda

Angel Puss 44 Chuck Jones

Angel River 86 Sergio Olhovich Greene

Angel Skin 83 Jean-Louis Daniel

Angel Street 39 Thorold Dickinson

Angel III: The Final Chapter 88 Tom DeSimone

Angel Town 90 Eric Karson

Angel Unchained 70 Lee Madden

Angel Who Pawned Her Harp, The 54 Alan Bromly

Angel with One Wing, An 86 Toshio Masuda

Angel with the Trumpet, The 49 Anthony Bushell

Angel Wore Red, The 60 Nunnally Johnson

Angela 55 Dennis O'Keefe

Angela 77 Boris Sagal

Angela Markado 80 Lino Brocka

Angela—Portrait of a Revolutionary 71 Yolande Du Luart

Angela's Sweet Skin 87 Andrea Bianchi

Angèle 34 Marcel Pagnol

Ángeles y Querubines 71 Rafael Corkidi

Angelic Conversation, The 85 Derek Jarman

Angelic Conversations 85 Derek Jarman

Angelic Servant, An 07 Georges Méliès

Angelika 51 Rolf Hansen

Angelika Urban, Salesgirl, Engaged 70 Helma Sanders-Brahms

Angelika Urban, Verkäuferin, Verlobt 70 Helma Sanders-Brahms

Angelina 47 Luigi Zampa

Angelina's Birthday Present 09 Joe Rosenthal

Angélique 64 Bernard Borderie

Angélique, Marquise des Anges 64 Bernard Borderie

Angelita 35 Louis King

Angelo 51 Francesco De Robertis

Angelo della Alpi, L' 57 Carlo Campogalliani

Angelo e il Diavolo, L' 46 Mario Camerini

Angelo È Sceso a Brooklyn, Un 57 Ladislas Vajda

Angelo in the Crowd 52 Leonardo De Mitri

Angelo, My Love 82 Robert Duvall

Angelo per Satana, Un 66 Camillo Mastrocinque

Angelos 82 Yorgos Katakouzinos

Angels 76 Spencer Compton

Angels' Alley 48 William Beaudine

Angels and the Pirates, The 51 Clarence Brown

Angels' Brigade 79 Greydon Clark

Angels Die Hard 70 Richard Compton

Angels' Door 71 Stan Brakhage

Angels for Kicks 71 Richard Kanter

Angels from Hell 68 Bruce Kessler

Angel's Holiday 37 James Tinling

Angels in Disguise 49 Jean Yarbrough

Angels in the Outfield 51 Clarence Brown

Angels of Darkness 53 Giuseppe Amato

Angels of Mons, The 15 L. C. MacBean, Fred Paul

Angels of the Street 36 Mou-che Yen

Angels of the Streets 43 Robert Bresson

Angels One Five 52 George More O'Ferrall

Angels Over Broadway 40 Lee Garmes, Ben Hecht

Angel's Pit, The 37 Carlo Ludovico Bragaglia

Angels Unawares 12 Edwin S. Porter

Angels Wash Their Faces 39 Ray Enright

Angels' Wild Women 72 Al Adamson

Angels with Broken Wings 41 Bernard Vorhaus

Angels with Dirty Faces 38 Michael Curtiz

Angélus, L' 00 Alice Guy-Blaché

Angelus, The 37 Thomas Bentley

Angelus Novus 87 Pasquale Misuraca

Angemaeul 82 Kwon-taek Im

Anger of the Golem 66 Herbert J. Leder

Anges du Péché, Les 43 Robert Bresson

Anges Gardiens 64 François Reichenbach*

Angestellte, Der 72 Helma Sanders-Brahms

Angi Vera 78 Pál Gábor

Angkor-Cambodia Express 81 Lek Kitiparaporn

Anglais Tel Que Max le Parle, L' 14 Max Linder

Änglar, Finns Dom... 60 Lars-Magnus Lindgren

Anglers, The 14 Charlie Chase

Angler's Dream, The 06 James A. Williamson

Angler's Nightmare, or A Policeman's Troubles, The 05 Georges Méliès

Angoissante Aventure, L' 20 Yakov Protazanov

Angoisse, L' 13 Louis Feuillade

Angoisse 17 André Hugon

Angoisse au Foyer, L' 15 Louis Feuillade

Angora Love 29 Lewis R. Foster

Angriff der Gegenwart auf die Übrige Zeit, Der 85 Alexander Kluge

Angriffsschlachter, Der 71 Alexander Kluge

Angry Boy 50 Alexander Hammid

Angry Breed, The 69 David Commons

Angry Ghost, The 43 Minoru Shibuya

Angry God, The 48 Van Campen Heilner

Angry Harvest 85 Agnieszka Holland

Angry Hills, The 59 Robert Aldrich

Angry Island 60 Seiji Hisamatsu

Angry Man, The 79 Claude Pinoteau

Angry Red Planet, The 59 Ib Melchior

Angry Sea, The 44 Tadashi Imai

Angry Silence, The 59 Guy Green

Angry Street, The 49 Mikio Naruse

Angst, Die 54 Roberto Rossellini

Angst des Tormanns beim Elfmeter, Die 71 Wim Wenders

Angst Essen Seele Auf 73 Rainer Werner Fassbinder

Angst vor der Angst 75 Rainer Werner Fassbinder

Anguish 74 Pedro Olea

Anguish 86 Bigas Luna

Angustia 47 José Antonio Nieves Conde

Angustia 86 Bigas Luna

Angyalföldi Fiatalok 55 Miklós Jancsó

Angyalok Földje 62 György Révész

Ani Imōto 53 Mikio Naruse

Ani Imōto 76 Tadashi Imai

Ani Ohev Otach Rosa 71 Moshe Mizrahi

Ani to Sono Imōto 39 Yasujiro Shimazu

Aniki-Bobo 42 Manoel De Oliveira

Anikina Vremena 54 Vladimir Pogačić

Anima Nera 62 Roberto Rossellini

Anima Persa 76 Dino Risi

Anima Tormentata 19 Mario Caserini

Animal, The 13 Allan Dwan

Animal, L' 77 Claude Zidi

Animal Behavior 85 Jenny Bowen, Kjehl Rasmussen

Animal Cracker Circus 38 Ben Harrison

Animal Crackers 30 Victor Heerman

Animal Farm 54 Joy Batchelor, John Halas

Animal House 78 John Landis

Animal Imitations 06 Arthur Gilbert

Animal Kingdom, The 32 George Cukor, Edward H. Griffith

Animal Within, The 12 Allan Dwan

Animal World, The 56 Irwin Allen

Animaland 47 David Hand

Animali Pazzi 39 Carlo Ludovico Bragaglia

Animals, The 63 Frédéric Rossif

Animals, The 70 Ron Joy

Animals and Humans 22 Julian Ollendorff

Animals and the Brigands, The 46 Jiří Trnka

Animals Are Beautiful People 74 Jamie Uys

Animals Film, The 81 Victor Schonfeld

Animals of Eden and After, The 70 Stan Brakhage

Animalympics 79 Steven Lisberger

Ánimas Trujano 61 Ismael Rodríguez

Animated Clown Portrait 1898 George Albert Smith

Animated Costumes, The 04 Georges Méliès

Animated Cotton 09 Walter R. Booth

Animated Crosswords No. 1 25 Bert Green

Animated Dress Stand, The 06 Tom Green

Animated Genesis 52 Joan Foldes, Peter Foldes

Animated Grouch Chaser, The 15 Raoul Barré

Animated Luncheon 00 Edwin S. Porter

Animated Matches 08 Émile Cohl

Animated Matches 08 Arthur Cooper

Animated Painting 04 Edwin S. Porter

Animated Pillar Box, The 07 Arthur Cooper

Animated Poster, The 03 Edwin S. Porter

Animated Putty 11 Walter R. Booth

Animated Self-Portraits 89 Jan Švankmajer

Animated Snowballs 08 Edwin S. Porter

Animated Technical Drawing 18 E. Dean Parmelee

Animated Toys 12 Walter R. Booth

Animaux, Les 63 Frédéric Rossif

Anime Buie 15 Emilio Ghione

Anioły Spadają 59 Roman Polanski
Anita—Dances of Vice 87 Rosa von
  Praunheim
Anita G. 66 Alexander Kluge
Anita Garibaldi 51 Goffredo Alessandrini,
  Francesco Rosi, Franco Rossi
Anita—Tänze des Lasters 87 Rosa von
  Praunheim
Anita's Butterfly 15 John Francis Dillon
Anjaam 87 Hariharan
Anjangarh 48 Bimal Roy
Anjo-Ke no Butōkai 47 Kozaburo Yoshi-
  mura
Anjos da Noite 87 Wilson Barros
Anjos do Arrabalde 87 Carlos Reichen-
  bach
Anjou 77 Roger Leenhardt
Anjuman 87 Muzaffar Ali
Anjuta the Dancer 16 Mauritz Stiller
Anka 31 Boris Barnet
Ankara, Heart of Turkey 34 Lev Arn-
  shtam, Sergei Yutkevich
Ankara Postası 29 Ertuğrul Muhsin
Ankara, Serdtsye Turkiye 34 Lev Arn-
  shtam, Sergei Yutkevich
Ankles Away 38 Charlie Chase
Ankles Preferred 27 John G. Blystone
Ankur 74 Shyam Benegal
Ann Carver's Profession 33 Edward Buz-
  zell
Ann Szabó 49 Félix Máriássy
Ann Vickers 33 John Cromwell
Anna 18 Henry Edwards
Anna 36 Ivan Pyriev
Anna 51 Giuseppe Berto, Alberto Lat-
  tuada, Dino Risi
Anna 57 Zoltán Fábri
Anna 70 Jörn Donner
Anna 81 Márta Mészáros
Anna 87 Yurek Bogayevicz
Anna and the King of Siam 46 John
  Cromwell
Anna and the Wolves 72 Carlos Saura
Anna Ascends 22 Victor Fleming
Anna Boleyn 20 Ernst Lubitsch
Anna Christie 23 Kenji Mizoguchi
Anna Christie 23 John Griffith Wray
Anna Christie 29 Jacques Feyder
Anna Christie 30 Clarence Brown
Anna Contract, The 78 David Percy
Anna Cross, The 54 I. Annensky
Anna di Brooklyn 58 Reginald Denham,
  Carlo Lasticati
Anna Garibaldi 10 Mario Caserini
Anna Karenina 14 J. Gordon Edwards
Anna Karenina 14 Vladimir Gardin
Anna Karenina 27 Edmund Goulding
Anna Karenina 35 Clarence Brown
Anna Karenina 47 Julien Duvivier
Anna Karenina 67 Alexander Zarkhi
Anna Karénine 47 Julien Duvivier
Anna Klara and Her Brothers 23 Per
  Lindberg
Anna la Bonne 59 Claude Jutra
Anna Lans 43 Rune Carlsten
Anna Lucasta 49 Irving Rapper
Anna Lucasta 58 Arnold Laven
Anna och Eva 69 Arne Mattsson
Anna of Brooklyn 58 Reginald Denham,
  Carlo Lasticati

Anna of Rhodes 50 Michael Gazlades,
  John Philippou
Anna Pavlova—A Woman for All Time 85
  Emil Lotyanu
Anna Szabó 49 Félix Máriássy
Anna the Adventuress 20 Cecil M. Hep-
  worth
Anna to the Infinite Power 83 Robert
  Wiemer
Anna und Elisabeth 33 Frank Wisbar
Annabel Lee 21 William J. Scully
Annabel Takes a Tour 38 Lew Landers
Annabelle Lee 72 Harold Daniels
Annabelle's Affairs 31 Alfred L. Werker
Annabel's Romance 16 Louis Gasnier
Annapolis 28 Christy Cabanne
Annapolis Farewell 35 Alexander Hall
Annapolis Salute 37 Christy Cabanne
Annapolis Story, An 55 Don Siegel
Annapurna 53 Marcel Ichac
Anne Against the World 29 Duke Worne
Anne and Eve 69 Arne Mattsson
Anne and Muriel 71 François Truffaut
Anne Boleyn 20 Ernst Lubitsch
Anne Devlin 84 Pat Murphy
Anne-Marie 36 Raymond Bernard
Anne of Green Gables 19 William Des-
  mond Taylor
Anne of Green Gables 34 George
  Nicholls, Jr.
Anne of Little Smoky 21 Edward Connor
Anne of the Indies 51 Jacques Tourneur
Anne of the Thousand Days 69 Charles
  Jarrott
Anne of Windy Poplars 40 Jack Hively
Anne of Windy Willows 40 Jack Hively
Anne One Hundred 33 Henry Edwards
Anne ou La Mort d'un Pilote 74 Jacques
  Doniol-Valcroze
Anne Trister 86 Léa Pool
Anneau Fatal, L' 12 Louis Feuillade
Anneaux d'Or de Mahdia, Les 60 René
  Vautier
Année Dernière à Marienbad, L' 61 Alain
  Resnais
Année des Méduses, L' 84 Christopher
  Frank
Année Prochaine Si Tout Va Bien, L' 81
  Jean-Loup Hubert
Années 80, Les 83 Chantal Akerman
Années Lumières, Les 80 Alain Tanner
Années Sandwiches, Les 88 Pierre Boutron
Années 25, Les 66 Nelly Kaplan
Annelie 41 Josef von Baky
Annemarie, die Braut der Kompanie 32
  Carl Boese
Annette in Paradise 36 Max Obal
Annexing Bill 18 Albert Parker
Anni Difficili 48 Luigi Zampa
Anni Facili 53 Luigi Zampa
Anni Ruggenti, Gli 62 Luigi Zampa
Annibale 59 Carlo Ludovico Bragaglia,
  Edgar G. Ulmer
Annie 82 John Huston
Annie Bell 11 August Blom
Annie-for-Spite 17 James Kirkwood
Annie Get Your Gun 50 George Sidney
Annie Hall 77 Woody Allen
Annie Hall: A Nervous Romance 77
  Woody Allen

Annie Laurie 16 Cecil M. Hepworth
Annie Laurie 27 John S. Robertson
Annie Laurie 36 Walter Tennyson
Annie, Leave the Room! 35 Leslie Hiscott
Annie Mae, Brave-Hearted Woman 79 Lan
  Brooks Ritz
Annie Moved Away 34 Walter Lantz
Annie Oakley 35 George Stevens
Annie's Coming Out 84 Gil Brealey
Annihilators, The 85 Charles E. Sellier
Anniversaire, L' 16 Georges Monca
Anniversary, The 67 Roy Ward Baker
Anniversary of the Revolution 19 Dziga
  Vertov
Anno Scorso a Marienbad, L' 61 Alain
  Resnais
Anno Uno 74 Roberto Rossellini
Ann's Finish 18 Lloyd Ingraham
Annual Parade, New York Fire Depart-
  ment 04 Edwin S. Porter
Annual Trip of the Mothers' Meeting,
  The 05 Lewin Fitzhamon
Annular Eclipse 75 Satsuo Yamamoto
Annushka 59 Boris Barnet
Ano Ang Kulay ng Mukha ng Diyos? 85
  Lino Brocka
Año de la Peste, El 78 Felipe Cazals
Año de las Luces, El 86 Fernando Trueba
Año del Conejo, El 87 Fernando Ayala
Año Siete 66 Santiago Álvarez
Ano Te Kono Te 52 Kon Ichikawa
Año Uno 72 Sara Gómez
Anónimo, El 32 Fernando De Fuentes
Anonimo Veneziano 70 Enrico Maria
  Salerno
Anonyme 58 Alexander Alexeïeff, Claire
  Parker
Anonymous Avenger, The 76 Enzo G.
  Castellari
Anonymous Venetian, The 70 Enrico
  Maria Salerno
Anoop and the Elephant 73 David Eady
Another Bottle, Doctor 26 Dave Fleischer
Another Chance 14 Donald Crisp
Another Chance 52 Gordon Parry
Another Chance 87 Jesse Vint
Another Country 84 Marek Kanievska
Another Dawn 37 William Dieterle
Another Day 87 Silvano Agosti
Another Experience 39 Carmine Gallone
Another Face 35 Christy Cabanne
Another Fallen Idol 15 L. M. Glackens
Another Fine Mess 30 James Parrott
Another 48 HRS. 90 Walter Hill
Another Island 87 Grażyna Kędzielawska
Another Job for the Undertaker 01 Edwin
  S. Porter
Another Language 33 Edward H. Griffith
Another Love Story 86 Américo Ortiz De
  Zarate
Another Man, Another Chance 77 Claude
  Lelouch
Another Man, Another Woman 77 Claude
  Lelouch
Another Man's Boots 22 William James
  Craft
Another Man's Poison 51 Irving Rapper
Another Man's Shoes 22 Jack Conway
Another Man's Wife 12 Allan Dwan
Another Man's Wife 15 Harold Weston

Apache Trail *42* Richard Thorpe
Apache Uprising *66* R. G. Springsteen
Apache War Smoke *52* Harold F. Kress
Apache Warrior *57* Elmo Williams
Apache Woman *55* Roger Corman
Apachen, Die *19* E. A. Dupont
Apachentanz *06* Oskar Messter
Apaches, Les *04* Georges Méliès
Apache's Gratitude, An *13* William Duncan
Apache's Last Battle *64* Hugo Fregonese
Apaches of Athens, The *30* Dimitrios Gaziadis
Apaches of Paris, The *15* Robert Ellis
Apaches of Paris *28* Nikolai Malikoff
Apaches Pas Veinards, Les *03* Alice Guy-Blaché
Apachides ton Athinon, I *30* Dimitrios Gaziadis
Apan Gharey *87* Pinaki Chowdhury
Apando, El *75* Felipe Cazals
Aparadhi *31* Debaki Kumar Bose
Aparadhi Kaun *58* Bimal Roy
Aparajito *56* Satyajit Ray
Apariencias Engañan, Las *82* Jaime Humberto Hermosillo
Aparoopa *82* Jahnu Barua
Apart from You *32* Mikio Naruse
Apartment, The *60* Billy Wilder
Apartment Above *38* Leon Trystan
Apartment for Peggy *48* George Seaton
Apartment House Story *79* Věra Chytilová
Apartment in Moscow *62* Victor Eisimont
Apartment on the Thirteenth Floor, The *72* Eloy De la Iglesia
Apartment 29 *17* Paul Scardon
Apartment Zero *88* Martin Donovan
Ape, The *28* Beverly C. Rule
Ape, The *34* William Nigh
Ape, The *40* William Nigh
Ape and Super Ape *72* Bert Haanstra
Ape Creature *68* Alfred Vohrer
Ape Man, The *43* William Beaudine
Ape Man of the Jungle *62* Charlie Foster
Ape Regina, L' *63* Marco Ferreri
Ape Woman, The *64* Marco Ferreri
Apeksha *84* Jahnu Barua
Apenas un Delincuente *47* Hugo Fregonese
Ape's Devotion, An *13* Wilfred Noy
Apes of Wrath *59* Friz Freleng
Apfel Ist Ab, Der *48* Helmut Käutner
Aphrodite *82* Robert Fuest
Aphrodite, Goddess of Love *62* Mario Bonnard
Aphrousa *71* Evangelos Joannides
Aplagueur, L' *76* Philippe Labro
Apna Ghar *41* Debaki Kumar Bose
Apocalipse Cannibal *80* Antonio Margheriti
Apocalipsis Caníbal *81* Bruno Mattei
Apocalisse Domani *80* Antonio Margheriti
Apocalisse sull' Fiume Giallo *59* William Dieterle
Apocalypse de Saint-Sévres, L' *49* Jean Grémillon
Apocalypse Domani *80* Antonio Margheriti
Apocalypse Now *79* Francis Ford Coppola
Apocalypse 3:16 *64* Martin Charlot

Apollo *20* Gregory La Cava
Apollo Goes on Holiday *68* Georges Skalenakis
Apólogo, Um *39* Humberto Mauro
Apology for Murder *45* Sam Newfield
Apostasy *48* Keisuke Kinoshita
Apostasy, The *61* Kon Ichikawa
Apostle of Vengeance, The *16* Reginald Barker
Apothecary, The *16* Michael Curtiz
Apotheosis *70* John Lennon, Yoko Ono
Apousies *87* Yorgos Katakouzinos
Appaloosa, The *66* Sidney J. Furie
Apparition, The *03* Georges Méliès
Apparition, or Mr. Jones' Comical Experiences with a Ghost, The *03* Georges Méliès
Apparitions Fantômatiques *10* Georges Méliès
Apparitions Fugitives, Les *04* Georges Méliès
Appartement des Filles, L' *63* Michel Deville
Appassionata, L' *29* Audre Liabel, Léon Mathot
Appassionata *44* Olof Molander
Appassionata *59* Jiří Weiss
Appassionata *85* Gian Luigi Calderone
Appearance of Evil *18* Lawrence C. Windom
Appearance of Supergiant, The *56* Teruo Ishii
Appearances *21* Donald Crisp
Appearances *45* Kamel Salim
Appel du Sang, L' *19* Louis Mercanton
Appel du Silence, L' *36* Léon Poirier
Appentis, L' *14* Émile Chautard
Appetite and Love *14* Anders Wilhelm Sandberg
Applause *29* Rouben Mamoulian
Applause *43* George Tzavellas
Apple, The *61* George Dunning
Apple, The *80* Menahem Golan
Apple Dumpling Gang, The *74* Norman Tokar
Apple Dumpling Gang Rides Again, The *79* Vincent McEveety
Apple Fell, The *48* Helmut Käutner
Apple Game, The *76* Věra Chytilová
Apple Is Picked, The *48* Helmut Käutner
Apple of Discord, The *07* Walter R. Booth
Apple-Tree Girl, The *17* Alan Crosland
Apple Woman, The *04* Alf Collins
Applejoy's Ghost *27* Andrew L. Stone
Apples *09* Walter R. Booth
Apples to You *32* Leigh Jason
Appointment, The *69* Sidney Lumet
Appointment, The *71* Chuck Vincent
Appointment by Telephone *02* Edwin S. Porter
Appointment for Love *41* William A. Seiter
Appointment for Murder *54* Baccio Bandini
Appointment in Berlin *43* Alfred E. Green
Appointment in Bray *71* André Delvaux
Appointment in Honduras *53* Jacques Tourneur

Appointment in London *53* Philip Leacock
Appointment in Persia *47* William Freshman, Giacomo Gentilomo
Appointment in Tokyo *45* Jack Hively
Appointment with a Shadow *57* Richard Carlson
Appointment with a Shadow *57* Joseph Pevney
Appointment with Crime *45* John Harlow
Appointment with Danger *49* Lewis Allen
Appointment with Death *88* Michael Winner
Appointment with Fear *85* Ramzi Thomas
Appointment with Murder *48* Jack Bernhard
Appointment with Venus *51* Ralph Thomas
Apprenti Salaud, L' *76* Michel Deville
Apprentice Heel, The *76* Michel Deville
Apprentice to Murder *87* Ralph L. Thomas
Apprenticeship of Duddy Kravitz, The *74* Ted Kotcheff
Apprentis, Les *64* Alain Tanner
Apprentis Militaires, Les *1897* Georges Méliès
Apprentissages de Boireau, Les *07* Albert Capellani
Apprezzato Professionista di Sicuro Avvenire, Un *71* Giuseppe De Santis
Approach of Autumn, The *60* Mikio Naruse
Appuntamento a Liverpool *88* Marco Tullio Giordana
Appunti di Federico Fellini *68* Federico Fellini
Appunti per un Romanzo dell'Immondeza *70* Pier Paolo Pasolini
Appunti per un'Film Indiano *68* Pier Paolo Pasolini
Appunti per un'Film sull'India *68* Pier Paolo Pasolini
Appunti per un'Orestiade Africana *69* Pier Paolo Pasolini
Appunti su un Fatto di Cronaca *51* Luchino Visconti
Âpre Lutte, L' *17* Robert Boudrioz
Après l'Amour *24* Léonce Perret
Après l'Amour *31* Léonce Perret
Après l'Amour *47* Maurice Tourneur
Après le Bal *1897* Georges Méliès
Après le Guerre *89* Jean-Loup Hubert
Après le Pluie *89* Camille De Casabianca
Après-Midi avec des Motos, Un *72* Claude Lelouch
April *16* Donald MacDonald
April *61* Otar Ioseliani
April, April *35* Douglas Sirk
April Blossoms *34* Paul Stein
April 1st, 2000 *52* Wolfgang Liebeneiner
April Folly *19* Robert Z. Leonard
April Fool *26* Nat Ross
April Fools *57* Zoltán Fábri
April Fools, The *69* Stuart Rosenberg
April Fool's Day *86* Fred Walton
April in Paris *52* David Butler
April in Vietnam in the Year of the Cat *75* Santiago Álvarez
April Is a Deadly Month *87* Laurent Heynemann

April Love *57* Henry Levin
April of Giron, The *66* Santiago Álvarez
April 1, 2000 *52* Wolfgang Liebeneiner
April Romance *34* Paul Stein
April Showers *23* Tom Forman
April Showers *48* James V. Kern
April 16th 1989 *88* David Byrne
Apron Fools *36* Widgey R. Newman
Apt Pupil *88* Alan Bridges
Apu Sansar *58* Satyajit Ray
Apur Sansar *58* Satyajit Ray
Apuros de Claudina, Los *40* Miguel Caronatto Paz
Aqua-Duck *63* Robert McKimson
Aqua Sex, The *62* John Lamb
Aquarian *74* Stan Brakhage
Aquarium *1895* Louis Lumière
Aquarium *56* Ernest Pintoff
Aquasanta Joe *71* Mario Gariazzo
Aquatic Artistry *36* David Miller
Aquella Casa en las Afueras *80* Eugenio Martin
Aquella Noche de Varsovia *41* Brian Desmond Hurst
Aquellarre de Vampiros *71* José María Elorrieta
Aquellos Años *72* Felipe Cazals
Aquila Nera *46* Riccardo Freda
Arab, The *15* Cecil B. DeMille
Arab, The *24* Rex Ingram
A'rab *88* Fadhel Jaibi, Fadhel Jaziri
Arab Conspiracy, The *76* Richard C. Sarafian
Arab-Israeli Dialogue *74* Lionel Rogosin
Arabe, L' *24* Rex Ingram
Arabella *16* Aleksander Hertz
Arabella *24* Karl Grüne
Arabella *67* Mauro Bolognini
Arabella and the Soft Soap *15* James Read
Arabella in Society *15* James Read
Arabella Meets Raffles *15* James Read
Arabella Out of a Job *15* James Read
Arabella Sells Soft Soap *15* James Read
Arabella Spies Spies *15* James Read
Arabella the Lady Slavey *15* James Read
Arabella vs. Lynxeye *15* James Read
Arabella's Frightfulness *15* James Read
Arabella's Motor *15* James Read
Arabesk *89* Ertam Egilmaz
Arabeski na Temu Pirosmani *85* Dodo Abashidze, Sergei Paradzhanov
Arabesque *28* Germaine Dulac
Arabesque *66* Stanley Donen
Arabesque *89* Ertam Egilmaz
Arabesques on the Pirosmani Theme *85* Dodo Abashidze, Sergei Paradzhanov
Arabia *22* Lynn Reynolds
Arabian Adventure *79* Kevin Connor
Arabian Jewish Dance *03* Edwin S. Porter
Arabian Knight, An *20* Charles Swickard
Arabian Knight, An *29* R. E. Jeffrey
Arabian Knights *31* Stephen Roberts
Arabian Love *22* Jerome Storm
Arabian Nights *42* John Rawlins
Arabian Nights, The *74* Pier Paolo Pasolini
Arabian Tragedy, An *12* Sidney Olcott
Arabics *82* Stan Brakhage
Arabie Inconnue *37* René Clément
Arabie Interdite, L' *37* René Clément

Arab's Curse, The *15* A. Kiralfy
Arachnophobia *90* Frank Marshall
Arakure *57* Mikio Naruse
Arañas Infernales *66* Federico Curiel
Aranyakam *88* Hariharan
Aranyásó *14* Michael Curtiz
Aranyember, Az *18* Alexander Korda
Aranyember *37* Béla Gaál
Aranyer Din Ratri *69* Satyajit Ray
Aranysárkány *66* László Ranódy
Arashi *56* Hiroshi Inagaki
Arashi Ga Oka *88* Kiju Yoshida
Arashi no Naka no Otoko *69* Senkichi Taniguchi
Arat az Orosházi "Dózsa" *53* Miklós Jancsó
Araucaima Mansion, The *86* Carlos Mayolo
Araumi no Oja *59* Tetsu Taguchi
Araya *58* Margot Benacerraf
Arbeit Macht Frei *32* Walter Ruttmann
Arbeit Macht Glücklich *32* Walter Ruttmann
Arbejdet Adler *14* August Blom
Arbejdet Kalder *41* Bjarne Henning-Jensen
Arbetaren *13* Victor Sjöström
Árboles de Buenos-Aires, Los *57* Leopoldo Torre-Nilsson
Arbre de Noël, L' *69* Terence Young
Arbre Généalogique *47* George Dunning, Evelyn Lambert
Arbres aux Champignons *51* Gregory Markopoulos
Arcade Attack *82* Michael Wallington
Arcadia Revisited *19* Frank Miller
Arcadian Maid, An *10* D. W. Griffith
Arcadians, The *27* Victor Saville
Arcady *16* Arcady Boytler
Arch of Triumph *48* Lewis Milestone
Archa Pana Servadaca *68* Karel Zeman
Archanděl Gabriel a Paní Husa *64* Jiří Trnka
Archangel Gabriel and Mother Goose, The *64* Jiří Trnka
Archangel Gabriel and Mrs. Goose, The *64* Jiří Trnka
Archangelos tou Pathous *87* Nicos Vergitsis
Archangels, The *63* Enzo Battaglia
Arche, Die *19* Richard Oswald
Arche II, Die *19* Richard Oswald
Archibald in a Tangle *14* Joe Evans
Archibald's Egg Diet *14* Joe Evans
Archimède *62* Pietro Francisci
Archimède le Clochard *58* Gilles Grangier
Archimède the Tramp *58* Gilles Grangier
Architecte Maudit, Claude-Nicolas Ledoux, L' *54* Pierre Kast
Architects Ayorou *71* Jean Rouch
Architects of Fear *86* Peter Rowe
Architectural Millinery *54* Sidney Peterson
Architecture et Lumière *53* Henri Colpi, J. P. Ganancia
Arcidiavolo, L' *66* Ettore Scola
Arctic Adventure *22* Chester Withey
Arctic Antics *30* Ubbe Iwerks
Arctic Flight *52* Lew Landers
Arctic Fury *49* Norman Dawn, Fred R. Feitshans, Jr.

Arctic Giant, The *42* Dave Fleischer
Arctic Harvest *46* Lewis Gilbert
Arctic Heat *86* Renny Harlin
Arctic Journey *40* Leonid Varmalov
Arctic Manhunt *49* Ewing Scott
Ard, El *68* Youssef Chahine
Ardent Heart, The *62* Otakar Vávra
Ardh Satya *83* Govind Nihalani
Ardoise, L' *69* Claude Bernard-Aubert
Are All Men Alike? *20* Phil Rosen
Are Children to Blame? *22* Paul Price
Are ga Minato no Hi Da *61* Tadashi Imai
Are Husbands Necessary? *42* Norman Taurog
Are Parents People? *25* Malcolm St. Clair
Are the Children to Blame? *22* Paul Price
Are These Our Children? *31* Wesley Ruggles
Are These Our Children? *32* Gregory La Cava
Are These Our Parents? *44* William Nigh
Are We All Murderers? *52* André Cayatte
Are We Civilized? *34* Edwin Carewe
Are We Prepared for the International Trade Hunt? *16* A. D. Reed
Are You a Failure? *23* Tom Forman
Are You a Mason? *15* Thomas Heffron
Are You a Mason? *34* Henry Edwards
Are You Afraid? *70* Henning Carlsen
Are You Afraid? Of What? *70* Henning Carlsen
Are You Among Them? *54* Jerzy Hoffman
Are You Being Served? *77* Bob Kellett
Are You Dying Young Man? *70* James Kelly
Are You John Brown? *10* Lewin Fitzhamon
Are You Legally Married? *19* Robert Thornby
Are You Listening? *32* Harry Beaumont
Are You Married? *20* Henry D. Bailey
Are You Sincere? *07* Arthur Gilbert
Are You There? *01* James A. Williamson
Are You There? *30* Hamilton MacFadden
Are You With It? *48* Jack Hively
Areias Escaldantes *87* Francisco De Paula
Arena *53* Richard Fleischer
Arena *67* Samson Samsonov
Arena, The *73* Steve Carver
Arena *88* Peter Manoogian
Árendás Zsidó, Az *17* Michael Curtiz
Arénicole *65* Jean Painlevé
Aren't Men Beasts! *36* Graham Cutts
Aren't We All? *32* Harry Lachman, Rudolph Maté
Aren't We Wonderful? *58* Kurt Hoffmann
Argent, L' *27* Marcel L'Herbier
Argent, L' *82* Robert Bresson
Argent de Poche, L' *75* François Truffaut
Argentine Love *24* Allan Dwan
Argentine Nights *40* Albert S. Rogell
Argila *40* Humberto Mauro, Carmen Santos
Argonauti, Gli *60* Riccardo Freda
Argonauts of California *16* Henry Kabierske
Argyle Case, The *17* Ralph Ince
Argyle Case, The *29* Howard Bretherton
Argyle Secrets, The *48* Cy Endfield

Århus by Night 89 Nils Malmros

Ari no Machi no Maria 58 Heinosuke Gosho

Aria 87 Robert Altman, Bruce Beresford, Bill Bryden, Jean-Luc Godard, Derek Jarman, Franc Roddam, Nicolas Roeg, Ken Russell, Charles Sturridge, Julien Temple

Aria del Continente, L' 39 Gennaro Righelli

Ariadne in Hoppegarten 28 Robert Dinesen

Ariane 31 Paul Czinner

Ariane, Russian Maid 31 Paul Czinner

Arie Prerie 49 Jiří Trnka

Ariel 88 Aki Kaurismäki

Arigatōsan 37 Hiroshi Shimizu

Arise, My Love 40 Mitchell Leisen

Aristide Maillol, Sculpteur 42 Jean Lods

Aristo, L' 34 André Berthomieu

Aristo-Cat, The 43 Chuck Jones

Aristocats, The 70 Wolfgang Reitherman

Aristocracy 14 Thomas Heffron

Aristocrates, Les 55 Denys De la Patellière

Aristocrats, The 55 Denys De la Patellière

Aristocrat's Stairs 59 Kozaburo Yoshimura

Aristotele 71 Jiří Brdečka, Max Massimino Garnier

Aristotle 71 Jiří Brdečka, Max Massimino Garnier

Arizona 13 Lawrence McGill

Arizona 18 Douglas Fairbanks, Albert Parker

Arizona 31 George B. Seitz

Arizona 40 Wesley Ruggles

Arizona Badman 35 S. Roy Luby

Arizona Bill 09 Jean Durand

Arizona Bill 11 George Melford, Robert Vignola

Arizona Bill 64 Mario Bava

Arizona Bound 27 John Waters

Arizona Bound 41 Spencer G. Bennet

Arizona Bushwhackers 67 Lesley Selander

Arizona Catclaw, The 19 William Bertram

Arizona Colt 65 Michele Lupo

Arizona Colt Si Scateno e Li Fece 70 Sergio Martino

Arizona Cowboy, The 50 R. G. Springsteen

Arizona Cyclone 28 Edgar Lewis

Arizona Cyclone 34 Robert E. Tansey

Arizona Cyclone 41 Joseph H. Lewis

Arizona Days 28 John P. McGowan

Arizona Days 37 John English

Arizona Express 24 Thomas Buckingham

Arizona Frontier 40 Albert Herman

Arizona Gangbusters 40 Sam Newfield

Arizona Gunfighter 37 Sam Newfield

Arizona Heat 88 John G. Thomas

Arizona Kid, The 29 Horace B. Carpenter

Arizona Kid, The 30 Alfred Santell

Arizona Kid, The 39 Joseph Kane

Arizona Legion 39 David Howard

Arizona Mahoney 36 James P. Hogan

Arizona Manhunt 51 Fred C. Brannon

Arizona Mission 56 Andrew V. McLaglen

Arizona Nights 27 Lloyd Ingraham

Arizona Nights 34 Bernard B. Ray

Arizona Raiders, The 36 James P. Hogan

Arizona Raiders 65 William Witney

Arizona Ranch Hands 41 Spencer G. Bennet

Arizona Ranger, The 48 John Rawlins

Arizona Rangers 48 John Rawlins

Arizona Romeo 25 Edmund Mortimer

Arizona Roundup 42 Robert E. Tansey

Arizona Speed 28 Robert J. Horner

Arizona Stagecoach 42 S. Roy Luby

Arizona Story, The 44 William Beaudine

Arizona Streak, The 26 Robert De Lacey

Arizona Sunset 48 Lambert Hillyer

Arizona Sweepstakes, The 26 Clifford Smith

Arizona Territory 50 Wallace Fox

Arizona Terror, The 31 Phil Rosen

Arizona Terrors 42 George Sherman

Arizona to Broadway 33 James Tinling

Arizona Trail 43 Vernon Keays

Arizona Trails 35 Alvin J. Neitz

Arizona Whirlwind, The 27 William James Craft

Arizona Whirlwind 44 Robert E. Tansey

Arizona Wildcat, The 27 Roy William Neill

Arizona Wildcat 38 Herbert I. Leeds

Arizonian, The 35 Charles Vidor

Ark of the Sun God, The 83 Antonio Margheriti

Arkadaş 74 Yılmaz Güney

Arkansas Judge 41 Frank McDonald

Arkansas Swing, The 48 Ray Nazarro

Arkansas Traveler, The 38 Alfred Santell

Arlequin et Charbonnier 1897 Georges Méliès

Arlésienne, L' 09 André Calmettes

Arlésienne, L' 12 Albert Capellani

Arlésienne, L' 22 André Antoine

Arlésienne, L' 30 Jacques De Baroncelli

Arlésienne, L' 42 Marc Allégret

Arm, The 87 Ben Bolt

Arm Drenthe 28 Joris Ivens

Arm of the Law 32 Louis King

Arm Wie eine Kirchenmaus 31 Richard Oswald

Arma, L' 78 Pasquale Squitieri

Arma Bianca 36 Ferdinando Maria Poggioli

Arma de Dos Filos, Un 67 Samuel Fuller

Armageddon 23 H. Bruce Woolfe

Armageddon 77 Alain Jessua

Armaguedon 77 Alain Jessua

Armata Azzurra, La 37 Gennaro Righelli

Armata Brancaleone, L' 65 Mario Monicelli

Armchair Detective, The 52 Brendan Stafford

Arme à Gauche, L' 65 Claude Sautet

Arme Eva 14 A. Berger, Robert Wiene

Arme Jenny, Die 12 Urban Gad

Arme Kleine Hedwig 25 Lupu Pick

Arme Millionär, Der 39 Joe Stöckel

Arme Violetta 20 Paul Stein

Armed and Dangerous 77 Vladimir Vainstok

Armed and Dangerous 86 Mark L. Lester

Armed Nation, An 61 Joris Ivens

Armed People, An 61 Joris Ivens

Armed Response 86 Fred Olen Ray

Armée d'Agenor, L' 09 Émile Cohl

Armee der Liebenden oder Aufstand der Perversen 78 Rosa von Praunheim

Armée des Ombres, L' 68 Jean-Pierre Melville

Armée Populaire Arme le Peuple, L' 69 Joris Ivens*

Armistice 29 Victor Saville

Armoire des Frères Davenport, L' 02 Georges Méliès

Armoire Volante, L' 48 Carlo-Rim

Armon 88 Malis Abzalov

Armor of Death 14 Yevgeni Bauer

Armored Attack 43 Lewis Milestone

Armored Car 37 Lewis R. Foster

Armored Car Robbery 50 Richard Fleischer

Armored Command 61 Byron Haskin

Armored Vault 25 Lupu Pick

Armour of God, The 86 Jackie Chan

Arms and the Girl 17 Joseph Kaufman

Arms and the Girl 35 Sidney Lanfield

Arms and the Gringo 14 Christy Cabanne

Arms and the Man 32 Cecil Lewis

Arms and the Man 58 Franz Peter Wirth

Arms and the Woman 16 George Fitzmaurice

Arms and the Woman 44 Alfred E. Green

Armstrong's Trick War Incidents 15 Charles Armstrong

Armstrong's Wife 15 George Melford

Army, The 44 Keisuke Kinoshita

Army Air Force Band, The 42 Jean Negulesco

Army Bound 52 Paul Landres

Army Brat 45 Fred Zinnemann

Army Cap, The 05 Harold Jeapes

Army Capers 52 William Witney

Army Game, The 61 Claude De Givray, François Truffaut

Army Girl 38 B. Reeves Eason, George Nicholls, Jr.

Army in the Shadows, The 68 Jean-Pierre Melville

Army of Shadows, The 68 Jean-Pierre Melville

Army of Two — An Incident During the American Revolution, The 08 Edwin S. Porter

Army Show 43 Jean Negulesco

Army Surgeon, The 12 Francis Ford

Army Surgeon 42 A. Edward Sutherland

Army Wives 44 Phil Rosen

Arnaud, Les 67 Léo Joannon

Arnauds, The 67 Léo Joannon

Arnelo Affair, The 47 Arch Oboler

Arnold 73 Georg Fenady

Arnold's Wrecking Co. 73 Steve De Souza

Arnulf Rainer 60 Peter Kubelka

Arohan 82 Shyam Benegal

Aroma of the South Seas 30 Will P. Kellino

Aroma tis Violettas, To 85 Maria Gavala

Around a Star 06 Gaston Velle

Around Is Around 50 Evelyn Lambert, Norman McLaren

Around the Corner 30 Bert Glennon

Around the Pyramids 22 Raoul Barré, Charles Bowers

Around the Town 38 Herbert Smith

Around the World 23 B. Reeves Eason

Around the World 43 Allan Dwan

Artist's Dream, The *1898* Georges Méliès
Artist's Dream, An *00* Edwin S. Porter
Artist's Hoax, The *10* H. Oceano Martinek
Artist's Model, The *07* Lewin Fitzhamon
Artist's Model, The *24* Earl Hurd
Artists of Antwerp *55* Paul Haesaerts
Artist's Revenge, The *09* Van Dyke Brooke
Artist's Ruse, The *10* H. Oceano Martinek
Artists Under the Big Top: Perplexed *67* Alexander Kluge
Artist's Wife, The *15* Elmer Clifton
Arts Cuba *77* Claude Jutra
Arts of Village India *70* Bruce Beresford
Artur Rubinstein *41* Jules Dassin
Artur Rubinstein — L'Amour de la Vie *68* S. Gerard Patris, François Reichenbach
Artur Rubinstein — The Love of Life *68* S. Gerard Patris, François Reichenbach
Arturo's Island *62* Damiano Damiani
Aru Eiga Kantoku no Shōgai: Mizoguchi Kenji *75* Kaneto Shindo
Aru Eiga Kantoku no Shōgai: Mizoguchi Kenji no Kiroku *75* Kaneto Shindo
Aru Sōnan *61* Toshio Sugie
Aru yo Futatabi *56* Heinosuke Gosho
Aru yo no Tonosama *46* Teinosuke Kinugasa
Arunata Pera *86* Amarnath Jayatilaka
Arupusu no Wakadaishō *66* Kengo Furusawa
Árvácska *76* László Ranódy
Arvottomat *82* Mika Kaurismäki
Aryan, The *16* William S. Hart, Clifford Smith
Arzt aus Halberstadt, Ein *69* Alexander Kluge
Arzt Ohne Gewissen *59* Falk Harnack
Arzt Stellt Fest, Der *66* Aleksander Ford
Arzt von St. Pauli, Der *69* Rolf Olsen
Arzt von Stalingrad, Der *58* Géza von Radványi
Ärztekongress *61* Edgar Reitz
As a Man Lives *23* J. Searle Dawley
As a Man Sows *14* Bert Haldane
As a Man Sows, or An Angel of the Slums *14* Bert Haldane
As a Man Thinks *19* George Irving
As a Wife, As a Woman *61* Mikio Naruse
As a Woman Sows *16* William F. Haddock
As an Umpire Nosey Ned Is an Onion *16* Harry S. Palmer
As des As, L' *82* Gérard Oury
As Distant As My Childhood *68* Jean Eustache, Marilu Parolini
As du Turf, Les *35* Serge De Poligny
As Fate Ordained *15* Christy Cabanne
As God Made Her *20* B. E. Doxat-Pratt
As Good As Married *37* Edward Buzzell
As Good As New *33* Graham Cutts
As He Was Born *19* Wilfred Noy
As Husbands Go *33* Hamilton MacFadden
As If It Were Raining *63* José Monter
As If It Were Yesterday *80* Myriam Abramowicz
As in a Looking Glass *11* D. W. Griffith
As in a Looking Glass *16* Frank Crane
As in Days of Yore *17* Maurice Sandground

As It Is in Life *10* D. W. Griffith
As It Might Have Been *14* Del Henderson
As Long As There Are Women *87* Didier Kaminka
As Long As They're Happy *55* J. Lee-Thompson
As Long As You're Healthy *65* Pierre Etaix
As Long As You're Near Me *54* Harald Braun
As Man Desires *25* Irving Cummings
As Man Made Her *17* George Archainbaud
As Men Love *17* E. Mason Hopper
As Negro, El *43* René Cardona
As No Man Has Loved *25* Rowland V. Lee
As Old As the Century *60* Samson Samsonov
As Old As the Hills *50* John Halas
As Prescribed by the Doctor *10* Dave Aylott
As Seen Through a Telescope *00* George Albert Smith
As Sparrows See Us *05* Alf Collins
As Tears Go By *88* Kar-wai Wong
As the Beast Dieth *86* Hilmar Oddsson
As the Bells Rang Out! *10* D. W. Griffith
As the Clouds Scatter *61* Heinosuke Gosho
As the Devil Commands *33* Roy William Neill, Keane Thompson
As the Earth Turns *34* Alfred E. Green
As the Fly Flies *44* Howard Swift
As the Sea Rages *60* Horst Haechler
As the Sparks Fly Upward *13* Hay Plumb
As the Sun Went Down *15* Frank Wilson
As the Sun Went Down *19* E. Mason Hopper
As the Wind Blows *14* Frank Lloyd
As Time Goes By *87* Barry Peak
As We Forgive *37* Vernon Sewell
As We Lie *27* Miles Mander
As Ye Repent *15* Lawrence Trimble
As Ye Sow *11* Edwin S. Porter
As Ye Sow *14* Frank Crane
As You Desire Me *32* George Fitzmaurice
As You Like It *12* J. Stuart Blackton, James Young
As You Like It *36* Paul Czinner
As You Please *27* Mario Camerini
As You Were *19* Alfred Santell
As You Were! *51* Fred Guiol
As Young As We Are *58* Bernard Girard
As Young As You Feel *31* Frank Borzage
As Young As You Feel *51* Harmon Jones
Asa Branca — Um Sonho Brasileiro *88* Djalma Limongi Batista
Asa no Hamon *52* Heinosuke Gosho
Asa no Namikimichi *36* Mikio Naruse
Asahi wa Kagayaku *29* Seichi Ina, Kenji Mizoguchi
Asamblea General *59* Tomás Gutiérrez Alea
Asani Sanket *73* Satyajit Ray
Asase *88* N. T. Jayarama Reddy
Ascendancy *82* Edward Bennett
Ascending Scale *82* Shyam Benegal
Ascenseur pour l'Échafaud *57* Louis Malle
Ascension de la Rosière, L' *08* Georges Méliès

Ascension d'un Ballon *1897* Georges Méliès
Ascent, The *76* Larissa Shepitko
Ascent, The *82* Shyam Benegal
Ascent to Heaven *51* Luis Buñuel
Aschenbrödel *14* Urban Gad
Aschenputtel *22* Lotte Reiniger
Aschermittwoch *35* Johannes Meyer
Ascot: A Race Against Time *60* Kevin Brownlow
Ase *29* Tomu Uchida
Asegure a Su Mujer *34* Lewis Seiler
Ases de Contrabando, Los *86* Fernando Durán
Asesino de Muñecas, El *74* Miguel Madrid
Asesino Invisible, El *64* René Cardona
Asesino Loco y el Sexo, El *69* René Cardona
Asfalto Selvagem *66* J. B. Tanko
Asfour, Al *73* Youssef Chahine
Ash Can Fleet, The *39* Fred Zinnemann
Ash Can, or Little Dick's First Adventure, The *15* Chester M. Franklin, Sidney Franklin
Ash Wednesday *35* Johannes Meyer
Ash Wednesday *73* Larry Peerce
Ash Wednesday Confession *60* William Dieterle
Ashad ka Ek Din *71* Mani Kaul
Ashamed of His Wife *13* Ernest G. Batley
Ashamed of Parents *21* Horace G. Plympton
Ashani Sanket *73* Satyajit Ray
Ashanti *79* Richard Fleischer
Ashanti: Land of No Mercy *79* Richard Fleischer
Asheke, Al *86* Mohamed Mournir Fanari
Ashes *22* Gilbert M. Anderson
Ashes *30* Frank Birch
Ashes *65* Andrzej Wajda
Ashes and Diamonds *58* Andrzej Wajda
Ashes and Embers *82* Haile Gerima
Ashes of Desire *19* Frank Borzage
Ashes of Embers *16* Joseph Kaufman
Ashes of Hope *17* Walter Edwards
Ashes of Revenge, The *15* Harold M. Shaw
Ashes of the Past *14* James Kirkwood
Ashes of Three *13* Allan Dwan
Ashes of Vengeance *23* Frank Lloyd
Ashi ni Sawatta Kōun *30* Yasujiro Ozu
Ashi ni Sawatta Onna *52* Kon Ichikawa
Ashik Kerib *88* Dodo Abashidze, Sergei Paradzhanov
Ashita *89* Kazuo Kuroki
Ashita Aru Kagiri *62* Shiro Toyoda
Ashita no Odoriko *39* Kozaburo Yoshimura
Ashiya Kara no Hikō *63* Michael Anderson
Ashizuri Misaki *54* Kozaburo Yoshimura
Ashley Green Goes to School *43* John Eldridge
Ashridge Castle — The Monmouth Rebellion *26* Charles C. Calvert
Así Como Habían Sido *87* Andrés Linares
Así Es la Mujer *36* José Bohr
Así Es la Vida *40* Francisco Mujica
Así Es Mi Tierra *39* Arcady Boytler
Así Se Quiere en Jalisco *42* Fernando De Fuentes

Asia 28 Alexander Ivanovsky
Asia Calling 33 Tomu Uchida
Asian Sun, The 21 Edmund Heuberger
Asignatura Aprobada 87 José Luis García Agraz
Asignatura Pendiente 76 José Luis García Agraz
Asılacak Kadin 86 Başar Sabuncu
Asilo di Polizia 86 Filippo Ottoni
Asilo Muito Louco, Um 69 Nelson Pereira Dos Santos
Ask a Policeman 38 Marcel Varnel
Ask Any Girl 59 Charles Walters
Ask Beccles 33 Redd Davis
Ask Dad 27 Sam Newfield
Ask the C.A.B. 42 Henry Cass
Asking for Trouble 14 Edwin J. Collins
Asking for Trouble 41 Oswald Mitchell
Asking for Trouble 87 Richard Attenborough
Asleep at the Switch 23 Roy Del Ruth
Aspern 81 Eduardo De Gregorio
Asphalt 29 Joe May
Asphalt Jungle, The 50 John Huston
Asphalte 59 Hervé Bromberger
Asphyx, The 72 Peter Newbrook
Ass and the Stick, The 74 Joy Batchelor
Assa 88 Sergei Soloviev
Assalto ao Trem Pagador 62 Roberto Farias
Assam Garden, The 85 Mary McMurray
Assassin, The 47 George Waggner
Assassin, The 52 Ralph Thomas
Assassin, The 60 Elio Petri
Assassin, The 64 Masahiro Shinoda
Assassin 73 Peter Crane
Assassin A Peur de la Nuit, L' 42 Jean Delannoy
Assassin Connaît la Musique, L' 63 Pierre Chénal
Assassin Est dans l'Annuaire, L' 61 Léo Joannon
Assassin for Hire 51 Michael McCarthy
Assassin Habite au 21, L' 41 Henri-Georges Clouzot
Assassin of Youth 37 Elmer Clifton
Assassinat de la Rue du Temple, L' 04 Alice Guy-Blaché
Assassinat du Courrier de Lyon, L' 04 Alice Guy-Blaché
Assassinat du Duc de Guise, L' 08 André Calmettes, Charles Le Bargy
Assassinat du McKinley, L' 01 Ferdinand Zecca
Assassinat du Père Noël, L' 40 Christian-Jaque
Assassination 64 Masahiro Shinoda
Assassination 86 Peter R. Hunt
Assassination Bureau, The 68 Basil Dearden
Assassination in Sarajevo 76 Veljko Bulajić
Assassination of the Duke de Guise, The 08 André Calmettes, Charles Le Bargy
Assassination of the King and Queen of Servia, The 03 Dicky Winslow
Assassination of Trotsky, The 72 Joseph Losey
Assassinio a Sarajevo 68 Carlo Lizzani
Assassinio di Trotsky, L' 72 Joseph Losey
Assassino, L' 60 Elio Petri

Assassino al Cimitero Etrusco 82 Christian Plummer
Assassino È Costretto ad Uccidere Ancora, L' 76 Luigi Cozzi
Assassins de l'Ordre, Les 71 Marcel Carné
Assassins d'Eau Douce 47 Jean Painlevé
Assassins du Dimanche, Les 56 Alex Joffé
Assassins et Voleurs 56 Sacha Guitry
Assassins of Order, The 71 Marcel Carné
Assassins of Rome 72 Damiano Damiani
Assault 70 Sidney Hayers
Assault, The 86 Fons Rademakers
Assault and Peppered 65 Robert McKimson
Assault Force 79 Andrew V. McLaglen
Assault in Broad Daylight 58 Ladislas Vajda
Assault in the Park 59 Joyce Wieland*
Assault of the Killer Bimbos 88 Anita Rosenberg
Assault of the Present Upon the Rest of Time, The 85 Alexander Kluge
Assault of the Rebel Girls 57 Barry Mahon
Assault on a Queen 66 Jack Donohue
Assault on Agathon 74 Laslo Benedek
Assault on Paradise 77 Richard Compton
Assault on Precinct 13 76 John Carpenter
Assault with a Deadly Weapon 83 Walter Gaines
Assaut d'Escrime—École de Joinville 1898 Georges Méliès
Assayer of Lone Gap, The 15 B. Reeves Eason
Assedio dell'Alcazar, L' 40 Augusto Genina
Assedio di Siracusa, L' 62 Pietro Francisci
Assembly of Love 64 Pier Paolo Pasolini
Assiettes Tournantes 1895 Louis Lumière
Assignation, The 53 Curtis Harrington
Assigned to Danger 48 Budd Boetticher
Assignment, The 76 Mats Arehn
Assignment Abroad 55 Arthur Dreifuss
Assignment in Brittany 43 Jack Conway
Assignment in China 48 Sam Newfield
Assignment in Paris 52 Robert Parrish, Vincent Sherman
Assignment Istanbul 68 Jesús Franco
Assignment K 67 Val Guest
Assignment: Kill Castro 80 Chuck Workman
Assignment Outer Space 60 Antonio Margheriti
Assignment—Paris! 52 Robert Parrish, Vincent Sherman
Assignment Redhead 56 Maclean Rogers
Assignment Terror 69 Tulio Demicheli, Hugo Fregonese
Assignment to Kill 68 Sheldon Reynolds
Assisi 32 Alessandro Blasetti
Assisi Underground, The 85 Alexander Ramati
Assistant, The 69 John Dooley
Assistant, The 82 Zoro Zahon
Assistant to His Highness 33 Martin Frič
Assisted Elopement, An 12 Allan Dwan
Associate, The 80 René Gainville
Association des Malfaiteurs, L' 87 Claude Zidi
Association of Wrongdoers, The 87 Claude Zidi

Associé, L' 80 René Gainville
Assoluto Naturale, L' 69 Mauro Bolognini, Antonio Pietrangeli
Assommoir, L' 09 Albert Capellani
Assommoir, L' 21 Charles De Marsan, Charles Maudru
Asszony a Telepen 62 Imre Fehér
Asszonyfaló 18 Béla Balázs
Astérie, L' 58 Jean Painlevé
Asterix chez les Bretons 86 Pino van Lamsweerde
Asterix et la Surprise de César 85 Gaetan Brizzi, Paul Brizzi
Asterix in Britain 86 Pino van Lamsweerde
Asterix the Gaul 85 Gaetan Brizzi, Paul Brizzi
Asterix vs. Caesar 85 Gaetan Brizzi, Paul Brizzi
Astero 29 Dimitrios Gaziadis
Astero 60 Dinos Dimopoulos
Asthore 17 Wilfred Noy
Astonished 88 Jeff Kahn, Travis Preston
Astonished Heart, The 49 Anthony Darnborough, Terence Fisher
Astonishing Frame, The 04 Georges Méliès
Astounding She-Monster, The 57 Ronnie Ashcroft
Astragale, L' 68 Guy Casaril
Astral Factor, The 76 John Florea
Astral Man 57 Stan Vanderbeek
Astro-Duck 66 Robert McKimson
Astro-Zombies 67 Ted V. Mikels
Astrologer, The 75 Craig Denney
Astrologer, The 79 James Glickenhaus
Astrologie 51 Jean Grémillon
Astrologie ou Le Miroir de la Vie 51 Jean Grémillon
Astromati 63 Dušan Vukotić
Astromuts 63 Dušan Vukotić
Astronautas, Los 60 Miguel Zacarías
Astronautes, Les 59 Walerian Borowczyk, Chris Marker
Astronauts, The 60 Kurt Mätzig
Astronomer's Dream, The 1898 Georges Méliès
Astuto Barone, L' 48 Riccardo Freda
Asu Aru Kagiri 62 Shiro Toyoda
Asu no Taiyō 59 Nagisa Oshima
Asu o Tsukuru Hitobito 46 Akira Kurosawa, Hideo Sekigawa, Kajiro Yamamoto
Asya 77 Josef Heifits
Asya's Happiness 66 Andrei Mikhalkov-Konchalovsky
Asylum 72 Roy Ward Baker
Asylum 72 Peter Robinson
Asylum Erotica 71 Fernando Di Leo
Asylum of Blood 74 Stephen Weeks
Asylum of Horror 31 Richard Oswald
Asylum of Satan 72 William Girdler
Asylum of the Insane 72 Peter Walker
Asymvivastos 79 Andreas Thomopoulos
@ 79 Stan Brakhage
At 82 Ali Özgentürk
At a High Cost 57 Mark Donskoi
At a High Price 57 Mark Donskoi
At Avret Silah 66 Yılmaz Güney
At Bay 15 George Fitzmaurice
At Close Range 86 James Foley

At Coney Island *12* Mack Sennett
At Cripple Creek *12* James Hallek Reid
At Dawn *28* Aleksander Ford
At Dawn We Die *42* George King
At Devil's Gorge *23* Ashton Dearholt
At Ease *27* Norman Taurog
At First Sight *17* Robert Z. Leonard
At First Sight *83* Diane Kurys
At 5:40 *38* André De Toth
At Five O'Clock in the Afternoon *60* Juan Antonio Bardem
At Good Old Siwash *40* Theodore Reed
At Great Cost *57* Mark Donskoi
At Gunpoint *55* Alfred L. Werker
At Home *34* Roman Karmen
At Home *68* Martin Lavut
At Home Among Strangers *74* Nikita Mikhalkov
At Home Among Strangers, a Stranger at Home *74* Nikita Mikhalkov
At It Again *12* Mack Sennett
At It Again *14* Charles Chaplin
At It Again *16* Charles Wilhelm
At It Again *28* Norman Taurog
At Land *44* Maya Deren
At Last! That Awful Tooth *02* George Albert Smith
At Long Last Love *75* Peter Bogdanovich
At Middle Age *85* Yu Sun, Qimin Wang
At Midnight *57* György Révész
At Piney Ridge *16* William Robert Daly
At 6 P.M. After the War *44* Ivan Pyriev
At Stalling Speed *89* Karst van der Meulen
At Sword's Point *49* Lewis Allen
At Sword's Point *52* Carlo Ludovico Bragaglia
At Swords' Points *18* Alfred Santell
At the Altar *09* D. W. Griffith
At the Beginning of Glorious Deeds *81* Sergei Gerasimov
At the Circus *39* Edward Buzzell
At the Crossroads *37* Mou-che Yen
At the Earth's Core *76* Kevin Connor
At the Edge of a Palm Grove *38* Raphael J. Sevilla
At the Edge of the World *27* Karl Grüne
At the Eleventh Hour *12* August Blom
At the Eleventh Hour *12* Warwick Buckland
At the End of the World *21* Penrhyn Stanlaws
At the Foot of the Scaffold *13* Warwick Buckland
At the French Ball *08* Wallace McCutcheon
At the Front *18* Raoul Barré, Charles Bowers
At the Grey House *23* Arthur von Gerlach
At the Havana *40* Richard Mishiku
At the Hotel Mix-Up *08* Georges Méliès
At the Hour of Three *12* Wilfred Noy
At the Lake *69* Sergei Gerasimov
At the Lörinc Spinnery *71* Márta Mészáros
At the Meeting with Joyous Death *72* Juan Buñuel
At the Mercy of His Wife *25* Alexander Butler
At the Mercy of Men *18* Charles Miller
At the Mercy of the Tide *10* Dave Aylott

At the Mercy of Tiberius *20* Fred LeRoy Granville
At the Moment of Trial *15* Victor Sjöström
At the Ol' Swimmin' Hole *19* Wallace A. Carlson
At the Old Crossed Roads *14* Frank L. Dear
At the Phone *12* Alice Guy-Blaché
At the Photographer's *59* Vatroslav Mimica
At the Prison Gates *10* August Blom
At the Prompting of the Devil *13* Frank Wilson
At the Ridge *31* John P. McCarthy
At the Risk of My Life *70* Masaki Kobayashi
At the River Galga *54* Miklós Jancsó
At the Sign of Jack O'Lantern *22* Lloyd Ingraham
At the Stage Door *21* Christy Cabanne
At the Strassburg *36* Franz Osten
At the Stroke of Nine *34* Richard Thorpe
At the Stroke of Nine *57* Lance Comfort
At the Stroke of Twelve *41* Jean Negulesco
At the Terminal Station *56* Ján Kadár, Elmar Klos
At the Torrent's Mercy *15* H. Oceano Martinek
At the Villa Rose *20* Maurice Elvey
At the Villa Rose *30* Leslie Hiscott
At the Villa Rose *39* Walter Summers
At 3:25 *23* René Clair
At Twelve O'Clock *13* Mack Sennett
At War with the Army *50* Hal Walker
At Yale *27* Edward H. Griffith
At Your Doorstep *63* Vassily Ordynski
At Your Orders, Madame *40* Mario Mattòli
At Your Service *35* Walter Lantz
At Your Service Madame *36* Friz Freleng
Ať Žije Nebožtík *35* Martin Frič
Ať Žije Republika! *65* Karel Kachyňa
Atacan las Brujas *65* José Díaz Morales
Atalante, L' *34* Jean Vigo
Atalia *85* Akiva Teveth
Ataliva Uzhvii *57* Sergei Paradzhanov
¡Átame! *90* Pedro Almodóvar
Ataque de los Muertos Sin Ojos, El *73* Amando De Ossorio
Ataragon *63* Inoshiro Honda
Ataúd del Muerto, El *57* Fernando Méndez, Paul Nagle
Ataúd del Vampiro, El *57* Fernando Méndez, Paul Nagle
Atchi wa Kotchi *62* Yoji Kuri
Atelier d'Artiste, Farce de Modèles *1898* Georges Méliès
Atelier de Fernand Léger *54* Walerian Borowczyk
Ateliers de La Ciotat *1895* Louis Lumière
Ateljé Interiör *56* Peter Weiss
Atención Prenatal *72* Sara Gómez
Athalie *10* Albert Capellani
Athena *54* Richard Thorpe
Athens, 1982 *82* Theodoros Angelopoulos
Ätherbräusch *88* Klaus Gengnagel
Athiratha Maharath *88* Perala
Athlete, The *32* Walter Lantz
Athlète Incomplet, L' *32* Claude Autant-

Lara
Athletics and Women *22* Julian Ollendorff
Atithi *66* Tapan Sinha
Atividades Políticas *50* Nelson Pereira Dos Santos
Atividades Políticas em São Paulo *50* Nelson Pereira Dos Santos
Atlantic *29* E. A. Dupont
Atlantic Adventure *35* Albert S. Rogell
Atlantic City *44* Ray McCarey
Atlantic City *80* Louis Malle
Atlantic City, U.S.A. *80* Louis Malle
Atlantic Convoy *42* Lew Landers
Atlantic Episode *37* Roy Kellino
Atlantic Ferry *41* Walter Forde
Atlantic Flight *37* William Nigh
Atlantic Story, An *54* Wanda Jakubowska
Atlantide, L' *21* Jacques Feyder
Atlantide, L' *32* G. W. Pabst
Atlantide, L' *61* Frank Borzage, Giuseppe Masini, Edgar G. Ulmer
Atlantide—Antinea, l'Amante della Città Sepolta, L' *61* Frank Borzage, Giuseppe Masini, Edgar G. Ulmer
Atlantik *29* E. A. Dupont
Atlantis *13* August Blom
Atlantis *30* E. A. Dupont*
Atlantis *48* John Brahm, Arthur Ripley, Douglas Sirk, Gregg Tallas
Atlantis the Lost Continent *48* John Brahm, Arthur Ripley, Douglas Sirk, Gregg Tallas
Atlantis, the Lost Continent *60* George Pal
Atlantis the Lost Continent *61* Frank Borzage, Giuseppe Masini, Edgar G. Ulmer
Atlantis the Lost Kingdom *61* Frank Borzage, Giuseppe Masini, Edgar G. Ulmer
Atlas *60* Roger Corman
Atlas Against the Cyclops *61* Antonio Leonviola
Atlas Against the Czar *64* Tanio Boccia
Atleta Fantasma, L' *19* Raimondo Scotti
Atma Bandhulu *88* Dasari Narayan Rao
Ato da Primavera *60* Manoel De Oliveira
Atoll K *50* John Berry, Léo Joannon
Atom, The *18* William Dowlan
Atom Age Vampire *60* Richard McNamara, Anton Giulio Majano
Atom Man vs. Superman *50* Spencer G. Bennet
Atome Qui Vous Veut du Bien, Une *59* Henri Gruel
Atomic Agent *59* Henri Decoin
Atomic Brain, The *64* Joseph Mascelli
Atomic Cafe, The *82* Jayne Loader, Kevin Rafferty, Pierce Rafferty
Atomic Cathedral, An *86* Jaroslav Balík
Atomic City, The *52* Jerry Hopper
Atomic Kid, The *54* Leslie Martinson
Atomic Man, The *53* Ken Hughes
Atomic Monster *41* George Waggner
Atomic Rocketship *36* Frederick Stephani
Atomic Rulers of the World, The *57* Koreyoshi Akasaka, Teruo Ishii, Akira Mitsuwa
Atomic Submarine, The *59* Spencer G. Bennet
Atomic War Bride *60* Veljko Bulajić

Atomová Katedrála 86 Jaroslav Balík
Atonement 20 William Humphrey
Atonement of Gösta Berling, The 23
Mauritz Stiller
Ator 83 David Hills
Ator, the Fighting Eagle 83 David Hills
Ator the Invincible 83 David Hills
Atoragon 63 Inoshiro Honda
Atout Cœur à Tokyo pour OSS
117 66 Michel Boisrond
Atraco al Hampa 67 Maurice Cloche
Atragon 63 Inoshiro Honda
Atragon the Flying Supersub 63 Inoshiro
Honda
Âtre, L' 23 Robert Boudrioz
Atroce Menace 34 Christian-Jaque
Atsui Yoru 68 Kozaburo Yoshimura
Att Älska 64 Jörn Donner
Att Segla Är Nödvändigt 38 Pál Fejős,
Åke Leijonhufvud
Atta Baby 27 Charles Lamont
Atta Boy! 26 Edward H. Griffith
Atta Boy's Last Race 16 George Siegmann
Attack! 56 Robert Aldrich
Attack and Retreat 64 Giuseppe De Santis
Attack Force Z 81 Tim Burstall
Attack from Space 58 Teruo Ishii
Attack from the Sea 53 Mikhail Romm
Attack in the Forest 67 Santiago Álvarez
Attack in the Rear 06 Harold Hough
Attack of the Crab Monsters 56 Roger
Corman
Attack of the Enemy Planes, An 43 Koza-
buro Yoshimura
Attack of the Fifty Foot Woman 58
Nathan Juran
Attack of the Flying Saucers 57 Koreyoshi
Akasaka, Teruo Ishii, Akira Mitsuwa
Attack of the Giant Leeches 59 Bernard
Kowalski
Attack of the Killer Tomatoes 78 John De
Bello
Attack of the Mayan Mummy 57 Rafael
Portillo
Attack of the Mayan Mummy 63 Jerry
Warren
Attack of the Monsters 69 Noriyaki Yuasa
Attack of the Moors 60 Mario Costa
Attack of the Mushroom People 63 Ino-
shiro Honda
Attack of the Normans 61 Mario Bava
Attack of the Puppet People 57 Bert I.
Gordon
Attack of the Rebel Girls 57 Barry Mahon
Attack of the Robots 67 Jesús Franco
Attack on a China Mission Station 00
James A. Williamson
Attack on a Chinese Mission — Bluejackets
to the Rescue 00 James A. Williamson
Attack on a Japanese Convoy 04 Frank
Mottershaw
Attack on a Picquet 1899 Robert Ashe
Attack on a Russian Outpost 04 Harold
Hough
Attack on an English Blockhouse 1897
Georges Méliès
Attack on the Agent, The 06 Tom Green
Attack on the Iron Coast 67 Paul Wend-
kos
Attack Squadron 63 Shue Matsubayashi

Attack! The Battle of New Britain 44
Robert Presnell
Attaco alla Piovra 84 Damiano Damiani
Attaque d'un Diligence, L' 04 Alice Guy-
Blaché
Attaque d'un Poste Anglais 1897 Georges
Méliès
Attaque d'un Train, L' 09 Jean Durand
Attaque Nocturne 31 Marc Allégret
Attempt to Kill 61 Royston Morley
Attempt to Smash a Bank, An 09 Theo
Bouwmeester
Attempted Elopement, An 10 Edwin S.
Porter
Attempted Murder in a Railway Train 04
Percy Stow
Attempted Nobbling of the Derby Favour-
ite 05 Tom Green
Attentat, L' 72 Yves Boisset
Attention 85 Giovanni Soldati
Attention Bandits 86 Claude Lelouch
Attention! Hélicoptères 62 Pierre
Schöndörffer
Attention Hooligans 55 Jerzy Hoffman
Attention! The Kids Are Watching 78
Serge Leroy
Attention! Une Femme Peut en Cacher
une Autre 83 Georges Lautner
Attento Gringo…e Tornato Sabata 72 A.
Bragan
Attenzione, L' 85 Giovanni Soldati
Atti Atrocissima de Amore e di Vendetta
79 Sergio Corbucci
Atti degli Apostoli 68 Roberto Rossellini
Attic, The 79 George Edwards
Attica 74 Cinda Firestone
Attila 54 Pietro Francisci
Attila 81 Robert Liddle
Attila, Flagello di Dio 54 Pietro Francisci
Attila il Flagello di Dio 17 Febo Mari
Attila '74 75 Michael Cacoyannis
Attila 1974 — The Rape of Cyprus 75
Michael Cacoyannis
Attila the Hun 54 Pietro Francisci
Attitudes 89 Vladimír Balco
Attore Scomparso, L' 41 Luigi Zampa
Attorney for the Defense 32 Irving
Cummings
Attorney for the Defense, The 35 Gero
Zambuto
Attorney for the Defense 42 Jean Yar-
brough
Attractive Catch, An 08 Lewin Fitzhamon
Attrait du Bouge, L' 12 Louis Feuillade
Au Bal de Flore 00 Alice Guy-Blaché
Au Bois Piget 56 Jean Dewever
Au Bonheur des Dames 29 Julien
Duvivier
Au Bonheur des Dames 43 André Cayatte
Au Bonheur des Dames 79 Nelly Kaplan
Au Cabaret 00 Alice Guy-Blaché
Au Carrefour de la Vie 49 Henri Storck
Au Clair de la Lune 04 Georges Méliès
Au Clair de la Lune ou Pierrot Malheureux
04 Georges Méliès
Au Cœur de la Vie 62 Robert Enrico
Au Cœur de la Ville 69 Claude Jutra
Au Cœur de l'Île-de-France 53 Jean
Grémillon
Au Cœur de l'Orage 47 Jean-Paul Le

Chanois
Au-Delà des Grilles 49 René Clément
Au-Delà des Lois Humaines 20 Gaston
Roudes
Au-Delà des Murs 68 Arthur Lamothe
Au Fil d'une Rivière 55 Georges Franju
Au Fou! 66 Yoji Kuri
Au Grand Balcon 49 Henri Decoin
Au Gré des Flots 13 Louis Feuillade
Au Hasard, Balthazar 66 Robert Bresson
Au Large des Côtes Tunisiennes 49
Jacques-Yves Cousteau
Au Nom de la Loi 32 Maurice Tourneur
Au Pair Girls 72 Val Guest
Au Paradis des Enfants 18 Charles Burguet
Au Pays de Georges Sand 26 Jean Epstein
Au Pays de Porgy and Bess 57 François
Reichenbach
Au Pays des Grandes Causses 52 Jean
Mitry
Au Pays des Jouets 08 Georges Méliès
Au Pays des Lions 12 Louis Feuillade
Au Pays des Mages Noirs 47 Pierre Ponty,
Jean Rouch, Jean Sauvy
Au Pays du Roi Lépreux 27 Jacques Feyder
Au Pays Noir 04 Ferdinand Zecca
Au Petit Bonheur 45 Marcel L'Herbier
Au Poulailler! 05 Alice Guy-Blaché
Au Ravissement des Dames 13 Alfred
Machin
Au Réfectoire 1898 Alice Guy-Blaché
Au Rendez-Vous de la Mort Joyeuse 72
Juan Buñuel
Au Revoir les Enfants 87 Louis Malle
Au Royaume des Cieux 49 Julien Duvivier
Au Rythme de Mon Cœur 83 Jean-Pierre
Lefèbvre
Au Secours! 23 Abel Gance
Au Service des Prisonniers 42 Charles
Dekeukeleire
Au Service du Diable 71 Jean Brismée
Au Seuil du Harem 22 Luitz-Morat
Auandar Anapu 74 Rafael Corkidi
Aube, L' 86 Miklós Jancsó
Auberge du Bon Repos, L' 03 Georges
Méliès
Auberge du Dragon Volant, L' 81 Calvin
Floyd
Auberge Ensorcelée, L' 1897 Georges
Méliès
Auberge Rouge, L' 23 Jean Epstein
Auberge Rouge, L' 51 Claude Autant-Lara
Aubervilliers 46 Eli Lotar
Aubrey's Birthday 14 Edwin J. Collins
Aubusson 46 Jean Lods
Aubusson et Jean Lurçat 46 Jean Lods
Aucassin et Nicolette 76 Lotte Reiniger
Auch Zwerge Haben Klein Angefangen 68
Werner Herzog
Auction, The 19 Frank Miller
Auction Block, The 17 Lawrence Trimble
Auction Block, The 25 Hobart Henley
Auction in Souls 33 Victor Schertzinger
Auction Mart, The 20 Duncan Macrae
Auction of Souls 22 Oscar Apfel
Auction of Virtue, The 17 Herbert Blaché
Auctioneer, The 27 Alfred E. Green
Audace Colpo dei Soliti Ignoti 59 Nanni
Loy
Audaces du Cœur, Les 13 Louis Feuillade

Audacious Mr. Squire, The *23* Edwin Greenwood

Audience, The *71* Marco Ferreri

Audition *63* Miloš Forman

Auditorium *57* Michel Drach

Audrey *16* Robert Vignola

Audrey Rose *77* Robert Wise

Auf der Suche nach einer Praktisch-Realistischen Haltung *83* Alexander Kluge

Auf Eis Geführt *14* Ernst Lubitsch

Auf Immer und Ewig *86* Christel Buschmann

Auf Wiedersehen, Franziska *41* Helmut Käutner

Auf Wiedersehen, Franziska Monpti *56* Helmut Käutner

Aufbruche *88* Hartmut Horst

Aufforderung zum Tanz *35* Rudolf von der Noss

Aufruhr des Blutes *29* Victor Trivas

Aufruhr in Damaskus *39* Gustav Ucicky

Aufstand, Der *80* Peter Lilienthal

Aufzeichnungen zu Kleidern und Städten *89* Wim Wenders

Auge der Toten, Das *22* Carl Boese

Augen aus einem Anderen Land *75* Alexander Kluge

Augen der Mumie Mâ, Die *18* Ernst Lubitsch

Augen des Ole Brandis, Die *14* Stellan Rye, Paul Wegener

Augen Wollen Sich Nicht zu Jeder Zeit Schliessen, oder Vielleicht eines Tages Wird Rom Sich Erlauben Seinerseits zu Wählen, Die *69* Danièle Huillet, Jean-Marie Straub

Augenblick des Friedens *65* Tadeusz Konwicki*

August der Starke *35* Paul Wegener

August 14 *47* Ilya Kopalin, Irina Setkina

August 14 — One Day in the U.S.S.R. *47* Ilya Kopalin, Irina Setkina

August Rhapsody, An *39* Arne Sucksdorff

August Week-End *36* Charles Lamont

August Without the Emperor *78* Satsuo Yamamoto

Auguste and Bibb *1897* Georges Méliès

Auguste et Bibb *1897* Georges Méliès

Augustine of Hippo *72* Roberto Rossellini

Augustirapsodi *39* Arne Sucksdorff

Auld Lang Syne *17* Sidney Morgan

Auld Lang Syne *25* Alexander Butler

Auld Lang Syne *29* George Pearson

Auld Lang Syne *37* James A. Fitzpatrick

Auld Robin Gray *17* Meyrick Milton

Auliban *65* Youssef Chahine

Aunt Clara *54* Anthony Kimmins

Aunt Emma Paints the Town *42* Jean Yarbrough

Aunt Matilda's Nephew *29* Stuart Legg

Aunt Rachel *20* Albert Ward

Aunt Sallie's Wonderful Bustle *01* Edwin S. Porter

Aunt Sally *33* Tim Whelan

Aunt Susan's Way *14* Percy Stow

Aunt Tabitha's Visit *11* A. E. Coleby

Aunt Zita *67* Robert Enrico

Auntie and the Cowboys *11* Allan Dwan

Auntie Mame *58* Morton Da Costa

Auntie's Ante *27* Sam Newfield

Auntie's Antics *29* Wilfred Gannon

Auntie's Cycling Lesson *05* Alf Collins

Auntie's Dilemma *14* Edwin J. Collins

Auntie's Fantasies *41* Martin Frič

Auntie's Mistake *29* Charles Lamont

Auntie's Parrot *11* Dave Aylott

Auntie's Secret Sorrow *13* Percy Stow

Auntie's Wedding Present *22* Bert Haldane

Aunt's in the Pants *30* Mark Sandrich

Auprès de Ma Blonde *43* George Dunning

Aura *66* Damiano Damiani

Aura No. 1 *30* Walter West

Aura No. 2 *30* Walter West

Aurat *39* Ramjankhan Mehboobkhan

Aurelia *86* Giorgio Molteni

Aurelia Steiner *79* Marguerite Duras

Aurora *66* François Reichenbach

Aurora *85* Maurizio Ponzi

Aurora Encounter, The *85* Jim McCullough

Aus dem Leben der Marionetten *80* Ingmar Bergman

Aus den Erinnerungen eines Frauenarztes II *21* Lupu Pick

Aus den Wolken Kommt das Glück *35* Reinhold Schünzel, Albert Valentin

Aus der Familie der Panzereschen *84* Wim Wenders

Aus einem Deutschen Leben *77* Theodor Kotulla

Aus Unseren Tage *49* Andrew Thorndike*

Ausgekochter Junge, Ein *32* Erich Schönfelder

Ausgestossener, Ein *13* Joe May

Ausgestossener 1. Teil: Der Junge Chef, Ein *13* Joe May

Ausschweifende Leben des Marquis de Sade, Das *69* Roger Corman, Cy Endfield, Gordon Hessler

Aussi Loin Que l'Amour *71* Frédéric Rossif

Aussi Loin Que Mon Enfance *68* Jean Eustache, Marilu Parolini

Aussi Longue Absence, Une *61* Henri Colpi

Austeria *82* Jerzy Kawalerowicz

Austerlitz *59* Abel Gance, Roger Richebé

Austernprinzessin, Die *19* Ernst Lubitsch

Australian Dream *86* Jackie McKimmie

Australian Made *87* Richard Lowenstein

Australian Wine *31* John Grierson, Paul Rotha

Austreibung, Die *23* F. W. Murnau

Austreibung — Die Macht der Zweiten Frau, Die *23* F. W. Murnau

Austria 1700 *69* Michael Armstrong

Ausweg Los *69* Reinhard Hauff

Authentique Procès de Carl Emmanuel Jung, L' *67* Marcel Hanoun

Author! Author! *82* Arthur Hiller

Authority *38* Pramatesh Chandra Barua

Auto, The *13* Émile Cohl

Auto Clinic, The *38* Manny Gould, Ben Harrison

Auto Maniac, The *09* J. Stuart Blackton

Auto Race, Lakeside *12* Allan Dwan

Auto Show *33* Dick Huemer

Auto Suggestion *29* Manny Gould, Ben Harrison

Autobahn *79* John Halas

Autobiography of a Princess *75* James Ivory

Autobiography of Miss Jane Pittman, The *74* John Korty

Autocrat, The *19* Tom Watts

Autocrat of Flapjack Junction, The *13* George D. Baker

Autograph, The *84* Peter Lilienthal

Autograph Hunter, The *34* Manny Gould, Ben Harrison

Automania 2000 *63* John Halas

Automat na Přání *67* Josef Pinkava

Autómatas de la Muerte, Los *60* Federico Curiel

Automate, L' *08* Émile Cohl

Automatic Monkey, The *09* Émile Cohl

Automatic Motorist, The *11* Walter R. Booth

Automatic Riveter, The *21* J. D. Leventhal

Automatic Weather Prophet, The *01* Edwin S. Porter

Automation *58* Alexander Alexeïeff, Claire Parker

Automobile, The *70* Jan Lenica

Automobile Ride, The *20* Dave Fleischer

Automobile Thieves, The *05* J. Stuart Blackton

Automobiles Starting on a Race *1896* Georges Méliès

Automobilisme et Autorité *1899* Georges Méliès

Automóvil Gris, El *19* Joachim Coss, Enrique Rosas

Autopsy, The *47* Christy Cabanne

Autopsy *74* Armando Crispino

Autopsy of a Criminal *62* Riccardo Blasco

Autostop *77* Pasquale Festa Campanile

Autour de l'Argent *28* Jean Dréville

Autour de Minuit *86* Bertrand Tavernier

Autour de Napoléon *27* Abel Gance

Autour du Mystère *20* Henri Desfontaines

Autour d'un Berceau *25* Georges Monca

Autour d'un Récif *49* Jacques-Yves Cousteau

Autre, L' *17* Louis Feuillade

Autre Aile, L' *24* Henri Andréani

Autre Homme, une Autre Chance, Un *77* Claude Lelouch

Autre Nuit, L' *88* Jean-Pierre Limosin

Autumn *16* Oscar A. C. Lund

Autumn *29* Ubbe Iwerks

Autumn *40* Friedrich Ermler, I. Menaker

Autumn *56* Walerian Borowczyk

Autumn *74* Andrei Smirnov

Autumn Afternoon, An *62* Yasujiro Ozu

Autumn Child *71* William A. Fraker

Autumn Crocus *34* Basil Dean

Autumn in Badacsony *54* Miklós Jancsó

Autumn in Rome *54* William Cameron Menzies

Autumn Leaves *56* Robert Aldrich

Autumn Marathon *78* Georgy Danelia

Autumn of Pride, The *21* Will P. Kellino

Autumn of the Kohayagawa Family, The *61* Yasujiro Ozu

Autumn Roses *12* H. Oceano Martinek

Autumn Sonata *78* Ingmar Bergman

Autumn Star *62* András Kovács
Autumn's Tale, An *87* Yuen Ting Chueng
Auvergne, L' *25* Jean Grémillon
Aux Deux Colombes *49* Sacha Guitry
Aux Frontières de l'Homme *53* Jean Rostand, Nicole Védrès
Aux Jardins de Murcie *23* René Hervil, Louis Mercanton
Aux Lions les Chrétiens *11* Louis Feuillade
Aux Purs Tout Est Pur *68* Michel Boisrond
Aux Quatre Coins *49* Jacques Rivette
Aux Yeux du Souvenir *48* Jean Delannoy
Av Zamanı *88* Erden Kiral
Availing Prayer, The *14* Donald Crisp
Avalanche, The *15* Will S. Davis
Avalanche, The *19* George Fitzmaurice
Avalanche! *23* Michael Curtiz
Avalanche *28* Otto Brower
Avalanche *30* Arnold Fanck
Avalanche *37* Mikio Naruse
Avalanche *46* Irving Allen
Avalanche *52* Kaneto Shindo
Avalanche *56* Satsuo Yamamoto
Avalanche *75* Frederic Goode
Avalanche *78* Corey Allen
Avalanche Express *78* Monte Hellman, Mark Robson
Avale Nanna Hendthi *88* Prabhakar-Umesh
Avaleuses, Les *73* Jesús Franco
Avalon *88* John J. Anderson
Avalon *90* Barry Levinson
Avant le Déluge *53* André Cayatte
Avanti! *72* Billy Wilder
Avanti C'È Posto *42* Mario Bonnard
Avanti Popolo *86* Raphi Bukaee
Avanzi di Galera *54* Vittorio Cottafavi
Avare, L' *08* Georges Méliès
Avare, L' *10* André Calmettes
Avare, L' *60* James Blue, R. Hermeantier
Avarice *58* Heinosuke Gosho
Avaricious Monk, The *12* Warwick Buckland
Avasthe *88* Krishna Masadi
Avatar *15* Carmine Gallone
Ave Caesar! *19* Alexander Korda
Ave Maria *06* Arthur Gilbert
Ave Maria *18* Wilfred Noy
Ave Maria *28* J. Steven Edwards, H. B. Parkinson
Ave Maria *37* Johannes Riemann
Ave Maria *84* Jacques Richard
Ave Maria de Schubert *36* Max Ophüls
Ave Sin Rumbo *38* R. O'Quigley
Avec André Gide *51* Marc Allégret
Avec la Peau des Autres *66* Jacques Deray
Avec l'Assurance *35* Roger Capellani
Avec le Sourire *36* Maurice Tourneur
Avec Passion Bosch ou Le Jardin des Délits de Jérôme Bosch *80* Jean Eustache
Avenger, The *15* Mauritz Stiller
Avenger, The *24* Charles R. Seeling
Avenger, The *31* Roy William Neill
Avenger, The *33* Edwin L. Marin
Avenger, The *47* Salah Abu Saif
Avenger, The *60* Karl Anton
Avenger, The *62* Giorgio Rivalta
Avenger, The *66* Ferdinando Baldi
Avenger of the Seven Seas *61* Domenico

Paolella
Avenger of Venice *63* Riccardo Freda
Avengers, The *42* Harold French
Avengers, The *50* John H. Auer
Avenging, The *81* Lyman Dayton
Avenging Angel *85* Robert Vincent O'Neil
Avenging Arrow, The *21* William J. Bowman, W. S. Van Dyke
Avenging Conscience, The *14* D. W. Griffith
Avenging Conscience, or Thou Shalt Not Kill, The *14* D. W. Griffith
Avenging Fangs *27* Ernest van Pelt
Avenging Force *86* Sam Firstenberg
Avenging Hand, The *15* Charles C. Calvert
Avenging Hand, The *36* Joseph Losey
Avenging Rider, The *28* Wallace Fox
Avenging Rider, The *43* Sam Nelson
Avenging Shadow, The *28* Ray Taylor
Avenging Spirit *77* Michael Anderson
Avenging Trail, The *18* Francis Ford
Avenging Waters *36* Spencer G. Bennet
Avenir d'Émilie, L' *84* Helma Sanders-Brahms
Avenir Dévoile par les Lignes des Pieds, L' *14* Émile Cohl
Aventura al Centro de la Tierra *65* Alfredo B. Crevenna
Aventura Peligrosa, Una *40* Ramón Peón
Aventuras de Quinque y Arturo el Robot *65* Pascual Cervera
Aventuras de Robinson Crusoe, Las *52* Luis Buñuel
Aventuras del Barbero de Sevilla *54* Ladislas Vajda
Aventuras del Vizconde, Las *67* Maurice Cloche
Aventure, Une *22* Victor Tourjansky
Aventure, L' *23* Marco De Gastyne
Aventure à Paris *36* Marc Allégret
Aventure C'Est l'Aventure, L' *72* Claude Lelouch
Aventure de Cabassou, L' *45* Gilles Grangier
Aventure de Guy, L' *36* Alain Resnais
Aventure des Millions, L' *16* Louis Feuillade
Aventure Malgache *44* Alfred Hitchcock
Aventure Sauvage, L' *66* Sidney Hayers
Aventures à l'Île de Madère *84* Raúl Ruiz
Aventures au Radio-Circus *53* André Michel
Aventures d'Arsène Lupin, Les *56* Jacques Becker
Aventures de Casanova, Les *47* Jean Boyer
Aventures de Clementine, Les *16* Émile Cohl*
Aventures de Don Quichotte *08* Georges Méliès
Aventures de la Famille Carre, Les *65* John Halas*
Aventures de Maltracé *13* Émile Cohl
Aventures de Rabbi Jacob, Les *73* Gérard Oury
Aventures de Reinette et Mirabelle, Les *86* Eric Rohmer
Aventures de Robert Macaire, Les *25* Jean Epstein
Aventures de Robinson Crusoe, Les *02*

Georges Méliès
Aventures de Salavin, Les *63* Pierre Granier-Deferre
Aventures de Till L'Espiègle, Les *56* Joris Ivens, Gérard Philipe
Aventures des Pieds-Nickelés, Les *16* Émile Cohl, Benjamin Rabier
Aventures du Baron de Münchausen, Les *10* Georges Méliès
Aventures du Vicomte, Les *67* Maurice Cloche
Aventures d'un Bout de Papier, Les *11* Émile Cohl
Aventures d'un Voyageur Trop Pressé, Les *03* Alice Guy-Blaché
Aventures Extraordinaires de Cervantes, Les *67* Vincent Sherman
Aventurier, Un *21* Charles De Marsan, Charles Maudru
Aventurier, L' *24* Maurice Mariaud
Aventurier, L' *34* Marcel L'Herbier
Aventurière, L' *12* Louis Feuillade
Aventurière, Dame de Compagnie, L' *11* Louis Feuillade
Aventuriers, Les *67* Robert Enrico
Äventyret *15* Mauritz Stiller
Avenue de l'Opera *00* Alice Guy-Blaché
Average Husband *30* Mack Sennett
Average Woman, The *23* Christy Cabanne
Aveu, L' *69* Costa-Gavras
Aveugle, L' *1897* Alice Guy-Blaché
Aveugle, L' *00* Alice Guy-Blaché
Aveugle de Jérusalem, L' *09* Louis Feuillade
Aveux les Plus Doux, Les *70* Édouard Molinaro
Aviatikeren og Journalistens Hustru *11* August Blom
Aviation Vacation *41* Tex Avery
Aviator, The *29* Roy Del Ruth
Aviator, The *85* George (Trumbull) Miller
Aviator and the Journalist's Wife, The *11* August Blom
Aviator Spy, The *14* Charles C. Calvert
Aviators, The *35* Yuli Raizman
Aviator's Generosity, The *11* Urban Gad
Aviator's Wife, The *80* Eric Rohmer
Avion de Minuit, L' *38* Dmitri Kirsanov
Avisen *54* Jørgen Roos
Avocat, L' *25* Gaston Ravel
Avocat d'Amour *38* Raoul Ploquin
Avoir Seize Ans *78* Jean-Pierre Lefèbvre
Avrianos Polemistis *81* Michael Papas
Avril Brise *87* Liria Begeja
Avventura, L' *59* Michelangelo Antonioni
Avventura ad Algeri *53* Ray Enright
Avventura di Dio, L' *20* Augusto Genina
Avventura di Giacomo Casanova *38* Carlo Bassoli
Avventura di Salvator Rosa, Un' *39* Alessandro Blasetti
Avventura di un Italiano in Cina, L' *61* Riccardo Freda, Hugo Fregonese, Piero Pierotti
Avventure di Bijou, Le *19* Augusto Genina
Avventure di Cartouche, Le *54* Steve Sekely, Gianni Vernuccio
Avventure di Dox, Le *61* Riccardo Freda
Avventure di Giacomo Casanova, Le *54* Steno

Avventure di Mandrin, Le *52* Mario Soldati

Avventure di Pinocchio, Le *71* Luigi Comencini

Avventure di Topo Gigio, Le *61* Federico Caldura, Luca De Rico

Avventure di Ulisse, Le *69* Franco Rossi

Avventure e gli Amori di Miguel Cervantes, Le *67* Vincent Sherman

Avventuriero, L' *67* Terence Young

Avventuriero a Tahiti, Un *66* Jean Becker

Avvocato del Diavolo, L' *77* Guy Green

Avvocato Difensore, L' *35* Gero Zambuto

Aw, Nurse *34* Art Davis, Sid Marcus

Awaiting the Pallbearers *86* Alejandro Doria

Awakening, The *09* D. W. Griffith

Awakening, The *15* Ralph Ince

Awakening, The *17* George Archainbaud

Awakening, The *28* Victor Fleming

Awakening, The *34* Aleksander Ford, Wanda Jakubowska

Awakening, The *38* Alfonse Frenguelli

Awakening, The *56* Mario Camerini

Awakening, The *80* Mike Newell

Awakening Hour, The *57* Donovan Winter

Awakening of Bess Morton, The *16* Otis B. Thayer

Awakening of Helena Richie, The *16* John W. Noble

Awakening of Jim Burke, The *35* Lambert Hillyer

Awakening of John Bond, The *11* Charles Brabin

Awakening of Norah, The *14* Lawrence Trimble

Awakening of Ruth, The *17* Edward H. Griffith

Awakening of Spring, The *29* Richard Oswald

Awakenings *90* Penny Marshall

Awara *51* Raj Kapoor

Award Presentation to Andy Warhol *64* Jonas Mekas

Awards and Decorations *74* Jan Łomnicki

Away All Boats! *56* Joseph Pevney

Away from It All *79* John Cleese, Clare Taylor

Away from It All *81* Nikolai Gubenko

Away Goes Prudence *20* John S. Robertson

Away Out West *10* Gilbert M. Anderson

Awdat al Ibn al Dhal *75* Youssef Chahine

Awdat Mowatin *86* Mohamed Khan

Awdit el Roh *69* Salah Abu Saif

Awesome Lotus *83* David O'Malley

Awful Dr. Orloff, The *61* Jesús Franco

Awful Moment, The *08* D. W. Griffith

Awful Orphan, The *48* Chuck Jones

Awful Skate, An *07* Gilbert M. Anderson

Awful Sleuth, The *51* Richard Quine

Awful Spook, The *21* Gregory La Cava, Vernon Stallings

Awful Truth, The *25* Paul Powell

Awful Truth, The *29* Marshall Neilan

Awful Truth, The *37* Leo McCarey

Awkward Anarchists *15* Dave Aylott

Awkward Horseman, The *05* Alf Collins

Awkward Sign Writer, The *1897* George

Albert Smith

Awkward Situation, An *07* Percy Stow

Awlad el Shareh *51* Youssef Wahby

Axe, The *77* Frederick R. Friedel

Axe and the Lamp, The *63* John Halas

Axe for the Honeymoon, An *69* Mario Bava

Axe Me Another *34* Dave Fleischer

Axiliad *87* Witold Leszczyński

¡Ay, Carmela! *90* Carlos Saura

Ay Jalisco No Te Rajes *43* Joselito Rodríguez

Ayahku *89* Aguy Elias

Ayah's Revenge, The *08* James A. Williamson

Ayamonn the Terrible *60* Francis Ford Coppola

Aylwin *20* Henry Edwards

Ayodhyecha Raja *32* Rajaram Vanakudre Shantaram

Aysa! *65* Jorge Sanjinés

Ayúdame a Vivir *36* José A. Ferreyra

Až do Konce *86* Antonín Kopřiva

Až Přijde Kocour *63* Vojtěch Jasný

Azaïs *31* René Hervil

Azima, El *40* Kamel Salim

Azit the Paratrooper Dog *72* Boaz Davidson

Aziza *80* Abdel-Latif Ben Ammar

Azra *88* Mirza Idrizović

Aztec Mummy, The *57* Rafael Portillo

Aztec Mummy vs. the Human Robot, The *57* Rafael Portillo

Azur Express *38* Béla Balázs

Azure Express *38* Béla Balázs

BBC: Droitwich *34* Edgar Anstey, Harry Watt

BBC—The Voice of Britain *34* Stuart Legg

B.F.'s Daughter *47* Robert Z. Leonard

BMX Bandits *83* Brian Trenchard-Smith

B-Movie *88* Kathy Milani

B Must Die *74* José Luis Borau

B.O.R.N. *89* Ross Hagen

B.S. I Love You *71* Steven Hilliard Stern

Baal *69* Volker Schlöndorff

Baap Beti *51* Bimal Roy

Baar Phir, Ek *80* Vinod Pande

Baara *78* Souleymane Cissé

Baath Omar *65* Mario Ruspoli

Bab el Hadid *57* Youssef Chahine

Bab Sama Maftouh *88* Farida Benlyazid

Bab the Fixer *17* Sherwood MacDonald

Baba *71* Yılmaz Güney

Baba Amin *50* Youssef Chahine

Baba Felunath, Joi *78* Satyajit Ray

Baba Yaga *73* Corrado Farina

Babar: The Movie *89* Alan Bunce

Babatou ou Les Trois Conseils *76* Boubou Hama, Jean Rouch

Babatu *76* Boubou Hama, Jean Rouch

Babbage *68* Charles Eames, Ray Eames

Babbitt *24* Harry Beaumont

Babbitt *34* William Keighley

Babbling Bess *16* Harry S. Palmer

Babbling Tongues *17* William Humphrey

Babe and Puppies *04* Edwin S. Porter

Babe Comes Home *27* Ted Wilde

Babe Ruth Story, The *48* Roy Del Ruth

Babel Opera *85* André Delvaux

Babel-Opéra *85* André Delvaux

Babel-Opéra ou La Répétition de Don Juan *85* André Delvaux

Babes and Boobs *18* Larry Semon

Babes in Arms *39* Busby Berkeley

Babes in Bagdad *52* Edgar G. Ulmer

Babes in the Wood, The *05* Lewin Fitzhamon

Babes in the Woods *17* Chester M. Franklin, Sidney Franklin

Babes in the Woods, The *25* Walter Lantz

Babes in Toyland *34* Gus Meins, Charles Rogers

Babes in Toyland *61* Jack Donohue

Babes on Broadway *41* Busby Berkeley

Babes on Swing Street *44* Edward Lilley

Babette *17* Charles Brabin

Babette Goes to War *59* Christian-Jaque

Babette S'en Va-t-en Guerre *59* Christian-Jaque

Babette's Feast *87* Gabriel Axel

Babettes Gæstebud *87* Gabriel Axel

Babies for Sale *40* Charles Barton

Babo 73 *63* Robert Downey

Baboona *35* Martin E. Johnson

Bab's Burglar *17* J. Searle Dawley

Bab's Candidate *20* Edward H. Griffith

Bab's Diary *17* J. Searle Dawley

Bab's Matinee Idol *17* J. Searle Dawley

Babula *87* Sadhu Meher

Baby, The *13* F. Martin Thornton

Baby, The *15* Chester M. Franklin, Sidney Franklin

Baby *15* Harry C. Myers

Baby *32* Karel Lamač

Baby, The *72* Ted Post

Baby, The *75* Peter Sasdy

Baby *85* B. W. L. Norton

Baby and the Ape, The *03* George Albert Smith

Baby and the Battleship, The *56* Jay Lewis

Baby and the Bomb, The *11* Bert Haldane

Baby and the Stork, The *11* D. W. Griffith

Baby and Young Girls *1896* Georges Méliès

Baby Be Good *25* Charles Lamont

Baby Be Good *35* Dave Fleischer

Baby Be Good *39* Ray Enright

Baby Blue Marine *75* John Hancock

Baby Boogie *55* Paul Julian

Baby Boom *87* Charles Shyer

Baby Bottleneck *46* Robert Clampett

Baby Buggy Bunny *54* Chuck Jones

Baby Butch *54* Joseph Barbera, William Hanna

Baby Carriage, The *56* Tomotaka Tasaka

Baby Carriage, The *62* Bo Widerberg

Baby Cart at the River Styx *72* Kenji Misumi

Baby Cyclone, The *28* A. Edward Sutherland

Baby Day *13* Mack Sennett

Baby Doll *56* Elia Kazan

Baby Doll *88* Jon Bang Carlsen

Baby Dolls *82* Ernst R. von Theumer

Baby Face *33* Alfred E. Green

Baby Face *35* Raoul Walsh

Baby Face Harrington *35* Raoul Walsh

Baby Face Morgan *42* Arthur Dreifuss

Baby Face Nelson *57* Don Siegel

Baby Feud 28 Manny Gould, Ben Harrison
Baby Ghana 57 Jean Rouch
Baby, It's You 83 John Sayles
Baby Kong 77 Mario Bava
Baby Love 68 Alastair Reid
Baby Love 83 Dan Wolman
Baby Maker, The 70 James Bridges
Baby Mine 17 John S. Robertson
Baby Mine 27 Robert Z. Leonard
Baby Mother, The 28 John Harvey
Baby on the Barge, The 15 Cecil M. Hepworth
Baby Puss 43 Joseph Barbera, William Hanna
Baby Review, The 03 Edwin S. Porter
Baby...Secret of the Lost Legend 85 B. W. L. Norton
Baby Show, The 11 Frank Wilson
Baby Show, The 28 Mannie Davis
Baby-Sitter, La 75 René Clément
Baby Sitter—Un Maledetto Pasticcio 75 René Clément
Baby Snakes 79 Frank Zappa
Baby Take a Bow 34 Harry Lachman
Baby, the Boy and the Teddy-Bear, The 10 H. Oceano Martinek
Baby, the Rain Must Fall 64 Robert Mulligan
Baby Vanishes, The 41 Gordon Douglas
Baby Wants a Bottleship 42 Dave Fleischer
Babylas à Hérité d'une Panthère 11 Alfred Machin
Babylas Explorateur 11 Alfred Machin
Babylon 80 Franco Rosso
Baby's Chum 09 Charles Raymond
Baby's Photograph 13 Will P. Kellino
Baby's Playmate 08 Lewin Fitzhamon
Baby's Power, A 10 Lewin Fitzhamon
Baby's Revenge 09 J. B. McDowell
Baby's Shoe, A 09 D. W. Griffith
Babysitter, The 69 Don Henderson
Babysitter, The 75 René Clément
Bacall to Arms 46 Robert Clampett
Bacchanale 70 John Amero, Lem Amero
Bacchantes, The 61 Giorgio Ferroni
Bach and Broccoli 87 André Melançon
Bach et Bottine 87 André Melançon
Bachelor and the Bobby-Soxer, The 47 Irving Reis
Bachelor Apartment 31 Lowell Sherman
Bachelor Apartments 20 Johnny Walker
Bachelor Babies 26 Charles Lamont
Bachelor Bait 34 George Stevens
Bachelor Bait 48 John Cromwell, Richard Wallace
Bachelor Blues 48 Leslie Goodwins
Bachelor Brides 26 William K. Howard
Bachelor Daddy, The 22 Alfred E. Green
Bachelor Daddy 41 Harold Young
Bachelor Father, The 30 Robert Z. Leonard
Bachelor Father 34 Gustaf Molander
Bachelor Father 39 Richard Harlan
Bachelor Flat 61 Frank Tashlin
Bachelor Girl, The 29 Richard Thorpe
Bachelor Girl 87 Rivka Hartman
Bachelor Girl Apartment 66 Robert Ellis Miller

Bachelor Girls 46 Andrew L. Stone
Bachelor Husband, A 20 Kenelm Foss
Bachelor in Paradise 61 Jack Arnold
Bachelor in Paris 52 John Guillermin
Bachelor Knight 47 Irving Reis
Bachelor Mother 33 Charles Hutchinson
Bachelor Mother 39 Garson Kanin
Bachelor of Arts 34 Louis King
Bachelor of Arts 69 Harry Booth
Bachelor of Hearts 58 Wolf Rilla
Bachelor Party, The 57 Delbert Mann
Bachelor Party 84 Neal Israel
Bachelor's Affairs 31 Alfred L. Werker
Bachelor's Babies, A 15 Cecil Birch
Bachelor's Baby, A 22 Arthur H. Rooke
Bachelor's Baby, The 27 Frank R. Strayer
Bachelor's Baby 32 Harry Hughes
Bachelors Beware 30 Heinosuke Gosho
Bachelor's Brides 26 William K. Howard
Bachelor's Children, A 18 Paul Scardon
Bachelors' Club, The 21 A. V. Bramble
Bachelor's Club, The 29 Noel Mason Smith
Bachelor's Daughters, The 46 Andrew L. Stone
Bachelor's Folly 31 T. Hayes Hunter, Victor Saville
Bachelor's Love Story, A 14 George Loane Tucker
Bachelor's Paradise, The 01 Georges Méliès
Bachelor's Paradise 28 George Archainbaud
Bachelors' Paradise 40 Kurt Hoffmann
Bachelor's Piece of Wedding Cake, The 07 Alf Collins
Bachelor's Ward, The 12 Warwick Buckland
Bachelor's Wife, A 19 Emmett J. Flynn
Bacio di Cirano, Il 13 Carmine Gallone
Bacio di Cirano, Il 20 Carmine Gallone
Bacio di Giuda, Il 88 Paolo Benvenuti
Back Alley Oproar 48 Friz Freleng
Back and Forth 69 Michael Snow
Back at the Front 52 George Sherman
Back at Three 12 Fred Rains
Back Door to Heaven 39 William K. Howard
Back Door to Hell 64 Monte Hellman
Back Fire 22 Alvin J. Neitz
Back from Eternity 56 John Farrow
Back from Shanghai 29 Noel Mason Smith
Back from the Dead 57 Charles Marquis Warren
Back Home and Broke 22 Alfred E. Green
Back in Circulation 37 Ray Enright
Back in the Country 39 Carl Boese
Back in the Saddle 41 Lew Landers
Back of the Man 17 Reginald Barker
Back Page, The 31 Roscoe Arbuckle
Back Page 34 Anton Lorenze
Back Pay 22 Frank Borzage
Back Pay 30 William A. Seiter
Back Roads 80 Martin Ritt
Back Room Boy 42 Herbert Mason
Back Stage 19 Roscoe Arbuckle
Back Street 32 John M. Stahl
Back Street 41 Robert Stevenson
Back Street 61 David Miller
Back Streets of Paris 48 Marcel Blistène
Back to Back 90 John Kincade

Back to Backing 26 William C. Nolan
Back to Bataan 45 Edward Dmytryk
Back to Broadway 14 Ralph Ince
Back to God's Country 19 David M. Hartford
Back to God's Country 27 Irvin Willat
Back to God's Country 53 Joseph Pevney
Back to Liberty 27 Bernard F. McEveety
Back to Life 13 Allan Dwan
Back to Life 25 Whitman Bennett
Back to Nature 36 James Tinling
Back to School 86 Alan Metter
Back to the Balkans 18 Raoul Barré, Charles Bowers
Back to the Beach 87 Lyndall Hobbs
Back to the Future 85 Robert Zemeckis
Back to the Future Part II 89 Robert Zemeckis
Back to the Future Part III 90 Robert Zemeckis
Back to the Trees 26 Edwin Greenwood
Back to the Wall 57 Édouard Molinaro
Back to the Woods 18 George Irving
Back to the Woods 37 Preston Black
Back to Yellow Jacket 22 Ben F. Wilson
Back Trail, The 24 Clifford Smith
Back Trail 48 Christy Cabanne
Backbiters 24 Albert Dieudonné
Backbone 23 Edward Sloman
Backfire 47 Lambert Hillyer
Backfire 50 Vincent Sherman
Backfire 61 Paul Almond
Backfire 64 Jean Becker
Backfire 87 Gilbert Cates
Backgammon Game 1895 Louis Lumière
Background 53 Daniel Birt
Background to Danger 43 Raoul Walsh
Backlash 47 Eugene Forde
Backlash 56 John Sturges
Backlash 86 Bill Bennett
Backroads 77 Phillip Noyce
Backstage 27 Phil Goldstone
Backstage 35 Herbert Wilcox
Backstage 86 Jonathan Hardy
Backstage at the Kirov 83 Derek Hart
Backstage Mystery 34 E. Mason Hopper
Backstairs 21 Leopold Jessner, Paul Leni
Backstreet Dreams 90 Rupert Hitzig
Backtrack 69 Earl Bellamy
Backtrack 89 Dennis Hopper
Backwoods Bunny 59 Robert McKimson
Backwoods Massacre 81 John Russo
Backyard 50 Gösta Werner
Backyard, The 80 Dariush Mehrjui
Backyard Front, The 40 Andrew Buchanan
Backyard Theatre 72 Jean-Pierre Lefèbvre
Bacon Grabbers, The 29 Lewis R. Foster
Bad 87 Martin Scorsese
Bad and the Beautiful, The 52 Vincente Minnelli
Bad aur Badnam 88 Firoze Chinoy
Bad Bascomb 45 S. Sylvan Simon
Bad Blonde 51 Reginald LeBorg
Bad Blood 33 Alexander Esway, Billy Wilder
Bad Blood 36 Herbert Mason
Bad Blood 81 Mike Newell
Bad Blood 82 Paul Nicholas, Maurice Smith
Bad Blood 86 Leos Carax

Bad Blood 89 Chuck Vincent
Bad Boy 25 Leo McCarey
Bad Boy, A 32 Mervyn LeRoy
Bad Boy 35 John G. Blystone
Bad Boy 36 Lawrence Huntington
Bad Boy 39 Herbert Meyer
Bad Boy 49 Kurt Neumann
Bad Boy, The 50 Andrzej Wajda
Bad Boy Billy 15 Charles H. Weston
Bad Boys 17 Chester Withey
Bad Boys 60 Susumu Hani
Bad Boys 83 Richard Rosenthal
Bad Boys' Joke on the Nurse 04 Edwin S. Porter
Bad Buck of Santa Ynez, The 15 William S. Hart
Bad Bunch, The 76 Greydon Clark
Bad Charleston Charlie 73 Ivan Nagy
Bad Cigar, A 00 George Albert Smith
Bad Companions, The 32 John Orton
Bad Company 25 Edward H. Griffith
Bad Company 31 Tay Garnett
Bad Company 46 Paul Barralet
Bad Company 63 Jean Eustache
Bad Company 72 Robert Benton
Bad Company 86 José Santiso
Bad Daughter 49 Mikio Naruse
Bad Day at Black Rock 54 John Sturges
Bad Day at Cat Rock 65 Chuck Jones
Bad Day for Levinsky, A 09 T. J. Gobbett
Bad Dreams 88 Andrew Fleming
Bad Eggs 46 Arne Mattsson
Bad for Each Other 53 Irving Rapper
Bad Genius, The 32 Dick Huemer
Bad Georgia Road 76 John Broderick
Bad Girl 31 Frank Borzage
Bad Girl, The 49 Mikio Naruse
Bad Girl 56 Herbert Wilcox
Bad Girls 75 Roberto Bianchi Montero
Bad Girls Don't Cry 59 Mauro Bolognini
Bad Girls Go to Hell 65 Doris Wishman
Bad Good Man, The 73 Josef Heifits
Bad Goody, The 73 Josef Heifits
Bad Guy 37 Edward L. Cahn
Bad Guys 86 Joel Silberg
Bad Housekeeping 37 Leslie Goodwins
Bad Influence 90 Curtis Hanson
Bad Investment, A 12 Allan Dwan
Bad Jim 90 Clyde Ware
Bad Joke, A 65 Alexander Alov, Vladimir Naumov
Bad Lands, The 25 Del Henderson
Bad Lands 39 Lew Landers
Bad Little Angel 39 Wilhelm Thiele
Bad Little Good Man, A 17 William Beaudine
Bad Lord Byron, The 49 David Mac-Donald
Bad Luck 34 Hiroshi Inagaki
Bad Luck 52 Arne Skouen
Bad Luck 59 Andrzej Munk
Bad Luck Blackie 49 Tex Avery
Bad Man, The 23 Edwin Carewe
Bad Man, The 30 Clarence Badger
Bad Man, The 40 Richard Thorpe
Bad Man and Others, A 15 Raoul Walsh
Bad Man and the Ranger, The 12 Allan Dwan
Bad Man from Bodie 41 Spencer G. Bennet

Bad Man from Red Butte 40 Ray Taylor
Bad Man of Brimstone, The 37 J. Walter Ruben
Bad Man of Harlem 37 Sam Newfield
Bad Man of Wyoming 40 Richard Thorpe
Bad Manners 84 Robert Houston
Bad Man's Bluff 26 Alvin J. Neitz
Bad Man's Money 29 John P. McGowan
Bad Man's River 71 Eugenio Martin
Bad Medicine 36 Jean Yarbrough
Bad Medicine 85 Harvey Miller
Bad Men of Missouri 41 Ray Enright
Bad Men of the Border 45 Wallace Fox
Bad Men of the Hills 42 William Berke
Bad Men of Thunder Gap 43 Albert Herman
Bad Men of Tombstone 48 Kurt Neumann
Bad Men's Money 29 John P. McGowan
Bad News Bears, The 76 Michael Ritchie
Bad News Bears Go to Japan, The 78 John Berry
Bad News Bears in Breaking Training, The 77 Michael Pressman
Bad Night 85 Gus Van Sant, Jr.
Bad Ol' Puddy Tat 49 Friz Freleng
Bad One, The 30 George Fitzmaurice
Bad One, The 57 Roger Corman
Bad Penny 79 Chuck Vincent
Bad Seed, The 55 Mervyn LeRoy
Bad Shilling, The 07 Arthur Cooper
Bad Sir Brian Botany 28 Frank Miller
Bad Sister 31 Hobart Henley
Bad Sister 47 Bernard Knowles
Bad Sixpence, The 07 Arthur Cooper
Bad Sleep Well, The 60 Akira Kurosawa
Bad Son, A 80 Claude Sautet
Bad Taste 88 Peter Jackson
Bad Timing 79 Nicolas Roeg
Bad Timing / A Sensual Obsession 79 Nicolas Roeg
Bada alla Tua Pelle Spirito Santo 72 Roberto Mauri
Baddegama 80 Lester James Peries
Baddesley Manor 26 Maurice Elvey
Baddesley Manor — The Phantom Gambler 26 Maurice Elvey
Baden-Powell Junior 11 Percy Stow
Badge of Honor 34 Spencer G. Bennet
Badge of Marshal Brennan, The 57 Albert C. Gannaway
Badge 373 73 Howard W. Koch
Badger's Green 34 Adrian Brunel
Badger's Green 49 John Irwin
Badjao 62 Lamberto Avellana
Badlanders, The 58 Delmer Daves
Badlands 73 Terrence Malick
Badlands of Dakota 41 Alfred E. Green
Badlands of Montana 57 Daniel B. Ullman
Badly Managed Hotel, A 1896 Georges Méliès
Badman of Deadwood 41 Joseph Kane
Badman's Country 58 Fred F. Sears
Badman's Gold 51 Robert E. Tansey
Badman's Territory 46 Tim Whelan
Badness of Burglar Bill, The 13 Frank Wilson
Baffled 24 John P. McGowan
Baffled Burglar, The 07 Walter R. Booth
Bag and Baggage 23 Finis Fox

Bag de Ens Facader 61 Peter Weiss
Bag of Fleas, A 62 Věra Chytilová
Bag of Monkey Nuts, A 11 A. E. Coleby
Bagarres 48 Henri Calef
Bagdad 49 Charles Lamont
Bagdad Cafe 87 Percy Adlon
Bagful of Fleas, A 62 Věra Chytilová
Bagged 12 Dave Aylott
Bagged 34 John Harlow
Baghe Sangui 76 Parviz Kimiavi
Bagnaia Paese Italico 49 Francesco Maselli
Bagne de Femmes 37 Douglas Sirk
Bagnosträfling, Der 49 Gustav Fröhlich
Bagpipes 60 John Halas*
Bague, La 47 Alain Resnais
Bague Qui Tue, La 15 Louis Feuillade
Bahama Passage 41 Edward H. Griffith
Bahia 77 Marcel Camus
Baie des Anges, La 62 Jacques Demy
Baignade dans le Torrent 1897 Alice Guy-Blaché
Baignade en Mer 1895 Louis Lumière
Baignade en Mer 1896 Georges Méliès
Baignade Impossible, La 01 Ferdinand Zecca
Baignoire, La 14 Émile Cohl
Bail Jumper 89 Christian Faber
Bailiff, The 54 Kenji Mizoguchi
Bailiff and the Dressmakers, The 09 Theo Bouwmeester
Bailiffs, The 32 Frank Cadman
Bailiff's Little Weakness, The 11 Lewin Fitzhamon
Bailout at 43,000 57 Francis D. Lyon
Bain de la Parisienne, Le 1897 Georges Méliès
Bain d'X 56 Alexander Alexeïeff, Claire Parker
Bairoletto 86 Attilio Polverini
Baiser de Feu, Une 37 Augusto Genina
Baiser de l'Empereur, Le 13 Alfred Machin
Baisers, Les 63 Claude Berri, Bertrand Tavernier
Baisers Volés 68 François Truffaut
Baishey Sravana 60 Mrinal Sen
Bait, The 16 William J. Bowman
Bait, The 20 Jack Gilbert, Maurice Tourneur
Bait 50 Frank Richardson
Bait 54 Hugo Haas
Baited Trap 26 Stuart Paton
Baited Trap, The 58 Norman Panama
Baiting the Bobby 09 Lewin Fitzhamon
Baixo Gavea 87 Haroldo Marinho Barbosa
Baja Oklahoma 88 Bobby Roth
Bajaderens Hævn 14 Forest Holger-Madsen
Bajaja 50 Jiří Trnka
Bajazzo 50 F. W. Murnau
Báječní Muži s Klikou 78 Jiří Menzel
Bajka 52 Andrzej Munk
Bajka w Ursusie 52 Andrzej Munk
Bajo el Cielo de México 37 Fernando De Fuentes
Bajo la Metralla 83 Felipe Cazals
Bakaruhában 57 Imre Fehér
Bakayaroo! (Watakushi Okotteimasu) 88 Takahita Hara, Tetsuya Nakajima, Yukihiko Tsutsumi, Eriko Watanabe
Baked Potato Festival, The 77 Yuri Ilyenko

Baker and Boy 02 Alf Collins
Baker and the Sweep, The 1898 George Albert Smith
Baker Boy, The 10 Van Dyke Brooke
Baker County U.S.A. 82 William Fruet
Baker's Bread 76 Erwin Keusch
Baker's Hawk 76 Lyman Dayton
Bakers in Trouble 07 Georges Méliès
Baker's Wife, The 38 Marcel Pagnol
Bakery, The 21 Norman Taurog*
Bakhshesh 77 Dariush Mehrjui
Bakintsy 38 Victor Turin
Baksmälla 72 Jörn Donner
Bakushū 50 Yasujiro Ozu
Bakusō 67 Hiroshi Teshigahara
Bal, Le 31 Wilhelm Thiele
Bal, Le 82 Ettore Scola
Bal de Nuit 59 Maurice Cloche
Bal des Pompiers, Le 49 André Berthomieu
Bal des Voyous, Le 69 Jean-Claude Dague, Louis Soulanes
Bal du Comte d'Orgel, Le 69 Marc Allégret
Bal du Gouverneur, Le 90 Marie-France Pisier
Bal na Vodi 86 Jovan Acin
Bal Tabarin 52 Philip Ford
Bala 76 Satyajit Ray
Balaclava 28 Maurice Elvey, Milton Rosmer
Balada da Praia dos Cães, A 86 José Fonseca e Costa
Balada o Trubi i Oblaku 61 France Štiglić
Balalaika 39 André De Toth
Balalaika 39 Reinhold Schünzel
Balance, The 74 Krzysztof Zanussi
Balance, La 81 Bob Swaim
Balaoo 13 Victorin Jasset
Balaoo ou Des Pas au Plafond 13 Victorin Jasset
Balaoo the Demon Baboon 13 Victorin Jasset
Balarasa 50 José Antonio Nieves Conde
Balata de Maipo 11 Mario Gallo
Balatum 38 Alexander Alexeïeff, Claire Parker
Balboa 82 James Polakoff
Balcón de la Luna, El 61 Luis Saslavsky
Balcón Sobre el Infierno, Un 63 François Villiers
Balcony, The 63 Joseph Strick
Bald Story, A 12 Percy Stow
Baldvins Bröllop 38 Emil A. Pehrsson, Gideon Wahlberg
Baldwin's Wedding 38 Emil A. Pehrsson, Gideon Wahlberg
Balettprimadonnan 16 Mauritz Stiller
Balıkçı Güzeli 53 Baha Gelenbevi
Balint Fabian Meets God 79 Zoltán Fábri
Baliseurs du Désert, Les 85 Nacer Khemir
Balked at the Altar 08 D. W. Griffith
Ball, Der 31 Wilhelm Thiele
Ball at Savoy 36 Joseph Losey
Ball at the Anjo House, A 47 Kozaburo Yoshimura
Ball at the Castle 39 Massimiliano Nuefeld
Ball im Metropol 37 Frank Wisbar
Ball im Savoy 34 Steve Sekely

Ball of Fire 41 Howard Hawks
Ball of Fortune, The 26 Hugh Croise
Ball of Suet, A 34 Mikhail Romm
Ball of the Anjo Family, The 47 Kozaburo Yoshimura
Ball-Trap on the Côte Sauvage 89 Jack Gold
Ballad, The 57 Sergei Paradzhanov
Ballad 68 Gösta Ågren
Ballad in Blue 64 Paul Henreid
Ballad of a Gunfighter 63 Bill Ward
Ballad of a Hussar, The 62 Eldar Ryazanov
Ballad of a Soldier 59 Grigori Chukhrai
Ballad of a Workman 62 Keisuke Kinoshita
Ballad of a Young Workman 62 Keisuke Kinoshita
Ballad of Ben and Charlie, The 72 Michele Lupo
Ballad of Berlin, The 48 Robert A. Stemmle
Ballad of Billie Blue 72 Kent Osborne
Ballad of Cable Hogue, The 70 Sam Peckinpah
Ballad of Cossack Gloota, The 37 Igor Savchenko
Ballad of Dickie Jones, The 71 George Bekes
Ballad of Dogs' Beach, The 86 José Fonseca e Costa
Ballad of Eva, The 86 Francesco Longo
Ballad of Gavilan 68 William J. Jugo
Ballad of Genkai Sea 86 Masanobu Deme
Ballad of Gregorio Cortez, The 82 Robert M. Young
Ballad of Joe Hill, The 71 Bo Widerberg
Ballad of Josie, The 67 Andrew V. McLaglen
Ballad of Love, A 66 Mikhail Bogin
Ballad of Narayama, The 58 Keisuke Kinoshita
Ballad of Narayama, The 83 Shohei Imamura
Ballad of Orin, The 77 Masahiro Shinoda
Ballad of Pony 86 Seijiro Koyama
Ballad of Tam-Lin, The 70 Roddy McDowall
Ballad of the Little Soldier 84 Werner Herzog
Ballad of the Narayama 58 Keisuke Kinoshita
Ballad of the Top Hat 36 Max De Haas
Ballad of the Trumpet and the Cloud, The 61 France Štiglić
Ballada o Soldatye 59 Grigori Chukhrai
Ballade pour un Voyou 63 Jean-Claude Bonnardot
Ballade vom Kleinen Soldaten 84 Werner Herzog
Ballata del Boia, La 63 Luis García Berlanga
Ballata di Eva, La 86 Francesco Longo
Ballata per un Pistolero 67 Alfio Caltabiano
Balle au Cœur, Une 65 Jean-Daniel Pollet
Balle dans le Canon, Une 58 Michel Deville, Charles Gérard
Ballerina, The 16 Mauritz Stiller
Ballerina 37 Jean Benoît-Lévy
Ballerina 50 Ludwig Berger

Ballerina 56 G. W. Pabst
Ballerine 36 Gustav Machatý
Ballerup Boulevard 86 Linda Wendel
Ballet Adagio 72 Norman McLaren
Ballet Dancer, The 11 August Blom, Urban Gad
Ballet Dancer's Love, A 11 August Blom, Urban Gad
Ballet de France 55 Richard Blareau
Ballet de Singe 07 Alice Guy-Blaché
Ballet do Brasil 62 Nelson Pereira Dos Santos
Ballet Girl, The 16 George Irving
Ballet Girl, The 18 Ernst Lubitsch
Ballet Girl 54 Astrid Henning-Jensen
Ballet Japonais 00 Alice Guy-Blaché
Ballet Libella 1897 Alice Guy-Blaché
Ballet Master's Dream, The 03 Georges Méliès
Ballet Mécanique, Le 24 Fernand Léger
Ballet of Othello, The 64 V. Chabukiani
Ballet of Romeo and Juliet, The 55 Lev Arnshtam, Leonid Lavrovsky
Ballet-Oops 54 Robert Cannon
Ballet Primadonna, The 16 Mauritz Stiller
Ballet Tales 56 V. Chabukiani, S. Managadze
Balletdanserinden 11 August Blom, Urban Gad
Balleten Danser 38 Svend Gade
Ballets de Niger, Les 62 Jean Rouch
Ballettens Børn 54 Astrid Henning-Jensen
Ballettens Datter 13 Forest Holger-Madsen
Ballhaus Barmbek 88 Christel Buschmann
Ballo al Castello 39 Massimiliano Nuefeld
Ballon Rouge, Le 55 Albert Lamorisse
Balloon, The 46 Nils Poppe
Balloon 60 Richard Leacock, D. A. Pennebaker
Balloon Ascension, A 1897 Georges Méliès
Balloon Goes Up, The 42 Redd Davis
Balloon Land 35 Ubbe Iwerks
Balloon Vendor, The 74 Mario Gariazzo
Balloonatic, The 23 Edward F. Cline, Buster Keaton
Balloonatics 23 Edward F. Cline, Buster Keaton
Balloonist's Mishap, The 00 Georges Méliès
Balloons 23 Dave Fleischer
Ballot Box Bunny 51 Friz Freleng
Ballyhoo Buster, The 28 Richard Thorpe
Balmat 34 Arnold Fanck
Balsamus 68 Pupi Avati
Balsamus l'Uomo di Satana 68 Pupi Avati
Balthazar 66 Robert Bresson
Baltic Deputy 36 Josef Heifits, Alexander Zarkhi
Baltic Express 59 Jerzy Kawalerowicz
Baltic Rhapsody 36 Leonard Buczkowski
Baltic Tragedy, A 71 Johan Bergenstråhle
Baltimore Bullet, The 80 Robert Ellis Miller
Bamba 48 Miguel Torres Contreras
Bambi 42 David Hand
Bambina 74 Alberto Lattuada
Bambini 51 Francesco Maselli
Bambini al Cinema 56 Francesco Maselli
Bambini Ci Guardano, I 42 Vittorio De Sica

Bar 51 *86* Amos Guttman
Bar 51—Sister of Love *86* Amos Guttman
Bar L Ranch *30* Harry S. Webb
Bar Mitzvah Boy *76* Michael Tuchner
Bar Nothin' *21* Edward Sedgwick
Bar Sinister, The *17* Edgar Lewis
Bar Sinister, The *55* Herman Hoffman
Bar 20 *43* Lesley Selander
Bar 20 Justice *38* Lesley Selander
Bar 20 Rides Again *35* Howard Bretherton
Bar Z Bad Men *37* Sam Newfield
Bara en Kypare *60* Alf Kjellin
Bara en Mor *49* Alf Sjöberg
Bara Gassen *49* Mikio Naruse
Bara Ikutabi *55* Teinosuke Kinugasa
Bara per lo Sceriffo, Una *65* Mario Caiano
Barabba *52* Alf Sjöberg
Barabba *61* Richard Fleischer
Barabbas *52* Alf Sjöberg
Barabbas *61* Richard Fleischer
Barabbas the Robber *49* Donald Taylor
Barajas, Aeropuerto Internacional *50* Juan Antonio Bardem
Bärande Hav *51* Arne Mattsson
Barão de Altamira, O *85* Artur Semedo
Barb Wire *22* Francis J. Grandon
Barbablù *41* Carlo Ludovico Bragaglia
Barbados Quest *55* Bernard Knowles
Barbagia *69* Carlo Lizzani
Barbara *61* Frank Wisbar
Barbara *70* Walter Burns
Barbara Broadcast *77* Radley Metzger
Barbara Elopes *21* Fred Paul, Jack Raymond
Barbara Frietchie *08* J. Stuart Blackton
Barbara Frietchie *15* Alice Guy-Blaché, Clarence J. Harris
Barbara Frietchie *24* Lambert Hillyer
Barbara Hepworth at the Tate *68* Bruce Beresford
Barbara in America *39* Márton Keleti
Barbara's Blindness *65* Joyce Wieland*
Barbarella *67* Roger Vadim
Barbarella, Queen of the Galaxy *67* Roger Vadim
Barbarian, The *20* Donald Crisp
Barbarian, The *33* Sam Wood
Barbarian and the Geisha, The *58* John Huston
Barbarian and the Lady, The *38* Adrian Brunel, Albert De Courville, Alexis Granowsky
Barbarian Ingomar, The *08* D. W. Griffith
Barbarian Queen *85* Héctor Olivera
Barbarians, The *57* Ferrucio Cerio
Barbarians, The *59* Rudolph Maté
Barbarians, The *87* Ruggero Deodato
Barbarians and Co., The *87* Ruggero Deodato
Barbaric Beast of Boggy Creek, Part Two, The *85* Charles B. Pierce
Bárbaro del Ritmo, El *63* Santiago Álvarez
Barbaros Hayrettin Paşa *51* Baha Gelenbevi
Barbarosa *82* Fred Schepisi
Barbarous Wedding, The *87* Marion Hansel
Barbary Coast *35* Howard Hawks
Barbary Coast Bunny *56* Chuck Jones

Barbary Coast Gent *44* Roy Del Ruth
Barbary Pirate *49* Lew Landers
Barbary Sheep *17* Maurice Tourneur
Barbe-Bleue *01* Georges Méliès
Barbe-Bleue *36* René Bertrand, Jean Painlevé
Barbe-Bleue *51* Christian-Jaque
Barbe-Bleue *72* Edward Dmytryk
Barbecue Brawl *55* Joseph Barbera, William Hanna
Barbed Wire *22* Francis J. Grandon
Barbed Wire *27* Rowland V. Lee, Mauritz Stiller
Barbed Wire *52* George Archainbaud
Barber and the Farmer, The *1897* Georges Méliès
Barber of Red Gap *45* Sam Newfield
Barber of Seville, The *13* Luigi Maggi
Barber of Seville, The *46* Mario Costa
Barber of Seville *49* Jean Loubignac
Barber of Seville, The *73* Ernst Wild
Barber of Seville, or The Useless Precaution, The *04* Georges Méliès
Barber of Stamford Hill, The *62* Caspar Wrede
Barber Shop, The *33* Arthur Ripley
Barberina *32* Fred Zelnik
Barberina die Tänzerin von Sans-Souci *32* Fred Zelnik
Barbero de Napoleon, El *30* Sidney Lanfield
Barberousse *16* Abel Gance
Barber's Daughter, The *29* Mack Sennett
Barber's Shop, The *39* Richard Llewellyn
Barbier de Séville, Le *04* Georges Méliès
Barbier de Séville, Le *36* Jean Kemm
Barbiere di Siviglia, Il *13* Luigi Maggi
Barbiere di Siviglia, Il *46* Mario Costa
Barboni *46* Dino Risi
Barbora Hlavsová *42* Martin Frič
Barbos the Dog and a Cross-Country Run *61* Leonid Gaidai
Barbouzes, Les *64* Georges Lautner
Barcarole *35* Gerhard Lamprecht
Barcelona *27* J. Steven Edwards
Bar-cel-ona *87* Ferrán Llagostera i Colli
Barcelona, Vieja Amiga *61* Jorge Grau
Bardelys the Magnificent *26* King Vidor
Bare Faced Flatfoot *51* Pete Burness
Bare-Fisted Gallagher *19* Joseph Franz
Bare Fists *19* John Ford
Bare Idea, The *20* Raoul Barré, Charles Bowers
Bare Knees *28* Erle C. Kenton
Bare Knuckles *21* James P. Hogan
Bare Knuckles *77* Don Edmonds
Baree, Son of Kazan *18* David Smith
Baree, Son of Kazan *25* David Smith
Barefoot Battalion *54* Gregg Tallas
Barefoot Boy *14* Robert Vignola
Barefoot Boy, The *23* David Kirkland
Barefoot Boy *38* Karl Brown
Barefoot Contessa, The *54* Joseph L. Mankiewicz
Barefoot Eagle, The *67* Alfonso Arau
Barefoot Executive, The *71* Robert Butler
Barefoot in the Park *66* Gene Saks
Barefoot Mailman, The *51* Earl McEvoy
Barefoot Savage *52* Clemente Fracassi
Barenhäuter, Der *87* Walter Beck

Barfly *87* Barbet Schroeder
Bargain, The *14* Reginald Barker
Bargain, The *21* Henry Edwards
Bargain, The *31* Robert Milton
Bargain Basement *35* Leslie Hiscott
Bargain of the Century, The *33* Charlie Chase
Bargee, The *64* Duncan Wood
Bargee's Daughter, The *11* Stuart Kinder
Bargee's Daughter, The *15* Ethyle Batley
Bargee's Revenge, The *12* Frank R. Growcott
Bargekeeper's Daughter, The *45* Alexander Esway
Bari, Al *85* Atef El Tayeb
Bari Theke Paliye *59* Ritwik Ghatak
Bari Thekey Pauye *59* Ritwik Ghatak
Bariera *66* Jerzy Skolimowski
Bariloche *39* Hugo Fregonese
Barker, The *17* J. A. Richmond
Barker, The *28* George Fitzmaurice
Barkleys of Broadway, The *49* Charles Walters
Barn av Solen *55* Arne Skouen
Barn Dance, The *28* Walt Disney, Ubbe Iwerks
Barn of the Naked Dead *73* Alan Rudolph
Barnaby *19* Jack Denton
Barnaby and Me *77* Norman Panama
Barnaby—Father Dear Father *62* John Halas
Barnaby—Overdue Dues Blues *62* John Halas
Barnaby Rudge *11* Charles Kent
Barnaby Rudge *15* Thomas Bentley
Barnacle Bill *30* Dave Fleischer
Barnacle Bill *35* Harry Hughes
Barnacle Bill *41* Richard Thorpe
Barnacle Bill *57* Charles Frend
Barnacle Bill the Sailor *30* Dave Fleischer
Barndommens Gade *86* Astrid Henning-Jensen
Barnes Murder Case, The *24* Sinclair Hill
Barnet *12* Mauritz Stiller
Barnet *14* Forest Holger-Madsen
Barnet *40* Benjamin Christensen
Barnets Magt *14* Forest Holger-Madsen
Barney Oldfield's Race for a Life *13* Mack Sennett
Barnstormer, The *22* Charles Ray
Barnstormers, The *15* Bert Haldane
Barnstormers, The *15* James W. Horne
Barnum Was Right *29* Del Lord
Barnum Was Wrong *30* Mark Sandrich
Barnvagnen *62* Bo Widerberg
Barnyard, The *23* Larry Semon
Barnyard Artists *28* Hugh Shields
Barnyard Babies *40* Sid Marcus
Barnyard Battle, The *29* Walt Disney, Ubbe Iwerks
Barnyard Brat *39* Dave Fleischer
Barnyard Broadcast, The *31* Burton Gillett
Barnyard Concert, The *30* Walt Disney
Barnyard Five *36* Walter Lantz
Barnyard Follies *40* Frank McDonald
Barnyard Hamlet, A *17* W. E. Stark
Barnyard Lodge Number One *28* Frank Moser
Barnyard Mixup, A *15* Vincent Whitman

Barnyard Olympics *32* Wilfred Jackson
Barnyard Politics *28* Hugh Shields
Baro, Il *62* Christian Marquand
Barocco *25* Charles Burguet
Barocco *76* André Téchiné
Baron, The *11* Mack Sennett
Baron Blood *72* Mario Bava
Baron de Crac, Le *10* Émile Cohl
Baron de l'Écluse, Le *59* Jean Delannoy
Barón del Terror, El *61* Chano Urueta
Baron Fantôme, Le *43* Serge De Poligny
Baron Münchausen's Dream *10* Georges Méliès
Baron Münchausen *40* Martin Frič
Baron Münchausen *43* Josef von Baky
Baron Münchausen *61* Karel Zeman
Baron of Arizona, The *49* Samuel Fuller
Baron Prášil *40* Martin Frič
Baron Prášil *61* Karel Zeman
Baron X *64* Risto Jarva, Jaakko Pakkasvirta, Spede Pasasen
Baroness and the Butler, The *38* Walter Lang
Baron's African War, The *43* Spencer G. Bennet
Baroque *89* Paul Leduc
Baroud *31* Rex Ingram, Alice Terry
Barque Sortant du Port *1895* Louis Lumière
Barque Sortant du Port de Trouville *1896* Georges Méliès
Barquero! *69* Gordon Douglas
Barrabas *19* Louis Feuillade
Barraca, La *44* Roberto Gavaldón
Barracuda *78* Harry Kerwin
Barrage Contre le Pacifique *57* René Clément
Barrage de l'Aigle, Le *46* Roger Leenhardt
Barrage du Chatelot *53* Henri Colpi
Barranco *32* André Berthomieu
Barravento *61* Glauber Rocha
Barred from a Bar *17* William Beaudine
Barred Road, The *58* Salah Abu Saif
Barren Gain, The *15* B. Reeves Eason
Barren Ground, The *77* Satsuo Yamamoto
Barren Lives *63* Nelson Pereira Dos Santos
Barretts of Wimpole Street, The *34* Sidney Franklin
Barretts of Wimpole Street, The *56* Sidney Franklin
Barricade, The *17* Edwin Carewe
Barricade, The *21* Christy Cabanne
Barricade *39* Gregory Ratoff
Barricade *50* Peter Godfrey
Barrier, The *26* George W. Hill
Barrier, The *37* Lesley Selander
Barrier *66* Jerzy Skolimowski
Barrier of Faith, The *15* Van Dyke Brooke
Barrier of the Law *50* Piero Costa
Barrière, La *15* Louis Feuillade
Barrières *49* Christian-Jaque
Barriers Burned Away *24* W. S. Van Dyke
Barriers of Folly *22* Edward Kull
Barriers of Society *16* Lloyd B. Carleton
Barriers of the Law *25* John P. McGowan
Barrings, Die *55* Rolf Thiele
Barrio *47* Ladislas Vajda
Barrister, The *28* Hugh Croise
Barroco *89* Paul Leduc
Barry Lyndon *75* Stanley Kubrick

Barry McKenzie Holds His Own *74* Bruce Beresford
Bars and Stripes *31* Manny Gould, Ben Harrison
Bars and Stripes Forever *39* Cal Dalton, Ben Hardaway
Bars of Hate *36* Albert Herman
Bars of Iron *20* F. Martin Thornton
Barsaat *49* Raj Kapoor
Bartered Bride, The *13* Max Urban
Bartered Bride, The *32* Max Ophüls
Bartholomew Versus the Wheel *64* Robert McKimson
Bartleby *70* Anthony Friedmann
Bartók Béla: Az Éjszaka Zenéje *70* István Gaál
Barton Mystery, The *20* Harry Roberts
Barton Mystery, The *32* Henry Edwards
Baruch *23* E. A. Dupont
Barwy Orchronne *76* Krzysztof Zanussi
Bas de Laine, Le *11* Louis Feuillade
Bas-Fonds, Les *36* Jean Renoir
Bas ya Bahar *71* Khalid Siddik
Basae *64* Jean-Daniel Pollet
Basættelse *44* Bodil Ipsen
Basanti Apa *88* S. K. Kalim
Base Deceivers, The *18* Maurice Sandground
Baseball *20* Hy Mayer
Baseball Bugs *46* Friz Freleng
Bashful Bachelor, The *41* Malcolm St. Clair
Bashful Buccaneer *25* Harry Joe Brown
Bashful Buzzard, The *45* Robert Clampett
Bashful Elephant, The *62* Dorrell McGowan, Stuart McGowan
Bashful Jim *25* Edward F. Cline
Bashful Suitor, The *21* Herbert Blaché
Bashnya *88* Viktor Tregubovich
Bashu, the Little Stranger *90* Bahram Beizai
Basic English *44* Len Lye
Basic Training *71* Frederick Wiseman
Basic Training *83* Andrew Sugerman
Basil the Great Mouse Detective *86* Ron Clements, Burny Mattinson, Dave Michener, John Musker
Basileus Quartet *82* Fabio Carpi
Basilischi, I *63* Lina Wertmuller
Basilisk, The *14* Cecil M. Hepworth
Basis des Make-Up, Die *84* Heinz Emigholz
Basket Case *81* Frank Henenlotter
Basket Case 2 *90* Frank Henenlotter
Basketball Fix, The *51* Felix E. Feist
Bassae *64* Jean-Daniel Pollet
Basta Che Non Si Sappia in Giro! *76* Luigi Comencini, Nanni Loy, Luigi Magni
Basta Guardarla *71* Luciano Salce
Bastard Brother of God, The *86* Benito Rabal
Bastardi, I *68* Duccio Tessari
Bastardo...Vamos a Matar *71* L. Mangini
Bastille *85* Rudolf van den Berg
Baston, La *85* Jean-Claude Missiaen
Bat, The *26* Roland West
Bat, The *48* Géza von Bolváry
Bat, The *58* Crane Wilbur
Bat People *74* Jerry Jameson
Bat 21 *88* Peter Markle

Bat Whispers, The *30* Roland West
Bataan *43* Tay Garnett
Bataille, La *23* Édouard E. Violet
Bataille d'Austerlitz, La *09* Émile Cohl
Bataille de Boules de Neige *00* Alice Guy-Blaché
Bataille de Confettis *1897* Georges Méliès
Bataille de France, La *63* Jean Aurel
Bataille de la Somme, La *16* Alfred Machin
Bataille de la Vie, La *49* Louis Daquin
Bataille de l'Eau Lourde, La *47* Jean Dréville, Titus Vibé-Müller
Bataille de San Sebastian, La *67* Henri Verneuil
Bataille de Verdun, La *17* Alfred Machin
Bataille des Dix Millions, La *70* Chris Marker, Valérie Mayoux
Bataille d'Oreillers *00* Alice Guy-Blaché
Bataille du Rail, La *45* René Clément
Bataille sur le Grand Fleuve *51* Roger Rosfelder, Jean Rouch
Batailles de la Vie, Les *12* Victorin Jasset
Batailles de l'Argent, Les *11* Louis Feuillade
Bataillon Élastique, Le *01* Georges Méliès
Batalla de Chile, La *76* Patricio Guzmán
Batallas en el Desierto, Las *87* Alberto Isaac
Batarcherjee *43* Bimal Roy
Bateau d'Émile, Le *62* Denys De la Patellière
Bateau-Mouche sur la Seine *1896* Georges Méliès
Bateau sur l'Herbe, Le *71* Gérard Brach
Båten *61* Jan Troell
Bath, The *14* Émile Cohl
Bath *62* Anatoly Karanovich, Sergei Yutkevich
Bath Harem, The *29* Heinosuke Gosho
Bath House, The *62* Anatoly Karanovich, Sergei Yutkevich
Bath of the Transitory World *29* Heinosuke Gosho
Bathers, The *00* Cecil M. Hepworth
Bather's Difficulties, A *06* Tom Green
Bathers' Revenge, The *04* William Haggar
Bathers Will Be Prosecuted *05* Lewin Fitzhamon
Bathing Beauty *44* George Sidney
Bathing in the Sea *1895* Louis Lumière
Bathing Not Allowed *05* William Haggar
Bathroom, The *70* Yoji Kuri
Bathroom Problem, A *13* Fred Evans, Joe Evans
Bâtir à Notre Âge *56* Sidney Jézéquel, Roger Leenhardt
Bâtisseurs, Les *38* Jean Epstein
Batman *43* Lambert Hillyer
Batman *66* Leslie Martinson
Batman *89* Tim Burton
Batman and Robin *49* Spencer G. Bennet
Batman Dracula *64* Andy Warhol
Batmen of Africa *36* B. Reeves Eason, Joseph Kane
Baton Bunny *59* Chuck Jones
Baton Rouge *85* Rachid Bouchareb
Baton Rouge *88* Rafael Moleón
Battaglia di Alamo, La *59* John Wayne
Battaglia di Algeri, La *65* Gillo Pontecorvo

Battaglia di Fort Apache, La *64* Hugo Fregonese
Battaglia di Maratona, La *59* Mario Bava, Jacques Tourneur, Bruno Vailati
Battaglia di Napoli, La *62* Nanni Loy
Battalion Shot, The *12* H. Oceano Martinek
Battant, Le *83* Alain Delon
Battellieri del Volga, I *59* Victor Tourjansky
Battements de Cœur *39* Henri Decoin
Batter Up *27* Stephen Roberts
Batteries Dogon: Éléments pour une Étude des Rythmes *66* Jean Rouch, Gilbert Rouget
*batteries not included *87* Matthew Robbins
Batteuse à Vapeur *1896* Georges Méliès
Batticuore *38* Mario Camerini
Battle, The *11* D. W. Griffith
Battle, The *15* Cecil M. Hepworth
Battle, The *23* Dave Fleischer
Battle, The *34* Nicolas Farkas
Battle at Apache Pass, The *51* George Sherman
Battle at Bloody Beach, The *61* Herbert Coleman
Battle at Elderbush Gulch, The *13* D. W. Griffith
Battle at Tsaritsyn *19* Dziga Vertov
Battle Beneath the Earth *67* Montgomery Tully
Battle Beneath the Sea *67* Montgomery Tully
Battle Beyond the Stars *68* Kinji Fukasaku
Battle Beyond the Stars *79* Jimmy T. Murakami
Battle Beyond the Sun *63* Francis Ford Coppola, Mikhail Karyukov, Alexander Kozyr
Battle Circus *52* Richard Brooks
Battle Cry, The *18* Ralph Ince
Battle Cry *54* Raoul Walsh
Battle Cry *75* Kihachi Okamoto
Battle Cry of Peace, The *15* J. Stuart Blackton, Wilfred North
Battle Flame *59* R. G. Springsteen
Battle for a Bottle, A *42* Frank Tashlin
Battle for Anzio, The *67* Edward Dmytryk
Battle for Berlin *71* Yuri Ozerov
Battle for China *50* Leonid Varmalov
Battle for Freedom, The *42* Basil Wright
Battle for Music *43* Donald Taylor
Battle for Our Soviet Ukraine, The *43* Yakiv Avdiyenko, Yulia Solntseva
Battle for the Planet of the Apes *73* J. Lee-Thompson
Battle for Tsaritsyn *19* Dziga Vertov
Battle Force *78* Umberto Lenzi
Battle Ground *88* David A. Prior
Battle Hell *56* Michael Anderson
Battle Hymn *56* Douglas Sirk
Battle Hymn of the Republic, The *11* Lawrence Trimble
Battle in Outer Space *59* Inoshiro Honda
Battle in the Clouds, The *09* Walter R. Booth
Battle Inferno *59* Frank Wisbar
Battle of Algiers, The *65* Gillo Pontecorvo
Battle of Austerlitz, The *09* Émile Cohl

Battle of Austerlitz, The *59* Abel Gance, Roger Richebé
Battle of Ballots, The *15* Frank B. Coigne
Battle of Billy's Pond, The *76* Harley Cokliss
Battle of Blood Island *60* Joel Rapp
Battle of Britain *43* Frank Capra, Anthony Veiller
Battle of Britain, The *68* Guy Hamilton
Battle of Broadway *38* George Marshall
Battle of Bunker Hill, The *11* J. Searle Dawley
Battle of Cauliflowers, A *05* Lewin Fitzhamon
Battle of Chemulpo Bay *04* Edwin S. Porter
Battle of Chile, The *76* Patricio Guzmán
Battle of China *43* Frank Capra, Anatole Litvak
Battle of El Alamein *68* Giorgio Ferroni
Battle of Gallipoli, The *30* Anthony Asquith, Geoffrey Barkas
Battle of Gettysburg, The *13* Charles Giblyn, Thomas Ince
Battle of Gettysownback, The *14* Fred Evans, Joe Evans
Battle of Glencoe, The *1899* Robert Ashe
Battle of Greed *34* Howard Higgin
Battle of Hearts *12* August Blom
Battle of Hearts *16* Oscar Apfel
Battle of Jutland, The *21* H. Bruce Woolfe
Battle of Kawanakajima, The *41* Teinosuke Kinugasa
Battle of Kolberg, The *45* Jerzy Bossak, Aleksander Ford
Battle of Kolobrzeg, The *45* Jerzy Bossak, Aleksander Ford
Battle of Leningrad *43* Aleksander Ford
Battle of Life, The *16* James Vincent
Battle of Love, The *23* Thomas Bentley
Battle of Love's Return, The *71* Lloyd Kaufman
Battle of Marathon, The *59* Mario Bava, Jacques Tourneur, Bruno Vailati
Battle of Mareth, The *78* Umberto Lenzi
Battle of Midway, The *42* John Ford
Battle of Midway, The *76* Jack Smight
Battle of Mons, The *26* Walter Summers
Battle of Neretva, The *69* Veljko Bulajić
Battle of New Orleans, The *60* Bob Godfrey
Battle of Pao Shan, The *38* Seto Waimon
Battle of Paris, The *29* Robert Florey
Battle of Powder River *50* George Sherman
Battle of Rogue River *54* William Castle
Battle of Roses, The *49* Mikio Naruse
Battle of Russia *44* Frank Capra, Anatole Litvak
Battle of San Pietro, The *44* John Huston
Battle of Santiago Bay, The *1898* J. Stuart Blackton
Battle of Shiloh, The *14* John Ince
Battle of Sokol, The *42* Alexander Rasumny
Battle of Stalingrad *69* Grigori Chukhrai
Battle of Stalingrad, Part One *49* Vladimir Petrov
Battle of Stalingrad, Part Two *50* Vladimir

Petrov
Battle of the Amazons *73* Alfonso Brescia
Battle of the Astros *65* Inoshiro Honda
Battle of the Barn *32* Dick Huemer
Battle of the Bulge, The *65* Ken Annakin
Battle of the Century, The *27* Clyde Bruckman
Battle of the Commandos *69* Umberto Lenzi
Battle of the Coral Sea *59* Paul Wendkos
Battle of the Giants *26* Victor Turin
Battle of the Neretva *69* Veljko Bulajić
Battle of the Rails *45* René Clément
Battle of the Red Men, The *12* Thomas Ince
Battle of the River Plate *56* Michael Powell, Emeric Pressburger
Battle of the Sexes, The *14* D. W. Griffith
Battle of the Sexes, The *27* D. W. Griffith
Battle of the Sexes, The *59* Charles Crichton
Battle of the Somme, The *16* Geoffrey H. Malins
Battle of the Ten Millions, The *70* Chris Marker, Valérie Mayoux
Battle of the V1, The *58* Vernon Sewell
Battle of the Villa Fiorita, The *64* Delmer Daves
Battle of the Worlds *61* Antonio Margheriti
Battle of Trafalgar, The *11* J. Searle Dawley
Battle of Tsaritsyn, The *19* Dziga Vertov
Battle of Waterloo, The *13* Charles H. Weston
Battle of Who Run, The *13* Mack Sennett
Battle of Wills, The *13* Allan Dwan
Battle on the Beach *61* Herbert Coleman
Battle on the River Neretva *69* Veljko Bulajić
Battle Royal, The *18* F. Richard Jones
Battle Royal *36* Walter Lantz
Battle Shock *56* Paul Henreid
Battle Stations *44* Garson Kanin
Battle Stations *56* Lewis Seiler
Battle Stripe *50* Fred Zinnemann
Battle Taxi *55* Herbert L. Strock
Battle Under the Walls of Kerchenetz *71* Ivan Ivanov-Vano
Battle with Confetti *1897* Georges Méliès
Battle Without Arms *60* Satsuo Yamamoto
Battle Zone *52* Lesley Selander
Battleaxe, The *62* Godfrey Grayson
Battlefield *85* Jan Budkiewicz
Battleground, The *12* Allan Dwan
Battleground *49* William A. Wellman
Battler, The *19* Frank Reicher
Battler, The *25* Robert North Bradbury
Battles in the Shadow *39* Domenico Gambino
Battles of Chief Pontiac *52* Felix E. Feist
Battles of Ivan, The *47* Sergei Eisenstein
Battles of the Coronel and Falkland Islands, The *27* Walter Summers
Battleship Maine *1898* Georges Méliès
Battleship Potemkin, The *25* Sergei Eisenstein
Battleships *11* Allan Dwan
Battlestar Galactica *78* Richard A. Colla

Battletruck *81* Harley Cokliss
Battling Bates *23* Webster Cullison
Battling Bellboy, The *17* William Beaudine
Battling Bellhop *37* Michael Curtiz
Battling Brewster *24* Del Henderson
Battling British, The *14* Maurice Elvey
Battling Brown of Birmingham *14* Charles H. Weston
Battling Bruisers *25* Adrian Brunel
Battling Buckaroo *32* Armand Schaefer
Battling Buddy *24* Richard Thorpe
Battling Bunyon *25* Paul Hurst
Battling Butler *26* Buster Keaton
Battling Charlie *15* Charles Chaplin
Battling Fool, The *24* W. S. Van Dyke
Battling for Barleycorn *26* William C. Nolan
Battling Hoofer *37* Victor Schertzinger
Battling Jane *18* Elmer Clifton
Battling Kelly *12* A. E. Coleby
Battling Kid *26* Paul Hurst
Battling King *22* P. D. Sargent
Battling Marshal *50* Oliver Drake
Battling Mason *24* William James Craft, Jack Nelson
Battling Orioles, The *24* Fred Guiol, Ted Wilde
Battling with Buffalo Bill *31* Ray Taylor
Batty Baseball *44* Tex Avery
Bauen und Heiraten *32* Alexis Granowsky
Baúl Macabro, El *36* Miguel Zacarías
Baule les Pins, La *90* Diane Kurys
Baumwolle *59* Edgar Reitz
Bavu *23* Stuart Paton
Bawbs o' Blue Ridge *16* Charles Miller
Bawdy Adventures of Tom Jones, The *75* Cliff Owen
Bawdy Tales *73* Sergio Citti
Baxter *72* Lionel Jeffries
Baxter *89* Jerome Boivin
Baxter Millions, The *35* Edward Ludwig
Baxter, Vera Baxter *76* Marguerite Duras
Baxter's Millions *46* Erle C. Kenton
Bay Boy, The *84* Daniel Petrie
Bay of Angels *62* Jacques Demy
Bay of Blood *71* Mario Bava
Bay of Gold *55* Břetislav Pojar
Bay of St. Michel, The *63* John Ainsworth
Bay of Seven Islands, The *15* Frank Lloyd
Bay of Seven Isles, The *15* Frank Lloyd
Bay of the Angels *62* Jacques Demy
Baya el Khawatim *65* Youssef Chahine
Bayadere's Revenge, The *14* Forest Holger-Madsen
Bayan Ko *84* Lino Brocka
Bayan Ko—Kapit sa Patalim *84* Lino Brocka
Bayan Ko: My Own Country *84* Lino Brocka
Bayaya *50* Jiří Trnka
Bayen Idek *59* Youssef Chahine
Bayn el Samaa wa el Ard *59* Salah Abu Saif
Bayn Idayk *59* Youssef Chahine
Bayou *57* Harold Daniels
Bayya al Khawatim *65* Youssef Chahine
Bbong *85* Doo-yong Lee
Be a Little Sport *19* Scott R. Dunlap
Be Beautiful But Shut Up *57* Marc Allé-gret

Be Big *30* James Parrott
Be Careful, Mr. Smith *35* Max Mack
Be Good Until Death *60* László Ranódy
Be Great! *32* Mikio Naruse
Be Happy *32* Dimitrios Gaziadis
Be Human *36* Dave Fleischer
Be Kind to Aminals *35* Dave Fleischer
Be Mine Tonight *32* Anatole Litvak
Be My Guest *65* Lance Comfort
Be My Valentine or Else... *81* Boaz Davidson
Be My Wife *21* Max Linder
Be Patient, Patient *44* Bob Wickersham
Be Reasonable *21* Roy Del Ruth
Be Safe or Be Sorry *55* Lester James Peries
Be Sick...It's Free! *68* Luigi Zampa
Be Sure and Insure *13* Percy Stow
Be Sure Your Sins *15* Cecil M. Hepworth
Be Up to Date *38* Dave Fleischer
Be Your Age *26* Leo McCarey
Be Yourself! *30* Thornton Freeland
Beach, The *53* Alberto Lattuada
Beach and Pier at Trouville, Part One *1896* Georges Méliès
Beach and Pier at Trouville, Part Two *1896* Georges Méliès
Beach at Villiers in a Gale, The *1896* Georges Méliès
Beach Ball *65* Lennie Weinrib
Beach Balls *88* Joe Ritter
Beach Blanket Bingo *65* William Asher
Beach Boys: An American Band, The *85* Malcolm Leo
Beach Bunnies *77* A. C. Stephen
Beach Casanova *63* Vittorio Sala
Beach Club, The *28* Harry Edwards
Beach Comber, The *16* Phil Rosen
Beach Comber, The *20* Rex Ingram
Beach Combers *36* Walter Lantz
Beach Girls, The *82* Pat Townsend
Beach Girls and the Monster, The *65* Jon Hall
Beach Guard in Winter, The *76* Goran Paskaljević
Beach House, The *67* Joe Sarno
Beach House *82* John A. Gallagher
Beach House Party *65* Maury Dexter
Beach of Dreams *21* William Parke
Beach Pajamas *31* Roscoe Arbuckle
Beach Party, The *31* Burton Gillett
Beach Party *63* William Asher
Beach Party, Italian Style *63* Camillo Mastrocinque
Beach Recovery *46* Ken Hughes
Beach Red *67* Cornel Wilde
Beachcomber, The *38* Erich Pommer
Beachcomber, The *54* Muriel Box
Beaches *88* Garry Marshall
Beaches and Peaches *18* Archie Mayo
Beaches and Scream *28* Manny Gould, Ben Harrison
Beachhead *54* Stuart Heisler
Beacon *41* Mark Donskoi
Beads of One Rosary, The *79* Kazimierz Kutz
Beaks *87* René Cardona, Jr.
Beale Street Mama *46* Spencer Williams
Beans *18* John Francis Dillon
Beans and Bullets *16* William Beaudine

Beanstalk Bunny *55* Chuck Jones
Bear, The *60* Edmond Séchan
Bear, The *70* Janusz Majewski
Bear, The *84* Richard C. Sarafian
Bear, The *88* Jean-Jacques Annaud
Bear and the Beavers, The *42* Rudolf Ising
Bear and the Doll, The *69* Michel Deville
Bear Cats *26* Charles Lamont
Bear Escape, A *12* Mack Sennett
Bear Facts *20* Gregory La Cava
Bear Facts, The *25* Charles Bowers
Bear Facts *38* Gordon Douglas
Bear Feat *49* Chuck Jones
Bear for Punishment, A *51* Chuck Jones
Bear Hug *64* Joseph Barbera, William Hanna
Bear Hunt in Rockies *09* Edwin S. Porter
Bear Island *79* Don Sharp
Bear Knees *28* Mark Sandrich
Bear Knuckles *64* Joseph Barbera, William Hanna
Bear-Skinned Man *87* Walter Beck
Bear That Couldn't Sleep, The *39* Rudolf Ising
Bear That Wasn't, The *67* Chuck Jones
Bear Up! *63* Joseph Barbera, William Hanna
Bearcat, The *22* Edward Sedgwick
Beard of Strength *31* Mikio Naruse
Bearded Lady, The *19* Raoul Barré, Charles Bowers
Bearded Youth *11* Mack Sennett
Bearly Able *62* Joseph Barbera, William Hanna
Bears and Bad Men *18* Larry Semon
Bears and I, The *74* Bernard McEveety
Bear's Tale, The *40* Tex Avery
Bears Versus Yudenich, The *25* Grigori Kozintsev, Leonid Trauberg
Bear's Wedding, The *26* Konstantin Eggert, Vladimir Gardin
Beast, The *15* Aleksander Hertz
Beast, The *16* Richard Stanton
Beast, The *59* Zoltán Fábri
Beast, The *75* Walerian Borowczyk
Beast, The *88* Kevin Reynolds
Beast and the Magic Sword, The *83* Jacinto Molina
Beast at Bay, A *12* D. W. Griffith
Beast from Haunted Cave, The *59* Monte Hellman
Beast from the Haunted Cave *59* Monte Hellman
Beast from 20,000 Fathoms, The *53* Eugène Lourié
Beast in the Cellar, The *70* James Kelly
Beast Must Die, The *69* Claude Chabrol
Beast Must Die, The *74* Paul Annett
Beast of Babylon Against the Son of Hercules, The *63* Siro Marcellini
Beast of Blood *70* Eddie Romero
Beast of Borneo *35* Harry Garson
Beast of Budapest, The *58* Harmon Jones
Beast of Hollow Mountain, The *56* Edward Nassour, Ismael Rodríguez
Beast of Morocco, The *66* Frederic Goode
Beast of Paradise Island *53* Harold Daniels
Beast of Paradise Isle *53* Harold Daniels
Beast of the City, The *32* Charles Brabin
Beast of the Dead *70* Eddie Romero

Beast of the Himalayas 34 Andrew Marton
Beast of the Yellow Night 70 Eddie Romero
Beast of Yucca Flats, The 61 Coleman Francis
Beast That Killed Women, The 62 Barry Mahon
Beast with a Million Eyes, The 55 David Kramarsky
Beast with Five Fingers, The 45 Robert Florey
Beast Within, The 81 Philippe Mora
Beastmaster, The 82 Don Coscarelli
Beasts 72 Eddie Romero
Beasts' Carnival, The 80 Jacinto Molina
Beasts of Berlin 39 Sam Newfield
Beasts of Marseilles, The 57 Hugo Fregonese
Beasts of Prey 48 Jiří Weiss
Beasts of the Jungle, The 13 Alice Guy-Blaché
Beat, The 86 Paul Mones
Beat Generation, The 59 Charles Haas
Beat Girl 59 Edmond T. Gréville
Beat Street 84 Stan Lathan
Beat the Band 46 John H. Auer
Beat the Devil 53 John Huston
Beat the Monster on Page One 72 Marco Bellocchio
Beat 13 45 Martin Frič
Beate 48 Carl Boese
Beaten 24 Harry G. Moody
Beaten by a Hare 20 Vernon Stallings
Beaten Kochiyama, The 34 Teinosuke Kinugasa
Beating He Needed, The 12 Mack Sennett
Beating the Book 26 Walter West
Beating the Game 21 Victor Schertzinger
Beating the Odds 19 Paul Scardon
Beatlemania 81 Joseph Manduke
Beatlemania—The Movie 81 Joseph Manduke
Beatles in New York, The 64 Albert Maysles, David Maysles, Charlotte Zwerin
Beatnik et le Minet, Le 66 Roger Leenhardt
Beatniks, The 58 Paul Frees
Beatrice 20 Herbert Brenon
Béatrice 86 Bertrand Tavernier
Beatrice Cenci 09 Mario Caserini
Beatrice Cenci 10 Ugo Falena
Beatrice Cenci 26 Baldassare Negroni
Beatrice Cenci 55 Riccardo Freda
Beatrice Cenci 69 Lucio Fulci
Beatsville 59 Gene Fowler, Jr.
Beau and Arrows 32 Walter Lantz
Beau Bandit 30 Lambert Hillyer
Beau Beste 33 Walter Lantz
Beau Bosko 33 Friz Freleng, Hugh Harman
Beau Broadway 28 Malcolm St. Clair
Beau Brocade 16 Thomas Bentley
Beau Brummel 13 J. Stuart Blackton, James Young
Beau Brummel 24 Harry Beaumont
Beau Brummel 54 Kurt Bernhardt
Beau Chumps 31 James W. Horne
Beau Geste 26 Herbert Brenon
Beau Geste 39 William A. Wellman

Beau Geste 66 Douglas Heyes
Beau Hunks 31 James W. Horne
Beau Ideal 31 Herbert Brenon
Beau James 57 Melville Shavelson
Beau Mariage, Le 81 Eric Rohmer
Beau-Père 81 Bertrand Blier
Beau Plaisir, Le 69 Pierre Perrault
Beau Revel 21 John Griffith Wray
Beau Sabreur 28 John Waters
Beau Serge, Le 58 Claude Chabrol
Beau Temps, Mais Orageux en Fin de Journée 86 Gérard Frot-Coutaz
Beaucoup Trop pour un Seul Homme 66 Pietro Germi
Beauf, Le 87 Yves Amoureux
Beauté du Diable, La 49 René Clair
Beauté Fatale 16 André Hugon
Beauté Qui Meurt 17 Georges Lacroix
Beauties Beware 29 Stephen Roberts
Beauties of the Night 52 René Clair
Beautiful Adventure, The 17 Del Henderson
Beautiful Adventure 32 Reinhold Schünzel
Beautiful and the Damned, The 22 William A. Seiter
Beautiful Bachelor, The 41 Malcolm St. Clair
Beautiful Blonde from Bashful Bend, The 49 Preston Sturges
Beautiful But Broke 44 Charles Barton
Beautiful But Dangerous 52 Lloyd Bacon
Beautiful But Dangerous 55 Robert Z. Leonard
Beautiful But Deadly 73 Richard Fleischer
Beautiful But Dumb 28 Elmer Clifton
Beautiful But Poor 57 Dino Risi
Beautiful Cheat, The 26 Edward Sloman
Beautiful Cheat, The 43 Irving Cummings
Beautiful Cheat, The 45 Charles Barton
Beautiful City, The 25 Kenneth Webb
Beautiful Days 55 Masaki Kobayashi
Beautiful Fraud, The 27 Richard Wallace
Beautiful Gambler, The 21 William Worthington
Beautiful Garden of Roses, A 14 Toby Cooper
Beautiful Jim 14 Maurice Elvey
Beautiful Kitty 23 Walter West
Beautiful Lady Without Pity, The 20 Germaine Dulac
Beautiful Liar, The 21 Wallace Worsley
Beautiful Lie, The 17 John W. Noble
Beautiful Margaret, The 10 Émile Cohl
Beautiful Model, The 20 Raoul Barré, Charles Bowers
Beautiful Mrs. Reynolds, The 18 Arthur Ashley
Beautiful People 74 Jamie Uys
Beautiful People II 83 Jamie Uys
Beautiful Prisoner, The 82 Alain Robbe-Grillet
Beautiful Rebel, The 24 E. Mason Hopper
Beautiful Sinner, The 15 Richard Oswald
Beautiful Sinner, The 24 W. S. Van Dyke
Beautiful Stranger, The 54 David Miller
Beautiful Swindlers, The 63 Claude Chabrol, Jean-Luc Godard, Ugo Gregoretti, Hiromichi Horikawa, Roman Polanski

Beautiful Voice, The 11 Mack Sennett
Beautiful Women and the Hydrogen Man 58 Inoshiro Honda
Beautiful Women Walking Around Town 86 Želimir Žilnik
Beautiful Years, The 55 Masaki Kobayashi
Beautifully Trimmed 20 Marcel De Sano
Beauty 33 Richard Boleslawski
Beauty and Bullets 28 Ray Taylor
Beauty and the Bad Man 25 William Worthington
Beauty and the Bandit 46 William Nigh
Beauty and the Barge 37 Henry Edwards
Beauty and the Bargee 14 Harold M. Shaw
Beauty and the Beach 26 Julian Ollendorff
Beauty and the Beast 05 Percy Stow
Beauty and the Beast 12 Edwin S. Porter
Beauty and the Beast 22 Guy Newall
Beauty and the Beast 24 Herbert M. Dawley
Beauty and the Beast 34 Friz Freleng
Beauty and the Beast 45 Jean Cocteau
Beauty and the Beast 49 René Clair
Beauty and the Beast 62 Edward L. Cahn
Beauty and the Beast 76 Fielder Cook
Beauty and the Beast, The 83 Nils Malmros
Beauty and the Beast 87 Eugene Marner
Beauty and the Boat 13 Lewin Fitzhamon
Beauty and the Body 63 Paul Mart
Beauty and the Bolshevik 23 Alexander Rasumny
Beauty and the Boss 32 Roy Del Ruth
Beauty and the Brain 60 Albert Zugsmith
Beauty and the Bullfighter 53 Georges Rouquier
Beauty and the Devil 49 René Clair
Beauty and the Dragon 55 Kozaburo Yoshimura
Beauty and the Robot, The 60 Albert Zugsmith
Beauty and the Rogue 18 Henry King
Beauty Care in the Jungle 37 Pál Fejös
Beauty Competition, The 08 Lewin Fitzhamon
Beauty Doctor, The 36 L. C. Beaumont
Beauty for Sale 33 Richard Boleslawski
Beauty for the Asking 39 Glenn Tryon
Beauty from Nivernaise, The 23 Jean Epstein
Beauty in Chains 18 Elsie Jane Wilson
Beauty Jungle, The 64 Val Guest
Beauty Market, The 19 Colin Campbell
Beauty #2 65 Andy Warhol
Beauty of Nivers, The 23 Jean Epstein
Beauty of the Pusta 37 Steve Sekely
Beauty of Vice, The 86 Živko Nikolić
Beauty on Parade 50 Lew Landers
Beauty Parade, The 30 Sam Newfield
Beauty Parlor, The 32 Richard Thorpe
Beauty Prize, The 24 Lloyd Ingraham
Beauty Proof 19 Paul Scardon
Beauty Salon in the Jungle 37 Pál Fejös
Beauty Secret, The 55 Vassily Ordynski
Beauty Shop, The 22 Edward Dillon
Beauty Shoppe 36 Walter Lantz
Beauty Shoppers, The 27 Louis Gasnier
Beauty Unadorned 13 L. Rogers Lytton, James Young
Beauty's Daughter 35 Allan Dwan

Beauty's Sorrows *31* Yasujiro Ozu
Beauty's Worth *22* Robert Vignola
Beaux-Arts de Jocko, Les *09* Émile Cohl
Beaux Arts Mystérieux, Les *10* Émile Cohl
Beaux Jours, Les *35* Marc Allégret
Beaux Souvenirs, Les *82* Francis Mankie-
   wicz
Beaver Coat, The *39* Jürgen von Alten
Beaver Valley *50* James Algar
Bébé Apache *10* Louis Feuillade
Bébé Embarrassant, Le *05* Alice Guy-
   Blaché
Bébé en Vacances *13* Louis Feuillade
Bébé et Fillettes *1896* Georges Méliès
Bébé Fume *10* Louis Feuillade
Bébé Pêcheur *10* Louis Feuillade
Bébert and the Train *63* Yves Robert
Bébert et l'Omnibus *63* Yves Robert
Bebo's Girl *63* Luigi Comencini
Because *18* Sidney Morgan
Because *19* Albert G. Frenguelli, Edith
   Mellor
Because He Loved Her *16* Del Henderson
Because I Love *28* Heinosuke Gosho
Because I Love *54* Tadashi Imai, Kozaburo
   Yoshimura
Because I Love You *27* J. Steven Edwards
Because I Loved You *30* Rudolf Walther-
   Fein
Because of a Woman *17* Jack Conway
Because of a Woman *62* Michel Deville
Because of Eve *48* Howard Bretherton
Because of Her Love *13* Mauritz Stiller
Because of Him *46* Richard Wallace
Because of Love *13* Mauritz Stiller
Because of My Hot Youth *52* Arne Matts-
   son
Because of the Cats *73* Fons Rademakers
Because of the Woman *17* Jack Conway
Because of You *52* Joseph Pevney
Because They're Young *60* Paul Wendkos
Because We Do Not Forget *62* Ján Kadár,
   Elmar Klos
Because You're Mine *52* Alexander Hall
Becket *23* George Ridgwell
Becket *63* Peter Glenville
Becket Affair, The *66* Osvaldo Civirani
Beckoning Flame, The *16* Walter Edwards
Beckoning Roads *20* Howard Hickman
Beckoning Trail, The *16* Jack Conway
Beckwith's Gun *10* Will Barker
Becky *27* John P. McCarthy
Becky Sharp *35* Rouben Mamoulian
Becoming Aware *85* Alejandro Doria
Becsapott Újságíró, A *14* Alexander Kor-
   da, Gyula Zilahy
Bed, The *53* Henri Decoin, Jean Delan-
   noy, Gianni Franciolini, Ralph Habib
Bed, The *67* James Broughton
Bed and Board *70* François Truffaut
Bed and Breakfast *30* Walter Forde
Bed and Breakfast *36* Walter West
Bed and Breakfast Two Shillings *04* Alf
   Collins
Bed and How They Made It, The *66* Joe
   Sarno
Bed and Sofa *26* Abram Room, Sergei
   Yutkevich
Bed of Fire *63* Antonio Santean
Bed of Grass *57* Gregg Tallas

Bed of Roses *33* Gregory La Cava
Bed of Violence *66* Joe Sarno
Bed Sitting Room, The *68* Richard Lester
Bedaya, Al *86* Salah Abu Saif
Bedaya wa Nehayat *60* Salah Abu Saif
Bedazzled *67* Stanley Donen
Bedelia *30* Dave Fleischer
Bedelia *46* Lance Comfort
Bedevilled *55* Mitchell Leisen, Richard
   Thorpe
Bedevilled Rabbit *57* Robert McKimson
Bedford Incident, The *65* James B. Harris
Bedknobs and Broomsticks *71* Ward Kim-
   ball, Robert Stevenson
Bedlam *46* Mark Robson
Bedouin's Love Song, The *07* Arthur Gil-
   bert
Bedrock *30* Carlyle Blackwell
Bedroom Blunder, A *17* Edward F. Cline
Bedroom Eyes *84* William Fruet
Bedroom Eyes II *90* Chuck Vincent
Bedroom Vendetta *59* Claude Autant-Lara
Bedroom Window, The *24* William De-
   Mille
Bedroom Window, The *86* Curtis Hanson
Beds, Baths and Bedlam *17* J. L. V. Leigh
Bedside *33* Robert Florey
Bedside Manner *45* Andrew L. Stone
Bedstemoders Vuggevise *12* August Blom
Bedtime *23* Dave Fleischer
Bedtime *67* John Irvin
Bedtime at the Zoo *29* Arthur Woods*
Bedtime for Bonzo *51* Frederick De
   Cordova
Bedtime for Sniffles *40* Chuck Jones
Bedtime Stories *26* Walter Lantz
Bedtime Story, A *33* Norman Taurog
Bedtime Story *38* Donovan Pedelty
Bedtime Story *41* Alexander Hall
Bedtime Story *64* Ralph Levy
Bedtime with Rosie *74* Wolf Rilla
Będzie Lepiej *37* Michael Waszyński
Bee Cause *27* Manny Gould, Ben Harrison
Bee-Deviled Bruin, The *48* Chuck Jones
Bee-Eater, The *86* George Ogilvie
Beef-Fore and After *62* Joseph Barbera,
   William Hanna
Beekeeper, The *86* Theodoros Angelopou-
   los
Beekeeper's Scrapbook *58* Dušan Makave-
   jev
Beelzebub's Daughters *03* Georges Méliès
Been Down So Long It Looks Like Up to
   Me *71* Jeffrey Young
Beep Beep *52* Chuck Jones
Beep Prepared *61* Chuck Jones
Beer *85* Patrick Kelly
Beer and Pyjamas *14* Toby Cooper
Beer Drinker's Guide to Fitness and Film-
   making, The *87* Fred G. Sullivan
Beer Parade, The *33* Dick Huemer
Beer Twopence a Glass *06* Percy Stow
Bees, The *78* Alfredo Zacharias
Bee's Buzz, The *29* Mack Sennett
Bees in Paradise *43* Val Guest
Beethoven *36* Abel Gance
Beethoven Concerto *37* M. Gavronsky, V.
   Schmidthof
Beethoven Story, The *51* Karl Hartl,
   Walter Kolm-Veltee

Beethoven Third Symphony, "Eroica" *67*
   Henri Colpi
Beethoven's Great Love *36* Abel Gance
Beethoven's Nephew *85* Paul Morrissey
Beetle, The *19* Alexander Butler
Beetle *87* Eric van Zuylen
Beetle Goes Flat Out, A *72* Rudolf Zehet-
   gruber
Beetle in Overdrive, A *73* Rudolf Zehet-
   gruber
Beetlejuice *88* Tim Burton
Befehl Ist Befehl *36* Alwin Elling
Before and After *85* Aziz Ghazal
Before Dawn *31* Teinosuke Kinugasa
Before Dawn *33* Irving Pichel
Before Dawn *53* Kozaburo Yoshimura
Before Election *53* Miklós Jancsó
Before God and Man *68* Károly Makk
Before Him All Rome Trembled *46* Car-
   mine Gallone
Before Hindsight *77* Jonathan Lewis
Before I Hang *40* Nick Grindé
Before I Wake *54* Albert S. Rogell
Before It's Too Late *57* Yuri Fogelman,
   Vytautas Zalakevicius
Before Midnight *25* John G. Adolfi
Before Midnight *33* Lambert Hillyer
Before Morning *33* Arthur Hoerl
Before October *65* Grigori Alexandrov
Before Spring *57* Joris Ivens
Before Stonewall *84* Robert Rosenberg,
   Greta Schiller
Before the Dawn *53* Kozaburo Yoshimura
Before the Dawn *86* Amarnath Jayatilaka
Before the Fact *71* Mario Bava
Before the Fair *62* Charles Eames, Ray
   Eames
Before the Flood *53* André Cayatte
Before the Judgment of History *64* Fried-
   rich Ermler
Before the Nickelodeon *82* Charles Musser
Before the Raid *43* Jiří Weiss
Before the Revolution *64* Bernardo Ber-
   tolucci
Before the White Man Came *20* John E.
   Maple
Before Winter Comes *68* J. Lee-Thompson
Befreite Hände *40* Hans Schweikert
Beg, Borrow or Steal *37* Wilhelm Thiele
Beggar Child, The *14* William Desmond
   Taylor
Beggar Girl's Wedding, The *15* Leedham
   Bantock
Beggar in Purple, A *20* Edgar Lewis
Beggar Maid, The *21* Herbert Blaché
Beggar Maiden, The *05* Georges Méliès
Beggar Man of Paris, The *16* Forest Hol-
   ger-Madsen
Beggar of Cawnpore, The *16* Charles
   Swickard
Beggar on Horseback *25* James Cruze
Beggar Prince, The *20* William Worth-
   ington
Beggar Princess, The *15* Forest Holger-
   Madsen
Beggar Student, The *31* John Harvel,
   Joseph Losey
Beggar Student, The *36* Georg Jacoby
Beggar Student, The *58* Werner Jacobs
Beggars, The *87* Benoît Jacquot

Beggar's Deceit, The *00* Cecil M. Hepworth

Beggar's Dream, The *1899* Georges Méliès

Beggar's Holiday *34* Sam Newfield

Beggars in Ermine *34* Phil Rosen

Beggars of Life *28* William A. Wellman

Beggar's Opera, The *31* G. W. Pabst

Beggar's Opera, The *53* Peter Brook

Beggar's Uproar, The *60* John Halas*

Begging the Ring *79* Colin Gregg

Begierde *28* G. W. Pabst

Beginners, The *68* James Neilson

Beginner's Luck *51* Edward L. Cahn

Beginner's Luck *83* Caroline Ahlfors Mouris, Frank Mouris

Beginners Three, The *68* James Neilson

Beginning, The *70* Gleb Panfilov

Beginning and the End, The *60* Salah Abu Saif

Beginning of the End *57* Bert I. Gordon

Beginning or the End?, The *46* Norman Taurog

Beginning Was Sin, The *62* Franz Cap

Beglets *32* Vladimir Petrov

Begone Dull Care *49* Evelyn Lambert, Norman McLaren

Begstvo Puankare *32* Alexander Ptushko

Beguiled, The *70* Don Siegel

Beguines, The *72* Guy Casaril

Begynnelsen på en Historie *88* Margrete Robsahm

Behave Yourself! *51* George Beck

Behave Yourself *62* Michael Winner

Behemoth the Sea Monster *59* Douglas Hickox, Eugène Lourié

Behind City Lights *45* John English

Behind Closed Doors *29* Roy William Neill

Behind Closed Doors *44* Budd Boetticher

Behind Closed Doors *60* Dino Risi

Behind Closed Shutters *50* Luigi Comencini

Behind Convent Walls *77* Walerian Borowczyk

Behind Enemy Lines *86* Gideon Amir

Behind Green Lights *35* Christy Cabanne

Behind Green Lights *45* Otto Brower

Behind Jury Doors *32* B. Reeves Eason

Behind Locked Doors *48* Budd Boetticher

Behind Locked Doors *76* Charles Romine

Behind Masks *21* Frank Reicher

Behind Office Doors *31* Melville Brown

Behind Prison Bars *37* Raymond Cannon

Behind Prison Gates *39* Charles Barton

Behind Prison Walls *43* Steve Sekely

Behind Southern Lines *52* Thomas Carr

Behind Stone Walls *32* Frank R. Strayer

Behind That Curtain *29* Irving Cummings

Behind the Altar *27* William Dieterle

Behind the Criminal *37* Harold S. Bucquet

Behind the Curtain *15* Frank Wilson

Behind the Curtain *24* Chester M. Franklin

Behind the Curtain *37* Kamel Salim

Behind the Door *19* Irvin Willat

Behind the Door *40* Nick Grindé

Behind the Eight Ball *42* Edward F. Cline

Behind the Evidence *35* Lambert Hillyer

Behind the Front *26* A. Edward Sutherland

Behind the Great Wall *58* Carlo Lizzani

Behind the Green Lights *35* Christy Cabanne

Behind the Guns *40* Montgomery Tully

Behind the Headlines *37* Richard Rosson

Behind the Headlines *53* Maclean Rogers

Behind the Headlines *56* Charles Saunders

Behind the High Wall *56* Abner Biberman

Behind the Iron Curtain *48* William A. Wellman

Behind the Iron Mask *77* Ken Annakin

Behind the Lines *16* Henry MacRae

Behind the Makeup *30* Dorothy Arzner, Robert Milton

Behind the Map *17* William Beaudine

Behind the Mask *17* Alice Guy-Blaché

Behind the Mask *32* John Francis Dillon

Behind the Mask *46* Phil Karlson

Behind the Mask *58* Brian Desmond Hurst

Behind the Meatball *45* Frank Tashlin

Behind the Mike *37* Sidney Salkow

Behind the News *40* Joseph Santley

Behind the Rising Sun *43* Edward Dmytryk

Behind the Scenes *1897* Georges Méliès

Behind the Scenes *04* Alf Collins

Behind the Scenes *08* D. W. Griffith

Behind the Scenes *10* Bert Haldane

Behind the Scenes *13* Wilfred Noy

Behind the Scenes *14* James Kirkwood

Behind the Scenes of the Circus *21* Hy Mayer

Behind the Scenes, or Algy's Mishap *04* Alf Collins

Behind the Scenes: Where All Is Not Gold That Glitters *08* D. W. Griffith

Behind the Screen *16* Charles Chaplin

Behind the Shop Window *55* Samson Samsonov

Behind the Shutters *72* Juan Antonio Bardem

Behind the Signs on Broadway *20* J. D. Leventhal

Behind the Spanish Lines *38* Sidney Cole, Thorold Dickinson

Behind the Stockade *11* Thomas Ince, George Loane Tucker

Behind the Tabs *38* R. A. Hopwood

Behind the Veil *14* Phillips Smalley, Lois Weber

Behind the Wall *71* Krzysztof Zanussi

Behind Two Guns *24* Robert North Bradbury

Behind Uniform Facades *61* Peter Weiss

Behind Your Back *37* Donovan Pedelty

Behinderte Zukunft *70* Werner Herzog

Behold a Pale Horse *63* Fred Zinnemann

Behold My Wife *20* George Melford

Behold My Wife *35* Mitchell Leisen

Behold the Man *21* Spencer G. Bennet*

Behold the Man *51* Walter Rilla

Behold This Mother *30* Tomotaka Tasaka

Behold This Woman *24* J. Stuart Blackton

Behold Thy Son *57* Heinosuke Gosho

Behold We Live *33* Elliott Nugent

Bei Aiqing Yiwangde Jiaoluo *86* Ya-lin Li, Qi Zhang

Bei der Blonden Katherin *34* Franz Seitz

Bei Vollmond Mord *61* Paolo Heusch

Beiden Seehunde, Die *35* Fred Sauer

Beijing Watermelon *89* Nobuhiko Obayashi

Beijo na Boca *87* Paulo Sérgio De Almeida

Beijo no Asfalto, O *84* Bruno Barreto

Beilis Case, The *17* Josef Soifer

Being, The *80* Jackie Kong

Being and Doing *84* Ken McMullen

Being Respectable *24* Phil Rosen

Being There *79* Hal Ashby

Being Two Isn't Easy *62* Kon Ichikawa

Beispiellose Verteidigung der Festung Deutschkreuz, Die *66* Werner Herzog

Beiss Mich, Liebling *70* Helmut Förnbacher

Bejalai *87* Stephen Teo

Bekännelsen på Dödsbädden *12* Victor Sjöström

Bekçi *85* Ali Özgentürk

Béke Útja, A *17* Michael Curtiz

Bekenntnis der Ina Kahr, Das *54* G. W. Pabst

Bekötött Szemmel *74* András Kovács

Bel Âge, Le *59* Pierre Kast

Bel Ami *19* Augusto Genina

Bel Ami *39* Willi Forst

Bel Ami *54* Louis Daquin

Bel Ami 2000 oder Wie Verführt Man einen Playboy? *66* Michael Pfleghar

Bel Indifférent, Le *57* Jacques Demy

Bel Paese, Il *77* Luciano Salce

Béla Bartók: The Night's Music *70* István Gaál

Bela Lugosi Meets a Brooklyn Gorilla *52* William Beaudine

Belanın Yedi Türlüsü *69* Mahinur Ergün

Belated Flowers *72* Abram Room

Belges et la Mer, Les *54* Henri Storck

Belgian, The *17* Sidney Olcott

Belgique Nouvelle, La *37* Henri Storck

Beli Djavo *58* Riccardo Freda

Believe in Me *71* Stuart Hagmann

Believe It or Else *39* Tex Avery

Believe Me Xantippe *18* Donald Crisp

Believers, The *87* John Schlesinger

Belinda *72* Richard Franklin

Belinda *87* Pamela Gibbons

Belinda and the Eggs *15* Ethyle Batley

Belinda Makes a Bloomer *15* Ernest G. Batley

Belinda's Dream *13* Stuart Kinder

Belinda's Elopement *13* Dave Aylott

Belinsky *53* Grigori Kozintsev

Beliye Nochi *59* Ivan Pyriev

Belizaire the Cajun *86* Glen Pitre

Bell, Bare and Beautiful *63* Herschell Gordon Lewis

Bell, Book and Candle *58* Richard Quine

Bell-Bottom George *43* Marcel Varnel

Bell Boy, The *18* Roscoe Arbuckle

Bell Boy 13 *23* William A. Seiter

Bell Diamond *86* Jon Jost

Bell for Adano, A *45* Henry King

Bell from Hell, A *73* Claudio Guerín Hill

Bell Hop, The *21* Larry Semon, Norman Taurog

Bell Hoppy *54* Robert McKimson

Bell Hops, The *17* Raoul Barré, Charles Bowers

Bell Jar, The *79* Larry Peerce

Bell of Hell, The *73* Claudio Guerín Hill

Bell of Nirvana, The *83* Choi-su Park

Bella Addormentata, La *42* Luigi Chiarini

Bella di Roma, La *55* Luigi Comencini

Bella Donna *15* Hugh Ford, Edwin S. Porter

Bella Donna *23* George Fitzmaurice

Bella Donna *83* Peter Keglevic

Bella Fioraia, La *58* Luis César Amadori

Bella Grinta, Una *65* Giuliano Montaldo

Bella Mugnaia!, La *55* Mario Camerini

Belladonna *34* Robert Milton

Belladonna *89* Beth B

Bellamy Trial, The *28* Monta Bell

Bell'Antonio, Il *60* Mauro Bolognini

Bella's Beau *12* Phillips Smalley

Bellavista Mystery, The *85* Luciano De Crescenzo

Bellboy, The *60* Jerry Lewis

Bellboy and the Playgirls, The *61* Francis Ford Coppola, Fritz Umgelter

Belle *73* André Delvaux

Belle Américaine, La *61* Robert Dhéry

Belle au Bois Dormant, La *02* Ferdinand Zecca

Belle au Bois Dormant, La *29* Georgy Vasiliev, Sergei Vasiliev

Belle au Bois Dormant, La *35* Alexander Alexeïeff, Claire Parker

Belle aux Cheveux d'Or, La *16* Léonce Perret

Belle Aventure, La *32* Reinhold Schünzel

Belle Aventure, La *42* Marc Allégret

Belle Captive, La *82* Alain Robbe-Grillet

Belle Dame Sans Merci, La *20* Germaine Dulac

Belle de Cadix, La *53* Raymond Bernard

Belle de Jour *66* Luis Buñuel

Belle dell'Aria, Le *57* Mario Costa

Belle des Belles, La *55* Robert Z. Leonard

Belle Équipe, La *35* Julien Duvivier

Belle et la Bête, La *45* Jean Cocteau

Belle et le Cavalier, La *67* Francesco Rosi

Belle Étoile, La *38* Jacques De Baroncelli

Belle Famiglie, Le *64* Ugo Gregoretti

Belle Fille Comme Moi, Une *72* François Truffaut

Belle Hélène, La *57* Lotte Reiniger

Belle Journée, Une *72* Jean-Charles Tacchella

Belle le Grande *51* Allan Dwan

Belle Ma Povere *57* Dino Risi

Belle Madame Moyse, La *31* Edmond T. Gréville

Belle Marinière, La *32* Harry Lachman

Belle Mentalité *53* André Berthomieu

Belle Meunière, La *48* Marcel Pagnol*

Belle Nivernaise, La *23* Jean Epstein

Belle o Brutte Si Sposan Tutte *39* Carlo Ludovico Bragaglia

Belle of Alaska *22* Chester Bennett

Belle of Bettws-y-Coed, The *12* Sidney Northcote

Belle of Broadway, The *26* Harry Hoyt

Belle of Crystal Palace, The *14* James Youngdeer

Belle of New York, The *19* Julius Steger

Belle of New York, The *51* Charles Walters

Belle of North Wales, The *12* Sidney Northcote

Belle of Old Mexico *50* R. G. Springsteen

Belle of the Bowery *45* Ralph Murphy

Belle of the Gambling Den *21* H. B. Parkinson

Belle of the Nineties *34* Leo McCarey

Belle of the Season, The *19* Sidney Rankin Drew

Belle of the Yukon *44* William A. Seiter

Belle Peur, Une *58* Georges Rouquier

Belle Que Voilà, La *50* Jean-Paul Le Chanois

Belle Russe, La *18* Charles Brabin

Belle Sommers *62* Elliot Silverstein

Belle Starr *41* Irving Cummings

Belle Starr's Daughter *47* Lesley Selander

Belle Vie, La *63* Robert Enrico

Belle Who Talks, The *09* S. Wormald

Belles and Ballets *60* Louis Cuny

Belles Conduites, Les *64* Michel Drach

Belles-de-Nuit, Les *52* René Clair

Belles of St. Clement's, The *36* Ivar Campbell

Belles of St. Trinian's, The *54* Frank Launder

Belles on Their Toes *52* Henry Levin

Bellezze in Bicicletta *51* Carlo Campogalliani

Bellifreschi *87* Enrico Oldoini

Bellissima *51* Luchino Visconti

Bellissimo: Images of the Italian Cinema *87* Gianfranco Mingozzi

Bellissimo Novembre, Un *68* Mauro Bolognini

Bellman, The *44* Christian-Jaque

Bellman and True *87* Richard Loncraine

Bello, il Brutto, il Cretino, Il *67* Giovanni Grimaldi

Bello Ma Dannato *79* Pasquale Festa Campanile

Bello Onesto Emigrato Australia Sposerebbe Compaesana Illibata *71* Luigi Zampa

Bells, The *13* Oscar Apfel

Bells, The *18* Ernest C. Warde

Bells, The *23* Edwin Greenwood

Bells, The *26* James Young

Bells, The *31* Harcourt Templeman, Oscar M. Werndorff

Bells *81* Michael Anderson

Bells Are Ringing *60* Vincente Minnelli

Bells Go Down, The *43* Basil Dearden

Bells Have Gone to Rome, The *58* Miklós Jancsó

Bells May Also Toll Tomorrow, The *83* Santiago Álvarez

Bells of Atlantis *52* Len Lye

Bells of Capistrano *42* William Morgan

Bells of Coronado *50* William Witney

Bells of Rheims, The *14* Maurice Elvey

Bells of Rosarita *45* Frank McDonald

Bells of St. Mary's, The *28* Redd Davis

Bells of St. Mary's, The *37* James A. Fitzpatrick

Bells of St. Mary's, The *45* Leo McCarey

Bells of San Angelo *47* William Witney

Bells of San Fernando, The *47* Terry Morse

Bells of San Juan *22* Scott R. Dunlap

Belly of an Architect, The *87* Peter Greenaway

Belonging *22* F. Martin Thornton

Beloved, The *27* Robert Wiene

Beloved *33* Victor Schertzinger

Beloved *49* Emilio Fernández

Beloved, The *71* George Pan Cosmatos

Beloved Adventuress, The *17* George Cowl

Beloved Bachelor, The *31* Lloyd Corrigan

Beloved Blackmailer, The *18* Del Henderson

Beloved Bozo *25* Edward F. Cline

Beloved Brat, The *38* Arthur Lubin

Beloved Brute, The *24* J. Stuart Blackton

Beloved Cheater, The *19* Christy Cabanne

Beloved Enemy *36* H. C. Potter

Beloved Imposter, The *18* Joseph Gleason

Beloved Imposter *36* Joseph Losey

Beloved Infidel *59* Henry King

Beloved Jim *17* Stuart Paton

Beloved Rogue, The *27* Alan Crosland

Beloved Rogues *17* Alfred Santell

Beloved Traitor, The *18* William Worthington

Beloved Vagabond, The *15* Edward José

Beloved Vagabond, The *23* Fred LeRoy Granville

Beloved Vagabond, The *34* Kurt Bernhardt

Below the Belt *80* Robert Fowler

Below the Border *42* Howard Bretherton

Below the Dead Line *21* John P. McGowan

Below the Deadline *29* John P. McGowan

Below the Deadline *36* Charles Lamont

Below the Deadline *46* William Beaudine

Below the Hill *74* Angus Bailey

Below the Line *25* Herman Raymaker

Below the Rio Grande *23* Neal Hart

Below the Sahara *53* Armand Denis

Below the Sea *33* Albert S. Rogell

Below the Surface *20* Irvin Willat

Below Zero *25* Norman Taurog

Below Zero *30* James Parrott

Below Zero *87* Gian Luigi Polidoro

Belphegor the Mountebank *21* Bert Wynne

Belstone Fox, The *73* James Hill

Belt, The *89* Giuliana Gamba

Belt and Suspenders Man, The *70* Don Levy

Belva, La *70* Mario Costa

Ben *72* Phil Karlson

Ben Blair *16* William Desmond Taylor

Ben Bolt *13* Alice Guy-Blaché

Ben Gets a Duck and Is Ducked *07* Gilbert M. Anderson

Ben-Gurion *69* David Perlov

Ben-Gurion Remembers *72* Simon Hesera

Ben-Hur *07* Sidney Olcott, Frank Oakes Rose

Ben-Hur *25* Ferdinand P. Earle, Fred Niblo

Ben-Hur *59* William Wyler

Ben-Hur—A Tale of the Christ *25* Ferdinand P. Earle, Fred Niblo

Ben-Hur: A Tale of the Christ *59* William Wyler

Best Little Girl in the World, The 06 Lewin Fitzhamon

Best Little Whorehouse in Texas, The 82 Colin Higgins

Best Man, The 14 Charles Brabin

Best Man, The 17 Bertram Bracken

Best Man, The 19 Thomas Heffron

Best Man, The 28 Harry Edwards

Best Man, The 64 Franklin J. Schaffner

Best Man, The 86 Joe Mahon

Best Man Loses, The 18 Gregory La Cava

Best Man Wins, The 09 Gilbert M. Anderson

Best Man Wins, The 12 Christy Cabanne, Allan Dwan

Best Man Wins, The 34 Erle C. Kenton

Best Man Wins, The 48 John Sturges

Best Mouse Loses, The 20 Vernon Stallings

Best of All, The 23 John W. Brunius

Best of Benny Hill, The 74 John Robins

Best of Enemies 33 Rian James

Best of Enemies, The 61 Guy Hamilton

Best of Everything, The 59 Jean Negulesco

Best of Friends, The 27 Harry Edwards

Best of Luck, The 20 Ray C. Smallwood

Best of Luck, The 21 Wallace A. Carlson

Best of the Badmen 51 William D. Russell

Best of the Best 89 Bob Radler

Best of the Blues 38 Raoul Walsh

Best of Times, The 86 Roger Spottiswoode

Best Pair of Legs in the Business, The 73 Christopher Hodson

Best People, The 25 Sidney Olcott

Best Policy, The 12 Allan Dwan

Best Seller 87 John Flynn

Best Shot 86 David Anspaugh

Best Things in Life Are Free, The 56 Michael Curtiz

Best Way, The 76 Claude Miller

Best Way to Walk, The 76 Claude Miller

Best Wishes 27 William C. Nolan

Best Wishes 88 Tereza Trautman

Best Woman of My Life, The 68 Martin Frič

Best Years of Our Lives, The 46 William Wyler

Bestia 15 Aleksander Hertz

Bestia, La 71 Gianfranco De Bosio

Bestia Uccide a Sangue Freddo, La 71 Fernando Di Leo

Bestia y la Espada Mágica, La 83 Jacinto Molina

Bestia y los Samurais, La 83 Jacinto Molina

Bestioles Artistes, Les 11 Émile Cohl

Bestione, Il 74 Sergio Corbucci

Besuch, Der 64 Bernhard Wicki

Besuch am Abend 37 Georg Jacoby

Bet That Didn't Come Off, The 07 Harold Hough

Beta Som 62 Charles Frend, Bruno Vailati

Bête, La 75 Walerian Borowczyk

Bête à l'Affût, La 59 Pierre Chénal

Bête Humaine, La 38 Jean Renoir

Bête Lumineuse, La 82 Pierre Perrault

Bête Noire, La 56 Georges Rouquier

Bête Traquée, La 23 René Le Somptier

Bêtes...Comme les Hommes 23 Alfred Machin, Henri Wuhlschleger

Bethanien 75 Edgar Reitz

Bethsabée 46 Léonide Moguy

Bethune 77 Eric Till

Bethune: The Making of a Hero 88 Phillip Borsos

Betrayal, The 28 Walter Summers

Betrayal 29 Lewis Milestone

Betrayal 32 Reginald Fogwell

Betrayal 37 Fedor Ozep

Betrayal, The 48 Oscar Micheaux

Betrayal, The 58 Ernest Morris

Betrayal, The 68 Alberto Lattuada

Betrayal 81 Gordon Punter

Betrayal, The 81 Vibeke Løkkeberg

Betrayal 83 David Jones

Betrayal from the East 45 William Berke

Betrayed 16 Howard Mitchell

Betrayed 17 Raoul Walsh

Betrayed 26 Charles Barnett

Betrayed 44 William Castle

Betrayed 54 Gottfried Reinhardt

Betrayed 88 Costa-Gavras

Betrayed by a Hand Print 08 D. W. Griffith

Betrayed by Hand Prints 08 D. W. Griffith

Betrayed Women 55 Edward L. Cahn

Betrayer 61 Albert C. Gannaway

Betrayer, The 61 Roberto Rossellini

Betrogen 85 Harun Farocki

Betrogen Bis zum Jüngsten Tag 57 Kurt Jung-Alsen

Betrothed, The 40 Mario Camerini

Betrothed 55 Erik Blomberg

Betrüger des Volkes 22 Reinhold Schünzel

Betsy, The 78 Daniel Petrie

Betsy Ross 17 George Cowl, Travers Vale

Betsy's Burglar 17 Paul Powell

Betsy's Wedding 90 Alan Alda

Bett einer Jungfrau, Das 66 Edward Dein

Betta Betta 71 William Byron Hillman

Betta the Gypsy 18 Charles Raymond

Bettelgräfin, Die 18 Joe May, Bruno Ziener

Bettelstudent, Der 22 Hans Steinhoff

Bettelstudent, Der 33 Viktor Jansen

Bettelstudent, Der 36 Georg Jacoby

Better a Widow 68 Duccio Tessari

Better Bet, The 16 Cecil Birch

Better Days 27 Frank S. Mattison

Better Half, The 18 John S. Robertson

Better Kiss a Cobra 86 Massimo Pirri

Better Late Than Never 14 Stuart Kinder

Better Late Than Never 82 Bryan Forbes

Better Man, The 15 John W. Noble

Better Man, The 21 Wilfred Lucas

Better Man, The 26 Scott R. Dunlap

Better Man, A 86 Nagisa Oshima

Better Man Wins, The 22 Frank S. Mattison, Marcel Perez

Better Off Dead 85 Savage Steve Holland

Better 'Ole, The 18 George Pearson

Better 'Ole, The 26 Charles Reisner

Better 'Ole, or The Romance of Old Bill, The 18 George Pearson

Better Than Bread 87 Alfredo B. Crevenna

Better Times 19 King Vidor

Better Tomorrow, A 45 Alexander Hammid

Better Tomorrow, A 85 John Woo

Better Tomorrow II, A 88 John Woo

Better Way, The 09 D. W. Griffith

Better Way, The 14 Christy Cabanne

Better Way, The 26 Ralph Ince

Better Wife, The 19 William P. S. Earle

Better Woman, The 15 Joseph A. Golden

Bettina Loved a Soldier 16 Rupert Julian

Betty and the Buccaneers 17 Rollin Sturgeon

Betty Be Good 17 Sherwood MacDonald

Betty Blue 86 Jean-Jacques Beineix

Betty Boop and Grampy 35 Dave Fleischer

Betty Boop and Little Jimmy 36 Dave Fleischer

Betty Boop and the Little King 36 Dave Fleischer

Betty Boop for President 32 Dave Fleischer

Betty Boop Limited, The 32 Dave Fleischer

Betty Boop, M.D. 32 Dave Fleischer

Betty Boop, with Henry, the Funniest Living American 35 Dave Fleischer

Betty Boop's Bamboo Isle 32 Dave Fleischer

Betty Boop's Big Boss 33 Dave Fleischer

Betty Boop's Birthday Party 33 Dave Fleischer

Betty Boop's Bizzy Bee 32 Dave Fleischer

Betty Boop's Crazy Inventions 33 Dave Fleischer

Betty Boop's Hallowe'en Party 33 Dave Fleischer

Betty Boop's Ker-Choo 33 Dave Fleischer

Betty Boop's Lifeguard 34 Dave Fleischer

Betty Boop's Little Pal 34 Dave Fleischer

Betty Boop's May Party 33 Dave Fleischer

Betty Boop's Museum 32 Dave Fleischer

Betty Boop's Penthouse 33 Dave Fleischer

Betty Boop's Prize Show 34 Dave Fleischer

Betty Boop's Rise to Fame 34 Dave Fleischer

Betty Boop's Trial 34 Dave Fleischer

Betty Boop's Ups and Downs 32 Dave Fleischer

Betty Co-Ed 31 Dave Fleischer

Betty Co-Ed 46 Arthur Dreifuss

Betty in Blunderland 34 Dave Fleischer

Betty of Greystone 16 Allan Dwan

Betty Slow Drag 53 Ernest Borneman

Betty Takes a Hand 18 John Francis Dillon

Betty to the Rescue 17 Frank Reicher

Betty's Birthday 14 Will P. Kellino

Betty's Night Out 16 Wilfred Noy

Between Brothers 16 Robert Dinesen

Between Calais and Dover 1897 Georges Méliès

Between Dangers 27 Richard Thorpe

Between Eleven and Midnight 48 Henri Decoin

Between Fighting Men 32 Forrest K. Sheldon

Between Friends 24 J. Stuart Blackton

Between Friends 73 Donald Shebib

Between Heaven and Earth 59 Salah Abu Saif

Between Heaven and Hell 56 Richard Fleischer

Between Knee and Knee 84 Chang-ho Lee

Between Love and Duty *60* Claude Autant-Lara
Between Men *16* Reginald Barker, William S. Hart
Between Men *35* Robert North Bradbury
Between Midnight and Dawn *50* Gordon Douglas
Between One and Two A.M. *07* Arthur Cooper
Between Showers *14* Henry Lehrman
Between the Acts *19* Larry Semon
Between the Cup and the Lip *87* Zbigniew Kuźmiński
Between the Lines *77* Joan Micklin Silver
Between the Parents *38* Hans Hinrich
Between Three and Five Minutes *72* Jan Němec
Between Time and Eternity *56* Arthur Maria Rabenalt
Between Two Hearts *36* Herbert Selpin
Between Two Wars *77* Harun Farocki
Between Two Women *37* George B. Seitz
Between Two Women *44* Willis Goldbeck
Between Two Worlds *21* Fritz Lang
Between Two Worlds *37* Goffredo Alessandrini
Between Two Worlds *44* Edward A. Blatt
Between Two Worlds *65* Marco Bellocchio
Between Two Worlds *66* Lester James Peries
Between Two Worlds *68* Rangel Vulchanov
Between Us Girls *42* Henry Koster
Between Us Thieves *45* Olof Molander
Between Wife and Lady *76* Kon Ichikawa, Shiro Toyoda
Between Women and Wives *76* Kon Ichikawa, Shiro Toyoda
Between Your Hands *59* Youssef Chahine
Betzilo Shel Halem Krav *88* Yoel Sharon
Beverly Hills Brats *89* Jim Sotos
Beverly Hills Cop *84* Martin Brest
Beverly Hills Cop II *87* Tony Scott
Beverly Hills Nightmare *72* Larry Cohen
Beverly Hills Vamp *89* Fred Olen Ray
Beverly of Graustark *26* Sidney Franklin
Beware *19* William Nigh
Beware *46* Bud Pollard
Beware My Brethren *71* Robert Hartford-Davis
Beware, My Lovely *52* Harry Horner
Beware of a Holy Whore *70* Rainer Werner Fassbinder
Beware of Bachelors *28* Roy Del Ruth
Beware of Barnacle Bill *35* Dave Fleischer
Beware of Blondes *28* George B. Seitz
Beware of Blondie *50* Edward Bernds
Beware of Children *60* Gerald Thomas
Beware of Ladies *36* Irving Pichel
Beware of Married Men *28* Archie Mayo
Beware of Pity *46* Maurice Elvey
Beware of Strangers *18* Colin Campbell
Beware of the Brethren *71* Robert Hartford-Davis
Beware of the Bride *20* Howard Mitchell
Beware of the Bull *08* Percy Stow
Beware of the Dog *23* Gregory La Cava
Beware of the Dog *64* Philip Ford
Beware of the Holy Whore *70* Rainer Werner Fassbinder

Beware of the Law *22* W. A. Douglas
Beware of the Raffled Turkey *05* Tom Green
Beware of Widows *27* Wesley Ruggles
Beware of Women *33* George King
Beware—Spooks! *39* Edward Sedgwick
Beware the Black Widow *68* Larry Crane
Beware! The Blob *71* Larry Hagman
Beware the Brethren *71* Robert Hartford-Davis
Beware the Holy Whore *70* Rainer Werner Fassbinder
Bewildering Cabinet, The *07* Georges Méliès
Bewildering Transformations *12* F. Percy Smith
Bewitched *45* Arch Oboler
Bewitched *81* Zhihong Gui
Bewitched *87* Francesco Nuti
Bewitched Boxing Gloves, The *10* Walter R. Booth
Bewitched Bunny *54* Chuck Jones
Bewitched Dungeon, The *00* Georges Méliès
Bewitched Inn, The *1897* Georges Méliès
Bewitched Matches *14* Émile Cohl
Bewitched Traveller, The *04* Lewin Fitzhamon, Cecil M. Hepworth
Bewitched Trunk, The *04* Georges Méliès
Bewitching Kisses *37* José A. Ferreyra
Bewitching Scatterbrain *63* Édouard Molinaro
Beyaz Mendil *55* Lütfü Akat
Beyond *21* William Desmond Taylor
Beyond, The *80* Lucio Fulci
Beyond a Reasonable Doubt *56* Fritz Lang
Beyond All Limits *57* Roberto Gavaldón
Beyond All Odds *26* Alvin J. Neitz
Beyond and Back *78* James L. Conway
Beyond Atlantis *73* Eddie Romero
Beyond Bengal *34* Harry Schenck
Beyond Control *71* Anthony Baker
Beyond Death's Door *79* Henning Schellerup
Beyond Decay *23* Teinosuke Kinugasa
Beyond Evil *77* Liliana Cavani
Beyond Evil *80* Herb Freed
Beyond Fear *77* Yannik Andrei
Beyond Forty *82* Anne Claire Poirier
Beyond Glory *48* John Farrow
Beyond Good and Evil *77* Liliana Cavani
Beyond London Lights *28* Tom Terriss
Beyond Mombasa *56* George Marshall
Beyond Obsession *82* Liliana Cavani
Beyond Our Horizon *39* Norman Walker
Beyond Passion *86* Jesús Garay
Beyond Price *21* J. Searle Dawley
Beyond Price *47* Cecil H. Williamson
Beyond Reason *77* Telly Savalas
Beyond Reasonable Doubt *80* John Laing
Beyond Silence *87* César Bolívar
Beyond Sing the Woods *49* Paul Ostermayer
Beyond Terror *79* Tomás Aznar
Beyond the Barricade *19* Forest Holger-Madsen
Beyond the Blue Horizon *42* Alfred Santell
Beyond the Border *25* Scott R. Dunlap
Beyond the Cities *30* Carlyle Blackwell

Beyond the Crossroads *22* Lloyd B. Carleton
Beyond the Curtain *60* Compton Bennett
Beyond the Darkness *79* Aristide Massaccesi
Beyond the Door *74* Sonia Assonitis, Roberto d'Ettore Piazzoli
Beyond the Door *82* Liliana Cavani
Beyond the Door II *76* Lamberto Bava, Mario Bava
Beyond the Dreams of Avarice *20* Thomas Bentley
Beyond the Fog *72* James O'Connolly
Beyond the Forest *49* King Vidor
Beyond the Gate *79* Gregory Goodell
Beyond the Gates *49* René Clément
Beyond the Grave *73* Jesús Franco
Beyond the Horizon *60* Zahari Zhandov
Beyond the Last Frontier *43* Howard Bretherton
Beyond the Law *18* Theodore Marston
Beyond the Law *30* John P. McGowan
Beyond the Law *34* D. Ross Lederman
Beyond the Law *67* Giorgio Stegani
Beyond the Law *68* Norman Mailer
Beyond the Limit *83* John Mackenzie
Beyond the Line of Duty *71* Per Berglund
Beyond the Living *77* Al Adamson
Beyond the Mist *86* Manoochehr Asgari-Nasab
Beyond the Moon *64* William Beaudine, Hollingsworth Morse
Beyond the Ocean *90* Ben Gazzara
Beyond the Pecos *44* Lambert Hillyer
Beyond the Poseidon Adventure *79* Irwin Allen
Beyond the Purple Hills *50* John English
Beyond the Rainbow *22* Christy Cabanne
Beyond the Reef *79* Frank C. Clark
Beyond the Rio Grande *30* Harry S. Webb
Beyond the Rising Moon *88* Philip Cook
Beyond the River *22* Ludwig Czerny
Beyond the River *56* Henry Hathaway
Beyond the Rockies *26* Jack Nelson
Beyond the Rockies *32* Fred Allen
Beyond the Rocks *22* Sam Wood
Beyond the Sacramento *40* Lambert Hillyer
Beyond the Seven Seas *44* Lambert Hillyer
Beyond the Shadows *18* J. W. McLaughlin
Beyond the Sierras *28* Nick Grindé
Beyond the Square *55* Márta Mészáros
Beyond the Time Barrier *59* Edgar G. Ulmer
Beyond the Time of Duty *42* Lewis Seiler
Beyond the Trail *26* Albert Herman
Beyond the Valley of the Dolls *70* Russ Meyer
Beyond the Veil *25* Sinclair Hill
Beyond the Wall *21* Fritz Lang
Beyond the Walls *84* Uri Barbash
Beyond Therapy *86* Robert Altman
Beyond This Place *59* Jack Cardiff
Beyond Tomorrow *40* A. Edward Sutherland
Beyond Victory *31* Edward H. Griffith, John S. Robertson
Bez Bebek *88* Engin Ayca
Bez Końca *84* Krzysztof Kieślowski

Bez Obav *55* Vojtěch Jasný
Bez Solntsa *88* Yuli Karasik
Bez Svidetelei *83* Nikita Mikhalkov
Bez Viny Vinovatye *45* Vladimir Petrov
Bez Znieczulenia *78* Andrzej Wajda
Bezhin Lug *35* Sergei Eisenstein
Bezhin Meadow *35* Sergei Eisenstein
Bezúčelná Procházka *30* Alexander Hammid
Bhagya Chakra *35* Nitin Bose
Bhai ka Dushman Bhai *88* Sudesh Issar
Bhale Mogudu *88* Relangi Narasimah Rao
Bhama Kalapam *88* Relangi Narasimah Rao
Bharat Mata *57* Ramjankhan Mehboobkhan
Bhargava Ramudu *87* A. Kothandarami Reddy
Bhasamur Mohini *13* D. G. Phalke
Bhatak Bhawani *88* Dinkar Patil
Bhavni Bhavai *80* Ketan Mehta
Bhopali *30* Rajaram Vanakudre Shantaram
Bhowani Junction *55* George Cukor
Bhumika *77* Shyam Benegal
Bhuvan Shome *69* Mrinal Sen
Bi and the Ba, The *86* Maurizio Nichetti
Bi Chamd Khayrtay *86* B. Baljinnyam
Bi e il Ba, Il *86* Maurizio Nichetti
Biały Mazur *73* Wanda Jakubowska
Bianca *84* Nanni Moretti
Bianchi Pascoli *47* Luciano Emmer, Enrico Gras
Bianco, il Giallo, il Nero, Il *75* Sergio Corbucci
Bianco, Rosso e... *71* Alberto Lattuada
Bianco, Rosso e Verdone *81* Carlo Verdone
Bianco, Rosso, Giallo, Rosa *66* Massimo Mida
Bibbi, Elin and Christina *86* Egil Kolstø
Bibbia, La *65* John Huston
Biberpelz, Der *39* Jürgen von Alten
Bibi *73* Joe Sarno
Bibi la Purée *34* Léo Joannon
Bible, The *65* John Huston
Bible, La *76* Marcel Carné
Bible, The *76* Marcel Carné
Bible...In the Beginning, The *65* John Huston
Bibliothèques, Les *63* Walerian Borowczyk
Biches, Les *67* Claude Chabrol
Bicycle Race, The *20* Raoul Barré, Charles Bowers
Bicycle Race *54* Jerzy Bossak
Bicycle Thief, The *48* Vittorio De Sica
Bicycle Thieves *48* Vittorio De Sica
Bicycles Repaired *08* Lewin Fitzhamon
Bicyclettes de Belsize, Les *68* Douglas Hickox
Bid for Bounty, A *15* Cecil Birch
Bid for Fortune, A *11* Bert Haldane
Bid for Fortune, A *17* Sidney Morgan
Bidasses en Folie, Les *72* Claude Zidi
Bidasses S'en Vont en Guerre, Les *74* Claude Zidi
Biddy *83* Christine Edzard
Bidon d'Or, Le *31* Christian-Jaque
Bidone, Il *55* Federico Fellini
Bidrohi *87* Anjan Chowdhury
Bien Aimée, La *66* Jacques Doniol-Valcroze

Bien Amada, La *51* Emilio Fernández
Bienfaiteur, Le *42* Henri Decoin
Bienfaits du Cinématographe, Les *04* Alice Guy-Blaché
¡Bienvenido, Sr. Marshall! *52* Luis García Berlanga
Bière, La *24* Jean Grémillon
Bièvre, La *39* René Clément
Bièvre, Fille Perdue, La *39* René Clément
Bièvre, Lost Girl, La *39* René Clément
Biff Bang Buddy *24* Frank L. Inghram
Biff! Bang!! Wallop!!! *14* Dave Aylott
Big *88* Penny Marshall
Big Adventure, The *21* B. Reeves Eason
Big and Small *56* Vladimir Pogačić
Big and the Bad, The *71* Maurizio Lucidi
Big Bad John *90* Burt Kennedy
Big Bad Mama *74* Steve Carver
Big Bad Mama II *87* Jim Wynorski
Big Banana Feet *77* Murray Grigor, Patrick Higson
Big Bang, Le *87* Jean-Marc Picha
Big Bang, The *87* Jean-Marc Picha
Big Bang, The *89* James Toback
Big Bankroll, The *61* Joseph M. Newman
Big Beat, The *58* Will Cowan
Big Ben Calling *35* Ivar Campbell
Big Ben's Dream of Greatness *12* A. E. Coleby
Big Bet, The *86* Bert I. Gordon
Big Bird Cage, The *72* Jack Hill
Big Birdcast, The *38* Charles Mintz
Big Blockade, The *41* Charles Frend
Big Blue, The *88* Luc Besson
Big Blue, The *89* Andrew Horn
Big Bluff, The *33* Reginald Denny
Big Bluff, The *37* Georg Jacoby
Big Bluff, The *55* W. Lee Wilder
Big Bonanza, The *44* George Archainbaud
Big Boodle, The *57* Richard Wilson
Big Boss, The *41* Charles Barton
Big Boss, The *72* Wei Lo
Big Bounce, The *69* Alex March
Big Boy *30* Alan Crosland
Big Boy Rides Again *35* Albert Herman
Big Brain, The *33* George Archainbaud
Big Brawl, The *80* Robert Clouse
Big Break, The *53* Joseph Strick
Big Broadcast, The *32* Frank Tuttle
Big Broadcast of 1936, The *35* Norman Taurog
Big Broadcast of 1937, The *36* Mitchell Leisen
Big Broadcast of 1938, The *37* Mitchell Leisen
Big Brother *23* Allan Dwan
Big Brown Eyes *36* Raoul Walsh
Big Bus, The *76* James Frawley
Big Business *29* James W. Horne
Big Business *30* Oscar M. Sheridan
Big Business *34* Cyril Gardner
Big Business *37* Frank R. Strayer
Big Business *88* Jim Abrahams
Big Business Girl *31* William A. Seiter
Big Bust-Out, The *73* Richard Jackson
Big Cage, The *33* Kurt Neumann
Big Calibre *35* Robert North Bradbury
Big Caper, The *57* Robert Stevens
Big Carnival, The *51* Billy Wilder
Big Cat, The *49* Phil Karlson

Big Catch, The *68* Laurence Henson
Big Chance, The *33* Albert Herman
Big Chance, The *57* Peter Graham Scott
Big Chase, The *54* Arthur Hilton
Big Chief, The *58* Henri Verneuil
Big Chief Ko-Ko *25* Dave Fleischer
Big Chief Little Pimple *14* Fred Evans, Joe Evans
Big Chief Ugh-Amugh-Ugh *38* Dave Fleischer
Big Chill, The *83* Lawrence Kasdan
Big Circus, The *59* Joseph M. Newman
Big City, The *27* Tod Browning
Big City, The *37* Frank Borzage
Big City *48* Norman Taurog
Big City, The *63* Satyajit Ray
Big City, The *66* Carlos Diegues
Big City Blues *32* Mervyn LeRoy
Big Clock, The *48* John Farrow
Big Combo, The *54* Joseph H. Lewis
Big Country, The *58* William Wyler
Big Cube, The *69* Tito Davison
Big Daddy *69* Carl K. Hittleman
Big Dame Hunting *32* George Marshall
Big Dan *23* William A. Wellman
Big Day, The *47* Jacques Tati
Big Day, The *60* Peter Graham Scott
Big Deadly Game *54* Daniel Birt
Big Deal, The *49* Edward Bernds
Big Deal *56* Mario Monicelli
Big Deal at Dodge City *66* Fielder Cook
Big Deal on Madonna Street *56* Mario Monicelli
Big Deal on Madonna Street...Twenty Years Later *85* Amanzio Todini
Big Decision, The *51* Felix E. Feist
Big Diamond Robbery, The *29* Eugene Forde
Big Dig, The *69* Ephraim Kishon
Big Dis, The *90* Gordon Eriksen, John O'Brien
Big Doll House, The *71* Jack Hill
Big Duel in the North Sea *66* Jun Fukuda
Big Dust-Up, The *70* Alexander Kluge
Big Easy, The *86* Jim McBride
Big Enough and Old Enough *68* Joseph Prieto
Big Executive *33* Erle C. Kenton
Big Fair, The *60* Jean Mitry
Big Family, The *54* Josef Heifits
Big Feast, The *73* Marco Ferreri
Big Fella *37* J. Elder Wills
Big Fibber, The *33* George Marshall
Big Fight, The *30* Walter Lang
Big Fish, The *55* Břetislav Pojar
Big Fisherman, The *59* Frank Borzage
Big Fix, The *47* James Flood
Big Fix, The *78* Jeremy Paul Kagan
Big Foot *73* Robert F. Slatzer
Big Foot and the Hendersons *87* William Dear
Big Forest *30* Heinosuke Gosho
Big Frame, The *52* David MacDonald
Big Freeze, The *61* Géza von Cziffra
Big Fun Carnival, The *57* Marc Daniels
Big Gamble, The *31* Fred Niblo
Big Gamble, The *60* Richard Fleischer, Elmo Williams
Big Game *21* Dallas M. Fitzgerald
Big Game *24* Charles Lamont

Big Game, The 28 Henry D. Bailey
Big Game, The 36 George Nicholls, Jr.
Big Game, The 53 Robert Siodmak
Big Game, The 72 Robert Day
Big Game George 27 Sam Newfield
Big Game Hunt 68 Alex Lovy
Big Game Hunter, The 25 George Marshall
Big Grab, The 62 Henri Verneuil
Big Gundown, The 66 Sergio Sollima
Big Guns 72 Duccio Tessari
Big Gusher, The 51 Lew Landers
Big Guy, The 39 Arthur Lubin
Big Hand for the Little Lady, A 66 Fielder Cook
Big Hangover, The 50 Norman Krasna
Big Happiness 20 Colin Campbell
Big Heart, The 47 George Seaton
Big-Hearted Herbert 34 William Keighley
Big Heat, The 53 Fritz Lang
Big Heel Watha 44 Tex Avery
Big Hop, The 28 James W. Horne
Big House 30 Pál Fejös
Big House, The 30 George W. Hill
Big House Blues 47 Howard Swift
Big House Bunny 50 Friz Freleng
Big House, U.S.A. 55 Howard W. Koch
Big Hug, A 40 Gustaf Edgren
Big Hurt, The 86 Barry Peak
Big Idea, The 18 Hal Mohr
Big Jack 48 Richard Thorpe
Big Jake 71 George Sherman
Big Jewel Case, The 30 Stephen Roberts
Big Jim Garrity 16 George Fitzmaurice
Big Jim McLain 52 Edward Ludwig
Big Job, The 65 Gerald Thomas
Big Joys, Small Sorrows 86 Keisuke Kinoshita
Big Jump, The 27 Arnold Fanck
Big Killing, The 28 F. Richard Jones
Big Knife, The 55 Robert Aldrich
Big Land, The 44 Sergei Gerasimov
Big Land, The 57 Gordon Douglas
Big Leaguer, The 53 Robert Aldrich
Big Li, Young Li and Old Li 62 Jin Xie
Big Lift, The 50 George Seaton
Big Little Person, The 19 Robert Z. Leonard
Big Lobby, The 84 Harry Hurwitz
Big Mac 85 Sigi Rothemund
Big Man, The 90 David Leland
Big Meat Eater 82 Chris Windsor
Big Mess, The 70 Alexander Kluge
Big Mo 73 Daniel Mann
Big Money 18 Harry Lorraine
Big Money 30 Russell Mack
Big Money 36 Pat Jackson, Harry Watt
Big Money, The 56 John Paddy Carstairs
Big Mouse Take 65 Joseph Barbera, William Hanna
Big Mouth, The 67 Jerry Lewis
Big News 29 Gregory La Cava
Big Night, The 51 Joseph Losey
Big Night, The 60 Sidney Salkow
Big Noise, The 28 Allan Dwan
Big Noise, The 36 Alex Bryce
Big Noise, The 36 Frank Lloyd
Big Noise, The 44 Malcolm St. Clair
Big North, The 51 Andrew Marton
Big Operator, The 59 Charles Haas

Big Pal 25 John G. Adolfi
Big Palooka, The 29 Mack Sennett
Big Parade, The 25 King Vidor
Big Parade, The 86 Kaige Chen
Big Party, The 30 John G. Blystone
Big Payoff, The 32 Ford Beebe
Big Payoff, The 75 Richard Bailey
Big Picture, The 89 Christopher Guest
Big Pond, The 30 Hobart Henley
Big Punch, The 20 John Ford
Big Punch, The 48 Sherry Shourds
Big Race, The 30 John Cromwell
Big Race, The 33 Fred Newmeyer
Big Race, The 37 Walter Lantz
Big Race, The 81 Jerzy Domaradzki
Big Red 62 Norman Tokar
Big Red One, The 79 Samuel Fuller
Big Red Riding Hood 25 Leo McCarey
Big Risk, The 59 Claude Sautet
Big Road, The 63 Yuri Ozerov
Big Road, The 87 Jean-Loup Hubert
Big Scare, The 64 Jean-Pierre Mocky
Big Score, The 83 Fred Williamson
Big Search, The 57 Arnold Belgard, Edoardo Capolino
Big Shakedown, The 34 John Francis Dillon
Big Shave, The 67 Martin Scorsese
Big Shot, The 31 Ralph Murphy
Big Shot, The 37 Edward Killy
Big Shot, The 42 Lewis Seiler
Big Shots, The 65 Robert Enrico
Big Shots 87 Robert Mandel
Big Show, The 26 Julian Ollendorff
Big Show, The 26 George Terwilliger
Big Show, The 29 Bobby Harman
Big Show, The 36 Mack V. Wright
Big Show, The 48 Anthony Gilkison
Big Show, The 61 James B. Clark
Big Show-Off, The 45 Howard Bretherton
Big Silence, The 67 Sergio Corbucci
Big Sister, The 16 John B. O'Brien
Big Sky, The 52 Howard Hawks
Big Sleep, The 46 Howard Hawks
Big Sleep, The 77 Michael Winner
Big Snatch, The 62 Henri Verneuil
Big Snooze, The 46 Robert Clampett
Big Sombrero, The 49 Frank McDonald
Big Splash, The 34 Leslie Hiscott
Big Squeal, The 33 Charles Lamont
Big Stakes 22 Clifford S. Elfelt
Big Stampede, The 32 Tenny Wright
Big Steal, The 49 Don Siegel
Big Store, The 41 Charles Reisner
Big Story, The 57 Richard Carlson
Big Street, The 42 Irving Reis
Big Strong Man, The 22 George A. Cooper
Big Swallow, The 01 James A. Williamson
Big Sweat, The 89 Ulli Lommel
Big Swim, The 26 Charles Bowers
Big Switch, The 68 Peter Walker
Big T.N.T. Show, The 66 Larry Peerce
Big Thrill, The 33 Leigh Jason
Big Timber 17 William Desmond Taylor
Big Timber 24 William James Craft
Big Timber 50 Jean Yarbrough
Big Time 29 Kenneth Hawks
Big Time 77 Andrew Georgias
Big Time 88 Chris Blum

Big Time 89 Howard Cummings, Jan Egleson
Big Time Operators 57 Basil Dearden
Big Time or Bust 33 Sam Newfield
Big Timer, The 32 Edward Buzzell
Big Timers 47 Bud Pollard
Big Tip Off, The 55 Frank McDonald
Big Top Bunny 51 Robert McKimson
Big Top Pee-wee 88 Randal Kleiser
Big Town 32 Arthur Hoerl
Big Town 47 William C. Thomas
Big Town, The 87 Ben Bolt
Big Town After Dark 47 William C. Thomas
Big Town Czar 39 Arthur Lubin
Big Town Girl 37 Frank R. Strayer
Big Town Ideas 21 Carl Harbaugh
Big Town Roundup 21 Lynn Reynolds
Big Town Scandal 48 William C. Thomas
Big Trail, The 30 Raoul Walsh
Big Trees, The 52 Felix E. Feist
Big Tremaine 16 Henry Otto
Big Trouble 84 John Cassavetes
Big Trouble in Little China 86 John Carpenter
Big Truck and Poor Clare 72 Robert Ellis Miller
Big Wash!, The 68 Jean-Pierre Mocky
Big Wave, The 60 Tad Danielewski
Big Wednesday 78 John Milius
Big Wheel, The 49 Edward Ludwig
Big Wheels and Sailor 80 Doug Aitken
Big Wilderness 86 Don Coscarelli
Big Zapper 73 Lindsay Shonteff
Bigamist, The 16 Herbert Brenon
Bigamist, The 21 Guy Newall
Bigamist, The 53 Ida Lupino
Bigamist, The 56 Luciano Emmer
Bigamo, Il 56 Luciano Emmer
Bigfoot — The Mysterious Monsters 75 Robert Guenette
Bigger Man, The 15 John W. Noble
Bigger Splash, A 74 Jack Hazan
Bigger Than Barnum's 26 Ralph Ince
Bigger Than Life 56 Nicholas Ray
Biggest Battle, The 78 Umberto Lenzi
Biggest Battle on Earth, The 65 Inoshiro Honda
Biggest Bundle of Them All, The 67 Ken Annakin
Biggest Fight on Earth, The 65 Inoshiro Honda
Biggest Show on Earth, The 18 Jerome Storm
Biggles 86 John Hough
Biggles: Adventures in Time 86 John Hough
Bij de Beesten Af 72 Bert Haanstra
Bijilee aur Toofan 88 S. R. Pratap
Bijin Aishū 31 Yasujiro Ozu
Bijō to Ekitai Ningen 58 Inoshiro Honda
Bijō to Kairyū 55 Kozaburo Yoshimura
Bijomaru Sword 45 Kenji Mizoguchi
Bijomaru the Noted Sword 45 Kenji Mizoguchi
Bijou 72 Wakefield Poole
Bijoutiers du Clair de Lune, Les 57 Roger Vadim
Bijstere Land van Veluwen, Het 48 Herman van den Horst

Bike Boy 67 Andy Warhol
Bikini Beach 64 William Asher
Bikini Genie 87 Chuck Vincent
Bikini Paradise 67 Gregg Tallas
Bikini Shop, The 85 David Wechter
Bikutsi Water Blues 88 Jean Marie Teno
Bílá Nemoc 36 Hugo Haas
Bílá Spona 60 Martin Frič
Bilans Kwartalny 74 Krzysztof Zanussi
Bilbao—Una Historia del Amor 78 Bigas
  Luna
Bild der Zeit, Ein 22 Fritz Lang
Bildnis, Das 25 Jacques Feyder
Bildnis des Dorian Gray, Das 17 Richard
  Oswald
Bildnis des Dorian Gray, Das 70 Massimo
  Dallamano
Bildnis des Doriana Gray, Das 76 Jesús
  Franco
Bildnis einer Unbekannten 54 Helmut
  Käutner
Bildschnitzer vom Walsertal, Der 50 Ed-
  mond T. Gréville
Bilitis 76 David Hamilton
Biljett till Paradiset 62 Arne Mattsson
Bill and Coo 31 John Orton
Bill and Coo 47 Dean Riesner
Bill and Ted's Excellent Adventure 88
  Stephen Herek
Bill Apperson's Boy 19 James Kirkwood
Bill Apperson's Son 19 James Kirkwood
Bill Bailey's Return 04 Alf Collins
Bill Brennan's Claim 17 George Marshall
Bill Bumper's Boy 13 Percy Stow
Bill Cosby, Himself 82 Bill Cosby
Bill Cracks Down 37 William Nigh
Bill for Divorcement, A 22 Denison Clift
Bill Henry 19 Jerome Storm
Bill il Taciturno 67 Massimo Pupillo
Bill of Divorcement, A 32 George Cukor
Bill of Divorcement, A 40 John Farrow
Bill of Hare 62 Robert McKimson
Bill Poster, The 1899 C. Goodwin Norton
Bill Poster, The 33 Manny Gould, Ben
  Harrison
Bill Poster's Revenge, The 01 George
  Albert Smith
Bill Sykes Up to Date 03 Arthur Cooper
Billard Cassé, Le 16 Jacques Feyder
Billboard Frolics 35 Friz Freleng
Billet de Banque, Le 06 Louis Feuillade
Billeted 19 John S. Robertson
Billets 25 Leslie Hiscott
Billiards Mad 12 Frank Wilson
Billie 65 Don Weis
Billie "Bow-Wow" 15 Rowland Moore
Billie's Baby 14 Frank Lloyd
Billie's Bugle 08 Dave Aylott
Billie's Rose 22 Challis Sanderson
Billiken Revolts 13 Dave Aylott
Billion Dollar Brain 67 Ken Russell
Billion Dollar Caper, The 68 Francis D.
  Lyon
Billion Dollar Hobo, The 77 Stuart Mc-
  Gowan
Billion Dollar Limited 42 Dave Fleischer
Billion Dollar Scandal 32 Harry Joe Brown
Billion for Boris, A 85 Alexander Grass-
  hoff
Billionaire, A 54 Kon Ichikawa

Billionaire, The 55 John Halas*
Billions 20 Ray C. Smallwood
Bill's Legacy 31 Harry Revier
Bill's Monicker 15 Will P. Kellino
Bill's Reformation 12 Bert Haldane
Bill's Rise in the World 14 Percy Nash
Bill's Temptation 12 Bert Haldane
Billy and the Big Stick 17 Edward H.
  Griffith
Billy Borntired 08 A. E. Coleby
Billy Boy 54 Tex Avery
Billy Budd 62 Peter Ustinov
Billy Bungler the Silent Burglar 12 Dave
  Aylott
Billy Galvin 86 John Gray
Billy in the Lowlands 79 Jan Egleson
Billy Jack 71 Tom Laughlin
Billy Jack Goes to Washington 77 Tom
  Laughlin
Billy Jim 22 Frank Borzage
Billy Liar! 63 John Schlesinger
Billy Rose's Casa Mañana Review 38
  George Sidney
Billy Rose's Diamond Horseshoe 45
  George Seaton
Billy Rose's Jumbo 62 Charles Walters
Billy Strikes Oil 17 Will P. Kellino
Billy Sunday's Tabernacle 17 F. M. Follett
Billy the Kid 30 King Vidor
Billy the Kid 41 David Miller
Billy the Kid and the Green Baize Vam-
  pire 85 Alan Clarke
Billy the Kid in Blazing Frontier 43 Sam
  Newfield
Billy the Kid in Cattle Stampede 43 Sam
  Newfield
Billy the Kid in Fugitive of the Plains 43
  Sam Newfield
Billy the Kid in Law and Order 42 Sam
  Newfield
Billy the Kid in Santa Fe 41 Sam Newfield
Billy the Kid in Texas 40 Sam Newfield
Billy the Kid in The Mysterious Rider 42
  Sam Newfield
Billy the Kid in The Renegade 43 Sam
  Newfield
Billy the Kid in Western Cyclone 43 Sam
  Newfield
Billy the Kid Outlawed 40 Sam Newfield
Billy the Kid Returns 38 Joseph Kane
Billy the Kid Rides Again 43 Sam New-
  field
Billy the Kid, Sheriff of Sage Valley 42
  Sam Newfield
Billy the Kid Trails West 41 Sam Newfield
Billy the Kid Trapped 42 Sam Newfield
Billy the Kid vs. Dracula 65 William
  Beaudine
Billy the Kid Wanted 41 Sam Newfield
Billy the Kid's Fighting Pals 41 Sam New-
  field
Billy the Kid's Gun Justice 40 Sam
  Newfield
Billy the Kid's Range War 41 Sam New-
  field
Billy the Kid's Roundup 41 Sam Newfield
Billy the Kid's Smoking Guns 42 Sam
  Newfield
Billy the Truthful 17 Will P. Kellino
Billy Two Hats 72 Ted Kotcheff

Billy ze Kick 85 Gérard Mordillat
Billy's Bible 11 Dave Aylott
Billy's Birthday Present 13 William Dun-
  can
Billy's Book on Boxing 11 H. Oceano
  Martinek
Billy's Boxing Gloves 13 Dave Aylott
Billy's Bulldog 10 A. E. Coleby
Billy's Burglar 12 Van Dyke Brooke
Billy's Rival 14 William Desmond Taylor
Billy's Spanish Love Spasm 15 Will P.
  Kellino
Billy's Stormy Courtship 16 Will P. Kel-
  lino
Billy's Stratagem 11 D. W. Griffith
Bilo, The 36 Pál Fejös
Biloxi Blues 88 Mike Nichols
Bim 49 Albert Lamorisse
Bim 76 Hugh Robertson
Bim, le Petit Âne 49 Albert Lamorisse
Bimbi Lontani 20 Baldassare Negroni
Bimbo the Great 61 Harald Philipp
Bimbo's Express 31 Dave Fleischer
Bimbo's Initiation 31 Dave Fleischer
Bimi 30 B. Reeves Eason, Richard Thorpe
Binata si Mister, Balaga si Misis 81 Lino
  Brocka
Binding Sentiments 68 Márta Mészáros
Binding Ties 68 Márta Mészáros
Bindle 68 Peter Saunders
Bindle at the Party 26 H. B. Parkinson
Bindle in Charge 26 H. B. Parkinson
Bindle Introduced 26 H. B. Parkinson
Bindle, Matchmaker 26 H. B. Parkinson
Bindle, Millionaire 26 H. B. Parkinson
Bindle (One of Them Days) 68 Peter
  Saunders
Bindle's Cocktail 26 H. B. Parkinson
Binettoscope, Le 10 Émile Cohl
Bing Bang Boom 22 Fred J. Butler
Bing Presents Oreste 55 Edward Dmytryk
Bingle's Nightmare 13 Ralph Ince
Bingo 74 Jean-Claude Lord
Bingo Bongo 83 Pasquale Festa Campanile
Bingo, Bridesmaids and Braces 88 Gillian
  Armstrong
Bingo Crosbyana 36 Cal Dalton, Sandy
  Walker
Bingo Long Traveling All-Stars and Motor
  Kings, The 76 John Badham
Binks' Wife's Uncle 13 Bert Haldane
Bint el Hawa 53 Youssef Wahby
Bint Sabatashar 59 Salah Abu Saif
Bio-Hazard 84 Fred Olen Ray
Biografía de un Carnaval 83 Santiago
  Álvarez
Biography of a Bachelor Girl 34 Edward
  H. Griffith
Biography of a Festival 83 Santiago Ál-
  varez
Biography of Madame Fashion, The 19 L.
  M. Glackens
Bionic Boy, The 77 Leody M. Díaz
Bip Goes to Town 41 Joris Ivens
Biquefarre 83 Georges Rouquier
Bir Avuç Cennet 86 Muammar Ozer
Bir Çirkin Adam 69 Yılmaz Güney
Bir Udum Sevgi 85 Atıf Yılmaz
Biraghin 46 Carmine Gallone
Biraj Bahu 54 Bimal Roy

Birbi 22 Hans Steinhoff
Birch Interval 75 Delbert Mann
Birch Wood, The 70 Andrzej Wajda
Bird 78 Stan Brakhage
Bird 88 Clint Eastwood
Bird Came C.O.D., The 41 Chuck Jones
Bird Fancier, The 20 Sidney Goldin
Bird in a Bonnet, A 58 Friz Freleng
Bird in a Guilty Cage 52 Friz Freleng
Bird in the Hand Is Worth..., A 87 Jesús Fragoso Montoya
Bird Man, The 35 Manny Gould, Ben Harrison
Bird Missing Spring, The 59 Keisuke Kinoshita
Bird of Freedom, A 08 Charles Raymond
Bird of Heaven, A 57 Imre Fehér
Bird of Mercy, The 27 Kenji Mizoguchi
Bird of Paradise 32 King Vidor
Bird of Paradise 51 Delmer Daves
Bird of Prey, A 16 Eugene Nowland
Bird of Prey, The 18 Edward J. LeSaint
Bird of Prey 33 Marcel L'Herbier
Bird of Springs Past, The 59 Keisuke Kinoshita
Bird of the Lighthouse, The 71 Santiago Álvarez
Bird on a Wire 74 Tony Palmer
Bird on a Wire 90 John Badham
Bird Store, The 32 Wilfred Jackson
Bird Stuffer 36 Manny Gould, Ben Harrison
Bird Watch, The 83 Jean-Pierre Denis
Bird with the Crystal Plumage, The 69 Dario Argento
Bird with the Glass Feathers, The 69 Dario Argento
Birdman of Alcatraz 61 John Frankenheimer
Birdmen, The 71 Philip Leacock
Birds, The 63 Alfred Hitchcock
Birds, The 63 Kazimierz Karabasz
Birds and the Bees, The 47 Fred M. Wilcox
Birds and the Bees, The 56 Norman Taurog
Birds Anonymous 57 Friz Freleng
Birds at Sunrise 72 Joyce Wieland
Birds, Bees and Storks 64 John Halas
Birds, Bees and the Italians, The 65 Pietro Germi
Birds' Christmas Carol, The 17 Lule Warrenton
Birds Come to Die in Peru, The 68 Romain Gary
Birds Do It 65 Andrew Marton
Birds Do It, Bees Do It 74 Nicholas Noxon
Bird's-Eye View of St. Helier, Jersey 1899 Georges Méliès
Birds in Love 36 Charles Mintz
Birds in Peru 68 Romain Gary
Birds of a Father 61 Robert McKimson
Birds of a Feather 31 Burton Gillett
Birds of a Feather 31 Ben R. Hart
Birds of a Feather 35 John Baxter
Birds of a Feather 78 Édouard Molinaro
Birds of a Feather Plot Together 14 Cecil Birch
Birds of Italy 85 Ciro Ippolito

Birds of Our Hopes, The 77 Elior Ishmukhamedov
Birds of Prey 27 William James Craft
Birds of Prey 30 Basil Dean
Birds of Prey 68 José Giovanni
Birds of Prey 73 William A. Graham
Birds of Prey 86 Jorge Montesi
Birds of Prey 87 René Cardona, Jr.
Birds of Prey 88 Gil Portes
Birds, the Bees and the Italians, The 65 Pietro Germi
Birdsville 86 Carl Schultz
Birdy 84 Alan Parker
Birdy and the Beast 44 Robert Clampett
Birgit Haas Must Be Killed 81 Laurent Heynemann
Birmingham Girl's Last Hope, A 17 Bert Haldane
Biro ve Diğerleri 88 Tunc Basaran
Birth 81 Robert Kramer
Birth of a Baby 38 Al Christie
Birth of a Nation, The 15 D. W. Griffith
Birth of a Notion, The 47 Robert McKimson
Birth of a Race 19 John W. Noble
Birth of a Robot 36 Humphrey Jennings, Len Lye
Birth of a Soul, The 20 Edwin L. Hollywood
Birth of a Town, The 59 Jan Łomnicki
Birth of Character, The 16 E. Mason Hopper
Birth of Frankenstein 56 Terence Fisher
Birth of Jazz 32 Manny Gould, Ben Harrison
Birth of Krishna, The 18 D. G. Phalke
Birth of Our Saviour, The 14 Charles Brabin
Birth of Patriotism, The 17 E. Magnus Ingleton
Birth of the Beatles 79 Richard Marquand
Birth of the Blues 41 Victor Schertzinger
Birth of the Robot, The 36 Humphrey Jennings, Len Lye
Birth of the Witch, The 81 Wilfried Minks
Birthday 22 Dave Fleischer
Birthday Cake, The 60 John Halas*
Birthday Gift, The 12 August Blom
Birthday Party, The 31 Burton Gillett
Birthday Party, The 37 Walter Lantz
Birthday Party, The 68 William Friedkin
Birthday Present, The 57 Pat Jackson
Birthday That Mattered, The 12 Bert Haldane
Birthday Town 87 Takis Papayannidis
Birthday Umbrella, The 05 Alf Collins
Birthmark 76 Richard Donner
Birthplace of the Hootenanny 63 Jack O'Connell
Birthright 24 Oscar Micheaux
Birthright 39 Oscar Micheaux
Birthright 52 Bill Clifford
Biruma no Tategoto 56 Kon Ichikawa
Biruma no Tategoto 85 Kon Ichikawa
Bis zum Ende Aller Tage 61 Franz Peter Wirth
Bis zur Bitteren Neige 75 Gerd Oswald
Bisbetica Domata, La 42 Ferdinando Maria Poggioli

Bisbetica Domata, La 66 Franco Zeffirelli
Biscuit Eater, The 40 Stuart Heisler
Biscuit Eater, The 72 Vincent McEveety
Bishop Misbehaves, The 33 E. A. Dupont
Bishop Murder Case, The 29 David Burton, Nick Grindé
Bishop of the Ozarks, The 23 Finis Fox
Bishop's Bathe, The 12 Hay Plumb
Bishop's Emeralds, The 19 John B. O'Brien
Bishop's Misadventures, The 33 E. A. Dupont
Bishop's Room, The 77 Dino Risi
Bishop's Silence, The 14 Charles H. Weston
Bishop's Wife, The 47 Henry Koster
Bismarck 40 Wolfgang Liebeneiner
Bisturi: La Mafia Bianca 73 Luigi Zampa
Bit o' Heaven, A 17 Lule Warrenton
Bit of Black Stuff, A 21 Fred Paul
Bit of Heaven, A 28 Clifford Wheeler
Bit of Jade, A 18 Edward Sloman
Bit of Kindling, A 17 Sherwood MacDonald
Bit Part, The 87 Brendan Maher
Bitch, The 31 Jean Renoir
Bitch 65 Andy Warhol
Bitch, The 79 Gerry O'Hara
Bite and Run 72 Dino Risi
Bite Me, Darling 70 Helmut Förnbacher
Bite the Bullet 75 Richard Brooks
Bite to Eat, A 59 Jan Němec
Biter Bit, The 09 A. E. Coleby
Biter Bit, The 20 S. Vanderlyn
Biter Bit, The 37 Redd Davis
Biter Bitten, The 04 William Haggar
Biting Husband 39 Márton Keleti
Bits of Broadway 30 Nick Grindé
Bits of Life 21 Marshall Neilan
Bitten Biter, The 20 Cecil Mannering
Bitter Apples 27 Harry Hoyt
Bitter Cane 84 Jacques Arcelin
Bitter Cherry 83 Gregory Dark
Bitter Coffee 86 Teguh Karya
Bitter Creek 54 Thomas Carr
Bitter Grass 65 Živka Mitrović
Bitter Harvest 62 Peter Graham Scott
Bitter Honeymoon 39 Béla Balázs
Bitter Reunion 58 Claude Chabrol
Bitter Rice 48 Giuseppe De Santis
Bitter Spears 56 Attilio Gatti
Bitter Spirit, The 61 Keisuke Kinoshita
Bitter Springs 50 Ralph Smart
Bitter Sweet 16 Jack Conway
Bitter Sweet 33 Herbert Wilcox
Bitter Sweet 40 W. S. Van Dyke
Bitter Sweet 59 Robert Siodmak
Bitter Sweets 28 Charles Hutchinson
Bitter Taste in the Morning 86 Miguel Mora
Bitter Tea of General Yen, The 32 Frank Capra
Bitter Tears of Petra von Kant, The 72 Rainer Werner Fassbinder
Bitter Truth, The 17 Kenean Buel
Bitter Truth, The 86 Zoltán Várkonyi
Bitter Victory 48 William Dieterle
Bitter Victory 57 Nicholas Ray
Bittere Ernte 85 Agnieszka Holland
Bittere Kruid, Het 85 Kees van Oostrum

Bitteren Tränen der Petra von Kant, Die 72 Rainer Werner Fassbinder
Bittersweet Love 76 David Miller
Bitva na Neretvi 69 Veljko Bulajić
Bitva za Nashu Radyansku Ukrayinu 43 Yakiv Avdiyenko, Yulia Solntseva
Bitva za Nashu Sovetskayu Ukrainu 43 Yakiv Avdiyenko, Yulia Solntseva
Bitwa o Kołobrzeg 45 Jerzy Bossak, Aleksander Ford
Bitwa pod Leninem 43 Aleksander Ford
Bitwa pod Lenino 43 Aleksander Ford
Bivouac, Le 1896 Georges Méliès
Bivouac, The 1896 Georges Méliès
Bizalom 79 István Szabó
Bizarre 69 Antony Balch
Bizarre, Bizarre 36 Marcel Carné
Bizet's Carmen 83 Francesco Rosi
Bjorn's Inferno 64 Allan King
Blå Natviol, Den 11 August Blom
Blå Undulater, De 65 Astrid Henning-Jensen
Black Abbot, The 34 George A. Cooper
Black Abbot, The 63 Franz-Josef Gottlieb
Black Ace, The 28 Leo D. Maloney
Black Aces 37 Buck Jones, Lesley Selander
Black Alleycats, The 74 Henning Schellerup
Black and Blue Market 43 Paul Sommer
Black and White 08 Émile Cohl
Black and White 10 Will Barker
Black and White 12 Christy Cabanne
Black and White 13 Stuart Kinder
Black and White 27 William C. Nolan
Black and White 29 R. E. Jeffrey
Black and White 29 Alfred Machin
Black and White 30 Alexander Oumansky
Black and White 86 Claire Devers
Black and White in Color 76 Jean-Jacques Annaud
Black and White Like Day and Night 78 Wolfgang Petersen
Black and White Magic 87 Naum Birman
Black and Without Sugar 86 Lutz Konermann
Black Angel, The 46 Roy William Neill
Black Angel 67 Jesús Franco
Black Angel 80 Roger Christian
Black Angels, The 70 Laurence Merrick
Black Arrow 44 Lew Landers
Black Arrow, The 48 Gordon Douglas
Black Arrow, The 87 Sergei Tarasov
Black Arrow Strikes, The 48 Gordon Douglas
Black Art 1897 Georges Méliès
Black Bag, The 22 Stuart Paton
Black Bandit 38 George Waggner
Black Bart 48 George Sherman
Black Bart, Highwayman 48 George Sherman
Black Beauty 06 Lewin Fitzhamon
Black Beauty 10 Lewin Fitzhamon
Black Beauty 21 David Smith
Black Beauty 33 Phil Rosen
Black Beauty 46 Max Nosseck
Black Beauty 71 James Hill
Black-Bellied Tarantula, The 71 Paolo Cavara
Black Belly of the Tarantula, The 71 Paolo Cavara

Black Belt Jones 74 Robert Clouse
Black Bird, The 25 Tod Browning
Black Bird, The 75 David Giler
Black Book, The 29 Spencer G. Bennet, Thomas Storey
Black Book, The 49 Anthony Mann
Black Boomerang, The 25 William H. Clifford
Black Bounty Killer, The 74 Jack Arnold
Black Box, The 15 Otis Turner
Black Brood 77 Manuel Gutiérrez Aragón
Black Buccaneer, The 61 Mario Costa
Black Bunch, The 73 Henning Schellerup
Black Butterflies 28 James W. Horne
Black Butterfly, The 16 Burton L. King
Black Caesar 72 Larry Cohen
Black Camel, The 31 Hamilton MacFadden
Black Cannon Incident, The 85 Jianxin Huang
Black Captain, The 20 Pál Fejős
Black Cargoes of the South Seas 29 Norman Dawn
Black Carrion 84 John Hough
Black Castle, The 52 Nathan Juran
Black Cat, The 34 Edgar G. Ulmer
Black Cat, The 41 Albert S. Rogell
Black Cat, The 66 Harold Hoffman
Black Cat 67 Kaneto Shindo
Black Cat, The 80 Lucio Fulci
Black Cat in the Bush, A 67 Kaneto Shindo
Black Cauldron, The 85 Ted Berman, Richard Rich
Black Chancellor, The 12 August Blom
Black Chapel 59 Ralph Habib
Black Chariot 71 Robert L. Goodwin
Black Christmas 63 Mario Bava
Black Christmas 74 Bob Clark
Black Circle, The 19 Frank Reicher
Black Circle Gang, The 16 Ernest G. Batley
Black Cobra, The 64 Rudolf Zehetgruber
Black Coffee 31 Leslie Hiscott
Black Coin, The 36 Albert Herman
Black Connection, The 74 Michael J. Finn
Black Corsair, The 39 Amleto Palermi
Black Cream 72 Michael Schultz
Black Crook, The 16 Robert Vignola
Black Cross 60 Aleksander Ford
Black Cross Gang, The 14 James Youngdeer
Black Crown, The 50 Luis Saslavsky
Black Cyclone 25 Fred Jackman
Black Dakotas, The 54 Ray Nazarro
Black Dawn 87 Carlos Lemos
Black Devils of Kali, The 55 Ralph Murphy
Black Diamond Express, The 27 Howard Bretherton
Black Diamonds 32 Charles Hanmer
Black Diamonds 40 Christy Cabanne
Black Diamonds 44 Ken Annakin
Black Doll, The 38 Otis Garrett
Black Dossier, The 55 André Cayatte
Black Dragon, The 87 Gio Lo
Black Dragon of Manzanar 43 William Witney
Black Dragons 42 William Nigh
Black Duke, The 61 Pino Mercanti

Black Eagle, The 46 Riccardo Freda
Black Eagle 48 Robert Gordon
Black Eagle 88 Eric Karson
Black Eagle of Santa Fe 64 Ernst Hofbauer
Black Eye 73 Jack Arnold
Black Eye, A 87 Serge Meynard
Black-Eyed Susan 08 Alf Collins
Black-Eyed Susan 13 Percy Nash
Black-Eyed Susan 14 Maurice Elvey
Black Eyes 39 Herbert Brenon
Black Eyes 87 Nikita Mikhalkov
Black Fantasy 72 Lionel Rogosin
Black Fear 15 John W. Noble
Black Feather 28 John Ince
Black Fist, The 18 Gregory La Cava
Black Fist 76 Timothy Galfas, Richard Kaye
Black Flag 86 Pedro Olea
Black Flowers for the Bride 70 Harold Prince
Black Forest, The 54 Gene Martel
Black Fox, The 62 Louis Clyde Stoumen
Black Frankenstein 73 William A. Levey
Black Friday 16 Lloyd B. Carleton
Black Friday 40 Arthur Lubin
Black Fury 35 Michael Curtiz
Black Gate, The 19 Theodore Marston
Black Gestapo, The 75 R. Lee Frost
Black Girl 65 Ousmane Sembène
Black Girl 72 Ossie Davis
Black Girl from..., The 65 Ousmane Sembène
Black Glove, The 54 Terence Fisher
Black God and the Blond Devil, The 64 Glauber Rocha
Black God and the White Devil, The 64 Glauber Rocha
Black God, White Devil 64 Glauber Rocha
Black Godfather, The 74 John Evans
Black Gold 24 Forrest K. Sheldon
Black Gold 47 Phil Karlson
Black Gold 63 Leslie Martinson
Black Gravel 60 Helmut Käutner
Black Gunn 72 Robert Hartford-Davis
Black Hand 49 Richard Thorpe
Black Hand Gang, The 30 Monty Banks
Black Hanky Panky 86 Thomas Gilou
Black Harvest 73 Christian Blackwood
Black Harvest of Countess Dracula, The 70 Leon Klimovsky
Black Harvest of Countess Dracula, The 73 Carlos Aured
Black Heat 76 Al Adamson
Black Hills 29 Norman Dawn
Black Hills 47 Ray Taylor
Black Hills Ambush 52 Harry Keller
Black Hills Express 43 John English
Black Hole, The 79 Gary Nelson
Black Holiday 73 Marco Leto
Black Hooker 74 Arthur Robertson
Black Horde, The 19 Yakov Protazanov
Black Horizons 36 Pál Fejős
Black Horse Canyon 54 Jesse Hibbs
Black Ice, The 57 Godfrey Grayson
Black Imp, The 05 Georges Méliès
Black in the Face 55 John Irwin
Black Is White 20 Charles Giblyn
Black Island 79 Ben Bolt
Black Jack 27 Orville Dull

Black Jack *49* Julien Duvivier
Black Jack *68* Gianfranco Baldanello
Black Jack *71* William T. Naud
Black Jack *79* Kenneth Loach
Black Jesus *67* Valerio Zurlini
Black-Jet Family, The *84* Sogo Ishii
Black Journal *77* Mauro Bolognini
Black Joy *77* Anthony Simmons
Black King *32* Bud Pollard
Black Kitten, The *10* Lewin Fitzhamon
Black Klansman, The *66* Ted V. Mikels
Black Knight, The *54* Tay Garnett
Black Lash, The *52* Ron Ormond
Black Legend *48* Alan Cooke, John Schlesinger
Black Legion *36* Archie Mayo
Black Lightning *24* James P. Hogan
Black Like Me *64* Carl Lerner
Black Limelight *38* Paul Stein
Black List, The *16* William DeMille
Black List, The *16* W. C. Morris
Black Lizard *68* Kinji Fukasaku
Black Lolita *75* Stephen Gibson
Black Love *72* Herschell Gordon Lewis
Black Love–White Love *67* Herbert Danska
Black Magic *1898* Georges Méliès
Black Magic *21* Henry D. Bailey
Black Magic *29* George B. Seitz
Black Magic *44* Phil Rosen
Black Magic *49* Gregory Ratoff, Orson Welles
Black Magic Rites–Reincarnations *73* Renato Polselli
Black Mama, White Mama *72* Eddie Romero
Black Marble, The *79* Harold Becker
Black Market Babies *45* William Beaudine
Black Market Rustlers *43* S. Roy Luby
Black Mask, The *06* Viggo Larsen
Black Mask *35* Ralph Ince
Black Masks, The *12* Mauritz Stiller
Black Masses of Exorcism, The *79* Jesús Franco
Black Memory *47* Oswald Mitchell
Black Mic-Mac *86* Thomas Gilou
Black Mic-Mac 2 *88* Marco Pauly
Black Midnight *49* Budd Boetticher
Black Mitt, Der *18* Gregory La Cava
Black Monocle, The *61* Georges Lautner
Black Moon *34* Roy William Neill
Black Moon *75* Louis Malle
Black Moon Rising *86* Harley Cokliss
Black Moritz *16* Ernst Lubitsch
Black Narcissus *46* Michael Powell, Emeric Pressburger
Black Night, The *16* Harold Weston
Black Nightmare *86* Fabrizio Rampelli
Black Oak Conspiracy *77* Robert Kelljan
Black on White *67* Jörn Donner
Black on White *69* Tinto Brass
Black Orchid *52* Charles Saunders
Black Orchid, The *58* Martin Ritt
Black Orchids *16* Rex Ingram
Black Orpheus *58* Marcel Camus
Black Oxen *23* Frank Lloyd
Black Palm Trees, The *67* Lars-Magnus Lindgren
Black Panther, The *77* Ian Merrick
Black Panther of Ratana *63* Jürgen Roland

Black Panthers *68* Agnès Varda
Black Panther's Cub, The *21* Émile Chautard
Black Parachute, The *44* Lew Landers
Black Paradise *26* Roy William Neill
Black Patch *57* Allen H. Miner
Black Pearl, The *28* Scott Pembroke
Black Pearl, The *77* Saul Swimmer
Black Peter *22* George Ridgwell
Black Peter *63* Miloš Forman
Black Pirate, The *26* Donald Crisp, Albert Parker
Black Pirates, The *54* Allen H. Miner
Black Pit, The *58* Fernando Méndez
Black Pit of Dr. M, The *58* Fernando Méndez
Black Planet, The *82* Paul Williams
Black Rain *88* Shohei Imamura
Black Rain *89* Ridley Scott
Black Rainbow, The *16* Michael Curtiz
Black Rainbow *66* Michael Zuckerman
Black Rainbow *89* Michael Hodges
Black Raven, The *43* Sam Newfield
Black Report *63* Yasuzo Masumura
Black Rider, The *54* Wolf Rilla
Black Rider, The *76* Larry Spangler
Black River *57* Masaki Kobayashi
Black River, The *64* Zahari Zhandov
Black Rodeo *72* Jeff Kanew
Black Roderick the Poacher *14* H. Oceano Martinek
Black Room, The *35* Roy William Neill
Black Room, The *82* Elly Kenner, Norman Thaddeus Vane
Black Room Mystery, The *35* Roy William Neill
Black Roots *70* Lionel Rogosin
Black Rose, The *49* Henry Hathaway
Black Rose *69* Kinji Fukasaku
Black Roses *21* Colin Campbell
Black Roses *32* Gustaf Molander
Black Roses *35* Paul Martin
Black Roses *45* Rune Carlsten
Black Roses *87* John Fasano
Black Rudolf *28* Gustaf Edgren
Black Sabbath *63* Mario Bava
Black Sail, The *28* Sergei Yutkevich
Black Samson *74* Chuck Bail
Black Samurai *77* Al Adamson
Black Scorpion, The *57* Edward Ludwig
Black Sea Fighters *43* Vasily Belyaev
Black Sea Mutiny, The *31* A. Kordium
Black Secret, The *19* George B. Seitz
Black Shack Alley *83* Euzhan Palcy
Black Shadow, The *42* Lambert Hillyer
Black Shadows *20* Howard Mitchell
Black Shadows *49* André Cauvin
Black Shampoo *76* Greydon Clark
Black Sheep, The *09* Gilbert M. Anderson
Black Sheep, The *12* D. W. Griffith
Black Sheep, A *15* Thomas Heffron
Black Sheep, The *20* Sidney Morgan
Black Sheep *21* Paul Hurst
Black Sheep *32* Dick Huemer
Black Sheep *35* Allan Dwan
Black Sheep, The *68* Luciano Salce
Black Sheep, The *87* Román Chalbaud
Black Sheep of the Family, The *16* Jay Hunt
Black Sheep of Whitehall, The *41* Basil

Dearden, Will Hay
Black Shield of Falworth, The *54* Rudolph Maté
Black Side of Blackie, The *87* Benjamín Escamilla Espinosa, Ángel Rodríguez Vázquez
Black Six, The *74* Matt Cimber
Black Skull, The *34* Edwin Greenwood
Black Sleep, The *56* Reginald LeBorg
Black Smoke *20* René Coiffart, Louis Delluc
Black Snow *90* Fei Xie
Black Spider, The *20* William Humphrey
Black Spider, The *83* Mark M. Rissi
Black Spot, The *14* George Loane Tucker
Black Spurs *65* R. G. Springsteen
Black Stallion, The *48* Ray Taylor
Black Stallion, The *79* Carroll Ballard
Black Stallion Returns, The *83* Robert Dalva
Black Star *66* Giovanni Grimaldi
Black Starlet *74* Chris Munger
Black Streetfighter, The *76* Timothy Galfas, Richard Kaye
Black Sun *66* Denys De la Patellière
Black Sun *78* Arne Mattsson
Black Sun, The *79* Otakar Vávra
Black Sun 731 *89* T. F. Mous
Black Sunday *60* Mario Bava
Black Sunday *76* John Frankenheimer
Black Sunlight *23* J. A. Norling
Black Swan, The *24* Millard Webb
Black Swan, The *42* Henry King
Black Swan, The *52* Leonard Reeve
Black Swans *84* Ivan Nichev
Black Tanner, The *86* Xavier Koller
Black Tears *27* John Gorman
Black Tent, The *56* Brian Desmond Hurst
Black 13 *53* Ken Hughes
Black Thursday *74* Michel Mitrani
Black Tide *54* So Yamamura
Black Tide *58* C. M. Pennington-Richards
Black Tights *60* Terence Young
Black Torment, The *64* Robert Hartford-Davis
Black Trash *78* Chris Rowley
Black Triangles, The *16* Percy Stow
Black Tuesday *54* Hugo Fregonese
Black Tulip, The *21* Frank Richardson
Black Tulip, The *37* Alex Bryce
Black Tulip, The *63* Christian-Jaque
Black Tunnel *86* Federico Bruno
Black Veil for Lisa, A *68* Massimo Dallamano
Black Viper, The *08* D. W. Griffith
Black Vision *65* Stan Brakhage
Black Watch, The *29* John Ford, Lumsden Hare
Black Waters *29* Marshall Neilan
Black Waters *55* Youssef Chahine
Black Werewolf *74* Paul Annett
Black Whip, The *56* Charles Marquis Warren
Black Widow, The *46* Spencer G. Bennet, Fred C. Brannon
Black Widow *51* Vernon Sewell
Black Widow *54* Nunnally Johnson
Black Widow *86* Bob Rafelson
Black Windmill, The *74* Don Siegel
Black Wolf, The *16* Frank Reicher

Black Zoo 63 Robert Gordon
Blackbeard the Pirate 52 Raoul Walsh
Blackbeard's Ghost 67 Robert Stevenson
Blackbird 88 Miloš Radivojević
Blackbird Descending 77 Malcolm Le Grice
Blackbird Descending: Tense Alignment 77 Malcolm Le Grice
Blackbirds 20 John Francis Dillon
Blackboard Jungle, The 55 Richard Brooks
Blackboard Massacre 76 Renee Daalder
Blackboard Revue 40 Ubbe Iwerks
Blackened Hills 12 Allan Dwan
Blackenstein 73 William A. Levey
Blackguard, The 25 Graham Cutts
Blackhawk 52 Spencer G. Bennet, Fred F. Sears
Blackie 62 Richard Leacock*
Blackie and the Law 46 D. Ross Lederman
Blackie Booked on Suspicion 45 Arthur Dreifuss
Blackie Goes Hollywood 42 Michael Gordon
Blackie Goes to Hollywood 42 Michael Gordon
Blackie's Redemption 19 John Ince
Blackie's Rendezvous 45 Arthur Dreifuss
Blackjack 78 John Evans
Blackjack Ketchum, Desperado 56 Earl Bellamy
Blackmail 12 Edwin J. Collins
Blackmail 20 Dallas M. Fitzgerald
Blackmail 29 Alfred Hitchcock
Blackmail 39 H. C. Potter
Blackmail 47 Lesley Selander
Blackmailed 50 Marc Allégret
Blackmailer, The 07 Frank Mottershaw
Blackmailer, The 16 Rupert Julian
Blackmailer, The 19 Frank Carlton
Blackmailer, The 36 Gordon Wiles
Blackmailers, The 15 A. E. Coleby
Blackmailers, The 63 Rafael Gil
Blackout 40 Michael Powell, Emeric Pressburger
Blackout 50 Robert S. Baker, Monty Berman, John Gilling
Blackout 54 Terence Fisher
Blackout 78 Eddy Matalon
Blackout 85 Erik Gustavsen
Blackout 88 Doug Adams
Blackout Time 39 Nigel Byass
Blacks and Whites in Days and Nights 60 Stan Vanderbeek
Blacks Britannica 78 David Koff
Black's Mysterious Box 15 Raoul Barré
Blacksmith, The 21 Buster Keaton, Malcolm St. Clair
Blacksmith in His Workshop 1896 Georges Méliès
Blacksmiths 1895 Louis Lumière
Blacksnake 73 Russ Meyer
Blacktop 51 Charles Eames, Ray Eames
Blackwell Story, The 57 James Neilson
Blackwell's Island 39 William McGann
Blacula 72 William Crain
Blade 73 Ernest Pintoff
Blade af Satans Bog 19 Carl Theodor Dreyer
Blade in the Body, The 66 Domenico De Felice, Elio Scardamaglia

Blade in the Dark, A 83 Lamberto Bava
Blade Master, The 83 David Hills
Blade o' Grass 15 Burton George
Blade Runner 82 Ridley Scott
Blades 90 Thomas R. Rondinella
Blades of the Musketeers 53 Budd Boetticher
Bladys of the Stewpony 19 L. C. MacBean
Blago u Srebrnom Jezeru 62 Harald Reinl
Blaho Lásky 65 Jiří Brdečka
Blaise Pascal 72 Roberto Rossellini
Blåjackor 64 Arne Mattsson
Blake Edwards' That's Life! 86 Blake Edwards
Blake of Scotland Yard 27 Robert F. Hill
Blake of Scotland Yard 39 Robert F. Hill
Blake the Lawbreaker 28 George A. Cooper
Blakes Slept Here, The 54 Jacques Brunius, Richard Massingham
Blame It on Paradise 85 Francesco Nuti
Blame It on Rio 83 Stanley Donen
Blame It on the Night 84 Gene Taft
Blame the Woman 32 Maurice Elvey, Fred Niblo
Blanc Comme Neige 48 André Berthomieu
Blanc de Chine 88 Pierre Granier-Deferre
Blanc et le Noir, Le 30 Marc Allégret, Robert Florey
Blanche 70 Walerian Borowczyk
Blanche Comme Neige 08 Émile Cohl
Blanche et Marie 85 Jacques Rénard
Blanche Fury 47 Marc Allégret
Blanchette 21 René Hervil
Blancheville Monster 63 Alberto De Martino
Blanchisserie Américaine, La 15 Émile Cohl
Blanchisseuses, Les 1896 Georges Méliès
Blank Generation 79 Ulli Lommel
Blanke Slavin, De 69 Renee Daalder
Blanket Game, The 1895 Louis Lumière
Blarney 17 John McDonagh
Blarney 26 Marcel De Sano
Blarney 38 Harry O'Donovan
Blarney Kiss, The 33 Tom Walls
Blarney Stone, The 33 Tom Walls
Blason, Le 15 Louis Feuillade
Blasphemer, The 21 O. E. Goebel
Blast, The 69 Jules Bricken
Blast of Silence 61 Allen Baron
Blast Off 67 Don Sharp
Blast-Off Girls 67 Herschell Gordon Lewis
Blasted Hopes 24 Arthur Rosson
Blastfighter 84 Lamberto Bava
Blastfighter 85 Michel Gérard
Blatt Papier, Ein 16 Joe May
Blaubart 51 Christian-Jaque
Blaubart 84 Krzysztof Zanussi
Blaue Engel, Der 30 Josef von Sternberg
Blaue Licht, Das 32 Béla Balázs, Leni Riefenstahl
Blaue Strohut, Der 49 Victor Tourjansky
Blaue Stunde, Die 52 Veidt Harlan
Blaue vom Himmel, Das 34 Viktor Jansen
Blaufuchs, Der 38 Victor Tourjansky
Blaze, The 52 Alessandro Blasetti
Blaze 89 Ron Shelton
Blaze Away 22 William Hughes Curran

Blaze o' Glory 29 George Crone, Renaud Hoffman
Blaze of Glory, A 28 Mannie Davis
Blaze of Glory 50 John Rawlins
Blaze of Glory 63 Robert Lynn
Blaze of Noon 47 John Farrow
Blazes 61 Robert Breer
Blazing Across the Pecos 48 Ray Nazarro
Blazing Arrows 22 Henry McCarthy
Blazing Arrows 31 Otto Brower, David Burton
Blazing Away 28 Norman Taurog
Blazing Barriers 23 Del Henderson
Blazing Barriers 37 Aubrey H. Scotto
Blazing Bullets 51 Wallace Fox
Blazing Caravan, The 54 Ken Hughes
Blazing Days 27 William Wyler
Blazing Forest, The 52 Edward Ludwig
Blazing Frontier 43 Sam Newfield
Blazing Guns 35 Ray Heinz
Blazing Guns 43 Robert E. Tansey
Blazing Guns 50 Thomas Carr
Blazing Guns 72 Giuliano Carmineo
Blazing Justice 36 Albert Herman
Blazing Love 16 Kenean Buel
Blazing Magnum 76 Alberto De Martino
Blazing Saddles 73 Mel Brooks
Blazing Sand 60 Raphael Nussbaum
Blazing Six Shooters 40 Joseph H. Lewis
Blazing Sixes 37 Noel Mason Smith
Blazing Sky, The 52 Youssef Chahine
Blazing Stewardesses 75 Al Adamson
Blazing Sun, The 50 John English
Blazing Sun, The 52 Youssef Chahine
Blazing the Overland Trail 56 Spencer G. Bennet
Blazing the Trail 12 Thomas Ince
Blazing the Western Trail 45 Vernon Keays
Blazing Trail, The 21 Robert Thornby
Blazing Trail, The 49 Ray Nazarro
Bláznova Kronika 64 Karel Zeman
Blé en Herbe, Le 53 Claude Autant-Lara
Bleak House 18 Maurice Elvey
Bleak House 22 H. B. Parkinson
Bleak House 85 Ross Devenish
Bleak Moments 71 Mike Leigh
Blechtrommel, Die 79 Volker Schlöndorff
Bled, Le 29 Jean Renoir
Bleeding Snows 27 Grigori Kozintsev, Leonid Trauberg
Bleep 71 Richard Erdman
Bleierne Zeit, Die 81 Margarethe von Trotta
Błękitny Krzyż 55 Andrzej Munk
Bless 'Em All 49 Robert Jordan Hill
Bless 'Em All 84 Sig Shore
Bless the Beasts and Children 71 Stanley Kramer
Bless Their Little Hearts 84 Billy Woodberry
Bless This House 72 Gerald Thomas
Blessed Event 32 Roy Del Ruth
Blessings of the Earth 86 Karin Brandauer
Blessure, La 25 Marco De Gastyne
Blessure d'Amour 16 Georges Monca
Blessure 1985 85 Michel Gérard
Bleu Comme l'Enfer 85 Yves Boisset
Bleus de l'Amour, Les 18 Henri Desfontaines

Bleus du Ciel, Les *33* Henri Decoin
Bliggs Family at the Zoo, The *12* H. Oceano Martinek
Bliggs on the Briny *13* Charles Raymond
Blighty *26* Adrian Brunel
Blind *30* Mikhail Kalatozov
Blind *86* Frederick Wiseman
Blind Adventure, The *18* Wesley Ruggles
Blind Adventure *33* Ernest B. Schoedsack
Blind Alibi *38* Lew Landers
Blind Alley *39* Charles Vidor
Blind Alley *74* Alexander Kluge, Edgar Reitz
Blind Alley *83* Larry Cohen
Blind Alleys *27* Frank Tuttle
Blind Bargain, A *22* Wallace Worsley
Blind Beast, The *69* Yasuzo Masumura
Blind Bird *62* Boris Dolin
Blind Boy, The *17* Jack Clare, Edwin J. Collins
Blind Chance *81* Krzysztof Kieslowski
Blind Circumstances *22* Milburn Morante
Blind Corner *63* Lance Comfort
Blind Date *34* Roy William Neill
Blind Date *59* Joseph Losey
Blind Date *84* Nico Mastorakis
Blind Date *87* Blake Edwards
Blind Dead, The *71* Amando De Ossorio
Blind Desire *45* Jean Delannoy
Blind Devotion *61* Teinosuke Kinugasa
Blind Director, The *85* Alexander Kluge
Blind Dogs *39* Anthony Asquith
Blind Endeavor *86* Livia Gyarmathy
Blind Fate *14* Cecil M. Hepworth
Blind Fate *15* August Blom
Blind Folly *39* Reginald Denham
Blind Fury *89* Phillip Noyce
Blind Goddess, The *26* Victor Fleming
Blind Goddess, The *47* Harold French
Blind Hearts *21* Rowland V. Lee
Blind Heroine, The *12* Bert Haldane
Blind Husbands *19* Erich von Stroheim
Blind Justice *15* Benjamin Christensen
Blind Justice *34* Bernard Vorhaus
Blind Love *12* D. W. Griffith
Blind Love, The *20* Oliver D. Bailey
Blind Man, The *09* Theo Bouwmeester
Blind Man of Verdun, The *16* A. V. Bramble
Blind Man's Bluff *03* Arthur Cooper
Blind Man's Bluff *36* Albert Parker
Blind Man's Bluff *52* Charles Saunders
Blind Man's Bluff *67* Santos Alcocer
Blind Man's Bluff *77* Gerry O'Hara
Blind Man's Buff *05* Percy Stow
Blind Man's Buff *14* Ernst Lubitsch
Blind Man's Buff *67* Santos Alcocer
Blind Man's Child, The *05* Alf Collins
Blind Man's Dog, The *12* Lewin Fitzhamon
Blind Man's Eyes *19* John Ince
Blind Man's Holiday *17* Martin Justice
Blind Man's Luck *17* George Fitzmaurice
Blind Owl, The *87* Raúl Ruiz
Blind Princess and the Poet, The *11* D. W. Griffith
Blind Rage *78* Efren C. Piñon
Blind Shot *88* Peter Walker
Blind Spot *32* John Daumery
Blind Spot *47* Robert Gordon

Blind Spot *58* Peter Maxwell
Blind Swordsman's Rescue, The *67* Satsuo Yamamoto
Blind Terror *71* Richard Fleischer
Blind Trail *26* Leo D. Maloney
Blind Venus *40* Abel Gance
Blind Violinist, The *07* Arthur Gilbert
Blind White Duration *67* Malcolm Le Grice
Blind Wives *20* Charles Brabin
Blind Wives *30* John M. Stahl
Blind Woman's Curse, The *70* Teruo Ishii
Blind Youth *20* Edward Sloman
Blinde Kuh *14* Ernst Lubitsch
Blinde Leidenschaften *88* Sven Severin
Blinde Passagier *37* Frem Saver
Blinde Skæbne, Den *15* August Blom
Blindfold *28* Charles Klein
Blindfold *65* Philip Dunne
Blindfold *74* András Kovács
Blindfolded *18* Raymond B. West
Blindfolded *78* Carlos Saura
Blinding Trail, The *19* Paul Powell
Blindman *71* Ferdinando Baldi
Blindness of Devotion *15* J. Gordon Edwards
Blindness of Divorce, The *18* Frank Lloyd
Blindness of Fortune, The *17* Frank Wilson
Blindness of Love, The *16* Charles T. Horan
Blindness of Virtue, The *15* Joseph Byron Totten
Blindside *87* Paul Lynch
Blinkende Fenster, Das *19* Piel Jutzi
Blinker's Spy Spotter *71* Jack Stephens
Blinkeyes *26* George Pearson
Blinkity Blank *54* Norman McLaren
Blinky *23* Edward Sedgwick
Bliss *67* Gregory Markopoulos
Bliss *85* Ray Lawrence
Bliss of Love, The *65* Jiří Brdečka
Bliss of Mrs. Blossom, The *68* Joseph McGrath
Blithe Spirit *44* David Lean
Blitz on Britain *60* Harry Booth
Blitz Wolf, The *42* Tex Avery
Blizzard, The *24* Mauritz Stiller
Blob, The *58* Irvin S. Yeaworth, Jr.
Blob, The *88* Chuck Russell
Block Busters *44* Wallace Fox
Block 15 *59* Evald Schorm
Block-Heads *38* John G. Blystone
Block Notes—Appunti di un Regista *68* Federico Fellini
Block-Notes di un Regista *68* Federico Fellini
Block Signal, The *26* Frank O'Connor
Blockade *28* Geoffrey Barkas, Michael Barringer
Blockade *28* George B. Seitz
Blockade *38* William Dieterle
Blocked Trail, The *43* Elmer Clifton
Blockhouse, The *73* Clive Rees
Blodets Röst *12* Victor Sjöström
Blödiga Tiden, Den *59* Ingemar Ejve, Erwin Leiser, Tore Sjöberg
Bloedverwanten *77* Wim Lindner
Blok 15 *59* Evald Schorm
Blomstertid, Den *39* Alf Sjöberg

Blond Dolly *87* Gerrit van Elst
Blonde Alibi *46* Will Jason
Blonde at the Bar, The *86* Ventura Pons
Blonde Bait *56* Elmo Williams
Blonde Bandit, The *49* Harry Keller
Blonde Blackmailer *55* Charles Deane
Blonde Bombshell, The *33* Victor Fleming
Blonde Captive *32* Clinton Childs, Paul C. Withington
Blonde Carmen, Die *39* Viktor Jansen
Blonde Cheat *38* Joseph Santley
Blonde Christl, Die *34* Franz Seitz
Blonde Comet, The *41* William Beaudine
Blonde Crazy *31* Roy Del Ruth
Blonde de Pekin, Le *67* Nicolas Gessner
Blonde Dream, A *32* Paul Martin
Blonde Dynamite *49* William Beaudine
Blonde Émoustillante, Une *80* Jiří Menzel
Blonde Fever *44* Richard Whorf
Blonde for a Day *46* Sam Newfield
Blonde for a Night, A *28* E. Mason Hopper
Blonde for Danger *48* Horace Shepherd
Blonde for Danger *57* Marc Allégret
Blonde Frau des Maharadscha, Die *62* Veidt Harlan
Blonde from Brooklyn, The *45* Del Lord
Blonde from Peking, The *67* Nicolas Gessner
Blonde from Singapore, The *41* Edward Dmytryk
Blonde Goddess *82* Bill Eagle
Blonde Ice *49* Jack Bernhard
Blonde in a White Car *58* Robert Hossein
Blonde in Love, A *65* Miloš Forman
Blonde Inspiration *40* Busby Berkeley
Blonde Nachtigall, Die *31* Johannes Meyer
Blonde Nightingale *31* Johannes Meyer
Blonde or Brunette *27* Richard Rosson
Blonde Pickup *55* Robert C. Dertano
Blonde Pressure *31* Edward Buzzell
Blonde Ransom *45* William Beaudine
Blonde Reporter, The *31* Alfred Santell
Blonde Saint, The *26* Svend Gade
Blonde Savage *47* Steve Sekely
Blonde Sinner *56* J. Lee-Thompson
Blonde Trouble *37* George Archainbaud
Blonde Vampire, The *22* Wray Physioc
Blonde Venus *32* Josef von Sternberg
Blonder Traum, Ein *32* Paul Martin
Blondes at Work *38* Frank McDonald
Blondes Beware *28* Norman Taurog
Blondes by Choice *27* Hampton Del Ruth
Blondes for Danger *38* Jack Raymond
Blondes Prefer Bonds *31* Lewis R. Foster
Blonde's Revenge, A *26* Edward F. Cline
Blondie *38* Frank R. Strayer
Blondie Brings Up Baby *39* Frank R. Strayer
Blondie for Victory *42* Frank R. Strayer
Blondie Goes Latin *41* Frank R. Strayer
Blondie Goes to College *42* Frank R. Strayer
Blondie Has Servant Trouble *40* Frank R. Strayer
Blondie Hits the Jackpot *49* Edward Bernds
Blondie in Society *41* Frank R. Strayer

Blondie in the Dough 47 Abby Berlin
Blondie Johnson 33 Ray Enright
Blondie Knows Best 46 Abby Berlin
Blondie Meets the Boss 39 Frank R. Strayer
Blondie of the Follies 32 Edmund Goulding
Blondie on a Budget 40 Frank R. Strayer
Blondie Plays Cupid 40 Frank R. Strayer
Blondie Takes a Vacation 39 Frank R. Strayer
Blondie's Anniversary 47 Abby Berlin
Blondie's Big Deal 49 Edward Bernds
Blondie's Big Moment 47 Abby Berlin
Blondie's Blessed Event 42 Frank R. Strayer
Blondie's Hero 50 Edward Bernds
Blondie's Holiday 47 Abby Berlin
Blondie's Lucky Day 46 Abby Berlin
Blondie's Reward 48 Abby Berlin
Blondie's Secret 48 Edward Bernds
Blood 71 Mario Caiano
Blood 74 Andy Milligan
Blood 75 Alexis Krasilovsky
Blood Alley 55 William A. Wellman
Blood and Black Lace 64 Mario Bava
Blood and Bosh 13 Hay Plumb
Blood and Defiance 62 Nick Nostro
Blood and Fire 45 Anders Henrikson
Blood and Guns 79 Giulio Petroni
Blood and Guts 78 Paul Lynch
Blood and Lace 70 Philip Gilbert
Blood and Roses 60 Roger Vadim
Blood and Sand 22 Fred Niblo
Blood and Sand 41 Rouben Mamoulian
Blood and Sand 87 Jeanne Labrune
Blood and Sand 89 Javier Elorrieta
Blood and Soul 22 Kenji Mizoguchi
Blood and Steel 25 John P. McGowan
Blood and Steel 59 Bernard Kowalski
Blood and Thunder 30 George Stevens
Blood and Water 13 Alice Guy-Blaché
Blood Arrow 58 Charles Marquis Warren
Blood Baron, The 72 Mario Bava
Blood Barrier, The 20 J. Stuart Blackton
Blood Barrier 79 Christopher Leitch
Blood Bath 66 Jack Hill, Stephanie Rothman
Blood Bath 71 Mario Bava
Blood Bath 76 Joel M. Reed
Blood Beach 80 Jeffrey Bloom
Blood Beast from Hell 67 Vernon Sewell
Blood Beast from Outer Space 65 John Gilling
Blood Beast Terror, The 67 Vernon Sewell
Blood Bond 37 Carmine Gallone
Blood Brides 69 Mario Bava
Blood Brother, The 32 Harry Fraser
Blood Brothers 29 Walter Lang
Blood Brothers 53 Robert Snyder
Blood Ceremony 72 Jorge Grau
Blood Couple 73 Bill Gunn
Blood Creature 59 Gerry De Leon, Eddie Romero
Blood Crowd, The 69 Alf Kjellin
Blood Cult of Shangri-La, The 75 Terry Becker
Blood Demon, The 67 Harald Reinl
Blood Diner 87 Jackie Kong
Blood Doctor 68 Gerry De Leon, Eddie

Romero
Blood Drinkers, The 66 Gerry De Leon
Blood Feast, The 59 Leopoldo Torre-Nilsson
Blood Feast 63 Herschell Gordon Lewis
Blood Feast 76 Emilio Miraglia
Blood Feud 79 Lina Wertmuller
Blood Fiend, The 66 Samuel Gallu
Blood for Blood, Death for Death 41 Dziga Vertov
Blood for Blood, Life for Life 41 Dziga Vertov
Blood for Dracula 73 Antonio Margheriti, Paul Morrissey
Blood from the Mummy's Tomb 71 Michael Carreras, Seth Holt
Blood Hook 87 James Mallon
Blood in the Streets 75 Sergio Sollima
Blood Is My Heritage 57 Herbert L. Strock
Blood Island 66 David Greene
Blood Kin 69 Sidney Lumet
Blood Legacy 71 Carl Monson
Blood Legacy 78 Andy Milligan
Blood Mad 78 Ross Hagen
Blood Mania 70 Robert Vincent O'Neil
Blood Money 21 Fred Goodwins
Blood Money 33 Rowland Brown
Blood Money 62 Ralph Nelson
Blood Money 74 Antonio Margheriti
Blood Monster 71 Ray Dennis Steckler
Blood Need Not Be Spilled 17 Yakov Protazanov
Blood of a Poet, The 30 Jean Cocteau
Blood of Animals, The 48 Georges Franju
Blood of Brothers 86 Govind Nihalani
Blood of Dr. Jekyll, The 81 Walerian Borowczyk
Blood of Dracula 57 Herbert L. Strock
Blood of Dracula's Castle 67 Al Adamson, Jean Hewitt
Blood of Frankenstein 70 Al Adamson
Blood of Fu Manchu, The 68 Jesús Franco
Blood of Ghastly Horror 65 Al Adamson
Blood of Heroes, The 90 David Peoples
Blood of His Fathers 17 Harrish Ingraham
Blood of His Fathers 17 Harrish Ingraham
Blood of Hussein, The 81 Jamil Dehlavi
Blood of Jesus 41 Spencer Williams
Blood of Minas 28 Humberto Mauro
Blood of Nostradamus, The 59 Federico Curiel, Alberto Mariscal
Blood of Others, The 83 Claude Chabrol
Blood of the Beasts 48 Georges Franju
Blood of the Condor 69 Jorge Sanjinés
Blood of the Demon 57 Herbert L. Strock
Blood of the Iron Maiden 69 Ben Benoit
Blood of the Man Devil 65 Harold Daniels, Reginald LeBorg
Blood of the Trevors 18 William P. S. Earle
Blood of the Undead 76 Peter Walker
Blood of the Vampire 58 Henry Cass
Blood on Easter Sunday 49 Giuseppe De Santis
Blood on His Lips 59 Thomas Bontross, Gianbatista Cassarino, Robert Clarke
Blood on His Sword 61 André Hunebelle
Blood on My Hands 48 Norman Foster
Blood on Satan's Claw, The 70 Piers Haggard
Blood on the Arrow 64 Sidney Salkow

Blood on the Balcony 64 Pasquale Prunas
Blood on the Land 65 Vassilis Georgiades
Blood on the Moon 48 Robert Wise
Blood on the Moon 87 James B. Harris
Blood on the Sun 45 Frank Lloyd
Blood Orange 53 Terence Fisher
Blood Orgy 71 Herschell Gordon Lewis
Blood Orgy of the She-Devils 72 Ted V. Mikels
Blood Queen 72 Radley Metzger
Blood Red 88 Peter Masterson
Blood Red Roses 86 John McGrath
Blood Reincarnation 74 Shan-hsi Ting
Blood Relations 77 Wim Lindner
Blood Relations 88 Graeme Campbell
Blood Relatives 77 Claude Chabrol
Blood Rites 68 Andy Milligan
Blood River 67 Giuseppe Colizzi
Blood River 68 George Breakston
Blood Rose, The 69 Claude Mulot
Blood Ruby, The 14 Maurice Costello
Blood Salvage 90 Tucker Johnston
Blood Seedling, The 15 Tom Santschi
Blood Seekers, The 69 Kent Osborne
Blood Seekers, The 71 Al Adamson
Blood Shack 71 Ray Dennis Steckler
Blood Ship, The 27 George B. Seitz
Blood Simple 84 Joel Coen
Blood Sisters 72 Brian DePalma
Blood Sisters 87 Roberta Findlay
Blood Song 82 Alan J. Levi
Blood-Spattered Bride, The 69 Vicente Aranda
Blood-Splattered Bride, The 69 Vicente Aranda
Blood Stain, The 12 Alice Guy-Blaché
Blood Suckers, The 64 Freddie Francis
Blood Suckers, The 67 David L. Hewitt
Blood, Sweat and Fear 75 Stevio Massi
Blood Sword of the 99th Virgin, The 59 Morihei Magatani
Blood Tells 16 Edwin J. Collins
Blood Tells, or The Anti-Frivolity League 16 Edwin J. Collins
Blood Test 23 Don Marquis
Blood Thirst 65 Newton Arnold
Blood Tide 80 Richard Jeffries
Blood Ties 86 Giacomo Battiato
Blood Tracks 87 Mats Olsson
Blood Virgin, The 74 José Ramón Larraz
Blood Waters of Dr. Z 82 Don Barton
Blood Wedding 73 Claude Chabrol
Blood Wedding 81 Carlos Saura
Blood Will Have Blood 71 Peter Sykes
Blood Will Tell 27 Ray Flynn
Bloodbath at the House of Death 83 Ray Cameron
Bloodbrothers 78 Robert Mulligan
Bloodeaters 79 Chuck McCrann
Bloodfist 89 Terence H. Winkless
Bloodhound, The 25 William James Craft
Bloodhounds of Broadway 52 Harmon Jones
Bloodhounds of Broadway 89 Howard Brookner
Bloodhounds of the North 13 Allan Dwan
Bloodless Vampire, The 65 Michael Du Pont
Bloodline 79 Terence Young
Bloodlust 59 Ralph Brooke

Blue Squadron, The *34* George King
Blue Squadron, The *38* Nelo Cosini
Blue Steel *34* Robert North Bradbury
Blue Steel *89* Kathryn Bigelow
Blue Streak, The *17* William Nigh
Blue Streak, The *26* Noel Mason Smith
Blue Streak McCoy *20* B. Reeves Eason
Blue Streak O'Neil *26* Paul Hurst
Blue Summer *71* Chuck Vincent
Blue Sunday *21* Charlie Chase
Blue Sunshine *76* Jeff Lieberman
Blue Thunder *82* John Badham
Blue Tunes *60* Robert Henryson
Blue Veil, The *42* Jean Stelli
Blue Veil, The *51* Kurt Bernhardt
Blue Velvet *86* David Lynch
Blue Water, White Death *71* Peter Gimbel, James Lipscomb
Blue Wet-Nurse, The *86* Markku Lehmuskallio
Blue White *65* Stan Brakhage
Blue, White and Perfect *41* Herbert I. Leeds
Bluebeard *01* Georges Méliès
Bluebeard *09* J. Searle Dawley
Bluebeard *44* Edgar G. Ulmer
Bluebeard *51* Christian-Jaque
Bluebeard *62* Claude Chabrol
Bluebeard *72* Edward Dmytryk
Bluebeard *84* Krzysztof Zanussi
Bluebeard Junior *22* Scott R. Dunlap
Bluebeard's Castle *64* Michael Powell
Bluebeard's Eighth Wife *23* Sam Wood
Bluebeard's Eighth Wife *38* Ernst Lubitsch
Bluebeard's Seven Wives *25* Alfred Santell
Bluebeard's Ten Honeymoons *60* W. Lee Wilder
Blueberry Hill *88* Strathford Hamilton
Bluebird's Baby *38* Charles Mintz
Bluebottles *28* Ivor Montagu
Bluefin Fury *55* Vittorio De Seta
Blueprint for Danger *52* Morton M. Lewis
Blueprint for Murder, A *53* Andrew L. Stone
Blueprint for Robbery *61* Jerry Hopper
Blues Accordin' to Lightnin' Hopkins, The *68* Les Blank
Blues Band, The *81* Peter Sykes
Blues Brothers, The *80* John Landis
Blues Busters *50* William Beaudine
Blues della Domenica, I *51* Valerio Zurlini
Blues for Lovers *64* Paul Henreid
Blues in the Night *41* Anatole Litvak
Blues Lahofesh Hagodol *87* Renen Schorr
Blues Metropolitano *85* Salvatore Piscicelli
Blues Pattern *56* Ernest Pintoff
Bluff *15* Arthur Backner
Bluff, Le *16* Jacques Feyder
Bluff *21* Geoffrey H. Malins
Bluff *24* Sam Wood
Bluff, Storie di Truffe e di Imbraglione *75* Sergio Corbucci
Bluffer, The *19* Travers Vale
Bluffer, The *30* Mack Sennett
Bluffers, The *15* B. Reeves Eason
Blum Affair, The *48* Erich Engel
Blume in Love *73* Paul Mazursky
Blume von Hawaii, Die *33* Richard Oswald
Blumen aus Nizza *36* Augusto Genina

Blumen für den Mann im Mond *75* Rolf Losansky
Blumenfrau von Lindenau, Die *31* Georg Jacoby
Blunden Harbor *52* Sidney Peterson
Blunder Below *42* Dave Fleischer
Blundering Boob, The *14* Charles Chaplin
Blunderland of Big Game, The *25* Adrian Brunel
Blunders of Mr. Butterbun: Trips and Tribunals, The *18* Fred Rains
Blunders of Mr. Butterbun: Unexpected Treasure, The *18* Fred Rains
Blusenkönig, Der *17* Ernst Lubitsch
Blushing Bride, The *21* Jules G. Furthman
Blushing Brides *30* Harry Beaumont
Blushing Charlie *70* Vilgot Sjöman
Blut an den Lippen *70* Harry Kümel
Blut und Boden *33* Walter Ruttmann
Blüten, Gauner und Die Nacht von Nizza *66* Jean-Paul Le Chanois
Blutgeld, Das *13* Friedrich Feher
Blutige Seide *64* Mario Bava
Blutigen Geier von Alaska, Die *73* Harald Reinl
Boadicea *26* Sinclair Hill
Boarding House, The *17* Raoul Barré, Charles Bowers
Boarding House *84* John Wintergate
Boarding House Blues *48* Josh Binney
Boarding House Mystery, A *12* Edwin S. Porter
Boarding House Scandal, A *16* Joe Evans
Boarding School, The *69* Narciso Ibáñez Serrador
Boarding School *77* André Farwagi
Boarding School Girls *05* Edwin S. Porter
Boardwalk *79* Stephen Verona
Boaster, The *07* Lewin Fitzhamon
Boaster, The *26* Duke Worne
Boasts and Boldness *17* Larry Semon
Boat, The *21* Edward F. Cline, Buster Keaton
Boat, The *56* Kaneto Shindo
Boat, The *61* Jan Troell
Boat, The *81* Wolfgang Petersen
Boat from Shanghai *31* Guy Newall
Boat Is Full, The *80* Markus Imhoof
Boat Leaving the Harbor *1895* Louis Lumière
Boat Leaving the Harbor of Trouville *1896* Georges Méliès
Boat People *82* Ann Hui
Boating Incident, A *05* William Haggar
Boatniks, The *70* Norman Tokar
Boatswain's Daughter, The *13* Theo Bouwmeester
Boatswain's Mate, The *24* H. Manning Haynes
Bob & Carol & Ted & Alice *69* Paul Mazursky
Bob and Sally *48* Erle C. Kenton
Bob Downe's Schooldays *16* Dave Aylott
Bob Hampton of Placer *21* Marshall Neilan
Bob Kick, l'Enfant Terrible *03* Georges Méliès
Bob Kick, the Mischievous Kid *03* Georges Méliès
Bob le Flambeur *55* Jean-Pierre Melville

Bob Marley and the Wailers Live *78* Keith MacMillan
Bob Mathias Story, The *54* Francis D. Lyon
Bob, Son of Battle *47* Louis King
Bob the Coster's Pony *12* A. E. Coleby
Bob, the Gambler *55* Jean-Pierre Melville
Boba Shahnai *88* Ajit Ganguly
Bobbed Hair *22* Thomas Heffron
Bobbed Hair *25* Alan Crosland
Bobbie Jo and the Outlaw *76* Mark L. Lester
Bobbie of the Ballet *16* Joseph De Grasse
Bobbikins *59* Robert Day
Bobbikins and the Bathing Belles *16* Dave Aylott
Bobby *74* Raj Kapoor
Bobby Bumps *20* Earl Hurd
Bobby Bumps Adopts a Turtle *17* Earl Hurd
Bobby Bumps' Adventures *15* Earl Hurd
Bobby Bumps' Amusement Park *17* Earl Hurd
Bobby Bumps and Co. *25* Earl Hurd
Bobby Bumps and Fido's Birthday Party *17* Earl Hurd
Bobby Bumps and His Goatmobile *16* Earl Hurd
Bobby Bumps and His Pointer Pup *16* Earl Hurd
Bobby Bumps and the Detective Story *16* Earl Hurd
Bobby Bumps and the Fly Swatter *16* Earl Hurd
Bobby Bumps and the Hypnotic Eye *19* Earl Hurd
Bobby Bumps and the Sand Lizard *19* Earl Hurd
Bobby Bumps and the Speckled Death *18* Earl Hurd
Bobby Bumps and the Stork *16* Earl Hurd
Bobby Bumps at School *22* Earl Hurd
Bobby Bumps at the Circus *16* Earl Hurd
Bobby Bumps at the Dentist *18* Earl Hurd
Bobby Bumps, Baseball Champion *17* Earl Hurd
Bobby Bumps Becomes an Ace *18* Earl Hurd
Bobby Bumps Caught in the Jamb *18* Earl Hurd
Bobby Bumps Checkmated *21* Earl Hurd
Bobby Bumps, Chef *17* Earl Hurd
Bobby Bumps, Daylight Camper *17* Earl Hurd
Bobby Bumps' Detective Story *16* Earl Hurd
Bobby Bumps' Disappearing Gun *18* Earl Hurd
Bobby Bumps, Early Shopper *17* Earl Hurd
Bobby Bumps' Eel-ectric Launch *19* Earl Hurd
Bobby Bumps' Fight *18* Earl Hurd
Bobby Bumps Films a Fire *18* Earl Hurd
Bobby Bumps' Fly Swatter *16* Earl Hurd
Bobby Bumps' Fourth *17* Earl Hurd
Bobby Bumps Gets a Substitute *16* Earl Hurd
Bobby Bumps Gets Pa's Goat *15* Earl Hurd

Bobby Bumps Goes Fishing *16* Earl Hurd
Bobby Bumps Goes Shopping *17* Earl Hurd
Bobby Bumps Helps Out a Book Agent *16* Earl Hurd
Bobby Bumps in Before and After *18* Earl Hurd
Bobby Bumps in Hunting and Fishing *21* Earl Hurd
Bobby Bumps in Shadow Boxing *21* Earl Hurd
Bobby Bumps in The Great Divide *17* Earl Hurd
Bobby Bumps' Incubator *18* Earl Hurd
Bobby Bumps' Last Smoke *19* Earl Hurd
Bobby Bumps Loses His Pup *16* Earl Hurd
Bobby Bumps' Lucky Day *19* Earl Hurd
Bobby Bumps' Night Out with Some Night Owls *19* Earl Hurd
Bobby Bumps, Office Boy *17* Earl Hurd
Bobby Bumps on the Doughnut Trail *18* Earl Hurd
Bobby Bumps on the Road *18* Earl Hurd
Bobby Bumps' Orchestra *20* Earl Hurd
Bobby Bumps Out West *18* Earl Hurd
Bobby Bumps Outwits the Dogcatcher *17* Earl Hurd
Bobby Bumps' Pup Gets the Flea-enza *19* Earl Hurd
Bobby Bumps Puts a Beanery on the Bum *18* Earl Hurd
Bobby Bumps Queers the Choir *16* Earl Hurd
Bobby Bumps, Sharpshooter *18* Earl Hurd
Bobby Bumps Starts a Lodge *16* Earl Hurd
Bobby Bumps Starts for School *17* Earl Hurd
Bobby Bumps, Submarine Chaser *17* Earl Hurd
Bobby Bumps, Surf Rider *17* Earl Hurd
Bobby Bumps' Tank *17* Earl Hurd
Bobby Bumps the Cave Man *20* Earl Hurd
Bobby Bumps Throwing the Ball *19* Earl Hurd
Bobby Bumps Volunteers *17* Earl Hurd
Bobby Bumps Working on an Idea *21* Earl Hurd
Bobby Bumps' World Serious *17* Earl Hurd
Bobby Deerfield *77* Sydney Pollack
Bobby, Movie Director *17* Wesley Ruggles
Bobby, Philanthropist *17* Wesley Ruggles
Bobby the Boy Scout, or The Boy Detective *09* Percy Stow
Bobby the Coward *11* D. W. Griffith
Bobby, the Pacifist *17* Wesley Ruggles
Bobby Ware Is Missing *55* Thomas Carr
Bobby Wideawake *09* Walter R. Booth
Bobby's Birthday *07* James A. Williamson
Bobby's Bravery *17* Wesley Ruggles
Bobby's Downfall, The *04* Frank Mottershaw
Bobby's Kodak *08* Wallace McCutcheon
Bobby's Letter *12* A. E. Coleby
Bobby's Nightmare, The *05* Alf Collins
Bóbita *64* Márta Mészáros
Bobo, The *67* Robert Parrish
Bobo *86* Melvin Frank
Bobo, O *87* José Alvaro Morais
Bobosse *59* Étienne Périer

Bobs *28* Jean Grémillon
Bob's Deception *12* Edwin S. Porter
Bob's Your Uncle *41* Oswald Mitchell
Boca de Ouro, A *62* Nelson Pereira Dos Santos
Boca del Lobo, La *88* Francisco José Lombardi
Bocal aux Poissons Rouges *1895* Louis Lumière
Boccaccio *20* Michael Curtiz
Boccaccio *36* Herbert Maisch
Boccaccio in Hungary *81* Miklós Jancsó
Boccaccio '70 *62* Vittorio De Sica, Federico Fellini, Mario Monicelli, Luchino Visconti
Bockbierfest *30* Carl Boese
Boda del Acordeonista, La *86* Luis Fernando Bottia
Bodakungen *20* Gustaf Molander
Bodas de Sangre *39* Edmundo Guibourg
Bodas de Sangre *81* Carlos Saura
Boden's Boy *23* Henry Edwards
Bødes Der For, Det *11* August Blom
Bodiam Castle *26* A. V. Bramble
Bodiam Castle and Eric the Slender *26* A. V. Bramble
Bodies Bear Traces of Carnal Violence, The *73* Sergio Martino
Body, The *70* Roy Battersby
Body and Soul *20* Charles Swickard
Body and Soul *24* Oscar Micheaux
Body and Soul *27* Reginald Barker
Body and Soul *31* Alfred Santell
Body and Soul *45* Delmer Daves
Body and Soul *47* Robert Rossen
Body and Soul *81* George Bowers
Body and the Whip, The *63* Mario Bava
Body Beat *86* Ted Mather
Body Beautiful *28* Yasujiro Ozu
Body Beautiful *53* Max Nosseck
Body Beneath, The *70* Andy Milligan
Body Chemistry *90* Kristine Peterson
Body Count *88* Paul Leder
Body Disappears, The *41* D. Ross Lederman
Body Double *84* Brian DePalma
Body Fever *69* Ray Dennis Steckler
Body Heat *81* Lawrence Kasdan
Body in the Library, The *87* Silvio Narizzano
Body in the Web *59* Fritz Böttger
Body Is a Shell, The *57* Merle S. Gould
Body Is Missing, The *62* Jean Girault
Body Punch, The *29* Leigh Jason
Body Rock *84* Marcelo Epstein
Body Said No!, The *50* Val Guest
Body Slam *86* Hal Needham
Body Snatcher, The *45* Robert Wise
Body Stealers, The *69* Gerry Levy
Body Vanishes, The *39* Walter Tennyson
Bodyguard *44* Joseph Barbera, William Hanna
Bodyguard *48* Richard Fleischer
Bodyguard, The *61* Akira Kurosawa
Bodyguard, The *76* Simon Nuchtern
Bodyhold *49* Seymour Friedman
Boefje *39* Douglas Sirk
Boeing Boeing *65* John Rich
Boeing — The Leading Edge *66* Charles Eames, Ray Eames

Boer Boersen, Jr. *39* Toralf Sandø
Boer War, The *14* George Melford
Boesman and Lena *74* Ross Devenish
Bœuf sur la Langue, Le *33* Christian-Jaque
Boevoi Kinosbornik 1 *41* Sergei Gerasimov
Boevoi Kinosbornik 2 *41* Grigori Kozintsev
Boevoi Kinosbornik 3 *41* Boris Barnet
Boevoi Kinosbornik 9 *41* Mark Donskoi
Boevoi Kinosbornik 10 *42* Boris Barnet
Boevoi Kinosbornik 13 *43* Lev Kuleshov
Bof *72* Claude Faraldo
Bofors Gun, The *68* Jack Gold
Bog *78* Don Keeslar
Bogard *75* Timothy Galfas
Bogataya Nevesta *38* Ivan Pyriev
Bogdan Khmelnitsky *41* Igor Savchenko
Bogey Man, The *80* Ulli Lommel
Boggy Creek II *85* Charles B. Pierce
Bogus Bandits *33* Hal Roach, Charles Rogers
Bogus House Agent, The *26* F. W. Engholm
Bogus Motor Elopement, A *09* Walter R. Booth
Bohater Roku *87* Feliks Falk
Bohaterstwo Polskiego Skauta *19* Richard Boleslawski
Bohème, La *16* Albert Capellani
Bohème, La *26* King Vidor
Bohème, La *65* Franco Zeffirelli
Bohème, La *87* Luigi Comencini
Bohemian Dancer *29* Fred Zelnik
Bohemian Girl, The *22* Harley Knoles
Bohemian Girl, The *27* H. B. Parkinson
Bohemian Girl, The *35* James W. Horne, Charles Rogers
Bohemian Rapture *48* Václav Krška
Bohemios *35* R. Portas
Boi pod Tsaritsinom *19* Dziga Vertov
Boia di Lilla, Il *52* Vittorio Cottafavi
Boia Scarlatto, Il *65* Massimo Pupillo
Boiler Room, The *87* John Golden
Boilesk *33* Dave Fleischer
Boiling Point, The *32* George Melford
Boiling Sea, The *85* King Hu
Boin-n-g *63* Herschell Gordon Lewis
Bois de Boulogne *1896* Georges Méliès
Bois de Boulogne — Porte de Madrid *1896* Georges Méliès
Bois des Amants, Le *60* Claude Autant-Lara
Bois Noirs, Les *89* Jacques Deray
Boîte à Malice, La *03* Georges Méliès
Boîte à Musique *61* Walerian Borowczyk, Jan Lenica
Boîte à Soleil, La *88* Jean-Pierre Lefèbvre
Boîte aux Rêves, La *43* Yves Allégret, Jean Choux
Boîte Diabolique, La *11* Émile Cohl
Boj om Moskva *85* Yuri Ozerov
Boje Sanjaju *58* Dušan Makavejev
Bokays and Brickbatz *25* William C. Nolan
Bokhandlaren Som Slutade Bada *68* Jarl Kulle
Boks *61* Jerzy Skolimowski
Bokser *67* Julian Dziedzina
Boku no Marumage *33* Mikio Naruse
Bokutō Kaidan *60* Shiro Toyoda

Bol d'Air à Loué, Un *62* François
Reichenbach
Bolchaia Semia *54* Josef Heifits
Bold Adventure, The *56* Joris Ivens,
Gérard Philipe
Bold Adventuress, A *15* Walter West
Bold and the Brave, The *56* Lewis R.
Foster
Bold Bad Man, A *18* Gregory La Cava
Bold Caballero, The *36* Wells Root
Bold Cavalier, The *36* Wells Root
Bold Emmett, Ireland's Martyr *15* Sidney
Olcott
Bold Frontiersman, The *48* Philip Ford
Bold Ones, The *50* Konstantin Yudin
Bold Seven, The *36* Sergei Gerasimov
Bold Venture, A *12* Warwick Buckland
Boldest Job in the West, The *71* José An-
tonio De la Loma
Bolero *34* Wesley Ruggles
Boléro *42* Jean Boyer
Boléro *81* Claude Lelouch
Bolero *84* John Derek
Bolero: An Adventure in Ecstasy *84* John
Derek
Bolibar *28* Walter Summers
Boliche *35* Francisco Elías
Bolivia Advances *64* Jorge Sanjinés
Bolivia Avanza *64* Jorge Sanjinés
Bolly *68* Joy Batchelor
Bolond Április *57* Zoltán Fábri
Bolondos Vakáció *67* Károly Makk
Bolshaya Semya *54* Josef Heifits
Bolshaya Zemlya *44* Sergei Gerasimov
Bolshaya Zhizn I *40* Leonid Lukov
Bolshevism on Trial *19* Harley Knoles
Bolshoi Ballet, The *57* Paul Czinner
Bolshoi Ballet '67 *66* Leonid Lavrovsky,
Alexander Shelenkov
Bolshoi Koncert *51* Vera Stroyeva
Bolt from the Blue, A *10* Dave Aylott
Bolted Door, The *23* William Worthing-
ton
Bolts of Melody *54* Stan Brakhage, Joseph
Cornell
Bolwieser *77* Rainer Werner Fassbinder
Bomarzo *49* Michelangelo Antonioni
Bomb, The *19* Rune Carlsten
Bomb at 10:10 *66* Charles Damic
Bomb Boy, The *14* George Fitzmaurice
Bomb for a Dictator, A *57* Alex Joffé
Bomb Hour *25* Kajiro Yamamoto
Bomb Idea, The *20* Vernon Stallings
Bomb in the High Street *61* Peter
Bezencenet, Terry Bishop
Bomb Was Stolen, A *61* Ion Popescu-
Gopo
Bomba, La *66* Pietro Germi
Bomba and the African Treasure *52* Ford
Beebe
Bomba and the Elephant Stampede *51*
Ford Beebe
Bomba and the Hidden City *50* Ford
Beebe
Bomba and the Jungle Girl *52* Ford Beebe
Bomba and the Lion Hunters *51* Ford
Beebe
Bomba and the Lost Volcano *50* Ford
Beebe
Bomba and the Safari Drums *53* Ford

Beebe
Bomba on Panther Island *49* Ford Beebe
Bomba, the Jungle Boy *49* Ford Beebe
Bombardier *43* Richard Wallace
Bombardment of Mafeking, The *1899*
Robert Ashe
Bombardment of Monte Carlo, The *31*
Hans Schwarz
Bombardment of Port Arthur, The *04*
Harold Hough
Bombay Clipper *41* John Rawlins
Bombay Mail *33* Edwin L. Marin
Bombay Our City *85* Anand Patwardhan
Bombay Talkie *70* James Ivory
Bomben auf Monte Carlo *31* Hans
Schwarz
Bombers B-52 *57* Gordon Douglas
Bomber's Moon *43* Robert Florey, Edward
Ludwig, Harold Schuster
Bombomania *59* Břetislav Pojar
Bombomanie *59* Břetislav Pojar
Bombs and Boobs *26* Charles Bowers
Bombs and Bums *26* Charles Bowers
Bombs Away *85* Bruce Wilson
Bombs Over Burma *42* Joseph H. Lewis
Bombs Over China *51* Lewis R. Foster
Bombs Over Japan *51* Allan Dwan
Bombs Over London *37* Sinclair Hill
Bombshell *33* Victor Fleming
Bombsight Stolen *41* Anthony Asquith
Bon Appetit *81* Chuck Vincent
Bon Baisers à Lundi *74* Michel Audiard
Bon Bon Parade *35* Charles Mintz
Bon Dieu Sans Confession, Le *53* Claude
Autant-Lara
Bon et les Méchants, Le *75* Claude Le-
louch
Bon, la Brute et le Truand, Le *66* Sergio
Leone
Bon Lit, Un *1899* Georges Méliès
Bon Petit Diable, Un *1896* Georges Méliès
Bon Petit Diable, Un *23* René Leprince
Bon Petit Diable, Un *83* Jean-Claude
Brialy
Bon Plaisir, Le *84* Françoise Giroud
Bon Propriétaire, Le *13* Louis Feuillade
Bon Roi Dagobert, Le *84* Dino Risi
Bon Samaritain, Un *76* René Gainville
Bon Voyage *44* Alfred Hitchcock
Bon Voyage! *62* James Neilson
Bon Voyage, Charlie Brown *80* Bill
Melendez
Bon Voyage, Charlie Brown (And Don't
Come Back!) *80* Bill Melendez
Bona *80* Lino Brocka
Bonanza Buckaroo, The *26* Richard
Thorpe
Bonanza Bunny *59* Robert McKimson
Bonanza Town *51* Fred F. Sears
Bonaparte et la Révolution *71* Abel Gance
Bonaventure *51* Douglas Sirk
Bonbast *77* Parviz Sayyad
Bonchi *60* Kon Ichikawa
Bond, The *18* Charles Chaplin
Bond Between, The *17* Donald Crisp
Bond Boy, The *22* Henry King
Bond of Fear *17* Jack Conway
Bond of Fear *56* Henry Cass
Bond Street *47* Gordon Parry
Bond Within, The *16* Edward Sloman

Bondage *17* Ida May Park
Bondage *33* Alfred Santell
Bondage *68* Félix Máriássy
Bondage of Barbara, The *19* Emmett J.
Flynn
Bondage of Fear, The *17* Travers Vale
Bonded Woman, The *22* Phil Rosen
Bondman, The *16* Edgar Lewis
Bondman, The *28* Herbert Wilcox
Bonds of Hate *19* August Blom
Bonds of Honor *19* William Worthington
Bonds of Honour *34* Fred Newmeyer
Bonds of Love *19* Reginald Barker
Bonds That Chafe *20* Mauritz Stiller
Bone *72* Larry Cohen
Bone Dry *27* Clyde Geronimi
Bone for a Bone, A *51* Friz Freleng
Bone of Contention, The *20* Paul Terry
Bone Sweet Bone *48* Art Davis
Bone Trouble *40* Jack Kinney
Boneyard Blues *24* Earl Hurd
Bonfire of the Vanities *90* Brian DePalma
Bonheur, Le *34* Marcel L'Herbier
Bonheur, Le *64* Agnès Varda
Bonheur A Encore Frappé, Le *86* Jean-Luc
Trotignon
Bonheur Conjugal, Le *22* Robert Saidreau
Bonheur des Autres, Le *18* Germaine
Dulac
Bonheur d'Être Aimée, Le *62* Henri Storck
Bonheur du Jour, Le *27* Gaston Ravel
Bonheur Perdu, Le *12* Henri Fescourt
Bonheur Toi-Même *80* Claude Goretta
Bonhomme de Neige *17* Georges Monca
Bonita of El Cajón *11* Allan Dwan
Bonitinha Mas Ordinária *65* J. P. De
Carvalho
Bonjour l'Angoisse *88* Pierre Tchernia
Bonjour Monsieur la Bruyère *56* Jacques
Doniol-Valcroze
Bonjour New York! *28* Robert Florey
Bonjour Sourire *55* Claude Sautet
Bonjour Tristesse *57* John Palmer, Otto
Preminger
Bonne, La *86* Salvatore Samperi
Bonne Absinthe, La *00* Alice Guy-Blaché
Bonne Année *13* Louis Feuillade
Bonne Année, La *72* Claude Lelouch
Bonne Aventure, La *32* Henri Diamant-
Berger
Bonne Bergère et la Méchante Princesse,
La *08* Georges Méliès
Bonne Chance *35* Sacha Guitry
Bonne Chance Charlie *62* Jean-Louis
Richard
Bonne Étoile, La *43* Jean Boyer
Bonne Farce, Une *1896* Georges Méliès
Bonne Farce avec Ma Tête, Une *04*
Georges Méliès
Bonne Hôtesse, La *18* Georges Monca
Bonne Occase, La *64* Michel Drach
Bonne Soupe, La *63* Robert Thomas
Bonne Surprise, Une *04* Georges Méliès
Bonne Tisane, La *58* Hervé Bromberger
Bonnes à Tuer *54* Henri Decoin
Bonnes Causes, Les *63* Christian-Jaque
Bonnes Femmes, Les *59* Claude Chabrol
Bonnes Manières, Les *51* Yves Robert
Bonnie and Clyde *67* Arthur Penn
Bonnie Annie Laurie *18* Harry Millarde

Bonnie, Bonnie Lassie *19* Tod Browning
Bonnie Brier Bush, The *21* Donald Crisp
Bonnie Mary *18* A. V. Bramble
Bonnie May *20* Joseph De Grasse, Ida May Park
Bonnie Parker Story, The *58* William Witney
Bonnie Prince Charlie *23* Charles C. Calvert
Bonnie Prince Charlie *48* Anthony Kimmins, Alexander Korda, Robert Stevenson
Bonnie Scotland *35* James W. Horne
Bonnie's Kids *73* Arthur Marks
Bons Baisers de Bangkok *64* Louis Malle
Bons Débarras!, Les *78* Francis Mankiewicz
Bons Vivants, Les *65* Gilles Grangier, Georges Lautner
Bonsoirs Russes *10* Émile Cohl
Bony a Klid *88* Vít Olmer
Bony Parts *22* Raoul Barré, Charles Bowers
Bonzo Goes to College *52* Frederick De Cordova
Boo, Boo, Theme Song *33* Dave Fleischer
Boob, The *26* William A. Wellman
Boob for Luck, A *17* William Beaudine
Boobs and Bricks *13* Allan Dwan
Boobs in the Woods *25* Harry Edwards
Boobs in the Woods *50* Robert McKimson
Boob's Romance, A *15* Robert Z. Leonard
Boob's Victory, The *16* Robert Z. Leonard
Booby Hatched *44* Frank Tashlin
Booby Socks *45* Howard Swift, Bob Wickersham
Booby Trap *57* Henry Cass
Booby Traps *44* Robert Clampett
Boogens, The *81* James L. Conway
Boogeyman, The *80* Ulli Lommel
Boogeyman II *82* Ulli Lommel, Bruce Starr
Boogie Doodle *40* Norman McLaren
Boogie Man Will Get You, The *42* Lew Landers
Boogie Woogie Bugle Boy of Company B, The *41* Walter Lantz
Book, The *13* Warwick Buckland
Book Agent, The *17* Otis Turner
Book and the Sword, The *87* Ann Hui
Book Bargain *35* Pat Jackson, Norman McLaren
Book of Days *88* Meredith Monk
Book of Love *90* Robert Shaye
Book of Numbers *73* Raymond St. Jacques
Book Revue *46* Robert Clampett
Booked on Suspicion *45* Arthur Dreifuss
Bookmaker, The *07* J. H. Martin
Books and Crooks *20* Jack Ross
Bookseller Who Gave Up Bathing, The *68* Jarl Kulle
Bookworms *20* Adrian Brunel
Booloo *38* Clyde E. Elliott
Boom, Il *63* Vittorio De Sica
Boom! *68* Joseph Losey
Boom Boom *36* Jack King
Boom Goes the Groom *39* Charlie Chase
Boom in the Moon *46* Jaime Salvador
Boom Town *40* Jack Conway
Boom Town *61* Veljko Bulajić
Boom Town Badmen *49* Oliver Drake
Boomer Bill's Awakening *17* George

Clardy
Boomerang, The *13* Thomas Ince
Boomerang, The *19* Bertram Bracken
Boomerang, The *25* Louis Gasnier
Boomerang *34* Arthur Maude
Boomerang *47* Elia Kazan
Boomerang *60* Alfred Weidenmann
Boomerang *79* Ivan Nichev
Boomerang Bill *22* Tom Terriss
Boomerang Boomerang *89* Hans W. Geissendörfer
Boomerang Justice *22* Edward Sedgwick
Boon, The *77* Shyam Benegal
Boop-Oop-a-Doop *32* Dave Fleischer
Boost, The *88* Harold Becker
Boot, Das *81* Wolfgang Petersen
Boot Hill *69* Giuseppe Colizzi
Boot Hill Bandits *42* S. Roy Luby
Boot Ist Voll, Das *80* Markus Imhoof
Boot Polish *58* Prakash Arora
Boothill Brigade *37* Sam Newfield
Bootleggers, The *22* Roy Sheldon
Bootleggers *61* Leonid Gaidai
Bootleggers *74* Charles B. Pierce
Bootleggers' Angel *74* Charles B. Pierce
Bootlegger's Daughter, The *22* Victor Schertzinger
Bootle's Baby *14* Harold M. Shaw
Boots *19* Elmer Clifton
Boots and Saddles *37* Joseph Kane
Boots, Boots *34* Bert Tracy
Boots from Bootle *16* Edwin J. Collins
Boots Malone *51* William Dieterle
Boots? Not 'Arf *15* Edwin J. Collins
Boots of Destiny *37* Arthur Rosson
Boots Turner *73* Edward J. Lakso
Bop Girl *57* Howard W. Koch
Bop Girl Goes Calypso *57* Howard W. Koch
Boquitas Pintadas *74* Leopoldo Torre-Nilsson
Bør Børsen, Jr. *39* Toralf Sandø
Boran — Time to Aim *87* Daniel Zuta
Boran — Zeit zum Zielen *87* Daniel Zuta
Borba Gigantov *26* Victor Turin
Borcsa Amerikában *39* Márton Keleti
Bordella *75* Pupi Avati
Bordello *85* Nikos Koundouros
Border, The *79* Christopher Leitch
Border, The *81* Tony Richardson
Border Badmen *45* Sam Newfield
Border Bandits *45* Lambert Hillyer
Border Blackbirds *27* Leo D. Maloney
Border Brigands *35* Nick Grindé
Border Buckaroos *43* Oliver Drake
Border Caballero *36* Sam Newfield
Border Cafe *37* Lew Landers
Border Cavalier, The *27* William Wyler
Border Devils *32* William Nigh
Border Fence *51* H. W. Kier, Norman Sheldon
Border Feud, The *13* Mauritz Stiller
Border Feud *47* Ray Taylor
Border Flight *36* Otho Lovering
Border G-Man *38* David Howard
Border Guns *34* Jack Nelson
Border Incident *49* Anthony Mann
Border Incident *53* Thorold Dickinson
Border Intrigue *25* John P. McGowan
Border Justice *25* B. Reeves Eason

Border Law *31* Louis King
Border Legion, The *18* T. Hayes Hunter
Border Legion, The *24* William K. Howard
Border Legion, The *30* Otto Brower, Edwin H. Knopf
Border Legion, The *40* Joseph Kane
Border Menace, The *34* Jack Nelson
Border of Life, The *53* Jean Rostand, Nicole Védrès
Border Outlaws *50* Richard Talmadge
Border Patrol, The *28* James P. Hogan
Border Patrol *35* John P. McCarthy
Border Patrol *43* Lesley Selander
Border Patrolman, The *36* David Howard
Border Phantom *37* S. Roy Luby
Border Radio *87* Allison Anders, Dean Lent, Kurt Voss
Border Raiders, The *18* Stuart Paton
Border Ranger, The *11* Gilbert M. Anderson
Border Rangers *50* William Berke
Border Rider, The *24* Frederick Reel, Jr.
Border River *54* George Sherman
Border Romance *30* Richard Thorpe
Border Roundup *42* Sam Newfield
Border Saddlemates *52* William Witney
Border Scouts, The *22* Bert Hall
Border Sheriff, The *26* Robert North Bradbury
Border Shootout *90* J. McIntyre
Border Showdown *56* Richard L. Bare
Border Street *48* Aleksander Ford
Border Treasure *50* George Archainbaud
Border Vengeance *25* Harry S. Webb
Border Vengeance *35* Ray Heinz
Border Vigilantes *41* Derwin Abrahams
Border Whirlwind, The *26* John P. McCarthy
Border Wildcat, The *29* Ray Taylor
Border Wireless, The *18* William S. Hart
Border Wolves *17* George Marshall
Border Wolves *38* Joseph H. Lewis
Border Women *24* Alvin J. Neitz
Borderland *22* Paul Powell
Borderland *33* Boris Barnet
Borderland *37* Nate Watt
Borderline *50* William A. Seiter
Borderline *80* Jerrold Freedman
Borderline *88* Houchang Allahyari
Borderlines *63* Hall Bartlett
Bordertown *34* Archie Mayo
Bordertown Gunfighters *43* Howard Bretherton
Bordertown Trail *44* Lesley Selander
Bore of a Boy, A *13* Lewin Fitzhamon
Bored *16* Harry Buss
Bored of Education *36* Gordon Douglas
Bōrei Kaibyō Yashiki *58* Nobuo Nakagawa
Borghese Piccolo Piccolo, Un *77* Mario Monicelli
Borgis *81* Lino Brocka
Borgne, Le *80* Raúl Ruiz
Borinage *33* Joris Ivens, Henri Storck
Boring Afternoon, A *65* Ivan Passer
Boris Godunov *55* Vera Stroyeva
Boris Godunov *86* Sergei Bondarchuk
Born Again *78* Irving Rapper
Born American *86* Renny Harlin

Born Anew *33* E. Gryaznof
Born Bad *58* Richard L. Bare
Born for Glory *35* Anthony Asquith, Walter Forde
Born for Trouble *42* B. Reeves Eason
Born for Trouble *55* Desmond Davis
Born Free *65* James Hill
Born in East L.A. *87* Cheech Marin
Born in Flames *82* Lizzie Borden
Born Losers *67* Tom Laughlin
Born Lucky *32* Michael Powell
Born 1944 *64* Kazimierz Karabasz
Born of Fire *87* Jamil Dehlavi
Born of the Sea *48* Anthony Mavrogordato
Born on the Fourth of July *89* Oliver Stone
Born Reckless *30* Andrew Bennison, John Ford
Born Reckless *37* Malcolm St. Clair
Born Reckless *59* Howard W. Koch
Born Rich *24* William Nigh
Born That Way *36* Randall Faye
Born to Battle *26* Robert De Lacey
Born to Battle *27* Alvin J. Neitz
Born to Battle *35* Harry S. Webb
Born to Be Bad *34* Lowell Sherman
Born to Be Bad *50* Nicholas Ray
Born to Be Kissed *34* Jack Conway
Born to Be Loved *59* Hugo Haas
Born to Be Wild *38* Joseph Kane
Born to Boogie *72* Ringo Starr
Born to Dance *36* Roy Del Ruth
Born to Fight *38* Charles Hutchinson
Born to Gamble *35* Phil Rosen
Born to Kill *47* Robert Wise
Born to Kill *74* Monte Hellman
Born to Lose *71* Ivan Passer
Born to Love *31* Paul Stein
Born to Peck *52* Walter Lantz
Born to Race *87* James Fargo
Born to Run *76* Don Chaffey
Born to Sing *41* Edward Ludwig
Born to Sing *62* Steve Previn
Born to Speed *47* Edward L. Cahn
Born to the Saddle *29* Josef Levigard
Born to the Saddle *53* William Beaudine
Born to the West *26* John Waters
Born to the West *37* Charles Barton
Born to Win *71* Ivan Passer
Born Tough *33* William Nigh
Born Wild *68* Maury Dexter
Born Yesterday *50* George Cukor
Børnenes Synd *16* Forest Holger-Madsen
Borneo *37* Martin E. Johnson
Bornéo *54* Serge Bourguignon
Børnevennerne *14* Forest Holger-Madsen
Bōrō no Kesshitai *42* Tadashi Imai
Borom Sarret *63* Ousmane Sembène
Borotalco *81* Carlo Verdone
Borrah Minnevitch and His Harmonica School *42* Jean Negulesco
Borrow a Million *34* Reginald Denham
Borrowed Babies *14* Michael Curtiz
Borrowed Baby, The *11* Frank Wilson
Borrowed Castle, The *37* Ladislas Vajda
Borrowed Clothes *18* Phillips Smalley, Lois Weber
Borrowed Clothes *34* Arthur Maude
Borrowed Finery *25* Oscar Apfel
Borrowed Hero *41* Lewis D. Collins

Borrowed Husbands *24* David Smith
Borrowed Plumage *17* Raymond B. West
Borrowed Trouble *48* George Archainbaud
Borrowed Wives *30* Frank R. Strayer
Borrowing Trouble *37* Frank R. Strayer
Borsalino *70* Jacques Deray
Borsalino and Co. *74* Jacques Deray
Börse, Die *39* Hans Richter
Borsos Miklós *66* Márta Mészáros
Boryets i Kloun *57* Boris Barnet, Konstantin Yudin
Bōryoku *52* Kozaburo Yoshimura
Bōryoku no Machi *50* Satsuo Yamamoto
Boş Beşik *52* Baha Gelenbevi
Bosambo *35* Zoltán Korda
Bosch *48* Luciano Emmer, Enrico Gras
Bosch with Passion, or The Garden of Delights of Hieronymous Bosch *80* Jean Eustache
Boschi sul Mare *42* Mario Chiari
Boscombe Valley Mystery, The *22* George Ridgwell
Bosh! *15* Edwin J. Collins
Bosko in Dutch *33* Friz Freleng, Hugh Harman
Bosko in Person *33* Friz Freleng, Hugh Harman
Bosko the Drawback *33* Hugh Harman
Bosko the Musketeer *33* Hugh Harman
Bosko the Sheep Herder *33* Hugh Harman
Bosko the Speed King *33* Hugh Harman
Bosko's Dizzy Date *33* Hugh Harman
Bosko's Knightmare *33* Hugh Harman
Bosko's Mechanical Man *33* Hugh Harman
Bosko's Picture Show *33* Friz Freleng, Hugh Harman
Bosko's Woodland Daze *33* Hugh Harman
Bosque Animado, El *87* José Luis Cuerda
Bosque de Ancines, El *68* Pedro Olea
Bosque del Lobo, El *68* Pedro Olea
Boss, The *15* Émile Chautard
Boss, The *56* Byron Haskin
Boss *74* Jack Arnold
Boss Cowboy *34* Victor Adamson
Boss Didn't Say Good Morning, The *37* Jacques Tourneur
Boss Lady *82* Chris Warfield
Boss Nigger *74* Jack Arnold
Boss of Big Town *42* Arthur Dreifuss
Boss of Boomtown *44* Ray Taylor
Boss of Bullion City *41* Ray Taylor
Boss of Camp 4, The *22* W. S. Van Dyke
Boss of Gun Creek, The *36* Lesley Selander
Boss of Hangtown Mesa *42* Joseph H. Lewis
Boss of Lonely Valley *37* Ray Taylor
Boss of Rawhide *43* Elmer Clifton
Boss of Rustler's Roost, The *28* Leo D. Maloney
Boss of the Family, The *17* William Beaudine
Boss of the Lazy Y, The *18* Clifford Smith
Boss Rider of Gun Creek, The *36* Lesley Selander
Boss Said "No," The *42* Frank R. Strayer
Boss' Son, The *78* Bobby Roth
Boss' Wife, The *86* Ziggy Steinberg
Bossu, Le *44* Jean Delannoy
Bossu, Le *59* André Hunebelle

Boston Beany *47* Sid Marcus
Boston Blackie *23* Scott R. Dunlap
Boston Blackie and the Law *46* D. Ross Lederman
Boston Blackie Booked on Suspicion *45* Arthur Dreifuss
Boston Blackie Goes Hollywood *42* Michael Gordon
Boston Blackie's Chinese Venture *49* Seymour Friedman
Boston Blackie's Little Pal *18* E. Mason Hopper
Boston Blackie's Rendezvous *45* Arthur Dreifuss
Boston Quackie *57* Robert McKimson
Boston Strangler, The *68* Richard Fleischer
Boston Tea Party, The *08* Edwin S. Porter
Bostonians, The *84* James Ivory
Bosun's Mate, The *14* Harold M. Shaw
Bosun's Mate, The *53* Richard Warren
Botan *63* Yoji Kuri
Botan Doru *68* Satsuo Yamamoto
Botany Bay *53* John Farrow
Both Barrels Blazing *45* Derwin Abrahams
Both Ends of the Candle *57* Michael Curtiz
Both Sides of the Law *53* Muriel Box
Both You and I *46* Mikio Naruse
Bother About a Bomb, A *14* Hay Plumb
Bothered Bathers, The *07* J. H. Martin
Bothered by a Beard *46* E. V. H. Emmett
Boticelli *49* Luciano Emmer, Enrico Gras
Botta di Vita, Una *88* Enrico Oldoini
Botta e Risposta *50* Mario Soldati
Bottle, The *15* Cecil M. Hepworth
Bottle Imp, The *17* Marshall Neilan
Bottle Party *36* R. A. Hopwood
Bottled Courage *13* Mark Melford
Bottled Sun *86* Edmund Valladares
Bottleneck *79* Luigi Comencini
Bottom Line, The *82* Georges Lautner
Bottom of the Bottle, The *56* Henry Hathaway
Bottom of the Sea, The *14* Vincent Whitman
Bottom of the Well, The *17* John S. Robertson
Bottoms Up *34* David Butler
Bottoms Up! *60* Mario Zampi
Bouassa, El *44* Kamel Salim
Bouba *87* Zeev Revah
Boucher, Le *69* Claude Chabrol
Bouclette *18* René Hervil, Louis Mercanton
Bouclier, Le *60* Georges Rouquier
Boudoir Diplomat *30* Malcolm St. Clair
Boudoir Secrets *02* Alf Collins
Boudu Sauvé des Eaux *32* Jean Renoir
Boudu Saved from Drowning *32* Jean Renoir
Bought *31* Archie Mayo
Bought and Paid For *16* Harley Knoles
Bought and Paid For *22* William DeMille
Boukoki *73* Jean Rouch
Boulanger de Valorgue, Le *52* Henri Verneuil
Boulangère de Monceau, La *62* Eric Rohmer
Boulangère de Monceau: Six Contes Moraux: 1, La *62* Eric Rohmer
Boulangerie Modèle, La *07* Georges Méliès

Boulder Dam *36* Frank McDonald
Boulder Wham *65* Rudy Larriva
Boule de Gomme *31* Georges Lacombe
Boule de Suif *34* Mikhail Romm
Boule de Suif *45* Christian-Jaque
Boulevard *60* Julien Duvivier
Boulevard des Italiens *1896* Georges Méliès
Boulevard du Rhum *71* Robert Enrico
Boulevard Nights *79* Michael Pressman
Boulevard of Broken Dreams *88* Pino Amenta
Boulevardier from the Bronx *36* Friz Freleng
Boulevards d'Afrique *88* Tam-Sir Doueb, Jean Rouch
Boum, La *81* Claude Pinoteau
Boum II, La *82* Claude Pinoteau
Bouncer Breaks Up *52* Don Chaffey
Bound and Gagged *19* George B. Seitz
Bound for Cairo *40* Benito Perojo
Bound for Glory *76* Hal Ashby
Bound for the Rio Grande *48* David Hand
Bound in Morocco *18* Allan Dwan
Bound in Spaghetti *19* Raoul Barré, Charles Bowers
Boundaries of the Heart *88* Lex Marinos
Boundary House *18* Cecil M. Hepworth
Bounding Bertie's Bungalow *13* Hay Plumb
Bountiful Summer *51* Boris Barnet
Bounty, The *84* Roger Donaldson
Bounty Hunter, The *54* André De Toth
Bounty Hunters, The *70* Gianfranco Parolini
Bounty Killer, The *65* Spencer G. Bennet
Bounty Killer a Trinità, Un *72* Oskar Faradine
Bounty Killers, The *66* Eugenio Martin
Bouquet d'Illusions *00* Georges Méliès
Bouquetière des Innocents, La *22* Jacques Robert
Bouquets from Nicholas *39* Maurice Cammage
Bourasque, La *20* Charles De Marsan, Charles Maudru
Bourbon Street *64* Oscar Daley
Bourbon Street Shadows *58* James Wong Howe, Ben Parker, John Sledge
Bourgeoise, La *79* Pierre Granier-Deferre
Bourgogne, La *36* Jean Epstein
Bourreau, Le *35* Jacques Becker
Bourreau Turc, Le *04* Georges Méliès
Bourse, La *09* Émile Cohl
Bourse et la Vie, La *65* Jean-Pierre Mocky
Bourse ou la Vie, La *61* Jerzy Skolimowski
Bout-de-Zan et la Torpille *16* Louis Feuillade
Bout-de-Zan Revient du Cirque *12* Louis Feuillade
Boutique, La *67* Luis García Berlanga
Boutique, The *67* Luis García Berlanga
Boutique de l'Orfèvre, La *88* Michael Anderson
Boutique des Miracles, La *75* Nelson Pereira Dos Santos
Bow Bells *54* Anthony Simmons
Bow Your Head *87* Leonid Osyka
Bowery, The *14* Raoul Walsh
Bowery, The *33* Raoul Walsh

Bowery at Midnight *42* Wallace Fox
Bowery Battalion *51* William Beaudine
Bowery Bimboes *30* Walter Lantz
Bowery Bishop, The *24* Colin Campbell
Bowery Blitzkrieg *41* Wallace Fox
Bowery Bombshell *46* Phil Karlson
Bowery Boy *40* William Morgan
Bowery Boys *45* Wallace Fox
Bowery Boys *55* William Beaudine
Bowery Boys Meet the Monsters, The *54* Edward Bernds
Bowery Buckaroos *47* William Beaudine
Bowery Bugs *49* Art Davis
Bowery Champs *44* William Beaudine
Bowery Cinderella *27* Burton L. King
Bowery Daze *34* Manny Gould, Ben Harrison
Bowery Leathernecks *52* William Beaudine
Bowery Thrush *50* William Beaudine
Bowery to Bagdad *54* Edward Bernds
Bowery to Broadway *44* Charles Lamont
Bowler and the Bonnet, The *69* Sean Connery
Bowling Alley, The *20* Raoul Barré, Charles Bowers
Bowling Alley Cat, The *42* Joseph Barbera, William Hanna
Bowling Bimboes *30* Walter Lantz
Bowling Match, The *13* Mack Sennett
Box Car Bill Falls in Luck *17* Bill Cause
Box of Real Turkish, A *14* Dave Aylott
Boxcar Bertha *72* Martin Scorsese
Boxer, The *67* Julian Dziedzina
Boxer, The *71* Franco Prosperi
Boxer *77* Shuji Terayama
Boxer, The *77* Shuji Terayama
Boxer a Smrt *62* Peter Solan
Boxer and Death, The *62* Peter Solan
Boxer's Omen, The *83* Zhihong Gui
Boxing *61* Jerzy Skolimowski
Boxing Fever *09* A. E. Coleby
Boxing Kangaroo, The *1896* Birt Acres
Boxing Kangaroo, The *20* Dave Fleischer
Boxing Match *1896* Birt Acres
Boxing Match *1897* Georges Méliès
Boxing Match, or Glove Contest *1896* Birt Acres
Boxing Waiter, The *09* Alf Collins
Boxoffice *82* Josef Bogdanovich
Boy *69* Nagisa Oshima
Boy...a Girl, A *68* John Derek
Boy, a Girl and a Bike, A *47* Ralph Smart
Boy, a Girl and a Dog, A *46* Herbert Kline
Boy, a Gun and Birds, A *40* Ben Harrison
Boy and a Pigeon, A *60* Andrei Mikhalkov-Konchalovsky
Boy and His Dog, A *36* Charles Mintz
Boy and His Dog, A *46* LeRoy Prinz
Boy and His Dog, A *75* L. Q. Jones
Boy and His Kite, The *09* Lewin Fitzhamon
Boy and His Kite, A *61* Jan Troell, Bo Widerberg
Boy and the Bridge, The *59* Kevin McClory
Boy and the Cheese, The *14* A. V. Bramble
Boy and the Convict, The *09* Dave Aylott
Boy and the Kite, The *61* Jan Troell, Bo Widerberg

Boy and the Law, The *14* John M. Stahl
Boy and the Pelican, The *64* Geoffrey Gurrin
Boy and the Physic, The *10* Fred Rains
Boy and the Pigeon, The *60* Andrei Mikhalkov-Konchalovsky
Boy and the Pirates, The *60* Bert I. Gordon
Boy and the Sea, The *53* Stan Brakhage
Boy Crazy *21* William A. Seiter
Boy Cried Murder, The *66* George Breakston
Boy Detective, The *08* Wallace McCutcheon
Boy, Did I Get a Wrong Number! *66* George Marshall
Boy Friend, The *26* Monta Bell
Boy Friend, The *28* Leo McCarey
Boy Friend *39* James Tinling
Boy Friend, The *71* Ken Russell
Boy from Barnardo's, The *38* Sam Wood
Boy from Calabria, A *87* Luigi Comencini
Boy from Ebalus, The *87* Giuseppe Schito
Boy from Indiana *50* John Rawlins
Boy from Oklahoma, The *53* Michael Curtiz
Boy from Stalingrad, The *43* Sidney Salkow
Boy from the Navy, The *26* Kenji Mizoguchi
Boy Girl, The *17* Edwin Stevens
Boy Goes to Biskra, The *24* Adrian Brunel
Boy in a Tree, The *60* Arne Sucksdorff
Boy in Blue, The *19* F. W. Murnau
Boy in Blue, The *85* Charles Jarrott
Boy in the Tree, The *60* Arne Sucksdorff
Boy Like the Others, A *86* Gianni Minello
Boy Meets Girl *38* Lloyd Bacon
Boy Meets Girl *84* Leos Carax
Boy Messenger, The *20* Maurice Sandground
Boy Millionaire, The *36* Anders Wilhelm Sandberg
Boy Named Charlie Brown, A *68* Bill Melendez
Boy Next Door, The *71* Buzz Kulik
Boy of Flanders, A *24* Victor Schertzinger
Boy of Mine *23* William Beaudine
Boy of the Sea, The *26* Kenji Mizoguchi
Boy of the Streets, A *27* Charles J. Hunt
Boy of the Streets *37* William Nigh
Boy of Two Worlds *59* Astrid Henning-Jensen, Bjarne Henning-Jensen
Boy on a Dolphin *57* Jean Negulesco
Boy Rents Girl *87* Steve Rash
Boy Rider, The *27* Louis King
Boy Scouts *22* Bernard Dudley
Boy Scouts Be Prepared *17* Percy Nash
Boy Scout's Dream, or How Billie Captured the Kaiser, A *17* Bert Haldane
Boy Scouts to the Rescue *17* Percy Nash
Boy Slaves *38* P. J. Wolfson
Boy Soldier *86* Karl Francis
Boy Ten Feet Tall, A *62* Alexander Mackendrick
Boy Trouble *38* George Archainbaud
Boy! What a Girl! *46* Arthur Leonard
Boy Who Caught a Crook, The *61* Edward L. Cahn

Boy Who Could Fly, The *86* Nick Castle

Boy Who Cried Werewolf, The *73* Nathan Juran

Boy Who Cried Wolf, The *17* Edward H. Griffith

Boy Who Had Everything, The *84* Stephen Wallace

Boy Who Never Was, The *80* Frank Godwin

Boy Who Stole a Million, The *60* Charles Crichton

Boy Who Turned Yellow, The *72* Michael Powell

Boy with a Flute *64* Montgomery Tully

Boy with Green Hair, The *48* Joseph Losey

Boy with the Big Black Dog, The *87* Hannelore Unterberg

Boy with Two Heads, The *74* Jonathan Ingrams

Boy Woodburn *22* Guy Newall

Boycott *86* Mohsen Makhmal Baf

Boyd's Shop *59* Henry Cass

Boyfriend School, The *90* Malcolm Mowbray

Boyfriends and Girlfriends *86* Eric Rohmer

Boyhood Daze *57* Chuck Jones

Boyichi and the Supermonster *67* Noriyaki Yuasa

Boys, The *59* Marco Ferreri

Boys, The *61* Sidney J. Furie

Boys and Girls Together *80* Ralph Lawrence Marsden

Boys and the Purse, The *09* Frank Wilson

Boys from Brazil, The *78* Franklin J. Schaffner

Boys from Brooklyn, The *52* William Beaudine

Boys from Fengkuei, The *83* Hsiao-hsien Hou

Boys from Leningrad, The *55* Semen Timoshenko

Boys from Syracuse, The *40* A. Edward Sutherland

Boys from the Sea, The *26* Kenji Mizoguchi

Boys from the West Coast *50* Astrid Henning-Jensen, Bjarne Henning-Jensen

Boys' Half Holiday, The *07* Arthur Cooper

Boys in Blue *64* Arne Mattsson

Boys in Blue, The *83* Val Guest

Boys in Brown *49* Montgomery Tully

Boys in Company C, The *77* Sidney J. Furie

Boys in the Band, The *70* William Friedkin

Boys Next Door, The *85* Penelope Spheeris

Boys' Night Out *62* Michael Gordon

Boys of Fengkuei, The *83* Hsiao-hsien Hou

Boys of Paul Street, The *68* Zoltán Fábri

Boys of the City *40* Joseph H. Lewis

Boys of the Old Brigade, The *16* Ernest G. Batley

Boys of the Otter Patrol *18* Percy Nash

Boys' Ranch *46* Roy Rowland

Boys' Reformatory *39* Howard Bretherton

Boys' School *38* Christian-Jaque

Boys Town *38* Norman Taurog

Boys Will Be Boys *03* James A. Williamson

Boys Will Be Boys *04* Frank Mottershaw

Boys Will Be Boys *11* Theo Bouwmeester

Boys Will Be Boys *21* Clarence Badger

Boys Will Be Boys *32* George Stevens

Boys Will Be Boys *35* William Beaudine

Boys Will Be Girls *37* Gilbert Pratt

Božská Ema *79* Jiří Krejčík

Bra Flicka Reder Sig Själv *14* Victor Sjöström

Braća Po Materi *88* Zdravko Šotra

Braccia Aperte, Le *22* Carmine Gallone

Brace Up *18* Elmer Clifton

Bracelet de la Marquise, Le *11* Louis Feuillade

Bracelets *31* Sewell Collins

Braconniers, Les *03* Alice Guy-Blaché

Braddock: Missing in Action III *88* Aaron Norris

Brady's Escape *83* Pál Gábor

Brahma Diamond, The *09* D. W. Griffith

Brahmane et le Papillon, Le *01* Georges Méliès

Brahmin and the Butterfly, The *01* Georges Méliès

Brain, The *62* Freddie Francis

Brain, The *69* Gérard Oury

Brain, The *88* Ed Hunt

Brain Damage *87* Frank Henenlotter

Brain Dead *90* Adam Simon

Brain Eaters, The *58* Bruno Ve Sota

Brain from Outer Space, The *59* Chogi Akasaka, Akira Miwa

Brain from Planet Arous, The *58* Nathan Juran

Brain Machine, The *53* Ken Hughes

Brain Machine, The *72* Joy Houck, Jr.

Brain of Blood, The *71* Al Adamson

Brain Storm *27* Stephen Roberts

Brain That Wouldn't Die, The *59* Giuseppe Vari

Brainiac, The *61* Chano Urueta

Brains Required *10* Émile Cohl

Brainsnatchers, The *36* Robert Stevenson

Brainstorm *65* William Conrad

Brainstorm *83* Douglas Trumbull

Brainwash *81* Bobby Roth

Brainwashed *60* Gerd Oswald

Brainwaves *82* Ulli Lommel

Bram Stoker's Count Dracula *70* Jesús Franco

Bram Stoker's Dracula *73* Dan Curtis

Bramble Bush, The *19* Tom Terriss

Bramble Bush, The *59* Daniel Petrie

Bramy Raju *67* Andrzej Wajda

Brancaleone alla Crusada *70* Mario Monicelli

Brancaleone alle Crociate *70* Mario Monicelli

Branches *70* Ed Emshwiller

Brand, The *12* Allan Dwan

Brand *15* Pavel Orlenev

Brand, The *19* Reginald Barker

Brand im Ozean *39* Günther Rittau

Brand in der Oper *30* Carl Fröhlich

Brand New Hero, A *14* Roscoe Arbuckle, Edward Dillon

Brand of Cain, The *35* Oscar Micheaux

Brand of California, The *13* Émile Cohl

Brand of Cowardice, The *16* John W. Noble

Brand of Cowardice *25* John P. McCarthy

Brand of Fear, The *11* Allan Dwan

Brand of Fear *49* Oliver Drake

Brand of Hate *34* Lewis D. Collins

Brand of Lopez, The *20* Joseph De Grasse

Brand of Man, The *15* Henry King

Brand of Satan, The *17* George Archainbaud

Brand of Shame *68* B. Ron Elliott

Brand of the Devil *44* Harry Fraser

Brand of the Outlaws *36* Robert North Bradbury

Brand X *70* Win Chamberlain

Branded *20* Charles C. Calvert

Branded *31* D. Ross Lederman

Branded *36* Lawrence Huntington

Branded *50* Rudolph Maté

Branded a Bandit *24* Paul Hurst

Branded a Coward *28* Christy Cabanne

Branded a Coward *35* Sam Newfield

Branded a Thief *24* Neal Hart

Branded Four, The *20* Duke Worne

Branded Man *28* Scott Pembroke

Branded Men *31* Phil Rosen

Branded Sombrero, The *28* Lambert Hillyer

Branded Soul, A *17* Bertram Bracken

Branded Soul, The *20* F. Martin Thornton

Branded Woman, The *20* Albert Parker

Brandende Straal, De *11* Joris Ivens

Branding *28* Mannus Franken, Joris Ivens

Branding a Bad Man *11* Allan Dwan

Branding Broadway *18* William S. Hart, Lambert Hillyer

Branding Iron, The *20* Reginald Barker

Brand's Daughter *17* Harry Harvey

Brandy Ashore *51* Derek Twist

Brandy, el Sheriff de Losatumba *63* José Luis Borau

Brandy for the Parson *51* John Eldridge

Brandy in the Wilderness *69* Stanton Kaye

Brandy, the Sheriff of Losatumba *63* José Luis Borau

Branle-Bas de Combat *42* Joris Ivens

Brannigan *74* Douglas Hickox

Bränningar *35* Ivar Johansson

Branquignol *49* Robert Dhéry

Branscombe's Pal *14* Harold M. Shaw

Bras Cubas *86* Julio Bressane

Bras de Fer *85* Gérard Vergez

Brasa Dormida *28* Humberto Mauro

Brasher Doubloon, The *47* John Brahm

Brasier Ardent, Le *23* Ivan Mozhukhin, Alexander Volkov

Brasil Ano 2.000 *68* Walter Lima Júnior

Brass *23* Sidney Franklin

Brass Bottle, The *14* Sidney Morgan

Brass Bottle, The *23* Maurice Tourneur

Brass Bottle, The *64* Harry Keller

Brass Bowl, The *24* Jerome Storm

Brass Buttons *19* Henry King

Brass Check, The *18* Will S. Davis

Brass Commandments *23* Lynn Reynolds

Brass Knuckles *27* Lloyd Bacon

Brass Legend, The *56* Gerd Oswald

Brass Monkey, The *47* Thornton Freeland

Brass Ring, The *75* Martin Beck

Brass Target *78* John Hough
Brat, The *19* Herbert Blaché
Brat, The *30* Louis Mercanton
Brat, The *31* John Ford
Brat, The *49* John English
Bratishka *26* Grigori Kozintsev, Leonid Trauberg
Brats *30* James Parrott
Bratya Karamazovy *68* Ivan Pyriev, Mikhail Ulyanov
Braut des Satans, Die *76* Peter Sykes
Bräutigam auf Kredit *21* Hans Steinhoff
Bräutigam, die Komödiantin und der Zuhälter, Der *68* Jean-Marie Straub
Bravados, The *58* Henry King
Brave and Bold *12* Mack Sennett
Brave and Bold *18* Carl Harbaugh
Brave and the Beautiful, The *55* Budd Boetticher
Brave Bulls, The *50* Robert Rossen
Brave Children, or The Little Thief Catchers *08* A. E. Coleby
Brave Cowards *27* Mark Sandrich
Brave Don't Cry, The *52* Philip Leacock
Brave Engineer, The *50* Jack Kinney
Brave Hare, The *55* Ivan Ivanov-Vano
Brave Hunter, The *12* Mack Sennett
Brave Lad's Reward, A *07* Charles Raymond
Brave Little Bat, The *41* Chuck Jones
Brave Little Dove *73* Raúl Ruiz
Brave Little Toaster, The *87* Jerry Rees
Brave One, The *56* Irving Rapper
Brave Seven, The *36* Sergei Gerasimov
Brave Soldat Schwejk, Der *60* Axel von Ambesser
Brave Soldier at Dawn, A *26* Teinosuke Kinugasa
Brave Sünder, Der *31* Fritz Kortner
Brave Tin Soldier, The *34* Ubbe Iwerks
Brave Toreador, The *20* Raoul Barré, Charles Bowers
Brave Warrior *52* Spencer G. Bennet
Brave Young Men of Weinberg, The *80* Robert Downey
Braveheart *25* Alan Hale
Braves Gens, Les *12* Louis Feuillade
Braves Petits Soldats de Plomb, Les *15* Émile Cohl
Bravest Girl in the South, The *10* Sidney Olcott
Bravest Way, The *18* George Melford
Bravestarr *88* Tom Tataranowicz
Bravo, The *28* Geoffrey H. Malins
Bravo di Venezia, Il *41* Carlo Campogalliani
Bravo Kilties! *14* F. Martin Thornton
Bravo, Mr. Strauss *43* George Pal
Brawn of the North *22* Lawrence Trimble
Brazen Beauty, The *18* Tod Browning
Brazil *44* Joseph Santley
Brazil *85* Terry Gilliam
Brazil: A Report on Torture *71* Saul Landau, Haskell Wexler
Brazza *40* Léon Poirier
Brazza *54* Folco Quilici
Breach in Breeches, A *12* Percy Stow
Breach of Contract *84* André Guttfreund
Breach of Faith, A *11* Edwin S. Porter
Breach of Promise *41* Harold Huth,

Roland Pertwee
Breach of Promise *42* Paul Stein
Breach of Promise Case, A *08* J. B. McDowell
Bread *18* Richard Boleslawski, Boris Suskevich
Bread *18* Ida May Park
Bread *24* Victor Schertzinger
Bread *36* Ramjankhan Mehboobkhan
Bread *53* Charles Eames, Ray Eames
Bread *59* Manoel De Oliveira
Bread *71* Stanley Long
Bread and Chocolate *74* Franco Brusati
Bread and Sulfur *56* Gillo Pontecorvo
Bread Cast Upon the Waters *13* Thomas Ince
Bread, Love and... *55* Dino Risi
Bread, Love and Dreams *53* Luigi Comencini
Bread, Love and Jealousy *54* Luigi Comencini
Bread of Love, The *53* Arne Mattsson
Bread Peddler, The *62* Maurice Cloche
Breadless Diet *84* Raúl Ruiz
Break, The *61* Jean-Claude Carrière, Pierre Etaix
Break, The *62* Lance Comfort
Break in the Circle *55* Val Guest
Break Loose *72* Robert Siegel
Break of Dawn *87* Isaac Artenstein
Break of Day *29* Mannie Davis
Break of Day *77* Ken Hannam
Break of Hearts *35* Philip Moeller
Break Out *84* Frank Godwin
Break the News *37* René Clair
Break to Freedom *53* Lewis Gilbert
Break-Up, The *30* L. Zamkovoy
Break-Up *65* Marco Ferreri
Break Up, The *70* Claude Chabrol
Break-Up *72* Maurice Pialat
Breakaway *56* Henry Cass
Breakaway *66* Bruce Conner
Breakdance *84* Joel Silberg
Breakdance II: Electric Boogaloo *84* Sam Firstenberg
Breakdancin' *84* Joel Silberg
Breakdown *53* Edmond Angelo
Breakdown *67* Bertrand Blier
Breakdown *81* Kathryn Bigelow
Breaker, The *16* Fred E. Wright
Breaker Breaker *77* Don Hulette
Breaker Morant *79* Bruce Beresford
Breakers, The *28* Mannus Franken, Joris Ivens
Breakers Ahead *18* Charles Brabin
Breakers Ahead *35* Anthony Gilkison
Breakers Ahead *37* Vernon Sewell
Breakfast *72* Michael Snow
Breakfast at Sunrise *27* Malcolm St. Clair
Breakfast at the Manchester Morgue *74* Jorge Grau
Breakfast at Tiffany's *61* Blake Edwards
Breakfast Club, The *85* John Hughes
Breakfast Food Industry, The *20* Raoul Barré, Charles Bowers
Breakfast for Two *37* Alfred Santell
Breakfast in Bed *63* Axel von Ambesser
Breakfast in Bed *78* William Haugse
Breakfast in Hollywood *45* Harold Schuster

Breakfast in Paris *82* John Lamond
Breakheart Pass *75* Tom Gries
Breakin' *84* Joel Silberg
Breakin' II: Electric Boogaloo *84* Sam Firstenberg
Breakin' and Enterin' *85* Topper Carew
Breakin' New York Style *86* Tony Roman
Breaking *85* Avi Nesher
Breaking All the Rules *85* James Orr
Breaking Away *79* Peter Yates
Breaking Glass *79* Brian Gibson
Breaking Home Ties *22* Frank N. Seltzer
Breaking In *89* Bill Forsyth
Breaking Into Society *23* Hunt Stromberg
Breaking It Up *67* John Berry
Breaking It Up at the Museum *60* D. A. Pennebaker
Breaking Loose *88* Rod Hay
Breaking of Bumbo, The *71* Andrew Sinclair
Breaking Point, The *14* Frank Wilson
Breaking Point, The *21* Paul Scardon
Breaking Point, The *24* Herbert Brenon
Breaking Point, The *50* Michael Curtiz
Breaking Point, The *60* Lance Comfort
Breaking Point *76* Bob Clark
Breaking the Habit *69* John Korty
Breaking the Ice *25* Lloyd Bacon
Breaking the Ice *38* Edward F. Cline
Breaking the Sound Barrier *52* David Lean, Anthony Squire
Breaking Through the Sound Barrier *52* David Lean, Anthony Squire
Breaking Up of the Territorial Army — France *1896* Georges Méliès
Breaking Up the Dance *57* Roman Polanski
Breaking Up the Party *57* Roman Polanski
Breakout *58* Peter Graham Scott
Breakout *59* Don Chaffey
Breakout *75* Tom Gries
Breakthrough *50* Lewis Seiler
Breakthrough, The *68* Yuri Ozerov
Breakthrough *78* Andrew V. McLaglen
Breakthrough *87* Dmitri Svetozarov
Breast of Russ Meyer, The *83* Russ Meyer
Breath of a Nation, The *19* Gregory La Cava
Breath of Life *62* J. Henry Piperno
Breath of Scandal, The *24* Louis Gasnier
Breath of Scandal *29* Lionel Barrymore
Breath of Scandal, A *59* Michael Curtiz, Mario Russo
Breath of the Gods, The *20* Rollin Sturgeon
Breathdeath *64* Stan Vanderbeek
Breathing *20* J. D. Leventhal
Breathing *63* Robert Breer
Breathless *59* Jean-Luc Godard
Breathless *83* Jim McBride
Breathless Moment, The *24* Robert F. Hill
Bred in Old Kentucky *26* Edward Dillon
Bred in the Bone *15* Paul Powell
Breed Apart, A *83* Philippe Mora
Breed o' the Mountains *14* Wallace Reid
Breed of Courage *27* Howard Mitchell
Breed of Men, The *19* William S. Hart, Lambert Hillyer
Breed of the Border, The *24* Harry Garson
Breed of the Border *33* Robert North Bradbury

Breed of the Sea 26 Ralph Ince
Breed of the Sunsets 28 Wallace Fox
Breed of the Treshams, The 20 Kenelm Foss
Breed of the West 30 Alvin J. Neitz
Breeders 86 Tim Kincaid
Breezes of Love 35 Heinosuke Gosho
Breezing Along 27 Norman Taurog
Breezing Home 37 Milton Carruth
Breezy 73 Clint Eastwood
Breezy Bill 30 John P. McGowan
Breezy Jim 19 Lorimer Johnston
Breite Weg, Der 17 Urban Gad
Brel 82 Frédéric Rossif
Brelan d'As 52 Henri Verneuil
Bremen Coffee 72 Rainer Werner Fassbinder
Bremen Town Musicians 35 Ubbe Iwerks
Bremer Freiheit 72 Rainer Werner Fassbinder
Brenda of the Barge 20 Arthur H. Rooke
Brenda Starr 86 Robert Ellis Miller
Brenda Starr, Reporter 45 Wallace Fox
Brendan Behan's Dublin 67 Norman Cohen
Brenn Hexe Brenn 69 Michael Armstrong
Brennende Acker, Der 22 F. W. Murnau
Brennende Betten 88 Pia Frankenberg
Brennende Blomster 86 Eva Dahr, Eva Isaksen
Brennende Gericht, Das 61 Julien Duvivier
Brennende Herz, Das 29 Ludwig Berger
Brennendes Geheimnis 33 Robert Siodmak
Brennus, Enemy of Rome 64 Giacomo Gentilomo
Bretagne, La 36 Jean Epstein
Brev från Sverige 87 Jörn Donner
Breva Stagione, Una 69 Renato Castellani
Breve Vacanza, Una 73 Vittorio De Sica
Brewster McCloud 70 Robert Altman
Brewster's Millions 14 Oscar Apfel, Cecil B. DeMille
Brewster's Millions 21 Joseph E. Henabery
Brewster's Millions 35 Thornton Freeland
Brewster's Millions 45 Allan Dwan
Brewster's Millions 85 Walter Hill
Brian's Song 72 Buzz Kulik
Bribe, The 48 Robert Z. Leonard
Brick Bradford 47 Spencer G. Bennet
Bricklayer's Day II 86 Gilberto Martínez Solares
Bridal Bail 34 George Stevens
Bridal Chair, The 19 George B. Samuelson
Bridal Couple Dodging Cameras 08 Edwin S. Porter
Bridal Path, The 58 Frank Launder
Bridal Suite 39 Wilhelm Thiele
Bride, The 29 Hugh Croise
Bride, The 73 Jean-Marie Pelissie
Bride, The 85 Franc Roddam
Bride and the Beast, The 58 Adrian Weiss
Bride by Mistake 44 Richard Wallace
Bride Came C.O.D., The 41 William Keighley
Bride Comes Home, The 35 Wesley Ruggles
Bride Comes to Yellow Sky, The 52 John

Brahm, Bretaigne Windust
Bride for Frank, A 56 Leonardo De Mitri
Bride for Henry, A 37 William Nigh
Bride for Sale 49 William D. Russell
Bride from Hades, The 68 Satsuo Yamamoto
Bride from Hell, The 68 Satsuo Yamamoto
Bride from Japan, The 59 Kaneto Shindo
Bride Goes Wild, The 48 Norman Taurog
Bride Is Much Too Beautiful, The 57 Fred Surin
Bride of Death, A 11 August Blom
Bride of Fear, The 18 Sidney Franklin
Bride of Fengriffen 73 Roy Ward Baker
Bride of Frankenstein, The 35 James Whale
Bride of Glomdal, The 25 Carl Theodor Dreyer
Bride of Hate, The 17 Walter Edwards
Bride of Lammermoor, The 22 Challis Sanderson
Bride of Re-Animator 90 Brian Yuzna
Bride of the Andes 66 Susumu Hani
Bride of the Atom 53 Edward D. Wood, Jr.
Bride of the Desert 29 Duke Worne
Bride of the Earth 68 Yılmaz Güney
Bride of the Gorilla 51 Curt Siodmak
Bride of the Lake 34 Maurice Elvey
Bride of the Monster 53 Edward D. Wood, Jr.
Bride of the Regiment 30 John Francis Dillon
Bride of the Storm 26 J. Stuart Blackton
Bride of Vengeance 49 Mitchell Leisen
Bride 68 29 Carmine Gallone
Bride sur le Cou, La 61 Jean Aurel, Jack Dunn Trop, Roger Vadim
Bride Talks in Her Sleep, The 33 Heinosuke Gosho
Bride Walks Out, The 36 Leigh Jason
Bride Was Very Beautiful, The 86 Pál Gábor
Bride Wasn't Willing, The 45 Charles Lamont
Bride with a Dowry 54 Tatiana Lukashevich, B. Ravenskikh
Bride Wore Black, The 67 François Truffaut
Bride Wore Boots, The 46 Irving Pichel
Bride Wore Crutches, The 41 Shepard Traube
Bride Wore Red, The 37 Dorothy Arzner
Bridegroom for Two 31 Richard Eichberg
Bridegroom in Sight 53 Juan Antonio Bardem, Luis García Berlanga
Bridegroom Talks in His Sleep, The 34 Heinosuke Gosho
Bridegroom, the Actress and the Pimp, The 68 Jean-Marie Straub
Bridegroom, the Comedienne and the Pimp, The 68 Jean-Marie Straub
Bridegrooms Beware 13 Maurice Elvey
Bridegroom's Dilemma, The 1899 Georges Méliès
Bridegroom's Mishaps, A 10 Edwin S. Porter
Brides Are Like That 36 William McGann
Bride's Awakening, The 18 Robert Z.

Leonard
Bride's Confession, The 21 Ivan Abramson
Brides of Blood 68 Gerry De Leon, Eddie Romero
Brides of Dr. Jekyll 64 Jesús Franco
Brides of Dracula, The 60 Terence Fisher
Brides of Fu Manchu, The 66 Don Sharp
Bride's Play, The 22 George Terwilliger
Bride's Relations, The 29 Mack Sennett
Bride's Silence, The 17 Henry King
Brides to Be 34 Reginald Denham
Bridge, The 28 Joris Ivens
Bridge, The 31 Charles Vidor
Bridge, The 42 Ben Maddow, Willard Van Dyke
Bridge, The 59 Bernhard Wicki
Bridge, The 86 José Luis Urquieta
Bridge Across No River 69 Tadashi Imai
Bridge Across the Sea 27 D. G. Phalke
Bridge Ahoy! 36 Dave Fleischer
Bridge at Remagen, The 69 John Guillermin
Bridge Destroyer, The 14 Frank Wilson
Bridge in the Jungle, The 70 Pancho Kohner
Bridge of Japan 56 Kon Ichikawa
Bridge of San Luis Rey, The 29 Charles Brabin
Bridge of San Luis Rey, The 44 Rowland V. Lee
Bridge of Sighs, The 24 Phil Rosen
Bridge of Sighs 36 Phil Rosen
Bridge of Storstrøm, The 50 Carl Theodor Dreyer
Bridge on the River Kwai, The 57 David Lean
Bridge Over the Ocean 27 D. G. Phalke
Bridge That Gap 65 Brian DePalma
Bridge to Nowhere 85 Ian Mune
Bridge to the Sun 61 Étienne Périer
Bridge to the Sun 86 Erdoğan Tokatli
Bridge Too Far, A 77 Richard Attenborough, Sidney Hayers
Bridge Wives 32 Roscoe Arbuckle
Bridges at Toko-Ri, The 54 Mark Robson
Bridges Burned 17 Perry N. Vekroff
Bridges-Go-Round 58 Shirley Clarke
Brief Authority 14 Warwick Buckland
Brief Ecstasy 37 Edmond T. Gréville
Brief Encounter 45 David Lean
Brief Encounters 67 Kira Muratova
Brief Moment 33 David Burton
Brief Rapture 52 Enzo Trapani
Brief Season, A 69 Renato Castellani
Brief Vacation, A 73 Vittorio De Sica
Briefträger Müller 53 Heinz Rühmann*
Brière, La 24 Léon Poirier
Brig, The 64 Adolfas Mekas, Jonas Mekas
Brigade des Mœurs 85 Max Pecas
Brigade No. 39 59 Károly Makk
Brigade Sauvage, La 38 Jean Dréville, Marcel L'Herbier
Brigada i Sverige 45 Bjarne Henning-Jensen
Brigadier Gerard 15 Bert Haldane
Brigadoon 54 Vincente Minnelli
Brigády 47 Karel Zeman
Brigand, The 52 Phil Karlson
Brigand Gentilhomme, Le 42 Joe Hamman

Brigand of Kandahar, The 65 John Gilling

Brigands, The 06 Lewin Fitzhamon

Brigand's Daughter, The 07 James A. Williamson

Brigand's Revenge, The 11 A. E. Coleby

Brigand's Wooing, A 13 Edwin J. Collins

Brigante, Il 61 Renato Castellani

Brigante di Tacca del Lupo, Il 52 Pietro Germi

Brigante Musolino, Il 50 Mario Camerini

Briganti Italiani, I 61 Mario Camerini

Briggs Family, The 40 Herbert Mason

Brigham Young 40 Henry Hathaway

Brigham Young—Frontiersman 40 Henry Hathaway

Bright College Years 71 Peter Rosen

Bright Day of My Life, The 48 Kozaburo Yoshimura

Bright Eyes 21 Malcolm St. Clair

Bright Eyes 34 David Butler

Bright Leaf 50 Michael Curtiz

Bright Lights 16 Roscoe Arbuckle

Bright Lights 24 Al Christie

Bright Lights 25 Robert Z. Leonard

Bright Lights 28 Walt Disney

Bright Lights 30 Michael Curtiz

Bright Lights 35 Busby Berkeley

Bright Lights, Big City 88 James Bridges

Bright Lights of Broadway 23 Webster Campbell

Bright Path 40 Grigori Alexandrov

Bright Prospects 40 Gustaf Molander

Bright Road, The 40 Grigori Alexandrov

Bright Road 53 Gerald Mayer

Bright Sea 63 Ko Nakahira

Bright Shawl, The 23 John S. Robertson

Bright Skies 20 Henry Kolker

Bright Victory 50 Mark Robson

Bright Young Things 27 George Dewhurst

Brighthaven Express 52 Maclean Rogers

Brightness 87 Souleymane Cissé

Brighton Beach Memoirs 86 Gene Saks

Brighton Mystery, The 24 Hugh Croise

Brighton Rock 47 John Boulting

Brighton Strangler, The 45 Max Nosseck

Brighty 67 Norman Foster

Brighty of the Grand Canyon 67 Norman Foster

Brigitte Horney 77 Krzysztof Zanussi

Brillantenschiff, Das 20 Fritz Lang

Brillantstjernen 12 August Blom

Brilliant Marriage 36 Phil Rosen

Brimade dans une Caserne 1895 Louis Lumière

Brimstone 49 Joseph Kane

Brimstone and Treacle 82 Richard Loncraine

Bring 'Em Back Alive 32 Clyde E. Elliott

Bring Him In 21 Robert Ensminger, Earle Williams

Bring Himself Back Alive 40 Dave Fleischer

Bring Me the Head of Alfredo Garcia 74 Sam Peckinpah

Bring Me the Vampire 60 Alfredo B. Crevenna

Bring On the Girls 45 Sidney Lanfield

Bring On the Night 85 Michael Apted

Bring Your Smile Along 55 Blake Edwards

Bringin' Home the Bacon 24 Richard Thorpe

Bringing Home Father 17 William Worthington

Bringing It Home 40 J. E. Lewis

Bringing It Home to Him 14 Toby Cooper

Bringing Up Baby 38 Howard Hawks

Bringing Up Betty 19 Oscar Apfel

Bringing Up Father 28 Jack Conway

Bringing Up Father 46 Edward F. Cline

Bringing Up Mother 54 William Hurtz

Brink, The 15 Walter Edwards

Brink of Hell 56 Mervyn LeRoy

Brink of Life 57 Ingmar Bergman

Brink's Job, The 78 William Friedkin

Brise-Glace 87 Jean Rouch, Raúl Ruiz

Bristet Lykke 13 August Blom

Brita in the Wholesaler's House 46 Åke Öhberg

Britain at Bay 40 Harry Watt

Britain Can Take It! 40 Humphrey Jennings, Harry Watt

Britain's Comet 52 James Hill

Britain's Naval Secret 15 Percy Moran

Britain's Secret Treaty 14 Charles Raymond

Britain's Tribute to Her Sons 01 Walter R. Booth

Britain's Welcome to Her Sons 00 Walter R. Booth

Britannia Hospital 81 Lindsay Anderson

Britannia Mews 49 Jean Negulesco

Britannia of Billingsgate 33 Sinclair Hill

British Agent 34 Michael Curtiz

British Bulldog Conquers, A 14 Alfred Lord

British Capturing a Maxim Gun 1899 Robert Ashe

British Family in Peace and War, A 40 George Pearson

British Intelligence 40 Terry Morse

British Lion Varieties 36 Herbert Smith

British Made 39 George Pearson

British Sounds 68 Jean-Luc Godard, Jean-Pierre Gorin

British Youth 41 George Pearson

Briton v. Boer 00 Arthur Cooper

Briton vs. Boer 00 Lewin Fitzhamon

Britons Awake! 15 Stuart Kinder

Britton of the Seventh 16 Lionel Belmore

Brivele der Mamen, A 39 Joseph Green

Broad Arrow, The 11 Bert Haldane

Broad Coalition, The 72 Simon Nuchtern

Broad Daylight 22 Irving Cummings

Broad-Minded 31 Mervyn LeRoy

Broad Road, The 23 Edmund Mortimer

Broadcast, The 68 Theodoros Angelopoulos

Broadcast News 87 James L. Brooks

Broadcasting 24 Earl Hurd

Broadcasting 25 Widgey R. Newman, Challis Sanderson

Broadway 29 Pál Fejös

Broadway 42 William A. Seiter

Broadway After Dark 24 Monta Bell

Broadway After Midnight 27 Fred Windermere

Broadway Ahead 41 Edward Dmytryk

Broadway and Home 20 Alan Crosland

Broadway Arizona 17 Lynn Reynolds

Broadway Babies 29 Mervyn LeRoy

Broadway Bad 33 Sidney Lanfield

Broadway Big Shot 42 William Beaudine

Broadway Bill 18 Fred J. Balshofer

Broadway Bill 34 Frank Capra

Broadway Billy 26 Harry Joe Brown

Broadway Blues 29 Mack Sennett

Broadway Boob, The 26 Joseph E. Henabery

Broadway Broke 23 J. Searle Dawley

Broadway Bubble, The 20 George L. Sargent

Broadway Butterfly, A 25 William Beaudine

Broadway Cowboy, The 20 Joseph Franz

Broadway Daddies 28 Fred Windermere

Broadway Daddies 29 Mervyn LeRoy

Broadway Danny Rose 84 Woody Allen

Broadway Drifter, The 27 Bernard F. McEveety

Broadway Fever 28 Edward F. Cline

Broadway Folly 30 Walter Lantz

Broadway Gallant, The 26 Noel Mason Smith

Broadway Gold 23 Edward Dillon

Broadway Gondolier 35 Lloyd Bacon

Broadway Hoofer, The 29 George Archainbaud

Broadway Hostess 35 Frank McDonald

Broadway Jones 17 Joseph Kaufman

Broadway Kid, The 27 Byron Haskin

Broadway Lady 25 Wesley Ruggles

Broadway Limited 41 Gordon Douglas

Broadway Love 17 Ida May Park

Broadway Madness 27 Burton L. King

Broadway Madonna, The 22 Harry Revier

Broadway Malady, The 33 Manny Gould, Ben Harrison

Broadway Melody, The 28 Harry Beaumont

Broadway Melody of 1936 35 Roy Del Ruth

Broadway Melody of 1938 37 Roy Del Ruth

Broadway Melody of 1940 40 Norman Taurog

Broadway Musketeers 38 John Farrow

Broadway Nights 27 Joseph C. Boyle

Broadway or Bust 24 Edward Sedgwick

Broadway Peacock, The 22 Charles Brabin

Broadway Rhythm 43 Roy Del Ruth

Broadway Rose 22 Robert Z. Leonard

Broadway Saint 19 Harry Hoyt

Broadway Scandal 18 Joseph De Grasse

Broadway Scandals 29 George Archainbaud

Broadway Serenade 39 Robert Z. Leonard

Broadway Singer 33 Alexander Hall, George Somnes

Broadway Sport, The 17 Carl Harbaugh

Broadway Through a Keyhole 33 Lowell Sherman

Broadway Thru a Keyhole 33 Lowell Sherman

Broadway to Cheyenne 32 Harry Fraser

Broadway to Hollywood 33 Willard Mack

Bröderna 13 Mauritz Stiller

Bröderna Karlsson 72 Vilgot Sjöman

Bröderna Mozart 86 Suzanne Osten

Broilers, The *20* Wallace A. Carlson
Broken April *87* Liria Begeja
Broken Arrow *50* Delmer Daves
Broken Barrier *17* George Bellamy
Broken Barriers *19* Charles E. Davenport
Broken Barriers *24* Reginald Barker
Broken Barriers *28* Burton L. King
Broken Blossoms *19* D. W. Griffith
Broken Blossoms *36* John Brahm
Broken Bottles *20* Leslie Henson
Broken Broom, The *04* Percy Stow
Broken Butterfly, The *19* Maurice Tourneur
Broken Chains *16* Yevgeni Bauer
Broken Chains *16* Robert Thornby
Broken Chains *22* Allen Holubar
Broken Chains *25* Yakov Protazanov
Broken Chisel, The *13* Charles H. Weston
Broken Cloud, A *15* B. Reeves Eason
Broken Coin, The *15* Francis Ford
Broken Commandment, The *61* Kon Ichikawa
Broken Commandments *19* Frank Beal
Broken Contract, A *20* Will P. Kellino
Broken Cross, The *11* D. W. Griffith
Broken Dishes *30* Mervyn LeRoy
Broken Doll, The *10* D. W. Griffith
Broken Doll, A *21* Allan Dwan
Broken Dreams *33* Robert Vignola
Broken Drum, The *49* Keisuke Kinoshita
Broken English *72* Derek Jarman
Broken English *81* Michie Gleason
Broken Faith *12* Dave Aylott
Broken Fetters *16* Rex Ingram
Broken Gate, The *20* Paul Scardon
Broken Gate, The *27* James McKay
Broken Hearted *29* Frank S. Mattison
Broken Hearts *26* Maurice Schwartz
Broken Hearts *33* Christy Cabanne
Broken Hearts and Noses *85* Sam Raimi
Broken Hearts of Broadway *23* Irving Cummings
Broken Hearts of Hollywood *26* Lloyd Bacon
Broken Homes *26* Hugh Dierker
Broken Horseshoe, The *52* Martyn Webster
Broken Images *86* Rafaat El Mihi
Broken in the Wars *18* Cecil M. Hepworth
Broken Journey *47* Ken Annakin
Broken Jug, The *38* Gustav Ucicky
Broken Lance *54* Edward Dmytryk
Broken Land, The *62* John Bushelman
Broken Law, The *15* Oscar Apfel
Broken Law, The *24* Bernard D. Russell
Broken Laws *24* Roy William Neill
Broken Leghorn, A *59* Robert McKimson
Broken Life, A *13* Edwin J. Collins
Broken Links *31* Erle C. Kenton
Broken Locket, The *09* D. W. Griffith
Broken Love *46* Guido Brignone
Broken Lullaby *31* Ernst Lubitsch
Broken Mask, The *28* James P. Hogan
Broken Melody, The *1896* Esme Collings
Broken Melody, The *07* Arthur Gilbert
Broken Melody, The *12* Lewin Fitzhamon
Broken Melody, The *16* Cavendish Morton
Broken Melody, The *20* William P. S. Earle
Broken Melody, The *29* Fred Paul

Broken Melody, The *34* Bernard Vorhaus
Broken Melody *38* Ken Hall
Broken Mirrors *84* Marleen Gorris
Broken Moon *86* Zheng Cao
Broken Noses *87* Bruce Weber
Broken Oath, The *13* Warwick Buckland
Broken Promise *83* Sandy Tung
Broken Rainbow *85* Maria Florio, Victoria Mudd
Broken Road, The *21* René Plaissetty
Broken Romance, A *29* J. Steven Edwards
Broken Rosary, The *34* Harry Hughes
Broken Sabre, The *65* Bernard McEveety
Broken Shadows *22* Albert Ward
Broken Shoes *34* Margarita Barskaya
Broken Silence, The *22* Del Henderson
Broken Sixpence, The *13* Warwick Buckland
Broken Sky *82* Ingrid Thulin
Broken Spell, The *13* Phillips Smalley
Broken Spur, The *21* Ben F. Wilson
Broken Star, The *56* Lesley Selander
Broken Strings *40* Bernard B. Ray
Broken Swords *69* Kazuo Ikehiro
Broken Threads *17* Henry Edwards
Broken Ties, The *12* Allan Dwan
Broken Ties *18* Arthur Ashley
Broken Toys *66* Manuel Summers
Broken Treaty at Battle Mountain *75* Joel L. Freedman
Broken Vase, The *13* Yakov Protazanov
Broken Victory *88* Gregory Strom
Broken Violin, The *08* Georges Méliès
Broken Violin, The *23* John Francis Dillon
Broken Violin, The *27* Oscar Micheaux
Broken Ways *13* D. W. Griffith
Broken Wedding Bells *30* Lewis R. Foster
Broken Wing, The *23* Tom Forman
Broken Wing, The *32* Lloyd Corrigan
Broken Wings, The *64* Yusuf Malouf
Brokiga Blad *31* Edvin Adolphson
Bröllopsbesvär *64* Åke Falck
Bröllopsresan *35* Gustaf Molander
Brolly, The *57* Břetislav Pojar
Bromley Case, The *20* Tom Collins
Bromo and Juliet *26* Leo McCarey
Bronc Buster, The *28* Leo D. Maloney
Bronc Stomper, The *28* Leo D. Maloney
Broncho Buster, The *27* Ernst Laemmle
Broncho Buster's Bride, The *11* Allan Dwan
Broncho Busting for Flying A Pictures *11* Allan Dwan
Broncho Pimple *14* Fred Evans, Joe Evans
Broncho Twister, The *27* Orville Dull
Bronco, El *86* Edgardo Gazcón
Bronco Billy *80* Clint Eastwood
Bronco Billy and the Revenue Agent *16* Gilbert M. Anderson
Bronco Billy Outwitted *12* Gilbert M. Anderson
Bronco Billy's Adventure *11* Gilbert M. Anderson
Bronco Billy's Indian Romance *14* Gilbert M. Anderson
Bronco Billy's Marriage *15* Gilbert M. Anderson
Bronco Billy's Oath *13* Gilbert M. Anderson
Bronco Billy's Redemption *10* Gilbert M.

Anderson
Bronco Billy's Vengeance *15* Gilbert M. Anderson
Bronco Bullfrog *70* Barney Platts-Mills
Bronco Buster, The *16* John R. Bray
Bronco Buster *35* Walter Lantz
Bronco Buster *52* Budd Boetticher
Bronenosets Potemkin *25* Sergei Eisenstein
Bronenosets Potyomkin *25* Sergei Eisenstein
Brontë *83* Delbert Mann
Brontë Sisters, The *78* André Téchiné
Bronx Warriors *82* Enzo G. Castellari
Bronze Bell, The *21* James W. Horne
Bronze Bride, The *17* Henry MacRae
Bronze Buckaroo, The *39* Richard Kahn
Bronze Idol, The *14* Frank Wilson
Brood, The *79* David Cronenberg
Brooding Eyes *26* Edward J. LeSaint
Brookfield Recreation Center, The *64* Bruce Baillie
Brooklyn Buckaroos *50* Leslie Goodwins
Brooklyn Orchid *42* Kurt Neumann
Broomstick Bunny *56* Chuck Jones
Brot des Bäckers, Das *76* Erwin Keusch
Broth for Supper *19* Thomas Ricketts
Broth of a Boy, A *59* George Pollock
Brother Alfred *32* Henry Edwards
Brother and His Younger Sister, A *39* Yasujiro Shimazu
Brother Brat *44* Frank Tashlin
Brother, Can You Spare a Dime? *75* Philippe Mora
Brother Carl *72* Susan Sontag
Brother, Cry for Me *70* William White
Brother from Another Planet, The *84* John Sayles
Brother John *70* James Goldstone
Brother, My Song *76* Christopher Cain
Brother of the Wind *72* Richard Robinson
Brother Officers *14* Charles C. Calvert
Brother Officers *15* Harold M. Shaw
Brother on the Run *73* Herbert L. Strock
Brother Orchid *40* Lloyd Bacon
Brother Rat *38* William Keighley
Brother Rat and a Baby *39* Ray Enright
Brother Sun, Sister Moon *72* Franco Zeffirelli
Brotherhood, The *26* Walter West
Brotherhood, The *68* Martin Ritt
Brotherhood *87* Stephen Shin
Brotherhood *90* Yang-ming Tsai
Brotherhood of Death *76* Bill Berry
Brotherhood of Man *47* Stephen Bosustow, Robert Cannon
Brotherhood of Satan, The *70* Bernard McEveety
Brotherhood of the Yakuza *74* Sydney Pollack
Brotherly Love *28* Charles Reisner
Brotherly Love *36* Dave Fleischer
Brotherly Love *69* J. Lee-Thompson
Brothers, The *10* Theo Bouwmeester
Brothers *12* D. W. Griffith
Brothers *13* Mauritz Stiller
Brothers, The *13* Allan Dwan
Brothers, The *14* Frank Wilson
Brothers, The *15* Ethyle Batley
Brothers *29* Walter Lang
Brothers *29* Scott Pembroke

Brothers, The 47 David MacDonald
Brothers 77 Arthur Barron
Brothers 84 Terry Bourke
Brothers, The 87 Jackie Chan
Brothers and Sisters 80 Richard Woolley
Brothers and Sisters of the Toda Family,
The 41 Yasujiro Ozu
Brother's Atonement, A 14 Bert Haldane
Brothers Carry Mouse Off 65 Chuck Jones
Brother's Devotion, A 10 J. Stuart Blackton
Brothers Divided 19 Frank Keenan
Brothers in Arms 89 George Jay Bloom III
Brothers in Law 56 Roy Boulting
Brothers in the Saddle 49 Lesley Selander
Brothers Karamazov, The 15 Victor Tourjansky
Brothers Karamazov, The 20 Dmitri Buchowetzki, Carl Fröhlich
Brothers Karamazov, The 31 Fedor Ozep
Brothers Karamazov, The 57 Richard Brooks
Brothers Karamazov, The 68 Ivan Pyriev, Mikhail Ulyanov
Brothers of the West 37 Sam Katzman
Brothers O'Toole, The 73 Richard Erdman
Brothers Rico, The 57 Phil Karlson
Brother's Sacrifice, A 12 Bert Haldane
Brothers Under the Skin 22 E. Mason Hopper
Brothers Wood 08 Émile Cohl
Brother's Wrong, A 09 Sidney Olcott
Brott och Straff 45 Erik Faustman
Brouillard sur la Ville, Le 16 Abel Gance
Brown Bewitched 11 A. E. Coleby
Brown Derby, The 26 Charles Hines
Brown of Harvard 17 Harry Beaumont
Brown of Harvard 26 Jack Conway
Brown on Resolution 35 Anthony Asquith, Walter Forde
Brown on Resolution 51 Roy Boulting
Brown Sugar 22 Fred Paul
Brown Sugar 31 Leslie Hiscott
Brown Wallet, The 36 Michael Powell
Browned Off 44 Donald Taylor
Brownie 42 Frank R. Strayer
Browning, Le 13 Louis Feuillade
Browning Version, The 50 Anthony Asquith
Brown's Day Off 12 Edwin J. Collins
Brown's Fishing Excursion 06 J. H. Martin
Brown's Half Holiday 05 James A. Williamson
Brown's Pudding 04 Alf Collins
Brown's Seance 12 Mack Sennett
Brubaker 80 Stuart Rosenberg
Bruce Gentry 48 Spencer G. Bennet, Thomas Carr
Bruce Gentry — Daredevil of the Skies 48 Spencer G. Bennet, Thomas Carr
Bruce Lee and I 76 Mar Lo
Bruce Lee — True Story 76 Ng See Yuen
Bruce Partington Plans, The 22 George Ridgwell
Brucia, Ragazzo, Brucia 70 Fernando Di Leo
Bruciati da Cocente Passione 76 Alberto Lattuada
Brücke, Die 59 Bernhard Wicki
Brüder Karamasoff, Die 20 Dmitri

Buchowetzki, Carl Fröhlich
Brüder Schellenberg, Die 26 Karl Grüne
Brug, De 28 Joris Ivens
Bruised by the Storms of Life 18 Josef Soifer
Bruiser, The 16 Charles E. Bartlett
Bruit, Le 55 Roger Leenhardt
Bruja, La 54 Chano Urueta
Bruja Sin Escoba, Una 67 José María Elorrieta
Brujas Mágicas 81 Mariano Ozores
Brûlure de Mille Soleils, La 64 Pierre Kast
Brumes d'Automne 28 Dmitri Kirsanov
Bruna Indiavolata, Una 51 Carlo Ludovico Bragaglia
Brune Que Voilà, La 60 Robert Lamoureux
Brunettes Prefer Gentlemen 27 Charles Lamont
Brunkul 41 Bjarne Henning-Jensen
Bruno, l'Enfant du Dimanche 68 Louis Grospierre
Bruno — Sunday's Child 68 Louis Grospierre
Brushfire! 61 Jack Warner, Jr.
Brussels Film Loops 58 Shirley Clarke, D. A. Pennebaker
Brussels Loops 58 Shirley Clarke, D. A. Pennebaker
Brussels-Transit 80 Samy Szlingerbaum
Brutal Justice 78 Umberto Lenzi
Brutal Master, A 09 Lewin Fitzhamon
Brutalität in Stein 60 Alexander Kluge, Peter Schamoni
Brutality 12 D. W. Griffith
Brutality in Stone 60 Alexander Kluge, Peter Schamoni
Brutality Rewarded 04 William Haggar
Brute, The 14 Sidney Olcott
Brute, The 21 Oscar Micheaux
Brute, The 27 Irving Cummings
Brute, The 52 Luis Buñuel
Brute, The 59 Zoltán Fábri
Brute, The 76 Gerry O'Hara
Brute, La 87 Claude Guillemot
Brute, The 87 Claude Guillemot
Brute and the Beast, The 66 Lucio Fulci, Terry Van Tell
Brute Breaker, The 19 Lynn Reynolds
Brute Corps 71 Jerry Jameson
Brute Force 13 D. W. Griffith
Brute Force 47 Jules Dassin
Brute Humaine, Une 14 Camille De Morlhon
Brute Man, The 46 Jean Yarbrough
Brute Master, The 20 Charles H. Kyson
Bruten Himmel 82 Ingrid Thulin
Brute's Revenge, A 12 A. E. Coleby
Bruto 10 Enrico Guazzoni
Bruto, El 52 Luis Buñuel
Brutti, Sporchi e Cattivi 76 Ettore Scola
Brutus 10 Enrico Guazzoni
Bruxelles-Transit 80 Samy Szlingerbaum
Bryant and the Speeches 13 Émile Cohl
Brzezina 70 Andrzej Wajda
Bu-Su 88 Jun Ichikawa
Bu Vatanın Çocukları 58 Atıf Yılmaz
Bubble, The 66 Arch Oboler
Bubbles 16 Herbert Brenon
Bubbles 20 Wayne Mack

Bubbles 22 Dave Fleischer
Bubbles of Trouble 16 Edward F. Cline
Bubbling Over 32 Leigh Jason
Bubù 70 Mauro Bolognini
Buccaneer, The 37 Cecil B. DeMille
Buccaneer, The 58 Anthony Quinn
Buccaneer Bunny 48 Friz Freleng
Buccaneer's Girl 50 Frederick De Cordova
Buchamukure Daihakken 69 Kengo Furusawa
Buchanan Rides Alone 58 Budd Boetticher
Buchanan's Wife 18 Charles Brabin
Bûcherons de la Manouane 62 Arthur Lamothe
Büchse der Pandora, Die 28 G. W. Pabst
Buck and the Preacher 71 Sidney Poitier
Buck Benny Rides Again 40 Mark Sandrich
Buck Privates 28 Melville Brown
Buck Privates 40 Arthur Lubin
Buck Privates Come Home 47 Charles Barton
Buck Rogers 39 Ford Beebe, Saul Goodkind
Buck Rogers in the Twenty-Fifth Century 79 Daniel Haller
Buckaroo 68 Adelchi Bianchi
Buckaroo Banzai 84 W. D. Richter
Buckaroo Broadcast, A 38 Jean Yarbrough
Buckaroo Bugs 44 Robert Clampett
Buckaroo from Powder River 47 Ray Nazarro
Buckaroo Kid, The 26 Lynn Reynolds
Buckaroo Sheriff of Texas 51 Philip Ford
Bucket of Blood 34 Brian Desmond Hurst
Bucket of Blood, A 59 Roger Corman
Buckeye and Blue 88 J. C. Compton
Bucking Broadway 17 John Ford
Bucking Horses 11 Allan Dwan
Bucking the Barrier 23 Colin Campbell
Bucking the Line 21 Carl Harbaugh
Bucking the Tiger 21 Henry Kolker
Bucking the Truth 26 Milburn Morante
Bucklige und die Tänzerin, Der 20 F. W. Murnau
Buck's Romance 13 William Duncan
Buckshot John 15 Hobart Bosworth
Buckskin 68 Michael Moore
Buckskin Frontier 43 Lesley Selander
Buckskin Lady, The 57 Carl K. Hittleman
Buckstone County Prison 78 Jimmy Huston
Bucktown 75 Arthur Marks
Buco, Il 59 Jacques Becker
Buco in Fronte, Un 68 Giuseppe Vari
Bucovina-Ukrainian Land 40 Yulia Solntseva
Bud Abbott and Lou Costello in Hollywood 45 S. Sylvan Simon
Bud and Susie 21 Frank Moser
Bud and Susie Join the Tecs 20 Frank Moser
Bud and Tommy Take a Day Off 20 Frank Moser
Bud Takes the Cake 20 Frank Moser
Budai Cukrászda 36 Béla Gaál
Budapest 55 Félix Máriássy
Budapest 85 Miklós Jancsó
Budapest, Amiért Szeretem 71 István Szabó*

Budapest Tales 76 István Szabó
Budapest: Why I Love It 71 István Szabó*
Budapesti Mesék 76 István Szabó
Budawanny 87 Bob Quinn
Buddenbrooks, Die 23 Gerhard Lam-
    precht
Buddenbrooks 59 Alfred Weidenmann
Buddha 65 Kenji Misumi
Buddha's Lock 87 Ho Yim
Buddies 76 Jan Halldoff
Buddies 83 Arch Nicholson
Buddies 85 Mats Arehn
Buddies 85 Arthur Bressan, Jr.
Buddy 26 Grigori Kozintsev, Leonid
    Trauberg
Buddy and Towser 34 Friz Freleng
Buddy Buddy 81 Billy Wilder
Buddy Holly Story, The 78 Steve Rash
Buddy in Africa 35 Ben Hardaway
Buddy of the Apes 34 Ben Hardaway
Buddy of the Legion 35 Ben Hardaway
Buddy Steps Out 35 Jack King
Buddy System, The 84 Glenn Jordan
Buddy the Dentist 35 Ben Hardaway
Buddy the Detective 34 Jack King
Buddy the Gee Man 35 Jack King
Buddy the Gob 34 Friz Freleng
Buddy the Woodsman 34 Jack King
Buddy's Adventures 35 Ben Hardaway
Buddy's Bearcats 34 Jack King
Buddy's Beer Garden 33 Earl Duvall
Buddy's Bug Hunt 35 Jack King
Buddy's Circus 34 Jack King
Buddy's Day Out 33 Jack King
Buddy's Garage 34 Earl Duvall
Buddy's Lost World 35 Jack King
Buddy's Pony Express 35 Ben Hardaway
Buddy's Show Boat 33 Jack King
Buddy's Theatre 35 Ben Hardaway
Buddy's Trolley Troubles 34 Friz Freleng
Büdös Víz 64 Frigyes Bán
Budujemy Nowe Wsie 46 Wanda Jaku-
    bowska
Buenaventura, La 34 William McGann
Bueno, el Feo y el Malo, El 66 Sergio
    Leone
Buenos Aires 22 José A. Ferreyra
Buenos Aires Rock '82 82 Héctor Olivera
Buenos Días Amor 57 Franco Rossi
Buffalo Bill 44 William A. Wellman
Buffalo Bill 62 Mario Costa
Buffalo Bill and the Indians, or Sitting
    Bull's History Lesson 76 Robert Altman
Buffalo Bill, Hero of the Far West 62
    Mario Costa
Buffalo Bill in Tomahawk Territory 52
    Bernard B. Ray
Buffalo Bill, l'Eroe del Far West 62 Mario
    Costa
Buffalo Bill on the Brain 11 Theo Bouw-
    meester
Buffalo Bill on the U.P. Trail 26 Frank S.
    Mattison
Buffalo Bill Rides Again 47 Bernard B.
    Ray
Buffalo Gun 61 Albert C. Gannaway
Buffalo Rider 78 George Lauris
Buffer Zone 81 István Gaál
Bufferin 66 Andy Warhol
Buffet Froid 79 Bertrand Blier

Bug 75 Jeannot Szwarc
Bug Parade, The 41 Tex Avery
Bug Vaudeville 16 Winsor McCay
Bugambilia 44 Emilio Fernández
Bugged By a Bee 69 Robert McKimson
Bugiarda, La 65 Luigi Comencini
Bugle Boy of Lancashire, The 14 Charles
    H. Weston
Bugle Call, The 16 Reginald Barker
Bugle Call, The 27 Edward Sedgwick
Bugle Sounds, The 41 S. Sylvan Simon
Bugler of Algiers, The 16 Rupert Julian
Bugles in the Afternoon 51 Roy Rowland
Bugs and Thugs 54 Friz Freleng
Bugs Bonnets 56 Chuck Jones
Bugs Bunny and the Three Bears 44
    Chuck Jones
Bugs Bunny Gets the Boid 42 Robert
    Clampett
Bugs Bunny Nips the Nips 44 Friz Freleng
Bugs Bunny Rides Again 48 Friz Freleng
Bugs Bunny/Road Runner Movie, The 79
    Chuck Jones, Phil Monroe
Bugs Bunny, Superstar 75 Larry Jackson
Bugs Bunny's 3rd Movie: 1001 Rabbit Tales
    82 Art Davis, David Detiege, Bill Perez
Bugsy and Mugsy 57 Friz Freleng
Bugsy Malone 76 Alan Parker
Build My Gallows High 47 Jacques
    Tourneur
Build Thy House 20 Fred Goodwins
Builders 42 Pat Jackson
Builders, The 54 Robert Altman
Builders of Castles 17 Ben Turbett
Building a Chicken House 14 F. L. Lynd-
    hurst
Building Made Easy, or How Mechanics
    Work in the Twentieth Century 01 Ed-
    win S. Porter
Building the Great Los Angeles Aqueduct
    13 Allan Dwan
Buildup, The 58 Yasuzo Masumura
Built on a Bluff 24 Charles Lamont
Buio in Sala 49 Dino Risi
Buio Omega 79 Aristide Massaccesi
Buisson Ardent, Le 55 Alexander Alex-
    eïeff, Claire Parker
Buisson Ardent 87 Laurent Perrin
Bukhta Smerti 26 Abram Room
Buki Naki Tatakai 60 Satsuo Yamamoto
Bukovyna-Zemlya Ukrayinska 40 Yulia
    Solntseva
Bulge of Fire, The 68 Yuri Ozerov
Bull and the Picnickers, The 02 Edwin S.
    Porter
Bull Durham 88 Ron Shelton
Bull Fight 59 Allan King
Bull Fighter, The 27 Edward F. Cline
Bull of the West, The 71 Jerry Hopper,
    Paul Stanley
Bull Rushes 30 Will P. Kellino
Bullamakanka 84 Simon Heath
Bulldog and the Baby, The 42 Alec Geiss
Bulldog Breed, The 60 Robert Asher
Bulldog Courage 22 Edward Kull
Bulldog Courage 35 Sam Newfield
Bulldog Drummond 23 Oscar Apfel
Bulldog Drummond 29 F. Richard Jones
Bulldog Drummond at Bay 37 Norman
    Lee

Bulldog Drummond at Bay 47 Sidney Sal-
    kow
Bulldog Drummond Comes Back 37 Louis
    King
Bulldog Drummond Escapes 37 James P.
    Hogan
Bulldog Drummond in Africa 38 Louis
    King
Bulldog Drummond Strikes Back 34 Roy
    Del Ruth
Bulldog Drummond Strikes Back 47 Frank
    McDonald
Bulldog Drummond's Bride 39 James P.
    Hogan
Bulldog Drummond's Peril 38 James P.
    Hogan
Bulldog Drummond's Revenge 37 Louis
    King
Bulldog Drummond's Secret Police 39
    James P. Hogan
Bulldog Drummond's Third Round 25
    Sidney Morgan
Bulldog Edition 36 Charles Lamont
Bulldog Grit 15 Ethyle Batley
Bulldog Jack 34 Walter Forde
Bulldog Pluck 27 Jack Nelson
Bulldog Sees It Through 40 Harold Huth
Bulldogs of the Trail, The 15 Kenneth
    MacDougall
Bulldozing the Bull 38 Dave Fleischer
Bulle und das Mädchen, Der 85 Peter
    Keglevic
Bulles de Savon 29 Slatan Dudow
Bulles de Savon Animées, Les 06 Georges
    Méliès
Bullet Code 40 David Howard
Bullet for a Badman 64 R. G. Springsteen
Bullet for a Stranger 71 Giuliano Car-
    mineo
Bullet for Billy the Kid 63 Rafael Baledón
Bullet for Joey, A 55 Lewis Allen
Bullet for Pretty Boy, A 70 Larry Buch-
    anan
Bullet for Sandoval, A 69 Julio Buchs
Bullet for Stefano 50 Duilio Coletti
Bullet for the General, A 66 Damiano
    Damiani
Bullet from the Past 57 Kenneth Hume
Bullet Is Waiting, A 54 John Farrow
Bullet Mark, The 28 Stuart Paton
Bullet-Proof 20 Lynn Reynolds
Bullet Scars 42 D. Ross Lederman
Bulleteers, The 42 Dave Fleischer
Bulletproof 87 Steve Carver
Bullets and Brown Eyes 16 Scott Sidney
Bullets and Bull 17 Gregory La Cava
Bullets and Bullion 41 S. Roy Luby
Bullets and Saddles 43 Anthony Marshall
Bullets Cannot Pierce Me 67 Yılmaz
    Güney
Bullets Cannot Touch Me, The 67 Yılmaz
    Güney
Bullets for Bandits 42 Wallace Fox
Bullets for O'Hara 41 William K. Howard
Bullets for Rustlers 40 Sam Nelson
Bullets or Ballots 36 William Keighley
Bullfight 51 Pierre Braunberger
Bullfight 55 Shirley Clarke
Bullfighter and the Lady, The 51 Budd
    Boetticher

Bullfighters, The *27* Edward F. Cline
Bullfighters, The *45* Malcolm St. Clair
Bullies *86* Paul Lynch
Bullin' the Bullsheviki *19* Frank P. Donovan
Bulling the Bolshevik *18* Raoul Barré, Charles Bowers
Bullitt *68* Peter Yates
Bull-oney *28* Walter Lantz, Tom Palmer
Bulloney *33* Ubbe Iwerks
Bulls and Bears *30* Mack Sennett
Bull's Eye *18* James W. Horne
Bullseye *86* Carl Schultz
Bullseye! *90* Michael Winner
Bullshot *83* Dick Clement
Bullwhip! *58* Harmon Jones
Bully, The *10* Theo Bouwmeester
Bully *32* Ubbe Iwerks
Bully *78* Peter H. Hunt
Bully and the Recruit, The *08* Jack Chart
Bully for Bugs *53* Chuck Jones
Bum Bandit, The *31* Dave Fleischer
Bum Steer, A *28* Manny Gould, Ben Harrison
Bum Voyage *34* Nick Grindé
Bumbles and the Bass *13* Will P. Kellino
Bumbles' Appetite *14* Will P. Kellino
Bumbles Becomes a Crook *13* Will P. Kellino
Bumbles' Blunder *15* Cecil Birch
Bumbles' Diminisher *13* Will P. Kellino
Bumbles' Electric Belt *13* Will P. Kellino
Bumbles Goes Butterflying *14* Will P. Kellino
Bumbles' Goose *13* Will P. Kellino
Bumbles' Holiday *13* Will P. Kellino
Bumbles, Photographer *13* Will P. Kellino
Bumbles' Radium Minstrels *13* Will P. Kellino
Bumbles' Walk to Brighton *13* Will P. Kellino
Bumerang *60* Alfred Weidenmann
Bumerang Bumerang *89* Hans W. Geissendörfer
Bummer *73* William Allen Castleman
Bump, The *20* Adrian Brunel
Bump in the Night *81* Andrew Davis
Bumping Into Broadway *19* Hal Roach
Bumpkin's Patent Spyopticon *10* A. E. Coleby
Bumps *28* Abram Room
Bumps and Things *22* Raoul Barré, Charles Bowers
Bumpstone *86* Franci Slak
Bun Mooi *82* Dennis Yu
Bunch of Keys, A *15* Richard Foster Baker
Bunch of Violets, A *16* Frank Wilson
Bunco Squad *50* Herbert I. Leeds
Buncoed Stage Johnnie *08* Georges Méliès
Bundfald *57* Palle Kjærulff-Schmidt
Bundle of Joy *56* Norman Taurog
Bundle of Trouble, A *42* Frank R. Strayer
Bundle of Trouble *47* Abby Berlin
Bungalow Boobs *24* Leo McCarey
Bungalow 13 *48* Edward L. Cahn
Bungawan Solo *51* Kon Ichikawa
Bungle Uncle *62* Joseph Barbera, William Hanna
Bungled Bungalow *50* Pete Burness
Bungling Burglars *12* Frank Wilson

Bunked and Paid For *17* Walt Mason
Bunker Bean *36* William Hamilton, Edward Killy
Bunker Hill Bunny *50* Friz Freleng
Bunker Palace Hotel *89* Enki Bilal
Bunkered *29* Redd Davis
Bunker's Patent Bellows *10* Dave Aylott
Bunnies Abundant *62* Joseph Barbera, William Hanna
Bunnies and Bonnets *33* Manny Gould, Ben Harrison
Bunny All at Sea *12* George D. Baker
Bunny and Claude *68* Robert McKimson
Bunny at the Derby *12* Lawrence Trimble
Bunny Blarneyed, or The Blarney Stone *13* Lawrence Trimble
Bunny Buys a Harem *14* George D. Baker
Bunny Caper, The *74* Jack Arnold
Bunny Hugged *51* Chuck Jones
Bunny in Bunnyland *15* Carl Francis Lederer
Bunny Lake Is Missing *65* Otto Preminger
Bunny-Mooning *37* Dave Fleischer
Bunny O'Hare *70* Gerd Oswald
Bunny's Birthday *14* George D. Baker
Bunny's Mistake *14* George D. Baker
Bunny's Scheme *14* George D. Baker
Bunting's Blink *15* Percy Nash
Buntkarierten, Die *49* Kurt Mätzig
Bunty Pulls the Strings *21* Reginald Barker
Bunty Wins a Pup *53* Victor M. Gover
Buon Funerale Amigos, Paga Sartana *70* Giuliano Carmineo
Buon Giorno Elefante *52* Gianni Franciolini
Buon Giorno Natura *55* Ermanno Olmi
Buon Natale, Buon Anno *89* Luigi Comencini
Buona Sera, Mrs. Campbell *68* Melvin Frank
Buone Notizie, Le *79* Elio Petri
Buono, il Brutto, il Cattivo, Il *66* Sergio Leone
Buque Maldito, El *74* Amando De Ossorio
Buraikan *70* Masahiro Shinoda
Burari Burabura Monogatari *63* Zenzo Matsuyama
Burbero, Il *87* Franco Castellano, Giuseppe Moccia
'burbs, The *89* Joe Dante
Burden of Dreams *82* Les Blank
Burden of Life *35* Heinosuke Gosho
Burden of Proof, The *18* Julius Steger
Bureau des Mariages, Le *62* Yannick Bellon
Bureau of Missing Persons *33* Roy Del Ruth
Burglar, The *05* Alf Collins
Burglar, The *17* Harley Knoles
Burglar, The *24* George Marshall
Burglar, The *28* Frank Capra
Burglar, The *56* Paul Wendkos
Burglar *87* Valery Ogorodnikov
Burglar *87* Hugh Wilson
Burglar Alarm, The *18* Raoul Barré, Charles Bowers
Burglar and Little Phyllis, The *10* Lewin Fitzhamon
Burglar and the Cat, The *06* Lewin Fitzhamon

Burglar and the Child, The *09* Theo Bouwmeester
Burglar and the Clock, The *08* Lewin Fitzhamon
Burglar and the Girl, The *28* Hugh Croise
Burglar and the Girls, The *04* Percy Stow
Burglar and the Judge, The *06* Lewin Fitzhamon
Burglar and the Lady, The *14* Herbert Blaché
Burglar As Father Christmas, The *11* Theo Bouwmeester
Burglar at the Ball, The *13* Hay Plumb
Burglar Bill *16* Alfonse Frenguelli, Lewis Gilbert
Burglar by Proxy *19* John Francis Dillon
Burglar Cupid, A *09* Edwin S. Porter
Burglar Expected, The *10* Percy Stow
Burglar for a Night, A *11* Bert Haldane
Burglar Helped, The *12* Hay Plumb
Burglar Lover, The *05* Alf Collins
Burglar on the Roof, The *1897* J. Stuart Blackton
Burglar, or The Hue and Cry, The *05* Alf Collins
Burglar-Proof *20* Maurice Campbell
Burglar Story, The *65* Satsuo Yamamoto
Burglars *18* Gregory La Cava
Burglars, The *71* Henri Verneuil
Burglars at the Ball *07* Lewin Fitzhamon
Burglar's Boy, The *05* Lewin Fitzhamon
Burglar's Child, The *13* Percy Nash
Burglar's Daughter, The *12* Lewin Fitzhamon
Burglar's Dilemma, The *12* D. W. Griffith
Burglars in the Wine Cellar, The *02* Georges Méliès
Burglar's Joke with the Automatic Doll, The *08* Alf Collins
Burglar's Misfortune, The *10* Fred Rains
Burglar's Mistake, A *09* D. W. Griffith
Burglar's Slide for Life, The *05* Edwin S. Porter
Burglar's Surprise, The *07* J. H. Martin
Burgomaster of Stilemonde, The *28* George J. Banfield
Burgtheater *36* Willi Forst
Burial Path *78* Stan Brakhage
Buridan—Le Héros de la Tour de Nesle *24* Pierre Marodon
Buried Alive *39* Victor Halperin
Buried Alive *51* Guido Brignone
Buried Alive *84* Michael Hodges
Buried Alive *84* Aristide Massaccesi
Buried Alive *90* Gérard Kikoine
Buried Gold *26* John P. McGowan
Buried Hand, The *15* Raoul Walsh
Buried Loot *35* George B. Seitz
Buried Secret, The *15* Forest Holger-Madsen
Buried Treasure *21* George D. Baker
Burke and Hare *71* Vernon Sewell
Burke & Wills *85* Graeme Clifford
Burlesk Queen *77* Celso Ad Castillo
Burlesque Highway Robbery in Gay Paree, A *04* Georges Méliès
Burlesque of Popular Composers *02* James A. Williamson
Burlesque Suicide *02* Edwin S. Porter

Burma Convoy *41* Noel Mason Smith
Burma Teak *31* John Grierson
Burma Victory *45* Roy Boulting
Burmese Harp, The *56* Kon Ichikawa
Burmese Harp, The *85* Kon Ichikawa
Burn! *68* Gillo Pontecorvo
Burn 'Em Up Barnes *21* George A. Beranger, Johnny Hines
Burn 'Em Up Barnes *34* Colbert Clark, Armand Schaefer
Burn 'Em Up O'Connor *39* Edward Sedgwick
Burn Out *75* Daniel Mann
Burn, Witch, Burn *61* Sidney Hayers
Burn, Witch, Burn *69* Michael Armstrong
Burndown *89* James Allen
Burned Hand, The *15* Tod Browning
Burnin' Love *87* John Moffitt
Burning, The *67* Stephen Frears
Burning, The *80* Tony Maylam
Burning Acre, The *22* F. W. Murnau
Burning an Illusion *81* Menelik Shabazz
Burning Angel *84* Lauri Törhönen
Burning Arrows *53* Lew Landers
Burning Bridges *28* James P. Hogan
Burning Bush *87* Laurent Perrin
Burning Court, The *61* Julien Duvivier
Burning Cross, The *47* Walter Colmes
Burning Cross, The *74* Terence Young
Burning Daylight *14* Hobart Bosworth
Burning Daylight *20* Edward Sloman
Burning Daylight *28* Charles Brabin
Burning Earth, The *22* F. W. Murnau
Burning Flowers *86* Eva Dahr, Eva Isaksen
Burning Gold *27* John W. Noble
Burning Gold *36* Sam Newfield
Burning Heart, The *29* Ludwig Berger
Burning Heart, The *62* Otakar Vávra
Burning Hearts *45* Veidt Harlan
Burning Hills, The *56* Stuart Heisler
Burning Home, The *09* Jack Smith
Burning Man, The *81* Quentin Masters
Burning of Durland's Riding Academy, The *02* Edwin S. Porter
Burning of Lanka, The *18* D. G. Phalke
Burning of St. Pierre *02* Edwin S. Porter
Burning Path, The *22* F. W. Murnau
Burning Question, The *36* Louis Gasnier
Burning Question, The *45* Ken Hughes
Burning Sands *22* George Melford
Burning Sands *87* Francisco De Paula
Burning Secret, The *33* Robert Siodmak
Burning Secret *88* Andrew Birkin
Burning Snow *88* Patrick Tam
Burning Soil *22* F. W. Murnau
Burning Stable, The *00* Cecil M. Hepworth
Burning the Candle *17* Harry Beaumont
Burning the Wind *29* Herbert Blaché, Henry MacRae
Burning Trail, The *25* Arthur Rosson
Burning Up *30* A. Edward Sutherland
Burning Up Broadway *28* Phil Rosen
Burning Words *23* Stuart Paton
Burning Years, The *79* Vittorio Sindoni
Burnout *79* Graham Meech-Burkestone
Burnt Evidence *54* Daniel Birt
Burnt Fingers *27* Maurice Campbell
Burnt In *20* Duncan Macrae
Burnt Offering *32* Frank Lloyd

Burnt Offerings *76* Dan Curtis
Burnt Up *27* William C. Nolan
Burnt Wings *16* Walter West
Burnt Wings *20* Christy Cabanne
Burroughs *84* Howard Brookner
Burr's Novelty Review No. 1 *22* R. E. Donahue, J. J. McManus
Burr's Novelty Review No. 2 *22* R. E. Donahue, J. J. McManus
Burr's Novelty Review No. 3 *22* R. E. Donahue, J. J. McManus
Burr's Novelty Review No. 4 *22* R. E. Donahue, J. J. McManus
Burr's Novelty Review No. 5 *22* R. E. Donahue, J. J. McManus
Burr's Novelty Review No. 6 *22* R. E. Donahue, J. J. McManus
Burschenlied aus Heidelberg, Ein *31* Karl Hartl
Burst City *82* Sogo Ishii
Burst of Lead *86* Pedro Galindo III
Bury Me an Angel *71* Barbara Peeters
Bury Me Dead *47* Bernard Vorhaus
Bury Me Not on the Lone Prairie *41* Ray Taylor
Bury Them Deep *68* Paolo Moffa
Burys *85* Alexei Simonov
Bus, The *65* Haskell Wexler
Bus, The *86* Yadollah Samadi
Bus *87* Takashi Komatsu
Bus Is Coming, The *71* Wendall James Franklin
Bus Number Three *80* Luo Tai, Jiayi Wang
Bus Riley's Back in Town *65* Harvey Hart
Bus Stop *56* Joshua Logan
Bus II *83* Bonnie Bass Parker, Tom Tyson, Haskell Wexler
Bush Christmas *46* Ralph Smart
Bush Christmas *83* Henri Safran
Bush Leaguer, The *27* Howard Bretherton
Bush Pilot *47* Sterling Campbell
Bushbaby, The *70* John Trent
Busher, The *19* Jerome Storm
Bushfire Moon *87* George (Trumbull) Miller
Bushido *63* Tadashi Imai
Bushido Blade, The *78* Tom Kotani
Bushido, Samurai Saga *63* Tadashi Imai
Bushidō Zankoku Monogatari *63* Tadashi Imai
Bushman *72* David Schikele
Bushranger, The *28* Chester Withey
Bushwhackers, The *51* Rod Amateau
Bushy Hare *50* Robert McKimson
Business and Pleasure *31* David Butler
Business As Usual *87* Lezli-An Barrett
Business As Usual During Alterations *13* Percy Stow
Business Is Booming *85* Janne Carlsson, Peter Schildt
Business Is Business *12* Wilfred Noy
Business Is Business *15* Otis Turner
Business Is Business *19* Gregory La Cava
Business Is Business *21* Erle C. Kenton
Business Is Business *71* Paul Verhoeven
Business Must Not Interfere *13* Émile Cohl
Business of Life, The *18* Tom Terriss
Business of Love, The *25* Irving Reis, Jess Robbins

Business People *63* Leonid Gaidai
Businessman's Lunch, The *68* Rolf Emyl
Busker's Revenge, The *14* Kelly Storrie
Busman's Holiday *36* Maclean Rogers
Busman's Honeymoon *40* Arthur Woods
Búsqueda, La *87* Juan Carlos De Sanzo
Busses Roar *42* D. Ross Lederman
Busted Hearts *14* Charles Chaplin
Busted Johnny, A *14* Henry Lehrman
Busted Up *86* Conrad E. Palmisano
Buster, The *23* Colin Campbell
Buster *88* David Green
Buster and Billie *74* Daniel Petrie
Buster Brown and His Dog Tige *04* Edwin S. Porter
Buster Keaton Story, The *57* Sidney Sheldon
Buster Minds the Baby *28* Sam Newfield
Buster Se Marie *30* Claude Autant-Lara
Buster Trains Up *28* Sam Newfield
Buster's Joke on Papa *03* Edwin S. Porter
Buster's Spooks *29* Sam Newfield
Buster's World *85* Bille August
Bustin' Loose *81* Oz Scott
Bustin' Thru *25* Clifford Smith
Busting *73* Peter Hyams
Busting Buster *28* Sam Newfield
Búsulni Nem Jó *38* Jenő Csepreghy
Busy Bakers *40* Cal Dalton, Ben Hardaway
Busy Barber, The *32* Walter Lantz
Busy Beavers, The *31* Wilfred Jackson
Busy Birds *27* William C. Nolan
Busy Bodies *33* Lloyd French
Busy Body, The *66* William Castle
Busy Buddies *56* Joseph Barbera, William Hanna
Busy Bus *34* Manny Gould, Ben Harrison
Busy Day, A *14* Charles Chaplin
Busy Kind of Bloke, A *80* Gillian Armstrong
Busy Man, The *07* Lewin Fitzhamon
Busybody, The *23* Gregory La Cava
Busybody, The *29* Edward Sloman
But a Butler *22* Alfred Santell
But It's Nothing Serious *36* Mario Camerini
But Not for Me *59* Walter Lang
But Not in Vain *48* Edmond T. Gréville
But the Flesh Is Weak *32* Jack Conway
But What Do These Women Want? *77* Coline Serreau
But Where Is Daniel Vax? *72* Avram Heffner
But You Were Dead *66* Gianni Vernuccio
Buta to Gunkan *61* Shohei Imamura
Butch and Sundance *79* Richard Lester
Butch and Sundance: The Early Days *79* Richard Lester
Butch Cassidy and the Sundance Kid *69* George Roy Hill
Butch Minds the Baby *42* Albert S. Rogell
Butch Minds the Baby *79* Peter Webb
Butcher, The *69* Claude Chabrol
Butcher and the Tramp, The *1899* C. Goodwin Norton
Butcher, Baker, Nightmare Maker *81* William Asher
Butcher Boy, The *17* Roscoe Arbuckle
Butcher Boy, The *32* Walter Lantz
Butcher's Boy and the Penny Dreadful, The *09* A. E. Coleby

Calhoun 87 Joseph L. Scanlan
Calibre 38 19 Edgar Lewis
Calibre 45 24 John P. McGowan
Calico Queen, The 69 J. Van Hearn
Caliente Love 33 George Marshall
California 27 W. S. Van Dyke
California 46 John Farrow
California 63 Hamil Petroff
California 78 Michele Lupo
California Axe Massacre 77 Frederick R.
  Friedel
California Conquest 52 Lew Landers
California Dolls, The 81 Robert Aldrich
California Dreaming 79 John Hancock
California Firebrand 48 Philip Ford
California Frontier 38 Elmer Clifton
California Girls 81 Al Music, Michael
  Sherman, William Webb
California Gold Rush 46 R. G. Spring-
  steen
California Holiday 66 Norman Taurog
California in 1878 30 William Nigh
California in '49 24 Jacques Jaccard
California Joe 43 Spencer G. Bennet
California Mail, The 29 Albert S. Rogell
California Mail, The 36 Noel Mason
  Smith
California or Bust 27 Phil Rosen
California Passage 50 Joseph Kane
California Reich, The 77 Keith F. Critch-
  low, Walter F. Parkes
California Romance, A 22 Jerome Storm
California Split 74 Robert Altman
California Straight Ahead 25 Harry A.
  Pollard
California Straight Ahead 37 Arthur
  Lubin
California Suite 78 Herbert Ross
California Trail, The 33 Lambert Hillyer
Californian, The 37 Gus Meins
Californian Junior Symphony 42 Jean
  Negulesco
California's Golden Beginning 48 Cecil B.
  DeMille
Caligari's Curse 83 Tom Palozola
Caligula 77 Tinto Brass
Caliph Storch 54 Lotte Reiniger
Caliph Stork 54 Lotte Reiniger
Caliph's Nights, The 86 José Luis García
  Agraz
Call, The 09 D. W. Griffith
Call, The 13 Ralph Ince
Call, The 14 Cecil M. Hepworth
Call, The 36 Léon Poirier
Call a Cop 21 Malcolm St. Clair
Call a Cop! 31 George Stevens
Call a Messenger 39 Arthur Lubin
Call for Arms, A 40 Brian Desmond
  Hurst
Call from Space 89 Richard Fleischer
Call from the Past, A 15 Frank Wilson
Call from the Wild, The 21 Wharton
  James
Call Girl 51 Reginald LeBorg
Call Girl 77 62 R. Lee Frost
Call Girls 57 Arthur Maria Rabenalt
Call Harry Crown 74 John Frankenheimer
Call Her Savage 32 John Francis Dillon
Call Him Mr. Shatter 74 Michael Carreras,
  Monte Hellman, Gordon Hessler, Seth

Holt
Call It a Day 37 Archie Mayo
Call It Luck 34 James Tinling
Call It Murder 34 Chester Erskine
Call Me 88 Sollace Mitchell
Call Me a Cab 63 Gerald Thomas
Call Me Bwana 63 Gordon Douglas
Call Me Genius 60 Robert Day
Call Me Madam 53 Walter Lang
Call Me Mame 33 John Daumery
Call Me Mister 51 Lloyd Bacon
Call Me Robert 67 Ilya Olshvanger
Call Northside 777 48 Henry Hathaway
Call of Courage, The 25 Clifford Smith
Call of Her People, The 17 John W.
  Noble
Call of Home, The 22 Louis Gasnier
Call of Motherhood, The 17 Abel Gance
Call of Siva, The 23 A. E. Coleby
Call of the Blood 47 John Clements, Lad-
  islas Vajda
Call of the Canyon, The 23 Victor Flem-
  ing
Call of the Canyon 42 Joseph Santley
Call of the Circus 30 Frank O'Connor
Call of the City, The 15 Harry Beaumont
Call of the Cuckoos 27 Clyde Bruckman
Call of the Cumberlands, The 15 Frank
  Lloyd
Call of the Dance, The 15 George L. Sar-
  gent
Call of the Desert 30 John P. McGowan
Call of the Drum, The 14 Harold Weston
Call of the East, The 17 George Melford
Call of the East, The 22 Bert Wynne
Call of the Flesh 30 Charles Brabin
Call of the Forest 49 John Link
Call of the Heart 19 John M. Stahl
Call of the Heart 28 Francis Ford
Call of the Hills, The 23 Fred Hornby
Call of the Jungle 44 Phil Rosen
Call of the Klondike, The 26 Oscar Apfel
Call of the Klondike 50 Frank McDonald
Call of the Mate 24 Alvin J. Neitz
Call of the Motherland, The 15 F. Martin
  Thornton
Call of the North, The 14 Oscar Apfel,
  Cecil B. DeMille
Call of the North, The 21 Joseph E. Hen-
  abery
Call of the Open Range, The 11 Allan
  Dwan
Call of the Pipes, The 17 Tom Watts
Call of the Prairie 36 Howard Bretherton
Call of the Ring, The 37 Irving Pichel
Call of the Road, The 20 A. E. Coleby
Call of the Rockies 31 Raymond K. John-
  son
Call of the Rockies 38 Alvin J. Neitz
Call of the Rockies 44 Lesley Selander
Call of the Savage, The 35 Lew Landers
Call of the Sea, The 15 Joseph Byron Tot-
  ten
Call of the Sea, The 15 J. Wallett Waller
Call of the Sea, The 30 Leslie Hiscott
Call of the Soul 19 Edward J. LeSaint
Call of the South Seas 44 John English
Call of the West 30 Albert Ray
Call of the Wild, The 08 D. W. Griffith
Call of the Wild, The 23 Fred Jackman

Call of the Wild, The 35 William A.
  Wellman
Call of the Wild, The 72 Ken Annakin
Call of the Wilderness, The 26 Jack Nel-
  son
Call of the Yukon 38 B. Reeves Eason*
Call of Youth, The 20 Hugh Ford
Call Out the Marines 42 William Hamil-
  ton, Frank Ryan
Call Surftide 77 62 R. Lee Frost
Call the Cops! 76 John Trent
Call the Mesquiteers 38 John English
Call to Arms, The 02 Cecil M. Hepworth
Call to Arms, The 10 D. W. Griffith
Call to Arms, The 13 Allan Dwan
Call to Arms 37 Alexander Macharet
Call Your Shots 28 Stephen Roberts
Callahans and the Murphys, The 27
  George W. Hill
Callan 74 Don Sharp
Callaway Went Thataway 51 Melvin
  Frank, Norman Panama
Callbox Mystery, The 32 George B.
  Samuelson
Calle Mayor 56 Juan Antonio Bardem
Called Back 11 Edwin S. Porter
Called Back 14 George Loane Tucker
Called Back 14 Otis Turner
Called Back 33 Reginald Denham, Jack
  Harris
Called to the Front 14 Charles H. Weston
Caller, The 87 Arthur Allan Seidelman
Calles de Buenos Aires 34 José A. Ferreyra
Calligraphy 53 Charles Eames, Ray Eames
Calling, The 81 Michael Anderson
Calling All Cars 35 Spencer G. Bennet
Calling All Cars 54 Maclean Rogers
Calling All Cats 58 Alfred Shaughnessy
Calling All Crooks 38 George Black
Calling All Doctors 37 Charles Lamont
Calling All G-Men 36 Albert S. Rogell
Calling All Husbands 40 Noel Mason Smith
Calling All Marines 39 John H. Auer
Calling All Ma's 37 Redd Davis
Calling All Stars 37 Herbert Smith
Calling Bulldog Drummond 51 Victor
  Saville
Calling Dr. Death 43 Reginald LeBorg
Calling Dr. Gillespie 42 Harold S. Buc-
  quet
Calling Dr. Kildare 39 Harold S. Bucquet
Calling Dr. Magoo 56 Pete Burness
Calling Dr. Porky 40 Friz Freleng
Calling Homicide 56 Edward Bernds
Calling Northside 777 48 Henry Hathaway
Calling of Dan Matthews, The 35 Phil
  Rosen
Calling of Jim Barton, The 14 Gilbert M.
  Anderson
Calling Paul Temple 48 Maclean Rogers
Calling Philo Vance 40 William Clemens
Calling the Tune 36 Reginald Denham
Calling Wild Bill Elliott 43 Spencer G.
  Bennet
Calliope 71 Matt Cimber
Calm Yourself! 35 George B. Seitz
Calmos 75 Bertrand Blier
Calomnie, La 17 Maurice Mariaud
Caltiki il Monstro Immortale 59 Mario
  Bava, Riccardo Freda

Canto do Mar, O *52* Alberto Cavalcanti

Cantor's Daughter, The *13* Avrom Yitskhok Kaminsky

Cantor's Son, The *37* Ilya Motylev

Canvas Kisser, The *25* Duke Worne

Canyon Ambush *52* Lewis D. Collins

Canyon City *43* Spencer G. Bennet

Canyon Crossroads *55* Alfred L. Werker

Canyon Dweller, The *12* Allan Dwan

Canyon Hawks *30* John P. McGowan

Canyon of Adventure, The *28* Albert S. Rogell

Canyon of Light, The *26* Ben Stoloff

Canyon of Missing Men, The *30* John P. McGowan

Canyon of the Fools *23* Val Paul

Canyon Pass *50* Edwin L. Marin

Canyon Passage *46* Jacques Tourneur

Canyon Raiders *51* Lewis D. Collins

Canyon River *56* Harmon Jones

Canyon Rustlers *25* Harry S. Webb

Canzone Appasionata *53* Giorgio C. Simonelli

Canzone del Cuore, La *55* Carlo Campogalliani

Canzone del Sole, La *36* Max Neufeld

Canzone di Primavera *50* Mario Costa

Canzoni nel Mondo *63* Vittorio Sala

Cap Canaille *83* Juliet Berto

Cap de l'Espérance, Le *51* Raymond Bernard

Cap du Sud *35* Henri Storck

Cap of Invisibility, The *11* Walter R. Booth, Theo Bouwmeester

Cap Perdu, Le *30* E. A. Dupont

Capablanca *86* Manuel Herrera

Cape Ashizuri *54* Kozaburo Yoshimura

Cape Canaveral Monsters *60* Phil Tucker

Cape Fear *61* J. Lee-Thompson

Cape Forlorn *30* E. A. Dupont

Cape Town Affair, The *67* Robert D. Webb

Capello da Prete, Il *43* Ferdinando Maria Poggioli

Caper of the Golden Bulls, The *65* Russell Rouse

Caperucita Roja, La *63* Roberto Rodríguez

Caperucita y Pulgarcito Contra los Monstruos *65* Roberto Rodríguez, Manuel San Fernando

Caperucita y Sus Tres Amigos *64* Roberto Rodríguez

Capitaine, Le *60* André Hunebelle

Capitaine Fracasse, Le *28* Alberto Cavalcanti

Capitaine Fracasse, Le *42* Abel Gance

Capitaine Mollenard *37* Robert Siodmak

Capitaine Morgan *60* André De Toth, Primo Zeglio

Capital Punishment *24* James P. Hogan

Capital Versus Labor *24* Edwin S. Porter

Capitán Aventurero, El *39* Arcady Boytler

Capitan Bianco *14* Nino Martoglio

Capitan Fracassa *09* Ernesto Maria Pasquali

Capitan Fracassa *17* Mario Caserini

Capitan Fuoco *58* Carlo Campogalliani

Capitano, Il *58* Wolfgang Staudte

Capitol, The *20* George Irving

Čapkovy Povídky *47* Martin Frič

Cap'n Abe's Niece *19* Tom Terriss

Cap'n Jericho *33* Grover Jones, William Slavens McNutt

Capone *75* Steve Carver

Caporal, El *21* Miguel Torres Contreras*

Caporal Épinglé, Le *62* Guy Lefranc, Jean Renoir

Caporale di Giornata *58* Carlo Ludovico Bragaglia

Cappello a Tre Punte, Il *34* Mario Camerini

Cappotto, Il *51* Alberto Lattuada

Cappuccino *89* Anthony Bowman

Cappy Ricks *21* Tom Forman

Cappy Ricks Returns *35* Mack V. Wright

Caprelles et Pantopèdes *30* Jean Painlevé

Capriccio *86* Tinto Brass

Capriccio all'Italiana *68* Mauro Bolognini, Mario Monicelli, Pier Paolo Pasolini, Steno

Capriccio Espagnol *42* Jean Negulesco

Caprice *13* J. Searle Dawley

Caprice *67* Frank Tashlin

Caprice *86* Tinto Brass

Caprice of Dear Caroline *50* Jean Devaivre

Caprice of the Mountains *16* John G. Adolfi

Caprices *41* Léo Joannon

Caprices de Marie, Les *69* Philippe de Broca

Caprices of Kitty, The *15* William Desmond Taylor

Capricieux, Les *84* Michel Deville

Capricious Ones, The *84* Michel Deville

Capricious Summer *68* Jiří Menzel

Capriciousness *80* Young-hyo Kim

Capricorn One *77* Peter Hyams

Capriolen *37* Gustaf Gründgens

Captain Adventure *52* Mario Soldati

Captain Alvarez *14* Rollin Sturgeon

Captain America *44* Elmer Clifton, John English

Captain Apache *71* Alexander Singer

Captain Applejack *31* Hobart Henley

Captain Barnacle's Courtship *11* George D. Baker

Captain Bill *35* Ralph Ceder

Captain Black Jack *49* Julien Duvivier

Captain Blood *24* David Smith

Captain Blood *35* Michael Curtiz

Captain Blood *60* André Hunebelle

Captain Blood, Fugitive *52* Ralph Murphy

Captain Boycott *47* Frank Launder

Captain Calamity *36* John Reinhardt

Captain Careless *28* Jerome Storm

Captain Carey U.S.A. *49* Mitchell Leisen

Captain Caution *40* Richard Wallace

Captain Celluloid vs. the Film Pirates *74* Louis A. McMahon

Captain China *49* Lewis R. Foster

Captain Clegg *61* Peter Graham Scott

Captain Courtesy *15* Hobart Bosworth

Captain Cowboy *29* John P. McGowan

Captain Cuff's Neighbours *12* Dave Aylott

Captain Dabac *59* Pal'o Bielek

Captain Dandy, Bushranger *12* Dave Aylott

Captain Dieppe *19* James Cruze

Captain Discovers the North Pole, Der *17* Gregory La Cava

Captain Eddie *45* Lloyd Bacon

Captain Eo *86* Francis Ford Coppola

Captain Falcon *58* Carlo Campogalliani

Captain Fly-by-Night *22* William K. Howard

Captain from Castile *47* Henry King

Captain from Cologne, The *56* Slatan Dudow

Captain from Koepenick *31* Richard Oswald

Captain from Koepenick, The *56* Helmut Käutner

Captain Fury *39* Hal Roach

Captain Goes A-Flivving, Der *17* Gregory La Cava

Captain Goes A-Swimming, Der *17* Gregory La Cava

Captain Goes A-Swimming, The *17* Gregory La Cava

Captain Grant's Children *39* D. Gutman, Vladimir Weinstock

Captain Hareblower *54* Friz Freleng

Captain Hates the Sea, The *34* Lewis Milestone

Captain Hits the Ceiling, The *35* Charles Lamont

Captain Horatio Hornblower *51* Raoul Walsh

Captain Horatio Hornblower, RN *51* Raoul Walsh

Captain Hurricane *35* John S. Robertson

Captain Hurricane *36* John Reinhardt

Captain Is a Lady, The *40* Robert B. Sinclair

Captain Is Examined for Insurance, Der *17* Gregory La Cava

Captain Jack VC *13* Hay Plumb

Captain January *24* Edward F. Cline

Captain January *36* David Butler

Captain Jinks of the Horse Marines *16* Fred E. Wright

Captain John Smith and Pocahontas *53* Lew Landers

Captain Khorshid *87* Nasser Taghvai

Captain Kid *25* Walter Lantz

Captain Kidd *22* John P. McGowan

Captain Kidd *45* Rowland V. Lee

Captain Kidd and the Slave Girl *54* Lew Landers

Captain Kidd, Jr. *18* William Desmond Taylor

Captain Kiddo *17* W. Eugene Moore

Captain Kidd's Kids *19* Hal Roach

Captain Kidd's Treasure *38* Leslie Fenton

Captain Kronos, Vampire Hunter *72* Brian Clemens

Captain Lash *29* John G. Blystone

Captain Lightfoot *54* Douglas Sirk

Captain Macklin *15* Jack Conway, John B. O'Brien

Captain McLean *14* Jack Conway

Captain Mephisto and the Transformation Machine *45* Spencer G. Bennet, Yakima Canutt, Wallace A. Grissell

Captain Midnight *42* James W. Horne

Captain Midnight *79* Beverly Sebastian, Ferd Sebastian

Captain Milkshake *70* Richard Crawford

Captain Moonlight *35* Henry Edwards

Captain Nemo and the Underwater City *69* James Hill

Captain Newman M.D. *63* David Miller
Captain Nighthawk *14* Gerald Lawrence
Captain of His Soul *18* Gilbert P. Hamilton
Captain of Koepenick, The *31* Richard Oswald
Captain of Koepenick, The *41* Richard Oswald
Captain of Koepenick, The *56* Helmut Käutner
Captain of the Forest, The *87* Attila Dargay
Captain of the Gray Horse Troop, The *17* William Wolbert
Captain of the Guard *30* Pál Fejös, John S. Robertson
Captain of "The Pilgrim" *87* Andrei Prachenko
Captain of the Pinafore *06* Arthur Gilbert
Captain Pirate *52* Ralph Murphy
Captain Salvation *27* John S. Robertson
Captain Scarlett *53* Thomas Carr
Captain Sinbad *63* Byron Haskin
Captain Sirocco *49* Edgar G. Ulmer
Captain Swagger *28* Edward H. Griffith
Captain Swift *14* Edgar Lewis
Captain Swift *20* Tom Terriss
Captain Thunder *30* Alan Crosland
Captain Tugboat Annie *45* Phil Rosen
Captain Video *51* Spencer G. Bennet, Wallace A. Grissell
Captain Yankee *84* Antonio Margheriti
Captain's Birthday, The *01* Walter R. Booth
Captain's Birthday, Der *18* Gregory La Cava
Captain's Captain, The *19* Tom Terriss
Captain's Courage, A *26* Louis Chaudet
Captains Courageous *37* Victor Fleming
Captain's Daughter, The *47* Mario Camerini
Captain's Daughter, The *59* V. Kaplunovsky
Captain's Kid, The *25* Walter Lantz
Captain's Kid, The *36* Nick Grindé
Captains of the Clouds *42* Michael Curtiz
Captain's Orders *37* Ivar Campbell
Captains Outrageous *52* Pete Burness
Captain's Paradise, The *53* Anthony Kimmins
Captain's Table, The *36* Percy Marmont
Captain's Table, The *58* Jack Lee
Captain's Valet, Der *17* Gregory La Cava
Captain's Wives, The *08* Percy Stow
Captivation *31* John Harvel
Captive, The *15* Cecil B. DeMille
Captive *75* Charles Trieschmann
Captive *86* Paul Mayersberg
Captive City, The *52* Robert Wise
Captive City, The *62* Joseph Anthony
Captive Girl *50* William Berke
Captive God, The *16* Reginald Barker, Charles Swickard
Captive Heart, The *46* Basil Dearden
Captive Hearts *87* Paul Almond
Captive of Billy the Kid *52* Fred C. Brannon
Captive Rage *88* Cedric Sundström
Captive Soul *12* Michael Curtiz
Captive Wild Woman *43* Edward

Dmytryk
Captive Women *52* Stuart Gilmore
Captives, The *62* Will Tremper
Captive's Island *66* Masahiro Shinoda
Captives of a Night Dance *89* Mahinur Ergün
Capture, The *50* John Sturges
Capture, The *55* Kevin Brownlow
Capture of Bigfoot, The *79* Bill Rebane
Capture of the Biddle Brothers *02* Edwin S. Porter
Capture of Yegg Bank Burglars *04* Edwin S. Porter
Capture That Capsule *61* Will Zens
Captured! *33* Roy Del Ruth
Captured! *81* Ted Kotcheff
Captured by Bedouins *12* Sidney Olcott
Captured by Consent *14* Stuart Kinder
Captured in Chinatown *35* Elmer Clifton
Car, The *77* Elliot Silverstein
Car Crash *81* Antonio Margheriti
Car Crazy *64* Frigyes Bán
Car 99 *35* Charles Barton
Car of Chance, The *17* William Worthington
Car of Dreams *35* Graham Cutts, Austin Melford
Car of Tomorrow, The *51* Tex Avery
Car Ride *03* Arthur Cooper
Car Trouble *85* David Green
Car-Tune Portrait, A *37* Dave Fleischer
Car Wash *76* Michael Schultz
Cara de Acelga *87* José Sacristán
Cara del Terror, La *62* Isidoro Martínez Ferry
Cara Sposa *77* Pasquale Festa Campanile
Carabelleria del Imperio *42* Miguel Torres Contreras
Carabina per Schut, Una *64* Robert Siodmak
Carabiniere, Il *11* Ernesto Maria Pasquali
Carabiniere a Cavallo, Il *61* Carlo Lizzani
Carabinieri Are Born *85* Mariano Laurenti
Carabinieri Si Nasce *85* Mariano Laurenti
Carabiniers, Les *63* Jean-Luc Godard
Caracas *89* Michael Scottenberg
Carambola *74* Ferdinando Baldi
Caramelle da uno Sconosciuto *87* Franco Ferrini
Carapate, La *78* Gérard Oury
Caraque Blonde, La *53* Jacqueline Audry
Carat *14* F. Martin Thornton
Caravaggio *40* Goffredo Alessandrini
Caravaggio *48* Umberto Barbaro, R. Longhi
Caravaggio *86* Derek Jarman
Caravan *34* Erik Charell
Caravan *46* Arthur Crabtree
Caravan of Courage *84* John Korty
Caravan pour Zagora *60* Edmon Agabra, Marco Ferreri
Caravan Sarai *86* Tassos Psarras
Caravan to Russia *59* Paul Delmer
Caravan to Vaccares *74* Geoffrey Reeve
Caravan Trail, The *46* Robert E. Tansey
Caravane d'Amour, La *70* François Reichenbach
Caravans *78* James Fargo
Caravans West *34* Charles Barton
Carbine Williams *52* Richard Thorpe

Carbon *41* Bjarne Henning-Jensen
Carbon Copy *81* Michael Schultz
Card, The *22* A. V. Bramble
Card, The *51* Ronald Neame
Card Game, The *20* Dave Fleischer
Card Manipulations *12* Walter R. Booth
Card of Fate *33* Jacques Feyder
Card of Fate *53* Robert Siodmak
Card Party, The *1895* Louis Lumière
Cardboard Baby, The *09* Sidney Olcott
Cardboard Box, The *23* George Ridgwell
Cardboard Cavalier *49* Walter Forde
Cardboard City *34* Louis King
Cardboard Lover, The *28* Robert Z. Leonard
Cardeuse de Matelas, La *06* Georges Méliès
Cardiac Arrest *80* Murray Mintz
Cardigan *22* John W. Noble
Cardigan's Last Case *32* George Archainbaud
Cardillac *69* Edgar Reitz
Cardinal, The *36* Sinclair Hill
Cardinal, The *63* Otto Preminger
Cardinal Richelieu *35* Rowland V. Lee
Cardinal Wolsey *12* J. Stuart Blackton, Lawrence Trimble
Cardinal's Conspiracy, The *09* D. W. Griffith, Frank Powell
Cardsharpers, The *10* Lewin Fitzhamon
Care and Affection *63* Márta Mészáros
Care Bears Adventure in Wonderland!, The *87* Raymond Jafelice
Care Bears Movie, The *85* Arna Selznick
Care Bears Movie II: A New Generation *86* Dale Schott
Career *39* Leigh Jason
Career *59* Joseph Anthony
Career Bed *72* Joel M. Reed
Career Girl *44* Wallace Fox
Career Girl *59* Harold David
Career of a Chambermaid, The *75* Dino Risi
Career of Catherine Bush, The *19* Roy William Neill
Career Woman *36* Lewis Seiler
Careers *29* John Francis Dillon
Carefree *38* Mark Sandrich
Carefree Goddesses *88* Teruhiko Kuze
Careful, He Might Hear You *83* Carl Schultz
Careful Please *26* Norman Taurog
Careful, Soft Shoulders *42* Oliver H. P. Garrett
Careless *33* Mikio Naruse
Careless *61* Mauro Bolognini
Careless Age, The *29* John Griffith Wray
Careless Cop, The *17* William Beaudine
Careless Hubby *27* Mark Sandrich
Careless Lady *32* Kenneth MacKenna
Careless Love *63* Robert Thomas
Careless Years, The *57* Arthur Hiller
Caress *33* Heinosuke Gosho
Caressed *64* Laurence L. Kent
Caretaker, The *63* Clive Donner
Caretakers, The *63* Hall Bartlett
Caretaker's Daughter, The *25* Leo McCarey
Caretaker's Daughter, The *52* Francis Searle

Carey Treatment, The 72 Blake Edwards
Carga de la Policía Montada, La 65 Ramón Torrado
Cargaison Blanche 37 Robert Siodmak
Cargaison Blanche, La 57 Georges Lacombe
Cargo from Jamaica 33 Basil Wright
Cargo of Innocents 42 Robert Z. Leonard
Cargo to Capetown 50 Earl McEvoy
Cargoes 38 Humphrey Jennings
Carhops 80 Peter Locke
Carib Gold 55 Harold Young
Caribbean 52 Edward Ludwig
Caribbean Gold 52 Edward Ludwig
Caribbean Hawk 63 Piero Regnoli
Caribbean Mystery, The 45 Robert D. Webb
Caribe 87 Paul Donovan, Michael Kennedy
Cariboo Trail 50 Edwin L. Marin
Caribou Trail, The 50 Edwin L. Marin
Carica del 70 Cavallegeri, La 64 Alberto De Martino
Carica Eroica 52 Francesco De Robertis
Carillon de Minuit, Le 22 Jacques De Baroncelli
Carillons, Les 36 Henri Storck
Carioca Serenaders 41 Jean Negulesco
Carl Hoff and His Band 42 Jean Negulesco
Carl Nielsen 1865–1931 78 Jørgen Roos
Carl Th. Dreyer 66 Jørgen Roos
Carleton-Browne of the F.O. 58 Roy Boulting, Jeffrey Dell
Carlos 71 Hans W. Geissendörfer
Carlos Marighela 75 Chris Marker
Carlos Monzón 74 François Reichenbach
Carlos und Elisabeth 24 Richard Oswald
Carmela 49 Flavio Calzavara
Carmelites, The 59 Philippe Agostini, R. Bruckberger
Carmen 07 Arthur Gilbert
Carmen 09 Ugo Falena
Carmen 14 Christy Cabanne
Carmen 15 Charles Chaplin
Carmen 15 Cecil B. DeMille
Carmen 15 Raoul Walsh
Carmen 18 Ernst Lubitsch
Carmen 22 George Wynn
Carmen 26 Jacques Feyder, Françoise Rosay
Carmen 27 H. B. Parkinson
Carmen 31 Cecil Lewis
Carmen 33 Lotte Reiniger
Carmen 42 Christian-Jaque
Carmen 43 Luis César Amadori
Carmen 49 Florian Rey
Carmen 83 Francesco Rosi
Carmen 83 Carlos Saura
Carmen, Baby 67 Radley Metzger
Carmen Comes Home 51 Keisuke Kinoshita
Carmen di Trastevere 62 Carmine Gallone
Carmen Jones 54 Otto Preminger
Carmen, La de Ronda 59 Tulio Demicheli
Carmen Nejen Podle Bizeta 67 Evald Schorm
Carmen Not According to Bizet 67 Evald Schorm
Carmen Not Only by Bizet 67 Evald

Schorm
Carmen of the Klondike 18 Reginald Barker
Carmen of the North 20 Maurits Binger
Carmen's Pure Love 52 Keisuke Kinoshita
Carmilla 63 Camillo Mastrocinque
Carnaby, M.D. 65 Ralph Thomas
Carnage 67 Robert Hartford-Davis
Carnage 71 Mario Bava
Carnage 83 Andy Milligan
Carnal Knowledge 71 Mike Nichols
Carnal Madness 75 Greg Corarito
Carnation Frank 61 Stanley Haynes
Carnation Kid, The 29 E. Mason Hopper
Carnaval 53 Henri Verneuil
Carnaval à la Nouvell-Orléans 57 François Reichenbach
Carnaval de las Bestias, El 80 Jacinto Molina
Carnaval des Vérités, Le 19 Marcel L'Herbier
Carnaval Sacre, Le 51 Henri Decaë
Carnavals 50 Henri Storck
Carne de Cabaret 31 Christy Cabanne
Carne de Horca 53 Ladislas Vajda
Carne de Tu Carne 84 Carlos Mayolo
Carné: L'Homme à la Caméra 80 Christian-Jaque
Carne per Frankenstein 73 Antonio Margheriti, Paul Morrissey
Carnegie Hall 47 Edgar G. Ulmer
Carnet de Bal, Un 36 Julien Duvivier
Carnet de Plongée 50 Jacques-Yves Cousteau
Carnet de Viaje 60 Joris Ivens
Carnets du Major Thompson, Les 55 Preston Sturges
Carnival, The 11 Sidney Olcott
Carnival 21 Harley Knoles
Carnival 31 Herbert Wilcox
Carnival 34 Walter Lang
Carnival 46 Stanley Haynes
Carnival 53 Henri Verneuil
Carnival Boat 32 Albert S. Rogell
Carnival Capers 32 Walter Lantz
Carnival Courage 45 Howard Swift
Carnival Crime, The 29 Willi Wolff
Carnival Girl, The 26 Cullen Tate
Carnival in Costa Rica 47 Gregory Ratoff
Carnival in Flanders 35 Jacques Feyder
Carnival in Moscow 56 Eldar Ryazanov
Carnival in the Clothes Cupboard 40 Joy Batchelor, John Halas
Carnival Lady 33 Howard Higgin
Carnival Magic 82 Al Adamson
Carnival Night 56 Eldar Ryazanov
Carnival Nights 34 Walter Lang
Carnival of Blood 71 Leonard Kirman
Carnival of Crime 29 Willi Wolff
Carnival of Sinners 42 Maurice Tourneur
Carnival of Souls 62 Herk Harvey
Carnival of the Night 82 Masashi Yamamoto
Carnival of Thieves 65 Russell Rouse
Carnival Queen 37 Nate Watt
Carnival Rock 57 Roger Corman
Carnival Story 54 Kurt Neumann
Carnival Week 27 John Foster
Carny 80 Robert Kaylor
Caro Gorbaciov 88 Carlo Lizzani

Caro Michele 76 Mario Monicelli
Caro Papa 79 Dino Risi
Čarobni Zvuci 57 Dušan Vukotić
Čarodějův Učeň 77 Karel Zeman
Carogne Si Nasce 68 Alfonso Brescia
Carol 70 Ed Emshwiller
Carolina 34 Henry King
Carolina Blues 44 Leigh Jason
Carolina Cannonball 55 Charles Lamont
Carolina Moon 40 Frank McDonald
Carolina Rediviva 20 Ivan Hedqvist
Caroline Chérie 51 Richard Pottier
Caroline Chérie 67 Denys De la Patellière
Caroline's Silver Yarn 87 Helle Murdmaa
Carolyn of the Corners 19 Robert Thornby
Carosello Napoletano 61 Ettore Giannini
Carousel 56 Henry King
Carousella 65 John Irvin
Čarovné Dědictví 85 Zdeněk Zelenka
Carpaccio 47 Umberto Barbaro, R. Longhi
Carpenter, The 32 Vladimir Petrov
Carpenter, The 88 David Wellington
Carpenter and Children 62 Tomotaka Tasaka
Carpet from Bagdad, The 15 Colin Campbell
Carpet of Horror, The 62 Harald Reinl
Carpetbaggers, The 63 Edward Dmytryk
Carquake 76 Paul Bartel
Carquenez Woods, The 16 Allan Dwan
Carrasco's Escape 87 Alfredo B. Crevenna
Carre Blanc 85 Michel Campioli, Gilles Delannoy
Carrefour 38 Kurt Bernhardt
Carrefour de l'Opéra 1898 Georges Méliès
Carrefour des Enfants Perdus, Le 43 Léo Joannon
Carriage Awaits, The 26 Paul M. Felton
Carriage to Vienna 66 Karel Kachyňa
Carrie 52 William Wyler
Carrie 76 Brian DePalma
Carrie Nation and Her Hatchet Brigade 01 Edwin S. Porter
Carrier, The 88 Nathan J. White
Carrière 21 Friedrich Feher
Carrière de Suzanne, La 63 Eric Rohmer
Carrière de Suzanne: Six Contes Moraux: 2, La 63 Eric Rohmer
Carringford School Mystery, The 58 William C. Hammond
Carrington V.C. 54 Anthony Asquith
Carrosse d'Or, Le 52 Jean Renoir
Carrot-Top 25 Julien Duvivier
Carrot-Top 32 Julien Duvivier
Carrots 17 Frank Wilson
Carrots & Peas 69 Hollis Frampton
Carrozza d'Oro, La 52 Jean Renoir
Carry It On 70 James Coyne, Robert Jones, Christopher Knight
Carry Me Back 82 John Reid
Carry On 18 George Pearson
Carry On 27 Victor Peers, Dinah Shurey
Carry On Abroad 72 Gerald Thomas
Carry On Admiral 57 Val Guest
Carry On Again, Doctor 69 Gerald Thomas
Carry On at Your Convenience 71 Gerald Thomas
Carry On Behind 75 Gerald Thomas
Carry On Cabbie 63 Gerald Thomas

Case of the Black Parrot, The *41* Noel Mason Smith

Case of the Curious Bride, The *35* Michael Curtiz

Case of the Elevator Duck, The *74* Joan Micklin Silver

Case of the 44's, The *64* Tom McCowen

Case of the Frightened Lady, The *40* George King

Case of the Full Moon Murders, The *73* Sean S. Cunningham, Brad Talbot

Case of the Howling Dog, The *34* Alan Crosland

Case of the Lost Sheep, The *35* Walter Lantz

Case of the Lucky Legs, The *35* Archie Mayo

Case of the Missing Blonde, The *38* Otis Garrett

Case of the Missing Brides, The *42* Wallace Fox

Case of the Missing Hare *42* Chuck Jones

Case of the Missing Man, The *35* D. Ross Lederman

Case of the Missing Scene, The *51* Don Chaffey

Case of the Missing Switchboard Operator, The *66* Dušan Makavejev

Case of the Mukkinese Battlehorn, The *56* Joseph Sterling

Case of the Old Rope Man, The *52* Darrell Catling

Case of the Red Monkey, The *53* Ken Hughes

Case of the River Morgue, The *56* Montgomery Tully

Case of the Smiling Stiffs, The *73* Sean S. Cunningham, Brad Talbot

Case of the Smiling Widow, The *57* Montgomery Tully

Case of the Stuttering Bishop, The *37* William Clemens

Case of the Stuttering Pig, The *37* Frank Tashlin

Case of the Three Million, The *26* Yakov Protazanov

Case of the Two Beauties, The *67* Jesús Franco

Case of the Velvet Claws, The *36* William Clemens

Case 68 *68* Salah Abu Saif

Case Van Geldern *32* Willi Wolff

Casey and His Neighbor's Goat *03* Edwin S. Porter

Casey at the Bat *16* Lloyd Ingraham

Casey at the Bat *27* Monte Brice

Casey Jones *27* Charles J. Hunt

Casey of the Coast Guard *26* William Nigh

Casey's Border Raid *17* George Marshall

Casey's Frightful Dream *04* Edwin S. Porter

Casey's Millions *22* John McDonagh

Casey's Shadow *77* Martin Ritt

Cash *32* Zoltán Korda

Cash and Carry *41* Edwin L. Marin

Cash and Marry *30* Lewis R. Foster

Cash McCall *59* Joseph Pevney

Cash on Delivery *26* Milton Rosmer

Cash on Delivery *54* Muriel Box

Cash on Demand *61* Quentin Lawrence

Cashier, The *22* Raoul Barré, Charles Bowers

Casino de Paree *35* Robert Florey, Archie Mayo

Casino de Paris *35* Robert Florey, Archie Mayo

Casino de Paris *57* André Hunebelle

Casino Murder Case, The *35* Edwin L. Marin

Casino Royale *67* Val Guest, Ken Hughes, John Huston, Joseph McGrath, Robert Parrish, Anthony Squire, Richard Talmadge

Casket for Living, A *25* Heinosuke Gosho

Caso Cerrado *85* Juan Cano Arecha

Caso de las Dos Bellezas, El *67* Jesús Franco

Caso Haller, Il *33* Alessandro Blasetti

Caso Mattei, Il *72* Tonino Guerra, Francesco Rosi

Caso Moro, Il *86* Giuseppe Ferrara

Caso Raoul, Il *75* Maurizio Ponzi

Caspar David Friedrich *87* Peter Schamoni

Caspian Oil Workers *53* Roman Karmen

Caspian Story *53* Roman Karmen

Caspians, The *44* Grigori Alexandrov

Casque d'Or *52* Jacques Becker

Cass Timberlane *47* George Sidney

Cassandra *87* Colin Eggleston

Cassandra Cat, The *63* Vojtěch Jasný

Cassandra Crossing, The *77* George Pan Cosmatos

Casse, Le *71* Henri Verneuil

Casse-Pieds, Les *48* Jean Dréville, Noël-Noël

Cassette de l'Émigrée, La *12* Louis Feuillade

Cassidy *17* Arthur Rosson

Cassidy of Bar 20 *38* Lesley Selander

Cassino to Korea *50* Edward Genock

Cassis *66* Jonas Mekas

Cassis Colank *59* Robert Breer

Cassowary *26* Teinosuke Kinugasa

Cast a Dark Shadow *55* Lewis Gilbert

Cast a Giant Shadow *65* Melville Shavelson

Cast a Long Shadow *59* Thomas Carr

Cast Adrift *17* Maurice Sandground

Cast Iron *30* George Cukor, Louis Gasnier

Cast-Iron *64* Otar Ioseliani

Cast-Off, The *59* Yasuzo Masumura

Cast Thy Bread Upon the Waters *10* Bert Haldane

Casta Diva *35* Carmine Gallone

Casta Diva *54* Carmine Gallone

Castagne Sono Buone, Le *70* Pietro Germi

Castaway, The *31* Wilfred Jackson

Castaway, The *45* Joseph Kane

Castaway *86* Nicolas Roeg

Castaway Cowboy, The *74* Vincent McEveety

Castaways, The *15* Geoffrey H. Malins

Castaways, The *62* Robert Stevenson

Caste *15* Lawrence Trimble

Caste *30* Campbell Gullan

Castel Sant'Angelo *45* Alessandro Blasetti

Castelli in Aria *38* Augusto Genina

Castello dei Morti Vivi, Il *64* Warren Keifer, Michael Reeves, Luciano Ricci

Castello della Malinconia, Il *20* Augusto Genina

Castello della Paura, Il *73* Robert H. Oliver

Castello delle Donne Maledette, Il *73* Robert H. Oliver

Castello dell'Orrore, El *73* Robert H. Oliver

Castello di Artena, Il *65* Massimo Pupillo

Castello di Fu Manchu, Il *68* Jesús Franco

Castello in Svezia, Il *63* Roger Vadim

Castighi *86* Giorgio Losego, Lidia Montanari

Castilian, The *63* Javier Seto

Castillo de Fu Manchu, El *68* Jesús Franco

Castillo de la Pureza, El *72* Arturo Ripstein

Castillo de los Monstruos, El *57* Julián Soler

Castillos de Castilla *33* Fernando Mantilla, Carlos Velo

Castillos en el Aire *38* Jaime Salvador

Castle *17* Lawrence Trimble

Castle, The *68* Rudolf Noelte

Castle, The *86* Jaakko Pakkasvirta

Castle in Greece *60* T. Meritzis

Castle in Sweden *63* Roger Vadim

Castle in the Air *52* Henry Cass

Castle in the Air *52* Richard Quine

Castle in the Carpathians *57* Alberto Cavalcanti

Castle in the Desert *42* Harry Lachman

Castle Keep *68* Sydney Pollack

Castle of Blood *63* Sergio Corbucci, Antonio Margheriti

Castle of Bloody Lust *67* Adrian Hoven

Castle of Carnage, The *52* Teinosuke Kinugasa

Castle of Crimes *40* Harold French

Castle of Doom *31* Carl Theodor Dreyer

Castle of Dreams *19* Wilfred Noy

Castle of Evil *66* Francis D. Lyon

Castle of Fu Manchu, The *68* Jesús Franco

Castle of Lust *67* Adrian Hoven

Castle of Purity *72* Arturo Ripstein

Castle of Terror *63* Sergio Corbucci, Antonio Margheriti

Castle of Terror *63* Richard McNamara, Antonio Margheriti

Castle of the Doomed *67* Jesús Franco

Castle of the Living Dead *63* Richard McNamara, Antonio Margheriti

Castle of the Living Dead *64* Warren Keifer, Michael Reeves, Luciano Ricci

Castle of the Monsters *57* Julián Soler

Castle of the Spider's Web, The *57* Akira Kurosawa

Castle of the Walking Dead *67* Harald Reinl

Castle of Unholy Desires, The *67* Adrian Hoven

Castle on the Hudson *40* Anatole Litvak

Castle One *66* Malcolm Le Grice

Castle Sinister *32* Widgey R. Newman

Castle Sinister *48* Oscar Burn

Castle Two *68* Malcolm Le Grice

Castle Vogelöd *21* F. W. Murnau

Castle Within a Castle *54* Carl Theodor Dreyer, Jørgen Roos

Castles for Two *17* Frank Reicher

Caught *48* Max Ophüls
Caught *49* John Berry
Caught *87* James F. Collier
Caught Bending *14* Hay Plumb
Caught Bluffing *22* Lambert Hillyer
Caught by Television *36* Del Lord
Caught by the Tide *06* Percy Stow
Caught by Wireless *08* Wallace McCutcheon
Caught Cheating *31* Frank R. Strayer
Caught in a Cabaret *14* Charles Chaplin, Mabel Normand
Caught in a Kilt *15* Will P. Kellino
Caught in Her Own Trap *11* Stuart Kinder
Caught in His Own Net *12* Edwin J. Collins
Caught in His Own Trap *12* August Blom
Caught in the Act *18* Harry Millarde
Caught in the Act *41* Jean Yarbrough
Caught in the Act *82* Lino Brocka
Caught in the Draft *41* David Butler
Caught in the Fog *28* Howard Bretherton
Caught in the Net *60* John Haggarty
Caught in the Rain *14* Charles Chaplin
Caught in the Web *25* Edwin Greenwood, Will P. Kellino
Caught Napping *10* Fred Rains
Caught Napping *13* Charles C. Calvert
Caught Plastered *31* William A. Seiter
Caught Short *30* Charles Reisner
Caught with the Goods *11* Mack Sennett
Cauldron of Blood *67* Santos Alcocer
Cauldron of Death, The *79* Tulio Demicheli
Causa Kaiser *32* Franz Wenzler
Causa Králík *79* Jaromil Jireš
Cause Commune, La *40* Alberto Cavalcanti
Cause for Alarm *50* Tay Garnett
Cause for Divorce *23* Hugh Dierker
Cause of All the Trouble, The *23* Edward D. Roberts
Cause of the Great European War, The *14* George Pearson
Cause Toujours...Tu M'Intéressés! *79* Édouard Molinaro
Cause We Serve, The *58* Josef Heifits
Cavalca e Uccidi *63* José Luis Borau
Cavalcade *32* Frank Lloyd
Cavalcade d'Amour *40* Raymond Bernard
Cavalcade of Song *54* Domenico Paolella
Cavalcade of the Dance *43* Jean Negulesco
Cavalcade of the Stars *38* Geoffrey Benstead
Cavalcade of the West *36* Harry Fraser
Cavalcade of Variety *40* Thomas Bentley
Cavalcata Ardente, La *23* Carmine Gallone
Cavalcata d'Eroi *49* Mario Costa
Cavaleur, Le *78* Philippe de Broca
Cavalier, The *28* Irvin Willat
Cavalier in Devil's Castle *59* Mario Costa
Cavalier Noir, Le *44* Gilles Grangier
Cavalier of the Golden Star *50* Yuli Raizman
Cavalier of the Streets, The *37* Harold French
Cavalier of the West *31* John P. McCarthy
Cavaliere Constante Nicosia Demoniaco ovvero Dracula in Brianza, Il *75* Lucio

Fulci
Cavaliere di Ferro, Il *49* Riccardo Freda
Cavaliere di Maison Rouge, Il *53* Vittorio Cottafavi
Cavaliere, la Morte e il Diavolo, Il *85* Beppe Cino
Cavaliere Misterioso, Il *47* Riccardo Freda
Cavalieri della Regina, I *54* Mauro Bolognini
Cavalieri di Rodi, I *12* Mario Caserini
Cavaliers de l'Orage, Les *84* Gérard Vergez
Cavaliers Rouges, Les *64* Hugo Fregonese
Cavalier's Wife, The *08* Percy Stow
Cavalleria *36* Goffredo Alessandrini
Cavalleria Commandos *63* Eddie Romero
Cavalleria Rusticana *17* Ugo Falena
Cavalleria Rusticana *47* Amleto Palermi
Cavalleria Rusticana *52* Carmine Gallone
Cavalry *36* Robert North Bradbury
Cavalry Charge *65* Ramón Torrado
Cavalry Command *63* Eddie Romero
Cavalry Scout *51* Lesley Selander
Cavanaugh of the Forest Rangers *18* William Wolbert
Cavar un Foso *66* Leopoldo Torre-Nilsson
Cavatori di Marmo *50* Piero Nelli
Cave, Un *72* Gilles Grangier
Cave Dwellers, The *40* D. W. Griffith, Hal Roach, Hal Roach, Jr.
Cave Girl, The *21* Joseph Franz
Cave-In, The *36* Louis King
Cave Man *34* Ubbe Iwerks
Cave Man *40* D. W. Griffith, Hal Roach, Hal Roach, Jr.
Cave Man's Bride, The *19* Raoul Barré, Charles Bowers
Cave of Outlaws *51* William Castle
Cave of Sharks, The *78* Tonino Ricci
Cave of the Demons, The *1898* Georges Méliès
Cave of the Living Dead *64* Ákos von Ráthonyi
Cave Se Rebiffe, Le *61* Gilles Grangier
Cavegirl *85* David Oliver
Cavell Case, The *18* John G. Adolfi
Caveman, The *14* Charles Chaplin
Caveman, The *25* Theodore Marston
Caveman, The *25* Lewis Milestone
Caveman *81* Carl Gottlieb
Caveman Inki *50* Chuck Jones
Cavern, The *64* Edgar G. Ulmer
Cavern Spider, The *24* Thomas Bentley
Caverne Maudite, La *1898* Georges Méliès
Caves of La Jolla *11* Allan Dwan
Caviar Rouge, Le *85* Robert Hossein
Čavka *88* Miloš Radivojević
Cayenne-Palace *87* Alain Maline
Cayman Triangle, The *77* Anderson Humphreys
Caza, La *65* Carlos Saura
Cazador de la Muerte, El *83* John Watson
Cazadores, Los *74* Peter Collinson
Ce Cochon de Morin *24* Victor Tourjansky
Ce Corps Tant Désiré *58* Luis Saslavsky
Ce Joli Monde *57* Carlo-Rim
Ce Pauvre Chéri *23* Jean Kemm
Ce Que Je Vois dans Mon Télescope *02* Ferdinand Zecca
Ce Que les Flots Racontent *15* Abel Gance

Ce Qu'On Voit de la Bastille *05* Ferdinand Zecca
Ce Répondeur Ne Prend Pas de Messages *79* Alain Cavalier
Ce Sacre Grand-Père *68* Jacques Poitrenaud
C'È Sartana...Vendi la Pistola e Comprati la Bara *70* Giuliano Carmineo
C'È Sempre un Ma... *42* Luigi Zampa
Ce Soir-Là, Gilles Vigneault *68* Arthur Lamothe
Ce Soir les Jupons Volent *56* Dmitri Kirsanov
Ce Soir ou Jamais *60* Michel Deville
Cease Fire *53* Owen Crump
Cease Fire *85* David Nutter
Cease Firing *34* Jacques De Baroncelli
Cebo para una Adolescente *73* Francisco Lara Polop
Cech Panen Kutnohorských *38* Otakar Vávra
Cécile Est Morte *43* Maurice Tourneur
Cecilia of the Pink Roses *18* Julius Steger
Cecilia Valdés *82* Humberto Solás
Ceddo *76* Ousmane Sembène
Cedric Sharpe and His Sextette *36* Horace Shepherd
Ceiling, The *62* Věra Chytilová
Ceiling Hero *40* Tex Avery
Ceiling Zero *35* Howard Hawks
Ceinture Électrique, La *07* Romeo Rosetti
Čekání na Déšť *78* Karel Kachyňa
Cela S'Appelle l'Aurore *55* Luis Buñuel
Celebrated Case, A *14* George Melford
Celebrated Scandal, A *15* J. Gordon Edwards
Celebration at Big Sur *71* Baird Bryant, Johanna Demetrakas
Célébrations, Les *79* Yves Simoneau
Celebrity *28* Tay Garnett
Celery Stalks at Midnight *58* John Whitney
Céleste *81* Percy Adlon
Celeste of the Ambulance Corps *16* Burton George
Celestial City, The *29* John Orton
Celestial Code, The *15* Raoul Walsh
Celestial Palace, The *66* Khwaja Ahmad Abbas
Celestina *53* Antonio Pietrangeli
Celestina, La *64* Carlo Lizzani
Celestina P... R..., La *64* Carlo Lizzani
Celia *49* Francis Searle
Celia *89* Ann Turner
Célimène—La Poupée de Montmartre *25* Michael Curtiz
Céline and Julie Go Boating *73* Jacques Rivette
Céline et Julie Vont en Bateau *73* Jacques Rivette
Cell 2455—Death Row *55* Fred F. Sears
Cellar Dweller *88* John Buechler
Cellar of Death, The *16* Charles C. Calvert
Cellbound *55* Tex Avery, Michael Lah
Celle Qui Domine *27* Carmine Gallone*
Cellulose *54* Jerzy Kawalerowicz
Celos *36* Arcady Boytler
Celtic Trilogy, A *79* Kathleen Dowdey
Celui Qui Doit Mourir *57* Jules Dassin

Chaliapin *69* Mark Donskoi
Chalice of Courage, The *15* Rollin Sturgeon
Chalice of Sorrow *16* Rex Ingram
Chalk Garden, The *63* Ronald Neame
Chalk Line, The *71* Ed Emshwiller
Chalk Marks *24* John G. Adolfi
Chalk River Ballet *50* René Jodoin, Norman McLaren
Challenge, The *16* Donald Mackenzie
Challenge, The *22* Dave Fleischer
Challenge, The *22* Tom Terriss
Challenge, The *31* Clarence Badger
Challenge, The *32* Friedrich Ermler, Sergei Yutkevich
Challenge, The *37* Milton Rosmer, Luis Trenker
Challenge, The *48* Jean Yarbrough
Challenge, The *50* Fred F. Sears
Challenge, The *51* Jack Arnold
Challenge, The *58* Francesco Rosi
Challenge, The *60* John Gilling
Challenge *74* Martin Beck
Challenge, The *75* Herbert Kline
Challenge, The *81* John Frankenheimer
Challenge—A Tribute to Modern Art, The *75* Herbert Kline
Challenge Accepted, The *18* Edwin L. Hollywood
Challenge for Robin Hood, A *67* C. M. Pennington-Richards
Challenge in the Snow *68* Claude Lelouch, François Reichenbach
Challenge of Chance, The *19* Harry Revier
Challenge of Greatness, The *75* Herbert Kline
Challenge of Rin-Tin-Tin, The *58* Robert Walker
Challenge of the Gladiator *65* Domenico Paolella
Challenge of the Law, The *20* Scott R. Dunlap
Challenge of the Mackennas *69* Leon Klimovsky
Challenge of the Range *49* Ray Nazarro
Challenge of the Wild *54* Frank Graham
Challenge the Wild *54* Frank Graham
Challenge to Be Free *72* Ford Beebe, Tay Garnett
Challenge to Lassie *49* Richard Thorpe
Challenge to Life *87* Rafael Baledón
Challenge to Live *64* Eizo Sugawa
Challenge to Survive *75* Kent Bateman
Challengers, The *68* Leslie Martinson
Chalutzim *33* Aleksander Ford
Chamaco *67* Leopoldo Savona
Chamade, La *68* Alain Cavalier
Chambara Fūfu *29* Mikio Naruse
Chamber of Horrors, The *12* Maurice Costello
Chamber of Horrors, The *17* Raoul Barré, Charles Bowers
Chamber of Horrors *29* Walter Summers
Chamber of Horrors *40* Norman Lee
Chamber of Horrors *44* Erle C. Kenton
Chamber of Horrors *66* Hy Averback
Chamber of Mystery, The *20* Abraham S. Schomer
Chamber of Tortures *72* Mario Bava
Chamberlain, The *13* Mauritz Stiller

Chambermaid's Revenge, The *19* Raoul Barré, Charles Bowers
Chambre, La *72* Chantal Akerman
Chambre Ardente, La *61* Julien Duvivier
Chambre Blanche, La *69* Jean-Pierre Lefèbvre
Chambre en Ville, Une *82* Jacques Demy
Chambre Obscure, La *69* Tony Richardson
Chambre 666 *82* Wim Wenders
Chambre Verte, La *78* François Truffaut
Chameleon *78* Jon Jost
Chameleon Man, The *1899* Georges Méliès
Champ, The *31* King Vidor
Champ, The *79* Franco Zeffirelli
Champ d'Honneur *87* Jean-Pierre Denis
Champ for a Day *53* William A. Seiter
Champagne *28* Alfred Hitchcock
Champagne Charlie *15* Charles Chaplin
Champagne Charlie *36* James Tinling
Champagne Charlie *44* Alberto Cavalcanti
Champagne for Breakfast *35* Melville Brown
Champagne for Caesar *50* Richard Whorf
Champagne for Everybody *53* Claude Binyon
Champagne Murders, The *66* Claude Chabrol
Champagne Waltz *37* A. Edward Sutherland
Champi-Tortu *21* Jacques De Baroncelli
Champignon des Carpates, Les *89* Jean-Claude Biette
Champion, The *13* Henry Lehrman
Champion, The *15* Charles Chaplin
Champion, The *23* Paul M. Felton
Champion *49* Mark Robson
Champion Charlie *15* Charles Chaplin
Champion du Jeu à la Mode, Le *10* Émile Cohl
Champion Loser, The *20* Charles Reisner
Champion of Death *76* Kazuhiko Yamaguchi
Champion of Lost Causes, The *25* Chester Bennett
Champions *22* Julian Ollendorff
Champions *83* John Irvin
Champions Forever *89* Dimitri Logothetis
Champs-Elysées *28* Jean Lods
Champs-Elysées *38* Sacha Guitry
Chams *86* Najib Sefrioui
Chan Is Missing *81* Wayne Wang
Chance, La *32* René Guissart
Chance at Heaven *33* William A. Seiter
Chance Deception, A *12* Christy Cabanne, D. W. Griffith
Chance et l'Amour, La *64* Claude Berri, Bertrand Tavernier
Chance Meeting *36* Igor Savchenko
Chance Meeting *54* Anthony Asquith
Chance Meeting *59* Joseph Losey
Chance Meeting *64* Samuel Goldwyn, Jr.
Chance Meeting on the Atlantic *79* Jerzy Kawalerowicz
Chance Meeting on the Ocean *79* Jerzy Kawalerowicz
Chance of a Lifetime, The *16* Bertram Phillips
Chance of a Lifetime, The *43* William Castle

Chance of a Lifetime *50* Bernard Miles, Alan Osbiston
Chance of a Night Time *31* Ralph Lynn, Herbert Wilcox
Chance Passengers *87* Mikhail Ordovsky
Chances *31* Allan Dwan
Chances Are *89* Emile Ardolino
Chandamama Raave *88* Movli
Chandidas *32* Debaki Kumar Bose
Chandler *71* Paul Magwood
Chandu the Magician *32* William Cameron Menzies, Marcel Varnel
Chanel Solitaire *81* George Kaczender
Chang *27* Merian C. Cooper, Ernest B. Schoedsack
Chang-Yu Chu-Hai *85* King Hu
Change for a Sovereign *37* Maurice Elvey
Change of Habit *68* William A. Graham
Change of Heart, A *09* D. W. Griffith
Change of Heart *34* John G. Blystone
Change of Heart *37* James Tinling
Change of Heart *43* Albert S. Rogell
Change of Heart *51* Peter Whale
Change of Heart, A *61* Freddie Francis
Change of Mind *69* Robert Stevens
Change of Seasons, A *80* Richard Lang
Change of Spirit, A *11* D. W. Griffith
Change Partners *65* Robert Lynn
Changed Identity *41* Roy Rowland
Changed Man *39* Victor Gertler
Changeling, The *28* Geoffrey H. Malins
Changeling, The *79* Peter Medak
Changes *69* Hall Bartlett
Changes in the Village *64* Lester James Peries
Changing Countryside, The *64* Lester James Peries
Changing Earth, The *53* Bert Haanstra
Changing Husbands *24* Paul Iribe, Frank Urson
Changing Trains *43* Hasse Ekman
Changing Woman, The *18* David Smith
Changing Year, The *32* Mary Field
Changing Years, The *58* Don Sharp
Channel Crossing *33* Milton Rosmer
Channel Incident *40* Anthony Asquith
Channing of the Northwest *22* Ralph Ince
Channings, The *20* Edwin J. Collins
Chanson d'Armor *33* Jean Epstein
Chanson des Peupliers, La *31* Jean Epstein
Chanson du Feu, La *17* Georges Monca
Chanson du Souvenir, La *36* Douglas Sirk
Chanson Filmées *18* Roger Lion
Chant de la Mine et du Feu, Le *31* Jean Benoît-Lévy
Chant de l'Amour Triomphant, Le *23* Victor Tourjansky
Chant des Ondes, Le *43* Roger Leenhardt
Chant du Marin, Le *31* Carmine Gallone
Chant du Monde, Le *65* Marcel Camus
Chant du Styrène, Le *58* Alain Resnais
Chant of Jimmie Blacksmith, The *78* Fred Schepisi
Chante-Louve *21* Georges Monca
Chantecoq *16* Henri Pouctal
Chanteur de Minuit, Le *36* Léo Joannon
Chanteur Inconnu, Le *31* Victor Tourjansky
Chanteur Inconnu, Le *46* André Cayatte
Chanticler Hat, A *10* Lewin Fitzhamon

Chantier en Ruines, Le *45* Roger Leen-hardt

Chaos *84* Paolo Taviani, Vittorio Taviani

Chapayev *34* Georgy Vasiliev, Sergei Vasiliev

Chapayev Is with Us *41* Vladimir Petrov

Chapayev s Nami *41* Vladimir Petrov

Chapeau à Surprises, Le *01* Georges Méliès

Chapeau de Max, Le *13* Max Linder

Chapeau de Paille d'Italie, Un *27* René Clair

Chapeaux à Transformations *1895* Louis Lumière

Chapeaux des Belles Dames, Les *09* Émile Cohl

Chaperone, The *12* Stuart Kinder

Chaperone, The *16* Arthur Berthelet

Chaperons *29* Sam Newfield

Chapetan Meitanos: I Ikona enas Mythikou Prosopou *87* Dimos Theos

Chaplet of Pearls, The *13* H. Oceano Martinek

Chaplinesque, My Life and Hard Times *72* Harry Hurwitz

Chapman Report, The *61* George Cukor

Chappaqua *66* Conrad Rooks

Chappy, That's All *24* Thomas Bentley

Chapter in Her Life, A *23* Lois Weber

Chapter Two *79* Robert Moore

Character As Revealed by the Ear *17* Paul Terry

Character As Revealed by the Eye *17* Paul Terry

Character As Revealed by the Mouth *17* Paul Terry

Character As Revealed by the Nose *17* Paul Terry

Charade *52* Roy Kellino

Charade *63* Stanley Donen

Charandas Chor *75* Shyam Benegal

Charandas the Thief *75* Shyam Benegal

Charcoal Burner, The *55* Julio García Espinosa, Tomás Gutiérrez Alea

Charcoal Man's Reception, The *1897* Georges Méliès

Charcuterie Mécanique *1895* Auguste Lumière, Louis Lumière

Chardons du Baragan, Les *57* Louis Daquin

Charge at Feather River, The *53* Gordon Douglas

Charge Is Murder, The *63* Boris Sagal

Charge It *21* Harry Garson

Charge It to Me *19* Roy William Neill

Charge of the Black Lancers *61* Giacomo Gentilomo

Charge of the Gauchos, The *28* Albert Kelley

Charge of the Lancers *53* William Castle

Charge of the Light Brigade, The *12* J. Searle Dawley

Charge of the Light Brigade, The *36* Michael Curtiz

Charge of the Light Brigade, The *68* Tony Richardson

Charge of the Model T's, The *79* Jim McCullough

Charge of the Seventh Cavalry, The *64* Alberto De Martino

Charge of the Uhlans *1895* Birt Acres

Charing Cross Road *35* Albert De Cour-ville

Chariot Race, The *07* Sidney Olcott, Frank Oakes Rose

Chariots of Fire *81* Hugh Hudson

Chariots of the Gods? *69* Harald Reinl

Chariots of the Sky *18* Forest Holger-Madsen

Charité du Prestidigitateur, La *05* Alice Guy-Blaché

Charity? *16* Frank Powell

Charity *19* Rex Wilson

Charity Ann *15* Maurice Elvey

Charity Castle *17* Lloyd Ingraham

Charity Covers a Multitude of Sins *05* Lewin Fitzhamon

Charlatan, Le *01* Georges Méliès

Charlatan, The *16* Sidney Morgan

Charlatan, The *17* Michael Curtiz

Charlatan, The *29* George Melford

Charlemagne *35* Pierre Colombier

Charles and Lucie *79* Nelly Kaplan

Charles Augustus Milverton *22* George Ridgwell

Charles Aznavour: Breaking America *83* Christian Blackwood

Charles Bukowski Tapes, The *85* Barbet Schroeder

Charles Chaplin in a Liberty Loan Appeal *18* Charles Chaplin

Charles, Dead or Alive *69* Alain Tanner

Charles et Lucie *79* Nelly Kaplan

Charles, Mort ou Vif *69* Alain Tanner

Charles Peace *05* William Haggar

Charles Peace, King of Criminals *14* Ernest G. Batley

Charles Rogers in The Movie Man *28* Archie Mayo

Charles VI *11* Louis Feuillade

Charles XII *25* John W. Brunius

Charles XII *33* Victor Sjöström

Charleston *26* Jean Renoir

Charleston *78* Marcello Fondato

Charleston Chain Gang *02* Edwin S. Porter

Charleston Dance *27* S. H. Johnson

Charleston-Parade *26* Jean Renoir

Charley *86* Theo van Gogh

Charley and the Angel *72* Vincent Mc-Eveety

Charley in the New Mines *47* Joy Batchelor, John Halas

Charley in the New Schools *47* Joy Batchelor, John Halas

Charley in the New Towns *47* Joy Batchelor, John Halas

Charley in "Your Very Good Health" *47* Joy Batchelor, John Halas

Charley Junior's Schooldays *47* Joy Batchelor, John Halas

Charley Moon *56* Guy Hamilton

Charley My Boy *26* Leo McCarey

Charley One-Eye *72* Don Chaffey

Charley Smiler Competes in a Cycle *11* Dave Aylott

Charley Smiler Is Robbed *11* Dave Aylott

Charley Smiler Is Stage Struck *11* A. E. Coleby

Charley Smiler Joins the Boy Scouts *11* Dave Aylott

Charley Smiler Loses His Watch *11* Dave Aylott

Charley Smiler Takes Brain Food *11* Dave Aylott

Charley Smiler Takes Up Ju-Jitsu *11* Dave Aylott

Charley Varrick *73* Don Siegel

Charley's American Aunt *41* Archie Mayo

Charley's Aunt *25* Scott Sidney

Charley's Aunt *30* Al Christie

Charley's Aunt *41* Archie Mayo

Charley's Big-Hearted Aunt *40* Walter Forde

Charley's March of Time *47* Joy Batchelor, John Halas

Charlie and a Half *73* Boaz Davidson

Charlie and the Perfect Lady *15* Charles Chaplin

Charlie and the Sausages *14* Charles Chaplin, Mabel Normand

Charlie at the Bank *15* Charles Chaplin

Charlie at the Races *14* Charles Chaplin

Charlie at the Show *15* Charles Chaplin

Charlie Bubbles *67* Albert Finney

Charlie Chan and the Curse of the Dragon Queen *80* Clive Donner

Charlie Chan and the Golden Eye *48* William Beaudine

Charlie Chan at Monte Carlo *38* Eugene Forde

Charlie Chan at the Circus *36* Harry Lachman

Charlie Chan at the Olympics *37* H. Bruce Humberstone

Charlie Chan at the Opera *36* H. Bruce Humberstone

Charlie Chan at the Race Track *36* H. Bruce Humberstone

Charlie Chan at the Wax Museum *40* Lynn Shores

Charlie Chan at Treasure Island *39* Norman Foster

Charlie Chan Carries On *31* Hamilton MacFadden

Charlie Chan: Happiness Is a Warm Clue *71* Leslie Martinson

Charlie Chan in Alcatraz *46* Phil Karlson

Charlie Chan in Black Magic *44* Phil Rosen

Charlie Chan in City in Darkness *39* Herbert I. Leeds

Charlie Chan in Dangerous Money *46* Terry Morse

Charlie Chan in Egypt *35* Louis King

Charlie Chan in Honolulu *38* H. Bruce Humberstone

Charlie Chan in London *34* Eugene Forde

Charlie Chan in Meeting at Midnight *44* Phil Rosen

Charlie Chan in Mexico *45* Phil Rosen

Charlie Chan in Panama *40* Norman Foster

Charlie Chan in Paris *35* Lewis Seiler

Charlie Chan in Reno *39* Norman Foster

Charlie Chan in Rio *41* Harry Lachman

Charlie Chan in Secret Service *44* Phil Rosen

Charlie Chan in Shanghai *35* James Tinling

Charlie Chan in the Chinese Cat *44* Phil Rosen

Charlie Chan in the City of Darkness *39* Herbert I. Leeds

Charlie Chan in the Secret Service *44* Phil Rosen

Charlie Chan on Broadway *37* Eugene Forde

Charlie Chan's Chance *32* John G. Blystone

Charlie Chan's Courage *34* Eugene Forde, George Hadden

Charlie Chan's Greatest Case *33* Hamilton MacFadden

Charlie Chan's Murder Cruise *40* Eugene Forde

Charlie Chan's Secret *35* Gordon Wiles

Charlie Chaplin's Burlesque on Carmen *15* Charles Chaplin

Charlie Dingo *87* Gilles Behat

Charlie in Turkey *19* Pat Sullivan

Charlie Loco *87* Gilles Behat

Charlie McCarthy — Detective *39* Frank Tuttle

Charlie on the Ocean *15* Charles Chaplin

Charlie on the Spree *15* Charles Chaplin

Charlie Smiler Asks Papa *12* Dave Aylott

Charlie Smiler at the Picnic *12* Dave Aylott

Charlie Smiler Catches a Tartar *12* Dave Aylott

Charlie Smiler's Love Affair *12* Dave Aylott

Charlie Spencer's Been Robbed *86* Francis Huster

Charlie the Burglar *16* Charles Chaplin

Charlie the Hobo *15* Charles Chaplin

Charlie the Lonesome Cougar *67* Winston Hibler

Charlie the Sailor *15* Charles Chaplin

Charlie Treats 'Em Rough *19* Pat Sullivan

Charlie's Day Out *15* Charles Chaplin

Charlotte *17* Oscar Eagle

Charlotte *74* Roger Vadim

Charlotte: A Girl Murdered *74* Roger Vadim

Charlotte and Her Steak *51* Eric Rohmer

Charlotte and Lulu *85* Claude Miller

Charlotte et Son Jules *58* Jean-Luc Godard

Charlotte et Son Steak *51* Eric Rohmer

Charlotte et Véronique *57* Jean-Luc Godard

Charlotte et Véronique ou Tous les Garçons S'Appellent Patrick *57* Jean-Luc Godard

Charlotte Forever *86* Serge Gainsbourg

Charlotte Löwensköld *30* Gustaf Molander

Charlotte's Web *72* Charles A. Nichols, Iwao Takamoto

Charly *68* Ralph Nelson

Charly der Wunderaffe *15* Joe May

Charly's Web *86* Simon Heath

Charm Bracelet, The *39* Art Davis, Sid Marcus

Charm of La Bohème, The *38* Géza von Bolváry

Charm School, The *20* James Cruze

Charm School, The *35* Ralph Murphy

Charm That Charmed, The *15* Dave Aylott

Charmant FrouFrou *01* Alice Guy-Blaché

Charmant Voyages de Noces *1899* Georges Méliès

Charmants Garçons *57* Henri Decoin

Charme Discret de la Bourgeoisie, Le *72* Luis Buñuel

Charmer, The *17* Jack Conway

Charmer, The *25* Sidney Olcott

Charmer, The *37* Lothar Mendes

Charmes de l'Existence, Les *49* Jean Grémillon, Pierre Kast

Charming Deceiver, The *21* George L. Sargent

Charming Deceiver, The *33* Monty Banks

Charming Sinners *29* Dorothy Arzner, Robert Milton

Charming Sounds *57* Dušan Vukotić

Charrette Fantôme, La *39* Julien Duvivier

Charro! *69* Charles Marquis Warren

Charron, Le *43* Georges Rouquier

Charter Pilot *40* Eugene Forde

Charter Trip II — Snow Roller *85* Lasse Åberg

Chartres *23* Jean Grémillon

Chartreuse de Parme, La *47* Christian-Jaque

Chartroose Caboose *60* William Reynolds

Charulata *64* Satyajit Ray

Chase, The *13* Allan Dwan

Chase, The *46* Arthur Ripley

Chase, The *65* Arthur Penn

Chase, The *65* Carlos Saura

Chase *87* David A. Prior

Chase a Crooked Shadow *58* Michael Anderson

Chase for the Golden Needles, The *74* Robert Clouse

Chase Me *20* Roy Del Ruth

Chase Me Charlie *17* Langford Reed

Chase of Death, The *14* B. Harold Brett

Chase of Death *49* Irving Allen

Chased Bride, The *23* Al Christie

Chased by Dogs *04* Alf Collins

Chased Into Love *17* Charlie Chase

Chaser, The *28* Harry Langdon

Chaser, The *33* Jack Conway

Chaser, The *38* Edwin L. Marin

Chaser Chased, The *06* Harold Hough

Chaser on the Rocks *65* Rudy Larriva

Chasers, The *59* Jean-Pierre Mocky

Chasers, The *60* Roy Rowland

Chases of Pimple Street, The *34* Charlie Chase

Chasing a Rainbow *11* Edwin S. Porter

Chasing Danger *39* Ricardo Cortez

Chasing Dreams *81* Therese Conte, Sean Roche

Chasing Rainbows *19* Frank Beal

Chasing Rainbows *29* Charles Reisner

Chasing the Moon *22* Edward Sedgwick

Chasing Through Europe *29* David Butler, Alfred L. Werker

Chasing Trouble *26* Milburn Morante

Chasing Trouble *40* Howard Bretherton

Chasing Two Hares *63* Victor Ivanov

Chasing Yesterday *35* George Nicholls, Jr.

Chasse à Courre, Une *51* Dmitri Kirsanov

Chasse à Courre à Villiers-Cotterets, Une *51* Dmitri Kirsanov

Chasse à la Fortune, La *30* Rochus Gliese, Karl Koch

Chasse à la Panthère *09* Alfred Machin

Chasse à l'Hippopotame, La *51* Roger Rosfelder, Jean Rouch

Chasse à l'Hippopotame sur le Nil Bleu *08* Alfred Machin

Chasse à l'Homme, La *53* Pierre Kast

Chasse à l'Homme, La *64* Édouard Molinaro

Chasse au Bonheur, La *30* Rochus Gliese, Karl Koch

Chasse au Cambrioleur, La *04* Alice Guy-Blaché

Chasse au Lion à l'Arc, La *65* Jean Rouch

Chasse Garde *86* Jean-Claude Biette

Chasse Royale, La *68* François Leterrier

Chasses de la Comtesse Zaroff, Les *73* Jesús Franco

Chasseur, Le *71* François Reichenbach

Chasseur de Chez Maxim's, Le *27* Roger Lion

Chasseur de Chez Maxim's, Le *53* Henri Diamant-Berger

Chasseurs de Lions, Les *13* Louis Feuillade

Chaste Suzanne, La *37* André Berthomieu

Chastity *23* Victor Schertzinger

Chastity *69* Alessio De Paola

Chastity Belt, The *67* Pasquale Festa Campanile

Chastnaya Zhizn *82* Yuli Raizman

Chastnyi Sluchai *34* Ilya Trauberg

Chat, Le *71* Pierre Granier-Deferre

Chat Botté, Le *03* Ferdinand Zecca

Chat Botté, Le *08* Albert Capellani

Chat dans le Sac, Le *64* Gilles Groulx

Chat et la Souris, Le *75* Claude Lelouch

Château de la Mort Lente, Un *25* Donatien

Château de la Peur, Le *12* Louis Feuillade

Château de Verre, Le *50* René Clément

Château des Morts Vivants, Le *64* Warren Keifer, Michael Reeves, Luciano Ricci

Château en Suède *63* Roger Vadim

Château Hanté, Le *1896* Georges Méliès

Château Historique *23* Henri Desfontaines

Château in Sweden *63* Roger Vadim

Château Life *65* Jean-Paul Rappeneau

Châteaux de France *48* Alain Resnais

Châteaux en Espagne *54* René Wheeler

Châtelaine du Liban, La *26* Marco De Gastyne

Châtelaine du Liban, La *33* Jean Epstein

Chato's Land *71* Michael Winner

Chattahoochee *90* Mick Jackson

Chattanooga Choo Choo *84* Bruce Bilson

Chatte, La *58* Henri Decoin

Chatte Métamorphosée en Femme, La *09* Louis Feuillade

Chatte Sort Ses Griffes, La *59* Henri Decoin

Chattel, The *16* Frederick Thompson

Chatterbox *35* George Nicholls, Jr.

Chatterbox *43* Joseph Santley

Chatterbox *77* Tom DeSimone

Chaud Lapin, Le *74* Pascal Thomas

Chaudron Infernal, Le *03* Georges Méliès

Chaudronnier, Le *49* Georges Rouquier

Chauffeur de Mademoiselle, Le *27* Henri Chomette

Chauffeur's Dream, The *08* Walter R. Booth

Chauffören *14* Victor Sjöström

Cherry Blossoms *72* Lino Brocka
Cherry Country *41* Minoru Shibuya
Cherry, Harry and Raquel! *69* Russ Meyer
Cherry Hill High *77* Alex E. Goitein
Cherry Picker, The *74* Peter Curran
Cherry Ripe *21* Kenelm Foss
Cherry 2000 *86* Steve De Jarnatt
Cheryomushki *63* Herbert Rappaport
Chess Fever *25* Vsevolod I. Pudovkin, Nikolai Shpikovsky
Chess-Nuts *32* Dave Fleischer
Chess Player, The *27* Raymond Bernard
Chess Player, The *30* Henri Dupuy-Mazuel
Chess Player, The *38* Jean Dréville
Chess Players, The *77* Satyajit Ray
Chess Queen, The *16* C. Allen Gilbert
Chesscetera *57* Hans Richter
Chester Forgets Himself *24* Andrew P. Wilson
Chester's Cat *21* Wallace A. Carlson
Chesty *70* John Ford
Chesty—A Tribute to a Legend *70* John Ford
Chesty Anderson, USN *76* Ed Forsyth
Chesty Anderson, US Navy *76* Ed Forsyth
Chetan, Indian Boy *73* Hark Böhm
Chetnik *43* Sergei Nolbandov
Chetniks *42* Louis King
Chetniks—The Fighting Guerrillas *42* Louis King
Cheval d'Orgeuil, Le *79* Claude Chabrol
Chevalier de Gaby, Le *20* Charles Burguet
Chevalier de Maupin, Le *65* Mauro Bolognini
Chevalier de Ménilmontant *54* Jacques Baratier
Chevalier Démontable et le Géneral Boum, Le *01* Georges Méliès
Chevalier des Neiges, Le *10* Georges Méliès
Chevalier Mystère, Le *1899* Georges Méliès
Chevalier Mystère, Le *07* Segundo De Chomón
Chevaliers, Les *72* Gilles Carle
Chevaliers du Chloroforme, Les *05* Georges Méliès
Chevauchée, La *64* Serge Bourguignon
Chevauchée Blanche, La *23* Donatien
Chevaux de Bois, Les *1896* Georges Méliès
Chevaux du Vercors, Les *43* Jacqueline Audry
Cheveaux d'Hollywood, Les *64* François Reichenbach
Chèvre, La *81* Francis Veber
Chèvre aux Pieds d'Or, La *26* Jacques Robert
Chevy Van *76* Sam Grossman
Chew-Chew Land *10* J. Stuart Blackton
Chewin' Bruin, The *40* Robert Clampett
Chewing Gum Industry, The *20* Raoul Barré, Charles Bowers
Cheyenne *29* Albert S. Rogell
Cheyenne *47* Raoul Walsh
Cheyenne Autumn *64* John Ford
Cheyenne Cyclone, The *32* Armand Schaefer
Cheyenne Kid, The *30* Jacques Jaccard
Cheyenne Kid, The *33* Robert F. Hill
Cheyenne Kid, The *40* Raymond K.

Johnson
Cheyenne Rides Again *37* Robert F. Hill
Cheyenne Roundup *43* Ray Taylor
Cheyenne Social Club, The *70* Gene Kelly
Cheyenne Takes Over *47* Ray Taylor
Cheyenne Tornado *35* William A. O'Connor
Cheyenne Trails *28* Robert J. Horner
Cheyenne Wildcat *44* Lesley Selander
Cheyenne's Pal *17* John Ford
Chez la Sorcière *01* Georges Méliès
Chez le Magnétiseur *1898* Alice Guy-Blaché
Chez le Maréchal-Ferrant *00* Alice Guy-Blaché
Chez le Photographe *00* Alice Guy-Blaché
Chhannachchara *88* Anjan Mukherjee
Chhou Dances of Purulia *70* Ritwik Ghatak
Chi C'È C'È *87* Piero Natoli
Chi È Dio? *48* Mario Soldati
Chi È Più Felice Di Me? *40* Guido Brignone
Chi Lavora È Perduto *63* Tinto Brass
Chi l'Ha Visto? *43* Goffredo Alessandrini
Chi o Suu Bara *75* Michio Yamamoto
Chi o Suu Me *71* Michio Yamamoto
Chi o Suu Ningyō *70* Michio Yamamoto
Chi Sei? *74* Sonia Assonitis, Roberto d'Ettore Piazzoli
Chi to Rei *22* Kenji Mizoguchi
Chi to Suna *66* Kihachi Okamoto
Chi Trovo un Amico, Trova un Tesoro *81* Sergio Corbucci
Chiamavano Cosetta, Lo *17* Carmine Gallone
Chiamavano King, Lo *71* Renato Savino
Chiamavano Tresette...Giocava Sempre col Morto, Lo *73* Giuliano Carmineo
Chiamavano Trinità, Lo *70* Enzo Barboni
Chiamavano Verità, Lo *72* Luigi Perelli
Chiameremo Andrea, Lo *72* Vittorio De Sica
Chiara e lo Scuro, La *83* Maurizio Ponzi
Chiave, La *84* Tinto Brass
Chibusa o Daku Musumetachi *62* Satsuo Yamamoto
Chica de la Calle Florida, La *21* José A. Ferreyra
Chica del Lunes, La *66* Leopoldo Torre-Nilsson
Chicago *27* Frank Urson
Chicago After Midnight *28* Ralph Ince
Chicago Blues *72* Harley Cokliss
Chicago Calling *51* John Reinhardt
Chicago, Chicago *69* Norman Jewison
Chicago Confidential *57* Sidney Salkow
Chicago Deadline *49* Lewis Allen
Chicago Fire, The *24* W. S. Van Dyke
Chicago Joe and the Showgirl *90* Bernard Rose
Chicago Kid, The *45* Frank McDonald
Chicago Masquerade *51* Frederick De Cordova
Chicago '70 *70* Kerry Feltham
Chicago Syndicate *55* Fred F. Sears
Chicano Connection, The *86* Luis Quintanilla Rico
Chicherin *86* Alexander Zarkhi
Chichi Ariki *42* Yasujiro Ozu

Chichi to Ko *69* Zenzo Matsuyama
Chichi yo Haha yo *80* Keisuke Kinoshita
Chichinette et Clé *21* Henri Desfontaines
Chicho o Mientras el Cuerpo Aguante *82* Fernando Trueba
Chick *28* A. V. Bramble
Chick *36* Michael Hankinson
Chick Carter, Detective *46* Derwin Abrahams
Chick for Cairo, A *85* Arend Aghte
Chick That Was Not Eggs-tinct, The *14* Hay Plumb
Chicken à la King *28* Henry Lehrman
Chicken à la King *37* Dave Fleischer
Chicken and Duck Talk *89* Clifton Ko
Chicken and Fries *87* Luis Rego
Chicken Casey *17* Raymond B. West
Chicken Chaser, The *26* William C. Nolan
Chicken Chronicles, The *77* Francis Simon
Chicken Dressing *23* Earl Hurd
Chicken Every Sunday *49* George Seaton
Chicken Fancier, The *21* Henry D. Bailey
Chicken Fraca-See *62* Joseph Barbera, William Hanna
Chicken Hearted *15* Percy Nash
Chicken-Hearted Jim *16* Francis Ford
Chicken Hearted Wolf *63* Joseph Barbera, William Hanna
Chicken in the Case, The *21* Victor Heerman
Chicken Jitters *39* Robert Clampett
Chicken Ranch *83* Nicholas Broomfield, Sandi Sissel
Chicken Real *70* Les Blank
Chicken Reel *34* Walter Lantz
Chicken Thief, The *21* Wallace A. Carlson
Chicken Thief, The *21* Grim Natwick
Chicken Wagon Family *39* Herbert I. Leeds
Chickens *21* Jack Nelson
Chickens Come Home *31* James W. Horne
Chickie *25* John Francis Dillon
Chico Rei *86* Walter Lima Júnior
Chicos, Los *59* Marco Ferreri
Chicot, Dentiste Américain *1897* Georges Méliès
Chidambaram *86* G. Aravindan
Chido Guan *84* Alfonso Arau
Chiedi Perdono a Dio Non a Me *68* Glenn Vincent Davis
Chiedo Asilo *79* Marco Ferreri
Chief, The *33* Charles Reisner
Chief Crazy Horse *55* George Sherman
Chief of the Horse Farm, The *78* András Kovács
Chief Wants No Survivors, The *63* Hans Albin, Peter Berneis
Chief Zabu *88* Neil Cohen, Howard Zuker
Chiefs *69* Richard Leacock, Noel Parmentel
Chief's Blanket, The *12* D. W. Griffith
Chief's Daughter, The *11* D. W. Griffith
Chief's Predicament, The *13* Mack Sennett
Chief's Son Is Dead, The *37* Pál Fejös
Chieko-Shō *67* Noboru Nakamura
Chien Andalou, Un *28* Luis Buñuel, Salvador Dali
Chien de Pique, La *60* Yves Allégret

Chien Jouant à la Balle 05 Alice Guy-Blaché

Ch'ien-Nu Yu-Hin 59 Han-hsiang Li

Chienne, La 31 Jean Renoir

Chiens, Les 78 Alain Jessua

Chiens dans la Nuit, Les 66 Willy Rozier

Chiens Perdus Sans Collier 55 Jean Delannoy

Chiens Savants, Les 02 Alice Guy-Blaché

Chiesa, La 89 Michele Soavi

Chiffonnier, Le 1896 Georges Méliès

Chiffonnier, Le 00 Alice Guy-Blaché

Chiffonnier de Paris, Le 24 Serge Nadejdine

Chiffy Kids, The 77 David Bracknell

Chiffy Kids II, The 78 David Bracknell

Chignon d'Or 16 André Hugon

Chiheisen 84 Kaneto Shindo

Chiisai Tōbōsha 66 Eduard Bocharov, Teinosuke Kinugasa

Chiisana Bōken Ryokō 64 Nagisa Oshima

Chiisana Kūkan 64 Yoji Kuri

Chiisana Sasayaki 66 Yoji Kuri

Chiisana Tōbōsha 66 Eduard Bocharov, Teinosuke Kinugasa

Chijō 57 Kozaburo Yoshimura

Chikagai Nijūyojikan 47 Tadashi Imai, Kiyoshi Kusuda, Hideo Sekigawa

Chikamatsu Monogatari 54 Kenji Mizoguchi

Chikamauga 61 Robert Enrico

Chikumagawa Zesshō 67 Shiro Toyoda

Chikuzan 77 Kaneto Shindo

Chikuzan Hitori Tabi 77 Kaneto Shindo

Chikuzan Travels Alone 77 Kaneto Shindo

Chikyū Bōeigun 57 Inoshiro Honda

Chikyū Saidai no Kessen 65 Inoshiro Honda

Chikyū wa Mawaru 28 Tomotaka Tasaka, Tomu Uchida

Child, The 12 Mauritz Stiller

Child, The 14 Forest Holger-Madsen

Child, The 40 Benjamin Christensen

Child, The 77 Robert Voskanian

Child, a Dog, a Vagabond, A 34 Arthur Maria Rabenalt

Child, a Wand and a Wish, A 12 H. Oceano Martinek

Child Accuser, The 07 Harold Hough

Child and the Fiddler, The 10 Theo Bouwmeester

Child and the Fiddler, The 17 Bert Haldane

Child and the Killer, The 59 Max Varnel

Child Bride 37 Harry Revier

Child Detective, The 12 Bert Haldane

Child for Sale, A 20 Ivan Abramson

Child God, The 86 Uptlendu Chakraborty

Child in Blue, The 19 F. W. Murnau

Child in Judgement, A 15 Carlton S. King

Child in the House 56 Charles De Lautour, Cy Endfield

Child Is a Wild Thing, A 76 Peter Skinner

Child Is Born, A 39 Lloyd Bacon

Child Is Waiting, A 62 John Cassavetes

Child Mother, The 13 Ethyle Batley

Child o' My Heart 14 Harold M. Shaw

Child of a Suffragette, The 13 F. Martin Thornton

Child of Destiny, The 16 William Nigh

Child of Divorce 46 Richard Fleischer

Child of Fate, The 12 Alice Guy-Blaché

Child of God, A 15 John G. Adolfi

Child of Man 46 Bjarne Henning-Jensen

Child of Manhattan 33 Edward Buzzell

Child of M'sieu 19 Harrish Ingraham

Child of Mystery, A 16 Hobart Henley

Child of Paris, A 16 Lloyd Ingraham

Child of Satan 76 Peter Sykes

Child of the Big City 14 Yevgeni Bauer

Child of the Ghetto, A 10 D. W. Griffith

Child of the Night 71 James Kelly

Child of the Palenque 86 Rubén Galindo, Jr.

Child of the Paris Streets, A 16 Lloyd Ingraham

Child of the Prairie, A 15 Tom Mix

Child of the Sea, A 15 Frank Wilson

Child of the Streets, A 15 Ernest G. Batley

Child of the Streets 67 Shyam Benegal

Child of the Wild, A 17 John G. Adolfi

Child Psykolojiky 41 Dave Fleischer

Child Sock-cology 61 Joseph Barbera, William Hanna

Child Thou Gavest Me, The 20 John M. Stahl

Child Under a Leaf 74 George Bloomfield

Child Went Forth, A 41 John Ferno, Joseph Losey

Childbirth Dream 78 Alexis Krasilovsky

Childhood Days 43 Jean Negulesco

Childhood of Gorky 38 Mark Donskoi

Childhood of Ivan 62 Andrei Tarkovsky

Childhood of Maxim Gorky, The 38 Mark Donskoi

Childhood Scenes of Provincial Life 86 Tomasz Żygaldo

Childish Things 66 John Derek, David Nelson

Children, The 49 Rolf Husberg

Children, The 66 Edgar Reitz

Children, The 80 Max Kalmanowicz

Children, The 84 Marguerite Duras, Jean Mascolo, Jean-Marc Turine

Children, The 90 Tony Palmer

Children and Cars 71 John Halas

Children and the Lions, The 00 George Green

Children and the Statue of Buddha 52 Hiroshi Shimizu

Children Are Watching Us, The 42 Vittorio De Sica

Children at School 36 Basil Wright

Children, Books 62 Márta Mészáros

Children, Flowers of Life 19 Yuri Zhelyabuzhsky

Children Galore 54 Terence Fisher

Children Hand in Hand 48 Hiroshi Inagaki

Children Hand in Hand 62 Susumu Hani

Children in the Classroom 54 Susumu Hani

Children in the House, The 16 Chester M. Franklin, Sidney Franklin

Children in the Wind 37 Hiroshi Shimizu

Children in Torment 38 Hiroshi Shimizu

Children in Uniform 58 Géza von Radványi

Children Must Laugh 36 Aleksander Ford

Children Must Learn, The 40 Willard Van Dyke

Children Mustn't Smoke 11 Lewin Fitzhamon

Children Not Wanted 20 Paul Scardon

Children of a Desired Sex 87 Mira Nair

Children of a Lesser God 86 Randa Haines

Children of Angyalföld 55 Miklós Jancsó

Children of Babylon 80 Lennie Little-White

Children of Banishment 19 Norval MacGregor

Children of Bullerby Village, The 86 Lasse Hallström

Children of Chance 30 Alexander Esway

Children of Chance 48 Luigi Zampa

Children of Chaos 43 Léo Joannon

Children of Courage 21 A. E. Coleby

Children of Darkness 22 E. A. Dupont

Children of Destiny 20 George Irving

Children of Divorce 27 Frank Lloyd, Josef von Sternberg

Children of Divorce 39 Benjamin Christensen

Children of Dreams 31 Alan Crosland

Children of Dust 23 Frank Borzage

Children of Fate 14 Wallace Reid

Children of Gibeon, The 20 Sidney Morgan

Children of God's Earth 83 Laila Mikkelsen

Children of Hiroshima 52 Kaneto Shindo

Children of Jazz 23 Jerome Storm

Children of Montmartre 32 Jean Benoît-Lévy, Marie Epstein

Children of Nagasaki 83 Keisuke Kinoshita

Children of No Importance 26 Gerhard Lamprecht

Children of Paradise 44 Marcel Carné

Children of Pleasure 30 Harry Beaumont

Children of Rage 75 Arthur Allan Seidelman

Children of Sanchez, The 78 Hall Bartlett

Children of the Atomic Bomb 52 Kaneto Shindo

Children of the Beehive 48 Hiroshi Shimizu

Children of the Century 15 Yevgeni Bauer

Children of the Cold War 85 Gonzalo Justiniano

Children of the Corn 84 Fritz Kiersch

Children of the Damned 63 Anton Leader

Children of the Dust 23 Frank Borzage

Children of the Earth 46 Khwaja Ahmad Abbas

Children of the Feud 16 Joseph E. Henabery

Children of the Fog 35 Leopold Jessner, John Quin

Children of the Forest 12 Lewin Fitzhamon

Children of the Ghetto 15 Frank Powell

Children of the New Day 30 Vladimir Petrov

Children of the Night 21 John Francis Dillon

Children of the Night No. 1 25 Charles C. Calvert

Children of the Night No. 2 25 Charles C. Calvert

Children of the Revolution 36 A. Maslyukov

Children of the Ritz 29 John Francis Dillon

Children of the Sea 26 Kenji Mizoguchi

Children of the Soviet Arctic 41 Mark Donskoi

Children of the Storm 26 Friedrich Ermler, Eduard Johansen

Children of the Streets 14 Victor Sjöström

Children of the Streets 51 Youssef Wahby

Children of the Sun 17 Anders Wilhelm Sandberg

Children of the Sun 60 John Hubley

Children of the Swallow, The 87 Costas Vrettakos

Children of the Whirlwind 25 Whitman Bennett

Children of the Wild 40 Charles Hutchinson, Vin Moore

Children of Theater Street, The 77 Robert Dornhelm, Earle Mack

Children of This Country, The 58 Atıf Yılmaz

Children of Villa Emma 83 Nissim Dayan

Children on Trial 46 Jack Lee

Children Paddling at the Seaside 1897 George Albert Smith

Children Pay, The 16 Lloyd Ingraham

Children Playing on the Beach 1896 Georges Méliès

Children Shouldn't Play with Dead Things 72 Bob Clark

Children Upstairs, The 54 Lindsay Anderson

Children vs. Earthquakes — Earthquakes Preferred 05 Lewin Fitzhamon

Children Were Watching, The 61 Richard Leacock*

Children Who Draw 55 Susumu Hani

Children's Cabaret 54 Olive Negus

Children's Corner 35 Marcel L'Herbier

Children's Friend, The 09 D. W. Griffith

Children's Games 1895 Louis Lumière

Children's Games 69 Walter Welebit

Children's Home, The 21 Walter C. Rowden

Children's Hour, The 61 William Wyler

Children's Quarrel 1895 Louis Lumière

Children's Thoughts for the Future 12 F. Martin Thornton

Child's Dream of Christmas, A 12 Gilbert Southwell

Child's Faith, A 10 D. W. Griffith

Child's First Adventure, A 64 Nagisa Oshima

Child's Impulse, A 10 D. W. Griffith

Child's Message to Heaven, A 10 T. J. Gobbett

Child's Play 54 Margaret Thomson

Child's Play 72 Sidney Lumet

Child's Play 84 Val Guest

Child's Play 88 Tom Holland

Child's Play 2 90 John Lafia

Child's Prayer, A 10 Percy Stow

Child's Remorse, A 12 D. W. Griffith

Child's Sacrifice, A 10 Alice Guy-Blaché

Child's Stratagem, A 10 D. W. Griffith

Child's Strategy, A 12 Ernest G. Batley

Childstealers 87 Alberto Bojorquez

Chile Con Carmen 30 Walter Lantz

Chili Corn Corny 65 Robert McKimson

Chili Weather 63 Friz Freleng

Chillers 88 Daniel Boyd

Chilling, The 89 Deland Nuse, Jack A. Sunseri

Chilly Days 28 Charles Lamont

Chilly Nights 85 Wen Que

Chilly Scenes of Winter 79 Joan Micklin Silver

Chilly Willy 53 Alex Lovy

Chilly Willy in the Legend of Rock-a-Bye Point 55 Tex Avery

Chillysmith Farm 82 Dan Jury, Mark Jury

Chiltern Country, The 38 Alberto Cavalcanti

Chiltern Hundreds, The 49 John Paddy Carstairs

Chimbella 39 José A. Ferreyra

Chimère 89 Claire Devers

Chimes, The 14 Thomas Bentley

Chimes, The 14 Herbert Blaché, Tom Terriss

Chimes at Midnight 65 Orson Welles

Chimimorya 71 Ko Nakahira

Chimiste Repopulateur, Le 01 Georges Méliès

Chimmie Fadden 15 Cecil B. DeMille

Chimmie Fadden Out West 15 Cecil B. DeMille

Chimney Sweep, The 06 Georges Méliès

Chimney Sweeps, The 63 Dudley Birch

Chimney's Secret, The 15 Lon Chaney

Chimp, The 32 James Parrott

Chimp and Zee 68 Alex Lovy

Chimpmates 76 Harold Orton

Chimpmates II 77 Harold Orton

Chimpmates III 78 Harold Orton

Chin Chin Chinaman 31 Guy Newall

Chin Nu Yu Hun 65 Han-hsiang Li

China 31 Walter Lantz

China 43 John Farrow

China 72 Michelangelo Antonioni

China Awakened 17 Hy Mayer

China Bound 29 Charles Reisner

China Caravan 41 George B. Seitz

China Clipper 36 Ray Enright

China Corsair 51 Ray Nazarro

China Defends Herself 38 Roman Karmen

China Doll 58 Frank Borzage

China Express 29 Ilya Trauberg

China Gate 57 Samuel Fuller

China Girl 42 Henry Hathaway

China Girl 87 Abel Ferrara

China Is Near 66 Marco Bellocchio, Franco Cristaldi

China Jones 59 Robert McKimson

China Liberated 50 Ivan Dukinsky, Sergei Gerasimov, Irina Setkina, M. Slavinsky, Sao-bin Sui, Elena Svilovoi

China, My Sorrow 89 Sijie Dai

China 9, Liberty 37 77 Monte Hellman

China Passage 37 Edward Killy

China Peril, The 24 Gaston Quiribet

China Plate, The 31 Wilfred Jackson

China Seas 35 Tay Garnett

China Sky 45 Ray Enright

China Slaver 29 Frank S. Mattison

China Story 61 Leo McCarey

China Syndrome, The 79 James Bridges

China Tea 66 Malcolm Le Grice

China Venture 53 Don Siegel

China Versus Allied Powers 01 Georges Méliès

Chinaman, The 20 Dave Fleischer

Chinaman's Chance 33 Ubbe Iwerks

China's 400 Million 38 John Ferno, Joris Ivens

China's Little Devils 45 Monta Bell

Chinatown 74 Roman Polanski

Chinatown After Dark 31 Stuart Paton

Chinatown at Midnight 49 Seymour Friedman

Chinatown Charlie 28 Charles Hines

Chinatown My Chinatown 29 Dave Fleischer

Chinatown Mystery, The 28 John P. McGowan

Chinatown Mystery 32 Dick Huemer

Chinatown Nights 29 William A. Wellman

Chinatown Nights 38 Anthony Frenguelli

Chinatown Squad 35 Murray Roth

Chinchero 71 Dennis Hopper

Chine: Die Künste, der Alltag 85 Ulrike Ottinger

Chine Ma Douleur 89 Sijie Dai

Chinese Adventure 49 Seymour Friedman

Chinese Adventures in China 65 Philippe de Broca

Chinese Are Coming, The 87 Manfred Stelzer

Chinese Boxes 84 Christopher Petit

Chinese Bungalow, The 26 Sinclair Hill

Chinese Bungalow, The 30 Arthur W. Barnes, J. B. Williams

Chinese Bungalow, The 39 George King

Chinese Cabaret 36 Buddy Harris

Chinese Cat, The 44 Phil Rosen

Chinese Connection, The 73 Wei Lo

Chinese Den 39 George King

Chinese Ghost Story, A 85 Hark Tsui, Ching Siu Tung

Chinese Ghost Story II, A 87 Hark Tsui

Chinese Ghost Story III, A 90 Hark Tsui

Chinese Girl, The 67 Jean-Luc Godard

Chinese Honeymoon, The 20 Gregory La Cava, Vernon Stallings

Chinese Magic 00 Walter R. Booth

Chinese Moon 27 J. Steven Edwards

Chinese Moon, A 28 Karl Freund

Chinese Parrot, The 27 Paul Leni

Chinese Puzzle, The 19 Fred Goodwins

Chinese Puzzle, The 32 Guy Newall

Chinese Question, The 20 Vernon Stallings

Chinese Ring, The 47 William Beaudine

Chinese Room, The 66 Albert Zugsmith

Chinese Roulette 76 Rainer Werner Fassbinder

Chinese Shadows 82 Raúl Ruiz

Chinese Vase, The 13 August Blom

Chinesen Kommen, Die 87 Manfred Stelzer

Chinesischen Götze, Der 16 Richard Oswald

Chinesisches Roulett 76 Rainer Werner Fassbinder
Ching Lin Foo Outdone 00 Edwin S. Porter
Chink at Golden Gulch, The 10 D. W. Griffith
Chinmoku 71 Masahiro Shinoda
Chinnathambi Periyathambi 87 Manivarnan
Chino 73 John Sturges
Chinois à Paris, Les 73 Jean Yanne
Chinoise, La 67 Jean-Luc Godard
Chinoise ou Plutôt à la Chinoise: Un Film en Train de Se Faire, La 67 Jean-Luc Godard
Chintao Yōsai Bakugeki Meirei 63 Kengo Furusawa
Chiny i Lyudi 29 Mikhail Doller, Yakov Protazanov
Chip of the Empire, A 29 Friedrich Ermler
Chip of the Flying U 14 Colin Campbell
Chip of the Flying U 26 Lynn Reynolds
Chip of the Flying U 39 Ralph Staub
Chip Off the Old Block, A 15 Dave Aylott
Chip Off the Old Block, A 15 Cecil Birch
Chip Off the Old Block, A 19 Wallace A. Carlson
Chip Off the Old Block 44 Charles Lamont
Chipmunk Adventure, The 86 Janice Karman
Chips 38 Edward Godal
Chips Are Down, The 47 Jean Delannoy
Chiquito Pero Picoso 67 Miguel Delgado
Chiriakhana 67 Satyajit Ray
Chirrokkrotimata, Ta 43 George Tzavellas
Chirurgie Correctrice et Réparatrice, La 39 Jean Painlevé
Chirurgie de l'Avenir, La 01 Georges Méliès
Chirurgie Fin de Siècle 00 Alice Guy-Blaché
Chirurgie Fin de Siècle 02 Georges Méliès
Chirurgien Américain 1897 Georges Méliès
Chirurgien Distrait, Un 09 Émile Cohl
Chiseler, The 31 Mack Sennett
Chismosa, La 40 Enrique T. Susini
Chistoye Nebo 61 Grigori Chukhrai
Chisum 70 Andrew V. McLaglen
Chitrakkathi 77 Mani Kaul
Chitty Chitty Bang Bang 68 Ken Hughes
Chivalrous Charley 21 Robert Ellis
Chivato 61 Albert C. Gannaway
Chiyari Fuji 55 Tomu Uchida
Chkatulka iz Kreposti 87 Gulbeniz Azimzade
Chlen Pravitelstva 37 Josef Heifits, Alexander Zarkhi
Chloe 34 Marshall Neilan
Chloë in the Afternoon 72 Eric Rohmer
Chloe, Love Is Calling You 34 Marshall Neilan
Chloroform Fiends, The 05 Georges Méliès
Chnouf 54 Henri Decoin
Chobizenesse 75 Jean Yanne
Chobotnice z II. Patra 87 Jindřich Polák
Chobun 77 Doo-yong Lee

Choca, La 73 Emilio Fernández
Chocolat 88 Claire Denis
Chocolate Factory 52 Sidney Peterson
Chocolate Girl 32 Mikio Naruse
Chocolate Inspector 87 Philip Chan
Chocolate Soldier, The 15 Walter Morton
Chocolate Soldier, The 41 Roy Del Ruth
Chocolate War, The 88 Keith Gordon
Choice, The 25 Alexander Butler
Choice, The 70 Youssef Chahine
Choice, The 87 Idrissa Ouedraogo
Choice Chance Woman Dance 71 Ed Emshwiller
Choice of a Goal, The 74 Igor Talankin
Choice of Arms 76 Kevin Connor
Choice of Arms 81 Alain Corneau
Choice of Weapons, A 76 Kevin Connor
Choices 81 Silvio Narizzano
Choirboys, The 77 Robert Aldrich
Choke Canyon 86 Chuck Bail
Chōken Yasha 28 Teinosuke Kinugasa
Chokoreito Garu 32 Mikio Naruse
Cholly Polly 42 Alec Geiss
Cholpon — Utrennyaya Zvezda 62 Roman Tikhomirov
Chômeur de Clochemerle, Le 57 Jean Boyer
Choose Life 62 Erwin Leiser
Choose Me 84 Alan Rudolph
Choose Your Partner 40 S. Sylvan Simon
Choose Your Partners 35 Charles Lamont
Choose Your Weppins 35 Dave Fleischer
Choosing a Husband 09 D. W. Griffith
Choosing the Wallpaper 09 George Albert Smith
Chopin 57 Jean Mitry
Chopin Nocturne, A 13 Yakov Protazanov
Chopin's Funeral March 07 Georges Méliès
Chopin's Funeral March Burlesqued 07 Georges Méliès
Chopper, The 71 Ray Dennis Steckler
Chopper 86 Nabyendu Chatterjee
Choppers, The 61 Leigh Jason
Chopping Mall 86 Jim Wynorski
Chōraku no Kanata 23 Teinosuke Kinugasa
Choral Cameos 30 R. E. Jeffrey
Choral von Leuten, Der 33 Carl Fröhlich
Choreography for Camera 45 Maya Deren
Chorros 87 Jorge Coscia, Guillermo Saura
Chorus 74 Mrinal Sen
Chorus Call 79 Antonio Shepherd
Chorus, Gentlemen 06 Arthur Gilbert
Chorus Girl, The 12 Phillips Smalley
Chorus Girl 48 Randolph Tomson
Chorus Girl's Romance, A 20 William Dowlan
Chorus Girl's Thanksgiving, The 14 Frank Lloyd
Chorus Kid, The 28 Howard Bretherton
Chorus Lady, The 15 Frank Reicher
Chorus Lady, The 24 Ralph Ince
Chorus Line, A 85 Richard Attenborough
Chorus of Disapproval, A 88 Michael Winner
Chorus of Tokyo, The 31 Yasujiro Ozu
Chosen, The 77 Alberto De Martino
Chosen, The 81 Jeremy Paul Kagan
Chosen Survivors 74 Sutton Roley
Choses de la Vie, Les 69 Claude Sautet

Chotard et Cie 33 Jean Renoir
Chouans, Les 47 Henri Calef
Chouans! 87 Philippe de Broca
Chouchou Poids Plume 25 Gaston Ravel
Chouchou Poids Plume 32 Léon Poirier
Chouette Aveugle, La 87 Raúl Ruiz
Chouquette et Son As 20 Georges Monca
Chow Hound 51 Chuck Jones
Choze Ahava 86 Dan Wolman
Chr. IV Som Bygherre 41 Bjarne Henning-Jensen
Chris and the Wonderful Lamp 17 Alan Crosland
Chris Columbus, Jr. 34 Walter Lantz
Chriss-Crossed 31 Edward Buzzell
Chris's Mrs. 29 Wilfred Gannon
Christ en Croix, Le 10 Louis Feuillade
Christ in Bronze 55 Minoru Shibuya
Christ Marchant sur les Eaux, Le 1899 Georges Méliès
Christ Marchant sur les Eaux ou Le Miracle des Flots, Le 1899 Georges Méliès
Christ Marchant sur les Flots, Le 1899 Georges Méliès
Christ Stopped at Eboli 79 Francesco Rosi
Christ Walking on the Water 1899 Georges Méliès
Christa 71 Jack O'Connell
Christabel 88 Adrian Shergood
Christening Party 67 István Gaál
Christian, The 14 Frederick Thompson
Christian, The 15 George Loane Tucker
Christian, The 23 Maurice Tourneur
Christian 39 Martin Frič
Christian 89 Gabriel Axel
Christian Dior 69 François Reichenbach
Christian Licorice Store, The 71 James Frawley
Christian IV: Master Builder 41 Bjarne Henning-Jensen
Christian the Lion 71 James Hill, Bill Travers
Christian Wahnschaffe 21 Urban Gad
Christiane F. 81 Ulrich Edel
Christiane F. Wir Kinder vom Bahnhof Zoo 81 Ulrich Edel
Christians Awake! 07 Arthur Gilbert
Christie Johnstone 21 Norman MacDonald
Christina 29 William K. Howard
Christina 51 Arthur Maria Rabenalt
Christina 74 Paul Krasny
Christine 36 Julien Duvivier
Christine 58 Pierre Gaspard-Huit
Christine 83 John Carpenter
Christine Jorgensen Story, The 70 Irving Rapper
Christine Keeler Affair, The 64 Robert Spafford
Christine of the Big Tops 26 Archie Mayo
Christine of the Hungry Heart 24 George Archainbaud
Christmas 22 Malcolm St. Clair
Christmas Adventure, A 12 Wilfred Noy
Christmas Angel, The 05 Georges Méliès
Christmas Burglars, The 08 D. W. Griffith
Christmas Card, or The Story of Three Homes, A 05 J. H. Martin
Christmas Carol, A 10 J. Searle Dawley
Christmas Carol, A 11 Charles Kent

Christmas Carol, A *14* Harold M. Shaw
Christmas Carol, A *16* Rupert Julian
Christmas Carol, A *38* Edwin L. Marin
Christmas Carol, A *40* Gregory Markopoulos
Christmas Carol, A *51* Brian Desmond Hurst
Christmas Carol, A *60* Robert Hartford-Davis
Christmas Carol *65* Agnès Varda
Christmas Carol, A *71* Richard Williams
Christmas Comes But Once a Year *36* Dave Fleischer
Christmas Day in the Workhouse *14* George Pearson
Christmas Dream, The *00* Georges Méliès
Christmas Dream, The *45* Karel Zeman*
Christmas Eve *13* Władysław Starewicz
Christmas Eve *15* Alfonse Frenguelli
Christmas Eve *47* Edwin L. Marin
Christmas Eve *66* H. Amiradzibi, Jerzy Stefan Stawiński
Christmas Evil *80* Lewis Jackson
Christmas Feast *74* John Halas
Christmas Greeting Film *11* Walter Speer
Christmas Holiday *44* Robert Siodmak
Christmas in Connecticut *45* Peter Godfrey
Christmas in July *40* Preston Sturges
Christmas Kid, The *67* Rudolf Zehetgruber
Christmas Memories *17* Robert Z. Leonard
Christmas Mountain *80* Pierre De Moro
Christmas Party, The *31* Charles Reisner
Christmas Present *86* Pupi Avati
Christmas Raffle, A *08* Alf Collins
Christmas Slippers *45* Nadezhda Kasheverova, Mikhail Shapiro
Christmas Story, A *83* Bob Clark
Christmas Strike, The *13* Warwick Buckland
Christmas That Almost Wasn't, The *66* Rossano Brazzi
Christmas Tree, The *66* Jim Clark
Christmas Tree, The *69* Terence Young
Christmas Tree *75* Claude Chagrin
Christmas Under Fire *41* Harry Watt
Christmas Visitor, The *58* John Halas
Christmas Waifs, or High Life Below Stairs, The *03* Alf Collins
Christmas with Elizabeth *68* Karel Kachyňa
Christmas Without Daddy *14* Ernest G. Batley
Christophe Colomb *19* Gérard Bourgeois
Christophe Colomb *39* Abel Gance
Christopher Bean *33* Sam Wood
Christopher Colombus *49* David MacDonald
Christopher Crumpet *53* Robert Cannon
Christopher Crumpet's Playmate *55* Robert Cannon
Christopher Plummer *64* William Brayne, Allan King
Christopher Strong *33* Dorothy Arzner
Christophorus *86* Andrzej Miakar
Christo's Valley Curtain *72* Ellen Giffard, Albert Maysles, David Maysles
Christus *17* Giulio Antamoro
Chromata tis Iridas, Ta *74* Nikos Panayotopoulos

Chrome and Hot Leather *71* R. Lee Frost
Chronic Innocence *85* Edward Fleming
Chronicle *68* István Gaál
Chronicle of a Death Foretold *86* Francesco Rosi
Chronicle of a Love *50* Michelangelo Antonioni
Chronicle of a Love Affair *85* Andrzej Wajda
Chronicle of a Single Day *63* Vytautas Zalakevicius
Chronicle of a Summer *60* Edgar Morin, Jean Rouch
Chronicle of Amorous Accidents, A *85* Andrzej Wajda
Chronicle of Anna Magdalena Bach *67* Jean-Marie Straub
Chronicle of Flaming Years *61* Yulia Solntseva
Chronicle of Love Affairs, A *85* Andrzej Wajda
Chronicle of May Rain, A *24* Kenji Mizoguchi
Chronicle of Poor Lovers *54* Carlo Lizzani
Chronicle of the Burning Years *75* Mohammed Lakhdar-Hamina
Chronicle of the May Rain *24* Kenji Mizoguchi
Chronicle of the Years of Embers *75* Mohammed Lakhdar-Hamina
Chronicle of the Years of the Brazier *75* Mohammed Lakhdar-Hamina
Chronicles of Bloom Center, The *15* Marshall Neilan
Chronicles of the Grey House, The *23* Arthur von Gerlach
Chronik der Anna Magdalena Bach *67* Jean-Marie Straub
Chronique d'un Été *60* Edgar Morin, Jean Rouch
Chronique Provincial *58* Jean-Paul Rappeneau
Chronopolis *82* Piotr Kamler
Chroussousis, O *52* George Tzavellas
Chrysalide et le Papillon d'Or, Le *01* Georges Méliès
Chrysalis *73* Ed Emshwiller, Alwin Nikolais
Chrysanthème Rouge, Le *11* Léonce Perret
Chrysanthemums *14* Pyotr Chardynin
Chrzesniak *86* Henryk Bielski
Chto Delat' *28* Alexander Ptushko
Chto u Senjki Bylo *86* Radomir Vassilevsky
Chu Chin Chow *23* Herbert Wilcox
Chu Chin Chow *34* Walter Forde
Chu Chu and the Philly Flash *81* David Lowell Rich
Chubasco *68* Allen H. Miner
Chucho el Roto *35* Gabriel Soria
Chuck Berry Hail! Hail! Rock 'n' Roll *87* Taylor Hackford
Chudá Holka *29* Martin Frič
Chudý Lidé *39* Elmar Klos
Chuji Kunisada *33* Hiroshi Inagaki
Chuji Kunisada *35* Sadao Yamanaka
Chuji Tabinikki *28* Daisuke Ito
Chuji's Early Days *25* Teinosuke Kinugasa
Chuk and Gek *53* I. Lubinsky

Chuka *67* Gordon Douglas
Chulas Fronteras *76* Les Blank
Chull Bumbai Chull *88* Mira Nair
Chumlum *64* Ron Rice
Chump at Oxford, A *40* Alfred Goulding
Chump Champ, The *50* Tex Avery
Chumps *12* George D. Baker
Chumps, The *30* Mack Sennett
Chums *14* Will P. Kellino
Chum's Treachery, A *10* Bert Haldane
Chung Kuo *72* Michelangelo Antonioni
Chung Lieh T'u *74* King Hu
Chung-Shen Ta-Shih *81* King Hu
Chuntao *89* Zhifeng Ling
Chuquiago *77* Antonio Eguino
Church, The *89* Michele Soavi
Church and Stage *12* Warwick Buckland
Church Mouse, The *34* Monty Banks
Church Parade from "The Catch of the Season" *07* John Morland
Churning, The *76* Shyam Benegal
Chūshingura *32* Teinosuke Kinugasa
Chūshingura *62* Hiroshi Inagaki
Chut! *72* Jean-Pierre Mocky
Chute, La *78* Ruy Guerra, Nelson Xavier
Chute de Cinq Étages, Une *06* Georges Méliès
Chute de la Maison Usher, La *28* Luis Buñuel, Jean Epstein
Chuvas de Verão *77* Carlos Dieguês
Chuzhaja, Belaja i Rjaboj *86* Sergei Soloviev
Chuzhie Deti *58* Tenghiz Abuladze, Revas Djaparidze
Chuzhie Igry *88* Nerses Oganisyan
Chuzhie Zdes Ne Khodyat *87* Anatoly Vokhotko, Roman Yershov
Chuzhoi Bereg *30* Mark Donskoi
Chyornaya Strela *87* Sergei Tarasov
Chyorni Parus *28* Sergei Yutkevich
Chyortovo Koleso *26* Grigori Kozintsev, Leonid Trauberg
Ci Risiamo Vero Provvidenza *73* Alberto De Martino
Ci Troviamo in Galleria *53* Mauro Bolognini
Ciak Mull, l'Uomo della Vendetta *69* Enzo Barboni
Ciao *67* David Tucker
Ciao Ma *88* Giandomenico Curi
Ciao! Manhattan *72* John Palmer, David Weisman
Ciao Maschio *78* Marco Ferreri
Cible, La *25* Serge Nadejdine
Cible Humaine *04* Alice Guy-Blaché
Ciboulette *33* Claude Autant-Lara
Čiča Tomina Koliba *65* Géza von Radványi
Cicada Is Not an Insect, The *68* Daniel Tinayre
Cicala, La *79* Alberto Lattuada
Cicernacchio *15* Emilio Ghione
Ciclón *63* Santiago Álvarez
Cid, Il *10* Mario Caserini
Cidade Mulher *34* Humberto Mauro
Cidade Oculta *87* Chico Botelho
Cieca di Sorrento, La *36* Nunzio Malasomma
Cieco, Il *71* Ferdinando Baldi
Ciel Est à Vous, Le *43* Jean Grémillon

City of Masks, The 20 Thomas Heffron
City of Mice 86 M. Boroomand, Ali Talebi
City of Missing Girls 41 Elmer Clifton
City of My Dreams, The 77 Ingvar Skogsberg
City of Pain 49 Mario Bonnard
City of Pirates 83 Raúl Ruiz
City of Play 29 Denison Clift
City of Purple Dreams 18 Colin Campbell
City of Purple Dreams 28 Duke Worne
City of Sadness 89 Hsiao-hsien Hou
City of Secrets 55 Fritz Kortner
City of Shadows 29 Norman Lee
City of Shadows 55 William Witney
City of Silent Men, The 21 Tom Forman
City of Silent Men 42 William Nigh
City of Sin 59 John Cromwell
City of Song, The 31 Carmine Gallone
City of Songs 30 Richard Oswald
City of Tears, The 18 Elsie Jane Wilson
City of Temptation 29 Walter Niebuhr
City of the Dead 15 Charles Swickard
City of the Dead, The 60 John Llewellyn Moxey
City of the Living Dead 80 Lucio Fulci
City of the Walking Dead 80 Umberto Lenzi
City of Torment 47 Josef von Baky
City of Women 79 Federico Fellini
City of Youth, The 28 Charles C. Calvert
City of Youth 38 Sergei Gerasimov
City on a Hunt 53 Charles Bennett
City on Fire 79 Alvin Rakoff
City on Fire 87 Ringo Lam
City on Trial 52 Luigi Zampa
City Out of Time 59 Colin Low
City Out of Wilderness 73 Alexander Hammid
City Park 34 Richard Thorpe
City Prepares, A 39 Pat Jackson, Humphrey Jennings, Harry Watt
City Rats 87 Valentín Trujillo
City Reborn, A 45 John Eldridge
City Sentinel 32 Charles Brabin
City Slicker, The 38 Art Davis, Sid Marcus
City Slickers 28 Henry D. Bailey
City Sparrow, A 20 Sam Wood
City Speaks, A 47 Paul Rotha
City Stands Trial, The 52 Luigi Zampa
City Story 54 William Beaudine
City Streets 31 Rouben Mamoulian
City Streets 38 Albert S. Rogell
City Symphony 29 Kenji Mizoguchi
City That Never Sleeps, The 24 James Cruze
City That Never Sleeps, The 53 John H. Auer
City Tramp, The 65 Rainer Werner Fassbinder
City Under the Sea, The 65 Jacques Tourneur
City Without Jews, The 28 Carl von Santer
City Without Men 43 Sidney Salkow
City Woman 34 Humberto Mauro
City's Edge, The 83 Ken Quinnell
Ciudad de Cartón, La 34 Louis King
Ciudad de Ensueño 22 José A. Ferreyra
Ciudad y el Campo, La 35 Fernando Mantilla, Carlos Velo

Ciudad y los Perros, La 85 Francisco José Lombardi
Ciulinii Bǎrǎganului 57 Louis Daquin
Civil Defense 50 Henning Carlsen
Civil Engineering 46 John Eldridge*
Civil War, The 90 Ken Burns
Civilforsvaret 50 Henning Carlsen
Civilian Clothes 20 Hugh Ford
Civilisation à Travers les Âges, Le 07 Georges Méliès
Civilization 16 Reginald Barker, Walter Edwards, David M. Hartford, Jay Hunt, Thomas Ince, J. Parker Read, Raymond B. West
Civilization and Its Discontents 64 Paul Morrissey
Civilization Through the Ages 07 Georges Méliès
Civilization's Child 16 Charles Giblyn
Cizím Vstup Povolen 87 Josef Pinkava
Cjamango 67 Eduardo Mulargia
Claim, The 18 Frank Reicher
Claim Jumpers, The 11 Allan Dwan
Clair de Femme 79 Costa-Gavras
Clair de Lune 32 Henri Diamant-Berger
Clair de Lune Espagnol 09 Émile Cohl
Claire Lust 72 Kjell Grede
Claire's Knee 70 Eric Rohmer
Clairvoyant, The 34 Maurice Elvey
Clairvoyant, The 82 Armand Mastroianni
Clambake 67 Arthur H. Nadel
Clan, The 84 Mika Kaurismäki
Clan des Siciliens, Le 68 Henri Verneuil
Clan of the Cave Bear, The 86 Michael Chapman
Clancarty 14 Harold M. Shaw
Clancy 74 Stan Brakhage
Clancy at the Bat 29 Mack Sennett
Clancy in Wall Street 30 Edward Small, Ted Wilde
Clancy of the Mounted 33 Ray Taylor
Clancy Street Boys 43 William Beaudine
Clancy's Kosher Wedding 27 Arvid E. Gillstrom
Clandestine 48 André E. Chotin
Clandestines, Les 61 Raoul André
Clandestinos Destinos 87 Jaime Humberto Hermosillo
Clandestins, Les 48 André E. Chotin
Clansman, The 15 D. W. Griffith
Clap Hands 35 Frank Dormand
Clap Vocalism 61 Yoji Kuri
Clara and Her Mysterious Toys 14 Émile Cohl
Clara Cleans Her Teeth 26 Walt Disney
Clara de Montargis 51 Henri Decoin
Clara's Heart 88 Robert Mulligan
Clarence 22 William DeMille
Clarence 37 George Archainbaud
Clarence and Angel 80 Robert Gardner
Clarence the Cross-Eyed Lion 65 Andrew Marton
Claretta and Ben 83 Gian Luigi Polidoro
Clarion, The 16 James Durkin
Clarissa 41 Gerhard Lamprecht
Claro! 75 Glauber Rocha
Clash by Night 51 Fritz Lang
Clash by Night 63 Montgomery Tully
Clash of Steel 62 Bernard Borderie

Clash of the Swords 84 Stephen Weeks
Clash of the Titans 81 Desmond Davis
Clash of the Wolves 25 Noel Mason Smith
Class 20 Chester M. Franklin
Class, The 57 John Schlesinger
Class 83 Lewis John Carlino
Class Action 90 Michael Apted
Class and No Class 21 Will P. Kellino
Class Enemy 84 Peter Stein
Class of '84 81 Mark L. Lester
Class of '44 73 Paul Bogart
Class of Miss MacMichael, The 78 Silvio Narizzano
Class of 1984 81 Mark L. Lester
Class of 1999 90 Mark L. Lester
Class of Nuke 'Em High 85 Richard W. Haines, Lloyd Kaufman
Class of '74, The 72 Mack Bing, Arthur Marks
Class Relations 84 Danièle Huillet, Jean-Marie Straub
Classe de Luttes 70 Chris Marker*
Classe Operaia Va in Paradiso, La 71 Elio Petri
Classe Tous Risques 59 Claude Sautet
Classic Centaur, The 23 Herbert M. Dawley
Classic Fairy Tales 66 Joy Batchelor
Classic vs. Jazz 30 Alexander Oumansky
Classical Chinese Opera, The 54 Vojtěch Jasný, Karel Kachyňa
Classification of Plants 82 Raúl Ruiz
Classifications des Plantes 82 Raúl Ruiz
Classified 25 Alfred Santell
Classmates 08 Wallace McCutcheon
Classmates 14 James Kirkwood
Classmates 24 John S. Robertson
Claude 66 Claude Berri
Claude Deputises 30 R. E. Jeffrey
Claude Duval 24 George A. Cooper
Claude-Nicolas Ledoux, Architecte Maudit 54 Pierre Kast
Claudelle Inglish 61 Gordon Douglas
Claudia 43 Edmund Goulding
Claudia and David 46 Walter Lang
Claudina's Troubles 40 Miguel Caronatto Paz
Claudine 40 Serge De Poligny
Claudine 74 John Berry
Clause in the Will, A 10 Edwin S. Porter
Clavillazo en la Luna 60 Rogelio A. González
Claw, The 18 Robert Vignola
Claw, The 27 Sidney Olcott
Claw Monsters, The 55 Franklin Adreon
Claw Strikes, The 46 Vernon Keays
Claws 77 Richard Bansbach, Robert E. Pierson
Claws for Alarm 54 Chuck Jones
Claws in the Lease 63 Robert McKimson
Claws of the Hun, The 18 Victor Schertzinger
Clay 20 Victor Sjöström
Clay 40 Humberto Mauro, Carmen Santos
Clay 64 Giorgio Manglamele
Clay Dollars 21 George Archainbaud
Clay Heart, The 15 Forest Holger-Madsen
Clay Pigeon, The 49 Richard Fleischer
Clay Pigeon 71 Lane Slate, Tom Stern
Clay Town 24 Dave Fleischer

Claydon Treasure Mystery, The 38 H. Manning Haynes
Clayton and Catherine 77 Monte Hellman
Clé de Voûté, La 25 Roger Lion
Clé sur la Porte, La 78 Yves Boisset
Clean and Sober 88 Glenn Gordon Caron
Clean Gun, The 17 Harry Harvey
Clean Heart, The 24 J. Stuart Blackton
Clean Loving...Never Stays That Way for Long 85 Martin Veyron
Clean Pastures 37 Friz Freleng
Clean Shaven Man, A 36 Dave Fleischer
Clean Slate 81 Bertrand Tavernier
Clean Sweep, A 58 Maclean Rogers
Clean-Up, The 17 William Worthington
Clean Up, The 23 William Parke
Clean-Up, The 29 Bernard F. McEveety
Clean-Up Man, The 28 Ray Taylor
Clean Words About Dirt 62 Henning Carlsen
Clean Your Feet 21 Frank Moser
Cleaning Up 26 Roscoe Arbuckle
Cleaning Up 33 Leslie Hiscott
Cleansing of a Dirty Dog, The 14 Langford Reed
Clear! 75 Glauber Rocha
Clear All Wires 33 George W. Hill
Clear Skies 61 Grigori Chukhrai
Clear Sky, A 61 Grigori Chukhrai
Clear the Decks 29 Joseph E. Henabery
Clear the Way 24 Charles Lamont
Cleared for Action 37 Edvin Adolphson
Clearing the Range 31 Otto Brower
Clearing the Trail 28 B. Reeves Eason
Clegg 69 Lindsay Shonteff
Clemenceau Case, The 15 Herbert Brenon
Clement Meadmore 63 Bruce Beresford
Clementine Tango 84 Caroline Roboh
Cleo 89 Chuck Vincent
Cléo de 5 à 7 61 Agnès Varda
Cleo from 5 to 7 61 Agnès Varda
Cleopatra 1899 Georges Méliès
Cleopatra 13 Charles L. Gaskill
Cleopatra 17 J. Gordon Edwards
Cleopatra 20 Raoul Barré, Charles Bowers
Cleopatra 28 Roy William Neill
Cleopatra 34 Cecil B. DeMille
Cleopatra 63 Joseph L. Mankiewicz
Cleopatra and Her Easy Mark 23 W. E. Stark
Cleopatra Jones 73 Jack Starrett
Cleopatra Jones and the Casino of Gold 75 Chuck Bail
Cleopatra's Daughter 60 Fernando Cerchio, Richard McNamara
Cléopâtre 1899 Georges Méliès
Clérambard 69 Yves Robert
Clergyman, The 13 Victor Sjöström
Clergyman from Uddarbo, The 58 Kenne Fant
Clerk's Downfall, The 10 Charles Raymond
Clever and Comic Cycle Act 00 James A. Williamson
Clever Egg Conjuring 12 Walter R. Booth
Clever Girl Takes Care of Herself, A 14 Victor Sjöström
Clever Illusions and How to Do Them 11 Percy Stow
Clever Mrs. Carfax, The 17 Donald Crisp

Clever One, The 14 Charles H. Weston
Clickety-Clack 70 Akira Kurosawa
Clicking of Cuthbert, The 24 Andrew P. Wilson
Client Sérieux, Un 32 Claude Autant-Lara
Cliff, The 60 Tadashi Imai
Cliff Edwards and His Buckaroos 41 Jean Negulesco
Cliff Face 44 Arne Sucksdorff
Cliff of Sin, The 52 Roberto Bianchi Montero
Climats 62 Stellio Lorenzi
Climax, The 15 Harold Weston
Climax, The 30 Renaud Hoffman
Climax, The 44 George Waggner
Climax, The 66 Pietro Germi
Climb, The 86 Donald Shebib
Climb Up the Wall 60 Michael Winner
Climber, The 17 Henry King
Climbers, The 15 Barry O'Neil
Climbers, The 19 Tom Terriss
Climbers, The 27 Paul Stein
Climbers, The 58 Yves Allégret
Climbing High 38 Carol Reed
Climbing the Matterhorn 47 Irving Allen
Climbing to the Sky 51 Luis Buñuel
Clin d'Œil 85 Jorge Amat
Clinging Vine, The 26 Paul Sloane
Clinic, The 82 David Stevens
Clinic of Stumble 47 Sidney Peterson
Clinic Xclusive 71 Don Chaffey
Clint il Solitario 67 Alfonso Balcazar
Clipped Wings 38 Stuart Paton
Clipped Wings 53 Edward Bernds
Clippetty Clobbered 66 Rudy Larriva
Clive of India 34 Richard Boleslawski
Cloak, The 26 Grigori Kozintsev, Leonid Trauberg
Cloak, The 59 Alexei Batalov
Cloak and Dagger 46 Fritz Lang
Cloak & Dagger 84 Richard Franklin
Cloak Without Dagger 56 Joseph Sterling
Clochard, Le 58 Gilles Grangier
Clochemerle 47 Pierre Chénal
Cloches de Corneville, Les 17 Thomas Bentley
Cloches de Paques, Les 12 Louis Feuillade
Clock, The 17 William Worthington
Clock, The 45 Vincente Minnelli
Clock Goes Round and Round, The 37 Art Davis, Sid Marcus
Clock Store, The 31 Wilfred Jackson
Clock Strikes Eight, The 35 Elliott Nugent
Clock Strikes Eight, The 46 Ronald Haines
Clock Strikes Eight, The 58 Michael Winner
Clock Strikes Three, The 61 Edward L. Cahn
Clockmaker, The 73 Bertrand Tavernier
Clockmaker of St. Paul, The 73 Bertrand Tavernier
Clockmaker's Dream, The 04 Georges Méliès
Clockwise 86 Christopher Morahan
Clockwork Orange, A 71 Stanley Kubrick
Clod, The 12 Thomas Ince
Clodhopper, The 17 Victor Schertzinger
Cloister and the Hearth, The 13 Hay Plumb

Cloistered 36 Robert Alexandre
Cloister's Touch, The 09 D. W. Griffith
Clones, The 73 Lamar Card, Paul Hunt
Clonus Horror, The 78 Robert S. Fiveson
Cloportes 65 Pierre Granier-Deferre
Close Call, A 12 Mack Sennett
Close Call, A 42 James P. Hogan
Close Call for Boston Blackie, A 46 Lew Landers
Close Call for Ellery Queen, A 42 James P. Hogan
Close Encounters of the Third Kind 77 Steven Spielberg
Close Friends 54 Mikhail Kalatozov
Close Harmony 29 John Cromwell, A. Edward Sutherland
Close Harmony 44 Lew Landers
Close Quarters 43 Jack Lee
Close Quarters, with a Notion of the Motion of the Ocean 02 James A. Williamson
Close Shave, A 20 Gregory La Cava
Close Shave 81 Robert Hendrickson
Close Shaves 26 Charles Lamont
Close to Home 86 Ric Beairsto
Close to My Heart 51 William Keighley
Close to Nature 67 Shyam Benegal
Close to the Wind 69 Stellan Olsson
Close-Up 48 Jack Donohue
Close Up 79 Louis Malle
Close-Up: The Blood 66 Miklós Jancsó
Closed Circuit 86 Rahman Rezaie
Closed Circuit 89 Václav Matějka
Closed Door 39 Luis Saslavsky
Closed Doors 21 Gustav von Seyffertitz
Closed Doors 33 Martin Frič
Closed Gates 27 Phil Rosen
Closed Road, The 16 Maurice Tourneur
Closed Shutters 72 Jean-Claude Brialy
Closely Observed Trains 66 Jiří Menzel
Closely Watched Trains 66 Jiří Menzel
Closer, The 90 Dimitri Logothetis
Closer to Life 51 Andrzej Munk
Closest of Kin, The 70 John Hayes
Closet, The 65 Andy Warhol
Closet Casanova, The 79 Ted Roter
Closin' In 18 J. W. McLaughlin
Closing Hour, The 60 Otakar Vávra
Closing Hours at Vibert's Perfume Factory 1896 Georges Méliès
Closing Net, The 15 Edward José
Clothes 20 Fred Sittenham
Clothes and the Woman 37 Albert De Courville
Clothes Make the Man 40 Helmut Käutner
Clothes Make the Pirate 25 Maurice Tourneur*
Clothes Make the Woman 28 Tom Terriss
Clothes of Deception 51 Kozaburo Yoshimura
Cloud-Capped Star, The 60 Ritwik Ghatak
Cloud Dancer 77 Barry Brown
Cloud Dodger, The 28 Bruce Mitchell
Cloud in Love 89 Muammar Ozer
Cloud in the Sky 40 Edgar G. Ulmer
Cloud of Andromeda, The 68 Yevgeny Sherstobitov
Cloud Patrol, The 28 Harry Joe Brown

Cloud Rider, The *25* Bruce Mitchell
Cloudburst *51* Francis Searle
Clouded Crystal, The *48* Alan Cullimore
Clouded Mind, A *23* Austin O. Huhn
Clouded Name, The *19* Caryl S. Fleming
Clouded Name, A *23* Austin O. Huhn
Clouded Yellow, The *50* Ralph Thomas
Cloudless Vacation, A *67* Károly Makk
Clouds *17* W. S. Van Dyke
Clouds at Sunset *67* Masahiro Shinoda
Clouds at Twilight *56* Keisuke Kinoshita
Clouds Over Borsk *61* Vassily Ordynski
Clouds Over Europe *37* Tim Whelan, Arthur Woods
Clouds Over Israel *62* Ivan Lengyel
Clouds Will Roll Away, The *50* Vojtěch Jasný, Karel Kachyňa
Cloudy Romance, A *25* Lewis Seiler
Člověk Pod Vodou *61* Jiří Brdečka, Ladislav Čapek
Clover's Rebellion *17* Wilfred North
Clown, The *16* William DeMille
Clown, The *16* Anders Wilhelm Sandberg
Clown, The *26* Anders Wilhelm Sandberg
Clown, The *27* William James Craft
Clown, The *31* Walter Lantz
Clown, The *50* Cecil H. Williamson
Clown, The *52* Robert Z. Leonard
Clown, The *75* Vojtěch Jasný
Clown and Automobile, The *1899* Georges Méliès
Clown and His Donkey, The *10* Charles Armstrong
Clown and Motor Car, The *1899* Georges Méliès
Clown and Policeman *00* Cecil M. Hepworth
Clown and the Alchemist, The *00* Edwin S. Porter
Clown and the Automaton, The *1897* Georges Méliès
Clown and the Kid, The *61* Edward L. Cahn
Clown and the Kids, The *68* Mende Brown
Clown aus Liebe *24* Max Linder, Édouard E. Violet
Clown Barber, The *1898* James A. Williamson
Clown en Sac *04* Alice Guy-Blaché
Clown Ferdinand and the Rocket *62* Jindřich Polák
Clown George *32* Alexander Soloviev
Clown Murders, The *75* Martyn Burke
Clown Must Laugh, A *36* Karl Grüne
Clown, Pantaloon and Bobby *02* Alf Collins
Clown Princes *39* George Sidney
Clown Versus Satan, The *01* Georges Méliès
Clownesse Fantôme, La *02* Georges Méliès
Clowns, Les *02* Alice Guy-Blaché
Clowns, I *70* Federico Fellini
Clowns, The *70* Federico Fellini
Clowns, The *85* Elisabeta Bostan
Clown's Crime, A *10* A. E. Coleby
Clowns de Dieu, Les *86* Jean Schmidt
Clown's Little Brother, The *20* Dave Fleischer
Clowns of Europe, The *14* Fred Evans, Joe Evans

Clowns of God, The *86* Jean Schmidt
Clown's Opinions, A *75* Vojtěch Jasný
Clown's Pup, The *19* Dave Fleischer
Clown's Telegram, The *04* James A. Williamson
Clown's Triumph, The *12* Herbert Brenon
Club, The *80* Bruce Beresford
Club de Femmes *37* Jacques Deval
Club de Rencontres *87* Michel Lang
Club Dead *72* Bud Townsend
Club Earth *87* Gorman Bechard
Club Extinction *89* Claude Chabrol
Club Havana *45* Edgar G. Ulmer
Club Life *86* Norman Thaddeus Vane
Club Méditerranée *76* François Reichenbach
Club of Pharos, The *15* Dave Aylott
Club of the Big Deed, The *27* Grigori Kozintsev, Leonid Trauberg
Club of the Great Deed, The *27* Grigori Kozintsev, Leonid Trauberg
Club Paradise *45* Christy Cabanne
Club Paradise *86* Harold Ramis
Clubman and the Tramp, The *08* D. W. Griffith
Clue, The *15* James Neill
Clue, The *50* Ray Nazarro
Clue *85* Jonathan Lynn
Clue of the Cigar Band, The *15* H. Oceano Martinek
Clue of the Missing Ape, The *52* James Hill
Clue of the New Pin, The *29* Arthur Maude
Clue of the New Pin, The *60* Allan Davis
Clue of the Oak Leaf, The *26* A. E. Coleby
Clue of the Pigtail, The *23* A. E. Coleby
Clue of the Second Goblet, The *28* George A. Cooper
Clue of the Silver Key *61* Gerard Glaister
Clue of the Twisted Candle *60* Allan Davis
Clumsy Mason, A *1898* Georges Méliès
Clunked on the Corner *29* Harry Edwards
Cluny Brown *46* Ernst Lubitsch
Clutch of Circumstance, The *18* Henri Houry
Clutching a Knife in Desperation *84* Lino Brocka
Clutching Hand, The *16* Fred Evans, Joe Evans
Clutching Hand, The *36* Albert Herman
C'mon, Let's Live a Little *67* David Butler
Co-Optimists, The *29* Laddie Cliff, Edwin Greenwood
Co-Respondent, The *17* Ralph Ince
Co Se Šepta *38* Hugo Haas
Coach *78* Bud Townsend
Coach Holdup in Dick Turpin's Days, A *03* Frank Mottershaw
Coach to Vienna *66* Karel Kachyňa
Coal *13* Émile Cohl
Coal and Cold Feet *18* Raoul Barré, Charles Bowers
Coal Black and de Sebben Dwarfs *42* Robert Clampett
Coal Face *35* Alberto Cavalcanti
Coal King, The *15* Percy Nash

Coal Miner's Daughter *79* Michael Apted
Coal Shortage, The *20* Frank Miller
Coals of Fire *10* Bert Haldane
Coals of Fire *18* Victor Schertzinger
Coast Guard *39* Edward Ludwig
Coast of Folly, The *25* Allan Dwan
Coast of Opportunity, The *20* Ernest C. Warde
Coast of Skeletons *35* Zoltán Korda
Coast of Skeletons *64* Robert Lynn
Coast of Terror *76* Christopher Fraser
Coast Patrol, The *25* Bud Barsky
Coast to Coast *28* Frank Moser
Coast to Coast *80* Joseph Sargent
Coastal Command *43* J. B. Holmes
Coastguard, The *22* Julian Ollendorff
Coastguard's Haul, The *13* H. Oceano Martinek
Coastguard's Sister, The *13* Charles Brabin
Coast's Happy Cavaliers, The *39* Ragnar Arvedson
Coastwatcher *89* Martin Wragge
Coax Me *19* Gilbert P. Hamilton
Cobarde, El *39* René Cardona
Cobbler, The *15* A. E. Coleby
Cobbler Stay at Your Bench *15* Victor Sjöström
Cobbler Stick to Your Last *15* Victor Sjöström
Cobblers of Umbrage, The *72* Ned Sherrin, Ian Wilson
Cobra *25* Joseph E. Henabery
Cobra, El *68* Mario Sequi
Cobra, Il *68* Mario Sequi
Cobra, The *68* Mario Sequi
Cobra *86* George Pan Cosmatos
Cobra Mission *86* Fabrizio De Angelis
Cobra Strikes, The *48* Charles Reisner
Cobra Thunderbolt *87* Tanong Srichua
Cobra Verde *87* Werner Herzog
Cobra Woman *43* Robert Siodmak
Cobre *58* Jorge Sanjinés
Cobweb, The *16* Cecil M. Hepworth
Cobweb, The *55* Vincente Minnelli
Cobweb *86* Zdeněk Zaoral
Cobweb Castle *57* Akira Kurosawa
Cobweb Hotel, The *36* Dave Fleischer
Coca-Cola Kid, The *85* Dušan Makavejev
Cocagne *61* Maurice Cloche
Cocaine *22* Graham Cutts
Cocaine Cowboys *79* Ulli Lommel
Cocaine Fiends, The *36* William A. O'Connor
Cocaine Wars *86* Héctor Olivera
Cochecito, El *59* Marco Ferreri
Cocher de Fiacre Endormi, Le *1898* Alice Guy-Blaché
Cochon, Le *70* Jean-Michel Barjol, Jean Eustache
Cock Crows Again, The *54* Heinosuke Gosho
Cock Crows Twice, The *54* Heinosuke Gosho
Cock-Eyed World, The *29* Raoul Walsh
Cock-Fighting *89* Jingqin Hu
Cock o' the North *35* Oswald Mitchell, Challis Sanderson
Cock o' the Walk *15* Hay Plumb
Cock o' the Walk *30* Walter Lang, Roy William Neill

Cock of the Air *32* Thomas Buckingham
Cockaboody *73* Faith Hubley, John Hubley
Cock-a-Doodle Dog *51* Tex Avery
Cock-a-Doodle-Doo *10* Percy Stow
Cockatoos for Two *47* Bob Wickersham
Cocked Gun *87* Rafael Villaseñor Kuri
Cockeyed Cavaliers *34* Mark Sandrich
Cockeyed Cowboys of Calico County *70* Anton Leader
Cockeyed Miracle, The *46* S. Sylvan Simon
Cockfighter *74* Monte Hellman
Cockleshell Heroes, The *55* Alex Bryce, José Ferrer
Cockney Spirit in the War No. 1, The *30* Castleton Knight
Cockney Spirit in the War No. 2, The *30* Castleton Knight
Cockney Spirit in the War No. 3, The *30* Castleton Knight
Cocksucker Blues *72* Robert Frank
Cocksure's Clever Ruse *10* Frank Wilson
Cocktail *36* L. C. Beaumont
Cocktail *88* Roger Donaldson
Cocktail Hostesses, The *76* A. C. Stephen
Cocktail Hour *33* Victor Schertzinger
Cocktail Molotov *79* Diane Kurys
Cocktails *28* Monty Banks
Cocktails in the Kitchen *54* J. Lee-Thompson
Cocky Bantam, The *43* Paul Sommer
Cocoa Industry *08* Edwin S. Porter
Cocoanut Grove *38* Alfred Santell
Cocoanuts, The *29* Robert Florey, Joseph Santley
Cocoon *85* Ron Howard
Cocoon: The Return *88* Daniel Petrie
Cocorico, Monsieur Poulet *74* Lam Ibrahim Dia, Jean Rouch, Damouré Zika
Cocotier, Le *62* Jean Rouch
Cocotiers, Les *62* Jean Rouch
Cocotte d'Azur, La *59* Agnès Varda
Cocu Magnifique, Le *64* Antonio Pietrangeli
Co'd in His Head, A *14* Toby Cooper
Coda *87* Craig Lahiff
Coda del Diavolo, La *87* Giorgio Treves
Code, The *66* Wojciech Has
Code Name: Emerald *85* Jonathan Sanger
Code Name: Operation Crossbow *64* Michael Anderson
Code Name, Red Roses *69* Fernando Di Leo
Code Name Tiger *64* Claude Chabrol
Code Name: Trixie *72* George Romero
Code Name Zebra *87* Giuseppe Tornatore
Code of Honor, The *16* Frank Borzage
Code of Honor *19* John M. Stahl
Code of Honor *30* John P. McGowan
Code of Marcia Gray, The *16* Frank Lloyd
Code of Scotland Yard, The *46* George King
Code of Silence *60* Ernst R. von Theumer
Code of Silence *85* Andrew Davis
Code of the Air *28* James P. Hogan
Code of the Cactus *39* Sam Newfield
Code of the Cow Country *27* Oscar Apfel
Code of the Fearless *39* Raymond K.

Johnson
Code of the Lawless *45* Wallace Fox
Code of the Mounted *35* Sam Newfield
Code of the Northwest *26* Frank S. Mattison
Code of the Outlaw *42* John English
Code of the Plains *43* Sam Newfield
Code of the Prairie *44* Spencer G. Bennet
Code of the Range *27* Bennett Cohn, Morris R. Schlank
Code of the Range *36* C. C. Coleman, Jr.
Code of the Rangers *38* Sam Newfield
Code of the Saddle *47* Thomas Carr
Code of the Scarlet *28* Harry Joe Brown
Code of the Sea, The *24* Victor Fleming
Code of the Secret Service *39* Noel Mason Smith
Code of the Silver Sage *50* Fred C. Brannon
Code of the Streets *39* Harold Young
Code of the West *25* William K. Howard
Code of the West *29* John P. McGowan
Code of the West *47* William Berke
Code of the Wilderness *24* David Smith
Code of the Yukon *19* Bertram Bracken
Code of Women *59* Kon Ichikawa, Yasuzo Masumura, Kozaburo Yoshimura
Code 7...Victim 5 *64* Robert Lynn
Code 645 *47* Fred C. Brannon, Yakima Canutt
Code Two *53* Fred M. Wilcox
Codename: The Soldier *82* James Glickenhaus
Codename Vengeance *88* David Winters
Codename: Wildgeese *84* Antonio Margheriti
Codfish and Aloes *15* Cecil Birch
Codice Privato *88* Francesco Maselli
Codicil, The *12* Warwick Buckland
Codine *62* Henri Colpi
Cody of the Pony Express *50* Spencer G. Bennet
Cœur Battant, Le *60* Jacques Doniol-Valcroze
Cœur de Coq *47* Maurice Cloche
Cœur de Cristal *57* Henri Gruel
Cœur de Gueux *36* Jean Epstein
Cœur de la France, Le *62* Roger Leenhardt
Cœur de Lilas *31* Anatole Litvak
Cœur de Paris, Le *31* Jean Benoît-Lévy, Marie Epstein
Cœur de Titi *24* Henri Étiévant
Cœur des Gueux, Le *25* Alfred Machin, Henri Wuhlschleger
Cœur et l'Argent, Le *12* Louis Feuillade
Cœur Fidèle *23* Jean Epstein
Cœur Fou, Le *70* Jean-Gabriel Albicocco
Cœur Froid, Le *77* Henri Helman
Cœur Gros Comme Ça, Un *61* François Reichenbach
Cœur Léger *23* Robert Saidreau
Cœur Musicien, Le *87* Frédéric Rossif
Cœur sur la Main, Le *49* André Berthomieu
Cœurs Croisés *87* Stephanie De Mareuil
Cœurs Farouches *23* Julien Duvivier
Cœurs Verts, Les *66* Édouard Luntz
Coevals *59* Vassily Ordynski
Coffee and Cigarettes *86* Jim Jarmusch

Coffee and Cigarettes Part Two *88* Jim Jarmusch
Coffee Fortune Teller, The *61* Alekos Sakelarios
Coffee House, The *70* Rainer Werner Fassbinder
Coffin, The *66* Lars-Magnus Lindgren
Coffin from Hong Kong, A *64* Manfred Kohler
Coffin House, The *66* Jan Švankmajer
Coffin Maker, The *27* Robert Florey
Coffin of Terror *63* Sergio Corbucci, Antonio Margheriti
Coffin of Terror *66* Massimo Pupillo
Coffins on Wheels *41* Joseph M. Newman
Coffre Enchanté, Le *04* Georges Méliès
Coffre-Fort, Le *08* Émile Cohl
Coffret de Jade, Le *21* Léon Poirier
Coffret de Tolède, Le *14* Louis Feuillade
Coffy *73* Jack Hill
Cognasse *32* Louis Mercanton
Cohen and Tate *88* Eric Red
Cohen at Coney Island *12* Mack Sennett
Cohen Collects a Debt *12* Mack Sennett
Cohen Saves the Flag *13* Mack Sennett
Cohen's Advertising Scheme *04* Edwin S. Porter
Cohens and Kellys, The *26* Harry A. Pollard
Cohens and Kellys in Africa, The *30* Vin Moore
Cohens and Kellys in Atlantic City, The *29* William James Craft
Cohens and Kellys in Hollywood, The *32* John Francis Dillon
Cohens and Kellys in Scotland, The *30* William James Craft
Cohens and Kellys in Trouble, The *33* George Stevens
Cohens and the Kellys, The *26* Harry A. Pollard
Cohens and the Kellys in Atlantic City, The *29* William James Craft
Cohens and the Kellys in Paris, The *28* William Beaudine
Cohen's Fire Sale *07* Edwin S. Porter
Cohen's Generosity *10* Edwin S. Porter
Cohen's Luck *15* John H. Collins
Cohen's Outing *13* Mack Sennett
Coiffeur pour Dames *32* René Guissart
Coiffeur pour Dames *52* Jean Boyer
Coin, The *63* Alexander Alov, Vladimir Naumov
Coin des Enfants, Le *36* Marcel L'Herbier
Coin Tranquille à la Campagne, Un *68* Elio Petri
Coincidence *21* Chester Withey
Coiners, The *04* Frank Mottershaw
Coiner's Den, The *12* Frank Wilson
Col Cuore in Gola *67* Tinto Brass
Col Ferro e Col Fuoco *61* Fernando Cerchio
Cold and Its Consequences, A *09* A. E. Coleby
Cold Blood *69* Stuart McGowan
Cold Comfort *57* James Hill
Cold Cuts *79* Bertrand Blier
Cold Days *66* András Kovács
Cold Deck, The *17* William S. Hart
Cold Feast, The *30* Vladimir Petrov

Cold Feet *30* Walter Lantz
Cold Feet *84* Bruce Van Dusen
Cold Feet *89* Robert Dornhelm
Cold Heat *88* Ulli Lommel
Cold in Columbia *85* Dieter Schidor
Cold Journey *75* Martin De Falco
Cold Nerve *25* John P. McGowan
Cold River *78* Fred G. Sullivan
Cold Shivers *29* Stephen Roberts
Cold Steel *12* Edwin J. Collins
Cold Steel *21* Leonard Franchon
Cold Steel *87* Dorothy Ann Puzo
Cold Summer of 1953 *88* Alexander Prochkin
Cold Sweat *70* Terence Young
Cold Tea *21* Raoul Barré, Charles Bowers
Cold Turkey *22* Raoul Barré, Charles Bowers
Cold Turkey *25* Edward F. Cline
Cold Turkey *29* Walter Lantz
Cold Turkey *69* Norman Lear
Cold Wind in August, A *61* Alexander Singer
Colditz Story, The *54* Guy Hamilton
Cole Younger—Gunfighter *58* R. G. Springsteen
Coleccionista de Cadáveres, El *67* Santos Alcocer
Colère des Dieux, La *47* Karel Lamač
Colère Froide *62* André Haguet, Jean-Paul Sassy
Colette *13* Henri Pouctal
Colette *50* Yannick Bellon
Colinot Trousse Chemise *73* Nina Companeez
Collage *61* Alexander Hammid
Collants Noirs, Les *60* Terence Young
Collapsible Metal Tubes *42* Len Lye
Collar and the Bracelet, The *86* Khairy Bishara
Colle Universelle, La *07* Georges Méliès
Collection Particulière, Une *73* Walerian Borowczyk
Collectionneuse, La *66* Eric Rohmer
Collectionneuse: Six Contes Moraux: 3, La *66* Eric Rohmer
Collections Privées *79* Walerian Borowczyk, Just Jaeckin, Shuji Terayama
Collective Ways *53* Miklós Jancsó*
Collector, The *64* William Wyler
Collector, The *66* Eric Rohmer
Colleen *27* Frank O'Connor
Colleen *36* Alfred E. Green
Colleen Bawn, The *11* Sidney Olcott
Colleen Bawn, The *24* Will P. Kellino
Colleen of the Pines *22* Chester Bennett
College *27* James W. Horne
College *31* Walter Lantz
College *34* Erich Engel
College Boob, The *26* Harry Garson
College Chums *07* J. Searle Dawley, Edwin S. Porter
College Chums *11* Lewin Fitzhamon
College Coach *33* William A. Wellman
College Confidential! *60* Albert Zugsmith
College Coquette, The *29* George Archainbaud
College Days *26* Richard Thorpe
College Flirt, The *26* Clarence Badger
College Hero, The *27* Walter Lang

College Holiday *36* Frank Tuttle
College Humor *33* Wesley Ruggles
College Is a Nice Place *36* Yasujiro Ozu
College Love *29* Nat Ross
College Lovers *30* John G. Adolfi
College Orphan, The *15* William Dowlan
College Rhythm *34* Norman Taurog
College Scandal *35* Elliott Nugent
College Sweethearts *42* William Nigh
College Swing *38* Raoul Walsh
College Swing *46* André Berthomieu
College Vamp, The *31* William Beaudine
College Widow, The *15* Barry O'Neil
College Widow, The *27* Archie Mayo
Collegiate *26* Del Andrews
Collegiate *35* Ralph Murphy
Collégiennes, Les *57* André Hunebelle
Collier de la Reine, Le *09* Louis Feuillade
Collier de Perles, Le *15* Louis Feuillade
Collier Vivant, Le *15* Jean Durand
Collina degli Stivali, La *69* Giuseppe Colizzi
Collision *32* George B. Samuelson
Collision and Shipwreck at Sea *1898* Georges Méliès
Collision Course *68* Frank Telford
Collision Course *88* Lewis Teague
Collision et Naufrage en Mer *1898* Georges Méliès
Colloque de Chiens *77* Raúl Ruiz
Colmena, La *82* Mario Camus
Colombes, Les *72* Jean-Claude Lord
Colombo Plan *67* Joy Batchelor
Colonel, The *17* Michael Curtiz
Colonel Blimp *43* Michael Powell, Emeric Pressburger
Colonel Blood *34* W. P. Lipscomb
Colonel Bogey *48* Terence Fisher
Colonel Bontemps, Le *15* Louis Feuillade
Colonel Chabert *47* René Le Haneff
Colonel Effingham's Raid *45* Irving Pichel
Col. Heeza Liar and the Bandits *16* John R. Bray
Col. Heeza Liar and the Ghost *23* Vernon Stallings
Col. Heeza Liar and the Pirates *16* John R. Bray
Col. Heeza Liar and the Torpedo *15* John R. Bray
Col. Heeza Liar and the Zeppelin *15* John R. Bray
Col. Heeza Liar at the Bat *15* John R. Bray
Col. Heeza Liar at the Front *15* John R. Bray
Col. Heeza Liar at the Vaudeville Show *16* John R. Bray
Col. Heeza Liar, Bull Thrower *24* Vernon Stallings
Col. Heeza Liar Captures Villa *16* John R. Bray
Col. Heeza Liar, Cave Man *24* Vernon Stallings
Col. Heeza Liar, Daredevil *24* Vernon Stallings
Col. Heeza Liar, Detective *17* John R. Bray
Col. Heeza Liar, Detective *23* Vernon Stallings
Col. Heeza Liar, Dog Fancier *15* John R.

Bray
Col. Heeza Liar, Explorer *14* John R. Bray
Col. Heeza Liar, Farmer *14* John R. Bray
Col. Heeza Liar Foils the Enemy *15* John R. Bray
Col. Heeza Liar Gets Married *16* John R. Bray
Col. Heeza Liar, Ghost Breaker *15* John R. Bray
Col. Heeza Liar, Ghost Breaker: Second Night *15* John R. Bray
Col. Heeza Liar, Hobo *16* John R. Bray
Col. Heeza Liar in Africa *13* John R. Bray
Col. Heeza Liar in Mexico *14* John R. Bray
Col. Heeza Liar in the African Jungles *23* Vernon Stallings
Col. Heeza Liar in the Haunted Castle *15* John R. Bray
Col. Heeza Liar in the Trenches *15* John R. Bray
Col. Heeza Liar in the Wilderness *14* John R. Bray
Col. Heeza Liar in Uncle Tom's Cabin *23* Vernon Stallings
Col. Heeza Liar Invents a New Kind of Shell *15* John R. Bray
Col. Heeza Liar, Naturalist *14* John R. Bray
Col. Heeza Liar, Nature Faker *15* John R. Bray
Col. Heeza Liar, Nature Faker *24* Vernon Stallings
Col. Heeza Liar on Strike *16* John R. Bray
Col. Heeza Liar on the Jump *17* John R. Bray
Col. Heeza Liar Plays Hamlet *16* John R. Bray
Col. Heeza Liar Runs the Blockade *15* John R. Bray
Col. Heeza Liar Shipwrecked *14* John R. Bray
Col. Heeza Liar Signs the Pledge *15* John R. Bray
Col. Heeza Liar, Sky Pilot *24* Vernon Stallings
Col. Heeza Liar, Spy Dodger *17* John R. Bray
Col. Heeza Liar, Strikebreaker *23* Vernon Stallings
Col. Heeza Liar the Lyin' Tamer *24* Vernon Stallings
Col. Heeza Liar, War Aviator *15* John R. Bray
Col. Heeza Liar, War Dog *15* John R. Bray
Col. Heeza Liar Wins the Pennant *16* John R. Bray
Col. Heeza Liar's African Hunt *14* John R. Bray
Col. Heeza Liar's Ancestors *24* Walter Lantz
Col. Heeza Liar's Bachelor Quarters *16* John R. Bray
Col. Heeza Liar's Big Game Hunt *14* John R. Bray
Col. Heeza Liar's Burglar *23* Vernon Stallings
Col. Heeza Liar's Courtship *16* John R. Bray
Col. Heeza Liar's Forbidden Fruit *23* Walter Lantz

Col. Heeza Liar's Horseplay 24 Vernon Stallings
Col. Heeza Liar's Knighthood 24 Walter Lantz
Col. Heeza Liar's Mysterious Case 24 Vernon Stallings
Col. Heeza Liar's Romance 24 Vernon Stallings
Col. Heeza Liar's Temperance Lecture 17 John R. Bray
Col. Heeza Liar's Treasure Island 22 Vernon Stallings
Col. Heeza Liar's Vacation 23 Walter Lantz
Col. Heeza Liar's Waterloo 16 John R. Bray
Colonel March Investigates 52 Cy Endfield
Colonel Newcome the Perfect Gentleman 20 Fred Goodwins
Colonel Redl 84 István Szabó
Colonel Wolodyjowski 69 Jerzy Hoffman
Colonello Chabert, Il 20 Carmine Gallone
Colonel's Daughter, The 11 Edwin S. Porter
Colonel's Peril, The 12 Thomas Ince
Colonel's Shower Bath, The 02 Georges Méliès
Colonel's Son, The 12 Thomas Ince
Colonel's Ward, The 12 Thomas Ince
Colonia Penal, La 70 Raúl Ruiz
Colonial Virginia — Historical Scenes and Incidents Connected with the Founding of Jamestown, Va. 07 Edwin S. Porter
Colonna Traiana, La 49 Luciano Emmer, Enrico Gras
Colony Under Ground 51 Zoltán Fábri
Color Box, A 35 Len Lye
Color Cry 52 Len Lye
Color Escondido 88 Raúl De la Torre
Color Fields 77 Stan Vanderbeek
Color Me Blood Red 64 Herschell Gordon Lewis
Color of Destiny, The 87 Jorge Duran
Color of Money, The 86 Martin Scorsese
Color of Pomegranates, The 68 Sergei Paradzhanov
Color Purple, The 85 Steven Spielberg
Color Rhythm 42 Oskar Fischinger
Colorado 15 Norval MacGregor
Colorado 21 B. Reeves Eason
Colorado 40 Joseph Kane
Colorado Ambush 51 Lewis D. Collins
Colorado Charlie 65 Robert Johnson
Colorado Kid, The 37 Sam Newfield
Colorado Legend 59 Stan Brakhage
Colorado Legend and the Ballad of the Colorado Ute, The 59 Stan Brakhage
Colorado Pioneers 45 R. G. Springsteen
Colorado Pluck 21 Jules G. Furthman
Colorado Ranger 50 Thomas Carr
Colorado Serenade 46 Robert E. Tansey
Colorado Sundown 51 William Witney
Colorado Sunset 39 George Sherman
Colorado Territory 49 Raoul Walsh
Colorado Trail, The 38 Sam Nelson
Colorado Trail, The 40 Albert Herman
Coloratura 32 Oskar Fischinger
Colorful China 57 Miklós Jancsó
Colors 88 Dennis Hopper
Colors Are Dreaming 58 Dušan Makavejev

Colors of China 57 Miklós Jancsó
Colors of Vásárhely 61 Márta Mészáros
Coloso de Rodas, El 60 Sergio Leone
Colosseum and Juicy Lucy 70 Tony Palmer
Colosso di Rodi, Il 60 Sergio Leone
Colossus and the Amazon Queen 60 Vittorio Sala
Colossus and the Amazons 60 Vittorio Sala
Colossus and the Headhunters 60 Guido Malatesta
Colossus and the Huns 62 Roberto Bianchi Montero
Colossus 1980 69 Joseph Sargent
Colossus of New York, The 58 Eugène Lourié
Colossus of Rhodes, The 60 Sergio Leone
Colossus of the Arena 62 Michele Lupo
Colossus: The Forbin Project 69 Joseph Sargent
Colour Box 35 Len Lye
Colour Cocktail 35 Norman McLaren
Colour Cry 52 Len Lye
Colour Flight 38 Len Lye
Colour Me Dead 69 Eddie Davis
Colours of Iris, The 74 Nikos Panayotopoulos
Colpa e la Pena, La 61 Marco Bellocchio
Colpi di Luce 85 Enzo G. Castellari
Colpire al Cuore 82 Gianni Amelio
Colpo di Fulmine 85 Marco Risi
Colpo di Pistola, Un 41 Renato Castellani
Colpo di Stato 68 Luciano Salce
Colpo Gobbo all'Italiana 62 Lucio Fulci
Colpo Grosso a Galata Bridge 66 Antonio Isamendi
Colpo Grosso a Parigi 65 Pierre Grimblat
Colpo Grosso Ma Non Troppo 65 Gérard Oury
Colpo Segreto di D'Artagnan, Il 62 Siro Marcellini
Colt, The 61 V. Fetin
Colt Cantarono la Morte È Fu: Tempo di Massacro, Le 66 Lucio Fulci, Terry Van Tell
Colt Comrades 43 Lesley Selander
Colt — Flight 802 87 Hanro Mohr
Colt .45 50 Edwin L. Marin
Colt in Pugno al Diavolo, Una 67 Sergio Bergonzelli
Coltelli del Vendicatore, I 65 Mario Bava
"Columbia" and "Shamrock II" 01 Edwin S. Porter
"Columbia" Winning the Cup 1899 Edwin S. Porter
Columbo: Dagger of the Mind 72 Richard Quine
Columbus 23 Edwin L. Hollywood
Columbus Discovers a New Whirl 23 W. E. Stark
Column South 53 Frederick De Cordova
Com Licenca, Eu Vou a Luta 86 Lui Farias
Coma 77 Michael Crichton
Comanche 56 George Sherman
Comanche Blanco 67 José Briz
Comanche Station 60 Budd Boetticher
Comanche Territory 50 George Sherman
Comancheros, The 61 Michael Curtiz
Comandos Comunales 72 Patricio Guzmán
Comata, the Sioux 09 D. W. Griffith

Combat, The 16 Ralph Ince
Combat, The 26 Lynn Reynolds
Combat 27 Albert Hiatt
Combat dans l'Île, Le 62 Alain Cavalier
Combat dans une Rue aux Indes 1897 Georges Méliès
Combat de Boxe 27 Charles Dekeukeleire
Combat de Coqs 1899 Georges Méliès
Combat Naval Devant Manille 1898 Georges Méliès
Combat Naval en Grèce 1897 Georges Méliès
Combat Sans Haine 48 André Michel
Combat Shock 86 Buddy Giovinazzo
Combat Squad 53 Cy Roth
Combined Cadets 44 Ken Annakin
Combined Operations 46 Graham Cutts
Come Across 29 Ray Taylor
Come Across 38 Harold S. Bucquet
Come Again 83 Sam Auster
Come Again Smith 19 E. Mason Hopper
Come and Get It 29 Wallace Fox
Come and Get It 36 Howard Hawks, Richard Rosson, William Wyler
Come and Get It 80 Ernest Pintoff
Come and See 85 Elem Klimov
Come-Back, The 16 Fred J. Balshofer
Come Back 82 Roger Vadim
Come Back Africa 58 Lionel Rogosin
Come Back Baby 68 David Allen Greene
Come Back, Charleston Blue 72 Mark Warren
Come Back, Little Sheba 52 Daniel Mann
Come Back, Little Shicksa 49 Jerry Lewis
Come Back of Percy, The 15 Marshall Neilan
Come Back Peter 52 Charles Saunders
Come Back Peter 69 Donovan Winter
Come Back to Erin 14 Sidney Olcott
Come Back to Hearing 14 Kelly Storrie
Come Back to Me 45 Lewis Seiler
Come Back to the 5 & Dime Jimmy Dean, Jimmy Dean 82 Robert Altman
Come Blow Your Horn 63 Bud Yorkin
Come Clean 31 James W. Horne
Come Closer, Folks 36 D. Ross Lederman
Come, Come, Come Upward 89 Kwontaek Im
Come Dance with Me 50 Mario Zampi
Come Dance with Me! 59 Michel Boisrond
Come Drink with Me 65 King Hu
Come È Dura l'Avventura 88 Flavio Mogherini
Come Easy, Go Slow 28 Manny Gould, Ben Harrison
Come Fill the Cup 51 Gordon Douglas
Come Fly with Me 63 Henry Levin
Come Have Coffee with Us 70 Alberto Lattuada
Come Home with Me 41 Benjamin Christensen
Come Inguaiammo l'Esercito 65 Lucio Fulci
Come Into My Parlour 32 John Longden
Come la Vida Misma 86 Victor Casaus
Come le Foglie 34 Mario Camerini
Come le Foglie 38 Angelo Besozzi
Come Live with Me 40 Clarence Brown
Come My Lad and Be a Soldier 08 Arthur Gilbert

Come Next Spring 56 R. G. Springsteen
Come-On, The 56 Russell Birdwell
Come On Children 72 Allan King
Come On Cowboys! 24 Ward Hayes
Come On, Cowboys! 37 Joseph Kane
Come On Danger! 32 Robert F. Hill
Come On Danger 42 Edward Killy
Come On George 39 Anthony Kimmins
Come On In 18 John Emerson
Come On, Leathernecks! 38 James Cruze
Come On Marines! 34 Henry Hathaway
Come On Out 61 Francis Ford Coppola
Come On Over 22 Alfred E. Green
Come On, Ponciano 37 Gabriel Soria
Come On, Rangers! 38 Joseph Kane
Come On, Tarzan 32 Alvin J. Neitz
Come One, Come All 70 Sebastian
  Gregory
Come Out, Come Out 69 Linda Yellen
Come Out Fighting 45 William Beaudine
Come Out of the Kitchen 19 John S.
  Robertson
Come Out of the Pantry 35 Jack Raymond
Come Play with Me 67 Salvatore Samperi
Come Play with Me 77 George Harrison
  Marks
Come Prima 58 Rudolph Maté
Come, Quando e con Chi 68 Antonio
  Pietrangeli
Come Ride the Wild Pink Horse 66 Joe
  Sarno
Come Rubammo la Bomba Atomica 67
  Lucio Fulci
Come See the Paradise 90 Alan Parker
Come September 61 Robert Mulligan
Come Spy with Me 67 Marshall Stone
Come Svaligiammo la Banca d'Italia 66
  Lucio Fulci
Come Take a Trip in My Airship 25 Dave
  Fleischer
Come Take a Trip in My Airship 30 Dave
  Fleischer
Come Through 17 Jack Conway
Come to My House 27 Alfred E. Green
Come to Papa 28 Charles Lamont
Come to the Stable 49 Henry Koster
Come una Rosa al Naso 76 Franco Rossi
Come Unto Dawn 81 Chang-ho Lee
Come Up Smiling 36 Ray Enright
Come with Me My Love 81 Chris Caras
Come with Us 38 Alexander Hammid
Comeback, The 17 George Marshall
Comeback, The 77 Peter Walker
Comeback 82 Hall Bartlett
Comeback Trail, The 71 Harry Hurwitz
Comedia Fantasticā 75 Ion Popescu-Gopo
Comedian and the Flypaper, The 02
  George Albert Smith
Comedian Paulus Singing "Coquin de
  Printemps" 1897 Georges Méliès
Comedian Paulus Singing "Derrière l'Om-
  nibus" 1897 Georges Méliès
Comedian Paulus Singing "Duelliste Mar-
  seillais" 1897 Georges Méliès
Comedians 41 G. W. Pabst
Comedians 53 Juan Antonio Bardem
Comedians, The 67 Peter Glenville
Comédie 87 Jacques Doillon
Comédie d'Été 89 Daniel Vigne
Comédie du Bonheur, La 39 Marcel
  L'Herbier
Comédie du Travail, La 88 Luc Moullet
Comédien, Le 47 Sacha Guitry
Comedienne 84 Katherine Matheson
Comedy 87 Jacques Doillon
Comedy Cartoons 07 Walter R. Booth
Comedy-Graph, The 10 Émile Cohl
Comedy in Black and White, A 08 Edwin
  S. Porter
Comedy Man, The 63 Alvin Rakoff
Comedy of Errors, A 15 Cecil Birch
Comedy of Happiness, The 39 Marcel
  L'Herbier
Comedy of Terrors, The 63 Jacques
  Tourneur
Comedy Tale of Fanny Hill, A 65 Leslie
  Goodwins
Comenzó a Retumbar el Momotombo 81
  Santiago Álvarez
Comes a Horseman 78 Alan J. Pakula
Comet Over Broadway 38 Busby Berkeley
Cometogether 71 Saul Swimmer
Comets 30 Sascha Geneen
Comfort and Joy 84 Bill Forsyth
Comfort of Strangers, The 90 Paul
  Schrader
Comic, The 69 Carl Reiner
Comic Barber 1897 George Albert Smith
Comic Book Confidential 88 Ron Mann
Comic Duel, A 06 Tom Green
Comic Face 1897 George Albert Smith
Comic Golf 13 G. Fletcher Hewitt
Comic Grimacer, The 01 Cecil M.
  Hepworth
Comic History of Aviation, A 58 Jiří
  Brdečka
Comic Magazine 86 Yojiro Takita
Comic Shaving 1897 George Albert Smith
Comic Strip, The 83 Julien Temple
Comic Strip Hero 67 Alain Jessua
Comical Conjuring 03 Georges Méliès
Cómicos 53 Juan Antonio Bardem
Comin' At Ya! 81 Ferdinando Baldi
Comin' Round the Mountain 36 Mack V.
  Wright
Comin' Round the Mountain 40 George
  Archainbaud
Comin' Round the Mountain 51 Charles
  Lamont
Comin' Thro' the Rye 16 Cecil M. Hep-
  worth
Comin' Thro' the Rye 22 Cecil M. Hep-
  worth
Comin' Thro' the Rye 47 Walter C. My-
  croft
Coming, The 81 Bert I. Gordon
Coming an' Going 26 Richard Thorpe
Coming Apart 69 Milton Moses Ginsberg
Coming Attractions 80 Ira Miller
Coming-Back of Kit Denver, The 12 War-
  wick Buckland
Coming Home 13 Wilfred Noy
Coming Home 77 Hal Ashby
Coming of Age 38 H. Manning Haynes
Coming of Age in Ibiza 64 Allan King
Coming of Amos, The 25 Paul Sloane
Coming of Angelo, The 13 D. W. Griffith
Coming of Columbus, The 12 Colin
  Campbell
Coming of the Dial, The 33 Stuart Legg
Coming of the Law, The 19 Lynn Rey-
  nolds
Coming Out Party 34 John G. Blystone
Coming-Out Party, A 61 Ken Annakin
Coming Power, The 14 Edward Mackey
Coming Through 25 A. Edward Suther-
  land
Coming Through 85 Peter Barber-Fleming
Coming Through the Rye 26 Dave
  Fleischer
Coming to America 88 John Landis
Coming to the Point 13 Percy Stow
Coming Up Roses 86 Stephen Bayly
Comizi d'Amore 64 Pier Paolo Pasolini
Command, The 54 David Butler
Command Decision 48 Sam Wood
Command Performance 31 Walter Lang
Command Performance 37 Sinclair Hill
Commander, The 85 Antonio Margheriti
Commander Lamin 87 Eddie Nicart
Commanding Officer, The 15 Allan Dwan
Commando 62 Frank Wisbar
Commando 85 Mark L. Lester
Commando Cody 53 Franklin Adreon,
  Fred C. Brannon, Harry Keller
Commando Leopard 85 Antonio
  Margheriti
Commando Squad 86 Fred Olen Ray
Commandos 68 Armando Crispino
Commandos Strike at Dawn, The 42 John
  Farrow
Commare Secca, La 62 Bernardo Ber-
  tolucci
Comme Il Est Bon Mon Français 71 Nel-
  son Pereira Dos Santos
Comme la Nuit 85 Luc Monheim
Comme Mars en Carême 67 Henri Lanoë
Comme On Fait Son Lit On Se Couche 04
  Alice Guy-Blaché
Comme sur des Roulettes 77 Nina Com-
  paneez
Comme un Boomerang 76 José Giovanni
Comme un Poisson dans l'Eau 61 André
  Michel
Comme un Pot de Fraises 74 Jean Aurel
Comme une Lettre à la Poste 38 Henri
  Storck
Commedia Fra i Pazzi, Una 37 Gennaro
  Righelli
Comment Ça Va 75 Jean-Luc Godard*
Comment Détruire la Réputation du Plus
  Célèbre Agent Secret du Monde 73
  Philippe de Broca
Comment Epouser un Premier Ministre 64
  Michel Boisrond
Comment Fabien Devient Architecte 00
  Ferdinand Zecca
Comment Faire l'Amour avec un Nègre
  Sans Se Fatiguer 89 Jacques W. Benoît
Comment Max Fait le Tour du Monde 13
  Max Linder
Comment Monsieur Prend Son Bain 03
  Alice Guy-Blaché
Comment Naissent les Méduses 60 Jean
  Painlevé
Comment On Disperse les Foules 04 Alice
  Guy-Blaché
Comment On Dort à Paris! 05 Alice Guy-
  Blaché
Comment Réussir dans la Vie Quand On

Confessions of the Naughty Nymphos 80 Anwar Kawadri

Confessions of the Night 75 Jean-Pierre Lefèbvre

Confessions of Tom Harris 66 John Derek, David Nelson

Confessions of Winifred Wagner, The 75 Hans-Jürgen Syberberg

Confessor 73 Edward Bergman, Alan Soffin

Confetti 27 Graham Cutts

Confetti al Pepe 63 Jacques Baratier

Confidence 09 D. W. Griffith

Confidence 13 Émile Cohl

Confidence 22 Harry A. Pollard

Confidence 33 Walter Lantz

Confidence 79 István Szabó

Confidence Girl 51 Andrew L. Stone

Confidence Man, The 24 Victor Heerman

Confidence Trick, The 04 Lewin Fitzhamon

Confidence Trick, The 26 F. W. Engholm

Confidences pour Confidences 78 Pascal Thomas

Confidencias 84 Jaime Humberto Hermosillo

Confident de Ces Dames, Le 59 Jean Boyer

Confidential 35 Edward L. Cahn

Confidential 86 Bruce Pittman

Confidential Agent 45 Herman Shumlin

Confidential Lady 39 Arthur Woods

Confidential Report 55 Orson Welles

Confidentially Connie 52 Edward Buzzell

Confidentially Yours 82 François Truffaut

Confirm or Deny 41 Fritz Lang, Archie Mayo

Conflagration 58 Kon Ichikawa

Conflict 16 Ralph Ince

Conflict, The 21 Stuart Paton

Conflict 30 Edward F. Cline

Conflict 36 David Howard

Conflict 38 Léonide Moguy

Conflict 45 Kurt Bernhardt

Conflict 55 Yuli Raizman

Conflict 65 Daniel Mann

Conflict in the Congo 60 Leonid Varmalov

Conflict of Wings 53 John Eldridge, Don Sharp

Conflicts of Life 13 Victor Sjöström, Mauritz Stiller

Conflit 38 Léonide Moguy

Conformist, The 69 Bernardo Bertolucci

Conformista, Il 69 Bernardo Bertolucci

Confort et l'Indifférence, Le 82 Denys Arcand

Confrontation, The 68 Miklós Jancsó

Confrontation 70 Arthur Hiller

Confrontation 87 Valery Kremnev

Confusión Cotidiana, Una 50 Nestor Almendros, Tomás Gutiérrez Alea

Confusions of a Nutsy Spy 42 Norm McCabe

Conga Swing 41 Frank R. Strayer

Congestion 18 Alexander Panteleyev

Congiuntura, La 64 Ettore Scola

Congiura de Spie 66 Édouard Molinaro

Congo Bill 48 Spencer G. Bennet, Thomas Carr

Congo Crossing 56 Joseph Pevney

Congo Express 40 Eduard von Borsody

Congo Express 86 Armand De Hesselle, Luk Gubbles

Congo Maisie 39 H. C. Potter

Congo Pongo 45 Sam Newfield

Congolaise 50 Jacques Dupont

Congorilla 32 Martin E. Johnson

Congratulatory Speech 86 Tomio Kuriyama

Congregation, The 51 William Beaudine

Congres der Vakverenigingen 29 Joris Ivens

Congrès des Nations en Chine 01 Georges Méliès

Congress Dances 31 Erik Charell

Conjugal Bed, The 63 Marco Ferreri

Conjure Woman, The 26 Oscar Micheaux

Conjurer, The 00 George Albert Smith

Conjurer's House, The 21 Joseph E. Henabery

Conjurer's Return 86 Antonín Kachlík

Conjuring 1896 Georges Méliès

Conjuring Clown, The 05 J. H. Martin

Conjuror and the Boer, The 1899 Cecil M. Hepworth

Conjuror As a Good Samaritan, The 12 Walter R. Booth

Conjuror Making Ten Hats in Sixty Seconds 1896 Georges Méliès

Conjuror with a Hundred Tricks, The 00 Georges Méliès

Conjurors, The 22 Bernard Dudley

Conjuror's Pupil, The 06 Walter R. Booth

Connecticut Yankee, A 31 David Butler

Connecticut Yankee, A 48 Tay Garnett

Connecticut Yankee at King Arthur's Court, A 21 Emmett J. Flynn

Connecticut Yankee in King Arthur's Court, A 48 Tay Garnett

Connecting Rooms 69 Franklin Gollings

Connection, The 60 Shirley Clarke

Conquérant de l'Inutile, Le 67 Marcel Ichac

Conquérants Solitaires, Les 52 Claude Vermorel

Conquered City, The 62 Joseph Anthony

Conquered Hearts 18 Francis J. Grandon

Conquered Seas 59 Roman Karmen

Conquering Cask, The 10 Lewin Fitzhamon

Conquering Horde, The 31 Edward Sloman

Conquering Power, The 21 Rex Ingram

Conquering the Woman 21 King Vidor

Conqueror, The 16 Reginald Barker

Conqueror, The 17 Raoul Walsh

Conqueror, The 55 Dick Powell

Conqueror of Atlantis 63 Alfonso Brescia

Conqueror of Corinth 62 Mario Costa

Conqueror of Maracaibo 61 Eugenio Martin

Conqueror of the Orient 61 Tanio Boccia

Conqueror Worm, The 68 Michael Reeves

Conquerors, The 32 William A. Wellman

Conquerors of the Night 33 Adolph Minkin, Igor Sorokhtin

Conquerors of Time 86 Kamel El Sheik

Conquest 28 Roy Del Ruth

Conquest 30 John Grierson, Basil Wright

Conquest 37 Clarence Brown

Conquest 65 Kaneto Shindo

Conquest 83 Lucio Fulci

Conquest in the Dry Zone 54 Lester James Peries

Conquest of a Germ 45 John Eldridge

Conquest of Canaan, The 21 Roy William Neill

Conquest of Cheyenne 46 R. G. Springsteen

Conquest of Cochise 53 William Castle

Conquest of Constantinople 54 A. Arakon

Conquest of Everest, The 53 Thomas Stobart

Conquest of Mycene 63 Giorgio Ferroni

Conquest of Oil 19 Victor Saville

Conquest of Paradise, The 81 Eliseo Subiela

Conquest of Siberia 08 Vasili M. Goncharov

Conquest of Space 54 Byron Haskin

Conquest of the Air 36 Alexander Esway, Lee Garmes, Zoltán Korda, William Cameron Menzies, John Monk Saunders, Alexander Shaw, Donald Taylor

Conquest of the Caucasus 13 L. Chorny, S. Esadze

Conquest of the Dry Zone 54 Lester James Peries

Conquest of the Earth 80 Barry Crane, Sidney Hayers, Sigmund Neufeld, Jr.

Conquest of the Planet of the Apes 72 J. Lee-Thompson

Conquest of the Pole, The 10 Georges Méliès

Conquest of the Skies 38 Hans Richter

Conquests of Peter the Great, The 39 Vladimir Petrov

Conquête d'Angleterre, La 35 Émile Cohl

Conquête de l'Air, La 01 Ferdinand Zecca

Conquête de l'Angleterre, La 55 Roger Leenhardt

Conquête des Gaules, La 22 Léonce-Henri Burel*

Conquista 72 Michael Syson

Conquista dei Diamanti 16 Augusto Genina

Conquista del Paraíso, La 81 Eliseo Subiela

Conquistador de la Luna, El 60 Rogelio A. González

Conquistatore di Corinto, Il 62 Mario Costa

Conquistatori, I 20 Luigi Maggi

Conrack 73 Martin Ritt

Conrad in Quest of His Youth 20 William DeMille

Conrad the Sailor 41 Chuck Jones

Conscience 10 Van Dyke Brooke

Conscience 11 D. W. Griffith

Conscience 12 Maurice Costello

Conscience 15 Stuart Paton

Conscience 17 Bertram Bracken

Conscience Bay 60 Norman Thaddeus Vane

Conscience de Prêtre 06 Alice Guy-Blaché

Conscience of Hassan Bey, The 13 Christy Cabanne

Conscription 15 Dave Aylott

Conseil d'Ami, Un 16 Jacques Feyder

Conseil de Famille 86 Costa-Gavras

Convicts No. 10 and No. 13 *11* August Blom
Convict's Sacrifice, A *09* D. W. Griffith
Convict's Sister, The *11* Bert Haldane
Convoy *27* Joseph C. Boyle, Lothar Mendes
Convoy *33* Leonid Lukov
Convoy *40* Pen Tennyson
Convoy *78* Sam Peckinpah
Convoy Buddies *77* Arthur Pitt
Conway the Kerry Dancer *12* Sidney Olcott
Coo-Coo Bird Dog *49* Sid Marcus
Coocoonut Grove, The *36* Friz Freleng
Coogan's Bluff *68* Don Siegel
Cook, The *14* Charles Chaplin
Cook, The *17* Gregory La Cava, Vernon Stallings
Cook, The *18* Roscoe Arbuckle
Cook in Trouble, The *04* Georges Méliès
Cook of Canyon Camp, The *17* Donald Crisp
Cook, the Thief, His Wife and Her Lover, The *89* Peter Greenaway
Cookie *88* Susan Seidelman
Cooking Up Trouble *44* D. Ross Lederman
Cooks *42* Ken Annakin
Cook's Bid for Fame *12* Frank Wilson
Cook's Dream, The *07* J. H. Martin
Cook's Lovers *04* Alf Collins
Cook's Revenge, The *00* Georges Méliès
Cooks vs. Chefs: The Phable of Olaf and Louie *16* Gregory La Cava
Cool and the Crazy, The *58* William Witney
Cool Breeze *72* Barry Pollack
Cool, Calm and Collected *75* Bertrand Blier
Cool Cat *67* Alex Lovy
Cool Change *85* George (Trumbull) Miller
Cool Hand Luke *67* Stuart Rosenberg
Cool It, Carol! *70* Peter Walker
Cool Mikado, The *63* Michael Winner
Cool Ones, The *67* Gene Nelson
Cool Sound from Hell, A *58* Sidney J. Furie
Cool World, The *63* Shirley Clarke
Coolangatta Gold, The *84* Igor Auzins
Cooler, The *82* Lol Colne, Kevin Godley
Cooley High *75* Michael Schultz
Coonskin *74* Ralph Bakshi
Cooperativas Agrícolas: El Agua *60* Manuel Octavio Gómez
Coordinates of Death *87* Samvel Gasparov, Nguyen Shang Tyan
Cop, The *28* Donald Crisp
Cop, The *60* Luigi Zampa
Cop, The *70* Yves Boisset
Cop, A *72* Jean-Pierre Melville
Cop, Le *84* Claude Zidi
Cop *87* James B. Harris
Cop au Vin *84* Claude Chabrol
Cop Fools the Sergeant, The *04* Edwin S. Porter
Cop Hater *58* William Berke
Cop Killers *83* Roberto Faenza
Cop-Out *67* Pierre Rouve
Copacabana *47* Alfred E. Green
Copacabana Palace *62* Steno

Copains, Les *64* Yves Robert
Copak Je To Za Vojáka? *88* Petr Tuček
Copenhagen *60* Jørgen Roos
Copie Conforme *47* Jean Dréville
Copla de la Dolores, La *49* Benito Perojo
Coplan, Agent Secret *64* Maurice Cloche
Coplan FX 18 Casse Tout *65* Riccardo Freda
Coplan III *67* Riccardo Freda
Coplan Sauve Sa Peau *68* Yves Boisset
Coppelia *00* Georges Méliès
Coppelia ou La Poupée Animée *00* Georges Méliès
Coppelia the Animated Doll *00* Georges Méliès
Copper, The *30* Richard Eichberg
Copper *58* Jorge Sanjinés
Copper Beeches, The *12* Georges Treville
Copper Beeches, The *21* Maurice Elvey
Copper Canyon *50* John Farrow
Copper Coin King, The *26* Kenji Mizoguchi
Copper Cylinder, The *26* A. E. Coleby
Copper King, The *26* Kenji Mizoguchi
Copper Sky *57* Charles Marquis Warren
Copperhead, The *20* Charles Maigne
Coppers and Cutups *15* Dave Aylott
Copper's Revenge, The *12* Lewin Fitzhamon
Coppia Tranquilla, Una *68* Francesco Maselli
Coppie, Le *70* Vittorio De Sica, Mario Monicelli, Alberto Sordi
Copping the Coppers *09* Dave Aylott
Cops *22* Edward F. Cline, Buster Keaton
Cops and Robbers *51* Mario Monicelli, Steno
Cops and Robbers *73* Aram Avakian
Cop's Honour *85* José Pinheiro
Cops Is Always Right *38* Dave Fleischer
Cops Suey *26* William C. Nolan
Copter Kids, The *76* Ronald Spencer
Copy Cat *41* Dave Fleischer
Coquette *29* Sam Taylor
Coquille et le Clergyman, La *27* Germaine Dulac
Cor, Le *31* Jean Epstein
Cor do Seu Destino, A *87* Jorge Duran
Cora *15* Edwin Carewe
Coração, O *58* Manoel De Oliveira
Coraggio di Parlare, Il *87* Leandro Castellani
Coraje del Pueblo, El *71* Jorge Sanjinés
Coral *15* Henry MacRae
Coralie et Cie *33* Alberto Cavalcanti
Corazón Bandolero *35* Raphael J. Sevilla
Corazón de Niño *40* Alejandro Galindo
Corazón del Bosque, El *78* Manuel Gutiérrez Aragón
Corazón Sobre la Tierra, El *86* Constante Diego
Corazones en Derrota *34* Rubén Navarro
Corbari *70* Valentino Orsini
Corbeau, Le *43* Henri-Georges Clouzot
Corbeille Enchantée, La *03* Georges Méliès
Corbusier, l'Architecte du Bonheur, Le *56* Pierre Kast
Cord of Life, The *09* D. W. Griffith
Corde au Cou, La *26* Robert Saidreau
Corde Raide, La *60* Jean-Charles

Dudrumet
Corde, un Colt, Une *68* Robert Hossein
Cordelia *80* Jean Beaudin
Cordelia the Magnificent *23* George Archainbaud
Cordillera *65* Monte Hellman
Cordobés, El *66* François Reichenbach
Corentin ou Les Infortunes Conjugales *88* Jean Marbœuf
Corethre *35* Jean Painlevé
Corinna Darling *58* Eduard von Borsody
Corinthian Jack *21* Walter C. Rowden
Coriolan *50* Jean Cocteau
Corky *51* Edward Bernds
Corky *71* Leonard Horn
Corky of Gasoline Alley *51* Edward Bernds
Cormorant *86* Anton Tomašić
Corn *43* Bjarne Henning-Jensen
Corn Is Green, The *45* Irving Rapper
Corn on the Cop *65* Irv Spector
Corn Plastered *51* Robert McKimson
Cornbread, Earl and Me *75* Joseph Manduke
Corne Perdere una Moglie È Trovare un'Amante *78* Pasquale Festa Campanile
Corner, The *16* Walter Edwards
Corner Grocer, The *17* George Cowl
Corner House Burglary, The *14* H. Oceano Martinek
Corner in Colleens, A *16* Charles Miller, Roy William Neill
Corner in Cotton, A *16* Fred J. Balshofer, Howard Truesdell
Corner in Wheat, A *09* D. W. Griffith
Corner Man, The *21* Einar J. Bruun
Corner of Great Tokyo, A *30* Heinosuke Gosho
Cornered *24* William Beaudine
Cornered *32* B. Reeves Eason
Cornered *45* Edward Dmytryk
Cornet, Der *55* Walter Reisch
Corni, Ti Scaveranno la Fossa, I *71* Ignacio F. Iquino
Corniaud, Le *65* Gérard Oury
Cornish Idyll, A *36* Francis Searle
Cornish Romance, A *12* Sidney Northcote
Cornue Infernale, La *06* Georges Méliès
Cornwall *49* David Hand
Corny Concerto, A *43* Robert Clampett
Corona di Ferro, La *40* Alessandro Blasetti
Corona Negra, La *50* Luis Saslavsky
Coronado *35* Norman Z. McLeod
Coronation of a Village Maiden *1896* Georges Méliès
Coronation of Edward VII, The *02* Georges Méliès, George Albert Smith, Charles Urban
Coronation of King Edward VII, The *01* Cecil M. Hepworth
Coronation of Their Majesties King Edward VII and Queen Alexandra, The *02* Georges Méliès, George Albert Smith, Charles Urban
Coronation Parade, The *53* Henry Hathaway
Coroner Creek *48* Ray Enright
Corot *65* Roger Leenhardt
Corpi Presentano Tracce di Violenza Carnale, I *73* Sergio Martino

Corporal Dolan, A.W.O.L. *46* Allan Dwan

Corporal Kate *26* Paul Sloane

Corporal's Kiddies, The *14* Warwick Buckland

Corporate Affairs *90* Terence H. Winkless

Corps Célestes, Les *73* Gilles Carle

Corps de Mon Ennemi, Le *76* Henri Verneuil

Corps et Biens *86* Benoît Jacquot

Corps et le Fouet, Le *63* Mario Bava

Corps Profond *63* Igor Barrière, Étienne Lalou

Corps Z'à Corps *88* André Halimi

Corpse, The *69* Viktors Ritelis

Corpse Came C.O.D., The *47* Henry Levin

Corpse Collectors, The *67* Santos Alcocer

Corpse Grinders, The *71* Ted V. Mikels

Corpse in the Morgue *38* Otis Garrett

Corpse Mania *81* Zhihong Gui

Corpse of Beverly Hills, The *65* Michael Pfleghar

Corpse Vanished, The *43* Steve Sekely

Corpse Vanishes, The *42* Wallace Fox

Corpus Christi Bandits *45* Wallace A. Grissell

Corral *54* Colin Low

Correction Please, or How We Got Into Pictures *80* Noel Burch

Corregidor *43* William Nigh

Corri, Uomo, Corri *68* Sergio Sollima

Corrida di Sposa, Il *62* Gian Vittorio Baldi

Corrida of Love *76* Nagisa Oshima

Corridor, The *68* Jan Halldoff

Corridor of Mirrors *48* Terence Young

Corridors of Blood *58* Robert Day

Corringa *73* Antonio Margheriti

Corrumpus, Les *66* Bill Catching, James Hill

Corrupción *87* Ismael Rodríguez, Jr.

Corrupción de Chris Miller, La *72* Juan Antonio Bardem

Corrupt, The *63* Jacques Deray

Corrupt *83* Roberto Faenza

Corrupt Ones, The *66* Bill Catching, James Hill

Corrupted Woman, A *67* Kozaburo Yoshimura

Corruption *17* John Gorman

Corruption *33* Charles E. Roberts

Corruption *50* Tso-lin Wang

Corruption *67* Robert Hartford-Davis

Corruption *87* Ismael Rodríguez, Jr.

Corruption of Chris Miller, The *72* Juan Antonio Bardem

Corruption of the Damned *65* George Kuchar

Corruzione, La *63* Mauro Bolognini

Corsair, The *14* Edward José

Corsair *31* Roland West

Corsaire, Le *39* Marc Allégret

Corsaires du Bois de Boulogne, Les *54* Norbert Carbonneaux

Corsaro, Il *23* Carmine Gallone, Augusto Genina

Corsaro Nero, Il *39* Amleto Palermi

Corsican Brothers, The *1897* George Albert Smith

Corsican Brothers, The *02* Dicky Winslow

Corsican Brothers, The *16* André Antoine

Corsican Brothers, The *19* Colin Campbell

Corsican Brothers, The *20* Louis Gasnier

Corsican Brothers, The *41* Gregory Ratoff

Corsican Brothers, The *61* Anton Giulio Majano

Corsican Brothers, The *84* Thomas Chong

Corso Rouge, Le *13* Maurice Tourneur

Corta Notte delle Bambole di Vetro, La *72* Aldo Lado

Corte de Faraón, La *85* José Luis García Sánchez

Cortège de la Mi-Carême *1897* Georges Méliès

Cortège de Tzar Allant à Versailles *1896* Georges Méliès

Cortège de Tzar au Bois de Boulogne *1896* Georges Méliès

Cortège du Bœuf Gras Boulevard des Italiens *1897* Georges Méliès

Cortège du Bœuf Gras Passant Place de la Concorde *1897* Georges Méliès

Cortigiana di Babilonia, La *55* Carlo Ludovico Bragaglia

Cortile *30* Carlo Campogalliani

Cortile Cascino *62* Michael Roemer, Robert M. Young

Cortile Cascino, Italy *62* Michael Roemer, Robert M. Young

Cortili *47* Dino Risi

Corvée de Quartier Accidenté *1898* Georges Méliès

Corvette K-225 *43* Howard Hawks, Richard Rosson

Corvette Port Arthur *42* Joris Ivens

Corvette Summer *78* Matthew Robbins

Corvini Inheritance *84* Gabrielle Beaumont

Cosacchi, I *59* Giorgio Rivalta, Victor Tourjansky

Cose da Pazzi *53* G. W. Pabst

Cose di Cosa Nostra *71* Steno

Cosh Boy *52* Lewis Gilbert

Così Come Sei *78* Alberto Lattuada

Così Sia *72* Alfio Caltabiano

Cosmic Eye, The *85* Faith Hubley

Cosmic Man, The *59* Herbert Greene

Cosmic Man Appears in Tokyo, The *56* Koji Shima

Cosmic Monster, The *57* Gilbert Gunn

Cosmic Monsters *57* Gilbert Gunn

Cosmic Ray *61* Bruce Conner

Cosmic Voyage, The *35* Vasili Zhuravlev

Cosmo Jones—Crime Smasher *43* James Tinling

Cosmo Jones in The Crime Smasher *43* James Tinling

Cosmo 2000: Planet Without a Name *77* Alfonso Brescia

Cosmonauts on Venus *62* Pavel Klushantsev

Cosmonauts Street *63* Grigori Roshal

Cosmos: War of the Planets *77* Alfonso Brescia

Cosmos: War of the Planets *77* Jun Fukuda

Cossack Beyond the Danube, A *54* Vasil Lapoknysh

Cossack Whip, The *16* John H. Collins

Cossacks, The *28* Clarence Brown, George W. Hill

Cossacks, The *59* Giorgio Rivalta, Victor Tourjansky

Cossacks Across the Danube, The *39* Edgar G. Ulmer

Cossacks in Exile *39* Edgar G. Ulmer

Cossacks of the Don *31* Olga Preobrazhenskaya

Cossacks of the Kuban *49* Ivan Pyriev

Cost, The *20* Harley Knoles

Cost of a Kiss, The *17* Adrian Brunel

Cost of Beauty, The *24* Walter Summers

Cost of Dying, The *68* Sergio Merolle

Cost of Hatred, The *17* George Melford

Costa Azzura *59* Vittorio Sala

Costa Brava '59 *59* Jorge Grau

Costanza della Regione, La *64* Pasquale Festa Campanile

Costaud des Épinettes, Le *23* Raymond Bernard

Costaud des P.T.T., Le *31* Rudolph Maté

Costello Case, The *30* Walter Lang

Costello Murder Case, The *30* Walter Lang

Coster and His Donkey, The *02* Percy Stow

Coster Bill *12* A. E. Coleby

Coster Bill of Paris *22* Jacques Feyder

Coster Burglar and His Dog, The *05* Tom Green

Coster Joe *13* Percy Stow

Coster Joe *15* Alfonse Frenguelli

Coster's Christening, The *05* Alf Collins

Coster's Honeymoon, The *12* Will P. Kellino

Coster's Phantom Fortune, The *10* Alf Collins

Coster's Revenge, The *06* Percy Stow

Coster's Wedding, The *04* Alf Collins

Coster's Wedding, The *04* Lewin Fitzhamon

Coster's Wedding, The *10* Theo Bouwmeester

Coster's Wedding, The *13* Percy Stow

Costly Gift, A *10* A. E. Coleby

Costumes Animés, Les *04* Georges Méliès

Costumi e Bellezze d'Italia *48* Dino Risi

Côte d'Azur, La *48* Roger Leenhardt

Coton, Le *35* Henri Storck

Cottage Near the Woods, A *76* Jiří Menzel

Cottage on Dartmoor, A *29* Anthony Asquith

Cottage to Let *41* Anthony Asquith

Cotter *72* Paul Stanley

Cotton *59* Edgar Reitz

Cotton and Cattle *21* Leonard Franchon

Cotton Club, The *84* Francis Ford Coppola

Cotton Comes to Harlem *70* Ossie Davis

Cotton King, The *15* Oscar Eagle

Cotton Queen *37* Bernard Vorhaus

Cottonpickin' Chickenpickers *67* Larry Jackson

Couch, The *62* Owen Crump

Couch *64* Andy Warhol

Couch Trip, The *87* Michael Ritchie

Coucher de la Mariée, Le *01* Ferdinand Zecca

Coucher de la Mariée ou Triste Nuit de Noce, Le *1899* Georges Méliès

Coucher d'une Parisienne *00* Alice Guy-Blaché

Coucher d'Yvette *1897* Alice Guy-Blaché

Coughing Horror, The *24* Fred Paul

Could I But Live *65* Zenzo Matsuyama

Couldn't Possibly Happen *35* Otto Brower, B. Reeves Eason

Couleur de Feu *57* Henri Storck

Couleur du Vent, La *88* Pierre Granier-Deferre

Couleur Encerclée, La *87* Jean Gagne, Serge Gagne

Coulomb Force Constant *59* Richard Leacock

Coulomb's Law *59* Richard Leacock

Council of the Gods *50* Kurt Mätzig

Counsel for Crime *37* John Brahm

Counsel for Romance *38* Raoul Ploquin

Counsel for the Defense *12* Van Dyke Brooke

Counsel for the Defense *25* Burton L. King

Counsel on de Fence *34* Arthur Ripley

Counsellor at Law *33* William Wyler

Counsel's Opinion *33* Allan Dwan

Count, The *16* Charles Chaplin

Count Down Clown *61* Joseph Barbera, William Hanna

Count Downe *74* Freddie Francis

Count Dracula *70* Jesús Franco

Count Dracula and His Vampire Bride *73* Alan Gibson

Count Dracula's Great Love *72* Javier Aguirre

Count 'Em *15* Ralph Ince

Count Five and Die *58* Victor Vicas

Count Me Out *38* Cal Dalton, Ben Hardaway

Count of Bragelonne, The *54* Fernando Cerchio

Count of Brechard, The *38* Mario Bonnard

Count of Luxembourg, The *26* Arthur Gregor

Count of Monte Cristo, The *12* Colin Campbell

Count of Monte Cristo, The *13* Joseph A. Golden, Edwin S. Porter

Count of Monte Cristo, The *34* Rowland V. Lee

Count of Monte Cristo, The *54* Robert Vernay

Count of Monte Cristo, The *61* Claude Autant-Lara

Count of Monte Cristo, The *74* David Greene

Count of No Account, The *21* George Dunstall

Count of St. Elmo, The *53* Guido Brignone

Count of Ten, The *28* James Flood

Count of the Monk's Bridge, The *34* Edvin Adolphson, Sigurd Wallen

Count of the Old Town, The *34* Edvin Adolphson, Sigurd Wallen

Count of Twelve *55* Paul Gerrard

Count on Me *48* Leslie Barber

Count Tacchia *82* Sergio Corbucci

Count Takes the Count, The *36* Charlie Chase, Harold Law

Count the Hours *53* Don Siegel

Count Three and Pray *55* George Sherman

Count to Ten *86* Oscar Barney Finn

Count Ugolin *49* Riccardo Freda

Count Vim's Last Exercise *67* Peter Weir

Count Yorga, Vampire *70* Robert Kelljan

Count Your Blessings *59* Jean Negulesco

Count Your Blessings *87* Pieter Verhoeff

Count Your Bullets *72* William A. Graham

Countdown *67* Robert Altman

Countdown *85* Pál Erdöss

Countdown at Kusini *76* Ossie Davis

Countdown to Danger *67* Peter Seabourne

Counted Out *27* Ralph Graves

Counter-Attack *45* Zoltán Korda

Counter-Attack *87* N. Chandra

Counter-Espionage *42* Edward Dmytryk

Counter Investigation *49* Jean Faurez

Counter-Strike *87* Vladimir Shevchenko

Counter Tenors, The *63* Pasquale Festa Campanile, Massimo Franciosa

Counterattack of the Monster *59* Hugo Grimaldi, Motoyoshi Odo

Counterblast *48* Paul Stein

Counterfeit *19* George Fitzmaurice

Counterfeit *36* Erle C. Kenton

Counterfeit Cat *49* Tex Avery

Counterfeit Coin, The *54* George Tzavellas

Counterfeit Commandos *78* Enzo G. Castellari

Counterfeit Constable, The *64* Robert Dhéry

Counterfeit Cowboy, The *15* Cecil Birch

Counterfeit Killer, The *68* Josef Leytes, Stuart Rosenberg

Counterfeit Lady *37* D. Ross Lederman

Counterfeit Love *23* Ralph Ince, Roy Sheldon

Counterfeit Plan, The *56* Montgomery Tully

Counterfeit Traitor, The *62* George Seaton

Counterfeiters, The *15* Charles Raymond

Counterfeiters, The *48* Daniel Mann, Sam Newfield

Counterfeiters, The *53* Franco Rossi

Counterfeiters, The *61* Gilles Grangier

Counterfeiters of Paris, The *61* Gilles Grangier

Counterplan *32* Friedrich Ermler, Sergei Yutkevich

Counterplot *59* Kurt Neumann

Counterpoint *67* Ralph Nelson

Counterspy *53* Vernon Sewell

Counterspy Meets Scotland Yard *50* Seymour Friedman

Countess Charming, The *17* Donald Crisp

Countess Donelli *24* G. W. Pabst

Countess Dracula *70* Peter Sasdy

Countess Dracula *72* Jorge Grau

Countess Dracula *73* Luigi Batzella

Countess from Hong Kong, A *66* Charles Chaplin

Countess' Honor, The *18* August Blom

Countess of Monte Cristo, The *33* Karl Freund

Countess of Monte Cristo, The *48* Frederick De Cordova

Countess of Parma, The *37* Alessandro Blasetti

Countess of Summacount, The *17* Frank Wilson

Country *84* Richard Pearce

Country Beyond, The *26* Irving Cummings

Country Beyond, The *36* Eugene Forde

Country Blue *75* Jack Conrad

Country Boy, The *15* Frederick Thompson

Country Boy, The *35* Friz Freleng

Country Boy *66* Joseph Kane

Country Bride *38* Ivan Pyriev

Country Bumpkin, The *36* Edwin L. Marin

Country Comes to Town, The *31* John Grierson, Basil Wright

Country Cousin, The *19* Alan Crosland

Country Cupid, A *11* D. W. Griffith

Country Dance *69* J. Lee-Thompson

Country Doctor, The *09* D. W. Griffith

Country Doctor, The *27* Rupert Julian

Country Doctor, The *36* Henry King

Country Doctor, The *51* Sergei Gerasimov

Country Doctor, The *60* Hiroshi Inagaki

Country Doctor, The *61* Karel Kachyňa

Country Doctor, The *63* Jorge Brum Do Canto

Country Excursion *36* Jean Renoir

Country Fair, The *34* Walter Lantz

Country Fair *41* Frank McDonald

Country Flapper, The *22* F. Richard Jones

Country Gentlemen *36* Ralph Staub

Country Girl, A *08* Lewin Fitzhamon

Country Girl, The *54* George Seaton

Country Girls, The *45* Youssef Wahby

Country Girls, The *83* Desmond Davis

Country Girl's Seminary Life and Experiences, A *08* Edwin S. Porter

Country God Forgot, The *16* Marshall Neilan

Country Hero, A *17* Roscoe Arbuckle

Country Holiday, A *12* Stuart Kinder

Country Husband, The *55* James Neilson

Country Kid, The *23* William Beaudine

Country Lass, A *12* Edwin J. Collins

Country Life *17* J. Stuart Blackton

Country Lovers, The *11* Mack Sennett

Country Mouse, The *14* Phillips Smalley

Country Mouse, The *35* Friz Freleng

Country Music *72* Robert Hinkle

Country Music Daughter *76* Gus Trikonis

Country Music Holiday *58* Alvin Ganzer

Country Music, U.S.A. *66* Arthur C. Pierce

Country of Countries, The *62* Evald Schorm

Country of the Mariachi, The *38* Raúl De Anda

Country of the Soviets, The *37* Esther Shub

Country School, The *31* Walter Lantz

Country Store *37* Walter Lantz

Country That God Forgot, The *16* Marshall Neilan

Country to Country *62* Evald Schorm

Country Town *71* Peter Maxwell

Cove of Missing Men 18 Frederick Sullivan

Čovek Nije Tica 65 Dušan Makavejev

Čovek sa Fotografije 63 Vladimir Pogačić

Covenant with Death, A 66 Lamont Johnson

Cover Girl 43 Charles Vidor

Cover Girl Killer 59 Terry Bishop

Cover Girl Models 75 Cirio Santiago

Cover Me Babe 70 Noel Black

Cover-Up 49 Alfred E. Green

Cover Up 84 Peter Crane

Covered Flagon, The 25 Wesley Ruggles

Covered Tracks 38 Veidt Harlan

Covered Trail, The 24 Jack Nelson

Covered Trailer, The 39 Gus Meins

Covered Wagon, The 23 James Cruze

Covered Wagon Days 40 George Sherman

Covered Wagon Raid 50 R. G. Springsteen

Covered Wagon Trails 30 John P. McGowan

Covered Wagon Trails 40 Raymond K. Johnson

Covergirl 84 Jean-Claude Lord

Covert Action 78 Romolo Guerrieri

Covert Action 87 Les Rose

Coverup: Behind the Iran-Contra Affair 88 Barbara Trent

Coveted Coat, The 24 Gaston Quiribet

Cow, The 68 Dariush Mehrjui

Cow and I, The 58 Henri Verneuil

Cow Belles 29 Manny Gould, Ben Harrison

Cow Country 53 Curtis Bishop, Lesley Selander

Cow Milker, The 21 Milt Gross

Cow on the Moon, The 59 Dušan Vukotić

Cow Town 50 John English

Coward, The 11 Wilfred Noy

Coward, The 12 Allan Dwan

Coward, The 14 Charles C. Calvert

Coward, The 14 Boris Glagolin, R. Ungern

Coward, The 15 Reginald Barker, Thomas Ince

Coward! 15 Frank Wilson

Coward, The 27 Alfred Raboch

Coward, The 39 René Cardona

Coward, The 61 Jiří Weiss

Coward and the Holy Man, The 65 Satyajit Ray

Coward and the Saint, The 65 Satyajit Ray

Cowardice Court 19 William Dowlan

Cowards, The 70 Simon Nuchtern

Coward's Courage, A 09 Theo Bouwmeester

Cowboy, The 54 Elmo Williams

Cowboy 58 Delmer Daves

Cowboy, Le 85 Georges Lautner

Cowboy Ace, A 21 Leonard Franchon

Cowboy and the Artist, The 11 Allan Dwan

Cowboy and the Bandit, The 35 Albert Herman

Cowboy and the Blonde, The 41 Ray McCarey

Cowboy and the Countess, The 26 Roy William Neill

Cowboy and the Flapper, The 24 Alvin J. Neitz

Cowboy and the Girl, The 43 Henry Hathaway, William A. Seiter

Cowboy and the Indians, The 49 John English

Cowboy and the Kid, The 36 Ray Taylor

Cowboy and the Lady, The 22 Charles Maigne

Cowboy and the Lady, The 38 H. C. Potter

Cowboy and the Outlaw, The 11 Allan Dwan

Cowboy and the Outlaw, The 29 John P. McGowan

Cowboy and the Prizefighter, The 49 Lewis D. Collins

Cowboy and the Schoolmarm, The 08 Edwin S. Porter

Cowboy and the Señorita, The 44 Joseph Kane

Cowboy and the Squaw, The 10 Gilbert M. Anderson

Cowboy Blues 46 Ray Nazarro

Cowboy Canteen 44 Lew Landers

Cowboy Cavalier, The 28 Richard Thorpe

Cowboy Cavalier 48 Derwin Abrahams

Cowboy Clem 15 Bert Haldane

Cowboy Commandos 43 S. Roy Luby

Cowboy Cop, The 26 Robert De Lacey

Cowboy Counsellor 32 George Melford

Cowboy Courage 25 Robert J. Horner

Cowboy Coward, The 11 Gilbert M. Anderson

Cowboy from Brooklyn 38 Lloyd Bacon

Cowboy from Lonesome River 44 Benjamin Kline

Cowboy from Sundown, The 40 Spencer G. Bennet

Cowboy Holiday 34 Robert F. Hill

Cowboy in Africa 67 Andrew Marton

Cowboy in Manhattan 43 Frank Woodruff

Cowboy in the Clouds 43 Benjamin Kline

Cowboy Jimmy 57 Dušan Vukotić

Cowboy Kid, The 28 Clyde Carruth

Cowboy King, The 22 Charles R. Seeling

Cowboy Millionaire, The 35 Edward F. Cline

Cowboy Musketeer, The 25 Robert De Lacey

Cowboy Prince, The 24 Francis Ford

Cowboy Quarterback, The 39 Noel Mason Smith

Cowboy Roundup 36 Lesley Selander

Cowboy Serenade 42 William Morgan

Cowboy Socialist, The 12 Allan Dwan

Cowboy Star, The 36 David Selman

Cowboy Village, The 15 J. L. V. Leigh

Cowboys, The 24 Lewis Seiler*

Cowboys, The 71 Mark Rydell

Cowboy's Courtships 10 Edwin S. Porter

Cowboy's Deliverance, The 11 Allan Dwan

Cowboys Don't Cry 88 Anne Wheeler

Cowboys from Texas 39 George Sherman

Cowboy's Ruse, The 11 Allan Dwan

Cowgirl Queen, The 22 Hugh Croise

Cowherd's Flute, The 64 Wei Te

Cowpunchers, The 20 Raoul Barré, Charles Bowers

Cows and Caws 17 Raoul Barré, Charles Bowers

Cow's Husband, The 19 Raoul Barré, Charles Bowers

Cow's Husband, A 28 Mark Sandrich

Cow's Husband, The 31 Dave Fleischer

Cowslips 31 Mark Sandrich

Coy Decoy, A 41 Robert Clampett

Coyote Fangs 24 Harry S. Webb

Coyote Trails 35 Bernard B. Ray

Což Takhle Dát Si Špenát 76 Miloš Macourek, Václav Vorlíček

Crab, The 17 Walter Edwards

Crab-Canning Ship, The 53 So Yamamura

Crabe Tambour, Le 77 Pierre Schöndörffer

Crabes, Les 29 Jean Painlevé

Crabs Are Crabs 18 Gregory La Cava

Crabs Iss Crabs 18 Gregory La Cava

Crack, El 81 José Luis García Agraz

Crack II, El 83 José Luis García Agraz

Crack House 89 Michael Fischa

Crack in the Mirror 60 Richard Fleischer

Crack in the Mirror 87 Robby Benson

Crack in the World 65 Andrew Marton

Crack o' Dawn 25 Albert S. Rogell

Crack-Up 36 Malcolm St. Clair

Crack-Up 46 Irving Reis

Cracked 85 Hideo Gosha

Cracked Ice 38 Frank Tashlin

Cracked Ice Man, The 33 Charlie Chase, Eddie Dunn

Cracked Nut, The 41 Walter Lantz

Cracked Nuts 31 Edward F. Cline

Cracked Nuts 41 Edward F. Cline

Cracked Quack 52 Friz Freleng

Cracked Shots 34 George Stevens

Crackerjack, The 25 Charles Hines

Crackerjack 38 Albert De Courville

Crackers 83 Louis Malle

Cracking Up 77 Rowby Goren, Chuck Staley

Cracking Up 82 Jerry Lewis

Crackle of Death 74 Alexander Grasshoff, Don Weis

Crackpot Quail, The 41 Tex Avery

Cracks, Les 68 Alex Joffé

Crackshot 68 Josef Leytes, Stuart Rosenberg

Cracksman, The 63 Peter Graham Scott

Cracksman's Daughter, The 13 Charles C. Calvert

Cracksmen and the Black Diamonds, The 08 Charles Raymond

Cradle, The 22 Paul Powell

Cradle Buster, The 22 Frank Tuttle

Cradle of Courage, The 20 Lambert Hillyer

Cradle of Crime 37 William Wyler

Cradle of Genius 59 Paul Rotha

Cradle Snatchers, The 27 Howard Hawks

Cradle Song 33 Mitchell Leisen

Crafty Usurper and the Young King, The 09 Percy Stow

Cragmire Tower 24 Fred Paul

Craig's Wife 28 William DeMille

Craig's Wife 35 Dorothy Arzner

Crainquebille 22 Jacques Feyder

Crainquebille 33 Jacques De Baroncelli

Cramps 16 Charles Bowers

Cran d'Arrêt 70 Yves Boisset

Cranes Are Flying, The 57 Mikhail Kalatozov

Craneur, Le 55 Dmitri Kirsanov
Crash, The 28 Edward F. Cline
Crash, The 32 William Dieterle
Crash! 77 Charles Band
Crash Dive 43 Archie Mayo
Crash Donovan 36 William Nigh
Crash Drive 59 Max Varnel
Crash Landing 57 Fred F. Sears
Crash of Silence 52 Alexander Mackendrick
Crashin' Through 24 Alvin J. Neitz
Crashin' Thru 23 Val Paul
Crashin' Thru 39 Elmer Clifton
Crashin' Thru Danger 38 Sam Newfield
Crashing Broadway 33 John P. McCarthy
Crashing Courage 23 Harry G. Moody
Crashing Hollywood 37 Lew Landers
Crashing Las Vegas 56 Jean Yarbrough
Crashing Through 28 Thomas Buckingham
Crashing Thru 39 Elmer Clifton
Crashing Thru 49 Ray Taylor
Crashout 55 Lewis R. Foster
Crater Lake Monster, The 77 William R. Stromberg
Craving, The 16 Charles E. Bartlett
Craving, The 18 Francis Ford, John Ford
Crawling Eye, The 58 Quentin Lawrence
Crawling Hand, The 63 Herbert L. Strock
Crawling Monster, The 64 John Sherwood
Crawling Terror, The 57 Gilbert Gunn
Crawlspace 86 David Schmoeller
Craze 73 Freddie Francis
Crazed Fruit 56 Ko Nakahira
Crazed Vampire, The 71 Jean Rollin
Crazies, The 72 George Romero
Craziest Asylum, The 69 Nelson Pereira Dos Santos
Crazy Boys 87 Peter Kern
Crazy Composer, A 05 Georges Méliès
Crazy Cruise 41 Tex Avery, Robert Clampett
Crazy Dandy 38 Arturo S. Mom
Crazy Day, A 60 Mauro Bolognini
Crazy Days 62 James M. Anderson
Crazy Desire 62 Luciano Salce
Crazy Family, The 84 Sogo Ishii
Crazy for Love 52 Jean Boyer
Crazy Horse 89 Stephen Withrow
Crazy Horse of Paris, The 81 Alain Bernardin
Crazy House 40 Walter Lantz
Crazy House 43 Edward F. Cline
Crazy House 73 Peter Sykes
Crazy Idea, A 21 Raoul Barré, Charles Bowers
Crazy in the Noodle 57 Maurice Regamey
Crazy Jack and the Boy 74 John Korty
Crazy Joe 74 Carlo Lizzani
Crazy Knights 44 William Beaudine
Crazy Legs 87 Bill Berry
Crazy Like a Fox 26 Leo McCarey
Crazy Love 87 Dominique Deruddere
Crazy Mama 75 Jonathan Demme
Crazy Mixed-Up Pup 54 Tex Avery
Crazy Moon 85 Allan Eastman
Crazy Musician, The 39 Luis Saslavsky
Crazy Nut, The 29 Charles Lamont
Crazy Ones, The 67 Hugo Haas
Crazy Over Horses 51 William Beaudine

Crazy Page, A 26 Teinosuke Kinugasa
Crazy Paradise 65 Gabriel Axel
Crazy People 34 Leslie Hiscott
Crazy People 90 Tony Bill
Crazy Pete 65 Jean-Luc Godard
Crazy Quilt 65 John Korty
Crazy Radio 86 Francesc Bellmunt
Crazy Ray, The 23 René Clair
Crazy That Way 30 Hamilton MacFadden, Marion Orth
Crazy Thunder Road 80 Sogo Ishii
Crazy to Kill 43 Willis Goldbeck
Crazy to Marry 21 James Cruze
Crazy Town 32 Dave Fleischer
Crazy Uproar 50 Minoru Shibuya
Crazy World 63 Gualtiero Jacopetti, Franco Prosperi
Crazy World 68 Yoji Kuri
Crazy World of Julius Vrooder, The 74 Arthur Hiller
Crazylegs 53 Francis D. Lyon
Crazylegs, All-American 53 Francis D. Lyon
Creaking Stairs 19 Rupert Julian
Cream — Last Concert 68 Tony Palmer
Cream of the Earth 28 Melville Brown
Cream Puff Romance, A 16 Roscoe Arbuckle
Creampuffs & Lollipops 87 Li Vilstrup
Created and Consumed by Light 76 Alexis Krasilovsky
Created to Kill 76 Ralph Nelson
Creation 22 Humberston Wright
Creation 79 Stan Brakhage
Création d'Ulcères Artificiels chez le Chien 34 Henri Storck
Creation of the Humanoids 62 Wesley Barry
Créations Spontanées 1898 Georges Méliès
Creator 85 Ivan Passer
Creature 85 William Malone
Creature Called Man, The 70 Kiyoshi Nishimura
Creature from Another World, The 58 Quentin Lawrence
Creature from Black Lake, The 75 Joy Houck, Jr.
Creature from the Black Lagoon, The 54 Jack Arnold
Creature from the Haunted Sea 60 Roger Corman
Creature of Destruction 67 Larry Buchanan
Creature of the Devil 43 Sam Newfield
Creature of the Walking Dead 60 Fernando Cortez, Jerry Warren
Creature Walks Among Us, The 56 John Sherwood
Creature Wasn't Nice, The 81 Bruce Kimmel
Creature with the Atom Brain 55 Edward L. Cahn
Creature with the Blue Hand 70 Alfred Vohrer
Créatures, Les 66 Agnès Varda
Creatures, The 66 Agnès Varda
Creatures, The 73 Kevin Connor
Creatures from Beyond the Grave, The 73 Kevin Connor
Creatures of Clay 14 Frank Wilson

Creatures of Darkness 69 Bill Williams
Creatures of Evil 70 Gerry De Leon
Creatures of Habit 14 Lawrence Trimble
Creatures of the Prehistoric Planet 70 Al Adamson, George Joseph
Creatures of the Red Planet 70 Al Adamson, George Joseph
Creature's Revenge, The 71 Al Adamson
Creatures the World Forgot 70 Don Chaffey
Credevano uno Stingo di Santo, Lo 72 Juan Bosch
Credo 23 Julien Duvivier
Credo ou La Tragédie de Lourdes 23 Julien Duvivier
Creeper, The 48 Jean Yarbrough
Creeper, The 78 Peter Carter
Creepers, The 66 Terence Fisher
Creepers, The 70 Sidney Hayers
Creepers 84 Dario Argento
Creeping Flesh, The 72 Freddie Francis
Creeping Shadows 31 John Orton
Creeping Terror, The 64 John Sherwood
Creeping Unknown, The 55 Val Guest
Creepozoids 87 David DeCoteau
Creeps 26 Norman Taurog
Creeps 80 Ed Hunt
Creeps 80 Wojciech Marczewski
Creepshow 82 George Romero
Creepshow II 87 Michael Gornick
Creepy Time Pal 60 Joseph Barbera, William Hanna
Creezy 74 Pierre Granier-Deferre
Crémation, La 1899 Georges Méliès
Cremator, The 68 Juraj Herz
Cremators, The 72 Harry Essex
Crème Simon, La 37 Alexander Alexeïeff, Claire Parker
Creo en Dios 40 Fernando De Fuentes
Creole Moon 40 Raphael J. Sevilla
Creole's Love Story, A 13 Charles Raymond
Creosoot 31 Joris Ivens
Creosote 31 Joris Ivens
Crepo Tue...Che Vivo 67 Massimo Dallamano
Crepúscolo de un Dios, El 68 Emilio Fernández
Crepuscolo di un Mondo 53 Piero Nelli
Crépuscule de Cœur, Le 16 Maurice Mariaud
Crépuscule d'Épouvante 21 Henri Étiévant
Crescendo 43 Curtis Harrington
Crescendo 69 Alan Gibson
Crest of the Wave 53 John Boulting, Roy Boulting
Crevettes, Les 29 Jean Painlevé
Crew, The 27 Maurice Tourneur
Crew Racing 36 David Miller
Cri de la Chair, Le 64 José Benazeraf
Cri du Cormoran le Soir Au-Dessus des Jonques, Le 70 Michel Audiard
Cri du Hibou, Le 87 Claude Chabrol
¡Cría! 75 Carlos Saura
Cría Cuervos 75 Carlos Saura
Cricca Dorata, La 13 Emilio Ghione
Cricket, The 17 Elsie Jane Wilson
Cricket on the Hearth, The 09 D. W. Griffith
Cricket on the Hearth, The 14 Alice Guy-Blaché

Cricket on the Hearth, The 23 Lorimer Johnston
Cries and Whispers 72 Ingmar Bergman
Cries in the Night 61 Jesús Franco
Cries in the Night 81 William Fruet
Criez-Le sur les Toits 35 Karl Anton
Crime, A 40 Anders Henrikson
Crime, The 57 Roman Polanski
Crime à Été Commis, Un 19 André Hugon
Crime Afloat 37 Elmer Clifton
Crime Against Joe 56 Lee Sholem
Crime and Passion 75 Ivan Passer
Crime and Punishment 11 Vasili M. Goncharov
Crime and Punishment 13 I. Vronsky
Crime and Punishment 17 Lawrence McGill
Crime and Punishment 23 Robert Wiene
Crime and Punishment 35 Pierre Chénal, Jean Renoir
Crime and Punishment 35 Josef von Sternberg
Crime and Punishment 45 Erik Faustman
Crime and Punishment 56 Georges Lampin
Crime and Punishment 69 Lev Kulidzhanov
Crime and Punishment 83 Aki Kaurismäki
Crime and Punishment, U.S.A. 59 Denis Sanders
Crime and the Penalty 16 R. Harley West
Crime at a Girls' School 65 Jiří Menzel*
Crime at Blossoms, The 33 Maclean Rogers
Crime at Porta Romana 80 Bruno Corbucci
Crime at the Mill 13 Stuart Kinder
Crime at the Nightclub 68 Jiří Menzel
Crime au Cimetière Étrusque 82 Christian Plummer
Crime au Concert Mayol 61 Pierre Mère
Crime Boss 72 Alberto De Martino
Crime Busters 76 Enzo Barboni
Crime by Night 44 William Clemens
Crime Casebook 75 David Eady
Crime d'Antoine, Le 89 Marc Rivière
Crime de Grand-Père, Le 10 Léonce Perret
Crime de la Rue de Cherche-Midi à Quatorze Heures, Le 08 Georges Méliès
Crime de la Rue du Temple, Le 04 Alice Guy-Blaché
Crime de Lord Arthur Saville, Le 22 René Hervil
Crime de Monsieur Lange, Le 35 Jean Renoir
Crime de Sylvestre Bonnard, Le 30 André Berthomieu
Crime des Hommes, Le 23 Gaston Roudes
Crime Doctor, The 34 John S. Robertson
Crime Doctor 43 Michael Gordon
Crime Doctor's Courage, The 45 George Sherman
Crime Doctor's Diary, The 49 Seymour Friedman
Crime Doctor's Gamble 47 William Castle
Crime Doctor's Man Hunt 46 William Castle
Crime Doctor's Strangest Case 43 Eugene

Forde
Crime Doctor's Vacation, The 47 George Archainbaud
Crime Doctor's Warning 45 William Castle
Crime Does Not Pay 62 Gérard Oury
Crime Does Not Pay 72 R. Tulsi Ramsay, Shyam Ramsay
Crime d'Ovide Plouffe, Le 84 Denys Arcand, Gilles Carle
Crime du Bouif, Le 21 Henri Pouctal
Crime et Châtiment 35 Pierre Chénal, Jean Renoir
Crime et Châtiment 56 Georges Lampin
Crime Gives Orders 38 Louis King
Crime in a Girls' School 65 Jiří Menzel*
Crime in a Nightclub 68 Jiří Menzel
Crime in the Maginot Line 39 Félix Gandéra
Crime in the Nightclub 68 Jiří Menzel
Crime in the Streets 56 Don Siegel
Crime, Inc. 41 Phil Rosen
Crime, Inc. 45 Lew Landers
Crime Lab 48 Edward Montagne
Crime Ne Paie Pas, Le 62 Gérard Oury
Crime Nobody Saw, The 37 Charles Barton
Crime of Cuenca, The 80 Pilar Miró
Crime of Dr. Crespi, The 35 John H. Auer
Crime of Dr. Forbes, The 36 George Marshall
Crime of Dr. Hallet, The 38 S. Sylvan Simon
Crime of Helen Stanley, The 34 D. Ross Lederman
Crime of Honor 85 John Goldschmidt
Crime of Honour 58 Montgomery Tully
Crime of Lord Arthur Saville, The 19 Pál Fejős
Crime of Monsieur Lange, The 35 Jean Renoir
Crime of Ovide Plouffe, The 84 Denys Arcand, Gilles Carle
Crime of Passion 57 Gerd Oswald
Crime of Peter Frame, The 38 Albert Parker
Crime of the Century, The 33 William Beaudine
Crime of the Century 46 Philip Ford
Crime of the Century, The 52 Alfred L. Werker
Crime of the Hour 18 Thomas Ricketts
Crime of Voodoo 35 George Terwilliger
Crime on the Hill 33 Bernard Vorhaus
Crime Over London 36 Alfred Zeisler
Crime Passionel, Un 31 Edmond T. Gréville
Crime Patrol, The 36 Eugene Cummings
Crime Pays 86 Christopher Monger
Crime Rave 39 Jean Yarbrough
Crime Reporter 42 Jean Yarbrough
Crime Reporter 47 Ben R. Hart
Crime Ring 38 Leslie Goodwins
Crime School 38 Lewis Seiler
Crime Smasher 43 James Tinling
Crime Squad 53 Ray Enright
Crime Takes a Holiday 38 Lewis D. Collins
Crime Unlimited 35 Ralph Ince

Crime Wave 53 André De Toth
Crime Without Passion 34 Ben Hecht, Charles MacArthur
Crime Zone 88 Luis Llosa
Crimebusters, The 61 Boris Sagal
Crimen 60 Mario Camerini
Crimen a las Tres 35 Luis Saslavsky
Crimen de Cuenca, El 80 Pilar Miró
Crimen de Doble Filo 64 José Luis Borau
Crimen de Medianoche, El 36 Bernard B. Ray
Crimen de Oribe, El 49 Leopoldo Torre-Nilsson, Leopoldo Torres Ríos
Crimen y Castigo 50 Fernando De Fuentes
Crimes 86 Sergio Pastore
Crimes 87 Giovanna Lenzi
Crimes and Misdemeanors 89 Woody Allen
Crimes at the Dark House 39 George King
Crime's End 39 Charles Barton
Crimes in the Wax Museum 69 Bud Townsend
Crimes of a Drifter 86 John Dwyer
Crimes of Dr. Mabuse, The 32 Fritz Lang
Crimes of Passion 84 Ken Russell
Crimes of Stephen Hawke, The 36 George King, Paul White
Crimes of the Black Cat, The 72 Sergio Pastore
Crimes of the Future 70 David Cronenberg
Crimes of the Heart 86 Bruce Beresford
Crime's Triangle 15 King Baggot
Crimewave 85 Sam Raimi
Criminal, The 15 Van Dyke Brooke
Criminal, The 16 Reginald Barker, Roy William Neill
Criminal, The 60 Joseph Losey
Criminal at Large 32 T. Hayes Hunter
Criminal Career of Klaus Barbie, The 87 Marcel Ophüls
Criminal Cargo 39 Lewis D. Collins
Criminal Code, The 30 Howard Hawks
Criminal Conversation 80 Kieran Hickey
Criminal Court 46 Robert Wise
Criminal Cried, The 07 John Morland
Criminal Hypnotist, The 08 D. W. Griffith
Criminal Investigator 42 Jean Yarbrough
Criminal Is Born, A 38 Leslie Fenton
Criminal Law 88 Martin Campbell
Criminal Lawyer 36 Christy Cabanne
Criminal Lawyer 51 Seymour Friedman
Criminal Life of Archibaldo de la Cruz, The 55 Luis Buñuel
Criminal Women 68 Teruo Ishii
Criminali della Galassia, I 65 Antonio Margheriti
Criminals 13 Allan Dwan
Criminals 33 Abram Room
Criminals, The 71 Yılmaz Güney
Criminals of the Air 37 C. C. Coleman, Jr.
Criminals of the Galaxy, The 65 Antonio Margheriti
Criminals Within 41 Joseph H. Lewis
Crimson Altar, The 68 Vernon Sewell
Crimson Blade, The 63 John Gilling
Crimson Canary, The 45 John Hoffman

Crimson Candle, The *34* Bernerd Mainwaring

Crimson Canyon, The *28* Ray Taylor

Crimson Challenge, The *22* Paul Powell

Crimson Circle, The *22* George Ridgwell

Crimson Circle, The *29* Sinclair Hill, Fred Zelnik

Crimson Circle, The *36* Reginald Denham

Crimson City, The *28* Archie Mayo

Crimson Cross, The *21* George Everett

Crimson Cult *68* Vernon Sewell

Crimson Curtain, The *52* Alexandre Astruc

Crimson Dove, The *17* Romaine Fielding

Crimson Dynasty *34* Maurice Tourneur

Crimson Executioner, The *65* Massimo Pupillo

Crimson Gardenia, The *19* Reginald Barker

Crimson Ghost, The *46* Fred C. Brannon, William Witney

Crimson Gold *23* Clifford S. Elfelt

Crimson Key, The *47* Eugene Forde

Crimson Kimono, The *59* Samuel Fuller

Crimson Permanent Assurance, The *83* Terry Gilliam

Crimson Pirate, The *52* Robert Siodmak

Crimson Romance *34* David Howard

Crimson Runner, The *25* Tom Forman

Crimson Sails *61* Alexander Ptushko

Crimson Shoals, The *19* Francis Ford

Crimson Stain Mystery, The *16* T. Hayes Hunter

Crimson Trail, The *35* Alfred Raboch

Crimson Triangle, The *15* Dave Aylott

Crimson Wing, The *15* Elisha H. Calvert

Crimson Wings *58* Ko Nakahira

Crin Blanc *52* Albert Lamorisse

Crin Blanc le Cheval Sauvage *52* Albert Lamorisse

Crinoline, La *06* Alice Guy-Blaché

Crinoline and Romance *23* Harry Beaumont

Cripple Creek *52* Ray Nazarro

Cripple Girl, The *15* August Blom

Cripple of Ypres, The *15* F. C. S. Tudor

Crippled Hand, The *15* David Kirkland, Robert Z. Leonard

Cripples Go Christmas, The *88* Ralf Hüttner

Cripta e l'Incubo, La *63* Camillo Mastrocinque

Crisantemi per un Branco di Carogne *68* Sergio Pastore

Crise du Logement, La *55* Jean Dewever

Crise Est Finie, La *34* Robert Siodmak

Crisi *21* Augusto Genina

Crisis, The *12* Thomas Ince

Crisis, The *15* Colin Campbell

Crisis *28* G. W. Pabst

Crisis *38* Herbert Kline

Crisis *45* Ingmar Bergman

Crisis *50* Richard Brooks

Crisis, A *54* Jin Xie

Crisis *63* Richard Leacock, D. A. Pennebaker

Crisis—A Film of the Nazi Way *38* Herbert Kline

Crisis: Behind a Presidential Commitment *63* Richard Leacock, D. A. Pennebaker

Crisis en el Caribe *62* Santiago Álvarez

Crisis Mundial *37* Benito Perojo

Criss Cross *48* Robert Siodmak

Cristeaux *28* Abel Gance

Cristo Proibito, Il *50* Curzio Malaparte

Cristo Si È Fermato a Eboli *79* Francesco Rosi

Cristoforo Colombo *37* Carmine Gallone

Cristoforo Columbus *83* Alberto Lattuada

Critic, The *63* Mel Brooks, Ernest Pintoff

Critical Age, The *23* Henry MacRae

Critical Condition *87* Michael Apted

Critico, Il *12* Febo Mari

Critic's Choice *63* Don Weis

Critters *85* Stephen Herek

Critters II *88* Mick Garris

Critters II: The Main Course *88* Mick Garris

Croce dalle Sette Pietre, La *86* Marco Antonio Andolfi

Crockette Doodle-Doo *60* Robert McKimson

Crocodile *79* Sompote Sands

Crocodile, Le *85* Philippe de Broca

"Crocodile" Dundee *86* Peter Faiman

"Crocodile" Dundee II *88* John Cornell

Croisade, La *20* René Le Somptier

Croisée des Chemins, La *42* André Berthomieu

Croisière de l'Atalante, La *26* Jean Grémillon

Croisière Noire, La *26* Léon Poirier

Croisières Sidérales *41* André Zwoboda

Croix de Bois, Les *32* Raymond Bernard

Croix des Cimes, La *34* Edmond T. Gréville

Croix des Vivants, La *63* Yvan Govar

Crollo di Roma, Il *62* Antonio Margheriti

Cromwell *70* Ken Hughes

Cronaca di un Amore *50* Michelangelo Antonioni

Cronaca di una Morte Annunciata *86* Francesco Rosi

Cronaca Familiare *62* Valerio Zurlini

Cronache di Poveri Amanti *54* Carlo Lizzani

Cronache di un Convento *61* Edward Dmytryk

Crónica de Familia *86* Diego López

Cronos Children, The *85* Giorgos Korras

Crook, The *70* Claude Lelouch

Crook Buster *25* William Wyler

Crook of Dreams *19* Oscar Apfel

Crook Who Cried Wolf *63* Joseph Barbera, William Hanna

Crooked Alley *23* Robert F. Hill

Crooked Billet, The *29* Adrian Brunel

Crooked Circle, The *32* H. Bruce Humberstone

Crooked Circle, The *57* Joseph Kane

Crooked Lady, The *32* Leslie Hiscott

Crooked Man, The *23* George Ridgwell

Crooked Mirror *56* Karel Kachyňa

Crooked Mix-Up, A *16* William Beaudine

Crooked River *50* Thomas Carr

Crooked Road, The *11* D. W. Griffith

Crooked Road *32* Louis King

Crooked Road, The *40* Phil Rosen

Crooked Road, The *64* Don Chaffey

Crooked Romance, A *17* William Parke

Crooked Sky, The *56* Henry Cass

Crooked Straight *19* Jerome Storm

Crooked Streets *20* Paul Powell

Crooked Trail, The *36* S. Roy Luby

Crooked Way, The *49* Robert Florey

Crooked Web, The *55* Nathan Juran

Crooks *87* Jorge Coscia, Guillermo Saura

Crooks and Coronets *69* James O'Connolly

Crooks Anonymous *62* Ken Annakin

Crooks Can't Win *28* George M. Arthur

Crooks' Honor *66* Wolfgang Staudte

Crooks in Cloisters *63* Jeremy Summers

Crooks in Clover *33* W. S. Van Dyke

Crook's Tour *40* John Baxter

Crooky *15* C. Jay Williams

Crooner *32* Lloyd Bacon

Crop Chasers *39* Ubbe Iwerks

Croque la Vie *81* Jean-Charles Tacchella

Croquemitaine et Rosalie *16* Émile Cohl

Croquette *27* Louis Mercanton

Croqueuses, Les *73* Jesús Franco

Crosby Case, The *34* Edwin L. Marin

Crosby Murder Case, The *34* Edwin L. Marin

Cross *87* Philippe Setbon

Cross and Mauser *25* Vladimir Gardin

Cross and the Switchblade, The *70* Don Murray

Cross and the Sword, The *34* Frank R. Strayer

Cross Bearer, The *18* George Archainbaud

Cross Breed *27* Noel Mason Smith

Cross Channel *55* R. G. Springsteen

Cross Country *83* Paul Lynch

Cross Country Cruise *34* Edward Buzzell

Cross Country Detours *40* Tex Avery

Cross Country Romance *40* Frank Woodruff

Cross Country Run, A *28* Henry D. Bailey

Cross Country Runner *69* Puriša Djordjević

Cross Creek *83* Martin Ritt

Cross Currents *16* Francis J. Grandon

Cross Currents *35* Adrian Brunel

Cross Examination *32* Richard Thorpe

Cross-Eyed Fortune *59* Andrzej Munk

Cross-Eyed Submarine, The *17* William Beaudine

Cross in the Plaza, A *58* Glauber Rocha

Cross My Heart *37* Bernerd Mainwaring

Cross My Heart *46* John Berry

Cross My Heart *87* Armyan Bernstein

Cross of Iron *77* Sam Peckinpah

Cross of Lorraine, The *43* Tay Garnett

Cross of the Living *63* Yvan Govar

Cross of the Seven Stones, The *86* Marco Antonio Andolfi

Cross of Valor, The *59* Kazimierz Kutz

Cross Purposes *13* Wallace Reid, Willis Robards

Cross Roads *22* Francis Ford

Cross Streets *34* Frank R. Strayer

Cross-Up *55* John Gilling

Cross with the Seven Stones, The *86* Marco Antonio Andolfi

Crossbeam *66* Jörn Donner

Crossed Signals *26* John P. McGowan

Crossed Swords *52* Nato De Angelis, Milton Krims, Arthur Villiesid

Crossed Swords 77 Richard Fleischer
Crossed Trails 24 John P. McGowan
Crossed Trails 48 Lambert Hillyer
Crossed Wires 23 King Baggot
Crosseyed Luck 59 Andrzej Munk
Crossfire 33 Otto Brower
Crossfire 47 Edward Dmytryk
Crossing Delancey 88 Joan Micklin Silver
Crossing Ice Bridge at Niagara Falls 04 Edwin S. Porter
Crossing of the Rhine, The 60 André Cayatte
Crossing the American Prairies in the Early Fifties 11 D. W. Griffith
Crossing the Great Sagrada 24 Adrian Brunel
Crossing Trails 21 Clifford Smith
Crossing Watchman of the Mountains, The 23 Yasujiro Shimazu
Crossover Dreams 85 León Ichaso
Crossplot 69 Alvin Rakoff
Crossroad Gallows, The 58 Montgomery Tully
Crossroads 28 Teinosuke Kinugasa
Crossroads 30 Reginald Fogwell
Crossroads 38 Kurt Bernhardt
Crossroads 42 Jack Conway
Crossroads 55 John Fitchen
Crossroads 76 Bruce Conner
Crossroads 86 Walter Hill
Crossroads for a Nun 70 Julio Buchs
Crossroads of Life, The 15 Forest Holger-Madsen
Crossroads of New York, The 22 F. Richard Jones
Crossroads of Passion 51 Jacques Companeez
Crossroads South Africa 80 Jonathan Wacks
Crossroads to Crime 60 Gerry Anderson
Crosstalk 82 Mark Egerton
Crosstrap 61 Robert Hartford-Davis
Crossways 28 Teinosuke Kinugasa
Crosswinds 51 Lewis R. Foster
Crouching Beast, The 35 Joseph Losey
Crow, The 19 B. Reeves Eason
Crow, The 43 Henri-Georges Clouzot
Crow Hollow 52 Michael McCarthy
Crow on the Tower 39 A. Endre Rodriguez
Crowd, The 27 King Vidor
Crowd for Lisette, A 61 R. John Hugh
Crowd Inside, The 71 Al Waxman
Crowd Outside, or Waiting for You, The 13 Percy Stow
Crowd Roars, The 32 Howard Hawks
Crowd Roars, The 38 Richard Thorpe
Crowd Snores, The 32 Walter Lantz
Crowded Day, The 54 John Guillermin
Crowded Hour, The 25 E. Mason Hopper
Crowded Paradise 56 Fred Pressburger
Crowded Sky, The 60 Joseph Pevney
Crowded Streetcar, The 57 Kon Ichikawa
Crowded Train, The 57 Kon Ichikawa
Crowing Pains 47 Robert McKimson
Crown Caper, The 68 Norman Jewison
Crown Jewels 18 Roy Clements
Crown of Lies, The 26 Dmitri Buchowetzki
Crown of Thorns 23 Robert Wiene

Crown Prince's Double, The 16 Van Dyke Brooke
Crown Trial 38 John Ruffin
Crown vs. Stevens 34 Michael Powell
Crowning Experience, The 60 Marion Clayton Anderson
Crowning Gift, The 67 Norman Walker
Crowning Touch, The 59 David Eady
Crown's Cavaliers, The 30 Gustaf Edgren
Crows and Scarecrows 21 Raoul Barré, Charles Bowers
Crows and Sparrows 49 Junli Zheng
Crow's Feat 62 Friz Freleng
Crow's Fete 65 Joseph Barbera, William Hanna
Crow's Nest, The 22 Paul Hurst
Croxley Master, The 21 Percy Nash
Crucial Moment, The 38 Ladislas Vajda
Crucial Test, The 16 John Ince, Robert Thornby
Crucible, The 14 Hugh Ford, Edwin S. Porter
Crucible, The 57 Raymond Rouleau
Crucible of Horror 69 Viktors Ritelis
Crucible of Life, The 18 Harry Lambart
Crucible of Terror, The 71 Ted Hooker
Crucified Lovers, The 54 Kenji Mizoguchi
Crucified Woman, The 54 Kenji Mizoguchi
Crucifix, The 34 George B. Samuelson
Crucifix of Destiny, The 20 R. Dale Armstrong
Crudeli, I 66 Sergio Corbucci
Cruel Embrace, The 87 Marion Hansel
Cruel Fate 86 Gerardo Vallejo
Cruel Ghost Legend 68 Kazuo Hase
Cruel Ones, The 71 Tonino Cervi
Cruel Passion 78 Chris Boger
Cruel Revenge, A 14 John Ince
Cruel Sea 44 Tadashi Imai
Cruel Sea, The 52 Charles Frend
Cruel Sea, The 71 Khalid Siddik
Cruel Story of the Samurai's Way 63 Tadashi Imai
Cruel Story of Youth 60 Nagisa Oshima
Cruel Swamp 55 Roger Corman
Cruel Tower, The 56 Lew Landers
Cruel Truth, The 27 Phil Rosen
Crueles, Las 71 Tonino Cervi
Cruise, The 67 John Hubley
Cruise Cat 52 Joseph Barbera, William Hanna
Cruise in the Albertina, A 40 Per Axel-Branner
Cruise Missile 78 Leslie Martinson
Cruise of the Hellion, The 27 Duke Worne
Cruise of the Jasper B, The 26 James W. Horne
Cruise of the Makebelieve, The 18 George Melford
Cruise of the Zaca 46 Errol Flynn
Cruiser Emden 31 Louis Ralph
Cruisin' Down the River 53 Richard Quine
Cruisin' 57 75 Toby Ross
Cruisin' High 75 John Bushelman
Cruising 80 William Friedkin
Cruising Casanovas 52 R. G. Springsteen
Cruiskeen Lawn 22 John McDonagh
Crunch 70 Marran Gosov

Crunch! 81 Mark Warren
Crusade Against Rackets 37 Elmer Clifton
Crusader, The 22 William K. Howard, Howard Mitchell
Crusader, The 32 Frank R. Strayer
Crusades, The 35 Cecil B. DeMille
Crushing the Drug Traffic 22 H. B. Parkinson
Crusoe 88 Caleb Deschanel
Cruz Brothers and Miss Malloy, The 79 Kathleen Collins
Cruz de Diablo, La 74 John Gilling
Cruz Diablo 34 Fernando De Fuentes
Cruz na Praça, A 58 Glauber Rocha
Cruz y la Espada, La 34 Frank R. Strayer
Cruzada ABC 66 Nelson Pereira Dos Santos
Crveni i Crni 86 Miroslav Mukiljan
Cry, The 57 Michelangelo Antonioni
Cry, The 63 Jaromil Jireš
Cry-Baby 90 John Waters
Cry Baby Killer, The 58 Jus Addiss
Cry Blood, Apache 70 Jack Starrett
Cry Danger 51 Robert Parrish
Cry Demon 78 Gus Trikonis
Cry, Dr. Chicago 71 George Manupelli
Cry Doublecross 60 Alfred Weidenmann
Cry for Happy 61 George Marshall
Cry for Help, A 12 D. W. Griffith
Cry for Justice, The 19 Albert G. Frenguelli
Cry for Me, Billy 72 William A. Graham
Cry Freedom 59 Lamberto Avellana
Cry Freedom 87 Richard Attenborough
Cry from the Mountain 86 James F. Collier
Cry from the Streets, A 58 Lewis Gilbert
Cry from the Wilderness, A 09 Edwin S. Porter
Cry Havoc! 43 Richard Thorpe
Cry in the Dark, A 88 Fred Schepisi
Cry in the Night, A 15 Ernest G. Batley
Cry in the Night, A 56 Frank Tuttle
Cry Murder 36 Jack Glenn
Cry of Battle 63 Irving Lerner
Cry of the Banshee 70 Gordon Hessler
Cry of the Bewitched 57 Alfredo B. Crevenna
Cry of the Captive, The 14 Frank Wilson
Cry of the City 48 Robert Siodmak
Cry of the Hunted 53 Joseph H. Lewis
Cry of the Nighthawk, The 23 A. E. Coleby
Cry of the Owl, The 87 Claude Chabrol
Cry of the Penguins 71 Roy Boulting, Arne Sucksdorff, Al Viola
Cry of the People, The 72 Humberto Ríos
Cry of the Weak, The 18 George Fitzmaurice
Cry of the Werewolf 44 Henry Levin
Cry of the Wild 72 Bill Mason
Cry Terror! 58 Andrew L. Stone
Cry, the Beloved Country 51 Zoltán Korda
Cry to the Wind 79 Robert W. Davidson
Cry Tough 59 Paul Stanley
Cry Uncle! 70 John G. Avildsen
Cry Vengeance 54 Mark Stevens
Cry Wilderness 87 Jay Schlossberg Cohen
Cry Wolf 47 Peter Godfrey
Cry Wolf 68 John Davis

Cupid, the Cowpuncher 20 Clarence Badger
Cupid Through a Keyhole 13 Van Dyke Brooke
Cupid Through Padlocks 12 Allan Dwan
Cupid Throws a Brick 13 Allan Dwan
Cupid vs. Money 14 Van Dyke Brooke
Cupid vs. Women's Rights 13 Maurice Costello
Cupid's Advice 20 Gregory La Cava
Cupid's Brand 21 Rowland V. Lee
Cupid's Carnival 20 Will P. Kellino
Cupid's Day Off 18 Edward F. Cline
Cupid's Fireman 23 William A. Wellman
Cupid's Joke 11 Mack Sennett
Cupid's Knockout 26 Bruce Mitchell
Cupid's Loaf 09 Lewin Fitzhamon
Cupid's Message Goes Astray 10 Frank Wilson
Cupid's Roundup 18 Edward J. LeSaint
Cupid's Rustler 24 Francis Ford
Cupid's Victory 25 Charles Lamont
Cups of San Sebastian, The 67 Richard Rush
Curate at the Races, The 09 Lewin Fitzhamon
Curate's Bride, The 13 Hay Plumb
Curate's Courtship, The 08 Lewin Fitzhamon
Curate's Dilemma, The 06 J. H. Martin
Curate's Double, The 07 Walter R. Booth
Curate's Honeymoon, The 08 Arthur Cooper
Curate's Love Story, A 12 Lewin Fitzhamon
Curate's New Year Gifts, The 10 Percy Stow
Cure, The 17 Charles Chaplin
Cure, The 24 Dave Fleischer
Cure, The 50 Michael Law, Richard Massingham
Cure, The 83 Gregory Dark
Cure for Love, The 49 Robert Donat
Cure for Lumbago, A 06 Lewin Fitzhamon
Cure That Failed, The 13 Mack Sennett
Cured 11 Mack Sennett
Curée, La 66 Roger Vadim
Curfew 89 Gary Winick
Curfew Breakers 57 Alex Wells
Curfew Must Not Ring Tonight 12 Hay Plumb
Curfew Must Not Ring Tonight 23 Edwin J. Collins
Curfew Shall Not Ring 16 Harry S. Palmer
Curfew Shall Not Ring Tonight 06 Alf Collins
Curfew Shall Not Ring Tonight 07 Arthur Gilbert
Curfew Shall Not Ring Tonight 12 James Hallek Reid
Curfew Shall Not Ring Tonight 26 Frank Tilley
Curieuse Évasion 04 Georges Méliès
Curing a Jealous Wife 07 Jack Smith
Curing the Blind 07 Percy Stow
Curio Shop, The 33 Manny Gould, Ben Harrison
Curiosité Punie, La 08 Georges Méliès
Curiosity 11 Mack Sennett

Curiosity Punished 08 Georges Méliès
Curious Conduct of Judge Legarde, The 15 Will S. Davis
Curious Dr. Humpp, The 67 Emilio Vieyra
Curious Dream, A 07 J. Stuart Blackton
Curious Female, The 69 Paul Rapp
Curious Mr. Curio 08 Edwin S. Porter
Curious Puppy, The 39 Chuck Jones
Curley 47 Bernard Carr
Curley and His Gang in the Haunted Mansion 48 Bernard Carr
Curly 58 George Romero
Curly Top 35 Irving Cummings
Curly's Holiday 17 J. F. Carr
Curlytop 24 Maurice Elvey
Current 63 István Gaál
Curse, The 74 Ousmane Sembène
Curse, The 87 David Keith
Curse and the Coffin, The 61 Julien Duvivier
Curse of Bigfoot, The 72 Don Fields
Curse of Dark Shadows 71 Dan Curtis, Alex Stevens
Curse of Dracula, The 58 Paul Landres
Curse of Drink, The 22 Harry Hoyt
Curse of Eve, The 17 Frank Beal
Curse of Frankenstein, The 56 Terence Fisher
Curse of Iku, The 17 Frank Borzage
Curse of Kilimanjaro 78 Edward A. Kuplerski
Curse of Melissa 71 Don Henderson
Curse of Money, The 09 Theo Bouwmeester
Curse of Nostradamus, The 59 Federico Curiel, Alberto Mariscal
Curse of Ravenscroft, The 26 A. E. Coleby
Curse of Simba 64 Lindsay Shonteff
Curse of the Allenbys, The 46 Jean Yarbrough
Curse of the Aztec Mummy, The 57 Rafael Portillo
Curse of the Blood 68 Kazuo Hase
Curse of the Blood Ghouls 61 Roberto Mauri
Curse of the Cat People, The 44 Günther von Fritsch, Robert Wise
Curse of the Coffin, The 61 Julien Duvivier
Curse of the Crimson Altar 68 Vernon Sewell
Curse of the Crying Woman, The 60 Rafael Baledón
Curse of the Dead 66 Mario Bava
Curse of the Demon 57 Jacques Tourneur
Curse of the Devil 73 Carlos Aured
Curse of the Doll People 60 Benito Alazraki, Paul Nagle
Curse of the Faceless Man 58 Edward L. Cahn
Curse of the Fly, The 65 Don Sharp
Curse of the Full Moon 72 Andy Milligan
Curse of the Ghosts, The 69 Issei Mori
Curse of the Golem, The 66 Herbert J. Leder
Curse of the Green Eyes, The 64 Ákos von Ráthonyi
Curse of the Headless Horseman 72 John

Kirkland
Curse of the Hidden Vault, The 64 Franz-Josef Gottlieb
Curse of the Karnsteins, The 63 Camillo Mastrocinque
Curse of the Living Corpse, The 63 Del Tenney
Curse of the Living Dead 66 Mario Bava
Curse of the Mayan Temple 77 Bill Burrud
Curse of the Mummy's Tomb, The 64 Michael Carreras
Curse of the Mushroom People 63 Inoshiro Honda
Curse of the One-Eyed Corpse 65 Tsuneo Kobayashi
Curse of the Pink Panther 83 Blake Edwards
Curse of the Stone Hand 65 Carlos Hugo Christensen, Carl Schleipper, Jerry Warren
Curse of the Swamp Creature 66 Larry Buchanan
Curse of the Undead 59 Edward Dein
Curse of the Vampire 60 Piero Regnoli
Curse of the Vampires 70 Gerry De Leon
Curse of the Vampyr, The 71 José María Elorrieta
Curse of the Voodoo 64 Lindsay Shonteff
Curse of the Werewolf, The 61 Terence Fisher
Curse of the Wraydons, The 46 Victor M. Gover
Curse of the Yellow Snake, The 63 Franz-Josef Gottlieb
Curse of Westacott, The 21 Fred Paul, Jack Raymond
Cursed Medallion, The 74 Massimo Dallamano
Cursed Millions 17 Yakov Protazanov
Curses Jack Dalton 15 Vincent Whitman
Curses of the Ghouls 61 Roberto Mauri
Curses of the Knife 90 Hung-wei Yeh
Curtain, The 14 Warwick Buckland
Curtain 20 James Young
Curtain at Eight 34 E. Mason Hopper
Curtain Call 40 Frank Woodruff
Curtain Call at Cactus Creek 49 Charles Lamont
Curtain Falls, The 34 Charles Lamont
Curtain Pole, The 08 D. W. Griffith
Curtain Razor 49 Friz Freleng
Curtain Rises, The 38 Marc Allégret
Curtain Up 52 Ralph Smart
Curtains 82 Richard Ciupka
Curtain's Secret, The 15 Frank Wilson
Curtiss' School of Aviation 12 Allan Dwan
Curucu, Beast of the Amazon 56 Curt Siodmak
Cuspidore, Il 21 Wallace A. Carlson
Cuspidorée, Le 21 Wallace A. Carlson
Custard Cup 22 Herbert Brenon
Custer Massacre, The 65 Sidney Salkow
Custer of the West 66 Irving Lerner, Robert Siodmak
Custer's Last Fight 12 Thomas Ince
Custer's Last Raid 12 Thomas Ince
Custer's Last Stand 36 Elmer Clifton
Custody 87 Ian Munro
Customary Two Weeks, The 17 Saul Harrison

Damoiselle et Son Revenant, La *51* Marc Allégret
Damon and Pythias *14* Otis Turner
Damon and Pythias *61* Kurt Bernhardt
Dämon der Berge, Der *34* Andrew Marton
Dämon des Meeres *31* Michael Curtiz, William Dieterle
Dämon und Mensch *15* Richard Oswald
Damortis *84* Briccio Santos
Damp Deed, A *13* Hay Plumb
Dams and Waterways *11* Allan Dwan
Damsel in Distress, A *19* George Archainbaud
Damsel in Distress, A *37* George Stevens
Damy *54* Lev Kulidzhanov, Genrikh Oganisyan, Yakov Segel
Dan Backs a Winner *13* Stuart Kinder
Dan Candy's Law *73* Claude Fournier
Dan Leno's Cricket Match *00* Arthur Cooper
Dan Matthews *35* Phil Rosen
Dan Nolan's Cross *12* Fred Rains
Dan, the Dandy *11* D. W. Griffith
Danaids' Barrel, The *00* Georges Méliès
Dança dos Bonecos, A *87* Helvécio Ratton
Dance, The *87* Samson Samsonov
Dance Band *35* Marcel Varnel
Dance Black America *85* Chris Hegedus, D. A. Pennebaker
Dance, Charlie, Dance *37* Frank McDonald
Dance Chromatic *59* Ed Emshwiller
Dance Contest, The *34* Dave Fleischer
Dance Contest in Esira *37* Pál Fejös
Dance Craze *81* Joe Massot
Dance, Fools, Dance *30* Harry Beaumont
Dance, Girl, Dance *33* Frank R. Strayer
Dance, Girl, Dance *40* Dorothy Arzner
Dance Goes On, The *30* William Dieterle
Dance Hall *29* Melville Brown
Dance Hall *41* Irving Pichel
Dance Hall *50* Charles Crichton
Dance Hall Hostess *33* B. Reeves Eason
Dance Hall Marge *31* Mack Sennett
Dance Hall Racket *53* Phil Tucker
Dance in the Rain *61* Boštjan Hladnik
Dance in the Sun, A *53* Shirley Clarke
Dance Little Lady *54* Val Guest
Dance Macabre *57* László Ranódy
Dance Madness *25* Robert Z. Leonard
Dance Magic *27* Victor Halperin
Dance Movie *63* Andy Warhol
Dance of Death *16* Yakov Protazanov
Dance of Death *19* Otto Rippert
Dance of Death, The *28* George J. Banfield, Leslie Eveleigh
Dance of Death, The *38* Gerald Blake
Dance of Death *59* Jacques Nahum
Dance of Death, The *68* David Giles
Dance of Life, The *29* John Cromwell, A. Edward Sutherland
Dance of Life, The *51* Walter Strate
Dance of the Damned *88* Katt Shea Ruben
Dance of the Dolls *87* Helvécio Ratton
Dance of the Dwarfs *83* Gus Trikonis
Dance of the Heron, The *66* Fons Rademakers
Dance of the Jungle, The *37* Pál Fejös
Dance of the Looney Spoons *59* Stan Vanderbeek

Dance of the Vampire *14* Yakov Protazanov
Dance of the Vampires *67* Roman Polanski
Dance of the Widow *83* Chang-ho Lee
Dance or Die *23* Erle C. Kenton
Dance or Die *88* Richard Munchkin
Dance, Pretty Lady *31* Anthony Asquith
Dance Program, A *36* Julien Duvivier
Dance Programme, The *36* Julien Duvivier
Dance Squared *63* Norman McLaren
Dance Team *31* Sidney Lanfield
Dance Training *24* Teinosuke Kinugasa
Dance with a Stranger *85* Mike Newell
Dance with Me Henry *56* Charles Barton
Dancer, The *51* Mikio Naruse
Dancer, The *89* Masahiro Shinoda
Dancer and the King, The *14* E. Artaud
Dancer and the Vampire, The *59* Renato Polselli
Dancer of Barcelona, The *27* Robert Wiene
Dancer of Izu *33* Heinosuke Gosho
Dancer of Paris, The *26* Alfred Santell
Dancer of the Nile, The *23* William P. S. Earle
Dancers, The *25* Emmett J. Flynn
Dancers, The *30* Chandler Sprague
Dancers *87* Herbert Ross
Dancer's Dream, The *05* J. H. Martin
Dancer's Dream, The *12* Stuart Kinder
Dancers in the Dark *32* David Burton
Dancers of Tomorrow *39* Kozaburo Yoshimura
Dancer's Peril, The *17* Travers Vale
Dancer's Revenge, The *15* Forest Holger-Madsen
Dancer's Strange Dream, A *15* Forest Holger-Madsen
Dances in Japan *58* Susumu Hani
Dances with Wolves *90* Kevin Costner
Dancin' Fool, The *20* Sam Wood
Dancing, El *35* Moglia Barth
Dancing Bull *90* Allen Fong
Dancing Cheat, The *24* Irving Cummings
Dancing Co-Ed *39* S. Sylvan Simon
Dancing Days *26* Albert Kelley
Dancing Doll *12* Dave Fleischer
Dancing Dynamite *31* Noel Mason Smith
Dancing Feet *29* George Archainbaud
Dancing Feet *36* Joseph Santley
Dancing Fool, The *32* Dave Fleischer
Dancing Fool, The *34* Murray Roth
Dancing Girl, The *08* Alf Collins
Dancing Girl, The *12* Edwin J. Collins
Dancing Girl, The *15* Allan Dwan
Dancing Girl *51* Mikio Naruse
Dancing Girl from Izu *33* Heinosuke Gosho
Dancing Girl of Butte, The *10* D. W. Griffith
Dancing Girls *1896* Birt Acres
Dancing Girls, Jardin de Paris *1897* Georges Méliès
Dancing Girls of Izu *33* Heinosuke Gosho
Dancing Heart, The *58* Wolfgang Liebeneiner
Dancing in a Harem *1897* Georges Méliès

Dancing in Manhattan *44* Henry Levin
Dancing in the Dark *49* Irving Reis
Dancing in the Dark *86* Leon Marr
Dancing Ladies *45* Will Jason
Dancing Lady *33* Robert Z. Leonard
Dancing Lesson, The *15* Harry S. Palmer
Dancing Mad *25* Alexander Korda
Dancing Man *34* Albert Ray
Dancing Masters, The *43* Malcolm St. Clair
Dancing Midget, The *01* Georges Méliès
Dancing Mothers *26* Herbert Brenon
Dancing Niggers *1899* C. Goodwin Norton
Dancing on a Dime *40* Joseph Santley
Dancing on the Moon *35* Dave Fleischer
Dancing on Water *86* Jovan Acin
Dancing Paradise *82* Pupi Avati
Dancing Partner, The *31* Jack Conway
Dancing Pirate, The *36* Lloyd Corrigan
Dancing Princess *51* Mikio Naruse
Dancing Romeo *44* Cy Endfield
Dancing Sweeties *30* Ray Enright
Dancing Tabloids *09* A. E. Coleby
Dancing Thru *46* Victor M. Gover
Dancing Vienna *29* Fred Zelnik
Dancing with Crime *46* John Paddy Carstairs
Dancing Years, The *49* Harold French
Dandelion *86* Juzo Itami
Dandin *88* Roger Planchon
Dandy Dick *34* William Beaudine
Dandy Dick of Bishopsgate *11* Theo Bouwmeester
Dandy Donovan the Gentleman Cracksman *14* J. Wallett Waller
Dandy in Aspic, A *67* Laurence Harvey, Anthony Mann
Dandy Lion, The *40* Dave Fleischer
Dandy, the All-American Girl *76* Jerry Schatzberg
Danfoss *59* Henning Carlsen
Danfoss, Jorden Rundt Døgnet Rundt *59* Henning Carlsen
Danger *23* Clifford S. Elfelt
Danger Ahead *21* Rollin Sturgeon
Danger Ahead *23* William K. Howard
Danger Ahead *35* Albert Herman
Danger Ahead *40* Ralph Staub
Danger Area *43* Henry Cass
Danger by My Side *62* Charles Saunders
Danger de Mort *47* Gilles Grangier
Danger: Diabolik *67* Mario Bava
Danger Flight *39* Howard Bretherton
Danger Game, The *18* Harry A. Pollard
Danger Girl, The *16* Clarence Badger
Danger Girl, The *26* Edward Dillon
Danger, Go Slow *18* Robert Z. Leonard
Danger Grows Wild *66* Terence Young
Danger in Paris *36* Paul Stein
Danger in the House *84* Michel Deville
Danger in the Middle East *59* Michel Clément
Danger in the Pacific *42* Lewis D. Collins
Danger Is a Woman *52* Emil E. Reinert
Danger Island *31* Ray Taylor
Danger Island *38* Herbert I. Leeds
Danger Lights *30* George B. Seitz
Danger Line, The *24* Édouard E. Violet
Danger List *57* Leslie Arliss

Danger—Love at Work *36* Otto Preminger
Danger Man, The *30* Bud Pollard
Danger Mark, The *18* Hugh Ford
Danger on Dartmoor *80* David Eady
Danger on the Air *38* Otis Garrett
Danger on the Danube *61* György Révész
Danger on the River *42* John Rawlins
Danger on Wheels *39* Christy Cabanne
Danger Path, The *16* Francis J. Grandon
Danger Patrol *28* Duke Worne
Danger Patrol *37* Lew Landers
Danger Point, The *22* Lloyd Ingraham
Danger Point *71* John Davis
Danger Quest *26* Harry Joe Brown
Danger Rider, The *28* Henry MacRae
Danger Rides the Range *39* George Sherman
Danger Route *67* Seth Holt
Danger Signal, The *15* George Kleine
Danger Signal, The *24* Erle C. Kenton
Danger Signal *45* Robert Florey
Danger Stalks Near *57* Keisuke Kinoshita
Danger Street *28* Ralph Ince
Danger Street *47* Lew Landers
Danger Tomorrow *60* Terry Bishop
Danger Trail, The *17* Frederick Thompson
Danger Trail *28* Noel Mason Smith
Danger Trails *35* Robert F. Hill
Danger Valley *37* Robert North Bradbury
Danger Vient de l'Espace, Le *58* Paolo Heusch
Danger Within *18* Rea Berger
Danger Within *59* Don Chaffey
Danger Woman *46* Lewis D. Collins
Danger! Women at Work *43* Sam Newfield
Danger Zone, The *18* Frank Beal
Danger Zone, The *25* Robert North Bradbury
Danger Zone *51* William Berke
Danger Zone, The *87* Henry Vernon
Danger Zone II: Reaper's Revenge *89* Geoffrey G. Bowers
Dangerous *35* Alfred E. Green
Dangerous Acquaintance *41* Horace Shepherd
Dangerous Adventure, A *20* Jack Warner, Sam Warner
Dangerous Adventure, A *37* D. Ross Lederman
Dangerous Adventure, The *40* Ramón Peón
Dangerous Affair, A *19* Charles Miller
Dangerous Affair, A *31* Edward Sedgwick
Dangerous Afternoon *61* Charles Saunders
Dangerous Age, The *11* August Blom
Dangerous Age, The *22* John M. Stahl
Dangerous Age *33* William A. Wellman
Dangerous Age, A *38* Arthur Lubin
Dangerous Age, A *57* Sidney J. Furie
Dangerous Agent *53* Jean Sacha
Dangerous Assignment *50* Ben R. Hart
Dangerous Blonde, The *24* Robert F. Hill
Dangerous Blondes *43* Leigh Jason
Dangerous Business *20* Roy William Neill
Dangerous Business *46* D. Ross Lederman
Dangerous Cargo *39* Harold Huth
Dangerous Cargo *54* John Harlow
Dangerous Charter *62* Robert Gottschalk
Dangerous Charter *64* John Sherwood

Dangerous Comment *40* John Paddy Carstairs
Dangerous Companions *34* A. N. C. Macklin
Dangerous Corner *34* Phil Rosen
Dangerous Coward, The *24* Albert S. Rogell
Dangerous Crossing *53* Joseph M. Newman
Dangerous Crossroads *33* Lambert Hillyer
Dangerous Curve Ahead *21* E. Mason Hopper
Dangerous Curves *29* Lothar Mendes
Dangerous Curves *88* David Lewis
Dangerous Curves Behind *25* Edward F. Cline
Dangerous Dan McFoo *39* Tex Avery
Dangerous Davies, the Last Detective *80* Val Guest
Dangerous Days *20* Reginald Barker
Dangerous Days *33* William A. Wellman
Dangerous Dub, The *26* Richard Thorpe
Dangerous Dude, The *26* Harry Joe Brown
Dangerous Encounter—First Kind *80* Hark Tsui
Dangerous Enemy *34* Spencer G. Bennet
Dangerous Exile *57* Brian Desmond Hurst
Dangerous Female *31* Roy Del Ruth
Dangerous Fingers *37* Norman Lee
Dangerous Flirt, The *24* Tod Browning
Dangerous Flirtation, A *24* Tod Browning
Dangerous Friend, A *71* Barry Shear
Dangerous Friends *26* Finis Fox
Dangerous Game, A *22* King Baggot
Dangerous Game, A *41* John Rawlins
Dangerous Game *88* Stephen Hopkins
Dangerous Games *58* Pierre Chénal
Dangerous Golfers *05* Percy Stow
Dangerous Ground *32* Richard Thorpe
Dangerous Ground *34* Norman Walker
Dangerous Holiday *37* Nicholas Barrows
Dangerous Hour *23* William Hughes Curran
Dangerous Hours *19* Fred Niblo
Dangerous Houses *52* Curtis Harrington
Dangerous Inheritance *50* Lew Landers
Dangerous Innocence *25* William A. Seiter
Dangerous Intrigue *36* David Selman
Dangerous Intruder *45* Vernon Keays
Dangerous Kiss, The *61* Yuzo Kawashima
Dangerous Lady *41* Bernard B. Ray
Dangerous Liaisons *59* Roger Vadim
Dangerous Liaisons *88* Stephen Frears
Dangerous Liaisons 1960 *59* Roger Vadim
Dangerous Lies *21* Paul Powell
Dangerous Little Demon, The *22* Clarence Badger
Dangerous Love *88* Marty Ollstein
Dangerous Love Affairs *59* Roger Vadim
Dangerous Lunatic, The *00* Georges Méliès
Dangerous Maid, The *23* Victor Heerman
Dangerous Man, A *35* Richard Kahn
Dangerous Medicine *38* Arthur Woods
Dangerous Millions *46* James Tinling
Dangerous Mission *54* Louis King
Dangerous Mists *44* Lew Landers
Dangerous Moment, The *21* Marcel De

Sano
Dangerous Money *24* Frank Tuttle
Dangerous Money *46* Terry Morse
Dangerous Moonlight *41* Brian Desmond Hurst
Dangerous Moves *83* Richard Dembo
Dangerous Nan McGrew *30* Malcolm St. Clair
Dangerous Number *36* Richard Thorpe
Dangerous Orphans *86* John Laing
Dangerous Paradise, The *20* William P. S. Earle
Dangerous Paradise *30* William A. Wellman
Dangerous Paradise *31* Rune Carlsten
Dangerous Partners *45* Edward L. Cahn
Dangerous Pass, Mont Blanc, A *1897* Georges Méliès
Dangerous Passage *44* William Berke
Dangerous Pastime *21* James W. Horne
Dangerous Paths *21* Duke Worne
Dangerous Play, A *12* Edward Schnedler-Sørensen
Dangerous Pleasure *25* Harry Revier
Dangerous Profession, A *49* Ted Tetzlaff
Dangerous Relations *73* J. Ford Bell
Dangerous Roads *42* Anders Henrikson
Dangerous Seas *31* Edward Dryhurst
Dangerous Secrets *38* Edmond T. Gréville
Dangerous Spring *48* Arne Mattsson
Dangerous Summer, A *81* Quentin Masters
Dangerous Talent, The *20* George L. Cox
Dangerous to Know *38* Robert Florey
Dangerous to Live *39* Anthony Hankey, Leslie Norman
Dangerous to Men *20* William Dowlan
Dangerous Toys *21* Samuel Bradley
Dangerous Traffic *26* Bennett Cohn
Dangerous Trails *23* Alvin J. Neitz
Dangerous Venture *47* George Archainbaud
Dangerous Voyage *54* Vernon Sewell
Dangerous Waters *19* Joseph Franz
Dangerous Waters *36* Lambert Hillyer
Dangerous When Wet *53* Charles Walters
Dangerous Woman, A *29* Rowland V. Lee
Dangerous Years *47* Arthur Pierson
Dangerous Youth *53* Lau Lauritzen, Jr.
Dangerous Youth *57* Herbert Wilcox
Dangerously Close *86* Albert Pyun
Dangerously They Live *41* Robert Florey
Dangerously Yours *33* Frank Tuttle
Dangerously Yours *37* Malcolm St. Clair
Dangers de l'Alcoolisme, Les *1896* Alice Guy-Blaché
Dangers of the Canadian Mounted *48* Fred C. Brannon, Yakima Canutt
Dangers of the Engagement Period *29* Fred Sauer
Daniel *83* Sidney Lumet
Daniel and the Devil *40* William Dieterle
Daniel Boone *07* Edwin S. Porter
Daniel Boone *36* David Howard
Daniel Boone—Frontier Trail Rider *66* George Sherman
Daniel Boone Thru the Wilderness *26* Robert North Bradbury, Frank S. Mattison
Daniel Boone, Trail Blazer *56* Albert C. Gannaway, Ismael Rodríguez

Daniel Deronda *21* Walter C. Rowden
Daniel Takes a Train *83* Pál Sándor
Daniele Cortis *47* Mario Soldati
Daniella by Night *62* Max Pecas
Danilo Treles, o Fimismenos Andalousianos Mousikos *86* Stavros Tornes
Danilo Treles, the Famous Andalusian Musician *86* Stavros Tornes
Danish Brigade in Sweden *45* Bjarne Henning-Jensen
Danish Design *60* Jørgen Roos
Danish Island *44* Bjarne Henning-Jensen
Danish Motorboat Story *53* Henning Carlsen
Danish Village Church, The *47* Carl Theodor Dreyer
Daniya, Jardín del Harem *88* Carlos Mira
Danjuro Sandai *44* Kenji Mizoguchi
Dann Ist Nichts Mehr Wie Vorher *87* Gerd Roman Forsch
Dann Schon Lieber Lebertran *30* Max Ophüls
Dannati della Terra, I *68* Valentino Orsini
D'Annunzio *87* Sergio Nasca
Danny *79* Gene Feldman
Danny Boy *34* Oswald Mitchell, Challis Sanderson
Danny Boy *41* Oswald Mitchell
Danny Boy *46* Terry Morse
Danny Boy *82* Neil Jordan
Danny Jones *72* Jules Bricken
Danny the Dragon *66* C. M. Pennington-Richards
Danny Travis *78* Roy Boulting
Danryū *39* Kozaburo Yoshimura
Dans la Brousse *12* Louis Feuillade
Dans la Nuit *29* Charles Vanel
Dans la Poussière du Soleil *71* Richard Balducci
Dans la Rafale *16* Georges Lacroix
Dans la Vallée d'Ossau *12* Émile Cohl
Dans la Vie *11* Louis Feuillade
Dans la Ville Blanche *82* Alain Tanner
Dans le Vent *63* Jacques Rozier
Dans le Ventre du Dragon *88* Yves Simoneau
Dans les Coulisses *1897* Georges Méliès
Dans les Coulisses *00* Alice Guy-Blaché
Dans les Griffes du Maniaque *65* Jesús Franco
Dans les Remous *18* Mauritz Stiller
Dans les Rues *33* Victor Trivas
Dans l'Ouragan de la Vie *16* Germaine Dulac
Dan's Motel *82* Jerry R. Barrish
Dans un Miroir *84* Raúl Ruiz
Dans une Île Perdue *30* Alberto Cavalcanti
Dans van de Reiger, De *66* Fons Rademakers
Danse au Sérail *1897* Georges Méliès
Danse Basque *01* Alice Guy-Blaché
Danse de l'Ivresse *00* Alice Guy-Blaché
Danse des Saisons, La *00* Alice Guy-Blaché
Danse du Feu, La *1899* Georges Méliès
Danse du Papillon *00* Alice Guy-Blaché
Danse du Pas des Foulards par des Almées *00* Alice Guy-Blaché
Danse du Ventre, La *01* Alice Guy-Blaché

Danse Fleur de Lotus *1897* Alice Guy-Blaché
Danse Macabre *32* Widgey R. Newman
Danse Macabre, La *63* Sergio Corbucci, Antonio Margheriti
Danse Mauresque *02* Alice Guy-Blaché
Danse Serpentine *1896* Georges Méliès
Danserinden *13* Forest Holger-Madsen
Danserindens Hævn *15* Forest Holger-Madsen
Danserindens Kærlighedsdrøm *15* Forest Holger-Madsen
Danses *00* Alice Guy-Blaché
Danses *28* Abel Gance
Danses Espagnoles *00* Louis Lumière
Danseuse de Marrakech, La *49* Léon Mathot
Danseuse Microscopique, La *01* Georges Méliès
Danseuse Orchidée, La *28* Léonce Perret
Danseuse Voilée, La *17* Maurice Mariaud
Danseuses au Jardin de Paris *1897* Georges Méliès
Danseuses da la Mer, Les *60* Jean Painlevé
Danske Politi i Sverige, Det *45* Astrid Henning-Jensen
Danske Sydhavsøer, De *44* Bjarne Henning-Jensen
Danstävlingen i Esira *37* Pál Fejös
Dante e Beatrice *12* Mario Caserini
Dante's Inferno *24* Henry Otto
Dante's Inferno *35* Harry Lachman
Danton *21* Dmitri Buchowetzki
Danton *31* Hans Behrendt
Danton *82* Andrzej Wajda
Danube — Fishes — Birds, The *71* István Szabó
Danube Waves, The *63* Liviu Ciulei
Danulon Gyártás *61* Márta Mészáros
Danulon Production *61* Márta Mészáros
Danun *24* Kajiro Yamamoto
Danza delle Ore, La *20* Luigi Maggi
Danza Macabra, La *63* Sergio Corbucci, Antonio Margheriti
Danzatrice della Taverna Nera *14* Emilio Ghione
Dao Ma Dan *86* Hark Tsui
Daoma Zei *85* Zhuangzhuang Tian
Daphné *09* Léonce Perret
Daphne *36* Roberto Rossellini
Daphne, The *67* Yasuke Chiba
Daphne and the Dean *13* Fred Rains
Daphne and the Pirate *16* Christy Cabanne
Daphnie, La *25* Jean Painlevé
Daphnis and Chloe *30* Orestes Laskos
Daraku Suru Onna *67* Kozaburo Yoshimura
Dařbuján a Pandrhola *60* Martin Frič
Darby and Joan *19* Percy Nash
Darby and Joan *37* Syd Courtenay
Darby O'Gill and the Little People *58* Robert Stevenson
Darby's Rangers *57* William A. Wellman
Dare-Deviltry *36* David Miller
Dare to Say No *76* Khodzhakuli Narliev
Daredevil, The *18* Francis J. Grandon
Daredevil *19* M. Narokov, Nikandr Turkin
Daredevil, The *19* Edward J. LeSaint
Daredevil, The *20* James P. Hogan

Daredevil, The *20* Tom Mix
Daredevil, The *32* Richard Eichberg
Daredevil, The *71* Robert W. Stringer
Daredevil Dick *31* Noel Mason Smith
Daredevil Drivers, The *38* B. Reeves Eason
Daredevil Droopy *51* Tex Avery
Daredevil in the Castle *61* Hiroshi Inagaki
Daredevil Jack *19* W. S. Van Dyke
Daredevil Kate *16* Kenean Buel
Daredevils of Earth *36* Bernard Vorhaus
Daredevils of the Clouds *48* George Blair
Daredevils of the Red Circle *39* John English, William Witney
Daredevils of the West *43* John English
Daredevil's Reward *28* Eugene Forde
Dárek *46* Jiří Trnka
Daring Caballero, The *49* Wallace Fox
Daring Chances *24* Clifford Smith
Daring Circus Youth *53* S. Gurov, Yuri Ozerov
Daring Danger *22* Clifford Smith
Daring Danger *32* D. Ross Lederman
Daring Daughters *33* Christy Cabanne
Daring Daylight Burglary, A *03* Frank Mottershaw
Daring Days *25* John B. O'Brien
Daring Deeds *27* Duke Worne
Daring Dobermans, The *73* Byron Chudnow
Daring Game, The *67* Laslo Benedek
Daring Hearts *19* Henri Houry
Daring Love *24* Roland G. Edwards
Daring of Diana, The *16* Sidney Rankin Drew
Daring Years, The *23* Kenneth Webb
Daring Young Man, The *35* William A. Seiter
Daring Young Man, The *42* Frank R. Strayer
Daring Youth *24* William Beaudine
Dariya Dil *88* K. Ravishankar
Dark, The *69* Michael Armstrong
Dark, The *79* John Cardos
Dark Age *86* Arch Nicholson
Dark Alibi *46* Phil Karlson
Dark Angel, The *25* George Fitzmaurice
Dark Angel, The *35* Sidney Franklin
Dark Angel *90* Craig R. Baxley
Dark at the Top of the Stairs, The *60* Delbert Mann
Dark August *75* Martin Goldman
Dark Avenger, The *55* Henry Levin
Dark Before Dawn *88* Robert Totten
Dark Castle, The *15* Willy Zehn
Dark Circle *82* Chris Beaver, Judy Irving, Ruth Landy
Dark City *50* William Dieterle
Dark Command *40* Raoul Walsh
Dark Corner, The *46* Henry Hathaway
Dark Crystal, The *82* Jim Henson, Frank Oz
Dark Delusion *47* Willis Goldbeck
Dark Dreams of August *67* Miguel Picazo
Dark End of the Street, The *81* Jan Egleson
Dark Endeavour *33* Elmer Clifton
Dark Enemy *84* Colin Finbow
Dark Eyes *35* Victor Tourjansky
Dark Eyes *80* James Polakoff
Dark Eyes *87* Nikita Mikhalkov

Dark Eyes of London *39* Walter Summers
Dark Eyes of London, The *61* Alfred Vohrer
Dark Forces *80* Simon Wincer
Dark Glow of the Mountains, The *84* Werner Herzog
Dark Habits *83* Pedro Almodóvar
Dark Hazard *34* Alfred E. Green
Dark Horse, The *32* Alfred E. Green
Dark Horse, The *46* Will Jason
Dark Hour, The *36* Charles Lamont
Dark Interlude *55* Paul Wendkos
Dark Interval *50* Charles Saunders
Dark Intruder *65* Harvey Hart
Dark Is the Night *45* Boris Barnet
Dark Journey *37* Victor Saville
Dark Lantern, A *20* John S. Robertson
Dark Light, The *51* Vernon Sewell
Dark Magic *39* Roy Rowland
Dark Man, The *50* Jeffrey Dell
Dark Manhattan *37* Harry Fraser
Dark Mirror, The *20* Charles Giblyn
Dark Mirror *46* Robert Siodmak
Dark Mountain *44* William Berke
Dark Moves *74* Austin Hunt
Dark Night *86* Fred Tan
Dark Obsession *89* Nicholas Broomfield
Dark Odyssey *61* William Kyriakys, Radley Metzger
Dark of the Night *85* Gaylene Preston
Dark of the Sun *67* Jack Cardiff
Dark Page, The *31* John Cromwell
Dark Page, The *51* Phil Karlson
Dark Passage *47* Delmer Daves
Dark Past, The *48* Rudolph Maté
Dark Places *72* Don Sharp
Dark Purpose *63* George Marshall, Vittorio Sala
Dark Rapture *38* Armand Denis
Dark Red Roses *29* Sinclair Hill
Dark River *52* Hugo Del Carril
Dark Road, The *17* Charles Miller
Dark Road, The *48* Alfred Goulding
Dark Room of Damocles, The *63* Fons Rademakers
Dark Sands *37* Thornton Freeland
Dark Secret *49* Maclean Rogers
Dark Secrets *23* Victor Fleming
Dark Shadows *44* Paul Burnford
Dark Shadows *70* Dan Curtis
Dark Side of the Moon, The *86* Erik Clausen
Dark Side of the Moon *90* D. J. Webster
Dark Side of Tomorrow, The *70* Jacques Deerson, Barbara Peeters
Dark Silence, The *16* Albert Capellani
Dark Skies *30* Harry Hoyt, Harry S. Webb
Dark Stairway, The *38* Arthur Woods
Dark Stairway, The *53* Ken Hughes
Dark Stairways *24* Robert F. Hill
Dark Star, The *19* Allan Dwan
Dark Star *74* John Carpenter
Dark Streets *29* Frank Lloyd
Dark Streets of Cairo *40* Leslie Kardos
Dark Sun, The *90* Damiano Damiani
Dark Sunday *78* Jimmy Huston
Dark Sunlight *66* Denys De la Patellière
Dark Swan, The *24* Millard Webb
Dark Tower, The *43* John Harlow
Dark Tower *87* Freddie Francis

Dark Venture *56* John Calvert
Dark Victory *39* Edmund Goulding
Dark Warrior *84* Robert Clouse
Dark Water *80* Andrew Bogle
Dark Waters *44* André De Toth
Dark World *35* Bernard Vorhaus
Darkened Rooms *29* Louis Gasnier
Darkened Skies *30* Harry Hoyt, Harry S. Webb
Darkening Trail, The *15* William S. Hart, Clifford Smith
Darker Than Amber *70* Robert Clouse
Darkest Africa *21* Raoul Barré, Charles Bowers
Darkest Africa *36* B. Reeves Eason, Joseph Kane
Darkest Hour, The *20* Paul Scardon
Darkest Hour, The *55* Frank Tuttle
Darkest London *15* Bert Haldane
Darkest London, or The Dancer's Romance *15* Bert Haldane
Darkest Russia *17* Travers Vale
Darkman *90* Sam Raimi
Darkness *23* George A. Cooper
Darkness and Daylight *23* Albert Plummer
Darkness at Noon *56* Tadashi Imai
Darkness in Daytime *63* Zoltán Fábri
Darktown Belle, The *13* Mack Sennett
Darktown Strutters *75* William Witney
Darlin' *22* Alfred E. Green
Darling *34* Martin Frič
Darling *65* John Schlesinger
Darling, Do You Love Me? *69* Martin Sharp, Bob Whittaker
Darling Dolly Gray *26* Dave Fleischer
Darling, How Could You? *51* Mitchell Leisen
Darling I Am Growing Younger *52* Howard Hawks
Darling, I Surrender *43* Gustaf Molander
Darling Lili *69* Blake Edwards
Darling Lili, Where Were You the Night I Shot Down Baron Von Richthofen? *69* Blake Edwards
Darling Mine *20* Lawrence Trimble
Darling of New York, The *23* King Baggot
Darling of Paris, The *17* J. Gordon Edwards
Darling of the Gods *30* Hans Schwarz
Darling of the Rich, The *22* John G. Adolfi
Darling Puggy *05* Alf Collins
Darò un Milione *35* Mario Camerini
Darse Cuenta *85* Alejandro Doria
Darskab, Dyd og Driveri *23* Forest Holger-Madsen
D'Artagnan *16* Charles Swickard
Darts Are Trumps *38* Maclean Rogers
Darwaza *78* R. Tulsi Ramsay, Shyam Ramsay
Darwin Adventure, The *72* Jack Couffer
Darwin Was Right *24* Lewis Seiler
Darwin's Theory of Evolution *25* Max Fleischer
Darya *64* Ebrahim Golestan
Das War Buffalo Bill *62* Mario Costa
Dash for Help, A *09* Dave Aylott
Dash for Liberty, A *08* Dave Aylott

Dash for Liberty, A *13* August Blom
Dash for Liberty, or The Convict's Escape and Capture, A *03* William Haggar
Dash of Courage, A *16* Charlie Chase
Dash Through the Clouds, A *12* Mack Sennett
Dash with the Despatches, A *04* Frank Mottershaw
Dashing North *21* Frank Moser
Date at Midnight *59* Godfrey Grayson
Date Bait *60* O'Dale Ireland
Date for Marriage *56* Kozaburo Yoshimura
Date in the Milky Way, The *87* Ianas Streitch
Date to Skate, A *38* Dave Fleischer
Date with a Dream, A *48* Dicky Leeman
Date with a Lonely Girl, A *71* Herbert Ross
Date with an Angel, A *42* Charles Lamont
Date with an Angel *87* Tom McLoughlin
Date with Death, A *59* Harold Daniels
Date with Death, A *64* Ralph Thomas
Date with Destiny, A *40* Tim Whelan
Date with Destiny, A *48* Joseph H. Lewis
Date with Disaster *57* Charles Saunders
Date with Dizzy, A *58* John Hubley
Date with Duke, A *46* George Pal
Date with Judy, A *48* Richard Thorpe
Date with the Falcon, A *41* Irving Reis
Dateline Diamonds *65* Jeremy Summers
Dauda Sorko *67* Jean Rouch
Daughter, A *26* Heinosuke Gosho
Daughter, The *49* Lotte Reiniger
Daughter, The *78* Alberto Lattuada
Daughter Angele *18* William Dowlan
Daughter-in-Law, The *72* Khodzhakuli Narliev
Daughter in Revolt, A *27* Harry Hughes
Daughter of a Werewolf *76* Salvatore Di Silvestro
Daughter of Belgium, A *14* F. Martin Thornton
Daughter of Brahma, A *18* August Blom
Daughter of Cleopatra *60* Fernando Cerchio, Richard McNamara
Daughter of Darkness *47* Lance Comfort
Daughter of Dawn, The *20* Norbert Myles
Daughter of Deceit *51* Luis Buñuel
Daughter of Destiny *17* George Irving
Daughter of Destiny, A *27* Henryk Galeen
Daughter of Dr. Jekyll *57* Edgar G. Ulmer
Daughter of Don Q *46* Spencer G. Bennet*
Daughter of England, A *15* Leedham Bantock
Daughter of Eve, A *19* Walter West
Daughter of Evil *30* Richard Oswald
Daughter of France, A *18* Edmund Lawrence
Daughter of Frankenstein, The *71* Miguel Delgado
Daughter of Frankenstein, The *71* Ernst R. von Theumer
Daughter of Garcia, Brigand, The *14* Dave Aylott
Daughter of Horror *55* John Parker
Daughter of Israel, A *14* Van Dyke Brooke
Daughter of Israel, A *26* Edward José

Daughter of Liberty, A *11* Allan Dwan
Daughter of Love, A *25* Walter West
Daughter of Love *53* Youssef Wahby
Daughter of Luxury, A *22* Paul Powell
Daughter of Luxury *31* Jack Conway, Robert Z. Leonard
Daughter of MacGregor, The *16* Sidney Olcott
Daughter of Madame X, The *17* Aleksander Hertz
Daughter of Maryland, A *17* John B. O'Brien
Daughter of Mata Hari *54* Carmine Gallone, Renzo Merusi
Daughter of Mine *19* Clarence Badger
Daughter of Romany, The *13* Charles Brabin
Daughter of Rosie O'Grady, The *42* Jean Negulesco
Daughter of Rosie O'Grady, The *50* David Butler
Daughter of Satan, A *14* Edwin J. Collins
Daughter of Shanghai *37* Robert Florey
Daughter of the City, A *15* Elisha H. Calvert
Daughter of the Confederacy *13* George Melford, Sidney Olcott
Daughter of the Congo, A *30* Oscar Micheaux
Daughter of the Don, The *17* Henry Kabierske
Daughter of the Dragon *31* Lloyd Corrigan
Daughter of the Fortune Teller, The *11* August Blom
Daughter of the Gods, A *16* Herbert Brenon
Daughter of the High Mountain *14* Victor Sjöström
Daughter of the Hills, A *13* J. Searle Dawley
Daughter of the Jungle *49* George Blair
Daughter of the Law, A *21* Jack Conway
Daughter of the Mountain *14* Victor Sjöström
Daughter of the Navajos, A *11* Alice Guy-Blaché
Daughter of the Night—Psalm 69, A *27* Charles Barnett
Daughter of the Nile *87* Hsiao-hsien Hou
Daughter of the Old South, A *18* Émile Chautard
Daughter of the Orient *37* Robert Florey
Daughter of the Peaks *14* Victor Sjöström
Daughter of the People, A *15* J. Searle Dawley
Daughter of the Poor, A *17* Edward Dillon
Daughter of the Railway, The *11* August Blom
Daughter of the Regiment *27* H. B. Parkinson
Daughter of the Revolution, A *11* Edwin S. Porter
Daughter of the Sands *48* André Zwoboda
Daughter of the Sea, A *15* Charles M. Seay
Daughter of the Sioux, A *25* Ben F. Wilson
Daughter of the Storm *54* Leopold Lindt-

berg
Daughter of the Sun *62* Herschell Gordon Lewis
Daughter of the Sun God *62* Kenneth Herts
Daughter of the Tong *39* Raymond K. Johnson
Daughter of the West, A *18* William Bertram
Daughter of the West *49* Harold Daniels
Daughter of the Wilds *17* Frank Wilson
Daughter of the Wolf *19* Irvin Willat
Daughter of Two Worlds *20* James Young
Daughter Pays, The *20* Robert Ellis
Daughters Courageous *39* Michael Curtiz
Daughters, Daughters *75* Moshe Mizrahi
Daughters of China *49* Zhifeng Ling, Jiang Zhai
Daughters of Darkness *70* Harry Kümel
Daughters of Desire *29* Burton L. King
Daughters of Destiny *52* Christian-Jaque, Jean Delannoy, Marcello Pagliero
Daughters of Dracula *74* José Ramón Larraz
Daughters of Fire *78* Walter Hugo Khouri
Daughters of Men *14* George Terwilliger
Daughters of Pleasure *24* William Beaudine
Daughters of Satan *72* Hollingsworth Morse
Daughters of Señor Lopez, The *12* Allan Dwan
Daughters of the Night *24* Elmer Clifton
Daughters of the Rich *23* Louis Gasnier
Daughters of the Vampire *60* Piero Regnoli
Daughters of Today *24* Rollin Sturgeon
Daughters of Today *33* F. W. Krämer
Daughters of Yoshiwara *55* Heinosuke Gosho
Daughter's Strange Inheritance, A *15* Van Dyke Brooke
Daughters Who Pay *25* George Terwilliger
Daughters, Wives and a Mother *60* Mikio Naruse
Daughters, Wives and Mothers *60* Mikio Naruse
Daumier *58* Roger Leenhardt
Dauphine Java, La *60* Alexander Alexeïeff, Claire Parker
Dauphins et Cétacés *49* Jacques-Yves Cousteau
Dav Pech *89* Kamal Sharma
Davanti a Lui Tremava Tutta Roma *46* Carmine Gallone
Dave Craggs, Detective *10* Lewin Fitzhamon
Dave's Love Affair *11* Mack Sennett
Davey Jones' Locker *66* Frederic Goode
David *51* Paul Dickson
David *61* Richard Leacock, D. A. Pennebaker
David *79* Peter Lilienthal
David and Bathsheba *51* Henry King
David and Goliath *60* Ferdinando Baldi, Richard Pottier
David and Golightly *61* James Hill
David and Jonathan *20* Alexander Butler
David and Lisa *62* Frank Perry
David-Bek *44* Amo Bek-Nazarov

David Copperfield *13* Thomas Bentley
David Copperfield *22* Anders Wilhelm Sandberg
David Copperfield *34* George Cukor
David Copperfield *70* Delbert Mann
David e Golia *60* Ferdinando Baldi, Richard Pottier
David Garrick *12* Percy Nash
David Garrick *13* Leedham Bantock
David Garrick *13* Hay Plumb
David Garrick *16* Frank Lloyd
David Garrick *28* George J. Banfield, Leslie Eveleigh
David Golder *30* Julien Duvivier
David Gorelick *31* Grigori Roshal
David Harding, Counterspy *50* Ray Nazarro
David Harum *15* Allan Dwan
David Harum *34* James Cruze
David Holzman's Diary *67* Jim McBride
David Livingstone *36* James A. Fitzpatrick
David Lynn's Sculpture *61* Bruce Baillie
Davy *57* Michael Relph
Davy Crockett *16* William Desmond Taylor
Davy Crockett and the River Pirates *55* Norman Foster
Davy Crockett at the Fall of the Alamo *26* Robert North Bradbury
Davy Crockett, Indian Scout *49* Lew Landers
Davy Crockett—King of the Wild Frontier *54* Norman Foster
Davy Jones *33* Ubbe Iwerks
Dawandeh *85* Amir Naderi
Dawn, The *14* Donald Crisp
Dawn *17* H. Lisle Lucoque
Dawn *19* J. Stuart Blackton
Dawn *28* Herbert Wilcox
Dawn *33* Yu Sun
Dawn, The *36* Thomas G. Cooper
Dawn *44* Arne Sucksdorff
Dawn, The *56* Mrinal Sen
Dawn *71* István Szabó
Dawn *79* Ken Hannam
Dawn, The *86* Miklós Jancsó
Dawn at Socorro *54* George Sherman
Dawn Breakers *76* Laurence Boulting
Dawn Comes Late *53* John Christian
Dawn Express, The *42* Albert Herman
Dawn Guard *41* Roy Boulting
Dawn in Manchuria *32* Kenji Mizoguchi
Dawn in Paris *37* Grigori Roshal
Dawn in the Boulevard *36* Mikio Naruse
Dawn Killer, The *59* Donald Taylor
Dawn Maker, The *16* William S. Hart
Dawn of a New Day *64* Youssef Chahine
Dawn of a Tomorrow *15* James Kirkwood
Dawn of a Tomorrow, The *24* George Melford
Dawn of Freedom, The *16* Theodore Marston, Paul Scardon
Dawn of Hope, The *86* Süreyya Duru
Dawn of India *56* Roman Karmen
Dawn of Life, The *32* James Flood, Elliott Nugent
Dawn of Love, The *16* Edwin Carewe
Dawn of Manchukuo and Mongolia, The *32* Kenji Mizoguchi
Dawn of Manchuria and Mongolia, The *32* Kenji Mizoguchi

Dawn of Mongolia, The *32* Kenji Mizoguchi
Dawn of Passion, The *12* Allan Dwan
Dawn of Revenge *22* Bernard Sievel
Dawn of the Dead *77* George Romero
Dawn of the Doomed Gold Mine, The *87* Arya Dashiev
Dawn of the East *21* Edward H. Griffith
Dawn of the Founding of Manchukuo and Mongolia, The *32* Kenji Mizoguchi
Dawn of the Great Divide *42* Howard Bretherton
Dawn of the Mummy *81* Frank Agrama, Armand Weston
Dawn of Truth, The *20* L. C. MacBean
Dawn of Understanding, The *18* David Smith
Dawn on the Great Divide *42* Howard Bretherton
Dawn Over France *45* André Hugon
Dawn Over Ireland *36* Thomas G. Cooper
Dawn Over Russia *47* Sergei Yutkevich
Dawn Patrol, The *30* Howard Hawks
Dawn Patrol, The *38* Edmund Goulding
Dawn Rider, The *35* Robert North Bradbury
Dawn to Dawn *33* Josef Berne
Dawn Trail, The *30* Christy Cabanne
Dawning, The *88* Robert Knights
Dawns Are Quiet Here, The *72* Stanislav Rostotsky
Day, The *60* Peter Finch, Yolande Turner
Day After, The *09* D. W. Griffith
Day After, The *65* Robert Parrish
Day After Day *43* Mikhail Slutsky
Day After Halloween, The *79* Simon Wincer
Day After the Divorce, The *40* Paul Verhoeven
Day After Tomorrow, The *45* Arch Oboler
Day After Trinity: J. Robert Oppenheimer and the Atomic Bomb, The *81* Jon Else
Day and Night *86* Jean-Bernard Menoud
Day and the Hour, The *62* René Clément
Day at Brighton, A *04* Alf Collins
Day at the Beach, A *70* Simon Hesera
Day at the Circus, A *01* Edwin S. Porter
Day at the Races, A *37* Sam Wood
Day at the Zoo, A *39* Tex Avery
Day Before, The *87* Giuliano Montaldo
Day Dreams *18* Clarence Badger
Day Dreams *21* Hy Mayer
Day Dreams *22* Edward F. Cline, Buster Keaton
Day Dreams *28* Ivor Montagu
Day Duty *07* A. E. Coleby
Day for Night *73* François Truffaut
Day in Camp, A *17* Raoul Barré, Charles Bowers
Day in Camp with the Volunteers, A *02* James A. Williamson
Day in Court, A *53* Steno
Day in Jerusalem, A *12* Sidney Olcott
Day in London, A *12* Lewin Fitzhamon
Day in Moscow, A *57* R. Grigoryev, I. M. Poselsky
Day in the Country, A *12* Lewin Fitzhamon
Day in the Country, A *36* Jean Renoir
Day in the Death of Joe Egg, A *70* Peter Medak
Day in the Life, A *46* Alessandro Blasetti
Day in the Life of a Dog, A *17* Will Anderson
Day in the New World, A *40* Roman Karmen
Day It Came to Earth, The *79* Harry Thomason
Day It Rained, The *59* Gerd Oswald
Day Kelly Came Home, The *60* Charles Davis
Day Mars Invaded Earth, The *62* Maury Dexter
Day Nurse *32* Walter Lantz
Day of Anger *67* Tonino Valerii
Day of Darkness *89* Alexander Sokurov
Day of Days, The *14* Daniel Frohman
Day of Faith, The *23* Tod Browning
Day of Fire *68* Paolo Bianchini
Day of Freedom *35* Leni Riefenstahl
Day of Fury, A *56* Harmon Jones
Day of Grace *57* Francis Searle
Day of Happiness, A *63* Josef Heifits
Day of Life, A *46* Alessandro Blasetti
Day of Marriage *56* Kozaburo Yoshimura
Day of Reckoning, The *15* B. Reeves Eason
Day of Reckoning *33* Charles Brabin
Day of Rest, A *15* Toby Cooper
Day of Rest *70* Jim Clark
Day of Sin, A *60* Mauro Bolognini
Day of the Animals *77* William Girdler
Day of the Assassin, The *81* Brian Trenchard-Smith
Day of the Bad Man *58* Harry Keller
Day of the Cobra, The *80* Enzo G. Castellari
Day of the Dead *57* Charles Eames, Ray Eames
Day of the Dead *83* George Romero
Day of the Dolphin, The *73* Mike Nichols
Day of the Evil Gun *68* Jerry Thorpe
Day of the Fight *49* Stanley Kubrick
Day of the Great Adventure, The *36* Josef Leytes
Day of the Hanging, The *63* William F. Claxton
Day of the Jackal, The *73* Fred Zinnemann
Day of the Landgrabbers *68* Nathan Juran
Day of the Locust, The *75* John Schlesinger
Day of the Nightmare *65* John Bushelman
Day of the Nitemare *65* John Bushelman
Day of the Outlaw *59* André De Toth
Day of the Owl, The *68* Damiano Damiani
Day of the Panther, The *87* Brian Trenchard-Smith
Day of the Shoot—Costa-Gavras' "L'Aveu", The *69* Chris Marker
Day of the Triffids, The *62* Freddie Francis, Steve Sekely
Day of the Trumpet, The *57* Eddie Romero
Day of the Victorious Country, The *47* Ilya Kopalin, Irina Setkina
Day of the Wolves *73* Ferde Grofé, Jr.
Day of the Woman *78* Meir Zarchi
Day of Triumph *54* John T. Coyle, Irving
Pichel
Day of Wrath *43* Carl Theodor Dreyer
Day of Wrath *86* Sulambek Mamilov
Day of Youth *30* Joris Ivens
Day Off, A *28* John Foster
Day on His Own, A *06* James A. Williamson
Day on Rollers, A *13* Lewin Fitzhamon
Day on the Grand Canal with the Emperor of China, A *88* Philip Haas
Day Our Lives Shine, The *48* Kozaburo Yoshimura
Day Santa Claus Cried, The *80* Philip Otto
Day Shall Dawn, A *44* Hasse Ekman
Day She Paid, The *19* Rex Ingram
Day Stars *66* Igor Talankin
Day That Shook the World, The *76* Veljko Bulajić
Day the Bookies Wept, The *39* Leslie Goodwins
Day the Clown Cried, The *72* Jerry Lewis
Day the Earth Caught Fire, The *61* Val Guest
Day the Earth Froze, The *59* Holger Harrivirta, Alexander Ptushko, Gregg Sebelious
Day the Earth Got Stoned, The *78* Richard Patterson
Day the Earth Stood Still, The *51* Robert Wise
Day the Fish Came Out, The *67* Michael Cacoyannis
Day the Hot Line Got Hot, The *68* Étienne Périer
Day the Lord Got Busted, The *76* Burt Topper
Day the Rains Came, The *59* Gerd Oswald
Day the Screaming Stopped, The *77* Peter Walker
Day the Sky Exploded, The *58* Paolo Heusch
Day the Sky Fell In, The *61* Barry Shawzin
Day the Sun Rose, The *69* Tetsuya Yamanouchi
Day the War Ended, The *61* Yakov Segel
Day the World Changed Hands, The *69* Joseph Sargent
Day the World Ended, The *55* Roger Corman
Day the World Ended, The *79* James Goldstone
Day They Gave Babies Away, The *57* Allen Reisner
Day They Robbed America, The *87* Manuel Cinco
Day They Robbed the Bank of England, The *60* John Guillermin
Day Time Ended, The *78* John Cardos
Day-Time Wife *39* Gregory Ratoff
Day to Remember, A *53* Ralph Thomas
Day to Wed, The *56* Kozaburo Yoshimura
Day When Love Returns, The *22* Kenji Mizoguchi
Day Will Come, A *60* Rudolf Jügert
Day Will Dawn, The *42* Harold French
Day with Governor Whitman, A *16* D. W. Griffith

Day with Mary Pickford, A *16* D. W. Griffith

Day with Poachers, A *12* Stuart Kinder

Day with the Fresh Air Fiend, A *05* Alf Collins

Day Without Sun, A *59* Kazimierz Karabasz*

Day You Love Me, The *35* John Reinhardt

Day You Love Me, The *86* Sergio Dow

Daybreak *17* Albert Capellani

Daybreak *31* Jacques Feyder

Daybreak *39* Marcel Carné

Daybreak *46* Compton Bennett

Daybreak and Whiteye *57* Stan Brakhage

Daybreak Express *53* D. A. Pennebaker

Daybreak in Udi *49* Terry Bishop

Daydream, The *65* Mrinal Sen

Daydreamer, The *66* Jules Bass

Daydreamer, The *75* Pierre Richard

Daydreams *13* Edwin J. Collins

Dayereh Mina *74* Dariush Mehrjui

Daylight Burglar, The *12* Christy Cabanne

Daylight Gold Robbery, The *20* Charles Raymond

Daylight Robbery *13* Charles C. Calvert

Daylight Robbery *64* Michael Truman

Daylight Saving Bill, The *16* Ethyle Batley

Dayoch Radio! *24* S. Grunberg, Sergei Yutkevich

Days, The *63* Aleksandar Petrović

Days and Nights *44* Alexander Stolper

Days and Nights in the Forest *69* Satyajit Ray

Days and Nights of Leningrad *42* Roman Karmen*

Days Are Numbered *61* Elio Petri

Days Are Passing, The *80* Goran Paskaljević

Day's Bread, A *70* Mani Kaul

Day's Holiday, A *08* James A. Williamson

Days in the Trees *76* Marguerite Duras

Days of Being Wild *90* Kar-wai Wong

Days of Buffalo Bill *46* Thomas Carr

Days of Evil Women *58* Minoru Shibuya

Days of '49 *13* Thomas Ince

Days of Glory *43* Jacques Tourneur

Days of Glory *45* Giuseppe De Santis, Mario Serandrei, Luchino Visconti

Days of Hate *54* Leopoldo Torre-Nilsson

Days of Hatred *54* Leopoldo Torre-Nilsson

Days of Heaven *78* Terrence Malick

Days of Hell *86* Tonino Ricci

Days of Hope *39* André Malraux

Days of Jesse James *39* Joseph Kane

Days of June, The *85* Alfredo Fischerman

Days of Love *54* Giuseppe De Santis

Days of October, The *58* Sergei Vasiliev

Days of Old *22* Charlie Chase

Days of Old Cheyenne, The *43* Elmer Clifton

Days of Our Life *14* Vladimir Gardin

Days of Our Years *51* Denise Tual, Roland Tual

Days of 36 *72* Theodoros Angelopoulos

Days of Thunder *90* Tony Scott

Days of Treason *73* Otakar Vávra

Days of Violence *67* Alfonso Brescia

Days of Volochayev, The *37* Georgy Vasiliev, Sergei Vasiliev

Days of Water *72* Manuel Octavio Gómez

Days of Whisky Gap *61* Colin Low

Days of Wine and Roses *62* Blake Edwards

Days of Youth *29* Yasujiro Ozu

Day's Pleasure, A *19* Charles Chaplin

Day's Sport, A *12* Mark Melford

Days to Remember *87* Jeanine Meerapfel

Daytime Wives *23* Émile Chautard

Daytona Beach Weekend *65* Robert Welby

Dayton's Devils *68* Jack Shea

Daze of the West *27* William Wyler

Dazzling Miss Davison, The *17* Frank Powell

Dcery Eviny *28* Karel Lamač

De América Soy Hijo...y a Ella Me Debo *72* Santiago Álvarez

De-Aş Fi Harap Alb *65* Ion Popescu-Gopo

De Cierta Manera *74* Sara Gómez

De Danadan *88* Mahesh Kothari

De Forest Phonofilms *27* Bertram Phillips

De Forest Phonofilms *28* Widgey R. Newman

De Gais Lurons en Congrès *58* Michel Brault, Gilles Groulx

De Gaulle Sketch *59* Charles Eames, Ray Eames

De Grey — Le Banc de Désolation *73* Claude Chabrol

De Guerre Lasse *88* Robert Enrico

De Hombre a Hombre *49* Hugo Fregonese

De Kom Tillbaka *62* Jan Troell

De la Jungle à l'Écran *29* Alfred Machin

De la Part des Copains *70* Terence Young

De la Veine à Revendre *59* Andrzej Munk

De l'Amour *63* Jean Aurel

De l'Argentine *86* Werner Schroeter

De l'Autre Côté de l'Image *85* Jean-François Laguionie

De Luxe Annie *18* Roland West

De Mayerling à Sarajevo *40* Max Ophüls

De Montréal à Manicouagan *63* Arthur Lamothe

De Mujer a Mujer *87* Mauricio Walerstein

De Nåede Færgen *48* Carl Theodor Dreyer, Jørgen Roos

De Notre Temps *62* Frédéric Rossif

De Quoi Tu Te Mêles, Daniéla! *62* Max Pecas

De Sable et de Sang *87* Jeanne Labrune

De Sade *69* Roger Corman, Cy Endfield, Gordon Hessler

De Sade 70 *70* Jesús Franco

De Tal Pedro, Tal Astilla *87* Luis Felipe Bernaza

De Todos Modos Juan Te Llamas *76* Marcela Fernández Violante

De Tout pour Faire un Monde *62* Jean Cayrol, Claude Durand

Deacon Outwitted, The *13* Mack Sennett

Deacon's Daughter, The *10* Sidney Olcott

Deacon's Troubles, The *12* Mack Sennett

Dead, The *60* Stan Brakhage

Dead, The *87* John Huston

Dead Aim *90* William van der Kloot

Dead Alive, The *16* Henry J. Vernot

Dead and Buried *81* Gary Sherman

Dead and the Deadly, The *83* Ma Wu

Dead Are Alive, The *72* Armando Crispino

Dead-Bang *88* John Frankenheimer

Dead Calm *88* Phillip Noyce

Dead Cat, The *02* Alf Collins

Dead Cert, A *19* Rowland Whiting

Dead Cert *73* Tony Richardson

Dead Certainty, A *20* George Dewhurst

Dead Country, The *71* István Gaál

Dead Don't Dream, The *48* George Archainbaud

Dead Drifter, A *59* Hideo Sekigawa

Dead Embers *28* Humberto Mauro

Dead End *37* William Wyler

Dead End *77* Parviz Sayyad

Dead End *80* Alan Birkinshaw

Dead End Creek *64* Pat Jackson

Dead End Drive-In *86* Brian Trenchard-Smith

Dead End Kids *86* JoAnne Akalaitis

Dead End Kids: A Story of Nuclear Power *86* JoAnne Akalaitis

Dead End Kids at Military School *39* William Clemens, Noel Mason Smith

Dead End Kids on Dress Parade *39* William Clemens, Noel Mason Smith

Dead End Street *82* Yaky Yosha

Dead Eye Jeff *20* Raoul Barré, Charles Bowers

Dead Eyes of London *61* Alfred Vohrer

Dead Game *23* Edward Sedgwick

Dead Heart, The *14* Hay Plumb

Dead Heat *26* Charles Barnett

Dead Heat *88* Mark Goldblatt

Dead Heat on a Merry-Go-Round *66* Bernard Girard

Dead Image *64* Paul Henreid

Dead Kids *81* Michael Laughlin

Dead Landscape *71* István Gaál

Dead Line, The *19* Del Henderson

Dead Line, The *26* Jack Nelson

Dead Lucky *60* Montgomery Tully

Dead Man, The *14* Alexander Tairov

Dead Man Died, The *39* Alejandro Galindo

Dead Man Walking *87* Gregory Brown

Dead Man's Chest *65* Patrick Dromgoole

Dead Man's Curve *28* Richard Rosson

Dead Man's Evidence *62* Francis Searle

Dead Man's Eyes *44* Reginald LeBorg

Dead Man's Float *80* Peter Sharp

Dead Man's Gold *48* Ray Taylor

Dead Man's Gulch *43* John English

Dead Man's Shoes *13* Wallace Reid

Dead Man's Shoes *39* Thomas Bentley

Dead Man's Trail *52* Lewis D. Collins

Dead March, The *37* Bud Pollard

Dead Mate *89* Straw Weisman

Dead Melody *38* Victor Tourjansky

Dead Men Are Dangerous *38* Harold French

Dead Men Don't Wear Plaid *82* Carl Reiner

Dead Men Ride *71* Aldo Florio

Dead Men Tell *41* Harry Lachman

Dead Men Tell No Tales *14* F. Martin Thornton

Dead Men Tell No Tales *20* Tom Terriss

Dead Men Tell No Tales *38* David Mac-Donald

Dead Men Walk *43* Sam Newfield

Dead Mountaineer Hotel, The *79* Grigori Kromarov

Dead of Night 45 Alberto Cavalcanti, Charles Crichton, Basil Dearden, Robert Hamer

Dead of Night 72 Bob Clark

Dead of Summer 70 Nelo Risi

Dead of Winter 86 Arthur Penn

Dead on Course 52 Terence Fisher

Dead on Time 55 Don Chaffey

Dead on Time 83 Lyndall Hobbs

Dead One, The 61 Barry Mahon

Dead Ones, The 48 Gregory Markopoulos

Dead or Alive 21 Del Henderson

Dead or Alive 44 Elmer Clifton

Dead or Alive 67 Franco Giraldi

Dead Past Recalled, The 14 F. Martin Thornton

Dead People 72 Willard Huyck

Dead Pigeon on Beethoven Street 72 Samuel Fuller

Dead Pit 90 Brett Leonard

Dead Poets Society 89 Peter Weir

Dead Pool, The 88 Buddy Van Horn

Dead Queen, The 45 José Leitão De Barros

Dead Reckoning 47 John Cromwell

Dead Ringer 64 Paul Henreid

Dead Ringer 82 Allan Nicholls

Dead Ringers 88 David Cronenberg

Dead Run 67 Christian-Jaque

Dead-Shot Baker 17 William Duncan

Dead Souls 60 René Allio

Dead Souls 60 Leonid Trauberg

Dead Speak, The 35 Gabriel Soria

Dead That Walk, The 57 Edward L. Cahn

Dead, the Devil and the Flesh, The 73 José María Oliveira

Dead, the Flesh and the Devil, The 73 José María Oliveira

Dead to the World 61 Nicholas Webster

Dead Woman's Kiss, A 51 Guido Brignone

Dead Zone, The 83 David Cronenberg

Deadfall 67 Bryan Forbes

Deadhead Miles 71 Vernon Zimmerman

Deadlier Sex, The 20 Robert Thornby

Deadlier Than the Male 55 Julien Duvivier

Deadlier Than the Male 66 Ralph Thomas

Deadliest Sin, The 53 Ken Hughes

Deadline, The 31 Lambert Hillyer

Deadline 48 Oliver Drake

Deadline 52 Richard Brooks

Deadline 80 Mario Azzopardi

Deadline 87 Nathaniel Gutman

Deadline at Dawn 46 Harold Clurman

Deadline at Eleven 20 George Fawcett

Deadline Auto Theft 83 H. B. Halicki

Deadline for Murder 46 James Tinling

Deadline Midnight 59 Jack Webb

Deadline U.S.A. 52 Richard Brooks

Deadlock! 31 George King

Deadlock 43 Ronald Haines

Deadlock 57 Don Weis

Deadlock 61 Edmond O'Brien

Deadlock 70 Roland Klick

Deadly Affair, The 66 Sidney Lumet

Deadly and the Beautiful, The 74 Robert Vincent O'Neil

Deadly Bees, The 66 Freddie Francis

Deadly Blessing 81 Wes Craven

Deadly China Doll 73 Feng Huang

Deadly Circle, The 64 Irwin Meyer

Deadly Companion 80 George Bloomfield

Deadly Companions, The 61 Sam Peckinpah

Deadly Decision 54 Alfred Weidenmann

Deadly Decoy, The 62 Maurice Labro

Deadly Dreams 88 Kristine Peterson

Deadly Drug, The 15 Cecil M. Hepworth

Deadly Duo 62 Reginald LeBorg

Deadly Encounter 75 R. John Hugh

Deadly Eyes 82 Robert Clouse

Deadly Females, The 76 Donovan Winter

Deadly Force 83 Paul Aaron

Deadly Friend 86 Wes Craven

Deadly Game, A 24 Michael Curtiz

Deadly Game, The 41 Phil Rosen

Deadly Game, The 54 Daniel Birt

Deadly Game, The 74 Wray Davis

Deadly Games 80 Scott Mansfield

Deadly Games 82 George Schaefer

Deadly Gas, The 16 Abel Gance

Deadly Glass of Beer, The 16 Tod Browning

Deadly Harvest 72 Timothy Bond

Deadly Hero 76 Ivan Nagy

Deadly Honeymoon 73 Elliot Silverstein

Deadly Illusion 86 Ola Solum

Deadly Illusion 87 Larry Cohen, William Tannen

Deadly Impact 83 Fabrizio De Angelis

Deadly Intent 88 Nigel Dick

Deadly Invention, The 57 Karel Zeman

Deadly Is the Female 49 Joseph H. Lewis

Deadly Mantis, The 56 Nathan Juran

Deadly Model, The 15 H. Oceano Martinek

Deadly Nightshade 51 Kon Ichikawa

Deadly Nightshade 53 John Gilling

Deadly Obsession 89 Jeno Hodi

Deadly Passion 85 Larry Larson

Deadly Peacemaker 55 Richard Wilson

Deadly Possession 89 Craig Lahiff

Deadly Prey 87 David A. Prior

Deadly Ray from Mars, The 38 Ford Beebe, Robert F. Hill

Deadly Record 59 Lawrence Huntington

Deadly Reef 78 John Randall

Deadly Silence, The 70 Lawrence Dobkin, Robert L. Friend

Deadly Spawn, The 83 Douglas McKeown, Tim Sullivan

Deadly Sting 87 Kenneth J. Hall

Deadly Strangers 74 Sidney Hayers

Deadly Thief, The 78 Krishna Shah

Deadly Trackers, The 73 Barry Shear

Deadly Trap, The 71 René Clément

Deadly Treasure of the Piranha 78 Antonio Margheriti, Herbert V. Theiss

Deadly Twins 88 Joe Oaks

Deadly Weapon 87 Michael Miner

Deadly Weapons 74 Doris Wishman

Deadtime Stories 86 Jeffrey S. Delman

Deadwood Coach, The 24 Lynn Reynolds

Deadwood Dick 40 James W. Horne

Deadwood Dick and the Mormons 15 L. C. MacBean, Fred Paul

Deadwood Dick Spoils Brigham Young 15 L. C. MacBean, Fred Paul

Deadwood Dick's Detective Pard 15 L. C. MacBean, Fred Paul

Deadwood Dick's Red Ally 15 L. C. MacBean, Fred Paul

Deadwood Dick's Vengeance 15 L. C. MacBean, Fred Paul

Deadwood Pass 33 John P. McGowan

Deadwood '76 65 James Landis

Deaf 86 Frederick Wiseman

Deaf Burglar, A 13 Mack Sennett

Deaf Smith and Johnny Ears 72 Paolo Cavara

Deaf to the City 87 Mireille Dansereau

Deafula 75 Peter Wechsberg

Deal 77 Robert M. Young

Deal, The 87 Mikhail Vedyshev

Deal in Broken China, A 10 H. Oceano Martinek

Deal in Crockery, A 12 H. Oceano Martinek

Deal of the Century 83 William Friedkin

Deal with the Devil, A 14 Forest Holger-Madsen

Deal with the Devil, A 16 Frank Wilson

Dealers 89 Colin Bucksey

Dealing, or The Berkeley-to-Boston Forty-Brick Lost-Bag Blues 72 Paul Williams

Dear America: Letters Home from Vietnam 87 Bill Couturie

Dear Boys 81 Paul De Lussanet

Dear Boys Home for the Holidays, The 03 James A. Williamson

Dear Brat 51 William A. Seiter

Dear Brigitte 65 Henry Koster

Dear Cardholder 87 Bill Bennett

Dear Caroline 50 Jean Devaivre

Dear, Dead Delilah 72 John Farris

Dear Detective 77 Philippe de Broca

Dear Eva 14 A. Berger, Robert Wiene

Dear Father 79 Dino Risi

Dear Fool, A 21 Harold M. Shaw

Dear Heart 64 Delbert Mann

Dear Inspector 77 Philippe de Broca

Dear Irene 71 Christian Braad Thomsen

Dear John 64 Lars-Magnus Lindgren

Dear John 88 Catherine Ord

Dear Liar, A 25 Fred LeRoy Granville

Dear Little Teacher, The 12 Warwick Buckland

Dear Maestro 83 Luciano Odorisio

Dear Martha 69 Leonard Kastle

Dear Michael 76 Mario Monicelli

Dear Mr. Prohack 49 Thornton Freeland

Dear Mr. Wonderful 82 Peter Lilienthal

Dear Murderer 47 Arthur Crabtree

Dear Octopus 43 Harold French

Dear Old Dog, The 09 Percy Stow

Dear Phone 77 Peter Greenaway

Dear Relatives 33 Gustaf Molander

Dear Ruth 47 William D. Russell

Dear Summer Sister 72 Nagisa Oshima

Dear Wife 49 Richard Haydn

Dearest Love 71 Louis Malle

Dearie 27 Archie Mayo

Dearly Loved Face, A 41 Mikio Naruse

Dearly Purchased Friendship 12 August Blom

Dearth of a Salesman 57 Leslie Arliss

Death, A 79 Ron Norman

Death and Destiny 85 Paul Cox

Death and the Devil 72 Mario Bava, Alfred Leone

Death's Marathon *13* D. W. Griffith
Deathshead Vampire, The *67* Vernon Sewell
Deathsport *78* Allan Arkush, Henry Suso
Deathstalker *83* John Watson
Deathstalker II *86* Jim Wynorski
Deathstalker II: Duel of the Titans *86* Jim Wynorski
Deathstalker III *89* Alfonso Corona Blake
Deathstalker III: The Warriors from Hell *89* Alfonso Corona Blake
Deathstalker and the Warriors from Hell *89* Alfonso Corona Blake
Deathtrap *82* Sidney Lumet
Deathwatch *66* Vic Morrow
Debajo del Mundo *86* Beda Ocampo Feijoo, Juan Bautista Stagnaro
Débarquement de Voyageurs, Port de Granville *1899* Georges Méliès
Débarquement des Congressistes à Neuville-sur-Saône *1895* Louis Lumière
Debauched Life of Gerard Floque, The *87* Georges Lautner
Debauchery Is Wrong *28* Heinosuke Gosho
Debeli i Mršavi *86* Svetislav Bata Prelić
Debito d'Odio *19* Augusto Genina
Débrouille-Toi *17* Louis Feuillade
Debshishu *86* Uptlendu Chakraborty
Debt, The *17* Frank Powell
Debt, The *19* William Worthington
Debt, The *88* Miguel Pereira
Debt of Gambling, The *13* Bert Haldane
Debt of Honor, A *16* William Nigh
Debt of Honor *18* Oscar A. C. Lund
Debt of Honour, A *22* Maurice Elvey
Debt of Honour *36* Norman Walker
Deburau *50* Sacha Guitry
Debut, The *70* Gleb Panfilov
Début de Siècle *68* Marc Allégret
Debut of Thomas Katt, The *20* John R. Bray
Débutant, Le *86* Daniel Janneau
Debuts *70* Gleb Panfilov
Débuts de Max au Cinéma, Les *10* Max Linder
Décade Prodigieuse, La *70* Claude Chabrol
Decadent Influence, The *64* Claude Lelouch
Decameron, The *70* Pier Paolo Pasolini
Decameron Nights *24* Herbert Wilcox
Decameron Nights *52* Hugo Fregonese
Decameron 3 *73* Antonio Margheriti
Decamerone, Il *70* Pier Paolo Pasolini
Decathlon Champion—The Story of Glenn Morris *37* Felix E. Feist
Deceit *21* Oscar Micheaux
Deceiver, The *20* Jean Hersholt, Lewis H. Moomaw
Deceiver, The *31* Louis King
Deceivers, The *66* Victor Stoloff
Deceivers, The *88* Nicholas Meyer
Deceivers Both *13* Hay Plumb
Deceiving Costume *51* Kozaburo Yoshimura
Deceiving Uncle *13* Ethyle Batley
December 7th *42* John Ford, Gregg Toland
December 7th: The Movie *42* John Ford, Gregg Toland

December 12, 1972 *72* Pier Paolo Pasolini*
December 31 *88* Mabobala
Décembre—Mois des Enfants *56* Henri Storck
Decembrists *27* Alexander Ivanovsky
Deception, The *09* D. W. Griffith
Deception, The *12* Bert Haldane
Deception *18* A. C. Hunter
Deception *20* Ernst Lubitsch
Deception *32* Lewis Seiler
Deception *46* Irving Rapper
Deceptions *85* Luigi Faccini
Déchaînes, Les *50* Leonard Kiegel
Décharge, La *70* Jacques Baratier
Déchargement de Bateaux—Le Havre *1896* Georges Méliès
Deciding Kiss, The *18* Tod Browning
Deciduous Tree, A *87* Kaneto Shindo
Decima Vittima, La *65* Elio Petri
Decimals of Love, The *60* Hasse Ekman
Decimo Clandestino, Il *89* Lina Wertmuller
Decision Against Time *56* Charles Crichton
Decision at Midnight *65* Lewis Allen
Decision at Sundown *57* Budd Boetticher
Decision Before Dawn *51* Anatole Litvak
Decision of Christopher Blake, The *48* Peter Godfrey
Decisive Battle *44* Teruo Hagiyama, Kozaburo Yoshimura
Decks Ran Red, The *58* Andrew L. Stone
Declaratie de Dragoste *85* Nicolae Corjos
Declaration of Fools *83* Chang-ho Lee
Declaration of Love *77* Ilya Averbakh
Declaration of Love *85* Nicolae Corjos
Déclassée *25* Robert Vignola
Déclic, Le *85* Jean-Louis Richard
Déclin de l'Empire Américain, Le *86* Denys Arcand
Decline and Fall *68* John Krish
Decline and Fall of a Bird Watcher *68* John Krish
Decline of the American Empire, The *86* Denys Arcand
Decline of Western Civilization, The *80* Penelope Spheeris
Decline of Western Civilization Part II: The Metal Years, The *88* Penelope Spheeris
Décolleté dans le Dos, Le *75* Jan Němec
Decoy, The *16* George W. Lederer
Decoy, The *18* Raoul Barré, Charles Bowers
Decoy *45* Derwin Abrahams
Decoy *46* Jack Bernhard
Decoy *62* C. M. Pennington-Richards
Decoy for Terror *70* Erick Santamaria
Decoyed *04* Lewin Fitzhamon
Decree of Destiny, A *10* D. W. Griffith
Dědáček *68* Jaromil Jireš
Dédale, Le *17* Jean Kemm
Dédale, Le *27* Gaston Roudes
Dede Mamata *88* Rodolfo Brandão
Dědeček Automobil *56* Alfred Radok
Dédée *47* Yves Allégret
Dédée d'Anvers *47* Yves Allégret
Dedee de Montmartre *42* André Berthomieu

Dedication of the Great Buddha, The *52* Teinosuke Kinugasa
Dedicato a una Stella *78* Luigi Cozzi
Dedo del Destino, El *67* Richard Rush
Dedo en el Gatillo, El *65* Rudolf Zehetgruber
Dédoublement Cabalistique *1898* Georges Méliès
Deduce You Say *56* Chuck Jones
Deeds Men Do, The *27* Walter Summers
Deeds of Daring *24* Charles R. Seeling
Deemster, The *17* Howell Hansel
Deep, The *77* Peter Yates
Deep at Heart *83* Yan Chang
Deep Blue Night *84* Chang-ho Bae
Deep Blue Sea, The *55* Anatole Litvak
Deep Desire of Gods *68* Shohei Imamura
Deep End *70* Jerzy Skolimowski
Deep Illusion *87* Marcos Altberg
Deep in My Heart *54* Stanley Donen
Deep in the Heart *82* Tony Garnett
Deep in the Heart of Texas *42* Elmer Clifton
Deep Inside *66* Joe Sarno
Deep Love *75* Chang-ho Lee
Deep Purple *15* James Young
Deep Purple, The *20* Raoul Walsh
Deep Red *75* Dario Argento
Deep Red Hatchet Murders *75* Dario Argento
Deep River Savages *72* Umberto Lenzi
Deep Sea Panic, A *24* Roy Del Ruth
Deep Six, The *57* Rudolph Maté
Deep South *36* Leslie Goodwins
Deep Space *87* Fred Olen Ray
Deep Thoughts *81* Jack Regis
Deep Throat *72* Gerard Damiano
Deep Throat II *73* Joe Sarno
Deep Thrust—The Hand of Death *73* Feng Huang
Deep Valley *47* Jean Negulesco
Deep Water *81* Michel Deville
Deep Waters *20* Maurice Tourneur
Deep Waters *48* Henry King
Deep Waters *79* David Eady
DeepStar Six *89* Sean S. Cunningham
Deer Hunter, The *78* Michael Cimino
Deerslayer, The *13* James Hallek Reid, Lawrence Trimble
Deerslayer *43* Lew Landers
Deerslayer, The *57* Kurt Neumann
Déesse, La *66* Jean Cayrol
Def by Temptation *90* James Bond III
Def-Con 4 *84* Paul Donovan
Defeat of Hannibal, The *37* Carmine Gallone
Defeat of Japan, The *45* Josef Heifits, Alexander Zarkhi
Defeat of the City, The *17* Thomas R. Mills
Defeat of the German Armies Near Moscow *42* Ilya Kopalin, Leonid Varmalov
Defeated People, A *45* Humphrey Jennings
Defective Detective, The *13* Hay Plumb
Defective Detective, The *15* Dave Aylott
Defector, The *66* Raoul Lévy
Defence of the Realm *85* David Drury
Defend My Love *55* Vincent Sherman

Desert Wedding *48* André Zwoboda

Desert Wooing, A *18* Fred Niblo

Deserted at the Altar *22* William K. Howard, Albert Kelley

Deserter, The *03* James A. Williamson

Deserter, The *08* Lewin Fitzhamon

Deserter, The *12* Thomas Ince

Deserter, The *16* Walter Edwards

Deserter, The *33* Vsevolod I. Pudovkin

Deserter, The *65* Jiří Brdečka

Deserter, The *70* Burt Kennedy

Deserter and the Nomads, The *68* Juraj Jakubisko

Deserters *83* Jack Darcus

Deserters, The *87* Janusz Majewski

Déserteur, Le *06* André Heuze

Déserteur, Le *39* Léonide Moguy

Déserteuse, La *17* Louis Feuillade

Deserto dei Tartari, Il *76* Valerio Zurlini

Deserto Rosso, Il *64* Michelangelo Antonioni

Desertore e i Nomadi, Il *68* Juraj Jakubisko

Desert's Crucible, The *22* Roy Clements

Desert's Price, The *25* W. S. Van Dyke

Desert's Sting, The *14* Wilfred Lucas

Desert's Toll, The *26* Clifford Smith

Déshabillage Impossible, Le *00* Georges Méliès

Desheredados, Los *36* Guillermo Baqueriza

Desiderando Giulia *86* Andrea Barzini

Desideria, la Vita Interiore *80* Gianni Barcelloni

Desiderio *43* Marcello Pagliero, Roberto Rossellini

Design for Death *47* Richard Fleischer

Design for Dying *60* Kozaburo Yoshimura

Design for Leaving *54* Robert McKimson

Design for Living *33* Ernst Lubitsch

Design for Loving *62* Godfrey Grayson

Design for Murder *39* Roy Boulting

Design for Scandal *41* Norman Taurog

Design for Spring *38* Humphrey Jennings

Design of a Human Being *49* Kon Ichikawa

Designing Woman *57* Vincente Minnelli

Designing Women *34* Ivar Campbell

Désir et l'Amour, Le *51* Henri Decoin

Desirable *34* Archie Mayo

Desire *20* George Edwardes Hall

Desire *23* Rowland V. Lee

Desire *28* G. W. Pabst

Desire *36* Frank Borzage

Désiré *37* Sacha Guitry

Desire *58* Heinosuke Gosho

Desire *58* Vojtěch Jasný

Desire *83* Eddie Romero

Desire *89* Stuart Marshall

Desire in the Dust *60* William F. Claxton

Desire Me *47* Jack Conway, George Cukor, Mervyn LeRoy

Desire of Night *30* Heinosuke Gosho

Desire of the Moth *17* Rupert Julian

Desire, the Interior Life *80* Gianni Barcelloni

Desire to Watch, The *86* Aristide Massaccesi

Desire Under the Elms *57* Delbert Mann

Desire Under the Palms *68* Joe Sarno

Desired Woman, The *18* Paul Scardon

Desired Woman, The *27* Michael Curtiz

Desirée *54* Henry Koster

Desirée *84* Felix de Rooy

Desires *53* Kozaburo Yoshimura

Desires *54* Rolf Hansen

Desires of the Vampire *60* Piero Regnoli

Desiring Giulia *86* Andrea Barzini

Desistfilm *53* Stan Brakhage

Desk Set, The *57* Walter Lang

Désordre *49* Jacques Baratier

Désordre, Le *62* Franco Brusati

Désordre *86* Olivier Assayas

Désordre A Vingt Ans, Le *67* Jacques Baratier

Désordre et la Nuit, Le *58* Gilles Grangier

Despair *77* Rainer Werner Fassbinder

Despegue a las 18:00 *69* Santiago Álvarez

Desperado, The *10* Gilbert M. Anderson

Desperado, The *54* Thomas Carr

Desperado, El *67* Franco Rossetti

Desperado City *81* Vadim Glowna

Desperado Trail, The *65* Harald Reinl

Desperadoes, The *42* Charles Vidor

Desperadoes Are in Town, The *56* Kurt Neumann

Desperadoes of Dodge City *48* Philip Ford

Desperadoes of the West *50* Fred C. Brannon

Desperadoes' Outpost *52* Philip Ford

Desperados, The *68* Henry Levin

Desperate *47* Anthony Mann

Desperate Adventure, A *24* John P. McGowan

Desperate Adventure, A *38* John H. Auer

Desperate Cargo *41* William Beaudine

Desperate Chance *26* John P. McGowan

Desperate Chance, A *42* James P. Hogan

Desperate Chance for Ellery Queen, A *42* James P. Hogan

Desperate Characters *71* Frank D. Gilroy

Desperate Courage *28* Richard Thorpe

Desperate Crime, A *06* Georges Méliès

Desperate Decision *52* Yves Allégret

Desperate Footpads *07* William Haggar

Desperate for Love *68* Nelson Pereira Dos Santos

Desperate Game, The *26* Joseph Franz

Desperate Hero, The *20* Wesley Ruggles

Desperate Hours, The *55* William Wyler

Desperate Hours *90* Michael Cimino

Desperate Journey *42* Raoul Walsh

Desperate Living *77* John Waters

Desperate Lover, A *12* Mack Sennett

Desperate Man, The *59* Peter Maxwell

Desperate Men *48* Ray Nazarro

Desperate Men, The *57* Paul Rotha

Desperate Moment, A *26* Jack Dawn

Desperate Moment *53* Compton Bennett

Desperate Moves *80* Ovidio Assonitis

Desperate Odds *25* Horace B. Carpenter

Desperate Ones, The *68* Alexander Ramati

Desperate Ones, The *71* Yılmaz Güney

Desperate Poaching Affray *03* William Haggar

Desperate Road, The *86* Ömer Kavur

Desperate Search *52* Joseph H. Lewis

Desperate Siege *50* Henry Hathaway

Desperate Stratagem, A *14* H. Oceano

Martinek

Desperate Trails *21* John Ford

Desperate Trails *39* Albert Ray

Desperate Youth *21* Harry B. Harris

Desperately Seeking Susan *85* Susan Seidelman

Desperation *16* Maurice Elvey

Desperation: The Last Frenzy *89* Xiaowen Zhou

Despertar da Redentora, O *42* Humberto Mauro

Despiadados, Los *66* Sergio Corbucci

Despised and Rejected *14* Frank Wilson

Despoiler, The *15* Thomas Ince

Despotic Fiancé, The *12* Mauritz Stiller

Dessinateur: Chamberlain *1896* Georges Méliès

Dessinateur Express: M. Thiers *1896* Georges Méliès

Dessinateur: Reine Victoria *1896* Georges Méliès

Dessinateur: Von Bismark *1897* Georges Méliès

Dessins et Merveilles *66* Nelly Kaplan

Dessous des Cartes, Les *47* André Cayatte

Destin *26* Dmitri Kirsanov

Destin des Mères, Le *11* Louis Feuillade

Destin Est Maître, Le *20* Jean Kemm

Destin Fabuleux de Désirée Clary, Le *41* Sacha Guitry

Destination Big House *50* George Blair

Destination Danger *53* Paul Landres

Destination Death *56* Montgomery Tully

Destination Death *61* Jürgen Roland

Destination Fury *61* Giorgio Bianchi

Destination Gobi *52* Robert Wise

Destination Inner Space *66* Francis D. Lyon

Destination Magoo *54* Pete Burness

Destination Meatball *51* Walter Lantz

Destination Milan *54* John Gilling*

Destination Moon *50* Irving Pichel

Destination Murder *50* Edward L. Cahn

Destination Rio *49* Åke Öhberg

Destination Saturn *39* Ford Beebe, Saul Goodkind

Destination 60,000 *57* George Waggner

Destination Tokyo *43* Delmer Daves

Destination Unknown *33* Tay Garnett

Destination Unknown *42* Ray Taylor

Destinazione Roma *77* Fred Williamson

Destinée *26* Henri Roussel

Destinées *52* Christian-Jaque, Jean Delannoy, Marcello Pagliero

Destino, Il *38* Mario Mattòli

Destino d'Amore *43* Luciano Emmer, Enrico Gras, Tatiana Grauding

Destino di Donna *37* Guido Brignone

Destino e il Timoniere, Il *19* Carmine Gallone

Destins *26* Dmitri Kirsanov

Destins de Manoel, Les *85* Raúl Ruiz

Destiny *15* Edwin Carewe

Destiny *19* Rollin Sturgeon

Destiny *21* Fritz Lang

Destiny *38* Mario Mattòli

Destiny *44* Julien Duvivier, Reginald LeBorg

Destiny *87* Gregory Nava

Destiny of a Man *59* Sergei Bondarchuk

Devil and Dr. Frankenstein, The *73* Antonio Margheriti, Paul Morrissey

Devil and Flesh *50* Luis Buñuel

Devil and Max Devlin, The *81* Steven Hilliard Stern

Devil and Miss Jones, The *41* Sam Wood

Devil and the Angel, The *46* Pierre Chénal

Devil and the Cornet, The *08* Lewin Fitzhamon

Devil and the Dead, The *72* Mario Bava, Alfred Leone

Devil and the Deep, The *32* Marion Gering

Devil and the Flesh, The *50* Luis Buñuel

Devil and the Nun, The *60* Jerzy Kawalerowicz

Devil and the Statue, The *01* Georges Méliès

Devil and the Ten Commandments, The *62* Julien Duvivier

Devil at 4 O'Clock, The *61* Mervyn LeRoy

Devil at His Elbow, The *16* Burton L. King

Devil at My Heels *65* Jean-Daniel Pollet

Devil Bat, The *40* Jean Yarbrough

Devil Bat's Daughter *46* Frank Wisbar

Devil Bear *77* Richard Bansbach, Robert E. Pierson

Devil by the Tail, The *68* Philippe de Broca

Devil Commands, The *41* Edward Dmytryk

Devil Dancer, The *27* Fred Niblo, Fred Niblo, Jr.

Devil Dodger, The *17* Clifford Smith

Devil Dogs *28* Fred Windermere

Devil Dogs of the Air *35* Lloyd Bacon

Devil-Doll, The *36* Tod Browning

Devil Doll, The *63* Lindsay Shonteff

Devil Doll Men *60* Benito Alazraki, Paul Nagle

Devil Foetus *83* Honquan Liu

Devil Girl from Mars *54* David MacDonald

Devil Goddess *55* Spencer G. Bennet

Devil Got Angry, The *66* Kimiyoshi Yasuda

Devil Has Seven Faces, The *77* Osvaldo Civirani

Devil Horse, The *26* Fred Jackman

Devil Horse, The *32* Otto Brower, Richard Talmadge

Devil in a Convent, The *1899* Georges Méliès

Devil in Evening Dress *73* George Miller

Devil in Love, The *66* Ettore Scola

Devil in Miss Jones, The *73* Gerard Damiano

Devil in My Flesh *68* Hideo Sekigawa

Devil in Silk *68* Rolf Hansen

Devil in the Castle *61* Hiroshi Inagaki

Devil in the Flesh, The *46* Claude Autant-Lara

Devil in the Flesh *86* Scott Murray

Devil in the Flesh, The *86* Marco Bellocchio

Devil in the Streets, The *24* Germaine Dulac

Devil in the Studio, The *01* Walter R. Booth

Devil Inside, The *60* Cliff Owen

Devil Is a Sissy, The *36* W. S. Van Dyke

Devil Is a Woman, The *35* Josef von Sternberg

Devil Is a Woman, The *72* Damiano Damiani

Devil Is an Empress, The *38* Jean Dréville

Devil Is Driving, The *32* Ben Stoloff

Devil Is Driving, The *37* Harry Lachman

Devil Lurks Among Bar-Girls, The *87* Miguel Delgado

Devil Made a Woman, The *59* Tulio Demicheli

Devil Makes Three, The *52* Andrew Marton

Devil May Care *29* Sidney Franklin

Devil May Care *69* José Briz

Devil May Hare *54* Robert McKimson

Devil McCare *19* Lorimer Johnston

Devil Men from Space, The *65* Antonio Margheriti

Devil Monster *46* S. Edwin Graham

Devil Never Sleeps, The *61* Leo McCarey

Devil of a Fellow, A *38* Georg Jacoby

Devil of a Honeymoon, A *15* Walter R. Booth

Devil of a Woman, A *66* Georg Tressler

Devil of the Desert *54* Youssef Chahine

Devil of the Desert Against the Son of Hercules *65* Antonio Margheriti

Devil of the Springs, The *45* Jiří Brdečka, Jiří Trnka

Devil on Deck *32* Wallace Fox

Devil on Horseback *36* Crane Wilbur

Devil on Horseback *54* Cyril Frankel

Devil on Springs, The *45* Jiří Brdečka, Jiří Trnka

Devil on Wheels *39* Lloyd Bacon

Devil on Wheels, The *47* Crane Wilbur

Devil Pays Off, The *41* John H. Auer

Devil Plays, The *31* Richard Thorpe

Devil, Probably, The *77* Robert Bresson

Devil Resuscitation *80* Kinji Fukasaku

Devil Riders *43* Sam Newfield

Devil Rides Out, The *67* Terence Fisher

Devil Ship *47* Lew Landers

Devil-Ship Pirates, The *64* Don Sharp

Devil Stone, The *17* Cecil B. DeMille

Devil Strikes at Night, The *57* Robert Siodmak

Devil Takes the Count, The *36* W. S. Van Dyke

Devil, the Saint and the Fool, The *87* Rafael Villaseñor Kuri

Devil, the Servant and the Man, The *16* Frank Beal

Devil Thumbs a Ride, The *47* Felix E. Feist

Devil Tiger *34* Clyde E. Elliott

Devil Times Five *74* Sean McGregor

Devil to Pay, The *15* Edwin J. Collins

Devil to Pay, The *20* Ernest C. Warde

Devil to Pay, The *30* George Fitzmaurice

Devil to Pay, The *62* Bruce Beresford

Devil Witch, The *73* Corrado Farina

Devil with Hitler, The *42* Gordon Douglas

Devil with Women, A *30* Irving Cummings

Devil Within, The *21* Bernard J. Durning

Devil Within Her, The *74* Sonia Assonitis, Roberto d'Ettore Piazzoli

Devil Within Her, The *75* Peter Sasdy

Devil Wolf of Shadow Mountain, The *64* Gary Kent

Devil Woman *64* Kaneto Shindo

Devil Woman *76* Felix Vilars, Albert Yu

Devilish Magic *1897* Georges Méliès

Devilish Plank, The *04* Georges Méliès

Devilman Story *67* Paolo Bianchini

Devils, The *71* Ken Russell

Devil's Advocate, The *77* Guy Green

Devil's Agent, The *62* John Paddy Carstairs

Devil's Angel, The *20* Lejaren A'Hiller

Devil's Angels *67* Daniel Haller

Devil's Apple Tree, The *29* Elmer Clifton

Devil's Assistant, The *17* Harry A. Pollard

Devil's Bait, The *17* Harry Harvey

Devil's Bait *59* Peter Graham Scott

Devil's Banknotes *60* Hideo Sekigawa

Devil's Bargain *08* A. E. Coleby

Devil's Bed, The *78* Helmut Pfandler

Devil's Bedroom, The *64* L. Q. Jones

Devil's Bondman, The *15* Percy Nash

Devil's Bondswoman, The *16* Lloyd B. Carleton

Devil's Bouncing Ball Song, The *77* Kon Ichikawa

Devil's Bowl, The *23* Neal Hart

Devil's Bride, The *67* Terence Fisher

Devil's Brigade, The *68* Andrew V. McLaglen

Devil's Brother, The *33* Hal Roach, Charles Rogers

Devil's Cabaret, The *31* Nick Grindé

Devil's Cage, The *28* Wilfred Noy

Devil's Camera, The *63* Herschell Gordon Lewis

Devil's Canyon *35* Clifford Smith

Devil's Canyon *53* Alfred L. Werker

Devil's Cargo, The *25* Victor Fleming

Devil's Cargo *48* John Link

Devil's Castle, The *1896* Georges Méliès

Devil's Chaplain *29* Duke Worne

Devil's Children, The *62* James Sheldon

Devil's Circus, The *25* Benjamin Christensen

Devil's Claim, The *20* Charles Swickard

Devil's Commandments, The *54* Riccardo Freda

Devil's Confession, The *21* John S. Lopez

Devil's Cross, The *34* Fernando De Fuentes

Devil's Cross, The *74* John Gilling

Devil's Daffodil, The *61* Ákos von Ráthonyi

Devil's Daughter, The *15* Frank Powell

Devil's Daughter, The *39* Arthur Leonard

Devil's Daughter *46* Henri Decoin

Devil's Daughter *49* Maurice Saurel

Devil's Dice *26* Tom Forman

Devil's Disciple, The *26* Oscar Micheaux

Devil's Disciple, The *58* Guy Hamilton, Alexander Mackendrick

Devil's Doll *59* William Hole, Jr.

Devil's Doorway *50* Anthony Mann

Devil's Dooryard, The *23* Louis King

Devil's Double, The *16* William S. Hart

Devil's Eight, The 68 Burt Topper
Devil's Elixir, The 76 Manfred Purzer
Devil's Envoys, The 42 Marcel Carné
Devil's Express 75 Barry Rosen
Devil's Eye, The 60 Ingmar Bergman
Devil's Feud Cake 63 Friz Freleng
Devil's Foot, The 21 Maurice Elvey
Devils from Space, The 65 Antonio Margheriti
Devil's Gambit 82 Ted V. Mikels
Devil's Garden, The 20 Kenneth Webb
Devil's General, The 55 Helmut Käutner
Devil's Godmother, The 38 Ramón Peón
Devil's Gulch, The 26 Jack Nelson
Devil's Hairpin, The 57 Cornel Wilde
Devil's Hand, The 42 Maurice Tourneur
Devil's Hand, The 59 William Hole, Jr.
Devil's Harbor 54 Montgomery Tully
Devil's Henchman, The 49 Seymour Friedman
Devil's Holiday, The 30 Edmund Goulding
Devil's Honey, The 86 Lucio Fulci
Devil's Imposter, The 72 Michael Anderson
Devil's in Love, The 33 William Dieterle
Devil's Island 26 Frank O'Connor
Devil's Island 39 William Clemens
Devil's Island, The 77 Kon Ichikawa
Devil's Island 80 Masahiro Shinoda
Devil's Ivy 73 Pierre De Moro
Devil's Jest, The 54 Alfred Goulding
Devil's Left Hand, The 66 Ko Nakahira
Devil's Longest Night, The 71 Jean Brismée
Devil's Lottery 32 Sam Taylor
Devil's Man, The 67 Paolo Bianchini
Devil's Manor, The 1896 Georges Méliès
Devil's Mask, The 46 Henry Levin
Devil's Masterpiece, The 27 John P. McCarthy
Devil's Mate 33 Phil Rosen
Devil's Maze, The 29 V. Gareth Gundrey
Devil's Men, The 76 Costas Carayiannis
Devil's Messenger, The 61 Herbert L. Strock
Devil's Mill, The 50 Jiří Trnka
Devil's Mistress, The 68 Orville Wanzer
Devil's Money Bags, The 02 Georges Méliès
Devil's Needle, The 16 Chester Withey
Devil's Nightmare, The 71 Jean Brismée
Devil's Odds 87 Beau Bridges
Devil's Odds 90 John Crowther, Michael Schroeder
Devils of Darkness 64 Lance Comfort
Devil's Own, The 16 George Marshall
Devil's Own, The 66 Cyril Frankel
Devil's Paradise, The 87 Vadim Glowna
Devil's Partner, The 23 Caryl S. Fleming
Devil's Partner, The 58 Charles R. Rondeau
Devil's Party, The 38 Ray McCarey
Devil's Pass, The 57 D'Arcy Conyers
Devil's Pass Key, The 20 Erich von Stroheim
Devil's Pawn, The 22 Paul Stein
Devil's Payday, The 17 William Worthington
Devil's People, The 76 Costas Carayiannis

Devil's Pipeline, The 40 Christy Cabanne
Devil's Pit, The 30 Lewis D. Collins
Devil's Pitchfork, The 52 Josef von Sternberg
Devil's Playground, The 18 Harry McRae Webster
Devil's Playground 37 Erle C. Kenton
Devil's Playground, The 46 George Archainbaud
Devil's Playground, The 76 Fred Schepisi
Devil's Plot 48 Paul Stein
Devil's Point 54 Montgomery Tully
Devil's Power, The 49 Aldo Vergano*
Devil's Price, The 42 Wallace Fox
Devil's Prize, The 16 Marguerite Bertsch
Devil's Profession, The 15 F. C. S. Tudor
Devil's Protégé, The 15 Forest Holger-Madsen
Devil's Rain, The 75 Robert Fuest
Devil's Riddle, The 19 Frank Beal
Devil's Rock 38 Germain Burger
Devil's Saddle, The 27 Albert S. Rogell
Devil's Saddle Legion, The 37 Bobby Connolly
Devil's Sisters, The 66 William Grefé
Devil's Skipper, The 28 John G. Adolfi
Devil's Sleep, The 51 W. Merle Connell
Devil's Song of Ball, The 77 Kon Ichikawa
Devil's Spawn, The 61 Lindsay Shonteff
Devil's Squadron 36 Erle C. Kenton
Devil's Tail, The 87 Giorgio Treves
Devil's Temple 69 Kenji Misumi
Devil's Toll, The 26 Clifford Smith
Devil's Tower 28 John P. McGowan
Devil's Toy, The 16 Harley Knoles
Devil's Toy, The 66 Claude Jutra
Devil's Trademark, The 28 James Leo Meehan
Devil's Trail, The 19 Stuart Paton
Devil's Trail, The 42 Lambert Hillyer
Devil's Trap, The 64 František Vláčil
Devil's Twin, The 27 Leo D. Maloney
Devil's Undead, The 72 Peter Sasdy
Devil's Wanton, The 48 Ingmar Bergman
Devil's Wedding Night, The 73 Luigi Batzella
Devil's Weed 49 Sam Newfield
Devil's Wheel, The 18 Edward J. LeSaint
Devil's Wheel, The 26 Grigori Kozintsev, Leonid Trauberg
Devil's Widow, The 70 Roddy McDowall
Devil's Woman, The 62 Joseph Losey
Devil's Woman, The 70 Roddy McDowall
Devon Whey 50 David Hand
Devonsville Terror, The 83 Ulli Lommel
Devoradora, La 46 Fernando De Fuentes
Devoted Ape, The 10 Dave Aylott
Devotee, The 33 Debaki Kumar Bose
Devotion 21 Burton George
Devotion 31 Robert Milton
Devotion 43 Kurt Bernhardt
Devotion 50 Augusto Genina
Devotion 55 K. Pyriev
Dévouement d'un Gosse, Le 11 Alfred Machin
Devuchka s Korobkoi 27 Boris Barnet
Devushka s Korobkoi 27 Boris Barnet
Devyat Dnei Odnogo Goda 61 Mikhail Romm
Dewdrop Braves the Floods of Maidenhead

15 Ernest G. Batley
Dexterity 36 David Miller
Dezertér 65 Jiří Brdečka
Dezertir 33 Vsevolod I. Pudovkin
D'Fightin' Ones 61 Friz Freleng
Dharam Shatru 88 Harmesh Malhotra
Dharmaga Tongjoguro Kan Kkadalgun? 89 Yong-kyun Bae
Dharti ke Lal 46 Khwaja Ahmad Abbas
D'Homme à Hommes 48 Christian-Jaque
Dhoorapu Kondalu 88 Prasad Nallam Reddy
Dhrupad 83 Mani Kaul
Di 77 Glauber Rocha
Di Che Segno Sei? 76 Sergio Corbucci
Di Padre in Figlio 83 Vittorio Gassman
Di Que Me Quieres 39 Robert Snody
Di Tresette Ce N'È Uno Tutti gli Altri Son Nessuno 74 Giuliano Carmineo
Día de los Albaniles II, El 86 Gilberto Martínez Solares
Día de Noviembre, Un 72 Humberto Solás
Día de Vida, Un 50 Emilio Fernández
Dia na Rampa, Um 57 Luiz Paulino Dos Santos, Glauber Rocha
Día Que Me Quieras, El 35 John Reinhardt
Día Que Me Quieras, El 86 Sergio Dow
Diable au Cœur, Le 27 Marcel L'Herbier
Diable au Corps, Le 46 Claude Autant-Lara
Diable au Couvent, Le 1899 Georges Méliès
Diable Boiteux, Le 48 Sacha Guitry
Diable dans la Ville, Le 24 Germaine Dulac
Diable et les Dix Commandements, Le 62 Julien Duvivier
Diable Géant ou Le Miracle de la Madone, Le 01 Georges Méliès
Diable Noir, Le 05 Georges Méliès
Diable par la Queue, Le 68 Philippe de Broca
Diable, Probablement, Le 77 Robert Bresson
Diable Soufflé, Le 47 Edmond T. Gréville
Diablesses, Les 73 Jean Rollin
Diablesses, Les 74 Antonio Margheriti
Diablo, el Santo y el Tonto, El 87 Rafael Villaseñor Kuri
Diablo Se Lleva a los Muertos, El 72 Mario Bava, Alfred Leone
Diablos del Terror, Los 58 Fernando Méndez
Diabolic Tenant, The 09 Georges Méliès
Diabolic Wedding 72 Gene Nash
Diabolical Dr. Mabuse, The 60 Fritz Lang
Diabolical Dr. Z, The 65 Jesús Franco
Diabolical Invention, The 57 Karel Zeman
Diabolical Pact 68 Jaime Salvador
Diabolical Paradise 39 Tsou-sen Tsai
Diabolical Shudder 71 Jorge Martin
Diabolically Yours 67 Julien Duvivier
Diabolici, I 20 Augusto Genina
Diabólico Dr. Mabuse, El 60 Fritz Lang
Diabolik 67 Mario Bava
Diabolique 54 Henri-Georges Clouzot
Diabolique Docteur Mabuse, Le 60 Fritz Lang

Diaboliquement Vôtre 67 Julien Duvivier
Diaboliques, Les 54 Henri-Georges Clouzot
Diabolo Mad 08 A. E. Coleby
Diabolo Menthe 77 Diane Kurys
Diabolo Nightmare 07 Walter R. Booth
Diafanoidi Portano la Morte, I 65 Antonio Margheriti
Diafanoidi Vengono da Morte, I 65 Antonio Margheriti
Diagnosis: Murder 74 Sidney Hayers
Diagonal Sinfonie 24 Viking Eggeling
Diagonal Symphony 24 Viking Eggeling
Diagonale du Fou, La 83 Richard Dembo
Dial: Help 88 Ruggero Deodato
Dial M for Murder 54 Alfred Hitchcock
Dial 999 38 Lawrence Huntington
Dial 999 55 Montgomery Tully
Dial 1119 50 Gerald Mayer
Dial Rat for Terror 72 Larry Cohen
Dial Red O 55 Daniel B. Ullman
Dial 17 52 Michael Anderson
Dialog 68 Jerzy Skolimowski*
Diálogo de Exiliados 74 Raúl Ruiz
Dialogo di Roma, Il 83 Marguerite Duras
Dialogue 63 János Herskó
Dialogue 68 Jerzy Skolimowski*
Dialogue des Carmélites, Le 59 Philippe Agostini, R. Bruckberger
Dialogue d'Exilés 74 Raúl Ruiz
Dialogue of Exiles 74 Raúl Ruiz
Dialogue 20-40-60 68 Jerzy Skolimowski*
Diamant, Le 70 Paul Grimault
Diamant du Sénéchal, Le 14 Louis Feuillade
Diamant Noir, Le 13 Alfred Machin
Diamant Noir 22 André Hugon
Diamant Noir, Le 39 Jean Delannoy
Diamant Vert, Le 17 Pierre Marodon
Diamantes à Go-Go 68 Giuliano Montaldo
Diamond, The 54 Dennis O'Keefe, Montgomery Tully
Diamond Bandit, The 24 Francis Ford
Diamond Brooch, The 12 J. Stuart Blackton
Diamond Carlisle 22 Milburn Morante
Diamond City 49 David MacDonald
Diamond Country 67 Bernard Glasser
Diamond Crown, The 13 J. Searle Dawley
Diamond Cut Diamond 14 Warwick Buckland
Diamond Cut Diamond 15 Dave Aylott
Diamond Cut Diamond 16 Fred Evans, Joe Evans
Diamond Cut Diamond 32 Maurice Elvey, Fred Niblo
Diamond Earrings 53 Max Ophüls
Diamond from the Sky, The 15 Jacques Jaccard, William Desmond Taylor
Diamond Frontier 40 Harold Schuster
Diamond Hand, The 69 Leonid Gaidai
Diamond Handcuffs 28 John P. McCarthy
Diamond Head 62 Guy Green
Diamond Horseshoe 45 George Seaton
Diamond Hunters 67 Bernard Glasser
Diamond Jim 35 A. Edward Sutherland
Diamond Maker, The 09 J. Stuart Blackton
Diamond Man, The 24 Arthur H. Rooke

Diamond Master, The 29 Jack Nelson
Diamond Mercenaries, The 75 Val Guest
Diamond Necklace, The 21 Denison Clift
Diamond Queen, The 21 Edward Kull
Diamond Queen, The 53 John Brahm
Diamond Runners, The 16 John P. McGowan
Diamond Safari 58 Gerald Mayer
Diamond Ship, The 20 Fritz Lang
Diamond Skulls 89 Nicholas Broomfield
Diamond Smugglers, The 11 Allan Dwan
Diamond Star, The 10 D. W. Griffith
Diamond Star, The 13 Edwin J. Collins
Diamond Stud 70 Greg Corarito
Diamond Thieves, The 08 Charles Raymond
Diamond 33 66 Dariush Mehrjui
Diamond Trail, The 32 Harry Fraser
Diamond Wizard, The 54 Dennis O'Keefe, Montgomery Tully
Diamonds 75 Menahem Golan
Diamonds Adrift 21 Chester Bennett
Diamonds and Crime 43 Andrew L. Stone
Diamonds and Dimples 18 Fred Rains
Diamonds and Pearls 17 George Archainbaud
Diamonds Are Forever 71 Guy Hamilton
Diamond's Edge 88 Stephen Bayly
Diamonds for Breakfast 68 Christopher Morahan
Diamonds of the Night 64 Jan Němec
Diamonds on Wheels 72 Jerome Courtland
Diana and Destiny 16 F. Martin Thornton
Diana of the Crossways 22 Denison Clift
Diana's Dress Reform 13 Ralph Ince
Diane 55 David Miller
Diane of Star Hollow 21 Oliver L. Sellers
Diane of the Follies 16 Christy Cabanne
Diane of the Green Van 19 Wallace Worsley
Diane's Body 69 Jean-Louis Richard
Diapason 86 Jorge Polaco
Diaries, Notes and Sketches 68 Jonas Mekas
Diaries, Notes and Sketches—Volume I, Reels 1-6: Lost Lost Lost 75 Jonas Mekas
Diaries of the Peasants 52 Andrzej Munk
Diario de Invierno 88 Francisco Regueiro
Diario de la Guerra del Cerdo 75 Leopoldo Torre-Nilsson
Diario di un Italiano 72 Sergio Capogna
Diario di una Amata, Il 36 Henry Koster
Diario di una Cameriera, Il 63 Luis Buñuel
Diario di una Schizofrenica 70 Nelo Risi
Diario Segreto di un Carcere Femminile 77 Salvatore Di Silvestro
Diary for My Children 82 Márta Mészáros
Diary for My Father and Mother 90 Márta Mészáros
Diary for My Love 87 Márta Mészáros
Diary for My Loved Ones 87 Márta Mészáros
Diary for Timothy, A 45 Humphrey Jennings
Diary of a Bachelor 64 Sandy Howard
Diary of a Bad Girl 56 Léonide Moguy
Diary of a Bride 48 John H. Auer
Diary of a Chambermaid 46 Jean Renoir

Diary of a Chambermaid, The 63 Luis Buñuel
Diary of a Cloistered Nun 73 Domenico Paolella
Diary of a Country Priest 50 Robert Bresson
Diary of a Drunkard, The 24 Daisuke Ito
Diary of a High School Bride 59 Burt Topper
Diary of a Lost Girl, The 29 G. W. Pabst
Diary of a Mad Housewife 70 Frank Perry
Diary of a Mad Old Man 87 Lili Rademakers
Diary of a Madman 63 Reginald LeBorg
Diary of a Madman 65 Richard Williams
Diary of a Madman, The 87 Roger Coggio
Diary of a Married Woman, The 53 Josef von Baky
Diary of a Murderer 16 Harry S. Palmer
Diary of a Nazi, The 42 Mark Donskoi, Igor Savchenko
Diary of a Revolutionist 32 J. I. Urinov
Diary of a Schizophrenic Girl 70 Nelo Risi
Diary of a Sergeant 45 Joseph M. Newman
Diary of a Shinjuku Burglar 68 Nagisa Oshima
Diary of a Shinjuku Thief 68 Nagisa Oshima
Diary of a Space Virgin 75 Derek Ford
Diary of a Teacher 72 Vittorio De Seta
Diary of a Tired Man 68 Masaki Kobayashi
Diary of a Voyage in the South Pacific 61 Franco Rossi
Diary of an Innocent Boy, The 66 Michel Deville
Diary of an Italian 72 Sergio Capogna
Diary of an Unknown Soldier 59 Peter Watkins
Diary of Anne Frank, The 59 George Stevens
Diary of Chuji's Travels, A 28 Daisuke Ito
Diary of Forbidden Dreams 73 Roman Polanski
Diary of Major Thompson, The 55 Preston Sturges
Diary of Oharu 52 Kenji Mizoguchi
Diary of One Week 66 István Szabó
Diary of Sueko, The 59 Shohei Imamura
Diary of the Pig War 75 Leopoldo Torre-Nilsson
Diary of Yunbogi, The 65 Nagisa Oshima
Diary of Yunbogi Boy 65 Nagisa Oshima
Días de Amor, Los 71 Alberto Isaac
Días de Junio, Los 85 Alfredo Fischerman
Días de Odio 54 Leopoldo Torre-Nilsson
Días del Cometa, Los 89 Luis Arino
Días Difíciles 88 Alejandro Pelayo Rangel
Dias Melhores Virão 90 Carlos Diegués
Días Perdidos, Los 63 Victor Erice
Diavoli della Spazio, I 65 Antonio Margheriti
Diavolo, Il 63 Gian Luigi Polidoro
Diavolo Bianco, Il 48 Nunzio Malasomma
Diavolo e i Morti, Il 72 Mario Bava, Alfred Leone
Diavolo e il Morto, Il 72 Mario Bava, Alfred Leone
Diavolo in Corpo, Il 86 Marco Bellocchio

Diavolo Innamorato, Il 66 Ettore Scola

Dice of Destiny 20 Henry King

Dice Player's Last Throw, The 03 Walter R. Booth

Dice Rules 90 Jay Dubin

Dice Woman, The 27 Edward Dillon

Dich Hab Ich Geliebt 30 Rudolf Walther-Fein

Diciottenni al Sole 63 Camillo Mastrocinque

Dick Barton at Bay 50 Godfrey Grayson

Dick Barton, Special Agent 48 Alfred Goulding

Dick Barton Strikes Back 49 Godfrey Grayson

Dick Carson Wins Through 17 Henry Edwards

Dick Deadeye 75 Bill Melendez

Dick Deadeye, or Duty Done 75 Bill Melendez

Dick Down Under 75 Richard Franklin

Dick the Kisser 08 Dave Aylott

Dick Tracy 37 Alvin J. Neitz, Ray Taylor

Dick Tracy 45 William Berke

Dick Tracy 90 Warren Beatty

Dick Tracy, Detective 45 William Berke

Dick Tracy Meets Gruesome 47 John Rawlins

Dick Tracy Meets Karloff 47 John Rawlins

Dick Tracy Returns 38 John English, William Witney

Dick Tracy vs. Crime, Inc. 41 John English, William Witney

Dick Tracy vs. Cueball 46 Gordon Douglas

Dick Tracy's Amazing Adventure 47 John Rawlins

Dick Tracy's Dilemma 47 John Rawlins

Dick Tracy's G-Men 39 John English, William Witney

Dick Turpin 25 John G. Blystone

Dick Turpin 33 Joseph Losey, John Stafford

Dick Turpin, Highwayman 56 David Paltenghi

Dick Turpin's Last Ride to York 06 Charles Raymond

Dick Turpin's Ride 51 Ralph Murphy

Dick Turpin's Ride to York 06 Lewin Fitzhamon

Dick Turpin's Ride to York 13 Charles Raymond

Dick Turpin's Ride to York 22 Maurice Elvey

Dick Whittington 1899 George Albert Smith

Dick Whittington and His Cat 12 Alice Guy-Blaché

Dick Whittington's Cat 36 Ubbe Iwerks

Dicke Turpin's Ride to Yorke 13 Fred Evans, Joe Evans

Dickens Up to Date 23 Bertram Phillips

Dickensian Fantasy, A 33 Aveling Ginever

Dick's Fairy 21 Bert Wynne

Dicky Monteith 22 Kenelm Foss

Dictator, The 15 Edwin S. Porter

Dictator, The 22 James Cruze

Dictator, The 35 Alfred Santell, Victor Saville

Dictator's Guns, The 65 Claude Sautet

Dictionary of Sex 64 Radley Metzger

Dictionnaire de Joachim, Le 65 Walerian Borowczyk

Did He? The Brute! 15 Percy Nash

Did I Betray? 35 Paul Martin

Did Mother Get Her Wish? 12 Mack Sennett

Did Sherman Say Law or War? 16 Ashley Miller

Did Somebody Laugh? 78 Henning Carlsen

Did You Hear the One About the Traveling Saleslady? 68 Don Weis

Dida Ibsens Geschichte 18 Richard Oswald

Diddled 12 Charles C. Calvert

Didn't You Hear? 83 Skip Sherwood

Didums and a Policeman 12 Wilfred Noy

Didums and the Bathing Machine 11 Wilfred Noy

Didums and the Christmas Pudding 11 Wilfred Noy

Didums and the Haddock 11 Wilfred Noy

Didums and the Monkey 12 Wilfred Noy

Didums As an Artist 12 Wilfred Noy

Didums at School 12 Wilfred Noy

Didums on His Holidays 12 Wilfred Noy

Die, Beautiful Maryanne 69 Peter Walker

Die Bian 79 Hark Tsui

Die! Die! My Darling 64 Silvio Narizzano

Die Hard 88 John McTiernan

Die Hard 2 90 Renny Harlin

Die Hard 2 — Die Harder 90 Renny Harlin

Die Is Cast, The 47 Jean Delannoy

Die Laughing 80 Jeff Werner

Die, Monster, Die! 65 Daniel Haller

Die oder Keine 32 Carl Fröhlich

Die Screaming, Marianne 69 Peter Walker

Die Sich Verkaufen 19 Richard Oswald

Die, Sister, Die 78 Randall Hood

Die vom Niederrhein 35 Max Obal

Die vom Rummelplatz 30 Karel Lamač

Dieci Italiani per un Tedesca 62 Filippo Walter Maria Ratti

10,000 Dollari per un Massacro 66 Romolo Guerrieri

Died on a Rainy Sunday 86 Joel Santoni

Dienst Ist Dienst 31 Carl Boese

Dies Irae 43 Carl Theodor Dreyer

Diesel 42 Gerhard Lamprecht

Diesel 85 Robert Kramer

Dieses Lied Bleibt bei Dir 54 Willi Forst

Dieu A Besoin des Hommes 49 Jean Delannoy

Dieu du Hasard, Le 18 Henri Pouctal

Dieux du Feu, Les 61 Henri Storck

Dieux et les Morts, Les 70 Ruy Guerra

Dieux Ont Soif, Les 26 Pierre Marodon

Dieux S'Amusent, Les 35 Reinhold Schünzel

Difendo il Mio Amore 55 Vincent Sherman

Different Sons 62 Yasuke Chiba

Different Story, A 78 Paul Aaron

Difficult Courtship, A 10 Lewin Fitzhamon

Difficult Days 88 Alejandro Pelayo Rangel

Difficult Life, A 61 Dino Risi

Difficult Love, A 66 Jiří Menzel

Difficult People 64 András Kovács

Difficult Shave, A 05 Tom Green

Difficult Way, The 14 George Loane Tucker

Difficult Years 48 Luigi Zampa

Dig That Juliet 61 Peter Ustinov

Dig That Uranium 56 Edward Bernds

Diga di Maghmod, La 29 Goffredo Alessandrini

Diga sul Ghiaccio, La 53 Ermanno Olmi

Diga sul Pacifico, La 57 René Clément

Digby — The Biggest Dog in the World 73 Joseph McGrath

Digging for Gold 36 R. A. Hopwood

Digging for Victory 42 Joy Batchelor, John Halas

Digital Dreams 83 Robert Dornhelm

Dignity 85 Roman Wionczek

Digterkongen 19 Forest Holger-Madsen

Digue, La 11 Abel Gance

Digue ou Pour Sauver la Hollande, La 11 Abel Gance

Dijkbouw 52 Bert Haanstra

Dike, The 11 Abel Gance

Dike Builders 52 Bert Haanstra

Dikie Lebedi 88 Helle Karis

Dilan 87 Erden Kiral

Dilemma, The 12 Christy Cabanne

Dilemma 62 Henning Carlsen

Dilemma 62 Peter Maxwell

Diles Que No Me Maten 85 Freddy Siso

Diligencia de los Condenados, La 70 Juan Bosch

Dill Jones and His All-Stars 60 Robert Henryson

Dillinger 45 Max Nosseck

Dillinger 73 John Milius

Dillinger È Morto 68 Marco Ferreri

Dillinger Is Dead 68 Marco Ferreri

Dilly and Dally 27 Widgey R. Newman

Dim Little Island, The 49 Humphrey Jennings

Dim Sum 84 Wayne Wang

Dim Sum: A Little Bit of Heart 84 Wayne Wang

Dimanche à la Campagne, Un 83 Bertrand Tavernier

Dimanche à Pékin 55 Chris Marker

Dimanche de la Vie, Le 65 Jean Herman

Dimanche Matin, Un 55 Andrzej Munk

Dimanches de Ville d'Avray, Les 62 Serge Bourguignon

Dimboola 79 John Duigan

Dime to Retire 55 Robert McKimson

Dime with a Halo 63 Boris Sagal

Dimension 4 66 Franklin Adreon

Dimension 5 66 Franklin Adreon

Dimensions in Death 63 Sergio Corbucci, Antonio Margheriti

Dimensions of Dialogue 82 Jan Švankmajer

Dimenticare Palermo 90 Francesco Rosi

Dimenticare Venezia 79 Franco Brusati

Dimenticati, I 59 Vittorio De Seta

Dimitri Arakishvili 52 Tenghiz Abuladze, Revaz Chkeidze

Dimka 64 Ilya Frez

Dimples 16 Edgar Jones

Dimples 36 William A. Seiter

Dimples and Tears 29 Jack Harrison

Din Achanak, Ek 88 Mrinal Sen

Din Prati Din, Ek 79 Mrinal Sen

Din Tillvaros Land 40 Arne Sucksdorff

Dinah 33 Dave Fleischer

Dinamite Jim 66 Alfonso Balcazar

Dinamite Joe 66 Antonio Margheriti

Dinarathrangal 88 Joshi

Diner 82 Barry Levinson

Dîner Impossible, Le 04 Georges Méliès

Ding Dong Daddy 42 Friz Freleng

Ding Dong Doggie 37 Dave Fleischer

Ding Dong Williams 46 William Berke

Dingaka 65 Jamie Uys

Dinky 35 Howard Bretherton, D. Ross Lederman

Dinky Doodle and the Bad Man 25 Walter Lantz

Dinky Doodle and the Little Orphan 26 Walter Lantz

Dinky Doodle in Egypt 26 Walter Lantz

Dinky Doodle in Lost and Found 26 Walter Lantz

Dinky Doodle in the Arctic 26 Walter Lantz

Dinky Doodle in the Army 26 Walter Lantz

Dinky Doodle in the Circus 25 Walter Lantz

Dinky Doodle in the Hunt 25 Walter Lantz

Dinky Doodle in the Restaurant 25 Walter Lantz

Dinky Doodle in the Wild West 26 Walter Lantz

Dinky Doodle in Uncle Tom's Cabin 26 Walter Lantz

Dinky Doodle's Bedtime Story 26 Walter Lantz

Dinner at Eight 33 George Cukor

Dinner at the Ritz 37 Harold Schuster

Dinner for Adele 78 Oldřich Lipský

Dinner Hour 06 Alf Collins

Dinner Hour 35 Edgar Anstey

Dinner Time 28 John Foster

Dinner Time 62 Friedrich Ermler

Dinner Under Difficulties, A 1898 Georges Méliès

Dino 57 Thomas Carr

Dinosaur...Secret of the Lost Legend 85 B. W. L. Norton

Dinosaurus! 60 Irvin S. Yeaworth, Jr.

Dinty 20 John McDermott, Marshall Neilan

Dio Chiamato a Dorian, Il 70 Massimo Dallamano

Dio Disse a Caino... 69 Antonio Margheriti

Dio in Cielo...Arizona in Terra 72 Ignacio F. Iquino

Dio Li Crea...Io Li Ammazzo 68 Paolo Bianchini

Dio Mio, Come Sono Caduta in Basso 74 Luigi Comencini

Dio Non Paga il Sabato 67 Tanio Boccia

Dio Perdona...Io No! 67 Giuseppe Colizzi

Dio Perdoni la Mia Pistola 69 Mario Gariazzo, Leopoldo Savona

Dio Serpente, Il 70 Piero Vivarelli

Dion Brothers, The 74 Jack Starrett

Dionysus 84 Jean Rouch

Dionysus in '69 68 Brian DePalma, Robert Fiore, Bruce Rubin

Dip 'Em and Do 'Em, Ltd. 14 Will P. Kellino

Diplomacy 16 Sidney Olcott

Diplomacy 26 Marshall Neilan

Diplomaniacs 33 William A. Seiter

Diplomatic Corpse, The 58 Montgomery Tully

Diplomatic Courier 52 Henry Hathaway

Diplomatic Lover, The 34 Anthony Kimmins

Diplomatic Mission 18 Jack Conway

Diplomatic Passport 54 Gene Martel

Diplomatic Pouch, The 27 Alexander Dovzhenko

Diplomats, The 29 Norman Taurog

Diplomat's Mansion, The 61 Shiro Toyoda

Diploteratology or Bardo Folly 67 George Landow

Dipper, The 17 Walt Mason

Dippy's Plight 11 A. E. Coleby

Dipsy Gipsy 41 George Pal

Diptych 67 Walerian Borowczyk

Diptyque 67 Walerian Borowczyk

Diputado, El 77 Eloy De la Iglesia

Dir Gehört Mein Herz 38 Carmine Gallone

Dire Straits Presents Making Movies 81 Lester Bookbinder

Direct au Cœur 33 Roger Lion, Marcel Pagnol

Directed by Andrei Tarkovsky 88 Michał Leszczyłowski

Directed by John Ford 70 Peter Bogdanovich

Directed by William Wyler 86 Aviva Slesin

Direction d'Acteur par Jean Renoir, La 68 Jean Renoir

Direction—Nowa Huta 51 Andrzej Munk

Direction of Main Strike, The 70 Yuri Ozerov

Director's Block Notes, A 68 Federico Fellini

Director's Notebook, A 68 Federico Fellini

Direktørens Datter 12 August Blom

Dirge 57 Heinosuke Gosho

Dirigeable Fantastique, Le 06 Georges Méliès

Dirigeable Fantastique ou Le Cauchemar d'un Inventeur, Le 06 Georges Méliès

Dirigible 31 Frank Capra

Dirnenmörderer von London, Der 76 Jesús Franco

Dirt 79 Eric Karson, Cal Naylor

Dirt Bike Kid, The 86 Hoite Caston

Dirt Gang, The 72 Jerry Jameson

Dirtiest Girl I Ever Met, The 73 Peter Walker

Dirty Dancing 87 Emile Ardolino

Dirty Dingus Magee 70 Burt Kennedy

Dirty Dishes 78 Joyce Buñuel

Dirty Dozen, The 67 Robert Aldrich

Dirty Duck 77 Charles Swenson

Dirty Face Dan 15 Chester M. Franklin, Sidney Franklin

Dirty Game, The 65 Christian-Jaque, Werner Klingler, Carlo Lizzani, Terence Young

Dirty Gerty from Harlem, U.S.A. 46 Spencer Williams

Dirty Girls, The 61 Shohei Imamura

Dirty Girls, The 65 Radley Metzger

Dirty Hands 51 Fernand Rivers

Dirty Hands 74 Claude Chabrol

Dirty Harry 71 Don Siegel

Dirty Heroes 69 Alberto De Martino

Dirty Knights' Work 76 Kevin Connor

Dirty Laundry 86 William Webb

Dirty Lilly 78 Chuck Vincent

Dirty Little Billy 72 Stan Dragoti

Dirty Looks 83 Chuck Vincent

Dirty Mary 69 Nelly Kaplan

Dirty Mary, Crazy Larry 74 John Hough

Dirty Money 72 Jean-Pierre Melville

Dirty O'Neil 74 Howard Freen, Lewis Teague

Dirty Outlaws, The 67 Franco Rossetti

Dirty Rebel 87 Aleksandar Petković

Dirty Rotten Scoundrels 88 Frank Oz

Dirty Story, A 77 Jean Eustache

Dirty Story 84 Jörn Donner

Dirty Tricks 80 Alvin Rakoff

Dirty War, The 65 Christian-Jaque, Werner Klingler, Carlo Lizzani, Terence Young

Dirty Work 33 Lloyd French

Dirty Work 34 Tom Walls

Dirty Work in a Laundry 15 Charlie Chase

Dirtymouth 70 Herbert S. Altman

Dis-Moi 80 Chantal Akerman

Dis-Moi Que Tu M'Aime 74 Michel Boisrond

Dis-Moi Qui Tuer 65 Étienne Périer

Disabled Motor, The 00 James A. Williamson

Disamistade 89 Gianfranco Cabiddu

Disappearance, The 77 Stuart Cooper

Disappearance of Lady Frances Carfax, The 23 George Ridgwell

Disappearance of the Judge, The 19 Alexander Butler

Disappeared, The 79 Sergio Castilla

Disappointed Suitor's Strategy and Reward, The 05 Tom Green

Disarmament 17 Forest Holger-Madsen

Disarmament Conference 31 Manny Gould, Ben Harrison

Disaster 48 William Pine

Disbarred 37 Robert Florey

Disc Jockey 51 Will Jason

Disc Jockey Jamboree 57 Roy Lockwood

Disc 927 28 Germaine Dulac

Discard, The 16 Lawrence C. Windom

Discarded Lovers 32 Fred Newmeyer

Discarded Woman, The 20 Burton L. King

Discarnates, The 89 Nobuhiko Obayashi

Disciple, The 15 William S. Hart, Clifford Smith

Disciple of Darwin, A 12 Frank Wilson

Disciple of Death 72 Tom Parkinson

Disciple of Dracula 65 Terence Fisher

Disciples, The 85 Géza Beremenyi

Disciples of Death 72 Frank Q. Dobbs

Disciples' Offerings to the Priest 86 Dayal Nihalani

Discipline 35 Lawrence Barrett, John Gladstone, A. B. Imeson, James Riddell

Disco Fever 78 Lamar Card

Disco 9000 *77* D'Urville Martin
Disco Volante, Il *64* Tinto Brass
Discomania *80* Oscar Riesel
Disconnected *84* Gorman Bechard
Discontent *16* Lois Weber
Discontented Husbands *24* Edward J. LeSaint
Discontented Wives *21* John P. McGowan
Discopříběh *87* Jaroslav Soukup
Discord *26* Gustaf Molander
Discord *33* Henry Edwards
Discord *55* László Ranódy
Discord and Harmony *14* Allan Dwan
Discord in Three Flats *15* Edwin J. Collins
Discoteca del Amor, La *80* Adolfo Aristarain
Discours de Bienvenue de McLaren *60* Norman McLaren
Discoveries *39* Redd Davis
Discovery Bay *87* William Webb
Discovery of Brazil, The *32* Humberto Mauro
Discovery of Sergei Radonezhsky's Remains *19* Dziga Vertov
Discovery of Zero, The *63* Yoji Kuri
Discovery, Penicillin *64* George Dunning
Discreet Charm of the Bourgeoisie, The *72* Luis Buñuel
Discretion with Honor *39* Johannes Meyer
Discussion de M. Janssen et de M. Lagrange *1895* Louis Lumière
Discussion Politique *01* Ferdinand Zecca
Disembodied, The *57* Walter Grauman
Disgraced! *33* Erle C. Kenton
Dish Ran Away with the Spoon, The *33* Rudolf Ising
Dishevelled Hair *61* Teinosuke Kinugasa
Dishonest Barber, The *08* Lewin Fitzhamon
Dishonorable Discharge *58* Bernard Borderie
Dishonored *31* Josef von Sternberg
Dishonored *50* Guido Brignone
Dishonored Lady *47* Robert Stevenson
Dishonored Medal, The *14* Christy Cabanne
Dishonour Bright *36* Tom Walls
Disillusion *49* Mario Bonnard
Disillusioned Bluebird *44* Howard Swift
Disinherited Nephew, The *12* Bert Haldane
Disk-o-Tek Holiday *63* Douglas Hickox
Diskret Ophold *46* Ole Palsbo
Diskretion-Ehrensache *39* Johannes Meyer
Dislocation Extraordinary *01* Georges Méliès
Dislocation Mystérieuse *01* Georges Méliès
Dislocations Mystérieuses *01* Georges Méliès
Disobedience *58* Yasuzo Masumura
Disobedient *53* Charles Frank
Disobedient Robot, The *56* Dušan Vukotić
Disorder *62* Franco Brusati
Disorder *86* Olivier Assayas
Disorder and Early Torment *77* Franz Seitz
Disorder by the Kuroda Clan *56* Tomu Uchida
Disorder Is Twenty Years Old *67* Jacques Baratier
Disorderlies *87* Michael Schultz
Disorderly Conduct *32* John W. Considine, Jr.
Disorderly Orderly, A *27* Sam Newfield
Disorderly Orderly, The *64* Frank Tashlin
Disordine, Il *62* Franco Brusati
Disorganized Crime *89* Jim Kouf
Disparus de Saint-Agil, Les *38* Christian-Jaque
Dispatch from Reuters, A *40* William Dieterle
Dispersing Clouds *51* Heinosuke Gosho
Disprezzo, Il *63* Jean-Luc Godard
Disputado Voto del Sr. Cayo, El *86* Antonio Gimenez-Rico
Disputed Passage *39* Frank Borzage
Disputed Vote of Mr. Cayo, The *86* Antonio Gimenez-Rico
Disque 413 *36* Richard Pottier
Disque 927 *28* Germaine Dulac
Disraeli *16* Charles C. Calvert, Percy Nash
Disraeli *21* Henry Kolker
Disraeli *29* Alfred E. Green
Dissolved Government, The *10* F. Percy Smith
Dissolving the Government *09* F. Percy Smith
Distance, La *18* Robert Boudrioz
Distance *75* Anthony Lover
Distance *86* Jesús Díaz
Distant Clouds *55* Keisuke Kinoshita
Distant Cry from Spring, A *80* Yoji Yamada
Distant Drums *51* Raoul Walsh
Distant Harmony *87* DeWitt Sage
Distant Journey *49* Alfred Radok
Distant Lights *87* Aurelio Chiesa
Distant Relative, The *12* Allan Dwan
Distant Thunder *73* Satyajit Ray
Distant Thunder *88* Richard Rosenthal
Distant Trumpet *52* Terence Fisher
Distant Trumpet, A *64* Raoul Walsh
Distant Voices, Still Lives *88* Terence Davies
Distinta Famiglia, Una *43* Mario Bonnard
Distortions *87* Armand Mastroianni
Distracted Bather, The *1899* C. Goodwin Norton
Distrait, Le *75* Pierre Richard
District Attorney, The *15* Barry O'Neil
Disturbance, The *90* Cliff Guest
Disturbing His Rest *07* Percy Stow
Dites-Cariatides, Les *84* Agnès Varda
Dites-Lui Que Je l'Aime *77* Claude Miller
Dites 33 *56* Camillo Mastrocinque
Ditirambo *67* Gonzalo Suárez
Ditte: Child of Man *46* Bjarne Henning-Jensen
Ditte Menneskebarn *46* Bjarne Henning-Jensen
Ditto *37* Charles Lamont
Ditya Bolshova Goroda *14* Yevgeni Bauer
Diva *80* Jean-Jacques Beineix
Dive Bomber *41* Michael Curtiz
Divergent Views, No.s 41 and 42 John Street *14* Toby Cooper
Divers at Work on a Wreck Under the Sea *1898* Georges Méliès
Divers at Work on the Wreck of the Maine
1898 Georges Méliès
Diver's Diversions *09* Dave Aylott
Diversion *80* James Dearden
Diver-sions *09* Dave Aylott
Divertissement, Le *52* Jacques Rivette
Divertissement *60* Alexander Alexeïeff, Claire Parker
Divetta del Regimento, La *16* Mario Caserini
Divide and Conquer *42* Frank Capra, Anatole Litvak
Divided Heart, The *54* Charles Crichton
Divided Love *88* Helma Sanders-Brahms
Divided Trail, The *80* Jerry Aronson, Mical Goldman
Divided We Fall *82* Jeff Burr*
Divided World, A *48* Arne Sucksdorff
Dividend, The *16* Walter Edwards
Dividing Line, The *49* Joseph Losey
Dividing Wall, The *51* Shih-ling Chu
Divinas Palabras *87* José Luis García Sánchez
Divine *35* Max Ophüls
Divine Creature *79* Giuseppe Patroni Griffi
Divine Croisière, La *28* Julien Duvivier
Divine Damnation, The *67* Gregory Markopoulos
Divine Emma, The *79* Jiří Krejčík
Divine Enfant *89* Jean-Pierre Mocky
Divine Gift, The *18* Thomas Bentley
Divine Jetta, The *37* Erich Waschneck
Divine Lady, The *29* Frank Lloyd
Divine Love *32* Lewis Seiler
Divine Madness *80* Michael Ritchie
Divine Mr. J, The *74* Peter Alexander
Divine Nymph *79* Giuseppe Patroni Griffi
Divine Sacrifice, The *18* George Archainbaud
Divine Sinner *28* Scott Pembroke
Divine Spark, The *35* Carmine Gallone
Divine Woman, The *27* Victor Sjöström
Divine Words *87* José Luis García Sánchez
Diviners, The *83* Robert Altman
Diving Fool, A *24* Charles Lamont
Diving for Treasure *00* Walter R. Booth
Diving Girl, The *11* Mack Sennett
Diving Girls' Island, The *63* Marion Gering
Diving Girls of Japan *63* Marion Gering
Divino Boemo, Il *75* Jaromil Jireš
Divisions de la Nature, Les *78* Raúl Ruiz
Divisions of Nature, The *78* Raúl Ruiz
Dívka s Třemi Velbloudy *68* Václav Krška
Dívka v Modrém *39* Otakar Vávra
Divorce *23* Chester Bennett
Divorce *28* Roy William Neill
Divorce *45* William Nigh
Divorce à la Carte *31* Charles Lamont
Divorce American Style *67* Bud Yorkin
Divorce Among Friends *30* Roy Del Ruth
Divorce and the Daughter *16* Frederick Sullivan
Divorce Coupons *22* Webster Campbell
Divorce Courtship, A *33* George Stevens
Divorce Game, The *17* Travers Vale
Divorce Heureux, Un *74* Henning Carlsen
Divorce in the Family *32* Charles Reisner
Divorce—Italian Style *61* Pietro Germi
Divorce Made Easy *29* Al Christie

Docteur Jekyll et les Femmes *81* Walerian Borowczyk

Docteur Justice *75* Christian-Jaque

Docteur Laënnec *48* Maurice Cloche

Docteur M *89* Claude Chabrol

Docteur Popaul *72* Claude Chabrol

Doctor, The *11* J. Searle Dawley

Doctor, The *16* Michael Curtiz

Doctor, The *86* Vojko Duletić

Dr. Alien *88* David DeCoteau

Dr. and Mrs. Jekyll *79* Steno

Doctor and the Bricklayer, The *18* Edward José

Doctor and the Debutante, The *41* W. S. Van Dyke

Doctor and the Devils, The *85* Freddie Francis

Doctor and the Girl, The *49* Kurt Bernhardt

Doctor and the Monkey, The *01* Georges Méliès

Doctor and the Quack, The *57* Mario Monicelli

Doctor and the Woman, The *18* Phillips Smalley, Lois Weber

Doctor at Large *57* Ralph Thomas

Doctor at Sea *55* Ralph Thomas

Doctor Beware *41* Vittorio De Sica

Dr. Black and Mr. Hyde *76* William Crain

Dr. Black, Mr. Hyde *76* William Crain

Doctor Blood's Coffin *60* Sidney J. Furie

Doctor Bluebird *36* Charles Mintz

Dr. Breedlove *64* Russ Meyer

Dr. Brian Pellie and the Bank Robbery *11* Wilfred Noy

Dr. Brian Pellie and the Baronet's Bride *11* Wilfred Noy

Dr. Brian Pellie and the Secret Despatch *12* Wilfred Noy

Dr. Brian Pellie and the Spanish Grandees *12* Wilfred Noy

Dr. Brian Pellie and the Wedding Gifts *13* Wilfred Noy

Dr. Brian Pellie Escapes from Prison *12* Wilfred Noy

Dr. Brian Pellie, Thief and Coiner *10* Wilfred Noy

Dr. Broadway *42* Anthony Mann

Doctor Bull *33* John Ford

Dr. Butcher, M.D. *79* Marino Girolami

Dr. Cadman's Secret *56* Reginald LeBorg

Dr. Caligari *90* Stephen Sayadian

Dr. Christian Meets the Women *40* William McGann

Dr. Coppelius *66* Ted Kneeland

Dr. Crimen *53* Chano Urueta

Dr. Crippen *62* Robert Lynn

Dr. Cut'emup *04* Alf Collins

Dr. Cyclops *40* Ernest B. Schoedsack

Dr. Death *73* Eddie Saeta

Dr. Death: Seeker of Souls *73* Eddie Saeta

Doctor Detroit *83* Michael Pressman

Doctor Devil and Mister Hare *64* Robert McKimson

Dr. Dolittle *28* Lotte Reiniger

Doctor Dolittle *67* Richard Fleischer, Herbert Ross

Dr. Dosem's Deputy *14* Will P. Kellino

Dr. Ehrlich's Magic Bullet *40* William Dieterle

Dr. Engel, Child Specialist *37* Johannes Riemann

Dr. Epameinondas *38* Toga Mizrahi

Doctor Faustus *67* Richard Burton, Nevill Coghill

Dr. Fenton's Ordeal *14* Frank Wilson

Dr. Frankenstein *73* Jack Smight

Dr. Frankenstein on Campus *67* Gilbert W. Taylor

Doctor from Halberstadt, A *69* Alexander Kluge

Doctor from Seven Dials, The *58* Robert Day

Dr. G. and the Bikini Machine *65* Norman Taurog

Dr. G. and the Love Bombs *66* Mario Bava

Dr. Gillespie's Criminal Case *43* Willis Goldbeck

Dr. Gillespie's New Assistant *42* Willis Goldbeck

Dr. Glas *42* Rune Carlsten

Dr. Glas *67* Mai Zetterling

Dr. Goldfoot and the Bikini Machine *65* Norman Taurog

Dr. Goldfoot and the Girl Bombs *66* Mario Bava

Dr. Hackenstein *88* Richard Clark

Dr. Heckyl and Mr. Hype *80* Charles B. Griffith

Dr. Holl *51* Rolf Hansen

Doctor in Clover *65* Ralph Thomas

Doctor in Distress *63* Ralph Thomas

Doctor in Love *60* Ralph Thomas

Doctor in the House *53* Ralph Thomas

Doctor in the Village *58* Fons Rademakers

Doctor in Trouble *70* Ralph Thomas

Doctor Jack *22* Fred Newmeyer

Dr. Jeckill y el Hombre Lobo *71* Leon Klimovsky

Dr. Jekyll *81* Walerian Borowczyk

Dr. Jekyll and Miss Osbourne *81* Walerian Borowczyk

Dr. Jekyll and Mr. Blood *72* Andy Milligan

Dr. Jekyll and Mr. Hyde *08* Sidney Olcott

Dr. Jekyll and Mr. Hyde *10* Viggo Larsen

Dr. Jekyll and Mr. Hyde *12* Lucius Henderson

Dr. Jekyll and Mr. Hyde *13* Herbert Brenon

Dr. Jekyll and Mr. Hyde *20* F. W. Murnau

Dr. Jekyll and Mr. Hyde *20* John S. Robertson

Dr. Jekyll and Mr. Hyde *31* Rouben Mamoulian

Dr. Jekyll and Mr. Hyde *41* Victor Fleming

Dr. Jekyll and Mr. Hyde *73* David Winters

Dr. Jekyll and Mr. Mouse *47* Joseph Barbera, William Hanna

Dr. Jekyll and Mr. Zip *20* Gregory La Cava

Doctor Jekyll and Sister Hyde *71* Roy Ward Baker

Dr. Jekyll and the Werewolf *71* Leon Klimovsky

Dr. Jekyll and the Wolfman *71* Leon Klimovsky

Dr. Jekyll and the Women *81* Walerian Borowczyk

Dr. Jekyll, Jr. *79* Steno

Dr. Jekyll y el Hombre Lobo *71* Leon Klimovsky

Dr. Jekyll's Dungeon of Death *78* James Wood

Dr. Jekyll's Mistress *64* Jesús Franco

Dr. Jerkyl's Hide *54* Friz Freleng

Dr. Jim *21* William Worthington

Dr. Josser KC *31* Norman Lee

Dr. Justice *75* Christian-Jaque

Dr. Kildare Goes Home *40* Harold S. Bucquet

Dr. Kildare's Crisis *40* Harold S. Bucquet

Dr. Kildare's Strange Case *40* Harold S. Bucquet

Dr. Kildare's Victory *41* W. S. Van Dyke

Dr. Kildare's Wedding Day *41* Harold S. Bucquet

Dr. Killjoy *21* Raoul Barré, Charles Bowers

Dr. Knock *33* Roger Goupillières, Louis Jouvet

Dr. Knock *55* Guy Lefranc

Dr. Korczak *90* Andrzej Wajda

Dr. M *58* Fernando Méndez

Dr. M *89* Claude Chabrol

Dr. Mabuse der Spieler — Part II: Inferno *22* Fritz Lang

Dr. Mabuse, King of Crime *22* Fritz Lang

Dr. Mabuse, Part One *22* Fritz Lang

Dr. Mabuse, Part Two *22* Fritz Lang

Doctor Mabuse, the Gambler *22* Fritz Lang

Dr. Mabuse, the Gambler — Part One: Ein Bild der Zeit *22* Fritz Lang

Dr. Mabuse the Gambler, Part Two *22* Fritz Lang

Dr. Mabuse vs. Scotland Yard *63* Paul Ostermayer

Dr. Mabuse's Rays of Death *64* Hugo Fregonese

Dr. MacDonald's Sanatorium *20* Willy Zehn

Dr. Maniac *36* Robert Stevenson

Dr. Maniac *73* Ray Austin

Dr. Mason's Temptation *15* Frank Lloyd

Dr. Minx *75* Hikmet Avedis

Dr. Monica *34* William Dieterle, William Keighley

Doctor Monko *15* Harry S. Palmer

Dr. Morelle *49* Godfrey Grayson

Dr. Morelle — The Case of the Missing Heiress *49* Godfrey Grayson

Dr. Neighbor *16* Lloyd B. Carleton

Dr. No *62* Terence Young

Dr. O'Dowd *39* Herbert Mason

Doctor of Doom *62* René Cardona

Doctor of St. Paul, The *69* Rolf Olsen

Dr. Orloff's Monster *64* Jesús Franco

Doctor Oswald *35* Walter Lantz

Dr. Otto and the Riddle of the Gloom Beam *83* John R. Cherry III

Dr. Paul Joseph Goebbels *44* Alfred Zeisler

Dr. Paxton's Last Crime *14* Sidney Morgan

Dr. Phibes Rises Again *72* Robert Fuest

Dr. Popaul *72* Claude Chabrol

Dr. Pulder Sows Poppies *75* Bert Haanstra

Dr. Rameau *15* Will S. Davis
Dr. Renault's Secret *42* Harry Lachman
Doctor Rhythm *38* Frank Tuttle
Dr. Russell's Lie *12* A. E. Coleby
Doctor Satan's Robot *40* John English, William Witney
Doctor Says, The *66* Aleksander Ford
Dr. Sin Fang *37* Anthony Frenguelli
Dr. Skinum *07* Wallace McCutcheon
Dr. Socrates *35* William Dieterle
Doctor Speaks Out, The *66* Aleksander Ford
Dr. Strangelove, or How I Learned to Stop Worrying and Love the Bomb *63* Stanley Kubrick
Dr. Sun Yatsen *87* Yinnan Sing
Dr. Sunshine *23* Clarence Badger
Dr. Syn *37* Roy William Neill
Dr. Syn *61* Peter Graham Scott
Dr. Syn *62* James Neilson
Dr. Syn Alias the Scarecrow *62* James Neilson
Doctor Takes a Wife, The *40* Alexander Hall
Dr. Tarr's Torture Dungeon *72* Juan López Moctezuma
Dr. Terror's Gallery of Horrors *67* David L. Hewitt
Dr. Terror's House of Horrors *64* Freddie Francis
Dr. Trimball's Verdict *13* Frank Wilson
Dr. Violet Dearing *15* Cecil Birch
Dr. Wake's Patient *16* Fred Paul
Dr. Who and the Daleks *65* Gordon Flemyng
Doctor Without Scruples *59* Falk Harnack
Dr. X *15* Robert Dinesen
Doctor X *31* Michael Curtiz
Doctor, You've Got to Be Kidding *67* Peter Tewksbury
Doctor Zhivago *64* David Lean
Dr. Zippy Opens a Sanatorium *16* Charles E. Howell
Doctored Affair, A *13* Mack Sennett
Doctored Beer, The *06* J. H. Martin
Doctored Dinner Pail, The *09* Edwin S. Porter
Doctors, The *56* Ralph Habib
Doctors, The *63* Ted V. Mikels
Doctor's Alibi *41* Lambert Hillyer
Doctors and Nurses *83* Maurice Murphy
Doctor's Apprentice *87* Boris Rytsarev
Doctor's Courage, The *45* George Sherman
Doctor's Crime, The *14* Charles H. Weston
Doctor's Diary, A *37* Charles Vidor
Doctor's Dilemma, The *11* Percy Stow
Doctor's Dilemma, The *58* Anthony Asquith
Doctor's Dodge, The *08* Lewin Fitzhamon
Doctors Don't Tell *41* Jacques Tourneur
Doctor's Gamble, The *47* William Castle
Doctor's Horrible Experiment, The *59* Jean Renoir
Doctor's Legacy, The *14* August Blom
Doctor's Orders *34* Norman Lee
Doctor's Round *81* Karel Kachyňa
Doctor's Sacrifice, The *32* Phil Rosen
Doctor's Secret, The *09* Georges Méliès

Doctor's Secret, The *13* Van Dyke Brooke
Doctor's Secret, The *29* William DeMille
Doctor's Secret, The *30* John W. Brunius
Doctors Should Have Patience *20* Gregory La Cava
Doctor's Warning, The *45* William Castle
Doctors Wear Scarlet *70* Robert Hartford-Davis
Doctors' Wives *31* Frank Borzage
Doctors' Wives *71* George Schaefer
Doctor's Women, The *27* Gustaf Molander
Document: Fanny and Alexander *86* Ingmar Bergman
Document of the Dead *80* Roy Frumkes
Document Secret *16* Gaston Ravel
Documental a Propósito del Tránsito, Un *71* Sara Gómez
Documentator, The *89* István Darday, György Szalai
Documenteur *81* Agnès Varda
Documenteur: An Emotion Picture *81* Agnès Varda
Documento, Il *39* Mario Camerini
Documento Fatale, Il *39* Mario Camerini
Documents Secrets *40* Léo Joannon
Doddington Diamonds, The *22* Jack Denton
Dödens Besegrare *15* Victor Sjöström
Dødens Brud *11* August Blom
Dødens Kontrakt *16* Forest Holger-Madsen
Dødes Halsbånd, Den *10* August Blom
Dödes' Kaden *70* Akira Kurosawa
Dødes Røst, Den *14* Forest Holger-Madsen
Dødes Sjæl, Den *15* Forest Holger-Madsen
Dōdesu Kaden *70* Akira Kurosawa
Dodge City *39* Michael Curtiz
Dodge City Trail *36* C. C. Coleman, Jr.
Dodgers Dodged, The *07* Frank Mottershaw
Dodging a Million *18* George Loane Tucker
Dodging the Dole *36* John E. Blakeley
Dodging the Landlord *13* Ernest Lepard
12 Dicembre *72* Pier Paolo Pasolini*
Dodici Dicembre *72* Pier Paolo Pasolini*
Dodici Dicembre 1972 *72* Pier Paolo Pasolini*
Dødsdrømmen *11* August Blom
Dødsdrømte, Den *15* Forest Holger-Madsen
Dödskyssen *16* Victor Sjöström
Dödspolare *85* Mats Arehn
Dodsworth *36* William Wyler
Doea Tanda Mata *86* Teguh Karya
Does, The *67* Claude Chabrol
Does It Pay? *23* Charles T. Horan
Dog, The *77* Juan Antonio Bardem
Dog, a Mouse and a Sputnik, A *58* Jean Dréville
Dog and the Bone, The *09* Frank Wilson
Dog and the Diamonds, The *53* Ralph Thomas
Dog Blight *36* Jean Yarbrough
Dog Came Back, The *09* Lewin Fitzhamon
Dog, Cat and Canary, The *45* Howard Swift
Dog Catcher's Love, The *17* Edward F. Cline
Dog Chaperone, The *10* Frank Wilson
Dog Collared *51* Robert McKimson

Dog Day *83* Yves Boisset
Dog Day Afternoon *75* Sidney Lumet
Dog Days *19* Charles Reisner
Dog Days *71* Jan Halldoff
Dog Daze *25* Charles Lamont
Dog Daze *37* Friz Freleng
Dog Daze *39* George Sidney
Dog Detective, The *06* Harold Hough
Dog Eat Dog *64* Ray Nazarro, Albert Zugsmith
Dog Factory *04* Edwin S. Porter
Dog Gone *26* Charles Bowers
Dog-Gone Clever *20* Charles Reisner
Dog Gone Dog Catcher *55* John Halas*
Dog Gone It *27* Walter Lantz
Dog Gone Modern *38* Chuck Jones
Dog Gone South *50* Chuck Jones
Dog-Gone Tough Luck *19* Raoul Barré, Charles Bowers
Dog Heads *54* Martin Frič
Dog House *52* Joseph Barbera, William Hanna
Dog House Builders, The *13* James Young
Dog in the Orchard, A *40* Jean Negulesco
Dog Justice *28* Jerome Storm
Dog Law *28* Jerome Storm
Dog Meets Dog *42* Frank Tashlin
Dog of Flanders, A *35* Edward Sloman
Dog of Flanders, A *59* James B. Clark
Dog of the Regiment, A *27* D. Ross Lederman
Dog Outwits the Kidnapper, The *08* Lewin Fitzhamon
Dog Pound, The *16* Charles Bowers
Dog Pounded *53* Friz Freleng
Dog Shy *26* Leo McCarey
Dog Snatcher, The *31* Dick Huemer
Dog Snatcher *52* Pete Burness
Dog Soldiers *78* Karel Reisz
Dog Star Man *64* Stan Brakhage
Dog Tags *90* Romano Scavolini
Dog Tales *58* Robert McKimson
Dog That Liked Trains, The *78* Goran Paskaljević
Dog Thief, The *08* Lewin Fitzhamon
Dog Tired *41* Chuck Jones
Dog Who Stopped the War, The *84* André Melançon
Događaj *69* Vatroslav Mimica
Doggone Cats *47* Art Davis
Doggone Mix-Up, A *38* Charles Lamont
Doggone People *60* Robert McKimson
Doggone Tired *49* Tex Avery
Doggy and the Four *54* Jiří Weiss
Dogodilo Se na Današnji Dan *88* Miroslav Lekić
Dogpound Shuffle *74* Jeffrey Bloom
Dogs *76* Burt Brinckerhoff
Dogs, The *78* Alain Jessua
Dogs and People *70* Evald Schorm
Dogs and the Desperado, The *13* Frank Wilson
Dogs' Beach *86* José Fonseca e Costa
Dogs Behind Bars *54* Gillo Pontecorvo
Dog's Best Friend, A *59* Edward L. Cahn
Dog's Devotion, The *08* Dave Aylott
Dog's Devotion, The *11* Lewin Fitzhamon
Dogs' Dialog *77* Raúl Ruiz
Dogs, Do You Want to Live Forever? *59* Frank Wisbar

Don Bosco *35* Goffredo Alessandrini
Don Caesar de Bazan *15* Robert Vignola
Don Camillo *51* Julien Duvivier
Don Camillo e i Giovani d'Oggi *72* Mario Camerini
Don Camillo e l'Onorevole Peppone *55* Carmine Gallone
Don Camillo Monsignore Ma Non Troppo *61* Carmine Gallone
Don Camillo's Last Round *55* Carmine Gallone
Don Carlos *10* André Calmettes
Don Carlos und Elisabeth *24* Richard Oswald
Don Cesare di Bazan *42* Riccardo Freda
Don Chicago *45* Maclean Rogers
Don Coo-Coo *25* Wesley Ruggles
Don Cossack Chorus, The *42* Jean Negulesco
Don Dare Devil *25* Clifford Smith
Don Daredevil Rides Again *51* Fred C. Brannon
Don del Mar, El *57* Jorge Grau
Don Desperado *27* Leo D. Maloney
Don Diego and Pelageya *27* Yakov Protazanov
Don Diego i Pelageya *27* Yakov Protazanov
Don Giovanni *55* Paul Czinner, Alfred Travers
Don Giovanni *79* Joseph Losey
Don Giovanni in Sicilia *67* Alberto Lattuada
Don Go On *27* William C. Nolan
Don Is Dead, The *73* Richard Fleischer
Don Juan *07* Albert Capellani
Don Juan *22* Edwin J. Collins
Don Juan *24* Fortunio Bonanova
Don Juan *26* Alan Crosland
Don Juan *34* Alexander Korda
Don Juan *55* John Berry
Don Juan *56* Walter Kolm-Veltee
Don Juan de Serralonga *13* Ricardo De Baños
Don Juan Diplomático *31* George Melford
Don Juan et Faust *22* Marcel L'Herbier
Don Juan Était une Femme *73* Roger Vadim
Don Juan in der Mädchenschule *28* Reinhold Schünzel
Don Juan, My Love *90* Antonio Mercero
Don Juan 1973 *73* Roger Vadim
Don Juan 1973, or If Don Juan Were a Woman *73* Roger Vadim
Don Juan 1973 ou Si Don Juan Était une Femme *73* Roger Vadim
Don Juan Quilligan *45* Frank Tuttle
Don Juan 68 *68* Jaromil Jireš
Don Juan Tenorio *10* Ricardo De Baños
Don Juan Tenorio *21* Ricardo De Baños
Don Juan Tenorio *37* René Cardona
Don Juan Tenorio *49* Luis César Amadori
Don Juan und die Drei Marien *22* Reinhold Schünzel
Don Juan's Night of Love *52* Mario Soldati
Don Juan's Three Nights *26* John Francis Dillon
Don-Kikhot *57* Grigori Kozintsev
Don Lorenzo *53* Carlo Ludovico Bragaglia

Don Mike *27* Lloyd Ingraham
Don Pietro Caruso *16* Emilio Ghione
Don Q and the Artist *12* H. Oceano Martinek
Don Q—How He Outwitted Don Luis *12* H. Oceano Martinek
Don Q—How He Treated the Parole of Gevil Hay *12* H. Oceano Martinek
Don Q, Son of Zorro *25* Donald Crisp
Don Quichotte *03* Ferdinand Zecca
Don Quichotte *09* Émile Cohl
Don Quichotte *32* G. W. Pabst
Don Quickshot of the Rio Grande *23* George Marshall
Don Quintín el Amargado *51* Luis Buñuel
Don Quintin the Bitter *51* Luis Buñuel
Don Quixote *09* Émile Cohl
Don Quixote *16* Edward Dillon
Don Quixote *23* Maurice Elvey
Don Quixote *32* G. W. Pabst
Don Quixote *34* Ubbe Iwerks
Don Quixote *49* Rafael Gil
Don Quixote *57* Grigori Kozintsev
Don Quixote *73* Robert Helpmann, Rudolf Nureyev
Don Quixote's Dream *08* Lewin Fitzhamon
Don Ricardo Returns *46* Terry Morse
Don Sanche *69* Jan Švankmajer
Don Winslow of the Navy *42* Ford Beebe, Ray Taylor
Don X *25* Forrest K. Sheldon
Doña Bárbara *43* Fernando De Fuentes
Dona Flor and Her Two Husbands *76* Bruno Barreto
Dona Flor e Seus Dois Maridos *76* Bruno Barreto
Doña Francisquita *35* Hans Behrendt
Doña Francisquita *52* Ladislas Vajda
Doña Herlinda and Her Son *85* Jaime Humberto Hermosillo
Doña Herlinda and Her Two Sons *85* Jaime Humberto Hermosillo
Doña Herlinda y Su Hijo *85* Jaime Humberto Hermosillo
Doña Juana *27* Paul Czinner
Donatella *55* Mario Monicelli
Donde Mueren las Palabras *46* Hugo Fregonese
Dondi *61* Albert Zugsmith
Dong Kingman *55* James Wong Howe
Donga Kapuram *88* Kodi Ramakrishna
Donga Pelli *88* Raviraja Pinisetty
Donga Ramudu *88* K. Raghavendra Rao
Dongagaru Swagatham *88* G. Ram Mohan Rao
Dongdong de Jiaqui *84* Hsiao-hsien Hou
Dongo Horendi *66* Jean Rouch
Dongo Hori *73* Jean Rouch
Dongo Yenendi *66* Jean Rouch
Dongoduchhadu *87* Kodi Ramakrishna
Donkey and the Serpentine Dancer, The *02* George Albert Smith
Donkey Comes on a Tank, The *64* Yoji Yamada
Donkey Party, The *01* Edwin S. Porter
Donkey Skin, The *18* Michael Curtiz
Donkey Skin *70* Jacques Demy
Donkey That Drank the Moon, The *88* Marie-Claude Treilhou

Donna a Ucciso, Una *51* Vittorio Cottafavi
Donna Abandonata, La *17* Baldassare Negroni
Donna Che Venne dal Mare, La *56* Francesco De Robertis
Donna Chiamata Apache, Una *77* George McRoots
Donna da Scoprire, Una *87* Riccardo Sesani
Donna dei Faraoini, La *60* Giorgio Rivalta, Victor Tourjansky
Donna del Fiume, La *54* Mario Soldati
Donna del Giorno, La *56* Francesco Maselli
Donna del Lago, La *65* Luigi Bazzoni, Franco Rossellini
Donna del Mondo, La *62* Paolo Cavara, Gualtiero Jacopetti, Franco Prosperi
Donna del Traghetto, La *87* Amedeo Fago
Donna della Domenica, La *75* Luigi Comencini
Donna della Luna, La *88* Vito Zagarrio
Donna della Montagna, La *43* Renato Castellani
Donna delle Meraviglie, La *85* Alberto Bevilacqua
Donna di Vita *60* Jacques Demy
Donna Donna! *87* Hans van Beek, Luc van Beek
Donna Duende, La *45* Luis Saslavsky
Donna d'Una Notte, La *30* Marcel L'Herbier
Donna È Donna, La *60* Jean-Luc Godard
Donna e il Cadavere, La *19* Augusto Genina
Donna È una Cosa Meravigliosa, La *64* Mauro Bolognini*
Donna Fra Due Mondi, Una *37* Goffredo Alessandrini
Donna Libera, Una *54* Vittorio Cottafavi
Donna Nuda, La *13* Carmine Gallone
Donna Passò, Una *22* Augusto Genina
Donna per Ringo, Una *66* Rafael Romero Marchent
Donna Più Bella del Mondo, La *55* Robert Z. Leonard
Donna Rosebud *86* J. P. Somersaulter
Donna Scimmia, La *64* Marco Ferreri
Donna Senza Nome, Una *86* Luigi Russo
Donna Spezzata, La *88* Marco Leto
Donne alla Frontiera *66* Rudolf Zehetgruber
Donne…Botte e Bersaglieri *68* Ruggero Deodato
Donne e Briganti *50* Mario Soldati
Donne, Mitra e Diamanti *64* Christian-Jaque
Donne Proibite *53* Giuseppe Amato
Donne Senza Nome *49* Géza von Radványi
Donne Sole *56* Vittorio Sala
Donnez-Moi Ma Chance *57* Léonide Moguy
Donnez-Moi Tes Yeux *42* Sacha Guitry
Donogoo *36* Henri Chomette
Donogoo Tonka *36* Reinhold Schünzel
Donovan Affair, The *29* Frank Capra
Donovan's Brain *53* Felix E. Feist
Donovan's Kid *31* Fred Niblo
Donovan's Reef *63* John Ford

Don's Party 76 Bruce Beresford
Don't! 25 Alfred Goulding
Don't Answer the Phone 80 Robert Hammer
Don't Axe Me 58 Robert McKimson
Don't Be a Dummy 32 Frank Richardson
Don't Be Blue 69 Philippe Labro
Don't Be Like That 36 Jean Yarbrough
Don't Believe in Monuments 58 Dušan Makavejev
Don't Bet on Blondes 35 Robert Florey
Don't Bet on Love 33 Murray Roth
Don't Bet on Women 31 William K. Howard
Don't Bite Your Dentist 30 Edward F. Cline
Don't Blame the Stork 54 Ákos von Ráthonyi
Don't Bother to Knock 52 Roy Ward Baker
Don't Bother to Knock 61 Cyril Frankel
Don't Build Your Happiness on Your Wife and Child 17 Josef Soifer
Don't Call It Love 23 William DeMille
Don't Call Me a Con Man 66 Kengo Furusawa
Don't Call Me Little Girl 21 Joseph E. Henabery
Don't Change Your Husband 18 Cecil B. DeMille
Don't Cry for Me Little Mother 72 Radley Metzger
Don't Cry, It's Only Thunder 81 Peter Werner
Don't Cry, Peter 64 France Štiglić
Don't Cry, Pretty Girls 70 Márta Mészáros
Don't Cry with Your Mouth Full 73 Pascal Thomas
Don't Doubt Your Husband 24 Harry Beaumont
Don't Doubt Your Wife 22 James W. Horne
Don't Drink the Water 69 Howard Morris
Don't Ever Leave Me 49 Arthur Crabtree
Don't Ever Marry 20 Victor Heerman, Marshall Neilan
Don't Fail 24 Lloyd Bacon
Don't Fence Me In 45 John English
Don't Fool Thyself, Heart 36 Miguel Torres Contreras
Don't Gamble with Love 36 Dudley Murphy
Don't Gamble with Strangers 46 William Beaudine
Don't Get Me Wrong 37 Reginald Purdell, Arthur Woods
Don't Get Personal 22 Clarence Badger
Don't Get Personal 36 William Nigh
Don't Get Personal 41 Charles Lamont
Don't Give Up the Sheep 52 Chuck Jones
Don't Give Up the Ship 59 Norman Taurog
Don't Go in the House 80 Joseph Ellison
Don't Go in the Woods 80 James Bryant
Don't Go Near the Park 81 Lawrence Foldes
Don't Go Near the Water 57 Charles Walters
Don't Go to the Law 07 A. E. Coleby
Don't Grieve 69 Georgy Danelia, R. Gabriadze

Don't Interfere with a Coalheaver 04 Lewin Fitzhamon
Don't Jump to Conclusions 15 Cecil Birch
Don't Just Lie There, Say Something! 73 Bob Kellett
Don't Just Stand There 68 Ron Winston
Don't Keep Off the Grass 60 Károly Makk
Don't Knock the Rock 56 Fred F. Sears
Don't Knock the Twist 62 Oscar Rudolph
Don't Leave the Door Open 33 Frank R. Strayer
Don't Leave Your Husband 21 Samuel Bradley
Don't Let It Kill You 67 Jean-Pierre Lefèbvre
Don't Let the Angels Fall 68 George Kaczender
Don't Let Them Shoot the Kite 89 Tunc Basaran
Don't Look Back 67 D. A. Pennebaker
Don't Look in the Basement 73 S. F. Brownrigg
Don't Look Now 36 Tex Avery
Don't Look Now 66 Gérard Oury
Don't Look Now 73 Nicolas Roeg
Don't Look Now...We're Being Shot At! 66 Gérard Oury
Don't Lose Your Head 66 Gerald Thomas
Don't Make War, Make Love 66 Franco Rossi
Don't Make Waves 67 Leigh Hunt, Alexander Mackendrick
Don't Marry 28 James Tinling
Don't Marry for Money 23 Clarence Brown
Don't Mess with My Sister 83 Meir Zarchi
Don't Move! 00 Georges Méliès
Don't Neglect Your Wife 21 Wallace Worsley
Don't Open the Window 74 Jorge Grau
Don't Open Till Christmas 83 Al McGoohan, Edmund Purdom
Don't Panic Chaps! 59 George Pollock
Don't Play Hookey 23 Archie Mayo
Don't Play Us Cheap 73 Melvin Van Peebles
Don't Play with Love 26 G. W. Pabst
Don't Play with Martians 67 Henri Lanoë
Don't Pull Your Punches 37 B. Reeves Eason
Don't Raise the Bridge, Lower the River 68 Jerry Paris
Don't Rush Me 36 Norman Lee
Don't Say 73 Malcolm Le Grice
Don't Say Die 50 Vivian Milroy
Don't Scream, Doris Mays 65 John Bushelman
Don't Shoot! 22 Jack Conway
Don't Shoot 26 William Wyler
Don't Take It to Heart 44 Jeffrey Dell
Don't Talk! 42 Joseph M. Newman
Don't Talk to Strange Men 62 Pat Jackson
Don't Tease the Mosquito 67 Lina Wertmuller
Don't Tell Everything 21 Cecil B. DeMille, Sam Wood
Don't Tell Her It's Me 90 Malcolm Mowbray
Don't Tell the Wife 27 Paul Stein
Don't Tell the Wife 37 Christy Cabanne

Don't Tempt the Devil 63 Christian-Jaque
Don't Torture the Duckling 72 Lucio Fulci
Don't Touch It 12 Percy Stow
Don't Touch My Sister 63 Antonio Santean
Don't Touch the Loot 53 Jacques Becker
Don't Touch the White Woman 73 Marco Ferreri
Don't Trust Your Husband 48 Lloyd Bacon
Don't Turn 'Em Loose 36 Ben Stoloff
Don't Turn the Other Cheek 71 Duccio Tessari
Don't Weaken 20 Malcolm St. Clair
Don't Worry 38 Jenő Csepreghy
Don't Worry, We'll Think of a Title 66 Harmon Jones
Don't Write Letters 22 George D. Baker
Don't You Cry 70 John Newland
Don't You Hear the Dogs Bark? 74 Noel Howard, François Reichenbach
Döntö Pillanat 38 Ladislas Vajda
Donzoko 57 Akira Kurosawa
Dood Wasser 34 Gerard Rutten
Dooley's Scheme 11 Mack Sennett
Doolins of Oklahoma, The 49 Gordon Douglas
Doom Asylum 88 Richard Friedman
Doomed 52 Akira Kurosawa
Doomed at Sundown 37 Sam Newfield
Doomed Battalion, The 31 Karl Hartl, Luis Trenker
Doomed Battalion, The 32 Cyril Gardner
Doomed Caravan 41 Lesley Selander
Doomed Cargo 36 Albert De Courville
Doomed to Die 40 William Nigh
Doomed to Die 80 Umberto Lenzi
Doomsday 28 Rowland V. Lee
Doomsday at Eleven 63 Theodore Zichy
Doomsday Flight, The 66 William A. Graham
Doomsday Machine, The 67 Harry Hope, Lee Sholem
Doomsday Voyage 72 John Vidette
Doomwatch 72 Peter Sasdy
Door, The 68 Ken Mundie
Door 88 Banmei Takahashi
Door Between, The 17 Rupert Julian
Door in the Wall, The 56 Glenn H. Alvey, Jr.
Door Knocker, The 32 Edward F. Cline
Door That Has No Key, The 21 Frank Crane
Door That Has No Lock, The 21 Hy Mayer
Door to Door 84 Patrick Bailey
Door-to-Door Maniac 61 Bill Karn
Door to the Open Sea 35 Marcel L'Herbier
Door Will Open, A 39 George Sidney
Door with Seven Locks, The 40 Norman Lee
Door with Seven Locks, The 62 Alfred Vohrer
Doorsteps 15 Henry Edwards
Doorway of Destruction, The 15 Francis Ford
Doorway to Hell 30 Archie Mayo
Dop Doctor, The 15 L. C. MacBean, Fred Paul
Dope 14 Christy Cabanne

Dope Addict 36 Louis Gasnier
Doped Youth 36 Louis Gasnier
Dopo il Veglione 14 Augusto Genina
Dopo una Notte d'Amore 35 Guido Brignone
Doppelbräutigam, Der 34 Martin Frič
Doppelgänger 69 Robert Parrish
Doppelte Lottchen, Das 50 Josef von Baky
Doppia Ferita, La 15 Augusto Genina
Doppia Taglia per Minnesota Stinky 71 D. Fidani
Doppio Delitto 78 Steno
Dora 09 Sidney Olcott
Dora 10 Bert Haldane
Dora 12 H. Oceano Martinek
Dora 27 Widgey R. Newman
Dora Nelson 39 Alessandro Blasetti, Mario Soldati
Dora Thorne 15 Lawrence Marston
Dorado, El 21 Marcel L'Herbier
Dorado, El 87 Carlos Saura
Dorado de Pancho Villa, Un 66 Emilio Fernández
Dōraku Goshinan 28 Heinosuke Gosho
Dorfsgolem, Der 21 Julius Somogyi
Dorian Gray 70 Massimo Dallamano
Dorian's Divorce 16 Oscar A. C. Lund
Doris Eddy 85 Deb Ellis
Dorm That Dripped Blood, The 82 Stephen Carpenter, Jeffrey Obrow
Dormant Power, The 17 Travers Vale
Dormire 85 Niklas Schilling
Dornröschen 17 Paul Leni
Dornröschen 22 Lotte Reiniger
Dornröschen 65 Fritz Genschow
Doro no Kawa 81 Kohei Oguri
Dorogaya Yelena Sergeevna 88 Eldar Ryazanov
Dorogoi Moi Chelovek 58 Josef Heifits
Dorogoi Tsenoi 57 Mark Donskoi
Dorotea 1897 Fructuoso Gelabert
Dorothea Angermann 58 Robert Siodmak
Dorothée Cherche l'Amour 45 Edmond T. Gréville
Dorothy Vernon of Haddon Hall 24 Marshall Neilan, Mary Pickford
Dorothys Bekenntnis 20 Michael Curtiz
Dorothy's Dream 02 George Albert Smith
Dorothy's Motor Car 10 Joe Rosenthal
Dorp aan de Rivier 58 Fons Rademakers
Dorst 88 Willy Breebaart
Dortoir des Grandes 53 Henri Decoin
Dos au Mur, Le 57 Édouard Molinaro
Dos Cosmonautas a la Fuerza 67 Lucio Fulci
Dos Más Uno Dos 34 John Reinhardt
Dos Mil Dolares per Coyote 66 Leon Klimovsky
Dos Monjes 34 Juan Bustillo Oro
Dos Mujeres y Un Don Juan 34 José Buchs
Dos Noches 33 Carlos Borcosque
Dos Orillas, Las 87 Juan Sebastián Bollain
Dos Putas, o Historia de Amor Que Termina en Boda 74 Pedro Almodóvar
Dos Viajeros del Espacio 60 Miguel Zacarías
Doss House 33 John Baxter
Dossier 51 78 Michel Deville
Dossier 51, Le 78 Michel Deville

Dossier Noir, Le 55 André Cayatte
Dot and Carrie 27 Widgey R. Newman
Dot and Keeto 86 Yoram Gross
Dot and the Bunny 83 Yoram Gross
Dot and the Koala 85 Yoram Gross
Dot and the Line, The 65 Chuck Jones
Dot and the Whale 86 Yoram Gross
Dot Goes to Hollywood 87 Yoram Gross
Dotanba 57 Tomu Uchida
Dotheboys Hall 03 Alf Collins
Dotheboys Hall, or Nicholas Nickleby 03 Alf Collins
Dotknięci 88 Wiesław Saniewski
Dotō Ichiman Kairi 67 Jun Fukuda
Dots 40 Norman McLaren
Dots and Dashes 20 Vernon Stallings
Dots and Dashes 26 William C. Nolan
Dotted Line, The 25 Paul Powell
Dottor Antonio, Il 37 Enrico Guazzoni
Dottor Jekyll e Gentile Signora 79 Steno
Dottore Jekill, Jr., Il 79 Steno
Dotyky 88 Vladimír Drha
Douaniers et Contrebandiers 05 Alice Guy-Blaché
Double, The 16 V. Demert
Double, The 63 Lionel Harris
Double, The 80 Akira Kurosawa
Double Action Daniels 25 Richard Thorpe
Double Adventure 20 W. S. Van Dyke
Double Affair, The 65 John Newland
Double Agent 73 74 Doris Wishman
Double Agents, The 59 Robert Hossein
Double Alibi 36 David MacDonald
Double Alibi 40 Phil Rosen
Double Alibi, The 42 Sam Newfield
Double Amour, Le 25 Jean Epstein
Double and Quits 15 Toby Cooper
Double-Barrelled Detective Story 65 Adolfas Mekas
Double Bed, The 65 Jean Delannoy, François Dupont-Midi, Gianni Puccini
Double-Bedded Room, The 03 Alf Collins
Double Bluff 33 R. E. Jeffrey
Double Bunk 60 C. M. Pennington-Richards
Double Chaser 42 Friz Freleng
Double Con, The 73 Larry Yust
Double Confession 50 Ken Annakin
Double Crime in the Maginot Line 39 Félix Gandéra
Double Cross 41 Albert Kelley
Double Cross 49 Riccardo Freda
Double Cross Roads 30 George E. Middleton, Alfred L. Werker
Double Crossbones 50 Charles Barton
Double Crossed 17 Émile Chautard, Robert Vignola
Double Crossed 26 William C. Nolan
Double Danger 38 Lew Landers
Double Daring 26 Richard Thorpe
Double Daring 39 Lew Landers
Double Date 41 Glenn Tryon
Double Deal 39 Arthur Dreifuss
Double Deal 50 Abby Berlin
Double Deal 81 Brian Kavanagh
Double Deal in Pork, A 15 Frank Lloyd
Double Dealing 23 Henry Lehrman
Double Dealing 28 Geoffrey H. Malins
Double Dealing 32 Leslie Hiscott
Double Deception, A 11 Lewin Fitzhamon

Double Deception 60 Serge Friedman
Double Diving 37 Felix E. Feist
Double Door, The 34 Charles Vidor
Double Down 83 James L. Wilson
Double Dribble 46 Jack Hannah
Double Dukes 17 Archie Mayo*
Double-Dyed Deceiver, A 20 Alfred E. Green
Double Dynamite 48 Irving Cummings
Double-Edged Murder 64 José Luis Borau
Double Elopement, The 11 Lewin Fitzhamon
Double Event, The 14 Warwick Buckland
Double Event, The 21 Kenelm Foss
Double Event, The 34 Leslie Howard Gordon
Double Existence de Lord Samsey, La 24 Georges Monca
Double Exposure, A 14 Edwin J. Collins
Double Exposure 44 William Berke
Double Exposure 54 John Gilling
Double Exposure 77 William Webb
Double Exposure 82 William Byron Hillman
Double Exposure 87 Nico Mastorakis
Double Exposures 37 John Paddy Carstairs
Double Face 69 Riccardo Freda
Double Fiance, The 34 Martin Frič
Double Fisted 25 Harry S. Webb
Double Gentlemen 86 Jean-François Stévenin
Double Harness 33 John Cromwell
Double Hit 76 Richard C. Sarafian
Double Indemnity 44 Billy Wilder
Double Initiation 70 Carlos Tobalina
Double Jeopardy 55 R. G. Springsteen
Double Jeopardy 83 Ulli Lommel
Double Jeu, Le 16 Louis Feuillade
Double Knot, The 13 Raoul Walsh
Double Life, A 06 Percy Stow
Double Life, A 12 Warwick Buckland
Double Life, A 13 Bert Haldane
Double Life, A 20 Henry D. Bailey
Double Life, A 47 George Cukor
Double Life of Mr. Alfred Burton, The 19 Arthur H. Rooke
Double Love 25 Jean Epstein
Double Man, The 67 Franklin J. Schaffner
Double McGuffin, The 79 Joe Camp
Double Messieurs 86 Jean-François Stévenin
Double Negative 80 George Bloomfield
Double Nickels 77 Jack Vacek
Double O, The 21 Roy Clements
002 Agenti Segretissimi 64 Lucio Fulci
00-2 Most Secret Agents 64 Lucio Fulci
002 Operazione Luna 66 Lucio Fulci
Double or Mutton 55 Chuck Jones
Double or Nothing 37 Theodore Reed
Double or Quits 38 Roy William Neill
Double Possession 73 Bill Gunn
Double Punch, The 42 William Berke
Double Reward, A 12 Thomas Ince
Double Room Mystery, The 17 Hobart Henley
Double Speed 19 Sam Wood
Double Standard, The 17 Phillips Smalley
Double-Stop 67 Gerald Seth Sindell
Double Suicide 25 Teinosuke Kinugasa
Double Suicide 69 Masahiro Shinoda

Drácula *31* George Melford
Dracula *58* Terence Fisher
Dracula *73* Dan Curtis
Dracula *73* Antonio Margheriti, Paul Morrissey
Dracula *79* John Badham
Dracula, A.D. 1972 *72* Alan Gibson
Dracula Against Frankenstein *72* Jesús Franco
Dracula and Son *76* Édouard Molinaro
Dracula and the 7 Golden Vampires *73* Roy Ward Baker
Dracula Blows His Cool *79* Carlo Ombra
Dracula Cerca Sangue di Vergine e...Mori di Sete *73* Antonio Margheriti, Paul Morrissey
Dracula Chases the Mini Girls *72* Alan Gibson
Dracula Chelsea 72 *72* Alan Gibson
Drácula Contra el Dr. Frankenstein *72* Jesús Franco
Drácula Contra Frankenstein *72* Jesús Franco
Dracula Has Risen from the Grave *68* Freddie Francis
Dracula im Schloss des Schreckens *70* Antonio Margheriti
Dracula in the Castle of Blood *70* Antonio Margheriti
Dracula in the Provinces *75* Lucio Fulci
Dracula Is Alive and Well and Living in London *73* Alan Gibson
Dracula Is Dead...and Well and Living in London *73* Alan Gibson
Dracula Jagt Frankenstein *69* Tulio Demicheli, Hugo Fregonese
Dracula Père et Fils *76* Édouard Molinaro
Dracula — Prince of Darkness *65* Terence Fisher
Dracula, Prisonnier de Frankenstein *72* Jesús Franco
Dracula Rises from the Coffin *82* Hyoung Pyo Lee
Dracula 71 *70* Jesús Franco
Dracula Sucks *79* Philip Marshak
Dracula (The Dirty Old Man) *69* William Edwards
Dracula the Terror of the Living Dead *72* José Luis Merino
Dracula Today *72* Alan Gibson
Dracula ton Exarchia *83* Nikos Zervos
Dracula vs. Frankenstein *69* Tulio Demicheli, Hugo Fregonese
Dracula vs. Frankenstein *70* Al Adamson
Dracula vs. Frankenstein *72* Jesús Franco
Dracula Vuole Vivere: Cerca Sangue di Vergine! *73* Antonio Margheriti, Paul Morrissey
Dracula's Castle *67* Al Adamson, Jean Hewitt
Dracula's Daughter *36* Lambert Hillyer
Dracula's Desire *52* John Gilling
Dracula's Disciple *84* Allen Schaaf
Dracula's Dog *77* Alfredo Antonini
Dracula's Great Love *72* Javier Aguirre
Dracula's Last Rites *80* Domonic Paris
Dracula's Lust for Blood *71* Michio Yamamoto
Dracula's Revenge *68* Freddie Francis
Dracula's Saga *72* Leon Klimovsky

Dracula's Virgin Lovers *72* Javier Aguirre
Dracula's Widow *87* Christopher Coppola
Draegerman Courage *36* Louis King
Draft Board, The *18* Raoul Barré, Charles Bowers
Draft Horse, The *41* Chuck Jones
Draft 258 *17* Christy Cabanne
Draftee Daffy *45* Robert Clampett
Drag *29* Frank Lloyd
Drag Harlan *20* J. Gordon Edwards
Drag Net, The *28* Josef von Sternberg
Drag Racer *74* John Cardos
Dragalong Droopy *53* Tex Avery
Dragão da Maldade Contra o Santo Guerreiro, O *69* Glauber Rocha
Dragées au Poivre *63* Jacques Baratier
Dragers Juveler *12* Victor Sjöström
Dragnet, The *47* Leslie Goodwins
Dragnet *54* Jack Webb
Dragnet *87* Tom Mankiewicz
Dragnet Girl *33* Yasujiro Ozu
Dragnet Night *31* Carmine Gallone
Dragnet Patrol *32* Frank R. Strayer
Dragon, The *16* Harry A. Pollard
Dragon Chow *87* Jan Schütte
Dragon Flies, The *75* Brian Trenchard-Smith
Dragon-Fly, The *01* Georges Méliès
Dragon Gate Inn *66* King Hu
Dragon Inn *66* King Hu
Dragon Lady *71* Joel M. Reed
Dragon Lord *82* Jackie Chan
Dragon Master *70* Paul Wendkos
Dragon Murder Case, The *34* H. Bruce Humberstone
Dragon of Evil Against the Holy Warrior, The *69* Glauber Rocha
Dragon of Komodo, The *37* Pál Fejös
Dragon of Pendragon Castle, The *50* John Baxter
Dragon Painter, The *19* William Worthington
Dragon Rapide *86* Jaime Camino
Dragon Seed *43* Harold S. Bucquet, Jack Conway, W. S. Van Dyke
Dragon Sky *62* Marcel Camus
Dragones de Ha-Long, Los *76* Santiago Álvarez
Dragonfly, The *55* S. Dolidze
Dragonfly *76* Gilbert Cates
Dragonfly Squadron *54* Lesley Selander
Dragonnades Sous Louis XIV, Les *09* Victorin Jasset
Dragon's Blood, The *59* Giacomo Gentilomo
Dragon's Claw, The *22* Joe May
Dragon's Food *87* Jan Schütte
Dragon's Gold *53* Jack Pollexfen, Aubrey Wisberg
Dragons of Ha-Long, The *76* Santiago Álvarez
Dragonslayer *81* Matthew Robbins
Dragonwyck *46* Joseph L. Mankiewicz
Dragoon Wells Massacre *57* Harold Schuster
Dragotsennye Zerna *48* Josef Heifits, Alexander Zarkhi
Dragstrip Girl *57* Edward L. Cahn
Dragstrip Riot *58* David Bradley
Dragueurs, Les *59* Jean-Pierre Mocky

Drake Case, The *29* Edward Laemmle
Drake of England *35* Arthur Woods
Drake the Pirate *35* Arthur Woods
Draken på Komodo *37* Pál Fejös
Drake's Love Story *13* Hay Plumb
Drama at the Château d'Acre *14* Abel Gance
Drama by Telephone *14* Yakov Protazanov
Drama de Luxe *27* Norman Taurog
Drama della Corona *16* Augusto Genina
Drama of Jealousy, A *70* Ettore Scola
Drama of Jealousy (And Other Things), A *70* Ettore Scola
Drama of the Rich *74* Mauro Bolognini
Drama on the Threshing Floor *37* Georg Jacoby
Drama von Mayerling, Das *24* Alexander Korda
Dramatic Life of Abraham Lincoln, The *24* Phil Rosen
Dramatic School *38* Robert B. Sinclair
Dramatic Story of the Vote, The *13* Wilfred Noy
Drame à Venise, Un *07* Ferdinand Zecca*
Drame au Château d'Acre, Un *14* Abel Gance
Drame au Château d'Acre ou Les Morts Reviennent-Ils?, Un *14* Abel Gance
Drame au Fond de la Mer *00* Ferdinand Zecca
Drame au Pays Basque, Un *13* Louis Feuillade
Drame chez les Fantoches, Un *08* Émile Cohl
Drame de Shanghai, Le *37* G. W. Pabst
Drame Sous Napoléon, Un *21* Gérard Bourgeois
Drame sur la Planche à Chaussures, Un *15* Émile Cohl
Dramma a 16 Anni, Un *29* Augusto Genina
Dramma al Circo, Un *38* Carmine Gallone
Dramma della Gelosia (Tutti i Particolari in Cronaca) *70* Ettore Scola
Dramma di Cristo, Il *48* Luciano Emmer, Enrico Gras
Dramma di una Notte, Il *17* Mario Caserini
Dramma Ignorato, Un *16* Emilio Ghione
Drango *57* Hall Bartlett, Jules Bricken
Drapeau Blanc d'Oxala, Le *69* Pierre Kast
Drapeau Noir Flotte sur la Marmite, Le *71* Michel Audiard
Drastic Demise *45* Kenneth Anger
Draufgänger, Der *32* Richard Eichberg
Draught, The *40* René Clément
Draughtsman's Contract, The *82* Peter Greenaway
Draughtsman's Revenge, The *12* Bert Haldane
Dravci *48* Jiří Weiss
Draw-Back, The *27* Norman Taurog
Drawing Lesson, or The Living Statue, The *03* Georges Méliès
Drawing the Line *12* Edwin S. Porter
Drawing the Line *15* B. Reeves Eason
Drawn Blind, The *10* Ernest G. Batley
Drawn Blind, The *14* Ethyle Batley
Drayton Case, The *53* Ken Hughes

Dreaded Mafia, The *61* Francesco Rosi
Dreaded Persuasion, The *58* Robert W. Larsen
Dreadnought to the Rescue *09* Joe Rosenthal
Dream, The *11* Thomas Ince, George Loane Tucker
Dream, A *14* Charles Chaplin
Dream *43* Mikhail Romm
Dream, The *85* Pieter Verhoeff
Dream a Little Dream *89* Marc Rocco
Dream Bad, Luck Ditto *15* Edwin J. Collins
Dream Ballerina *50* Ludwig Berger
Dream Castle, The *86* Petter Vennerød, Svend Wam
Dream Cheater, The *20* Ernest C. Warde
Dream Come True, A *63* Mikhail Karyukov, Otar Koberidze
Dream Comes True, or The Valise, A *87* Earnest Yasan
Dream Demon, The *88* Harley Cokliss
Dream Doctor, The *36* R. W. Lotinga
Dream Doll, The *17* Howard S. Moss
Dream Faces *26* Hugh Croise
Dream Flights *83* Roman Balajan
Dream Girl, The *16* Cecil B. DeMille
Dream Girl *48* Mitchell Leisen
Dream Kids, The *44* Bob Wickersham
Dream Lady, The *18* Elsie Jane Wilson
Dream Lover *86* Alan J. Pakula
Dream Lovers *86* Tony Au
Dream Machine, The *82* Derek Jarman
Dream Maker, The *63* Don Sharp
Dream Melody, The *29* Burton L. King
Dream Mother *32* Richard Thorpe
Dream, N.Y.C., the Return, the Flower, The *76* Stan Brakhage
Dream No More *50* Joseph Krumgold
Dream of a Cossack *50* Yuli Raizman
Dream of a Hindu Beggar, The *01* Georges Méliès
Dream of a Rarebit Fiend, The *06* Edwin S. Porter
Dream of a Rose, The *86* Zoran Tadić
Dream of Allan Gray, The *31* Carl Theodor Dreyer
Dream of an Opium Fiend, The *07* Georges Méliès
Dream of Butterfly, The *39* Carmine Gallone
Dream of Death, A *11* August Blom
Dream of Eugene Aram, The *23* Edwin Greenwood
Dream of Freedom, A *69* Jan Halldoff
Dream of Glory, A *13* A. E. Coleby
Dream of Kings, A *69* Daniel Mann
Dream of Kings, A *70* Lester James Peries
Dream of Life *32* James Flood, Elliott Nugent
Dream of Love *28* Fred Niblo
Dream of Love, A *38* James A. Fitzpatrick
Dream of My People, The *34* A. J. Blume
Dream of Northern Lights *86* Lasse Glomm
Dream of Olwen *47* John Harlow
Dream of Passion, A *77* Jules Dassin
Dream of Schoenbrunn *33* Johannes Meyer
Dream of the Ballet Master, The *03* Georges Méliès

Dream of the Red Chamber, The *66* Ping Wang
Dream of Tomorrow, A *14* Lawrence Cowen
Dream On *81* Ed Harker
Dream One *84* Arnaud Selignac
Dream or Two Ago, A *16* James Kirkwood
Dream Paintings *12* Elwin Neame
Dream Path of Youth, The *22* Kenji Mizoguchi
Dream/Slap *86* Deb Ellis
Dream Street *21* D. W. Griffith
Dream Stuff *34* William Beaudine
Dream Team, The *89* Howard Zieff
Dream That Came True, The *19* Frank Miller
Dream Town *73* Johannes Schaaf
Dream Valley *47* Arne Sucksdorff
Dream Walking, A *34* Dave Fleischer
Dream Wife *53* Sidney Sheldon
Dream Woman, The *14* Alice Guy-Blaché
Dream World of Harrison Marks, The *67* George Harrison Marks
Dreamaniac *87* David DeCoteau
Dreamboat *52* Claude Binyon
Dreamchild *85* Gavin Millar
Dreamer, The *70* Dan Wolman
Dreamer *79* Noel Nosseck
Dreamers, The *33* Frank Cadman
Dreamers *87* Uri Barbash
Dreamers of Glory *38* Miguel Torres Contreras
Dreamer's Walk, A *57* Lars-Magnus Lindgren
Dreamhouse *81* Al Beresford
Dreaming *44* John Baxter
Dreaming *80* Stan Vanderbeek
Dreaming, The *88* Mario Andreacchio
Dreaming Lips *32* Paul Czinner
Dreaming Lips *37* Paul Czinner, Lee Garmes
Dreaming Lips *52* Josef von Baky
Dreaming Out Loud *40* Harold Young
Dreamland *83* Nancy Baker, Joel Schulman, Oz Scott
Dreamland Adventures *07* Walter R. Booth
Dreams *40* Felix E. Feist
Dreams *54* Ingmar Bergman
Dreams *61* Allan King
Dreams *70* Max Fischer
Dreams *90* Akira Kurosawa
Dreams and Realities *62* Jorge Sanjinés
Dreams Come True *36* Reginald Denham
Dreams in a Drawer *57* Renato Castellani
Dreams of Glass *69* Robert Clouse
Dreams of Gold *85* José Luis García Agraz, Eric Weston
Dreams of Love *54* Christian Stengel
Dreams of Monte Carlo *26* Christy Cabanne
Dreams of Thirteen *74* Nicholas Ray*
Dreams of Toyland *08* Arthur Cooper
Dreams of Youth *22* Kenji Mizoguchi
Dreams of Youth *28* Yasujiro Ozu
Dreams of Youth *43* Kamel Salim
Dreams on Ice *39* Sid Marcus
Dreams That Money Can Buy *46* Man Ray, Hans Richter
Dreamscape *84* Joseph Ruben

Dreamwood *72* James Broughton
Dreamworld *84* Jean-Claude Lord
Dreamy Dud at the Ole Swimmin' Hole *15* Wallace A. Carlson
Dreamy Dud Cowboy *15* Wallace A. Carlson
Dreamy Dud Goes Bear Hunting *15* Wallace A. Carlson
Dreamy Dud Has a Laugh on the Boss *16* Wallace A. Carlson
Dreamy Dud in King Koo Koo's Kingdom *15* Wallace A. Carlson
Dreamy Dud in Love *15* Wallace A. Carlson
Dreamy Dud in the African War Zone *16* Wallace A. Carlson
Dreamy Dud in the Swim *15* Wallace A. Carlson
Dreamy Dud Joyriding with Princess Zlim *16* Wallace A. Carlson
Dreamy Dud Lost at Sea *16* Wallace A. Carlson
Dreamy Dud Resolves Not to Smoke *15* Wallace A. Carlson
Dreamy Dud Sees Charlie Chaplin *15* Wallace A. Carlson
Dreamy Dud Up in the Air *15* Wallace A. Carlson
Dreamy Eyes *05* Arthur Gilbert
Dreamy Jimmy Dreams Again *14* Dave Aylott
Dreary House *28* Andrew L. Stone
Dreckschleuder, Die *87* Niki List
Dregs *57* Palle Kjærulff-Schmidt
Drei Amerikanische LPs *69* Wim Wenders
Drei Blaue Jungs, Ein Blondes Mädel *36* Carl Boese
Drei Gegen Drei *85* Dominik Graf
Drei Kaiserjäger *35* Franz Hofler, Robert Land
Drei Kuckucksuhren, Die *26* Lothar Mendes
Drei Mäorl um Schubert *37* E. W. Emo
Drei Marien und der Herr von Marana, Die *22* Reinhold Schünzel
Drei Nächte *20* Carl Boese
Drei Tage Liebe *31* Heinz Hilpert
Drei Tage Mittelarrest *33* Carl Boese
Drei Tänze der Mary Wilford, Die *20* Robert Wiene
Drei um Christine, Die *40* Hans Deppe
Drei Unteroffiziere *39* Werner Hochbaum
Drei Vater um Anna *40* Carl Boese
Drei Vaterunser für Vier Halunken *72* Giancarlo Santi
Drei von der Kavallerie *32* Carl Boese
Drei von der Tankstelle, Die *30* Wilhelm Thiele
Drei von der Tankstelle, Die *55* Hans Wolff
Dreigroschenoper, Die *31* G. W. Pabst
Dreigroschenoper, Die *63* Wolfgang Staudte
Dreikland *38* Hans Hinrich
Dreimäderlhaus, Das *18* Richard Oswald
Dreimäderlhaus, Das *61* Ernst Marischka
Dreimal Komödie *45* Victor Tourjansky
Dreizehn Oktober, Der *49* Andrew Thorndike
Dreizehn Sklavinnen des Dr. Fu Manchu, Die *66* Don Sharp

Dreptate în Lanţuri 83 Dan Piţa
Dresden Doll, The 22 Dave Fleischer
Dress, The 64 Vilgot Sjöman
Dress, The 85 Eva Sereny
Dress Parade 27 Donald Crisp
Dress Parade 39 William Clemens, Noel Mason Smith
Dress Rehearsal 35 Alex Brown
Dressage 85 Pierre B. Reinhard
Dressed to Kill 28 Irving Cummings
Dressed to Kill 41 Eugene Forde
Dressed to Kill 46 Roy William Neill
Dressed to Kill 80 Brian DePalma
Dressed to Thrill 35 Harry Lachman
Dresser, The 83 Peter Yates
Dressmaker, The 88 Jim O'Brien
Dressmaker from Paris, The 25 Paul Bern
Dreszcze 80 Wojciech Marczewski
Drevo Zhelanya 76 Tenghiz Abuladze
Dreyfus 30 Richard Oswald
Dreyfus 31 F. W. Krämer, Milton Rosmer
Dreyfus 40 Richard Oswald
Dreyfus Affair, The 1899 Georges Méliès
Dreyfus Case, The 1899 Georges Méliès
Dreyfus Case, The 31 F. W. Krämer, Milton Rosmer
Dreyfus Case, The 40 Richard Oswald
Dreyfus Court Martial 1899 Georges Méliès
Drift Fence 36 Otho Lovering
Drifter, The 16 Richard Garrick
Drifter, The 29 Robert De Lacey
Drifter, The 32 William A. O'Connor
Drifter, The 44 Sam Newfield
Drifter, The 66 Alex Matter
Drifter 75 Pat Rocco
Drifter, The 88 Larry Brand
Drifters, The 19 Jesse D. Hampton
Drifters 29 John Grierson
Drifters, The 66 Santos Alcocer
Driftin' Kid, The 41 Robert E. Tansey
Driftin' River 46 Robert E. Tansey
Driftin' Sands 28 Wallace Fox
Driftin' Thru 26 Scott R. Dunlap
Drifting 23 Tod Browning
Drifting 32 Morris R. Schlank
Drifting 84 Amos Guttman
Drifting Along 46 Derwin Abrahams
Drifting Clouds 51 Heinosuke Gosho
Drifting Souls 32 Louis King
Drifting Weeds 59 Yasujiro Ozu
Drifting Westward 39 Robert F. Hill
Driftwood 12 Allan Dwan
Driftwood 16 Marshall Farnum
Driftwood 28 Christy Cabanne
Driftwood 47 Allan Dwan
Driller Killer 79 Abel Ferrara
Drink 07 Lewin Fitzhamon
Drink 17 Sidney Morgan
Drink! A Great Temperance Story 07 Georges Méliès
Drink and Repentance 05 Tom Green
Drink Cure, A 07 A. E. Coleby
Drink's Lure 12 Christy Cabanne, D. W. Griffith
Dripalong Daffy 51 Chuck Jones
Dripping Deep Red 75 Dario Argento
Dripping Water 69 Michael Snow, Joyce Wieland
Dritte Generation, Die 79 Rainer Werner Fassbinder

Dritte Geschlecht, Das 57 Veidt Harlan
Drive a Crooked Road 54 Richard Quine
Drive for a Life 09 D. W. Griffith
Drive for Life, The 09 D. W. Griffith
Drive, He Said 71 Jack Nicholson
Drive-In 76 Rod Amateau
Drive-In Massacre 76 Stuart Segall
Driven 16 Maurice Elvey
Driven 23 Charles Brabin
Driven by Hunger 15 Fred Evans
Driven from Home 23 F. W. Murnau
Driven from Home 25 Alexander Butler
Driven from Home 27 James Young
Driver, The 78 Walter Hill
Drivers in Hell 61 Ray Dennis Steckler
Driver's Seat, The 73 Giuseppe Patroni Griffi
Drivers to Hell 61 Ray Dennis Steckler
Drivin' Fool, The 23 Robert Thornby
Driving Force 88 Rolf De Heer
Driving Home the Cows 12 Sidney Olcott
Driving Miss Daisy 89 Bruce Beresford
Droeven 81 Jean-Jacques Andrien
Droga do Nieba 58 Wincenty Ronisz, Krzysztof Zanussi
Droga Młodych 36 Aleksander Ford
Droit à la Vie, Le 16 Abel Gance
Droit de Tuer, Le 20 Charles De Marsan, Charles Maudru
Drôle de Dimanche, Un 58 Marc Allégret
Drôle de Drame 36 Marcel Carné
Drôle de Jeu 68 Pierre Kast
Drôle de Noce 51 Léo Joannon
Drôle de Paroissien, Un 63 Jean-Pierre Mocky
Drôle de Samedi 85 Bay Okan
Drôle d'Endroit pour une Rencontre 88 François Dupeyron
Droll Stories 53 G. W. Pabst
Dröm om Frihet, En 69 Jan Halldoff
Drömda Dalen, Den 47 Arne Sucksdorff
Drömmares Vandring, En 57 Lars-Magnus Lindgren
Drömmen om Amerika 76 Jörn Donner
Drømmeslottet 86 Petter Vennerød, Svend Wam
Droom, De 85 Pieter Verhoeff
Droopy's Double Trouble 51 Tex Avery
Droopy's Good Deed 51 Tex Avery
Drop Dead 68 Pasquale Festa Campanile
Drop Dead, Darling 66 Ken Hughes
Drop Dead My Love 68 Pasquale Festa Campanile
Drop Kick, The 27 Millard Webb
Drop Them or I'll Shoot 69 Sergio Corbucci
Drop Too Much, A 1899 Georges Méliès
Dropout 70 Tinto Brass
Droppel Bloed, De 13 Alfred Machin
Droppington's Family Tree 15 J. Farrell MacDonald
Drops of Blood 60 Giorgio Ferroni
Drowned 56 Vytautas Zalakevicius
Drowning by Numbers 87 Peter Greenaway
Drowning Pool, The 75 Stuart Rosenberg
Drowsy Dick Dreams He's a Burglar 10 H. Oceano Martinek
Drowsy Dick's Dream 09 H. Oceano

Martinek
Drug 88 Leonid Kvinikhidze
Drug Store Cowboy 25 Park Frame
Drug Traffic, The 23 Irving Cummings
Drugaya Zhizn 88 Rasim Odzhagov
Drugged Waters 16 William Dowlan
Druggist's Dilemma, The 33 Mark Sandrich
Drugstore Cowboy 89 Gus Van Sant, Jr.
Druhá Směna 40 Martin Frič
Druhý Tah Pěsce 85 Vít Olmer
Druides, Les 06 Alice Guy-Blaché
Drum, The 24 Sinclair Hill
Drum, The 38 Zoltán Korda
Drum 76 Steve Carver, Burt Kennedy
Drum Beat 54 Delmer Daves
Drum Crazy 59 Don Weis
Drum-Sticked 63 Joseph Barbera, William Hanna
Drum Taps 33 John P. McGowan
Drummer of the 8th, The 13 Thomas Ince
Drummer of Vengeance 74 Robert Paget
Drummer's Vacation, The 12 Mack Sennett
Drums 38 Zoltán Korda
Drums 61 Hans G. Casparius
Drums Across the River 54 Nathan Juran
Drums Along the Amazon 48 John H. Auer
Drums Along the Mohawk 39 John Ford
Drums in the Deep South 51 William Cameron Menzies
Drums o' Voodoo 34 Arthur Hoerl
Drums of Africa 63 James B. Clark
Drums of Destiny 37 Ray Taylor
Drums of Fate 23 Charles Maigne
Drums of Fu Manchu 40 John English, William Witney
Drums of Jeopardy, The 23 Edward Dillon
Drums of Jeopardy, The 31 George B. Seitz
Drums of Love 27 D. W. Griffith
Drums of Tabu, The 67 Javier Seto
Drums of Tahiti 53 William Castle
Drums of the Congo 42 Christy Cabanne
Drums of the Desert 27 John Waters
Drums of the Desert 40 George Waggner
Drums of the Jungle 35 George Terwilliger
Drunk 65 Andy Warhol
Drunk Driving 39 David Miller
Drunkard, The 49 George Tzavellas
Drunkard and Inventor 02 Georges Méliès
Drunkards, The 1897 Georges Méliès
Drunkard's Conversion, The 01 Walter R. Booth
Drunkard's Dream, A 1897 Georges Méliès
Drunkard's Dream, The 08 Alf Collins
Drunkard's Reformation, A 09 D. W. Griffith
Drunkard's Son, A 09 Lewin Fitzhamon
Drunken Angel 48 Akira Kurosawa
Drunken Motorcyclist, The 07 Alf Collins
Drunken Night 86 Bernard Nauer
Drunkenness and Its Consequences 13 A. Dvoretsky
Drunter und Drüber 32 Max Neufeld
Drusilla with a Million 25 F. Harmon Weight

Dry Earth *60* Yoshishige Yoshida
Dry Lake *60* Masahiro Shinoda
Dry Martini *28* Harry D'Abbadie D'Arrast
Dry Rot *56* Maurice Elvey
Dry Summer *64* David Durston, Erkan Metin, Ismail Metin
Dry White Season, A *89* Euzhan Palcy
Dry Wood *73* Les Blank
Drying Up the Streets *78* Robin Spry
Drylanders *63* Don Haldane
Držanje za Vazduh *86* Zdravko Sotra
Dschingis Khan *65* Henry Levin
Dschungel Ruft, Der *37* Harry Piel
Du-beat-e-o *84* Alan Sacks
Du Bist die Welt für Mich *53* Ernst Marischka
Du Bist Mein—Ein Deutsches Tagebuch *69* Andrew Thorndike, Annelie Thorndike
Du Bist Mein Glück *40* Karl Heinz Martin
Du Charbon et des Hommes *52* Roger Leenhardt
Du Côté de la Côte *58* Agnès Varda
Du Côté d'Orouët *71* Jacques Rozier
Du Fil à l'Aiguille *24* Jean Grémillon
Du Gamla, Du Fria *39* Gunnar Olsson
Du Haut en Bas *33* G. W. Pabst
Du Mich Auch *87* Helmut Berger, Anja Franke, Dani Levy
Du Mouron pour les Petits Oiseaux *62* Marcel Carné
Du Plaisir à la Joie *78* Roger Leenhardt
Du Rififi à Paname *66* Denys De la Patellière
Du Rififi chez les Femmes *59* Alex Joffé
Du Rififi chez les Hommes *54* Jules Dassin
Du Rire aux Larmes *17* Gaston Ravel
Du Sang de la Volupté et de la Mort *47* Gregory Markopoulos
Du Skal Ære Din Hustru *25* Carl Theodor Dreyer
Du Skal Elske Din Næste *15* August Blom
Du Soleil Plein les Yeux *70* Michel Boisrond
Du Sollst Nicht Ehebrechen! *28* Jacques Feyder
Du und Mancher Kameraden *56* Andrew Thorndike, Annelie Thorndike
Dual Alibi *47* Alfred Travers
Dual Control *32* Walter Summers
Dub, The *18* James Cruze
DuBarry, La *14* Edoardo Bencivenga
DuBarry *15* George Kleine
DuBarry, La *54* Christian-Jaque
DuBarry von Heute, Eine *26* Alexander Korda
DuBarry Was a Lady *43* Roy Del Ruth
DuBarry, Woman of Passion *30* Sam Taylor
Dublin Nightmare *58* John Pomeroy
Dublyor Nachinaet Deystvovat *87* Earnest Yasan
Dubrovsky *36* Alexander Ivanovsky
Dubrowsky *58* William Dieterle
Duchess and the Dirtwater Fox, The *76* Melvin Frank
Duchess of Broadway *46* George Sherman
Duchess of Buffalo, The *26* Sidney Franklin
Duchess of Doubt, The *17* George D.

Baker
Duchess of Idaho *50* Robert Z. Leonard
Duchess of Seven Dials, The *19* Fred Paul
Duchess Satanella *20* Michael Curtiz
Duchesse de Langeais, La *42* Jacques De Baroncelli
Duck à l'Orange *75* Dino Risi
Duck Amuck *53* Chuck Jones
Duck Doctor *52* Joseph Barbera, William Hanna
Duck Dodgers in the 24th½ Century *53* Chuck Jones
Duck Hunt, The *32* Burton Gillett
Duck Hunt *37* Walter Lantz
Duck Hunter, The *22* Roy Del Ruth
Duck in Orange Sauce *76* Luciano Salce
Duck! Rabbit! *53* Chuck Jones
Duck, Rabbit, Duck *53* Chuck Jones
Duck Rings at Half Past Seven, The *69* Rolf Thiele
Duck Soup *33* Leo McCarey
Duck Soup to Nuts *44* Friz Freleng
Duck, You Sucker! *71* Sergio Leone
Ducking Stool, The *05* Arthur Cooper
Ducking the Devil *57* Robert McKimson
Ducks and Drakes *21* Maurice Campbell
Ducks on Sale or Return *04* Arthur Cooper
Ducksters, The *50* Chuck Jones
DuckTales: The Movie—Treasure of the Lost Lamp *90* Bob Hathcock
Ducktators, The *42* Norm McCabe
Duckweed Story *55* Satsuo Yamamoto
Duckweed Story, The *59* Yasujiro Ozu
Dud Cheque Chicanery *26* F. W. Engholm
Dud Leaves Home *19* Wallace A. Carlson
Dud Perkins Gets Mortified *19* Wallace A. Carlson
Dud the Circus Performer *19* Wallace A. Carlson
Dud the Lion Tamer *20* Wallace A. Carlson
Dude Bandit, The *33* George Melford
Dude Cowboy, The *26* Jack Nelson
Dude Cowboy *41* David Howard
Dude Goes West, The *48* Kurt Neumann
Dude Ranch *31* Frank Tuttle
Dude Ranch, The *34* Edward F. Cline
Dude Ranger, The *34* Edward F. Cline
Dude Wrangler, The *30* Richard Thorpe
Dudek na Froncie *36* Michael Waszyński
Dudes *87* Penelope Spheeris
Dudes Are Pretty People *42* Hal Roach, Jr.
Duds *20* Thomas R. Mills
Dud's Geography Lesson *19* Wallace A. Carlson
Dud's Greatest Cirkus on Earth *19* Wallace A. Carlson
Dud's Haircut *20* Wallace A. Carlson
Dud's Home Run *19* Wallace A. Carlson
Due Carabinieri, I *84* Carlo Verdone
Due Colonelli, I *62* Steno
Due Croci a Danger Pass *67* Rafael Romero Marchent
Due Crocifissi, I *18* Augusto Genina
Due Cuori Felici *32* Baldassare Negroni
Due Cuori Sotto Sequestro *41* Carlo Ludovico Bragaglia

Due della Legione, I *62* Lucio Fulci
Due Dozzine di Rose Scarlatte *39* Giuseppe Amato, Vittorio De Sica
Due Evasi di Sing Sing, I *64* Lucio Fulci
Due Facce del Dollaro, I *67* Roberto Bianchi Montero
Due Figli di Ringo, I *66* Giorgio C. Simonelli
Due Figli di Trinità, I *72* Osvaldo Civirani
Due Fratelli in un Posto Chiamato Trinità *72* James London
Due Gondolieri, I *58* Dino Risi
Due Gringos nel Texas *67* Marino Girolami
Due Lettere Anonime *45* Mario Camerini
Due Madri, Le *40* Amleto Palermi
Due Mafiosi dell' F.B.I., I *66* Mario Bava
Due Mafiosi nel Far West *64* Giorgio C. Simonelli
Due Marescialli, I *61* Sergio Corbucci
Due Marines e un Generale *67* Luigi Scattini
Due Milioni per un Sorriso *39* Carlo Borghesio, Mario Soldati
Due Mille Diciannove *84* Sergio Martino
2019: Dopo la Caduta di New York *84* Sergio Martino
2019: I Nuovi Barbari *82* Enzo G. Castellari
Due Mogli Sono Troppe *50* Mario Camerini
Due Nemici, I *61* Guy Hamilton
Due Notti con Cleopatra *53* Mario Mattòli
Due Occhi Diabolici *90* Dario Argento, George Romero
Due Once di Piombo *66* Maurizio Lucidi
Due Orfanelle, Le *42* Carmine Gallone
Due Para', I *66* Lucio Fulci
Due Pericoli Pubblici, I *65* Lucio Fulci
Due Pistole e un Vigliacco *67* Giorgio Ferroni
2 + 5: Missione Hydra *66* Pietro Francisci
Due Sergenti, I *08* Ernesto Maria Pasquali
Due Sergenti, I *36* Enrico Guazzoni
Due Sergenti del Generale Custer, I *65* Giorgio C. Simonelli
Due Soldi di Speranza *51* Renato Castellani
Due Vite di Mattia Pascal, Le *85* Mario Monicelli
Duel, The *05* Lewin Fitzhamon
Duel, The *12* Mack Sennett
Duel, The *22* Vladimir Gardin
Duel, Le *27* Jacques De Baroncelli
Duel, The *57* Vladimir Petrov
Duel, The *64* Tatyana Berezantseva, Lev Rudnik
Duel *71* Steven Spielberg
Duel at Apache Wells *57* Joseph Kane
Duel at Dawn, A *15* Clarence Badger
Duel at Diablo *66* Ralph Nelson
Duel at Ezo *70* Kengo Furusawa
Duel at Ganryu Island *67* Hiroshi Inagaki
Duel at Hannya-Zaka *43* Daisuke Ito
Duel at Ichijoji Temple, The *64* Tomu Uchida
Duel at Rio Bravo *64* Tulio Demicheli
Duel at Silver Creek *52* Don Siegel
Duel at the Rio Grande *62* Mario Caiano
Duel de Max, Le *13* Max Linder

Duel in Durango *57* Sidney Salkow
Duel in the Forest *58* Helmut Käutner
Duel in the Jungle *53* George Marshall
Duel in the Sun *46* Otto Brower, William Dieterle, B. Reeves Eason, Sidney Franklin, William Cameron Menzies, David Selznick, Josef von Sternberg, King Vidor
Duel of a Snowy Night *54* Teinosuke Kinugasa
Duel of Champions *61* Ferdinando Baldi, Terence Young
Duel of Fire *62* Umberto Lenzi
Duel of the Candles, The *11* Allan Dwan
Duel of the Gargantuas *66* Inoshiro Honda
Duel of the Space Monsters *65* Robert Gaffney
Duel of the Titans *61* Sergio Corbucci
Duel on the Mississippi *55* William Castle
Duel Personalities *39* George Sidney
Duel Personality *66* Chuck Jones
Duel Politique *1899* Georges Méliès
Duel Scene from "The Two Orphans" *02* William Haggar
Duel Tragique *04* Alice Guy-Blaché
Duel with Death *49* Paul Ostermayer
Duel Without End *62* Tomu Uchida
Duel Without Honor *53* Camillo Mastrocinque
Duell in den Bergen *49* Luis Trenker
Duell mit dem Tod *49* Paul Ostermayer
Duell vor Sonnenuntergang *65* Leopold Lahola
Duelle *75* Jacques Rivette
Duellists, The *77* Ridley Scott
Duello nel Texas *63* Riccardo Blasco
Duelo a Río Bravo *64* Tulio Demicheli
Duelo en las Montañas *49* Emilio Fernández
Dueño del Sol, El *87* Rodolfo Mortola
Dueños del Silencio, Los *87* Carlos Lemos
Duet for Cannibals *69* Susan Sontag
Duet for Four *81* Tim Burstall
Duet for One *86* Andrei Mikhalkov-Konchalovsky
Duffy *68* Robert Parrish
Duffy of San Quentin *53* Walter Doniger
Duffy's Tavern *45* Hal Walker
Dugan of the Badlands *31* Robert North Bradbury
Dugan of the Dugouts *28* Robert Ray
Dugi Brodovi *63* Jack Cardiff
Duguejo *66* Giuseppe Vari
Duke Comes Back, The *37* Irving Pichel
Duke Dolittle's Jungle Fizzle *17* Charles Saxon
Duke for a Day, A *34* James Parrott
Duke Is Tops, The *38* William Nolte
Duke of Chicago *49* George Blair
Duke of Chimney Butte, The *21* Frank Borzage
Duke of the Navy *42* William Beaudine
Duke of West Point, The *38* Alfred E. Green
Duke Steps Out, The *29* James Cruze
Duke Wore Jeans, The *58* Gerald Thomas
Duke's Good Joke, The *08* Georges Méliès
Duke's Plan, The *09* D. W. Griffith
Duke's Son *20* Franklin Dyall

Dukkestuen *50* Henning Carlsen
Dulces Horas *81* Carlos Saura
Dulcie's Adventure *16* James Kirkwood
Dulcima *70* Frank Nesbitt
Dulcimer Street *48* Sidney Gilliat
Dulcinea *62* Vicente Escriva
Dulcy *23* Sidney Franklin
Dulcy *40* S. Sylvan Simon
Dull Clang *52* Arne Mattsson
Dull Razor, The *00* George Albert Smith
Dulscy *76* Jan Rybkowski
Dům pro Dva *88* Miloš Zábranský
Duma Vez por Todas *85* Joaquim Leitão
Dumb Bell, The *22* Charlie Chase
Dumb But Disciplined *79* Claude Zidi
Dumb Cluck, The *37* Walter Lantz
Dumb Comrades *10* Lewin Fitzhamon
Dumb Conscious Mind, The *42* John Hubley, Paul Sommer
Dumb Daddies *28* Leo McCarey
Dumb Dicks *86* Filippo Ottoni
Dumb Dora Discovers Tobacco *45* Charles Hawtrey
Dumb Girl of Portici, The *16* Phillips Smalley, Lois Weber
Dumb Hounded *42* Tex Avery
Dumb Man of Manchester, The *08* William Haggar
Dumb Man's Evidence, The *15* Ernest G. Batley
Dumb Matchmaker, A *12* Bert Haldane
Dumb Patrol, The *64* Gerry Chinquy
Dumb Sagacity *07* Lewin Fitzhamon
Dumb Waiter, A *28* Harry Edwards
Dumb Waiter, The *79* Robert Bierman
Dumbbells in Derbies *31* Lewis R. Foster
Dumbbells in Ermine *30* John G. Adolfi
Dumbo *41* Ben Sharpsteen
Dumb's the Word *37* Leslie Goodwins
Dumka *57* Sergei Paradzhanov
Dummkopf, Der *20* Lupu Pick
Dummy, The *16* Will P. Kellino
Dummy, The *17* Francis J. Grandon
Dummy, The *29* Robert Milton
Dummy Ache *36* Leslie Goodwins
Dummy Owner, The *38* Jean Yarbrough
Dummy Talks, The *43* Oswald Mitchell
Dummy Trouble *40* William Beaudine
Dun-Huang *86* Junya Sato
Duna Bull, The *72* Laurence Henson
Duna—Halak—Madarak *71* István Szabó
Duna-Parti Randevú *37* Steve Sekely
Dune *84* David Lynch
Dunera Boys, The *85* Sam Lewin
Dung-Aw *75* Lino Brocka
Dungeon, The *22* Oscar Micheaux
Dungeon, The *50* E. A. Dupont
Dungeon of Death, The *15* Charles H. Weston
Dungeonmaster, The *85* David Allen, Charles Band, John Buechler, Steve Ford, Peter Manoogian, Ted Nicolaou, Rose Marie Turko
Dungeons of Harrow *64* Pat Boyette
Dungeons of Horror *64* Pat Boyette
Duniya Na Mane *37* Rajaram Vanakudre Shantaram
Dunja *55* Josef von Baky
Dunkel bei Tageslicht *63* Zoltán Fábri
Dunki-Schott *86* Hans Liechti, Tobias

Wyss
Dunkirk *58* Leslie Norman
Dunoyer de Segonzac *65* Monique Lepeuve, François Reichenbach
Dunwich Horror, The *69* Daniel Haller
Duo *87* Patrice Leconte
Duomo di Milano, Il *46* Alessandro Blasetti
Dupe, The *16* Frank Reicher
Dupe, The *65* Hideo Sekigawa
Duped *25* John P. McGowan
Duped by Determination *12* Fred Rains
Duped Journalist, The *14* Alexander Korda, Gyula Zilahy
Duped Othello, The *09* Jack Smith
Duped Till Doomsday *57* Kurt Jung-Alsen
Duplicity *78* Stan Brakhage
Duplicity II *78* Stan Brakhage
Duplicity III *80* Stan Brakhage
Duplicity of Hargraves, The *17* Thomas R. Mills
Dupont la Joie *75* Yves Boisset
Dupont Lajoie *75* Yves Boisset
Dura Lex *26* Lev Kuleshov
Durand of the Bad Lands *17* Richard Stanton
Durand of the Bad Lands *25* Lynn Reynolds
Durango Kid, The *40* Lambert Hillyer
Durango Valley Raiders *38* Sam Newfield
Durant Affair, The *62* Godfrey Grayson
Durante l'Estate *70* Ermanno Olmi
Duration *72* Malcolm Le Grice
Durbargati Padma *71* Ritwik Ghatak
Durch die Wälder, Durch die Auen *56* G. W. Pabst
Durchlaucht Hyperchonder *17* E. A. Dupont
Dürfen Wir Schweigen? *26* Richard Oswald
During One Night *60* Sidney J. Furie
During the Plague *13* Forest Holger-Madsen
During the Round Up *13* D. W. Griffith
During the Summer *70* Ermanno Olmi
Dusk to Dawn *22* King Vidor
Dusks and Dawns *61* Miklós Jancsó
Dusky Melodies *30* Alexander Oumansky
Duşman *79* Zeki Ökten
Düsseldorf *35* Walter Ruttmann
Dust *16* Edward Sloman
Dust *85* Marion Hansel
Dust and Gold *55* John Guillermin
Dust Be My Destiny *39* Lewis Seiler
Dust Flower, The *21* Rowland V. Lee
Dust in the Wind *87* Hsiao-hsien Hou
Dust of Desire *19* Perry N. Vekroff
Dust of Egypt, The *15* George D. Baker
Dustbin Parade *41* Joy Batchelor, John Halas
Dustforough *88* Mohsen Makhmal Baf
Dustman's Nightmare, The *15* Will P. Kellino
Dustman's Wedding, The *16* Will P. Kellino
Dustmen's Holiday, The *13* Will P. Kellino
Dustmen's Outing, The *16* Will P. Kellino
Dusts *54* Georges Franju

Dusty 82 John Richardson
Dusty and Sweets McGee 71 Floyd Mutrux
Dusty Bates 47 Darrell Catling
Dusty Dick's Awakening 11 A. E. Coleby
Dusty Ermine 36 Bernard Vorhaus
Dusty Gets a Shock 11 A. E. Coleby
Dutch Courage 22 George Dunstall
Dutch Gold Mine, A 11 Mack Sennett
Dutch Treat 86 Boaz Davidson
Dutchman 66 Anthony Harvey
Duty 14 Harold M. Shaw
Duty and Love 27 A. Gavronsky, Yuli
    Raizman
Duty and the Beast 43 Alec Geiss
Duty First 22 Marcel Perez
Duty Free Marriage 80 János Zsombolyai
Duty's Reward 27 Bertram Bracken
Dúvad 59 Zoltán Fábri
Duvar 82 Yılmaz Güney
Duvidha 73 Mani Kaul
Dva, Bouldej, Dva 29 Nina Agadzhanova-
    Shutko, Lev Kuleshov
Dva-Buldi-Dva 29 Nina Agadzhanova-
    Shutko, Lev Kuleshov
Dva Mrazíci 54 Jiří Trnka
Dva Mušketýři 64 Karel Zeman
Dvadtsat Dnei Bez Voini 76 Alexei
    Gherman
Dvadtsat Dva Neschastya 30 Sergei
    Bartenev, Sergei Gerasimov
Dvadtsat Shest Komissarov 33 Nikolai
    Shengelaya
Dvakrát Kaučuk 40 Alexander Hammid
Dvanáct Křesel 33 Martin Frič*
Dvoe Pod Odnim Zontom 87 Georgy
    Ungwald-Khilkevich
Dvoryanskoye Gnezdo 69 Andrei Mikhal-
    kov-Konchalovsky
Dwadzat Schest Dnej is Shisni Dostojew-
    skogo 81 Alexander Zarkhi
Dwaj Ludzie z Szafą 58 Roman Polanski
Dwarf and the Giant, The 02 Georges
    Méliès
Dwelling Place of Light, The 20 Jack
    Conway
Dyadya Vanya 70 Andrei Mikhalkov-
    Konchalovsky
Dybbuk 37 Michael Waszyński
Dybbuk, The 37 Michael Waszyński
D'Ye Ken John Peel? 08 Arthur Gilbert
D'Ye Ken John Peel? 35 Henry Edwards
Dyetstvo Gorkovo 38 Mark Donskoi
Dying Detective, The 21 Maurice Elvey
Dying for a Smoke 66 John Halas
Dying of Thirst 07 Lewin Fitzhamon
Dýmky 65 Vojtěch Jasný
Dynamique de l'Évolution de l'Œuf de
    Pieuvre 67 Jean Painlevé
Dynamite 29 Cecil B. DeMille
Dynamite 47 Åke Öhberg
Dynamite 48 William Pine
Dynamite Allen 21 Del Henderson
Dynamite Anchorage 54 Edgar G. Ulmer
Dynamite Brothers, The 74 Al Adamson
Dynamite Canyon 41 Robert E. Tansey
Dynamite Chicken 71 Ernest Pintoff
Dynamite Dan 24 Bruce Mitchell
Dynamite Delaney 38 Joseph Rothman
Dynamite Denny 32 Frank R. Strayer
Dynamite Jack 61 Jean Bastia

Dynamite Jim 66 Alfonso Balcazar
Dynamite Joe 66 Antonio Margheriti
Dynamite Johnson 78 Bobby A. Suarez
Dynamite Man from Glory Jail 71 Andrew
    V. McLaglen
Dynamite Pass 50 Lew Landers
Dynamite Ranch 32 Forrest K. Sheldon
Dynamite Smith 24 Ralph Ince
Dynamite Women 76 Michael Pressman
Dynamiters, The 12 William Duncan
Dynamiters, The 56 Terence Fisher, Fran-
    cis Searle
Dyplomatyczna Żona 38 Carl Boese,
    Mieczysław Krawicz
Dyrekøbt Glimmer 11 Urban Gad
Dyrekøbt Venskab 12 August Blom
Dyrygent 79 Andrzej Wajda
Dzhoi and His Friends 28 M. Khukhun-
    ashvili, Vladimir Petrov
Dzhoi i Druzhok 28 M. Khukhunashvili,
    Vladimir Petrov
Dzieje Grzechu 75 Walerian Borowczyk
Dzień Upragniony 39 Henryk Szaro
Dziesięciu z Pawiaka 32 Richard Ordynski
Dziewczęta z Nowolipku 38 Josef Leytes
Dzingis-Kan 65 Henry Levin
Dziś w Nocy Umrze Miasto 61 Jan Ryb-
    kowski
Dzusovy Roman 88 Fero Fenic
E alla Fine lo Chiamarono Jerusalemme
    l'Implacabile 72 Toni Secchi
È Arrivato il Cavaliere 50 Mario Monicelli,
    Steno
È Arrivato Mio Fratello 85 Franco Castel-
    lano, Giuseppe Moccia
ECS 62 Charles Eames, Ray Eames
...E Chiamavano Spirito Santo 71 Giu-
    liano Carmineo
E Continuano a Fregarsi il Milione di Dol-
    lari 71 Eugenio Martin
E Continuavano a Chiamarlo Figlio di...
    72 Rafael Romero Marchent
E Così Divennero i Tre Supermen del West
    73 I. Marinego
E Dio Disse a Caino... 69 Antonio
    Margheriti
E Divenne il Più Spietato Bandito del Sud
    67 Julio Buchs
E Flat 61 Ritwik Ghatak
E Flat Man, The 35 Charles Lamont
E la Nave Va... 83 Federico Fellini
È l'Amor Che Mi Rovina 51 Mario Soldati
E' Lollipop 76 Ashley Lazarus
E Lucean le Stelle 34 Carmine Gallone
E per Tetto un Cielo di Stelle 68 Giulio
    Petroni
E' Permesso Maresciallo? 58 Carlo Ludo-
    vico Bragaglia
È Più Facile Che un Cammello 50 Luigi
    Zampa
...E Pri lo Chiamavano il Magnifico 72
    Enzo Barboni
È Primavera 49 Renato Castellani
ESD 87 Anna Sokołowska
E.T., the Extra-Terrestrial 82 Steven Spiel-
    berg
E' Tornato Sabata...Hai Chiuso un'Altro
    Volto 71 Gianfranco Parolini
E Tu Vivrai nel Terrore! L'Aldilà 80 Lucio
    Fulci

...E Venne il Tempo di Uccidere 68 Vin-
    cent Eagle
E Venne l'Alba...Ma Tinto di Rosse 70
    Antonio Margheriti
E Venne un Uomo 64 Ermanno Olmi
E Vennero in Quattro per Uccidere Sartana
    69 D. Fidani
E Vissero per Sempre Felici e Ammazzati
    73 Marc Meyer
Each According to His Faith 55 William
    Beaudine
Each Dawn I Crow 49 Friz Freleng
Each Dawn I Die 39 William Keighley
Each Goes His Own Way 48 Hasse Ekman
Each Heart Has Its Own Story 53 Bror
    Bugler
Each Man for Himself 68 Giorgio Capitani
Each One for Himself 68 Giorgio Capitani
Each Other 79 Michal Bat-Adam
Each Pearl a Tear 16 George Melford
Each to His Kind 17 Edward J. LeSaint
Each Within His Shell 55 Tomu Uchida
Eadie Was a Lady 34 Jack Conway
Eadie Was a Lady 43 Arthur Dreifuss
Eager Beaver, The 45 Chuck Jones
Eager Beavers 75 Gus Trikonis
Eager Lips 27 Wilfred Noy
Eagle, The 18 Elmer Clifton
Eagle, The 25 Clarence Brown
Eagle, The 86 Don Hulette
Eagle and the Hawk, The 33 Mitchell
    Leisen, Stuart Walker
Eagle and the Hawk, The 50 Lewis R.
    Foster
Eagle Has Landed, The 76 John Sturges
Eagle Has Two Heads, The 47 Jean Coc-
    teau
Eagle in a Cage 70 Fielder Cook
Eagle of the Caucasus, The 32 Boris Mik-
    hin
Eagle of the Sea, The 26 Frank Lloyd
Eagle Over London 70 Enzo G. Castellari
Eagle Rock 64 Henry Geddes
Eagle Squadron 42 Arthur Lubin
Eagle with Two Heads, The 47 Jean Coc-
    teau
Eagles Attack at Dawn 74 Menahem
    Golan
Eagle's Brood, The 35 Howard Bretherton
Eagles' Cemetery, The 39 Luis Lezama
Eagle's Claw, The 24 Charles R. Seeling
Eagle's Feather, The 23 Edward Sloman
Eagle's Mate, The 14 James Kirkwood
Eagle's Nest 15 Romaine Fielding
Eagles of the Fleet 50 Cyril Frankel
Eagles of the Fleet 52 Lesley Selander
Eagles Over London 70 Enzo G. Castellari
Eagle's Tail, The 41 Daisuke Ito
Eagle's Wing 78 Anthony Harvey
Eagle's Wings, The 16 Robert Z. Leonard
Eames Lounge Chair 56 Charles Eames,
    Ray Eames
Ear, The 20 F. Lyle Goldman
Earl Carroll Sketchbook 46 Albert S.
    Rogell
Earl Carroll Vanities 45 Joseph Santley
Earl of Camelot, The 14 Henry Wilson
Earl of Chicago, The 39 Richard Thorpe
Earl of Pawtucket, The 15 Harry C. Myers
Earl of Puddlestone 40 Gus Meins

Early Autumn *61* Yasujiro Ozu
Early Bird, The *25* Charles Hines
Early Bird, The *28* John Foster
Early Bird, The *36* Donovan Pedelty
Early Bird, The *38* Art Davis, Sid Marcus
Early Bird, The *65* Robert Asher
Early Bird Dood It, The *42* Tex Avery
Early Birds *06* Harold Jeapes
Early Birds *23* Albert Brouett
Early Days of Communication *58* John Halas
Early Spring *56* Yasujiro Ozu
Early Spring *57* Joris Ivens
Early Summer *50* Yasujiro Ozu
Early to Bed *28* Emmett J. Flynn
Early to Bed *33* Ludwig Berger
Early to Bed *36* Norman Z. McLeod
Early to Bet *51* Robert McKimson
Early to Wed *26* Frank Borzage
Early Works *69* Želimir Žilnik
Early Worm, The *11* Lewin Fitzhamon
Early Worm Gets the Bird, The *39* Tex
   Avery
Earring, The *15* Ethyle Batley
Earrings of Madame de . . . , The *53* Max
   Ophüls
Ears Between the Teeth *87* Patrick Schul-
   mann
Ears of Experience *38* Leslie Goodwins
Earth *30* Alexander Dovzhenko
Earth, The *39* Tomu Uchida
Earth *57* Zahari Zhandov
Earth, The *68* Youssef Chahine
Earth Cries Out, The *49* Duilio Coletti
Earth Defense Force *57* Inoshiro Honda
Earth Dies Screaming, The *64* Terence
   Fisher
Earth Entranced *66* Glauber Rocha
Earth Girls Are Easy *88* Julien Temple
Earth in Chains *28* Fedor Ozep
Earth in Labour *50* John Halas
Earth Is a Sinful Song, The *73* Rauni
   Mollberg
Earth Sings, The *33* Karel Plicka
Earth Smiles, The *25* Kenji Mizoguchi
Earth Thirsts, The *30* Yuli Raizman
Earth Trembles, The *47* Luchino Visconti
Earth II *71* Tom Gries
Earth vs. the Flying Saucers *56* Fred F.
   Sears
Earth vs. the Spider *58* Bert I. Gordon
Earth Will Tremble, The *47* Luchino
   Visconti
Earth Woman, The *26* Walter Lang
Earthbottom *56* George Romero
Earthbound *20* T. Hayes Hunter
Earthbound *40* Irving Pichel
Earthbound *81* James L. Conway
Earthling, The *80* Peter Collinson
Earthly Rituals *59* Kon Ichikawa
Earthquake *74* Mark Robson
Earthquake in Chile *74* Helma Sanders-
   Brahms
Earthquake Motor, The *17* Karl Heinz
   Wolff
Earth's Cap, The *55* Alexander Alexeïeff,
   Claire Parker
Earth's Final Fury *79* James Goldstone
Earth's Revenge, The *15* Forest Holger-
   Madsen
Earthworm Tractors *36* Ray Enright

Easiest Profession, The *60* Jean Boyer
Easiest Way, The *17* Albert Capellani
Easiest Way, The *31* Jack Conway
East African Safari *65* François Reichen-
   bach
East and West *20* Charles Raymond
East China Sea *69* Tadahiko Isomi
East End Chant *34* Alexander Hall
East Is Best *26* William C. Nolan
East Is East *13* Dave Aylott
East Is East *16* Henry Edwards
East Is West *22* Sidney Franklin
East Is West *30* Monta Bell
East Lynne *02* Dicky Winslow
East Lynne *13* Arthur Charrington
East Lynne *13* Bert Haldane
East Lynne *16* Bertram Bracken
East Lynne *21* Hugo Ballin
East Lynne *25* Emmett J. Flynn
East Lynne *30* Frank Lloyd
East Lynne on the Western Front *31*
   George Pearson
East Lynne with Variations *19* Edward F.
   Cline
East Meets West *36* Herbert Mason
East of Borneo *31* George Melford
East of Broadway *24* William K. Howard
East of Eden *55* Elia Kazan
East of Elephant Rock *76* Don Boyd
East of Fifth Avenue *33* Albert S. Rogell
East of Fifth Avenue *33* Ben Stoloff
East of Java *35* George Melford
East of Java *49* H. Bruce Humberstone
East of Kilimanjaro *57* Arnold Belgard,
   Edoardo Capolino
East of Ludgate Hill *37* H. Manning
   Haynes
East of Piccadilly *40* Harold Huth
East of Shanghai *32* Alfred Hitchcock
East of Singapore *27* Geoffrey H. Malins
East of Sudan *64* Nathan Juran
East of Suez *25* Martin E. Johnson
East of Suez *25* Raoul Walsh
East of Sumatra *53* Budd Boetticher
East of the Bowery *44* William Beaudine
East of the Rising Sun *49* Richard Thorpe
East of the River *40* Alfred E. Green
East of the Wall *86* Wieland Speck
East 103rd Street *83* Chris Menges
East River Novelty *03* Edwin S. Porter
East Side Kids *40* Robert F. Hill
East Side Kids Meet Bela Lugosi, The *43*
   William Beaudine
East Side New York *20* Hy Mayer
East Side of Heaven *39* David Butler
East Side Rascals *46* Sam Newfield
East Side Sadie *29* Sidney Goldin
East Side Urchins Bathing in a Foun-
   tain *03* Edwin S. Porter
East Side, West Side *23* Irving Cummings
East Side, West Side *26* Dave Fleischer
East Side, West Side *27* Allan Dwan
East Side, West Side *49* Mervyn LeRoy
East Wind *69* Daniel Cohn-Bendit, Jean-
   Luc Godard, Jean-Pierre Gorin
Easter Celebration at Jerusalem *12* Sidney
   Olcott
Easter in Sicily *55* Vittorio De Seta
Easter Parade *48* Charles Walters
Easter Sunday *80* Jackie Kong

Easter Yeggs *47* Robert McKimson
Eastern Condors *87* Samo Hung
Eastern Cowboy, The *11* Allan Dwan
Eastern Flower, An *13* Allan Dwan
Eastern Girl, The *12* Allan Dwan
Eastern Nigerian Newsreel No. 30 *65*
   Bruce Beresford
Eastern Westerner, An *20* Hal Roach
Eastern Wind *82* Daniel Wachsmann
Easterner, The *07* J. Stuart Blackton
Eastward Ho! *19* Emmett J. Flynn
Easy Alley *39* Kajiro Yamamoto
Easy Come, Easy Go *28* Frank Tuttle
Easy Come, Easy Go *47* John Farrow
Easy Come, Easy Go *67* John Rich
Easy Down There! *71* Jacques Deray
Easy Go *30* Edward Sedgwick
Easy Going *26* Richard Thorpe
Easy Going Gordon *25* Duke Worne
Easy in Mind *89* Mary Jiménez
Easy Life *44* Walter Hart
Easy Life, The *62* Dino Risi
Easy Life, The *71* Francis Warin
Easy Living *37* Mitchell Leisen
Easy Living *49* Jacques Tourneur
Easy Millions *33* Fred Newmeyer
Easy Money *17* Travers Vale
Easy Money *25* Albert S. Rogell
Easy Money *34* Redd Davis
Easy Money *36* Phil Rosen
Easy Money *48* Bernard Knowles
Easy Money *83* James Signorelli
Easy on the Eye *33* George Marshall
Easy Peckins *53* Robert McKimson
Easy Pickings *27* George Archainbaud
Easy Riches *38* Maclean Rogers
Easy Rider *69* Dennis Hopper
Easy Road, The *21* Tom Forman
Easy Road *79* Andreas Thomopoulos
Easy Street *16* Charles Chaplin
Easy Street *28* Oscar Micheaux
Easy to Get *20* Walter Edwards
Easy to Look At *45* Ford Beebe
Easy to Love *33* William Keighley
Easy to Love *53* Charles Walters
Easy to Make Money *19* Edwin Carewe
Easy to Take *36* Glenn Tryon
Easy to Wed *46* Edward Buzzell
Easy Virtue *27* Alfred Hitchcock
Easy Way, The *51* Norman Taurog
Easy Wheels *89* David O'Malley
Easy Years *53* Luigi Zampa
Eat *63* Andy Warhol
Eat a Bowl of Tea *89* Wayne Wang
Eat and Run *86* Christopher Hart
Eat My Dust! *76* Charles B. Griffith
Eat the Peach *86* Peter Ormrod
Eat the Rich *87* Peter Richardson
Eaten Alive *76* Tobe Hooper
Eaten Alive *80* Umberto Lenzi
Eaten Alive by the Cannibals *80* Umberto
   Lenzi
Eatin' on the Cuff *42* Robert Clampett
Eating *90* Henry Jaglom
Eating Out with Tommy *41* Desmond
   Dickinson
Eating Raoul *82* Paul Bartel
Eating Too Fast *66* Andy Warhol
Eau, L' *66* Alexander Alexeïeff, Claire
   Parker

Eleventh Commandment, The *35* Martin Frič

Eleventh Hour, The *16* Ernest G. Batley

Eleventh Hour, The *18* Fred O'Donovan

Eleventh Hour, The *22* George Ridgwell

Eleventh Hour, The *23* Bernard J. Durning

Eleventh Hour, The *57* Tomu Uchida

Eleventh Year, The *28* Dziga Vertov

Elf Jahre und ein Tag *63* Gottfried Reinhardt

Elf Teufel, Die *27* Carl Boese, Zoltán Korda

Eli, Eli *40* Joseph Seiden

Éliane *19* Camille De Morlhon

Éliette ou Instants de la Vie d'une Femme *71* François Reichenbach

Eliminator, The *67* Seth Holt

Eliminators *86* Peter Manoogian

Elinor Norton *34* Hamilton MacFadden

Eliot Feld: Artistic Director *70* Christian Blackwood

Elippathayam *81* Adoor Gopalakrishnan

Elisa, My Life *77* Carlos Saura

Elisa, My Love *77* Carlos Saura

Elisa, Vida Mía *77* Carlos Saura

Elisabeth of Austria *31* Adolf Trotz

Élisabeth Reine d'Angleterre *12* Henri Desfontaines, Louis Mercanton

Elisabeth und der Narr *33* Thea von Harbou

Elisabeth von Österreich *31* Adolf Trotz

Elise *87* Claus Ploug

Élise ou La Vraie Vie *70* Michel Drach

Elisir d'Amore, L' *39* Lotte Reiniger

Elisir d'Amore *46* Mario Costa

Eliso *28* Nikolai Shengelaya

Elite Ball, The *13* Mack Sennett

Elitélt, Az *17* Béla Balázs

Elixiere des Teufels, Die *76* Manfred Purzer

Elixir of Life, The *01* James A. Williamson

Elixirs of the Devil, The *76* Manfred Purzer

Eliza Comes to Stay *36* Henry Edwards

Eliza Fraser *76* Tim Burstall

Elizabeth and Essex *39* Michael Curtiz

Elizabeth and Mary *64* D. A. Pennebaker

Elizabeth Is Queen *53* Terry Ashwood

Elizabeth of England *35* Arthur Woods

Elizabeth of Ladymead *48* Herbert Wilcox

Elizabeth the Queen *39* Michael Curtiz

Elizabethan Romance, An *11* Theo Bouwmeester

Eliza's Horoscope *75* Gordon Sheppard

Eliza's Romeo *22* Bert Haldane

Ella Cinders *26* Alfred E. Green

Elle à Passe Tant d'Heures Sous les Sunlights *85* Philippe Garrel

Elle Boit Pas, Elle Fume Pas, Elle Drague Pas. . .Mais Elle Cause! *70* Michel Audiard

Elle Cause Plus. . .Elle Flingue *72* Michel Audiard

Elle Est Bicimidine *27* Edmond T. Gréville

Ellehammer *57* Jørgen Roos

Ellen *50* James V. Kern

Ellery Queen and the Murder Ring *41* James P. Hogan

Ellery Queen and the Perfect Crime *41* James P. Hogan

Ellery Queen — Master Detective *40* Kurt Neumann

Ellery Queen's Penthouse Mystery *41* James P. Hogan

Elles Étaient Douze Femmes *40* Georges Lacombe

Ellie *84* Peter Wittman

Elliot Fauman, Ph.D. *90* Ric Klass

Elliott Carter *80* D. A. Pennebaker

Ellis Island *36* Phil Rosen

Elmer *77* Christopher Cain

Elmer and Elsie *34* Gilbert Pratt

Elmer Gantry *60* Richard Brooks

Elmer the Great *32* Mervyn LeRoy

Elmer, the Great Dane *35* Walter Lantz

Elmer's Candid Camera *40* Chuck Jones

Elmer's Pet Rabbit *41* Chuck Jones

Elmo the Fearless *20* John P. McGowan

Elnémult Harangok *16* Béla Balázs

Elnök Kisasszony *35* Andrew Marton

Elogio della Pazzia *86* Roberto Aguerre

Elokuu *56* Matti Kassila

Elope If You Must *22* C. R. Wallace

Elopement, The *11* Frank Powell

Elopement *51* Henry Koster

Elopements on Double L Ranch, The *11* Allan Dwan

Eloping with Aunty *09* D. W. Griffith

Elsa *66* Agnès Varda

Elsa, Elsa *85* Yehuda Ne'eman

Elsa la Rose *66* Agnès Varda

Elsa Maxwell's Hotel for Women *39* Gregory Ratoff

Elsa's Brother *15* Van Dyke Brooke

Else von Erlenhof *19* Fritz Kortner

Elsie the Gamekeeper's Daughter *11* Bert Haldane

Elsie's Nightmare *13* Edgar Rogers

Elskovsleg *13* August Blom, Forest Holger-Madsen

Elskovsmagt *12* August Blom, Forest Holger-Madsen

Elso Kétszáz Évem *85* Gyula Maar

Elstree Calling *30* Adrian Brunel, André Charlot, Alfred Hitchcock, Jack Hulbert, Paul Murray

Elstree Story, The *52* Gilbert Gunn

Eltávozott Nap *68* Márta Mészáros

Élteto Tisza-Víz *54* Miklós Jancsó

Elton John in Central Park *81* Mike Mansfield

Élus de la Mer, Les *25* Gaston Roudes

Elusive Corporal, The *62* Guy Lefranc, Jean Renoir

Elusive Idea, The *17* Harry S. Palmer

Elusive Isabel *16* Stuart Paton

Elusive Jan, The *42* I. Annensky, Vladimir Petrov

Elusive Pimpernel, The *19* Maurice Elvey

Elusive Pimpernel, The *50* Michael Powell, Emeric Pressburger

Elvarázsolt Dollár, Az *85* István Bujtor

Elveszett Paradicsom *62* Károly Makk

Elvira Madigan *43* Åke Öhberg

Elvira Madigan *67* Bo Widerberg

Elvira: Mistress of the Dark *88* James Signorelli

Elvis *79* John Carpenter

Elvis, Elvis *77* Kay Pollak

Elvis Gratton, le King des Kings *86* Pierre Falardeau

Elvis Gratton, the King of Kings *86* Pierre Falardeau

Elvis Hansen — En Samfundshjælper *88* Jan Hertz

Elvis-Kissan Jäljillä *87* Claes Olsson

Elvis on Tour *72* Robert Abel, Pierre Adidge

Elvis: That's the Way It Is *70* Denis Sanders

Elysia *33* Bryan Foy

Elysium *86* Erika Szántó

Em Portugal Já Se Fazem Automóveis *38* Manoel De Oliveira

Emak Bakia *26* Man Ray

Emanon *86* Stuart Paul

Emanuelle e gli Ultimi Cannibali *77* Aristide Massaccesi

Emanuelle in America *77* Aristide Massaccesi

Embajador de la India, El *88* Mario Ribero

Embalmer, The *65* Dino Tavella

Embarrassed Bridegroom, An *13* William Duncan

Embarrassing Moments *30* William James Craft

Embarrassing Moments *34* Edward Laemmle

Embarrassment of Riches, The *18* Edward Dillon

Embassy *72* Gordon Hessler

Embassy Girl *32* Sidney Lanfield

Ember a Híd Alatt *36* Ladislas Vajda

Ember Néha Téved, Az *38* Béla Gaál

Emberek! Ne Engedjétek! *54* Miklós Jancsó*

Embers *16* Arthur Maude

Embezzled Heaven *59* Ernst Marischka

Embezzler, The *14* Allan Dwan

Embezzler, The *54* John Gilling

Embodied Thought, The *16* Edward Sloman

Embraceable You *48* Felix Jacoves

Embracers, The *66* Gary Graver

Embrassez-Moi *32* Léon Mathot

Embrióák *85* Pál Zolnay

Embrogynèse d'Orizias Latipes *59* Jean Painlevé

Embroidery Extraordinary *10* Cecil M. Hepworth

Embryo *76* Ralph Nelson

Embryos *85* Pál Zolnay

Embun *56* Osman Ismai

Emerald City *89* Michael Jenkins

Emerald Forest, The *85* John Boorman

Emerald of Death *19* F. W. Murnau

Emerald of the East *28* Jean De Kuharski

Emergency! *52* Lewis Gilbert

Emergency *62* Francis Searle

Emergency Call *33* Edward L. Cahn

Emergency Call *52* Lewis Gilbert

Emergency Calls *85* Miloš Zábranský

Emergency Hospital *56* Lee Sholem

Emergency Landing *41* William Beaudine

Emergency Squad *39* Edward Dmytryk

Emergency Ward *72* Blake Edwards

Emergency Wedding *50* Edward Buzzell

Emerson, Lake and Palmer in Concert *81* Ron Kantor

Emigrant, The *10* T. J. Gobbett

Émigrante, L' *38* Yves Allégret, Léo Joannon

Émigrante, L' *73* Pasquale Festa Campanile

Emigrantes *49* Aldo Fabrizi

Emigrants, The *21* Mauritz Stiller

Emigrants, The *70* Jan Troell

Emigrata, L' *18* Augusto Genina

Emil *34* Milton Rosmer

Emil and the Detectives *31* Gerhard Lamprecht

Emil and the Detectives *34* Milton Rosmer

Emil and the Detectives *54* Robert A. Stemmle

Emil and the Detectives *64* Peter Tewksbury

Emil Coleman and His Orchestra *42* Jean Negulesco

Emil und die Detektive *31* Gerhard Lamprecht

Emiliano Zapata *70* Felipe Cazals

Emilie Högqvist *39* Gustaf Molander

Emilio Varela's Band *87* Ralph Portillo

Emily *64* Arthur Hiller

Emily *76* Henry Herbert

Emily *79* Malcolm Le Grice

Emir's Secret Voyage, The *87* Fardi Davletshin

Émission, L' *68* Theodoros Angelopoulos

Emitai *71* Ousmane Sembène

Emlékezz, Ifjúság! *55* Miklós Jancsó

Emma *31* Clarence Brown

Emma *65* Anthony Perry

Emma Hamilton *68* Christian-Jaque

Emma Mae *76* Jamaa Fanaka

Emmanuelle *74* Just Jaeckin

Emmanuelle—The Joys of a Woman *76* Francis Giacobetti

Emmanuelle in Soho *81* David Hughes

Emmanuelle IV *83* Francis Leroy, Iris Letans

Emmanuelle V *87* Walerian Borowczyk

Emmanuelle 6 *88* Bruno Zincone

Emmanuell's Silver Tongue *81* Mauro Ivaldi, Guido Leoni

Emma's Shadow *88* Søren Kragh-Jacobsen

Emma's War *86* Clytie Jessop

Emmerdeur, L' *73* Édouard Molinaro

Emmy *34* Steve Sekely

Emmy of Stork's Nest *15* William Nigh

Emotional Education, An *46* Mark Donskoi

Emperor, The *67* George Lucas

Emperor and a General, The *67* Kihachi Okamoto

Emperor and His Baker, The *51* Martin Frič

Emperor and the General, The *67* Kihachi Okamoto

Emperor and the Golem, The *51* Martin Frič

Emperor and the Nightingale, The *48* Miloš Macourek, Jiří Trnka

Emperor Jones, The *33* Dudley Murphy

Emperor of California, The *36* Luis Trenker

Emperor of Peru, The *81* Fernando Arrabal

Emperor of Portugal, The *44* Gustaf Molander

Emperor of the North *73* Robert Aldrich

Emperor of the North Pole, The *73* Robert Aldrich

Emperor Waltz, The *47* Billy Wilder

Emperor's Baker, The *51* Martin Frič

Emperor's Baker and the Baker's Emperor, The *51* Martin Frič

Emperor's Candlesticks, The *37* George Fitzmaurice

Emperor's Messenger, The *12* Hay Plumb

Emperor's New Clothes, The *53* Ted Parmelee

Emperor's New Clothes, The *87* David Irving

Emperor's Nightingale, The *48* Miloš Macourek, Jiří Trnka

Empire *64* Andy Warhol

Empire d'Alexandre, L' *73* Alain Resnais

Empire de la Nuit, L' *63* Pierre Grimblat

Empire de la Passion, L' *78* Nagisa Oshima

Empire des Sens, L' *76* Nagisa Oshima

Empire du Diament, L' *20* Léonce Perret

Empire of Diamonds, The *20* Léonce Perret

Empire of Dracula, The *66* Federico Curiel

Empire of Night, The *63* Pierre Grimblat

Empire of Passion, The *78* Nagisa Oshima

Empire of the Ants *77* Bert I. Gordon

Empire of the Passions *76* Nagisa Oshima

Empire of the Senses *76* Nagisa Oshima

Empire of the Sun *55* Mario Craveri, Enrico Gras

Empire of the Sun *87* Steven Spielberg

Empire Sonhrai, L' *63* Ousmane Sembène

Empire State *87* Ron Peck

Empire State Express, the Second, Taking Water on the Fly *05* Edwin S. Porter

Empire Strikes Back, The *80* Irvin Kershner

Empire Timber *31* John Grierson

Employee, The *72* Helma Sanders-Brahms

Employees *84* Pupi Avati

Employees' Entrance *33* Roy Del Ruth

Employment with Investment and the Masked Fraud *26* F. W. Engholm

Empreinte, L' *16* André Hugon

Empreinte des Géants, L' *79* Robert Enrico

Empreinte du Dieu, L' *40* Léonide Moguy

Empress, The *17* Alice Guy-Blaché

Empress and I, The *33* Friedrich Hollände

Empress Josephine, or Wife of a Demigod *23* Edwin Greenwood

Empress' Love Letter, The *16* Robert Wiene

Empress Wu *65* Han-hsiang Li

Empress Yang Kwei Fei *55* Kenji Mizoguchi

Emprise, L' *24* Henri Diamant-Berger

Emptied-Out Grocer's Shop, The *33* Martin Frič

Empty Arms *20* Frank Reicher

Empty Beach, The *85* Chris Thomson

Empty Cab, The *18* Douglas Gerrard

Empty Canvas, The *63* Damiano Damiani

Empty Cradle, The *23* Burton L. King

Empty Cradle, The *38* Miguel Zacarías

Empty Hands *24* Victor Fleming

Empty Hearts *24* Alfred Santell

Empty Holsters *37* B. Reeves Eason

Empty House, The *21* Maurice Elvey

Empty Pillow, The *57* Salah Abu Saif

Empty Pockets *17* Herbert Brenon

Empty Quarter *85* Raymond Depardon

Empty Saddle, The *25* Harry S. Webb

Empty Saddles *36* Lesley Selander

Empty Socks *27* Walt Disney

Empty Star, The *62* Emilio Gómez Muriel

Empty Table, The *85* Masaki Kobayashi

En av de Många *14* Victor Sjöström

En Bateau *51* Jean Mitry

En Blandt Mange *61* Astrid Henning-Jensen, Bjarne Henning-Jensen

En Cabinet Particulier *1897* Georges Méliès

En Cas de Malheur *58* Claude Autant-Lara

En Classe *1898* Alice Guy-Blaché

En Cours de Route *79* Márta Mészáros

En Crête Sans les Dieux *34* Roger Leenhardt, René Zuber

En de Zee Was Niet Meer *55* Bert Haanstra

En Effeuillant la Marguerite *56* Marc Allégret

En el Aire *88* Pastor Vega

En el Nombre del Hijo *87* Jorge Polaco

En el País de los Pies Ligeros *83* Marcela Fernández Violante

En el Río *61* José Luis Borau

En el Viejo Tampico *47* Luis Buñuel

En Enda Natt *38* Gustaf Molander

En Este Pueblo No Hay Ladrones *65* Alberto Isaac

En Faction *02* Alice Guy-Blaché

En Fluga Gör Ingen Sommar *47* Hasse Ekman

En Grève *11* Louis Feuillade

Én XX. Századom, Az *89* Ildikó Enyedi

En la Otra Isla *68* Sara Gómez

En la Palma de Tu Mano *50* Roberto Gavaldón

En la Terraza *61* Victor Erice

Én Lányom Nem Olyan, Az *37* Ladislas Vajda

En Lisant le Journal *32* Alberto Cavalcanti

En, Men ett Lejon *40* Gustaf Molander

En Natt *31* Gustaf Molander

En och En *78* Erland Josephson, Sven Nykvist, Ingrid Thulin

En Passant *43* Alexander Alexeïeff, Claire Parker

En Passant par la Lorraine *50* Georges Franju

En Penumbra *86* José Luis Lozano

En Plain Cirage *61* Georges Lautner

En Plein Midi *57* Sidney Jézéquel, Roger Leenhardt

En Plo *85* Stavros Konstantarakos

En Plongée *27* Jacques Robert

En Rade *27* Alberto Cavalcanti

En Retirada *84* Juan Carlos De Sanzo

En Route *10* Émile Cohl

En Scène *47* Sacha Guitry

En Svala Gör Ingen Sommar *47* Hasse Ekman

En to Iu Onna *71* Tadashi Imai
En Toute Innocence *88* Alain Jessua
En un Lugar de Castilla *36* Carlos Velo
Én XX. Századom, Az *89* Ildikó Enyedi
Enamorada *46* Emilio Fernández
Enas Erodios via tin Germania *88* Stavros Tornes
Encarnação de Demônio *81* José Mojica Marins
Enchanté *88* Édouard Molinaro
Enchanted April *35* Harry Beaumont
Enchanted Barn, The *19* David Smith
Enchanted Basket, The *03* Georges Méliès
Enchanted Castle in Dudinci, The *51* Dušan Vukotić
Enchanted Cottage, The *24* John S. Robertson
Enchanted Cottage, The *45* John Cromwell
Enchanted Cup, The *02* Walter R. Booth
Enchanted Desna, The *64* Yulia Solntseva
Enchanted Dollars, The *85* István Bujtor
Enchanted Drawing, The *00* J. Stuart Blackton
Enchanted Flute, The *29* Frank Moser
Enchanted Forest, The *45* Lew Landers
Enchanted Forest, The *87* José Luis Cuerda
Enchanted Hill, The *26* Irvin Willat
Enchanted House, The *39* Otakar Vávra
Enchanted Island, The *27* William G. Crosby
Enchanted Island *58* Allan Dwan
Enchanted Island *76* Lester James Peries
Enchanted Mirror, The *59* James Komisarjevsky, L. Kristy
Enchanted Sedan Chair, The *05* Georges Méliès
Enchanted Shadow *59* Han-hsiang Li
Enchanted Toymaker, The *04* Arthur Cooper
Enchanted Valley, The *48* Robert E. Tansey
Enchanted Walk *54* Arne Mattsson
Enchanted Well, The *03* Georges Méliès
Enchanter, The *03* Georges Méliès
Enchanteur Alcofrisbas, L' *03* Georges Méliès
Enchanting Shadow, The *65* Han-hsiang Li
Enchantment *16* Frank Borzage
Enchantment *20* Einar J. Bruun
Enchantment *21* Robert Vignola
Enchantment *48* Irving Reis
Enchantress, The *85* Manoussos Manoussakis
Encircling of Color, The *87* Jean Gagne, Serge Gagne
Enclos, L' *60* Armand Gatti
Enclosure, The *60* Armand Gatti
Encore *51* Harold French, Pat Jackson, Anthony Pelissier
Encore (Once More) *88* Paul Vecchiali
Encore Paris *63* Frédéric Rossif
Encounter *51* Joseph Losey
Encounter of the Spooky Kind *80* Samo Hung
Encounter with France *60* Sergei Yutkevich
Encounter with the Unknown *73* Harry Thomason
Encounters at Dusk *57* Alf Kjellin
Encounters in Salzburg *64* Max Friedman
Encounters in the Dark *60* Wanda Jakubowska
Encrucijada para una Monja *70* Julio Buchs
Encuentro: La Salación, El *65* Manuel Octavio Gómez
Encyclopédie de Grand'maman en 13 Volumes, L' *63* Walerian Borowczyk
Encyclopédie Filmée, L' *51* Jean Grémillon, Pierre Kast, Marcello Pagliero
Encyclopédie Filmée—Alchimie, Azur, Absence, L' *51* Jean Grémillon, Pierre Kast, Marcello Pagliero
End, The *68* Bruce Beresford
End, The *78* Burt Reynolds
End, The *86* Ali Talebi
End As a Man *57* Jack Garfein
End of a Day, The *38* Julien Duvivier
End of a Priest, The *68* Evald Schorm
End of a Prolonged Journey *54* Teinosuke Kinugasa
End of All Things, The *1897* George Albert Smith
End of an Era *83* Lester James Peries
End of August *74* Gary Alexander Young
End of August, The *81* Bob Graham
End of August at the Hotel Ozone, The *66* Jan Schmidt
End of Bad Luck, The *33* Dimitrios Gaziadis
End of Battle Fire, The *50* Kozaburo Yoshimura
End of Belle, The *60* Édouard Molinaro
End of Civilization, The *85* Piotr Szulkin
End of Dawn, The *64* Andy Warhol
End of der Limit, Der *17* Gregory La Cava
End of Desire *58* Alexandre Astruc
End of Engagement *40* Satsuo Yamamoto
End of Innocence *57* Leopoldo Torre-Nilsson
End of Innocence, The *90* Dyan Cannon
End of Milton Levy, The *80* Nissim Dayan
End of Mrs. Cheney, The *63* Franz Josef Wild
End of Operation "Resident", The *87* Veniamin Dorman
End of Our World, The *64* Wanda Jakubowska
End of St. Petersburg, The *27* Mikhail Doller, Vsevolod I. Pudovkin
End of Summer, The *61* Yasujiro Ozu
End of Term *77* David Grant
End of the Act, The *34* George B. Samuelson
End of the Affair, The *54* Edward Dmytryk
End of the Art World *71* Alexis Krasilovsky
End of the Day, The *38* Julien Duvivier
End of the Dialogue *70* Nana Mahomo
End of the Feud, The *12* Allan Dwan
End of the Feud, The *14* Allan Dwan
End of the Game, The *19* Jesse D. Hampton
End of the Game *75* Maximilian Schell
End of the Good Old Days, The *89* Jiří Menzel
End of the Line, The *57* Charles Saunders
End of the Line *86* Pierre-William Glenn
End of the Line *87* Jay Russell
End of the Rainbow, The *16* Lynn Reynolds
End of the Rainbow *47* Allan Dwan
End of the River, The *47* Derek Twist
End of the Road, The *15* Thomas Ricketts
End of the Road, The *19* Edward H. Griffith
End of the Road, The *36* Alex Bryce
End of the Road *44* George Blair
End of the Road, The *54* Wolf Rilla
End of the Road, The *58* Jan Łomnicki
End of the Road, The *70* Aram Avakian
End of the Rope *23* Charles R. Seeling
End of the Tour, The *17* George D. Baker
End of the Trail, The *16* Oscar Apfel
End of the Trail, The *32* D. Ross Lederman
End of the Trail *36* Erle C. Kenton
End of the Trouble, The *06* Harold Jeapes
End of the War, The *86* Dragan Kresoja
End of the World, The *15* August Blom
End of the World, The *30* Abel Gance
End of the World *62* Ray Milland
End of the World *77* John Hayes
End of the World in Our Usual Bed in a Night Full of Rain, The *78* Lina Wertmuller
End of War Disasters *50* Kozaburo Yoshimura
End Play *75* Tim Burstall
End Without End *86* Prakash Jha
Endangered Species *82* Alan Rudolph
Endelig Alene *14* Forest Holger-Madsen
Endemoniada, La *74* Amando De Ossorio
Endgame *84* Steven Benson
Endişe *74* Şerif Gören, Yılmaz Güney
Endless Desire *58* Shohei Imamura
Endless Dream *86* Lauro Escorel Filho
Endless Game, The *89* Bryan Forbes
Endless Land of Alexis, The *81* Jean-Jacques Andrien
Endless Love *81* Franco Zeffirelli
Endless Night, The *63* Will Tremper
Endless Night *71* Sidney Gilliat
Endless Passion *49* Kon Ichikawa
Endless Summer, The *66* Bruce Brown
Endlose Nacht, Die *63* Will Tremper
Endstation *37* E. W. Emo
Endstation Freiheit *80* Reinhard Hauff
Endstation Liebe *57* Georg Tressler
Endstation 13—Sahara *62* Seth Holt
Enemies, The *38* Alexander Ivanovsky
Enemies, A Love Story *89* Paul Mazursky
Enemies of Children *23* Lillian Ducey, John M. Voshell
Enemies of Progress *34* Nikolai Beresnyef
Enemies of Society *33* George Archainbaud
Enemies of the Law *31* Lawrence C. Windom
Enemies of the Public *31* William A. Wellman
Enemies of Women, The *23* Alan Crosland
Enemies of Youth *25* Arthur Berthelet
Enemigo Principal, El *73* Jorge Sanjinés
Enemigos *34* Chano Urueta

Enemy, The *16* Paul Scardon
Enemy, The *27* Fred Niblo
Enemy, The *65* Živojin Pavlović
Enemy, The *68* John Boorman
Enemy, The *79* Zeki Ökten
Enemy Agent *40* Lew Landers
Enemy Agent *40* Terry Morse
Enemy Agents Meet Ellery Queen *42* James P. Hogan
Enemy Air Attack *43* Kozaburo Yoshimura
Enemy Amongst Us, The *16* Ernest G. Batley
Enemy Below, The *57* Dick Powell
Enemy from Space *57* Val Guest
Enemy General, The *60* George Sherman
Enemy in Our Midst, The *14* Wilfred Noy
Enemy in the Blood *31* Walter Ruttmann
Enemy in the Camp, An *08* Lewin Fitzhamon
Enemy Mine *85* Wolfgang Petersen
Enemy of Men, An *25* Frank R. Strayer
Enemy of the Law *45* Harry Fraser
Enemy of the People, An *46* Tadashi Imai
Enemy of the People, An *77* George Schaefer
Enemy of the People, An *89* Satyajit Ray
Enemy of the Police *33* George King
Enemy of the Republic *31* William A. Wellman
Enemy of Women *44* Alfred Zeisler
Enemy Round-Up *42* Roy Mack
Enemy Sex, The *24* James Cruze
Enemy Sisters *15* Germaine Dulac
Enemy Territory *87* Peter Manoogian
Enemy the Sea, The *63* Kon Ichikawa
Enemy to Society, An *15* Edgar Jones
Enemy to the King, An *16* Frederick Thompson
Enemy Within, The *14* Dave Aylott
Enemy Within, The *49* R. G. Springsteen
Énergie Électrique *39* René Clément
Énergie et Vous, L' *61* Henri Storck
Energizer *08* Wallace McCutcheon
Energy and How to Get It *80* Robert Frank
Energy First *55* Lindsay Anderson
Enfagh *77* Dariush Mehrjui
Enfance de l'Art, L' *10* Émile Cohl
Enfance de l'Art, L' *88* Françoise Giroud
Enfance Nue, L' *67* Maurice Pialat
Enfant Aimé, L' *71* Chantal Akerman
Enfant dans la Foule, Un *77* Gérard Blain
Enfant de la Barricade, L' *07* Alice Guy-Blaché
Enfant de la Roulotte, L' *14* Louis Feuillade
Enfant de l'Amour, L' *29* Marcel L'Herbier
Enfant de Paris, L' *13* Léonce Perret
Enfant d'Hiver, L' *89* Olivier Assayas
Enfant du Carnaval, L' *18* Ivan Mozhukhin
Enfant Prodigue, L' *01* Ferdinand Zecca
Enfant Roi, L' *23* Joe Hamman
Enfant Sauvage, L' *69* François Truffaut
Enfants, Les *84* Marguerite Duras, Jean Mascolo, Jean-Marc Turine
Enfants aux Jouets *1895* Louis Lumière
Enfants de l'Amour, Les *53* Léonide Moguy

Enfants de Néant, Les *67* Michel Brault, Annie Tresgot
Enfants du Désordre, Les *89* Yannick Bellon
Enfants du Miracle, Les *04* Alice Guy-Blaché
Enfants du Paradis, Les *44* Marcel Carné
Enfants du Silence, Les *62* Michel Brault, Claude Jutra
Enfants Gâtés, Les *77* Bertrand Tavernier
Enfants Jouant sur la Plage *1896* Georges Méliès
Enfants Terribles, Les *49* Jean-Pierre Melville
Enfer, L' *64* Henri-Georges Clouzot
Enfer des Anges, L' *39* Christian-Jaque
Enforcer, The *50* Raoul Walsh, Bretaigne Windust
Enforcer, The *76* James Fargo
Engagement, The *62* Ermanno Olmi
Engagement, The *70* Paul Joyce
Engagement in Zurich *56* Helmut Käutner
Engagement Italiano *66* Alfredo Giannetti
Engagement of Convenience, An *14* Hay Plumb
Engagement Ring, The *12* Mack Sennett
Engagement Ring *50* Keisuke Kinoshita
Engel auf Erden, Ein *59* Géza von Radványi
Engel mit dem Saitenspiel, Der *44* Heinz Rühmann
Engel mit Kleinen Fehler *36* Carl Boese
Engelchen *21* Richard Oswald
Engelein *13* Urban Gad
Engeleins Hochzeit *14* Urban Gad
Engineer Garin's Death Ray *65* Alexander Gintsburg
Engineer Prite's Project *18* Lev Kuleshov
Engineering Problem, An *16* J. D. Leventhal
Engineer's Thumb, The *23* George Ridgwell
England Expects *14* George Loane Tucker
England Invaded *09* Leo Stormont
England Made Me *72* Peter Duffell
England's Call *14* Dave Aylott
England's Future Safeguard *16* Ethyle Batley
England's Menace *14* Harold M. Shaw
England's Warrior King *15* Eric Williams
Englische Heirat, Die *34* Reinhold Schünzel
English Criminal Justice *46* Ken Annakin
English Girl Abroad, The *79* Peter Shillingford
English Harvest *38* Humphrey Jennings
English Jig *1896* Georges Méliès
English Oil Wells *39* Francis Searle
English Potter, The *33* Robert Flaherty
English Rose, The *20* Fred Paul
English Without Tears *44* Harold French
Englishman Abroad, An *83* John Schlesinger
Englishman and the Girl, The *10* D. W. Griffith
Englishman's Home, An *14* Ernest G. Batley
Englishman's Home, An *39* Albert De Courville

Englishman's Trip to Paris from London, An *04* Lewin Fitzhamon
Engrenage, L' *19* Louis Feuillade
Engrenage, L' *23* Georges Monca
Enhörningen *55* Gustaf Molander
Enid Is Sleeping *90* Maurice Phillips
Enigma *29* Kurt Bernhardt
Enigma *82* Jeannot Szwarc
Enigma *87* Alberto Chiantaretto, Marco Di Castri, Daniele Pianciola, Jean Rouch
Enigma de Muerte *68* Federico Curiel
Enigma of Kaspar Hauser, The *74* Werner Herzog
Enigma para Demonios *74* Carlos Hugo Christensen
Enigma Variations, The *70* James Archibald
Énigmatique Monsieur Parkes, L' *30* Louis Gasnier
Énigme, L' *19* Louis Feuillade
Énigme, L' *19* Jean Kemm
Énigme aux Folies-Bergère *59* Jean Mitry
Énigme de Dix Heures, L' *14* Abel Gance
Énigme du Mont Agel, L' *24* Alfred Machin, Henri Wuhlschleger
Enjō *58* Kon Ichikawa
Enjôleuse, L' *52* Luis Buñuel
Enkel Resa *88* Hans Iveberg
Enlèvement de Déjanire Goldebois, L' *14* Émile Cohl
Enlèvement en Automobile et Mariage Précipité *03* Alice Guy-Blaché
Enlèvement en Hydroplane, Un *13* Max Linder
Enlevez-Moi *32* Léonce Perret
Enlighten Thy Daughter *17* Ivan Abramson
Enlighten Thy Daughter *34* John Varley
Enligt Lag *57* Peter Weiss
Enlisted Man's Honor, An *11* Alice Guy-Blaché
Ennemi Public, Un *37* Henri Storck
Ennemi Public No. 1, L' *53* Henri Verneuil
Ennemis, Les *61* Édouard Molinaro
Ennemis de la Mafia, Les *88* Claude Goretta
Ennemis Intimes *87* Denis Amar
Ennui et Sa Diversion, l'Érotisme, L' *63* Damiano Damiani
Enoch Arden *14* Percy Nash
Enoch Arden *15* Christy Cabanne
Enoch Arden, Part I *11* D. W. Griffith
Enoch Arden, Part II *11* D. W. Griffith
Enormous Changes at the Last Minute *82* Mirra Bank, Ellen Hovde
Enough Cuts for a Murder *79* Christopher Monger
Enough for Happiness *52* Lloyd Bacon
Enough of It *14* Forest Holger-Madsen
Enough Rope *62* Claude Autant-Lara
Enough to Eat *35* Edgar Anstey
Enquiry Into General Practice *59* Paul Dickson
Enragés, Les *85* Pierre-William Glenn
Enrico *56* Paul Grimault
Enrico IV *84* Marco Bellocchio
Ens Hustru *11* August Blom
Ensayo de un Crimen *55* Luis Buñuel
Ensign Pulver *64* Joshua Logan

Ernest Goes to Jail *90* John R. Cherry III

Ernest Hemingway's Adventures of a Young Man *62* Martin Ritt

Ernest Hemingway's The Killers *64* Don Siegel

Ernest le Rebelle *38* Christian-Jaque

Ernest Maltravers *20* Jack Denton

Ernest Saves Christmas *88* John R. Cherry III

Ernesto *79* Salvatore Samperi

Ernie and Rose *82* John W. Huckert

Ernie Game, The *67* Don Owen

Ernst Fuchs *76* Vojtěch Jasný

Ernst Ist das Leben *16* Fern Andra

Ernst Thalmann *55* Kurt Mätzig

Eroberung der Zitadelle, Die *77* Bernhard Wicki

Eroberung des Himmels, Die *38* Hans Richter

Eröd, Az *79* Miklós Szinetár

Erode il Grande *59* Arnaldo Genoino

Eroe dei Nostri Tempi, Un *55* Mario Monicelli

Eroe Sono Io, L' *51* Carlo Ludovico Bragaglia, Andrea Checchi

Erogami no Onryō *30* Yasujiro Ozu

Erogeny *76* James Broughton

Eroi, Gli *72* Duccio Tessari

Eroi del West, Gli *63* Steno

Eroi della Domenica, Gli *52* Mario Camerini

Eroi di Fort Worth, Gli *64* Alberto De Martino

Eroica, L' *19* Febo Mari

Eroica *51* Karl Hartl, Walter Kolm-Veltee

Eroica *57* Andrzej Munk

Eroica *59* Michael Cacoyannis

Eroica — Polen 44 *57* Andrzej Munk

Eros ke Kimata *28* Dimitrios Gaziadis

Eros, o Basileas *67* Gregory Markopoulos

Erosion *71* Peter Greenaway

Erotic Adventures of Zorro, The *72* Robert Freeman

Erotic Fantasies *72* Mike Leigh

Erotic Inferno *75* Trevor Wren

Erotica *61* Russ Meyer

Erotica *62* Alberto Bonucci, Nino Manfredi, Sergio Sollima

Eroticon *61* Russ Meyer

Erotikon *20* Mauritz Stiller

Erotikon *29* Gustav Machatý

Erotikon *63* Boštjan Hladnik

Érotique, L' *60* Jerzy Skolimowski

Érotique *69* Jean-François Davy

Erotissimo *68* Gérard Pirès

Erotyk *60* Jerzy Skolimowski

Errand, The *81* Nigel Finch

Errand Boy, The *61* Jerry Lewis

Erratic Power *10* Dave Aylott

Erreur de Jeunesse *89* Radovan Tadić

Erreur de Poivrot *04* Alice Guy-Blaché

Erreur Judiciaire *00* Alice Guy-Blaché

Erreur Tragique *13* Louis Feuillade

Erroneous Practice *32* Mikio Naruse

Errors of Youth, The *89* Boris Frumin

Ersatz *61* Dušan Vukotić

Erste Liebe *38* S. Innemann

Erste Liebe *70* Maximilian Schell

Erste Patient, Der *15* Ernst Lubitsch

Erste Walzer, Der *78* Doris Dörrie

1. April 2000 *52* Wolfgang Liebeneiner

Erstwhile Susan *19* John S. Robertson

Erszebet *70* Harry Kümel

Eruption, The *59* Liviu Ciulei

Éruption du Mont Pelé, L' *02* Georges Méliès

Eruption of Mount Pelee, The *02* Georges Méliès

Éruption Volcanique à la Martinique *02* Georges Méliès

Ervinka *74* Ephraim Kishon

Erzebeth *70* Harry Kümel

Érzékeny Búcsú a Fejedelemtől *86* László Vitézy

Es Blasen die Trompeten *26* Carl Boese

Es Cosa con Plumas *88* Oscar Ladoire

Es Geht um Mein Leben *38* Richard Eichberg

Es Geschah am Hellichten Tag *58* Ladislas Vajda

Es Geschah am 20. Juli *55* G. W. Pabst

Es Geschehen Noch Wunder *51* Willi Forst

Es Gibt Nur Eine Liebe *37* Johannes Meyer

Es Hilft Nicht Wo Gewalt Herrscht *65* Jean-Marie Straub

Es Ist Nicht Leicht ein Gott zu Sein *89* Peter Fleischmann

Es Kommt ein Tag *60* Rudolf Jügert

Es Leuchten die Sterne *38* Hans Zerlett

Es Mi Vida — El Noa Noa 2 *86* Gonzalo Martínez Ortega

Es War eine Rauschende Ballnacht *39* Carl Fröhlich

Es War Einmal ein Walzer *34* Viktor Jansen

Es Werde Licht! *17* E. A. Dupont, Richard Oswald

Es Wird Schon Wieder Besser *34* Kurt Gerron

Esa Pareja Feliz *51* Juan Antonio Bardem, Luis García Berlanga

Escala en la Ciudad *36* Luis Saslavsky

Escalada del Chantaje, La *65* Santiago Álvarez

Escalation of Blackmail *65* Santiago Álvarez

Escale *59* Serge Bourguignon

Escale à Orly *55* Jean Dréville

Escalier C *85* Jean-Charles Tacchella

Escalier de Service *55* Carlo-Rim

Escalier Sans Fin, L' *43* Georges Lacombe

Escalofrío Diabólico *71* Jorge Martin

Escambray *61* Santiago Álvarez, Jorge Fraga

Escamotage d'une Dame chez Robert-Houdin *1896* Georges Méliès

Escándalo, El *34* Chano Urueta

Escapade *32* Richard Thorpe

Escapade *35* Robert Z. Leonard

Escapade *50* John Berry, Léo Joannon

Escapade *55* Philip Leacock

Escapade de Filoche, L' *15* Louis Feuillade

Escapade in Florence *62* Steve Previn

Escapade in Japan *57* Arthur Lubin

Escapades of Estelle, The *16* Harry S. Palmer

Escapades of Eva, The *39* Martin Frič

Escapades of Teddy Bear, The *09* Jack Smith

Escape, The *14* D. W. Griffith

Escape, The *26* Edwin Greenwood

Escape, The *26* Milburn Morante

Escape, The *28* Richard Rosson

Escape *30* Basil Dean

Escape, The *39* Ricardo Cortez

Escape *40* Mervyn LeRoy

Escape *48* Joseph L. Mankiewicz

Escape *79* Eduardo Mulargia

Escape Artist, The *81* Caleb Deschanel

Escape Attempt *76* Vojtěch Jasný

Escape by Night *37* Hamilton MacFadden

Escape by Night *53* John Gilling

Escape by Night *60* Roberto Rossellini

Escape by Night *63* Montgomery Tully

Escape Dangerous *47* Digby Smith

Escape Episode *44* Kenneth Anger

Escape from Alcatraz *79* Don Siegel

Escape from Andersonville *09* Sidney Olcott

Escape from Angola *76* Leslie Martinson

Escape from Bad Girls' Dormitory *85* Tim Kincaid

Escape from Broadmoor *13* Charles H. Weston

Escape from Broadmoor *48* John Gilling

Escape from Crime *42* D. Ross Lederman

Escape from Devil's Island *35* Albert S. Rogell

Escape from East Berlin *62* Robert Siodmak

Escape from El Diablo *83* Gordon Hessler

Escape from Fort Bravo *53* John Sturges

Escape from Hell *79* Eduardo Mulargia

Escape from Hell Island *63* Mark Stevens

Escape from Hong Kong *42* William Nigh

Escape from New York *81* John Carpenter

Escape from Red Rock *58* Edward Bernds

Escape from Sahara *57* Wolfgang Staudte

Escape from Saigon *57* Maurice Labro

Escape from San Quentin *57* Fred F. Sears

Escape from Segovia *84* Imanol Uribe

Escape from Terror *60* George Coogan, Jackie Coogan

Escape from the Bronx *85* Enzo G. Castellari

Escape from the Dark *76* Charles Jarrott

Escape from the Planet of the Apes *71* Don Taylor

Escape from the Sea *68* Peter Seabourne

Escape from Yesterday *34* Julien Duvivier

Escape from Yesterday *38* Alfred E. Green

Escape from Zahrain *61* Ronald Neame

Escape If You Can *51* Edgar G. Ulmer

Escape in the Desert *44* Edward A. Blatt, Robert Florey

Escape in the Fog *45* Budd Boetticher

Escape in the Sun *56* George Breakston

Escape Into Dreams *50* Pietro Francisci

Escape Libre *64* Jean Becker

Escape Me Never *35* Paul Czinner

Escape Me Never *47* Peter Godfrey

Escape of Hugo van Groot, The *12* Alfred Machin

Escape of Jim Dolan, The *13* William Duncan

Escape of Megagodzilla, The *75* Inoshiro Honda

Escape of Princess Charming, The *34* Maurice Elvey

Escape of the Amethyst 56 Michael Anderson

Escape of the Birdmen 71 Philip Leacock

Escape Route 52 Seymour Friedman, Peter Graham Scott

Escape Route 67 Seth Holt

Escape to Athena 79 George Pan Cosmatos

Escape to Berlin 62 Will Tremper

Escape to Burma 54 Allan Dwan

Escape to Danger 43 Lance Comfort, Max Greene, Joseph Losey

Escape to Entebbe 76 David Grant, Joseph McGrath

Escape to Freedom 86 Leo Penn

Escape to Glory 40 John Brahm

Escape to Happiness 39 Gregory Ratoff

Escape to Justice 42 C. Pattinson Knight

Escape to Nowhere 60 Steven Spielberg

Escape to Nowhere 73 Claude Pinoteau

Escape to Paradise 39 Erle C. Kenton

Escape to the Sun 72 Menahem Golan

Escape to Victory 81 John Huston

Escape to Witch Mountain 74 John Hough

Escape 2000 81 Brian Trenchard-Smith

Escaped from Dartmoor 29 Anthony Asquith

Escaped from Hell 29 Georg Asagaroff

Escaped the Law, But... 14 August Blom

Escapement 57 Montgomery Tully

Escapes 85 David Steensland

Escapes Home 80 Jaromil Jireš

Escarpins de Max, Les 13 Max Linder

Esclave, L' 53 Yves Ciampi

Escondida, La 56 Roberto Gavaldón

Escondido 67 Franco Giraldi

Escopeta Nacional, La 78 Luis García Berlanga

Escort for Hire 60 Godfrey Grayson

Escort Girl 86 Bob Swaim

Escort Girls 73 Donovan Winter

Escort West 59 Francis D. Lyon

Escot, L' 87 Antoni Verdaguer

Escrito en la Niebla 82 Silvio F. Balbuena

Escrocs, Les 65 Édouard Molinaro

Escuadrón Azul, El 38 Nelo Cosini

Escuadrón de la Muerte 86 Alfredo Gurrola

Escuela de Sordomudos 67 Patricio Guzmán

Ese Loco Loco Hospital 86 Julio Ruiz Llaneza

Esercito di 5 Uomini, Un 69 Don Taylor

Eserov Trial, The 22 Dziga Vertov

Esfinge de Cristal, La 67 Kamel El Sheik, Luigi Scattini

Eskadrilya N5 39 Abram Room

Eskimo 33 W. S. Van Dyke

Eskimo Nell 75 Martin Campbell

Eskimo Village 34 Edgar Anstey

Esmeralda, La 05 Alice Guy-Blaché

Esmeralda 15 James Kirkwood

Esmeralda 17 Ugo Falena

Esmeralda 22 Edwin J. Collins

Esop 69 Rangel Vulchanov

Esorcista n.2, L' 76 Elo Pannaccio

Esos Hombres 37 Rolando Aguilar

Esotika, Erotika, Psicotika Fab 75 Radley Metzger

Espace d'une Vie, L' 49 Charles Dekeukeleire

Espada del Zorro, La 61 Joaquín Luis Romero Marchent

Espadachines de la Reina, Los 63 Roberto Rodríguez

Espagne 37 37 Luis Buñuel

Espaldos Nojaldas 53 Alejandro Galindo

¡España Leal en Armas! 37 Luis Buñuel

Espanto Surge de la Tumba, El 72 Carlos Aured

Espectro de la Guerra, El 88 Ramiro Lacayo-Deshon

Espectro de la Novia, El 43 René Cardona

Espectro del Terror, El 72 José María Elorrieta

Espejo de la Bruja, El 60 Chano Urueta

Espérame 33 Louis Gasnier

Espérame en el Cielo 88 Antonio Mercero

Esperando la Carroza 86 Alejandro Doria

Espion, L' 66 Raoul Lévy

Espionage 37 Kurt Neumann

Espionage Agent 39 Lloyd Bacon

Espionne, L' 23 Henri Desfontaines

Espionne aux Yeux Noirs, L' 26 Henri Desfontaines

Espions, Les 57 Henri-Georges Clouzot

Espions a l'Affût 66 Max Pecas

Espions Meurent à Beyrouth, Les 65 Mario Donen

Espiritismo 61 Benito Alazraki

Espíritu de la Colmena, El 73 Victor Erice

Espoir, L' 39 André Malraux

Espontáneo, El 63 Jorge Grau

Essai de Simulation de Délire Cinématographique 35 André Breton, Paul Éluard, Man Ray

Essai sur l'Agression 74 Jacques Rivette

Essanay-Chaplin Revue of 1916, The 16 Charles Chaplin

Essay on Rehearsing, An 76 Evald Schorm

Essence, The 86 Shyam Benegal

Essene 72 Frederick Wiseman

Essential Spark of Jewishness, The 12 A. Slavinsky

Esso 54 Alexander Alexeïeff, Claire Parker

Esta Noche Cena Pancho (Despedida de Soltero) 87 Víctor Manuel Castro

Esta Noite Encarnarei No Teu Cadáver 66 José Mojica Marins

Esta Tierra Es Mía 60 Hugo Del Carril

Esta Tierra Nuestra 59 Tomás Gutiérrez Alea

Estación Central 89 J. A. Salgot

Estación del Regreso, La 87 Leonardo Kocking

Estamboul '65 66 Antonio Isamendi

Estampida, La 71 Santiago Álvarez

Estanquera de Vallecas, La 87 Eloy De la Iglesia

Estate Sta Finito, L' 87 Bruno Cortini

Estate Violenta 59 Valerio Zurlini

Estátuas de Lisboa 31 Manoel De Oliveira

Estelle and the Movie Hero 16 Harry S. Palmer

Esterina 59 Carlo Lizzani

Esther 10 Louis Feuillade

Esther 16 Maurice Elvey

Esther 86 Amos Gitai

Esther and the King 60 Raoul Walsh

Esther e il Re 60 Raoul Walsh

Esther Redeemed 15 Sidney Morgan

Esther Waters 47 Ian Dalrymple, Peter Proud

Estigma 81 José Ramón Larraz

Estrada da Vida 80 Nelson Pereira Dos Santos

Estrangero de la Calle Cruz del Sur, El 86 Jordi Grau

Estranguladores, Los 06 Antonio Leal

Estranha Hospedaria dos Prazeres, A 76 Marcelo Motta

Estranho Mundo de Zé do Caixão, O 68 José Mojica Marins

Estrela Sobe, A 74 Bruno Barreto

Estrella, El 76 Pedro Almodóvar

Estrella Vacía, La 62 Emilio Gómez Muriel

Estrellita 39 René Cardona

Estudios para un Retrato 78 Paul Leduc

Estupro, O 78 José Mojica Marins

Et Ár med Henry 67 Jørgen Roos

Et Dieu...Créa la Femme 56 Roger Vadim

...Et Mourir de Plaisir 60 Roger Vadim

Et Si Nous Buvions un Coup 08 Émile Cohl

Et Si On Faisant l'Amour 68 Vittorio Caprioli

Età del Malessere, L' 70 Giuliano Biagetti

Età dell'Amore, L' 53 Lionello De Felice

Età di Cosimo de'Medici, L' 72 Roberto Rossellini

Étalon, L' 69 Jean-Pierre Mocky

État de Grâce, L' 86 Jacques Rouffio

État de Siège 72 Costa-Gavras

État Sauvage, L' 78 Françoise Giroud

États d'Âme 86 Jacques Fansten

Étau, L' 20 Maurice Mariaud

Etc. 75 Robert Breer

Été à Saint-Tropez, Un 83 David Hamilton

Été de la Saint-Martin, L' 20 Georges Champavert

Été Dernier à Tanger, L' 87 Alexandre Arcady

Été en Pente Douce, L' 87 Gérard Krawczyk

Été Indien, L' 57 François Reichenbach

Été Meurtrier, L' 83 Jean Becker

Été Prochain, L' 84 Nadine Trintignant

Été Sauvage, Un 70 Marcel Camus

Été Torride, Un 65 Walerian Borowczyk

Ete und Ali 85 Peter Kahane

Été Violent 59 Valerio Zurlini

Eterna Femmina 53 Marc Allégret, Edgar G. Ulmer

Eterna Mártir 38 Juan Orol

Eternal Bond, The 47 Rune Carlsten

Eternal Chains 56 Anton Giulio Majano

Eternal City, The 15 Hugh Ford, Edwin S. Porter

Eternal City, The 23 George Fitzmaurice

Eternal Conflict, The 12 Edwin S. Porter

Eternal Evil 85 George Mihalka

Eternal Feminine, The 31 Arthur Varney-Serrao

Eternal Flame, The 22 Frank Lloyd

Eternal Generation, The 54 Keisuke Kinoshita

Eternal Grind, The 16 John B. O'Brien

Faces *23* Hy Mayer
Faces *34* Sidney Morgan
Faces *68* John Cassavetes
Faces in a Famine *86* Robert H. Lieberman
Faces in the Dark *60* David Eady
Faces in the Fire *18* Santry
Faces in the Fog *44* John English
Faces in the Shadows *56* Christer Strömholm, Peter Weiss
Faces of America *65* Ed Emshwiller
Faces of Children *23* Jacques Feyder, Françoise Rosay
Faces of Israel *67* Michael Roemer
Faces of Love *78* Michel Soutter
Faces of Women *83* Desiré Écaré
Facial Expression *02* Edwin S. Porter
Facing the Enemy *14* Charles H. Weston
Facing the Music *33* Harry Hughes
Facing the Music *41* Maclean Rogers
Facing the Wind *29* Josef Heifits, Alexander Zarkhi
Facteur de Saint-Tropez, Le *85* Richard Balducci
Facteur S'en Va-t-en Guerre, Le *66* Claude Bernard-Aubert
Facteur Trop Ferré, Un *07* Louis Feuillade
Factory Family *43* Len Lye
Factory Front *40* Alberto Cavalcanti
Factory Girl, The *09* Sidney Olcott
Factory Girl's Honour, A *12* B. Harold Brett
Factory Magdalene, A *14* Elwood Bostwick
Factory to Consumer *21* Raoul Barré, Charles Bowers
Facts and Figures *35* Vernon Sewell
Facts of Life, The *48* Ken Annakin, Arthur Crabtree, Harold French, Ralph Smart
Facts of Life, The *60* Melvin Frank
Facts of Love, The *45* Henry Cass
Facts of Murder, The *57* Pietro Germi
Fada, La *32* Léonce-Henri Burel
Fade-In *68* Jud Taylor
Fade to Black *80* Vernon Zimmerman
Fadeaway, The *26* Dave Fleischer
Faded Flower, The *16* Ivan Abramson
Faded Lilies, The *09* D. W. Griffith
Fader og Søn *11* August Blom
Fadern *69* Alf Sjöberg
Fadern, Sonen och den Helige Ande *87* Marie-Louise de Geer Bergenstrahle
Fádní Odpoledne *65* Ivan Passer
Fædrenes Synd *14* August Blom
Fag End *45* Charles Hawtrey
Fagasa *28* Raymond Wells
Fagin *22* H. B. Parkinson
Fagin's Freshmen *39* Cal Dalton, Ben Hardaway
Fagyosszentek *62* György Révész
Fahrendes Volk *37* Jacques Feyder
Fahrenheit 451 *66* François Truffaut
Fährmann Maria *36* Frank Wisbar
Fahrt in die Jugend, Die *35* Carl Boese
Fahrt ins Glück *45* Erich Engel
Fahrt ins Grüne, Die *36* Max Obal
Fai in Fretta ad Uccidermi...Ho Freddo! *68* Francesco Maselli
Faibles Femmes *59* Michel Boisrond
Fail Safe *63* Sidney Lumet

Failure, The *11* D. W. Griffith
Failure, The *15* Christy Cabanne
Failure, The *17* Henry Edwards
Failure, The *86* Hans de Ridder
Failure's Song Is Sad *22* Kenji Mizoguchi
Faim du Monde, La *58* Paul Grimault
Faim...L'Occasion...L'Herbe Tendre, La *04* Alice Guy-Blaché
Faint Heart *22* Gregory La Cava
Faint Perfume *25* Louis Gasnier
Fainting Lover *31* Mack Sennett
Fair and Warmer *19* Henry Otto
Fair and Wormer *46* Chuck Jones
Fair Barbarian, The *17* Robert Thornby
Fair Cheat, The *23* Burton L. King
Fair Co-Ed, The *27* Sam Wood
Fair Enough *18* Edward Sloman
Fair Exchange, A *09* D. W. Griffith
Fair Exchange, A *14* Charles Chaplin
Fair Exchange *36* Ralph Ince
Fair Game *14* Frank Wilson
Fair Game *85* Christopher Fitchett
Fair Game *86* Mario Andreacchio
Fair-Haired Hare *51* Friz Freleng
Fair Imposter, A *16* Alexander Butler
Fair Lady *22* Kenneth Webb
Fair Maid of Perth, The *23* Edwin Greenwood
Fair Maid of Perth, The *26* Miles Mander
Fair Play *25* Frank Crane
Fair Pretender, The *18* Charles Miller
Fair Sussex *13* George Pearson
Fair Today *41* Walter Lantz
Fair Warning *25* Stephen Roberts
Fair Warning *30* Alfred L. Werker
Fair Warning *37* Norman Foster
Fair Weather *26* Julian Ollendorff
Fair Weather Friend *47* Joseph Barbera, William Hanna
Fair Week *24* Robert Wagner
Fair Wind to Java *53* Joseph Kane
Fairfax Avenue *49* Jerry Lewis
Fairground *60* Wolfgang Staudte
Fairies, The *66* Mauro Bolognini, Mario Monicelli, Antonio Pietrangeli, Luciano Salce
Fairies' Revenge, The *13* Hay Plumb
Fairport Convention and Matthews Southern Comfort *70* Tony Palmer
Fairy and the Waif, The *15* Mary Hubert Frohman, George Irving
Fairy Bottle, The *13* Dave Aylott
Fairy Doll, The *12* Laurence Caird
Fairy Godmother, The *06* Arthur Cooper
Fairy of Solbakken, The *19* John W. Brunius
Fairy Tale About Tiny, A *85* Gunars Piesis
Fairy Tales *78* Harry Hurwitz
Fairy Tales Under Snow *85* Zdeněk Smetana
Fairyland *16* H. Lisle Lucoque
Fairyland, or The Kingdom of the Fairies *03* Georges Méliès
Fairy's Sword, The *08* Lewin Fitzhamon
Fairytale for 17-Year-Olds *88* Nguyen Xuan Son
Faiseurs de Pluie, Les *51* Roger Rosfelder, Jean Rouch
Faisons un Rêve *36* Sacha Guitry
Fait Divers *23* Claude Autant-Lara

Faites-Moi Confiance *53* Gilles Grangier
Faites Vos Jeux, Mesdames *64* Marcel Ophüls
Faith *11* Edwin S. Porter
Faith *16* James Kirkwood
Faith *19* Charles Swickard
Faith *19* Rex Wilson
Faith *20* Howard Mitchell
Faith and Endurin' *18* Clifford Smith
Faith and Fortune *15* Frank McGlynn
Faith Healer, The *11* Bert Haldane
Faith Healer, The *21* George Melford
Faith, Hope and Charity *84* Bille August
Faith of a Child, The *15* F. Martin Thornton
Faith of the Strong, The *19* Robert North Bradbury
Faithful *10* D. W. Griffith
Faithful *36* Paul Stein
Faithful City *52* Josef Leytes
Faithful Clock, The *09* Lewin Fitzhamon
Faithful Heart, The *22* Fred Paul
Faithful Heart, The *23* Jean Epstein
Faithful Heart, The *32* Victor Saville
Faithful Hearts *32* Victor Saville
Faithful in My Fashion *46* Sidney Salkow
Faithful Indian, The *11* Gilbert M. Anderson
Faithful River, The *87* Tadeusz Chmielewski
Faithful to the Rescue *56* Olive Negus
Faithful Unto Death *12* August Blom
Faithful Wives *26* Norbert Myles
Faithful Woman, A *76* Roger Vadim
Faithless *32* Harry Beaumont
Faithless Friend, A *08* Lewin Fitzhamon
Faithless Lover *28* Lawrence C. Windom
Faithless Sex, The *22* Henry J. Napier
Faith's Reward *16* Henry King
Faits d'Hiver *51* Henri Decaë
Faits Divers *56* Émile Degelin
Faits Divers à Paris *49* Dmitri Kirsanov
Faja Lobbi *60* Herman van den Horst
Fajr Yawm Jadid *64* Youssef Chahine
Fake, The *27* Georg Jacoby
Fake, The *53* Godfrey Grayson
Fake? *73* François Reichenbach, Orson Welles
Fake Blind Man, The *06* Charles Raymond
Fake-Diamond Swindler, A *08* Georges Méliès
Fake Girl *27* Heinosuke Gosho
Fake Out *82* Matt Cimber
Fake Russian Prophet, The *04* Georges Méliès
Fake Spiritualism Exposed *26* A. E. Coleby
Fakelos Polk stin Aera *87* Dionyssis Grigoratos
Faker, The *29* Phil Rosen
Fakers, The *70* Al Adamson
Fake's Progress *50* Kenneth Fairbairn
Faking of the President, The *76* Alan Abel, Jeanne Abel
Faking with Society *14* Charles Chaplin, Mabel Normand
Fakir—A Hindoo Mystery, The *1896* Georges Méliès
Fakir and the Footpads, The *06* J. H. Martin

False Wireless, The 14 H. Oceano Martinek

False Witness 35 Edward Buzzell

False Witness 70 Richard A. Colla

False Witness 81 Volker Schlöndorff

False Women 21 R. Dale Armstrong

Falsely Accused 05 Lewin Fitzhamon

Falsely Accused 15 Ethyle Batley

Falsk Som Vatten 85 Hans Alfredson

Falska Greta 34 John W. Brunius

Falskt Alarm 12 Victor Sjöström

Falstaff 65 Orson Welles

Falstaff the Tavern Knight 23 Edwin Greenwood

Falu Rossza, A 37 Béla Pásztor

Famalicão 40 Manoel De Oliveira

Fame 36 Leslie Hiscott

Fame 80 Alan Parker

Fame and Fortune 18 Lynn Reynolds

Fame Is the Spur 46 Roy Boulting

Fame Street 32 Louis King

Famiglia, La 86 Ettore Scola

Famiglia Impossibile, Una 40 Carlo Ludovico Bragaglia

Famiglia Passaguai, La 51 Aldo Fabrizi

Familia Dressel, La 35 Fernando De Fuentes

Familia Pichilín, La 78 Octavio Getino

Familiar, El 73 Octavio Getino

Familiaridades 69 Felipe Cazals

Familie Benthin 50 Slatan Dudow, Kurt Mätzig

Familie Buchholz 44 Carl Fröhlich

Familie Schimek 39 E. W. Emo

Familiebilleder 64 Henning Carlsen

Familien Gyldenkål 75 Gabriel Axel

Familien Schmidt 50 Ole Palsbo

Familienanschluss 41 Carl Boese

Familienparade 37 Fritz Wendhausen

Familjen Andersson 39 Sigurd Wallen

Familjen Som Var en Karusell 37 S. Bauman

Familjens Hemlighet 36 Gustaf Molander

Famille Fenouillard, La 61 Yves Robert

Famille Lefrançois, La 39 André Hugon

Famille Pont-Biquet, La 35 Christian-Jaque

Family, A 42 Minoru Shibuya

Family, A 43 Grigori Alexandrov

Family, The 70 Sergio Sollima

Family, The 74 Satsuo Yamamoto

Family, The 86 Raymond Fung

Family, The 86 Ettore Scola

Family Adopt a Camel, The 15 Harry S. Palmer

Family Affair, A 16 Clarence Badger

Family Affair, A 20 Gregory La Cava, Vernon Stallings

Family Affair, A 37 George B. Seitz

Family Affair 53 Val Guest

Family Album 23 Julian Ollendorff

Family Album 26 Paul M. Felton

Family Album, The 26 Hy Mayer

Family Album 54 Jacques Brunius, Richard Massingham

Family Business 86 Costa-Gavras

Family Business 89 Sidney Lumet

Family Centered Maternity Care 61 Alexander Hammid

Family Chronicle, A 86 Diego López

Family Circus, The 51 Art Babbitt

Family Closet, The 21 John B. O'Brien

Family Council 86 Costa-Gavras

Family Cupboard, The 15 Frank Crane

Family Diary 38 Satsuo Yamamoto

Family Diary 62 Valerio Zurlini

Family Doctor 58 Derek Twist

Family Dressel, The 35 Fernando De Fuentes

Family Enforcer 75 Ralph De Vito

Family Entrance, The 25 Leo McCarey

Family Game, The 83 Yoshimitsu Morita

Family Group, The 28 Leo McCarey*

Family Home 14 Charles Chaplin

Family Honeymoon 48 Claude Binyon

Family Honor, The 17 Émile Chautard

Family Honor, The 20 King Vidor

Family Honor 73 Clark Worswick

Family in Mexico, The 15 Harry S. Palmer

Family Jewels, The 65 Jerry Lewis

Family Killer 75 Vittorio Schiraldi

Family Life 70 Krzysztof Zanussi

Family Life 71 Kenneth Loach

Family Mixup, A 12 Mack Sennett

Family Next Door, The 39 Joseph Santley

Family of Chimps, The 84 Bert Haanstra

Family Plot 76 Alfred Hitchcock

Family Portrait 50 Humphrey Jennings

Family Portraits 64 Henning Carlsen

Family Relations 81 Nikita Mikhalkov

Family Secret, The 24 William A. Seiter

Family Secret, The 36 Gustaf Molander

Family Secret, The 51 Henry Levin

Family Skeleton, The 18 Victor Schertzinger

Family Solicitor, The 14 Wilfred Noy

Family Stain, The 15 Will S. Davis

Family Story, A 44 William Beaudine

Family Traditions 20 Rune Carlsten

Family Tree 47 George Dunning, Evelyn Lambert

Family Tree Book, The 78 Kwon-taek Im

Family Troubles 32 George Stevens

Family Upstairs, The 26 John G. Blystone

Family Viewing 87 Atom Egoyan

Family Visits Florida, The 16 Harry S. Palmer

Family Way, The 66 Roy Boulting

Family's Taste in Modern Furniture, The 15 Harry S. Palmer

Famous Box Trick, The 1898 Georges Méliès

Famous Ferguson Case, The 32 Lloyd Bacon

Famous Illusion of De Kolta, The 01 Walter R. Booth

Famous Men 22 Julian Ollendorff

Famous Men of Today 15 Sidney Olcott

Famous Mrs. Fair, The 23 Fred Niblo

Famous Rulers of the World 15 Sidney Olcott

Famous Scenes from Shakespeare—Julius Caesar 45 Henry Cass

Famous Scenes from Shakespeare—Macbeth 45 Henry Cass

Famous Soviet Heroes 38 Dziga Vertov

Famous Sword Bijomaru, The 45 Kenji Mizoguchi

Fan, The 49 Otto Preminger

Fan, The 81 Edward Bianchi

Fan Fan 18 Chester M. Franklin, Sidney Franklin

Fanatic 64 Silvio Narizzano

Fanatic 81 David Winters

Fanatics 17 Raymond Wells

Fanatics, The 57 Alex Joffé

Fanatics, The 61 Károly Makk

Fanatiques, Les 57 Alex Joffé

Fanchon the Cricket 15 James Kirkwood

Fanciulla di Portici, La 40 Mario Bonnard

Fanciulla, il Poeta e la Laguna, La 20 Carmine Gallone

Fanciulle di Lusso 52 Bernard Vorhaus

Fanciullo del West, Il 43 Giorgio Ferroni

Fancy Baggage 29 John G. Adolfi

Fancy Dress 19 Kenelm Foss

Fancy Dress Ball, The 09 Lewin Fitzhamon

Fancy Pants 50 George Marshall

Fandango 70 John Hayes

Fandango 85 Kevin Reynolds

Fando and Lis 70 Alejandro Jodorowsky

Fandy Ó Fandy 82 Karel Kachyňa

Fanella me to Ennia, I 88 Pantelis Voulgaris

Fanfan la Tulipe 07 Alice Guy-Blaché

Fanfan la Tulipe 51 Christian-Jaque

Fanfan the Tulip 51 Christian-Jaque

Fanfare 58 Bert Haanstra

Fanfare for a Death Scene 67 Leslie Stevens

Fanfare for Figleaves 52 Compton Bennett

Fang and Claw 35 Frank Buck

Fange Nr. 1 35 Pál Fejös

Fange Nr. 113 16 Forest Holger-Madsen

Fängelse 48 Ingmar Bergman

Fangerfamilie i Thuledistriktet, En 67 Jørgen Roos

Fangio 77 Hugh Hudson

Fangs 74 Arthur A. Names

Fangs of Death 27 Edwin Greenwood

Fangs of Destiny 27 Stuart Paton

Fangs of Fate 25 Horace B. Carpenter

Fangs of Fate 28 Noel Mason Smith

Fangs of Justice 26 Noel Mason Smith

Fangs of the Arctic 53 Rex Bailey

Fangs of the Living Dead 68 Amando De Ossorio

Fangs of the Wild 28 Jerome Storm

Fangs of the Wild 54 William F. Claxton

Fangs of the Wolf 24 Joseph A. Golden, Harry Hoyt

Fangschuss, Der 76 Volker Schlöndorff

Fanny 32 Marc Allégret

Fanny 61 Joshua Logan

Fanny and Alexander 82 Ingmar Bergman

Fanny by Gaslight 44 Anthony Asquith

Fanny Foley Herself 31 Melville Brown

Fanny Hawthorne 27 Maurice Elvey, Victor Saville

Fanny Hill 64 Russ Meyer

Fanny Hill 83 Gerry O'Hara

Fanny Hill Meets Dr. Erotico 67 Barry Mahon

Fanny Hill Meets Lady Chatterley 67 Barry Mahon

Fanny Hill Meets the Red Baron 67 Barry Mahon

Fanny Hill: Memoirs of a Woman of Pleasure 64 Russ Meyer

Fanny och Alexander 82 Ingmar Bergman
Fanny's Conspiracy 13 Van Dyke Brooke
Fänrik Stals Sägner 26 John W. Brunius
Fan's Notes, A 72 Eric Till
Fantaisie de Milliardaire 19 Édouard E. Violet
Fantaisies d'Agenor Maltrace, Les 11 Émile Cohl
Fantaisies Truquées 15 Émile Cohl
Fantasia 40 Ben Sharpsteen
Fantasia Sottomarina 39 Roberto Rossellini
Fantasie: Dresden China 13 Walter R. Booth
Fantasies 73 John Derek
Fantasist, The 86 Robin Hardy
Fantasm 76 Richard Franklin
Fantasma 14 Charles M. Seay
Fantasma d'Amore 81 Dino Risi
Fantasma de la Casa Roja, El 54 Miguel Delgado
Fantasma del Convento, El 34 Fernando De Fuentes
Fantasmagorie 08 Émile Cohl
Fantasmi a Roma 61 Antonio Pietrangeli
Fantasmi del Mare 48 Francesco De Robertis
Fantassin Guignard, La 05 Alice Guy-Blaché
Fantastic Comedy, A 75 Ion Popescu-Gopo
Fantastic Disappearing Man, The 58 Paul Landres
Fantastic Invasion of Planet Earth 66 Arch Oboler
Fantastic Invention, The 57 Karel Zeman
Fantastic Night, The 42 Marcel L'Herbier
Fantastic Planet 73 René Laloux
Fantastic Tale of Naruto, A 57 Teinosuke Kinugasa
Fantastic Three, The 67 Gianfranco Parolini
Fantastic Voyage 66 Richard Fleischer
Fantastica 80 Gilles Carle
Fantastical Airship, The 06 Georges Méliès
Fantastical Illusions 1898 Georges Méliès
Fantastical Meal, A 00 Georges Méliès
Fantastici Tre Supermen, I 67 Gianfranco Parolini
Fantástico Mundo del Dr. Coppelius, El 66 Ted Kneeland
Fantasy 27 Andrew L. Stone
Fantasy Film Worlds of George Pal, The 86 Arnold Leibovit
Fantasy for Piano 72 Yoji Kuri
Fantasy Man 84 John Meagher
Fantasy of the Monastery, The 34 Fernando De Fuentes
Fantasy on Ireland, A 49 David Hand
Fantasy on London Life, A 50 David Hand
Fantee 20 Lewis Willoughby
Fantoche Cherche un Logement 16 Émile Cohl
Fantômas 13 Louis Feuillade
Fantômas II 13 Louis Feuillade
Fantômas III 13 Louis Feuillade
Fantômas IV 14 Louis Feuillade
Fantômas V 14 Louis Feuillade
Fantomas 21 Edward Sedgwick
Fantomas 31 Pál Fejős

Fantômas 36 Alain Resnais
Fantômas 64 André Hunebelle
Fantômas 66 André Hunebelle
Fantômas Against Scotland Yard 66 André Hunebelle
Fantômas Contre Fantômas 14 Louis Feuillade
Fantômas Contre Scotland Yard 66 André Hunebelle
Fantômas Se Déchaîne 65 André Hunebelle
Fantômas Strikes Back 65 André Hunebelle
Fantôme d'Alger, Le 06 Georges Méliès
Fantôme de la Liberté, Le 74 Luis Buñuel
Fantôme du Moulin-Rouge, Le 24 René Clair
Fantômes du Chapelier, Les 81 Claude Chabrol
Fantorro le Dernier Justicier 72 Jan Lenica
Fantorro the Last Just Man 72 Jan Lenica
Fapados Szerelem 59 Félix Máriássy
Far Call, The 29 Allan Dwan
Far Country, The 54 Anthony Mann
Far Cry, The 26 Silvano Balboni
Far East, The 21 Raoul Barré, Charles Bowers
Far East 37 Georgy Vasiliev, Sergei Vasiliev
Far East 82 John Duigan
Far East Martial Court, The 83 Masaki Kobayashi
Far Freedom 45 Pal'o Bielek
Far from Dallas 72 Philippe Toledano
Far from Home 89 Meiert Avis
Far from Moscow 50 Alexander Stolper
Far from Poland 83 Susan Delson, Jill Godmilow, Mark Magill, Andrzej Tymowski
Far from the Madding Crowd 15 Lawrence Trimble
Far from the Madding Crowd 67 John Schlesinger
Far from Vietnam 66 Jacques Demy, Jean-Luc Godard, Ruy Guerra, Joris Ivens, William Klein, Claude Lelouch, Louis Malle, Chris Marker, Alain Resnais, Agnès Varda
Far from War 87 Mei Hu
Far Frontier, The 48 William Witney
Far Horizons, The 55 Rudolph Maté
Får Jag Låna Din Fru? 59 Arne Mattsson
Far North, The 21 Raoul Barré, Charles Bowers
Far North, The 38 Sergei Gerasimov
Far North 88 Sam Shepard
Far Out Man 90 Thomas Chong
Far Road, The 77 Sachiko Hidari
Far Shore, The 76 Joyce Wieland
Far Side of the Sun, The 69 Robert Parrish
Far Western Trails 29 Robert J. Horner
Faraon 65 Jerzy Kawalerowicz
Farářův Konec 68 Evald Schorm
Faraway Fields 12 Edwin S. Porter
Farce de Marmitons 00 Georges Méliès
Farces de Cuisinière 02 Alice Guy-Blaché
Farces de Jocko, Les 1898 Alice Guy-Blaché
Farceur, Le 60 Philippe de Broca

Fare-Play 32 Dick Huemer
Fares Please 25 Stephen Roberts*
Farewell 30 Robert Siodmak
Farewell, The 81 Elem Klimov
Farewell, The 82 Tuija-Maija Niskanen
Farewell Again 37 Tim Whelan
Farewell Cream 68 Tony Palmer
Farewell Doves 60 Yakov Segel
Farewell Friend 68 Jean Herman
Farewell, Goodbye 87 Anssi Mänttäri
Farewell Green Summer 87 Elior Ishmukhamedov
Farewell Illusion 84 Petter Vennerød, Svend Wam
Farewell My Beloved 69 Hideo Oba
Farewell My Love 56 Youssef Chahine
Farewell My Lovely 44 Edward Dmytryk
Farewell, My Lovely 75 Dick Richards
Farewell Performance 63 Robert Tronson
Farewell Scarlet 76 Chuck Vincent
Farewell to Arms, A 32 Frank Borzage
Farewell to Arms, A 57 Charles Vidor
Farewell to Childhood 50 Hereward Jansz, Lester James Peries
Farewell to Cinderella 37 Maclean Rogers
Farewell to Dreams 56 Keisuke Kinoshita
Farewell to False Paradise 89 Tevfik Baser
Farewell to Fame 41 Jean Yarbrough
Farewell to Love 31 Carmine Gallone
Farewell to Majorca 81 Elem Klimov
Farewell to Matyora 81 Elem Klimov
Farewell to Summer Light 68 Yoshishige Yoshida
Farewell to the Channel 88 Jen Wan
Farewell to the Devil 56 Wanda Jakubowska
Farewell to the King 88 John Milius
Farewell to the Land 82 Mitsuo Yanagimachi
Farewell to the President 87 Matti Kassila
Farewell to You 87 Sándor Simon
Farewell to Your Love 56 Youssef Chahine
Farewell, Uncle Tom 72 Gualtiero Jacopetti, Franco Prosperi
Farewells 58 Wojciech Has
Fargo 52 Lewis D. Collins
Fargo 64 Brian G. Hutton
Fargo Express 33 Alvin J. Neitz
Fargo Kid, The 40 Edward Killy
Fari nella Nebria 41 Gianni Franciolini
Farkas, A 16 Michael Curtiz
Farlig Forbryder, En 13 August Blom
Farlig Pant, En 20 Victor Sjöström
Farlig Vår 48 Arne Mattsson
Farlige Alder, Den 11 August Blom
Farligt Spil, Et 12 Edward Schnedler-Sørensen
Farm, The 87 David Keith
Farm Calendar 55 Roman Kroitor
Farm Efficiency 20 Raoul Barré, Charles Bowers
Farm Frolics 41 Robert Clampett
Farm Girl 65 John Hayes
Farm Hand, The 27 Clyde Geronimi
Farm in the Fens, A 45 Ken Annakin
Farm of the Year 88 Gary Sinise
Farm of Tomorrow 54 Tex Avery
Farm Relief 29 Manny Gould, Ben Harrison
Farm Yard, A 1897 Georges Méliès

Farmer, The *31* Walter Lantz
Farmer, The *77* David Berlatsky
Farmer Al Falfa and His Wayward Pup *17* Paul Terry
Farmer Al Falfa Invents a New Kite *16* Paul Terry
Farmer Al Falfa Sees New York *16* Paul Terry
Farmer Al Falfa's Blind Pig *16* Paul Terry
Farmer Al Falfa's Bride *23* Paul Terry
Farmer Al Falfa's Catastrophe *16* Paul Terry
Farmer Al Falfa's Egg-citement *16* Paul Terry
Farmer Al Falfa's Pet Cat *23* Paul Terry
Farmer Al Falfa's Prune Plantation *16* Paul Terry
Farmer Al Falfa's Revenge *16* Paul Terry
Farmer Al Falfa's Scientific Diary *16* Paul Terry
Farmer Al Falfa's Tentless Circus *16* Paul Terry
Farmer Al Falfa's Watermelon Patch *16* Paul Terry
Farmer Al Falfa's Wolfhound *16* Paul Terry
Farmer and the Bad Boys, The *01* Edwin S. Porter
Farmer aus Texas, Der *25* Joe May
Farmer, Feast or Famine, The *65* Roger Barlow, Willard Van Dyke
Farmer Giles and His Portrait *00* Arthur Cooper
Farmer Giles in London *09* Theo Bouwmeester
Farmer Has a Wife, The *87* Edvard Laine
Farmer in the Dell, The *36* Ben Holmes
Farmer Spudd and His Missus Take a Trip to Town *15* J. L. V. Leigh
Farmer Takes a Wife, The *35* Victor Fleming
Farmer Takes a Wife, The *53* Henry Levin
Farmer's Daughter, The *10* Lewin Fitzhamon
Farmer's Daughter, The *12* Edwin J. Collins
Farmer's Daughter, The *28* Arthur Rosson, Norman Taurog
Farmer's Daughter, The *40* James P. Hogan
Farmer's Daughter, The *47* H. C. Potter
Farmer's Goat, The *29* John Foster
Farmer's Other Daughter, The *65* John Hayes
Farmer's Two Sons, The *10* Bert Haldane
Farmer's Wife, The *28* Alfred Hitchcock
Farmer's Wife, The *40* Leslie Arliss, Norman Lee
Farming Fools *36* Walter Lantz
Farmyard Follies *20* Roy Del Ruth
Farmyard Follies *28* Rollin Hamilton, Walter Lantz
Faro da Padre, Le *74* Alberto Lattuada
Fårö Document, The *69* Ingmar Bergman
Fårö Document 1979, The *79* Ingmar Bergman
Fårö—Dokument *69* Ingmar Bergman
Fårö—Dokument 1979 *79* Ingmar Bergman
Faro Jack *41* Sam Nelson

Fårö 1979 *79* Ingmar Bergman
Fårödokument *69* Ingmar Bergman
Fårödokument 1979 *79* Ingmar Bergman
Farrebique *46* Georges Rouquier
Farrier Summer, The *1895* Louis Lumière
Fars Sorg *16* Forest Holger-Madsen
Fasching in Wien *39* Hubert Marischka
Fascinating Game, A *08* Lewin Fitzhamon
Fascinating Mrs. Francis, The *09* D. W. Griffith
Fascinating Vamp, A *28* Karl Freund
Fascinating Youth *26* Sam Wood
Fascination *22* Robert Z. Leonard
Fascination *31* Miles Mander
Fascination *79* Jean Rollin
Fascination, The *87* Serge Bourguignon
Fascino Sottile del Peccato, Il *87* Nini Grassia
Fascism Will Be Destroyed *41* Esther Shub
Fascist, The *61* Luciano Salce
Fashion *60* Yoji Kuri
Fashion Follies of 1934 *33* William Dieterle
Fashion House of Death *64* Mario Bava
Fashion Madness *28* Louis Gasnier
Fashion Model, The *13* Mauritz Stiller
Fashion Model *45* William Beaudine
Fashion Row *23* Robert Z. Leonard
Fashionable Fakers *23* William Worthington
Fashions *33* William Dieterle
Fashions for Women *27* Dorothy Arzner
Fashions in Love *29* Victor Schertzinger
Fashions of 1934 *33* William Dieterle
Fashizm Budet Razbit *41* Esther Shub
Fasshon *60* Yoji Kuri
Fast and Fearless *24* Richard Thorpe
Fast and Furious *24* Norman Taurog
Fast and Furious *27* Melville Brown
Fast and Furious *31* Charles Lamont
Fast and Furious *39* Busby Berkeley
Fast and Furry-ous *49* Chuck Jones
Fast and Loose *30* Fred Newmeyer
Fast and Loose *39* Edwin L. Marin
Fast and Loose *54* Gordon Parry
Fast and Sexy *58* Reginald Denham, Carlo Lasticati
Fast and the Furious, The *54* John Ireland, Edwards Sampson
Fast Break *79* Jack Smight
Fast Buck Duck *63* Ted Bonnicksen, Robert McKimson
Fast Bullets *36* Harry S. Webb
Fast Charlie and the Moonbeam *79* Steve Carver
Fast Charlie the Moonbeam Rider *79* Steve Carver
Fast Companions *32* Kurt Neumann
Fast Company *18* Lynn Reynolds
Fast Company *29* Edwin H. Knopf, A. Edward Sutherland
Fast Company *38* Edward Buzzell
Fast Company *53* John Sturges
Fast Company *78* David Cronenberg
Fast Express, The *24* William Duncan
Fast, Fast *80* Carlos Saura
Fast Fightin' *25* Richard Thorpe
Fast Food *89* Michael A. Simpson
Fast Fortune *74* Aram Avakian, Anthony Squire

Fast Forward *85* Sidney Poitier
Fast Freight *21* Raoul Barré, Charles Bowers
Fast Freight, The *21* James Cruze
Fast Gun *87* Cirio Santiago
Fast Kill, The *72* Lindsay Shonteff
Fast Lady, The *62* Ken Annakin
Fast Life *29* John Francis Dillon
Fast Life *32* Harry A. Pollard
Fast Mail, The *18* George Marshall
Fast Mail, The *22* Bernard J. Durning
Fast Male, The *25* Wesley Ruggles
Fast on the Draw *50* Thomas Carr
Fast Play *38* George Archainbaud
Fast Set, The *24* William DeMille
Fast Talking *83* Ken Cameron
Fast Times *82* Amy Heckerling
Fast Times at Ridgemont High *82* Amy Heckerling
Fast-Walking *81* James B. Harris
Fast Worker, The *24* William A. Seiter
Fast Workers *33* Tod Browning
Faster Pussycat! Kill! Kill! *65* Russ Meyer
Fasters Miljoner *34* Gustaf Molander
Fastest Guitar Alive, The *67* Michael Moore
Fastest Gun, The *64* Sidney Salkow
Fastest Gun Alive, The *56* Russell Rouse
Fastest with the Mostest, The *60* Chuck Jones
Fästmö Uthyres *51* Gustaf Molander
Fastnachtsbeichte, Die *60* William Dieterle
Fat and Furious *17* Gregory La Cava
Fat and Lean Wrestling Match *00* Georges Méliès
Fat and the Lean, The *60* Roman Polanski
Fat and Thin *86* Svetislav Bata Prelić
Fat Angels *80* Manuel Summers
Fat Chance *75* Peter Hyams
Fat Chance *80* Manuel Summers
Fat City *71* John Huston
Fat Guy Goes Nutzoid *83* John Golden
Fat Man, The *51* William Castle
Fat Man and Little Boy *89* Roland Joffé
Fat Spy, The *65* Joseph Cates
Fat Wives for Thin *30* Mack Sennett
Fata Morgana *69* Werner Herzog
Fatal Alarm *32* Karl Brown
Fatal Appetiser, The *09* Lewin Fitzhamon
Fatal Assassin *76* Peter Collinson
Fatal Attraction *80* Michael Grant
Fatal Attraction *87* Adrian Lyne
Fatal Beauty *87* Tom Holland
Fatal Black Bean, The *15* Raoul Walsh
Fatal Card, The *30* Norman Taurog
Fatal Chase *87* Mario Azzopardi
Fatal Chocolate, The *12* Mack Sennett
Fatal Desire *52* Carmine Gallone
Fatal Fingers *16* A. V. Bramble, Eliot Stannard
Fatal Fingertips *46* Phil Karlson
Fatal Flower, The *18* William A. Seiter
Fatal Formula, The *15* Frank Stather
Fatal Glass of Beer, The *16* Tod Browning
Fatal Glass of Beer, The *33* Clyde Bruckman
Fatal Hand, The *07* J. H. Martin
Fatal Hour, The *08* D. W. Griffith
Fatal Hour, The *20* George Terwilliger

Fatal Hour, The *37* George Pearson
Fatal Hour, The *40* William Nigh
Fatal Journey *54* Paul Gherzo
Fatal Kiss, The *39* Fernando Rivero
Fatal Lady *36* Edward Ludwig
Fatal Leap, The *06* Lewin Fitzhamon
Fatal Lie, A *11* August Blom
Fatal Mallet, The *14* Charles Chaplin, Mack Sennett
Fatal Marriage, The *15* Christy Cabanne
Fatal Marriage, The *18* Henry Lehrman
Fatal Mirror, The *12* Allan Dwan
Fatal Mistake, The *24* Scott R. Dunlap
Fatal Necklace, The *05* J. H. Martin
Fatal Night, The *48* Mario Zampi
Fatal Orchids, The *16* Rex Ingram
Fatal Passions, Part One, The *22* Fritz Lang
Fatal Passions, Part Two, The *22* Fritz Lang
Fatal Plunge, The *24* Harry Hoyt
Fatal Promise, The *16* Rex Ingram
Fatal Pulse *88* Anthony J. Christopher
Fatal Ring, The *17* George B. Seitz
Fatal Telephone, The *87* Damjan Kozole
Fatal 30, The *21* John J. Hayes
Fatal Warning, The *29* Richard Thorpe
Fatal Wedding, The *13* Christy Cabanne, Lawrence Marston
Fatal Wig, The *04* Alf Collins
Fatal Witness, The *45* Lesley Selander
Fatale Méprise *00* Georges Méliès
Fatalidad, La *10* Segundo De Chomón
Fatalna Klatwa *13* Avrom Yitskhok Kaminsky
Fatawa, El *56* Salah Abu Saif
Fate *11* Theo Bouwmeester
Fate *11* Edwin S. Porter
Fate *12* D. W. Griffith, Frank Powell
Fate *43* Ramjankhan Mehboobkhan
Fate, Le *66* Mauro Bolognini, Mario Monicelli, Antonio Pietrangeli, Luciano Salce
Fate and the Child *17* Edward Sloman
Fate and the Woman *11* A. E. Coleby
Fate and the Woman *16* Fred W. Durrant
Fate Is the Hunter *64* Ralph Nelson
Fate of a Family *85* Masaki Kobayashi
Fate of a Flirt, The *25* Frank R. Strayer
Fate of a King, The *13* A. E. Coleby
Fate of a Man *59* Sergei Bondarchuk
Fate of an Opera *58* Edgar Reitz
Fate of Lee Khan, The *72* King Hu
Fate Takes a Hand *61* Max Varnel
Fate's Alibi *15* Frank Lloyd
Fate's Boomerang *16* Frank Crane
Fate's Fathead *34* Charlie Chase
Fate's Interception *12* D. W. Griffith
Fate's Plaything *20* B. E. Doxat-Pratt
Fate's Turning *10* D. W. Griffith
Father *22* Yasujiro Shimazu
Father *66* István Szabó
Father, The *69* Alf Sjöberg
Father, The *71* Yılmaz Güney
Father Amin *50* Youssef Chahine
Father and His Child *29* Heinosuke Gosho
Father and His Son *29* Heinosuke Gosho
Father and Master *77* Paolo Taviani, Vittorio Taviani
Father and Son *10* Wilfred Noy

Father and Son *11* August Blom
Father and Son *29* Erle C. Kenton
Father and Son *30* Victor Sjöström
Father and Son *34* Monty Banks
Father and Son *81* Allen Fong
Father and the Bookmaker *06* Tom Green
Father and the Boys *15* Joseph De Grasse
Father Brown *54* Robert Hamer
Father Brown—Detective *35* Edward Sedgwick
Father Brown, Detective *54* Robert Hamer
Father Buys a Lawn Roller *07* Alf Collins
Father Buys a Picture *08* A. E. Coleby
Father Buys a Screen *10* Lewin Fitzhamon
Father Buys an Armchair *09* Joe Rosenthal
Father Buys Some Linoleum *07* Alf Collins
Father Buys the Fireworks *09* T. J. Gobbett
Father Came Too *63* Peter Graham Scott
Father, Dear Father *73* William G. Stewart
Father Frost *24* Yuri Zhelyabuzhsky
Father Gets in the Game *08* D. W. Griffith
Father Gets Into the Movies *16* Gregory La Cava
Father Goose *64* Ralph Nelson
Father Hold My Wool *09* A. E. Coleby
Father in the Kitchen *05* Alf Collins
Father Is a Bachelor *50* Abby Berlin, Norman Foster
Father Is a Prince *40* Noel Mason Smith
Father Knish's Gang *24* Alexander Rasumny
Father Knows Best *35* Fritz Schulz, Andor Zsoldos
Father Makes Good *50* Jean Yarbrough
Father Makes Love to the Pump *05* Alf Collins
Father, Master *77* Paolo Taviani, Vittorio Taviani
Father Minds the Baby *10* Alf Collins
Father o' Nine *38* Roy Kellino
Father of a Soldier *65* Revaz Chkeidze
Father of His Country, The *38* Giovacchino Forzano
Father of More Than Four *39* R. O'Quigley
Father of the Bride *50* Vincente Minnelli
Father O'Flynn *19* Tom Watts
Father O'Flynn *35* Wilfred Noy, Walter Tennyson
Father Serge *78* Igor Talankin
Father Sergius *18* Yakov Protazanov
Father Sorrow *16* Forest Holger-Madsen
Father Steps Out *37* Maclean Rogers
Father Steps Out *41* Jean Yarbrough
Father Takes a Wife *41* Jack Hively
Father Takes the Air *51* Frank McDonald
Father Takes the Baby Out *13* Frank Wilson
Father Thames' Temperance Cure *02* Walter R. Booth
Father, the Son and the Holy Ghost, The *87* Marie-Louise de Geer Bergenstrahle
Father to Be *79* Lasse Hallström
Father Tom *21* John B. O'Brien
Father Vojtěch *28* Martin Frič
Father Vojtěch *36* Martin Frič

Father Wanted *47* Arne Mattsson
Father Was a Fullback *49* John M. Stahl
Father Wins a Turkey *08* Alf Collins
Fatherhood *15* Hobart Bosworth
Fatherland *86* Kenneth Loach
Fatherly Love *21* Wallace A. Carlson
Fatherly Love *21* William C. Nolan
Fathers and Sons *30* Victor Sjöström
Fathers and Sons *57* Mario Monicelli
Fathers and Sons *60* Adolph Bergunker, Natalia Rashevskaya
Father's Baby Boy *09* Percy Stow
Father's Birthday Cheese *05* Percy Stow
Father's Birthday Party *04* Alf Collins
Father's Choice *13* Mack Sennett
Father's Coat to the Rescue *12* Gilbert Southwell
Father's Day *30* Sam Wood
Father's Derby Tip *06* Tom Green
Father's Dilemma *50* Alessandro Blasetti
Father's Doing Fine *52* Henry Cass
Father's Estate *80* Hrafn Gunnlaugsson
Father's Favorite *12* Allan Dwan
Father's Fighting Fever *14* Dave Aylott
Father's First Baby *08* Frank Mottershaw
Father's Flirtation *14* George D. Baker
Father's Forty Winks *12* Arthur Cooper
Father's Hat, or Guy Fawkes' Day *04* Percy Stow
Father's Hatband *13* Van Dyke Brooke
Father's Legacy—A Goat *10* Joe Rosenthal
Father's Lesson *08* Lewin Fitzhamon
Father's Lesson *12* Christy Cabanne
Father's Little Dividend *50* Vincente Minnelli
Father's Little Flutter *13* Frank Wilson
Father's Love, A *09* S. Wormald
Father's Love, A *78* Robert Mulligan
Father's Mistake, A *09* Theo Bouwmeester
Fathers of Men *16* William Humphrey
Father's on a Business Trip *85* Emir Kusturica
Father's Sacrifice, A *12* Charles Raymond
Father's Saturday Afternoon *11* A. E. Coleby
Father's Son *31* William Beaudine
Father's Son *41* D. Ross Lederman
Father's Vengeance, A *07* Lewin Fitzhamon
Father's Wild Game *50* Herbert I. Leeds
Fathom *67* Leslie Martinson
Fatia Negra *59* Frigyes Bán
Fatiche di Ercole, Le *57* Pietro Francisci
Fatso *80* Anne Bancroft
Fatti di Gente Perbene *74* Mauro Bolognini
Fatto di Sangue Fra Due Uomini per Causa di una Vedova (Si Sospettano Moventi Politici) *79* Lina Wertmuller
Fatto su Misura *85* Francesco Laudadio
Fatty Again *14* Roscoe Arbuckle
Fatty and Mabel Adrift *16* Roscoe Arbuckle
Fatty and Mabel at the San Diego Exposition *15* Roscoe Arbuckle
Fatty and Mabel Viewing the World's Fair at San Francisco *15* Roscoe Arbuckle, Mabel Normand
Fatty and Mabel's Simple Life *15* Roscoe Arbuckle, Mabel Normand

Fatty and Minnie He-Haw 14 Roscoe Arbuckle, Edward Dillon

Fatty and the Broadway Stars 15 Roscoe Arbuckle, Edward Dillon

Fatty and the Heiress 14 Roscoe Arbuckle, Edward Dillon

Fatty at Coney Island 17 Roscoe Arbuckle

Fatty at San Diego 13 Henry Lehrman

Fatty Finn 80 Maurice Murphy

Fatty Joins the Force 13 Henry Lehrman

Fatty on the Job 13 Ralph Ince

Fatty's Affair of Honor 13 Ralph Ince

Fatty's Chance Acquaintance 15 Roscoe Arbuckle

Fatty's Debut 14 Roscoe Arbuckle, Edward Dillon

Fatty's Faithful Fido 15 Roscoe Arbuckle, Edward Dillon

Fatty's Finish 14 Roscoe Arbuckle

Fatty's Gift 14 Roscoe Arbuckle, Edward Dillon

Fatty's Jonah Day 14 Roscoe Arbuckle, Edward Dillon

Fatty's Magic Pants 14 Roscoe Arbuckle, Edward Dillon

Fatty's New Role 15 Roscoe Arbuckle, Charles Avery, Edward Dillon

Fatty's Overtime 22 Edward D. Roberts

Fatty's Plucky Pup 15 Roscoe Arbuckle

Fatty's Reckless Fling 15 Roscoe Arbuckle

Fatty's Sweetheart 14 Ralph Ince

Fatty's Tintype Tangle 15 Roscoe Arbuckle

Fatty's Wine Party 14 Roscoe Arbuckle, Edward Dillon

Faubourg Montmartre 24 Charles Burguet

Faubourg Montmartre 32 Raymond Bernard

Faubourg Saint-Martin 86 Jean-Claude Guiguet

Faulty Pronoun Reference, Comparison, and Punctuation of the Restrictive or Non-Restrictive Element 61 George Landow

Faun 17 Alexander Korda

Fauno, Il 16 Febo Mari

Faunovo Velmi Pozdní Odpoledne 84 Věra Chytilová

Fausse Alerte 40 Jacques De Baroncelli

Fausse Maîtresse, La 42 André Cayatte

Fausses Ingénues 64 Giuseppe Bennati

Fausses Nouvelles 37 René Clair

Faust 04 Georges Méliès

Faust 07 Arthur Gilbert

Faust 09 J. Searle Dawley

Faust 10 Henri Andréani

Faust 10 David Barnett

Faust 11 Cecil M. Hepworth

Faust 12 Antonín Pech

Faust 22 Gérard Bourgeois

Faust 22 Challis Sanderson

Faust 23 Bertram Phillips

Faust 26 F. W. Murnau

Faust 27 H. B. Parkinson

Faust 36 Albert Hopkins

Faust 63 Peter Gorski

Faust 64 Michael Suman

Faust and Marguerite 1897 Georges Méliès

Faust and Marguerite 00 Edwin S. Porter

Faust and Marguerite 04 Georges Méliès

Faust and Mephistopheles 1898 George Albert Smith

Faust and the Devil 48 Carmine Gallone

Faust aux Enfers 03 Georges Méliès

Faust aux Enfers ou La Damnation du Faust 03 Georges Méliès

Faust et Marguerite 1897 Georges Méliès

Faust et Marguerite 04 Georges Méliès

Faust et Méphistophélès 03 Alice Guy-Blaché

Faust Family of Acrobats 01 Edwin S. Porter

Faust XX 66 Ion Popescu-Gopo

Faustine and the Beautiful Summer 71 Nina Companeez

Faustine et le Bel Été 71 Nina Companeez

Faustrecht der Freiheit 74 Rainer Werner Fassbinder

Faustus XX 66 Ion Popescu-Gopo

Faut Pas Prendre les Enfants du Bon Dieu pour des Canards Sauvages 68 Michel Audiard

Faute de l'Abbé Mouret, La 70 Georges Franju

Faute de Monique, La 28 Maurice Gleize

Faute d'Odette Maréchal, La 20 Henri Roussel

Faute d'Orthographe, La 19 Jacques Feyder

Fauteuil 47, La 26 Gaston Ravel

Faux-Cul, Le 75 Roger Hanin

Faux Magistrat, Le 14 Louis Feuillade

Favela dos Meus Amores 34 Humberto Mauro

Favela of My Loves 34 Humberto Mauro

Favola del Cappello 49 Valerio Zurlini

Favor to a Friend, A 19 John Ince

Favored Son, The 12 Allan Dwan

Favoris de la Lune, Les 84 Otar Ioseliani

Favorita, La 52 Cesare Barlacchi

Favorite Fool, A 15 Edwin Frazee, Del Henderson

Favorite Son, The 13 Francis Ford

Favorite Wife of the Maharaja, The 18 August Blom

Favors 90 Brooks Bushnell

Favourite for the Jamaica Cup, The 13 Charles Raymond

Favourites of the Moon 84 Otar Ioseliani

Fazil 27 Howard Hawks

Fe, Esperanza y Caridad 73 Luis Alcoriza*

Fear, The 12 Allan Dwan

Fear 27 Edwin Greenwood

Fear 45 Robert Cannon

Fear 46 Alfred Zeisler

Fear 54 Roberto Rossellini

Fear 65 Ritwik Ghatak

Fear, The 67 Costas Manoussakis

Fear 78 Lee Madden

Fear 80 Riccardo Freda

Fear, The 80 Lucio Fulci

Fear 87 Gunar Tselinsky

Fear 88 Robert A. Ferretti

Fear and Desire 53 Stanley Kubrick

Fear and Peter Brown 40 Richard Massingham

Fear, Anxiety and Depression 89 Todd Solondz

Fear-Bound 25 William Nigh

Fear Chamber, The 68 Jack Hill, Juan Ibáñez

Fear City 84 Abel Ferrara

Fear Eats the Soul 73 Rainer Werner Fassbinder

Fear Fighter, The 25 Albert S. Rogell

Fear in the City of the Living Dead 80 Lucio Fulci

Fear in the Night 47 Maxwell Shane

Fear in the Night 72 Jimmy Sangster

Fear Is the Key 72 Michael Tuchner

Fear Market, The 20 Kenneth Webb

Fear No Evil 49 Giuseppe M. Scotese

Fear No Evil 80 Frank LaLoggia

Fear No More 61 Bernard Wiesen

Fear Not 17 Allen Holubar

Fear o' God 26 Alfred Hitchcock

Fear of Fear 75 Rainer Werner Fassbinder

Fear Ship, The 33 J. Steven Edwards

Fear Strikes Out 56 Robert Mulligan

Fear Woman, The 19 John A. Barry

Fearless 55 Vojtěch Jasný

Fearless Fagan 52 Stanley Donen

Fearless Frank 67 Philip Kaufman

Fearless Hyena, The 79 Jackie Chan

Fearless Lover, The 24 Henry MacRae

Fearless Rider, The 28 Edgar Lewis

Fearless Vampire Killers, The 67 Roman Polanski

Fearless Vampire Killers, or Pardon Me But Your Teeth Are in My Neck, The 67 Roman Polanski

Fearmakers, The 58 Jacques Tourneur

Feast 67 Heinosuke Gosho

Feast at Zhirmunka 41 Mikhail Doller, Vsevolod I. Pudovkin

Feast of Flesh 68 George Romero

Feast of Flesh 76 Emilio Miraglia

Feast of Harmony, A 30 R. E. Jeffrey

Feast of Life, The 16 Albert Capellani

Feast of Mayrun, The 67 Youssef Chahine

Feast of St. Jorgen, The 30 Yakov Protazanov

Feather, The 29 Leslie Hiscott

Feather Bed, The 33 Bertram Fryer

Feather Bluster 58 Robert McKimson

Feather Duster 55 Robert McKimson

Feather Finger 66 Robert McKimson

Feather in Her Hat, A 33 Alfred Santell

Feather in His Cap, A 07 Lewin Fitzhamon

Feather in His Hare, A 48 Chuck Jones

Feather Pushers 26 William C. Nolan

Feather Your Nest 37 William Beaudine

Feathered Serpent, The 34 Maclean Rogers

Feathered Serpent, The 48 William Beaudine

Feathertop 16 Henry J. Vernot

Febbre da Cavallo 77 Steno

February 29 12 Allan Dwan

Fécondité 29 Henri Étiévant

Fede 16 Carmine Gallone

Federal Agent 36 Sam Newfield

Federal Agent at Large 50 George Blair

Federal Agents vs. Underworld, Inc. 49 Fred C. Brannon

Federal Bullets 37 Karl Brown

Federal Fugitives 41 William Beaudine

Federal Man 50 Robert E. Tansey

Federal Man-Hunt 39 Nick Grindé

Federal Operator 99 45 Spencer G. Bennet, Yakima Canutt, Wallace A. Grissell

Felix the Ghost Breaker 23 Pat Sullivan
Felix the Globe Trotter 23 Pat Sullivan
Felix the Goat Getter 23 Pat Sullivan
Felix the Hypnotist 21 Pat Sullivan
Felix the Landlord 20 Pat Sullivan
Felix Tries for Treasure 23 Pat Sullivan
Felix Tries the Trades 25 Pat Sullivan
Felix Tries to Rest 24 Pat Sullivan
Felix Trifles with Time 25 Pat Sullivan
Felix Trips Thru Toyland 25 Pat Sullivan
Felix Trumps the Ace 26 Pat Sullivan
Felix Turns the Tide 23 Pat Sullivan
Felix Uses His Head 26 Pat Sullivan
Felix Wakes Up 22 Pat Sullivan
Felix Weathers the Weather 26 Pat Sullivan
Felix Wins and Loses 25 Pat Sullivan
Felix Wins Out 23 Pat Sullivan
Feliz Ano Velho 88 Roberto Gervitz
Fella with the Fiddle, The 37 Friz Freleng
Feller Needs a Friend 32 Harry A. Pollard
Fellini Casanova 76 Federico Fellini
Fellini Satyricon 69 Federico Fellini
Fellini's Amarcord 73 Federico Fellini
Fellini's Casanova 76 Federico Fellini
Fellini's Interview 87 Federico Fellini
Fellini's Roma 72 Federico Fellini
Fellini's Scrapbook 68 Federico Fellini
Fellow Americans 42 Garson Kanin
Fellow Clerks 09 Theo Bouwmeester
Fellow from Our Town, A 42 Boris Ivanov, Alexander Stolper
Fellow Students 30 Sam Newfield
Fellow Traveler 89 Philip Saville
Fellows Who Ate the Elephant, The 47 Kozaburo Yoshimura
Fellowship of the Frog 59 Harald Reinl
Fem Kopier 13 August Blom
Fem Raske Piger 33 Anders Wilhelm Sandberg
Female, The 24 Sam Wood
Female 33 Michael Curtiz, William Dieterle
Female 56 Franz Eichhorn
Female, The 58 Julien Duvivier
Female, The 62 Leopoldo Torre-Nilsson
Female and the Flesh 55 Georges Lacombe
Female Animal, The 58 Harry Keller
Female Bunch, The 69 Al Adamson, John Cardos
Female Butcher, The 72 Jorge Grau
Female Cabbie, The 87 Víctor Manuel Castro
Female Correspondent 41 Alfred E. Green
Female Demon, The 13 Robert Dinesen
Female Demon 28 Teinosuke Kinugasa
Female Facial Expressions 02 Edwin S. Porter
Female Fiend, The 66 Samuel Gallu
Female Fiends 58 Montgomery Tully
Female Fugitive 38 William Nigh
Female Impersonator, The 14 Charles Chaplin
Female Jungle, The 55 Bruno Ve Sota
Female of the Species, The 12 D. W. Griffith
Female of the Species, The 13 Lois Weber
Female of the Species, The 16 Raymond B. West
Female on the Beach 55 Joseph Pevney

Female Prince, The 66 See-loke Chou
Female Prisoner, The 68 Henri-Georges Clouzot
Female Rebellion 86 Hyeong-myeong Kim
Female Response, The 72 Tim Kincaid
Female Swindler, The 16 Albert Ward
Female Times Three 57 Steno
Female Trap, The 68 Gunnar Hellström
Female Trouble 74 John Waters
Females Is Fickle 40 Dave Fleischer
Feme 27 Richard Oswald
Femeile Zilelor Noastre 58 Márta Mészáros
Femina 17 Augusto Genina
Féminin-Féminin 73 Henri Calef
Féminin Fleur, La 65 Jan Lenica
Feminine Touch 30 Richard Thorpe
Feminine Touch, The 41 W. S. Van Dyke
Feminine Touch, The 56 Pat Jackson
Femme à Sa Fenêtre, Une 76 Pierre Granier-Deferre
Femme au Corbeau, La 28 Frank Borzage
Femme aux Bottes Rouges, La 74 Juan Buñuel
Femme aux Deux Visages, La 20 Pierre Marodon
Femme Coquette, Une 55 Jean-Luc Godard
Femme d'à Côté, La 81 François Truffaut
Femme dans la Nuit, Une 41 Abel Gance, Edmond T. Gréville
Femme de Jean, La 73 Yannick Bellon
Femme de l'Aviateur, La 80 Eric Rohmer
Femme de l'Aviateur: Comédies et Proverbes: 1, La 80 Eric Rohmer
Femme de Ma Vie, La 86 Régis Wargnier
Femme de Mon Pôte, La 82 Bertrand Blier
Femme de Nulle Part, La 22 Louis Delluc
Femme de Paille, La 89 Suzanne Schiffman
Femme de Papier 89 Suzanne Schiffman
Femme de Rose Hill, La 89 Alain Tanner
Femme Disparaît, Une 39 Jacques Feyder
Femme Douce, Une 69 Robert Bresson
Femme du Boulanger, La 38 Marcel Pagnol
Femme du Bout du Monde, La 37 Jean Epstein
Femme du Gange, La 73 Marguerite Duras
Femme d'Une Nuit, La 30 Marcel L'Herbier
Femme Écarlate, La 69 Jean Valère
Femme en Blanc Se Revolte, Une 66 Claude Autant-Lara
Femme en Bleu, La 72 Michel Deville
Femme en Homme, La 31 Augusto Genina
Femme Entre Chien et Loup 79 André Delvaux
Femme Est une Femme, Une 60 Jean-Luc Godard
Femme et le Pantin, La 29 Jacques De Baroncelli
Femme et le Pantin, La 58 Julien Duvivier
Femme Fatale, La 17 Louis Feuillade
Femme Fatale, La 45 Jean Boyer
Femme Fidèle, Une 76 Roger Vadim
Femme Fleur, La 65 Jan Lenica
Femme Flic, La 80 Yves Boisset
Femme Idéale, La 34 André Berthomieu

Femme Inconnue, La 16 Abel Gance
Femme Inconnue, Une 18 Gaston Ravel
Femme Inconnue, La 23 Jacques De Baroncelli
Femme Infidèle, La 68 Claude Chabrol
Femme Invisible, La 33 Georges Lacombe
Femme Mariée, La 64 Jean-Luc Godard
Femme Mariée, Une 64 Jean-Luc Godard
Femme Nikita, La 90 Luc Besson
Femme Nue, La 26 Léonce Perret
Femme Nue, La 33 Jean-Paul Paulin
Femme Nue, La 49 André Berthomieu
Femme ou Deux, Une 85 Daniel Vigne
Femme Revée, La 29 Jean Durand
Femme Secrète, La 86 Sebastien Grall
Femme Spectacle, La 63 Claude Lelouch
Femme Su Voisin, La 29 Jacques De Baroncelli
Femme Volante, La 02 Georges Méliès
Femmes, Les 69 Jean Aurel
Femmes, Les 69 Jean-Claude Dague, Louis Soulanes
Femmes au Soleil 74 Lilliane Dreyfus
Femmes Collantes, Les 20 Georges Monca
Femmes de Paris 53 Jean Loubignac
Femmes de Personne 84 Christopher Frank
Femmes des Autres, Les 20 Pierre Marodon
Femmes du Louvre, Les 51 Pierre Kast
Femmes d'un Été 64 Gianni Franciolini
Femmes Fatales 75 Bertrand Blier
Femmes Fatales 79 Bertrand Tavernier
Femmes Sont Folles, Les 50 Gilles Grangier
Femmes Sont Marrantes, Les 58 André Hunebelle
Femmes Vampires, Les 67 Jean Rollin
Femmina 17 Augusto Genina
Femmina 53 Marc Allégret, Edgar G. Ulmer
Femmina 66 Georges Lautner
Femmine di Lusso 64 Giorgio Bianchi
Femmine Tre Volte 57 Steno
Fence Riders 50 Wallace Fox
Fencing at the Joinville School 1898 Georges Méliès
Fencing Master, The 15 Raoul Walsh
Fenêtre Ouverte, La 52 Henri Storck
Feng-Kuei-Lai-Tejen 83 Hsiao-hsien Hou
Fengriffen 73 Roy Ward Baker
Fengslende Dager for Christina Berg 88 Egil Kolstø
Fenomenal e il Tesori di Tutankamen 68 Ruggero Deodato
Fényes Szelek 68 Miklós Jancsó
Fer à Cheval, Le 15 Louis Feuillade
Ferda the Aunt 44 Hermina Tyrlova
Ferestadeh 83 Parviz Sayyad
Férfi Mind Örült, A 37 Victor Gertler
Férfiarckép 64 István Gaál
Ferghana Canal, The 39 Sergei Eisenstein
Feriebørn 52 Jørgen Roos
Ferien Vom Ich 35 Hans Deppe
Ferme du Choquart, Le 22 Jean Kemm
Ferme du Pendu, La 46 Jean Dréville
Fermière à Montfauçon 67 Eric Rohmer
Fern the Red Deer 77 Jan Darnley-Smith
Fernandel the Dressmaker 56 Jean Boyer
Feroce Saladino, Il 37 Mario Bonnard

Field of Honor *87* Jean-Pierre Denis
Field of Honour, The *22* Percy Moran
Field of Red, The *58* Peter Watkins
Field Poppy, The *35* Kenji Mizoguchi
Fielder's Field *37* Lambert Hillyer
Fields of Honor *18* Ralph Ince
Fields of Honor *65* Andrew V. McLaglen
Fiend, The *71* Robert Hartford-Davis
Fiend *80* Donald M. Dohler
Fiend of Dope Island *61* Nate Watt
Fiend Who Walked the West, The *58* Gordon Douglas
Fiend with the Atomic Brain, The *65* Al Adamson
Fiend with the Electronic Brain, The *65* Al Adamson
Fiend with the Synthetic Brain, The *65* Al Adamson
Fiend Without a Face *57* Arthur Crabtree
Fiendish Ghouls, The *59* John Gilling
Fiendish Plot of Dr. Fu Manchu, The *80* Piers Haggard
Fiendish Plot of Fu Manchu, The *80* Piers Haggard
Fiends, The *54* Henri-Georges Clouzot
Fiends of Hell, The *14* Charles C. Calvert
Fieras en Brama *87* Gilberto De Anda
Fierce Charger and the Knight, The *01* Georges Méliès
Fierce One, The *73* Tolomush Okeyev
Fiercest Heart, The *61* George Sherman
Fiery Autumn *78* Masaki Kobayashi
Fiery Deeds of the Terrible Two, The *14* Joe Evans
Fiery Fireman *28* Friz Freleng, Rudolf Ising
Fiery Hand, The *23* A. E. Coleby
Fiery Love *60* Herman van den Horst
Fiery Miles *57* Samson Samsonov
Fiery Spur *68* R. Lee Frost
Fiery Transport, The *29* Alexander Ivanov
Fiesco *20* Paul Leni
Fiesta *41* LeRoy Prinz
Fiesta *47* Richard Thorpe
Fiesta Brava *56* Vittorio Cottafavi
Fiesta Fiasco *67* Alex Lovy
Fiesta Time *45* Bob Wickersham
Fièvre *21* Louis Delluc
Fièvre Monte à El Pao, La *59* Luis Buñuel
Fièvres *41* Jean Delannoy
Fifi la Plume *64* Albert Lamorisse
Fifi Tambour *15* Louis Feuillade
Fifres et Tambours d'Entre-Sambre-et-Meuse *74* Henri Storck
15/18, Le *73* Chantal Akerman, Samy Szlingerbaum
Fifteen from Rome *63* Dino Risi
15 Malden Lane *36* Allan Dwan
15 Minutes on 15 Years *65* Márta Mészáros
15 Perc 15 Évröl *65* Márta Mészáros
Fifteen Scaffolds for a Killer *68* Nunzio Malasomma
Fifteen Wives *34* Frank R. Strayer
15-Year-Old Girl, The *89* Jacques Doillon
15ème Prélude de Chopin, Le *22* Victor Tourjansky
Fifth Avenue *16* George Fitzmaurice
Fifth Avenue *26* Robert Vignola
Fifth Avenue Girl *39* Gregory La Cava
Fifth Avenue Models *25* Svend Gade

Fifth Chair, The *45* Richard Wallace
Fifth Column Mouse, The *43* Friz Freleng
Fifth Day of Peace, The *72* Giuliano Montaldo
Fifth Floor, The *80* Hikmet Avedis
Fifth Form at St. Dominics, The *21* A. E. Coleby
Fifth Horseman, The *24* E. M. McMahon
Fifth Horseman Is Fear, The *65* Zbyněk Brynych
Fifth Man, The *14* Francis J. Grandon
5th Monkey, The *90* Eric Rochant
Fifth Musketeer, The *77* Ken Annakin
Fifth Round, The *38* Howard Bretherton
Fifth Seal, The *76* Zoltán Fábri
Fifty Candles *21* Irvin Willat
Fifty Fantastics and Fifty Personalities *65* Andy Warhol
Fifty Fathoms Deep *31* Roy William Neill
Fifty-Fifty *16* Allan Dwan
Fifty-Fifty *16* Ashley Miller
Fifty-Fifty *20* Frank Moser
Fifty-Fifty *23* Robert Florey
Fifty-Fifty *25* Henri Diamant-Berger
50/50 *86* Uwe Brandner
Fifty-Fifty *89* Peter Timm
Fifty-Fifty Girl, The *28* Clarence Badger
55 Days at Peking *63* Noel Howard, Andrew Marton, Nicholas Ray
Fifty Mile Auto Contest *12* Allan Dwan
$50 Million Can't Be Wrong *33* Joseph Santley
Fifty Million Frenchmen *31* Lloyd Bacon
Fifty Roads to Town *37* Norman Taurog
52nd Street *37* Harold Young
Fifty-Shilling Boxer *37* Maclean Rogers
50,000 B.C. (Before Clothing) *63* Warner Rose
Fifty Thousand Dollar Reward *24* Clifford S. Elfelt
52 Miles to Midnight *64* John Brahm
52 Miles to Terror *64* John Brahm
52 Pick-Up *86* John Frankenheimer
Fifty Years After *12* Fred Evans
Fig Leaves *26* Howard Hawks
Figaro *29* Gaston Ravel
Figaro e la Sua Gran'Giornata *31* Mario Camerini
Figaro et l'Auvergnant *1897* Georges Méliès
Figaro Qua, Figaro La *50* Carlo Ludovico Bragaglia
Figaro's Big Day *31* Mario Camerini
Fight, The *15* George W. Lederer
Fight, The *24* George Marshall
Fight, The *61* Michel Brault, Marcel Carrière, Claude Fournier, Claude Jutra
Fight and Win *24* Erle C. Kenton
Fight Between a Miller and a Sweep *1899* Arthur Cooper
Fight for Freedom, The *08* D. W. Griffith
Fight for Freedom, or Exiled to Siberia, A *14* Herbert Blaché
Fight for His Heart, The *16* Mauritz Stiller
Fight for Honor, A *24* Henry MacRae
Fight for Honour, A *08* A. E. Coleby
Fight for Life, A *12* Bert Haldane
Fight for Life, A *15* Will P. Kellino
Fight for Life, The *40* Pare Lorentz
Fight for Love, A *19* John Ford

Fight for Millions, The *13* Herbert Blaché
Fight for Millions, A *18* William Duncan
Fight for Our Soviet Ukraine, The *43* Yakiv Avdiyenko, Yulia Solntseva
Fight for Right, The *13* Oscar Apfel
Fight for Rome, The *69* Robert Siodmak
Fight for the Glory *70* Hirokazu Ichimura
Fight for the Red Cow, The *87* Jarl Friis Mikkelsen, Ole Stephensen
Fight for the Ultimatum Factory *23* Dmitri Bassaligo
Fight for Us *89* Lino Brocka
Fight for Your Lady *37* Ben Stoloff
Fight for Your Life *77* Robert Endelson
Fight Goes On, The *41* Gustaf Molander
Fight in a Thieves' Kitchen *21* Edward R. Gordon
Fight Is Right *36* Jean Yarbrough
Fight On for Old *56* Ernest Pintoff
Fight On, Marines! *42* Louis Gasnier
Fight Pest, The *28* Leo McCarey*
Fight to the Finish, A *25* B. Reeves Eason
Fight to the Finish, A *37* C. C. Coleman, Jr.
Fight to the Last *38* Y. C. Cheng
Fight with Fire, A *11* Lewin Fitzhamon
Fight with Sledgehammers *02* Dicky Winslow
Fight with the Dragon, The *39* Franz Seitz
Fighter, The *21* Henry Kolker
Fighter, The *51* Herbert Kline
Fighter Attack *53* Lesley Selander
Fighter Squadron *48* Raoul Walsh
Fighter's Paradise *24* Alvin J. Neitz
Fightin' Comeback, The *27* Tenny Wright
Fightin' Devil *22* Robert McKenzie
Fightin' Mad *21* Joseph Franz
Fightin' Odds *25* Bennett Cohn
Fightin' Ones, D' *61* Friz Freleng
Fightin' Pals *40* Dave Fleischer
Fightin' Redhead, The *28* Louis King
Fightin' Thru *24* Roy M. Hughes
Fightin' Thru *30* William Nigh
Fighting American, The *24* Tom Forman
Fighting Back *17* Raymond Wells
Fighting Back *48* Malcolm St. Clair
Fighting Back *82* Michael Caulfield
Fighting Back *82* Lewis Teague
Fighting Bill Carson *45* Sam Newfield
Fighting Bill Fargo *41* Ray Taylor
Fighting Billy *15* Will P. Kellino
Fighting Blade, The *23* John S. Robertson
Fighting Blood *11* D. W. Griffith
Fighting Blood *16* Oscar Apfel
Fighting Blood *23* Malcolm St. Clair
Fighting Blood of Jerry McDub, The *17* H. M. Freck
Fighting Bob *15* John W. Noble
Fighting Boob, The *26* Jack Nelson
Fighting Breed, The *21* Wilfred Lucas
Fighting Brothers, The *19* John Ford
Fighting Buckaroo, The *26* Roy William Neill
Fighting Buckaroo, The *43* William Berke
Fighting Caballero *35* Elmer Clifton
Fighting Caravans *31* Otto Brower, David Burton
Fighting Champ, The *32* John P. McCarthy

Fighting Chance, The 20 Charles Maigne
Fighting Chance, The 55 William Witney
Fighting Cheat, The 26 Richard Thorpe
Fighting Coast Guard 51 Joseph Kane
Fighting Cobbler, The 15 A. E. Coleby
Fighting Code, The 33 Lambert Hillyer
Fighting Colleen, A 19 David Smith
Fighting Command 43 John Rawlins
Fighting Courage 25 Clifford S. Elfelt
Fighting Coward, The 24 James Cruze
Fighting Cowboy, The 33 Victor Adamson
Fighting Cressy 19 Robert Thornby
Fighting Cub, The 25 Paul Hurst
Fighting Curate, The 08 Frank Motter-shaw
Fighting Death 14 Herbert Blaché
Fighting Demon, The 25 Arthur Rosson
Fighting Deputy, The 37 Sam Newfield
Fighting Dervishes, The 12 Sidney Olcott
Fighting Destiny 19 Paul Scardon
Fighting Devil Dogs 38 John English, William Witney
Fighting Doctor, The 26 Robert North Bradbury
Fighting Dude, The 25 Roscoe Arbuckle
Fighting Eagle, The 27 Donald Crisp
Fighting Edge, The 26 Henry Lehrman
Fighting Engineers, The 43 B. Reeves Eason
Fighting Failure, The 26 E. G. Boyle
Fighting Fate 21 William Duncan
Fighting Fate 25 Albert S. Rogell
Fighting Father Dunne 48 Ted Tetzlaff
Fighting Film Album No. 1: Meeting with Maxim 41 Sergei Gerasimov
Fighting Film Album No. 2 41 Grigori Kozintsev
Fighting Film Album No. 3 41 Boris Barnet
Fighting Film Album No. 9: Beacon 41 Mark Donskoi
Fighting Film Album No. 10 42 Boris Barnet
Fighting Film Album No. 13 43 Lev Kuleshov
Fighting Fluid 25 Leo McCarey
Fighting Fool, The 29 Jack Harrison
Fighting Fool, The 32 Lambert Hillyer
Fighting Fools 49 Reginald LeBorg
Fighting for Gold 19 Edward J. LeSaint
Fighting for Justice 24 Walter De Courcy
Fighting for Justice 32 Otto Brower
Fighting for Love 16 Raymond Wells
Fighting Friends 29 Yasujiro Ozu
Fighting Friends, Japanese Style 29 Yasu-jiro Ozu
Fighting Frontier 42 Lambert Hillyer
Fighting Frontiersman, The 46 Derwin Abrahams
Fighting Fury 24 Clifford Smith
Fighting Gentleman, The 17 Edward Sloman
Fighting Gentleman, The 32 Fred New-meyer
Fighting Gladiator, The 26 Geoffrey H. Malins, H. B. Parkinson
Fighting Gob, The 26 Harry Fraser
Fighting Grin, The 18 Joseph De Grasse
Fighting Gringo, The 17 Fred A. Kelsey
Fighting Gringo, The 39 David Howard

Fighting Guardsman, The 44 Henry Levin
Fighting Guide, The 22 Don Clark, William Duncan
Fighting Heart, The 18 B. Reeves Eason
Fighting Heart, A 24 Jack Nelson
Fighting Heart, The 25 John Ford
Fighting Hearts 16 Alexander Korda
Fighting Hero 34 Harry S. Webb
Fighting His Battles Over Again 02 James A. Williamson
Fighting Hombre, The 27 Jack Nelson
Fighting Hope, The 15 George Melford
Fighting in the Streets in India 1897 Georges Méliès
Fighting Instinct 18 Forest Holger-Madsen
Fighting Jack 21 Walter C. Rowden
Fighting Jack 26 Louis Chaudet
Fighting Jim Grant 23 W. Adcock
Fighting Kentuckian, The 49 George Waggner
Fighting Kentuckians, The 20 J. Harrison Edwards
Fighting Lady 35 Carlos Borcosque
Fighting Lady, The 43 William Wyler
Fighting Lawman, The 53 Thomas Carr
Fighting Legion, The 30 Harry Joe Brown
Fighting Line, The 19 B. Reeves Eason
Fighting Love 27 Nils Olaf Chrisander
Fighting Lover, The 21 Fred LeRoy Gran-ville
Fighting Luck 26 John P. McGowan
Fighting Mad 17 Edward J. LeSaint
Fighting Mad 39 Sam Newfield
Fighting Mad 48 Reginald LeBorg
Fighting Mad 57 Denis Kavanagh
Fighting Mad 76 Jonathan Demme
Fighting Mad 77 Cirio Santiago
Fighting Man of the Plains 49 Edwin L. Marin
Fighting Marine, The 26 Spencer G. Bennet
Fighting Marines, The 35 B. Reeves Eason, Joseph Kane
Fighting Marshal, The 31 D. Ross Led-erman
Fighting Marshal 40 Lesley Selander
Fighting Men, The 50 Camillo Mastro-cinque
Fighting Mustang 48 Oliver Drake
Fighting Near Tsaritsyn 19 Dziga Vertov
Fighting Odds, The 17 Allan Dwan
Fighting O'Flynn, The 49 Arthur Pierson
Fighting Parson, The 12 George Gray, Bert Haldane
Fighting Parson, The 33 Harry Fraser
Fighting Peacemaker, The 26 Clifford Smith
Fighting Phantom, The 33 Fred Allen
Fighting Pilot 35 Noel Mason Smith
Fighting Pimpernel, The 41 Leslie Howard
Fighting Pimpernel, The 50 Michael Powell, Emeric Pressburger
Fighting Pioneers 35 Harry Fraser
Fighting Playboy 37 Robert F. Hill
Fighting Prince of Donegal, The 66 Michael O'Herlihy
Fighting Ranger 26 Paul Hurst
Fighting Ranger, The 34 George B. Seitz
Fighting Ranger, The 48 Lambert Hillyer
Fighting Rats of Tobruk 45 Charles Chau-

vel
Fighting Redhead, The 49 Lewis D. Collins
Fighting Renegade, The 39 Sam Newfield
Fighting Romeo, The 25 Al Ferguson
Fighting Rookie, The 34 Spencer G. Bennet
Fighting Roosevelts, The 19 William Nigh
Fighting Sap, The 24 Albert S. Rogell
Fighting Schoolmaster, The 21 Charles Maigne
Fighting Seabees, The 44 Edward Ludwig, Howard Lydecker
Fighting Selina 15 Dave Aylott
Fighting 7th, The 51 Charles Marquis Warren
Fighting Shadows 35 David Selman
Fighting Shepherdess, The 20 Edward José
Fighting Sheriff, The 25 John P. Mc-Gowan
Fighting Sheriff, The 31 Louis King
Fighting 69th, The 40 William Keighley
Fighting 69th½, The 41 Friz Freleng
Fighting Smile, The 25 Jay Marchant
Fighting Snub Reilly 24 Andrew P. Wilson
Fighting Spirit 42 Charles Barton
Fighting Stallion, The 26 Ben F. Wilson
Fighting Stallion, The 50 Robert E. Tansey
Fighting Stock 35 Tom Walls
Fighting Strain, The 23 Neal Hart
Fighting Strain of Old England, The 14 Dave Aylott
Fighting Stranger, The 21 Webster Cullison
Fighting Streak, The 22 Arthur Rosson
Fighting Sullivans, The 44 Lloyd Bacon
Fighting Terror, The 29 John P. Mc-Gowan
Fighting Texan, The 37 Charles Abbott
Fighting Texan, The 46 Lambert Hillyer
Fighting Texans, The 33 Armand Schaefer
Fighting the Flames 24 B. Reeves Eason
Fighting Thoroughbreds 26 Harry Joe Brown
Fighting Thoroughbreds 39 Sidney Salkow
Fighting Three, The 27 Albert S. Rogell
Fighting Through 18 Christy Cabanne
Fighting Through 30 William Nigh
Fighting Through 34 Harry Fraser
Fighting to Live 34 Edward F. Cline
Fighting Tools 43 Robert Clampett
Fighting Trail, The 17 William Duncan
Fighting Trooper, The 34 Ray Taylor
Fighting Trouble 56 George Blair
Fighting Valley 43 Oliver Drake
Fighting Vigilantes, The 47 Ray Taylor
Fighting Washerwomen 04 Percy Stow
Fighting Westerner, The 34 David Selman
Fighting Westerner, The 35 Charles Barton
Fighting Wildcats 57 Arthur Crabtree
Fighting with Buffalo Bill 26 Ray Taylor
Fighting with Kit Carson 33 Colbert Clark, Armand Schaefer
Fighting Youth 25 B. Reeves Eason
Fighting Youth 35 Hamilton MacFadden
Figleaf 66 Félix Máriássy
Figli Non Si Vendono, I 52 Mario Bonnard

Figlia del Capitano, La *47* Mario Camerini

Figlia del Corsaro Verde, La *40* Enrico Guazzoni

Figlia del Mare, La *19* Carmine Gallone

Figlia del Tempesta, La *20* Carmine Gallone

Figlia dello Sceicco, La *58* Goffredo Alessandrini, Fernando Cerchio, Leon Klimovsky, Ricardo Muñoz Suay, Gianni Vernuccio

Figlia di Frankenstein, La *71* Ernst R. von Theumer

Figlia di Mata Hari, La *54* Carmine Gallone, Renzo Merusi

Figlio del Capitano Blood, Il *62* Tulio Demicheli

Figlio del Corsaro Rosso, Il *60* Primo Zeglio

Figlio della Guerra, Il *15* Ugo Falena

Figlio delle Stelle *79* Carlo Vanzina

Figlio di D'Artagnan, Il *49* Riccardo Freda

Figlio di Django, Il *67* Osvaldo Civirani

Figlio di Madame Sans-Gêne, Il *22* Baldassare Negroni

Figlio di Spartacus, Il *62* Sergio Corbucci

Figlio Mio Infinitamente Caro *85* Valentino Orsini

Figurants du Nouveau Monde, Les *69* Philippe de Broca

Figurehead, The *20* Robert Ellis

Figurehead, The *53* Joy Batchelor, John Halas

Figures de Cire *12* Maurice Tourneur

Figures de Cire et Têtes de Bois *16* Émile Cohl

Figures Don't Lie *27* A. Edward Sutherland

Figures in a Landscape *70* Joseph Losey

Fil à la Patte, Un *14* Henri Pouctal

Fil à la Patte, Un *24* Robert Saidreau

File No. 113 *32* Chester M. Franklin

File of the Golden Goose, The *68* Sam Wanamaker

File on Thelma Jordan, The *49* Robert Siodmak

File 113 *32* Chester M. Franklin

Filer *88* Roman Balajan

Files from Scotland Yard *51* Anthony Squire

Filha de Drácula, A *72* Jesús Franco

Filhas do Fogo, As *78* Walter Hugo Khouri

Fille à la Valise, La *60* Valerio Zurlini

Fille aux Yeux d'Or, La *61* Jean-Gabriel Albicocco

Fille Bien Gardée, La *24* Louis Feuillade

Fille d'Artiste *16* Camille De Morlhon

Fille de Delft, La *14* Alfred Machin

Fille de Dracula, La *72* Jesús Franco

Fille de Feu, La *64* Alfred Rodé

Fille de Hambourg, La *58* Yves Allégret

Fille de Jephté, La *10* Louis Feuillade

Fille de Jephté, La *13* Henri Andréani

Fille de la Rizière, La *63* Raffaello Matarazzo

Fille de l'Eau, La *24* Jean Renoir

Fille de Mata Hari, La *54* Carmine Gallone, Renzo Merusi

Fille de Pachas, La *26* Joe Hamman*

Fille de Quinze Ans, La *89* Jacques Doillon

Fille de Rien *21* André Hugon

Fille des Chiffonniers, La *22* Henri Desfontaines

Fille du Boche, La *15* Henri Pouctal

Fille du Diable, La *46* Henri Decoin

Fille du Diable, La *49* Maurice Saurel

Fille du Juge d'Instruction, La *11* Louis Feuillade

Fille du Margrave, La *12* Louis Feuillade

Fille du Peuple, La *20* Camille De Morlhon

Fille du Puisatier, La *40* Marcel Pagnol

Fille et Des Fusils, Une *64* Claude Lelouch

Fille et le Garçon, La *32* Wilhelm Thiele

Fille pour l'Été, Une *59* Édouard Molinaro

Fille Sage, La *64* Walerian Borowczyk

Filléres Gyönyör *33* Béla Gaál

Filles de Feu, Les *75* Jacques Rivette

Filles de la Concierge, Les *34* Jacques Tourneur

Filles de la Nuit, Les *57* Maurice Cloche

Filles du Cantonnier, Les *09* Louis Feuillade

Filles du Diable, Les *03* Georges Méliès

Filles du Soleil, Les *49* Jacques Baratier

Filles Sement le Vent, Les *61* Louis Soulanes

Filles Traquées *80* Jean Rollin

Filling His Own Shoes *17* Harry Beaumont

Filling the Gap *41* Joy Batchelor, John Halas

Fillmore *72* Richard T. Heffron

Film *79* David Rayner Clark

Film About a Woman Who... *74* Yvonne Rainer

Film About Love, A *70* István Szabó

Film About the Book *62* Dušan Makavejev

Film Actress *87* Kon Ichikawa

Film and Reality *42* Alberto Cavalcanti

Film aus dem Süden, Ein *23* E. A. Dupont

Film 100% Brasileiro, Um *87* José Sette

Film Comme les Autres, Un *68* Jean-Luc Godard, Jean-Pierre Gorin

Film-Concert Dedicated to the 25th Anniversary of the Red Army *43* Yefim Dzigan, Sergei Gerasimov, Mikhail Kalatozov

Film-Concert for the Red Army's 25th Anniversary *43* Yefim Dzigan, Sergei Gerasimov, Mikhail Kalatozov

Film d'Amore e d'Anarchia *73* Lina Wertmuller

Film d'Amore e d'Anarchia, ovvero Stamattina alle 10 in Via dei Fiori nella Nota Casa di Toleranza *73* Lina Wertmuller

Film de Jean, Le *53* Marc Allégret

Film der Menschlichkeit, Ein *23* Robert Wiene

Film Fan, The *39* Robert Clampett

Film Fare *37* Alec Hopkins

Film Favourites *14* Lawrence Trimble

Film Favourites *24* Cecil M. Hepworth

Film for Guitar *65* Bruce Beresford

Film for Maria, A *62* Jack Smith

Film Form No. 1 *70* Stan Vanderbeek

Film Form No. 2 *70* Stan Vanderbeek

Film Gegen die Volkskrankheit Krebs — Jeder Achte..., Ein *41* Walter Ruttmann

Film Hour *68* Edgar Reitz

Film in Which There Appear Sprocket Holes, Edge Lettering, Dirt Particles, Etc. *65* George Landow

Film Is Rhythm *21* Hans Richter

Film Ist Rhythmus *21* Hans Richter

Film Johnnie, A *14* Mack Sennett

Film Like All the Others, A *68* Jean-Luc Godard, Jean-Pierre Gorin

Film Like Any Other, A *68* Jean-Luc Godard, Jean-Pierre Gorin

Film Magazine of the Arts *63* Jonas Mekas

Film Noir, Le *83* Marc Silverman

Film Novel, Three Sisters *78* István Darday, György Szalai

Film o Knjizi A.B.C. *62* Dušan Makavejev

Film of Love and Anarchy, or This Morning at 10 in the Via dei Fiori at the Well Known House of Tolerance *73* Lina Wertmuller

Film Ohne Titel *47* Rudolf Jügert

Film 100% Brasileiro, Um *87* José Sette

Film Pie *20* Neville Bruce, Geoffrey H. Malins

Film Report on the War No. 4 *41* Grigori Alexandrov

Film Star's Perfect Day, The *21* Neville Bruce

Film Study *25* Hans Richter

Film Study of an Arabesque *28* Germaine Dulac

Film That Rises to the Surface of Clarified Butter, The *68* George Landow

Film-Truth *23* Dziga Vertov

Film with Three Dancers *70* Ed Emshwiller

Film Without a Name *47* Rudolf Jügert

Film Without a Title *47* Rudolf Jügert

Film Without Title *47* Rudolf Jügert

Filme Demência *86* Carlos Reichenbach

Filming of Othello, The *77* Orson Welles

Filming Othello *77* Orson Welles

Filmmaker *68* George Lucas

Filmnotities uit de Sovjet-Unie *30* Joris Ivens

Filmograph Cartoons *13* Hy Mayer

Filmprimadonna, Die *13* Urban Gad

Films by Stan Brakhage: An Avant-Garde Home Movie *61* Stan Brakhage

Filmstudie 25 *25* Hans Richter

Filmstudy, Zeedijk *27* Joris Ivens

Filmstunde *68* Edgar Reitz

Filo della Vita, Il *18* Mario Caserini

Filofax *90* Arthur Hiller

Filosofská Historie *37* Otakar Vávra

Filou *88* Samir

Fils, Le *73* Pierre Granier-Deferre

Fils d'Amérique, Le *25* Henri Fescourt

Fils d'Amérique, Un *32* Carmine Gallone

Fils de Flibustier, Le *22* Louis Feuillade

Fils de l'Eau, Les *55* Suzanne Baron, Jean Rouch

Fils de Locuste, Le *11* Louis Feuillade

Fils de Rajah, Le *31* Claude Autant-Lara

Fils de Sunamite, Le *11* Louis Feuillade

Fils du Garde-Chasse, Le *06* Alice Guy-Blaché

Filumena Marturano *51* Eduardo De Filippo

Fimpen 73 Bo Widerberg
Fin de Don Juan, La 11 Victorin Jasset
Fin de Fiesta 59 Leopoldo Torre-Nilsson
Fin de Journée 68 Gilles Grangier
Fin de Monte, La 27 Henri Étiévant
Fin de Réveillon 10 Georges Méliès
Fin de Semana para los Muertos 74 Jorge Grau
Fin du Jour, La 38 Julien Duvivier
Fin du Monde, La 30 Abel Gance
Fin d'un Alcoolique, La 07 Georges Méliès
Fin 'n' Catty 43 Chuck Jones
Final Accord 36 Douglas Sirk
Final Appointment 54 Terence Fisher
Final Arrangement, The 87 Veikko Aaltonen
Final Assignment 80 Paul Almond
Final Chapter, Walking Tall 77 Jack Starrett
Final Chord, The 36 Douglas Sirk
Final Close-Up, The 19 Walter Edwards
Final Column, The 55 David MacDonald
Final Comedown, The 72 Oscar Williams
Final Conflict, The 81 Graham Baker
Final Countdown, The 79 Don Taylor
Final Crash, The 73 Alan Myerson
Final Curtain 87 Edward Fleming
Final Cut, The 80 Ross Dimsey
Final Edition, The 32 Howard Higgin
Final Exam 81 Jimmy Huston
Final Executioner, The 83 Romolo Guerrieri
Final Extra, The 27 James P. Hogan
Final Hour, The 36 D. Ross Lederman
Final Hour, The 62 Robert Douglas
Final Judgment, The 15 Edwin Carewe
Final Justice 85 Greydon Clark
Final Lie, The 57 Michael Cacoyannis
Final Mission 86 Cirio Santiago
Final Option, The 82 Ian Sharp
Final Pardon, The 12 Edwin S. Porter
Final Payment, The 17 Frank Powell
Final Problem, The 23 George Ridgwell
Final Programme, The 73 Robert Fuest
Final Reckoning, The 32 John Argyle
Final Settlement, The 10 D. W. Griffith
Final Shot, The 70 Sergio Sollima
Final Take 86 Yoji Yamada
Final Take: The Golden Age of Movies 86 Yoji Yamada
Final Take: The Golden Days of Movies 86 Yoji Yamada
Final Terror, The 81 Andrew Davis
Final Test, The 52 Anthony Asquith
Final Test, The 87 Kin Lo
Final Verdict, The 14 Raoul Walsh
Final War, The 60 Shigeaki Hidaka
Final War, The 62 Shue Matsubayashi
Finally Sunday! 82 François Truffaut
Finalmente...Le Mille e Una Notte 72 Antonio Margheriti
Finances of the Grand Duke, The 23 F. W. Murnau
Finanzen des Grossherzogs, Die 23 F. W. Murnau
Finanzen des Grossherzogs, Die 34 Gustaf Gründgens
Finchè C'È Guerra C'È Speranza 74 Alberto Sordi
Finchè Dura la Tempesta 62 Charles

Frend, Bruno Vailati
Fincho 65 Sam Zebba
Find a Place to Die 68 Giuliano Carmineo
Find, Fix and Strike 41 Compton Bennett
Find the Blackmailer 43 D. Ross Lederman
Find the Lady 36 Roland Gillett
Find the Lady 56 Charles Saunders
Find the Lady 76 John Trent
Find the Witness 37 David Selman
Find the Woman 18 Tom Terriss
Find the Woman 22 Tom Terriss
Find the Woman 26 Geoffrey H. Malins, H. B. Parkinson
Find Your Man 24 Malcolm St. Clair
Finders Keepers 21 Otis B. Thayer
Finders Keepers 28 Wesley Ruggles
Finders Keepers 51 Frederick De Cordova
Finders Keepers 66 Sidney Hayers
Finders Keepers 84 Richard Lester
Finders Keepers, Lovers Weepers! 68 Russ Meyer
Findhord 76 Peter Werner
Finding His Voice 29 Max Fleischer*
Finding Mary March 88 Ken Pittman
Finding the Lost World 26 Luis Seel
Findling, Der 67 George Moorse
Fine and Dandy 50 Roy Del Ruth
Fine Clothes 25 John M. Stahl
Fine Feathered Friend 42 Joseph Barbera, William Hanna
Fine Feathers 12 Edwin S. Porter
Fine Feathers 15 Maurice Elvey
Fine Feathers 21 Fred Sittenham
Fine Feathers 26 Roy Del Ruth
Fine Feathers 37 Leslie Hiscott
Fine Feathers, The 41 Andrew Buchanan
Fine Feathers Make Fine Birds 05 Percy Stow
Fine Feathers Make Fine Friends 05 Percy Stow
Fine Madness, A 66 Irvin Kershner
Fine Manners 26 Richard Rosson
Fine Mess, A 86 Blake Edwards
Fine Pair, A 68 Francesco Maselli
Fine Points 33 George Marshall
Fine Snow 83 Kon Ichikawa
Fine Weather, But Storms Due Towards Evening 86 Gérard Frot-Coutaz
Fine Windy Days 80 Chang-ho Lee
Finer Things, The 13 Allan Dwan
Finest Hours, The 64 Peter Baylis
Finestra sul Luna Park, La 56 Luigi Comencini
Finestre 50 Francesco Maselli
Finestre, Il 62 Gianfranco Mingozzi
Fingal's Cave 46 Slavko Vorkapich
Finger Man 55 Harold Schuster
Finger Man, The 62 Jean-Pierre Melville
Finger of Destiny, The 14 Charles Raymond
Finger of Fate, The 11 Wilfred Noy
Finger of Guilt 55 Joseph Losey
Finger of Suspicion, The 16 Ethyle Batley
Finger on the Trigger 65 Rudolf Zehetgruber
Finger Points, The 31 John Francis Dillon
Finger Prints 23 Joseph Levering
Finger Prints 26 Lloyd Bacon
Fingerprints 31 Ray Taylor

Fingerprints Don't Lie 51 Sam Newfield
Fingers 40 Herbert Mason
Fingers 77 James Toback
Fingers at the Window 42 Charles Lederer
Finian's Rainbow 68 Francis Ford Coppola
Finie la Crise 34 Robert Siodmak
Finis Hominis 70 José Mojica Marins
Finis Terrae 29 Jean Epstein
Finish of Bridget McKeen, The 01 Edwin S. Porter
Finish of Michael Casey, or Blasting Rocks in Harlem, The 01 Edwin S. Porter
Finished 23 George A. Cooper
Finished Actor, A 27 Mack Sennett
Finishing School 34 George Nicholls, Jr., Wanda Tuchock
Finishing School 52 Bernard Vorhaus
Finishing Touch, The 28 Clyde Bruckman, Leo McCarey
Finishing Touch, The 32 George Stevens
Finn and Hattie 30 Norman Z. McLeod, Norman Taurog
Finnegan's Ball 27 James P. Hogan
Finnegan's Chin 83 Malcolm Le Grice
Finnegans Wake 65 Mary Ellen Bute
Finney 69 Bill Hare
Fino a Farti Male 69 Jean-Daniel Simon
Finyé 82 Souleymane Cissé
Fiole Enchantée, La 02 Alice Guy-Blaché
Fior d'Amore 20 Mario Caserini
Fior di Male 15 Carmine Gallone
Fiore delle Mille e Una Notte, Il 74 Pier Paolo Pasolini
Fiori, I 52 Francesco Maselli
Fiori di Zucca 88 Stefano Pomilia
Fioriture 15 Abel Gance
Fioritures ou La Source de Beauté 15 Abel Gance
Fire! 01 James A. Williamson
Fire 26 William Nigh
Fire 30 Mark Donskoi
Fire 48 Raj Kapoor
Fire 61 Ebrahim Golestan
Fire 68 Gian Vittorio Baldi
Fire Alarm 32 Karl Brown
Fire Alarm, The 36 Jack King
Fire and Flames at Luna Park 04 Edwin S. Porter
Fire and Ice 63 Alain Cavalier
Fire and Ice 82 Ralph Bakshi
Fire and Ice 87 Willy Bogner
Fire and Steel 27 Bertram Bracken
Fire and Sword 14 T. Hayes Hunter
Fire and Sword 82 Veith von Fürstenberg
Fire at Will 64 Marcel Ophüls
Fire Away 25 Stephen Roberts
Fire Barrier 26 William Wyler
Fire Bird, The 52 Hasse Ekman
Fire Bride, The 22 Arthur Rosson
Fire Brigade, The 26 William Nigh
Fire Bugs 30 Dave Fleischer
Fire Cat, The 21 Norman Dawn
Fire Cheese 41 Dave Fleischer
Fire Detective, The 29 Spencer G. Bennet
Fire Djævele, De 11 Robert Dinesen
Fire Down Below 57 Robert Parrish
Fire Eater, The 21 B. Reeves Eason
Fire Festival 85 Mitsuo Yanagimachi
Fire Fighters, The 30 Burton Gillett
Fire Fighters 38 Joseph Kane

Fire! Fire! *32* Ubbe Iwerks
Fire! Fire! *67* Miloš Forman
Fire Flingers, The *19* Rupert Julian
Fire Has Been Arranged, A *35* Leslie Hiscott
Fire in Eden *86* Tara Hawkins Moore
Fire in the Flesh *64* Alfred Rodé
Fire in the Night *86* John Steven Soet
Fire in the Opera House *30* Carl Fröhlich
Fire in the Stone, The *83* Gary Conway
Fire in the Straw *39* Jean Benoît-Lévy
Fire Maidens from Outer Space *55* Cy Roth
Fire Maidens of Outer Space *55* Cy Roth
Fire Monster, The *59* Hugo Grimaldi, Motoyoshi Odo
Fire of a Thousand Suns, The *64* Pierre Kast
Fire of Life, The *11* Edward Schnedler-Sørensen
Fire of Waters *65* Stan Brakhage
Fire on Board *22* Victor Sjöström
Fire Over Africa *54* Richard Sale
Fire Over England *36* William K. Howard
Fire Over the Women's Castle *87* Hideo Gosha
Fire Patrol, The *24* Hunt Stromberg
Fire Plug, The *37* Art Davis, Sid Marcus
Fire Proof *29* Charles Lamont
Fire Raisers, The *33* Michael Powell
Fire Sale *77* Alan Arkin
Fire Under Her Skin *54* Marcel Blistène
Fire with Fire *86* Duncan Gibbins
Fire Within, The *63* Louis Malle
Fireball, The *50* Tay Garnett
Fireball 500 *66* William Asher
Fireball Jungle *68* Joseph Prieto
Firebird, The *34* William Dieterle
Firebird *78* Kon Ichikawa
Firebird 2015 A.D. *81* David Robertson
Firebirds *90* David Green
Firebrand, The *18* Edmund Lawrence
Firebrand, The *22* Alvin J. Neitz
Firebrand, The *62* Maury Dexter
Firebrand Johnson *30* Alvin J. Neitz
Firebrand Jordan *30* Alvin J. Neitz
Firebrand Trevision *20* Thomas Heffron
Firebrands of Arizona *44* Lesley Selander
Firebugs, The *13* Mack Sennett
Firechasers, The *70* Sidney Hayers
Firecracker *81* Cirio Santiago
Firecreek *68* Vincent McEveety
Fired Wife *43* Charles Lamont
Firefall, The *04* Georges Méliès
Firefight *63* Steven Spielberg
Firefighters, The *75* Jonathan Ingrams
Firefighters: Bringing Out the Pump, Getting Ready, Attacking the Fire, the Rescue *1895* Louis Lumière
Fireflies, The *58* Heinosuke Gosho
Fireflies of the North *85* Hideo Gosha
Firefly, The *37* Robert Z. Leonard
Firefly *89* Koichi Kajima
Firefly Light *58* Heinosuke Gosho
Firefly of France, The *18* Donald Crisp
Firefly of Tough Luck *17* E. Mason Hopper
Firefox *82* Clint Eastwood
Firehouse *87* J. Christian Ingvordsen
Firehouse Honeymoon, A *32* George

Marshall
Firelight *66* John Carpenter
Fireman, The *07* Arthur Gilbert
Fireman, The *16* Charles Chaplin
Fireman, The *31* Walter Lantz
Fireman, The *85* Neri Parenti
Fireman E. A. Winterstein *68* Alexander Kluge
Fireman Save My Child *18* Hal Roach
Fireman Save My Child *19* Raoul Barré, Charles Bowers
Fireman Save My Child *27* A. Edward Sutherland
Fireman Save My Child *32* Lloyd Bacon
Fireman Save My Child *54* Leslie Goodwins
Fireman's Ball, The *67* Miloš Forman
Fireman's Daughter, The *08* Charles Raymond
Fireman's Daughter, The *11* Lewin Fitzhamon
Fireman's Picnic *37* Walter Lantz
Fireman's Snapshot, The *1899* Arthur Cooper
Fireman's Song, The *06* Arthur Gilbert
Fireman's Story, A *05* Frank Mottershaw
Fireman's Wedding, The *10* Charles Raymond
Firemen on Parade *1897* Georges Méliès
Firemen to the Rescue *03* Cecil M. Hepworth
Firepower *79* Michael Winner
Fires of Baku *50* Josef Heifits, R. Takhmasib, Alexander Zarkhi
Fires of Conscience *14* Wallace Reid
Fires of Conscience, The *16* Oscar Apfel
Fires of Faith *19* Edward José
Fires of Fate *13* Wallace Reid, Willis Robards
Fires of Fate *23* Tom Terriss
Fires of Fate *32* Norman Walker
Fires of Innocence *22* Sidney Morgan
Fires of Rebellion *17* Ida May Park
Fires of Youth, The *17* Émile Chautard
Fires of Youth *18* Rupert Julian
Fires of Youth, The *31* Monta Bell
Fires on the Plain *59* Kon Ichikawa
Fires Were Started *43* Humphrey Jennings
Fireside Reminiscences *08* Edwin S. Porter
Firestarter *84* Mark L. Lester
Firetrap, The *35* Burt Lynwood
Firewalker *86* J. Lee-Thompson
Fireworks *47* Kenneth Anger
Fireworks *87* Leslie Stevens
Fireworks Over the Sea *51* Keisuke Kinoshita
Firing Line, The *19* Charles Maigne
Firm Friends *54* Mikhail Kalatozov
Firm Man, The *75* John Duigan
Firm of Girdlestone, The *15* Harold M. Shaw
First a Girl *35* Victor Saville
First Aid *31* Stuart Paton
First Aid Flirtations *11* Percy Stow
First and the Last, The *37* Basil Dean
First Auto, The *27* Roy Del Ruth
First Baby, The *36* Lewis Seiler
First Bad Man, The *55* Tex Avery
First Blood *82* Ted Kotcheff
First Born, The *21* Colin Campbell

First Born, The *28* Miles Mander
First Charge of the Machete *69* Manuel Octavio Gómez
First Chronicles of Don Q – The Dark Brothers of the Civil Guard, The *12* H. Oceano Martinek
First Circle, The *72* Aleksander Ford
First Comes Courage *43* Dorothy Arzner
First Communion *50* Alessandro Blasetti
First Cornet Streshnev *28* Mikhail Chiaureli, Yefim Dzigan
First Date *89* Peter Wang
First Day, The *58* Friedrich Ermler
First Day of Freedom, The *64* Aleksander Ford
First Day of Peace, The *61* Yakov Segel
First Day on the Spot *43* Francis Searle
First Days, The *39* Pat Jackson, Humphrey Jennings, Harry Watt
First Days *51* Jan Rybkowski
First Deadly Sin, The *80* Brian G. Hutton
First Degree, The *23* Edward Sedgwick
First Delegate, The *75* Santiago Álvarez
First Division *41* Hasse Ekman
First Echelon, The *55* Mikhail Kalatozov
First Family *80* Buck Henry
First Flyer, The *18* L. M. Glackens
First Front, The *49* Vladimir Petrov
First Gentleman, The *47* Alberto Cavalcanti
First Great Train Robbery, The *78* Michael Crichton
First Hello, The *80* Harvey Hart
First Hundred Years, The *38* Richard Thorpe
First Kiss, The *28* Rowland V. Lee
First Kiss, The *55* Mikio Naruse*
First Lad, The *58* Sergei Paradzhanov
First Lady *37* Stanley Logan
First Law, The *18* Lawrence McGill
First Left Past Aden *61* Compton Bennett
First Legion, The *50* Douglas Sirk
First Lesson *59* Vladimir Petrov, Rangel Vulchanov
First Line of Defence *47* Joy Batchelor, John Halas
First Love *21* Maurice Campbell
First Love *25* Heinosuke Gosho
First Love *38* S. Innemann
First Love *39* Henry Koster
First Love *50* Minoru Shibuya
First Love *58* Mario Camerini
First Love *70* Maximilian Schell
First Love *77* Joan Darling
First Love *78* Dino Risi
First Man Into Space *58* Robert Day
First Man to the Moon, The *20* Dave Fleischer
First Marines *50* Will Price
First Marriage *80* Josef Heifits
First Mass, The *61* Lima Barreto
First Men in the Moon, The *19* J. L. V. Leigh
First Men in the Moon *64* Nathan Juran
First Monday in October *81* Ronald Neame
First Mrs. Fraser, The *32* Sinclair Hill
First Name: Carmen *82* Jean-Luc Godard
First Night, The *27* Richard Thorpe
First Night *37* Donovan Pedelty

First Night, The 58 Georges Franju

First Ninety-Nine, The 58 Joy Batchelor

First Notch, The 77 Gil Ward

First Nudie Musical, The 76 Mark Haggard, Bruce Kimmel

First of the Few, The 42 Leslie Howard

First Offence 36 Herbert Mason

First Offenders 39 Frank McDonald

First on the Road 60 Joseph Losey

First 100 Years, The 24 F. Richard Jones

First Opera Film Festival 48 E. Cancellieri

First Position 73 William Richert

First Power, The 90 Robert Resnikoff

First Prize 27 Mark Sandrich

First Rebel, The 39 William A. Seiter

First Rescue Party, The 59 Otakar Vávra

First Season, The 89 Ralph L. Thomas

First Shrine, The 26 Daisuke Ito

First Son 84 Doo-yong Lee

First Spaceship on Venus 60 Kurt Mätzig

First Start, The 51 Leonard Buczkowski

First Steeplechase, The 13 Lewin Fitzhamon

First Steps, The 62 Kazimierz Karabasz

First Steps Ashore 32 Yasujiro Shimazu

First Taste of Love 62 Henry Zaphiratos

First Teacher, The 65 Andrei Mikhalkov-Konchalovsky

First Texan, The 56 Byron Haskin

First Time, The 51 Herbert Kline

First Time, The 51 Frank Tashlin

First Time, The 68 James Neilson

First Time, The 76 Claude Berri

First Time, The 83 Charles Loventhal

First Time 'Round 72 J. Brian

First to Fight 67 Christian Nyby

First Traveling Saleslady, The 56 Arthur Lubin

First Trip to the Stars 61 Ilya Kopalin

First Turn-On, The 84 Michael Herz, Lloyd Kaufman

First Waltz, The 78 Doris Dörrie

First Wife 63 John Rich

First Woman, The 22 Glen Lyons

First Woman Into Space 65 Leonard Katzman

First World War, The 34 Louis De Rochemont III

First Yank Into Tokyo 45 Gordon Douglas

First Year, The 26 Frank Borzage

First Year, The 32 William K. Howard

First Year, The 70 Patricio Guzmán

First Year of the Meiji Era, The 32 Daisuke Ito

First Years, The 47 Joris Ivens

Firstborn 84 Michael Apted

Fischio al Naso, Il 67 Ugo Tognazzi

Fischke der Drume 39 Edgar G. Ulmer

Fischke the Cripple 39 Edgar G. Ulmer

Fischke the Lame 39 Edgar G. Ulmer

Fischke the Lame One 39 Edgar G. Ulmer

Fish, The 21 Dave Fleischer

Fish 36 William McGann

Fish and Milligan 66 Christopher Mason

Fish and Slips 62 Robert McKimson

Fish and the Ring, The 13 R. H. Callum, F. Martin Thornton

Fish Called Wanda, A 88 Charles Crichton

Fish Hawk 80 Donald Shebib

Fish Out of Water 76 Derek Burbidge

Fish Story, A 20 Gregory La Cava

Fish Tales 36 Jack King

Fish That Saved Pittsburgh, The 79 Gilbert Moses

Fishe da Krin 39 Edgar G. Ulmer

Fisher Folks 11 D. W. Griffith

Fisher Maid, The 11 Thomas Ince

Fishergirl of Cornwall, The 12 Sidney Northcote

Fishergirl's Folly, A 13 George Pearson

Fishergirl's Love, A 13 Edwin J. Collins

Fisherless Cartoon, A 18 Raoul Barré, Charles Bowers

Fisherman, The 31 Walter Lantz

Fisherman of Bally David, The 11 Sidney Olcott

Fisherman's Daughter, The 11 Theo Bouwmeester

Fisherman's Infatuation, A 12 J. Wallett Waller

Fisherman's Infatuation, A 15 J. Wallett Waller

Fisherman's Love Story, A 12 Lewin Fitzhamon

Fisherman's Luck 00 Jack Smith

Fisherman's Luck 13 Bert Haldane

Fisherman's Luck 16 John R. Bray

Fisherman's Luck 18 Gregory La Cava

Fisherman's Luck 20 Raoul Barré, Charles Bowers

Fisherman's Perfect Day, The 21 Neville Bruce

Fisherman's Wharf 39 Bernard Vorhaus

Fishermen 57 Vittorio De Seta

Fishin' Around 31 Burton Gillett

Fishing 20 Raoul Barré, Charles Bowers

Fishing 21 Dave Fleischer

Fishing Banks of Skye, The 33 John Grierson

Fishing Boat, The 56 Kaneto Shindo

Fishing for Goldfish 1895 Louis Lumière

Fishing Grounds of the World 47 Lewis Gilbert

Fishing Village, The 19 Mauritz Stiller

Fishmonger's Apprentice, The 13 F. Martin Thornton

Fishy Affair, A 13 Mack Sennett

Fishy Story, A 13 Edwin J. Collins

Fishy Tales 37 Gordon Douglas

Fiske Torpedo Plane 17 J. D. Leventhal

Fiskebyn 19 Mauritz Stiller

Fist Fight 64 Robert Breer

Fist Fighter 89 Frank Zuniga

Fist in His Pocket 65 Marco Bellocchio

Fist of Fear, Touch of Death 80 Matthew Mallinson

Fist-Right of Freedom 74 Rainer Werner Fassbinder

Fistful of Chopsticks, A 82 Elliot Hong

Fistful of Dollars, A 64 Sergio Leone

Fistful of Dynamite, A 71 Sergio Leone

Fistful of Rawhide 70 W. G. Beggs

Fistic Mystic, The 69 Robert McKimson

Fisticuffs 38 David Miller

Fists in the Pocket 65 Marco Bellocchio

Fists of Fury 72 Wei Lo

Fists of Steel 89 Jerry Schafer

Fit for a King 37 Edward Sedgwick

Fit to Be Tied 52 Joseph Barbera, William Hanna

Fit to Be Untied 74 Silvano Agosti, Marco Bellocchio, Sandro Petraglia, Stefano Rulli

Fit to Fight 18 Edward H. Griffith

Fit to Win 19 Edward H. Griffith

Fits and Misfits 10 Lewin Fitzhamon

Fitting Gift, A 20 Gregory La Cava

Fitzcarraldo 82 Werner Herzog

Fitznoodle's Hunt for Wealth 14 Charles C. Calvert

Fitznoodle's Wooing 11 Frank Wilson

Fitzwilly 67 Delbert Mann

Fitzwilly Strikes Back 67 Delbert Mann

Fiume del Grande Caimano, Il 79 Sergio Martino

Fiume della Rivolta, Il 64 Tinto Brass

Fiume di Dollari, Un 66 Carlo Lizzani

Fiume Giallo, Il 58 Carlo Lizzani

Five 51 Arch Oboler

Five, The 70 Joy Batchelor

Five Acres of Land 69 Lester James Peries

Five Against the House 55 Phil Karlson

Five and Dime 33 Walter Lantz

Five and Ten 31 Jack Conway, Robert Z. Leonard

Five and Ten Cent Annie 28 Roy Del Ruth

Five Angles on Murder 50 Anthony Asquith

Five Angry Women 75 Kent Osborne

Five Ashore in Singapore 68 Bernard Toublanc-Michel

Five Bad Men 35 Clifford Smith

Five Bloody Days to Tombstone 69 Al Adamson

Five Bloody Graves 69 Al Adamson

Five Bold Women 59 Jorge López-Portillo

Five Boys from Barska Street 53 Aleksander Ford

Five Boys of Barska Street 53 Aleksander Ford

Five Branded Women 59 Martin Ritt

Five Brides, Then a Sweetheart 87 Leila Gordeladze

Five Brothers and Sisters 39 Kozaburo Yoshimura

Five Came Back 39 John Farrow

Five Card Stud 68 Henry Hathaway

Five Cent Trolley Ride, A 05 Edwin S. Porter

Five Clues to Fortune 57 Joe Mendoza

Five Copies 13 August Blom

Five Corners 87 Tony Bill

Five Day Lover, The 61 Philippe de Broca

Five Days 54 Montgomery Tully

Five Days, Five Nights 61 Lev Arnshtam

Five Days from Home 77 George Peppard

Five Days Home 72 Richard Compton

Five Days in June 89 Michel Legrand

Five Days One Summer 82 Fred Zinnemann

Five Days to Live 22 Norman Dawn

Five Dollar Baby, The 22 Harry Beaumont

Five Dolls for an August Moon 70 Mario Bava

Five Easy Pieces 70 Bob Rafelson

Five Evenings 78 Nikita Mikhalkov

Five Faults of Flo, The 16 George Foster Platt

Five Finger Exercise *62* Daniel Mann
Five Fingers *52* Joseph L. Mankiewicz
Five Fingers of Death *62* Gene Nelson
Five Fingers of Death *73* Cheng Chang Ho
Five Fires *87* Hariharan
Five for Four *42* Norman McLaren
Five from Barska Street *53* Aleksander Ford
Five Gates to Hell *59* James Clavell
Five Giants from Texas *66* Aldo Florio
Five Girls and a Rope *90* Hung-wei Yeh
Five Girls Equals a Millstone Round One's Neck *66* Evald Schorm
Five Girls Like a Millstone Round One's Neck *66* Evald Schorm
Five Girls to Cope With *66* Evald Schorm
Five Golden Dragons *67* Jeremy Summers
Five Golden Hours *61* Mario Zampi
Five Graves for a Medium *66* Massimo Pupillo
Five Graves to Cairo *43* Billy Wilder
Five Guineas a Week *56* Donald Monat
Five Guns to Tombstone *61* Edward L. Cahn
Five Guns West *54* Roger Corman
Five Have a Mystery to Solve *64* Ernest Morris
Five Hours *11* Edwin S. Porter
500 Hats of Bartholomew Cubbins, The *43* George Pal
500 Miles on a Gallon of Gas *19* Raoul Barré, Charles Bowers
504 et les Foudroyers, La *74* Lam Ibrahim Dia, Jean Rouch, Damouré Zika
$500,000 Reward *11* Mack Sennett
Five Last Days *82* Percy Adlon
Five Little Peppers and How They Grew *39* Charles Barton
Five Little Peppers at Home *40* Charles Barton
Five Little Peppers in Trouble *40* Charles Barton
Five Little Widows *17* Al Christie
Five Man Army, The *69* Don Taylor
Five Men in the Circus *35* Mikio Naruse
Five Men of Edo *51* Daisuke Ito
Five Miles to Midnight *62* Anatole Litvak
$5,000,000 Counterfeiting Plot, The *14* Bertram Harrison
Five Million Years to Earth *67* Roy Ward Baker
Five Millions Seek an Heir *38* Carl Boese
Five Minutes of Freedom *73* Ivan Nagy
Five Minutes to Live *61* Bill Karn
Five Minutes to Love *63* John Hayes
Five Nerds Take Las Vegas *87* Alfredo B. Crevenna
Five Nights *15* Bert Haldane
Five O'Clock Finish *54* John Irwin
Five O'Clock Girl, The *29* Alfred E. Green
Five of a Kind *38* Herbert I. Leeds
Five of the Jazzband *32* Erich Engel
Five on a Treasure Island *57* Gerald Landau
Five on the Black Hand Side *73* Oscar Williams
Five Pennies, The *59* Melville Shavelson
Five Postcards from Capital Cities *67* Peter Greenaway

£5 Man, The *37* Albert Parker
Five Pound Note, The *10* A. E. Coleby
Five Pounds Reward *13* Stuart Kinder
Five Pounds Reward *20* Adrian Brunel
Five Savage Men *70* Ron Joy
Five Scouts *38* Tomotaka Tasaka
Five Sinister Stories *19* Richard Oswald
Five Sinners *61* Wolfgang Glück
5 Squadron *39* Abram Room
Five Star Final *31* Mervyn LeRoy
Five Steps to Danger *56* Henry S. Kesler
Five-Storied Pagoda, The *44* Heinosuke Gosho
Five the Hard Way *69* Gus Trikonis
5-30 Collection, The *07* Arthur Cooper
Five Thousand an Hour *18* Ralph Ince
5000 Dollar für den Kopf von Johnny R *65* José Luis Madrid
$5,000 Reward *18* Douglas Gerrard
Five Thousand Dollar Reward *28* Eugene Forde
$5,000 Reward, Dead or Alive *11* Allan Dwan
5,000 Fingers of Dr. T, The *52* Roy Rowland
Five to One *63* Gordon Flemyng
Five Towns *47* Terry Bishop
Five Ways to Kill Yourself *87* Gus Van Sant, Jr.
Five Weeks in a Balloon *62* Irwin Allen
Five Wild Girls *66* Max Pecas
Five Wild Kids *66* Max Pecas
Five Wishes, The *16* Wilfred Noy
Five Women Around Utamaro *46* Kenji Mizoguchi
Five Year Plan, The *30* Abram Room
Five Years of Struggle and Victory *23* Dziga Vertov
Fix, The *85* Will Zens
Fixation *67* Bob Clark
Fixed Bayonets! *51* Samuel Fuller
Fixed by George *20* Eddie Lyons, Lee Moran
Fixer, The *29* Charles Lamont
Fixer, The *68* John Frankenheimer
Fixer Dugan *39* Lew Landers
Fixer-Uppers, The *35* Charles Rogers
Fixing the Swing *04* Alf Collins
Fizessen Nagység *37* Ákos von Ráthonyi
14 Dage i Jernalderen *77* Jørgen Roos
Flăcări pe Comori *88* Nicolae Mărgineanu
Flag *88* Jacques Santi
Flag Lieutenant, The *19* Percy Nash
Flag Lieutenant, The *25* Maurice Elvey
Flag Lieutenant, The *32* Henry Edwards
Flag of Humanity, The *40* Jean Negulesco
Flag Speaks, The *40* David Miller
Flagrant Désir *86* Claude Faraldo
Flagrant Desire *86* Claude Faraldo
Flags of Dawn, The *84* Jorge Sanjinés
Flambeau au Pays des Surprises *16* Émile Cohl*
Flambeau aux Lignes *16* Émile Cohl*
Flambeau, Chien Perdu *16* Émile Cohl*
Flambée, La *16* Henri Pouctal
Flambée de Rêves, La *24* Jacques De Baroncelli
Flamberede Hjerter *86* Helle Ryslinge
Flambierte Frau, Die *82* Robert Van Ackeren

Flamboyant Sex, The *63* Barbro Roman
Flame, The *20* F. Martin Thornton
Flame, The *47* John H. Auer
Flame *74* Richard Loncraine
Flame and the Arrow, The *50* Jacques Tourneur
Flame and the Fire *65* Pierre-Dominique Gaisseau
Flame and the Flesh *54* Richard Brooks
Flame Barrier, The *58* Paul Landres
Flame in My Heart, A *87* Alain Tanner
Flame in the Heather *35* Donovan Pedelty
Flame in the Streets *61* Roy Ward Baker
Flame of Araby *51* Charles Lamont
Flame of Calcutta *53* Seymour Friedman
Flame of Hellgate, The *20* George E. Middleton
Flame of Life, The *18* Mauritz Stiller
Flame of Life, The *23* Hobart Henley
Flame of Love, The *30* Richard Eichberg, Walter Summers
Flame of My Love *49* Kenji Mizoguchi
Flame of New Orleans, The *40* René Clair
Flame of Passion, The *15* Tom Terriss
Flame of Sacramento *46* Joseph Kane
Flame of Stamboul *51* Ray Nazarro
Flame of the Argentine *26* Edward Dillon
Flame of the Barbary Coast *45* Joseph Kane
Flame of the Desert *19* Reginald Barker
Flame of the Islands *55* Edward Ludwig
Flame of the West *45* Lambert Hillyer
Flame of the Yukon, The *17* Charles Miller, Roy William Neill
Flame of the Yukon, The *26* George Melford
Flame of Torment *58* Kon Ichikawa
Flame of Youth, The *17* Elmer Clifton
Flame of Youth *20* Howard Mitchell
Flame of Youth *49* R. G. Springsteen
Flame Over India *59* J. Lee-Thompson
Flame Over Vietnam *67* José María Elorrieta
Flame Top *80* Pirjo Honkasalo, Pekka Lehto
Flame Within, The *35* Edmund Goulding
Flamenca la Gitane *28* Henri Andréani
Flamenco *54* Edgar Neville
Flames *17* Maurice Elvey
Flames *26* Lewis H. Moomaw
Flames *32* Karl Brown
Flames in the Dark *42* Hasse Ekman
Flames of Chance, The *18* Raymond Wells
Flames of Desire *24* Denison Clift
Flames of Fear *30* Charles Barnett
Flames of Johannis, The *16* Edgar Lewis
Flames of Passion *22* Graham Cutts
Flames of Passion *23* Harry G. Moody
Flames of the Flesh *20* Edward J. LeSaint
Flames on the Volga *29* Yuri Tarich
Flames on the Volga *55* Grigori Roshal
Flames Over Baku *50* Josef Heifits, R. Takhmasib, Alexander Zarkhi
Flames Over the Adriatic *68* Alexandre Astruc
Flaming Arrow *11* Joris Ivens
Flaming Barriers *24* George Melford
Flaming Borders *86* Sahib Haddad
Flaming Bullets *45* Harry Fraser

Flaming Clue, The *20* Edwin L. Hollywood
Flaming Desire *62* Norman C. Chaitin
Flaming Disc, The *20* Robert F. Hill
Flaming Feather *51* Ray Enright
Flaming Forest, The *26* Reginald Barker
Flaming Forties, The *24* George Archainbaud, Tom Forman
Flaming Frontier, The *26* Edward Sedgwick
Flaming Frontier *45* Lambert Hillyer
Flaming Frontier *58* Sam Newfield
Flaming Frontier *65* Alfred Vohrer
Flaming Frontiers *38* Alvin J. Neitz, Ray Taylor
Flaming Fury *26* James P. Hogan
Flaming Fury *49* George Blair
Flaming Gold *33* Ralph Ince
Flaming Guns *32* Arthur Rosson
Flaming Hearts *22* Clifford S. Elfelt
Flaming Hearts *86* Helle Ryslinge
Flaming Hour, The *22* Edward Sedgwick
Flaming Lead *39* Sam Newfield
Flaming Love *25* J. K. McDonald
Flaming Omen, The *17* William Wolbert
Flaming Passion *23* Jack Conway
Flaming Romance *26* Stephen Roberts
Flaming Signal *33* George Jeske, Charles E. Roberts
Flaming Star *60* Don Siegel
Flaming Sword, The *15* August Blom
Flaming Teen-Age, The *56* Charles Edwards, Irvin S. Yeaworth, Jr.
Flaming Torch, The *54* Francis D. Lyon
Flaming Waters *25* F. Harmon Weight
Flaming Years, The *61* Yulia Solntseva
Flaming Youth *23* John Francis Dillon
Flamingo Affair, The *48* Horace Shepherd
Flamingo Kid, The *84* Garry Marshall
Flamingo Road *49* Michael Curtiz
Flamme, Die *22* Ernst Lubitsch
Flamme, La *25* René Hervil
Flamme, La *36* André Berthomieu
Flamme Blanche *28* Charles Dekeukeleire
Flamme Cache, La *18* Roger Lion, Musidora
Flamme dans Mon Cœur, Une *87* Alain Tanner
Flamme Merveilleuse, La *03* Georges Méliès
Flammes Sur l'Adriatique *68* Alexandre Astruc
Flammesværdet *15* August Blom
Flanagan *85* Scott Goldstein
Flanagan Boy, The *51* Reginald LeBorg
Flannelfoot *53* Maclean Rogers
Flap *70* Carol Reed
Flapjacks *20* Raoul Barré, Charles Bowers
Flapper, The *20* Alan Crosland
Flapper and the Curates, The *12* Lewin Fitzhamon
Flapper Wives *24* Justin H. McCloskey, Jane Murfin
Flappers and the Colonel, The *13* Lewin Fitzhamon
Flappers and the Nuts, The *13* Lewin Fitzhamon
Flapper's Elopement, The *12* Lewin Fitzhamon
Flare-Up Sal *18* Roy William Neill

Flareup *69* James Neilson
Flash, The *23* William James Craft
Flash *86* Doron Eran
Flash and the Firecat *75* Beverly Sebastian, Ferd Sebastian
Flash Gordon *36* Frederick Stephani
Flash Gordon *36* Frederick Stephani
Flash Gordon *80* Michael Hodges
Flash Gordon Conquers the Universe *40* Ford Beebe, Ray Taylor
Flash Gordon: Mars Attacks the World *38* Ford Beebe, Robert F. Hill
Flash Gordon's Trip to Mars *38* Ford Beebe, Robert F. Hill
Flash in the Dark, A *14* Wallace Reid
Flash of an Emerald, The *15* Albert Capellani
Flash of Fate, The *18* Elmer Clifton
Flash of Green, A *84* Victor Nuñez
Flash of Light, A *10* D. W. Griffith
Flash of Lightning, A *13* Charles Raymond
Flash O'Lightning *25* Leo D. Maloney
Flash Pimple the Master Crook *15* Fred Evans, Joe Evans
Flash the Sheepdog *67* Laurence Henson
Flashback *90* Franco Amurri
Flashbacks *38* R. E. Jeffrey
Flashdance *83* Adrian Lyne
Flashdance Fever *83* Alan Roberts
Flashing Fangs *26* Henry McCarthy
Flashing Guns *47* Lambert Hillyer
Flashing Spurs *24* B. Reeves Eason
Flashing Steeds *25* Horace B. Carpenter
Flashlight, The *17* Ida May Park
Flashpoint *72* Brian Hannant
Flashpoint *84* William Tannen
Flat, The *21* Fred Paul
Flat, The *68* Jan Švankmajer
Flat Charleston, The *26* Dudley Ponting
Flat Foot Stooges *38* Charlie Chase
Flat Hatting *46* John Hubley
Flat Hunting *20* Wallace A. Carlson
Flat No. 3 *33* Leslie Hiscott
Flat No. 9 *32* Frank Richardson
Flat Top *52* Lesley Selander
Flat 2 *62* Alan Cooke
Flatfoot *74* Steno
Flatfoot on the Nile *78* Steno
Flatliners *90* Joel Schumacher
Flattery *25* Tom Forman
Flavia la Monaca Musulmana *74* Gianfranco Mingozzi
Flavia la Nonne Musulmane *74* Gianfranco Mingozzi
Flavia, Priestess of Violence *74* Gianfranco Mingozzi
Flavor of Green Tea Over Rice, The *52* Yasujiro Ozu
Flaw, The *33* Norman Walker
Flaw, The *55* Terence Fisher
Flaxfield, The *84* Jan Gruyaert
Flaxy Martin *49* Richard L. Bare
Flea Circus, The *54* Tex Avery
Flea in Her Ear, A *68* Jacques Charon
Flebus *57* Ernest Pintoff
Flecha Envenenada, La *57* Rafael Baledón
Flèche d'Argent *38* René Clément
Fledermaus, Die *31* Karel Lamač
Fledermaus, Die *48* Géza von Bolváry
Fledermaus, Die *64* Géza von Cziffra

Fledermaus '55 *55* Michael Powell, Emeric Pressburger
Fledglings *65* Norman Thaddeus Vane
Fleet That Came to Stay, The *45* Budd Boetticher
Fleet's In, The *28* Malcolm St. Clair
Fleet's In, The *42* Victor Schertzinger, Hal Walker
Fleets of Stren'th *42* Dave Fleischer
Fleetwing *28* Lambert Hillyer
Fleming Faloon *63* George Landow
Flemish Farm, The *43* Jeffrey Dell
Flesh *31* John Ford
Flesh *68* Paul Morrissey
Flesh and Blood *12* Alice Guy-Blaché
Flesh and Blood *22* Irving Cummings
Flesh and Blood *49* Anthony Kimmins
Flesh + Blood *85* Paul Verhoeven
Flesh and Blood Show, The *72* Peter Walker
Flesh and Desire *55* Jean Josipovici
Flesh and Fantasy *43* Julien Duvivier
Flesh and Flame *58* Hugo Haas
Flesh and Fury *51* Joseph Pevney
Flesh and Lace *65* Joe Sarno
Flesh and Spirit *22* Joseph Levering
Flesh and the Devil *26* Clarence Brown
Flesh and the Fiends, The *59* John Gilling
Flesh and the Spur *56* Edward L. Cahn
Flesh and the Woman *53* Robert Siodmak
Flesh and Woman *53* Robert Siodmak
Flesh Creatures, The *70* Al Adamson, George Joseph
Flesh Creatures of the Red Planet *70* Al Adamson, George Joseph
Flesh Eaters, The *64* Jack Curtis
Flesh Feast *70* Brad F. Ginter
Flesh for Frankenstein *73* Antonio Margheriti, Paul Morrissey
Flesh Gordon *74* Michael Benveniste, Howard Ziehm
Flesh Is Hot, The *61* Shohei Imamura
Flesh Is Weak, The *57* Don Chaffey
Flesh Is Weak, The *57* Ko Nakahira
Flesh Merchant, The *56* W. Merle Connell
Flesh of Morning *56* Stan Brakhage
Flesh of Your Flesh *84* Carlos Mayolo
Flesh Will Surrender *47* Alberto Lattuada
Fleshburn *84* George Gage
Fletch *84* Michael Ritchie
Fletch Lives *89* Michael Ritchie
Fleur d'Amour *27* Marcel Vandal
Fleur dans les Ronces, Une *21* Camille De Morlhon
Fleur de Fougère *50* Władysław Starewicz
Fleur de l'Âge, La *64* Gian Vittorio Baldi, Michel Brault, Jean Rouch, Hiroshi Teshigahara
Fleur de l'Âge ou Les Adolescentes, La *64* Gian Vittorio Baldi, Michel Brault, Jean Rouch, Hiroshi Teshigahara
Fleur de Paris *16* André Hugon
Fleur des Ruines, La *15* Abel Gance
Fleur d'Oseille *67* Georges Lautner
Fleur Sanglante, La *12* Alfred Machin
Fleurs du Miel, Les *76* Claude Faraldo
Fleurs du Soleil, Les *69* Vittorio De Sica
Fleurs Sauvages, Les *81* Jean-Pierre Lefèbvre
Fleuve, Le *52* Jean Mitry

Fleuve d'Argent, Le 56 Pierre Chénal
Flic, Un 72 Jean-Pierre Melville
Flic Story 75 Jacques Deray
Flick 67 Gilbert W. Taylor
Flicka och Hyacinter 50 Hasse Ekman
Flickan från Tredje Raden 49 Hasse Ekman
Flickan i Frack 56 Arne Mattsson
Flickan i Regnet 55 Alf Kjellin
Flickan och Djävulen 44 Erik Faustman
Flicker Fever 35 Mack Sennett
Flicker Flashbacks 43 Richard Fleischer
Flicker Flicker Little Star 20 Wallace A. Carlson
Flicker Memories 41 George Sidney
Flickers 40 Lawrence Huntington
Flickorna 68 Mai Zetterling
Flickorna från Gamla Stan 34 S. Bauman
Flicks 81 Peter Winograd
Fliegende Koffer, Der 21 Lotte Reiniger
Fliegenden Ärzte von Ostafrika, Die 68 Werner Herzog
Flieger, Der 87 Erwin Keusch
Fliehende Schatten 22 Gerhard Lamprecht
Fliehendes Pferd, Ein 86 Peter Beauvais
Flies, The 08 A. E. Coleby
Flies 22 Dave Fleischer
Flies Ain't Human 41 Dave Fleischer
Flight 29 Frank Capra
Flight, The 42 Albert Mertz, Jørgen Roos
Flight 60 Louis Bispo
Flight, The 71 Alexander Alov, Vladimir Naumov
Flight 74 Stan Brakhage
Flight Angels 40 Lewis Seiler
Flight at Midnight 39 Sidney Salkow
Flight Command 40 Frank Borzage
Flight Commander, The 27 Maurice Elvey
Flight Commander 30 Howard Hawks
Flight for Freedom 43 Lothar Mendes
Flight from Ashiya 63 Michael Anderson
Flight from Destiny 41 Vincent Sherman
Flight from Folly 44 Herbert Mason
Flight from Glory 37 Lew Landers
Flight from Justice 39 Nick Grindé
Flight from Life, The 19 Forest Holger-Madsen
Flight from Singapore 62 Dudley Birch
Flight from Terror 61 Leo McCarey
Flight from the Millions 33 Pál Fejös
Flight from Vienna 56 Denis Kavanagh
Flight Into Darkness 35 Anatole Litvak
Flight Into France 48 Mario Soldati
Flight Into Nowhere 38 Lewis D. Collins
Flight Lieutenant 42 Sidney Salkow
Flight North 86 Ingemo Engstrom
Flight Nurse 53 Allan Dwan
Flight of Mr. McKinley, The 65 Grigori Roshal
Flight of Pigeons 78 Shyam Benegal
Flight of Rainbirds, A 81 Ate de Jong
Flight of the Doves 71 Ralph Nelson
Flight of the Duchess, The 16 Eugene Nowland
Flight of the Eagle, The 78 Jan Troell
Flight of the King, The 22 George Ridgwell
Flight of the Lost Balloon 60 Nathan Juran
Flight of the Navigator 86 Randal Kleiser

Flight of the Phoenix, The 65 Robert Aldrich
Flight of the Sandpiper, The 65 Vincente Minnelli
Flight of the Spruce Goose, The 86 Lech Majewski
Flight of the White Stallions, The 62 Arthur Hiller
Flight of Wealth, The 13 Will P. Kellino
Flight That Disappeared, The 61 Reginald LeBorg
Flight That Failed, The 25 William C. Nolan
Flight That Failed, The 28 Hugh Shields
Flight That Vanished, The 61 Reginald LeBorg
Flight to Berlin 84 Christopher Petit
Flight to Fame 38 C. C. Coleman, Jr.
Flight to Fury 65 Monte Hellman
Flight to Hong Kong 56 Joseph M. Newman
Flight to Mars 51 Lesley Selander
Flight to Nowhere 46 William Rowland
Flight to Tangier 53 Charles Marquis Warren
Flight 222 86 Sergei Mikaelyan
Flim Flam Man, The 67 Yakima Canutt, Irvin Kershner
Flip Flops 23 Roy Del Ruth
Flipotte 20 Jacques De Baroncelli
Flipper 63 James B. Clark
Flipper and the Pirates 64 Leon Benson
Flipper's New Adventure 64 Leon Benson
Flip's Circus 21 Winsor McCay
Flip's Lunch Room 33 Ubbe Iwerks
Flirt, The 12 Edwin S. Porter
Flirt, The 16 Phillips Smalley, Lois Weber
Flirt, The 17 Hal Roach
Flirt, The 22 Hobart Henley
Flirtation at Sea, A 13 Charles Raymond
Flirtation Walk 34 Frank Borzage
Flirtations of Phyllis, The 21 Fred Paul, Jack Raymond
Flirting Husband, The 12 Mack Sennett
Flirting in the Park 33 George Stevens
Flirting Widow, The 30 William A. Seiter
Flirting with Danger 34 Vin Moore
Flirting with Death 17 Elmer Clifton
Flirting with Fate 16 Christy Cabanne
Flirting with Fate 38 Frank McDonald
Flirting with Love 24 John Francis Dillon
Flirting Wives 31 Norman Walker
Flirty Birdy 45 Joseph Barbera, William Hanna
Flirty Four-Flushers 26 Edward F. Cline
Flitterwochen in der Hölle 60 Johannes Kai
Flivvering 21 Raoul Barré, Charles Bowers
Flivver's Art of Mystery 15 Fred Evans, Joe Evans
Flivver's Dilemma 15 Fred Evans, Joe Evans
Flivver's Famous Cheese Hound 15 Charles H. Weston
Flivver's Good Turn 15 Fred Evans, Joe Evans
Flivver's Still Alarm 15 Fred Evans, Joe Evans
Flivver's Terrible Past 15 Charles H. Weston

Flo the Flapper 12 Lewin Fitzhamon
Float Like a Butterfly, Sting Like a Bee 69 William Klein
Floating Clouds 55 Mikio Naruse
Floating College, The 28 George Crone
Floating Dutchman, The 53 Vernon Sewell
Floating Vessel 57 Teinosuke Kinugasa
Floating Weeds 59 Yasujiro Ozu
Floch 72 Dan Wolman
Flock 72 Dan Wolman
Flock, The 78 Zeki Ökten
Flodder 86 Dick Maas
Flood 15 Pyotr Chardynin
Flood, The 23 Louis Delluc
Flood, The 26 Irving Cummings
Flood 27 Yevgeni Ivanov-Barkov
Flood, The 31 James Tinling
Flood, The 46 Jerzy Bossak
Flood, The 58 Martin Frič
Flood, The 63 Frederic Goode
Flood of Love, The 16 Joseph M. Kerrigan
Flood Tide 34 John Baxter
Flood Tide 58 Abner Biberman
Flooded Mine, The 12 Wilfred Noy
Flooded Out 61 Fernando Birri
Floodgates 24 George Irving
Floods of Fear 58 Charles Crichton
Floodstage 86 David Dawkins
Floodtide, The 13 Charles Brabin
Floodtide 49 Frederick Wilson
Floor Above, The 14 James Kirkwood
Floor Below, The 18 Clarence Badger
Floor Show 78 Richard Myers
Floor Treatment 55 Henning Carlsen
Floorwalker, The 16 Charles Chaplin
Flop Goes the Weasel 43 Chuck Jones
Flop House 32 Dick Huemer
Flor de Mayo 57 Roberto Gavaldón
Flor del Irupe, La 65 Albert Dubois
Flor do Mar, A 86 João Cesar Monteiro
Flor Silvestre 43 Emilio Fernández
Flora 48 Alex Lovy
Floradas na Serra 53 Luciano Salce
Floradora Girl, The 30 Harry Beaumont
Floraison, La 13 Léonce-Henri Burel
Floral Studies 10 Émile Cohl
Florence—Days of Destruction 65 Franco Zeffirelli
Florence Nightingale 15 Maurice Elvey
Florence Turner Impersonates Film Favorites 14 Lawrence Trimble
Florentine Dagger, The 35 Robert Florey
Florentiner Hut, Der 39 Wolfgang Liebeneiner
Flores del Miedo, Las 72 José María Oliveira
Flores y Perlas 10 Segundo De Chomón
Florette e Patapon 13 Mario Caserini
Florian 40 Edwin L. Marin
Florida Crackers 08 Sidney Olcott
Florida Enchantment, A 14 Sidney Rankin Drew
Florida Feud, A 08 Sidney Olcott
Florida Special 36 Ralph Murphy
Florine la Fleur du Valois 26 Donatien
Floss der Toten, Das 21 Carl Boese
Flötenkonzert von Sanssouci, Das 31 Gustav Ucicky
Flotilla the Flirt 14 Lawrence Trimble

Flotsam *21* Edmund Blake
Flourishes *15* Abel Gance
Flower *41* Kozaburo Yoshimura
Flower, The *67* Yoji Kuri
Flower Blooms, A *48* Kon Ichikawa
Flower Drum Song *61* Henry Koster
Flower in His Mouth, The *75* Luigi Zampa
Flower of Doom, The *17* Rex Ingram
Flower of Faith, The *16* Burton L. King
Flower of Night *25* Paul Bern
Flower of No Man's Land, The *16* John H. Collins
Flower of the Arabian Nights, The *74* Pier Paolo Pasolini
Flower of the Dusk *18* John H. Collins
Flower of the North *21* David Smith
Flower of the Ranch, The *10* Gilbert M. Anderson
Flower of the Ruins, The *15* Abel Gance
Flower of the Tisza *39* Géza von Bolváry
Flower on the Stone *62* Sergei Paradzhanov
Flower Path, The *68* Shyam Benegal
Flower Thief, The *60* Ron Rice
Flower Woman, The *65* Jan Lenica
Flower Woman of Lindenau, The *31* Georg Jacoby
Flowergirl's Romance, A *10* Bert Haldane
Flowering Time *39* Alf Sjöberg
Flowers, The *64* Nikos Koundouros
Flowers and Trees *32* Burton Gillett
Flowers Are Late, The *17* Boris Suskevich
Flowers for Madame *35* Friz Freleng
Flowers for the Man in the Moon *75* Rolf Losansky
Flowers from Nice *36* Augusto Genina
Flowers in the Attic *87* Jeffrey Bloom
Flowers of Asphalt *49* Gregory Markopoulos
Flowers of Hell *57* Daisuke Ito
Flowers of St. Francis *49* Roberto Rossellini
Flowers That Bloom in the Spring, The *06* Arthur Gilbert
Flowers That Bloom in the Spring, The *07* John Morland
Flowing *56* Mikio Naruse
Flowing Gold *21* Leonard Franchon
Flowing Gold *24* Joseph De Grasse
Flowing Gold *40* Alfred E. Green
Flowing Night *60* Yuzo Kawashima, Mikio Naruse
Fluch der Grünen Augen, Der *64* Ákos von Ráthonyi
Flucht in den Norden *86* Ingemo Engstrom
Flucht in die Dolomiten *55* Luis Trenker
Flucht nach Berlin *62* Will Tremper
Fluchtgefahr *74* Markus Imhoof
Flüchtling aus Chicago, Der *36* Johannes Meyer
Flüchtlinge *34* Gustav Ucicky
Fluchtversuch *76* Vojtěch Jasný
Fluchtweg St. Pauli *71* Wolfgang Staudte
Fluchtweg St. Pauli — Grossalarm für die Davidswache *71* Wolfgang Staudte
Fluffy *65* Earl Bellamy
Flügel und Fesseln *84* Helma Sanders-Brahms
Flugten *42* Albert Mertz, Jørgen Roos

Flugten fra Livet *19* Forest Holger-Madsen
Flugten fra Millionerne *33* Pál Fejös
Flugten Gennem Skyerne *12* August Blom
Fluke in the 'Fluence, A *15* Edwin J. Collins
Flunking Out *76* José Luis García Agraz
Flunky, Work Hard *31* Mikio Naruse
Flurina *70* John Halas
Flush *81* Andrew J. Kuehn
Flusspiraten des Mississippi, Die *63* Jürgen Roland
Flûte à Six Schtroumpfs, La *84* José Dutillieu, John Rust
Flute and the Arrow, The *57* Arne Sucksdorff
Flûte Magique, La *46* Paul Grimault
Fly, The *58* Kurt Neumann
Fly, The *71* John Lennon, Yoko Ono
Fly, The *86* David Cronenberg
Fly II, The *89* Chris Walas
Fly About the House *49* Joy Batchelor, John Halas
Fly Ann *07* John Morland
Fly-Away Baby *37* Frank McDonald
Fly Away Peter *48* Charles Saunders
Fly Ball, The *18* William A. Seiter
Fly by Night *42* Robert Siodmak
Fly Catchers *04* Frank Mottershaw
Fly Cop, The *20* Mort Peebles, Larry Semon, Norman Taurog
Fly God, The *18* Clifford Smith
Fly Guy, The *20* Gregory La Cava
Fly in the Ointment, The *43* Paul Sommer
Fly Me *73* Cirio Santiago
Fly Me, Savage! *73* Cirio Santiago
Fly Me to the Bank *73* Clive Donner
Fly Now, Pay Later *69* B. H. Dial
Fly Paper *08* Edwin S. Porter
Fly, Raven, Fly *65* Alan S. Lee
Fly with Money, A *54* Ion Popescu-Gopo
Flyer, The *87* Erwin Keusch
Flyers *35* Yuli Raizman
Flyin' Buckaroo, The *28* Richard Thorpe
Flyin' Cowboy, The *28* B. Reeves Eason
Flyin' Thru *25* Bruce Mitchell
Flying *86* Paul Lynch
Flying Aces *39* A. Edward Sutherland
Flying Age, The *28* John Foster
Flying Blind *41* Frank McDonald
Flying Blind *88* Vincent DiPersio
Flying Buckaroo, The *28* Richard Thorpe
Flying Cadets *41* Erle C. Kenton
Flying Carpet, The *26* Luis Seel
Flying Carpet, The *60* Gennady Kazansky
Flying Cat *51* Joseph Barbera, William Hanna
Flying Circus, The *33* Russell Birdwell
Flying Circus *68* Alex Lovy
Flying Classroom, The *58* Kurt Hoffmann
Flying Colors *17* Frank Borzage
Flying Dane, The *57* Jørgen Roos
Flying Despatch, The *12* Stuart Kinder
Flying Deuces, The *39* A. Edward Sutherland
Flying Devils *33* Russell Birdwell
Flying Disc Men from Mars *51* Fred C. Brannon
Flying Doctor, The *36* Miles Mander
Flying Doctors of East Africa, The *68*

Werner Herzog
Flying Down to Rio *33* Thornton Freeland
Flying Dutchman, The *23* Lloyd B. Carleton
Flying Dutchman, The *66* Joris Ivens
Flying Elephants *27* Fred J. Butler, Hal Roach
Flying Elephants *39* Harry Watt
Flying Eye, The *55* William C. Hammond
Flying Fifty-Five, The *23* A. E. Coleby
Flying Fifty-Five *39* Reginald Denham
Flying Fish Over Hollywood *83* Christopher Petit
Flying Fists *30* Ubbe Iwerks
Flying Fists, The *38* Robert F. Hill
Flying Fleet, The *28* George W. Hill
Flying Fontaines, The *59* George Sherman
Flying Fool *25* Frank S. Mattison
Flying Fool, The *28* Tay Garnett
Flying Fool, The *31* Walter Summers
Flying Fortress *42* Walter Forde
Flying Fox in a Freedom Tree *89* Martyn Anderson
Flying from Justice *13* Arthur Charrington
Flying from Justice *15* Percy Nash
Flying G-Men *39* James W. Horne, Ray Taylor
Flying Guillotine, The *75* Meng-hau Ho
Flying High *26* Charles Hutchinson
Flying High *31* Charles Reisner
Flying Hoofs *25* Clifford Smith
Flying Hoofs *28* Henry D. Bailey
Flying Horseman, The *26* Orville Dull
Flying Hostess *36* Murray Roth
Flying House, The *20* Robert McCay, Winsor McCay
Flying Irishman, The *39* Leigh Jason
Flying Lariats *31* Alvin J. Neitz
Flying Leathernecks *51* Nicholas Ray
Flying Luck *27* Herman Raymaker
Flying Machine, The *01* Ferdinand Zecca
Flying Mail, The *26* Noel Mason Smith
Flying Man, The *62* George Dunning
Flying Marine, The *29* Albert S. Rogell
Flying Matchmaker, The *66* Israel Becker
Flying Missile, The *50* Henry Levin
Flying Padre *51* Stanley Kubrick
Flying Pat *20* F. Richard Jones
Flying Romeos *28* Mervyn LeRoy
Flying Saucer, The *50* Mikel Conrad
Flying Saucer, The *64* Tinto Brass
Flying Saucers Coming! *77* Jaromil Jireš
Flying Saucers Over Our Town *77* Jaromil Jireš
Flying Scot, The *57* Compton Bennett
Flying Scotsman, The *29* Castleton Knight
Flying Serpent, The *45* Sam Newfield
Flying Sex *81* Marino Girolami
Flying Sorcerer, The *74* Harry Booth
Flying Sorceress *55* Joseph Barbera, William Hanna
Flying Squad, The *29* Arthur Maude
Flying Squad, The *32* F. W. Krämer
Flying Squad, The *40* Herbert Brenon
Flying Squadron, The *40* Herbert Brenon
Flying Squadron *52* Luigi Capuano
Flying Supersub, The *63* Inoshiro Honda
Flying Tigers *42* David Miller
Flying Torpedo, The *16* Christy Cabanne, John B. O'Brien

Flying Trapeze *51* Jacques Baratier
Flying U Ranch, The *27* Robert De Lacey
Flying Wild *41* William West
Flying with Music *42* George Archainbaud
Flying Yeast *29* Manny Gould, Ben Harrison
Flyktningar Finner en Hamn *45* Astrid Henning-Jensen, Bjarne Henning-Jensen
Flynn's Birthday Celebrations *04* William Haggar
Flypaper *06* Alf Collins
Fly's Revenge, The *11* Frank Wilson
Flyveren og Journalisten *11* August Blom
Flyveren og Journalistens Hustru *11* Urban Gad
Focolare Spento, Il *25* Augusto Genina
Fødselsdagsgaven *12* August Blom
Foes *77* John Coats
Fog *13* Ashley Miller
Fog, The *23* Paul Powell
Fog *33* Albert S. Rogell
Fog *65* James Hill
Fog, The *79* John Carpenter
Fog and Rain *24* Teinosuke Kinugasa
Fog Bound *23* Irvin Willat
Fog for a Killer *62* Montgomery Tully
Fog Island *45* Terry Morse
Fog Over Frisco *34* William Dieterle, Daniel Reed
Foggy Harbor *23* Kenji Mizoguchi
Foghorn Leghorn, The *48* Robert McKimson
Foglio di Via *54* Carlo Campogalliani
Fogo e Paixão *88* Márcio Kogan, Isay Weinfeld
Fohnforscher, Die *85* Herbert Achternbusch
Foiled *32* Walter Lantz
Foiled Again *32* Charles Lamont
Foiled by a Girl *12* Wilfred Noy
Foiled by a Woman, or Falsely Accused *06* Tom Green
Foiled by Fido *15* Roscoe Arbuckle
Foiling Fickle Father *13* Mabel Normand, Mack Sennett
Foire aux Cancres, La *63* Louis Daquin
Foire aux Chimères, La *46* Pierre Chénal
Foire Internationale de Bruxelles, La *40* Henri Storck
Föld Embere, A *17* Michael Curtiz
Folie des Grandeurs, La *71* Gérard Oury
Folie des Miens, La *77* Claude Chabrol
Folie des Vaillants, La *25* Germaine Dulac
Folie du Docteur Tube, La *14* Abel Gance
Folie du Doute, La *23* René Leprince
Folie Ordinaire d'une Fille de Cham *88* Jean Rouch
Folies Bergère *35* Roy Del Ruth
Folies Bergère *56* Henri Decoin
Folies Bourgeoises *76* Claude Chabrol
Folies Masquées *01* Alice Guy-Blaché
Folk Dances of the USSR *39* Mikhail Kaufman
Folk og Røvere i Kardemomme By *88* Bente Erichsen
Folk Tale, A *80* Ketan Mehta
Folketingsvalg *45* Astrid Henning-Jensen, Bjarne Henning-Jensen
Folkets Ven *18* Forest Holger-Madsen
Folks at Red Wolf Inn, The *72* Bud Townsend

Folks at the Red Wolf Inn, The *72* Bud Townsend
Folks from Way Down East *24* Lee Beggs
Folks of the Fair *16* Ethyle Batley
Folle à Tuer, Une *75* Yves Boisset
Folle, Folle, Fólleme, Tim *78* Pedro Almodóvar
Folle Nuit, La *32* Léon Poirier
Føllet *43* Bjarne Henning-Jensen
Follie per l'Opera *47* Mario Costa
Follies Girl, The *18* John Francis Dillon
Follies Girl *43* William Rowland
Follow a Star *59* Robert Asher
Follow Me *69* Gene McCabe
Follow Me! *71* Carol Reed
Follow Me *89* Maria Knilli
Follow Me, Boys! *66* Norman Tokar
Follow Me Quietly *49* Richard Fleischer, Anthony Mann
Follow My Gaze *86* Jean Curtelin
Follow Teacher *28* Charles Lamont
Follow That Bird *85* Ken Kwapis
Follow That Camel *67* Gerald Thomas
Follow That Car *81* Daniel Haller
Follow That Dream *62* Gordon Douglas
Follow That Horse *60* Alan Bromly
Follow That Man *61* Jerome Epstein
Follow That Woman *45* Lew Landers
Follow the Arrow *38* Felix E. Feist
Follow the Band *43* Jean Yarbrough
Follow the Boys *44* A. Edward Sutherland
Follow the Boys *63* Richard Thorpe
Follow the Fleet *36* Mark Sandrich
Follow the Girl *17* Louis Chaudet
Follow the Hunter *54* William F. Claxton
Follow the Lady *33* Adrian Brunel
Follow the Leader *01* Edwin S. Porter
Follow the Leader *30* Norman Taurog
Follow the Leader *44* William Beaudine
Follow the Leader *54* William F. Claxton
Follow the Music *47* Arthur Dreifuss
Follow the Sun *51* Sidney Lanfield
Follow Thru *30* Lloyd Corrigan, Laurence Schwab
Follow Your Dreams *82* Robert Mandel
Follow Your Heart *36* Aubrey H. Scotto
Follow Your Leader *14* Hay Plumb
Follow Your Leader and the Master Follows Last *08* Percy Stow
Follow Your Star *38* Sinclair Hill
Following in Father's Footsteps *06* Walter R. Booth
Following in Father's Footsteps *08* Arthur Gilbert
Following in Mother's Footsteps *08* Walter R. Booth
Following Mother's Footsteps *11* Theo Bouwmeester
Following the Führer *84* Erwin Leiser
Following the Trail *14* Toby Cooper
Folly of Desire, The *16* George Loane Tucker
Folly of Desire, or The Shulamite, The *16* George Loane Tucker
Folly of the Brave, The *25* Germaine Dulac
Folly of Vanity, The *24* Maurice Elvey, Henry Otto
Folly to Be Wise *52* Frank Launder

Folterkammer des Dr. Fu Manchu, Die *68* Jesús Franco
Foma Gordeyev *59* Mark Donskoi
Fome de Amor *68* Nelson Pereira Dos Santos
Fond de l'Air Est Rouge, Le *77* Chris Marker
Fond Farewell to the Prince, A *86* László Vitézy
Fond Memories *82* Francis Mankiewicz
Fondateur, Le *47* Charles Dekeukeleire
Fonderies Martin, Les *38* Alexander Alexeïeff, Claire Parker
Foney Fables *42* Friz Freleng
Fontaine d'Aréthuse, La *36* Dmitri Kirsanov
Fontaine de Vaucluse *53* Louis Malle
Fontaine des Amours, La *24* Roger Lion
Fontaine Merveilleuse, La *08* Georges Méliès
Fontaine Sacrée ou La Vengeance de Boudha, La *01* Georges Méliès
Fontamara *80* Carlo Lizzani
Fontana di Trevi *60* Carlo Campogalliani
Fontána pre Zuzanu *85* Dušan Rapos
Fontane Effi Briest *74* Rainer Werner Fassbinder
Fonte da Saudade *87* Marcos Altberg
Food for Scandal *20* James Cruze
Food for Thought *40* Adrian Brunel
Food Gamblers, The *17* Albert Parker
Food of the Gods, The *76* Bert I. Gordon
Food of the Gods II *89* Damian Lee
Fool, The *13* George Pearson
Fool, The *25* Harry Millarde
Fool and His Money, A *11* Bert Haldane
Fool and His Money, A *14* Lois Weber
Fool and His Money, A *20* Robert Ellis
Fool and His Money, A *24* Erle C. Kenton
Fool and the Princess, The *48* William C. Hammond
Fool Coverage *38* Leslie Goodwins
Fool Coverage *52* Robert McKimson
Fool for Love *85* Robert Altman
Fool Killer, The *65* Servando González
Fool There Was, A *14* Frank Powell
Fool There Was, A *22* Emmett J. Flynn
Foolin' Around *78* Richard T. Heffron
Foolish Age, The *19* F. Richard Jones
Foolish Age, The *21* William A. Seiter
Foolish Bunny, The *38* Art Davis
Foolish Husbands *41* Marcel L'Herbier
Foolish Matrons, The *21* Clarence Brown, Maurice Tourneur
Foolish Men and Smart Women *24* Fred Newmeyer
Foolish Monte Carlo *22* William Humphrey
Foolish Virgin, The *17* Albert Capellani
Foolish Virgin, The *24* George W. Hill
Foolish Wives *22* Erich von Stroheim
Foolproof *36* Edward L. Cahn
Fools *70* Tom Gries
Fools and Riches *23* Herbert Blaché
Fools and Their Money *19* Herbert Blaché
Fools Awake *48* John English
Fool's Awakening, A *24* Harold M. Shaw
Fool's Errand, A *27* William C. Nolan
Fool's Fancy *11* A. E. Coleby
Fools First *22* Marshall Neilan

Fools for Luck *17* Lawrence C. Windom
Fools for Luck *28* Charles Reisner
Fools for Scandal *38* Mervyn LeRoy
Fool's Gold *19* Lawrence Trimble
Fool's Gold *46* George Archainbaud
Fools' Highway *24* Irving Cummings
Fools in the Dark *24* Alfred Santell
Fool's Luck *26* Roscoe Arbuckle
Fool's Mate *89* Matthieu Carrière
Fools of Desire *41* Bernard B. Ray
Fools of Fashion *26* James McKay
Fools of Fate *09* D. W. Griffith
Fools of Fortune *22* A. Byron Davis
Fools of Fortune *90* Pat O'Connor
Fools of Passion *26* Rudolph Biebrach
Fools' Parade *71* Andrew V. McLaglen
Fool's Paradise *21* Cecil B. DeMille
Fool's Revenge, A *09* D. W. Griffith
Fool's Revenge, The *16* Will S. Davis
Fools Rush In *49* John Paddy Carstairs
Fools Step In *38* Nigel Byass
Fools Who Made History — "The Story of Charles Goodyear" *39* Jan Leman
Fools Who Made History — "The Story of Elias Howe" *39* Jan Leman
Foot, The *24* Teinosuke Kinugasa
Foot and Mouth *55* Lindsay Anderson
Foot Film *67* Yvonne Rainer
Football *61* Robert Drew, Richard Leacock
Football Coach *33* William A. Wellman
Football Daft *21* Victor W. Rowe
Football Favourite, A *22* George Wynn
Football Fever *37* Walter Lantz
Football Fun *22* Bernard Dudley
Football Romeo *38* George Sidney
Football Teamwork *35* Felix E. Feist
Football Toucher Downer, The *37* Dave Fleischer
Footballer's Honour, A *14* Lewin Fitzhamon
Footbridge, The *61* Leonard Kiegel
Footfalls *21* Charles Brabin
Footlight Fever *41* Irving Reis
Footlight Glamour *27* John Ford
Footlight Glamour *43* Frank R. Strayer
Footlight Parade *33* Lloyd Bacon, Busby Berkeley, William Keighley
Footlight Ranger, The *23* Scott R. Dunlap
Footlight Serenade *42* Gregory Ratoff
Footlight Varieties *51* Hal Yates
Footlights *21* John S. Robertson
Footlights *37* R. A. Hopwood
Footlights and Fakers *17* Larry Semon
Footlights and Fools *29* William A. Seiter
Footlights and Shadows *20* John W. Noble
Footlights of Fate, The *16* William Humphrey
Footloose *84* Herbert Ross
Footloose Heiress, The *37* William Clemens
Footloose Widows *26* Roy Del Ruth
Footnotes *67* Edgar Reitz
Footprints *60* Jaromil Jireš
Footrot Flats *86* Murray Ball
Footsteps *73* Alan Parker
Footsteps in the Dark *41* Lloyd Bacon, Hugh MacMullen
Footsteps in the Fog *55* Arthur Lubin
Footsteps in the Night *31* Maurice Elvey

Footsteps in the Night *57* Jean Yarbrough
Foozle Takes Up Golf *11* Frank Wilson
Fop, The *29* Mark Donskoi
For a Baby's Sake *11* Lewin Fitzhamon
For a Dollar in the Teeth *66* Luigi Vanzi
For a Few Bullets More *67* Enzo G. Castellari
For a Few Dollars Less *66* Mario Mattòli
For a Few Dollars More *64* Sergio Leone
For a Fistful of Dollars *64* Sergio Leone
For a Joyful Life *51* Vojtěch Jasný, Karel Kachyňa
For a Night of Love *88* Dušan Makavejev
For a Thousand Dollars a Day *66* Silvio Amadio
For a Wife's Honor *08* D. W. Griffith
For a Woman's Eyes *26* Geoffrey H. Malins, H. B. Parkinson
For a Woman's Fair Name *16* Harry Davenport
For a Woman's Honor *10* Sidney Olcott
For Alimony Only *26* William DeMille
For All Eternity *17* A. E. Coleby, Arthur H. Rooke
For All Mankind *89* Al Reinert
For Another Woman *24* David Kirkland
For Any Occasion *22* Paul M. Felton
För Att Inte Tala Om Alla Dessa Kvinnor *64* Ingmar Bergman
For Baby's Sake *08* A. E. Coleby
For Baby's Sake *12* Bert Haldane
For Beauty's Sake *41* Shepard Traube
For Better, for Worse *19* Cecil B. DeMille
For Better, for Worse *54* J. Lee-Thompson
For Better for Worse *59* Joy Batchelor, John Halas
For Better, for Worse *74* Jan Troell
For Better or for Worse *75* Claude Jutra
For Better or for Worse *90* Gene Quintano
For Better or Worse *11* Bert Haldane
For Better or Worser *35* Dave Fleischer
For Big Stakes *22* Lynn Reynolds
For Bitter or for Verse *19* Raoul Barré, Charles Bowers
For Cash *15* Lon Chaney
For Crimes Not Theirs *39* Eugene Bodo
For Crime's Sake *27* Manny Gould, Ben Harrison
For de Andre *15* August Blom
For Dear Life *26* Paul M. Felton
For East Is East *11* Dave Aylott
For Every Child *53* William Beaudine
For Exchange *85* Juan Carlos Tabio
For Fifty Thousand Pounds *13* Alexander Butler
For France *17* Wesley Ruggles
For Freedom *18* Frank Lloyd
For Freedom *40* Maurice Elvey
For Freedom and Love *38* Fritz Peter Buch
For Freedom of Cuba *12* Thomas Ince
For Fun, for Play *77* Volker Schlöndorff
For Heaven's Sake *26* Sam Taylor
For Heaven's Sake *50* George Seaton
For Her Brother's Sake *11* Thomas Ince
For Her Brother's Sake *15* Fred Evans
For Her Country's Sake *37* Erich Waschneck
For Her Father's Sake *21* Alexander Butler
For Her Mother's Sake *12* Wilfred Noy

For Her Mother's Sake *13* Edwin J. Collins
For Her People *14* Lawrence Trimble
For Her Sake *09* Dave Aylott
For Her Sister's Sake *12* August Blom
For He's a Jolly Bad Fellow *63* Don Chaffey
For His Child's Sake *08* Dave Aylott
For His Country's Honor *15* August Blom
For His Sake *22* John S. Lawrence
For His Son *11* D. W. Griffith
For His Superior's Honor *14* Frank Lloyd
For Home and Country *14* Harold M. Shaw
For Husbands Only *17* Phillips Smalley, Lois Weber
For Kayako *86* Kohei Oguri
For Keeps *88* John G. Avildsen
For King and Country *14* Arthur Finn
For Ladies Only *27* Henry Lehrman, Scott Pembroke
For Liberty *17* Bertram Bracken
For Lizzie's Sake *13* Mack Sennett
For Love Alone *86* Stephen Wallace
For Love and Life *12* Hay Plumb
For Love and Money *67* Don Davis
For Love and the King *12* F. Martin Thornton
For Love...for Magic *67* Duccio Tessari
For Love of a Queen *35* Alfred Santell, Victor Saville
For Love of Gold *08* D. W. Griffith
For Love of Gold: A Story of the Underworld *08* D. W. Griffith
For Love of Him *13* Warwick Buckland
For Love of Ivy *68* Daniel Mann
For Love of Mabel *13* Henry Lehrman
For Love of Man *72* Sergei Gerasimov
For Love of Money *67* Don Davis
For Love of Service *22* Milburn Morante
For Love of You *33* Carmine Gallone
For Love or Money *32* Zoltán Korda
For Love or Money *39* Albert S. Rogell
For Love or Money *63* Michael Gordon
For Marion's Sake *13* Warwick Buckland
For Me and My Gal *32* Raoul Walsh
For Me and My Gal *42* Busby Berkeley
For Members Only *60* Ramsey Herrington
For Men Only *39* Guido Brignone
For Men Only *51* Paul Henreid
För Min Heta Ungdoms Skull *52* Arne Mattsson
For Mother's Sake *14* A. Ray
For My Lady's Happiness *26* Geoffrey H. Malins
For Old Times' Sake *48* Paul Barralet
For 1,000 Dollars a Day *66* Silvio Amadio
For Pete's Sake! *66* James F. Collier
For Pete's Sake *74* Peter Yates
For Queen and Country *88* Martin Stellman
For Reward of Service *17* Alfred E. Green
For Richer for Poorer *80* Gerard Damiano
For Sale *18* Fred E. Wright
For Sale *24* George Archainbaud
For Sale: A Baby *09* Georges Méliès
For Scent-imental Reasons *49* Chuck Jones
For Sin Faders Skyld *16* Forest Holger-Madsen
För Sin Kärleks Skull *13* Mauritz Stiller
For Singles Only *68* Arthur Dreifuss

For Sit Lands Ære *15* August Blom
For Such Is the Kingdom of Heaven *13* Warwick Buckland
For the Cause *12* Christy Cabanne
For the Cause *13* Thomas Ince
For the Cause of Suffrage *09* Georges Méliès
For the Common Defense *42* Allen Kenward
For the Defense *16* Frank Reicher
For the Defense *22* Paul Powell
For the Defense *30* John Cromwell
For the Empire *14* Harold M. Shaw
For the Empire *16* George Pearson
For the First Time *58* Rudolph Maté
For the Freedom of the East *18* Ira M. Lowry
For the Freedom of the World *17* F. J. Carroll, Ira M. Lowry
For the Good of Her Men *12* Allan Dwan
For the Hand of a Princess *04* Lewin Fitzhamon
For the Honour of Belgium *14* Edwin J. Collins
For the Honour of the House *13* Warwick Buckland
For the Little Lady's Sake *08* Lewin Fitzhamon
For the Living *46* Josef Heifits, Alexander Zarkhi
For the Love o' Lil *30* James Tinling
For the Love o' Pete *26* Walter Lantz
For the Love of Ada *72* Ronnie Baxter
For the Love of Benji *77* Joe Camp
For the Love of Lil *30* James Tinling
For the Love of Man *72* Sergei Gerasimov
For the Love of Mary *48* Frederick De Cordova
For the Love of Mike *27* Frank Capra
For the Love of Mike *32* Monty Banks
For the Love of Mike *60* George Sherman
For the Love of Rusty *47* John Sturges
For the Rich *87* Sergio Corbucci
For the Sake of the Little Ones at Home *11* Frank Wilson
For the Service *36* Buck Jones
For the Soul of Rafael *20* Harry Garson
For Them That Trespass *48* Alberto Cavalcanti
For Those I Loved *83* Robert Enrico
For Those in Peril *43* Charles Crichton
For Those Unborn *13* Christy Cabanne
For Those We Love *21* Arthur Rosson
For Those Who Think Young *64* Leslie Martinson
For Valour *17* Albert Parker
For Valour *28* George B. Samuelson
For Valour *37* Tom Walls
For We Too Do Not Forgive *62* Ján Kadár, Elmar Klos
For Whom the Bell Tolls *43* Sam Wood
For Whom the Larks Sing *59* László Ranódy
For Wives Only *26* Victor Heerman
For Woman's Favor *24* Oscar A. C. Lund
For You Alone *37* Robert Riskin
For You Alone *44* Geoffrey Faithfull
For You at the Kazakhstan Front *43* Dziga Vertov
For You I Die *47* John Reinhardt

For You My Boy *23* William L. Roubert
For Your Daughter's Sake *20* Burton L. King
For Your Entertainment *52* Colin Bell
For Your Eyes Only *81* John Glen
For Your Heart Only *85* Raymond Fung
For Your Love Only *76* Wolfgang Petersen
Forager, The *10* Sidney Olcott
Forajidos en la Mira *87* Alberto Mariscal
Forbidden *19* Phillips Smalley, Lois Weber
Forbidden *31* Frank Capra
Forbidden *48* George King
Forbidden *53* Rudolph Maté
Forbidden *54* Mario Monicelli
Forbidden *85* Anthony Page
Forbidden Adventure, The *15* Charles Swickard
Forbidden Adventure *31* Norman Taurog
Forbidden Alliance, The *34* Sidney Franklin
Forbidden Arabia *37* René Clément
Forbidden Box, The *18* Phillips Smalley, Lois Weber
Forbidden Cargo *25* Thomas Buckingham
Forbidden Cargo *54* Harold French
Forbidden Cargoes *25* Fred LeRoy Granville
Forbidden Christ, The *50* Curzio Malaparte
Forbidden City, The *18* Sidney Franklin
Forbidden Company *32* Richard Thorpe
Forbidden Dance, The *90* Greydon Clark
Forbidden Fire *19* Arthur Rosson
Forbidden Fruit *16* Ivan Abramson
Forbidden Fruit *20* Cecil B. DeMille
Forbidden Fruit *52* Henri Verneuil
Forbidden Games *51* René Clément
Forbidden Grass *28* E. M. Eldridge
Forbidden Ground *68* Pál Gábor
Forbidden Heaven *36* Reginald Barker
Forbidden Hours *28* Harry Beaumont
Forbidden Island *59* Charles B. Griffith
Forbidden Journey *50* Richard Jarvis, Cecil Maiden
Forbidden Jungle *50* Robert E. Tansey
Forbidden Love *21* Philip Van Loan
Forbidden Love *27* Graham Cutts
Forbidden Love *32* Tod Browning
Forbidden Love *40* Jacques De Baroncelli
Forbidden Love *65* Yoshishige Yoshida
Forbidden Love Affair *66* J. B. Tanko
Forbidden Love Affair *76* Ashley Lazarus
Forbidden Lover, The *1898* James A. Williamson
Forbidden Lover *23* Nat C. Deverich
Forbidden Melody *33* Frank R. Strayer
Forbidden Music *36* Walter Forde
Forbidden Paradise *22* Herbert Brenon
Forbidden Paradise *24* Ernst Lubitsch
Forbidden Paradise *79* Jan Troell
Forbidden Passage *41* Fred Zinnemann
Forbidden Path, The *18* J. Gordon Edwards
Forbidden Paths *17* Robert Thornby
Forbidden Planet *56* Fred M. Wilcox
Forbidden Range, The *23* Neal Hart
Forbidden Relations *83* Zsolt Kézdi-Kovács
Forbidden Room, The *14* Allan Dwan
Forbidden Room, The *19* Lynn Reynolds

Forbidden Room, The *76* Dino Risi
Forbidden Songs *47* Leonard Buczkowski
Forbidden Street *49* Jean Negulesco
Forbidden Sun *89* Zelda Barron
Forbidden Territory *34* Phil Rosen
Forbidden Thing, The *20* Allan Dwan
Forbidden Trail, The *23* Robert North Bradbury
Forbidden Trail, The *32* Lambert Hillyer
Forbidden Trails *20* Scott R. Dunlap
Forbidden Trails *28* Robert J. Horner
Forbidden Trails *41* Robert North Bradbury
Forbidden Under the Censorship of the King *73* Barry R. Kerr
Forbidden Valley *20* J. Stuart Blackton
Forbidden Valley *38* Whyndham Gittens
Forbidden Volcano *65* Haroun Tazieff
Forbidden Waters *26* Alan Hale
Forbidden Woman, The *20* Harry Garson
Forbidden Woman, The *27* Paul Stein
Forbidden World *81* Allan Holzman
Forbidden Zone *80* Richard Elfman
Forbin Project, The *69* Joseph Sargent
Forbrydelsens Element *84* Lars von Trier
Forca per un Bastardo, Una *68* Amasi Damiani
Force *71* Helma Sanders-Brahms
Force Beyond, The *78* William Sachs
Force Beyond, The *78* Gus Trikonis
Force de la Vie *20* René Leprince
Force de l'Enfant, La *08* Émile Cohl
Force Doit Rester à la Loi *1899* Georges Méliès
Force et le Droit, La *70* Marcel Carné
Force: Five *81* Robert Clouse
Force Four *75* Michael Fink
Force Majeure *89* Pierre Jolivet
Force of Arms *51* Michael Curtiz
Force of Circumstance *90* Liza Bear
Force of Destiny, The *49* Carmine Gallone
Force of Evil *48* Abraham Polonsky, Don Weis
Force of Impulse *61* Saul Swimmer
Force of One, A *79* Paul Aaron
Force of the Hungarian Soil, The *16* Michael Curtiz
Force 10 from Navarone *78* Guy Hamilton
Forced Bravery *13* Mack Sennett
Forced Confession, The *12* Wilfred Noy
Forced Entry *75* Jim Sotos
Forced Labor *28* Yuli Raizman
Forced Landing *35* Melville Brown
Forced Landing *41* Gordon Wiles
Forced March *89* Rick King
Forced to Consent *08* Lewin Fitzhamon
Forced Vengeance *82* James Fargo
Forces' Sweetheart *53* Maclean Rogers
Ford Fairlane *90* Renny Harlin
Fordington Twins, The *20* Will P. Kellino
Foreclosure, The *12* Allan Dwan
Foreign Affair, A *48* Billy Wilder
Foreign Affaires *35* Tom Walls
Foreign Agent *42* William Beaudine
Foreign Body *86* Ronald Neame
Foreign City, A *88* Didier Goldschmidt
Foreign Correspondent *40* Alfred Hitchcock
Foreign Devils *27* W. S. Van Dyke
Foreign Harbor *48* Erik Faustman

Foreign Intrigue *56* Sheldon Reynolds
Foreign Legion, The *28* Edward Sloman
Foreign Skies *86* Lindsay Anderson
Foreign Spies, The *14* Arthur Finn
Foreign Spy, The *11* Bert Haldane
Foreign Spy, The *13* Charles C. Calvert
Foreign Spy, The *13* Wallace Reid
Foreigner, The *28* Archie Mayo
Foreigner, The *78* Amos Poe
Foreman Hassan *52* Salah Abu Saif
Foreman of the Jury, The *13* Mack Sennett
Foreman Went to France, The *41* Charles Frend
Foreman's Fixup, The *11* Allan Dwan
Foreman's Treachery, The *14* Charles Brabin
Foreplay *74* John G. Avildsen, Robert McCarty, Bruce Malmuth
Forest, The *31* Sergei Gerasimov
Forest, The *73* Girish Karnad
Forest, The *83* Don Jones
Forest Havoc *26* Stuart Paton
Forest King, The *22* Ferris G. Hartman
Forest Murmurs *47* Slavko Vorkapich
Forest of Fear *79* Chuck McCrann
Forest of Hanged Men *65* Liviu Ciulei
Forest of Little Bear *87* Toshio Goto
Forest of the Hanged, The *65* Liviu Ciulei
Forest on the Hill, The *19* Cecil M. Hepworth
Forest Primeval, The *81* Andrew Davis
Forest Ranger, The *10* Gilbert M. Anderson
Forest Rangers, The *42* George Marshall
Forest Ring, The *30* David Gaither, Kyra Markham
Forest Rivals, The *19* Harry Hoyt
Forest Symphony *67* Alexander Zguridi
Forestalled *39* Joseph H. Lewis
Forester Made King, A *07* Georges Méliès
Forester's Remedy, The *08* Georges Méliès
Forester's Song *66* Jiří Brdečka
Forêt Qui Tue, La *24* René Le Somptier
Forêt Sacrée *54* Pierre-Dominique Gaisseau
Forêt Secrète d'Afrique *68* Henri Storck
Forever *21* George Fitzmaurice
Forever *41* Kamel Salim
Forever After *26* F. Harmon Weight
Forever Amber *47* Otto Preminger
Forever and a Day *43* René Clair, Edmund Goulding, Cedric Hardwicke, Frank Lloyd, Victor Saville, Kent Smith, Robert Stevenson, Herbert Wilcox
Forever and Always *86* Christel Buschmann
Forever, Darling *55* Alexander Hall
Forever England *35* Anthony Asquith, Walter Forde
Forever Female *53* Irving Rapper
Forever in Love *45* Delmer Daves
Forever, Lulu *86* Amos Kollek
Forever My Heart *54* Leslie Arliss, Bernard Knowles
Forever My Love *55* Ernst Marischka
Forever Young *84* David Drury
Forever Young, Forever Free *76* Ashley Lazarus
Forever Yours *34* Stanley Irving, Zoltán Korda

Forever Yours *45* William Nigh
Forever Yours *58* Youssef Chahine
Forfaiture *37* Marcel L'Herbier
Forfeit, The *19* Frank Powell
Forfejlet Spring, Et *13* August Blom
Forfølgelsen *81* Anja Breien
Forged Bride, The *20* Douglas Gerrard
Forged Passport *39* John H. Auer
Forged Will, The *49* Ray Nazarro
Forger, The *28* George B. Samuelson
Forger, The *47* Derwin Abrahams
Forger of London *61* Harald Reinl
Forgerons *1895* Louis Lumière
Forgerons, Les *1896* Georges Méliès
Forgers of Peace *62* Santiago Álvarez
Forgery, The *81* Volker Schlöndorff
Forgery of the One Pound Notes, The *16* Ethyle Batley
Forges *53* Jean Brismée, André Delvaux
Forget-Me-Not *22* W. S. Van Dyke
Forget Me Not *34* Stanley Irving, Zoltán Korda
Forget-Me-Nots *17* Émile Chautard
Forget Mozart *85* Miloslav Luther
Forget That Case *86* Krassimir Spassov
Forget Venice *79* Franco Brusati
Forging Ahead *33* Norman Walker
Forgive and Forget *23* Howard Mitchell
Forgive Me *87* Ernest Jassan
Forgive Me for Your Betrayal *86* Braz Chediak
Forgive Me, Son *37* Ramón Peón
Forgive Us Our Trespasses *19* L. C. MacBean
Forgiven *10* Edwin S. Porter
Forgiven, or The Jack o' Diamonds *14* William Robert Daly
Forgiven Sinner, The *61* Jean-Pierre Melville
Forgotten, The *12* Avrom Yitskhok Kaminsky
Forgotten *14* Stuart Kinder
Forgotten *33* Richard Thorpe
Forgotten, The *50* Luis Buñuel
Forgotten Children *49* Hiroshi Inagaki
Forgotten Commandments *32* Louis Gasnier, William Schorr
Forgotten Cove, The *58* Bruno Gebel
Forgotten Faces *28* Victor Schertzinger
Forgotten Faces *36* E. A. Dupont
Forgotten Faces *36* Robert Florey
Forgotten Faces *46* George Tzavellas
Forgotten Faces, The *61* Peter Watkins
Forgotten Girls *40* Phil Rosen
Forgotten Hero *37* William Nigh
Forgotten Law, The *22* James W. Horne
Forgotten Men *35* Norman Lee
Forgotten Prayer, The *16* Frank Borzage
Forgotten Ship, The *38* Leslie Fenton
Forgotten Tune for the Flute, A *88* Eldar Ryazanov
Forgotten Victory *39* Fred Zinnemann
Forgotten Village, The *40* Herbert Kline
Forgotten War, The *67* Santiago Álvarez
Forgotten Woman *21* Park Frame
Forgotten Woman, The *39* Harold Young
Forgotten Women *27* George B. Seitz
Forgotten Women *31* William Beaudine
Forgotten Women *31* Richard Thorpe
Forgotten Women *49* William Beaudine

Forjadores de la Paz *62* Santiago Álvarez
Forlorn River *26* John Waters
Forlorn River *37* Charles Barton
Form Phases I *52* Robert Breer
Form Phases II and III *53* Robert Breer
Form Phases IV *54* Robert Breer
Formel eins Film, Der *85* Wolfgang Buld
Formerly You Had a Big Time *82* Bert Haanstra
Forms of Love *89* Rudolph Thome
Formula, The *80* John G. Avildsen
Formula for a Murder *86* Alberto De Martino
Formula for Murder *86* Alberto De Martino
Fornaretto di Venezia, Il *14* Luigi Maggi
Fornaretto di Venezia, Il *63* Duccio Tessari
Fornarina, La *42* Enrico Guazzoni
Føroyar Færøerne *61* Jørgen Roos
Forró Vizet a Kopaszra *77* Péter Bacsó
Forsaken, The *13* Warwick Buckland
Forsaken Garden, The *63* Richard Rush
Forsaking All Others *22* Émile Chautard
Forsaking All Others *34* W. S. Van Dyke
Förseglade Läppar *27* Gustaf Molander
Första Divisionen *41* Hasse Ekman
Første Honorar, Det *12* August Blom
Første Kærlighed, Den *12* August Blom
Første Kreds, Den *72* Aleksander Ford
Forsyte Saga, The *49* Compton Bennett
Fort, The *49* Ray Nazarro
Fort Algiers *53* Lesley Selander
Fort Apache *48* John Ford, Cliff Lyons
Fort Apache, the Bronx *81* Daniel Petrie
Fort Bowie *58* Howard W. Koch
Fort Courageous *65* Lesley Selander
Fort Defiance *51* John Rawlins
Fort Dobbs *57* Gordon Douglas
Fort Dodge Stampede *51* Harry Keller
Fort du Fou *62* Léo Joannon
Fort Frayne *26* Ben F. Wilson
Fort Graveyard *66* Kihachi Okamoto
Fort Massacre *58* Joseph M. Newman
Fort Osage *52* Lesley Selander
Fort Saganne *84* Alain Corneau
Fort Savage Raiders *51* Ray Nazarro
Fort Ti *53* William Castle
Fort Utah *67* Lesley Selander
Fort Vengeance *53* Lesley Selander
Fort Worth *51* Edwin L. Marin
Fort Worth Robbery *15* King Vidor
Fort Yuma *55* Lesley Selander
Fort Yuma Gold *66* Giorgio Ferroni
Forteresse, La *47* Fedor Ozep
40th Door, The *24* George B. Seitz
Fortini/Cani *76* Danièle Huillet, Jean-Marie Straub
Fortress, The *79* Miklós Szinetár
Fortress *81* Bruce Beresford
Fortress in the Sun *78* George Rowe
Fortress on the Volga *42* Alexei Ginsburg
Förtrollad Vandring *54* Arne Mattsson
Fortuna *69* Yuri Ozerov
Fortuna *69* Menahem Golan
Fortuna di Essere Donna, La *55* Alessandro Blasetti
Fortunat *60* Alex Joffé
Fortunate Fool, The *33* Norman Walker
Fortune, The *74* Mike Nichols

Four Flights to Love *38* Abel Gance
Four Flusher, The *23* Norman Taurog
Four-Footed Ranger, The *28* Stuart Paton
Four for Texas *63* Robert Aldrich
Four for the Morgue *62* John Sledge
Four Friends *81* Arthur Penn
Four Frightened People *33* Cecil B. De-Mille
Four from Nowhere, The *25* Francis Ford
Four from the Infantry *30* G. W. Pabst
Four Girls in Town *56* Jack Sher
Four Girls in White *38* S. Sylvan Simon
Four Guns to the Border *54* Richard Carlson
Four Hands *87* Hans Fels
Four Hearts *22* Leonard Wheeler
Four Hearts *46* Konstantin Yudin
Four Hits and a Mister *62* Douglas Hickox
Four Hooligans, The *06* Alf Collins
Four Horsemen of the Apocalypse, The *21* Rex Ingram
Four Horsemen of the Apocalypse, The *61* Vincente Minnelli
Four Hours to Kill *35* Mitchell Leisen
400 Blows, The *58* François Truffaut
400 Million, The *38* John Ferno, Joris Ivens
400 Million Miles from the Earth *17* Forest Holger-Madsen
491 *63* Vilgot Sjöman
Four in a Jeep *51* Leopold Lindtberg
Four in the Afternoon *51* James Broughton
Four in the Morning *53* James Ivory
Four in the Morning *65* Anthony Simmons
Four Jacks and a Jill *41* Jack Hively
Four Jills in a Jeep *44* William A. Seiter
Four Jolly Sailor Boys from "The Princess of Kensington" *07* John Morland
Four Journeys Into Mystic Time *80* Shirley Clarke
Four Just Men, The *21* George Ridgwell
Four Just Men, The *39* Walter Forde
Four Kinds of Love *64* Mauro Bolognini, Luigi Comencini, Dino Risi, Franco Rossi
Four Little Tailors, The *10* Émile Cohl
Four Love Stories *47* Teinosuke Kinugasa, Mikio Naruse
Four Masked Men *34* George Pearson
Four Men and a Prayer *38* John Ford
Four Men in a Van *21* Hugh Croise
Four Monks, The *62* Carlo Ludovico Bragaglia
Four Moods *70* King Hu, Han-hsiang Li, Shing Lu, Ching-jui Pai
Four Mothers *41* William Keighley
Four Musicians of Bremen, The *22* Walt Disney
Four Musketeers, The *35* Heinz Paul
Four Musketeers, The *63* Carlo Ludovico Bragaglia
Four Musketeers, The *73* Richard Lester
Four Musketeers: The Revenge of Milady, The *73* Richard Lester
Four Nights of a Dreamer *71* Robert Bresson
Four Orphans, The *23* Gregory La Cava
Four Parts *34* Charlie Chase, Eddie Dunn

Four Patches of Grey Velvet *71* Dario Argento
Four-Poster, The *52* Irving Reis
Four Rode Out *69* John Peyser
Four Seasons, The *46* Georges Rouquier
Four Seasons, The *81* Alan Alda
Four Seasons of Children *39* Hiroshi Shimizu
Four Seasons of Love, The *58* Ko Nakahira
Four Seasons of Tateshina *66* Kaneto Shindo
Four Seasons of Woman, The *50* Shiro Toyoda
Four Sided Triangle *53* Terence Fisher
Four Skulls of Jonathan Drake, The *59* Edward L. Cahn
Four Soldiers from Stalingrad *57* Alexander Ivanov
Four Sons *28* John Ford
Four Sons *40* Archie Mayo
Four-Star Boarder, The *36* Charlie Chase
**** *67* Andy Warhol
Four Stars *67* Andy Warhol
Four Steps in the Clouds *42* Alessandro Blasetti
Four Times About Bulgaria *58* Karel Kachyňa
Four Times That Night *72* Mario Bava
Four Tomboys, The *09* Alf Collins
Four Troublesome Heads, The *1898* Georges Méliès
Four Truths, The *62* Alessandro Blasetti, Hervé Bromberger, René Clair, Luis García Berlanga
Four Visits of Samuel Vulf, The *34* Alexander Stolper
Four Wall Duration *73* Malcolm Le Grice
Four Walls *28* William Nigh
Four Ways Out *51* Pietro Germi
Four Wheels and No Brake *55* Ted Parmelee
Four Winds Island *61* David Villiers
Four Wives *39* Michael Curtiz
Four Women for One Hero *62* Leopoldo Torre-Nilsson
Fourberies de Pingouin, Les *16* Louis Feuillade
Fourchambault, Les *29* Georges Monca
4ème Pouvoir, Le *85* Serge Leroy
Fourflusher, The *19* Harry Franklin
Fourflusher, The *28* Wesley Ruggles
Four's a Crowd *38* Michael Curtiz
14, The *73* David Hemmings
14 Carrot Rabbit *52* Friz Freleng
14 Dage i Jernalderen *77* Jørgen Roos
14-18 *62* Jean Aurel
Fourteen Hours *51* Henry Hathaway
Fourteen Lives *54* Zoltán Fábri
Fourteen Lives in Danger *54* Zoltán Fábri
Fourteen Lives Saved *54* Zoltán Fábri
Fourteen Numara *86* Sinan Cetin
14-18 *62* Jean Aurel
14 Year Old Girl, The *65* Andy Warhol
Fourteen's Good, Eighteen's Better *80* Gillian Armstrong
Fourteenth Lover, The *21* Harry Beaumont
Fourteenth Man, The *20* Joseph E. Henabery
Fourteenth of July, The *32* René Clair

Fourth, The *73* Alexander Stolper
Fourth Alarm, The *30* Phil Whitman
Fourth Commandment, The *27* Emory Johnson
Fourth Estate, The *16* Frank Powell
Fourth Estate, The *39* Paul Rotha
Fourth for Marriage, A *64* Bob Wehling
Fourth Horseman, The *32* Hamilton Mac-Fadden
Fourth Man, The *82* Paul Verhoeven
Fourth Marriage of Dame Margaret, The *20* Carl Theodor Dreyer
Fourth Musketeer, The *23* William K. Howard
Fourth Protocol, The *86* John Mackenzie
Fourth Square, The *61* Allan Davis
Fourth War, The *90* John Frankenheimer
Fourth Wish, The *75* Don Chaffey
Fous de Bassan, Les *87* Yves Simoneau
Fous du Stade, Les *72* Claude Zidi
Fovos, O *67* Costas Manoussakis
Fowl Ball, The *30* Walter Lantz
Fowl Brawl *47* Howard Swift
Fowl Play *37* Dave Fleischer
Fowl Proceeding, A *25* Leslie Hiscott
Fowl Weather *53* Friz Freleng
Fox, The *21* Robert Thornby
Fox, The *39* Minoru Shibuya
Fox, The *67* Mark Rydell
Fox *74* Rainer Werner Fassbinder
Fox, The *86* Claes Lindberg
Fox Affair, The *78* Fereidun G. Jorjani
Fox and His Friends *74* Rainer Werner Fassbinder
Fox and the Grapes, The *41* Frank Tashlin
Fox and the Hound, The *81* Ted Berman, Richard Rich, Art Stevens
Fox and the Rabbit, The *35* Walter Lantz
Fox Chase, The *28* Walt Disney
Fox Chase, The *52* Len Lye
Fox Farm *22* Guy Newall
Fox Fire Child Watch *71* Stan Brakhage
Fox Fire Light *81* Allen Baron
Fox Hunt, The *31* Wilfred Jackson
Fox in a Fix, A *51* Robert McKimson
Fox in the Chicken Coop *78* Ephraim Kishon
Fox Movietone Follies *29* David Butler, Marcel Silver
Fox Movietone Follies of 1929 *29* David Butler, Marcel Silver
Fox Movietone Follies of 1930 *30* Ben Stoloff
Fox Pop *42* Chuck Jones
Fox Style *73* Clyde Houston
Fox Tales *27* Stephen Roberts
Fox Terror *57* Robert McKimson
Fox with Nine Tails, The *69* Shinichi Yagi
Fox Woman, The *15* Lloyd Ingraham
Foxbat *77* Po-chih Leong
Foxes *80* Adrian Lyne
Foxes of Harrow, The *47* John M. Stahl
Foxey Flatfoots *46* Bob Wickersham
Foxfire *55* Joseph Pevney
Foxhole in Cairo *60* John Llewellyn Moxey
Foxholes *48* Pal'o Bielek
Foxhunt *37* Anthony Gross, Hector Hoppin
Foxiest Girl in Paris, The *56* Christian-Jaque

Foxtrap *86* Fred Williamson
Foxtrot *75* Arturo Ripstein
Foxtrot *88* Jón Tryggvason
Foxy Brown *74* Jack Hill
Foxy by Proxy *52* Friz Freleng
Foxy Duckling, A *47* Art Davis
Foxy Hunter, The *37* Dave Fleischer
Foxy Lady *71* Ivan Reitman
Foxy Pup, The *37* Ubbe Iwerks
F'r Safety Sake *50* Joseph Barbera, William Hanna
Fra Diavolo *12* Alice Guy-Blaché
Fra Diavolo *22* Challis Sanderson
Fra Diavolo *31* Mario Bonnard
Fra Diavolo *33* Hal Roach, Charles Rogers
Fra' Diavolo *41* Luigi Zampa
Fra Diavolo *62* Leopoldo Savona
Fra Fyrste til Knejpevært *13* Forest Holger-Madsen
Fra Piazza del Popolo *25* Anders Wilhelm Sandberg
Fra Vincenti *09* Louis Feuillade
Fracchia Contro Dracula *85* Neri Parenti
Fracchia vs. Dracula *85* Neri Parenti
Fractured Leghorn, A *50* Robert McKimson
Frage 7 *61* Stuart Rosenberg
Fragilité — Ton Nom Est Femme *65* Nadine Trintignant
Fragment of an Empire *29* Friedrich Ermler
Fragment of Fear *70* Richard C. Sarafian
Fragment of Seeking *46* Curtis Harrington
Fragrance of Wild Flowers, The *77* Srđan Karanović
Fraidy Cat, The *42* Joseph Barbera, William Hanna
Frail Women *32* Maurice Elvey
Frailty *16* Sidney Morgan
Frailty *21* F. Martin Thornton
Fram för Lilla Märta *45* Hasse Ekman
Frame of Mind *65* Jan Rybkowski
Frame-Up, The *15* Otis Turner
Frame-Up, The *17* Edward Sloman
Frame Up, The *23* Harry G. Moody
Frame-Up, The *37* D. Ross Lederman
Framed *26* Stephen Roberts
Framed *27* Charles Brabin
Framed *30* George Archainbaud
Framed *39* Harold Schuster
Framed *47* Richard Wallace
Framed *74* Phil Karlson
Framed Cat *50* Joseph Barbera, William Hanna
Frames of Reference *59* Richard Leacock
Framing Father *36* Leslie Goodwins
Framing Framers *18* Ferris G. Hartman, Philip Hurn
Framing Youth *37* Gordon Douglas
Främmande Hamn *48* Erik Faustman
Fran *85* Glenda Hambly
Från Yttersta Skären *31* Gustaf Molander
Française et l'Amour, La *60* Michel Boisrond, Christian-Jaque, René Clair, Henri Decoin, Jean Delannoy, Jean-Paul Le Chanois, Henri Verneuil
Françaises Veillez *15* Léonce Perret
France Est un Jardin, La *53* Roger Leenhardt
France et Angleterre Forever *15* Léonce Perret

France Is a Garden *53* Roger Leenhardt
France Liberated *44* Sergei Yutkevich
France Société Anonyme *74* Alain Corneau
France sur Mer *69* François Reichenbach
France sur un Caillou, La *60* Claude Fournier, Gilles Groulx
Frances *82* Graeme Clifford
Francesca *86* Verena Rudolph
Francesca da Rimini *07* J. Stuart Blackton
Francesca da Rimini *13* Ugo Falena
Francesca È Mia *86* Roberto Russo
Francesca Is Mine *86* Roberto Russo
Francesco *89* Liliana Cavani
Francesco d'Assisi *66* Liliana Cavani
Francesco, Giullare di Dio *49* Roberto Rossellini
Franches Lippées *33* Jean Delannoy
Franchette: Les Intrigues *69* Arlo Shiffen
Franchise Affair, The *50* Lawrence Huntington
Francis *49* Arthur Lubin
Francis Bacon *78* Paul Leduc
Francis Covers the Big Town *53* Arthur Lubin
Francis, God's Jester *49* Roberto Rossellini
Francis Goes to the Races *51* Arthur Lubin
Francis Goes to West Point *52* Arthur Lubin
Francis in the Haunted House *56* Charles Lamont
Francis in the Navy *55* Arthur Lubin
Francis Joins the WACs *54* Arthur Lubin
Francis of Assisi *61* Michael Curtiz
Francis the First *36* Christian-Jaque
Francisca *81* Manoel De Oliveira
Franciscain de Bourges, Le *67* Claude Autant-Lara
Franck Aroma *37* Alexander Alexeïeff, Claire Parker
Franco de Port *37* Dmitri Kirsanov
François Mauriac *54* Roger Leenhardt
François Ier *36* Christian-Jaque
François Ier et Triboulet *07* Georges Méliès
François Reichenbach's Japan *81* François Reichenbach
François Villon *50* André Zwoboda
Françoise *63* André Cayatte
Françoise Steps Out *53* Jacques Becker
Frank Buck's Jungle Cavalcade *41* Armand Denis, Clyde E. Elliott
Frankenhooker *90* Frank Henenlotter
Frankenstein *10* J. Searle Dawley
Frankenstein *31* James Whale
Frankenstein *69* Tulio Demicheli, Hugo Fregonese
Frankenstein *73* Mario Mancini
Frankenstein *73* Antonio Margheriti, Paul Morrissey
Frankenstein all'Italiana *76* Armando Crispino
Frankenstein and the Giant Lizard *64* Inoshiro Honda
Frankenstein and the Monster from Hell *72* Terence Fisher
Frankenstein Conquers the World *64* Inoshiro Honda
Frankenstein Created Woman *65* Terence Fisher
Frankenstein '88 *85* Jean-Claude Lord

Frankenstein, el Vampiro y Cía. *61* Benito Alazraki
Frankenstein, el Vampiro y Compañía *61* Benito Alazraki
Frankenstein Experiment, The *73* Antonio Margheriti, Paul Morrissey
Frankenstein General Hospital *88* Deborah Roberts
Frankenstein Island *81* Jerry Warren
Frankenstein, Italian Style *76* Armando Crispino
Frankenstein Made Woman *65* Terence Fisher
Frankenstein Meets the Space Monster *65* Robert Gaffney
Frankenstein Meets the Spacemen *65* Robert Gaffney
Frankenstein Meets the Wolf Man *43* Roy William Neill
Frankenstein Must Be Destroyed! *69* Terence Fisher
Frankenstein 1970 *58* Howard W. Koch
Frankenstein 1980 *73* Mario Mancini
Frankenstein 90 *84* Alain Jessua
Frankenstein: The True Story *73* Jack Smight
Frankenstein, the Vampire and Co. *61* Benito Alazraki
Frankenstein Unbound *90* Roger Corman
Frankenstein vs. the Giant Devilfish *64* Inoshiro Honda
Frankenstein's Bloody Terror *67* Enrique L. Equiluz
Frankenstein's Castle of Freaks *73* Robert H. Oliver
Frankenstein's Daughter *58* Richard Cunha
Frankenstein's Great-Aunt Tillie *85* Myron J. Gold
Frankenstein's Island *81* Jerry Warren
Frankenstein's Monster *20* Eugenio Testa
Frankie and Johnny *35* John H. Auer, Chester Erskine
Frankie and Johnny *66* Frederick De Cordova
Frank's Greatest Adventure *67* Philip Kaufman
Frånskild *51* Gustaf Molander
Frantic *57* Louis Malle
Frantic *88* Roman Polanski
Franz Lehar *23* Wilhelm Thiele, Hans Torre
Franza *86* Xaver Schwarzenberger
Frasier the Sensuous Lion *73* Pat Shields
Frasquita *34* Karel Lamač
Fratelli Miracolosi, I *49* Luciano Emmer, Enrico Gras
Fratello Sole, Sorella Luna *72* Franco Zeffirelli
Fraternally Yours *33* William A. Seiter
Fraternity Row *77* Thomas J. Tobin
Fraternity Sweetheart *43* Arthur Dreifuss
Fraternity Vacation *85* James Frawley
Frau am Scheidewege, Die *38* Josef von Baky
Frau auf der Folter, Die *28* Robert Wiene
Frau Blackburn, Born 5 Jan. 1872, Is Filmed *67* Alexander Kluge
Frau Blackburn, Geb. 5 Jan. 1872, Wird Gefilmt *67* Alexander Kluge

Frau Blackburn Wird Gefilmt 67 Alexander Kluge

Frau Cheneys Ende 63 Franz Josef Wild

Frau Die Weiss Was Sie Will, Eine 36 Viktor Jansen

Frau Dorothys Bekenntnis 20 Michael Curtiz

Frau Dorothy's Confession 20 Michael Curtiz

Frau Eva 14 A. Berger, Robert Wiene

Frau für 24 Stunden, Die 25 Reinhold Schünzel

Frau Hölle 85 Juraj Jakubisko

Frau im Besten Mannesalter 59 Bernhard Wicki

Frau im Feuer, Die 24 Carl Boese

Frau im Mond, Die 28 Fritz Lang

Frau im Strom 39 Gerhard Lamprecht

Frau Lehmanns Töchter 33 Karl Heinz Wolff

Frau mit dem Schlechten Ruf, Die 24 Benjamin Christensen

Frau Nach der Mann Sich Sehnt, Die 29 Kurt Bernhardt

Frau Nach Mass 40 Helmut Käutner

Frau Ohne Bedeutung, Eine 36 Hans Steinhoff

Frau Sylvelin 39 Herbert Maisch

Frau Über Bord 45 Wolfgang Staudte

Frau von Der Man Spricht, Die 33 Viktor Jansen

Frau von Vierzig Jahren, Die 25 Richard Oswald

Frau Warrens Gewerbe 60 Ákos von Ráthonyi

Frau Wie Du, Eine 33 Carl Boese

Frau Wie Du, Eine 39 Victor Tourjansky

Fraud That Failed, The 12 Allan Dwan

Fraudulent Beggar, The 1898 James A. Williamson

Fraudulent Solicitor, The 07 Lewin Fitzhamon

Fraudulent Spiritualism Exposed 13 Charles Raymond

Fraudulent Spiritualistic Seance, The 20 Charles Raymond

Frauen Die Durch die Hölle Gehen 66 Rudolf Zehetgruber

Frauen im Liebeslager 77 Jesús Franco

Frauen in New York 77 Rainer Werner Fassbinder

Frauen Sind Keine Engel 43 Willi Forst

Frauen um den Sonnenkönig 35 Carl Fröhlich

Frauen vom Tannhof, Die 36 Franz Seitz

Frauengefängnis 75 Jesús Franco

Frauenhaus von Rio, Das 27 Hans Steinhoff

Frauenleid 37 Augusto Genina

Frauenliebe 37 Augusto Genina

Frauenopfer 22 Karl Grüne

Frauenparadies, Das 39 Arthur Maria Rabenalt

Frauenschicksal 29 Arthur Robison

Frauenschicksale 52 Slatan Dudow

Fräulein 58 Henry Koster

Fräulein Doktor 68 Alberto Lattuada

Fräulein Else 29 Paul Czinner

Fräulein Falsch Verbunden! 34 E. W. Emo

Fräulein Frau 34 Carl Boese

Fräulein Liselott 35 Johannes Guter

Fräulein Seifenschaum 14 Ernst Lubitsch

Fräulein von Amt, Das 25 Carl Heinz Schroth

Fräulein Zahnarzt 19 Joe May

Freak Barber, The 05 J. H. Martin

Freak from Suckweasel Mountain, The 83 Nick Zedd

Freak Patents: The Balloon R.R. 17 J. D. Leventhal

Freakmaker, The 73 Jack Cardiff

Freaks 32 Tod Browning

Freaks 66 Byron Mabe

Freaky Friday 76 Gary Nelson

Freccia, La 43 Alberto Lattuada

Freccia d'Oro, La 62 Antonio Margheriti

Freccia nel Fianco, La 43 Alberto Lattuada

Frechdachs, Der 34 Carl Boese, Heinz Hille

Freckled Rascal, The 29 Louis King

Freckles 17 Marshall Neilan

Freckles 28 James Leo Meehan

Freckles 35 William Hamilton, Edward Killy

Freckles 60 Andrew V. McLaglen

Freckles Comes Home 42 Jean Yarbrough

Fred Barry, Comédien 59 Claude Jutra

Fredaines de Pierrette, Les 00 Alice Guy-Blaché

Freda's Photo 13 Wilfred Noy

Freddie Steps Out 46 Arthur Dreifuss

Freddy Martin and His Orchestra 41 Jean Negulesco

Freddy und das Lied der Prärie 64 Hugo Fregonese

Freddy Unter Fremden Sternen 62 Wolfgang Schleif

Freddy's Dumb Playmates 13 Lewin Fitzhamon

Freddy's Little Love Affair 08 A. E. Coleby

Frédéric Chopin 61 Philip Wrestler

Fredlös 35 Pál Fejös

Free Air 22 Edward H. Griffith

Free and Easy 30 Edward Sedgwick

Free and Easy 41 George Sidney

Free and Easy 60 Robert Henryson

Free, Blonde and Twenty-One 40 Ricardo Cortez

Free Breathing 73 Márta Mészáros

Free Enterprise 86 John Dixon

Free Fall 67 Stan Vanderbeek

Free for All 49 Charles Barton

Free Grass 69 Bill Brame

Free House 42 Henry Cass

Free Kisses 26 William Nigh

Free Lips 28 Wallace MacDonald

Free Love 30 Hobart Henley

Free Lunch 21 Pat Sullivan

Free Pardon, A 08 Lewin Fitzhamon

Free Radicals 57 Len Lye

Free Ride, A 03 Percy Stow

Free Ride 86 Tom Trbovich

Free School 51 Kozaburo Yoshimura

Free Soul, A 31 Clarence Brown

Free Spirit 73 James Hill

Free Time at La Roca 81 Santiago Álvarez

Free to Live 38 George Cukor

Free to Love 25 Frank O'Connor

Free Trade Branch, The 03 George Albert Smith

Free, White and Twenty-One 63 Larry Buchanan

Free Wind 61 A. Tontichkin, Leonid Trauberg

Free Woman, A 71 Volker Schlöndorff

Freebie and the Bean 74 Richard Rush

Freebooters, The 08 A. E. Coleby

Freed Bird 13 Yevgeni Bauer

Freed 'Em and Weep 29 Leo McCarey

Freed Hands 40 Hans Schweikert

Freedom Committee 45 Bjarne Henning-Jensen

Freedom for Us 31 René Clair

Freedom Must Have Wings 41 Compton Bennett

Freedom of the Press 28 George Melford

Freedom of the Seas 34 Marcel Varnel

Freedom Radio 40 Anthony Asquith

Freedom Road 79 Ján Kadár

Freedom to Die 61 Francis Searle

Freelance 70 Francis Megahy

Freeway 88 Francis Delia

Freeway Maniac, The 89 Paul Winters

Freewheelin' 76 Scott Dittrich

Freeze Bomb 80 Al Adamson

Freeze—Die—Come to Life 90 Vitaly Kanevski

Freeze Out, The 21 John Ford

Freezing Mixture, The 10 Walter R. Booth

Freezing Point 66 Satsuo Yamamoto

Frei Geboren 65 James Hill

Freight Investigation 18 Raoul Barré, Charles Bowers

Freight Prepaid 21 James Cruze

Freighters of Destiny 31 Fred Allen

Freiheit 65 George Lucas

Freischutz, Der 70 Joachim Hess

Freiwild 28 Forest Holger-Madsen

Frelsende Film, Den 15 Forest Holger-Madsen

Fremd im Sudetenland 38 H. Wassermann

Fremde Fürst, Der 18 Paul Wegener*

Fremde Vogel, Der 11 Urban Gad

Fremmed Banker på, En 63 Johan Jacobsen

French, The 81 William Klein

French Are a Funny Race, The 55 Preston Sturges

French Cancan 54 Jean Renoir

French Connection, The 71 William Friedkin

French Connection II, The 75 John Frankenheimer

French Conspiracy, The 72 Yves Boisset

French Cops Learning English 08 Georges Méliès

French Detective, The 75 Pierre Granier-Deferre

French Doll, The 23 Robert Z. Leonard

French Downstairs, The 16 Lois Weber

French Dressing 27 Allan Dwan

French Dressing 63 Ken Russell

French Duel, The 09 D. W. Griffith

French Game, The 60 Jacques Doniol-Valcroze

French Heels 22 Edwin L. Hollywood

French Interpreter Policeman 08 Georges Méliès

French Key, The 46 Walter Colmes
French Kiss, The 87 Paulo Sérgio De Almeida
French Kisses 30 Stephen Roberts
French Leave 30 Sam Newfield
French Leave 30 Jack Raymond
French Leave 37 Norman Lee
French Leave 48 Frank McDonald
French Lesson 84 Brian Gilbert
French Lieutenant's Woman, The 81 Karel Reisz
French Line, The 53 Lloyd Bacon
French Mistress, The 60 Roy Boulting
French Officers' Meeting 1896 Georges Méliès
French Peep Show, The 50 Russ Meyer
French Postcards 79 Willard Huyck
French Provincial 74 André Téchiné
French Quarter 77 Dennis Kane
French Rarebit, The 51 Robert McKimson
French Regiment Going to the Parade 1896 Georges Méliès
French Revolution, The 89 Robert Enrico, Richard T. Heffron
French Spy, The 12 Lawrence Trimble
French They Are a Funny Race, The 55 Preston Sturges
French Touch, The 52 Jean Boyer
French vs. English 12 Gilbert Southwell
French Way, The 40 Jacques De Baroncelli
French Way, The 73 Michel Deville
French White Cargo 37 Robert Siodmak
French Without Tears 39 Anthony Asquith
French Woman, The 79 Just Jaeckin
Frenchie 50 Louis King
Frenchman's Creek 44 Mitchell Leisen
Frenchman's Farm 87 Ron Way
Frenchy Discovers America 20 Milt Gross
Frenesi de l'Estate 63 Luigi Zampa
Frenesia 39 Mario Bonnard
Frenzied Flames 26 Stuart Paton
Frenzy 28 Andrew L. Stone
Frenzy 39 Mario Bonnard
Frenzy 44 Alf Sjöberg
Frenzy 45 Vernon Sewell
Frenzy, The 63 Giovanni Guareschi, Pier Paolo Pasolini
Frenzy 72 Alfred Hitchcock
Fréquence Meurtre 88 Elisabeth Rappeneau
Frère de Lait, Le 16 Jacques Feyder
Frères Bouquinquant, Les 47 Louis Daquin
Frères Boutdebois, Les 08 Émile Cohl
Frères Corses, Les 16 André Antoine
Frères Pétard, Les 86 Hervé Palud
Frescos on the White 68 Emil Lotyanu
Fresh Air 39 Martin Frič
Fresh Airedale 45 Chuck Jones
Fresh Every Hour 28 William James Craft
Fresh Fish 22 Earl Hurd
Fresh Fish 39 Tex Avery
Fresh from Paris 55 Leslie Goodwins
Fresh Hare 42 Friz Freleng
Fresh Horses 88 David Anspaugh
Fresh Paint 1898 Georges Méliès
Fresh Vegetable Mystery, The 39 Dave Fleischer

Freshie, The 22 William Hughes Curran
Freshman, The 25 Fred Newmeyer, Sam Taylor
Freshman, The 58 Wolf Rilla
Freshman, The 90 Andrew Bergman
Freshman Love 36 William McGann
Freshman Year 38 Frank McDonald
Freud 62 John Huston
Freud — The Secret Passion 62 John Huston
Freudlose Gasse, Die 25 G. W. Pabst
Freudy Cat 64 Robert McKimson
Freundin eines Grossen Mannes, Die 34 Paul Wegener
Freundin So Goldig Wie Du, Eine 30 Karel Lamač
Freundschaft Siegt 51 Joris Ivens, Ivan Pyriev
Freut Euch des Lebens 34 Hans Steinhoff
Friars Road 86 Marc C. Tropia
Fric, Le 59 Maurice Cloche
Fric-Frac 39 Claude Autant-Lara, Maurice Lehmann
Frida 84 Paul Leduc
Frida: Naturaleza Vida 84 Paul Leduc
Frida's Song 30 Gustaf Molander
Fridas Visor 30 Gustaf Molander
Friday Evening 45 Kamel Salim
Friday Foster 75 Arthur Marks
Friday on My Mind 70 Wayne A. Schotten
Friday Rose 38 Ladislas Vajda
Friday the Thirteenth 16 Émile Chautard
Friday the Thirteenth 33 Victor Saville
Friday the Thirteenth 53 Pal'o Bielek
Friday the 13th 80 Sean S. Cunningham
Friday the 13th Part 2 81 Steve Miner
Friday the 13th Part 3 82 Steve Miner
Friday the 13th — The Final Chapter 84 Joseph Zito
Friday the 13th Part V: A New Beginning 85 Danny Steinmann
Friday the 13th Part VI: Jason Lives 86 Tom McLoughlin
Friday the 13th Part VII — The New Blood 88 John Buechler
Friday the 13th Part VIII: Jason Takes Manhattan 89 Rob Hedden
Friday the Thirteenth...The Orphan 79 John Ballard
Fridericus 39 Johannes Meyer
Frieda 47 Basil Dearden
Friedensfahrt 1952 52 Joris Ivens
Friederike von Barring 56 Rolf Thiele
Friedhof der Lebenden, Der 21 Gerhard Lamprecht
Friend, The 74 Yılmaz Güney
Friend Husband 18 Clarence Badger
Friend in Blue, The 14 H. Oceano Martinek
Friend in Need, A 09 Lewin Fitzhamon
Friend in Need, A 14 Frank Wilson
Friend Indeed, A 37 Fred Zinnemann
Friend of a Jolly Devil, The 87 Jerzy Łukaszewicz
Friend of Cupid, A 25 Leslie Hiscott
Friend of the Family, The 09 D. W. Griffith
Friend of the Family 49 James Hill
Friend of the Family 65 Robert Thomas

Friend of the People, A 18 Forest Holger-Madsen
Friend or Foe 82 John Krish
Friend Will Come Tonight, A 46 Raymond Bernard
Friend Wilson's Daughter 15 Langdon West
Friendliest Girls in the World, The 63 Henry Levin
Friendly Enemies 25 George Melford
Friendly Enemies 42 Allan Dwan
Friendly Husband 23 John G. Blystone
Friendly Killer, The 70 Teruo Ishii
Friendly Neighbors 40 Nick Grindé
Friendly Persuasion 56 William Wyler
Friends 12 D. W. Griffith
Friends 71 Lewis Gilbert
Friends 88 Jan Němec
Friends and Husbands 82 Margarethe von Trotta
Friends and Lovers 31 Victor Schertzinger
Friends and Lovers 69 Harvey Cort
Friends and Neighbours 59 Gordon Parry
Friends for Life 55 Franco Rossi
Friends Forever 87 Stefan Henszelman
Friends, Lovers & Lunatics 89 Stephen Withrow
Friends of Eddie Coyle, The 73 Peter Yates
Friends of Mr. Sweeney, The 34 Edward Ludwig
Friends, Romans and Leo 17 Alan Crosland
Friends vs. Foes 14 Arrigo Bocchi
Friendship 40 Oreste Biancoli
Friendship of Beaupère, The 18 Alfred E. Green
Friendship, Secrets and Lies 79 Marlena Laird, Ann Zane Shanks
Friendship Tour 1952 52 Joris Ivens
Friendship Triumphs 51 Joris Ivens, Ivan Pyriev
Friendship's Death 87 Peter Wollen
Friesennot 36 Peter Hagen, Werner Kortwich
Fright 56 W. Lee Wilder
Fright 71 Peter Collinson
Fright, The 81 Jean-Claude Lord
Fright House 90 Len Anthony
Fright Night 85 Tom Holland
Fright Night — Part II 88 Tommy Lee Wallace
Frightened Bride, The 52 Terence Young
Frightened City 50 Earl McEvoy
Frightened City, The 61 John Lemont
Frightened Freddy and the Desperate Alien 11 Percy Stow
Frightened Freddy and the Murderous Marauder 11 Percy Stow
Frightened Freddy — How Freddy Won a Hundred Pounds 10 Percy Stow
Frightened Freddy the Fearful Policeman 10 Percy Stow
Frightened Lady, The 32 T. Hayes Hunter
Frightened Lady 40 George King
Frightened Man, The 52 John Gilling
Frightened Marksman, The 54 Vojtěch Jasný, Karel Kachyňa
Frightmare 74 Peter Walker
Frightmare 83 Norman Thaddeus Vane

Frontier Fighters *43* Sam Newfield
Frontier Fremont *76* Richard Friedenberg
Frontier Fugitives *45* Harry Fraser
Frontier Fury *41* Sam Newfield
Frontier Fury *43* William Berke
Frontier Gal *45* Charles Lamont
Frontier Gambler *56* Sam Newfield
Frontier Gun *58* Paul Landres
Frontier Gunlaw *46* Derwin Abrahams
Frontier Hellcat *64* Alfred Vohrer
Frontier Horizon *39* George Sherman
Frontier Investigator *49* Fred C. Brannon
Frontier Justice *36* Robert McGowan
Frontier Law *43* Elmer Clifton
Frontier Marshal *33* Lewis Seiler
Frontier Marshal *39* Allan Dwan
Frontier Marshal *49* Fred C. Brannon
Frontier Marshal in Prairie Pals *42* Sam
    Newfield
Frontier of the Stars *21* Charles Maigne
Frontier Outlaws *44* Sam Newfield
Frontier Outpost *49* Ray Nazarro
Frontier People *13* Mauritz Stiller
Frontier Phantom, The *52* Ron Ormond
Frontier Pony Express *39* Joseph Kane
Frontier Rangers *59* Jacques Tourneur
Frontier Revenge *48* Ray Taylor
Frontier Scout *38* Sam Newfield
Frontier Scout *56* Lesley Selander
Frontier Town *38* Ray Taylor
Frontier Trail, The *26* Scott R. Dunlap
Frontier Uprising *39* George Sherman
Frontier Uprising *61* Edward L. Cahn
Frontier Vengeance *39* Nate Watt
Frontier Woman *56* Ron Ormond
Frontière, La *61* Jean Cayrol, Claude
    Durand
Frontiers of '49 *39* Joseph Levering
Frontiers of News *64* Willard Van Dyke
Frontiersman, The *27* Reginald Barker
Frontiersman, The *38* Lesley Selander
Frontiersman, The *68* Michael Moore
Frontline Cameras, 1935-1965 *65* Willard
    Van Dyke
Frosty Roads *86* Massoud Jafari Jozani
Frosty the Snowman *73* Arthur Rankin, Jr.
Frou Frou *38* Richard Thorpe
Frou Frou *55* Augusto Genina
Frozen Affair *37* Arthur Dreifuss
Frozen Alive *64* Bernard Knowles
Frozen Dead, The *66* Herbert J. Leder
Frozen Fate *29* St. John L. Clowes, Ben R.
    Hart
Frozen Ghost, The *45* Harold Young
Frozen Justice *29* Allan Dwan
Frozen Leopard, The *86* Lars Oskarsson
Frozen Limits, The *39* Marcel Varnel
Frozen North, The *19* Raoul Barré,
    Charles Bowers
Frozen North, The *22* Edward F. Cline,
    Buster Keaton
Frozen River *29* F. Harmon Weight
Frozen Scream *80* Frank Roach
Frozen Warning, The *18* Oscar Eagle
Fru Potifar *11* August Blom
Frühling im Wien *37* J. A. Hübler-Kahla
Frühlingserwachen *29* Richard Oswald
Frühlingsmärchen *34* Carl Fröhlich
Frühlingsrauschen *29* William Dieterle
Frühlingssinfonie *83* Peter Schamoni

Frühlingsstimmen *33* Pál Fejős
Frühreifen, Die *58* Josef von Baky
Fruit Défendu, Le *52* Henri Verneuil
Fruit Is Ripe, The *61* Louis Soulanes
Fruit Machine, The *88* Philip Saville
Fruit of Divorce, The *28* Roy William
    Neill
Fruit of Evil, The *14* Wallace Reid
Fruit of Paradise, The *69* Věra Chytilová
Fruit of the Trees of Paradise, The *69* Věra
    Chytilová
Fruitful Farm *29* John Foster
Fruitful Vine, The *21* Maurice Elvey
Fruits Amers *66* Jacqueline Audry
Fruits de la Passion, Les *81* Shuji Tera-
    yama
Fruits de l'Été, Les *55* Raymond Bernard
Fruits de Saison *02* Alice Guy-Blaché
Fruits et Légumes Animés *15* Émile Cohl
Fruits et Légumes Vivants *12* Émile Cohl
Fruits of Desire, The *16* Oscar Eagle
Fruits of Love, The *26* Alexander Dovz-
    henko
Fruits of Matrimony, The *04* Alf Collins
Fruits of Passion *19* George Ridgwell
Fruits of Passion, The *81* Shuji Terayama
Fruits of Summer *55* Raymond Bernard
Fruits of Vengeance *10* J. Stuart Blackton
Fruits Sauvages, Les *54* Hervé Bromberger
Frullo del Passero, Il *89* Gianfranco Min-
    gozzi
Frusna Leoparden, Den *86* Lars Oskarsson
Frusta e il Corpo, La *63* Mario Bava
Frustrated *12* Gilbert Southwell
Frustrated Elopement, The *02* Percy Stow
Frustrated Future *70* Werner Herzog
Frustration *47* Ingmar Bergman
Frustrations *67* Georges Combret
Frutto Acerbo *34* Carlo Ludovico Bragaglia
Fu Manchu and the Kiss of Death *68* Jesús
    Franco
Fu Manchu y el Beso de la Muerte *68* Jesús
    Franco
Fu Manchu's Castle *68* Jesús Franco
Fu Mattia Pascal, Il *37* Pierre Chénal
Fuchsjagd auf Skiern Durchs Engadin,
    Eine *22* Arnold Fanck
Fuck *68* Paul Morrissey, Andy Warhol
Fuck Off! – Images of Finland *71* Jörn
    Donner, Erkki Seiro, Jaakko Talaskivi
Fuddy Duddy Buddy *51* John Hubley
Fudget's Budget *54* Robert Cannon
Fuefuki-Gawa *60* Keisuke Kinoshita
Fuego *64* Julio Coll
Fuegos *87* Alfredo Arias
Fuel for Battle *44* John Eldridge
Fuel of Life *17* Walter Edwards
¡Fuera de Aquí! *77* Jorge Sanjinés
Fuera de la Ley *40* Manuel Romero
Fuerte Perdido *64* José María Elorrieta
Fuerza del Destino, La *10* Ricardo De
    Baños
Fuerzas Vivas, Las *75* Luis Alcoriza
Fūfu *53* Mikio Naruse
Fuga, La *37* Luis Saslavsky
Fuga, La *44* Norman Foster
Fuga *60* Carlos Diegués*
Fuga, La *66* Paolo Spinola
Fuga a Due Voci *43* Carlo Ludovico
    Bragaglia

Fuga dall'Arcipelago Maladetto *82*
    Antonio Margheriti
Fuga de Carrasco, La *87* Alfredo B.
    Crevenna
Fuga degli Amanti, La *14* Augusto Genina
Fuga in Città *50* Dino Risi
Fuga in Francia *48* Mario Soldati
Fügefalevél *66* Félix Máriássy
Fugitif, La *18* André Hugon
Fugitifs, Les *86* Francis Veber
Fugitive, The *10* D. W. Griffith
Fugitive, The *13* Allan Dwan
Fugitive, The *16* Frederick Sullivan
Fugitive, The *25* Ben F. Wilson
Fugitive, The *32* Vladimir Petrov
Fugitive, The *33* Harry Fraser
Fugitive, The *39* Brian Desmond Hurst
Fugitive, The *47* John Ford
Fugitive, The *50* Mario Camerini
Fugitive Apparitions *04* Georges Méliès
Fugitive at Large *39* Lewis D. Collins
Fugitive from a Prison Camp *40* Lewis D.
    Collins
Fugitive from Justice, A *40* Terry Morse
Fugitive from Matrimony, A *19* Henry
    King
Fugitive from Sonora *43* Howard Brether-
    ton
Fugitive from the Past *64* Tomu Uchida
Fugitive from Time *43* William Berke
Fugitive Futurist, The *24* Gaston Quiribet
Fugitive Girls *75* Stephen C. Apostolof
Fugitive in Saigon *56* Marcel Camus
Fugitive in the Sky *36* Nick Grindé
Fugitive Killer *75* Emile A. Harvard
Fugitive Kind, The *59* Sidney Lumet
Fugitive Lady *34* Albert S. Rogell
Fugitive Lady *49* Marino Girolami, Sidney
    Salkow
Fugitive Lovers *33* Richard Boleslawski
Fugitive of the Plains *43* Sam Newfield
Fugitive Road *34* Frank R. Strayer
Fugitive Sheriff, The *36* Spencer G.
    Bennet
Fugitive Valley *41* R. Finkel, S. Roy Luby,
    John Vlamos
Fugitives, The *12* August Blom
Fugitives *29* William Beaudine
Fugitives, The *71* Yılmaz Güney
Fugitives, The *86* Francis Veber
Fugitives Find Shelter *45* Astrid Henning-
    Jensen, Bjarne Henning-Jensen
Fugitives for a Night *38* Leslie Goodwins
Fugue de Lily, La *17* Louis Feuillade
Fugue de Mahmoud, La *50* Roger Leen-
    hardt
Führer's Face, Der *43* Jack Kinney
Führmann Henschel *18* Ernst Lubitsch
Führmann Henschel *56* Josef von Baky
Fuite de Gaz, La *12* Max Linder
Fuji *74* Robert Breer
Fukeiki Jidai *30* Mikio Naruse
Fukkatsu no Hi *79* Kinji Fukasaku
Fukushū Suruwa Wareni Ari *79* Shohei
    Imamura
Fukuyō Koikaze *35* Heinosuke Gosho
Fulaninha *86* David Neves
Fulfilled Dreams *39* N. Brazybulski
Fulfilment of the Law, The *14* Ethyle
    Batley

Further Exploits of Sexton Blake—The Mystery of the S.S. Olympic, The 19 Harry Lorraine

Further Prophecies of Nostradamus 42 David Miller

Further Tales from the Crypt 72 Roy Ward Baker

Further Than Fear 79 Tomás Aznar

Further Up the Creek! 58 Val Guest

Furtivos 75 José Luis Borau

Furusato 22 Kenji Mizoguchi

Furusato 30 Kenji Mizoguchi

Furusato no Uta 25 Kenji Mizoguchi

Fury 22 Henry King

Fury 36 Fritz Lang

Fury 48 Phil Karlson

Fury 73 Antonio Calenda

Fury, The 78 Brian DePalma

Fury and the Woman 37 Lewis D. Collins

Fury at Furnace Creek 48 H. Bruce Humberstone

Fury at Gunsight Pass 56 Fred F. Sears

Fury at Showdown 57 Gerd Oswald

Fury at Smugglers' Bay 60 John Gilling

Fury Below 38 Harry Fraser

Fury in Paradise 55 Rolando Aguilar, George Bruce

Fury in the Pacific 45 Bonney Powell

Fury Is a Woman 61 Andrzej Wajda

Fury of Achilles 62 Marino Girolami

Fury of Hercules, The 60 Gianfranco Parolini

Fury of Samson, The 60 Gianfranco Parolini

Fury of the Apaches 63 José María Elorrieta

Fury of the Congo 51 William Berke

Fury of the Jungle 33 Roy William Neill

Fury of the Pagans 62 Guido Malatesta

Fury of the Succubus 80 James Polakoff

Fury of the Vikings 61 Mario Bava

Fury of the Wild 29 Leon D'Usseau

Fury of the Wolf Man, The 70 José María Zabalza

Fury River 58 Alan Crosland, Jr., Otto Lang, Jacques Tourneur, George Waggner

Fury Unleashed 58 Lew Landers

Furyō Shōjo 49 Mikio Naruse

Furyō Shōnen 60 Susumu Hani

Fūryū Fukagawa 60 So Yamamura

Fūryū Katsujinken 34 Sadao Yamanaka

Fusée, La 33 Jacques Tourneur

Fushichō 47 Keisuke Kinoshita

Fushin no Toki 68 Tadashi Imai

Fusillamiento de Dorrego, El 08 Mario Gallo

Fusillier Wipf 38 Leopold Lindtberg*

Fusils, Les 63 Ruy Guerra

Fusils de la Liberté, Les 62 Mohammed Lakhdar Amina, Jamal Chanderli

Fusion 67 Ed Emshwiller, Alwin Nikolais

Fuss and Feathers 09 Edwin S. Porter

Fuss and Feathers 18 Fred Niblo

Fuss Over Feathers 53 John Eldridge, Don Sharp

Fussgänger, Der 74 Maximilian Schell

Fussnoten 67 Edgar Reitz

Füst 70 Miklós Jancsó

Futari de Aruita Ikuharuaki 62 Keisuke Kinoshita

Futari de Aruita Ikushunjū 62 Keisuke Kinoshita

Futari no Musuko 62 Yasuke Chiba

Futatsu Doro 33 Teinosuke Kinugasa

Futatsu no Yakizakana 68 Yoji Kuri

Futtock's End 69 Bob Kellett

Future Cop 84 Charles Band

Future Hackenschmidts 04 Alf Collins

Future Is a Woman, The 84 Marco Ferreri

Future Is Woman, The 84 Marco Ferreri

Future-Kill 85 Ronald W. Moore

Future of Emily, The 84 Helma Sanders-Brahms

Future Revealed by the Lines of the Feet, The 14 Émile Cohl

Future Women 70 Jesús Franco

Future's in the Air, The 36 Paul Rotha

Futures Vedettes 54 Marc Allégret

Futureworld 76 Richard T. Heffron

Futurismo 23 Marcel L'Herbier

Futuro È Donna, Il 84 Marco Ferreri

Futz 69 Tom O'Horgan

Fuyuki Shinju 34 Teinosuke Kinugasa

Fūzen no Tomoshibi 57 Keisuke Kinoshita

Fuzi Qing 81 Allen Fong

Fuzis, Os 63 Ruy Guerra

Fuzz 72 Richard A. Colla

Fuzzy Pink Nightgown, The 57 Norman Taurog

Fuzzy Settles Down 44 Sam Newfield

4 x 4 65 Jan Troell*

491 63 Vilgot Sjöman

Fyre 79 Richard Grand

G. G. Passion 66 David Bailey

G.I. Blues 60 Norman Taurog

G.I. Executioner, The 71 Joel M. Reed

G.I. Honeymoon 44 Phil Karlson

G.I. Jane 50 Reginald LeBorg

G.I. Joe 45 William A. Wellman

G.I. War Brides 46 George Blair

G.L.O.W. 87 Matt Cimber

G.m.b.H. Tenor, Der 16 Ernst Lubitsch

G-Man's Wife 35 Nick Grindé

G-Men 35 William Keighley

G-Men Never Forget 47 Fred C. Brannon, Yakima Canutt

G-Men vs. the Black Dragon 43 William Witney

G.O.R.P. 80 Joseph Ruben

G. P. As Basil the Brainless 15 G. P. Huntley

GUM 22 Dziga Vertov

Gå med Mig Hjem 41 Benjamin Christensen

Gabbia, La 85 Giuseppe Patroni Griffi

Gabbiano, Il 77 Marco Bellocchio

Gabby Goes Fishing 41 Dave Fleischer

Gable and Lombard 76 Sidney J. Furie

Gables Mystery, The 31 Harry Hughes

Gables Mystery, The 38 Harry Hughes

Gabriel Grub 04 James A. Williamson

Gabriel Grub the Surly Sexton 04 James A. Williamson

Gabriel Over the White House 33 Gregory La Cava

Gabriela 83 Bruno Barreto

Gabriele Dambrone 43 Hans Steinhoff

Gabriella 74 Mack Bing

Gabrielle 54 Hasse Ekman

Gaby 56 Kurt Bernhardt

Gaby—A True Story 87 Luis Mandoki

Gadbad Ghotala 87 Raja Bargir

Gadflies 76 Stan Brakhage

Gadfly, The 55 Alexander Feinzimmer, Samson Samsonov

Gado Bravo 33 Max Nosseck

Gæst fra en Anden Verden, En 14 August Blom

Gaétan ou Le Commis Audacieux 22 Louis Feuillade

Gaffeur, Le 85 Serge Penard

Gage d'Amour 04 Alice Guy-Blaché

Gagnant, Le 35 Yves Allégret

Gai Dimanche 35 Jacques Tati

Gai Savoir, Le 67 Jean-Luc Godard

Gaieté Parisienne 42 Jean Negulesco

Gaietés de l'Escadron, Les 13 Maurice Tourneur

Gaietés de l'Escadron, Les 32 Maurice Tourneur

Gaiety Duet, A 09 Arthur Gilbert

Gaiety George 45 Freddie Carpenter, George King, Leontine Sagan

Gaiety Girl, The 24 King Baggot

Gaiety Girls, The 37 Thornton Freeland

Gaijo no Sukechi 25 Kenji Mizoguchi*

Gaily, Gaily 69 Norman Jewison

Gaines Roussel, Les 39 Alexander Alexeïeff, Claire Parker

Gaitō no Kishi 28 Heinosuke Gosho

Gakusō o Idete 25 Kenji Mizoguchi

Gal Who Took the West, The 49 Frederick De Cordova

Gal Young 'Un 79 Victor Nuñez

Gala 61 Jean-Daniel Pollet

Gala Day 63 John Irvin

Gala Dinner 56 György Révész

Galactic Gigolo 87 Gorman Bechard

Galápagos Islands 38 Richard Leacock

Galatée 10 Georges Méliès

Galathea 35 Lotte Reiniger

Galavorstellung, Die 33 Fred Zelnik

Galaxie 66 Gregory Markopoulos

Galaxina 80 William Sachs

Galaxy Express 82 Taro Rin

Galaxy of Terror 81 Bruce Clark

Galerie des Monstres, La 24 Jaque Catelain

Galeries de Malgovert, Les 50 Georges Rouquier

Galette du Roi, La 86 Jean-Michel Ribes

Galga Mentén 54 Miklós Jancsó

Galgamannen 45 Gustaf Molander

Galia 65 Georges Lautner

Galicia y Compostela 33 Fernando Mantilla, Carlos Velo

Galiläer, Der 21 Dmitri Buchowetzki

Galileo 68 Liliana Cavani

Galileo 73 Joseph Losey

Galileo Galilei 08 Luigi Maggi

Gall of the North, The 32 Edward Buzzell

Gallant Bess 46 Andrew Marton

Gallant Blade, The 48 Henry Levin

Gallant Defender 35 David Selman

Gallant Festivals 65 René Clair

Gallant Fool, The 26 Duke Worne

Gallant Fool, The 33 Robert North Bradbury

Gallant Gringo, The 27 Victor Tourjansky, W. S. Van Dyke

Gallant Hours, The 60 Robert Montgomery

Gallant Journey 46 William A. Wellman

Gallant Lady 33 Gregory La Cava

Gallant Lady 42 William Beaudine

Gallant Legion, The 48 Joseph Kane

Gallant Little Tailor, The 54 Lotte Reiniger

Gallant One, The 64 Aaron Stell

Gallant Sons 40 George B. Seitz

Gallery Murders, The 69 Dario Argento

Gallery of Horrors 67 David L. Hewitt

Galley Slave, The 15 J. Gordon Edwards

Gallina Clueca, La 41 Fernando De Fuentes

Gallina Vogelbirdae 63 Jiří Brdečka

Gallipoli 81 Peter Weir

Galloper, The 15 Donald Mackenzie

Gallopin' Gals 40 Joseph Barbera, William Hanna

Gallopin' Gaucho, The 28 Walt Disney, Ubbe Iwerks

Gallopin' Through 23 Robert North Bradbury

Galloping Ace, The 24 Robert North Bradbury

Galloping Bungalows 24 Edward F. Cline

Galloping Cowboy, The 26 William James Craft

Galloping Devil, The 20 Nate Watt

Galloping Devils 20 Nate Watt

Galloping Dude 20 Nate Watt

Galloping Dynamite 37 Harry Fraser

Galloping Fish 24 Del Andrews

Galloping Fury 27 B. Reeves Eason

Galloping Gallagher 24 Albert S. Rogell

Galloping Ghost, The 31 B. Reeves Eason

Galloping Gobs, The 27 Richard Thorpe

Galloping Hoofs 24 George B. Seitz

Galloping Jinx 25 Robert Eddy

Galloping Justice 27 William Wyler

Galloping Kid, The 22 Nat Ross

Galloping Kid, The 32 Robert E. Tansey

Galloping Major, The 50 Henry Cornelius

Galloping On 25 Richard Thorpe

Galloping Romeo 13 William Duncan

Galloping Romeo 33 Robert North Bradbury

Galloping Thru 23 Robert North Bradbury

Galloping Thru 31 Lloyd Nosler

Galloping Thunder 27 Scott Pembroke

Galloping Thunder 46 Ray Nazarro

Galloping Vengeance 25 William James Craft

Galops 28 Abel Gance

Galoše Štastia 86 Juraj Herz

Gals, Inc. 43 Leslie Goodwins

Galvanic Fluid 08 J. Stuart Blackton

Gambara vs. Barugon 66 Shigeo Tanaka

Gamberge, La 62 Norbert Carbonneaux

Gambit 66 Ronald Neame

Gamble for Love, A 17 Frank Wilson

Gamble in Lives, A 20 George Ridgwell

Gamble in Souls, A 16 Walter Edwards, Roy William Neill

Gamble with Hearts, A 23 Edwin J. Collins

Gambler, The 58 Claude Autant-Lara

Gambler, The 74 Karel Reisz

Gambler and the Lady, The 52 Patrick Jenkins, Sam Newfield

Gambler from Natchez, The 54 Henry Levin

Gambler Wore a Gun, The 61 Edward L. Cahn

Gamblers, The 05 Percy Stow

Gamblers, The 14 Barry O'Neil

Gamblers, The 19 Paul Scardon

Gamblers, The 29 Michael Curtiz

Gamblers, The 48 Elmer Clifton

Gamblers, The 69 Ron Winston

Gamblers All 19 Dave Aylott

Gambler's Choice 44 Frank McDonald

Gambler's Luck 66 Yoji Yamada

Gambler's Nightmare, The 06 Charles Raymond

Gambler's Villainy, A 11 Theo Bouwmeester

Gambler's Wife, The 1899 George Albert Smith

Gambler's Wife, The 13 Forest Holger-Madsen

Gamblin' Man 74 Monte Hellman

Gambling 34 Rowland V. Lee

Gambling Daughters 41 Max Nosseck

Gambling Fool, The 25 John P. McGowan

Gambling Hell 39 Jean Delannoy

Gambling Hell 50 John Rossi

Gambling House 50 Ted Tetzlaff

Gambling in Souls 19 Harry Millarde

Gambling Lady 34 Archie Mayo

Gambling on the High Seas 40 George Amy

Gambling Samurai, The 66 Senkichi Taniguchi

Gambling Sex, The 32 Fred Newmeyer

Gambling Ship 33 Louis Gasnier, Max Marcin

Gambling Ship 39 Aubrey H. Scotto

Gambling Terror, The 37 Sam Newfield

Gambling with Souls 36 Elmer Clifton

Gambling with the Gulf Stream 23 J. A. Norling

Gambling Wives 24 Del Henderson

Game, The 68 Jerzy Kawalerowicz

Game, The 90 Curtis Brown

Game Chicken, The 22 Chester M. Franklin

Game Chicken, The 26 H. B. Parkinson

Game Fighter, A 24 Tom Gibson

Game for Life, A 10 Edwin S. Porter

Game for Six Lovers, A 59 Jacques Doniol-Valcroze

Game for Three Losers 63 Gerry O'Hara

Game for Two, A 21 Fred Paul, Jack Raymond

Game for Vultures 79 James Fargo

Game in the Sand 64 Werner Herzog

Game Is Over, The 66 Roger Vadim

Game of Bluff, A 14 Cecil Birch

Game of Chance, A 32 Charles Barnett

Game of Chess and Kisses, A 1899 George Albert Smith

Game of Danger 54 Lance Comfort

Game of Death, A 45 Robert Wise

Game of Death 79 Robert Clouse

Game of Liberty, The 16 George Loane Tucker

Game of Life, The 22 George B. Samuelson

Game of Love, The 53 Claude Autant-Lara

Game of Love, The 59 Jacques Doniol-Valcroze

Game of Luck 65 Risto Jarva

Game of Poker, A 13 Mack Sennett

Game of Snowballing, A 1899 C. Goodwin Norton

Game of Survival 86 Roberta Findlay

Game of Truth, The 61 Robert Hossein

Game of Wits, A 17 Henry King

Game Old Knight, A 15 F. Richard Jones

Game Pass 72 Rainer Werner Fassbinder

Game Show Models 77 David Neil Gottlieb

Game That Kills, The 37 D. Ross Lederman

Game with Fate, A 18 Paul Scardon

Gamekeeper, The 80 Kenneth Loach

Gamekeeper's Daughter, The 10 Dave Aylott

Gamekeeper's Dog, The 07 Harold Hough

Gamekeeper's Revenge, The 12 Wilfred Noy

Gamera 66 Noriyaki Yuasa

Gamera Tai Barugon 66 Shigeo Tanaka

Gamera Tai Daimaju Jaiga 70 Noriyaki Yuasa

Gamera Tai Gaos 67 Noriyaki Yuasa

Gamera Tai Guiron 69 Noriyaki Yuasa

Gamera Tai Shinkai Kaijū Jigura 71 Noriyaki Yuasa

Gamera Tai Uchūkaijū Bairasu 68 Noriyaki Yuasa

Gamera Tai Viras 68 Noriyaki Yuasa

Gamera the Invincible 66 Noriyaki Yuasa

Gamera vs. Barugon 66 Shigeo Tanaka

Gamera vs. Gaos 67 Noriyaki Yuasa

Gamera vs. Guiron 69 Noriyaki Yuasa

Gamera vs. Gyaos 67 Noriyaki Yuasa

Gamera vs. Jiger 70 Noriyaki Yuasa

Gamera vs. Monster X 70 Noriyaki Yuasa

Gamera vs. Outer Space Monster Viras 68 Noriyaki Yuasa

Gamera vs. the Deep Sea Monster Zigra 71 Noriyaki Yuasa

Gamera vs. Viras 68 Noriyaki Yuasa

Gamera vs. Zigra 71 Noriyaki Yuasa

Games 67 Curtis Harrington

Games, The 69 Michael Winner

Games for Schoolchildren 87 Arvo Ikho, Lejda Lajus

Games for Six Lovers 59 Jacques Doniol-Valcroze

Games Girls Play, The 74 Jack Arnold

Games Men Play, The 68 Daniel Tinayre

Games of Artifice 87 Virginie Thevenet

Games of Desire 68 Hans Albin

Games of Love 16 Anders Wilhelm Sandberg

Games of the Angels, The 64 Walerian Borowczyk

Games That Lovers Play 70 Mike Leigh

Game's Up, The 19 Elsie Jane Wilson

Games Women Play 82 Chuck Vincent

Gamesters, The 20 George L. Cox

Gamila Bohraid 58 Youssef Chahine

Gamila Buhrayd 58 Youssef Chahine

Gamin de Paris, Le 23 Louis Feuillade
Gamin's Gratitude, A 09 Lewin Fitz-
hamon
Gamla Kvarnen, Den 62 Jan Troell
Gamle, De 61 Henning Carlsen
Gamle Bænk, Den 13 Forest Holger-
Madsen
Gamle Købmandshus, Det 11 August
Blom
Gamlet 63 Grigori Kozintsev
Gamma People, The 56 John Gilling
Gamma Sango Uchū Daisakusen 68 Kinji
Fukasaku
Gamma 693 81 Joel M. Reed
Gammelion 67 Gregory Markopoulos
Gammera 66 Noriyaki Yuasa
Gammera the Invincible 66 Noriyaki
Yuasa
Gamperaliya 64 Lester James Peries
Ganashatru 89 Satyajit Ray
Gancheros, Los 55 Luis García Berlanga
Gancia 64 Walerian Borowczyk
Gandahar 87 René Laloux, Harvey
Weinstein
Gander at Mother Goose, A 40 Tex Avery
Gandhi 82 Richard Attenborough
Gang, The 37 Alfred Goulding
Gang, Le 76 Jacques Deray
Gang 79 Robert Collins
Gang Bullets 38 Lambert Hillyer
Gang Buster, The 31 A. Edward
Sutherland
Gang Busters 42 Ford Beebe, Noel Mason
Smith, Ray Taylor
Gang Busters 55 Bill Karn
Gang des Otages, Le 72 Édouard Molinaro
Gang in die Nacht, Der 20 F. W. Murnau
Gang Made Good, The 41 Frank McDon-
ald
Gang of Four, The 89 Jacques Rivette
Gang of Three Forever 89 Wei-yen Yu
Gang Show, The 37 Alfred Goulding
Gang Show 39 George A. Cooper
Gang That Couldn't Shoot Straight, The
71 James Goldstone
Gang War 28 Bert Glennon
Gang War 40 Leo C. Popkin
Gang War 46 Carol Reed
Gang War 58 Gene Fowler, Jr.
Gang War 62 Frank Marshall
Gang Wars 75 Barry Rosen
Ganga 61 Rajen Tarafder
Ganga Bruta 32 Humberto Mauro
Ganga Vataren 32 D. G. Phalke
Ganga Zumba 63 Carlos Diegués
Gangs 88 Ah Mon Lawrence
Gang's All Here, The 39 Thornton Free-
land
Gang's All Here, The 41 Jean Yarbrough
Gang's All Here, The 43 Busby Berkeley
Gangs, Inc. 41 Phil Rosen
Gangs of Chicago 40 Arthur Lubin
Gangs of New York 38 James Cruze
Gangs of Sonora 41 John English
Gangs of the Waterfront 45 George Blair
Gangster, The 13 Mack Sennett
Gangster, The 47 Gordon Wiles
Gangster, El 64 Luis Alcoriza
Gangster Boss 58 Henri Verneuil
Gangster Story 59 Walter Matthau

Gangster VIP, The 68 Toshio Masuda
Gangster We Made, The 50 Robert Florey
Gangsterpremiere 51 Curd Jürgens
Gangsters and Philanthropists 62 Jerzy
Hoffman
Gangster's Boy 38 William Nigh
Gangster's Bride 37 Howard Bretherton
Gangster's Den 45 Sam Newfield
Gangster's Enemy No. 1 35 Robert North
Bradbury
Gangsters of New York, The 13 Christy
Cabanne
Gangsters of the Frontier 44 Elmer Clifton
Gangsters of the Sea 32 Charles Hutchin-
son
Gangster's Revenge 60 Charles Davis
Gangway 37 Sonnie Hale
Gangway for Tomorrow 43 John H. Auer
Ganito Kami Noon, Paano Kayo Ngayon?
76 Eddie Romero
Ganja and Hess 73 Bill Gunn
Ganovenehre 33 Richard Oswald
Ganovenehre 66 Wolfgang Staudte
Gans von Sedan, Die 59 Helmut Käutner
Gänsemagd, Die 67 Fritz Genschow
Ganze Welt Dreht Sich Um Liebe, Die 35
Victor Tourjansky
Ganzer Kerl, Ein 36 Carl Boese
Gaol Break 35 Ralph Ince
Gaolbreak 62 Francis Searle
Gap, The 37 Donald Carter
Gap, The 70 John G. Avildsen
Gap-Toothed Women 87 Les Blank
Gappa the Trifibian Monster 67 Haruyasu
Noguchi
Garage, The 19 Roscoe Arbuckle
Garage, The 75 Vilgot Sjöman
Garaget 75 Vilgot Sjöman
Garakuta 64 Hiroshi Inagaki
Garantiere Rolland, Il 10 Luigi Maggi
Garbage Boys, The 86 Cheik Omar
Sissoko
Garbage Man, The 63 Eric Sayers
Garbage Man Cometh, The 63 Eric Sayers
Garbage Pail Kids Movie, The 87 Rod
Amateau
Garbo Talks 84 Sidney Lumet
Garçon! 83 Claude Sautet
Garçon Divorcé, Le 32 Alberto Cavalcanti
Garçon Sauvage, Le 51 Jean Delannoy
Garçonne, La 57 Jacqueline Audry
Garçonnière, La 60 Giuseppe De Santis
Garçons, Les 59 Mauro Bolognini
Garde à Vue 81 Claude Miller
Garde-Chasse, Le 51 Henri Decaë
Garden 68 Jan Švankmajer
Garden, The 90 Derek Jarman
Garden Gaieties 35 Manny Gould, Ben
Harrison
Garden Gopher 50 Tex Avery
Garden Murder Case, The 36 Edwin L.
Marin
Garden of Allah, The 16 Colin Campbell
Garden of Allah, The 27 Rex Ingram
Garden of Allah, The 36 Richard Bole-
slawski
Garden of Allah, The 89 David Neves
Garden of Deception, The 86 Ferruccio
Casati
Garden of Delights, The 70 Carlos Saura

Garden of Earthly Delights, The 70 Carlos
Saura
Garden of Earthly Delights, The 81 Stan
Brakhage
Garden of Eden, The 28 Lewis Milestone
Garden of Eden, The 54 Max Nosseck
Garden of Evil 54 Henry Hathaway
Garden of Lies, The 15 Augustus Thomas
Garden of Resurrection, The 19 Arthur H.
Rooke
Garden of Stones 76 Parviz Kimiavi
Garden of the Dead 72 John Hayes
Garden of the Finzi-Continis, The 70
Vittorio De Sica
Garden of the Moon 38 Busby Berkeley
Garden of Weeds, The 24 James Cruze
Garden of Women, The 54 Keisuke Kino-
shita
Gardener, The 1895 Louis Lumière
Gardener, The 12 Victor Sjöström
Gardener, The 72 James H. Kay III
Gardener Burning Weeds 1896 Georges
Méliès
Gardener of Eden, The 81 James Brough-
ton
Gardener's Daughter, The 13 Wilfred Noy
Gardener's Hose, The 14 Frank Wilson
Gardener's Nap, The 05 Alf Collins
Gardens of Stone 87 Francis Ford Coppola
Gardeoffizier, Der 25 Robert Wiene
Gardez le Sourire 33 Pál Fejős
Gardien, Le 21 Joe Hamman
Gardien de la Nuit 86 Jean-Pierre Limosin
Gardienne du Feu, La 13 Louis Feuillade
Gardiens de Phare 29 Jean Grémillon
Gardin du Feu, Le 24 Gaston Ravel
Gare Centrale 57 Youssef Chahine
Gare Saint-Lazare, La 1896 Georges Méliès
Gargon Terror, The 59 Tom Graeff
Garibah no Uchū Ryokō 66 Yoshio
Kuroda
Garibaldi 07 Mario Caserini
Garibaldi 60 Roberto Rossellini
Garibaldian in the Convent, A 41 Vittorio
De Sica
Garibaldino al Convento, Un 41 Vittorio
De Sica
Garland of Song, A 34 Horace Shepherd
Garlic Is As Good As Ten Mothers 80 Les
Blank
Garm Hava 73 M. S. Sathyu
Garment Center, The 57 Robert Aldrich,
Vincent Sherman
Garment Jungle, The 57 Robert Aldrich,
Vincent Sherman
Garments of Truth 21 George D. Baker
Garmon 34 Igor Savchenko
Garnet Bracelet, The 65 Abram Room
Garou-Garou le Passe-Muraille 50 Jean
Boyer
Garras de Lorelei, Las 72 Amando De
Ossorio
Garret in Bohemia, A 15 Harold M. Shaw
Garringo 69 Rafael Romero Marchent
Garrison Follies 40 Maclean Rogers
Garrison's Finish 23 Arthur Rosson
Garrotting a Motor Car 04 Harold Hough
Garryowen 20 George Pearson
Gars des Vues, Le 75 Jean-Pierre Lefèbvre
Garter Colt 67 Gian Andrea Rocco

Garter Girl, The *20* Edward H. Griffith
Garu the Mad Monk *71* Andy Milligan
Gas *70* Roger Corman
Gas *81* Les Rose
Gas House Kids *46* Sam Newfield
Gas House Kids Go West *47* William Beaudine
Gas House Kids in Hollywood *47* Edward L. Cahn
Gas-Oil *55* Gilles Grangier
Gas, Oil and Water *22* Charles Ray
Gas! or It Became Necessary to Destroy the World in Order to Save It *70* Roger Corman
Gas Pump Girls *79* Joel Bender
Gasbags *40* Walter Forde, Marcel Varnel
Gasherbrum — Der Leuchtende Berg *85* Werner Herzog
Gaslight *39* Thorold Dickinson
Gaslight *44* George Cukor
Gasoline Alley *51* Edward Bernds
Gasoline Cowboy *26* Frederick Reel, Jr.
Gasoline Engine, The *17* J. D. Leventhal
Gasoline Gus *21* James Cruze
Gasoloons *35* Arthur Ripley
Gaspard et Fils *88* François Labonte
Gasparone *38* Georg Jacoby
Gasschen zum Paradies, Das *36* Martin Frič
Gassenhauer *31* Lupu Pick
Gas-s-s-s! *70* Roger Corman
Gas-s-s-s, or It Became Neccessary to Destroy the World in Order to Save It *70* Roger Corman
Gas-s-s-s, or It May Become Neccessary to Destroy the World in Order to Save It *70* Roger Corman
Gastone *59* Mario Bonnard
Gasu Ningen Daiichigo *60* Inoshiro Honda
Gatan *49* Gösta Werner
Gatans Barn *14* Victor Sjöström
Gate, The *87* Tibor Takacs
Gate Crasher, The *28* William James Craft
Gate No. 6 *52* Pan Liu
Gate of Flesh *64* Seijun Suzuki
Gate of Heaven, The *44* Vittorio De Sica
Gate of Hell *53* Teinosuke Kinugasa
Gate of Lilacs *57* René Clair
Gategutter *49* Ulf Greber, Arne Skouen
Gates of Alcatraz, The *39* Charles Vidor
Gates of Brass *19* Ernest C. Warde
Gates of Doom, The *17* Charles Swickard
Gates of Doom, The *19* Sidney Goldin
Gates of Duty *19* Randle Ayrton
Gates of Eden, The *16* John H. Collins
Gates of Flesh, The *88* Hideo Gosha
Gates of Gladness *18* Harley Knoles
Gates of Heaven, The *67* Andrzej Wajda
Gates of Heaven *78* Errol Morris
Gates of Hell, The *80* Lucio Fulci
Gates of Night *46* Marcel Carné
Gates of Paris *57* René Clair
Gates of the Louvre, The *74* Michel Mitrani
Gates of the Night *46* Marcel Carné
Gates to Paradise *67* Andrzej Wajda
Gateway *38* Alfred L. Werker
Gateway of the Moon, The *28* John Griffith Wray

Gateway to Glory *70* Mitsuo Murayama
Gateway to the South *81* Micky Dolenz
Gathering Coconuts *21* Raoul Barré, Charles Bowers
Gathering of Eagles, A *63* Delbert Mann
Gatling Gun, The *71* Robert Gordon
Gato con Botas, El *64* Manuel San Fernando
Gator *76* Burt Reynolds
Gator Bait *76* Beverly Sebastian, Ferd Sebastian
Gator Bait II: Cajun Justice *88* Beverly Sebastian, Ferd Sebastian
Gatto, Il *77* Luigi Comencini
Gatto a Nove Code, Il *70* Dario Argento
Gatto di Park Lane, Il *80* Lucio Fulci
Gatto Nero, Il *80* Lucio Fulci
Gatto Rossi in un Labirinto do Vetro *78* Umberto Lenzi
Gattopardo, Il *62* Luchino Visconti
Gaucho, The *27* F. Richard Jones
Gaucho, Il *64* Dino Risi
Gaucho, The *64* Dino Risi
Gaucho Chivalry *38* Sebastián Naon
Gaucho Serenade *40* Frank McDonald
Gauchos of El Dorado *41* Les Orlebeck
Gaudeamus Igitur *37* Otakar Vávra
Gauguin *50* Alain Resnais
Gauguin: Wolf at the Door *86* Henning Carlsen
Gauloises Bleues, Les *68* Michel Cournot
Gaunt Stranger, The *31* Walter Forde
Gaunt Stranger, The *38* Walter Forde
Gauntlet, The *20* Edwin L. Hollywood
Gauntlet, The *77* Clint Eastwood
Gautama the Buddha *55* Rajbans Khanna, Bimal Roy
Gav *68* Dariush Mehrjui
Gavea Girls *87* Haroldo Marinho Barbosa
Gaven *12* August Blom
Gavilán, El *40* Ramón Pereda
Gavilan *68* William J. Jugo
Gavilán o Paloma *86* Alfredo Gurrola
Gavotte, La *02* Alice Guy-Blaché
Gavotte *67* Walerian Borowczyk
Gawain and the Green Knight *72* Stephen Weeks
Gay Adventure, The *36* Sinclair Hill
Gay Adventure, The *49* Gordon Parry
Gay Adventure, The *53* Anatole De Grunwald
Gay Amigo, The *49* Wallace Fox
Gay and Devilish *22* William A. Seiter
Gay Anties, The *47* Friz Freleng
Gay Back Alley *39* Kozaburo Yoshimura
Gay Blades *46* George Blair
Gay Bride, The *34* Jack Conway
Gay Buckaroo, The *32* Phil Rosen
Gay Caballero, The *32* Alfred L. Werker
Gay Caballero, The *40* Otto Brower
Gay Canary, The *29* Lev Kuleshov
Gay Cavalier, The *46* William Nigh
Gay City, The *40* Ralph Murphy
Gay Confessions *80* Richard Gaylor
Gay Corinthian, The *24* Arthur H. Rooke
Gay Deceiver, The *26* John M. Stahl
Gay Deceivers, The *16* Dave Aylott
Gay Deceivers, The *69* Bruce Kessler
Gay Deception, The *35* William Wyler
Gay Defender, The *27* Gregory La Cava

Gay Desperado, The *36* Rouben Mamoulian
Gay Diplomat, The *31* Richard Boleslawski
Gay Divorce, The *34* Mark Sandrich
Gay Divorcee, The *34* Mark Sandrich
Gay Dog, The *54* Maurice Elvey
Gay Duellist, The *46* Peter Cresswell, Thornton Freeland
Gay Falcon, The *41* Irving Reis
Gay Huskies, The *26* Urban Gad
Gay Imposters, The *37* Ray Enright
Gay Intruders, The *44* Maurice Elvey
Gay Intruders, The *48* Ray McCarey
Gay Knighties, The *41* George Pal
Gay Lady, The *29* Robert Florey
Gay Lady, The *35* Alan Crosland
Gay Lady *49* Brian Desmond Hurst
Gay Lord Ducie, The *11* Lewin Fitzhamon
Gay Lord Quex, The *17* Maurice Elvey
Gay Lord Quex, The *19* Harry Beaumont
Gay Lord Waring, The *16* Otis Turner
Gay Love *34* Leslie Hiscott
Gay Masquerade, The *28* Teinosuke Kinugasa
Gay Masquerade, The *58* Daisuke Ito
Gay Mrs. Trexel, The *39* George Cukor
Gay Nighties, The *31* Mark Sandrich
Gay Nineties, The *30* Harry Beaumont
Gay Nineties, The *42* Reginald LeBorg
Gay Old Bird, The *27* Herman Raymaker
Gay Old Dog, The *19* Hobart Henley
Gay Old Dog *35* George King
Gay Parisian, The *42* Jean Negulesco
Gay Purr-ee *62* Abe Levitow
Gay Ranchero, The *48* William Witney
Gay Retreat, The *27* Ben Stoloff
Gay Señorita, The *45* Arthur Dreifuss
Gay Shoe Clerk, The *03* Edwin S. Porter
Gay Sisters, The *42* Irving Rapper
Gay Swordsman, The *49* Riccardo Freda
Gay Vagabond, The *41* William Morgan
Gayest of the Gay, The *24* Bertram Phillips
Gaynor and the Night Clubs *13* Émile Cohl
Gaz Mortels, Les *16* Abel Gance
Gaz Mortels ou Le Brouillard sur la Ville, Les *16* Abel Gance
Gazebo, The *59* George Marshall
Gdy Spadają Anioły *59* Roman Polanski
Gdziekolwiek Jesteś, Jeśliś Jest *88* Krzysztof Zanussi
Géant à la Cour de Kublai Khan, Le *61* Riccardo Freda
Géant de la Vallée des Rois, Le *60* Carlo Campogalliani
Geared to Go *24* Albert S. Rogell
Gebissen Wird Nur Nachts *70* Freddie Francis
Gebroken Spiegels *84* Marleen Gorris
Geburt der Hexe *81* Wilfried Minks
Gece Dansı Tutsakları *89* Mahinur Ergün
Gece Yolculuğu *88* Ömer Kavur
Gee Whiz! *20* F. Richard Jones
Gee Whiz-z-z *56* Chuck Jones
Geek Maggot Bingo *83* Nick Zedd
Gefährliches Spiel, Ein *19* Robert Wiene
Gefangene des Königs, Der *35* Carl Boese
Gefangene des Maharadscha, Die *53* Veidt Harlan

Gefangene Frauen *80* Jesús Franco

Gefangene von Shanghai, Die *27* Géza von Bolváry, Augusto Genina

Gege Bellavita *79* Pasquale Festa Campanile

Geheimcode Wildganse *84* Antonio Margheriti

Geheimnis der Drei Dschunken, Das *65* Ernst Hofbauer

Geheimnis der Gelden Narzizzen, Das *61* Ákos von Ráthonyi

Geheimnis der Lederschlinge, Das *64* Luigi Capuano

Geheimnis der Leeren Wasserflasche, Das *17* Joe May

Geheimnis der Schwarzen Handschuhe, Das *69* Dario Argento

Geheimnis der Todeninsel, Das *66* Ernst R. von Theumer

Geheimnis des Abbé X, Das *27* William Dieterle

Geheimnis des Amerika-Docks, Das *17* E. A. Dupont

Geheimnisse einer Seele *25* G. W. Pabst

Geheimnisse in Golden Nylons *67* Christian-Jaque

Geheimnisse Villa, Die *13* Joe May

Geheimnisse von London, Die *20* Richard Oswald

Geheimnisse von London *61* Alfred Vohrer

Geheimnisvolle Mister X, Der *39* J. A. Hübler-Kahla

Geheimnisvolle Spiegel, Der *27* Karl Hoffmann, Prof. Teschner

Geheimnisvolle Tiefen *49* G. W. Pabst

Geheimnisvolle Villa, Die *13* Joe May

Geheimskretär, Der *15* Joe May

Gehenu Lamai *77* Sumitra Peries

Gehetzte Frauen *27* Richard Oswald

Gehetzte Menschen *32* Friedrich Feher

Geido Ichidai Otoko *40* Kenji Mizoguchi

Geierwally, Der *21* E. A. Dupont

Geierwally, Die *40* Hans Steinhoff

Geierwally *88* Walter Bockmayer

Geiger, Der *43* Günther Rittau

Geiger von Florenz, Der *26* Paul Czinner

Geisha, A *53* Kenji Mizoguchi

Geisha Boy, The *58* Frank Tashlin

Geisha Girl *52* George Breakston, Ray Stahl

Geisha Girl Ginko *53* Kaneto Shindo

Geisha in the Old City, A *57* Hiroshi Inagaki

Geisha und der Samurai, Der *19* Carl Boese

Geisha Who Saved Japan, The *09* Sidney Olcott

Geisha's Suicide, A *55* Kaneto Shindo

Gejagten der Sierra Nevada, Die *65* Alfonso Balcazar

Gekka no Kyōjin *26* Teinosuke Kinugasa

Gekkō Kamen *58* Tsuneo Kobayashi

Gelbe Flagge, Die *37* Gerhard Lamprecht

Gelbe Haus des King-Fu, Das *31* Karl Grüne

Geld *89* Doris Dörrie

Geld auf der Strasse, Das *22* Reinhold Schünzel

Geld auf der Strasse *30* Georg Jacoby

Geld, Geld, Geld *27* Marcel L'Herbier

Geld Regiert die Welt *34* Max Neufeld

Gelegenheitsarbeit einer Sklavin *73* Alexander Kluge

Geliebte, Die *27* Robert Wiene

Geliebte, Die *39* Gerhard Lamprecht

Geliebte Bestie *61* Arthur Maria Rabenalt

Geliebte des Gouverneurs, Die *27* Friedrich Feher

Geliebte Roswolskys, Die *21* Felix Basch

Geliebtes Leben *53* Rolf Thiele

Gelignite Gang, The *56* Terence Fisher, Francis Searle

Gelöbt Sei Was Hart Macht *72* Rolf Thiele

Gelosia *15* Augusto Genina

Gelosia *42* Ferdinando Maria Poggioli

Gelosia *53* Pietro Germi

Gem Jams *43* Lambert Hillyer

Gemelli del Texas, I *63* Steno

Gemini Affair *75* Matt Cimber

Gemini Strain, The *78* Ed Hunt

Gemini: The Twin Stars *88* Jaques Sandoz

Gemini Twins, The *71* John Hough

Gemischte Frauenchor, Der *16* Ernst Lubitsch

Gemma Orientale dei Papi, La *46* Alessandro Blasetti

Gemütlich beim Kaffee *1898* Oskar Messter

Gen to Fudōmyōō *61* Hiroshi Inagaki

Genbaku no Ko *52* Kaneto Shindo

Genbaku no Zu *51* Tadashi Imai

Gendai no Joō *24* Kenji Mizoguchi

Gendarme de Saint-Tropez, Le *66* Jean Girault

Gendarme Est Sans Culotte, Le *14* Louis Feuillade

Gendarme Est Sans Pitié, Le *32* Claude Autant-Lara

Gendarme Est Sans Pitié, Le *34* Jacques Becker, Pierre Prévert

Gendarme et les Extraterrestres, Le *78* Jean Girault

Gendarme of St. Tropez, The *66* Jean Girault

Gendarmes, Les *07* Alice Guy-Blaché

Gendre de Monsieur Poirier, Le *33* Marcel Pagnol

Gene Autry and the Mounties *51* John English

Gene Krupa Story, The *59* Don Weis

General, The *26* Clyde Bruckman, Buster Keaton

General, The *30* Nick Grindé

General, The *40* Tadashi Imai

General Assembly *59* Tomás Gutiérrez Alea

General Babka *24* Michael Curtiz

General Confusion *40* Arthur Maria Rabenalt

General Crack *29* Alan Crosland

General Custer at Little Big Horn *26* Harry Fraser

General Della Rovere *59* Roberto Rossellini

General Died at Dawn, The *36* Lewis Milestone

General Ginsburg *30* Mark Sandrich

General Goes Too Far, The *36* Thorold Dickinson

General Housecleaning *38* Karel Lamač

General Idi Amin Dada *74* Barbet Schroeder

General in Red Robe, The *73* Doo-yong Lee

General John Regan *21* Harold M. Shaw

General John Regan *33* Henry Edwards

General Line, The *29* Grigori Alexandrov, Sergei Eisenstein

General Massacre *73* Burr Jerger

General Nogi and Kuma-San *25* Kenji Mizoguchi

General Post *20* Thomas Bentley

General Spanky *36* Gordon Douglas, Fred Newmeyer

General Speidel *57* Andrew Thorndike, Annelie Thorndike

General Suvorov *40* Mikhail Doller, Vsevolod I. Pudovkin

General von Dobeln *42* Olof Molander

Generale d'Acciaio, Il *69* Franklin J. Schaffner

Generale Della Rovere, Il *59* Roberto Rossellini

Generalnaya Linya *29* Grigori Alexandrov, Sergei Eisenstein

Generals of Tomorrow *38* Kurt Neumann

General's Only Son, The *11* Theo Bouwmeester

General's Son, The *90* Kwon-taek Im

Generals Without Buttons *38* Jacques Daroy

Generation, A *54* Andrzej Wajda

Generation *69* George Schaefer

Generation of Conquerors, A *36* Vera Stroyeva

Génération Spontanée *09* Émile Cohl

Générations Comiques, Les *09* Émile Cohl

Generations of Resistance *80* Peter Davis

Generosity *11* Urban Gad

Generosity of Mr. Smith, The *12* Warwick Buckland

Generous Summer *51* Boris Barnet

Genesis *86* Mrinal Sen

Genesis—A Band in Concert *77* Tony Maylam

Genesung *55* Konrad Wolf

Geneviève *23* Léon Poirier

Genevieve *53* Henry Cornelius

Geneviève *66* Michel Brault

Genghis Khan *52* Lou Salvador

Genghis Khan *65* Henry Levin

Genie, The *53* Lance Comfort, Lawrence Huntington

Génie des Cloches, Le *08* Georges Méliès

Génie du Feu, Le *07* Georges Méliès

Genie of Fire, The *07* Georges Méliès

Genio, Due Compari e un Pollo, Un *75* Sergio Corbucci, Damiano Damiani, Sergio Leone

Genius, The *14* Del Henderson

Genius *70* Gregory Markopoulos

Genius, The *75* Sergio Corbucci, Damiano Damiani, Sergio Leone

Genius at Work *46* Leslie Goodwins

Genius in the Family, A *46* Frank Ryan

Genji Monogatari *51* Kozaburo Yoshimura

Genkai Tsurezure Bushi *86* Masanobu Deme

George's False Alarm *28* Sam Newfield
George's Joy Ride *14* Percy Stow
George's School Daze *27* Sam Newfield
Georgi Saakadze I *42* Mikhail Chiaureli
Georgi Saakadze II *43* Mikhail Chiaureli
Georgia *88* Ben Lewin
Georgia, Georgia *72* Stig Björkman
Georgia Rose *30* Harry A. Gant
Georgian State Dancing Company, The *54* Tenghiz Abuladze, Revaz Chkeidze
Georgia's Friends *81* Arthur Penn
Georgie and the Dragon *51* Robert Cannon
Georgy Girl *66* Silvio Narizzano
Gerald Cranston's Lady *24* Emmett J. Flynn
Gerald McBoing Boing *50* Robert Cannon, John Hubley
Gerald McBoing Boing on the Planet Moo *56* Robert Cannon
Gerald McBoing Boing's Symphony *53* Robert Cannon
Geraldine *29* Melville Brown
Geraldine *53* R. G. Springsteen
Geraldine's First Year *22* George A. Cooper
Gerald's Butterfly *11* Theo Bouwmeester
Gerald's Symphony *53* Robert Cannon
Gerard Malanga Reads Poetry *66* Andy Warhol
Gerla di Papa Martin, La *09* Mario Caserini
Germ, The *23* P. S. McGreeney
Germaine *23* Augusto Genina
German Diary, A *69* Andrew Thorndike, Annelie Thorndike
German Manpower *43* Garson Kanin, Robert Parrish
German Sisters, The *81* Margarethe von Trotta
German Spy Peril, The *14* Bert Haldane
German Story, The *56* Andrew Thorndike, Annelie Thorndike
German Tanks *40* Walter Ruttmann
German Trick That Failed, A *18* Leighton Budd
Germania, Anno Zero *47* Roberto Rossellini
Germanin im Banne des Monte Miracolo *45* Luis Trenker
Germans Strike Again, The *49* Alekos Sakelarios
Germany Calling *42* Len Lye
Germany in Autumn *78* Heinrich Böll, Alf Brustellin, Hans Peter Cloos, Rainer Werner Fassbinder, Alexander Kluge, Maximiliane Mainka, Beate Mainka-Jellinghaus, Edgar Reitz, Katja Rupé, Volker Schlöndorff, Peter Schubert, Bernhard Sinkel
Germany, Pale Mother *79* Helma Sanders-Brahms
Germany, Year Zero *47* Roberto Rossellini
Germinal *13* Albert Capellani
Germinal *62* Yves Allégret
Germination d'un Haricot *28* Germaine Dulac
Germination of a Bean *28* Germaine Dulac
Gerō *27* Daisuke Ito

Gerō no Kubi *55* Daisuke Ito
Geroi Shipki *54* Sergei Vasiliev
Geroite na Shipka *54* Sergei Vasiliev
Gerónima *86* Raúl Tosso
Geronimo! *39* Paul Sloane
Geronimo *62* Arnold Laven
Geronimo's Last Raid *12* John Emerson
Geronimo's Revenge *62* Harry Keller, James Neilson
Geroy Yeyo Romana *87* Yuri Gorkovenko
Gert and Daisy Clean Up *42* Maclean Rogers
Gert and Daisy's Weekend *41* Maclean Rogers
Gertie *14* Winsor McCay
Gertie on Tour *17* Winsor McCay
Gertie the Dinosaur *14* Winsor McCay
Gertie the Dinosaurus *14* Winsor McCay
Gertie the Trained Dinosaur *14* Winsor McCay
Gertrud *64* Carl Theodor Dreyer
Gerusalemme Liberata, La *11* Enrico Guazzoni
Gerusalemme Liberata, La *17* Enrico Guazzoni
Gerusalemme Liberata *57* Carlo Ludovico Bragaglia
Gervaise *55* René Clément
Geschichte der Stillen Mühle, Die *14* Richard Oswald
Geschichte des Kleinen Muck, Die *53* Wolfgang Staudte
Geschichte des Prinzen Achmed, Die *26* Lotte Reiniger
Geschichte einer Kleine Pariserin, Die *27* Augusto Genina
Geschichte einer Reichen Erbin, Die *24* Reinhold Schünzel
Geschichte von Fünf Städten *51* Géza von Cziffra, Romolo Marcellini, Emil E. Reinert, Wolfgang Staudte, Montgomery Tully
Geschichten aus dem Wienerwald *35* Georg Jacoby
Geschichten aus dem Wienerwald *78* Maximilian Schell
Geschichten aus den Hunsrückdorfern *81* Edgar Reitz
Geschichten vom Kübelkind *70* Edgar Reitz, Ula Stöckl
Geschichtsunterricht *72* Danièle Huillet, Jean-Marie Straub
Geschlecht in Fesseln *28* William Dieterle
Geschlecht in Fesseln—Die Sexualnot der Gefangenen *28* William Dieterle
Geschlossene Kette, Die *20* Paul Stein
Geschminkte Jugend *29* Carl Boese
Geschminkte Jugend *60* Max Nosseck
Geschwader Fledermaus *59* Erich Engel
Gesetz der Mine, Das *15* Joe May
Gesolei *23* Walter Ruttmann
Gespenst, Das *83* Herbert Achternbusch
Gespensterschiff, Das *21* Paul Leni
Gespensterstunde, Die *17* Urban Gad
Gespensteruhr, Die *16* Joe May
Geständnis einer Sechzehnjährigen *60* Georg Tressler
Geständnis Unter Vier Angen *54* André Michel
Gestapo *40* Carol Reed

Gestehen Sie Dr. Corda! *58* Josef von Baky
Gestes du Silence, Les *60* Henri Storck
Gesticulador, El *57* Emilio Fernández
Gestiefelte Kater, Der *67* Herbert B. Fredersdorf
Gestohlene Herz, Das *34* Lotte Reiniger
Gesù di Nazareth *76* Franco Zeffirelli
Gesunkenen, Die *25* William Dieterle*
Gesuzza la Sposa Garibaldina *33* Alessandro Blasetti
Get a Coffin Ready *68* Ferdinando Baldi
Get Back *73* Donald Shebib
Get Carter *70* Michael Hodges
Get Charlie Tully *72* Cliff Owen
Get Cracking *42* Marcel Varnel
Get Crazy *83* Allan Arkush
Get Down and Boogie *75* William Witney
Get Going *43* Jean Yarbrough
Get Hep to Love *42* Charles Lamont
Get In and Get Out *14* Charles H. Weston
Get Married, Mother *62* Heinosuke Gosho
Get Me a Step Ladder *08* J. Stuart Blackton
Get Mean *76* Ferdinando Baldi
Get Off My Back *65* Richard Quine
Get Off My Foot *35* William Beaudine
Get On with It *61* C. M. Pennington-Richards
Get Out and Get Under *20* Hal Roach
Get Out of Town *60* Charles Davis
Get Out Your Handkerchiefs *77* Bertrand Blier
Get Outta Town *60* Charles Davis
Get Rich Quick *13* Henry Lehrman
Get Rich Quick Porky *37* Robert Clampett
Get-Rich-Quick Wallingford *15* Fred Niblo
Get-Rich-Quick Wallingford *21* Frank Borzage
Get-Rich-Quick Wallingford *31* Sam Wood
Get That Girl *32* George Crone
Get That Girl *36* Bernard B. Ray
Get That Man *35* Spencer G. Bennet
Get the Terrorists *87* Dominic Elmo Smith
Get to Know Your Rabbit *72* Brian De-Palma
Get to Work *20* Wallace A. Carlson
Get Well Soon *81* Jean-Claude Lord
Get Your Diploma First *76* Maurice Pialat
Get Your Man! *21* George W. Hill, William K. Howard
Get Your Man *27* Dorothy Arzner
Get Your Man *34* George King
Get Yourself a College Girl *64* Sidney Miller
Getaway, The *41* Edward Buzzell
Getaway, The *72* Sam Peckinpah
Getaway Kate *18* George B. Seitz
Getaway Life, The *79* Daniel Duval
Geteilte Himmel, Der *64* Konrad Wolf
Geteilte Liebe *88* Helma Sanders-Brahms
Geträumte Stunden *67* Jesús Franco
Getting a Story, or The Origins of the Shimmie *19* Pat Sullivan
Getting Acquainted *14* Charles Chaplin
Getting Ahead *22* Raoul Barré, Charles Bowers

Getting Away with Murder *75* Maximilian Schell
Getting Dad's Consent *11* Percy Stow
Getting Even *09* D. W. Griffith
Getting Even *22* Raoul Barré, Charles Bowers
Getting Even *81* Mark Feldberg
Getting Even *81* Harvey Hart
Getting Even *86* Dwight H. Little
Getting Evidence *06* Edwin S. Porter
Getting Father's Consent *09* A. E. Coleby
Getting Gertie's Garter *27* E. Mason Hopper
Getting Gertie's Garter *45* Allan Dwan
Getting His Change *07* Harold Hough
Getting His Goat *14* Charles Chaplin
Getting His Own Back *12* Walter R. Booth
Getting His Own Back *13* Charles C. Calvert
Getting His Own Back *14* Hay Plumb
Getting It On *83* William Olsen
Getting It Right *89* Randal Kleiser
Getting Mary Married *19* Allan Dwan
Getting of Wisdom, The *77* Bruce Beresford
Getting on His Nerves *15* Cecil Birch
Getting Over *81* Bernie Rollins
Getting Rid of His Dog *07* James A. Williamson
Getting Straight *70* Richard Rush
Getting Theirs *21* Frank Moser
Getting Together *76* David Secter
Getting Up Made Easy *03* Percy Stow
Gewalt *71* Helma Sanders-Brahms
Gewisser Herr Gran, Ein *34* Gerhard Lamprecht
Gewitter im Mai *38* Hans Deppe
Gezeichneten, Die *21* Carl Theodor Dreyer
Gezeichneten, Die *47* Fred Zinnemann
Gezin Van Paemel, Het *86* Paul Cammermans
Ghame Afghan *86* Zmarai Kasi, Mark M. Rissi
Ghanat *71* Dariush Mehrjui
Ghar ka Sukh *88* Kalptaru
Ghar Mein Ram Gali Mein Shyam *88* Subhash Sonik
Gharam wa Intikam *44* Youssef Wahby
Gharbar *63* James Ivory
Ghare-Baire *82* Satyajit Ray
Gharib al Saghir, Al *62* Georges M. Nasser
Gharibeh-Va-Meh *74* Bahram Beizai
Ghashiram Kotwol *76* Mani Kaul
Ghashiram the Police Chief *76* Mani Kaul
Ghastly Ones, The *68* Andy Milligan
Ghastly Orgies of Count Dracula, The *73* Renato Polselli
Ghengis Khan *65* Henry Levin
Ghetto, The *28* Norman Taurog
Ghetto Freaks *70* Robert J. Emery
Ghetto Shamrock, The *26* Francis Ford
Ghetto Terezín *49* Alfred Radok
Ghettoblaster *89* Alan L. Stewart
Ghidora the Three-Headed Monster *65* Inoshiro Honda
Ghidorah Sandai Kaijū Chikyū Saidai no Kessen *65* Inoshiro Honda

Ghidrah *65* Inoshiro Honda
Ghidrah the Three-Headed Monster *65* Inoshiro Honda
Ghosks Is the Bunk *39* Dave Fleischer
Ghost, The *11* Mack Sennett
Ghost, The *33* Ramón Peón
Ghost, The *63* Riccardo Freda
Ghost, The *71* Yoon Kyo Park
Ghost *90* Jerry Zucker
Ghost Against Ghost *80* Samo Hung
Ghost and Mr. Chicken, The *66* Alan Rafkin
Ghost and Mrs. Muir, The *47* Joseph L. Mankiewicz
Ghost and the Candle, The *03* Georges Méliès
Ghost and the Guest, The *43* William Nigh
Ghost at Noon, A *63* Jean-Luc Godard
Ghost Baron, The *27* Gustaf Edgren
Ghost Beauty *68* Satsuo Yamamoto
Ghost Breaker, The *14* Oscar Apfel, Cecil B. DeMille
Ghost Breaker, The *22* Alfred E. Green
Ghost Breakers, The *40* George Marshall
Ghost Camera, The *33* Bernard Vorhaus
Ghost Catchers, The *44* Edward F. Cline
Ghost Chasers *50* William Beaudine
Ghost City *21* William Bertram
Ghost City *32* Harry Fraser
Ghost Comes Home, The *40* Wilhelm Thiele
Ghost Crazy *44* William Beaudine
Ghost Creeps, The *40* Joseph H. Lewis
Ghost Dad *90* Sidney Poitier
Ghost Dance *82* Peter Bufa
Ghost Dance *83* Ken McMullen
Ghost Diver *57* Richard Einfeld, Merrill G. White
Ghost Fakir, The *26* William C. Nolan
Ghost Fever *85* Lee Madden
Ghost Flower, The *17* Frank Borzage
Ghost for Sale, A *52* Victor M. Gover
Ghost Galleon, The *74* Amando De Ossorio
Ghost Goes Gear, The *66* Hugh Gladwish
Ghost Goes West, The *35* René Clair
Ghost Goes Wild, The *47* George Blair
Ghost Guns *44* Lambert Hillyer
Ghost House, The *17* William DeMille
Ghost in the Garret, The *21* F. Richard Jones
Ghost in the Invisible Bikini, The *66* Don Weis
Ghost in the Mirror *74* Cunshou Song
Ghost in the Noonday Sun *73* Peter Medak
Ghost of a Chance, A *68* Jan Darnley-Smith
Ghost of Crossbones Canyon, The *52* Frank McDonald
Ghost of Dragstrip Hollow, The *59* William Hole, Jr.
Ghost of Folly, The *26* Edward F. Cline
Ghost of Frankenstein, The *41* Erle C. Kenton
Ghost of Hidden Valley *46* Sam Newfield
Ghost of John Holling, The *34* William Nigh
Ghost of Kasane, The *57* Nobuo

Nakagawa
Ghost of Love *81* Dino Risi
Ghost of Monk's Island, The *66* Jeremy Summers
Ghost of Old Morro, The *17* Richard Ridgely
Ghost of Otamage-Ike, The *60* Yoshihiro Ichikawa
Ghost of Rashmon Hall, The *48* Denis Kavanagh
Ghost of Rosy Taylor, The *18* Edward Sloman
Ghost of St. Michael's, The *41* Marcel Varnel
Ghost of the China Sea *58* Fred F. Sears
Ghost of the Hunchback, The *65* Hajime Sato
Ghost of the One-Eyed Man *65* Tsuneo Kobayashi
Ghost of the Rancho, The *18* William Worthington
Ghost of the Snow Girl *68* Tokuzo Tanaka
Ghost of the Twisted Oaks, The *15* Sidney Olcott
Ghost of the Variety, The *10* August Blom
Ghost of Tolston's Manor, The *22* Oscar Micheaux
Ghost of Yotsuya, The *59* Nobuo Nakagawa
Ghost of Yotsuya, The *65* Shiro Toyoda
Ghost of Yotsuya — New Version, The *49* Keisuke Kinoshita
Ghost of Zorro *49* Fred C. Brannon
Ghost Parade *31* Mack Sennett
Ghost Patrol, The *23* Nat Ross
Ghost Patrol *36* Sam Newfield
Ghost Rider, The *35* Jack Jevne
Ghost Rider, The *43* Wallace Fox
Ghost Ship, The *43* Mark Robson
Ghost Ship *52* Vernon Sewell
Ghost Steps Out, The *46* Charles Barton
Ghost Stories *64* Masaki Kobayashi
Ghost Story *74* Stephen Weeks
Ghost Story *81* John Irvin
Ghost Story of Peonies and Stone Lanterns, A *68* Satsuo Yamamoto
Ghost Story of Yotsuya in Tokaido *59* Nobuo Nakagawa
Ghost Story of Youth *55* Kon Ichikawa
Ghost Story — The Kasane Swamp *57* Nobuo Nakagawa
Ghost Tales Retold *38* Widgey R. Newman
Ghost Talks, The *29* Lewis Seiler
Ghost That Never Returns, The *29* Abram Room
Ghost That Walks Alone, The *43* Lew Landers
Ghost That Will Not Return, The *29* Abram Room
Ghost Town *36* Harry Fraser
Ghost Town *52* Lewis D. Collins
Ghost Town *56* Allen H. Miner
Ghost Town *88* Richard Governor
Ghost Town Gold *36* Joseph Kane
Ghost Town Law *42* Howard Bretherton
Ghost Town Renegades *47* Ray Taylor
Ghost Town Riders *38* George Waggner

Ghost Train, The *27* Géza von Bolváry
Ghost Train, The *31* Walter Forde
Ghost Train, The *41* Walter Forde
Ghost Train Murder, The *59* Peter Maxwell
Ghost Valley *32* Fred Allen
Ghost Valley, The *87* Alain Tanner
Ghost Valley Raiders *40* George Sherman
Ghost Walks, The *34* Frank R. Strayer
Ghost Walks, The *35* Walter Tennyson
Ghost Wanted *40* Chuck Jones
Ghost Warrior *84* J. Larry Carroll
Ghostbusters *84* Ivan Reitman
Ghostbusters II *89* Ivan Reitman
Ghosthouse *89* Umberto Lenzi
Ghostly Affair, A *14* Hay Plumb
Ghostly Wallop, A *22* Raoul Barré, Charles Bowers
Ghosts *12* Hay Plumb
Ghosts *14* Elwin Neame
Ghosts *15* John Emerson, George Nicholls
Ghosts *15* Vladimir Gardin
Ghosts Before Breakfast *28* Hans Richter
Ghosts Before Noon *28* Hans Richter
Ghosts Can't Do It *90* John Derek
Ghosts' Holiday, The *07* Lewin Fitzhamon
Ghosts in Rome *61* Antonio Pietrangeli
Ghosts in the Night *41* Phil Rosen
Ghosts in the Night *43* William Beaudine
Ghosts, Italian Style *67* Renato Castellani
Ghosts of Berkeley Square, The *47* Vernon Sewell
Ghosts of Rome *61* Antonio Pietrangeli
Ghosts of the Civil Dead *88* John Hillcoat
Ghosts of Yesterday *18* Charles Miller
Ghosts on Parade *68* Yoshiyuki Kuroda
Ghosts on the Loose *41* Phil Rosen
Ghosts on the Loose *43* William Beaudine
Ghosts That Still Walk *77* James T. Flocker
Ghoul, The *33* T. Hayes Hunter
Ghoul, The *74* Freddie Francis
Ghoul in a Girl's Dormitory *61* Paolo Heusch
Ghoul in School, The *61* Paolo Heusch
Ghoulies *84* Luca Bercovici
Ghoulies II *88* Alfredo Antonini
Ghulami ki Zanjeer *87* Chander Sharma
Ghurka's Revenge, The *14* A. E. Coleby
Giacomo l'Idealista *42* Alberto Lattuada
Giallo *33* Mario Camerini
Giallo Napoletano *79* Sergio Corbucci
Giant *56* George Stevens
Giant Behemoth, The *59* Douglas Hickox, Eugène Lourié
Giant Claw, The *57* Fred F. Sears
Giant from the Unknown *58* Richard Cunha
Giant Gila Monster, The *59* Ray Kellogg
Giant Killer, The *24* Walter Lantz
Giant Killer, The *61* Nathan Juran
Giant Leeches, The *59* Bernard Kowalski
Giant Monster *60* Pierre Chénal
Giant of Marathon, The *59* Mario Bava, Jacques Tourneur, Bruno Vailati
Giant of Metropolis, The *62* Umberto Scarpelli
Giant of the Evil Island *64* Piero Pierotti
Giant Spider Invasion, The *75* Bill Rebane
Giants A'Fire *41* Lambert Hillyer

Giants of the Steppes *42* Grigori Roshal
Giants of Thessaly, The *60* Riccardo Freda
Giarabub *42* Goffredo Alessandrini
Giardino degli Inganni, Il *86* Ferruccio Casati
Giardino dei Finzi-Contini, Il *70* Vittorio De Sica
Giarrettiera Colt *67* Gian Andrea Rocco
Gibel Sensaty *35* Alexander Andreievsky
Gibraltar *32* Basil Wright
Gibraltar *38* Fedor Ozep
Gibraltar Adventure *52* James Hill
Gibson Goddess, The *09* D. W. Griffith
Giddy Goats, The *07* Dave Aylott
Giddy Golightly *17* Cecil Mannering
Giddy Yapping *44* Howard Swift
Giddyap *50* Art Babbitt
Gideon of Scotland Yard *58* John Ford
Gideon's Day *58* John Ford
Gidget *59* Paul Wendkos
Gidget Goes Hawaiian *61* Paul Wendkos
Gidget Goes to Rome *63* Paul Wendkos
Gidgette Goes to Hell *72* Jonathan Demme*
Gift, The *13* Jack Hulcup
Gift, The *46* Jiří Trnka
Gift *66* Knud Leif Thomsen
Gift *72* Stan Brakhage
Gift, The *82* Michel Lang
Gift for Heidi, A *58* George Templeton
Gift for Music *57* Maria Fyodorova
Gift Girl, The *17* Rupert Julian
Gift o' Gab *17* W. S. Van Dyke
Gift of Gab, The *34* Karl Freund
Gift of God, The *82* Gaston J. M. Kaboré
Gift of Green, The *50* David Flaherty
Gift of Love, The *58* Jean Negulesco
Gift Supreme, The *20* Oliver L. Sellers
Gift Wrapped *52* Friz Freleng
Giftas *51* Anders Henrikson
Giftpilen *15* August Blom
Gig, The *85* Frank D. Gilroy
Gigante di Metropolis, Il *62* Umberto Scarpelli
Gigantes Interplanetarios *65* Alfredo B. Crevenna
Gigantes Planetarios *65* Alfredo B. Crevenna
Giganti della Tessaglia, I *60* Riccardo Freda
Giganti di Roma, I *64* Antonio Margheriti
Gigantic Devil, The *01* Georges Méliès
Gigantic Marionettes *13* Percy Stow
Gigantis *59* Hugo Grimaldi, Motoyoshi Odo
Gigantis the Fire Monster *59* Hugo Grimaldi, Motoyoshi Odo
Gigi *48* Jacqueline Audry
Gigi *58* Vincente Minnelli
Gigolette *20* Henri Pouctal
Gigolette *35* Charles Lamont
Gigolettes *32* Roscoe Arbuckle
Gigolettes of Paris *33* Alphonse Martel
Gigolo *26* William K. Howard
Gigolo, Le *60* Jacques Deray
Gigot *62* Gene Kelly
Gigue Merveilleuse, La *09* Georges Méliès
Gilbert and Sullivan *53* Sidney Gilliat
Gilbert Dying to Die *15* Maurice Elvey

Gilbert Gets Tiger-Itis *15* Maurice Elvey
Gilbert Harding Speaks of Murder *53* Paul Dickson
Gilda *46* Charles Vidor
Gilda Live *80* Mike Nichols
Gilded Butterfly, The *26* John Griffith Wray
Gilded Cage, The *16* Harley Knoles
Gilded Cage, The *54* John Gilling
Gilded Dream, The *20* Rollin Sturgeon
Gilded Fool, A *15* Edgar Lewis
Gilded Highway, The *25* J. Stuart Blackton
Gilded Lies *21* William P. S. Earle
Gilded Lily, The *21* Robert Z. Leonard
Gilded Lily, The *35* Wesley Ruggles
Gilded Spider, The *16* Joseph De Grasse
Gilded Youth, A *17* George L. Sargent
Gildersleeve on Broadway *43* Gordon Douglas
Gildersleeve's Bad Day *43* Gordon Douglas
Gildersleeve's Ghost *44* Gordon Douglas
Gilding the Lily *37* David Miller
Giles' First Visit to London *11* H. Oceano Martinek
Giles Has His Fortune Told *11* Walter R. Booth
Gilgi, Eine von Uns *37* Johannes Meyer
Giliap *76* Roy Andersson
Gill Woman *65* Peter Bogdanovich, Pavel Klushantsev
Gill Women of Venus *65* Peter Bogdanovich, Pavel Klushantsev
Gillekop *16* August Blom
Gilsodom *85* Kwon-taek Im
Gimme *23* Rupert Hughes
Gimme an F *84* Paul Justman
Gimme Shelter *70* Albert Maysles, David Maysles, Charlotte Zwerin
Gimmie *23* Rupert Hughes
Gin-Shinju *55* Kaneto Shindo
Gina *56* Luis Buñuel
Gina *75* Denys Arcand
Ginepro Fatto Uomo *62* Marco Bellocchio
Ginga-Tetsudō no Yoru *86* Gisaburo Sugii
Ginger *19* Burton George
Ginger *35* Lewis Seiler
Ginger *47* Oliver Drake
Ginger *71* Don Schain
Ginger and Fred *84* Federico Fellini
Ginger Bread Boy, The *34* Walter Lantz
Ginger e Fred *84* Federico Fellini
Ginger in the Morning *73* Gordon Wiles
Ginger Nutt's Bee Bother *49* David Hand
Ginger Nutt's Christmas Circus *49* David Hand
Ginger Nutt's Forest Dragon *50* David Hand
Ginger Seeks a Situation *14* Will P. Kellino
Ginger Snaps *20* Milt Gross
Ginger Snaps *29* Charles Lamont
Gingerbread *09* Dave Aylott
Gingerbread House *71* Curtis Harrington
Gingerbread Hut *51* Břetislav Pojar
Gingham Girl, The *27* David Kirkland
Ginko the Geisha *53* Kaneto Shindo
Ginpei from Koina *33* Teinosuke Kinugasa

Ginsberg the Great *27* Byron Haskin
Ginza Cosmetics *51* Mikio Naruse
Ginza Geshō *51* Mikio Naruse
Ginza no Mosa *60* Kon Ichikawa
Ginza no Onna *55* Kozaburo Yoshimura
Ginza no Yanagi *32* Heinosuke Gosho
Ginza Sanshiro *50* Kon Ichikawa
Ginza Tomboy *60* Kajiro Yamamoto
Ginza Veteran, A *60* Kon Ichikawa
Giocare col Fuoco *74* Alain Robbe-Grillet
Giocare d'Azzardo *82* Cinzia H. Torrini
Giocattolo, Il *78* Giuliano Montaldo
Giochi d'Estate *85* Bruno Cortini
Giochi di Colonia *58* Ermanno Olmi
Gioco al Massacro *89* Damiano Damiani
Gioco di Massacro *89* Damiano Damiani
Gioco di Società *88* Nanni Loy
Gioconda, La *11* Luigi Maggi
Gioconda, La *58* Giacinto Solito
Gioia's Photograph *87* Lamberto Bava
Gion Bayashi *53* Kenji Mizoguchi
Gion Festival *33* Kenji Mizoguchi
Gion Festival Music *53* Kenji Mizoguchi
Gion Matsuri *33* Kenji Mizoguchi
Gion Matsuri *69* Tetsuya Yamanouchi
Gion Music *53* Kenji Mizoguchi
Gion Music Festival *53* Kenji Mizoguchi
Gion no Shimai *36* Kenji Mizoguchi
Giordano Bruno *08* Giovanni Pastrone
Giordano Bruno *73* Giuliano Montaldo
Giordano Bruno, Eroe di Valmy *08* Giovanni Pastrone
Giornata Balorda, La *60* Mauro Bolognini
Giornata Speciale, Una *77* Ettore Scola
Giorni Contati, I *61* Elio Petri
Giorni d'Amore *54* Giuseppe De Santis
Giorni del Commissario Ambrosio, I *88* Sergio Corbucci
Giorni della Violenza, I *67* Alfonso Brescia
Giorni dell'Inferno, I *86* Tonino Ricci
Giorni dell'Ira, I *67* Tonino Valerii
Giorni di Fuoco *64* Harald Reinl
Giorni di Gloria *45* Giuseppe De Santis, Mario Serandrei, Luchino Visconti
Giorni di Sangue *68* Enzo Gicca
Giorno da Leoni, Un *61* Nanni Loy
Giorno della Civetta, Il *68* Damiano Damiani
Giorno e l'Ora, Il *62* René Clément
Giorno in Barbagia, Un *58* Vittorio De Seta
Giorno in Pretura, Un *53* Steno
Giorno nella Vita, Un *46* Alessandro Blasetti
Giorno Più Corto, Il *63* Sergio Corbucci
Giorno Prima, Il *87* Giuliano Montaldo
Giotto *40* Luciano Emmer, Enrico Gras, Tatiana Grauding
Giovane Attila, Il *71* Miklós Jancsó
Giovane Normale, Il *69* Dino Risi
Giovane Toscanini, Il *88* Franco Zeffirelli
Giovani Mariti *57* Mauro Bolognini
Giovanna d'Arco *08* Mario Caserini
Giovanna d'Arco al Rogo *54* Roberto Rossellini
Giovanni de Medici — The Leader *37* Luis Trenker
Giovanni delle Bande Nere *10* Mario Caserini

Giovanni Episcopo *47* Alberto Lattuada
Giovanni Senzapensieri *86* Marco Colli
Giovedi, Il *62* Dino Risi
Gioventù Perduta *47* Pietro Germi
Giovinezza, Giovinezza *69* Franco Rossi
Giperboloid Ingenera Garina *65* Alexander Gintsburg
Gipfelstürmer, Der *37* Franz Wenzler
Gipsies at Home *1896* Georges Méliès
Gipsy Blood *22* Bert Haldane
Gipsy Blood *31* Cecil Lewis
Gipsy Cavalier, A *22* J. Stuart Blackton
Gipsy Child, The *09* Lewin Fitzhamon
Gipsy Fortune Teller, The *05* Alf Collins
Gipsy Girl's Honour, A *12* Lewin Fitzhamon
Gipsy Hate *13* Lewin Fitzhamon
Gipsy Nan *11* Lewin Fitzhamon
Gipsy Talisman, The *12* Christy Cabanne
Giraffe's Long Neck, The *26* Clyde Geronimi
Girara *64* Kazui Nihonmatsu
Girasoli, I *69* Vittorio De Sica
Girdle of Gold *52* Montgomery Tully
Girl, The *68* Márta Mészáros
Girl, The *87* Arne Mattsson
Girl, a Guy and a Gob, A *41* Richard Wallace
Girl Across the Way, The *12* Christy Cabanne
Girl Against Napoleon, A *59* Tulio Demicheli
Girl Alaska, The *19* Albert Smith
Girl Alone, A *12* Bert Haldane
Girl and Her Trust, The *12* D. W. Griffith
Girl and Some Guns, A *64* Claude Lelouch
Girl and the Boy, The *32* Wilhelm Thiele
Girl and the Bronco Buster, The *11* Alice Guy-Blaché
Girl and the Bugler, The *67* Alexander Mitta
Girl and the Crisis, The *17* William V. Mong
Girl and the Devil, The *44* Erik Faustman
Girl and the Gambler, The *39* Lew Landers
Girl and the Game, The *16* John P. McGowan
Girl and the General, The *66* Pasquale Festa Campanile
Girl and the Gold Mine, The *14* Dalton Somers
Girl and the Gorilla, The *44* Sam Newfield
Girl and the Gun, The *12* Allan Dwan
Girl and the Judge, The *18* John B. O'Brien
Girl and the Legend, The *57* Josef von Baky
Girl and the Outlaw, The *08* D. W. Griffith
Girl and the Palio, The *57* Luigi Zampa
Girl Angle, The *17* Edgar Jones
Girl at Bay, A *19* Thomas R. Mills
Girl at Dojo Temple, A *46* Kon Ichikawa
Girl at Home, The *17* Marshall Neilan
Girl at Lancing Mill, The *13* Warwick Buckland

Girl at the Ironing Board, The *34* Friz Freleng
Girl at the Lodge, The *12* Bert Haldane
Girl Back Home, The *12* Allan Dwan
Girl Boy Scout, The *14* Ethyle Batley
Girl by the Roadside, The *17* Theodore Marston
Girl Can't Help It, The *56* Frank Tashlin
Girl Can't Stop, The *66* Willy Rozier
Girl Crazy *29* Mack Sennett
Girl Crazy *32* William A. Seiter
Girl Crazy *43* Norman Taurog
Girl Crazy *65* Alvin Ganzer
Girl Divers from Spook Mansion *59* Morihei Magatani
Girl Dodger, The *19* Jerome Storm
Girl Downstairs, The *38* Norman Taurog
Girl Fever *61* Yevsie Petrushansky, Sherman Price
Girl Field Marshal, The *68* Steno
Girl for Joe, A *51* Michael Curtiz
Girl Friend, The *26* Heinosuke Gosho
Girl Friend, The *35* Edward Buzzell
Girl Friends *36* Lev Arnshtam
Girl Friends, The *55* Michelangelo Antonioni
Girl from Alaska, The *42* Nick Grindé
Girl from Avenue A *40* Otto Brower
Girl from Beyond, The *18* William Wolbert
Girl from Bohemia, The *18* Lawrence McGill
Girl from Calgary *32* Leon D'Usseau, Phil Whitman
Girl from Carthage, The *24* Scemana Chikly
Girl from Chicago, The *27* Ray Enright
Girl from Chicago, The *27* Oscar Micheaux
Girl from China, The *29* John S. Robertson
Girl from Corfu, The *57* J. Petropoulakis
Girl from Downing Street, The *18* Geoffrey H. Malins
Girl from Everywhere, The *27* Edward F. Cline
Girl from 5000 A.D., The *58* Robert Gurney, Jr.
Girl from Flanders, The *55* Helmut Käutner
Girl from Gay Paree, The *27* Phil Goldstone
Girl from God's Country, The *21* Nell Shipman
Girl from God's Country *40* Sidney Salkow
Girl from Hamburg, The *58* Yves Allégret
Girl from Havana, The *29* Ben Stoloff
Girl from Havana *40* Lew Landers
Girl from His Town, The *15* Harry A. Pollard
Girl from Hong Kong, The *61* Franz Peter Wirth
Girl from Hunan *86* Lan Niao, Fei Xie
Girl from Ireland, The *37* Norman Lee
Girl from Jones Beach, The *49* Peter Godfrey
Girl from Leningrad, The *41* Victor Eisimont
Girl from Lorraine, A *80* Claude Goretta

Girl from Mandalay, The *36* Howard Bretherton

Girl from Manhattan, The *48* Alfred E. Green

Girl from Mani, The *86* Paul Annett

Girl from Maxim's, The *33* Alexander Korda

Girl from Mexico, The *29* Erle C. Kenton

Girl from Mexico, The *39* Leslie Goodwins

Girl from Missouri, The *34* Jack Conway

Girl from Monterey, The *43* Wallace Fox

Girl from Montmartre, The *26* Alfred E. Green

Girl from Nowhere, The *19* Wilfred Lucas, Bess Meredyth

Girl from Nowhere, The *21* George Archainbaud

Girl from Nowhere, The *28* Harry Edwards

Girl from Nowhere *39* Lambert Hillyer

Girl from Paris, The *36* Leigh Jason

Girl from Petrovka, The *74* Robert Ellis Miller

Girl from Poltava *36* M. J. Gann, E. Kavaleridze, Edgar G. Ulmer

Girl from Porcupine, The *21* Del Henderson

Girl from Prosperity, The *14* Ralph Ince

Girl from Rio, The *27* Tom Terriss

Girl from Rio, The *39* Lambert Hillyer

Girl from Rocky Point, The *22* Fred G. Becker

Girl from San Lorenzo, The *50* Derwin Abrahams

Girl from Scotland Yard, The *37* Robert Vignola

Girl from Scotland Yard, The *48* Paul Barralet

Girl from Starship Venus, The *75* Derek Ford

Girl from State Street, The *28* Archie Mayo

Girl from Stormycroft, The *17* Victor Sjöström

Girl from Swabia, The *19* Ernst Lubitsch

Girl from 10th Avenue, The *35* Alfred E. Green

Girl from Texas, The *48* William Castle

Girl from the Dead Sea, The *67* Menahem Golan

Girl from the Department Store, The *33* Anders Henrikson*

Girl from the Factory, A *70* Gleb Panfilov

Girl from the Gallery, The *49* Hasse Ekman

Girl from the Marsh Croft *17* Victor Sjöström

Girl from the Marsh Croft, The *35* Douglas Sirk

Girl from the Mountain Village, The *48* Anders Henrikson

Girl from the Outside, The *19* Reginald Barker

Girl from the Sky, The *14* Elwin Neame

Girl from the Stormy Croft *17* Victor Sjöström

Girl from the West *23* Wallace MacDonald

Girl from Tobacco Row, The *66* Ron Ormond

Girl from Trieste, The *83* Pasquale Festa Campanile

Girl from Valladolid *58* Luis César Amadori

Girl from Woolworth's, The *29* William Beaudine

Girl Game *62* Steno

Girl-Getters, The *64* Michael Winner

Girl Glory, The *17* Roy William Neill

Girl Grabbers *68* Simon Nuchtern

Girl Grief *32* James Parrott

Girl Habit, The *31* Edward F. Cline

Girl Happy *65* Boris Sagal

Girl He Didn't Buy, The *28* Dallas M. Fitzgerald

Girl He Left Behind, The *56* David Butler

Girl Hunters, The *60* Roy Rowland

Girl I Abandoned, The *70* Kiriro Urayama

Girl I Left Behind Me, The *15* Lloyd B. Carleton

Girl I Loved, The *23* Joseph De Grasse

Girl I Loved, The *46* Keisuke Kinoshita

Girl I Made, The *33* Harry Beaumont

Girl in a Bikini *56* Dino Risi

Girl in a Boot *83* Herbert Ballman

Girl in a Dresscoat *56* Arne Mattsson

Girl in a Million, A *46* Francis Searle

Girl in a Swing, The *89* Gordon Hessler

Girl in Australia, A *71* Luigi Zampa

Girl in Black, The *55* Michael Cacoyannis

Girl in Black Stockings, The *57* Howard W. Koch

Girl in Blue, The *73* George Kaczender

Girl in Bohemia, A *19* Howard Mitchell

Girl in Danger *34* D. Ross Lederman

Girl in Distress *41* Harold French

Girl in Every Port, A *28* Howard Hawks

Girl in Every Port, A *52* Chester Erskine

Girl in 419, The *33* Alexander Hall, George Somnes

Girl in Gold Boots, The *68* Ted V. Mikels

Girl in His House, The *18* Thomas R. Mills

Girl in His Pocket *57* Pierre Kast

Girl in His Room, The *22* Edward José

Girl in Lover's Lane, The *60* Charles R. Rondeau

Girl in Mourning, The *63* Manuel Summers

Girl in Number 29, The *20* John Ford

Girl in Overalls, The *43* Norman Z. McLeod

Girl in Pawn, The *34* Alexander Hall

Girl in Possession, The *34* Monty Banks

Girl in Room 13 *61* Richard Cunha

Girl in Room 17, The *53* Arnold Laven

Girl in the Armchair, The *13* Alice Guy-Blaché

Girl in the Bikini, The *52* Willy Rozier

Girl in the Case, The *44* William Berke

Girl in the Checkered Coat, The *17* Joseph De Grasse

Girl in the Crowd, The *34* Michael Powell

Girl in the Dark, The *18* Stuart Paton

Girl in the Flat, The *34* Redd Davis

Girl in the Glass Cage, The *29* Ralph Dawson

Girl in the Headlines *63* Michael Truman

Girl in the Invisible Bikini, The *66* Don Weis

Girl in the Kremlin, The *57* Russell Birdwell

Girl in the Leather Suit *69* Maury Dexter

Girl in the Limousine, The *24* Larry Semon

Girl in the Mist *59* Hideo Suzuki

Girl in the Moon, The *28* Fritz Lang

Girl in the News, The *40* Carol Reed

Girl in the Night, The *31* Henry Edwards

Girl in the Painting, The *48* Terence Fisher

Girl in the Picture, The *56* Don Chaffey

Girl in the Picture, The *85* Cary Parker

Girl in the Pullman, The *27* Erle C. Kenton

Girl in the Rain, The *20* Rollin Sturgeon

Girl in the Rain *55* Alf Kjellin

Girl in the Red Velvet Swing, The *55* Richard Fleischer

Girl in the Rumor, The *35* Mikio Naruse

Girl in the Show, The *29* Edgar Selwyn

Girl in the Taxi, The *21* Lloyd Ingraham

Girl in the Taxi, The *37* André Berthomieu

Girl in the Trunk, The *73* Georges Lautner

Girl in the Web, The *20* Robert Thornby

Girl in the Window, The *60* Luciano Emmer

Girl in the Woods, The *58* Tom Gries

Girl in 313 *40* Ricardo Cortez

Girl in Trouble *63* Brandon Chase

Girl in White, The *52* John Sturges

Girl Is Mine, The *50* Marjorie Deans

Girl Isn't Allowed to Love, A *55* Teinosuke Kinugasa

Girl Journalist, The *27* Lev Kuleshov

Girl Like That, A *17* Del Henderson

Girl Loves Boy *37* Duncan Mansfield

Girl Madness *61* Coleman Francis

Girl Merchants *57* Maurice Cloche

Girl Missing *32* Robert Florey

Girl Most Likely, The *57* Mitchell Leisen

Girl Must Live, A *39* Carol Reed

Girl Named Mary, The *19* Walter Edwards

Girl Named Tamiko, A *62* John Sturges

Girl Next Door, The *13* Lewin Fitzhamon

Girl Next Door, The *14* Arthur Finn

Girl Next Door, The *23* W. S. Van Dyke

Girl Next Door, The *53* Richard Sale

Girl No. 217 *44* Mikhail Romm

Girl o' My Dreams *34* Ray McCarey

Girl of Glenbeigh, A *18* John McDonagh

Girl of Gold, The *25* John Ince

Girl of Good Family, A *86* Jianxin Huang

Girl of Last Night, The *38* Peter Paul Brauer

Girl of London, A *25* Henry Edwards

Girl of Lost Lake, The *16* Lynn Reynolds

Girl of My Dreams, The *18* Louis Chaudet

Girl of My Dreams *33* Edwin L. Marin

Girl of My Heart, The *15* Leedham Bantock

Girl of My Heart *20* Edward J. LeSaint

Girl of Seventeen, A *59* Salah Abu Saif

Girl of the Bersagliere, The *66* Alessandro Blasetti

Girl of the Golden West, The *14* Cecil B. DeMille

Girl of the Golden West, The *23* Edwin Carewe

Girl of the Golden West, The *30* John Francis Dillon

Girl of the Golden West, The *38* Robert Z. Leonard

Girl of the Gypsy Camp, The *15* Langdon West

Girl of the Limberlost, A *24* James Leo Meehan

Girl of the Limberlost, A *34* Christy Cabanne

Girl of the Limberlost, The *45* Mel Ferrer

Girl of the Meiji Era, A *68* Heinosuke Gosho

Girl of the Meiji Period, A *68* Heinosuke Gosho

Girl of the Moors, The *61* Gustav Ucicky

Girl of the Mountains *58* Orestes Laskos

Girl of the Night *60* Joseph Cates

Girl of the Nile, The *67* Rudolf Zehetgruber

Girl of the Ozarks *36* William Shea

Girl of the Port *30* Bert Glennon

Girl of the Ranch, The *11* Allan Dwan

Girl of the Rio *32* Herbert Brenon

Girl of the Sea *20* J. Winthrop Kelley

Girl of the Timber Claims, The *17* Paul Powell

Girl of the West *25* Alvin J. Neitz

Girl of the Year *50* Henry Levin

Girl of Tin, The *70* Marcello Aliprandi

Girl of Today *18* John S. Robertson

Girl of Yesterday, A *15* Allan Dwan

Girl on a Chain Gang *66* Jerry Gross

Girl on a Motorcycle, The *68* Jack Cardiff

Girl on Approval *61* Charles Frend

Girl on the Barge, The *29* Edward Sloman

Girl on the Boat, The *61* Henry Kaplan

Girl on the Bridge *51* Hugo Haas

Girl on the Canal, The *45* Charles Crichton

Girl on the Front Page, The *36* Harry Beaumont

Girl on the Moon, The *28* Fritz Lang

Girl on the Pier *53* Lance Comfort

Girl on the Run *58* Richard L. Bare

Girl on the Run *61* Arthur J. Beckhard, Joseph Lee

Girl on the Spot *46* William Beaudine

Girl on the Stairs, The *24* William Worthington

Girl on the Third Floor, The *58* Pierre Gaspard-Huit

Girl on the Train, The *27* Erle C. Kenton

Girl on the Underground, The *89* Romano Scandariato

Girl Overboard *29* Wesley Ruggles

Girl Overboard *37* Sidney Salkow

Girl Philippa, The *17* Sidney Rankin Drew

Girl Problem, The *19* Kenneth Webb

Girl Refugee, The *38* Demetre Bogris

Girl Reporter, The *13* Phillips Smalley

Girl Rosemarie, The *58* Rolf Thiele

Girl Rush *44* Gordon Douglas

Girl Rush, The *55* Robert Pirosh

Girl Said No, The *30* Sam Wood

Girl Said No, The *36* Andrew L. Stone

Girl School Screamers *86* John P. Finegan

Girl Scout, The *09* Sidney Olcott

Girl Sellers, The *57* Maurice Cloche

Girl Shy *24* Fred Newmeyer, Sam Taylor

Girl-Shy Cowboy *28* R. Lee Hough

Girl Smugglers *67* Barry Mahon

Girl Spy Before Vicksburg, The *10* Sidney Olcott

Girl Strike Leader, The *10* Edwin S. Porter

Girl Stroke Boy *71* Bob Kellett

Girl Swappers, The *61* Freddie Francis

Girl That I Love, The *46* Keisuke Kinoshita

Girl, the Body and the Pill, The *67* Herschell Gordon Lewis

Girl Thief, The *34* Paul Merzbach

Girl Trouble *33* Bernard B. Ray

Girl Trouble *34* Edward F. Cline

Girl Trouble *42* Bernard B. Ray

Girl Trouble *42* Harold Schuster

Girl Was Young, The *37* Alfred Hitchcock

Girl Who Came Back, The *18* Robert Vignola

Girl Who Came Back, The *21* Edward R. Gordon

Girl Who Came Back, The *23* Tom Forman

Girl Who Came Back, The *35* Charles Lamont

Girl Who Couldn't Grow Up, The *17* Harry A. Pollard

Girl Who Couldn't Quite, The *49* Norman Lee

Girl Who Couldn't Say No, The *68* Franco Brusati

Girl Who Dared, The *10* Edwin S. Porter

Girl Who Dared, The *19* Allen Holubar

Girl Who Dared, The *20* Clifford Smith

Girl Who Dared, The *44* Howard Bretherton

Girl Who Did Not Care, The *16* Ivan Abramson

Girl Who Didn't Care, The *16* Fred W. Durrant

Girl Who Didn't Think, The *17* William F. Haddock

Girl Who Doesn't Know, The *17* Charles E. Bartlett

Girl Who Forgot, The *39* Adrian Brunel

Girl Who Had Everything, The *53* Richard Thorpe

Girl Who Joined the Bushrangers, The *09* Lewin Fitzhamon

Girl Who Knew Too Much, The *69* Francis D. Lyon

Girl Who Liked Purple Flowers, The *73* Steve Sekely

Girl Who Lived in Straight Street, The *14* Warwick Buckland

Girl Who Loves a Soldier, The *16* Alexander Butler

Girl Who Played the Game, The *14* Warwick Buckland

Girl Who Ran Wild, The *22* Rupert Julian

Girl Who Stayed at Home, The *19* D. W. Griffith

Girl Who Took the Wrong Turning, The *15* Leedham Bantock

Girl Who Won Out, The *17* W. Eugene Moore

Girl Who Wouldn't Quit, The *18* Edgar Jones

Girl Who Wouldn't Work, The *25* Marcel De Sano

Girl Who Wrecked His Home, The *16* Albert Ward

Girl with a Gun *67* Mario Monicelli

Girl with a Jazz Heart, The *20* Lawrence C. Windom

Girl with a Pistol, The *67* Mario Monicelli

Girl with a Suitcase, The *60* Valerio Zurlini

Girl with Green Eyes, The *63* Desmond Davis

Girl with Hyacinths *50* Hasse Ekman

Girl with Ideas, A *37* S. Sylvan Simon

Girl with No Regrets, The *19* Harry Millarde

Girl with the Champagne Eyes, The *18* Chester M. Franklin

Girl with the Fabulous Box, The *69* Charles Nisbet

Girl with the Golden Eyes, The *61* Jean-Gabriel Albicocco

Girl with the Green Eyes, The *16* Herbert Blaché, Alice Guy-Blaché

Girl with the Guitar, The *60* Alexander Feinzimmer

Girl with the Hatbox, The *27* Boris Barnet

Girl with the Jazz Heart, The *20* Lawrence C. Windom

Girl with the Red Hair, The *81* Ben Verbong

Girl with Three Camels, The *68* Václav Krška

Girl Without a Room *33* Ralph Murphy

Girl Without a Soul, The *17* John H. Collins

Girl Without an Address, The *57* Eldar Ryazanov

Girl Woman, The *19* Thomas R. Mills

Girlfriends, The *67* Claude Chabrol

Girlfriends *78* Claudia Weill

Girlfriends and Boyfriends *86* Eric Rohmer

Girlhood of a Queen *36* Erich Engel

Girlies Behave *28* Charles Lamont

Girls *19* Walter Edwards

Girls, Les *57* George Cukor

Girls, The *59* Claude Chabrol

Girls, The *68* Mai Zetterling

Girls, The *77* Sumitra Peries

Girls *80* Just Jaeckin

Girls About Town *31* George Cukor

Girls Among the Flowers *53* Kajiro Yamamoto

Girls and a Daddy, The *08* D. W. Griffith

Girls and Daddy, The *08* D. W. Griffith

Girls Are for Loving *73* Don Schain

Girls Are Willing, The *59* Gabriel Axel

Girls at Sea *58* Gilbert Gunn

Girls' Aunt, The *39* Juan Bustillo Oro

Girls Behind Bars *50* Alfred Braun

Girl's Best Years, A *37* Reginald LeBorg

Girls Can Play *37* Lambert Hillyer

Girls Come First *75* Joseph McGrath

Girls Demand Excitement *31* Seymour Felix

Girl's Desire, A *22* David Divad

Girls Disappear *58* Édouard Molinaro

Girls Don't Gamble *21* Fred J. Butler

Girls' Dormitory *36* Irving Cummings

Girls' Dormitory *53* Henri Decoin

Girl's Folly, A *17* Maurice Tourneur
Girls for Men Only *66* Peter Walker
Girls for Rent *74* Al Adamson
Girls for the Summer *59* Édouard Molinaro
Girls from Thunder Strip, The *66* David L. Hewitt
Girls from Wilko, The *78* Andrzej Wajda
Girls! Girls! Girls! *62* Norman Taurog
Girls Gone Wild *29* Lewis Seiler
Girls He Left Behind, The *43* Busby Berkeley
Girls in Action *59* Louis Clyde Stoumen
Girls in Arms *59* Gilbert Gunn
Girls in Chains *43* Edgar G. Ulmer
Girls in One Umbrella, The *03* Georges Méliès
Girls in Prison *56* Edward L. Cahn
Girls in the Harbor *45* Åke Öhberg
Girls in the Night *53* Jack Arnold
Girls in the Shadows *61* Ladislas Vajda
Girls in the Street *37* Herbert Wilcox
Girls in Uniform *31* Leontine Sagan
Girls in Uniform *58* Géza von Radványi
Girls, Inc. *60* Barry Mahon
Girls Just Want to Have Fun *85* Alan Metter
Girl's Love-Letter, A *11* Bert Haldane
Girls Marked Danger *52* Luigi Comencini
Girls Men Forget *24* Maurice Campbell
Girls Never Tell *51* Seymour Friedman
Girls Next Door, The *79* James Hong
Girls' Night Out *84* Robert Deubel
Girls of 42nd Street *74* Andy Milligan
Girls of France, The *38* Yves Allégret
Girls of Izu, The *45* Heinosuke Gosho
Girls of Latin Quarter *60* Alfred Travers
Girls of Nowolipek *38* Josef Leytes
Girls of Okinawa, The *53* Tadashi Imai
Girls of Pleasure Island, The *53* Alvin Ganzer, F. Hugh Herbert
Girls of Spider Island *59* Fritz Böttger
Girls of Summer, The *88* Joan Freeman
Girls of the Big House *45* George Archainbaud
Girls of the Night *57* Maurice Cloche
Girls of the Piazza di Spagna *52* Luciano Emmer
Girls of the Road *40* Nick Grindé
Girls of the Village, The *17* Maurice Sandground
Girls on Probation *38* William McGann, Harry Seymour
Girls on the Beach, The *65* William Witney
Girls on the Loose *58* Paul Henreid
Girl's Own Story, A *83* Jane Campion
Girls Please *34* Jack Raymond
Girls' School *38* John Brahm
Girls' School *50* Lew Landers
Girl's Stratagem, A *13* D. W. Griffith
Girls Town *42* Victor Halperin
Girls Town *59* Charles Haas
Girls Under 21 *40* Max Nosseck
Girls Who Dare *29* Frank S. Mattison
Girls Will Be Boys *34* Marcel Varnel
Girltalk *87* Kate Davis
Girly *69* Freddie Francis
Giro City *82* Karl Francis
Girolimoni, il Mostro di Roma *72*

Damiano Damiani
Girovaghi, I *56* Hugo Fregonese
Girth of a Nation, The *18* Kenneth M. Anderson
Giselle *52* Henry Caldwell
Giselle *82* Victori Di Mello
Giselle *87* Herbert Ross
Gishiki *71* Nagisa Oshima
Git! *65* Ellis Kadison
Git Along, Little Dogies *37* Joseph Kane
Git Along, Little Wifie *33* Charles Lamont
Gita Scolastica, Una *83* Pupi Avati
Gitan, Le *75* José Giovanni
Gitane, La *85* Philippe de Broca
Gitanella, La *14* Louis Feuillade
Gitanella *24* André Hugon
Gitanes *24* Jacques De Baroncelli
Gitanos et Papillons *54* Henri Gruel
Gitta Entdeckt Ihr Herz *32* Carl Fröhlich
Giù la Testa *71* Sergio Leone
Giù le Mani... Carogna *71* Lucky Dickinson
Giuditta e Oloferne *29* Baldassare Negroni
Giuditta e Oloferne *58* Fernando Cerchio
Giudizio Universale, Il *61* Vittorio De Sica
Giulia e Giulia *87* Peter Del Monte
Giuliano de' Medici *40* Ladislas Vajda
Giulietta degli Spiriti *65* Federico Fellini
Giulietta e Romeo *54* Renato Castellani
Giulietta e Romeo *64* Riccardo Freda
Giulio Cesare il Conquistatore delle Gallie *63* Tanio Boccia
Giulli *27* Nikolai Shengelaya*
Giumenta Verda, La *59* Claude Autant-Lara
Giuro Che Ti Amo *86* Nino D'Angelo
Giuro... e Li Uccise ad Uno ad Uno *68* Guido Celano
Giuseppe Venduto dai Fratelli *60* Irving Rapper, Luciano Ricci
Giuseppe Verdi *38* Carmine Gallone
Giuseppe Verdi *53* Raffaello Matarazzo
Giuseppina *60* James Hill
Give a Dog a Bone *67* Henry Cass
Give a Girl a Break *53* Stanley Donen
Give and Take *28* William Beaudine
Give and Take *46* Del Lord
Give and Tyke *56* Joseph Barbera, William Hanna
Give 'Em Hell *54* John Berry
Give 'Em Hell, Harry *75* Steve Binder
Give 'Er the Gas *21* Wallace A. Carlson
Give Her a Ring *34* Arthur Woods
Give Her the Moon *69* Philippe de Broca
Give Me a Sailor *38* Elliott Nugent
Give Me Liberty *37* B. Reeves Eason
Give Me My Chance *57* Léonide Moguy
Give Me the Stars *44* Maclean Rogers
Give Me Your Hand My Love *56* Karl Hartl
Give Me Your Heart *35* Marcel Varnel
Give Me Your Heart *36* Archie Mayo
Give My Regards to Broad Street *84* Peter Webb
Give My Regards to Broadway *48* Lloyd Bacon
Give Out, Sisters *42* Edward F. Cline
Give Till It Hurts *37* Felix E. Feist
Give Us Air *24* Dziga Vertov
Give Us Radio! *24* S. Grunberg, Sergei

Yutkevich
Give Us the Moon *44* Val Guest
Give Us This Day *13* Victor Sjöström
Give Us This Day *49* Edward Dmytryk
Give Us This Night *36* Alexander Hall
Give Us Tomorrow *78* Donovan Winter
Give Us Wings *36* Jiří Weiss
Give Us Wings *40* Charles Lamont
Given Word, The *61* Anselmo Duarte
Giving Becky a Chance *17* Howard Estabrook
Gizmo *77* Howard Smith
Glace à Trois Faces, La *27* Jean Epstein
Glacier Fox, The *78* Koreyoshi Kurahara
Glad Eye, The *20* Kenelm Foss
Glad Eye, The *27* Maurice Elvey
Glad Rag Doll, The *29* Michael Curtiz
Glad Rags to Riches *33* Charles Lamont
Glad Tidings *53* Wolf Rilla
Gladiador Invencible, El *62* Anthony Momplet
Gladiator, The *38* Edward Sedgwick
Gladiator of Rome *62* Mario Costa
Gladiatore di Roma, Il *62* Mario Costa
Gladiatore Invincibile, Il *62* Anthony Momplet
Gladiatorerna *68* Peter Watkins
Gladiators *68* Peter Watkins
Gladiators Seven *64* Pedro Lazaga Sabater
Gladiola *15* John H. Collins
Glaive et la Balance, Le *62* André Cayatte
Glamis Castle *26* Maurice Elvey
Glamorous Night *37* Brian Desmond Hurst
Glamour *31* Seymour Hicks, Harry Hughes
Glamour *34* William Wyler
Glamour *85* François Merlet
Glamour Boy *40* Leslie Goodwins
Glamour Boy *40* Ralph Murphy
Glamour for Sale *40* D. Ross Lederman
Glamour Girl *38* Arthur Woods
Glamour Girl *47* Arthur Dreifuss
Glance at the Pupil of the Sun, A *66* Veljko Bulajić
Glas *58* Bert Haanstra
Glas Wasser, Ein *23* Ludwig Berger
Glas Wasser, Das *60* Helmut Käutner
Glasberget *53* Gustaf Molander
Gläserne Himmel, Der *88* Nina Grosse
Gläserne Kugel, Die *39* Peter Stanchina
Gläserne Turm, Der *57* Harald Braun
Glasgow Orpheus Choir *51* George Hoellering
Glass *58* Bert Haanstra
Glass Alibi, The *46* W. Lee Wilder
Glass Ball, The *39* Peter Stanchina
Glass Bottom Boat, The *66* Frank Tashlin
Glass Cage, The *55* Montgomery Tully
Glass Cage, The *63* Antonio Santean
Glass Castle, The *50* René Clément
Glass Cell, The *77* Hans W. Geissendörfer
Glass Heaven, The *88* Nina Grosse
Glass House, The *72* Tom Gries
Glass Houses *21* Harry Beaumont
Glass Houses *70* Alexander Singer
Glass Key, The *35* Frank Tuttle
Glass Key, The *42* Stuart Heisler
Glass Menagerie, The *50* Irving Rapper
Glass Menagerie, The *87* Paul Newman

Glass Mountain, The 48 Henry Cass
Glass of Beer, A 55 Félix Máriássy
Glass of Goat's Milk, A 09 Percy Stow
Glass of Water, A 60 Helmut Käutner
Glass Slipper, The 54 Charles Walters
Glass Sphinx, The 67 Kamel El Sheik, Luigi Scattini
Glass Tomb, The 55 Montgomery Tully
Glass Tower, The 57 Harald Braun
Glass Wall, The 53 Maxwell Shane
Glass Web, The 53 Jack Arnold
Glassmakers of England, The 33 Robert Flaherty
Glastonbury Fair, The 71 Nicolas Roeg
Glastonbury Fayre 73 Peter Neal
Glastonbury Past and Present 22 H. Oceano Martinek
Glaube und Wahrung 80 Werner Herzog
Gleam O'Dawn 22 John Francis Dillon
Gleaming the Cube 88 Graeme Clifford
Gleisdreieck 38 Robert A. Stemmle
Glembajevi 88 Anton Vrdoljak
Glen and Randa 71 Jim McBride
Glen Gray and His Casa Loma Band 42 Jean Negulesco
Glen or Glenda? 53 Edward D. Wood, Jr.
Glenister of the Mounted 26 Harry Garson
Glenn Gould—Off the Record 60 Wolf Koenig, Roman Kroitor
Glenn Gould—On the Record 60 Wolf Koenig, Roman Kroitor
Glenn Miller Story, The 53 Anthony Mann
Glenrowan Affair, The 51 Rupe Kathner
Gli Fumavano le Colt...Lo Chiamavano Camposanto 71 Giuliano Carmineo
Glimpse of Los Angeles, A 14 Wilfred Lucas
Glimpse of Paradise, A 34 Ralph Ince
Glimpses of the Moon, The 23 Allan Dwan
Glimpses of U.S.A. 59 Charles Eames, Ray Eames, John Whitney
Glinka 46 Lev Arnshtam
Glinka 52 Grigori Alexandrov
Glissements Progressifs du Plaisir 73 Alain Robbe-Grillet
Glitch 87 Nico Mastorakis
Glitter Dome, The 84 Stuart Margolin
Glitterball, The 77 Harley Cokliss
Glittering Sword, The 29 Ronald Gow
Glittering You 86 Tokihisa Morikawa
Global Affair, A 63 Jack Arnold
Globe Trotters, The 26 Charles Bowers
Globe Trotting with Hy Mayer 16 Hy Mayer
Gloire Rouge 23 Albert Dieudonné
Glomdalsbruden 25 Carl Theodor Dreyer
Gloom Chaser, The 28 Charles Lamont
Gloom Chasers, The 35 Art Davis, Sid Marcus
Gloria, La 12 Baldassare Negroni
Gloria, La 13 Augusto Genina
Gloria, La 16 Febo Mari
Gloria 32 Hans Behrendt
Gloria 77 Claude Autant-Lara
Gloria 80 John Cassavetes
Gloria Mundi 75 Nikos Papatakis
Gloria Scott, The 23 George Ridgwell

Gloriana 16 E. Mason Hopper
Glorifying the American Girl 29 John Harkrider, Millard Webb
Glorious Adventure, The 18 Hobart Henley
Glorious Adventure, The 21 J. Stuart Blackton
Glorious Betsy 28 Alan Crosland
Glorious Fool, The 22 E. Mason Hopper
Glorious Lady 19 George Irving
Glorious Musketeers, The 73 John Halas
Glorious Nights 38 Rolando Aguilar
Glorious Road, The 51 Ilya Kopalin*
Glorious Sacrifice 36 Lynn Shores
Glorious Trail, The 28 Albert S. Rogell
Glorious Youth 28 Graham Cutts
Glory 17 Francis J. Grandon, Burton L. King
Glory 55 David Butler
Glory 89 Edward Zwick
Glory Alley 52 Raoul Walsh
Glory and Misery of Human Life, The 89 Matti Kassila
Glory at Sea 52 Compton Bennett
Glory Boy 71 Edwin Sherin
Glory Brigade, The 53 Robert D. Webb
Glory for Me 46 William Wyler
Glory Guys, The 65 Arnold Laven
Glory of a Nation, The 17 J. Stuart Blackton
Glory of Clementina, The 22 Émile Chautard
Glory of Faith, The 38 Georges Pallu
Glory of Love, The 20 Maurice Tourneur
Glory of Yolanda, The 17 Marguerite Bertsch
Glory on the Summit 62 Masahiro Shinoda
Glory on the Summit: Burning Youth 62 Masahiro Shinoda
Glory Stompers, The 67 Anthony M. Lanza
Glory Trail, The 36 Lynn Shores
Glove, The 78 Ross Hagen
Glove: Lethal Terminator, The 78 Ross Hagen
Glove Taps 36 Gordon Douglas
Gloves 87 Rafi Adar
Gloves of Ptames, The 14 Dave Aylott
Glow, Little Glow Worm, Glow 07 Arthur Gilbert
Glow of Life, The 18 Norimasa Kaeriyama
Glow Worm, The 30 Dave Fleischer
Głowa 53 Walerian Borowczyk
Glowing Autumn 78 Masaki Kobayashi
Glu, La 13 Albert Capellani
Glu, La 27 Henri Fescourt
Glück auf dem Lande 40 Carl Boese
Glückliche Reise 33 Alfred Abel
Glücklichen Jahre der Thorwalds, Die 62 John Olden, Wolfgang Staudte
Glücklichste Ehe von Wien, Die 38 Karl Heinz Martin
Glückskinder 37 Paul Martin
Glückspilze 36 Robert A. Stemmle
Glückszylinder, Der 34 Rudolf Bernauer
Glue Factory, The 21 Raoul Barré, Charles Bowers
Glue-my Affair, A 13 C. Borup
Glumov's Film Diary 23 Sergei Eisenstein

GLUMP 72 Carl Monson
Glutton for Punishment, A 20 Raoul Barré, Charles Bowers
Glutton's Nightmare, The 01 Percy Stow
Gnat Gets Estelle's Goat, The 16 Harry S. Palmer
Gnaw: Food of the Gods II 89 Damian Lee
Gnev Dionisa 14 Yakov Protazanov
Gnome-Mobile, The 66 Robert Stevenson
Go and Get It 20 Marshall Neilan, Henry Symonds
Go and See 85 Elem Klimov
Go Away Stowaway 67 Alex Lovy
Go-Between, The 70 Joseph Losey
Go Chase Yourself 38 Edward F. Cline
Gô chez les Oiseaux 39 Paul Grimault
Go Down Death 44 Spencer Williams
Go Fly a Kite 57 Chuck Jones
Go for a Take 72 Harry Booth
Go for Broke! 51 Robert Pirosh
Go for the Gold 84 Jackie Cooper
Go Get 'Em Garringer 19 Ernest Traxler
Go-Get-'Em Haines 36 Sam Newfield
Go Get 'Em Hutch 22 George B. Seitz
Go-Getter, The 23 Edward H. Griffith
Go Getter, The 37 Busby Berkeley
Go Go Amigo 65 Robert McKimson
Go Go Big Beat 64 Kenneth Hume
Go Go Mania 65 Frederic Goode
Go-Go Set 64 Sidney Miller
Go Into Your Dance 35 Robert Florey, Archie Mayo
Go, Johnny, Go! 58 Paul Landres
Go Kart Go! 64 Jan Darnley-Smith
Go, Man, Go! 54 James Wong Howe
Go Masters, The 82 Ji-shun Duan, Junya Sato
Go Naked in the World 60 Ranald MacDougall
Go Straight 21 William Worthington
Go Straight 25 Frank O'Connor
Go Tell It on the Mountain 84 Stan Lathan
Go Tell the Spartans 77 Ted Post
Go to Blazes 42 Walter Forde
Go to Blazes 61 Michael Truman
Go to Nowhere 66 Ivan Ivanov-Vano
Go West 25 Buster Keaton
Go West 40 Edward Buzzell
Go West, Young Lady 40 Frank R. Strayer
Go West, Young Man 19 Harry Beaumont
Go West, Young Man 36 Henry Hathaway
Go with Matt Monro 67 Bertram Tyrer
Goal! 67 Ross Devenish, Abidine Dino
Goal in the Clouds 39 Wolfgang Liebeneiner
Goal Keeper 37 Semen Timoshenko
Goal Rush 32 Ubbe Iwerks
Goal! World Cup 1966 67 Ross Devenish, Abidine Dino
Goalie's Anxiety at the Penalty Kick, The 71 Wim Wenders
Goalkeeper's Fear of the Penalty Kick, The 71 Wim Wenders
Goat, The 18 Donald Crisp
Goat, The 21 Buster Keaton, Malcolm St. Clair
Goat, The 81 Francis Veber

Goat Getter *25* Albert S. Rogell
Goat Horn, The *72* Metodi Andonov
Goat's Whiskers, The *26* Clyde Geronimi
Gobbo, Il *60* Carlo Lizzani
Goben no Tsubaki *65* Yoshitaro Nomura
Goblins *87* Robert Short
Gobots: Battle of the Rock Lords *86* Ray Patterson
Gobs and Gals *52* R. G. Springsteen
Gobsek *37* Konstantin Eggert
God and His Servants, A *59* Arne Skouen
God and the Gypsy *54* Erik Faustman
God and the Man *18* Edwin J. Collins
God Bless Dr. Shagetz *77* Edward Collins, Larry Spiegel, Peter S. Traynor
God Bless Our Red, White and Blue *18* Rex Wilson
God Devyatnadtsatyi *38* Ilya Trauberg
God Does Not Believe in Us Anymore *81* Axel Corti
God Forgives, I Don't *67* Giuseppe Colizzi
God Game, The *68* Guy Green
God Gave Him a Dog *40* Stuart Heisler
God Gave Me Twenty Cents *26* Herbert Brenon
God in the Garden, The *21* Edwin J. Collins
God Is My Co-Pilot *44* Robert Florey
God Is My Partner *57* William F. Claxton
God Is My Witness *31* Berthold Viertel
God Is on Our Side *54* Ahmed Badrakhan
God King, The *75* Lester James Peries
God, Man and Devil *49* Joseph Seiden
God Needs Men *50* Jean Delannoy
God of Gold, The *12* Colin Campbell
God of Little Children *17* Richard Ridgely
God of Mankind *28* Grover Jones
God Respects Us When We Work But Loves Us When We Dance *68* Les Blank
God Shiva *55* Bert Haanstra
God Snake, The *70* Piero Vivarelli
God Speaks Today *57* Norman Walker
God Speed You, Black Emperor *76* Mitsuo Yanagimachi
God Told Me To *76* Larry Cohen
God Within, The *12* D. W. Griffith
Godard on Godard *69* D. A. Pennebaker, Mark Woodcock
Godard's Passion *81* Jean-Luc Godard
Goddag Børn! *53* Jørgen Roos
Goddag Dyr! *47* Albert Mertz, Jørgen Roos
Goddess, The *14* Ralph Ince
Goddess *34* Yonggang Wu
Goddess, The *58* John Cromwell
Goddess, The *60* Satyajit Ray
Goddess of Lost Lake, The *18* Wallace Worsley
Goddess of Love *60* Victor Tourjansky
Goddess of Sagebrush Gulch, The *12* D. W. Griffith
Goddess of Vengeance *63* Mario Camerini
Godelureaux, Les *60* Claude Chabrol
Godfather, The *72* Francis Ford Coppola
Godfather, Part II, The *74* Francis Ford Coppola
Godfather, Part III, The *90* Francis Ford Coppola
Godfather of Harlem *72* Larry Cohen

Godless Girl, The *28* Cecil B. DeMille
Godless Men *21* Reginald Barker
Godmother, The *12* Ralph Ince
Godność *85* Roman Wionczek
Godovshchine Revolyutsiye *19* Dziga Vertov
Gods and the Dead, The *70* Ruy Guerra
God's Angry Man *80* Werner Herzog
God's Autumn Star *62* András Kovács
God's Bloody Acre *75* Harry Kerwin
God's Clay *19* Arthur H. Rooke
God's Clay *28* Graham Cutts
God's Country *31* John P. McCarthy
God's Country *46* Robert E. Tansey
God's Country *85* Louis Malle
God's Country and the Law *21* Sidney Olcott
God's Country and the Man *31* John P. McCarthy
God's Country and the Man *37* Robert North Bradbury
God's Country and the Woman *16* Rollin Sturgeon
God's Country and the Woman *36* William Keighley
God's Crucible *16* Lynn Reynolds
God's Crucible *21* Henry MacRae
God's Gift to Women *31* Michael Curtiz
God's Gold *21* Webster Cullison
God's Good Man *19* Maurice Elvey
God's Great Wilderness *27* David M. Hartford
God's Gun *76* Gianfranco Parolini
God's Half Acre *16* Edwin Carewe
God's Law and Man's *17* John H. Collins
God's Little Acre *57* Anthony Mann
God's Man *17* George Irving
Gods Must Be Crazy, The *79* Jamie Uys
Gods Must Be Crazy II, The *88* Jamie Uys
Gods of Bali *52* Nikola Drakulić
Gods of Fate, The *16* John H. Pratt
Gods of the Plague *69* Rainer Werner Fassbinder
Gods of the Street *49* Ulf Greber, Arne Skouen
God's Outlaw *18* Christy Cabanne
God's Partner *87* Federico García
God's Prodigal *23* Edward José, Bert Wynne
God's Stepchildren *37* Oscar Micheaux
God's Thunder *65* Denys De la Patellière
God's Unfortunate *12* Allan Dwan
God's Way *19* Victor Sjöström
Godsend, The *79* Gabrielle Beaumont
Godson, The *67* Jean-Pierre Melville
Godson, The *86* Henryk Bielski
Godspell *73* David Greene
Goduria, La *76* Luigi Comencini, Nanni Loy, Mario Monicelli
Gody Molodiye *61* Alexei Mishurin
Godzilla *54* Inoshiro Honda, Terry Morse
Godzilla Fights the Giant Moth *64* Inoshiro Honda
Godzilla, King of the Monsters *54* Inoshiro Honda, Terry Morse
Godzilla 1985 *85* Koji Hashimoto, R. J. Kizer
Godzilla on Monster Island *72* Jun Fukuda
Godzilla Raids Again *59* Hugo Grimaldi,

Motoyoshi Odo
Godzilla Tai Mothra *64* Inoshiro Honda
Godzilla—The Legend Is Reborn *85* Koji Hashimoto, R. J. Kizer
Godzilla vs. Gigan *72* Jun Fukuda
Godzilla vs. Hedora *71* Yoshimitsu Banno
Godzilla vs. Mechagodzilla *74* Jun Fukuda
Godzilla vs. Megalon *73* Jun Fukuda
Godzilla vs. Monster Zero *65* Inoshiro Honda
Godzilla vs. Mothra *64* Inoshiro Honda
Godzilla vs. the Bionic Monster *74* Jun Fukuda
Godzilla vs. the Cosmic Monster *74* Jun Fukuda
Godzilla vs. the Giant Moth *64* Inoshiro Honda
Godzilla vs. the Sea Monster *66* Jun Fukuda
Godzilla vs. the Smog Monster *71* Yoshimitsu Banno
Godzilla vs. the Thing *64* Inoshiro Honda
Godzilla's Counterattack *59* Hugo Grimaldi, Motoyoshi Odo
Godzilla's Revenge *69* Inoshiro Honda
Goémons *47* Yannick Bellon
Goethes Jugendgeliebte *32* Hans Tintner
Goforth *68* Joseph Losey
Gog *54* Herbert L. Strock
Gøglerblod *13* August Blom
Gøgleren *12* August Blom, Forest Holger-Madsen
Goha *57* Jacques Baratier
Goin' All the Way *82* Robert Freedman
Goin' Coconuts *78* Howard Morris
Goin' Down the Road *70* Donald Shebib
Goin' Home *76* Chris Prentiss
Goin' South *78* Jack Nicholson
Goin' to Heaven on a Mule *34* Friz Freleng
Goin' to San Francisco *68* D. A. Pennebaker
Goin' to Town *35* Alexander Hall
Goin' to Town *44* Leslie Goodwins
Going and Coming Back *84* Claude Lelouch
Going Ape *70* Carl Reiner
Going Ape! *81* Jeremy Joe Kronsberg
Going Ashore *49* Arne Sucksdorff
Going Astray in an Orientation Course *86* Julius Matula
Going Bananas *87* Boaz Davidson
Going Berserk *83* David Steinberg
Going Bye-Bye *34* Charles Rogers
Going Crazy *26* Charles Lamont
Going Crooked *26* George Melford
Going Ga-Ga *28* Leo McCarey
Going Gay *33* Carmine Gallone
Going, Going, Gone *15* Edwin J. Collins
Going! Going! Gosh! *52* Chuck Jones
Going Great *25* Norman Taurog
Going Highbrow *35* Robert Florey
Going Hollywood *33* Raoul Walsh
Going Hollywood—The 30's *84* Julian Schlossberg
Going Hollywood—The War Years *88* Julian Schlossberg
Going Home *71* Herbert Leonard
Going Home *88* Terry Ryan
Going in Style *79* Martin Brest

Going My Way 44 Leo McCarey
Going Places 29 Stephen Roberts
Going Places 38 Ray Enright
Going Places 73 Bertrand Blier
Going Sane 86 Michael Robertson
Going Some 20 Harry Beaumont
Going Steady 58 Fred F. Sears
Going Steady 81 Boaz Davidson
Going Straight 16 Chester M. Franklin, Sidney Franklin
Going Straight 33 John Rawlins
Going the Limit 25 Duke Worne
Going the Limit 26 Chester Withey
Going to Bed Under Difficulties 00 Georges Méliès
Going to Blazes 33 Walter Lantz
Going to Town 49 Charles Lamont
Going Undercover 84 James Kenelm Clarke
Going Up 23 Lloyd Ingraham
Going Wild 30 William A. Seiter
Gojira 54 Inoshiro Honda, Terry Morse
Gojira no Gyakushū 59 Hugo Grimaldi, Motoyoshi Odo
Gojira no Musuko 67 Jun Fukuda
Gojira Tai Gaigan 72 Jun Fukuda
Gojira Tai Gigan 72 Jun Fukuda
Gojira Tai Hedora 71 Yoshimitsu Banno
Gojira Tai Megalon 73 Jun Fukuda
Gojira Tai Megaro 73 Jun Fukuda
Gojira Tai Meka-Gojira 74 Jun Fukuda
Gojira Tai Mosura 64 Inoshiro Honda
Gojū no Tō 44 Heinosuke Gosho
Gojūman-Nin no Isan 64 Toshiro Mifune
Goke, Bodysnatcher from Hell 68 Hajime Sato
Goke the Vampire 68 Hajime Sato
Gōkiburi 90 Hiroaki Yoshida
Gokumon 77 Kon Ichikawa
Gold 26 Kenji Mizoguchi
Gold 32 Otto Brower
Gold 34 Karl Hartl
Gold 55 Colin Low
Gold 62 Wojciech Has
Gold 74 John Glen, Peter R. Hunt
Gold and Glitter 12 D. W. Griffith
Gold and Grit 24 Richard Thorpe
Gold and the Dross 16 B. C. Gibbs
Gold and the Girl 25 Edmund Mortimer
Gold and the Woman 16 James Vincent
Gold Bricks 28 Manny Gould, Ben Harrison
Gold Bullets 51 Wallace Fox
Gold Cure, The 19 John H. Collins
Gold Cure, The 25 Will P. Kellino
Gold Diggers, The 23 Harry Beaumont
Gold Diggers, The 84 Sally Potter
Gold Diggers in Paris 37 Ray Enright
Gold Diggers of Broadway, The 29 Roy Del Ruth
Gold Diggers of 1933 33 Mervyn LeRoy
Gold Diggers of 1935 35 Busby Berkeley
Gold Diggers of 1937 36 Lloyd Bacon
Gold Dreams 62 Wojciech Has
Gold Dredgers, The 21 Frank Urson
Gold Dust Gertie 31 Lloyd Bacon
Gold Express, The 55 S. G. Ferguson
Gold Fever 52 Leslie Goodwins
Gold Fever 65 Jacques Deray
Gold for the Caesars 62 Sabatino Ciuffini,

André De Toth, Riccardo Freda
Gold from the Gutter 12 August Blom
Gold from the Sea 32 Jean Epstein
Gold from Weepah 27 William Bertram
Gold Getters 35 Art Davis, Sid Marcus
Gold Ghost, The 34 Charles Lamont
Gold, Glory and Custer 63 George Waggner
Gold Grabbers 22 Francis Ford
Gold Guitar, The 66 J. Hunter Todd
Gold Heels 24 W. S. Van Dyke
Gold Hunters, The 25 Paul Hurst
Gold Is Not All 10 D. W. Griffith
Gold Is Where You Find It 38 Michael Curtiz
Gold Is Where You Find It 68 Francis Searle
Gold Lust, The 11 Allan Dwan
Gold Madness 23 Robert Thornby
Gold Mine in the Sky 38 Joseph Kane
Gold Necklace, A 10 D. W. Griffith
Gold of Christobal, The 39 Jacques Becker, Jean Stelli
Gold of Naples, The 54 Vittorio De Sica
Gold of the Seven Saints 61 Gordon Douglas
Gold Racket, The 37 Louis Gasnier
Gold Raiders 51 Edward Bernds
Gold-Rimmed Glasses, The 87 Giuliano Montaldo
Gold Route, The 32 Edino Cominetti
Gold Rush, The 25 Charles Chaplin
Gold Rush Daze 39 Cal Dalton, Ben Hardaway
Gold Rush Maisie 40 Edwin L. Marin
Gold Seekers, The 10 D. W. Griffith
Gold, Silver, Bad Luck 82 Peque Gallaga
Gold Spectacles, The 87 Giuliano Montaldo
Gold Struck 26 William C. Nolan
Gold von Sam Cooper, Das 68 Giorgio Capitani
Goldbergs, The 50 Walter Hart
Golden Age, The 30 Luis Buñuel, Salvador Dali
Golden Apples of the Sun 71 Barrie Angus McLean
Golden Arrow, The 36 Alfred E. Green
Golden Arrow 49 Gordon Parry
Golden Arrow, The 62 Antonio Margheriti
Golden Ballot, The 20 Frank Miller
Golden Bed, The 24 Cecil B. DeMille
Golden Bird, The 18 John S. Robertson
Golden Blade, The 53 Nathan Juran
Golden Boat, The 90 Raúl Ruiz
Golden Box, The 70 Don Davis
Golden Boy 39 Rouben Mamoulian
Golden Bracken 63 Jiří Weiss
Golden Braid, The 90 Paul Cox
Golden Breed 68 Dale Davis
Golden Bullet 69 Richard Benedict
Golden Cage, The 33 Ivar Campbell
Golden Calf, The 30 Millard Webb
Golden Century 53 Paul Haesaerts
Golden Chance, The 13 Percy Nash
Golden Chance, The 15 Cecil B. DeMille
Golden Chance, The 15 Frank Stather
Golden Child, The 86 Michael Ritchie
Golden Claw, The 15 Reginald Barker

Golden Clown, The 26 Anders Wilhelm Sandberg
Golden Coach, The 52 Jean Renoir
Golden Cocoon, The 25 Millard Webb
Golden Dawn, The 21 Ralph Dewsbury
Golden Dawn 30 Ray Enright
Golden Demon, The 23 Teinosuke Kinugasa
Golden Demon 53 Koji Shima
Golden Disc, The 58 Don Sharp
Golden Dreams 22 Benjamin B. Hampton
Golden Dreams 62 Wojciech Has
Golden Earrings 47 Mitchell Leisen
Golden Eighties, The 83 Chantal Akerman
Golden Eye, The 48 William Beaudine
Golden Fern, The 63 Jiří Weiss
Golden Fetter, The 17 Edward J. LeSaint
Golden Fingernails 90 Zhifang Bao
Golden Fish, The 51 Jiří Trnka
Golden Fleece, The 18 Gilbert P. Hamilton
Golden Fleece, The 71 Edgar Reitz*
Golden Fleecing, The 40 Leslie Fenton
Golden Fortress, The 74 Satyajit Ray
Golden Gallows, The 22 Paul Scardon
Golden Gate, The 69 Yulia Solntseva
Golden Gate Girl 41 Esther Eng
Golden Gift, The 22 Maxwell Karger
Golden Girl 51 Lloyd Bacon
Golden Gloves 39 Edward Dmytryk
Golden Gloves 39 Phil Rosen
Golden Gloves 61 Gilles Groulx
Golden Gloves Story, The 50 Felix E. Feist
Golden Goal, The 18 Paul Scardon
Golden Goddess of Rio Beni 64 Eugenio Martin
Golden Goose, The 14 William H. Clifford, Thomas Ince
Golden Hands 57 Sergei Paradzhanov
Golden Hands of Kurigal 49 Fred C. Brannon
Golden Harvest 33 Ralph Murphy
Golden Hawk, The 52 Sidney Salkow
Golden Head, The 64 Richard Thorpe
Golden Heist, The 75 Peter Duffell
Golden Helmet 52 Jacques Becker
Golden Honey 28 N. Bersenev, Vladimir Petrov
Golden Hoofs 41 Lynn Shores
Golden Horde, The 51 George Sherman
Golden Horde of Genghis Khan, The 51 George Sherman
Golden Hour, The 41 George Marshall
Golden Idiot, The 17 Arthur Berthelet
Golden Idol, The 54 Ford Beebe
Golden Ivory 54 George Breakston
Golden Key, The 39 Alexander Ptushko
Golden Kite, The 66 László Ranódy
Golden Lady 46 Derwin Abrahams
Golden Lady, The 79 José Ramón Larraz
Golden Lake, The 19 Fritz Lang
Golden Link, The 54 Charles Saunders
Golden Louis 09 D. W. Griffith
Golden Madonna, The 49 Ladislas Vajda
Golden Mahmudia, The 87 Kazimierz Tarnas
Golden Marie 52 Jacques Becker
Golden Mask, The 52 Jack Lee

Golden Mistress, The *54* Abner Biberman
Golden Mountains *31* Sergei Yutkevich
Golden Mountains *58* Gabriel Axel
Golden Needles *74* Robert Clouse
Golden Nymphs, The *64* Irwin Meyer
Golden Pavement, The *15* Cecil M. Hepworth
Golden Pince-Nez, The *22* George Ridgwell
Golden Pippin Girl, The *20* A. C. Hunter
Golden Plague, The *54* John Brahm
Golden Pomegranates, The *24* Fred Paul
Golden Positions, The *70* James Broughton
Golden Prince *24* Ernest B. Schoedsack
Golden Princess, The *25* Clarence Badger
Golden Rabbit, The *62* David MacDonald
Golden Rendezvous *77* Freddie Francis, Ashley Lazarus
Golden Rennet, The *65* Otakar Vávra
Golden River, The *86* Jaime Chavarri
Golden Rosary, The *17* Tom Van Plack
Golden Rule Kate *17* Reginald Barker
Golden Salamander, The *49* Ronald Neame
Golden Sea, The *19* Fritz Lang
Golden Seal, The *83* Frank Zuniga
Golden Shackles *28* Dallas M. Fitzgerald
Golden Shawl *67* Lester James Peries
Golden Shovel, The *14* Michael Curtiz
Golden Shower, The *19* John W. Noble
Golden Silence *23* Paul Hurst
Golden Smile, The *33* Pál Fejős
Golden Smile, The *35* Pál Fejős
Golden Snare, The *21* David M. Hartford
Golden Spoon Mary *17* Paul Terry
Golden Spurs, The *26* Walter West
Golden Stallion, The *49* William Witney
Golden Strain, The *25* Victor Schertzinger
Golden Stuff, The *71* Edgar Reitz*
Golden Supper, The *10* D. W. Griffith
Golden Taiga *35* Vladimir Schneiderhof
Golden Touch, The *35* Walt Disney
Golden Trail, The *20* Jean Hersholt, Lewis H. Moomaw
Golden Trail, The *37* Mack V. Wright
Golden Trail, The *40* Albert Herman
Golden Valley *37* Nikolai Shengelaya
Golden Virgin *57* David Miller
Golden Voyage of Sinbad, The *73* Gordon Hessler
Golden Wall, The *18* Del Henderson
Golden Web, The *20* Geoffrey H. Malins
Golden Web, The *26* Walter Lang
Golden West, The *32* David Howard
Golden Woman, The *87* Viktor Kobzev
Golden Yeggs *50* Friz Freleng
Golden Yukon, The *27* Nell Shipman
Goldene Ding, Das *71* Edgar Reitz*
Goldene Pest, Die *54* John Brahm
Goldene Schmetterling, Der *26* Michael Curtiz
Goldene See, Der *19* Fritz Lang
Goldene Stadt, Die *42* Veidt Harlan
Goldengirl *79* Joseph Sargent
Goldfinger *64* Guy Hamilton
Goldfish, The *24* Jerome Storm
Goldfish Bowl *1895* Louis Lumière
Goldie *31* Ben Stoloff
Goldie Gets Along *33* Malcolm St. Clair

Goldie Locks and the Three Bears *22* Walt Disney
Goldielocks and the Three Bears *34* Walter Lantz
Goldiggers of '49 *36* Tex Avery
Goldilocks *56* Hermina Tyrlova
Goldilocks and the Jivin' Bears *44* Friz Freleng
Goldilocks and the Three Bares *63* Herschell Gordon Lewis
Goldilocks and the Three Bears *22* Walt Disney
Goldilocks' Three Chicks *63* Herschell Gordon Lewis
Goldimouse and the Three Cats *60* Friz Freleng
Goldstein *64* Philip Kaufman, Benjamin Manaster
Goldsucher von Arkansas, Die *64* Alberto Cardone, Paul Martin
Goldtown Ghost Raiders *53* George Archainbaud
Goldtown Ghost Riders *53* George Archainbaud
Goldwyn Follies, The *38* George Marshall, H. C. Potter
G'Ole! *83* Tom Clegg
Golem, Der *14* Henryk Galeen, Paul Wegener
Golem, The *14* Henryk Galeen, Paul Wegener
Golem, Der *20* Carl Boese, Paul Wegener
Golem, The *20* Carl Boese, Paul Wegener
Golem, Der *35* Julien Duvivier
Golem, Le *35* Julien Duvivier
Golem, The *35* Julien Duvivier
Golem *79* Piotr Szulkin
Golem, The *79* Piotr Szulkin
Golem: How He Came Into the World, The *20* Carl Boese, Paul Wegener
Golem—The Legend of Prague, The *35* Julien Duvivier
Golem und die Tänzerin, Der *17* Rochus Gliese, Paul Wegener
Golem: Wie Er in die Welt Kam, Der *20* Carl Boese, Paul Wegener
Golem's Last Adventure, The *21* Julius Somogyi
Golems Letzte Abenteuer, Der *21* Julius Somogyi
Golf *16* Harry S. Palmer
Golf Chumps *39* Manny Gould, Ben Harrison
Golf Mistakes *37* Felix E. Feist
Golf Nut, The *27* Harry Edwards
Golf Socks *29* Manny Gould, Ben Harrison
Golf Specialist, The *30* Monte Brice
Golf Widows *28* Erle C. Kenton
Golfer, The *21* Edward F. Cline*
Golfers, The *29* Mack Sennett
Golfers, The *37* Walter Lantz
Golfing *13* G. Fletcher Hewitt
Golfing *22* Raoul Barré, Charles Bowers
Golfing Extraordinary *1896* Birt Acres
Golfing Extraordinary, Five Gentlemen *1896* Birt Acres
Golfo *58* Orestes Laskos
Golfo de Vizcaya *85* Javier Rebollo
Golfo, Girl of the Mountains *58* Orestes

Laskos
Golfos, Los *59* Carlos Saura
Golgotha *35* Julien Duvivier
Goliat Contra los Gigantes *61* Guido Malatesta
Goliath *64* Félix Máriássy
Goliath Against the Giants *61* Guido Malatesta
Goliath and the Barbarians *59* Carlo Campogalliani
Goliath and the Dragon *60* Vittorio Cottafavi
Goliath and the Giants *61* Guido Malatesta
Goliath and the Golden City *61* Riccardo Freda
Goliath and the Island of Vampires *61* Sergio Corbucci, Giacomo Gentilomo
Goliath and the Sins of Babylon *63* Michele Lupo
Goliath and the Vampires *61* Sergio Corbucci, Giacomo Gentilomo
Goliath at the Conquest of Damascus *64* Domenico Paolella
Goliath Contro i Giganti *61* Guido Malatesta
Goliath the Rebel Slave *63* Mario Caiano
Goliathon *79* Homer Gaugh
Gollocks, There's Plenty of Room in New Zealand *74* Dennis Abey
Gollywog's Motor Accident *12* Walter R. Booth, F. Martin Thornton
Golod...Golod...Golod *21* Vladimir Gardin, Vsevolod I. Pudovkin
Golondrina, La *38* Miguel Torres Contreras
Golpe de Estado, El *76* Patricio Guzmán
Golpeando en la Selva *67* Santiago Álvarez
Golu Hadawatha *68* Lester James Peries
Goluboi Ekspress *29* Ilya Trauberg
Golubye Gory Ely Nepravdopodobnaya Istoria *83* Eldar Shengelaya
Gólyakalifa, A *17* Alexander Korda
Gomar the Human Gorilla *68* René Cardona
Gömlek *89* Bilge Olgac
Gommes, Les *72* Alain Robbe-Grillet
Gōmon Hyakunenshi *75* Koji Wakamatsu
Gondola *87* Chisho Itoh
Gondola del Diavolo, La *47* Carlo Campogalliani
Gondole aux Chimères, La *36* Augusto Genina
Gondoviselés *87* Pál Erdöss
Gone Are the Days *63* Nicholas Webster
Gone Batty *54* Robert McKimson
Gone in 60 Seconds *74* H. B. Halicki
Gone to Earth *50* Rouben Mamoulian, Michael Powell, Emeric Pressburger
Gone to the Dogs *28* Fred V. Merrick
Gone to the Dogs *39* Ken Hall
Gone with the Mind *87* Janne Kuusi
Gone with the West *75* Bernard Girard
Gone with the Wind *39* George Cukor, Victor Fleming, Sidney Franklin, William Cameron Menzies, Sam Wood
Gong Cried Murder, The *46* Ronald Haines
Gong Show Movie, The *80* Chuck Barris

Gonin no Hanzaisha *59* Teruo Ishii
Gonin no Kyōdai *39* Kozaburo Yoshimura
Gonka za Samogonkoi *24* Abram Room
Gonks Go Beat *65* Robert Hartford-Davis
Gonza the Spearman *85* Masahiro Shinoda
Gonzague *22* Henri Diamant-Berger
Gonzague *33* Jean Grémillon
Gonzague ou L'Accordeur *33* Jean Grémillon
Gonzales' Tamales *57* Friz Freleng
Goo Goo Eyes *03* Edwin S. Porter
Goo Goo Goliath *54* Friz Freleng
Gooa, El *86* Ali Badrakhan
Good and Bad at Games *83* Jack Gold
Good and Naughty *26* Malcolm St. Clair
Good and the Bad, The *75* Claude Lelouch
Good As Gold *27* Scott R. Dunlap
Good Bad Boy, The *24* Edward F. Cline
Good Bad Girl, The *24* Alfred E. Green
Good Bad Girl, The *31* Roy William Neill
Good Bad Man, The *16* Allan Dwan
Good-Bad Wife, The *21* Vera McCord
Good Beginning, The *53* Gilbert Gunn
Good Bunch, The *35* Julien Duvivier
Good Business Deal, A *15* B. Reeves Eason
Good Companions, The *32* Victor Saville
Good Companions, The *56* J. Lee-Thompson
Good Dame *34* Marion Gering
Good Day for a Hanging *58* Nathan Juran
Good Day for Fighting, A *66* Irving Lerner, Robert Siodmak
Good Die Young, The *54* Lewis Gilbert
Good Dissonance Like a Man, A *77* Theodore W. Timreck
Good Earth, The *36* Victor Fleming, Sidney Franklin, George W. Hill, Gustav Machatý, Fred Niblo, W. S. Van Dyke
Good Egg, The *39* Chuck Jones
Good Fairy, The *35* William Wyler
Good Fairy, The *50* Keisuke Kinoshita
Good Father, The *86* Mike Newell
Good Fellows, The *43* Jo Graham
Good Fight, The *83* Noel Buckner, Mary Dore, Sam Sills
Good Financial Situation *35* Heinosuke Gosho
Good for Evil *13* Charles C. Calvert
Good-for-Nothing, The *14* Charles Chaplin
Good for Nothing, The *17* Carlyle Blackwell
Good for Nothing *37* Mieczysław Krawicz
Good-for-Nothing *60* Yoshishige Yoshida
Good for the Gout *13* Edwin J. Collins
Good Girl *34* Marion Gering
Good Girl Keeps Herself in Order, A *14* Victor Sjöström
Good Girl Should Solve Her Own Problems, A *14* Victor Sjöström
Good Girls Go to Paris *39* Alexander Hall
Good Glue Sticks *07* Georges Méliès
Good Gracious Annabelle *19* George Melford
Good Guys Always Win, The *73* John Flynn
Good Guys and the Bad Guys, The *69*

Burt Kennedy
Good Guys Wear Black *77* Ted Post
Good Heavens *59* Hasse Ekman
Good Hope, The *86* Guido Pieters
Good Humor Man, The *50* Lloyd Bacon
Good Indian, The *13* William Duncan
Good Intentions *30* William K. Howard
Good Joke, A *1896* Georges Méliès
Good Joke, A *1899* George Albert Smith
Good Kick-Off, A *10* Frank Wilson
Good King Dagobert, The *84* Dino Risi
Good Liar, A *17* Otto Messmer
Good Life, The *87* Fernando Colomo
Good Little Devil, A *13* J. Searle Dawley, Edwin S. Porter
Good Little Pal, A *15* Cecil Birch
Good Loser, The *18* Dick Donaldson
Good Love and the Bad, The *12* Allan Dwan
Good Luck, Miss Wyckoff *79* Marvin Chomsky
Good Luck, Mr. Yates *43* Ray Enright
Good Luck of a Souse, The *07* Georges Méliès
Good Marriage, A *81* Eric Rohmer
Good Men and Bad *23* William Merrill McCormick
Good Men and True *22* Val Paul
Good Morning *59* Yasujiro Ozu
Good Morning...and Goodbye! *67* Russ Meyer
Good Morning, Babilonia *86* Paolo Taviani, Vittorio Taviani
Good Morning, Babylon *86* Paolo Taviani, Vittorio Taviani
Good Morning, Boys *36* William Beaudine
Good Morning, Boys *37* Marcel Varnel
Good Morning, Doctor *41* Wesley Ruggles
Good Morning Judge *28* William A. Seiter
Good Morning, Judge *43* Jean Yarbrough
Good Morning Madam *25* Lloyd Bacon
Good Morning, Miss Dove *55* Henry Koster
Good Morning, Poland *69* Aleksander Ford
Good Morning, Vietnam *87* Barry Levinson
Good Mother, The *88* Leonard Nimoy
Good Mothers *42* Carl Theodor Dreyer
Good Neighbor Sam *64* David Swift
Good News *30* Nick Grindé, Edgar J. McGregor
Good News *47* Charles Walters
Good News *79* Elio Petri
Good News for Jones *11* Dave Aylott
Good Night *1898* C. Goodwin Norton
Good Night Elmer *40* Chuck Jones
Good Night Nurse *18* Roscoe Arbuckle
Good Night Nurse *19* Gregory La Cava
Good Night, Rusty *43* George Pal
Good Noose *62* Robert McKimson
Good Old Days, The *39* Roy William Neill
Good Old Days, The *89* Klaus Gietinger, Leo Hiemer
Good Old Schooldays *40* Theodore Reed
Good Old Siwash *40* Theodore Reed
Good Old Soak, The *37* J. Walter Ruben

Good Ole Country Music *56* Ernest Pintoff
Good Provider, The *22* Frank Borzage
Good Pull-Up, A *53* Don Chaffey
Good Queen Bess *13* Walter R. Booth
Good References *20* Roy William Neill
Good Riddance! *78* Francis Mankiewicz
Good Sam *47* Leo McCarey
Good Scout *34* Ubbe Iwerks
Good Scout Buster *28* Sam Newfield
Good Shepherdess and the Evil Princess, The *08* Georges Méliès
Good Ship Nellie, The *28* Frank Moser
Good Soldier, The *82* Franco Brusati
Good Soldier Schweik, The *26* Karel Lamač
Good Soldier Schweik *31* Martin Frič
Good Soldier Schweik, The *54* Jiří Trnka
Good Soldier Schweik, The *60* Axel von Ambesser
Good Soup, The *63* Robert Thomas
Good Spirits *25* Archie Mayo
Good Sport *31* Kenneth MacKenna
Good Stories *1899* George Albert Smith
Good Story, A *01* George Albert Smith
Good Sunday, A *86* Cesare Bastelli
Good, the Bad and the Ugly, The *66* Sergio Leone
Good Time Charley *27* Michael Curtiz
Good Time Girl *48* David MacDonald
Good Times *67* William Friedkin
Good Times, Wonderful Times *65* Lionel Rogosin
Good to Go *86* Blaine Novak
Good Tonic, A *12* Frank Wilson
Good Trick, A *01* Georges Méliès
Good Wife, The *86* Ken Cameron
Good Women *21* Louis Gasnier
Goodbye *17* Maurice Elvey
Goodbye Again *33* Michael Curtiz
Goodbye Again *61* Anatole Litvak
Goodbye and Amen *78* Damiano Damiani
Goodbye and Good Day *59* Kon Ichikawa
Goodbye Bill *18* John Emerson
Goodbye Broadway *38* Ray McCarey
Goodbye Bruce Lee: His Last Game of Death *79* Robert Clouse
Goodbye, Charlie *64* Vincente Minnelli
Goodbye, Children *87* Louis Malle
Goodbye, Columbus *69* Larry Peerce
Goodbye Cruel World *82* David Irving
Goodbye! Duman River *61* Kwon-taek Im
Goodbye Emmanuelle *78* François Leterrier
Goodbye Flickmania *79* Masato Harada
Goodbye Franklin High *78* Mike MacFarland
Goodbye Gemini *70* Alan Gibson
Goodbye Girl, The *77* Herbert Ross
Goodbye Girls *23* Jerome Storm
Goodbye, Good Day *59* Kon Ichikawa
Goodbye, Hello *59* Kon Ichikawa
Goodbye Kiss, The *28* Mack Sennett
Goodbye Legs *30* Mack Sennett
Goodbye Little Sister *08* Arthur Gilbert
Goodbye Love *33* H. Bruce Humberstone
Goodbye, Mr. Chips *39* Sam Wood
Goodbye, Mr. Chips *69* Herbert Ross
Goodbye Mr. Moth *42* Walter Lantz

Goodbye Moscow 68 Hiromichi Horikawa
Goodbye My Fancy 51 Vincent Sherman
Goodbye My Girl 33 Heinosuke Gosho
Goodbye, My Lady 56 William A. Wellman
Goodbye My Lady Love 24 Dave Fleischer
Goodbye My Lady Love 29 Dave Fleischer
Goodbye, New York 85 Amos Kollek
Goodbye Norma Jean 76 Larry Buchanan
Goodbye Paradise 82 Carl Schultz
Goodbye People, The 84 Herb Gardner
Goodbye Pork Pie 80 Geoff Murphy
Goodbye Summer 14 Van Dyke Brooke
Goodbye Sweet Marie 06 Arthur Gilbert
Goodbye to All That 30 R. E. Jeffrey
Goodbye to the Hill 69 Daniel Haller
Goodbye to the Past 61 Wojciech Has
GoodFellas 90 Martin Scorsese
Goodie Two Shoes 83 Ian Emes
Goodness Gracious, or Movies As They Shouldn't Be 14 James Young
Goodnight, Ladies and Gentlemen 76 Leonardo Benvenuti, Luigi Comencini, Piero De Bernardi, Nanni Loy, Ruggero Maccari, Luigi Magni, Mario Monicelli, Ugo Pirro, Ettore Scola
Goodnight Paul 18 Walter Edwards
Goodnight Sweetheart 44 Joseph Santley
Goodnight Vienna 32 Herbert Wilcox
Goodrich Dirt Among the Beach Nuts 17 Wallace A. Carlson
Goodrich Dirt and the Duke de Whatanob 18 Wallace A. Carlson
Goodrich Dirt and the $1,000 Reward 17 Wallace A. Carlson
Goodrich Dirt at the Amateur Show 17 Wallace A. Carlson
Goodrich Dirt at the Seashore 17 Wallace A. Carlson
Goodrich Dirt at the Training Camp 17 Wallace A. Carlson
Goodrich Dirt Bad Man Tamer 18 Wallace A. Carlson
Goodrich Dirt Coin Collector 18 Wallace A. Carlson
Goodrich Dirt Cowpuncher 18 Wallace A. Carlson
Goodrich Dirt Hypnotist 19 Wallace A. Carlson
Goodrich Dirt in a Difficult Delivery 19 Wallace A. Carlson
Goodrich Dirt in Darkest Africa 18 Wallace A. Carlson
Goodrich Dirt in Spot Goes Romeoing 18 Wallace A. Carlson
Goodrich Dirt in the Barber Business 18 Wallace A. Carlson
Goodrich Dirt King of Spades 18 Wallace A. Carlson
Goodrich Dirt Lunch Detective 17 Wallace A. Carlson
Goodrich Dirt Mat Artist 18 Wallace A. Carlson
Goodrich Dirt Millionaire 18 Wallace A. Carlson
Goodrich Dirt the Cop 18 Wallace A. Carlson
Goodrich Dirt the Dark and Stormy Knight 18 Wallace A. Carlson
Goodrich Dirt When Wishes Come True 18 Wallace A. Carlson
Goodrich Dirt's Amateur Night 17 Wallace A. Carlson
Goodrich Dirt's Bear Facts 18 Wallace A. Carlson
Goodrich Dirt's Bear Hunt 18 Wallace A. Carlson
Goodwill to All Dogs 60 John Halas*
Goodwin Sands 29 Castleton Knight
Goodwin Sands, The 48 Rudall C. Hayward
Goofballs 87 Brad Turner
Goofer Trouble 40 Maurice Elvey
Goofy Gondolas 34 Manny Gould, Ben Harrison
Goofy Gophers, The 47 Robert Clampett, Art Davis
Goofy Groceries 41 Robert Clampett
Goofy News Views 45 Sid Marcus
Goole by Numbers 76 Peter Greenaway
Goona-Goona 32 Armand Denis, André Roosevelt
Goonies, The 85 Richard Donner
Goonj 89 Jalal Agha
Goonland 38 Dave Fleischer
Goopi and Bagha 68 Satyajit Ray
Goopi Gyne Bagha Byne 68 Satyajit Ray
Goose and Stuffing 26 Frank Miller
Goose and the Gander, The 35 Alfred E. Green
Goose Boy, The 51 Kálmán Nadasdy
Goose Flesh 27 Norman Taurog
Goose Girl, The 15 Cecil B. DeMille, Frederick Thompson
Goose Girl, The 67 Fritz Genschow
Goose Goes South 41 Joseph Barbera, William Hanna
Goose Hangs High, The 25 James Cruze
Goose Step 39 Sam Newfield
Goose Steps Out, The 42 Basil Dearden, Will Hay
Goose Woman, The 25 Clarence Brown
Gooseberry Pie 43 George Pal
Gooseland 26 Edward F. Cline
Goosey Goosey 73 John Beech
Gopher Broke 58 Robert McKimson
Gopher Goofy 42 Norm McCabe
Gopher Trouble 36 Walter Lantz
Gor 87 Fritz Kiersch
Gorąca Linia 65 Wanda Jakubowska
Gorączka 80 Agnieszka Holland
Gorath 62 Inoshiro Honda
Gorbals Story, The 50 David MacKane
Gordeyev Family, The 59 Mark Donskoi
Gordian der Tyrann 37 Fred Sauer
Gordon il Pirata Nero 61 Mario Costa
Gordon of Ghost City 33 Ray Taylor
Gordon of Ghost Town 33 Ray Taylor
Gordon Sisters Boxing 01 Edwin S. Porter
Gordon's War 73 Ossie Davis
Gore-Gore Girls, The 71 Herschell Gordon Lewis
Gorge Between Love and Hate, The 34 Kenji Mizoguchi
Gorge Between Love and Hate, The 37 Kenji Mizoguchi
Gorgeous Bird Like Me, A 72 François Truffaut
Gorgeous Hussy, The 36 Clarence Brown
Gorgo, Il 18 Emilio Ghione
Gorgo 59 Eugène Lourié
Gorgon, The 63 Terence Fisher
Gorgona, La 14 Mario Caserini
Gorilla, The 27 Alfred Santell
Gorilla, The 30 Bryan Foy
Gorilla, The 39 Allan Dwan
Gorilla 44 Sam Newfield
Gorilla 55 George Romero
Gorilla 56 Sven Nykvist, Lars Henrik Ottoson
Gorilla at Large 54 Harmon Jones
Gorilla Greets You, The 58 Bernard Borderie
Gorilla Hunt, The 39 Ubbe Iwerks
Gorilla Man, The 42 D. Ross Lederman
Gorilla My Dreams 48 Robert McKimson
Gorilla Mystery, The 30 Burton Gillett
Gorilla Ship 32 Frank R. Strayer
Gorilla Strikes, The 43 William Beaudine
Gorillas in the Mist 88 Michael Apted
Gorille à Mordu l'Archevêque, Le 62 Maurice Labro
Gorille Vous Salue Bien, Le 58 Bernard Borderie
Gorizont 32 Lev Kuleshov
Gorizont 61 Josef Heifits
Gorky Park 83 Michael Apted
Gorky's Childhood 38 Mark Donskoi
Gorp 80 Joseph Ruben
Gorrod Zero 89 Karen Shakhnazarov
Goryachie Deneki 35 Josef Heifits, Mikhail Shapiro, Alexander Zarkhi
Gosh 74 Tom Scheuer
Gosh Darn Mortgage, The 26 Edward F. Cline
Goskino Journal 25 Dziga Vertov
Goskino Kalendar 25 Dziga Vertov
Gospel 82 David Leivick, Frederick Ritzenberg
Gospel According to St. Matthew, The 64 Pier Paolo Pasolini
Gospel According to Vic, The 85 Charles Gormley
Gospel Road, The 73 Robert Elfstrom
Gospoda Avantyuristy 87 Bidzina Chkeidze
Gospoda Skotininy 26 Grigori Roshal
Gospođica Doktor — Špijunka Bez Imena 68 Alberto Lattuada
Gospodin Oformitel 88 Oleg Teptsov
Gospodin za Edin Den 85 Nikolai Volev
Gosseline, La 23 Louis Feuillade
Gossette 23 Germaine Dulac
Gossip 23 King Baggot
Gossiper, The 40 Enrique T. Susini
Gossipy Plumber, The 31 Charles Lamont
Gost 88 Aleksandr Kaidanovski
Gost o Ostrova Svobody 63 Roman Karmen
Gösta Berlings Saga 23 Mauritz Stiller
Gosti iz Galaksije 81 Dušan Vukotić
Got a Match? 12 Mack Sennett
Got a Penny Stamp? 08 Percy Stow
Got 'Em Again 13 Charles C. Calvert
Got It Made 73 James Kenelm Clarke
Got What She Wanted 30 James Cruze
Gotcha! 85 Jeff Kanew
Gothic 86 Ken Russell
Goto, Island of Love 68 Walerian Borowczyk

Goto, l'Île d'Amour 68 Walerian Borowczyk

Gott Mit Uns 69 Giuliano Montaldo

Götter der Pest 69 Rainer Werner Fassbinder

Götterdämmerung 69 Luchino Visconti

Gottes Mühlen Mahlen Langsam 39 J. Medeolti

Gottesgeissel, Die 19 Michael Curtiz

Goumbé des Jeunes Noceurs, La 65 Jean Rouch

Goupi-Mains-Rouges 43 Jacques Becker

Gourmand, The 17 Harry S. Palmer

Goût de la Farine, Le 76 Pierre Perrault

Goût de la Violence, Le 60 Robert Hossein

Goûter de Bébé, Le 1895 Louis Lumière

Goutte de Sang, La 24 Jean Epstein, Maurice Mariaud

Gouty Patient, The 00 Georges Méliès

Gouverneur, Der 39 Victor Tourjansky

Government Agents vs. the Phantom Legion 51 Fred C. Brannon

Government Girl 43 Dudley Nichols

Government Vessel, The 26 Teinosuke Kinugasa

Governor, The 77 Stan Brakhage

Governor Bradford 38 Hugh Parry

Governor William Bradford 38 Hugh Parry

Governor's Boss, The 15 Charles E. Davenport

Governor's Daughter, The 09 Sidney Olcott

Governor's Daughter, The 12 August Blom

Governor's Daughters, The 15 Victor Sjöström

Governor's Decision, The 16 Herbert Brenon

Governor's Lady, The 23 Harry Millarde

Govorit Moskva 87 Renita Grigoryeva, Yuri Grigoryeva

Gow the Headhunter 28 Merian C. Cooper, Ernest B. Schoedsack

Gown of Destiny, The 18 Lynn Reynolds

Gown Shop, The 23 Larry Semon

Goya 50 Luciano Emmer

Goya 51 Jean Grémillon, Pierre Kast

Goya, oder Der Arge Weg zur Erkenntnis 70 Konrad Wolf

Goya ou Les Désastres de la Guerre 51 Jean Grémillon, Pierre Kast

Goyescas 44 Benito Perojo

Goyōkin 69 Hideo Gosha

Goyosen 26 Teinosuke Kinugasa

Gozaresh-e Yek Ghatl 87 Mohammed Ali Nadjafi

Gozenchū no Jikanwari 72 Susumu Hani

Gra 68 Jerzy Kawalerowicz

Grå Dame, Den 09 Viggo Larsen

Graal, Le 74 Robert Bresson

Grabbers, The 69 R. Lee Frost

Grace Moore Story, The 53 Gordon Douglas

Grace Quigley 83 Anthony Harvey

Gracias, Santiago 84 Santiago Álvarez

Gracie Allen Murder Case, The 39 Alfred E. Green

Graciela 56 Leopoldo Torre-Nilsson

Grad Night 80 John Tenorio

Gradenico e Tiepolo ovvero Amori e Congiure a Venezia 11 Enrico Guazzoni

Graduate, The 67 Mike Nichols

Graduate First 76 Maurice Pialat

Graduation, The 81 Joseph Zito

Graduation Day 81 Herb Freed

Graduation Day in Bugland 31 Dave Fleischer

Graduation Exercises 35 Art Davis, Sid Marcus

Graduation Party 85 Pupi Avati

Graf Bobby, der Schrecken des Wilden Westens 65 Paul Martin

Graf Cohn 23 Carl Boese

Graf Dracula Beisst Jetzt in Oberbayern 79 Carlo Ombra

Graf von Cagliostro, Der 20 Reinhold Schünzel

Graf von Carabas, Der 34 Lotte Reiniger

Graf von Charolais, Der 22 Karl Grüne

Grafen Pocci, Die 67 Hans-Jürgen Syberberg

Grafen Pocci — Einige Kapitel zur Geschichte einer Familie, Die 67 Hans-Jürgen Syberberg

Graffiti Blackboard 59 Kaneto Shindo

Graffiti Bridge 90 Prince

Gräfin Donelli 24 G. W. Pabst

Gräfin Mariza 25 Hans Steinhoff

Gräfin Mariza 32 Richard Oswald

Gräfin von Monte Cristo, Die 19 Joe May

Gräfin von Paris, Die 22 Dmitri Buchowetzki

Graft 13 Émile Cohl

Graft 31 Christy Cabanne

Grafters 17 Arthur Rosson

Grail, The 23 Colin Campbell

Grail, The 74 Robert Bresson

Grain 35 I. Pravov, Olga Preobrazhenskaya

Grain de Sable, Le 64 Pierre Kast

Grain of Dust, A 18 Harry Revier

Grain of Dust, The 28 George Archainbaud

Grain of Sand, A 17 Frank Wilson

Grain of Wheat, A 58 Kozaburo Yoshimura

Gramps Is a Great Guy 87 Michel Drach

Grampy's Indoor Outing 36 Dave Fleischer

Gran Amor del Conde Drácula, El 72 Javier Aguirre

Gran Bollito 77 Mauro Bolognini

Gran Calavera, El 49 Luis Buñuel

Gran Casino 47 Luis Buñuel

Gran Cruz, La 37 Raphael J. Sevilla

Gran Fiesta, La 86 Marcos Zurinaga

Gran Salto al Vacío, El 79 Santiago Álvarez

Gran Serafín, El 87 José María Ulloque

Gran Varietà 55 Domenico Paolella

Granada, My Granada 67 Roman Karmen

Granaderos del Amor 34 John Reinhardt

Granatovyi Braslet 65 Abram Room

Grand Amour, Le 68 Pierre Etaix

Grand Amour de Beethoven, Un 36 Abel Gance

Grand Babylon Hotel, The 16 Frank Wilson

Grand Barrage, Le 60 Ermanno Olmi

Grand Bazar, Le 73 Claude Zidi

Grand Bleu, Le 88 Luc Besson

Grand Blond avec Une Chaussure Noire, Le 72 Yves Robert

Grand Bounce, The 37 Jacques Tourneur

Grand Canary 34 Irving Cummings

Grand Canyon 49 Paul Landres

Grand Canyon Trail 48 William Witney

Grand Central Murder 42 S. Sylvan Simon

Grand Chef, Le 58 Henri Verneuil

Grand Chemin, Le 87 Jean-Loup Hubert

Grand Christmas Harlequinade 14 Will P. Kellino

Grand Concert, The 51 Vera Stroyeva

Grand Concert, The 60 John Halas*

Grand Dadais, Le 67 Pierre Granier-Deferre

Grand Duchess and the Waiter, The 26 Malcolm St. Clair

Grand Duel, The 72 Giancarlo Santi

Grand Duel in Magic 66 Tetsuya Yamaguchi

Grand Duke and Mr. Pimm, The 62 David Swift

Grand Duke's Finances, The 23 F. W. Murnau

Grand Duke's Finances, The 34 Gustaf Gründgens

Grand Élan, Le 38 Christian-Jaque

Grand Embouteillage, Le 79 Luigi Comencini

Grand Escapade, The 46 John Baxter

Grand Exit 35 Erle C. Kenton

Grand Finale 36 Ivar Campbell

Grand Guignol 87 Jean Marbœuf

Grand Harlequinade 12 Will P. Kellino

Grand Highway, The 87 Jean-Loup Hubert

Grand Hotel 32 Edmund Goulding

Grand Hotel Babylon, Das 19 E. A. Dupont

Grand Illusion 37 Jean Renoir

Grand Illusion, The 86 Tuija-Maija Niskanen

Grand Jeu, Le 33 Jacques Feyder

Grand Jeu, Le 53 Robert Siodmak

Grand Journal Illustré, Un 27 Edmond T. Gréville

Grand Junction Case, The 61 Peter Duffell

Grand Jury 36 Albert S. Rogell

Grand Jury 76 Christopher Cain

Grand Jury Secrets 39 James P. Hogan

Grand Khan 61 Riccardo Freda, Hugo Fregonese, Piero Pierotti

Grand Larceny 22 Wallace Worsley

Grand Machin et le Petit Chose, Le 10 Émile Cohl

Grand Maneuver, The 55 René Clair

Grand Meaulnes, Le 67 Jean-Gabriel Albicocco

Grand Méchant Loup Appelle 64 Ralph Nelson

Grand Méliès, Le 52 Georges Franju

Grand National Night 53 Bob McNaught

Grand Old Girl 35 John S. Robertson

Grand Ole Opry 40 Frank McDonald

Grand Olympics, The 64 Romolo Marcellini

Grand Parade, The 30 Fred Newmeyer, Frank Reicher

Grand Passion, The *18* Ida May Park
Grand Patron, Un *51* Yves Ciampi
Grand Paysage d'Alexis Droeven, Le *81* Jean-Jacques Andrien
Grand Prix *34* St. John L. Clowes
Grand Prix *66* John Frankenheimer
Grand Rendez-Vous, Le *49* Jean Dréville
Grand Slam *33* William Dieterle
Grand Slam *68* Giuliano Montaldo
Grand Slam Opera *36* Charles Lamont
Grand Street *53* Jonas Mekas
Grand Street Boys *43* William Beaudine
Grand Substitution, The *65* Chun Yen
Grand Sud, Le *56* François Reichenbach
Grand Theft Auto *77* Ron Howard
Grand Uproar, The *30* Dave Fleischer
Grandad Rudd *35* Ken Hall
Grandad's Exile *12* Charles C. Calvert
Grandchild's Devotion, A *06* Lewin Fitzhamon
Grande Abbuffata, La *73* Marco Ferreri
Grande Appello, Il *36* Mario Camerini
Grande Blek, Il *87* Giuseppe Piccioni
Grande Bouffe, La *73* Marco Ferreri
Grande Bouffe, The *73* Marco Ferreri
Grande Bourgeoise, La *74* Mauro Bolognini
Grande-Bretagne et les États-Unis de 1896 à 1900, La *68* Marc Allégret
Grande Caccia, La *57* Arnold Belgard, Edoardo Capolino
Grande Chartreuse, La *38* René Clément
Grande Cidade, A *66* Carlos Diegués
Grande Duello, Il *72* Giancarlo Santi
Grande Épreuve, La *27* Joe Hamman*
Grande Fille Toute Simple, Une *49* Jacques Manuel
Grande Foire, La *60* Jean Mitry
Grande Frousse, La *64* Jean-Pierre Mocky
Grande Guerra, La *59* Mario Monicelli
Grande Guerre, La *59* Mario Monicelli
Grande Illusion, La *37* Jean Renoir
Grande Lessive, La *68* Jean-Pierre Mocky
Grande Luce, La *38* Carlo Campogalliani
Grande Lutte des Mineurs, La *48* Louis Daquin
Grande Notte di Ringo, La *65* Mario Maffei
Grande Paese d'Acciaio, Il *60* Ermanno Olmi
Grande Pagaille, La *60* Luigi Comencini
Grande Passion, La *28* André Hugon
Grande Pastorale, La *43* René Clément
Grande Rinuncia, La *51* Aldo Vergano
Grande Rue *56* Juan Antonio Bardem
Grande Sauterelle, La *66* Georges Lautner
Grande Silenzio, Il *67* Sergio Corbucci
Grande Speranza, La *54* Duilio Coletti
Grande Strada, La *48* Vittorio Cottafavi, Michael Waszyński
Grande Strada Azzurra, La *56* Gillo Pontecorvo
Grande Tormenta, La *20* Carmine Gallone
Grande Vadrouille, La *66* Gérard Oury
Grande Vergogna, La *16* Emilio Ghione
Grande Vie, La *34* Henri Diamant-Berger
Grande Vie, La *59* Julien Duvivier
Grandes Familles, Les *58* Denys De la Patellière
Grandes Gueules, Les *65* Robert Enrico
Grandes Manœuvres *1896* Georges Méliès

Grandes Manœuvres, Les *55* René Clair
Grandes Pelouses, Les *61* Marcel Moussy
Grandes Personnes, Les *60* Jean Valère
Grandeur and Decadence of a Small-Time Film Company *86* Jean-Luc Godard
Grandeur et Décadence *23* Raymond Bernard
Grandeur et Décadence *37* Jacques Natanson
Grandeur et Décadence d'un Petit Commerce de Cinéma *86* Jean-Luc Godard
Grandeur Nature *73* Philippe Agostini, Luis García Berlanga
Grandfather, The *86* Majid Gharizadeh
Grandfather Smallweed *28* Hugh Croise
Grandfather Trilogy *81* Allen Ross
Grandfather's Birthday, or The Last Roll-Call *08* A. E. Coleby
Grandfather's Clock *12* Edwin S. Porter
Grandfather's Follies *44* Jean Negulesco
Grandfather's Old Boots *12* Frank Wilson
Grandfather's Tormentors *05* Arthur Cooper
Grandi Magazzini, I *39* Mario Camerini
Grandi Magazzini *86* Franco Castellano, Giuseppe Moccia
Grandma and the Eight Children *77* Espen Thorstenson
Grandma Moses *50* Jerome Hill
Grandma Threading Her Needle *00* George Albert Smith
Grandma's Boy *21* Fred Newmeyer
Grandma's Buoys *36* Leslie Goodwins
Grandma's Encyclopedia *63* Walerian Borowczyk
Grandma's Girl *30* Mack Sennett
Grandma's Pet *32* Walter Lantz
Grandma's Reading Glass *00* George Albert Smith
Grandma's Sleeping Draught *12* Percy Stow
Grand'mères — Odette Robert *80* Jean Eustache
Grandmother, The *16* Alexander Korda
Grandmother, The *70* David Lynch
Grandmother *89* Idrissa Ouedraogo
Grandmother Had No Worries *35* Aleksander Ford, Michael Waszyński
Grandmother Sabella *57* Dino Risi
Grandmothers *80* Jean Eustache
Grandmother's House *89* Peter Rader
Grandmother's Story *08* Georges Méliès
Grandmother's War Story *11* Sidney Olcott
Grandpa *68* Jaromil Jireš
Grandpa and the Butterfly *05* Alf Collins
Grandpa Goes to Town *40* Gus Meins
Grandpa Planted a Beet *45* Jiří Trnka
Grandpa's Boy *27* Charles Lamont
Grandpa's Forty Winks *08* Arthur Cooper
Grandpa's Pension Day *08* Arthur Cooper
Grandpa's Will *14* Percy Stow
Grands, Les *24* Henri Fescourt
Grands Chemins, Les *62* Christian Marquand
Grands Feux *37* Alexander Alexeïeff, Claire Parker
Grands Moments, Les *65* Claude Lelouch
Grands Moyens, Les *76* Hubert Cornfield
Grandview, U.S.A. *84* Randal Kleiser
Granite Hotel *40* Dave Fleischer

Granny *14* Christy Cabanne
Granny General *86* Melo Absalov
Granny Get Your Gun *39* George Amy
Gränsfolken *13* Mauritz Stiller
Granton Trawler *33* Edgar Anstey, John Grierson
Grape Nutty *49* Alex Lovy
Grapes Are Ripe, The *52* Erich Engel
Grapes of Wrath, The *40* John Ford
Grasp of Greed, The *16* Joseph De Grasse
Grass *25* Merian C. Cooper, Marguerite Harrison, Ernest B. Schoedsack
Grass *68* Malcolm Le Grice
Grass — A Nation's Battle for Life *25* Merian C. Cooper, Marguerite Harrison, Ernest B. Schoedsack
Grass Eater, The *61* John Hayes
Grass Is Greener, The *60* Stanley Donen
Grass Is Singing, The *81* Michael Raeburn
Grass Orphan, The *22* Frank Crane
Grass — The Epic of a Lost Tribe *25* Merian C. Cooper, Marguerite Harrison, Ernest B. Schoedsack
Grass Whistle *55* Shiro Toyoda
Grass Widowers *21* William Drury
Grasshopper, The *55* Alexander Feinzimmer, Samson Samsonov
Grasshopper, The *70* Jerry Paris
Grasshopper and the Ant, The *1897* Georges Méliès
Grasshopper and the Ant, The *54* Lotte Reiniger
Grateful Dead, The *77* Jerry Garcia
Grateful Dog, A *08* Charles Raymond
Gratitude of Wanda, The *13* Wallace Reid
Gratitude to the Emperor *27* Kenji Mizoguchi
Gratuités *27* Jean Grémillon
Graue Dame, Die *38* Erich Engel
Graue Haus, Das *26* Friedrich Feher
Graue Herr, Der *15* Viggo Larsen
Grausame Freundin, Die *32* Karel Lamač
Grausame Job, Der *66* Édouard Molinaro
Grausige Nächte *21* Lupu Pick
Graustark *15* Fred E. Wright
Graustark *25* Dmitri Buchowetzki
Grave Desires *68* Gerry De Leon, Eddie Romero
Grave New World *72* Steve Turner
Grave of the Living Dead, The *82* Jesús Franco
Grave of the Vampire *72* John Hayes
Grave Robbers from Outer Space *56* Edward D. Wood, Jr.
Graves of Our Fathers, The *37* Pál Fejös
Graveside Story, The *63* Jacques Tourneur
Graveyard, The *73* Don Chaffey
Graveyard of Horror *71* Miguel Madrid
Graveyard Shift *85* Gerard Ciccoritti
Graveyard Shift *90* Ralph S. Singleton
Graveyard Shift II *89* Gerard Ciccoritti
Graveyard Tramps *73* Denis Sanders
Gravy Train, The *74* Jack Starrett
Gray Automobile, The *19* Joachim Coss, Enrique Rosas
Gray Dawn, The *22* Jean Hersholt, Eliot Howe
Gray Dawn *59* Grigori Roshal
Gray Gardens *75* Ellen Hovde, Muffie Meyer

Gray Horizon, The *19* William Worthington
Gray Lady, The *38* Erich Engel
Gray Lady Down *77* David Greene
Gray Towers Mystery, The *19* John W. Noble
Gray Wolf's Ghost, The *19* Park Frame, Joseph Franz
Grayeagle *77* Charles B. Pierce
Grazie Commissario *88* Sergio Corbucci
Grazie Zia *67* Salvatore Samperi
Graziella *26* Marcel Vandal
Grease *78* Randal Kleiser
Grease II *82* Patricia Birch
Greased Lightning *19* Jerome Storm
Greased Lightning *28* Ray Taylor
Greased Lightning *77* Michael Schultz
Greased Pole, The *18* Leighton Budd
Greaser, The *15* Raoul Walsh
Greaser and the Weakling, The *12* Allan Dwan
Greaser's Gauntlet, The *08* D. W. Griffith
Greaser's Palace *72* Robert Downey
Great Accident, The *20* Harry Beaumont
Great Administrator, The *54* Teinosuke Kinugasa
Great Adventure, The *15* Lawrence Trimble
Great Adventure, The *18* Alice Guy-Blaché
Great Adventure, The *21* Kenneth Webb
Great Adventure, The *50* David Mac-Donald
Great Adventure, The *53* Arne Sucksdorff
Great Adventure, The *75* Gianfranco Baldanello
Great Adventures of Captain Kidd, The *53* Derwin Abbe, Charles S. Gould
Great Adventures of Wild Bill Hickok, The *38* Sam Nelson, Mack V. Wright
Great Air Robbery, The *19* Jacques Jaccard
Great Alaskan Mystery, The *44* Lewis D. Collins, Ray Taylor
Great Albanian Warrior Skanderbeg, The *53* Sergei Yutkevich
Great Alligator, The *79* Sergio Martino
Great Alligator River *79* Sergio Martino
Great Alone, The *22* James Colwell, Jacques Jaccard
Great Amateur, The *58* Hasse Ekman
Great American Broadcast, The *41* Archie Mayo
Great American Bugs Bunny/Road Runner Chase, The *79* Chuck Jones, Phil Monroe
Great American Chase, The *79* Chuck Jones, Phil Monroe
Great American Cowboy, The *74* Kieth Merrill
Great American Massacre, The *84* Mark G. Gilhuis
Great American Mug, The *45* Cy Endfield
Great American Pastime, The *56* Herman Hoffman
Great American Pie Company, The *35* Nick Grindé
Great Americans *15* Harry S. Palmer
Great Americans Past and Present *15* Sidney Olcott
Great Anarchist Mystery, The *12* Charles Raymond

Great Armored Car Swindle, The *60* Lance Comfort
Great Awakening, The *41* Reinhold Schünzel
Great Balloon Adventure, The *78* Richard A. Colla
Great Balls of Fire! *89* Jim McBride
Great Bank Hoax, The *77* Joseph Jacoby
Great Bank Robbery, The *69* Hy Averback
Great Bank Sensation, The *15* Wilfred Noy
Great Bargain Sale, The *08* James A. Williamson
Great Barrier, The *37* Geoffrey Barkas, Milton Rosmer
Great Battle, The *74* Yuri Ozerov
Great Battle, The *78* Umberto Lenzi
Great Battle of the Volga, The *63* Mia Slavenska
Great Bear Hunt, Der *17* Gregory La Cava
Great Beginning, The *37* Josef Heifits, Alexander Zarkhi
Great Bet, The *15* Harry Piel
Great Big Bunch of You, A *33* Rudolf Ising
Great Big Thing, A *67* Eric Till
Great Big World and Little Children, The *62* Anna Sokołowska
Great Bird Mystery, The *32* Dick Huemer
Great Bodhisattva Pass, The *57* Tomu Uchida
Great Bradley Mystery, The *17* Richard Ridgely
Great Brain, The *78* Sidney Levin
Great Brain Machine, The *53* Ken Hughes
Great British Striptease, The *80* Doug Smith
Great British Train Robbery, The *65* John Olden, Claus Peter Witt
Great Buldis, The *29* Nina Agadzhanova-Shutko, Lev Kuleshov
Great Bullion Robbery, The *13* Alexander Butler
Great Bunch of Girls, A *78* Mary Ann Braubach, Tracy Tynan
Great Cargoes *33* Paul Rotha
Great Carrot Train Robbery, The *69* Robert McKimson
Great Caruso, The *51* Richard Thorpe
Great Catherine *67* Gordon Flemyng
Great Chartreuse, The *38* René Clément
Great Cheese Robber, The *20* Gregory La Cava, Vernon Stallings
Great Cheeze Mystery, The *41* Art Davis
Great Cheque Fraud, The *15* Charles Raymond
Great Chess Movie, The *82* Gilles Carle, Camille Coudari
Great Chicago Conspiracy Circus, The *70* Kerry Feltham
Great Citizen, The *39* Friedrich Ermler
Great City, The *63* Satyajit Ray
Great Clean Up, The *20* Frank Moser
Great Clown, The *51* Youssef Chahine
Great Commandment, The *39* Irving Pichel
Great Concert *51* Vera Stroyeva
Great Consoler, The *33* Lev Kuleshov
Great Conway, The *40* S. E. Reynolds

Great Coup, A *19* George Dewhurst
Great Dan Patch, The *49* Joseph M. Newman
Great Dawn, The *38* Mikhail Chiaureli
Great Dawn, The *47* Giuseppe M. Scotese
Great Day, The *20* Hugh Ford
Great Day *45* Lance Comfort
Great Day, The *52* Oscar Burn
Great Day, The *77* Ettore Scola
Great Day in the Morning *55* Jacques Tourneur
Great Deception, The *26* Howard Higgin
Great Decide, The *25* Wesley Ruggles
Great Decision, The *32* Ralph Ince
Great Defender, The *34* Thomas Bentley
Great Diamond Mystery, The *24* Denison Clift
Great Diamond Robbery, The *14* Daniel V. Arthur
Great Diamond Robbery, The *53* Robert Z. Leonard
Great Dictator, The *40* Charles Chaplin
Great Director, The *66* John Boorman
Great Divide, The *16* Edgar Lewis
Great Divide, The *24* Reginald Barker
Great Divide, The *29* Reginald Barker
Great Dream, The *66* Gary Graver
Great Earth, The *44* Sergei Gerasimov
Great Ecstasy of the Sculptor Steiner, The *74* Werner Herzog
Great Ecstasy of Woodcarver Steiner, The *74* Werner Herzog
Great Escape, The *63* John Sturges
Great Expectations *17* Joseph Kaufman, Robert Vignola
Great Expectations *21* Anders Wilhelm Sandberg
Great Expectations *34* Stuart Walker
Great Expectations *46* David Lean
Great Expectations *74* Joseph Hardy
Great Expectations *81* Julian Amyes
Great Expectations — The Australian Story *86* Tim Burstall
Great Expectations — The Untold Story *86* Tim Burstall
Great Expedition, The *59* Donovan Winter
Great Experience, The *40* Tsou-sen Tsai
Great Experiment, The *34* Art Davis, Sid Marcus
Great Family, The *54* Josef Heifits
Great Fear *58* Dušan Vukotić
Great Feed, The *73* Marco Ferreri
Great Fields, The *61* Marcel Moussy
Great Fight at All-Sereno, The *10* Walter R. Booth
Great Finale to Act 1 of "The Yeoman of the Guard" *07* John Morland
Great Flamarion, The *45* Anthony Mann
Great Flirtation, The *34* Ralph Murphy
Great Force, The *49* Friedrich Ermler
Great Gabbo, The *29* James Cruze
Great Gambini, The *37* Charles Vidor
Great Gambler, The *22* Fritz Lang
Great Game, The *18* A. E. Coleby
Great Game, The *30* Jack Raymond
Great Game, The *45* Henry Cass
Great Game, The *52* Maurice Elvey
Great Garrick, The *37* James Whale
Great Gatsby, The *26* Herbert Brenon

Great Gatsby, The *49* Elliott Nugent
Great Gatsby, The *74* Jack Clayton
Great Gay Road, The *20* Norman Mac-Donald
Great Gay Road, The *31* Sinclair Hill
Great Generation, The *86* Ferenc András
Great Georgia Bank Hoax, The *77* Joseph Jacoby
Great German North Sea Tunnel, The *14* Frank Newman
Great Gilbert and Sullivan, The *53* Sidney Gilliat
Great Gildersleeve, The *42* Gordon Douglas
Great Glinka, The *46* Lev Arnshtam
Great God Gold *35* Arthur Lubin
Great Gold Robbery, The *13* Maurice Elvey
Great Gundown, The *77* Paul Hunt
Great Gunfighter, The *63* Frank McDonald
Great Guns *27* Walt Disney
Great Guns *41* Monty Banks
Great Guy *36* John G. Blystone
Great Handicap, The *19* Gregory La Cava
Great Hansom Cab Mystery, The *17* Gregory La Cava
Great Harmony, The *13* Allan Dwan
Great Heart, The *38* David Miller
Great Hope, The *54* Duilio Coletti
Great Hora, The *58* Emil Lotyanu
Great Hospital Mystery, The *37* James Tinling
Great Hotel Murder, The *34* Eugene Forde
Great Hotel Mystery, The *34* Eugene Forde
Great Hunger Duel, The *22* Kenneth Graeme
Great Impersonation, The *21* George Melford
Great Impersonation, The *35* Alan Crosland
Great Impersonation, The *42* John Rawlins
Great Imposter, The *18* F. Martin Thornton
Great Imposter, The *60* Robert Mulligan
Great Is My Country *58* Roman Karmen
Great: Isambard Kingdom Brunel *75* Bob Godfrey
Great Jasper, The *33* J. Walter Ruben
Great Jesse James Raid, The *53* Reginald LeBorg
Great Jewel Robber, The *50* Peter Godfrey
Great Jewel Robbery, The *25* John Ince
Great John L., The *45* Frank Tuttle
Great Junction Hotel, The *31* William Beaudine
Great K & A Train Robbery, The *26* Lewis Seiler
Great Land *44* Sergei Gerasimov
Great Land of Small, The *86* Vojtěch Jasný
Great Leap, The *14* Christy Cabanne
Great Leap Into Space, The *79* Santiago Álvarez
Great Lester Boggs, The *75* Harry Thomason
Great Lie, The *41* Edmund Goulding

Great Life, Part One, A *40* Leonid Lukov
Great Life, Part Two, A *46* Leonid Lukov
Great Light, The *38* Carlo Campogalliani
Great Locomotive Chase, The *56* Francis D. Lyon
Great London Mystery, The *20* Charles Raymond
Great Long For Husband, The *63* Kwon-taek Im
Great Love, The *17* D. W. Griffith
Great Love, The *25* Marshall Neilan
Great Love, The *31* Otto Preminger
Great Love, The *38* Anders Henrikson
Great Love, The *68* Pierre Etaix
Great Lover, The *20* Frank Lloyd
Great Lover, The *31* Harry Beaumont
Great Lover, The *49* Alexander Hall
Great Macarthy, The *75* David Baker
Great Madcap, The *49* Luis Buñuel
Great Magaraz, The *15* Victor Tourjansky
Great Mail Robbery, The *27* George B. Seitz
Great Man, The *56* José Ferrer
Great Man Votes, The *39* Garson Kanin
Great Manhunt, The *49* Gordon Douglas
Great Manhunt, The *50* Sidney Gilliat
Great Man's Lady, The *41* William A. Wellman
Great Marshall Jewel Case *10* Edwin S. Porter
Great McGinty, The *40* Preston Sturges
Great McGonagall, The *74* Joseph McGrath
Great Meadow, The *31* Charles Brabin
Great Meddler, The *40* Fred Zinnemann
Great Medicine Ball Caravan, The *70* François Reichenbach
Great Méliès, The *52* Georges Franju
Great Men Among Us *15* William Parke
Great Mike, The *44* Wallace Fox
Great Mine Disaster, The *13* George Pearson
Great Missouri Raid, The *50* Gordon Douglas
Great Mistake, A *10* Joe Rosenthal
Great Mr. Handel, The *42* Norman Walker
Great Mr. Nobody, The *41* Ben Stoloff
Great Moment, The *21* Sam Wood
Great Moment, The *43* Preston Sturges
Great Monkey Rip-Off, The *79* Thomas Stobart
Great Monster Yongkari *67* Kiduck Kim
Great Morgan, The *46* Nat Perrin
Great Motor Bus Outrage, The *15* Wilfred Noy
Great Mouse Detective, The *86* Ron Clements, Burny Mattinson, Dave Michener, John Musker
Great Movie Robbery, The *86* Oldřich Lipský, Zdeněk Podskalský
Great Muppet Caper, The *81* Jim Henson
Great Mystery, The *20* Raoul Barré, Charles Bowers
Great Night, The *22* Howard Mitchell
Great Northfield Minnesota Raid, The *71* Philip Kaufman
Great Offensive, The *17* Gregory La Cava
Great O'Malley, The *37* William Dieterle
Great Outdoors, The *88* Howard Deutch

Great Pants Mystery, The *31* Norman Taurog
Great Pastorale, The *43* René Clément
Great Patriotic War, The *65* Roman Karmen
Great Pearl Tangle, The *16* Del Henderson
Great Physician, The *13* Richard Ridgely
Great Pickle Robbery, The *20* Raoul Barré, Charles Bowers
Great Piggy Bank Robbery, The *46* Robert Clampett
Great Plains, The *57* Roman Kroitor
Great Plane Robbery, The *40* Lewis D. Collins
Great Plane Robbery, The *50* Edward L. Cahn
Great Poison Mystery, The *14* Frank Wilson
Great Pony Raid, The *68* Frederic Goode
Great Power, The *29* Joe Rock
Great Power *49* Friedrich Ermler
Great Prince Shan, The *24* A. E. Coleby
Great Problem, The *16* Rex Ingram
Great Profile, The *40* Walter Lang
Great Profligate, The *49* Luis Buñuel
Great Python Robbery, The *14* Arthur Finn
Great Race, The *64* Blake Edwards
Great Radio Mystery, The *34* Phil Rosen
Great Radium Mystery, The *19* Robert F. Hill, Robert Roadwell
Great Red War, The *16* Ethyle Batley
Great Redeemer, The *20* Clarence Brown, Maurice Tourneur
Great Ride *78* Don Hulette
Great Riviera Bank Robbery, The *79* Francis Megahy
Great Road, The *27* Esther Shub
Great Rock 'n' Roll Swindle, The *79* Julien Temple
Great Romance, The *19* Henry Otto
Great Ruby, The *15* Barry O'Neil
Great Rupert, The *50* Irving Pichel
Great St. Louis Bank Robbery, The *59* Charles Guggenheim, John Stix
Great St. Trinian's Train Robbery, The *66* Sidney Gilliat, Frank Launder
Great Santini, The *79* Lewis John Carlino
Great Schnozzle, The *34* Ben Stoloff
Great Scot on Wheels *11* Percy Stow
Great Scout and Cathouse Thursday, The *76* Don Taylor
Great Sea Serpent, The *04* James A. Williamson
Great Secret, The *16* Christy Cabanne
Great Sensation, The *25* Jay Marchant
Great Seraph, The *87* José María Ulloque
Great Servant Question, The *04* Lewin Fitzhamon
Great Shadow, The *20* Harley Knoles
Great Sinner, The *49* Robert Siodmak
Great Sioux Massacre, The *65* Sidney Salkow
Great Sioux Uprising, The *53* Lloyd Bacon
Great Ski Caper, The *72* George Englund
Great Skycopter Rescue, The *82* Lawrence Foldes
Great Smokey Roadblock, The *76* John Leone

Great Snakes 20 Gerald Ames, Gaston Quiribet

Great Spy Chase, The 64 Georges Lautner

Great Spy Mission, The 64 Michael Anderson

Great Spy Raid, The 14 Sidney Morgan

Great Stagecoach Robbery, The 45 Lesley Selander

Great Stone Face, The 68 Vernon Becker

Great Strength 49 Friedrich Ermler

Great Stuff 33 Leslie Hiscott

Great Swindle, The 41 Lewis D. Collins

Great Telephone Robbery, The 72 Menahem Golan

Great Temptation, A 06 Harold Hough

Great Temptation, The 35 Marcel L'Herbier

Great Terror, The 22 George Ridgwell

Great Test, The 28 A. Duges, Alexandre Ryder

Great Texas Dynamite Chase, The 76 Michael Pressman

Great Theatres of the World 87 Herbert Kline

Great Tiger Ruby, The 12 Charles C. Calvert

Great Train Robbery, The 03 Edwin S. Porter

Great Train Robbery, The 41 Joseph Kane

Great Train Robbery, The 78 Michael Crichton

Great Turf Mystery, The 24 Walter West

Great Turning Point, The 46 Friedrich Ermler

Great Umbrella Mystery, The 20 Gregory La Cava

Great Universal Mystery, The 14 Allan Dwan

Great Vacuum Robbery, The 15 F. Richard Jones

Great Van Robbery, The 59 Max Varnel

Great Victor Herbert, The 39 Andrew L. Stone

Great Victory, The 33 Mikhail Kaufman

Great Victory—Wilson or the Kaiser?, The 18 Charles Miller

Great Waldo Pepper, The 75 George Roy Hill

Great Wall, The 65 Shigeo Tanaka

Great Wall, A 85 Peter Wang

Great Wall Is a Great Wall, The 85 Peter Wang

Great Wall of China, The 70 Joel Tuber

Great Waltz, The 33 Alfred Hitchcock

Great Waltz, The 38 Julien Duvivier, Victor Fleming, Josef von Sternberg

Great Waltz, The 72 Andrew L. Stone

Great War, The 59 Mario Monicelli

Great Warrior, The 53 Sergei Yutkevich

Great Warrior Skanderbeg, The 53 Sergei Yutkevich

Great Well, The 24 Henry Kolker

Great White, The 81 Enzo G. Castellari

Great White Hope, The 70 Martin Ritt

Great White North, The 28 H. A. Snow, Sidney Snow

Great White Tower, The 66 Satsuo Yamamoto

Great White Trail, The 17 Leopold Wharton

Great White Way, The 24 E. Mason Hopper

Great Who Dood It, The 52 Walter Lantz

Great World Power Rising, A 38 Hiroshi Inagaki

Great Yearning, The 30 Steve Sekely

Great Ziegfeld, The 36 Robert Z. Leonard

Greater Advisor, The 40 Joseph Seiden

Greater Christian, The 12 Edwin S. Porter

Greater Claim, The 21 Wesley Ruggles

Greater Devotion, The 14 Wallace Reid

Greater Duty, The 22 Gilbert M. Anderson

Greater Glory, The 26 Curt Rehfeld

Greater Law, The 17 Lynn Reynolds

Greater Love, The 12 Edwin S. Porter

Greater Love, The 13 Allan Dwan

Greater Love, The 19 Geoffrey H. Malins

Greater Love, The 31 John P. McCarthy

Greater Love Hath No Man 13 Alexander Butler

Greater Love Hath No Man 15 Herbert Blaché, Alice Guy-Blaché

Greater Need, The 16 Ralph Dewsbury

Greater Profit, The 21 William Worthington

Greater Promise, A 36 Vladimir Korsh-Sablin

Greater Sinner, The 19 A. J. Blume

Greater Than a Crown 25 Roy William Neill

Greater Than Art 15 John H. Collins

Greater Than Fame 20 Alan Crosland

Greater Than Love 19 Fred Niblo, John M. Stahl

Greater Than Marriage 24 Victor Halperin

Greater War, The 26 Jack Raymond

Greater Wealth 12 Colin Campbell

Greater Will, The 15 Harley Knoles

Greater Woman, The 17 Frank Powell

Greatest, The 77 Tom Gries

Greatest Battle, The 78 Umberto Lenzi

Greatest Battle on Earth, The 65 Inoshiro Honda

Greatest Challenge of All, The 67 Yoji Yamada

Greatest in the World, The 19 Forest Holger-Madsen

Greatest Kidnapping in the West, The 67 Maurizio Lucidi

Greatest Love, The 14 August Blom

Greatest Love, The 20 Henry Kolker

Greatest Love, The 51 Roberto Rossellini

Greatest Love of All, The 24 George Beban

Greatest Menace, The 23 Albert S. Rogell

Greatest of These, The 11 Lewin Fitzhamon

Greatest of These, The 26 Charles Barnett

Greatest of These, The 34 George B. Samuelson

Greatest Power, The 17 Edwin Carewe

Greatest Question, The 19 D. W. Griffith

Greatest Show on Earth, The 16 Harry S. Palmer

Greatest Show on Earth, The 51 Cecil B. DeMille

Greatest Story Ever Told, The 65 George Stevens

Greatest Thing in Life, The 17 D. W.

Griffith

Greatest Truth, The 22 Joe May

Greatest Wish in the World, The 18 Maurice Elvey

Greatheart 21 George Ridgwell

Greco, El 64 Luciano Salce

Greed 17 Theodore Marston

Greed 24 Erich von Stroheim

Greed in the Sun 63 Henri Verneuil

Greed of William Hart, The 48 Oswald Mitchell

Greedy Billy 05 Alf Collins

Greedy Boy's Dream, The 49 Richard Massingham

Greedy for Tweety 57 Friz Freleng

Greedy Girl, The 08 Lewin Fitzhamon

Greedy Humpty Dumpty 36 Dave Fleischer

Greedy Neighbor, The 14 Émile Cohl

Greek Interpreter, The 22 George Ridgwell

Greek Miracle, The 21 Dimitrios Gaziadis

Greek Sculpture 59 Michael Ayrton, Basil Wright

Greek Street 30 Sinclair Hill

Greek Testament 42 Alberto Cavalcanti

Greek Tycoon, The 78 J. Lee-Thompson

Greeks Had a Word for Them, The 32 Lowell Sherman

Green and Pleasant Land 54 Lindsay Anderson

Green Archer, The 25 Spencer G. Bennet

Green Archer, The 40 James W. Horne

Green Archer, The 61 Jürgen Roland

Green Berets, The 68 Ray Kellogg, Mervyn LeRoy, John Wayne

Green Bird, The 79 István Szabó

Green Buddha, The 54 John Lemont

Green Caravan, The 22 Edwin J. Collins

Green Card 90 Peter Weir

Green Carnation, The 54 John Lemont

Green Carnation, The 60 Ken Hughes

Green Cobra 87 Werner Herzog

Green Cockatoo, The 37 William K. Howard, William Cameron Menzies

Green Dolphin Street 47 Victor Saville

Green Dragon, The 07 Lewin Fitzhamon

Green Eye of the Yellow God, The 13 Richard Ridgely

Green-Eyed Blonde, The 57 Bernard Girard

Green-Eyed Monster, The 12 Allan Dwan

Green-Eyed Monster, The 15 Cecil Birch

Green-Eyed Monster, The 16 J. Gordon Edwards

Green-Eyed Woman 42 Mitchell Leisen

Green Eyes 18 Roy William Neill

Green Eyes 34 Richard Thorpe

Green Fields 37 Jacob Ben-Ami, Edgar G. Ulmer

Green Fingers 46 John Harlow

Green Fire 54 Andrew Marton

Green Flame, The 20 Ernest C. Warde

Green Flood 65 István Gaál

Green for Danger 46 Sidney Gilliat

Green Ghost, The 29 Lionel Barrymore

Green Glove, The 51 Rudolph Maté

Green Glow of the Mountains, The 84 Werner Herzog

Green God, The 18 Paul Scardon

Green Goddess, The *23* Sidney Olcott
Green Goddess, The *30* Alfred E. Green
Green Grass of Wyoming *48* Louis King
Green Grass Widows *28* Alfred Raboch
Green, Green Grass of Home *82* Hsiao-hsien Hou
Green Grow the Rushes *51* Derek Twist
Green Hell, The *39* Eduard von Borsody
Green Hell *40* James Whale
Green Helmet, The *61* Michael Forlong
Green Horizon, The *81* Susumu Hani*
Green Hornet, The *40* Ford Beebe, Ray Taylor
Green Hornet Strikes Again, The *40* Ford Beebe, John Rawlins
Green Ice *81* Ernest Day
Green Leather Note Case, The *34* George B. Samuelson
Green Light, The *37* Frank Borzage
Green Light for the 1964 Sugar Crop *64* Santiago Álvarez
Green Magic *55* Gian Gaspare Napolitano
Green Man, The *56* Robert Day
Green Mansions *59* Mel Ferrer
Green Manuela, The *23* E. A. Dupont
Green Mare, The *59* Claude Autant-Lara
Green Mare's Nest, The *59* Claude Autant-Lara
Green Men from Outer Space *86* Hans Hatwig
Green Mist, The *24* Fred Paul
Green Monkey *87* William Fruet
Green Mountain Land *50* David Flaherty
Green Necklace, The *12* Charles Magnusson
Green Orchard, The *16* Harold Weston
Green Pack, The *34* T. Hayes Hunter
Green Pastures, The *36* Marc Connelly, William Keighley
Green Promise, The *49* William D. Russell
Green Ray, The *85* Eric Rohmer
Green Room, The *78* François Truffaut
Green Scarf, The *54* George More O'Ferrall
Green Shoes, The *68* Ian Brims
Green Slime, The *68* Kinji Fukasaku
Green Spider, The *16* Alexander Volkov
Green Spot Mystery, The *31* Henry MacRae
Green Stockings *16* Wilfred North
Green Swamp, The *16* Scott Sidney
Green Temptation, The *22* William Desmond Taylor
Green Terror, The *19* Will P. Kellino
Green Tree, The *65* Joseph Roland
Green Wall, The *69* Armando Robles Godoy
Green Wall, The *85* Cecile Tang Shu Shuen
Green Years, The *46* Victor Saville
Green Years, The *65* István Gaál
Green Years *85* Milan Muchna
Greene Felde *37* Jacob Ben-Ami, Edgar G. Ulmer
Greene Murder Case, The *28* Frank Tuttle
Greene Murder Case, The *36* E. A. Dupont
Greengage Summer, The *61* Lewis Gilbert
Greenhouse, The *85* Vangelis Serdaris

Greenland's Icy Mountains *16* L. M. Glackens
Green's Goose *08* Arthur Cooper
Greenwich Village *20* Hy Mayer
Greenwich Village *44* Walter Lang
Greenwich Village Story *63* Jack O'Connell
Greenwood Tree, The *29* Harry Lachman
Greetings *68* Brian DePalma
Greetings Bait! *43* Friz Freleng
Greetings Moscow! *45* Sergei Yutkevich
Greetings to the Swallows *72* Jaromil Jireš
Gregor Marold *18* Fritz Kortner
Gregorio *85* María Barea, Fernando Espinosa, Stefan Kaspar, Alejandro Legaspi, Susana Pastor
Gregorio Cortez *82* Robert M. Young
Gregory's Girl *80* Bill Forsyth
Greh *62* Franz Cap
Greifer, Der *30* Richard Eichberg
Grekh *16* Georgy Azagarov, Yakov Protazanov
Grêle de Feu *52* Haroun Tazieff
Grell Mystery, The *17* Paul Scardon
Gremlins *84* Joe Dante
Gremlins 2: The New Batch *90* Joe Dante
Grenadiers of Love *34* John Reinhardt
Grendel Grendel Grendel *80* Alexander Stitt
Grenoble *68* Claude Lelouch, François Reichenbach
Grenzfeuer *36* Hans Beck-Gaden
Gretchen, the Greenhorn *16* Chester M. Franklin, Sidney Franklin
Gretel *73* Gillian Armstrong
Gretel and Liesel *31* Wilhelm von Kaufmann
Gretl Zieht das Grosse Los *35* Carl Boese
Gretna Green *12* Mark Melford
Gretna Green *15* Hugh Ford, Thomas Heffron
Grève, La *04* Ferdinand Zecca
Grève des Apaches, La *08* Louis Feuillade
Grevinde Hjerteløs *15* Forest Holger-Madsen
Grevindens Ære *18* August Blom
Grey Dame, The *09* Viggo Larsen
Grey Devil, The *26* Bennett Cohn
Grey Fox, The *82* Phillip Borsos
Grey Gardens *75* Albert Maysles, David Maysles
Grey Gold *80* Raúl Ruiz
Grey Hounded Hare, The *49* Robert McKimson
Grey Lady, The *09* Viggo Larsen
Grey Parasol, The *18* Lawrence C. Windom
Grey Vulture, The *26* Forrest K. Sheldon
Greyeagle *77* Charles B. Pierce
Greyfriars Bobby *61* Don Chaffey
Greyhound, The *14* Lawrence McGill
Greyhound Limited, The *29* Howard Bretherton
Greystoke: The Legend of Tarzan *84* Hugh Hudson
Greystoke: The Legend of Tarzan, Lord of the Apes *84* Hugh Hudson
Greystoke: The Legend of Tarzan of the Apes *84* Hugh Hudson
Greywater Park *24* Fred Paul

Gribiche *25* Jacques Feyder
Gribouille *37* Marc Allégret
Gribushin Family, The *23* Alexander Rasumny
Gricheux, Les *09* Émile Cohl
Grid Iron Demons *28* Frank Moser
Grid-Iron Hero, A *16* Gregory La Cava, Vernon Stallings
Grid Ironed *27* Manny Gould, Ben Harrison
Gridiron Flash *34* Glenn Tryon
Grido, Il *57* Michelangelo Antonioni
Grido della Città, Il *48* Dino Risi
Grido della Terra, Il *49* Duilio Coletti
Grief Street *31* Richard Thorpe
Grievous Bodily Harm *88* Mark Joffe
Grif Starovo Bortza *16* Yevgeni Bauer
Griff nach den Sternen *55* Helmut Käutner
Griff Swims the Channel *19* Maurice Sandground
Griffon of an Old Warrior *16* Yevgeni Bauer
Griff's Lost Love *19* Maurice Sandground
Grifters, The *90* Stephen Frears
Grigsby *70* Gordon Flemyng
Grijpstra and de Gier *83* Wim Verstappen
Griller, Der *68* George Moorse
Grim Comedian, The *21* Frank Lloyd
Grim Game, The *19* Irvin Willat
Grim Justice *16* Lawrence Trimble
Grim Pastures *43* George Dunning
Grim Prairie Tales *90* Wayne Coe
Grim Reaper, The *62* Bernardo Bertolucci
Grim Reaper, The *80* Aristide Massaccesi
Grimace, La *66* Bertrand Blier
Grimaci Parizhi *24* Dziga Vertov
Grimaldi *14* Charles Vernon
Grin and Bear It *33* George Stevens
Gringalet *46* André Berthomieu
Gringo *63* Riccardo Blasco
Gringo *85* Lech Kowalski
Gringo Getta il Fucile *66* Joaquín Luis Romero Marchent
Gringo Mojado *84* Ricardo Franco
Gringos Non Perdonano, I *65* Alberto Cardone
Gringo's Pitiless Colt *66* José Luis Madrid
Grinning Guns *27* Albert S. Rogell
Griot Badye, Le *77* Ousseini, Jean Rouch
Grip, The *13* A. E. Coleby
Grip *15* Maurice Elvey
Grip of Ambition, The *14* Frank Wilson
Grip of Fear, The *62* Blake Edwards
Grip of Iron, The *13* Arthur Charrington
Grip of Iron, The *20* Bert Haldane
Grip of Jealousy, The *16* Joseph De Grasse, Ida May Park
Grip of the Past, The *14* Edwin J. Collins
Grip of the Strangler *58* Robert Day
Grip of the Yukon, The *28* Ernst Laemmle
Grisbi *53* Jacques Becker
Grissly's Millions *44* John English
Grissom Gang, The *70* Robert Aldrich
Grit *24* Frank Tuttle
Grit of a Dandy, The *14* Hubert von Herkomer
Grit of a Jew, The *17* Maurice Elvey
Grit Wins *29* Josef Levigard

Guerre aux Sauterelles, La *31* Edmond T. Gréville

Guerre Continue, La *62* Leopoldo Savona

Guerre de Troie, La *62* Giorgio Ferroni

Guerre des Boutons, La *62* Yves Robert

Guerre du Silence, La *59* Claude Lelouch

Guerre d'un Seul Homme, La *81* Edgardo Cozarinsky

Guerre en Dentelles, La *52* Pierre Kast

Guerre Est Finie, La *66* Alain Resnais

Guerre Oubliée, La *88* Richard Boutet

Guerre Planetari *61* Antonio Margheriti

Guerre Populaire au Laos, La *68* Antoine Bonfanti, Emmanuele Castro, Suzanne Fen, Joris Ivens, Marceline Loridan, Bernard Ortion, Anne Rullier, Jean-Pierre Sergent

Guerre Secrète, La *65* Christian-Jaque, Werner Klingler, Carlo Lizzani, Terence Young

Guerriere del Sno Nuda, Le *73* Terence Young

Guerrieri *42* Luciano Emmer, Enrico Gras, Tatiana Grauding

Guerrieri del Bronx, I *82* Enzo G. Castellari

Guerrieri dell'Anno 2072, I *83* Lucio Fulci

Guerrilla, The *08* D. W. Griffith

Guerrilla, The *73* Mrinal Sen

Guerrilla Brigade *39* Igor Savchenko

Guerrilla Fighter, The *73* Mrinal Sen

Guerrilla Girl *53* John Christian

Guerrilla—Los Desastres de la Guerra *83* Mario Camus

Guerrillas in Pink Lace *64* George Montgomery

Guess What? *69* John G. Avildsen

Guess What Happened to Count Dracula *70* Laurence Merrick

Guess What We Learned in School Today? *69* John G. Avildsen

Guess Who's Coming to Dinner *67* Stanley Kramer

Guest, The *63* Clive Donner

Guest, The *84* Ross Devenish

Guest at Steenkampskraal, The *77* Ross Devenish

Guest Came, A *47* Arne Mattsson

Guest from the Island of Freedom, A *63* Roman Karmen

Guest House, The *31* Stuart Paton

Guest in One's Own Home, A *57* Stig Olin

Guest in the House, A *44* John Brahm, André De Toth, Lewis Milestone

Guest of Honour *34* George King

Guest of the Evening, The *14* Frank Wilson

Guest of the Regiment, The *15* Wilfred Noy

Guest on Freedom Island *63* Roman Karmen

Guest Wife *45* Sam Wood

Guestless Dinner Party, The *14* August Blom

Guests Are Coming *65* Romuald Drobażyński, Jan Rutkiewicz, Gerard Zalewski

Guests of the Hotel Astoria, The *89* Reza Alamehzadeh

Guests of the Nation *35* Denis Johnston

Guet-Apens, Le *13* Louis Feuillade

Gueule d'Amour *37* Jean Grémillon

Gueule d'Ange *62* Marcel Blistène

Gueule Ouverte, La *73* Maurice Pialat

Guglielmo Oberdan il Martire di Trieste *15* Emilio Ghione

Gugusse and the Automaton *1897* Georges Méliès

Gugusse et Belzebuth *01* Georges Méliès

Gugusse et l'Automate *1897* Georges Méliès

Gui an Yan *83* Henry Chan

Gui Da Gui *80* Samo Hung

Guichets du Louvre, Les *74* Michel Mitrani

Guidance to the Indulgent *28* Heinosuke Gosho

Guide, The *65* Tad Danielewski

Guide Dogs for the Blind *39* Anthony Asquith

Guide for the Married Man, A *67* Gene Kelly

Guided Muscle *55* Chuck Jones

Guiding Conscience *16* Forest Holger-Madsen

Guilala *64* Kazui Nihonmatsu

Guild of the Kutna Hora Virgins *38* Otakar Vávra

Guild of the Virgins of Kutna Hora, The *38* Otakar Vávra

Guile of Women *21* Clarence Badger

Guillaume *1896* Émile Reynaud

Guillaume Tell et le Clown *1898* Georges Méliès

Guilt *30* Reginald Fogwell

Guilt *67* Lars Görling

Guilt Is My Shadow *50* Roy Kellino

Guilt Is Not Mine *68* Giuseppe Masini

Guilt of Janet Ames, The *47* Henry Levin

Guilt of Silence, The *18* Elmer Clifton

Guilt Redeemed *14* Victor Sjöström

Guilty? *30* George B. Seitz

Guilty, The *47* John Reinhardt

Guilty? *56* Edmond T. Gréville

Guilty As Charged *32* Erle C. Kenton

Guilty As Hell *32* Erle C. Kenton

Guilty Assignment *47* William C. Thomas

Guilty Bystander *50* Joseph Lerner

Guilty Conscience, A *21* David Smith

Guilty Generation, The *31* Rowland V. Lee

Guilty Hands *31* W. S. Van Dyke

Guilty Love *15* August Blom

Guilty Man, The *18* Irvin Willat

Guilty Melody *36* Richard Potter

Guilty of Love *20* Harley Knoles

Guilty of Treason *49* Felix E. Feist

Guilty One, The *24* Joseph E. Henabery

Guilty or Not Guilty *32* Albert Ray

Guilty Parents *34* Jack Townley

Guilty Party, The *62* Lionel Harris

Guilty Passion *13* Yevgeni Bauer

Guilty Though Guiltless *45* Vladimir Petrov

Guilty Though Innocent *45* Vladimir Petrov

Guilty Though Innocent *53* Jørgen Roos

Guilty Trails *38* George Waggner

Guima Zhiduo Zing *81* Hark Tsui

Guinea Entertainer, The *06* Arthur Cooper

Guinea Pig, The *48* Roy Boulting

Guinguette *58* Jean Delannoy

Guirara *64* Kazui Nihonmatsu

Guirlande Merveilleuse, La *03* Georges Méliès

Guitare et la Jazz Band, La *22* Gaston Roudes

Guitarrita, La *58* Jorge Sanjinés

Guitars of Love *54* Werner Jacobs

Gül Baba *40* Kálmán Nadasdy

Gula Bilen, Den *63* Arne Mattsson

Gulag *85* Roger Young

Guld og Grønne Skove *58* Gabriel Axel

Guldet og Vort Hjerte *12* Forest Holger-Madsen

Guldets Gift *15* Forest Holger-Madsen

Guldmønten *12* August Blom

Guldregn *88* Søren Kragh-Jacobsen

Gulf Between, The *17* Herbert T. Kalmus

Gulf Between, The *18* Wray Physioc

Gulf Stream *39* Alexander Alexeïeff, Claire Parker

Gull! *44* Arne Sucksdorff

Gullible Canary, The *42* Alec Geiss

Gulliver in Lilliput *23* Albert Mourlan, Raymond Villette

Gulliver no Uchū Ryokō *66* Yoshio Kuroda

Gulliver's Travels *02* Georges Méliès

Gulliver's Travels *39* Dave Fleischer

Gulliver's Travels *76* Peter R. Hunt

Gulliver's Travels Among the Lilliputians and the Giants *02* Georges Méliès

Gulliver's Travels Beyond the Moon *66* Yoshio Kuroda

Gulls and Buoys *72* Robert Breer

Gülsusan *86* Bilge Olgac

Gulvbehandling *55* Henning Carlsen

Gum Shoe Work *20* Raoul Barré, Charles Bowers

Gumball Rally, The *76* Chuck Bail

Gumbo Ya-Ya *62* Norman Taurog

Gumising Ka, Maruja *78* Lino Brocka

Gums *76* Robert J. Kaplan

Gumshoe *71* Stephen Frears

Gumshoe Kid, The *90* Joseph Manduke

Gumshoe Magoo *58* Gil Turner

Gun, The *78* Pasquale Squitieri

Gun Battle at Monterey *57* Sidney Franklin, Jr., Carl K. Hittleman

Gun Belt *53* Ray Nazarro

Gun Brothers *56* Sidney Salkow

Gun Bus *86* Zoran Perisic

Gun Code *40* Sam Newfield

Gun Crazy *49* Joseph H. Lewis

Gun Crazy *68* Richard Quine

Gun Duel in Durango *57* Sidney Salkow

Gun Fever *58* Mark Stevens

Gun Fight *61* Edward L. Cahn

Gun Fight at High Noon *63* Joaquín Luis Romero Marchent

Gun for a Coward *57* Abner Biberman

Gun Fury *53* Raoul Walsh

Gun Glory *57* Roy Rowland

Gun Gospel *27* Harry Joe Brown

Gun Grit *36* William Berke

Gun Hand, The *64* R. G. Springsteen

Gun-Hand Garrison *27* Edward R. Gordon

Gun Hawk, The *63* Edward Ludwig
Gun in His Hand, A *45* Joseph Losey
Gun Justice *27* William Wyler
Gun Justice *33* Alvin J. Neitz
Gun Law *19* John Ford
Gun Law *29* John Burch
Gun Law *33* Lewis D. Collins
Gun Law *38* David Howard
Gun Law Justice *49* Lambert Hillyer
Gun Lords of Stirrup Basin *37* Sam Newfield
Gun Moll *49* Fletcher Markle
Gun Packer, The *19* John Ford
Gun Packer *38* Wallace Fox
Gun Play *35* Albert Herman
Gun Pusher, The *19* John Ford
Gun Ranger, The *37* Robert North Bradbury
Gun Riders *69* Al Adamson
Gun Runner, The *28* Edgar Lewis
Gun Runner *49* Lambert Hillyer
Gun Runner, The *56* Gordon Douglas
Gun Runner *69* Richard Compton
Gun Runners, The *58* Don Siegel
Gun Shy *22* Alvin J. Neitz
Gun Shy *42* Bernard B. Ray
Gun Smoke *31* Edward Sloman
Gun Smoke *36* Bartlett Carre
Gun Smoke *45* Howard Bretherton
Gun Smugglers *48* Frank McDonald
Gun Street *61* Edward L. Cahn
Gun Talk *47* Lambert Hillyer
Gun That Won the West, The *55* William Castle
Gun the Man Down *56* Andrew V. McLaglen
Gun Town *46* Wallace Fox
Gun Woman, The *18* Frank Borzage
Gunboat Ginsburg *30* Mark Sandrich
Güneşe Köprü *86* Erdoğan Tokatli
Güney's The Wall *82* Yılmaz Güney
Gunfight, A *70* Lamont Johnson
Gunfight at Abilene *67* William Hale
Gunfight at Comanche Creek *63* Frank McDonald
Gunfight at Dodge City, The *59* Joseph M. Newman
Gunfight at Red Sands *63* Riccardo Blasco
Gunfight at Sandoval *61* Harry Keller
Gunfight at the O.K. Corral *57* John Sturges
Gunfight in Abilene *67* William Hale
Gunfighter, The *17* William S. Hart
Gunfighter, The *23* Lynn Reynolds
Gunfighter, The *50* Henry King
Gunfighters *47* George Waggner
Gunfighters *77* Monte Hellman
Gunfighters of Abilene *60* Edward L. Cahn
Gunfighters of Casa Grande, The *64* Roy Rowland
Gunfighters of the Northwest *53* Spencer G. Bennet
Gunfightin' Gentleman, A *19* John Ford
Gunfire *35* Harry Fraser
Gunfire *50* William Berke
Gunfire at Indian Gap *57* Joseph Kane
Gung Ho! *43* Ray Enright
Gung Ho *86* Ron Howard
Gunga Din *39* George Stevens

Gungala la Pantera Nuda *68* Ruggero Deodato
Gunless Bad Man, The *26* William Wyler
Gunman, The *11* Allan Dwan
Gunman, The *13* Raoul Walsh
Gunman, The *52* Lewis D. Collins
Gunman from Bodie, The *41* Spencer G. Bennet
Gunman Has Escaped, A *48* Richard Grey
Gunman in the Streets *50* Frank Tuttle
Gunman in Town *70* Giuliano Carmineo
Gunman's Code *46* Wallace Fox
Gunman's Walk *58* Phil Karlson
Gunmen from Laredo *59* Wallace MacDonald
Gunmen of Abilene *50* Fred C. Brannon
Gunmen of the Rio Grande *64* Tulio Demicheli
Gunn *66* Blake Edwards
Gunnar Hedes Saga *22* Mauritz Stiller
Gunners and Guns *35* Jerry Callahan
Gunning for Justice *48* Ray Taylor
Gunning for Vengeance *46* Ray Nazarro
Gunplay *51* Lesley Selander
Gunpoint! *55* Alfred L. Werker
Gunpoint *66* Earl Bellamy
Gunpowder *87* Norman J. Warren
Gunpowder Plot, The *00* Cecil M. Hepworth
Gunrunner, The *83* Nardo Castillo
Gunrunners, The *69* Richard Compton
Guns, The *63* Ruy Guerra
Guns *80* Robert Kramer
Guns A-Blazing *32* Edward L. Cahn
Guns Along the Border *52* Lewis D. Collins
Guns and Guitars *36* Joseph Kane
Guns and the Fury, The *82* Tony M. Zarindast
Guns at Batasi *64* John Guillermin
Guns for Hire *32* Lewis D. Collins
Guns for San Sebastian *67* Henri Verneuil
Guns for the Dictator *65* Claude Sautet
Guns, Girls and Gangsters *58* Edward L. Cahn
Guns in the Afternoon *61* Sam Peckinpah
Guns in the Dark *37* Sam Newfield
Guns in the Heather *68* Robert Butler
Guns of a Stranger *73* Robert Hinkle
Guns of August, The *64* Nathan Kroll
Guns of Darkness *62* Anthony Asquith
Guns of Diablo *64* Boris Sagal
Guns of Fort Petticoat, The *57* George Marshall
Guns of Hate *48* Lesley Selander
Guns of Justice *50* Thomas Carr
Guns of Loos, The *27* Sinclair Hill
Guns of Navarone, The *61* J. Lee-Thompson
Guns of San Sebastian, The *67* Henri Verneuil
Guns of the Black Witch *61* Lee Kresel, Domenico Paolella
Guns of the Law *44* Elmer Clifton
Guns of the Magnificent Seven *68* Paul Wendkos
Guns of the Pecos *37* Noel Mason Smith
Guns of the Timberland *60* Robert D. Webb
Guns of the Trees *61* Jonas Mekas

Guns of Wrath *48* Lesley Selander
Guns of Wyoming *63* Tay Garnett
Guns, Sin and Bathtub Gin *79* Lewis Teague
Gunsaulus Mystery, The *21* Oscar Micheaux
Gunsight Ridge *57* Francis D. Lyon
Gunslinger, The *56* Roger Corman
Gunslingers *50* Wallace Fox
Gunsmoke *47* Fred King
Gunsmoke! *52* Nathan Juran
Gunsmoke in Tucson *58* Thomas Carr
Gunsmoke Mesa *44* Harry Fraser
Gunsmoke on the Guadalupe *35* Bartlett Carre
Gunsmoke Ranch *37* Joseph Kane
Gunsmoke Range *52* Lewis D. Collins
Gunsmoke Trail *38* Sam Newfield
Guru, The *68* James Ivory
Guru *89* Umesh Mehra
Guru Dakshina *86* Dayal Nihalani
Guru das Siete Cidades *72* Carlos Bini
Guru the Mad Monk *71* Andy Milligan
Gus *76* Vincent McEveety
Gusanos, Los *77* Camilo Vila
Gusarskaya Ballada *62* Eldar Ryazanov
Gusher, The *21* Raoul Barré, Charles Bowers
Gustaf Wasa *26* John W. Brunius
Gustav Mond...Du Gehst So Stille *27* Reinhold Schünzel
Gustav Vigeland *68* Jørgen Roos
Gustave Est Médium *21* Louis Feuillade
Gustave Moreau *61* Nelly Kaplan
Gutai Kenkai *31* Heinosuke Gosho
Guts in the Sun *58* Claude Bernard-Aubert
Gutter *54* Kaneto Shindo
Gutter Girls *63* Robert Hartford-Davis
Gutter Magdalene, The *16* George Melford
Guttersnipe, The *22* Dallas M. Fitzgerald
Guttersnipes *49* Ulf Greber, Arne Skouen
Guvernørens Datter *12* August Blom
Guv'nor, The *35* Milton Rosmer
Guy, a Gal and a Pal, A *45* Budd Boetticher
Guy Called Caesar, A *62* Frank Marshall
Guy Could Change, A *45* William K. Howard
Guy Fawkes *23* Maurice Elvey
Guy Fawkes and the Gunpowder Plot *13* Ernest G. Batley
Guy from Harlem, The *77* René Martínez, Jr.
Guy Named Joe, A *43* Victor Fleming
Guy of Warwick *26* Fred Paul
Guy Who Came Back, The *51* Joseph M. Newman
Guy with a Grin *40* William Keighley
Guyana, Crime of the Century *80* René Cardona, Jr.
Guyana, Cult of the Damned *80* René Cardona, Jr.
Guys and Dolls *55* Joseph L. Mankiewicz
Guys of the Sea *57* Kaneto Shindo
Gvozd v Sapogye *32* Mikhail Kalatozov
Gwendoline *84* Just Jaeckin
Gwiazda Piołun *88* Henryk Kluba
Gwiazdy Muszą Płonąć *54* Witold Lesiewicz, Andrzej Munk

Gwyneth of the Welsh Hills 21 F. Martin Thornton
Gyakufunsha Kazoku 84 Sogo Ishii
Gyakuten Ryokō 70 Shoji Segawa
Gyalog a Mennyországba 59 Imre Fehér
Gyarmat a Föld Alatt 51 Zoltán Fábri
Gycklarnas Afton 53 Ingmar Bergman
Gyermekek, Könyvek 62 Márta Mészáros
Gyermekrablás a Palánk Utcában 85 Sándor Mihályfy
Gyertek El a Névnapomra 83 Zoltán Fábri
Gyimesi Vadvirág 39 Ákos von Ráthonyi
Gyldne Smil, Det 35 Pál Fejős
Gym Dandy, A 27 Sam Newfield
Gym Jams 22 Raoul Barré, Charles Bowers
Gym Jams 38 Manny Gould, Ben Harrison
Gymkata 85 Robert Clouse
Gymnasium Jim 22 Roy Del Ruth
Gymnastics, Indian Club Performer 1897 George Albert Smith
Gymnasts, The 61 Bruce Baillie
Gyppo Loggers 57 Allan King
Gypsies 36 M. Goldblatt, Eugene Schneider
Gypsies 62 István Gaál
Gypsy 36 Roy William Neill
Gypsy 62 Mervyn LeRoy
Gypsy, The 85 Philippe de Broca
Gypsy and the Gentleman, The 57 Joseph Losey
Gypsy Baron, The 54 Arthur Maria Rabenalt
Gypsy Blood 11 Urban Gad
Gypsy Blood 14 Robert Dinesen
Gypsy Blood 18 Ernst Lubitsch
Gypsy Blood 50 Rouben Mamoulian, Michael Powell, Emeric Pressburger
Gypsy Caravan, The 88 Emir Kusturica
Gypsy Colt 53 Andrew Marton
Gypsy Courage 26 Geoffrey H. Malins, H. B. Parkinson
Gypsy Fury 49 Christian-Jaque
Gypsy Girl 65 John Mills
Gypsy Joe 16 Clarence Badger*
Gypsy Land 30 Alexander Oumansky
Gypsy Lover, The 09 Lewin Fitzhamon
Gypsy Melody 36 Edmond T. Gréville
Gypsy Moths, The 69 John Frankenheimer
Gypsy of the North 28 Scott Pembroke
Gypsy Passion 20 Louis Mercanton
Gypsy Queen, The 13 Mack Sennett
Gypsy Romance, A 14 Wallace Reid
Gypsy Trail, The 18 Walter Edwards
Gypsy Ways 40 Géza von Bolváry
Gypsy Wildcat 44 Roy William Neill
Gypsy's Baby, The 09 Lewin Fitzhamon
Gypsy's Curse, The 14 Will P. Kellino
Gypsy's Trust, The 17 Edward Sloman
Gyurkovics, The 20 John W. Brunius
Gyurkovisarna 20 John W. Brunius
H.A.R.M. Machine, The 65 Gerd Oswald
H.E.A.L.T.H. 79 Robert Altman
H. G. Wells' New Invisible Man 57 Alfredo B. Crevenna
H. G. Wells' The Shape of Things to Come 79 George McCowan
H. M. Pulham, Esq. 41 King Vidor
H.M.S. Defiant 61 Lewis Gilbert
HMS Minelayer 41 Henry Cass

H-Man, The 58 Inoshiro Honda
H.O. 66 Arturo Ripstein
H.O.G. 79 Donald Wrye
H.O.T.S. 79 Gerald Seth Sindell
H. P. Lovecraft's Re-Animator 85 Stuart Gordon
H.R. Pufnstuf 70 Hollingsworth Morse
H2O 29 Ralph Steiner
Ha! Ha! Ha! 34 Dave Fleischer
Haagschool, Den 62 André Delvaux
Haakon VII 52 Henning Carlsen, Titus Vibé-Müller
Habañera, La 37 Douglas Sirk
Habeas Corpus 28 James Parrott
Habit 21 Edwin Carewe
Habit Ne Fait Pas le Moine, L' 08 Georges Méliès
Habit of Happiness, The 16 Allan Dwan
Habit Rabbit 63 Joseph Barbera, William Hanna
Habit Troubles 64 Joseph Barbera, William Hanna
Habitación de Alquilar 60 Miguel Picazo
Habla Mudita 73 Manuel Gutiérrez Aragón
Habricha el Hashemesh 72 Menahem Golan
Haceldama 19 Julien Duvivier
Haceldama ou Le Prix du Sang 19 Julien Duvivier
Hacha para la Luna de Miel, Una 69 Mario Bava
Hack 'Em High 87 Gorman Bechard
Hadaka no Jūkyū-Sai 70 Kaneto Shindo
Hadaka no Machi 37 Tomu Uchida
Hadaka no Shima 60 Kaneto Shindo
Hadaka no Taishō 64 Hiromichi Horikawa
Hadda 86 Mohamed Aboulouakar
Haddem Baad's Elopement 16 L. M. Glackens
Hadduta Misriya 82 Youssef Chahine
Hadimrsku Doesn't Know 31 Martin Frič, Karel Lamač
Hadley's Rebellion 84 Fred Walton
Hadota Misreya 82 Youssef Chahine
Hævnen 11 August Blom
Hævnens Nat 15 Benjamin Christensen
Hævnet 11 August Blom
Hagbard and Signe 67 Gabriel Axel
Haggard's "She" — The Pillar of Fire 1899 Georges Méliès
Hagiographia 71 Gregory Markopoulos
Hagiva 55 Thorold Dickinson
Hägringen 59 Peter Weiss
Haha 62 Kaneto Shindo
Haha Ko Gusa 59 So Yamamura
Haha no Kyoku 37 Satsuo Yamamoto
Haha o Kōwazu-Ya 34 Yasujiro Ozu
Haha wa Shinazu 42 Mikio Naruse
Haha yo Kimi no Na o Kegasu Nakare 28 Heinosuke Gosho
Haha yo Koishi 26 Heinosuke Gosho
Hai-T'an-Shang-Te Yi T'ien 83 Edward Yang
Hai zi Wang 87 Kaige Chen
Haie und Kleine Fische 57 Frank Wisbar
Haikyo no Naka 23 Kenji Mizoguchi
Hail 73 Fred Levinson
Hail and Farewell 36 Ralph Ince
Hail Brother! 35 Leigh Jason

Hail Days 62 György Révész
Hail! Hail! Rock 'n' Roll 87 Taylor Hackford
Hail Hero! 69 David Miller
Hail, Mafia 65 Raoul Lévy
Hail, Mary 83 Jean-Luc Godard
Hail the Conquering Hero 44 Preston Sturges
Hail the Hero 24 James W. Horne
Hail, the Princess 30 Stephen Roberts
Hail the Woman 21 John Griffith Wray
Hail to the Chief 73 Fred Levinson
Hail to the Rangers 43 William Berke
Haine, La 14 Henri Pouctal
Haine 18 Georges Lacroix
Hair 79 Miloš Forman
Hair of the Dog 61 Terry Bishop
Hair Raiser 25 William C. Nolan
Hair-Raising Episode, A 15 Ernest G. Batley
Hair-Raising Episode in One Splash, A 14 Edwin J. Collins
Hair Raising Hare 45 Chuck Jones
Hair Restorer 07 Lewin Fitzhamon
Hair Trigger Baxter 26 Jack Nelson
Hair Trigger Casey 16 Frank Borzage
Hair-Trigger Casey 36 Harry Fraser
Hair Trigger Stuff 20 B. Reeves Eason
Hairbreadth Escape of Jack Sheppard, The 00 Walter R. Booth
Haircut 63 Andy Warhol
Hairdresser No. 3 47 Tso-lin Wang
Hairpin Trail, The 14 Ethyle Batley
Hairpins 20 Fred Niblo
Hairspray 88 John Waters
Hairy Ape, The 44 Alfred Santell
Hairy Hercules 60 John Halas*
Haiti Dreams of Democracy 88 Jonathan Demme, Jo Menell
Haitian Corner 88 Raoul Peck
Haizan no Uta wa Kanashi 22 Kenji Mizoguchi
Hajen Som Visste För Mycket 89 Claes Eriksson
Hajnal 71 István Szabó
Hajnali Háztetők 86 János Domolky
Hakai 48 Keisuke Kinoshita
Hakai 61 Kon Ichikawa
Hakaitz Shel Avia 88 Eli Cohen
Hakarka Ha a Dom 53 Thorold Dickinson
Hakoiri Musume 34 Yasujiro Ozu
Hakone Fūunroke 51 Satsuo Yamamoto
Hakrav al Hava'ad 86 Avi Cohen
Hakuchi 51 Akira Kurosawa
Hakuchū no Tōrima 66 Nagisa Oshima
Hakugin no Ōza 35 Tomu Uchida
Hakuja Den 61 Kazuhiko Okabe, Taiji Yabushita
Hal, El 81 Ahmed El Maanouni
Hal Kemp and His Orchestra 41 Jean Negulesco
Halahaka 78 Avi Nesher
Halálcsengő, A 17 Michael Curtiz
Halálos Csönd 18 Béla Balázs
Halbblut 19 Fritz Lang
Halbseide 25 Richard Oswald
Halbstarken, Die 56 Georg Tressler
Halcón y la Presa, El 66 Sergio Sollima
Haldane of the Secret Service 23 Harry Houdini

Haleurs de Bateaux, Les *1896* Georges Méliès
Half a Bride *28* Gregory La Cava
Half a Century of Songs *54* Domenico Paolella
Half a Chance *20* Robert Thornby
Half-a-Dollar Bill *23* W. S. Van Dyke
Half a Hero *53* Don Weis
Half a House *79* Brice Mack
Half a Lifetime *86* Daniel Petrie
Half a Man *65* Vittorio De Seta
Half a Rogue *16* Henry Otto
Half a Sinner *34* Kurt Neumann
Half a Sinner *40* Al Christie
Half a Sixpence *67* George Sidney
Half a Truth *22* Sinclair Hill
Half an Hour *20* Harley Knoles
Half Angel *36* Sidney Lanfield
Half Angel *51* Richard Sale
Half Back Buster *28* Sam Newfield
Half-Baked Relations *34* Charles Lamont
Half Breed *13* Victor Sjöström
Half-Breed, The *16* Allan Dwan
Half Breed *19* Fritz Lang
Half Breed, The *22* Charles Taylor
Half-Breed, The *52* Stuart Gilmore
Half Caste *19* Fritz Lang
Half-Day Excursion, The *35* A. L. Dean
Half-Duan Qing *85* Guoxi Chen
Half Fare Hare *56* Robert McKimson
Half Human *55* Kenneth Crane, Inoshiro Honda
Half-Man *86* Sogo Ishii
Half Man Half Monster *62* George Breakston, Kenneth Crane
Half Marriage *29* William Cowen
Half Million Bribe, The *16* Edgar Jones
Half Moon Street *86* Bob Swaim
Half Naked Truth, The *32* Gregory La Cava
Half of Heaven *86* Manuel Gutiérrez Aragón
Half of Love *86* Mary Jiménez
Half Past Midnight *48* William F. Claxton
Half Pint, The *60* Erven Jourdan
Half-Pint Hero, A *27* Charles Lamont
Half-Pint Pygmy *48* Tex Avery
Half Right, Half Left *85* Sergio Martino
Half Shot at Sunrise *30* Paul Sloane
Half-Truth *83* Govind Nihalani
Half Way to Heaven *29* George Abbott
Half Way to Hollywood *38* Charlie Chase
Half Way to Shanghai *42* John Rawlins
Halfbreed's Gratitude, A *11* Lewin Fitzhamon
Halfway Girl, The *25* John Francis Dillon
Halfway House, The *43* Basil Dearden
Halhatatlanság *59* Miklós Jancsó
Halka *38* Julius Gardan
Hall of Lost Steps, The *60* Jaromil Jireš
Hall of the Crying Deer, The *86* Kon Ichikawa
Hallelujah! *29* King Vidor
Hallelujah, I'm a Bum *33* Lewis Milestone
Hallelujah, I'm a Tramp *33* Lewis Milestone
Hallelujah the Hills *63* Adolfas Mekas
Hallelujah Trail, The *65* John Sturges
Halliday Brand, The *57* Joseph H. Lewis
Halló Budapest! *35* Ladislas Vajda

Hallo Caesar! *26* Reinhold Schünzel
Hallo Everybody! *33* Hans Richter
Hallo! Hallo! Hier Spricht Berlin *31* Julien Duvivier
Halloween *61* Tadeusz Konwicki
Halloween *78* John Carpenter
Halloween II *81* Richard Rosenthal
Halloween III: Season of the Witch *82* Tommy Lee Wallace
Halloween IV: The Return of Michael Myers *88* Dwight H. Little
Halloween 5 *89* Dominique Othénin-Girard
Halloween 5: The Revenge of Michael Myers *89* Dominique Othénin-Girard
Halloween Night at the Seminary *04* Edwin S. Porter
Halls of Anger *70* Paul Bogart
Halls of Montezuma, The *50* Lewis Milestone
Hallucinated Alchemist, An *1897* Georges Méliès
Hallucination *19* Pál Fejös
Hallucination de l'Alchimiste, L' *1897* Georges Méliès
Hallucination Generation *66* Santos Alcocer
Hallucinationer *52* Peter Weiss
Hallucinations *52* Peter Weiss
Hallucinations du Baron de Münchausen, Les *10* Georges Méliès
Hallucinations Pharmaceutiques *08* Georges Méliès
Hallucinators, The *70* William Grefé
Halodhia Choraye Baodhan Khai *88* Jahnu Barua
Hälsningar *34* Ivar Johansson
Halvblod *13* Victor Sjöström
Ham and Eggs *27* Roy Del Ruth
Ham and Eggs *33* Walter Lantz
Ham and Eggs at the Front *27* Roy Del Ruth
Ham Artist, The *14* Charles Chaplin
Ham in a Role, A *49* Robert McKimson
Ham the Lineman *14* Marshall Neilan
Ham the Piano Mover *14* Marshall Neilan
Hamagure no Komoriuta *73* Kozaburo Yoshimura
Hamara Shaher *85* Anand Patwardhan
Hamari Jung *87* Rajesh Bahaduri
Hamateur Night *38* Tex Avery
Hambone and Hillie *83* Roy Watts
¿Hambre Cómo Ves? *86* Paul Leduc
Hamburg *38* Walter Ruttmann
Hamburg *61* Jørgen Roos
Hamburg — Weltstrasse See *38* Walter Ruttmann
Hamburg — Weltstrasse Welthafen *38* Walter Ruttmann
Hamburger *86* Mike Marvin
Hamburger Hill *87* John Irvin
Hamburger Krankheit, Die *79* Peter Fleischmann
Hamburger...The Motion Picture *86* Mike Marvin
Hame'ahev *86* Michal Bat-Adam
Hamile *65* Terry Bishop
Hamilton in the Music Festival *61* John Halas
Hamilton the Musical Elephant *61* John

Halas
Hamles *60* Jerzy Skolimowski
Hamlet *07* Georges Méliès
Hamlet *10* August Blom
Hamlet *10* Mario Caserini
Hamlet *12* Charles Raymond
Hamlet *13* J. Stuart Blackton
Hamlet *13* Hay Plumb
Hamlet *15* Will P. Kellino
Hamlet *20* Svend Gade
Hamlet *48* Laurence Olivier
Hamlet *62* Franz Peter Wirth
Hamlet *63* Grigori Kozintsev
Hamlet *64* Bill Colleran, John Gielgud
Hamlet *69* Tony Richardson
Hamlet *76* Celestino Coronado
Hamlet *87* Aki Kaurismäki
Hamlet *90* Franco Zeffirelli
Hamlet Goes Business *87* Aki Kaurismäki
Hamlet Liikemaailmassa *87* Aki Kaurismäki
Hamlet, Prince de Danemark *07* Georges Méliès
Hamlet, Prince of Denmark *07* Georges Méliès
Hamlet's Castle *50* Jørgen Roos
Hammer *72* Bruce Clark
Hammer Against Witches, A *69* Otakar Vávra
Hammer the Toff *52* Maclean Rogers
Hammerhead *68* David Miller
Hammersmith Is Out *72* Peter Ustinov
Hammett *81* Wim Wenders
Hammond Mystery, The *42* John Brahm
Hämnaren *15* Mauritz Stiller
Hamnstad *48* Ingmar Bergman
Hamp *64* Joseph Losey
Hampelmann, Der *31* E. W. Emo
Hampels Abenteuer *15* Richard Oswald
Hampi *60* Jean Rouch
Hampton Court Palace *26* Bert Cann
Hams That Couldn't Be Cured, The *42* Walter Lantz
Hamsin *82* Daniel Wachsmann
Hamster, The *46* Karel Zeman
Hamster of Happiness, The *78* Hal Ashby
Hamsters of Happiness *78* Hal Ashby
Han Ye *85* Wen Que
Hana *41* Kozaburo Yoshimura
Hana *67* Yoji Kuri
Hana Hiraku *48* Kon Ichikawa
Hana Ichimomme *86* Toshiya Ito
Hana no Nagadosū *54* Teinosuke Kinugasa
Hana no Yoshiwara Hyakuningiri *60* Tomu Uchida
Hana to Namida to Honō *70* Umeji Inoue
Hanakago no Uta *37* Heinosuke Gosho
Hanamuko no Negoto *34* Heinosuke Gosho
Hanane Kadiet el Yom *44* Kamel Salim
Hanare Goze Orin *77* Masahiro Shinoda
Hanasake Jijii *23* Teinosuke Kinugasa
Hanasaku Minato *43* Keisuke Kinoshita
Hanauma Bay *85* Tommy Lee Wallace
Hanayome no Negoto *33* Heinosuke Gosho
Hanayome-San wa Sekai Ichi *59* Kaneto Shindo
Hand, The *60* Henry Cass

Hans le Marin 48 François Villiers
Hans Memling 38 André Cauvin
Hans Nåds Testamente 19 Victor Sjöström
Hans Rigtige Kone 16 Forest Holger-Madsen
Hans Trutz im Schlaraffenland 17 Paul Wegener
Hans Vanskeligste Rolle 12 August Blom
Hanseaten 25 Gerhard Lamprecht
Hansel and Gretel 09 J. Searle Dawley, Edwin S. Porter
Hansel and Gretel 54 John Paul
Hansel and Gretel 55 Lotte Reiniger
Hansel and Gretel 65 Walter Janssen
Hansel and Gretel 87 Len Talan
Hansel und Gretel 65 Walter Janssen
Hansom Driver, The 13 Mack Sennett
Hansu Kurishitan Anderusan no Sekai 68 Al Kilgore, Charles McCann, Kimio Yabuki
Hantise, La 12 Louis Feuillade
Hantise 22 Jean Kemm
Hanul dintre Dealuri 88 Christiana Nicolae
Hanussen 55 O. W. Fischer, Georg Marischka
Hanussen 87 István Szabó
Hány az Óra, Vekker Úr? 85 Péter Bacsó
Hapax Legomena I: Nostalgia 71 Hollis Frampton
Hapax Legomena II: Poetic Justice 71 Hollis Frampton
Hapax Legomena III: Critical Mass 71 Hollis Frampton
Hapax Legomena IV: Travelling Matte 71 Hollis Frampton
Hapax Legomena V: Ordinary Matter 72 Hollis Frampton
Hapax Legomena VI: Remote Control 72 Hollis Frampton
Hapax Legomena VII: Special Effects 72 Hollis Frampton
Ha'penny Breeze 49 Don Sharp, Frank Worth
Happening, The 67 Elliot Silverstein
Happening der Vampire 70 Freddie Francis
Happening in Africa 70 Zygmunt Sulistrowski
Happening of the Vampire, The 70 Freddie Francis
Happenings, The 79 Ho Yim
Happidrome 43 Phil Brandon
Happiest Days of Your Life, The 50 Frank Launder
Happiest Man on Earth, The 40 David Miller
Happiest Married Couple in Vienna, The 38 Karl Heinz Martin
Happiest Millionaire, The 67 Norman Tokar
Happily Buried 39 Felix E. Feist
Happily Ever After 67 Francesco Rosi
Happily Ever After 85 Bruno Barreto
Happily Ever After 90 John Howley
Happiness 17 Reginald Barker
Happiness 23 King Vidor
Happiness 34 Alexander Medvedkin
Happiness 64 Agnès Varda
Happiness 81 Kon Ichikawa

Happiness à la Mode 19 Walter Edwards
Happiness Ahead 28 William A. Seiter
Happiness Ahead 34 Mervyn LeRoy
Happiness C.O.D. 35 Charles Lamont
Happiness Cage, The 72 Bernard Girard
Happiness of Asya, The 66 Andrei Mikhalkov-Konchalovsky
Happiness of Others, The 18 Germaine Dulac
Happiness of Three Women, The 16 William Desmond Taylor
Happiness of Three Women, The 54 Maurice Elvey
Happiness of Us Alone 62 Zenzo Matsuyama
Happiness Strikes Again 86 Jean-Luc Trotignon
Happy 34 Fred Zelnik
Happy Alcoholic, The 84 Karl Francis
Happy Alexander 67 Yves Robert
Happy Anniversary 59 David Miller
Happy Anniversary 61 Jean-Claude Carrière, Pierre Etaix
Happy Anniversary 72 Claude Lelouch
Happy As Can Be 58 Jack Gold
Happy As the Grass Was Green 73 Charles Davis
Happy Asya 66 Andrei Mikhalkov-Konchalovsky
Happy Bachelors, The 85 Chong Song
Happy Bigamist 87 Chan Friend
Happy Birthday 29 James Parrott
Happy Birthday 38 Art Davis, Sid Marcus
Happy Birthday Blackie 63 Richard Leacock
Happy Birthday Davy 70 Richard Fontaine
Happy Birthday Gemini 80 Richard Benner
Happy Birthday to Me 80 J. Lee-Thompson
Happy Birthday, Wanda June 71 Mark Robson
Happy Butterfly 34 Art Davis, Sid Marcus
Happy Circus, The 50 Jiří Trnka
Happy Day 76 Pantelis Voulgaris
Happy Days 30 Ben Stoloff
Happy Days 36 Ubbe Iwerks
Happy Days Are Here Again 35 Norman Lee
Happy Days Revue 35 Norman Lee
Happy Daze 20 Charles Reisner
Happy Deathday 69 Henry Cass
Happy Din Don 86 Michael Hui
Happy Divorce, A 74 Henning Carlsen
Happy Dustmen, The 13 Will P. Kellino
Happy Dustmen Play Golf, The 14 Will P. Kellino
Happy Dustmen's Christmas, The 14 Will P. Kellino
Happy End 66 Oldřich Lipský
Happy End 88 Marcel Schupbach
Happy Ending, The 25 George A. Cooper
Happy Ending, The 31 Millard Webb
Happy Ending, The 69 Richard Brooks
Happy Event 39 Patrick Brunner
Happy Event in the Poorluck Family, A 11 Lewin Fitzhamon
Happy Ever After 32 Robert Stevenson
Happy Ever After 54 Mario Zampi
Happy Family, The 34 Alfred E. Green
Happy Family, A 35 Manny Gould, Ben

Harrison
Happy Family, The 36 Maclean Rogers
Happy Family 46 Ronald Haines
Happy Family, The 52 Muriel Box
Happy Gets the Razoo 17 Gregory La Cava
Happy Go Loopy 61 Joseph Barbera, William Hanna
Happy Go Lovely 51 H. Bruce Humberstone
Happy-Go-Lucky 14 James Young
Happy Go Lucky 33 Lewis Milestone
Happy Go Lucky 36 Aubrey H. Scotto
Happy Go Lucky 42 Kurt Bernhardt
Happy Go Lucky 55 Joseph Barbera, William Hanna
Happy-Go-Nutty 44 Tex Avery
Happy Gypsies 67 Aleksandar Petrović
Happy Homecoming, Comrade 86 Lefteris Xanthopoulos
Happy Hooker, The 75 Nicholas Sgarro
Happy Hooker Goes Hollywood, The 80 Alan Roberts
Happy Hooker Goes to Washington, The 77 William A. Levey
Happy Hooldini 20 Gregory La Cava
Happy Hooligan 00 J. Stuart Blackton
Happy Hooligan and His Airship 02 Edwin S. Porter
Happy Hooligan April-Fooled 01 Edwin S. Porter
Happy Hooligan at the Circus 17 Gregory La Cava
Happy Hooligan at the Picnic 17 Gregory La Cava
Happy Hooligan, Double Cross Nurse 17 Gregory La Cava
Happy Hooligan in a Trap 03 Edwin S. Porter
Happy Hooligan in Oil 20 William C. Nolan
Happy Hooligan in Soft 17 Gregory La Cava
Happy Hooligan in the Zoo 17 Gregory La Cava
Happy Hooligan Surprised 01 Edwin S. Porter
Happy Hooligan Tries the Movies Again 16 Gregory La Cava
Happy Hooligan Turns Burglar 02 Edwin S. Porter
Happy Hooligan's Interrupted Lunch 03 Edwin S. Porter
Happy Hour 85 John De Bello
Happy in the Morning 38 Pat Jackson*
Happy Is the Bride! 57 Roy Boulting
Happy Journey 43 Otakar Vávra
Happy Knowledge 67 Jean-Luc Godard
Happy Land 43 Irving Pichel
Happy Landing 31 Charles Reisner
Happy Landing 34 Robert North Bradbury
Happy Landing 38 Roy Del Ruth
Happy Life, A 51 Vojtěch Jasný, Karel Kachyňa
Happy Man, The 06 Arthur Cooper
Happy Mother's Day, A 63 Joyce Chopra, Richard Leacock
Happy Mother's Day...Love George 73 Darren McGavin
Happy Mother's Day Mrs. Fisher 63 Joyce Chopra, Richard Leacock

Happy New Year 72 Claude Lelouch
Happy New Year 85 John G. Avildsen
Happy New Year Caper, The 72 Claude Lelouch
Happy New Year '49 86 Štole Popov
Happy Old Man 23 Teinosuke Kinugasa
Happy Pair, The 21 Fred Paul
Happy Prisoner, The 24 Hugh Croise
Happy Rascals, The 26 Frank Miller
Happy Road, The 56 Gene Kelly
Happy Sunday, A 89 Olegario Barrera
Happy Thieves, The 61 George Marshall
Happy Tho' Married 36 Arthur Ripley
Happy Though Married 18 Fred Niblo
Happy Time, The 52 Richard Fleischer
Happy Times 49 Henry Koster
Happy Together 89 Mel Damski
Happy Tots 39 Ben Harrison
Happy Tots' Expedition, The 40 Ben Harrison
Happy Warrior, The 17 F. Martin Thornton
Happy Warrior, The 25 J. Stuart Blackton
Happy We 83 Lasse Hallström
Happy Years, The 50 William A. Wellman
Happy You and Merry Me 36 Dave Fleischer
Här Börjar Äventyret 65 Jörn Donner
Här Har Du Ditt Liv 66 Jan Troell
Har Jeg Ret til At Tage Mit Eget Liv? 19 Forest Holger-Madsen
Här Kommer Bärsärkarna 65 Arne Mattsson
Här Ni Något att Förtulla 12 Victor Sjöström
Hara-Kiri 19 Fritz Lang
Hara-Kiri 34 Nicolas Farkas
Harag Napja, A 53 Károly Makk
Harakiri 62 Masaki Kobayashi
Harald Handfaste 46 Erik Faustman
Harangok Rómába Mentek, A 58 Miklós Jancsó
Harangok Városa—Veszprém 66 Márta Mészáros
Harapós Férj 39 Márton Keleti
Harassed Hero, The 54 Maurice Elvey
Harbor in the Fog 23 Kenji Mizoguchi
Harbor in the Heart of Europe 40 Alexander Hammid
Harbor Light Yokohama 70 Meijiro Umezu
Harbor Lights 63 Maury Dexter
Harbor of Missing Men 50 R. G. Springsteen
Harbor Rats 57 Kaneto Shindo
Harbour Lights, The 14 Percy Nash
Harbour Lights, The 23 Tom Terriss
Harcerze na Złocie 52 Wojciech Has
Hard Asfalt 86 Sølve Skagen
Hard Asphalt 86 Sølve Skagen
Hard Boiled 19 Victor Schertzinger
Hard Boiled 25 Leo McCarey
Hard Boiled 26 John G. Blystone
Hard-Boiled Canary, The 41 Andrew L. Stone
Hard-Boiled Haggerty 27 Charles Brabin
Hard Boiled Mahoney 47 William Beaudine
Hard Boiled Rose 29 F. Harmon Weight

Hard Boiled Yeggs 30 Edward Buzzell
Hard Bunch, The 69 Greg Corarito
Hard Cash 21 Edwin J. Collins
Hard Choices 84 Rick King
Hard Contract 69 S. Lee Pogostin
Hard Country 81 David Greene
Hard Day for Archie, A 73 Jim McBride
Hard Day's Night, A 64 Richard Lester
Hard Driver 73 Lamont Johnson
Hard, Fast and Beautiful 51 Ida Lupino
Hard Feelings 81 Daryl Duke
Hard Fists 27 William Wyler
Hard Game 86 Ugo Giorgetti
Hard Guy 41 Elmer Clifton
Hard Hittin' Hamilton 24 Richard Thorpe
Hard Hombre 31 Otto Brower
Hard Is the Life of an Adventurer 41 Martin Frič
Hård Klang 52 Arne Mattsson
Hard Knocks 80 Don McLennan
Hard Knocks and Love Taps 21 Roy Del Ruth
Hard Labor on the River Douro 29 Manoel De Oliveira
Hard Life 28 Abram Room
Hard Life of an Adventurer, The 41 Martin Frič
Hard Lions 19 Raoul Barré, Charles Bowers
Hard Luck 21 Edward F. Cline, Buster Keaton
Hard Luck Santa Claus, A 20 Raoul Barré, Charles Bowers
Hard Man, The 57 George Sherman
Hard on the Trail 69 Greg Corarito
Hard Part Begins, The 73 Paul Lynch
Hard Ride, The 71 Burt Topper
Hard Road, The 70 Gary Graver
Hard Rock Breed, The 18 Raymond Wells
Hard Rock Harrigan 35 David Howard
Hard Rock Zombies 85 Krishna Shah
Hard Shell Game, A 21 Raoul Barré, Charles Bowers
Hard Steel 41 Norman Walker
Hard Ticket to Hawaii 87 Andy Sidaris
Hard Times 09 Percy Stow
Hard Times 15 Thomas Bentley
Hard Times 30 Mikio Naruse
Hard Times 75 Walter Hill
Hard Times 88 João Botelho
Hard Times for Dracula 59 Steno
Hard Times for Vampires 59 Steno
Hard to Be a God 89 Peter Fleischmann
Hard to Beat 09 Edwin S. Porter
Hard to Get 29 William Beaudine
Hard to Get 38 Ray Enright
Hard to Handle 32 Mervyn LeRoy
Hard to Handle 37 C. C. Coleman, Jr.
Hard to Hold 83 Larry Peerce
Hard to Kill 90 Bruce Malmuth
Hard Trail 69 Greg Corarito
Hard Traveling 85 Dan Bessie
Hard Way, The 16 Walter West
Hard Way, The 42 Vincent Sherman
Hard Way, The 80 Michael Dryhurst
Hard Wills 22 John W. Brunius
Hard Won Happiness 58 Alexander Stolper
Hårda Viljor 22 John W. Brunius
Hardbodies 84 Mark Griffiths

Hardbodies II 86 Mark Griffiths
Hardboiled 29 Ralph Ince
Hardcase and Fist 89 Tony M. Zarindast
Hardcore 77 James Kenelm Clarke
Hardcore 79 Paul Schrader
Hardcore Life, The 79 Paul Schrader
Hardcover 88 Tibor Takacs
Harder They Come, The 73 Perry Henzell
Harder They Fall, The 56 Mark Robson
Hardly a Criminal 47 Hugo Fregonese
Hardly Working 79 Jerry Lewis
Hardrock Dome Episode No. 1 19 Pat Sullivan
Hardrock Dome Episode No. 2 19 Pat Sullivan
Hardrock Dome Episode No. 3 19 Pat Sullivan
Hardship of Miles Standish 40 Friz Freleng
Hardships of Destiny 86 Gerardo Vallejo
Hardware 90 Richard Stanley
Hardworking Clerk 31 Mikio Naruse
Hardys Ride High, The 39 George B. Seitz
Hare Brained Hypnotist, The 42 Friz Freleng
Hare-Breadth Hurry 63 Chuck Jones
Hare Brush 55 Friz Freleng
Hare Conditioned 45 Chuck Jones
Hare-Do 49 Friz Freleng
Hare Force 44 Friz Freleng
Hare Grows in Manhattan, A 47 Friz Freleng
Hare Krishna 66 Jonas Mekas
Hare Lift 52 Friz Freleng
Hare Mail, The 31 Walter Lantz
Hare Remover 46 Frank Tashlin
Hare Ribbin' 44 Robert Clampett
Hare Splitter 48 Friz Freleng
Hare Tonic 45 Chuck Jones
Hare Trigger 45 Friz Freleng
Hare Trimmed 53 Friz Freleng
Hare-Way to the Stars 58 Chuck Jones
Hare We Go 51 Friz Freleng
Hare-abian Knights 59 Ken Harris
Haredevil Hare 47 Chuck Jones
Hare-less Wolf 58 Friz Freleng
Harem, L' 67 Marco Ferreri
Harem 85 Arthur Joffe
Harem Bunch, or War and Peace, The 69 Paul Hunt
Harem Bunch, or War and Piece, The 69 Paul Hunt
Harem Girl 52 Edward Bernds
Harem Holiday 65 Gene Nelson
Harem Knight, A 26 Edward F. Cline
Harem Scarem 27 Walt Disney
Haremseventyr, Et 14 Forest Holger-Madsen
Hare-um Scare-um 39 Cal Dalton, Ben Hardaway
Hari Hondal Bargadar 80 Shyam Benegal
Hari sa Hari, Lahi sa Lahi 87 Lili Chao, Hsiao Lang, Eddie Romero
Haricot, Le 62 Edmond Séchan
Harishandra 12 D. G. Phalke
Harlan County, U.S.A. 76 Barbara Kopple
Harlekin 31 Lotte Reiniger
Harlekin és Szerelmese 66 Imre Fehér

Hats Off 36 Boris Petroff
Hats Off to Rhythm 46 Albert S. Rogell
Hatsukoi 25 Heinosuke Gosho
Hatsukoi Jigokuhen 68 Susumu Hani
Hatter's Castle 41 Lance Comfort
Hatter's Ghosts, The 81 Claude Chabrol
Hatton Garden Robbery, The 15 Ethyle Batley
Haunted, The 57 Jacques Tourneur
Haunted, The 76 Michael A. DeGaetano
Haunted 83 Michael Roemer
Haunted and the Hunted, The 62 Francis Ford Coppola
Haunted Bedroom, The 07 Walter R. Booth
Haunted Bedroom, The 19 Fred Niblo
Haunted by Hawkeye 13 Hay Plumb
Haunted by His Mother-in-Law 13 Frank Wilson
Haunted Castle, The 1896 Georges Méliès
Haunted Castle, The 1897 George Albert Smith
Haunted Castle, The 21 F. W. Murnau
Haunted Castle, The 60 Kurt Hoffmann
Haunted Castle, The 69 Tokuzo Tanaka
Haunted Cave, The 59 Morihei Magatani
Haunted Cavern, The 1898 Georges Méliès
Haunted Curiosity Shop, The 01 Walter R. Booth
Haunted England 61 Michael Winner
Haunted Gold 32 Mack V. Wright
Haunted Harbor 44 Spencer G. Bennet, Wallace A. Grissell
Haunted Homestead, The 27 William Wyler
Haunted Honeymoon 40 Arthur Woods
Haunted Honeymoon 86 Gene Wilder
Haunted Hotel, The 06 J. Stuart Blackton
Haunted Hotel, The 18 Fred Rains
Haunted House, The 17 Albert Parker
Haunted House, The 21 Edward F. Cline, Buster Keaton
Haunted House, The 22 Erle C. Kenton
Haunted House, The 23 Abel Gance
Haunted House, The 28 Benjamin Christensen
Haunted House, The 29 Walt Disney, Ubbe Iwerks
Haunted House, The 40 Robert McGowan
Haunted House of Horror, The 69 Michael Armstrong
Haunted Houseboat, The 04 Alf Collins
Haunted Island 28 Robert F. Hill
Haunted Lady, The 29 Wesley Ruggles
Haunted Life of a Dragon-Tattooed Lass, The 70 Teruo Ishii
Haunted Man, The 66 Stanley Willis
Haunted Manor, The 16 Edwin Middleton
Haunted Mine, The 46 Derwin Abrahams
Haunted Mouse, The 41 Tex Avery
Haunted Mouse 65 Chuck Jones
Haunted Night, The 57 Ernest Pintoff
Haunted Oak, The 04 Lewin Fitzhamon
Haunted Pajamas 17 Fred J. Balshofer
Haunted Palace 49 Richard Fisher
Haunted Palace, The 63 Roger Corman
Haunted Picture Gallery, The 1899 George Albert Smith
Haunted Planet, The 65 Mario Bava

Haunted Ranch, The 26 Paul Hurst
Haunted Ranch, The 43 Robert E. Tansey
Haunted Range, The 26 Paul Hurst
Haunted Scene Painter, The 04 Walter R. Booth
Haunted Ship, The 27 Forrest K. Sheldon
Haunted Spooks 20 Hal Roach
Haunted Strangler, The 58 Robert Day
Haunted Summer 88 Ivan Passer
Haunted Trails 49 Lambert Hillyer
Haunted Valley 23 George Marshall
Haunters of the Deep 85 Andrew Bogle
Haunting, The 63 Robert Wise
Haunting of Castle Montego, The 66 Francis D. Lyon
Haunting of Hamilton High, The 87 Bruce Pittman
Haunting of Julia, The 76 Richard Loncraine
Haunting of M, The 79 Anna Thomas
Haunting of Morella, The 90 Jim Wynorski
Haunting of Silas P. Gould, The 15 Elwin Neame
Haunting Shadows 19 Henry King
Haunts 77 Herb Freed
Haunts for Rent 16 C. Allen Gilbert
Hauptdarsteller, Der 77 Reinhard Hauff
Hauptmann und Sein Held, Der 55 Max Nosseck
Hauptmann von Köln, Der 56 Slatan Dudow
Hauptmann von Köpenick, Der 31 Richard Oswald
Hauptmann von Köpenick, Der 56 Helmut Käutner
Haus am Fluss, Das 86 Roland Graf
Haus am Meer 72 Reinhard Hauff
Haus der Lüge, Das 25 Lupu Pick
Haus der Tausend Freuden 67 Jeremy Summers
Haus des Lebens 53 Karl Hartl
Haus in der Dragonergasse, Das 21 Richard Oswald
Haus in Montevideo, Das 63 Helmut Käutner
Haus Ohne Lachen, Das 23 Gerhard Lamprecht
Haut de Vent 42 Jacques De Baroncelli
Haut für Haut 61 Robert Hossein
Haut les Mains! 12 Louis Feuillade
Haut sur Ces Montagnes, La 45 Norman McLaren
Haute Infidélité 64 Mario Monicelli, Elio Petri, Franco Rossi, Luciano Salce
Haute Lisse 56 Jean Grémillon
Hauteterre 52 Jean Mitry
Havana 90 Sydney Pollack
Havana Rose 51 William Beaudine
Havana 1762 58 Tomás Gutiérrez Alea
Havana Widows 33 Ray Enright
Havárie 85 Antonín Kopřiva
Have a Cigar 14 Charles C. Calvert
Have a Heart 34 David Butler
Have a Nice Weekend 75 Michael Walters
Have It Out My Boy, Have It Out 11 A. E. Coleby
Have Rocket, Will Travel 59 David Lowell Rich
Have Some More Meat 15 Cecil Birch

Have You a Match? 13 Charles C. Calvert
Have You Got Any Castles? 38 Frank Tashlin
Have You Heard of the San Francisco Mime Troup? 68 Ronnie Davis, Don Lenzer, Fred Wardenburg
Have You Seen the Barefoot God? 86 Soo-gil Kim
Have You Thought of Talking to the Director? 62 Bruce Baillie
Havets Djävul 37 Pál Fejös
Havets Husmand 54 Henning Carlsen
Havets Melodi 34 John W. Brunius*
Havi 200 Fix 36 Béla Balázs
Havinck 87 Franz Weisz
Having a Go 83 Gillian Armstrong
Having a Wild Weekend 65 John Boorman
Having Wonderful Crime 45 A. Edward Sutherland
Having Wonderful Time 38 Alfred Santell, George Stevens
Havlandet 86 Lasse Glom
Havoc, The 16 Arthur Berthelet
Havoc 25 Rowland V. Lee
Havre 86 Juliet Berto
Havsgamarna 15 Victor Sjöström
Havsgammar 15 Victor Sjöström
Hawaii 66 George Roy Hill
Hawaii Beach Boy 61 Norman Taurog
Hawaii Calls 38 Edward F. Cline
Hawaiian Aye Aye 64 Gerry Chinquy
Hawaiian Birds 36 Dave Fleischer
Hawaiian Buckaroo 37 Ray Taylor
Hawaiian Nights 34 Paul Sloane
Hawaiian Nights 39 Albert S. Rogell
Hawaiian Nuts 17 William Beaudine
Hawaiians, The 70 Tom Gries
Hawk, The 17 Paul Scardon
Hawk, The 32 Fred Allen
Hawk, The 35 Edward Dmytryk
Hawk, The 40 Ramón Pereda
Hawk of Powder River, The 48 Ray Taylor
Hawk of the Hills 27 Spencer G. Bennet
Hawk of the Wilderness 38 John English, William Witney
Hawk of Wild River, The 52 Fred F. Sears
Hawk or Dove 86 Alfredo Gurrola
Hawk the Slayer 80 Terence Marcel
Hawken 86 Charles B. Pierce
Hawken's Breed 86 Charles B. Pierce
Hawkeye, Coastguard 12 Hay Plumb
Hawkeye, Hall Porter 14 Hay Plumb
Hawkeye Has to Hurry 13 Hay Plumb
Hawkeye, King of the Castle 15 Hay Plumb
Hawkeye Learns to Punt 11 Lewin Fitzhamon
Hawkeye Meets His Match 13 Hay Plumb
Hawkeye Rides in a Point-to-Point 13 Hay Plumb
Hawkeye, Showman 12 Hay Plumb
Hawks, The 68 Montgomery Tully
Hawks 88 Robert Ellis Miller
Hawks and Sparrows 66 Pier Paolo Pasolini
Hawks and the Sparrows, The 66 Pier Paolo Pasolini
Hawk's Nest, The 28 Benjamin Christensen

Headin' for the Rio Grande 36 Robert North Bradbury
Headin' for Trouble 31 John P. McGowan
Headin' Home 20 Lawrence C. Windom
Headin' North 21 Charles E. Bartlett
Headin' North 30 John P. McCarthy
Headin' South 18 Arthur Rosson
Headin' Through 24 Leo D. Maloney
Headin' West 22 William James Craft
Headin' Westward 29 John P. McGowan
Heading for Heaven 47 Lewis D. Collins
Heading West 46 Ray Nazarro
Headless Eyes, The 83 Kent Bateman
Headless Ghost, The 58 Peter Graham Scott
Headless Horseman, The 22 Edward D. Venturini
Headless Horseman, The 34 Ubbe Iwerks
Headless Rider, The 56 Chano Urueta
Headless Woman, The 43 René Cardona
Headleys at Home, The 39 Chris Beute
Headline 42 John Harlow
Headline Crasher 37 Leslie Goodwins
Headline Hunters 55 William Witney
Headline Hunters 68 Jonathan Ingrams
Headline Shooter 33 Otto Brower
Headline Woman, The 35 William Nigh
Headlines 25 Edward H. Griffith
Headlines of Destruction 55 John Berry
Headman's Vengeance, The 13 Edwin J. Collins
Headmaster, The 21 Kenelm Foss
Headquarters State Secret 62 Paul Man
Heads I Kill You—Tails You Die 71 Giuliano Carmineo
Heads I Win 63 Georges Robin
Heads or Tails 69 Piero Pierotti
Heads or Tails 80 Robert Enrico
Heads Up 25 Harry Garson
Heads Up 30 Victor Schertzinger
Heads Up, Charlie 26 Willi Wolff
Heads We Go 33 Monty Banks
Heads Win 19 Preston Kendall
Headwinds 25 Herbert Blaché
Heal Hitler 86 Herbert Achternbusch
Healer, The 35 Reginald Barker
Healing Water, The 64 Frigyes Bán
Health 79 Robert Altman
Health-Giving Waters of Tisza, The 54 Miklós Jancsó
Health in Industry 38 Harry Watt
Health in War 40 Pat Jackson
Healthy Eroticism 85 Péter Tímár
Healthy Neighborhood, A 13 Mack Sennett
Hear 'Em and Weep 33 Joseph Santley
Hear Me Good 57 Don McGuire
Hear the Pipers Calling 18 Tom Watts
Heard Over the Phone 08 Edwin S. Porter
Heard This One 30 R. E. Jeffrey
Hearse, The 80 George Bowers
Heart, The 54 Kon Ichikawa
Heart, The 58 Manoel De Oliveira
Heart 73 Kaneto Shindo
Heart 87 James Lemmo
Heart and Soul 17 J. Gordon Edwards
Heart and Soul 19 A. V. Bramble
Heart and Soul 50 Duilio Coletti
Heart Bandit, The 24 Oscar Apfel
Heart Beat 79 John Byrum

Heart Beats Again, The 56 Abram Room
Heart Beats of Long Ago 10 D. W. Griffith
Heart Bowed Down, The 06 Arthur Gilbert
Heart Buster, The 24 Jack Conway
Heart Condition 90 James D. Parriott
Heart in Pawn, A 19 William Worthington
Heart Into Hearts 90 Stephen Shin
Heart Is a Lonely Hunter, The 68 Robert Ellis Miller
Heart Knows No Frontiers, The 50 Luigi Zampa
Heart Like a Wheel 82 Jonathan Kaplan
Heart Line, The 21 Frederick Thompson
Heart o' the Hills 19 Sidney Franklin
Heart of a Bandit, The 24 Oscar Apfel
Heart of a Child, The 15 Harold M. Shaw
Heart of a Child, The 20 Ray C. Smallwood
Heart of a Child 40 Alejandro Galindo
Heart of a Child 58 Clive Donner
Heart of a Clown 26 Anders Wilhelm Sandberg
Heart of a Coward, The 26 Duke Worne
Heart of a Cowboy, The 09 Gilbert M. Anderson
Heart of a Cracksman, The 13 Wallace Reid, Willis Robards
Heart of a Dog 75 Alberto Lattuada
Heart of a Fishergirl, The 10 Lewin Fitzhamon
Heart of a Follies Girl, The 28 John Francis Dillon
Heart of a Fool 20 Allan Dwan
Heart of a Gipsy, The 19 Harry McRae Webster
Heart of a Girl, The 18 John G. Adolfi
Heart of a Gypsy Maid, The 13 Edwin J. Collins
Heart of a Hero, The 16 Émile Chautard
Heart of a Lion, The 17 Frank Lloyd
Heart of a Man, The 12 Gilbert Southwell
Heart of a Man, The 59 Herbert Wilcox
Heart of a Mother 66 Mark Donskoi
Heart of a Nation, The 40 Julien Duvivier
Heart of a Painted Woman, The 15 Alice Guy-Blaché
Heart of a Rose, The 19 Jack Denton
Heart of a Savage, The 11 D. W. Griffith
Heart of a Siren, The 25 Phil Rosen
Heart of a Temptress 25 Phil Rosen
Heart of a Texan, The 22 Paul Hurst
Heart of a Tyrant 81 Miklós Jancsó
Heart of a Woman, The 12 Warwick Buckland
Heart of a Woman, The 20 John H. Pratt
Heart of Alaska 24 Harold McCracken
Heart of Arizona 38 Lesley Selander
Heart of Blue Ridge, The 15 James Young
Heart of Britain, The 41 Humphrey Jennings
Heart of Broadway, The 28 Duke Worne
Heart of Dixie 89 Martin Davidson
Heart of Ezra Greer, The 17 Émile Chautard
Heart of General Robert E. Lee, The 28 Roy William Neill
Heart of Glass 76 Werner Herzog

Heart of Gold 19 Travers Vale
Heart of Humanity, The 18 Allen Holubar
Heart of Jennifer, The 15 James Kirkwood
Heart of Juanita 19 George E. Middleton
Heart of Lincoln, The 22 Francis Ford
Heart of Maryland, The 15 Herbert Brenon
Heart of Maryland, The 21 Tom Terriss
Heart of Maryland, The 27 Lloyd Bacon
Heart of Midlothian, The 14 Frank Wilson
Heart of Midnight 87 Matthew Chapman
Heart of New York, The 16 Walter P. MacNamara
Heart of New York, The 32 Mervyn LeRoy
Heart of New York, The 33 Lewis Milestone
Heart of Nora Flynn, The 16 Cecil B. DeMille
Heart of O Yama 08 D. W. Griffith
Heart of Oak 10 Lewin Fitzhamon
Heart of Oyama, The 08 D. W. Griffith
Heart of Paris 37 Marc Allégret
Heart of Paro, The 15 Tom Santschi
Heart of Rachael, The 18 Howard Hickman
Heart of Romance, The 18 Harry Millarde
Heart of Salome, The 27 Victor Schertzinger
Heart of Sister Anne, The 15 Harold M. Shaw
Heart of Solomon, The 32 Sergei Gerasimov, M. Kressin
Heart of Tara, The 16 William J. Bowman
Heart of Texas Ryan, The 17 E. A. Martin
Heart of the Blue Ridge, The 15 James Young
Heart of the Dragon 85 Samo Hung
Heart of the Golden West 42 Joseph Kane
Heart of the Hills, The 14 Wallace Reid
Heart of the Hills, The 16 Richard Ridgely
Heart of the Matter, The 53 George More O'Ferrall
Heart of the Mountains, The 66 Kozaburo Yoshimura
Heart of the North, The 21 Harry Revier
Heart of the North 38 Lewis Seiler
Heart of the Rio Grande 42 William Morgan
Heart of the Rockies 37 Joseph Kane
Heart of the Rockies 51 William Witney
Heart of the Stag 84 Michael Firth
Heart of the Sunset 18 Frank Powell
Heart of the West 36 Howard Bretherton
Heart of the Wilds 18 Marshall Neilan
Heart of the Yukon, The 26 W. S. Van Dyke
Heart of Twenty, The 20 Henry Kolker
Heart of Virginia 48 R. G. Springsteen
Heart of Wetona, The 18 Sidney Franklin
Heart of Youth, The 19 Robert Vignola
Heart on the Land, The 86 Constante Diego
Heart Punch, The 32 B. Reeves Eason
Heart Raider, The 23 Wesley Ruggles
Heart Royal 47 Robert Gordon
Heart Sings, The 58 G. Melik-Avakyan
Heart Snatcher, The 20 Roy Del Ruth*
Heart Song 33 Friedrich Holländer

Heart Specialist, The 22 Frank Urson
Heart Strings 20 J. Gordon Edwards
Heart Thief, The 27 Nils Olaf Chrisander
Heart Thief, The 38 Carl Boese
Heart to Heart 28 William Beaudine
Heart to Heart 38 Steve Sekely
Heart to Heart 78 Pascal Thomas
Heart to Let, A 21 Edward Dillon
Heart Trouble 28 Harry Langdon
Heart Within, The 57 David Eady
Heartaches 15 Joseph Kaufman
Heartaches 47 Basil Wrangell
Heartaches 81 Donald Shebib
Heartbeat 38 Mario Camerini
Heartbeat 38 Marcel Pagnol
Heartbeat 46 Sam Wood
Heartbeat 61 Márta Mészáros
Heartbeat 68 Alain Cavalier
Heartbeat 100 87 Kent Cheng, Kin Lo
Heartbeeps 81 Allan Arkush
Heartbound 25 Glen Lambert
Heartbreak 31 Alfred L. Werker
Heartbreak Hotel 88 Chris Columbus
Heartbreak Kid, The 72 Elaine May
Heartbreak Ridge 55 Jacques Dupont
Heartbreak Ridge 86 Clint Eastwood
Heartbeak Yakuza, The 87 Masato
Harada
Heartbreaker 83 Frank Zuniga
Heartbreakers, Die 83 Peter F. Bringmann
Heartbreakers, The 83 Peter F. Bringmann
Heartbreakers 84 Bobby Roth
Heartburn 86 Mike Nichols
Heartland 79 Richard Pearce
Heartland Reggae 80 J. P. Lewis
Heartless Grief 87 Alexander Sokurov
Heartless Husbands 25 Bertram Bracken
Heartless Mother, A 08 Lewin Fitzhamon
Hearts Adrift 13 Edwin S. Porter
Hearts Aflame 23 Reginald Barker
Hearts and Armour 82 Giacomo Battiato
Hearts and Dollars 23 Anatole Litvak
Hearts and Fists 26 Lloyd Ingraham
Hearts and Flowers 19 Edward F. Cline
Hearts and Flowers for Tora-San 82 Yoji
Yamada
Hearts and Horses 13 Allan Dwan, Wallace Reid
Hearts and Horses 18 Gregory La Cava
Hearts and Masks 14 Colin Campbell
Hearts and Masks 21 William A. Seiter
Hearts and Minds 73 Michele Lupo
Hearts and Minds 74 Peter Davis
Hearts and Planets 15 Mack Sennett
Hearts and Saddles 19 Walter West
Hearts and Spangles 26 Frank O'Connor
Hearts and Spurs 25 W. S. Van Dyke
Hearts and the Highway 15 Wilfred North
Hearts Are Thumps 37 Gordon Douglas
Hearts Are Trumps 20 Rex Ingram
Hearts Asleep 19 Howard Hickman
Heart's Desire 17 Francis J. Grandon
Heart's Desire 35 Paul Stein
Hearts Divided 36 Frank Borzage
Heart's Haven 22 Benjamin B. Hampton
Hearts in Bondage 36 Lew Ayres
Hearts in Dixie 29 Paul Sloane, A. H.
Van Buren
Hearts in Exile 15 James Young
Hearts in Exile 29 Michael Curtiz

Hearts in Love 39 Carl Boese
Hearts in Reunion 36 Norman Taurog
Hearts in Shadow 15 B. Reeves Eason
Hearts in Springtime 40 Ralph Murphy
Hearts o' the Range 21 Milburn Morante
Hearts of Age, The 34 William Vance,
Orson Welles
Hearts of Fire 87 Richard Marquand
Hearts of Gold 15 Geoffrey H. Malins
Hearts of Humanity 32 Christy Cabanne
Hearts of Humanity 36 John Baxter
Hearts of Love 18 J. Charles Haydon
Hearts of Men, The 12 Edwin J. Collins
Hearts of Men 15 Perry N. Vekroff
Hearts of Men 19 George Beban
Hearts of Men 28 James P. Hogan
Hearts of Oak 24 John Ford
Hearts of Oak 33 Graham Hewett, M. A.
Wetherell
Hearts of the West 75 Howard Zieff
Hearts of the Woods 21 Roy Calnek
Hearts of the World 17 D. W. Griffith
Hearts of Youth 20 Thomas N. Miranda,
Millard Webb
Hearts or Diamonds 18 Henry King
Heart's Revenge, A 18 Oscar A. C. Lund
Hearts That Are Human 15 A. V. Bramble
Hearts That Meet 14 Victor Sjöström
Hearts Trump Diamonds 25 Edwin
Greenwood, Will P. Kellino
Hearts Up! 20 Val Paul
Heart's Voice, The 12 Forest Holger-
Madsen
Heartsease 19 Harry Beaumont
Heartstone 90 Andrew J. Prowse
Heartstrings 17 Allen Holubar
Heartstrings 23 Edwin Greenwood
Heat 63 Larissa Shepitko
Heat 64 Kazimierz Kutz
Heat 70 Armando Bo, Jack Curtis
Heat 71 Paul Morrissey
Heat 87 Dick Richards
Heat and Dust 82 James Ivory
Heat and Mud 50 Kon Ichikawa
Heat and Sunlight 86 Rob Nilsson
Heat at Midnight 66 Max Pecas
Heat Haze 68 Kaneto Shindo
Heat Lightning 34 Mervyn LeRoy
Heat Line, The 88 Hubert-Yves Rose
Heat of Desire 80 Luc Béraud
Heat of Midnight 66 Max Pecas
Heat of the Summer 61 Louis Félix
Heat Wave, The 11 Frank Wilson
Heat Wave 35 Maurice Elvey
Heat Wave 54 Ken Hughes
Heat Wave Island 68 Kaneto Shindo
Heated Vengeance 85 Edward Murphy
Heathcliff: The Movie 86 Bruno Bianchi
Heathen Benefit, A 18 Gregory La Cava
Heather 38 Jerzy Starczewski
Heathers 89 Michael Lehmann
Heat's On, The 43 Gregory Ratoff
Heatwave 81 Phillip Noyce
Heave Away My Johnny 48 Joy Batchelor,
John Halas
Heave-Ho! 34 Martin Frič
Heave Two 33 Leslie Goodwins
Heaven 87 Diane Keaton
Heaven and Earth 90 Haruki Kadokawa

Heaven and Earth Magic 58 Harry Smith
Heaven and Hell 62 Akira Kurosawa
Heaven Avenges 11 D. W. Griffith
Heaven Bound 33 Sam Newfield
Heaven Can Wait 43 Ernst Lubitsch
Heaven Can Wait 78 Warren Beatty, Buck
Henry
Heaven Fell That Night 57 Roger Vadim
Heaven Help Us 85 Michael Dinner
Heaven Is Round the Corner 43 Maclean
Rogers
Heaven Knows, Mr. Allison 57 John
Huston
Heaven Linked with Love 32 Heinosuke
Gosho
Heaven on Earth 27 Phil Rosen
Heaven on Earth 31 Russell Mack
Heaven on Earth 60 Robert Spafford
Heaven Only Knows 47 Albert S. Rogell
Heaven Over the Marshes 49 Augusto
Genina
Heaven Scent 56 Chuck Jones
Heaven Sent 63 Jean-Pierre Mocky
Heaven with a Barbed Wire Fence 39
Ricardo Cortez
Heaven with a Gun 68 Lee H. Katzin
Heaven with No Love 61 Vladimir Pogačić
Heavenly Bodies 63 Russ Meyer
Heavenly Bodies 85 Lawrence Dane
Heavenly Body, The 43 Alexander Hall
Heavenly Days 44 Howard Estabrook
Heavenly Kid, The 85 Cary Medoway
Heavenly Pursuits 85 Charles Gormley
Heavenly Puss 49 Joseph Barbera, William
Hanna
Heavenly Twins, The 07 Lewin Fitzhamon
Heavenly Twins, The 12 Ernest G. Batley
Heavenly Twins at Lunch 03 Edwin S.
Porter
Heavenly Twins at Odds 03 Edwin S.
Porter
Heavens Above! 63 John Boulting
Heavens Call, The 59 Mikhail Karyukov,
Alexander Kozyr
Heaven's Gate 80 Michael Cimino
Heavily Married 37 Clayton Hutton
Heavy Armor 88 Avi Nesher
Heavy Cross, The 37 Raphael J. Sevilla
Heavy Load 75 Chuck Vincent
Heavy Metal 81 John Bruno, John Halas,
Pino van Lamsweerde, Jimmy T.
Murakami, Barrie Nelson, Gerald Potterton, Paul Sabella, Jack Stokes, Julian
Szuchopa, Harold Whitaker
Heavy Petting 88 Obie Benz
Heavy Traffic 73 Ralph Bakshi
Hebi Himesama 38 Teinosuke Kinugasa
Hechos Consumados 85 Luis R. Vera
Heckling Hare, The 41 Tex Avery
Hectic Days 35 Josef Heifits, Mikhail
Shapiro, Alexander Zarkhi
Hectic Honeymoon 38 Jean Yarbrough
Hector 87 Stijn Coninx
Hector Servadac's Ark 68 Karel Zeman
Hedda 75 Trevor Nunn
Hedda Gabler 17 Frank Powell
Hedda Gabler 19 Giovanni Pastrone
Hedy 65 Andy Warhol
Hedy the Shoplifter 65 Andy Warhol
Heedless Moths 21 Robert Z. Leonard

Heel of Italy, The *40* Alberto Cavalcanti

Heel Taps *25* Edwin Greenwood, Will P. Kellino

Hei Pao Shi Jian *85* Jianxin Huang

Hei Tai Yang 731 *89* T. F. Mous

Hei Tiki *35* Alexander Markey

Heidenlöcher *86* Wolfram Paulus

Heideschulmeister Uwe Karsten *34* Karl Heinz Wolff

Heidi *37* Allan Dwan

Heidi *52* Luigi Comencini

Heidi *65* Werner Jacobs

Heidi and Peter *54* Franz Schnyder

Heidi und Peter *54* Franz Schnyder

Heidi's Song *82* Robert Taylor

Heien *28* Joris Ivens

Heifer, The *84* Luis García Berlanga

Height *57* Alexander Zarkhi

Height A *41* Dziga Vertov

Height of Battle, The *50* Kozaburo Yoshimura

Heights, The *57* Alexander Zarkhi

Heights of Danger *53* Peter Bradford

Heights of Hazards, The *15* Harry Lambart

Heilige Berg, Der *26* Arnold Fanck

Heilige Flamme, Die *30* William Dieterle, Berthold Viertel

Heilige Lüge, Die *25* Forest Holger-Madsen

Heilige Simplizia, Die *20* Joe May

Heilige und Ihr Narr, Die *28* William Dieterle

Heilige und Ihr Narr, Die *35* Hans Deppe

Heilt Hitler *86* Herbert Achternbusch

Heimat *38* Carl Fröhlich

Heimat *83* Edgar Reitz

Heimat am Rhein *34* Fred Sauer

Heimat Ruft, Die *37* Douglas Sirk

Heimat und Fremde *13* Joe May

Heimatland *39* Ernst Martin

Heimkehr *28* Joe May

Heimlichkeiten *68* Wolfgang Staudte

Heinrich *76* Helma Sanders-Brahms

Heinzelmännchen *67* Erich Kobler

Heinze's Resurrection *13* Mack Sennett

Heir Conditioned *55* Friz Freleng

Heir-Loons *25* Grover Jones

Heir of Genghis Khan, The *28* Vsevolod I. Pudovkin

Heir of the Ages, The *17* Edward J. LeSaint

Heir to Genghis Khan, The *28* Vsevolod I. Pudovkin

Heir to Jenghiz Khan, The *28* Vsevolod I. Pudovkin

Heir to the Hoorah, The *16* William De-Mille

Heir to Trouble *35* Spencer G. Bennet

Heiratsschwindler *25* Carl Boese

Heiress, The *11* Edwin S. Porter

Heiress, The *49* William Wyler

Heiress, The *65* Tobe Hooper

Heiress at Coffee Dan's, The *17* Edward Dillon

Heiress for a Day, An *18* John Francis Dillon

Heiresses, The *80* Márta Mészáros

Heirloom Mystery, The *36* Maclean Rogers

Heirs *70* András Kovács

Heiss Weht der Wind *64* Rolf Olsen

Heisse Spur St. Pauli *71* Wolfgang Staudte

Heisser Sand auf Sylt *70* Jerzy Macc, Peter Savage

Heisses Blut *11* Urban Gad

Heisses Blut *36* Georg Jacoby

Heist, The *71* Richard Brooks

Heist, The *79* Sergio Gobbi

Heisters, The *70* Tobe Hooper

Hej *65* Jonas Cornell

Hej Rup! *34* Martin Frič

Hej, Te Eleven Fa... *63* Miklós Jancsó

Heja, Roland! *65* Bo Widerberg

Held by a Child *14* Dave Aylott

Held by the Enemy *20* Donald Crisp

Held by the Law *27* Edward Laemmle

Held for Ransom *13* Frank Wilson

Held for Ransom *38* Clarence Brown

Held in Trust *20* John Ince

Held in Trust *49* Cecil H. Williamson

Held Meiner Träume, Der *60* Arthur Maria Rabenalt

Held to Answer *23* Harold M. Shaw

Held to Ransom *06* Arthur Cooper

Held Up for the Makins *20* B. Reeves Eason

Helden *58* Franz Peter Wirth

Helden — Himmel und Hölle *64* Edgar G. Ulmer

Heldinnen *62* Dietrich Haugh

Heldorado *46* William Witney

Helen Keller in Her Story *54* Richard C. Wood

Helen la Belle *57* Lotte Reiniger

Helen Morgan Story, The *57* Michael Curtiz

Helen of Four Gates *20* Cecil M. Hepworth

Helen of Troy *27* Alexander Korda

Helen of Troy *51* Gustaf Edgren

Helen of Troy *53* Marc Allégret, Edgar G. Ulmer

Helen of Troy *55* Robert Wise

Helen — Queen of the Nautch Girls *73* James Ivory

Hélène *36* Jean Benoît-Lévy

Helene of the North *15* J. Searle Dawley

Helen's Babies *24* William A. Seiter

Helen's Marriage *12* Mack Sennett

Helga *67* Erich Bender, Terry Van Tell

Helicopter Spies, The *67* Boris Sagal

Heliotrope *20* George D. Baker

Hell *60* Nobuo Nakagawa

Hell *71* Jan Lenica

Hell and High Water *33* Grover Jones, William Slavens McNutt

Hell and High Water *53* Samuel Fuller

Hell Below *33* Jack Conway

Hell Below Zero *54* Mark Robson

Hell Bent *18* John Ford

Hell-Bent for Election *44* Stephen Bosustow, Chuck Jones

Hell Bent for 'Frisco *31* Stuart Paton

Hell Bent for Glory *57* William A. Wellman

Hell-Bent for Heaven *26* J. Stuart Blackton

Hell Bent for Leather *60* George Sherman

Hell Bent for Love *34* D. Ross Lederman

Hell Boats *69* Paul Wendkos

Hell Bound *31* Walter Lang

Hell Bound *57* William Hole, Jr.

Hell Canyon Outlaws *57* Paul Landres

Hell Cat, The *18* Reginald Barker

Hell Cat, The *34* Albert S. Rogell

Hell Comes to Frogtown *87* Donald G. Jackson, R. J. Kizer

Hell Creatures, The *57* Edward L. Cahn

Hell Diggers, The *21* Frank Urson

Hell Divers *31* George W. Hill

Hell Drivers *57* Cy Endfield

Hell Fire Austin *32* Forrest K. Sheldon

Hell Harbor *29* Henry King

Hell Has No Gates *80* Hark Tsui

Hell Hath No Fury *17* Charles E. Bartlett

Hell, Heaven and Hoboken *58* John Guillermin

Hell, Heaven or Hoboken *58* John Guillermin

Hell High *89* Douglas Grossman

Hell House *83* Andy Milligan

Hell House Girls *75* Robert Hartford-Davis

Hell Hunters *88* Ernst R. von Theumer

Hell in Korea *56* Julian Amyes

Hell in the City *58* Renato Castellani

Hell in the Heavens *34* John G. Blystone

Hell in the Pacific *68* John Boorman

Hell Is a City *59* Val Guest

Hell Is Empty *63* John Ainsworth, Bernard Knowles

Hell Is for Heroes! *62* Don Siegel

Hell Is Sold Out *51* Michael Anderson

Hell, Live *85* Ruggero Deodato

Hell Morgan's Girl *17* Joseph De Grasse

Hell Night *81* Tom DeSimone

Hell of Frankenstein, The *60* Rafael Baledón

Hell of the Living Dead *81* Bruno Mattei

Hell of the Living Death *81* Bruno Mattei

Hell on Devil's Island *57* Christian Nyby

Hell on Earth *31* Victor Trivas

Hell on Frisco Bay *55* Frank Tuttle

Hell on Wheels *67* Will Zens

Hell Raiders *65* Larry Buchanan

Hell Raiders of the Deep *54* Duilio Coletti

Hell Riders *85* James Bryant

Hell River *77* Stole Jankovic

Hell Roarin' Reform *19* Edward J. LeSaint

Hell Screen, The *69* Shiro Toyoda

Hell Ship, The *20* Scott R. Dunlap

Hell Ship, The *22* Victor Sjöström

Hell Ship Morgan *36* D. Ross Lederman

Hell Ship Mutiny *57* Lee Sholem, Elmo Williams

Hell Spit Flexion *83* Stan Brakhage

Hell Squad *58* Burt Topper

Hell Squad *83* Ken Hartford

Hell to Eternity *60* Phil Karlson

Hell to Macao *66* Bill Catching, James Hill

Hell-to-Pay Austin *16* Paul Powell

Hell Town *37* Charles Barton

Hell Unlimited *36* Helen Biggar, Norman McLaren

Hell Up in Harlem *73* Larry Cohen

Hell with Heroes, The *67* Joseph Sargent

Hellbenders, The *66* Sergio Corbucci

Hellborn *61* Edward D. Wood, Jr.
Hellbound: Hellraiser II *88* Tony Randel
Hellcamp *86* Eric Karson
Hellcat, The *28* Harry Hughes
Hellcats, The *68* Robert F. Slatzer
Hellcats of the Navy *57* Nathan Juran
Helldorado *34* James Cruze
Helldorado *46* William Witney
Hellé *71* Roger Vadim
Heller in Pink Tights *59* George Cukor
Heller Wahn *82* Margarethe von Trotta
Hellfighters *68* Andrew V. McLaglen
Hellfire *49* R. G. Springsteen
Hellfire *86* William Murray
Hellfire Club, The *60* Robert S. Baker,
  Monty Berman
Hellgate *52* Charles Marquis Warren
Hellhole *85* Pierre De Moro
Hellige Løgne *25* Forest Holger-Madsen
Hellion, The *19* George L. Cox
Hellion, The *24* Bruce Mitchell
Hellions, The *61* Ken Annakin
Hello Again *87* Frank Perry
Hello Annapolis *42* Charles Barton
Hello Baby *25* Leo McCarey
Hello Baby! *75* Johan Bergenstråhle
Hello! Beautiful *42* Norman Z. McLeod
Hello Budapest! *35* Ladislas Vajda
Hello Cheyenne *28* Eugene Forde
Hello Children *62* Mark Donskoi
Hello Cubans *63* Agnès Varda
Hello, Dolly! *69* Gene Kelly
Hello Down There *68* Jack Arnold
Hello Elephant *52* Gianni Franciolini
Hello Everybody! *32* William A. Seiter
Hello Exchange *16* Kelly Storrie
Hello, Frisco, Hello *43* H. Bruce
  Humberstone
Hello God *51* William Marshall
Hello Goodbye *25* Norman Taurog
Hello-Goodbye *70* Jean Negulesco
Hello Hollywood *25* Norman Taurog
Hello, How Am I? *39* Dave Fleischer
Hello Little Girl Hello *60* Arthur Gilbert
Hello London *58* Sidney Smith
Hello Mars *20* Dave Fleischer
Hello Mary Lou: Prom Night II *87* Bruce
  Pittman
Hello Moscow! *45* Sergei Yutkevich
Hello Out There *49* James Whale
Hello Pardners *23* Erle C. Kenton
Hello, Prosperity *34* Charles Lamont
Hello Sailor *27* Mark Sandrich
Hello Sister *30* Walter Lang
Hello, Sister! *33* Erich von Stroheim,
  Raoul Walsh, Alfred L. Werker
Hello, Sucker *41* Edward F. Cline
Hello Sweetheart *35* Monty Banks
Hello Thar *30* Edward Buzzell
Hello Trouble *18* Charlie Chase
Hello, Trouble *32* Lambert Hillyer
Hello Vera *67* János Herskó
Hello Young Lovers *81* Lino Brocka
Hellraiser *87* Clive Barker
Hell's Angels *30* Howard Hawks, Howard
  Hughes, Lewis Milestone, Marshall
  Neilan, Luther Reed, James Whale
Hell's Angels Forever *83* Richard Chase,
  Leon Gast, Kevin Keating
Hell's Angels on Wheels *67* Richard Rush

Hell's Angels '69 *69* Lee Madden
Hell's Belles *69* Maury Dexter
Hell's Bells *29* Ubbe Iwerks
Hell's Bloody Devils *70* Al Adamson
Hell's Cargo *33* Albert S. Rogell
Hell's Cargo *35* Walter Summers
Hell's Cargo *37* Léo Joannon
Hell's Cargo *39* Harold Huth
Hell's Chosen Few *68* David L. Hewitt
Hell's Crater *18* W. B. Pearson
Hell's Creatures *67* Enrique L. Equiluz
Hell's Crossroads *57* Franklin Adreon
Hell's Devils *39* Sam Newfield
Hell's End *18* J. W. McLaughlin
Hell's Fire *34* Ubbe Iwerks
Hell's Five Hours *57* Jack L. Copeland
Hell's 400 *26* John Griffith Wray
Hell's Gate Island *77* Kon Ichikawa
Hell's Half Acre *54* John H. Auer
Hell's Headquarters *32* Andrew L. Stone
Hell's Heels *30* Walter Lantz
Hell's Heroes *29* William Wyler
Hell's Highroad *24* Rupert Julian
Hell's Highway *32* Rowland Brown
Hell's Highway *58* Howard W. Koch
Hell's Hinges *16* Reginald Barker, William
  S. Hart, Clifford Smith, Charles Swick-
  ard
Hell's Hole *23* Emmett J. Flynn
Hell's Horizon *55* Tom Gries
Hell's House *32* Howard Higgin
Hell's Island *30* Edward Sloman
Hell's Island *54* Phil Karlson
Hell's Kitchen *39* E. A. Dupont, Lewis
  Seiler
Hell's Long Road *63* Charles Roberti
Hell's Oasis *20* Neal Hart
Hell's Outpost *54* Joseph Kane
Hell's Playground *67* Jesse Clark
Hell's River *22* Irving Cummings
Hell's Valley *31* Alvin J. Neitz
Hellseher, Der *33* Eugen Thiele
Hellship Bronson *28* Joseph E. Henabery
Hellstrom Chronicle, The *71* Walon
  Green
Hellyys *72* Jörn Donner
Hellzapoppin *41* H. C. Potter
Help *12* Robert Dinesen
Help! *23* Abel Gance
Help! *65* Richard Lester
Help! Help! *12* Mack Sennett
Help! Help! Hydrophobia! *13* Henry
  Lehrman
Help! Help! Police! *19* Edward Dillon
Help! I'm an Heiress *37* Steve Sekely
Help! I'm Invisible *52* E. W. Emo
Help Me Dream *81* Pupi Avati
Help Me...I'm Possessed *76* Charles
  Nizet
Help Me to Live *36* José A. Ferreyra
Help Wanted *17* F. M. Follett
Help Wanted! *39* Fred Zinnemann
Help Wanted—Male *20* Henry King
Help Yourself *20* Hugo Ballin
Help Yourself *32* John Daumery
Helpful Al *25* Charles Lamont
Helpful Hogan *23* Gregory La Cava
Helping Hand *08* Georges Méliès
Helping Hand, The *08* D. W. Griffith
Helping Hand, A *13* Warwick Buckland

Helping Himself *14* Charles Chaplin
Helping McAdoo *18* Raoul Barré, Charles
  Bowers
Helping Paw, A *41* Sid Marcus
Helpmates *31* James Parrott
Helsinki-Napoli: All Night Long *87* Mika
  Kaurismäki
Helsinki 62 *62* Evald Schorm
Helsinky 62 *62* Evald Schorm
Helt Vanlig Person, En *67* Arne Mattsson
Helter Skelter *29* Charles Lamont
Helter Skelter *49* Ralph Thomas
Helter Skelter *76* Tom Gries
Hem från Babylon *41* Alf Sjöberg
Hem Hayu Asar *61* Baruch Dienar
Hemingway's Adventures of a Young
  Man *62* Martin Ritt
Hemligt Giftermål, Ett *12* Victor Sjöström
Hemmelighedsfulde X, Det *13* Benjamin
  Christensen
Hemo, King of Jerusalem *87* Amos Gutt-
  man
Hemo the Magnificent *57* Frank Capra
Hemsöborna *55* Arne Mattsson
Hen Fruit *30* Walter Lantz
Hen Hop *42* Norman McLaren
Hen House Henery *49* Robert McKimson
Hen in the Wind, A *48* Yasujiro Ozu
Hen Will Squawk Again, A *54* Heinosuke
  Gosho
Hendes Ære *15* August Blom
Hendes Helt *17* Forest Holger-Madsen
Hendes Moders Løfte *16* Forest Holger-
  Madsen
Hendes Nåde Dragonen *25* August Blom
Henkel *38* Walter Ruttmann
Henkel—Ein Deutsches Werk in Seiner
  Arbeit *38* Walter Ruttmann
Henker, Frauen und Soldaten *40* Johannes
  Meyer
Henker von London, Der *63* Edwin
  Zbonek
Hennes Lilla Majestät *40* S. Bauman
Hennessy *75* Don Sharp
Henpecked *30* Walter Lantz
Henpecked *41* Frank R. Strayer
Henpecked Duck, The *41* Robert
  Clampett
Henpecked Hindoo, The *05* Alf Collins
Henpecked Hoboes *46* Tex Avery
Henpecked Husband, The *06* Alf Collins
Henpeck's Double *12* Dave Aylott
Henri *86* François Labonte
Henri Matisse ou Le Talent du Bonheur
  60 Marcel Ophüls
Henrietta Maria, or The Queen of Sorrow
  23 Edwin Greenwood
Henriette *52* Julien Duvivier
Henriette Jacoby *18* Richard Oswald
Henriette's Holiday *52* Julien Duvivier
Henry *54* Lindsay Anderson
Henry Aldrich, Boy Scout *44* Hugh Ben-
  nett
Henry Aldrich, Editor *42* Hugh Bennett
Henry Aldrich for President *41* Hugh
  Bennett
Henry Aldrich Gets Glamour *42* Hugh
  Bennett
Henry Aldrich Haunts a House *43* Hugh
  Bennett

Henry Aldrich Plays Cupid 44 Hugh Bennett

Henry Aldrich Swings It 43 Hugh Bennett

Henry Aldrich's Little Secret 44 Hugh Bennett

Henry and Dizzy 42 Hugh Bennett

Henry & June 90 Philip Kaufman

Henry B. Walthall in Retribution 28 Archie Mayo

Henry Busse and His Orchestra 40 Jean Negulesco

Henry Geldzahler 64 Andy Warhol

Henry Goes Arizona 39 Edwin L. Marin

Henry, King of Navarre 24 Maurice Elvey

Henry Limpet 63 Arthur Lubin

Henry: Portrait of a Serial Killer 86 John McNaughton

Henry Steps Out 40 Widgey R. Newman

Henry IV 84 Marco Bellocchio

Henry V 44 Reginald Beck, Laurence Olivier

Henry V 89 Kenneth Branagh

Henry VIII 11 Will Barker

Henry VIII 32 Alexander Korda

Henry VIII and His Six Wives 72 Waris Hussein

Henry, the Rainmaker 48 Jean Yarbrough

Henry W. Zippy Buys a Motor Boat 16 Charles E. Howell

Henry W. Zippy Buys a Pet Pup 16 Charles E. Howell

Hentai 66 Takashi Shiga

Hep Cat, The 42 Robert Clampett

Her Accidental Husband 23 Dallas M. Fitzgerald

Her Adventurous Night 46 John Rawlins

Her Alibi 89 Bruce Beresford

Her Ambition 26 Charles Lamont

Her American Husband 18 E. Mason Hopper

Her American Prince 16 D. H. Turner

Her Awakening 11 D. W. Griffith

Her Awakening 12 Hay Plumb

Her Awakening 14 Christy Cabanne

Her Awakening: The Punishment of Pride 11 D. W. Griffith

Her Bachelor Guardian 12 H. Oceano Martinek

Her Bachelor Husband 43 William Beaudine

Her Bashful Beau 30 Sam Newfield

Her Beloved Enemy 17 Ernest C. Warde

Her Beloved Villain 20 Sam Wood

Her Benny 20 A. V. Bramble

Her Better Self 12 Bert Haldane

Her Better Self 17 Robert Vignola

Her Big Adventure 26 John Ince

Her Big Night 26 Melville Brown

Her Big Story 13 Allan Dwan

Her Birthday Present 13 Mack Sennett

Her Bitter Cup 16 Joe King, Cleo Madison

Her Bleeding Heart 16 John H. Pratt

Her Body in Bond 18 Robert Z. Leonard

Her Bodyguard 33 William Beaudine

Her Boy 15 Frank Wilson

Her Boy 18 George Irving

Her Brother 60 Kon Ichikawa

Her Brother's Tutor 12 Edwin J. Collins

Her Cardboard Lover 29 Clayton Hutton

Her Cardboard Lover 42 George Cukor

Her Children 14 Harold M. Shaw

Her Chum's Brother 11 Sidney Olcott

Her Code of Honor 19 John M. Stahl

Her Condoned Sin 17 D. W. Griffith

Her Country First 18 Rollin Sturgeon

Her Country's Call 17 Lloyd Ingraham

Her Cross 19 A. V. Bramble

Her Crowning Glory 13 Warwick Buckland

Her Dancing Partner 22 George A. Cooper

Her Darkest Hour 11 Thomas Ince

Her Debt of Honor 16 William Nigh

Her Debt of Honour 10 Bert Haldane

Her Decision 18 Jack Conway

Her Dilemma 31 David Burton, Dudley Murphy

Her Double Life 16 J. Gordon Edwards

Her Elephant Man 20 Scott R. Dunlap

Her Enlisted Man 35 Sidney Lanfield

Her Excellency the Governor 17 Albert Parker

Her Face Value 21 Thomas Heffron

Her Faithful Companions 14 Lewin Fitzhamon

Her Fatal Hand 15 Dave Aylott

Her Fatal Millions 23 William Beaudine

Her Father Said No 27 Jack McKeown

Her Father's Daughter 40 Desmond Dickinson

Her Father's Gold 16 W. Eugene Moore

Her Father's Photograph 11 H. Oceano Martinek

Her Father's Pride 10 D. W. Griffith

Her Father's Silent Partner 14 Donald Crisp

Her Father's Son 16 William Desmond Taylor

Her Favorite Patient 45 Andrew L. Stone

Her Favourite Husband 50 Mario Soldati

Her Fighting Chance 17 Edwin Carewe

Her Filmland Hero 15 Chester M. Franklin, Sidney Franklin

Her Final Reckoning 18 Émile Chautard

Her First Adventure 08 Wallace McCutcheon

Her First Affair 41 Henri Decoin

Her First Affaire 32 Allan Dwan

Her First Attempt 07 Arthur Cooper

Her First Beau 16 Edward F. Cline

Her First Beau 41 Theodore Reed

Her First Biscuits 09 D. W. Griffith

Her First Cake 06 James A. Williamson

Her First Elopement 20 Sam Wood

Her First Experience 39 Josef von Baky

Her First Husband 15 Percy Nash

Her First Love Affair 12 August Blom

Her First Mate 33 William Wyler

Her First Pancake 07 Arthur Cooper

Her First Romance 39 Josef von Baky

Her First Romance 40 Edward Dmytryk

Her First Romance 51 Seymour Friedman

Her Five-Foot Highness 20 Harry Franklin

Her Fling 18 Ida May Park

Her Forgotten Past 33 Wesley Ford

Her Fortune at Stake 20 Charles Raymond

Her Friend the Bandit 14 Charles Chaplin, Mabel Normand

Her Friend the Enemy 07 Lewin Fitzhamon

Her Game 19 Frank Crane

Her Gilded Cage 22 Sam Wood

Her Golden Hair Was Hanging Down Her Back 25 Alexander Butler

Her Good Name 17 W. S. Van Dyke

Her Great Chance 18 Charles Maigne

Her Great Hour 16 Stanner E. V. Taylor

Her Great Mistake 25 Alexander Butler

Her Great Price 16 Edwin Carewe

Her Greater Gift 19 Fred Goodwins

Her Greatest Love 17 J. Gordon Edwards

Her Greatest Performance 16 Fred Paul

Her Greatest Success 39 Johannes Meyer

Her Guardian 11 Wilfred Noy

Her Happiness 15 Harry Beaumont

Her Heritage 19 Bannister Merwin

Her Hero 11 Van Dyke Brooke

Her Highness and the Bellboy 45 Richard Thorpe

Her Honor the Governor 26 Chester Withey

Her Honor the Mayor 20 Paul Cazeneuve

Her Hour 17 George Cowl

Her Hour of Retribution 14 B. Harold Brett

Her Husband Lies 37 Edward Ludwig

Her Husband's Affairs 47 S. Sylvan Simon

Her Husband's Friend 20 Fred Niblo

Her Husband's Honor 18 Burton L. King

Her Husband's Secret 25 Frank Lloyd

Her Husband's Secretary 37 Frank McDonald

Her Husband's Trademark 22 Sam Wood

Her Husky Hero 27 Norman Taurog

Her Imaginary Lover 33 George King

Her Indian Hero 09 Sidney Olcott

Her Innocent Marriage 13 Allan Dwan, Wallace Reid

Her Inspiration 18 George D. Baker

Her Invisible Husband 16 Matt Moore

Her Jungle Love 38 George Archainbaud

Her Kind of Man 46 Frederick De Cordova

Her Kingdom of Dreams 19 Marshall Neilan

Her Last Affaire 34 Michael Powell

Her Last Mile 44 Steve Sekely

Her Last Trip 38 Humphrey Jennings

Her Life and His 17 Frederick Sullivan

Her Life in London 15 R. Harley West

Her Little Majesty 40 S. Bauman

Her Little Pet 13 Frank Wilson

Her Lonely Lane 62 Mikio Naruse

Her Lonely Soldier 19 Percy Nash

Her Lord and Master 21 Edward José

Her Love Story 24 Allan Dwan

Her Lover's Honour 09 H. Oceano Martinek

Her Luck in London 14 Maurice Elvey

Her Lucky Night 45 Edward Lilley

Her Mad Bargain 21 Edwin Carewe

Her Mad Night 32 E. Mason Hopper

Her "Mail" Parent 12 Hay Plumb

Her Majesty 22 George Irving

Her Majesty, Love 31 William Dieterle

Her Man 18 Ralph Ince

Her Man 30 Tay Garnett

Her Man Gilbey 44 Harold French

Her Man o' War 26 Frank Urson

Her Market Value 25 Paul Powell
Her Marriage Lines 17 Frank Wilson
Her Marriage Vow 24 Millard Webb
Her Master's Voice 36 Joseph Santley
Her Maternal Right 16 John Ince, Robert Thornby
Her Mistake 18 Julius Steger
Her Moment 18 Frank Beal
Her Morning Dip 06 Alf Collins
Her Mother Interferes 11 Mack Sennett
Her Mother's Necklace 14 Donald Crisp
Her Mother's Oath 13 D. W. Griffith
Her Mother's Secret 15 Frederick Thompson
Her Mountain Home 12 Allan Dwan
Her Name Is Vasfiye 86 Atıf Yılmaz
Her Name of Venice in Calcutta Desert 75 Marguerite Duras
Her Nameless Child 15 Maurice Elvey
Her Nature Dance 17 Edward F. Cline
Her New Beau 13 Mack Sennett
Her New York 17 Oscar A. C. Lund
Her Night of Nights 22 Hobart Henley
Her Night of Romance 24 Sidney Franklin
Her Night Out 32 William McGann
Her Official Fathers 17 Elmer Clifton, Joseph E. Henabery
Her One Mistake 18 Edward J. LeSaint
Her One Redeeming Feature 15 Warwick Buckland
Her Only Pal 12 Lewin Fitzhamon
Her Only Son 12 Hay Plumb
Her Only Son 14 Gerald Lawrence
Her Only Way 18 Sidney Franklin
Her or Nobody 32 Carl Fröhlich
Her Own Country 12 Allan Dwan
Her Own Free Will 24 Paul Scardon
Her Own Money 22 Joseph E. Henabery
Her Own People 17 Scott Sidney
Her Own Story 26 Francis Ford
Her Own Way 15 Herbert Blaché
Her Painted Hero 15 F. Richard Jones
Her Panelled Door 50 George More O'Ferrall, Ladislas Vajda
Her Penalty 21 Einar J. Bruun
Her Pet 11 Mack Sennett
Her Pony's Love 13 Lewin Fitzhamon
Her Price 18 Edmund Lawrence
Her Primitive Way 44 Charles Lamont
Her Primitive Mate 27 Mervyn LeRoy
Her Private Affair 29 Paul Stein
Her Private Hell 68 Norman J. Warren
Her Private Life 29 Alexander Korda
Her Proper Place 15 Langdon West
Her Purchase Price 19 Howard Hickman
Her Redemption 24 Bertram Phillips
Her Relations 12 Percy Stow
Her Reputation 23 John Griffith Wray
Her Reputation 31 Sidney Morgan
Her Reputation 33 Sidney Lanfield
Her Resale Value 33 B. Reeves Eason
Her Right to Live 17 Paul Scardon
Her Rival's Necklace 07 Charles Raymond
Her Romance 21 Fred Paul
Her Rosary 13 Oscar Apfel
Her Sacrifice 11 D. W. Griffith
Her Sacrifice 12 Bert Haldane
Her Sacrifice 14 Colin Campbell
Her Sacrifice 17 Cheslav Sabinsky
Her Sacrifice 26 Wilfred Lucas

Her Sacrifice 34 Roy William Neill
Her Savings Saved 18 Henry Edwards
Her Second Chance 26 Lambert Hillyer
Her Second Husband 18 Del Henderson
Her Second Mother 40 Joseph Seiden
Her Secret 17 Perry N. Vekroff
Her Secret 19 Frederick S. Jensen
Her Secret 33 Warren Millais
Her Shattered Idol 15 John B. O'Brien
Her Shattered Idol 17 J. Searle Dawley
Her Silent Sacrifice 17 Edward José
Her Sister 11 Edwin S. Porter
Her Sister 17 John B. O'Brien
Her Sister from Paris 25 Sidney Franklin
Her Sister's Secret 46 Edgar G. Ulmer
Her Sister's Silence 12 A. E. Coleby
Her Social Value 21 Jerome Storm
Her Soldier Sweetheart 10 Sidney Olcott
Her Son 14 August Blom
Her Son 20 Walter West
Her Soul's Inspiration 17 Jack Conway
Her Splendid Folly 33 William A. O'Connor
Her Story 20 Alexander Butler
Her Story 22 Allyn B. Carrick
Her Strange Desire 31 Maurice Elvey
Her Strange Wedding 17 George Melford
Her Sturdy Oak 21 Thomas Heffron
Her Suitor's Suit 14 Warwick Buckland
Her Summer Hero 28 James Dugan
Her Surrender 16 Ivan Abramson
Her Sweetheart 33 Sam Wood
Her Teddy Bear 12 Charles Raymond
Her Temporary Husband 24 John McDermott
Her Temptation 17 Richard Stanton
Her Terrible Ordeal 09 D. W. Griffith
Her Twelve Men 54 Robert Z. Leonard
Her Unborn Child 33 Albert Ray
Her Uncle 15 George Loane Tucker
Her Unwilling Husband 20 Paul Scardon
Her Vocation 15 James W. Castle
Her Way 11 Edwin S. Porter
Her Way of Love 29 Dimitri Poznanski, Alexander Strizhak
Her Wayward Sister 16 Clay M. Greene
Her Wedding Night 30 Frank Tuttle
Her Wild Oat 27 Marshall Neilan
Her Winning Way 21 Joseph E. Henabery
Her Wonderful Lie 47 Carmine Gallone
Herakles 62 Werner Herzog
Herb Alpert and the Tijuana Brass Double Feature 66 Faith Hubley, John Hubley
Herbe Folle, L' 59 Carlo Lizzani
Herbie Anyone Lived in a Pretty Hometown 66 George Lucas
Herbie Goes Bananas 80 Vincent McEveety
Herbie Goes to Monte Carlo 76 Vincent McEveety
Herbie Rides Again 73 Robert Stevenson
Herbst-Manöver 39 Georg Jacoby
Herbstsonate 78 Ingmar Bergman
Hercegnő Pongyolában, A 14 Michael Curtiz
Hercule 37 Carlo-Rim, Alexander Esway
Hercule à la Conquête de l'Atlantide 61 Vittorio Cottafavi
Hercule Contre Moloch 63 Giorgio Ferroni
Hercules 57 Pietro Francisci
Hercules 62 Werner Herzog

Hercules 70 Arthur Allan Seidelman
Hercules 83 Luigi Cozzi
Hercules II 83 Luigi Cozzi
Hercules Against Rome 60 Piero Pierotti
Hercules Against the Moon Men 64 Giacomo Gentilomo
Hercules Against the Sons of the Sun 63 Osvaldo Civirani
Hercules and the Big Stick 10 Émile Cohl
Hercules and the Captive Women 61 Vittorio Cottafavi
Hercules and the Conquest of Atlantis 61 Vittorio Cottafavi
Hercules and the Haunted Women 61 Vittorio Cottafavi
Hercules and the Hydra 60 Carlo Ludovico Bragaglia
Hercules and the Masked Rider 63 Piero Pierotti
Hercules and the Queen of Lydia 59 Pietro Francisci
Hercules and the Ten Avengers 64 Alberto De Martino
Hercules and the Treasure of the Incas 61 Piero Pierotti
Hercules and the Tyrants of Babylon 64 Domenico Paolella
Hercules at the Center of the Earth 61 Mario Bava
Hercules Conquers Atlantis 61 Vittorio Cottafavi
Hercules Goes Bananas 70 Arthur Allan Seidelman
Hercules in New York 70 Arthur Allan Seidelman
Hercules in the Centre of the Earth 61 Mario Bava
Hercules in the Haunted World 61 Mario Bava
Hercules in the Vale of Woe 62 Mario Mattòli
Hercules of the Desert 64 Tanio Boccia
Hercules' Pills 60 Nino Manfredi, Luciano Salce
Hercules, Prisoner of Evil 64 Antonio Margheriti
Hercules, Samson and Ulysses 64 Pietro Francisci
Hercules—The Movie 70 Arthur Allan Seidelman
Hercules Unchained 59 Pietro Francisci
Hercules vs. Kung Fu 74 Antonio Margheriti
Hercules vs. the Giant Warriors 64 Alberto De Martino
Hercules vs. the Vampires 61 Mario Bava
Hercules vs. Ulysses 61 Mario Caiano
Herd, The 78 Zeki Ökten
Herdeiros, Os 69 Carlos Diegues
Herdsman, The 82 Jin Xie
Herdsmen of the Sun 88 Werner Herzog
Here and There 19 Raoul Barré, Charles Bowers
Here and There 36 John Baxter
Here and There 62 Yoji Kuri
Here Are Ladies 71 John Quested
Here at the Water's Edge 60 Leo T. Hurwitz
Here Come the Co-Eds 45 Jean Yarbrough

Héroïsme de Paddy, L' 15 Abel Gance
Héros de Chipka, Les 54 Sergei Vasiliev
Héros de l'Yser, Les 15 Léonce Perret
Hero's Island 62 Leslie Stevens
Héros Sans Retour 62 Frank Wisbar
Héros Sont Fatigués, Les 55 Yves Ciampi
Hero's Way 86 Ümit Elçi
Herostratus 67 Don Levy
Herowork 77 Michael Adrian
Herr Arnes Pengar 19 Mauritz Stiller
Herr Arnes Pengar 54 Gustaf Molander
Herr Arnes Penningar 54 Gustaf Molander
Herr der Liebe, Der 19 Fritz Lang
Herr der Welt, Der 33 Harry Piel
Herr des Todes, Der 26 Hans Steinhoff
Herr Doktor 17 Louis Feuillade
Herr Kobin Geht auf Abenteuer 35 Hans
  Deppe
Herr Meets Hare 45 Friz Freleng
Herr Puntila and His Servant Matti 55
  Alberto Cavalcanti
Herr Puntila und Sein Knecht Matti 55
  Alberto Cavalcanti
Herr Storms Første Monokel 11 August
  Blom
Herr Über Leben und Tod 19 Lupu Pick
Herre i Kjole og Hvidt, En 42 Bodil Ipsen
Herren der Meere 21 Alexander Korda
Herren mit der Weissen Weste, Die 70
  Wolfgang Staudte
Herren och Hans Tjenere 59 Arne Skouen
Herrenpartie 64 Wolfgang Staudte
Herrin der Welt, Die 20 Joe May
Herrin der Welt 59 William Dieterle
Herrin und Ihr Knecht, Die 29 Richard
  Oswald
Herrin vom Maxim, Die 32 Carl Boese
Herrin von Atlantis, Die 32 G. W. Pabst
Herrin von Brinkenhof 22 Svend Gade
Herring Murder Case, The 31 Dave
  Fleischer
Herring Murder Mystery, The 43 Don
  Roman
Herring on the Trail, A 13 Frank Wilson
Herringbone Clouds 58 Mikio Naruse
Herrscher, Der 37 Veidt Harlan
Herrscher Ohne Krone 56 Harald Braun
Hers to Hold 43 Frank Ryan
Herself 18 Percy Nash
Hersenschimmen 88 Heddy Honigmann
Herşeye Rağman 88 Orhan Oğuz
Herthas Erwachen 33 Gerhard Lamprecht
Herz aus Glas 76 Werner Herzog
Herz einer Königin, Das 40 Carl Fröhlich
Herz Ist Trumpf 34 Carl Boese
Herz Ohne Gnade 58 Victor Tourjansky
Herzblut 32 Constantin J. David
Herzbube 71 Jerzy Skolimowski
Herzensdieb, Die 38 Carl Boese
Herzl 67 Alberto Cavalcanti
Herzog Ferrantes Ende 22 Paul Wegener*
Herzog von Reichstadt, Der 31 Victor
  Tourjansky
Herzogin Satanella 20 Michael Curtiz
Herztrumpf 20 E. A. Dupont
He's a Cockeyed Wonder 50 Peter God-
  frey
He's a Prince 25 A. Edward Sutherland
He's My Girl 87 Gabrielle Beaumont
He's My Guy 43 Edward F. Cline

He's My Pal 24 Lewis Seiler
Hesper of the Mountains 16 Wilfred
  North
Hessian Renegades, The 09 D. W.
  Griffith
Hest på Sommerferie 59 Astrid Henning-
  Jensen
Hesten 43 Bjarne Henning-Jensen
Hesten på Kongens Nytorv 41 Bjarne
  Henning-Jensen
Hester Street 75 Joan Micklin Silver
Heterodyne 67 Hollis Frampton
Heterosexuals, The 67 Claude Chabrol
Hets 44 Alf Sjöberg
Heure de la Vérité, L' 64 Henri Calef
Heure de Rêve, L' 14 Léonce Perret
Heure Tragique, L' 16 Georges Lacroix
Heures, Les 09 Louis Feuillade
Heures Chaudes 63 Louis Félix
Heureuse Intervention 19 Robert Florey
Heureux Anniversaire 61 Jean-Claude Car-
  rière, Pierre Etaix
Heureux Mort, L' 24 Serge Nadejdine
Heureux Qui Comme Ulysse 69 Henri
  Colpi
Heute Ist der Schönste Tag in Meinem
  Leben 36 Richard Oswald
Heute Nacht Eventuell 33 E. W. Emo
Hex 73 Leo Garen
Hex 80 Zhihong Gui
Hexen Bis aufs Blut Gequält 69 Michael
  Armstrong
Hexen Geschandet und zu Tode Gequält
  72 Adrian Hoven
Hexentöter von Blackmoor, Der 69 Jesús
  Franco
Hexer, Der 32 Karel Lamač
Hexer, Der 64 Alfred Vohrer
Hey Babe! 80 Rafal Zielinski
Hey Babu Riba 86 Jovan Acin
Hey Boy! Hey Girl! 59 David Lowell Rich
Hey Diddle Diddle 30 George Marshall
Hey Good Lookin' 75 Ralph Bakshi
Hey, Hey, Chela 86 Bebe Kamin
Hey! Hey! Cowboy 27 Lynn Reynolds
Hey! Hey! U.S.A. 38 Marcel Varnel
Hey, Let's Twist! 61 Greg Garrison
Hey Maestro! 88 Nodar Managadze
Hey Rookie 44 Charles Barton
Hey Rube! 28 George B. Seitz
Hey Sailor 34 Lloyd Bacon
Hey There, It's Yogi Bear 64 Joseph
  Barbera, William Hanna
Hey, You're As Funny As Fozzie
  Bear! 88 Jim Henson
Heya 67 Yoji Kuri
Hi Beautiful! 44 Leslie Goodwins
Hi, Buddy 43 Harold Young
Hi-De-Ho 47 Josh Binney
Hi Diddle Diddle 27 J. Steven Edwards
Hi Diddle Diddle 43 Andrew L. Stone
Hi-Fi 87 Vladimir Blazevski
Hi! Gang 41 Marcel Varnel
Hi, Gaucho 35 Thomas Atkins
Hi, Good Lookin' 44 Edward Lilley
Hi in the Cellar 70 Theodore J. Flicker
Hi-Jack 57 Cecil H. Williamson
Hi-Jacked 50 Sam Newfield
Hi-Jackers, The 63 James O'Connolly
Hi-Jacking Rustlers 26 Bennett Cohn

Hi mo Tsuki mo 69 Noboru Nakamura
Hi, Mom! 70 Brian DePalma
Hi, Neighbor! 42 Charles Lamont
Hi, Nellie! 34 Mervyn LeRoy
Hi no Hate 54 Satsuo Yamamoto
Hi no Tori 78 Kon Ichikawa
Hi no Tori 2772 79 Suguru Sugiyama,
  Osamu Tezuku
Hi Rasta, Ek 41 Ramjankhan Mehboob-
  khan
Hi-Riders, The 78 Greydon Clark
Hi! Stop Those Barrels 08 Lewin Fitz-
  hamon
Hi-Yo Silver! 38 John English, William
  Witney
Hiawatha 03 Joe Rosenthal
Hiawatha 52 Kurt Neumann
Hiawatha's Rabbit Hunt 41 Friz Freleng
Hibana 22 Teinosuke Kinugasa
Hibana 56 Teinosuke Kinugasa
Hibari no Takekurabe 55 Heinosuke
  Gosho
Hibernatus 68 Édouard Molinaro
Hibiscus Town 86 Jin Xie
Hic-Cups the Champ 32 Manny Gould,
  Ben Harrison
Hick, The 21 Larry Semon, Norman
  Taurog
Hick, a Slick and a Chick, A 48 Art Davis
Hick Chick, The 46 Tex Avery
Hick-Cup Pup 54 Joseph Barbera, Wil-
  liam Hanna
Hickey and Boggs 72 Robert Culp
Hickory Hill 68 Richard Leacock, George
  Plimpton
Hicks in Nightmareland 15 Raoul Barré
Hickville to Broadway 21 Carl Harbaugh
Hidari Uchiwa 35 Heinosuke Gosho
Hidden, The 87 Jack Sholder
Hidden Aces 27 Howard Mitchell
Hidden Agenda 90 Kenneth Loach
Hidden Children, The 17 Oscar Apfel
Hidden City, The 15 Francis Ford
Hidden City 36 B. Reeves Eason, Joseph
  Kane
Hidden City, The 50 Ford Beebe
Hidden City 87 Chico Botelho
Hidden City 87 Stephen Poliakoff
Hidden Code, The 20 Richard Le Strange
Hidden Danger 48 Ray Taylor
Hidden Enemy 40 Howard Bretherton
Hidden Evidence 34 Lambert Hillyer
Hidden Eye, The 45 Richard Whorf
Hidden Face 54 Edward D. Wood, Jr.
Hidden Face, The 65 Patrick Dromgoole
Hidden Fear 57 André De Toth
Hidden Fires 18 George Irving
Hidden Fortress, The 58 Akira Kurosawa
Hidden Gold 32 Arthur Rosson
Hidden Gold 40 Lesley Selander
Hidden Guns 56 Albert C. Gannaway
Hidden Hand, The 16 Lawrence Cowen
Hidden Hand, The 42 Ben Stoloff
Hidden Heart, The 53 William Beaudine
Hidden Hero, The 79 Kwon-taek Im
Hidden Hoard, The 08 Lewin Fitzhamon
Hidden Homicide 59 Anthony Young
Hidden Letters, The 14 Van Dyke Brooke
Hidden Light, The 12 Edwin S. Porter
Hidden Light 20 Abraham S. Schomer

Hidden Loot *25* Robert North Bradbury
Hidden Menace, The *25* Charles Hutchinson
Hidden Menace *38* Albert De Courville
Hidden Pearls, The *18* George Melford
Hidden Power *39* Lewis D. Collins
Hidden River *47* Emilio Fernández
Hidden Room, The *48* Edward Dmytryk
Hidden Room of 1,000 Horrors, The *60* Ernest Morris
Hidden Scar, The *16* Barry O'Neil
Hidden Secret *52* Wallace A. Grissell
Hidden Spring, The *17* E. Mason Hopper
Hidden Star, The *60* Ritwik Ghatak
Hidden Trail, The *11* Thomas Ince
Hidden Treasure *11* Frank Wilson
Hidden Truth, The *19* Julius Steger
Hidden Valley, The *16* Ernest C. Warde
Hidden Valley *32* Robert North Bradbury
Hidden Valley Outlaws *44* Howard Bretherton
Hidden Vision *90* Jag Mohan Mundhra
Hidden Way, The *26* Joseph De Grasse
Hidden Wealth *12* J. Wallett Waller
Hidden Witness, The *14* H. Oceano Martinek
Hidden Woman, The *22* Allan Dwan
Hidden Woman, The *56* Roberto Gavaldón
Hide and Go Shriek *87* Skip Schoolnik
Hide and Seek *13* Mack Sennett
Hide and Seek *22* Martin Walker
Hide and Seek *32* Dave Fleischer
Hide and Seek *62* Cy Endfield
Hide and Seek *63* Lars-Magnus Lindgren
Hide and Seek *72* David Eady
Hide and Seek *76* Leopoldo Torre-Nilsson
Hide and Seek *80* Dan Wolman
Hide and Seek Detectives *18* Edward F. Cline
Hide and Shriek *38* Gordon Douglas
Hide in Plain Sight *80* James Caan
Hide-Out *34* W. S. Van Dyke
Hideaway *37* Richard Rosson
Hideaway Girl *36* George Archainbaud
Hideaways, The *73* Fielder Cook
Hideg Napok *66* András Kovács
Hideko no Shashō-San *41* Mikio Naruse
Hideko the Bus Conductor *41* Mikio Naruse
Hideous Sun Demon, The *59* Thomas Bontross, Gianbatista Cassarino, Robert Clarke
Hideout *30* Reginald Barker
Hideout *48* Fergus McDonnell
Hideout *49* Philip Ford
Hideout, The *56* Peter Graham Scott
Hideout, The *61* Raoul André
Hideout in the Alps *36* Bernard Vorhaus
Hideouts *86* Wolfram Paulus
Hiding Out *87* Bob Giraldi
Hiding Place, The *75* James F. Collier
Hier et Aujourd'hui *18* Dominique Bernard-Deschamps
Higanbana *58* Yasujiro Ozu
Higashi Shinakai *69* Tadahiko Isomi
Higashikara Kita Otoko *61* Umeji Inoue
Hige no Chikara *31* Mikio Naruse
Higgins Family, The *38* Gus Meins
Higgins Family, The *40* Malcolm St. Clair

High *68* Laurence L. Kent
High and Dizzy *20* Hal Roach
High and Dry *53* Alexander Mackendrick
High and Handsome *25* Harry Garson
High and Low *13* Allan Dwan
High and Low *33* G. W. Pabst
High and Low *62* Akira Kurosawa
High and the Flighty, The *56* Robert McKimson
High and the Mighty, The *54* William A. Wellman
High Anxiety *77* Mel Brooks
High-Ballin' *78* Peter Carter
High Barbaree *47* Jack Conway
High Beer Pressure *36* Lesiie Goodwins
High, Bright Sun, The *64* Ralph Thomas
High Command, The *36* Thorold Dickinson
High Commissioner, The *68* Ralph Thomas
High Conquest *47* Irving Allen
High Cost, A *57* Mark Donskoi
High Cost of Living, The *16* Ashley Miller
High Cost of Living, The *19* Raoul Barré, Charles Bowers
High Cost of Loving, The *58* José Ferrer
High Country, The *80* Harvey Hart
High Crime *73* Enzo G. Castellari
High Desert Kill *90* Harry Falk
High Diving Hare *49* Friz Freleng
High Encounters of the Ultimate Kind *80* Thomas Chong
High Explosive *43* Frank McDonald
High Fidelity *88* Allan Miller
High Fidelity: The Adventures of the Guarneri String Quartet *88* Allan Miller
High Finance *17* Otis Turner
High Finance *33* George King
High Flies the Hawk *49* Jiří Weiss
High Flight *57* John Gilling
High Flyer, The *26* Harry Joe Brown
High Flyers *37* Edward F. Cline
High Flyin' George *27* Sam Newfield
High Frequency *88* Faliero Rosati
High Fury *47* Harold French
High Game *08* A. E. Coleby
High Gear *24* Archie Mayo
High Gear *31* George Stevens
High Gear *33* Leigh Jason
High Gear *46* Del Lord
High Gear Jeffrey *17* Edward Sloman
High Hand, The *15* William Desmond Taylor
High Hand, The *26* Leo D. Maloney
High Hat *27* James Ashmore Creelman
High Hat *29* Joseph Santley
High Hat *37* Clifford Sanforth
High Heels *21* Lee Kohlmar
High Heels! *72* Claude Chabrol
High Hell *58* Burt Balaban
High Hopes *88* Mike Leigh
High Infidelity *64* Mario Monicelli, Elio Petri, Franco Rossi, Luciano Salce
High Jinks in Society *49* John Guillermin, Robert Jordan Hill
High Jinx, A *25* Lewis Seiler
High Jump *59* Godfrey Grayson
High Kukus *73* James Broughton
High Life on a Farm *16* Hy Mayer
High Life Taylor *08* Georges Méliès

High Lonesome *50* Alan LeMay
High Noon *52* Fred Zinnemann
High Note, The *60* Chuck Jones
High Peril *34* Michael Curtiz
High Places *43* Mario Soldati
High Plains Drifter *72* Clint Eastwood
High Play *17* Edward Sloman
High Pockets *19* Ira M. Lowry
High Powered *45* William Berke
High-Powered Rifle, The *60* Maury Dexter
High Pressure *32* Mervyn LeRoy
High Rise Donkey *80* Michael Forlong
High Risk *81* Stewart Raffill
High Road, The *15* John W. Noble
High Road, The *30* Sidney Franklin
High Road to China *82* Brian G. Hutton
High Rolling *77* Igor Auzins
High Rolling in a Hot Corvette *77* Igor Auzins
High School *40* George Nicholls, Jr.
High School *53* Luciano Emmer
High School *68* Frederick Wiseman
High School Big Shot *59* Joel Rapp
High School Caesar *60* O'Dale Ireland
High School Confidential! *58* Jack Arnold
High School Girl *35* Crane Wilbur
High School Girls *90* Kuo-fu Chen
High School Hellcats *58* Edward Bernds
High School Hero *27* David Butler
High School Hero *46* Arthur Dreifuss
High School Honeymoon *60* Richard Rush
High Sea Blues *26* Stephen Roberts
High Seas *28* Mannie Davis
High Seas *29* Denison Clift
High Seas Hijack *76* John Bushelman
High Season *87* Clare Peploe
High Sierra *41* Raoul Walsh
High Sign, The *17* Elmer Clifton
High Sign, The *20* Edward F. Cline, Buster Keaton
High Society *29* Wesley Ruggles
High Society *32* John Rawlins
High Society *55* William Beaudine
High Society *56* Charles Walters
High Society Blues *30* David Butler
High Society Limited *82* Ottokar Runze
High Speed *17* Elmer Clifton, George L. Sargent
High Speed *20* Charles Miller
High Speed *24* Herbert Blaché
High Speed *32* D. Ross Lederman
High Speed *86* Monique Dartonne, Michel Kaptur
High Speed Lee *23* Dudley Murphy
High-Spirited Blonde, A *80* Jiří Menzel
High Spirits *88* Neil Jordan
High Spots *27* Stephen Roberts
High Stake, A *12* August Blom
High Stakes *18* Arthur Hoyt
High Stakes *27* Hugh Shields
High Stakes *28* George B. Seitz
High Stakes *31* Lowell Sherman
High Stakes *46* Ray Nazarro
High Stakes *87* Laurence L. Kent
High Stakes *89* Amos Kollek
High Steel *66* Don Owen
High Steppers *26* Edwin Carewe
High Strung *28* Mark Sandrich
High Tension *36* Allan Dwan
High Tension *50* Ingmar Bergman

High Terrace, The *56* Henry Cass
High Tide *18* Gilbert P. Hamilton
High Tide *47* John Reinhardt
High Tide *87* Gillian Armstrong
High Tide at Noon *57* Philip Leacock
High Time *60* Blake Edwards
High Treason *29* Maurice Elvey
High Treason *35* Henry Edwards
High Treason *51* Roy Boulting
High Up *28* Rollin Hamilton, Rudolf Ising
High Velocity *77* Remi Kramer
High Venture *51* Lewis R. Foster
High Vermilion *51* Byron Haskin
High Voltage *29* Howard Higgin
High Wall *47* Kurt Bernhardt
High Wall, The *64* Karel Kachyňa
High, Wide and Handsome *37* Rouben Mamoulian
High Wind in Jamaica, A *65* Alexander Mackendrick
High Window, The *47* John Brahm
High Yellow *65* Larry Buchanan
Highbinders, The *15* Tod Browning
Highbinders, The *26* George Terwilliger
Higher and Higher *43* Tim Whelan
Higher Education *87* John Sheppard
Higher Law, The *23* Frank Borzage
Higher Patriotism, A *37* Mou-che Yen
Higher Power, A *16* Ethyle Batley
Highest Bid, The *16* William Russell
Highest Bidder, The *21* Wallace Worsley
Highest Bidder, The *72* Eddie Romero
Highest Honour, The *82* Peter Maxwell
Highest Honour — A True Story, The *82* Peter Maxwell
Highest Law, The *21* Ralph Ince
Highest Trump, The *19* James Young
Highland Fling *36* H. Manning Haynes
Highlander, The *11* Theo Bouwmeester
Highlander *86* Russell Mulcahy
Highly Dangerous *50* Roy Ward Baker
Highpoint *79* Peter Carter
Highriders *87* Clark Henderson
Highs *76* Stan Brakhage
Highway, The *34* Yu Sun
Highway Dragnet *54* Nathan Juran
Highway of Hope, The *17* Howard Estabrook
Highway Patrol *38* C. C. Coleman, Jr.
Highway Patrol *50* Sam Newfield
Highway Pickup *63* Julien Duvivier
Highway Runnery *65* Rudy Larriva
Highway Sings, The *37* Alexander Hammid
Highway Snobbery *36* Manny Gould, Ben Harrison
Highway 13 *48* William Berke
Highway 301 *50* Andrew L. Stone
Highway to Battle *60* Ernest Morris
Highway to Freedom *41* Richard Thorpe
Highway to Hell *84* Mark Griffiths
Highway West *41* William McGann
Highwayman, The *51* Lesley Selander
Highwayman Hal *13* Hay Plumb
Highwayman Rides, The *30* King Vidor
Highwayman's Honour, A *14* Siegfried von Herkomer
Highways by Night *42* Peter Godfrey
Hija de Frankenstein, La *71* Miguel Delgado

Hija del Engaño, La *51* Luis Buñuel
Hijack, The *52* Ján Kadár, Elmar Klos
Hi-Jack *57* Cecil H. Williamson
Hijack *75* Michael Forlong
Hijack Highway *55* Gilles Grangier
Hi-Jacked *50* Sam Newfield
Hi-Jackers, The *63* James O'Connolly
Hijacking, The *52* Ján Kadár, Elmar Klos
Hi-Jacking Rustlers *26* Bennett Cohn
Hijas del Cid, Las *62* Miguel Iglesias Bonns
Hijo de Pedro Navajas, El *87* Alfonso Rosas Priego
Hijo del Barrio, El *40* José A. Ferreyra
Hijo del Capitán Blood, El *62* Tulio Demicheli
Hijo del Crack, El *53* Leopoldo Torre-Nilsson, Leopoldo Torres Ríos
Hijo del Palenque *86* Rubén Galindo, Jr.
Hijo del Pistolero, El *64* Paul Landres
Hijos de Fierro, Los *76* Fernando Solanas
Hijos de la Guerra Fría, Los *85* Gonzalo Justiniano
Hijos de María Morales, Los *52* Fernando De Fuentes
Hijösen no Onna *33* Yasujiro Ozu
Hikari *28* Tomu Uchida
Hikaru Onna *87* Shinji Somai
Hiken *63* Hiroshi Inagaki
Hiken Yaburi *69* Kazuo Ikehiro
Hiking with Mademoiselle *33* Edward Nakhimoff
Hikinige *66* Mikio Naruse
Hikkoshi Fūfu *28* Yasujiro Ozu
Hikuidori *26* Teinosuke Kinugasa
Hilal, Al *32* Ramjankhan Mehboobkhan
Hilarious Posters, The *06* Georges Méliès
Hilarities by Hy Mayer *13* Hy Mayer
Hilarity on Board Ship *02* George Albert Smith
Hilary's Blues *83* Peter Jensen
Hilda Crane *56* Philip Dunne
Hilda Routs the Enemy *15* Cecil Birch
Hilda's Busy Day *15* Cecil Birch
Hilda's Lovers *11* Bert Haldane
Hilde Petersen, Postlagernd *37* Viktor Jansen
Hilde Warren and Death *16* Joe May
Hilde Warren und der Tod *16* Joe May
Hildur and the Magician *69* Larry Jordan
Hilfe! Ich Bin Unsichtbar *52* E. W. Emo
1001 Crtež *61* Dušan Vukotić
Hill, The *65* Sidney Lumet
Hill Billies *35* Walter Lantz
Hill Billy *18* John Ford
Hill Billy, The *24* George W. Hill
Hill in Korea, A *56* Julian Amyes
Hill of Death *62* Veljko Bulajić
Hill on the Dark Side of the Moon, A *83* Lennart Hjulström
Hill 24 Doesn't Answer *55* Thorold Dickinson
Hill 171 *87* Romeo Montaya
Hillbilly, The *35* Walter Lantz
Hillbilly Blitzkrieg *42* Roy Mack
Hillbilly Goat *37* Leslie Goodwins
Hillbilly Hare *50* Robert McKimson
Hillbillys in a Haunted House *67* Jean Yarbrough

Hillcrest Mystery, The *18* George Fitzmaurice
Hill's Angels *78* Bruce Bilson
Hills Are Calling, The *14* Cecil M. Hepworth
Hills Have Eyes, The *77* Wes Craven
Hills Have Eyes Part II, The *83* Wes Craven
Hills of Donegal, The *47* John Argyle
Hills of Home *48* Fred M. Wilcox
Hills of Ireland, The *51* Harry Dugan
Hills of Kentucky *27* Howard Bretherton
Hills of Missing Men *22* John P. McGowan
Hills of Oklahoma *50* R. G. Springsteen
Hills of Old Wyomin', The *36* Dave Fleischer
Hills of Old Wyoming *37* Nate Watt
Hills of Peril *27* Lambert Hillyer
Hills of the Brave *50* Ray Nazarro
Hills of Utah *51* John English
Hills Run Red, The *66* Carlo Lizzani
Him *52* Luis Buñuel
Himalaya *50* Marcel Ichac
Himatsuri *85* Mitsuo Yanagimachi
Himeyuri Lily Tower *53* Tadashi Imai
Himeyuri Lily Tower *82* Tadashi Imai
Himeyuri no Tō *53* Tadashi Imai
Himeyuri no Tō *82* Tadashi Imai
Himiko *74* Masahiro Shinoda
Himlaspelet *42* Alf Sjöberg
Himmat aur Mehnat *88* K. Bappiah
Himmel auf Erden, Der *35* E. W. Emo
Himmel och Pannkaka *59* Hasse Ekman
Himmel og Helvede *88* Morten Arnfred
Himmel Ohne Sterne *55* Helmut Käutner
Himmel Über Berlin, Der *87* Wim Wenders
Himmelskibet *17* Forest Holger-Madsen
Himmo, King of Jerusalem *87* Amos Guttman
Himmo Melech Yerushalaim *87* Amos Guttman
Hims Ancient and Modern *22* Edward D. Roberts
Himself As Herself *67* Gregory Markopoulos
Hind, The *58* Atıf Yılmaz
Hindenburg, The *75* Robert Wise
Hindered *74* Stephen Dwoskin
Hindle Wakes *18* Maurice Elvey
Hindle Wakes *27* Maurice Elvey, Victor Saville
Hindle Wakes *31* Victor Saville
Hindle Wakes *51* Arthur Crabtree
Hindoo Dagger, The *08* D. W. Griffith
Hindoo Jugglers *00* Walter R. Booth
Hindoo's Treachery, The *10* Dave Aylott
Hindu, The *53* Frank Ferrin
Hindu Image, The *13* Raoul Walsh
Hindu Tomb, The *21* Fritz Lang, Joe May
Hindu Tomb, The *58* Fritz Lang
Hing Lou Meng *66* Ping Wang
Hinges on the Bar Room Door, The *21* Vernon Stallings
Hinter den Zahlen *39* Walter Ruttmann
Hintertreppe *21* Leopold Jessner, Paul Leni
Hintónjáró Szerelem *54* László Ranódy
Hinton's Double *17* Ernest C. Warde

Hints on Horsemanship *24* Geoffrey Benstead
Hinugot sa Langit *86* Lino Brocka
Hip Action *33* George Marshall
Hip, Hip, Hooray! *87* Kjell Grede
Hip, Hip, Hurrah! *87* Kjell Grede
Hip, Hip—Hurry! *58* Chuck Jones
Hipnosis *62* Eugenio Martin
Hipólito, El de Santa *49* Fernando De Fuentes
Hippetty Hopper *49* Robert McKimson
Hippie Revolt, The *67* Edgar Beatty
Hippocampe, L' *33* Jean Painlevé
Hippodrome *61* Arthur Maria Rabenalt
Hippodrome Races, Dreamland, Coney Island *05* Edwin S. Porter
Hippolyt the Lackey *32* Steve Sekely
Hippydrome Tiger *68* Alex Lovy
Hips Hips Hooray *34* Mark Sandrich
Hiram's Bride *09* Sidney Olcott
Hire a Hall *27* William C. Nolan
Hired and Fired *29* Norman Taurog
Hired Gun, The *57* Ray Nazarro
Hired Gun *61* Lindsay Shonteff
Hired Guns *52* Thomas Carr
Hired Hand, The *71* Peter Fonda
Hired Killer, The *67* Franco Prosperi
Hired Man, The *18* Victor Schertzinger
Hired Wife *34* George Melford
Hired Wife *40* William A. Seiter
Hireling, The *73* Alan Bridges
Hirok Rajar Deshe *79* Satyajit Ray
Hiroku Kaibyōden *69* Tokuzo Tanaka
Hiroku Onna-Rō *67* Akira Inoue
Hiroshima *53* Hideo Sekigawa
Hiroshima Heartache *62* Kozaburo Yoshimura
Hiroshima, Mon Amour *59* Alain Resnais
Hirsekorn *31* Andrew Marton
Hirsekorn Greift Ein *32* Rudolf Bernauer
His Actress Daughter *12* Bert Haldane
His Affair *37* William A. Seiter
His Alibi *16* Roscoe Arbuckle
His Ancestors *14* Émile Cohl
His and Hers *60* Brian Desmond Hurst
His and His *64* Henry Levin
His Apologies *35* Widgey R. Newman
His Back Against the Wall *22* Rowland V. Lee
His Best Friend *38* Harry Piel
His Best Girl *21* Charlie Chase
His Best Man *36* William McGann
His Better Half *27* Norman Taurog
His Better Self *11* Alice Guy-Blaché
His Birthright *18* William Worthington
His Bitter Half *50* Friz Freleng
His Bitter Lesson *15* Ethyle Batley
His Bonded Wife *18* Charles Brabin
His Bread and Butter *16* Edward F. Cline
His Bridal Night *19* Kenneth Webb
His Brother's Ghost *45* Sam Newfield
His Brother's Keeper *21* Wilfred North
His Brother's Keeper *39* Roy William Neill
His Brother's Wife *15* Warwick Buckland
His Brother's Wife *16* Harley Knoles
His Brother's Wife *36* W. S. Van Dyke
His Buddy's Wife *25* Tom Terriss
His Burglar Brother *12* A. E. Coleby
His Busted Trust *16* Edward F. Cline

His Busy Day *18* Fred Rains
His Butler's Sister *43* Frank Borzage
His Call *25* Yakov Protazanov
His Captive *15* Frank Lloyd
His Captive Woman *29* George Fitzmaurice
His Cheap Watch *07* Frank Mottershaw
His Children's Children *23* Sam Wood
His Choice *13* Hubert von Herkomer
His Chum the Baron *13* Mack Sennett
His Coming-Out Party *17* William Beaudine
His Conscience *11* Theo Bouwmeester
His Country *28* William K. Howard
His Country Cousin *20* Gregory La Cava
His Country's Bidding *14* Cecil M. Hepworth
His Country's Honour *14* Charles C. Calvert
His Crooked Career *13* Mack Sennett
His Dark Past *18* Gregory La Cava
His Darker Self *24* John W. Noble
His Daughter *11* D. W. Griffith
His Daughter and His Gold *06* Lewin Fitzhamon
His Daughter Is Peter *38* Heinz Helbig
His Daughter's Dilemma *16* Ralph Dewsbury
His Daughter's Voice *07* Walter R. Booth
His Day Off *18* Gregory La Cava
His Dearest Possession *19* Henry Edwards
His Debt *19* William Worthington
His Divorced Wife *19* Douglas Gerrard
His Dog *27* Karl Brown
His Double Life *33* William DeMille, Arthur Hopkins
His Duty *09* D. W. Griffith, Frank Powell
His Duty *12* Fred Rains
His Enemy the Law *18* Raymond Wells
His Enemy's Daughter *17* W. Eugene Moore
His English Wife *26* Gustaf Molander
His Error *30* Stephen Roberts
His Evil Genius *13* Frank Wilson
His Excellency *27* Grigori Roshal
His Excellency *44* Hasse Ekman
His Excellency *51* Robert Hamer
His Exciting Night *38* Gus Meins
His Eyes *16* Vyacheslav Viskovsky
His Family Tree *35* Charles Vidor
His Fatal Beauty *17* William Beaudine
His Father's Bridegroom *13* William Duncan
His Father's Footsteps *15* Charlie Chase, Ford Sterling
His Father's Sin *15* Will P. Kellino
His Father's Son *17* George D. Baker
His Father's Voice: Mrs. Kelly *13* Walter R. Booth
His Father's Wife *19* Frank Crane
His Ferocious Pal *34* Spencer G. Bennet
His Fighting Blood *15* Tom Santschi
His Fighting Blood *35* John English
His First Car *30* Monty Banks
His First Cigar, Probably His Last *02* George Albert Smith
His First Command *29* Gregory La Cava
His First Flame *27* Harry Edwards
His First Job *08* Georges Méliès
His First Monocle *11* August Blom

His First Patient *12* August Blom
His First Silk Hat *06* Frank Mottershaw
His First Sovereign *12* Mark Melford
His First Top Hat *07* J. H. Martin
His Foreign Wife *27* John P. McCarthy
His Forgotten Wife *24* William A. Seiter
His Girl Friday *39* Howard Hawks
His Glorious Night *29* Lionel Barrymore
His Grace Gives Notice *24* Will P. Kellino
His Grace Gives Notice *33* George A. Cooper
His Grace's Last Testament *19* Victor Sjöström
His Grace's Will *19* Victor Sjöström
His Grandson *13* Ernest G. Batley
His Great Adventure *38* Fernando De Fuentes
His Great Moment *27* Miles Mander
His Great Opportunity *14* Warwick Buckland
His Great Triumph *16* William Nigh
His Greatest Battle *25* Robert J. Horner
His Greatest Bluff *27* Henryk Galeen, Harry Piel
His Greatest Gamble *34* John S. Robertson
His Greatest Sacrifice *21* J. Gordon Edwards
His Guardian Angel *20* August Blom
His Hare Raising Tale *51* Friz Freleng
His Head *29* Jean Epstein
His Hereafter *16* F. Richard Jones
His, Hers and Theirs *68* Melville Shavelson
His Highness the Dragon *25* August Blom
His Honour at Stake *12* Bert Haldane
His Hour *24* King Vidor
His House in Order *20* Hugh Ford
His House in Order *28* Randle Ayrton
His Innocent Dupe *15* Forest Holger-Madsen
His Inspiration *13* Christy Cabanne
His Jazz Bride *26* Herman Raymaker
His Just Deserts *14* Gerald Lawrence
His Kind of Woman *51* John Farrow, Richard Fleischer
His Lady *26* Alan Crosland
His Land *67* James F. Collier
His Last Adventure *32* Armand Schaefer
His Last Bow *23* George Ridgwell
His Last Burglary *10* D. W. Griffith
His Last Burglary *11* Theo Bouwmeester
His Last Defence *19* Geoffrey Wilmer
His Last Dollar *10* D. W. Griffith
His Last Fight *13* Ralph Ince
His Last Fling *35* Charles Lamont
His Last Haul *28* Marshall Neilan
His Last Legs *20* Gregory La Cava
His Last Race *23* B. Reeves Eason
His Last Serenade *15* Frank Lloyd
His Last Trick *15* Frank Lloyd
His Last Twelve Hours *50* Luigi Zampa
His Last Will *18* Gregory La Cava
His Late Excellency *27* Wilhelm Thiele
His Lesson *12* D. W. Griffith
His Life to Live *63* Evald Schorm
His Little Lordship *15* Tom Watts
His Little Page *14* Van Dyke Brooke
His Little Son Was with Him All the Time *10* Percy Stow

His Lordship *15* George Loane Tucker
His Lordship *32* Michael Powell
His Lordship *36* Herbert Mason
His Lordship Goes to Press *38* Maclean Rogers
His Lordship Regrets *38* Maclean Rogers
His Lordship's Last Will *19* Victor Sjöström
His Lordship's White Feather *12* Alice Guy-Blaché
His Lost Love *09* D. W. Griffith
His Lucky Day *29* Edward F. Cline
His Lying Heart *16* Ford Sterling
His Maiden Aunt *13* H. Oceano Martinek
His Majesty and Co. *35* Anthony Kimmins
His Majesty, Bunker Bean *18* William Desmond Taylor
His Majesty Bunker Bean *25* Harry Beaumont
His Majesty Bunker Bean *36* William Hamilton, Edward Killy
His Majesty King Ballyhoo *31* Carl Boese
His Majesty Mr. Jones *50* Alessandro Blasetti
His Majesty O'Keefe *53* Byron Haskin
His Majesty the American *19* Joseph E. Henabery
His Majesty the Outlaw *24* Jacques Jaccard
His Majesty the Scarecrow of Oz *14* J. Farrell MacDonald
His Majesty Will Have to Wait *45* Gustaf Edgren
His Majesty's Dates *64* Károly Makk
His Majesty's Guests Steal a Holiday *10* Will Barker
His Master's Voice *10* H. Oceano Martinek
His Master's Voice *25* Renaud Hoffman
His Meal Ticket *21* Edward F. Cline
His Message *11* Thomas Ince
His Most Difficult Part *12* August Blom
His Mother *12* Sidney Olcott
His Mother's Boy *17* Victor Schertzinger
His Mother's Necklace *10* Walter R. Booth
His Mother's Portrait, or The Soldier's Vision *00* Lewin Fitzhamon
His Mother's Sacrifice *15* Ethyle Batley
His Mother's Scarf *11* D. W. Griffith
His Mother's Son *13* D. W. Griffith
His Mouse Friday *51* Joseph Barbera, William Hanna
His Musical Career *14* Charles Chaplin
His Musical Soup *20* Raoul Barré, Charles Bowers
His Mysterious Adventure *23* Benjamin Christensen
His Mystery Girl *23* Robert F. Hill
His Name Is Robert *67* Ilya Olshvanger
His Name Is Sukhe-Bator *42* Josef Heifits, Alexander Zarkhi
His Neighbor's Wife *13* Edwin S. Porter
His Nemesis *12* Thomas Ince
His New Job *15* Charles Chaplin
His New Lid *10* D. W. Griffith
His New Mama *10* Lewin Fitzhamon
His New Mamma *24* Roy Del Ruth
His New Profession *14* Charles Chaplin
His New York Wife *26* Albert Kelley
His Nibs *21* Gregory La Cava
His Night Out *35* Max Mack

His Night Out *35* William Nigh
His Noisy Still *20* Roy Del Ruth
His Official Fiancée *18* Robert Vignola
His Old-Fashioned Mother *13* Allan Dwan
His Only Daughter *10* Theo Bouwmeester
His Only Friend *09* Lewin Fitzhamon
His Only Pair of Trousers *07* A. E. Coleby
His Other Wife *21* Percy Nash
His Other Woman *57* Walter Lang
His Own Fault *12* Mack Sennett
His Own Home Town *18* Victor Schertzinger
His Own Law *20* J. Parker Read
His Own People *18* William P. S. Earle
His Parisian Wife *19* Émile Chautard
His People *25* Edward Sloman
His Pest Friend *38* Leslie Goodwins
His Phantom Burglar *15* Dave Aylott
His Phantom Sweetheart *15* Ralph Ince
His Picture in the Papers *16* John Emerson
His Pipe Dreams *15* Vincent Whitman
His Prehistoric Past *14* Charles Chaplin
His Pride and Shame *16* Charlie Chase, Ford Sterling
His Private Life *26* Roscoe Arbuckle
His Private Life *28* Frank Tuttle
His Private Secretary *33* Phil Whitman
His Puppy Love *21* Charles Reisner
His Real Wife *16* Forest Holger-Madsen
His Reformation *14* Arthur Holmes-Gore
His Regeneration *15* Gilbert M. Anderson
His Rest Day *27* George A. Cooper
His Return *15* Raoul Walsh
His Rise to Fame *27* Bernard F. McEveety
His Robe of Honor *18* Rex Ingram
His Royal Highness *18* Carlyle Blackwell
His Royal Highness *32* F. W. Thring
His Royal Slyness *19* Hal Roach
His Salad Days *18* Fred Rains
His Scarlet Cloak *58* Satsuo Yamamoto
His Second Childhood *14* Charles C. Calvert
His Second Wife *13* Ralph Ince
His Secret Sin *12* A. E. Coleby
His Secretary *25* Hobart Henley
His Silver Bachelorhood *13* Van Dyke Brooke
His Sister-in-Law *10* D. W. Griffith*
His Sister's Champion *16* John H. Collins
His Sister's Honour *14* Bert Haldane
His Sister's Sweetheart *11* Alice Guy-Blaché
His Smothered Love *18* Edward F. Cline, F. Richard Jones
His Son *11* Bert Haldane
His Superior Officer *04* Lewin Fitzhamon
His Superior's Honor *15* Frank Lloyd
His Supreme Moment *25* George Fitzmaurice
His Supreme Sacrifice *22* Bert Wynne
His Sweetheart *17* Donald Crisp
His Sweetheart When a Boy *07* Arthur Cooper
His Talented Wife *14* Mack Sennett
His Temporary Wife *20* Joseph Levering
His Tiger Lady *28* Hobart Henley
His Trail *17* Paul Terry
His Trust *10* D. W. Griffith
His Trust Fulfilled *10* D. W. Griffith
His Trysting Place *14* Charles Chaplin

His Two Daughters *20* Ernst Lubitsch
His Two Loves *52* Carmine Gallone
His Uncle's Heir *17* Dave Aylott
His Unknown Rival *15* Frederick J. Allen
His Unlucky Job *21* Ray Enright*
His Ups and Downs *13* Mack Sennett
His Vindication *15* Ralph Dewsbury
His Ward's Love *09* D. W. Griffith
His Washing Day *05* Arthur Cooper
His Wedding Morn *08* A. E. Coleby
His Wedding Night *15* Mauritz Stiller
His Wedding Night *17* Roscoe Arbuckle
His Week-End *32* Edward F. Cline
His Week's Pay *10* Percy Stow
His Wife *15* George Foster Platt
His Wife's Brother *10* Theo Bouwmeester
His Wife's Brother *12* A. E. Coleby
His Wife's Friend *19* Joseph De Grasse
His Wife's Good Name *16* Ralph Ince
His Wife's Habit *70* Joy Houck, Jr.
His Wife's Husband *13* Avrom Yitskhok Kaminsky
His Wife's Husband *22* George A. Cooper
His Wife's Husband *22* Kenneth Webb
His Wife's Lover *31* Sidney Goldin
His Wife's Mistake *16* Roscoe Arbuckle
His Wife's Money *20* Ralph Ince
His Wife's Mother *09* D. W. Griffith
His Wife's Mother *32* Harry Hughes
His Wife's Past *15* Mauritz Stiller
His Wife's Visitor *09* D. W. Griffith
His Wild Oats *16* Clarence Badger, Ford Sterling
His Woman *31* Edward Sloman
His Wonderful Lamp *13* Edwin J. Collins
His Wooden Wedding *25* Leo McCarey
His Work or His Wife *09* Percy Stow
His Young Wife *45* Mario Soldati
His Younger Brother *13* Charles C. Calvert
His Younger Sister *76* Tadashi Imai
Hiss and Make Up *43* Friz Freleng
Hisshōka *45* Kenji Mizoguchi*
Histoire Comique *42* Marc Allégret
Histoire d'A, L' *74* Charles Belmont
Histoire d'Adèle H., L' *75* François Truffaut
Histoire d'Aimer *69* Claude Lelouch
Histoire d'Amour, Une *32* Pál Fejős
Histoire d'Amour, Une *33* Max Ophüls
Histoire d'Amour, Une *51* Robert Clavel
Histoire de Brigands, Une *20* Donatien
Histoire de Chapeaux *10* Émile Cohl
Histoire de Lourdes *32* Charles Dekeukeleire
Histoire de Minna Claessens *12* Alfred Machin
Histoire de Puce *09* Louis Feuillade
Histoire de Rire *41* Marcel L'Herbier
Histoire de Vent, Une *88* Joris Ivens, Marceline Loridan
Histoire d'Eau, Une *58* Jean-Luc Godard, François Truffaut
Histoire d'Éléphants, Une *58* Frédéric Rossif
Histoire des Crevettes *64* Jean Painlevé
Histoire d'Odessa *35* Jean Lods
Histoire du Costume *39* René Clément
Histoire du Palais Idéale *54* Jacques Baratier

Histoire du Soldat Inconnu *32* Henri Storck

Histoire d'un Crime *01* Ferdinand Zecca

Histoire d'un Crime, L' *06* Georges Méliès

Histoire d'un Petit Garçon Devenu Grand *63* François Reichenbach

Histoire d'un Pierrot *13* Baldassare Negroni

Histoire d'un Poisson Rouge, L' *58* Edmond Séchan

Histoire d'un P'tit Gars, L' *12* Alfred Machin

Histoire d'une Pépite *62* Pierre Hébert

Histoire Grise *62* Pierre Hébert

Histoire Immortelle, Une *68* Orson Welles

Histoire Simple, Une *78* Claude Sautet

Histoires d'Amérique *88* Chantal Akerman

Histoires Extraordinaires *67* Federico Fellini, Louis Malle, Roger Vadim

Historia de Amor, Una *67* Jorge Grau

Historia de Tres Amores *53* Vincente Minnelli, Gottfried Reinhardt

Historia de una Batalla *62* Manuel Octavio Gómez

Historia de una Chica Sola *69* Jorge Grau

Historia de una Mala Mujer *48* Luis Saslavsky

Historia de una Noche *41* Luis Saslavsky

Historia del 900 *49* Hugo Del Carril

História do Brasil *74* Marcos Medeiros, Glauber Rocha

Historia Naturae *68* Jan Švankmajer

Historia Oficial, La *85* Luis Puenzo

Historia Współczesna *60* Wanda Jakubowska

Historia Żółtej Ciżemki *61* Sylwester Chęciński

Historias de la Revolución *60* Tomás Gutiérrez Alea

Historias Prohibidas de Pulgarcito *79* Paul Leduc

Historical Fan *09* Émile Cohl

Historie Fíkového Listu *38* Alexander Hammid

Historien om Barbara *67* Palle Kjærulff-Schmidt

Historien om en Mand *44* Jørgen Roos*

Historien om en Moder *12* August Blom

Historien om et Slot *51* Jørgen Roos

History *40* Tomu Uchida

History *70* Ernie Gehr

History *86* Luigi Comencini

History and Romance of Transportation, The *41* Sidney Meyers*

History Is Made at Night *37* Frank Borzage

History Lessons *72* Danièle Huillet, Jean-Marie Straub

History of a Battle *62* Manuel Octavio Gómez

History of Albertfalva, A *55* Márta Mészáros

History of Brazil *74* Marcos Medeiros, Glauber Rocha

History of Love, The *55* Kajiro Yamamoto

History of Mr. Polly, The *49* Anthony Pelissier

History of Motion in Motion, The *67* Stan Vanderbeek

History of Postwar Japan As Told by a Bar Hostess *70* Shohei Imamura

History of the Burning Years *61* Yulia Solntseva

History of the Cinema, The *57* John Halas

History of the Civil War *21* Dziga Vertov

History of the Fig Leaf *38* Alexander Hammid

History of the World—Part I *81* Mel Brooks

Hit! *73* Sidney J. Furie

Hit, The *84* Stephen Frears

Hit and Run *24* Edward Sedgwick

Hit and Run *57* Hugo Haas

Hit and Run *66* Mikio Naruse

Hit and Run *81* Robin Spry

Hit and Run *82* Charles Braverman

Hit and Run Driver *35* Edward L. Cahn

Hit Him Again *14* Charles Chaplin, Mack Sennett

Hit List *89* William Lustig

Hit Man *72* George Armitage

Hit Me Again *33* Robert Florey

Hit of the Show *28* Ralph Ince

Hit or Miss *19* Del Henderson

Hit Parade, The *37* Gus Meins

Hit Parade of 1941 *40* John H. Auer

Hit Parade of 1943 *43* Albert S. Rogell

Hit Parade of 1947 *47* Frank McDonald

Hit Parade of 1951 *50* John H. Auer

Hit Parade of the Gay Nineties, The *43* Jean Negulesco

Hit the Deck *30* Luther Reed

Hit the Deck *55* Roy Rowland

Hit the Hay *45* Del Lord

Hit the Ice *43* Erle C. Kenton, Charles Lamont

Hit the Road *41* Joe May

Hit the Saddle *37* Mack V. Wright

Hit-the-Trail Holliday *18* Marshall Neilan

Hitch-Hike Lady *35* Aubrey H. Scotto

Hitch-Hiker, The *53* Ida Lupino

Hitch in Time, A *78* Jan Darnley-Smith

Hitcher, The *86* Robert Harmon

Hitchhike to Happiness *45* Joseph Santley

Hitchhike to Heaven *36* Frank R. Strayer

Hitchhike to Hell *78* Irvin Berwick

Hitchhikers, The *72* Beverly Sebastian, Ferd Sebastian

Hitchin' Posts *20* John Ford

Hitchy-Coo *16* Dave Aylott

Hitchy-Koo *13* Edwin J. Collins

Hither and Thither *22* Raoul Barré, Charles Bowers

Hitler *61* Stuart Heisler

Hitler: A Film from Germany *77* Hans-Jürgen Syberberg

Hitler—Beast of Berlin *39* Sam Newfield

Hitler...Connais Pas! *62* Bertrand Blier

Hitler—Dead or Alive *42* Nick Grindé

Hitler: Ein Film aus Deutschland *77* Hans-Jürgen Syberberg

Hitler Gang, The *44* John Farrow

Hitler Lives? *45* Don Siegel

Hitler: The Last Ten Days *73* Ennio De Concini

Hitlerjunge Quex *33* Hans Steinhoff

Hitler's Children *42* Edward Dmytryk

Hitler's Executioners *58* Felix von Podmanitzky

Hitler's Gold *75* Peter Duffell

Hitler's Hangman *42* Douglas Sirk

Hitler's Madman *42* Douglas Sirk

Hitler's SS: Portrait in Evil *85* Jim Goddard

Hitler's Son *78* Rod Amateau

Hitler's Women *43* Steve Sekely

Hitman *85* Bobby A. Suarez

Hito Hada Kannon *37* Teinosuke Kinugasa

Hito no Isshō *27* Kenji Mizoguchi

Hito no Yo Sugata *28* Heinosuke Gosho

Hitokiri *70* Hideo Gosha

Hitori Musuko *36* Yasujiro Ozu

Hitotsubu no Mugi *58* Kozaburo Yoshimura

Hittebarnet *15* Forest Holger-Madsen

Hitter, The *79* Christopher Leitch

Hittin' the Trail *37* Robert North Bradbury

Hitting a New High *37* Raoul Walsh

Hitting Home *88* Robin Spry

Hitting the Headlines *42* Joseph Santley

Hitting the High Spots *18* Raoul Barré, Charles Bowers

Hitting the High Spots *18* Charles Swickard

Hitting the Jackpot *49* Edward Bernds

Hitting the Trail *18* Del Henderson

Hiuch ha'Gdi *86* Shimon Dotan

Hivatalnok Urak *18* Béla Balázs

Hiver, L' *69* Marcel Hanoun

Hi'Ya, Chum *43* Harold Young

Hi'Ya, Sailor *43* Jean Yarbrough

Hjärtan Som Mötas *14* Victor Sjöström

Hjärtats Triumf *29* Gustaf Molander

Hjärter Knekt *50* Hasse Ekman

Hjerte af Guld, Et *12* August Blom

Hjerternes Kamp *12* August Blom

Hjertestorme *15* August Blom

Hjertets Guld *12* August Blom

Hjertetyven *43* Albert Mertz, Jørgen Roos

Hledám Dům Holubů *85* Věra Plívová-Šimková

Ho! *68* Robert Enrico

Ho! Criminal Face *68* Robert Enrico

Ho Perduto Mio Marito *36* Enrico Guazzoni

Ho Scelto l'Amore *53* Mario Zampi

Ho Visto Brillare le Stelle *39* Enrico Guazzoni

Hoa-Binh *70* Raoul Coutard

Hoarded Assets *18* Paul Scardon

Hoax, The *72* Robert Anderson

Hob fee Baghdad *86* Abdul Hadi Al Rawi

Hobbs in a Hurry *18* Henry King

Hobby Horse Laffs *42* Norm McCabe

Hobo Bobo *47* Robert McKimson

Hobo Gadget Band, The *39* Cal Dalton, Ben Hardaway

Hoboes, The *38* Karel Lamač

Hoboes in Paradise *50* René Le Haneff

Hoboken Nightingale, The *24* Earl Hurd

Hobson's Choice *20* Percy Nash

Hobson's Choice *31* Thomas Bentley

Hobson's Choice *53* David Lean

Hochtourist, Der *34* Alfred Zeisler

Hochzeit am Wolfgangsee *34* Hans Behrendt

Hochzeit des Figaro, Die *70* Joachim Hess

Hochzeit im Exzentric-Club, Die *17* Joe May

Hochzeitshotel, Das *44* Carl Boese

Hochzeitsreise, Die *39* Karl Ritter

Hochzeitstraum, Ein *36* Erich Engel

Hock Shop, The *16* Charles Bowers

Hockey Night *84* Paul Shapiro

Hocking the Kaiser *18* Kenneth M. Anderson

Hocus Pocus Powwow *68* Alex Lovy

Hocuspocus *30* Gustav Ucicky

Hocussing of Cigarette, The *24* Hugh Croise

Hodja fra Pjort *85* Brita Wielopolska

Hoedown *50* Ray Nazarro

Hōen Danu *27* Tomu Uchida

Hoffman *70* Alvin Rakoff

Hoffmanns Erzählungen *11* Jakob Fleck, Anton Kolm, Luise Kolm, Claudius Valtée

Hoffmanns Erzählungen *15* Richard Oswald

Hoffmanns Erzählungen *23* Max Neufeld

Hoffmeyer's Legacy *12* Mack Sennett

Hoffnungsloser Fall, Ein *39* Erich Engel

Hofintrige, En *12* August Blom

Hofkonzert, Das *36* Douglas Sirk

Hog Wild *30* James Parrott

Hog Wild *80* Les Rose

Hogan the Porter *15* Charles Avery

Hogan's Alley *25* Roy Del Ruth

Hogan's Mussy Job *15* Charles Avery

Hogar Muy Decente, Un *87* Alberto Isaac

Hogaraka ni Ayume *30* Yasujiro Ozu

Högfjällets Dotter *14* Victor Sjöström

Hogs and Warships *61* Shohei Imamura

Hogueras en la Noche *37* Arturo Porchet

Hogy Állunk, Fiatalember? *63* György Révész

Hohe Schule *34* Erich Engel

Hohelied der Kraft, Das *30* Oskar Fischinger

Höhenfeuer *85* Fredi M. Murer

Höhere Befehl, Der *36* Gerhard Lamprecht

Hohoemu Jinsei *30* Heinosuke Gosho

Højt Spil *13* August Blom

Hokus Focus *33* Mark Sandrich

Hokusai *53* Hiroshi Teshigahara

Hokusai Manga *82* Kaneto Shindo

Hokusai, Ukiyoe Master *82* Kaneto Shindo

Hol Volt Hol Nem Volt... *87* Gyula Gazdag

Holcroft Covenant, The *85* John Frankenheimer

Hold Autumn in Your Hand *45* Jean Renoir

Hold Back the Dawn *41* Mitchell Leisen

Hold Back the Night *56* Allan Dwan

Hold Back Tomorrow *55* Hugo Haas

Hold 'Em Jail! *32* Norman Taurog

Hold 'Em Navy *37* Kurt Neumann

Hold 'Em Yale! *27* Edward H. Griffith

Hold 'Em Yale *35* Sidney Lanfield

Hold 'Er Sheriff *26* Stephen Roberts

Hold 'Er Sheriff *31* Mack Sennett

Hold Everything *30* Roy Del Ruth

Hold Fast *27* Mark Sandrich

Hold It! *38* Dave Fleischer

Hold Me Tight *32* David Butler

Hold My Hand *38* Thornton Freeland

Hold On! *65* Arthur Lubin

Hold That Baby! *49* Reginald LeBorg

Hold That Bear *27* Mark Sandrich

Hold That Blonde *45* George Marshall

Hold That Co-Ed *38* George Marshall

Hold That Ghost *41* Arthur Lubin

Hold That Girl *34* Hamilton MacFadden

Hold That Girl *38* George Marshall

Hold That Hypnotist! *57* Austen Jewell

Hold That Kiss *38* Edwin L. Marin

Hold That Line *52* William Beaudine

Hold That Lion *26* William Beaudine

Hold That Lion *50* Joseph Barbera, William Hanna

Hold That Pose *27* Edward F. Cline

Hold That Woman! *40* Sam Newfield

Hold the Lion, Please *41* Chuck Jones

Hold the Press *33* Phil Rosen

Hold the Wire *36* Dave Fleischer

Hold-Up, The *11* Alice Guy-Blaché

Hold Up *29* Joseph Santley

Hold-Up *85* Alexandre Arcady

Hold-Up à la Milanaise *59* Nanni Loy

Hold-Up au Crayon, Le *71* François Reichenbach

Hold-Up in a Country Store *04* Edwin S. Porter

Hold Your Breath *24* Scott Sidney

Hold Your Hat *26* Stephen Roberts

Hold Your Horses *21* E. Mason Hopper

Hold Your Man *29* Emmett J. Flynn

Hold Your Man *33* Sam Wood

Holdudvar, A *68* Márta Mészáros

Hole, The *57* Kon Ichikawa

Hole, The *59* Jacques Becker

Hole, The *62* John Hubley

Hole, The *64* Kaneto Shindo

Hole Cheese, The *22* Raoul Barré, Charles Bowers

Hole Idea, The *55* Robert McKimson

Hole in the Head, A *59* Frank Capra

Hole in the Wall, The *21* Maxwell Karger

Hole in the Wall, A *28* Robert Florey

Hole Lot of Trouble, A *70* Francis Searle

Holi *84* Ketan Mehta

Holiday *30* Edward H. Griffith

Holiday *38* George Cukor

Holiday *47* Jacques Tati

Holiday, The *73* Vittorio De Sica

Holiday Affair *49* Don Hartman

Holiday Camp *47* Ken Annakin

Holiday for Drumsticks *49* Art Davis

Holiday for Henrietta *52* Julien Duvivier

Holiday for Lovers *59* Henry Levin

Holiday for Shoestrings *46* Friz Freleng

Holiday for Sinners *52* Gerald Mayer

Holiday Highlights *40* Tex Avery

Holiday Husband, The *20* A. C. Hunter

Holiday in Havana *49* Jean Yarbrough

Holiday in Mexico *46* George Sidney

Holiday in Spain *60* Jack Cardiff

Holiday in Tokyo *58* Kajiro Yamamoto

Holiday Inn *42* Mark Sandrich

Holiday Island *51* John Argyle

Holiday Island *57* Mario Camerini

Holiday Land *34* Art Davis, Sid Marcus

Holiday Lovers *32* Jack Harrison

Holiday Night *54* Yuri Ozerov

Holiday of St. Jorgen *30* Yakov Protazanov

Holiday on Ischia *57* Mario Camerini

Holiday on Sylt *57* Andrew Thorndike, Annelie Thorndike

Holiday on the Buses *73* Bryan Izzard

Holiday Rhythm *50* Jack Scholl

Holiday Week *51* Arthur Crabtree

Holiday's End *36* John Paddy Carstairs

Holidays with Pay *48* John E. Blakeley

Hölle von Macao, Die *66* Bill Catching, James Hill

Hölle von Manitoba, Die *64* Sheldon Reynolds

Höllenjagd auf Heisse Ware *66* Giorgio Ferroni

Höllenspuk in Sechs Akten, Ein *20* Richard Oswald

Höllische Nacht *21* Robert Wiene

Hollow, The *75* George T. Nierenberg

Hollow of Her Hand, The *18* Charles Maigne

Hollow Triumph *48* Steve Sekely

Holloway's Treasure *24* Sinclair Hill

Holly and the Ivy, The *52* George More O'Ferrall

Hollweird *81* Peter Winograd

Hollywood *23* James Cruze

Hollywood *30* Walter Lantz

Hollywood and Vine *45* Alexis Thurn-Taxis

Hollywood Babies *33* Dick Huemer

Hollywood Barn Dance *47* Bernard B. Ray

Hollywood Boulevard *36* Robert Florey

Hollywood Boulevard *76* Allan Arkush, Joe Dante

Hollywood Bound *23* Charles Lamont

Hollywood Canine Canteen *46* Robert McKimson

Hollywood Canteen *44* Delmer Daves

Hollywood Capers *35* Jack King

Hollywood Cavalcade *39* Irving Cummings, Malcolm St. Clair

Hollywood Chainsaw Hookers *87* Fred Olen Ray

Hollywood, Ciudad de Ensueño *34* George Crane

Hollywood Cop *88* Amir Shervan

Hollywood Cowboy *37* Ewing Scott

Hollywood Cowboy *75* Howard Zieff

Hollywood Daffy *46* Friz Freleng

Hollywood Detour, A *42* Frank Tashlin

Hollywood Dreaming *86* James L. Wilson

Hollywood Extra, A *27* Robert Florey, Slavko Vorkapich

Hollywood Extra! *36* Felix E. Feist

Hollywood Goes Krazy *32* Manny Gould, Ben Harrison

Hollywood Graduation *38* Art Davis

Hollywood Half Backs *31* Charles Lamont

Hollywood Handicap, The *32* Charles Lamont

Hollywood Handicap *38* Buster Keaton

Hollywood Happenings *31* Mack Sennett

Hollywood Harry *85* Robert Forster

Hollywood Hero, A *27* Harry Edwards

Hollywood High *76* Patrick Wright

Hollywood High, Part Two *84* Caruth C. Byrd, Lee Thornburg

Hollywood Hobbies *39* George Sidney

Hollywood Hoodlum *34* B. Reeves Eason

Hollywood Hot Tubs *84* Chuck Vincent
Hollywood Hot Tubs II: Educating Crystal *90* Ken Raich
Hollywood Hotel *37* Busby Berkeley
Hollywood Kid, The *24* Roy Del Ruth
Hollywood Kids *32* Charles Lamont
Hollywood Knight *79* David Worth
Hollywood Knights, The *80* Floyd Mutrux
Hollywood Luck *32* Roscoe Arbuckle
Hollywood Man, The *76* Jack Starrett
Hollywood Matador *42* Walter Lantz
Hollywood Meatcleaver Massacre *75* Evan Lee
Hollywood Monster *87* Roland Emmerich
Hollywood Mystery *34* B. Reeves Eason
Hollywood 90028 *73* Christina Hornisher
Hollywood North *87* Zale Dalen
Hollywood on Trial *76* David Helpern, Jr.
Hollywood or Bust *56* Frank Tashlin
Hollywood Party *34* Richard Boleslawski, Allan Dwan, Edmund Goulding, Roy Rowland, George Stevens, Sam Wood
Hollywood Party in Technicolor *37* Roy Rowland
Hollywood Reporter, The *26* Bruce Mitchell
Hollywood Revue of 1929, The *29* Charles Reisner
Hollywood Rhapsody *27* Robert Florey, Slavko Vorkapich
Hollywood Roundup *37* Ewing Scott
Hollywood Runaround *32* Charles Lamont
Hollywood Screen Test *37* S. Sylvan Simon
Hollywood Shuffle *87* Robert Townsend
Hollywood Speaks *32* Edward Buzzell
Hollywood Stadium Mystery *38* David Howard
Hollywood Star, A *29* Mack Sennett
Hollywood Steps Out *41* Tex Avery
Hollywood Story *50* William Castle
Hollywood Strangler, The *80* Robert Hammer
Hollywood Strangler Meets the Skid Row Slasher, The *79* Ray Dennis Steckler
Hollywood Stunt Man *53* Bernard B. Ray
Hollywood Sweepstakes *39* Ben Harrison
Hollywood Ten, The *50* John Berry
Hollywood — The Second Step *36* Felix E. Feist
Hollywood Theme Song, A *30* William Beaudine
Hollywood Thrill-Makers *53* Bernard B. Ray
Hollywood Varieties *50* Paul Landres
Hollywood Vice Squad *86* Penelope Spheeris
Hollywood Zap *86* David Cohen
Holocaust 2000 *77* Alberto De Martino
Holster Full of Law, A *61* James Neilson
Holt of the Secret Service *41* James W. Horne
Holt Vidék *71* István Gaál
Holy Apes, The *67* Andrzej Wajda
Holy Innocents, The *84* Mario Camus
Holy Matrimony *43* John M. Stahl
Holy Mountain, The *73* Alejandro Jodorowsky
Holy Orders *17* A. E. Coleby, Arthur H. Rooke

Holy Smoke *63* Walerian Borowczyk
Holy Terror, A *31* Irving Cummings
Holy Terror, The *36* James Tinling
Holy Terror, The *63* Yves Robert
Holy Terror *76* Alfred Sole
Holy Veil, The *26* Jean Benoît-Lévy
Holy Year 1950 *50* Anthony Muto
Holzapfel Weiss Alles *33* Viktor Jansen
Homa Vaftike Kokkino, To *65* Vassilis Georgiades
Homage at Siesta Time *62* Leopoldo Torre-Nilsson
Homage to Chagall: The Colors of Love *75* Harry Rasky
Homage to Jean Tinguely's Homage to New York *60* Robert Breer
Homage to the Siesta *62* Leopoldo Torre-Nilsson
Hombori *49* Jean Rouch
Hombre *66* Martin Ritt
Hombre de Éxito, Un *86* Humberto Solás
Hombre de la Deuda Externa, El *87* Pablo Olivo
Hombre de los Hongos, El *76* Roberto Gavaldón
Hombre Desnudo, El *87* Rogelio A. González, Jr.
Hombre Invisible, El *57* Alfredo B. Crevenna
Hombre Lobo, El *67* Enrique L. Equiluz
Hombre Mirando al Sudeste *81* Eliseo Subiela
Hombre o Demonio *33* Miguel Torres Contreras
Hombre Peligroso, Un *35* Richard Kahn
Hombre Que Ganó la Razón, El *86* Alejandro Agresti
Hombre Que Logró Ser Invisible, El *57* Alfredo B. Crevenna
Hombre Que Mató a Billy el Niño, El *67* Julio Buchs
Hombre Que Se Reía del Amor, El *35* Benito Perojo
Hombre Que Vino de Ummo, El *69* Tulio Demicheli, Hugo Fregonese
Hombre Sin Patria, El *22* Miguel Torres Contreras
Hombre Sin Rostro, El *50* Juan Bustillo Oro
Hombre Vino a Matar, Un *68* Leon Klimovsky
Hombre Violente, Un *86* Valentín Trujillo
Hombre y el Monstruo, El *58* Rafael Baledón
Hombre y la Bestia, El *51* Mario Soffici
Hombres de Mar *38* Chano Urueta
Home *15* Maurice Elvey
Home *16* Charles Miller
Home *19* Lois Weber
Home Again My Cherry Blossom *07* Arthur Gilbert
Home Alone *90* Chris Columbus
Home and Away *56* Vernon Sewell
Home and the World, The *82* Satyajit Ray
Home at Seven *51* Ralph Richardson
Home Beautiful, The *13* Percy Stow
Home Before Dark *58* Mervyn LeRoy
Home Before Midnight *79* Peter Walker
Home Brew *20* Raoul Barré, Charles Bowers

Home Comforts *16* Kelly Storrie
Home Construction *26* Widgey R. Newman, Challis Sanderson
Home Early *39* Roy Rowland
Home for Tanya, A *59* Lev Kulidzhanov
Home for the Holidays *13* Lewin Fitzhamon
Home Free All *83* Stewart Bird
Home from Babylon *41* Alf Sjöberg
Home from Home *39* Herbert Smith
Home from the Hill *60* Vincente Minnelli
Home from the Sea *15* Raoul Walsh
Home from the Sea *62* Lester James Peries
Home from the Sea *72* Yoji Yamada
Home Front *85* Paul Aaron, Terry Winsor
Home Guard *41* Ivan Moffat
Home in Indiana *44* Henry Hathaway
Home in Oklahoma *36* Mack V. Wright
Home in Oklahoma *46* William Witney
Home in San Antone *49* Ray Nazarro
Home in Wyomin' *42* William Morgan
Home Influence *20* Cecil Mannering
Home Is Calling *37* Douglas Sirk
Home Is the Hero *59* Fielder Cook
Home Is Where the Hart Is *87* Rex Bromfield
Home Is Where the Heart Is *86* Daniel Petrie
Home James *18* Alfred Santell
Home James *28* William Beaudine
Home-Keeping Hearts *21* Carlyle Ellis
Home Made *27* Charles Hines
Home-Made Car, The *64* James Hill
Home Made Man, A *28* Norman Taurog
Home Maker, The *19* George Dewhurst
Home Maker, The *25* King Baggot
Home Movies *79* Brian DePalma
Home Murders *82* Marc Lobet
Home of the Brave *49* Mark Robson
Home of the Brave *86* Laurie Anderson
Home of Your Own, A *64* Jay Lewis
Home on the Prairie *39* Jack Townley
Home on the Range *35* Arthur Jacobson
Home on the Range *46* R. G. Springsteen
Home Plums *31* John Grierson
Home Remedy *88* Maggie Greenwald
Home Spun Folks *20* John Griffith Wray
Home Stretch, The *21* Jack Nelson
Home Struck *27* Ralph Ince
Home Stuff *21* Albert Kelley
Home, Sweet Home *14* D. W. Griffith
Home Sweet Home *17* Wilfred Noy
Home Sweet Home *20* Raoul Barré, Charles Bowers
Home Sweet Home *21* H. B. Parkinson
Home Sweet Home *33* George A. Cooper
Home Sweet Home *45* John E. Blakeley
Home Sweet Home *81* Nettie Pena
Home Sweet Homicide *46* Lloyd Bacon
Home Talent *21* James E. Abbe, Mack Sennett
Home to Danger *50* Terence Fisher
Home to Our Mountains *06* Arthur Gilbert
Home Town *22* Kenji Mizoguchi
Home Town *30* Kenji Mizoguchi
Home Town Girl, The *19* Robert Vignola
Home Town Story *51* Arthur Pierson
Home Towners, The *28* Bryan Foy
Home Trail, The *18* William Wolbert

Home Trail, The *27* William Wyler
Home Tweet Home *50* Friz Freleng
Home Wanted *19* Tefft Johnson
Home Without Mother *06* J. H. Martin
Homebodies *74* Larry Yust
Homeboy *76* Timothy Galfas, Richard Kaye
Homeboy *88* Michael Seresin
Homeboys *78* Bill Yahraus
Homebreaker, The *19* Victor Schertzinger
Homecoming *28* Joe May
Homecoming *48* Martin Frič
Homecoming *48* Mervyn LeRoy
Homecoming *57* Alexander Rasumny
Homecoming, The *73* Peter Hall
Homecoming *84* Ho Yim
Homecoming Song *40* Sergio Miró
Homefolks *11* D. W. Griffith
Homeland *39* Ernst Martin
Homeland *83* Edgar Reitz
Homeless Hare *49* Chuck Jones
Homeless Homer *28* Friz Freleng, Rudolf Ising
Homem da Capa Preta, O *86* Sérgio Rezende
Homem Lobo, O *71* Raffaele Rossi
Homenaje *75* Pedro Almodóvar
Homenaje a la Hora de la Siesta *62* Leopoldo Torre-Nilsson
Homenaje para Adriana *68* Miguel Picazo
Homer *70* John Trent
Homer & Eddie *89* Andrei Mikhalkov-Konchalovsky
Homer Comes Home *20* Jerome Storm
Homesdale *71* Peter Weir
Homesick *28* Henry Lehrman
Homespun Vamp, A *22* Frank O'Connor
Homesteader, The *19* Oscar Micheaux
Homesteader Droopy *54* Tex Avery
Homesteaders, The *53* Lewis D. Collins
Homesteaders of Paradise Valley *47* R. G. Springsteen
Homestretch, The *47* H. Bruce Humberstone
Hometown *30* Kenji Mizoguchi
Hometown Song *25* Kenji Mizoguchi
Hometown U.S.A. *79* Max Baer
Hometowners *40* Noel Mason Smith
Homeward Bound *23* Ralph Ince
Homework *79* James Beshears
Homicidal *61* William Castle
Homicide *49* Felix Jacoves
Homicide Bureau *38* C. C. Coleman, Jr.
Homicide for Three *48* George Blair
Homicide Squad *31* Edward L. Cahn, George Melford
Hommage à Albert Einstein *55* Jean Lods
Hommage à Debussy *63* Marcel L'Herbier
Hommage à Marcel Mauss: Germaine Dieterlen *77* Jean Rouch
Hommage à Marcel Mauss: Marcel Levy *77* Jean Rouch
Hommage à Marcel Mauss: Taro Okamoto *73* Jean Rouch
Homme à Détruire, Un *51* Joseph Losey
Homme à la Buick, L' *66* Gilles Grangier
Homme à la Pipe, L' *62* Roger Leenhardt
Homme à la Tête de Caoutchouc, L' *01* Georges Méliès
Homme à la Valise, L' *83* Chantal Aker-

man
Homme à l'Hispano, L' *26* Julien Duvivier
Homme à l'Hispano, L' *32* Jean Epstein
Homme à l'Imperméable, L' *56* Julien Duvivier
Homme Aimanté, L' *07* Louis Feuillade
Homme Amoureux, Un *87* Diane Kurys
Homme au Cerveau Greffé, L' *72* Jacques Doniol-Valcroze
Homme au Chapeau Rond, L' *46* Pierre Billon
Homme au Crâne Rasé, L' *65* André Delvaux
Homme au Foulard à Pois, L' *16* Jacques Feyder
Homme au Gants Blancs, L' *08* Albert Capellani
Homme aux Cent Trucs, L' *00* Georges Méliès
Homme aux Clefs d'Or, L' *56* Léo Joannon
Homme aux Mille Inventions, L' *10* Georges Méliès
Homme aux Yeux d'Argent, L' *85* Pierre Granier-Deferre
Homme Blesse, L' *83* Patrice Chereau
Homme Comme Il Faut, Un *10* Georges Méliès
Homme dans la Lune, L' *1898* Georges Méliès
Homme de Cendres, L' *86* Nouri Bouzid
Homme de Compagnie, L' *16* Jacques Feyder
Homme de Londres, L' *43* Henri Decoin
Homme de Marrakech, L' *65* Jacques Deray
Homme de New York, L' *67* Marcel Camus
Homme de Nulle Part, L' *37* Pierre Chénal
Homme de Proie, L' *12* Louis Feuillade
Homme de Rio, L' *63* Philippe de Broca
Homme de Tête, Un *1898* Georges Méliès
Homme des Baleares, L' *25* André Hugon
Homme des Poisons, L' *16* Louis Feuillade
Homme d'Istambul, L' *66* Antonio Isamendi
Homme du Jour, L' *35* Julien Duvivier
Homme du Large, L' *20* Marcel L'Herbier
Homme du Minnesota, L' *64* Sergio Corbucci
Homme du Niger, L' *40* Jacques De Baroncelli
Homme du Train 117, L' *23* Charles De Marsan, Charles Maudru
Homme en Colère, L' *79* Claude Pinoteau
Homme en Or, Un *34* Jean Dréville
Homme Est Mort, Un *72* Jacques Deray
Homme et Femme *38* Pál Fejős, Gunnar Skoglund
Homme et la Poupée, L' *21* Maurice Mariaud
Homme et Son Boss, Un *70* Guy Borremans, Arthur Lamothe
Homme et une Femme, Un *66* Claude Lelouch
Homme et une Femme: Vingt Ans Déjà, Un *86* Claude Lelouch
Homme Inusable, L' *23* Raymond Bernard
Homme Invisible, L' *09* Ferdinand Zecca

Homme Marche dans la Ville, Un *49* Marcello Pagliero
Homme Merveilleux, L' *22* Louis Mercanton
Homme-Mouche, L' *02* Georges Méliès
Homme Mystérieux, L' *33* Maurice Tourneur
Homme Noir, L' *27* Alfred Machin, Henri Wuhlschleger
Homme-Orchestre, L' *00* Georges Méliès
Homme Passe, Un *17* Henri Roussel
Homme Pressé, L' *77* Édouard Molinaro
Homme Protée, L' *1899* Georges Méliès
Homme Qui A des Roues dans la Tête, L' *00* Georges Méliès
Homme Qui Aimait les Femmes, L' *77* François Truffaut
Homme Qui Assassina, L' *17* Henri Andréani
Homme Qui Assassina, L' *30* Kurt Bernhardt
Homme Qui Me Plaît, Un *69* Claude Lelouch
Homme Qui Ment, L' *67* Alain Robbe-Grillet
Homme Qui Revient de Lion, L' *17* Gaston Ravel
Homme Qui Valait des Milliards, L' *67* Michel Boisrond
Homme Sans Cœur, L' *37* Léo Joannon
Homme Sans Tête, L' *12* Émile Cohl
Homme Sans Visage, L' *18* Louis Feuillade
Homme Sans Visage, L' *73* Georges Franju
Homme sur la Voie, Un *56* Andrzej Munk
Homme Voile, L' *87* Maroun Bagdadi
Hommes, Les *73* Daniel Vigne
Hommes Bleus, Les *31* Rex Ingram, Alice Terry
Hommes de la Baleine, Les *56* Chris Marker, Mario Ruspoli
Hommes de la Croix Bleue, Les *55* Andrzej Munk
Hommes de Las Vegas, Les *68* Antonio Isamendi
Hommes du Champagne, Les *50* Roger Leenhardt
Hommes en Blanc, Les *56* Ralph Habib
Hommes Ne Pensent Qu'à Ça, Les *54* Yves Robert
Hommes Nouveaux, Les *35* Marcel L'Herbier
Hommes Préférent les Grosses, Les *81* Jean-Marie Poire
Hommes Qui Font la Pluie, Les *51* Roger Rosfelder, Jean Rouch
Hommes Veulent Vivre, Les *62* Léonide Moguy
Homo Eroticus *73* Marco Vicario
Homo Immanis *19* Paul Czinner
Homoman, L' *64* Jean-Pierre Lefèbvre
Homunculus *16* Otto Rippert
Hon Dansade En Sommar *51* Arne Mattsson
Hon, den Enda *26* Gustaf Molander
Hon Kom Som en Vind *52* Erik Faustman
Hon Segrade *15* Victor Sjöström
Hon. William's Donah, The *14* Elwin Neame
Hondo *53* John Farrow
Hondo and the Apaches *67* Lee H. Katzin

Honest Book Agent, The *19* Raoul Barré, Charles Bowers
Honest, Decent and True *85* Les Blair
Honest Fool *64* Yoji Yamada
Honest Fool — Sequel *64* Yoji Yamada
Honest Hutch *20* Clarence Badger
Honest Injun *26* Norman Taurog
Honest Jockey, The *20* Raoul Barré, Charles Bowers
Honest John *45* Vernon Keays
Honest Love and True *38* Dave Fleischer
Honest Man, An *18* Frank Borzage
Honest Thief, The *18* George B. Seitz
Honesty Is the Best Policy *08* Edwin S. Porter
Honesty Is the Best Policy *26* F. W. Engholm
Honesty — The Best Policy *26* Chester Bennett
Honey *30* Wesley Ruggles
Honey *81* Gian Franco Angelucci
Honey Bee, The *20* Rupert Julian
Honey, I Shrunk the Kids *89* Joe Johnston
Honey Moon *78* Bille August
Honey Pot, The *66* Joseph L. Mankiewicz
Honeybaby, Honeybaby *74* Michael Schultz
Honeybunch *88* Ruud van Hemert
Honeychile *51* R. G. Springsteen
Honeycomb, The *69* Carlos Saura
Honeymoon, The *17* Charles Giblyn
Honeymoon *28* Robert Golden
Honeymoon, The *39* Karl Ritter
Honeymoon *47* William Keighley
Honeymoon *58* Michael Powell
Honeymoon *85* Patrick Jamain
Honeymoon Academy *90* Gene Quintano
Honeymoon Adventure, A *31* Maurice Elvey
Honeymoon Ahead *27* Tim Whelan
Honeymoon Ahead *45* Reginald LeBorg
Honeymoon at Niagara Falls, The *06* Edwin S. Porter
Honeymoon Deferred *40* Lew Landers
Honeymoon Deferred *51* Mario Camerini
Honeymoon Express, The *26* James Flood
Honeymoon: First, Second and Third Class, The *04* Lewin Fitzhamon
Honeymoon Flats *28* Millard Webb
Honeymoon for Five *50* Jean Yarbrough
Honeymoon for Three, A *15* Maurice Elvey
Honeymoon for Three *35* Leo Mittler
Honeymoon for Three *41* Lloyd Bacon
Honeymoon Hate *27* Luther Reed
Honeymoon Hotel *25* Richard Wallace
Honeymoon Hotel *34* Earl Duvall
Honeymoon Hotel *46* John E. Blakeley
Honeymoon Hotel *64* Henry Levin
Honeymoon in a Balloon *08* Georges Méliès
Honeymoon in Bali *39* Edward H. Griffith
Honeymoon Killers, The *69* Leonard Kastle
Honeymoon Lane *31* William James Craft
Honeymoon Limited *35* Arthur Lubin
Honeymoon Lodge *43* Edward Lilley
Honeymoon Machine, The *61* Richard Thorpe
Honeymoon Merry-Go-Round *36* Alfred

Goulding
Honeymoon of Horror *64* Irwin Meyer
Honeymoon of Terror *61* Peter Perry
Honeymoon Ranch *20* Robert H. Townley
Honeymoon Trio *31* Roscoe Arbuckle
Honeymoon Trip, The *35* Gustaf Molander
Honeymoon Zeppelin *30* Mack Sennett
Honeymooners, The *14* George D. Baker
Honeymooniacs *29* Stephen Roberts
Honeymoon's Over, The *39* Eugene Forde
Honeymoons Will Kill You *67* Mario Amendola
Honeymousers, The *56* Robert McKimson
Honeypot, The *20* Fred LeRoy Granville
Honey's Money *62* Friz Freleng
Honeysuckle *39* Luis César Amadori
Honeysuckle Rose *80* Jerry Schatzberg
Hong Gaoliang *87* Yimou Zhang
Hong Kong *51* Lewis R. Foster
Hong Kong Affair *58* Paul F. Heard
Hong Kong and Onward *67* Robert H. Lieberman
Hong Kong Confidential *58* Edward L. Cahn
Hong Kong Graffiti *85* Terry Tong
Hong Kong, Hong Kong *85* Clifford Choi
Hong Kong Hot Harbor *62* Jürgen Roland
Hong Kong Nights *35* E. Mason Hopper
Hong Kong 1941 *85* Po-chih Leong
Honjin Satsujin Jiken *75* Yoichi Takabayashi
Honkers, The *71* Steve Ihnat
Honkon no Hoshi *62* Yasuke Chiba
Honkon no Shiroibara *65* Jun Fukuda
Honkon no Yoru *61* Yasuke Chiba
Honky *71* William A. Graham
Honky Tonk *29* Lloyd Bacon
Honky Tonk *41* Jack Conway
Honky Tonk Freeway *81* John Schlesinger
Honkytonk Man *82* Clint Eastwood
Honneur d'Artiste *17* Jean Kemm
Honneur du Corse, L' *06* Alice Guy-Blaché
Honneur Est Satisfait, L' *06* Georges Méliès
Honneurs de la Guerre, Les *61* Jean Dewever
Honning Måne *78* Bille August
Honnō *66* Kaneto Shindo
Honolulu *38* Edward Buzzell
Honolulu Lu *41* Charles Barton
Honolulu-Tokyo-Hong Kong *63* Yasuke Chiba
Honolulu Wiles *30* Manny Gould, Ben Harrison
Honor *26* Amo Bek-Nazarov
Honor *29* A. Shirvanzada
Honor Among Lovers *31* Dorothy Arzner
Honor Among Men *24* Denison Clift
Honor Among Thieves *68* Jean Herman
Honor Bound *20* Jacques Jaccard
Honor Bound *28* Alfred E. Green
Honor First *22* Jerome Storm
Honor Guard, The *78* Burt Kennedy
Honor of His Family, The *09* D. W. Griffith
Honor of His House, The *18* William DeMille
Honor of Mary Blake, The *16* Edwin Stevens

Honor of Men, The *17* George Marshall
Honor of the District Attorney, The *15* B. Reeves Eason
Honor of the Family *31* Lloyd Bacon
Honor of the Mounted *14* Allan Dwan
Honor of the Mounted *32* Harry Fraser
Honor of the Press *32* B. Reeves Eason
Honor of the Range, The *20* Ford Beebe, Leo D. Maloney
Honor of the Range *34* Alvin J. Neitz
Honor of the West *39* George Waggner
Honor of Thieves, The *08* D. W. Griffith
Honor System, The *16* Raoul Walsh
Honor System, The *43* William Beaudine
Honor the Sabbath Day *88* Krzysztof Kieślowski
Honor Thy Father *15* Robert Vignola
Honor Thy Father *73* Paul Wendkos
Honor Thy Father and Thy Mother *88* Krzysztof Kieślowski
Honor Thy Name *16* Charles Giblyn
Honorable Algernon, The *13* Van Dyke Brooke
Honorable Algy, The *16* Raymond B. West
Honorable Catherine, L' *42* Marcel L'Herbier
Honorable Catherine, The *48* Georges Lampin
Honorable Friend, The *16* Edward J. LeSaint
Honorary Consul, The *83* John Mackenzie
Honoring the Russian Flag *13* Yakov Protazanov
Honor's Altar *16* Raymond B. West
Honor's Cross *18* Wallace Worsley
Honors Easy *35* Herbert Brenon
Honour Among Thieves *12* Dave Aylott
Honour Among Thieves *15* Ernest G. Batley
Honour Among Thieves *16* Wilfred Noy
Honour Among Thieves *53* Jacques Becker
Honour in Pawn *16* Harold Weston
Honourable Event, The *13* Lawrence Trimble
Honourable Member for Outside Left, The *24* Sinclair Hill
Honourable Mr. Wong, The *32* William A. Wellman
Honourable Murder, An *59* Godfrey Grayson
Honours Even *08* Alf Collins
Honrarás a Tus Padres *37* Juan Orol
Honryū *26* Heinosuke Gosho
Hooch *77* Santos Alcocer
Hooch Ball, The *20* Gregory La Cava
Hoodlum, The *19* Sidney Franklin
Hoodlum, The *51* Max Nosseck
Hoodlum, The *70* Claude Lelouch
Hoodlum Empire *51* Joseph Kane
Hoodlum Priest, The *61* Irvin Kershner
Hoodlum Saint, The *45* Norman Taurog
Hoodlum Soldier, The *65* Yasuzo Masumura
Hoodlums' Honor *66* Wolfgang Staudte
Hoodman Blind *13* James Gordon
Hoodman Blind *16* Oscar Apfel
Hoodman Blind *23* John Ford
Hoodoo Ann *16* D. W. Griffith, Lloyd Ingraham

Hoodoo Ranch 26 William Bertram
Hoodwink 81 Claude Whatham
Hoof Marks 27 Tenny Wright
Hoofbeats of Vengeance 29 Henry MacRae
Hook, The 63 George Seaton
Hook and Hand 14 Herbert Blaché
Hook and Ladder 24 Edward Sedgwick
Hook and Ladder No. 9 27 F. Harmon Weight
Hook, Line and Sinker 30 Edward F. Cline
Hook, Line and Sinker 68 George Marshall
Hook, Line and Stinker 58 Chuck Jones
Hooked Generation, The 68 William Grefé
Hooker Cult Murders, The 72 Harvey Hart
Hoola Boola 41 George Pal
Hooligans, The 59 Carlos Saura
Hoop van Zegen, Op 86 Guido Pieters
Hooper 78 Hal Needham
Hoop-la 19 Louis Chaudet
Hoopla 33 Frank Lloyd
Hooray for Love 35 Walter Lang
Hoosegow, The 29 James Parrott
Hoosier Holiday 43 Frank McDonald
Hoosier Romance, A 18 Colin Campbell
Hoosier Schoolboy, The 37 William Nigh
Hoosier Schoolmaster, The 24 Oliver L. Sellers
Hoosier Schoolmaster, The 35 Lewis D. Collins
Hoosiers 86 David Anspaugh
Hoot Mon 19 Hal Roach
Hoot Mon 22 Raoul Barré, Charles Bowers
Hootch and Mootch in A Steak at Stake 21 Earl Hurd
Hootenanny Hoot 62 Gene Nelson
Hoots Mon 39 Roy William Neill
Hop and Go 43 Norm McCabe
Hop Harrigan 46 Derwin Abrahams
Hop, Look and Listen 48 Robert McKimson
Hop, Skip and a Chump 42 Friz Freleng
Hop, Skip and Jump 22 Raoul Barré, Charles Bowers
Hop — The Devil's Brew 16 Phillips Smalley, Lois Weber
Hopalong Cassidy 35 Howard Bretherton
Hopalong Cassidy Enters 35 Howard Bretherton
Hopalong Cassidy Returns 36 Nate Watt
Hopalong Casualty 60 Chuck Jones
Hopalong Rides Again 37 Lesley Selander
Hope 19 Rex Wilson
Hope, The 20 Herbert Blaché
Hope, The 59 Nuri Habib
Hope 63 Karel Kachyňa
Hope 70 Yılmaz Güney
Hope and Glory 87 John Boorman
Hope and Pain 88 Yoji Yamada
Hope Avenue 53 Dino Risi
Hope Chest, The 18 Elmer Clifton
Hope of His Side, The 35 Jack Raymond
Hope of Youth, The 42 Kajiro Yamamoto
Hopeless Ones, The 65 Miklós Jancsó
Hopeless Ones, The 71 Yılmaz Güney
Hopeless Passion, A 11 Frank Wilson
Hopelessly Lost 72 Georgy Danelia

Hopes of Blind Alley, The 14 Allan Dwan
Hopi Legend, A 13 Wallace Reid
Hopper, The 18 Thomas Heffron
Hoppity Goes to Town 41 Dave Fleischer
Hoppity Pop 46 Norman McLaren
Hoppy Daze 61 Robert McKimson
Hoppy Go Lucky 52 Robert McKimson
Hoppy Serves a Writ 43 George Archainbaud
Hoppy's Holiday 47 George Archainbaud
Hopscotch 80 Ronald Neame
Hør, Var Der Ikke En, Som Lo? 78 Henning Carlsen
Hora Bruja, La 85 Jaime De Armiñán
Hora da Estrela, A 85 Suzana Amaral
Hora de la Verdad 44 Norman Foster
Hora de los Hornos, La 66 Santiago Álvarez, Octavio Getino, Fernando Solanas
Hora de los Niños, La 69 Arturo Ripstein
Hora Téxaco, La 85 Eduardo Barberena
Horace Earns a Halo 19 Arthur H. Rooke
Horace's Triumph 19 Arthur H. Rooke
Horatio 61 Ferdinando Baldi, Terence Young
Horatio's Deception 20 Cecil Mannering
Hordubal Brothers, The 37 Martin Frič
Hordubalové 37 Martin Frič
Hordubals, The 37 Martin Frič
Horečka 58 Jaromil Jireš
Horendi 72 Jean Rouch
Hoří, Má Panenko 67 Miloš Forman
Horizon 32 Lev Kuleshov
Horizon, The 61 Josef Heifits
Horizon 71 Pál Gábor
Horizon, The 84 Kaneto Shindo
Horizon — The Wandering Jew 32 Lev Kuleshov
Horizons 83 Ron Norman
Horizons Noirs 36 Pál Fejős
Horizons Sans Fin 53 Jean Dréville
Horizons West 52 Budd Boetticher
Horizont 71 Pál Gábor
Horizontal Lieutenant, The 62 Richard Thorpe
Horká Kaše 88 Radovan Urban
Horká Zima 72 Karel Kachyňa
Horla, The 63 Reginald LeBorg
Horla, Le 67 Jean-Daniel Pollet
Horloger de Saint-Paul, L' 73 Bertrand Tavernier
Horn Blows at Midnight, The 45 Raoul Walsh
Hörn i Norr, Ett 50 Arne Sucksdorff
Hornet's Nest 19 James Young
Hornet's Nest 23 Walter West
Hornet's Nest, The 55 Charles Saunders
Hornet's Nest 70 Phil Karlson
Hōrōki 62 Mikio Naruse
Horoscope 50 Boro Drašković
Horoscope for a Child 69 Shyam Benegal
Horoskop 50 Boro Drašković
Horoucí Srdce 62 Otakar Vávra
Horowitz Plays Mozart 87 Susan Froemke, Albert Maysles, Charlotte Zwerin
Horrible Dr. Hichcock, The 62 Riccardo Freda
Horrible Dr. Orloff, L' 61 Jesús Franco
Horrible House on the Hill, The 74 Sean McGregor

Horrible Midnight 58 Hideo Sekigawa
Horrible Mill Women, The 60 Giorgio Ferroni
Horrible Orgies of Count Dracula, The 73 Renato Polselli
Horrible Sexy Vampire, The 70 José Luis Madrid
Horriplante Bestia Humana, La 68 René Cardona
Horror! 63 Anton Leader
Horror Castle 63 Richard McNamara, Antonio Margheriti
Horror Chamber of Dr. Faustus, The 59 Georges Franju
Horror Creatures of the Prehistoric Planet 70 Al Adamson, George Joseph
Horror Creatures of the Red Planet 70 Al Adamson, George Joseph
Horror Dream 47 Sidney Peterson
Horror Express 72 Eugenio Martin
Horror Film One 70 Malcolm Le Grice
Horror Film Two 72 Malcolm Le Grice
Horror High 73 Larry N. Stouffer
Horror Hospital 73 Antony Balch
Horror Hotel 60 John Llewellyn Moxey
Horror Hotel 76 Tobe Hooper
Horror Hotel Massacre 76 Tobe Hooper
Horror House 69 Michael Armstrong
Horror in the Midnight Sun 60 Virgil Vogel, Jerry Warren
Horror Island 40 George Waggner
Horror Maniacs 48 Oswald Mitchell
Horror of a Deformed Man 69 Teruo Ishii
Horror of an Ugly Woman 70 Kimiyoshi Yasuda
Horror of Death, The 72 Peter Newbrook
Horror of Dracula 58 Terence Fisher
Horror of Frankenstein, The 70 Jimmy Sangster
Horror of It All, The 63 Terence Fisher
Horror of Malformed Men, The 69 Teruo Ishii
Horror of Party Beach, The 64 Del Tenney
Horror of the Blood Monsters 70 Al Adamson, George Joseph
Horror of the Stone Women 60 Giorgio Ferroni
Horror of the Zombies 74 Amando De Ossorio
Horror on Snape Island 72 James O'Connolly
Horror Planet 80 Norman J. Warren
Horror Rises from the Tomb 72 Carlos Aured
Horror Show, The 89 James Isaac
Horror Star, The 83 Norman Thaddeus Vane
Horror Story 72 Manuel Esteba Gallego
Horror y Sexo 68 René Cardona
Horrores del Bosque Negro, Los 64 Rafael Baledón
Horrors of Drink, The 01 Walter R. Booth
Horrors of Spider Island 59 Fritz Böttger
Horrors of the Black Museum 59 Arthur Crabtree
Horrors of the Black Zoo 63 Robert Gordon
Hors la Loi 85 Robin Davis
Horse 41 Kajiro Yamamoto

Horse 65 Andy Warhol
Horse, La 69 Pierre Granier-Deferre
Horse, The 82 Ali Özgentürk
Horse! A Horse!, A 13 Percy Stow
Horse and Carriage 57 Dinos Dimopoulos
Horse and Mrs. Grundy, A 11 Lewin Fitzhamon
Horse Ate the Hat, The 27 René Clair
Horse Called Jester, A 80 Kenneth Fairbairn
Horse Feathers 32 Norman Z. McLeod
Horse for Horse 40 Juan Bustillo Oro
Horse Hare 60 Friz Freleng
Horse in the Gray Flannel Suit, The 68 Larry Lansburgh, Norman Tokar
Horse, My Horse 82 Ali Özgentürk
Horse Named Comanche, A 58 Lewis R. Foster
Horse of Pride, The 79 Claude Chabrol
Horse Over Tea Kettle 62 Robert Breer
Horse Play 24 Walter Lantz
Horse Play 27 William C. Nolan
Horse Play 33 Edward Sedgwick
Horse Play 37 Jean Yarbrough
Horse Race 31 Walter Lantz
Horse Sense 24 Ward Hayes
Horse Sense 38 Widgey R. Newman
Horse Shoes 27 Clyde Bruckman
Horse Shoo 65 Joseph Barbera, William Hanna
Horse Soldiers, The 59 John Ford
Horse Stealer, or A Casual Acquaintance, The 05 Tom Green
Horse Tale, A 28 Rollin Hamilton, Tom Palmer
Horse That Ate the Baby, The 06 Percy Stow
Horse That Cried, The 57 Mark Donskoi
Horse, the Woman and the Gun, The 66 Yilmaz Güney
Horse Thief, The 12 Allan Dwan
Horse Thief, The 13 Wilfred Lucas
Horse Thief 85 Zhuangzhuang Tian
Horse Thief's Bigamy, The 11 Allan Dwan
Horse Thistle, The 26 Teinosuke Kinugasa
Horse Trader, The 26 William Wyler
Horse Without a Head, The 63 Don Chaffey
Horsefly Fleas, A 48 Robert McKimson
Horseman of the Plains, A 28 Ben Stoloff
Horseman, the Woman and the Moth, The 68 Stan Brakhage
Horsemasters, The 61 William Fairchild
Horsemen, The 51 Konstantin Yudin
Horsemen, The 70 John Frankenheimer
Horsemen of the Sierras 49 Fred F. Sears
Horses 43 Bjarne Henning-Jensen
Horses 65 Tolomush Okeyev
Horses and Their Ancestors 62 John Hubley
Horses' Collars 34 Clyde Bruckman
Horses in Winter 88 Rick Raxlen, Patrick Vallely
Horse's Mouth, The 52 C. M. Pennington-Richards
Horse's Mouth, The 58 Ronald Neame
Horses on the Merry-Go-Round 38 Ubbe Iwerks
Horseshoe for Luck, A 46 Karel Zeman
Horseshoe Luck 24 Joseph Franz

Horsie 51 Arthur Lubin
Horst Wessel 39 Franz Wenzler
Horton Hatches the Egg 42 Robert Clampett
Horvatov Izbor 86 Eduard Galić
Horvat's Choice 86 Eduard Galić
Horyū-Ji 58 Susumu Hani
Horyu Temple 58 Susumu Hani
Hospital 70 Frederick Wiseman
Hospital, The 71 Arthur Hiller
Hospital Massacre 81 Boaz Davidson
Hospital of Terror 77 Al Adamson
Hospital Orderlies 18 Raoul Barré, Charles Bowers
Hospitaliky 37 Dave Fleischer
Hospitalities 29 Manny Gould, Ben Harrison
Hosszú az Út Hazáig 60 Félix Máriássy
Host, The 23 Lloyd Bacon
Hostage, The 17 Robert Thornby
Hostage, The 56 Harold Huth
Hostage, The 66 Russell Doughton, Jr.
Hostage 83 Frank Shields
Hostage 87 Hanro Mohr
Hostage: Dallas 86 Dwight H. Little
Hostage of the Embassy, The 16 August Blom
Hostage Syndrome 87 Dominic Elmo Smith
Hostage: The Christine Maresch Story 83 Frank Shields
Hostages 43 Frank Tuttle
Hostages, The 72 Édouard Molinaro
Hostages, The 75 David Eady
Hostile Country 50 Thomas Carr
Hostile Guns 67 R. G. Springsteen
Hostile Takeover 88 George Mihalka
Hostile Wind, The 56 Mikhail Kalatozov
Hostile Witness 67 Ray Milland
Höstsonaten 78 Ingmar Bergman
Hot Air Salesman, The 37 Dave Fleischer
Hot and Bothered 30 Edward Buzzell
Hot and Bothered 31 Charles Lamont
Hot and Cold 33 Walter Lantz
Hot and Cold 89 Ted Kotcheff
Hot and Deadly 81 Elliot Hong
Hot—and How! 30 Stephen Roberts
Hot Angel, The 58 Joe Parker
Hot Blood 55 Nicholas Ray
Hot Box, The 72 Joe Viola
Hot Bridge 30 Mark Sandrich
Hot Bubblegum 81 Boaz Davidson
Hot Car Girl 56 Leslie Martinson
Hot Car Girl 58 Bernard Kowalski
Hot Cargo 46 Lew Landers
Hot Cars 56 Donald McDougall
Hot Child in the City 87 John Florea
Hot Chili 85 William Sachs
Hot Cross Bunny 48 Robert McKimson
Hot Curves 30 Norman Taurog
Hot Dog 28 Walt Disney
Hot Dog 30 Dave Fleischer
Hot Dog...The Movie 84 Peter Markle
Hot Doggie 25 Al Christie
Hot Dogs 14 Charles Chaplin, Mabel Normand
Hot Dogs 20 Raoul Barré, Charles Bowers
Hot Dogs 25 William C. Nolan
Hot Dogs on Ice 38 Manny Gould, Ben Harrison

Hot Enough for June 63 Ralph Thomas
Hot Feet 31 Walter Lantz
Hot Foot Lights 45 Howard Swift
Hot for Hollywood 30 Walter Lantz
Hot for Paris 29 Raoul Walsh
Hot Frustrations 67 Georges Combret
Hot Girls, The 74 Laurence Barnett, John Lindsay
Hot Girls for Men Only 66 Peter Walker
Hot Heels 28 William James Craft
Hot Heir 30 Will P. Kellino
Hot Heiress, The 31 Clarence Badger
Hot Horse 58 Hal Kanter
Hot Hours 63 Louis Félix
Hot House 49 James Whitney, John Whitney
Hot Ice 52 Kenneth Hume
Hot in Paradise 59 Fritz Böttger
Hot Lead 51 Stuart Gilmore
Hot Lead 56 Samuel Fuller
Hot Lead and Cold Feet 78 Robert Butler
Hot Lightning 27 Stephen Roberts
Hot Line, The 65 Wanda Jakubowska
Hot Line 68 Étienne Périer
Hot Luck 28 Charles Lamont
Hot Marshland, The 50 Kon Ichikawa
Hot Millions 68 Eric Till
Hot Money 36 William McGann, Harry Seymour
Hot Money Girl 59 Alvin Rakoff
Hot Month of August, The 69 Sokrates Kapsakis
Hot Moves 84 Jim Sotos
Hot News 28 Clarence Badger
Hot News 36 Will P. Kellino
Hot News 53 Edward Bernds
Hot Night, A 68 Kozaburo Yoshimura
Hot Off the Press 35 Albert Herman
Hot One, The 78 Matthew Robbins
Hot or Cold 28 Stephen Roberts
Hot Pearls 41 Edward Dmytryk
Hot Pepper 33 John G. Blystone
Hot Pepper 73 Les Blank
Hot Pickles 10 Lewin Fitzhamon
Hot Pie 06 Alf Collins
Hot Potato 76 Oscar Williams
Hot Property 84 Lino Brocka
Hot Pursuit 81 James West
Hot Pursuit 87 Steven Lisberger
Hot Resort 85 John Robins
Hot Rhythm 44 William Beaudine
Hot Rock, The 72 Peter Yates
Hot Rod 50 Lewis D. Collins
Hot Rod and Reel 59 Chuck Jones
Hot Rod Gang 58 Lew Landers
Hot Rod Girl 56 Leslie Martinson
Hot Rod Hullabaloo 66 William T. Naud
Hot Rod Rumble 57 Leslie Martinson
Hot Rods to Hell 64 John Brahm
Hot Saturday 32 William A. Seiter
Hot Seat 87 Waldemar Korzeniowsky
Hot Shots 56 Jean Yarbrough
Hot Soup 27 Mark Sandrich
Hot Spell 58 George Cukor, Daniel Mann
Hot Spot 41 H. Bruce Humberstone
Hot Spot, The 90 Dennis Hopper
Hot Spur 68 R. Lee Frost
Hot Steel 40 Christy Cabanne
Hot Streak 82 Don Siegel
Hot Stuff 12 Mack Sennett

Hot Stuff 29 Mervyn LeRoy
Hot Stuff 79 Dom DeLuise
Hot Summer in Barefoot County 74 Will Zens
Hot Summer Night 56 David Friedkin
Hot Summer Week 73 Thomas J. Schmidt
Hot T-Shirts 79 Chuck Vincent
Hot Target 85 Denis Lewiston
Hot Time in Punkville, A 15 Vincent Whitman
Hot Time in the Gym, A 17 Gregory La Cava
Hot Time in the Old Town Tonight, A 30 Dave Fleischer
Hot Times 29 Stephen Roberts
Hot Times 73 Jim McBride
Hot Tip 35 James Gleason, Ray McCarey
Hot to Trot 88 Michael Dinner
Hot Tomorrows 77 Martin Brest
Hot Touch, The 80 Roger Vadim
Hot Water 24 Fred Newmeyer, Sam Taylor
Hot Water 37 Frank R. Strayer
Hot Wind 34 Tomu Uchida
Hot Wind 43 Satsuo Yamamoto
Hot Wind 82 Daniel Wachsmann
Hot Winds 73 M. S. Sathyu
Hot Winter 72 Karel Kachyňa
Hotaru 89 Koichi Kajima
Hotarubi 58 Heinosuke Gosho
Hotarugawa 87 Eizo Sugawa
Hotcha Melody 35 Manny Gould, Ben Harrison
Hotel 67 Richard Quine
Hotel, The 68 Daniel Tinayre
Hotel Adlon 55 Josef von Baky
Hotel at Osaka 54 Heinosuke Gosho
Hotel Berlin 45 John Gage, Peter Godfrey
Hotel Blue Star, The 41 Martin Frič
Hotel Colonial 87 Cinzia H. Torrini
Hotel Continental 32 Christy Cabanne
Hôtel de France 87 Patrice Chereau
Hotel de Gink 15 Harry S. Palmer
Hôtel de la Gare, L' 14 Louis Feuillade
Hôtel de le Plage, L' 77 Michel Lang
Hotel de los Chiflados, El 39 Antonio Helu
Hotel de Mutt 18 Raoul Barré, Charles Bowers
Hôtel des Amériques 82 André Téchiné
Hôtel des Étudiants 32 Victor Tourjansky
Hôtel des Invalides 51 Georges Franju
Hôtel des Voyageurs de Commerce, L' 06 Georges Méliès
Hôtel du Libre-Échange, L' 33 Marc Allégret, Christian-Jaque
Hôtel du Nord 38 Marcel Carné
Hôtel du Paradis 86 Jana Bokova
Hôtel du Silence, L' 08 Émile Cohl
Hotel Eléctrico 05 Segundo De Chomón
Hôtel Empoisonné, L' 1896 Georges Méliès
Hotel for Women 39 Gregory Ratoff
Hotel Haywire 37 George Archainbaud
Hotel Honeymoon 12 Alice Guy-Blaché
Hotel Imperial 26 Mauritz Stiller
Hotel Imperial 38 Robert Florey
Hotel Modrá Hvězda 41 Martin Frič
Hotel Monterey 72 Chantal Akerman
Hotel Mouse, The 23 Fred Paul

Hotel New Hampshire, The 84 Tony Richardson
Hotel New York 85 Jackie Raynal
Hotel Paradiso 66 Peter Glenville
Hotel Reserve 44 Lance Comfort, Max Greene, Joseph Losey
Hotel Sacher 39 Erich Engel
Hotel Sahara 51 Ken Annakin
Hotel Splendide 32 Michael Powell
Hotel Sunrise 37 Béla Gaál
Hotel Terminus: Klaus Barbie, His Life and Times 87 Marcel Ophüls
Hotel Terminus: The Life and Times of Klaus Barbie 87 Marcel Ophüls
Hotel Variety 33 Raymond Cannon
Hotelgeheimnisse 28 Friedrich Feher
Hothead 63 Santos Alcocer
Hothead 79 Jean-Jacques Annaud
Hothouse, The 87 Peter Gödel
Hothouse Venus, The 85 Martin Tapak
Hotlips Jasper 44 George Pal
Hotohira no Yuki 86 Kichitaro Negishi
Hototogisu 32 Heinosuke Gosho
Hôtreal 87 Ildikó Szabó
Hotshot 86 Rick King
Hotsprings Holiday 70 Hirokazu Ichimura
Hotsy Footsy 52 William Hurtz
Hotsy Totsy 25 Edward F. Cline
Hottentot, The 22 James W. Horne
Hottentot, The 29 Roy Del Ruth
Hottentot and the Gramophone, The 08 Lewin Fitzhamon
Hotter Than Hot 29 Lewis R. Foster
Hotwire 80 Frank Q. Dobbs
Houdini 53 George Marshall
Houghland Murder Case, The 35 Clifford Sanforth
Hound Dog Man, The 59 Don Siegel
Hound for Trouble, A 51 Chuck Jones
Hound Hunters 47 Tex Avery
Hound of Silver Creek, The 28 Stuart Paton
Hound of the Baskervilles, The 14 Rudolf Meinert
Hound of the Baskervilles, The 15 Richard Oswald
Hound of the Baskervilles, The 20 Willy Zehn
Hound of the Baskervilles, The 21 Maurice Elvey
Hound of the Baskervilles, The 29 Richard Oswald
Hound of the Baskervilles, The 31 V. Gareth Gundrey
Hound of the Baskervilles, The 39 Sidney Lanfield
Hound of the Baskervilles, The 58 Terence Fisher
Hound of the Baskervilles, The 77 Paul Morrissey
Hound of the Baskervilles, The 83 Douglas Hickox
Hound of the Baskervilles: The Dark Castle, The 15 Willy Zehn
Hound That Thought He Was a Racoon, The 60 Tom McGowan
Hounded 49 Ted Tetzlaff
Hounds of Notre Dame, The 80 Zale Dalen
Hounds of Zaroff, The 32 Irving Pichel,

Ernest B. Schoedsack
Houp-la 28 Frank Miller
Hour Before Dawn, An 13 J. Searle Dawley
Hour Before the Dawn, The 44 Frank Tuttle
Hour for Lunch, An 38 Roy Rowland
Hour of Decision 57 C. M. Pennington-Richards
Hour of Fear, The 29 Andrew Marton
Hour of Glory 48 Michael Powell, Emeric Pressburger
Hour of Reckoning, The 14 Thomas Ince
Hour of Reckoning, The 27 John Ince
Hour of the Assassin 87 Luis Llosa
Hour of the Furnaces, The 66 Santiago Álvarez, Octavio Getino, Fernando Solanas
Hour of the Gun 67 John Sturges
Hour of the Star, The 85 Suzana Amaral
Hour of the Wolf 67 Ingmar Bergman
Hour of 13, The 52 Harold French
Hour of Trial 15 Victor Sjöström
Hour of Trial, The 20 A. E. Coleby
Hour of Truth 64 Henri Calef
Hour with Chekhov, An 29 Mikhail Doller, Yakov Protazanov
Hourglass Sanatorium, The 73 Wojciech Has
Hours Between, The 31 Marion Gering
Hours of Hope 56 Jan Rybkowski
Hours of Loneliness 30 Guarino G. Glavany
Hours of Love, The 63 Luciano Salce
Hours of Wedlock, The 87 Kichitaro Negishi
House 55 Charles Eames, Ray Eames
House 58 Walerian Borowczyk, Jan Lenica
House, The 62 Louis Van Gastern
House 77 Nobuhiko Obayashi
House, The 82 Egill Edvardsson
House 86 Steve Miner
House II: The Second Story 87 Ethan Wiley
House 87 Chart Gobjitti, Egalag Gobjitti
House Across the Bay, The 40 Archie Mayo
House Across the Lake, The 54 Ken Hughes
House Across the Street, The 36 Christian-Jaque
House Across the Street, The 49 Richard L. Bare
House at the End of the World, The 65 Daniel Haller
House at the Terminus, The 56 Ján Kadár, Elmar Klos
House Behind the Cedars, The 23 Oscar Micheaux
House Broken 36 Michael Hankinson
House Builder Upper, The 38 Dave Fleischer
House Built Upon Sand, The 17 Edward Morrissey
House by the Cemetery, The 81 Lucio Fulci
House by the Lake, The 76 William Fruet
House by the River, The 49 Fritz Lang
House by the River, The 86 Roland Graf
House Calls 78 Howard Zieff

House Cat, The *48* David Hand
House Cleaning *33* Manny Gould, Ben Harrison
House Cleaning Blues *37* Dave Fleischer
House Committee Rivalry *86* Avi Cohen
House Divided, A *13* Alice Guy-Blaché
House Divided, A *19* J. Stuart Blackton
House Divided, A *31* William Wyler
House Hunting Mice *47* Chuck Jones
House I Live In, The *45* Mervyn LeRoy
House I Live In, The *57* Lev Kulidzhanov, Yakov Segel
House I Wish to Build, The *55* Henning Carlsen
House in Marsh Road, The *59* Montgomery Tully
House in Nightmare Park, The *73* Peter Sykes
House in Rue Rapp, The *46* Ronald Haines
House in the Snowdrifts, The *28* Friedrich Ermler
House in the Square, The *51* Roy Ward Baker
House in the Woods, The *57* Maxwell Munden
House in Which They Live, The *16* John R. Bray
House Is Not a Home, A *64* Russell Rouse
House Next Door, The *14* Barry O'Neil
House of a Thousand Candles, The *15* Thomas Heffron
House of a Thousand Candles, The *36* Arthur Lubin
House of a Thousand Pleasures *77* Antonio Margheriti
House of Angel, The *57* Leopoldo Torre-Nilsson
House of Bamboo *55* Samuel Fuller
House of Bernarda Alba, The *87* Mario Camus
House of Blackmail *53* Maurice Elvey
House of Cards *16* Alice Guy-Blaché
House of Cards *34* Ivar Campbell
House of Cards *68* John Guillermin
House of Connelly *34* Henry King
House of Crazies *72* Roy Ward Baker
House of Danger *34* Charles Hutchinson
House of Dark Shadows *70* Dan Curtis
House of Darkness, The *13* D. W. Griffith
House of Darkness *48* Oswald Mitchell
House of Death *16* Yakov Protazanov
House of Death *32* V. F. Federov
House of Deceit, The *28* Phil Rosen
House of Discord, The *13* James Kirkwood
House of Distemperley, The *14* Fred Evans, Joe Evans
House of Doom *34* Edgar G. Ulmer
House of Doom *73* Carlos Aured
House of Dracula *45* Erle C. Kenton
House of Dreams *33* Anthony Frenguelli
House of Dreams *63* Robert Berry
House of Errors *42* Bernard B. Ray
House of Evil *68* Jack Hill, Juan Ibáñez
House of Evil *82* Mark Rosman
House of Exorcism, The *72* Mario Bava, Alfred Leone
House of Fate, The *36* Charles Vidor
House of Fear, The *14* John Ince
House of Fear, The *15* Arnold Daly, Ashley Miller
House of Fear, The *39* Joe May
House of Fear, The *45* Roy William Neill
House of Flickers *25* Roy Del Ruth*
House of Fortescue, The *16* Frank Wilson
House of Frankenstein *44* Erle C. Kenton
House of Freaks, The *73* Robert H. Oliver
House of Fright *60* Mario Bava
House of Fright *60* Terence Fisher
House of Games *87* David Mamet
House of Glass, The *18* Émile Chautard
House of God, The *79* Donald Wrye
House of Gold, The *18* Edwin Carewe
House of Greed *34* Alexander Ivanovsky
House of Hanging *79* Kon Ichikawa
House of Hate, The *18* George B. Seitz
House of Horror, The *28* Benjamin Christensen
House of Horrors *46* Jean Yarbrough
House of Insane Women *71* Rafael Moreno Alba
House of Intrigue, The *19* Lloyd Ingraham
House of Intrigue, The *59* Duilio Coletti
House of Lies, The *16* William Desmond Taylor
House of Life *53* Karl Hartl
House of Light, The *69* Jean-Pierre Lefèbvre
House of Long Shadows, The *82* Peter Walker
House of Lovers, The *57* Julien Duvivier
House of Madness *72* Juan López Moctezuma
House of Magic *37* Walter Lantz
House of Marney, The *26* Cecil M. Hepworth
House of Menace *35* George B. Seitz
House of Mirrors, The *16* Marshall Farnum
House of Mirth, The *18* Albert Capellani
House of Mortal Sin *75* Peter Walker
House of Mystery, The *01* Georges Méliès
House of Mystery, The *13* Wilfred Noy
House of Mystery, The *20* Charles Raymond
House of Mystery *31* Kurt Neumann
House of Mystery, The *34* William Nigh
House of Mystery *38* Lewis D. Collins
House of Mystery *39* Walter Summers
House of Mystery *42* Ford Beebe*
House of Mystery *61* Vernon Sewell
House of Numbers *57* Russell Rouse
House of 1,000 Dolls *67* Jeremy Summers
House of Peril, The *22* Kenelm Foss
House of Pleasure *51* Max Ophüls
House of Psychotic Women, The *73* Carlos Aured
House of Ricordi *54* Carmine Gallone
House of Rothschild *34* Alfred L. Werker
House of Scandal, The *28* King Baggot
House of Science *62* Charles Eames, Ray Eames
House of Secrets *29* Edmund Lawrence
House of Secrets *37* Roland Reed
House of Secrets *56* Guy Green
House of Settlement *49* Gordon Douglas, Henry Levin
House of Seven Corpses, The *72* Paul Harrison
House of Seven Gables, The *40* Joe May
House of Seven Joys *68* Phil Karlson
House of Shadows *77* Richard Wulicher
House of Shame, The *28* Burton Young
House of Shame, A *67* Tomotaka Tasaka
House of Silence, The *18* Donald Crisp
House of Silence *33* Rune Carlsten
House of Silence, The *37* R. K. Neilson-Baxter
House of Strange Loves, The *69* Tan Ida
House of Strangers *49* Joseph L. Mankiewicz
House of Tao Ling, The *46* James Tinling
House of Tears, The *15* Edwin Carewe
House of Temperley, The *13* Harold M. Shaw
House of Terror *59* Gilberto Martínez Solares, Jerry Warren
House of Terrors *65* Hajime Sato
House of the Angel, The *57* Leopoldo Torre-Nilsson
House of the Arrow, The *30* Leslie Hiscott
House of the Arrow, The *40* Harold French
House of the Arrow, The *52* Michael Anderson
House of the Black Death *65* Harold Daniels, Reginald LeBorg
House of the Damned *62* Maury Dexter
House of the Dark Stairway *83* Lamberto Bava
House of the Golden Windows, The *16* George Melford
House of the Good Return, The *86* Beppe Cino
House of the Hanging on Hospital Hill, The *79* Kon Ichikawa
House of the Living Dead *73* Ray Austin
House of the Long Shadows *82* Peter Walker
House of the Lost Court, The *15* Charles Brabin
House of the Lute *79* Cheng-han Liu
House of the Ogre, The *38* Fernando De Fuentes
House of the Psychotic Women *73* Carlos Aured
House of the Rising Sun *85* Chuck Vincent
House of the Seven Gables, The *40* Joe May
House of the Seven Hawks, The *59* Richard Thorpe
House of the Sleeping Virgins, The *68* Kozaburo Yoshimura
House of the Spaniard, The *36* Reginald Denham
House of the Three Girls, The *61* Ernst Marischka
House of the Tolling Bell, The *20* J. Stuart Blackton
House of Three Girls, The *61* Ernst Marischka
House of Tomorrow, The *49* Tex Avery
House of Toys, The *20* George L. Cox
House of Trent, The *33* Norman Walker
House of Unclaimed Women *68* Robert Hartford-Davis
House of Unrest, The *31* Leslie Howard Gordon
House of Usher *60* Roger Corman
House of Usher, The *88* Alan Birkinshaw

House of Wax 53 André De Toth
House of Whipcord 74 Peter Walker
House of Whispers, The 20 Ernest C. Warde
House of Women 53 Erik Faustman
House of Women 60 Walter Doniger, Crane Wilbur
House of Wooden Blocks, The 68 Yasuzo Masumura
House of Youth, The 24 Ralph Ince
House on a Volcano, The 28 Amo Bek-Nazarov
House on Carroll Street, The 87 Peter Yates
House on Cedar Hill, The 26 Carlton Moss
House on Chelouche Street, The 73 Moshe Mizrahi
House on 56th Street, The 33 Robert Florey
House on Fire 86 Kinji Fukasaku
House on Haunted Hill 58 William Castle
House on Marsh Road, The 59 Montgomery Tully
House on 92nd Street, The 45 Henry Hathaway
House on Skull Mountain, The 73 Ron Honthaner
House on Sorority Row, The 82 Mark Rosman
House on Stournara Street, The 60 Dinos Dimopoulos
House on Straw Hill, The 75 James Kenelm Clarke
House on Sullivan Street, The 87 Peter Yates
House on Telegraph Hill, The 51 Robert Wise
House on the Brink, A 86 Antonietta De Lillo, Giorgio Magliulo
House on the Dune, The 34 Pierre Billon
House on the Edge of the Park, The 80 Ruggero Deodato
House on the Front Line, The 63 Alexander Galich, Stanislav Rostotsky
House on the Marsh, The 19 Fred Paul
House on the River, The 86 Roland Graf
House on the Riverside, The 86 Roland Graf
House on the Sand 67 Tony M. Zarindast
House on the Square, The 51 Roy Ward Baker
House on the Wastelands 49 Jan Rybkowski
House on the Waterfront, The 54 Edmond T. Gréville
House on Trubnaya Square, The 28 Boris Barnet
House Opposite, The 17 Frank Wilson
House Opposite, The 31 Walter Summers
House Outside the Cemetery, The 81 Lucio Fulci
House Party 90 Reginald Hudlin
House That Cried Murder, The 73 Jean-Marie Pelissie
House That Dinky Built, The 25 Walter Lantz
House That Dripped Blood, The 70 Peter Duffell
House That Jack Built, The 00 George

Albert Smith
House That Jack Built, The 11 Allan Dwan
House That Jack Built, The 39 Sid Marcus
House That Jazz Built, The 21 Penrhyn Stanlaws
House That Jerry Built, The 13 Frank Wilson
House That Screamed, The 69 Narciso Ibáñez Serrador
House That Vanished, The 73 José Ramón Larraz
House to Let 06 J. H. Martin
House Under the Rocks, The 58 Károly Makk
House Warmers 29 Bobby Harman
House Warming 54 Shih-ling Chu
House Where Death Lives, The 80 Alan Beattie
House Where Evil Dwells, The 82 Kevin Connor
House Where I Live, The 57 Lev Kulidzhanov, Yakov Segel
House with an Attic, The 64 Yakov Bazelian
House with Closed Shutters, The 10 D. W. Griffith
House with the Closed Shutters, The 10 D. W. Griffith
House Without a Christmas Tree 72 Paul Bogart
House Without a Key, The 26 Spencer G. Bennet
House Without Children, The 19 Samuel Brodsky
House Without Windows 75 Earl Bellamy
Houseboat 58 Melville Shavelson
Houseboat Mystery, The 14 B. Harold Brett
Houseful of Happiness, A 60 János Herskó
Householder, The 63 James Ivory
Housekeeper, The 86 Ousama Rawi
Housekeeper's Daughter, The 39 Hal Roach
Housekeeping 87 Bill Forsyth
Housemaster, The 38 Herbert Brenon
Housewarming, The 83 Zoltán Fábri
Housewife 34 Alfred E. Green
Housewife 72 Larry Cohen
Housewives, Inc. 60 Barry Mahon
Housing 20 Frank Miller
Housing Problems 35 Edgar Anstey, Arthur Elton
Houslový Koncert 62 Jaromil Jireš*
Houston Story, The 56 William Castle
Houston Texas 56 François Reichenbach
Houston Texas 80 François Reichenbach
Houwen Zo 53 Herman van den Horst
Hövdingens Son Är Död 37 Pál Fejős
Hoverbug 70 Jan Darnley-Smith
How a Burglar Feels 07 J. H. Martin
How a French Nobleman Got a Wife Through the New York "Herald" Personal Columns 04 Edwin S. Porter
How a Housekeeper Lost Her Character 13 Fred Rains
How a Mosquito Operates 12 Winsor McCay
How a Young Man Lives 64 Vasili Shuksin

How About Us? 63 Henning Carlsen
How Animated Cartoons Are Made 19 John R. Bray
How 'Arry Sold His Seeds 12 Charles Raymond
How Baby Caught Cold 06 Percy Stow
How Baxter Butted In 25 William Beaudine
How Billy Kept His Word 14 Frank Wilson
How Bridget's Lover Escaped 07 Georges Méliès
How Broad Is Our Country 58 Roman Karmen
How Brown Brought Home the Goose 05 Alf Collins
How Cecil Played the Game 13 Edwin J. Collins
How Charlie Captured the Kaiser 18 Pat Sullivan
How Come Nobody's on Our Side? 75 Richard Michaels
How Could William Tell? 19 Gregory La Cava
How Could You, Caroline? 18 Frederick Thompson
How Could You, Jean? 18 William Desmond Taylor
How Could You, Uncle? 18 Maurice Sandground
How Dizzy Joe Got to Heaven 16 L. M. Glackens
How Do I Know It's Sunday? 34 Friz Freleng
How Do I Love Thee? 70 Michael Gordon
How Do You Do? 45 Ralph Murphy
How Do You Like Them Bananas? 66 Lionel Rogosin
How Doooo You Do? 45 Ralph Murphy
How Eve Helped the War Fund 18 J. L. V. Leigh
How Far and Yet How Near 72 Tadeusz Konwicki
How Father Killed the Cat 06 Percy Stow
How Fine, How Fresh the Roses Were 13 Yakov Protazanov
How Funny Can Sex Be? 73 Dino Risi
How Grandpa Changed Till Nothing Was Left 52 Jiří Trnka
How Green Was My Valley 41 John Ford
How He Lied to Her Husband 30 Cecil Lewis
How He Missed His Train 01 Georges Méliès
How Hiram Won Out 13 Mack Sennett
How I Became Krazy 21 Vernon Stallings
How I Began 26 Widgey R. Newman, Challis Sanderson
How I Cook-ed Peary's Record 09 Walter R. Booth
How I Got Into College 89 Savage Steve Holland
How I Was Systematically Destroyed by an Idiot 84 Slobodan Šijan
How I Won the Belt 14 Harcourt Brown
How I Won the War 67 Richard Lester
How Is It Done? 13 Frank Wilson
How Isaacs Won the Cup 06 Harold Hough
How It Feels 22 Hy Mayer

How It Feels to Be Run Over *00* Cecil M. Hepworth

How It Happened *25* Alexander Butler

How Jones Got a New Suit *08* A. E. Coleby

How Jones Lost His Roll *05* Edwin S. Porter

How Jones Saw the Derby *05* Charles Raymond

How Kico Was Born *51* Dušan Vukotić

How Kitchener Was Betrayed *21* Percy Nash

How Kutasek and Kutilka Got Up in the Morning *52* Jiří Trnka

How Lieutenant Pimple Captured the Kaiser *14* Fred Evans, Joe Evans

How Lieutenant Rose RN Spiked the Enemy's Guns *15* Percy Stow

How Love Came *16* Charles C. Calvert

How Low Can You Fall? *74* Luigi Comencini

How Man Learned to Fly *58* Jiří Brdečka

How Many Roads? *69* Robert Alan Aurthur

How Mary Decided *11* A. E. Coleby

How Men Love Women *15* Percy Moran

How Molly and Polly Got Pa's Consent *12* Bert Haldane

How Molly Made Good *15* Lawrence McGill

How Molly Malone Made Good *15* Lawrence McGill

How Much Loving Does a Normal Couple Need? *67* Russ Meyer

How Much Wood Would a Woodchuck Chuck *76* Werner Herzog

How My Vacation Spent Me *20* Milt Gross

How Not to Rob a Department Store *65* Pierre Grimblat

How Not to Succeed in Business *75* John Halas

How Now Boing Boing *54* Robert Cannon

How Now Sweet Jesus? *70* Ned Bosnick

How Old Is Ann? *03* Edwin S. Porter

How Pimple Saved Kissing Cup *13* Fred Evans, Joe Evans

How Pimple Won the Derby *14* Fred Evans, Joe Evans

How Potts Backed the Winner *09* A. E. Coleby

How Puny Peter Became Strong *11* A. E. Coleby

How Richard Harris Became Known As Deadwood Dick *15* L. C. MacBean, Fred Paul

How Robinson Was Created *61* Eldar Ryazanov

How Scroggins Found the Comet *10* Dave Aylott

How She Triumphed *11* D. W. Griffith

How Smiler Raised the Wind *12* Dave Aylott

How Spotted Duff Saved the Squire *14* Will P. Kellino

How Sweet It Is! *68* Jerry Paris

How Tasty Was My Little Frenchman *71* Nelson Pereira Dos Santos

How the Artful Dodger Secured a Meal *08* A. E. Coleby

How the Baby's Soul Sobs *13* Yakov Protazanov

How the Bear Got His Short Tail *25* Walter Lantz

How the Bulldog Paid the Rent *09* Charles Raymond

How the Burglar Tricked the Bobby *01* Cecil M. Hepworth

How the Camel Got His Hump *25* Clyde Geronimi

How the Dutch Beat the Irish *01* Edwin S. Porter

How the Elector Will Vote *37* Sergei Yutkevich

How the Elephant Got His Trunk *25* Walter Lantz

How the F-100 Got Its Tail *55* Richard Leacock

How the Giraffe Got His Long Neck *26* Clyde Geronimi

How the Office Boy Saw the Ball Game *06* Edwin S. Porter

How the Old Woman Caught the Omnibus *03* Percy Stow

How the Poor Help the Poor *05* Alf Collins

How the Steel Was Tempered *42* Mark Donskoi

How the Tramps Tricked the Motorist *05* Lewin Fitzhamon

How the West Was Won *62* John Ford, Henry Hathaway, George Marshall, Richard Thorpe

How They Do Things on the Bowery *02* Edwin S. Porter

How They Got the Vote *13* Ashley Miller

How They Made a Man of Billy Brown *09* Jack Chart

How Things Do Develop *14* Hay Plumb

How to Be a Detective *36* Felix E. Feist

How to Be Happy *87* Yuri Chuliukin

How to Be Loved *62* Wojciech Has

How to Be Very, Very Popular *55* Nunnally Johnson

How to Beat the High Co$t of Living *80* Robert Scheerer

How to Behave *36* Arthur Ripley

How to Commit Marriage *69* Norman Panama

How to Destroy the Reputation of the Greatest Secret Agent *73* Philippe de Broca

How to Eat *39* Roy Rowland

How to Educate a Wife *24* Monta Bell

How to Figure Income Tax *38* Roy Rowland

How to Fire a Lewis Gun *18* Max Fleischer

How to Fire a Stokes Mortar *18* Max Fleischer

How to Frame a Figg *70* Alan Rafkin

How to Get Ahead in Advertising *88* Bruce Robinson

How to Handle Women *28* William James Craft

How to Keep the Red Lamp Burning *65* Gilles Grangier, Georges Lautner

How to Make a Doll *67* Herschell Gordon Lewis

How to Make a Monster *58* Herbert L. Strock

How to Make It *68* Roger Corman

How to Make Love to a Negro Without Getting Tired *89* Jacques W. Benoît

How to Make Time Fly *06* J. H. Martin

How to Marry a Millionaire *53* Jean Negulesco

How to Murder a Rich Uncle *57* Nigel Patrick, Max Varnel

How to Murder Your Wife *64* Richard Quine

How to Operate Behind Enemy Lines *42* John Ford

How to Play Football *49* Jack Kinney

How to Raise a Baby *38* Roy Rowland

How to Read *38* Roy Rowland

How to Read an Army Map *18* Max Fleischer

How to Rob a Bank *58* Henry Levin

How to Save a Marriage...and Ruin Your Life *67* Fielder Cook

How to Score with Girls *80* Ogden Lowell

How to Seduce a Playboy *66* Michael Pfleghar

How to Seduce a Virgin *73* Jesús Franco

How to Seduce a Woman *74* Charles Martin

How to Sleep *35* Nick Grindé

How to Start the Day *37* Roy Rowland

How to Steal a Diamond in Four Uneasy Lessons *72* Peter Yates

How to Steal a Million *66* William Wyler

How to Steal the World *66* Sutton Roley

How to Stop a Motor Car *02* Percy Stow

How to Stuff a Wild Bikini *65* William Asher

How to Sub-Let *38* Roy Rowland

How to Succeed in Business Without Really Trying *67* David Swift

How to Succeed with Sex *70* Bert I. Gordon

How to Train a Dog *36* Arthur Ripley

How to Undress in Front of Your Husband *37* Dwain Esper

How to Undress in Public Without Undue Embarrassment *65* Compton Bennett

How to Vote *36* Felix E. Feist

How to Watch Football *38* Roy Rowland

How Troy Was Collared *23* W. E. Stark

How Vandyck Won His Wife *12* Bert Haldane

How, Why and What For Is a General Assassinated? *71* Santiago Álvarez

How Willingly You Sing *75* Garry Patterson

How Willy Joined Barnum Bill *13* Will P. Kellino

How Winky Fought for a Bride *14* Cecil Birch

How Winky Whacked the Germans *14* Cecil Birch

How Women Love *22* Kenneth Webb

How You See *20* J. D. Leventhal

How Young We Were Then *85* Mikhail Belikov

How Yukong Moved the Mountains *76* Joris Ivens, Marceline Loridan

Howard, a New Breed of Hero *86* Willard Huyck

Howard Case, The *36* Frank Richardson

Howard the Duck *86* Willard Huyck

Howards of Virginia, The *40* Frank Lloyd

Howdy Duke 27 Norman Taurog
Howdy Partner 20 Wallace A. Carlson
Howlin' Jones 13 William Duncan
Howling, The 80 Joe Dante
Howling II: Your Sister Is a Werewolf 85 Philippe Mora
Howling III 87 Philippe Mora
Howling IV: The Original Nightmare 88 John Hough
Howling V: The Rebirth 89 Neal Sundström
How's About It? 43 Erle C. Kenton
How's Chances? 34 Anthony Kimmins
How's My Baby? 30 Stephen Roberts
How's Your Poor Wife? 17 Will P. Kellino
Howzer 73 Ken Laurence
Hoy Comienza la Vida 36 Alex Phillips
Hr. Storms Første Monokel 11 August Blom
Hra na Krále 67 Jaromil Jireš
Hra o Jablko 76 Věra Chytilová
Hra o Život 56 Jiří Weiss
Hrafninn Flýgur 85 Hrafn Gunnlaugsson
Hranjenik 70 Vatroslav Mimica
Hrdina Jedné Noci 35 Martin Frič
Hrst Plná Vody 69 Ján Kadár, Elmar Klos
Hrudaya Pallavi 88 R. N. Jayagopal
Hry pro Mírně Pokročilé 86 Oto Koval
Hsi Nu Ai Le 70 King Hu, Han-hsiang Li, Shing Lu, Ching-jui Pai
Hsia Nu 68 King Hu
Hu-Man 75 Jerome Laperrousaz
Hu-Yueh-Te Ku-Shih 81 Ann Hui
Hua Mu-Lan 65 Feng Yueh
Hua Pi 66 Zhifang Bao
Huajie Shidai 86 Angie Chan
Huang Tudi 84 Kaige Chen
Huanle Dingdang 86 Michael Hui
Huanle Yingziong 89 Ziniu Wu
Huapango 38 Juan Bustillo Oro
Hub Bahdala, El 51 Salah Abu Saif
Hub Ilal Abad 58 Youssef Chahine
Hubbun Ila'l Abad 58 Youssef Chahine
Hubby Goes to the Races 12 Frank Wilson
Hubby's Beano 14 Kelly Storrie
Hubby's Letter 12 Lewin Fitzhamon
Huck and Tom 18 William Desmond Taylor
Huckleberry Finn 20 William Desmond Taylor
Huckleberry Finn 31 John Cromwell, Norman Taurog
Huckleberry Finn 39 Richard Thorpe
Huckleberry Finn 60 Michael Curtiz
Huckleberry Finn 74 J. Lee-Thompson
Hucksters, The 47 Jack Conway
Hud 62 Martin Ritt
Hud 86 Vibeke Løkkeberg
Hudba z Marsu 53 Ján Kadár, Elmar Klos
Huddle 32 Sam Wood
Hudodelci 88 Franci Slak
Hudson's Bay 40 Irving Pichel
Hue and Cry 46 Charles Crichton
Huella 40 Moglia Barth
Huella Macabra, La 62 Alfredo B. Crevenna
Huey 68 Agnès Varda
Huey Lewis and the News: Be-Fore! 86 Les Blank

Huey Long 85 Ken Burns
Huggers 85 Allan Eastman
Huggetts Abroad, The 49 Ken Annakin
Hughes and Harlow: Angels in Hell 78 Larry Buchanan
Hughie at the Victory Derby 19 George Pearson
Hugo and Josefin 67 Kjell Grede
Hugo and Josephine 67 Kjell Grede
Hugo och Josefin 67 Kjell Grede
Hugo the Hippo 75 William Feigenbaum
Hugon the Mighty 18 Rollin Sturgeon
Hugs and Kisses 66 Jonas Cornell
Huguan 89 Jun Zhao Zhang
Huguenot, Le 09 Louis Feuillade
Huie's Predigt 80 Werner Herzog
Huilor 37 Alexander Alexeïeff, Claire Parker
Huis Clos 54 Jacqueline Audry
Huis Clos 62 Tad Danielewski
Huitième Jour, Le 59 Marcel Hanoun
Huk! 56 John Barnwell
Hula 27 Victor Fleming
Hula Hula Cabaret, The 19 Raoul Barré, Charles Bowers
Hula Hula Town 20 Raoul Barré, Charles Bowers
Hulda from Holland 16 John B. O'Brien
Hulda Rasmussen 11 Urban Gad
Hullabaloo 40 Edwin L. Marin
Hullabaloo 55 Vassily Ordynski, Yakov Segel
Hullabaloo Over Georgie and Bonnie's Pictures 78 James Ivory
Hullo Everybody 14 Charles Chaplin
Hullo Fame 40 Andrew Buchanan
Hullo Moscow! 45 Sergei Yutkevich
Hullo! Who's Your Lady Friend? 17 Will P. Kellino
Hülyeség Nem Akadály 85 János Xantus
Hum Bhi Insaan Hain 89 Mani Vannan
Hum Farishte Nahin 88 Jatin Kumar
Huma Gun Anmogaldi 46 Ramjankhan Mehboobkhan
Humain, Trop Humain 72 Louis Malle
Human Beast, The 38 Jean Renoir
Human Being, The 25 Kenji Mizoguchi
Human Being 61 Kaneto Shindo
Human Bullet, The 68 Kihachi Okamoto
Human Cargo 29 J. Steven Edwards
Human Cargo 36 Allan Dwan
Human Collateral 20 Lawrence C. Windom
Human Comedy, The 43 Clarence Brown
Human Condition, The 59 Masaki Kobayashi
Human Condition, A 72 Louis Malle
Human Condition, Part One, The 59 Masaki Kobayashi
Human Condition, Part One: No Greater Love, The 59 Masaki Kobayashi
Human Condition II, The 59 Masaki Kobayashi
Human Condition II: Road to Eternity, The 59 Masaki Kobayashi
Human Condition III, The 61 Masaki Kobayashi
Human Condition III: A Soldier's Prayer, The 61 Masaki Kobayashi
Human Desire, The 19 Wilfred North

Human Desire 54 Fritz Lang
Human Desires 24 Burton George
Human Driftwood 15 Émile Chautard, Maurice Tourneur
Human Duplicators, The 65 Hugo Grimaldi
Human Dutch, The 63 Bert Haanstra
Human Experiments 79 Gregory Goodell
Human Face Is a Monument, The 65 Stan Vanderbeek
Human Factor, The 74 Edward Dmytryk
Human Factor, The 79 Otto Preminger
Human Fish, The 33 Clyde Bruckman
Human Fly, The 02 Georges Méliès
Human Ghost, The 39 Walter Summers
Human Hearts 22 King Baggot
Human Highway 82 Dean Stockwell, Neil Young
Human Interest Story, The 51 Billy Wilder
Human Jungle, The 54 Joseph M. Newman
Human Kindness 13 Allan Dwan
Human Lanterns 82 Sun Chung
Human Law 26 Maurice Elvey
Human Monster, The 39 Walter Summers
Human Orchid, The 16 C. C. Field
Human Passions 19 Jacques Tyrol
Human Patterns 49 Kon Ichikawa
Human Pawn, A 16 Rex Ingram
Human Pyramid, The 1899 Georges Méliès
Human Sabotage 42 B. Reeves Eason
Human Side, The 34 Edward Buzzell
Human Skin Lantern, The 82 Sun Chung
Human Sparrows 26 William Beaudine
Human Stuff 20 B. Reeves Eason
Human Suffering 23 Kensaku Suzuki
Human Targets 32 John P. McGowan
Human, Too Human 72 Louis Malle
Human Tornado, The 25 Ben F. Wilson
Human Tornado, The 76 Cliff Roquemore
Human Vapor, The 60 Inoshiro Honda
Human Wall, The 59 Satsuo Yamamoto
Human Wreckage 23 John Griffith Wray
Human Zoo 61 Yoji Kuri
Humanity 25 Kenji Mizoguchi
Humanity 33 John Francis Dillon
Humanity and Paper Balloons 37 Sadao Yamanaka
Humanity, or Only a Jew 13 Bert Haldane, John Lawson
Humanity Through the Ages 07 Georges Méliès
Humanity's Hope 48 Sen Fou
Humanoid, The 79 George B. Lewis
Humanoids from the Deep 80 Barbara Peeters
Humanoids of the Deep 80 Barbara Peeters
Humble Man and the Singer, The 24 E. A. Dupont
Humdinger, The 26 Norman Taurog
Humdrum Brown 18 Rex Ingram
Hummel-Hummel 39 Alwin Elling
Humming Bird, The 24 Sidney Olcott
Humongous 81 Paul Lynch
Humoreska 39 Otakar Vávra
Humoresque 20 Frank Borzage
Humoresque 39 Otakar Vávra

Humoresque 46 Jean Negulesco
Humoresques 24 Dziga Vertov
Humorous Phases of Funny Faces 06 J. Stuart Blackton
Humors of Summer 13 Hy Mayer
Humour Noir 64 Claude Autant-Lara*
Humours of a River Picnic, The 06 Tom Green
Humpbacked Horse, The 76 Ivan Ivanov-Vano
Humphrey Takes a Chance 50 Jean Yarbrough
Humpty Dumpty 35 Ubbe Iwerks
Humpty Dumpty Man, The 89 Paul Hogan
Humrahi 45 Bimal Roy
Humunqus Hector 76 Pasquale Festa Campanile
Hun Within, The 18 Chester Withey
Hunan Girl Xiaoxiao 86 Lan Niao, Fei Xie
Hunch, The 21 George D. Baker
Hunch, The 67 Sarah Erulkar
Hunchback, The 11 A. E. Coleby
Hunchback, The 14 Christy Cabanne
Hunchback, The 14 Frank Wilson
Hunchback and the Dancer, The 20 F. W. Murnau
Hunchback of Notre Dame, The 11 Albert Capellani
Hunchback of Notre Dame, The 22 Edwin J. Collins
Hunchback of Notre Dame, The 23 Wallace Worsley
Hunchback of Notre Dame, The 39 William Dieterle
Hunchback of Notre Dame, The 56 Jean Delannoy
Hunchback of Rome, The 60 Carlo Lizzani
Hunchback of the Morgue, The 72 Javier Aguirre
Hund von Baskerville, Der 14 Rudolf Meinert
Hund von Baskerville, Der 15 Richard Oswald
Hund von Baskerville, Der 20 Willy Zehn
Hund von Baskerville, Der 29 Richard Oswald
Hund von Baskerville: Das Dunkle Schloss, Der 15 Willy Zehn
Hund von Baskerville III, Der 15 Richard Oswald
Hunde, Wollt Ihr Ewig Leben? 59 Frank Wisbar
Hundimiento de la Casa Usher, El 83 Jesús Franco
Hundra 84 Matt Cimber
Hundred Days in Burma, A 57 Leonid Varmalov
Hundred for One, A 41 Herbert Rappaport
Hundred Ghost Stories, The 68 Kimiyoshi Yasuda
Hundred Horsemen, The 64 Vittorio Cottafavi
Hundred Hour Hunt, The 52 Lewis Gilbert
Hundred Meters with Chaplin, A 67 Patricio Guzmán

Hundred Monsters, The 68 Kimiyoshi Yasuda
Hundred Pound Window, The 43 Brian Desmond Hurst
Hundred Thousand Children, A 55 Lindsay Anderson
Hundred to One 33 Walter West
Hundred to One Shot 06 J. Stuart Blackton
Hundredth Chance, The 20 Maurice Elvey
Hung Without Evidence 25 Alexander Butler
Hungarian Fairy Tale, A 87 Gyula Gazdag
Hungarian Nights 30 Viktor Jansen
Hungarian Rhapsody 29 Hans Schwarz
Hungarian Rhapsody 78 Miklós Jancsó
Hungarians, The 77 Zoltán Fábri
Hunger 32 Leo T. Hurwitz
Hunger 66 Henning Carlsen
Hunger, The 83 Tony Scott
Hunger 86 Ali Badrakhan
Hunger for Love 68 Nelson Pereira Dos Santos
Hunger...Hunger...Hunger 21 Vladimir Gardin, Vsevolod I. Pudovkin
Hunger in Waldenburg 28 Piel Jutzi
Hunger of the Blood, The 21 Nate Watt
Hunger Straits 64 Tomu Uchida
Hunger Stroke, A 28 Manny Gould, Ben Harrison
Hunger's Curse 10 Bert Haldane
Hungry Countryman, The 1899 George Albert Smith
Hungry Dog, The 60 John Halas*
Hungry Eyes 18 Rupert Julian
Hungry for Love 60 Antonio Pietrangeli
Hungry Heart, A 17 Émile Chautard
Hungry Heart, The 17 Robert Vignola
Hungry Hearts 22 E. Mason Hopper
Hungry Hill 46 Brian Desmond Hurst
Hungry Hoboes 28 Walt Disney
Hungry i Reunion 80 Thomas Cohen
Hungry Lions and Tender Hearts 20 Roy Del Ruth, Malcolm St. Clair
Hungry Mosquito, The 12 Winsor McCay
Hungry Pets 72 Carl Monson
Hungry Wives 72 George Romero
Hungry Wolves, The 69 Yılmaz Güney
Hunk 87 Lawrence Bassoff
Hunky and Spunky 38 Dave Fleischer
Huns, The 60 Sergio Grieco
Huns of the North Sea 14 Sidney Morgan
Hunt, The 15 Charlie Chase, Ford Sterling
Hunt, The 24 George Marshall
Hunt, The 60 Manoel De Oliveira
Hunt, The 65 Carlos Saura
Hunt for a Collar, The 10 Walter R. Booth
Hunt for Red October, The 90 John McTiernan
Hunt the Man Down 50 George Archainbaud
Hunt to Kill 77 J. Lee-Thompson
Hunted 44 William Berke
Hunted, The 48 Jack Bernhard
Hunted, The 51 Charles Crichton
Hunted, The 58 Nikos Koundouros
Hunted 72 Peter Crane
Hunted, The 74 Douglas Fifthian
Hunted in Holland 61 Derek Williams

Hunted Men 30 John P. McGowan
Hunted Men 38 Louis King
Hunted Through the Everglades 11 Sidney Olcott
Hunted Woman, The 16 Sidney Rankin Drew
Hunted Woman, The 25 Jack Conway
Hunter, The 31 Walter Lantz
Hunter, The 80 Buzz Kulik
Hunter in the Dark 70 Hideo Gosha
Hunter of the Apocalypse 80 Antonio Margheriti
Hunters, The 58 Dick Powell
Hunters, The 60 Bruce Beresford
Hunters, The 77 Theodoros Angelopoulos
Hunter's Blood 86 Robert Hughes
Hunter's Diary, A 64 Ko Nakahira
Hunters of the Golden Cobra, The 82 Antonio Margheriti
Huntin' Trouble 24 Leo D. Maloney
Hunting Absurdity, A 14 Vincent Whitman
Hunting African Animals 23 Martin E. Johnson
Hunting Big Game 20 Burton Gillett
Hunting Flies 69 Andrzej Wajda
Hunting in Siberia 62 Gleb Nifontov
Hunting of the Hawk, The 17 George Fitzmaurice
Hunting Party, The 70 Don Medford
Hunting Rifle 61 Heinosuke Gosho
Hunting the Dragon 87 Latif Faiziyev
Hunting the Hunter 29 Stephen Roberts
Hunting the Teddy Bear 08 Georges Méliès
Hunting the U-Boats 18 Raoul Barré, Charles Bowers
Hunting Trouble 33 George Stevens
Huntingtower 27 George Pearson
Huntress, The 23 Lynn Reynolds
Huntress of Men, The 16 Lucius Henderson
Huntsman, The 28 Frank Moser
Huntsmen, The 77 Theodoros Angelopoulos
Huomenna 86 Juha Rosma
Huphyokwi Yanyo 81 In Soo Kim
Hurá za Ním 88 Radim Cvrček
Hurdes, Las 32 Luis Buñuel
Hurdes, Tierra Sin Pan, Las 32 Luis Buñuel
Hurdy Gurdy 29 Walter Lantz
Hurdy Gurdy 29 Leo McCarey
Hurdy Gurdy, The 58 Alekos Sakelarios
Hurdy Gurdy Hare 50 Robert McKimson
Hurle, La 21 Georges Champavert
Hurlevent 85 Jacques Rivette
Hurling 36 David Miller
Hurra! Ein Junge! 32 Georg Jacoby
Hurra! Ich Bin Papa 40 Kurt Hoffmann
Hurra! Ich Lebe! 28 Wilhelm Thiele
Hurrah for Soldiers, A 63 Bruce Baillie
Hurrah! I'm a Papa 40 Kurt Hoffmann
Hurrah! I'm Alive! 28 Wilhelm Thiele
Hurricane, The 26 Fred Caldwell
Hurricane 29 Ralph Ince
Hurricane, The 37 John Ford, Stuart Heisler
Hurricane 63 Santiago Álvarez
Hurricane, The 64 George Fraser

Hurricane 79 Jan Troell
Hurricane Express, The 32 John P. Mc-
  Gowan, Armand Schaefer
Hurricane Horseman 25 Robert Eddy
Hurricane Horseman 31 Armand Schaefer
Hurricane Hutch 21 George B. Seitz
Hurricane Hutch in Many Adventures 24
  Charles Hutchinson
Hurricane in Galveston 13 King Vidor*
Hurricane Island 51 Lew Landers
Hurricane Kid, The 24 Edward Sedgwick
Hurricane Rosy 79 Mario Monicelli
Hurricane Smith 41 Bernard Vorhaus
Hurricane Smith 52 Jerry Hopper
Hurricane's Gal 22 Allen Holubar
Hurried Man, The 77 Édouard Molinaro
Hurry Call, A 32 Mark Sandrich
Hurry, Charlie, Hurry 41 Charles E. Rob-
  erts
Hurry, Doctor 31 Dave Fleischer
Hurry, Hurry 80 Carlos Saura
Hurry Sundown 66 Otto Preminger
Hurry Up or I'll Be 30 73 Joseph Jacoby
Hurvinek Circus, The 55 Jiří Trnka
Husaren Heraus 38 Georg Jacoby
Husassistenten 14 Forest Holger-Madsen
Husband and How to Train It, A 07 Har-
  old Hough
Husband and Wife 16 Barry O'Neil
Husband and Wife 52 Eduardo De
  Filippo
Husband and Wife 53 Mikio Naruse
Husband for Anna, A 53 Giuseppe De
  Santis
Husband Hater 18 George Marshall
Husband Hunter, The 20 Fred W.
  Durrant
Husband Hunter, The 20 Howard
  Mitchell
Husband Hunters 27 John G. Adolfi
Husbands 70 John Cassavetes
Husbands and Lovers 24 John M. Stahl
Husbands and Wives 20 Joseph Levering
Husbands Are So Jealous 34 George B.
  Samuelson
Husbands Beware 07 Harold Hough
Husband's Chastity, A 37 Kajiro Yama-
  moto
Husbands for Rent 27 Henry Lehrman
Husband's Holiday 31 Robert Milton
Husband's Love, A 14 Toby Cooper
Husbands or Lovers 24 Paul Czinner
Husbands or Lovers? 39 Edward H.
  Griffith
Husbands' Reunion 33 George Marshall
Husbands Wanted 24 Archie Mayo
Huse til Mennesker 72 Jørgen Roos
Hush 21 Harry Garson
Hush...Hush, Sweet Charlotte 64 Robert
  Aldrich
Hush Money 21 Charles Maigne
Hush Money 31 Sidney Lanfield
Hush My Mouse 45 Chuck Jones
Hush-a-Bye Murder 70 John Newland
Hushed Hour, The 20 Edmund Mortimer
Husid 82 Egill Edvardsson
Huskors, Et 14 Forest Holger-Madsen
Hussar Ballad, The 62 Eldar Ryazanov
Hussards, Les 55 Alex Joffé
Hussards et Grisettes 01 Alice Guy-Blaché

Hussars of Fehérvári 39 Márton Keleti
Hussite Trilogy, Part One 54 Otakar Vávra
Hussite Trilogy, Part Two 54 Otakar Vávra
Hussite Trilogy, Part Three 57 Otakar
  Vávra
Hussite Warrior, The 54 Otakar Vávra
Hussy 79 Matthew Chapman
Hustle 75 Robert Aldrich
Hustled Wedding, A 11 Frank Wilson
Hustler, The 21 Charlie Chase
Hustler, The 61 Robert Rossen
Hustler Squad 73 Ted V. Mikels
Hustruer 75 Anja Breien
Hustruer II 85 Anja Breien
Hustruer — Ti År Efter 85 Anja Breien
Hustruer — Ti År Etter 85 Anja Breien
Húsz Évre Egymástól 62 Imre Fehér
Húsz Óra 64 Zoltán Fábri
Huszárszerelem 35 Steve Sekely
Huta 59 59 Jan Łomnicki
Hutch of the U.S.A. 24 James Chapin
Hutch Stirs 'Em Up 23 Frank Crane
Hutch — U.S.A. 24 James Chapin
Hutterites, The 63 Colin Low
Hvad med Os? 63 Henning Carlsen
Hvem Er Gentlemantyven? 15 Forest
  Holger-Madsen
Hvem Er Han? 14 August Blom
Hvem Var Forbryderen? 12 August Blom
Hvězda Zvaná Pelyněk 64 Martin Frič
Hvide Dame, Den 13 Forest Holger-
  Madsen
Hvide Djævel, Den 15 Forest Holger-
  Madsen
Hvide Slavehandel I, Den 10 August
  Blom
Hvide Slavehandel II, Den 11 August
  Blom
Hvide Slavehandel III, Den 12 Urban Gad
Hvo Som Elsker Sin Fader 15 Forest Hol-
  ger-Madsen
Hvor Bjergene Sejler 55 Bjarne Henning-
  Jensen
Hvor Er Magten Blevet Af? 68 Henning
  Carlsen
Hvor Sorgerne Glemmes 15 Forest Holger-
  Madsen
Hwang Jin-i 86 Chang-ho Bae
Hy Mayer: His Merry Pen 13 Hy Mayer
Hy Mayer's Cartoons 13 Hy Mayer
Hyakuman-Nin no Musumetachi 63
  Heinosuke Gosho
Hyas, Le 29 Jean Painlevé
Hyas et Sténorinque 29 Jean Painlevé
Hyde and Go Tweet 60 Friz Freleng
Hyde and Hare 55 Friz Freleng
Hyde Park 34 Randall Faye
Hyde Park Corner 35 Sinclair Hill
Hyde Park Pop 73 George McIndoe*
Hydro, The 20 Maurice Sandground
Hydrothérapie Fantastique 09 Georges
  Méliès
Hyena's Laugh, The 27 Clyde Geronimi,
  Walter Lantz
Hymn of Energy, The 30 Oskar Fischinger
Hymn of the Nations 44 Alexander Ham-
  mid
Hymn to a Tired Man 68 Masaki Koba-
  yashi
Hymn to Her 74 Stan Brakhage

Hyōten 66 Satsuo Yamamoto
Hyp-nut-tist, The 35 Dave Fleischer
Hyper Sapien 86 Peter R. Hunt
Hyper Sapien: People from Another Star
  86 Peter R. Hunt
Hyperboloid of Engineer Garin, The 65
  Alexander Gintsburg
Hyperspace 86 Todd Durham
Hypnosis 62 Eugenio Martin
Hypnotic Eye, The 60 George Blair
Hypnotic Hooch 20 Grim Natwick
Hypnotic Portrait, The 22 Kenneth
  Graeme
Hypnotic Suggestion 09 Dave Aylott
Hypnotist, The 20 Raoul Barré, Charles
  Bowers
Hypnotist, The 21 Dave Fleischer
Hypnotist, The 21 Pat Sullivan
Hypnotist, The 27 Tod Browning
Hypnotist, The 57 Montgomery Tully
Hypnotist and the Convict, The 11 Walter
  R. Booth, Theo Bouwmeester
Hypnotist at Work, A 1897 Georges
  Méliès
Hypnotist's Joke, The 08 Arthur Cooper
Hypnotist's Revenge 09 Georges Méliès
Hypnotized 32 Mack Sennett
Hypochondri-Cat, The 50 Chuck Jones
Hypocrisy 16 Kenean Buel
Hypocrite, The 21 Oscar Micheaux
Hypocrites 14 Lois Weber
Hypocrites, The 16 George Loane Tucker
Hypocrites, The 23 Charles Giblyn
Hypothèse du Tableau Volé, L' 78 Raúl
  Ruiz
Hypothesis of a Stolen Painting, The 78
  Raúl Ruiz
Hypothesis of the Stolen Painting, The 78
  Raúl Ruiz
Hyppolit a Lakáj 32 Steve Sekely
Hysteria 64 Freddie Francis
Hysterical 83 Chris Bearde
Hysterical High Spots in American History
  41 Walter Lantz
I 66 Peter Kylberg
I 87 Walter Hugo Khouri
I, a Lover 68 Börje Nyberg
I, a Man 67 Andy Warhol
I, a Negro 56 Jean Rouch
I, a Woman 66 Mac Ahlberg
I Accuse! 16 William F. Haddock
I Accuse! 18 Abel Gance
I Accuse! 37 Abel Gance
I Accuse! 57 José Ferrer
I Accuse My Parents 44 Sam Newfield
I Adore You 33 George King
I Adore You 86 B. Baljinnyam
I Aim at the Stars 60 J. Lee-Thompson
I Ain't Got Nobody 32 Dave Fleischer
I Am a Camera 55 Henry Cornelius
I Am a Cat 36 Kajiro Yamamoto
I Am a Cat 75 Kon Ichikawa
I Am a Criminal 38 William Nigh
I Am a Dancer 72 Bryan Forbes, Pierre
  Jourdan
I Am a Fugitive 31 Mervyn LeRoy
I Am a Fugitive from a Chain Gang 31
  Mervyn LeRoy
I Am a Fugitive from the Chain Gang 31
  Mervyn LeRoy

I Am a Groupie 70 Derek Ford
I Am a Paranormal Phenomenon 85 Sergio Corbucci
I Am a Son of America...and I Am Indebted to It 72 Santiago Álvarez
I Am a Thief 34 Robert Florey
I Am Afraid 77 Damiano Damiani
I Am Blushing 81 Vilgot Sjöman
I Am Cuba 62 Mikhail Kalatozov
I Am Curious (Blue) 68 Vilgot Sjöman
I Am Curious Gay 70 Richard Fontaine
I Am Curious (Yellow) 67 Vilgot Sjöman
I Am Eight 56 Humberto Mauro
I Am Frigid...Why? 73 Max Pecas
I Am Guilty 21 Jack Nelson
I Am Not Afraid 39 Crane Wilbur
I Am Not Me 85 Václav Vorlíček
I Am Photogenic 80 Dino Risi
I Am Snub-Nosed But I Can Smell 39 Miguel Zacarías
I Am Suzanne! 33 Rowland V. Lee
I Am the Cheese 83 Robert Jiras
I Am the Law 22 Edwin Carewe
I Am the Law 38 Alexander Hall
I Am the Lord Thy God 88 Krzysztof Kieślowski
I Am the Man 24 Ivan Abramson
I Am the Woman 21 Francis Ford
I Am Twenty Years Old 65 Marlen Khutsiev
I Am Two 62 Kon Ichikawa
I Am With You 49 Gösta Stevens
I and My Love 65 Georges Lautner
I and My Lovers 65 Georges Lautner
I Ask for the Floor 75 Gleb Panfilov
I Ask to Speak 75 Gleb Panfilov
IBM at the Fair 65 Charles Eames, Ray Eames
IBM Fair Presentation Film, Part I 62 Charles Eames, Ray Eames
IBM Fair Presentation Film, Part II 63 Charles Eames, Ray Eames
IBM Mathematics Peep Show 61 Charles Eames, Ray Eames
IBM Museum 67 Charles Eames, Ray Eames
IBM Puppet Shows 65 Charles Eames, Ray Eames
I Became a Criminal 47 Alberto Cavalcanti
I Beg Your Pardon 87 Vytautas Zalakevicius
I Believe 16 George Loane Tucker
I Believe in You 51 Basil Dearden, Michael Relph
I Believed in You 34 Irving Cummings
I Bombed Pearl Harbor 60 Shue Matsubayashi
I Bury the Living 58 Alfredo Antonini
ICOGRADA Congress 66 John Halas
I Can Explain 22 George D. Baker
I Can Get It for You Wholesale 51 Michael Gordon
I Can't Escape 34 Otto Brower
I Can't Escape from You 36 Dave Fleischer
I Can't Give You Anything But Love, Baby 40 Albert S. Rogell
I Can't...I Can't 69 Piers Haggard
I Carry the World 88 Lino Brocka

I Changed My Sex 53 Edward D. Wood, Jr.
I Cheated the Law 48 Edward L. Cahn
I Come in Peace 90 Craig R. Baxley
I...Comme Icare 79 Henri Verneuil
I Confess 52 Alfred Hitchcock
I Conquer the Sea 36 Victor Halperin
I Could Go On Singing 62 Ronald Neame
I Could Never Have Sex with Any Man Who Has So Little Respect for My Husband 73 Robert McCarty
I Cover Big Town 47 William C. Thomas
I Cover Chinatown 36 Norman Foster
I Cover the Underworld 47 William C. Thomas
I Cover the Underworld 55 R. G. Springsteen
I Cover the War 37 Arthur Lubin
I Cover the Waterfront 33 James Cruze
I Crossed the Color Line 66 Ted V. Mikels
I Crossed the Line 66 Ted V. Mikels
I Deal in Danger 66 Walter Grauman
I Demand Payment 38 Clifford Sanforth
I den Grønne Skov 68 Palle Kjærulff-Schmidt
I den Store Pyramide 74 Jørgen Roos
I Did It 72 Alberto Lattuada
I Did It, Mama 09 D. W. Griffith
I Didn't Do It 45 Marcel Varnel
I Died a Thousand Times 55 Stuart Heisler
I Dismember Mama 72 Paul Leder
I Do 21 Fred Newmeyer, Sam Taylor
I Do 'Em In 87 Rafael Baledón
I Do Like a Joke 16 Frank Wilson
I Do Like to Be Beside the Seaside 25 Alexander Butler
I Dödens Väntrum 46 Hasse Ekman
I-Don't-Care Girl, The 52 Lloyd Bacon
I Don't Give a Damn 87 Shmuel Imberman
I Don't Know You But I Love You 35 Géza von Bolváry
I Don't Think I'll Tell Them 85 Franco Rossetti
I Don't Understand You Any More 80 Sergio Corbucci
I Don't Want to Be a Man 18 Ernst Lubitsch
I Don't Want to Be Born 75 Peter Sasdy
I Don't Want to Make History 36 Dave Fleischer
I Dood It! 43 Vincente Minnelli
I Dream of Jeannie 52 Allan Dwan
I Dream Too Much 35 John Cromwell
I Dreamed of My Elk 87 Siegfried Kühn
I...Dreaming 88 Stan Brakhage
I Drink Your Blood 70 David Durston
I Eat Your Skin 64 Del Tenney
I Eats My Spinach 33 Dave Fleischer
I Entrust My Wife to You 39 János Vaszary
I Escaped from Devil's Island 73 William Witney
I Escaped from the Gestapo 43 Harold Young
I Even Knew Happy Gypsies 67 Aleksandar Petrović
I Even Met Happy Gypsies 67 Aleksandar Petrović

I Even Met Some Happy Gypsies 67 Aleksandar Petrović
IFO 86 Ulli Lommel
I. F. Stone's Weekly 73 Jerry Bruck, Jr.
I Failed, But... 30 Yasujiro Ozu
I Feel Like a Feather in the Breeze 36 Dave Fleischer
I Flunked, But... 30 Yasujiro Ozu
I Formerlære 49 Henning Carlsen
I Found a Dog 49 Lew Landers
I Found Stella Parish 35 Mervyn LeRoy
I Get Dizzy When I Do That Twostep Dance 08 Arthur Gilbert
I Give My Heart 35 Marcel Varnel
I Give My Heart 36 Archie Mayo
I Give My Life 41 Nicolas Farkas
I Give My Love 34 Karl Freund
I Go to Tokyo 86 Tomio Kuriyama
I Go Toward the Sun 55 Andrzej Wajda
I Gopher You 54 Friz Freleng
I Got Plenty of Mutton 44 Frank Tashlin
I Graduated, But... 29 Yasujiro Ozu
I, Grandmother, Illiko & Illarion 63 Tenghiz Abuladze
I Had My Brother's Wife 64 David Durston, Erkan Metin, Ismail Metin
I Had Seven Daughters 54 Jean Boyer
I Hate Actors 86 Gérard Krawczyk
I Hate Blondes 81 Giorgio Capitani
I Hate My Body 75 Leon Klimovsky
I Hate Women 34 Aubrey H. Scotto
I Hate Your Guts! 61 Roger Corman
I Have a New Master 48 Jean-Paul Le Chanois
I Have Faith in You 79 Santiago Álvarez
I Have Lived 33 Richard Thorpe
I Have Lost My Husband 36 Enrico Guazzoni
I Have No Mouth But I Must Scream 73 Roy Ward Baker
I Have Seven Daughters 54 Jean Boyer
I Have Sinned 37 S. Goskind
I Haven't Got a Hat 35 Friz Freleng
I Hear You Calling Me 19 A. E. Coleby
I Heard 33 Dave Fleischer
I Heard It Through the Grape Vine 82 Richard Fontaine, Pat Harley
I Hired a Contract Killer 90 Aki Kaurismäki
I, Jane Doe 48 John H. Auer
I Killed 43 Olof Molander
I Killed Einstein 69 Oldřich Lipský
I Killed Einstein, Gentlemen 69 Oldřich Lipský
I Killed Geronimo 50 John Hoffman
I Killed Rasputin 65 Don Sharp
I Killed Rasputin 67 Robert Hossein
I Killed That Man 41 Phil Rosen
I Killed the Count 39 Fred Zelnik
I Killed Wild Bill Hickok 56 Richard Talmadge
I Kiss Your Hand, Madame 32 Robert Land
I Knew Her Well 65 Antonio Pietrangeli
I Know Where I'm Going! 45 Michael Powell, Emeric Pressburger
I Lagens Namn 86 Kjell Sundvall
I Led Two Lives 53 Edward D. Wood, Jr.
I Like Babies and Infinks 37 Dave Fleischer

I Like Birds 66 Peter Walker
I Like Her 85 Enrico Montesano
I Like It That Way 34 Harry Lachman
I Like Money 61 Peter Sellers
I Like Mountain Music 33 Dave Fleischer
I Like Mountain Music 33 Rudolf Ising
I Like to Hunt People 85 Donald G. Jackson
I Like Your Nerve 31 William McGann
I Live for Love 35 Busby Berkeley
I Live for You 35 Busby Berkeley
I Live in Fear 55 Akira Kurosawa
I Live in Grosvenor Square 45 Herbert Wilcox
I Live My Life 35 W. S. Van Dyke
I Live on Danger 42 Sam White
I Lived with You 33 Maurice Elvey
I Livets Brænding 15 Forest Holger-Madsen
I Look for a House of Pigeons 85 Věra Plívová-Šimková
I Love 36 Leonid Lukov
I Love a Bandleader 45 Del Lord
I Love a Lassie 07 Arthur Gilbert
I Love a Lassie 25 Dave Fleischer
I Love a Lassie 31 George Pearson
I Love a Mystery 45 Henry Levin
I Love a Parade 33 Rudolf Ising
I Love a Soldier 44 Mark Sandrich
I Love Melvin 52 Don Weis
I Love My Wife 70 Mel Stuart
I Love N.Y. 87 Gianni Bozzacchi
I Love That Man 33 Harry Joe Brown
I Love to Be a Sailor 31 George Pearson
I Love to Singa 36 Tex Avery
I Love Trouble 47 S. Sylvan Simon
I Love You 18 Walter Edwards
I Love You 74 Pierre Duceppe
I Love You 81 Arnaldo Jabor
I Love You 86 Eduardo Calcagno
I Love You 86 Marco Ferreri
I Love You 87 Li Vilstrup
I Love You Again 40 W. S. Van Dyke
I Love You Alice B. Toklas 68 Hy Averback
I Love You I Kill You 71 Uwe Brandner
I Love You, I Love You Not 79 Armenia Balducci
I Love, You Love 60 Alessandro Blasetti
I Love You Love 68 Stig Björkman
I Love You, Rosa 71 Moshe Mizrahi
I Love You to Death 90 Lawrence Kasdan
I Loved a Woman 33 Alfred E. Green
I Loved You More Than Life 87 Rasim Izmailov
I Loved You Wednesday 33 Henry King, William Cameron Menzies
I, Madman 89 Tibor Takacs
I Married a Communist 49 Robert Stevenson
I Married a Doctor 36 Archie Mayo
I Married a Monster from Outer Space 58 Gene Fowler, Jr.
I Married a Nazi 40 Irving Pichel
I Married a Shadow 82 Robin Davis
I Married a Spy 37 Edmond T. Gréville
I Married a Vampire 83 Jay Raskin
I Married a Werewolf 61 Paolo Heusch
I Married a Witch 42 René Clair
I Married a Woman 56 Hal Kanter

I Married an Angel 41 W. S. Van Dyke
I Married for Love 37 Steve Sekely
I Married Too Young 62 George Moskov
I Married You for Fun 67 Luciano Salce
I, Maureen 78 Janine Manatis
I May Be Anything, But I Love You 86 Carlos Galettini
I Met a Murderer 39 Roy Kellino
I Met Him in Paris 37 Wesley Ruggles
I Met My Love Again 37 George Cukor, Joshua Logan, Arthur Ripley
I Miss Sonia Henie 72 Dušan Makavejev
I Miss You, Hugs and Kisses 78 Murray Markowitz
I, Mobster 58 Roger Corman
I, Monster 70 Stephen Weeks
I Morgen Er Det Slut 88 Sigfred Aagaard
I.N.R.I. 23 Robert Wiene
I Natt eller Aldrig 41 Gustaf Molander
I Need a Mustache 86 Manuel Summers
I Never Changes My Altitude 37 Dave Fleischer
I Never Forget the Wife 07 Charles Raymond
I Never Promised You a Rose Garden 77 Anthony Page
I Never Sang for My Father 70 Gilbert Cates
I Nikto na Svete 87 Vladimir Dovgan
I Only Arsked! 58 Montgomery Tully
I Only Have Eyes for You 37 Tex Avery
I Only Want You to Love Me 76 Rainer Werner Fassbinder
I Ought to Be in Pictures 81 Herbert Ross
I Passed for White 60 Fred M. Wilcox
I Played It for You 85 Ronee Blakley
I Promise 87 Vyacheslav Maksakov
I Promise to Pay 37 D. Ross Lederman
I Promised to Pay 61 Sidney Hayers
I Prövningens Stund 15 Victor Sjöström
I Remember Love 81 Norbert Meisel
I Remember Mama 47 George Stevens
I Remember You 85 Ali Khamrayev
I Ring Doorbells 45 Frank R. Strayer
I Sailed to Tahiti with an All Girl Crew 68 Richard L. Bare
I Saw What You Did 65 William Castle
I See a Dark Stranger 46 Frank Launder
I See Everybody Naked 69 Dino Risi
I See Ice 38 Anthony Kimmins
I Sell Anything 34 Robert Florey
I Sent a Letter to My Love 80 Moshe Mizrahi
I Senzo Dio 71 Roberto Bianchi Montero
I Shall Live Again 40 Roberto Rodríguez
I Shall Not Yield 18 Alexander Ivanovsky
I Shall Return 50 Fritz Lang
I Shan't Be Long 42 Otakar Vávra
I Shot Billy the Kid 50 William Berke
I Shot Jesse James 48 Samuel Fuller
I Should Have Stood in Bedlam 49 Jerry Lewis
I Should Say So 14 Dave Aylott
I Should Worry 15 Vincent Colby
I-Ski Love-Ski You-Ski 36 Dave Fleischer
Í Skugga Hrafnsins 88 Hrafn Gunnlaugsson
Í Som Här Inträdden 45 Arne Mattsson
I Spit on Your Grave 62 Michael Gast
I Spit on Your Grave 78 Meir Zarchi
I Spy 33 Allan Dwan

I Spy, You Spy 66 Don Sharp
I Stand Accused 38 John H. Auer
I Stand Condemned 35 Anthony Asquith
I Start Counting 69 David Greene
I Stole a Million 39 Frank Tuttle
I Surrender Dear 31 Mack Sennett
I Surrender Dear 48 Arthur Dreifuss
I Survived Certain Death 60 Vojtěch Jasný
I Survived My Death 60 Vojtěch Jasný
I Swear I Love You 86 Nino D'Angelo
I Take This Oath 40 Sam Newfield
I Take This Woman 31 Marion Gering, Slavko Vorkapich
I Take This Woman 39 Frank Borzage, Josef von Sternberg, W. S. Van Dyke
I Taw a Puddy Tat 48 Friz Freleng
I Thank a Fool 62 Robert Stevens
I Thank You 41 Marcel Varnel
I, the Body 65 Arne Mattsson
I the Executioner 87 Valentín Trujillo
I, the Jury 53 Harry Essex
I, the Jury 81 Richard T. Heffron
I Think We're Being Followed 67 Robert Day
I...Thou...and...She 33 John Reinhardt
I To Će Proći 86 Nenad Dizdarević
I Too Am Only a Woman 63 Alfred Weidenmann
I. Vor Pittfalks 67 Richard Williams
I Wake Up Screaming 41 H. Bruce Humberstone
I Walk Alone 47 Byron Haskin
I Walk the Line 70 John Frankenheimer
I Walk to the Sun 55 Andrzej Wajda
I Walked with a Zombie 43 Jacques Tourneur
I Wanna Be a Lifeguard 36 Dave Fleischer
I Wanna Be a Sailor 37 Tex Avery
I Wanna Hold Your Hand 77 Robert Zemeckis
I Wanna Mink 60 John Halas*
I Wanna Play House (With You) 36 Friz Freleng
I Want a Divorce 40 Ralph Murphy
I Want a Husband 19 Aleksander Hertz
I Want Her Dead 74 Richard Quine
"I Want My Hat!" 09 D. W. Griffith
I Want My Man 25 Lambert Hillyer
I Want the Floor 75 Gleb Panfilov
I Want to Be a Mother 37 George Roland
I Want to Be an Actress 37 Art Davis, Sid Marcus
I Want to Be an Actress 43 Paul Barralet
I Want to Forget 18 James Kirkwood
I Want to Go Home 89 Alain Resnais
I Want to Live! 58 Robert Wise
I Want to Play House 36 Friz Freleng
I Want What I Want 71 John Dexter
I Want You 51 Mark Robson
I Wanted Wings 41 Mitchell Leisen
I Was a Communist for the FBI 51 Gordon Douglas
I Was a Convict 39 Aubrey H. Scotto
I Was a Criminal 41 Richard Oswald
I Was a Criminal 43 Kurt Neumann
I Was a Dancer 49 Frank Richardson
I Was a Fireman 43 Humphrey Jennings
I Was a Male War Bride 49 Howard Hawks

I Was a Parish Priest *52* Rafael Gil
I Was a Prisoner on Devil's Island *41* Lew Landers
I Was a Shoplifter *49* Charles Lamont
I Was a Spy *33* Victor Saville
I Was a Teenage Alien *80* Bob Cooper
I Was a Teenage Boy *85* Paul Schneider
I Was a Teenage Frankenstein *57* Herbert L. Strock
I Was a Teenage Sex Mutant *87* David DeCoteau
I Was a Teenage TV Terrorist *85* Stanford Singer
I Was a Teenage Thumb *63* Chuck Jones
I Was a Teenage Werewolf *57* Gene Fowler, Jr.
I Was a Teenage Zombie *87* John Elias Michalakias
I Was a Zombie for the FBI *82* Marius Penczner
I Was an Adventuress *40* Gregory Ratoff
I Was an American Spy *51* Lesley Selander
I Was Born, But... *32* Yasujiro Ozu
I Was Caught in the Night *85* Juraj Herz
I Was Faithless *32* King Vidor
I Was Framed *42* D. Ross Lederman
I Was Happy Here *65* Desmond Davis
I Was Monty's Double *58* John Guillermin
I Was 19 *67* Konrad Wolf
I Went to the Dance *89* Les Blank, Chris Strachwitz
I Will *19* Kenelm Foss, Hubert Herrick
I Will...I Will...for Now *75* Norman Panama
I Will Repay *17* William P. S. Earle
I Will Repay *23* Henry Kolker
I Wish I Had Wings *33* Rudolf Ising
I Wish to Speak *75* Gleb Panfilov
I Wished on the Moon *35* Dave Fleischer
I Wonder Who's Killing Her Now *75* Steven Hilliard Stern
I Wonder Who's Kissing Her Now *31* Dave Fleischer
I Wonder Who's Kissing Her Now *47* Lloyd Bacon
I Won't Forget That Night *62* Kozaburo Yoshimura
I Would Like to Marry You *07* John Morland
I Wouldn't Be in Your Shoes *48* William Nigh
I Yam Love Sick *38* Dave Fleischer
I Yam What I Yam *33* Dave Fleischer
I...You...He...She *74* Chantal Akerman
Ib and Little Christina *08* Percy Stow
Iba Den *89* Kvetoslav Hečko, Michal Ruttkay, Vladimir Stric
Ibáñez' Torrent *25* Monta Bell, Mauritz Stiller
Ibis Bleu, L' *19* Camille De Morlhon
Ibis Rouge, L' *75* Jean-Pierre Mocky
Ibn al Nil *51* Youssef Chahine
İbret *71* Şerif Gören, Yılmaz Güney
Ibun Sarutobi Sasuke *65* Masahiro Shinoda
Ibunda *87* Teguh Karya
Icarus *60* Brian DePalma
Icarus XB-1 *63* Jindřich Polák

Ice *70* Robert Kramer
Ice Antics *39* David Miller
Ice Boating on the North Shrewsbury, Red Bank, N.J. *04* Edwin S. Porter
Ice Box Episodes *20* Wallace A. Carlson
Ice Boxed *28* Manny Gould, Ben Harrison
Ice Break *81* Michael Wallington
Ice-Breaker Krassnin, The *28* Georgy Vasiliev, Sergei Vasiliev
Ice-Capades *41* Joseph Santley
Ice-Capades Revue *42* Bernard Vorhaus
Ice Castles *78* Donald Wrye
Ice Cold in Alex *58* J. Lee-Thompson
Ice Cream Jack, The *07* Alf Collins
Ice Flood, The *26* George B. Seitz
Ice Follies of 1939 *39* Reinhold Schünzel
Ice House, The *69* Stuart McGowan
Ice Man's Luck *29* Walter Lantz
Ice Palace *60* Vincent Sherman
Ice Palace, The *87* Per Blom
Ice Pirates, The *83* Stewart Raffill
Ice Skating in Central Park, N.Y. *04* Edwin S. Porter
Ice Station Zebra *68* John Sturges
Icebound *24* William DeMille
Iced *88* Jeff Kwitny
Iced Bullet, The *17* Reginald Barker
Iceland *42* H. Bruce Humberstone
Iceman *84* Fred Schepisi
Iceman Cometh, The *73* John Frankenheimer
Iceman Ducketh, The *64* Phil Monroe
Iceman's Ball, The *32* Mark Sandrich
Ich bei Tag und Du bei Nacht *32* Ludwig Berger
Ich Bin Auch Nur eine Frau *63* Alfred Weidenmann
Ich Bin ein Antistar... *76* Rosa von Praunheim
Ich Bin ein Elefant, Madame *68* Peter Zadek
Ich Bin Nur eine Frau *62* Alfred Weidenmann
Ich Bin Sebastian Otto *39* V. Becker, Willi Forst
Ich Geh' Aus und Du Bleibst Da *32* Hans Behrendt
Ich Glaub' Nie Mehr an eine Frau *33* Max Reichmann
Ich Hab' von Dir Geträumt *44* Wolfgang Staudte
Ich Kenn' Dich Nicht und Liebe Dich *35* Géza von Bolváry
Ich Klage An *41* Wolfgang Liebeneiner
Ich Lebe für Dich *29* William Dieterle
Ich Liebe Alle Frauen *35* Karel Lamač
Ich Liebe Dich *25* Paul Stein
Ich Liebe Dich Ich Töte Dich *71* Uwe Brandner
Ich Möchte Kein Mann Sein *18* Ernst Lubitsch
Ich Sehne Mich nach Dir *36* Johannes Riemann
Ich Sing Mich in Dein Herz Hinein *35* Fritz Kampers
Ich Suche Dich *56* O. W. Fischer
Ich und die Kaiserin *33* Friedrich Holländer
Ich und Er *88* Doris Dörrie
Ich War Jack Mortimer *35* Carl Fröhlich

Ich War 19 *67* Konrad Wolf
Ich Werde Dich auf Händen Tragen *58* Veidt Harlan
Ich Will Doch Nur, Dass Ihr Mich Liebt *76* Rainer Werner Fassbinder
Ich Will Nicht Wissen Wer Du Bist *33* Géza von Bolváry
Ichabod and Mr. Toad *49* James Algar, Clyde Geronimi, Jack Kinney, Ben Sharpsteen
Ichhapuran *70* Mrinal Sen
Ichiban Utsukushiku *44* Akira Kurosawa
Ichijoji no Kettō *67* Hiroshi Inagaki
Ichinichi 240 Jikan *70* Hiroshi Teshigahara
Ici et Ailleurs *74* Jean-Luc Godard*
Icicle Thief, The *89* Maurizio Nichetti
Iconoclast, The *09* Edwin S. Porter
Iconoclast, The *10* D. W. Griffith
Iconostasis *69* Todor Dinov, Hristo Hristov
Icy Breasts *74* Georges Lautner
Id al Mayrun *67* Youssef Chahine
I'd Climb the Highest Mountain *31* Dave Fleischer
I'd Climb the Highest Mountain *51* Henry King
I'd Give My Life *36* Edwin L. Marin
I'd Love to Take Orders from You *36* Tex Avery
I'd Rather Be Rich *64* Jack Smight
Ida Regénye *34* Steve Sekely
Idade da Terra, A *80* Glauber Rocha
Idaho *25* Robert F. Hill
Idaho *43* Joseph Kane
Idaho Kid *36* Robert F. Hill
Idaho Red *29* Robert De Lacey
Idaho Transfer *73* Peter Fonda
Ida's Christmas *12* Van Dyke Brooke
Idę do Słońca *55* Andrzej Wajda
Idę ku Słońcu *55* Andrzej Wajda
Idea di un'Isola *67* Roberto Rossellini
Idea di un'Isola: La Sicilia *67* Roberto Rossellini
Idea Fissa, L' *64* Mino Guerrini, Gianni Puccini
Idea Girl *46* Will Jason
Ideaalmaastik *86* Peeter Simm
Ideal Crossword Puzzles No. 1 *25* John Colman Terry
Ideal Crossword Puzzles No. 2 *25* John Colman Terry
Ideal Crossword Puzzles No. 3 *25* John Colman Terry
Ideal Crossword Puzzles No. 4 *25* John Colman Terry
Ideal Crossword Puzzles No. 5 *25* John Colman Terry
Ideal Crossword Puzzles No. 6 *25* John Colman Terry
Ideal Crossword Puzzles No. 7 *25* John Colman Terry
Ideal Crossword Puzzles No. 8 *25* John Colman Terry
Ideal Crossword Puzzles No. 9 *25* John Colman Terry
Ideal Crossword Puzzles No. 10 *25* John Colman Terry
Ideal Husband, An *47* Alexander Korda
Ideal Husband, An *81* Viktor Georgiyev
Ideal Landscape *86* Peeter Simm
Ideal Lodger, The *56* Wolf Schmidt

Ideale Frau, Die *59* Josef von Baky
Ideale Untermieter, Der *56* Wolf Schmidt
Idealer Gatte, Ein *37* Herbert Selpin
Idealny Muzh *81* Viktor Georgiyev
Idée à l'Eau, Une *39* Jean-Paul Le Chanois
Idée de Françoise, L' *23* Robert Saidreau
Ideiglenes Paradicsom *81* András Kovács
Identification Marks: None *64* Jerzy Skolimowski
Identification of a Woman *82* Michelangelo Antonioni
Identificazione di una Donna *82* Michelangelo Antonioni
Identikit *73* Giuseppe Patroni Griffi
Identité Judiciaire *51* Hervé Bromberger
Identities *73* Ed Emshwiller
Identity Crisis *89* Melvin Van Peebles
Identity Parade *34* Howard Higgin
Identity Unknown *45* Walter Colmes
Identity Unknown *60* Frank Marshall
Ideological Problem, The *50* Ting Li, Tsolin Wang
Idi Amin Dada *74* Barbet Schroeder
Idi i Smotri *85* Elem Klimov
Idillio Tragico *12* Baldassare Negroni
Idiot, The *20* Lupu Pick
Idiot, L' *46* Georges Lampin
Idiot, The *46* Georges Lampin
Idiot, The *51* Akira Kurosawa
Idiot, The *57* Ivan Pyriev
Idiot in Love, An *67* Yasuzo Masumura
Idiot of the Mountains, The *09* Theo Bouwmeester
Idiot's Delight *38* Clarence Brown
Idiots May Apply *85* János Xantus
Idle Class, The *21* Charles Chaplin
Idle Hands *21* Frank Reicher
Idle on Parade *59* John Gilling
Idle Rich, The *21* Maxwell Karger
Idle Rich, The *29* William DeMille
Idle Tongues *24* Lambert Hillyer
Idle Wives *16* Phillips Smalley, Lois Weber
Idler, The *15* Lloyd B. Carleton
Idler *27* Tomu Uchida
Idlers That Work *49* Lindsay Anderson
Idő Ablaka, Az *69* Tamás Fejér
Idő Kereke, Az *60* Miklós Jancsó
Idő Van *85* Péter Gothár
Ido Zero Daisakusen *69* Inoshiro Honda
Idol, The *66* Daniel Petrie
Idol Dancer, The *20* D. W. Griffith
Idol of Paris, The *14* Maurice Elvey
Idol of Paris *48* Leslie Arliss
Idol of the Crowd *37* Arthur Lubin
Idol of the North, The *21* Roy William Neill
Idol of the Stage, The *16* Richard Garrick
Idol on Parade *59* John Gilling
Idolators *17* Walter Edwards
Idole Brisée, L' *20* Maurice Mariaud
Idolmaker, The *80* Taylor Hackford
Ídolo, El *49* Pierre Chénal
Idolo Infranto *13* Emilio Ghione
Ídolos de la Radio *35* Eduardo Morera
Idols in the Dust *51* David Miller
Idols of Clay *15* Robert Z. Leonard
Idols of Clay *20* George Fitzmaurice
Idylle *1897* Alice Guy-Blaché
Idylle à la Ferme, Une *12* Max Linder

Idylle à la Plage, Une *31* Henri Storck
Idylle Interrompue *1898* Alice Guy-Blaché
Idylle Sous un Tunnel *01* Ferdinand Zecca
Ie *77* Nobuhiko Obayashi
Iéna Bridge *00* Louis Lumière
Ieraishan *51* Kon Ichikawa
Ieri, Oggi, Domani *63* Vittorio De Sica
Ieri, Oggi e Domani *63* Vittorio De Sica
If... *16* Stuart Kinder
If... *68* Lindsay Anderson
If a Comrade Calls *63* Alexander Ivanov
If a Man Answers *62* Henry Levin
If a Picture Tells a Story *24* Gaston Quiribet
If All the Guys in the World... *55* Christian-Jaque
If Don Juan Were a Woman *73* Roger Vadim
If Dreams Come True *12* Edwin S. Porter
If England Were Invaded *14* Fred W. Durrant
If Ever I See You Again *78* Joseph Brooks
If Four Walls Told *22* Fred Paul
If He Hollers Let Him Go *68* Charles Martin
If I Had a Million *32* James Cruze, H. Bruce Humberstone, Ernst Lubitsch, Norman Z. McLeod, Lothar Mendes, Stephen Roberts, William A. Seiter, Norman Taurog
If I Had Four Dromedaries *66* Chris Marker
If I Had My Way *40* David Butler
If I Had to Do It Again *76* Claude Lelouch
If I Had to Do It All Over Again *76* Claude Lelouch
If I Lose You *61* Atıf Yılmaz
If I Love You? *34* Sergei Gerasimov
If I Marry Again *25* John Francis Dillon
If I Were a Spy *67* Bertrand Blier
If I Were Boss *38* Maclean Rogers
If I Were Free *33* Elliott Nugent
If I Were King *10* Georges Méliès
If I Were King *20* J. Gordon Edwards
If I Were King *30* Ludwig Berger
If I Were King *38* Frank Lloyd
If I Were Queen *22* Wesley Ruggles
If I Were Rich *32* Zoltán Korda
If I Were Rich *36* Randall Faye
If I Were Single *27* Roy Del Ruth
If I'm Lucky *46* Lewis Seiler
If It's Tuesday This Must Be Belgium *69* Mel Stuart
If Looks Could Kill *86* Chuck Vincent
If Marriage Fails *25* John Ince
If Matches Struck *22* Gaston Quiribet
If My Country Should Call *16* Joseph De Grasse
'If Only' Jim *21* Jacques Jaccard
If Paris Were Told to Us *55* Sacha Guitry
If the Cap Fits *47* Ken Hughes
If the Sun Never Returns *87* Claude Goretta
If There Was No Music *63* Miloš Forman
If This Be Love *61* Yuli Raizman
If This Be Sin *49* Gregory Ratoff
If This Isn't Love *34* Leigh Jason
If Thou Wert Blind *17* F. Martin Thornton

If War Comes Tomorrow *38* G. Berezko, Yefim Dzigan, N. Karmazinski
If We All Were Angels *36* Carl Fröhlich
If We Reversed *23* Milt Gross
If We Went to the Moon *20* J. D. Leventhal
If Winter Comes *23* Harry Millarde
If Winter Comes *47* Victor Saville
If Women Only Knew *21* Edward H. Griffith
If Women Were Policemen *08* Percy Stow
If You Believe It, It's So *22* Tom Forman
If You Could Only Cook *35* William A. Seiter
If You Could See What I Hear *82* Eric Till
If You Could Shrink *20* Dave Fleischer
If You Don't Stop It, You'll Go Blind *77* Keefe Brasselle, Bob Levy
If You Feel Like Singing *50* Charles Walters
If You Knew Susie *48* Gordon Douglas
If You Like It *28* Heinosuke Gosho
If You Love Me *54* Tadashi Imai, Kozaburo Yoshimura
If You Want to Know Who We Are *07* John Morland
If You Want to Live...Shoot *68* Sergio Garrone
If Your Home Is Dear to You *67* Vassily Ordynski
If Youth But Knew *26* George A. Cooper
Igdenbu *30* Amo Bek-Nazarov
Igen *64* György Révész
'Igh Art *15* Cecil Birch
Igloo *32* Ewing Scott
Ignace *50* Pierre Colombier
Ignorance *16* J. A. Fitzgerald
Igor Bulichov *53* Yulia Solntseva
Igor Stravinsky: A Portrait *64* Richard Leacock*
Igorota *70* Luis Nepomuceno
Igorota, the Legend of the Tree of Life *70* Luis Nepomuceno
Igra *62* Dušan Vukotić
Igry Dlja Detej Sko'nogo Vozrasta *87* Arvo Ikho, Lejda Lajus
Iguana *88* Monte Hellman
Iguana dalla Lingua di Fuoco, L' *71* Riccardo Freda
Így Jöttem *64* Miklós Jancsó
Ihmiselon Ihanuus ja Kurjuus *89* Matti Kassila
Ihr Erstes Erlebnis *39* Josef von Baky
Ihr Grosses Geheimnis *18* Joe May
Ihr Grösster Erfolg *39* Johannes Meyer
Ihr Junge *31* Friedrich Feher
Ihre Durchlacht, die Verkäuferin *33* Karl Hartl
Ihre Hoheit Befiehlt *31* Hans Schwarz
Ihre Majestät die Liebe *30* Joe May
Ijintachi Tono Natsu *89* Nobuhiko Obayashi
Ikari no Machi *49* Mikio Naruse
Ikari no Umi *44* Tadashi Imai
Ikaria XB-1 *63* Jindřich Polák
Ikarie XB-1 *63* Jindřich Polák
Ikeru Ningyō *29* Tomu Uchida
Ikh Tsartsvo *28* Nutsa Gogoberidze, Mikhail Kalatozov

In Gollywog Land *12* Walter R. Booth, F. Martin Thornton

In Harm's Way *64* Otto Preminger

In Heaven There Is No Beer!? *84* Les Blank

In Her Own Time *85* Lynne Littman

In High Gear *24* Robert North Bradbury

In His Brother's Place *19* Harry Franklin

In His Grip *21* Charles C. Calvert

In His Steps *36* Karl Brown

In Holland *29* Norman Taurog

In Hollywood with Potash and Perlmutter *24* Alfred E. Green

In Honor's Web *19* Paul Scardon

In Hot Weather *22* Paul M. Felton

In il Nome del Padre *71* Marco Bellocchio

In Jenen Tagen *47* Helmut Käutner

In Jest and Earnest *11* Lewin Fitzhamon

In Judgment of... *18* Will S. Davis

In Laughland with Hy Mayer *13* Hy Mayer

In-Laws, The *79* Arthur Hiller

In Life's Cycle *10* D. W. Griffith

In Like Flint *67* Gordon Douglas

In Line of Duty *31* Bert Glennon

In Little Italy *09* D. W. Griffith

In London's Toils *13* Alexander Butler

In Love *69* Elior Ishmukhamedov

In Love *80* Steven Paul

In Love *82* Chuck Vincent

In Love and War *13* Allan Dwan

In Love and War *58* Philip Dunne

In Love at 40 *35* Arthur Ripley

In Love with a Fireman *16* William Beaudine

In Love with a Picture Girl *09* Percy Stow

In Love with an Actress *11* Frank Wilson

In Love with Life *34* Frank R. Strayer

In Love with Love *24* Rowland V. Lee

In Love's Laboratory *17* Edward H. Griffith

In Lunyland *16* Leighton Budd

In MacArthur Park *77* Bruce R. Schwartz

In Memoriam László Mészáros *69* Márta Mészáros

In Memory of Sergei Ordzhonikidzye *37* Dziga Vertov

In Mizzoura *19* Hugh Ford

In Montezuma from "The Belle of Mayfair" *06* Arthur Gilbert

In Mother's Footsteps *11* Theo Bouwmeester

In My Merry Oldsmobile *31* Dave Fleischer

In 'n' Out *84* Ricardo Franco

In Name der Menschlichkeit *47* G. W. Pabst

In Name Only *39* John Cromwell

In 1998 AD: The Automatic Reducing Machine *19* Leighton Budd

In Nome del Popolo Italiano *71* Dino Risi

In Nome della Legge *48* Pietro Germi

In Old Amarillo *51* William Witney

In Old Arizona *28* Irving Cummings, Raoul Walsh

In Old Caliente *39* Joseph Kane

In Old California *10* D. W. Griffith

In Old California *29* Burton L. King

In Old California *42* William McGann

In Old Cheyenne *31* Stuart Paton

In Old Cheyenne *41* Joseph Kane

In Old Chicago *37* H. Bruce Humberstone, Henry King, Robert D. Webb

In Old Colorado *41* Howard Bretherton

In Old Florida *11* Sidney Olcott

In Old Heidelberg *15* John Emerson

In Old Heidelberg *27* Ernst Lubitsch

In Old Kentucky *09* D. W. Griffith

In Old Kentucky *19* Alfred E. Green, Marshall Neilan

In Old Kentucky *27* John M. Stahl

In Old Kentucky *35* George Marshall

In Old Kentucky: A Stirring Episode of the Civil War *09* D. W. Griffith

In Old Los Angeles *48* Joseph Kane

In Old Madrid *11* Thomas Ince

In Old Madrid *21* Harry D. Leonard

In Old Mexico *38* Edward D. Venturini

In Old Missouri *40* Frank McDonald

In Old Montana *39* Raymond K. Johnson

In Old Monterey *39* Joseph Kane

In Old New Mexico *45* Phil Rosen

In Old Oklahoma *43* Albert S. Rogell

In Old Sacramento *46* Joseph Kane

In Old Santa Fe *34* David Howard

In Old Wyoming *45* Robert E. Tansey

In Olden Days *52* Alessandro Blasetti

In Our Alley *06* Alf Collins

In Our Time *33* Aveling Ginever

In Our Time *44* Vincent Sherman

In Our Time *82* Edward Yang*

In Paradise *41* Per Lindberg

In Paris, A.W.O.L. *36* Roland Reed

In Paris Parks *54* Shirley Clarke

In Pawn *14* Dalton Somers

In Peace and War *14* Wilfred Noy

In Person *35* William A. Seiter

In Pieno Sole *59* René Clément

In Praise of Folly *86* Roberto Aguerre

In Praise of Older Women *78* George Kaczender

In Prehistoric Days *13* D. W. Griffith

In Pursuit of Fashion *10* Lewin Fitzhamon

In Pursuit of Polly *18* Chester Withey

In Quest of Health *07* Arthur Cooper

In Relation with Vassilis *86* Stavros Tsiolis

In Retirement *84* Juan Carlos De Sanzo

In Room 111 *38* Steve Sekely

In Rosie's Room *44* Joseph Santley

In Rough Style *39* A. Martin De Lucenay

In Saigon, Some May Live *67* Vernon Sewell

În Sat la Noi *51* Jean Georgescu, Victor Iliu

In Search of a Golden Sky *83* Charles E. Sellier

In Search of a Hero *26* Duke Worne

In Search of a Husband *15* Wilfred Noy

In Search of a Sinner *20* David Kirkland

In Search of a Thrill *23* Oscar Apfel

In Search of Anna *78* Esben Storm

In Search of Arcady *19* Bertram Bracken

In Search of Famine *80* Mrinal Sen

In Search of Gregory *69* Peter Wood

In Search of Happiness *40* Grigori Roshal, Vera Stroyeva

In Search of Historic Jesus *79* Henning Schellerup

In Search of Noah's Ark *76* James L. Conway

In Search of the Bride *87* Goderdzi Chokheli

In Search of the Castaways *62* Robert Stevenson

In Self Defence *21* Mauritz Stiller

In Self Defense *47* Jack Bernhard

In Slumberland *17* Irvin Willat

In Society *44* Jean Yarbrough

In Spite of Danger *35* Lambert Hillyer

In Spring One Plants Alone *81* Vincent Ward

In Strange Company *31* Stuart Paton

In Such Trepidation I Creep Off Tonight to the Evil Battle *77* Alexander Kluge

In the Aisles of the Wild *12* D. W. Griffith

In the Balance *17* Paul Scardon

In the Barber Shop *07* Georges Méliès

In the Belly of the Dragon *88* Yves Simoneau

In the Belly of the Whale *84* Doris Dörrie

In the Big City *27* Mikhail Averbakh, Mark Donskoi

In the Bishop's Carriage *13* J. Searle Dawley, Edwin S. Porter

In the Black Mountains *41* Nikolai Shengelaya

In the Blood *15* Wilfred Noy

In the Blood *23* Walter West

In the Bogie Man's Cave *07* Georges Méliès

In the Bonds of Passion *13* Forest Holger-Madsen

In the Border States *10* D. W. Griffith

In the Castle of Bloody Lust *67* Adrian Hoven

In the Cellar *60* John Halas*

In the Club *63* Kazimierz Karabasz

In the Clutches of the Gang *14* George Nicholls, Mack Sennett

In the Clutches of the Hun *15* Joe Evans

In the Clutches of the Ku Klux Klan *13* Sidney Olcott

In the Cool of the Day *63* Robert Stevens

In the Country *66* Robert Kramer

In the Course of Time *75* Wim Wenders

In the Dark *28* Frank Miller

In the Days of '49 *11* D. W. Griffith

In the Days of Robin Hood *13* F. Martin Thornton

In the Days of Saint Patrick *20* Norman Whitten

In the Days of the Missions *16* Lloyd B. Carleton

In the Days of the Thundering Herd *14* Colin Campbell

In the Days of the Thundering Herd *33* Henry Hathaway

In the Days of Trafalgar *14* Maurice Elvey

In the Dead Man's Room *13* Charles C. Calvert

In the Dear Old Summertime *22* Hy Mayer

In the Depths of the Sea *38* Boris Dolin, Alexander Zguridi

In the Devil's Bowl *23* Neal Hart

In the Devil's Garden *70* Sidney Hayers

In the Diplomatic Service *16* Francis X. Bushman

In the Dog House *34* Arthur Ripley

In the Doghouse *61* D'Arcy Conyers

In the Environment of Liquids and Nasals a Parasitic Vowel Sometimes Develops *75* George Landow

In the Fall of '55 Eden Cried 67 Fred Johnson
In the Far East 37 David Marian
In the First Degree 27 Phil Rosen
In the French Style 62 Robert Parrish
In the Front Line 41 Dziga Vertov
In the Gloaming 18 Edwin J. Collins
In the Good Old Days 10 Lewin Fitzhamon
In the Good Old Summertime 26 Dave Fleischer
In the Good Old Summertime 30 Dave Fleischer
In the Good Old Summertime 49 Robert Z. Leonard
In the Good Old Times 05 Arthur Cooper
In the Good Old Times 05 James A. Williamson
In the Grasp of the Law 15 Frank Lloyd
In the Green of the Woods 68 Palle Kjærulff-Schmidt
In the Grip of Death 13 H. Oceano Martinek
In the Grip of Spies 14 H. Oceano Martinek
In the Grip of the Law 15 Frank Lloyd
In the Grip of the Spider 70 Antonio Margheriti
In the Grip of the Sultan 15 Leon Bary
In the Hands of Imposters 11 August Blom
In the Hands of the Enemy 10 Theo Bouwmeester
In the Hands of the London Crooks 13 Alexander Butler
In the Hands of the Spoilers 16 Leon Bary
In the Headlines 29 John G. Adolfi
In the Heart of a Fool 20 Allan Dwan
In the Heart of the City 69 Claude Jutra
In the Heat of the Night 67 Norman Jewison
In the Hollow of Her Hand 18 Charles Maigne
In the Hour of His Need 13 Warwick Buckland
In the Hour of Trial 15 Victor Sjöström
In the Icy Ocean 52 Alexander Zguridi
In the Jungle 60 John Halas*
In the King of Prussia 82 Emile De Antonio
In the Kingdom of Oil and Millions 16 B. Svetlov
In the Land of Nod 08 Arthur Cooper
In the Land of the Headhunters 14 Edward S. Curtis
In the Land of the War Canoes 14 Edward S. Curtis
In the Line of Duty 31 Bert Glennon
In the Line of Fire—Film Reporters 41 Dziga Vertov
In the Long Ago 13 Colin Campbell
In the Meantime, Darling 44 Otto Preminger
In the Money 19 Raoul Barré, Charles Bowers
In the Money 34 Frank R. Strayer
In the Money 57 William Beaudine
In the Month of May 70 Marlen Khutsiev
In the Mood 87 Phil Alden Robinson
In the Mountains of Ala-Tau 44 Dziga

Vertov
In the Mountains of Yugoslavia 46 Abram Room
In the Mouth of the Wolf 88 Francisco José Lombardi
In the Movies 22 Charlie Chase
In the Name of Life 46 Josef Heifits, Alexander Zarkhi
In the Name of Love 25 Howard Higgin
In the Name of the Father 71 Marco Bellocchio
In the Name of the Fatherland 43 Vsevolod I. Pudovkin, Dmitri Vasiliev
In the Name of the Homeland 43 Vsevolod I. Pudovkin, Dmitri Vasiliev
In the Name of the Italian People 71 Dino Risi
In the Name of the Law 22 Emory Johnson
In the Name of the Law 48 Pietro Germi
In the Name of the Law 86 Kjell Sundvall
In the Name of the People 84 Frank Christopher
In the Name of the People 87 Živko Nikolić
In the Name of the Pope King 77 Luigi Magni
In the Name of the Prince of Peace 14 J. Searle Dawley
In the Name of the Son 87 Jorge Polaco
In the Navy 41 Arthur Lubin
In the Next Room 30 Edward F. Cline
In the Nick 60 Ken Hughes
In the Night 20 Frank Richardson
In the Night 31 Walter Ruttmann
In the Night 41 Jean Yarbrough
In the Nikitsky Botanical Garden 52 Yuri Ozerov
In the North Woods 12 D. W. Griffith
In the October Days 58 Sergei Vasiliev
In the Outskirts of the City 57 Miklós Jancsó
In the Pacific 57 Alexander Zguridi
In the Palace of the King 15 Fred E. Wright
In the Palace of the King 23 Emmett J. Flynn
In the Park 15 Charles Chaplin
In the Pillory 24 Amo Bek-Nazarov
In the Power of the Ku Klux Klan 13 Sidney Olcott
In the Presence of Life 14 Yakov Protazanov
In the Prime of Life 11 August Blom
In the Python's Den 13 Dave Aylott
In the Rain 86 Seyfollah Dad
In the Ranks 14 Percy Nash
In the Rapture 76 William H. Wiggins, Jr.
In the Realm of Passion 78 Nagisa Oshima
In the Realm of the Senses 76 Nagisa Oshima
In the Rear of the Enemy 42 Eugene Schneider
In the Red Rays of the Sleeping Sun 25 Kenji Mizoguchi*
In the River 61 José Luis Borau
In the Ruins 23 Kenji Mizoguchi
In the Sands of Central Asia 43 Alexander

Zguridi
In the Season of Buds 10 D. W. Griffith
In the Season of the Buds 10 D. W. Griffith
In the Secret State 85 Christopher Morahan
In the Service of the King 09 Lewin Fitzhamon
In the Shade of the Old Apple Sauce 31 Dave Fleischer
In the Shade of the Old Apple Tree 30 Dave Fleischer
In the Shadow 15 Harry Handworth
In the Shadow of Big Ben 14 Frank Wilson
In the Shadow of Darkness 13 Bert Haldane
In the Shadow of Kilimanjaro 84 Raju Patel
In the Shadow of the Rope 12 Percy Nash
In the Shadow of the Sea 12 Curt A. Stark
In the Shadow of the Sun 81 Derek Jarman
In the Shadow of the Wind 87 Yves Simoneau
In the Shadows 16 C. Allen Gilbert
In the Signal Box 22 H. B. Parkinson
In the Silly Summertime 21 Hy Mayer
In the Smuggler's Grip 13 Edwin J. Collins
In the Soup 36 Henry Edwards
In the South China Countryside 57 Miklós Jancsó
In the Spider's Web 24 Robert Boudrioz
In the Spirit 90 Sandra Seacat
In the Springtime of Life 26 Humberto Mauro
In the Steps of Our Ancestors 61 Alexander Zguridi
In the Storm 52 Vatroslav Mimica
In the Stretch 14 Phil Scovelle
In the Sultan's Garden 11 Thomas Ince
In the Summer Time 06 Lewin Fitzhamon
In the Summertime 70 Ermanno Olmi
In the Theatrical Business 17 Raoul Barré, Charles Bowers
In the Toils of the Blackmailer 13 Bert Haldane
In the Toils of the Temptress 13 Hay Plumb
In the Town of S 66 Josef Heifits
In the Waiting Room of Death 46 Hasse Ekman
In the Wake of a Stranger 58 David Eady
In the Wake of the Bounty 33 Charles Chauvel
In the Watches of the Night 09 D. W. Griffith
In the Web of the Grafters 16 Murdock MacQuarrie
In the West 23 George Holt
In the Whirlwind of Revolution 22 Alexander Chargonin
In the White City 82 Alain Tanner
In the Wild Mountains 86 Xueshu Yan
In the Wilderness 87 Rafael Fuster Pardo
In the Window Recess 09 D. W. Griffith
In the Woods 50 Akira Kurosawa
In the World 39 Mark Donskoi
In the Year of the Pig 68 Emile De Antonio

Indian Jealousy *12* Allan Dwan
Indian Love Call *36* W. S. Van Dyke
Indian Love Lyrics, The *23* Sinclair Hill
Indian Massacre, The *12* Thomas Ince
Indian Mother, The *10* Sidney Olcott
Indian Paint *64* Norman Foster
Indian Runner's Romance, The *09* D. W. Griffith
Indian Scarf, The *63* Alfred Vohrer
Indian Scout *49* Lew Landers
Indian Scout's Vengeance, An *10* Sidney Olcott
Indian Sorcerer, The *08* Georges Méliès
Indian Squaw's Sacrifice *10* Edwin S. Porter
Indian Story *61* Miklós Jancsó
Indian Summer, An *11* D. W. Griffith
Indian Summer *49* Boris Ingster
Indian Summer *68* Jiří Menzel
Indian Summer *87* Don Cato
Indian Summer *87* Timothy Forder
Indian Summer of Dry Valley Johnson, The *17* Martin Justice
Indian Territory *50* John English
Indian Tomb, The *18* August Blom
Indian Tomb, The *21* Fritz Lang, Joe May
Indian Tomb, The *58* Fritz Lang
Indian Trailer, The *09* Gilbert M. Anderson
Indian Uprising *51* Ray Nazarro
Indian Vendetta, An *12* Lewin Fitzhamon
Indian Village *51* Arne Sucksdorff
Indian Woman's Pluck, The *12* Frank Wilson
Indian Youth: An Exploration *68* Shyam Benegal
Indiana Jones and the Last Crusade *89* Steven Spielberg
Indiana Jones and the Temple of Doom *84* Steven Spielberg
Indianapolis Speedway *39* Lloyd Bacon
Indians Are Coming, The *30* Henry MacRae
Indian's Friendship, An *12* Gilbert M. Anderson
Indians Gambling for Furs — Is It War or Peace? *03* Joe Rosenthal
Indian's Loyalty, The *13* D. W. Griffith
Indian's Recompense, An *12* F. Martin Thornton
Indian's Romance, An *08* Frank Mottershaw
Indiántörténet *61* Miklós Jancsó
Indifferenti, Gli *63* Francesco Maselli
Indigestion, Une *02* Georges Méliès
Indio, El *39* Armando Vargas de la Maza
Indio *88* Antonio Margheriti
Indio Black *70* Gianfranco Parolini
Indio Black, Sai Che Ti Dico: Sei un Gran Figlio di . . . *70* Gianfranco Parolini
Indische Grabmal, Das *21* Fritz Lang, Joe May
Indische Grabmal, Das *58* Fritz Lang
Indiscreet *31* Leo McCarey
Indiscreet *58* Stanley Donen
Indiscreet Corinne *17* John Francis Dillon
Indiscret aux Bains de Mer, L' *1897* Georges Méliès
Indiscrète, L' *69* François Reichenbach
Indiscretion *17* Wilfred North

Indiscretion *21* Will S. Davis
Indiscretion *45* Peter Godfrey
Indiscretion *53* Vittorio De Sica
Indiscretion of an American Wife *53* Vittorio De Sica
Indiscretions *39* Sacha Guitry
Indiscretions of Eve *32* Cecil Lewis
Indiscrets, Les *1897* Georges Méliès
Indisk By *51* Arne Sucksdorff
Indiskrete Frau, Die *27* Carl Boese
Indomitable Leni Peickert, The *69* Alexander Kluge
Indomitable Teddy Roosevelt, The *83* Harrison Engle
Indonesia Calling *46* Joris Ivens
Indonesia Today *55* V. Nikosa
Industrial Britain *31* Robert Flaherty, John Grierson
Industrial Investigation *15* Harry S. Palmer
Industrial Reserve Army, The *71* Helma Sanders-Brahms
Industrial Symphony *31* Joris Ivens
Industrie de la Tapisserie et du Meuble Sculpté, L' *35* Henri Storck
Industrie du Verre, L' *13* Léonce-Henri Burel
Industrielle Reservearmee, Die *71* Helma Sanders-Brahms
Industry *66* Krzysztof Zanussi
Indvielse af Storstrømsbroen *37* Anders Wilhelm Sandberg
Inesorabili, Gli *50* Camillo Mastrocinque
Inevitable, The *13* Frank Wilson
Inevitable, The *17* Ben Goetz
Inevitable, The *18* Henry Edwards
Inexhaustible Cab, The *1899* George Albert Smith
Inexperienced Angler, An *09* Frank Wilson
Inez from Hollywood *24* Alfred E. Green
Infamia Araba *12* Mario Caserini
Infamous, The *16* Forest Holger-Madsen
Infamous *61* William Wyler
Infamous Conduct *66* Richard Martin
Infamous Crimes *47* William Beaudine
Infamous Lady, The *28* Geoffrey Barkas, Michael Barringer
Infamous Miss Revell, The *21* Dallas M. Fitzgerald
Infanzia, Vocazione e Prima Esperienze di Giacomo Casanova — Veneziano *69* Luigi Comencini
Infatuation *25* Irving Cummings
Infatuation *30* Sascha Geneen
Infatuation *85* Guoxi Chen
Infedeli, Le *52* Mario Monicelli, Steno
Infelice *15* L. C. MacBean, Fred Paul
Inferior Sex, The *20* Joseph E. Henabery
Infernal Cakewalk, The *03* Georges Méliès
Infernal Caldron, The *03* Georges Méliès
Infernal Cauldron, The *03* Georges Méliès
Infernal Cauldron and the Phantasmal Vapours, The *03* Georges Méliès
Infernal Idol, The *73* Freddie Francis
Infernal Machine *33* Marcel Varnel
Infernal Machine, The *48* Roberto Rossellini
Infernal Triangle, The *35* Gordon Douglas
Inferno *20* Paul Czinner
Inferno *22* Fritz Lang

Inferno *53* Roy Ward Baker
Inferno, The *62* Michael Roemer, Robert M. Young
Inferno *78* Dario Argento
Inferno *81* Tatsumi Kumashiro
Inferno — A Play About People of Our Time *22* Fritz Lang
Inferno Addosso, L' *66* Gianni Vernuccio
Inferno de Almas *58* Benito Alazraki
Inferno dei Morti-Viventi *81* Bruno Mattei
Inferno del Deserto, L' *69* Nanni Loy
Inferno dell'Amore, L' *27* Carmine Gallone
Inferno des Verbrechens *22* Fritz Lang
Inferno di Amore *27* Carmine Gallone
Inferno — Ein Spiel von Menschen Unserer Zeit *22* Fritz Lang
Inferno Giallo *42* Géza von Radványi
Inferno in Diretta *85* Ruggero Deodato
Inferno — Men of the Time *22* Fritz Lang
Inferno — Menschen der Zeit *22* Fritz Lang
Inferno of First Love *68* Susumu Hani
Inferno — People of the Time *22* Fritz Lang
Infidel, The *22* James Young
Infidelidad *39* Boris Malcon
Infidelity *17* Ashley Miller
Infidelity *52* Alessandro Blasetti
Infidelity *61* Philippe de Broca
Infierno de Frankenstein, El *60* Rafael Baledón
Infiltrator, The *55* Pierre Foucaud
Infinite Sorrow *22* Alexander Panteleyev
Infinitos *35* Fernando Mantilla, Carlos Velo
Infirmière, L' *15* Henri Pouctal
Inflation *27* Hans Richter
Influence de la Lumière sur les Mouvements de l'Œuf de Truite *57* Jean Painlevé
Information *66* Hollis Frampton
Information Kid *32* Kurt Neumann
Information Machine, The *57* Charles Eames, Ray Eames
Information Received *61* Robert Lynn
Informer, The *12* D. W. Griffith
Informer, The *29* Arthur Robison
Informer, The *31* Martin Frič, Karel Lamač
Informer, The *35* John Ford
Informer, The *86* Bernhard Giger
Informers, The *63* Ken Annakin
Infortunes d'un Explorateur, Les *00* Georges Méliès
Infra-Man *75* Hua-Shan
Infra Superman, The *75* Hua-Shan
Inga *67* Joe Sarno
Inga II *69* Joe Sarno
Ingagi *31* William Campbell
Inganni *85* Luigi Faccini
Inge Bliver Voksen *54* Jørgen Roos
Inge Larsen *23* Hans Steinhoff
Inge und Die Millionen *33* Erich Engel
Ingeborg Holm *13* Victor Sjöström
Ingen Kan Älska Som Vi *88* Staffan Hildebrand
Ingen Morgondag *57* Arne Mattsson
Ingen Så Tokig Som Jag *55* Erik Faustman
Ingenious Revenge, An *08* A. E. Coleby
Ingenious Safe Deposit, An *09* Percy Stow
Ingenjör Andrees Luftfärd *78* Jan Troell

Investigation, The *78* Étienne Périer
Investigation, The *86* Damiano Damiani
Investigation of a Citizen Above Suspicion *70* Elio Petri
Investigation of Murder, An *73* Stuart Rosenberg
Invigorating Electricity *10* Lewin Fitzhamon
Invincibili Sette, Gli *66* Alberto De Martino
Invincibili Tre, Gli *64* Gianfranco Parolini
Invincible, The *42* Sergei Gerasimov, Mikhail Kalatozov
Invincible Brothers Machiste, The *65* Roberto Mauri
Invincible Gladiator, The *62* Anthony Momplet
Invincible Six, The *68* Jean Negulesco
Invisibili, Gli *88* Pasquale Squitieri
Invisibility *09* Lewin Fitzhamon, Cecil M. Hepworth
Invisible Adversaries *77* Valie Export
Invisible Agent *42* Edwin L. Marin
Invisible Army, The *50* Johan Jacobsen
Invisible Asset, The *63* Norman Harrison
Invisible Avenger *58* James Wong Howe, Ben Parker, John Sledge
Invisible Bond, The *19* Charles Maigne
Invisible Boy, The *57* Herman Hoffman
Invisible Button, The *08* Dave Aylott
Invisible Creature, The *59* Montgomery Tully
Invisible Divorce, The *20* Nat C. Deverich, Thomas R. Mills
Invisible Dr. Mabuse, The *61* Harald Reinl
Invisible Dog, The *09* Walter R. Booth
Invisible Enemy *38* John H. Auer
Invisible Fear, The *21* Edwin Carewe
Invisible Fluid, The *08* Wallace McCutcheon
Invisible Ghost, The *41* Joseph H. Lewis
Invisible Horror, The *61* Harald Reinl
Invisible Informer *46* Philip Ford
Invisible Ink *21* Dave Fleischer
Invisible Invaders *59* Edward L. Cahn
Invisible Kid, The *88* Avery Crounse
Invisible Killer, The *39* Sam Newfield
Invisible Man, The *33* James Whale
Invisible Man, The *57* Alfredo B. Crevenna
Invisible Man, The *63* Raphael Nussbaum
Invisible Man, The *87* Ulf Miehe
Invisible Man Goes Through the City, An *33* Harry Piel
Invisible Man Returns, The *40* Joe May
Invisible Maniac, The *90* Rif Coogan
Invisible Man's Revenge, The *44* Ford Beebe
Invisible Menace, The *37* John Farrow
Invisible Message, The *35* Albert Herman
Invisible Monster, The *50* Fred C. Brannon
Invisible Mouse *47* Joseph Barbera, William Hanna
Invisible Opponent *33* Rudolf Katscher
Invisible Power, The *14* George Melford
Invisible Power, The *21* Frank Lloyd
Invisible Power *32* James Cruze
Invisible Ray, The *20* Harry A. Pollard
Invisible Ray, The *35* Lambert Hillyer

Invisible Revenge *25* Charles Bowers
Invisible Silvia, The *04* Georges Méliès
Invisible Strangler *76* John Florea
Invisible Stripes *39* Lloyd Bacon
Invisible Terror, The *63* Raphael Nussbaum
Invisible Thief, An *09* Ferdinand Zecca
Invisible Wall, The *44* Gustaf Molander
Invisible Wall, The *47* Eugene Forde
Invisible Web, The *21* Beverly C. Rule
Invisible Woman, The *41* A. Edward Sutherland
Invisibles, Los *61* Jaime Salvador
Invitados, Los *87* Víctor Barrera
Invitata, L' *69* Vittorio De Seta
Invitation *51* Gottfried Reinhardt
Invitation, L' *73* Claude Goretta
Invitation, The *73* Claude Goretta
Invitation and an Attack, An *15* Charles Brabin
Invitation au Voyage, L' *27* Germaine Dulac
Invitation au Voyage *82* Peter Del Monte
Invitation to a Gunfighter *64* Richard Wilson
Invitation to a Hanging *63* William F. Claxton
Invitation to Happiness *39* Wesley Ruggles
Invitation to Magic *56* Harold Baim
Invitation to Murder *62* Robert Lynn
Invitation to the Dance *35* Rudolf von der Noss
Invitation to the Dance *56* Gene Kelly
Invitation to the Inside *78* Andrzej Wajda
Invitation to the Interior *78* Andrzej Wajda
Invitation to the Voyage *27* Germaine Dulac
Invitation to the Voyage *82* Peter Del Monte
Invitation to the Waltz *35* Paul Merzbach
Invitation to the Wedding *84* Joseph Brooks
Invité de la Onzième Heure, L' *45* Maurice Cloche
Invite Monsieur à Dîner *32* Claude Autant-Lara
Invited, The *69* Vittorio De Seta
Invited, The *87* Víctor Barrera
Invitée, L' *69* Vittorio De Seta
Invités de M. Latourte, Les *04* Georges Méliès
Invito a Pranzo, Un *07* Enrico Guazzoni
Invocation of My Demon Brother *69* Kenneth Anger
Io Amo, Tu Ami *60* Alessandro Blasetti
Io e Caterina *80* Alberto Sordi
Io e Lui *73* Luciano Salce
Io e Mia Sorella *87* Carlo Verdone
Io, Io, Io...e gli Altri *65* Alessandro Blasetti
Io La Conoscevo Bene *65* Antonio Pietrangeli
Io, Mammeta e Tu *58* Carlo Ludovico Bragaglia
Io Non Perdono...Uccido *68* Rafael Romero Marchent
Io Non Vedo Tu Non Parli Lui Non Sente *71* Mario Camerini

Io So Che Tu Sai Che Io So *82* Alberto Sordi
Io Sono un Autarchico *76* Nanni Moretti
Io Suo Padre *38* Mario Bonnard
Io Ti Amo *68* Antonio Margheriti
Iolanta *64* Vladimir Gorikker
Iola's Promise *12* D. W. Griffith
Ipcress File, The *65* Sidney J. Furie
Iphigenia *76* Michael Cacoyannis
Ipnosi *62* Eugenio Martin
Ipotesi *70* Elio Petri*
Ippodromi all'Alba *50* Alessandro Blasetti
Ippon-Gatana Dohyōiri *31* Hiroshi Inagaki
Ippon-Gatana Dohyōiri *34* Teinosuke Kinugasa
Ira di Dio, L' *68* Alberto Cardone
Iran *71* Claude Lelouch
Iré a Santiago *64* Sara Gómez
Ireland the Oppressed *12* Sidney Olcott
Ireland—The Tear and the Smile *60* Willard Van Dyke
Ireland's Border Line *38* Harry O'Donovan
Irene *26* Alfred E. Green
Irene *36* Reinhold Schünzel
Irene *40* Herbert Wilcox
Irene Irene *75* Peter Del Monte
Irgendwo in Berlin *46* Gerhard Lamprecht
Irgendwo in Europa *47* Géza von Radványi
Irina Kirsanova *15* Yevgeni Bauer
Iris *15* Cecil M. Hepworth
Iris *46* Alf Sjöberg
Iris *87* Mady Saks
Iris and the Lieutenant *46* Alf Sjöberg
Iris och Löjtnantshjärta *46* Alf Sjöberg
Iris Perdue et Retrouvée *33* Louis Gasnier
Irish and Proud of It *34* Leonard Fields
Irish and Proud of It *36* Donovan Pedelty
Irish Destiny *25* I. J. Eppel
Irish Emigrant, The *26* Hugh Croise
Irish Eyes *18* William Dowlan
Irish Eyes Are Smiling *44* Gregory Ratoff
Irish for Luck *36* Arthur Woods
Irish Girl, The *17* John McDonagh
Irish Girl's Love, An *12* Sidney Olcott
Irish Gringo, The *35* William L. Thompson
Irish Hearts *27* Byron Haskin
Irish Hearts *34* Brian Desmond Hurst
Irish Honeymoon, The *11* Sidney Olcott
Irish in America, The *15* Sidney Olcott
Irish in Us, The *35* Lloyd Bacon
Irish Luck *25* Victor Heerman
Irish Luck *38* Howard Bretherton
Irish Medley, An *38* Hayford Hobbs
Irish Melody *50* Paul Barralet
Irish Mother, An *25* I. J. Eppel
Irish Whiskey Rebellion *72* Chester Erskine
Irishman, The *78* Donald Crombie
Irishman and the Button, The *02* George Albert Smith
Irith, Irith *85* Naftali Alter
Irma la Douce *63* Billy Wilder
Irma la Mala *36* Raphael J. Sevilla
Iro *69* Shinji Murayama
Iron and Silk *89* Shirley Sun
Iron Angel *64* Ken Kennedy
Iron Bread *70* Vivian Pei
Iron Claw, The *16* Edward José, George B. Seitz

Iron Claw, The *41* James W. Horne
Iron Collar, The *63* R. G. Springsteen
Iron Cross, The *14* Richard Oswald
Iron Crown, The *40* Alessandro Blasetti
Iron Curtain, The *48* William A. Wellman
Iron Duke, The *34* Victor Saville
Iron Eagle *86* Sidney J. Furie
Iron Eagle II *88* Sidney J. Furie
Iron Eagle II: The Battle Beyond the Flag *88* Sidney J. Furie
Iron Earth, Copper Sky *87* Ömer Zülfü Livaneli
Iron Field, The *87* Yaropolk Lapshin
Iron Fist *26* John P. McGowan
Iron Fist *35* Lambert Hillyer
Iron Flower, The *57* János Herskó
Iron Gate *57* Youssef Chahine
Iron Glove, The *54* William Castle
Iron Hand, The *16* Ulysses Davis
Iron Heart, The *17* Paul Cazeneuve, Denison Clift
Iron Heart, The *17* George Fitzmaurice
Iron Heel, The *19* Vladimir Gardin
Iron Horse, The *24* John Ford
Iron Justice *15* Sidney Morgan
Iron Kiss, The *63* Samuel Fuller
Iron Maiden, The *62* Gerald Thomas
Iron Major, The *43* Ray Enright
Iron Man, The *25* William Bennett
Iron Man, The *31* Tod Browning
Iron Man *51* Joseph Pevney
Iron Mask, The *29* Allan Dwan
Iron Master, The *13* Christy Cabanne
Iron Master, The *33* Chester M. Franklin
Iron Men, The *82* Chang-ho Bae
Iron Mistress, The *52* Gordon Douglas
Iron Mountain Trail *53* William Witney
Iron Petticoat, The *56* Ralph Thomas
Iron Rider, The *20* Scott R. Dunlap
Iron Ring, The *17* George Archainbaud
Iron Ring *72* Kaneto Shindo
Iron Road, The *43* Lesley Selander
Iron Sheriff, The *57* Sidney Salkow
Iron Stair, The *20* F. Martin Thornton
Iron Stair, The *32* Leslie Hiscott
Iron Strain, The *15* Reginald Barker
Iron Swordsman, The *49* Riccardo Freda
Iron Test, The *18* Robert North Bradbury, Paul Hurst
Iron to Gold *22* Bernard J. Durning
Iron Trail, The *21* Roy William Neill
Iron Triangle, The *89* Eric Weston
Iron Warrior *87* Alfonso Brescia
Iron Wills *22* John W. Brunius
Iron Woman, The *16* Carl Harbaugh
Ironie du Destin, L' *23* Dmitri Kirsanov
Ironie du Sort, L' *24* Georges Monca
Ironie du Sort, L' *74* Édouard Molinaro
Ironmaster *82* Umberto Lenzi
Ironweed *87* Hector Babenco
Irony of Fate, The *12* Bert Haldane
Irony of Fate, The *23* Dmitri Kirsanov
Irony of Fate, The *75* Eldar Ryazanov
Iroquois Trail, The *50* Phil Karlson
Irreconcilable Differences *84* Charles Shyer
Irrende Seelen *22* Carl Fröhlich
Irresistible *57* Dino Risi
Irresistible Flapper, The *19* Frank Wilson
Irresistible Lover, The *27* William Beaudine

Irresistible Man, The *37* Géza von Bolváry
Irrésistible Rebelle, L' *39* Jean-Paul Le Chanois
Irrgarten der Leidenschaft *25* Alfred Hitchcock
Irritable Model, An *1897* Georges Méliès
Irritarono...e Sartana Fece Piazza Pulita, Lo *70* Rafael Romero Marchent
Is a Mother to Blame? *22* Roy Sheldon
Is Divorce a Failure? *23* Wallace Worsley
Is Everybody Happy? *29* Archie Mayo
Is Everybody Happy? *43* Charles Barton
Is It Easy to Be Young? *82* Yuri Podniek
Is It You? *86* Henry Jaglom
Is Life Worth Living? *21* Alan Crosland
Is Love Everything? *24* Christy Cabanne
Is Marriage a Failure? *21* Clarence Brown, Maurice Tourneur
Is Marriage the Bunk? *25* Leo McCarey
Is Matrimony a Failure? *22* James Cruze
Is Money Everything? *23* Glen Lyons
Is My Face Red? *32* William A. Seiter
Is My Palm Read *33* Dave Fleischer
Is Paris Burning? *65* René Clément
Is-Slottet *87* Per Blom
Is That Nice? *26* Del Andrews
Is There a Doctor in the Mouse? *64* Chuck Jones
Is There Intelligent Life on Earth? *63* Joy Batchelor, John Halas
Is There Justice? *31* Stuart Paton
Is There Sex After Death? *71* Alan Abel, Jeanne Abel
Is This Trip Really Necessary? *69* Ben Benoit
Is Your Daughter Safe? *27* Louis King, Leon Lee
Is Your Honeymoon Really Necessary? *53* Maurice Elvey
Is Zat So? *27* Alfred E. Green
Isaac in America *86* Amram Nowak
Isaac in America: A Journey with Isaac Bashevis Singer *86* Amram Nowak
Isaac Littlefeathers *84* Les Rose
Isaacs As a Broker's Man *13* Charles C. Calvert
Isabel *68* Paul Almond
Isabel, Duchess of the Devils *69* Bruno Corbucci
Isabella d'Aragon *10* Ernesto Maria Pasquali
Isabella, Duchessa dei Diavoli *69* Bruno Corbucci
Isabella Stewart Gardner *77* Richard Leacock, Pamela Wise
Isadora *67* Karel Reisz
Isar *76* Dariush Mehrjui
Ischia Operazione Amore *66* Vittorio Sala
Isen Brydes *47* Poul Bang, Jørgen Roos
Isewixer *79* Markus Imhoof
Ishchu Druga Zhizni *88* Mikhail Yershov
Ishimatsu of Mori *49* Kozaburo Yoshimura
Ishimatsu of the Forest *37* Sadao Yamanaka
Ishimatsu of the Forest *49* Kozaburo Yoshimura
Ishinaka Sensei Gyōjōki *50* Mikio Naruse
Ishtar *87* Elaine May

Isichos Thanatos, Enas *86* Frieda Liappa
Isidore à la Déveine *19* Robert Florey
Isidore sur le Lac *19* Robert Florey
Iska Worreh *17* Gregory La Cava
Iskandariya...Lih? *78* Youssef Chahine
Iskindirya Kaman Oue Kaman *90* Youssef Chahine
Iskindirya—Leh? *78* Youssef Chahine
Iskrenne Vash... *87* Alla Surikova
Iskushenie Don Zhuana *87* Grigori Koltunov, Vasily Levin
Isla de la Muerte, La *66* Ernst R. von Theumer
Isla de la Pasión, La *41* Emilio Fernández
Isla de los Muertos, La *68* Jack Hill, Juan Ibáñez
Isla del Tesoro *69* Sara Gómez
Isla del Tesoro, La *72* John Hough
Isla Maldita, La *35* Boris Malcon
Island, The *60* Kaneto Shindo
Island, The *64* Alf Sjöberg
Island, The *80* Michael Ritchie
Island, The *85* Po-chih Leong
Island *89* Paul Cox
Island Affair *62* Giorgio Bianchi
Island at the Top of the World, The *74* Robert Stevenson
Island Captives *37* Glenn Kershner
Island Claws *80* Hernán Cárdenas
Island Escape *62* Richard Goldstone, John Monks, Jr.
Island in Flight *30* Alexander Rasumny
Island in the Sky *38* Herbert I. Leeds
Island in the Sky *53* William A. Wellman
Island in the Sun *57* Robert Rossen
Island Jess *14* F. C. S. Tudor
Island (Life and Death), The *85* Po-chih Leong
Island Man *38* Richard Bird
Island of Adventure, The *81* Anthony Squire
Island of Allah *56* Richard Lyford
Island of Death *75* Narciso Ibáñez Serrador
Island of Death *75* Nico Mastorakis
Island of Desire, The *17* Otis Turner
Island of Desire *30* Joseph E. Henabery
Island of Desire *52* Stuart Heisler
Island of Despair, The *26* Henry Edwards
Island of Dr. Moreau, The *77* Don Taylor
Island of Doom *33* Semen Timoshenko
Island of Doomed Men *40* Charles Barton
Island of Evil Spirits *80* Masahiro Shinoda
Island of Flame *60* Roman Karmen
Island of Hell *77* Kon Ichikawa
Island of Horrors *77* Kon Ichikawa
Island of Intrigue, The *19* Henry Otto
Island of Living Horror *68* Gerry De Leon, Eddie Romero
Island of Lost Men *39* Kurt Neumann
Island of Lost Souls *32* Erle C. Kenton
Island of Lost Women *58* Frank Tuttle
Island of Love *63* Morton Da Costa
Island of Monte Cristo *52* Harold Daniels
Island of Naked Scandal *31* Heinosuke Gosho
Island of Passion, The *84* Juan Buñuel
Island of Procida, The *52* Mario Sequi
Island of Regeneration, The *15* Harry Davenport

It's a Great Life! *35* Edward F. Cline
It's a Great Life *43* Frank R. Strayer
It's a Hap-Hap-Happy Day *41* Dave Fleischer
It's a Have *06* Alf Collins
It's a Joke, Son *47* Ben Stoloff
It's a King *32* Jack Raymond
It's a Long Long Way to Tipperary *14* Maurice Elvey
It's a Long Time That I've Loved You *79* Jean-Charles Tacchella
It's a Long Way Home *60* Félix Máriássy
It's a Long Way to Tipperary *14* Maurice Elvey
It's a Lovely Day *49* David Hand
It's a Mad, Mad, Mad, Mad World *63* Stanley Kramer
It's a Pipe *26* George Marshall
It's a Pleasure! *45* William A. Seiter
It's a Small World *35* Irving Cummings
It's a Small World *50* William Castle
It's a Trad, Dad! *61* Richard Lester
It's a 2'6" Above the Ground World *72* Ralph Thomas
It's a Wise Child *31* Robert Z. Leonard
It's a Wonderful Day *49* Hal Wilson
It's a Wonderful Life *46* Frank Capra
It's a Wonderful World *39* W. S. Van Dyke
It's a Wonderful World *56* Val Guest
It's Alive *68* Larry Buchanan
It's Alive! *74* Larry Cohen
It's Alive II *78* Larry Cohen
It's Alive III: Island of the Alive *87* Larry Cohen
It's All Happening *63* Don Sharp
It's All in Your Mind *38* Bernard B. Ray
It's All Over Town *63* Douglas Hickox
It's All True *42* Orson Welles
It's All Yours *37* Elliott Nugent
It's Always Fair Weather *55* Stanley Donen, Gene Kelly
It's Always the Woman *16* Wilfred Noy
It's an Ill Wind *39* Cal Dalton, Ben Hardaway
It's Best to Be Natural *13* Percy Stow
It's Easy to Become a Father *29* Erich Schönfelder
It's Easy to Make Money *19* Edwin Carewe
It's Easy to Remember *35* Dave Fleischer
It's Forever Springtime *49* Renato Castellani
It's Great to Be Alive *33* Alfred L. Werker
It's Great to Be Young *46* Del Lord
It's Great to Be Young! *55* Cyril Frankel
It's Happiness That Counts *18* Bertram Phillips
It's Hard to Be Good *48* Jeffrey Dell
It's Hot in Hell *62* Henri Verneuil
It's Hot in Paradise *59* Fritz Böttger
It's Hummertime *50* Robert McKimson
It's in the Air *35* Charles Reisner
It's in the Air *38* Anthony Kimmins
It's in the Bag *32* Pierre Prévert
It's in the Bag *36* William Beaudine
It's in the Bag *43* Herbert Mason
It's in the Bag *45* Richard Wallace
It's in the Blood *38* Gene Gerrard
It's in the Stars *38* David Miller
It's Just My Luck *08* Arthur Cooper

It's Love Again *36* Victor Saville
It's Love I'm After *37* Archie Mayo
It's Love That Makes the World Go Round *13* Percy Stow
It's Magic *48* Michael Curtiz
It's Me Here, Bellett *64* Nagisa Oshima
It's My Fault *26* Kenji Mizoguchi
It's My Life *62* Jean-Luc Godard
It's My Life—El Noa Noa 2 *86* Gonzalo Martínez Ortega
It's My Model *46* Gustaf Molander
It's My Turn *80* Claudia Weill
It's Never Too Late *56* Michael McCarthy
It's Never Too Late *77* Jaime De Armiñán
It's Never Too Late to Mend *17* Dave Aylott
It's Never Too Late to Mend *22* George Wynn
It's Never Too Late to Mend *37* David MacDonald
It's Nice to Have a Mouse Around the House *65* Friz Freleng
It's No Laughing Matter *14* Lois Weber
It's No Use Crying Over Spilt Milk *00* Arthur Cooper
It's Not Always Cloudy *50* Vojtěch Jasný, Karel Kachyňa
It's Not Cricket *37* Ralph Ince
It's Not Cricket *48* Roy Rich, Alfred Roome
It's Not Just You, Murray! *64* Martin Scorsese
It's Not the Size That Counts *74* Ralph Thomas
It's Only Money *48* Irving Cummings
It's Only Money *62* Frank Tashlin
It's Sam Small Again *37* Alfred Goulding
It's That Man Again *42* Walter Forde
It's the Cats *26* Dave Fleischer
It's the Natural Thing to Do *39* Dave Fleischer
It's the Old Army Game *26* A. Edward Sutherland
It's the Only Way to Go *69* Ray Austin
It's Tough to Be Famous *32* Alfred E. Green
It's Trad, Dad! *61* Richard Lester
It's Turned Out Nice Again *41* Marcel Varnel
It's Up to You *36* Christy Cabanne
It's Up to You *41* Elia Kazan
It's Up to You *69* Stellan Olsson
It's What's Happening *67* Elliot Silverstein
It's You I Want *36* Ralph Ince
It's Your Move *68* Robert Fiz
It's Your Thing *70* Mike Garguilo
Itsuwareru Seisō *51* Kozaburo Yoshimura
Itto *34* Jean Benoît-Lévy, Marie Epstein
Itto d'Afrique *34* Jean Benoît-Lévy, Marie Epstein
Iumoreski *24* Dziga Vertov
Ivailo the Great *64* Nikola Vulcev
Ivan *32* Alexander Dovzhenko
Ivan Grozny *44* Sergei Eisenstein
Ivan Grozny II—Boyarskii Zagovor *46* Sergei Eisenstein
Ivan Grozny III *47* Sergei Eisenstein
Ivan il Terribile *15* Enrico Guazzoni
Ivan Kupala's Eve *68* Yuri Ilyenko
Ivan Nikulin, Russian Sailor *43* Igor

Savchenko
Ivan Pavlov *49* Grigori Roshal
Ivan, Son of the White Devil *54* Guido Brignone
Ivan the Terrible, Part One *44* Sergei Eisenstein
Ivan the Terrible, Part Two *46* Sergei Eisenstein
Ivan the Terrible, Part Two: The Boyars' Plot *46* Sergei Eisenstein
Ivan the Terrible, Part Three *47* Sergei Eisenstein
Ivan Vassilievich Changes His Profession *73* Leonid Gaidai
Ivanhoe *13* Leedham Bantock
Ivanhoe *13* Herbert Brenon
Ivanhoe *52* Richard Thorpe
Ivanov Kater *88* Mark Ossepijan
Ivanovo Detstvo *62* Andrei Tarkovsky
Ivan's Childhood *62* Andrei Tarkovsky
I've Always Loved You *46* Frank Borzage
I've Been Around *34* Philip Cahn
I've Got a Horse *38* Herbert Smith
I've Got Rings on My Fingers *29* Dave Fleischer
I've Got to Sing a Torch Song *33* Tom Palmer
I've Got You, You've Got Me by the Chin Hairs *79* Jean Yanne
I've Got Your Number *34* Ray Enright
I've Gotta Horse *65* Kenneth Hume
I've Heard the Mermaids Singing *87* Patricia Rozema
I've Lived Before *56* Richard Bartlett
Ivory Coast Adventure *64* Christian-Jaque
Ivory Hand, The *15* Wilfred Noy
Ivory-Handled Gun, The *35* Ray Taylor
Ivory Hunter *51* Harry Watt
Ivory Hunters, The *51* Harry Watt
Ivory Snuff Box, The *15* Maurice Tourneur
Ivrognes, Les *1897* Georges Méliès
Ivy *47* Sam Wood
Ivy and John *65* Andy Warhol
Ivy League Killers *62* William Davidson
Ivy's Elopement *14* Elwin Neame
Iwan Koschula *14* Richard Oswald
Iwashigumo *58* Mikio Naruse
Iz Zhizni Nachalnika Ugolovnogo Rozyska *87* Stepan Puchinyan
Iz Zhizni Potapova *87* Nikolai Skuybin
Izbavitelj *77* Krsto Papić
Izhaar *89* Yash Pal
Izotópok a Gyógyászatban *59* Miklós Jancsó
Izu no Musumetachi *45* Heinosuke Gosho
Izu no Odoriko *33* Heinosuke Gosho
Izumi *56* Masaki Kobayashi
Izvinite Pozhaluysta *87* Vytautas Zalakevicius
Izzy Able the Detective *21* Milt Gross
J. A. Martin Photographe *76* Jean Beaudin
J & S—Storia Criminale del Far West *73* Sergio Corbucci
J.C. *72* William McGaha
J.D. and the Salt Flat Kid *78* Alexander Grasshoff
J.D.'s Revenge *76* Arthur Marks
J. F. Willumsen *51* Jørgen Roos
J.J. Garcia *84* John Randall

J.J. McCulloch 75 Max Baer
J-Men Forever! 79 Richard Patterson
J.R. 67 Martin Scorsese
J. Th. Arnfred 74 Jørgen Roos
J. W. Coop 71 Cliff Robertson
Ja, Ja, Mein General, But Which Way to
    the Front? 70 Jerry Lewis
Já Nejsem Já 85 Václav Vorlíček
Já Prosím Slovo 75 Gleb Panfilov
Já Se Fabricam Automóveis em Portugal
    38 Manoel De Oliveira
Ja, Treu Ist die Soldatenliebe 34 Georg
    Jacoby
Jäähyväiset 82 Tuija-Maija Niskanen
Jäähyväiset Presidentille 87 Matti Kassila
Jääkärin Morsian 39 Risto Orko
Jään Kääntöpiiri 87 Lauri Törhönen
Jabberwocky 71 Jan Švankmajer
Jabberwocky 76 Terry Gilliam
Jacaré 42 Charles E. Ford
J'Accuse! 18 Abel Gance
J'Accuse! 37 Abel Gance
Jáchymov 34 Alexander Hammid
Jack 25 Robert Saidreau
Jack Ahoy! 34 Walter Forde
Jack and Jill 05 Harold Jeapes
Jack and Jill 17 William Desmond Taylor
Jack and Jill 80 Chuck Vincent
Jack and Jill II 84 Chuck Vincent
Jack and Jim 03 Georges Méliès
Jack and the Beanstalk 02 Edwin S. Porter
Jack and the Beanstalk 17 Chester M.
    Franklin, Sidney Franklin
Jack and the Beanstalk 22 Walt Disney
Jack and the Beanstalk 24 Herbert M.
    Dawley
Jack and the Beanstalk 24 Walter Lantz
Jack and the Beanstalk 31 Dave Fleischer
Jack and the Beanstalk 33 Ubbe Iwerks
Jack and the Beanstalk 52 Jean Yarbrough
Jack and the Beanstalk 55 Lotte Reiniger
Jack and the Beanstalk 70 Barry Mahon
Jack and the Beanstalk 74 Gisaburo Sugii
Jack and the Fairies 12 Stuart Kinder
Jack Armstrong 47 Wallace Fox
Jack Chanty 15 Max Figman
Jack el Destripador de Londres 71 José
    Luis Madrid
Jack et Jim 03 Georges Méliès
Jack Frost 23 Charlie Chase
Jack Frost 34 Ubbe Iwerks
Jack Frost 66 Alexander Rou
Jack in the Letterbox 08 Lewin Fitzhamon
Jack Jaggs and Dum Dum 03 Georges
    Méliès
Jack Johnson 71 William Cayton
Jack Kerouac's America 85 John Antonelli
Jack-Knife Man, The 20 King Vidor
Jack le Ramoneur 06 Georges Méliès
Jack London 43 Alfred Santell
Jack London's Adventures in the South
    Seas 12 Martin E. Johnson
Jack London's Klondike Fever 80 Peter
    Carter
Jack McCall—Desperado 53 Sidney Salkow
Jack o' Clubs 24 Robert F. Hill
Jack o' Hearts 26 David M. Hartford
Jack of All Trades 35 Jack Hulbert, Robert
    Stevenson
Jack of Diamonds 12 Allan Dwan

Jack of Diamonds, The 49 Vernon Sewell
Jack of Diamonds 67 Don Taylor
Jack of Hearts 19 B. Reeves Eason
Jack of Hearts 26 David M. Hartford
Jack of Hearts 50 Hasse Ekman
Jack Pot 40 Roy Rowland
Jack Rider, The 21 Charles R. Seeling
Jack, Sam and Pete 19 Percy Moran
Jack Sheppard 03 Frank Mottershaw
Jack Sheppard 12 Percy Nash
Jack Sheppard 23 Henry Cockraft Taylor
Jack Slade 53 Harold Schuster
Jack Spratt As a Blackleg Waiter 14 Toby
    Cooper
Jack Spratt As a Bricklayer 14 Toby Cooper
Jack Spratt As a Bus Conductor 14 Toby
    Cooper
Jack Spratt As a Dude 14 Toby Cooper
Jack Spratt As a Gardener 14 Toby Cooper
Jack Spratt As a Policeman 14 Toby
    Cooper
Jack Spratt As a Special Constable 14 Toby
    Cooper
Jack Spratt As a War Lord 14 Toby
    Cooper
Jack Spratt As a Wounded Prussian 14
    Toby Cooper
Jack Spratt's Parrot 15 Toby Cooper
Jack Spratt's Parrot As the Artful Dodger
    16 Toby Cooper
Jack Spratt's Parrot Getting His Own Back
    16 Toby Cooper
Jack Spratt's Parrot in Putting the Lid on
    It 16 Toby Cooper
Jack Spurlock, Prodigal 18 Carl Harbaugh
Jack Straw 20 William DeMille
Jack Tar 15 Bert Haldane
Jack the Giant Killer 16 L. M. Glackens
Jack the Giant Killer 25 Herbert M. Daw-
    ley
Jack the Giant Killer 55 Lotte Reiniger
Jack the Giant Killer 61 Nathan Juran
Jack the Handy Man 12 Gilbert Southwell
Jack the Kisser 07 J. Searle Dawley, Edwin
    S. Porter
Jack the Mangler of London 71 José Luis
    Madrid
Jack the Ripper 58 Robert S. Baker, Monty
    Berman
Jack the Ripper 71 José Luis Madrid
Jack the Ripper 76 Jesús Franco
Jack Trent Investigates 57 Olive Negus
Jack Wabbit and the Beanstalk 43 Friz
    Freleng
Jackal of Nahueltoro, The 69 Miguel Lit-
    tin
Jackal Trap 87 Mukadas Mahmudov
Jackals, The 67 Robert D. Webb
Jackals 86 Gary Grillo
Jackass Mail 41 Norman Z. McLeod
Jackboot Mutiny 55 G. W. Pabst
Jackie 21 John Ford
Jackie and the Beanstalk 29 Bobby Har-
    man
Jackie Chan's Police Story 85 Jackie Chan
Jackie Cooper's Christmas 31 Charles Reis-
    ner
Jackie Robinson Story, The 50 Alfred E.
    Green
Jackie's Nightmare 29 Bobby Harman

Jacknife 89 David Jones
Jackpot, The 50 Walter Lang
Jackpot 60 Montgomery Tully
Jackpot 75 Terence Young
Jackpot 82 John Goodell
Jackpot 86 Giancarlo Giannini
Jackpot Jitters 49 William Beaudine
Jack's Back 88 Rowdy Herrington
Jack's Return 05 Alf Collins
Jack's Rival 04 Alf Collins
Jack's Sister 11 Bert Haldane
Jack's the Boy 32 Walter Forde
Jack's Wife 72 George Romero
Jack's Word 12 Allan Dwan
Jackson County Jail 76 Michael Miller
Jacktown 62 William Martin
Jackville 65 Jean Rouch
Jacob 88 Mircea Daneliuc
Jacob the Liar 74 Frank Beyer
Jacob Two-Two Meets the Hooded Fang
    77 Theodore J. Flicker
Jacob's Ladder 42 Gustaf Molander
Jacob's Ladder 90 Adrian Lyne
Jacobs Stege 42 Gustaf Molander
Jacqueline 56 Roy Ward Baker
Jacqueline Kennedy's Asian Journey 62
    Leo Seitzer
Jacqueline, or Blazing Barriers 23 Del
    Henderson
Jacqueline Susann's Once Is Not Enough
    74 Guy Green
Jacques and November 85 Jean Beaudry,
    François Bouvier
Jacques Brel Is Alive and Well and Living
    in Paris 75 Denis Héroux
Jacques Callot, Correspondant du Guerre
    52 Pierre Kast
Jacques et Novembre 85 Jean Beaudry,
    François Bouvier
Jacques-Henri Lartigue 80 François
    Reichenbach
Jacques Landauze 19 André Hugon
Jacques of the Silver North 19 Norval
    MacGregor
Jacula 73 Jesús Franco
Jadą Goście Jadą 65 Romuald Drobażyń-
    ski, Jan Rutkiewicz, Gerard Zalewski
Jade 34 George B. Samuelson
Jade Box, The 30 Ray Taylor
Jade Casket, The 21 Léon Poirier
Jade Cup, The 26 Frank Crane
Jade Heart, The 15 Dave Aylott
Jade Love 86 Yi Zhang
Jade Mask, The 44 Phil Rosen
Jadup und Böl 81 Rainer Simon
Jaffery 15 George Irving
Jag Älskar Dig, Karlsson 47 Lau Lauritz-
    en, Jr., John Zacharias
Jag Är Nyfiken—Blå 68 Vilgot Sjöman
Jag Är Nyfiken—Gul 67 Vilgot Sjöman
Jag Rodnar 81 Vilgot Sjöman
Jaga wa Hashitta 70 Kiyoshi Nishimura
Jagd nach dem Glück, Die 30 Rochus
    Gliese, Karl Koch
Jagd nach der Wahrheit, Die 20 Karl
    Grüne
Jäger von Fall, Der 37 Hans Deppe
Jagged Edge 85 Richard Marquand
Jaggers Breaks All Records 09 T. J.
    Gobbett

Jagirdar *42* Ramjankhan Mehboobkhan
Jags and Jealousy *16* William Beaudine
Jagte Raho *57* Raj Kapoor
Jagten på Gentlemanrøveren *10* August Blom
Jaguar *56* George Blair
Jaguar *67* Jean Rouch
Jaguar *79* Lino Brocka
Jaguar, The *87* Sebastián Alarcón
Jaguar Lives! *79* Ernest Pintoff
Jaguar's Claws, The *17* Marshall Neilan
Jahre Vergehen, Die *44* Günther Rittau
J'Ai 17 Ans *45* André Berthomieu
J'Ai Été au Bal *89* Les Blank, Chris Strachwitz
J'Ai Faim, J'Ai Froid *84* Chantal Akerman
J'Ai Quelque Chose à Vous Dire *30* Marc Allégret
J'Ai 17 Ans *45* André Berthomieu
J'Ai Tant Danse *43* George Dunning
J'Ai Tout Donné *71* François Reichenbach
J'Ai Tué *24* Roger Lion
J'Ai Tué Raspoutine *67* Robert Hossein
J'Ai un Hanneton dans Mon Pantalon *06* Alice Guy-Blaché
Jaidev *87* Shyamal Mukherjee
Jail Bait *37* Charles Lamont
Jail Bait *54* Edward D. Wood, Jr.
Jail Bait *72* Rainer Werner Fassbinder
Jail Bird and How He Flew, The *06* J. Stuart Blackton
Jail Birds *23* Albert Brouett
Jail Birds *31* Ubbe Iwerks
Jail Break *35* Ralph Ince
Jail Break *46* Ray Nazarro
Jail Busters *55* William Beaudine
Jail House Blues *42* Albert S. Rogell
Jailbird, The *13* Edwin J. Collins
Jailbird, The *20* Lloyd Ingraham
Jailbird in Borrowed Feathers *10* Theo Bouwmeester
Jailbird, or The Bishop and the Convict, The *05* Charles Raymond
Jailbird Rock *88* Phillip Schuman
Jailbirds *31* James Parrott
Jailbirds *39* Oswald Mitchell
Jailbreak *36* Nick Grindé
Jailbreak *61* Luigi Comencini
Jailbreakers, The *60* Alexander Grasshoff
Jailhouse Rock *57* Richard Thorpe
J'Aime Toutes les Femmes *35* Karel Lamač
J'Aime, Tu Aimes *60* Alessandro Blasetti
Jaisi Karni Waisi Bharani *89* Vimal Kumar
Jaje *59* Vatroslav Mimica
Jak Básníkům Voní Život? *88* Dušan Klein
Jak Być Kochaną *62* Wojciech Has
Jak Se Člověk Naučil Létat *58* Jiří Brdečka
Jak Stařeček Měnil Až Vyměnil *52* Jiří Trnka
Jakarta *88* Charles Kaufman
Jake Speed *86* Andrew Lane
Jake the Plumber *27* Edward I. Luddy
Jake's Daughter *10* Theo Bouwmeester
Jako Jed *85* Vít Olmer
Jakob der Lügner *74* Frank Beyer
Jakob Hinter der Blauen Tür *88* Haro Senft
Jalisco Canta en Sevilla *48* Fernando De Fuentes
Jalisco Never Loses *37* Chano Urueta

Jalisco Nunca Pierde *37* Chano Urueta
Jalna *35* John Cromwell
Jalopy *53* William Beaudine
Jalousie de Barbouillé, La *27* Alberto Cavalcanti
Jalousie 1976 *76* Nadine Trintignant
Jalsaghar *58* Satyajit Ray
Jalwa *87* Punkaj Parashar
Jam Now in Season *06* Alf Collins
Jam Session *44* Charles Barton
Jama Masjid Street Journal *79* Mira Nair
Jamaica Inn *39* Alfred Hitchcock
Jamaica Run *53* Lewis R. Foster
Jamaican Gold *71* Henry Levin
Jamais Plus Toujours *75* Yannick Bellon
Jamboree *41* Joseph Santley
Jamboree *57* Roy Lockwood
Jambul *53* Yefim Dzigan
James and Gems *25* William C. Nolan
James Brothers, The *56* Nicholas Ray
James Brothers of Missouri, The *50* Fred C. Brannon
James Dean Story, The *57* Robert Altman, George W. George
James Joyce's Women *85* Michael Pearce
Jamestown *23* Edwin L. Hollywood
Jamestown Baloos *57* Robert Breer
Jamila el Gazairia *58* Youssef Chahine
Jamila the Algerian *58* Youssef Chahine
Jamila the Algerian Girl *58* Youssef Chahine
Jamilya *70* Irina Poplavskaya
Jan Garber and His Orchestra *41* Jean Negulesco
Jan Hus *54* Otakar Vávra
Jan Konstantin *61* Evald Schorm
Jan of the Big Snows *22* Charles M. Seay
Jan Petru's Return *86* Martin Tapak
Jan Žižka *54* Otakar Vávra
Jan Žižka z Trocnova *54* Otakar Vávra
Jana-Aranya *75* Satyajit Ray
Jana—Das Mädchen aus dem Böhmerwald *36* Emil Synek
Jane *15* Frank Lloyd
Jane *62* Robert Drew, Richard Leacock
Jane and the Lost City *87* Terence Marcel
Jane Austen in Manhattan *80* James Ivory
Jane B. by Agnès V. *88* Agnès Varda
Jane B. par Agnès V. *88* Agnès Varda
Jane Eyre *14* Martin J. Faust
Jane Eyre *21* Hugo Ballin
Jane Eyre *34* Christy Cabanne
Jane Eyre *44* Robert Stevenson
Jane Eyre *83* Julian Amyes
Jane Goes A'Wooing *18* George Melford
Jane Gray *11* Mario Caserini
Jane on the Warpath *06* Alf Collins
Jane Shore *11* Frank Powell
Jane Shore *15* Bert Haldane, F. Martin Thornton
Jane Shore *22* Edwin J. Collins
Jane Steps Out *38* Paul Stein
Jane's Engagement Party *26* Sam Newfield
Janes Gode Ven *19* Forest Holger-Madsen
Jane's Honeymoons *26* Charles Lamont
Jane's Predicament *26* Sam Newfield
Jane's Sleuth *27* Sam Newfield
Janet of the Chorus *15* Van Dyke Brooke
Janetana Sogand *88* Kishore Vyas
Janet's Flirtation *11* Lewin Fitzhamon

Jangle, Jangle Sound the Bells *55* Rajaram Vanakudre Shantaram
Jangnam *85* Doo-yong Lee
Janice *73* Joseph Strick
Janice Meredith *24* E. Mason Hopper
Janie *44* Michael Curtiz
Janie Gets Married *46* Vincent Sherman
Janis *74* Howard Alk, Seaton Findlay
Janitor, The *80* Peter Yates
Janitor in Trouble, A *1896* Georges Méliès
Janitors, The *17* Raoul Barré, Charles Bowers
Janitor's Vendetta, A *16* William Beaudine
Janitor's Wife's Temptation, A *15* Del Henderson
Jänken *70* Lars Forsberg
Janko the Musician *60* Jan Lenica
János Tornyai *62* Márta Mészáros
János Vitéz *39* Béla Gaál
Jánošík *35* Martin Frič
Jánošík I *62* Pal'o Bielek
Jánošík II *63* Pal'o Bielek
January Man, The *88* Pat O'Connor
January Ororma *87* Chandrakant Joshi
Janus-Faced *20* F. W. Murnau
Janus Head, The *20* F. W. Murnau
Januskopf, Der *20* F. W. Murnau
Janyo-Nok *85* Jin-woo Chung
Japan and the Japanese *70* Kon Ichikawa
Japan Sinks *73* Andrew Meyer, Shiro Moritani
Japanerin, Die *17* E. A. Dupont
Japanese Acrobats *04* Edwin S. Porter
Japanese Fantasy, A *09* Émile Cohl
Japanese Grandmothers *62* Tadashi Imai
Japanese House *55* Sidney Peterson
Japanese Idyll, A *12* Edwin S. Porter
Japanese Magic *09* Émile Cohl
Japanese Magic *12* Stuart Kinder
Japanese Nightingale, The *18* George Fitzmaurice
Japanese Summer: Double Suicide *67* Nagisa Oshima
Japanese Tragedy, A *45* Fumio Kamei
Japanese Tragedy, A *53* Keisuke Kinoshita
Japanese War Bride *51* King Vidor
Japon de Fantaisie *09* Émile Cohl
Japon, d'Hiver et d'Aujourd'hui *59* Pierre Kast*
Japon Insolite, Le *81* François Reichenbach
Japula *71* Michio Yamamoto
Jar Je Priya *88* Salil Datta
Jardim de Allah *89* David Neves
Jardín de la Tía Isabel, El *71* Felipe Cazals
Jardín de las Delicias, El *70* Carlos Saura
Jardín Secreto, El *85* Carlos Suárez
Jardin sur l'Oronte, Le *25* René Leprince
Jardinier, Le *1895* Louis Lumière
Jardinier Brûlant des Herbes *1896* Georges Méliès
Jardinier d'Argenteuil, Le *66* Jean-Paul Le Chanois
Jardins d'Arabie *63* Maurice Pialat
Jardins de Paris, Les *48* Alain Resnais
Jarnac's Treacherous Blow *09* Émile Cohl
Jarrapellejos *88* Antonio Gimenez-Rico
Járvány *75* Pál Gábor
Jascha Heifetz Master Class *62* Alexander Hammid, Francis Thompson

Jeff's Downfall *12* Bert Haldane

Jeff's Toothache *16* Charles Bowers

Jeg Elsker Dig *87* Li Vilstrup

Jeg et Hus Mig Bygge Vil *55* Henning Carlsen

Jeg Skal Ha' Briller *68* Jørgen Roos

Jego Wielka Miłość *36* Mieczysław Krawicz, S. Perzanowska

Jehanne *56* Robert Enrico

Jekyll and Hyde *10* Viggo Larsen

Jekyll and Hyde Portfolio, The *72* Eric Jeffrey Haims

Jekyll and Hyde...Together Again *82* Jerry Belson

Jekyll, Jr. *79* Steno

Jekyll's Inferno *60* Terence Fisher

Jelenlét *65* Miklós Jancsó

Jelf's *15* George Loane Tucker

Jelly Fish, The *26* Stephen Roberts*

Jemima and Johnny *66* Lionel Ngakane

Jemima and the Editor *12* Lewin Fitzhamon

Jemné Umění Obrany *88* Jana Semschová

Jenatsch *87* Daniel Schmid

Jenifer Hale *37* Bernerd Mainwaring

Jennie *40* David Burton

Jennie *48* William Dieterle

Jennie Gerhardt *33* Marion Gering

Jennie Lees Ha una Nuova Pistola *64* Tulio Demicheli

Jennie, Wife/Child *68* Robert Carl Cohen, James Landis

Jennifer *53* Joel Newton

Jennifer *64* Brian DePalma

Jennifer *78* Brice Mack

Jennifer on My Mind *71* Noel Black

Jennifer (The Snake Goddess) *78* Brice Mack

Jenny *36* Marcel Carné

Jenny *69* George Bloomfield

Jenny Be Good *20* William Desmond Taylor

Jenny Kissed Me *85* Brian Trenchard-Smith

Jenny Lamour *47* Henri-Georges Clouzot

Jenny Lind *30* Sidney Franklin

Jenny Lind *30* Arthur Robison

Jenny Omroyd of Oldham *20* Frank Etheridge

Jenny's Diary *75* Clive Donner

Jenny's Pearls *13* Mack Sennett

Jenseits des Rheins *60* André Cayatte

Jeopardy *52* John Sturges

Jephtah's Daughter *19* Robert Dinesen

Jeremiah Johnson *72* Sydney Pollack

Jeremy *73* Arthur Barron

Jericho *37* Thornton Freeland

Jéricho *46* Henri Calef

Jerk, The *79* Carl Reiner

Jerky Turkey *45* Tex Avery

Jernbanens Datter *11* August Blom

Jérôme Perreau, Héros des Barricades *35* Abel Gance

Jerrico the Wonder Clown *54* Joseph Pevney

Jerry *24* Carmine Gallone

Jerry and Jumbo *53* Joseph Barbera, William Hanna

Jerry and the Five Fifteen Train *20* Vernon Stallings

Jerry and the Goldfish *51* Joseph Barbera, William Hanna

Jerry and the Lion *50* Joseph Barbera, William Hanna

Jerry Builders, The *30* Monty Banks

Jerry-Built House, The *06* Lewin Fitzhamon

Jerry Jerry Quite Contrary *66* Chuck Jones

Jerry McDub Collects Some Accident Insurance *16* H. M. Freck

Jerry Saves the Navy *17* Gregory La Cava, Vernon Stallings

Jerry Ships a Circus *16* Gregory La Cava, Vernon Stallings

Jerry the Giant *26* Mark Sandrich, Lesley Selander

Jerry's Cousin *51* Joseph Barbera, William Hanna

Jerry's Diary *49* Joseph Barbera, William Hanna

Jerusalem File, The *71* John Flynn

Jerusalem Set Free *57* Carlo Ludovico Bragaglia

Jes' Call Me Jim *20* Clarence Badger

Jesień *56* Walerian Borowczyk

Jesse and Lester—Two Brothers in a Place Called Trinity *72* James London

Jesse James *27* Lloyd Ingraham

Jesse James *38* Henry King

Jesse James As the Outlaw *21* Franklin B. Coates

Jesse James at Bay *41* Joseph Kane

Jesse James, Jr. *42* George Sherman

Jesse James Meets Frankenstein's Daughter *66* William Beaudine

Jesse James Rides Again *47* Fred C. Brannon, Thomas Carr

Jesse James Under the Black Flag *21* Franklin B. Coates

Jesse James vs. the Daltons *53* William Castle

Jesse James' Women *54* Donald Barry

Jessica *61* Jean Negulesco, Oreste Palella

Jessica *67* J. L. Anderson

Jessica's First Prayer *08* Dave Aylott

Jessica's First Prayer *21* Bert Wynne

Jessie's Girls *75* Al Adamson

Jessy *61* Wolf Rilla

Jest, The *21* Fred Paul

Jest of God, A *68* Paul Newman

Jester, The *87* José Alvaro Morais

Jester and the Queen, The *88* Věra Chytilová

Jester's Joke, The *12* Walter R. Booth

Jester's Tale, The *64* Karel Zeman

Jesus *79* John Krish, Peter Sykes

Jesus Christ Superstar *73* Norman Jewison

Jésus de Montréal *89* Denys Arcand

Jesus of Montreal *89* Denys Arcand

Jesus of Nazareth *76* Franco Zeffirelli

Jesus Trip, The *71* Russ Mayberry

Jet Attack *58* Edward L. Cahn

Jet Cage, The *62* Friz Freleng

Jet Job *52* William Beaudine

Jet Men of the Air *51* Joseph Pevney

Jet Over the Atlantic *59* Byron Haskin

Jet Pilot *50* Jules G. Furthman, Josef von Sternberg

Jet Squad *58* Edward L. Cahn

Jet Storm *59* Cy Endfield

J'Étais une Aventurière *38* Raymond Bernard

Jetée, La *62* Chris Marker

Jetée et Plage de Trouville, 1ère Partie *1896* Georges Méliès

Jetée et Plage de Trouville, 2ème Partie *1896* Georges Méliès

Jetlag *81* Gonzalo Herraldo

Jetsons: The Movie *90* Joseph Barbera, William Hanna

Jetstream *59* Cy Endfield

Jettchen Gebert *18* Richard Oswald

Jetty, The *62* Chris Marker

Jeu avec le Feu, Le *74* Alain Robbe-Grillet

Jeu de la Vérité, Le *61* Robert Hossein

Jeu de l'Oie, Le *79* Raúl Ruiz

Jeu de Massacre *67* Alain Jessua

Jeu Si Simple, Un *64* Gilles Groulx

Jeu 1 *62* François Reichenbach, Dirk Sanders

Jeudi On Chantera Comme Dimanche *66* Henri Storck

Jeugddag *30* Joris Ivens

Jeune Fille, La *60* Luis Buñuel

Jeune Fille Assassinée, La *74* Roger Vadim

Jeune Fille au Jardin, La *36* Dmitri Kirsanov

Jeune Fille de France *38* Yves Allégret

Jeune Fille d'une Nuit, La *34* Reinhold Schünzel

Jeune Fille et les Leçons de l'Enfer, La *85* François Mimet

Jeune Fille un Seul Amour, Une *59* Robert Siodmak

Jeune Folle, La *52* Yves Allégret

Jeune Homme, Un *63* Jean-Pierre Melville

Jeune Homme et la Mort, Le *53* Kenneth Anger

Jeune Magicien, Le *87* Waldemar Dziki

Jeune Marie, Le *83* Bernard Stora

Jeune Morte, La *70* Claude Faraldo

Jeune Patriarche *57* Serge Bourguignon

Jeunes Filles de France *40* Marc Allégret*

Jeunes Filles en Détresse *39* G. W. Pabst

Jeunes Filles en Uniforme *58* Géza von Radványi

Jeunes Filles Impudiques *73* Jean Rollin

Jeunes Gens a Marier *12* Émile Cohl

Jeunes Loups, Les *67* Marcel Carné

Jeunes Mariés *53* Gilles Grangier

Jeunes Timides *42* Yves Allégret

Jeunesse *34* Georges Lacombe

Jeunesse de France *68* Marc Allégret

Jeunesses Musicales, Les *56* Claude Jutra

Jeux *62* François Reichenbach, Dirk Sanders

Jeux d'Adultes *67* Nanni Loy

Jeux Dangereux *58* Pierre Chénal

Jeux d'Artifices *87* Virginie Thevenet

Jeux de Cartes *16* Émile Cohl

Jeux de Femmes *46* Maurice Cloche

Jeux de l'Amour, Les *59* Philippe de Broca

Jeux de l'Été et de la Mer, Les *36* Henri Storck

Jeux d'Enfants *13* Henri Fescourt

Jeux d'Enfants *46* Jean Painlevé

Jeux des Anges, Les *64* Walerian Borowczyk

Jeux des Reflets et de la Vitesse *23* Henri Chomette

Jeux Interdits, Les *51* René Clément
Jeux Précoces *60* Damiano Damiani
Jeux Sont Faits, Les *47* Jean Delannoy
Jew at War, A *31* Grigori Roshal
Jew Suss *34* Lothar Mendes
Jew Suss *40* Veidt Harlan
Jewel *15* Phillips Smalley, Lois Weber
Jewel, The *33* Reginald Denham
Jewel Box from a Castle, A *87* Gulbeniz Azimzade
Jewel in Pawn, A *17* Jack Conway
Jewel in the Crown, The *84* Christopher Morahan, Jim O'Brien
Jewel of the Nile, The *85* Lewis Teague
Jewel Robbery *32* William Dieterle
Jewel Thieves, The *09* Lewin Fitzhamon
Jewel Thieves Outwitted, The *13* Frank Wilson
Jeweller's Shop, The *88* Michael Anderson
Jewels and Fine Clothes *12* Hugh Moss
Jewels and Jimjams *15* Dave Aylott
Jewels of Brandenburg *47* Eugene Forde
Jewels of Desire *27* Paul Powell
Jewels of Sacrifice *13* Allan Dwan
Jewish Daughter *33* George Roland
Jewish Father *34* Henry Lynn
Jewish King Lear *35* Harry Thomashefsky
Jewish Luck *25* Alexis Granowsky
Jewish Melody, The *40* Joseph Seiden
Jew's Christmas, The *13* Phillips Smalley, Lois Weber
Jews in Poland *57* B. Ladowicz
Jezebel *38* William Wyler
Jezebelles, The *75* Jack Hill
Jezebels, The *75* Jack Hill
Jezebel's Kiss *90* Harvey Keith
Jezioro Bodeńskie *86* Janusz Zaorski
Jézus Krisztus Horoszkópja *89* Miklós Jancsó
Jhanak, Jhanak Payal Baje *55* Rajaram Vanakudre Shantaram
Jhanjhaar *87* V. Shantaram
Jhoothi *87* Hrishikesh Mukherjee
Jíbaro *86* Daniel Díaz Torres
Jibun no Ana no Nakade *55* Tomu Uchida
Jiggin' on the Old Sod *21* Julian Ollendorff
Jiggs and Maggie in Court *48* William Beaudine, Edward F. Cline
Jiggs and Maggie in Jackpot Jitters *49* William Beaudine
Jiggs and Maggie in Society *47* Edward F. Cline
Jiggs and Maggie Out West *50* William Beaudine
Jigoku *60* Nobuo Nakagawa
Jigoku *81* Tatsumi Kumashiro
Jigokuhen *69* Shiro Toyoda
Jigokumon *53* Teinosuke Kinugasa
Jigsaw *44* Henry Cass
Jigsaw *49* Fletcher Markle
Jigsaw *62* Val Guest
Jigsaw *68* James Goldstone
Jigsaw Man, The *83* Terence Young
Jihi Shincho *27* Kenji Mizoguchi
Jikan no Kyōfu *60* Shigeaki Hidaka
Jill and the Old Fiddle *15* Hay Plumb
Jilt, The *09* D. W. Griffith
Jilt, The *22* Irving Cummings

Jilted *61* Gordon Douglas
Jilted *87* Bill Bennett
Jilted and Jolted *21* Wallace A. Carlson
Jilted Janet *18* Lloyd Ingraham
Jilted Woman's Revenge, A *08* Charles Raymond
Jim All-Alone *12* Warwick Buckland
Jim and the Pirates *87* Hans Alfredson
Jim Bludso *17* Tod Browning, Wilfred Lucas
Jim Bougne Boxeur *23* Henri Diamant-Berger
Jim Buck *77* Allan A. Buckhantz
Jim Grimsby's Boy *16* Reginald Barker
Jim Hanvey, Detective *37* Phil Rosen
Jim la Houlette, Roi des Voleurs *26* Pierre Colombier
Jim och Piraterna Blom *87* Hans Alfredson
Jim of the Mounted Police *11* Lewin Fitzhamon
Jim the Conqueror *27* George B. Seitz
Jim the Fireman *14* Bert Haldane
Jim the Man *67* Max Katz
Jim the Penman *15* Hugh Ford
Jim the Penman *21* Kenneth Webb
Jim the Penman *47* Frank Chisnell
Jim the Scorpion *15* H. Oceano Martinek
Jim the Signalman *06* J. H. Martin
Jim — The World's Greatest *76* Don Coscarelli, Craig Mitchell
Jim Thorpe — All American *51* Michael Curtiz
Jim Vaus Story, The *56* Dick Ross
Jimi *86* D. A. Pennebaker
Jimi Hendrix *73* Joe Boyd, John Head, Gary Weis
Jimi Plays Monterey *86* D. A. Pennebaker
Jiminy Crickets *25* Richard Wallace
Jimmie Higgins *33* George Tassin
Jimmie's Millions *25* James P. Hogan
Jimmy *16* A. V. Bramble, Eliot Stannard
Jimmy and Joe and the Water Spout *05* Percy Stow
Jimmy and Sally *33* James Tinling
Jimmy Boy *35* John Baxter
Jimmy Bruiteur *30* Jean Benoît-Lévy, Marie Epstein
Jimmy Lester, Convict and Gentleman *12* Warwick Buckland
Jimmy Orpheus *66* Roland Klick
Jimmy Reardon *87* William Richert
Jimmy the Boy Wonder *66* Herschell Gordon Lewis
Jimmy the Gent *34* Michael Curtiz
Jimmy the Kid *82* Gary Nelson
Jimmy Valentine *28* Jack Conway
Jimmy Valentine *36* Lewis D. Collins
Jimson Joins the Anarchists *11* Fred Rains
Jimson Joins the Piecans *11* Fred Rains
Jin *88* Ya-lin Li
Jinchōge *67* Yasuke Chiba
Jinete Sin Cabeza, El *56* Chano Urueta
Jingcha Gushi *85* Jackie Chan
Jingle Bells *27* Dave Fleischer
Jingle Bells *27* Walter Lantz
Jinks Joins the Temperance Club *11* Mack Sennett
Jinkyō *24* Kenji Mizoguchi
Jinpu Group, The *33* Kenji Mizoguchi

Jinpu-Ren *33* Kenji Mizoguchi
Jinruigaku Nyūmon *66* Shohei Imamura
Jinsei Gekijō *36* Tomu Uchida
Jinsei Gekijō — Hishakaku to Kiratsune *68* Tomu Uchida
Jinsei no Onimotsu *35* Heinosuke Gosho
Jinsei o Mitsumete *23* Teinosuke Kinugasa
Jinsei Tombogaeri *46* Tadashi Imai
Jinx, The *19* Victor Schertzinger
Jinx Money *48* William Beaudine
Jinxed! *82* Don Siegel
Jiny Vzduch *39* Martin Frič
Jinye Xingguang Canlan *89* Ann Hui
J'Irai Cracher sur Vos Tombes *62* Michael Gast
Jiro Monogatari *55* Hiroshi Shimizu
Jis Desh Men Ganga Behti *61* Raj Kapoor
Jitney Elopement, A *15* Charles Chaplin
Jitney Jack and Gasolena *16* Jay Evans
Jittemai *87* Hideo Gosha
Jitterbug Knights *39* Sid Marcus
Jitterbugs *43* Malcolm St. Clair
Jitters, The *38* Leslie Goodwins
Jitters, the Butler *32* Mark Sandrich
Jivaro *53* Edward Ludwig
Jive *79* Robert Downey
Jive Junction *43* Edgar G. Ulmer
Jive Turkey *76* Bill Brame
Jivin' and Jammin' *48* Frank Gardner
Jiyū Gakkyū *51* Kozaburo Yoshimura
Jó az Öreg a Háznál *35* Fritz Schulz, Andor Zsoldos
Jo Jo Dancer, Your Life Is Calling *86* Richard Pryor
Jo la Romance *49* Gilles Grangier
Jo the Crossing Sweeper *18* Alexander Butler
Jo the Wanderer's Boy *12* Warwick Buckland
Joachim's Dictionary *65* Walerian Borowczyk
Joan at the Stake *54* Roberto Rossellini
Joan, Carry It On *70* James Coyne, Robert Jones, Christopher Knight
Joan Lui: But One Monday I Arrive in Town *85* Adriano Celentano
Joan Lui: Ma un Giorno nel Paese Arrivo Io di Lunedi *85* Adriano Celentano
Joan Medford Is Missing *46* Jean Yarbrough
Joan of Arc *00* Georges Méliès
Joan of Arc *08* Albert Capellani
Joan of Arc *08* Mario Caserini
Joan of Arc *48* Victor Fleming
Joan of Arc at the Stake *54* Roberto Rossellini
Joan of Flanders *16* Herbert Brenon
Joan of Ozark *42* Joseph Santley
Joan of Paris *42* Robert Stevenson
Joan of Plattsburg *18* William Humphrey, George Loane Tucker
Joan of the Angels *60* Jerzy Kawalerowicz
Joan of the Woods *18* Travers Vale
Joan the Woman *16* Cecil B. DeMille
Joana a Francesa *73* Carlos Diegues
Joanna *25* Edwin Carewe
Joanna *68* Michael Sarne
João de Barro *55* Humberto Mauro
Joaquín Murrieta *58* Miguel Torres Contreras

Joaquín Murrieta *64* George Sherman

Joaquin Murrieta *70* Earl Bellamy

Job, The *61* Hasse Ekman

Job, The *61* Ermanno Olmi

Jób Lázadása *83* Imre Gyöngyössy, Barna Kabay

Job Offer *79* Jean Eustache

Jobard a Tue Sa Belle-Mère *11* Émile Cohl

Jobard Amoureux Timide *11* Émile Cohl

Jobard Change de Bonne *11* Émile Cohl

Jobard Chauffeur *11* Émile Cohl

Jobard Est Demande en Mariage *11* Émile Cohl

Jobard Fiancé par Intérim *11* Émile Cohl

Jobard Garçon de Recettes *11* Émile Cohl

Jobard Ne Peut Pas Rire *11* Émile Cohl

Jobard Ne Peut Pas Voir les Femmes Travailler *11* Émile Cohl

Jobard Portefaux par Amour *11* Émile Cohl

Jobson's Luck *13* H. Oceano Martinek

Jocaste *27* Gaston Ravel

Jocelyn *22* Léon Poirier

Jock Petersen *74* Tim Burstall

Jockey, The *14* F. L. Lyndhurst

Jockey of Death, The *16* M. Lind

Jocko Musicien *03* Alice Guy-Blaché

Jocko the Artist *09* Émile Cohl

Jocks *84* Steve Carver

Joconde, La *14* Louis Feuillade

Joconde, La *57* Henri Gruel

Jocular Winds, The *13* Allan Dwan

Joe *70* John G. Avildsen

Joe and Ethel Turp Call on the President *39* Robert B. Sinclair

Joe and Maxi *80* Maxi Cohen, Joel Gold

Joe Boko Breaking Into the Big League *14* Wallace A. Carlson

Joe Boko in a Close Shave *15* Wallace A. Carlson

Joe Boko in Canimated Nooz Pictorial No. 8 *16* Wallace A. Carlson

Joe Boko in Saved by Gasoline *15* Wallace A. Carlson

Joe Boko's Adventures *16* Wallace A. Carlson

Joe Butterfly *57* Jesse Hibbs

Joe, Cercati un Posto per Morire *68* Giuliano Carmineo

Joe Cocker, Mad Dogs and Englishmen *70* Pierre Adidge

Joe Dakota *57* Richard Bartlett

Joe el Implacable *66* Sergio Corbucci

Joe Glow, the Firefly *41* Chuck Jones

Joe Hill *71* Bo Widerberg

Joe Kidd *72* John Sturges

Joe l'Implacabile *66* Antonio Margheriti

Joe Louis Story, The *53* Robert Gordon

Joe Macbeth *55* Ken Hughes

Joe Named Palooka, A *48* Reginald LeBorg

Joe Navidad *67* Rudolf Zehetgruber

Joe Palooka *34* Ben Stoloff

Joe Palooka, Champ *46* Reginald LeBorg

Joe Palooka in Fighting Mad *48* Reginald LeBorg

Joe Palooka in Humphrey Takes a Chance *50* Jean Yarbrough

Joe Palooka in The Big Fight *49* Cy Endfield

Joe Palooka in The Counterpunch *49* Reginald LeBorg

Joe Palooka in The Knockout *47* Reginald LeBorg

Joe Palooka in the Squared Circle *50* Reginald LeBorg

Joe Palooka in Triple Cross *50* Reginald LeBorg

Joe Palooka in Winner Take All *48* Reginald LeBorg

Joe Palooka Meets Humphrey *50* Jean Yarbrough

Joe Panther *76* Paul Krasny

Joe Reichmann and His Orchestra *40* Jean Negulesco

Joe Smith, American *41* Richard Thorpe

Joe Valachi: I Segreti di Cosa Nostra *72* Terence Young

Joe Versus the Volcano *90* John Patrick Shanley

Jōen *59* Teinosuke Kinugasa

Jōen no Chimata *22* Kenji Mizoguchi

Joe's Bed-Stuy Barbershop: We Cut Heads *82* Spike Lee

Joey *77* Horace Jackson

Joey *85* Joseph Ellison

Joey *85* Roland Emmerich

Joey and Sam *65* Roy Benson

Joey Boy *65* Frank Launder

Joey Knows a Villain *60* James Richards

Joey Leads the Way *60* James Richards

Joey the Showman *16* Joe Evans

Joey Walks in His Sleep *16* Joe Evans

Joey's Apache Mania *16* Joe Evans

Joey's Aunt *16* Joe Evans

Joey's Automatic Furniture *16* Joe Evans

Joey's Black Defeat *16* Joe Evans

Joey's Dream *16* Joe Evans

Joey's High Jinks *16* Joe Evans

Joey's Liar Meter *16* Joe Evans

Joey's Night Escapade *16* Joe Evans

Joey's No Ass *60* James Richards

Joey's Permit *16* Joe Evans

Joey's Pluck *16* Joe Evans

Joey's Twenty-First Birthday *15* Joe Evans

Jofroi *33* Marcel Pagnol

Jōgashima *24* Daisuke Ito

Jogo Duro *86* Ugo Giorgetti

Jogo Perigoso *66* Luis Alcoriza, Arturo Ripstein

Johan *20* Arthur Nordeen, Mauritz Stiller

Johan Ekberg *64* Jan Troell

Johan Sebastian Bach *61* Philip Wrestler

Johan Ulfstjerna *23* John W. Brunius

Johan Ulfstjerna *36* Gustaf Edgren

Johann Mouse *53* Joseph Barbera, William Hanna

Johann the Coffin Maker *27* Robert Florey

Johanna d'Arc of Mongolia *89* Ulrike Ottinger

Johanna Enlists *18* William Desmond Taylor

Johannes Feuer *40* Arthur Maria Rabenalt

Johannes, Fils de Johannes *18* André Hugon

Johannes Hemmelighed *85* Åke Sandgren

Johannes Jørgensen i Assissi *50* Jørgen Roos

Johannes Jørgensen i Svendborg *54* Jørgen Roos

Johannes Larsen *57* Jørgen Roos

Johannes V. Jensen *47* Jørgen Roos

Johannesnacht *35* Willy Reiber

Johansson and Vestman *46* Olof Molander

Johansson Gets Scolded *45* Sigurd Wallen

John and Julie *55* William Fairchild

John and Mary *69* Peter Yates

John and the Magic Music Man *76* Ciarin Scott

John and the Missus *87* Gordon Pinsent

John Barleycorn *14* Hobart Bosworth

John Bull's Fireside *03* George Albert Smith

John Bull's Hearth *03* George Albert Smith

John Carter's Double *16* Ernest G. Batley

John Citizen *27* Widgey R. Newman

John Dillinger, Killer *45* Max Nosseck

John Doe, Dynamite *41* Frank Capra

John Ericsson Victor of Hampton Roads *37* Gustaf Edgren

John Ermine of Yellowstone *17* Francis Ford

John F. Kennedy: Years of Lightning, Day of Drums *64* Bruce Herschensohn

John Forrest Finds Himself *20* Henry Edwards

John Gilpin *08* Percy Stow

John Gilpin *51* John Halas

John Gilpin's Ride *08* Lewin Fitzhamon

John Glayde's Honor *15* George Irving

John Goldfarb, Please Come Home *64* J. Lee-Thompson

John Halifax, Gentleman *15* George Pearson

John Halifax, Gentleman *38* George King

John Henry and the Inky Poo *46* George Pal

John Heriot's Wife *20* B. E. Doxat-Pratt

John il Bastardo *67* Armando Crispino

John Linworth's Atonement *14* Frank Wilson

John Loves Mary *49* David Butler

John Meade's Woman *37* Richard Wallace

John Needham's Double *16* Phillips Smalley, Lois Weber

John of the Fair *52* Michael McCarthy

John Paul Jones *59* John Farrow

John Pawkson's Brutality *15* Edwin J. Collins

John Pellet's Dream *16* Rupert Julian

John Petticoats *19* Lambert Hillyer

John Rance, Gentleman *14* Van Dyke Brooke

John Smith *22* Victor Heerman

John Smith Wakes Up *40* Jiří Weiss

John the Bastard *67* Armando Crispino

John the Hero *39* Béla Gaál

John the Soldier, or Vengeance *39* Louis Gasnier

John the Tenant *17* Michael Curtiz

John the Younger Brother *19* Michael Curtiz

John Tobin's Sweetheart *13* George D. Baker

John Wesley *54* Norman Walker

Johnny Allegro *49* Ted Tetzlaff

Johnny Angel *45* Edwin L. Marin

Johnny Apollo *40* Henry Hathaway

Johnny Banco *66* Yves Allégret

Johnny Banco — Geliebter Taugenichts 66 Yves Allégret
Johnny Be Good 88 Bud Smith
Johnny Belinda 48 Jean Negulesco
Johnny Cash: The Man, His World, His Music 69 Robert Elfstrom
Johnny Come Lately 43 William K. Howard
Johnny Comes Flying Home 46 Ben Stoloff
Johnny Concho 56 Don McGuire
Johnny Cool 63 William Asher
Johnny Dangerously 84 Amy Heckerling
Johnny Dark 54 George Sherman
Johnny Doesn't Live Here Any More 44 Joe May
Johnny Doughboy 42 John H. Auer
Johnny Eager 41 Mervyn LeRoy
Johnny Firecloud 75 William Allen Castleman
Johnny Frenchman 45 Charles Frend
Johnny Get Your Gun 19 Donald Crisp
Johnny Get Your Hair Cut 26 B. Reeves Eason, Archie Mayo
Johnny Got His Gun 71 Dalton Trumbo
Johnny Guitar 54 Nicholas Ray
Johnny Hallyday 71 François Reichenbach
Johnny Hamlet 68 Enzo G. Castellari
Johnny Handsome 89 Walter Hill
Johnny Holiday 49 Willis Goldbeck
Johnny in the Clouds 45 Anthony Asquith
Johnny Monroe 87 Renaud Saint-Pierre
Johnny Nobody 61 Nigel Patrick
Johnny North 64 Don Siegel
Johnny O'Clock 47 Robert Rossen
Johnny on the Run 52 Lewis Gilbert, Vernon Harris
Johnny-on-the-Spot 19 Harry Franklin
Johnny on the Spot 54 Maclean Rogers
Johnny One-Eye 49 Robert Florey
Johnny Oro 66 Sergio Corbucci
Johnny Reno 66 R. G. Springsteen
Johnny Ring and the Captain's Sword 21 Norman L. Stevens
Johnny Rocco 58 Paul Landres
Johnny Shiloh 63 James Neilson
Johnny Smith and Poker Huntas 38 Tex Avery
Johnny Steals Europe 32 Harry Piel
Johnny Stool Pigeon 49 William Castle
Johnny the Giant Killer 53 Charles Frank, Jean Image
Johnny Tiger 66 Paul Wendkos
Johnny Tremain 57 Robert Stevenson
Johnny Trouble 57 John H. Auer
Johnny Vagabond 43 William K. Howard
Johnny Vik 73 Charles Nauman
Johnny West il Mancino 65 Gianfranco Parolini
Johnny, You're Wanted 56 Vernon Sewell
Johnny Yuma 66 Romolo Guerrieri
Johnny's Days 71 François Reichenbach
Johnny's Gun 07 Lewin Fitzhamon
Johnny's Rim 07 Frank Mottershaw
Johnny's Romeo 16 Harry S. Palmer
Johnny's Stepmother and the Cat 16 Harry S. Palmer
Johnson at the Wedding 11 Theo Bouwmeester

Johnson's Strong Ale 11 Fred Rains
Johnstown Flood, The 26 Irving Cummings
Johnstown Monster, The 71 Olaf Pooley
Joi Baba Felunath 78 Satyajit Ray
Jōi-Uchi 67 Masaki Kobayashi
Joie de Revivre, La 47 Henri Storck
Joie de Vivre 34 Anthony Gross, Hector Hoppin
Join Our Ranks 59 Gleb Panfilov
Join the Marines 37 Ralph Staub
Joining the Tanks 18 Raoul Barré, Charles Bowers
Joining Up 28 Hugh Croise
Joint Affair, A 29 Manny Gould, Ben Harrison
Joint Brothers, The 86 Hervé Palud
Joke, The 68 Jaromil Jireš
Joke in Jerks, A 14 Dave Aylott
Joke of Destiny, A 83 Lina Wertmuller
Joke of Destiny Lying in Wait Around the Corner Like a Robber, A 83 Lina Wertmuller
Joke of Destiny Lying in Wait Around the Corner Like a Street Bandit, A 83 Lina Wertmuller
Joke on Grandma 01 Edwin S. Porter
Joke on the Gardener, A 1898 George Albert Smith
Joke on the Joker, The 12 Mack Sennett
Joke on the Motorist, A 04 Charles Raymond
Joke That Failed, The 04 Percy Stow
Joke That Failed, The 17 Frank Wilson
Joke That Failed, The 21 Fred Paul, Jack Raymond
Jokei 59 Kon Ichikawa, Yasuzo Masumura, Kozaburo Yoshimura
Joker, The 60 Philippe de Broca
Joker, Der 88 Peter Patzak
Joker Is Wild, The 57 Charles Vidor
Jokers, The 66 Michael Winner
Joker's Banquet, The 41 Alessandro Blasetti
Joker's Mistake, The 12 Walter R. Booth
Jokes My Folks Never Told Me 79 Gerry Woolery
Joko Invoca Dio...e Muori 68 Antonio Margheriti
Jokyō 59 Kon Ichikawa, Yasuzo Masumura, Kozaburo Yoshimura
Jokyū Aishi 30 Heinosuke Gosho
Jola 20 Władysław Starewicz
Jolanda — La Figlia del Corsaro Nero 52 Mario Soldati
Joli Mai, Le 63 Chris Marker
Jolifou Inn 55 Colin Low
Jolly Bad Fellow, A 63 Don Chaffey
Jolly, Clown da Circo 23 Mario Camerini
Jolly Farmers, The 30 R. E. Jeffrey
Jolly Fellows 34 Grigori Alexandrov
Jolly Genie, The 64 Wesley Barry
Jolly Jilter, The 27 Edward F. Cline
Jolly Jottings by Hy Mayer 13 Hy Mayer
Jolly Little Elves 34 Walter Lantz
Jolly Old Couple, A 00 George Albert Smith
Jolly Old Higgins 40 Gus Meins
Jolly Tars 26 Norman Taurog
Jolly Whirl, The 10 Émile Cohl

Jollyboy's Dream 14 Dave Aylott
Jolson Sings Again 49 Henry Levin
Jolson Story, The 46 Alfred E. Green, Joseph H. Lewis
Jolt, The 21 George Marshall
Jolt for General Germ, A 31 Dave Fleischer
Jom 82 Ababacar Samb Makharam
Jom: Ou, L'Histoire d'un Peuple 82 Ababacar Samb Makharam
Jon az Öcsém 19 Michael Curtiz
Jonah Man, The 04 Lewin Fitzhamon, Cecil M. Hepworth
Jonah Man, or The Traveller Bewitched, The 04 Lewin Fitzhamon, Cecil M. Hepworth
Jonah Who Will Be 25 in the Year 2000 75 Alain Tanner
Jonas 59 Ottomar Domnick
Jonáš, Dejme Tomu ve Středu 86 Vladimír Sís
Jonas Qui Aura 25 Ans en l'An 2000 75 Alain Tanner
Jonas, Say, for Instance, on Wednesday 86 Vladimír Sís
Jonas 39.5 C 89 Vladimír Sís
Jonathan 69 Hans W. Geissendörfer
Jonathan Livingston Seagull 73 Hall Bartlett
Jonathan — Vampiren Sterben Nicht 69 Hans W. Geissendörfer
Jones and His New Neighbors 09 D. W. Griffith
Jones and the Lady Book Agent 09 D. W. Griffith
Jones at the Ball 08 D. W. Griffith
Jones' Birthday 07 Harold Hough
Jones Boys' Sister, The 23 W. E. Stark
Jones' Burglar 09 D. W. Griffith
Jones Buys China 10 Fred Rains
Jones Dresses for the Pageant 10 Fred Rains
Jones Entertains 08 D. W. Griffith
Jones Family in Hollywood, The 39 Malcolm St. Clair
Jones Family in Quick Millions, The 39 Malcolm St. Clair
Jones Junior, or Money for Nothing 10 Fred Rains
Jones' Lottery Prize — A Husband 10 Fred Rains
Jones' Mistake 12 Edwin J. Collins
Jones' Nightmare 11 Fred Rains
Jones Tests His Wife's Courage 10 Frank Wilson
Joneses Have Amateur Theatricals, The 09 D. W. Griffith
Jōnetsu no Ichiya 29 Heinosuke Gosho
Joni 80 James F. Collier
Joniko 69 Ford Beebe
Joniko and the Kush Ta Ka 69 Ford Beebe
Jonker Diamond, The 36 Jacques Tourneur
Jonny Rettet Nebrador 53 Rudolf Jügert
Jonny Roova 85 John Olsson
Jonny Stiehlt Europa 32 Harry Piel
Jönsson Gang Turns Up Again, The 86 Mikael Ekman
Jönssonligan Dyker Upp Igen 86 Mikael Ekman

Jonube Shahr *59* Farrokh Ghaffary
Jōō Bachi *78* Kon Ichikawa
Jord *87* Petter Vennerød, Svend Wam
Jordan Is a Hard Road *15* Allan Dwan
Jordens Hævn *15* Forest Holger-Madsen
Jorge, a Brazilian *89* Paulo Thiago
Jorge Amado no Cinema *79* Glauber
   Rocha
Jorge um Brasileiro *89* Paulo Thiago
Jørgen Roos Zeigt Hamburg *61* Jørgen
   Roos
Jorjamado no Cinema *79* Glauber Rocha
Jorobado de la Morgue, El *72* Javier
   Aguirre
Jory *72* Jorge Fons
José Torres *59* Hiroshi Teshigahara
José Torres II *65* Hiroshi Teshigahara
Josef Drenters *60* Allan King
Josef und Seine Brüder *22* Carl Fröhlich
Josei ni Kansuru Jūnishō *54* Kon Ichikawa
Josei no Shōri *46* Kenji Mizoguchi
Josei wa Tsuyoshi *24* Kenji Mizoguchi
Joseph and His Brethren *22* Carl Fröhlich
Joseph and His Brethren *60* Irving Rap-
   per, Luciano Ricci
Joseph Andrews *77* Tony Richardson
Joseph Desa *61* Edward Dmytryk
Joseph in the Land of Egypt *14* W.
   Eugene Moore
Joseph in the Land of Egypt *32* George
   Roland
Joseph Kilián *63* Pavel Juráček, Jan
   Schmidt
Joseph Mánes *52* Břetislav Pojar
Joseph Schmidt Story, The *33* Richard
   Oswald
Joseph Sold by His Brothers *60* Irving
   Rapper, Luciano Ricci
Josepha *82* Christopher Frank
Josephine and Her Lovers *10* Lewin Fitz-
   hamon
Josephine and Men *55* Roy Boulting
Josette *36* Christian-Jaque
Josette *38* Allan Dwan
Joshilaay *89* Sibte Hasan Rizvi
Josh's Suicide *11* Mack Sennett
Joshua *76* Larry Spangler
Joshua, a Nigerian Portrait *62* Allan King
Joshua—Joshua *87* Avi Cohen
Joshua Then and Now *85* Ted Kotcheff
Jóslat *20* Pál Fejős
Josselyn's Wife *19* Howard Hickman
Josselyn's Wife *26* Richard Thorpe
Josser in the Army *32* Norman Lee
Josser Joins the Navy *32* Norman Lee
Josser, K.C. *29* Hugh Croise
Josser on the Farm *34* T. Hayes Hunter
Josser on the River *32* Norman Lee
Jōtai *69* Yasuzo Masumura
Jōtai Sambashi *59* Teruo Ishii
Jouet, Le *76* Francis Veber
Jouets Animés, Les *12* Émile Cohl
Jouets Vivants, Les *08* Segundo De
   Chomón
Joueur, Le *38* Louis Daquin, Gerhard
   Lamprecht
Joueur, Le *58* Claude Autant-Lara
Joueur d'Échecs, Le *27* Raymond Bernard
Joueur d'Échecs, Le *30* Henri Dupuy-
   Mazuel

Joueur d'Échecs, Le *38* Jean Dréville
Joujoux Savants, Les *12* Émile Cohl
Joukovsky *50* Vsevolod I. Pudovkin,
   Dmitri Vasiliev
Jour Comme les Autres, Un *52* Georges
   Rouquier
Jour de Fête *47* Jacques Tati
Jour de Fête *49* Joseph Strick
Jour de Marché à Trouville *1896* Georges
   Méliès
Jour de Tournage *69* Chris Marker
Jour des Parques, Le *70* Claude Chabrol
Jour du Frotteur, Le *32* Alberto Cavalcanti
Jour du Terme, Le *04* Alice Guy-Blaché
Jour et l'Heure, Le *62* René Clément
Jour et Nuit *86* Jean-Bernard Menoud
Jour Pina M'à Demandé, Un *88* Chantal
   Akerman
Jour "S"..., Le *84* Jean-Pierre Lefèbvre
Jour Se Lève, Le *39* Marcel Carné
Journal Animé, Le *08* Émile Cohl
Journal de la Résistance *45* Jean Grémillon
Journal d'un Curé de Campagne *50* Rob-
   ert Bresson
Journal d'un Fou, Le *87* Roger Coggio
Journal d'un Scélérat *50* Eric Rohmer
Journal d'une Femme de Chambre, Le *63*
   Luis Buñuel
Journal d'une Femme en Blanc, Le *65*
   Claude Autant-Lara
Journal of a Crime *34* William Keighley
Journal of an Exhausted Man *68* Masaki
   Kobayashi
Journal of the Orange Flower *59* Heino-
   suke Gosho
Journal Tombe à Cinq Heures, Le *42*
   Georges Lacombe
Journalist *27* Lev Kuleshov
Journalist, The *66* Sergei Gerasimov
Journée Bien Remplié, Une *73* Jean-Louis
   Trintignant
Journée de Flambeau, La *16* Émile Cohl*
Journée Naturelle *47* Alain Resnais
Journey, The *58* Anatole Litvak
Journey *72* Paul Almond
Journey, The *73* Vittorio De Sica
Journey, The *86* Markus Imhoof
Journey, The *86* Peter Watkins
Journey Ahead *47* Peter Mills
Journey Among Women *77* Tom Cowan
Journey Back to Oz *64* Hal Sutherland
Journey Beneath the Desert *61* Frank Bor-
   zage, Giuseppe Masini, Edgar G. Ulmer
Journey Beyond Three Seas *57* Khwaja
   Ahmad Abbas, Vassili M. Pronin
Journey by Way of the Hand, A *83* Raúl
   Ruiz
Journey for Jeremy *47* James Hill
Journey for Margaret *42* W. S. Van Dyke
Journey from Berlin 1971 *80* Yvonne
   Rainer
Journey from the Shadows *38* Jiří Weiss
Journey Into Autumn *54* Ingmar Bergman
Journey Into Darkness *68* James Hill,
   Peter Sasdy
Journey Into Fear *42* Norman Foster, Or-
   son Welles
Journey Into Fear *75* Daniel Mann
Journey Into Light *51* Stuart Heisler
Journey Into Medicine *46* Willard Van

Dyke
Journey Into Midnight *68* Roy Ward
   Baker, Alan Gibson
Journey Into Nowhere *63* Denis Scully
Journey Into Prehistory, A *54* Karel
   Zeman
Journey Into Primeval Times, A *54* Karel
   Zeman
Journey Into the Night *20* F. W. Murnau
Journey of a Thousand and One Nights *36*
   Hiroshi Inagaki
Journey of a Young Composer *86* Georgy
   Shengelaya
Journey of Dr. Kotnis, The *46* Rajaram
   Vanakudre Shantaram
Journey of Hope *90* Xavier Koller
Journey of Natty Gann, The *85* Jeremy
   Paul Kagan
Journey of Vincenc Moštek and Simon Pešl
   of Vlčnov to Prague, 1969 A.D., The *69*
   Jaromil Jireš
Journey Out *45* Alf Sjöberg
Journey Round My Skull *70* György
   Révész
Journey Through Rosebud *72* Tom Gries
Journey Through the Past *72* Neil Young
Journey to Cythera *84* Theodoros Angelo-
   poulos
Journey to Freedom *57* Robert C. Dertano
Journey to Italy *53* Roberto Rossellini
Journey to Jerusalem, A *68* Michael Mind-
   lin, Jr.
Journey to Love *53* Giorgio Pastina
Journey to Primeval Times, A *54* Karel
   Zeman
Journey to Shiloh *68* William Hale
Journey to Spirit Island *88* László Pál
Journey to the Beginning of Time *54*
   Karel Zeman
Journey to the Center of the Earth *59*
   Henry Levin
Journey to the Center of the Earth *87*
   Rusty Lemorande
Journey to the Center of Time *67* David
   L. Hewitt
Journey to the Far Side of the Sun *69*
   Robert Parrish
Journey to the Lost City *58* Fritz Lang
Journey to the Middle of the Earth, A *09*
   Segundo De Chomón
Journey to the Outer Limits *74* Alexander
   Grasshoff
Journey to the Seventh Planet *61* Rudolf
   Zehetgruber
Journey to You, The *53* Stig Olin
Journey Together *45* John Boulting
Journey with Father *68* Vilgot Sjöman
Journey with Jacob *73* Pál Gábor
Journey's End *18* Travers Vale
Journey's End, The *21* Hugo Ballin
Journey's End *30* James Whale
Jours de Fête à Moscou *57* Jean Valère
Jours de 36 *72* Theodoros Angelopoulos
Jours de Volotchaiev, Les *37* Georgy
   Vasiliev, Sergei Vasiliev
Jours d'Octobre, Les *58* Sergei Vasiliev
Jours Tranquilles à Clichy *90* Claude
   Chabrol
Jovanka e l'Altri *59* Martin Ritt
Joven, La *60* Luis Buñuel

Jovencito Drácula, El 75 Carlos Benito Parra
Jóvenes, Los 60 Luis Alcoriza
Jovial Expressions 05 Tom Green
Jovial Fluid, The 13 Will P. Kellino
Jovial Monks No. 1, The 1899 James A. Williamson
Jovial Monks No. 2 — Tit for Tat, The 1899 James A. Williamson
Jovita 70 Janusz Morgenstern
Jowita 70 Janusz Morgenstern
Joy 83 Sergio Bergonzelli
Joy and Joan 85 Jacques Saurel
Joy and the Dragon 16 Henry King
Joy Girl, The 27 Allan Dwan
Joy House 63 René Clément
Joy in the Morning 65 Alex Segal
Joy of Learning, The 67 Jean-Luc Godard
Joy of Living 38 Tay Garnett
Joy of Loving 54 Marc Allégret
Joy of Sex 84 Martha Coolidge
Joy Parade, The 37 William A. Seiter
Joy Ride 35 Harry Hughes
Joy Ride 58 Edward Bernds
Joy Ride to Nowhere 78 Ernst R. von Theumer
Joy Street 29 Raymond Cannon
Joy Tonic 29 Charles Lamont
Joyeaux Microbes, Les 09 Émile Cohl
Joyeuse Prison, La 56 André Berthomieu
Joyeux Prophète Russe, Le 04 Georges Méliès
Joyeux Tromblons, Les 75 Henri Storck
Joyful Wisdom, The 67 Jean-Luc Godard
Joyless Street, The 25 G. W. Pabst
Joyous Adventures of Aristide Pujol, The 20 Frank Miller
Joyous Eve, The 60 Fons Rademakers
Joyous Heroes, The 89 Ziniu Wu
Joyous Liar, The 19 Ernest C. Warde
Joyous Troublemakers, The 20 J. Gordon Edwards
Joyride 77 Joseph Ruben
Joys Elope, The 16 Gregory La Cava
Joys of Torture, The 68 Teruo Ishii
Joysticks 82 Greydon Clark
Joyū 47 Teinosuke Kinugasa
Joyū 56 Kaneto Shindo
Joyū Sumako no Koi 47 Kenji Mizoguchi
Joyū to Shijin 35 Mikio Naruse
Jsi Falešný Hráč 86 Zdeněk Zelenka
Ju Dou 89 Yimou Zhang
Ju-Jitsu 07 Alf Collins
Ju-Jitsu to the Rescue 13 Charles Raymond
Juan José 17 Ricardo De Baños
Juan Moreira 09 Mario Gallo
Juan Soldado, o Venganza 39 Louis Gasnier
Juana Gallo 61 Miguel Zacarías
Juana la Cantinera 87 Pepe Loza
Juana the Saloon Keeper 87 Pepe Loza
Juarez 39 William Dieterle
Juárez and Maximillian 33 Miguel Torres Contreras
Juárez y Maximiliano 33 Miguel Torres Contreras
Jubal 56 Delmer Daves
Jubiabá 85 Nelson Pereira Dos Santos
Jubilation Street 44 Keisuke Kinoshita
Jubilee 44 Vladimir Petrov

Jubilee 62 Kazimierz Karabasz
Jubilee 78 Christopher Hobbs, Derek Jarman
Jubilee Story 59 Andrzej Munk
Jubilee Trail 54 Joseph Kane
Jubilee Window 35 George Pearson
Jubilej G. Ikla 55 Vatroslav Mimica
Jubilo 19 Clarence Badger
Jucklins, The 20 George Melford
Jud 71 Gunther Collins
Jud Süss 40 Veidt Harlan
Júdás 18 Michael Curtiz
Judas 30 Yevgeni Ivanov-Barkov
Judas 37 Manuel R. Ojeda
Judas City 65 Marshall Smith
Judas Money 15 Victor Sjöström
Judas von Tirol, Der 35 Franz Osten
Judas Was a Woman 38 Jean Renoir
Judaspengar 15 Victor Sjöström
Judaspengene 15 Victor Sjöström
Judex 16 Louis Feuillade
Judex 33 Maurice Champreux
Judex 63 Georges Franju
Judge, The 48 Elmer Clifton
Judge, The 60 Alf Sjöberg
Judge and the Assassin, The 75 Bertrand Tavernier
Judge and the Sinner, The 64 Paul Verhoeven
Judge Brown's Justice 17 King Vidor
Judge for a Day 35 Dave Fleischer
Judge Hardy and Son 39 George B. Seitz
Judge Hardy's Children 38 George B. Seitz
Judge Her Not 21 George Edwardes Hall
Judge Jefferson Remembers 45 Ronald Haines
Judge Not 14 Victor Sjöström
Judge Not 15 Robert Z. Leonard
Judge Not 20 Einar J. Bruun
Judge Not, or The Woman of Mona Diggins 15 Robert Z. Leonard
Judge Pimple 15 Fred Evans, Joe Evans
Judge Priest 34 John Ford
Judge Rummy in Bear Facts 20 Gregory La Cava
Judge Rummy's Miscue 19 Gregory La Cava
Judge Rummy's Off Day 18 Gregory La Cava
Judge Steps Out, The 49 Boris Ingster
Judged by Appearances 14 Hay Plumb
Judged by Appearances 16 Hugh Croise
Judge's Crossword Puzzles No. 1 25 John Colman Terry
Judge's Crossword Puzzles No. 2 25 John Colman Terry
Judge's Crossword Puzzles No. 3 25 John Colman Terry
Judge's Crossword Puzzles No. 4 25 John Colman Terry
Judge's Crossword Puzzles No. 5 25 John Colman Terry
Judge's Crossword Puzzles No. 6 25 John Colman Terry
Judge's Crossword Puzzles No. 7 25 John Colman Terry
Judge's Crossword Puzzles No. 8 25 John Colman Terry
Judge's Crossword Puzzles No. 9 25 John

Colman Terry
Judge's Crossword Puzzles No. 10 25 John Colman Terry
Judge's Friend, The 79 Fons Rademakers
Judgment 09 Gilbert M. Anderson
Judgment 16 Ernest G. Batley
Judgment, The 22 Mauritz Stiller
Judgment at Nuremberg 61 Stanley Kramer
Judgment Book, The 35 Charles Hutchinson
Judgment Deferred 51 John Baxter
Judgment House, The 17 J. Stuart Blackton
Judgment in Berlin 86 Leo Penn
Judgment in Stone, A 86 Ousama Rawi
Judgment in the Sun 63 Martin Ritt
Judgment of the Guilty 16 Jack Conway
Judgment of the Hills 27 James Leo Meehan
Judgment of the Mad 62 Grigori Roshal
Judgment of the People 47 Roman Karmen
Judgment of the Storm 24 Del Andrews
Judith 65 Daniel Mann
Judith and Holophernes 58 Fernando Cerchio
Judith et Holopherne 09 Louis Feuillade
Judith of Bethulia 13 D. W. Griffith
Judith of the Cumberlands 16 John P. McGowan
Judith Trachtenberg 20 Henryk Galeen
Judo Saga 43 Akira Kurosawa
Judo Saga 65 Seiichiro Uchikawa
Judo Saga II 45 Akira Kurosawa
Judo Showdown 66 Masateru Nishiyama
Judou 89 Yimou Zhang
Judy Buys a Horse 39 Lance Comfort
Judy Forgot 15 T. Hayes Hunter
Judy Goes to Town 41 Joseph Santley
Judy of Rogues' Harbor 20 William Desmond Taylor
Judy's Little No-No 69 Sherman Price
Jue Xiang 86 Zeming Zhang
Juego de la Muerte, El 86 Alfredo Gurrola
Juego de la Oca, El 64 Manuel Summers
Juego Más Divertido, El 88 Emilio Martínez-Lazaro
Juego Peligroso 66 Luis Alcoriza, Arturo Ripstein
Jueves Milagro, Los 57 Luis García Berlanga
Juez Sangriento, El 69 Jesús Franco
Juge et l'Assassin, Le 75 Bertrand Tavernier
Juge Fayard Dit le "Sheriff," Le 77 Yves Boisset
Jugement de Dieu, Le 52 Raymond Bernard
Jugement de Salomon, Le 16 Jacques De Baroncelli
Jugement des Pierres, Le 14 Léon Poirier
Jugement du Garde-Champêtre, Le 08 Georges Méliès
Jugend 38 Veidt Harlan
Jugend und Tollheit 12 Urban Gad
Jugend von Heute 38 Peter Paul Brauer
Jugendrichter, Der 64 Paul Verhoeven
Juggernaut, The 15 Ralph Ince
Juggernaut 36 Henry Edwards

Juggernaut *74* Bryan Forbes, Richard Lester, Don Medford
Juggins' Motor *03* James A. Williamson
Juggins' Motor Skates *09* Percy Stow
Juggler, The *53* Edward Dmytryk
Juggling Mad *13* Will P. Kellino
Juggling on the Brain *10* Walter R. Booth
Juggling with Fate *13* William Duncan
Juguetes Rotos *66* Manuel Summers
Juha *35* Nyrki Tapiovaara
Juif Errant, Le *04* Georges Méliès
Juif Errant, Le *26* Luitz-Morat
Juif Polonais, Le *37* Jean Kemm
Juillet en Septembre *88* Sebastien Japrisot
Juilliard *71* Christian Blackwood
Jūjin Yūkiotoko *55* Kenneth Crane, Inoshiro Honda
Jūjiro *28* Teinosuke Kinugasa
Juke Box Jenny *42* Harold Young
Juke Box Racket *60* Barry Mahon
Juke Box Rhythm *59* Arthur Dreifuss
Juke Girl *42* Kurt Bernhardt
Juke Joint *47* Spencer Williams
Jukti, Takko ar Gappo *74* Ritwik Ghatak
Jūku no Haru *33* Heinosuke Gosho
1999 — Nen no Natsu Yasumi *89* Shusuke Kaneko
Jūku-Sai no Haru *33* Heinosuke Gosho
Jules and Jim *61* François Truffaut
Jules et Jim *61* François Truffaut
Jules of the Strong Heart *18* Donald Crisp
Jules Verne's Rocket to the Moon *67* Don Sharp
Julia *77* Fred Zinnemann
Julia and Julia *87* Peter Del Monte
Julia, Du Bist Zauberhaft *62* Alfred Weidenmann
Julia Jubilerar *38* Lau Lauritzen, Jr., Alice O'Fredericks
Julia Misbehaves *48* Jack Conway
Julia und die Geister *65* Federico Fellini
Juliana *88* Fernando Espinosa, Alejandro Legaspi
Julias Geheim *87* Hans Hylkema
Julie *56* Andrew L. Stone
Julie Darling *82* Paul Nicholas, Maurice Smith
Julie la Rousse *59* Claude Boissol
Julie Pot de Colle *77* Philippe de Broca
Julie the Redhead *59* Claude Boissol
Juliet and Her Romeo *23* Bertram Phillips
Juliet Buys a Baby *35* Louis King
Juliet of the Spirits *65* Federico Fellini
Juliet, or The Key to Dreams *51* Marcel Carné
Julieta Compra un Hijo *35* Louis King
Juliet's Secret *87* Hans Hylkema
Julietta *53* Marc Allégret
Juliette des Esprits *65* Federico Fellini
Juliette la Fille au Sexe Brillant *75* Jesús Franco
Juliette, or The Key of Dreams *51* Marcel Carné
Juliette ou La Clé des Songes *51* Marcel Carné
Julika, Die *39* Géza von Bolváry
Julius Caesar *14* George Kleine
Julius Caesar *26* George A. Cooper
Julius Caesar *45* Compton Bennett
Julius Caesar *49* David Bradley

Julius Caesar *53* Joseph L. Mankiewicz
Julius Caesar *69* Stuart Burge
July 14 *32* René Clair
July Fourteenth *32* René Clair
July Pork Bellies *74* Peter Yates
July Rain *67* Marlen Khutsiev
Jumbo *62* Charles Walters
Jumeau, Le *84* Yves Robert
Jument Verte, La *59* Claude Autant-Lara
Jump *71* Joseph Manduke
Jump for Glory *37* Raoul Walsh
Jump Into Hell *55* David Butler
Jumpin' Jack Flash *86* Penny Marshall
Jumpin' Jupiter *55* Chuck Jones
Jumping *86* Jean-Pierre De Decker
Jumping Ash *76* Po-chih Leong
Jumping Beans *22* Dave Fleischer
Jumping for Joy *55* John Paddy Carstairs
Jumping Jacks *52* Norman Taurog
Jumping Over Puddles Again *70* Karel Kachyňa
Jumping the Puddles Again *70* Karel Kachyňa
Junai Monogatari *57* Tadashi Imai
Junction City *52* Ray Nazarro
June Bride *48* Bretaigne Windust
June Friday *15* Duncan Macrae
June Madness *22* Harry Beaumont
June Moon *31* A. Edward Sutherland
June Night *40* Per Lindberg
June's Birthday Party *05* Edwin S. Porter
Jung on Film *57* John W. Meaney
Jungal ki Beti *88* R. Thakur
Jungbaaz *89* Mehul Kumar
Junge Graf, Der *35* Karel Lamač
Junge Lord, Der *70* Gustav R. Sellner
Junge Medardus, Der *23* Michael Curtiz
Junge mit dem Grossen Schwarzen Hund, Der *87* Hannelore Unterberg
Junge Monch, Der *78* Herbert Achternbusch
Junge Schrie Mord, Ein *66* George Breakston
Junge Törless, Der *66* Volker Schlöndorff
Jungfrau auf dem Dach, Die *53* Otto Preminger
Jungfrau Gegen Mönch *35* E. W. Emo
Jungfrau und die Peitsche, Die *70* Jesús Franco
Jungfrukällan *59* Ingmar Bergman
Jungle, The *14* Augustus Thomas
Jungle, The *52* William Berke
Jungle Adventures *21* Martin E. Johnson
Jungle Attack *51* Lewis R. Foster
Jungle Book *42* André De Toth, Zoltán Korda
Jungle Book, The *67* Wolfgang Reitherman
Jungle Bride *33* Harry Hoyt, Albert Kelley
Jungle Captive *45* Harold Young
Jungle Cat *59* James Algar
Jungle Cavalcade *41* Frank Buck, Armand Denis, Clyde E. Elliott
Jungle Child, The *16* Walter Edwards
Jungle Dance *37* Pál Fejös
Jungle Days *28* John Foster
Jungle Drums of Africa *53* Fred C. Brannon
Jungle Fighters *60* Leslie Norman
Jungle Flight *47* Sam Newfield

Jungle Gents *54* Edward Bernds, Austen Jewell
Jungle Girl *41* John English, William Witney
Jungle Girl *52* Ford Beebe
Jungle Goddess *48* Lewis D. Collins
Jungle Gold *44* Spencer G. Bennet, Wallace A. Grissell
Jungle Heat *27* Stephen Roberts
Jungle Heat *57* Howard W. Koch
Jungle Heat *83* Gus Trikonis
Jungle Hell *56* Norman A. Cerf
Jungle Island *38* Elmer Clifton
Jungle Jim *37* Ford Beebe, Clifford Smith
Jungle Jim *48* William Berke
Jungle Jim in the Forbidden Land *52* Lew Landers
Jungle Jingles *29* Walter Lantz
Jungle Jitters *34* Ubbe Iwerks
Jungle Jitters *38* Friz Freleng
Jungle Jumble *19* Gregory La Cava
Jungle Jumble, A *32* Walter Lantz
Jungle Justice *53* B. Reeves Eason
Jungle Lovers, The *15* Lloyd B. Carleton
Jungle Man *41* Harry Fraser
Jungle Man-Eaters *54* Lee Sholem
Jungle Manhunt *51* Lew Landers
Jungle Menace *37* Harry Fraser, George Melford
Jungle Moon Men *55* Charles S. Gould
Jungle Mystery, The *32* Ray Taylor
Jungle of Chang *38* Pál Fejös, Gunnar Skoglund
Jungle Pals *23* Lewis Seiler, Ben Stoloff
Jungle Patrol *48* Joseph M. Newman
Jungle Princess, The *36* Wilhelm Thiele
Jungle Queen *45* Lewis D. Collins, Ray Taylor
Jungle Raiders *45* Lesley Selander
Jungle Raiders *84* Antonio Margheriti
Jungle Rampage *62* Henry Hathaway, Phil Karlson
Jungle Rhythm *29* Walt Disney, Ubbe Iwerks
Jungle Siren *42* Sam Newfield
Jungle Stampede *50* George Breakston
Jungle Street *61* Charles Saunders
Jungle Street Girls *61* Charles Saunders
Jungle Terror *68* Joseph Prieto
Jungle Track *59* Alexander Zguridi
Jungle Trail *19* Richard Stanton
Jungle Trail of the Son of Tarzan, The *23* Arthur J. Flaven, Harry Revier
Jungle Triangle, A *28* Mannie Davis
Jungle Warfare *43* Joy Batchelor, John Halas
Jungle Warriors *84* Ernst R. von Theumer
Jungle Woman, The *26* Frank Hurley
Jungle Woman *44* Reginald LeBorg
Jungle Woman, The *44* Sam Newfield
Juninatten *40* Per Lindberg
Junior *88* Gus Van Sant, Jr.
Junior Army *42* Lew Landers
Junior Bonner *72* Sam Peckinpah
Junior G-Men *40* Ford Beebe, John Rawlins
Junior G-Men of the Air *42* Lewis D. Collins, Ray Taylor
Junior Miss *45* George Seaton
Junior Prom *46* Arthur Dreifuss**

Junjō 29 Mikio Naruse
Junk Man, The 27 Mannie Davis
Junket 89 70 Peter Plummer
Junkman 82 H. B. Halicki
Junkopia 81 Chris Marker
Juno and the Paycock 30 Alfred Hitchcock
Juno Helps Out 53 William C. Hammond
Juno Home Help 53 William C. Hammond
Juno Makes Friends 57 Barbara Woodhouse
Junoon 78 Shyam Benegal
Juntos 87 Rafael Rosales Durán
Juntos Pero No Revueltos 39 Fernando Rivero
Jupiter 52 Gilles Grangier
Jupiter Menace, The 82 Lee Auerbach, Peter Matulavich
Jupiter's Darling 54 George Sidney
Jupiter's Thigh 79 Philippe de Broca
Jupiter's Thunderbolts 03 Georges Méliès
Jupiter's Thunderbolts, or The Home of the Muses 03 Georges Méliès
Jupon Rouge, Le 87 Geneviève Lefèbvre
Jury of Fate, The 17 Tod Browning
Jury of One 74 André Cayatte
Jury of the Jungle 33 Roy William Neill
Jury's Evidence 36 Ralph Ince
Jury's Secret, The 37 Edward Sloman
Jus Prima Noctis 72 Pasquale Festa Campanile
Jusqu'à la Nuit 85 Didier Martiny
Jusqu'à la Victoire 70 Jean-Luc Godard, Jean-Pierre Gorin
Jusqu'au Cœur 68 Jean-Pierre Lefèbvre
Just a Big, Simple Girl 49 Jacques Manuel
Just a Few Lines 18 Pat Sullivan
Just a Gigolo 31 Jack Conway
Just a Gigolo 32 Dave Fleischer
Just a Gigolo 78 David Hemmings
Just a Girl 13 Charles H. Weston
Just a Girl 16 Alexander Butler
Just a Little Piece of Cloth 06 J. H. Martin
Just a Movie 85 Pál Sándor
Just a Nut 14 Charles H. Weston
Just a Pain in the Parlor 32 George Marshall
Just a Pal 30 Norman Taurog
Just a Song at Twilight 22 Carlton S. King
Just a Wife 20 Howard Hickman
Just a Wolf at Heart 63 Joseph Barbera, William Hanna
Just a Woman 25 Irving Cummings
Just Across the Street 52 Joseph Pevney
Just Another Blonde 26 Alfred Santell
Just Another Day at the Races 75 Richard Bailey
Just Another Miracle 85 Charles Gormley
Just Another Murder 35 Mack Sennett
Just Another War 70 Francesco Rosi
Just Around the Corner 21 Frances Marion
Just Around the Corner 38 Irving Cummings
Just Ask for Diamond 88 Stephen Bayly
Just Be There 77 David Feldshuh
Just Before Dawn 46 William Castle
Just Before Dawn 80 Jeff Lieberman
Just Before Nightfall 70 Claude Chabrol

Just Between Friends 86 Allan Burns
Just Brown's Luck 13 Mack Sennett
Just Dandy 28 Stephen Roberts
Just Deception, A 17 A. E. Coleby
Just Ducky 53 Joseph Barbera, William Hanna
Just for a Song 30 V. Gareth Gundrey
Just for Fun 21 Julian Ollendorff
Just for Fun 41 Marcel L'Herbier
Just for Fun 63 Gordon Flemyng
Just for Fun, Just for Play 77 Volker Schlöndorff
Just for Luck 13 Hy Mayer
Just for the Hell of It 68 Herschell Gordon Lewis
Just for Tonight 18 Charles Giblyn
Just for Tonight 35 Patrick K. Heale
Just for You 52 Elliott Nugent
Just for You 56 Michael Carreras
Just for You 63 Douglas Hickox
Just Gold 13 D. W. Griffith
Just Great 71 Jean-Luc Godard, Jean-Pierre Gorin
Just Imagine 30 David Butler
Just in Time 06 Lewin Fitzhamon
Just in Time 07 James A. Williamson
Just in Time 15 Percy Nash
Just Jim 15 Oscar A. C. Lund
Just Joe 59 Maclean Rogers
Just Kids 13 Henry Lehrman
Just Lads 27 David Butler
Just Like a Mother 13 Bert Haldane
Just Like a Woman 12 D. W. Griffith
Just Like a Woman 16 Gregory La Cava
Just Like a Woman 23 Scott R. Beal, Hugh McClung
Just Like a Woman 38 Paul Stein
Just Like a Woman 66 Robert Fuest
Just Like America 87 Péter Gothár
Just Like at Home 78 Márta Mészáros
Just Like Heaven 30 Roy William Neill
Just Like the Weather 86 Allen Fong
Just Married 28 Frank R. Strayer
Just Me 50 Marc-Gilbert Sauvajon
Just Mickey 30 Walt Disney
Just My Luck 33 Jack Raymond
Just My Luck 36 Ray Heinz
Just My Luck 57 John Paddy Carstairs
Just Nuts 15 Hal Roach
Just Off Broadway 24 Edmund Mortimer
Just Off Broadway 29 Frank O'Connor
Just Off Broadway 42 Herbert I. Leeds
Just Once More 63 Gunnar Hellström
Just One Day 89 Kvetoslav Hečko, Michal Ruttkay, Vladimir Stric
Just One More 63 Gunnar Hellström
Just One More Chance 32 Dave Fleischer
Just One More Time 63 Francis Megahy
Just One More Time 74 Maurice Hamblin
Just One of the Guys 85 Lisa Gottlieb
Just One Word 29 Joseph Santley
Just Out of College 20 Alfred E. Green
Just Out of Reach 79 Linda Blagg
Just Outside the Door 21 George Irving
Just Pals 20 John Ford
Just Plain Folks 25 Robert North Bradbury
Just Plane Beep 65 Rudy Larriva
Just Show People 13 Van Dyke Brooke
Just Smith 33 Tom Walls
Just Spooks 25 Walter Lantz

Just Squaw 19 George E. Middleton
Just Suppose 26 Kenneth Webb
Just Sylvia 18 Travers Vale
Just Tell Me What You Want 79 Sidney Lumet
Just Tell Me You Love Me 79 Tony Mordente
Just the Two of Us 75 Barbara Peeters
Just the Way You Are 84 Édouard Molinaro
Just This Once 51 Don Weis
Just to Be Loved 70 Jerzy Macc, Peter Savage
Just Tony 22 Lynn Reynolds
Just Travelin' 27 Horace B. Carpenter
Just William 39 Graham Cutts
Just William's Luck 47 Val Guest
Just You and Me, Kid 79 Leonard Stern
Juste Avant la Nuit 70 Claude Chabrol
Justice 14 Frank Wilson
Justice 17 Maurice Elvey
Justice and Caryl Chessman 60 Quentin Reynolds, Ed Spiegel
Justice Cain 69 Kent Osborne
Justice d'Abord 21 Yakov Protazanov
Justice Est Faite 50 André Cayatte
Justice for Sale 32 W. S. Van Dyke
Justice Has Been Done 50 André Cayatte
Justice Is Done 50 André Cayatte
Justice of the Far North 25 Norman Dawn
Justice of the Range 35 David Selman
Justice of the Sage 12 Allan Dwan
Justice Rides Again 32 Ben Stoloff
Justice Takes a Holiday 33 Spencer G. Bennet
Justice Victorious 17 Forest Holger-Madsen
Justiceiro, O 67 Nelson Pereira Dos Santos
Justices 78 André Cayatte
Justicier, Le 67 Nelson Pereira Dos Santos
Justicière, La 25 Maurice Gleize
Justiciero, El 67 Nelson Pereira Dos Santos
Justifiable Deception, A 15 Ethyle Batley
Justin de Marseille 34 Maurice Tourneur
Justine 68 George Cukor, Joseph Strick
Justine 69 Jesús Franco
Justinian's Human Torches 07 Georges Méliès
Jutro 67 Puriša Djordjević
Juve Contre Fantômas 13 Louis Feuillade
Juvenile Barbers, The 06 Will Barker
Juvenile Court 38 D. Ross Lederman
Juvenile Court 73 Frederick Wiseman
Juvenile Hypnotist, A 11 Walter R. Booth
Juvenile Jungle 58 William Witney
Juvenile Pranks 11 Walter R. Booth
Juvenile Scientist, A 07 Walter R. Booth
Juvenizer, The 81 King Hu
Juventud a la Intemperie 61 Ignacio F. Iquino
Juventude 50 Nelson Pereira Dos Santos
Južná Pošta 88 Stanislav Parnicky
KGB—The Secret War 86 Dwight H. Little
K-God 80 Rick Friedberg
K-9 89 Rod Daniel
K.O. Va e Uccidi 66 G. Ferrero
K.S.E. 32 Esther Shub
K.Sh.E. 32 Esther Shub
K the Hunchback 13 Yevgeni Bauer
K—The Unknown 24 Harry A. Pollard

K und K Balletmädel 28 Max Neufeld
Kaadu 73 Girish Karnad
Kaalchakra 88 Dilip Shankar
Kaatil 53 Lütfü Akat
Kabe Atsuki Heya 53 Masaki Kobayashi
Kabe no Naka no Himegoto 63 Koji Wakamatsu
Kabine 27 45 Wolfgang Staudte
Kabinett des Dr. Caligari, Das 19 Robert Wiene
Kabinett des Dr. Larifari, Das 31 Robert Wohlmuth
Kabocha 28 Yasujiro Ozu
Kabuliwala 61 Bimal Roy
Kaçaklar 71 Yılmaz Güney
Kaçamak 88 Başar Sabuncu
Kāchan Kekkon Shiroyo 62 Heinosuke Gosho
Kāchan to Jūichi-Nin no Kodomo 66 Heinosuke Gosho
Kadaicha 88 James Bogle
Kaddish 84 Steve Brand
Kadetten 33 Georg Jacoby
Kadoyng 72 Ian Shand
Kaeranu Sasabue 26 Heinosuke Gosho
Kære Irene 71 Christian Braad Thomsen
Kære Legetøj, Det 68 Gabriel Axel
Kærlighed Gør Blind 12 August Blom
Kærlighed på Kredit 55 Astrid Henning-Jensen
Kærlighed på Rulleskøjter 43 Albert Mertz, Jørgen Roos
Kærligheden Varer Længst 67 Jørgen Roos
Kærlighedens Magt 11 August Blom
Kærlighedens Styrke 11 August Blom
Kærlighedens Triumf 14 Forest Holger-Madsen
Kærligheds Længsel 15 August Blom
Kærligheds Væddemålet 14 August Blom
Kaette Kita Yopparai 68 Nagisa Oshima
Käfer auf Extratour, Ein 73 Rudolf Zehetgruber
Käfer Geht aufs Ganze, Ein 71 Rudolf Zehetgruber
Käfer Gibt Vollgas, Ein 72 Rudolf Zehetgruber
Kaffeehaus, Das 70 Rainer Werner Fassbinder
Kafuku 37 Mikio Naruse
Kagemusha 80 Akira Kurosawa
Kagemusha the Shadow Warrior 80 Akira Kurosawa
Kagerō 68 Kaneto Shindo
Kagerō Ezu 59 Teinosuke Kinugasa
Kagi 59 Kon Ichikawa
Kagi no Kag 64 Senkichi Taniguchi
Kagirinaki Hodo 34 Mikio Naruse
Kagirinaki Zenshin 36 Tomu Uchida
Kahan Kahan se Guzar Gaya 86 M. S. Sathyu
Kahir Elzaman 86 Kamel El Sheik
Kahuna 81 Frank Sillman
Kaibyō Otamage-Ike 60 Yoshihiro Ichikawa
Kaidan 64 Masaki Kobayashi
Kaidan Botan Doru 68 Satsuo Yamamoto
Kaidan Kasanegafuchi 57 Nobuo Nakagawa
Kaidan Kasanegafuchi 70 Kimiyoshi Yasuda

Kaidan Katame no Otoko 65 Tsuneo Kobayashi
Kaidan Noboriryū 70 Teruo Ishii
Kaidan Semushi Otoko 65 Hajime Sato
Kaidan Yukigoro 68 Tokuzo Tanaka
Kaidan Zankoku Monogatari 68 Kazuo Hase
Kaidō no Kishi 28 Heinosuke Gosho
Kaigun Tokubetsu Shōnen Hei 72 Tadashi Imai
Kaijū Daisensō 65 Inoshiro Honda
Kaijū Sōshingeki 68 Inoshiro Honda
Kaikoku Danji 26 Kenji Mizoguchi
Kaikokuki 28 Teinosuke Kinugasa
Kainszeichen, Das 19 Richard Oswald
Kaintuck 12 James Hallek Reid
Kairyū Daikessen 66 Tetsuya Yamaguchi
Kaisen no Zenya 43 Kozaburo Yoshimura
Kaiser, The 18 Rupert Julian
Kaiser Captures Pimple, The 15 Fred Evans, Joe Evans
Kaiser Case, The 32 Franz Wenzler
Kaiser—The Beast of Berlin, The 18 Rupert Julian
Kaiser von Kalifornien, Der 36 Luis Trenker
Kaiserjäger 56 Willi Forst
Kaiserliebchen 31 Hans Tintner
Kaiser's Finish, The 18 John Harvey, Clifford P. Saum
Kaiser's Lackey, The 49 Wolfgang Staudte
Kaiser's New Dentist, The 18 Raoul Barré, Charles Bowers
Kaiser's Present, The 15 Dave Aylott
Kaiser's Shadow, The 18 Roy William Neill
Kaiser's Spies, The 14 Charles Raymond
Kaiser's Surprise Party, The 18 Leighton Budd
Kaiserwalzer 34 Fred Zelnik
Kaisha-In Seikatsu 29 Yasujiro Ozu
Kaitei Daisensō 66 Hajime Sato
Kaitei Gunkan 63 Inoshiro Honda
Kaja, Ubit Ću Te 67 Vatroslav Mimica
Kak Boudet Golosovat Izbiratel 37 Sergei Yutkevich
Kak Doma, Kak Dela? 88 Samvel Gasparov
Kak Khoroshi, Kak Svezhi Byli Rozi 13 Yakov Protazanov
Kak Molody My Byli 85 Mikhail Belikov
Kak Rydala Dusha Rebenka 13 Yakov Protazanov
Kak Stat Schastlyvym 87 Yuri Chuliukin
Kak Zakalyalas Stal 42 Mark Donskoi
Kakita Akanishi 36 Mansaku Itami
Kakka 40 Tadashi Imai
Kakothikavile Appuppan Thadigal 88 Kamal
Kaku and Tsune 68 Tomu Uchida
Kakushi Toride no San-Akunin 58 Akira Kurosawa
Kalaa, El 88 Mohamed Chouikh
Kaláliuvit 70 Jørgen Roos
Kalamazoo 80 Marc-André Forcier
Kalamita 80 Věra Chytilová
Kalankini Nayika 88 Suven Sarkar
Kald Mig Miriam 68 Astrid Henning-Jensen
Kaldırım Çiçeği 53 Baha Gelenbevi

Kaleidoscope 35 Len Lye
Kaleidoscope 61 Charles Eames, Ray Eames
Kaleidoscope 66 Jack Smight
Kaleidoscope, The 81 Mrinal Sen
Kaleidoscope Shop 61 Charles Eames, Ray Eames
Kaleidoskop 77 Volker Schlöndorff
Kaleidoskop: Valeska Gert, Nur zum Spass—Nur zum Spiel 77 Volker Schlöndorff
Kalemites Visit Gibraltar, The 12 Sidney Olcott
Kali Patritha, Syntrofe 86 Lefteris Xanthopoulos
Kali Yug, Goddess of Vengeance 63 Mario Camerini
Kali Yug—La Dea della Vendetta 63 Mario Camerini
Kalidaa 18 Augusto Genina
Kalina Krasnaya 74 Vasili Shuksin
Kalinin, the Elder Statesman of All Russians 20 Dziga Vertov
Kaliya Maradan 19 D. G. Phalke
Kaliyuga Krishnu 88 Krishna
Kaliyugaya 82 Lester James Peries
Kalkmalerier 54 Jørgen Roos
Kalle på Spången 40 Emil A. Pehrsson
Kallelsen 74 Sven Nykvist
Kalpana 48 Uday Shankar
Kalpiki Lira, I 54 George Tzavellas
Kalt in Kolumbien 85 Dieter Schidor
Kalte Mamsell, Die 35 Carl Boese
Kalte Paradies, Das 88 Bernard Safarik
Kalyana Thambulam 87 Bapu
Kalyug 80 Shyam Benegal
Kam Doskáče Ranní Ptáče 86 Drahomíra Králová
Kam Pánové, Kam Jdete? 88 Karel Kachyňa
Kamæleonen 16 Forest Holger-Madsen
Kamarád do Deště 88 Jaroslav Soukup
Kamaszváros 63 Márta Mészáros
Kamata Kōshinkyoku 80 Kinji Fukasaku
Kamata March 80 Kinji Fukasaku
Kameliendame, Die 87 John Neumeier
Kamenny Tsvetok 46 Alexander Ptushko
Kamerad Hedwig 45 Gerhard Lamprecht
Kameraden auf See 39 Heinz Paul
Kameradschaft 31 G. W. Pabst
Kami e no Michi 28 Heinosuke Gosho
Kamigami no Fukaki Yokubō 68 Shohei Imamura
Kamikaze 82 Wolf Gremm
Kamikaze 86 Luc Besson, Didier Grousset
Kamikaze '89 82 Wolf Gremm
Kamikaze Group, The 33 Kenji Mizoguchi
Kamikaze Hearts 86 Juliet Bashore
Kamikaze 1989 82 Wolf Gremm
Kamikaze-Ren 33 Kenji Mizoguchi
Kamikazen—Ultima Notte a Milano 88 Gabriel Salvatores
Kamilla 81 Vibeke Løkkeberg
Kamilla and the Thief 87 Grete Salomonsen
Kamilla og Tyven 87 Grete Salomonsen
Kaminingyō Haru no Sasayaki 26 Kenji Mizoguchi
Kamla 85 Jag Mohan Mundhra

Kammarjunkaren *13* Mauritz Stiller
Kammermusik *25* Carl Fröhlich
Kamong Sentosa *52* B. Reeves Eason
Kamouraska *72* Claude Jutra
Kampen Mod Kræften *47* Carl Theodor Dreyer
Kampen mod Uretten *48* Ole Palsbo
Kampen om den Røde Ko *87* Jarl Friis Mikkelsen, Ole Stephensen
Kampen om Hans Hjärta *16* Mauritz Stiller
Kampf, Der *36* Gustav Wangenheim
Kampf des Unabhängigen Gegen den Kommerziellen Film *29* Sergei Eisenstein, Ivor Montagu, Hans Richter
Kampf mit dem Drachen, Der *39* Franz Seitz
Kampf um Rom, Der *69* Robert Siodmak
Kampf ums Matterhorn, Der *28* Mario Bonnard, Nunzio Malasomma
Kämpfende Herzen *20* Fritz Lang
Kämpfende Welten *22* E. A. Dupont
Kamu Onna *88* Tatsumi Kumashiro
Kamyabi *88* Pervez Mehta
Kan Pi *75* Rom Bunnag
Kanał *56* Andrzej Wajda
Kanashiki Hakuchi *24* Kenji Mizoguchi
Kanashimi wa Onna Dake Ni *58* Kaneto Shindo
Kanawa *72* Kaneto Shindo
Kanchana Seetha *88* Dasari Narayan Rao
Kanchanjangha *62* Satyajit Ray
Kanchenjungha *62* Satyajit Ray
Kanchō Imada Shisezu *42* Kozaburo Yoshimura
Kandidat, Der *80* Alexander Kluge, Volker Schlöndorff
Kandy Perahera *71* Lester James Peries
Kandyland *87* Robert Allen Schnitzer
Kane *26* Kenji Mizoguchi
Kangaroo *20* Dave Fleischer
Kangaroo *52* Lewis Milestone
Kangaroo *86* Tim Burstall
Kangaroo Complex, The *86* Pierre Jolivet
Kangaroo Courting *54* Pete Burness
Kangaroo Kid, The *38* Ben Harrison
Kangaroo Kid, The *50* Lesley Selander
Kango Fire Brigade, The *14* Toby Cooper
Kanikōsen *53* So Yamamura
Kankana Bhagya *88* Perala
Kanko no Machi *44* Keisuke Kinoshita
Kankon Sōsai *59* Kon Ichikawa
Kannibal Kapers *35* Manny Gould, Ben Harrison
Kanojo *26* Heinosuke Gosho
Kanojo to Kare *63* Susumu Hani
Kanojo to Unmei *24* Teinosuke Kinugasa
Kanonen-Serenade *58* Wolfgang Staudte
Kanraku no Onna *24* Kenji Mizoguchi
Kansan, The *43* George Archainbaud
Kansas *88* David Stevens
Kansas City Bomber *72* Jerrold Freedman
Kansas City Confidential *52* Phil Karlson
Kansas City Kitty *44* Del Lord
Kansas City Princess *34* William Keighley
Kansas Cyclone *41* George Sherman
Kansas Pacific *53* Ray Nazarro
Kansas Raiders *50* Ray Enright
Kansas Saloon Smashers *01* Edwin S. Porter

Kansas Territory *52* Lewis D. Collins
Kansas Terrors, The *39* George Sherman
Kantō *23* Kenji Mizoguchi
Kantor Ideál *32* Martin Frič
Kantorowitz *23* Walter Ruttmann
Kao *63* Yoji Kuri
Kaos *84* Paolo Taviani, Vittorio Taviani
Kapax del Amazonas *86* Miguel Ángel Rincón
Kapax of the Amazon *86* Miguel Ángel Rincón
Kaphetzou *61* Alekos Sakelarios
Kapit sa Palatim *84* Lino Brocka
Kapitan Dabac *59* Pal'o Bielek
Kapitan "Piligrima *87* Andrei Prachenko
Kapitanleutnant Prien — Der Stier von Scapa Flow *58* Harald Reinl
Kapkan dlya Shakalov *87* Mukadas Mahmudov
Kapò *59* Gillo Pontecorvo
Kaptain Discovers the North Pole, Der *17* Gregory La Cava
Kaptain Goes A-Flivving, Der *17* Gregory La Cava
Kaptain Goes A-Swimming, Der *17* Gregory La Cava
Kaptain Is Examined for Insurance, Der *17* Gregory La Cava
Kaptain's Birthday, Der *18* Gregory La Cava
Kaptain's Valet, Der *17* Gregory La Cava
Käpt'n Bay-Bay *52* Helmut Käutner
Kapurush-o-Mahapurush *65* Satyajit Ray
Käpy Selän Alla *67* Mikko Niskanen
Kára Plná Bolesti *85* Stanislav Parnicky
Kara Sevdeli Bulut *89* Muammar Ozer
Kära Släkten *33* Gustaf Molander
Karacaoğlanin Kara Sevdası *59* Atıf Yılmaz
Karacaoğlan's Mad Love *59* Atıf Yılmaz
Karađorđe *10* Jules Barry
Karakoram *36* Marcel Ichac
Karakuri Musume *27* Heinosuke Gosho
Karamaneh *24* Fred Paul
Karamazov *31* Fedor Ozep
Karambol *64* Félix Máriássy
Karami-Ai *62* Masaki Kobayashi
Karatachi Nikki *59* Heinosuke Gosho
Karate *61* Joel Holt
Karate Kid, The *84* John G. Avildsen
Karate Kid Part II, The *86* John G. Avildsen
Karate Kid Part III, The *89* John G. Avildsen
Karate Killers, The *67* Barry Shear
Karate, the Hand of Death *61* Joel Holt
Karayuki-San *73* Shohei Imamura
Karayuki-San: The Making of a Prostitute *73* Shohei Imamura
Kard és Kocka *59* Imre Fehér
Käre John *64* Lars-Magnus Lindgren
Karen, the Lovemaker *70* Zygmunt Sulistrowski
Kárhozat *88* Béla Tarr
Karin, Daughter of Ingmar *19* Victor Sjöström
Karin, Daughter of Man *53* Alf Sjöberg
Karin, Ingmar's Daughter *19* Victor Sjöström
Karin Ingmarsdotter *19* Victor Sjöström

Karin Mansdotter *53* Alf Sjöberg
Karins Ansikte *83* Ingmar Bergman
Karin's Face *83* Ingmar Bergman
Karl-Fredrik Reigns *34* Gustaf Edgren
Karl Marx *63* Grigori Roshal
Karl May *74* Hans-Jürgen Syberberg
Karl XII *25* John W. Brunius
Karla *68* Joe Sarno
Kärlek *52* Gustaf Molander
Kärlek och Journalistik *16* Mauritz Stiller
Kärlek och Kassabrist *32* Gustaf Molander
Kärlek 65 *65* Bo Widerberg
Kärlek Starkare Än Hat *13* Victor Sjöström
Kärleken Segrar *49* Gustaf Molander
Kärlekens Bröd *53* Arne Mattsson
Kärlekens Decimaler *60* Hasse Ekman
Kärlekens Ögon *22* John W. Brunius
Kärleks Ön *77* Joe Sarno
Karlovy Vary *34* Alexander Hammid
Karlsson Brothers, The *72* Vilgot Sjöman
Karma *33* J. L. Freer-Hunt
Karma *86* Ho Quang Minh
Karma *88* Doo-yong Lee
Karmnik Jankowy *54* Wojciech Has
Karneval und Liebe *34* Karel Lamač
Karnival Kid, The *29* Walt Disney, Ubbe Iwerks
Karnstein *63* Camillo Mastrocinque
Karnstein Curse, The *63* Camillo Mastrocinque
Károly-Bakák *18* Zoltán Korda, Miklós Pásztory
Karosszék *39* Béla Balázs
Karthauzi, A *16* Michael Curtiz
Kartofler *45* Ole Palsbo
Karumen Junjōsu *52* Keisuke Kinoshita
Karumen Kokyō ni Kaeru *51* Keisuke Kinoshita
Karusel na Bazarnoy Ploshchadi *87* Nikolai Stambula
Karussell *55* Zoltán Fábri
Karussell des Lebens, Das *23* Dmitri Buchowetzki
Kas, Al *86* Mohamed Damak
Kasař *73* Jaromil Jireš
Kaseki *74* Masaki Kobayashi
Kaseki no Mori *73* Masahiro Shinoda
Käsekönig Holländer *16* Ernst Lubitsch
Kashimanada no Onna *59* So Yamamura
Kashmiri Run *69* John Peyser
Kaspichy *44* Grigori Alexandrov
Kasset Gharam *46* Ahmed Abdel Jawad, Kamel Salim
Kastrull Resan *50* Arne Mattsson
Kasturi *88* J. H. Sattar
Katakomby *40* Martin Frič
Kataku no Hito *86* Kinji Fukasaku
Katayoku Dake no Tenshi *86* Toshio Masuda
Katchem Kate *12* Mack Sennett
Kate Plus Ten *38* Reginald Denham
Katei no Jijō *62* Kozaburo Yoshimura
Katerina Ismailova *66* Mikhail Shapiro
Katerina Izmailova *66* Mikhail Shapiro
Katerlampe *36* Veidt Harlan
Kathakku Pinnil *87* K. G. George
Katharina die Letzte *35* Henry Koster
Katherina die Grosse *20* Reinhold Schünzel

Katherine Knie 29 Karl Grüne
Katherine Reed Story, The 65 Robert Altman
Kathleen 37 Norman Lee
Kathleen 41 Harold S. Bucquet
Kathleen Mavourneen 06 Edwin S. Porter
Kathleen Mavourneen 13 Herbert Brenon
Kathleen Mavourneen 19 Charles Brabin
Kathleen Mavourneen 30 Albert Ray
Kathleen Mavourneen 37 Norman Lee
Kathryn Reed Story, The 65 Robert Altman
Kathy O 58 Jack Sher
Kathy's Love Affair 47 Herbert Wilcox
Katia 38 Maurice Tourneur
Katia 59 Robert Siodmak
Katie Did It 51 Frederick De Cordova
Katie's Passion 75 Paul Verhoeven
Katina 42 H. Bruce Humberstone
Katinka 87 Max von Sydow
Katja 59 Robert Siodmak
Katka 50 Ján Kadár
Katka Bumazhnyi Ranyot 26 Friedrich Ermler, Eduard Johansen, Andrei Moskin
Katka the Apple Girl 26 Friedrich Ermler, Eduard Johansen, Andrei Moskin
Katka's Reinette Apples 26 Friedrich Ermler, Eduard Johansen, Andrei Moskin
Katnip Kollege 38 Cal Dalton, Ben Hardaway
Katnips of 1940 34 Manny Gould, Ben Harrison
Katok i Skripka 60 Andrei Tarkovsky
Katorga 28 Yuli Raizman
Katrina 43 Gustaf Edgren
Kats Is Kats 20 Vernon Stallings
Kattorna 64 Henning Carlsen
Katya 50 Ján Kadár
Katya 59 Robert Siodmak
Katz and Karasso 71 Menahem Golan
Kätze, Die 88 Dominik Graf
Katzelmacher 69 Rainer Werner Fassbinder
Katzensteg, Der 27 Gerhard Lamprecht
Katzensteg 38 Fritz Peter Buch
Kaukasierin, Die 18 Jens W. Krafft, Joe May
Kaun Jeeta? Kaun Hara? 88 Rakesh Kumar
Kavaler Zolotoi Zvezdy 50 Yuli Raizman
Kavi 49 Debaki Kumar Bose
Kawa no Aru Shitamachi no Hanashi 55 Teinosuke Kinugasa
Kawa no Ue no Taiyō 34 Tomu Uchida
Kawaita Hana 63 Masahiro Shinoda
Kawaita Mizuumi 60 Masahiro Shinoda
Kawanakajima Kassen 41 Teinosuke Kinugasa
Kaya 67 Vatroslav Mimica
Kaya, I'll Kill You 67 Vatroslav Mimica
Kazablan 73 Menahem Golan
Kazahana 59 Keisuke Kinoshita
Kazakhstan Front, The 43 Dziga Vertov
Kazakhstan Frontu 43 Dziga Vertov
Kazaks—Minorité Nationale—Sinkiang, Les 77 Joris Ivens, Marceline Loridan
Kazan 21 Bertram Bracken
Kazan 49 Will Jason

Każdemu Wolno Kochać 33 Mieczysław Krawicz, J. Warnecki
Každý Den Odvahu 64 Evald Schorm
Kaze no Naka no Mendori 48 Yasujiro Ozu
Kazhdyy Okhotnik Zhelaet Znat 87 Mikhail Ilyenko
Kazoku Geimu 83 Yoshimitsu Morita
Kdo Chce Zabít Jessu? 65 Václav Vorlíček
Kdo Hledá Zlaté Dno 74 Jiří Menzel
Kdo Se Bojí Utíká 86 Dušan Klein
Kdo Své Nebe Neunese 59 Evald Schorm
Kdyby Ty Muziky Nebyly 63 Miloš Forman
Když v Ráji Pršelo 88 Magdalena Pivoňková
Ke Dyo Avga Tourkias 87 Aris Foriadis
Ke Tu Chiu Hen 90 Ann Hui, Hark Tsui
Kean 24 Alexander Volkov
Kean 54 Vittorio Gassman, Francesco Rosi
Kean, Genius or Scoundrel? 54 Vittorio Gassman, Francesco Rosi
Kean—The Madness of Genius 24 Alexander Volkov
Kechimbō Nagaya 27 Tomu Uchida
Keeler Affair, The 64 Robert Spafford
Keep, The 83 Michael Mann
Keep an Eye on Amelia 49 Claude Autant-Lara
Keep Busy 75 Robert Frank
Keep 'Em Flying 41 Arthur Lubin
Keep 'Em Home 22 Malcolm St. Clair
Keep 'Em Rolling 34 George Archainbaud
Keep 'Em Sailing 42 Basil Wrangell
Keep 'Em Slugging 43 Christy Cabanne
Keep Fit 37 Anthony Kimmins
Keep Going 26 John Harvey
Keep Him Alive 40 Lewis D. Collins
Keep in Style 34 Dave Fleischer
Keep It Clean 56 David Paltenghi
Keep It Cool 58 Harry Foster
Keep It Dark 15 Toby Cooper
Keep It Quiet 34 Leslie Hiscott
Keep It Up Downstairs 76 Robert M. Young
Keep It Up Jack! 74 Derek Ford
Keep Laughing 32 Roscoe Arbuckle
Keep Moving 15 George Kleine
Keep My Grave Open 80 S. F. Brownrigg
Keep Off, Keep Off 75 Shelley Berman
Keep On Rockin' 70 D. A. Pennebaker
Keep On Smoking, Ladányi 38 Márton Keleti
Keep Our Lad's Home Going 16 Ethyle Batley
Keep Punching 39 John Clein
Keep Smiling 25 Albert Austin, Gilbert Pratt
Keep Smiling 38 Monty Banks
Keep Smiling 38 Herbert I. Leeds
Keep Smiling, Baby 86 Arvo Ikho, Lejda Lajus
Keep Talking, Baby 61 Guy Lefranc
Keep the Home Fires Burning 16 Ethyle Batley
Keep to Your Trade 15 Victor Sjöström
Keep Walking 83 Ermanno Olmi
Keep Your Fingers Crossed 71 Dick Clement
Keep Your Mouth Shut 44 George Dun-

ning, Norman McLaren
Keep Your Powder Dry 44 Edward Buzzell
Keep Your Right Up 87 Jean-Luc Godard
Keep Your Seats Please 36 Monty Banks
Keeper, The 76 Tom Drake
Keeper of the Bees, The 25 James Leo Meehan
Keeper of the Bees, The 35 Christy Cabanne
Keeper of the Bees 47 John Sturges
Keeper of the Door 19 Maurice Elvey
Keeper of the Flame 42 George Cukor
Keeper of the Lions, The 37 Walter Lantz
Keepers, The 58 Georges Franju
Keepers of the Flock 13 Charles Brabin
Keepers of the Night 53 Harald Braun
Keepers of Youth 31 Thomas Bentley
Keeping Company 30 Edward Buzzell
Keeping Company 40 S. Sylvan Simon
Keeping Man Interested 22 George A. Cooper
Keeping On 81 Barbara Kopple
Keeping Track 86 Robin Spry
Keeping Up with Lizzie 21 Lloyd Ingraham
Keeps Rainin' All the Time 34 Dave Fleischer
Keetje Tippel 75 Paul Verhoeven
Kegyelet 67 István Szabó
Kei Wong 90 Hark Tsui
Kein Wort von Liebe 38 Alwin Elling
Keine Angst vor Liebe 36 Hans Steinhoff
Keine Feier Ohne Meyer 31 Carl Boese
Keiraku Hichō 28 Teinosuke Kinugasa
Keiro's Cat 05 Alf Collins
Keisatsukan 33 Tomu Uchida
Keisatsukan to Boroyuku-Dan 59 Kon Ichikawa
Keith of the Border 18 Clifford Smith
Kejsaren av Portugallien 44 Gustaf Molander
Kék Bálvány, A 31 Lajos Lázár
Kekarmeni, I 87 Dimitris Makris
Kekkon 47 Keisuke Kinoshita
Kekkon-Gaku Nyūmon 30 Yasujiro Ozu
Kekkon Kōshinkyoku 51 Kon Ichikawa
Kekkon no Seitai 40 Tadashi Imai
Kelcy Gets His Man 27 William Wyler
Kelly 81 Christopher Chapman
Kelly and Me 56 Robert Z. Leonard
Kelly of the Emerald Isle 13 Alice Guy-Blaché
Kelly of the Secret Service 36 Robert F. Hill
Kelly of the U.S.A. 34 Leonard Fields
Kelly the Second 36 Gus Meins
Kelly's Heroes 70 Brian G. Hutton
Kempō Samurai 64 Seiichiro Uchikawa
Kempy 29 E. Mason Hopper
Ken Death Gets Out of Jail 87 Gus Van Sant, Jr.
Kenilworth Castle 26 Maurice Elvey
Kenilworth Castle and Amy Robsart 26 Maurice Elvey
Kennedy Square 16 Del Henderson
Kennedy's Castle 38 Leslie Goodwins
Kennel Murder Case, The 33 Michael Curtiz
Kenner 68 Steve Sekely

Kenny & Co. 76 Don Coscarelli
Keno Bates—Liar 15 William S. Hart, Clifford Smith
Kensington Mystery, The 24 Hugh Croise
Kent the Fighting Man 16 A. E. Coleby
Kentish Industries 13 George Pearson
Kentuckian, The 55 Burt Lancaster
Kentuckians, The 21 Charles Maigne
Kentucky 38 David Butler
Kentucky Bells 31 Walter Lantz
Kentucky Blue Streak 35 Raymond K. Johnson
Kentucky Cinderella, A 17 Rupert Julian
Kentucky Colonel, The 20 William A. Seiter
Kentucky Courage 28 Alfred Santell
Kentucky Days 23 David Soloman
Kentucky Derby, The 22 King Baggot
Kentucky Feud, A 12 Edwin S. Porter
Kentucky Fried Movie, The 77 John Landis
Kentucky Handicap 26 Harry Joe Brown
Kentucky Jubilee 51 Ron Ormond
Kentucky Kernels 34 George Stevens
Kentucky Kith and Kin 72 Christian Blackwood
Kentucky Minstrels 34 John Baxter
Kentucky Moonshine 38 David Butler
Kentucky Pride 25 John Ford
Kentucky Rifle 56 Carl K. Hittleman
Kentucky Woman 83 Walter Doniger
Kenya, Africa 61 Richard Leacock, Albert Maysles, David Maysles
Kenya 61 61 Richard Leacock, Albert Maysles, David Maysles
Kenya, South Africa 61 Richard Leacock, Albert Maysles, David Maysles
Keoma 76 Enzo G. Castellari
Képek egy Város Életéböl 75 István Gaál
Képi, Le 05 Alice Guy-Blaché
Kept Husbands 31 Lloyd Bacon
Képvadászok 85 András Szurdi, Miklós Szurdi
Keresztelö 67 István Gaál
Kermesse Héroïque, La 35 Jacques Feyder
Kerouac 85 John Antonelli
Kerry Gow, The 12 Sidney Olcott
Kes 69 Kenneth Loach
Keserü Igazság 86 Zoltán Várkonyi
Keserü Mézeshetek 39 Béla Balázs
Kessen 44 Teruo Hagiyama, Kozaburo Yoshimura
Kessen Nankai no Daikaijū 70 Inoshiro Honda
Kesudano Rang 88 Vivakar Mehta
Két Arckép 65 András Kovács
Két Félidö a Pokolban 61 Zoltán Fábri
Két Fogoly 37 Steve Sekely
Két Lány az Utcán 38 André De Toth
Két Történet a Félmúltból 79 Károly Makk
Két Választás Magyarországon 87 András Kovács
Keto and Kote 54 S. Ghedevanshvili, V. Tabliashvili
Kétszer Kettö Néha Öt 54 György Révész
Kétszínü Férfi, A 16 Alexander Korda
Kettar, Al 86 Ahmed Fouad
Kettévált Mennyezet 82 Pál Gábor
Kettle Creek 30 Harry Joe Brown

Kettles in the Ozarks, The 56 Charles Lamont
Kettles on Old MacDonald's Farm, The 57 Virgil Vogel
Kettö Ganryū Jima 67 Hiroshi Inagaki
Keufs, Les 87 Josiane Balasko
Kew Gardens 37 Philip Leacock
Kewi 49 Debaki Kumar Bose
Key, The 34 Michael Curtiz
Key, The 58 Carol Reed
Key, The 59 Kon Ichikawa
Key, The 84 Tinto Brass
Key and the Ring, The 47 Anders Henrikson
Key Exchange 85 Barnet Kellman
Key Largo 48 John Huston
Key Man, The 54 Montgomery Tully
Key of Keys 64 Senkichi Taniguchi
Key of the World, The 18 J. L. V. Leigh
Key to Harmony 35 Norman Walker
Key to Power, The 18 William Parke
Key to the City 49 George Sidney
Key Witness 47 D. Ross Lederman
Key Witness 60 Phil Karlson
Keyhole, The 33 Michael Curtiz
Keyhole Katie 33 Charles Lamont
Keys of Heaven, The 08 Arthur Gilbert
Keys of Heaven, The 28 Karl Freund
Keys of the Kingdom 44 John M. Stahl
Keys of the Righteous, The 18 Jerome Storm
Keys to Happiness 13 Vladimir Gardin, Yakov Protazanov
Kezünkbe Vettük a Béke Ügyét 50 Miklós Jancsó*
Kfafot 87 Rafi Adar
Khabarda 31 Mikhail Chiaureli
Khandar 83 Mrinal Sen
Khareba i Gogi 88 Georgy Shengelaya
Kharidar 88 Kartik Mehta
Kharij 82 Mrinal Sen
Khartoum 66 Yakima Canutt, Basil Dearden, Eliot Elisofon
Khatyal Sasu Nathal Soon 88 N. S. Vaidya
Khaz-Push 27 Amo Bek-Nazarov
Khazdeni za Tri Morya 57 Khwaja Ahmad Abbas, Vassili M. Pronin
Khel Mohabbat Ka 88 Satish Duggal
Khet, Al 37 S. Goskind
Khleb 18 Richard Boleslawski, Boris Suskevich
Kholodni Mart 88 Igor Minaev
Kholodnoe Leto Piatdesiat Tretiego 88 Alexander Prochkin
Khoon Baha Ganga Mein 88 Parveen Bhatt
Khovanschina 59 Vera Stroyeva
Khoziain 86 Bagrat Oganisyan
Khrani Menio Moi Talisman 86 Roman Balajan
Khronika-Molniya 24 Dziga Vertov
Khun-e Siaavash 66 Ferydoun Rahnema
Khveska 20 Alexander Ivanovsky
Khyber Patrol 54 Seymour Friedman
Kiállítás Képei, Egy 54 Miklós Jancsó
Kiáltás és Kiáltás 88 Zsolt Kézdi-Kovács
Kiáltó 64 Márta Mészáros
Kibitzer, The 29 Edward Sloman
Kick Back, The 22 Val Paul

Kick In 17 George Fitzmaurice
Kick In 22 George Fitzmaurice
Kick In 31 Richard Wallace
Kick in Time, A 40 Dave Fleischer
Kick Me, I'm Bill Bailey 05 Jasper Redfern
Kick-Off, The 26 Wesley Ruggles
Kick-Off!, The 31 George Stevens
Kickapoo Juice 44 Howard Swift
Kickboxer 89 Mark DiSalle, David Worth
Kickin' the Conga 'Round 42 Dave Fleischer
Kicking the Moon Around 38 Walter Forde
Kico 51 Dušan Vukotić
Kid, The 10 Frank Powell
Kid, The 16 Wilfred North
Kid, The 20 Charles Chaplin
Kid, The 86 Alain Corneau
Kid 88 Mark Robinson
Kid and the Cowboy, The 19 B. Reeves Eason
Kid Auto Races at Venice 14 Henry Lehrman
Kid Blue 73 James Frawley
Kid Boots 26 Frank Tuttle
Kid Brother, The 27 J. A. Howe, Lewis Milestone, Ted Wilde
Kid Brother 56 Alexander Hammid
Kid Brother, The 87 Claude Gagnon
Kid Canfield the Reform Gambler 22 Kid Canfield
Kid Casey the Champion 16 Frank Moser
Kid Colossus, The 54 Harold Young
Kid Colter 85 David O'Malley
Kid Comes Back, The 37 B. Reeves Eason
Kid Courageous 35 Robert North Bradbury
Kid Dynamite 43 Wallace Fox
Kid for Two Farthings, A 54 Carol Reed
Kid from Amarillo, The 51 Ray Nazarro
Kid from Arizona, The 31 Robert J. Horner
Kid from Broken Gun, The 52 Fred F. Sears
Kid from Brooklyn, The 46 Norman Z. McLeod
Kid from Canada, The 57 Kay Mander
Kid from Cleveland, The 49 Herbert Kline
Kid from Gower Gulch, The 50 Oliver Drake
Kid from Kansas, The 41 William Nigh
Kid from Kokomo, The 39 Lewis Seiler
Kid from Left Field, The 53 Harmon Jones
Kid from Not-So-Big, The 78 William Crain
Kid from Santa Fe, The 40 Raymond K. Johnson
Kid from Spain, The 32 Leo McCarey
Kid from Texas, The 39 S. Sylvan Simon
Kid from Texas, The 49 Kurt Neumann
Kid Galahad 37 Michael Curtiz
Kid Galahad 62 Phil Karlson
Kid Glove Killer 42 Fred Zinnemann
Kid Gloves 29 Ray Enright
Kid Hayseed 28 Charles Lamont
Kid il Monello del West 73 T. Good
Kid Is Clever, The 18 Paul Powell
Kid Magicians, The 15 Chester M. Franklin, Sidney Franklin

Kid Millions 34 Roy Del Ruth, Willy Pogany
Kid Monk Baroni 52 Harold Schuster
Kid 'n Hollywood 33 Charles Lamont
Kid Nightingale 39 George Amy
Kid Ranger, The 36 Robert North Bradbury
Kid Rides Again, The 43 Sam Newfield
Kid Rodelo 66 Richard Carlson
Kid Sister, The 27 Ralph Graves
Kid Sister, The 45 Sam Newfield
Kid Snatchers 17 Archie Mayo
Kid Speed 24 Larry Semon, Noel Mason Smith
Kid Tricks 27 Charles Lamont
Kid Vengeance 77 Joseph Manduke
Kidco 82 Ronald F. Maxwell
Kiddie 11 Bert Haldane
Kiddie Review 36 Walter Lantz
Kiddies in the Ruins, The 18 George Pearson
Kiddie's Kitty, A 55 Friz Freleng
Kiddies on Parade 35 Stewart B. Moss
Kiddin' the Kitten 52 Robert McKimson
Kidding Captain Kidd 23 W. E. Stark
Kidnap 52 Ján Kadár, Elmar Klos
Kidnap of Mary Lou, The 74 Umberto Lenzi
Kidnap Syndicate 75 Fernando Di Leo
Kidnapped 07 Lewin Fitzhamon
Kidnapped 17 Alan Crosland
Kidnapped 33 Alexander Hall
Kidnapped 38 Otto Preminger, Alfred L. Werker
Kidnapped 48 William Beaudine
Kidnapped 52 Ján Kadár, Elmar Klos
Kidnapped 60 Robert Stevenson
Kidnapped 69 Alberto Cardone
Kidnapped 71 Delbert Mann
Kidnapped 86 Hikmet Avedis
Kidnapped Child, The 04 Charles Raymond
Kidnapped for Revenge 13 Ernest G. Batley
Kidnapped King, The 15 Joe Evans
Kidnapped Servant, The 10 Fred Rains
Kidnapper, The 58 Leopoldo Torre-Nilsson
Kidnapper and the Child, The 06 Lewin Fitzhamon
Kidnappers, The 53 Philip Leacock
Kidnappers, The 64 Eddie Romero
Kidnapping of the President, The 80 George Mendeluk
Kids Are Alright, The 79 Jeff Stein
Kid's Clever, The 28 William James Craft
Kids Find Candy's Catching, The 20 Frank Moser
Kids in the Shoe, The 35 Dave Fleischer
Kids Is Kids 20 Charlie Chase
Kid's Kite, The 10 H. Oceano Martinek
Kids' Last Fight, The 33 Charles Lamont
Kids' Last Fight, The 33 Archie Mayo
Kid's Last Ride, The 41 S. Roy Luby
Kids Together 19 Will Scott
Kié a Müvészet? 75 András Kovács
Kiedy Ty Śpisz 50 Andrzej Wajda
Kierunek Nowa Huta 51 Andrzej Munk
Kiev Comedy, A 63 Victor Ivanov
Kiff Tebbi 27 Mario Camerini

Kiffer's High Finance 19 Frank Miller
Kiga Kaikyō 64 Tomu Uchida
Kigeki Dai Shōgeki 70 Hirokazu Ichimura
Kiiroi Karasu 57 Heinosuke Gosho
Kiki 26 Clarence Brown
Kiki 31 Sam Taylor
Kiki 32 Karel Lamač
Kiku and Isamu 58 Tadashi Imai
Kiku to Isamu 58 Tadashi Imai
Kil 1 62 Arnold Louis Miller
Kildare of Storm 18 Harry Franklin
Kilenc Hónap 76 Márta Mészáros
9-es Kórterem 55 Károly Makk
Kilencvenkilenc 18 Michael Curtiz
Kill 68 Kihachi Okamoto
Kill, The 68 Gary Graver
Kill 71 Romain Gary
Kill a Dragon 67 Michael Moore
Kill and Go Hide 77 Robert Voskanian
Kill and Kill Again 81 Ivan Hall
Kill, Baby, Kill 66 Mario Bava
Kill Barbara with Panic 73 Celso Ad Castillo
Kill Castro 80 Chuck Workman
Kill City 87 Peter Lindholm
Kill Her Gently 57 Charles Saunders
Kill Him for Me 50 Roberto Gavaldón
Kill Johnny Ringo 66 Gianfranco Baldanello
Kill-Joy, The 17 Fred E. Wright
Kill! Kill! Kill! 71 Romain Gary
Kill Me Again 89 John Dahl
Kill Me, Cop 89 Jacek Bromski
Kill Me Quick, I'm Cold 68 Francesco Maselli
Kill Me Tomorrow 57 Terence Fisher
Kill-Off, The 90 Maggie Greenwald
Kill or Be Killed 42 Len Lye
Kill or Be Killed 50 Max Nosseck
Kill or Be Killed 66 Tanio Boccia
Kill or Be Killed 80 Ivan Hall
Kill or Cure 28 Hugh Shields
Kill or Cure 62 George Pollock
Kill or Die 87 Rafael Villaseñor Kuri
Kill Patrice, un Shérif Pas Comme les Autres 69 François Reichenbach
Kill Squad 81 Patrick G. Donahue
Kill That Fly 14 Cecil Birch
Kill That Rat 41 Terry Bishop
Kill the Dragon 89 Mark Zakharov
Kill the Golden Goose 79 Elliot Hong
Kill the Umpire! 50 Lloyd Bacon
Kill Them All and Come Back Alone 68 Enzo G. Castellari
Kill Zone 85 David A. Prior
Killbots 86 Jim Wynorski
Killed at War 62 Gleb Panfilov
Killer, The 21 Jack Conway, Howard Hickman
Killer, The 32 David Howard
Killer! 69 Claude Chabrol
Killer, The 73 Yuan Chu
Killer, The 89 John Woo
Killer, Adiós 68 Primo Zeglio
Killer Ape 53 Spencer G. Bennet
Killer at Large 36 David Selman
Killer at Large 47 William Beaudine
Killer Bait 49 Byron Haskin
Killer Bats 40 Jean Yarbrough
Killer Behind the Mask, The 76 David

Paulsen
Killer Calibre 32 67 Alfonso Brescia
Killer Calibro 32 67 Alfonso Brescia
Killer Dill 47 Lewis D. Collins
Killer Diller 48 Josh Binney
Killer Dino 57 Thomas Carr
Killer-Dog 36 Jacques Tourneur
Killer Elite, The 75 Sam Peckinpah
Killer Fish 78 Antonio Margheriti, Herbert V. Theiss
Killer Force 75 Val Guest
Killer Grizzly 76 William Girdler
Killer Inside Me, The 75 Burt Kennedy
Killer Instinct 87 Cirio Santiago
Killer Is Loose, The 55 Budd Boetticher
Killer Kid, The 67 Leopoldo Savona
Killer Klowns 88 Stephen Chiodo
Killer Klowns from Outer Space 88 Stephen Chiodo
Killer Leopard 54 Ford Beebe, Edward Morey, Jr.
Killer Lives at 21, The 41 Henri-Georges Clouzot
Killer Man 72 José Giovanni
Killer McCoy 47 Roy Rowland
Killer Nun 78 Giulio Berruti
Killer of Killers 72 Michael Winner
Killer of Sheep 77 Charles Burnett
Killer on a Horse 66 Burt Kennedy
Killer Orphan 79 John Ballard
Killer Party 86 William Fruet
Killer per Sua Maestà, Un 68 Maurice Cloche, Richard Owens
Killer Shark 50 Budd Boetticher
Killer Shrews, The 59 Ray Kellogg
Killer Spy 58 Georges Lampin
Killer That Stalked New York, The 50 Earl McEvoy
Killer Walks, A 52 Ronald Drake
Killer Whale 76 Michael Anderson, Folco Quilici
Killer with a Label 50 Erle C. Kenton
Killer Workout 87 David A. Prior
Killers, The 46 Robert Siodmak
Killers, The 64 Don Siegel
Killers, The 81 Patrick Roth
Killers Are Challenged 65 Mario Donen
Killers' Cage 60 Ernst R. von Theumer
Killer's Carnival 65 Alberto Cardone, Robert Lynn, Sheldon Reynolds
Killer's Delight 78 Jeremy Hoenack
Killers from Kilimanjaro 59 Richard Thorpe
Killers from Space 54 W. Lee Wilder
Killer's Kiss 55 Stanley Kubrick
Killer's Moon 78 Alan Birkinshaw
Killer's Nocturne 87 Lai-choi Nam
Killers of Kilimanjaro 59 Richard Thorpe
Killers of the East 54 Gian Paolo Callegari, Ralph Murphy
Killers of the Prairie 38 Samuel Diege
Killers of the Sea 37 Ray Friedgin
Killers of the Wild 40 Charles Hutchinson, Vin Moore
Killers on Parade 61 Masahiro Shinoda
Killers Three 68 Bruce Kessler
Killing, The 56 Stanley Kubrick
Killing Affair, A 85 David Saperstein
Killing at Monte Carlo 60 Mario Camerini
Killing Cars 86 Michael Verhoeven

Killing 'Em Softly *85* Max Fischer
Killing Fields, The *84* Roland Joffé
Killing Floor, The *84* Bill Duke
Killing Game, The *67* Alain Jessua
Killing Game, The *88* Joseph Merhi
Killing Heat *81* Michael Raeburn
Killing Hour, The *82* Armand Mastroianni
Killing Kind, The *73* Curtis Harrington
Killing Machine *83* José Antonio De la Loma
Killing of a Chinese Bookie, The *76* John Cassavetes
Killing of America, The *82* Sheldon Renan
Killing of Angel Street, The *81* Donald Crombie
Killing of Santa Claus, The *40* Christian-Jaque
Killing of Satan, The *86* Efren C. Piñon
Killing of Sister George, The *68* Robert Aldrich
Killing Time, The *87* Rick King
Killing to Live *31* Vladimir Korolevitch
Killing Urge, The *59* Cy Endfield
Killing with Kindness *88* Evald Schorm
Killpoint *84* Frank Harris
Kilmeny *15* Oscar Apfel
Kilroy on Deck *48* Frank McDonald
Kilroy Was Here *47* Phil Karlson
Kilties *27* Norman Taurog
Kilties Are Coming, The *51* Robert Jordan Hill
Kilties Three *18* Maurice Sandground
Kim *50* Victor Saville
Kim Jest Ten Człowiek *85* Ewa Petelska, Czesław Petelski
Kimberley Jim *65* Emil Nofal
Kimi ga Kagayaku Toki *86* Tokihisa Morikawa
Kimi to Iku Michi *36* Mikio Naruse
Kimi to Wakarete *32* Mikio Naruse
Kimi to Yuku Michi *36* Mikio Naruse
Kimi wa Hadashi no Kami o Mitaka *86* Soo-gil Kim
Kimiko *35* Mikio Naruse
Kin *26* Kenji Mizoguchi
Kin-Dza-Dza *87* Georgy Danelia
Kína Vendégei Voltunk *57* Miklós Jancsó
Kind, ein Hund, ein Vagabond, Ein *34* Arthur Maria Rabenalt
Kind Hearted Percival *11* Frank Wilson
Kind Hearts and Coronets *49* Robert Hamer
Kind Hearts Are More Than Coronets *13* Wilfred Noy
Kind Lady *35* George B. Seitz
Kind Lady *51* John Sturges
Kind Millionaire, The *49* Martin Frič
Kind of English, A *86* Ruhul Amin
Kind of Loving, A *62* John Schlesinger
Kind Ruft, Das *14* Urban Gad
Kind Stepmother *35* Béla Balázs
Kindar the Invulnerable *64* Osvaldo Civirani
Kinder, Die *66* Edgar Reitz
Kinder der Finsternis *22* E. A. Dupont
Kinder der Strasse *28* Carl Boese
Kinder des Generals, Die *12* Urban Gad
Kinder, Mütter und ein General *55* Laslo

Benedek
Kindergarten *72* Yevgeny Yevtushenko
Kindergarten Cop *90* Brian Grazer, Ivan Reitman
Kinderseelen Klagen An *27* Kurt Bernhardt
Kinderseelen Klagen Euch An *27* Kurt Bernhardt
Kindertragödie *27* Piel Jutzi
Kindled Courage *23* William Worthington
Kindling *15* Cecil B. DeMille
Kindly Remove Your Hat, or She Didn't Mind *13* Percy Stow
Kindly Scram *43* Alec Geiss
Kindred, The *86* Stephen Carpenter, Jeffrey Obrow
Kindred of the Dust *22* Raoul Walsh
Kinema Girl, The *14* Percy Stow
Kinema no Tenchi *86* Yoji Yamada
Kinemacolor Puzzle *09* George Albert Smith
Kinemacolor Songs *11* Theo Bouwmeester
Kinesiske Vase, Den *13* August Blom
Kinetic Art Show, Stockholm *61* Robert Breer
Kineto's Side-Splitters No. 1 *15* Walter R. Booth
Kinfolk *70* John Hayes
Kinfolk *81* Nikita Mikhalkov
King, The *41* Pierre Colombier
King, The *50* Marc-Gilbert Sauvajon
King: A Filmed Record, Montgomery to Memphis *69* Sidney Lumet, Joseph L. Mankiewicz
King and Country *64* Joseph Losey
King and Four Queens, The *56* Raoul Walsh
King and His Movie, A *86* Carlos Sorin
King and I, The *56* Walter Lang
King and Mr. Bird, The *67* Paul Grimault
King and the Chorus Girl, The *37* Mervyn LeRoy
King and the Jester, The *07* Georges Méliès
King Arthur Was a Gentleman *42* Marcel Varnel
King Blank *83* Michael Oblowitz
King Charles *13* Wilfred Noy
King Charlie *14* Charles Chaplin
King Chico *86* Walter Lima Júnior
King Cobra *79* Bob Claver
King Cowboy *28* Robert De Lacey
King Creole *58* Michael Curtiz
King David *85* Bruce Beresford
King Dinosaur *55* Bert I. Gordon
King Elephant *72* Simon Trevor
King for a Day *40* Dave Fleischer
King for a Day *85* Nikolai Volev
King for a Night *33* Kurt Neumann
King Frat *79* Ken Wiederhorn
King Game, The *67* Jaromil Jireš
King Goes Forth to France, The *86* Anssi Mänttäri
King Gun *71* Robert Gordon
King Haakon VII *52* Henning Carlsen, Titus Vibé-Müller
King in New York, A *57* Charles Chaplin
King in Shadow *56* Harald Braun
King Kelly of the U.S.A. *34* Leonard

Fields
King Klunk *33* Walter Lantz
King Kong *33* Merian C. Cooper, Ernest B. Schoedsack
King Kong *76* John Guillermin
King Kong Escapes *67* Inoshiro Honda, Arthur Rankin, Jr.
King Kong Lives *86* John Guillermin
King Kong no Gyakushū *67* Inoshiro Honda, Arthur Rankin, Jr.
King Kong Tai Godzilla *63* Inoshiro Honda, Thomas Montgomery
King Kong Tai Gojira *63* Inoshiro Honda, Thomas Montgomery
King Kong vs. Godzilla *63* Inoshiro Honda, Thomas Montgomery
King Kong's Counterattack *67* Inoshiro Honda, Arthur Rankin, Jr.
King Lavra *50* Karel Zeman
King Lear *16* Ernest C. Warde
King Lear *69* Peter Brook
King Lear *70* Grigori Kozintsev
King Lear *87* Jean-Luc Godard
King Lear *87* Anssi Mänttäri
King Matthew I *57* Wanda Jakubowska
King Midas, Junior *42* John Hubley, Paul Sommer
King Monster *77* Richard Martin
King Murder, The *32* Richard Thorpe
King, Murray *69* Jonathan Gordon, David Hoffman
King Oedipus *57* Tyrone Guthrie
King of a Penny *26* Kenji Mizoguchi
King of Africa *67* Sandy Howard
King of Alcatraz *37* Robert Florey
King of Ayodhya, The *32* Rajaram Vanakudre Shantaram
King of Boda *20* Gustaf Molander
King of Burlesque *35* Sidney Lanfield
King of Chess *48* Daisuke Ito
King of Chess *90* Hark Tsui
King of Children *87* Kaige Chen
King of Chinatown *39* Nick Grindé
King of Clubs, The *05* J. H. Martin
King of Coins *03* Alf Collins
King of Comedy, The *82* Martin Scorsese
King of Crime, The *14* Sidney Northcote
King of Diamonds, The *18* Paul Scardon
King of Dodge City *41* Lambert Hillyer
King of Endings *87* Živorad Tomić
King of Gamblers *37* Robert Florey
King of Hearts *36* Oswald Mitchell, Walter Tennyson
King of Hearts *66* Philippe de Broca
King of Hockey *36* Noel Mason Smith
King of Indigo, The *11* Theo Bouwmeester
King of Jazz *30* John Murray Anderson, Pál Fejös
King of Kings, The *26* Cecil B. DeMille
King of Kings *61* Nicholas Ray
King of Kings *63* Martin Frič
King of Kong Island *78* Robert Morris
King of Marvin Gardens, The *72* Bob Rafelson
King of New York *90* Abel Ferrara
King of Paris, The *17* Yevgeni Bauer
King of Paris, The *34* Jack Raymond
King of Rio *86* Fabio Barreto
King of Seven Dials, The *14* Charles H. Weston

King of Sharpshooters, The 05 Georges Méliès

King of Smugglers 85 Sune Lund-Sørensen

King of the Alcatraz 37 Robert Florey

King of the Arena 33 Alvin J. Neitz

King of the Bandits 47 Christy Cabanne

King of the Beasts, The 26 Clyde Geronimi

King of the Bullwhip 50 Ron Ormond

King of the Carnival 55 Franklin Adreon

King of the Castle 25 Henry Edwards

King of the Castle 36 Redd Davis

King of the Children 87 Kaige Chen

King of the Circus 20 John P. McGowan

King of the Circus 24 Max Linder, Édouard E. Violet

King of the City 86 Norman Thaddeus Vane

King of the Congo 52 Spencer G. Bennet, Wallace A. Grissell

King of the Coral Sea 56 Noel Monkman, Lee Robinson

King of the Cowboys 43 Joseph Kane

King of the Criminals, The 68 Paolo Bianchini

King of the Damned 35 Walter Forde

King of the Forest Rangers 46 Spencer G. Bennet, Fred C. Brannon

King of the Gamblers, The 37 Robert Florey

King of the Gamblers 48 George Blair

King of the Grizzlies 70 Ron Kelly

King of the Gypsies, The 33 Frank R. Strayer

King of the Gypsies 78 Frank Pierson

King of the Herd 27 Frank S. Mattison

King of the Ice Rink 36 Noel Mason Smith

King of the Jungle 33 H. Bruce Humberstone, Max Marcin

King of the Jungleland 36 B. Reeves Eason, Joseph Kane

King of the Keyboard 43 Horace Shepherd

King of the Khyber Rifles 29 John Ford, Lumsden Hare

King of the Khyber Rifles 53 Henry King

King of the Kongo 29 Richard Thorpe

King of the Lumberjacks 40 William Clemens

King of the Mardi Gras 35 Dave Fleischer

King of the Mongols 64 Kato Tai

King of the Mountain 64 Ralph Levy

King of the Mountain 81 Noel Nosseck

King of the Mounties 42 William Witney

King of the Newsboys 38 Bernard Vorhaus

King of the Night 75 Hector Babenco

King of the Pack 26 Frank Richardson

King of the Pecos 36 Joseph Kane

King of the People, A 17 Percy Nash

King of the Ragpickers, The 85 Fabrice Cazeneuve

King of the Ritz 33 Carmine Gallone

King of the Roaring Twenties 61 Joseph M. Newman

King of the Roaring Twenties—The Story of Arnold Rothstein 61 Joseph M. Newman

King of the Rocket Men 49 Fred C. Brannon

King of the Rodeo 29 Henry MacRae

King of the Royal Mounted 36 Howard Bretherton

King of the Royal Mounted 40 John English, William Witney

King of the Saddle 26 William James Craft

King of the Sierras 38 Samuel Diege

King of the Stallions 42 Edward Finney

King of the Streets 86 Ed Hunt

King of the Sumava, The 59 Karel Kachyňa

King of the Texas Rangers 41 John English, William Witney

King of the Turf, The 26 James P. Hogan

King of the Turf 39 Alfred E. Green

King of the Underworld 38 Lewis Seiler

King of the Underworld 52 Victor M. Gover

King of the Vikings 60 Luis Lucia

King of the White Elephant, The 41 Sunh Vasudhara

King of the Wild 30 B. Reeves Eason, Richard Thorpe

King of the Wild 33 Earl Haley

King of the Wild Horses, The 24 Fred Jackman

King of the Wild Horses, The 33 Earl Haley

King of the Wild Horses 47 George Archainbaud

King of the Wild Stallions 59 R. G. Springsteen

King of the Zombies 41 Jean Yarbrough

King of Thieves, The 61 Atıf Yılmaz

King of Whales, The 34 Challis Sanderson

King of Wild Horses 33 Earl Haley

King on Horseback 57 Georges Lampin

King on Main Street, The 25 Monta Bell

King, Queen and Knave 71 Jerzy Skolimowski

King, Queen, Joker 21 Sydney Chaplin

King, Queen, Knave 71 Jerzy Skolimowski

King Rat 65 Bryan Forbes

King Richard and the Crusaders 54 David Butler

King Robert of Sicily 12 Hay Plumb

King Robot 52 John Gilling

King-Size Canary 47 Tex Avery

King Size Woman 66 Bruce Beresford

King Social Briars 18 Henry King

King Solomon of Broadway 35 Alan Crosland

King Solomon's Mines 37 Geoffrey Barkas, Robert Stevenson

King Solomon's Mines 50 Compton Bennett, Andrew Marton

King Solomon's Mines 85 J. Lee-Thompson

King Solomon's Treasure 77 Alvin Rakoff

King Spruce 20 Roy Clements

King Steps Out, The 36 Josef von Sternberg

King Tut-Ankh-Amen's Eighth Wife 23 Andrew Remo

King Ubu 76 Jan Lenica

King Without a Crown, The 37 Jacques Tourneur

Kingdom of Diamonds, The 79 Satyajit Ray

Kingdom of Human Hearts, The 21 Wilbert Leroy Cosper

Kingdom of Love, The 17 Frank Lloyd

Kingdom of the Fairies, The 03 Georges Méliès

Kingdom of the Spiders 77 John Cardos

Kingdom of Twilight, The 29 Alexander MacDonald

Kingdom of Youth, The 18 Clarence Badger

Kingdom on the Waters, A 52 Ivan Nagy

Kingdom Within, The 22 Victor Schertzinger

Kingfish Caper, The 75 Dirk DeVilliers

Kingfisher Caper, The 75 Dirk DeVilliers

Kingfisher's Roost, The 22 Louis Chaudet, Paul Hurst

Kings and Desperate Men 81 Alexis Kanner

Kings and Queens 56 Paul Czinner

King's Breakfast, The 28 Frank Miller

King's Breakfast, The 36 Lotte Reiniger

King's Breakfast, The 63 Wendy Toye

King's Cake, The 86 Jean-Michel Ribes

King's Creek Law 23 Leo D. Maloney, Bob Williamson

King's Cup, The 32 Alan Cobham, Robert Cullen, Donald Macardle, Herbert Wilcox

King's Daughter, The 16 Maurice Elvey

King's Game, The 16 Ashley Miller, George B. Seitz

Kings Go Forth 58 Delmer Daves

King's Highway, The 27 Sinclair Hill

King's Jester, The 35 Manny Gould, Ben Harrison

King's Jester, The 41 Mario Bonnard

King's Minister, The 14 Harold M. Shaw

King's Move in the City, The 14 Charles Brabin

Kings of Crime 88 Yuri Kara

Kings of the Forest 12 Colin Campbell

Kings of the Hill 76 Michael Dmytryk

Kings of the Road 75 Wim Wenders

Kings of the Sun 63 J. Lee-Thompson

Kings or Better 31 Edward Buzzell

King's Outcast, The 15 Ralph Dewsbury

King's Pardon, The 08 Edwin S. Porter

King's Pardon, The 11 Dave Aylott

King's People, The 37 John S. Stumar

King's Peril, The 11 H. Oceano Martinek

King's Pirate, The 67 Don Weis

King's Ransom 85 Cirio Santiago

King's Rhapsody 55 Herbert Wilcox

King's Romance, The 14 Ernest G. Batley

King's Row 41 Sam Wood

King's Story, A 67 Harry Booth

King's Thief, The 55 Robert Z. Leonard

King's Vacation, The 33 John G. Adolfi

King's Whore, The 90 Axel Corti

Kingsajz 88 Juliusz Machulski

Kinigi, I 77 Theodoros Angelopoulos

Kinjite 89 J. Lee-Thompson

Kinjite: Forbidden Subjects 89 J. Lee-Thompson

Kinkaid, Gambler 16 Raymond Wells

Kinky Coaches and the Pom-Pom Pussycats, The 81 Mark Warren

Kinnō Jidai 26 Teinosuke Kinugasa

Kino-Concert 1941 41 I. Menaker, Adolph

Klabautermanden 69 Henning Carlsen
Kladivo na Čarodějnice 69 Otakar Vávra
Klänningen 64 Vilgot Sjöman
Klansman, The 74 Terence Young
Klapperstorchverband, Der 38 Carl Boese
Klart til Drabbning 37 Edvin Adolphson
Klass und Datsch die Pechvögel 26 Piel
Jutzi
Klassenverhältnisse 84 Danièle Huillet,
Jean-Marie Straub
Klatsche, Die 39 Edgar G. Ulmer
Klaun Ferdinand a Raketa 62 Jindřich
Polák
Kleider Machen Leute 22 Hans Steinhoff
Kleider Machen Leute 40 Helmut Käutner
Klein Dorrit 34 Karel Lamač
Kleine Chaos, Das 66 Rainer Werner Fass-
binder
Kleine Melodie aus Wien 48 E. W. Emo
Kleine Mutti 34 Henry Koster
Kleine Nachtmusik, Eine 40 Leopold
Hainisch
Kleine Schornsteinfeger, Der 35 Lotte
Reiniger
Kleine Schwindlerin, Die 37 Johannes
Meyer
Kleine Seitensprung, Der 31 Reinhold
Schünzel
Kleine Staatsanwalt, Der 87 Hark Böhm
Kleine Sünderin, Die 38 Carl Boese
Kleine und die Grosse Liebe, Die 38 Josef
von Baky
Kleine Welt im Dunkelen, Eine 38 Hans
Richter
Kleiner Film einer Grossen Stadt: Die
Stadt Düsseldorf am Rhein 35 Walter
Ruttmann
Kleiner Film einer Grossen Stadt: Düssel-
dorf 35 Walter Ruttmann
Kleines Bezirksgericht 39 Alwin Elling
Kleines Zeit und Grosse Liebe 64 Rainer
Geis
Kleinhoff Hotel 77 Carlo Lizzani
Kleinstadtpoet, Der 40 Josef von Baky
Kleptomania Tablets 12 Ernest G. Batley
Kleptomaniac, The 05 Edwin S. Porter
Kleptomaniac, The 14 Warwick Buckland
Kleptomaniacs 49 David Miller
Kleptomanin, Die 18 Urban Gad
Klima, Reina de las Amazonas 75 Miguel
Iglesias Bonns
Klima von Vancourt, Das 17 Joe May
Klinkart 57 Paul Meyer
Klios 87 Costas Coutsomitis
Kliou the Killer 37 Henry De la Falaise
Klondike 32 Phil Rosen
Klondike Annie 36 Raoul Walsh
Klondike Fever 80 Peter Carter
Klondike Fury 42 William K. Howard
Klondike Kate 43 William Castle
Klondike Victory 42 William K. Howard
Klosterfriede 17 Urban Gad
Klosterjäger, Der 36 Max Obal
Klostret i Sendomir 19 Victor Sjöström
Klovnen 16 Anders Wilhelm Sandberg
Klovnen 26 Anders Wilhelm Sandberg
Klubvennen 16 Forest Holger-Madsen
Kluge Schwiegermutter, Die 39 Hans
Deppe
Klugen Frauen, Die 35 Jacques Feyder

Klute 71 Alan J. Pakula
Kluven Värld, En 48 Arne Sucksdorff
Klyatva 46 Mikhail Chiaureli
Klyatva Molodykh 44 Dziga Vertov
Klyatva Timura 42 Alexandra Khokhlova,
Lev Kuleshov
Klyuchi Shchastya 13 Vladimir Gardin,
Yakov Protazanov
Kmo Ty, Vsadnik? 88 Amangheldy
Tazhbayev
Knabe in Blau, Der 19 F. W. Murnau
Knack, The 65 Richard Lester
Knack...and How to Get It, The 65
Richard Lester
Knave of Diamonds, The 21 René Plais-
setty
Knave of Hearts, The 19 F. Martin Thorn-
ton
Knave of Hearts 54 René Clément
Knee Action 36 Charles Lamont
Knee Deep in Daisies 26 Miles Mander
Knickerbocker Buckaroo, The 19 Albert
Parker
Knickerbocker Holiday 44 Harry Joe
Brown
Knife, The 18 Robert Vignola
Knife, The 60 Fons Rademakers
Knife, The 66 Živka Mitrović
Knife for the Ladies, A 73 Larry Spangler
Knife in the Body, The 66 Domenico De
Felice, Elio Scardamaglia
Knife in the Head 78 Reinhard Hauff
Knife in the Water 61 Roman Polanski
Knife of the Party, The 34 Leigh Jason
Knife to Grind, A 13 Will P. Kellino
Kniga v Derevne 29 Alexander Ptushko
Knight, Death and the Devil, The 85
Beppe Cino
Knight Errant, A 07 J. H. Martin
Knight Errant, The 22 George Ridgwell
Knight in Armour, A 14 Toby Cooper
Knight in London, A 27 Lupu Pick
Knight-Mare Hare 55 Chuck Jones
Knight of Black Art, The 07 Georges
Méliès
Knight of the Dragon, The 86 Fernando
Colomo
Knight of the Gold Star, The 50 Yuli
Raizman
Knight of the Plains 38 Sam Newfield
Knight of the Range, A 16 Jacques Jaccard
Knight of the Road, A 11 D. W. Griffith
Knight of the Road, A 14 Warwick Buck-
land
Knight of the Snows, The 10 Georges
Méliès
Knight of the Street 28 Heinosuke Gosho
Knight of the Sword, The 69 Leopoldo
Torre-Nilsson
Knight of the West, A 21 Robert McKen-
zie
Knight Without Armour 37 Jacques Fey-
der
Knightriders 79 George Romero
Knights and Emeralds 86 Ian Emes
Knights and Ladies 28 Frank Miller
Knights Before Xmas 30 Lewis R. Foster
Knights Electric 81 Barney Broom
Knights for a Day 36 Walter Lantz
Knights for a Day 37 Aveling Ginever,

Norman Lee
Knights Must Fall 49 Friz Freleng
Knights of the Black Cross 60 Aleksander
Ford
Knights of the City 85 Dominic Orlando
Knights of the Range 40 Lesley Selander
Knights of the Round Table 53 Richard
Thorpe
Knights of the Square Table 17 Alan
Crosland
Knights of the Square Table, or The Grail
17 Alan Crosland
Knights of the Teutonic Order 60 Alek-
sander Ford
Knights Out 29 Norman Taurog
Knighty Knight Bugs 58 Friz Freleng
Kniplinger 18 August Blom
Kniplinger 26 Forest Holger-Madsen
Knive 54 Henning Carlsen
Knives 54 Henning Carlsen
Knives of the Avenger 65 Mario Bava
Knivstikkeren 13 August Blom
Knock 26 René Hervil
Knock 33 Roger Goupillières, Louis Jouvet
Knock 55 Guy Lefranc
Knock, Knock 40 Walter Lantz
Knock on Any Door 48 Nicholas Ray
Knock on the Door, The 23 William
Hughes Curran
Knock on Wood 54 Melvin Frank, Nor-
man Panama
Knock-Out 35 Karel Lamač, Hans Zerlett
Knock-Out 86 Pavlos Tassios
Knock-Out Blow, The 19 Jerome Storm
Knocker and the Naughty Boys, The 03
Percy Stow
Knocking at Heaven's Door 80 John
Linton
Knocking on the Door, The 23 A. E.
Coleby
Knocking the "H" Out of Heinie 19
Gregory La Cava
Knocking the "I" Out of Kaiser 18 Pat
Sullivan
Knocknagow 18 Fred O'Donovan
Knockout, The 23 Alexander Butler
Knockout, The 25 Lambert Hillyer
Knockout 40 Lloyd Bacon
Knockout 41 William Clemens
Knockout 42 Carmine Gallone
Knockout, The 47 Reginald LeBorg
Knockout Blow, The 12 F. Martin
Thornton
Knockout Blow, The 17 Walter West
Knockout Cop, The 74 Steno
Knockout Drops 35 Charles Lamont
Knockout Kid, The 25 Albert S. Rogell
Knockout Kisses 33 George Marshall
Knockout Reilly 27 Malcolm St. Clair
Knocturne 72 George Kuchar, Mike
Kuchar
Knot, The 86 Kiril Čenevski
Knot in the Plot, A 10 D. W. Griffith
Knotty Problem, A 59 Henning Carlsen
Know Your Ally: Britain 43 Frank Capra
Know Your Enemy: Germany 45 Frank
Capra
Know Your Enemy: Japan 45 Frank
Capra, Joris Ivens
Know Your Man 21 Charles Giblyn

Kurobe no Taiyō *68* Kei Kumai
Kuroda Seichūroku *38* Teinosuke Kinugasa
Kuroda Sōdō *56* Tomu Uchida
Kuroi Ame *88* Shohei Imamura
Kuroi Jūnin no Onna *61* Kon Ichikawa
Kuroi Kawa *57* Masaki Kobayashi
Kuroi Ushio *54* So Yamamura
Kuroneko *67* Kaneto Shindo
Kurragömma *63* Lars-Magnus Lindgren
Kurşun Ata Ata Biter *86* Ümit Elçi
Kurşunların Kanunu *69* Mahinur Ergün
Kurukshetra *88* Bhargava
Kurukshetra *88* Sriram Panda
Kurutta Ippeiji *26* Teinosuke Kinugasa
Kuruzsló, A *17* Michael Curtiz
Kurve Kriegen, Die *85* Monica Teuber
Kusha Laila *40* Debaki Kumar Bose
Kustens Glada Kavaljerer *39* Ragnar Arvedson
Kustom Kar Kommandos *64* Kenneth Anger
Kutásek a Kutilka Jak Ráno Vstávali *52* Jiří Trnka
Kutasek and Kutilka *52* Jiří Trnka
Kutsū *27* Tomu Uchida
Kutsukate Tokijiro *34* Teinosuke Kinugasa
Kutuzov *44* Vladimir Petrov
Kuu On Vaarallinen *63* Toivo Särkkä
69 *69* Jörn Donner
Kuutamosonaatti *88* Olli Soinio
Kuyucaklı Yusuf *86* Feyzi Tuna
Kuzmich *59* Igor Talankin
Kvarnen *21* John W. Brunius
Kvarteret Korpen *62* Bo Widerberg
Kvartetten Som Sprängdes *50* Gustaf Molander
Kvindedyr *64* Henning Carlsen
Kvinna i Vitt *49* Arne Mattsson
Kvinna Utan Ansikte *47* Gustaf Molander
Kvinnan Bakom Allt *51* Erik Faustman
Kvinnas Ansikte, En *37* Gustaf Molander
Kvinnas Slav, En *12* Mauritz Stiller
Kvinnodröm *54* Ingmar Bergman
Kvinnohuset *53* Erik Faustman
Kvinnorna på Taket *89* Carl-Gustaf Nykvist
Kvinnors Väntan *52* Ingmar Bergman
Kwaidan *64* Masaki Kobayashi
Kweer Kuss, A *15* Dave Aylott
Kybernetická Babička *62* Jiří Trnka
Kyeoul Nagune *87* Chi-gyoon Kwak
Kyō mo Mata Kakute Arinan *59* Keisuke Kinoshita
Kyōfu Kikei Ningen *69* Teruo Ishii
Kyokubadan no Joō *24* Kenji Mizoguchi
Kyomo Ware Ōzorani Ari *65* Kengo Furusawa
Kyōnetsu no Kisetsu *63* Koreyoshi Kurahara
Kyōren no Butō *24* Teinosuke Kinugasa
Kyōren no Onna Shishō *26* Kenji Mizoguchi
Kyōshitsu no Kodomotachi *54* Susumu Hani
Kyoshu *88* Takehiro Nakajima
Kyōsō Mikka-Kan *27* Tomu Uchida
Kyōtō *68* Kon Ichikawa
Kyriakatiko Xyprima *53* Michael Cacoyannis

Kyritz-Pyritz *32* Karl Heinz Wolff
Kyssen på Kryssen *50* Arne Mattsson
Kyūbi no Kitsune to Tobimaru *69* Shin-ichi Yagi
Kyūjū-Kyūhonme no Kimusume *59* Morihei Magatani
Kyūketsu Dokurosen *68* Hiroshi Matsuno
Kyūketsuki Gokemidoro *68* Hajime Sato
Kyvaldo, Jáma a Naděje *83* Jan Švankmajer
L.A. Bounty *89* Worth Keeter
L.A. Crackdown *88* Joseph Merhi
L.A. Crackdown II *88* Joseph Merhi
L.A. Heat *89* Joseph Merhi
L.A. Streetfighters *86* Richard Park
L.A.X. *80* Fabrice Ziolkowski
LBJ *68* Santiago Álvarez
LMNO *78* Robert Breer
LO-LKP *48* Max De Haas
LSD—I Hate You! *66* Albert Zugsmith
L-Shaped Room, The *62* Bryan Forbes
La Anam *57* Salah Abu Saif
La Bamba *87* Luis Valdez
La Conga Nights *40* Lew Landers
La Cucaracha *34* Lloyd Corrigan
La Cucaracha *59* Ismael Rodríguez
Là dalle Ardenne all'Inferno *69* Alberto De Martino
La La Lucille *20* Eddie Lyons, Lee Moran
La Paloma *30* Dave Fleischer
La Paloma *36* Karl Heinz Martin
La Paloma *37* Miguel Torres Contreras
La Paloma *44* Helmut Käutner
La Paloma *74* Daniel Schmid
La Tutfi el Shems *61* Salah Abu Saif
Laastste Reis, De *88* Kees Hin
Labbra Rosse *64* Giuseppe Bennati
Labda Varázsa, A *62* Márta Mészáros
Labedzi Spiew *88* Robert Glinski
Laberinto de Pasiones *82* Pedro Almodóvar
Lábios Sem Beijos *30* Humberto Mauro
Labirintus *76* András Kovács
Labirynt *62* Jan Lenica
Laboratory of Mephistopheles *1897* Georges Méliès
Labour Leader, The *17* Thomas Bentley
Labour of Love, A *82* Margarethe von Trotta
Laburnum Grove *36* Carol Reed
Labyrinth, The *15* E. Mason Hopper
Labyrinth *59* Rolf Thiele
Labyrinth *62* Jan Lenica
Labyrinth *71* William A. Fraker
Labyrinth *76* András Kovács
Labyrinth *86* Jim Henson
Labyrinth der Leidenschaft *59* Rolf Thiele
Labyrinth des Grauens *20* Michael Curtiz
Labyrinth of Horror *20* Michael Curtiz
Labyrinth of Passion *82* Pedro Almodóvar
Lac aux Dames *34* Marc Allégret
Lac d'Argent, Le *22* Gaston Roudès
Lac des Morts Vivants, Le *80* Jean Rollin
Lac Enchanté, Le *08* Georges Méliès
Lace *18* August Blom
Lace *28* Sergei Yutkevich
Lace Rope, The *64* Joe Sarno
Lacemaker, The *77* Claude Goretta
Lachdoktor, Der *38* Fred Sauer
Lache, Bajazzo *14* Richard Oswald

Lachende Dritte, Der *38* Georg Zoch
Lachende Erben, Die *31* Max Ophüls
Lachende Grauen, Das *20* Lupu Pick
Lâches Vivent d'Espoir, Les *60* Claude Bernard-Aubert
Lackey and the Lady, The *19* Thomas Bentley
Lacombe, Lucien *73* Louis Malle
Lacrime e Sorrisi *36* Raffaello Matarazzo
Lad, The *35* Henry Edwards
Lad: A Dog *61* Aram Avakian, Leslie Martinson
Lad and the Lion, The *17* Alfred E. Green
Lad from Old Ireland, The *09* Sidney Olcott
Lad from Our Town, A *42* Boris Ivanov, Alexander Stolper
Lad-in Bagdad, A- *38* Cal Dalton, Cal Howard
Lad in His Lamp, A *48* Robert McKimson
Ladder, The *67* George Dunning
Ladder Jinx, The *22* Jess Robbins
Ladder of Lies, The *20* Tom Forman
Ladder of Success, The *58* Kozaburo Yoshimura
Laddie *20* Bannister Merwin
Laddie *26* James Leo Meehan
Laddie *35* George Stevens
Laddie *40* Jack Hively
Laddie Be Good *28* Bennett Cohn
Ladies *54* Lev Kulidzhanov, Genrikh Oganisyan, Yakov Segel
Ladies and Gentlemen…The Fabulous Stains *81* Lou Adler
Ladies and Gentlemen, the Rolling Stones *75* Rollin Binzer
Ladies and Ladies *67* Luigi Zampa
Ladies at Ease *27* Jerome Storm
Ladies at Play *26* Alfred E. Green
Ladies Be Careful of Your Sleeves *32* Mikio Naruse
Ladies Beware *27* Charles Giblyn
Ladies' Club, The *84* Janet Greek
Ladies Courageous *44* John Rawlins
Ladies Crave Excitement *35* Nick Grindé
Ladies' Day *43* Leslie Goodwins
Ladies First *63* Raoul André
Ladies in Distress *38* Gus Meins
Ladies in Love *30* Edgar Lewis
Ladies in Love *36* Edward H. Griffith
Ladies in Retirement *41* Charles Vidor
Ladies in the Green Hats, The *37* Maurice Cloche
Ladies in Washington *44* Louis King
Ladies' Journal, The *11* August Blom
Ladies Last *30* George Stevens
Ladies Love Brutes *30* Rowland V. Lee
Ladies Love Danger *35* H. Bruce Humberstone
Ladies' Man *31* Lothar Mendes
Ladies' Man *47* William D. Russell
Ladies' Man *60* Bernard Borderie
Ladies' Man, The *61* Jerry Lewis
Ladies Must Dress *27* Victor Heerman
Ladies Must Live *21* George Loane Tucker
Ladies Must Live *40* Noel Mason Smith
Ladies Must Love *33* E. A. Dupont
Ladies Must Play *30* Raymond Cannon
Ladies' Night *28* Edward F. Cline
Ladies' Night in a Turkish Bath *28* Edward F. Cline

Ladies Not Allowed *32* Joseph Santley
Ladies of Leisure *26* Thomas Buckingham
Ladies of Leisure *30* Frank Capra
Ladies of the Big House *31* Marion Gering
Ladies of the Bois de Boulogne, The *45* Robert Bresson
Ladies of the Chorus *46* Sam Newfield
Ladies of the Chorus *48* Phil Karlson
Ladies of the Jury *32* Lowell Sherman
Ladies of the Lotus *87* Douglas C. Nicolle, Lloyd A. Simandl
Ladies of the Mob *28* William A. Wellman
Ladies of the Mob *60* Walter Doniger, Crane Wilbur
Ladies of the Night Club *28* George Archainbaud
Ladies of the Park *45* Robert Bresson
Ladies of Washington *44* Louis King
Ladies on the Rocks *83* Christian Braad Thomsen
Ladies Only *34* Christian-Jaque
Ladies Preferred *28* Charles Lamont
Ladies Should Listen *34* Frank Tuttle
Ladies They Talk About *33* Howard Bretherton, William Keighley
Ladies to Board *24* John G. Blystone
Ladies Who Do *63* C. M. Pennington-Richards
Ladoumègue *32* Jean Lods
Ladra, La *55* Mario Bonnard
Ladri, I *59* Lucio Fulci
Ladri di Biciclette *48* Vittorio De Sica
Ladri di Saponette *89* Maurizio Nichetti
Ladro di Bagdad, Il *60* Arthur Lubin
Ladro di Donne *36* Abel Gance
Ladro di Venezia, Il *50* John Brahm
Ladro Lui, Ladro Lei *58* Luigi Zampa
Ladrón de Cadáveres, El *56* Fernando Méndez
Ladros de Niños *57* Benito Alazraki
Lads and Lasses on Parade *51* Robert Jordan Hill
Lads of the Village, The *19* Harry Lorraine
Lady, The *25* Frank Borzage
Lady, The *87* Jordi Cadena
Lady and Gent *32* Stephen Roberts
Lady and Her Favorites, The *30* Yasujiro Ozu
Lady and the Bandit, The *51* Ralph Murphy
Lady and the Beard, The *30* Yasujiro Ozu
Lady and the Burglar, The *15* Herbert Blaché
Lady and the Doctor, The *44* George Sherman
Lady and the Mob, The *39* Ben Stoloff
Lady and the Monster, The *44* George Sherman
Lady and the Mouse, The *13* D. W. Griffith
Lady and the Outlaw, The *72* Ted Kotcheff
Lady and the Tramp *55* Clyde Geronimi, Wilfred Jackson, Hamilton Luske
Lady Angela and the Boy *12* Warwick Buckland
Lady at Midnight *48* Sam Newfield
Lady Audley's Secret *20* Jack Denton
Lady Avenger *87* David DeCoteau

Lady Baffles and Detective Duck *15* Allen Curtis
Lady Barber, The *1898* George Albert Smith
Lady Barnacle *17* John H. Collins
Lady Be Careful *36* Theodore Reed
Lady Be Gay *39* Albert S. Rogell
Lady Be Good *28* Richard Wallace
Lady Be Good *41* Norman Z. McLeod
Lady Be Kind *41* Rodney Ackland
Lady, Be Not Wronged *23* Teinosuke Kinugasa
Lady Beaulay's Necklace *11* Theo Bouwmeester
Lady Behave *38* Lloyd Corrigan
Lady Beware *32* Albert Ray
Lady Beware *87* Karen Arthur
Lady Bodyguard *42* William Clemens
Lady by Choice *34* David Burton
Lady Candale's Diamonds *10* S. Wormald
Lady Caroline Lamb *72* Robert Bolt
Lady Charlie *14* Charles Chaplin
Lady Chaser *46* Sam Newfield
Lady Chatterley's Lover *55* Marc Allégret
Lady Chatterley's Lover *81* Just Jaeckin
Lady Chatterly vs. Fanny Hill *70* Mike Leigh
Lady Clare, The *13* Ashley Miller
Lady Clare, The *19* Wilfred Noy
Lady Cocoa *75* Matt Cimber
Lady Confesses, The *45* Sam Newfield
Lady Consents, The *36* Stephen Roberts
Lady Craved Excitement, The *50* Francis Searle
Lady Dances, The *34* Ernst Lubitsch
Lady Detective, The *15* Joe Evans
Lady Doctor *56* Camillo Mastrocinque
Lady Dracula *72* Jorge Grau
Lady Dracula *73* Richard Blackburn
Lady Dracula *77* Franz-Josef Gottlieb
Lady Escapes, The *37* Eugene Forde
Lady Eve, The *41* Preston Sturges
Lady Fights Back, The *37* Milton Carruth
Lady for a Day *33* Frank Capra
Lady for a Night *42* Leigh Jason
Lady Frankenstein *71* Ernst R. von Theumer
Lady Frederick *19* Herbert Blaché
Lady from Boston, The *51* Bernard Vorhaus
Lady from Cheyenne, The *41* Frank Lloyd
Lady from Chungking *42* William Nigh
Lady from Constantinople, The *68* Judit Elek
Lady from Hell, The *26* Stuart Paton
Lady from Lisbon, The *42* Leslie Hiscott
Lady from Longacre, The *21* George Marshall
Lady from Louisiana *41* Bernard Vorhaus
Lady from Musashino, The *51* Kenji Mizoguchi
Lady from Nowhere, The *31* Richard Thorpe
Lady from Nowhere *36* Gordon Wiles
Lady from Paris, The *27* Manfred Noa
Lady from Shanghai, The *46* Orson Welles
Lady from Texas, The *51* Joseph Pevney
Lady from the Sea, The *29* Castleton Knight

Lady Gambles, The *49* Michael Gordon
Lady Gangster *41* Robert Florey
Lady General, The *65* Feng Yueh
Lady Godiva *28* George J. Banfield, Leslie Eveleigh
Lady Godiva *55* Arthur Lubin
Lady Godiva of Coventry *55* Arthur Lubin
Lady Godiva Rides *69* A. C. Stephen
Lady Godiva Rides Again *51* Frank Launder
Lady Grey *80* Worth Keeter
Lady Hamilton *21* Richard Oswald
Lady Hamilton *41* Alexander Korda
Lady Hamilton *68* Christian-Jaque
Lady Hamilton — Zwischen Schmach und Liebe *68* Christian-Jaque
Lady Has No Alibi, The *57* Kon Ichikawa
Lady Has Plans, The *42* Sidney Lanfield
Lady Helen's Escapade *09* D. W. Griffith
Lady Ice *73* Tom Gries
Lady in a Cage *64* Walter Grauman
Lady in a Jam *42* Gregory La Cava
Lady in Black, The *21* Edward R. Gordon
Lady in Black, The *58* Arne Mattsson
Lady in Cement *68* Gordon Douglas
Lady in Danger *34* Tom Walls
Lady in Distress *39* Herbert Mason
Lady in Ermine, The *27* James Flood
Lady in Furs, The *25* Edwin Greenwood, Will P. Kellino
Lady in High Heels, The *25* Edwin Greenwood, Will P. Kellino
Lady in Jewels, The *25* Edwin Greenwood, Will P. Kellino
Lady in Lace, The *25* Edwin Greenwood, Will P. Kellino
Lady in Love, A *20* Walter Edwards
Lady in Question, The *40* Charles Vidor
Lady in Red, The *35* Friz Freleng
Lady in Red, The *79* Lewis Teague
Lady in Scarlet, The *35* Charles Lamont
Lady in Silk Stockings, The *25* Edwin Greenwood, Will P. Kellino
Lady in the Car with Glasses and a Gun, The *69* Anatole Litvak
Lady in the Dark *44* Mitchell Leisen
Lady in the Death House *44* Steve Sekely
Lady in the Fog *52* Sam Newfield
Lady in the Iron Mask *52* Ralph Murphy
Lady in the Lake *46* Robert Montgomery
Lady in the Library, The *17* Edgar Jones
Lady in the Morgue, The *38* Otis Garrett
Lady in the Train, The *51* Youssef Chahine
Lady in White, The *40* Mario Mattòli
Lady in White *62* Arne Mattsson
Lady in White *87* Frank LaLoggia
Lady Is a Square, The *59* Herbert Wilcox
Lady Is Fickle, The *48* Mario Mattòli
Lady Is Waiting, The *56* Richard Quine
Lady Is Willing, The *33* Gilbert Miller
Lady Is Willing, The *42* Mitchell Leisen
Lady Jane *85* Trevor Nunn
Lady Jane Grey *36* Robert Stevenson
Lady Jane Grey, or The Court of Intrigue *23* Edwin Greenwood
Lady Jennifer *15* James Warry Vickers
Lady Killer *33* Roy Del Ruth
Lady Knows a Little of It, from the Devil, The *14* Yakov Protazanov

Lady L *65* Peter Ustinov
Lady Letmere's Jewellery *08* George R. Sims
Lady, Let's Dance *43* Frank Woodruff
Lady Lies, The *29* Hobart Henley
Lady Lion, A *28* Mark Sandrich
Lady Love *18* Maurice Tourneur
Lady Luck *36* Charles Lamont
Lady Luck *37* Gennaro Righelli
Lady Luck *40* William Beaudine
Lady Luck *46* Edwin L. Marin
Lady Lucy Runs Away *11* Wilfred Noy
Lady Luna(tic)'s Hat, The *08* Jack Smith
Lady Macbeth *18* Enrico Guazzoni
Lady Macbeth of Mtsensk *61* Andrzej Wajda
Lady Macbeth of Mtsensk *66* Mikhail Shapiro
Lady Macbeth of Siberia *61* Andrzej Wajda
Lady Macbeth of the Mtsensk District *89* Roman Balajan
Lady Makbet Mitsenskovo Uezda *89* Roman Balajan
Lady Marion *12* Victor Sjöström
Lady Marions Sommarflirt *12* Victor Sjöström
Lady Marion's Summer Flirtation *12* Victor Sjöström
Lady Mary's Love *11* August Blom
Lady Mislaid, A *58* David MacDonald
Lady Musashino *51* Kenji Mizoguchi
Lady Noggs *20* Sidney Morgan
Lady Noggs, Peeress *20* Sidney Morgan
Lady Objects, The *38* Erle C. Kenton
Lady of Burlesque *43* William A. Wellman
Lady of Chance, A *28* Hobart Henley, Robert Z. Leonard
Lady of Deceit *47* Robert Wise
Lady of Lebanon Castle, The *56* Richard Pottier
Lady of Lyons, The *13* Leon Bary
Lady of Monza, The *70* Eriprando Visconti
Lady of Mystery *46* Lew Landers
Lady of Quality, A *13* J. Searle Dawley
Lady of Quality, A *24* Hobart Henley
Lady of Red Butte, The *19* Victor Schertzinger
Lady of Scandal *30* Sidney Franklin
Lady of Secrets *36* Marion Gering
Lady of Shallot, The *12* Elwin Neame
Lady of the Boulevards *34* Dorothy Arzner
Lady of the Camellias, The *22* Edwin J. Collins
Lady of the Camellias, The *25* Olof Molander
Lady of the Camellias, The *80* Mauro Bolognini
Lady of the Camellias *87* John Neumeier
Lady of the Dugout *18* W. S. Van Dyke
Lady of the Harem, The *26* Raoul Walsh
Lady of the Lake, The *12* J. Stuart Blackton
Lady of the Lake, The *28* James A. Fitzpatrick
Lady of the Night *24* Monta Bell
Lady of the Night *29* D. W. Griffith
Lady of the Night *33* William A. Wellman

Lady of the Night, The *86* Piero Schivazappa
Lady of the Pavements *29* D. W. Griffith
Lady of the Photograph, The *17* Ben Turbett
Lady of the Rose *30* John Francis Dillon
Lady of the Shadows *62* Francis Ford Coppola, Roger Corman, Monte Hellman, Jack Hill, Dennis Jacob, Jack Nicholson
Lady of the Train, The *51* Youssef Chahine
Lady of the Tropics *36* W. S. Van Dyke
Lady of the Tropics *39* Jack Conway
Lady of Vengeance *57* Burt Balaban
Lady of Victories, The *28* Roy William Neill
Lady on a Train *45* Charles David
Lady on the Bus *78* Neville D'Almedia
Lady on the Tracks, The *68* Ladislav Rychman
Lady on the Train *51* Youssef Chahine
Lady or the Lions, The *08* S. Wormald
Lady or the Tiger?, The *41* Fred Zinnemann
Lady Oscar *78* Jacques Demy
Lady Owner, The *23* Walter West
Lady Paname *51* Henri Jeanson
Lady Pays Off, The *51* Douglas Sirk
Lady Peggy's Escape *13* Sidney Olcott
Lady Plumpton's Motor *04* Lewin Fitzhamon
Lady Possessed *52* Roy Kellino, William Spier
Lady President, The *52* Pietro Germi
Lady Raffles *28* Roy William Neill
Lady Refuses, The *31* George Archainbaud
Lady Reporter *36* Charles Lamont
Lady Robinhood *25* Ralph Ince
Lady Rose's Daughter *20* Hugh Ford
Lady Says No, The *51* Frank Ross
Lady Scarface *41* Frank Woodruff
Lady Seeks Room *37* Béla Balázs
Lady Sings the Blues *72* Sidney J. Furie
Lady Slavey, The *16* Bert Haldane
Lady Stay Dead *82* Terry Bourke
Lady Surrenders, A *30* John M. Stahl
Lady Surrenders, A *44* Leslie Arliss
Lady Takes a Chance, A *43* Henry Hathaway, William A. Seiter
Lady Takes a Flyer, The *57* Jack Arnold
Lady Takes a Sailor, The *49* Michael Curtiz
Lady Tetley's Decree *20* Fred Paul
Lady Thief and the Baffled Bobbies, The *03* Percy Stow
Lady to Love, A *29* Victor Sjöström
Lady Tubbs *35* Alan Crosland
Lady Vanishes, The *38* Alfred Hitchcock
Lady Vanishes, The *79* Anthony Page
Lady Wants Mink, The *52* William A. Seiter
Lady Who Dared, The *31* William Beaudine
Lady Who Lied, The *25* Edwin Carewe
Lady Windermere's Fan *16* Fred Paul
Lady Windermere's Fan *25* Ernst Lubitsch
Lady Windermere's Fan *49* Otto Preminger
Lady with a Dog, The *59* Josef Heifits

Lady with a Lamp, The *51* Herbert Wilcox
Lady with a Little Dog, The *59* Josef Heifits
Lady with a Past *32* Edward H. Griffith
Lady with Red Hair, The *40* Kurt Bernhardt
Lady with Sunflowers, The *18* Michael Curtiz
Lady with the Black Gloves, The *19* Michael Curtiz
Lady with the Colored Gloves, The *42* Benjamin Christensen
Lady with the Dog, The *59* Josef Heifits
Lady with the Lamp, The *51* Herbert Wilcox
Lady with the Light Gloves, The *42* Benjamin Christensen
Lady with the Little Dog, The *59* Josef Heifits
Lady Without Camellias, The *53* Michelangelo Antonioni
Lady Without Passport, A *50* Joseph H. Lewis
Ladybird, The *27* Walter Lang
Ladybug, Ladybug *63* Frank Perry
Ladyfingers *21* Bayard Veiller
Ladyhawke *85* Richard Donner
Ladykiller from Rome, The *60* Elio Petri
Ladykiller of Rome, The *60* Elio Petri
Ladykillers, The *55* Alexander Mackendrick
Lady's First Lesson on the Bicycle, A *02* James A. Williamson
Lady's from Kentucky, The *39* Alexander Hall
Lady's Morals, A *30* Sidney Franklin
Lady's Name, A *18* Walter Edwards
Lady's Profession, A *33* Norman Z. McLeod
Lady's Tailor, A *19* Erle C. Kenton*
Lægens Hustru *13* Forest Holger-Madsen
Længslernes Nat *29* Forest Holger-Madsen
Læreår, Et *14* August Blom
Lafayette *61* Jean Dréville
Lafayette Escadrille *57* William A. Wellman
Lafayette (Una Spada per Due Bandiere) *61* Jean Dréville
Lafayette, We Come! *18* Léonce Perret
Laffin' Fool, The *27* Bennett Cohn
Lagartija con Piel de Mujer, Una *71* Lucio Fulci
Lager SSadis Kastrat Kommandantur *76* Sergio Garrone
Lager SS5 — L'Inferno delle Donne *76* Sergio Garrone
Laggiu nella Giungla *88* Stefano Reali
Lago de las Vírgenes, El *81* Jesús Franco
Lago de los Muertos Vivientes, El *80* Jean Rollin
Lago di Satana, Il *65* Michael Reeves
Lago Maldito *82* Ivan Cardozo
Lågor i Dunklet *42* Hasse Ekman
Lagourdette, Gentleman Cambrioleur *16* Louis Feuillade
Lahing Pilipino *77* Lino Brocka
Lahire ou Le Valet de Cœur *22* Louis Feuillade
Lahoma *20* Edgar Lewis
Laila *62* Rolf Husberg

Landsflyktige, De *21* Mauritz Stiller

Landshövdingens Döttrar *15* Victor Sjöström

Landslide *37* Donovan Pedelty

Landslide! *65* Jorge Sanjinés

Landslides *87* Sarah Gibson, Susan Lambert

Landstreicher, Die *38* Karel Lamač

Lane That Has No Turning, The *22* Victor Fleming

Langage de l'Écran *47* Jacques Rozier

Langage des Fleurs, Le *59* Jan Lenica

Langage du Sourire, Le *56* Serge Bourguignon

Langdon's Legacy *15* Otis Turner

Lange Hosen, Kurze Haare *59* Georg Tressler

Langer Ritt nach Eden, Ein *72* Günther Hendel

Langford Reed's Limericks *35* A. F. C. Barrington

Längtan *65* Mai Zetterling

Längtan till Havet *31* John W. Brunius

Language All My Own, A *35* Dave Fleischer

Language of Faces *63* John Korty

Languedocienne, La *76* Roger Leenhardt

Lanka Dahan *18* D. G. Phalke

Lantern, The *60* Teinosuke Kinugasa

Lantern Under a Full Moon *51* Teinosuke Kinugasa

Lanterna del Diavolo, La *31* Carlo Campogalliani

Lanterne Magique, La *03* Georges Méliès

Lanton Mills *72* Terrence Malick

Lao Jing *87* Tianming Wu

Laoniang Gou Sao *86* Kei Shu

Laos, the Forgotten War *67* Santiago Álvarez

Lapicque *65* François Reichenbach

Lapin, Petit Lapin *74* Jean Rouch

Lappflickan *14* Victor Sjöström

Laputa *86* Helma Sanders-Brahms

Laputa: The Castle in the Sky *87* Hayao Miyazaki

Laramie *49* Ray Nazarro

Laramie Kid, The *35* Harry S. Webb

Laramie Mountains *52* Ray Nazarro

Laramie Trail, The *44* John English

Larceny *48* George Sherman

Larceny in Her Heart *46* Sam Newfield

Larceny, Inc. *42* Lloyd Bacon

Larceny Lane *31* Roy Del Ruth

Larceny on the Air *37* Irving Pichel

Larceny Street *36* Tim Whelan

Larceny with Music *43* Edward Lilley

Laredo, Costa de Esmeralda *61* Jorge Grau

Large Rope, The *53* Wolf Rilla

Large Rope, The *61* William Witney

Lariat Kid, The *29* B. Reeves Eason

Lariats and Sixshooters *31* Alvin J. Neitz

Larissa *80* Elem Klimov

Lark Still Sings, The *54* Hugh Wedderburn

Larks in Toyland *13* Arthur Cooper

Larks on a String *69* Jiří Menzel

Larks on a Thread *69* Jiří Menzel

Larmes de Crocodile *16* Maurice Mariaud

Larmes du Pardon, Les *19* René Leprince

Larry's Recent Behaviour *63* Joyce Wieland

Larry's Revenge *13* Charles C. Calvert

Lars Harde *48* Erik Faustman

Larsen, Wolf of the Seven Seas *74* Giuseppe Vari

Larsson i Andra Giftet *35* S. Bauman

Las Vegas by Night *63* Walon Green, Mitchell Leisen

Las Vegas 500 Millones *68* Antonio Isamendi

Las Vegas 500 Millions *68* Antonio Isamendi

Las Vegas Free-for-All *68* Takashi Tsuboshima

Las Vegas Hillbillys *66* Arthur C. Pierce

Las Vegas Lady *76* Noel Nosseck

Las Vegas Nights *40* Ralph Murphy

Las Vegas Shakedown *55* Sidney Salkow

Las Vegas Story, The *52* Robert Stevenson

Las Vegas Weekend *85* Dale Trevillion

Lasca *19* Norman Dawn

Lasca of the Rio Grande *31* Edward Laemmle

Lasciviousness of the Viper, The *20* Norimasa Kaeriyama

Laserblast *78* Michael Rae

Laserman, The *88* Peter Wang

Lash, The *16* James Young

Lash, The *30* Frank Lloyd

Lash, The *34* Henry Edwards

Lash of Destiny, The *16* George Terwilliger

Lash of Fate, The *12* Edwin S. Porter

Lash of Jealousy, The *17* Léonce Perret

Lash of Lust *62* Joe Sarno

Lash of Pinto Pete, The *24* Francis Ford

Lash of Power, The *17* Harry Solter

Lash of the Czar, The *28* Yakov Protazanov

Lash of the Penitentes *36* Harry Revier

Lash of the Whip *24* Francis Ford

Láska *72* Karel Kachyňa

Láska Mezi Kapkami Deště *79* Karel Kachyňa

Láska v Barvách Karnevalu *74* Evald Schorm*

Lásky Jedné Plavovlásky *65* Miloš Forman

Lass from the Stormy Croft *17* Victor Sjöström

Lass o' the Looms, A *19* Jack Denton

Lass of Gloucester, The *13* Lewin Fitzhamon

Lass of the Lumberlands *16* Paul Hurst, John P. McGowan

Lasse-Maja *43* Gunnar Olsson

Lassie Come Home *43* Fred M. Wilcox

Lassie from Lancashire *38* John Paddy Carstairs

Lassie the Voyager *66* Jack Hively, Dick Moder

Lassie's Great Adventure *63* William Beaudine

Lassie's Greatest Adventure *63* William Beaudine

Lassiter *84* Roger Young

Lässt Uns Töten, Compañeros *70* Sergio Corbucci

Last Abdication, The *45* Hiroshi Inagaki

Last Act of Martin Weston, The *70* Michael Jacot

Last Adventure, The *67* Robert Enrico

Last Adventure, The *75* Jan Halldoff

Last Adventure of Arsène Lupin, The *21* Pál Fejös

Last Adventurers, The *37* Roy Kellino

Last Adventures of Sherlock Holmes, The *23* George Ridgwell

Last Affair, The *76* Henri Charbakshi

Last Alarm, The *26* Oscar Apfel

Last Alarm, The *40* William West

Last American Hero, The *73* Lamont Johnson

Last American Preppie, The *84* Dorian Walker

Last American Virgin, The *82* Boaz Davidson

Last Angry Man, The *59* Daniel Mann

Last Appeal, The *21* Fred Paul

Last Aristocrats, The *89* Jin Xie

Last Assault, The *71* Yuri Ozerov

Last Assault, The *86* Sergiu Nicolaescu

Last Assignment, The *36* Dan Milner

Last Attraction, The *29* Olga Preobrazhenskaya

Last Bandit, The *49* Joseph Kane

Last Barricade, The *38* Alex Bryce

Last Battle, The *83* Luc Besson

Last Bend, The *39* Pierre Chénal

Last Betrothal, The *73* Jean-Pierre Lefèbvre

Last Blitzkrieg, The *58* Arthur Dreifuss

Last Bohemian, The *12* Michael Curtiz

Last Bomb, The *46* Frank Lloyd

Last Bottle at the Club, The *01* George Albert Smith

Last Bridge, The *53* Helmut Käutner

Last Bullet, The *50* Thomas Carr

Last But One, The *63* Károly Makk

Last Call, The *29* Pál Fejös

Last Call *85* Emmerich Oross

Last Call *90* Jag Mohan Mundhra

Last Cannibal World, The *76* Ruggero Deodato

Last Card, The *21* Bayard Veiller

Last Card, The *26* Richard Thorpe

Last Cartridges, The *1897* Georges Méliès

Last Castle, The *75* Don Taylor

Last Challenge, The *16* Harold M. Shaw

Last Challenge, The *67* Richard Thorpe

Last Chance, The *21* Webster Cullison

Last Chance, The *26* Horace B. Carpenter

Last Chance, The *37* Thomas Bentley

Last Chance, The *45* Leopold Lindtberg

Last Chance, The *68* Niny Rosati

Last Chance for a Born Loser *75* Maurizio Lucidi

Last Chants for a Slow Dance *77* Jon Jost

Last Chapter, The *15* William Desmond Taylor

Last Chapter, The *66* Benjamin Rothman, Lawrence Rothman

Last Chapter, The *74* David Tringham

Last Charge, The *62* Leopoldo Savona

Last Chase, The *81* Martyn Burke

Last Circus Show, The *74* Mario Gariazzo

Last Command, The *28* Josef von Sternberg

Last Command, The *42* Arthur Ripley, Edgar G. Ulmer

Last Command, The *55* Frank Lloyd

Last Company, The *30* Kurt Bernhardt

Last of the Black Hand Gang, The *12* Hay Plumb
Last of the Blue Devils, The *79* Bruce Ricker
Last of the Buccaneers *50* Lew Landers
Last of the Carnabys, The *17* William Parke
Last of the Cavalry, The *38* B. Reeves Eason, George Nicholls, Jr.
Last of the Clintons, The *35* Harry Fraser
Last of the Comancheros *71* Al Adamson
Last of the Comanches, The *52* André De Toth
Last of the Cowboys, The *76* John Leone
Last of the Dandy, The *10* Dave Aylott
Last of the Desperadoes *55* Sam Newfield
Last of the Duanes, The *19* J. Gordon Edwards
Last of the Duanes *24* Lynn Reynolds
Last of the Duanes *30* Alfred L. Werker
Last of the Duanes *41* James Tinling
Last of the Fast Guns, The *58* George Sherman
Last of the Finest, The *89* John Mackenzie
Last of the Ingrahams, The *17* Walter Edwards
Last of the Knucklemen, The *79* Tim Burstall
Last of the Line, The *14* Thomas Ince
Last of the Lone Wolf *30* Richard Boleslawski
Last of the Maffia, The *15* Sidney Goldin
Last of the Mobile Hot-Shots *69* Sidney Lumet
Last of the Moe Higgins, The *31* Edward Buzzell
Last of the Mohicans, The *20* Clarence Brown, Maurice Tourneur
Last of the Mohicans, The *32* Ford Beebe, B. Reeves Eason
Last of the Mohicans, The *36* George B. Seitz
Last of the Nomads *58* Per Holst
Last of the Pagans *35* Richard Thorpe
Last of the Pony Riders *53* George Archainbaud
Last of the Red Hot Lovers *72* Gene Saks
Last of the Redmen *47* George Sherman
Last of the Redskins *47* George Sherman
Last of the Renegades *64* Harald Reinl
Last of the Secret Agents?, The *66* Norman Abbott
Last of the Ski Bums *69* Dick Barrymore
Last of the Vikings, The *60* Giacomo Gentilomo
Last of the Warrens *36* Robert North Bradbury
Last of the Wild Horses *48* Robert L. Lippert
Last Original B-Movie, The *69* Ray Dennis Steckler
Last Outlaw, The *19* John Ford
Last Outlaw, The *27* Arthur Rosson
Last Outlaw, The *36* Christy Cabanne
Last Outpost, The *35* Charles Barton, Louis Gasnier
Last Outpost, The *51* Lewis R. Foster
Last Page, The *52* Terence Fisher
Last Pair Out *55* Alf Sjöberg
Last Parade, The *31* Erle C. Kenton

Last Paradise, The *56* Folco Quilici
Last Payment, The *21* Georg Jacoby
Last Performance, The *29* Pál Fejös
Last Picture Show, The *71* Peter Bogdanovich
Last Plane Out *83* David Nelson
Last Porno Flick, The *74* Ray Marsh
Last Posse, The *53* Alfred L. Werker
Last Post, The *29* Dinah Shurey
Last Prey of the Vampire, The *60* Piero Regnoli
Last Rebel, The *18* Gilbert P. Hamilton
Last Rebel, The *61* Miguel Torres Contreras
Last Rebel, The *71* Denys McCoy
Last Remake of Beau Geste, The *77* Marty Feldman
Last Resort *86* Zane Buzby
Last Reunion, The *80* Jay Wertz
Last Rhino, The *61* Henry Geddes
Last Ride, The *32* Duke Worne
Last Ride, The *44* D. Ross Lederman
Last Ride to Santa Cruz, The *63* Rolf Olsen
Last Rites *80* Domonic Paris
Last Rites *88* Donald P. Bellisario
Last Road, The *87* Leonid Menaker
Last Roll Call, The *36* Mario Camerini
Last Roman, The *69* Robert Siodmak
Last Romance *87* José María Forque
Last Romantic Lover, The *80* Just Jaeckin
Last Rose of Summer, The *20* Gregory La Cava
Last Rose of Summer, The *20* Albert Ward
Last Rose of Summer, The *37* James A. Fitzpatrick
Last Round, The *14* Bert Haldane
Last Round-Up, The *29* John P. McGowan
Last Round-Up, The *34* Henry Hathaway
Last Round-Up, The *47* John English
Last Run, The *71* Richard Fleischer, John Huston
Last Safari, The *67* Henry Hathaway
Last Sentence, The *17* Ben Turbett
Last Shot, The *22* Raoul Barré, Charles Bowers
Last Shot, The *26* Charles Barnett
Last Shot, The *50* Jiří Weiss
Last Shot, The *58* Jan Rybkowski
Last Shot You Hear, The *68* Gordon Hessler
Last Song *86* Denis Berry
Last Song, The *87* Pisarn Akarasainee
Last Song in Paris *86* Chor Yuen
Last Stage, The *47* Wanda Jakubowska
Last Stagecoach West *57* Joseph Kane
Last Stake, The *23* Thomas Bentley
Last Stand, The *38* Joseph H. Lewis
Last Starfighter, The *84* Nick Castle
Last Stop, The *47* Wanda Jakubowska
Last Stop, The *56* Tom Gries
Last Stop on the Night Train *76* Evans Isle
Last Straw, The *10* Edwin S. Porter
Last Straw, Der *17* Gregory La Cava
Last Straw, The *20* Denison Clift, Charles Swickard
Last Straw, The *87* Giles Walker
Last Summer, The *37* Alexander Hammid
Last Summer *69* Frank Perry

Last Summer in Tangiers *87* Alexandre Arcady
Last Sunset, The *61* Robert Aldrich
Last Supper, The *76* Tomás Gutiérrez Alea
Last Survivor, The *76* Ruggero Deodato
Last Tango in Acapulco, The *75* Carlos Tobalina
Last Tango in Paris *72* Bernardo Bertolucci
Last Temptation *56* Mario Camerini
Last Temptation of Christ, The *88* Martin Scorsese
Last Ten Days, The *55* G. W. Pabst
Last Ten Days of Adolf Hitler, The *55* G. W. Pabst
Last Thrill, The *73* Jesús Franco
Last Tide, The *31* John Argyle
Last Time I Saw Archie, The *61* Jack Webb
Last Time I Saw Paris, The *53* Richard Brooks
Last Tomahawk, The *65* Harald Reinl
Last Tomb of Ligeia, The *64* Roger Corman
Last Trail, The *21* Emmett J. Flynn
Last Trail, The *27* Lewis Seiler
Last Trail, The *33* James Tinling
Last Train, The *60* Geoffrey Muller
Last Train from Bombay *52* Fred F. Sears
Last Train from Gun Hill *59* John Sturges
Last Train from Madrid, The *37* James P. Hogan
Last Trick, The *64* Jan Švankmajer
Last Trump, The *42* Jacques Becker
Last Tycoon, The *75* Elia Kazan
Last Unicorn, The *82* Jules Bass, Arthur Rankin, Jr.
Last Vacation, The *47* Roger Leenhardt
Last Valley, The *70* James Clavell
Last Victim, The *75* Jim Sotos
Last Victim of the Vampire, The *60* Piero Regnoli
Last Volunteer, The *14* Oscar Apfel
Last Voyage, The *59* Andrew L. Stone
Last Wager, The *87* Costas Zirinis
Last Wagon, The *56* Delmer Daves
Last Waltz, The *27* Arthur Robison
Last Waltz, The *34* Georg Jacoby
Last Waltz, The *36* Gerald Barry, Leo Mittler
Last Waltz, The *58* Arthur Maria Rabenalt
Last Waltz, The *78* Martin Scorsese
Last War, The *60* Shigeaki Hidaka
Last War, The *62* Shue Matsubayashi
Last Warning, The *28* Paul Leni
Last Warning, The *38* Albert S. Rogell
Last Warrior, The *70* Carol Reed
Last Warrior, The *83* Romolo Guerrieri
Last Warrior, The *89* Martin Wragge
Last Wave, The *77* Peter Weir
Last White Man, The *24* Frank S. Mattison
Last Will of Dr. Mabuse, The *32* Fritz Lang
Last Winter, The *83* Riki Shelach Nissimoff
Last Winters, The *71* Jean-Charles Tacchella
Last Wish, The *49* Sam Lee
Last Witness, The *25* Fred Paul

Last Witness, The 60 Wolfgang Staudte
Last Woman, The 76 Marco Ferreri
Last Woman of Shang, The 64 Feng Yueh
Last Woman on Earth, The 58 Roger Corman
Last Word, The 16 Winsor McCay
Last Word, The 78 Roy Boulting
Last Word, The 86 Bernard Dubois
Last Words 67 Werner Herzog
Last Year at Marienbad 61 Alain Resnais
Last Year's Timetable 09 Lewin Fitzhamon
Laster, Das 15 Richard Oswald
Late at Night 46 Michael Chorlton
Late Autumn 60 Yasujiro Ozu
Late Christopher Bean, The 33 Sam Wood
Late Chrysanthemums 54 Mikio Naruse
Late Edwina Black, The 51 Maurice Elvey
Late Extra 35 Albert Parker
Late Flowering Love 81 Charles Wallace
Late for Work 04 Frank Mottershaw
Late George Apley, The 46 Joseph L. Mankiewicz
Late Great Planet Earth, The 77 Robert Amram
Late Liz, The 71 Dick Ross
Late Mathias Pascal, The 24 Marcel L'Herbier
Late Mathias Pascal, The 37 Pierre Chénal
Late Matthew Pascal, The 24 Marcel L'Herbier
Late Night Final 54 Montgomery Tully
Late Season 67 Zoltán Fábri
Late Show, The 76 Robert Benton
Late Spring 49 Yasujiro Ozu
Late Summer Blues 87 Renen Schorr
Late Superimpositions 65 Harry Smith
Latent Image 88 Pablo Perelman
Latest from Paris, The 28 Sam Wood
Latest in Underwear, The 18 Gregory La Cava
Latest in Underwear, The 20 Raoul Barré, Charles Bowers
Latidos de Pánico 83 Jacinto Molina
Látigo, El 39 José Bohr
Latin Love 30 Sinclair Hill
Latin Lovers 52 Mervyn LeRoy
Latin Lovers 61 Gian Vittorio Baldi, Marco Ferreri, Francesco Maselli, Lorenza Mazzetti, Gianfranco Mingozzi, Piero Nelli, Florestano Vancini
Latin Lovers 65 Mario Costa
Latin Quarter 45 Vernon Sewell
Latin Quarter Frenzy 45 Vernon Sewell
Latin Roulette 88 Maurice Hatton
Latino 85 Haskell Wexler
Latitude Zero 69 Inoshiro Honda
Lauaxeta 87 José A. Zorrilla
Läufer von Marathon, Der 33 E. A. Dupont
Laugh and Get Rich 31 Gregory La Cava
Laugh and the World Laughs 16 Allan Dwan
Laugh and the World Laughs with You 25 Alexander Butler
Laugh Back, The 30 Stephen Roberts
Laugh, Bajazzo 14 Richard Oswald
Laugh, Clown, Laugh 28 Herbert Brenon
Laugh Doctor, The 38 Fred Sauer
Laugh It Off 39 Albert S. Rogell
Laugh It Off 40 John Baxter, Wallace

Orton
Laugh Pagliacci 48 Giuseppe Fatigati
Laugh Your Blues Away 42 Charles Barton
Laughing Anne 53 Herbert Wilcox
Laughing at Danger 24 James W. Horne
Laughing at Danger 40 Howard Bretherton
Laughing at Death 29 Wallace Fox
Laughing at Life 33 Ford Beebe
Laughing at Trouble 37 Frank R. Strayer
Laughing Bill Hyde 18 Hobart Henley
Laughing Boy 34 W. S. Van Dyke
Laughing Cavalier, The 17 A. V. Bramble, Eliot Stannard
Laughing Gas 07 J. Searle Dawley, Edwin S. Porter
Laughing Gas 14 Charles Chaplin
Laughing Gas 22 Erle C. Kenton
Laughing Gas 31 Ubbe Iwerks
Laughing Girl Murder, The 73 David Eady
Laughing Gravy 31 James W. Horne
Laughing in the Sunshine 53 Daniel Birt
Laughing Irish Eyes 36 Joseph Santley
Laughing Lady, The 29 Victor Schertzinger
Laughing Lady, The 46 Paul Stein
Laughing Nigger, The 07 Arthur Gilbert
Laughing Policeman, The 73 Stuart Rosenberg
Laughing Rembrandt 88 Jon Jost
Laughing Saskia, The 16 Alexander Korda
Laughing Sinners 31 Harry Beaumont
Laughter 30 Harry D'Abbadie D'Arrast, Alexander Korda
Laughter and Tears 12 Victor Sjöström
Laughter and Tears 21 B. E. Doxat-Pratt
Laughter and Tears 28 H. B. Parkinson
Laughter in Hell 33 Edward L. Cahn
Laughter in Paradise 51 Mario Zampi
Laughter in the Air 33 Al Boasberg
Laughter in the Dark 69 Tony Richardson
Laughter of Fools, The 33 Adrian Brunel
Laughter Sticks to Your Heels 86 Hynek Bocan
Laughter Through the Tears 33 G. Gricher-Cherikover
Laughterhouse 84 Richard Eyre
Launching of a Ship at La Ciotat 1895 Louis Lumière
Laundromat, The 85 Robert Altman
Laundry, The 20 Charles Reisner
Laundry 23 Dave Fleischer
Laundry, The 85 Håkan Alexandersson
Laundry Girl, The 19 Albert G. Frenguelli, Edith Mellor
Laundryman's Mistake, The 10 Frank Wilson
Laura 44 Otto Preminger
Laura 79 David Hamilton
Laura 87 Géza Boszormenyi
Laura 88 Gonzalo Herraldo
Laura Comstock's Bag Punching Dog 01 Edwin S. Porter
Laura Laur 89 Brigitte Sauriol
Laura — Les Ombres de l'Été 79 David Hamilton
Laura's Toys 75 Joe Sarno
Laurel and Hardy in Toyland 34 Gus

Meins, Charles Rogers
Laurel and Hardy Murder Case, The 30 James Parrott
Laurels 09 Émile Cohl
Lausbubengeschichten 64 Helmut Käutner
Lautary 72 Emil Lotyanu
Lauter Liebe 40 Heinz Rühmann
Lauter Lügen 38 Heinz Rühmann
Lautlose Waffen 66 Raoul Lévy
Lava 89 Tadeusz Konwicki
Lavatory Moderne 01 Alice Guy-Blaché
Lavender and Old Lace 21 Lloyd Ingraham
Lavender Bath Lady, The 22 King Baggot
Lavender Hill Mob, The 50 Charles Crichton
Lavirint Smrti 65 Alfred Vohrer
Law, The 40 Ray Taylor
Law, The 58 Jules Dassin
Law and Disorder 40 David MacDonald
Law and Disorder 56 Henry Cornelius, Charles Crichton
Law and Disorder 74 Ivan Passer
Law and Jake Wade, The 58 John Sturges
Law and Lawless 32 Armand Schaefer
Law and Lead 36 Robert F. Hill
Law and Order 32 Edward L. Cahn
Law and Order 36 Spencer G. Bennet
Law and Order 36 Harry S. Webb
Law and Order 40 Ray Taylor
Law and Order 42 Sam Newfield
Law and Order 53 Nathan Juran
Law and Order 69 Frederick Wiseman
Law and Order on Bar L Ranch 11 Allan Dwan
Law and the Fist, The 64 Jerzy Hoffman
Law and the Lady, The 24 John L. McCutcheon
Law and the Lady, The 51 Edwin H. Knopf
Law and the Man 28 Scott Pembroke
Law and the Outlaw, The 13 William Duncan
Law and the Woman, The 22 Penrhyn Stanlaws
Law and Tombstone, The 67 John Sturges
Law Beyond the Range 35 Ford Beebe
Law Bringers, The 20 Ralph Ince
Law Comes to Gunsight, The 47 Lambert Hillyer
Law Comes to Texas, The 39 Joseph Levering
Law Commands, The 37 William Nigh
Law Decides, The 16 William P. S. Earle
Law Demands, The 24 Harry Hoyt
Law Divine, The 20 H. B. Parkinson, Challis Sanderson
Law for Tombstone 37 B. Reeves Eason, Buck Jones
Law Forbids, The 24 Jess Robbins
Law Hustlers, The 23 Louis King
Law in Her Hands, The 36 William Clemens
Law in Their Own Hands, The 13 Frank Wilson
Law Is the Law, The 57 Christian-Jaque
Law Men 44 Lambert Hillyer
Law of Compensation, The 17 Joseph A. Golden, Julius Steger
Law of Desire 86 Pedro Almodóvar
Law of Fear 28 Jerome Storm

Law of God, The *12* Allan Dwan
Law of Gravitation, The *16* Ashley Miller
Law of Life, The *40* Boris Ivanov, Alexander Stolper
Law of Men, The *19* Fred Niblo
Law of Nature, The *19* David G. Fischer
Law of Survival, The *66* José Giovanni
Law of the Badlands *51* Lesley Selander
Law of the Barbary Coast *49* Lew Landers
Law of the Canyon *47* Ray Nazarro
Law of the 45s *35* John P. McCarthy
Law of the Golden West *49* Philip Ford
Law of the Great Love, The *45* Boris Dolin
Law of the Great Northwest, The *18* Raymond Wells
Law of the Jungle *42* Jean Yarbrough
Law of the Land, The *17* Maurice Tourneur
Law of the Lash *47* Ray Taylor
Law of the Lawless, The *23* Victor Fleming
Law of the Lawless *63* William F. Claxton
Law of the Mountains, The *09* Sidney Olcott
Law of the Mounted *28* John P. McGowan
Law of the North, The *17* Burton George
Law of the North, The *18* Irvin Willat
Law of the North *32* Harry Fraser
Law of the Northwest *43* William Berke
Law of the Pampas *39* Nate Watt
Law of the Panhandle *50* Lewis D. Collins
Law of the Plains *38* Sam Nelson
Law of the Range, The *27* William Nigh
Law of the Range *41* Ray Taylor
Law of the Ranger *37* Spencer G. Bennet
Law of the Rio Grande *31* Bennett Cohn, Forrest K. Sheldon
Law of the Saddle *43* Melville DeLay
Law of the Sea *32* Otto Brower
Law of the Siberian Taiga *30* M. Bolshintsov
Law of the Snow Country, The *26* Paul Hurst
Law of the Texan *38* Elmer Clifton
Law of the Timber *41* Bernard B. Ray
Law of the Tong *31* Lewis D. Collins
Law of the Tropics *41* Ray Enright
Law of the Underworld *38* Lew Landers
Law of the Valley *44* Howard Bretherton
Law of the West, The *12* Thomas Ince
Law of the West *32* Robert North Bradbury
Law of the West *49* Ray Taylor
Law of the Wild, The *34* B. Reeves Eason, Armand Schaefer
Law of the Wild *41* Raymond K. Johnson
Law of the Wolf *41* Raymond K. Johnson
Law of the Yukon, The *20* Charles Miller
Law or Loyalty *26* Lawson Harris
Law Rides, The *36* Robert North Bradbury
Law Rides Again, The *43* Alvin J. Neitz
Law Rides West, The *30* Otto Brower, Edwin H. Knopf
Law Rustlers, The *23* Louis King
Law That Divides, The *19* Howard Mitchell
Law They Forgot, The *38* José A. Ferreyra
Law Unto Himself, A *16* Robert R. Broadwell
Law vs. Billy the Kid, The *54* William

Castle
Law West of Tombstone, The *38* Glenn Tryon
Lawa *89* Tadeusz Konwicki
Lawbreakers, The *60* Joseph M. Newman
Lawet el Hub *59* Salah Abu Saif
Lawful Cheaters *25* Frank O'Connor
Lawful Holdup, The *11* Allan Dwan
Lawful Larceny *23* Allan Dwan
Lawful Larceny *30* Lowell Sherman
Lawine, Die *23* Michael Curtiz
Lawless, The *49* Joseph Losey
Lawless, The *58* Nikos Koundouros
Lawless Border *35* John P. McCarthy
Lawless Breed, The *46* Wallace Fox
Lawless Breed, The *52* Raoul Walsh
Lawless Clan *46* Wallace Fox
Lawless Code *49* Oliver Drake
Lawless Cowboys *51* Lewis D. Collins
Lawless Eighties, The *57* Joseph Kane
Lawless Empire *45* Vernon Keays
Lawless Frontier, The *34* Robert North Bradbury
Lawless Land *37* Albert Ray
Lawless Legion, The *29* Harry Joe Brown
Lawless Love *18* Robert Thornby
Lawless Men *24* Neal Hart
Lawless Nineties, The *36* Joseph Kane
Lawless Plainsmen *42* William Berke
Lawless Range, The *35* Robert North Bradbury
Lawless Rider, The *54* Yakima Canutt
Lawless Riders *35* Spencer G. Bennet
Lawless Street, A *55* Joseph H. Lewis
Lawless Trails *26* Forrest K. Sheldon
Lawless Valley *32* John P. McGowan
Lawless Valley *38* David Howard
Lawless Woman, The *31* Richard Thorpe
Lawman *70* Michael Winner
Lawman Is Born, A *37* Sam Newfield
Lawrence of Arabia *62* David Lean
Law's Lash, The *28* Noel Mason Smith
Law's Outlaw, The *18* Clifford Smith
Lawton Story, The *49* William Beaudine, Harold Daniels
Lawyer, The *68* Sidney J. Furie
Lawyer Man *32* William Dieterle
Lawyer Quince *14* Harold M. Shaw
Lawyer Quince *24* H. Manning Haynes
Lawyer Suhasini *87* Vamsi
Lawyer's Message, The *11* Lewin Fitzhamon
Lawyer's Secret, The *31* Louis Gasnier, Max Marcin
Laxdale Hall *52* John Eldridge
Lay Down Your Arms *14* Forest Holger-Madsen
Lay That Rifle Down *55* Charles Lamont
Layout, The *68* Joe Sarno
Layout for Five Models *73* John Gaudioz
Lazarillo *59* César Ardavin
Lazarillo de Tormes, El *59* César Ardavin
Lazy Bones *34* Dave Fleischer
Lazy Boy, The *09* Lewin Fitzhamon
Lazy Jim's Luck *08* Charles Raymond
Lazy Lightning *26* William Wyler
Lazy River *34* George B. Seitz
Lazy Sa Pohli *52* Pal'o Bielek
Lazy Workmen *05* Frank Mottershaw
Lazybones *25* Frank Borzage

Lazybones *33* Lewis Milestone
Lazybones *35* Michael Powell
Lazzarella *57* Carlo Ludovico Bragaglia
Le Ho Amate Tutte *65* Damiano Damiani
Le Mans *70* Lee H. Katzin
Lea Lyon *15* Alexander Korda, Miklós Pásztory
Lead, Kindly Light *18* Rex Wilson
Lead Kindly Light *28* J. Steven Edwards, H. B. Parkinson
Lead Law *36* S. Roy Luby
Lead Shoes, The *49* Sidney Peterson
Leadbelly *76* Gordon Parks
Leaden Times *81* Margarethe von Trotta
Leader *64* Bruce Conner
Leader of the Band *87* Nessa Hyams
Leader of the Pack *72* Vernon Zimmerman
Leader Saladin, The *62* Youssef Chahine
Leaders of Tomorrow *43* René Clément
Leading Edge, The *87* Michael Firth
Leading Lizzie Astray *14* Roscoe Arbuckle, Edward Dillon
Leading Man, The *12* Mack Sennett
Leading Man, The *25* H. B. Parkinson
Leadville Gunslinger *52* Harry Keller
League of Frightened Men, The *37* Alfred E. Green
League of Gentlemen, The *59* Basil Dearden
League of Nations, The *20* Raoul Barré, Charles Bowers
League of Nations *24* Dave Fleischer
Leah Kleschna *13* J. Searle Dawley
Leah the Forsaken *12* Herbert Brenon
Leah's Suffering *17* Josef Soifer
Leak, The *17* William Beaudine
Leak, The *18* Raoul Barré, Charles Bowers
Lean on Me *89* John G. Avildsen
Leányportré *71* István Szabó
Leányvári Boszorkány *39* Victor Gertler
Leap, The *68* Kazimierz Kutz
Leap Into Life *24* Johannes Guter
Leap Into the Void *79* Marco Bellocchio
Leap of Faith *31* Edwin Greenwood
Leap to Fame *18* Carlyle Blackwell
Leap Year *21* James Cruze
Leap Year *32* Tom Walls
Leap Year Cowboy, The *12* Allan Dwan
Leapfrog As Seen by the Frog *00* Cecil M. Hepworth
Leaping Luck *28* Stephen Roberts
Learn, Baby, Learn *69* Gordon Parks
Learn from Experience *37* Mikio Naruse
Learn Polikeness *38* Dave Fleischer
Learnin' of Jim Benton, The *17* Clifford Smith
Learning Modules for Rural Children *75* Shyam Benegal
Learning to Love *25* Sidney Franklin
Learning Tree, The *69* Gordon Parks
Lease of Life *54* Charles Frend
Leather and Nylon *66* Jean Delannoy
Leather Boys, The *63* Sidney J. Furie
Leather Burners, The *43* Joseph E. Henabery
Leather Gloves *48* William Asher, Richard Quine
Leather Necker, The *34* Arthur Ripley
Leather Pushers, The *40* John Rawlins

Legend of the Lost 57 Henry Hathaway
Legend of the Mountain 78 King Hu
Legend of the Sea Wolf 74 Giuseppe Vari
Legend of the Seven Golden Vampires,
The 73 Roy Ward Baker
Legend of the Suburbs, A 57 Félix Mári-
ássy
Legend of the Suram Fortress, The 84
Dodo Abashidze, Sergei Paradzhanov
Legend of the Tree of Life, The 70 Luis
Nepomuceno
Legend of the True Cross 49 Luciano Em-
mer, Enrico Gras
Legend of the Werewolf 74 Freddie Fran-
cis
Legend of the Witches 70 Mike Leigh
Legend of the Wolfwoman 76 Salvatore
Di Silvestro
Legend of Tianyuan Mountain, The 81 Jin
Xie
Legend of Tichborne Dole, The 26 Hugh
Croise
Legend of Till Eulenspiegel, The 76 Alex-
ander Alov, Vladimir Naumov
Legend of Tom Dooley, The 59 Ted Post
Legend of William Tell, The 35 Heinz
Paul
Legend of Wisely, The 87 Teddy Robin
Legend of Witch Hollow 69 William O.
Brown
Legend of Young Dick Turpin, The 65
James Neilson
Legend, or Was It?, A 63 Keisuke Kino-
shita
Legenda o Krásné Julice 68 Ivan Passer
Legenda o Ledyanom 57 A. Sakharov,
Eldar Shengelaya
Legenda Serebryanogo Ozera 87 Eldar
Kuliev
Legenda Suramskoi Kreposti 84 Dodo
Abashidze, Sergei Paradzhanov
Legendary Champions, The 68 Harry
Chapin
Legendary Curse of Lemora, The 73 Rich-
ard Blackburn
Légende de la Fileuse, La 07 Louis Feuill-
lade
Légende de l'Aigle, La 11 Émile Chautard
Légende de Polichinelle, La 07 Ferdinand
Zecca
Légende de Rip Van Winkle, La 05
Georges Méliès
Légende de Sœur Béatrix, La 23 Jacques
De Baroncelli
Légende des Phares, La 09 Louis Feuillade
Légende du Fantôme, La 07 Segundo De
Chomón
Legende von der Heiligen Simplizia 20 Joe
May
Legende von Sünde und Strafe 22 Michael
Curtiz
Legends About Anika 54 Vladimir Pogačić
Legends of Anika 54 Vladimir Pogačić
Legge, La 58 Jules Dassin
Leggenda del Piave, La 52 Riccardo Freda
Leggenda del Rubino Malese, La 84 An-
tonio Margheriti
Leggenda del Santo Bevitore, La 88 Er-
manno Olmi
Leggenda della Croce, La 49 Luciano Em-

mer, Enrico Gras
Leggenda di Enea, La 62 Giorgio Rivalta
Leggenda di Faust, La 48 Carmine Gal-
lone
Leggenda di Sant'Orsola, La 48 Luciano
Emmer, Enrico Gras
Leggenda Sinfonica 47 Mario Bava, M.
Melani
Leghorn Blows at Midnight, The 50 Rob-
ert McKimson
Leghorn Hat, The 39 Wolfgang Liebe-
neiner
Leghorn Swoggled 51 Robert McKimson
Legion of Death, The 18 Tod Browning
Legion of Honor, The 28 A. Duges, Alex-
andre Ryder
Legion of Lost Flyers 39 Christy Cabanne
Legion of Missing Men, The 37 Hamilton
MacFadden
Legion of Terror 36 C. C. Coleman, Jr.
Legion of the Condemned, The 28 Wil-
liam A. Wellman
Legion of the Damned 69 Umberto Lenzi
Legion of the Doomed 58 Thor Brooks
Legion of the Lawless, The 40 David
Howard
Legion of the Street 32 Aleksander Ford
Legion of the Streets 32 Aleksander Ford
Légion Saute sur Kolwezi, La 79 Raoul
Coutard
Legion Ulicy 32 Aleksander Ford
Legioni di Cleopatra, Le 59 Vittorio Cot-
tafavi
Légionnaire, La 14 Henri Pouctal
Legionnaires in Paris 27 Arvid E. Gill-
strom
Legions of the Nile 59 Vittorio Cottafavi
Legittima Difesa 40 A. Giacalone
Legong 35 Henry De la Falaise
Legs 70 John Lennon, Yoko Ono
Légy Jó Mindhalálig 36 Steve Sekely
Légy Jó Mindhalálig 60 László Ranódy
Lehigh Valley Black Diamond Express 03
Edwin S. Porter
Lehrer im Wandel 63 Alexander Kluge,
Karen Kluge
Leibgardist, Der 25 Robert Wiene
Leichte Kavallerie 36 Werner Hochbaum
Leidenschaft 40 Walter Janssen
Leif 87 Claes Eriksson
Leila and the Wolves 84 Heiny Srour
Leila Diniz 87 Luiz Carlos Lacerda
Leise Flehen Meine Lieder 33 Anthony As-
quith, Willi Forst
Lejanía 86 Jesús Díaz
Lejonsommar 69 Torbjörn Axelman
Lekkamraterna 14 Mauritz Stiller
Lekko 54 Herman van den Horst
Lektion, En 11 August Blom
Lektion i Kärlek, En 53 Ingmar Bergman
Lel Hab Kessa Akhira 86 Rafaat El Mihi
Léleklátó Sugár 18 Alfréd Deesy
Lem Hawkins' Confession 35 Oscar Mich-
eaux
Lemon Drop Kid, The 34 Marshall Neilan
Lemon Drop Kid, The 50 Sidney Lanfield,
Frank Tashlin
Lemon (For Robert Huot) 69 Hollis
Frampton
Lemon Grove Kids Meet the Monsters, The

66 Ray Dennis Steckler
Lemon Hearts 62 Vernon Zimmerman
Lemon Popsicle 81 Boaz Davidson
Lemon Popsicle II 81 Boaz Davidson
Lemon Popsicle III 81 Boaz Davidson
Lemon Popsicle IV 82 Boaz Davidson
Lemon Popsicle V 83 Dan Wolman
Lemon Popsicle VI 85 Dan Wolman
Lemon Sisters, The 89 Joyce Chopra
Lemon Sky 87 Jan Egleson
Lemonade Joe 64 Oldřich Lipský
Lemora—A Child's Tale of the Super-
natural 73 Richard Blackburn
Lemora—Lady Dracula 73 Richard Black-
burn
Lemora, the Lady Dracula 73 Richard
Blackburn
Lena and the Geese 11 D. W. Griffith
Lena Rivers 25 Whitman Bennett
Lena Rivers 32 Phil Rosen
Lend Me Your Ear 42 William Beaudine
Lend Me Your Husband 24 Christy
Cabanne
Lend Me Your Husband 35 Frederick
Hayward
Lend Me Your Name 18 Fred J. Balshofer
Lend Me Your Wife 35 Will P. Kellino
Lenin 48 Vasily Belyaev, Mikhail Romm
Lenin in 1918 38 Mikhail Romm
Lenin in October 37 Mikhail Romm,
Dmitri Vasiliev
Lenin in Paris 81 Sergei Yutkevich
Lenin in Poland 61 Grigori Alexandrov
Lenin in Poland 64 Sergei Yutkevich
Lenin in Polsce 61 Grigori Alexandrov
Lenin in Switzerland 66 Grigori Alex-
androv
Lenin v 1918 38 Mikhail Romm
Lenin v 1918 Godu 38 Mikhail Romm
Lenin v Octyabre 37 Mikhail Romm,
Dmitri Vasiliev
Lenin v Oktiabrye 37 Mikhail Romm,
Dmitri Vasiliev
Lenin v Paridzhe 81 Sergei Yutkevich
Lenin v Polshe 64 Sergei Yutkevich
Lenin v Shveitzarii 66 Grigori Alexandrov
Lenin v 1918 38 Mikhail Romm
Lenin v 1918 Godu 38 Mikhail Romm
Lenin w Polsce 64 Sergei Yutkevich
Leningrad Cowboys Go America 89 Aki
Kaurismäki
Leningrad in Combat 42 Roman Karmen*
Leningrad Music Hall 41 I. Menaker,
Adolph Minkin, Herbert Rappaport,
Mikhail Shapiro, Semen Timoshenko,
M. Tsekhanovsky
Leningrad Segodnya 27 Ilya Trauberg
Leningrad Symphony 58 Z. Agranenko
Leningrad Today 27 Ilya Trauberg
Leningrad v Borbye 42 Roman Karmen*
Leninist Film-Truth 25 Dziga Vertov
Lenin's Address 29 Vladimir Petrov
Leninskaya Kino-Pravda 25 Dziga Vertov
Lenka and Prim 61 Karel Kachyňa
Lenny 74 Bob Fosse
Lenny Bruce Without Tears 72 Fred Baker
Lensman 84 Kazuyuki Hirokawa, Yoshiaki
Kawajiri
Lenz 71 George Moorse
Lenz 87 András Szirtes

Leo and Loree 80 Jerry Paris
Léo la Lune 57 Robert Giraud, Alain Jessua
Leo Reishmann and His Orchestra 42 Jean Negulesco
Leo the Last 69 John Boorman
Leo the Moon 57 Robert Giraud, Alain Jessua
Leo Tolstoy 84 Sergei Gerasimov
Léon Morin Prêtre 61 Jean-Pierre Melville
Léon Morin, Priest 61 Jean-Pierre Melville
Leonard Part 6 87 Paul Weiland
Leonardo da Vinci 52 Luciano Emmer, Lauro Venturi
Leonardo da Vinci 71 Renato Castellani
Leonardo's Diary 88 Jan Švankmajer
Leonardův Deník 88 Jan Švankmajer
Leone di San Marco, Il 63 Luigi Capuano, Richard McNamara
Leone Have Sept Cabeças, Der 70 Glauber Rocha
Leoni al Sole 61 Vittorio Caprioli
Leonor 75 Juan Buñuel
Leonski Incident, The 86 Philippe Mora
Leontines Ehemänner 28 Robert Wiene
Leopard, The 62 Luchino Visconti
Léopard, Le 84 Jean-Claude Sussfeld
Leopard, The 84 Jean-Claude Sussfeld
Leopard in the Snow 78 Gerry O'Hara
Leopard Lady, The 28 Rupert Julian
Leopard Man, The 43 Jacques Tourneur
Leopard Woman, The 20 Wesley Ruggles
Leopardess, The 23 Henry Kolker
Leopard's Spots, The 18 Cecil M. Hepworth
Leopard's Spots, The 25 Clyde Geronimi
Léopold le Bien-Aimé 33 Marcel Pagnol
Leper 76 Jerzy Hoffman
Lepke 75 Menahem Golan
Lepota Poroka 86 Živko Nikolić
Lerhjertet 15 Forest Holger-Madsen
Lermontov 87 Nikolai Burlyayev
Les Girls 57 George Cukor
Les Patterson Saves the World 87 George (Trumbull) Miller
Lesbian Twins 70 Ray Austin
Lesbian Vampires 70 Jesús Franco
Leslie Jeffries and His Orchestra 36 Horace Shepherd
Lesnaya Pesnya 63 Viktor Ivchenko
Less Than Kin 18 Donald Crisp
Less Than the Dust 16 John Emerson
Less Than Zero 87 Marek Kanievska
Lesser Evil, The 12 D. W. Griffith
Lesson, The 10 D. W. Griffith
Lesson, The 13 Warwick Buckland
Lesson, The 17 Charles Giblyn
Lesson, The 28 Mikhail Averbakh, Mark Donskoi
Lesson in Electricity, A 09 Percy Stow
Lesson in History, A 57 Lev Arnshtam, Hristo Piskov
Lesson in Life, A 55 Yuli Raizman
Lesson in Love, A 53 Ingmar Bergman
Lesson in Mechanics, A 14 Christy Cabanne
Lesson Number 1 29 James Parrott
Lesson of Life 55 Yuli Raizman
Lessons for Wives 27 Allan Dwan
Lessons in Love 21 Chester Withey

Lest We Forget 14 Maurice Elvey
Lest We Forget 18 Léonce Perret
Lest We Forget 34 John Baxter
Lest We Forget 37 Henry Hathaway
Lest We Forget 42 Fritz Lang
Lest We Forget 54 Leonid Lukov
Lester Persky Story, The 64 Andy Warhol*
Let 'Em Have It 35 Sam Wood
Let 'Er Buck 25 Edward Sedgwick
Let 'Er Go Gallegher 28 Elmer Clifton
Let Freedom Ring 39 Jack Conway
Let George Do It 38 Ken Hall
Let George Do It 40 Marcel Varnel
Let Him Buck 24 Frank Morrow
Let It Be 69 Michael Lindsay-Hogg
Let It Be Me 36 Friz Freleng
Let It Rain 27 Edward F. Cline
Let It Ride 89 Joe Pytka
Let Joy Reign Supreme 74 Bertrand Tavernier
Let Justice Be Done 50 André Cayatte
Let Katie Do It 15 Chester M. Franklin, Sidney Franklin
Let Me Call You Sweetheart 32 Dave Fleischer
Let Me Dream Again 00 George Albert Smith
Let Me Explain, Dear 32 Gene Gerrard, Frank Miller
Let Me Make a Complaint 64 Eldar Ryazanov
Let My People Go 60 John Krish
Let My People Live 39 Edgar G. Ulmer
Let My Puppets Come 77 Gerard Damiano
Let No Man Put Asunder 24 J. Stuart Blackton
Let No Man Write My Epitaph 59 Philip Leacock
Let Sleeping Cops Lie 88 José Pinheiro
Let Sleeping Dogs Lie 10 Frank Wilson
Let the Balloon Go 77 Oliver Howes
Let the Good Times Roll 73 Robert Abel, Sidney Levin
Let the People Laugh 37 Redd Davis
Let the People Sing 42 John Baxter
Let Them Kill Me Once and for All 86 Oscar Blancarte
Let Them Live 37 Donald Gallagher, Harold Young
Let Them Rest 67 Carlo Lizzani
Let There Be Light! 17 E. A. Dupont, Richard Oswald
Let There Be Light 45 John Huston
Let Us Be Gay 30 Robert Z. Leonard
Let Us Live 39 John Brahm
Let Women Alone 25 Paul Powell
Letcher 74 Chuck Vincent
Lethal 86 Dwight H. Little
Lethal Obsession 88 Peter Patzak
Lethal Weapon 87 Richard Donner
Lethal Weapon 2 89 Richard Donner
Let's All Sing Like the Birdies Sing 34 Dave Fleischer
Let's Be Famous 39 Walter Forde
Let's Be Fashionable 20 Lloyd Ingraham
Let's Be Happy 56 Henry Levin
Let's Be Ritzy 34 Edward Ludwig
Let's Celebrake 38 Dave Fleischer
Let's Dance 35 David Miller

Let's Dance 50 Norman Z. McLeod
Let's Do It 69 Sherman Price
Let's Do It Again 53 Alexander Hall
Let's Do It Again 75 Sidney Poitier
Let's Eat 32 Walter Lantz
Let's Elope 19 John S. Robertson
Let's Face It 43 Sidney Lanfield
Let's Fall in Love 33 David Burton
Let's Fall in Love 34 Constantin Bakaleinikoff
Let's Get a Divorce 18 Charles Giblyn
Let's Get Harry 85 Stuart Rosenberg
Let's Get Laid 77 James Kenelm Clarke
Let's Get Lost 88 Bruce Weber
Let's Get Married 26 Gregory La Cava
Let's Get Married 37 Alfred E. Green
Let's Get Married 60 Peter Graham Scott
Let's Get Movin' 36 Dave Fleischer
Let's Get Tough! 42 Wallace Fox
Let's Go! 23 William K. Howard
Let's Go Collegiate 41 Jean Yarbrough
Let's Go Crazy 51 Alan Cullimore
Let's Go Gallagher 25 Robert De Lacey
Let's Go Native 30 Leo McCarey
Let's Go Navy! 51 William Beaudine
Let's Go Places 29 Frank R. Strayer
Let's Go Steady 45 Del Lord
Let's Go, Wakadaisho! 67 Katsumi Iwauchi
Let's Go with Pancho Villa 35 Fernando De Fuentes
Let's Go, Young Guy! 67 Katsumi Iwauchi
Let's Have a Dream 67 Yoji Yamada
Let's Have a Murder 50 John E. Blakeley
Let's Have Fun 42 Charles Barton
Let's Hope It's a Girl 85 Mario Monicelli
Let's Kill Uncle 66 William Castle
Let's Live a Little 48 Richard Wallace
Let's Live Again 48 Herbert I. Leeds
Let's Live Tonight 35 Victor Schertzinger
Let's Love and Laugh 31 Richard Eichberg
Let's Make a Million 37 Ray McCarey
Let's Make a Night of It 37 Graham Cutts
Let's Make It Legal 51 Richard Sale
Let's Make Love 60 George Cukor
Let's Make Music 40 Leslie Goodwins
Let's Make Up 54 Herbert Wilcox
Let's Make Whoopee 28 Raymond Cannon
Let's Paint 24 Gaston Quiribet
Let's Play 31 Stephen Roberts
Let's Pretend 20 James Reardon
Let's Pretend 22 Fred Paul
Let's Ring Doorbells 35 Art Davis, Sid Marcus
Let's Rock! 58 Harry Foster
Let's Scare Jessica to Death 71 John Hancock
Let's Sing Again 36 Kurt Neumann
Let's Spend the Night Together 82 Hal Ashby
Let's Talk About Men 65 Lina Wertmuller
Let's Talk About Women 64 Ettore Scola
Let's Talk It Over 34 Kurt Neumann
Let's Talk Turkey 39 Felix E. Feist
Let's Try Again 34 Worthington Miner
Let's You and Him Fight 34 Dave Fleischer
Letter, The 29 Jean De Limur
Letter, The 40 William Wyler

Letter Box Thief, The *09* James A. Williamson

Letter for Evie, A *45* Jules Dassin

Letter from an Unknown Woman *47* Max Ophüls

Letter from an Unknown Woman *62* Salah Abu Saif

Letter from Columbia *63* James Blue

Letter from East Anglia, A *53* Cynthia Whitby

Letter from Home, A *41* Carol Reed

Letter from Korea *51* Lew Landers

Letter from Siberia *57* Chris Marker

Letter from the Isle of Wight, A *54* Brian Salt

Letter from the Wife *74* Purnendu Pattrea

Letter from Ulster, A *42* Brian Desmond Hurst

Letter from Wales, A *53* George Lloyd

Letter in the Sand, A *07* Lewin Fitzhamon

Letter M, The *63* Jiří Brdečka

Letter of Introduction, A *38* John M. Stahl

Letter of Warning, A *32* John Daumery

Letter That Never Came Out, The *14* Charles Brabin

Letter That Was Never Sent, The *60* Mikhail Kalatozov

Letter That Wasn't Sent, The *60* Mikhail Kalatozov

Letter to Brezhnev, A *85* Chris Bernard

Letter to Jane *72* Jean-Luc Godard, Jean-Pierre Gorin

Letter to Jane: Investigation of a Still *72* Jean-Luc Godard, Jean-Pierre Gorin

Letter to the Princess, A *12* Ashley Miller

Letter to Three Husbands, A *50* Irving Reis

Letter to Three Wives, A *48* Joseph L. Mankiewicz

Lettera Aperta a un Giornale della Sera *70* Francesco Maselli

Lettere a Sottemente *43* Goffredo Alessandrini

Lettere di una Novizia *60* Alberto Lattuada

Letters, The *22* George A. Cooper

Letters from a Dead Man *86* Konstantin Lopushansky

Letters from a Novice *60* Alberto Lattuada

Letters from America *72* Lakis Papastathis

Letters from Capri *86* Tinto Brass

Letters from China *57* Joris Ivens

Letters from Marusia *75* Miguel Littin

Letters from My Windmill *54* Marcel Pagnol

Letters from the Park *88* Tomás Gutiérrez Alea

Letters Home *86* Chantal Akerman

Letters of Credit *21* Fred Paul

Letters to an Unknown Lover *85* Peter Duffell

Letti Sbagliati *65* Steno

Letti Selvaggi *79* Luigi Zampa

Lettie Limelight in Her Lair *03* George Albert Smith

Letting in the Sunshine *33* Lupino Lane

Lettino Vuoto, Il *13* Enrico Guazzoni

Letto, Il *53* Henri Decoin, Jean Delannoy, Gianni Franciolini, Ralph Habib

Letto a Tre Piazze *60* Steno

Lettre, La *30* Louis Mercanton

Lettre à Freddy Buache *82* Jean-Luc Godard

Lettre à Jane *72* Jean-Luc Godard, Jean-Pierre Gorin

Lettre de Paris *45* Roger Leenhardt

Lettre de Sibérie *57* Chris Marker

Lettre Ouverte à un Mari *53* Alex Joffé

Lettres, Les *14* Louis Feuillade

Lettres d'Amour *42* Claude Autant-Lara

Lettres de Chine *57* Joris Ivens

Lettres de Mon Moulin, Les *54* Marcel Pagnol

Letty Lynton *32* Clarence Brown

Letun *31* Ilya Trauberg

Letyat Zhuravli *57* Mikhail Kalatozov

Letzte Akt, Der *55* G. W. Pabst

Letzte Anzug, Der *15* Ernst Lubitsch

Letzte Brücke, Die *53* Helmut Käutner

Letzte Chance, Die *45* Leopold Lindtberg

Letzte Droschke von Berlin, Die *26* Carl Boese

Letzte Fort, Das *27* Kurt Bernhardt

Letzte Fünf Tage *82* Percy Adlon

Letzte Fussgänger, Der *60* Wilhelm Thiele

Letzte Geheimnis, Das *59* Falk Harnack

Letzte Geschichte von Schloss Königswald, Die *88* Peter Schamoni

Letzte Kompanie, Die *30* Kurt Bernhardt

Letzte Kugel Traf den Besten, Die *65* Joaquín Luis Romero Marchent

Letzte Liebe *38* Fritz Schulz

Letzte Mann, Der *24* F. W. Murnau

Letzte Mohikaner, Der *65* Harald Reinl

Letzte Rechnung Zählst Du Selbst, Die *67* Giorgio Stegani

Letzte Ritt nach Santa Cruz, Der *63* Rolf Olsen

Letzte Rose *36* Karl Anton

Letzte Stunde, Die *20* Dmitri Buchowetzki

Letzte Walzer, Der *27* Arthur Robison

Letzte Walzer, Der *34* Georg Jacoby

Letzte Worte *67* Werner Herzog

Letzte Zeuge, Der *60* Wolfgang Staudte

Letzten Menschen, Die *19* Richard Oswald

Letzten Tage von Gomorrah, Die *74* Helma Sanders-Brahms

Letzten Zwei vom Rio Bravo, Die *65* Manfred Rieger

Leuchtfeuer *54* Wolfgang Staudte

Leur Dernière Nuit *53* Georges Lacombe

Leute mit Flügeln *60* Konrad Wolf

Leutnant auf Befehl *15* Ernst Lubitsch

Lev s Bílou Hřívou *86* Jaromil Jireš

Lev Tolstoi *84* Sergei Gerasimov

Lev Tolstoi and the Russia of Nikolai II *28* Esther Shub

Lévi et Goliath *86* Gérard Oury

Léviathan *61* Leonard Kiegel

Leviathan *89* George Pan Cosmatos

Levity and Laity *22* William Drury

Lèvres Closes *06* Alice Guy-Blaché

Lèvres de Sang *75* Jean Rollin

Lèvres Entrouvertes *77* Jean Rollin

Lèvres Rouges et Bottes Noires *75* Jesús Franco

Levsha *87* Sergei Ovcharov

Levy and Goliath *86* Gérard Oury

Lévy et Goliath *86* Gérard Oury

Lew Tyler's Wives *26* Harley Knoles

Lexington Experience, The *71* Lawrence J. Schiller

Ley del Deseo, La *86* Pedro Almodóvar

Ley del Forastero, La *64* Roy Rowland

Ley Que Olvidaron, La *38* José A. Ferreyra

Leyenda de Bandido, La *45* Fernando Méndez

Lezione di Chimica *47* Mario Mattòli

Li-Hang le Cruel *20* Édouard E. Violet

Li Oke *25* Pan Liu

Liaga, La *37* Ramón Peón

Liaisons Amoureuses, Les *60* Pierre Kast

Liaisons Dangereuses, Les *59* Roger Vadim

Liaisons Dangereuses 1960, Les *59* Roger Vadim

Liana *55* Boris Barnet

Lianbron *64* Sven Nykvist

Liane, Jungle Goddess *56* Eduard von Borsody

Liang Jia Funu *86* Jianxin Huang

Liang Shan-Po and Chu Ying-T'ai *63* King Hu, Han-hsiang Li

Liang Shan-Po yu Chu Ying-T'ai *63* King Hu, Han-hsiang Li

Lianna *82* John Sayles

Liar, The *12* Allan Dwan

Liar, The *18* Edmund Lawrence

Liar and the Nun, The *67* Joseph Czech, Rolf Thiele

Liar Bird *28* Manny Gould, Ben Harrison

Liars, The *61* Edmond T. Gréville

Liar's Dice *80* Issam B. Makdissy

Liar's Moon *81* David Fisher

Libel! *59* Anthony Asquith

Libeled Lady *36* Jack Conway

Libellule, La *01* Georges Méliès

Libera, Amore Mio! *73* Mauro Bolognini

Liberated China *50* Ivan Dukinsky, Sergei Gerasimov, Irina Setkina, M. Slavinsky, Sao-bin Sui, Elena Svilovoi

Liberated Czechoslovakia *46* Pera Atasheva, Ilya Kopalin

Liberated France *44* Sergei Yutkevich

Liberated Land *51* Frigyes Bán

Liberation *37* Pramatesh Chandra Barua

Liberation *40* Alexander Dovzhenko, Yulia Solntseva

Libération des Territoriaux *1896* Georges Méliès

Liberation of L. B. Jones, The *69* William Wyler

Liberation of Prague *77* Otakar Vávra

Liberation, Part One *68* Yuri Ozerov

Liberation, Part Two *68* Yuri Ozerov

Liberation, Part Three *70* Yuri Ozerov

Liberation, Part Four *71* Yuri Ozerov

Liberation, Part Five *71* Yuri Ozerov

Liberté *50* Jean Mitry

Liberté *61* Yves Ciampi, Chris Marker

Liberté Chérie *31* René Clair

Liberté, Égalité, Choucroute *85* Jean Yanne

Liberté en Croupe, La *70* Édouard Molinaro

Libertine, The *16* Joseph A. Golden, Julius Steger

Libertine, The *68* Pasquale Festa Campanile

Liberty 29 Leo McCarey
Liberty Belles 14 Del Henderson
Liberty Crown 67 Bruce Conner
Liberty, Equality, Sauerkraut 85 Jean Yanne
Liberty Hall 14 Harold M. Shaw
Libido 66 Ernesto Gastaldi, Vittorio Salerno
Libido 67 Kaneto Shindo
Libido 73 David Baker, Tim Burstall, John B. Murray, Fred Schepisi
Library of Congress 45 Alexander Hammid
Lição de Taxiderma 50 Humberto Mauro
Liceeni 86 Nicolae Corjos
Licence to Kill 89 John Glen
License to Drive 88 Greg Beeman
License to Kill 64 Henri Decoin
Licensed to Kill 65 Lindsay Shonteff
Licensed to Love and Kill 79 Lindsay Shonteff
Lichnoye Delo 31 Georgy Vasiliev, Sergei Vasiliev
Lichnoye Delo Sudyi Ivanovoy 87 Ilya Frez
Licht in der Finsternis 56 G. W. Pabst
Licht Scheuen..., Das 20 Piel Jutzi
Lichtenstein in London 68 Bruce Beresford
Lichtkonzert No. 2 35 Oskar Fischinger
Lichtstrahl im Dunkel, Ein 17 Joe May
Lick Observatory 68 Charles Eames, Ray Eames
Lickerish Quartet, The 70 Radley Metzger
Lickety Splat 61 Chuck Jones
Licking Hitler 77 David Hare
Lidé Jednoho Srdce 53 Vojtěch Jasný, Karel Kachyňa
Lidé na Kolečkách 66 Martin Frič
Lidé na Křse 37 Martin Frič
Lidé z Maringotek 66 Martin Frič
Lidé z Metra 74 Jaromil Jireš
Lidércnyomás 19 Pál Fejős
Lido Mystery, The 42 James P. Hogan
Lidoire 32 Maurice Tourneur
Liduška of the Stage 40 Martin Frič
Lie, The 13 Allan Dwan
Lie, The 14 Frank Wilson
Lie, The 17 Yevgeni Bauer
Lie, The 18 J. Searle Dawley
Lie, The 70 Alan Bridges
Lie Detector, The 46 Lew Landers
Lie of Nina Petrovna, The 37 Victor Tourjansky
Lie That Became the Truth, The 15 Ethyle Batley
Liebe 26 Paul Czinner
Liebe Augustin, Der 60 Rolf Thiele
Liebe der Hetty Raymond, Die 17 Joe May
Liebe der Jeanne Ney, Die 27 G. W. Pabst
Liebe der Mitsu, Die 37 Arnold Fanck
Liebe des Maharadscha, Die 36 Arthur Maria Rabenalt
Liebe des Van Royk, Die 18 Lupu Pick
Liebe im Dreiviertel Takt 38 Hubert Marischka
Liebe im Gleitflug 38 Gustaf Gründgens
Liebe im Ring 30 Reinhold Schünzel
Liebe in Deutschland, Eine 83 Andrzej Wajda
Liebe in Uniform 34 Georg Jacoby

Liebe Ist Kälter Als der Tod 69 Rainer Werner Fassbinder
Liebe Ist Liebe 32 Paul Martin
Liebe Kann Wie Gift Sein 58 Veidt Harlan
Liebe Macht Blind 25 Lothar Mendes
Liebe mit Zwanzig 62 Shintaro Ishihara, Marcel Ophüls, Renzo Rossellini, François Truffaut, Andrzej Wajda
Liebe Muss Verstanden Sein 34 Hans Steinhoff
Liebe Ohne Illusion 55 Erich Engel
Liebe, Schmerz und das Ganze Verdammte Zeug 72 Alan J. Pakula
Liebe, Tod und Teufel 35 Heinz Hilpert, Reinhardt Steinbicker
Liebe und die Erste Eisenbahn, Die 35 Hassa Preis
Liebe und So Weiter 68 George Moorse
Liebe und Trompetenklang 34 Gustav Fröhlich
Liebelei 13 August Blom, Forest Holger-Madsen
Liebelei 32 Max Ophüls
Liebenstraum 28 Andrew L. Stone
Liebes-Korridor, Der 20 Urban Gad
Liebes Pilgerfahrt 23 Yakov Protazanov
Liebesbrief der Königin, Die 16 Robert Wiene
Liebesbriefe aus dem Engadin 38 Luis Trenker
Liebesbriefe der Baronin von S..., Die 24 Henryk Galeen
Liebesbriefe einer Portugiesischen Nonne, Die 76 Jesús Franco
Liebesexpress, Der 31 Robert Wiene
Liebesfeuer 25 Paul Stein
Liebesgeschichten 43 Victor Tourjansky
Liebeshölle 27 Carmine Gallone
Liebeskarnaval 28 Augusto Genina
Liebeskarussell, Das 65 Rolf Thiele
Liebeskommando 32 Géza von Bolváry
Liebesleute 36 Erich Waschneck
Liebesnacht, Eine 33 Joe May
Liebespremier 43 Arthur Maria Rabenalt
Liebesquelle, Die 68 Ernst Hofbauer
Liebesroman im Hause Hapsburg, Ein 36 Willi Wolff
Liebesspiel 31 Oskar Fischinger
Liebesspiele 67 Curt Siodmak
Liebesspiele im Schnee 67 Curt Siodmak
Liebestraum 32 Widgey R. Newman
Liebeswalzer 30 Wilhelm Thiele, Carl Winston
Liebeswüste, Die 86 Lothar Lambert
Liebling der Götter 30 Hans Schwarz
Liebling der Matrosen 37 Douglas Sirk
Liebling Schöner Frauen, Der 39 Willi Forst
Liebling von Wien, Der 33 Géza von Bolváry
Liebschaften des Hektor Dalmore, Die 21 Richard Oswald
Lied der Matrosen, Das 58 Kurt Mätzig*
Lied der Ströme 54 Joris Ivens
Lied der Wüste, Das 40 Paul Martin
Lied, ein Kuss, ein Mädel, Ein 36 Géza von Bolváry
Lied einer Nacht, Das 32 Anatole Litvak
Lied für Dich, Ein 33 Joe May

Lied Geht Um die Welt, Ein 33 Richard Oswald
Lied Ist Aus, Das 32 Géza von Bolváry
Lied vom Glück, Das 33 Carl Boese
Lied vom Leben, Das 31 Alexis Granowsky
Lien de Parente 86 Willy Rameau
Lien Lien Fung Chen 87 Hsiao-hsien Hou
Liens du Sang, Les 77 Claude Chabrol
Lies 63 Teinosuke Kinugasa, Kozaburo Yoshimura
Lies 83 Jim Wheat, Ken Wheat
Lies My Father Told Me 60 Don Chaffey
Lies My Father Told Me 73 Ján Kadár
Lieu du Crime, Le 86 André Téchiné
Lieut. Danny U.S.A. 16 Walter Edwards
Lieutenant by Command 15 Ernst Lubitsch
Lieutenant Craig, Missing 51 Giacomo Gentilomo
Lieutenant Danny U.S.A. 16 Walter Edwards
Lieutenant Daring, Aerial Scout 14 Ernest G. Batley
Lieutenant Daring and the Dancing Girl 13 Charles Raymond
Lieutenant Daring and the International Jewel Thieves 13 Charles H. Weston
Lieutenant Daring and the Labour Riots 13 Charles Raymond
Lieutenant Daring and the Mystery of Room 41 13 Charles H. Weston
Lieutenant Daring and the Photographing Pigeon 12 H. Oceano Martinek
Lieutenant Daring and the Plans of the Minefields 12 H. Oceano Martinek
Lieutenant Daring and the Ship's Mascot 12 Dave Aylott
Lieutenant Daring and the Stolen Invention 14 Ernest G. Batley
Lieutenant Daring Avenges an Insult to the Union Jack 12 Dave Aylott
Lieutenant Daring Defeats the Middleweight Champion 12 Charles Raymond
Lieutenant Daring Quells a Rebellion 12 Charles Raymond
Lieutenant Daring, RN 35 Reginald Denham
Lieutenant Daring RN and the Secret Service Agents 11 Dave Aylott
Lieutenant Daring RN and the Water Rats 24 Edward R. Gordon, Percy Moran, James Youngdeer
Lieutenant Daring RN Saves H.M.S. Medina 11 Dave Aylott
Lieutenant Geranium and the Stealed Orders 14 Dave Aylott
Lieutenant Lilly and the Plans of the Divided Skirt 12 Hay Plumb
Lieutenant Lilly and the Splodge of Opium 13 Hay Plumb
Lieutenant Nekrasov's Fault 87 Roald Batyrov
Lieutenant of Rákóczi, The 53 Frigyes Bán
Lieutenant of the Carabinieri, The 86 Maurizio Ponzi
Lieutenant Pie's Love Story 13 Hay Plumb
Lieutenant Pimple and the Stolen Invention 14 Fred Evans, Joe Evans
Lieutenant Pimple and the Stolen Submarine 14 Fred Evans, Joe Evans

Light That Failed, The *10* Percy Stow
Light That Failed, The *16* Edward José
Light That Failed, The *23* George Melford
Light That Failed, The *39* William A. Wellman
Light Touch, The *51* Richard Brooks
Light Touch, The *55* Michael Truman
Light Up the Sky! *60* Lewis Gilbert
Light Within, The *18* Lawrence Trimble
Light Within, The *21* Fritz Lang
Light Woman, A *20* George L. Cox
Light Woman, A *28* Adrian Brunel
Light Years *87* René Laloux, Harvey Weinstein
Light Years Away *80* Alain Tanner
Lightblast *85* Enzo G. Castellari
Lighter Burden, A *13* George Pearson
Lighter Than Hare *60* Friz Freleng
Lighter That Failed, The *27* James Parrott
Lighthorsemen, The *87* Simon Wincer
Lighthouse *46* Frank Wisbar
Lighthouse, The *57* Keisuke Kinoshita
Lighthouse by the Sea, The *24* Malcolm St. Clair
Lighthouse in the Fog *41* Gianni Franciolini
Lighthouse Keepers *29* Jean Grémillon
Lighthouse Keeper's Daughter, The *52* Willy Rozier
Lighthouse Keeper's Family, The *86* Keisuke Kinoshita
Lighthouse Keeping *32* Manny Gould, Ben Harrison
Lighthouse Mouse *55* Robert McKimson
Lightnin' *25* John Ford
Lightnin' *30* Henry King
Lightnin' Bill Carson *36* Sam Newfield
Lightnin' Carson Rides Again *38* Sam Newfield
Lightnin' Crandall *37* Sam Newfield
Lightnin' in the Forest *48* George Blair
Lightnin' Shot *28* John P. McGowan
Lightnin' Smith Returns *31* Jack Irwin
Lightning *20* J. D. Leventhal
Lightning *27* James McKay
Lightning *52* Mikio Naruse
Lightning Bill *26* Louis Chaudet
Lightning Bolt, The *13* Wallace Reid
Lightning Bolt *65* Antonio Margheriti
Lightning Change Artist, The *1899* Georges Méliès
Lightning Conductor, The *14* Walter Hale
Lightning Conductor *38* Maurice Elvey
Lightning Express, The *30* Henry MacRae
Lightning Flyer, The *31* William Nigh
Lightning Guns *50* Fred F. Sears
Lightning Lariats *27* Robert De Lacey
Lightning Liver Cure, The *20* Will P. Kellino
Lightning Over Braddock: A Rust Bowl Fantasy *89* Tony Buba
Lightning Over Water *80* Nicholas Ray, Wim Wenders
Lightning Postcard Artist, The *08* Walter R. Booth
Lightning Raider, The *18* George B. Seitz
Lightning Raiders *45* Sam Newfield
Lightning Range *34* Victor Adamson
Lightning Reporter *26* John W. Noble
Lightning Rider, The *24* Lloyd Ingraham

Lightning Romance *24* Albert S. Rogell
Lightning Sketch: Chamberlain, A *1896* Georges Méliès
Lightning Sketch: H.M. Queen Victoria, A *1896* Georges Méliès
Lightning Sketch: Mr. Thiers, A *1896* Georges Méliès
Lightning Sketch: Von Bismark, A *1897* Georges Méliès
Lightning Sketches *07* J. Stuart Blackton
Lightning Sketches by Hy Mayer *13* Hy Mayer
Lightning Speed *28* Robert North Bradbury
Lightning Strikes Twice *34* Ben Holmes
Lightning Strikes Twice *50* King Vidor
Lightning Strikes West *40* Harry Fraser
Lightning Swords of Death *72* Kenji Misumi
Lightning, the White Stallion *86* William A. Levey
Lightning Triggers *35* S. Roy Luby
Lightning Warrior, The *31* Benjamin Kline, Armand Schaefer
Lights *87* Solomon Shuster
Lights and Shadows *29* Albert Kelley, Robert Ober
Lights Fantastic *42* Friz Freleng
Lights from Circus Life *24* August Blom
Lights o' London, The *14* Bert Haldane
Lights o' London, The *22* Edwin J. Collins
Lights o' London, The *23* Charles C. Calvert
Lights of Baku, The *50* Josef Heifits, R. Takhmasib, Alexander Zarkhi
Lights of Home, The *20* Fred Paul
Lights of London *23* Charles C. Calvert
Lights of My Shoes *73* Luis Puenzo
Lights of New York, The *16* Van Dyke Brooke
Lights of New York, The *22* Charles Brabin
Lights of New York *28* Bryan Foy
Lights of Night *58* Shohei Imamura
Lights of Old Broadway *25* Monta Bell
Lights of Old Santa Fe *44* Frank McDonald
Lights of the Desert *22* Harry Beaumont
Lights of Variety *50* Federico Fellini, Alberto Lattuada
Lights Out *23* Alfred Santell
Lights Out *50* Mark Robson
Lights Out in Europe *39* Herbert Kline
Lightship, The *85* Jerzy Skolimowski
Lightweight Lover, A *20* Roy Del Ruth
Ligne de Chaleur, La *88* Hubert-Yves Rose
Ligne de Démarcation, La *66* Claude Chabrol
Ligne Turbulent, Le *09* Émile Cohl*
Lignes Horizontales *62* Evelyn Lambert, Norman McLaren
Lignes Verticales *60* Evelyn Lambert, Norman McLaren
Liguero Mágico, El *80* Mariano Ozores
Liian Iso Keikka *87* Ere Kokkonen
Lijden van der Scheepsjongen, Het *12* Alfred Machin
Lijepe Žene Prolaze Kroz Grad *86* Želimir Žilnik

Lika, Chekov's Love *68* Sergei Yutkevich
Lika le Grand Amour de Tchekov *68* Sergei Yutkevich
Lika, Lyubov Chekhova *68* Sergei Yutkevich
Like a Bird on a Wire *74* Rainer Werner Fassbinder
Like a Crow on a June Bug *72* Lawrence Dobkin
Like a House on Fire *67* Miloš Forman
Like a Turtle on Its Back *78* Luc Béraud
Like a Wife, Like a Woman *61* Mikio Naruse
Like Father and Son *83* Eric Weston
Like Father, Like Daughter *87* Luis Felipe Bernaza
Like Father, Like Son *57* Mario Monicelli
Like Father Like Son *61* Tom Laughlin
Like Father, Like Son *87* Rod Daniel
Like Life Itself *86* Victor Casaus
Like Most People *44* Hasse Ekman
Like Most Wives *14* Lois Weber
Like Night and Day *69* Jonas Cornell
Like Poison *85* Vít Olmer
Like the Changing Heart of a Bird *27* Kenji Mizoguchi
Like the Leaves *38* Angelo Besozzi
Like Two Drops of Water *63* Fons Rademakers
Like Wildfire *17* Stuart Paton
Likely Lads, The *76* Michael Tuchner
Likely Story, A *47* H. C. Potter
Likeness of the Night, The *21* Percy Nash
Likewise *88* Elliott Kastner, Arthur Sherman
Liköre *23* Walter Ruttmann
Li'l Abner *40* Albert S. Rogell
Li'l Abner *59* Melvin Frank
Li'l Anjil *36* Manny Gould, Ben Harrison
Lil Hob Kessa Akhira *86* Rafaat El Mihi
Li'l Louisiana Belle *41* Albert Herman
Lil o' London *14* Harold M. Shaw
Lila *62* Rolf Husberg
Lila *68* William Rotsler
Lila Akác *34* Steve Sekely
Lila — Love Under the Midnight Sun *62* Rolf Husberg
Lilac *31* Anatole Litvak
Lilac Domino, The *37* Fred Zelnik
Lilac Girl, The *86* Flavio Mogherini
Lilac Sunbonnet, The *22* Sidney Morgan
Lilac Time *28* George Fitzmaurice
Lilacs in the Spring *54* Herbert Wilcox
Lileia *60* Vasil Lapoknysh, Vakhtang Vronsky
Lili *52* Charles Walters
Lili Marleen *80* Rainer Werner Fassbinder
Lili Marlene *50* Arthur Crabtree
Lilies of the Field *24* John Francis Dillon
Lilies of the Field *29* Alexander Korda
Lilies of the Field *34* Norman Walker
Lilies of the Field *63* Ralph Nelson
Lilies of the Streets *25* Joseph Levering
Liliom *19* Michael Curtiz
Liliom *30* Frank Borzage
Liliom *33* Fritz Lang
Liliomfi *54* Károly Makk
Lilith *63* Robert Rossen
Lilith and Ly *19* Drich Kober
Lilith und Ly *19* Drich Kober

Lilla Märta Kommer Tillbaka 48 Hasse Ekman
Lille Chauffør, Den 14 August Blom
Lilli Marlene 50 Arthur Crabtree
Lillian Gish 84 Jeanne Moreau
Lillian Roth and Her Piano Boys 29 Robert Florey
Lillian Russell 40 Irving Cummings
Lilliputian Minuet, The 05 Georges Méliès
Lilly Turner 33 William A. Wellman
Lily, The 26 Victor Schertzinger
Lily and the Rose, The 15 Paul Powell
Lily Christine 32 Paul Stein
Lily den Suffragetten 13 Mauritz Stiller
Lily in Love 85 Károly Makk
Lily of Killarney, The 22 Challis Sanderson
Lily of Killarney 27 H. B. Parkinson
Lily of Killarney 29 George Ridgwell
Lily of Killarney 34 Maurice Elvey
Lily of Laguna 38 Oswald Mitchell
Lily of Letchworth Lock 12 H. Oceano Martinek, Percy Moran
Lily of the Alley 23 Henry Edwards
Lily of the Dust 24 Dmitri Buchowetzki
Lily of the Harbor 52 George Tzavellas
Lily of the Tenements, The 10 D. W. Griffith
Lily of the Tenements: A Story of the East Side of New York, The 10 D. W. Griffith
Lily of the Valley, The 14 Colin Campbell
Lily, Tomboy 15 Cecil Birch
Lily Tomlin 86 Nicholas Broomfield, Joan Churchill
Lily's Birthday 15 Cecil Birch
Lily's Lovers 12 Mack Sennett
Limani ton Dacrion, To 28 Dimitrios Gaziadis
Limbo 67 Martin B. Cohen
Limbo 72 Mark Robson
Limbo Line, The 68 Samuel Gallu
Lime Juice Nights 31 Lewis R. Foster
Limehouse 26 Herbert Wilcox
Limehouse Blues 34 Alexander Hall
Limelight 35 Herbert Wilcox
Limelight 52 Charles Chaplin
Limfjorden 61 Henning Carlsen
Limit, The 72 Yaphet Kotto
Limit Fire Brigade, The 11 Dave Aylott
Limit Up 89 Richard Martini
Limite 30 Mario Peixoto
Limited Mail, The 25 George W. Hill
Limonádový Joe 64 Oldřich Lipský
Limousine Life 18 John Francis Dillon
Limousine Love 28 Leo McCarey*
Limping Man, The 31 John Orton
Limping Man, The 36 Walter Summers
Limping Man, The 53 Charles De Lautour, Cy Endfield
Lina Braake 75 Bernhard Sinkel
Linceul N'A Pas de Poches, Un 74 Jean-Pierre Mocky
Lincoln Conspiracy, The 77 James L. Conway
Lincoln Cycle, The 17 John M. Stahl
Lincoln Highwayman, The 19 Emmett J. Flynn
Lincoln the Lover 14 Ralph Ince
Lincoln's Gettysburg Address 12 J. Stuart

Blackton, James Young
Linda 29 Dorothy Davenport
Linda 60 Don Sharp
Linda and Abilene 69 Herschell Gordon Lewis
Linda Be Good 47 Frank McDonald
Linda Lovelace for President 75 Claudio Guzmán
Lindenbaum, Der 89 Kazuhiko Yamaguchi
Lindenwirtin vom Rhein, Die 31 Georg Jacoby
Line 61 Nils Reinhardt Christensen
Line 69 Yvonne Rainer
Line, The 80 Robert Siegel
Line Engaged 35 Bernerd Mainwaring
Line of Destiny, The 56 Lester James Peries
Line of Duty 62 Edward L. Cahn
Line of Life, The 56 Lester James Peries
Line to Tcherva Hut, The 36 Alberto Cavalcanti
Line to Tschierva Hut, The 36 Alberto Cavalcanti
Line-Up, The 34 Howard Higgin
Línea del Cielo, La 83 Fernando Colomo
Liner Cruising South 33 Basil Wright
Lines Horizontal 62 Evelyn Lambert, Norman McLaren
Lines of White on a Sullen Sea 09 D. W. Griffith
Lines Vertical 60 Evelyn Lambert, Norman McLaren
Lineup, The 58 Don Siegel
Lingerie 28 George Melford
Lingner Werke 35 Alexander Alexeïeff, Claire Parker
Linie 1 88 Reinhard Hauff
Link 86 Richard Franklin
Link Missing, A 25 Charles Bowers
Link That Binds, The 14 Frank Lloyd
Linked by Fate 19 Albert Ward
Links of Justice 58 Max Varnel
Links of Love 12 Percy Stow
Linkshändige Frau, Die 77 Peter Handke
Linna 86 Jaakko Pakkasvirta
Linus 79 Vilgot Sjöman
Linus and the Mysterious Red Brick House 79 Vilgot Sjöman
Linus eller Tegelhusets Hemlighet 79 Vilgot Sjöman
Liolà 63 Alessandro Blasetti
Lion, The 48 David Hand
Lion, The 62 Jack Cardiff
Lion and the Horse, The 52 Louis King
Lion and the Lamb, The 31 George B. Seitz
Lion and the Mouse, The 14 Barry O'Neil
Lion and the Mouse, The 19 Tom Terriss
Lion and the Mouse, The 28 Lloyd Bacon
Lion at World's End, The 71 James Hill, Bill Travers
Lion des Mogols, Le 24 Jean Epstein
Lion Has Seven Heads, The 70 Glauber Rocha
Lion Has Wings, The 39 Adrian Brunel, Brian Desmond Hurst, Alexander Korda, Michael Powell
Lion Hunters, The 21 Raoul Barré, Charles Bowers

Lion Hunters, The 51 Ford Beebe
Lion Hunters, The 65 Jean Rouch
Lion in Winter, The 68 Anthony Harvey
Lion Is in the Streets, A 53 Raoul Walsh
Lion Man, The 36 John P. McCarthy
Lion Man 64 Lindsay Shonteff
Lion Nommé l'Américain, Un 68 Jean Rouch
Lion of St. Mark, The 63 Luigi Capuano, Richard McNamara
Lion of Sparta 62 Rudolph Maté
Lion of the Desert 79 Moustapha Akkad
Lion of the Moguls, The 24 Jean Epstein
Lion of Thebes, The 64 Giorgio Ferroni
Lion Savant, Le 02 Alice Guy-Blaché
Lion Tamer, The 28 Frank Miller
Lion Tamer, The 60 John Halas*
Lion Tamers, The 19 Raoul Barré, Charles Bowers
Lionel Lion 44 Paul Sommer
Lionheart 68 Michael Forlong
Lionheart 87 Franklin J. Schaffner
Lionheart 90 Sheldon Lettich
Lions Are Loose, The 61 Henri Verneuil
Lion's Breath, The 16 Horace Davey
Lion's Busy, The 50 Friz Freleng
Lion's Cubs, The 15 Ralph Dewsbury
Lion's Dance 53 Daisuke Ito
Lion's Den, The 19 George D. Baker
Lion's Den, The 36 Sam Newfield
Lion's Love 69 Agnès Varda
Lion's Mouse, The 22 Oscar Apfel
Lion's Roar, The 28 Mack Sennett
Lions Sont Lâchés, Les 61 Henri Verneuil
Lipotakis 88 Giorgos Korras, Christos Voupouras
Lips of Blood 72 Ken Ruder
Lips Without Kisses 30 Humberto Mauro
Lipsky's Christmas Dinner 34 George B. Samuelson
Lipstick 60 Damiano Damiani
Lipstick 76 Lamont Johnson
Liquéfaction des Corps Durs 09 Segundo De Chomón
Liqueur du Couvent, La 03 Alice Guy-Blaché
Liquid Electricity 07 J. Stuart Blackton
Liquid Gold 19 Aubrey M. Kennedy
Liquid Sky 82 Slava Tsukerman
Liquid Sunshine 19 Victor Saville
Liquidator, The 65 Jack Cardiff
Lis de Mer, Le 70 Jacqueline Audry
Lisa 61 Philip Dunne
Lisa 77 Frederick R. Friedel
Lisa 90 Gary Sherman
Lisa and the Devil 72 Mario Bava, Alfred Leone
Lisa e il Diavolo 72 Mario Bava, Alfred Leone
Lisa, the Greek Tosca 61 Sokrates Kapsakis
Lisa, Tosca of Athens 61 Sokrates Kapsakis
Lisboa Cultural 83 Manoel De Oliveira
Lisbon 56 Ray Milland
Lisbon Story 46 Paul Stein
Lise e il Diavolo 72 Mario Bava, Alfred Leone
Lisette 61 R. John Hugh
Lisi and the General 86 Mark M. Rissi
Lisi und der General 86 Mark M. Rissi
Lisice 70 Krsto Papić

Lismonimena Prossopa *46* George Tzavellas

Lisolette von der Pfalz *35* Carl Fröhlich

Lissy *57* Konrad Wolf

List of Adrian Messenger, The *63* John Huston

Listen Children *28* Norman Taurog

Listen, Darling *38* Edwin L. Marin

Listen, Lester *24* William A. Seiter

Listen, Let's Make Love *68* Vittorio Caprioli

Listen to Britain *41* Humphrey Jennings, Stewart McAllister

Listen to Me *89* Douglas Day Stewart

Listen to My Music *61* Robert Henryson

Listen to the Bands *44* Jean Negulesco

Listen to the City *84* Ron Mann

Listen to the Roar of the Ocean *50* Hideo Sekigawa

Listen Up: The Lives of Quincy Jones *90* Ellen Weissbrod

Listening In *26* Widgey R. Newman, Challis Sanderson

Listopad *35* Otakar Vávra

Listopad *66* Otar Ioseliani

Liszt Rhapsody *35* Carmine Gallone

Lisztomania *75* Ken Russell

Lit à Deux Places, Le *65* Jean Delannoy, François Dupont-Midi, Gianni Puccini

Lit Lantern, The *83* Agassi Aivasian

Liten Ida *81* Laila Mikkelsen

Litet Bo *56* Arne Mattsson

Litsom k Litsu *88* Anatoli Bobrovsky

Little Accident, The *30* William James Craft

Little Accident *39* Charles Lamont

Little Adventures *40* Flavio Calzavara

Little Adventuress, The *27* William DeMille

Little Adventuress, The *38* D. Ross Lederman

Little American, The *17* Cecil B. DeMille

Little Angel *35* Louis King

Little Angel *61* Roberto Rodríguez, Ken Smith

Little Angel of Canyon Creek, The *14* Rollin Sturgeon

Little Angels of Luck *10* D. W. Griffith

Little Annie Rooney *25* William Beaudine

Little Annie Rooney *31* Dave Fleischer

Little Ark, The *72* James B. Clark

Little Australians *40* Arthur Greville Collins

Little Ballerina, The *47* Lewis Gilbert

Little Beau Pepe *52* Chuck Jones

Little Beau Porky *36* Frank Tashlin

Little Bet, A *20* Cecil Mannering

Little Big Horn *27* Harry Fraser

Little Big Horn *51* Charles Marquis Warren

Little Big Man *70* Arthur Penn

Little Big Shot *35* Michael Curtiz

Little Big Shot *52* Jack Raymond

Little Billie and the Bellows *13* Frank Wilson

Little Bit of Bluff, A *35* Maclean Rogers

Little Bit of Fluff, A *19* Kenelm Foss

Little Bit of Fluff, A *28* Wheeler Dryden, Jess Robbins

Little Bit of Heaven *28* Clifford Wheeler

Little Bit of Heaven, A *40* Andrew Marton

Little Bit of Sugar for the Birds, A *06* Harold Jeapes

Little Blabbermouse *40* Friz Freleng

Little Black Pom, The *11* Lewin Fitzhamon

Little Black Sambo *35* Ubbe Iwerks

Little Blonde in Black *15* Robert Z. Leonard

Little Blue Cap, The *10* Lewin Fitzhamon

Little Bo Bopped *59* Joseph Barbera, William Hanna

Little Bootblack, A *16* Ethyle Batley

Little Boss, The *19* David Smith

Little Boy Blue *16* Rupert Julian

Little Boy Blue *36* Ubbe Iwerks

Little Boy Boo *54* Robert McKimson

Little Boy Bountiful *14* Warwick Buckland

Little Boy Lost *53* George Seaton

Little Boy Scout, The *17* Francis J. Grandon

Little Boy That Santa Claus Forgot, The *38* Harold Simpson

Little Boy with a Big Horn, The *53* Robert Cannon

Little Boys *87* Ere Kokkonen

Little Boys Next Door, The *11* Percy Stow

Little Breadwinner, The *16* Wilfred Noy

Little Broadcast, The *42* George Pal

Little Brother, The *17* Charles Miller

Little Brother *26* Grigori Kozintsev, Leonid Trauberg

Little Brother of God *22* F. Martin Thornton

Little Brother of the Rich, A *15* Hobart Bosworth, Otis Turner

Little Brother of the Rich, A *19* Lynn Reynolds

Little Brother Rat *39* Chuck Jones

Little Buckaroo, The *28* Louis King

Little Buckaroo *38* Manny Gould, Ben Harrison

Little Bull, The *84* Luis García Berlanga

Little Bunch, The *83* Michel Deville

Little Caesar *30* Mervyn LeRoy

Little Chaos, The *66* Rainer Werner Fassbinder

Little Chauffeur, The *14* August Blom

Little Chevalier, The *17* Alan Crosland

Little Child Shall Lead Them, A *13* Alexander Butler

Little Child Shall Lead Them, A *14* Ethyle Batley

Little Child Shall Lead Them, A *19* Bertram Phillips

Little Child Shall Lead Them, A *22* J. Searle Dawley

Little Chimney Sweep, The *35* Lotte Reiniger

Little Church Around the Corner, The *23* William A. Seiter

Little Cigars *73* Chris Christenberry

Little Circus, The *62* Joris Ivens

Little City of Dreams, The *21* Hy Mayer

Little Clown, The *21* Thomas Heffron

Little Colonel, The *35* David Butler

Little Comrade *19* Chester Withey

Little Convict, The *80* Yoram Gross

Little Corporal, The *22* Baldassare Negroni

Little Country Court *39* Alwin Elling

Little Country Mouse, The *14* Donald Crisp

Little Coxswain of the Varsity Eight, The *08* Edwin S. Porter

Little Cupids, The *15* Chester M. Franklin, Sidney Franklin

Little Damozel, The *16* Wilfred Noy

Little Damozel, The *32* Herbert Wilcox

Little Darling, The *09* D. W. Griffith

Little Darlings, The *14* Toby Cooper

Little Darlings *80* Ronald F. Maxwell

Little Daughter's Letter, The *11* Theo Bouwmeester

Little Dears, The *20* William A. Seiter

Little Devil, A *1896* Georges Méliès

Little Devils *45* Monta Bell

Little Dick's First Adventure *15* Chester M. Franklin, Sidney Franklin

Little Dick's First Case *15* Chester M. Franklin, Sidney Franklin

Little Diplomat, The *19* Stuart Paton

Little Doctor, The *01* George Albert Smith

Little Doctor and the Sick Kitten, The *01* George Albert Smith

Little Dog for Roger *67* Malcolm Le Grice

Little Doggerel, A *13* Percy Stow

Little Dolly Daydream *25* Alexander Butler

Little Dolly Daydream *38* Oswald Mitchell

Little Door Into the World, The *23* George Dewhurst

Little Dorrit *20* Sidney Morgan

Little Dorrit *24* Anders Wilhelm Sandberg

Little Dorrit *87* Christine Edzard

Little Dragons, The *80* Curtis Hanson

Little Drummer Girl, The *84* George Roy Hill

Little Duchess, The *17* Harley Knoles

Little Dutch Girl, The *15* Émile Chautard

Little Dutch Mill *34* Dave Fleischer

Little Dutch Plate *35* Friz Freleng

Little Egypt *51* Frederick De Cordova

Little Egypt Malone *15* Al Christie

Little Elsie *13* Bert Haldane

Little Emily *11* Frank Powell

Little Eva Ascends *22* George D. Baker

Little Eva Egerton *16* Robert Z. Leonard

Little Fairground Swing *55* Zoltán Fábri

Little Fantasy on a Nineteenth Century Painting, A *46* Norman McLaren

Little Fauss and Big Halsy *70* Sidney J. Furie

Little Fella *32* William McGann

Little Feller, The *79* Colin Eggleston

Little Firebrand, The *27* Charles Hutchinson

Little Flames *85* Peter Del Monte

Little Flower Girl, The *08* Frank Mottershaw

Little Flower Girl's Christmas, The *09* Lewin Fitzhamon

Little Flower of Jesus, The *38* Georges Chaperot

Little Fool, The *21* Phil Rosen

Little Foxes, The *41* William Wyler

Little 'Fraid Lady, The *20* John G. Adolfi

Little French Girl, The *25* Herbert Brenon

Little Friend *34* Berthold Viertel

Little Fruits of Love, The 26 Alexander Dovzhenko

Little Fugitive, The 53 Ray Ashley, Morris Engel, Ruth Orkin

Little Gel 36 Oswald Mitchell, Walter Tennyson

Little General, The 12 Fred Evans

Little German Band 04 Edwin S. Porter

Little Giant, The 26 William Nigh

Little Giant, The 33 Roy Del Ruth

Little Giant 46 William A. Seiter

Little Girl, Big Tease 77 Roberto Mitrotti

Little Girl in a Big City, A 25 Burton L. King

Little Girl Next Door, The 23 W. S. Van Dyke

Little Girl of the Attic, The 15 Frank Lloyd

Little Girl Who Did Not Believe in Santa Claus, A 07 J. Searle Dawley, Edwin S. Porter

Little Girl Who Lives Down the Lane, The 76 Nicolas Gessner

Little God, The 14 Langford Reed

Little Gold Mine, A 12 Frank Wilson

Little Gray Lady, The 14 Francis Powers

Little Grey Mouse, The 20 James P. Hogan

Little Guitar, The 58 Jorge Sanjinés

Little Gypsy, The 15 Oscar Apfel

Little Herman 15 Paul Terry

Little Hero, A 13 Mack Sennett

Little Home in the West, The 15 Tom Watts

Little Hour of Peter Wells, The 20 B. E. Doxat-Pratt

Little Housekeeper, The 10 Lewin Fitzhamon

Little Humpbacked Horse, The 47 Ivan Ivanov-Vano

Little Humpbacked Horse, The 62 Alexander Radunsky

Little Hunchback, The 13 Alice Guy-Blaché

Little Hut, The 56 Mark Robson

Little Ida 81 Laila Mikkelsen

Little Intruder, The 19 Oscar Apfel

Little Iodine 46 Reginald LeBorg

Little Irish Girl, The 26 Roy Del Ruth

Little Island, The 58 Richard Williams

Little Island 69 Yoji Kuri

Little Italy 21 George Terwilliger

Little Jim 09 A. E. Coleby

Little Jim, or The Cottage Was a Thatched One 02 Dicky Winslow

Little Joe the Wrangler 42 Lewis D. Collins

Little Johnny Jet 53 Tex Avery

Little Johnny Jones 23 Charles Hines, Arthur Rosson

Little Johnny Jones 29 Mervyn LeRoy

Little Journey, A 26 Robert Z. Leonard

Little Jungle Boy 69 Mende Brown

Little Kidnappers, The 53 Philip Leacock

Little Knowledge, A 13 Warwick Buckland

Little Lady Eileen 16 J. Searle Dawley

Little Lady Lafayette 11 Walter R. Booth, Theo Bouwmeester

Little Lady Next Door, The 15 B. Reeves Eason

Little Lambkin 40 Dave Fleischer

Little Lamby 37 Dave Fleischer

Little Laura and Big John 73 Luke Moberly, Bob Woodburn

Little Letter to Mother, A 39 Joseph Green

Little Liar, The 16 Lloyd Ingraham

Little Liar, The 53 Ion Popescu-Gopo

Little Lillian, Toe Danseuse 03 Edwin S. Porter

Little Lion Hunter, The 39 Chuck Jones

Little Lise, The 30 Jean Grémillon

Little Lord Fauntleroy 14 F. Martin Thornton

Little Lord Fauntleroy 21 Alfred E. Green, Jack Pickford

Little Lord Fauntleroy 36 John Cromwell

Little Lord Fauntleroy 80 Jack Gold

Little Lost Sister 17 Alfred E. Green

Little MacArthurs 42 Wallace Fox

Little Mademoiselle, The 15 Oscar Eagle

Little Magician, The 59 Jorge Sanjinés

Little Major, The 11 Edwin S. Porter

Little Malcolm 74 Stuart Cooper

Little Malcolm and His Struggle Against the Eunuchs 74 Stuart Cooper

Little Man, The 48 Luigi Zampa

Little Man, What Now? 34 Frank Borzage

Little Marie 15 Tod Browning

Little Märta Returns 48 Hasse Ekman

Little Martyr, The 42 Vittorio De Sica

Little Mary Fix-It 17 Jack Conway

Little Mary Sunshine 16 Henry King

Little Match Girl, The 14 Percy Nash

Little Match Girl, The 28 Jean Renoir, Jean Tedesco

Little Match Seller, The 02 James A. Williamson

Little Match-Seller, The 28 Jean Renoir, Jean Tedesco

Little Mayoress, The 16 Fred W. Durrant

Little Meena's Romance 16 Paul Powell

Little Meg and the Wonderful Lamp 06 Lewin Fitzhamon

Little Meg's Children 21 Bert Wynne

Little Melody from Vienna 48 E. W. Emo

Little Men 34 Phil Rosen

Little Men 40 Norman Z. McLeod

Little Mermaid, The 76 Karel Kachyňa

Little Mermaid, The 89 Ron Clements, John Musker

Little Mickey Grogan 27 James Leo Meehan

Little Micky the Mesmerist 13 Walter R. Booth

Little Milliner and the Thief, The 09 Lewin Fitzhamon

Little Minister, The 13 James Young

Little Minister, The 15 Percy Nash

Little Minister, The 21 Penrhyn Stanlaws

Little Minister, The 22 David Smith

Little Minister, The 34 Richard Wallace

Little Miss Big 46 Erle C. Kenton

Little Miss Broadway 38 Irving Cummings

Little Miss Broadway 47 Arthur Dreifuss

Little Miss Brown, The 15 James Young

Little Miss Demure 12 Fred Rains

Little Miss Devil 51 Mohammed Ragaky

Little Miss Fortune 17 Joseph Levering

Little Miss Grown-Up 18 Sherwood Mac-Donald

Little Miss Happiness 16 John G. Adolfi

Little Miss Hawkshaw 21 Carl Harbaugh

Little Miss Hoover 18 John S. Robertson

Little Miss Innocence 73 Chris Warfield

Little Miss London 29 Harry Hughes

Little Miss Marker 34 Alexander Hall

Little Miss Marker 80 Walter Bernstein

Little Miss Molly 38 Alex Bryce

Little Miss No-Account 18 William P. S. Earle

Little Miss Nobody 17 Harry Millarde

Little Miss Nobody 23 Wilfred Noy

Little Miss Nobody 33 John Daumery

Little Miss Nobody 36 John G. Blystone

Little Miss Optimist 17 Robert Thornby

Little Miss Rebellion 20 George Fawcett

Little Miss Roughneck 38 Aubrey H. Scotto

Little Miss Smiles 22 John Ford

Little Miss Somebody 37 Walter Tennyson

Little Miss Thoroughbred 38 John Farrow

Little Mr. Fixer 15 Frank Lloyd

Little Mr. Jim 45 Fred Zinnemann

Little Mobsters 43 Wallace Fox

Little Monsters 89 Richard Greenberg

Little Mook 53 Wolfgang Staudte

Little Moritz Soldat d'Afrique 12 Alfred Machin

Little Mother, The 08 James A. Williamson

Little Mother, The 12 A. E. Coleby

Little Mother, The 13 Ethyle Batley

Little Mother, The 15 Warwick Buckland

Little Mother, The 22 A. V. Bramble

Little Mother 34 Henry Koster

Little Mother 72 Radley Metzger

Little Mothers 38 Joseph Green, Konrad Tom

Little Moth's Big Flame 38 Sid Marcus

Little Murders 70 Alan Arkin

Little Murmurs 66 Yoji Kuri

Little Napoleon, The 23 Georg Jacoby

Little Napoleon 33 Adrian Brunel

Little Napoleon 43 Gustaf Edgren

Little Nell 06 Arthur Gilbert

Little Nell and Burglar Bill 03 Alf Collins

Little Nellie Kelly 40 Norman Taurog

Little Nell's Tobacco 10 Thomas Ince

Little Nemo 09 J. Stuart Blackton, Winsor McCay

Little Night Music, A 77 Harold Prince

Little Nightingale 36 Nikolai Ekk

Little Nikita 88 Richard Benjamin

Little Nobody 36 Dave Fleischer

Little Nuns, The 63 Luciano Salce

Little of What You Fancy, A 68 Robert D. Webb

Little Old-Fashioned World 41 Mario Soldati

Little Old New York 23 Sidney Olcott

Little Old New York 40 Henry King

Little Old World 41 Mario Soldati

Little Ones, The 65 James O'Connolly

Little Organ Player of San Juan, The 12 Colin Campbell

Little Orphan, The 10 Theo Bouwmeester

Little Orphan 15 John Gorman

Little Orphan, The 17 Jack Conway

Little Orphan 30 Ubbe Iwerks

Little Orphan 49 Joseph Barbera, William Hanna
Little Orphan Airedale 47 Chuck Jones
Little Orphan Annie 19 Colin Campbell
Little Orphan Annie 32 John S. Robertson
Little Orphan Annie 38 Ben Holmes
Little Orphant Annie 19 Colin Campbell
Little Orvie 40 Ray McCarey
Little Pal 15 James Kirkwood
Little Pal 35 Reginald Barker
Little Pancho Vanilla 38 Frank Tashlin
Little Paper People 35 Margaret Hoyland
Little Patriot, A 17 William Bertram
Little Peacemaker, The 08 Georges Méliès
Little People, The 26 George Pearson
Little People 35 Harold S. Bucquet
Little Pest, The 31 Dick Huemer
Little Phantasy, A 46 Norman McLaren
Little Picture Producer, The 14 Edgar Rogers, F. Martin Thornton
Little Pippin 15 G. P. Huntley
Little Pirate, The 17 Elsie Jane Wilson
Little Place of One's Own, A 56 Arne Mattsson
Little Poacher, The 12 Bert Haldane
Little Poacher, The 20 Maurice Sandground
Little Prince, The 74 Stanley Donen
Little Prince and the Eight-Headed Dragon, The 63 Yugo Serikawa
Little Princess, The 17 Marshall Neilan
Little Princess, The 39 Walter Lang
Little Prosecutor, The 87 Hark Böhm
Little Quacker 50 Joseph Barbera, William Hanna
Little Railroad Queen, The 11 August Blom
Little Rain, A 76 Camilo Vila
Little Ranger, The 38 Gordon Douglas
Little Rebel, The 13 Sidney Olcott
Little Rebels, The 55 Jean Delannoy
Little Red Decides 18 Jack Conway
Little Red Hen, The 34 Ubbe Iwerks
Little Red Monkey 53 Ken Hughes
Little Red Riding Hood 01 Georges Méliès
Little Red Riding Hood 11 A. E. Coleby
Little Red Riding Hood 22 Walt Disney
Little Red Riding Hood 25 Walter Lantz
Little Red Riding Hood 29 Alberto Cavalcanti
Little Red Riding Hood 63 Roberto Rodríguez
Little Red Riding Hood 87 Adam Brooks
Little Red Riding Hood and Her Friends 64 Roberto Rodríguez
Little Red Riding Hood and Her Three Friends 64 Roberto Rodríguez
Little Red Riding Hood and the Monsters 65 Roberto Rodríguez, Manuel San Fernando
Little Red Riding Hood: The Year 2000 88 Márta Mészáros
Little Red Riding Rabbit 44 Friz Freleng
Little Red Rodent Hood 52 Friz Freleng
Little Red Schoolhouse, The 23 John G. Adolfi
Little Red Schoolhouse 36 Charles Lamont
Little Red Walking Hood 37 Tex Avery
Little Revenge 86 Olegario Barrera
Little Rita in the West 67 Ferdinando

Baldi
Little Rita nel West 67 Ferdinando Baldi
Little Robinson Corkscrew 24 F. Richard Jones
Little Robinson Crusoe 24 Edward F. Cline
Little Romance, A 79 George Roy Hill
Little Rowdy 19 Harry Beaumont
Little Rube, The 27 Norman Taurog
Little Runaway, The 18 William P. S. Earle
Little Runaway 52 Joseph Barbera, William Hanna
Little Runaway, The 66 Eduard Bocharov, Teinosuke Kinugasa
Little Rural Red Riding Hood 49 Tex Avery
Little Rural Riding Hood 49 Tex Avery
Little Saint Anthony 86 Pepe Sánchez
Little Samaritan, The 17 Joseph Levering
Little Savage, The 29 Louis King
Little Savage, The 59 Byron Haskin
Little School Ma'am, The 16 Chester M. Franklin, Sidney Franklin
Little School Mistress, The 38 Guido Brignone
Little School Mouse 54 Joseph Barbera, William Hanna
Little Sea Nymph, The 76 Karel Kachyňa
Little Sex, A 82 Bruce Paltrow
Little Shepherd of Bargain Row, The 16 Fred E. Wright
Little Shepherd of Kingdom Come, The 20 Wallace Worsley
Little Shepherd of Kingdom Come, The 28 Alfred Santell
Little Shepherd of Kingdom Come, The 61 Andrew V. McLaglen
Little Shoes 17 Arthur Berthelet
Little Shop in Fore Street, The 26 Frank Miller
Little Shop of Horrors, The 60 Roger Corman
Little Shop of Horrors 86 Frank Oz
Little Sinner, The 38 Carl Boese
Little Siren, The 80 Roger Andrieux
Little Sister 11 Sidney Olcott
Little Sister 69 Paul Bogart
Little Sister, The 85 Jan Egleson
Little Sister of Everybody, A 18 Robert Thornby
Little Sisters 72 Alex De Renzy
Little Smite and the Scamps 86 Miklós Markos
Little Snob, The 28 John G. Adolfi
Little Snow Waif, The 13 Charles H. Weston
Little Soap and Water, A 35 Dave Fleischer
Little Soldier, The 60 Jean-Luc Godard
Little Soldier of '64, The 11 Sidney Olcott
Little Spreewald Maiden, The 10 Sidney Olcott
Little Stranger, A 08 Arthur Cooper
Little Stranger 34 George King
Little Stranger, The 36 Dave Fleischer
Little Sugar House, The 80 Karel Kachyňa
Little Swee' Pea 36 Dave Fleischer
Little Sweetheart 88 Anthony Simmons
Little Teacher, The 09 D. W. Griffith

Little Teacher, The 15 Mack Sennett
Little Tease, The 13 D. W. Griffith
Little Tenderfoot 38 Albert Herman
Little Terror, The 17 Rex Ingram
Little Theater of Jean Renoir, The 69 Jean Renoir
Little Theatre, The 41 Art Davis, Sid Marcus
Little Theatre, The 82 Raúl Ruiz
Little Thief, The 89 Claude Miller
Little Tinker 47 Tex Avery
Little Tokyo U.S.A. 42 Otto Brower
Little Tom's Letter 11 Percy Stow
Little Tough Guy 38 Harold Young
Little Tough Guys in Society 38 Erle C. Kenton
Little Toys 33 Yu Sun
Little Trail, The 30 Manny Gould, Ben Harrison
Little Train Robbery, The 05 Edwin S. Porter
Little Treasure 85 Alan Sharp
Little Vegas 90 Perry Lang
Little Vera 88 Vasily Pichul
Little Vulgar Boy, The 13 Wilfred Noy
Little Waif and the Captain's Daughter, The 08 Percy Stow
Little Waitress 32 Widgey R. Newman
Little Wanderer, The 20 Howard Mitchell
Little Welsh Girl, The 20 Fred Paul
Little White Dove 73 Raúl Ruiz
Little White Savage, The 19 Paul Powell
Little Widow, The 19 Bert Roach, Malcolm St. Clair
Little Widow Is a Dangerous Thing, A 13 Frank Wilson
Little Wild Girl, The 28 Frank S. Mattison
Little Wildcat 22 David Divad
Little Wildcat, The 28 Ray Enright
Little Willie and the Mouse 01 George Albert Smith
Little Willie's Apprenticeships 13 Lewin Fitzhamon
Little Willie's Last Celebration 01 Edwin S. Porter
Little Witness, The 05 George Albert Smith
Little Women 17 Alexander Butler, George B. Samuelson
Little Women 18 Harley Knoles
Little Women 33 George Cukor
Little Women 48 Mervyn LeRoy
Little Wooden Soldier, The 11 Theo Bouwmeester
Little World of Don Camillo, The 51 Julien Duvivier
Little Yank, The 17 George Siegmann
Little Yellow House, The 28 James Leo Meehan
Littlest Hobo, The 58 Charles R. Rondeau
Littlest Horse Thieves, The 76 Charles Jarrott
Littlest Outlaw, The 55 Roberto Gavaldón
Littlest Rebel, The 35 David Butler
Littlest Scout, The 19 J. Stuart Blackton
Live a Little, Love a Little 68 Norman Taurog
Live a Little, Steal a Lot 74 Marvin Chomsky

Live Again 36 Arthur Maude
Live and Help Live 25 Paul M. Felton
Live and Laugh 33 Max Wilner
Live and Learn 20 Charlie Chase
Live and Let Die 73 Guy Hamilton
Live and Let Live 21 Christy Cabanne
Live Cowards 26 Stephen Roberts
Live Fast, Die Young 58 Paul Henreid
Live for Life 67 Claude Lelouch
Live Ghost, The 34 Charles Rogers
Live in Fear 47 Hugo Fregonese
Live in Fear 58 Hugo Fregonese
Live It Up 63 Lance Comfort
Live, Love and Learn 37 George Fitz-
  maurice
Live News 27 Charles Lamont
Live Now, Pay Later 62 Jay Lewis
Live Sparks 20 Ernest C. Warde
Live to Love 59 William Hole, Jr.
Live Today—Die Tomorrow 70 Kaneto
  Shindo
Live Today for Tomorrow 48 Michael
  Gordon
Live Wire, The 14 George Pearson
Live Wire, The 25 Charles Hines
Live Wire, The 37 Herbert Brenon
Live Wire Hick, A 20 Henry King
Live Wires 21 Edward Sedgwick
Live Wires 45 Phil Karlson
Live Your Own Way 70 Tokihisa Mori-
  kawa
Lively Alley 39 Kozaburo Yoshimura
Lively Cockfight 1899 Georges Méliès
Lively Day, A 21 Harry Granville
Lively Quarter Day, A 06 J. H. Martin
Lively Set, The 64 Jack Arnold
Lively Skeleton, A 10 S. Wormald
Liver Eaters, The 64 Jack Hill
Lives of a Bengal Lancer, The 34 Henry
  Hathaway
Lives of Performers 72 Yvonne Rainer
Livet Är Stenkul 67 Jan Halldoff
Livet på Hegnsgård 39 Arne Weel
Livets Bål 11 Edward Schnedler-Sørensen
Livets Gøglespil 16 Forest Holger-Madsen
Livets Konflikter 13 Victor Sjöström,
  Mauritz Stiller
Livets Storme 10 August Blom
Livets Vår 57 Arne Mattsson
Living, The 34 Heinosuke Gosho
Living 52 Akira Kurosawa
Living and the Dead, The 63 Alexander
  Stolper
Living Between Two Worlds 63 Bobby
  Johnson
Living Blackboard 08 Émile Cohl
Living by Their Wits 18 Maurice Sand-
  ground
Living Camera, The 62 Richard Leacock,
  Gregory Shuker
Living Coffin, The 58 Fernando Méndez
Living Corpse, A 18 Cheslav Sabinsky
Living Corpse, The 18 Richard Oswald
Living Corpse, The 28 Fedor Ozep
Living Corpse, The 36 Marcel L'Herbier
Living Dangerously 36 Herbert Brenon
Living Dangerously 87 Nicos Perakis
Living Dangerously 88 Fernando Pérez
Living Daylights, The 87 John Glen
Living Dead, The 18 Richard Oswald

Living Dead, The 31 Richard Oswald
Living Dead, The 33 Thomas Bentley
Living Dead, The 40 Richard Oswald
Living Dead at the Manchester Morgue,
  The 74 Jorge Grau
Living Dead Girl, The 82 Jean Rollin
Living Dead Man, The 24 Marcel
  L'Herbier
Living Death, The 15 Tod Browning
Living Death, The 28 Fred Paul
Living Death, The 68 Jack Hill, Juan
  Ibáñez
Living Desert, The 53 James Algar
Living Doll, A 29 Tomu Uchida
Living Earth, The 78 Alexander Hammid
Living Free 72 Jack Couffer
Living Ghost, The 42 William Beaudine
Living Head, The 61 Chano Urueta
Living Heroes 60 Vytautas Zalakevicius
Living Idol, The 56 Albert Lewin
Living in a Big Way 47 Gregory La Cava
Living Is Better 56 Fumio Kamei
Living It Up 54 Norman Taurog
Living Jazz 60 Jack Gold
Living Legend 80 Worth Keeter
Living Lies 22 Émile Chautard
Living Machine, The 61 Roman Kroitor
Living Magoroku, The 43 Keisuke Kino-
  shita
Living Nightmare 55 France Štiglic
Living on Love 37 Lew Landers
Living on Tokyo Time 86 Steven Okazaki
Living on Velvet 34 Frank Borzage
Living One's Life 63 Evald Schorm
Living Orphan, The 39 Joseph Seiden
Living Playing Cards, The 05 Georges
  Méliès
Living Russia, or The Man with the Cam-
  era 28 Dziga Vertov
Living Sea, The 58 Susumu Hani
Living Skeleton 68 Hiroshi Matsuno
Living Statues 00 Jack Smith
Living Stream, The 50 Arne Sucksdorff
Living Sugoroku, The 43 Heinosuke
  Gosho
Living Tree... 63 Miklós Jancsó
Living Venus 60 Herschell Gordon Lewis
Living with Fear 74 Christian Blackwood
Livingstone 25 M. A. Wetherell
Livre Magique, Le 00 Georges Méliès
Livro, O 54 Lima Barreto
Livsfare-Miner 46 Ole Palsbo
Livsfarlig Film 88 Suzanne Osten
Liza 71 Marco Ferreri
Liza on the Stage 15 Joe Evans
Lizard in a Woman's Skin, A 71 Lucio
  Fulci
Lizards, The 63 Lina Wertmuller
Liza's Legacy 15 Joe Evans
Lizzie 57 Hugo Haas
Lizzie and the Iceman 14 Phillips Smalley
Lizzie's Last Lap 24 Gaston Quiribet
Ljepotica 62 62 Dušan Makavejev
Ljubavna Pisma s Predumišljajem 86
  Zvonimir Berković
Ljubavni Slučaj 66 Dušan Makavejev
Ljubavni Slučaj ili Tragedija Službenice
  P.T.T. 66 Dušan Makavejev
Ljubavni Slučaj, Tragedija Službenice
  P.T.T. 66 Dušan Makavejev

Ljubazan 86 Rajko Ranfl
Ljusnande Framtid, Den 40 Gustaf
  Molander
Ljuvlig Är Sommernatten 61 Arne
  Mattsson
Llamada del Vampiro, La 71 José María
  Elorrieta
Llano Kid, The 39 Edward D. Venturini
Llanto por un Bandido 64 Carlos Saura
Llegada de Noche 48 José Antonio Nieves
  Conde
Llegaron los Marcianos 64 Franco Castel-
  lano, L. Martin, Giuseppe Moccia
Llorona, La 33 Ramón Peón
Llorona, La 59 René Cardona
Lloyd of the C.I.D. 31 Henry MacRae
Lloyds of London 36 Henry King
Llucsi Caimanta 77 Jorge Sanjinés
Lo del César 87 Felipe Cazals
Lo Que Importa Es Vivir (El Amante
  Eficaz) 87 Luis Alcoriza
Lo Que Vendrá 88 Gustavo Mosquera
Lo Sam Zayin 87 Shmuel Imberman
Lo, the Poor Buffal 48 Alex Lovy
Loaded Dice 18 Herbert Blaché
Loaded Dice 37 Bernerd Mainwaring
Loaded Door, The 22 Harry A. Pollard
Loaded Pistols 48 John English
Loaf, The 59 Jan Němec
Loaf of Bread 59 Jan Němec
Loafers, The 53 Federico Fellini
Loan Shark 52 Seymour Friedman
Loba, La 64 Rafael Baledón
Lobishomem, O 71 Raffaele Rossi
Lobishomem, O 74 Elyseu Visconti Caval-
  heiro
Lobster Nightmare, The 23 Herbert M.
  Dawley
Local Bad Man, The 32 Otto Brower
Local Boy Makes Good 31 Mervyn LeRoy
Local Color 78 Mark Rappaport
Local Hero 83 Bill Forsyth
Local Train Mystery, The 37 Anthony
  Baerlin
Locandiera, La 43 Luigi Chiarini
Locataire, Le 76 Roman Polanski
Locataire Diabolique, Le 09 Georges
  Méliès
Locataires d'à Côté, Les 09 Émile Cohl
Locations 67 Wim Wenders
Loch Ness Horror, The 82 Larry Buchanan
Lochinvar 15 Leslie Seldon-Truss
Lochs and Bonds 37 Leslie Goodwins
Lock & Seal 87 Heidi Ulmke
Lock 17 86 Sebastian Lentz
Lock Up 89 John Flynn
Lock Up Your Daughters! 69 Peter Coe
Lock Your Doors 43 William Beaudine
Locked Door, The 26 A. E. Coleby
Locked Door, The 29 George Fitzmaurice
Locked Doors 25 William DeMille
Locked Heart, The 18 Henry King
Locked Lips 20 William Dowlan
Lockende Ziel, Das 30 Max Reichmann
Locker 69 62 Norman Harrison
Locket, The 12 Allan Dwan
Locket, The 15 Wilfred Noy
Locket, The 46 John Brahm
Locksmith and Chancellor 23 Vladimir
  Gardin

Lockspitzel Asew *35* Piel Jutzi
Lockvogel *34* Hans Steinhoff
Loco Lindo *38* Arturo S. Mom
Loco Lobo *47* Howard Swift
Loco Luck *27* Clifford Smith
Loco Motifs *27* Manny Gould, Ben Harrison
Loco Serenata, El *39* Luis Saslavsky
Locomotive No. 10006 *26* Lev Kuleshov
Locomotives *34* Humphrey Jennings
Locura de Amor *11* Ricardo De Baños
Locura de Amor *50* Juan De Orduna
Locus *63* Yoji Kuri
Lodge in the Wilderness, The *26* Henry McCarthy
Lodger, The *26* Alfred Hitchcock
Lodger, The *31* Maurice Elvey
Lodger, The *44* John Brahm
Lodger — A Story of the London Fog, The *26* Alfred Hitchcock
Lodger Had the Haddock, The *07* Arthur Cooper
Lodger Who Wasn't Exactly a Paying Guest, The *19* Frank Miller
Lodgers *87* Dariush Mehrjui
Lodging for the Knight, A *12* D. W. Griffith
Lodging for the Night, A *12* D. W. Griffith
Lodging House Comedy, A *06* Alf Collins
Lodgings to Let *05* Lewin Fitzhamon
Łódz *45* Leonard Buczkowski
Łódz — The Polish Manchester *28* Aleksander Ford
Loffe the Vagabond *48* Gösta Werner
Lofoten *40* David MacDonald
Löft *85* Eckhart Schmidt
Log Cabin, The *65* Jaromil Jireš
Logan's Run *75* Michael Anderson
Logis de l'Horreur, Le *22* Julien Duvivier
Loha *87* Raj Sippy
Loi, La *58* Jules Dassin
Loi...C'Est la Loi, La *57* Christian-Jaque
Loi du Nord, La *39* Jacques Feyder
Loi du Survivant, La *66* José Giovanni
Loi du 21 Juin 1907, La *42* Sacha Guitry
Loi Re Trai Tren Duong Mon *86* Huy Thanh
Loin de Manhattan *81* Jean-Claude Biette
Loin du Viêt-nam *66* Jacques Demy, Jean-Luc Godard, Ruy Guerra, Joris Ivens, William Klein, Claude Lelouch, Louis Malle, Chris Marker, Alain Resnais, Agnès Varda
Löjen och Tårar *12* Victor Sjöström
Lokis *70* Janusz Majewski
Lola *14* James Young
Lola *32* Phil Rosen
Lola *60* Jacques Demy
Lola *69* Richard Donner
Lola *81* Rainer Werner Fassbinder
Lola *86* Bigas Luna
Lola Colt *67* Siro Marcellini
Lola Montès *55* Max Ophüls
Lola Montez *55* Max Ophüls
Lola's Kidnapping — Lola the Trucker II *86* Raúl Fernández
Lola's Mistake *60* Richard L. Bare
Lolita *61* Stanley Kubrick
Lollipop *66* J. B. Tanko

Lollipop *76* Ashley Lazarus
Lollipop Cover, The *64* Everett Chambers
Lollipops and Posies *17* Frank Wilson
Lolly Madonna War, The *72* Richard C. Sarafian
Lolly Madonna XXX *72* Richard C. Sarafian
Lombardi Ltd. *19* Jack Conway
Lomelin *65* François Reichenbach
London *26* Herbert Wilcox
London *38* Hayford Hobbs
London After Midnight *27* Tod Browning
London Belongs to Me *48* Sidney Gilliat
London Blackout Murders, The *42* George Sherman
London by Night *13* Alexander Butler
London by Night *37* Wilhelm Thiele
London Calling *58* Sidney Smith
London Can Take It! *40* Humphrey Jennings, Harry Watt
London Connection, The *79* Robert Clouse
London Drag *70* Richard Benner
London Entertains *51* E. J. Fancey
London Flat Mystery, A *15* Walter West
London Love *26* H. Manning Haynes
London Melody *30* Geoffrey H. Malins, Donald Stuart
London Melody *37* Herbert Wilcox
London Mystery, A *14* Charles C. Calvert
London Nighthawks *15* Percy Moran
London — 1942 *42* Ken Annakin
London Nobody Knows, The *67* Norman Cohen
London Pop *64* George Moorse
London Pride *20* Harold M. Shaw
London Rock and Roll Show, The *73* Peter Clifton
London Scene, The *67* Peter Brook*
London — Through My Eyes *70* Charles Crichton
London Town *46* Wesley Ruggles
Londonderry Air, The *38* Alex Bryce
Londoners, The *39* Philip Leacock*
London's Enemies *16* Percy Moran
London's Underworld *14* Harry Lorraine
London's Yellow Peril *15* Maurice Elvey
Londra Chiama Polo Nord *59* Duilio Coletti
Lone Avenger, The *33* Alvin J. Neitz
Lone Bandit, The *34* John P. McGowan
Lone Chance, The *24* Howard Mitchell
Lone Climber, The *50* William C. Hammond
Lone Cowboy, The *15* Raoul Walsh
Lone Cowboy, The *34* Paul Sloane
Lone Defender, The *30* Richard Thorpe
Lone Eagle, The *27* Emory Johnson
Lone Fighter *23* Albert Russell
Lone Gun, The *54* Ray Nazarro
Lone Hand, The *20* Clifford Smith
Lone Hand, The *22* B. Reeves Eason
Lone Hand, The *53* George Sherman
Lone Hand Saunders *26* B. Reeves Eason
Lone Hand Texan, The *47* Ray Nazarro
Lone Hand Wilson *20* L. S. McKee, Harry G. Moody
Lone Hazel, The *87* Frunze Dovlatyan
Lone Horseman, The *23* Fred Caldwell
Lone Horseman, The *29* John P. Mc-

Gowan
Lone Journey, The *55* Hiroshi Inagaki
Lone Mountie, The *38* Manny Gould, Ben Harrison
Lone Prairie, The *42* William Berke
Lone Ranger, The *38* John English, William Witney
Lone Ranger, The *55* Stuart Heisler
Lone Ranger *67* John Halas*
Lone Ranger and the Lost City of Gold, The *58* Lesley Selander
Lone Ranger Rides Again, The *39* John English, William Witney
Lone Rider, The *22* Victor Adamson
Lone Rider, The *30* Louis King
Lone Rider, The *34* Robert E. Tansey
Lone Rider Ambushed, The *41* Sam Newfield
Lone Rider and the Bandit, The *42* Sam Newfield
Lone Rider Crosses the Rio, The *41* Sam Newfield
Lone Rider Fights Back, The *41* Sam Newfield
Lone Rider in Border Roundup, The *42* Sam Newfield
Lone Rider in Cheyenne, The *42* Sam Newfield
Lone Rider in Death Rides the Plains, The *43* Sam Newfield
Lone Rider in Frontier Fury, The *41* Sam Newfield
Lone Rider in Ghost Town, The *41* Sam Newfield
Lone Rider in Law of the Saddle, The *43* Melville DeLay
Lone Rider in Outlaws of Boulder Pass, The *42* Sam Newfield
Lone Rider in Overland Stagecoach, The *42* Sam Newfield
Lone Rider in Texas Justice, The *42* Sam Newfield
Lone Rider in Wild Horse Rustlers, The *43* Sam Newfield
Lone Rider Rides On, The *41* Sam Newfield
Lone Runner, The *86* Ruggero Deodato
Lone Scout, The *29* J. H. Martin Cross
Lone Shark, The *29* Manny Gould, Ben Harrison
Lone Star *16* Edward Sloman
Lone Star, The *27* William Wyler
Lone Star *51* Vincent Sherman
Lone Star Country *83* Caruth C. Byrd, Lee Thornburg
Lone Star Law *41* Robert E. Tansey
Lone Star Law Men *41* Robert E. Tansey
Lone Star Lawman *51* Lewis D. Collins
Lone Star Moonlight *46* Ray Nazarro
Lone Star Pioneers *39* Joseph Levering
Lone Star Raiders *40* George Sherman
Lone Star Ranger, The *19* J. Gordon Edwards
Lone Star Ranger, The *23* Lambert Hillyer
Lone Star Ranger *30* A. F. Erickson
Lone Star Ranger, The *42* James Tinling
Lone Star Rush, The *15* Edmund Mitchell
Lone Star Stranger, The *31* Edward Buzzell
Lone Star Trail, The *43* Ray Taylor

Lone Star Vigilantes, The *42* Wallace Fox
Lone Stranger and Porky, The *39* Robert Clampett
Lone Texan *59* Paul Landres
Lone Texas Ranger *45* Spencer G. Bennet
Lone Trail, The *32* Forrest K. Sheldon, Harry S. Webb
Lone Troubador, The *39* Raymond K. Johnson
Lone Wagon, The *24* Frank S. Mattison
Lone White Sail, The *37* Vladimir Legoshin
Lone Wolf, The *17* Herbert Brenon
Lone Wolf, The *24* Stanner E. V. Taylor
Lone Wolf and His Lady, The *49* John Hoffman
Lone Wolf in London, The *47* Leslie Goodwins
Lone Wolf in Mexico, The *47* D. Ross Lederman
Lone Wolf in Paris, The *38* Albert S. Rogell
Lone Wolf Keeps a Date, The *41* Sidney Salkow
Lone Wolf McQuade *83* Steve Carver
Lone Wolf Meets a Lady, The *40* Sidney Salkow
Lone Wolf Returns, The *26* Ralph Ince
Lone Wolf Returns, The *35* Roy William Neill
Lone Wolf Spy Hunt, The *39* Peter Godfrey
Lone Wolf Strikes, The *40* Sidney Salkow
Lone Wolf Takes a Chance, The *41* Sidney Salkow
Lone Wolf's Daughter, The *19* William P. S. Earle
Lone Wolf's Daughter, The *28* Albert S. Rogell
Lone Wolf's Daughter, The *39* Peter Godfrey
Lone World Sail *60* John Halas*
Lonedale Operator, The *11* D. W. Griffith
Loneliness of Neglect, The *12* Allan Dwan
Loneliness of the Long Distance Runner, The *62* Tony Richardson
Lonely Are the Brave *62* David Miller
Lonely Boy *62* Wolf Koenig, Roman Kroitor
Lonely 15 *82* David Lai
Lonely Guy, The *84* Arthur Hiller
Lonely Heart *21* John B. O'Brien
Lonely Heart Bandits *50* George Blair
Lonely Hearts *81* Paul Cox
Lonely Hearts *81* Kon Ichikawa
Lonely Hearts Bandits *50* George Blair
Lonely Hearts Killer, The *69* Leonard Kastle
Lonely Hearts Killers, The *69* Leonard Kastle
Lonely Hoodlum *27* Heinosuke Gosho
Lonely House, The *56* Montgomery Tully
Lonely Inn, The *12* A. E. Coleby
Lonely Lady, The *53* Roberto Rossellini
Lonely Lady, The *82* Peter Sasdy
Lonely Lady of Grosvenor Square, The *22* Sinclair Hill
Lonely Lane *62* Mikio Naruse
Lonely Man, The *57* Henry Levin
Lonely Man *69* Al Adamson

Lonely Night, The *54* Irving Jacoby
Lonely Passion of Judith Hearne, The *87* Jack Clayton
Lonely Range, The *11* Allan Dwan
Lonely Road, The *21* Alfred Vanderbosch
Lonely Road, The *23* Victor Schertzinger
Lonely Road, The *36* James Flood
Lonely Roughneck, The *27* Heinosuke Gosho
Lonely Stage, The *62* Ronald Neame
Lonely Trail, The *36* Joseph Kane
Lonely Villa, The *09* D. W. Griffith
Lonely Village *24* Teinosuke Kinugasa
Lonely White Sail *37* Vladimir Legoshin
Lonely Wife, The *64* Satyajit Ray
Lonely Wives *31* Russell Mack
Lonely Woman, The *18* Thomas Heffron
Lonely Woman, The *53* Roberto Rossellini
Lonely Woman Is Looking for a Life Companion, A *87* Vyacheslav Krishtofovich
Lonely Woman Seeks Life Companion *87* Vyacheslav Krishtofovich
Lonely Woman Seeks Lifetime Companion *87* Vyacheslav Krishtofovich
Lonelyhearts *58* Vincent J. Donehue
Lonelyhearts Club *87* Michel Lang
Loner, The *81* Max Kleven
Loner *87* William Byron Hillman
Loner, The *87* Jacques Deray
Loners, The *72* Sutton Roley
Lonesome *28* Pál Fejős
Lonesome Chap, The *17* Edward J. LeSaint
Lonesome Corners *22* Edgar Jones
Lonesome Cowboys *68* Andy Warhol
Lonesome Farm *22* George Dewhurst
Lonesome Heart *15* William Desmond Taylor
Lonesome Ladies *27* Joseph E. Henabery
Lonesome Lenny *46* Tex Avery
Lonesome Luke *15* J. Farrell MacDonald
Lonesome Luke on Tin Can Alley *17* Hal Roach
Lonesome Luke's Movie Muddle *16* Hal Roach
Lonesome Mouse *43* Joseph Barbera, William Hanna
Lonesome Town *16* Thomas Heffron
Lonesome Trail, The *30* Bruce Mitchell
Lonesome Trail *45* Oliver Drake
Lonesome Trail, The *55* Richard Bartlett
Long Absence, The *61* Henri Colpi
Long Ago Tomorrow *70* Bryan Forbes
Long and Short of It, The *02* Georges Méliès
Long and the Short and the Tall, The *60* Leslie Norman
Long Arm, The *56* Charles Frend
Long Arm of Law and Order, The *16* John R. Bray
Long Arm of Mannister, The *19* Bertram Bracken
Long Arm of the Law *84* Johnny Mak
Long Blue Road, The *56* Gillo Pontecorvo
Long Chance, The *15* Edward J. LeSaint
Long Chance, A *18* Jack Conway
Long Chance, The *22* Jack Conway
Long Coats, The *86* Gilles Behat
Long Corridor *63* Samuel Fuller
Long Count, The *28* Manny Gould, Ben

Harrison
Long Dark Hall, The *51* Reginald Beck, Anthony Bushell
Long Dark Night, The *77* Robert Clouse
Long Day's Dying, The *68* Peter Collinson
Long Day's Journey Into Night *62* Sidney Lumet
Long des Trottoirs, Le *56* Léonide Moguy
Long Distance *59* Alvin Rakoff
Long Distance Wireless Photography *07* Georges Méliès
Long Duel, The *66* Ken Annakin
Long Good Friday, The *80* John Mackenzie
Long Goodbye, The *71* Kira Muratova
Long Goodbye, The *73* Robert Altman
Long Gray Line, The *55* John Ford
Long Hair of Death, The *64* Antonio Margheriti
Long-Haired Hare *48* Chuck Jones
Long Haul, The *57* Ken Hughes
Long Hole, The *24* Andrew P. Wilson
Long, Hot Summer, The *57* Martin Ritt
Long Is the Road *48* Herbert B. Fredersdorf, Marek Goldstein
Long John Silver *54* Byron Haskin
Long John Silver Returns to Treasure Island *54* Byron Haskin
Long Knife, The *58* Montgomery Tully
Long Lane's Turning, The *19* Louis Chaudet
Long Live Ghosts *79* Oldřich Lipský
Long Live Kindness *35* Martin Frič
Long Live Life *84* Claude Lelouch
Long Live the Air *24* Dziga Vertov
Long Live the Bride and Groom *69* Luis García Berlanga
Long Live the Deceased *35* Martin Frič
Long Live the King *22* Raoul Barré, Charles Bowers
Long Live the King *23* Victor Schertzinger
Long Live the King *26* Leo McCarey
Long Live the King *33* William McGann
Long Live the Lady! *87* Ermanno Olmi
Long Live the Newlyweds *69* Luis García Berlanga
Long Live the Republic! *65* Karel Kachyňa
Long Live Your Death *71* Duccio Tessari
Long, Long Trail, The *29* Arthur Rosson
Long, Long Trail, The *42* Robert E. Tansey
Long, Long Trailer, The *53* Vincente Minnelli
Long Loop, The *27* Leo D. Maloney
Long Loop on the Pecos, The *27* Leo D. Maloney
Long Lost Father *34* Ernest B. Schoedsack
Long March, The *66* Alexandre Astruc
Long Memory, The *52* Robert Hamer
Long Night, The *47* Anatole Litvak
Long Night, The *76* Woodie King, Jr.
Long Night of '43, The *60* Florestano Vancini
Long Night of Terror, The *63* Sergio Corbucci, Antonio Margheriti
Long Odds *22* A. E. Coleby
Long Pants *27* Frank Capra
Long Path, The *56* Leonid Gaidai, V. Nevzorov
Long Ride, The *83* Pál Gábor

Long Ride from Hell, A 68 Camillo Bazzoni
Long Ride Home, The 67 Roger Corman, Phil Karlson
Long Riders, The 80 Walter Hill
Long Rifle and the Tomahawk, The 56 Sam Newfield, Sidney Salkow
Long Road, The 11 D. W. Griffith
Long Rope, The 61 William Witney
Long Run, The 83 Pál Gábor
Long Shadow, The 61 Peter Maxwell
Long Ships, The 63 Jack Cardiff
Long Shot, The 38 Charles Lamont
Long Shot, The 76 Peter Collinson
Long Shot 78 Maurice Hatton
Long Strider 87 Rafael Moreno Alba
Long Strike, The 12 Herbert Brenon
Long Sunday, The 61 Roman Polanski
Long, the Short and the Tall, The 60 Leslie Norman
Long Tomorrow, The 72 William A. Graham
Long Trail, The 17 Howell Hansel
Long Voyage Home, The 40 John Ford
Long Wait, The 54 Victor Saville
Long Walk Home, The 90 Richard Pearce
Long Way, The 14 Charles Brabin
Long Way Home, The 89 Michael Apted
Long Weekend 78 Colin Eggleston
Longest Day, The 62 Ken Annakin, Andrew Marton, Gerd Oswald, Bernhard Wicki
Longest Day in Japan, The 67 Kihachi Okamoto
Longest Hunt, The 68 Bruno Corbucci
Longest Night, The 36 Errol Taggart
Longest Spur, The 68 R. Lee Frost
Longest Yard, The 74 Robert Aldrich
Longhorn, The 51 Lewis D. Collins
Longing 20 F. W. Murnau
Longing 35 Heinosuke Gosho
Longing for Love 66 Koreyoshi Kurahara
Longing for the Sea 31 John W. Brunius
Longs Manteaux, Les 86 Gilles Behat
Longshot 81 E. W. Swackhamer
Longshot, The 86 Paul Bartel
Longtime Companion 90 Norman René
Longue Marche, La 66 Alexandre Astruc
Lonnie 63 William Hale
Look at Life 65 George Lucas
Look Back in Anger 58 Tony Richardson
Look Before You Laugh 59 Lance Comfort
Look Before You Leap 13 Hay Plumb
Look Before You Love 48 Harold Huth
Look Down and Die 80 Steve Carver
Look for the Silver Lining 49 David Butler
Look in Any Window 61 William Alland
Look Out! 59 Jiří Brdečka
Look Out Below 29 Stephen Roberts
Look Out for Love 37 Herbert Wilcox
Look Out for the Cars 66 Eldar Ryazanov
Look Out Girl, The 28 Dallas M. Fitzgerald
Look Out Mr. Haggis 35 Redd Davis
Look Out Sister 48 Bud Pollard
Look Pleasant Please 19 Raoul Barré, Charles Bowers
Look Up and Laugh 35 Basil Dean
Look Who's Laughing 41 Allan Dwan
Look Who's Talking 89 Amy Heckerling

Look Who's Talking Too 90 Amy Heckerling
Look Your Best 23 Rupert Hughes
Looker 81 Michael Crichton
Lookin' for Someone 46 Ray Nazarro
Lookin' Good 71 Leonard Horn
Lookin' to Get Out 81 Hal Ashby
Looking for Danger 57 Austen Jewell
Looking for Eileen 87 Rudolf van den Berg
Looking for His Murderer 30 Robert Siodmak, Carl Winston
Looking for John Smith 06 Wallace McCutcheon
Looking for Lodgings at the Seaside 10 Fred Rains
Looking for Love 64 Don Weis
Looking for Mr. Goodbar 77 Richard Brooks
Looking for Mushrooms 67 Bruce Conner
Looking for Sally 25 Leo McCarey
Looking for Trouble 26 Robert North Bradbury
Looking for Trouble 31 Ralph Murphy, Albert S. Rogell
Looking for Trouble 33 William A. Wellman
Looking for Trouble 51 William C. Hammond
Looking Forward 33 Clarence Brown
Looking Glass War, The 69 Frank Pierson
Looking on the Bright Side 31 Graham Cutts, Basil Dean
Looking Up 77 Linda Yellen
Looks and Smiles 81 Kenneth Loach
Looming Shadow, A 85 Kazimierz Karabasz
Looney Balloonists 36 Art Davis, Sid Marcus
Looney, Looney, Looney Bugs Bunny Movie, The 81 Friz Freleng
Loonies on Broadway 45 Gordon Douglas
Loony Tom 51 James Broughton
Loony Tom, the Happy Lover 51 James Broughton
Looped for Life 24 Park Frame
Loophole 54 Harold Schuster
Loophole 80 John Quested
Looping the Loop 28 Arthur Robison
Loops 40 Norman McLaren
Loops 58 Shirley Clarke, D. A. Pennebaker
Loopy's Hare-Do 61 Joseph Barbera, William Hanna
Loose Ankles 30 Ted Wilde
Loose Cannons 89 Bob Clark
Loose Connections 83 Richard Eyre
Loose Ends 30 Norman Walker
Loose Ends 75 David Burton Morris
Loose in London 53 Edward Bernds
Loose Joints 81 Peter Winograd
Loose Pleasures 64 Claude De Givray
Loose Screws 85 Rafal Zielinski
Loose Shoes 80 Ira Miller
Loosened Plank, The 14 Lewin Fitzhamon
Loot 19 William Dowlan
Loot 70 Silvio Narizzano
Looters, The 55 Abner Biberman
Looters of Liege, The 14 F. Martin Thornton

Løperjenten 81 Vibeke Løkkeberg
Lorca and the Outlaws 85 Roger Christian
Lorca, la Muerte de un Poeta 87 Juan Antonio Bardem
Lord Algy's Beauty Show 08 A. E. Coleby
Lord and Lady Algy 19 Harry Beaumont
Lord Arthur Saville's Crime 19 Pál Fejös
Lord Babs 32 Walter Forde
Lord Blend's Love Story 10 Theo Bouwmeester
Lord Byron 22 Conrad Veidt
Lord Byron of Broadway 29 Harry Beaumont, William Nigh
Lord Camber's Ladies 32 Benn W. Levy
Lord Chumley 14 James Kirkwood
Lord Edgware Dies 34 Henry Edwards
Lord Epping Returns 51 Leslie Goodwins
Lord Feathertop 08 Edwin S. Porter
Lord for a Night 46 Teinosuke Kinugasa
Lord Gave, The 15 Sidney Morgan
Lord High Executioner, The 06 Arthur Gilbert
Lord High Executioner, The 07 John Morland
Lord Jeff 38 Sam Wood
Lord Jim 25 Victor Fleming
Lord Jim 64 Richard Brooks
Lord Love a Duck 66 George Axelrod
Lord Loveland Discovers America 16 Arthur Maude
Lord Loves the Irish, The 19 Ernest C. Warde
Lord Mountdrago 54 David Eady, George More O'Ferrall, Wendy Toye
Lord of the Brothels 87 Shohei Imamura
Lord of the Flies 62 Peter Brook
Lord of the Flies 90 Harry Hook
Lord of the Jungle 55 Ford Beebe
Lord of the Manor 33 Henry Edwards
Lord of the Rings, The 78 Ralph Bakshi
Lord Ouverier, Le 15 Henri Diamant-Berger
Lord Richard in the Pantry 30 Walter Forde
Lord Shango 75 Ray Marsh
Lord Shiva's Dream 54 Kenneth Anger
Lördagskvällar 36 S. Bauman
Lords of Discipline, The 82 Franc Roddam
Lords of Flatbush, The 74 Martin Davidson, Stephen Verona
Lords of High Decision, The 16 John Harvey
Lords of Magick, The 90 David Marsh
Lords of the Deep 89 Mary Ann Fisher
Lords of Treason 84 Robert Altman
Lorelei of the Sea 17 Henry Otto
Lorelei's Grasp, The 72 Amando De Ossorio
Lorenzino de Medici 36 Guido Brignone
Lorgnon Accusateur, Le 05 Alice Guy-Blaché
Lörinci Fonóban, A 71 Márta Mészáros
Lorna 64 Russ Meyer
Lorna Doone 12 Wilfred Noy
Lorna Doone 15 J. Farrell MacDonald
Lorna Doone 20 H. Lisle Lucoque
Lorna Doone 22 Robert Thornby, Maurice Tourneur
Lorna Doone 34 Basil Dean
Lorna Doone 51 Phil Karlson

Lorna l'Exorciste 72 Jesús Franco
Lorraine of the Lions 25 Edward Sedgwick
Lorsque l'Enfant Paraît 56 Michel Bois-
rond
Lorsqu'une Femme Vent 19 Georges
Monca
Los de Abajo 40 Chano Urueta
Los Que Viven Donde Sopla el Viento
Suave 73 Felipe Cazals
Loser Take All 48 William Asher, Richard
Quine
Loser Take All 88 James Scott
Loser Takes All 56 Ken Annakin
Loser, the Hero, The 85 Peter Mak
Loser Wins, The 15 Ernest G. Batley
Losers, The 68 Edward Montoro, James
Somich
Losers, The 70 Jack Starrett
Loser's End 34 Bernard B. Ray
Losin' It 83 Curtis Hanson
Losing Fight, The 14 Colin Campbell
Losing Game, A 15 Hay Plumb
Losing Game, The 30 Lowell Sherman
Losing Ground 82 Kathleen Collins
Losing Winner, The 17 Carter DeHaven
Loss of Feeling 35 Alexander Andreievsky
Loss of Innocence 61 Lewis Gilbert
Loss of the Birkenhead, The 14 Maurice
Elvey
Lost 55 Guy Green
Lost 85 Peter Rowe
Lost, a Leg of Mutton 06 Alf Collins
Lost, a Monkey 10 H. Oceano Martinek
Lost: A Wife 25 William DeMille
Lost and Found 17 Alfred E. Green
Lost and Found 23 Raoul Walsh
Lost and Found 79 Melvin Frank
Lost and Found on a South Sea Island 23
Raoul Walsh
Lost and Found—The Story of Cook's An-
chor 79 David Lean*
Lost and Foundling 44 Chuck Jones
Lost and Foundry 37 Dave Fleischer
Lost and Won 15 Lawrence Trimble
Lost and Won 17 Frank Reicher
Lost Angel 43 Roy Rowland
Lost Angels 89 Hugh Hudson
Lost Army, The 65 Andrzej Wajda
Lost at Sea 26 Louis Gasnier
Lost at the Front 27 Del Lord
Lost Atlantis 21 Jacques Feyder
Lost Atlantis 32 G. W. Pabst
Lost Bag, The 13 August Blom
Lost Battalion, The 19 Burton L. King
Lost Battalion 61 Eddie Romero
Lost Boundaries 49 Alfred L. Werker
Lost Boys, The 87 Joel Schumacher
Lost Bridegroom, The 16 James Kirkwood
Lost Canyon 42 Lesley Selander
Lost Child, The 04 Wallace McCutcheon
Lost Child, The 54 Khwaja Ahmad Abbas
Lost Chord, The 16 Wilfred Noy
Lost Chord, The 28 J. Steven Edwards, H.
B. Parkinson
Lost Chord, The 33 Maurice Elvey
Lost City, The 35 Harry Revier
Lost City, The 82 Robert Dukes
Lost City of the Jungle 46 Lewis D. Col-
lins, Ray Taylor
Lost Collar Stud, The 14 F. Martin Thorn-
ton

Lost Command, The 66 Mark Robson
Lost Continent, The 51 Sam Newfield
Lost Continent, The 54 Leonardo Bonzi,
Mario Craveri, Enrico Gras, Giorgio
Moser, Folco Quilici
Lost Continent, The 68 Michael Carreras,
Leslie Norman
Lost Empire, The 24 Ernest B. Schoedsack
Lost Empire, The 84 Jim Wynorski
Lost Express, The 17 John P. McGowan
Lost Express, The 26 John P. McGowan
Lost Face, The 65 Pavel Hobl
Lost Forest, The 65 Liviu Ciulei
Lost Happiness 48 Filippo Walter Maria
Ratti
Lost Honeymoon 47 Leigh Jason
Lost Honor of Katharina Blum, The 75
Volker Schlöndorff, Margarethe von
Trotta
Lost Horizon 37 Frank Capra
Lost Horizon 72 Charles Jarrott
Lost Hours, The 52 David MacDonald
Lost House, The 15 Christy Cabanne
Lost Illusion, The 48 Carol Reed
Lost Illusions 11 Edwin S. Porter
Lost Illusions 82 Gyula Gazdag
Lost in a Big City 23 George Irving
Lost in a Harem 44 Charles Reisner
Lost in Alaska 52 Jean Yarbrough
Lost in America 85 Albert Brooks
Lost in Cuddihy 66 Ira Schneider
Lost in Prague 48 Martin Frič
Lost in the Alps 07 Edwin S. Porter
Lost in the Arctic 28 H. A. Snow, Sidney
Snow
Lost in the Dark 14 Nino Martoglio
Lost in the Dark 49 Camillo Mastrocinque
Lost in the Desert 71 Jamie Uys
Lost in the Jungle 15 Wallace A. Carlson
Lost in the Legion 34 Fred Newmeyer
Lost in the Snow 06 Frank Mottershaw
Lost in the Stars 74 Daniel Mann
Lost in the Stratosphere 34 Melville Brown
Lost in the Wilderness 86 Junya Sato
Lost in the Woods 12 Frank Wilson
Lost in Transit 17 Donald Crisp
Lost Island of Kioga 38 John English,
William Witney
Lost Jungle, The 34 David Howard, Ar-
mand Schaefer
Lost Kingdom, The 61 Frank Borzage,
Giuseppe Masini, Edgar G. Ulmer
Lost Lady, A 24 Harry Beaumont
Lost Lady, The 31 William A. Wellman
Lost Lady, A 34 Alfred E. Green
Lost Lagoon 58 John Rawlins
Lost Leader, A 22 George Ridgwell
Lost Leg of Mutton, The 06 Alf Collins
Lost Letters 66 Mikhail Romm
Lost Limited, The 27 John P. McGowan
Lost, Lonely and Vicious 58 Frank Myers
Lost Lost Lost 75 Jonas Mekas
Lost Love Letter, The 12 Wilfred Noy
Lost Luck 30 Yasujiro Ozu
Lost Man, The 69 Robert Alan Aurthur
Lost Memory, The 09 Lewin Fitzhamon
Lost Men 31 Edward L. Cahn, George
Melford
Lost Millionaire, The 13 Ralph Ince

Lost Missile, The 58 William Berke
Lost Moment, The 47 Martin Gabel
Lost Money 19 Edmund Lawrence
Lost on the Ice 37 Martin Frič
Lost on the Western Front 37 Maurice
Elvey
Lost One, The 47 Carmine Gallone
Lost One, The 51 Peter Lorre
Lost One Wife 27 Miles Mander
Lost Over London 34 Rex Graves
Lost Paradise, The 14 Oscar Apfel
Lost Paradise, The 62 Károly Makk
Lost Paradise, The 86 Basilio Martín
Patino
Lost Patrol, The 29 Walter Summers
Lost Patrol, The 34 John Ford
Lost People, The 49 Muriel Box, Bernard
Knowles
Lost Photograph, The 60 Lev Kulidzhanov
Lost Planet, The 53 Spencer G. Bennet
Lost Planet Airmen 49 Fred C. Brannon
Lost Princess, The 19 Scott R. Dunlap
Lost Property 49 Christian-Jaque
Lost Ranch 37 Sam Katzman
Lost Ring, or Johnson's Honeymoon, The
11 Theo Bouwmeester
Lost River 50 Ray Nazarro
Lost Romance, The 21 William DeMille
Lost Sex 66 Kaneto Shindo
Lost Shadow, The 21 Rochus Gliese, Paul
Wegener
Lost Shuttlecock, The 04 Alf Collins
Lost Son, The 34 Luis Trenker
Lost Son, The 74 Lotte Reiniger
Lost Soul 76 Dino Risi
Lost Souls 16 Roland West
Lost Souls 61 Adelchi Bianchi, Roberto
Mauri
Lost Special, The 32 Henry MacRae
Lost Spring 32 Mikio Naruse
Lost Squadron, The 32 George Archain-
baud
Lost Stage Valley 50 Ralph Murphy
Lost, Stolen or Strayed 05 Lewin Fitz-
hamon
Lost, Stolen or Strayed 21 Edward R.
Gordon
Lost Track, The 56 Karel Kachyňa
Lost Trail, The 26 John P. McGowan
Lost Trail, The 45 Lambert Hillyer
Lost Trail, The 56 Karel Kachyňa
Lost Treasure 27 Humberto Mauro
Lost Treasure of the Amazon 53 Edward
Ludwig
Lost Treasure of the Aztecs 61 Piero
Pierotti
Lost Tribe, The 49 William Berke
Lost Tribe, The 83 John Laing
Lost Volcano, The 50 Ford Beebe
Lost Watch, The 12 Allan Dwan
Lost Wedding Veil 70 Doo-yong Lee
Lost Weekend, The 45 Billy Wilder
Lost Will, The 12 Lewin Fitzhamon
Lost with All Hands 86 Benoît Jacquot
Lost Women 49 Ron Ormond, Herbert
Tevos
Lost Women of Zarpa 49 Ron Ormond,
Herbert Tevos
Lost World, The 25 William Dowlan,
Harry Hoyt

Lost World, The *60* Irwin Allen
Lost World of Sinbad, The *64* Senkichi Taniguchi
Lost Youth *47* Pietro Germi
Lost Zeppelin, The *29* Edward Sloman
Lot of Bull, A *18* Raoul Barré, Charles Bowers
Lotna *59* Andrzej Wajda
Lotte *28* Carl Fröhlich
Lotte in Italia *69* Jean-Luc Godard, Jean-Pierre Gorin
Lotte nell'Ombra *39* Domenico Gambino
Lotteriseddel No. 22152 *15* August Blom
Lottery Bride, The *30* Paul Stein
Lottery Lover *35* Wilhelm Thiele
Lottery Man, The *19* James Cruze
Lottery Prince, The *37* Stanisław Szwebgo, Konrad Tom
Lottery Ticket No. 66 *11* Bert Haldane
Lotti Ezredes *17* Béla Balázs
Lottie's Pancakes *07* Arthur Cooper
Lotus Blossom *21* Francis J. Grandon
Lotus d'Or, Le *16* Louis Mercanton
Lotus Eater, The *21* Marshall Neilan
Lotus for Miss Kwen, A *67* Jürgen Roland
Lotus Lady *30* Phil Rosen
Lotus Woman, The *16* Harry Millarde
Lou Costello and His 30 Foot Bride *59* Sidney Miller
Loud Soup *29* Lewis R. Foster
Loud Speaker, The *26* Widgey R. Newman, Challis Sanderson
Loudest Whisper, The *61* William Wyler
Loudspeaker, The *34* Joseph Santley
Loudwater Mystery, The *21* Walter West
Louie, There's a Crowd Downstairs *69* Bud Yorkin
Louis Capet *54* Roger Leenhardt, Jean-Pierre Vivet
Louis Malle's India *69* Louis Malle
Louis XI ou La Naissance d'un Roi *77* Alexandre Astruc
Louis XVI *54* Roger Leenhardt, Jean-Pierre Vivet
Louisa *50* Alexander Hall
Louise *38* Abel Gance
Louise *72* Philippe de Broca
Louisiana *19* Robert Vignola
Louisiana *47* Phil Karlson
Louisiana Gal *37* Irvin Willat
Louisiana Hayride *44* Charles Barton
Louisiana Hussy *60* Lee Sholem
Louisiana Purchase *41* Irving Cummings
Louisiana Story *48* Robert Flaherty
Louisiana Territory *53* Harry W. Smith
Louisiane *84* Philippe de Broca
Loulou *79* Maurice Pialat
Loup Garou, Le *32* Friedrich Feher
Loup Y Es-Tu? *83* Eric Rohmer
Loupe de Grand-Mère, La *00* Ferdinand Zecca
Loupe de Gran'maman, La *00* Ferdinand Zecca
Loups dans la Bergerie, Les *60* Hervé Bromberger
Loups Entre Eux, Les *85* José Giovanni
Lourdes *58* Ken Russell
Lourdes et Ses Miracles *54* Georges Rouquier
Louss *89* Mohamed Rachid Benhadj

Louves, Les *25* Robert Boudrioz
Louves, Les *57* Luis Saslavsky
Louves, Les *85* Peter Duffell
Louvre Come Back to Me *62* Chuck Jones
Lovable and Sweet *31* William James Craft
Lovable Cheat, The *49* Richard Oswald
Lovable Tramp, The *66* Yoji Yamada
Love *14* Yakov Protazanov
Love *16* L. C. MacBean
Love *19* Roscoe Arbuckle
Love *20* Wesley Ruggles
Love *24* Teinosuke Kinugasa
Love *27* Edmund Goulding
Love *48* Marcel Pagnol, Jean Renoir, Roberto Rossellini
Love *52* Gustaf Molander
Love *62* Yoji Kuri
Love *71* Károly Makk
Love *72* Karel Kachyňa
Love *81* Annette Cohen, Nancy Dowd, Liv Ullmann, Mai Zetterling
Love à la Carte *60* Antonio Pietrangeli
Love à la Mode *30* Stephen Roberts
Love Affair *32* Thornton Freeland
Love Affair *38* Leo McCarey
Love Affair *66* Dušan Makavejev
Love Affair in Toyland, A *08* Émile Cohl
Love Affair of Ima Knut, The *17* Otto Messmer
Love Affair of the Dictator, The *35* Alfred Santell, Victor Saville
Love Affair, or The Case of the Missing Switchboard Operator *66* Dušan Makavejev
Love Aflame *17* Raymond Wells
Love Among the Millionaires *30* Frank Tuttle
Love Among the Roses *10* D. W. Griffith
Love Among the Ruins *75* George Cukor
Love and a Burglar *13* Hay Plumb
Love and a Legacy *15* Cecil Birch
Love and a Savage *15* Al Christie
Love and a Sewing Machine *11* Lewin Fitzhamon
Love and a Tub *14* Will P. Kellino
Love and a Warrior *25* Teinosuke Kinugasa
Love and a Whirlwind *22* Duncan Macrae, Harold M. Shaw
Love and Ambition *17* Edward Warren
Love and Anarchy *73* Lina Wertmuller
Love and Anger *67* Marco Bellocchio, Bernardo Bertolucci, Jean-Luc Godard, Carlo Lizzani, Pier Paolo Pasolini
Love and Bullets *14* Dave Aylott
Love and Bullets *78* Stuart Rosenberg
Love and Cameras *15* Cecil Birch
Love and Chatter *57* Alessandro Blasetti
Love and Courage *13* Mack Sennett
Love and Curses *38* Cal Dalton, Ben Hardaway
Love and Death *32* Rosario Romeo
Love and Death *75* Woody Allen
Love and Deficit *32* Gustaf Molander
Love and Die *88* Gerard Ciccoritti
Love and Doughnuts *21* Roy Del Ruth
Love and Fear *88* Margarethe von Trotta
Love and 'Fluence *16* Cecil Birch
Love and Gasoline *14* Mack Sennett
Love and Glory *24* Rupert Julian

Love and Greed *64* Yasuzo Masumura
Love and Hate *16* James Vincent
Love and Hate *24* Thomas Bentley
Love and Hisses *37* Sidney Lanfield
Love and Journalism *16* Mauritz Stiller
Love and Kisses *25* Edward F. Cline
Love and Kisses *65* Ozzie Nelson
Love and Larceny *59* Dino Risi
Love and Learn *28* Frank Tuttle
Love and Learn *47* Frederick De Cordova
Love and Lemons *12* Allan Dwan
Love and Lies *81* Ilya Frez
Love and Life *61* Yasuzo Masumura
Love and Lobster *18* Fred Rains
Love and Lobsters *16* Roscoe Arbuckle
Love and Loot *16* Larry Semon
Love and Lunch *14* Charles Chaplin, Mabel Normand
Love and Lunch *17* Gregory La Cava, Vernon Stallings
Love and Magic *14* Walter R. Booth
Love and Marriage *64* Mino Guerrini, Gianni Puccini
Love and Marriage *71* Terry Gould
Love and Molasses *08* Georges Méliès
Love and Money *80* James Toback
Love and Other Crimes *76* John Korty
Love and Pain *13* Mack Sennett
Love and Pain and the Whole Damn Thing *72* Alan J. Pakula
Love and Pain and the Whole Darn Thing *72* Alan J. Pakula
Love and Pledge *45* Tadashi Imai
Love and Rubbish *13* Henry Lehrman
Love and Sacrifice *24* D. W. Griffith
Love and Sacrifice *36* George Roland
Love and Separation in Sri Lanka *76* Keisuke Kinoshita
Love and Spanish Onions *15* Edwin J. Collins
Love and the Boxing Gloves *14* Cecil Birch
Love and the Devil *29* Alexander Korda
Love and the Dirigible *47* Jiří Brdečka
Love and the First Railroad *35* Hassa Preis
Love and the Frenchwoman *60* Michel Boisrond, Christian-Jaque, René Clair, Henri Decoin, Jean Delannoy, Jean-Paul Le Chanois, Henri Verneuil
Love and the Journalist *16* Mauritz Stiller
Love and the Law *13* Wallace Reid
Love and the Law *19* Edgar Lewis
Love and the Midnight Auto Supply *78* James Polakoff
Love and the Varsity *13* Percy Stow
Love and the Warrior *25* Teinosuke Kinugasa
Love and the Whirlwind *20* Harold M. Shaw
Love and the Woman *19* Tefft Johnson
Love and War *1899* James White
Love and War *11* A. E. Coleby
Love and War *14* Forest Holger-Madsen
Love and War in Toyland *13* Edgar Rogers, F. Martin Thornton
Love Around the Corner *86* Alberto Cortés Calderón
Love at Arms *12* Fred Rains
Love at First Bite *79* Stan Dragoti
Love at First Flight *28* Edward F. Cline
Love at First Sight *28* Edward F. Cline

Love at First Sight 30 Edgar Lewis
Love at First Sight 74 Rex Bromfield
Love at First Sight 85 Marco Risi
Love at Large 90 Alan Rudolph
Love at Night 61 Pierre Mère
Love at Sea 36 Adrian Brunel
Love at Second Sight 34 Paul Merzbach
Love at Stake 87 John Moffitt
Love at the Circus 14 Ethyle Batley
Love at the Top 73 Michel Deville
Love at the Wheel 21 Bannister Merwin
Love at Twenty 62 Shintaro Ishihara,
    Marcel Ophüls, Renzo Rossellini, Fran-
    çois Truffaut, Andrzej Wajda
Love Auction, The 19 Edmund Lawrence
Love Ban, The 72 Ralph Thomas
Love Bandit, The 24 Del Henderson
Love Before Breakfast 36 Walter Lang
Love Begins at Twenty 36 Frank Mc-
    Donald
Love Between the Raindrops 79 Karel
    Kachyňa
Love Bewitched, A 85 Carlos Saura
Love Birds 34 William A. Seiter
Love Blackmailer, The 66 Ted Leversuch
Love Blinds Us 25 Lothar Mendes
Love Boids 45 Joseph Barbera, William
    Hanna
Love Bound 32 Robert F. Hill
Love Box, The 72 Billy White, Teddy
    White
Love Brand, The 23 Stuart Paton
Love Brokers, The 18 E. Mason Hopper
Love Bug, The 68 Robert Stevenson
Love Burglar, The 19 James Cruze
Love Butcher, The 75 Mikel Angel, Don
    Jones
Love by the Light of the Moon 01 Edwin
    S. Porter
Love Cage, The 63 René Clément
Love Call, The 19 Louis Chaudet
Love Camp 81 Christian Anders
Love Camp Seven 68 R. Lee Frost
Love Captive, The 34 Max Marcin
Love Charm, The 21 Thomas Heffron
Love Chastised 55 Kenne Fant
Love Cheat, The 18 George Archainbaud
Love Child 82 Larry Peerce
Love Children 68 Richard Rush
Love Circle, The 69 Giuseppe Patroni
    Griffi
Love Comes Along 30 Rupert Julian
Love Comes to Magoo 58 Tom McDonald
Love Commandment, The 28 Viktor Jan-
    sen
Love Commands 40 Augusto Cesar
    Vatteone
Love Commune 70 Robert J. Emery
Love Conquers 11 Theo Bouwmeester
Love Conquers Crime 12 Fred Rains
Love Contract, The 32 Herbert Selpin
Love Contract, The 86 Dan Wolman
Love Crazy 41 Jack Conway
Love Crisis 33 Kajiro Yamamoto
Love Cycles 69 Georges Skalenakis
Love, Death 73 Theodore Gershuny
Love Defender, The 19 Tefft Johnson
Love Doctor, The 17 Paul Scardon
Love Doctor, The 29 Melville Brown
Love Doll 73 Philippe Agostini, Luis Gar-

cía Berlanga
Love Dossier, or The Tragedy of a Switch-
    board Operator 66 Dušan Makavejev
Love Dream 88 Charles Finch
Love 'Em and Feed 'Em 27 Clyde Bruck-
    man
Love 'Em and Leave 'Em 26 Frank Tuttle
Love Epidemic, The 75 Brian Trenchard-
    Smith
Love Eternal 43 Jean Delannoy
Love Eterne, The 63 King Hu, Han-
    hsiang Li
Love Expert, The 20 David Kirkland
Love Factory 66 Massimo Mida
Love Feast, The 66 Hans Dieter Bove
Love Fever 85 René Cardona, Jr.
Love Film 70 István Szabó
Love Finds a Way 08 D. W. Griffith
Love Finds a Way 30 George Archainbaud
Love Finds Andy Hardy 38 George B.
    Seitz
Love Flower, The 20 D. W. Griffith
Love, Fog and Rain 24 Teinosuke Kinu-
    gasa
Love for Love 40 Carlos Navarro
Love-Forsaken Corner, A 86 Ya-lin Li, Qi
    Zhang
Love from a Stranger 36 Rowland V. Lee
Love from a Stranger 47 Richard Whorf
Love from Paris 56 Helmut Käutner
Love Gamble, The 25 Edward J. LeSaint
Love Gambler, The 22 Joseph Franz
Love Game, The 59 Philippe de Broca
Love Game, The 59 Kenne Fant
Love Games 31 Oskar Fischinger
Love Girl, The 16 Robert Z. Leonard
Love God?, The 69 Nat Hiken
Love Habit, The 31 Harry Lachman
Love Happy 49 David Miller
Love Has Many Faces 65 Alexander Singer
Love Hate 70 Jean-Pierre Mocky
Love, Hate and a Woman 21 Charles T.
    Horan
Love, Hate, Death 18 Ivan Perestiani
Love, Honor and ? 19 Charles Miller
Love, Honor and Behave 20 F. Richard
    Jones, Erle C. Kenton
Love, Honor and Behave 38 Stanley Logan
Love, Honor and Goodbye 45 Albert S.
    Rogell
Love, Honor and He Pays 32 Edward
    Buzzell
Love, Honor and Obey 19 Alfred E.
    Green
Love, Honor and Obey 20 Leander De
    Cordova
Love, Honor and Oh Baby! 33 Edward
    Buzzell
Love, Honor and Oh Baby! 40 Charles
    Lamont
Love Hour, The 25 Herman Raymaker
Love Hunger, The 19 William P. S. Earle
Love Hunger 65 Albert Dubois
Love Hungry 28 Victor Heerman
Love Hurts 90 Bud Yorkin
Love Image, The 22 John Ford
Love in a Boarding House 13 Lewin Fitz-
    hamon
Love in a Bungalow 37 Ray McCarey
Love in a Fallen City 84 Ann Hui

Love in a Four Letter World 70 John Sone
Love in a Goldfish Bowl 61 Jack Sher
Love in a Hammock 01 Edwin S. Porter
Love in a Hot Climate 53 Georges Rou-
    quier
Love in a Hurry 19 Del Henderson
Love in a Laundry 12 Frank Wilson
Love in a Minefield 87 Pastor Vega
Love in a Mist 16 Cecil M. Hepworth
Love in a Taxi 80 Robert Sickinger
Love in a Teashop 13 Hubert von Herko-
    mer
Love in a Wood 15 Maurice Elvey
Love in an Apartment Hotel 12 D. W.
    Griffith
Love in an Attic 23 Edwin Greenwood
Love in Baghdad 86 Abdul Hadi Al Rawi
Love in Bloom 35 Elliott Nugent
Love in Cold Blood 69 Stuart McGowan
Love in Exile 36 Alfred L. Werker
Love in Four Dimensions 65 Mino Guer-
    rini, Massimo Mida, Gianni Puccini, Jac-
    ques Romain
Love in Germany, A 83 Andrzej Wajda
Love in High Gear 32 Frank R. Strayer
Love in Jerusalem 67 Menahem Golan
Love in Las Vegas 64 George Sidney
Love in Mardi Gras Colors 74 Evald
    Schorm*
Love in Morocco 31 Rex Ingram, Alice
    Terry
Love in Pawn 53 Charles Saunders
Love in Quarantine 38 Amleto Palermi
Love in Question 78 André Cayatte
Love in Rome 60 Dino Risi
Love in September 36 Edward F. Cline
Love in Stunt Flying 38 Gustaf Gründgens
Love in Suspense 16 William Beaudine
Love in the Afternoon 57 Billy Wilder
Love in the Afternoon 72 Eric Rohmer
Love in the Army 35 Mieczysław Krawicz
Love in the City 53 Michelangelo Anto-
    nioni, Federico Fellini, Alberto Lat-
    tuada, Carlo Lizzani, Francesco Maselli,
    Dino Risi, Cesare Zavattini
Love in the Dark 22 Harry Beaumont
Love in the Desert 29 George Melford
Love in the Hills 11 D. W. Griffith
Love in the Rough 30 Charles Reisner
Love in the Tropics 11 August Blom
Love in the Welsh Hills 21 Bernard Dud-
    ley
Love in the Wilderness 20 Alexander
    Butler
Love in Tokyo 32 Heinosuke Gosho
Love in Waiting 48 Douglas Pierce
Love in Waltz Time 38 Hubert Marischka
Love-Ins, The 67 Arthur Dreifuss
Love Insurance 19 Donald Crisp
Love Is a Ball 62 David Swift
Love Is a Carousel 70 Roy P. Cheverton
Love Is a Day's Work 60 Mauro Bolognini
Love Is a Dog from Hell 87 Dominique
    Deruddere
Love Is a Fat Woman 87 Alejandro
    Agresti
Love Is a Funny Thing 69 Claude Lelouch
Love Is a Headache 37 Richard Thorpe
Love Is a Many Splendored Thing 55
    Henry King

Love Is a Racket *32* William A. Wellman
Love Is a Scandal *51* Salah Abu Saif
Love Is a Splendid Illusion *70* Tom Clegg
Love Is a Weapon *54* Phil Karlson
Love Is a Woman *65* Frederic Goode
Love Is an Awful Thing *22* Victor Heerman
Love Is Better Than Ever *51* Stanley Donen
Love Is Blind *09* Edwin S. Porter
Love Is Blind *12* August Blom
Love Is Blind *13* Allan Dwan
Love Is Blonde *28* Mark Sandrich*
Love Is Colder Than Death *69* Rainer Werner Fassbinder
Love Is Dangerous *33* Richard Thorpe
Love Is Ever Young *86* Moshe Mizrahi
Love Is Like That *30* Scott Pembroke
Love Is Like That *33* Richard Thorpe
Love Is Love *19* Scott R. Dunlap
Love Is Love *32* Paul Martin
Love Is My Profession *58* Claude Autant-Lara
Love Is News *37* Tay Garnett
Love Is on the Air *37* Nick Grindé
Love Is Strength *30* Mikio Naruse
Love Is When You Make It *59* Pierre Kast
Love Island *52* Bud Pollard
Love, Italian Style *64* Giorgio Bianchi
Love Kiss, The *30* Robert Snody
Love Knows No Obstacle *61* Hossein Mabrouk
Love Krazy *32* Manny Gould, Ben Harrison
Love Laughs at Andy Hardy *46* Willis Goldbeck
Love Letter, The *23* King Baggot
Love Letter *53* Kinuyo Tanaka
Love Letter *86* Tatsumi Kumashiro
Love Letter *87* Yoichi Higashi
Love Letters, The *05* Percy Stow
Love Letters *17* Roy William Neill
Love Letters *24* David Soloman
Love Letters *45* William Dieterle
Love Letters *83* Amy Jones
Love Letters from the Engadine *38* Luis Trenker
Love Letters of a Star *36* Milton Carruth, Lewis R. Foster
Love Letters with Intent *86* Zvonimir Berković
Love Liar, The *16* Crane Wilbur
Love Lies *31* Lupino Lane
Love, Life and Laughter *23* George Pearson
Love, Life and Laughter *34* Maurice Elvey
Love, Life and Laughter at Swaythling Court *26* Adrian Brunel
Love Light, The *21* Frances Marion
Love, Live and Laugh *29* William K. Howard
Love Lottery, The *54* Charles Crichton
Love, Luck and Gasoline *14* J. Stuart Blackton
Love, Lust and Ecstasy *81* Ilia Milonako
Love Machine, The *71* Jack Haley, Jr.
Love-Mad Tutoress, The *26* Kenji Mizoguchi
Love Madness *20* Joseph E. Henabery
Love Madness *36* Louis Gasnier

Love Maggy *21* Fred LeRoy Granville
Love Makes 'Em Wild *27* Albert Ray
Love Makes Us Blind *25* Lothar Mendes
Love Mania *24* Al St. John
Love Maniac, The *65* Al Adamson
Love Mart, The *27* George Fitzmaurice
Love Mask, The *16* Frank Reicher
Love Master, The *24* Lawrence Trimble
Love Match, The *55* David Paltenghi
Love Match *74* Claude Chabrol
Love Mates, The *70* Roger Kahane
Love Me *18* Roy William Neill
Love Me! *86* Kay Pollak
Love Me and the World Is Mine *27* E. A. Dupont
Love Me Deadly *72* Jacques Lacerte
Love Me Forever *35* Victor Schertzinger
Love Me Forever or Never *86* Arnaldo Jabor
Love Me Little, Love Me Long *15* Frank Wilson
Love Me, Love Me, Love Me *62* Richard Williams
Love Me, Love My Biscuits *17* William Beaudine
Love Me, Love My Dog *10* Lewin Fitzhamon
Love Me, Love My Mouse *66* Chuck Jones, Ben Washam
Love Me or Leave Me *55* Charles Vidor
Love Me Tender *56* Robert D. Webb
Love Me Tonight *32* Rouben Mamoulian
Love Meetings *64* Pier Paolo Pasolini
Love Merchant, The *66* Joe Sarno
Love Merchants *66* Joe Sarno
Love Microbe, The *07* Wallace McCutcheon
Love, Mirth, Melody *34* Bert Tracy
Love, Mother *87* János Rózsa
Love Nest, The *22* Wray Physioc
Love Nest, The *23* Edward F. Cline, Buster Keaton
Love Nest, The *33* Thomas Bentley
Love Nest *51* Joseph M. Newman
Love Nest on Wheels *37* Charles Lamont
Love Net, The *18* Tefft Johnson
Love Never Dies *16* William Worthington
Love Never Dies *21* King Vidor
Love Never Dies *28* George Fitzmaurice
Love Not Again *61* Tomu Uchida
Love Now...Pay Later *66* Don Rolos
Love Now...Pay Later *66* Gianni Vernuccio
Love Odyssey *87* Pim de la Parra
Love of a Clown *48* Mario Costa
Love of a Gypsy, The *08* Charles Raymond
Love of a Nautch Girl, The *09* Percy Stow
Love of a Romany Lass, The *09* Joe Rosenthal
Love of a State Councillor *15* Pyotr Chardynin
Love of Actress Sumako, The *47* Kenji Mizoguchi
Love of an Actress, The *14* Wilfred Noy
Love of Jeanne Ney, The *27* G. W. Pabst
Love of Lady Irma, The *10* Frank Powell
Love of Life *68* S. Gerard Patris, François Reichenbach
Love of Sport *38* Zoltán Farkas, Leslie

Kardos
Love of Sumako the Actress, The *47* Kenji Mizoguchi
Love of Sunya, The *27* Albert Parker
Love of the West, The *11* Allan Dwan
Love of Their Lives, The *15* Percy Nash
Love of Three Queens *53* Marc Allégret, Edgar G. Ulmer
Love of Women, The *15* Joseph Smiley
Love of Women *24* Whitman Bennett
Love, Old and New *61* Masahiro Shinoda
Love on a Bet *36* Leigh Jason
Love on a Budget *38* Herbert I. Leeds
Love on a Pillow *62* Roger Vadim
Love on Credit *55* Astrid Henning-Jensen
Love on Skates *16* Clarence Badger
Love on Skis *33* Ladislas Vajda
Love on Tap *39* George Sidney
Love on the Dole *41* John Baxter
Love on the Ground *84* Jacques Rivette
Love on the Range *37* George Pal
Love on the Riviera *24* W. H. Sheppard
Love on the Riviera *64* Gianni Franciolini
Love on the Run *36* W. S. Van Dyke
Love on the Run *79* François Truffaut
Love on the Spot *32* Graham Cutts
Love on the Wing *37* Norman McLaren
Love on Toast *37* E. A. Dupont
Love on Wheels *32* Victor Saville
Love One Another *21* Carl Theodor Dreyer
Love or a Kingdom *37* Josef Leytes
Love or an Empire *16* Herbert Brenon
Love or Justice *17* Walter Edwards
Love or Money *20* Burton L. King
Love or Money *88* Todd Hallowell
Love or Riches *11* Theo Bouwmeester
Love Over Night *28* Edward H. Griffith
Love Pains *32* James W. Horne
Love Parade, The *29* Ernst Lubitsch
Love Piker, The *23* E. Mason Hopper
Love Pill, The *71* Kenneth Turner
Love Pirate, The *23* Richard Thomas
Love Play *61* Fabien Collin, François Moreuil
Love, Poetry and Paint *14* Dave Aylott
Love Problems *70* Giuliano Biagetti
Love Race, The *31* Lupino Lane, Pat Morton
Love Race *34* Ray McCarey
Love Racket, The *29* William A. Seiter
Love Rebellion, The *66* Joe Sarno
Love Redeemed *32* Frank R. Strayer
Love Requited *57* Walerian Borowczyk, Jan Lenica
Love Rewarded *57* Walerian Borowczyk, Jan Lenica
Love Riot, A *16* F. Richard Jones
Love Robots, The *65* Koji Wakamatsu
Love Romance of Admiral Sir Francis Drake, The *13* Hay Plumb
Love Romance of the Girl Spy, The *10* Sidney Olcott
Love Root, The *65* Alberto Lattuada
Love Route, The *15* Allan Dwan
Love Scenes *84* Bud Townsend
Love Should Be Guarded *77* Josef Heifits
Love Sick *25* Charles Lamont
Love Sickness at Sea *13* Mack Sennett
Love 65 *65* Bo Widerberg

Love Slaves of the Amazon *57* Curt Siodmak

Love, Soldiers and Women *52* Christian-Jaque, Jean Delannoy, Marcello Pagliero

Love Song, The *06* Arthur Gilbert

Love Song, The *26* Dmitri Buchowetzki

Love Songs *84* Elie Chouraqui

Love Special, The *21* Frank Urson

Love Specialist, The *57* Luigi Zampa

Love Starved *32* William A. Seiter

Love Storm, The *30* E. A. Dupont

Love Story *43* Claude Autant-Lara

Love Story *44* Leslie Arliss

Love Story *51* Robert Clavel

Love Story *70* Arthur Hiller

Love Story *88* Shinichiro Sawai

Love Story of Aliette Brunton, The *24* Maurice Elvey

Love Story of Charles II, A *11* Theo Bouwmeester

Love Story One *71* Malcolm Le Grice

Love Story Two *71* Malcolm Le Grice

Love Story Three *72* Malcolm Le Grice

Love, Strange Love *85* Walter Hugo Khouri

Love Streams *83* John Cassavetes

Love Stronger Than Hate *13* Victor Sjöström

Love Struck *87* Richard Masur

Love Sublime, A *17* Tod Browning, Wilfred Lucas

Love Sundae, A *26* Edward F. Cline

Love Sunk *28* Manny Gould, Ben Harrison

Love Swindle, The *18* John Francis Dillon

Love—Tahiti Style *61* Franco Rossi

Love Takes Flight *37* Conrad Nagel

Love Test, The *35* Michael Powell

Love That Brute *50* Alexander Hall

Love That Dares, The *19* Harry Millarde

Love That Doesn't Return *38* Bruno Valetti

Love That Lives, The *17* Robert Vignola

Love That Lives, The *19* Forest Holger-Madsen

Love That Pup *49* Joseph Barbera, William Hanna

Love, the Italian Way *64* Giorgio Bianchi

Love the Magician *85* Carlos Saura

Love, the Only Law *17* Victor Sjöström

Love Thief, The *14* Charles Chaplin

Love Thief, The *16* Richard Stanton

Love Thief, The *26* John McDermott

Love Thrill, The *27* Millard Webb

Love Thy Neighbor *34* Dave Fleischer

Love Thy Neighbor *40* Mark Sandrich

Love Thy Neighbour *14* Toby Cooper

Love Thy Neighbour *73* John Robins

Love Till First Blood *85* György Dobray, Péter Horváth

Love Time *34* James Tinling

Love Today *87* Ernesto Del Río

Love Token, The *08* Lewin Fitzhamon

Love Toy, The *26* Erle C. Kenton

Love Trader, The *30* Joseph E. Henabery

Love Trail, The *15* L. C. MacBean, Fred Paul

Love Trap, The *23* John Ince

Love Trap, The *29* William Wyler

Love Trap, The *60* Jean-Pierre Mocky

Love Travels by Coach *54* László Ranódy

Love Under Fire *37* George Marshall

Love Under the Crucifix *60* Kinuyo Tanaka

Love Unto Death *84* Alain Resnais

Love Unto Waste *87* Stanley Kwan

Love Up the Pole *36* Clifford Gulliver

Love Variations *70* Terry Gould

Love vs. Pride *13* Percy Stow

Love vs. Science *09* Jack Smith

Love Wager, The *27* Clifford Wheeler

Love Wager, The *33* A. Cyran

Love Waltz, The *30* Wilhelm Thiele, Carl Winston

Love Watches *18* Henri Houry

Love Will Conquer *49* Gustaf Molander

Love Will Find a Way *07* Charles Raymond

Love Will Find a Way *08* Edwin S. Porter

Love Wins in the End *12* Warwick Buckland

Love with the Perfect Stranger *86* Jianming Lu

Love with the Proper Stranger *63* Robert Mulligan

Love Without Pity *89* Eric Rochant

Love Without Question *20* B. A. Rolfe

Love You to Death *87* Larry Cohen, William Tannen

Lovebound *23* Henry Otto

Lovechild, The *87* Robert Smith

Loved by Two *15* Michael Curtiz

Loved Child, The *71* Chantal Akerman

Loved One, The *40* Ivan Pyriev

Loved One, The *64* Tony Richardson

Loveland *73* Richard Franklin

Loveless, The *81* Kathryn Bigelow, Monty Montgomery

Loveletters from Teralba Road *77* Stephen Wallace

Lovelines *84* Rod Amateau

Lovelock *87* Chantal Picault

Lovelorn, The *27* John P. McCarthy

Lovelorn Geisha, The *60* Yuzo Kawashima, Mikio Naruse

Lovelorn Leghorn *51* Robert McKimson

Lovely and Fresh *87* Enrico Oldoini

Lovely But Deadly *83* David Sheldon

Lovely Flute and Drum *67* Keisuke Kinoshita

Lovely Mary *16* Edgar Jones

Lovely to Look At *37* Sidney Lanfield

Lovely to Look At *51* Mervyn LeRoy, Vincente Minnelli

Lovely Way to Die, A *68* David Lowell Rich

Lovely Way to Go, A *68* David Lowell Rich

Lovemaker, The *56* Juan Antonio Bardem

Lovemakers, The *60* Mauro Bolognini

Lovemaking *68* Stan Brakhage

Lovemates *60* Lars-Magnus Lindgren

Lover, The *51* Kon Ichikawa

Lover, The *53* Kon Ichikawa

Lover, The *86* Michal Bat-Adam

Lover, The *86* Mohamed Mournir Fanari

Lover and His Lass, A *75* Lasse Hallström

Lover Boy *54* René Clément

Lover Boy *77* Bernard Queysanne

Lover Come Back *31* Erle C. Kenton

Lover Come Back *46* William A. Seiter

Lover Come Back *61* Delbert Mann

Lover Divine *33* Anthony Asquith, Willi Forst

Lover for Love *87* Tatyana Berezantseva

Lover for the Summer, A *59* Édouard Molinaro

Lover of Camille, The *24* Harry Beaumont

Lover Who Took the Cake, The *13* Hay Plumb

Lover, Wife *77* Marco Vicario

Loverboy *89* Joan Micklin Silver

Lovers? *27* John M. Stahl

Lovers, The *53* Kon Ichikawa

Lovers, The *58* Louis Malle

Lovers, The *72* Luciano Ricci

Lovers *84* Fred Tan

Lovers and Liars *78* Lee Kresel, Mario Monicelli

Lovers and Lollipops *55* Morris Engel, Ruth Orkin

Lovers and Luggers *38* Ken Hall

Lovers and Other Strangers *70* Cy Howard

Lovers and Thieves *56* Sacha Guitry

Lovers Arrive, The *56* George Tzavellas

Lovers Beyond the Tomb *65* Mario Caiano

Lover's Call *60* Youssef Chahine

Lovers' Charm, The *07* Arthur Cooper

Lovers, Coal Box and Fireplace, The *01* Edwin S. Porter

Lovers Courageous *32* Robert Z. Leonard

Lover's Crime, The *04* Lewin Fitzhamon

Lovers from Beyond the Tomb *65* Mario Caiano

Lovers, Happy Lovers! *54* René Clément

Lover's Hazing, A *08* Georges Méliès

Lovers in Araby *23* Adrian Brunel

Lovers in Limbo *68* Gunnar Hellström

Lovers in Quarantine *25* Frank Tuttle

Lover's Island *25* Henri Diamant-Berger

Lovers' Lane *23* William Beaudine, Phil Rosen

Lovers Like Us *75* Jean-Paul Rappeneau

Lovers Must Learn *62* Delmer Daves

Lovers' Net *54* Henri Verneuil

Lover's Oath, A *25* Ferdinand P. Earle

Lovers of Lisbon, The *54* Henri Verneuil

Lovers of Montparnasse, The *57* Jacques Becker

Lovers of Paris *57* Julien Duvivier

Lovers of Teruel, The *12* Ricardo De Baños

Lovers of Teruel, The *61* Raymond Rouleau

Lovers of the Lord of the Night, The *83* Isela Vega

Lovers of Toledo, The *52* Henri Decoin

Lovers of Verona, The *48* André Cayatte

Lovers on a Tightrope *60* Jean-Charles Dudrumet

Lovers on the Sands *04* Alf Collins

Lover's Predicament, The *06* J. H. Martin

Lover's Quarrel, A *07* Lewin Fitzhamon

Lover's Return, A *46* Christian-Jaque

Lovers' Rock *66* Pan Lei

Lover's Romance, A *74* Andrei Mikhalkov-Konchalovsky

Lover's Ruse, The *04* Lewin Fitzhamon

Lover's Troubles, A *03* Alf Collins

Lovers' Wind, The *70* Albert Lamorisse

Love's a Luxury *52* Francis Searle
Loves and Adventures in the Life of Shakespeare *14* Frank R. Growcott, J. B. McDowell
Loves and Death of a Scoundrel, The *56* Charles Martin
Loves and Times of Scaramouche, The *75* Enzo G. Castellari
Love's Battle *20* William James Craft
Love's Berries *26* Alexander Dovzhenko
Love's Berry *26* Alexander Dovzhenko
Love's Blindness *26* John Francis Dillon
Love's Boomerang *22* Tom Geraghty, John S. Robertson
Love's Confusion *58* Slatan Dudow
Love's Conquest *18* Edward José
Love's Cross Roads *16* Joseph A. Golden
Love's Crucible *16* Émile Chautard
Love's Crucible *20* Victor Sjöström
Love's Devotee *13* August Blom, Forest Holger-Madsen
Love's False Faces *19* F. Richard Jones
Love's Family Tree *61* Heinosuke Gosho
Love's Flame *20* Carl Louis Gregory
Love's Four Stone Walls *12* Edwin S. Porter
Love's Frontiers *34* Frank R. Strayer
Love's Greatest Mistake *27* A. Edward Sutherland
Love's Harvest *20* Howard Mitchell
Love's Influence *22* William S. Charlton, Edward R. Gordon
Love's Labor Lost *20* Vernon Stallings
Love's Labors Lost *16* Raoul Barré
Love's Labour Lost *04* Charles Raymond
Love's Lariat *16* Harry Carey, George Marshall
Love's Law *17* Tefft Johnson
Love's Law *18* Francis J. Grandon
Love's Legacy *15* James Warry Vickers
Love's Masquerade *22* William P. S. Earle
Love's Mockery *20* F. W. Murnau
Loves of a Blonde *65* Miloš Forman
Loves of a Dictator, The *35* Alfred Santell, Victor Saville
Loves of a Greek in Paris *60* C. Kyriakopoulos
Loves of a Kabuki Actor, The *38* Kajiro Yamamoto
Loves of an Actress *28* Rowland V. Lee
Loves of Ariane, The *31* Paul Czinner
Loves of Carmen, The *27* Raoul Walsh
Loves of Carmen, The *48* Charles Vidor
Loves of Casanova, The *27* Alexander Volkov
Loves of Casanova *47* Jean Boyer
Loves of Colleen Bawn, The *24* Will P. Kellino
Loves of Don Juan, The *48* Dino Falconi
Loves of Edgar Allan Poe, The *42* Harry Lachman
Loves of Hercules, The *60* Carlo Ludovico Bragaglia
Loves of Isadora, The *67* Karel Reisz
Loves of Joanna Godden, The *47* Charles Frend
Loves of Letty, The *19* Frank Lloyd
Loves of Madame DuBarry, The *35* Marcel Varnel
Loves of Mary Queen of Scots, The *23* Denison Clift

Loves of Omar Khayyam, The *57* William Dieterle
Loves of Ondine, The *67* Andy Warhol
Loves of Pharaoh, The *21* Ernst Lubitsch
Loves of Ricardo, The *26* George Beban
Loves of Robert Burns, The *30* Herbert Wilcox
Loves of Salammbo, The *62* Sergio Grieco
Loves of Three Queens *53* Marc Allégret, Edgar G. Ulmer
Loves of Zero, The *27* Robert Florey
Love's Old Dream *14* George D. Baker
Love's Old Sweet Song *17* F. Martin Thornton
Love's Old Sweet Song *23* Oscar A. C. Lund
Love's Old Sweet Song *27* S. H. Johnson
Love's Old Sweet Song *33* H. Manning Haynes
Love's Option *28* George Pearson
Love's Pay Day *18* E. Mason Hopper
Love's Penalty *21* Jack Gilbert
Love's Pilgrimage to America *15* Harry C. Myers
Love's Polka *46* Igor Savchenko
Love's Premier *43* Arthur Maria Rabenalt
Love's Prisoner *19* John Francis Dillon
Love's Redemption *21* Eugene V. Brewster
Love's Redemption *21* Albert Parker
Love's Sacrifice *14* William H. Clifford, Thomas Ince
Love's Strategy *08* A. E. Coleby
Love's Strategy *10* Lewin Fitzhamon
Love's Strategy *11* Theo Bouwmeester
Love's Toll *16* John H. Pratt
Love's Triumph *38* Mario Mattòli
Love's Western Flight *14* Wallace Reid
Love's Whirlpool *24* Bruce Mitchell
Love's Wilderness *24* Robert Z. Leonard
Lovesick *37* Walter Lantz
Lovesick *83* Marshall Brickman
Lovesick Alex *86* Boaz Davidson
Lovespell *79* Tom Donovan
Lovetime *21* Howard Mitchell
Lovey Mary *26* King Baggot
Lovin' Fool, The *26* Horace B. Carpenter
Lovin' Molly *73* Sidney Lumet
Lovin' the Ladies *30* Melville Brown
Loving *56* Stan Brakhage
Loving *70* Irvin Kershner
Loving Couples *64* Mai Zetterling
Loving Couples *80* Jack Smight
Loving Feeling *69* Norman J. Warren
Loving Fool, The *26* Horace B. Carpenter
Loving in the Rain *74* Jean-Claude Brialy
Loving Lies *24* W. S. Van Dyke
Loving Memory *70* Anthony Scott
Loving Touch, The *70* Robert Vincent O'Neil
Loving Walter *83* Stephen Frears
Loving You *57* Hal Kanter
Low Blow *86* Frank Harris
Low-Cut Back, The *75* Jan Němec
Lower Depths, The *36* Jean Renoir
Lower Depths, The *48* Tso-lin Wang
Lower Depths, The *57* Akira Kurosawa
Lower Rhine Folks *35* Max Obal
Lowland *54* Leni Riefenstahl
Lowland Cinderella, A *21* Sidney Morgan

Loyal 47, The *42* Kenji Mizoguchi
Loyal 47 of the Genroku Era, The *42* Kenji Mizoguchi
Loyal 47 Ronin, The *32* Teinosuke Kinugasa
Loyal 47 Ronin, The *34* Daisuke Ito
Loyal 47 Ronin, The *39* Kajiro Yamamoto
Loyal 47 Ronin, The *42* Kenji Mizoguchi
Loyal 47 Ronin, The *62* Hiroshi Inagaki
Loyal 47 Ronin of the Genroku Era, The *42* Kenji Mizoguchi
Loyal Heart *46* Oswald Mitchell
Loyal Lives *23* Charles Giblyn
Loyal Soldier of Pancho Villa, A *66* Emilio Fernández
Loyalism at Kuroda *38* Teinosuke Kinugasa
Loyalties *33* Basil Dean
Loyalties *86* Anne Wheeler
Loyalty *18* John H. Pratt
Loyalty of Love *37* Guido Brignone
Loyola the Soldier Saint *52* José Díaz Morales
Lśnisty Anioł *85* Maciej Wojtyszko
Lu, a Kokott *18* Michael Curtiz
Lu, the Cocotte *18* Michael Curtiz
Lu, the Coquette *18* Michael Curtiz
Luanda Is No Longer St. Paul's *76* Santiago Álvarez
Luanda Ya No Es de San Pablo *76* Santiago Álvarez
Luca il Contrabbandiere *80* Lucio Fulci
Lucas *86* David Seltzer
Lucciola *17* Augusto Genina
Luce negli Impressionisti, La *38* Vittorio Sala
Lucerna *25* Karel Lamač
Lucertola con la Pelle di Donna, Una *71* Lucio Fulci
Luces de Barriada *40* Robert Quigley
Luces y Sombras *88* Jaime Camino
Lucette *24* Maurice Champreux, Louis Feuillade
Luch Smerti *25* Lev Kuleshov, Vsevolod I. Pudovkin
Luchadoras Contra el Médico Resino, Las *62* René Cardona
Luchadoras Contra el Robot Asesino, Las *69* René Cardona
Luchadoras Contra la Momia, Las *64* René Cardona
Luci del Varietà *50* Federico Fellini, Alberto Lattuada
Luci Iontane *87* Aurelio Chiesa
Luci Sommerse *36* Adelqui Millar
Lucía *68* Humberto Solás
Lucia di Lammermoor *10* Giovanni Pastrone
Lucia di Lammermoor *47* Piero Ballerini
Luciano *60* Gian Vittorio Baldi
Luciano Serra Pilota *38* Goffredo Alessandrini
Lucie de Trécœur *22* Augusto Genina
Lucifer Complex, The *78* Ken Hartford, David L. Hewitt
Lucifer Project, The *78* Harry Kerwin
Lucifer Rising *80* Kenneth Anger
Lucifer's Women *78* Paul Aratow
Lucille Love, the Girl of Mystery *14* Francis Ford

Lying Lips *21* John Griffith Wray
Lying Lips *39* Oscar Micheaux
Lying Truth, The *22* Marion Fairfax
Lying Wives *25* Ivan Abramson
Lykkehjulet *26* Urban Gad
Lykkelig Skilsmisse, En *74* Henning Carlsen
Lykken *16* Forest Holger-Madsen
Lykken Dræber *13* Forest Holger-Madsen
Lynmouth *13* George Pearson
Lynn Seymour *64* Allan King
Lynxeye on the Prowl *15* James Read
Lynxeye Trapped *15* James Read
Lynxeye's Night Out *15* James Read
Lyodolom *31* Boris Barnet
Lyon Lea *15* Alexander Korda, Miklós Pásztory
Lyon, Place Bellecour *1895* Louis Lumière
Lyon, Place des Cordeliers *1895* Louis Lumière
Lyons in Paris, The *55* Val Guest
Lyons Mail, The *16* Fred Paul
Lyons Mail, The *31* Arthur Maude
Lyotchiki *35* Yuli Raizman
Lys Rouge, Le *20* Charles De Marsan, Charles Maudru
Lyset i Natten *53* Jørgen Roos
Lysistrata *48* Alfred Stoger
Lysten Styret *14* Forest Holger-Madsen
Lyubit Cheloveka *72* Sergei Gerasimov
Lyubliyu Li Tebya *34* Sergei Gerasimov
Lyubovyu za Lyubov *87* Tatyana Berezantseva
Lyudi *66* Grigori Chukhrai
Lyudi i Zveri *62* Sergei Gerasimov, Lutz Kohlert
Lyudi na Mostu *59* Alexander Zarkhi
M *31* Fritz Lang
M *50* Joseph Losey
M.A.R.S. *23* Roy William Neill
M*A*S*H *69* Robert Altman
MBKS *73* Malcolm Le Grice
M. Hire *89* Patrice Leconte
MMM 83 *65* Sergio Bergonzelli
M.P. Case, The *60* Bert Haanstra
M3: The Gemini Strain *78* Ed Hunt
MUSE Concert: No Nukes, The *80* Dan Goldberg, Anthony Potenza, Julian Schlossberg, Haskell Wexler
Ma and Pa *22* Roy Del Ruth
Ma and Pa Kettle *48* Charles Lamont
Ma and Pa Kettle at Home *54* Charles Lamont
Ma and Pa Kettle at the Fair *52* Charles Barton
Ma and Pa Kettle at Waikiki *55* Lee Sholem
Ma and Pa Kettle Back on the Farm *51* Edward Sedgwick
Ma and Pa Kettle Go to Paris *52* Charles Lamont
Ma and Pa Kettle Go to Town *49* Charles Lamont
Ma and Pa Kettle on Vacation *52* Charles Lamont
Ma Barker's Killer Brood *60* Bill Karn
Ma Cousine de Varsovie *31* Carmine Gallone
Ma Drives a Car *16* Harry S. Palmer
Ma és Holnap *12* Michael Curtiz

Ma Femme Est Formidable *51* André Hunebelle
Ma Femme, Ma Gosse et Moi *57* Marc Allégret
Ma! He's Making Eyes at Me *40* Harold Schuster
Ma l'Amor *13* Mario Caserini
Ma l'Amor Mio Non Muore *38* Giuseppe Amato
Ma no Ike *23* Teinosuke Kinugasa
Ma Non È una Cosa Seria *36* Mario Camerini
Ma Nuit chez Maud *68* Eric Rohmer
Ma Nuit chez Maud: Six Contes Moraux: 4 *68* Eric Rohmer
Ma Pomme *50* Marc-Gilbert Sauvajon
Ma Sœur de Lai *38* Jean Boyer
Ma Tante d'Honfleur *23* Robert Saidreau
Ma Tries to Reduce *15* Harry S. Palmer
Ma vagy Holnap *65* András Kovács
Maa *51* Bimal Roy
Maa On Syntinen Laulu *73* Rauni Mollberg
Maarakat Alger *65* Gillo Pontecorvo
Maarakat Madinat al Jazaer *65* Gillo Pontecorvo
Maavuri Magaadu *88* K. Bappiah
Mabel and Fatty Viewing the World's Fair at San Francisco *15* Roscoe Arbuckle, Mabel Normand
Mabel and Fatty's Married Life *15* Roscoe Arbuckle
Mabel and Fatty's Simple Life *15* Roscoe Arbuckle, Edward Dillon, Mabel Normand
Mabel and Fatty's Wash Day *15* Roscoe Arbuckle, Edward Dillon, Mabel Normand
Mabel at the Wheel *14* Mabel Normand, Mack Sennett
Mabel, Fatty and the Law *15* Roscoe Arbuckle
Mabel's Adventures *12* Mack Sennett
Mabel's Awful Mistake *13* Mack Sennett
Mabel's Busy Day *14* Charles Chaplin, Mabel Normand
Mabel's Dramatic Career *13* Mack Sennett
Mabel's Flirtation *14* Charles Chaplin, Mabel Normand
Mabel's Heroes *13* Mack Sennett
Mabel's Lovers *12* Mack Sennett
Mabel's Married Life *14* Charles Chaplin, Mabel Normand
Mabel's Nerve *14* Mabel Normand
Mabel's New Hero *13* Mack Sennett
Mabel's New Job *14* Mabel Normand
Mabel's Strange Predicament *14* Henry Lehrman, Mack Sennett
Mabel's Stratagem *12* Mack Sennett
Mabul *27* Yevgeni Ivanov-Barkov
Mac and Me *88* Stewart Raffill
Macabra *79* Alfredo Zacharias
Macabre *57* William Castle
Macabre *80* Lamberto Bava
Macabre Legacy, The *39* José Bohr
Macabre Trunk, The *36* Miguel Zacarías
Macabro *67* Romolo Marcellini
Macabro *80* Lamberto Bava
Macabro Dr. Scivano, O *71* Raul Calhado
Macadam *46* Marcel Blistène

Macao *52* Nicholas Ray, Josef von Sternberg
Macao *88* Clemens Klopfenstein
Macao, l'Enfer du Jeu *39* Jean Delannoy
Macario *60* Roberto Gavaldón
Macaroni *85* Ettore Scola
Macaroni Blues *86* Béla Csepcsányi, Fred Sassebo
Macaroni Feast, A *05* Alf Collins
MacArthur *77* Joseph Sargent
MacArthur: The Rebel General *77* Joseph Sargent
MacArthur's Children *84* Masahiro Shinoda
Macbeth *08* J. Stuart Blackton
Macbeth *09* André Calmettes
Macbeth *09* Mario Caserini
Macbeth *16* John Emerson
Macbeth *21* Richard Oswald
Macbeth *22* H. B. Parkinson
Macbeth *46* David Bradley
Macbeth *48* William Alland, Orson Welles
Macbeth *50* Katherine Stenholm
Macbeth *60* George Schaefer
Macbeth *71* Roman Polanski
Macbeth *87* Claude D'Anna
McCabe & Mrs. Miller *71* Robert Altman
Maccabei, I *10* Enrico Guazzoni
Maccheroni *85* Ettore Scola
Macchie Solari *74* Armando Crispino
Macchina Ammazzacattivi, La *48* Roberto Rossellini
Macchina Cinema, La *78* Marco Bellocchio
McConnell Story, The *55* Gordon Douglas
McCord *67* Franco Giraldi
McCullochs, The *75* Max Baer
MacDonald of the Canadian Mounties *51* Joseph M. Newman
MacDougal's Aeroplane *15* James Read
Mace *87* William van der Kloot
McFadden's Flats *27* Richard Wallace
McFadden's Flats *35* Ralph Murphy
McGlusky the Sea Rover *35* Walter Summers
McGuerins from Brooklyn, The *42* Kurt Neumann
McGuffin, The *85* Colin Bucksey
McGuire, Go Home! *64* Ralph Thomas
McGuire of the Mounted *23* Richard Stanton
Mach a Šebestová, k Tabuli! *85* Adolf Born, Jaroslav Doubrava, Miloš Macourek
Mach and Sebestova, Come to the Blackboard Please! *85* Adolf Born, Jaroslav Doubrava, Miloš Macourek
Mach' Mich Glücklich *35* Arthur Robison
McHale's Navy *64* Edward Montagne
McHale's Navy Joins the Air Force *65* Edward Montagne
Machete *58* Kurt Neumann
Machi no Hitobito *26* Heinosuke Gosho
Machi no Irezumi Mono *35* Sadao Yamanaka
Machi to Gesui *53* Susumu Hani
Machibuse *70* Hiroshi Inagaki
Machine, The *73* Helma Sanders-Brahms
Machine à Découdre, La *85* Jean-Pierre Mocky

Machine à Refaire la Vie, La 24 Julien Duvivier, Henri Lepage

Machine à Refaire la Vie, La 33 Julien Duvivier

Machine Age, The 80 Shyam Benegal

Machine et l'Homme, La 56 Jean Mitry

Machine for Recreating Life, The 24 Julien Duvivier, Henri Lepage

Machine for Recreating Life, The 33 Julien Duvivier

Machine Gun Kelly 58 Roger Corman

Machine Gun Mama 44 Harold Young

Machine Gun McCain 68 Giuliano Montaldo

Machine Mon Ami 60 Louis Daquin

Machine of Eden, The 70 Stan Brakhage

Machine That Kills Bad People, The 48 Roberto Rossellini

Machismo—40 Graves for 40 Guns 70 Paul Hunt

Machiste Against Hercules in the Vale of Woe 62 Mario Mattòli

Machiste Against the Czar 64 Tanio Boccia

Machiste Against the Vampires 61 Sergio Corbucci, Giacomo Gentilomo

Machiste at the Court of the Great Khan 61 Riccardo Freda

Machiste in Hell 26 Guido Brignone

Machiste in Hell 62 Riccardo Freda

Machiste in King Solomon's Mines 64 Martin Andrews

Machiste, Strongest Man in the World 61 Antonio Leonviola

Machiste—The Mighty 60 Carlo Campogalliani

Machiste vs. the Vampire 61 Sergio Corbucci, Giacomo Gentilomo

Machnower Schleusen, Die 27 Piel Jutzi

Macho, El 77 Marcello Andrei

Macho Callahan 70 Bernard Kowalski

Macho Dancer 87 Lino Brocka

Macho y Hembra 85 Mauricio Walerstein

Machorka-Muff 63 Jean-Marie Straub

Macht der Berge, Die 38 Gustav Ucicky

Macht der Finsternis, Die 23 Conrad Wiene

Macht der Gefühle, Die 83 Alexander Kluge

Macht der Männer Ist die Geduld der Frauen, Die 78 Cristina Perincioli

Macht des Goldes, Die 11 Urban Gad

Maciste 15 Giovanni Pastrone

Maciste alla Corte del Gran Khan 61 Riccardo Freda

Maciste all'Inferno 62 Riccardo Freda

Maciste Alpino 16 Romano Borgnetto, Luigi Maggi, Giovanni Pastrone

Maciste Atleta 19 Giovanni Pastrone

Maciste Contre les Hommes de Pierre 64 Giacomo Gentilomo

Maciste Contro gli Uomini della Luna 64 Giacomo Gentilomo

Maciste Contro il Vampiro 61 Sergio Corbucci, Giacomo Gentilomo

Maciste Contro lo Sceicco 25 Mario Camerini

Maciste e la Regina di Samar 64 Giacomo Gentilomo

Maciste—L'Eroe Più Grande del Mondo 63 Michele Lupo

Maciste nella Terra dei Ciclopi 61 Antonio Leonviola

Maciste nella Valle dei Re 60 Carlo Campogalliani

Maciste und die Chinesische Truhe 23 Carl Boese

Mack, The 73 Michael Campus

Mack at It Again 14 Mack Sennett

Mack the Knife 89 Menahem Golan

McKenna of the Mounted 32 D. Ross Lederman

MacKenna's Gold 68 J. Lee-Thompson

McKenzie Break, The 70 Lamont Johnson

Mackerel Fishing 22 Julian Ollendorff

Mackintosh and T.J. 75 Marvin Chomsky

Mackintosh Man, The 73 James Arnett, John Huston

McKlusky 73 Joseph Sargent

McLintock! 63 Andrew V. McLaglen

Maclovia 48 Emilio Fernández

McMasters, The 69 Alf Kjellin

McMasters...Tougher Than the West Itself, The 69 Alf Kjellin

McNab's Visit to London 05 Arthur Cooper

Macomber Affair, The 47 Zoltán Korda

Macon County Line 74 Richard Compton

Maçon Maladroit, Le 1898 Georges Méliès

Maçons, Les 05 Alice Guy-Blaché

McQ 74 John Sturges

Macskafogó 87 Béla Ternovszky

Macskajaték 74 Károly Makk

Macumba 69 Pierre Kast

Macumba Love 60 Douglas Fowley

Macumba Sexual 81 Jesús Franco

Macunaima 70 Joaquim Pedro De Andrade

Macushlah 37 Alex Bryce

McVicar 80 Tom Clegg

Mad About Men 54 Ralph Thomas

Mad About Money 37 Melville Brown

Mad About Music 38 Norman Taurog

Mad About Opera 47 Mario Costa

Mad Adventures of Rabbi Jacob, The 73 Gérard Oury

Mad As a Mars Hare 63 Chuck Jones

Mad at the World 55 Harry Essex

Mad Atlantic, The 67 Jun Fukuda

Mad Bomber, The 73 Bert I. Gordon

Mad Bull 77 Walter Doniger, Len Steckler

Mad Butcher, The 71 Guido Zurli

Mad Butcher of Vienna, The 71 Guido Zurli

Mad Cage, The 78 Édouard Molinaro

Mad Checkmate 68 Robert Fiz

Mad Dancer 25 Burton L. King

Mad Doctor, The 40 Tim Whelan

Mad Doctor of Blood Island 68 Gerry De Leon, Eddie Romero

Mad Doctor of Market Street, The 41 Joseph H. Lewis

Mad Dog, The 06 Dave Aylott

Mad Dog, The 32 Burton Gillett

Mad Dog 76 Philippe Mora

Mad Dog Coll 61 Burt Balaban

Mad Dog Morgan 76 Philippe Mora

Mad Dogs and Englishmen 70 Pierre Adidge

Mad Emperor, The 37 Maurice Tourneur

Mad Empress, The 33 Miguel Torres Contreras

Mad Executioners, The 63 Edwin Zbonek

Mad Game, The 33 Irving Cummings

Mad Genius, The 31 Michael Curtiz

Mad Ghoul, The 43 James P. Hogan

Mad Hatter, The 40 Sid Marcus

Mad Hatter, The 45 Harold Schuster

Mad Hatters, The 35 Ivar Campbell

Mad Holiday 36 George B. Seitz

Mad Hour, The 28 Joseph C. Boyle

Mad Infatuation, A 10 Theo Bouwmeester

Mad Little Island 57 Michael Relph

Mad Love 21 Dmitri Buchowetzki

Mad Love 35 Karl Freund

Mad Lover, The 17 Léonce Perret

Mad Lover 44 Alfred Zeisler

Mad, Mad Movie Makers, The 74 Ray Marsh

Mad Maestro, The 39 Hugh Harman

Mad Magazine Presents Up the Academy 80 Robert Downey

Mad Magazine's Up the Academy 80 Robert Downey

Mad Magician, The 54 John Brahm

Mad Marriage, The 21 Rollin Sturgeon

Mad Marriage, The 25 Frank P. Donovan

Mad Martindales, The 42 Alfred L. Werker

Mad Masquerade 32 Charles Brabin

Mad Max 79 George Miller

Mad Max II 81 George Miller

Mad Max Beyond Thunderdome 85 George Miller, George Ogilvie

Mad Men of Europe 39 Albert De Courville

Mad Miss Manton, The 38 Leigh Jason

Mad Mission IV 86 Ringo Lam

Mad Mokes and Motors 15 Edwin J. Collins

Mad Monk, The 65 Don Sharp

Mad Monkey, The 11 A. E. Coleby

Mad Monkey, The 89 Fernando Trueba

Mad Monster, The 42 Sam Newfield

Mad Monster Party 67 Jules Bass

Mad Musician, The 09 Frank Mottershaw

Mad Parade, The 31 William Beaudine

Mad Queen, The 50 Juan De Orduna

Mad Room, The 69 Bernard Girard

Mad Sex 73 Dino Risi

Mad Souls 17 Germaine Dulac

Mad Trapper, The 72 Ford Beebe, Tay Garnett

Mad Trapper of the Yukon 72 Ford Beebe, Tay Garnett

Mad Wednesday 46 Preston Sturges

Mad Whirl, The 25 William A. Seiter

Mad Youth 40 Willis Kent

Madagascar 30 Léon Poirier

Madalena 65 Dinos Dimopoulos

Madam Sans Gin 25 Wesley Ruggles

Madama Arlecchino 18 Mario Caserini

Madama Butterfly 55 Carmine Gallone

Madame 61 Christian-Jaque

Madame Aki 63 Shiro Toyoda

Madame and Wife 31 Heinosuke Gosho

Madame Behave 25 Scott Sidney

Madame Blaubart 33 Conrad Wiene

Madame Bovary 34 Jean Renoir

Madame Bovary 37 Gerhard Lamprecht

Madame Bovary 49 Vincente Minnelli
Madame Butterfly 15 Sidney Olcott
Madame Butterfly 19 Fritz Lang
Madame Butterfly 32 Marion Gering
Madame Butterfly 55 Carmine Gallone
Madame Claude 79 Just Jaeckin
Madame Conduit 59 Claude Lelouch
Madame Curie 43 Mervyn LeRoy
Madame de... 53 Max Ophüls
Madame de Thèbes 15 Mauritz Stiller
Madame Death 68 Jaime Salvador
Madame DuBarry 17 J. Gordon Edwards
Madame DuBarry 19 Ernst Lubitsch
Madame DuBarry 28 Roy William Neill
Madame DuBarry 34 William Dieterle
Madame DuBarry 54 Christian-Jaque
Madame et le Mort 42 Louis Daquin
Madame et Son Filleul 19 Georges Monca
Madame Flirt 18 Baldassare Negroni
Madame Flirt 23 Henri Desfontaines
Madame Frankenstein 71 Ernst R. von Theumer
Madame Guillotine 31 Reginald Fogwell
Madame Hat Ausgang 31 Wilhelm Thiele
Madame Jealousy 18 Robert Vignola
Madame Julie 31 Victor Schertzinger
Madame la Presidente 16 Frank Lloyd
Madame Louise 51 Maclean Rogers
Madame Musashino 51 Kenji Mizoguchi
Madame Olga's Pupils 81 Joseph L. Bronstein
Madame Peacock 20 Ray C. Smallwood
Madame Pimpernel 45 Gregory Ratoff
Madame Pompadour 27 Herbert Wilcox
Madame Potiphar 11 August Blom
Madame President 16 Frank Lloyd
Madame Q 29 Leo McCarey
Madame Racketeer 32 Harry Wagstaff Gribble, Alexander Hall
Madame Récamier 28 Gaston Ravel
Madame Récamier, or The Price of Virtue 23 Edwin Greenwood
Madame Rex 11 D. W. Griffith
Madame Rosa 77 Moshe Mizrahi
Madame Sans-Gêne 11 André Calmettes, Henri Pouctal
Madame Sans-Gêne 21 Baldassare Negroni
Madame Sans-Gêne 25 Léonce Perret
Madame Sans-Gêne 45 Luis César Amadori
Madame Sans-Gêne 61 Christian-Jaque
Madame Satan 30 Cecil B. DeMille
Madame Se Meurt 61 Jean Cayrol, Claude Durand
Madame Shall Not Know 37 Minoru Shibuya
Madame Sherry 17 Ralph Dean
Madame Sin 71 David Greene
Madame Sousatzka 88 John Schlesinger
Madame Sphinx 18 Thomas Heffron
Madame Spy 18 Douglas Gerrard
Madame Spy 33 Karl Freund
Madame Spy 42 Roy William Neill
Madame Tallien 16 Enrico Guazzoni
Madame Wang's 81 Paul Morrissey
Madame Wants No Children 26 Alexander Korda
Madame White Snake 56 Shiro Toyoda
Madame White Snake 63 Feng Yueh
Madame Who? 17 Reginald Barker

Madame Wünscht Keine Kinder 26 Alexander Korda
Madame Wünscht Keine Kinder 33 Hans Steinhoff
Madame X 16 George F. Marion
Madame X 20 Frank Lloyd
Madame X 29 Lionel Barrymore
Madame X 37 Sam Wood
Madame X 60 Orestes Laskos
Madame X 65 David Lowell Rich
Madamigella di Maupin 65 Mauro Bolognini
Madamu to Nyōbo 31 Heinosuke Gosho
Madcap, The 16 William Dowlan
Madcap 37 Robert F. Hill
Madcap Betty 15 Phillips Smalley
Madcap Madge 17 Raymond B. West
Madcap Magoo 55 Pete Burness
Madcap of the House 50 Juan Bustillo Oro
Mädchen auf dem Brett, Das 67 Kurt Mätzig
Mädchen aus der Ackerstrasse 21 Reinhold Schünzel
Mädchen aus Flandern, Ein 55 Helmut Käutner
Mädchen für Alles 37 Carl Boese
Mädchen für die Mambobar 68 Wolfgang Glück
Mädchen im Tigerfell, Das 61 Arthur Maria Rabenalt
Mädchen in Uniform 31 Leontine Sagan
Mädchen in Uniform 58 Géza von Radványi
Mädchen Irene, Das 36 Reinhold Schünzel
Mädchen Johanna, Das 35 Gustav Ucicky
Mädchen mit den Feuerzeugen, Das 88 Ralf Hüttner
Mädchen mit den Fünf Nullen, Das 27 Kurt Bernhardt
Mädchen Ohne Grenzen 55 Géza von Radványi
Mädchen Ohne Vaterland, Das 12 Urban Gad
Mädchen Rosemarie, Das 58 Rolf Thiele
Mädchen vom Moorhof, Das 35 Douglas Sirk
Mädchen vom Moorhof, Das 61 Gustav Ucicky
Mädchen von Gestern Nacht, Das 38 Peter Paul Brauer
Mädchen Wie das Meer, Ein 66 Georges Lautner
Mädchenhirt, Der 19 Karl Grüne
Mädchenjahre einer Königin 36 Erich Engel
Mädchenrauber 36 Fred Sauer
Maddalena 53 Augusto Genina
Maddalena, Zero for Conduct 40 Vittorio De Sica
Maddalena, Zero in Condotta 40 Vittorio De Sica
Maddest Car in the World, The 74 Rudolf Zehetgruber
Maddest Story Ever Told, The 64 Jack Hill
Made 72 John Mackenzie
Made a Coward 13 William Duncan
Made for Each Other 39 John Cromwell
Made for Each Other 71 Robert B. Bean
Made for Laughs 52 James M. Anderson

Made for Love 26 Paul Sloane
Made in Argentina 87 Juan José Jusid
Made in Germany 14 Ernest G. Batley
Made in Hawaii 85 Tommy Lee Wallace
Made in Heaven 21 Victor Schertzinger
Made in Heaven 52 John Paddy Carstairs
Made in Heaven 87 Alan Rudolph
Made in Italy 65 Nanni Loy
Made in Paris 65 Boris Sagal
Made in Sweden 69 Johan Bergenstråhle
Made in U.S.A. 66 Jean-Luc Godard
Made in U.S.A. 86 Ken Friedman
Made Manifest 80 Stan Brakhage
Made on Broadway 33 Harry Beaumont
Made to Measure 85 Francesco Laudadio
Made-to-Order Hero, A 28 Edgar Lewis
Mädel aus U.S.A., Das 30 Karel Lamač
Mädel der Strasse, Ein 32 Hans Steinhoff
Mädel mit Tempo, Ein 37 Robert A. Stemmle
Mädel vom Ballett, Das 18 Ernst Lubitsch
Mädel vom Ballett, Ein 36 Karel Lamač
Mädel von der Reeperbahn, Das 31 Karl Anton
Madeleine 28 Karl Freund
Madeleine 50 David Lean
Madeleine 58 Kurt Meisel
Madeleine Is 71 Sylvia Spring
Madeleine und der Legionär 57 Wolfgang Staudte
Madeline 52 Robert Cannon
Madelon, La 55 Jean Boyer
Mademoiselle 65 Tony Richardson
Mademoiselle, Age 39 56 Alekos Sakelarios
Mademoiselle Cents Millions 13 Maurice Tourneur
Mademoiselle de la Seiglière 20 André Antoine
Mademoiselle de Maupin 65 Mauro Bolognini
Mademoiselle Désirée 41 Sacha Guitry
Mademoiselle Docteur 36 G. W. Pabst
Mademoiselle Docteur 37 Edmond T. Gréville
Mademoiselle Fifi 21 Raoul Barré, Charles Bowers
Mademoiselle Fifi 44 Robert Wise
Mademoiselle France 42 Jules Dassin
Mademoiselle from Armentières 26 Maurice Elvey
Mademoiselle Gobette 52 Pietro Germi
Mademoiselle Josette Ma Femme 26 Gaston Ravel
Mademoiselle Josette Ma Femme 33 André Berthomieu
Mademoiselle Ma Mère 37 Henri Decoin
Mademoiselle Midnight 24 Robert Z. Leonard
Mademoiselle Modiste 26 Robert Z. Leonard
Mademoiselle Parley-Voo 28 Maurice Elvey
Mademoiselle Paulette 18 Raymond Wells
Mademoiselle Pimple 15 Fred Evans, Joe Evans
Mademoiselle S'Amuse 48 Jean Boyer
Mademoiselle Striptease 56 Marc Allégret
Mademoiselle Tiptoes 18 Henry King
Madhouse, The 29 Stephen Roberts
Madhouse 72 Jim Clark

Madhouse *81* Ovidio Assonitis
Madhouse *84* Marek Koterski
Madhouse *90* Tom Ropelawski
Madhouse Mansion *74* Stephen Weeks
Madhumati *58* Bimal Roy
Madigan *67* Don Siegel
Madigan's Millions *67* Dan Ash, Giorgio Gentili, L. Lelli
Madison Avenue *61* H. Bruce Humberstone
Madison Square Garden *32* Harry Joe Brown
Madly *70* Roger Kahane
Madman, The *70* Claude Goretta
Madman *78* Dan Cohen
Madman *82* Joe Giannone
Madman at War *85* Dino Risi
Madman in the Dark *38* Martin Frič
Madman of Lab 4, The *67* Jacques Besnard
Madman on the Cliff, The *15* Abel Gance
Madman's Bride, The *07* Lewin Fitzhamon
Madman's Defense, A *76* Kjell Grede
Madman's Fate, The *06* J. H. Martin
Madmen of Mandoras *63* David Bradley
Madness *19* Conrad Veidt
Madness of Dr. Tube, The *14* Abel Gance
Madness of Helen, The *16* Travers Vale
Madness of Love, The *22* Wray Physioc
Madness of the Heart *49* Charles Bennett
Madness of Youth *23* Jerome Storm
Mado *65* Yoji Kuri
Mado *76* Claude Sautet
Madol Duwa *76* Lester James Peries
Madone des Sleepings, La *28* Maurice Gleize
Madonna Che Silenzio C'E' Stasera *82* Maurizio Ponzi
Madonna Grazia *17* Carmine Gallone
Madonna in Ketten *49* Gerhard Lamprecht
Madonna Mann, Der *88* Hans-Christof Blumenberg
Madonna of Avenue A, The *29* Michael Curtiz
Madonna of the Cells, A *25* Fred Paul
Madonna of the Desert *48* George Blair
Madonna of the Seven Moons *44* Arthur Crabtree
Madonna of the Sleeping Cars, The *28* Maurice Gleize
Madonna of the Storm, The *13* D. W. Griffith
Madonna of the Streets *24* Edwin Carewe
Madonna of the Streets *30* John S. Robertson
Madonna, Wo Bist Du? *36* Georg Jacoby
Madonnas and Men *20* B. A. Rolfe
Madonna's Secret, The *46* Wilhelm Thiele
Madre Folle, La *22* Carmine Gallone
Madre Querida *35* Juan Orol
Madres de Plaza de Mayo, Las *85* Susan Muñoz
Madres del Mundo *36* Rolando Aguilar
Madreselva *39* Luis César Amadori
Madrid *87* Basilio Martín Patino
Madrid en el Año 2000 *25* Manuel Noriega
Madrid in the Year 2000 *25* Manuel Noriega

Madriguera, La *69* Carlos Saura
Madrina del Diablo, La *38* Ramón Peón
Madron *70* Jerry Hopper
Madwoman of Chaillot, The *69* Bryan Forbes, John Huston
Mælkehygiejne *54* Henning Carlsen
Maelstrom, The *17* Paul Scardon
Mae'n Talu Withe *86* Christopher Monger
Maestrina, La *38* Guido Brignone
Maestro, El *58* Aldo Fabrizi, Carol Riethof, Peter Riethof
Maestro, Il *58* Aldo Fabrizi, Carol Riethof, Peter Riethof
Maestro, The *64* John Halas*
Maestro di Don Giovanni, Il *52* Nato De Angelis, Milton Krims, Arthur Villiesid
Maestro di Vigevano, Il *63* Elio Petri
Maestro Do-mi-sol-do, Le *06* Georges Méliès
Maestro e Margherita, Il *72* Aleksandar Petrović
Maestro Leuita, El *40* Luis César Amadori
Maeva *61* Umberto Bonsignori
Maeva—Portrait of a Tahitian Girl *61* Umberto Bonsignori
Maffia, La *71* Leopoldo Torre-Nilsson
Maffia Fait la Loi, La *68* Damiano Damiani
Mafia *48* Pietro Germi
Mafia, The *62* Alberto Lattuada
Mafia *68* Damiano Damiani
Mafia, The *71* Leopoldo Torre-Nilsson
Mafia Girls, The *69* Rossano Brazzi
Mafia Junction *77* Massimo Dallamano
Mafia No! *67* John Irvin
Mafia Uccide *65* Raoul Lévy
Mafioso, Il *62* Alberto Lattuada
Mafu Cage, The *78* Karen Arthur
Mag Wheels *78* Bethel Buckalew
Maga Lesz a Férjem *38* Béla Gaál
Magasiskola *70* István Gaál
Magda *12* Ricardo De Baños
Magda *17* Émile Chautard
Magda *38* Carl Fröhlich
Magda Is Expelled *38* Ladislas Vajda
Magdalena *70* Jerzy Kawalerowicz
Magdalena Viraga *87* Nina Menkes
Magdalene *90* Monica Teuber
Magdalene of the Hills, A *17* John W. Noble
Magdana's Donkey *55* Tenghiz Abuladze, Revaz Chkeidze
Magdan's Donkey *55* Tenghiz Abuladze, Revaz Chkeidze
Magdát Kicsapják *38* Ladislas Vajda
Maggie, The *53* Alexander Mackendrick
Maggie Pepper *19* Chester Withey
Mágia *17* Alexander Korda
Magia a Prezzi Modici *50* Riccardo Freda
Magia Chyornaya i Byelaya *87* Naum Birman
Magia Negra, La *57* Miguel Delgado
Magic *17* Alexander Korda
Magic *78* Richard Attenborough
Magic Alphabet, The *42* Jacques Tourneur
Magic Bag, The *86* Hans Otto Nicolayssen
Magic Book, The *00* Georges Méliès
Magic Book *60* John Halas*
Magic Bottle, The *06* Walter R. Booth
Magic Bow, The *46* Bernard Knowles

Magic Box, The *08* Jack Smith
Magic Box, The *51* John Boulting
Magic Boy *60* Akira Daikubara, Sanae Yamamoto
Magic Bullet, The *40* William Dieterle
Magic Canvas *48* John Halas
Magic Carpet, The *09* Walter R. Booth
Magic Carpet, The *25* Walter Lantz
Magic Carpet, The *51* Lew Landers
Magic Cartoons *09* Émile Cohl
Magic Christian, The *69* Joseph McGrath
Magic Christmas Tree, The *64* Richard C. Parish
Magic Circus, The *77* Evald Schorm*
Magic City *54* Nikos Koundouros
Magic Cup, The *21* John S. Robertson
Magic Donkey, The *70* Jacques Demy
Magic Eggs *09* Émile Cohl
Magic Extinguisher, The *01* James A. Williamson
Magic Eye, The *18* Rea Berger
Magic Face, The *51* Frank Tuttle
Magic Fan *09* Émile Cohl
Magic Fan, The *11* Walter R. Booth
Magic Feature, The *58* Harry Smith
Magic Fire *55* William Dieterle
Magic Flame, The *27* Henry King
Magic Fluke, The *48* John Hubley
Magic Flute, The *74* Ingmar Bergman
Magic Fountain, The *61* Allan David
Magic Fountain, The *61* Fernando Lamas
Magic Fountain Pen, The *07* J. Stuart Blackton
Magic Garden, The *27* James Leo Meehan
Magic Garden, The *52* Donald Swanson
Magic Garden of Stanley Sweetheart, The *70* Leonard Horn
Magic Glass, The *14* Hay Plumb
Magic Hand, The *13* Hy Mayer
Magic Hat, The *52* Alfred Radok
Magic Heritage, A *85* Zdeněk Zelenka
Magic Hoop *08* Émile Cohl
Magic Horse, The *47* Ivan Ivanov-Vano
Magic Horse, The *53* Lotte Reiniger
Magic in Music *41* Andrew L. Stone
Magic Isle of the Pacific *11* Allan Dwan
Magic Jazzbo, The *17* Alfred Santell
Magic Lamp, The *24* Walter Lantz
Magic Lantern, The *03* Georges Méliès
Magic Lantern II *59* Ján Kadár, Elmar Klos
Magic Marble, The *51* Darrell Catling
Magic Mountains *62* Robert Enrico
Magic Night *32* Herbert Wilcox
Magic of Catchy Songs *08* Georges Méliès
Magic of Lassie, The *78* Don Chaffey
Magic of Love *10* Percy Stow
Magic of the Diamond *58* Jørgen Roos
Magic on a Stick *45* Cy Endfield
Magic on Broadway *37* Dave Fleischer
Magic Plus Fours, The *24* Andrew P. Wilson
Magic Pony *76* Ivan Ivanov-Vano
Magic Prague of Rudolph II, The *82* Jaromil Jireš
Magic Ring, The *06* Lewin Fitzhamon
Magic Ring, The *11* Theo Bouwmeester
Magic Ring, The *56* Olive Negus
Magic Rug, The *25* Walter Lantz
Magic Serpent, The *66* Tetsuya Yamaguchi

Magic Shop, The *82* Ian Emes
Magic Show, The *83* Norman Campbell
Magic Skin, The *15* Richard Ridgely
Magic Skin, The *20* George Edwardes Hall
Magic Snowman, The *87* C. Stanner
Magic Spectacles *61* Bob Wehling
Magic Squares *14* Louis Nikola
Magic Sticks *87* Peter Keglevic
Magic Strength *44* Bob Wickersham
Magic Sword, The *01* Walter R. Booth
Magic Sword, The *52* Volslav Nanovich
Magic Sword, The *62* Bert I. Gordon
Magic Sword, or A Medieval Mystery, The *01* Walter R. Booth
Magic Through the Ages *06* Georges Méliès
Magic Touch, The *66* Joe Sarno
Magic Town *47* William A. Wellman
Magic Toyshop, The *86* David Wheatley
Magic Voyage of Sinbad, The *53* James Landis, Alexander Ptushko
Magic Waltz *18* Michael Curtiz
Magic Wand, The *22* George Wynn
Magic Weaver, The *60* Alexander Rou
Magic World of Topo Gigio, The *61* Federico Caldura, Luca De Rico
Magical Maestro, The *51* Tex Avery
Magical Mysteries *14* Walter R. Booth
Magical Press, The *07* Walter R. Booth
Magical Spectacles *61* Bob Wehling
Magician, The *1898* Georges Méliès
Magician, The *26* Rex Ingram
Magician, The *26* Walter Lantz
Magician, The *58* Ingmar Bergman
Magician of Lublin, The *79* Menahem Golan
Magician's Cavern, The *01* Georges Méliès
Magician's Daughter, The *38* Felix E. Feist
Magicians of the Silver Screen *78* Jiří Menzel
Magicien, Le *1898* Georges Méliès
Magicien, Le *59* Walerian Borowczyk
Magiciens, Les *75* Claude Chabrol
Magiciens de Wanzerbé, Les *48* Marcel Griaule, Jean Rouch
Magiciens Noirs, Les *48* Marcel Griaule, Jean Rouch
Magie à Travers les Âges, La *06* Georges Méliès
Magie Diabolique *1897* Georges Méliès
Magie du Diamant *58* Jørgen Roos
Magie Noire *04* Alice Guy-Blaché
Magiko Viali, To *88* Maria Gavala
Magino—Mura Monogatari *87* Shinsuke Ogawa
Magirama *56* Abel Gance, Nelly Kaplan
Magistrate, The *21* Bannister Merwin
Magistrate, The *59* Luigi Zampa
Magistrate's Daughter, The *18* Maurice Sandground
Magistrato, Il *59* Luigi Zampa
Magliari, I *59* Francesco Rosi
Mágnás Miska *16* Alexander Korda
Magnat *87* Filip Bajon
Magnate, The *87* Filip Bajon
Magnet, The *49* Charles Frend
Magnet Laboratory *59* Richard Leacock
Magnet of Doom *63* Jean-Pierre Melville
Magnetic Maid, The *13* Hy Mayer
Magnetic Monster, The *53* Curt Siodmak

Magnetic Squirt, The *09* Georges Hatot
Magnetic Telescope, The *42* Dave Fleischer
Magnétiseur, Le *1897* Georges Méliès
Magnificent Adventurer, The *63* Riccardo Freda
Magnificent Ambersons, The *42* Freddie Fleck, Orson Welles, Robert Wise
Magnificent Bandits, The *69* Giovanni Fago
Magnificent Brute, The *21* Robert Thornby
Magnificent Brute, The *36* John G. Blystone
Magnificent Concubine, The *64* Han-hsiang Li
Magnificent Cuckold, The *64* Antonio Pietrangeli
Magnificent Doll *46* Frank Borzage
Magnificent Dope, The *42* Walter Lang
Magnificent Flirt, The *28* Harry D'Abbadie D'Arrast
Magnificent Four, The *65* Primo Zeglio
Magnificent Fraud, The *39* Robert Florey
Magnificent Islands *65* Alexander Zguridi
Magnificent Lie, The *31* Berthold Viertel
Magnificent Lover, The *86* Aline Issermann
Magnificent Matador, The *55* Budd Boetticher
Magnificent Meddler, The *17* William Wolbert
Magnificent Obsession *35* John M. Stahl
Magnificent Obsession *54* Douglas Sirk
Magnificent One, The *73* Philippe de Broca
Magnificent Outcast *38* Leslie Goodwins
Magnificent Rebel, The *60* Georg Tressler
Magnificent Rogue, The *46* Albert S. Rogell
Magnificent Roughnecks *56* Sherman Rose
Magnificent Seven, The *54* Akira Kurosawa
Magnificent Seven, The *60* John Sturges
Magnificent Seven Deadly Sins, The *71* Graham Stark
Magnificent Seven Ride!, The *72* George McCowan
Magnificent Showman, The *64* Henry Hathaway
Magnificent Sinner *59* Robert Siodmak
Magnificent Six and ½, The *68* Harry Booth
Magnificent 6 and ½, The *69* Harry Booth
Magnificent Six and a Half, The *71* Peter Graham Scott
Magnificent Three, The *63* Joaquín Luis Romero Marchent
Magnificent Tramp, The *58* Gilles Grangier
Magnificent Two, The *67* Cliff Owen
Magnificent Warriors *87* David Chung
Magnificent Yankee, The *50* John Sturges
Magnifico Avventuriero, Il *63* Riccardo Freda
Magnifico Cornuto, Il *64* Antonio Pietrangeli
Magnifico Straniero, Il *65* Herschel Daugherty

Magnifico Texano, Il *67* Luigi Capuano
Magnifico West, Il *72* G. Crea
Magnifique, Le *73* Philippe de Broca
Magnifi-Sinner *59* Robert Siodmak
Magnum Force *73* Ted Post
Magnum Thrust *81* Earl Bellamy
Magoichi Saga, The *70* Kenji Misumi
Magokoro *39* Mikio Naruse
Magokoro *53* Masaki Kobayashi
Magoo Beats the Heat *56* Pete Burness
Magoo Breaks Par *57* Pete Burness
Magoo Goes Overboard *57* Pete Burness
Magoo Goes Skiing *54* Pete Burness
Magoo Goes West *56* Pete Burness
Magoo Makes News *55* Pete Burness
Magoo Saves the Bank *57* Pete Burness
Magoo Slept Here *53* Pete Burness
Magoo's Caine Mutiny *56* Pete Burness
Magoo's Check Up *55* Pete Burness
Magoo's Cruise *58* Rudy Larriva
Magoo's Express *55* Pete Burness
Magoo's Glorious Fourth *57* Pete Burness
Magoo's Homecoming *59* Gil Turner
Magoo's Lodge Brother *59* Rudy Larriva
Magoo's Masquerade *57* Rudy Larriva
Magoo's Masterpiece *53* Pete Burness
Magoo's Moose Hunt *57* Robert Cannon
Magoo's Private War *57* Rudy Larriva
Magoo's Problem Child *56* Pete Burness
Magoo's Puddle Jumper *56* Pete Burness
Magoo's Three-Point Landing *58* Pete Burness
Magoo's Young Manhood *58* Pete Burness
Magoroku Is Still Alive *43* Keisuke Kinoshita
Magot de Joséfa, Le *63* Claude Autant-Lara
Magpie's Strategy, The *87* Zlatko Lavanić
Maguito, El *59* Jorge Sanjinés
Magus, The *68* Guy Green
Magus *88* František Vláčil
Magyar Föld Ereje, A *16* Michael Curtiz
Magyar Ugaron, A *72* András Kovács
Magyarok *77* Zoltán Fábri
Mahabharata, The *89* Peter Brook
Mahanagar *63* Satyajit Ray
Maharadjæns Yndlingshustru *16* Svend Gade
Maharadjæns Yndlingshustru II *18* August Blom
Maharajah's Favorite, The *18* August Blom
Maharajah's Love, The *36* Arthur Maria Rabenalt
Maharshi *88* Vamsi
Mahatma and the Mad Boy *72* James Ivory, Ismael Merchant
Mahiru no Ankoku *56* Tadashi Imai
Mahiru no Enbukyoku *49* Kozaburo Yoshimura
Mahler *73* Ken Russell
Mahlzeiten *67* Edgar Reitz
Mahogany *75* Berry Gordy
Mahuliena, Zlatá Panna *86* Miloslav Luther
Mai con le Donne *85* Giovanni Fago
Maid Among Maids, A *24* John W. Brunius
Maid and the Man, The *12* Allan Dwan
Maid and the Martian, The *64* Don Weis
Maid and the Money, The *14* Hay Plumb

Maid for Murder *61* Robert Asher
Maid Happy *33* Mansfield Markham
Maid in Morocco *25* Charles Lamont
Maid in Paris *57* Pierre Gaspard-Huit
Maid in the Garden, The *1897* George Albert Smith
Maid of Belgium, A *17* George Archainbaud
Maid of Cefn Ydfa, The *08* William Haggar
Maid of Cefn Ydfa, The *14* William Haggar, Jr.
Maid of Formosa *49* Fei-kwong Ho
Maid of Salem *37* Frank Lloyd
Maid of the Alps, A *12* Alf Collins
Maid of the Mountains, The *32* Lupino Lane
Maid of the Silver Sea, A *22* Guy Newall
Maid of the West *21* Philo McCullough, C. R. Wallace
Maid to Order *31* Elmer Clifton
Maid to Order *87* Amy Jones
Maidanek *44* Jerzy Bossak, Aleksander Ford
Maiden, The *61* Alfred Rodé
Maiden and Men *12* Allan Dwan
Maiden for a Prince, A *65* Pasquale Festa Campanile
Maiden for the Prince, A *65* Pasquale Festa Campanile
Maiden in the Storm *33* Yasujiro Shimazu
Maiden of the Woods, The *87* Nicolae Mărgineanu
Maiden Voyage *39* Wilhelm Thiele
Maiden vs. Monk *35* E. W. Emo
Maidens from Wilko *78* Andrzej Wajda
Maidens of Kashima Sea, The *59* So Yamamura
Maiden's Paradise, A *01* Georges Méliès
Maids, The *74* Christopher Miles
Maid's Kid, The *55* Tomotaka Tasaka
Maid's Night Out *38* Ben Holmes
Maidstone *70* Norman Mailer
Maigret et l'Affaire Saint-Fiacre *58* Jean Delannoy
Maigret Lays a Trap *57* Jean Delannoy
Maigret Sets a Trap *57* Jean Delannoy
Maigret Tend un Piège *57* Jean Delannoy
Maigret Voit Rouge *63* Gilles Grangier
Maihime *51* Mikio Naruse
Maijiki Poli, I *54* Nikos Koundouros
Mail and Female *37* Gordon Douglas
Mail and Technology *61* Edgar Reitz
Mail Early *41* Norman McLaren
Mail Early for Christmas *59* Norman McLaren
Mail Order Bride *63* Burt Kennedy
Mail Train *40* Walter Forde
Mail Van Murder, The *57* John Knight
Mailbag Robbery *57* Compton Bennett
Maillol *42* Jean Lods
Mailman, The *23* Emory Johnson
Mailman, The *70* Dariush Mehrjui
Main à Couper, La *74* Étienne Périer
Main Actor, The *77* Reinhard Hauff
Main Attraction, The *62* Daniel Petrie
Main Chance, The *64* John Knight
Main Chaude, La *59* Gérard Oury
Main Cuirassée, La *1898* Georges Méliès
Main de Fer *12* Léonce Perret

Main du Diable, La *42* Maurice Tourneur
Main du Professeur Hamilton ou Le Roi des Dollars, La *03* Alice Guy-Blaché
Main Event, The *27* William K. Howard
Main Event, The *38* Daniel Dare
Main Event, The *79* Howard Zieff
Main Mystérieuse, La *16* Émile Cohl
Main 1-2-3 *18* Alfred Santell
Main Qui à Tue, La *24* Maurice Gleize
Main Secourable, La *08* Georges Méliès
Main Street *23* Harry Beaumont
Main Street *36* Archie Mayo
Main Street *56* Juan Antonio Bardem
Main Street After Dark *44* Edward L. Cahn
Main Street Girl *38* Elmer Clifton
Main Street Girl *45* Christy Cabanne
Main Street Kid, The *47* R. G. Springsteen
Main Street Lawyer *39* Dudley Murphy
Main Street to Broadway *53* Tay Garnett
Main Tera Dushman *89* Vijay Reddy
Main Thing Is to Love, The *75* Andrzej Żuławski
Maine-Océan *86* Jacques Rozier
Maine-Océan Express *86* Jacques Rozier
Mainland, The *44* Sergei Gerasimov
Mains d'Orlac, Les *59* Edmond T. Gréville
Mains du Futur, Les *69* François Reichenbach
Mains Flétries, Les *20* Édouard E. Violet
Mains Nettes, Les *58* Claude Jutra
Mains Sales, Les *51* Fernand Rivers
Mainspring, The *16* Jack Conway
Maintain the Right *40* Joseph M. Newman
Mais N'Te Promène Donc Pas Toute Nue *36* Léo Joannon
Mais Où et Donc Ornicar *79* Bertrand Van Effenterre
Mais Qu'Est-Ce Qu'Elles Veulent? *77* Coline Serreau
Mais Toi Tu Es Pierre *71* Maurice Cloche
Maisie *39* Edwin L. Marin
Maisie Gets Her Man *42* Roy Del Ruth
Maisie Goes to Reno *44* Harry Beaumont
Maisie Was a Lady *40* Edwin L. Marin
Maisie's Marriage *23* Alexander Butler
Maison Assassinée, La *88* Georges Lautner
Maison aux Images, La *55* Jean Grémillon
Maison Bonnadieu, La *51* Carlo-Rim
Maison dans la Dune, La *34* Pierre Billon
Maison dans la Dune, La *52* Georges Lampin
Maison d'Argile, La *18* Gaston Ravel
Maison de Danses *30* Maurice Tourneur
Maison de Jade, La *88* Nadine Trintignant
Maison de Jeanne, La *88* Magali Clément
Maison de la Flèche, La *32* Henri Fescourt
Maison de l'Espoir, La *15* Jacques De Baroncelli
Maison d'en Face, La *36* Christian-Jaque
Maison des Bories, La *69* Jacques Doniol-Valcroze
Maison des Lions, La *12* Louis Feuillade
Maison du Fantoche, La *16* Émile Cohl
Maison du Maltais, La *27* Henri Fescourt
Maison du Maltais, La *38* Pierre Chénal
Maison du Soleil, La *29* Gaston Roudes
Maison Hantée, La *07* Segundo De Chomón

Maison Jaune, La *32* Karl Grüne
Maison Sous la Mer, La *47* Henri Calef
Maison Sous les Arbres, La *71* René Clément
Maison Tranquille, La *00* Georges Méliès
Maison Vide, La *21* Raymond Bernard
Maisons *48* Charles Dekeukeleire
Maisons de la Misère, Les *37* Henri Storck
Maître Après Dieu *50* Louis Daquin
Maître chez Soi *32* Edmond T. Gréville
Maître de Forges, Le *33* Abel Gance
Maître de la Foudre, Le *16* Louis Feuillade
Maître de Montpelier, Le *60* Roger Leenhardt
Maître de Musique, Le *88* Gérard Corbiau
Maître d'École, Le *81* Claude Berri
Maître du Temps, Le *69* Jean-Daniel Pollet
Maître Évora *21* Gaston Roudes
Maître-Nageur, Le *79* Jean-Louis Trintignant
Maîtres du Temps, Les *82* René Laloux
Maîtres Fous, Les *55* Jean Rouch
Maîtresse *75* Barbet Schroeder
Maja Desnuda, La *59* Henry Koster, Mario Russo
Majd a Zsuzsi *38* Béla Gaál
Majdanek *44* Jerzy Bossak, Aleksander Ford
Majdanek, Cmentarzysko Europy *44* Jerzy Bossak, Aleksander Ford
Majdanek, Extermination Camp *44* Jerzy Bossak, Aleksander Ford
Majdhar *84* Ahmed A. Jamal
Majesty of the Law, The *15* Julia Ivers
Majha Pati Karodpati *88* Sachin
Majin *66* Kimiyoshi Yasuda
Majin Strikes Again *66* Issei Mori
Majin the Hideous Idol *66* Kimiyoshi Yasuda
Majin the Monster of Terror *66* Kimiyoshi Yasuda
Majnu *87* Dasari Narayan Rao
Major and the Minor, The *42* Billy Wilder
Major Barbara *41* Harold French, David Lean, Gabriel Pascal
Major Dundee *65* Sam Peckinpah
Major from Ireland, The *12* Sidney Olcott
Major League *89* David S. Ward
Major Lied Till Dawn, The *38* Frank Tashlin
Major the Red Cross Dog *11* Theo Bouwmeester
Majordôme, Le *64* Jean Delannoy
Majorettes, The *88* Bill Hinzman
Majority of One, A *61* Mervyn LeRoy
Majorka-Muff *63* Jean-Marie Straub
Majster Kat *65* Pal'o Bielek
Május 1 *52* Miklós Jancsó
Mak p 100 *88* Antonio Bito
Makai Tensho *81* Kinji Fukasaku
Make a Face *71* Karen Sperling, Avraham Tau
Make a Funny Face *72* Alexander Mitta
Make a Million *35* Lewis D. Collins
Make a Wish *37* Kurt Neumann
Make and Break *67* Peter Brook
Make Believe Ballroom *49* Joseph Santley
Make-Believe Wife, The *18* John S. Robertson

Make Fruitful the Land 45 Ken Annakin
Make Haste to Live 54 William A. Seiter
Make It Snappy 24 Charles Lamont
Make It Three 38 David MacDonald
Make Like a Thief 64 Richard Long, Palmer Thompson
Make Love Not War 66 Franco Rossi
Make Me a Star 32 William Beaudine
Make Me a Woman 69 Errikos Andreou
Make Me an Offer! 54 Cyril Frankel
Make Mine a Double 59 D'Arcy Conyers
Make Mine a Million 59 Lance Comfort
Make Mine Freedom 55 Joseph Barbera, William Hanna
Make Mine Laughs 48 Richard Fleischer, Hal Yates
Make Mine Mink 60 Robert Asher
Make Mine Music 46 Robert Cormack, Clyde Geronimi, Jack Kinney, Hamilton Luske, Joshua Meador
Make Them Die Slowly 81 Umberto Lenzi
Make-Up 37 Alfred Zeisler
Make Up 85 Kazuo Ikehiro
Make Way for a Lady 36 David Burton
Make Way for Lila 62 Rolf Husberg
Make Way for Tomorrow 37 Leo McCarey
Make Your Own Bed 44 Peter Godfrey
Maker of Diamonds, A 09 J. Stuart Blackton
Maker of Men 31 Edward Sedgwick
Makers of Men 25 Forrest K. Sheldon
Maki Állást Vállal 16 Béla Balázs
Making a Living 14 Henry Lehrman
Making a Man 22 Joseph E. Henabery
Making a Man of Him 12 F. Martin Thornton
Making a Splash 84 Peter Greenaway
Making Contact 85 Roland Emmerich
Making Friends 36 Dave Fleischer
Making Good 21 Sidney Olcott
Making Good 32 Walter Lantz
Making Good Resolutions 22 Bernard Dudley
Making It 71 John Erman
Making It 73 Bertrand Blier
Making It Move 77 John Halas
Making Love 81 Arthur Hiller
Making Michael Jackson's Thriller 83 John Landis
Making Mr. Right 87 Susan Seidelman
Making Moving Pictures 08 J. Stuart Blackton
Making Music 60 Robert Henryson
Making of a Lady, The 68 Christian-Jaque
Making of a Man, The 11 D. W. Griffith
Making of a Man, The 25 Hy Mayer
Making of Bobby Burnit, The 14 Oscar Apfel
Making of Gordon's, The 22 Challis Sanderson
Making of Maddalena, The 16 Frank Lloyd
Making of O'Malley, The 25 Lambert Hillyer
Making Over of Geoffrey Manning, The 15 Harry Davenport
Making Paper Money 22 Bernard Dudley
Making Photoplays in Egypt 12 Sidney Olcott
Making Sausages 1897 George Albert Smith

Making Stars 35 Dave Fleischer
Making the Grade 21 Fred J. Butler
Making the Grade 29 Alfred E. Green
Making the Grade 47 Horace Shepherd
Making the Grade 84 Dorian Walker
Making the Headlines 38 Lewis D. Collins
Making the Varsity 28 Clifford Wheeler
Making Whoopee 28 Charles Lamont
Makin's of an Artist, The 24 Hy Mayer
Makioka Sisters, The 83 Kon Ichikawa
Makk Hetes 16 Michael Curtiz
Makkers Staakt Uw Wild Geraas 60 Fons Rademakers
Mako: The Jaws of Death 76 William Grefé
Makom Le'Yad Hayam 88 Rafael Rebibo
Makwayela 77 Jean Rouch
Mal, El 66 Gilberto Gazcón
Mal d'Aimer, Le 86 Giorgio Treves
Mal de Mer, Le 12 Max Linder
Mal des Todes, Das 85 Peter Handke
Mal du Siècle, Le 53 Claude Lelouch
Mala Hronika 62 Vatroslav Mimica
Malá Mořská Víla 76 Karel Kachyňa
Mala Noche 85 Gus Van Sant, Jr.
Mala Ordina, La 73 Fernando Di Leo
Mala Pianta, La 11 Mario Caserini
Mala the Magnificent 33 W. S. Van Dyke
Mala Vida, La 73 Hugo Fregonese
Malabrigo 86 Alberto Durant
Malacca 86 Vilgot Sjöman
Malachias 61 Bernhard Wicki
Malachi's Cove 73 Henry Herbert
Malade Hydrophobe, Le 00 Georges Méliès
Malade Hydrophobe ou L'Homme Qui A des Roues dans la Tête, Le 00 Georges Méliès
Malade Imaginaire, Le 1897 Georges Méliès
Maladie d'Amour 87 Jacques Deray, André Téchiné, Andrzej Żuławski
Malady of Love, The 86 Giorgio Treves
Malady of Love 87 Jacques Deray, André Téchiné, Andrzej Żuławski
Malaga 54 Richard Sale
Malaga 59 Laslo Benedek
Malakeen, The 64 John Irvin
Malakhov Burial Mound, The 44 Josef Heifits, Alexander Zarkhi
Malakhov Kirgan 44 Josef Heifits, Alexander Zarkhi
Malakov Hill 44 Josef Heifits, Alexander Zarkhi
Malamondo 64 Paolo Cavara
Malandro 86 Ruy Guerra
Malarek: A Street Kid Who Made It 89 Roger Cardinal
Mälarpirater 23 Gustaf Molander
Mälarpirater 87 Allan Edwall
Malastrana 72 Aldo Lado
Malatesta's Carnival 73 Christopher Speeth
Malaventura 88 Manuel Gutiérrez Aragón
Malay Nights 33 E. Mason Hopper
Malaya 49 Richard Thorpe
Malayunta 86 José Santiso
Malchik i Golub 60 Andrei Mikhalkov-Konchalovsky
Malchik s Palchik 85 Gunars Piesis
Malcolm 86 Nadia Tass

Malcolm Strauss' Salome 23 Malcolm Strauss
Malcolm X: Struggle for Freedom 68 John Taylor
Maldeniye Simion 87 D. B. Nihalsingha
Maldición de Frankenstein, La 72 Jesús Franco
Maldición de la Bestia, La 75 Miguel Iglesias Bonns
Maldición de la Llorona, La 60 Rafael Baledón
Maldición de la Momia Azteca, La 57 Rafael Portillo
Maldición de los Karnstein, La 63 Camillo Mastrocinque
Maldición de Nostradamus, La 59 Federico Curiel, Alberto Mariscal
Malditas Sean las Mujeres 36 Juan Bustillo Oro
Maldonne 27 Jean Grémillon
Maldonne 87 John Berry
Male and Female 19 Cecil B. DeMille
Male and Female 61 Carlos Rinaldi
Male and Female Since Adam and Eve 61 Carlos Rinaldi
Male Animal, The 42 Elliott Nugent
Male Companion 64 Philippe de Broca
Male du Siècle, Le 75 Claude Berri
Male Game, The 89 Jan Švankmajer
Male Hunt 64 Édouard Molinaro
Male Man, The 31 Dave Fleischer
Male of the Century, The 75 Claude Berri
Male Oscuro, Il 90 Mario Monicelli
Male Service 66 Arch Hudson
Male Vampire, The 59 Nobuo Nakagawa
Maledette Pistole di Dallas, Le 64 José María Zabalza
Maledetti, I 55 Riccardo Freda
Maledetto Imbroglio, Un 57 Pietro Germi
Malediction de Frankenstein, La 72 Jesús Franco
Maledizione dei Karnstein, La 63 Camillo Mastrocinque
Maléfice, Le 12 Louis Feuillade
Maléfices 61 Henri Decoin
Maleficio II, El 86 Raúl Araiza
Malencontre 20 Germaine Dulac
Malenka 68 Amando De Ossorio
Malenka—La Nipote del Vampiro 68 Amando De Ossorio
Malenka—La Sobrina del Vampiro 68 Amando De Ossorio
Malenka the Vampire 68 Amando De Ossorio
Malenkaya Vera 88 Vasily Pichul
Malenki Beglyets 66 Eduard Bocharov, Teinosuke Kinugasa
Mâles, Les 70 Gilles Carle
Malevil 81 Christian De Chalonge
Malfray 48 Alain Resnais*
Malgache Adventure, The 44 Alfred Hitchcock
Malgovert 50 Georges Rouquier
Malheur N'Arrive Jamais Seul, Un 03 Georges Méliès
Malheur Qui Passe, Le 16 Louis Feuillade
Malheurs de la Guerre, Les 62 Henri Storck
Malheurs de Sophie, Les 45 Jacqueline Audry

Mali Mestieri, Il *63* Gianfranco Mingozzi
Malia *45* Giuseppe Amato
Malibran, La *42* Sacha Guitry
Malibu *34* Chester M. Franklin
Malibu Beach *78* Robert J. Rosenthal
Malibu Beach Party *40* Friz Freleng
Malibu Bikini Shop, The *85* David Wechter
Malibu Express *84* Andy Sidaris
Malibu High *79* Irvin Berwick
Malice *73* Salvatore Samperi
Malice in Slumberland *42* Alec Geiss
Malicious *73* Salvatore Samperi
Malizia *73* Salvatore Samperi
Malkat Hakita *86* Itzhak Yeshurun
Malkat Hakvish *70* Menahem Golan
Mallarmé *60* Jean Lods
Malle au Mariage, La *12* Max Linder
Malom a Pokolban *87* Gyula Maar
Malombra *16* Carmine Gallone
Malombra *42* Mario Soldati
Malone *87* Harley Cokliss
Maloola from Paloona *15* Dave Aylott
Malou *80* Jeanine Meerapfel
Malpas Mystery, The *60* Sidney Hayers
Malpertuis *71* Harry Kümel
Malpertuis: Histoire d'une Maison Maudite *71* Harry Kümel
Malpractice *89* Bill Bennett
Malquerida, La *49* Emilio Fernández
Malta Story *53* Brian Desmond Hurst
Maltese Bippy, The *69* Norman Panama
Maltese Falcon, The *31* Roy Del Ruth
Maltese Falcon, The *41* John Huston
Malu Tianshi *37* Muzhi Yuan
Malva *24* Robert Dinesen
Malva *57* Vladimir Braun
Mam-Mō Kenkoku no Reimei *32* Kenji Mizoguchi
Mamá *33* Benito Perojo
Mama Behave *26* Leo McCarey
Mamá Cumple Cien Años *79* Carlos Saura
Mama Dracula *79* Boris Szulzinger
Mama Ich Lebe *77* Konrad Wolf
Mama Is Boos! *86* Ruud van Hemert
Mama Is Mad! *86* Ruud van Hemert
Mama Loves Papa *31* George Stevens
Mama Loves Papa *33* Norman Z. McLeod
Mama Loves Papa *45* Frank R. Strayer
Mama, Papa, the Maid and I *54* Jean-Paul Le Chanois
Mama Runs Wild *38* Ralph Staub
Mama Steps Out *37* George B. Seitz
Mama, There's a Man in Your Bed *88* Coline Serreau
Mama Turns 100 *79* Carlos Saura
Maman Colibri *29* Julien Duvivier
Maman Colibri *37* Jean Dréville
Maman et la Putain, La *73* Jean Eustache
Maman Poupée *18* Carmine Gallone
Mama's Affair *21* Victor Fleming
Mama's Baby Boy *23* Archie Mayo
Mama's D-E-A-R *15* Cecil Birch
Mama's Dirty Girls *74* John Hayes
Mamba *30* Albert S. Rogell
Mamba *88* Mario Orfini
Mambo *54* Robert Rossen
Mambrú Se Fué a la Guerra *86* Fernando Fernán Gómez
Mambru Went to War *86* Fernando Fer-

nán Gómez
Mame *74* Gene Saks
Mamele *38* Joseph Green, Konrad Tom
Mami *38* János Vaszary
Mamie Rose *11* August Blom
Mamma Ebe *85* Carlo Lizzani
Mamma Mia È Arrivato Così Sia *72* Alfio Caltabiano
Mamma Roma *62* Pier Paolo Pasolini
Mammals *62* Roman Polanski
Mammame *85* Raúl Ruiz
Mamma's Affair *21* Victor Fleming
Mammy *30* Michael Curtiz
Mammy Water *53* Jean Rouch
Mammy's Rose *16* Frank Borzage, James Douglass
Mamsell Nitouche *31* Karel Lamač
Mamy Water *53* Jean Rouch
Mam'zelle Bonaparte *41* Maurice Tourneur
Mam'zelle Nitouche *31* Marc Allégret
Mam'zelle Nitouche *33* Charles David
Mam'zelle Nitouche *53* Yves Allégret
Mam'zelle Pigalle *56* Michel Boisrond
Man, The *10* D. W. Griffith
Man, The *25* Kenji Mizoguchi
Man, The *61* Kaneto Shindo
Man, The *72* Joseph Sargent
Man, a Woman and a Bank, A *79* Noel Black
Man, a Woman and a Killer, A *75* Richard A. Richardson, Richard R. Schmidt, Wayne Wang
Man About the House, A *47* Leslie Arliss
Man About the House *74* John Robins
Man About Town *32* John Francis Dillon
Man About Town *39* Mark Sandrich
Man About Town *47* René Clair
Man Above the Law *18* Raymond Wells
Man Accused *59* Montgomery Tully
Man Afraid *57* Harry Keller
Man Against Man *61* Senkichi Taniguchi
Man Against Woman *32* Irving Cummings
Man Alive *45* Ray Enright
Man Alone, The *23* William H. Clifford
Man Alone, A *46* Robert Siodmak
Man Alone, A *55* Ray Milland
Man Although a Thief, A *05* Frank Mottershaw
Man Among Men, A *55* Kajiro Yamamoto
Man and a Serving Maid, A *12* Hay Plumb
Man and a Woman, A *16* F. L. Lyndhurst
Man and a Woman, A *66* Claude Lelouch
Man and a Woman: 20 Years Later, A *86* Claude Lelouch
Man and Beast *17* Henry MacRae
Man and Boy *72* E. W. Swackhamer
Man and Child *57* Raoul André
Man and His Angel *16* Burton L. King
Man and His Bees, A *09* Lewin Fitzhamon
Man and His Bottle, The *08* Lewin Fitzhamon
Man and His Dog Out for Air, A *57* Robert Breer
Man and His Kingdom *21* Maurice Elvey
Man and His Mate, A *15* John G. Adolfi
Man and His Mate *40* D. W. Griffith, Hal Roach, Hal Roach, Jr.

Man and His Money, A *19* Harry Beaumont
Man and His Soul *16* John W. Noble
Man and His Tools *62* John Hubley
Man and His Wife, A *34* Jean Dréville
Man and His Woman *20* J. Stuart Blackton
Man and His World *67* Stan Vanderbeek
Man and Maid *25* Victor Schertzinger
Man and the Beast, The *51* Mario Soffici
Man and the Girl, The *09* Sidney Olcott
Man and the Latchkey, The *08* Lewin Fitzhamon
Man and the Moment, The *18* Arrigo Bocchi
Man and the Moment, The *29* George Fitzmaurice
Man and the Monster, The *58* Rafael Baledón
Man and the Snake, The *72* Sture Rydman
Man and the Woman, The *08* D. W. Griffith
Man and the Woman, A *17* Herbert Blaché, Alice Guy-Blaché
Man and Wife *23* John L. McCutcheon
Man and Wife *70* Matt Cimber
Man and Woman *20* Charles Logue
Man and Woman *38* Pál Fejős, Gunnar Skoglund
Man at Large *41* Eugene Forde
Man at Six, The *31* Harry Hughes
Man at the Carlton Tower *61* Robert Tronson
Man at the Crossroads, The *23* William Dieterle
Man at the Gate, The *40* Norman Walker
Man at the Top *73* Mike Vardy
Man at the Wheel, The *16* Frank Wilson
Man Bait *26* Donald Crisp
Man Bait *52* Terence Fisher
Man Beast *55* Jerry Warren
Man, Beast and Virtue *53* Steno
Man Behind the Curtain, The *16* Courtlandt J. Van Deusen
Man Behind the Door, The *14* Wally Van
Man Behind the Gun, The *52* Felix E. Feist
Man Behind the Mask, The *14* Warwick Buckland
Man Behind the Mask, The *36* Michael Powell
Man Behind the Times, The *17* Frank Wilson
Man Beneath, The *19* William Worthington
Man Betrayed, A *37* John H. Auer
Man Betrayed, A *41* John H. Auer
Man Between, The *23* Finis Fox
Man Between, The *53* Carol Reed
Man Braucht Kein Geld *31* Carl Boese
Man Burde Ta' Sig af Det *52* Ole Palsbo
Man by the Roadside, The *23* William Dieterle
Man Called Adam, A *66* Leo Penn
Man Called Back, The *32* Robert Florey
Man Called Dagger, A *67* Richard Rush
Man Called Flintstone, The *66* Joseph Barbera, William Hanna
Man Called Gannon, A *68* James Goldstone

Man from Yesterday, The 49 Oswald Mitchell
Man Getter, The 22 Francis Ford
Man Goes Through the Wall, A 59 Ladislas Vajda
Man He Found, The 51 William Cameron Menzies
Man Housemaid, A 09 A. E. Coleby
Man Hunt 11 Allan Dwan
Man Hunt, The 18 Travers Vale
Man Hunt 33 Irving Cummings
Man Hunt 36 William Clemens
Man Hunt 41 Fritz Lang
Man Hunter, The 19 Frank Lloyd
Man Hunter, The 30 D. Ross Lederman
Man Hunter, The 80 Jesús Franco
Man Hunters of the Caribbean 38 André Roosevelt, Ewing Scott
Man I Killed, The 31 Ernst Lubitsch
Man I Love, The 29 William A. Wellman
Man I Love, The 46 John Maxwell, Raoul Walsh
Man I Married, The 40 Irving Pichel
Man I Marry, The 36 Ralph Murphy
Man I Want, The 34 Leslie Hiscott
Man in a Cocked Hat 58 Roy Boulting, Jeffrey Dell
Man in a Hurry 77 Édouard Molinaro
Man in a Hurry 86 Kinji Fukasaku
Man in Black, The 49 Francis Searle
Man in Blue, The 25 Edward Laemmle
Man in Blue, The 37 Milton Carruth
Man in Grey, The 43 Leslie Arliss
Man in Half Moon Street, The 44 Ralph Murphy
Man in Hiding 53 Terence Fisher
Man in Hiding 61 Edmond O'Brien
Man in His Place, The 16 Ernest G. Batley
Man in Hobbles, The 28 George Archainbaud
Man in Love, A 87 Diane Kurys
Man in Mommy's Bed, A 68 Howard Morris
Man in Motley, The 16 Ralph Dewsbury
Man in My Life, The 61 Youssef Chahine
Man in Outer Space 61 William Hole, Jr., Oldřich Lipský
Man in Polar Regions 67 Shirley Clarke
Man in Possession, The 15 Cecil Birch
Man in Possession, The 15 Will P. Kellino
Man in Possession, The 31 Sam Wood
Man in Possession, The 37 W. S. Van Dyke
Man in Silence 59 John Halas*
Man in the Attic, The 15 Ralph Dewsbury
Man in the Attic 53 Hugo Fregonese, Robert L. Jacks
Man in the Back Seat, The 61 Vernon Sewell
Man in the Barn, The 37 Jacques Tourneur
Man in the Dark 53 Lew Landers
Man in the Dark 63 Lance Comfort
Man in the Dinghy, The 50 Herbert Wilcox
Man in the Glass Booth, The 74 Arthur Hiller
Man in the Gray Flannel Suit, The 55 Nunnally Johnson

Man in the Hispano-Suiza, The 32 Jean Epstein
Man in the Iron Mask, The 28 George J. Banfield, Leslie Eveleigh
Man in the Iron Mask, The 39 James Whale
Man in the Middle 59 Peter Bourne
Man in the Middle, The 63 Guy Hamilton
Man in the Mirror, The 36 Maurice Elvey
Man in the Moon, The 1898 Georges Méliès
Man in the Moon, The 09 Émile Cohl
Man in the Moon 60 Basil Dearden
Man in the Moon, The 86 Erik Clausen
Man in the Moonlight, The 19 Paul Powell
Man in the Moonlight Mask, The 58 Tsuneo Kobayashi
Man in the Net, The 59 Michael Curtiz
Man in the North, The 57 Kon Ichikawa
Man in the Open, A 19 Ernest C. Warde
Man in the Raincoat, The 56 Julien Duvivier
Man in the Road, The 56 Lance Comfort
Man in the Rough 28 Wallace Fox
Man in the Saddle, The 26 Lynn Reynolds, Clifford Smith
Man in the Saddle, The 28 Widgey R. Newman
Man in the Saddle 51 André De Toth
Man in the Shadow, The 26 David M. Hartford
Man in the Shadow 57 Jack Arnold
Man in the Shadow 57 Montgomery Tully
Man in the Shadows, The 15 Charles McEvoy
Man in the Silk Hat, The 83 Maud Linder
Man in the Sky, The 56 Charles Crichton
Man in the Steel Mask, The 73 Jack Gold
Man in the Storm, The 69 Senkichi Taniguchi
Man in the Street, The 14 Charles Brabin
Man in the Street, The 26 Thomas Bentley
Man in the Trunk, The 42 Malcolm St. Clair
Man in the Vault 55 Andrew V. McLaglen
Man in the Water, The 63 Mark Stevens
Man in the White Suit, The 51 Alexander Mackendrick
Man in the Wilderness 71 Richard C. Sarafian
Man Inside, The 16 John G. Adolfi
Man Inside, The 58 John Gilling
Man Inside, The 90 Bobby Roth
Man Is Armed, The 56 Franklin Adreon
Man Is Born, A 56 Vassily Ordynski
Man Is Not a Bird 65 Dušan Makavejev
Man Is Ten Feet Tall, A 56 Martin Ritt
Män Kan Inte Våltas 78 Jörn Donner
Man Killer 33 Michael Curtiz
Man Life Passed By, The 23 Victor Schertzinger
Man Like Eva, A 83 Radu Gabrea
Man Looking Southeast 81 Eliseo Subiela
Man Mad 58 Albert C. Gannaway
Man Made Monster 41 George Waggner
Man Missing 61 Edward L. Cahn
Man Must Live, A 25 Paul Sloane

Man Named John, A 64 Ermanno Olmi
Man Named Rocca, A 61 Jean Becker
Man Next Door, The 13 Mack Sennett
Man Next Door, The 23 Victor Schertzinger
Man Next Door, The 65 Yoji Kuri
Man Nobody Knows, The 25 Errett LeRoy Kenepp
Man och Kvinna 38 Pál Fejős, Gunnar Skoglund
Man of a Thousand Faces 57 Joseph Pevney
Man of Action, A 23 James W. Horne
Man of Action 33 George Melford
Man of Affairs 36 Herbert Mason
Man of Africa 53 Cyril Frankel
Man of Aran 34 Robert Flaherty
Man of Ashes 86 Nouri Bouzid
Man of Bronze, The 18 David M. Hartford
Man of Bronze 51 Michael Curtiz
Man of Bronze, The 75 Michael Anderson
Man of Conflict 53 Hal Makelim
Man of Conquest 39 George Nicholls, Jr.
Man of Courage 34 Giovacchino Forzano
Man of Courage 43 Alexis Thurn-Taxis
Man of Earth 86 Agim Sopi
Man of Evil 44 Anthony Asquith
Man of Flowers 83 Paul Cox
Man of His Word, A 15 George Loane Tucker
Man of Honor, A 19 Fred J. Balshofer
Man of Iron, A 25 William Bennett
Man of Iron 35 William McGann
Man of Iron 55 Pietro Germi
Man of Iron 80 Andrzej Wajda
Man of La Mancha 72 Arthur Hiller
Man of Legend 71 Sergio Grieco
Man of Letters 27 Sam Newfield
Man of Marble 72 Andrzej Wajda
Man of Mayfair 31 Louis Mercanton
Man of Might 19 William Duncan
Man of Music 52 Grigori Alexandrov
Man of Mystery, A 12 Frank Wilson
Man of Mystery, The 17 Frederick Thompson
Man of Mystery 26 Thomas Bentley
Man of Nerve, A 25 Louis Chaudet
Man of Passion, A 89 José Antonio De la Loma
Man of Position, A 23 Archie Mayo
Man of Quality, A 26 Wesley Ruggles
Man of Sentiment, A 33 Richard Thorpe
Man of Shame, The 15 Harry C. Myers
Man of Sorrow 16 Oscar Apfel
Man of Stone, The 21 George Archainbaud
Man of Stone, The 35 Julien Duvivier
Man of Straw 57 Pietro Germi
Man of the Century 60 Samson Samsonov
Man of the Cross, The 42 Roberto Rossellini
Man of the Day, The 35 Julien Duvivier
Man of the East 72 Enzo Barboni
Man of the Family 43 Charles Lamont
Man of the Foreign Debt, The 87 Pablo Olivo
Man of the Forest 26 John Waters
Man of the Forest 33 Henry Hathaway
Man of the Hour, The 14 Maurice Tourneur

Man of the Hour *35* Julien Duvivier
Man of the Hour *45* Irving Pichel
Man of the Moment, The *32* Kenji Mizoguchi
Man of the Moment *35* Monty Banks
Man of the Moment *55* John Paddy Carstairs
Man of the North *57* Kon Ichikawa
Man of the Open Seas *20* Marcel L'Herbier
Man of the People *37* Edwin L. Marin
Man of the Right Moment, The *32* Kenji Mizoguchi
Man of the Sea *48* Roberto De Ribon, B. L. Randone
Man of the Soil, The *17* Michael Curtiz
Man of the West, The *26* Albert S. Rogell
Man of the West *58* Anthony Mann
Man of the World *31* Edward Goodman, Richard Wallace
Man of the Year *73* Marco Vicario
Man of Tin *40* Art Davis, Sid Marcus
Man of Two Worlds *33* J. Walter Ruben
Man of Violence *70* Peter Walker
Man on a Mission *65* Robert Gardner
Man on a String *60* André De Toth
Man on a Swing *74* Frank Perry
Man on a Tightrope *53* Elia Kazan, Gerd Oswald
Man on America's Conscience, The *42* William Dieterle
Man on Fire *57* Ranald MacDougall
Man on Fire *87* Elie Chouraqui
Man on the Beach, A *55* Joseph Losey
Man on the Box, The *14* Oscar Apfel, Wilfred Buckland, Cecil B. DeMille
Man on the Box, The *25* Charles Reisner
Man on the Case, The *14* Allan Dwan
Man on the Cliff, The *55* Robert Hartford-Davis
Man on the Eiffel Tower, The *49* Burgess Meredith
Man on the Flying Trapeze, The *34* Dave Fleischer
Man on the Flying Trapeze, The *35* Clyde Bruckman
Man on the Flying Trapeze, The *47* Ken Hughes
Man on the Flying Trapeze, The *54* Ted Parmelee
Man on the Line, The *85* Julius Matula
Man on the Phone, The *85* Julius Matula
Man on the Prowl *57* Art Napoleon
Man on the Roof, The *76* Bo Widerberg
Man on the Run *49* Lawrence Huntington
Man on the Run *64* Eddie Romero
Man on the Staircase *70* Roy Cannon
Man on the Tracks *56* Andrzej Munk
Man or Gun *58* Albert C. Gannaway
Man or His Money, The *13* Warwick Buckland
Man Outside, The *33* George A. Cooper
Man Outside *65* Joseph Marzano
Man Outside, The *67* Samuel Gallu
Man Outside *86* Mark Stouffer
Man Overboard *72* Khodzhakuli Narliev
Man Power *27* Clarence Badger
Man-Proof *37* Richard Thorpe
Man Proposes God Disposes *25* Alexander Butler

Man Rustlin' *26* Del Andrews
Man She Brought Back, The *22* Charles Miller
Man Sku' Være Noget ved Musikken *72* Henning Carlsen
Man-Slashing Horse-Piercing Sword *29* Daisuke Ito
Man Sometimes Errs *38* Béla Gaál
Man Spielt Nicht mit der Liebe *26* G. W. Pabst
Man Spricht Deutsch *88* Hanns Christian Müller
Man Steigt Nach *27* Ernö Metzner
Man Stolen *33* Max Ophüls
Man Tamer, The *21* Harry B. Harris
Man the Army Made, A *17* Bertram Phillips
Man the Lifeboat *04* Harold Hough
Man There Was, A *16* Victor Sjöström
Man They Could Not Hang, The *39* Nick Grindé
Man They Couldn't Arrest, The *31* T. Hayes Hunter
Man to Man *22* Stuart Paton
Man to Man *30* Allan Dwan
Man to Man *58* Grigori Alexandrov
Man to Man Talk *58* Luis Saslavsky
Man to Men *48* Christian-Jaque
Man to Remember, A *38* Garson Kanin
Man Trackers, The *21* Edward Kull
Man Trail, The *15* Elisha H. Calvert
Man Trailer, The *34* Lambert Hillyer
Man Trap, The *17* Elmer Clifton
Man-Trap *61* Edmond O'Brien
Man Trouble *30* Berthold Viertel
Man Unconquerable, The *22* Joseph E. Henabery
Man Under Cover, The *22* Tod Browning
Man Under Suspicion *84* Norbert Kuckelmann
Man Under the Bridge, The *36* Ladislas Vajda
Man Under Water *61* Jiří Brdečka, Ladislav Čapek
Man Upstairs, The *26* Roy Del Ruth
Man Upstairs, The *58* Don Chaffey
Man Vanishes, A *67* Shohei Imamura
Man Wanted *22* John Francis Dillon
Man Wanted *32* William Dieterle
Man Who, The *21* Maxwell Karger
Man Who Assassinated Ryoma, The *87* Kosaku Yamashita
Man Who Bought London, The *16* F. Martin Thornton
Man Who Broke the Bank at Monte Carlo, The *35* Stephen Roberts
Man Who Came Back, The *21* H. B. Parkinson
Man Who Came Back, The *24* Emmett J. Flynn
Man Who Came Back, The *31* Raoul Walsh
Man Who Came Back, The *41* Jean Renoir
Man Who Came for Coffee, The *70* Alberto Lattuada
Man Who Came from Ummo, The *69* Tulio Demicheli, Hugo Fregonese
Man Who Came to Dinner, The *41* William Keighley
Man Who Changed, The *34* Henry Edwards
Man Who Changed His Mind, The *28*

Ronald Gow, Captain Mee
Man Who Changed His Mind, The *36* Robert Stevenson
Man Who Changed His Name, The *28* A. V. Bramble
Man Who Changed His Name, The *34* Henry Edwards
Man Who Cheated Himself, The *50* Felix E. Feist
Man Who Cheated Life, The *26* Henryk Galeen
Man Who Could Cheat Death, The *58* Terence Fisher
Man Who Could Not Commit Suicide, The *07* Lewin Fitzhamon
Man Who Could Walk Through Walls, The *59* Ladislas Vajda
Man Who Could Work Miracles, The *36* Lothar Mendes
Man Who Couldn't Beat God, The *15* Maurice Costello, Robert Gaillard
Man Who Couldn't Get Enough, The *75* Alan Birkinshaw
Man Who Couldn't Laugh, The *10* Percy Stow
Man Who Couldn't Walk, The *60* Henry Cass
Man Who Cried Wolf, The *37* Lewis R. Foster
Man Who Dared, The *20* Emmett J. Flynn
Man Who Dared, The *33* Hamilton MacFadden
Man Who Dared, The *39* Crane Wilbur
Man Who Dared, The *46* John Sturges
Man Who Dared God, The *17* Lois Weber
Man Who Died Twice, The *58* Joseph Kane
Man Who Disappeared, The *13* Charles Brabin
Man Who Envied Women, The *85* Yvonne Rainer
Man Who Fell to Earth, The *76* Nicolas Roeg
Man Who Fights Alone, The *24* Wallace Worsley
Man Who Finally Died, The *62* Quentin Lawrence
Man Who Forgot, The *16* Ernest G. Batley
Man Who Forgot, The *17* Émile Chautard
Man Who Forgot, The *19* F. Martin Thornton
Man Who Found Himself, The *15* Frank Crane
Man Who Found Himself, The *25* Alfred E. Green
Man Who Found Himself, The *37* Lew Landers
Man Who Gained Reason, The *86* Alejandro Agresti
Man Who Had Everything, The *20* Alfred E. Green
Man Who Had His Hair Cut Short, The *65* André Delvaux
Man Who Had Power Over Women, The *70* John Krish
Man Who Haunted Himself, The *70* Basil Dearden
Man Who Kept Silent, The *11* Bert Haldane

Man Who Killed Billy the Kid, The 67 Julio Buchs

Man Who Knew Too Much, The 34 Alfred Hitchcock

Man Who Knew Too Much, The 56 Alfred Hitchcock

Man Who Laughs, The 27 Paul Leni

Man Who Laughs, The 66 Sergio Corbucci

Man Who Learned to Fly, The 08 Lewin Fitzhamon

Man Who Left His Will on Film, The 70 Nagisa Oshima

Man Who Lies, The 67 Alain Robbe-Grillet

Man Who Liked Funerals, The 59 David Eady

Man Who Liked Lemons, The 23 George A. Cooper

Man Who Lived Again, The 36 Robert Stevenson

Man Who Lived Twice, The 36 Harry Lachman

Man Who Lost Himself, The 20 George D. Baker

Man Who Lost Himself, The 41 Edward Ludwig

Man Who Lost His Way, The 42 Jack Conway

Man Who Loved Cat Dancing, The 73 Richard C. Sarafian

Man Who Loved Redheads, The 54 Harold French

Man Who Loved Women, The 77 François Truffaut

Man Who Loved Women, The 83 Blake Edwards

Man Who Made Diamonds, The 37 Ralph Ince

Man Who Made Good, The 17 Dave Aylott

Man Who Made Good, The 17 Arthur Rosson

Man Who Made the Army, The 17 George Pearson

Man Who Married His Own Wife, The 22 Stuart Paton

Man Who Murdered, The 31 Kurt Bernhardt

Man Who Never Was, The 55 Ronald Neame

Man Who Paid, The 22 Oscar Apfel

Man Who Pawned His Soul, The 34 Hobart Henley

Man Who Played God, The 22 F. Harmon Weight

Man Who Played God, The 32 John G. Adolfi

Man Who Played Square, The 24 Alfred Santell

Man Who Reclaimed His Head, The 34 Edward Ludwig

Man Who Returned to Life, The 42 Lew Landers

Man Who Saw Tomorrow, The 22 Alfred E. Green

Man Who Saw Tomorrow, The 81 Robert Guenette

Man Who Seeks His Own Murderer, The 30 Robert Siodmak, Carl Winston

Man Who Seeks the Truth, The 41 Alexander Esway

Man Who Shot Christmas, The 85 Diana Patrick

Man Who Shot Liberty Valance, The 61 John Ford

Man Who Skied Down Everest, The 75 Bruce Nyznik

Man Who Stayed at Home, The 15 Cecil M. Hepworth

Man Who Stayed at Home, The 19 Herbert Blaché

Man Who Stole the Sun, The 48 Zdenek Miler

Man Who Stole the Sun, The 80 Kazuhiko Hasegawa

Man Who Stood Still, The 16 Frank Crane

Man Who Talked Too Much, The 40 Vincent Sherman

Man Who Tamed the Victors, The 18 Forest Holger-Madsen

Man Who Thought He Was Poisoned, The 10 Frank Wilson

Man Who Thought Life, The 69 Jens Ravn

Man Who Took a Chance, The 17 William Worthington

Man Who Turned to Stone, The 57 Leslie Kardos

Man Who Turned White, The 19 Park Frame

Man Who Understood Women, The 59 Nunnally Johnson

Man Who Wagged His Tail, The 57 Ladislas Vajda

Man Who Waited, The 22 Edward I. Luddy

Man Who Walked Alone, The 45 Christy Cabanne

Man Who Walked Through the Wall, The 59 Ladislas Vajda

Man Who Was Afraid, The 17 Fred E. Wright

Man Who Was Nobody, The 60 Montgomery Tully

Man Who Was Sherlock Holmes, The 37 Karl Hartl

Man Who Wasn't, The 15 Hay Plumb

Man Who Wasn't There, The 83 Bruce Malmuth

Man Who Watched Trains Go By, The 52 Harold French

Man Who Went, The 15 Ethyle Batley

Man Who Woke Up, The 18 J. W. McLaughlin

Man Who Won, The 18 Rex Wilson

Man Who Won, The 19 Paul Scardon

Man Who Won, The 23 William A. Wellman

Man Who Won, The 32 Norman Walker

Man Who Would Be King, The 75 John Huston

Man Who Would Not Die, The 16 William Russell

Man Who Would Not Die, The 75 Robert Arkless

Man Who Wouldn't Die, The 42 Herbert I. Leeds

Man Who Wouldn't Talk, The 40 David Burton

Man Who Wouldn't Talk, The 58 Herbert Wilcox

Man Who Wouldn't Tell, The 18 James Young

Man with a Cloak, The 51 Fletcher Markle

Man with a Conscience, The 42 Edgar G. Ulmer

Man with a Dog 58 Leslie Arliss

Man with a Gun, The 38 Sergei Yutkevich

Man with a Gun 58 Montgomery Tully

Man with a Hundred Faces, The 38 Albert De Courville

Man with a Married Woman's Hairdo, A 33 Mikio Naruse

Man with a Million 53 Ronald Neame

Man with a Movie Camera, The 28 Dziga Vertov

Man with a Package, The 17 William Beaudine

Man with a Rifle, The 38 Sergei Yutkevich

Man with a Suitcase 83 Chantal Akerman

Man with an Umbrella, The 46 Ingmar Bergman

Man with Bogart's Face, The 80 Robert Day

Man with Connections, The 70 Claude Berri

Man with Four Heads, The 1898 Georges Méliès

Man with My Face, The 51 Edward Montagne

Man with Nine Fingers, The 16 Anders Wilhelm Sandberg

Man with Nine Lives, The 40 Nick Grindé

Man with One Red Shoe, The 85 Stan Dragoti

Man with the Accordion, The 87 Nikolai Dostal

Man with the Axe, The 78 Mrinal Sen

Man with the Balloons, The 65 Marco Ferreri

Man with the Black Coat, The 86 Sérgio Rezende

Man with the Deadly Lens, The 82 Richard Brooks

Man with the Electric Voice, The 34 Frank R. Strayer

Man with the Golden Arm, The 55 Otto Preminger

Man with the Golden Gun, The 74 Guy Hamilton

Man with the Golden Keys, The 56 Léo Joannon

Man with the Golden Touch, The 18 Alexander Korda

Man with the Green Carnation, The 54 John Lemont

Man with the Green Carnation, The 60 Ken Hughes

Man with the Grey Glove, The 53 Camillo Mastrocinque

Man with the Gun, The 38 Sergei Yutkevich

Man with the Gun, The 55 Richard Wilson

Man with the Hispano, The 32 Jean Epstein

Man with the Limp, The 23 A. E. Coleby

Man with the Magnetic Eyes, The 45 Ronald Haines

Man with the Movie Camera, The *28* Dziga Vertov

Man with the Rubber Head, The *01* Georges Méliès

Man with the Scar, The *15* Frank Wilson

Man with the Shaven Head, The *65* André Delvaux

Man with the Steel Whip, The *54* Franklin Adreon

Man with the Synthetic Brain, The *65* Al Adamson

Man with the Transplanted Brain, The *72* Jacques Doniol-Valcroze

Man with the Twisted Lip, The *21* Maurice Elvey

Man with the Twisted Lip, The *51* Richard Grey

Man with the Yellow Eyes, The *61* Romano Ferrara

Man with Thirty Sons, The *50* John Sturges

Man with Three Coffins, The *87* Chang-ho Lee

Man with Two Brains, The *83* Carl Reiner

Man with Two Faces, The *34* Archie Mayo

Man with Two Faces, The *62* Peter Maxwell

Man with Two Heads, The *72* Andy Milligan

Man with Two Hearts, The *16* Alexander Korda

Man with Two Lives, The *42* Phil Rosen

Man with Two Lives, The *64* Stanley Goulder

Man with Two Mothers, The *22* Paul Bern

Man with Two Shadows, The *70* Terence Young

Man with Wheels in His Head, The *00* Georges Méliès

Man with X-Ray Eyes, The *63* Roger Corman

Man Within, The *14* Wallace Reid

Man Within, The *47* Bernard Knowles

Man Without a Body, The *57* Charles Saunders, W. Lee Wilder

Man Without a Case, The *32* Vera Stroyeva

Man Without a Conscience, The *25* James Flood

Man Without a Country, The *17* Ernest C. Warde

Man Without a Country, The *25* Rowland V. Lee

Man Without a Country *51* Kon Ichikawa

Man Without a Face, The *28* Spencer G. Bennet

Man Without a Face, The *35* George King

Man Without a Face, The *50* Juan Bustillo Oro

Man Without a Face *64* Julio Coll

Man Without a Face *73* Jack Gold

Man Without a Face, The *73* Georges Franju

Man Without a Future, The *15* Forest Holger-Madsen

Man Without a Gun *55* Richard Wilson

Man Without a Heart, The *24* Burton L. King

Man Without a Map, The *68* Hiroshi Teshigahara

Man Without a Nationality, The *51* Kon Ichikawa

Man Without a Soul, The *16* George Loane Tucker

Man Without a Star *54* King Vidor

Man Without Desire, The *23* Adrian Brunel

Man Without Skirts *30* Lewis R. Foster

Man, Woman and Child *82* Dick Richards

Man, Woman and Dog *64* Yoji Kuri

Man, Woman and Sin *27* Monta Bell

Man, Woman and Wife *29* Edward Laemmle

Man, Woman, Marriage *21* Allen Holubar

Man Worth While, The *21* Romaine Fielding

Man You Love to Hate, The *79* Patrick Montgomery

Managed Money *34* Charles Lamont

Manager of the B & A, The *16* John P. McGowan

Mañana de Cobre *86* Miguel Mora

Mañana Seré Libre *88* Vicente Aranda

Manaschi *65* Bolotbek Shamshiev

Manavidu Osthannadu *88* Kodi Ramakrishna

Manche et la Belle, Une *57* Henri Verneuil

Manchester Man, The *20* Bert Wynne

Manchi Donga *88* K. Raghavendra Rao

Manchu Eagle Murder Caper Mystery, The *73* Dean Hargrove

Manchurian Avenger *85* Ed Warnick

Manchurian Candidate, The *62* John Frankenheimer

Mandabi *68* Ousmane Sembène

Mandacaru Vermelho *61* Nelson Pereira Dos Santos

Mandala *81* Kwon-taek Im

Mandaladheesudu *87* Prabhakara Reddy

Mandalay *34* Michael Curtiz

Mandarin Mystery, The *36* Ralph Staub

Mandarin Secret, The *46* Terry Morse

Mandarine, La *71* Édouard Molinaro

Mandarin's Gold *19* Oscar Apfel

Mandat, Le *68* Ousmane Sembène

Manden Der Sejrede *18* Forest Holger-Madsen

Manden Der Tankte Ting *69* Jens Ravn

Manden i Månen *86* Erik Clausen

Manden Uden Fremtid *15* Forest Holger-Madsen

Manden Uden Smil *16* Forest Holger-Madsen

Mandi *83* Shyam Benegal

Mandingo *75* Richard Fleischer

Mandragola, La *65* Alberto Lattuada

Mandragola — The Love Root *65* Alberto Lattuada

Mandragora *45* Gustaf Molander

Mandragore *27* Henryk Galeen

Mandragore *52* Arthur Maria Rabenalt

Mandrake *27* Henryk Galeen

Mandrake, The *65* Alberto Lattuada

Mandrake, the Magician *39* Norman Deming, Sam Nelson

Mandrin *23* Henri Fescourt

Mandrin *62* Jean-Paul Le Chanois

Mandrin, Bandit Gentilhomme *62* Jean-Paul Le Chanois

Mandy *52* Alexander Mackendrick

Maneater *67* Samuel Fuller

Maneater *73* Vincent Edwards

Maneaters of Hydra, The *66* Ernst R. von Theumer

Manège *28* Max Reichmann

Manège *38* Carmine Gallone

Manèges *49* Yves Allégret

Måneprinsessen *16* Forest Holger-Madsen

Manet ou le Novateur Malgré Lui *80* Roger Leenhardt

Maneuver *79* Frederick Wiseman

Maneuvers of the French Army *1896* Georges Méliès

Manewry Miłosne *36* Jan Nowina-Przybylski

Manfish *56* W. Lee Wilder

Manganinnie *80* John Honey

Mangeclous *88* Moshe Mizrahi

Mangiati Vivi *80* Umberto Lenzi

Mangiati Vivi dai Cannibali *80* Umberto Lenzi

Mango Tree, The *77* Kevin Dobson

Mangryongui Kok *80* Yoon Kyo Park

Mangryongui Wechingturesu *81* Yoon Kyo Park

Manhandled *24* Allan Dwan

Manhandled *49* Lewis R. Foster

Manhandlers, The *75* Lee Madden

Manhatta *21* Paul Strand*

Manhattan *24* R. H. Burnside

Manhattan *79* Woody Allen

Manhattan Angel *48* Arthur Dreifuss

Manhattan Baby *82* Lucio Fulci

Manhattan Butterfly *35* Lewis D. Collins

Manhattan Cocktail *28* Dorothy Arzner

Manhattan Cowboy *28* John P. McGowan

Manhattan Heartbeat *40* David Burton

Manhattan Knight *20* George A. Beranger

Manhattan Knights *28* Burton L. King

Manhattan Love Song *34* Leonard Fields

Manhattan Madness *16* Allan Dwan

Manhattan Madness *25* John McDermott

Manhattan Madness *36* Edward Ludwig

Manhattan Madness *41* Harold Huth, Roland Pertwee

Manhattan Melodrama *34* W. S. Van Dyke

Manhattan Merry-Go-Round *37* Charles Reisner

Manhattan Monkey Business *35* Charlie Chase, Harold Law

Manhattan Moon *35* Stuart Walker

Manhattan Music Box *37* Charles Reisner

Manhattan Parade *31* Lloyd Bacon

Manhattan Project, The *86* Marshall Brickman

Manhattan Project: The Deadly Game *86* Marshall Brickman

Manhattan Serenade *45* Joseph Barbera, William Hanna

Manhattan Shakedown *39* Leon Barsha

Manhattan Tower *32* Frank R. Strayer

Manhole Covers *54* Sidney Peterson

Manhood *39* Mikhail Kalatozov

Manhood *41* Boris Barnet

Manhunt *58* Henry Hathaway

Manhunt *73* Fernando Di Leo

Manhunt, The *84* Fabrizio De Angelis

Manhunt in Space *54* Walter Grauman

Manhunt in the Jungle *58* Tom McGowan
Manhunt of Mystery Island *45* Spencer G. Bennet, Yakima Canutt, Wallace A. Grissell
Manhunter *83* Martin Beck
Manhunter *86* Michael Mann
Mani di Pistolero *65* Rafael Romero Marchent
Mani sulla Città, Le *63* Francesco Rosi
Mania *59* John Gilling
Mania *85* George Panoussopoulos
Mania *86* Paul Lynch, D. M. Robertson, John Sheppard
Maniac *34* Dwain Esper
Maniac *62* Michael Carreras
Maniac *72* Jürgen Goslar
Maniac *77* Richard Compton
Maniac *80* William Lustig
Maniac Chase *04* Edwin S. Porter
Maniac Cook, The *08* D. W. Griffith
Maniac Cop *87* William Lustig
Maniac Mansion *72* Jürgen Goslar
Maniaci, I *63* Vittorio Caprioli
Maniaci, I *64* Lucio Fulci
Maniacs Are Loose, The *64* Ray Dennis Steckler
Maniac's Guillotine, The *02* William Haggar
Maniacs on Wheels *48* Jack Lee, R. Q. McNaughton
Manicure Girl, The *25* Frank Tuttle
Manicure Lady, The *11* Mack Sennett
Manicurist, The *16* Ford Sterling
Manifesto *88* Dušan Makavejev
Manila Calling *42* Herbert I. Leeds
Manila, in the Claws of Light *75* Lino Brocka
Manila: In the Claws of Neon *75* Lino Brocka
Manila, Open City *67* Eddie Romero
Manin Densha *57* Kon Ichikawa
Manina *52* Willy Rozier
Manina la Fille Sans Voile *52* Willy Rozier
Manipulator, The *79* Dusty Nelson
Manitas de Plata *66* François Reichenbach
Manitou, The *77* William Girdler
Manitou Trail, The *25* Geoffrey Barkas
Manji *64* Yasuzo Masumura
Mankiller *47* André De Toth
Mankillers *87* David A. Prior
Mankinda *57* Stan Vanderbeek
Manly Education *86* Usman Saparov
Manly Man, A *11* Thomas Ince
Manmade Woman *28* Paul Stein
Manmade Women *28* Paul Stein
Manmohan *40* Ramjankhan Mehboobkhan
Mann auf den Schienen, Der *56* Andrzej Munk
Mann auf der Mauer, Der *82* Reinhard Hauff
Mann aus Neapel, Der *18* E. A. Dupont
Mann Dem Man den Namen Stahl, Der *45* Wolfgang Staudte
Mann Der den Mord Beging, Der *31* Kurt Bernhardt
Mann Der Nicht Lieben Darf, Der *27* William Dieterle
Mann Der Nicht Nein Sagen Kann, Der *37* Mario Camerini
Mann Der Seinen Mörder Sucht, Der *30*

Robert Siodmak, Carl Winston
Mann Der Sherlock Holmes War, Der *37* Karl Hartl
Mann Der Sich Verkaufte, Der *59* Josef von Baky
Mann Geht Durch die Wand, Ein *59* Ladislas Vajda
Mann im Keller, Der *14* Joe May
Mann im Spiegel, Der *16* Robert Wiene
Mann in Fesseln, Der *29* Reinhold Schünzel
Mann Ohne Gedächtnis *84* Kurt Gloor
Mann Ohne Schlaf, Der *26* Carl Boese
Mann Über Bord *21* Karl Grüne
Mann um Mitternacht, Der *24* Forest Holger-Madsen
Mann von Oberzalzberg—Adolf und Marlene, Der *76* Ulli Lommel
Mann Wie Eva, Ein *83* Radu Gabrea
Mann Will nach Deutschland, Ein *34* Paul Wegener
Mannaja *78* Sergio Martino
Mannekäng i Rött *58* Arne Mattsson
Mannekängen *13* Mauritz Stiller
Mannen från Mallorca *84* Bo Widerberg
Männen i Mörker *55* Arne Mattsson
Mannen på Taket *76* Bo Widerberg
Mannequin *26* James Cruze
Mannequin *33* George A. Cooper
Mannequin *37* Frank Borzage
Mannequin *76* Claude Pessis
Mannequin *87* Michael Gottlieb
Mannequin in Red *58* Arne Mattsson
Mannequins de Paris *56* André Hunebelle
Männer *85* Doris Dörrie
Männer Müssen So Sein *39* Arthur Maria Rabenalt
Männer Müssen So Sein *61* Arthur Maria Rabenalt
Männer um Lucie, Die *31* Alexander Korda
Männer vom Blauen Kreuz, Die *55* Andrzej Munk
Männer Vor der Ehe *36* Carl Boese
Mannesmann *37* Walter Ruttmann
Människor i Stad *47* Arne Sucksdorff
Människor Mötas och Ljuv Musik Uppstär i Hjärtat *67* Henning Carlsen
Manny's Orphans *78* Sean S. Cunningham
Mano a Mano *33* Arcady Boytler
Mano della Morta, La *49* Carlo Campogalliani
Mano dello Straniero, La *53* Mario Soldati
Mano en la Trampa, La *61* Leopoldo Torre-Nilsson
Mano Spietata della Legge, La *73* Mario Gariazzo
Manoel dans l'Île des Merveilles *85* Raúl Ruiz
Manoel on the Isle of Wonders *85* Raúl Ruiz
Manoeuvre *79* Frederick Wiseman
Manoir de la Peur, Le *27* Alfred Machin, Henri Wuhlschleger
Manoir du Diable, Le *1896* Georges Méliès
Manolescu *29* Victor Tourjansky
Manolescus Memoiren *20* Richard Oswald
Manolete *50* Florian Rey
Manolis *62* Paul H. Crosfield
Manon *48* Henri-Georges Clouzot

Manon *86* Román Chalbaud
Manon de Montmartre *14* Louis Feuillade
Manon des Sources *52* Marcel Pagnol
Manon des Sources *86* Claude Berri
Manon: Finestra 2 *56* Ermanno Olmi
Manon Lescaut *10* Giovanni Pastrone
Manon Lescaut *26* Arthur Robison
Manon Lescaut *39* Carmine Gallone
Manon of the Spring *86* Claude Berri
Manon of the Springs *52* Marcel Pagnol
Manon 70 *68* Jean Aurel
Manone il Ladrone *74* Antonio Margheriti
Manor of the Devil, The *1896* Georges Méliès
Manos—The Hands of Fate *66* Hal P. Warren
Manpower *40* Raoul Walsh
Manrape *78* Jörn Donner
Mans, Le *70* Lee H. Katzin
Man's Affair, A *49* Jay Lewis
Man's Best Friend *35* Edward Kull
Man's Best Friend *41* Walter Lantz
Man's Calling *12* Allan Dwan
Man's Castle, A *33* Frank Borzage
Man's Country, A *19* Henry Kolker
Man's Country *38* Robert F. Hill
Man's Desire *19* Lloyd Ingraham
Man's Duty, A *12* James Hallek Reid
Man's Favorite Sport? *63* Howard Hawks
Man's Game, A *34* D. Ross Lederman
Man's Genesis *11* D. W. Griffith
Man's Great Adversary *12* August Blom, Forest Holger-Madsen
Man's Greatest Friend *38* Joseph M. Newman
Man's Heart *25* Heinosuke Gosho
Man's Heritage *39* Joseph Santley
Man's Home, A *21* Ralph Ince
Man's Hope *39* André Malraux
Man's House, A *21* Ralph Ince
Man's Land, A *32* Phil Rosen
Man's Law, A *17* Harry Davenport
Man's Law and God's *22* Finis Fox
Man's Life, A *27* Kenji Mizoguchi
Man's Lust for Gold *11* D. W. Griffith
Man's Making, The *15* John H. Pratt
Man's Man, A *17* Oscar Apfel
Man's Man, A *23* Oscar Apfel
Man's Man, A *29* James Cruze
Man's Mate, A *24* Edmund Mortimer
Man's Past, A *27* George Melford
Man's Plaything *20* Charles T. Horan
Man's Prerogative, A *15* George Nicholls
Man's Shadow, A *12* Edwin J. Collins
Man's Shadow, A *20* Sidney Morgan
Man's Size, A *23* Howard Mitchell
Man's Solitary Voice *78* Alexander Sokurov
Man's Value *28* Mikhail Averbakh, Mark Donskoi
Man's Woman *17* Travers Vale
Man's Word, A *12* Allan Dwan
Man's World, A *18* Herbert Blaché
Man's World, A *25* Frank Borzage
Man's World, A *42* Charles Barton
Man's Worldly Appearance *28* Heinosuke Gosho
Mansfield Park *86* David Giles
Mansión de Araucaima, La *86* Carlos Mayolo

Mansión de la Locura, La *72* Juan López Moctezuma
Mansión de la Niebla, La *70* Francisco Lara Polop
Mansión de los Muertos Vivientes, La *82* Jesús Franco
Mansion of Aching Hearts, The *25* James P. Hogan
Mansion of Madness, The *72* Juan López Moctezuma
Mansion of the Doomed *75* Michael Pataki
Manslaughter *22* Cecil B. DeMille
Manslaughter *30* George Abbott
Manson Massacre, The *76* Kentucky Jones
Manster, The *62* George Breakston, Kenneth Crane
Manster—Half Man, Half Monster, The *62* George Breakston, Kenneth Crane
Mantan Messes Up *46* Sam Newfield
Manteau Rouge, Le *55* Giuseppe M. Scotese
Mantello Rosso, Il *55* Giuseppe M. Scotese
Mantenuto, Il *61* Ugo Tognazzi
Manthan *76* Shyam Benegal
Mantis in Lace *68* William Rotsler
Mantis Stalks the Cicada, The *88* Jingqin Hu
Mantle of Charity *18* Edward Sloman
Mantra-Mugdha *49* Bimal Roy
Mantrap *26* Victor Fleming
Mantrap, The *43* George Sherman
Mantrap *53* Terence Fisher
Mantrap *84* Julien Temple
Manual of Arms *66* Hollis Frampton
Manuela *57* Guy Hamilton
Manuela *65* Humberto Solás
Manuela's Loves *87* Geneviève Lefèbvre
Manulescu *33* Willi Wolff
Manuscript Found in Saragossa *64* Wojciech Has
Manuscripts *87* Mehrzad Minoui
Manutara *66* Lawrence Huntington
Manxman, The *16* George Loane Tucker
Manxman, The *29* Alfred Hitchcock
Many a Sip *31* Mark Sandrich
Many a Slip *11* Lewin Fitzhamon
Many a Slip *20* Eric Harrison
Many a Slip *31* Vin Moore
Many Happy Returns *13* Hay Plumb
Many Happy Returns *16* Edwin J. Collins
Many Happy Returns *34* Norman Z. McLeod
Many Is the Time *08* Arthur Gilbert
Many Phases of Life, The *86* M. S. Sathyu
Many Rivers to Cross *54* Roy Rowland
Many Tanks *42* Dave Fleischer
Many Tanks Mr. Atkins *38* Roy William Neill
Many Wars Ago *70* Francesco Rosi
Many Waters *31* Milton Rosmer
Manzana de la Discordia, La *68* Felipe Cazals
Maos Sangrentas Assassinos *62* Carlos Hugo Christensen
Mapantsula *88* Oliver Schmitz
Maputo: Meridiano Noveno *76* Santiago Álvarez
Maputo: The Ninth Meridian *76* Santiago Álvarez

Mar y Tú, El *51* Emilio Fernández
Mara Maru *52* Gordon Douglas
Mara of the Wilderness *65* Frank McDonald
Maracaibo *58* Cornel Wilde
Maramao *88* Giovanni Veronesi
Marana Homann *88* A. Kothandarami Reddy
Maranhão *66* Glauber Rocha
Maranhão 66 *66* Glauber Rocha
Maraschino Cherry *77* Radley Metzger
Marat/Sade *66* Peter Brook
Marathon Family, The *84* Slobodan Šijan
Marathon Man *76* John Schlesinger
Marathon Runner, The *33* E. A. Dupont
Marâtre, La *06* Alice Guy-Blaché
Marauders, The *12* Allan Dwan
Marauders *47* George Archainbaud
Marauders, The *55* Gerald Mayer
Marauders, The *61* Samuel Fuller
Marble Heart, The *16* Herbert Brenon, Kenean Buel
Marble Returns, The *51* Darrell Catling
Marc Chagall *62* Henri Langlois
Marca del Hombre Lobo, La *67* Enrique L. Equiluz
Marca del Muerto, La *60* Fernando Cortez, Jerry Warren
Marcados, Los *72* Alberto Mariscal
Marcantonio e Cleopatra *13* Enrico Guazzoni
Marcantonio e Cleopatra *16* Enrico Guazzoni
Marcelino *55* Ladislas Vajda
Marcelino, Pan y Vino *55* Ladislas Vajda
Marcella *20* Carmine Gallone
Marcella *40* Carmine Gallone
Marcellini Millions, The *17* Donald Crisp
Marcello, I'm So Bored *67* John Milius
Marcey *68* Joe Sarno
March, The *63* James Blue
March Hare, The *19* Frank Miller
March Hare, The *21* Maurice Campbell
March Hare, The *56* George More O'Ferrall
March of the Amazons, The *02* George Albert Smith
March of the Light Cavalry *07* Arthur Gilbert
March of the Monsters, The *68* Inoshiro Honda
March of the Movies *38* Howard Gaye
March of the Movies, The *65* E. J. Fancey
March of the Spring Hare *69* Jack Baran
March of the Toys *34* Gus Meins, Charles Rogers
March of the Wooden Soldiers *34* Gus Meins, Charles Rogers
March On, Marines *40* B. Reeves Eason
March on Paris, 1914, of Generaloberst Alexander von Klück and His Memory of Jessee Holladay, The *77* Walter Gutman
March or Die *77* Dick Richards
March to Aldermaston *59* Lindsay Anderson, Karel Reisz
March to Rome, The *62* Dino Risi
March to Washington, The *63* James Blue
March Towards the Sun *55* Andrzej Wajda

March Winds *08* A. E. Coleby
Marcha o Muere *62* Frank Wisbar
Marchand d'Amour *35* Edmond T. Gréville
Marchand de Ballons, Le *02* Alice Guy-Blaché
Marchand de Coco, Le *00* Alice Guy-Blaché
Marchand de Notes, Le *42* Paul Grimault
Marchand de Plaisir, Le *23* Jaque Catelain
Marchandes d'Illusions *61* Raoul André
Marchands de Filles *57* Maurice Cloche
Marché à la Volaille *00* Alice Guy-Blaché
Marche des Machines, La *28* Eugene Deslaw
Marche des Rois, La *13* Louis Feuillade
Marche du Destin, La *24* Henri Diamant-Berger
Marche Funèbre de Chopin, La *07* Georges Méliès
Marche Nuptiale, La *29* André Hugon
Marche ou Crève *59* Georges Lautner
Marche Triomphale, La *16* Maurice Mariaud
Marche Triomphale, La *75* Marco Bellocchio
Märchen aus Alt-Wien *23* Wilhelm Thiele
Marchese del Grillo, Il *81* Mario Monicelli
Marcheurs de Sainte Rolende, Les *75* Henri Storck
Marchi Rosso, Il *18* Carlo Campogalliani
Marching Along *52* Henry Koster
Marcia *78* David Grant
Marcia Nuziale *15* Carmine Gallone
Marcia Nuziale *34* Mario Bonnard
Marcia Nuziale *65* Marco Ferreri
Marcia o Crepa *62* Frank Wisbar
Marcia su Roma, La *62* Dino Risi
Marcia Trionfale *75* Marco Bellocchio
Marco *73* Seymour Robbie
Marco le Magnifique *64* Christian-Jaque, Denys De la Patellière, Noel Howard, Cliff Lyons
Marco Polo *61* Riccardo Freda, Hugo Fregonese, Piero Pierotti
Marco Polo *64* Christian-Jaque, Denys De la Patellière, Noel Howard, Cliff Lyons
Marco Polo Junior *73* Eric Porter
Marco the Magnificent *64* Christian-Jaque, Denys De la Patellière, Noel Howard, Cliff Lyons
Marco Visconti *08* Mario Caserini
Marco Visconti *13* Ugo Falena
Marco Visconti *40* Mario Bonnard
Marcus Garland *25* Oscar Micheaux
Mardi and the Monkey *53* Kay Mander
Mardi Gras *58* Edmund Goulding
Mardi Gras Massacre *78* Jack Weis
Mare, Il *62* Giuseppe Patroni Griffi
Mare, The *86* Ali Jekan
Mare di Guai, Un *40* Carlo Ludovico Bragaglia, Luigi Zampa
Mare di Napoli, Il *19* Carmine Gallone
Mare Matto *62* Renato Castellani
Mare Nostrum *25* Rex Ingram
Maréchal-Ferrant, Le *1895* Louis Lumière
Marée Montante sur Brise-Lames *1896* Georges Méliès
Margaret Day *13* Victor Sjöström
Margaret of Cortona *50* Mario Bonnard

Marito per Anna Zaccheo, Un *53* Giuseppe De Santis

Marius *31* Alexander Korda

Marius, Amateur de Cidre *31* Edmond T. Gréville

Marius et Olive à Paris *35* Jean Epstein

Mariutch *30* Dave Fleischer

Marizinia *62* Zygmunt Sulistrowski

Marizinia, the Witch Beneath the Sea *62* Zygmunt Sulistrowski

Marizza, Called the Smugglers' Madonna *21* F. W. Murnau

Marizza, Gennant die Schmugglermadonna *21* F. W. Murnau

Marjoe *72* Sarah Kernochan, Howard Smith

Marjolin ou La Fille Manquée *21* Louis Feuillade

Marjorie Morningstar *58* Irving Rapper

Marjory's Goldfish *14* Stuart Kinder

Mark, The *60* Guy Green

Mark It Paid *33* D. Ross Lederman

Mark of Cain, The *16* Joseph De Grasse

Mark of Cain, The *17* George Fitzmaurice

Mark of Cain, The *47* Brian Desmond Hurst

Mark of Cain, The *85* Bruce Pittman

Mark of Terror *31* George B. Seitz

Mark of the Apache *56* Lesley Selander

Mark of the Avenger *38* Lesley Selander

Mark of the Beast *23* Thomas Dixon

Mark of the Beast *80* Frank LaLoggia

Mark of the Claw *47* John Rawlins

Mark of the Devil *69* Michael Armstrong

Mark of the Devil, Part Two *72* Adrian Hoven

Mark of the Gorilla *50* William Berke

Mark of the Hawk *57* Michael Audley, Gilbert Gunn

Mark of the Lash *48* Ray Taylor

Mark of the Phoenix *56* Maclean Rogers

Mark of the Renegade *51* Hugo Fregonese

Mark of the Spur *32* John P. McGowan

Mark of the Vampire *35* Tod Browning

Mark of the Vampire *57* Paul Landres

Mark of the West *59* Edward Dein

Mark of the Whistler, The *44* William Castle

Mark of the Witch *70* Tom Moore

Mark of the Wolfman, The *67* Enrique L. Equiluz

Mark of Zorro, The *20* Fred Niblo

Mark of Zorro, The *40* Rouben Mamoulian

Mark Turbyfill *66* Gregory Markopoulos

Mark Twain *85* Will Vinton

Mark Twain, American *76* Robert Wilbor

Marked Bullet, The *41* Lambert Hillyer

Marked Cards *18* Henri D'Elba

Marked for Death *90* Dwight H. Little

Marked for Murder *45* Elmer Clifton

Marked Girls *49* Francis De Carco

Marked Man, A *16* Frank Miller

Marked Man, A *17* John Ford

Marked Man, The *44* William Castle

Marked Men *19* John Ford

Marked Men *40* Sam Newfield

Marked Money *28* Spencer G. Bennet

Marked One, The *63* Francis Searle

Marked Time-Table, The *10* D. W. Griffith

Marked Trails *44* John P. McCarthy

Marked Woman, The *14* Oscar A. C. Lund

Marked Woman *37* Lloyd Bacon

Market Day–Trouville *1896* Georges Méliès

Market of Human Flesh *23* Yasujiro Shimazu

Market of Miracles *66* Jerzy Hoffman

Market of Souls *19* Joseph De Grasse

Market of the Humble, The *86* René Cardona, Jr.

Market of Vain Desire, The *16* Reginald Barker

Market Square, The *28* Frank Miller

Market Woman's Mishap, The *04* Frank Mottershaw

Markéta Lazarová *66* František Vláčil

Marketplace, The *83* Shyam Benegal

Marko Polo *64* Christian-Jaque, Denys De la Patellière, Noel Howard, Cliff Lyons

Markopoulos Passion, The *67* Gregory Markopoulos

Marksman, The *53* Lewis D. Collins

Markurells i Wadköping *30* Victor Sjöström

Markurells of Wadköping, The *30* Victor Sjöström

Marlene *83* Maximilian Schell

Marley *85* Gary Weis

Marlie the Killer *28* Noel Mason Smith

Marlowe *69* Paul Bogart

Marmaduke and His Angel *15* Frank Wilson

Marmalade Revolution, The *79* Erland Josephson, Sven Nykvist

Marmeladupproret *79* Erland Josephson, Sven Nykvist

Marnie *64* Alfred Hitchcock

Maroc d'Aujourd'hui *49* André Michel

Maroc 7 *66* Gerry O'Hara

Marooned *33* Leslie Hiscott

Marooned *69* John Sturges

Marooned Hearts *20* George Archainbaud

Marquis de Sade: Justine *69* Jesús Franco

Marquis d'Eon, der Spion der Pompadour *28* Karl Grüne

Marquis d'Or *20* Reinhold Schünzel

Marquis Preferred *29* Frank Tuttle

Marquise d'O..., La *76* Eric Rohmer

Marquise of O..., The *76* Eric Rohmer

Marquise von O..., Die *76* Eric Rohmer

Marquise von Pompadour, Die *36* Willi Wolff

Marquitta *27* Jean Renoir

Marrakesh *66* Don Sharp

Marriage *27* Roy William Neill

Marriage *45* I. Annensky

Marriage *47* Keisuke Kinoshita

Marriage *74* Claude Lelouch

Marriage, A *83* Sandy Tung

Marriage Agency, The *12* Victor Sjöström

Marriage Bargain, The *35* Albert Ray

Marriage Bond, The *16* Lawrence Marston

Marriage Bond, The *32* Maurice Elvey

Marriage Broker, The *39* Edgar G. Ulmer

Marriage Bureau, The *12* Victor Sjöström

Marriage by Contract *28* James Flood

Marriage by Motor *03* Alf Collins

Marriage Came Tumbling Down, The *68* Jacques Poitrenaud

Marriage Chance, The *22* Hampton Del Ruth

Marriage Cheat, The *21* John Griffith Wray

Marriage Circle, The *24* Ernst Lubitsch

Marriage Clause, The *26* Lois Weber

Marriage Counselor Tora-San *84* Yoji Yamada

Marriage for Convenience *19* Sidney Olcott

Marriage for Moderns *49* Alexander Hammid

Marriage Forbidden *37* Phil Goldstone

Marriage-Go-Round, The *60* Walter Lang

Marriage in the Moon, A *10* Enrico Novelli

Marriage in the Shadows *47* Kurt Mätzig

Marriage in Transit *25* Roy William Neill

Marriage Is a Private Affair *44* Robert Z. Leonard

Marriage, Italian Style *64* Vittorio De Sica

Marriage License? *26* Frank Borzage

Marriage Lie, The *18* Harvey Gates, Stuart Paton

Marriage Lines, The *21* Wilfred Noy

Marriage Maker, The *23* William DeMille

Marriage Market, The *17* Arthur Ashley

Marriage Market, The *23* Edward J. LeSaint

Marriage Morals *23* William Nigh

Marriage of a Young Stockbroker, The *71* Lawrence Turman

Marriage of Arthur, The *16* Rupert Julian

Marriage of Balzaminov, The *66* Konstantin Voinov

Marriage of Convenience, A *14* Forest Holger-Madsen

Marriage of Convenience *34* George Melford

Marriage of Convenience *60* Clive Donner

Marriage of Convenience *86* Albert Mkrtchyan

Marriage of Corbal, The *36* Karl Grüne

Marriage of Figaro, The *13* Luigi Maggi

Marriage of Figaro *50* Georg Wildhagen

Marriage of Figaro, The *63* Jean Meyer

Marriage of Figaro, The *70* Joachim Hess

Marriage of Kitty, The *15* George Melford

Marriage of Maria Braun, The *78* Rainer Werner Fassbinder

Marriage of Molly-O, The *16* Paul Powell

Marriage of Muggins VC and a Further Exploit, The *10* Dave Aylott

Marriage of the Bear, The *26* Konstantin Eggert, Vladimir Gardin

Marriage of William Ashe, The *16* Cecil M. Hepworth

Marriage of William Ashe, The *21* Edward Sloman

Marriage on Approval *33* Howard Higgin

Marriage on the Rocks *65* Jack Donohue

Marriage Pit, The *20* Frederick Thompson

Marriage Playground, The *29* Lothar Mendes

Marriage Price, The *19* Émile Chautard

Marriage Ring, The *18* Fred Niblo

Marriage Rows *31* Roscoe Arbuckle

Marriage Speculation, The *17* Ashley Miller

Marriage Symphony *34* Worthington Miner
Marriage, Tel Aviv Style *79* Joel Silberg
Marriage Time *61* Kozaburo Yoshimura
Marriage Trap, The *26* Alexander Dovzhenko
Marriage Under Terror *27* Anders Wilhelm Sandberg
Marriage War, The *32* Charles Lamont
Marriage Whirl, The *25* Alfred Santell
Marriage Wows *30* Dave Fleischer
Marriage Wrestler, The *64* Hasse Ekman
Marriageable Age *61* Kozaburo Yoshimura
Marriages Are Made *18* Carl Harbaugh
Married? *26* George Terwilliger
Married Alive *27* Emmett J. Flynn
Married and in Love *40* John Farrow
Married Bachelor *41* Edward Buzzell
Married Before Breakfast *37* Edwin L. Marin
Married Bliss *05* Alf Collins
Married—But Single *40* Alexander Hall
Married Couple, A *69* Allan King
Married Flapper, The *22* Stuart Paton
Married Flirts *24* Robert Vignola
Married for Love *10* A. E. Coleby
Married for Money *15* Leon Bary
Married in Haste *10* Lewin Fitzhamon
Married in Haste *10* Edwin S. Porter
Married in Haste *12* Fred Rains
Married in Haste *15* Charles Chaplin
Married in Haste *19* Arthur Rosson
Married in Haste *31* Paul Sloane
Married in Haste *33* Howard Higgin
Married in Hollywood *29* Marcel Silver
Married in Name Only *17* Edmund Lawrence
Married Lady Borrows Money, A *36* Heinosuke Gosho
Married Life *20* Erle C. Kenton
Married Life *21* Georges Treville
Married Life *26* Olof Molander
Married Life *40* Tadashi Imai
Married Life *51* Anders Henrikson
Married Life, A *51* Mikio Naruse
Married Life, the Second Year *14* Charles H. Weston
Married Love *23* Alexander Butler
Married Neighbors *25* Charles Lamont
Married Ones, The *13* Aleksander Hertz
Married People *22* Hugo Ballin
Married to a Mormon *22* H. B. Parkinson
Married to the Mob *88* Jonathan Demme
Married Too Young *62* George Moskov
Married Virgin, The *18* Emmett J. Flynn
Married Woman, A *64* Jean-Luc Godard
Married Woman, The *64* Jean-Luc Godard
Married Woman Needs a Husband, A *35* James Tinling
Marry in Haste *24* Duke Worne
Marry Me *25* James Cruze
Marry Me *32* Wilhelm Thiele
Marry Me *49* Terence Fisher
Marry Me Again *53* Frank Tashlin
Marry Me! Marry Me! *68* Claude Berri
Marry the Boss' Daughter *41* Thornton Freeland
Marry the Girl *28* Phil Rosen
Marry the Girl *35* Maclean Rogers
Marry the Girl *37* William McGann

Marry the Poor Girl *21* Lloyd Ingraham
Marrying Gretchen *14* William Duncan
Marrying Kind, The *52* George Cukor
Marrying Money *15* James Young
Marrying Under Difficulties *08* Lewin Fitzhamon
Marrying Widows *34* Sam Newfield
Mars *08* Segundo De Chomón
Mars *30* Walter Lantz
Mars Attacks the World *38* Ford Beebe, Robert F. Hill
Mars Calling *23* Roy William Neill
Mars Invades Puerto Rico *65* Robert Gaffney
Mars Needs Women *66* Larry Buchanan
Marschier oder Kreiper *62* Frank Wisbar
Marse Covington *15* Edwin Carewe
Marseillaise, La *12* Émile Cohl
Marseillaise, La *20* Henri Desfontaines
Marseillaise, La *30* Pál Fejős, John S. Robertson
Marseillaise, La *37* Jean Renoir
Marseillaise, The *37* Jean Renoir
Marseille Contract, The *74* Robert Parrish
Marshal of Amarillo *48* Philip Ford
Marshal of Cedar Rock *53* Harry Keller
Marshal of Cripple Creek *47* R. G. Springsteen
Marshal of Gunsmoke *44* Vernon Keays
Marshal of Heldorado *50* Thomas Carr
Marshal of Laredo *45* R. G. Springsteen
Marshal of Mesa City, The *39* David Howard
Marshal of Moneymint, The *22* Roy Clements
Marshal of Reno *44* Wallace A. Grissell
Marshal's Daughter, The *53* William Berke
Marshals in Disguise *54* Frank McDonald
Marshmallow Moon *52* Claude Binyon
Marsupials: The Howling III, The *87* Philippe Mora
Marta of the Lowlands *14* J. Searle Dawley
Marter der Liebe *27* Carmine Gallone
Martha *22* George Wynn
Martha *23* Walt Disney
Martha *27* H. B. Parkinson
Martha *74* Rainer Werner Fassbinder
Martha Clarke, Light and Dark *81* Joyce Chopra
Martha Jellneck *88* Kai Wessel
Martha, Ruth & Edie *88* Norma Bailey, Deepa Mehta Saltzman, Danièle J. Suissa
Martha's Vindication *15* Chester M. Franklin, Sidney Franklin
Marthe *19* Gaston Roudes
Marthe Richard *37* Raymond Bernard
Martial Arts of Shaolin *86* Kar-leung Lau
Martian in Moscow *65* John Halas
Martian in Paris, A *61* Jean-Daniel Daninos
Martian Thru Georgia *62* Chuck Jones
Martians Come Back, The *56* Ernest Pintoff
Martians Go Home! *90* David Odell
Martien à Paris, Un *61* Jean-Daniel Daninos
Martin *76* George Romero
Martin Agrippa *69* Bruce Beresford

Martin Andersen Nexøs Sidste Rejse *54* Jørgen Roos
Martin Eden *42* Sidney Salkow
Martin et Gaston *53* Henri Gruel
Martin et Lea *78* Alain Cavalier
Martín Fierro *68* Leopoldo Torre-Nilsson
Martín Garatuza *35* Gabriel Soria
Martin Lowe, Financier *15* Frank Lloyd
Martin Lowe, Fixer *15* Frank Lloyd
Martin Luther *53* Irving Pichel
Martin Missil Quarterly Reports *57* Stan Brakhage
Martin of the Mounted *26* William Wyler
Martin Roumagnac *46* Georges Lacombe
Martin Soldat *66* Michel Deville
Martinache Marriage, The *17* Bertram Bracken
Martin's Day *84* Alan Gibson
Marty *55* Delbert Mann
Martyr, The *11* Edwin S. Porter
Martyr, The *73* Aleksander Ford
Martyr Sex, The *24* Duke Worne
Martyrdom of Adolf Beck, The *09* George R. Sims
Martyrdom of Phillip Strong, The *16* Richard Ridgely
Martyrdom of Thomas a Becket, The *08* Percy Stow
Martyre *26* Charles Burguet
Martyre de l'Obèse, Le *33* Pierre Chénal
Martyre de Ste. Maxence, La *27* Donatien
Martyred Presidents *01* Edwin S. Porter
Märtyrer, Der *73* Aleksander Ford
Martyrium, Das *20* Paul Stein
Martyrs of Love *66* Jan Němec
Martyrs of the Alamo, The *15* Christy Cabanne
Maruja *19* Park Frame, Joseph Franz
Marusa no Onna *87* Juzo Itami
Marusa no Onna II *88* Juzo Itami
Marusia *38* Leo Bulgakov
Marvada Carne *86* André Klotzel
Marvellous Egg Producing with Surprising Developments *01* Georges Méliès
Marvellous Hair Restorer, The *01* James A. Williamson
Marvellous Hoop, The *03* Georges Méliès
Marvellous Suspension and Evolution *02* Georges Méliès
Marvellous Syringe, The *03* Alf Collins
Marvellous Wreath, The *03* Georges Méliès
Marvels of Ski *20* Arnold Fanck*
Marvels of the Bull Ring *43* Raphael J. Sevilla
Marvin and Tige *83* Eric Weston
Marx Brothers at the Circus, The *39* Edward Buzzell
Marx Brothers Go West, The *40* Edward Buzzell
Mary *30* Alfred Hitchcock
Mary Ann *18* Alexander Korda
Mary Burns—Fugitive *35* William K. Howard
Mary Ellen Comes to Town *20* Elmer Clifton
Mary Find-the-Gold *21* George Pearson
Mary Girl *17* Maurice Elvey
Mary Had a Little. . . *61* Edward Buzzell
Mary Had a Lovely Voice *10* Percy Stow

Mary Has Her Way *12* Hay Plumb
Mary Is Dry *05* William Haggar
Mary Jane's Loves *09* Frank Wilson
Mary Jane's Mishap *01* George Albert Smith
Mary Jane's Mishap, or Don't Fool with the Paraffin *01* George Albert Smith
Mary Jane's Pa *17* Charles Brabin
Mary Jane's Pa *35* William Keighley
Mary, Keep Your Feet Still *16* Jack Conway
Mary Latimer, Nun *20* Bert Haldane
Mary Lawson's Secret *17* John B. O'Brien
Mary Lou *48* Arthur Dreifuss
Mary, Mary *63* Mervyn LeRoy
Mary, Mary, Bloody Mary *74* Juan López Moctezuma
Mary Millington's World Striptease Extravaganza *82* Roy Deverell, David Sullivan
Mary Moreland *17* Frank Powell
Mary My Dearest *83* Jaime Humberto Hermosillo
Mary Names the Day *41* Harold S. Bucquet
Mary of Briarwood Dell *13* Bert Haldane
Mary of Scotland *36* John Ford
Mary of the Movies *23* John McDermott
Mary of the Stars *89* Thomas Mauch
Mary Pickford's Kiss *27* Sergei Komarov
Mary Poppins *64* Robert Stevenson
Mary, Queen of Scots *22* Edwin Greenwood
Mary, Queen of Scots *71* Charles Jarrott
Mary Regan *19* Lois Weber
Mary Ryan, Detective *49* Abby Berlin
Mary Stevens, M.D. *33* Lloyd Bacon
Mary Stuart *13* J. Searle Dawley
Mary the Coster *10* Lewin Fitzhamon
Mary the Fishergirl *14* Sidney Northcote
Mary the Flower Girl *13* A. E. Coleby
Mary Was a Housemaid *10* Percy Stow
Marya-Iskusnitsa *60* Alexander Rou
Maryjane *67* Maury Dexter
Maryjka *34* Jan Nowina-Przybylski
Maryland *40* Henry King
Mary's Ankle *20* Lloyd Ingraham
Mary's Birthday *49* Lotte Reiniger
Mary's Lamb *15* Donald Mackenzie
Mary's Little Lamb *35* Ubbe Iwerks
Mary's Little Lobster *20* Edward F. Cline
Mary's New Blouse *14* Ethyle Batley
Mary's Policeman *12* Frank Wilson
Mary's Work *21* Fred Paul, Jack Raymond
Maryse *17* Camille De Morlhon
Marziani Hanno Dodici Mani, I *64* Franco Castellano, L. Martin, Giuseppe Moccia
Marzipan of the Shapes *20* A. C. Hunter
Más Allá de la Muerta *36* Ramón Peón
Más Allá de la Pasión *86* Jesús Garay
Más Allá de las Montañas *68* Alexander Ramati
Más Allá del Silencio *87* César Bolívar
Más Allá del Sol *75* Hugo Fregonese
Más Allá del Terror *79* Tomás Aznar
Más Buenas Que el Pan *87* Alfredo B. Crevenna
Más Fabuloso Golpe del Far West, El *71* José Antonio De la Loma
Más Vale Pájaro en Mano... *87* Jesús Fragoso Montoya

Ma's Wipe Your Feet Campaign *21* Frank Moser
Masada *80* Boris Sagal
Mascara *87* Patrick Conrad
Maschenka *87* John Goldschmidt
Maschera, La *88* Fiorella Infascelli
Maschera del Demonio, La *60* Mario Bava
Maschera di Ferro, La *09* Giovanni Pastrone
Maschera di Misterio *16* Mario Caserini
Maschera e il Volto, La *19* Augusto Genina
Maschiaccio *17* Augusto Genina
Maschine, Die *73* Helma Sanders-Brahms
Mascot, The *30* Aleksander Ford
Mascot of Troop C, The *11* Alice Guy-Blaché
Mascotte *30* Aleksander Ford
Mascotte des Poilus, La *18* Charles De Marsan, Charles Maudru
Masculin-Féminin *66* Jean-Luc Godard
Masculin-Féminin — 15 Faits Precis *66* Jean-Luc Godard
Masculine Feminine *66* Jean-Luc Godard
Masculine Mystique, The *85* John Smith, Giles Walker
Mashenka *42* Yuli Raizman, Dmitri Vasiliev
Masher, The *10* Mack Sennett
Masher and the Nursemaid, The *05* Frank Mottershaw
Masher's Dilemma, The *04* Alf Collins
Másik Ember, A *88* Ferenc Kósa
Mask, The *18* Thomas Heffron
Mask, The *21* Bertram Bracken
Mask, The *53* Don Chaffey
Mask, The *61* Julian Roffman
Mask *85* Peter Bogdanovich
Mask, The *88* Fiorella Infascelli
Mask and the Sword, The *49* Christian-Jaque
Mask of Comedy, The *26* Monta Bell
Mask of Diijon, The *46* Lew Landers
Mask of Dimitrios, The *44* Jean Negulesco
Mask of Dust *54* Terence Fisher
Mask of Fu Manchu, The *32* Charles Brabin, Charles Vidor
Mask of Fu Manchu, The *65* Don Sharp
Mask of Fury *45* Gordon Douglas
Mask of Horror, The *12* Abel Gance
Mask of Korea *50* John Rossi
Mask of Lopez, The *24* Albert S. Rogell
Mask of Riches *18* Thomas Heffron
Mask of the Avenger *51* Phil Karlson
Mask of the Demon *60* Mario Bava
Mask of the Dragon *51* Sam Newfield
Mask of the Himalayas *51* Laslo Benedek, Andrew Marton, Herbert L. Strock
Maskarad *41* Sergei Gerasimov
Maskarada *87* Janusz Kijowski
Mask-a-Raid *31* Dave Fleischer
Maske, Die *19* E. A. Dupont
Maske Fällt, Die *30* William Dieterle
Masked Angel *28* Frank O'Connor
Masked Avenger, The *22* Frank Fanning
Masked Ball, The *21* Wallace A. Carlson
Masked Bride, The *25* Christy Cabanne, Josef von Sternberg
Masked Conqueror, The *62* Luigi Capuano

Masked Dancer, The *24* Burton L. King
Masked Emotions *27* David Butler, Kenneth Hawks
Masked Heart, The *17* Edward Sloman
Masked Lover, The *40* Otakar Vávra
Masked Man Against the Pirates, The *65* Vertunio De Angelis
Masked Marvel, The *24* Roy Del Ruth
Masked Marvel, The *43* Spencer G. Bennet
Masked Pirate, The *49* Edgar G. Ulmer
Masked Raiders *49* Lesley Selander
Masked Rider, The *16* Fred J. Balshofer
Masked Rider, The *22* Challis Sanderson
Masked Rider, The *41* Ford Beebe
Masked Smuggler, The *12* Edwin J. Collins
Masked Stranger, The *40* Lambert Hillyer
Masked Woman, The *27* Silvano Balboni
Maskerade *34* Willi Forst
Maskerage *52* Max De Haas
Maskierte Schrecken, Der *19* Piel Jutzi
Maskovaná Milenka *40* Otakar Vávra
Masks *66* Ingmar Bergman
Masks and Faces *17* Fred Paul
Masks of Death, The *84* Roy Ward Baker
Masks of the Devil *28* Victor Sjöström
Maskulinum-Femininum *66* Jean-Luc Godard
Masnadieri, I *61* Mario Bonnard
Masoch *80* Franco Taviani
Mason of the Mounted *32* Harry Fraser
Masque de Fer, Le *62* Henri Decoin
Masque d'Horreur, Le *12* Abel Gance
Masque of the Red Death, The *64* Roger Corman
Masque of the Red Death *89* Larry Brand
Masque Raid, The *37* Manny Gould, Ben Harrison
Masquerade, The *13* Émile Cohl
Masquerade, The *24* Dave Fleischer
Masquerade *29* Russell Birdwell, Lumsden Hare
Masquerade *41* Sergei Gerasimov
Masquerade *64* Basil Dearden
Masquerade, The *87* Janusz Kijowski
Masquerade *88* Bob Swaim
Masquerade Bandit, The *26* Robert De Lacey
Masquerade in Mexico *45* Mitchell Leisen
Masquerade in Vienna *34* Willi Forst
Masquerade Party, The *34* Manny Gould, Ben Harrison
Masquerader, The *14* Charles Chaplin
Masquerader, The *22* James Young
Masquerader, The *33* Richard Wallace
Masqueraders, The *15* James Kirkwood
Masques *52* Alexander Alexeïeff, Claire Parker
Masques *87* Claude Chabrol
Mass Appeal *84* Glenn Jordan
Mass for the Dakota Sioux *64* Bruce Baillie
Mass Is Ended, The *85* Nanni Moretti
Mass Mouse Meeting *43* Alec Geiss
Mass Production of Eggs *62* Márta Mészáros
Mass Struggle *34* E. Kavaleridze
Massacre, The *12* D. W. Griffith
Massacre *33* Alan Crosland

Massacre 56 Louis King
Massacre, Le 69 François Reichenbach
Massacre at Central High 76 Renee Daalder
Massacre at Fort Grant 64 José María Elorrieta
Massacre at Fort Holman 72 Tonino Valerii
Massacre at Fort Perdition 64 José María Elorrieta
Massacre at Grand Canyon 64 Alfredo Antonini, Sergio Corbucci
Massacre at Marble City 64 Alberto Cardone, Paul Martin
Massacre at the Rosebud, The 65 Sidney Salkow
Massacre Canyon 54 Fred F. Sears
Massacre en Dentelles 52 André Hunebelle
Massacre Harbor 68 John Peyser
Massacre Hill 48 Harry Watt
Massacre in Crete 1897 Georges Méliès
Massacre in Dinosaur Valley 85 Michele Tarantini
Massacre in Rome 73 George Pan Cosmatos
Massacre River 49 John Rawlins
Massacre Valley 50 Wallace Fox
Massacres en Crète 1897 Georges Méliès
Massacro al Grande Canyon 64 Alfredo Antonini, Sergio Corbucci
Massaggiatrici, Le 62 Lucio Fulci
Masseur's Curse, The 70 Kimiyoshi Yasuda
Massey Sahib 86 Pradip Krishen
Massimamente Folle 85 Marcello Troiani
Massive Retaliation 84 Thomas Cohen
Massnahmen Gegen Fanatiker 69 Werner Herzog
Master, The 14 Mauritz Stiller
Master, The 84 William Byron Hillman
Master, The 86 Bagrat Oganisyan
Master and His Servants, The 59 Arne Skouen
Master and Man 15 Percy Nash
Master and Man 29 George A. Cooper
Master and Man 34 John Harlow
Master and Margarita, The 72 Aleksandar Petrović
Master Cracksman, The 14 Harry Carey
Master Crook, The 13 Charles H. Weston
Master Crook Outwitted by a Child, The 14 Ernest G. Batley
Master Crook Turns Detective, The 14 Ernest G. Batley
Master Gunfighter, The 75 Tom Laughlin
Master Hand 73 Hiromichi Horikawa
Master Ideal 32 Martin Frič
Master Key, The 14 Robert Z. Leonard
Master Key, The 45 Lewis D. Collins, Ray Taylor
Master Man, The 19 Ernest C. Warde
Master Mind, The 14 Oscar Apfel, Cecil B. DeMille
Master Mind, The 20 Kenneth Webb
Master Minds 49 Jean Yarbrough
Master, Mistress and Maid 1897 George Albert Smith
Master Mystery, The 18 Burton L. King
Master Nikifor 56 Jan Łomnicki

Master of Ballantrae, The 53 William Keighley
Master of Bankdam 47 Walter Forde
Master of Craft, A 22 Thomas Bentley
Master of Gray, The 18 Tom Watts
Master of His Home 17 Walter Edwards
Master of Horror 59 Irvin S. Yeaworth, Jr.
Master of Horror, The 60 Enrique Carreras
Master of Lassie 48 Fred M. Wilcox
Master of Love, The 19 Fritz Lang
Master of Men, A 13 A. E. Coleby
Master of Men, A 17 Wilfred Noy
Master of Men 33 Lambert Hillyer
Master of Merripit, The 15 Wilfred Noy
Master of Terror, The 59 Irvin S. Yeaworth, Jr.
Master of the House 25 Carl Theodor Dreyer
Master of the Islands 70 Tom Gries
Master of the Vineyard, The 11 Allan Dwan
Master of the World 33 Harry Piel
Master of the World 61 William Witney
Master of Winter Sports 55 Martin Frič
Master Passion, The 17 Richard Ridgely
Master Plan, The 54 Cy Endfield
Master Race, The 44 Herbert J. Biberman, Madeleine Dmytryk
Master Samuel 20 Victor Sjöström
Master Shakespeare, Strolling Player 16 Frederick Sullivan
Master Spy, The 14 Charles H. Weston
Master Spy 63 Montgomery Tully
Master Stroke, A 20 Chester Bennett
Master Swordsman 54 Hiroshi Inagaki
Master Thief, The 15 Mauritz Stiller
Master Touch, The 73 Michele Lupo
Master Will Shakespeare 36 Jacques Tourneur
Master Zoard 17 Michael Curtiz
Masterblaster 87 Glenn R. Wilder
Mästerkatten i Stövlar 18 John W. Brunius
Mästerman 20 Victor Sjöström
Mastermind 76 Alex March
Masterpieces of Horror 60 Enrique Carreras
Masters of Men 23 David Smith
Masters of the Congo Jungle 58 Henry Brandt, Heinz Seilmann, Henri Storck
Masters of the Sea 21 Alexander Korda
Masters of the Universe 87 Gary Goddard
Masters of Venus 62 Ernest Morris
Master's Razor, The 06 Tom Green
Mastership 34 Aveling Ginever
Masterson of Kansas 54 William Castle
Mästertjuven 15 Mauritz Stiller
Masterwork 77 Miklós Jancsó
Masterworks of Terror 60 Enrique Carreras
Mastery of the Sea 41 Alberto Cavalcanti
Mat 26 Vsevolod I. Pudovkin
Mat 55 Mark Donskoi
Mat That Mattered, The 14 Dave Aylott
Mata Au Hi Made 32 Yasujiro Ozu
Mata Au Hi Made 50 Tadashi Imai
Mata Hari 27 Friedrich Feher
Mata Hari 32 George Fitzmaurice
Mata Hari 64 Jean-Louis Richard
Mata Hari 85 Curtis Harrington
Mata Hari, Agent H21 64 Jean-Louis Richard

Mata Hari, Agente Segreto H21 64 Jean-Louis Richard
Mata Hari the Red Dancer 27 Friedrich Feher
Mata Hari's Daughter 54 Carmine Gallone, Renzo Merusi
Matador 86 Pedro Almodóvar
Matador Magoo 57 Pete Burness
Matalo! 70 Cesare Canevari
Mátalos y Vuelve 68 Enzo G. Castellari
Matango 63 Inoshiro Honda
Matango Fungus of Terror 63 Inoshiro Honda
Matanza en Matamoros 86 José Luis Urquieta
Matar o Morir 87 Rafael Villaseñor Kuri
Matarah Tiran, Ha' 68 Raphael Nussbaum
Matatabi 73 Kon Ichikawa
Match, The 88 Carlo Vanzina
Match-Breaker, The 21 Dallas M. Fitzgerald
Match Contre la Mort 59 Claude Bernard-Aubert
Match de Boxe — École de Joinville 1897 Georges Méliès
Match de Prestidigitation 04 Georges Méliès
Match Factory Girl, The 90 Aki Kaurismäki
Match Girl 66 Andrew Meyer
Match Kid, The 33 Dick Huemer
Match King, The 32 Howard Bretherton, William Keighley
Match-Makers, The 16 George Ridgwell
Match Play 30 Mack Sennett
Matchball 69 Duccio Tessari
Matche de Boxe Entre Patineurs à Roulettes 12 Max Linder
Matches 13 Allan Dwan
Matching Dreams 16 B. Reeves Eason
Matchless 66 Alberto Lattuada
Matchless 74 John Papadopoulos
Matchmaker, The 40 Amleto Palermi
Matchmaker, The 58 Joseph Anthony
Matchmaking Mamas 29 Harry Edwards
Matchmaking of Anna, The 72 Pantelis Voulgaris
Máte Doma Lva? 66 Pavel Hobl
Mate of the John M, The 11 J. Stuart Blackton
Mate of the Sally Ann, The 17 Henry King
Matelas Alcoolique, Le 06 Alice Guy-Blaché
Mater Dolorosa 09 Louis Feuillade
Mater Dolorosa 12 Mario Caserini
Mater Dolorosa 17 Abel Gance
Mater Dolorosa 32 Abel Gance
Mater Nostra 36 Gabriel Soria
Materi i Docheri 74 Sergei Gerasimov
Material Evidence 48 Darrell Catling
Material Witness, The 65 Geoffrey Nethercott
Matériaux Nouveaux, Demeures Nouvelles 56 Henri Colpi
Maternal Spark, The 17 Gilbert P. Hamilton
Maternelle, La 25 Gaston Roudes
Maternelle, La 32 Jean Benoît-Lévy, Marie Epstein

Maternelle, La 48 Henri Diamant-Berger
Maternité 27 Jean Benoît-Lévy, Marie Epstein
Maternité 37 Jean Choux
Maternity 17 John B. O'Brien
Maternity 27 Jean Benoît-Lévy, Marie Epstein
Matewan 87 John Sayles
Mathias Kneissl 71 Reinhard Hauff
Mathias Sandorf 20 Henri Fescourt
Mathias Sandorf 62 Georges Lampin
Mati Balidan ki 88 Shiv Kumar
Matières Nouvelles 64 Henri Storck
Matilda 78 Daniel Mann
Matin Comme les Autres, Un 54 Yannick Bellon
Matinée 78 Jaime Humberto Hermosillo
Matinee Idol, The 28 Frank Capra
Matinee Idol 33 George King
Matinee Idol 55 John Halas*
Matinee Ladies 27 Byron Haskin
Mating, The 15 Scott Sidney
Mating, The 18 Frederick Thompson
Mating Call, The 28 James Cruze
Mating Game, The 58 George Marshall
Mating of Marcella, The 18 Roy William Neill
Mating of Marcus, The 24 Will P. Kellino
Mating of Millie, The 48 Henry Levin
Mating of the Sabine Women, The 62 Alberto Gout
Mating Season, The 51 Mitchell Leisen
Matins Infidèles, Les 89 François Bouvier
Matira Manisha 67 Mrinal Sen
Matisse 60 Marcel Ophüls
Matisse, or The Talent for Happiness 60 Marcel Ophüls
Matisse ou Le Talent du Bonheur 60 Marcel Ophüls
Matj (Zaprechtchionnye Lioudi) 88 Gleb Panfilov
Matka Joanna od Aniołów 60 Jerzy Kawalerowicz
Matka Królów 87 Janusz Zaorski
Matou, Le 86 Jean Beaudin
Matrero, El 40 Orestes Caviglia
Matriarca, La 68 Pasquale Festa Campanile
Matrimaniac, The 16 Paul Powell
Matrimonial Announcement 55 Gösta Werner
Matrimonial Bed, The 30 Michael Curtiz
Matrimonial Bliss 16 Kelly Storrie
Matrimonial Criminals, The 63 Valentino Orsini, Paolo Taviani, Vittorio Taviani
Matrimonial Deluge, A 13 William Duncan
Matrimonial Maneuvers 13 Maurice Costello
Matrimonial Muddle, A 12 Percy Stow
Matrimonial Problem, A 30 Michael Curtiz
Matrimonial Web, The 21 Edward José
Matrimonio alla Modo 51 Luciano Emmer
Matrimonio all'Italiana 64 Vittorio De Sica
Matrimonio di Caterina, Il 82 Luigi Comencini
Matrimonio di Figaro, Il 13 Luigi Maggi
Matrimonio Ideale, Un 39 Camillo Mastrocinque
Matrimonio Interplanetario, Un 10 Enrico Novelli

Matrimony 15 Scott Sidney
Matrimony's Speed Limit 13 Alice Guy-Blaché
Matrix 71 John Whitney
Matrix and Joseph's Coat 73 Malcolm Le Grice
Matt 18 A. E. Coleby
Matt Riker: Mutant Hunt 86 Tim Kincaid
Mattatore, Il 59 Dino Risi
Mattatore: L'Homme aux Cent Visages, Il 59 Dino Risi
Mattei Affair, The 72 Tonino Guerra, Francesco Rosi
Matter of Choice, A 63 Vernon Sewell
Matter of Conviction, A 61 John Frankenheimer
Matter of Days, A 68 Yves Ciampi
Matter of Dignity, A 57 Michael Cacoyannis
Matter of Honor, A 88 Sergio Cabrera
Matter of Innocence, A 67 Guy Green
Matter of Life and Death, A 46 Michael Powell, Emeric Pressburger
Matter of Life and Death, A 86 Marianne Ahrne
Matter of Love, A 79 Chuck Vincent
Matter of Morals, A 60 John Cromwell
Matter of Murder, A 49 John Gilling
Matter of Pride, A 61 Allan King
Matter of Resistance, A 65 Jean-Paul Rappeneau
Matter of Time, A 76 Vincente Minnelli
Matter of WHO, A 61 Don Chaffey
Matti da Slegare 74 Silvano Agosti, Marco Bellocchio, Sandro Petraglia, Stefano Rulli
Mau Mau 55 Elwood Price
Maud 11 Wilfred Noy
Maud the Educated Mule 16 Gregory La Cava
Maudie's Adventure 13 Percy Stow
Maudite Galette, La 72 Denys Arcand
Maudite Soit la Guerre 10 Louis Feuillade
Maudite Soit la Guerre 13 Alfred Machin
Maudits, Les 47 René Clément
Maudits Sauvages, Les 71 Jean-Pierre Lefèbvre
Maulkorb, Der 38 Erich Engel
Maulkorb, Der 58 Wolfgang Staudte
Mauprat 26 Jean Epstein
Mauri 87 Merata Mita
Maurice 87 James Ivory
Maurie 73 Daniel Mann
Maurizius Case, The 53 Julien Duvivier
Mauro the Gypsy 73 Laurence Henson
Mausoleum 81 Michael Dugan
Mauvais Cœur Puni 04 Alice Guy-Blaché
Mauvais Coups, Les 61 François Leterrier
Mauvais Fils, Un 80 Claude Sautet
Mauvais Garçon, Le 21 Henri Diamant-Berger
Mauvais Garçon, Un 36 Jean Boyer
Mauvais Œil, Le 38 Charles Dekeukeleire
Mauvais Sang 86 Leos Carax
Mauvaise Conduite 84 Nestor Almendros, Orlando Jiménez-Leal
Mauvaise Graine 33 Alexander Esway, Billy Wilder
Mauvaise Plaisanterie, Une 01 Georges

Méliès
Mauvaise Soupe, La 00 Alice Guy-Blaché
Mauvaises Fréquentations, Les 63 Jean Eustache
Mauvaises Rencontres, Les 55 Alexandre Astruc
Maverick, The 52 Thomas Carr
Maverick Queen, The 56 Joseph Kane
Max 70 Claude Sautet
Max à Monaco 13 Max Linder
Max a Peur de l'Eau 13 Max Linder
Max à un Duel 11 Max Linder
Max Aeronaute 10 Max Linder
Max Amoureux de la Teinturière 11 Max Linder
Max and His Taxi 17 Max Linder
Max and Moritz 78 John Halas
Max Assassiné 13 Max Linder
Max Asthmatique 13 Max Linder
Max au Couvent 13 Max Linder
Max Bandit par Amour 12 Max Linder
Max Boxeur par Amour 12 Max Linder
Max Cocher de Fiacre 12 Max Linder
Max Collectionneur de Chaussures 12 Max Linder
Max Comes Across 17 Max Linder
Max Contre Nick Winter 12 Max Linder
Max Cuisinier par Amour 11 Max Linder
Max dans les Aires 14 Max Linder
Max dans Sa Famille 11 Max Linder
Max Décoré 14 Max Linder
Max Devrait Porter des Bretelles 15 Max Linder
Max Dugan Returns 82 Herbert Ross
Max Émule de Tartarin 12 Max Linder
Max en Convalescence 11 Max Linder
Max Entre Deux Femmes 16 Max Linder
Max Entre Deux Feux 16 Max Linder
Max Escamoteur 12 Max Linder
Max Est Charitable 11 Max Linder
Max Est Distrait 11 Max Linder
Max et Jane en Voyage de Noces 11 Max Linder
Max et Jane Font des Crêpes 11 Max Linder
Max et la Doctoresse 14 Max Linder
Max et la Main-Qui-Étreint 16 Max Linder
Max et le Bâton de Rouge 14 Max Linder
Max et le Billet Doux 13 Max Linder
Max et le Commissaire 14 Max Linder
Max et le Mari Jaloux 14 Max Linder
Max et le Sac 15 Max Linder
Max et l'Entente Cordiale 12 Max Linder
Max et les Femmes 12 Max Linder
Max et les Ferrailleurs 70 Claude Sautet
Max et l'Espion 15 Max Linder
Max et Son Âne 11 Max Linder
Max et Son Chien Dick 11 Max Linder
Max Fait des Conquêtes 13 Max Linder
Max Fait du Ski 10 Louis Gasnier
Max Has a Birthday 15 Ernest G. Batley
Max Havelaar 76 Fons Rademakers
Max Illusioniste 14 Max Linder
Max in a Taxi 17 Max Linder
Max Jockey par Amour 12 Max Linder
Max Lance la Mode 11 Max Linder
Max Linder Contre Nick Winter 12 Max Linder
Max Maître d'Hôtel 14 Max Linder
Max Médecin Malgré Lui 14 Max Linder

Max, Mon Amour 86 Nagisa Oshima
Max, My Love 86 Nagisa Oshima
Max N'Aime Pas les Chats 13 Max Linder
Max Part en Vacances 13 Max Linder
Max Pédicure 14 Max Linder
Max Peintre par Amour 12 Max Linder
Max Pratique Tous les Sports 12 Max Linder
Max Professeur de Tango 12 Max Linder
Max Reprend Sa Liberté 11 Max Linder
Max Sauveteur 14 Max Linder
Max Se Marié 10 Max Linder
Max the Gentleman 37 Mario Camerini
Max Toréador 12 Max Linder
Max Veut Faire du Théâtre 11 Max Linder
Max Veut Grandir 12 Max Linder
Max Victime du Quinquina 11 Max Linder
Max Virtuose 13 Max Linder
Max Wall, Funny Man 75 John Scoffield
Max Wants a Divorce 17 Max Linder
Maxie 85 Paul Aaron
Maxim at Vyborg 38 Grigori Kozintsev, Leonid Trauberg
Maxime 58 Henri Verneuil
Maximka 53 L. Braun
Maximum Overdrive 86 Stephen King
Maximum Thrust 88 Tim Kincaid
Maxplatte, Maxplatten 65 Jiří Trnka
Maxwell Archer, Detective 39 John Paddy Carstairs
Maxwell's Demon 68 Hollis Frampton
May and December 07 A. E. Coleby
May and December 10 D. W. Griffith
May Blossom 15 Allan Dwan
May Blossom 17 Edward José
May Events 51 Vaclav Berdych, Martin Frič
May Fairy Tales 40 Otakar Vávra
May First 38 Grigori Alexandrov
May-Fly, The 16 Forest Holger-Madsen
May Fools 90 Louis Malle
May, Hundred Years After 87 Kalie Kiysk
May I Borrow Your Wife? 59 Arne Mattsson
May I Have the Floor? 75 Gleb Panfilov
May Morning 70 Ugo Liberatore
May Night 53 Alexander Rou
May Rain and Silk Paper 24 Kenji Mizoguchi
Maya 36 Pramatesh Chandra Barua
Maya 49 Raymond Bernard
Maya 64 John Berry
Maya 82 Agust Agustsson, Ruth Schell
Maya from Tskhneti 60 Revaz Chkeidze
Maya iz Tskhneti 60 Revaz Chkeidze
Mayakovsky Laughs 75 Anatoly Karanovich, Sergei Yutkevich
Mayakovsky Smeyotsia 75 Anatoly Karanovich, Sergei Yutkevich
Maybe Darwin Was Right 42 B. Reeves Eason
Maybe I'm a Loser, But I Love You 86 Carlos Galettini
Maybe It's Love 30 William A. Wellman
Maybe It's Love 35 William McGann
Maybe September 70 José Briz
Mayerling 24 Alexander Korda
Mayerling 35 Anatole Litvak
Mayerling 68 Terence Young
Mayerling to Sarajevo 40 Max Ophüls
Mayfair Girl 33 George King

Mayfair Melody 37 Arthur Woods
Mayhem 69 Joseph Adler
Maynila: Jaguar 79 Lino Brocka
Maynila, sa mga Kuko ng Liwanag 75 Lino Brocka
Mayor, The 39 Gilberto Martínez Solares
Mayor of Casterbridge, The 21 Sidney Morgan
Mayor of Filbert, The 18 Christy Cabanne
Mayor of 44th Street, The 42 Alfred E. Green
Mayor of Hell, The 33 Archie Mayo
Mayordomo, El 61 Ismael Rodríguez
Mayor's Dilemma, The 39 Raymond Bernard
Mayor's Nest, The 32 Maclean Rogers
Mayor's Nest, The 41 Lambert Hillyer
Maytime 23 Louis Gasnier
Maytime 37 Robert Z. Leonard, William von Wymetal
Maytime in Mayfair 49 Herbert Wilcox
Mazaher, El 45 Kamel Salim
Maze, The 53 William Cameron Menzies
Mazel Tov, Jews 41 Joseph Seiden
Mazel Tov ou Le Mariage 68 Claude Berri
Mazepa 68 Walerian Borowczyk
Mazeppa 08 Frank Dudley
Mazeppa 09 Vasili M. Goncharov
Mazes and Monsters 82 Steven Hilliard Stern
Mazlíček 34 Martin Frič
Mazo 39 Hiroshi Inagaki
Mazur File, The 60 Jacques Panijel, Jean-Paul Sassy
Mazurka 35 Willi Forst
Mazurka del Barone della Santa e del Fico Fiorone, La 74 Pupi Avati
Mazurka di Papa, La 40 Oreste Biancoli
Mazzetta, La 78 Sergio Corbucci
M'Blimey 31 J. Elder Wills
Me 67 Maurice Pialat
Me and Captain Kid 19 Oscar Apfel
Me and Gott 18 Kenneth M. Anderson
Me and Gott 18 Whyndham Gittens
Me and Him 88 Doris Dörrie
Me and Marlborough 35 Victor Saville
Me and Me Moke 16 Harold M. Shaw
Me and M'Pal 16 Harold M. Shaw
Me and My Brother 68 Robert Frank
Me and My Gal 32 Raoul Walsh
Me and My Girl 21 George Pearson
Me and My Girl 32 Raoul Walsh
Me and My Pal 33 Lloyd French, Charles Rogers
Me and My Pal 39 Thomas Bentley
Me and My Sister 87 Carlo Verdone
Me and My Two Pals 06 Charles Raymond
Me and Myself 30 Lincoln Stoll
Me and the Boys 29 Victor Saville
Me and the Colonel 58 Peter Glenville
Me and You 68 Astrid Henning-Jensen
Me, Gangster 28 Raoul Walsh
Me, Grandma, Iliko and Hillarion 63 Tenghiz Abuladze
Me Hace Falta un Bigote 86 Manuel Summers
Me, Me, Me...and the Others 65 Alessandro Blasetti
Me, Mother and You 58 Carlo Ludovico Bragaglia

Me, Natalie 69 Fred Coe
Me und Gott 18 Whyndham Gittens
Me und Gott 18 L. M. Glackens
Mea Culpa 19 Georges Champavert
Me'Achorei Hasoragim 84 Uri Barbash
Meadow, The 79 Paolo Taviani, Vittorio Taviani
Meal, The 75 R. John Hugh
Mealtimes 67 Edgar Reitz
Mean Dog Blues 78 Mel Stuart
Mean Frank and Crazy Tony 73 Michele Lupo
Mean Johnny Barrows 76 Fred Williamson
Mean Machine, The 74 Robert Aldrich
Mean Season, The 85 Phillip Borsos
Mean Streets 73 Martin Scorsese
Meanest Gal in Town, The 34 Russell Mack
Meanest Man in the World, The 23 Edward F. Cline
Meanest Man in the World, The 43 Sidney Lanfield
Meanest Man on Earth, The 09 Lewin Fitzhamon
Meanest Men in the West, The 67 Samuel Fuller
Means and Ends 85 Gerald Michenaud
Meantime 83 Mike Leigh
Meanwhile, Back at the Ranch 67 Andrew V. McLaglen
Meanwhile, Far from the Front 67 Jack Smight
Measure for Measure 51 Marco Elter
Measure of a Man, The 11 Edwin S. Porter
Measure of a Man, The 16 Jack Conway
Measure of a Man, The 24 Arthur Rosson
Measures Against Fanatics 69 Werner Herzog
Meat 76 Frederick Wiseman
Meat Is Meat 71 Guido Zurli
Meatballs 79 Ivan Reitman
Meatballs Part II 84 Ken Wiederhorn
Meatballs III 86 George Mendeluk
Meatballs III: Summer Job 86 George Mendeluk
Meatcleaver Massacre 75 Evan Lee
Meatless Flyday 44 Friz Freleng
Mecánica Nacional 71 Luis Alcoriza
Mécaniciens de l'Armée de l'Air, Les 59 Claude Lelouch
Mechanic, The 72 Michael Winner
Mechanical Butcher, The 1895 Auguste Lumière, Louis Lumière
Mechanical Cow, The 27 Walt Disney
Mechanical Flea, The 64 Ivan Ivanov-Vano
Mechanical Handy Man, The 37 Walter Lantz
Mechanical Husband, A 10 S. Wormald
Mechanical Legs, The 08 Alf Collins
Mechanical Man 32 Walter Lantz
Mechanical Man, The 58 Ritwik Ghatak
Mechanical Mary Anne, The 10 Lewin Fitzhamon
Mechanical Monsters, The 41 Dave Fleischer
Mechanical Operation of British Tanks 17 J. D. Leventhal
Mechanical Principle 31 Ralph Steiner
Mechanical Saw, The 13 Forest Holger-Madsen

Mechanical Statue and the Ingenious Servant, The *07* J. Stuart Blackton

Mechanics of the Brain *26* Vsevolod I. Pudovkin

Mechanizacja Robót Ziemnych *51* Wojciech Has

Mechta *43* Mikhail Romm

Med Dej i Mina Armar *40* Hasse Ekman

Med Folket för Fosterlandet *39* Sigurd Wallen

Med Glorian på Sned *57* Hasse Ekman

Med Kærlig Hilsen *71* Gabriel Axel

Med Livet Som Insats *39* Alf Sjöberg

Med Mord i Bagaget *61* Tom Younger

Medaglione Insanguinato, Il *74* Massimo Dallamano

Médaille de Sauvetage, La *14* Max Linder

Medal for Benny, A *45* Irving Pichel

Medal for the General *44* Maurice Elvey

Medals *29* John Cromwell, Richard Wallace

Medals *54* Minoru Shibuya

Medan Porten Var Stängd *46* Hasse Ekman

Meddler, The *25* Arthur Rosson

Meddlers, The *12* Allan Dwan

Meddlesome Mike *14* Edwin J. Collins

Meddlin' Stranger, The *27* Richard Thorpe

Meddling Policeman, The *04* William Haggar

Meddling Women *24* Ivan Abramson

Medea *69* Pier Paolo Pasolini

Médecin des Sols *53* Serge Bourguignon

Médecins et Médecins *76* Ousseini, Jean Rouch

Mediator, The *16* Otis Turner

Medical Congress *61* Edgar Reitz

Medical Mystery, A *25* Harcourt Templeman

Medicine Ball Caravan *70* François Reichenbach

Medicine Bend *16* John P. McGowan

Medicine Bottle, The *09* D. W. Griffith

Medicine Man, The *17* Clifford Smith

Medicine Man, The *20* Raoul Barré, Charles Bowers

Medicine Man, The *30* Scott Pembroke

Medicine Man, The *33* Redd Davis

Medicine Man *46* Ray Nazarro

Medicine Men, The *29* Norman Taurog

Medicine Show, The *32* Manny Gould, Ben Harrison

Medico della Mutua, Il *68* Luigi Zampa

Medico e lo Stregone, Il *57* Mario Monicelli

Medico of Painted Springs, The *41* Lambert Hillyer

Medico per Forza *31* Carlo Campogalliani

Medieval Dutch Sculpture *51* Bert Haanstra

Medikus, A *16* Michael Curtiz

Medio Siglo en un Pincel *60* Jorge Grau

Mediocres, Los *62* Servando González

Meditation on Violence *48* Maya Deren

Mediterranean Holiday *64* Hermann Leitner, Rudolph Nussgruber

Méditerranée *63* Jean-Daniel Pollet

Medium, The *34* Vernon Sewell

Medium, Il *51* Alexander Hammid, Gian Carlo Menotti

Medium, The *51* Alexander Hammid, Gian Carlo Menotti

Medium *85* Jacek Koprowicz

Medium Cool *69* Haskell Wexler

Medium Exposed, The *06* J. H. Martin

Među Jastrebovima *64* Alfred Vohrer

Medusa *73* Gordon Hessler

Medusa Against the Son of Hercules *63* Marcello Baldi

Medusa Touch, The *78* Jack Gold

Meet Boston Blackie *40* Robert Florey

Meet Danny Wilson *51* Joseph Pevney

Meet Dr. Christian *39* Bernard Vorhaus

Meet John Doe *41* Frank Capra

Meet John Doughboy *41* Robert Clampett

Meet Marlon Brando *65* Albert Maysles, David Maysles

Meet Maxwell Archer *39* John Paddy Carstairs

Meet Me After the Show *51* Richard Sale

Meet Me at Dawn *46* Peter Cresswell, Thornton Freeland

Meet Me at the Fair *52* Jack Daniels, Douglas Sirk

Meet Me in Las Vegas *55* Roy Rowland

Meet Me in Moscow *66* Georgy Danelia

Meet Me in St. Louis *44* Vincente Minnelli

Meet Me on Broadway *46* Leigh Jason

Meet Me Tonight *52* Anthony Pelissier

Meet Miss Bobby Socks *44* Glenn Tryon

Meet Miss Marple *61* George Pollock

Meet Miss Mozart *37* Yvan Noe

Meet Mr. Beat *61* George Ivan Barnett

Meet Mr. Callaghan *54* Charles Saunders

Meet Mr. Lucifer *52* Anthony Pelissier

Meet Mr. Malcolm *54* Daniel Birt

Meet Mr. Penny *38* David MacDonald

Meet Mother Magoo *56* Pete Burness

Meet My Girl *26* Lloyd Bacon

Meet My Sister *32* John Daumery

Meet My Wife *17* George Marshall

Meet Nero Wolfe *36* Herbert J. Biberman

Meet Peter Foss *58* Wolfgang Becker

Meet Sexton Blake *44* John Harlow

Meet Simon Cherry *49* Godfrey Grayson

Meet the Baron *33* Walter Lang

Meet the Boy Friend *37* Ralph Staub

Meet the Boyfriend *30* Norman Taurog

Meet the Chump *41* Edward F. Cline

Meet the Duke *49* James Corbett

Meet the Fleet *40* B. Reeves Eason

Meet the Folks *27* Al Christie

Meet the Girls *38* Eugene Forde

Meet the Hollowheads *89* Tom Burman

Meet the Mayor *38* Ralph Ceder

Meet the Missus *37* Joseph Santley

Meet the Missus *40* Malcolm St. Clair

Meet the Mob *42* Jean Yarbrough

Meet the Navy *46* Alfred Travers

Meet the Nelsons *52* Frederick De Cordova

Meet the People *44* Charles Reisner

Meet the Pioneers *48* Lindsay Anderson

Meet the Prince *26* Joseph E. Henabery

Meet the Stewarts *42* Alfred E. Green

Meet the Wife *31* Leslie Pearce

Meet the Wildcat *40* Arthur Lubin

Meet Whiplash Willie *66* Billy Wilder

Meeting, The *64* Mamoun Hassan

Meeting at Midnight *44* Phil Rosen

Meeting Hearts *14* Victor Sjöström

Meeting in America *60* Leonid Varmalov

Meeting in July *77* Karel Kachyňa

Meeting in Warsaw *55* Jerzy Bossak*

Meeting Life *52* Gösta Werner

Meeting on the Atlantic *79* Jerzy Kawalerowicz

Meeting on the Elbe *49* Grigori Alexandrov

Meeting Ships *15* Victor Sjöström

Meeting Theda Bara *18* Raoul Barré, Charles Bowers

Meeting with France *60* Sergei Yutkevich

Meeting with Maxim *41* Sergei Gerasimov

Meeting with President Ho Chi Minh *68* Joris Ivens, Marceline Loridan

Meetings and Partings *74* Elior Ishmukhamedov

Meetings of Anna, The *78* Chantal Akerman

Meetings with Remarkable Men *79* Peter Brook

Meetings with Warsaw *65* Jan Łomnicki

Méfiez-Vous de Votre Bonne *20* Robert Saidreau

Méfiez-Vous des Blondes *50* André Hunebelle

Méfiez-Vous Fillettes *57* Yves Allégret

Méfiez-Vous Mesdames *63* André Hunebelle

Mefisto Funk *87* Marco Poma

Meg *26* Walter Shaw

Még Kér a Nép *72* Miklós Jancsó

Meg o' the Woods *18* Bertram Phillips

Meg the Lady *16* Maurice Elvey

Megaforce *82* Hal Needham

Meg'Alexandros, O *80* Theodoros Angelopoulos

Megáll az Idő *81* Péter Gothár

Mégano, El *55* Julio García Espinosa, Tomás Gutiérrez Alea

Megara *75* Sakis Maniatis, Yorgos Tsemberopoulos

Mégère Récalcitrante, Le *00* Ferdinand Zecca

Megfagyott Gyermek, A *21* Béla Balázs

Megfelelő Ember, A *59* György Révész

Megfelelő Ember Kényes Feladatra *85* János Kovácsi

Meghe Dhaka Tara *60* Ritwik Ghatak

Meghey Dhaaka Taara *60* Ritwik Ghatak

Meglio Baciare un Cobra *86* Massimo Pirri

Meglio Vedova *68* Duccio Tessari

Megszállottak *61* Károly Makk

Meia Noite Levarei a Sua Alma, A *66* José Mojica Marins

Meier *86* Peter Timm

Meier aus Berlin *18* Ernst Lubitsch

Meigetsu Sōmatō *51* Teinosuke Kinugasa

Meiguo Xin *86* Allen Fong

Meiji Haru Aki *68* Heinosuke Gosho

Meilleur de la Vie, Le *85* Renaud Victor

Meilleure Bobonne, La *30* Marc Allégret

Meilleure Façon de Marcher, La *76* Claude Miller

Meilleure Maîtresse, La *29* René Hervil

Meilleure Part, La *55* Yves Allégret

Mein Herz Ruft nach Dir *34* Carmine Gallone

Mein Ist die Welt *33* Harry Piel

Mein Kampf *59* Ingemar Ejve, Erwin Leiser, Tore Sjöberg

Mein Kampf – My Crimes *40* Norman Lee

Mein Leben für Maria Isabell *35* Erich Waschneck

Mein Leopold *31* Hans Steinhoff

Mein Lieber Schatz *85* Beate Klockner

Mein Mann der Nachtredakteur *19* Urban Gad

Mein Schulfreund *60* Robert Siodmak

Mein Sohn der Herr Minister *37* Veidt Harlan

Mein Vater, der Schauspieler *56* Robert Siodmak

Mein Wille Ist Gesetz *19* Lupu Pick

Meine Cousine aus Warschau *31* Carl Boese

Meine Frau, die Filmschauspielerin *18* Ernst Lubitsch

Meine Frau die Hochstaplerin *32* Kurt Gerron

Meine Frau die Schützenkönigin *35* Carl Boese

Meine Freundin Barbara *38* Fritz Kirchhoff

Meine Tante, Deine Tante *39* Carl Boese

Meine Vier Jungen *44* Günther Rittau

Meines Vaters Pferde *54* Gerhard Lamprecht

Meir Ezofewicz *11* Aleksander Hertz

Meisje met het Rode Haar, Het *81* Ben Verbong

Meisterdetektiv, Der *34* Franz Seitz

Meistersinger *27* Ludwig Berger

Meistersinger von Nürnberg, Die *27* Ludwig Berger

Meitō Bijomaru *45* Kenji Mizoguchi

Mej och Dej *68* Astrid Henning-Jensen

Mekagojira no Gyakushū *75* Inoshiro Honda

Mekhanika Golovnovo Mozga *26* Vsevolod I. Pudovkin

Melancholia *89* Andi Engel

Melancólicas, Las *71* Rafael Moreno Alba

Melanie *82* Rex Bromfield

Melanie Rose *89* Amos Kollek

Melba *53* Lewis Milestone

Melbourne Rendezvous *57* M. Lucot

Melgarejo *37* Florencio Parravicini

Melinda *72* Hugh Robertson

Melissa of the Hills *17* James Kirkwood

Melissokomos, O *86* Theodoros Angelopoulos

Mellow Quartette, The *25* Earl Hurd

Mélo *32* Paul Czinner

Mélo *86* Alain Resnais

Melodía de Arrabal *33* Louis Gasnier

Melodía Prohibida, La *33* Frank R. Strayer

Melodie der Liebe *34* Georg Jacoby

Melodie der Welt *29* Walter Ruttmann

Mélodie en Sous-Sol *62* Henri Verneuil

Mélodie Éterne *40* Carmine Gallone

Melodies *26* Francis Ford

Melodies from Grand Hotel *52* Robert Henryson

Melodies of the Moment *38* Horace Shepherd

Melodies of the Veri Suburb *73* Georgy Shengelaya

Melody *71* Andrew Birkin, Waris Hussein

Melody and Moonlight *40* Joseph Santley

Melody and Romance *37* Maurice Elvey

Melody Club *49* Monty Berman

Melody Cruise *33* Mark Sandrich

Melody for Three *41* Erle C. Kenton

Melody for Two *37* Louis King

Melody Girl *40* Lew Landers

Melody Haunts My Memory, The *80* Rajko Grlić

Melody in F *32* Widgey R. Newman

Melody in Gray *77* Masahiro Shinoda

Melody in Spring *34* Norman Z. McLeod

Melody in the Dark *48* Robert Jordan Hill

Melody Inn *43* George Marshall

Melody Lane *29* Robert F. Hill

Melody Lane *41* Charles Lamont

Melody Lingers On, The *35* David Burton

Melody Maker, The *33* Leslie Hiscott

Melody Maker *46* William Berke

Melody Man *30* Roy William Neill

Melody of Death *22* F. Martin Thornton

Melody of Life *32* Gregory La Cava

Melody of Love *28* Arch Heath

Melody of Love *39* Stuart Heisler, Archie Mayo

Melody of Love *54* Mario Costa

Melody of My Heart *36* Wilfred Noy

Melody of the Heart *30* Hans Schwarz

Melody of the Plains *37* Sam Newfield

Melody of the Sea, The *34* John W. Brunius*

Melody of the World, The *29* Walter Ruttmann

Melody of Youth *39* Stuart Heisler, Archie Mayo

Melody Parade *43* Arthur Dreifuss

Melody Ranch *40* Joseph Santley

Melody Roundup *46* Robert E. Tansey

Melody Time *48* Clyde Geronimi, Wilfred Jackson, Jack Kinney, Hamilton Luske, Ben Sharpsteen

Melody Trail *35* Joseph Kane

Mélomane, Le *03* Georges Méliès

Melomaniac, The *03* Georges Méliès

Melon Affair, The *79* Art Lieberman

Melon-Drama, A *31* Mark Sandrich

Melons Baladeurs, Les *11* Émile Cohl

Melting Millions *17* Otis Turner

Melting Millions *27* Spencer G. Bennet

Melting Pot, The *15* Sidney Olcott

Melting Pot, The *46* Arthur Dreifuss

Melvin and Howard *80* Jonathan Demme

Melvin Purvis: G-Man *74* Dan Curtis

Melvin, Son of Alvin *84* John Eastway

Melvin's Revenge *49* Jerry Lewis

Member of Parliament *20* Yakov Protazanov

Member of Tattersall's, A *19* Albert Ward

Member of the Government *37* Josef Heifits, Alexander Zarkhi

Member of the Jury *37* Bernerd Mainwaring

Member of the Tattersall's, A *19* Albert Ward

Member of the Wedding, The *52* Fred Zinnemann

Memed My Hawk *83* Peter Ustinov

Memento Mei *63* Martin Charlot

Mementos *86* Teguh Karya

Memo for Joe *44* Richard Fleischer

Mémoire, La *82* Youssef Chahine

Mémoire de Simone *86* Chris Marker

Mémoire des Apparences *86* Raúl Ruiz

Mémoire des Apparences: La Vie Est un Songe *86* Raúl Ruiz

Mémoire Fertile, La *80* Michel Khleifi

Mémoire Tatouée, La *86* Ridha Behi

Mémoires d'un Juif Tropical *86* Joseph Morder

Memoirs *84* Bachar Chbib

Memoirs of a French Whore *79* Daniel Duval

Memoirs of a Sinner, The *86* Wojciech Has

Memoirs of a Survivor *81* David Gladwell

Memoirs of Prison *84* Nelson Pereira Dos Santos

Memorandum *67* Donald Brittain, John Spotton

Memorias del Subdesarrollo *68* Tomás Gutiérrez Alea

Memórias do Cárcere *84* Nelson Pereira Dos Santos

Memórias e Confissões *82* Manoel De Oliveira

Memorias y Olvidos *88* Simon Feldman

Memories *25* Arthur Backner

Memories *78* Wolfgang Staudte

Memories and Confessions *82* Manoel De Oliveira

Memories from the Boston Club *09* Charles Magnusson

Memories in Men's Souls *14* Van Dyke Brooke

Memories of a Marriage *89* Kaspar Rostrup

Memories of a Tropical Jew *86* Joseph Morder

Memories of Me *88* Henry Winkler

Memories of Prison *84* Nelson Pereira Dos Santos

Memories of the Great Sacrifice *29* R. E. Jeffrey

Memories of Underdevelopment *68* Tomás Gutiérrez Alea

Memories of Young Days *31* Heinosuke Gosho

Memories – Psalm 46 *27* Charles Barnett

Memories Within Miss Aggie *73* Gerard Damiano

Memory *14* Warwick Buckland

Memory *71* Grigori Chukhrai

Memory Expert, The *35* Clyde Bruckman

Memory for Two *45* Del Lord

Memory Lane *26* John M. Stahl

Memory of Appearances *86* Raúl Ruiz

Memory of Appearances: Life Is a Dream *86* Raúl Ruiz

Memory of His Mother, The *08* Percy Stow

Memory of Justice, The *75* Marcel Ophüls

Memory of Love *47* John Cromwell

Memory of Our Day, The *63* Jan Němec

Memory of Simone *86* Chris Marker

Memory of Us *74* H. Kaye Dyal

Memphis Belle, The *43* William Wyler

Memphis Belle *90* Michael Caton-Jones

Men *24* Dmitri Buchowetzki

Men, The *50* Fred Zinnemann

Men... *85* Doris Dörrie

Men Against the Sea *35* Vernon Sewell
Men Against the Sky *40* Leslie Goodwins
Men Against the Sun *53* Brendan Stafford
Men and Beasts *62* Sergei Gerasimov, Lutz Kohlert
Men and Jobs *33* Alexander Macharet
Men and Microbes *51* Max De Haas
Men and the Nile *72* Youssef Chahine
Men and Wolves *56* Giuseppe De Santis
Men and Women *14* James Kirkwood
Men and Women *25* William DeMille
Men Are Children Twice *53* Gilbert Gunn
Men Are Like That *29* Frank Tuttle
Men Are Like That *31* George B. Seitz
Men Are Not Gods *36* Walter Reisch
Men Are Such Fools *32* William Nigh
Men Are Such Fools *38* Busby Berkeley
Men Are Such Rascals *32* Mario Camerini
Men Are That Way *39* Arthur Maria Rabenalt
Men at Work *90* Emilio Estevez
Men Behind Bars *53* Walter Doniger
Men Behind the Meters *40* Arthur Elton
Men Behind the Sun *89* T. F. Mous
Men Call It Love *31* Edgar Selwyn
Men Can't Be Raped *78* Jörn Donner
Men Don't Leave *90* Paul Brickman
Men in Danger *37* Pat Jackson
Men in Darkness *55* Arne Mattsson
Men in Exile *37* John Farrow
Men in Fright *38* George Sidney
Men in Her Diary *45* Charles Barton
Men in Her Life *31* William Beaudine
Men in Her Life, The *41* Gregory Ratoff
Men in Love *90* Marc Huestis
Men in the Raw *23* George Marshall
Men in War *56* Anthony Mann
Men in White *34* Richard Boleslawski
Men Like These *31* Walter Summers
Men Must Fight *33* Edgar Selwyn
Men o' War *29* Lewis R. Foster
Men of Action *35* Alvin J. Neitz
Men of America *32* Ralph Ince
Men of Arnhem *44* Brian Desmond Hurst, Terence Young
Men of Baku *38* Victor Turin
Men of Boys Town *41* Norman Taurog
Men of Brazil *60* Carlos Anselmo, Otto Lopes Barbosa, Nelson Marcellino De Carvalho
Men of Chance *32* George Archainbaud
Men of Daring *27* Albert S. Rogell
Men of Destiny *42* Ray Enright
Men of Ireland *38* Richard Bird
Men of Marble *55* Gillo Pontecorvo
Men of Novgorod *43* Boris Barnet
Men of Rochdale *44* Compton Bennett
Men of San Quentin *42* William Beaudine
Men of Sherwood Forest *54* Val Guest
Men of Steel *26* George Archainbaud
Men of Steel *32* George King
Men of Steel *37* William Nigh
Men of Steel *80* Steve Carver
Men of Texas *42* Ray Enright
Men of the Alps *36* Harry Watt
Men of the Alps *39* Alberto Cavalcanti
Men of the Blue Cross *55* Andrzej Munk
Men of the Caspian *44* Grigori Alexandrov
Men of the Deep *45* Del Lord

Men of the Desert *17* W. S. Van Dyke
Men of the Fighting Lady *54* Andrew Marton
Men of the Hour *35* Lambert Hillyer
Men of the Lightship *40* David MacDonald
Men of the Mines *45* David MacKane
Men of the Night *26* Albert S. Rogell
Men of the Night *34* Lambert Hillyer
Men of the North *30* Hal Roach
Men of the Plains *36* Robert F. Hill
Men of the Rice Fields *57* Tadashi Imai
Men of the Sea *33* Carol Reed
Men of the Sea *38* Alexander Feinzimmer
Men of the Sea *38* Chano Urueta
Men of the Sea *40* Norman Walker
Men of the Sky *31* Alfred E. Green
Men of the Sky *42* B. Reeves Eason
Men of the Tenth *70* John Cardos
Men of the Timberland *41* John Rawlins
Men of Tohoku, The *57* Kon Ichikawa
Men of Tomorrow *32* Zoltán Korda, Leontine Sagan
Men of Tomorrow *59* Alfred Travers
Men of Two Worlds *46* Thorold Dickinson
Men of Yesterday *36* John Baxter
Men of Zanzibar, The *22* Rowland V. Lee
Men on Call *30* John G. Blystone
Men on Her Mind *35* Alfred E. Green
Men on Her Mind *36* William Dieterle
Men on Her Mind *44* Wallace Fox
Men on the Bridge *59* Alexander Zarkhi
Men on Wings *35* Yuli Raizman
Men Only Mean Trouble *86* Mihailo Vukobratović
Men Prefer Fat Girls *81* Jean-Marie Poire
Men She Married, The *16* Travers Vale
Men Were Deceivers Ever *11* Dave Aylott
Men Were Deceivers Ever *17* Bert Haldane
Men Who Forget *23* Reuben Gillmer
Men Who Have Made Love to Me *18* Arthur Berthelet
Men Who Tread on the Tiger's Tail *45* Akira Kurosawa
Men Will Deceive *14* Lewin Fitzhamon
Men with Steel Faces *35* Otto Brower, B. Reeves Eason
Men with Wings *38* William A. Wellman
Men Without Honour *39* Widgey R. Newman
Men Without Law *30* Louis King
Men Without Names *35* Ralph Murphy
Men Without Souls *40* Nick Grindé
Men Without Women *29* Andrew Bennison, John Ford
Men Without Women *83* Derek Burbidge
Men, Women and Money *19* George Melford
Men Women Love *31* James Cruze
Menace, The *13* Allan Dwan
Menace, La *15* Henri Fescourt
Menace, The *18* John S. Robertson
Menace, The *32* Roy William Neill
Menace *34* Adrian Brunel
Menace *34* Ralph Murphy
Menace, La *60* Gérard Oury
Menace, The *60* Gérard Oury
Menace, La *77* Alain Corneau
Menace in the Night *56* Lance Comfort
Menace of the Mute, The *15* Ashley Miller

Menace on the Mountain *72* Vincent McEveety
Menace to Carlotta, The *14* Allan Dwan
Ménaces *39* Edmond T. Gréville
Menacing Shadows *46* Derwin Abrahams
Ménage *86* Bertrand Blier
Ménage à Trois *82* Bryan Forbes
Menagerie, The *67* Satyajit Ray
Mended Lute, The *09* D. W. Griffith
Mender of Nets, The *12* D. W. Griffith
Mendiants, Les *87* Benoît Jacquot
Ménesgazda, A *78* András Kovács
Ménestrel de la Reine Anne, Le *13* Louis Feuillade
Meneur de Joies, Le *29* Charles Burguet
Mengzhong Ren *86* Tony Au
Ménilmontant *24* Dmitri Kirsanov
Mennesker Mødes og Sød Musik Opstår i Hjertet *67* Henning Carlsen
Men's Club, The *86* Peter Medak
Men's Outing *64* Wolfgang Staudte
Mens Pesten Raser *13* Forest Holger-Madsen
Mens Sagføreren Sover *45* Johan Jacobsen
Mensch am Wege, Der *23* William Dieterle
Mensch Gegen Mensch *24* Hans Steinhoff
Mensch Verstreut und Welt Verkehrt *75* Raúl Ruiz
Menschen am Sonntag *29* Robert Siodmak, Edgar G. Ulmer, Fred Zinnemann
Menschen Die das Stauferjahr Vorbereiten, Die *77* Alexander Kluge, Maximiliane Mainka
Menschen Die die Staufer-Ausstellung Vorbereiten, Die *77* Alexander Kluge, Maximiliane Mainka
Menschen Hinter Gittern *30* Pál Fejős
Menschen im Hotel *59* Gottfried Reinhardt
Menschen im Käfig *30* E. A. Dupont
Menschen im Netz *59* Franz Peter Wirth
Menschen im Sturm *34* Pál Fejős
Menschen im Werk *58* Gerhard Lamprecht
Menschen in Ketten *19* Karl Grüne, Fred Zelnik
Menschen Ohne Namen *32* Gustav Ucicky
Menschen und Tiere *62* Sergei Gerasimov, Lutz Kohlert
Menschen vom Varieté *39* Josef von Baky
Mensonge de Nina Petrovna, Le *37* Victor Tourjansky
Mensonges *58* Pierre Granier-Deferre
Mental Poise *38* Roy Rowland
Mental Suicide *13* Allan Dwan
Menteurs, Les *61* Edmond T. Gréville
Menteurs, Les *79* Claude Chabrol
Mentioned in Confidence *17* Edgar Jones
Mentiras Piadosas *89* Arturo Ripstein
Menuet Lilliputien, Le *05* Georges Méliès
Menzogna, La *16* Augusto Genina
Meoto Boshi *26* Teinosuke Kinugasa
Mephisto *12* Alfred De Manby, F. Martin Thornton
Mephisto *80* István Szabó
Mephisto Waltz, The *70* Paul Wendkos
Mephisto's Plight *11* A. E. Coleby
Mépris, Le *63* Jean-Luc Godard
Mépris N'Aura Qu'un Temps, Le *70* Arthur Lamothe

Mer des Corbeaux, La 30 Jean Epstein
Mer Om Oss Barn i Bullerbyn 87 Lasse
  Hallström
Mer Rouge, La 52 Jacques-Yves Cousteau
Mer Sera Haute à 16 Heures, La 54 Michel
  Drach
Mera Lahoo 87 Virendra
Mera Naam Joker 70 Raj Kapoor
Mera Suhaag 88 Ajay Shama
Meraviglie di Aladino, Le 61 Mario Bava,
  Henry Levin
Meravigliose Avventure di Marco Polo,
  Le 64 Christian-Jaque, Denys De la
  Patellière, Noel Howard, Cliff Lyons
Mercado de Humildes, El 86 René Car-
  dona, Jr.
Mercante di Venezia, Il 11 Ugo Falena
Mercato delle Facce, Il 52 Valerio Zurlini
Mercedes 35 José Castellvi
Mercenaire, Le 61 Baccio Bandini, Étienne
  Périer
Mercenari Raccontano, I 85 Sergio Pastore
Mercenaries, The 67 Jack Cardiff
Mercenaries, The 80 Chuck Workman
Mercenaries, The 85 Sergio Pastore
Mercenaries, The 87 Yoshimitsu Morita
Mercenario, Il 61 Baccio Bandini, Étienne
  Périer
Mercenario, Il 68 Sergio Corbucci
Mercenario, El 69 Dieter Müller
Mercenarios, Los 62 Piero Costa
Mercenary, The 68 Sergio Corbucci
Mercenary Fighters 88 Riki Shelach Nissi-
  moff
Mercenary Motive, A 25 Harcourt Tem-
  pleman
Merchant Homme, Le 21 Charles De Mar-
  san, Charles Maudru
Merchant Marine 54 Georges Franju
Merchant of Four Seasons, The 71 Rainer
  Werner Fassbinder
Merchant of Slaves 49 Duilio Coletti
Merchant of Venice, The 08 J. Stuart
  Blackton
Merchant of Venice, The 11 Ugo Falena
Merchant of Venice, The 14 Phillips
  Smalley, Lois Weber
Merchant of Venice, The 16 Walter West
Merchant of Venice, The 22 Challis San-
  derson
Merchant of Venice, The 27 Widgey R.
  Newman
Merci Monsieur Robertson 86 Pierre Levie
Merci, Natercia 60 Pierre Kast
Mercia the Flower Girl 13 Arthur Char-
  rington
Mercy Island 41 William Morgan
Mercy Plane 39 Richard Harlan
Mère du Moine, La 09 Louis Feuillade
Mère et l'Enfant, La 59 Jacques Demy,
  Jean Masson
Mère, une Fille, Une 81 Márta Mészáros
Merely Mary Ann 16 John G. Adolfi
Merely Mary Ann 20 Edward J. LeSaint
Merely Mary Ann 31 Henry King
Merely Mr. Hawkins 38 Maclean Rogers
Merely Mrs. Stubbs 17 Henry Edwards
Merely Players 18 Oscar Apfel
Mères Françaises 17 René Hervil, Louis
  Mercanton

Meres tou 36, I 72 Theodoros Angelopou-
  los
Meridian 90 Charles Band
Méridienne, La 88 Jean-François Amiguet
Merle, Le 58 Evelyn Lambert, Norman
  McLaren
Merlin the Magic Mouse 67 Alex Lovy
Merlo Maschio, Il 71 Pasquale Festa Cam-
  panile
Merlusse 35 Marcel Pagnol
Mermaid, The 04 Georges Méliès
Mermaid, The 12 Lewin Fitzhamon
Mermaid, The 60 Kao Li
Mermaids 90 Richard Benjamin
Mermaids of the Thames 14 Kelly Storrie
Mermaids of Tiburon, The 62 John Lamb
Merrie Old Soul, A 35 Friz Freleng
Merrill's Marauders 61 Samuel Fuller
Merrily We Go to... 32 Dorothy Arzner
Merrily We Go to Hell 32 Dorothy Arzner
Merrily We Live 38 Norman Z. McLeod
Merrily Yours 33 Charles Lamont
Merry Andrew 58 Michael Kidd
Merry Beggars, The 10 Lewin Fitzhamon
Merry Cafe, The 20 Raoul Barré, Charles
  Bowers
Merry Cafe 36 Manny Gould, Ben Harri-
  son
Merry Cavalier, The 26 Noel Mason Smith
Merry Chase, The 48 Giorgio Bianchi
Merry Christmas, Mr. Lawrence 82 Nagisa
  Oshima
Merry Christmas to All Our Friends, A 11
  Stuart Kinder
Merry Circus, The 50 Jiří Trnka
Merry Comes to Stay 37 George King
Merry Comes to Town 37 George King
Merry Dog 33 Walter Lantz
Merry Dwarfs, The 29 Walt Disney
Merry Frinks, The 34 Alfred E. Green
Merry Frolics of Satan, The 06 Georges
  Méliès
Merry-Go-Round, A 1896 Georges Méliès
Merry-Go-Round 19 Edmund Lawrence
Merry-Go-Round 23 Rupert Julian, Erich
  von Stroheim
Merry-Go-Round 48 Josh Binney
Merry-Go-Round 55 Zoltán Fábri
Merry-Go-Round 78 Jacques Rivette
Merry-Go-Round in a Market Square 87
  Nikolai Stambula
Merry-Go-Round of 1938 37 Irving Cum-
  mings
Merry Husband, The 19 Ernst Lubitsch
Merry Jail, A 17 Ernst Lubitsch
Merry Jester, The 12 Walter R. Booth
Merry Madcaps 43 Reginald LeBorg
Merry Mannequins 37 Ubbe Iwerks
Merry Men of Sherwood, The 32 Widgey
  R. Newman
Merry Microbes, The 09 Émile Cohl
Merry Minstrel Magoo 59 Rudy Larriva
Merry Monahans, The 44 Charles Lamont
Merry Night, A 14 Dave Aylott
Merry Old Soul, The 33 Walter Lantz
Merry Sea Trip, A 38 Alwin Elling
Merry Widow, The 18 Michael Curtiz
Merry Widow, The 25 Erich von Stroheim
Merry Widow, The 34 Ernst Lubitsch
Merry Widow, The 52 Kurt Bernhardt

Merry Widow Craze, The 08 Edwin S.
  Porter
Merry Widow Waltz Craze, The 08 Edwin
  S. Porter
Merry Widow's Ball, The 39 Alwin Elling
Merry Wisdom 67 Jean-Luc Godard
Merry Wives, The 38 Otakar Vávra
Merry Wives of Gotham 25 Monta Bell
Merry Wives of Pimple, The 16 Fred
  Evans, Joe Evans
Merry Wives of Reno, The 34 H. Bruce
  Humberstone
Merry Wives of Tobias Rourke, The 72
  John Board
Merry Wives of Windsor, The 52 Georg
  Wildhagen
Merry Wives of Windsor, The 65 Georg
  Tressler
Merrymakers 25 Lloyd Bacon
Merton of the Goofies 25 Wesley Ruggles
Merton of the Movies 24 James Cruze
Merton of the Movies 47 Robert Alton
Mertvye Dushi 60 Leonid Trauberg
Merveilleuse Vie de Jeanne d'Arc, La 29
  Marco De Gastyne
Merveilleuse Visite, La 74 Marcel Carné
Merveilleux Éventail Vivant, Le 04 Georges
  Méliès
Merzavets 88 Vaghif Mustafayev
Mes, Het 60 Fons Rademakers
Més-Estimations 29 Edmond T. Gréville
Mes Femmes Américaines 65 Gian Luigi
  Polidoro
Mes Petites Amoureuses 75 Jean Eustache
Mesa of Lost Women, The 49 Ron Or-
  mond, Herbert Tevos
Mésaventure de Shylock, Une 05 Georges
  Méliès
Mésaventure d'un Charbonnier 00 Alice
  Guy-Blaché
Mésaventures de M. Boit-Sans-Soif, Les 04
  Georges Méliès
Mésaventures d'un Aéronaute 00 Georges
  Méliès
Mésaventures d'une Tête de Veau, Les
  1898 Alice Guy-Blaché
Mesdames et Messieurs 65 Pietro Germi
Mese a Tizenkét Találatról 56 Károly
  Makk
Meseautó 36 Béla Gaál
Mesék az Írógépről 16 Alexander Korda
Meshes of the Afternoon 43 Maya Deren,
  Alexander Hammid
Meshi 51 Mikio Naruse
Meshte Nastreshu 63 Mikhail Karyukov,
  Otar Koberidze
Meshwar Omar 86 Mohamed Khan
Meskal le Contrebandier 08 Victorin Jasset
Mesmerian Experiment, A 05 Georges
  Méliès
Mesmerist, The 1898 George Albert Smith
Mesmerist, The 15 Percy Nash
Mesmerized 85 Michael Laughlin
Mesquite Buckaroo 39 Harry S. Webb
Messa da Requiem 69 Henri-Georges
  Clouzot
Messa È Finità, La 85 Nanni Moretti
Message, The 09 D. W. Griffith
Message, The 18 Henry Edwards
Message, The 30 Sewell Collins

Miami Blues *89* George Armitage
Miami Exposé *56* Fred F. Sears
Miami Golem *86* Alberto De Martino
Miami Rendezvous *63* Wynn Miles
Miami Story, The *54* Fred F. Sears
Miarka la Fille à l'Ours *20* Louis Mercanton
Miarka the Daughter of the Bear *20* Louis Mercanton
Mice and Men *16* J. Searle Dawley
Mice and Money *20* Frank Moser
Mice Follies *54* Joseph Barbera, William Hanna
Mice Follies *60* Robert McKimson
Mice Will Play, The *38* Tex Avery
Michael *24* Carl Theodor Dreyer
Michael and Mary *31* Victor Saville
Michael Kohlhaas *69* Volker Schlöndorff
Michael Kohlhaas—Der Rebell *69* Volker Schlöndorff
Michael Kohlhaas—The Rebel *69* Volker Schlöndorff
Michael McShane, Matchmaker *12* Lawrence Trimble
Michael O'Halloran *23* James Leo Meehan
Michael O'Halloran *37* Karl Brown
Michael O'Halloran *48* John Rawlins
Michael Shayne, Private Detective *40* Eugene Forde
Michael Strogoff *10* J. Searle Dawley
Michael Strogoff *14* Alice Guy-Blaché
Michael Strogoff *26* Victor Tourjansky
Michael Strogoff *37* George Nicholls, Jr.
Michael Strogoff *56* Carmine Gallone
Miche *32* Jean De Marguenat
Michel Strogoff *26* Victor Tourjansky
Michel Strogoff *36* Jacques De Baroncelli
Michel Strogoff *56* Carmine Gallone
Michel Strogoff *68* Georges Lautner
Michelangelo Antonioni *65* Gianfranco Mingozzi
Michelangelo Antonioni—Storia di un Autore *65* Gianfranco Mingozzi
Micheline *20* Jean Kemm
Michelino la B *56* Ermanno Olmi
Michelle *67* Henri Jacques
Michigan Kid, The *28* Irvin Willat
Michigan Kid, The *47* Ray Taylor
Michurin *47* Alexander Dovzhenko, Yulia Solntseva
Mickey *18* F. Richard Jones
Mickey *48* Ralph Murphy
Mickey Cuts Up *31* Burton Gillett
Mickey in Arabia *32* Wilfred Jackson
Mickey Magnate *49* Márton Keleti
Mickey Mouse Anniversary Show, The *68* Ward Kimball, Robert Stevenson
Mickey One *64* Arthur Penn
Mickey Steps Out *31* Burton Gillett
Mickey the Kid *36* Arthur Lubin
Mickey's Choo Choo *29* Walt Disney, Ubbe Iwerks
Mickey's Christmas Carol *83* Burny Mattinson
Mickey's Follies *29* Walt Disney, Ubbe Iwerks
Mickey's Orphans *31* Burton Gillett
Mickey's Pal *12* Alice Guy-Blaché
Mickey's Revue *32* Wilfred Jackson
Micki and Maude *84* Blake Edwards

Micki + Maude *84* Blake Edwards
Microbe, The *19* Henry Otto
Microchip Killer, The *88* Adolf Winkelmann
Microscope Mystery, The *16* Paul Powell
Microscopia *66* Richard Fleischer
Microscopie à Bord d'un Bateau de Pêche *36* Jean Painlevé
Microwave Massacre *79* Wayne Berwick
Micsoda Éjszaka *58* György Révész
Mid-Day Miss *68* Rolf Emyl
Mid-Day Mistress *68* Rolf Emyl
Mid-Lent Procession in Paris *1897* Georges Méliès
Mid-Nightly Wedding, The *14* Toby Cooper
Midaregami *61* Teinosuke Kinugasa
Midaregumo *67* Mikio Naruse
Midareru *64* Mikio Naruse
Midas Run *69* Alf Kjellin
Midas Touch, The *39* David MacDonald
Midchannel *20* Harry Garson
Midday *31* Josef Heifits, Alexander Zarkhi
Middle Age Crazy *80* John Trent
Middle Age Spread *79* John Reid
Middle Course, The *61* Montgomery Tully
Middle of Nowhere *61* Don Chaffey
Middle of the Night *59* Delbert Mann
Middle of the Road Is a Very Dead End, The *74* Alexander Kluge, Edgar Reitz
Middle of the World, The *74* Alain Tanner
Middle Passage *78* Tom Fielding
Middle Watch, The *30* Norman Walker
Middle Watch, The *39* Thomas Bentley
Middleman, The *15* George Loane Tucker
Middleman, The *75* Satyajit Ray
Middleton Family at the N.Y. World's Fair, The *39* Robert Snody
Midinette *17* René Hervil, Louis Mercanton
Midlanders, The *20* Joseph De Grasse, Ida May Park
Midnatsgæsten *24* Forest Holger-Madsen
Midnatsjægernen *27* Forest Holger-Madsen
Midnight *22* Maurice Campbell
Midnight *31* George King
Midnight *34* Chester Erskine
Midnight *39* Mitchell Leisen
Midnight *81* John Russo
Midnight *87* Ka On Yeung
Midnight *89* Norman Thaddeus Vane
Midnight Adventure, A *09* D. W. Griffith
Midnight Adventure, A *13* Frank Wilson
Midnight Adventure, The *28* Duke Worne
Midnight Alarm, The *23* David Smith
Midnight Alibi *34* Alan Crosland
Midnight Angel *41* Ralph Murphy
Midnight at Madame Tussaud's *36* George Pearson
Midnight at Maxim's *15* George L. Sargent
Midnight at the Wax Museum *36* George Pearson
Midnight Auto Supply *78* James Polakoff
Midnight Bell, A *21* Charles Ray
Midnight Bride, The *20* William Humphrey
Midnight Burglar, The *18* Robert Ensminger

Midnight Cabaret *23* Larry Semon
Midnight Caller, The *80* Percival Rubens
Midnight Canyon *64* Rolf Olsen
Midnight Club *33* Alexander Hall, George Somnes
Midnight Cop *89* Peter Patzak
Midnight Court *37* Frank McDonald
Midnight Cowboy *69* John Schlesinger
Midnight Crossing *88* Roger Holzberg
Midnight Cupid, A *10* D. W. Griffith
Midnight Daddies *29* Mack Sennett
Midnight Elopement, A *12* Mack Sennett
Midnight Episode, A *1899* Georges Méliès
Midnight Episode *50* Gordon Parry
Midnight Event, The *60* Břetislav Pojar
Midnight Express, The *24* George W. Hill
Midnight Express *78* Alan Parker
Midnight Faces *26* Bennett Cohn
Midnight Fires *26* Bennett Cohn
Midnight Flower, The *23* Leslie T. Peacock
Midnight Flyer, The *25* Tom Forman
Midnight Folly *61* Marc Allégret, Charles Gérard
Midnight Frolics *38* Ubbe Iwerks
Midnight Gambols *19* James McKay
Midnight Girl, The *25* Wilfred Noy
Midnight Guest, The *23* George Archainbaud
Midnight Hosts *24* Forest Holger-Madsen
Midnight in a Toy Shop *30* Wilfred Jackson
Midnight in Paris *42* Georges Lacombe
Midnight Intruder *04* Edwin S. Porter
Midnight Intruder *38* Arthur Lubin
Midnight Kiss, The *26* Irving Cummings
Midnight Lace *60* David Miller
Midnight Lady, The *32* Richard Thorpe
Midnight Life *28* Scott R. Dunlap
Midnight Limited *26* Oscar Apfel
Midnight Limited, The *40* Howard Bretherton
Midnight Lovers *26* John Francis Dillon
Midnight Madness *18* Rupert Julian
Midnight Madness *28* F. Harmon Weight
Midnight Madness *80* Michael Nankin, David Wechter
Midnight Madonna *37* James Flood
Midnight Mail, The *15* Warwick Buckland
Midnight Man, The *17* Elmer Clifton
Midnight Man, The *19* James W. Horne
Midnight Man, The *74* Roland Kibbee, Burt Lancaster
Midnight Manhunt *45* William C. Thomas
Midnight Marauders *12* Percy Stow
Midnight Mary *33* William A. Wellman
Midnight Meeting *61* Roger Leenhardt
Midnight Melody *46* John English
Midnight Menace *37* Sinclair Hill
Midnight Message, The *26* Paul Hurst
Midnight Molly *25* Lloyd Ingraham
Midnight Morals *32* E. Mason Hopper
Midnight Mystery *30* George B. Seitz
Midnight on the Barbary Coast *29* Robert J. Horner
Midnight Patrol, The *18* Irvin Willat
Midnight Patrol, The *32* Christy Cabanne
Midnight Patrol *33* Lloyd French
Midnight Phantom, The *35* Bernard B. Ray

Midnight Pleasures 75 Marcello Fondato
Midnight Raiders 44 Lewis D. Collins
Midnight Ride of Paul Revere, The 07 J. Searle Dawley, Edwin S. Porter
Midnight Ride of Paul Revere, The 14 Charles Brabin
Midnight Romance, A 19 Lois Weber
Midnight Rose 28 James Young
Midnight Run 88 Martin Brest
Midnight Secrets 24 Jack Nelson
Midnight Shadow 39 George Randol
Midnight Shadows 24 Francis Ford
Midnight Snack, The 41 Joseph Barbera, William Hanna
Midnight Special 31 Duke Worne
Midnight Stage, The 19 Ernest C. Warde
Midnight Story, The 57 Joseph Pevney
Midnight Summons, The 24 Fred Paul
Midnight Sun 13 Robert Dinesen
Midnight Sun, The 26 Dmitri Bucho-wetzki
Midnight Supper, A 09 Edwin S. Porter
Midnight Taxi, The 28 John G. Adolfi
Midnight Taxi 37 Eugene Forde
Midnight Trail, The 18 Edward Sloman
Midnight Warning 32 Spencer G. Bennet
Midnight Watch, The 24 Charles Lamont
Midnight Watch, The 27 Charles J. Hunt
Midnight Wedding, The 14 Ernest G. Batley
Midnightmare 61 Quifeng Yuan
Midnite in a Toy Shop 30 Wilfred Jackson
Midnite Spares 83 Quentin Masters
Midshipmaid, The 32 Albert De Courville
Midshipmaid Gob 32 Albert De Courville
Midshipman, The 25 Christy Cabanne
Midshipman Easy 15 Maurice Elvey
Midshipman Easy 33 Carol Reed
Midshipman Jack 33 Christy Cabanne
Midsommer 11 August Blom
Midst Woodland Shadows 14 Ralph Ince
Midstream 29 James Flood
Midsummer Day's Work, A 39 Alberto Cavalcanti
Midsummer Madness 20 William DeMille
Midsummer Mush 33 Charlie Chase
Midsummer Nightmare 57 John Halas
Midsummer Night's Dream, A 09 Charles Kent
Midsummer Night's Dream, A 28 Hans Neumann
Midsummer Night's Dream, A 35 William Dieterle, Max Reinhardt
Midsummer Night's Dream, A 59 Howard Sackler, Jiří Trnka
Midsummer Night's Dream, A 66 Dan Eriksen
Midsummer Night's Dream, A 68 Peter Hall
Midsummer Night's Dream, A 84 Celestino Coronado
Midsummer Night's Sex Comedy, A 82 Woody Allen
Midsummer Night's Steam, A 27 Mark Sandrich
Midsummer-Tide 11 August Blom
Midsummer-Time 11 August Blom
Midway 76 Jack Smight
Midwife, The 61 Alekos Sakelarios
Midwinter Sacrifice 46 Gösta Werner

Midwinter Trip to Los Angeles, A 11 Allan Dwan
Między Ustami a Brzegiem Pucharu 87 Zbigniew Kuźmiński
Miei Primi Quarant'Anni, I 87 Carlo Vanzina
Miele del Diavolo, Il 86 Lucio Fulci
Mientras Haya Luz 87 Felipe Vega
Mientras México Duerme 38 Alejandro Galindo
Mientre Buenos Aires Duerme 21 José A. Ferreyra
Miestä Ei Voi Raiskata 78 Jörn Donner
Mifanwy — A Tragedy 13 Elwin Neame
Mig og Dig 68 Astrid Henning-Jensen
Miggles' Maid 16 Frank Wilson
Might and Right 70 Marcel Carné
Might and the Man 17 Edward Dillon
Might Makes Right 74 Rainer Werner Fassbinder
Mighty, The 29 John Cromwell
Mighty Atom, The 11 A. E. Coleby
Mighty Barnum, The 34 Walter Lang
Mighty Crusaders, The 57 Carlo Ludovico Bragaglia
Mighty Gorga, The 69 David L. Hewitt
Mighty Hunters, The 40 Chuck Jones
Mighty Joe Young 49 Ernest B. Schoed-sack
Mighty Jungle, The 64 Arnold Belgard, David DaLie, Ismael Rodríguez
Mighty Lak' a Rose 23 Edwin Carewe
Mighty Like a Moose 26 Leo McCarey
Mighty McGurk, The 46 John Waters
Mighty Mouse in the Great Space Chase 83 Ed Friedman, Lou Kachivas, Marsh Lamore, Gwen Wetzler, Kay Wright, Lou Zukor
Mighty Navy, The 41 Dave Fleischer
Mighty Peking Man, The 79 Homer Gaugh
Mighty Quinn, The 89 Carl Schenkel
Mighty Stream 39 Sergei Eisenstein
Mighty Treve, The 37 Lewis D. Collins
Mighty Tundra, The 36 Norman Dawn
Mighty Ursus, The 60 Carlo Campogalliani
Mighty Warrior, The 62 Giorgio Ferroni
Mignon 12 Alice Guy-Blaché
Mignon 15 Alex E. Beyfuss
Mignon e Partita 88 Francesca Archibugi
Mignon or The Child of Fate 12 Alice Guy-Blaché
Migrants, The 74 Tom Gries
Migrating Birds 87 Latif Abdul Latif
Migratory Birds Under the Moon 51 Teinosuke Kinugasa
Mijn Vriend 79 Fons Rademakers
Mikado, The 39 Victor Schertzinger
Mikado, The 67 Stuart Burge
Mikaël 24 Carl Theodor Dreyer
Mikan no Taikyoku 82 Ji-shun Duan, Junya Sato
Mike 26 Marshall Neilan
Mike Alone in the Jungle 15 Dave Aylott
Mike and the Miser 16 Dave Aylott
Mike and the Zeppelin Raid 15 Dave Aylott
Mike Backs the Winner 16 Dave Aylott
Mike Joins the Force 14 Dave Aylott

Mike Murphy As a Picture Actor 14 Dave Aylott
Mike Murphy, Broker's Man 14 Dave Aylott
Mike Murphy, Mountaineer 14 Dave Aylott
Mike Murphy VC 14 Dave Aylott
Mike Murphy's Dream of Love and Riches 14 Dave Aylott
Mike Murphy's Dream of the Wild West 14 Dave Aylott
Mike Murphy's Marathon 15 Dave Aylott
Mike Wins the Championship 14 Dave Aylott
Mikela 65 Eldar Shengelaya
Mike's Gold Mine 15 Dave Aylott
Mike's Murder 82 James Bridges
Mikey and Nicky 76 Elaine May
Mikkel 48 Jørgen Roos
Miklós Borsos 66 Márta Mészáros
Mikres Afrodites 62 Nikos Koundouros
Mikroscop, Das 88 Rudolph Thome
Mil, Le 62 Jean Rouch
Mil Gritos Tiene la Noche 81 Juan Piquer Simon
Mil Huit Cent Quatorze 10 Louis Feuillade
Milady 22 Henri Diamant-Berger
Milady 75 François Leterrier
Milady o' the Bean Stalk 18 William Bertram
Milagro Beanfield War, The 87 Robert Redford
Milagro en Roma 88 Lisandro Duque Naranjo
Milan '83 83 Ermanno Olmi
Milano '83 83 Ermanno Olmi
Milarepa 74 Liliana Cavani
Milcząca Gwiazda 60 Kurt Mätzig
Mildred Pierce 45 Michael Curtiz
Mile a Minute 44 Wallace Fox
Mile-a-Minute Kendall 18 William Desmond Taylor
Mile-a-Minute Love 37 Elmer Clifton
Mile-a-Minute Man, The 26 Jack Nelson
Mile-a-Minute Monty 15 Leon Searl
Mile a Minute Morgan 24 Frank S. Mattison
Mile-a-Minute Romeo 23 Lambert Hillyer
Mile avec Jules Ladoumègue, Le 32 Jean Lods
Miles Against Minutes 24 Lee Morrison
Miles from Home 88 Gary Sinise
Miles of Fire 57 Samson Samsonov
Milestones 16 Thomas Bentley
Milestones 20 Paul Scardon
Milestones 75 John Douglas, Robert Kramer
Milieu du Monde, Le 74 Alain Tanner
Militaire et Nourrice 04 Alice Guy-Blaché
Militant Min 20 Wallace A. Carlson
Militant Suffragette 14 Charles Chaplin
Militare e Mezzo, Un 60 Steno
Militarism and Torture 69 Raúl Ruiz
Militarismo y Tortura 69 Raúl Ruiz
Military Academy 40 D. Ross Lederman
Military Academy 50 D. Ross Lederman
Military Academy with That 10th Avenue Gang 50 D. Ross Lederman
Military Apprentices 1897 Georges Méliès

Military Policemen *52* George Marshall
Military Secret *45* Vladimir Legoshin
Military Tactics *04* Alf Collins
Milizia Territoriale *35* Mario Bonnard
Milk *13* Émile Cohl
Milk & Honey *88* Glen Salzman, Rebecca Yates
Milk and Money *36* Tex Avery
Milk and Yeggs *21* Charles Reisner
Milk Hygiene *54* Henning Carlsen
Milk Made *27* Manny Gould, Ben Harrison
Milka *80* Rauni Mollberg
Milkmaid, The *05* Alf Collins
Milkmaid, The *59* Toivo Särkkä
Milkman, The *32* Ubbe Iwerks
Milkman, The *50* Charles Barton
Milkman's Wedding, The *07* Lewin Fitzhamon
Milky Waif, The *46* Joseph Barbera, William Hanna
Milky Way, The *22* W. S. Van Dyke
Milky Way, The *35* Leo McCarey
Milky Way, The *40* Rudolf Ising
Milky Way, The *68* Luis Buñuel
Mill, The *21* John W. Brunius
Mill, The *87* Atıf Yılmaz
Mill Girl, The *07* J. Stuart Blackton
Mill Girl, The *13* Warwick Buckland
Mill of Luck and Plenty, The *56* Victor Iliu
Mill of the Stone Maidens *60* Giorgio Ferroni
Mill of the Stone Women *60* Giorgio Ferroni
Mill on the Floss, The *15* W. Eugene Moore
Mill on the Floss, The *37* Tim Whelan
Mill on the Heath, The *13* Charles C. Calvert
Mill on the Po, The *49* Alberto Lattuada
Mill on the River, The *49* Alberto Lattuada
Mill Owner's Daughter, The *16* Fred W. Durrant
Millbrook Report, The *66* Jonas Mekas
Mille di Garibaldi, I *33* Alessandro Blasetti
Mille Dollari sul Nero *66* Alberto Cardone
Mille et Une Nuits, Les *61* Mario Bava, Henry Levin
Mille Milliards de Dollars *81* Henri Verneuil
1848 *48* Dino Risi
1860 *33* Alessandro Blasetti
1989 *63* Roger Leenhardt
1990: I Guerrieri del Bronx *82* Enzo G. Castellari
Millennium *89* Michael Anderson
Miller and the Sweep, The *1897* George Albert Smith
Miller's Beautiful Wife, The *55* Mario Camerini
Miller's Crossing *90* Joel Coen
Miller's Daughter, The *05* Edwin S. Porter
Miller's Daughter, The *34* Friz Freleng
Miller's Wife, The *55* Mario Camerini
Millerson Case, The *47* George Archainbaud
Millhouse: A White Comedy *71* Emile De

Antonio
Millhouse: A White House Comedy *71* Emile De Antonio
Millie *31* John Francis Dillon
Millie's Daughter *47* Sidney Salkow
Milling the Militants *13* Percy Stow
Million, Le *31* René Clair
Million, The *31* René Clair
Million a Minute, A *16* John W. Noble
Million Bid, A *13* Ralph Ince
Million Bid, A *27* Michael Curtiz
Million Daughters, A *63* Heinosuke Gosho
Million Dollar Baby *34* Joseph Santley
Million Dollar Baby *41* Kurt Bernhardt
Million Dollar Bid, A *14* J. Stuart Blackton
Million Dollar Cat *44* Joseph Barbera, William Hanna
Million Dollar Collar, The *29* D. Ross Lederman
Million Dollar Dollies, The *18* Léonce Perret
Million Dollar Handicap, The *25* Scott Sidney
Million Dollar Kid *44* Wallace Fox
Million Dollar Legs *32* Edward F. Cline
Million Dollar Legs *39* Edward Dmytryk, Nick Grindé
Million Dollar Manhunt *56* Maclean Rogers
Million Dollar Mermaid *52* Mervyn LeRoy
Million Dollar Mystery *27* Charles J. Hunt
Million Dollar Mystery *87* Richard Fleischer
Million Dollar Pursuit *51* R. G. Springsteen
Million Dollar Pursuit, The *68* Yoji Yamada
Million Dollar Racket *37* Robert F. Hill
Million Dollar Ransom *34* Murray Roth
Million Dollar Robbery, The *14* Herbert Blaché
Million Dollar Trio *52* Jules Dassin
Million Dollar Weekend *48* Gene Raymond
Million for Love, A *28* Robert F. Hill
Million for Mary, A *16* Rea Berger
Million Girls, A *63* Heinosuke Gosho
Million-Hare *63* Robert McKimson
Million in the Wedding Basket, A *87* Vsevolod Shilovsky
Million Pound Note, The *16* Alexander Korda
Million Pound Note, The *53* Ronald Neame
Million to Burn, A *23* William Parke
Million to One, A *37* Lynn Shores
Million v Brachnoy Korzine *87* Vsevolod Shilovsky
Millionærdrengen *13* Forest Holger-Madsen
Millionærdrengen *36* Anders Wilhelm Sandberg
Millionaire, The *21* Jack Conway
Millionaire, The *27* Oscar Micheaux
Millionaire, The *31* John G. Adolfi
Millionaire Baby, The *15* Lawrence Marston
Millionaire Cat, The *32* Mark Sandrich

Millionaire Cowboy *15* Anders Wilhelm Sandberg
Millionaire Cowboy, The *24* Harry Garson
Millionaire Droopy *56* Tex Avery
Millionaire for a Day, A *21* Wilfred North
Millionaire for a Day *34* Edward Ludwig
Millionaire for Christy, A *51* George Marshall
Millionaire Hobo *39* Art Davis, Sid Marcus
Millionaire in Trouble *78* Joel Silberg
Millionaire Kid *36* Bernard B. Ray
Millionaire Merry-Go-Round *38* Walter Forde
Millionaire Orphan, The *26* Robert J. Horner
Millionaire Pirate, The *19* Rupert Julian
Millionaire Playboy *37* David Howard
Millionaire Playboy *40* Leslie Goodwins
Millionaire Policeman, The *26* Edward J. LeSaint
Millionaire Vagrant, The *17* Victor Schertzinger
Millionaires *26* Herman Raymaker
Millionaire's Double, The *17* Harry Davenport
Millionaire's Express, The *86* Samo Hung
Millionaires in Prison *40* Ray McCarey
Millionaire's Nephew, The *11* Theo Bouwmeester
Millionairess, The *60* Anthony Asquith
Millionnaires d'un Jour *50* André Hunebelle
Millions *36* Leslie Hiscott
Millions de la Bonne, Les *13* Louis Feuillade
Millions de l'Oncle James, Les *24* Alfred Machin, Henri Wuhlschleger
Millions en Fuite, Les *33* Pál Fejös
Millions in Flight *33* Pál Fejös
Millions in the Air *35* Ray McCarey
Millions Like Us *43* Sidney Gilliat, Frank Launder
Millón de Madigan, El *67* Dan Ash, Giorgio Gentili, L. Lelli
Millónes de Chaflan, Los *38* Rolando Aguilar
Mills Brothers Story, The *86* Don McGlynn
Mills of Hell *87* Gyula Maar
Mills of the Gods, The *09* D. W. Griffith
Mills of the Gods *34* Roy William Neill
Mills of the Gods, The *39* J. Medeolti
Miłość Dwudziestolatków *62* Shintaro Ishihara, Marcel Ophüls, Renzo Rossellini, François Truffaut, Andrzej Wajda
Miłość Wszystko Zwycięża *36* Mieczysław Krawicz
Milou en Mai *90* Louis Malle
Milpitas Monster, The *80* Robert L. Burrill
Milwr Bychan *86* Karl Francis
Mimi *35* Paul Stein
Mimì Metallurgico Ferito nell'Onore *72* Lina Wertmuller
Mimi the Metalworker, Wounded in Honour *72* Lina Wertmuller
Mimi Trottin *22* Henri Andréani
Mimino *77* Georgy Danelia
Mimo Zhizni *14* Yakov Protazanov
Mimosa *10* Léonce Perret

Min and Bill *30* George W. Hill
Min Bedstefar Er en Stok *67* Astrid Henning-Jensen
Min Første Monokel *11* August Blom
Min Kära Är en Ros *63* Hasse Ekman
Min Pappa Är Tarzan *86* Judith Hollander
Min Van Balthazar *66* Robert Bresson
Min Ven Levy *14* Forest Holger-Madsen
Minami no Kaze *42* Kozaburo Yoshimura
Minami no Shima ni Yuki ga Fura *63* Seiji Hisamatsu
Minas Blood *28* Humberto Mauro
Mind Benders, The *63* Basil Dearden
Mind Cure, The *12* Phillips Smalley
Mind-Detecting Ray, The *18* Alfréd Deesy
Mind Field *90* Jean-Claude Lord
Mind Killer *87* Michael Krueger
Mind of Mr. Reeder, The *39* Jack Raymond
Mind of Mr. Soames, The *69* Alan Cooke
Mind Over Motor *23* Ward Lascelle
Mind Reader, The *33* Roy Del Ruth
Mind Shadows *88* Heddy Honigmann
Mind Snatchers, The *72* Bernard Girard
Mind the Paint *12* Percy Stow
Mind-the-Paint Girl, The *19* Wilfred North
Mind the Wet Paint *03* Alf Collins
Mind Your Own Business *07* Jack Smith
Mind Your Own Business *36* Norman Z. McLeod
Minden Kezdet Nehéz *66* György Révész
Mindennapi Történetek *55* Márta Mészáros
Mindent a Semmiért *34* Géza von Cziffra
Minding the Baby *31* Dave Fleischer
Minding the Baby *31* Dick Huemer
Mindwarp: An Infinity of Terror *81* Bruce Clark
Mine and the Minotaur, The *80* David Gowing
Mine in Vista *40* Francesco De Robertis
Mine of Missing Men *17* Lawrence Trimble
Mine Own Executioner *47* Anthony Kimmins
Mine Pilot, The *15* Mauritz Stiller
Mine to Keep *23* Ben F. Wilson
Mine with the Iron Door, The *24* Sam Wood
Mine with the Iron Door, The *36* David Howard
Mined and Counter-Mined *26* Frank Miller
Minefield! *44* Roy Boulting
Miners *34* Sergei Yutkevich
Miner's Daughter, The *05* John Codman
Miner's Daughter, The *06* James A. Williamson
Miner's Daughter, The *50* Robert Cannon
Miner's Mascot, The *12* Dave Aylott
Miners of the Don *51* Leonid Lukov
Miner's Wife, The *11* Allan Dwan
Minerva Traduce el Mar *62* Humberto Solás*
Mines and Matrimony *16* William Beaudine
Mines of Kilimanjaro, The *86* Mino Guerrini
Minesweeper *43* William Berke
Ming Green *66* Gregory Markopoulos
Ming, Ragazzi *73* Antonio Margheriti

Mingaloo *58* Theodore Zichy
Mingus *68* Thomas Reichman
Mini Affair, The *68* Robert Amram
Mini-Skirt Mob, The *68* Maury Dexter
Mini Weekend *67* Georges Robin
Miniature *50* Valerio Zurlini
Minière del Kilimangiaro, Le *86* Mino Guerrini
Minin and Pozharsky *39* Mikhail Doller, Vsevolod I. Pudovkin
Minin i Pozharsky *39* Mikhail Doller, Vsevolod I. Pudovkin
Minister's Magician, The *80* Simon Wincer
Ministry of Fear *43* Fritz Lang
Ministry of Vengeance *89* Peter Maris
Miniver Story, The *50* H. C. Potter
Minlotsen *15* Mauritz Stiller
Minne *50* Jacqueline Audry
Minne l'Ingénue Libertine *50* Jacqueline Audry
Minnesota Clay *64* Sergio Corbucci
Minnie *22* Marshall Neilan, Frank Urson
Minnie and Moskowitz *71* John Cassavetes
Minnie the Moocher *32* Dave Fleischer
Minor Love and the Real Thing *38* Josef von Baky
Minotaur *54* Hans Richter
Minotaur, The *61* Silvio Amadio
Minotaur *76* Costas Carayiannis
Minotaur — The Wild Beast of Crete, The *61* Silvio Amadio
Minotaur, Wild Beast of Crete *61* Silvio Amadio
Minshū no Teki *46* Tadashi Imai
Minstrel Boy, The *37* Sidney Morgan
Minstrel Man *44* Joseph H. Lewis
Minstrel Mishaps *06* Edwin S. Porter
Minstrel Show, The *32* Manny Gould, Ben Harrison
Minstrel's Song, The *63* Jiří Brdečka
Mint Spy, The *20* Raoul Barré, Charles Bowers
Mints of Hell, The *19* Park Frame
Minuet *82* Lili Rademakers
Minuit...Place Pigalle *28* René Hervil
Minute de Vérité, La *52* Jean Delannoy
Minute to Pray, a Second to Die, A *67* Franco Giraldi
Minutemen, The *72* Raúl Ruiz, Valeria Sarmiento
Minuteros, Los *72* Raúl Ruiz, Valeria Sarmiento
Minuto per Pregare, un Istante per Morire, Un *67* Franco Giraldi
Minx, The *69* Raymond Jacobs
Mio *70* Susumu Hani
Mio Amico Jeckyll, Il *60* Marino Girolami
Mio Corpo per un Poker, Il *68* Nathan Wich
Mio Figlio Nerone *56* Steno
Mio Figlio Professore *46* Renato Castellani
Mio, Moy Mio *87* Vladimir Grammatikov
Mio, My Mio *87* Vladimir Grammatikov
Mio Nome È Mallory: "M" Come Morte, Il *71* M. Moroni
Mio Nome È Nessuno, Il *73* Tonino Valerii
Mio Nome È Pecos *66* Maurizio Lucidi
Mio Nome È Shanghai Joe, Il *73* Mario Caiano

Mio Non Muore *13* Mario Caserini
Mioche, Le *36* Léonide Moguy
Miquette *49* Henri-Georges Clouzot
Miquette and Her Mother *49* Henri-Georges Clouzot
Miquette et Sa Mère *33* Henri Diamant-Berger
Miquette et Sa Mère *40* Jean Boyer
Miquette et Sa Mère *49* Henri-Georges Clouzot
Mir Kumen An *36* Aleksander Ford
Mir Vkhodyashchemu *61* Alexander Alov, Vladimir Naumov
Mira *70* Fons Rademakers
Miracle, The *12* Thomas Bentley
Miracle, The *12* Joseph Menchen
Miracle, The *13* Victor Sjöström
Miracle, The *23* A. E. Coleby
Miracle, Un *54* Robert Breer, Pontus Hulten
Miracle, The *59* Irving Rapper
Miracle, Le *86* Jean-Pierre Mocky
Miracle Baby, The *23* Val Paul
Miracle Can Happen, A *48* Leslie Fenton, John Huston, George Stevens, King Vidor
Miracle des Ailes, Le *56* Jean Mitry
Miracle des Loups, Le *24* Raymond Bernard
Miracle des Loups, Le *61* André Hunebelle
Miracle Healing, The *86* Jean-Pierre Mocky
Miracle in Harlem *37* Oscar Micheaux
Miracle in Harlem *47* Jack Kemp
Miracle in Milan *50* Vittorio De Sica
Miracle in Rome *88* Lisandro Duque Naranjo
Miracle in Soho *57* Julian Amyes
Miracle in the Rain *56* Rudolph Maté
Miracle in the Sand *36* Richard Boleslawski
Miracle Kid, The *41* William Beaudine
Miracle-Maker *22* Alexander Panteleyev
Miracle Makers, The *23* W. S. Van Dyke
Miracle Man, The *19* George Loane Tucker
Miracle Man, The *31* Norman Z. McLeod
Miracle Man, The *38* Michael Waszyński
Miracle Mile *88* Steve De Jarnatt
Miracle Money *38* Leslie Fenton
Miracle of Father Malachias, The *61* Bernhard Wicki
Miracle of Fatima *52* John Brahm
Miracle of Life, The *15* Harry A. Pollard
Miracle of Life, The *26* Stanner E. V. Taylor
Miracle of Life, The *34* King Vidor
Miracle of Love, A *16* Lloyd B. Carleton
Miracle of Love *19* Robert Z. Leonard
Miracle of Malachias, The *61* Bernhard Wicki
Miracle of Manhattan, The *21* George Archainbaud
Miracle of Marcelino, The *55* Ladislas Vajda
Miracle of Money, The *20* Hobart Henley
Miracle of Morgan's Creek, The *44* Preston Sturges
Miracle of Our Lady of Fatima, The *52* John Brahm
Miracle of Saint Thérèse *59* George Bernier

Miracle of San Sebastian *67* Henri Verneuil
Miracle of the Bells, The *48* Irving Pichel
Miracle of the Hills *59* Paul Landres
Miracle of the Vistula, The *20* Richard Boleslawski
Miracle of the White Stallions, The *62* Arthur Hiller
Miracle of the Wolves, The *24* Raymond Bernard
Miracle on Main Street, A *39* Steve Sekely
Miracle on 34th Street *47* George Seaton
Miracle Rider, The *35* B. Reeves Eason, Armand Schaefer
Miracle Song, The *40* Rolando Aguilar
Miracle Sous l'Inquisition, Un *04* Georges Méliès
Miracle Tree, The *76* Tenghiz Abuladze
Miracle Under the Inquisition, A *04* Georges Méliès
Miracle Woman, The *31* Frank Capra
Miracle Worker, The *62* Arthur Penn
Miracles *34* P. Petrov-Bytov
Miracles *84* Jim Kouf
Miracles Do Happen *38* Maclean Rogers
Miracles du Brahmane, Les *1899* Georges Méliès
Miracles for Sale *39* Tod Browning
Miracles N'Ont Lieu Qu'une Fois, Les *50* Yves Allégret
Miracles of Brahmin, The *1899* Georges Méliès
Miracles Still Happen *74* Giuseppe M. Scotese
Miracolo, Il *19* Mario Caserini
Miracolo a Firenze *53* Alessandro Blasetti
Miracolo a Milano *50* Vittorio De Sica
Miracolo di Sant'Antonio, Il *32* Nicola Fausto Neroni
Miracolul *88* Tudor Mărăscu
Miraculous Brothers, The *49* Luciano Emmer, Enrico Gras
Miraculous Journey *48* Sam Newfield
Miraculous Recovery, A *11* Wilfred Noy
Mirage, The *20* Arthur H. Rooke
Mirage, The *24* George Archainbaud
Mirage, The *59* Peter Weiss
Mirage *64* Edward Dmytryk
Mirage *72* Armando Robles Godoy
Mirage *81* Ernie Gehr
Mirage *87* Siu-ming Tsui
Mirages de Paris *33* Fedor Ozep
Mirages of Love *87* Tolomush Okeyev
Mirai no Shusse *27* Tomu Uchida
Mirakel, Das *12* Max Reinhardt
Miraklet *13* Victor Sjöström
Miramar, Beach of Roses *39* Manoel De Oliveira
Miramar, Praia de Rosas *39* Manoel De Oliveira
Miranda *48* Ken Annakin
Miranda *85* Tinto Brass
Mirandy Smiles *18* William DeMille
Mirazhi Lyubri *87* Tolomush Okeyev
Mirch Masala *86* Ketan Mehta
Mireille *06* Louis Feuillade, Alice Guy-Blaché
Mirele Efros *12* Andrzej Marek
Mirele Efros *39* Josef Berne
Miriam *28* Enrico Guazzoni

Miriam Rozella *24* Sidney Morgan
Miris Poljskog Cveća *77* Srđan Karanović
Miroir A Deux Faces, Le *58* André Cayatte
Miroir de Cagliostro, Le *1899* Georges Méliès
Miroir de la Vie, Le *51* Jean Grémillon
Miroir de Venise, Le *05* Georges Méliès
Miroir de Venise ou Les Mésaventures de Shylock, Le *05* Georges Méliès
Miroir Obscène, Le *73* Jesús Franco
Mironov Trial, The *19* Dziga Vertov
Mirror, The *17* Frank Powell
Mirror, A *71* István Szabó
Mirror, The *74* Andrei Tarkovsky
Mirror and Markheim, The *54* John Lemont
Mirror Animations *56* Harry Smith
Mirror Crack'd, The *80* Guy Hamilton
Mirror Has Two Faces, The *58* André Cayatte
Mirror of Holland *50* Bert Haanstra
Mirror with Two Faces, The *58* André Cayatte
Mirrored Reason *80* Stan Vanderbeek
Mirrors *78* Noel Black
Mirt Sost Shi Amit *72* Haile Gerima
Mirth and Melody *29* Frank R. Strayer
Mirth and Melody *51* Horace Shepherd
Mirth and Mystery *12* Stuart Kinder
Mirthful Mary—A Case for the Black List *03* William Haggar
Mirthful Mary in the Dock *04* William Haggar
Mirza Nowrouz' Shoes *86* Mohammad Motevasselani
Misadventure *20* Germaine Dulac
Misadventures of a Claim Agent, The *11* Allan Dwan
Misadventures of a Cycle Thief, The *09* S. Wormald
Misadventures of Bill the Plumber, The *11* H. Oceano Martinek
Misadventures of Merlin Jones, The *63* Robert Stevenson
Misadventures of Mike Murphy, The *13* Dave Aylott
Misadventures of Mr. Wilt, The *89* Michael Tuchner
Misadventures of the Bull Moose *16* John Colman Terry
Misappropriated Turkey, A *12* D. W. Griffith
Misbehavin' *81* Chuck Vincent
Misbehaving Husbands *40* William Beaudine
Misbehaving Ladies *31* William Beaudine
Misc. Happenings *62* Stan Vanderbeek
Mischances of a Drunkard, The *04* Georges Méliès
Mischances of a Photographer, The *08* Georges Méliès
Mischief *31* Jack Raymond
Mischief *69* Ian Shand
Mischief *85* Mel Damski
Mischief Maker, The *16* John G. Adolfi
Mischief Makers, The *57* François Truffaut
Mischievous Girls *07* Lewin Fitzhamon
Mischievous Margery *12* Stuart Kinder
Mischievous Puck *11* Walter R. Booth, Theo Bouwmeester

Mischievous Sketch, A *07* Georges Méliès
Mischievous Tutor, The *46* Otakar Vávra
Miscreants of the Motor World *26* F. W. Engholm
Mise à Sac *67* Alain Cavalier
Miser, The *08* Georges Méliès
Miser and the Child, The *09* Lewin Fitzhamon
Miser and the Maid, The *12* Warwick Buckland
Miser, or The Gold Country, The *00* Georges Méliès
Miserabili, I *46* Riccardo Freda
Misérables, Les *09* J. Stuart Blackton
Misérables, Les *11* Albert Capellani
Misérables, Les *18* Frank Lloyd
Misérables, Les *25* Henri Fescourt
Misérables, Les *34* Raymond Bernard
Misérables, Les *35* Richard Boleslawski
Misérables, Les *44* Kamel Salim
Miserables, Los *44* Fernando Rivero
Misérables, Les *46* Riccardo Freda
Misérables, Les *50* Daisuke Ito
Misérables, Les *52* Lewis Milestone
Misérables, Les *57* Jean-Paul Le Chanois
Misérables, Les *82* Robert Hossein
Misère au Borinage *33* Joris Ivens, Henri Storck
Miserère *06* Arthur Gilbert
Miséricorde *17* Camille De Morlhon
Misericordia *19* Lupu Pick
Miserie del Signor Travet, Le *45* Mario Soldati
Miser's Child, The *10* Sidney Olcott
Miser's Doom, The *1899* Walter R. Booth
Miser's Dream of Gold, The *00* Georges Méliès
Miser's Gift, The *16* Joseph M. Kerrigan
Miser's Heart, The *11* D. W. Griffith
Miser's Lesson, The *10* Bert Haldane
Misery *90* Rob Reiner
Misfit Brigade, The *87* Gordon Hessler
Misfit Earl, A *19* Ira M. Lowry
Misfit Wife, The *20* Edmund Mortimer
Misfits, The *13* Percy Stow
Misfits, The *60* John Huston
Misfits of Science *85* James D. Parriott
Misfortune Never Comes Alone *03* Georges Méliès
Misfortunes of an Explorer, The *00* Georges Méliès
Misfortunes of Love *45* Kajiro Yamamoto
Misguided Bobby, The *05* J. H. Martin
Mishaps of the N.Y.-Paris Race *08* Georges Méliès
Mishima *85* Paul Schrader
Mishima: A Life in Four Chapters *85* Paul Schrader
Mishka Against Yudenich *25* Grigori Kozintsev, Leonid Trauberg
Mishka Versus Yudenich *25* Grigori Kozintsev, Leonid Trauberg
Mishki Protiv Yudenicha *25* Grigori Kozintsev, Leonid Trauberg
Mishpachat Simchon *69* Joel Silberg
Miska the Great *16* Alexander Korda
Miska the Magnate *16* Alexander Korda
Misleading Lady, The *16* Arthur Berthelet
Misleading Lady, The *20* George Irving
Misleading Lady, The *32* Stuart Walker

Misleading Miss, A *14* Hay Plumb
Misleading Widow, The *19* John S. Robertson
Mislukking, De *86* Hans de Ridder
Mismates *26* Charles Brabin
Misplaced Husbands *28* Charles Lamont
Misplaced Jealousy *11* Mack Sennett
Misquelito *84* Lino Brocka
Miss Adventure *19* Lynn Reynolds
Miss Ambition *18* Henri Houry
Miss Annie Rooney *42* Edwin L. Marin
Miss Arizona *19* Otis B. Thayer
Miss Arizona *88* Pál Sándor
Miss Austen's Adventure *13* Charles C. Calvert
Miss Bluebeard *25* Frank Tuttle
Miss Bracegirdle Does Her Duty *26* Edwin Greenwood
Miss Bracegirdle Does Her Duty *36* Lee Garmes
Miss Brewster's Millions *26* Clarence Badger
Miss Catastrophe *56* Dmitri Kirsanov
Miss Catnip Goes to the Movies *17* Harry S. Palmer
Miss Charity *21* Edwin J. Collins
Miss Chic *59* Hasse Ekman
Miss Crusoe *19* Frank Crane
Miss De Vère *1896* Georges Méliès
Miss Death *65* Jesús Franco
Miss Death and Dr. Z *65* Jesús Franco
Miss Deceit *15* Frank Wilson
Miss Deception *17* Eugene Nowland
Miss Dorothy's Bekenntnis *20* Michael Curtiz
Miss Dorothy's Confession *20* Michael Curtiz
Miss Dulcie from Dixie *19* Joseph Gleason
Miss Edith, Duchesse *28* Donatien
Miss Ellen Terry at Home *00* George Albert Smith
Miss Europe *30* Augusto Genina
Miss Fane's Baby *33* Alexander Hall
Miss Fane's Baby Is Stolen *33* Alexander Hall
Miss Fatty's Seaside Lovers *15* Roscoe Arbuckle
Miss Firecracker *88* Thomas Schlamme
Miss Fix-It *38* Herbert I. Leeds
Miss George Washington *16* J. Searle Dawley
Miss Gladeye Slip's Vacation *13* Percy Stow
Miss Glory *36* Tex Avery
Miss Grant Goes to the Door *40* Brian Desmond Hurst
Miss Grant Takes Richmond *49* Lloyd Bacon
Miss Helyett *27* Georges Monca
Miss Hobbs *20* Donald Crisp
Miss Innocence *18* Harry Millarde
Miss Italy *52* Duilio Coletti
Miss Jackie of the Army *17* Lloyd Ingraham
Miss Jackie of the Navy *16* Harry A. Pollard
Miss Jessica Is Pregnant *67* J. L. Anderson
Miss Jessie Cameron, Champion Child Sword Dancer *03* Edwin S. Porter
Miss Jessie Dogherty, Champion Female

Highland Fling Dancer *03* Edwin S. Porter
Miss Jude *64* Richard Thorpe
Miss Julie *50* Alf Sjöberg
Miss Julie *72* John Glenister, Robin Phillips
Miss Knowall *40* Graham Cutts
Miss Leslie's Dolls *72* Joseph Prieto
Miss Lillian Shaffer and Her Dancing Horse *04* Edwin S. Porter
Miss Lina Esbrard Danseuse Cosmopolite et Serpentine *02* Alice Guy-Blaché
Miss London, Ltd. *43* Val Guest
Miss Lonelyhearts *83* Michael Dinner
Miss Lulu Bett *21* William DeMille
Miss Mactaggart Won't Lie Down *66* Francis Searle
Miss Madcap May *15* Cecil Birch
Miss Mary *86* María Luisa Bemberg
Miss Me Again *25* Wesley Ruggles
Miss Melody Jones *73* Bill Brame
Miss Mend *26* Boris Barnet, Fedor Ozep
Miss Millionersha *88* S. Rogozhkin
Miss Mink of 1949 *49* Glenn Tryon
Miss Mischief *19* Max Leder
Miss Mischief Maker *18* Sherwood MacDonald
Miss Mona *87* Mehdi Charef
Miss Muerte *65* Jesús Franco
Miss Nanny Goat at the Circus *17* Clarence Rigby
Miss Nanny Goat Becomes an Aviator *16* Clarence Rigby
Miss Nanny Goat on the Rampage *16* Clarence Rigby
Miss Nippon *31* Tomu Uchida
Miss Nobody *17* William Parke
Miss Nobody *20* Francis J. Grandon
Miss Nobody *26* Lambert Hillyer
Miss Nomination *16* John R. Bray
Miss Nymphet's Zap-In *70* Herschell Gordon Lewis
Miss Oyu *51* Kenji Mizoguchi
Miss Pacific Fleet *35* Ray Enright
Miss Peasant *16* Olga Preobrazhenskaya
Miss Petticoats *16* Harley Knoles
Miss Pilgrim's Progress *49* Val Guest
Miss Pimple, Suffragette *13* Fred Evans, Joe Evans
Miss Pinkerton *32* Lloyd Bacon
Miss Polly *41* Fred Guiol
Miss President *35* Andrew Marton
Miss Right *81* Paul Williams
Miss Robin Crusoe *54* E. A. Dupont, Eugene Frenke
Miss Robin Hood *52* John Guillermin
Miss Robinson Crusoe *17* Christy Cabanne
Miss Rovel *20* Jean Kemm
Miss Sadie Thompson *53* Kurt Bernhardt
Miss Sherlock Holmes *08* Edwin S. Porter
Miss Simpkins' Boarders *10* Percy Stow
Miss Snake Princess *38* Teinosuke Kinugasa
Miss Soapsuds *14* Ernst Lubitsch
Miss Sunbeam *48* Gösta Werner
Miss Susie Slagle's *44* John Berry
Miss Tatlock's Millions *48* Richard Haydn
Miss Tulip Stays the Night *55* Leslie Arliss
Miss Tutti Frutti *20* Michael Curtiz
Miss U.S.A. *17* Harry Millarde

Miss V from Moscow *42* Albert Herman
Miss Yugoslavia 62 *62* Dušan Makavejev
Missbrauchten Liebesbriefe, Die *40* Leopold Lindtberg
Misses Stooge, The *35* James Parrott
Missile *87* Frederick Wiseman
Missile Base at Taniak *53* Franklin Adreon
Missile Monsters *51* Fred C. Brannon
Missile to the Moon *58* Richard Cunha
Missiles from Hell *58* Vernon Sewell
Missing *18* J. Stuart Blackton, James Young
Missing *81* Costa-Gavras
Missing Admiralty Plans, The *14* Forest Holger-Madsen
Missing, Believed Married *37* John Paddy Carstairs
Missing Corpse, The *45* Albert Herman
Missing Daughters *24* William H. Clifford
Missing Daughters *39* C. C. Coleman, Jr.
Missing Evidence *39* Phil Rosen
Missing Girls *36* Phil Rosen
Missing Guest, The *38* John Rawlins
Missing Husbands *21* Jacques Feyder
Missing in Action *84* Joseph Zito
Missing in Action 2 — The Beginning *84* Lance Hool
Missing Juror, The *44* Budd Boetticher
Missing Lady, The *46* Phil Karlson
Missing Legacy, or The Story of a Brown Hat, The *06* Alf Collins
Missing Link, The *17* Will P. Kellino
Missing Link, The *27* Charles Reisner
Missing Links, The *15* Lloyd Ingraham
Missing Man, The *53* Ken Hughes
Missing Million, The *42* Phil Brandon
Missing Millions *22* Joseph E. Henabery
Missing Note, The *61* Michael Brandt
Missing One, The *16* Gregory La Cava, Vernon Stallings
Missing People *39* Jack Raymond
Missing Persons *33* Roy Del Ruth
Missing Persons *53* Alun Falconer
Missing Princess, The *54* Desmond Leslie, Alastair Scobie
Missing Rembrandt, The *32* Leslie Hiscott
Missing Ten Days *39* Tim Whelan
Missing the Tide *17* Walter West
Missing Three Quarter, The *23* George Ridgwell
Missing Tiara, The *12* Charles C. Calvert
Missing Witness, The *16* Herbert Brenon
Missing Witness, The *33* H. Manning Haynes
Missing Witness *37* William Clemens
Missing Witnesses *37* William Clemens
Missing Women *51* Philip Ford
Mission, The *83* Parviz Sayyad
Mission, The *86* Roland Joffé
Mission à Tanger *49* André Hunebelle
Mission Batangas *68* Keith Larsen
Mission Bloody Mary *67* Sergio Grieco
Mission Cobra *86* Fabrizio De Angelis
Mission Galactica: The Cylon Attack *79* Vincent Edwards, Christian Nyby II
Mission Hill *82* Robert Jones
Mission Kill *85* David Winters
Mission Mars *68* Nicholas Webster
Mission: Monte Carlo *81* Roy Ward Baker
Mission of a Flower, The *08* A. E. Coleby

Mission of Danger 59 Jacques Tourneur, George Waggner
Mission Over Korea 53 Fred F. Sears
Mission Stardust 68 Primo Zeglio
Mission to Hell 62 Arthur A. Jones
Mission to Hell with Secret Agent FX15 64 Gianfranco Parolini
Mission to Hong Kong 65 Ernst Hofbauer
Mission to Moscow 43 Michael Curtiz
Mission to Venice 63 André Versini
Missionaries in Darkest Africa 12 Sidney Olcott
Missionary, The 81 Richard Loncraine
Missionary's Daughter, The 08 Percy Stow
Missione Eroica 87 Giorgio Capitani
Missione Pianeta Errante 65 Antonio Margheriti
Missione Timiriazev 53 Gillo Pontecorvo
Missioner, The 22 George Ridgwell
Missioner's Plight, The 13 Frank Wilson
Missionnaire, Un 55 Maurice Cloche
Missions de France 39 Marcel Ichac
Mississippi 31 Russell Mack
Mississippi 35 A. Edward Sutherland
Mississippi Blues 83 Robert Parrish, Bertrand Tavernier
Mississippi Burning 88 Alan Parker
Mississippi Gambler, The 29 Reginald Barker
Mississippi Gambler 42 John Rawlins
Mississippi Gambler, The 53 Rudolph Maté
Mississippi Hare 48 Chuck Jones
Mississippi Mermaid, The 68 François Truffaut
Mississippi Moods 37 Leslie Goodwins
Mississippi Mud 28 Walter Lantz
Mississippi Rhythm 49 Derwin Abrahams
Mississippi Summer 68 William Bayer
Missouri Breaks, The 76 Arthur Penn
Missouri Hayride 46 Josef Berne
Missouri Outlaw, A 41 George Sherman
Missouri Traveler, The 58 Jerry Hopper
Missourians, The 50 George Blair
Mist 89 Ömer Zülfü Livaneli
Mist in the Valley 22 Cecil M. Hepworth
Mist of Errors, A 13 Warwick Buckland
Mistake, The 13 D. W. Griffith
Mistaken for a Burglar in His Own House 05 Tom Green
Mistaken Identity 06 J. H. Martin
Mistaken Identity, A 08 Georges Méliès
Mistaken Identity 09 Theo Bouwmeester
Mistaken Identity 10 Dave Aylott
Mistaken Identity 39 Walter Tennyson
Mistaken Masher, The 13 Mack Sennett
Mistaken Orders 26 John P. McGowan
Mr. Ace 46 Edwin L. Marin
Mr. Anatol's Hat 58 Jan Rybkowski
Mr. & Mrs. Bridge 90 James Ivory
Mr. and Mrs. Is the Name 35 Friz Freleng
Mr. and Mrs. North 41 Robert B. Sinclair
Mr. and Mrs. Piecan — The Giddy Husband 15 Joe Evans
Mr. and Mrs. Poorluck Separate 11 Lewin Fitzhamon
Mr. and Mrs. Smith 41 Alfred Hitchcock
Mr. and Mrs. Swordplay 29 Mikio Naruse
Mr. Antonio 29 James Flood, Frank Reicher

Mr. Arkadin 55 Orson Welles
Mr. Ashton Was Indiscreet 47 George S. Kaufman
Mr. Barnes of New York 14 Maurice Costello, Robert Gaillard
Mr. Barnes of New York 22 Victor Schertzinger
Mr. Beamish Goes South 53 Oscar Burn, John Wall
Mr. Belvedere Goes to College 49 Elliott Nugent
Mr. Belvedere Rings the Bell 51 Henry Koster
Mr. Big 43 Charles Lamont
Mr. Bill the Conqueror 32 Norman Walker
Mr. Billings Spends His Dime 23 Wesley Ruggles
Mr. Billion 76 Jonathan Kaplan
Mr. Bingle 22 Leopold Wharton
Mr. Blandings Builds His Dream House 48 H. C. Potter
Mr. Boggs Buys a Barrel 38 Gordon Wiles
Mr. Boggs Steps Out 38 Gordon Wiles
Mr. Bonehead Gets Wrecked 16 Harry S. Palmer
Mr. Borland Thinks Again 40 Paul Rotha
Mr. Bragg, a Fugitive 11 Mack Sennett
Mr. Breakneck's Invention 10 Percy Stow
Mr. Bride 32 James Parrott
Mr. Broadway 33 Edgar G. Ulmer
Mr. Brown 72 Roger Andrieux
Mr. Brown Comes Down the Hill 66 Henry Cass
Mr. Brown's Bathing Tent 05 Percy Stow
Mister Buddwing 65 Delbert Mann
Mr. Bug Goes to Town 41 Dave Fleischer
Mr. Celebrity 41 William Beaudine
Mr. Chedworth Steps Out 39 Ken Hall
Mr. Christmas Dinner 88 Anthony Perkins
Mr. Chump 38 William Clemens
Mr. Cinderella 26 Norman Taurog
Mister Cinderella 36 Edward Sedgwick
Mister Cinders 34 Fred Zelnik
Mr. Cohen Takes a Walk 35 William Beaudine
Mr. Common Peepul Investigates 17 Harry S. Palmer
Mister Cory 56 Blake Edwards
Mr. Dauber and the Whimsical Picture 05 Georges Méliès
Mr. Deeds Goes to Town 36 Frank Capra
Mr. Denning Drives North 51 Anthony Kimmins
Mr. Destiny 90 James Orr
Mr. Diddlem's Will 12 Percy Stow
Mr. District Attorney 41 William Morgan
Mr. District Attorney 46 Robert B. Sinclair
Mr. District Attorney in the Carter Case 41 Bernard Vorhaus
Mr. Dodd Takes the Air 37 Alfred E. Green
Mr. Dódek 69 Jerzy Bossak
Mr. Dolan of New York 17 Raymond Wells
Mr. Doodle Kicks Off 38 Leslie Goodwins
Mr. Drake's Duck 50 Val Guest
Mr. Drew 48 Alberto Cavalcanti
Mr. Dynamite 35 Alan Crosland

Mr. Dynamite 41 John Rawlins
Mr. Editor Is Crazy 38 H. Wencel
Mister 880 50 Edmund Goulding
Mr. Elephant Goes to Town 40 Art Davis
Mr. Emmanuel 44 Harold French
Mr. Fabre's Mill 86 Ahmed Rachedi
Mr. Faintheart 35 George Marshall
Mr. Fancy Car and the Eerie Manor 87 Janusz Kidawa
Mr. Fix-It 18 Allan Dwan
Mr. Fixer 12 Ralph Ince
Mr. Fixit 12 Ralph Ince
Mister Flow 36 Robert Siodmak
Mr. Forbush and the Penguins 71 Roy Boulting, Arne Sucksdorff, Al Viola
Mr. Fore by Fore 44 Howard Swift
Mr. 44 16 Henry Otto
Mister 420 55 Raj Kapoor
Mr. Fox of Venice 66 Joseph L. Mankiewicz
Mr. Freedom 68 William Klein
Mr. Frenhofer and the Minotaur 48 Sidney Peterson
Mister Frost 90 Philippe Setbon
Mr. Fuller Pep: An Old Bird Pays Him a Visit 17 F. M. Follett
Mr. Fuller Pep Breaks for the Beach 16 F. M. Follett
Mr. Fuller Pep Celebrates His Wedding Anniversary 17 F. M. Follett
Mr. Fuller Pep Dabbles in the Pond 16 F. M. Follett
Mr. Fuller Pep Does Some Quick Moving 17 F. M. Follett
Mr. Fuller Pep Goes to the Country 17 F. M. Follett
Mr. Fuller Pep Tries Mesmerism 16 F. M. Follett
Mr. Fuller Pep's Day of Rest 17 F. M. Follett
Mr. Fuller Pep's Wife Goes for a Rest 17 F. M. Follett
Mr. Gallagher and Mr. Shean 31 Dave Fleischer
Mr. Gilfil's Love Story 20 A. V. Bramble
Mr. Goode the Samaritan 16 Edward Dillon
Mr. Grex of Monte Carlo 15 Frank Reicher
Mr. Griggs Returns 46 S. Sylvan Simon
Mr. Grouch at the Seashore 11 Mack Sennett
Mr. Gullible 70 Dariush Mehrjui
Mr. H.C. Anderson 50 Ronald Haines
Mr. Hayashi 61 Bruce Baillie
Mr. Head 59 Henri Gruel, Jan Lenica
Mr. Henpeck's Dilemma 13 George Pearson
Mr. Henpeck's Quiet Bank Holiday 06 Charles Raymond
Mr. Hercules Against Karate 74 Antonio Margheriti
Mr. Hex 46 William Beaudine
Mr. Hobbs Takes a Vacation 62 Henry Koster
Mister Hobo 35 Milton Rosmer
Mr. Hobo 52 Lewis D. Collins
Mr. Hoover and I 89 Emile De Antonio
Mr. Horatio Knibbles 71 Robert Hird
Mr. Hot Shot 84 Garry Marshall
Mr. Hughes and His Christmas Turkey 04 John Codman

Mr. Hulot's Holiday 53 Jacques Tati
Mr. Ikla's Jubilee 55 Vatroslav Mimica
Mr. Ima Jonah's Home Brew 21 R. E. Donahue, J. J. McManus
Mr. Imperium 51 Don Hartman
Mr. India 87 Shekhar Kapur
Mr. Innocent 67 Elliot Silverstein
Mr. Invisible 70 Antonio Margheriti
Mr. Jefferson Green 13 Christy Cabanne
Mister Jericho 69 Sidney Hayers
Mr. Jim—American, Soldier and Gentleman 56 France Štiglić
Mr. Jocko from Jungletown 16 Harry S. Palmer
Mr. Jolly Lives Next Door 87 Stephen Frears
Mr. Jones at the Ball 08 D. W. Griffith
Mr. Jones' Burglar 09 D. W. Griffith
Mr. Jones Has a Card Party 08 D. W. Griffith
Mr. Jones Has a Tile Loose 08 Percy Stow
Mr. Justice Raffles 21 Gerald Ames, Gaston Quiribet
Mr. K—Green Street 60 Věra Chytilová
Mr. Kennedy, Mr. Reagan and the Big, Beautiful, Beleaguered American Dream 67 Clifford Solway
Mr. King på Eventyr 14 August Blom
Mr. Kingstreet's War 70 Percival Rubens
Mr. Kinky 67 Dino Risi
Mr. Klein 76 Joseph Losey
Mr. Know-How 61 George Dunning
Mr. Kobin Seeks Adventure 35 Hans Deppe
Mr. Lemon of Orange 31 John G. Blystone
Mister Lewis 65 Malcolm Craddock
Mr. Limpet 63 Arthur Lubin
Mr. Logan, U.S.A. 18 Lynn Reynolds
Mr. Lord Says No! 52 Muriel Box
Mr. Love 85 Roy Battersby
Mr. Lucky 43 H. C. Potter
Mr. Lucky 52 Kon Ichikawa
Mr. Lyndon at Liberty 15 Harold M. Shaw
Mr. Magoo 49 John Hubley
Mr. Magoo's Holiday Festival 70 Abe Levitow
Mr. Majestyk 74 Richard Fleischer
Mr. Max 37 Mario Camerini
Mr. Mean 77 Fred Williamson
Mr. Meek's Missus 14 Hay Plumb
Mr. Meek's Nightmare 14 Hay Plumb
Mr. Mike's Mondo Video 79 Michael O'Donoghue
Mr. Mom 83 Stan Dragoti
Mr. Moocher 44 Bob Wickersham
Mr. Mosenstein 04 Alf Collins
Mister Moses 64 Ronald Neame
Mr. Moto and the Persian Oil Case 65 Ernest Morris
Mr. Moto in Danger Island 38 Herbert I. Leeds
Mr. Moto on Danger Island 38 Herbert I. Leeds
Mr. Moto Takes a Chance 38 Norman Foster
Mr. Moto Takes a Vacation 38 Norman Foster
Mr. Moto's Gamble 38 James Tinling
Mr. Moto's Last Warning 39 Norman

Foster
Mr. Muggs Meets a Deadline 44 William Beaudine
Mr. Muggs Rides Again 45 Wallace Fox
Mr. Muggs Steps Out 43 William Beaudine
Mr. Mugwump and the Baby 10 Frank Wilson
Mr. Mugwump Takes Home the Washing 10 Frank Wilson
Mr. Mugwump's Banknotes 10 Frank Wilson
Mr. Mugwump's Clock 11 Frank Wilson
Mr. Mugwump's Hired Suit 10 Frank Wilson
Mr. Mugwump's Jealousy 10 Frank Wilson
Mr. Mum 83 Stan Dragoti
Mr. Music 50 Richard Haydn
Mr. Naive 70 Dariush Mehrjui
Mr. Nobody 27 Frank Miller
Mr. Nobody 36 Christian-Jaque
Mr. North 88 Danny Huston
Mr. Opp 17 Lynn Reynolds
Mr. Orchid 46 René Clément
Mr. Pastry Does the Laundry 50 Herbert Marshall
Mr. Patman 80 John Guillermin
Mr. Peabody and the Mermaid 48 Irving Pichel
Mr. Peck Goes Calling 11 Mack Sennett
Mr. Peek-a-Boo 50 Jean Boyer
Mr. Perrin and Mr. Traill 48 Lawrence Huntington
Mr. Pharaoh and His Cleopatra 59 Don Weis
Mr. Pickwick in a Double Bedded Room 13 Wilfred Noy
Mr. Pickwick's Christmas at Wardle's 01 Walter R. Booth
Mr. Pim Passes By 21 Albert Ward
Mr. Poo 53 Kon Ichikawa
Mr. Poorluck As an Amateur Detective 12 Frank Wilson
Mr. Poorluck Buys Some China 11 Lewin Fitzhamon
Mr. Poorluck Buys Some Furniture 10 Lewin Fitzhamon
Mr. Poorluck Gets Married 09 Lewin Fitzhamon
Mr. Poorluck, Journalist 13 Frank Wilson
Mr. Poorluck Repairs His House 13 Frank Wilson
Mr. Poorluck's Dream 10 Lewin Fitzhamon
Mr. Poorluck's IOUs 13 Frank Wilson
Mr. Poorluck's Lucky Horseshoe 10 Lewin Fitzhamon
Mr. Poorluck's River Suit 12 Hay Plumb
Mr. Potter of Texas 22 Leopold Wharton
Mr. Potts Goes to Moscow 52 Mario Zampi
Mr. Preedy and the Countess 25 George Pearson
Mr. Prokouk and the Red Tape 47 Karel Zeman
Mr. Prokouk in Temptation 47 Karel Zeman
Mr. Prokouk in the Office 47 Karel Zeman
Mr. Prokouk Is Filming 48 Karel Zeman
Mr. Prokouk Leaves for Volunteer Work

47 Karel Zeman
Mr. Prokouk Makes a Film 48 Karel Zeman
Mr. Prokouk on a Brigade 47 Karel Zeman
Mr. Prokouk the Acrobat 59 Z. Rozkopal
Mr. Prokouk the Animal Fancier 55 Karel Zeman
Mr. Prokouk the Animal Lover 55 Karel Zeman
Mr. Prokouk the Inventor 48 Karel Zeman
Mr. Proudfoot Shows a Light 41 Herbert Mason
Mr. Pulver and the Captain 64 Joshua Logan
Mister Quilp 75 Michael Tuchner
Mr. Quincey of Monte Carlo 33 John Daumery
Mr. Radish and Mr. Carrot 64 Minoru Shibuya
Mr. Reckless 48 Frank McDonald
Mr. Reeder in Room 13 38 Norman Lee
Mr. Ricco 74 Paul Bogart
Mister Roberts 54 John Ford, Mervyn LeRoy
Mr. Robinson Crusoe 32 A. Edward Sutherland
Mr. Rock and Roll 57 Charles Dubin
Mr. Sardonicus 61 William Castle
Mr. Satan 38 Arthur Woods
Mr. Scarface 77 Fernando Di Leo
Mister Scoutmaster 53 Henry Levin
Mr. Sebastian 67 David Greene
Mr. Selkie 79 Anthony Squire
Mr. Shepard and Mr. Milne 75 Andrew Holmes
Mr. Shome 69 Mrinal Sen
Mr. Silent Haskins 15 William S. Hart, Clifford Smith
Mr. Skeeter 85 Colin Finbow
Mr. Skeffington 44 Vincent Sherman
Mr. Skitch 33 James Cruze
Mr. Slotter's Jubilee 79 Bert Haanstra
Mr. Smith 76 Adrian Lyne
Mr. Smith Carries On 37 Lister Laurance
Mr. Smith Goes to Washington 39 Frank Capra
Mr. Smith Wakes Up 29 Jack Harrison
Mr. Smug 43 William Castle
Mr. Soft Touch 49 Gordon Douglas, Henry Levin
Mr. Strauss Takes a Walk 42 George Pal
Mr. Stringfellow Says No 37 Randall Faye
Mister Superinvisible 70 Antonio Margheriti
Mr. Sycamore 74 Pancho Kohner
Mr. Tau 88 Jindřich Polák
Mister Ten Percent 67 Peter Graham Scott
Mr. Tomkins Inside Himself 62 Stan Brakhage
Mr. Topaze 61 Peter Sellers
Mr. Troublesome 09 John Codman
Mr. Tubby's Triumph 10 Dave Aylott
Mr. Universe 51 Joseph Lerner
Mr. Universe 88 György Szomjas
Mister V 41 Leslie Howard
Mr. Valiant 54 Kajiro Yamamoto
Mr. Vampire 86 Kun Wai Lau
Mr. Walkie Talkie 52 Fred Guiol
Mr. Washington Goes to Town 40 William Beaudine, Jed Bruell

Mr. What's-His-Name *35* Ralph Ince
Mr. Winkle Goes to War *44* Alfred E.
  Green
Mr. Wise Guy *42* William Nigh
Mr. Wise, Investigator *11* E. Mason Hopper
Mr. Wonderbird *52* Paul Grimault
Mr. Wong at Headquarters *40* William
  Nigh
Mr. Wong, Detective *38* William Nigh
Mr. Wong in Chinatown *39* William Nigh
Mr. Wrong *85* Gaylene Preston
Mr. Wu *19* Maurice Elvey
Mr. Wu *27* William Nigh
Mister, You Are a Widower *71* Václav
  Vorlíček
Mr. Zervadac's Ark *68* Karel Zeman
Misteri della Giungla Nera, I *64* Luigi
  Capuano
Misterio *81* Marcela Fernández Violante
Misterio del Rostro Pálido, El *37* Juan
  Bustillo Oro
Misterio en la Isla de los Monstruos *80*
  Juan Piquer Simon
Misterios de Bosque Negro, Los *64* Rafael
  Baledón
Misterios de la Magia Negra *57* Miguel
  Delgado
Misterios del Rosario, Los *65* Joseph Breen
Misterios del Ultratumba *58* Fernando
  Méndez
Mistero dei Bauli Neri, Il *18* Luigi Maggi
Mistero dei Tre Continenti, Il *59* William
  Dieterle
Mistero del Tempio Indiano, Il *63* Mario
  Camerini
Mistero della Quattro Corona, Il *82* Ferdinando Baldi
Mistero di Bellavista, Il *85* Luciano De
  Crescenzo
Mistero di Oberwald, Il *79* Michelangelo
  Antonioni
Mistigri *32* Harry Lachman
Mistletoe Bough, The *04* Percy Stow
Mistletoe Bough, The *23* Edwin J. Collins
Mistletoe Bough, The *26* Charles C. Calvert
Mistons, Les *57* François Truffaut
Mistr Zimních Sportů *55* Martin Frič
Mistral, Le *65* Joris Ivens
Mistress, The *53* Leonid Lukov
Mistress, The *53* Shiro Toyoda
Mistress, The *62* Vilgot Sjöman
Mistress for the Summer, A *59* Édouard
  Molinaro
Mistress Nell *15* James Kirkwood
Mistress of a Foreigner *30* Kenji Mizoguchi
Mistress of Atlantis, The *32* G. W. Pabst
Mistress of Shenstone, The *21* Henry King
Mistress of the Apes *81* Larry Buchanan
Mistress of the Mountains *54* Fernando
  Cerchio
Mistress of the World *20* Joe May
Mistress of the World *59* William Dieterle
Mistress Pamela *73* James O'Connolly
Mistresses of Dr. Jekyll *64* Jesús Franco
Mistrovství Světa Leteckých Modelářů *57*
  Karel Kachyňa
Mistrz Nikifor *56* Jan Łomnicki

Misty *61* James B. Clark
Misty *75* Joe Sarno
Misunderstanding, The *12* Gilbert Southwell
Misunderstood *14* Forest Holger-Madsen
Misunderstood *66* Luigi Comencini
Misunderstood *82* Jerry Schatzberg
Misunderstood Boy, A *13* D. W. Griffith
Mit Csinált Felséged 3-tól 5-ig *64* Károly
  Makk
Mit Dir Durch Dick und Dünn *34* Franz
  Seitz
Mit Django Kam der Tod *68* Luigi Bazzoni
Mit Eva Fing die Sünde An *61* Francis
  Ford Coppola, Fritz Umgelter
Mit Livs Eventyr *55* Jørgen Roos
Mit Mir Will Keiner Spielen *76* Werner
  Herzog
Mit Versiegelter Order *38* Karl Anton
Mitad del Cielo, La *86* Manuel Gutiérrez
  Aragón
Mitasareta Seikatsu *62* Susumu Hani
Mitchell *75* Andrew V. McLaglen
Mitläufer, Die *84* Erwin Leiser
Mito, Il *65* Adimaro Sala
Mitrea Cocor *52* Victor Iliu
Mitsou *56* Jacqueline Audry
Mitt Hem Är Copacabana *65* Arne Sucksdorff
Mitt Hjärta Har Två Tungor *87* Mikael
  Wiström
Mitt Liv Som Hund *85* Lasse Hallström
Mitten ins Herz *83* Doris Dörrie
Mitternacht *18* E. A. Dupont
Mitternachtsliebe *31* Carl Fröhlich,
  Augusto Genina
Mittsu no Ai *54* Masaki Kobayashi
Mitya *27* Nikolai Pavlovich Okhlopkov
Mivtza Kahir *66* Menahem Golan
Mix Me a Person *61* Leslie Norman
Mix-Up in Raincoats, A *11* Mack Sennett
Mix-Up in the Gallery, A *06* Georges
  Méliès
Mixed Babies *05* Frank Mottershaw
Mixed Bathing *04* Alf Collins
Mixed Bathing at Home *05* Alf Collins
Mixed Blood *16* Charles Swickard
Mixed Blood *84* Paul Morrissey
Mixed Company *74* Melville Shavelson
Mixed Doubles *33* Sidney Morgan
Mixed Doubles *79* Christopher Coy
Mixed Faces *22* Rowland V. Lee
Mixed Ladies Chorus, The *16* Ernst
  Lubitsch
Mixed Master *56* Robert McKimson
Mixed Nuts *34* James Parrott
Mixed Relations *16* George Loane Tucker
Mixed Wives *19* William Beaudine
Mixing Business with Pleasure *20* Wallace
  A. Carlson
Mixing in Mexico *25* Charles Bowers
Miya Sama *07* John Morland
Miyamoto Musashi *40* Hiroshi Inagaki
Miyamoto Musashi *42* Kenji Mizoguchi
Miyamoto Musashi *54* Hiroshi Inagaki
Miyamoto Musashi I *61* Tomu Uchida
Miyamoto Musashi II *62* Tomu Uchida
Miyamoto Musashi III *63* Tomu Uchida
Miyamoto Musashi IV *64* Tomu Uchida

Miyamoto Musashi V *65* Tomu Uchida
Mizar *54* Francesco De Robertis
Mizící Svět *35* Vladimír Úleha
Mizpah, or Love's Sacrifice *15* Stuart Kinder
Mladé Víno *86* Václav Vorlíček
Mladý Muž a Bílá Velryba *78* Jaromil Jireš
M'liss *15* Oscar A. C. Lund
M'liss *18* Marshall Neilan
M'liss *36* George Nicholls, Jr.
Mlle. Conduit *59* Claude Lelouch
Mlle. Désirée *41* Sacha Guitry
Mlle. Irene the Great *31* Edward F. Cline
Mlle. Tiptoes *18* Henry King
Młodość Chopina *52* Aleksander Ford
Młody Las *34* Josef Leytes
M'Lord of the White Road *23* Arthur H.
  Rooke
Mme. Thora Fleming *14* Mauritz Stiller
Mo *83* Zhihong Gui
Mo' Better Blues *90* Spike Lee
Mo Tai *83* Honquan Liu
Mō Taku-To to Bunkadaika-Kumei *69*
  Nagisa Oshima
Moa *86* Anders Wahlgren
Moana *25* Frances Flaherty, Robert
  Flaherty
Moana—A Romance of the Golden Age
  25 Frances Flaherty, Robert Flaherty
Moana—The Love Life of a South Sea
  Siren *25* Frances Flaherty, Robert
  Flaherty
Moara cu Noroc *56* Victor Iliu
Mob, The *51* Robert Parrish
Mob Town *41* William Nigh
Mob War *89* J. Christian Ingvordsen
Mobilier Fidèle, Le *10* Émile Cohl
Mobs, Inc. *56* William Asher
Mobster, The *58* Roger Corman
Moby Dick *30* Lloyd Bacon
Moby Dick *31* Michael Curtiz, William
  Dieterle
Moby Dick *56* John Huston
Moby Duck *65* Robert McKimson
Moccasins *25* Robert North Bradbury
Mochuelo, El *05* Ricardo De Baños
Mock Auctioneer, The *26* F. W. Engholm
Mockery *27* Benjamin Christensen
Moço de 74 Anos, Um *63* Nelson Pereira
  Dos Santos
Mod *64* Brian DePalma
Mod Lyset *18* Forest Holger-Madsen
Mod Stjernerne *20* August Blom
Mode in France *85* William Klein
Mode Rêvée, La *38* Marcel L'Herbier
Model, The *13* Mauritz Stiller
Model, The *16* Harry Buss
Model *80* Frederick Wiseman
Model and the Marriage Broker, The *51*
  George Cukor
Model for Murder *58* Terry Bishop
Model from Montmartre, The *28* Léonce
  Perret
Model Husband, The *38* Wolfgang Liebeneiner
Model Muddle *55* John Halas*
Model Murder, The *45* William Beaudine
Model Murder Case, The *63* Michael Truman
Model Shop, The *68* Jacques Demy

Model Wife *41* Leigh Jason
Model Young Man, A *14* James Young
Modelage Express *03* Alice Guy-Blaché
Modèle Irascible, Le *1897* Georges Méliès
Modeling *21* Dave Fleischer
Modeling for Money *38* David Miller
Modella, La *20* Mario Caserini
Modelling Extraordinary *12* Walter R. Booth
Models and Wives *31* Charles Lamont
Model's Confession *18* Ida May Park
Models, Inc. *51* Reginald LeBorg
Models, Inc. *63* Gerry O'Hara
Modena, Città del Emilia Rossa *50* Carlo Lizzani
Moder, En *12* Victor Sjöström
Moderato Cantabile *60* Peter Brook
Modern Bill Adams, A *18* Pat Sullivan
Modern Bluebeard, A *46* Jaime Salvador
Modern Cinderella, A *08* Percy Stow
Modern Cinderella, A *10* J. Stuart Blackton
Modern Cinderella, A *17* John G. Adolfi
Modern Daughters *27* Charles J. Hunt
Modern Day Houdini *83* Eddie Beverly, Jr.
Modern Dick Whittington, A *13* Percy Stow
Modern Don Juan, A *07* Lewin Fitzhamon
Modern Don Juan, A *14* Dalton Somers
Modern DuBarry, A *26* Alexander Korda
Modern Enoch Arden, A *16* Charles Avery, Clarence Badger
Modern Fishing *22* Raoul Barré, Charles Bowers
Modern Galatea, A *07* Walter R. Booth
Modern George Washington, A *10* Dave Aylott
Modern Girls *86* Jerry Kramer
Modern Grace Darling, A *08* T. J. Gobbett
Modern Guide to Health *46* Joy Batchelor, John Halas
Modern Hero, A *11* Theo Bouwmeester
Modern Hero, A *34* Arthur Greville Collins, G. W. Pabst
Modern Hero, A *40* Lloyd Bacon
Modern Highwayman, A *14* Dalton Somers
Modern Hooligans *65* Ko Nakahira
Modern Husbands *19* Francis J. Grandon
Modern Jack the Ripper, A *13* August Blom
Modern Lorelei, A *17* Henry Otto
Modern Love *18* Robert Z. Leonard
Modern Love *29* Arch Heath
Modern Love *90* Robby Benson
Modern Love Potion, A *10* Lewin Fitzhamon
Modern Madness *36* Frank Lloyd
Modern Magdalene, A *15* Will S. Davis
Modern Marriage *23* Lawrence C. Windom
Modern Marriage, A *50* Paul Landres
Modern Marriage, A *62* Ben Parker
Modern Matrimony *23* Victor Heerman
Modern Miracle, The *39* Irving Cummings
Modern Monte Cristo, A *17* W. Eugene Moore
Modern Monte Cristo, A *41* Harold Schuster

Modern Mothers *28* Phil Rosen
Modern Musketeer, A *17* Allan Dwan
Modern Mystery, A *12* Walter R. Booth
Modern Oliver Twist, A *06* J. Stuart Blackton
Modern Othello, A *17* Léonce Perret
Modern Paul Pry, A *10* A. E. Coleby
Modern Pirates, The *06* Arthur Cooper
Modern Problems *81* Ken Shapiro
Modern Prodigal, The *10* D. W. Griffith
Modern Pygmalion and Galatea, The *11* Walter R. Booth, Theo Bouwmeester
Modern Rhythm *63* Robert Henryson
Modern Robinson, A *21* Rune Carlsten
Modern Romance *81* Albert Brooks
Modern Salome, A *19* Léonce Perret
Modern Slaves *12* Edwin S. Porter
Modern Snare, The *13* Wallace Reid
Modern Suffragette, The *13* Mauritz Stiller
Modern Thelma, A *16* John G. Adolfi
Modern Times *36* Charles Chaplin
Modern Youth *26* Jack Nelson
Moderna Suffragetten, Den *13* Mauritz Stiller
Moderne École *09* Émile Cohl*
Moderno Barba Azul, El *46* Jaime Salvador
Moderns, The *52* Minoru Shibuya
Moderns, The *88* Alan Rudolph
Moders Kærlighed, En *12* August Blom
Moders Kærlighed, En *14* August Blom
Modest Hero, A *13* D. W. Griffith
Modest Young Man, A *09* Edwin S. Porter
Modesty Blaise *66* Joseph Losey
Modigliani of Montparnasse *57* Jacques Becker
Mødrehjælpen *42* Carl Theodor Dreyer
Mods and Rockers *64* Kenneth Hume
Moeru Aki *78* Masaki Kobayashi
Moetsukita Chizu *68* Hiroshi Teshigahara
Mofles' Escapades *87* Javier Durán
Mofles y los Mecanicos, El *87* Víctor Manuel Castro
Mogambo *53* John Ford
Mögen Sie in Frieden Ruhen? *67* Carlo Lizzani
Mogli Pericolose *58* Luigi Comencini
Mogliamante *77* Marco Vicario
Moglie Americana, Una *65* Gian Luigi Polidoro
Moglie Bella, La *24* Augusto Genina
Moglie del Prete, La *70* Dino Risi
Moglie di Sua Eccellenza, La *13* Augusto Genina
Moglie in Pericolo, Una *40* Max Neufeld
Moglie, Marito e... *20* Augusto Genina
Moglie per una Notte *51* Mario Camerini
Moglie Più Bella, La *70* Damiano Damiani
Mohammad, Messenger of God *76* Moustapha Akkad
Mohan Joshi Haazir Ho *84* Saeed Akhtar Mirza
Mohawk *56* Kurt Neumann
Mohawk's Way, A *10* D. W. Griffith
Mohican's Daughter, The *22* Stanner E. V. Taylor
Mohre *88* Raghuvir Kul

Moi Aussi, J'Accuse *20* Alfred Machin, Henri Wuhlschleger
Moi Drug Ivan Lapshin *86* Alexei Gherman
Moi Je *73* Jean-Luc Godard
Moi Mladshii Brat *62* Alexander Zarkhi
Moi Pierre Rivière *76* René Allio
Moi, Pierre Rivière, Ayant Égorgé Ma Mère, Ma Sœur et Mon Frère *76* René Allio
Moi Rodina *32* Josef Heifits, Alexander Zarkhi
Moi, un Noir *56* Jean Rouch
Moi Universiteti *40* Mark Donskoi
Moi Vouloir Toi *85* Patrick Dewolf
Moi Y en Avoir des Sous *72* Jean Yanne
Moi Y'en A Vouloir des Sous *72* Jean Yanne
Moine, Le *72* Ado Kyrou
Moine et la Sorcière, La *87* Suzanne Schiffman
Moires *63* Jonas Mekas
Mois d'Avril Sont Meurtriers, Les *87* Laurent Heynemann
Moïse et l'Amour *62* Henri Gruel
Moïse Sauvé des Eaux *10* Henri Andréani
Moisson de l'Espoir, Les *69* François Reichenbach
Moitié de l'Amour, La *86* Mary Jiménez
Moitié de Polka *08* Georges Méliès
Moj Tata, Socialistički Kulak *88* Matjaz Klopčić
Mojado Power *80* Alfonso Arau
Mojave Firebrand *44* Spencer G. Bennet
Mojave Kid, The *27* Robert North Bradbury
Moje Miasto *48* Wojciech Has
Mōjū *69* Yasuzo Masumura
Mokey *42* Wells Root
Mokuseki *40* Heinosuke Gosho
Molba *67* Tenghiz Abuladze
Molchaniye Doktor Aivens *73* Budimir Metalnikov
Moldavian Fairy Tale *51* Sergei Paradzhanov
Moldavskaia Skazka *51* Sergei Paradzhanov
Molder's Apprentice *49* Henning Carlsen
Mole, The *71* Alejandro Jodorowsky
Mole Men Against the Son of Hercules *61* Antonio Leonviola
Mole People, The *56* Virgil Vogel
Molens die Juichen en Weenen, De *12* Alfred Machin
Molester, The *60* Cyril Frankel
Molière *10* Louis Feuillade, Léonce Perret
Molière *13* Léonce Perret
Molière *75* Ariane Mnouchkine
Molinos de Viento *40* Arthur Sánchez
Mollenard *37* Robert Siodmak
Molly *50* Walter Hart
Molly and I *20* Howard Mitchell
Molly and Lawless John *72* Gary Nelson
Molly and Me *29* Albert Ray
Molly and Me *45* Lewis Seiler
Molly Bawn *16* Cecil M. Hepworth
Molly Cures a Cowboy *40* Jean Yarbrough
Molly Entangled *17* Robert Thornby
Molly Go Get 'Em *18* Lloyd Ingraham
Molly Learns to Mote *12* Percy Stow

Molly Louvain 32 Michael Curtiz
Molly Maguires, The 68 Martin Ritt
Molly Make-Believe 16 J. Searle Dawley
Molly O 21 F. Richard Jones
Molly of the Follies 19 Edward Sloman
Mollycoddle, The 20 Victor Fleming
Molly's Burglar 13 Bert Haldane
Molodaya Gvardiya 47 Sergei Gerasimov
Molodost Nashi Stranyi 45 I. M. Poselsky, Ivan Venzher, Sergei Yutkevich
Molti Sogni per le Strade 48 Mario Camerini
Moltopren I-IV 61 Edgar Reitz
Mom and Dad 44 William Beaudine
Môme, Le 86 Alain Corneau
Môme aux Boutons, La 58 Georges Lautner
Môme Pigalle, La 61 Alfred Rodé
Moment, The 80 Astrid Henning-Jensen
Moment Before, The 16 Robert Vignola
Moment by Moment 78 Jane Wagner
Moment d'Égarement, Un 77 Claude Berri
Moment in Love, A 57 Shirley Clarke
Moment in the Stars, The 75 Lev Kulidzhanov
Moment of Danger 59 Laslo Benedek
Moment of Darkness, A 15 Cecil M. Hepworth
Moment of Decision 62 John Knight
Moment of Indiscretion 58 Max Varnel
Moment of Love, A 57 Shirley Clarke
Moment of Passion 60 Mary Plyta
Moment of Peace, A 65 Tadeusz Konwicki*
Moment of Terror 66 Mikio Naruse
Moment of Truth, The 52 Jean Delannoy
Moment of Truth 60 John Guillermin
Moment of Truth, The 64 Tonino Cervi, Francesco Rosi
Moment to Kill, The 68 Giuliano Carmineo
Moment to Moment 65 Mervyn LeRoy
Momento de la Verdad, El 64 Tonino Cervi, Francesco Rosi
Momento della Verità, Il 64 Tonino Cervi, Francesco Rosi
Momento di Uccidere, Il 68 Giuliano Carmineo
Momento Più Bello, Il 57 Luciano Emmer
Momentos 81 María Luisa Bemberg
Moments 74 Peter Crane
Moments 79 Michal Bat-Adam
Moments Without Proper Names 86 Gordon Parks
Momia, La 57 Rafael Portillo
Momia Azteca, La 57 Rafael Portillo
Momia Azteca Contra el Robot Humano, La 57 Rafael Portillo
Momia Nacional, La 81 José Ramón Larraz
Momie, La 13 Louis Feuillade
Momma Don't Allow 55 Karel Reisz, Tony Richardson
Momman, Little Jungle Boy 69 Mende Brown
Momma's Boy 81 William Asher
Mommie Dearest 81 Frank Perry
Mommy Loves Puppy 40 Dave Fleischer
Momo 86 Johannes Schaaf
Momotombo Begins to Rumble 81 Santiago Álvarez

Mon Ami le Traître 88 José Giovanni
Mon Ami Victor 31 André Berthomieu
Mon Amie Pierrette 67 Jean-Pierre Lefèbvre
Mon Amour, Mon Amour 67 Nadine Trintignant
Mon and Ino 76 Tadashi Imai
Mon Beau-Frère A Tué Ma Sœur 86 Jacques Rouffio
Mon Bel Amour, Ma Déchirure 87 José Pinheiro
Mon Cas 86 Manoel De Oliveira
Mon Cher Sujet 88 Anne-Marie Miéville
Mon Chien 55 Georges Franju
Mon Cœur au Ralenti 28 Marco De Gastyne
Mon Cœur Balance 33 René Guissart
Mon Cœur T'Appelle 34 Carmine Gallone
Mon Coquin de Père 58 Georges Lacombe
Mon Curé chez les Pauvres 25 Donatien
Mon Curé chez les Riches 25 Donatien
Mon Gosse de Père 31 Jean De la Muir
Mon Gosse de Père 52 Léon Mathot
Mon Journal 08 Émile Cohl
Mon Mari Est Merveilleux 53 André Hunebelle
Mon Œil 71 Jean-Pierre Lefèbvre
Mon Oncle 17 Louis Feuillade
Mon Oncle 25 Maurice Mariaud
Mon Oncle 58 Jacques Tati
Mon Oncle Américain 78 Alain Resnais
Mon Oncle Antoine 70 Claude Jutra
Mon Oncle Benjamin 23 René Leprince
Mon Oncle Benjamin 69 Édouard Molinaro
Mon Oncle d'Amérique 78 Alain Resnais
Mon Père Avait Raison 36 Sacha Guitry
Mon Premier Amour 78 Elie Chouraqui
Mona Kent 61 Charles Hundt
Mona, l'Étoile Sans Nom 66 Henri Colpi
Mona Lisa 57 Henri Gruel
Mona Lisa 86 Neil Jordan
Monaca di Monza, La 62 Carmine Gallone
Monaca di Monza, La 87 Luciano Odorisio
Monaca nel Peccato, La 86 Dario Donati
Monachine, Le 63 Luciano Salce
Monanieba 84 Tenghiz Abuladze
Monarki og Demokrati 77 Jørgen Roos
Monastery Garden 32 Maurice Elvey
Monastery of Sendomir, The 19 Victor Sjöström
Moncton 70 Michel Brault, Pierre Perrault
Monday Morning in a Coney Island Police Court 08 D. W. Griffith
Monday or Tuesday 66 Vatroslav Mimica
Monday, Tuesday, Wednesday, Thursday, Friday, Saturday, Sunday 76 Lino Brocka
Monday's Child 66 Leopoldo Torre-Nilsson
Monde de Paul Delvaux, Le 44 Henri Storck
Monde du Silence, Le 55 Jacques-Yves Cousteau, Louis Malle
Monde en Parade, Le 31 Eugene Deslaw
Monde Instantané, Le 60 Frédéric Rossif
Monde Jeune, Un 65 Vittorio De Sica
Monde Nouveau, Un 65 Vittorio De Sica
Monde Sans Soleil, Le 64 Jacques-Yves Cousteau

Monde Tremblera, Le 39 Richard Pottier
Mondo Cane 61 Gualtiero Jacopetti
Mondo Cane n.2 63 Gualtiero Jacopetti, Franco Prosperi
Mondo Cannibale 72 Umberto Lenzi
Mondo Cannibale 79 Jesús Franco
Mondo Condo 86 Avi Cohen
Mondo di Yor, Il 83 Antonio Margheriti
Mondo Insanity 63 Gualtiero Jacopetti, Franco Prosperi
Mondo nella Mia Tasca, Il 60 Alvin Rakoff
Mondo Nuovo, Un 65 Vittorio De Sica
Mondo Nuovo, Il 82 Ettore Scola
Mondo Pazzo 63 Gualtiero Jacopetti, Franco Prosperi
Mondo Senza Sole, Il 64 Jacques-Yves Cousteau
Mondo Teeno 67 Jörn Donner, Norman Herbert, Richard Lester
Mondo Topless 66 Russ Meyer
Mondo Trasho 69 John Waters
Monelle 47 Henri Decoin
Moneta 63 Alexander Alov, Vladimir Naumov
Money 15 James Keane
Money 21 Duncan Macrae
Money 26 Kenji Mizoguchi
Money 27 Marcel L'Herbier
Money 46 Nils Poppe
Money, The 75 Chuck Workman
Money 82 Robert Bresson
Money a Pickle 37 Norman McLaren
Money and Economy 54 Henning Carlsen
Money and the Woman 40 William K. Howard
Money and Three Bad Men 58 Kon Ichikawa
Money Changers, The 20 Jack Conway
Money Corral, The 19 William S. Hart, Lambert Hillyer
Money Dance, The 64 Kon Ichikawa
Money for Jam 43 Erle C. Kenton
Money for Nothing 13 Edwin J. Collins
Money for Nothing 16 Maurice Elvey
Money for Nothing 26 Adrian Brunel
Money for Nothing 32 Monty Banks
Money for Speed 33 Bernard Vorhaus
Money from Home 53 George Marshall
Money Habit, The 24 Walter Niebuhr
Money in My Pocket 62 Erven Jourdan
Money Isn't Everything 18 Edward Sloman
Money Isn't Everything 25 Thomas Bentley
Money Isn't Everything 39 Frank McDonald
Money Jungle, The 68 Francis D. Lyon
Money King 36 Enrico Guazzoni
Money Kings, The 12 Van Dyke Brooke
Money Mad 08 D. W. Griffith
Money Mad 18 Hobart Henley
Money Mad 34 Frank Richardson
Money Madness 17 Henry MacRae
Money Madness 48 Sam Newfield
Money Magic 17 William Duncan
Money-Making Coats 13 Will P. Kellino
Money Maniac, The 21 Léonce Perret
Money, Marbles and Chalk 73 Ivan Nagy
Money Master, The 15 George Fitzmaurice
Money Master, The 21 George Melford
Money Means Nothing 32 Harcourt Templeman, Herbert Wilcox

Moonlight Follies *21* King Baggot
Moonlight in Havana *42* Anthony Mann
Moonlight in Hawaii *41* Charles Lamont
Moonlight in Vermont *43* Edward Lilley
Moonlight Madness *26* Teinosuke Kinugasa
Moonlight Masquerade *42* John H. Auer
Moonlight Murder *36* Edwin L. Marin
Moonlight on the Prairie *35* D. Ross Lederman
Moonlight on the Range *37* Sam Newfield
Moonlight Raid *49* Ray Nazarro
Moonlight Serenade, or The Miser Punished, A *04* Georges Méliès
Moonlight Sonata, The *32* Widgey R. Newman
Moonlight Sonata *37* Lothar Mendes
Moonlighter, The *53* Roy Rowland
Moonlighting *82* Jerzy Skolimowski
Moonlighting Wives *64* Joe Sarno
Moonlit Swords *57* Tomu Uchida
Moonraker, The *58* David MacDonald
Moonraker *79* Lewis Gilbert
Moonrise *48* Frank Borzage
Moonrunners, The *74* Gy Waldron
Moon's Our Home, The *36* William A. Seiter
Moonshine *18* Roscoe Arbuckle
Moonshine County Express *77* Gus Trikonis
Moonshine Menace, The *21* John P. McGowan
Moonshine Mountain *64* Herschell Gordon Lewis
Moonshine Trail, The *19* J. Stuart Blackton
Moonshine Valley *22* Herbert Brenon
Moonshine War, The *70* Richard Quine
Moonshiner, The *04* Wallace McCutcheon
Moonshiners, The *16* Roscoe Arbuckle
Moonshiners, The *24* Abram Room
Moonshiner's Woman *68* Allan Davis
Moonshot *67* Robert Altman
Moonstone, The *15* Frank Crane
Moonstone, The *34* Reginald Barker
Moonstone of Fez, The *14* Maurice Costello, Robert Gaillard
Moonstruck *15* Cecil Birch
Moonstruck *60* John Halas*
Moonstruck *87* Norman Jewison
Moontide *42* Fritz Lang, Archie Mayo
Moontrap, The *62* Michel Brault, Pierre Perrault
Moontrap *89* Robert Dyke
Moonwalk One *72* Theo Kamecke
Moorland Tragedy, A *33* M. A. Wetherell
Moors and Christians *87* Luis García Berlanga
Moors and Minarets *23* Adrian Brunel
Moose Hunt, The *31* Burton Gillett
Mopping Up a Million *18* Gregory La Cava
Mor Defter *64* Mahinur Ergün
Mor och Dotter *12* Mauritz Stiller
Moral Code, The *17* Ashley Miller
Moral Courage *17* Romaine Fielding
Moral Deadline, The *19* Travers Vale
Moral der Ruth Halbfass, Die *71* Volker Schlöndorff
Moral '63 *63* Rolf Thiele

Moral Fabric, The *16* Raymond B. West
Moral Fibre *21* Webster Campbell
Moral Law *18* Bertram Bracken
Moral of Ruth Halbfass, The *71* Volker Schlöndorff
Moral Sinner, The *23* Ralph Ince
Moral '63 *63* Rolf Thiele
Moral Suicide *18* Ivan Abramson
Moralist, The *59* Giorgio Bianchi
Moralista, Il *59* Giorgio Bianchi
Morality Above All *37* Martin Frič
Morals *21* William Desmond Taylor
Morals for Men *25* Bernard Hyman
Morals for Women *31* Mort Blumenstock
Morals of Hilda, The *16* Lloyd B. Carleton
Morals of Marcus, The *35* Miles Mander
Morals of Ruth Halbfass, The *71* Volker Schlöndorff
Morals of Weybury, The *16* George Loane Tucker
Moran of the Lady Letty *22* George Melford
Moran of the Marines *28* Frank R. Strayer
Moran of the Mounted *26* Harry Joe Brown
Moranbong *59* Jean-Claude Bonnardot
Moravian Chronicle *68* Vojtěch Jasný
Morbidness *72* Gonzalo Suárez
Morbo *72* Gonzalo Suárez
Morbus *82* Ignasi P. Ferre Serra
Morbus, o Que Aproveche *82* Ignasi P. Ferre Serra
Mord Em'ly *21* George Pearson
Mord i Mörket *86* Sune Lund-Sørensen
Mord i Paradis *88* Sune Lund-Sørensen
Mord Ohne Täter *20* E. A. Dupont
Mord und Totschlag *67* Volker Schlöndorff
Mördaren *67* Arne Mattsson
Mordei ha'Or *64* Alexander Ramati
Mörder, Der *62* Claude Autant-Lara
Mörder Dimitri Karamasoff, Der *31* Fedor Ozep
Mörder Sind Unter Uns, Die *46* Wolfgang Staudte
Mörder Unter Uns *31* Fritz Lang
Morderstwo *57* Roman Polanski
Mordi e Fuggi *72* Dino Risi
Mordprozess Mary Dugan *31* Arthur Robison
Mords Pas, On T'Aime *76* Yves Allégret
More *69* Barbet Schroeder
More About Nostradamus *41* David Miller
More About the Children of Bullerby Village *87* Lasse Hallström
More Amazing Than a Fairy Tale *64* Boris Dolin
More American Graffiti *79* B. W. L. Norton
More Bad News *87* Adrian Edmondson
More Dead Than Alive *68* Robert Sparr
More Deadly Than the Male *19* Robert Vignola
More Deadly Than the Male *59* Robert Bucknell
More Eggs from Your Hens *42* Terry Bishop
More Excellent Way, The *17* Perry N. Vekroff
More for Peace *54* William Beaudine
More Fun with Liquid Electricity *08*

J. Stuart Blackton
More Human Mikado, A *07* John Morland
More Milk, Evette *65* Andy Warhol
More Milk Yvette *65* Andy Warhol
More Pay, Less Work *26* Albert Ray
More Pep *36* Dave Fleischer
More, Please *29* Dave Aylott
More Than a Kiss *31* William K. Howard
More Than a Miracle *67* Francesco Rosi
More Than a Secretary *36* Alfred E. Green
More Than He Bargained For *13* Frank Wilson
More Than He Bargained For *19* Arthur H. Rooke
More the Merrier, The *43* George Stevens
More Things Change, The *86* Robyn Nevin
More to Be Pitied Than Scorned *22* Edward J. LeSaint
More to Him Than Life *16* Wilfred Noy
More Trouble *18* Ernest C. Warde
More Truth Than Poetry *17* Burton L. King
More We Are Together, The *27* J. Steven Edwards
Moře Začíná za Vsí *88* Zdeněk Flídr
Morena *86* Anssi Mänttäri
Morena Clara *38* Florian Rey
Morfalous, Les *83* Henri Verneuil
Morgan! *65* Karel Reisz
Morgan—A Suitable Case for Treatment *65* Karel Reisz
Morgan il Pirata *60* André De Toth, Primo Zeglio
Morgan le Pirate *09* Victorin Jasset
Morgan Stewart's Coming Home *85* Paul Aaron, Terry Winsor
Morgan the Pirate *60* André De Toth, Primo Zeglio
Morganatic Marriage, The *09* Percy Stow
Morgane la Sirène *28* Léonce Perret
Morgane the Enchantress *28* Léonce Perret
Morgan's Cake *88* Richard R. Schmidt
Morgan's Last Raid *29* Nick Grindé
Morgan's Marauders *29* Fred Newmeyer
Morgan's Raiders *18* Wilfred Lucas, Bess Meredyth
Morganson's Finish *26* Fred Windermere
Morgen Grauen *84* L. E. Neiman, Peter Samann
Morgengrauen *54* Victor Tourjansky
Morgenrot *33* Gustav Ucicky
Mori no Ishimatsu *37* Sadao Yamanaka
Mori no Ishimatsu *49* Kozaburo Yoshimura
Mori to Mizuumi no Matsuri *58* Tomu Uchida
Morianerna *65* Arne Mattsson
Morianna *65* Arne Mattsson
Moriarty *22* Albert Parker
Móricz Zsigmond *56* Miklós Jancsó
Morir por la Patria Es Vivir *76* Santiago Álvarez
Morirai a Mezzanotte *86* Lamberto Bava
Morita *71* Fred Paul
Morituri *65* Bernhard Wicki
Moritz, Dear Moritz *78* Hark Böhm
Mørke Punkt, Det *11* August Blom
Mørke Punkt, Det *13* Forest Holger-Madsen

Mormon, The *12* Allan Dwan
Mormon Maid, A *17* Robert Z. Leonard
Mormon Peril, The *22* H. B. Parkinson
Mormonens Offer *11* August Blom
Morning *67* Puriša Djordjević
Morning *68* Ernie Gehr
Morning After, The *33* Allan Dwan
Morning After, The *86* Sidney Lumet
Morning Before Sleep, The *69* Dan Wolman
Morning Call *58* Arthur Crabtree
Morning Conflicts *52* Heinosuke Gosho
Morning Departure *49* Roy Ward Baker
Morning for the Osone Family *46* Keisuke Kinoshita
Morning Glory *33* Lowell Sherman
Morning in the City *54* Jörn Donner
Morning in the Town *33* Tsou-sen Tsai
Morning Judge *26* Dave Fleischer
Morning, Judge *37* Leslie Goodwins
Morning Man, The *87* Danièle J. Suissa
Morning, Noon and Night *33* Dave Fleischer
Morning, Noon and Nightclub *37* Dave Fleischer
Morning Patrol *87* Nikos Nikolaidis
Morning Schedule *72* Susumu Hani
Morning Spider, The *77* Claude Chagrin
Morning Star *62* Roman Tikhomirov
Morning Sun Shines, The *29* Seichi Ina, Kenji Mizoguchi
Morning Terror *84* L. E. Neiman, Peter Samann
Morning Wash, A *00* Jack Smith
Morning with the Osone Family, A *46* Keisuke Kinoshita
Morning's Tree-Lined Street *36* Mikio Naruse
Moro Affair, The *86* Giuseppe Ferrara
Moro Naba *57* Jean Rouch
Moro Witch Doctor *64* Gerry De Leon, Eddie Romero
Morocco *30* Josef von Sternberg
Morocco *58* Allan King
Morocco Nights *34* Edward F. Cline
Morons from Outer Space *85* Michael Hodges
Moros y Cristianos *87* Luis García Berlanga
Morozko *66* Alexander Rou
Morphia, the Death Drug *14* Cecil M. Hepworth
Morrhår och Ärtor *86* Gösta Ekman
Morsa, La *16* Baldassare Negroni
Morsel, The *59* Jan Němec
Mort, La *09* Louis Feuillade
Mort A Pondu un Œuf, La *69* Giulio Questi
Mort au Champ d'Honneur *15* Léonce Perret
Mort de Belle, La *60* Édouard Molinaro
Mort de Jules César, La *07* Georges Méliès
Mort de Lucrèce, La *13* Louis Feuillade
Mort de Mario Ricci, La *83* Claude Goretta
Mort de Mozart, La *09* Louis Feuillade
Mort de Robert Macaire et Bertrand *05* Alice Guy-Blaché
Mort de Vénus, La *30* Henri Storck
Mort du Cerf, La *51* Dmitri Kirsanov
Mort du Cygne, La *37* Jean Benoît-Lévy

Mort du Duc d'Enghien, La *09* Albert Capellani
Mort du Soleil, La *21* Germaine Dulac
Mort d'un Bûcheron, La *73* Gilles Carle
Mort d'un Pourri *77* Georges Lautner
Mort d'un Toréador, La *07* Louis Gasnier
Mort d'un Tueur, La *63* Robert Hossein
Mort en Ce Jardin, La *56* Luis Buñuel
Mort en Direct, La *79* Bertrand Tavernier
Mort en Fraude *56* Marcel Camus
Mort en Fuite, Le *36* André Berthomieu
Mort Interdite *41* Yves Ciampi
Mort, Où Est Ta Victoire? *64* Hervé Bromberger
Mort ou Vif *12* Jean Durand
Mort Qui Tue, Le *13* Louis Feuillade
Mort un Dimanche de Pluie *86* Joel Santoni
Mort Vivant, Le *12* Louis Feuillade
Mortadella, La *71* Mario Monicelli
Mortal Clay *20* Victor Sjöström
Mortal Sin, The *17* John H. Collins
Mortal Storm, The *40* Frank Borzage
Morte a Venezia *71* Luchino Visconti
Morte Civile, La *42* Ferdinando Maria Poggioli
Morte di un Amico *59* Franco Rossi
Morte di un Bandito *61* Giuseppe Amato
Morte Espreita no Mar, A *62* Luis Alcoriza
Morte Ha Fatto l'Uovo, La *69* Giulio Questi
Morte in Vaticano *81* Marcello Aliprandi
Morte negli Occhi del Gatto, La *73* Antonio Margheriti
Morte Non Conta i Dollari, La *67* Riccardo Freda
Morte Piagne, La *20* Mario Bonnard
Morte Risale a Ieri Sera, La *70* Duccio Tessari
Morte-Saison des Amours, La *60* Pierre Kast
Morte Salé in Ascenseur, La *63* Marcel Bluwal
Morte sull'Alta Coclina, La *69* Fred Ringoold
Morte Vestita di Dollari, La *64* Ray Nazarro, Albert Zugsmith
Morte Viene della Spazio, La *58* Paolo Heusch
Morte Vivante, La *82* Jean Rollin
Mortgaged Wife, The *18* Allen Holubar
Morti Non Si Contano, I *68* Rafael Romero Marchent
Mortmain *15* Theodore Marston
Morton of the Mounted *35* Robert E. Tansey
Morts Qui Parlent, Les *20* Pierre Marodon
Morts Reviennent-Ils?, Les *14* Abel Gance
Mortu Nega *88* Flora Gomes
Mortuary *83* Hikmet Avedis
Mortuary Academy *87* Michael Schroeder
Mor'Vran *30* Jean Epstein
Mosaic *65* Norman McLaren
Mosaic in Confidence *55* Peter Kubelka
Mosaici di Ravenna *53* Riccardo Freda
Mosaico *73* Mario Mancini
Mosaik im Vertrauen *55* Peter Kubelka
Mosaïque *65* Norman McLaren
Mosby's Marauders *66* Michael O'Herlihy

Mosca Addio *86* Mauro Bolognini
Moschettieri del Mare, I *62* Steno
Moscow *26* Mikhail Kaufman, Ilya Kopalin
Moscow *32* Roman Karmen
Moscow Builds the Metro *34* Esther Shub
Moscow Builds the Subway *34* Esther Shub
Moscow—Cassiopeia *74* Richard Viktorov
Moscow Distrusts Tears *79* Vladimir Menshov
Moscow Does Not Believe in Tears *79* Vladimir Menshov
Moscow Drama *09* Vasili M. Goncharov
Moscow Farewell *86* Mauro Bolognini
Moscow in October *27* Boris Barnet
Moscow, Kara Kum, Moscow *33* Roman Karmen
Moscow Laughs *34* Grigori Alexandrov
Moscow Music Hall *43* Yefim Dzigan, Sergei Gerasimov, Mikhail Kalatozov
Moscow My Love *74* Alexander Mitta, Kenji Yoshida
Moscow Nights *35* Anthony Asquith
Moscow Nights *38* Alexis Granowsky
Moscow Nights *44* Yuli Raizman
Moscow on the Hudson *84* Paul Mazursky
Moscow-Shanghai *36* Paul Wegener
Moscow Sky *44* Yuli Raizman
Moscow—Ten Years After *69* D. A. Pennebaker
Moscow Today *28* Dziga Vertov
Moses *76* Gianfranco De Bosio
Moses and Aaron *74* Danièle Huillet, Jean-Marie Straub
Moses Pendleton Presents Moses Pendleton *82* Robert Elfstrom
Moses the Lawgiver *76* Gianfranco De Bosio
Moses und Äron *74* Danièle Huillet, Jean-Marie Straub
Moskau-Shanghai *36* Paul Wegener
Moskva *26* Mikhail Kaufman, Ilya Kopalin
Moskva *32* Roman Karmen
Moskva—Kassiopeia *74* Richard Viktorov
Moskva Slezam Ne Verit *79* Vladimir Menshov
Moskva Stroyit Metro *34* Esther Shub
Moskva v Octyabr' *27* Boris Barnet
Mosquita Muerta *46* Luis César Amadori
Mosquito, The *13* Émile Cohl
Mosquito *22* Dave Fleischer
Mosquito Coast, The *86* Peter Weir
Mosquito der Schänder *76* Marijan Vajda
Mosquito Squadron *68* Boris Sagal
Moss Rose *47* Gregory Ratoff
Most Beautiful, The *44* Akira Kurosawa
Most Beautiful, The *51* Luchino Visconti
Most Beautiful Age, The *68* Jaroslav Papoušek
Most Beautiful Woman in the World, The *55* Robert Z. Leonard
Most Beautiful Woman in the World, The *65* Andy Warhol
Most Beautifully *44* Akira Kurosawa
Most Charming and Attractive, The *87* Gerald Bezhanov
Most Dangerous Game, The *32* Irving Pichel, Ernest B. Schoedsack
Most Dangerous Game, The *68* Pierre Kast

Most Dangerous Man Alive, The *58* Allan Dwan
Most Dangerous Man in the World, The *69* J. Lee-Thompson
Most Dangerous Sin, The *56* Georges Lampin
Most Immoral Lady, A *29* John Griffith Wray
Most Precious Thing, The *34* Lambert Hillyer
Most Precious Thing in Life, The *34* Lambert Hillyer
Most Unlikely Millionaire, The *65* Allan King
Most Useful Tree in the World, The *37* Pál Fejös
Most Wanted Man, The *53* Henri Verneuil
Most Wanted Man in the World, The *53* Henri Verneuil
Most Wonderful Evening of My Life, The *72* Ettore Scola
Most Wonderful Moment, The *57* Luciano Emmer
Mostri, I *63* Dino Risi
Mostro, Il *77* Luigi Zampa
Mostro dell'Isola, Il *53* Roberto Bianchi Montero
Mostro dell'Opera, Il *64* Renato Polselli
Mostro di Firenze, Il *86* Cesare Farrario
Mostro di Frankenstein, Il *20* Eugenio Testa
Mostro di Venezia, Il *65* Dino Tavella
Mostro È in Tavola...Barone Frankenstein, Il *73* Antonio Margheriti, Paul Morrissey
Mosura *61* Inoshiro Honda, Lee Kresel
Mosura Tai Gojira *64* Inoshiro Honda
Mot de Cambronne, Le *36* Sacha Guitry
Mot de l'Énigme, Le *19* Louis Feuillade
Möte i Natten *46* Hasse Ekman
Motel *83* Mike MacFarland
Motel *83* Luis Mandoki
Motel *89* Christian Blackwood
Motel Hell *80* Kevin Connor
Motel, the Operator *40* Joseph Seiden
Motele the Weaver *34* Vladimir Vilner
Möten i Skymningen *57* Alf Kjellin
Moth, The *17* Edward José
Moth, The *34* Fred Newmeyer
Moth and Rust *21* Sidney Morgan
Moth and the Flame, The *14* Sidney Olcott
Motheaten Spring *32* Mikio Naruse
Mother *13* Robert Dinesen
Mother *14* Maurice Tourneur
Mother *20* Alexander Rasumny
Mother *26* Vsevolod I. Pudovkin
Mother *27* James Leo Meehan
Mother *52* Mikio Naruse
Mother *55* Mark Donskoi
Mother *62* Kaneto Shindo
Mother *68* Don Joslyn
Mother *85* Choi-su Park
Mother *87* Teguh Karya
Mother, The *88* Gleb Panfilov
Mother, a Daughter, A *81* Márta Mészáros
Mother and Child *39* Minoru Shibuya
Mother-and-Child Grass *42* Tomotaka Tasaka

Mother and Daughter *12* Mauritz Stiller
Mother and Daughter *62* Yevgeni Brunchugin, Anatoly Bukovsky
Mother and Daughter *81* Márta Mészáros
Mother and Eleven Children *66* Heinosuke Gosho
Mother and Gun *58* Hideo Sekigawa
Mother and Her Children, A *59* So Yamamura
Mother and Son *31* John P. McCarthy
Mother and Son *67* Jan Němec
Mother and Sons *38* Mikhail Doller, Vsevolod I. Pudovkin
Mother and Sons of 1776, A *12* Lewin Fitzhamon
Mother and the Law, The *19* D. W. Griffith
Mother and the Whore, The *73* Jean Eustache
Mother Carey's Chickens *38* Rowland V. Lee
Mother Dear *82* Lino Brocka
Mother Didn't Tell Me *50* Claude Binyon
Mother Do Not Shame Your Name *28* Heinosuke Gosho
Mother Earth Rises *32* Tomu Uchida
Mother Eternal *21* Ivan Abramson
Mother, Get Married *62* Heinosuke Gosho
Mother Gets the Wrong Tonic *13* Charles C. Calvert
Mother Goose à Go-Go *66* Jack H. Harris
Mother Goose in Swingtime *39* Manny Gould
Mother Goose Land *25* Dave Fleischer
Mother Goose Land *33* Dave Fleischer
Mother Goose Melodies *31* Burton Gillett
Mother Goose Nursery Rhymes *02* George Albert Smith
Mother Goose on the Loose *42* Walter Lantz
Mother Goose Stories *88* Jim Henson
Mother Heart, The *21* Howard Mitchell
Mother Hen's Holiday *37* Charles Mintz
Mother Hubba-Hubba Hubbard *47* Bob Wickersham
Mother I Miss You *26* Heinosuke Gosho
Mother I Need You *18* Frank Beal
Mother in Exile, A *14* Charles H. Weston
Mother-in-Law Has All the Luck *09* Lewin Fitzhamon
Mother India *57* Ramjankhan Mehboobkhan
Mother Instinct, The *17* Roy William Neill
Mother Is a Freshman *48* Lloyd Bacon
Mother Joan of the Angels *60* Jerzy Kawalerowicz
Mother, Jugs and Speed *76* Peter Yates
Mother Knows Best *28* John G. Blystone, Charles Judels, Dave Stamper
Mother Knows Best *48* Lloyd Bacon
Mother Krause's Journey to Happiness *29* Piel Jutzi
Mother Kuster Goes to Heaven *75* Rainer Werner Fassbinder
Mother Kuster's Journey to Heaven *75* Rainer Werner Fassbinder
Mother Kuster's Trip to Heaven *75* Rainer Werner Fassbinder
Mother Lode *82* Joe Canutt, Charlton Heston

Mother Love *31* Georg Jacoby
Mother Love *40* Gustav Ucicky
Mother Love and the Law *17* George Siegmann
Mother Machree *27* John Ford
Mother, Mother, Mother, Pin a Rose on Me *24* Dave Fleischer
Mother Never Dies *42* Mikio Naruse
Mother, 1905 *26* Vsevolod I. Pudovkin
Mother o' Mine *17* Rupert Julian
Mother o' Mine *21* Fred Niblo
Mother of Dartmoor, The *16* George Loane Tucker
Mother of His Children, The *20* Edward J. LeSaint
Mother of Kings, The *87* Janusz Zaorski
Mother of Men, A *14* Sidney Olcott
Mother of Men *38* George Pearson
Mother of the Ranch, The *11* Allan Dwan
Mother on the Quay *76* Komuri Kenjiro
Mother Ought to Be Loved, A *34* Yasujiro Ozu
Mother Ought to Marry *61* Vincent Sherman
Mother Pin a Rose on Me *29* Dave Fleischer
Mother Riley Meets the Vampire *52* John Gilling
Mother Riley Runs Riot *52* John Gilling
Mother Riley's New Venture *49* John Harlow
Mother Should Be Loved, A *34* Yasujiro Ozu
Mother, Sir! *56* Edward Bernds
Mother Superior *66* Ida Lupino
Mother Teresa *85* Ann Petrie, Jeanette Petrie
Mother Was a Rooster *62* Robert McKimson
Mother Wore Tights *47* Walter Lang
Motherhood *14* Harry A. Pollard
Motherhood *15* Harold Weston
Motherhood *17* Percy Nash
Motherhood *17* Frank Powell
Motherhood Is Not Enough *38* Ramón Peón
Motherhood or Politics *13* Warwick Buckland
Mothering Heart, The *13* D. W. Griffith
Motherland *27* Rex Davis, George B. Samuelson
Motherland Hotel *87* Ömer Kavur
Motherless Waif, A *09* A. E. Coleby
Motherlove *16* Maurice Elvey
Motherly Pram, The *08* Lewin Fitzhamon
Mothers and Daughters *74* Sergei Gerasimov
Mother's Boy *11* Lewin Fitzhamon
Mother's Boy *13* Mack Sennett
Mother's Boy *25* Roy William Neill
Mother's Boy *29* Bradley Barker, James Seymour
Mothers Cry *30* Hobart Henley
Mother's Darling *21* Edward R. Gordon
Mother's Day *48* James Broughton
Mother's Day *80* Charles Kaufman
Mother's Day Out *12* Percy Stow
Mother's Devotion, A *66* Mark Donskoi
Mothers, Fathers and Lovers *73* Greydon Clark

Mother's Gratitude, A 10 Frank Wilson
Mother's Heart, A 66 Mark Donskoi
Mother's Holiday 32 Roscoe Arbuckle
Mothers-in-Law 23 Louis Gasnier
Mother's Influence, A 16 George Loane Tucker
Mothers' Love 26 Heinosuke Gosho
Mother's Loyalty, A 66 Mark Donskoi
Mother's Millions 31 James Flood
Mothers of Men 17 Willis Robards
Mothers of Men 20 Edward José, Sidney Olcott
Mothers of Today 39 Henry Lynn
Mother's Ordeal 17 W. S. Van Dyke
Mother's Secret, A 18 Douglas Gerrard
Mother's Sin, A 07 J. H. Martin
Mother's Sin, A 18 Thomas R. Mills
Mothlight 63 Stan Brakhage
Mothra 61 Inoshiro Honda, Lee Kresel
Mothra vs. Godzilla 64 Inoshiro Honda
Moths 13 Christy Cabanne
Motion Painting No. 1 47 Oskar Fischinger
Motion Pictures 55 Robert Breer
Motion to Adjourn, A 21 Roy Clements
Motive for Revenge 35 Burt Lynwood
Motive Was Jealousy, The 70 Ettore Scola
Motivos de Luz, Los 85 Felipe Cazals
Motocyclette, La 68 Jack Cardiff
Motor Bandits, The 12 Walter Speer
Motor Competition, The 05 Alf Collins
Motor Highwayman, The 05 Arthur Cooper
Motor Mad 25 Norman Taurog
Motor Madness 37 D. Ross Lederman
Motor Masquerade, A 05 Alf Collins
Motor Mat and His Fliv 16 Pat Sullivan
Motor Patrol 50 Sam Newfield
Motor Psycho 65 Russ Meyer
Motor Valet, The 06 Arthur Cooper
Motorbike Adventure, A 05 Alf Collins
Motorcar Apaches, The 15 Mauritz Stiller
Motorcart, The 59 Marco Ferreri
Motorcycle Elopement, A 14 Leedham Bantock
Motorcycle Gang 57 Edward L. Cahn
Motorcycle Squad 41 Albert Kelley
Motorcycles 49 Martin Frič
Motoring 26 Luis Seel
Motoring 27 George Dewhurst
"?" Motorist, The 06 Walter R. Booth
Motorist's Dream, The 15 Percy Nash
Motormania 51 Jack Kinney
Mots Ont un Sens, Les 67 Chris Marker
Mots pour le Dire, Les 83 José Pinheiro
Motte Flog zum Licht, Eine 15 Fern Andra
Motten im Licht 86 Urs Egger
Moucharde, La 61 Guy Lefranc
Mouche, La 04 Alice Guy-Blaché
Mouchette 66 Robert Bresson
Mouettes, Les 19 Maurice Mariaud
Moul Le Ya, Moul Le Ya 83 Doo-yong Lee
Moulai Hafid et Alphonse XIII 12 Émile Cohl
Moulders of Men 27 Ralph Ince
Moule, La 36 Jean Delannoy
Moulin des Supplices, Le 60 Giorgio Ferroni
Moulin Maudit, Le 13 Alfred Machin

Moulin Rouge 28 E. A. Dupont
Moulin Rouge 34 Sidney Lanfield
Moulin Rouge 44 Yves Mirande
Moulin Rouge 52 John Huston
Moulins Chantent et Pleurent, Les 12 Alfred Machin
Mount Vernon 49 Willard Van Dyke
Mountain, The 35 Travis Jackson
Mountain 44 René Clément
Mountain, The 56 Edward Dmytryk
Mountain Brigand 52 Mario Soldati
Mountain Cat, The 21 Ernst Lubitsch
Mountain Charlie 82 George Stapleford
Mountain Desperadoes 52 Ray Nazarro
Mountain Dew 17 Thomas Heffron
Mountain Eagle, The 26 Alfred Hitchcock
Mountain Ears 39 Manny Gould
Mountain Family Robinson 79 John Cotter
Mountain Fighters 43 B. Reeves Eason
Mountain Justice 30 Harry Joe Brown
Mountain Justice 36 Michael Curtiz
Mountain Kate 12 Allan Dwan
Mountain Madness 20 Lloyd B. Carleton
Mountain Man 77 David O'Malley
Mountain Mary 15 B. Reeves Eason
Mountain Men, The 79 Richard Lang
Mountain Moonlight 41 Nick Grindé
Mountain Music 37 Robert Florey
Mountain of Cannibal Gods 78 Sergio Martino
Mountain Pass of Love and Hate, The 34 Kenji Mizoguchi
Mountain Rat, The 14 James Kirkwood
Mountain Rhythm 39 B. Reeves Eason
Mountain Rhythm 42 Frank McDonald
Mountain Road, The 60 Daniel Mann
Mountain Woman, The 21 Charles Giblyn
Mountaineer, The 14 Wallace Reid
Mountaineer's Honor, The 09 D. W. Griffith
Mountaineer's Honor: A Story of the Kentucky Hills, The 09 D. W. Griffith
Mountaineer's Romance, The 12 Charles Raymond
Mountains Are Stirring, The 52 Pal'o Bielek
Mountains o' Mourne 38 Harry Hughes
Mountains of Gold 31 Sergei Yutkevich
Mountains of Manhattan 27 James P. Hogan
Mountains of Mourne 30 Herbert Wilcox
Mountains of the Moon 58 Willard Van Dyke
Mountains of the Moon 87 Paulo Rocha
Mountains of the Moon 90 Bob Rafelson
Mountaintop Motel Massacre 85 Jim McCullough
Mounted Fury 31 Stuart Paton
Mounted Gymnastics 1895 Louis Lumière
Mounted Stranger, The 30 Arthur Rosson
Moura Encantada, A 85 Manuel Costa e Silva
Mourir à Madrid 62 Frédéric Rossif
Mourir à Tue-Tête 79 Anne Claire Poirier
Mourir d'Aimer 70 André Cayatte
Mourning Becomes Electra 47 Dudley Nichols
Mourning Suit, The 75 Leonard Yakir
Mouse and Garden 60 Friz Freleng
Mouse and His Child, The 77 Charles

Swenson, Fred Wolf
Mouse and the Woman, The 81 Karl Francis
Mouse Cleaning 48 Joseph Barbera, William Hanna
Mouse Comes to Dinner, The 45 Joseph Barbera, William Hanna
Mouse Divided, A 53 Friz Freleng
Mouse for Sale 54 Joseph Barbera, William Hanna
Mouse in Manhattan 45 Joseph Barbera, William Hanna
Mouse in the Art School, The 01 George Albert Smith
Mouse in the House, A 47 Joseph Barbera, William Hanna
Mouse Mazurka 49 Friz Freleng
Mouse Menace 46 Art Davis
Mouse on 57th Street, The 61 Chuck Jones
Mouse on the Moon, The 63 Richard Lester
Mouse Place Kitten 59 Robert McKimson
Mouse That Jack Built, The 59 Robert McKimson
Mouse That Roared, The 59 Jack Arnold
Mouse to Dinner 45 Joseph Barbera, William Hanna
Mouse Trouble 44 Joseph Barbera, William Hanna
Mouse Warming 52 Chuck Jones
Mouse Wreckers 48 Chuck Jones
Mouse-merized Cat, The 46 Robert McKimson
Mouse-taken Identity 57 Friz Freleng
Mousey 74 Daniel Petrie
Mousquetaire de la Reine, Le 10 Georges Méliès
Mousquetaires de la Reine, Les 03 Georges Méliès
Moustachu, Le 87 Dominique Chaussois
Moutarde Me Monte au Nez, La 74 Claude Zidi
Mouth Agape, The 73 Maurice Pialat
Mouth of Gold, The 62 Nelson Pereira Dos Santos
Mouth to Mouth 78 John Duigan
Mouthpiece, The 32 James Flood, Elliott Nugent
Mouton A Cinq Pattes, Le 54 Henri Verneuil
Mouton Enragé, Le 73 Michel Deville
Mouvement Image par Image, Le 78 Norman McLaren
Mouvement Perpétuel 49 Michel Brault, Claude Jutra
Mouvements Intraprotoplasmiques de l'Élodéa Canadensis 29 Jean Painlevé
Mouvements Protoplasmiques dans les Cellules d'Élodéa Canadensis en Milieux Isotiniques, Hypertoniques, Hypotoniques 29 Jean Painlevé
Move 70 Stuart Rosenberg
Move Along 26 Norman Taurog
Move Over, Darling 63 Michael Gordon
Movers and Shakers 85 William Asher
Movidas del Mofles, Las 87 Javier Durán
Movie, A 58 Bruce Conner
Movie Actress 87 Kon Ichikawa
Movie Crazy 32 Clyde Bruckman

Movie Daredevil, The 23 Earl Hurd
Movie Fans 20 Erle C. Kenton
Movie Fantasy, A 23 Hy Mayer
Movie-Go-Round 49 Fred Weiss
Movie Hound, The 27 Mark Sandrich
Movie House Massacre 86 Alice Raley
Movie Mad 31 Ubbe Iwerks
Movie Maker, The 86 James L. Wilson
Movie Memories 48 Horace Shepherd
Movie Mixture 46 E. W. White
Movie Movie 78 Stanley Donen
Movie Night 29 Lewis R. Foster
Movie Star American Style, or LSD — I
  Hate You! 66 Albert Zugsmith
Movie Struck 33 Dick Huemer
Movie Struck 37 Edward Sedgwick
Movie Stuntmen 53 Bernard B. Ray
Movie-Town 31 Mack Sennett
Movie Trip Through Film Land, A 21 Paul
  M. Felton
Movieland 26 Norman Taurog
Moviemakers 70 John Pearse
Movies, The 25 Roscoe Arbuckle
Movies Take a Holiday, The 44 Hans
  Richter, Herman Weinberg
Movietone Follies of 1929 29 David
  Butler, Marcel Silver
Movietone Follies of 1930 30 Ben Stoloff
Moving 88 Alan Metter
Moving a Piano 14 F. L. Lyndhurst
Moving Day 07 James A. Williamson
Moving Day 15 Harry S. Palmer
Moving Day 17 Gregory La Cava, Vernon
  Stallings
Moving Finger, The 63 Larry Moyer
Moving Hazard, The 24 Andrew P. Wil-
  son
Moving Image, The 20 Fritz Lang
Moving In 08 Alf Collins
Moving in Society 41 Nick Grindé
Moving On 48 Arne Sucksdorff
Moving Out 82 Michael Pattinson
Moving Perspectives 67 Mrinal Sen
Moving Picture Cowboy, The 14 Tom Mix
Moving Picture Rehearsal, The 10 Theo
  Bouwmeester
Moving Spirit 51 John Halas*
Moving Target, The 66 Jack Smight
Moving Target 67 Sergio Corbucci
Moving Targets 87 Chris Langman
Moving Violation 76 Charles Dubin
Moving Violations 85 Neal Israel
Movini's Venom 72 Andrew Meyer
Moy Lyubimyy Kloun 87 Yuri Kushnerov
Moya Malenkaya Zhena 87 Raimundas Ba-
  nionis
Moyak s Aurora 26 Grigori Kozintsev,
  Leonid Trauberg
Moyse et Cohen, Businessmen 31 Edmond
  T. Gréville
Moyse, Marchand d'Habits 31 Edmond T.
  Gréville
Mozambique 64 Robert Lynn
Mozart 36 Basil Dean
Mozart 56 Karl Hartl
Mozart Brothers, The 86 Suzanne Osten
Mozart Rondo 49 James Whitney, John
  Whitney
Mozart Story, The 48 Karl Hartl, Frank
  Wisbar

Mozjukhin's Field Guard 87 Valery
  Lonskoy
Možnosti Dialogu 82 Jan Švankmajer
Mravenci Nesou Smrt 85 Zbyněk Brynych
Mravnost Nade Vše 37 Martin Frič
Mrigaya 76 Mrinal Sen
Mrlja na Savjesti 68 Dušan Vukotić
Mrs. and Mr. Duff 09 Georges Méliès
Mrs. Balfane 17 Frank Powell
Mrs. Black Is Back 14 J. Searle Dawley
Mrs. Brown Goes Home to Her Mother 06
  James A. Williamson
Mrs. Brown You've Got a Lovely Daughter
  68 Saul Swimmer
Mrs. Carfax the Clever 17 Donald Crisp
Mrs. Cassell's Profession 15 Fred W. Dur-
  rant
Mrs. Corney Makes Tea 13 Wilfred Noy
Mrs. Dane's Confession 22 Michael Curtiz
Mrs. Dane's Danger 22 Wilfred North
Mrs. Dane's Defence 33 A. V. Bramble
Mrs. Dane's Defense 18 Hugh Ford
Mrs. Erricker's Reputation 20 Cecil M.
  Hepworth
Mrs. Fitzherbert 47 Montgomery Tully
Mrs. Gibbons' Boys 62 Max Varnel
Mrs. Hyde 70 Jesús Franco
Mrs. Jones Entertains 08 D. W. Griffith
Mrs. Jones' Lover 09 D. W. Griffith
Mrs. Jones' Lover, or "I Want My Hat!" 09
  D. W. Griffith
Mrs. Leffingwell's Boots 18 Walter Ed-
  wards
Mrs. Letare Lets Apartments 13 Will P.
  Kellino
Mrs. Loring's Secret 46 Lewis Allen
Mrs. Mephistopheles 29 Hugh Croise
Mrs. Mike 49 Louis King
Mrs. Miniver 42 William Wyler
Mrs. O'Malley and Mr. Malone 50 Nor-
  man Taurog
Mrs. Parkington 44 Tay Garnett
Mrs. Plum's Pudding 15 Al Christie, Ed-
  win Frazee
Mrs. Pollifax — Spy 71 Leslie Martinson
Mrs. Pym of Scotland Yard 39 Fred Elles
Mrs. Rabbit's Husband Takes the Shill-
  ing 13 Percy Stow
Mrs. Raffles nee Pimple 15 Fred Evans, Joe
  Evans
Mrs. Scrubbs' Discovery 14 Harry Furniss
Mrs. Slacker 18 Hobart Henley
Mrs. Soffel 84 Gillian Armstrong
Mrs. Temple's Telegram 20 James Cruze
Mrs. Thompson 19 Rex Wilson
Mrs. Tutti Frutti 20 Michael Curtiz
Mrs. Warren's Profession 60 Ákos von
  Ráthonyi
Mrs. Wiggs of the Cabbage Patch 19 Hugh
  Ford
Mrs. Wiggs of the Cabbage Patch 34 Nor-
  man Taurog
Mrs. Wiggs of the Cabbage Patch 42
  Ralph Murphy
Ms. Don Juan 73 Roger Vadim
Ms. 45 80 Abel Ferrara
Ms. 45 — Angel of Vengeance 80 Abel
  Ferrara
Mt. Pelee in Eruption and Destruction of

St. Pierre 02 Edwin S. Porter
Mt. Pelee Smoking Before Eruption 02 Ed-
  win S. Porter
Mučedníci Lásky 66 Jan Němec
Much Ado About... 12 Dave Aylott
Much Ado About Mousing 64 Chuck
  Jones
Much Ado About Murder 73 Douglas
  Hickox
Much Ado About Nutting 53 Chuck Jones
Much Mystery 26 Stephen Roberts
Much Too Shy 42 Marcel Varnel
Muchachita de Chiclana 26 José A.
  Ferreyra
Muchachita de Valladolid 58 Luis César
  Amadori
Muchachos de la Ciudad 37 José A.
  Ferreyra
Mucho Mouse 56 Joseph Barbera, William
  Hanna
Muchos Locos 66 Robert McKimson
Mücke, Die 54 Walter Reisch
Muckrakers, The 87 Niki List
Mud 77 Jeffrey Bloom
Mud and Soldiers 39 Tomotaka Tasaka
Muddleton Fire Brigade, The 14 Cecil
  Birch
Muddy River 81 Kohei Oguri
Muddy Romance, A 13 Mack Sennett
Muddy Waters 53 Tadashi Imai
Müde Theodor, Der 36 Veidt Harlan
Müde Tod, Der 21 Fritz Lang
Müde Tod — Ein Deutsches Volkslied in
  Sechs Versen, Der 21 Fritz Lang
Mudhoney 65 Russ Meyer
Mudlark, The 50 Jean Negulesco
Mueda — Memória e Massacre 79 Ruy
  Guerra
Mueda — Memory and Massacre 79 Ruy
  Guerra
Muerte al Invasor 61 Santiago Álvarez,
  Tomás Gutiérrez Alea
Muerte Civil 10 Mario Gallo
Muerte Cruzó el Río Bravo, La 86 Her-
  nando Name
Muerte de Pío Baroja, La 57 Juan Antonio
  Bardem
Muerte de un Burócrata, La 66 Tomás
  Gutiérrez Alea
Muerte de un Ciclista 55 Juan Antonio
  Bardem
Muerte en Este Jardín, La 56 Luis Buñuel
Muerte Espera en Atenas, La 67 Sergio
  Grieco
Muerte Viviente, La 68 Jack Hill, Juan
  Ibáñez
Muertín, El 58 Manuel Summers
Muerto, El 75 Héctor Olivera
Muerto del Palomo, El 87 Pedro Galindo
  III
Muerto Falta a la Cita, El 44 Pierre
  Chénal
Muerto Murió, El 39 Alejandro Galindo
Muerto 4-3-2-1-0 67 Primo Zeglio
Muertos Hablan, Los 35 Gabriel Soria
Muertos, la Carne y el Diablo, Los 73 José
  María Oliveira
Muet Mélomane, Le 1899 Ferdinand Zecca
Muffler and the Mechanics 87 Víctor
  Manuel Castro

Muffler's Escapades 87 Javier Durán
Mug Town 43 Ray Taylor
Mugarem fi Ijaza 58 Salah Abu Saif
Mugger, The 58 William Berke
Muggins VC 09 Dave Aylott
Muggins VC – The Defence of Khuma Hospital, India 12 Dave Aylott
Muggsy Becomes a Hero 10 D. W. Griffith*
Muggsy's First Sweetheart 10 D. W. Griffith
Mughammarat Antar wa Abla 48 Salah Abu Saif
Mugsy's Girls 84 Kevin Brodie
Mugwump's Paying Guest 11 Frank Wilson
Muharraj al Kabir, Al 51 Youssef Chahine
Muhō Matsu no Isshō 43 Hiroshi Inagaki
Muhō Matsu no Isshō 58 Hiroshi Inagaki
Muhsin Bey 88 Yavuz Turgul
Muider Circle Lives Again, The 48 Bert Haanstra
Muider Group Revived, The 48 Bert Haanstra
Muiderkring Herleeft, De 48 Bert Haanstra
Muito Prazer 79 David Neves
Můj Hříšný Muž 86 Václav Matějka
Můj Přítel Fabián 53 Jiří Weiss
Mujer de Nadie, La 38 Adela Sequeiro
Mujer del Puerto, La 33 Arcady Boytler
Mujer Mexicana, La 38 Ramón Peón
Mujer Sin Alma, La 43 Fernando De Fuentes
Mujer Sin Amor, Una 51 Luis Buñuel
Mujer Sin Cabeza, La 43 René Cardona
Mujer Sin Cabeza, Una 48 Luis César Amadori
Mujer, un Hombre, una Ciudad, Una 78 Manuel Octavio Gómez
Mujer y la Bestia, La 58 Alfonso Corona Blake
Mujer y la Selva, La 41 José A. Ferreyra
Mujeres al Borde de un Ataque de Nervios 88 Pedro Almodóvar
Mujeres de Drácula, Las 66 Federico Curiel
Mujeres de Hoy 36 Ramón Peón
Mujeres de la Frontera 87 Iván Argüello
Mujeres los Prefieren Tantos, Las 66 Luis Saslavsky
Mujeres Mandan, Las 36 Fernando De Fuentes
Mujeres Que Trabajan 40 Manuel Romero
Mujeres Salvajes 87 Gabriel Retes
Mujeres Sin Alma 36 Ramón Peón
Mukhamukham 86 Adoor Gopalakrishnan
Mukōkūseki Mono 51 Kon Ichikawa
Mukōkūseki-Sha 51 Kon Ichikawa
Mukti 37 Pramatesh Chandra Barua
Mukunthetta, Sumitra Vilikkunnu 88 Priyadarshan
Mulberry Tree, The 85 Doo-yong Lee
Muldori Village 79 Doo-yong Lee
Mule Mates 17 William Beaudine
Mule Train 50 John English
Mulefeathers 77 Don von Mizener
Mule's Disposition, The 26 Walter Lantz
Mulhall's Great Catch 26 Harry Garson
Mulher 32 Humberto Mauro

Mulher de Verdade 54 Alberto Cavalcanti
Mulher do Próximo, A 89 José Fonseca e Costa
Mulino del Po, Il 49 Alberto Lattuada
Mulino delle Donne di Pietra, Il 60 Giorgio Ferroni
Mullaway 88 Don McLennan
Müller's Bureau 86 Niki List
Müllers Büro 86 Niki List
Multi-Handicapped 86 Frederick Wiseman
Multiple Maniacs 69 John Waters
Mumia, El 69 Shadi Abdelsalam
Mumming Birds 23 Albert Brouett
Mummy, The 12 A. E. Coleby
Mummy, The 23 Norman Taurog
Mummy, The 32 Karl Freund
Mummy, The 57 Rafael Portillo
Mummy, The 59 Terence Fisher
Mummy and the Hummingbird, The 15 James Durkin
Mummy o' Mine 26 Charles Bowers
Mummy Strikes, The 57 Rafael Portillo
Mummy's Boys 36 Fred Guiol
Mummy's Curse, The 44 Leslie Goodwins
Mummy's Ghost, The 44 Reginald LeBorg
Mummy's Hand, The 40 Christy Cabanne
Mummy's Revenge, The 73 Carlos Aured
Mummy's Shroud, The 66 John Gilling
Mummy's Tomb, The 42 Harold Young
Mummy's Vengeance, The 73 Carlos Aured
Mum's the Word 26 Leo McCarey
Mumsie 27 Herbert Wilcox
Mumsy, Nanny, Sonny & Girly 69 Freddie Francis
Mumu 61 Anatoli Bobrovsky, Yevgeni Teterin
München-Berlin Wanderung 27 Oskar Fischinger
Münchhausen 43 Josef von Baky
Münchhausens Abenteuer 43 Josef von Baky
Munchies 87 Bettina Hirsch
Mundo de los Vampiros, El 60 Alfonso Corona Blake
Mundo de Vampiros, El 60 Alfonso Corona Blake
Mundo Extraño 50 Franz Eichhorn
Mundo Mercado do Sexo 78 José Mojica Marins
Mundo para Mí, Un 64 José Antonio De la Loma, Louis Duchesne, Radley Metzger
Muñeca Reina, La 71 Sergio Olhovich
Muñecos Infernales 60 Benito Alazraki, Paul Nagle
Munekata Shimai 50 Yasujiro Ozu
Munekata Sisters, The 50 Yasujiro Ozu
Muñequitas Porteñas 31 José A. Ferreyra
Munich ou La Prix pour Cent Ans 67 Marcel Ophüls
Municipal Elections 70 Patricio Guzmán
Munition Conspiracy, The 15 Forest Holger-Madsen
Munition Girl's Romance, A 17 Frank Wilson
Munition Workers 12 Lewin Fitzhamon
Munka vagy Hivatás? 63 Márta Mészáros
Munkbrogreven 34 Edvin Adolphson, Sigurd Wallen

Munna 54 Khwaja Ahmad Abbas
Munster Go Home 66 Earl Bellamy
Muntakem, El 47 Salah Abu Saif
Muntz TV 53 Oskar Fischinger
Muppet Movie, The 79 James Frawley
Muppets Take Manhattan, The 84 Frank Oz
Mur, Le 1895 Louis Lumière
Mur, Le 82 Yılmaz Güney
Mur à Jérusalem, Un 68 Albert Knobler, Frédéric Rossif
Mur de l'Atlantique, Le 70 Marcel Camus
Mur Murs 80 Agnès Varda
Mura di Malapaga, Le 49 René Clément
Mura di Sana, Le 70 Pier Paolo Pasolini
Mura no Hanayome 27 Heinosuke Gosho
Muraglia Cinese, La 58 Carlo Lizzani
Mural Murals 80 Agnès Varda
Muralla Verde, La 69 Armando Robles Godoy
Murals 54 Jørgen Roos
Murals Without Walls 78 Richard Leacock
Murato, Il 49 Francesco De Robertis
Muratti Greift Ein 34 Oskar Fischinger
Muratti Marches On 34 Oskar Fischinger
Muratti Privat 34 Oskar Fischinger
Murder! 30 Alfred Hitchcock
Murder à la Carte 55 Julien Duvivier
Murder à la Mod 67 Brian DePalma
Murder Ahoy! 64 George Pollock
Murder Among Friends 41 Ray McCarey
Murder Anonymous 55 Ken Hughes
Murder at Covent Garden 32 Michael Barringer, Leslie Hiscott
Murder at Dawn 32 Richard Thorpe
Murder at 45 R.P.M. 60 Étienne Périer
Murder at Glen Athol 36 Frank R. Strayer
Murder at Malibu Beach 46 Howard Bretherton
Murder at Midnight 31 Frank R. Strayer
Murder at Monte Carlo 34 Ralph Ince
Murder at Scotland Yard 52 Victor M. Gover
Murder at Site Three 59 Francis Searle
Murder at Ten 35 Patrick K. Heale
Murder at the Baskervilles 37 Thomas Bentley
Murder at the Burlesque 49 Val Guest
Murder at the Cabaret 34 Reginald Fogwell
Murder at the Gallop 63 George Pollock
Murder at the Grange 52 Victor M. Gover
Murder at the Inn 34 George King
Murder at the Vanities 34 Mitchell Leisen
Murder at the Windmill 49 Val Guest
Murder at 3 A.M. 53 Francis Searle
Murder by Agreement 63 Denis Scully
Murder by an Aristocrat 36 Frank McDonald
Murder by Appointment 41 Phil Rosen
Murder by Confession 78 Anthony Page
Murder by Contract 58 Irving Lerner
Murder by Death 76 Robert Moore
Murder by Decree 78 Bob Clark
Murder by Illusion 85 Robert Mandel
Murder by Invitation 41 Phil Rosen
Murder by Mail 80 David Paulsen
Murder by Numbers 90 Paul Leder
Murder by Phone 81 Michael Anderson
Murder by Proxy 54 Terence Fisher

Murder by Rope *36* George Pearson
Murder by Signature *61* Erwin Leiser
Murder by Television *35* Clifford Sanforth
Murder by the Book *86* Mel Damski
Murder by the Clock *31* Edward Sloman
Murder by the Stars *41* Joseph H. Lewis
Murder Can Be Deadly *61* Lance Comfort
Murder Can Hurt You *70* Roger Duchowny
Murder Clinic, The *66* Domenico De Felice, Elio Scardamaglia
Murder, Czech Style *66* Jiří Weiss
Murder for Sale *30* Gustav Ucicky
Murder Game, The *65* Sidney Salkow
Murder Goes to College *37* Charles Reisner
Murder, He Says *45* George Marshall
Murder in Eden *61* Max Varnel
Murder in Greenwich Village *37* Albert S. Rogell
Murder in Limehouse, A *19* Frank Carlton
Murder in Mississippi *65* Joseph P. Mawra
Murder in Morocco *43* Fred Newmeyer
Murder in Reverse *45* Montgomery Tully
Murder in Soho *38* Norman Lee
Murder in Swingtime *37* Arthur Dreifuss
Murder in the Air *40* Lewis Seiler
Murder in the Air *49* Lesley Selander
Murder in the Big House *36* Nick Grindé
Murder in the Big House *42* B. Reeves Eason
Murder in the Blue Room *44* Leslie Goodwins
Murder in the Cathedral *51* George Hoellering
Murder in the Clouds *34* D. Ross Lederman
Murder in the Dark *86* Sune Lund-Sørensen
Murder in the Etruscan Cemetery *82* Christian Plummer
Murder in the Family *38* Albert Parker
Murder in the Family *44* William Beaudine
Murder in the Fleet *35* Edward Sedgwick
Murder in the Footlights *46* Maclean Rogers
Murder in the Museum *34* Melville Shyer
Murder in the Music Hall *46* John English
Murder in the Night *38* Norman Lee
Murder in the Old Red Barn *35* Milton Rosmer
Murder in the Private Car *34* Harry Beaumont
Murder in the Red Barn, A *13* Maurice Elvey
Murder in the Stratosphere *34* Melville Brown
Murder in Thornton Square, The *44* George Cukor
Murder in Times Square *43* Lew Landers
Murder in Trinidad *34* Louis King
Murder in Yoshiwara *60* Tomu Uchida
Murder, Inc. *50* Raoul Walsh, Bretaigne Windust
Murder, Inc. *60* Burt Balaban, Stuart Rosenberg
Murder Is a Murder...Is a Murder, A *72* Étienne Périer
Murder Is Announced, A *87* David Giles

Murder Is My Beat *54* Edgar G. Ulmer
Murder Is My Business *46* Sam Newfield
Murder Is News *39* Leon Barsha
Murder Is News *54* Douglas Pierce
Murder Lust *85* Don Jones
Murder Man, The *35* Tim Whelan
Murder Mansion, The *70* Francisco Lara Polop
Murder Men, The *61* John Peyser
Murder Mississippi *65* Joseph P. Mawra
Murder Most Foul *64* George Pollock
Murder, My Little Friend *55* Stig Olin
Murder, My Sweet *44* Edward Dmytryk
Murder Obsession *80* Riccardo Freda
Murder of Dr. Harrigan, The *35* Frank McDonald
Murder of Dmitri Karamazov, The *68* Ivan Pyriev, Mikhail Ulyanov
Murder of Father Christmas, The *40* Christian-Jaque
Murder of General Gryaznov, The *21* Ivan Perestiani
Murder of Karamazov *31* Fedor Ozep
Murder of Squire Jeffrey, The *13* Dave Aylott
Murder on a Bridle Path *36* William Hamilton, Edward Killy
Murder on a Honeymoon *35* Lloyd Corrigan
Murder on Approval *55* Bernard Knowles
Murder on Dante Street *56* Mikhail Romm
Murder on Diamond Row *37* William K. Howard
Murder on Lenox Avenue *41* Arthur Dreifuss
Murder on Monday *51* Ralph Richardson
Murder on the Air *49* Paul Stein
Murder on the Blackboard *34* George Archainbaud
Murder on the Bridge *75* Maximilian Schell
Murder on the Campus *34* Richard Thorpe
Murder on the Campus *61* Michael Winner
Murder on the Orient Express *74* Sidney Lumet
Murder on the Roof *29* George B. Seitz
Murder on the Rue Dante *56* Mikhail Romm
Murder on the Runaway Train *34* Harry Beaumont
Murder on the Second Floor *32* William McGann
Murder on the Set *35* Leslie Hiscott
Murder on the Waterfront *43* B. Reeves Eason
Murder on the Yukon *40* Louis Gasnier
Murder One *88* Graeme Campbell
Murder, Our Style *66* Jiří Weiss
Murder Over New York *40* Harry Lachman
Murder Party, The *33* Michael Powell
Murder Party *61* Helmuth Ashley
Murder Psalm *80* Stan Brakhage
Murder Rap *88* Kliff Kuehl
Murder Reported *57* Charles Saunders
Murder Ring, The *41* James P. Hogan
Murder, She Said *61* George Pollock

Murder She Sings *86* Fred Baker
Murder Society, The *66* Domenico De Felice, Elio Scardamaglia
Murder Syndrome *80* Riccardo Freda
Murder Tomorrow *38* Donovan Pedelty
Murder Will Out *1899* Georges Méliès
Murder Will Out *30* Clarence Badger
Murder Will Out *39* Roy William Neill
Murder Will Out *52* John Gilling
Murder with Music *41* George P. Quigley
Murder with Pictures *36* Charles Barton
Murder Without Cause *20* E. A. Dupont
Murder Without Crime *50* J. Lee-Thompson
Murder Without Tears *53* William Beaudine
Murderer, The *62* Claude Autant-Lara
Murderer, The *67* Arne Mattsson
Murderer Among Us *31* Fritz Lang
Murderer Dmitri Karamazov, The *31* Fedor Ozep
Murderer Lives at No. 21, The *41* Henri-Georges Clouzot
Murderer Lives at 21, The *41* Henri-Georges Clouzot
Murderers Among Us *46* Wolfgang Staudte
Murderers Are Among Us, The *46* Wolfgang Staudte
Murderers Are Amongst Us, The *46* Wolfgang Staudte
Murderers Are at Large *42* Vsevolod I. Pudovkin, Yuri Tarich
Murderers Are Coming, The *42* Vsevolod I. Pudovkin, Yuri Tarich
Murderers Are on Their Way *42* Vsevolod I. Pudovkin, Yuri Tarich
Murderers' Row *66* Henry Levin
Murderock, Uccide a Passo di Danza *84* Lucio Fulci
Murderous Obsession *80* Riccardo Freda
Murders in the Rue Morgue *32* Robert Florey
Murders in the Rue Morgue *71* Gordon Hessler
Murders in the Zoo *33* A. Edward Sutherland
Murdock Trial, The *14* Lawrence Trimble
Muri di Sana, I *70* Pier Paolo Pasolini
Muri Shinjū Nihon no Natsu *67* Nagisa Oshima
Muriel *63* Alain Resnais
Muriel, il Tempo di un Ritorno *63* Alain Resnais
Muriel, or The Time of Return *63* Alain Resnais
Muriel ou Le Temps d'un Retour *63* Alain Resnais
Muriel's Double *12* Bert Haldane
Murieron a Mitad del Río *87* José Nieto Ramírez
Murmur of the Heart *71* Louis Malle
Muro, El *47* Leopoldo Torre-Nilsson
Murph the Surf *74* Marvin Chomsky
Murphy and the Magic Cap *13* Dave Aylott
Murphy's IOU *13* Mack Sennett
Murphy's Law *86* J. Lee-Thompson
Murphy's Millions *14* Dave Aylott
Murphy's Romance *85* Martin Ritt

Murphy's Wake 03 Alf Collins
Murphy's War 70 Peter Yates
Murri Affair, The 74 Mauro Bolognini
Murrieta 64 George Sherman
Musashi Miyamoto 40 Hiroshi Inagaki
Musashi Miyamoto 42 Kenji Mizoguchi
Musashi Miyamoto 54 Hiroshi Inagaki
Musashino Fujin 51 Kenji Mizoguchi
Muscă cu Bani, O 54 Ion Popescu-Gopo
Muscle Beach 48 Irving Lerner, Joseph
  Strick
Muscle Beach Party 63 William Asher
Muscle Beach Tom 55 Joseph Barbera,
  William Hanna
Muscle Tussle 53 Robert McKimson
Muscles Mouse 51 Joseph Barbera, Wil-
  liam Hanna
Musée, Le 64 Walerian Borowczyk
Musée dans la Mer, Un 53 Jacques-Yves
  Cousteau
Musée des Grotesques, Le 11 Émile Cohl
Musée Grévin 58 Jacques Demy, Jean
  Masson
Musée Vivant, Le 65 Henri Storck
Musen Fusen 24 Kenji Mizoguchi
Museo dei Sogni, Il 48 Luigi Comencini
Museo del Crimen, El 44 René Cardona
Museum and the Fury, The 56 Leo T.
  Hurwitz
Museum Mystery 37 Clifford Gulliver
Musgrave Ritual, The 12 Georges Treville
Musgrave Ritual, The 22 George Ridgwell
Mushibameru Haru 32 Mikio Naruse
Mushroom Eater, The 76 Roberto
  Gavaldón
Mushroom Stew 15 Cecil Birch
Music 66 Marguerite Duras, Paul Seban
Music Academy, The 64 John Halas*
Music and Millions 36 Randall Faye
Music As a Hair Restorer 16 Harry S.
  Palmer
Music Box, The 32 James Parrott
Music Box 40 Denis Kavanagh
Music Box 89 Costa-Gavras
Music Box Kid, The 60 Edward L. Cahn
Music City U.S.A. 66 Preston Collins,
  James Dinet
Music for Madame 37 John G. Blystone
Music for Millions 44 Henry Koster
Music from Mars 53 Ján Kadár, Elmar
  Klos
Music Goes 'Round, The 36 Victor Schert-
  zinger
Music Hall 34 John Baxter
Music Hall Manager's Dilemma, The 04
  Walter R. Booth
Music Hall Parade 39 Oswald Mitchell
Music Hall Star, The 16 Forest Holger-
  Madsen
Music Hath Charms 11 Theo Bouwmeester
Music Hath Charms 17 Gregory La Cava
Music Hath Charms 35 Thomas Bentley,
  Alexander Esway, Walter Summers, Ar-
  thur Woods
Music Hath Charms 36 Walter Lantz
Music in Darkness 47 Ingmar Bergman
Music in Manhattan 44 John H. Auer
Music in My Heart 39 Joseph Santley
Music in the Air 34 Joe May
Music in the Dark 47 Ingmar Bergman

Music Is Magic 35 George Marshall
Music Lesson, The 32 Ubbe Iwerks
Music Lovers, The 70 Ken Russell
Music Machine, The 78 Ian Sharp
Music Made Simple 38 Roy Rowland
Music Maker, The 36 Horace Shepherd
Music Man, The 38 John Halas
Music Man 48 Will Jason
Music Man, The 62 Morton Da Costa
Music Master, The 27 Allan Dwan
Music Master, The 43 Fedor Ozep
Music Mice-tro 67 Rudy Larriva
Music Room, The 58 Satyajit Ray
Music Teacher, The 88 Gérard Corbiau
Music Will Tell 38 Jean Yarbrough
Music with Max Jaffa 59 Francis Searle
Musica, La 66 Marguerite Duras, Paul
  Seban
Musica in Piazza 36 Mario Mattòli
Musica Profana 19 Mario Caserini
Musica Proibita 43 Carlo Campogalliani
Musical Beauty Shop, The 30 Monty
  Banks
Musical Cocktail, A 41 Horace Shepherd
Musical Farmer 32 Wilfred Jackson
Musical Film Revues 33 Herbert Smith
Musical Madness 16 William Beaudine
Musical Masquerade 46 Horace Shepherd
Musical Medley 29 R. E. Jeffrey
Musical Medley 35 John E. Blakeley
Musical Medley No. 1 28 Hugh Croise
Musical Medley No. 5 27 George A.
  Cooper
Musical Medley No. 6 28 Hugh Croise
Musical Memories 35 Dave Fleischer
Musical Merrytone No. 1 36 Will Hammer
Musical Moments 29 R. E. Jeffrey
Musical Mountaineers 39 Dave Fleischer
Musical Paintbox 47 David Hand
Musical Passage 84 Jim Brown
Musical Poster No. 1 40 Len Lye
Musical Ride, The 01 Edwin S. Porter
Musical Romance 47 Horace Shepherd
Musical Story, A 40 Alexander Ivanovsky,
  Herbert Rappaport
Musical Tramps 14 Charles Chaplin
Musicians 60 Kazimierz Karabasz
Musician's Girl 40 Martin Frič
Musiciens du Ciel, Les 40 Georges
  Lacombe
Musicomanie, La 10 Émile Cohl
Musik i Mörker 47 Ingmar Bergman
Musique en Méditerranée 68 François
  Reichenbach
Musique et Danse des Chasseurs Gow 65
  Jean Rouch
Musketeers of Pig Alley, The 12 D. W.
  Griffith
Musketeers of the Queen, The 03 Georges
  Méliès
Musketeers of the Sea 60 Massimo Patrizi
Musketier Meier III 38 Joe Stöckel
Musolino the Bandit 50 Mario Camerini
Musorgsky 50 Grigori Roshal
Muss 'Em Up 36 Charles Vidor
Mussolini Speaks 33 Jack Cohn
Mussolini — Ultimo Atto 74 Carlo Lizzani
Mussorgsky 50 Grigori Roshal
Must We Marry? 28 Frank S. Mattison
Mustaa Valkoisella 67 Jörn Donner

Mustafa Kamel 53 Ahmed Badrakhan
Mustang 59 Peter Stephens
Mustang Country 76 John Champion
Mustergatte, Der 38 Wolfgang Liebe-
  neiner
Musuko no Seishun 52 Masaki Kobayashi
Musulman Rigolo, Le 1897 Georges Méliès
Musume 26 Heinosuke Gosho
Musume Dōjōji 46 Kon Ichikawa
Musume Kawaiya 28 Kenji Mizoguchi
Musume, Tsuma, Haha 60 Mikio Naruse
Mut 39 Mikhail Kalatozov
Mutant 81 Allan Holzman
Mutant 84 John Cardos
Mutant Hunt 86 Tim Kincaid
Mutant on the Bounty 89 Robert Torrance
Mutation, The 73 Jack Cardiff
Mutations, The 73 Jack Cardiff
Mutchan no Uta 86 Hiromichi Horikawa
Mute Appeal, A 17 Walter Edwin
Mute Witness, The 13 Allan Dwan
Muthers, The 76 Cirio Santiago
Mutige Seefahrer, Der 36 Hans Deppe
Mutilated 74 Michael Findlay
Mutilator, The 79 John Cardos
Mutilator, The 83 Buddy Cooper
Mutineers, The 49 Jean Yarbrough
Mutineers, The 61 Lewis Gilbert
Mutinés de l'Elseneur, Les 36 Pierre
  Chénal
Mutiny 17 Lynn Reynolds
Mutiny 24 F. Martin Thornton
Mutiny 52 Edward Dmytryk
Mutiny, The 62 Silvio Amadio
Mutiny Ahead 35 Thomas Atkins
Mutiny Ain't Nice 38 Dave Fleischer
Mutiny in Outer Space 58 Edward Bernds
Mutiny in Outer Space 65 Hugo Grimaldi
Mutiny in Space 88 David Winters
Mutiny in the Arctic 41 John Rawlins
Mutiny in the Big House 39 William
  Nigh
Mutiny in the Kitchen 08 A. E. Coleby
Mutiny of the Elsinore, The 20 Edward
  Sloman
Mutiny of the Elsinore, The 37 Roy Lock-
  wood
Mutiny on a Russian Battleship 05 Alf
  Collins
Mutiny on the Blackhawk 39 Christy
  Cabanne
Mutiny on the Body 39 Charlie Chase
Mutiny on the Bounty 35 Frank Lloyd
Mutiny on the Bounty 62 Lewis Milestone,
  Carol Reed
Mutiny on the Bunny 50 Friz Freleng
Mutiny on the Buses 72 Harry Booth
Mutiny on the Seas 39 Lewis D. Collins
Mutt and Jeff in Iceland 20 Raoul Barré,
  Charles Bowers
Mutt and Jeff in Spain 19 Raoul Barré,
  Charles Bowers
Mutt and Jeff in Switzerland 19 Raoul
  Barré, Charles Bowers
Mutt and Jeff in the Submarine 16 Charles
  Bowers
Mutt and Jeff's Nooze Weekly 20 Raoul
  Barré, Charles Bowers
Mutt in a Rutt, A 59 Robert McKimson
Mutt 'n' Bones 44 Paul Sommer

Mutt the Mutt Trainer *19* Raoul Barré, Charles Bowers

Mutter Courage und Ihr Kinder *55* Wolfgang Staudte

Mutter der Kompagnie, Die *34* Franz Seitz

Mutter Krausens Fahrt ins Glück *29* Piel Jutzi

Mutter Küsters Fahrt zum Himmel *75* Rainer Werner Fassbinder

Mutter und Kind *24* Carl Fröhlich

Mutter und Kind *33* Hans Steinhoff

Mutterliebe *40* Gustav Ucicky

Mutts to You *38* Charlie Chase

Muž Který Lže *67* Alain Robbe-Grillet

Muž na Drátě *85* Julius Matula

Muž z Neznáma *39* Martin Frič

Muž z Prvního Století *61* William Hole, Jr., Oldřich Lipský

Muzestvo *41* Boris Barnet

Muzhestvo *41* Boris Barnet

Muzikantská Liduška *40* Martin Frič

Mužné Hry *89* Jan Švankmajer

Muzsika *84* Miklós Jancsó

Muzskoe Vospitanie *86* Usman Saparov

Muzzle, The *58* Wolfgang Staudte

Muzzle Tough *54* Friz Freleng

My African Adventure *87* Boaz Davidson

My Ain Folk *44* Germain Burger

My Ain Folk *73* Bill Douglas

My American Cousin *85* Sandy Wilson

My American Uncle *78* Alain Resnais

My American Wife *22* Sam Wood

My American Wife *36* Harold Young

My Apple *50* Marc-Gilbert Sauvajon

My Apprenticeship *39* Mark Donskoi

My Artistical Temperature *37* Dave Fleischer

My Asylum *79* Marco Ferreri

My Aunt *86* Halit Refik

My Aunt Nora *89* Jorge Preloran

My Aunt's Millions *34* Gustaf Molander

My Baby *12* D. W. Griffith

My Baby Is Black *60* Claude Bernard-Aubert

My Baby Just Cares for Me *31* Dave Fleischer

My Bare Lady *62* Arthur Knight

My Beautiful Laundrette *85* Stephen Frears

My Beloved *58* Josef Heifits

My Beloved Child *26* Heinosuke Gosho

My Beloved Clown *87* Yuri Kushnerov

My Best Friend Is a Vampire *88* Jimmy Huston

My Best Friend's Girl *82* Bertrand Blier

My Best Gal *43* Anthony Mann

My Best Girl *27* Sam Taylor

My Bill *38* John Farrow

My Blood Runs Cold *65* William Conrad

My Bloody Valentine *81* George Mihalka

My Blue Heaven *50* Henry Koster

My Blue Heaven *90* Herbert Ross

My Body Hungers *67* Joe Sarno

My Bodyguard *80* Tony Bill

My Bonnie *25* Dave Fleischer

My Bonnie Lies Over the Ocean *25* Dave Fleischer

My Boy *21* Albert Austin, Victor Heerman

My Boys Are Good Boys *78* Bethel Bucka-lew

My Breakfast with Blassie *83* Andy Kaufman, Linda Lautrec

My Bride Is a Ghost *68* Satsuo Yamamoto

My Brilliant Career *78* Gillian Armstrong

My Brother *32* Heinosuke Gosho

My Brother Fidel *77* Santiago Álvarez

My Brother Has Bad Dreams *77* Robert J. Emery

My Brother-in-Law Has Killed My Sister *86* Jacques Rouffio

My Brother Jonathan *47* Harold French

My Brother Julio's Paintings *65* Manoel De Oliveira

My Brother Talks to Horses *46* Fred Zinnemann

My Brother the Outlaw *51* Elliott Nugent

My Brothers and I *64* Khodzhakuli Narliev

My Brother's Come to Stay *85* Franco Castellano, Giuseppe Moccia

My Brother's Keeper *48* Roy Rich, Alfred Roome

My Brother's Wedding *83* Charles Burnett

My Buddy *44* Steve Sekely

My Bunny Lies Over the Sea *48* Chuck Jones

My Candidate *38* Chano Urueta

My Case *86* Manoel De Oliveira

My Champion *81* Gwen Arner

My Chauffeur *85* David Beaird

My Childhood *72* Bill Douglas

My City *67* Ion Popescu-Gopo

My Country *32* Josef Heifits, Alexander Zarkhi

My Country *84* Lino Brocka

My Country First *16* Tom Terriss

My Country's Wings *40* Carlos Borcosque

My Cousin *18* Edward José

My Cousin Rachel *52* Henry Koster

My Dad *22* Clifford Smith

My Dad Is Tarzan *86* Judith Hollander

My Dark Lady *87* Frederick King Keller

My Darling Clementine *46* John Ford

My Darling, My Darling *86* Eduard Zahariev

My Darling, My Dearest *82* Sergio Corbucci

My Darling Shiksa *83* Menahem Golan

My Daughter *60* Victor Zhilin

My Daughter Is Different *37* Ladislas Vajda

My Daughter Joy *50* Gregory Ratoff

My Days with Jean-Marc *63* André Cayatte

My Dear Fellow *58* Josef Heifits

My Dear Friends, Act III *85* Nanni Loy

My Dear Love *11* Lewin Fitzhamon

My Dear Man *58* Josef Heifits

My Dear Miss Aldrich *37* George B. Seitz

My Dear Secretary *48* Charles Martin

My Dearest Señorita *72* Jaime De Armiñán

My Death Is a Mockery *52* Anthony Young

My Demon Lover *87* Charles Loventhal

My Dinner with André *81* Louis Malle

My Dog *55* Georges Franju

My Dog, Buddy *60* Ray Kellogg

My Dog Rusty *48* Lew Landers

My Dog Shep *46* Ford Beebe

My Dog, the Thief *69* Robert Stevenson

My Dolly *09* Jack Smith

My Dream Is Yours *48* Michael Curtiz

My Enemy the Sea *63* Kon Ichikawa

My Erotic Fantasies *73* Jim McBride

My Face, Red in the Sunset *61* Masahiro Shinoda

My Fair Lady *64* George Cukor

My Father *89* Aguy Elias

My Father, My Master *77* Paolo Taviani, Vittorio Taviani

My Fatherland *32* Josef Heifits, Alexander Zarkhi

My Father's Glory *90* Yves Robert

My Father's House *46* Herbert Kline

My Father's Mistress *68* Arne Mattsson

My Fault *26* Kenji Mizoguchi

My Fault, Continued *26* Kenji Mizoguchi

My Fault, New Version *26* Kenji Mizoguchi

My Favorite Blonde *42* Sidney Lanfield

My Favorite Brunette *47* Elliott Nugent

My Favorite Duck *42* Chuck Jones

My Favorite Spy *42* Tay Garnett

My Favorite Spy *51* Norman Z. McLeod

My Favorite Wife *40* Garson Kanin, Leo McCarey

My Favorite Year *82* Richard Benjamin

My Feelin's Is Hurt *40* Dave Fleischer

My Fighting Gentleman *17* Edward Sloman

My First Forty Years *87* Carlo Vanzina

My First Love *45* André Berthomieu

My First Love *78* Elie Chouraqui

My First Love Affair *55* Keisuke Kinoshita

My First Two Hundred Years *85* Gyula Maar

My First Wife *84* Paul Cox

My Foolish Heart *49* Mark Robson

My Forbidden Past *51* Robert Stevenson

My Four Years in Germany *18* William Nigh

My Friend *79* Fons Rademakers

My Friend Barbara *38* Fritz Kirchhoff

My Friend Fabian *53* Jiří Weiss

My Friend Flicka *43* Harold Schuster

My Friend from India *27* E. Mason Hopper

My Friend Irma *49* George Marshall

My Friend Irma Goes West *50* Hal Walker

My Friend Ivan Lapshin *86* Alexei Gherman

My Friend Jeckyll *60* Marino Girolami

My Friend Kolka *61* Alexander Mitta, A. Saltykov

My Friend Levy *14* Forest Holger-Madsen

My Friend the Devil *22* Harry Millarde

My Friend the Gypsy *53* Jiří Weiss

My Friend the King *31* Michael Powell

My Friend the Monkey *39* Dave Fleischer

My Friends *75* Pietro Germi, Mario Monicelli

My Friends, Act II *82* Mario Monicelli

My Friends Need Killing *84* Paul Leder

My Friends 2 *82* Mario Monicelli

My Gal Loves Music *44* Edward Lilley

My Gal Sal *30* Dave Fleischer

My Gal Sal *42* Irving Cummings

My Geisha *61* Jack Cardiff

My General *87* Jaime De Armiñán

My Girl Tisa *48* Elliott Nugent
My Girlfriend's Boyfriend *86* Eric Rohmer
My Girlfriend's Wedding *68* Jim McBride
My Grandfather's Clock *34* Felix E. Feist
My Green Fedora *35* Friz Freleng
My Gun Is Quick *57* Giorgio Bianchi, Phil Victor
My Hands Are Clay *48* Lionel Tomlinson
My Harem *30* Stephen Roberts
My Heart Belongs to Daddy *42* Robert Siodmak
My Heart Belongs to Thee *38* Carmine Gallone
My Heart Goes Crazy *46* Wesley Ruggles
My Heart Has Two Voices *87* Mikael Wiström
My Heart Is Calling *34* Carmine Gallone
My Heart Sings *54* Mario Mattòli
My Hero *12* D. W. Griffith
My Hero *20* Pat Sullivan
My Hero *48* Edward Sedgwick
My Hobo *63* Zenzo Matsuyama
My Home Is Copacabana *65* Arne Sucksdorff
My Home Town *28* Scott Pembroke
My Homeland *32* Josef Heifits, Alexander Zarkhi
My How Times Have Changed *19* Leighton Budd
My Husband Lies *13* Michael Curtiz
My Husband's Friend *18* Marshall Farnum, Jesse J. Ormont
My Husband's Other Wife *19* J. Stuart Blackton
My Husband's Wives *24* Maurice Elvey
My Hustler *65* Andy Warhol
My Indian Anna *07* Arthur Gilbert
My Infinitely Dear Son *85* Valentino Orsini
My Irish Molly *38* Alex Bryce
My Kid *26* Charles Lamont
My Kind of Town *84* Charles Wilkinson
My Kingdom for... *85* Budd Boetticher
My Kingdom for a Cook *43* Richard Wallace
My Kingdom for a Horse *86* Serge Bourguignon
My Lady Friends *21* Lloyd Ingraham
My Lady Incog *16* Sidney Olcott
My Lady Incognito *16* Sidney Olcott
My Lady of Whims *25* Dallas M. Fitzgerald
My Lady's Dress *17* Alexander Butler
My Lady's Garter *19* Maurice Tourneur
My Lady's Latchkey *21* Edwin Carewe
My Lady's Lips *25* James P. Hogan
My Lady's Revenge *07* J. H. Martin
My Lady's Slipper *16* Ralph Ince
My Last Duchess *66* Ken Hughes
My Learned Friend *43* Basil Dearden, Will Hay
My Left Foot *89* Jim Sheridan
My Life As a Dog *85* Lasse Hallström
My Life for Maria Isabell *35* Erich Waschneck
My Life for Zarah Leander *85* Christian Blackwood
My Life Is at Stake *38* Richard Eichberg
My Life Is Like Fire *61* Hideo Sekigawa
My Life Is Yours *41* Harold S. Bucquet

My Life Story *55* Jørgen Roos
My Life to Live *62* Jean-Luc Godard
My Life with Caroline *41* Lewis Milestone
My Lips Betray *33* John G. Blystone
My Little Boy *17* Elsie Jane Wilson
My Little Buckaroo *38* Friz Freleng
My Little Chickadee *40* Edward F. Cline
My Little Duckaroo *54* Chuck Jones
My Little Feller *37* Charles Lamont
My Little Girl *85* Constance Kaiserman
My Little Lady Bountiful *08* Lewin Fitzhamon
My Little Loves *75* Jean Eustache
My Little Mother *40* Francisco Elías
My Little Pony *86* Michael Joens
My Little Pony—The Movie *86* Michael Joens
My Little Sister *19* Kenean Buel
My Little Wife *87* Raimundas Banionis
My Lord Conceit *21* F. Martin Thornton
My Lord the Chauffeur *27* B. E. Doxat-Pratt
My Love *59* Heinosuke Gosho
My Love Burns *49* Kenji Mizoguchi
My Love Came Back *40* Kurt Bernhardt
My Love for Yours *39* Edward H. Griffith
My Love Has Been Burning *49* Kenji Mizoguchi
My Love Is a Rose *63* Hasse Ekman
My Love Letters *83* Amy Jones
My Love to the Swallows *72* Jaromil Jireš
My Lovely Daughter *28* Kenji Mizoguchi
My Lover, My Son *70* John Newland
My Loving Child *26* Heinosuke Gosho
My Loving Daughter *28* Kenji Mizoguchi
My Lucky Star *33* Louis Blattner, John Harlow
My Lucky Star *38* Roy Del Ruth
My Madonna *15* Alice Guy-Blaché
My Main Man from Stony Island *78* Andrew Davis
My Man *24* David Smith
My Man *28* Archie Mayo
My Man Adam *85* Roger Simon
My Man and I *52* William A. Wellman
My Man Godfrey *36* Gregory La Cava
My Man Godfrey *57* Henry Koster
My Man Jasper *44* George Pal
My Margo *67* Menahem Golan
My Marriage *35* George Archainbaud
My Michael *75* Dan Wolman
My Mistake *27* Sam Newfield
My Mother *32* Phil Rosen
My Mother-in-Law *04* Alf Collins
My Mother-in-Law's Visit *07* Charles Raymond
My Mother the General *81* Joel Silberg
My Motherland *32* Josef Heifits, Alexander Zarkhi
My Mother's Castle *90* Yves Robert
My Mother's Lovers *86* Radysław Piwowarski
My Name Ain't Suzie *86* Angie Chan
My Name Is Gatillo *87* Pedro Galindo III
My Name Is Ivan *62* Andrei Tarkovsky
My Name Is John *72* John Newland
My Name Is Joker *70* Raj Kapoor
My Name Is Julia Ross *45* Joseph H. Lewis
My Name Is Kerim *67* Yılmaz Güney
My Name Is King *71* Renato Savino

My Name Is Legend *75* Duke Kelly
My Name Is Nobody *73* Tonino Valerii
My Name Is Pecos *66* Maurizio Lucidi
My Name Is Rocco Papaleo *71* Ettore Scola
My Name Is Trinity *76* Ferdinando Baldi
My Neighbor's Wife *25* Clarence Geldert
My New Friends *87* Gus Van Sant, Jr.
My New Partner *84* Claude Zidi
My Night at Maud's *68* Eric Rohmer
My Night with Maud *68* Eric Rohmer
My Nights with Françoise *63* André Cayatte
My Obvinyaem *87* Timofei Levchuk
My Official Wife *14* James Young
My Official Wife *26* Paul Stein
My Old China *31* Will P. Kellino
My Old Duchess *33* Lupino Lane
My Old Dutch *15* Lawrence Trimble
My Old Dutch *26* Lawrence Trimble
My Old Dutch *34* Sinclair Hill
My Old Kentucky Home *22* Ray C. Smallwood
My Old Kentucky Home *26* Dave Fleischer
My Old Kentucky Home *38* Lambert Hillyer
My Old Man's a Fireman *33* Charles Reisner
My Old Man's Place *71* Edwin Sherin
My Other "Husband" *83* Georges Lautner
My Outlaw Brother *51* Elliott Nugent
My Own Country *84* Lino Brocka
My Own Pal *26* John G. Blystone
My Own True Love *48* Compton Bennett
My Own United States *18* John W. Noble
My Pal *25* Ward Hayes
My Pal Dr. Jeckyll *60* Marino Girolami
My Pal Gus *52* Robert Parrish
My Pal Paul *30* Walter Lantz
My Pal the King *32* Kurt Neumann
My Pal Trigger *46* Frank McDonald
My Pal Wolf *44* Alfred L. Werker
My Partner Master Davis *36* Claude Autant-Lara
My Partner Mr. Davis *36* Claude Autant-Lara
My Past *31* Roy Del Ruth
My Pleasure Is My Business *74* Al Waxman
My Pony Boy *29* Dave Fleischer
My Pop, My Pop *40* Dave Fleischer
My Reputation *46* Kurt Bernhardt
My Rural Relations *22* Clyde E. Elliott
My s Urala *44* Lev Kuleshov*
My Science Project *85* Jonathan Betuel
My Second Brother *59* Shohei Imamura
My Seven Little Sins *54* Jean Boyer
My Side of the Mountain *69* James B. Clark
My Sin *31* George Abbott
My Sister and I *48* Harold Huth
My Sister Eileen *42* Alexander Hall
My Sister Eileen *55* Richard Quine
My Sister, My Love *66* Vilgot Sjöman
My Sister, My Love *78* Karen Arthur
My Sister's Keeper *86* David Saperstein
My Six Convicts *52* Hugo Fregonese
My Six Loves *63* Gower Champion
My Son *14* Charles H. Weston
My Son *25* Edwin Carewe

My Son *39* Joseph Seiden
My Son *79* Keisuke Kinoshita
My Son Alone *42* William McGann
My Son Is a Criminal *39* C. C. Coleman, Jr.
My Son Is Guilty *39* Charles Barton
My Son John *51* Leo McCarey
My Son! My Son! *40* Charles Vidor
My Son Nero *56* Steno
My Son the Curate *08* Dave Aylott
My Son, the Hero *43* Edgar G. Ulmer
My Son, the Hero *61* Duccio Tessari
My Son the Professor *46* Renato Castellani
My Son the Vampire *52* John Gilling
My Song for You *34* Maurice Elvey
My Song Goes 'Round the World *34* Richard Oswald
My Son's Youth *52* Masaki Kobayashi
My Soul Runs Naked *65* James Landis
My Stars *26* Roscoe Arbuckle
My Stepmother Is an Alien *88* Richard Benjamin
My Stupid Brother *32* Heinosuke Gosho
My Sweet Charlie *70* Lamont Johnson
My Sweet Lady *75* Daniel Haller
My Sweet Little Village *85* Jiří Menzel
My Sweetheart *18* Meyrick Milton
My Tail Is My Ticket *59* Dušan Vukotić
My Teenage Daughter *56* Herbert Wilcox
My Therapist *82* Al Rossi
My Third Wife, by George *68* Harry Kerwin
My Third Wife George *68* Harry Kerwin
My True Love, My Wound *87* José Pinheiro
My True Story *51* Mickey Rooney
My Tutor *82* George Bowers
My 20th Century *89* Ildikó Enyedi
My Two Husbands *40* Wesley Ruggles
My Uncle *58* Jacques Tati
My Uncle Antoine *70* Claude Jutra
My Uncle from America *78* Alain Resnais
My Uncle, Mr. Hulot *58* Jacques Tati
My Uncle the Vampire *59* Steno
My Uncle's Legacy *88* Krsto Papić
My Universities *40* Mark Donskoi
My University *40* Mark Donskoi
My Unmarried Wife *17* George Siegmann
My Valet *15* Alfred Santell, Mack Sennett
My Way *74* Emil Nofal, Roy Sargent
My Way *74* Kaneto Shindo
My Way Home *64* Miklós Jancsó
My Way Home *78* Bill Douglas
My Weakness *33* David Butler
My White City *73* Emil Lotyanu
My Widow and I *50* Carlo Ludovico Bragaglia
My Wife *18* Del Henderson
My Wife and I *25* Millard Webb
My Wife Is a Panther *61* Raymond Bailly
My Wife, the Film Star *18* Ernst Lubitsch
My Wife the Miss *34* Steve Sekely
My Wife's a Teetotaler *06* Alf Collins
My Wife's Best Friend *52* Richard Sale
My Wife's Dog *08* James A. Williamson
My Wife's Enemy *67* Gianni Puccini
My Wife's Family *31* Monty Banks
My Wife's Family *41* Walter C. Mycroft
My Wife's Family *56* Gilbert Gunn
My Wife's Gone to the Country *31* Dave Fleischer

My Wife's Husband *16* Cecil Birch
My Wife's Husband *63* Gilles Grangier
My Wife's Lodger *52* Maurice Elvey
My Wife's Pet *12* Fred Rains
My Wife's Relations *22* Edward F. Cline, Buster Keaton
My Wife's Relatives *39* Gus Meins
My Wild Irish Rose *22* David Smith
My Wild Irish Rose *47* David Butler
My Will, I Will *87* Luk Kim Ming
My Woman *33* Victor Schertzinger
My Word, If I Catch You Smoking *09* A. E. Coleby
My Word, If You're Not Off *07* Frank Mottershaw
My World Dies Screaming *58* Harold Daniels
My Younger Brother *62* Alexander Zarkhi
My za Mir *51* Joris Ivens, Ivan Pyriev
My Zhdom Vas s Pobedoi *41* Alexander Medvedkin, Ilya Trauberg
Mya: La Mère *70* Jean Rouch
Myonuriui Han *71* Yoon Kyo Park
Myortvye Dushi *60* Leonid Trauberg
Myra Breckinridge *70* Michael Sarne
Myra Hess *45* Humphrey Jennings
Myriam *28* Enrico Guazzoni
Myrt and Marge *33* Al Boasberg
Myrte and the Demons *48* Bruno Paul Schreiber
Mystère *83* Carlo Vanzina
Mystère Alexina *85* René Feret
Mystère Barton, Le *49* Charles Spaak
Mystère de la Chambre Jaune, Le *13* Émile Chautard, Maurice Tourneur
Mystère de la Chambre Jaune, Le *30* Marcel L'Herbier
Mystère de la Tour Eiffel, Le *27* Julien Duvivier
Mystère de la Villa Rose, Le *29* Edmond T. Gréville
Mystère de la Villa Rose, Le *30* René Hervil, Louis Mercanton
Mystère de l'Atelier Quinze, Le *57* André Heinrich, Chris Marker, Alain Resnais
Mystère de Paris *34* Jacques De Baroncelli
Mystère d'une Vie *17* André Hugon
Mystère Koumiko, Le *65* Chris Marker
Mystère Picasso, Le *55* Henri-Georges Clouzot
Mystères d'Angkor, Les *59* William Dieterle
Mystères de la Tour Eiffel, Les *27* Julien Duvivier
Mystères de l'Ombre, Les *14* Léonce Perret
Mystères de Paris, Les *11* Albert Capellani
Mystères de Paris, Les *37* Félix Gandéra
Mystères de Paris, Les *43* Jacques De Baroncelli
Mystères de Paris, Les *62* André Hunebelle
Mystères du Château du Dé, Les *29* Man Ray
Mystères du Ciel, Les *20* Gérard Bourgeois
Mysterians, The *57* Inoshiro Honda
Mysteries *68* Gregory Markopoulos
Mysteries *78* Paul De Lussanet
Mysteries from Beyond the Grave *58* Fernando Méndez

Mysteries of Black Magic *57* Miguel Delgado
Mysteries of India *21* Fritz Lang, Joe May
Mysteries of London, The *15* A. E. Coleby
Mysteries of New York *16* Christy Cabanne
Mysteries of the Sea *80* Robert Elfstrom, Al Giddings
Mysteries of Warsaw, The *16* Aleksander Hertz
Mysterious Airman, The *28* Harry Revier
Mysterious Avenger, The *36* David Selman
Mysterious Box, The *03* Georges Méliès
Mysterious Bullet, The *55* Paul Gherzo
Mysterious Cabinet, The *02* Georges Méliès
Mysterious Cafe, The *01* Edwin S. Porter
Mysterious Client, The *18* Fred E. Wright
Mysterious Contragrav, The *15* Henry MacRae
Mysterious Crossing *36* Arthur Lubin
Mysterious Desperado, The *49* Lesley Selander
Mysterious Detective Morgan, The *61* Hideo Sekigawa
Mysterious Doctor, The *43* Ben Stoloff
Mysterious Dr. Fu Manchu, The *29* Rowland V. Lee
Mysterious Dr. Satan *40* John English, William Witney
Mysterious Footsteps *17* Anders Wilhelm Sandberg
Mysterious Goods *23* Charles R. Seeling
Mysterious Heads, The *02* Walter R. Booth
Mysterious House of Dr. C., The *76* Ted Kneeland
Mysterious Intruder *46* William Castle
Mysterious Invader *57* Ronnie Ashcroft
Mysterious Island, The *05* Georges Méliès
Mysterious Island, The *26* Benjamin Christensen, Lucien Hubbard, Maurice Tourneur
Mysterious Island *41* B. M. Chelintsev, E. A. Penzlin
Mysterious Island *51* Spencer G. Bennet
Mysterious Island *60* Cy Endfield
Mysterious Island, The *72* Juan Antonio Bardem, Henri Colpi
Mysterious Island of Captain Nemo, The *72* Juan Antonio Bardem, Henri Colpi
Mysterious Jug, The *37* Walter Lantz
Mysterious Knight, The *1899* Georges Méliès
Mysterious Lady, The *16* Forest Holger-Madsen
Mysterious Lady, The *28* Fred Niblo
Mysterious Lady's Companion, The *16* August Blom
Mysterious Lodger, The *14* Maurice Costello, Robert Gaillard
Mysterious Magician, The *64* Alfred Vohrer
Mysterious Mechanical Toy, The *03* Alf Collins
Mysterious Miss Terry, The *17* J. Searle Dawley
Mysterious Miss X, The *39* Gus Meins
Mysterious Mr. Davis, The *36* Claude Autant-Lara

Mysterious Mr. M, The *46* Lewis D. Collins, Vernon Keays
Mysterious Mr. Moto *38* Norman Foster
Mysterious Mr. Moto of Devil's Island *38* Norman Foster
Mysterious Mr. Nicholson, The *47* Oswald Mitchell
Mysterious Mr. Reeder, The *39* Jack Raymond
Mysterious Mr. Tiller, The *17* Rupert Julian
Mysterious Mr. Valentine, The *46* Philip Ford
Mysterious Mr. Wong, The *35* William Nigh
Mysterious Mr. X, The *39* J. A. Hübler-Kahla
Mysterious Monsters, The *75* Robert Guenette
Mysterious Mouse *30* Dave Fleischer
Mysterious Mrs. M, The *17* Lois Weber
Mysterious Mrs. Musslewhite, The *17* Lois Weber
Mysterious Mystery, The *32* Edward F. Cline
Mysterious Paper, The *1896* Georges Méliès
Mysterious Philanthropist, The *13* Warwick Buckland
Mysterious Pilot, The *37* Spencer G. Bennet
Mysterious Poacher, The *49* Don Chaffey
Mysterious Portrait, A *1899* Georges Méliès
Mysterious Princess, The *19* Herbert Brenon
Mysterious Retort, The *06* Georges Méliès
Mysterious Rider *21* Benjamin B. Hampton
Mysterious Rider, The *27* John Waters
Mysterious Rider, The *33* Fred Allen
Mysterious Rider, The *38* Lesley Selander
Mysterious Rider, The *42* Sam Newfield
Mysterious Rider, The *47* Riccardo Freda
Mysterious Rose, The *14* Francis Ford
Mysterious Satellite, The *56* Koji Shima
Mysterious Shadows *49* G. W. Pabst
Mysterious Shot, The *14* Donald Crisp
Mysterious Stranger, The *25* Roy Del Ruth
Mysterious Stranger, The *25* Jack Nelson
Mysterious Stranger, The *37* Howard Bretherton
Mysterious Stranger, The *45* Wallace Fox
Mysterious Stranger *82* Peter H. Hunt
Mysterious Vamp, The *20* Gregory La Cava
Mysterious Witness, The *23* Seymour Zeliff
Mysterious World, The *16* Yevgeni Bauer
Mysterious X, The *13* Benjamin Christensen
Mysterious Yarn, The *17* Gregory La Cava
Mysterium *79* Shirley Clarke
Mystery *33* Mario Camerini
Mystery at Monstein *54* Joe Mendoza
Mystery at Monte Carlo *33* B. Reeves Eason
Mystery at the Burlesque *49* Val Guest
Mystery at the Villa Rose *30* Leslie Hiscott
Mystery Box, The *22* J. A. Norling

Mystery Brand, The *27* Ben F. Wilson
Mystery Broadcast *43* George Sherman
Mystery Club, The *26* Herbert Blaché
Mystery Girl, The *18* William DeMille
Mystery House *38* Noel Mason Smith
Mystery in Mexico *48* Robert Wise
Mystery in Swing *40* Arthur Dreifuss
Mystery in the Mine *59* James Hill
Mystery Junction *51* Michael McCarthy
Mystery Lake *53* Larry Lansburgh
Mystery Liner *34* William Nigh
Mystery Man, The *35* Ray McCarey
Mystery Man *44* George Archainbaud
Mystery Mansion *84* David E. Jackson
Mystery Mountain *34* Otto Brower, B. Reeves Eason
Mystery of a Hansom Cab, The *15* Harold Weston
Mystery of a London Flat, The *15* Walter West
Mystery of Alexina, The *85* René Feret
Mystery of Blood, The *53* Martin Frič
Mystery of Boscombe Vale, The *12* Georges Treville
Mystery of Brudenell Court, The *24* Hugh Croise
Mystery of Compartment C, The *31* Spencer G. Bennet
Mystery of Diamond Island, The *35* Elmer Clifton
Mystery of Dogstooth Cliff, The *24* Hugh Croise
Mystery of Edwin Drood, The *09* Arthur Gilbert
Mystery of Edwin Drood, The *14* Herbert Blaché, Tom Terriss
Mystery of Edwin Drood, The *35* Stuart Walker
Mystery of Kaspar Hauser, The *74* Werner Herzog
Mystery of Marie Roget, The *42* Phil Rosen
Mystery of Mr. Bernard Brown, The *21* Sinclair Hill
Mystery of Mr. Marks, The *14* Warwick Buckland
Mystery of Mr. Wong, The *39* William Nigh
Mystery of Mr. X, The *34* Edgar Selwyn
Mystery of No. 47, The *17* Otis B. Thayer
Mystery of Oberwald, The *79* Michelangelo Antonioni
Mystery of Picasso, The *55* Henri-Georges Clouzot
Mystery of Pine Tree Camp, The *13* Sidney Olcott
Mystery of Room 13, The *15* George Ridgwell
Mystery of Room 13 *38* Norman Lee
Mystery of the Black Jungle *55* Ralph Murphy
Mystery of the Château of the Dice, The *29* Man Ray
Mystery of the Dancing Men, The *23* George Ridgwell
Mystery of the Diamond Belt, The *14* Charles Raymond
Mystery of the Double Cross, The *17* Louis Gasnier
Mystery of the £500,000 Pearl Necklace,

The *13* Harold Heath
Mystery of the Galvanised Iron Ash Can, The *20* Raoul Barré, Charles Bowers
Mystery of the Garrison *08* Georges Méliès
Mystery of the Golden Eye, The *48* William Beaudine
Mystery of the Grand Hotel *16* James W. Horne
Mystery of the Hindu Image, The *13* Raoul Walsh
Mystery of the Hooded Horsemen, The *37* Ray Taylor
Mystery of the Khaki Tunic, The *24* Hugh Croise
Mystery of the Landlady's Cat, The *14* Will P. Kellino
Mystery of the Leaping Fish, The *16* John Emerson
Mystery of the Lost Ranch, The *25* Tom Gibson, Harry S. Webb
Mystery of the Marie Celeste, The *35* Denison Clift
Mystery of the Mary Celeste *35* Denison Clift
Mystery of the Old Mill, The *14* H. Oceano Martinek
Mystery of the Pink Villa, The *30* Leslie Hiscott
Mystery of the Pirate Queen, The *87* Stepan Puchinyan
Mystery of the Riverboat *44* Lewis D. Collins, Ray Taylor
Mystery of the Silent Death, The *28* Leslie Eveleigh
Mystery of the Sleeper Trunk, The *09* Sidney Olcott
Mystery of the Snakeskin Belt, The *50* Frank Cadman
Mystery of the 13th Guest, The *43* William Beaudine
Mystery of the Wax Museum, The *33* Michael Curtiz
Mystery of the Wentworth Castle, The *40* William Nigh
Mystery of the White Handkerchief, The *47* Ken Hughes
Mystery of the White Room *39* Otis Garrett
Mystery of the Yellow Aster Mine, The *13* Wallace Reid
Mystery of the Yellow Room, The *19* Émile Chautard
Mystery of the Yellow Room, The *30* Marcel L'Herbier
Mystery of Thirteen, The *19* Francis Ford
Mystery of Thor Bridge, The *23* George Ridgwell
Mystery of Thug Island, The *64* Luigi Capuano
Mystery of Tut-Ankh-Amen's Eighth Wife, The *23* Andrew Remo
Mystery on Bird Island *54* John Haggarty
Mystery on Monster Island *80* Juan Piquer Simon
Mystery Plane *39* George Waggner
Mystery Ranch *32* David Howard
Mystery Ranch *34* Bernard B. Ray
Mystery Range *37* Robert F. Hill
Mystery Rider *28* Robert J. Horner
Mystery Road, The *21* Paul Powell

Mystery Sea Raider 40 Edward Dmytryk
Mystery Ship, The 17 Francis Ford, Harry Harvey
Mystery Ship 41 Lew Landers
Mystery Squadron 33 Colbert Clark, David Howard
Mystery Street 50 John Sturges
Mystery Submarine 50 Douglas Sirk
Mystery Submarine 62 C. M. Pennington-Richards
Mystery Train 31 Phil Whitman
Mystery Train 89 Jim Jarmusch
Mystery Trooper, The 31 Stuart Paton
Mystery Valley 28 John P. McGowan
Mystery Woman 34 Eugene Forde
Mystic, The 25 Tod Browning
Mystic Circle Murders 39 Frank O'Connor
Mystic Faces 18 E. Mason Hopper
Mystic Hour, The 17 Richard Ridgely
Mystic Hour, The 34 Melville DeLay
Mystic Jewel, The 15 Jack Conway
Mystic Manipulations 11 Walter R. Booth, Theo Bouwmeester
Mystic Mat, The 13 Dave Aylott
Mystic Mirror, The 27 Karl Hoffmann, Prof. Teschner
Mystic Moonstone, The 13 Dave Aylott
Mystic Mountain, The 33 Dmitri Kirsanov
Mystic Pizza 88 Donald Petrie
Mystic Ring, The 12 Dave Aylott
Mystic Shriner's Day 05 Edwin S. Porter
Mystic Swing, The 00 Edwin S. Porter
Mystical Flame, The 03 Georges Méliès
Mystical Love-Making 08 Émile Cohl
Mystical Maid of Jamasha Pass 12 Allan Dwan
Mystifiers, The 63 Jacques Deray
Mystike Fremmede, Den 14 Forest Holger-Madsen
Mystique 81 Bobby Roth
Mystiske Selskabsdame, Den 16 August Blom
Mysto Fox 46 Bob Wickersham
Myten 66 Jan Halldoff
Myth, The 65 Adimaro Sala
Myth, The 66 Jan Halldoff
N.I. Ni-C'Est Fini 08 Émile Cohl
N or NW 37 Len Lye
N.P. 68 Silvano Agosti
N.P. — The Secret 68 Silvano Agosti
N Stands for Nelly 11 Lewin Fitzhamon
N.U. 48 Michelangelo Antonioni
NVV Congres 29 Joris Ivens
Na Estrada da Vida 80 Nelson Pereira Dos Santos
Na-Insaafi 89 Mehul Kumar
Na Iskhode Nochi 88 Rodion Nakhapetov
Na Kometě 68 Karel Zeman
Na Krasnom Frontye 20 Lev Kuleshov
Na Linii Ognya — Operatory Kino-Khroniki 41 Dziga Vertov
Na Malkia Ostrov 58 Rangel Vulchanov
Na Pražském Hradě 32 Alexander Hammid
Na Primavera da Vida 26 Humberto Mauro
Na Putu za Katangu 87 Živojin Pavlović
Na Samotě u Lesa 76 Jiří Menzel
Na Semi Vetrakh 63 Alexander Galich, Stanislav Rostotsky

Na Srebrnym Globie 88 Andrzej Żuławski
Na Start 35 Eugeniesz Cekalski, Aleksander Ford, Wanda Jakubowska
Na Svojoj Zemlji 48 France Štiglić
Na Varshavskom Trakte 16 Władysław Starewicz
Nabat 17 Yevgeni Bauer
Nabat na Rassvete 87 Arkady Kordon
Nabbed 15 Edwin J. Collins
Nabbem Joins the Force 13 Edwin J. Collins
Nablyudatel 88 Arvo Ikho
Nabonga 44 Sam Newfield
Nacala 70 Gleb Panfilov
Nace un Amor 38 Luis Saslavsky
Nacer en Leningrado 77 Humberto Solás
Načeradec, Král Kibiců 31 Gustav Machatý
Nach Meinem Letzten Umzug 70 Hans-Jürgen Syberberg
Nachalo 70 Gleb Panfilov
Nachbar, Der 87 Markus Fischer
Nachmittag zu den Wettrennen 29 Hans Richter
Nachrichten von der Staufern 77 Alexander Kluge
Nachsaison 88 Wolfram Paulus
Nacht, Die 85 Hans-Jürgen Syberberg
Nacht an der Donau, Eine 35 Carl Boese
Nacht auf Goldenhall, Die 19 Conrad Veidt
Nacht-Bummler 30 Richard Eichberg
Nacht der Entscheidung, Die 31 Dmitri Buchowetzki
Nacht der Erkenntnis, Die 22 Arthur Robison
Nacht der Königin Isabeau, Die 20 Robert Wiene
Nacht der Vampire 70 Leon Klimovsky
Nacht des Grauens, Eine 21 F. W. Murnau
Nacht des Marders, Die 88 Maria Theresa Wagner
Nacht des Schicksals, Die 81 Helmer von Lützelburg
Nacht Fiel Über Gotenhaten 60 Frank Wisbar
Nacht Gehört Uns, Die 29 Carl Fröhlich
Nacht im Mai, Eine 38 Georg Jacoby
Nacht im Paradies, Eine 32 Karel Lamač
Nacht in London, Eine 27 Lupu Pick
Nacht in Venedig, Eine 34 Robert Wiene
Nacht mit dem Kaiser, Die 37 Erich Engel
Nacht Ohne Morgen 20 Karl Grüne
Nacht Ohne Pause, Die 31 Andrew Marton, Franz Wenzler
Nachtbesuch 20 Karl Grüne
Nächte des Grauens 16 Arthur Robison
Nächte von Port Said, Die 31 Dmitri Kirsanov*
Nachtfalter 11 Urban Gad
Nachtgestalten 20 Richard Oswald
Nachtgestalten 29 Hans Steinhoff
Nachtigall Mädel, Das 33 Leo Lasky
Nachtlokal zum Silbermond, Das 61 Wolfgang Glück
Nachtmeerfahrt, Die 86 Kitty Kino
Nachts, Wenn der Teufel Kam 57 Robert Siodmak
Nachts Wenn Dracula Erwacht 70 Jesús Franco

Nachtschatten 72 Niklas Schilling
Nación Clandestina, La 89 Jorge Sanjinés
Nacional III 83 Luis García Berlanga
Nackt Unter Wölfen 63 Frank Beyer
Nackte Mann auf dem Sportplatz, Der 77 Konrad Wolf
Nackte und der Satan, Die 59 Victor Trivas
Nad Niemnem 39 Wanda Jakubowska, Karol Szołowski
Nad Niemnem 87 Zbigniew Kuźmiński
Nad Ranem 28 Aleksander Ford
Nada 73 Claude Chabrol
Nada Gang, The 73 Claude Chabrol
Nada Más Que una Mujer 34 Harry Lachman
Nadare 37 Mikio Naruse
Nadare 52 Kaneto Shindo
Naděje 63 Karel Kachyňa
Nadezhda 55 Sergei Gerasimov
Nadezhda 73 Mark Donskoi
Nadia 84 Alan Cooke
Nadia 86 Amnon Rubinstein
Nadie Dijo Nada 71 Raúl Ruiz
Nadie Escuchaba 88 Nestor Almendros, Jorge Ulla
Nådige Frøken, Den 11 August Blom
Nadine 87 Robert Benton
Nadja à Paris 64 Eric Rohmer
Nadzór 81 Wiesław Saniewski
Nae-Shi 86 Doo-yong Lee
Naeb el Am, El 45 Ahmad Kamel Morsi
Naerata Ometi 86 Arvo Ikho, Lejda Lajus
Nafrat ki Aandhi 89 Mehul Kumar
Nag in the Bag, A 38 Charlie Chase
Nagana 33 Ernest L. Frank
Nagana 55 Hervé Bromberger
Nagareru 56 Mikio Naruse
Nagarik 52 Ritwik Ghatak
Nagaya no Shinshi Roku 47 Yasujiro Ozu
Nagooa 84 Amos Guttman
Några Sommarkvällar på Jorden 87 Gunnel Lindblom
Nagrodzone Uczucie 57 Walerian Borowczyk, Jan Lenica
Nagurareta Kochiyama 34 Teinosuke Kinugasa
Nagy Generáció, A 86 Ferenc András
Nagymama, A 16 Alexander Korda
Nagymama 35 István György
Nagyüzemi Tojástermelés 62 Márta Mészáros
Náhodou Je Prima! 88 Radovan Urban
Naidra the Dream Woman 14 George Kleine
Naïf aux Quarante Enfants, Le 57 Philippe Agostini
Nail, The 49 Rafael Gil
Nail Gun Massacre 87 Bill Leslie, Terry Lofton
Nail in the Boot, A 32 Mikhail Kalatozov
Nain, Le 12 Louis Feuillade
Nain et Géant 02 Georges Méliès
Näinä Päivinä 55 Jörn Donner
Nais 45 Marcel Pagnol
Nais 48 Raymond Laboursier
Naisenkuvia 70 Jörn Donner
Naissance 81 Robert Kramer
Naissance de la Photographie, La 64 Roger Leenhardt

Naissance des Cigognes, La *25* Jean Gré-
millon
Naissance des Heures, La *30* Edmond T.
Gréville
Naissance du Cinéma *46* Roger Leenhardt
Naissance d'une Cité *64* Louis Daquin
Naissance et Mont de Prométhée *74* Jac-
ques Rivette
Nakaw na Pag-Ibig *80* Lino Brocka
Naked Africa *57* Cedric Worth
Naked Alibi *54* Jerry Hopper
Naked Among the Wolves *63* Frank Beyer
Naked and the Dead, The *58* Raoul
Walsh
Naked Angels *69* Bruce Clark
Naked Ape, The *73* Donald Driver
Naked As Nature Intended *61* George
Harrison Marks
Naked Autumn *61* François Leterrier
Naked Brigade, The *65* Maury Dexter
Naked Cage, The *86* Paul Nicholas
Naked Came the Stranger *75* Radley
Metzger
Naked Camera *60* Russ Meyer
Naked Cell, The *88* John Crome
Naked Childhood *67* Maurice Pialat
Naked Citizen, The *86* Başar Sabuncu
Naked City, The *48* Jules Dassin
Naked Civil Servant, The *78* Jack Gold
Naked Country, The *85* Tim Burstall
Naked Dawn, The *55* Edgar G. Ulmer
Naked Earth, The *58* Vincent Sherman
Naked Edge, The *61* Michael Anderson
Naked Evil *66* Stanley Goulder
Naked Exorcism *76* Elo Pannaccio
Naked Eye, The *57* Louis Clyde Stoumen
Naked Face, The *83* Bryan Forbes
Naked Face of Night, The *58* Kozaburo
Yoshimura
Naked Flame, The *70* Larry Matanski
Naked Fog, The *64* Joe Sarno
Naked Fury *59* Charles Saunders
Naked Gals of the Golden West *62* Russ
Meyer
Naked General, The *64* Hiromichi Hori-
kawa
Naked Goddess, The *59* William Hole, Jr.
Naked Gun, The *56* Edward Dew
Naked Gun, The *88* David Zucker
Naked Gun: From the Files of Police
Squad!, The *88* David Zucker
Naked Heart, The *34* Julien Duvivier
Naked Heart, The *49* Marc Allégret
Naked Hearts *16* Rupert Julian
Naked Hearts *66* Édouard Luntz
Naked Hills, The *56* Josef Shaftel
Naked Hours, The *64* Marco Vicario
Naked in the Sun *57* R. John Hugh
Naked Island *60* Kaneto Shindo
Naked Jungle, The *53* Byron Haskin
Naked Kiss, The *63* Samuel Fuller
Naked Lovers, The *70* William Grefé
Naked Maja, The *59* Henry Koster, Mario
Russo
Naked Man, The *23* Henry Edwards
Naked Man, The *87* Rogelio A. González,
Jr.
Naked Man on the Athletic Field, The *77*
Konrad Wolf
Naked Murder Case of the Island *31*

Heinosuke Gosho
Naked Night, The *53* Ingmar Bergman
Naked Nineteen-Year-Old *70* Kaneto
Shindo
Naked Paradise *56* Roger Corman
Naked Prey, The *66* Cornel Wilde
Naked Revenge *72* William A. Graham
Naked River *77* William Diehl, Jr.
Naked Runner, The *67* Sidney J. Furie
Naked Sea *55* Allen H. Miner
Naked Spur, The *53* Anthony Mann
Naked Spur, The *68* R. Lee Frost
Naked Street, The *55* Maxwell Shane
Naked Temptress, The *61* Andy Milligan
Naked Town, The *37* Tomu Uchida
Naked Truth, The *19* Ralph Ince
Naked Truth, The *57* Mario Zampi
Naked Under Leather *68* Jack Cardiff
Naked Vampire, The *69* Jean Rollin
Naked Vengeance *86* Ted V. Mikels
Naked Vengeance *86* Cirio Santiago
Naked Warriors *73* Steve Carver
Naked Weekend, The *81* Bobby Roth
Naked Witch, The *61* Andy Milligan
Naked Woman, The *49* André Bertho-
mieu
Naked World of Harrison Marks, The *67*
George Harrison Marks
Naked Youth *59* John Schreyer
Naked Youth *60* Nagisa Oshima
Naked Youth: A Story of Cruelty *60*
Nagisa Oshima
Naked Zoo, The *70* William Grefé
Näkemiin, Hyvästi *87* Anssi Mänttäri
Nakusei Daisensō *77* Jun Fukuda
Nalla Thrachu *88* Nandakumar
Naloutai *52* Pierre-Dominique Gaisseau
Nam Angels *70* Jack Starrett
Namakemono *27* Tomu Uchida
Name, Age, Occupation *42* Pare Lorentz
Name der Rose, Der *86* Jean-Jacques
Annaud
Name for Evil, A *70* Bernard Girard
Name of the Game Is Kill, The *68* Gun-
nar Hellström
Name of the Rose, The *86* Jean-Jacques
Annaud
Name the Man *23* Victor Sjöström
Name the Woman *28* Elmer Harris, Erle
C. Kenton, Peter Milne
Name the Woman *34* Albert S. Rogell
Nameless *23* Michael Curtiz
Nameless *68* Alberto Lattuada
Nameless Men *28* Christy Cabanne
Nameless People *37* Heinosuke Gosho
Namenlos *23* Michael Curtiz
Namensheirat *33* Heinz Paul
Namida o Shishi no Tategami Ni *62*
Masahiro Shinoda
Namonaku Mazushiku Utsukushiku *62*
Zenzo Matsuyama
Namu, the Killer Whale *66* Laslo Benedek
Namus *26* Amo Bek-Nazarov
Nan, a Coster Girl's Romance *11* Charles
Raymond
Nan Good-for-Nothing *14* Arthur
Holmes-Gore
Nan in Fairyland *12* Edwin J. Collins
Nan o' the Backwoods *15* Sidney Olcott
Nan of Music Mountain *17* Cecil B. De-

Mille, George Melford
Nan of the North *21* Duke Worne
Nan Wild *27* George A. Cooper
Nana *26* Jean Renoir
Nana *34* Dorothy Arzner
Nana *54* Christian-Jaque
Nana *80* Dan Wolman
Nanami, Inferno of First Love *68* Susumu
Hani
Nanas, Les *85* Annick Lanoë
Nance *20* Albert Ward
Nancy *22* H. B. Parkinson
Nancy Comes Home *18* John Francis
Dillon
Nancy Drew and the Hidden Staircase *39*
William Clemens
Nancy Drew, Detective *38* William
Clemens, John Langan
Nancy Drew—Reporter *39* William
Clemens, John Langan
Nancy Drew—Troubleshooter *39* William
Clemens
Nancy from Nowhere *22* Chester M.
Franklin
Nancy Goes to Rio *49* Robert Z. Leonard
Nancy Keith *14* Forest Holger-Madsen
Nancy, or The Burglar's Daughter *08* Percy
Stow
Nancy Steele Is Missing *37* George Mar-
shall
Nancy's Birthright *16* Murdock Mac-
Quarrie
Nanette *39* Erich Engel
Nanette of the Wilds *16* Joseph Kaufman
Nanguila Tomorrow *60* Joris Ivens
Nanhi Munni Ladki Thi, Ek *70* R. Tulsi
Ramsay, Shyam Ramsay
Naniwa Elegy *36* Kenji Mizoguchi
Naniwa Ereji *36* Kenji Mizoguchi
Naniwa Hika *36* Kenji Mizoguchi
Naniwa no Koi no Monogatari *59* Tomu
Uchida
Naniwa Onna *40* Kenji Mizoguchi
Nankai no Daikaijū *70* Inoshiro Honda
Nankai no Daikettō *66* Jun Fukuda
Nanking *38* Fumio Kamei
Nanny *31* George Pearson
Nanny, The *65* Seth Holt
Nanook of the North *21* Robert Flaherty
Nanou *86* Conny Templeman
Nantas *24* Donatien
Nanto no Haru *25* Heinosuke Gosho
Nanu Sie Kennen Korff Noch Nicht? *39*
Fritz Holl
Naomi and Rufus Kiss *64* Andy Warhol
Nap *28* Hugh Croise
Naples au Baiser de Feu *25* Serge
Nadejdine
Naples au Baiser de Feu *37* Augusto
Genina
Naples Is a Battlefield *44* Jack Clayton
Naples That Never Dies *40* Amleto
Palermi
Napló Apámnak, Anyámnak *90* Márta
Mészáros
Napló Gyermekeimnek *82* Márta Mészáros
Napló Szerelmeimnek *87* Márta Mészáros
Napoléon *12* Louis Feuillade
Napoleon *20* Raoul Barré, Charles Bowers
Napoléon *26* Abel Gance

Natsu no Imōto 72 Nagisa Oshima
Natsukashi no Kao 41 Mikio Naruse
Natsukashiki Fueya Taiko 67 Keisuke Kinoshita
Natt i Hamn 43 Erik Faustman
Nattens Mysterium 16 Forest Holger-Madsen
Nattevandreren 16 Forest Holger-Madsen
Nattlek 65 Mai Zetterling
Nattmara 66 Arne Mattsson
Nattseilere 86 Tor M. Torstad
Nattsvardsgästerna 62 Ingmar Bergman
Natural, The 84 Barry Levinson
Natural Born Salesman, A 36 Ray Enright
Natural Colour Portraiture 09 George Albert Smith
Natural Enemies 79 Jeff Kanew
Natural Instinct 90 Ulli Lommel
Natural Law, The 17 Charles H. France
Natural Laws Reversed 05 Tom Green
Naturalists, The 21 Raoul Barré, Charles Bowers
Nature Girl, The 18 Oscar A. C. Lund
Nature Morte 70 Jan Lenica
Nature of the Beast, The 19 Cecil M. Hepworth
Nature of the Beast, The 88 Franco Rosso
Nature's Gentleman 18 F. Martin Thornton
Nature's Mistakes 32 Tod Browning
Nature's Playmates 62 Herschell Gordon Lewis
Nature's Triumph 15 Frank Lloyd
Nature's Workshop 33 Walter Lantz
Naufragatore, Il 15 Emilio Ghione
Naufrages de l'Île de la Tortue, Les 76 Jacques Rozier
Naufragio 78 Jaime Humberto Hermosillo
Naughty 27 Hampton Del Ruth
Naughty 71 Stanley Long
Naughty Arlette 48 Edmond T. Gréville
Naughty Baby 28 Mervyn LeRoy
Naughty Boy 27 Charles Lamont
Naughty But Mice 39 Chuck Jones
Naughty But Nice 27 Millard Webb
Naughty But Nice 39 Ray Enright
Naughty Cinderella 33 John Daumery
Naughty Duchess, The 28 Tom Terriss
Naughty Flirt, The 31 Edward F. Cline
Naughty Girl 56 Michel Boisrond
Naughty Girls 75 Peter Shillingford
Naughty Girls on the Loose 76 Morton M. Lewis
Naughty Husbands 30 Geoffrey Benstead
Naughty Marietta 35 W. S. Van Dyke
Naughty Martine 53 Emil E. Reinert
Naughty Nanette 27 James Leo Meehan
Naughty, Naughty! 18 Jerome Storm
Naughty Neighbors 39 Robert Clampett
Naughty Nineties, The 45 Jean Yarbrough
Naughty Nymphs 74 Franz Antel
Naughty School Girls 77 Jean Paul Scardino
Naughty Stewardesses, The 73 Al Adamson
Naughty Wife, The 19 John S. Robertson
Naughty Wives 73 Wolf Rilla
Nauka Bliżej Życia 51 Andrzej Munk
Naukari 54 Bimal Roy
Naulahka, The 18 George Fitzmaurice

Nausicaa 70 Agnès Varda
Navaho 07 Arthur Gilbert
Navajo 51 Norman Foster
Navajo Joe 66 Sergio Corbucci
Navajo Kid, The 45 Harry Fraser
Navajo Run 64 Johnny Seven
Navajo Trail, The 45 Howard Bretherton
Navajo Trail Raiders 49 R. G. Springsteen
Naval Academy 41 Erle C. Kenton
Naval Engagement, A 06 Harold Hough
Naval Review at Cherbourg, A 1896 Georges Méliès
Naval Treaty, The 22 George Ridgwell
Nave, La 11 Luigi Maggi
Nave Bianca, La 41 Roberto Rossellini
Nave de los Monstruos, La 59 Rogelio A. González
Nave delle Donne Maledette, La 63 Raffaello Matarazzo
Navel of the Moon, The 86 Jorge Prior
Navigation Marchande 54 Georges Franju
Navigator, The 24 Donald Crisp, Buster Keaton
Navigator, The 88 Vincent Ward
Navigator: A Medieval Odyssey, The 88 Vincent Ward
Navigator: An Odyssey Across Time, The 88 Vincent Ward
Navire des Hommes Perdus, Le 27 Maurice Tourneur
Navire Night, Le 78 Marguerite Duras
Návrat Domů 48 Martin Frič
Návrat Jana Petru 86 Martin Tapak
Návrat Ztraceného Syna 66 Evald Schorm
Navvy's Fortune, The 10 Fred Rains
Navy, The 30 Walter Lantz
Navy 43 Tomotaka Tasaka
Navy Beans 28 Charles Lamont
Navy Blue and Gold 37 Sam Wood
Navy Blues 29 Clarence Brown
Navy Blues 37 Ralph Staub
Navy Blues 41 Lloyd Bacon
Navy Born 36 Nate Watt
Navy Bound 51 Paul Landres
Navy Comes Through, The 42 A. Edward Sutherland
Navy Heroes 55 Wolf Rilla
Navy Lark, The 59 Gordon Parry
Navy SEALS 90 Lewis Teague
Navy Secrets 39 Howard Bretherton
Navy Spy 37 Joseph H. Lewis, Crane Wilbur
Navy Steps Out, The 41 Richard Wallace
Navy vs. the Night Monsters, The 65 Michael Hoey
Navy Way, The 44 William Berke
Navy Wife 35 Allan Dwan
Navy Wife 56 Edward Bernds
Nayak 66 Satyajit Ray
Nayakan 88 Mani Rathnam
Nazar Stodolya 37 G. M. Tassin
Nazar Stodolya 54 Grigori Chukhrai, Viktor Ivchenko
Nazaré 28 José Leitão De Barros
Nazarín 58 Luis Buñuel
Nazi Agent 41 Jules Dassin
Nazi Spy Ring 42 Albert Herman
Nazi Terror at Night 57 Robert Siodmak
Nazis Strike, The 42 Frank Capra, Anatole Litvak

Nazrana 87 Ravi Tandon
Nazty Nuisance 43 Glenn Tryon
Ne Bougeons Plus! 00 Georges Méliès
Ne Bougeons Plus 03 Alice Guy-Blaché
Ne de Père Inconnu 50 Maurice Cloche
Ne Jouez Pas avec les Martiens 67 Henri Lanoë
Ne Kérdezd Ki Voltom 41 Béla Balázs
Ne Kōfun Shicha Iyayo 31 Mikio Naruse
Ne Le Criez Pas sur les Toits 42 Jacques Daniel-Norman
Ne Me Demandez Pas Pourquoi 59 Jean Cocteau
Ne Nado Krovi 17 Yakov Protazanov
Ne Nous Fachons Pas 65 Georges Lautner
Ne Plači Petre 64 France Štiglić
Ne Prends Pas les Poulets pour des Pigeons 85 Jean Rollin
Ne Réveillez Pas un Flic Qui Dort 88 José Pinheiro
Ne Sírja Édesanyám 36 Georges Pallu
Ne Sois Pas Jalouse 32 Augusto Genina
Ne Tirez Pas Dolly! 37 Jean Delannoy
Ne Tuez Pas Dolly! 37 Jean Delannoy
Néa 76 Nelly Kaplan
Néa—A Young Emmanuelle 76 Nelly Kaplan
Neanderthal Man, The 53 E. A. Dupont
Neapolitan Carousel 61 Ettore Giannini
Neapolitan Heart 40 Amleto Palermi
Neapolitan Mouse 54 Joseph Barbera, William Hanna
Near and Far 76 Marianne Ahrne
Near Dark 87 Kathryn Bigelow
Near Death 89 Frederick Wiseman
Near Lady, The 23 Herbert Blaché
Near Relatives 35 Sølve Cederstrand
Near the Rainbow's End 30 John P. McGowan
Near the Trail's End 31 Trem Carr
Near to Earth 13 D. W. Griffith
Near-Tragedy, A 12 Mack Sennett
Nearer My God to Thee 17 Cecil M. Hepworth
Nearest and Dearest 73 John Robins
Nearing the End 22 Raoul Barré, Charles Bowers
Nearly a King 16 Frederick Thompson
Nearly a Lady 15 William Desmond Taylor
Nearly a Nasty Accident 61 Don Chaffey
Nearly Eighteen 43 Arthur Dreifuss
Nearly Married 17 Chester Withey
Neat Stuff...to Know and to Do 88 Jim Henson
'Neath Arizona Skies 34 Harry Fraser
'Neath Brooklyn Bridge 42 Wallace Fox
'Neath Canadian Skies 46 B. Reeves Eason
'Neath the Arizona Skies 34 Harry Fraser
'Neath Western Skies 29 John P. McGowan
Nebbia a Venezia 38 Vittorio Sala
Nebel und Sonne 16 Joe May
...Nebo Byt Zabit 85 Martin Holly
Nebo Moskvy 44 Yuli Raizman
Nebo Zovyot 59 Mikhail Karyukov, Alexander Kozyr
Nebo Zowet 59 Mikhail Karyukov, Alexander Kozyr
Nebraska il Pistolero 65 Antonio Roman

Nero and the Burning of Rome *53* Primo Zeglio

Nero—Hass War Sein Gebet, Il *69* Claudio Gora

Nero su Bianco *69* Tinto Brass

Nerone *30* Alessandro Blasetti

Nerone e Agrippina *13* Mario Caserini

Nero's Big Weekend *56* Steno

Nero's Mistress *56* Steno

Nero's Weekend *56* Steno

Nervo and Knox *26* Widgey R. Newman

Nervous Curate, The *10* Percy Stow

Nervous Wreck, The *26* Scott Sidney

Nervy Nat Kisses the Bride *04* Edwin S. Porter

Neskolko Dnei iz Zhizni I. I. Oblomova *79* Nikita Mikhalkov

Neskolko Intervyu po Lichnyam Voprosam *79* Lana Gogoberidze

Nessa Bala Rejal *52* Youssef Chahine

Nessie—Das Verrückteste Monster der Welt *85* Rudolf Zehetgruber

Nessuno o Tutti, Matti da Slegare *74* Silvano Agosti, Marco Bellocchio, Sandro Petraglia, Stefano Rulli

Nessuno Torna Indietro *43* Alessandro Blasetti

Nest, The *26* Jean Benoît-Lévy

Nest, The *27* William Nigh

Nest, The *43* Kenneth Anger

Nest, The *80* Jaime De Armiñán

Nest, The *88* Terence H. Winkless

Nest of Gentlefolk, A *69* Andrei Mikhalkov-Konchalovsky

Nest of Gentry, A *69* Andrei Mikhalkov-Konchalovsky

Nest of Noblemen, A *15* Vladimir Gardin

Nest of the Cuckoo Birds, The *65* Bert Williams

Nest of Vipers *79* Tonino Cervi

Nest on the Black Cliff, The *13* H. Oceano Martinek

Nestašni Robot *56* Dušan Vukotić

Nesterka *55* Alexander Zarkhi

Nesting, The *80* Armand Weston

Net, The *16* George Foster Platt

Net, The *23* J. Gordon Edwards

Net, The *52* Anthony Asquith

Net, The *53* Emilio Fernández

Netepichnaja Istoria *77* Grigori Chukhrai

Nethaji Palkar *26* Rajaram Vanakudre Shantaram

Netherlands, The *82* Bert Haanstra

Nets of Destiny *24* Arthur H. Rooke

Netsudeichi *50* Kon Ichikawa

Netsujō no Ichiya *29* Heinosuke Gosho

Nettezza Urbana *48* Michelangelo Antonioni

Nettoyage par le Vide *08* Louis Feuillade

Network *76* Sidney Lumet

Neue Dalila, Die *18* Urban Gad

Neue Nase, Die *16* Ernst Lubitsch

Neues Leben *30* Hans Richter

Neulovimyi Yan *42* I. Annensky, Vladimir Petrov

1914, die Letzten Tage Vor dem Weltbrand *31* Richard Oswald

Neunzig Minuten Nach Mitternacht *62* Jürgen Goslar

Neunzig Nächte und ein Tag *64* Edgar G. Ulmer

Neúplné Zatmění *82* Jaromil Jireš

Neurasthenia *29* Noah Galkin

Neutral Port *40* Walter Forde, Marcel Varnel

Neutralizer, The *74* Don Sharp

Neutrón Contra el Dr. Caronte *60* Federico Curiel

Neutrón el Enmascarado Negro *60* Federico Curiel

Neuvaine, La *14* Louis Feuillade

Neuvaine de Colette, La *25* Georges Champavert

Nevada *27* John Waters

Nevada *35* Charles Barton

Nevada *44* Edward Killy

Nevada *71* José Antonio De la Loma

Nevada Badmen *51* Lewis D. Collins

Nevada Buckaroo, The *31* John P. McCarthy

Nevada City *41* Joseph Kane

Nevada Smith *66* Henry Hathaway

Nevadan, The *50* Gordon Douglas

Never a Dull Moment *43* Edward Lilley

Never a Dull Moment *50* George Marshall

Never a Dull Moment *68* Jerry Paris

Never Again *10* D. W. Griffith

Never Again *15* Cecil Birch

Never Again *17* Harry S. Palmer

Never Again, Never *12* Lewin Fitzhamon

Never Back Losers *61* Robert Tronson

Never Complain to Your Laundress *07* Lewin Fitzhamon

Never Cry Devil *90* Rupert Hitzig

Never Cry Wolf *83* Carroll Ballard

Never Despair *15* Cecil Birch

Never Fear *49* Ida Lupino

Never Forget the Ring *13* Bert Haldane

Never Give a Sucker a Break *33* Jack Conway

Never Give a Sucker an Even Break *41* Edward F. Cline

Never Give an Inch *71* Richard A. Colla, Paul Newman

Never Kick a Woman *36* Dave Fleischer

Never Late, or The Conscientious Clerk *09* Percy Stow

Never Let Go *60* John Guillermin

Never Let Me Go *53* Delmer Daves

Never Lie to Your Wife *16* Al Christie

Never Look Back *52* Francis Searle

Never Love a Stranger *58* Robert Stevens

Never Mention Murder *64* John Nelson Burton

Never Mind the Quality, Feel the Width *73* Ronnie Baxter

Never Never Land *80* Paul Annett

Never Never Murder, The *61* Peter Duffell

Never on Sunday *59* Jules Dassin

Never on Tuesday *88* Adam Rifkin

Never Put It in Writing *63* Andrew L. Stone

Never Put Off Till Tomorrow *25* Alexander Butler

Never Say Die *20* Walter Forde

Never Say Die *24* George Crone

Never Say Die *39* Elliott Nugent

Never Say Die *50* Vivian Milroy

Never Say Die *88* Geoff Murphy

Never Say Goodbye *46* James V. Kern

Never Say Goodbye *55* Jerry Hopper, Douglas Sirk

Never Say Never Again *83* Irvin Kershner

Never Say Quit *19* Edward Dillon

Never Send a Man to Match a Ribbon *10* Lewin Fitzhamon

Never Should Have Told You *37* Dave Fleischer

Never So Few *59* John Sturges

Never Sock a Baby *39* Dave Fleischer

Never Steal Anything Small *58* Charles Lederer

Never Steal Anything Wet *67* Lee Sholem

Never Strike a Woman—Even with a Flower *66* Zdeněk Podskalský

Never Take Candy from a Stranger *60* Cyril Frankel

Never Take No for an Answer *51* Maurice Cloche, Ralph Smart

Never Take Sweets from a Stranger *60* Cyril Frankel

Never the Dames Shall Meet *27* James Parrott

Never the Twain Shall Meet *25* Maurice Tourneur

Never the Twain Shall Meet *31* W. S. Van Dyke

Never to Love *40* John Farrow

Never Too Late *25* Forrest K. Sheldon

Never Too Late *35* Bernard B. Ray

Never Too Late *65* Bud Yorkin

Never Too Old *19* F. Richard Jones

Never Too Young to Die *86* Gil Bettman

Never Too Young to Rock *75* Dennis Abey

Never Travel on a One-Way Ticket *87* Håkan Alexandersson

Never Trouble Trouble *31* Lupino Lane

Never Trust a Gambler *51* Ralph Murphy

Never Wave at a WAC *52* Norman Z. McLeod

Never Weaken *21* Fred Newmeyer, Sam Taylor

Never with Women *85* Giovanni Fago

NeverEnding Story, The *84* Wolfgang Petersen

NeverEnding Story II *90* George (Trumbull) Miller

NeverEnding Story II: The Next Chapter *90* George (Trumbull) Miller

Nevertheless They Go On *31* Kenji Mizoguchi

Nevető Szászkia, A *16* Alexander Korda

Neveu de Beethoven, Le *85* Paul Morrissey

Neveu Silencieux, Un *78* Robert Enrico

Nevinost Bez Zaštite *68* Dušan Makavejev

Nevjera *53* Vladimir Pogačić

New Adam and Eve, The *15* Richard Garrick

New Adventures of Baron Münchhausen *15* F. Martin Thornton

New Adventures of Batman and Robin, The *49* Spencer G. Bennet

New Adventures of Dr. Fu Manchu, The *30* Rowland V. Lee

New Adventures of Don Juan, The *48* Vincent Sherman

New Adventures of Get-Rich-Quick Wallingford, The *31* Sam Wood

New Adventures of Pippi Longstocking, The *88* Ken Annakin

New York by Heck *18* Hy Mayer
New York Caledonian Club's Parade *03* Edwin S. Porter
New York Chiam a Superdrago *66* Giorgio Ferroni
New York City in a Blizzard *02* Edwin S. Porter
New York City Police Parade *03* Edwin S. Porter
New York City Public Bath *03* Edwin S. Porter
New York Confidential *55* Russell Rouse
New York Eye and Ear Control *64* Michael Snow
New York Girl, A *14* Mack Sennett
New York Harbor Police Boat Patrol Capturing Pirates *03* Edwin S. Porter
New York Hat, The *12* D. W. Griffith
New York Idea, The *20* Herbert Blaché
New York Light Record *60* Norman McLaren
New York Lightboard *60* Norman McLaren
New York Luck *17* Edward Sloman
New York, New York *77* Martin Scorsese
New York Night Life *19* Raoul Barré, Charles Bowers
New York Nights *29* Lewis Milestone
New York Nights *81* Simon Nuchtern
New York Peacock, The *17* Kenean Buel
New York Ripper, The *81* Lucio Fulci
New York Stories *89* Woody Allen, Francis Ford Coppola, Martin Scorsese
New York sur Mer *63* Pierre-Dominique Gaisseau
New York Town *41* Preston Sturges, Charles Vidor
New York University *52* Willard Van Dyke
New York's Finest *88* Chuck Vincent
Newborn, The *53* Jørgen Roos
Newcomer, The *79* Richard De Meideros
Newcomers, The *70* Robert Totten
Newer Way, The *15* B. Reeves Eason
Newer Woman, The *14* Donald Crisp
Newest Profession, The *52* Norman Z. McLeod
Newly Rich *31* Norman Taurog
Newlydeads, The *88* Joseph Merhi
Newlywed Phable, A *16* Gregory La Cava
Newlyweds, The *10* D. W. Griffith
Newlyweds *57* Mauro Bolognini
Newlyweds' Visit *28* Sam Newfield
Newman's Law *74* Richard T. Heffron
Newport *72* Malcolm Le Grice
News for the Navy *37* Norman McLaren
News from Home *76* Chantal Akerman
News from the Soviet Union *30* Joris Ivens
News Hound *47* William Beaudine
News Hounds *47* William Beaudine
News Is Made at Night *39* Alfred L. Werker
News No. 3 *62* Bruce Baillie
News Parade, The *28* David Butler
News Reeling *28* Manny Gould, Ben Harrison
Newsboy's Christmas Dream, A *13* Edwin J. Collins
Newsboy's Debt, The *14* Donald Cornwallis

Newsboys' Home *38* Harold Young
Newsfront *78* Phillip Noyce
Newsie and the Lady, The *39* Luis César Amadori
Newslaffs No. 1 *27* William C. Nolan
Newslaffs No. 2 *27* William C. Nolan
Newslaffs No. 3 *27* William C. Nolan
Newslaffs No. 4 *27* William C. Nolan
Newslaffs No. 5 *27* William C. Nolan
Newslaffs No. 6 *27* William C. Nolan
Newslaffs No. 7 *27* William C. Nolan
Newslaffs No. 8 *27* William C. Nolan
Newslaffs No. 9 *27* William C. Nolan
Newslaffs No. 10 *28* William C. Nolan
Newslaffs No. 11 *28* William C. Nolan
Newslaffs No. 12 *28* William C. Nolan
Newslaffs No. 13 *28* William C. Nolan
Newslaffs No. 14 *28* William C. Nolan
Newslaffs No. 15 *28* William C. Nolan
Newslaffs No. 16 *28* William C. Nolan
Newslaffs No. 17 *28* William C. Nolan
Newslaffs No. 18 *28* William C. Nolan
Newslaffs No. 19 *28* William C. Nolan
Newslaffs No. 20 *28* William C. Nolan
Newslaffs No. 21 *28* William C. Nolan
Newslaffs No. 22 *28* William C. Nolan
Newslaffs No. 23 *28* William C. Nolan
Newslaffs No. 24 *28* William C. Nolan
Newspaper Boys, The *37* Ramón Peón
Newspaper Train *41* Len Lye
Newsreel Lightning *24* Dziga Vertov
Newsreel of Dreams No. 1 *68* Stan Vanderbeek
Newsreel of Dreams No. 2 *69* Stan Vanderbeek
Next *71* Sergio Martino
Next Cheech & Chong Movie, The *80* Thomas Chong
Next Corner, The *24* Sam Wood
Next Door Madame and My Wife *31* Heinosuke Gosho
Next Door Neighbors *09* Émile Cohl
Next Gentleman Please *27* John Greenidge, Russel Messel
Next in Line *42* William Berke
Next Man, The *76* Richard C. Sarafian
Next of Kin, The *08* S. Wormald
Next of Kin, The *42* Thorold Dickinson
Next of Kin *82* Tony Williams
Next of Kin *84* Atom Egoyan
Next of Kin *86* Willy Rameau
Next of Kin *89* John Irvin
Next One, The *82* Nico Mastorakis
Next Stop, Greenwich Village *75* Paul Mazursky
Next Summer *84* Nadine Trintignant
Next Time I Marry *38* Garson Kanin
Next Time We Live *36* Edward H. Griffith
Next Time We Love *36* Edward H. Griffith
Next to No Time *58* Henry Cornelius
Next Victim, The *71* Sergio Martino
Next Voice You Hear, The *50* William A. Wellman
Neylonovaya Yolka *87* Rezo Esadze
Nez, Le *63* Alexander Alexeïeff, Claire Parker
Nez de Cuir *51* Yves Allégret
Než Nám Narostla Křídla *58* Jiří Brdečka
Nezabyvayemi *68* Yulia Solntseva

Nezabyvayemi 1919 Godu *52* Mikhail Chiaureli
Nezbedný Bakalář *46* Otakar Vávra
Ngati *87* Barry Barclay
Ni Avec Toi, Ni Sans Toi *85* Alain Maline
Ni de Aquí, Ni de Allá *87* María Elena Velazco
Ni Liv *57* Arne Skouen
Ni Ljuger *69* Vilgot Sjöman
Ni-Lo-Ho Nu-Erh *87* Hsiao-hsien Hou
Ni Vu Ni Connu *58* Yves Robert
Niagara *53* Henry Hathaway
Niagara Falls *32* Roscoe Arbuckle
Niagara Falls *41* Gordon Douglas
Nianchan *59* Shohei Imamura
Niaye *64* Ousmane Sembène
Nibelungen, Die *66* Harald Reinl
Nibelungen—Part I: Siegfrieds Tod, Die *23* Fritz Lang
Nibelungen II, Die *24* Fritz Lang
Nibelungs, Part One, The *23* Fritz Lang
Nibelungs—Part II:Kriemhilds Rache, The *24* Fritz Lang
Nicaragua, September 1978 *78* Frank Diamond
Nice à Propos de Jean Vigo *84* Manoel De Oliveira
Nice and Friendly *22* Charles Chaplin
Nice Dreams *81* Thomas Chong
Nice Girl? *41* William A. Seiter
Nice Girl Like Me, A *69* Desmond Davis
Nice Girls Don't Explode *87* Chuck Martinez
Nice Little Bank That Should Be Robbed, A *58* Henry Levin
Nice People *22* William DeMille
Nice Plate of Spinach, A *76* Miloš Macourek, Václav Vorlíček
Nice Time *57* Claude Goretta, Alain Tanner
Nice Women *31* Edwin H. Knopf
Nichirin *25* Teinosuke Kinugasa
Nichirin *50* Teinosuke Kinugasa
Nicholas and Alexandra *71* Franklin J. Schaffner
Nicholas Nickleby *46* Alberto Cavalcanti
Nicht Versöhnt oder Es Hilft Nur Gewalt Wo Gewalt Herrscht *65* Jean-Marie Straub
Nichta me tin Silena, I *86* Demetris Panayotatos
Nick Carter *06* Victorin Jasset
Nick Carter Contre Paulin Broquet *11* Victorin Jasset
Nick Carter in Prague *78* Oldřich Lipský
Nick Carter—Master Detective *39* Jacques Tourneur
Nick Carter Va Tout Casser *64* Henri Decoin
Nick, Gentleman Detective *36* W. S. Van Dyke
Nick Harris *31* Spencer G. Bennet
Nick-of-Time Baby, The *17* Clarence Badger
Nicked Nags *28* Manny Gould, Ben Harrison
Nickel Mountain *83* Drew Denbaum
Nickel Queen, The *71* John McCallum
Nickel Ride, The *74* Robert Mulligan
Nickelodeon *76* Peter Bogdanovich

Nicklehausen Journey, The 70 Rainer Werner Fassbinder*

Nick's Film 80 Nicholas Ray, Wim Wenders

Nick's Knickers 29 Wilfred Gannon

Nick's Movie 80 Nicholas Ray, Wim Wenders

Nico Mastorakis' Glitch 87 Nico Mastorakis

Nid, Le 14 Léon Poirier

Nid, Le 26 Jean Benoît-Lévy

Nida al Ushaq 60 Youssef Chahine

Nidhanaya 70 Lester James Peries

Nido, El 80 Jaime De Armiñán

Nido del Ragno, Il 89 Gianfranco Giagni

Nie Wieder Liebe 31 Anatole Litvak

Niebo Nashevo Detstva 67 Tolomush Okeyev

Niebo Zowiet 59 Mikhail Karyukov, Alexander Kozyr

Niece of the Vampire, The 68 Amando De Ossorio

Niedorajda 37 Mieczysław Krawicz

Niedzielny Poranek 55 Andrzej Munk

Niemand Weiss Es 20 Lupu Pick

Niemandsland 31 Victor Trivas

Niet Tevergeefs 48 Edmond T. Gréville

Niet voor de Poesen 73 Fons Rademakers

Nieuwe Architectuur 28 Joris Ivens

Nieuwe Gronden 33 Joris Ivens

Niewinni Czarodzieje 60 Andrzej Wajda

Niezwykła Podróż Baltazara Kobera 88 Wojciech Has

Nifty Nurses 34 Leigh Jason

Niger—Jeune République, Le 60 Claude Jutra

Niger 60 60 Claude Jutra

Niggard, The 14 Donald Crisp

Nigger, The 15 Edgar Lewis

Nigger Boy's Revenge, The 04 Lewin Fitzhamon

Night, The 23 Kenji Mizoguchi

Night, The 60 Michelangelo Antonioni

Night, The 85 Hans-Jürgen Syberberg

Night Affair 58 Gilles Grangier

Night After Night 32 Archie Mayo

Night After Night 69 Lewis J. Force

Night After Night After Night 69 Lewis J. Force

Night Alarm, A 08 Charles Raymond

Night Alarm 34 Spencer G. Bennet

Night Alone, A 38 Thomas Bentley

Night Ambush 56 Michael Powell, Emeric Pressburger

Night and Day 32 Walter Forde

Night and Day 46 Michael Curtiz

Night and Day 62 Risto Jarva, Jaakko Pakkasvirta

Night and Fog 55 Alain Resnais

Night and Fog in Japan 60 Nagisa Oshima

Night and Morning 15 Wilfred Noy

Night and the City 50 Jules Dassin

Night Andy Came Home, The 72 Bob Clark

Night Angel, The 31 Edmund Goulding

Night Angel 90 Dominique Othénin-Girard

Night Angels 87 Wilson Barros

Night at Earl Carroll's, A 40 Kurt Neumann

Night at the Crossroads 32 Jean Renoir

Night at the Movies, A 37 Roy Rowland

Night at the Opera, A 35 Sam Wood

Night at the Ritz, A 35 William McGann

Night at the Troc, A 39 Arthur Dreifuss

Night at Varennes, The 82 Ettore Scola

Night Beat 31 George B. Seitz

Night Beat 47 Harold Huth

Night Beauties 52 Christian-Jaque

Night Beauties 52 René Clair

Night Before, The 21 Malcolm St. Clair

Night Before, The 86 Thom Eberhardt

Night Before Christmas, The 05 Edwin S. Porter

Night Before Christmas, The 41 Joseph Barbera, William Hanna

Night Before Christmas, A 63 Alexander Rou

Night Before the Divorce, The 42 Robert Siodmak

Night Before the War, The 43 Kozaburo Yoshimura

Night Bell, The 14 Frank Wilson

Night Bird, The 28 Fred Newmeyer

Night Birds 30 Richard Eichberg

Night Boat to Dublin 45 Lawrence Huntington

Night Bride, The 27 E. Mason Hopper

Night Butterflies 57 Kozaburo Yoshimura

Night Call Nurses 72 Jonathan Kaplan

Night Caller, The 65 John Gilling

Night Caller 74 Henri Verneuil

Night Caller from Outer Space 65 John Gilling

Night Cargo 36 Charles Hutchinson

Night Cargoes 62 Ernest Morris

Night Child, The 74 Massimo Dallamano

Night Club, The 25 Paul Iribe, Frank Urson

Night Club 28 Robert Florey

Night Club 35 Charles Lamont

Night Club Girl 44 Edward F. Cline

Night Club Hostess 39 Kurt Neumann

Night Club Lady, The 32 Irving Cummings

Night Club Murder 34 Lawrence Huntington

Night Club Queen 34 Bernard Vorhaus

Night Club Scandal 37 Ralph Murphy

Night Comes Too Soon 48 Denis Kavanagh

Night Court 32 W. S. Van Dyke

Night Crawlers, The 65 Michael Hoey

Night Creature 78 Lee Madden

Night Creatures 61 Peter Graham Scott

Night Crossing 57 Montgomery Tully

Night Crossing 81 Delbert Mann

Night Cry, The 26 Herman Raymaker

Night Digger, The 71 Alastair Reid

Night Does Strange Things, The 56 Jean Renoir

Night Drum 58 Tadashi Imai

Night Duty 04 Alf Collins

Night Duty, or A Policeman's Experiences 06 Tom Green

Night Editor 46 Henry Levin

Night Encounter 59 Robert Hossein

Night Evelyn Came Out of the Grave, The 71 Emilio Miraglia

Night Express, The 32 Christy Cabanne

Night Eyes 82 Robert Clouse

Night Eyes 90 Jag Mohan Mundhra

Night Ferry 77 David Eady

Night Fighters, The 60 Tay Garnett

Night Fighters 86 Lawrence Foldes

Night Flight 33 Clarence Brown

Night Flight 79 Desmond Davis

Night Flight from Moscow 72 Henri Verneuil

Night Flowers 79 Luis San Andrés

Night Flyer, The 28 Walter Lang

Night for Crime, A 42 Alexis Thurn-Taxis

Night Freight 55 Jean Yarbrough

Night Friend 88 Peter Gerretsen

Night Full of Rain, A 78 Lina Wertmuller

Night Game 89 Peter Masterson

Night Games 65 Mai Zetterling

Night Games 79 Roger Vadim

Night God Screamed, The 73 Lee Madden

Night Guardian 86 Jean-Pierre Limosin

Night Guest 61 Otakar Vávra

Night Hair Child 71 James Kelly

Night Has a Thousand Eyes, The 48 John Farrow

Night Has Eyes, The 42 Leslie Arliss

Night Hawk, The 21 John Gliddon

Night Hawk, The 24 Stuart Paton

Night Hawk, The 38 Sidney Salkow

Night Heat 59 Mauro Bolognini

Night Heaven Fell, The 57 Roger Vadim

Night Holds Terror, The 55 Andrew L. Stone

Night Horseman, The 21 Lynn Reynolds

Night Howls 28 Manny Gould, Ben Harrison

Night Hunt 68 Charles Martin

Night in Armour, A 10 Lewin Fitzhamon

Night in Bangkok 66 Yasuke Chiba

Night in Cairo, A 33 Sam Wood

Night in Casablanca, A 46 Archie Mayo

Night in Havana 57 Richard Wilson

Night in Heaven, A 83 John G. Avildsen

Night in Hong Kong, A 61 Yasuke Chiba

Night in June 40 Per Lindberg

Night in London, A 27 Lupu Pick

Night in May, A 10 Yakov Protazanov

Night in May, A 38 Georg Jacoby

Night in May, A 41 Nikolai Ekk

Night in Montmartre, A 31 Leslie Hiscott

Night in New Arabia, A 17 Thomas R. Mills

Night in New Orleans, A 42 William Clemens

Night in Paradise, A 46 Arthur Lubin

Night in September, A 39 Boris Barnet

Night in the Harbor 43 Erik Faustman

Night in the Life of Jimmy Reardon, A 87 William Richert

Night in the Show, A 15 Charles Chaplin

Night Into Morning 51 Fletcher Markle

Night Invader, The 42 Herbert Mason

Night Is Ending, The 43 Léonide Moguy

Night Is My Future 47 Ingmar Bergman

Night Is My Kingdom, The 51 Georges Lacombe

Night Is Ours, The 30 Henri Roussel

Night Is the Phantom 63 Mario Bava

Night Is Young, The 34 Dudley Murphy

Night Is Young, The 86 Leos Carax

Night Journey *38* Oswald Mitchell
Night Journey *55* Erik Faustman
Night Journey *60* Alexander Hammid
Night Key *37* Lloyd Corrigan
Night Legs *71* Peter Collinson
Night Life *27* George Archainbaud
Night Life in Hollywood *22* Fred Caldwell
Night Life in Reno *31* Raymond Cannon
Night Life of New York *25* Allan Dwan
Night Life of the Bugs *36* Walter Lantz
Night Life of the Gods *35* Lowell Sherman
Night Like This, A *32* Tom Walls
Night Magic *85* Lewis Furey
Night Mail *35* Herbert Smith
Night Mail *36* Harry Watt, Basil Wright
Night Mayor, The *32* Ben Stoloff
Night Message, The *24* Perley Poore Sheehan
Night Monster, The *42* Ford Beebe
'Night Mother *86* Tom Moore
Night Moves *75* Arthur Penn
Night Must Fall *37* Richard Thorpe
Night Must Fall *63* Karel Reisz
Night My Number Came Up, The *55* Leslie Norman
Night 'n' Gales *37* Gordon Douglas
Night Nurse *31* William A. Wellman
Night Nurse, The *77* Igor Auzins
Night of a Thousand Cats *72* René Cardona, Jr.
Night of Adventure, A *44* Gordon Douglas
Night of Anubis *68* George Romero
Night of Bloody Horror *69* Joy Houck, Jr.
Night of Counting the Years, The *69* Shadi Abdelsalam
Night of Dark Shadows *71* Dan Curtis, Alex Stevens
Night of Evil *62* Richard Galbreath
Night of Fame, A *48* Mario Monicelli, Steno
Night of Fear *64* Leon Klimovsky
Night of Great Love, The *37* Géza von Bolváry
Night of January 16th, The *41* William Clemens
Night of June 13th, The *32* Stephen Roberts
Night of Love, The *27* George Fitzmaurice
Night of Love *54* Mario Bonnard
Night of Love *65* José Benazeraf
Night of Lust *65* José Benazeraf
Night of Magic, A *44* Bert Wynne
Night of Mystery, A *28* Lothar Mendes
Night of Mystery *36* E. A. Dupont
Night of Nights, The *39* Lewis Milestone
Night of Passion, A *29* Heinosuke Gosho
Night of Passion *60* Sidney J. Furie
Night of Peril, A *12* Bert Haldane
Night of Remembrance, A *54* Jerzy Kawalerowicz
Night of Revenge, The *15* Benjamin Christensen
Night of San Juan, The *71* Jorge Sanjinés
Night of San Lorenzo, The *81* Paolo Taviani, Vittorio Taviani
Night of Sin, The *33* Miguel Torres Contreras
Night of Terror *33* Ben Stoloff

Night of Terrors, The *66* Domenico De Felice, Elio Scardamaglia
Night of the Askari *78* Jürgen Goslar
Night of the Beast *65* Harold Daniels, Reginald LeBorg
Night of the Big Heat *67* Terence Fisher
Night of the Blind Dead *71* Amando De Ossorio
Night of the Blood Beast *58* Bernard Kowalski
Night of the Blood Monster *69* Jesús Franco
Night of the Bloody Apes *68* René Cardona
Night of the Bride, The *67* Karel Kachyňa
Night of the Claw *80* Hernán Cárdenas
Night of the Cobra Woman *72* Andrew Meyer
Night of the Comet *84* Thom Eberhardt
Night of the Creeps *86* Fred Dekker
Night of the Cyclone *90* David Irving
Night of the Damned *71* Filippo Walter Maria Ratti
Night of the Dark Full Moon *72* Theodore Gershuny
Night of the Demon *57* Jacques Tourneur
Night of the Demon *71* Don Henderson
Night of the Demon *80* Jim Wasson
Night of the Demons *87* Kevin S. Tenney
Night of the Desperado, The *65* Mario Maffei
Night of the Devils *72* Giorgio Ferroni
Night of the Doomed *65* Mario Caiano
Night of the Eagle *61* Sidney Hayers
Night of the Flesh Eaters *68* George Romero
Night of the Following Day, The *68* Hubert Cornfield
Night of the Full Moon, The *54* Donald Taylor
Night of the Garter *33* Jack Raymond
Night of the Generals, The *66* Anatole Litvak
Night of the Ghouls *59* Edward D. Wood, Jr.
Night of the Great Attack, The *60* Giuseppe M. Scotese
Night of the Grizzly, The *66* Joseph Pevney
Night of the Howling Beast *75* Miguel Iglesias Bonns
Night of the Hunter, The *55* Charles Laughton
Night of the Iguana *64* John Huston
Night of the Juggler *80* Robert Butler
Night of the Killer *67* Nagisa Oshima
Night of the Knight, The *24* Gaston Quiribet
Night of the Laughing Dead *73* Peter Sykes
Night of the Lepus *72* William F. Claxton
Night of the Living Dead *68* George Romero
Night of the Living Dead *90* Tom Savini
Night of the Mayas *39* Chano Urueta
Night of the Party, The *33* Michael Powell
Night of the Pencils, The *86* Héctor Olivera
Night of the Prowler *62* Francis Searle
Night of the Prowler, The *78* Jim

Sharman
Night of the Pub, The *20* John Harvey
Night of the Quarter Moon *58* Hugo Haas
Night of the Seagull, The *70* Katsumi Iwauchi
Night of the Seagulls *75* Amando De Ossorio
Night of the Sharks *90* Tonino Ricci
Night of the Shooting Stars *81* Paolo Taviani, Vittorio Taviani
Night of the Silicates *66* Terence Fisher
Night of the Snakes, The *69* Giulio Petroni
Night of the Sorcerers, The *70* Amando De Ossorio
Night of the Strangler *75* Joy Houck, Jr.
Night of the Thousand Cats, The *72* René Cardona, Jr.
Night of the Tiger *66* Bernard McEveety
Night of the Vampire, The *70* Michio Yamamoto
Night of the Vampires *64* Ákos von Ráthonyi
Night of the Wehrmacht Zombies *81* Joel M. Reed
Night of the Witches *70* Keith Larsen
Night of the Zombies *81* Bruno Mattei
Night of the Zombies *81* Joel M. Reed
Night of Thought, A *66* Mikhail Romm
Night of Varennes, The *82* Ettore Scola
Night of Vengeance *15* Benjamin Christensen
Night of Witches *70* Keith Larsen
Night on a Bare Mountain *33* Alexander Alexeïeff, Claire Parker
Night on Bald Mountain *33* Alexander Alexeïeff, Claire Parker
Night on the Danube, A *35* Carl Boese
Night on the Town, A *86* Miguel Delgado
Night or Day *62* Risto Jarva, Jaakko Pakkasvirta
Night Out, A *15* Charles Chaplin
Night Out, A *16* George D. Baker
Night Owl, The *26* Harry Joe Brown
Night Owl *27* William C. Nolan
Night Owls *27* Mark Sandrich
Night Owls *29* Sam Newfield
Night Owls *30* James Parrott
Night Parade *29* Malcolm St. Clair
Night Passage *57* Anthony Mann, James Neilson
Night Paths *79* Krzysztof Zanussi
Night Patrol, The *26* Noel Mason Smith
Night Patrol, The *29* Norman Lee
Night Patrol *84* Jackie Kong
Night People *54* Nunnally Johnson
Night Plane from Chungking *42* Ralph Murphy
Night Plane to Amsterdam *55* Ken Hughes
Night Porter, The *30* Sewell Collins
Night Porter, The *74* Liliana Cavani
Night Raiders *52* Howard Bretherton
Night Rehearsal, The *80* Evald Schorm
Night Ride *30* John S. Robertson
Night Ride *37* John Paddy Carstairs
Night Rider, The *32* William Nigh
Night Riders, The *20* Alexander Butler
Night Riders, The *39* George Sherman
Night Riders *58* Fernando Méndez

Night Riders of Montana *51* Fred C. Brannon
Night River *56* Kozaburo Yoshimura
Night Rose, The *21* Wallace Worsley
Night Runner, The *57* Abner Biberman
Night School *80* Ken Hughes
Night Shadows *31* Albert De Courville
Night Shadows *84* John Cardos
Night She Arose from the Tomb, The *71* Emilio Miraglia
Night Shift *41* Garson Kanin
Night Shift *79* Tony Price
Night Shift *82* Ron Howard
Night Ship, The *25* Henry McCarthy
Night Song *47* John Cromwell
Night Spot *38* Christy Cabanne
Night Stage to Galveston *52* George Archainbaud
Night Stalker, The *85* Max Kleven
Night Star, Goddess of Electra *63* Giuseppe Vari
Night Stripes *43* Garson Kanin
Night Sun *90* Paolo Taviani, Vittorio Taviani
Night That Evelyn Left the Tomb, The *71* Emilio Miraglia
Night the Creatures Came, The *66* Terence Fisher
Night the Lights Went Out in Georgia, The *81* Ronald F. Maxwell
Night the Silicates Came, The *66* Terence Fisher
Night the Sun Came Out, The *70* Melvin Van Peebles
Night the World Exploded, The *57* Fred F. Sears
Night They Invented Striptease, The *68* William Friedkin
Night They Killed Rasputin, The *60* Pierre Chénal
Night They Raided Minsky's, The *68* William Friedkin
Night They Robbed Big Bertha's, The *75* Peter Kares
Night Tide *61* Curtis Harrington
Night Time in Nevada *48* William Witney
Night to Dismember, A *83* Doris Wishman
Night to Remember, A *42* Richard Wallace
Night to Remember, A *58* Roy Ward Baker
Night to Remember, A *62* Kozaburo Yoshimura
Night Train *40* Carol Reed
Night Train *59* Jerzy Kawalerowicz
Night Train *75* Charles R. Rondeau
Night Train for Inverness *59* Ernest Morris
Night Train for the Milky Way, The *86* Gisaburo Sugii
Night Train to Memphis *46* Lesley Selander
Night Train to Milan *63* Marcello Baldi
Night Train to Mundo Fine *66* Coleman Francis
Night Train to Munich *40* Carol Reed
Night Train to Paris *64* Robert Douglas
Night Train to Terror *85* John Carr, Jay Schlossberg Cohen, Tom McGowan, Philip Marshak, Gregg Tallas
Night Unto Night *47* Don Siegel
Night Vision *88* Michael Krueger
Night Visitor, The *70* Laslo Benedek
Night Visitor *90* Rupert Hitzig
Night Voyage *86* Tor M. Torstad
Night Waitress *36* Lew Landers
Night Walk, The *72* Bob Clark
Night Walker, The *64* William Castle
Night Warning *81* William Asher
Night Was Our Friend *51* Michael Anderson
Night Watch, The *26* Fred Caldwell
Night Watch, The *28* Alexander Korda
Night Watch *41* Donald Taylor
Night Watch, The *59* Jacques Becker
Night Watch *73* Brian G. Hutton
Night Watchman, The *38* Chuck Jones
Night We Dropped a Clanger, The *59* D'Arcy Conyers
Night We Got the Bird, The *60* D'Arcy Conyers
Night Wind *48* James Tinling
Night with Masqueraders in Paris, A *07* Georges Méliès
Night with Silena, The *86* Demetris Panayotatos
Night Without Pity *62* Theodore Zichy
Night Without Sleep *52* Roy Ward Baker
Night Without Stars *51* Terry Morse
Night Without Stars *51* Anthony Pelissier
Night Women *63* Claude Lelouch
Night Won't Talk, The *52* Daniel Birt
Night Work *30* Russell Mack
Night Work *39* George Archainbaud
Night Workers, The *17* J. Charles Haydon
Night World *32* Hobart Henley
Night Zoo *87* Jean-Claude Lauzon
Nightbeast *82* Donald M. Dohler
Nightbirds of London, The *15* Frank Wilson
Nightbreed *89* Clive Barker
Nightcats *56* Stan Brakhage
Nightclub Girl *47* Arthur Dreifuss
Nightcomers, The *71* Michael Winner
Nightfall *56* Jacques Tourneur
Nightfall *88* Paul Mayersberg
Nightflyers *87* Robert Collector
Nightforce *86* Lawrence Foldes
Nighthawks *78* Paul Hallam, Ron Peck
Nighthawks *81* Bruce Malmuth
Nightingale, The *14* Augustus Thomas
Nightingale *36* Nikolai Ekk
Nightingale *38* Shiro Toyoda
Nightingale Sang in Berkeley Square, A *79* Ralph Thomas
Nightingales *73* Clinton Kimbrough
NightKill *80* Ted Post
Nightkillers *83* Simon Nuchtern
Nightly Encounter *46* Hasse Ekman
Nightmail *36* Harry Watt, Basil Wright
Nightmare, A *1897* Georges Méliès
Nightmare *19* Pál Fejös
Nightmare *42* Tim Whelan
Nightmare *56* Maxwell Shane
Nightmare *63* Freddie Francis
Nightmare *66* Arne Mattsson
Nightmare *80* Umberto Lenzi
Nightmare *81* Romano Scavolini
Nightmare Alley *47* Edmund Goulding
Nightmare at Noon *87* Nico Mastorakis
Nightmare at Shadow Woods *84* John Grissmer
Nightmare Castle *65* Mario Caiano
Nightmare City *80* Umberto Lenzi
Nightmare County *77* Sean McGregor
Nightmare Honeymoon *73* Elliot Silverstein
Nightmare Hotel *70* Eugenio Martin
Nightmare in Blood *76* John Stanley
Nightmare in the Sun *64* Marc Lawrence
Nightmare in Wax *69* Bud Townsend
Nightmare Island *82* J. S. Cardone
Nightmare Maker *81* William Asher
Nightmare of the Glad-Eye, The *13* Edgar Rogers
Nightmare on Elm Street, A *84* Wes Craven
Nightmare on Elm Street 2: Freddy's Revenge, A *85* Jack Sholder
Nightmare on Elm Street 3: Dream Warriors, A *87* Chuck Russell
Nightmare on Elm Street 4: The Dream Master, A *88* Renny Harlin
Nightmare on Elm Street 5: The Dream Child, A *89* Stephen Hopkins
Nightmare Park *73* Peter Sykes
Nightmare Series *78* Stan Brakhage
Nightmare Weekend *86* Henry Sala
Nightmares *83* Joseph Sargent
Nightmares in a Damaged Brain *81* Romano Scavolini
Nightmares of the Devil *88* Yaphet Kotto
Nightmare's Passengers *86* Fernando Ayala
Nights at O'Rear's *80* Robert Mandel
Night's Dream, A *85* Vladimír Sís
Night's End *56* Mrinal Sen
Night's End *75* Shyam Benegal
Nights in a Harem *55* Ted Tetzlaff
Nights in Andalusia *38* Herbert Maisch
Nights in White Satin *87* Michael Barnard
Nights of Cabiria *56* Federico Fellini
Nights of Dracula, The *70* Jesús Franco
Nights of Lucretia Borgia, The *60* Sergio Grieco
Nights of Prague, The *68* Jiří Brdečka, Miloš Macourek, Evald Schorm
Nights of Rasputin, The *60* Pierre Chénal
Nights of Shame *61* Raoul André
Nights of Temptation *60* Sergio Grieco
Nights of the Caliph, The *86* José Luis García Agraz
Nights of the Full Moon *84* Eric Rohmer
Nights of the Werewolf *68* René Govar
Nights When the Devil Came *57* Robert Siodmak
Nightshade *72* Niklas Schilling
Nightshade Flower *51* Kon Ichikawa
Nightsongs *84* Marva Nabili
Nightstick *29* Roland West
Nightstick *87* Joseph L. Scanlan
Nightwars *87* David A. Prior
Nightwing *79* Arthur Hiller
Nightwish *89* Bruce Cook
Nigorie *53* Tadashi Imai
Nihiki no Sama *59* Yoji Kuri
Nihon Bridge, The *29* Kenji Mizoguchi
Nihon-Maru *76* Masahiro Shinoda
Nihon-Maru Ship *76* Masahiro Shinoda
Nihon no Buyō *58* Susumu Hani

Nitchevo *36* Jacques De Baroncelli
Nitwits, The *35* George Stevens
Nitwits *87* Nikolai van der Heyde
Nitwits on Parade, The *49* Robert Jordan Hill
Niwa no Kotori *22* Teinosuke Kinugasa
Niwatori wa Futatabi Naku *54* Heinosuke Gosho
Nix on Dames *29* Donald Gallagher
Nix on Hypnotricks *41* Dave Fleischer
Njeriu Prej Dheu *86* Agim Sopi
Nju *24* Paul Czinner
No *65* György Révész
No Babies Wanted *28* John Harvey
No Barking *54* Chuck Jones
No Basta Ser Madre *38* Ramón Peón
No Bathing Allowed *03* James A. Williamson
No Big Deal *79* Po-chih Leong
No Big Deal *83* Robert Charlton
No Biz Like Shoe Biz *60* Joseph Barbera, William Hanna
No Blade of Grass *70* Cornel Wilde
No Blood No Surrender *87* Rudy Dominguez
No Brakes *29* Tay Garnett
No Cheating *27* Stephen Roberts
No Children Wanted *18* Sherwood MacDonald
No Child's Land *79* Marco Ferreri
No Clouds in the Sky *25* Heinosuke Gosho
No Consultation Today *52* Minoru Shibuya
No Control *27* E. J. Babille, Scott Sidney
No Crossing Under Fire *68* Gleb Panfilov
No Cure Like Father's *14* Edwin J. Collins
No Dead Heroes *87* J. C. Miller
No Deadly Machine *61* Phil Karlson
No Defense *21* William Duncan
No Defense *29* Lloyd Bacon
No Dejes la Puerta Abierta *33* Frank R. Strayer
No Deposit, No Return *76* Norman Tokar
No Door to Hell *80* Hark Tsui
No Down Payment *57* Martin Ritt
No Drowning *87* Pierre Granier-Deferre
No Drums, No Bugles *71* Clyde Ware
No End *84* Krzysztof Kieslowski
No Escape *34* Ralph Ince
No Escape *36* Norman Lee
No Escape *43* Harold Young
No Escape *47* Ray Nazarro
No Escape *53* Charles Bennett
No Escape *58* Charles Brabant
No Escape, No Exit *36* Norman Lee
No Exit *30* Charles Saunders
No Exit *54* Jacqueline Audry
No Exit *62* Tad Danielewski
No Exit, No Panic *81* Helma Sanders-Brahms
No Eyes Today *29* Dave Fleischer
No Fare *28* Charles Lamont
No Father to Guide Him *25* Leo McCarey
No Fight Without Money *24* Kenji Mizoguchi
No Flies on Cis *13* Frank Wilson
No Fool Like an Old Fool *15* Cecil Birch
No Ford in the Fire *68* Gleb Panfilov
No Funny Business *33* Joseph Losey, John Stafford

No Good for Anything *08* Joe Rosenthal
No-Good Guy, The *16* Walter Edwards
No Good to Die for That *67* Jean-Pierre Lefèbvre
No Greater Glory *34* Frank Borzage
No Greater Glory *69* Ajay Kardar
No Greater Love *31* Albert S. Rogell
No Greater Love *32* Lewis Seiler
No Greater Love *43* Friedrich Ermler
No Greater Love *52* Harald Braun
No Greater Love *59* Masaki Kobayashi
No Greater Love Than This *69* Kenji Yoshida
No Greater Sin *41* William Nigh
No Greater Sin *57* Joe Parker
No-Gun Man, The *24* Harry Garson
No Habrá Más Penas ni Olvido *83* Héctor Olivera
No Hagas Planes con Marga *88* Rafael Alcazar
No Hands on the Clock *41* Frank McDonald
No Haunt for a Gentleman *52* Leonard Reeve
No Highway *51* Henry Koster
No Highway in the Sky *51* Henry Koster
No Holds Barred *52* William Beaudine
No Holds Barred *89* Thomas J. Wright
No Kidding *60* Gerald Thomas
No Knife *79* Robert Aldrich
No Lady *31* Lupino Lane
No Leave, No Love *46* Charles Martin
No Limit *31* Frank Tuttle
No Limit *35* Monty Banks
No Living Witness *32* E. Mason Hopper
No Longer Alone *78* Nicholas Webster
No Love for Johnnie *61* Ralph Thomas
No Love for Judy *55* Jacques de Lane Lea
No Man is an Island *62* Richard Goldstone, John Monks, Jr.
No Man of Her Own *32* Wesley Ruggles
No Man of Her Own *50* Mitchell Leisen
No Man Walks Alone *64* Carl Lerner
No Man's Daughter *76* László Ranódy
No Man's Gold *26* Lewis Seiler
No Man's Land *18* Will S. Davis
No Man's Land *27* Fred Jackman
No Man's Land *31* Victor Trivas
No Man's Land *35* Robert North Bradbury
No Man's Land *64* Russ Harvey
No Man's Land *85* Alain Tanner
No Man's Land *87* Peter Werner
No Man's Law *25* Del Andrews
No Man's Law *27* Fred Jackman
No Man's Range *35* Robert North Bradbury
No Man's Woman *21* Wayne Mack, Leo D. Maloney
No Man's Woman *55* Franklin Adreon
No Maps on My Taps *78* George T. Nierenberg
No Marriage Ties *33* J. Walter Ruben
No Mercy *86* Richard Pearce
No Mercy Man, The *73* Daniel J. Vance
No Mercy, No Future *81* Helma Sanders-Brahms
No Minor Vices *48* Lewis Milestone
No Money, No Fight *24* Kenji Mizoguchi
No Monkey Business *35* Marcel Varnel

No More Divorces *63* Jerzy Stefan Stawiński
No More Excuses *68* Robert Downey
No More God, No More Love *85* Tooru Murakawa
No More Hats Wanted *09* Lewin Fitzhamon
No More Ladies *35* George Cukor, Edward H. Griffith
No More Love *31* Anatole Litvak
No More Orchids *32* Walter Lang
No More West *34* Nick Grindé
No More Women *24* Lloyd Ingraham
No More Women *34* Albert S. Rogell
No Mother to Guide Her *23* Charles T. Horan
No Mother to Guide Him *19* Erle C. Kenton, Malcolm St. Clair
No, My Darling Daughter *61* Ralph Thomas
No Name on the Bullet *59* Jack Arnold
No! No! A Thousand Times No! *35* Dave Fleischer
No, No, Lady *31* Edward F. Cline
No, No, Nanette *30* Clarence Badger
No, No, Nanette *40* Herbert Wilcox
No Nukes *80* Dan Goldberg, Anthony Potenza, Julian Schlossberg, Haskell Wexler
No One in the World *87* Vladimir Dovgan
No One Is Crazier Than I Am *55* Erik Faustman
No One Man *32* Lloyd Corrigan
No One Turns Back *43* Alessandro Blasetti
No One Wanted to Die *65* Vytautas Zalakevicius
No One Will Play with Me *76* Werner Herzog
No Orchids for Lulu *62* Rolf Thiele
No Orchids for Miss Blandish *48* St. John L. Clowes
No Ordinary Summer *56* Vladimir Basov
No Other One *36* Dave Fleischer
No Other Woman *28* Lou Tellegen
No Other Woman *33* J. Walter Ruben
¿No Oyes Ladrar los Perros? *74* Noel Howard, François Reichenbach
No Parking *38* Jack Raymond
No Parking Hare *54* Robert McKimson
No Peace Among the Olives *49* Giuseppe De Santis
No Peace Under the Olives *49* Giuseppe De Santis
No Picnic *88* Philip Hartman
No Place for a Lady *43* James P. Hogan
No Place for Jennifer *49* Henry Cass
No Place Like Homicide! *61* Pat Jackson
No Place Like Rome *36* Reginald LeBorg
No Place to Go *27* Mervyn LeRoy
No Place to Go *39* Terry Morse
No Place to Hide *56* Josef Shaftel
No Place to Hide *75* Robert Allen Schnitzer
No Place to Land *58* Albert C. Gannaway
No Problems in Summer *63* Péter Bacsó
No Profanar el Sueño de los Muertos *74* Jorge Grau
No Questions Asked *51* Harold F. Kress
No Ransom *34* Fred Newmeyer

No Regrets for My Youth 46 Akira Kurosawa
No Regrets for Our Youth 46 Akira Kurosawa
No Resting Place 50 Paul Rotha
No Retreat, No Surrender 86 Corey Yuen
No Retreat, No Surrender II 89 Corey Yuen
No Return 26 Heinosuke Gosho
No Return Address 61 Alexander Grattan
No Road Back 56 Montgomery Tully
No Room at the Inn 48 Daniel Birt
No Room for Father 04 Alf Collins
No Room for the Groom 52 Douglas Sirk
No Room to Die 68 Sergio Garrone
No Room to Run 78 Robert Michael Lewis
No Roses for O.S.S. 117 67 André Hunebelle
No Sad Songs for Me 50 Rudolph Maté
No Safe Haven 86 Ronnie Rondell
No Safety Ahead 59 Max Varnel
No Sail 45 Jack Hannah
No Sex Please—We're British 73 Cliff Owen
"No Sir" Orison 75 George Landow
No Sleep on the Deep 34 Charles Lamont
No Sleep Till Dawn 57 Gordon Douglas
No Small Affair 84 Jerry Schatzberg
No Smoking 55 Henry Cass
No Somos de Piedra 68 Manuel Summers
No Sun in Venice 57 Roger Vadim
No Surrender 85 Peter K. Smith
No Survivors Please 63 Hans Albin, Peter Berneis
No Te Engañes Corazón 36 Miguel Torres Contreras
No Tickee No Shirtee 21 Henry D. Bailey
No Time for Breakfast 75 Jean-Louis Bertucelli
No Time for Comedy 40 William Keighley
No Time for Ecstasy 63 Jean-Jacques Vierne
No Time for Flowers 52 Don Siegel
No Time for Love 42 William Beaudine
No Time for Love 43 Mitchell Leisen
No Time for Sergeants 57 Mervyn LeRoy
No Time for Tears 51 Richard Quine
No Time for Tears 57 Cyril Frankel
No Time to Be Young 57 David Lowell Rich
No Time to Die! 57 Terence Young
No Time to Die 84 Helmuth Ashley, E. G. Bakker, Has Manan
No Time to Kill 61 Tom Younger
No Time to Marry 38 Harry Lachman
No Tomorrow 39 Max Ophüls
No Tomorrow 57 Salah Abu Saif
No Tomorrow 57 Arne Mattsson
No Toys for Christmas 65 John Derek
No Trace 50 John Gilling
No Tree in the Street 58 J. Lee-Thompson
No Trees in the Street 58 J. Lee-Thompson
No Trespassing 22 Edwin L. Hollywood
No Trifling with Love 08 Georges Méliès
No Vietnamese Ever Called Me Nigger 68 David Loeb Weiss
No Way Back 49 Stefan Osiecki
No Way Back 55 Victor Vicas
No Way Back 76 Fred Williamson

No Way Out 50 Joseph L. Mankiewicz
No Way Out 72 Duccio Tessari
No Way Out 86 Roger Donaldson
No Way to Treat a Lady 67 Jack Smight
No Wedding Bells 23 Larry Semon
No Woman Knows 21 Tod Browning
Noa at Seventeen 85 Itzhak Yeshurun
Noah und der Cowboy 86 Felix Tissi
Noah's Ark 28 Michael Curtiz
Noah's Ark 50 André Jacques
Noah's Ark Principle, The 84 Roland Emmerich
Noah's Lark 29 Dave Fleischer
Nob Hill 45 Henry Hathaway
Nobbler's Card Party 05 Alf Collins
Nobbling the Bridge 15 Edwin J. Collins
Nobby and the Pearl Mystery 13 Will P. Kellino
Nobby the Knut 14 Will P. Kellino
Nobby the New Waiter 13 Will P. Kellino
Nobby Wins the Cup 14 Will P. Kellino
Nobby's Ju-Jitsu Experiments 14 Will P. Kellino
Nobby's Stud 14 Will P. Kellino
Nobby's Tango Teas 14 Will P. Kellino
Nobi 59 Kon Ichikawa
Noble Art, The 20 Fred Goodwins
Noble Bachelor, The 21 Maurice Elvey
Noble Deception, A 14 Warwick Buckland
Noble Heart, A 11 Theo Bouwmeester
Noble Outcast, A 10 A. E. Coleby
Noble Revenge, A 11 H. Oceano Martinek
Nobleza Baturra 38 Florian Rey
Nobleza Gaucha 38 Sebastián Naon
Nobleza Ranchera 39 Alfredo De Diestro
Nobody 21 Roland West
Nobody Home 19 Elmer Clifton
Nobody Listened 88 Nestor Almendros, Jorge Ulla
Nobody Lives Forever 46 Jean Negulesco
Nobody Loves a Drunken Indian 70 Carol Reed
Nobody Loves a Flapping Eagle 70 Carol Reed
Nobody Ordered Love 71 Robert Hartford-Davis
Nobody Runs Forever 68 Ralph Thomas
Nobody Said Anything 71 Raúl Ruiz
Nobody Said Nothing 71 Raúl Ruiz
Nobody Waved Goodbye 64 Don Owen
Nobody's Baby 37 Gus Meins
Nobody's Bride 23 Herbert Blaché
Nobody's Business 26 Norman Taurog
Nobody's Child 13 Harold Heath
Nobody's Child 15 Ethyle Batley
Nobody's Child 19 George Edwardes Hall
Nobody's Children 26 Ugo Del Colle
Nobody's Children 40 Charles Barton
Nobody's Darling 43 Anthony Mann
Nobody's Daughter 15 August Blom
Nobody's Fool 21 King Baggot
Nobody's Fool 36 Arthur Greville Collins
Nobody's Fool 86 Evelyn Purcell
Nobody's Girl 20 Francis J. Grandon
Nobody's Kid 21 Howard Hickman
Nobody's Land 40 Mario Baffico
Nobody's Money 23 Wallace Worsley
Nobody's Perfect 68 Alan Rafkin
Nobody's Perfect 89 Robert Kaylor
Nobody's Perfekt 81 Peter Bonerz

Nobody's Son 17 Michael Curtiz
Nobody's Widow 27 Donald Crisp
Nobody's Wife 18 Edward J. LeSaint
Nobody's Wife 38 Adela Sequeiro
Nobody's Women 84 Christopher Frank
Noboriryū Tekkahada 70 Teruo Ishii
Noc Listopadowa 33 J. Warnecki
Noc Listopadowa 79 Andrzej Wajda
Noc Nevěsty 67 Karel Kachyňa
Noce au Lac Saint-Fargeau, Un 05 Alice Guy-Blaché
Noce au Village, Une 01 Georges Méliès
Noce en Galilée 87 Michel Khleifi
Noces Barbares, Les 87 Marion Hansel
Noces d'Argent, Les 15 Louis Feuillade
Noces de Sable 48 André Zwoboda
Noces Rouges, Les 73 Claude Chabrol
Noces Sanglantes, Les 16 Louis Feuillade
Noces Siciliennes, Les 12 Louis Feuillade
Noces Vénitiennes, Les 58 Alberto Cavalcanti
Noch Minderjährig 57 Georg Tressler
Noch v Sentyabr' 39 Boris Barnet
Noche de Juerga 86 Miguel Delgado
Noche de la Muerte Ciega, La 71 Amando De Ossorio
Noche de las Gaviotas, La 75 Amando De Ossorio
Noche de los Asesinos, La 74 Jesús Franco
Noche de los Brujos, La 70 Amando De Ossorio
Noche de los Diablos, La 72 Giorgio Ferroni
Noche de los Lapices, La 86 Héctor Olivera
Noche de los Mayas 39 Chano Urueta
Noche de los Mil Gatos, La 72 René Cardona, Jr.
Noche de los Vampiros, La 75 Leon Klimovsky
Noche de Terror 57 Julián Soler
Noche de Verano 62 Jorge Grau
Noche de Walpurgis, La 70 Leon Klimovsky
Noche del Buque Maldito, La 74 Amando De Ossorio
Noche del Hombrelobo, La 80 Jacinto Molina
Noche del Pecado, La 33 Miguel Torres Contreras
Noche del Terror Ciego, La 71 Amando De Ossorio
Noche Más Hermosa, La 84 Manuel Gutiérrez Aragón
Noche Oscura, La 89 Carlos Saura
Noches de Gloria 38 Rolando Aguilar
Noches de Paloma, Las 78 Alberto Isaac
Noches del Califas, Las 86 José Luis García Agraz
Noches del Hombre Lobo, Las 68 René Govar
Nochnoi Ekipazh 88 Boris Tokarev
Noční Host 61 Otakar Vávra
Noční Zkouška 80 Evald Schorm
Nocout 84 José Luis García Agraz
Nocturna 78 Harry Hurwitz
Nocturna Amor Que Te Vas 87 Marcela Fernández Violante
Nocturna, Granddaughter of Dracula 78 Harry Hurwitz

Nocturnal Love That Goes Away 87 Marcela Fernández Violante
Nocturnal Voyage, The 86 Kitty Kino
Nocturne, Le 17 Maurice Mariaud
Nocturne, Le 19 Louis Feuillade
Nocturne 46 Edwin L. Marin
Nocturne 54 Alexander Alexeïeff, Claire Parker, Georges Violet
Nocturno 34 Gustav Machatý
Nocturno der Liebe 18 Carl Boese
Noddy in Toyland 58 Maclean Rogers
Nodes 81 Stan Brakhage
Nödlanding 52 Arne Skouen
Noe Helt Annet 86 Morten Kolstad
Noël d'Artistes 08 Léonce Perret
Noël de Francesca, Le 12 Louis Feuillade
Noël de Poilu, Le 15 Louis Feuillade
Noël du Père Lathuile, Le 22 Pierre Colombier
Noël d'un Vagabond, Le 18 René Leprince
Nogent—Eldorado du Dimanche 29 Marcel Carné, Michel Sanvoisin
Nogent, the Sunday Eldorado 29 Marcel Carné, Michel Sanvoisin
Nogi Shōgun to Kuma-San 25 Kenji Mizoguchi
Nogi Taishō to Kuma-San 25 Kenji Mizoguchi
Nogiku no Gotoki Kimi Nariki 55 Keisuke Kinoshita
Noi Cei din Linia Intîi 86 Sergiu Nicolaescu
Noi Donne Siamo Fatte Così 71 Dino Risi
Noi Tre 84 Pupi Avati
Noi Uomini Duri 87 Maurizio Ponzi
Noi Vivi 42 Goffredo Alessandrini
Noia, La 63 Damiano Damiani
Noir et Blanc 86 Claire Devers
Noire de..., La 65 Ousmane Sembène
Noise Annoys Ko-Ko 29 Dave Fleischer
Noise from the Deep, A 13 Mack Sennett
Noise in Newboro, A 23 Harry Beaumont
Noisy Neighbors 29 Charles Reisner
Noita Palaa Elämään 52 Roland Af Hällström
Noix de Coco 39 Jean Boyer
Nomad Puppeteers, The 74 Mani Kaul
Nomadic Lives 77 Mark Obenhaus
Nomadie 31 Alexander Singelow
Nomads 85 John McTiernan
Nomads of the North 20 David M. Hartford
Nomisuke Kinshu Undō 28 Tomu Uchida
Non Aspettare Django Spara 67 Eduardo Mulargia
Non Canto Più 43 Riccardo Freda
Non C'È Pace Tra gli Ulivi 49 Giuseppe De Santis
Non Ci Resta Che Piangere 84 Roberto Benigni
Non Coupable 47 Henri Decoin
Non Credo Più all'Amore 54 Roberto Rossellini
Non Faccio la Guerra, Faccio l'Amore 66 Franco Rossi
Non Si Deve Profanare il Sonno dei Morti 74 Jorge Grau
Non Si Sevizia un Paperino 72 Lucio Fulci
Non Son Gelosia 33 Carlo Ludovico Bragaglia

Non Sono Superstizioso, Ma... 44 Carlo Ludovico Bragaglia
Non-Stop Flight, The 26 Emory Johnson
Non-Stop New York 37 Robert Stevenson
Non Stuzzicate la Zanzara 67 Lina Wertmuller
Non-Suited 14 Edwin J. Collins
Non Ti Pago! 42 Carlo Ludovico Bragaglia
Non Tirate il Diavolo per la Coda 68 Philippe de Broca
Non Toccate la Donna Bianca 73 Marco Ferreri
Non Uccidere 61 Claude Autant-Lara
Nona, La 78 Héctor Olivera
Nonconformist Parson, A 19 A. V. Bramble
None But the Brave 14 Charles H. Weston
None But the Brave 15 Will P. Kellino
None But the Brave 28 Albert Ray
None But the Brave 60 George Sherman
None But the Brave 63 Ken Richardson
None But the Brave 64 Frank Sinatra
None But the Lonely Heart 44 Clifford Odets
None But the Lonely Spy 64 Emimmo Salvi
None of That's Worth Love 31 Jacques Tourneur
None Shall Escape 44 André De Toth
None So Blind 23 Burton L. King
Nonentity, The 22 Sinclair Hill
Nonentity, The 86 Michel Deville
Nonna Sabella, La 57 Dino Risi
Nono Nénesse 75 Jacques Rozier, Pascal Thomas
Noon 31 Josef Heifits, Alexander Zarkhi
Noon 68 Puriša Djordjević
Noose, The 28 John Francis Dillon
Noose 48 Edmond T. Gréville
Noose, The 57 Wojciech Has
Noose, The 87 Costas Coutsomitis
Noose for a Gunman 60 Edward L. Cahn
Noose for a Lady 53 Wolf Rilla
Noose Hangs High, The 48 Charles Barton
Nor the Moon by Night 58 Ken Annakin
Nora 23 Berthold Viertel
Nora Helmer 73 Rainer Werner Fassbinder
Nora Inu 49 Akira Kurosawa
Nora Prentiss 47 Vincent Sherman
Norah Mayer the Quick-Change Dancer 1898 James A. Williamson
Norah O'Neale 34 Brian Desmond Hurst
Norah's Debt of Honour 12 Wilfred Noy
Nord Atlantique 39 Maurice Cloche
Nordpol-Ahoi! 32 Arnold Fanck, Andrew Marton
Noris 19 Augusto Genina
Norma Rae 78 Martin Ritt
Normal Young Man, The 69 Dino Risi
Normalsatz 81 Heinz Emigholz
Norman Conquest 53 Bernard Knowles
Norman...Is That You? 76 George Schlatter
Norman Loves Rose 81 Henri Safran
Norman Normal 68 Alex Lovy
Norman Rockwell's World—An American Dream 72 Robert Deubel
Normande 79 Gilles Carle
Normandie-Niémen 59 Jean Dréville

Normetal 59 Claude Fournier, Gilles Groulx
Noroi no Yakata-Chi wa Suu 71 Michio Yamamoto
Noroît 76 Jacques Rivette
Norseman, The 78 Charles B. Pierce
Norte, El 83 Gregory Nava
North Avenue Irregulars, The 78 Bruce Bilson
North Bridge 81 Jacques Rivette
North by Northwest 59 Alfred Hitchcock
North Dallas Forty 79 Ted Kotcheff
North East Corner 46 John Eldridge
North from Lone Star 40 Lambert Hillyer
North from the Lone Star 40 Lambert Hillyer
North of Alaska 24 Frank S. Mattison
North of Arizona 35 Harry S. Webb
North of 53 17 Richard Stanton, William Desmond Taylor
North of Hudson Bay 23 John Ford
North of Nevada 24 Albert S. Rogell
North of Nome 25 Raymond K. Johnson
North of Nome 36 William Nigh
North of Shanghai 39 D. Ross Lederman
North of the Border 46 B. Reeves Eason
North of the Great Divide 50 William Witney
North of the Rio Grande 22 Joseph E. Henabery
North of the Rio Grande 37 Nate Watt
North of the Rockies 42 Lambert Hillyer
North of the Yukon 23 John Ford
North of the Yukon 39 Sam Nelson
North of 36 24 Irvin Willat
North or Northwest 37 Len Lye
North Pole, The 20 Frank Moser
North Sea 38 Harry Watt
North Sea Hijack 79 Andrew V. McLaglen
North Sea Patrol 38 Norman Lee
North Shore 87 William Phelps
North Star 25 Paul Powell
North Star, The 43 Lewis Milestone
North Star, The 82 Pierre Granier-Deferre
North to Alaska 60 Henry Hathaway
North to the Klondike 42 Erle C. Kenton
North West Frontier 59 J. Lee-Thompson
North West Mounted Police 40 Cecil B. DeMille
North Wind 37 Mario Soffici
North Wind's Malice, The 20 Paul Bern, Carl Harbaugh
North Woods, The 20 Raoul Barré, Charles Bowers
North Woods 31 Walter Lantz
Northeast of Seoul 72 David Lowell Rich
Northeast to Seoul 72 David Lowell Rich
Northern Bridge, The 81 Jacques Rivette
Northern Code 25 Leon De la Mothe
Northern Frontier 35 Sam Newfield
Northern Lights 14 Edgar Lewis
Northern Lights 78 John Hanson, Rob Nilsson
Northern Mystery, The 24 Hugh Croise
Northern Patrol 53 Rex Bailey
Northern Pursuit 43 Raoul Walsh
Northern Star, The 82 Pierre Granier-Deferre
Northfield Cemetery Massacre, The 76 William Dear, Thomas L. Dyke

Northville Cemetery Massacre, The *76* William Dear, Thomas L. Dyke
Northwest *76* Jacques Rivette
Northwest Hounded Police *46* Tex Avery
Northwest Outpost *47* Allan Dwan
Northwest Passage *39* Jack Conway, King Vidor
Northwest Passage, Book One: Rogers' Rangers *39* Jack Conway, King Vidor
Northwest Passage, Part One: Rogers' Rangers *39* Jack Conway, King Vidor
Northwest Rangers *42* Joseph M. Newman
Northwest Stampede *48* Albert S. Rogell
Northwest Territory *51* Frank McDonald
Northwest Trail *45* Derwin Abrahams
Northwest U.S.A. *44* Willard Van Dyke
Northwest Wind *76* Jacques Rivette
Norway Replies *44* F. Herrick Herrick
Nor'west *76* Jacques Rivette
Norwood *70* Jack Haley, Jr.
Norwood Builder, The *22* George Ridgwell
Nos Ancêtres les Explorateurs *55* Pierre Kast
Nos Bons Étudiants *04* Alice Guy-Blaché
Nos Reímos de la Migra *87* Víctor Manuel Castro
Nose, The *63* Alexander Alexeïeff, Claire Parker
Nose Has It, The *42* Val Guest
Nosey Dobson *77* Michael Alexander
Nosey Ned *16* Harry S. Palmer
Nosey Ned and His New Straw Lid *16* Harry S. Palmer
Nosey Ned Commandeers an Army Mule *16* Harry S. Palmer
Nosey Parker *06* Alf Collins
Nosey Parker *13* Will P. Kellino
Nosférat ou Les Eaux Glacées du Calcul Égoïste, Le *74* Maurice Rabinowicz
Nosferatu *21* F. W. Murnau
Nosferatu—A Symphony of Horror *21* F. W. Murnau
Nosferatu—A Symphony of Terror *21* F. W. Murnau
Nosferatu a Venezia *88* Augusto Caminito
Nosferatu—Eine Symphonie des Grauens *21* F. W. Murnau
Nosferatu, Phantom der Nacht *78* Werner Herzog
Nosferatu the Vampire *21* F. W. Murnau
Nosferatu the Vampire *78* Werner Herzog
Nosferatu the Vampyre *78* Werner Herzog
Nosotros Dos *54* Emilio Fernández
Nostalghia *83* Andrei Tarkovsky
Nostalgia *83* Andrei Tarkovsky
Nostalgie *29* William Dieterle
Nostalgie *37* Victor Tourjansky
Nostalgie de Souna, La *75* Jean Rouch
Nostra Guerra, La *43* Alberto Lattuada
Nostra Patria, La *25* Emilio Ghione
Nostradamus *37* Juan Bustillo Oro
Nostradamus *38* David Miller
Nostradamus IV *44* Cy Endfield*
Nostradamus no Daiyogen *74* Toshio Masuda
Nostri Figli, I *52* Michelangelo Antonioni
Nostri Mariti, I *66* Luigi Filippo D'Amico, Dino Risi, Luigi Zampa
Nostri Sogni, I *43* Vittorio Cottafavi

Noszty Fiú Esete Tóth Marival *38* Steve Sekely
Not a Drum Was Heard *24* William A. Wellman
Not a Hope in Hell *60* Maclean Rogers
Not a Ladies' Man *42* Lew Landers
Not a Love Story *81* Bonnie Sherr Klein
Not a Pretty Picture *75* Martha Coolidge
Not a Word About Love *38* Alwin Elling
Not Against the Flesh *31* Carl Theodor Dreyer
Not As a Stranger *55* Stanley Kramer
Not As Bad As That *74* Claude Goretta
Not As Rehearsed *13* Frank Wilson
Not As Wicked As That *74* Claude Goretta
Not Blood Relations *32* Mikio Naruse
Not Built for Runnin' *24* Leo D. Maloney
Not Damaged *30* Chandler Sprague
Not Detained at the Office *06* Alf Collins
Not Everything Is True *86* Rogério Sganzerla
Not Exactly Gentlemen *31* Ben Stoloff
Not for Honor and Glory *66* Mark Robson
Not for Publication *27* Ralph Ince
Not for Publication *84* Paul Bartel
Not for Sale *24* Will P. Kellino
Not Guilty *08* Georges Méliès
Not Guilty *11* Lewin Fitzhamon
Not Guilty *13* Dave Aylott
Not Guilty *15* Joseph A. Golden
Not Guilty *19* Arrigo Bocchi
Not Guilty *21* Sidney Franklin
Not Guilty *47* Henri Decoin
Not In, or Out *18* Alexander Korda
Not Just a Pretty Face *83* Gillian Armstrong
Not Likely *14* Dave Aylott
Not Mine to Love *67* Uri Zohar
Not My Daughter *75* Jerry Schafer
Not My Sister *16* Charles Giblyn
Not Negotiable *18* Walter West
Not Now *36* Dave Fleischer
Not Now Comrade *77* Ray Cooney, Harold Snoad
Not Now Darling *72* Ray Cooney, David Croft
Not of This Earth *56* Roger Corman
Not of This Earth *88* Jim Wynorski
Not on Your Life *63* Morton Da Costa
Not on Your Life *63* Luis García Berlanga
Not One to Spare *24* Renaud Hoffman
Not Quite a Lady *28* Thomas Bentley
Not Quite Decent *29* Irving Cummings
Not Quite Jerusalem *84* Lewis Gilbert
Not Quite Paradise *84* Lewis Gilbert
Not Reconciled *65* Jean-Marie Straub
Not Reconciled, or Only Violence Helps Where It Rules *65* Jean-Marie Straub
Not Reconciled, or Only Violence Helps Where Violence Rules *65* Jean-Marie Straub
Not Since Casanova *88* Brett Thompson
Not So Bad As He Seemed *10* D. W. Griffith
Not So Dumb *29* King Vidor
Not So Dusty *36* Maclean Rogers
Not So Dusty *56* Maclean Rogers
Not So Long Ago *25* Sidney Olcott
Not So Quiet *30* Walter Lantz

Not So Quiet on the Western Front *30* Monty Banks
Not Such a Fool *12* Edwin J. Collins
Not Such a Fool As He Looks *07* Lewin Fitzhamon
Not Tonight, Darling *71* Anthony Sloman
Not Tonight Josephine *34* Edward F. Cline
Not Wanted *13* Percy Stow
Not Wanted *49* Elmer Clifton, Ida Lupino
Not Wanted on Voyage *36* Emil E. Reinert
Not Wanted on Voyage *57* Maclean Rogers
Not Wedded But a Wife *21* Raoul Barré, Charles Bowers
Not with My Wife You Don't! *66* Norman Panama
Note in the Shoe, The *09* D. W. Griffith
Notebook on Clothes and Cities, A *89* Wim Wenders
Notebooks of Major Thompson *55* Preston Sturges
Noted Sword, The *45* Kenji Mizoguchi
Notes and Notions *29* R. E. Jeffrey
Notes for a Film About Donna and Gail *66* Don Owen
Notes for a Lewd Novel *70* Pier Paolo Pasolini
Notes for an African Oresteia *69* Pier Paolo Pasolini
Notes for Jerome *81* Jonas Mekas
Notes on the Circus *66* Jonas Mekas
Notes on the Green Revolution *72* Shyam Benegal
Notes to You *41* Friz Freleng
Nothing Barred *61* D'Arcy Conyers
Nothing But a Man *64* Michael Roemer, Robert M. Young
Nothing But Girls *20* Raoul Barré, Charles Bowers
Nothing But Lies *20* Lawrence C. Windom
Nothing But the Best *63* Clive Donner
Nothing But the Night *72* Peter Sasdy
Nothing But the Tooth *48* Art Davis
Nothing But the Truth *20* David Kirkland
Nothing But the Truth *29* Victor Schertzinger
Nothing But the Truth *39* Weyler Hildebrand
Nothing But the Truth *41* Elliott Nugent
Nothing But the Truth *73* François Reichenbach, Orson Welles
Nothing But Trouble *44* Sam Taylor
Nothing Else Matters *20* George Pearson
Nothing Ever Happens *63* Juan Antonio Bardem
Nothing Flat *27* Stephen Roberts
Nothing in Common *86* Garry Marshall
Nothing in Order *73* Lina Wertmuller
Nothing Lasts Forever *84* Tom Schiller
Nothing Like Publicity *36* Maclean Rogers
Nothing Matters *26* Norman Taurog
Nothing Personal *80* George Bloomfield
Nothing Sacred *37* William A. Wellman
Nothing to Be Done *14* Edgar Jones
Nothing to Lose *52* Lewis Gilbert
Nothing to Wear *28* Erle C. Kenton
Nothing Unusual *57* Peter Weiss

Now or Never *21* Fred Newmeyer, Hal Roach, Sam Taylor
Now or Never *35* Bernard B. Ray
Now She Lets Him Go Out *13* Bert Haldane
Now That April's Here *58* William Davidson
Now That I Was Born a Woman *34* Heinosuke Gosho
Now That Summer Is Gone *38* Frank Tashlin
Now, Voyager *42* Irving Rapper
Now We Shall Be Happy *40* William Molte
Now We'll Call You Brother *71* Raúl Ruiz
Now We'll Tell One *33* James Parrott
Now We're in the Air *27* Frank R. Strayer
Now You See Him, Now You Don't *72* Robert Butler
Now You See It Now You Don't *16* John Colman Terry
Now You're Talking *40* John Paddy Carstairs
Nowhere to Go *58* Seth Holt
Nowhere to Hide *87* Mario Azzopardi
Nowhere to Run *89* Carl Franklin
Nowsreel *68* Haskell Wexler
Nowy Janko Muzykant *60* Jan Lenica
Noyade Interdite *87* Pierre Granier-Deferre
Nóż w Wodzie *61* Roman Polanski
Nozze di Sangue *41* Goffredo Alessandrini
Nozze d'Oro *11* Luigi Maggi
Nran Gouyne *68* Sergei Paradzhanov
N'Te Promène Donc Pas Toute Nue *06* Louis Feuillade
Nth Commandment, The *23* Frank Borzage
Ntturudu *86* Umban U'Kset
Nu Börjar Livet *48* Gustaf Molander
Nu Shi Zhang De Si Ren Sheng Hua *88* Yanjing Yang
Nuba *77* Leni Riefenstahl
Nuclear Terror *77* Freddie Francis, Ashley Lazarus
Nucleo Zero *84* Carlo Lizzani
Nude Bomb, The *79* Clive Donner
Nude Heat Wave *68* Robert Freeman
Nude in a White Car *58* Robert Hossein
Nude in Charcoal *62* Joe Sarno
Nude in His Pocket *57* Pierre Kast
Nude Odyssey *61* Franco Rossi
Nude Restaurant *67* Andy Warhol
Nude. . .Si Muore *68* Antonio Margheriti
Nudes of the World *61* Arnold Louis Miller
Nudes on Credit *66* Don Rolos
Nudes on the Rocks *63* Warner Rose
Nudist Paradise *59* Charles Saunders
Nudist Story, The *60* Ramsey Herrington
Nudo di Donna *81* Alberto Lattuada, Nino Manfredi
Nuestra Tierra de Paz *40* Arturo S. Mom
Nueva Canción Chilena *73* Raúl Ruiz
Nueva Sinfonía *82* Santiago Álvarez
Nuevitas *68* Manuel Octavio Gómez
Nuevo Viaje a la Luna *09* Segundo De Chomón
Nugget Jim's Pardner *16* Frank Borzage
Nugget Nell *19* Elmer Clifton

Nuisance, The *33* Jack Conway
Nuit, La *30* Henri Roussel
Nuit à l'Assemblée Nationale, Une *88* Jean-Pierre Mocky
Nuit à Tabarin, Une *47* Karel Lamač
Nuit Agitée, Une *1897* Alice Guy-Blaché
Nuit Agitée, Une *08* Louis Feuillade
Nuit Agitée, Une *12* Max Linder
Nuit Agitée, Une *20* Alfred Machin
Nuit Américaine, La *73* François Truffaut
Nuit avec Hortense, La *88* Jean Chabot
Nuit de Carnaval *07* Georges Méliès
Nuit de Cimetière *72* Jean Rollin
Nuit de Décembre *39* Kurt Bernhardt
Nuit de la Revanche, La *24* Henri Étiévant
Nuit de la Saint-Jean, La *29* William Dieterle
Nuit de Noël, La *11* Alfred Machin
Nuit de Saint-Germain des Prés, La *77* Bob Swaim
Nuit de Saint-Jean, La *22* Robert Saidreau
Nuit de Varennes, La *82* Ettore Scola
Nuit des Adieux, La *67* Jean Dréville
Nuit des Espions, La *59* Robert Hossein
Nuit des Généraux, La *66* Anatole Litvak
Nuit des Traquées, La *80* Jean Rollin
Nuit d'Été en Ville *90* Michel Deville
Nuit d'Ivresse *86* Bernard Nauer
Nuit Docile *87* Guy Gilles
Nuit du Carnaval, La *22* Victor Tourjansky
Nuit du Carrefour, La *32* Jean Renoir
Nuit du Cinéma, La *42* Sacha Guitry
Nuit du 11 Septembre, La *22* Dominique Bernard-Deschamps
Nuit du 13, La *21* Henri Fescourt
Nuit Électrique, La *30* Eugene Deslaw
Nuit Est à Nous, La *27* Roger Lion
Nuit Est à Nous, La *30* Henri Roussel
Nuit Est Mon Royaume, La *51* Georges Lacombe
Nuit et Brouillard *55* Alain Resnais
Nuit et Jour *76* Chantal Akerman
Nuit Fantastique, La *42* Marcel L'Herbier
Nuit Noire, Calcutta *64* Marin Karmitz
Nuit Porte Jarretelles, La *85* Virginie Thevenet
Nuit Rouge, La *24* Maurice Gleize
Nuit sur le Mont Chauve, Une *33* Alexander Alexeïeff, Claire Parker
Nuit Terrible, Une *1896* Georges Méliès
Nuits Andalouses *54* Maurice Cloche
Nuits Blanches *57* Luchino Visconti
Nuits Blanches de Saint-Pétersbourg, Les *38* Jean Dréville
Nuits d'Alerte *45* Léon Mathot
Nuits de Feu *36* Marcel L'Herbier
Nuits de la Pleine Lune, Les *84* Eric Rohmer
Nuits de l'Épouvante, Les *66* Domenico De Felice, Elio Scardamaglia
Nuits de Port Said, Les *31* Dmitri Kirsanov*
Nuits de Prince *28* Marcel L'Herbier
Nuits de Raspoutine, Les *60* Pierre Chénal
Nuits Rouges *73* Georges Franju
Nuke 'Em High *85* Richard W. Haines, Lloyd Kaufman
Nuke Trap, The *88* Francesco Laudadio
Nukiashi Sashiashi *34* Kozaburo Yoshi-

mura
Numazu Heigakkō *39* Tadashi Imai
Numazu Military Academy, The *39* Tadashi Imai
Number, The *78* Roy Boulting
No. 8 *54* Harry Smith
No. 11 *56* Harry Smith
No. 15 *66* Harry Smith
No. 5 *50* Harry Smith
Number 5 *69* John Lennon, Yoko Ono
Number 5 John Street *21* Kenelm Foss
No. 4 *50* Harry Smith
No. 14 *65* Harry Smith
Number Fourteen *86* Sinan Cetin
No. 9 *54* Harry Smith
No. 99 *20* Ernest C. Warde
Number 96 *74* Peter Bernados
No. 1 *39* Harry Smith
Number One *69* Tom Gries
Number One *84* Les Blair
Number 111 *19* Alexander Korda
Number 1 of the Secret Service *78* Lindsay Shonteff
Number One with a Bullet *87* Jack Smight
Number Our Days *77* Lynne Littman
Number, Please *20* Hal Roach
Number, Please *31* George King
No. 7 *51* Harry Smith
Number 7 Brick Row *22* Fred W. Durrant
Number 17 *20* George A. Beranger
Number Seventeen *28* Géza von Bolváry
Number Seventeen *32* Alfred Hitchcock
No. 6 *51* Harry Smith
Number Six *62* Robert Tronson
No. 16 *67* Harry Smith
No. 10 *56* Harry Smith
No. 13 *62* Harry Smith
No. 13 Demon Street *61* Herbert L. Strock
No. 3 *47* Harry Smith
No. 12 *58* Harry Smith
No. 2 *40* George Sidney
No. 2 *42* Harry Smith
Number Two *75* Jean-Luc Godard
Number Zero *71* Jean Eustache
Numbered Men *30* Mervyn LeRoy
Numbered Woman *38* Karl Brown
Numbers of Monte Carlo *34* William Nigh
Numbskull Emptybrook Back in the Country *87* Ere Kokkonen
Numéro Deux *75* Jean-Luc Godard
Numero 121, Il *17* Emilio Ghione
Numéro Zéro *71* Jean Eustache
Nun, The *07* Lewin Fitzhamon
Nun, The *65* Jacques Rivette
Nun and the Sergeant, The *62* Franklin Adreon
Nun at the Crossroads *70* Julio Buchs
Nun in the State of Sin, A *86* Dario Donati
Nun of Monza, The *70* Eriprando Visconti
Nun of Monza, The *87* Luciano Odorisio
Nunca Pasa Nada *63* Juan Antonio Bardem
1 2 3 Duan Mahaphai *77* Prinya Lilason, Narong Poomin, Vinai Poomin
Nuns on the Run *90* Jonathan Lynn
Nun's Story, The *58* Fred Zinnemann
Nunta de Piatră *73* Dan Pița, Mircea Veroiu

Objectif 500 Million *66* Pierre Schöndörf-fer

Objectif 500 Millions *66* Pierre Schöndörf-fer

Objection *85* Andrzej Trzos-Rastawiecki

Objections Overruled *12* Allan Dwan

Objective, Burma! *45* Raoul Walsh

Objective 500 Million *66* Pierre Schön-dörffer

Obligation to Assassinate, The *37* Antonio Helu

Obligin' Buckaroo, The *27* Richard Thorpe

Obliging Young Lady *41* Richard Wallace

Oblomok Imperii *29* Friedrich Ermler

Oblomov *79* Nikita Mikhalkov

Oblong Box, The *69* Gordon Hessler, Michael Reeves

Oboro yo no Onna *36* Heinosuke Gosho

Oborona Tsaritsina *42* Georgy Vasiliev, Sergei Vasiliev

Oboroten Tom *87* Eric Latsis

Obozhzhenniue Krylya *15* Yevgeni Bauer

Obras Maestras del Terror *60* Enrique Car-reras

Obryv *87* Vladimir Vengerov

Obscure Illness, The *90* Mario Monicelli

Obscured by Clouds *72* Barbet Schroeder

Observations Under the Volcano *84* Chris-tian Blackwood

Obsessed *51* Maurice Elvey

Obsessed *83* Henry Chan

Obsessed *88* Robin Spry

Obsession *33* Maurice Tourneur

Obsession *42* Luchino Visconti

Obsession *43* Julien Duvivier

Obsession *48* Edward Dmytryk

Obsession *54* Jean Delannoy

Obsession *60* Jiří Trnka

Obsession *68* Gunnar Höglund

Obsession *75* Brian DePalma

Obsession, The *78* Shyam Benegal

Obsession *89* Xiaowen Zhou

Obsitos *17* Béla Balázs

Obstacle, L' *18* Jean Kemm

Obvinyaetsya Svadba *87* Alexander Itygilov

Obvious Situation, An *30* Guarino G. Glavany

Obvious Thing, The *35* James Riddell

Obyasnenie v Lubvi *77* Ilya Averbakh

Obyknovennyi Fashizm *64* Mikhail Romm

Obyknovennyi Fazhism *64* Mikhail Romm

Obžalovaný *63* Ján Kadár, Elmar Klos

Occasional Work of a Female Slave *73* Alexander Kluge

Occasionally Yours *20* James W. Horne

Occhi, la Bocca, Gli *82* Marco Bellocchio

Occhi Senza Volto *59* Georges Franju

Occhiali d'Oro, Gli *87* Giuliano Montaldo

Occhio del Male, L' *82* Lucio Fulci

Occhio nel Labirinto, L' *71* Mario Caiano

Occhio per Occhio *67* Miguel Iglesias Bonns

Occhio Selvaggio, L' *68* Paolo Cavara

Occident, L' *27* Henri Fescourt

Occident, L' *37* Henri Fescourt

Occultism *18* Raoul Barré, Charles Bowers

Occultisme et la Magie, L' *52* Marc Allégret

Occupation in 26 Pictures, The *78* Lordan Zafranović

Occupational Hazards *67* André Cayatte

Occupe-Toi d'Amélie *49* Claude Autant-Lara

Occurrence at Owl Creek Bridge, An *61* Robert Enrico

Ocean Breakers *35* Ivar Johansson

Ocean Drive Weekend *84* Bryan Jones

Ocean Hop, The *27* Walt Disney

Ocean Swells *34* George Stevens

Ocean Waif, The *16* Alice Guy-Blaché

Oceano *71* Folco Quilici

Ocean's Eleven *60* Lewis Milestone

Oceans of Trouble *25* Charles Bowers

Och Alla Dessa Kvinnor *44* Arne Mattsson

Ocharcoaga *61* Jorge Grau

Ochazuke no Aji *52* Yasujiro Ozu

Ochen Khorosho Zhevyotsa *30* Mikhail Doller, Vsevolod I. Pudovkin

Ochnaya Stavka *87* Valery Kremnev

Oci Ciornie *87* Nikita Mikhalkov

Octagon, The *80* Eric Karson

Octaman *71* Harry Essex

Octaroon, The *03* Dicky Winslow

Octavia *84* David Beaird

October *27* Grigori Alexandrov, Sergei Eisenstein

October Days *58* Sergei Vasiliev

October Drive, The *31* Leonid Lukov

October 4th *25* Alexander Butler

October Man, The *47* Roy Ward Baker

October Moth *59* John Kruse

October Revolution, The *67* Frédéric Rossif

October Without Ilyich *25* Dziga Vertov

Octobre à Madrid *65* Marcel Hanoun

Octobre à Paris *62* Jacques Panijel

Octoman *71* Harry Essex

Octopus, The *15* Tom Santschi

Octopus Gang, The *15* H. Oceano Martinek

Octopuses Wish You a Merry Christmas, The *86* Jindřich Polák

Octopussy *83* John Glen

Octoroon, The *13* Sidney Olcott

Octubre de Todos, El *77* Santiago Álvarez

Od Petka do Petka *86* Anton Vrdoljak

Óda na Radost *86* Jaroslav Balík

Oda-Vissza *62* István Gaál

Odalisque, The *14* Christy Cabanne

Odd Affinity *69* Kaneto Shindo

Odd Angry Shot, The *79* Tom Jeffrey

Odd Birds *85* Jeanne Collachia

Odd Charges *16* Frank Miller

Odd Couple, The *68* Gene Saks

Odd Folk *70* Vasili Shuksin

Odd Freak, An *16* George Loane Tucker

Odd Freak, An *23* H. Manning Haynes

Odd Job, The *78* Peter Medak

Odd Job Man, The *12* Allan Dwan

Odd Jobs *84* Mark Story

Odd Man, The *78* Bill Forsyth

Odd Man Out *15* Edwin J. Collins

Odd Man Out *46* Carol Reed

Odd Numbers *29* R. E. Jeffrey

Odd Obsession *59* Kon Ichikawa

Odd Triangle, The *68* Joe Sarno

Odd Tricks *24* Fred Rains

Oddo *67* Joe Davis

Odds Against *15* Lawrence Trimble

Odds Against Her, The *19* Alexander Butler

Odds Against Tomorrow *59* Robert Wise

Odds and Ends *86* Alexander Kluge, Volker Schlöndorff

Ode to an Old Teacher *66* Minoru Shibuya

Ode to Billy Joe *76* Max Baer

Ode to Happiness *86* Jaroslav Balík

Odessa File, The *74* Ronald Neame

Odessa in Fiamme *42* Carmine Gallone

Odessa in Flames *42* Carmine Gallone

Odette *50* Herbert Wilcox

Odia il Prossimo Tuo *68* Ferdinando Baldi

Odinnadtsatyi *28* Dziga Vertov

Odinokaya Oreshina *87* Frunze Dovlatyan

Odinokaya Zhenchina Zhelaet Poznakomi-taya *87* Vyacheslav Krishtofovich

Odinokij Golos Celoveka *78* Alexander Sokurov

Odinotchnoye Plavaniye *86* Mikhail Tumanishvili

Odio *35* Richard Harlan

Odio *40* William Rowland

Odio le Bionde *81* Giorgio Capitani

Odio Mi Cuerpo *75* Leon Klimovsky

Odio per Odio *67* Domenico Paolella

Odipussi *88* Loriot

Odissea Nuda *61* Franco Rossi

Odkaz *65* Evald Schorm

Odna *31* Grigori Kozintsev, Leonid Trauberg

Odna Semya *43* Grigori Alexandrov

Odnazhdi Noch *45* Boris Barnet

Odongo *56* John Gilling

Odor of the Day *48* Art Davis

Odor-able Kitty, The *44* Chuck Jones

Odvahu pro Všední Den *64* Evald Schorm

Odyssea *85* Jiří Tyller

Odyssée d'Amour *87* Pim de la Parra

Odyssée du Capitaine Steve, L' *56* Marcello Pagliero

Odyssée Nue, L' *61* Franco Rossi

Odyssey *77* Gerard Damiano

Odyssey *85* Jiří Tyller

Odyssey of the North, An *14* Hobart Bosworth

Odyssey of the Pacific *81* Fernando Arrabal

Oedipus Rex *57* Tyrone Guthrie

Oedipus Rex *67* Pier Paolo Pasolini

Oedipus the King *67* Philip Saville

Œil au Beurre Noir, L' *87* Serge Meynard

Œil de Saint-Yves, L' *19* Georges Champavert

Œil du Maître, L' *57* Jacques Doniol-Valcroze

Œil du Malin, L' *61* Claude Chabrol

Œil du Monocle, L' *62* Georges Lautner

Œil pour Œil *56* André Cayatte

Œil Torve, L' *60* Jerzy Skolimowski

Œillet Blanc, L' *23* Henri Desfontaines

O'er Hill and Dale *31* Basil Wright

Oeste Nevada Joe *65* Ignacio F. Iquino

Œuf d'Épinoche *22* Jean Painlevé

Œuf du Sorcier, L' *01* Georges Méliès

Œuf Magique Prolifique, L' *01* Georges Méliès

Œufs Brouilles, Les *76* Joel Santoni

Œufs de l'Autruche, Les *57* Denys De la Patellière

Œuvre au Noir, L' *88* André Delvaux

Œuvre Immortelle, L' *23* Julien Duvivier

Œuvre Scientifique de Pasteur, L' *47* Jean Painlevé, Georges Rouquier

Of a Thousand Delights *65* Luchino Visconti

Of Beds and Broads *62* Marc Allégret, Claude Barma, Michel Boisrond, Jacques Poitrenaud

Of-Course-I-Can Brothers, The *13* Hay Plumb

Of Crystal or Cinders, Fire or Wind, As Long As It's Love *89* Lina Wertmuller

Of Feline Bondage *65* Chuck Jones

Of Flesh and Blood *62* Christian Marquand

Of Fox and Hounds *40* Tex Avery

Of Great Events and Ordinary People *78* Raúl Ruiz

Of Human Bondage *34* John Cromwell

Of Human Bondage *46* Edmund Goulding

Of Human Bondage *64* Bryan Forbes, Henry Hathaway, Ken Hughes

Of Human Hearts *38* Clarence Brown

Of Life and Love *54* Aldo Fabrizi, Giorgio Pastina, Mario Soldati, Luchino Visconti, Luigi Zampa

Of Love and Bandits *50* Mario Soldati

Of Love and Desire *63* Richard Rush

Of Love and Lust *51* Anders Henrikson

Of Men and Demons *69* Faith Hubley, John Hubley

Of Men and Music *50* Alexander Hammid, Irving Reis

Of Mice and Men *39* Lewis Milestone

Of Pups and Puzzles *41* George Sidney

Of Rice and Hen *53* Robert McKimson

Of Seals and Man *78* Mai Zetterling

Of Stars and Men *61* Faith Hubley, John Hubley

Of Thee I Sting *46* Friz Freleng

Of These Thousand Pleasures *65* Luchino Visconti

Of Unknown Origin *82* George Pan Cosmatos

Of Wayward Love *62* Alberto Bonucci, Nino Manfredi, Sergio Sollima

Ofelas *87* Nils Gaup

Ofelia Kommer til Byen *85* Jon Bang Carlsen

Off Beat *86* Michael Dinner

Off for the Holidays *04* Percy Stow

Off for the Holidays *10* Percy Stow

Off His Beat *25* Archie Mayo

Off His Trolley *24* Edward F. Cline

Off Limits *52* George Marshall

Off Limits *88* Cristopher Crowe

Off-Shore Pirate, The *21* Dallas M. Fitzgerald

Off the Beaten Track *42* Edward F. Cline

Off the Dole *35* Arthur Mertz

Off the Edge *77* Michael Firth

Off the Highway *25* Tom Forman

Off the Mark *87* Bill Berry

Off the Record *39* James Flood

Off the Scent *26* Charles Barnett

Off the Scent *34* George B. Samuelson

Off the Wall *77* Rich King

Off the Wall *83* Rick Friedberg

Off to Bedlam *01* Georges Méliès

Off to Bloomingdale Asylum *01* Georges Méliès

Off to Peoria *30* Mark Sandrich

Off to the Races *37* Frank R. Strayer

Off Your Rocker *80* Morley Markson, Larry Pall

Offbeat *60* Cliff Owen

Offence, The *73* Sidney Lumet

Offenders, The *24* Fenwicke L. Holmes

Offenders, The *80* Beth B, Scott B

Offener Hass Gegen Unbekannt *70* Reinhard Hauff

Offense, The *73* Sidney Lumet

Offering, The *66* David Secter

Offerings *89* Christopher Reynolds

Office Boy, The *32* Ubbe Iwerks

Office Boy's Dream, The *08* Dave Aylott

Office Boy's Revenge, The *03* Edwin S. Porter

Office Boy's Revenge, The *04* Alf Collins

Office Girl, The *31* Victor Saville

Office Girls *74* Ernst Hofbauer

Office Party, The *72* Jan Halldoff

Office Party, The *76* David Grant

Office Party *88* George Mihalka

Office Picnic, The *74* Tom Cowan

Office Scandal, The *29* Paul Stein

Office Wife, The *30* Lloyd Bacon

Office Wife, The *34* George King

Officer and a Gentleman, An *82* Taylor Hackford

Officer and the Lady, The *41* Sam White

Officer, Call a Cop *17* William Beaudine

Officer 444 *26* Francis Ford, Ben F. Wilson

Officer Jim *26* Wilbur F. McGaugh

Officer John Donovan *14* Van Dyke Brooke

Officer O'Brien *30* Tay Garnett

Officer Pooch *41* Joseph Barbera, William Hanna

Officer 666 *20* Harry Beaumont

Officer 13 *33* George Melford

Officer with a Rose *87* Dejan Sorak

Officer's Mess, The *31* H. Manning Haynes

Officers of the French Army Leaving Service 1896 Georges Méliès

Officer's Swordknot, The *15* Alexander Korda

Official History, The *85* Luis Puenzo

Official Story, The *85* Luis Puenzo

Official Version, The *85* Luis Puenzo

Offre d'Emploi *79* Jean Eustache

Offret *86* Andrei Tarkovsky

Offspring, The *89* Jeff Burr

Oficir s Ružom *87* Dejan Sorak

O'Flynn, The *49* Arthur Pierson

Often an Orphan *49* Chuck Jones

Oggi a Me...Domani a Te! *68* Tonino Cervi

Oggi, Domani e Dopodomani *64* Eduardo De Filippo, Marco Ferreri, Luciano Salce

Oglyanis *88* Aida Manassarova

Ognennye Versty *57* Samson Samsonov

Ogni *87* Solomon Shuster

Ogni Baku *50* Josef Heifits, R. Takhmasib, Alexander Zarkhi

Ognuno per Se *68* Giorgio Capitani

Ogon *30* Mark Donskoi

Ogre and the Girl, The *15* Clay M. Greene

Ogre of Athens, The *56* Nikos Koundouros

Ogresses, Les *66* Mauro Bolognini, Mario Monicelli, Antonio Pietrangeli, Luciano Salce

Ogro *79* Gillo Pontecorvo

Oh *68* Stan Vanderbeek

Oh! Alfie *75* Ken Hughes

Oh, Amelia! *49* Claude Autant-Lara

Oh Auntie! *16* Dave Aylott

Oh Baby! *26* Harley Knoles

Oh Babylon! *87* Costas Ferris

Oh Black Forest! Oh Home! *39* Carl Boese

Oh Boy! *19* Albert Capellani

Oh Boy! *37* Albert De Courville

Oh Bridget *25* Archie Mayo

Oh Brotherhood *77* Thomas J. Tobin

Oh! Calcutta! *72* Guillaume Martin Aucion

Oh! Ce Baiser *17* René Hervil, Louis Mercanton

Oh, Charlie *41* Arthur Lubin

Oh Come Sono Buoni i Bianchi *87* Marco Ferreri

Oh Dad, Poor Dad, Mama's Hung You in the Closet and I'm Feeling So Sad *66* Alexander Mackendrick, Richard Quine

Oh Dad, Poor Dad, Mamma's Hung You in the Closet and I'm Feelin' So Sad *66* Alexander Mackendrick, Richard Quine

Oh Daddy! *22* Roy Del Ruth

Oh Daddy! *35* Graham Cutts, Austin Melford

Oh Darling *30* Stephen Roberts

Oh Dear! *86* Vladimír Drha

Oh Dear Uncle! *39* Richard Llewellyn

Oh Doctor! *17* Roscoe Arbuckle

Oh Doctor! *24* Harry A. Pollard

Oh Doctor! *37* Ray McCarey

Oh Doctor! *43* Erle C. Kenton, Charles Lamont

Oh, Duchess! *36* Charles Lamont

Oh for a Man! *30* Hamilton MacFadden

Oh! For a Man! *57* Frank Tashlin

Oh for a Plumber! *33* Widgey R. Newman

Oh for a Smoke! *12* Hay Plumb

Oh Girls What Next *17* Leighton Budd

Oh, God! *77* Carl Reiner

Oh, God! Book Two *80* Gilbert Cates

Oh, God! You Devil *84* Paul Bogart

Oh, Heavenly Dog! *80* Joe Camp

Oh! How I Hate to Get Up in the Morning *32* Dave Fleischer

Oh, It's You! *11* Percy Stow

Oh! Jemimah! *20* Cecil Mannering

Oh, Jo! *21* F. Richard Jones

Oh, Johnny *19* Ira M. Lowry

Oh, Johnny, How You Can Love! *40* Charles Lamont

Oh, Kay! *28* Mervyn LeRoy

Oh Lady, Lady *20* Maurice Campbell

Oh! Les Femmes! *12* Max Linder

Oh, Mabel! *24* Dave Fleischer

Oh Mabel, Behave *21* Mack Sennett, Ford Sterling

Oh Mary Be Careful! *21* Arthur Ashley
Oh, Men! Oh, Women! *56* Nunnally Johnson
Oh! Mr. Porter *37* Marcel Varnel
Oh My! *15* Cecil Birch
Oh! My Aunt *13* Edwin J. Collins
Oh My Aunt! *14* Cecil M. Hepworth
Oh My Darling Clementine *43* Frank McDonald
Oh No Doctor! *34* George King
Oh! Qué Mambo! *58* John Berry
Oh Rosalinda! *55* Michael Powell, Emeric Pressburger
Oh Sabella! *57* Dino Risi
Oh! Sailor, Behave! *30* Archie Mayo
Oh Scissors! *11* Frank Wilson
Oh, Serafina! *76* Alberto Lattuada
Oh, Sun *70* Med Hondo
Oh, Susanna! *36* Joseph Kane
Oh, Susanna! *51* Joseph Kane
Oh Teacher *19* Raoul Barré, Charles Bowers
Oh, Teacher *27* Walt Disney
Oh, Teddy *30* Norman Taurog
Oh! That Awful Tooth *02* George Albert Smith
Oh That Cat! *07* Alf Collins
Oh That Collar Button! *02* George Albert Smith
Oh That Doctor's Boy! *06* J. H. Martin
Oh That Face! *15* Will P. Kellino
Oh That Hat! *06* Harold Jeapes
Oh That Limerick! *07* Frank Mottershaw
Oh That Molar! *07* Arthur Cooper
Oh That Woollen Undervest! *13* Will P. Kellino
Oh the Crocodile! *10* Joe Rosenthal
Oh Those Boys! *08* Arthur Cooper
Oh Those Eyes! *12* Mack Sennett
Oh! Those Most Secret Agents *64* Lucio Fulci
Oh to Be on the Bandwagon *72* Henning Carlsen
Oh, Tomorrow Night *19* John W. Brunius
Oh, Uncle! *09* D. W. Griffith
Oh What a Beautiful Dream *18* Kenneth M. Anderson
Oh What a Day! *14* Hay Plumb
Oh What a Duchess! *33* Lupino Lane
Oh, What a Knight *28* Walt Disney
Oh What a Knight! *37* Charlie Chase
Oh! What a Lovely War *69* Richard Attenborough
Oh, What a Night! *14* Charles Chaplin
Oh! What a Night *26* Lloyd Ingraham
Oh, What a Night! *35* Frank Richardson
Oh, What a Night! *44* William Beaudine
Oh! What a Nurse! *26* Charles Reisner
Oh What a Peach! *12* Edwin J. Collins
Oh! What a Surprise! *04* James A. Williamson
Oh, Wifey Will Be Pleased! *15* Frank Wilson
Oh, Yeah! *29* Tay Garnett
Oh, You Beautiful Doll *26* Dave Fleischer
Oh, You Beautiful Doll *29* Dave Fleischer
Oh, You Beautiful Doll! *49* John M. Stahl
Oh You Tony! *24* John G. Blystone
Oh You Women! *19* John Emerson

Ōhan *84* Kon Ichikawa
O'Hara As a Guardian Angel *13* Van Dyke Brooke
O'Hara Helps Cupid *13* Van Dyke Brooke
O'Hara, Squatter and Philosopher *12* Van Dyke Brooke
O'Hara's Wife *82* William S. Bartman
Oharu *52* Kenji Mizoguchi
Ohayō *59* Yasujiro Ozu
Ohm Krüger *41* Hans Steinhoff
Ohne Dich Wird Es Nacht *56* Curd Jürgens
Ohrfeigen *69* Rolf Thiele
Oil *77* Mircea Dragan
Oil and Romance *25* Harry Fraser
Oil and Water *12* D. W. Griffith
Oil for Aladdin's Lamp *42* Joris Ivens
Oil for the Lamps of China *35* Mervyn LeRoy
Oil Girls, The *71* Guy Casaril, Christian-Jaque
Oil on Troubled Waters *13* Allan Dwan
Oil on Troubled Waters *26* Charles Barnett
Oil Raider, The *34* Spencer G. Bennet
Oil Town *55* Robert Parrish
Oilfield, The *53* Bert Haanstra
Oil's Well *29* Walter Lantz
Oil's Well That Ends Well *19* Raoul Barré, Charles Bowers
Oily American, The *54* Robert McKimson
Oily Hare, The *52* Robert McKimson
Oiseau Blanc, L' *49* Louis Daquin
Oiseau de Paradis, L' *62* Marcel Camus
Oiseau Moquerr, L' *61* Robert Enrico
Oiseau Rare, L' *73* Jean-Claude Brialy
Oiseaux de Passage *25* Gaston Roudes
Oiseaux Vont Mourir au Pérou, Les *68* Romain Gary
8a. Bienal de São Paulo, A *65* Carlos Dieguês
Oito Universitários *67* Carlos Dieguês
Øjeblikket *80* Astrid Henning-Jensen
Ojo de la Cerradura, El *64* Leopoldo Torre-Nilsson
Ojo de la Muerte, El *61* Chano Urueta
Ōjo Kichiza *26* Teinosuke Kinugasa
Ojo por Ojo, Diente por Diente *86* Denis Amar
Ojos Azules de la Muñeca Rota, Los *73* Carlos Aured
Ojos Más Lindos del Mundo, Los *43* Luis Saslavsky
Ojos Tapatíos *39* Jorge M. Dada, Boris Malcon
Ojos Vendados, Los *78* Carlos Saura
Ojōsan *30* Yasujiro Ozu
Ojōsan Kampai *49* Keisuke Kinoshita
Ōk Ketten *77* Márta Mészáros
Oka Oorie Katha *77* Mrinal Sen
Ōka Seidan *28* Daisuke Ito
O'Kalems' Visit to Killarney, The *12* Sidney Olcott
Ōkame *27* Heinosuke Gosho
Ōkami *55* Kaneto Shindo
Ōkami to Buta to Ningen *72* Kinji Fukasaku
Okānda, Den *13* Mauritz Stiller
Okāsan *52* Mikio Naruse
Okasaretu Byūakui *67* Koji Wakamatsu

Okay America! *32* Tay Garnett
Okay Bill *68* John G. Avildsen
Okay for Sound *37* Marcel Varnel
Okay Nero *53* Lewis E. Cianelli
Okay Toots *36* Charlie Chase, William Terhune
Okefenokee *60* Roul Haig
Okhota na Drakona *87* Latif Faiziyev
Okichi, Mistress of a Foreigner *30* Kenji Mizoguchi
Okichi the Mistress *31* Teinosuke Kinugasa
Okichi the Stranger *30* Kenji Mizoguchi
Okinawa *52* Leigh Jason
Oklahoma *54* Oskar Fischinger
Oklahoma! *55* Fred Zinnemann
Oklahoma Annie *52* R. G. Springsteen
Oklahoma Badlands *48* Yakima Canutt
Oklahoma Blues *48* Lambert Hillyer
Oklahoma Bound *40* Albert Herman
Oklahoma Crude *73* Stanley Kramer
Oklahoma Cyclone *30* John P. McCarthy
Oklahoma Frontier *39* Ford Beebe
Oklahoma Jim *31* Harry Fraser
Oklahoma John *64* Jesús Jaime Balcazar, Harald Reinl
Oklahoma Justice *51* Lewis D. Collins
Oklahoma Kid, The *29* John P. McGowan
Oklahoma Kid, The *39* Lloyd Bacon
Oklahoma Outlaws *43* B. Reeves Eason
Oklahoma Outlaws *51* Lewis D. Collins
Oklahoma Raiders *44* Lewis D. Collins
Oklahoma Renegades *40* Nate Watt
Oklahoma Sheriff, The *30* John P. McGowan
Oklahoma Territory *60* Edward L. Cahn
Oklahoma Terror *39* Spencer G. Bennet
Oklahoma Woman, The *55* Roger Corman
Oklahoman, The *57* Francis D. Lyon
Oko Wykół *60* Jerzy Skolimowski
Okos Mama, Az *36* Emil Martonffy
Okoto and Sasuke *61* Teinosuke Kinugasa
Okoto to Sasuke *61* Teinosuke Kinugasa
Okouzlená *42* Otakar Vávra
Okraina *33* Boris Barnet
Oktoberfest *87* Dragan Kresoja
Októberi Vasárnap *79* András Kovács
Oktyabar *27* Grigori Alexandrov, Sergei Eisenstein
Oktyabr' *27* Grigori Alexandrov, Sergei Eisenstein
Oktyabr' Dni *58* Sergei Vasiliev
Okuman Chōja *54* Kon Ichikawa
Okuni and Gohei *52* Mikio Naruse
Okuni to Gohei *52* Mikio Naruse
Okupacija u 26 Slika *78* Lordan Zafranović
Okusama Shakuyōshō *36* Heinosuke Gosho
Ol' Swimmin' 'Ole, The *28* Walt Disney
Ola and Julia *67* Jan Halldoff
Ola och Julia *67* Jan Halldoff
Olaf, an Atom *13* D. W. Griffith
Olavine Aasare *88* K. V. Jayaram
Old Acquaintance *43* Vincent Sherman
Old Actor, The *12* D. W. Griffith
Old Actor, An *13* Colin Campbell
Old Actor's Story, The *22* H. B. Parkinson
Old Age Handicap *28* Frank S. Mattison
Old Age: The Wasted Years *66* Nell Cox, Richard Leacock

Old and New *29* Grigori Alexandrov, Sergei Eisenstein

Old and New Style Conjurors *06* Georges Méliès

Old and the New, The *29* Grigori Alexandrov, Sergei Eisenstein

Old Appointment, An *13* Ashley Miller

Old Armchair, The *12* Jack Conway

Old Armchair, The *20* Percy Nash

Old Barn, The *28* Mack Sennett

Old Barn Dance, The *38* Joseph Kane

Old Bill and Son *40* Ian Dalrymple

Old Bill of Paris *22* Jacques Feyder

Old Bill Through the Ages *24* Thomas Bentley

Old Bird Pays Him a Visit, An *17* F. M. Follett

Old Black Joe *26* Dave Fleischer

Old Black Joe *29* Dave Fleischer

Old Blackout Joe *42* John Hubley, Paul Sommer

Old Bones of the River *38* Marcel Varnel

Old Bookkeeper, The *11* D. W. Griffith

Old Boyfriends *78* Joan Tewkesbury

Old Bull, The *32* George Marshall

Old Capitol, The *63* Noboru Nakamura

Old Capitol, The *80* Kon Ichikawa

Old Chinese Opera *54* Vojtěch Jasný, Karel Kachyňa

Old Chisholm Trail, The *42* Elmer Clifton

Old Chorister, The *04* James A. Williamson

Old City, The *80* Kon Ichikawa

Old Clothes *25* Edward F. Cline

Old Code, The *28* Ben F. Wilson

Old College Badge, The *13* Charles Raymond

Old Colonel's Gratitude, The *12* A. E. Coleby

Old Composer and the Prima Donna, The *08* Percy Stow

Old Confectioner's Mistake, The *11* D. W. Griffith

Old Corral, The *36* Joseph Kane

Old Corral, The *36* John P. McCarthy

Old Country, The *21* A. V. Bramble

Old Country Where Rimbaud Died, The *77* Jean-Pierre Lefèbvre

Old Curiosity Shop, The *12* Frank Powell

Old Curiosity Shop, The *13* Thomas Bentley

Old Curiosity Shop, The *21* Thomas Bentley

Old Curiosity Shop, The *34* Thomas Bentley

Old Curiosity Shop, The *75* Michael Tuchner

Old Czech Legends *53* Jiří Trnka

Old Dad *20* Lloyd Ingraham

Old Dark House, The *32* James Whale, William Wyler

Old Dark House, The *62* William Castle

Old Doc Gloom *16* Gregory La Cava

Old Doc Yak *13* Sidney Smith

Old Doc Yak and the Artist's Dream *13* Sidney Smith

Old Doc Yak's Christmas *13* Sidney Smith

Old Doctor, The *40* Mario Soffici

Old Drac *74* Clive Donner

Old Dracula *74* Clive Donner

Old English *30* Alfred E. Green

Old Enough *84* Marisa Silver

Old Explorers *90* William Pohland

Old Faithful *35* Maclean Rogers

Old Fashioned Boy, An *20* Jerome Storm

Old Fashioned Girl, An *12* Edwin S. Porter

Old-Fashioned Girl, An *15* Donald Crisp

Old-Fashioned Girl, An *48* Arthur Dreifuss

Old Fashioned Scottish Reel *03* Edwin S. Porter

Old-Fashioned Way, The *34* William Beaudine

Old Fashioned Woman *74* Martha Coolidge

Old-Fashioned World *41* Mario Soldati

Old-Fashioned Young Man, An *17* Lloyd Ingraham

Old Favourite and the Ugly Golliwog, The *08* Percy Stow

Old Firehand *66* Alfred Vohrer

Old Flame, An *30* Manny Gould, Ben Harrison

Old Flynn's Fiddle *13* Charles C. Calvert

Old Folk Song, An *63* Miklós Jancsó

Old Folks at Home, The *07* John Morland

Old Folks at Home, The *16* Chester Withey

Old Folks at Home *25* Dave Fleischer

Old Fool, The *23* Edward D. Venturini

Old Footlight Favourite *08* Georges Méliès

Old Forest, The *85* Steven J. Ross

Old Frontier, The *50* Philip Ford

Old Gardener, The *12* H. Oceano Martinek

Old Glory *39* Chuck Jones

Old Gods Still Live, The *37* Gideon Wahlberg

Old Gray Mayor, The *48* Will Jason

Old Greatheart *31* William A. Seiter

Old Grey Hare, The *44* Robert Clampett

Old Gringo *88* Luis Puenzo

Old Grouchy *56* George Tzavellas

Old Guard, The *33* Alessandro Blasetti

Old Guard, The *41* Sergei Gerasimov

Old Gun, The *75* Robert Enrico

Old Hartwell's Cub *18* Thomas Heffron

Old Hat, The *11* Theo Bouwmeester

Old Heidelberg *15* John Emerson

Old Heidelberg *27* Ernst Lubitsch

Old Home Week *25* Victor Heerman

Old Homestead, The *16* James Kirkwood

Old Homestead, The *22* James Cruze

Old Homestead, The *35* William Nigh

Old Homestead, The *42* Frank McDonald

Old Homestead, or Saved from the Workhouse, The *05* Tom Green

Old Horseman, The *40* Boris Barnet

Old Hutch *36* J. Walter Ruben

Old Iron *38* Tom Walls

Old Ironsides *26* James Cruze

Old Jockey, The *40* Boris Barnet

Old Labor Song, An *63* Miklós Jancsó

Old Lady, The *59* Vladimir Petrov, Rangel Vulchanov

Old Lady 31 *20* John Ince

Old Lantern, The *60* Teinosuke Kinugasa

Old Lie and the New, The *06* J. H. Martin

Old Los Angeles *48* Joseph Kane

Old Louisiana *37* Irvin Willat

Old Love, An *40* Luis Lezama

Old Loves and New *26* Maurice Tourneur

Old Loves for New *18* Raymond Wells

Old Mac *61* Michael Winner

Old Maid, The *39* Edmund Goulding

Old Maid, The *72* Jean-Pierre Blanc

Old Maid and Fortune Teller *04* Edwin S. Porter

Old Maid Having Her Picture Taken, The *01* Edwin S. Porter

Old Maid in the Drawing Room, The *01* Edwin S. Porter

Old Maid in the Horse Carriage, The *01* Edwin S. Porter

Old Maid's Baby, The *19* William Bertram

Old Maids' Temperance Club *08* Edwin S. Porter

Old Maid's Valentine, The *00* George Albert Smith

Old Man, The *31* H. Manning Haynes

Old Man and the Boy, The *66* Claude Berri

Old Man and the Flower, The *62* Ernest Pintoff

Old Man and the Sea, The *58* Henry King, John Sturges, Fred Zinnemann

Old Man Is Coming, The *39* Per Lindberg

Old Man Motorcar *56* Alfred Radok

Old Man of the Mountain, The *33* Dave Fleischer

Old Man Rhythm *35* Edward Ludwig

Old Man's Pension Day, The *09* Joe Rosenthal

Old Man's Place, The *71* Edwin Sherin

Old Mansion, The *22* Mauritz Stiller

Old Mill, The *62* Jan Troell

Old Mother Hubbard *12* Arthur Cooper

Old Mother Hubbard *18* Henry Edwards

Old Mother Hubbard *35* Ubbe Iwerks

Old Mother Riley *37* Oswald Mitchell

Old Mother Riley *49* John Harlow

Old Mother Riley at Home *45* Oswald Mitchell

Old Mother Riley Catches a Quisling *38* Oswald Mitchell

Old Mother Riley, Detective *43* Lance Comfort

Old Mother Riley, Headmistress *50* John Harlow

Old Mother Riley in Business *40* John Baxter

Old Mother Riley in Paris *38* Oswald Mitchell

Old Mother Riley in Society *40* John Baxter

Old Mother Riley Joins Up *39* Maclean Rogers

Old Mother Riley MP *39* Oswald Mitchell

Old Mother Riley Meets the Vampire *52* John Gilling

Old Mother Riley Overseas *43* Oswald Mitchell

Old Mother Riley's Circus *41* Thomas Bentley

Old Mother Riley's Ghosts *41* John Baxter

Old Mother Riley's Jungle Treasure *51* Maclean Rogers

Old Mother Riley's New Venture *49* John Harlow

Old Music, The *85* Mario Camus
Old Nest, The *21* Reginald Barker
Old Nuisance, The *13* Hay Plumb
Old Oaken Bucket, The *21* May Tully
Old Oklahoma Plains *52* William Witney
Old Old Story, The *14* Ethyle Batley
Old Organist, The *12* Edwin S. Porter
Old Overland Trail *53* William Witney
Old People *61* Henning Carlsen
Old Pfool Pfancy at the Beach *16* Harry S. Palmer
Old Primer *87* Victor Prokhorov
Old Raid Mule, The *38* Charlie Chase
Old Rascals, The *71* Eldar Ryazanov
Old Reliable *14* Van Dyke Brooke
Old Rockin' Chair Tom *48* Joseph Barbera, William Hanna
Old Roses *35* Bernerd Mainwaring
Old Roué Visualizes, The *17* Harry S. Palmer
Old Sailor's Tale, The *38* Hayford Hobbs
Old St. Paul's *14* Wilfred Noy
Old San Francisco *27* Alan Crosland
Old School Tie, The *36* Joseph Santley
Old Shatterhand *64* Hugo Fregonese
Old Shoes *27* Frederick Stowers
Old Soak, The *26* Edward Sloman
Old Soldier, The *10* Theo Bouwmeester
Old Soldiers *38* George Pearson
Old Soldiers Never Die *31* Monty Banks
Old Songs and Memories *12* Colin Campbell
Old South, The *40* Fred Zinnemann
Old Spanish Custom, An *35* Adrian Brunel
Old Spanish Customers *32* Lupino Lane
Old Surehand *65* Alfred Vohrer
Old Surehand, Part One *65* Alfred Vohrer
Old Sweetheart of Mine, An *23* Harry Garson
Old Swimmin' Hole, The *21* Joseph De Grasse
Old Swimmin' Hole, The *40* Robert McGowan
Old Testament, The *63* Gianfranco Parolini
Old Texas Trail, The *44* Lewis D. Collins
Old Time Music Hall, An *29* Dave Aylott
Old Tire Man Diamond Cartoon Film *18* Paul M. Felton
Old Toymaker's Dream, The *04* Arthur Cooper
Old Toymaker's Dream, An *13* Arthur Cooper
Old Treasures from New China *77* Peter Wang
Old Well, The *87* Tianming Wu
Old West, The *52* George Archainbaud
Old Wives for New *18* Cecil B. DeMille
Old Wives' Tale, The *21* Denison Clift
Old Wives' Tales *46* Joy Batchelor, John Halas
Old Woman Ghost, The *76* Tadashi Imai
Old Women of Japan, The *62* Tadashi Imai
Old Wood Carver, The *13* Hubert von Herkomer
Old Wyoming Trail, The *37* Folmer Blangsted
Old Yeller *57* Robert Stevenson
Oldás és Kötés *62* Miklós Jancsó

Older Brother and Younger Sister *76* Tadashi Imai
Older Brother, Younger Sister *53* Mikio Naruse
Oldest Confession, The *61* George Marshall
Oldest Law, The *18* Harley Knoles
Oldest Profession, The *67* Claude Autant-Lara, Mauro Bolognini, Philippe de Broca, Jean-Luc Godard, Franco Indovina, Michael Pfleghar
Oldřich a Božena *86* Otakar Vávra
Oldrich and Bozena *86* Otakar Vávra
Öldürmek Hakkimdir *68* Mahinur Ergün
Ole Dole Doff *67* Jan Troell
Ole Opfinders Offer *24* Forest Holger-Madsen
Ole Rex *61* Robert Hinkle
Ole Swimmin' Hole, The *28* Walt Disney
O'Leary Night *54* Mario Zampi
Oleko Dundich *58* Leonid Lukov
Ölelkező Tekintetek *82* Károly Makk
Olga's Girls *64* Joseph P. Mawra
Olieveld, Het *53* Bert Haanstra
Olimpiada en México, La *68* Alberto Isaac
Olio for Jasper *46* George Pal
Olive Oyl and Water Don't Mix *42* Dave Fleischer
Olive Trees of Justice, The *62* James Blue
Oliver! *68* Carol Reed
Oliver and Company *88* George Scribner
Oliver Cromwell *11* Theo Bouwmeester
Oliver the Eighth *33* Lloyd French
Oliver Twist *09* J. Stuart Blackton
Oliver Twist *12* Thomas Bentley
Oliver Twist *16* James Young
Oliver Twist *20* Lupu Pick
Oliver Twist *22* Frank Lloyd
Oliver Twist *33* William Cowen
Oliver Twist *40* David Bradley
Oliver Twist *47* David Lean
Oliver Twist *85* Gareth Davies
Oliver Twist, Jr. *21* Millard Webb
Oliver Twisted *17* Fred Evans, Joe Evans
Oliver's Story *78* John Korty
Olive's Boithday Presink *41* Dave Fleischer
Olive's Sweepstakes Ticket *41* Dave Fleischer
Olivia *50* Jacqueline Audry
Olivia *83* Ulli Lommel
Oliviers de la Justice, Les *62* James Blue
Olle *67* Budd Boetticher
Olly Oakley *27* George A. Cooper
Olly, Olly, Oxen Free *78* Richard A. Colla
Ölmez Ağacı *86* Yusuf Kurcenli
Olor a Muerte *87* Ismael Rodríguez, Jr.
Ölprinz, Der *65* Harald Philipp
Olsen's Big Moment *33* Malcolm St. Clair
Olsen's Night Out *33* Malcolm St. Clair
Oltraggio al Pudore *66* Silvio Amadio
Oltre il Bene e il Male *77* Liliana Cavani
Oltre la Porta *82* Liliana Cavani
Oltre l'Amore *40* Carmine Gallone
Oltre l'Oblio *48* Michelangelo Antonioni
Ölüm Perdesi *60* Atıf Yılmaz
Olvidados, Los *50* Luis Buñuel
Olvidados de Dios, Los *40* Ramón Pereda
Olyan, Mint Otthon *78* Márta Mészáros
Olympia *30* Jacques Feyder
Olympia *38* Leni Riefenstahl

Olympia *59* Michael Curtiz, Mario Russo
Olympia 52 *52* Chris Marker
Olympiad *38* Leni Riefenstahl
Olympian, The *70* Gregory Markopoulos
Olympic Cavalcade *48* Joseph Lerner
Olympic Games, The *38* Leni Riefenstahl
Olympic Games of 1948, The *48* Castleton Knight
Olympic Hero, The *28* Roy William Neill
Olympic Honeymoon *36* Alfred Goulding
Olympic Visions *72* Miloš Forman, Kon Ichikawa, Claude Lelouch, Yuri Ozerov, Arthur Penn, Michael Pfleghar, John Schlesinger, Mai Zetterling
Olympics in Mexico, The *68* Alberto Isaac
Olympische Spiele *38* Leni Riefenstahl
Olympische Spiele 1936 *38* Leni Riefenstahl
Om Dar-B-Dar *88* Kamal Swaroop
Om Kärlek *87* Mats Arehn
Omaha Trail, The *42* Edward Buzzell
O'Malley of the Mounted *20* Lambert Hillyer
O'Malley of the Mounted *36* David Howard
O'Malley Rides Alone *30* John P. McGowan
Omar Khayyam *57* William Dieterle
Omar Mukhtar *79* Moustapha Akkad
Omar the Tentmaker *22* James Young
Omar's Journey *86* Mohamed Khan
Ombligo de la Luna, El *86* Jorge Prior
Ombra di un Trono, L' *21* Carmine Gallone
Ombra di Zorro, L' *62* Joaquín Luis Romero Marchent
Ombre, L' *48* André Berthomieu
Ombre Bianchi *59* Baccio Bandini, Nicholas Ray
Ombre Déchirée, L' *21* Léon Poirier
Ombre du Bonheur, L' *24* Gaston Roudes
Ombre du Péché, L' *22* Yakov Protazanov
Ombre d'une Chance, L' *73* Jean-Pierre Mocky
Ombre et Lumière *51* Henri Calef
Ombre et Lumière de Rome *59* Mario Ruspoli
Ombrellai *52* Francesco Maselli
Ombrellone, L' *65* Dino Risi
Ombres Chinoises, Les *07* Segundo De Chomón
Ombres Chinoises *82* Raúl Ruiz
Ombres Qui Passant, Les *24* Alexander Volkov
Ombyte av Tåg *43* Hasse Ekman
Ombyte Förnöjer *38* Gustaf Molander
Omega Connection, The *79* Robert Clouse
Omega Man, The *71* Boris Sagal
Omega, Omega *82* Miklós Jancsó
Omega Syndrome *86* Joseph Manduke
Omegans, The *68* W. Lee Wilder
Omelette Fantastique, L' *09* Émile Cohl
Omen, The *76* Richard Donner
Ömhet *72* Jörn Donner
Omicida, L' *62* Claude Autant-Lara
Omicron *63* Ugo Gregoretti
Omnibus des Toqués, L' *01* Georges Méliès
Omnibus des Toqués ou Les Échappés de Charenton, L' *01* Georges Méliès

On the Night Stage *15* Reginald Barker
On the Old Spanish Trail *47* William Witney
On the Other Side of the Arax *46* Esther Shub
On the Outskirts *87* Volker Führer
On the Outskirts of Town *57* Miklós Jancsó
On the Pole *60* Richard Leacock, D. A. Pennebaker
On the Quiet *18* Chester Withey
On the Red Front *20* Lev Kuleshov
On the Reef *09* D. W. Griffith
On the Reserve *20* Will P. Kellino
On the Right Track *81* Lee Philips
On the Riviera *51* Walter Lang
On the Road Again *80* Jerry Schatzberg
On the Road to Button Bay *62* Richard Leacock, D. A. Pennebaker
On the Road to Katanga *87* Živojin Pavlović
On the Roads of Fate *13* Victor Sjöström, Mauritz Stiller
On the Roofs *1897* Georges Méliès
On the Roofs of Budapest *61* András Kovács
On the Run *58* Ernest Morris
On the Run *63* Robert Tronson
On the Run *69* Pat Jackson
On the Run *83* Mende Brown
On the Russian Frontier *14* Charles H. Weston
On the Shelf *25* Paul Powell
On the Sidelines *76* Péter Szász
On the Spanish Main *17* Edward A. Salisbury
On the Spanish Trail *47* William Witney
On the Spot *40* Howard Bretherton
On-the-Square Girl, The *17* George Fitzmaurice
On the Steps of the Altar *16* R. Harley West
On the Stroke of Nine *34* Richard Thorpe
On the Stroke of Three *24* F. Harmon Weight
On the Stroke of Twelve *27* Charles J. Hunt
On the Sunny Side *36* Gustaf Molander
On the Sunny Side *42* Harold Schuster
On the Threshold *25* Renaud Hoffman
On the Threshold of Space *56* Robert D. Webb
On the Tiger's Back *61* Luigi Comencini
On the Town *49* Stanley Donen, Gene Kelly
On the Trail *27* William C. Nolan
On the Trail of Elvis the Cat *87* Claes Olsson
On the Trail of the Lonesome Pine *87* Jill Godmilow
On the Twelfth Day *56* Wendy Toye
On the Warsaw Highroad *16* Władysław Starewicz
On the Warsaw Highway *16* Władysław Starewicz
On the Waterfront *54* Elia Kazan
On the Way to Spider Gate *36* Mikio Naruse
On the Western Frontier *09* Edwin S. Porter

On the Wrong Trek *36* Charlie Chase, Harold Law
On the Yard *78* Raphael D. Silver
On Their Own *40* Otto Brower
On Thin Ice *25* Malcolm St. Clair
On Thin Ice *26* Charles Bowers
On Thin Ice *33* Bernard Vorhaus
On Thin Ice *61* Géza von Cziffra
On This Earth *57* Kozaburo Yoshimura
On Time *24* Henry Lehrman
On to Mars *53* Charles Lamont
On to Reno *27* James Cruze
On to the Front! *43* Dziga Vertov
On Top of Old Smoky *53* George Archainbaud
On Top of the Underworld *38* Mickey Delamar, Denis Kavanagh
On Top of the Whale *81* Raúl Ruiz
On Top of the World *36* Redd Davis
On Tour with Pina Bausch *83* Chantal Akerman
On Trial *17* James Young
On Trial *28* Archie Mayo
On Trial *39* Terry Morse
On Trial! *53* Julien Duvivier
On Ubivat Ne Khotel *67* Eldar Shengelaya
On Valentine's Day *86* Ken Harrison
On Velvet *38* Widgey R. Newman
On Vous Parle *60* Jean Cayrol, Claude Durand
On Vous Parle de Brésil *69* Chris Marker
On Watch in the Forest *66* Jiří Brdečka
On Wings of Song *35* Victor Schertzinger
On with the Dance *20* George Fitzmaurice
On with the Dance *27* J. Steven Edwards, H. B. Parkinson
On with the Motley *20* Carmine Gallone
On with the New *38* Dave Fleischer
On with the Show *29* Alan Crosland
On Your Back *30* Guthrie McClintic
On Your Toes *27* Fred Newmeyer
On Your Toes *39* Ray Enright
On ze Boulevard *27* Harry Millarde
Ona Zashchishchayet Rodinu *43* Friedrich Ermler
Once *74* Morton Heilig
Once a Crook *41* Herbert Mason
Once a Doctor *37* William Clemens
Once a Gentleman *30* James Cruze
Once a Hero *37* Harry Lachman
Once a Jolly Swagman *48* Jack Lee, R. Q. McNaughton
Once a Lady *31* Guthrie McClintic
Once a Plumber *20* Eddie Lyons, Lee Moran
Once a Rainy Day *68* Hideo Onchi
Once a Sinner *31* Guthrie McClintic
Once a Sinner *50* Lewis Gilbert
Once a Thief *35* George Pearson
Once a Thief *50* W. Lee Wilder
Once a Thief *61* George Marshall
Once a Thief *65* Ralph Nelson
Once a Week *37* Sándor Sziatinay
Once Aboard the Lugger *14* Hay Plumb
Once Aboard the Lugger *20* Gerald Ames, Gaston Quiribet
Once Again *80* Vinod Pande
Once Again *86* Amin Q. Chaudhri
Once Again *87* Alfredo Gurrola
Once and Forever *27* Phil Goldstone

Once Before I Die *65* John Derek
Once Bitten *32* Leslie Hiscott
Once Bitten *85* Howard Storm
Once in a Blue Moon *34* Ben Hecht, Charles MacArthur
Once in a Lifetime *25* Duke Worne
Once in a Lifetime *32* Russell Mack
Once in a Million *36* Arthur Woods
Once in a New Moon *35* Anthony Kimmins
Once in Paris *78* Frank D. Gilroy
Once Is Not Enough *74* Guy Green
Once More *47* Heinosuke Gosho
Once More, My Darling *49* Robert Montgomery
Once More, with Feeling! *59* Stanley Donen
Once por Cero *70* Santiago Álvarez
Once Somewhere *86* G. Aravindan
Once There Was a Girl *45* Victor Eisimont
Once There Was a War *66* Palle Kjærulff-Schmidt
Once to Every Bachelor *34* William Nigh
Once to Every Man *19* T. Hayes Hunter
Once to Every Man *25* John Ford
Once to Every Woman *20* Allen Holubar
Once to Every Woman *34* Lambert Hillyer
Once Too Often *04* Percy Stow
Once Upon a Coffee House *65* Shepard Traube
Once Upon a Dream *48* Ralph Thomas
Once Upon a Honeymoon *42* Leo McCarey
Once Upon a Horse *58* Hal Kanter
Once Upon a Night in Rome *60* Roberto Rossellini
Once Upon a Scoundrel *73* George Schaefer
Once Upon a Summer *63* Desmond Davis
Once Upon a Thursday *42* Jules Dassin
Once Upon a Time *13* Fred Evans, Joe Evans
Once Upon a Time *15* Cecil Birch
Once Upon a Time *18* Thomas Bentley
Once Upon a Time *22* Carl Theodor Dreyer
Once Upon a Time *22* Ruth Bryan Owen
Once Upon a Time *41* Horace Shepherd
Once Upon a Time *44* Alexander Hall
Once Upon a Time *57* Walerian Borowczyk, Jan Lenica
Once Upon a Time *67* Francesco Rosi
Once Upon a Time... *87* Gyula Gazdag
Once Upon a Time in America *83* Sergio Leone
Once Upon a Time in the Midwest *86* Benoit Ramampy
Once Upon a Time in the West *68* Sergio Leone
Once Upon a Time There Was a King *54* Bořivoj Zeman
Once Upon a Virgin *75* Jean Rollin
Once Upon a War *66* Palle Kjærulff-Schmidt
Once We Were Dreamers *87* Uri Barbash
Once You Kiss a Stranger *69* Robert Sparr
Onda, L' *55* Ermanno Olmi
Ondata di Calore *70* Nelo Risi
Ondata di Piacere, Una *75* Ruggero Deodato

Ondine 76 Rolf Thiele
Ondört Numara 86 Sinan Cetin
Ondskans Värdshus 81 Calvin Floyd
1A in Oberbayern 39 Franz Seitz
1A in Upper Bavaria 39 Franz Seitz
One A.M. 16 Charles Chaplin
1 A.M. 70 D. A. Pennebaker
One a Minute 21 Jack Nelson
One Afternoon in Koppánymonostor 55 Miklós Jancsó
One Against All 65 Antonio Del Amo
One Against Seven 45 Zoltán Korda
One Against the World 39 Fred Zinnemann
One American Movie 70 D. A. Pennebaker
One and One 78 Erland Josephson, Sven Nykvist, Ingrid Thulin
One and Only, The 75 Josef Heifits
One and Only, The 78 Carl Reiner
One and Only, The 86 Jerome Diamant-Berger
One and Only Genuine, Original Family Band, The 67 Michael O'Herlihy
One and Ten 34 Boris Barnet*
1. April 2000 52 Wolfgang Liebeneiner
One Arabian Night 20 Ernst Lubitsch
One Arabian Night 23 Sinclair Hill
One Armed Executioner 80 Bobby A. Suarez
One Away 75 Sidney Hayers
One Big Affair 52 Peter Godfrey
One Body Too Many 44 Frank McDonald
One Born Every Minute 67 Yakima Canutt, Irvin Kershner
One Brief Summer 69 John Mackenzie
One Busy Hour 09 D. W. Griffith
One, But a Lion 40 Gustaf Molander
One Cab's Family 52 Tex Avery
One Chance in a Million 27 Noel Mason Smith
One Christmas Eve 14 Edwin J. Collins
One Clear Call 22 John M. Stahl
One Colombo Night 23 George Ridgwell
One Colombo Night 26 Henry Edwards
One Company 43 John Harlow
One Could Laugh in Former Days 82 Bert Haanstra
One Crazy Summer 86 Savage Steve Holland
One Crowded Night 40 Irving Reis
One Damp Day 17 William Beaudine
One Dangerous Night 42 Michael Gordon
One Dark Night 39 Leo C. Popkin
One Dark Night 82 Tom McLoughlin
One Day 16 Hal Clarendon
One Day a Cat 63 Vojtěch Jasný
One Day at Summer's End 68 Yasuzo Masumura
One Day in Soviet Russia 41 Mikhail Slutsky
One Day in the Life of Ivan Denisovich 71 Caspar Wrede
One Day in the U.S.S.R. 47 Ilya Kopalin, Irina Setkina
One Day Last Summer 84 Mark Evans, Nigel Horne
One Day More, One Day Less 73 Zoltán Fábri
One Day, Paulino 62 Jorge Sanjinés

One Day, 240 Hours 70 Hiroshi Teshigahara
One Day with Russians 61 B. Bolkov, Roman Karmen
One Deadly Summer 83 Jean Becker
One Desire 55 Jerry Hopper
One Does Not Play with Love 26 G. W. Pabst
One Down, Two to Go 82 Fred Williamson
One Eighth Apache 22 Ben F. Wilson
One Embarrassing Night 30 Byron Haskin, Tom Walls
1 = 2? 75 Dolores Grassjan
One Excited Orphan 23 Bertram Phillips
One Exciting Adventure 34 Ernest L. Frank
One Exciting Night 22 D. W. Griffith
One Exciting Night 44 Walter Forde
One Exciting Night 45 William C. Thomas
One Exciting Week 46 William Beaudine
One Extra Day 56 William Fairchild
One-Eyed Dragon 42 Hiroshi Inagaki
One-Eyed Jacks 61 Marlon Brando
One-Eyed Man, The 80 Raúl Ruiz
One-Eyed Soldiers 66 Jean Christophe
One Fair Daughter 13 Warwick Buckland
One Family 30 Walter Creighton
One Family 43 Grigori Alexandrov
One Fatal Hour 31 Mervyn LeRoy
One Fatal Hour 36 William McGann
1-Film 29 Joris Ivens
One Fine Day 68 Ermanno Olmi
One Flew Over the Cuckoo's Nest 75 Miloš Forman
One Foot in Heaven 41 Irving Rapper
One Foot in Hell 60 James B. Clark
One for All 36 Phil Rosen
One for Sorrow, Two for Joy 89 John David Coles
One for the Book 47 Irving Rapper
1:42:08: A Man and His Car 66 George Lucas
One Friday to the Next 86 Anton Vrdoljak
One Frightened Night 35 Christy Cabanne
One Froggy Evening 55 Chuck Jones
One from the Heart 81 Francis Ford Coppola
One Girl's Confession 53 Hugo Haas
One Glass Too Many 53 Břetislav Pojar
One Glorious Day 22 James Cruze
One Glorious Night 24 Scott R. Dunlap
One Glorious Scrap 27 Edgar Lewis
One Good Turn 15 Frank Wilson
One Good Turn 31 James W. Horne
One Good Turn 36 Alfred Goulding
One Good Turn 51 Arthur Maude
One Good Turn 54 John Paddy Carstairs
One Good Turn Deserves Another 09 Theo Bouwmeester
One Grain of Barley 58 Kozaburo Yoshimura
One Ham's Family 43 Tex Avery
One Heavenly Night 30 George Fitzmaurice
One Honest Man 15 Ethyle Batley
One Horse Town 36 William A. Wellman

One Hour 17 Edwin L. Hollywood, Paul McAllister
One Hour Before Dawn 20 Henry King
One Hour Late 34 Ralph Murphy
One Hour of Happiness 29 William Dieterle
One Hour of Love 26 Robert Florey
One Hour Past Midnight 24 Beverly C. Rule
One Hour to Doom's Day 53 Budd Boetticher
One Hour to Doomsday 70 Irwin Allen
One Hour to Live 39 Harold Schuster
One Hour to Zero 77 Jeremy Summers
One Hour with You 32 George Cukor, Ernst Lubitsch
One Hundred a Day 73 Gillian Armstrong
One Hundred Cries of Terror 64 Ramón Obón
One Hundred Days of Napoleon 36 Giovacchino Forzano
One Hundred Dollars 31 Charles Lamont
$100 a Night 68 Wolfgang Glück
100 Fäuste und ein Vaterunser 72 Mario Siciliano
One Hundred Men and a Girl 37 Henry Koster
100,000,000 Women 42 Jiří Weiss
100% Brazilian Film, A 87 José Sette
One Hundred Per Cent Proof 20 Harry D. Leonard
100% Pure 34 Jack Conway
£100 Reward 08 James A. Williamson
100 Ragazze per un Playboy 66 Michael Pfleghar
100 Rifles 68 Tom Gries
100 Years Hence 08 J. Stuart Blackton
101 Dalmations 61 Clyde Geronimi, Hamilton Luske, Wolfgang Reitherman
111-es, A 19 Alexander Korda
111-es Szóbában 38 Steve Sekely
113, El 38 Raphael J. Sevilla
120 Decibels 87 Vassilis Vafeas
120 Kilometers an Hour 37 Leslie Kardos
125 Rooms of Comfort 74 Patrick Loubert
125 Rue Montmartre 59 Gilles Grangier
141 Minutes from the Unfinished Sentence 75 Zoltán Fábri
141 Perc a Befejezetlen Mondatból 75 Zoltán Fábri
150 na Godzinę 71 Wanda Jakubowska
One Hysterical Night 30 William James Craft
One in a Million 34 Frank R. Strayer
One in a Million 36 Sidney Lanfield
One Increasing Purpose 27 Harry Beaumont
One Is a Lonely Number 72 Mel Stuart
One Is Business, the Other Crime 12 D. W. Griffith
One Is Guilty 34 Lambert Hillyer
One Jump Ahead 55 Charles Saunders
One Just Man 55 David MacDonald
1K-Film 29 Joris Ivens
One Last Fling 49 Peter Godfrey
One Law for Both 17 Ivan Abramson
One Law for the Woman 24 Del Henderson
One Life 58 Alexandre Astruc

One Little Indian *73* Bernard McEveety
One Live Ghost *36* Leslie Goodwins
One Look—and Love Begins *86* Jutta Bruckner
One Mad Kiss *30* Marcel Silver, James Tinling
One Magic Christmas *85* Phillip Borsos
1 Maja *38* Grigori Alexandrov
One Man *77* Robin Spry
One Man Band, The *00* Georges Méliès
One Man Band *65* Bob Godfrey
One Man Dog, The *29* Leon D'Usseau
One Man Force *89* Dale Trevillion
One Man Game, A *27* Ernst Laemmle
One Man in a Million *21* George Beban
One Man Jury *78* Charles Martin
One Man Justice *37* Leon Barsha
One Man Law *31* Lambert Hillyer
One Man Mutiny *55* Otto Preminger
One Man Too Many *66* Costa-Gavras
One Man Trail *21* Bernard J. Durning
One Man's China *72* Felix Greene
One Man's Journey *33* John S. Robertson
One Man's Law *40* George Sherman
One Man's War *81* Edgardo Cozarinsky
One Man's Way *64* Denis Sanders
One Meat Brawl *47* Robert McKimson
One Mile from Heaven *37* Allan Dwan
One Million B.C. *40* D. W. Griffith, Hal Roach, Hal Roach, Jr.
$1,000,000 Duck *71* Vincent McEveety
$1,000,000 Pearl Mystery *13* Harold Heath
One Million Dollars *15* John W. Noble
One Million Dollars *64* Ettore Scola
1,000,000 Eyes of Sumuru, The *67* Lindsay Shonteff
One Million in Jewels *23* John P. McGowan
One Million Pound Note, The *16* Alexander Korda
One Million Years B.C. *66* Don Chaffey
One Minute to Midnight *88* Robert Michael Ingria
One Minute to Play *26* Sam Wood
One Minute to Zero *52* Tay Garnett
One Moment's Temptation *22* Arthur H. Rooke
One Month Later *87* Nouchka van Brakel
One More American *18* William DeMille
One More Chance *31* Mack Sennett
One More Chance *81* Sam Firstenberg
One More River *34* James Whale
One More Saturday *87* Sergio Vejar
One More Saturday Night *86* Dennis Klein
One More Spring *35* Henry King
One More Time *47* Heinosuke Gosho
One More Time *69* Jerry Lewis
One More Tomorrow *46* Peter Godfrey
One More Train to Rob *71* Andrew V. McLaglen
One Mysterious Night *44* Budd Boetticher
One New York Night *35* Jack Conway
One Night *31* Gustaf Molander
One Night *45* Boris Barnet
One Night...a Train *68* André Delvaux
One Night and Then... *09* D. W. Griffith
One Night at Susie's *30* John Francis Dillon

One Night in Lisbon *41* Edward H. Griffith
One Night in Paris *38* Walter Summers
One Night in Rome *24* Clarence Badger
One Night in the Tropics *40* A. Edward Sutherland
One Night of Fame *48* Mario Monicelli, Steno
One Night of Love *34* Victor Schertzinger
One Night of Passion *29* Heinosuke Gosho
One Night Only *83* Timothy Bond
One Night Stand *76* Pierre Rissient
One Night Stand *78* Allan King
One Night Stand *84* John Duigan
One Night with You *48* Terence Young
One of Many *17* Christy Cabanne
One of Millions *14* J. Searle Dawley
One of Our Aircraft Is Missing *41* Michael Powell, Emeric Pressburger
One of Our Dinosaurs Is Missing *75* Anthony Squire, Robert Stevenson
One of Our Girls *14* Thomas Heffron
One of Our Spies Is Missing *66* E. Darrell Hallenbeck
One of the Best *27* T. Hayes Hunter
One of the Bravest *25* Frank O'Connor
One of the Bulldog Breed *09* Joe Rosenthal
One of the Discard *14* Thomas Ince, C. Gardner Sullivan
One of the Finest *19* Harry Beaumont
One of the Many *14* Victor Sjöström
One of the Many *33* William Nigh
One of the Nuts *13* Charles C. Calvert
One of the Smiths *31* James Parrott
One of Them Days *68* Peter Saunders
One of Those Things *74* Erik Balling
One Ol' Cat *22* Earl Hurd
One on Ikey *15* Cecil Birch
One on One *77* Lamont Johnson
One Out of Many *14* Victor Sjöström
One Page of Love *79* Ted Roter
One Piece Bathing Suit, The *52* Mervyn LeRoy
1 + 1 *61* Arch Oboler
One Plus One *68* Jean-Luc Godard
One Plus One *78* Erland Josephson, Sven Nykvist, Ingrid Thulin
1 + 1 = 3 *79* Heidi Genée
1 + 1: Exploring the Kinsey Report *61* Arch Oboler
One Potato, Two Potato... *61* Dušan Makavejev
One Potato, Two Potato *64* Larry Peerce
One Precious Year *33* Henry Edwards
One Punch O'Day *26* Harry Joe Brown
One Quack Mind *55* Joseph Barbera, William Hanna
One Rainy Afternoon *36* Rowland V. Lee
One Rainy Night *86* Romeo Costantini
One Reel Feature, A *15* Vincent Whitman
One Romantic Night *30* George Fitzmaurice, Paul Stein
One-Room Tenants *60* Wojciech Has
One-Round Hogan *27* Howard Bretherton
One Round Jeff *20* Raoul Barré, Charles Bowers
One-Round O'Brien *12* Mack Sennett
One Run Elmer *35* Charles Lamont

One Russian Summer *73* Antonio Calenda
One Second in Montreal *69* Michael Snow
One Shall Be Taken *14* Ethyle Batley
One She Loved, The *12* D. W. Griffith
One Shocking Moment *64* Larry Cohen, Ted V. Mikels
One Shot Ross *17* Clifford Smith
One Silver Dollar *64* Giorgio Ferroni
One Single Night *38* Gustaf Molander
One Sings, the Other Doesn't *76* Agnès Varda
One Splendid Hour *29* Burton L. King
One Spy Too Many *65* Joseph Sargent
One Step Ahead of My Shadow *33* Rudolf Ising
One Step to Eternity *54* Henri Decoin
One Step to Hell *67* Sandy Howard
One Stolen Night *23* Robert Ensminger
One Stolen Night *29* Scott R. Dunlap
One Stormy Knight *22* Al Christie
One Straight and Two with Salt *87* Rafael Villaseñor Kuri
One Summer Love *76* Gilbert Cates
One Summer of Happiness *51* Arne Mattsson
One Summer's Day *17* Frank G. Bayley
One Sunday Afternoon *33* Stephen Roberts
One Sunday Afternoon *48* Raoul Walsh
One Sunday Morning *55* Andrzej Munk
One Swallow Doesn't Make a Summer *47* Hasse Ekman
One That Got Away, The *57* Roy Ward Baker
One Thing After Another *14* Lawrence Trimble
One-Thing-at-a-Time O'Day *19* John Ince
One Third of a Nation *39* Dudley Murphy
1000 Arabian Knights *59* Jack Kinney
1,000 Convicts and a Woman *71* Ray Austin
One Thousand Dollars *18* Kenneth Webb
$1,000 a Minute *35* Aubrey H. Scotto
$1,000 a Touchdown *39* James P. Hogan
$1,000 Reward *23* Charles R. Seeling
1,000 Female Shapes *63* Barry Mahon
1,000 Plane Raid, The *69* Boris Sagal
£1000 Reward *13* Harold Heath
1,000 Shapes of a Female *63* Barry Mahon
1,000 Years from Now *52* Stuart Gilmore
1001 Arabian Nights *59* Jack Kinney
1001 Crtež *61* Dušan Vukotić
1001 Drawings *61* Dušan Vukotić
1001 Nights with Toho *47* Kon Ichikawa*
One Thrilling Night *42* William Beaudine
1-100 *78* Peter Greenaway
One Too-Exciting Night *22* Gaston Quiribet
One Too Many *50* Erle C. Kenton
One Touch of Nature *08* D. W. Griffith
One Touch of Nature *17* Edward H. Griffith
One Touch of Sin *17* Richard Stanton
One Touch of Venus *48* Gregory La Cava, William A. Seiter
One-Trick Pony *80* Robert M. Young
One, Two, Three *12* Allan Dwan
One, Two, Three *61* André Smagghe, Billy Wilder
1-2-3 *70* John Whitney

1 2 3 Duan Mahaphai 77 Prinya Lilason, Narong Poomin, Vinai Poomin
1 2 3 Monster Express 77 Prinya Lilason, Narong Poomin, Vinai Poomin
One Way or Another 74 Sara Gómez
One Way or Another 76 Elio Petri
One Way Out 34 Lambert Hillyer
One Way Out 50 Henry Levin
One Way Out 55 Francis Searle
One Way Passage 31 Tay Garnett
One Way Pendulum 64 Peter Yates
One-Way Street 25 John Francis Dillon
One-Way Street 50 Hugo Fregonese
One Way Ticket 35 Herbert J. Biberman
One-Way Ticket, A 88 Agliberto Melendez
One-Way Ticket for Love 60 Masahiro Shinoda
One Way Ticket to Hell 55 Bamlet L. Price, Jr.
One-Way Ticket to Love 60 Masahiro Shinoda
One Way to Love 45 Ray Enright
One-Way Trail, The 20 Fred A. Kelsey
One Way Trail, The 31 Ray Taylor
One-Way Wahine 65 William O. Brown
One-Way Wahini 65 William O. Brown
One Week 20 Edward F. Cline, Buster Keaton
One Week of Happiness 34 Max Nosseck
One Week of Life 19 Hobart Henley
One Week of Love 22 George Archainbaud
One Week to Live 21 Sinclair Hill
One Week with Love 57 Mario Camerini
One Who Remembered 10 Fred Rains
One Wild Moment 77 Claude Berri
One Wild Night 38 Eugene Forde
One Wild Oat 51 Charles Saunders
One Wild Week 21 Maurice Campbell
One Winter's Night 14 Edwin J. Collins
One Wish Too Many 56 John Durst
One with the Fuzz, The 69 Garson Kanin
One Woman, The 18 Reginald Barker
One Woman Idea, The 29 Berthold Viertel
One Woman or Two 85 Daniel Vigne
One Woman to Another 27 Frank Tuttle
One Woman's Story 48 David Lean
One Wonderful Night 14 Elisha H. Calvert
One Wonderful Night 22 Stuart Paton
One Wonderful Sunday 47 Akira Kurosawa
One Yard to Go 31 William Beaudine
One Year Later 33 E. Mason Hopper
One Year of Freedom 60 Santiago Álvarez, Julio García Espinosa
One Year to Live 25 Irving Cummings
Oneichan Makari Toru 59 Toshio Sugie
O'Neil of the Glen 16 Joseph M. Kerrigan
Onestà del Peccato, L' 18 Augusto Genina
Oni Azami 26 Teinosuke Kinugasa
Oni no Sumu Yakata 69 Kenji Misumi
Oni Shli na Vostok 64 Giuseppe De Santis
Oni Srajalis za Rodinou 74 Sergei Bondarchuk
Oni Srazhalis za Rodinu 74 Sergei Bondarchuk

Onibaba 64 Kaneto Shindo
Onibaba — The Hole 64 Kaneto Shindo
Onimasa 82 Hideo Gosha
Onion Field, The 79 Harold Becker
Onion Hero, The 17 William Beaudine
Onion Pacific 40 Dave Fleischer
Onionhead 58 Norman Taurog
Oniro Aristeris Nichtas 87 Dinos Katsouridis
Oniros 67 Jean-Daniel Pollet
Onkel aus Amerika, Der 52 Carl Boese
Onkel og Nevø 11 August Blom
Onkel Toms Hutte 65 Géza von Radványi
Only a Coffin 66 Santos Alcocer
Only a Dancing Girl 27 Olof Molander
Only a Dart 08 Dave Aylott
Only a Face at the Window 03 Percy Stow
Only a Flower Girl 14 Warwick Buckland
Only a Girl 13 Charles H. Weston
Only a Limerick 07 A. E. Coleby
Only a Messenger Boy 15 Charlie Chase
Only a Mill Girl 19 Lewis Willoughby
Only a Mother 49 Alf Sjöberg
Only a Penny a Box 08 Alf Collins
Only a Room-er 16 Toby Cooper
Only a Shop Girl 22 Edward J. LeSaint
Only a Tramp 09 Theo Bouwmeester
Only a Waiter 60 Alf Kjellin
Only a Wedding 13 Stuart Kinder
Only a Woman 34 Harry Lachman
Only a Woman 41 Anders Henrikson
Only a Woman 62 Alfred Weidenmann
Only an Outcast 12 Bert Haldane
Only Angels Have Wings 39 Howard Hawks
Only Eight Hours 34 George B. Seitz
Only for Fun — Only for Play: Kaleidoscope Valeska Gert 77 Volker Schlöndorff
Only for Love 61 Jean Aurel, Jack Dunn Trop, Roger Vadim
Only for Thee 38 Carmine Gallone
Only Game in Town, The 68 George Stevens
Only Girl, The 33 Friedrich Holländer
Only God Knows 74 Peter Pearson
Only Her Brother 05 Lewin Fitzhamon
Only Her Husband 29 Charles Lamont
Only Life, The 41 Ramjankhan Mehboobkhan
Only Man, The 15 Will P. Kellino
Only Man, The 25 H. B. Parkinson
Only Once in a Lifetime 79 Alexander Grattan
Only One, The 75 Josef Heifits
Only One Girl, or A Boom in Sausages 10 Percy Stow
Only One New York 63 Pierre-Dominique Gaisseau
Only One Night 38 Gustaf Molander
Only One Pair 16 Percy Stow
Only Road, The 18 Frank Reicher
Only Saps Work 30 Cyril Gardner, Edwin H. Knopf
Only Son, The 14 Cecil B. DeMille, Thomas Heffron
Only Son, The 36 Yasujiro Ozu
Only Takes Two 78 Francis Megahy
Only the Best 51 Michael Gordon
Only the Brave 30 Frank Tuttle
Only the French Can 54 Jean Renoir

Only the Valiant 51 Gordon Douglas
Only Thing, The 25 Jack Conway
Only Thing You Know, The 71 Clarke Mackey
Only 38 23 William DeMille
Only Two Can Play 61 Sidney Gilliat
Only Two Little Shoes 10 H. Oceano Martinek
Only Way, The 25 Herbert Wilcox
Only Way, The 70 Bent Christensen
Only Way Home, The 72 G. D. Spradlin
Only Way Out, The 26 Charles Barnett
Only Way Out Is Dead, The 70 John Trent
Only When I Larf 67 Basil Dearden
Only When I Laugh 81 Glenn Jordan
Only Woman, The 24 Sidney Olcott
Only Women Have Trouble 58 Kaneto Shindo
Only Women Know Sorrow 58 Kaneto Shindo
Only Yesterday 33 John M. Stahl
Onna 48 Keisuke Kinoshita
Onna ga Kaidan o Agaru Toki 60 Mikio Naruse
Onna Goroshi Abura Jigoku 64 Hiromichi Horikawa
Onna Hitori Daichi o Iku 53 Fumio Kamei
Onna Kōsō Ie o Mamore 39 Kozaburo Yoshimura
Onna Kyūketsuki 59 Nobuo Nakagawa
Onna Niko 67 Akira Inoue
Onna no Isshō 49 Fumio Kamei
Onna no Isshō 53 Kaneto Shindo
Onna no Kao 49 Tadashi Imai
Onna no Kunshō 60 Kozaburo Yoshimura
Onna no Machi 40 Tadashi Imai
Onna no Mizuumi 66 Yoshishige Yoshida
Onna no Naka ni Iru Tanin 65 Mikio Naruse
Onna no Rekishi 63 Mikio Naruse
Onna no Saka 60 Kozaburo Yoshimura
Onna no Sono 54 Keisuke Kinoshita
Onna no Uzu to Fuchi to Nagare 64 Ko Nakahira
Onna no Za 62 Mikio Naruse
Onna to Misoshiru 68 Heinosuke Gosho
Onna to Umareta Karanya 34 Heinosuke Gosho
Onna Ukiyoburō 69 Tan Ida
Onna wa Tamoto o Goyōjin 32 Mikio Naruse
Onna yo Ayamaru Nakare 23 Teinosuke Kinugasa
Onna yo Kimi no Na o Kegasu Nakare 30 Heinosuke Gosho
Onnenpeli 65 Risto Jarva
Onno 23 88 Bea Reese
Onore e Sacrificio 50 Guido Brignone
Onorevole Angelina, L' 47 Luigi Zampa
Onsen Gerira Dai Shōgeki 70 Hirokazu Ichimura
Ont Staan en Vergaan 53 Bert Haanstra
Onward Christian Soldiers 06 Arthur Gilbert
Onward Christian Soldiers 18 Rex Wilson
Onyxknopf, Der 17 Joe May
Ooh...You Are Awful 72 Cliff Owen
Oohakachavadam 88 K. Madhu

Ooka's Trial 28 Daisuke Ito
Oompahs, The 51 Pete Burness, Robert Cannon
Op Hop 65 Pierre Hébert
Opal Stealers, The 13 A. E. Coleby
Opbrud 88 Claus Ploug
Open Air Museum, An 73 Tenghiz Abuladze
Open All Night 24 Paul Bern
Open All Night 34 George Pearson
Open at Night 31 Heinosuke Gosho
Open City 45 Roberto Rossellini
Open Country 22 Sinclair Hill
Open Door, The 14 Toby Cooper
Open Door, The 19 Dallas M. Fitzgerald
Open Doors 90 Gianni Amelio
Open During Alterations 13 Percy Stow
Open from Six to Midnight 88 Victor Dinenzon
Open Gate, The 09 D. W. Griffith
Open House 26 Charles Lamont
Open House 87 Jag Mohan Mundhra
Open Places 17 W. S. Van Dyke
Open Range 27 Clifford Smith
Open Road, The 40 Fernand Rivers
Open Road, The 48 Arne Sucksdorff
Open Season 74 Peter Collinson
Open Secret 48 John Reinhardt
Open Spaces 26 Charles Lamont
Open Switch, The 26 John P. McGowan
Open the Door and See All the People 64 Jerome Hill
Open Trail, The 25 Clifford Smith
Open Your Eyes 19 Gilbert P. Hamilton
Opened by Mistake 34 James Parrott
Opened by Mistake 41 George Archainbaud
Opened Shutters, The 14 Otis Turner
Opened Shutters 21 William Worthington
Opening Ceremonies, New York Subway, Oct. 27, 1904 04 Edwin S. Porter
Opening Day 38 Roy Rowland
Opening in Moscow 59 D. A. Pennebaker
Opening Night, The 27 Edward H. Griffith
Opening Night 35 Alex Brown
Opening Night 77 John Cassavetes
Opening of Belmont Park Race Course 05 Edwin S. Porter
Opening of Misty Beethoven, The 76 Radley Metzger
Opening of the Universal Exposition 00 Louis Lumière
Opening Speech 60 Norman McLaren
Opera 87 Dario Argento
Opera Ball 31 Max Neufeld
Opera Ball 40 Géza von Bolváry
Opera Cordis 68 Dušan Vukotić
Opéra de Quatre Pesos, L' 70 François Reichenbach
Opéra de Quat'Sous, L' 31 G. W. Pabst
Ópera do Malandro 86 Ruy Guerra
Opera in the Vineyard 81 Jaromil Jireš
Opéra-Mouffe, L' 58 Agnès Varda
Opéra Musette 42 René Lefèvre, Claude Renoir
Opera Prima 80 Fernando Trueba
Opera ve Vinici 81 Jaromil Jireš
Operabranden 12 August Blom
Operace Mé Dcery 86 Ivo Novák

Operación Abril del Caribe 82 Santiago Álvarez, Lázaro Buria
Operación Dalila 66 Luis De los Arcos
Operación Goldman 65 Antonio Margheriti
Operación Loto Azul 67 Sergio Grieco
Operación Marijuana 87 José Luis Urquieta
Operación Ogro 79 Gillo Pontecorvo
Operation Abduction 57 Jean Stelli
Operation Amsterdam 59 Michael McCarthy
Operation April in the Caribbean 82 Santiago Álvarez, Lázaro Buria
Operation Atlantis 65 Paul Fleming
Operation Belgrade 68 Živka Mitrović
Opération Béton 54 Jean-Luc Godard
Operation Bikini 63 Anthony Carras
Operation Blue Book 68 Frank Telford
Operation Bottleneck 61 Edward L. Cahn
Operation Bullshine 59 Gilbert Gunn
Operation C.I.A. 65 Christian Nyby
Operation Camel 60 Sven Methling, Jr.
Operation Caviar 59 Géza von Radványi
Operation Cicero 52 Joseph L. Mankiewicz
Operation Conspiracy 56 Joseph Sterling
Operation Cross Eagles 69 Richard Conte
Operation Crossbow 64 Michael Anderson
Operation Cupid 60 Charles Saunders
Operation Dames 59 Louis Clyde Stoumen
Operation Daybreak 75 Lewis Gilbert
Operation Delilah 66 Luis De los Arcos
Operation Diamond 48 Ronnie Pilgrim
Operation Diplomat 53 John Guillermin
Operation Diplomatic Passport 62 André Labrousse
Operation Disaster 49 Roy Ward Baker
Operation Eichmann 61 R. G. Springsteen
Operation Fear 66 Mario Bava
Operation Ganymed 77 Rainer Erler
Opération Gas-Oil 55 Philippe de Broca
Operation: Get Victor Corpus the Rebel Soldier 87 Pablo Santiago
Operation Gold Ingot 63 Georges Lautner
Operation Haylift 50 William Berke
Operation Heartbeat 71 Boris Sagal
Operation Hong Kong 64 Helmuth Ashley
Operation Hourglass 55 Alexander Hammid
Operation Kid Brother 67 Alberto De Martino
Opération La Fontaine 54 Jean Dewever
Operation Leontine 68 Michel Audiard
Operation Lotus Bleu 67 Sergio Grieco
Operation Lovebirds 67 Erik Balling
Operation M 70 Al Adamson
Operation Mad Ball 57 Richard Quine
Operation Malaya 53 David MacDonald
Operation Manhunt 54 Jack Alexander
Operation Marijuana 87 José Luis Urquieta
Operation Masquerade 64 Basil Dearden
Operation Mermaid 63 John Ainsworth
Operation Monsterland 68 Inoshiro Honda
Operation Murder 57 Ernest Morris
Operation Negligee 68 Kaneto Shindo
Operation of the K-13 Gunsight 44 John Hubley

Operation Ogre 79 Gillo Pontecorvo
Operation Ogro 79 Gillo Pontecorvo
Operation Overkill 82 Ted V. Mikels
Operation Overthrow 78 Martyn Burke
Operation Pacific 51 George Waggner
Operation Petticoat 59 Blake Edwards
Operation: Rabbit 52 Chuck Jones
Operation St. Peter's 68 Lucio Fulci
Operation San Gennaro 65 Dino Risi
Operation Secret 52 Lewis Seiler
Operation Snafu 61 Cyril Frankel
Operation Snafu 70 Nanni Loy
Operation Snatch 62 Robert Day
Operation Stadium 77 Dušan Vukotić
Operation Stogie 62 Ernest Morris
Operation Swallow 47 Jean Dréville, Titus Vibé-Müller
Operation Third Form 66 David Eady
Operation Thunderbolt 77 Menahem Golan
Operation Titanic 43 Anatole Litvak
Operation Undercover 74 Milton Katselas
Operation Violin Case 86 Günther Friedrich
Operation Warhead 61 Cyril Frankel
Operation X 50 Gregory Ratoff
Operation X 63 Kihachi Okamoto
Operation Y and Shurik's Other Adventures 65 Leonid Gaidai
Operator at Black Rock, The 14 John P. McGowan
Operator 13 33 Richard Boleslawski
Operazione Crossbow 64 Michael Anderson
Operazione Goldman 65 Antonio Margheriti
Operazione Ogro 79 Gillo Pontecorvo
Operazione Paradiso 66 Henry Levin, Dino Maiuri
Operazione Paura 66 Mario Bava
Operazione San Gennaro 65 Dino Risi
Operazione San Pietro 68 Lucio Fulci
Operetta 40 Willi Forst
Operette 40 Willi Forst
Opern-Ball, Der 31 Max Neufeld
Opernball 40 Géza von Bolváry
Opernina 35 Carmine Gallone
Opernredoute 31 Max Neufeld
Opernring 35 Carmine Gallone
Opfer 18 Joe May
Opfer der Helen, Das 21 Paul Stein
Opfergang 44 Veidt Harlan
Onkel og Nevø 11 August Blom
Ophelia 62 Claude Chabrol
Ophélie 62 Claude Chabrol
Opiate '67 63 Dino Risi
Opium 16 Robert Dinesen
Opium Cigarettes, The 14 Stuart Kinder
Opium Connection, The 66 Terence Young
Opium Den 11 Julius Jaenzon
Opium Dreams 14 Forest Holger-Madsen
Opium Smoker's Dream, The 14 Forest Holger-Madsen
Ópiumkeringö 43 Béla Balázs
Opiumsdrømmen 14 Forest Holger-Madsen
Opname 79 Marja Kok, Eric van Zuylen
Opowieść Atlantycka 54 Wanda Jakubowska

Original Old Mother Riley, The *37* Oswald Mitchell

Original Sin, The *48* Helmut Käutner

O'Riley's Luck *36* Charles Barton

Orin, a Blind Woman *77* Masahiro Shinoda

Orin the Abandoned Girl *77* Masahiro Shinoda

Orinoco — Prison of Sex *79* Eduardo Mulargia

Orion Nebula *87* Jurrien Rood

Orionnevel, De *87* Jurrien Rood

Orion's Belt *85* Ola Solum

Orions Belte *85* Ola Solum

Orizuru Osen *34* Kenji Mizoguchi

Orkestar Jedne Mladosti *86* Sveta Pavlović

Orlacs Hände *24* Robert Wiene

Orlak, El Infierno de Frankenstein *60* Rafael Baledón

Orlak, The Hell of Frankenstein *60* Rafael Baledón

Ormens Ägg *77* Ingmar Bergman

Ormens Väg på Hälleberget *86* Bo Widerberg

Ornament des Verliebten Herzens, Das *19* Lotte Reiniger

Ornament of the Loving Heart, The *19* Lotte Reiniger

Ornette: Made in America *85* Shirley Clarke

Oro dei Bravados, L' *70* Renato Savino

Oro di Napoli, L' *54* Vittorio De Sica

Oro di Roma, L' *61* Carlo Lizzani

Oro Nero *40* Enrico Guazzoni

Oro per i Cesari *62* Sabatino Ciuffini, André De Toth, Riccardo Freda

Oro, Plata, Mata *82* Peque Gallaga

Oro Sangre y Sol *25* Miguel Torres Contreras

Oro y Plata *34* Ramón Peón

Örök Titok, Az *40* István György

Örökbefogadás *75* Márta Mészáros

Örökösök *70* András Kovács

Örökség *80* Márta Mészáros

Örökségünk *75* István Gaál

Orologio a Cucu, L' *38* Camillo Mastrocinque

Oroszlán Ugrani Készül, Az *69* György Révész

O'Rourke of the Royal Mounted *54* Raoul Walsh

Orphan, The *12* A. E. Coleby

Orphan, The *20* J. Gordon Edwards

Orphan, The *67* George Moorse

Orphan, The *79* John Ballard

Orphan Boy of Vienna, An *37* Max Neufeld

Orphan of the Pecos *37* Sam Katzman

Orphan of the Ring *39* Lewis Seiler

Orphan of the Sage *28* Louis King

Orphan of the Wilderness *37* Ken Hall

Orphan Sally *22* Edward L. Hemmer

Orphans, The *07* James A. Williamson

Orphans *87* Alan J. Pakula

Orphan's Mine, The *13* Allan Dwan

Orphans of the North *40* Norman Dawn

Orphans of the Storm *21* D. W. Griffith

Orphans of the Street *38* John H. Auer

Orphée *49* Jean Cocteau

Orphelin de Paris, L' *23* Louis Feuillade

Orpheline, L' *21* Louis Feuillade

Orpheus *49* Jean Cocteau

Orpheus and Eurydice *85* István Gaál

Orpheus in the Underworld *10* Charles Magnusson

Orrechio, L' *46* Mario Bava

Orribile Segreto del Dottor Hichcock, L' *62* Riccardo Freda

Orrori del Castello di Norimberga, Gli *72* Mario Bava

Országutak Vándora *56* Márta Mészáros

Orthopedic Paradise *69* Patricio Guzmán

Oru Chi Diary Kurippu *88* K. Madhu

Oru Kaijū Daishingeki *69* Inoshiro Honda

Oru Maymasappulariyil *88* V. R. Gopinath

Oru Minnaminuginte Nurungu Vettam *88* Bharathan

Oru Muthassi Katha *88* Priyadarshan

Orzowei *75* Yves Allégret

Osa *85* Oleg Egorov

Ōsaka Elegy *36* Kenji Mizoguchi

Ōsaka-Jō Monogatari *61* Hiroshi Inagaki

Ōsaka Monogatari *56* Kenji Mizoguchi, Kozaburo Yoshimura

Ōsaka Monogatari *61* Hiroshi Inagaki

Ōsaka Natsu no Jin *37* Teinosuke Kinugasa

Ōsaka no Onna *58* Teinosuke Kinugasa

Ōsaka no Yado *54* Heinosuke Gosho

Osaka Story, An *56* Kenji Mizoguchi, Kozaburo Yoshimura

Ösbemutató *74* István Szabó

Oscar, The *65* Russell Rouse

Oscar *67* Édouard Molinaro

Oscar, Champion de Tennis *32* Jacques Tati

Oscar, Tennis Champion *32* Jacques Tati

Oscar Wilde *60* Gregory Ratoff

Oscillation *26* Widgey R. Newman, Challis Sanderson

Oscuros Sueños de Agosto *67* Miguel Picazo

Ösember, Az *17* Cornelius Hinter

Osen *40* Friedrich Ermler, I. Menaker

Osen of the Paper Cranes *34* Kenji Mizoguchi

Osenny Marafon *78* Georgy Danelia

Ošetřovna *69* Zbyněk Brynych

O'Shaughnessy's Boy *35* Richard Boleslawski

Oshikiri Shinkonki *30* Mikio Naruse

Ōshō *73* Hiromichi Horikawa

Oslo *63* Jørgen Roos

Osman the Infantryman *70* Şerif Gören, Yılmaz Güney

Osman the Wanderer *70* Şerif Gören, Yılmaz Güney

Osmjeh 61 *61* Dušan Makavejev

Osmosis *48* Willard Van Dyke

Ósmy Dzień Tygodnia *57* Aleksander Ford

Osobisty Pamiętnik Grzesznika Przez Niego Samego Spisany *86* Wojciech Has

Osone-Ke no Asa *46* Keisuke Kinoshita

Osorezan no Onna *64* Heinosuke Gosho

Ōsōshiki *84* Juzo Itami

Ospedale del Delitto, L' *48* Luigi Comencini

Ospite, L' *71* Liliana Cavani

Osram *56* Alexander Alexeïeff, Claire Parker

Oss Emellan *69* Stellan Olsson

Ossegg oder Die Wahrheit Über Hansel und Gretel *88* Thees Klahn

Ossessa, L' *74* Mario Gariazzo

Ossessione *42* Luchino Visconti

Ossessione Che Uccide, L' *80* Riccardo Freda

Ossi's Diary *17* Ernst Lubitsch

Ossis Tagebuch *17* Ernst Lubitsch

Ossuary, The *70* Jan Švankmajer

Osta Hassen, El *52* Salah Abu Saif

Ostacolo, L' *14* Baldassare Negroni

Ostatni Dzień Lata *58* Tadeusz Konwicki, Jan Laskowski

Ostatni Etap *47* Wanda Jakubowska

Ostende, Reine des Plages *30* Henri Storck

Osterman Weekend, The *83* Sam Peckinpah

Ostře Sledované Vlaky *66* Jiří Menzel

Ostrich, The *49* David Hand

Ostrich Feathers *37* Walter Lantz

Ostrich Has Two Eggs, The *57* Denys De la Patellière

Ostrich's Plumes, The *26* Clyde Geronimi

Ostrov Stříbrných Volavek *76* Jaromil Jireš

Ostrva *63* Jovan Živanović

Osudy Dobrého Vojáka Švejka *54* Jiří Trnka

Osvetnik *58* Dušan Vukotić

Osvobozhdeniye *40* Alexander Dovzhenko, Yulia Solntseva

Osvobozhdeniye Frantsye *44* Sergei Yutkevich

Osvobozhdeniye Kitai *50* Ivan Dukinsky, Sergei Gerasimov, Irina Setkina, M. Slavinsky, Sao-bin Sui, Elena Svilovoi

Osvobozhdennaya Frantsiya *44* Sergei Yutkevich

Oswego *43* Willard Van Dyke

Osynliga Muren, Den *44* Gustaf Molander

Ösz Badacsonyban *54* Miklós Jancsó

Öt Óra 40 *38* André De Toth

Otac na Službenom Putu *85* Emir Kusturica

Otages, Les *39* Raymond Bernard

Otália de Bahia *77* Marcel Camus

Otan o Syzygos Taxeideyei *39* Toga Mizrahi

Otar's Widow *57* Mikhail Chiaureli

Otchi Dom *59* Lev Kulidzhanov

Otchi Tchiornie *35* Victor Tourjansky

Otchi Tchiornie *87* Nikita Mikhalkov

Otel 'u Pogibshchego Alpinista *79* Grigori Kromarov

Otello *07* Mario Caserini

Otello *55* Sergei Yutkevich

Otello *86* Franco Zeffirelli

Otets Sergii *18* Yakov Protazanov

Otets Soldata *65* Revaz Chkeidze

Othello *07* Mario Caserini

Othello *09* Ugo Falena

Othello *22* Dmitri Buchowetzki

Othello *46* David MacKane

Othello *51* Orson Welles

Othello *55* Sergei Yutkevich

Othello *65* Stuart Burge, John Dexter

Othello Sapp's Wonderful Invention *21* Milt Gross

Other, The *12* Max Mack

Other, The *30* Robert Wiene
Other, The *72* Robert Mulligan
Other *80* Stan Brakhage
Other Cuba, The *85* Orlando Jiménez-Leal
Other Dog's Day, The *20* Cecil Mannering
Other Girl, The *16* Percy Winter
Other Half, The *19* King Vidor
Other Half of the Sky—A China Memoir, The *74* Shirley MacLaine, Claudia Weill
Other Halves *85* John Laing
Other Kind of Love, The *24* Duke Worne
Other Love, The *47* André De Toth
Other Man, The *16* Roscoe Arbuckle
Other Man, The *18* Paul Scardon
Other Man, The *88* Ferenc Kósa
Other Man's Wife, The *19* Carl Harbaugh
Other Men's Daughters *18* Carl Harbaugh
Other Men's Daughters *23* Ben F. Wilson
Other Men's Shoes *20* Edgar Lewis
Other Men's Wives *19* Victor Schertzinger
Other Men's Women *31* William A. Wellman
Other Mrs. Phipps, The *31* Guy Newall
Other One, The *67* René Allio
Other People, The *68* David Hart
Other People's Business *31* William A. Seiter
Other People's Money *16* William Parke
Other People's Passions *86* Ianas Streitch
Other People's Sins *31* Sinclair Hill
Other Person, The *21* B. E. Doxat-Pratt
Other Realms *83* John Cardos
Other Self, The *18* Fritz Freisler
Other Shore, The *30* Mark Donskoi
Other Side, The *22* Hugh Dierker
Other Side of Bonnie and Clyde, The *68* Larry Buchanan
Other Side of Midnight, The *77* Charles Jarrott
Other Side of Paradise, The *75* Arturo Ripstein
Other Side of the Door, The *16* Thomas Ricketts
Other Side of the Hedge, The *04* Lewin Fitzhamon
Other Side of the Image, The *85* Jean-François Laguionie
Other Side of the Medal, The *65* Fadil Hadžić
Other Side of the Mountain, The *74* Larry Peerce
Other Side of the Mountain Part 2, The *77* Larry Peerce
Other Side of the Underneath, The *72* Jane Arden
Other Side of the Wind, The *72* Orson Welles
Other Tomorrow, The *30* Lloyd Bacon
Other Voices *69* David Sawyer
Other Wise Man, The *12* Allan Dwan
Other Woman, The *18* Albert Parker
Other Woman, The *21* Edward Sloman
Other Woman, The *31* George B. Samuelson
Other Woman, The *54* Hugo Haas
Other Woman, The *61* Mikio Naruse
Other Woman's Story, The *25* B. F. Stanley
Other Women's Clothes *22* Hugo Ballin

Other Women's Husbands *26* Erle C. Kenton
Othon *69* Danièle Huillet, Jean-Marie Straub
Otklonenie *68* Grisha Ostrovski, Todor Stoyanov
Otley *68* Dick Clement
Ötödik Pecsét, Az *76* Zoltán Fábri
Otoko Gokoro *25* Heinosuke Gosho
Otoko Tai Otoko *61* Senkichi Taniguchi
Otoko to Onna to Inu *64* Yoji Kuri
Otoko wa Tsuraiyō *69* Yoji Yamada
Otoko wa Tsuraiyō: Shiawaseno Aoi Tori *86* Yoji Yamada
Otoko wa Tsuraiyō, Shibamata yori Ai o Komete *86* Yoji Yamada
Otoko wa Tsuraiyō Tōraijiro Kokoro no Tabiji *89* Yoji Yamada
Otome-Gokoro Sannin Shimai *34* Mikio Naruse
Otoshiana *61* Hiroshi Teshigahara
Otōto *60* Kon Ichikawa
Otra, La *46* Roberto Gavaldón
Otra Historia de Amor *86* Américo Ortiz De Zarate
Otra Vuelta de Tuerca *85* Eloy De la Iglesia
Otro, El *84* Arturo Ripstein
Otro Cristóbal, El *62* Armand Gatti
Otro Lado del Espejo, El *73* Jesús Franco
Otroki vo Vselennoi *75* Richard Viktorov
Otryad *85* Alexei Simonov
Otstupnik *88* Valery Rubinchik
Otto—Der Film *85* Xaver Schwarzenberger, Otto Waalkes
Otto—Der Neue Film *87* Xaver Schwarzenberger, Otto Waalkes
8½ *62* Federico Fellini
Otto e Mezzo *62* Federico Fellini
Otto Luck and Ruby Razmataz *17* Wallace A. Carlson
Otto Luck and the Ruby of Razmataz *17* Wallace A. Carlson
Otto Luck in the Movies *17* Wallace A. Carlson
Otto Luck to the Rescue *17* Wallace A. Carlson
Otto Luck's Flivvered Romance *17* Wallace A. Carlson
Otto—The New Film *87* Xaver Schwarzenberger, Otto Waalkes
Otvad Horizonta *60* Zahari Zhandov
Où Est Passé Tom? *71* José Giovanni
Où Êtes-Vous Donc? *69* Gilles Groulx
Ouanga *35* George Terwilliger
Ouanzerbé, Capitale de la Magie *48* Marcel Griaule, Jean Rouch
Oublié *27* Germaine Dulac
Oublié—La Princesse Mandane *27* Germaine Dulac
Oubliette, L' *12* Louis Feuillade
Ouch! *67* Gerard Bryant
Ouigours—Minorité Nationale—Sinkiang, Les *77* Joris Ivens, Marceline Loridan
Ouija Board, The *20* Dave Fleischer
Ouistiti de Totò, Le *14* Émile Cohl
Our Aggie *21* Jack Denton
Our Baby *14* Arthur Finn
Our Bessie *12* Bert Haldane
Our Better Selves *18* George Fitzmaurice

Our Betters *32* George Cukor
Our Bill of Rights *41* George Arthur Durlam
Our Blushing Brides *30* Harry Beaumont
Our Boyhood Days *06* Frank Mottershaw
Our Boys *15* Sidney Morgan
Our Champions *50* Mark Donskoi
Our Cissy *73* Alan Parker
Our Combat *39* Hugo Haas
Our Constitution *41* George Arthur Durlam
Our Country *44* John Eldridge
Our Countrymen *68* Vojtěch Jasný
Our Country's Youth *45* I. M. Poselsky, Ivan Venzher, Sergei Yutkevich
Our Courtyard *56* Revaz Chkeidze
Our Cousin from Abroad *08* Lewin Fitzhamon
Our Daily Bread *28* Piel Jutzi
Our Daily Bread *29* F. W. Murnau
Our Daily Bread *34* King Vidor
Our Daily Bread *46* Graham Cutts
Our Daily Bread *49* Slatan Dudow
Our Daily Water *76* Georgy Shengelaya
Our Dancing Daughters *28* Harry Beaumont
Our Declaration of Independence *41* George Arthur Durlam
Our Exploits at West Poley *86* Diarmid Lawrence
Our Father *85* Francisco Regueiro
Our Father's House *59* Lev Kulidzhanov
Our Fighting Navy *37* Norman Walker
Our Foolish Family *69* Karel Kachyňa
Our Forefathers *16* Harry S. Palmer
Our Four Days in Germany *18* Raoul Barré, Charles Bowers
Our Freedom of the Seas *41* George Arthur Durlam
Our Gang Follies of 1938 *37* Gordon Douglas
Our Girl Friday *53* Noel Langley
Our Girls and Their Physique *20* Geoffrey H. Malins
Our Great Mikado *07* John Morland
Our Heart *17* Vladimir Gardin
Our Heart *46* Alexander Stolper
Our Hearts Were Growing Up *46* William D. Russell
Our Hearts Were Young and Gay *44* Lewis Allen
Our Heritage *40* David MacDonald
Our Heritage *75* István Gaál
Our Hitler *77* Hans-Jürgen Syberberg
Our Hitler: A Film from Germany *77* Hans-Jürgen Syberberg
Our Hospitality *23* John G. Blystone, Buster Keaton
Our Husband *35* Patrick K. Heale
Our Husbands *66* Luigi Filippo D'Amico, Dino Risi, Luigi Zampa
Our Indonesian Friend *60* Roman Karmen
Our Instructor *39* Tadashi Imai
Our Intrepid Correspondent *11* Percy Stow
Our Lady of Fatima *52* John Brahm
Our Lady of the Paints *85* Claude Jutra
Our Land of Peace *40* Arturo S. Mom
Our Last Spring *59* Michael Cacoyannis
Our Leading Citizen *22* Alfred E. Green
Our Leading Citizen *39* Alfred Santell

Our Little Girl *35* John S. Robertson
Our Little Nell *17* W. S. Van Dyke
Our Little Nell *28* Frank Moser
Our Little Red Riding Hood *60* Jiří Brdečka
Our Little Wife *18* Edward Dillon
Our Louisiana Purchase *41* George Arthur Durlam
Our Love Is Slipping Away *65* Arnold Louis Miller
Our Man *86* Jože Pogačnik
Our Man Flint *65* Daniel Mann
Our Man in Havana *59* Carol Reed
Our Man in Jamaica *65* Richard Jackson
Our Man in Marrakesh *65* Jacques Deray
Our Man in Marrakesh *66* Don Sharp
Our Marriage *62* Masahiro Shinoda
Our Men in Bagdad *67* Paolo Bianchini
Our Merchant Marine *16* John Colman Terry
Our Miss Brooks *55* Al Lewis
Our Miss Fred *72* Bob Kellett
Our Mr. Sun *56* Frank Capra
Our Modern Maidens *28* Jack Conway
Our Monroe Doctrine *41* George Arthur Durlam
Our Moscow *39* Mikhail Kaufman
Our Mother's House *67* Jack Clayton
Our Mrs. McChesney *18* Ralph Ince
Our Mutual Friend *61* Ivan Pyriev
Our National Vaudeville *16* Harry S. Palmer
Our Neighbor *34* Yasujiro Shimazu
Our Neighbors, the Carters *39* Ralph Murphy
Our New Cook *03* Alf Collins
Our New Errand Boy *05* James A. Williamson
Our New Pillar Box *07* Arthur Cooper
Our New Policeman *06* Lewin Fitzhamon
Our Oath *52* Jerzy Bossak
Our Old Car *46* Cy Endfield
Our Palace *53* Tenghiz Abuladze, Revaz Chkeidze
Our "Pravda" *62* Leonid Varmalov
Our Red Riding Hood *60* Jiří Brdečka
Our Relations *36* Harry Lachman
Our Russian Front *41* Joris Ivens, Lewis Milestone
Our Sea *25* Rex Ingram
Our Seaside Holiday *06* Frank Mottershaw
Our Silent Love *69* Zenzo Matsuyama
Our Story *84* Bertrand Blier
Our Sweet Days of Youth *87* Chang-ho Bae
Our Teacher *39* Tadashi Imai
Our Teddy *19* William Nigh
Our Time *74* Peter Hyams
Our Times *53* Alessandro Blasetti
Our Town *40* Sam Wood
Our Very Own *50* David Miller
Our Village *51* Jean Georgescu, Victor Iliu
Our Village Club Holds a Marathon Race *08* Charles Raymond
Our Village Heroes *11* A. E. Coleby
Our Vines Have Tender Grapes *45* Roy Rowland
Our Virgin Island *58* Pat Jackson
Our Visit to China *57* Miklós Jancsó
Our War *43* Alberto Lattuada

Our Watch Dog *16* John R. Bray
Our Wealthy Nephew John *11* Bert Haldane
Our Wife *31* James W. Horne
Our Wife *41* John M. Stahl
Our Winning Season *78* Joseph Ruben
Our Wonderful Years *66* Heinosuke Gosho
Ouragan sur la Montagne, L' *22* Julien Duvivier
Ours, Un *21* Charles Burguet
Ours, L' *60* Edmond Séchan
Ours, L' *88* Jean-Jacques Annaud
Ours et la Poupée, L' *69* Michel Deville
Ours et la Sentinelle, L' *1899* Georges Méliès
Ourselves Alone *36* Brian Desmond Hurst, Walter Summers
Oursin dans la Poche, Un *77* Pascal Thomas
Oursins, Les *28* Jean Painlevé
Oursins, Les *53* Jean Painlevé
Out *82* Eli Hollander
Out Again, In Again *17* William Beaudine
Out All Night *27* William A. Seiter
Out All Night *33* Sam Taylor
Out an' In Again *19* Raoul Barré, Charles Bowers
Out and In *13* Mack Sennett
Out and Out Rout *66* Rudy Larriva
Out at Home *28* Sam Newfield
Out California Way *46* Lesley Selander
Out Cold *88* Malcolm Mowbray
Out for the Dough *17* William Beaudine
Out-Foxed *49* Tex Avery
Out from the Shadow *11* D. W. Griffith
Out in the World *39* Mark Donskoi
Out of a Clear Sky *18* Marshall Neilan
Out of Africa *85* Sydney Pollack
Out of Bounds *86* Richard Tuggle
Out of College *25* Kenji Mizoguchi
Out of Control *85* Allan Holzman
Out of Darkness *67* Valerio Zurlini
Out of Evil Cometh Good *12* Warwick Buckland
Out of Evil Cometh Good *14* Ethyle Batley
Out of Here! *77* Jorge Sanjinés
Out of His Element *12* A. E. Coleby
Out of It *69* Paul Williams
Out of Luck *19* Elmer Clifton
Out of Luck *23* Edward Sedgwick
Out of Order *83* Arthur Ellis
Out of Order *84* Carl Schenkel
Out of Order *87* Jonnie Turpie
Out of Rosenheim *87* Percy Adlon
Out of Season *75* Alan Bridges
Out of Sight *66* Lennie Weinrib
Out of Sight Out of Mind *25* Alexander Butler
Out of Singapore *32* Charles Hutchinson
Out of the Bag *17* Alfred Santell
Out of the Bandbox *53* Norman Redhead
Out of the Blue *31* Gene Gerrard, John Orton
Out of the Blue *47* Leigh Jason
Out of the Blue *80* Dennis Hopper
Out of the Body *88* Brian Trenchard-Smith

Out of the Box *44* Terry Bishop
Out of the Chorus *21* Herbert Blaché
Out of the Clouds *21* Leonard Franchon
Out of the Clouds *54* Basil Dearden, Michael Relph
Out of the Dark *88* Michael Schroeder
Out of the Darkness *58* Roger Corman
Out of the Darkness *78* Lee Madden
Out of the Darkness *85* John Krish
Out of the Depths *21* Edmund Cobb, Frank Reicher, Otis B. Thayer
Out of the Depths *45* D. Ross Lederman
Out of the Drifts *16* J. Searle Dawley
Out of the Dust *20* John P. McCarthy
Out of the Ether *33* Manny Gould, Ben Harrison
Out of the Fog *19* Albert Capellani
Out of the Fog *41* Anatole Litvak
Out of the Fog *62* Montgomery Tully
Out of the Frying Pan *14* Hay Plumb
Out of the Frying Pan *43* Edward H. Griffith
Out of the Inkwell *38* Dave Fleischer
Out of the Night *18* James Kirkwood
Out of the Night *20* Al Christie
Out of the Night *45* Edgar G. Ulmer
Out of the Past *12* Edwin J. Collins
Out of the Past *27* Dallas M. Fitzgerald
Out of the Past *33* Leslie Hiscott
Out of the Past *47* Jacques Tourneur
Out of the Ruins *15* Ashley Miller
Out of the Ruins *28* John Francis Dillon
Out of the Shadow *19* Émile Chautard
Out of the Shadow *61* Michael Winner
Out of the Silent North *22* William Worthington
Out of the Snows *20* Ralph Ince
Out of the Storm *20* William Parke
Out of the Storm *26* Louis Gasnier
Out of the Storm *48* R. G. Springsteen
Out of the Tiger's Mouth *62* Tim Whelan, Jr.
Out of the Underworld *16* Forest Holger-Madsen
Out of the Way! *31* Mikhail Chiaureli
Out of the West *26* Robert De Lacey
Out of the Wreck *17* William Desmond Taylor
Out of Thin Air *69* Gerry Levy
Out of This World *45* Hal Walker
Out-of-Towners, The *64* Delbert Mann
Out-of-Towners, The *69* Arthur Hiller
Out of True *51* Philip Leacock
Out of Work *09* Sidney Olcott
Out of Work for Years *75* Hiroshi Teshigahara
Out on Probation *59* Lou Place
Out on the Little Ranch *39* René Cardona
Out 1: Noli Me Tangere *71* Jacques Rivette
Out 1 Out 2 *72* Jacques Rivette
Out 1: Spectre *72* Jacques Rivette
Out-Stepping *31* Charles Lamont
Out-Takes from Maya Deren's Study in Choreography for Camera *75* Maya Deren
Out to Play *36* Philip Leacock*
Out to Win *23* Denison Clift
Out West *14* William Duncan
Out West *18* Roscoe Arbuckle

Pair of Antique Vases, A *11* A. E. Coleby
Pair of Bags, A *12* Frank Wilson
Pair of Briefs, A *62* Ralph Thomas
Pair of Cupids, A *18* Charles Brabin
Pair of Desperadoes, A *09* Lewin Fitz-
hamon
Pair of Desperate Swindlers, A *06* Charles
Raymond
Pair of Dummies, A *15* Cecil Birch
Pair of Gloves, A *20* Cecil Mannering
Pair of Handcuffs, A *12* Percy Stow
Pair of Hellions, A *24* Walter Willis
Pair of Kings, A *22* Norman Taurog*
Pair of New Boots, A *11* Percy Stow
Pair of Silk Stockings, A *18* Walter Ed-
wards
Pair of Sixes, A *18* Lawrence C. Windom
Pair of Socks, A *33* Charles Lamont
Pair of Spectacles, A *16* Alexander Butler
Pair of Stars, A *15* Cecil Birch
Pair of Tights, A *28* Leo McCarey
Pair of Trousers, A *12* A. E. Coleby
Pair of Truants, A *09* Lewin Fitzhamon
Paisà *46* Roberto Rossellini
Paisan *46* Roberto Rossellini
Paix chez Soi, La *21* Robert Saidreau
Pajama Game, The *57* George Abbott,
Stanley Donen
Pajama Party *64* Don Weis
Pajama Party in the Haunted House *66*
Don Weis
Pajamas *27* John G. Blystone
Pájaro del Faro, El *71* Santiago Álvarez
Pájaros de Baden-Baden, Los *74* Mario
Camus
Pak Slaag, Een *79* Bert Haanstra
Pal from Texas, The *39* Harry S. Webb
Pal Joey *57* George Sidney
Pal o' Mine *24* Edward J. LeSaint
Pal o' Mine *36* Widgey R. Newman
Pál Utcai Fiúk, A *17* Béla Balázs
Pál Utcai Fiúk *24* Béla Balázs
Pál Utcai Fiúk, A *68* Zoltán Fábri
Palace *84* Édouard Molinaro
Palace and Fortress *24* Alexander
Ivanovsky
Palace of Mystery, The *12* Stuart Kinder
Palace of Nudes *61* Pierre Mère
Palace of Pleasure, The *26* Emmett J.
Flynn
Palace of Shame *61* Pierre Mère
Palace of the Arabian Nights, The *05*
Georges Méliès
Palace of the Darkened Windows, The *20*
Henry Kolker
Palace Scandal *49* Paul Verhoeven
Palaces *27* Jean Durand
Palaces of a Queen *67* Michael Ingrams
Palaces of Peking *57* Miklós Jancsó
Paladini, I *82* Giacomo Battiato
Palais de Danse *28* Maurice Elvey
Palais des Mille et Une Nuits, Le *05*
Georges Méliès
Palais Royale *88* Martin Lavut
Palanquin, The *26* Teinosuke Kinugasa
Palanquin des Larmes, La *88* Jacques
Dorfmann
Palava Enkeli *84* Lauri Törhönen
Palaver *26* Geoffrey Barkas
Pale Arrow *57* George Waggner

Pale-Face *33* Ubbe Iwerks
Pale Face *85* Claude Gagnon
Pale Flower *63* Masahiro Shinoda
Pale Rider *85* Clint Eastwood
Paleface, The *21* Edward F. Cline, Buster
Keaton
Paleface, The *48* Norman Z. McLeod
Paleontologie *59* Bert Haanstra
Palermo *38* Arturo S. Mom
Palermo oder Wolfsburg *80* Werner
Schroeter
Palermo or Wolfsburg *80* Werner Schroe-
ter
Palestine *12* Sidney Olcott
Palindrome *69* Hollis Frampton
Palio *32* Alessandro Blasetti
Palipat-Lipat, Papalit-Palit *82* Lino Brocka
Palisade Street Kidnapping *85* Sándor
Mihályfy
Paliser Case, The *20* William Parke
Pallard the Punter *19* J. L. V. Leigh
Palle Alene i Verden *49* Astrid Henning-
Jensen
Palle Alone in the World *49* Astrid Hen-
ning-Jensen
Pallet on the Floor *84* Lynton Butler
Palm Beach *79* Albie Thoms
Palm Beach Girl, The *26* Erle C. Kenton
Palm Beach Story, The *42* Preston Sturges
Palm Court Orchestra, The *64* John Halas
Palm Springs *36* Aubrey H. Scotto
Palm Springs Affair *36* Aubrey H. Scotto
Palm Springs Weekend *63* Norman
Taurog
Palmier à l'Huile, Le *62* Jean Rouch
Palmy Days *31* A. Edward Sutherland
Paloma, La *30* Dave Fleischer
Paloma, La *36* Karl Heinz Martin
Paloma, La *37* Miguel Torres Contreras
Paloma, La *44* Helmut Käutner
Paloma, La *74* Daniel Schmid
Paloma Herida *63* Emilio Fernández
Palombella Rossa *89* Nanni Moretti
Palombière, La *83* Jean-Pierre Denis
Palomino, The *50* Ray Nazarro
Palomita Blanca *73* Raúl Ruiz
Palomita Brava *73* Raúl Ruiz
Palooka *34* Ben Stoloff
Palooka from Paducah *34* Charles Lamont
Pals *12* Allan Dwan
Pals *14* Frank Wilson
Pals *25* John P. McCarthy
Pals First *18* Edwin Carewe
Pals First *26* Edwin Carewe
Pals in Paradise *26* George B. Seitz
Pals in Peril *27* Richard Thorpe
Pals of the Golden West *51* William
Witney
Pals of the Pecos *41* Les Orlebeck
Pals of the Prairie *29* Louis King
Pals of the Range *10* Gilbert M. Anderson
Pals of the Range *35* Elmer Clifton
Pals of the Saddle *38* George Sherman
Pals of the Silver Sage *40* Albert Herman
Pal's Return *48* Leslie Goodwins
Paltoquet, Le *86* Michel Deville
Pályamunkások *57* István Gaál
Pam Kuso Kar *74* Jean Rouch
Pamela, Pamela You Are... *68* William
Rose

Pamela's Party *12* Hay Plumb
Pamiątka z Celulozą *54* Jerzy Kawalero-
wicz
Pamiętniki Chłopów *52* Andrzej Munk
Pampa Bárbara *43* Lucas Demare, Hugo
Fregonese
Pampas Salvaje *66* Hugo Fregonese
Pampered Youth *25* David Smith
Pamyat *71* Grigori Chukhrai
Pamyati Sergo Ordzhonikidzye *37* Dziga
Vertov
Pán *20* Pál Fejös
Pan *61* Herman van den Horst
Pan-American Exposition by Night *01* Ed-
win S. Porter
Pan-Americana *45* John H. Auer
Pan Chopali *61* Tadashi Imai
Pan Prokouk Akrobatem *59* Z. Rozkopal
Pan Prokouk Filmuje *48* Karel Zeman
Pan Prokouk Jede na Brigádu *47* Karel
Zeman
Pan Prokouk, Přítel Zvířátek *55* Karel
Zeman
Pan Prokouk Úřaduje *47* Karel Zeman
Pan Prokouk v Pokušení *47* Karel Zeman
Pan Prokouk Vynálezcem *48* Karel Zeman
Pan Redaktor Szaleje *38* H. Wencel
Pan Samochodzik i Niesamowity Dwór *87*
Janusz Kidawa
Pan the Piper *24* Herbert M. Dawley
Pan Twardowski *37* Henryk Szaro
Panama Canal, The *18* J. D. Leventhal
Panama Flo *32* Ralph Murphy
Panama Hattie *42* Norman Z. McLeod,
Vincente Minnelli
Panama Lady *39* Jack Hively
Panama Patrol *39* Charles Lamont
Panama Red *76* Robert C. Chinn
Panama Sal *57* William Witney
Panamint's Bad Man *38* Ray Taylor
Panchagni *87* Hariharan
Panchito Gang, The *86* Arturo Velazco
Pancho Villa *71* Eugenio Martin
Pancho Villa Returns *49* Miguel Torres
Contreras
Pancho's Hideaway *64* Friz Freleng
Panchvati *87* Basu Bhattacharya
Panda and the Magic Serpent *61* Kazuhiko
Okabe, Taiji Yabushita
Pandamonium *39* Widgey R. Newman
Pandavapuram *87* G. S. Panicker
Pandemonium *70* Toshio Matsumoto
Pandemonium *82* Alfred Sole
Pandemonium *88* Haydn Keenan
Pandevil *88* Gorman Bechard
Pandora and the Flying Dutchman *50* Al-
bert Lewin
Pandora's Box *28* G. W. Pabst
Pandora's Box *63* Joe Sarno
Pane, Amore e... *55* Dino Risi
Pane, Amore e Fantasia *53* Luigi Com-
encini
Pane, Amore e Gelosia *54* Luigi Com-
encini
Pane e Cioccolata *74* Franco Brusati
Pane e Zolfo *56* Gillo Pontecorvo
Pane, Vy Jste Vdova *71* Václav Vorlíček
Panel Story, The *79* Věra Chytilová
Paneless Window Washer, The *37* Dave
Fleischer

Paradies *86* Doris Dörrie
Paradies der Junggesellen *40* Kurt Hoffmann
Paradine Case, The *47* Alfred Hitchcock
Paradis de Satan, Le *38* Jean Delannoy, Félix Gandéra
Paradis des Pilotes Perdus, Le *49* Georges Lampin
Paradis Perdu, Le *38* Abel Gance
Paradis pour Tous *82* Alain Jessua
Paradise *26* Irvin Willat
Paradise *28* Denison Clift
Paradise *82* Stuart Gillard
Paradise *86* Doris Dörrie
Paradise Alley *31* John Argyle
Paradise Alley *57* Hugo Haas
Paradise Alley *78* Sylvester Stallone
Paradise Canyon *35* Carl Pierson
Paradise Express *37* Joseph Kane
Paradise for Three *37* Edward Buzzell
Paradise for Two *26* Gregory La Cava
Paradise for Two *37* Thornton Freeland
Paradise Garden *17* Fred J. Balshofer
Paradise, Hawaiian Style *66* Michael Moore
Paradise Hotel *17* Robert Dinesen
Paradise in Harlem *39* Joseph Seiden
Paradise Island *30* Bert Glennon
Paradise Isle *37* Arthur Greville Collins
Paradise Lagoon *57* Lewis Gilbert
Paradise Lost *11* D. W. Griffith
Paradise Lost, A *13* August Blom
Paradise Lost *38* Abel Gance
Paradise Motel *85* Cary Medoway
Paradise Not Yet Lost, or Oona's Fifth Year *80* Jonas Mekas
Paradise Now *70* Sheldon Rochlin
Paradise Place *77* Gunnel Lindblom
Paradise Road *36* Martin Frič
Paradise Road *69* Carl K. Hittleman
Paradise Without Adam *18* Victor Tourjansky
Paradiso Perduto, Il *48* Luciano Emmer, Enrico Gras
Paradiso Terrestre, Il *40* Luciano Emmer, Enrico Gras, Tatiana Grauding
Paradiso Terrestre *57* Luciano Emmer, Robert Enrico
Paradissos Anigi me Antiklidi, O *87* Vassilis Buduris
Paradistorg *77* Gunnel Lindblom
Paraguelia *80* Pavlos Tassios
Paraíso Ortopédico, El *69* Patricio Guzmán
Paraísos Perdidos, Los *86* Basilio Martín Patino
Parakh *60* Bimal Roy
Parallax View, The *74* Alan J. Pakula
Parallèles *62* Louis Daquin
Parallels *80* Mark Schoenberg
Parallels and Horizontal *24* Viking Eggeling
Paralytic, The *12* Alice Guy-Blaché
Param Dharam *88* Swaroop Kumar
Paramatta *37* Douglas Sirk
Paramedics *88* Stuart Margolin
Paramount on Parade *30* Dorothy Arzner, Otto Brower, Edmund Goulding, Victor Heerman, Edwin H. Knopf, Rowland V. Lee, Ernst Lubitsch, Lothar Mendes, Vic-

tor Schertzinger, A. Edward Sutherland, Frank Tuttle
Paraninfo, Il *40* Amleto Palermi
Paranoia *64* Eduardo De Filippo, Marco Ferreri, Luciano Salce
Paranoia *68* Umberto Lenzi
Paranoia *69* Umberto Lenzi
Paranoiac *62* Freddie Francis
Paranomi, I *58* Nikos Koundouros
Paraplíčko *57* Břetislav Pojar
Parapluie Fantastique, La *03* Georges Méliès
Parapluie Fantastique ou Dix Femmes Sous Une Ombrelle, La *03* Georges Méliès
Parapluies de Cherbourg, Les *64* Jacques Demy
Paras Pathar *57* Satyajit Ray
Parashuram *78* Mrinal Sen
Parasite, The *25* Louis Gasnier
Parasite *81* Charles Band
Parasite Murders, The *74* David Cronenberg
Parasites *29* Frank Lloyd
Parasites of Life *18* Yakov Protazanov
Parasol, El *65* Dino Risi
Parasol, The *65* Dino Risi
Parasuram *78* Mrinal Sen
Paratroop Command *59* William Witney
Paratrooper *53* Terence Young
Párbeszéd *63* János Herskó
Parcel Post Pete: Not All His Troubles Are Little Ones *16* Frank Moser
Parcels or the Baby *13* Will P. Kellino
Parchain *30* Rajaram Vanakudre Shantaram
Pardesi *41* Rajaram Vanakudre Shantaram
Pardesi *57* Khwaja Ahmad Abbas, Vassili M. Pronin
Pardessus de Demi-Saison, Le *17* Jacques Feyder
Pardessus le Mur *23* Pierre Colombier
Pardessus le Mur *59* Jean-Paul Le Chanois
Pardners *56* Norman Taurog
Pardon Me But Your Teeth Are in My Neck *67* Roman Polanski
Pardon Mon Affaire *76* Yves Robert
Pardon Mon Affaire, Too *77* Yves Robert
Pardon My Brush *64* John K. McCarthy
Pardon My French *21* Sidney Olcott
Pardon My French *51* Bernard Vorhaus
Pardon My Gun *30* Robert De Lacey
Pardon My Gun *42* William Berke
Pardon My Nerve! *22* B. Reeves Eason
Pardon My Past *45* Leslie Fenton
Pardon My Pups *34* Charles Lamont
Pardon My Rhythm *44* Felix E. Feist
Pardon My Sarong *42* Erle C. Kenton
Pardon My Stripes *42* John H. Auer
Pardon My Trunk *52* Gianni Franciolini
Pardon Our Nerve *39* H. Bruce Humberstone
Pardon Tévedtem *33* Géza von Bolváry, Steve Sekely
Pardon Us *31* James Parrott
Pardonnez-Nous Nos Offenses *56* Robert Hossein
Pareh, Song of the Rice *35* Mannus Franken
Parema, Creature from the Starworld *22* Mano Ziffer-Teschenbruck

Parent Trap, The *61* David Swift
Parentage *18* Hobart Henley
Parental Claim *86* Willy Rameau
Parenthood *89* Ron Howard
Parents *88* Bob Balaban
Parents, Awake *80* Keisuke Kinoshita
Parents on Trial *39* Sam Nelson
Parents Terribles, Les *48* Jean Cocteau
Parfum de la Dame en Noir, Le *30* Marcel L'Herbier
Parfum de la Dame en Noir, Le *49* Louis Daquin
Parfums, Les *24* Jean Grémillon
Parfums Revillon *69* François Reichenbach
Pari e Dispari *79* Sergio Corbucci
Pari Original, Un *12* Max Linder
Pariahs of Glory *63* Henri Decoin
Parias de la Gloire *63* Henri Decoin
Parigi È Sempre Parigi *51* Luciano Emmer
Parigi o Cara *62* Vittorio Caprioli
Parigine, Le *62* Marc Allégret, Claude Barma, Michel Boisrond, Jacques Poitrenaud
Parinati *88* Prakash Jha
Parinda *88* Vidhu Vinod Chopra
Parineeta *52* Bimal Roy
Paris *24* René Hervil
Paris *26* Edmund Goulding
Paris *29* Clarence Badger
Paris After Dark *23* Hans Wierendorf
Paris After Dark *43* Léonide Moguy
Paris Asleep *23* René Clair
Paris at Midnight *26* E. Mason Hopper
Paris au Mois d'Août *65* Pierre Granier-Deferre
Paris-Béguin *31* Augusto Genina
Paris Belongs to Us *60* Jacques Rivette
Paris Blues *61* Martin Ritt
Paris Bound *29* Edward H. Griffith
Paris Brûle-t-il? *65* René Clément
Paris by Night *88* David Hare
Paris Calling *41* Edwin L. Marin
Paris-Cinéma *29* Pierre Chénal, Jean Mitry
Paris Commune *37* Grigori Roshal
Paris-Deauville *35* Jean Delannoy
Paris des Mannequins, Le *62* François Reichenbach
Paris des Photographes, Le *62* François Reichenbach
Paris Does Strange Things *56* Jean Renoir
Paris en Cinq Jours *26* Pierre Colombier
Paris Erotika *63* José Benazeraf
Paris Est le Désert Français *57* Roger Leenhardt
Paris Exposition, 1900 *00* Georges Méliès
Paris Express *28* Marcel Duhamel, Pierre Prévert
Paris Express *52* Harold French
Paris Follies of 1956 *55* Leslie Goodwins
Paris Frills *45* Jacques Becker
Paris Girls *29* Henri Roussel
Paris Goes Away *80* Jacques Rivette
Paris Green *20* Jerome Storm
Paris Holiday *58* Gerd Oswald
Paris Honeymoon *38* Frank Tuttle
Paris Hotel *56* Henri Verneuil
Paris in August *65* Pierre Granier-Deferre
Paris in Spring *35* Lewis Milestone
Paris in the Month of August *65* Pierre Granier-Deferre

Partners of the Sunset *22* Robert H. Townley

Partners of the Sunset *48* Lambert Hillyer

Partners of the Tide *21* L. V. Jefferson

Partners of the Trail *31* Wallace Fox

Partners of the Trail *44* Lambert Hillyer

Partners Please *32* Lloyd Richards

Partners Three *19* Fred Niblo

Parts: The Clonus Horror *78* Robert S. Fiveson

Party, The *64* Robert Altman

Party, The *68* Blake Edwards

Party, The *81* Claude Pinoteau

Party, The *89* Ugo Giorgetti

Party and the Guests, The *66* Jan Němec

Party Animal, The *84* David Beaird

Party Camp *86* Gary Graver

Party Card, The *36* Ivan Pyriev

Party Cat *50* Joseph Barbera, William Hanna

Party Crashers, The *58* Bernard Girard

Party Fever *38* George Sidney

Party Girl *30* Victor Halperin

Party Girl *45* Christy Cabanne

Party Girl *58* Nicholas Ray

Party Girls *89* Chuck Vincent

Party Girls for the Candidate *64* Robert Angus

Party Husbands *31* Clarence Badger

Party Is Over, The *59* Leopoldo Torre-Nilsson

Party Line *88* William Webb

Party Party *83* Terry Winsor

Party Wire *35* Erle C. Kenton

Party's Over, The *34* Walter Lang

Party's Over, The *62* Guy Hamilton

Parvi Urok *59* Vladimir Petrov, Rangel Vulchanov

Pa's Comments on the Morning News *02* George Albert Smith

Pas de Caviar pour Tante Olga *65* Jean Becker

Pas de Deux *67* Norman McLaren

Pas de Femmes *32* Mario Bonnard

Pas de la Mule, Le *30* Jean Epstein

Pas de Mentalité *60* Alvin Rakoff

Pas de Roses pour O.S.S. 117 *67* André Hunebelle

Pas de Violence Entre Nous *72* Nelson Pereira Dos Santos

Pas Folle la Guêpe *72* Jean Delannoy

Pas Question le Samedi *65* Alex Joffé

Pas Si Bête *28* André Berthomieu

Pas Si Bête *47* André Berthomieu

Pas Si Méchant Que Ça... *74* Claude Goretta

Pasado Acusa, El *38* David Selman

Pasajeros de una Pesadilla *86* Fernando Ayala

Pasażerka *63* Witold Lesiewicz, Andrzej Munk

Pascali's Island *88* James Dearden

Pascoli Rossi, I *63* Alfredo Antonini

Paseo Sobre una Guerra Antigua *48* Juan Antonio Bardem, Luis García Berlanga

Pasha's Wives, The *42* Marc Sorkin

Pasht *65* Stan Brakhage

Paşi spre Lună *63* Ion Popescu-Gopo

Pasión Desnuda, La *52* Luis César Amadori

Pasión Según Berenice, La *77* Jaime Humberto Hermosillo

Pasionaria, La *56* Emilio Fernández

Paso Doble *86* Dan Pița

Pasodoble *88* José Luis García Sánchez

Pasodoble pre Troch *86* Vladimír Balco

Pasos Largos: El Último Bandido Andaluz *87* Rafael Moreno Alba

Pasqua in Sicilia *55* Vittorio De Seta

Pasquale *16* William Desmond Taylor

Pasqualino Settebellezze *75* Lina Wertmuller

Pass It On *13* Frank Wilson

Pass of Arms *72* Peter Elford

Pass the Ammo *87* David Beaird

Pass the Gravy *28* Leo McCarey

Pass to Romance *44* Leslie Goodwins

Pass Your Exam First *76* Maurice Pialat

Passa la Ruina *19* Mario Bonnard

Passa l'Amore *33* Amleto Palermi

Passa Sartana...e l'Ombra della Tua Morte *69* Sean O'Neal

Passado e o Presente, O *72* Manoel De Oliveira

Passage, The *40* Alexander Ivanov

Passage, The *78* J. Lee-Thompson

Passage, Le *86* René Manzor

Passage, The *86* René Manzor

Passage, The *87* Harry Thompson

Passage Dangereux, Mont Blanc *1897* Georges Méliès

Passage du Rhin, Le *60* André Cayatte

Passage from Hong Kong *41* D. Ross Lederman

Passage Home *55* Roy Ward Baker

Passage of Love *65* Desmond Davis

Passage Secret *85* Laurent Perrin

Passage to India, A *84* David Lean

Passage to London *37* Lawrence Huntington

Passage to Marseille *44* Michael Curtiz

Passage to Marseilles *44* Michael Curtiz

Passage West *51* Lewis R. Foster

Passager, Le *26* Jacques De Baroncelli

Passager de la Pluie, Le *69* René Clément

Passagère, La *63* Witold Lesiewicz, Andrzej Munk

Passagers, Les *76* Serge Leroy

Passagers de la Grande Ourse, Les *39* Paul Grimault

Passages from "Finnegans Wake" *65* Mary Ellen Bute

Passages from James Joyce's "Finnegans Wake" *65* Mary Ellen Bute

Passaggio del Reno, Il *60* André Cayatte

Passagier, Der *88* Thomas Brasch

Passagierin, Die *63* Witold Lesiewicz, Andrzej Munk

Passante, La *11* Victorin Jasset

Passante, La *51* Henri Calef

Passante, La *82* Jacques Rouffio

Passaporto Rosso *36* Guido Brignone

Passatore, Il *50* Duilio Coletti

Passé de Monique, Le *17* Louis Feuillade

Passe du Diable, La *57* Jacques Dupont, Pierre Schöndörffer

Passe Montagne *79* Jean-François Stévenin

Passe-Muraille, Le *50* Jean Boyer

Passé Simple, Le *77* Michel Drach

Passe Ton Bac d'Abord *76* Maurice Pialat

Passe Tous Bac *76* Maurice Pialat

Passenger, The *63* Witold Lesiewicz, Andrzej Munk

Passenger, The *74* Michelangelo Antonioni

Passenger to London *37* Lawrence Huntington

Passenger to Tokyo *54* Ken Hughes

Passengers Landing at Harbour of Granville *1899* Georges Méliès

Passerby, The *12* Oscar Apfel

Passerelle, La *88* Jean-Claude Sussfeld

Passers-By *16* Stanner E. V. Taylor

Passers-By *20* J. Stuart Blackton

Passing, The *83* John W. Huckert

Passing by the Lorraine *50* Georges Franju

Passing Clouds *40* John Harlow

Passing Fancy *33* Yasujiro Ozu

Passing of a Soul, The *15* Cecil M. Hepworth

Passing of Black Pete, The *14* Joe Evans

Passing of Evil, The *70* Jerry Paris

Passing of Love and Hate, The *34* Kenji Mizoguchi

Passing of Mr. Quin, The *28* Leslie Hiscott

Passing of the Beast *14* Wallace Reid

Passing of the Oklahoma Outlaws, The *15* William Tilghman

Passing of the Old Four-Wheeler, The *12* Warwick Buckland

Passing of the Third Floor Back, The *18* Herbert Brenon

Passing of the Third Floor Back, The *35* Berthold Viertel

Passing of Two-Gun Hicks, The *14* William S. Hart

Passing of Wolf MacLean, The *24* Paul Hurst

Passing Shadows *34* Leslie Hiscott

Passing Show, The *33* Raymond Cannon

Passing Stranger, The *54* John Arnold

Passing the Buck *19* Larry Semon

Passing the Course *87* José Luis García Agraz

Passing the Grip *17* William Beaudine

Passing the Hat *27* William C. Nolan

Passing Through *16* Allan Dwan

Passing Through *21* William A. Seiter

Passing Through *77* Larry Clark

Passing Thru *21* William A. Seiter

Passion, La *02* Lucien Nonguet, Ferdinand Zecca

Passion *17* Richard Ridgely

Passion *19* Ernst Lubitsch

Passion *40* Walter Janssen

Passion *51* Georges Lampin

Passion *54* Allan Dwan

Passion *60* Jiří Trnka

Passion *64* Yasuzo Masumura

Passion, A *69* Ingmar Bergman

Passion, En *69* Ingmar Bergman

Passion *81* Jean-Luc Godard

Passion *85* Sylvia Chang

Passion: A Letter in 16mm *86* Patricia Rozema

Passion and the Revenge *44* Youssef Wahby

Passion Béatrice, La *86* Bertrand Tavernier

Passion de Jeanne d'Arc, La *27* Carl Theodor Dreyer

Passion de Jésus, La *07* Segundo De Chomón
Passion Fire *47* Minoru Shibuya
Passion Flower, The *21* Herbert Brenon
Passion Flower *30* William DeMille
Passion Flower Hotel, The *77* André Farwagi
Passion for Life *48* Jean-Paul Le Chanois
Passion Fruit *21* John Ince
Passion Holiday *63* Wynn Miles
Passion in Hot Hollows *67* Joe Sarno
Passion in the Desert *31* Rex Ingram, Alice Terry
Passion in the Sun *64* Dale Berry
Passion Island *27* H. Manning Haynes
Passion Island *41* Emilio Fernández
Passion of a Woman Teacher, The *26* Kenji Mizoguchi
Passion of Anna, The *69* Ingmar Bergman
Passion of Beatrice, The *86* Bertrand Tavernier
Passion of Jesus, The *60* Manoel De Oliveira
Passion of Joan of Arc, The *27* Carl Theodor Dreyer
Passion of Love *81* Ettore Scola
Passion of Remembrance, The *86* Maureen Blackwood
Passion of St. Francis, The *32* Giulio Antamoro
Passion of Slow Fire, The *60* Édouard Molinaro
Passion of the Sun *64* Dale Berry
Passion Pit, The *65* Ebar Lobato
Passion Pits, The *69* Stuart McGowan
Passion Selon les Coras, La *73* François Reichenbach
Passion Song, The *28* Harry Hoyt
Passion Street *64* Oscar Daley
Passion Street U.S.A. *64* Oscar Daley
Passion Streets *64* Oscar Daley
Passion Without End *49* Kon Ichikawa
Passion Without Limit, The *49* Kon Ichikawa
Passionate Adventure, The *24* Graham Cutts
Passionate Affair *60* Henri Decoin
Passionate Demons, The *61* Nils Reinhardt Christensen
Passionate Friends, The *22* Maurice Elvey
Passionate Friends, The *48* David Lean
Passionate Heart, The *62* Otakar Vávra
Passionate Pastime *57* Hans Richter
Passionate Pilgrim, The *21* Robert Vignola
Passionate Plumber, The *32* Edward Sedgwick
Passionate Quest, The *26* J. Stuart Blackton
Passionate Sentry, The *52* Anthony Kimmins
Passionate Stranger, The *56* Muriel Box
Passionate Strangers, The *68* Eddie Romero
Passionate Summer *57* Charles Brabant
Passionate Summer *58* Rudolph Cartier
Passionate Sunday *61* William Kyriakys, Radley Metzger
Passionate Thief, The *60* Mario Monicelli
Passionate Youth *25* Dallas M. Fitzgerald
Passione d'Amore *81* Ettore Scola

Passione Tzigane *16* Ernesto Maria Pasquali
Passionelle *46* Edmond T. Gréville
Passionless Moments *84* Jane Campion
Passionnément *21* Georges Lacroix
Passions—He Had Three *13* Henry Lehrman
Passions of Men, The *13* Alexander Butler
Passions of Men, The *14* Wilfred Noy
Passions of the Sea *23* Raoul Walsh
Passion's Pathway *24* Bertram Bracken
Passion's Playground *20* John A. Barry
Passkey to Danger *46* Lesley Selander
Passover Miracle, A *14* Sidney Olcott
Passover Plot, The *76* Michael Campus
Passport for a Corpse *62* Mario Gariazzo
Passport Husband *38* James Tinling
Passport to Adventure *44* Ray McCarey
Passport to Alcatraz *40* Lewis D. Collins
Passport to China *60* Michael Carreras
Passport to Destiny *44* Ray McCarey
Passport to Fame *34* John Ford
Passport to Hell, A *32* Frank Lloyd
Passport to Hell *40* Lewis D. Collins
Passport to Hell *51* Pietro Germi
Passport to Oblivion *65* Val Guest
Passport to Paradise *32* George B. Seitz
Passport to Pimlico *48* Henry Cornelius
Passport to Shame *59* Alvin Rakoff
Passport to Suez *43* André De Toth
Passport to Treason *55* Robert S. Baker
Password Is Courage, The *62* Andrew L. Stone
Past *50* Martin Frič
Past and Present *72* Manoel De Oliveira
Past Caring *85* Richard Eyre
Past of Mary Holmes, The *33* Harlan Thompson, Slavko Vorkapich
Past Perfumance *55* Chuck Jones
Past, Present, Future *86* Shyam Benegal
Pastasciutta nel Deserto *61* Carlo Ludovico Bragaglia
Paste *16* Ralph Dewsbury
Pasteboard Crown, A *22* Travers Vale
Pasteboard Lover, The *28* Lawrence C. Windom
Pasteur *22* Jean Benoît-Lévy, Jean Epstein
Pasteur *35* Sacha Guitry
Pasteur *47* Jean Painlevé, Georges Rouquier
Pastor Hall *40* Roy Boulting
Pastor of Vejlby, The *31* George Schneevoigt
Pastoral *76* Otar Ioseliani
Pastores da Noite, Os *77* Marcel Camus
Pastori di Orgosolo *58* Vittorio De Seta
Pastor's Daughter, The *16* Forest Holger-Madsen
Pastor's End *68* Evald Schorm
Pat and Mike *52* George Cukor
Pat Garrett and Billy the Kid *73* Sam Peckinpah
Patagonia Rebelde, La *74* Héctor Olivera
Patakin *85* Manuel Octavio Gómez
Patate *65* Robert Thomas
Patates, Les *69* Claude Autant-Lara
Patayin Mo sa Sindak si Barbara *73* Celso Ad Castillo
Patch *67* Don Siegel, Robert Totten
Patch of Blue, A *65* Guy Green

Patched Coat, The *12* Edwin J. Collins
Patchwork Girl of Oz, The *14* J. Farrell MacDonald
Patent Ductus Arteriosus *47* Pat Jackson
Patent Leather Kid, The *27* Alfred Santell
Patent Leather Pug, The *26* Albert S. Rogell
Patent Medicine Kid, The *28* Manny Gould, Ben Harrison
Pater, Le *10* Louis Feuillade
Páter Vojtěch *28* Martin Frič
Páter Vojtěch *36* Martin Frič
Paternal Home, The *59* Lev Kulidzhanov
Paternal Instinct *26* Charles Barnett
Paternal Love *15* Frank Lloyd
Paternity *81* David Steinberg
Pater's Patent Painter *09* Percy Stow
Path of Glory, The *34* Dallas Bower
Path of Happiness, The *16* Elaine Sterne
Path of Hope, The *50* Pietro Germi
Path She Chose, The *20* Phil Rosen
Path to the Rainbow, The *15* Joseph Smiley
Pathar Dil *88* Surendra Mohan
Pathé Radio Music Hall *45* Fred Watts
Pather Panchali *55* Satyajit Ray
Pathetic Fallacy *58* Ritwik Ghatak
Pathetic Gazette, The *24* Adrian Brunel
Pathétone Parade *34* Fred Watts
Pathétone Parade of 1936 *36* Fred Watts
Pathétone Parade of 1938 *37* Fred Watts
Pathétone Parade of 1939 *39* Fred Watts
Pathétone Parade of 1940 *39* Fred Watts
Pathétone Parade of 1941 *41* Fred Watts
Pathétone Parade of 1942 *42* Fred Watts
Pathfinder, The *52* Sidney Salkow
Pathfinder *87* Nils Gaup
Paths of Glory *57* Stanley Kubrick
Paths of Hate *64* Marino Girolami
Paths to Paradise *25* Clarence Badger
Pati Parmeshwar *89* Madan Joshi
Patience *20* Paul Leni
Patient, The *30* Norman Taurog
Patient in Room 18, The *38* Bobby Connolly, Crane Wilbur
Patient Porky *40* Robert Clampett
Patient Vanishes, The *41* Lawrence Huntington
Pátio, O *58* Glauber Rocha
Patio, The *58* Glauber Rocha
Pâtissier et Ramoneur *04* Alice Guy-Blaché
Pâtres du Désordre, Les *67* Nikos Papatakis
Patria, Amore e Dovere *37* Alessandro Blasetti
Patria o Muerte *61* Jerzy Hoffman
Patriarch #1 and #2, The *77* Claude Jutra
Patricia Brent, Spinster *19* Geoffrey H. Malins
Patricia et Jean-Baptiste *66* Jean-Pierre Lefèbvre
Patricia Gets Her Man *37* Reginald Purdell
Patrick *78* Richard Franklin
Patrick Is Still Alive *80* Mario Landi
Patrick Still Lives *80* Mario Landi
Patrick the Great *44* Frank Ryan
Patrick Vive Ancora *80* Mario Landi

Patrie 13 Albert Capellani

Patrie 45 Louis Daquin

Patrimonio Nacional 80 Luis García Berlanga

Patriot, The 16 William S. Hart

Patriot, The 28 Ernst Lubitsch

Patriot, The 37 Maurice Tourneur

Patriot, The 79 Alexander Kluge

Patriot, The 86 Frank Harris

Patriot Game, The 78 Arthur Mac Caig

Patriote, Le 37 Maurice Tourneur

Patriotic Arabella 15 James Read

Patriotic English Girl, A 14 Leedham Bantock

Patriotic Mrs. Brown 16 Will P. Kellino

Patriotic Woman, The 79 Alexander Kluge

Patriotin, Die 79 Alexander Kluge

Patriotism 15 Flohri

Patriotism 64 Joyce Wieland

Patriots 33 Boris Barnet

Patriots 37 Karl Ritter

Patrioty 33 Boris Barnet

Patrolling the Ether 44 Paul Burnford

Patron Est Mort, Le 38 Henri Storck

Patronne, La 49 Robert Dhéry

Patrouille de Choc 56 Claude Bernard-Aubert

Pat's Birthday 62 Robert Breer, Claes Oldenburg

Pat's Day Off 12 Mack Sennett

Pat's Idea 13 Mark Melford

Patsy 17 John G. Adolfi

Patsy 21 John McDermott

Patsy, The 27 King Vidor

Patsy, The 64 Jerry Lewis

Patsy, The 83 Denis Amar

Pattern for Plunder 63 John Ainsworth

Pattern of Evil 62 Jerald Intrator

Patterns 56 Fielder Cook

Patterns of Power 56 Fielder Cook

Pattes Blanches 48 Jean Grémillon

Pattes de Mouche 36 Jean Grémillon

Patti Rocks 87 David Burton Morris

Patto Col Diavolo 48 Luigi Chiarini

Patto d'Amicizia 51 Piero Nelli

Patton 69 Franklin J. Schaffner

Patton: A Salute to a Rebel 69 Franklin J. Schaffner

Patton il Generale d'Acciaio 69 Franklin J. Schaffner

Patton: Lust for Glory 69 Franklin J. Schaffner

Pattuglia di Passo San Giacomo, La 54 Ermanno Olmi

Pattuglia Perduto, La 54 Piero Nelli

Patty Hearst 88 Paul Schrader

Patu 83 Merata Mita

Pauki 42 Ilya Trauberg, I. Zemgano

Paul and Michelle 74 Lewis Gilbert

Paul Bowles in Morocco 70 Gary Conklin

Paul Chevrolet and the Ultimate Hallucination 85 Pim de la Parra

Paul Chevrolet en de Ultieme Hallucinatie 85 Pim de la Parra

Paul Delvaux, or The Forbidden Woman 70 Henri Storck

Paul Delvaux ou Les Femmes Défendues 70 Henri Storck

Paul et Michele 74 Lewis Gilbert

Paul Gauguin 57 Folco Quilici

Paul Jones, Jr. 24 George Marshall

Paul Raymond's Erotica 81 Brian Smedley-Aston

Paul Sleuth and the Mystic Seven 13 Charles C. Calvert

Paul Sleuth, Crime Investigator — The Burglary Syndicate 12 Dave Aylott

Paul Sleuth, Investigator and the Burglary Syndicate 12 Dave Aylott

Paul Street Boys 24 Béla Balázs

Paul Street Boys, The 68 Zoltán Fábri

Paul Swan 65 Andy Warhol

Paul Temple Returns 52 Maclean Rogers

Paul Temple's Triumph 50 Maclean Rogers

Paul Tomkowitz, Railway Switchman 54 Roman Kroitor

Paul Valéry 59 Roger Leenhardt

Paula 15 Cecil Birch

Paula 47 Richard Wallace

Paula 52 Rudolph Maté

Paule Pauländer 75 Reinhard Hauff

Paulette 86 Claude Confortes

Paulina 1880 72 Jean-Louis Bertucelli

Paulina S'en Va 69 André Téchiné

Pauline à la Plage 83 Eric Rohmer

Pauline at the Beach 83 Eric Rohmer

Paul's Awakening 85 Michele Saponaro

Paulus Chantant "Coquin de Printemps" 1897 Georges Méliès

Paulus Chantant "Derrière l'Omnibus" 1897 Georges Méliès

Paulus Chantant "Duelliste Marseillais" 1897 Georges Méliès

Paulus Chantant "En Revenant d'la Revue" 1897 Georges Méliès

Paulus Chantant "Père la Victoire" 1897 Georges Méliès

Paumé, Le 71 Michel Audiard

Paunch 'n' Judy 40 Ben Harrison

Pauper Millionaire, The 22 Frank Crane

Paura, La 54 Roberto Rossellini

Paura e Amore 88 Margarethe von Trotta

Paura nella Città dei Morti Viventi 80 Lucio Fulci

Pauvre John ou Les Aventures d'un Buveur de Whiskey 07 Georges Méliès

Pauvre Pompier 06 Alice Guy-Blaché

Pauvres Gosses 09 Léonce Perret

Pavage Moderne 38 Roger Leenhardt

Pavane pour un Crétin Défunt 71 Jean-Pierre Mocky

Pavé, Le 05 Alice Guy-Blaché

Pavé de Paris, Le 60 Henri Decoin

Pavel Korchagin 56 Alexander Alov, Vladimir Naumov

Pavillon Brûle, Le 41 Jacques De Baroncelli

Pavlinka 52 Alexander Zarkhi

Pavlínka 74 Karel Kachyňa

Pavlova — A Woman for All Time 85 Emil Lotyanu

Pavučina 86 Zdeněk Zaoral

Paw 59 Astrid Henning-Jensen, Bjarne Henning-Jensen

Paw — Boy of Two Worlds 59 Astrid Henning-Jensen, Bjarne Henning-Jensen

Pawn, The 68 Jean Carmen Dillow

Pawn of Fate, The 16 Maurice Tourneur

Pawn of Fortune, The 14 Leopold Wharton

Pawn Ticket 210 22 Scott R. Dunlap

Pawnbroker, The 64 Sidney Lumet

Pawnbrokers, The 20 Raoul Barré, Charles Bowers

Pawnbroker's Heart, The 17 Edward F. Cline

Pawned 22 Irvin Willat

Pawnee 57 George Waggner

Pawns of Fate 15 Frank Lloyd

Pawns of Mars 15 Theodore Marston

Pawns of Passion 27 Carmine Gallone

Pawnshop, The 16 Charles Chaplin

Paws of the Bear 17 Reginald Barker

Pax Æterna 16 Forest Holger-Madsen

Pax Domine 23 René Leprince

Pay As You Enter 28 Lloyd Bacon

Pay As You Exit 36 Gordon Douglas

Pay Car, The 09 Sidney Olcott

Pay Day 18 Mrs. Sidney Drew, Sidney Rankin Drew

Pay Day 22 Charles Chaplin

Pay Day 22 Dave Fleischer

Pay Day 38 Leo T. Hurwitz, Paul Strand

Pay Dirt 16 B. Reeves Eason, Henry King

Pay Me 17 Joseph De Grasse

Pay-Off, The 26 Del Henderson

Pay-Off, The 30 Lowell Sherman

Pay-Off, The 35 Robert Florey

Pay-Off, The 43 William Berke

Pay-Off, The 59 Richard Harbinger

Pay or Die! 60 Richard Wilson

Pay the Devil 57 Jack Arnold

Pay Tribute to the Fire 72 Tolomush Okeyev

Payable on Demand 24 Leo D. Maloney

Payasada de la Vida 35 Miguel Zacarías

Paybox Adventure 36 Will P. Kellino

Payday 72 Daryl Duke

Paying Him Out 15 Will P. Kellino

Paying His Debt 18 Clifford Smith

Paying Off Old Scores 07 Percy Stow

Paying the Limit 24 Tom Gibson

Paying the Penalty 13 Warwick Buckland

Paying the Penalty 27 Josef von Sternberg

Paying the Piper 21 George Fitzmaurice

Paying the Price 16 Frank Crane

Paying the Price 27 David Selman

Paying the Rent 20 John McDonagh

Paymaster's Son, The 13 Thomas Ince

Payment, The 16 Raymond B. West

Payment Deferred 32 Lothar Mendes

Payment Guaranteed 21 George L. Cox

Payment in Blood 67 Enzo G. Castellari

Payment in Kind 67 Peter Duffell

Payment on Demand 51 Kurt Bernhardt

Payoff, The 42 Arthur Dreifuss

Payroll 61 Sidney Hayers

Pays Bassari 52 Pierre-Dominique Gaisseau

Pays Bleu, Le 77 Jean-Charles Tacchella

Pays de Cocagne 70 Pierre Etaix

Pays de la Terre Sans Arbre, Le 79 Pierre Perrault

Pays d'Octobre 83 Robert Parrish, Bertrand Tavernier

Pays d'Où Je Viens, Le 56 Marcel Carné

Pays Sans Bon Sens, Un 70 Pierre Perrault

Pays Sans Étoiles, Le 46 Georges Lacombe

Peer Gynt *39* Fritz Wendhausen
Peer Gynt *41* David Bradley
Peesua lae Dokmai *85* Euthana Mukdasnit
Peg o' My Heart *19* William DeMille
Peg o' My Heart *22* King Vidor
Peg o' My Heart *33* Robert Z. Leonard
Peg o' the Pirates *18* Oscar A. C. Lund
Peg o' the Sea *17* Eugene Nowland
Peg of Old Drury *35* Herbert Wilcox
Peg of the Pirates *18* Oscar A. C. Lund
Peg Woffington *12* A. E. Coleby
Pegeen *20* David Smith
Peggie and the Roundheads *12* A. E. Coleby
Peggy *16* Charles Giblyn
Peggy *50* Frederick De Cordova
Peggy As Peacemaker *13* Ethyle Batley
Peggy Becomes a Boy Scout *12* Ethyle Batley
Peggy Does Her Darndest *19* George D. Baker
Peggy Gets Rid of the Baby *12* Ethyle Batley
Peggy Leads the Way *17* Lloyd Ingraham
Peggy of the Secret Service *25* John P. McGowan
Peggy on a Spree *46* Arne Mattsson
Peggy på Vift *46* Arne Mattsson
Peggy Puts It Over *21* Gustav von Seyffertitz
Peggy Rebels *17* Henry King
Peggy Sue Got Married *86* Francis Ford Coppola
Peggy, the Will-o'-the-Wisp *17* Tod Browning
Peggy's Blue Skylight *64* Joyce Wieland
Peggy's Burglar *13* Ralph Ince
Peggy's New Papa *14* Ethyle Batley
Pègre de Paris, La *06* Alice Guy-Blaché
Pehla Admi *48* Bimal Roy
Pehlivan *64* Maurice Pialat
Peine d'Amour *14* Henri Fescourt
Peine du Talion, La *06* Albert Capellani
Peine du Talion, La *16* Louis Feuillade
Peintre Barbouillard et le Tableau Diabolique, Le *05* Georges Méliès
Peintre et Ivrogne *05* Alice Guy-Blaché
Peintre Neo-Impressioniste, Le *10* Émile Cohl
Pékin Central *86* Camille De Casabianca
Pekin Teki Suika *89* Nobuhiko Obayashi
Peking *38* Fumio Kamei
Peking Blonde *67* Nicolas Gessner
Peking Central *86* Camille De Casabianca
Peking Express *51* William Dieterle
Peking Medallion, The *66* Bill Catching, James Hill
Peking Opera Blues *86* Hark Tsui
Peking Palotái *57* Miklós Jancsó
Pekka As a Policeman *87* Visa Mäkinen
Pekka Puupää Poliisina *87* Visa Mäkinen
Pele *76* François Reichenbach
Pelea Cubana Contra los Demonios, Una *71* Tomás Gutiérrez Alea
Pelican, The *26* Frank Borzage
Pélican, Le *73* Gérard Blain
Pelican's Bill, The *26* Walter Lantz
Película del Rey, La *86* Carlos Sorin
Pelileo Earthquake *49* Richard Leacock
Pell Street Mystery, The *24* Joseph Franz

Pelle, La *81* Liliana Cavani
Pelle Erobreren *87* Bille August
Pelle Svanslös i Amerikatt *85* Jan Gissberg, Stig Lasseby
Pelle the Conqueror *87* Bille August
Pellegrini d'Amore *54* Joseph Losey
Pelo nel Mondo, Il *64* Antonio Margheriti, Marco Vicario
Peloton d'Exécution *45* André Berthomieu
Pelvis *77* Lew Mishkin
Pemberton Valley *57* Allan King
Pen and Inklings Around Jerusalem *16* Hy Mayer
Pen and Inklings in and Around Jerusalem *16* Hy Mayer
Pen Is Mightier Than the Sword, The *16* L. M. Glackens
Pen Laughs *14* Hy Mayer
Pen Point Percussion *50* Norman McLaren
Pen Talk *13* Hy Mayer
Pen Talks by Hy Mayer *13* Hy Mayer
Pen Trip to Palestine, A *16* Hy Mayer
Pena de Muerte *73* Jorge Grau
Penal Code, The *33* George Melford
Penal Colony, The *70* Raúl Ruiz
Penal Servitude *28* Yuli Raizman
Penalty, The *20* Wallace Worsley
Penalty, The *41* Harold S. Bucquet
Penalty of Beauty, The *09* Lewin Fitzhamon
Penalty of Fame, The *19* Forest Holger-Madsen
Penalty of Fame *32* Tay Garnett
Pendaison à Jefferson City *11* Jean Durand
Penderecki, Lutosławski, Baird *76* Krzysztof Zanussi
Pendler, Der *86* Bernhard Giger
Pendu, Le *06* Louis Gasnier
Pendulum *69* George Schaefer
Penelope *66* Arthur Hiller
Penelope Pulls It Off *75* Peter Curran
Pénétrations Vicieuses *79* Jean Rollin
Peng! Du Bist Tot! *87* Adolf Winkelmann
Pengabdi Setan *82* Sisworo Gautama Putra
Penge og Økonomi *54* Henning Carlsen
Pengene eller Livet *81* Henning Carlsen
Penguin, The *64* Jerzy Stefan Stawiński
Penguin Parade, The *38* Tex Avery
Penguin Pool Murder, The *32* George Archainbaud
Penguin Pool Mystery, The *32* George Archainbaud
Péniche Tragique, La *24* Lupu Pick
Penitent, The *86* Cliff Osmond
Penitente Murder Case, The *36* Harry Revier
Penitentes, The *15* Jack Conway
Penitentiary *38* John Brahm
Penitentiary *79* Jamaa Fanaka
Penitentiary II *82* Jamaa Fanaka
Penitentiary III *87* Jamaa Fanaka
Penn & Teller Get Killed *89* Arthur Penn
Penn of Pennsylvania *41* Lance Comfort
Pennies from Heaven *36* Norman Z. McLeod
Pennies from Heaven *81* Herbert Ross
Penniless Millionaire, The *21* Einar J. Bruun
Pennington's Choice *15* William J. Bow-

man
Penny and the Pownall Case *48* Slim Hand
Penny for Your Thoughts, or Birds, Dolls and Scratch—English Style, A *66* Donovan Winter
Penny from Panama *34* James Parrott
Penny Gold *73* Jack Cardiff
Penny Journey *38* Humphrey Jennings
Penny of Top Hill Trail *21* Arthur Berthelet
Penny Paradise *38* Basil Dean, Carol Reed
Penny Philanthropist, The *17* Guy W. McConnell
Penny Points to Paradise *51* Anthony Young
Penny Pool, The *37* George Black
Penny Princess *51* Val Guest
Penny Serenade *41* George Stevens
Penny Wisdom *37* David Miller
Penny's Party *38* David Miller
Pennywhistle Blues *52* Donald Swanson
Penrod *22* Marshall Neilan, Frank O'Connor
Penrod and His Twin Brother *38* William McGann
Penrod and Sam *23* William Beaudine
Penrod and Sam *31* William Beaudine
Penrod and Sam *37* William McGann
Penrod's Double Trouble *38* Lewis Seiler
Penseur, Le *19* Léon Poirier
Pension Groonen *24* Robert Wiene
Pension Mimosas *34* Jacques Feyder
Pension Schöller *32* Georg Jacoby
Pensionato, Il *55* Ermanno Olmi
Pensioners, The *12* Allan Dwan
Pente, La *28* Henri Andréani
Pente, La *31* Claude Autant-Lara
Péntek Rézi *38* Ladislas Vajda
Penthouse *33* W. S. Van Dyke
Penthouse, The *67* Peter Collinson
Penthouse Mouse *63* Chuck Jones
Penthouse Party *36* William Nigh
Penthouse Rhythm *44* Edward F. Cline
Pentito, Il *85* Pasquale Squitieri
People *60* Yoji Kuri
People! *66* Grigori Chukhrai
People, The *76* Ousmane Sembène
People Against O'Hara, The *51* John Sturges
People and Art *75* András Kovács
People and the Nile *72* Youssef Chahine
People and Their Guns, The *68* Joris Ivens, Marceline Loridan
People Are Bunny *59* Robert McKimson
People Are Funny *45* Sam White
People from the Empty Area *57* Kazimierz Karabasz*
People from the Metro *74* Jaromil Jireš
People in Luck *62* Philippe de Broca*
People in Slum Area *82* Chang-ho Bae
People in the Subway *74* Jaromil Jireš
People in the Sun *35* Jiří Weiss
People in the Town *26* Heinosuke Gosho
People Like Maria *58* Harry Watt
People Meet and Sweet Music Fills the Heart *67* Henning Carlsen
People Next Door, The *70* David Greene
People of France *36* Jean-Paul Le Chanois, Jean Renoir, André Zwoboda

Peril for the Guy 56 James Hill
Peril of Prussianism, The 18 Leighton Budd
Peril of the Fleet, The 09 S. Wormald
Peril of the Rail 26 John P. McGowan
Peril Within, The 18 Chester Withey
Perilous Holiday 46 Edward H. Griffith
Perilous Journey 39 Herbert Meyer
Perilous Journey, A 53 R. G. Springsteen
Perilous Valley 20 Harry Grossman
Perilous Waters 47 Jack Bernhard
Perils from the Planet Mongo 36 Frederick Stephani
Perils from the Planet Mongo 40 Ford Beebe, Ray Taylor
Perils of Divorce 16 Edwin August
Perils of Gwendoline, The 84 Just Jaeckin
Perils of Gwendoline in the Land of the Yik Yak, The 84 Just Jaeckin
Perils of Nyoka 42 William Witney
Perils of P.K., The 86 Giuseppe Vari
Perils of Paris 24 Edward José
Perils of Pauline, The 14 Louis Gasnier, Donald Mackenzie
Perils of Pauline, The 34 Ray Taylor
Perils of Pauline, The 47 George Marshall
Perils of Pauline, The 67 Herbert Leonard, Joshua Shelley
Perils of Pork Pie, The 16 Will P. Kellino
Perils of the Coast Guard 26 Oscar Apfel
Perils of the Darkest Jungle 44 Spencer G. Bennet, Wallace A. Grissell
Perils of the Jungle 53 George Blair
Perils of the Park 16 Del Henderson
Perils of the Royal Mounted 42 James W. Horne
Perils of the Sea, The 13 George Melford, Sidney Olcott
Perils of the Wilderness 56 Spencer G. Bennet
Perinbaba 85 Juraj Jakubisko
Period of Adjustment 62 George Roy Hill
Périscope, Le 15 Abel Gance
Periscope, The 15 Abel Gance
Perishing Solicitors 83 Charles Crichton
Periwinkle 17 James Kirkwood
Perjura 39 Raphael J. Sevilla
Perjurer, The 57 Edgar G. Ulmer
Perjury 21 Harry Millarde
Perkele! 71 Jörn Donner, Erkki Seiro, Jaakko Talaskivi
Perkele! — Kuvia Suomesta 71 Jörn Donner, Erkki Seiro, Jaakko Talaskivi
Perkins' Pheasants 16 Ethyle Batley
Perla, La 45 Emilio Fernández
Perle des Savants, La 07 Georges Méliès
Perlenhalsband, Das 17 E. A. Dupont
Perles de la Couronne, Les 37 Christian-Jaque, Sacha Guitry
Perličky na Dně 64 Věra Chytilová, Jaromil Jireš, Jiří Menzel, Jan Němec, Evald Schorm
Perlyotniye Ptit 87 Latif Abdul Latif
Permanent Record 88 Marisa Silver
Permanent Vacation 82 Jim Jarmusch
Permanent Wave 29 Walter Lantz
Permette? Rocco Papaleo 71 Ettore Scola
Permette Signora Che Ami Vostra Figlia 83 Gian Luigi Polidoro
Permian Strata 69 Bruce Conner

Permission, La 67 Melvin Van Peebles
Permission to Kill 75 Cyril Frankel
Permissive 70 Lindsay Shonteff
Permutations 68 John Whitney
Perníková Chaloupka 51 Břetislav Pojar
Perón: Actualización Política y Doctrinaria para la Toma del Poder 71 Octavio Getino, Fernando Solanas
Perón: La Revolución Justicialista 71 Octavio Getino, Fernando Solanas
Perpetua 22 Tom Geraghty, John S. Robertson
Perpetual Motion 20 Dave Fleischer
Perri 57 N. Paul Kenworthy, Jr., Ralph Wright
Perros de la Noche 86 Teo Kofman
Perry Rhodan — S.O.S. aus dem Weltall 67 Primo Zeglio
Persecución Hasta Valencia 68 Julio Coll
Persecution 73 Don Chaffey
Persecution and Assassination of Jean-Paul Marat As Performed by the Inmates of the Asylum of Charenton Under the Direction of the Marquis de Sade, The 66 Peter Brook
Persecution of Bob Pretty, The 16 Frank Miller
Persecution of Hasta Valencia, The 68 Julio Coll
Persevering Edwin 07 Lewin Fitzhamon
Persevering Peter 13 Charles C. Calvert
Persian Dance: Eightpence a Mile 13 Walter R. Booth
Persiane Chiuse 50 Luigi Comencini
Persistent Lovers, The 22 Guy Newall
Persistent Poet, The 11 Frank Wilson
Persistent Suitor, A 09 Edwin S. Porter
Persnickety Polly Ann 17 Charles Miller
Person to Bunny 60 Friz Freleng
Person Unknown 56 Montgomery Tully
Persona 66 Ingmar Bergman
Personaggi & Interpreti 87 Heinz Butler
Personal 04 Wallace McCutcheon
Personal Affair, A 31 Georgy Vasiliev, Sergei Vasiliev
Personal Affair, A 40 Alexander Rasumny
Personal Affair 53 Anthony Pelissier
Personal and Confidential 65 Geoffrey Nethercott
Personal Best 82 Robert Towne
Personal Choice 86 David Saperstein
Personal Column 39 Robert Siodmak
Personal Column 47 Douglas Sirk
Personal Foul 87 Ted Lichtenfeld
Personal History, Adventures, Experience and Observations of David Copperfield the Younger, The 34 George Cukor
Personal History of the Australian Surf, A 82 Michael Blakemore
Personal Honour 42 Charles Barton
Personal Maid 31 Monta Bell, Lothar Mendes
Personal Maid's Secret 35 Arthur Greville Collins
Personal Matter, A 31 Georgy Vasiliev, Sergei Vasiliev
Personal Property 37 W. S. Van Dyke
Personal Secretary 38 Otis Garrett
Personal Services 86 Terry Jones
Personality 30 Victor Heerman

Personality Kid, The 34 Alan Crosland
Personality Kid 46 George Sherman
Personals, The 81 Peter Markle
Personel 75 Krzysztof Kieslowski
Persons in Hiding 38 Louis King
Persons Unknown 56 Mario Monicelli
Persuader, The 57 Dick Ross
Persuaders, The 71 Val Guest
Persuading Papa 10 Lewin Fitzhamon
Persuasive Peggy 17 Charles Brabin
Perücke, Die 24 Berthold Viertel
Pervaya Vstrecha, Poslednaya Vstrecha 88 Vitaly Melnikov
Pervenche 21 Alfred Machin, Henri Wuhlschleger
Perversão 78 José Mojica Marins
Perverse 73 Jean Rollin
Perversión 74 Francisco Lara Polop
Pervert, The 34 John H. Auer
1 Maja 38 Grigori Alexandrov
Pervola 85 Orlow Seunke
Pervola: Tracks in the Snow 85 Orlow Seunke
Pervyi Den 58 Friedrich Ermler
Pervyi Den Mira 61 Yakov Segel
Pervyi Eshelon 55 Mikhail Kalatozov
Pervyi Paren 58 Sergei Paradzhanov
Pervyi Uchitel 65 Andrei Mikhalkov-Konchalovsky
Peryl 70 Roger Vadim
Pescado 51 Luis César Amadori
Pescados 34 Emilio Gómez Muriel, Fred Zinnemann
Pescatorella 46 Dino Risi
Pescherecci 57 Vittorio De Seta
Pesky Pup, A 17 Joseph Harwitz
Pesn Lyubvi Nedopetaya 18 Lev Kuleshov, Vitold Polonsky
Pesn o Gerojach 32 Joris Ivens
Pesn o Geroyazh 32 Joris Ivens
Pesn o Metallye 28 V. Granatman, Josef Heifits, Mikhail Shapiro, Alexander Zarkhi
Pesn Proshedshikh Dney 87 Albert Mkrtchyan
Pesn Torzhestvuyushchei Liubvi 15 Yevgeni Bauer
Pesni Abaya 45 E. Aron, Grigori Roshal
Pesn'Liubvi Nedopetaia 18 Lev Kuleshov, Vitold Polonsky
Pesnya Katorzhanina 11 Yakov Protazanov
Pesnya o Shchastye 34 Mark Donskoi, Vladimir Legoshin
Pest, The 17 Christy Cabanne
Pest in Florenz, Die 19 Otto Rippert
Pest in the House, A 47 Chuck Jones
Pest Pilot 41 Dave Fleischer
Pest That Came to Dinner, The 48 Art Davis
Pesti Háztetők 61 András Kovács
Pesti Mese 38 Béla Gaál
Pesti Szerelem 34 Géza von Bolváry
Pěsti ve Tmě 86 Jaroslav Soukup
Pesticide 78 Jean Rollin
Pestonjee 88 Vijaya Mehta
Pests for Guests 55 Friz Freleng
Pet, The 16 Winsor McCay
Pet Hen, The 14 Will P. Kellino
Pět Holek na Krku 66 Evald Schorm
Pet of the Regiment, The 14 Frank Wilson

Pet Parrot, The *16* Harry S. Palmer
Pet Peave *54* Joseph Barbera, William Hanna
Pet Sematary *89* Mary Lambert
Pet Shop, The *32* Dick Huemer
Petal on the Current, A *19* Tod Browning
Pete Hothead *52* Ted Parmelee
Pete Kelly's Blues *55* Jack Webb
Pete 'n' Tillie *72* Martin Ritt
Pete Roleum and His Cousins *39* Joseph Losey
Pete Seeger—A Song and a Stone *71* Robert Elfstrom
Peter *33* Henry Koster
Peter and Pavla *63* Miloš Forman
Peter der Grosse *22* Dmitri Buchowetzki
Peter der Matrose *29* Reinhold Schünzel
Peter Ibbetson *21* George Fitzmaurice
Peter Ibbetson *35* Henry Hathaway
Peter im Schnee *37* Karel Lamač
Peter-No-Tail in Americat *85* Jan Gissberg, Stig Lasseby
Peter Pan *24* Herbert Brenon
Peter Pan *53* Clyde Geronimi, Wilfred Jackson, Hamilton Luske
Peter Pan Handled *25* Walter Lantz
Peter, Paul und Nanette *39* Erich Engel
Peter Pens Poetry *13* Bert Haldane
Peter Pickles' Wedding *12* Bert Haldane
Peter Rabbit and Tales of Beatrix Potter *71* Reginald Mills
Peter Schlemihl *15* Stellan Rye
Peter Studies Form *64* Stan Strangeway
Peter Stuyvesant *24* Frank Tuttle
Peter the Barber *22* Bernard Dudley
Peter the Crazy *65* Jean-Luc Godard
Peter the First, Part One *37* Vladimir Petrov
Peter the First, Part Two *39* Vladimir Petrov
Peter the Great *10* Vasili M. Goncharov, Kai Hansen
Peter the Great *22* Dmitri Buchowetzki
Peter the Great, Part One *37* Vladimir Petrov
Peter the Great, Part Two *39* Vladimir Petrov
Peter the Pirate *24* Arthur Robison
Peter Tries Suicide *13* Bert Haldane
Peter Vinogradof *35* Alexander Macharet
Peter von Scholten *87* Palle Kjærulff-Schmidt
Peter Voss der Millionendieb *32* E. A. Dupont
Peter Voss Who Stole Millions *32* E. A. Dupont
Petering Out *27* Walter Lantz
Petermann 1st Dagegen *37* Frank Wisbar
Peter's Little Picnic *13* Hay Plumb
Peter's Rival *12* Edwin J. Collins
Petersburg Nights *34* Grigori Roshal, Vera Stroyeva
Petersburg Slums *15* Vladimir Gardin, Yakov Protazanov
Petersburgskaya Nochi *34* Grigori Roshal, Vera Stroyeva
Petersburgskiye Trushchobi *15* Vladimir Gardin, Yakov Protazanov
Petersen *74* Tim Burstall
Peterville Diamond, The *42* Walter Forde

Pete's Dragon *77* Don Chaffey
Pete's Haunted House *26* Walter Lantz
Pete's Party *26* Walter Lantz
Pete's Pow-Wow *27* Clyde Geronimi
Petey and Johnny *61* Richard Leacock*
Petey Wheatstraw *78* Cliff Roquemore
Pětistovka *49* Martin Frič
Petit à Petit *69* Jean Rouch
Petit Amour, Le *87* Agnès Varda
Petit Ange *20* Luitz-Morat
Petit Ange et Son Pantin *23* Luitz-Morat
Petit Babouin, Le *32* Jean Grémillon
Petit Baigneur, Le *68* Robert Dhéry
Petit Café, Le *19* Raymond Bernard
Petit Café, Le *62* François Reichenbach
Petit Chanteclair, Le *10* Émile Cohl
Petit Chaperon Rouge, Le *01* Georges Méliès
Petit Chaperon Rouge, Le *29* Alberto Cavalcanti
Petit Chapiteau, Le *62* Joris Ivens
Petit Chose, Le *23* André Hugon
Petit Chose, Le *38* Maurice Cloche
Petit Con *84* Gérard Lauzier
Petit Diable, Un *1896* Georges Méliès
Petit Discours de la Méthode *63* Claude Jutra, Pierre Patry
Petit Garçon de l'Ascenseur, Le *61* Pierre Granier-Deferre
Petit Hamlet, Le *60* Jerzy Skolimowski
Petit Hôtel à Louer *23* Pierre Colombier
Petit Jimmy, Le *30* Jean Benoît-Lévy, Marie Epstein
Petit Jules Verne, Le *07* Gaston Velle
Petit Matin, Le *71* Jean-Gabriel Albicocco
Petit Moineau de Paris, Le *23* Gaston Roudes
Petit Monde de Don Camillo, Le *51* Julien Duvivier
Petit Poucet, Le *12* Louis Feuillade
Petit Poucet, Le *65* Walerian Borowczyk
Petit Poucet, Le *72* Michel Boisrond
Petit Prof', Le *58* Carlo-Rim
Petit Roi, Le *33* Julien Duvivier
Petit Soldat, Le *08* Léonce Perret
Petit Soldat, Le *47* Paul Grimault
Petit Soldat, Le *60* Jean-Luc Godard
Petit Soldat Qui Devient Dieu, Le *08* Émile Cohl
Petit Théâtre, Le *82* Raúl Ruiz
Petit Théâtre de Jean Renoir, Le *69* Jean Renoir
Petite, La *78* Louis Malle
Petite Allumeuse, La *87* Danièle Dubroux
Petite Amie, La *88* Luc Béraud
Petite Andalouse, La *14* Louis Feuillade
Petite Bande, La *83* Michel Deville
Petite Bonne du Palace, La *26* Louis Mercanton
Petite Café, La *30* Ludwig Berger
Petite Chocolatière, La *27* René Hervil
Petite Chocolatière, La *31* Marc Allégret
Petite Chocolatière, La *50* André Berthomieu
Petite Danseuse, La *13* Louis Feuillade
Petite Fille *28* Pierre Colombier
Petite Fille et la Recherche du Printemps, La *71* Philippe Agostini
Petite Fille en Velours Bleu, La *78* Alan Bridges

Petite Lili, La *27* Alberto Cavalcanti, Jean Renoir
Petite Lise, La *30* Jean Grémillon
Petite Magicienne, La *00* Alice Guy-Blaché
Petite Main Qui Se Place, Une *22* Sacha Guitry
Petite Marchande d'Allumettes, La *28* Jean Renoir, Jean Tedesco
Petite Sirène, La *80* Roger Andrieux
Petites Apprenties, Les *11* Louis Feuillade
Petites du Quai aux Fleurs, Les *43* Marc Allégret
Petites Marionnettes, Les *18* Louis Feuillade
Petites Pensionnaires Impudiques *79* Jean Rollin
Petits, Les *25* Gaston Roudes
Petits, Les *36* Alfred Machard, Constant Remy
Petits Coupeurs de Bois Vert, Les *04* Alice Guy-Blaché
Petits Matins, Les *61* Jacqueline Audry
Petits Peintres, Les *04* Alice Guy-Blaché
Petits Vagabonds, Les *05* Ferdinand Zecca
Pětka s Hvězdičkov *85* Miroslav Balajka
Petla *57* Wojciech Has
Petomane, Il *83* Pasquale Festa Campanile
Petos *88* Taavi Kassila
Petrified Dog, The *48* Sidney Peterson
Petrified Forest, The *35* Archie Mayo
Petrified Forest, The *73* Masahiro Shinoda
Petrina Chronia *85* Pantelis Voulgaris
Petroleum Girls, The *71* Guy Casaril, Christian-Jaque
Pétroleuses, Les *71* Guy Casaril, Christian-Jaque
Pétrus *46* Marc Allégret
Pets *74* Raphael Nussbaum
Pets and Pearls *19* Raoul Barré, Charles Bowers
Pets' Tea Party, The *08* Lewin Fitzhamon
Pett and Pott *34* Alberto Cavalcanti
Pettersson & Bendel *34* Per Axel-Branner
Petticoat Fever *36* George Fitzmaurice
Petticoat Larceny *43* Ben Holmes
Petticoat Loose *22* George Ridgwell
Petticoat Perfidy *13* Hay Plumb
Petticoat Pilot, A *18* Rollin Sturgeon
Petticoat Pirates *61* David MacDonald
Petticoat Politics *40* Erle C. Kenton
Petticoats and Bluejeans *61* David Swift
Petticoats and Politics *18* Howard Mitchell
Pettigrew's Girl *19* George Melford
Pettin' in the Park *34* Bernard Brown
Petting Larceny *29* Manny Gould, Ben Harrison
Petty Girl, The *50* Henry Levin
Petulia *68* Richard Lester
Peu, Beaucoup, Passionnément, Un *71* Robert Enrico
Peu de Feu S.V.P., Un *04* Georges Méliès
Peu de Soleil dans l'Eau Froide, Un *71* Jacques Deray
Peuple Est Invincible, Le *69* Joris Ivens*
Peuple et Ses Fusils, Le *68* Joris Ivens, Marceline Loridan
Peuple Ne Peut Rien Sans Ses Fusils, Le *69* Joris Ivens*
Peuple Peut Tout, Le *69* Joris Ivens*

Peur des Coups, La *32* Claude Autant-Lara

Peur sur la Ville *74* Henri Verneuil

Peyton Place *57* Mark Robson

Peyvast Kolieh *78* Dariush Mehrjui

Pfarrer von St. Pauli, Der *70* Rolf Olsen

Phable of a Busted Romance, The *15* Gregory La Cava

Phable of a Phat Woman, The *16* Gregory La Cava

Phable of Sam and Bill, The *15* Gregory La Cava

Phaedra *61* Jules Dassin

Phantasm *78* Don Coscarelli

Phantasm II *88* Don Coscarelli

Phantasmes *18* Marcel L'Herbier

Phantasmes *75* Jean Rollin

Phantasmes Pornographiques *75* Jean Rollin

Phantasy, A *48* Norman McLaren

Phantom, The *16* Charles Giblyn

Phantom *22* F. W. Murnau

Phantom, The *43* B. Reeves Eason

Phantom Baron, The *43* Serge De Poligny

Phantom Broadcast, The *33* Phil Rosen

Phantom Buccaneer, The *16* J. Charles Haydon

Phantom Bullet, The *26* Clifford Smith

Phantom Buster, The *27* William Bertram

Phantom Carriage, The *20* Victor Sjöström

Phantom Carriage, The *39* Julien Duvivier

Phantom Carriage, The *58* Arne Mattsson

Phantom Chariot, The *20* Victor Sjöström

Phantom Chariot, The *58* Arne Mattsson

Phantom City, The *28* Albert S. Rogell

Phantom Cowboy, The *35* Robert J. Horner

Phantom Cowboy, The *41* George Sherman

Phantom Creeps, The *39* Ford Beebe, Saul Goodkind

Phantom Empire, The *35* Otto Brower, B. Reeves Eason

Phantom Empire *87* Fred Olen Ray

Phantom Express, The *25* John G. Adolfi

Phantom Express, The *32* Emory Johnson

Phantom Fiend, The *31* Maurice Elvey

Phantom Fiend *61* Harald Reinl

Phantom Flyer, The *28* Bruce Mitchell

Phantom Foe, The *26* Geoffrey H. Malins, H. B. Parkinson

Phantom Fortune, The *23* Robert F. Hill

Phantom Fortunes, The *16* Paul Scardon

Phantom from Space *53* W. Lee Wilder

Phantom from 10,000 Leagues, The *56* Dan Milner

Phantom Gold *38* Joseph Levering

Phantom Honeymoon, The *19* J. Searle Dawley

Phantom Horse, The *56* Koji Shima

Phantom Horseman, The *24* Robert North Bradbury

Phantom Horseman, The *50* Richard Talmadge

Phantom Husband, A *17* Ferris G. Hartman

Phantom in the House, The *29* Phil Rosen

Phantom India *69* Louis Malle

Phantom Justice *24* Richard Thomas

Phantom Kid, The *83* Peter Hammond

Phantom Killer, The *41* Joseph H. Lewis

Phantom Killer, The *42* William Beaudine

Phantom Lady *44* Robert Siodmak

Phantom Light, The *34* Michael Powell

Phantom Love *78* Nagisa Oshima

Phantom Lovers *61* Antonio Pietrangeli

Phantom Melody, The *20* Douglas Gerrard

Phantom of Chinatown *40* Phil Rosen

Phantom of Crestwood, The *32* J. Walter Ruben

Phantom of Death *88* Ruggero Deodato

Phantom of 42nd Street, The *45* Albert Herman

Phantom of Liberty, The *74* Luis Buñuel

Phantom of Love, The *78* Nagisa Oshima

Phantom of Paris, The *31* John S. Robertson

Phantom of Paris *42* Phil Rosen

Phantom of Santa Fe *37* Jacques Jaccard

Phantom of Soho, The *67* Franz-Josef Gottlieb

Phantom of Terror, The *69* Dario Argento

Phantom of the Air *33* Phil Rosen

Phantom of the Convent, The *34* Fernando De Fuentes

Phantom of the Desert *30* Harry S. Webb

Phantom of the Forest, The *26* Henry McCarthy

Phantom of the Jungle *55* Spencer G. Bennet

Phantom of the Mall: Eric's Revenge *89* Richard Friedman

Phantom of the Moulin Rouge, The *24* René Clair

Phantom of the North *29* Harry S. Webb

Phantom of the Opera, The *25* Rupert Julian, Ernst Laemmle, Edward Sedgwick

Phantom of the Opera *43* Arthur Lubin

Phantom of the Opera, The *62* Terence Fisher

Phantom of the Opera, The *89* Dwight H. Little

Phantom of the Paradise *74* Brian DePalma

Phantom of the Plains *45* Lesley Selander

Phantom of the Range *28* James Dugan

Phantom of the Range, The *36* Robert F. Hill

Phantom of the Red House, The *54* Miguel Delgado

Phantom of the Rue Morgue *54* Roy Del Ruth

Phantom of the Turf *28* Duke Worne

Phantom of the Violin *14* Francis Ford

Phantom of the West, The *31* D. Ross Lederman

Phantom Outlaw *27* William Wyler

Phantom Paradise *12* Alice Guy-Blaché

Phantom Patrol *36* Charles Hutchinson

Phantom Picture, The *16* Albert Ward

Phantom Plainsmen, The *42* John English

Phantom Planet, The *61* William Marshall

Phantom President, The *32* Norman Taurog

Phantom Raiders *40* Jacques Tourneur

Phantom Rancher *40* Harry Fraser

Phantom Ranger, The *28* Bruce Mitchell

Phantom Ranger, The *38* Sam Newfield

Phantom Rider, The *29* John P. McGowan

Phantom Rider, The *36* Ray Taylor

Phantom Rider, The *46* Spencer G. Bennet, Fred C. Brannon

Phantom Riders, The *18* John Ford

Phantom Shadows *25* Al Ferguson

Phantom Ship, The *08* A. E. Coleby, J. H. Martin

Phantom Ship *35* Denison Clift

Phantom Ship, The *36* Jack King

Phantom Shot, The *47* Mario Zampi

Phantom Shotgun, The *17* Harry Harvey

Phantom Speaks, The *45* John English

Phantom Stage, The *38* Drew Eberson

Phantom Stage, The *39* George Waggner

Phantom Stagecoach, The *57* Ray Nazarro

Phantom Stallion, The *54* Harry Keller

Phantom Stockman, The *53* Lee Robinson

Phantom Strikes, The *38* Walter Forde

Phantom Submarine, The *41* Charles Barton

Phantom Thief, The *46* D. Ross Lederman

Phantom Thunderbolt, The *33* Alvin J. Neitz

Phantom Tollbooth, The *69* Chuck Jones, Abe Levitow, David Monahan

Phantom Trail, The *28* Manny Gould, Ben Harrison

Phantom Valley *48* Ray Nazarro

Phantom von Soho, Das *67* Franz-Josef Gottlieb

Phantom Wagon, The *39* Julien Duvivier

Phantome des Glücks *29* Reinhold Schünzel

Phantoms, Inc. *45* Harold Young

Phantom's Secret, The *17* Charles Swickard

Phar Lap *83* Simon Wincer

Phar Lap—Heart of a Nation *83* Simon Wincer

Pharaoh *65* Jerzy Kawalerowicz

Pharaoh's Court *85* José Luis García Sánchez

Pharaoh's Curse *57* Lee Sholem

Pharaoh's Woman, The *60* Giorgio Rivalta, Victor Tourjansky

Pharmaceutical Hallucinations *08* Georges Méliès

Pharmacist, The *33* Arthur Ripley

Phase IV *73* Saul Bass

Phatikchand *83* Sandip Ray

Phénix, Le *05* Georges Méliès

Phenix City Story, The *55* Phil Karlson

Phénix ou Le Coffret de Cristal, Le *05* Georges Méliès

Phenomena *68* Jordan Belson

Phenomena *84* Dario Argento

Phenomenal Contortionist, A *01* Edwin S. Porter

Phenomenon No. 1 *64* Stan Vanderbeek

Phera *87* Buddhadep Dasgupta

Phfffft! *54* Mark Robson

Phfft *54* Mark Robson

Phil Blood's Leap *13* Wilfred Noy

Phil-for-Short *19* Oscar Apfel

Philadelphia Attraction, The *85* Péter Gardos

Philadelphia Experiment, The *84* Stewart Raffill

Philadelphia Here I Come 75 John Quested

Philadelphia Story, The 40 George Cukor

Philip 69 Richard C. Sarafian

Philip Holden, Waster 16 George L. Sargent

Philips-Radio 31 Joris Ivens

Philise Me Maritsa 31 Dimitrios Gaziadis

Philistine in Bohemia, A 20 Edward H. Griffith

Philly 81 Alan Myerson

Philo Vance Returns 47 William Beaudine

Philo Vance's Gamble 47 Basil Wrangell

Philo Vance's Secret Mission 47 Reginald LeBorg

Philosopher's Stone, The 1899 Georges Méliès

Philosopher's Stone, The 57 Satyajit Ray

Philosophical Story, A 37 Otakar Vávra

Philosophy in the Boudoir 70 Jesús Franco

Phobia 80 John Huston

Phobia 80 Armand Weston

Phobia 88 John Dingwall

Phoebe 88 Bettina Rathborne

Phoebe of the Inn 12 Bert Haldane

Phoebe Snow 05 Edwin S. Porter

Phoelix 79 Anna Ambrose

Phoenix 47 Keisuke Kinoshita

Phoenix, The 78 Kon Ichikawa

Phoenix, The 83 Sadamasa Arikawa, Richard Caan

Phoenix 2772 79 Suguru Sugiyama, Osamu Tezuku

Phone Call from a Stranger 52 Jean Negulesco

Phone Rings Every Night, The 62 Géza von Cziffra

Phoney Baloney 45 Bob Wickersham

Phoney Express 32 Ubbe Iwerks

Phoney Focus, The 22 Raoul Barré, Charles Bowers

Phonographe, Le 69 Walerian Borowczyk

Phony American, The 62 Ákos von Ráthonyi

Phoques du Rio d'Oro, Les 49 Jacques-Yves Cousteau

Phoques du Sahara, Les 49 Jacques-Yves Cousteau

Photo Finish 57 Norbert Carbonneaux

Photo Phonies 50 Leslie Goodwins

Photodram 21 Walter Ruttmann

Photogénie Mécanique, La 24 Jean Grémillon

Photogénies 25 Jean Epstein

Photograph, The 86 Nikos Papatakis

Photograph from an Area Window 01 George Albert Smith

Photographe 1896 Louis Lumière

Photographer 1896 Louis Lumière

Photographer, The 38 Jean Yarbrough

Photographer, The 47 Willard Van Dyke

Photographer, The 74 William Byron Hillman

Photographer's Flirtation, The 08 Lewin Fitzhamon

Photographer's Mishap, The 01 Edwin S. Porter

Photographia, I 86 Nikos Papatakis

Photographic Episode, A 03 Alf Collins

Photographic Expressions Illustrated 05 Harold Jeapes

Photographie Électrique à Distance, La 07 Georges Méliès

Photographies Vivantes 54 Walerian Borowczyk

Photographing a Country Couple 01 Edwin S. Porter

Photographing a Ghost 1898 George Albert Smith

Photography and the City 69 Charles Eames, Ray Eames

Photos d'Alix 80 Jean Eustache

Phototone Reels 28 John Harlow, James B. Sloan

Phrenological Burlesque, A 01 Georges Méliès

Phrénologique Burlesque, Le 01 Georges Méliès

Phrenologist and the Lively Skull, The 01 Georges Méliès

Phroso 22 Louis Mercanton

Phroso the Mysterious Mechanical Doll 03 Alf Collins

Phyllis and the Foreigner 15 Frank Wilson

Phyllis of the Follies 28 Ernst Laemmle

Phynx, The 70 Lee H. Katzin

Physical Culture 11 Frank Wilson

Physical Evidence 88 Michael Crichton

Physician, The 28 Georg Jacoby

Piaf 74 Guy Casaril

Piaf — The Early Years 74 Guy Casaril

Pianeta degli Uomini Spenti, Il 61 Antonio Margheriti

Pianeta Errante, Il 65 Antonio Margheriti

Pianeti Contro di Noi, I 61 Romano Ferrara

Piano, The 30 Boris Barnet

Piano in Midair, A 77 Péter Bacsó

Piano Mover 32 Manny Gould, Ben Harrison

Piano Movers, The 14 Charles Chaplin

Piano Players Rarely Ever Play Together 85 Stevenson J. Palfi

Pianorama 74 Richard Taylor

Pianos Mecanicos, Los 64 Juan Antonio Bardem

Pianos Mécaniques, Les 64 Juan Antonio Bardem

Pianto delle Zitelle, Il 58 Gian Vittorio Baldi

Piaobo Qiyu 82 Benzheng Yu

Piątka z Ulicy Barskiej 53 Aleksander Ford

Pibe Cabeza, El 74 Leopoldo Torre-Nilsson

Picador Porky 37 Tex Avery

Pícara Susanna, La 44 Fernando Cortez

Picardía Mexicana II 86 Rafael Villaseñor Kuri

Picari, I 87 Mario Monicelli

Picaros, The 87 Mario Monicelli

Picasso 54 Luciano Emmer

Picasso Mystery, The 55 Henri-Georges Clouzot

Picasso, Pablo 82 Frédéric Rossif

Picasso Summer, The 67 Serge Bourguignon

Picasso Trigger 87 Andy Sidaris

Picasso's Sculpture 67 Bruce Beresford

Piccadilly 28 E. A. Dupont

Piccadilly Incident 46 Herbert Wilcox

Piccadilly Jim 20 Wesley Ruggles

Piccadilly Jim 36 Robert Z. Leonard

Piccadilly Nights 30 Albert H. Arch

Piccadilly Playtime 36 Frank Green

Piccadilly Third Stop 60 Wolf Rilla

Piccola Posta 55 Steno

Piccoli Avventurieri 40 Flavio Calzavara

Piccoli Fuochi 85 Peter Del Monte

Piccolo 60 Dušan Vukotić

Piccolo Cerinaio, Il 14 Augusto Genina

Piccolo Diavolo, Il 88 Roberto Benigni

Piccolo Eroe 37 Alessandro Blasetti

Piccolo Martire, Il 42 Vittorio De Sica

Piccolo Mondo Antico 41 Mario Soldati

Piccolo Mondo di Don Camillo, Il 51 Julien Duvivier

Piccolo Sceriffo, Il 50 Vittorio Sala

Pick a Star 37 Edward Sedgwick

Pick-Me-Up Est un Sportsman 14 Émile Cohl

Pick-Pocket et Policeman 1899 Georges Méliès

Pick-Up 33 Marion Gering

Pick-Up 75 Bernie Hirschenson

Pick-Up Artist, The 87 James Toback

Pick-Up Summer 81 George Mihalka

Picked Romance, A 26 William C. Nolan

Picket Guard, The 13 Allan Dwan

Picketing for Love 38 Jean Yarbrough

Pickled Puss 48 Howard Swift

Pickles Make Me Cry 88 Peter Chow

Pickpocket, The 03 Alf Collins

Pickpocket 59 Robert Bresson

Pickpocket — A Chase Through London, The 03 Alf Collins

Pickup 51 Hugo Haas

Pickup Alley 57 John Gilling

Pickup in Rome 60 Mauro Bolognini

Pickup Is a Sportsman 13 Émile Cohl

Pickup on 101 72 John Florea

Pickup on South Street 52 Samuel Fuller

Pickwick Papers, The 13 Lawrence Trimble

Pickwick Papers, The 52 Noel Langley

Pickwick vs. Bardell 13 Wilfred Noy

Picnic, The 30 Burton Gillett

Picnic 48 Curtis Harrington

Picnic 55 Joshua Logan

Picnic 75 Edgar Reitz

Picnic at Hanging Rock 75 Peter Weir

Picnic Disturbed, A 04 Frank Mottershaw

Picnic for Two, A 18 Gregory La Cava

Picnic on the Grass 59 Jean Renoir

Picnic on the Island, The 13 Lewin Fitzhamon

Picnic Panic 46 Bob Wickersham

Picnics Are Fun and Dino's Serenade 59 Lew Keller

Picto Puzzles No. 1 17 Sam Lloyd

Picto Puzzles No. 2 17 Sam Lloyd

Picto Puzzles No. 3 17 Sam Lloyd

Picto Puzzles No. 4 17 Sam Lloyd

Picto Puzzles No. 5 17 Sam Lloyd

Picto Puzzles No. 6 17 Sam Lloyd

Picto Puzzles No. 7 17 Sam Lloyd

Pictorial Revue 36 Fred Watts

Pictorial Revue of 1943 43 Fred Watts

Pictura, an Adventure in Art 51 E. A. Dupont

Picture Brides 33 Phil Rosen

Picture Hunters, The 85 András Szurdi, Miklós Szurdi

Picture Mommy Dead *66* Bert I. Gordon
Picture of Dorian Gray, The *15* Vsevolod Meyerhold
Picture of Dorian Gray, The *16* Fred W. Durrant
Picture of Dorian Gray, The *17* Richard Oswald
Picture of Dorian Gray, The *44* Albert Lewin
Picture of Madame Yuki *50* Kenji Mizoguchi
Picture of the Time, A *22* Fritz Lang
Picture Palace Piecans *14* Will P. Kellino
Picture Show Man, The *77* John Power
Picture Snatcher *33* Lloyd Bacon
Picture Story *86* Mariano Laurenti
Picture Thieves, The *10* Theo Bouwmeester
Pictures *82* Michael Black
Pictures at an Exhibition *54* Miklós Jancsó
Pictures at an Exhibition *72* Alexander Alexeïeff, Claire Parker
Pictures at an Exhibition *72* Nicholas Ferguson
Pictures from the Life of a Town *75* István Gaál
Pictures in the Fire *18* Santry
Pictures of My Brother Julio *65* Manoel De Oliveira
Pictures of the Atom Bomb *51* Tadashi Imai
Pidgin Island *16* Fred J. Balshofer
Pie-Covered Wagon, The *32* Charles Lamont
Pie Curs *27* Manny Gould, Ben Harrison
Pie in the Sky *34* Elia Kazan, Ralph Steiner
Pie in the Sky *64* Allen Baron
Pie, Tramp and the Bulldog *01* Edwin S. Porter
Piebald *61* Karel Kachyňa
Piecan's Tonic *15* Joe Evans
Piece of Bread, A *59* Jan Němec
Piece of Cake, A *48* John Irwin
Piece of Pleasure, A *74* Claude Chabrol
Piece of the Action, A *77* Sidney Poitier
Pieces *81* Juan Piquer Simon
Pieces of Dreams *70* Daniel Haller
Pied Piper, The *07* Percy Stow
Pied Piper, The *24* Walter Lantz
Pied Piper, The *42* Irving Pichel
Pied Piper, The *68* Mende Brown
Pied Piper, The *71* Jacques Demy
Pied Piper Malone *24* Alfred E. Green
Pied Piper of Guadalupe, The *61* Friz Freleng, Hawley Pratt
Pied Piper of Hamelin, The *17* Rochus Gliese, Paul Wegener
Pied Piper of Hamelin, The *26* Frank Tilley
Pied Piper of Hamelin, The *57* Bretaigne Windust
Pied Piper of Hamelin, The *60* Lotte Reiniger
Pied Piper of Hamelin, The *71* Jacques Demy
Pied Piper of Hamelin, The *85* Jiří Barta
Pied Piper Porky *39* Robert Clampett
Pied Qui Étreint, Le *16* Jacques Feyder
Piedra Libre *76* Leopoldo Torre-Nilsson

Piedra Sobre Piedra *70* Santiago Álvarez
Piège *69* Jacques Baratier
Piège à Cons, Le *79* Jean-Pierre Mocky
Piège à Fourrure *77* Alain Robbe-Grillet
Piège pour Cendrillon *65* André Cayatte
Pièges *39* Robert Siodmak
Piel de Verano *61* Leopoldo Torre-Nilsson
Pieniądze Albo Życie *61* Jerzy Skolimowski
Pier, The *62* Chris Marker
Pier at Tréport During a Storm, The *1896* Georges Méliès
Pier 5, Havana *59* Edward L. Cahn
Pier 13 *32* Raoul Walsh
Pier 13 *40* Eugene Forde
Pier 23 *51* William Berke
Piera's Story *82* Marco Ferreri
Pierpin la Figlia Ritrovata *36* Duilio Coletti
Pierre and Jean *51* Luis Buñuel
Pierre et Djemila *87* Gérard Blain
Pierre et Jean *24* Donatien
Pierre et Jean *43* André Cayatte
Pierre et Paul *68* René Allio
Pierre of the Plains *42* George B. Seitz
Pierre Philosophale, La *1899* Georges Méliès
Pierre Philosophe, Le *12* Abel Gance
Pierre Vallières *72* Joyce Wieland
Pierres Chantantes d'Ayorou *68* Jean Rouch
Pierrette No. 1 *24* Oskar Fischinger
Pierrot and Pierrette *1896* Birt Acres
Pierrot and the Devil's Dice, The *05* J. H. Martin
Pierrot Assassin *04* Alice Guy-Blaché
Pierrot des Bois *54* Claude Jutra
Pierrot le Fou *65* Jean-Luc Godard
Pierrot Malheureux *04* Georges Méliès
Pierrot, Pierrette *24* Louis Feuillade
Pierścien i Róża *87* Jerzy Gruza
Pierwsze Dni *51* Jan Rybkowski
Pierwsze Lata *47* Joris Ivens
Pierwszy Dzień Wolności *64* Aleksander Ford
Pierwszy Plon *50* Wojciech Has
Pietà per Chi Cade *53* Mario Costa
Pietro der Korsar *24* Arthur Robison
Pietro Micca *37* Aldo Vergano
Piętro Wyżej *38* Leon Trystan
Piety *67* István Szabó
Pieuvre, La *26* Jean Painlevé
Pig, The *70* Jean-Michel Barjol, Jean Eustache
Pig Across Paris *56* Claude Autant-Lara
Pig Pen *69* Pier Paolo Pasolini
Pig Styles *28* Manny Gould, Ben Harrison
Piga Bland Pigor, En *24* John W. Brunius
Pigen fra Sydhavsøen *20* Anders Wilhelm Sandberg
Pigeon, The *29* Mark Donskoi
Pigeon That Took Rome, The *62* Melville Shavelson
Pigeons *70* John Dexter
Pigs *16* Harry S. Palmer
Pigs, The *72* Marc Lawrence
Pigs *84* Cathal Black
Pigs and Battleships *61* Shohei Imamura
Pigs and Pearls *80* Dušan Makavejev
Pigs and Warships *61* Shohei Imamura

Pigs Are Seldom Clean *73* Jean-Pierre Lefèbvre
Pig's Curly Tail, The *26* Walter Lantz
Pigs in a Polka *43* Friz Freleng
Pigs in Clover *19* Gregory La Cava
Pigs Is Pigs *14* George D. Baker
Pigs Is Pigs *37* Friz Freleng
Pigs Is Pigs *54* Jack Kinney
Pigskin Palooka, The *37* Gordon Douglas
Pigskin Parade *36* David Butler
Pigsty *69* Pier Paolo Pasolini
Pigtails and Peaches *19* Raoul Barré, Charles Bowers
Piker's Peak *57* Friz Freleng
Pikkupojat *87* Ere Kokkonen
Pikoló Világos, Egy *55* Félix Máriássy
Pikoo *81* Satyajit Ray
Pikoo's Day *81* Satyajit Ray
Pikovaya Dama *16* Yakov Protazanov
Pikovaya Dama *60* Roman Tikhomirov
Pilatus und Andere *72* Andrzej Wajda
Pile Driver, The *14* Charles Chaplin, Mack Sennett
Pilgrim, The *23* Charles Chaplin
Pilgrim, Farewell *80* Michael Roemer
Pilgrim Lady, The *47* Lesley Selander
Pilgrim Porky *40* Robert Clampett
Pilgrimage *33* William Collier, John Ford
Pilgrimage *72* Beni Montresor
Pilgrimage at Night *59* Shiro Toyoda
Pilgrimage for Peace, Pope Paul VI Visits America, A *66* Carl Allensworth
Pilgrimage to Kevlaar *21* Ivan Hedqvist
Pilgrimage to the Virgin *60* Vojtěch Jasný
Pilgrimage to the Virgin Mary *60* Vojtěch Jasný
Pilgrims of the Night *21* Edward Sloman
Pill, The *67* Herschell Gordon Lewis
Pill Maker's Mistake, The *06* Lewin Fitzhamon
Pill Pounder, The *23* Gregory La Cava
Pillage by Pillar Box *07* Lewin Fitzhamon
Pillanatnyi Pénzzavar *39* József Kanizsay
Pillar of Fire, The *63* Larry Frisch
Pillar of Flame, A *15* Van Dyke Brooke
Pillar of Mist, The *86* Choi-su Park
Pillar to Post *47* Philip Leacock
Pillars of Society *16* D. W. Griffith, Raoul Walsh
Pillars of Society *20* Rex Wilson
Pillars of Society *35* Douglas Sirk
Pillars of the Sky *56* George Marshall
Pillole di Ercole, Le *60* Nino Manfredi, Luciano Salce
Pillory, The *16* Frederick Sullivan
Pillow of Death *45* Wallace Fox
Pillow Talk *59* Michael Gordon
Pillow to Post *45* Vincent Sherman
Pills for Papa *20* Alfred Santell
Pilot, The *79* Cliff Robertson
Pilot Is Safe, The *41* Jack Lee
Pilot No. 5 *42* George Sidney
Pilot of Peace, The *15* W. C. Morris
Pilot Returns, A *42* Roberto Rossellini
Pilota Ritorna, Un *42* Roberto Rossellini
Pilote de Guerre, Pilote de Ligne *49* Yves Ciampi
Piloti *89* Otakar Fuka
Pilots, The *35* Yuli Raizman
Pilots *38* Leonid Varmalov

Pimple's Some Burglar *15* Fred Evans, Joe Evans

Pimple's Sporting Chance *13* Fred Evans, Joe Evans

Pimple's Storyette *15* Fred Evans, Joe Evans

Pimple's Tableaux Vivants *17* Fred Evans, Joe Evans

Pimple's Tenth Commandment *16* Fred Evans, Joe Evans

Pimple's The Case of Johnny Walker *15* Charles H. Weston

Pimple's The Whip *17* Fred Evans, Joe Evans

Pimple's The Woman Who Did *17* Fred Evans, Joe Evans

Pimple's Three *15* Fred Evans, Joe Evans

Pimple's Three Musketeers *22* Fred Evans, Joe Evans

Pimple's Three O'Clock Race *15* Fred Evans, Joe Evans

Pimple's Three Weeks *15* Charles H. Weston

Pimple's Three Weeks, Without the Option *15* Charles H. Weston

Pimple's Topical Gazette *20* Fred Evans, Joe Evans

Pimple's Trousers *14* Fred Evans, Joe Evans

Pimple's Uncle *15* Fred Evans, Joe Evans

Pimple's Vengeance *14* Fred Evans, Joe Evans

Pimple's Wife *13* Fred Evans, Joe Evans

Pimple's Willit-Wasit-Isit *15* Fred Evans, Joe Evans

Pimple's Wonderful Gramophone *13* Fred Evans, Joe Evans

Pimple's Zeppelin Scare *16* Fred Evans, Joe Evans

Pin *88* Sándor Stern

Pin Feathers *33* Walter Lantz

Pin Pricks *15* Cecil Birch

Pin Up Girl *44* H. Bruce Humberstone

Pinball Pick-Up *81* George Mihalka

Pinball Summer *81* George Mihalka

Pinch, The *15* Frank Lloyd

Pinch Hitter, The *17* Victor Schertzinger

Pinch Hitter, The *25* Joseph E. Henabery

Ping-Pong *02* James A. Williamson

Ping Pong *85* Po-chih Leong

Ping Pong Woo *15* Carl Francis Lederer

Pingwin *64* Jerzy Stefan Stawiński

Pinhamy *79* Lester James Peries

Pink and Blue Blues *52* Pete Burness

Pink Cadillac *89* Buddy Van Horn

Pink Chiquitas, The *86* Anthony Currie

Pink Elephants *26* Stephen Roberts

Pink Flamingos *72* John Waters

Pink Floyd—The Wall *82* Alan Parker

Pink Gods *22* Penrhyn Stanlaws

Pink Jungle, The *68* Delbert Mann

Pink Motel *83* Mike MacFarland

Pink Nights *85* Philip Koch

Pink Pajama Girl, The *12* J. Stuart Blackton

Pink Panther, The *63* Blake Edwards

Pink Panther Strikes Again, The *76* Blake Edwards

Pink String and Sealing Wax *45* Robert Hamer

Pink Telephone, The *75* Édouard Molinaro

Pink Tights *20* B. Reeves Eason

Pinkerton Pup's Portrait, The *18* C. T. Anderson

Pinky *49* John Ford, Elia Kazan

Pinky's Gang *86* Linda Wendel

Pinnacle, The *19* Erich von Stroheim

Pinnacle Rider, The *26* William Wyler

Pinne e Arpioni *52* Folco Quilici

Pinocchio *11* Enrico Guazzoni

Pinocchio *40* Hamilton Luske, Ben Sharpsteen

Pinocchio *69* Ron Merk

Pinocchio *71* Corey Allen

Pinocchio and the Emperor of the Night *87* Hal Sutherland

Pinocchio dans le Space *64* Ray Goosens

Pinocchio in Outer Space *64* Ray Goosens

Pinocchio's Adventure in Outer Space *64* Ray Goosens

Pinocchio's Storybook Adventures *79* Ron Merk

Pins and Needles *21* John Gliddon

Pinto *19* Victor Schertzinger

Pinto Bandit, The *44* Elmer Clifton

Pinto Ben *15* William S. Hart

Pinto Ben *24* William S. Hart

Pinto Canyon *40* Raymond K. Johnson

Pinto Kid, The *28* Louis King

Pinto Kid, The *40* Lambert Hillyer

Pinto Rustlers *36* Harry S. Webb

Pintor e a Cidade, O *56* Manoel De Oliveira

Pintura Mural Mexicana *53* Carlos Velo

Pinturas do Meu Irmão Julio, As *65* Manoel De Oliveira

Pioggia d'Estate *37* Mario Monicelli

Piombo e la Carne, Il *65* Marino Girolami

Pioneer Builders *32* William A. Wellman

Pioneer Days *30* Burton Gillett

Pioneer Days *40* Harry S. Webb

Pioneer Go Home *62* Gordon Douglas

Pioneer Justice *47* Ray Taylor

Pioneer Marshal *49* Philip Ford

Pioneer Scout, The *28* Lloyd Ingraham, Alfred L. Werker

Pioneer Trail *38* Joseph Levering

Pioneer Trails *23* David Smith

Pioneers, The *41* Albert Herman

Pioneers Crossing the Plains in '49 *08* Edwin S. Porter

Pioneers in Ingolstadt *70* Rainer Werner Fassbinder

Pioneers of the Frontier *40* Sam Nelson

Pioneers of the West *29* John P. McGowan

Pioneers of the West *40* Les Orlebeck

Pioniere in Ingolstadt *70* Rainer Werner Fassbinder

Pious Crooks *28* Marshall Neilan

Pip-Eye, Pup-Eye, Poop-Eye and Peep-Eye *42* Dave Fleischer

Pip from Pittsburgh, The *31* James Parrott

Pipe Dreams *76* Stephen Verona

Pipe the Whiskers *18* Hal Roach

Piper, The *22* Erle C. Kenton

Piper, The *68* Mende Brown

Piper's Price, The *16* Joseph De Grasse

Piper's Tune, The *62* Muriel Box

Pipes *65* Vojtěch Jasný

Pipes of Lucknow, The *26* Frank Tilley

Pipes of Pan, The *22* Cecil M. Hepworth

Pipi, Caca, Dodo *79* Marco Ferreri

Piping Hot *25* Charles Lamont

Piping Hot *59* Joy Batchelor, John Halas

Pippa Passes *09* D. W. Griffith

Pippi in the South Seas *74* Olle Hellbom

Pippi Långstrump på de Sju Haven *74* Olle Hellbom

Pippi on the Run *77* Olle Hellbom

Pippin Up to His Pranks *12* Bert Haldane

Pique Dame *22* Pál Fejős

Piqueurs de Fûts, Les *02* Georges Méliès

Pir v Zhirmunka *41* Mikhail Doller, Vsevolod I. Pudovkin

Pirañas, Las *67* Luis García Berlanga

Piranha *78* Joe Dante

Piranha d'Amour *85* Philippe de Broca

Piranha II: Flying Killers *81* Ovidio Assonitis, James Cameron

Piranha II: The Spawning *81* Ovidio Assonitis, James Cameron

Pirata dello Sparviero Nero, Il *58* Sergio Grieco

Pirate, The *09* Charles Magnusson

Pirate, The *47* Vincente Minnelli

Pirate and the Slave Girl, The *61* Piero Pierotti

Pirate de l'Épervier Noir, Le *58* Sergio Grieco

Pirate Gold *12* D. W. Griffith

Pirate Gold *20* George B. Seitz

Pirate Movie, The *82* Ken Annakin

Pirate of the Black Hawk *58* Sergio Grieco

Pirate Ship, The *06* Lewin Fitzhamon

Pirate Ship, The *08* Dave Aylott

Pirate Ship *49* Jean Yarbrough

Pirate Submarine *52* Georges Peclet

Pirate Treasure *34* Ray Taylor

Pirates *51* Hiroshi Inagaki

Pirates *86* Roman Polanski

Pirates Bold *15* Chester M. Franklin, Sidney Franklin

Pirates Bold *26* Luis Seel

Pirates du Rail, Les *37* Christian-Jaque

Pirate's Fiancée *69* Nelly Kaplan

Pirate's Gold, The *08* D. W. Griffith

Pirates ni Yoroshiku *88* Koichi Goto

Pirates of Blood River, The *61* John Gilling

Pirates of Capri, The *49* Edgar G. Ulmer

Pirates of Lake Mälaren *87* Allan Edwall

Pirates of Monterey *47* Alfred L. Werker

Pirates of 19..., The *11* Dave Aylott, A. E. Coleby

Pirates of 1920, The *11* Dave Aylott, A. E. Coleby

Pirates of Penzance, The *82* Wilford Leach

Pirates of Regent's Canal, The *06* Dave Aylott

Pirates of the Coast *60* Domenico Paolella

Pirates of the High Seas *50* Spencer G. Bennet, Thomas Carr

Pirates of the Mississippi, The *63* Jürgen Roland

Pirates of the Prairie *42* Howard Bretherton

Pirates of the Seven Seas *38* Harold Schuster

Pirates of the Skies *39* Joseph A. McDonough

Pirates of the Sky 27 Charles Andrews
Pirates of Tortuga 61 Robert D. Webb
Pirates of Tripoli 55 Felix E. Feist
Pirates on Horseback 41 Lesley Selander
Pirates on Lake Mälar 23 Gustaf Molander
Pirati della Malesia, I 41 Enrico Guazzoni
Pirati della Malesia, I 64 Umberto Lenzi
Pirati di Capri, I 49 Edgar G. Ulmer
Pire Nuri 68 Yılmaz Güney*
Piri Mindent Tud 32 Steve Sekely
Pirogov 47 Grigori Kozintsev
Piros Bugyelláris 38 Béla Pásztor
Pirosbetüs Hétköznapok 62 Félix Máriássy
Piroska és a Farkas 88 Márta Mészáros
Pirosmani 69 Georgy Shengelaya
Piscine, La 68 Jacques Deray
Píseň o Sletu 49 Jiří Weiss
Pisingana 86 Leopoldo Pinzón
Pisito, El 58 Marco Ferreri
Pisma Mertvogo Cheloveka 86 Konstantin Lopushansky
Pisma Myortvovo Chelovyeka 86 Konstantin Lopushansky
Pismak 85 Wojciech Has
Piso Pisello 81 Peter Del Monte
Pissarro 75 Roger Leenhardt
Piste du Nord, La 39 Jacques Feyder
Pistol for Ringo, A 65 Duccio Tessari
Pistol Harvest 51 Lesley Selander
Pistol Packin' Mama 43 Frank Woodruff
Pistol Shot, A 41 Renato Castellani
Pistola para Ringo, Una 65 Duccio Tessari
Pistola per Ringo, Una 65 Duccio Tessari
Pistolas No Discuten, Las 64 Mario Caiano
Pistole Non Discutono, Le 64 Mario Caiano
Pistolère, Le 71 Guy Casaril, Christian-Jaque
Pistolero 67 Richard Thorpe
Pistolero dell'Ave Maria, Il 69 Ferdinando Baldi
Pistolero of Red River, The 67 Richard Thorpe
Pistoleros, Los 61 Benito Alazraki
Pistoleros de Casa Grande, Los 64 Roy Rowland
Pistols 74 Jiří Tirl
Pistols Don't Say No 64 Mario Caiano
Pistols for Two 13 Charles C. Calvert
Pistonnée, Le 70 Claude Berri
Pit, The 14 Maurice Tourneur
Pit, The 57 Kon Ichikawa
Pit, The 62 Edward Abrahams
Pit, The 67 Roy Ward Baker
Pit, The 84 Louis Lehman
Pit and the Pendulum, The 13 Alice Guy-Blaché
Pit and the Pendulum, The 61 Roger Corman
Pit of Darkness 61 Lance Comfort
Pit of Loneliness 50 Jacqueline Audry
Pit Stop 69 Jack Hill
Pit, the Pendulum and Hope, The 83 Jan Švankmajer
Pita Putra 88 Munim Barua
Pitboy's Romance, A 17 A. E. Coleby, Arthur H. Rooke
Pitch o' Chance, The 15 Frank Borzage
Pitfall, The 15 James W. Horne
Pitfall 48 André De Toth

Pitfall, The 61 Hiroshi Teshigahara
Pitfalls of a Big City 19 Frank Lloyd
Pitfalls of Passion 27 Leonard Livingstone
Pits 28 Abram Room
Pittsburgh 42 Lewis Seiler
Pittsburgh Kid, The 41 Jack Townley
Pity the Poor Blind 07 J. H. Martin
Pity the Poor Rich 35 Ian Walker
Più Bella Serata della Mia Vita, La 72 Ettore Scola
Più Corto Giorno, Il 63 Sergio Corbucci
Più Grande Amore, Il 25 Augusto Genina
Più Grande Colpo del Secolo, Il 66 Jean Delannoy
Più Grande Rapina del West, La 67 Maurizio Lucidi
Pixote 80 Hector Babenco
Piyade Osman 70 Şerif Gören, Yılmaz Güney
Pizhon 29 Mark Donskoi
Pizza Connection, The 85 Damiano Damiani
Pizza Triangle, The 70 Ettore Scola
Pizza Tweety Pie, A 58 Friz Freleng
Pizzaiolo et Mozzarel 85 Christian Gion
Pizzicato Pussycat 55 Friz Freleng
Placard Infernal, Le 07 Georges Méliès
Place à Olivier Guimond 66 Gilles Carle
Place at the Coast, The 86 George Ogilvie
Place aux Jerolas 67 Gilles Carle
Place Beyond the Winds, The 16 Joseph De Grasse
Place Called Glory, A 64 Sheldon Reynolds
Place Called Today, A 72 Don Schain
Place de la Bastille 1896 Georges Méliès
Place de la Concorde 1896 Georges Méliès
Place de la Concorde 39 Karel Lamač
Place de la République 73 Louis Malle
Place de l'Opéra, 1st View 1896 Georges Méliès
Place de l'Opéra, 2nd View 1896 Georges Méliès
Place de l'Opéra, 3rd View 1898 Georges Méliès
Place de l'Opéra, 1er Aspect 1896 Georges Méliès
Place de l'Opéra, 2ème Aspect 1896 Georges Méliès
Place du Théâtre Français 1896 Georges Méliès
Place for Gold, A 60 Basil Wright
Place for Lovers, A 68 Vittorio De Sica
Place in the Sun, A 14 Ethyle Batley
Place in the Sun, A 16 Lawrence Trimble
Place in the Sun, A 51 George Stevens
Place in the Sun, A 88 Young Y. Jin
Place of Honour, The 21 Sinclair Hill
Place of One's Own, A 45 Bernard Knowles
Place of the Honeymoons, The 20 Kenean Buel
Place of Weeping, A 86 Darrell Roodt
Place Saint-Augustin 1896 Georges Méliès
Place to Go, A 63 Basil Dearden
Place Without Parents, A 74 Ken Handler
Placer de la Venganza, El 87 Hernando Name
Placer de Matar, El 88 Felix Rotoeta
Places in the Heart 84 Robert Benton

Plácido 61 Luis García Berlanga
Plácido 86 Sergio Giral
Placier Est Tenace, Le 10 Émile Cohl
¡Plaff! 88 Juan Carlos Tabio
Plage de Villiers par Gros Temps 1896 Georges Méliès
Plage du Désir, La 62 Ruy Guerra
Plague 78 Ed Hunt
Plague Dogs, The 82 Martin Rosen
Plague in Florence, The 19 Otto Rippert
Plague M3 78 Ed Hunt
Plague of the Zombies, The 65 John Gilling
Plagues and Puppy Love 17 Larry Semon
Plain and Fancy Girls 25 Leo McCarey
Plain Clothes 25 Harry Edwards
Plain Clothes 88 Martha Coolidge
Plain Jane 16 Charles Miller
Plain Man's Guide to Advertising, The 62 Bob Godfrey
Plain People 45 Grigori Kozintsev, Leonid Trauberg
Plain Song, A 10 D. W. Griffith
Plain Woman, A 27 Heinosuke Gosho
Plains, My Plains 57 Vera Stroyeva
Plains of Heaven, The 82 Ian Pringle
Plainsman, The 36 Cecil B. DeMille, Arthur Rosson
Plainsman, The 63 Herschel Daugherty
Plainsman, The 66 David Lowell Rich
Plainsman and the Lady, The 46 Joseph Kane
Plainsong 82 Ed Stabile
Plaisir, Le 51 Max Ophüls
Plaisir à Trois 73 Jesús Franco
Plaisirs de Paris 32 Edmond T. Gréville
Plaisirs Défendus 33 Alberto Cavalcanti
Plan for Destruction 43 Edward L. Cahn
Plan 9 from Outer Space 56 Edward D. Wood, Jr.
Plan of Great Works 30 Abram Room
Plan Velikikh Rabot 30 Abram Room
Planche du Diable, La 04 Georges Méliès
Plane Crazy 28 Walt Disney, Ubbe Iwerks
Plane Daffy 44 Frank Tashlin
Plane Dippy 36 Tex Avery
Planes, Trains and Automobiles 87 John Hughes
Planet of Blood 65 Mario Bava
Planet of Blood 66 Curtis Harrington, Mikhail Karyukov, Alexander Kozyr
Planet of Dinosaurs 78 James K. Shea
Planet of Horrors 81 Bruce Clark
Planet of Storms 62 Pavel Klushantsev
Planet of Terror, The 65 Mario Bava
Planet of the Apes 68 Franklin J. Schaffner
Planet of the Damned, The 65 Mario Bava
Planet of the Lifeless Men 61 Antonio Margheriti
Planet of the Vampires 65 Mario Bava
Planet on the Prowl 65 Antonio Margheriti
Planeta Burg 62 Pavel Klushantsev
Planeta Ciego 75 Amando De Ossorio
Planeta de las Mujeres Invasoras, El 65 Alfredo B. Crevenna
Planète Fauve, La 59 Jean Brismée, André Delvaux

Planète Sauvage, La *73* René Laloux
Planets Against Us, The *61* Romano Ferrara
Plank, The *67* Eric Sykes
Planned Crops *43* Len Lye
Plans of the Fortress, The *10* Theo Bouwmeester
Planter, The *17* Thomas Heffron, John Ince
Planter's Daughter, The *13* Charles Raymond
Planter's Wife, The *08* D. W. Griffith
Planter's Wife, The *52* Ken Annakin
Planton du Colonel, Le *1897* Alice Guy-Blaché
Plants Are Watching, The *78* Jonathan Sarno
Plastered in Paris *28* Ben Stoloff
Plastic Age, The *25* Wesley Ruggles
Plastic Bag, The *86* Hans Otto Nicolayssen
Plastic Dome of Norma Jean, The *66* Juleen Compton
Plastikkposen *86* Hans Otto Nicolayssen
Plastiques *63* Henri Storck
Plastposen *86* Hans Otto Nicolayssen
Plateau, Le *05* Alice Guy-Blaché
Platillos Voladores, Los *55* Julián Soler
Platinum Blonde *31* Frank Capra
Platinum High School *60* Charles Haas
Platinum Life, The *87* Claude Cadiou
Platonische Ehe, Die *19* Paul Leni
Platoon *86* Oliver Stone
Platoon Leader *88* Aaron Norris
Plato's Cave Inn *80* Stan Vanderbeek
Platos Voladores, Los *55* Julián Soler
Platypus, The *49* David Hand
Plavec *81* Irakli Kvirikadze
Play, The *62* Dušan Vukotić
Play *68* Jerzy Kawalerowicz
Play Ball *20* Frank Moser
Play Ball *21* Julian Ollendorff
Play Ball *25* Spencer G. Bennet
Play Ball *33* Ubbe Iwerks
Play...Boy *85* Joaquim Leitão
Play Dead *81* Peter Wittman
Play Dirty *68* André De Toth
Play Girl *28* Arthur Rosson
Play Girl *32* Ray Enright
Play Girl *40* Frank Woodruff
Play in Colors, A *34* Oskar Fischinger
Play in the Summer Breezes *39* Roger von Norman
Play It Again, Sam *72* Herbert Ross
Play It As It Lays *72* Frank Perry
Play It Cool *62* Michael Winner
Play It Cool *70* Yasuzo Masumura
Play It Cooler *61* Ken Hughes
Play Misty for Me *71* Clint Eastwood
Play Safe *27* Joseph E. Henabery
Play Safe *36* Dave Fleischer
Play Square *21* William K. Howard
Play Up the Band *35* Harry Hughes
Playa de los Perros, La *86* José Fonseca e Costa
Playa del Amor, La *79* Adolfo Aristarain
Playa Vacía, La *79* Roberto Gavaldón
Playback *62* Quentin Lawrence
Playbirds, The *78* Willy Roe
Playboy, The *38* Walter Forde
Playboy of Paris, The *30* Ludwig Berger

Playboy of the Western World, The *62* Brian Desmond Hurst
Players, The *41* G. W. Pabst
Players *79* Anthony Harvey
Players *80* Bruce Beresford
Players at the Gate of Love, The *37* Seto Waimon
Playful Pan *30* Burton Gillett
Playful Pest, The *43* Paul Sommer
Playful Polar Bears, The *38* Dave Fleischer
Playful Pup, The *37* Walter Lantz
Playful Robot, The *56* Dušan Vukotić
Playgirl *54* Joseph Pevney
Playgirl *68* Will Tremper
Playgirl After Dark *60* Terence Young
Playgirl and the War Minister, The *62* Anthony Kimmins
Playgirl Gang *75* Jack Hill
Playgirl Killer, The *70* Erick Santamaria
Playgirls *42* Jean Negulesco
Playgirls and the Bellboy, The *61* Francis Ford Coppola, Fritz Umgelter
Playgirls and the Vampire, The *60* Piero Regnoli
Playground, The *65* Richard Hilliard
Playground Express *55* John Irwin
Playhouse, The *21* Edward F. Cline, Buster Keaton
Playing Around *29* Mervyn LeRoy
Playing at Doctors *22* Bernard Dudley
Playing at Love *59* Philippe de Broca
Playing Away *86* Horace Ove
Playing Beatie Bow *86* Donald Crombie
Playing Cards *1896* Georges Méliès
Playing Dead *15* Sidney Rankin Drew
Playing Double *23* Dick Rush
Playing for Keeps *85* Károly Makk
Playing for Keeps *86* Bob Weinstein, Harvey Weinstein
Playing It Wild *23* William Duncan
Playing Politics *36* Art Davis, Sid Marcus
Playing the Deuce *15* Will P. Kellino
Playing the Game *18* Victor Schertzinger
Playing the Game *22* George Wynn
Playing the Game *31* Norman Z. McLeod
Playing the Pied Piper *41* Lou Lilly
Playing the Ponies *37* Charles Lamont
Playing Truant *10* H. Oceano Martinek
Playing Trumps *12* Alice Guy-Blaché
Playing with Fire *16* Francis J. Grandon
Playing with Fire *21* Dallas M. Fitzgerald
Playing with Fire *26* Charles Bowers
Playing with Souls *25* Ralph Ince
Playmates, The *14* Mauritz Stiller
Playmates *41* David Butler
Playmates *69* Jean-Claude Dague, Louis Soulanes
Plaything, The *29* Castleton Knight
Plaything of Broadway, The *21* John Francis Dillon
Playthings *18* Douglas Gerrard
Playthings of Desire *24* Burton L. King
Playthings of Destiny *21* Edwin Carewe
Playthings of Hollywood *31* William A. O'Connor
Playtime *61* Fabien Collin, François Moreuil
Playtime *67* Jacques Tati
Playtime for Workers *43* Harold Baim
Plaza Real *88* Herbert Vesely

Plaza Suite *70* Arthur Hiller
Plea, The *67* Tenghiz Abuladze
Plea for Passion, A *56* Luciano Emmer
Pleasant Breakfast, A *03* Alf Collins
Pleasantville *76* Kenneth Locker, Vicki Polon
Please Answer *40* Roy Rowland
Please Believe Me *50* Norman Taurog
Please Conductor, Don't Put Me Off the Train *07* Arthur Gilbert
Please Don't Eat My Mother! *72* Carl Monson
Please Don't Eat the Daisies *60* Charles Walters
Please Excuse Me *26* Sam Newfield
Please Get Married *19* John Ince
Please Go 'Way and Let Me Sleep *31* Dave Fleischer
Please Help Emily *17* Del Henderson
Please Keep Me in Your Dreams *37* Dave Fleischer
Please, Mr. Balzac *56* Marc Allégret
Please Murder Me! *56* Peter Godfrey
Please, Not My Mother *72* Carl Monson
Please, Not Now *61* Jean Aurel, Jack Dunn Trop, Roger Vadim
Please Release My Mother *72* Carl Monson
Please Sir *71* Mark Stuart
Please Stand By *72* Jack Milton, Joanna Milton
Please Teacher *37* Stafford Dickens
Please Turn Over *59* Gerald Thomas
Pleased to Meet Cha! *35* Dave Fleischer
Pleasure *33* Otto Brower
Pleasure, The *85* Aristide Massaccesi
Pleasure Before Business *27* Frank R. Strayer
Pleasure Bound *25* Norman Taurog
Pleasure Buyers, The *25* Chester Withey
Pleasure Crazed *29* Donald Gallagher, Charles Klein
Pleasure Cruise *33* Frank Tuttle
Pleasure Doing Business, A *79* Steven Vagnino
Pleasure Garden, The *25* Alfred Hitchcock
Pleasure Garden, The *52* James Broughton
Pleasure Garden *61* Alf Kjellin
Pleasure Girl *60* Valerio Zurlini
Pleasure Girls, The *65* Gerry O'Hara
Pleasure Lover *59* Charles Saunders
Pleasure Lovers, The *59* Charles Saunders
Pleasure Mad *23* Reginald Barker
Pleasure of His Company, The *61* George Seaton
Pleasure of Vengeance, The *87* Hernando Name
Pleasure Party *74* Claude Chabrol
Pleasure Planet *86* Albert Pyun
Pleasure Plantation *70* Jerry Denby
Pleasure Seekers, The *20* George Archainbaud
Pleasure Seekers, The *64* Jean Negulesco
Pleasures and Vices *62* Marcel Blistène
Pleasures of the Flesh, The *65* Nagisa Oshima
Pleasures of the Rich *26* Louis Gasnier
Plebei *15* Yakov Protazanov
Plebeian *15* Yakov Protazanov
Pledge, The *82* Digby Rumsey
Pledge to Bataan *43* David Griffin

Policy of Pinpricks, A *13* Hay Plumb
Polijuschka *58* Carmine Gallone
Polikushka *19* Alexander Sanin
Poliorkia *62* Claude Bernard-Aubert
Poliorkia ou Les Moutons de Praxos *62* Claude Bernard-Aubert
Polioty vo Sne Naiavou *83* Roman Balajan
Polis Paulus Påskasmäll *24* Gustaf Molander
Polish Blood *34* Karel Lamač
Polish Suite *62* Jan Łomnicki
Polish War Worker, The *86* Nico Hoffmann, Thomas Strittmater
Polishing Up *14* George D. Baker
Polite Lunatic, The *05* James A. Williamson
Polite Parson, The *09* Jack Smith
Politic Flapper, The *27* King Vidor
Political Asylum *75* Manuel Zecena Dieguez
Political Discussion, A *03* Alf Collins
Political Duel, A *1899* Georges Méliès
Political Party, A *33* Norman Lee
Political Portraits *69* Gregory Markopoulos
Politicians, The *20* Raoul Barré, Charles Bowers
Politician's Dream, The *11* George D. Baker
Politician's Love Story, The *09* D. W. Griffith
Politics *31* Charles Reisner
Politics and the Press *14* Van Dyke Brooke
Politimesteren *11* August Blom
Polizeiakte 909 *33* Robert Wiene
Polizeibericht Überfall *28* Ernö Metzner
Polizeifilm *68* Wim Wenders
Polizia Ringrazia, La *72* Steno
Polk County Pot Plane *77* James West
Polk File on the Air, The *87* Dionyssis Grigoratos
Polka Dot Puss *49* Joseph Barbera, William Hanna
Polka on the Brain *08* Walter R. Booth
Polly *21* Fred Paul
Polly Ann *17* Charles Miller
Polly Fulton *47* Robert Z. Leonard
Polly of the Circus *17* Edwin L. Hollywood, Charles T. Horan
Polly of the Circus *32* Alfred Santell
Polly of the Follies *22* John Emerson
Polly of the Movies *27* Scott Pembroke
Polly of the Storm Country *20* Arthur Rosson
Polly Put the Kettle On *16* Douglas Gerrard
Polly Redhead *17* Jack Conway
Polly the Girl Scout *11* A. E. Coleby
Polly the Girl Scout and Grandpa's Medals *13* Bert Haldane
Polly the Girl Scout and the Jewel Thieves *13* Bert Haldane
Polly the Girl Scout's Timely Aid *13* Bert Haldane
Polly-Tix in Washington *33* Charles Lamont
Polly Wants a Doctor *44* Howard Swift
Polly with a Past *20* Leander De Cordova
Pollyanna *20* Paul Powell
Pollyanna *60* David Swift
Polly's Day at Home *17* Harry S. Palmer

Polly's Excursion *08* A. E. Coleby
Polly's Progress *14* Lawrence Trimble
Polly's Two Fathers *36* Will Hammer
Polo *36* George Sidney
Polo Boat, The *13* Émile Cohl
Polo Champion, The *15* M. Hugon
Polo Joe *36* William McGann
Polonaise, La *71* Pierre Etaix
Polowanie na Muchy *69* Andrzej Wajda
Polownia Rains, The *24* Teinosuke Kinugasa
Polska Kronika Filmowa Nr 52 A-B *59* Andrzej Munk
Polterabend *40* Carl Boese
Poltergeist *82* Tobe Hooper
Poltergeist II *86* Brian Gibson
Poltergeist II: The Other Side *86* Brian Gibson
Poltergeist III *88* Gary Sherman
Polustanok *63* Boris Barnet
Polvere di Stelle *73* Alberto Sordi
Polyecran for International Exposition of Labor Turin *61* Jaromil Jireš*
Polyecran for the Brno Industrial Fair *60* Jaromil Jireš, Ján Kadár
Polyekrán pro BVV *60* Jaromil Jireš, Ján Kadár
Polyekrán pro Mezinárodní Výstavu Práce Turin *61* Jaromil Jireš*
Polyester *81* John Waters
Polyorchia *62* Claude Bernard-Aubert
Pom-Pom Girls, The *76* Joseph Ruben
Pomme, La *68* Charles Matton
Pomme d'Amour *32* Jean Dréville
Pommier, Le *02* Alice Guy-Blaché
Pomnalui Nunsogi *86* Chang Bom Rim, Ko Hak Rim
Pompadour, Die *35* Veidt Harlan, Heinz Helbig, Willy Schmidt-Gentner
Pompadourtasken *13* August Blom
Pompeii *86* Chuck Vincent
Pömperlys Kampf mit dem Schneeschuh *22* Arnold Fanck, Forest Holger-Madsen
Pompieri, I *85* Neri Parenti
Pompiers: Attaque du Feu *1895* Louis Lumière
Pompiers: Sortie de la Pompe, Mise en Batterie, Attaque du Feu, Sauvetage *1895* Louis Lumière
Pompon Malencontreux, Le *04* Alice Guy-Blaché
Pomsta *68* Jiří Brdečka, Evald Schorm
Poncomania *39* Arthur Leonard
Ponderoso Caballero *34* Max Nosseck
Ponedeljak ili Utorak *66* Vatroslav Mimica
Pong *85* Doo-yong Lee
Ponirah *83* Slamet Rahardjo
Ponirah Terpidana *83* Slamet Rahardjo
Ponjola *23* Donald Crisp
Ponky's Burglar *13* Stuart Kinder
Ponky's Houseboat *13* Stuart Kinder
Ponnu *88* P. G. Viswambaran
Pont d'Iéna, Le *00* Louis Lumière
Pont du Nord, Le *81* Jacques Rivette
Pont sur l'Abîme, Le *12* Louis Feuillade
Pontcarral, Colonel d'Empire *42* Jean Delannoy
Ponte dei Fantasmi, Il *12* Luigi Maggi
Ponte dei Sospiri, Il *40* Mario Bonnard
Ponte di Vetro, Il *40* Goffredo Alessand-

rini
Pontius Pilate *61* Gian Paolo Callegari, Irving Rapper
Pony Express *09* Edwin S. Porter
Pony Express, The *25* James Cruze
Pony Express *53* Jerry Hopper
Pony Express Boy, The *86* Franco Amurri
Pony Express Rider, The *10* Gilbert M. Anderson
Pony Express Rider *26* Robert J. Horner
Pony Express Rider *76* Robert Totten
Pony Post *40* Ray Taylor
Pony Soldier *51* Joseph M. Newman
Pony Who Paid the Rent, The *12* Lewin Fitzhamon
Ponzio Pilato *61* Gian Paolo Callegari, Irving Rapper
Pooch Parade *40* Art Davis, Sid Marcus
Pookie *69* Alan J. Pakula
Pool Hustlers, The *83* Maurizio Ponzi
Pool of Flame, The *16* Otis Turner
Pool of London *50* Basil Dearden
Poopdeck Pappy *40* Dave Fleischer
Poor Albert and Little Annie *72* Paul Leder
Poor Algy *05* Edwin S. Porter
Poor Aunt Matilda *08* Percy Stow
Poor Boob *19* Donald Crisp
Poor But Beautiful *56* Dino Risi
Poor But Handsome *56* Dino Risi
Poor Butterfly *24* Stephen Roberts
Poor Butterfly *86* Raúl De la Torre
Poor Cinderella *34* Dave Fleischer
Poor Clem *15* Bert Haldane
Poor Cow *67* Kenneth Loach
Poor, Dear Margaret Kirby *21* William P. S. Earle
Poor Drenthe *28* Joris Ivens
Poor Elmer *38* Sid Marcus
Poor Fish, A *22* Erle C. Kenton
Poor Fish, The *24* Leo McCarey
Poor Fish, A *31* Mack Sennett
Poor Fish, The *33* Joseph Santley
Poor Girl *29* Martin Frič
Poor Girls *27* William James Craft
Poor Girl's Romance, A *26* F. Harmon Weight
Poor Little Butterfly *38* Ben Harrison
Poor Little Chap He Was Only Dreaming *13* Émile Cohl
Poor Little Peppina *16* Sidney Olcott
Poor Little Rich Girl, The *17* Maurice Tourneur
Poor Little Rich Girl *36* Irving Cummings
Poor Little Rich Girl *65* Andy Warhol
Poor Men's Wives *23* Louis Gasnier
Poor Millionaire, The *30* George Melford
Poor Millionaire, The *39* Joe Stöckel
Poor Millionaires *58* Dino Risi
Poor Nut, The *27* Richard Wallace
Poor Old Bill *31* Monty Banks
Poor Old Mr. and Mrs. Brown in the Stocks *05* Arthur Cooper
Poor Old Piecan *15* Joe Evans
Poor Ones, The *75* Yılmaz Güney, Atıf Yılmaz
Poor Outlaws *65* Miklós Jancsó
Poor Pa, or Mother's Day Out *06* Tom Green
Poor Pa Pays *10* Joe Rosenthal

Poor Pa Pays *13* Dave Aylott
Poor Papa *28* Walt Disney
Poor Pa's Folly *07* James A. Williamson
Poor People *39* Elmar Klos
Poor Pérez *37* Luis César Amadori
Poor Pretty Eddie *75* Richard Robinson
Poor Princess, The *19* Anders Wilhelm Sandberg
Poor Relation, A *21* Clarence Badger
Poor Relations *19* King Vidor
Poor Rich, The *34* Edward Sedgwick
Poor Rich Man, The *18* Charles Brabin
Poor Schmaltz *15* Hugh Ford
Poor Si Keeler *16* Gregory La Cava
Poor Sick Men, The *11* D. W. Griffith
Poor Simp, The *20* Victor Heerman
Poor White Trash *57* Harold Daniels
Poor White Trash II *76* S. F. Brownrigg
Poorluck As a Messenger Boy *13* Frank Wilson
Poorluck Minds the Shop *14* Frank Wilson
Poorluck's Excursion Tickets *11* Lewin Fitzhamon
Poorlucks' First Tiff, The *10* Lewin Fitzhamon
Poorluck's Picnic *12* Hay Plumb
Poorlucks Take Part in a Pageant, The *10* Lewin Fitzhamon
Poovanam *68* Shyam Benegal
Poovizhi Vasalile *87* Fazil
Pop *27* Widgey R. Newman
Pop Always Pays *40* Leslie Goodwins
Pop and Mom in Wild Oysters *41* Dave Fleischer
Pop Buell, Hoosier Farmer in Laos *65* Willard Van Dyke
Pop Corn and Chips *85* Mariano Laurenti
Pop Corn and Potato Chips *85* Mariano Laurenti
Pop Corn e Patatine *85* Mariano Laurenti
Pop Gear *65* Frederic Goode
Pop Goes My Heart *34* Friz Freleng
Pop 'Im Pop *50* Robert McKimson
Pop Pirates *84* Jack Grossman
Popas în Tabăra de Vară *58* Márta Mészáros
Popcorn *69* Peter Clifton
Popcorn Story *50* Art Babbitt
Popdown *68* Fred Marshall
Pope Joan *72* Michael Anderson
Pope of Greenwich Village, The *84* Stuart Rosenberg
Pope Ondine Story, The *66* Andy Warhol
Popeye *80* Robert Altman
Popeye Meets Rip Van Winkle *41* Dave Fleischer
Popeye Meets William Tell *40* Dave Fleischer
Popeye Presents Eugene the Jeep *40* Dave Fleischer
Popeye the Sailor *33* Dave Fleischer
Popeye the Sailor Meets Ali Baba's Forty Thieves *37* Dave Fleischer
Popeye the Sailor Meets Sinbad the Sailor *36* Dave Fleischer
Popi *69* Arthur Hiller
Popiełusko *88* Agnieszka Holland
Popiół i Diament *58* Andrzej Wajda
Popioły *65* Andrzej Wajda
Poppies *14* Stuart Kinder

Poppies, The *35* Kenji Mizoguchi
Poppies Are Also Flowers *66* Terence Young
Poppies of Flanders *27* Arthur Maude
Poppy *17* Émile Chautard, Edward José
Poppy *35* Kenji Mizoguchi
Poppy *36* Stuart Heisler, A. Edward Sutherland
Poppy Girl *19* William S. Hart, Lambert Hillyer
Poppy Girl's Husband, The *19* William S. Hart, Lambert Hillyer
Poppy Is Also a Flower, The *66* Terence Young
Poppy Trail, The *20* Carl Harbaugh
Poprigunya *55* Alexander Feinzimmer, Samson Samsonov
Popsy Pop *70* Jean Herman
Popsy Wopsy *13* Maurice Elvey
Popular Melodies *33* Dave Fleischer
Popular Pieces *29* Dave Aylott
Popular Poetry, Theory and Practice *72* Raúl Ruiz
Popular Power, The *79* Patricio Guzmán
Popular Sin, The *26* Malcolm St. Clair
Population: One *86* Renee Daalder
Poputchik *88* Ivan Kiasashvili
Poquianchis, Las *76* Felipe Cazals
Por Buen Camino *36* Eduardo Morera
Por la Puerta Falsa *50* Fernando De Fuentes
Por la Tierra Ajena *69* Miguel Littin
Por los Caminos Verdes *87* Marilda Vera
Por Mis Pistolas *39* José Bohr
Por Mis Pistolas *69* Miguel Delgado
¿Por Qué Seguir Matando? *66* José Antonio De la Loma
¿Por Qué Te Engaña Tu Marido? *68* Manuel Summers
Por un Puñado de Dólares *64* Sergio Leone
Por un Vestido de Novia *86* Arturo Martínez
Porcelain Lamp, The *21* Ben Blake
Porcelaines Tendres *09* Émile Cohl
Porcile, Il *69* Pier Paolo Pasolini
Porgy and Bess *59* Otto Preminger
Pori *30* Baron A. von Dungern
Porion, Le *21* Georges Champavert
Pork Chop Hill *59* Lewis Milestone
Pork Chop Phooey *65* Joseph Barbera, William Hanna
Porkala *56* Jörn Donner
Porkuliar Piggy *44* Bob Wickersham
Porky and Daffy *38* Robert Clampett
Porky and Gabby *37* Ubbe Iwerks
Porky and Teabiscuit *39* Cal Dalton, Ben Hardaway
Porky at the Crocadero *38* Frank Tashlin
Porky Chops *49* Art Davis
Porky in Egypt *38* Robert Clampett
Porky in Wackyland *38* Robert Clampett
Porky of the Northwoods *36* Frank Tashlin
Porky Pig in Hollywood *86* Friz Freleng, Chuck Jones
Porky Pig's Feat *43* Frank Tashlin
Porky the Fireman *38* Frank Tashlin
Porky the Giant Killer *39* Cal Dalton, Ben Hardaway
Porky the Gob *38* Cal Dalton, Ben Hard-

away
Porky the Rainmaker *36* Tex Avery
Porky the Wrestler *36* Tex Avery
Porky's *81* Bob Clark
Porky's II: The Next Day *83* Bob Clark
Porky's Ant *41* Chuck Jones
Porky's Badtime Story *37* Robert Clampett
Porky's Baseball Broadcast *40* Friz Freleng
Porky's Bear Facts *41* Friz Freleng
Porky's Building *37* Frank Tashlin
Porky's Cafe *42* Chuck Jones
Porky's Double Trouble *37* Frank Tashlin
Porky's Duck Hunt *37* Tex Avery
Porky's Five and Ten *38* Robert Clampett
Porky's Garden *37* Tex Avery
Porky's Hare Hunt *38* Cal Dalton, Ben Hardaway
Porky's Hero Agency *37* Robert Clampett
Porky's Hired Hand *40* Friz Freleng
Porky's Hotel *39* Robert Clampett
Porky's Last Stand *40* Robert Clampett
Porky's Midnight Matinee *41* Chuck Jones
Porky's Movie Mystery *39* Robert Clampett
Porky's Moving Day *36* Jack King
Porky's Naughty Nephew *38* Robert Clampett
Porky's Party *38* Robert Clampett
Porky's Pastry Pirates *42* Friz Freleng
Porky's Pet *36* Jack King
Porky's Phoney Express *38* Cal Dalton, Cal Howard
Porky's Picnic *39* Robert Clampett
Porky's Pooch *41* Robert Clampett
Porky's Poor Fish *40* Robert Clampett
Porky's Poppa *38* Robert Clampett
Porky's Poultry Plant *36* Frank Tashlin
Porky's Preview *41* Tex Avery
Porky's Prize Pony *41* Chuck Jones
Porky's Railroad *37* Frank Tashlin
Porky's Revenge *85* James Komack
Porky's Road Race *37* Frank Tashlin
Porky's Romance *37* Frank Tashlin
Porky's Snooze Reel *41* Robert Clampett, Norm McCabe
Porky's Spring Planting *38* Frank Tashlin
Porky's Super Service *37* Ubbe Iwerks
Porky's Tire Trouble *39* Robert Clampett
Porn Flakes *76* Chuck Vincent
Porno Erotico Western *68* Gerald B. Lennox
Pornographer, The *66* Shohei Imamura
Pornographers, The *66* Shohei Imamura
Pornographers: Introduction to Anthropology, The *66* Shohei Imamura
Porridge *79* Dick Clement
Port Afrique *56* Rudolph Maté
Port Chicago *66* Bruce Baillie
Port du Désir, Le *54* Edmond T. Gréville
Port o' Dreams *29* Wesley Ruggles
Port of Call *48* Ingmar Bergman
Port of Desire *58* Yves Allégret
Port of Doom, The *13* J. Searle Dawley
Port of Escape *55* Anthony Young
Port of Flowers *43* Keisuke Kinoshita
Port of Forty Thieves, The *44* John English
Port of Freedom *44* Helmut Käutner
Port of Hate *39* Harry S. Webb
Port of Hell *54* Harold Schuster
Port of Lost Dreams *35* Frank R. Strayer

Pot Carriers, The 62 Peter Graham Scott
Pot Luck 36 Tom Walls
Pot Luck in the Army 18 Raoul Barré,
    Charles Bowers
Pot o' Gold 41 George Marshall
Pot, Parents, Police 75 Phillip Pine
Potage Indigeste 03 Alice Guy-Blaché
Potami, To 60 Nikos Koundouros
Potapov's Life 87 Nikolai Skuybin
Potash and Perlmutter 23 Clarence Badger
Potato Fritz 76 Peter Schamoni
Pote tin Kyriaki 59 Jules Dassin
Potemkin 05 Alf Collins
Potemkin 25 Sergei Eisenstein
Potent Lotion 55 John Halas*
Poteryalsya Slon 86 Yevgeni Ostashenko
Poteryannaya Fotografiya 60 Lev Kulid-
    zhanov
Pote's Poem 15 Will P. Kellino
Potifars Hustru 11 August Blom
Potiphar's Wife 17 Robert Dinesen
Potiphar's Wife 31 Maurice Elvey
Potlatch 87 Nicos Vergitsis
Potluck Pards 34 Bernard B. Ray
Poto and Cabengo 82 Jean-Pierre Gorin
Potomok Belogo Barssa 85 Tolomush
    Okeyev
Potomok Chingis-Khana 28 Vsevolod I.
    Pudovkin
Potpourri 63 Victor Jobin, Colin Low
Pots and Pans Peggie 17 W. Eugene
    Moore
Potselui Meri Pikford 27 Sergei Komarov
Potted Pantomimes 14 Will P. Kellino
Potted Plays No. 1 12 F. Martin Thornton
Potted Plays No. 2 13 F. Martin Thornton
Potted Plays No. 3 10 Walter R. Booth
Potted Psalm, The 46 James Broughton,
    Sidney Peterson
Potter of the Yard 52 Oscar Burn, John
    Wall
Potteries 81 István Gaál
Potters, The 27 Fred Newmeyer
Potter's Cart, The 1896 Georges Méliès
Potter's Clay 22 H. Grenville-Taylor,
    Douglas Payne
Pottery at Ilza 51 Andrzej Wajda
Pottery Girl's Romance, A 18 G. Fletcher
    Hewitt
Pottery Maker, The 25 Robert Flaherty
Pottery of Ilza, The 51 Andrzej Wajda
Potterymaker, A 1897 Georges Méliès
Potu Storonu Araksa 46 Esther Shub
Poudre de Vitesse 11 Émile Cohl
Poudre d'Escampette, La 70 Philippe de
    Broca
Poule et Frites 87 Luis Rego
Poule Fantaisiste, La 03 Alice Guy-Blaché
Poule Merveilleuse, La 02 Ferdinand Zecca
Poule Mouillée Qui Se Sèche, Une 12
    Émile Cohl
Poulet, Le 64 Claude Berri
Poulet au Vinaigre 84 Claude Chabrol
Poulette Grise 47 Norman McLaren
Poulot N'Est Pas Sage 12 Émile Cohl
Poultry Pirates 38 Friz Freleng
Pound 70 Robert Downey
Pound Foolish 40 Felix E. Feist
Pound Puppies and the Legend of Big
    Paw 88 Pierre DeCelles

Poupée, La 20 Henri Étiévant
Poupée, La 20 Meyrick Milton
Poupée, La 62 Jacques Baratier
Poupée Vivante, La 08 Georges Méliès
Poupées de Roseau 81 Jillali Ferhati
Pour Cent Briques, T'As Plus Rien Mainte-
    nant 82 Édouard Molinaro
Pour Clemence 77 Charles Belmont
Pour Don Carlos 21 Musidora*
Pour Épouser Gaby 17 Charles Burguet
Pour Être Aimée 33 Jacques Tourneur
Pour la Peau d'un Flic 81 Alain Delon
Pour la Suite du Monde 62 Michel Brault,
    Pierre Perrault
Pour le Meilleur et pour le Pire 75 Claude
    Jutra
Pour le Mérite 39 Karl Ritter
Pour le Mistral 65 Joris Ivens
Pour les P'tiots 08 Georges Méliès
Pour l'Espagne 63 Frédéric Rossif
Pour l'Étoile S.V.P. 08 Georges Méliès
Pour l'Honneur d'un Père 05 Ferdinand
    Zecca
Pour Sauver la Hollande 11 Abel Gance
Pour Secourer la Salade 02 Alice Guy-
    Blaché
Pour Service de Nuit 31 Henri Fescourt
Pour un Amour Lointain 67 Edmond
    Séchan
Pour un Maillot Jaune 65 Claude Lelouch
Pour un Sou d'Amour 31 Jean Grémillon
Pour une Éducation de Qualité 69 Arthur
    Lamothe
Pour une Étoile Sans Nom 66 Henri Colpi
Pour Une Nuit 21 Yakov Protazanov
Pour Une Nuit d'Amour 21 Yakov Pro-
    tazanov
Pour Une Nuit d'Amour 46 Edmond T.
    Gréville
Pour Vos Beaux Yeux 30 Henri Storck
Pourquoi 71 Kon Ichikawa
Pourquoi Israel? 73 Claude Lanzmann
Pourquoi l'Amérique? 69 Frédéric Rossif
Pourquoi l'Étrange Monsieur Zolock
    S'Intéressait-Il Tant à la Bande Dessi-
    née? 83 Yves Simoneau
Pourquoi Paris 62 Denys De la Patellière
Pourquoi Pas! 78 Coline Serreau
Pourquoi Viens-Tu Si Tard? 59 Henri
    Decoin
Pourvu Que Ce Soit une Fille 85 Mario
    Monicelli
Pourvu Qu'On Ait l'Ivresse 57 Jean-Daniel
    Pollet
Pousse Café, The 19 Raoul Barré, Charles
    Bowers
Pousse des Plantes, La 13 Léonce-Henri
    Burel
Poussière d'Ange 87 Édouard Niermans
Poussière sur la Ville 65 Arthur Lamothe
Poussières, Les 54 Georges Franju
Pouta 61 Karel Kachyňa
Poutníci 88 Zdeněk Zaoral
Pouvoir du Mal, Le 85 Krzysztof Zanussi
Pouvoir Intime 86 Yves Simoneau
Povere Bimbe 23 Giovanni Pastrone
Poveri Ma Belli 56 Dino Risi
Poveri Milionari 58 Dino Risi
Poveri Muoriono Prima, I 71 Bernardo
    Bertolucci

Poverty and Compassion 08 Theo Bouw-
    meester
Poverty and Nobility 54 Mario Mattòli
Poverty of Riches, The 21 Reginald Barker
Povest o Neftyanikakh Kaspiya 53 Roman
    Karmen
Povest' Plammennykh Let 61 Yulia
    Solntseva
Povodeň 58 Martin Frič
Powaqqatsi 88 Godfrey Reggio
Powder 16 Arthur Maude
Powder Flash of Death, The 13 Allan
    Dwan
Powder My Back 28 Roy Del Ruth
Powder River 53 Louis King
Powder River Rustlers 49 Philip Ford
Powder Town 42 Rowland V. Lee
Powdersmoke Range 35 Wallace Fox
Power 28 Howard Higgin
Power 34 Lothar Mendes
Power, The 67 Byron Haskin, George Pal
Power, The 83 Stephen Carpenter, Jeffrey
    Obrow
Power 86 Sidney Lumet
Power Among Men 58 Alexander Ham-
    mid*
Power and Glory 33 William K. Howard
Power and the Glory, The 18 Lawrence C.
    Windom
Power and the Glory, The 33 William K.
    Howard
Power and the Land, The 40 Joris Ivens
Power and the Prize, The 56 Henry Koster
Power Dive 41 James P. Hogan
Power Divine, The 23 William James
    Craft, Harry G. Moody
Power God, The 25 Ben F. Wilson
Power of a Lie, The 22 George Archain-
    baud
Power of Darkness, The 18 Cheslav
    Sabinsky
Power of Darkness 27 Robert Wiene
Power of Decision, The 17 John W. Noble
Power of Destiny 68 Jiří Brdečka
Power of Emotion, The 83 Alexander
    Kluge
Power of Evil, The 16 H. D. Horkheimer,
    H. M. Horkheimer
Power of Evil, The 29 P. Barkhoudian, M.
    Goldvani
Power of Evil, The 85 Krzysztof Zanussi
Power of Gold, The 11 Urban Gad
Power of Justice 40 Lambert Hillyer
Power of Life 38 Henry Lynn
Power of Life, The 40 Alexander Zguridi
Power of Love, The 11 August Blom
Power of Love, The 12 Allan Dwan
Power of Love, The 19 Anders Wilhelm
    Sandberg
Power of Love, The 22 Nat C. Deverich
Power of Men Is the Patience of Women,
    The 78 Cristina Perincioli
Power of Possession 45 Vernon Keays
Power of Right, The 19 F. Martin Thorn-
    ton
Power of Silence, The 28 Wallace Worsley
Power of the Mountains, The 38 Gustav
    Ucicky
Power of the Press, The 13 August Blom
Power of the Press, The 28 Frank Capra

Premier de Cordée *43* Louis Daquin
Premier Jour de Vacances de Poulot, Le *12* Émile Cohl
Premier Mai *58* Luis Saslavsky
Premier May *58* Luis Saslavsky
Premier Rendez-Vous *41* Henri Decoin
Premier Voyage *79* Nadine Trintignant
Premiere *38* Walter Summers
Première *74* István Szabó
Première Cigarette, La *04* Alice Guy-Blaché
Première Fois, La *76* Claude Berri
Première Gamelle, La *02* Alice Guy-Blaché
Première Idylle de Boucot, Le *20* Robert Saidreau
Première Nuit, La *58* Georges Franju
Première Sortie d'un Collégien, La *05* Louis Gasnier
Premières Armes *50* René Wheeler
Premières Armes de Rocambole, Les *24* Charles De Marsan, Charles Maudru
Premiers Désirs *83* David Hamilton
Premio della Bonta', Il *71* Elio Petri
Premonition *72* Alan Rudolph
Premonition, The *75* Robert Allen Schnitzer
Prends la Route *37* Jean Boyer
Prenez Garde à la Peinture *1898* Georges Méliès
Prenez Garde à la Peinture *33* Henri Chomette
Prénom Carmen *82* Jean-Luc Godard
Prenses *86* Sinan Cetin
Prep and Pep *28* David Butler
Prep School *81* Paul Almond
Preparati la Bara *68* Ferdinando Baldi
Prepared to Die *23* William Hughes Curran
Preparedness *17* Raoul Barré, Charles Bowers
Préparez Vos Mouchoirs *77* Bertrand Blier
Preppies *84* Chuck Vincent
Preppies *84* Dorian Walker
Près de Crime *21* Charles De Marsan, Charles Maudru
Presagio, Il *16* Augusto Genina
Presagio *74* Luis Alcoriza
Prescott Kid, The *34* David Selman
Prescription for Murder *58* Derek Twist
Prescription for Romance *37* S. Sylvan Simon
Prescription Murder *58* Derek Twist
Presence *65* Miklós Jancsó
Presence, The *72* Stan Brakhage
Présence Réelle, La *83* Raúl Ruiz
Present Arms *30* Edward F. Cline
Present for Her Husband, A *09* Lewin Fitzhamon
Present for Her Husband, A *12* Frank Wilson
Present for His Wife, A *10* Lewin Fitzhamon
Present from Father, A *13* Percy Stow
Present from India, A *11* Frank Wilson
Present from Uncle, A *13* Dave Aylott
Present Times *72* Péter Bacsó
Présentation *51* Eric Rohmer
Présentation ou Charlotte et Son Steak *51* Eric Rohmer

Presentiment *47* Otakar Vávra
Presenting Lily Mars *43* Norman Taurog
Presents *81* Michael Snow
Presepi, Il *32* Ferdinando Maria Poggioli
President, The *18* Carl Theodor Dreyer
Président, Le *60* Henri Verneuil
President McKinley and Escort Going to the Capitol *01* Edwin S. Porter
President McKinley's Funeral Cortege at Buffalo, NY *01* Edwin S. Porter
President McKinley's Funeral Cortege at Washington, DC *01* Edwin S. Porter
President Must Die, The *81* James L. Conway
President Roosevelt's Inauguration *05* Edwin S. Porter
President Vanishes, The *34* William A. Wellman
Presidentessa, La *52* Pietro Germi
Presidentessa, La *76* Luciano Salce
President's Analyst, The *67* Theodore J. Flicker
President's Death, The *77* Jerzy Kawalerowicz
President's Lady, The *53* Henry Levin
President's Mystery, The *36* Phil Rosen
President's Special, The *14* Charles Brabin
Presidio, The *88* Peter Hyams
Press for Time *66* Robert Asher
Press Illustrated, The *04* Lewin Fitzhamon
Pressens Magt *13* August Blom
Pressure *76* Horace Ove
Pressure of Guilt *61* Hiromichi Horikawa
Pressure of the Poster, The *15* Ethyle Batley
Pressure Point *62* Hubert Cornfield
Prestige *32* Tay Garnett
Presto Change-O *39* Chuck Jones
Prestupleniye i Nakazaniye *69* Lev Kulidzhanov
Presumed Innocent *90* Alan J. Pakula
Presumption of Stanley Hay, MP, The *25* Sinclair Hill
Prêté pour un Rendu, Un *04* Georges Méliès
Prêté pour un Rendu ou Une Bonne Farce avec Ma Tête, Un *04* Georges Méliès
Pretender, The *18* Clifford Smith
Pretender, The *47* W. Lee Wilder
Pretender, The *87* Jerzy Sztwiertnia
Pretenders, The *15* Robert Vignola
Pretenders, The *16* George D. Baker
Pretenders from Yesterday's Street *87* Janusz Kidawa
Pretora, La *76* Lucio Fulci
Pretty Baby *50* Bretaigne Windust
Pretty Baby *78* Louis Malle
Pretty Boy Floyd *60* Herbert J. Leder
Pretty But Wicked *65* J. P. De Carvalho
Pretty Clothes *27* Phil Rosen
Pretty Good for a Human Being *77* Rauni Mollberg
Pretty in Pink *86* Howard Deutch
Pretty Indian Girl, The *39* Antonio Helu
Pretty Ladies *25* Monta Bell
Pretty Maids All in a Row *71* Roger Vadim
Pretty Miss Schragg *37* Hans Deppe
Pretty Mrs. Smith *15* Hobart Bosworth
Pretty Poison *68* Noel Black
Pretty Polly *67* Guy Green

Pretty Sister of José, The *15* Allan Dwan
Pretty Smart *87* Dimitri Logothetis
Pretty Smooth *19* Rollin Sturgeon
Pretty Things, The *66* Caterina Arvat, Anthony West
Pretty Woman *90* Garry Marshall
Prettykill *87* George Kaczender
Pretzel Farming *20* Raoul Barré, Charles Bowers
Preuve, La *21* André Hugon
Preuve d'Amour *88* Miguel Courtois
Preview Murder Mystery, The *35* Robert Florey
Prey, The *20* George L. Sargent
Prey *77* Norman J. Warren
Prey, The *84* Edwin Brown
Prey for the Shadows *60* Alexandre Astruc
Prey of the Dragon, The *21* F. Martin Thornton
Prey of the Wind *26* René Clair
Přežil Jsem Svou Smrt *60* Vojtěch Jasný
Prezzo del Potere, Il *69* Tonino Valerii
Priča o Fabrika *48* Vladimir Pogačić
Price, The *11* Edwin S. Porter
Price, The *15* Joseph A. Golden
Price for Folly, A *15* George D. Baker
Price He Paid, The *16* Dave Aylott
Price Mark, The *17* Roy William Neill
Price of a Gift, The *14* Warwick Buckland
Price of a Good Sneeze, The *20* Raoul Barré, Charles Bowers
Price of a Good Time, The *17* Phillips Smalley, Lois Weber
Price of a Kiss, The *33* Marcel Silver
Price of a Party, The *24* Charles Giblyn
Price of a Song, The *35* Michael Powell
Price of Applause, The *18* Thomas Heffron
Price of Beauty, The *11* August Blom
Price of Betrayal, The *15* Victor Sjöström
Price of Bread, The *09* T. J. Gobbett
Price of Crime, The *47* Ray Nazarro
Price of Death, The *71* Enzo Gicca
Price of Deception, The *13* Bert Haldane
Price of Divorce, The *28* Sinclair Hill
Price of Fame, The *14* Warwick Buckland
Price of Fame, The *16* Charles Brabin
Price of Fear, The *28* Leigh Jason
Price of Fear, The *56* Abner Biberman
Price of Flesh, The *62* Walter Kapps
Price of Folly, The *37* Walter Summers
Price of Freedom, The *75* Lewis Gilbert
Price of Happiness, The *16* Edmund Lawrence
Price of Her Silence, The *14* Ernest G. Batley
Price of Her Soul, The *17* Oscar Apfel
Price of Honor, The *27* Edward H. Griffith
Price of Justice, The *14* Maurice Elvey
Price of Living, The *54* Tito Davison
Price of Love, The *84* Tonia Marketaki
Price of Malice, The *16* Oscar A. C. Lund
Price of Man, The *28* Mikhail Averbakh, Mark Donskoi
Price of Money, The *12* Edwin S. Porter
Price of Peace, The *12* Edwin S. Porter
Price of Pleasure, The *25* Edward Sloman
Price of Possession, The *21* Hugh Ford
Price of Power, The *15* Jack Conway

Price of Power, The *69* Tonino Valerii
Price of Pride, The *17* Harley Knoles
Price of Redemption, The *20* Dallas M. Fitzgerald
Price of Silence, The *16* Joseph De Grasse
Price of Silence, The *17* Frank Lloyd
Price of Silence, The *20* Fred LeRoy Granville
Price of Silence, The *60* Montgomery Tully
Price of Success, The *25* Antonio Gaudio
Price of the Necklace, The *14* Charles Brabin
Price of Things, The *30* Elinor Glyn
Price of Victory, The *13* John Ince
Price of Wisdom, The *35* Reginald Denham
Price of Youth, The *22* Ben F. Wilson
Price on His Head, A *14* Warwick Buckland
Price She Paid, The *17* Charles Giblyn
Price She Paid, The *24* Henry MacRae
Price Woman Pays, The *19* George Terwilliger
Priceless Beauty *87* Charles Finch
Priceless Day, A *79* Péter Gothár
Priceless Head, A *42* Boris Barnet
Prick Up Your Ears *87* Stephen Frears
Pride *17* Richard Ridgely
Pride and Prejudice *40* Robert Z. Leonard
Pride and Prejudice *85* Cyril Coke
Pride and the Man, The *16* Frank Borzage
Pride and the Man *17* Edward Sloman
Pride and the Passion, The *56* Stanley Kramer
Pride, Love and Suspicion *52* Alessandro Blasetti
Pride of Battery B, The *13* Wilfred Noy
Pride of Donegal, The *29* J. Steven Edwards
Pride of Jennico, The *14* J. Searle Dawley
Pride of Kentucky *49* David Butler
Pride of Lonesome *13* Wallace Reid
Pride of Maryland *51* Philip Ford
Pride of Nations, The *15* Claude Friese-Greene
Pride of New York, The *17* Raoul Walsh
Pride of Palomar, The *22* Frank Borzage
Pride of Pawnee, The *29* Robert De Lacey
Pride of St. Louis, The *52* Harmon Jones
Pride of Sunshine Alley *24* William James Craft
Pride of the Army *42* S. Roy Luby
Pride of the Blue Grass *39* William McGann
Pride of the Blue Grass *54* William Beaudine
Pride of the Bowery *41* Joseph H. Lewis
Pride of the Bowery, The *46* William Beaudine
Pride of the Clan, The *17* Maurice Tourneur
Pride of the Fancy, The *20* Albert Ward
Pride of the Force, The *25* Duke Worne
Pride of the Force, The *33* Norman Lee
Pride of the Legion, The *32* Ford Beebe
Pride of the Marines *36* D. Ross Lederman
Pride of the Marines *45* Delmer Daves
Pride of the Navy *39* Charles Lamont
Pride of the North, The *20* A. E. Coleby

Pride of the Plains *40* Wallace Fox
Pride of the South, The *13* Thomas Ince
Pride of the West *38* Lesley Selander
Pride of the Yankees, The *42* Sam Wood
Priehrada *50* Pal'o Bielek
Priest, The *13* Victor Sjöström
Priest and Empress *63* Teinosuke Kinugasa
Priest of Love *80* Christopher Miles
Priest of St. Pauli, The *70* Rolf Olsen
Priest of Wilderness, The *10* Sidney Olcott
Priest's End, The *68* Evald Schorm
Priest's Wife, The *70* Dino Risi
Prigioniera, La *68* Henri-Georges Clouzot
Prigionieri del Male *55* Mario Costa
Prigioniero della Montagna, Il *55* Luis Trenker
Prigioniero di Santa Cruz, Il *40* Carlo Ludovico Bragaglia
Prija Banhabi *40* Pramatesh Chandra Barua
Přijdu Hned *42* Otakar Vávra
Prijs de Maar *58* Herman van den Horst
Priklyuchenia na Malenkikh Ostrovekh *87* Usman Saparov
Prima Amore *58* Mario Camerini
Prima Angélica, La *73* Carlos Saura
Prima Communione *50* Alessandro Blasetti
Prima della Rivoluzione *64* Bernardo Bertolucci
Prima Donna's Dupes, The *12* Frank Wilson
Prima Donna's Husband, The *16* Joseph A. Golden, Julius Steger
Prima Notte, La *58* Alberto Cavalcanti
Prima Notte di Quiete, La *72* Valerio Zurlini
Prima Ti Perdono...Poi T'Ammazzo *70* Ignacio F. Iquino
Primal Call, The *11* D. W. Griffith
Primal Fear *79* Anne Claire Poirier
Primal Law, The *21* Bernard J. Durning
Primal Lure, The *16* William S. Hart
Primal Rage *90* Vittoria Rambaldi
Primal Scream *88* William Murray
Primanerinnen *51* Rolf Thiele
Primanerliebe *28* Robert Land
Primary *60* Robert Drew, Richard Leacock, Albert Maysles, D. A. Pennebaker
Primary Target *90* Clark Henderson
Primate *74* Frederick Wiseman
Prime Cut *72* Michael Ritchie
Prime Minister, The *41* Thorold Dickinson
Prime of Miss Jean Brodie, The *68* Ronald Neame
Prime Risk *84* Michael Farkas
Prime Time, The *60* Herschell Gordon Lewis
Primeira Missa, A *61* Lima Barreto
Primer Año, El *70* Patricio Guzmán
Primer Delegado, El *75* Santiago Álvarez
Primera Carga al Machete, La *69* Manuel Octavio Gómez
Primera Fundación de Buenos Aires, La *59* Fernando Birri
Primerose *18* Mario Caserini
Primitive Call, The *17* Bertram Bracken
Primitive Love *27* Frank E. Kleinschmidt
Primitive Love *66* Luigi Scattini
Primitive Lover, The *22* Sidney Franklin

Primitive Man *13* D. W. Griffith
Primitive Man's Career to Civilization, A *11* Cherry Kearton
Primitive Paradise *61* Lewis Cotlow
Primitive Woman, The *18* Lloyd Ingraham
Primitives, The *62* Alfred Travers
Primo Amore *41* Carmine Gallone
Primo Amore *78* Dino Risi
Primrose Path, The *15* Lawrence Marston
Primrose Path, The *25* Harry Hoyt
Primrose Path, The *34* Reginald Denham
Primrose Path, The *40* Gregory La Cava
Primrose Ring, The *17* Robert Z. Leonard
Primula Bianca, La *47* Carlo Ludovico Bragaglia
Prince and Betty, The *19* Robert Thornby
Prince and the Beggarmaid, The *21* A. V. Bramble
Prince and the Dancer *29* Max Neufeld
Prince and the Great Race *83* Henri Safran
Prince and the Pauper, The *09* J. Searle Dawley
Prince and the Pauper, The *15* Hugh Ford, Edwin S. Porter
Prince and the Pauper, The *20* Alexander Korda
Prince and the Pauper, The *37* William Keighley
Prince and the Pauper, The *62* Don Chaffey
Prince and the Pauper, The *69* Elliot Geisinger
Prince and the Pauper, The *77* Richard Fleischer
Prince and the Showgirl, The *57* Anthony Bushell, Laurence Olivier
Prince Azur, Le *08* Émile Cohl
Prince Bayaya *50* Jiří Trnka
Prince Chap, The *16* Marshall Neilan
Prince Chap *20* William DeMille
Prince Charmant, Le *25* Victor Tourjansky
Prince Charmant, Le *42* Jean Boyer
Prince Charming *12* James Kirkwood, George Loane Tucker
Prince Cuckoo *19* Paul Leni
Prince de Galles et Fallières, Le *12* Émile Cohl
Prince Dimitri *27* Edwin Carewe
Prince Embête *20* Georges Monca
Prince for Cynthia, A *53* Muriel Box
Prince Henry at Lincoln Monument, Chicago, Ill. German and American Tableau *02* Edwin S. Porter
Prince in a Pawnshop, A *16* Paul Scardon
Prince Jack *84* Bert Lovitt
Prince Jean, Le *28* René Hervil
Prince Jean, Le *36* Jean De Marguenat
Prince, King of Dogs *35* Felix E. Feist
Prince of a King, A *23* Albert Austin
Prince of Arcadia *33* Hans Schwarz
Prince of Avenue A, The *20* John Ford
Prince of Bavaria, A *14* Frank Lloyd
Prince of Broadway, The *26* John Gorman
Prince of Darkness *87* John Carpenter
Prince of Diamonds *30* Karl Brown, A. H. Van Buren
Prince of Evil, A *13* Ralph Ince
Prince of Fogo, The *87* Inge Tenvik
Prince of Foxes, The *49* Henry King

Prince of Graustark, The *16* Fred E. Wright

Prince of Headwaiters, The *27* John Francis Dillon

Prince of Hearts, The *29* Clifford Wheeler

Prince of His Race, The *26* Roy Calnek

Prince of India, A *14* Leopold Wharton

Prince of Lovers, A *22* Charles C. Calvert

Prince of Magicians, The *01* Georges Méliès

Prince of Peace *39* Donald Carter

Prince of Peace, The *49* William Beaudine, Harold Daniels

Prince of Peanuts *28* William James Craft

Prince of Pennsylvania, The *88* Ron Nyswaner

Prince of Pep, The *25* Jack Nelson

Prince of Pilsen, The *26* Paul Powell

Prince of Pirates *53* Sidney Salkow

Prince of Players *55* Philip Dunne

Prince of Rogues, The *27* Kurt Bernhardt

Prince of Space, The *59* Eijiro Wakabayashi

Prince of Tempters, The *26* Lothar Mendes

Prince of the Blue Grass *54* William Beaudine

Prince of the City *81* Sidney Lumet

Prince of the Plains *27* Robin E. Williamson

Prince of the Plains *49* Philip Ford

Prince of Thieves, The *48* Howard Bretherton

Prince or Clown *27* Alexander Rasumny

Prince Rupert's Drops *69* Hollis Frampton

Prince There Was, A *21* Tom Forman

Prince Valiant *54* Henry Hathaway

Prince Varmint *61* Friz Freleng

Prince Violent *61* Friz Freleng

Prince Who Was a Thief, The *50* Rudolph Maté

Prince Yang San *89* Sang-ok Shin

Prince Zilah *26* Gaston Roudes

Princes, Les *82* Tony Gatlif

Princes, The *82* Tony Gatlif

Princes in the Tower, The *13* Hay Plumb

Princes in the Tower, The *28* George J. Banfield, Leslie Eveleigh

Princess *70* Åke Falck

Princess, The *85* Pál Erdöss

Princess *86* Sinan Cetin

Princess Academy, The *87* Bruce Block

Princess and the Call Girl, The *84* Radley Metzger

Princess and the Magic Frog, The *65* Austin Green

Princess and the Pea, The *79* Keith Goddard

Princess and the Pirate, The *44* David Butler

Princess and the Plumber, The *30* Alexander Korda*

Princess Bride, The *87* Rob Reiner

Princess Charming *34* Maurice Elvey

Princess Clementina *11* Will Barker

Princess Comes Across, The *36* William K. Howard

Princess' Dilemma, The *13* Forest Holger-Madsen

Princess from Hoboken, The *27* Allan Dale

Princess from the Moon *87* Kon Ichikawa

Princess Impudence *19* Herbert Brenon

Princess Jones *21* Gustav von Seyffertitz

Princess' Necklace, The *17* Floyd France

Princess Nicotine, or The Smoke Fairy *09* J. Stuart Blackton*

Princess of Bagdad *13* Charles L. Gaskill

Princess of Broadway, The *27* Dallas M. Fitzgerald

Princess of Happy Chance, The *16* Maurice Elvey

Princess of New York, The *21* Donald Crisp

Princess of Park Row, The *17* Ashley Miller

Princess of Patches, The *17* Alfred E. Green

Princess of the Blood, A *15* Wilfred Noy

Princess of the Dark, A *17* Charles Miller, Fred Niblo

Princess of the Nile *54* Harmon Jones

Princess O'Hara *35* David Burton

Princess Olala *28* Robert Land

Princess O'Rourke *43* Norman Krasna

Princess Pongyola *14* Michael Curtiz

Princess Priscilla's Fortnight *28* Anthony Asquith, Frederick Wendhausen

Princess Romanoff *15* Frank Powell

Princess Tam-Tam *35* Edmond T. Gréville

Princess Virtue *17* Robert Z. Leonard

Princess with the Golden Star, The *59* Martin Frič

Princess Yang Kwei Fei *55* Kenji Mizoguchi

Princesse aux Clowns, La *25* André Hugon

Princesse de Clèves, La *60* Jean Delannoy

Princesse Lulu *24* Donatien

Princesse Mandane, La *27* Germaine Dulac

Princesse Masha *27* René Leprince

Princesse Muette, La *60* James Blue

Princesse Tam-Tam *35* Edmond T. Gréville

Princeton *48* Alexander Hammid

Princezna se Zlatou Hvězdou *59* Martin Frič

Principal, The *87* Christopher Cain

Principal Enemy, The *73* Jorge Sanjinés

Principe dell'Impossibile, Il *18* Augusto Genina

Príncipe Gondolero, El *33* Edward D. Venturini

Principessa di Bagdad, La *16* Baldassare Negroni

Principessa Misteriosa, La *19* Herbert Brenon

Principessa Tarakanova, La *37* Mario Soldati

Principles of Cinematography *73* Malcolm Le Grice

Prinsen fra Fogo *87* Inge Tenvik

Prinsessan *70* Åke Falck

Prinsesse Elena *13* Forest Holger-Madsen

Print of Death *57* Montgomery Tully

Printemps, Le *09* Louis Feuillade

Printemps, Le *68* Marcel Hanoun

Printemps d'Amour *27* Léonce Perret

Printemps de la Liberté, Le *48* Jean Grémillon

Printemps, l'Automne et l'Amour, Le *54* Gilles Grangier

Printer's Devil, The *23* William Beaudine

Prinz der Legende, Der *24* Alexander Korda

Prinz Kuckuck *19* Paul Leni

Prinz Sami *17* Ernst Lubitsch

Prinz und Bettelknabe *20* Alexander Korda

Prinz Verliebt Sich, Ein *32* Conrad Wiene

Prinzessin Sissy *39* Fritz Thiery

Prinzessin Turandot *34* Gerhard Lamprecht

Priorities on Parade *42* Albert S. Rogell

Priory School, The *21* Maurice Elvey

Prisca *21* Gaston Roudes

Priscilla and the Pesky Fly *16* Ashley Miller

Priscilla and the Umbrella *11* Mack Sennett

Priscilla's April Fool Joke *11* Mack Sennett

Priscilla's Capture *12* Mack Sennett

Priscillas Fahrt ins Glück *28* Anthony Asquith, Frederick Wendhausen

Prise de Pouvoir par Louis XIV, La *66* Roberto Rossellini

Prise de Tournavos, La *1897* Georges Méliès

Prisionero 13, El *33* Fernando De Fuentes

Prisioneros de la Tierra *39* Mario Soffici

Prism *71* Anitra Pivnick

Přísně Tajné Premiéry *67* Martin Frič

Prison *48* Ingmar Bergman

Prison *65* Andy Warhol

Prison *88* Renny Harlin

Prison Break *38* Arthur Lubin

Prison Breaker *36* Adrian Brunel

Prison Camp *40* Lewis D. Collins

Prison Farm *38* Louis King

Prison Girl *41* William Beaudine

Prison Girls *42* William Beaudine

Prison Mutiny *43* Phil Rosen

Prison Nurse *38* James Cruze

Prison on Fire *87* Ringo Lam

Prison Panic, The *30* Walter Lantz

Prison Reform *10* Dave Aylott, A. E. Coleby

Prison Sans Barreaux *33* Léonide Moguy

Prison Shadows *36* Robert F. Hill

Prison Ship *45* Arthur Dreifuss

Prison Ship: The Adventures of Taura, Part One *86* Fred Olen Ray

Prison sur le Gouffre, La *12* Louis Feuillade

Prison Taint, The *16* Forest Holger-Madsen

Prison Train *38* Gordon Wiles

Prison Warden *49* Seymour Friedman

Prison Without Bars *33* Léonide Moguy

Prison Without Bars *38* Brian Desmond Hurst, Maxwell Wray

Prison Without Walls, The *17* E. Mason Hopper

Prisoner, The *23* Jack Conway

Prisoner, The *55* Peter Glenville

Prisoner, The *68* Henri-Georges Clouzot

Prisoner in the Middle *74* John O'Connor

Prisoner 984 *79* Tibor Takacs

Prisoner No. 1 *35* Pál Fejös

Prisoner No. 113 *16* Forest Holger-Madsen

Prisoner of Corbal *36* Karl Grüne
Prisoner of Japan *42* Arthur Ripley, Edgar G. Ulmer
Prisoner of Mars *42* Kenneth Anger
Prisoner of Rio *87* Lech Majewski
Prisoner of Second Avenue, The *74* Melvin Frank
Prisoner of Shark Island, The *36* John Ford
Prisoner of the Cannibal God *78* Sergio Martino
Prisoner of the Caucasus *67* Leonid Gaidai
Prisoner of the Harem, A *12* Sidney Olcott
Prisoner of the Harem, The *14* Alice Guy-Blaché
Prisoner of the Iron Mask, The *60* Francesco De Feo, Lee Kresel
Prisoner of the Jungle *59* Willy Rozier
Prisoner of the Pines *18* Ernest C. Warde
Prisoner of the Skull *73* Jack Gold
Prisoner of the Volga *59* Victor Tourjansky
Prisoner of War *54* Andrew Marton
Prisoner of Zenda, The *13* Hugh Ford, Edwin S. Porter
Prisoner of Zenda, The *15* George Loane Tucker
Prisoner of Zenda, The *22* Rex Ingram
Prisoner of Zenda, The *37* John Cromwell, George Cukor, W. S. Van Dyke
Prisoner of Zenda, The *52* Richard Thorpe
Prisoner of Zenda, The *78* Richard Quine
Prisoners *29* William A. Seiter
Prisoners *37* Yevgeni Tcherviakov
Prisoners *73* William Bushnell, Jr.
Prisoners *84* Peter Werner
Prisoners in Petticoats *50* Philip Ford
Prisoners of Love *21* Arthur Rosson
Prisoners of the Casbah *53* Richard L. Bare
Prisoners of the Lost Universe *83* Terence Marcel
Prisoners of the Sea *29* M. Werner
Prisoners of the Sea *85* Joseph Pevney
Prisoners of the Storm *26* Lynn Reynolds
Prisoner's Song, The *11* Yakov Protazanov
Prisoner's Song *30* Dave Fleischer
Prisonnier de l'Araignée *70* Antonio Margheriti
Prisonnier Récalcitrant, Le *00* Georges Méliès
Prisonnière, La *68* Henri-Georges Clouzot
Prisonnières *88* Charlotte Silvera
Prisons à l'Américaine *69* François Reichenbach
Prisons de Femmes *58* Maurice Cloche
Přístav v Srdci Evropy *40* Alexander Hammid
Private Access *88* Francesco Maselli
Private Affairs *25* Renaud Hoffman
Private Affairs *33* Lewis D. Collins
Private Affairs *40* Albert S. Rogell
Private Affairs *88* Francesco Massaro
Private Affairs of Bel Ami, The *47* Albert Lewin
Private Afternoons of Pamela Mann, The *74* Radley Metzger
Private Angelo *49* Michael Anderson, Peter Ustinov
Private Bass Has Pass *19* L. M. Glackens

Private Benjamin *80* Howard Zieff
Private Bom *48* Lars-Eric Kjellgren
Private Buckaroo *42* Edward F. Cline
Private Classes *86* Pierre Granier-Deferre
Private Collection *72* Keith Salvat
Private Conversation, A *83* Nikita Mikhalkov
Private Conversations *85* Christian Blackwood
Private Detective *39* Noel Mason Smith
Private Detective 62 *33* Michael Curtiz
Private Detectives, The *20* Raoul Barré, Charles Bowers
Private Dinner, A *1897* Georges Méliès
Private Duty Nurses *71* George Armitage
Private Enterprise, A *75* Peter Smith
Private Entrance *56* Hasse Ekman
Private Eyes *53* Edward Bernds
Private Eyes, The *80* Lang Elliott
Private Files of J. Edgar Hoover, The *77* Larry Cohen
Private Film for the Duke of Sutherland *19* Victor Fleming
Private Function, A *84* Malcolm Mowbray
Private Hector, Gentleman *12* Dave Aylott
Private Hell 36 *54* Don Siegel
Private Information *52* Fergus McDonnell
Private Investigation *87* Wojciech Wójcik
Private Investigations *87* Nigel Dick
Private Ivan *57* B. Karevsky
Private Izzy Murphy *26* Lloyd Bacon
Private Jones *33* Russell Mack
Private Lesson, The *68* Michel Boisrond
Private Lessons *81* Alan Myerson
Private Life *61* Louis Malle
Private Life *82* Yuli Raizman
Private Life of a Cat, The *45* Maya Deren, Alexander Hammid
Private Life of an Actor, The *47* Sacha Guitry
Private Life of Dr. Paul Joseph Goebbels, The *44* Alfred Zeisler
Private Life of Don Juan, The *34* Alexander Korda
Private Life of Helen of Troy, The *27* Alexander Korda
Private Life of Henry VIII, The *32* Alexander Korda
Private Life of Louis XIV, The *35* Carl Fröhlich
Private Life of Mussolini, The *38* John Park
Private Life of Paul Joseph Goebbels, The *44* Alfred Zeisler
Private Life of Sherlock Holmes, The *70* Billy Wilder
Private Lives *31* Sidney Franklin
Private Lives of Adam and Eve, The *60* Mickey Rooney, Albert Zugsmith
Private Lives of Elizabeth and Essex, The *39* Michael Curtiz
Private Navy of Sergeant O'Farrell, The *68* Frank Tashlin
Private Number *36* Roy Del Ruth
Private Nurse *38* Karl Brown
Private Nurse *41* David Burton
Private Parts *72* Paul Bartel
Private Peat *18* Edward José
Private Pooley *62* Kurt Jung-Alsen
Private Popsicle *82* Boaz Davidson

Private Potter *62* Caspar Wrede
Private Property *60* Leslie Stevens
Private Property *85* Alan Roberts
Private Resort *85* George Bowers
Private Right, The *67* Michael Papas
Private Road *71* Barney Platts-Mills
Private Road (No Trespassing) *87* Raphael Nussbaum
Private Scandal, A *21* Chester M. Franklin
Private Scandal, A *32* Charles Hutchinson
Private Scandal *34* Ralph Murphy
Private School *83* Noel Black
Private Secretary, The *35* Henry Edwards
Private Show *85* Sixto Kayko
Private Snuffy Smith *42* Edward F. Cline
Private Vices and Public Virtues *76* Miklós Jancsó
Private Vices, Public Virtue *76* Miklós Jancsó
Private War of Major Benson, The *55* Jerry Hopper
Private Wives *33* Mark Sandrich
Private Wore Skirts, The *52* Norman Z. McLeod
Private Worlds *35* Gregory La Cava
Private's Affair, A *59* Raoul Walsh
Private's Job, The *38* Karl Ritter
Privates on Parade *82* Michael Blakemore
Private's Progress *55* John Boulting
Privatklinik Prof. Lund *59* Falk Harnack
Privatsekretärin Heiratet, Die *35* Henry Koster
Prividenie, Kotoroye Ne Vozvrashchayet-sya *29* Abram Room
Prividenya *31* Boris Barnet
Privilege *66* Derek Ware, Peter Watkins
Privilege, The *83* Andrea Findlay, Ian Knox
Privilege *90* Yvonne Rainer
Privileged *82* Michael Hoffman
Prix de Beauté *30* Augusto Genina
Prix du Danger, Le *83* Yves Boisset
Prix du Sang, Le *19* Julien Duvivier
Prix et Profits *32* Yves Allégret
Prize, The *50* Jean Boyer
Prize, The *63* Mark Robson
Prize Dance, The *20* Gregory La Cava
Prize Fight, A *19* Raoul Barré, Charles Bowers
Prize of Arms, A *61* Cliff Owen
Prize of Gold *55* Mark Robson
Prize of Peril, The *83* Yves Boisset
Prize Pest, The *51* Robert McKimson
Prized As a Mate *68* Yannis Dalianidis
Prizefighter, The *79* Michael Preece
Prizefighter and the Lady, The *33* W. S. Van Dyke
Prizemyavane *87* Roumyana Petrova
Prizzi's Honor *85* John Huston
Pro, The *69* Tom Gries
Pro Patria *14* August Blom
Próba Ciśnienia *64* Krzysztof Zanussi
Probabilità Zero *68* Dario Argento*
Probation *32* Richard Thorpe
Probation Wife, The *19* Sidney Franklin
Próbaút *60* Félix Máriássy
Problem Child *55* Tatiana Lukashevich
Problem Child *90* Dennis Dugan
Problem Girls *53* E. A. Dupont
Problem of the Day, The *44* Kamel Salim

Przhevalsky *51* Sergei Yutkevich
Przyjaciel Wesołego Diabła *87* Jerzy Łukaszewicz
Przypadek *81* Krzysztof Kieślowski
Przysięgam u Ziemi Polskiej *43* Aleksander Ford*
Psalm, The *66* Evald Schorm
Psexoanálisis *67* Héctor Olivera
Psi a Lidé *70* Evald Schorm
Psi Factor, The *80* Quentin Masters
Psohlavci *54* Martin Frič
Psy *80* Philippe de Broca
Psych-Out *68* Richard Rush
Psyche 59 *63* Alexander Singer
Psychedelirium *69* Kenneth Anger
Psychiatry in Russia *55* Albert Maysles
Psychic, The *68* Herschell Gordon Lewis
Psychic, The *77* Lucio Fulci
Psychic Killer *75* Ray Danton
Psychic Lover, The *66* Edward Dein
Psycho *60* Alfred Hitchcock
Psycho II *83* Richard Franklin
Psycho III *86* Anthony Perkins
Psycho à Go-Go! *65* Al Adamson
Psycho-Circus *66* John Llewellyn Moxey
Psycho from Texas *82* Jim Feazell
Psycho Girls *84* Gerard Ciccoritti
Psycho Killers *59* John Gilling
Psycho Lover *69* Robert Vincent O'Neil
Psycho Sex Fiend *73* José Ramón Larraz
Psycho Sisters *72* Reginald LeBorg
Psychodrame, Le *56* Roberto Rossellini
Psychomania *63* Richard Hilliard
Psychomania *71* Don Sharp
Psychopath, The *64* Freddie Francis
Psychopath *73* Larry Brown
Psychos in Love *86* Gorman Bechard
Psychotronic Man, The *80* Jack M. Sell
Psychout for Murder *69* Rossano Brazzi
Psycosissimo *61* Steno
P'Tang Yang Kipperbang *82* Michael Apted
P'tit Con *84* Gérard Lauzier
P'tite du Sixième, La *17* René Hervil, Louis Mercanton
P'tite Lili, La *27* Alberto Cavalcanti, Jean Renoir
Pū-San *53* Kon Ichikawa
Puberty Blues *81* Bruce Beresford
Public Affair, A *62* Bernard Girard
Public Be Damned *17* Stanner E. V. Taylor
Public Be Damned *32* Christy Cabanne
Public Be Hanged, The *32* Christy Cabanne
Public Benefactor, A *64* Satsuo Yamamoto
Public Cowboy No. 1 *37* Joseph Kane
Public Deb No. 1 *40* Gregory Ratoff
Public Defender *17* Burton L. King
Public Defender, The *31* J. Walter Ruben
Public Enemies *41* Albert S. Rogell
Public Enemy, The *31* William A. Wellman
Public Enemy No. 1 *53* Henri Verneuil
Public Enemy's Wife *35* Nick Grindé
Public Eye, The *71* Carol Reed
Public Ghost No. 1 *36* Charlie Chase, Harold Law
Public Hero No. 1 *35* J. Walter Ruben

Public Life of Henry the Ninth, The *34* Bernerd Mainwaring
Public Menace, The *35* Erle C. Kenton
Public Nuisance No. 1 *36* Marcel Varnel
Public Opinion *16* Frank Reicher
Public Opinion *35* Frank R. Strayer
Public Pays, The *36* Errol Taggart
Public Pigeon No. 1 *57* Norman Z. McLeod
Public Prosecutor *17* Yakov Protazanov
Public Prosecutor, The *45* Ahmad Kamel Morsi
Public Stenographer *33* Lewis D. Collins
Public Wedding *37* Nick Grindé
Publicity Madness *27* Albert Ray
Publicity Pays *24* Leo McCarey
Pubs and Beaches *66* Richard Williams
Puccini *52* Carmine Gallone
Puce Moment *49* Kenneth Anger
Puchar Tatr *48* Wojciech Has
Pucker Up and Bark Like a Dog *90* Paul S. Parco
Puck's Pranks on a Suburbanite *06* Walter R. Booth
Puddin' Head *41* Joseph Santley
Puddin' Head Wilson *16* Frank Reicher
Puddle Pranks *30* Ubbe Iwerks
Puddleton Police, The *14* Percy Stow
Pudd'nhead Wilson *16* Frank Reicher
Puddy Tat Twouble *51* Friz Freleng
Pudgy and the Lost Kitten *38* Dave Fleischer
Pudgy in Thrills and Chills *38* Dave Fleischer
Pudgy Picks a Fight *37* Dave Fleischer
Pudgy Takes a Bow-Wow *37* Dave Fleischer
Pudgy the Watchman *38* Dave Fleischer
Pudhche Paol *87* Raj Dutt
Pueblerina *48* Emilio Fernández
Pueblito *61* Emilio Fernández
Pueblo o El Amor *61* Emilio Fernández
Pueblo Armado *61* Joris Ivens
Pueblo en Armas *61* Joris Ivens
Pueblo Legend, A *12* D. W. Griffith
Pueblo Terror *31* Alvin J. Neitz
Puente, El *77* Juan Antonio Bardem
Puente, El *86* José Luis Urquieta
Puente Alsina *35* José A. Ferreyra
Puente de la Muerte, El *10* Segundo De Chomón
Puerta, La *68* Luis Alcoriza
Puerta Cerrada *39* Luis Saslavsky
Puerto Nuevo *36* Luis César Amadori
Pufnstuf *70* Hollingsworth Morse
Pugachev *38* P. Petrov-Bytov
Pugilatori *50* Valerio Zurlini
Pugilistic Potts *15* James Read
Pugni in Tasca, I *65* Marco Bellocchio
Puishka *34* Mikhail Romm
Puits aux Trois Vérités, Le *63* François Villiers
Puits de Jacob, Le *26* Edward José
Puits Fantastique, Le *03* Georges Méliès
Puits Mitoyen, Le *13* Maurice Tourneur
Pukkelryggede, Den *15* August Blom
Pukotina Raja *61* Vladimir Pogačić
Pulchérie et Ses Meubles *16* Émile Cohl
Pulcinella *25* Gaston Roudes
Pulga na Balança, Uma *53* Luciano Salce

Pulgarcito *11* Segundo De Chomón
Pulgarcito *58* René Cardona
Pull My Daisy *58* Robert Frank, Alfred Leslie
Pulling It Off *87* Gabrielle Beaumont
Pullman Bride, The *17* Clarence Badger
Půlnoční Příhoda *60* Břetislav Pojar
Pulp *72* Michael Hodges
Pulpo Humano, El *35* Jorge Bell
Pulsating Giant, The *71* Shyam Benegal
Pulse *88* Paul Golding
Pulse of Life, The *17* Rex Ingram
Pulsebeat *86* Marice Tobias
Pulsepounders *88* Charles Band
Puma Man, The *80* Alberto De Martino
Pump Up the Volume *90* Allan Moyle
Pumping Iron *77* George Butler, Robert Fiore
Pumping Iron II: The Women *85* George Butler
Pumpkin *28* Yasujiro Ozu
Pumpkin Eater, The *64* Jack Clayton
Pumpkinhead *87* Stan Winston
Punascha *61* Mrinal Sen
Punch and Judy *06* Tom Green
Punch and Judy *06* Georges Méliès
Punch and Judy Man, The *62* Jeremy Summers
Punch the Clock *22* William Beaudine
Punch Trunk *53* Chuck Jones
Punchline *88* David Seltzer
Punchy de Leon *49* John Hubley
Punchy Pancho *51* Leslie Goodwins
Punisher, The *87* Mark Goldblatt
Punishment, The *12* D. W. Griffith
Punishment *86* Giorgio Losego, Lidia Montanari
Punishment Battalion *60* Harald Philipp
Punishment Island *66* Masahiro Shinoda
Punishment of Anne, The *75* Radley Metzger
Punishment Park *71* Peter Watkins
Punishment Room *56* Kon Ichikawa
Punition, La *60* Jean Rouch
Punk Can Take It *79* Julien Temple
Punk Piper, A *20* Vernon Stallings
Punk Rock Movie, The *78* Don Letts
Punks Kommt aus Amerika *37* Karl Heinz Martin
Punt'a a Čtyřlístek *54* Jiří Weiss
Punta and the Four-Leaf Clover *54* Jiří Weiss
Punter's Mishap, The *1899* Cecil M. Hepworth
Punto Nero, Un *22* Augusto Genina
Può una Morta Rivivere per Amore? *67* Jesús Franco
Pupa del Gangster, La *74* Albert Maysles, David Maysles
Pupilla nell'Ombra *19* Mario Bonnard
Pupils of the Seventh Class *38* G. Levkoyer, Yakov Protazanov
Pupils of the Seventh Grade *38* G. Levkoyer, Yakov Protazanov
Puppe, Die *19* Ernst Lubitsch
Puppenheim, Ein *22* Berthold Viertel
Puppenmacher von Kiang-Ning, Der *23* Robert Wiene
Puppet Crown, The *15* George Melford
Puppet Man, The *21* Frank Crane

Puppet Murder Case, The *35* Art Davis, Sid Marcus
Puppet of Destiny *17* Yevgeni Bauer
Puppet on a Chain *70* Geoffrey Reeve, Don Sharp
Puppet Show, The *36* Walter Lantz
Puppetoon Movie, The *87* Arnold Leibovit
Puppets *16* Tod Browning
Puppets *26* George Archainbaud
Puppets *34* Yakov Protazanov
Puppet's Nightmare, The *08* Émile Cohl
Puppets of Fate *12* Frank Powell
Puppets of Fate *21* Frank Crane
Puppets of Fate *21* Dallas M. Fitzgerald
Puppets of Fate *33* George A. Cooper
Puppies *21* Hy Mayer
Puppy Express, The *27* Walter Lantz
Puppy Love *19* Roy William Neill
Puppy Love *28* Mannie Davis
Puppy Love *32* Ubbe Iwerks
Puppy Lovetime *26* Edward F. Cline
Puppy Tale *53* Joseph Barbera, William Hanna
Pup's Tale, A *26* Hy Mayer
Pur Sang *31* Claude Autant-Lara
Pura Sangre *83* Luis Ospina
Puran Bhagat *33* Debaki Kumar Bose
Purani Haveli *89* R. Tulsi Ramsay, Shyam Ramsay
Purchase Price, The *32* William A. Wellman
Pure Air *59* Jørgen Roos
Pure America *87* Péter Gothár
Pure and Simple *30* Lewis R. Foster
Pure Beauté *54* Alexander Alexeïeff, Claire Parker
Pure Blood *83* Luis Ospina
Pure Grit *23* Nat Ross
Pure Hell of St. Trinian's, The *60* Frank Launder
Pure Love *29* Mikio Naruse
Pure S *76* Bert Deling
Purgation, The *10* D. W. Griffith
Purgatory *75* Michael Meschke
Purgatory *88* Willi Hengstler
Purimspieler, Der *37* Joseph Green, Jan Nowina-Przybylski
Puritain, Le *37* Jeff Musso
Puritaine, La *86* Jacques Doillon
Puritan, The *14* John Ince
Puritan, The *37* Jeff Musso
Puritan Maid, The *11* H. Oceano Martinek
Puritan Maid and the Royalist Refugee, The *08* Percy Stow
Puritan Passions *23* Frank Tuttle
Puritans, The *24* Frank Tuttle
Purity *16* Rea Berger
Purity and After *78* Stan Brakhage
Purity Squad *45* Harold F. Kress
Purlie Victorious *63* Nicholas Webster
Purple Cipher, The *20* Chester Bennett
Purple Dawn *23* Charles R. Seeling
Purple Death from Outer Space *40* Ford Beebe, Ray Taylor
Purple Gang, The *60* Frank McDonald
Purple Haze *82* David Burton Morris
Purple Heart, The *44* Lewis Milestone
Purple Heart Diary *51* Richard Quine
Purple Hearts *83* Sidney J. Furie
Purple Hearts: A Vietnam Love Story *83*

Sidney J. Furie
Purple Highway, The *23* Henry Kolker
Purple Hills, The *61* Maury Dexter
Purple Is the Color *64* Jack Webb
Purple Lady, The *16* George A. Lessey
Purple Lily, The *18* George Kelson
Purple Mask, The *17* Francis Ford
Purple Mask, The *55* H. Bruce Humberstone
Purple Monster Strikes, The *45* Spencer G. Bennet, Fred C. Brannon
Purple Noon *59* René Clément
Purple People Eater *88* Linda Shayne
Purple Plain, The *54* Robert Parrish
Purple Rain *84* Albert Magnoli
Purple Riders, The *38* George Sherman
Purple Rose of Cairo, The *85* Woody Allen
Purple Stream, The *61* Clive Donner
Purple Taxi, The *77* Yves Boisset
Purple V, The *43* George Sherman
Purple Vigilantes, The *38* George Sherman
Purpur und Waschblau *32* Max Neufeld
Purse Strings *33* Henry Edwards
Pursued *25* Del Henderson
Pursued *34* Louis King
Pursued *47* Raoul Walsh
Pursued by Priscilla *12* Edwin J. Collins
Pursuers, The *61* Godfrey Grayson
Pursuing Mice *89* Jingqin Hu
Pursuing Vengeance, The *16* Martin Sabine
Pursuit, The *18* Donald Crisp
Pursuit *35* Edwin L. Marin
Pursuit *47* Giuseppe De Santis
Pursuit *75* Thomas Quillen
Pursuit *81* John Frankenheimer, Buzz Kulik, Roger Spottiswoode
Pursuit Across the Desert *60* Gilberto Gazcón
Pursuit at Dawn *50* Kon Ichikawa
Pursuit of D. B. Cooper, The *81* John Frankenheimer, Buzz Kulik, Roger Spottiswoode
Pursuit of Happiness, The *34* Alexander Hall
Pursuit of Happiness, The *62* Allan King
Pursuit of Happiness, The *70* Robert Mulligan
Pursuit of Happiness, The *87* Martha Ansara
Pursuit of Moonshine, The *24* Abram Room
Pursuit of Pamela, The *20* Harold M. Shaw
Pursuit of Polly *18* Chester Withey
Pursuit of the Graf Spee *56* Michael Powell, Emeric Pressburger
Pursuit of the Phantom, The *14* Hobart Bosworth
Pursuit of Venus, The *14* Edwin J. Collins
Pursuit to Algiers *45* Roy William Neill
Purushartham *88* K. R. Mohanan
Push-Button Kitty *52* Joseph Barbera, William Hanna
Pusher, The *60* Gene Milford
Pusher-in-the-Face, The *28* Robert Florey
Pushers, The *68* William Grefé
Pushka *34* Mikhail Romm

Pushover *54* Richard Quine
Pushover, The *65* Adimaro Sala
Pushpak *88* Singeetham Srinivas Rao
Puss and Boots *15* Edwin J. Collins
Puss Gets the Boot *40* Rudolf Ising
Puss in Boots *18* John W. Brunius
Puss in Boots *22* Walt Disney
Puss in Boots *34* Lotte Reiniger
Puss in Boots *53* Lotte Reiniger
Puss in Boots *87* Eugene Marner
Puss 'n Boots *03* Ferdinand Zecca
Puss 'n Boots *08* Albert Capellani
Puss 'n Boots *34* Ubbe Iwerks
Puss 'n Boots *64* Manuel San Fernando
Puss 'n Boots *67* Herbert B. Fredersdorf
Puss 'n Boots *83* Chuck Vincent
Puss 'n' Booty *43* Frank Tashlin
Puss 'n' Toots *42* Joseph Barbera, William Hanna
Puss och Kram *66* Jonas Cornell
Pussycat Alley *63* Wolf Rilla
Pussycat, Pussycat, I Love You *70* Rod Amateau
Pussyfoot Comedy *19* Maurice Sandground
Pussy's Breakfast *05* Alf Collins
Pusztai Szél *37* Steve Sekely
Put a Penny in the Slot *09* Percy Stow
Put 'Em Up *28* Edgar Lewis
Put Entuziastov *30* Nikolai Pavlovich Okhlopkov
Put Me Among the Girls *08* Dave Aylott
Put on the Spot *36* Robert F. Hill
Put on Your Old Gray Bonnet *29* Dave Fleischer
Put Out or Shut Up *68* Armando Bo
Put Pa Amongst the Girls *08* Alf Collins
Put Some Money in the Pot *49* Leslie Goodwins
Put Up or Shut Up *68* Armando Bo
Put Up Your Hands! *19* Edward Sloman
Putain Respectueuse, La *52* Charles Brabant, Marcello Pagliero
Putney Swope *69* Robert Downey
Puttin' on the Act *40* Dave Fleischer
Puttin' on the Dog *44* Joseph Barbera, William Hanna
Puttin' on the Ritz *30* Edward Sloman
Puttin' Out the Kitten *37* Art Davis, Sid Marcus
Putting Fritz on the Water Wagon *18* Leighton Budd
Putting It Over *19* Donald Crisp
Putting It Over *22* Grover Jones
Putting on the Dog *20* Raoul Barré, Charles Bowers
Putting on the 'Fluence *15* Cecil Birch
Putting One Over *14* Charles Chaplin
Putting One Over *19* Edward Dillon
Putting Pants on Philip *27* Clyde Bruckman
Putting the Bee in Herbert *17* Floyd France
Putting Volcanoes to Work *17* J. D. Leventhal
Putto, Il *63* Gianfranco Mingozzi
Putyovka v Zhizn *30* Nikolai Ekk, R. Yanushkevich
Puzzle, The *23* Dave Fleischer
Puzzle Maniac, The *06* Alf Collins
Puzzle of a Downfall Child *70* Jerry Schatzberg

Puzzle of Horrors 69 Riccardo Freda
Puzzle of the Red Orchid, The 62 Helmuth Ashley
Puzzled 13 Frank Wilson
Puzzled Bather and His Animated Clothes, The 01 James A. Williamson
Puzzled by Crosswords 25 Charles Lamont
Puzzles 29 Paul Leni
Pyar Karke Dekho 87 Babu D. Rajendra
Pyar ke Kabil 88 Anil Ganguly
Pyat Let Borby i Pobedy 23 Dziga Vertov
Pyat Nevest do Lyubimoy 87 Leila Gordeladze
Pyat' Vecherov 78 Nikita Mikhalkov
Pygmalion 35 Erich Engel
Pygmalion 38 Anthony Asquith, Leslie Howard
Pygmalion and Galatea 1898 Georges Méliès
Pygmalion and Galatea 12 Elwin Neame
Pygmalion et Galathée 1898 Georges Méliès
Pygmy Hunt 38 Friz Freleng
Pygmy Island 50 William Berke
Pyjamas Preferred 32 Val Valentine
Pylon 57 Douglas Sirk
Pyotr Pervyi I 37 Vladimir Petrov
Pyotr Pervyi II 39 Vladimir Petrov
Pyramide de Triboulet, La 1899 Georges Méliès
Pyramide des Sonnengottes, Die 65 Robert Siodmak
Pyramide Humaine, La 60 Jean Rouch
Pyramides Bleues, Les 88 Arielle Dombasle
Pyro 64 Julio Coll
Pyro — Man Without a Face 64 Julio Coll
Pyro — The Thing Without a Face 64 Julio Coll
Pyshka 34 Mikhail Romm
Pytel Blech 62 Věra Chytilová
Pythoness, The 51 John Halas
Pytlákova Schovanka 49 Martin Frič
Pyx, The 72 Harvey Hart
Q 82 Larry Cohen
Q&A 90 Sidney Lumet
Q Planes 37 Tim Whelan, Arthur Woods
Q-Ships 28 Geoffrey Barkas, Michael Barringer
Q — The Winged Serpent 82 Larry Cohen
Qasam Us Waqt ki 69 Ajay Kardar
Q-bec My Love 70 Jean-Pierre Lefèbvre
Qian Nu Youhun 85 Hark Tsui, Ching Siu Tung
Qingchun Ji 86 Luanxin Zhang
Qingchun Nuchao 86 Jiquang Cai
Qiu Deng Ye Yu 74 Fengpan Yao
Qivitoq 56 Erik Balling
Qiwang 88 Wenji Teng
Quack, The 14 Wallace Reid
Quack Shot 54 Robert McKimson
Quacker Tracker 67 Rudy Larriva
Quackodile Tears 62 Friz Freleng
Quackser Fortune Has a Cousin in the Bronx 70 Waris Hussein
Quacky Doodles As the Early Bird 17 F. M. Follett
Quacky Doodles' Food Crisis 17 F. M. Follett
Quacky Doodles' Picnic 17 F. M. Follett

Quacky Doodles Signs the Pledge 17 F. M. Follett
Quacky Doodles Soldiering for Fair 17 F. M. Follett
Quacky Doodles the Cheater 17 F. M. Follett
Quadrante d'Oro, Il 20 Emilio Ghione
Quadrate 34 Oskar Fischinger
Quadratonia 67 Jan Lenica
Quadratonien 67 Jan Lenica
Quadriga 67 Bernhard Wicki*
Quadrille 37 Sacha Guitry
Quadrille, Le 50 Jacques Rivette
Quadrille Réaliste 02 Alice Guy-Blaché
Quadroon 72 Jack Weis
Quadrophenia 79 Franc Roddam
Quai de Grenelle 52 Emil E. Reinert
Quai des Brumes 38 Marcel Carné
Quai des Orfèvres 47 Henri-Georges Clouzot
Quail Hunt, The 35 Walter Lantz
Quaint Q's, The 25 Gaston Quiribet
Quais à Marseille, Les 1896 Georges Méliès
Quais de la Havane 1898 Georges Méliès
Qualcosa di Biondo 85 Maurizio Ponzi
Qualen der Nacht 26 Kurt Bernhardt
Qualified Adventurer, The 25 Sinclair Hill
Quality of Faith, The 16 Richard Garrick
Quality of Mercy, The 14 Warwick Buckland
Quality Street 27 Sidney Franklin
Quality Street 37 George Stevens
Quand Je Vis 69 Jean-Pierre Lefèbvre
Quand la Femme S'en Mêle 57 Yves Allégret
Quand le Rideau Se Lève 57 Claude Lelouch
Quand le Siècle A Pris Formes 78 Chris Marker
Quand les Feuilles Tombent 11 Louis Feuillade
Quand Minuit Sonnera 36 Léo Joannon
Quand Nous Étions Deux 29 Léonce Perret
Quand On Est Belle 31 Arthur Robison
Quand Passent les Faisans 65 Édouard Molinaro
Quand Sonnera Midi 57 Edmond T. Gréville
Quand Tu Liras Cette Lettre 52 Jean-Pierre Melville
Quando il Sola Scotta 70 Georges Lautner
Quando le Donne Avevano la Coda 70 Pasquale Festa Campanile
Quando le Donne Perserano la Coda 72 Pasquale Festa Campanile
Quando Marta Urlo nella Tomba 70 Francisco Lara Polop
Quando o Carnaval Chegar 72 Carlos Dieguês
Quando os Deuses Adormecem 71 José Mojica Marins
Quando Si Ama 15 Carlo Campogalliani
Quante Volte...Quella Notte 72 Mario Bava
Quantez 57 Harry Keller
Quanto Costa Morire 68 Sergio Merolle
Quantrill's Raiders 58 Edward Bernds
45mo Parallelo 86 Attilio Concari
47, Morto Che Parla 51 Carlo Ludovico

Bragaglia
48, Avenue de l'Opéra 17 Dominique Bernard-Deschamps
Quarantine 89 Charles Wilkinson
Quarantined Rivals 27 Archie Mayo
Quare Fellow, The 62 Arthur Dreifuss
Quarrelsome Anglers, The 1898 Cecil M. Hepworth
Quarrelsome Couple, The 02 Percy Stow
Quarrelsome Neighbours 03 James A. Williamson
Quarry, The 66 Roger Vadim
Quarry Mystery, The 14 Cecil M. Hepworth
Quarter Day Episode, A 05 Tom Green
Quarter Hour of City Statistics, A 33 Oskar Fischinger
Quarterback, The 26 Fred Newmeyer
Quarterback, The 40 H. Bruce Humberstone
Quarterly Balance 74 Krzysztof Zanussi
Quartet 48 Ken Annakin, Arthur Crabtree, Harold French, Ralph Smart
Quartet 81 James Ivory
Quartet That Split Up, The 50 Gustaf Molander
Quartier Latin 29 Augusto Genina
Quartier Sans Soleil 39 Dmitri Kirsanov
Quartiere 87 Silvano Agosti
Quartieri Alti 43 Mario Soldati
Quatermass and the Pit 67 Roy Ward Baker
Quatermass Conclusion, The 79 Piers Haggard
Quatermass Experiment, The 55 Val Guest
Quatermass II 57 Val Guest
Quatermass Xperiment, The 55 Val Guest
14-18 62 Jean Aurel
Quatorze Juillet 32 René Clair
Quatorze Juillet, Le 53 Abel Gance
Quatre Aventures de Reinette et Mirabelle 86 Eric Rohmer
Quatre Cavaliers de l'Apocalypse, Les 17 Henri Diamant-Berger
Quatre Cent Farces du Diable, Les 06 Georges Méliès
Quatre Cents Coups, Les 58 François Truffaut
Quatre Charlots Mousquetaires, Les 74 André Hunebelle
Quatre Jours à Paris 55 André Berthomieu
Quatre Mains 87 Hans Fels
Quatre Mouches de Velours Gris 71 Dario Argento
Quatre Nuits d'un Rêveur 71 Robert Bresson
Quatre Saisons, Les 46 Georges Rouquier
Quatre Temps 56 Alexander Alexeïeff, Claire Parker
Quatres Petits Tailleurs, Les 10 Émile Cohl
Quatres Vagabonds, Les 31 Lupu Pick
Quatres Vérités, Les 62 Alessandro Blasetti, Hervé Bromberger, René Clair, Luis García Berlanga
Quatrevingt-Quatre Prend des Vacances, Le 49 Léo Joannon
Quatrevingt-Treize 14 Albert Capellani
Quatrevingt-Treize 21 André Antoine
4ème Pouvoir, Le 85 Serge Leroy

Quel Ragazzo della Curva "B" 87 Romano Scandariato
Quelé do Pajéu 69 Anselmo Duarte
Quella Piccola Differenza 69 Duccio Tessari
Quella Sporca Storia del West 68 Enzo G. Castellari
Quella Vecchia Canaglia 34 Carlo Ludovico Bragaglia
Quella Villa Accanto al Cimitero 81 Lucio Fulci
Quelle Drôle de Blanchisserie 12 Émile Cohl
Quelle Drôle de Gosse 35 Léo Joannon
Quelle Joie de Vivre! 61 René Clément
Quelle Sporche Anime Dannate 71 Luigi Batzella
Quelle Strane Occasioni 76 Luigi Comencini*
Quelli Che Non Muoiono 68 Giuseppe Masini
Quelli Che Soffrono per Noi 51 Alessandro Blasetti
Quelli del Casco 88 Luciano Salce
Quelli della Montagna 42 Aldo Vergano
Quelque Messieurs Trop Tranquilles 73 Georges Lautner
Quelque Part, Quelqu'un 72 Yannick Bellon
Quelques Jours avec Moi 88 Claude Sautet
Quelqu'un Derrière la Porte 71 Nicolas Gessner
Quem É Beta? 72 Nelson Pereira Dos Santos
Quem Tem Medo de Lobishomem 74 Reginaldo Faria
Quemando Tradiciones 71 Santiago Álvarez
Quentin Durward 55 Richard Thorpe
Quentin Quail 45 Chuck Jones
Querelle 82 Rainer Werner Fassbinder
Querelle—A Pact with the Devil 82 Rainer Werner Fassbinder
Querelle de Brest 82 Rainer Werner Fassbinder
Querelle de Jardins 82 Raúl Ruiz
Querelle Enfantine 1895 Louis Lumière
Querelly—Ein Pakt mit dem Teufel 82 Rainer Werner Fassbinder
Query 45 Montgomery Tully
Quest, The 15 Harry A. Pollard
Quest, The 86 Brian Trenchard-Smith
Qu'Est-Ce Qui Fait Courir David? 82 Elie Chouraqui
Qu'Est-Ce Qu'On Attend pour Être Heureux! 82 Coline Serreau
Quest for Fire 81 Jean-Jacques Annaud
Quest for Love 71 Ralph Thomas
Quest for Love 88 Helen Nogueira
Quest for the Lost City 55 Dana Lamb, Ginger Lamb
Quest of Life, The 16 Ashley Miller
Quest of the Sacred Gem, The 14 George Fitzmaurice
Questa È la Vita 54 Aldo Fabrizi, Giorgio Pastina, Mario Soldati, Luchino Visconti, Luigi Zampa
Questa Volta Parliamo di Uomini 65 Lina Wertmuller
Questi Fantasmi 54 Eduardo De Filippo

Questi Fantasmi 67 Renato Castellani
Question, The 16 Harry Handworth
Question, The 17 Perry N. Vekroff
Question, The 67 John Halas
Question, The 70 Ritwik Ghatak
Question, La 77 Laurent Heynemann
Question, The 77 Laurent Heynemann
Question d'Assurance, Une 59 Pierre Kast
"?" Motorist, The 06 Walter R. Booth
Question of Adultery, A 58 Don Chaffey
Question of Courage, A 14 Christy Cabanne
Question of Hairs, A 16 Percy Stow
Question of Honor, A 15 B. Reeves Eason
Question of Honor, A 22 Edwin Carewe
Question of Honor, A 65 Luigi Zampa
Question of Identity, A 13 Warwick Buckland
Question of Identity, A 14 Charles Brabin
Question of Loving, A 86 Louise Carré
Question of Principle, A 22 George A. Cooper
Question of Rape, A 67 Jacques Doniol-Valcroze
Question of Silence, A 82 Marleen Gorris
Question of Suspense, A 61 Max Varnel
Question of Today, The 28 Lloyd Bacon
Question of Trust, A 20 Maurice Elvey
Question 7 61 Stuart Rosenberg
Questione di Pelle 58 Claude Bernard-Aubert
Questione d'Onore, Una 65 Luigi Zampa
Questo e Quello 83 Sergio Corbucci
Questo Si' Che E'Amore 77 Filippo Ottoni
Qui? 70 Leonard Kiegel
Qui à Tiré Sur Nos Histoires d'Amour? 86 Louise Carré
Qui à Tué 19 Pierre Marodon
Qui à Tué Max? 13 Max Linder
Qui Commande aux Fusils 69 Joris Ivens*
Qui Êtes-Vous Monsieur Sorge? 60 Yves Ciampi
Qui Êtes-Vous Polly Maggoo? 66 William Klein
Qui Jin 83 Jin Xie
Qui Trop Embrasse 86 Jacques Davila
Qui Veut Tuer Carlos? 67 Christian-Jaque
Quick 32 Robert Siodmak
Quick Action 21 Edward Sloman
Quick and the Dead, The 63 Robert Totten
Quick, Before It Melts 64 Delbert Mann
Quick Billy 70 Bruce Baillie
Quick Change, A 20 Vernon Stallings
Quick Change 25 Del Henderson
Quick Change 90 Howard Franklin, Bill Murray
Quick-Change Mesmerist, A 08 Walter R. Booth
Quick, der Sieger 32 Robert Siodmak
Quick Gun, The 64 Sidney Salkow
Quick—König der Clowns 32 Robert Siodmak
Quick! Let's Get Married 63 William Dieterle
Quick Millions 31 Rowland Brown
Quick Millions 39 Malcolm St. Clair
Quick Money 37 Edward Killy
Quick on the Trigger 48 Ray Nazarro
Quick Shave and Brush Up, A 00 George

Albert Smith
Quick Trigger Lee 31 John P. McGowan
Quick Triggers 28 Ray Taylor
Quickening Flame, The 19 Travers Vale
Quicker Than the Eye 88 Nicolas Gessner
Quicker'n a Wink 40 George Sidney
Quicker'n Lightnin' 25 Richard Thorpe
Quicksand 50 Irving Pichel
Quicksands, The 14 Christy Cabanne
Quicksands 17 George Bellamy
Quicksands 18 Victor Schertzinger
Quicksands 23 Jack Conway
Quicksands of Life 15 J. L. V. Leigh
Quicksilver 86 Tom Donnelly
Quicksilver Pudding 09 Alf Collins
¿Quién Mató a Eva? 34 José Bohr
¿Quién Puede Matar a un Niño? 75 Narciso Ibáñez Serrador
¿Quién Sabe? 66 Damiano Damiani
Quiet Affair, A 33 Gustaf Molander
Quiet American, The 57 Joseph L. Mankiewicz
Quiet Cool 86 Clay Borris
Quiet Day at the End of the War, A 70 Nikita Mikhalkov
Quiet Day in Belfast, A 74 Milad Bessada
Quiet Day in the Country, A 16 Gregory La Cava
Quiet Days in Clichy 90 Claude Chabrol
Quiet Death, A 86 Frieda Liappa
Quiet Don, The 31 Olga Preobrazhenskaya
Quiet Duel, The 48 Akira Kurosawa
Quiet Earth, The 85 Geoff Murphy
Quiet Flows the Don 57 Sergei Gerasimov
Quiet Gun, The 57 William F. Claxton
Quiet Home, A 57 Frigyes Bán
Quiet Little Game, A 21 Wallace A. Carlson
Quiet Man, The 52 John Ford
Quiet One, The 49 Sidney Meyers
Quiet Place in the Country, A 68 Elio Petri
Quiet Place to Kill, A 69 Umberto Lenzi
Quiet Please 33 George Stevens
Quiet Please 38 Roy William Neill
Quiet Please! 45 Joseph Barbera, William Hanna
Quiet Please, Murder 42 John Larkin
Quiet! Pleeze 41 Dave Fleischer
Quiet Revolution 74 Shyam Benegal
Quiet Wedding 40 Anthony Asquith
Quiet Week in the House, A 69 Jan Švankmajer
Quiet Weekend 46 Harold French
Quiet Woman, The 51 John Gilling
Quiet Worker, The 28 Charles Lamont
Quigley Down Under 90 Simon Wincer
Qu'Il Était Bon Mon Petit Français 71 Nelson Pereira Dos Santos
Quiller Memorandum, The 66 Michael Anderson
Quilombo 84 Carlos Diegües
Quincannon, Frontier Scout 56 Lesley Selander
Quincy Adams Sawyer 22 Clarence Badger
Quindici Forche per un Assassino 68 Nunzio Malasomma
Quinine 17 Gregory La Cava, Vernon Stallings

Quinneys *19* Rex Wilson
Quinneys *27* Maurice Elvey
Quint City, U.S.A. *63* Joyce Chopra, Richard Leacock
Quintana *69* Glenn Vincent Davis
Quintet *78* Robert Altman
Quintrala, La *55* Hugo Del Carril
15/18, Le *73* Chantal Akerman, Samy Szlingerbaum
15ème Prélude de Chopin, Le *22* Victor Tourjansky
Quiproquo *08* Georges Méliès
Quit Ye Like Men *06* Harold Jeapes
Quits *11* H. Oceano Martinek
Quitter, The *16* Charles T. Horan
Quitter, The *29* Joseph E. Henabery
Quitter, The *34* Richard Thorpe
Quitter Grant *22* Edwin J. Collins
Quitters, The *34* Richard Thorpe
Quixote *65* Bruce Baillie
Quiz Crimes *43* Ronald Haines
Quo Vadis? *01* Ferdinand Zecca
Quo Vadis? *12* Enrico Guazzoni
Quo Vadis? *25* Arturo Ambrosio
Quo Vadis? *51* Mervyn LeRoy, Anthony Mann
Quoi de Neuf Pussycat? *65* Clive Donner
R.A.S. *73* Yves Boisset
R.C.M.P. and the Treasure of Genghis Khan *48* Fred C. Brannon, Yakima Canutt
R E D Spells Red *83* He Yong Lin
RN 37 *37* Roger Leenhardt
R.O.B.O.T. *86* Jim Wynorski
R.O.T.O.R. *88* Cullen Blaine
R-1 *27* Oskar Fischinger
R.P.M. *70* Stanley Kramer
R.R. *81* Stan Brakhage
R.S.V.P. *21* Charles Ray
R.S.V.P. *84* Lem Amero
RX Murder *58* Derek Twist
Ra Expeditions, The *71* Lennart Ehrenborg
Raat Bhore *56* Mrinal Sen
Raat ke Andhere Mein *88* Vinod Talwar
Raba Lubvi *76* Nikita Mikhalkov
Rabbi and the Shikse, The *76* Joel Silberg
Rabbia, La *63* Giovanni Guareschi, Pier Paolo Pasolini
Rabbit Case, The *79* Jaromil Jireš
Rabbit Every Monday *51* Friz Freleng
Rabbit Fire *51* Chuck Jones
Rabbit Hood *49* Chuck Jones
Rabbit of Seville, The *50* Chuck Jones
Rabbit Punch *47* Chuck Jones
Rabbit Rampage *55* Chuck Jones
Rabbit Romeo *57* Robert McKimson
Rabbit, Run *70* Jack Smight
Rabbit Seasoning *52* Chuck Jones
Rabbit Stew and Rabbits Too *69* Robert McKimson
Rabbit Test *78* Joan Rivers
Rabbit Transit *47* Friz Freleng
Rabbit Trap, The *58* Philip Leacock
Rabbit's Feat *60* Chuck Jones
Rabbit's Kin *52* Robert McKimson
Rabbit's Moon *50* Kenneth Anger
Rabbit's Moon *71* Kenneth Anger
Rabbitson Crusoe *56* Friz Freleng
Rabble, The *64* Hiroshi Inagaki
Rabia, La *63* Myron J. Gold

Rabid *76* David Cronenberg
Rabid Grannies *89* Emmanuel Kervyn
Rabindranath Tagore *60* Satyajit Ray
Rablélek *12* Michael Curtiz
Rabouilleuse, La *59* Louis Daquin
Racconti d'Estate *64* Gianni Franciolini
Racconti di Canterbury, I *71* Pier Paolo Pasolini
Racconto da una Affresco *40* Luciano Emmer, Enrico Gras, Tatiana Grauding
Racconto del Quartiere *49* Valerio Zurlini
Racconto della Stura, Il *55* Ermanno Olmi
Race, The *16* George Melford
Race, The *85* Amir Naderi
Race for a Bride, A *10* Dave Aylott
Race for a Bride, A *22* Challis Sanderson
Race for a Kiss, A *04* Lewin Fitzhamon
Race for a Rose, A *08* Alf Collins
Race for Bed, A *05* J. H. Martin
Race for Glory *89* Rocky Lang
Race for Life, A *28* D. Ross Lederman
Race for Life *54* Terence Fisher
Race for Life *55* Christian-Jaque
Race for Love, A *13* Lewin Fitzhamon
Race for Millions, A *07* J. Searle Dawley, Edwin S. Porter
Race for the Farmer's Cup, The *09* Lewin Fitzhamon
Race for the Yankee Zephyr *81* David Hemmings
Race for Your Life, Charlie Brown *77* Bill Melendez, Phil Roman
Race Gang *37* William K. Howard, William Cameron Menzies
Race Never Loses—It Smells Like Gas, The *87* Víctor Manuel Castro
Race of the Age, The *20* J. W. O'Mahoney
Race Riot *29* Walter Lantz
Race Street *48* Edwin L. Marin
Race Suicide *16* George Terwilliger
Race Symphony *29* Hans Richter
Race to the Yankee Zephyr *81* David Hemmings
Race Track, The *21* Hy Mayer
Race Wild *26* Oscar Apfel
Race with Death, The *15* Robert Dinesen
Race with the Devil *75* Jack Starrett
Racers, The *54* Henry Hathaway
Racetrack *32* James Cruze
Racetrack *85* Frederick Wiseman
Rache der Toten, Die *17* Richard Oswald
Rache des Banditen, Die *19* Piel Jutzi
Rache des Fu Manchu, Die *67* Jeremy Summers
Rache einer Frau, Die *20* Robert Wiene
Rachel and the Stranger *48* Norman Foster
Rachel Cade *60* Gordon Douglas
Rachel Papers, The *89* Damian Harris
Rachel, Rachel *68* Paul Newman
Rachel River *87* Sandy Smolan
Rachel's Man *74* Moshe Mizrahi
Rachel's Sin *11* Lewin Fitzhamon
Rächer, Der *60* Karl Anton
Rachmaninov's Prelude *32* Widgey R. Newman
Racing *61* Alexander Kluge, Paul Kruntorad
Racing Blood *26* Frank Richardson
Racing Blood *38* Rex Hale

Racing Blood *54* Wesley Barry
Racing Canines *36* David Miller
Racing Fever *64* William Grefé
Racing Fool, The *27* Harry Joe Brown
Racing for Life *24* Henry MacRae
Racing Hearts *23* Paul Powell
Racing Lady *37* Wallace Fox
Racing Luck *22* Arthur H. Rooke
Racing Luck *24* Herman Raymaker
Racing Luck *35* D. Ross Lederman
Racing Luck *35* Sam Newfield
Racing Luck *48* William Berke
Racing Mad *28* Stephen Roberts
Racing Romance *26* Harry Joe Brown
Racing Romance *37* Maclean Rogers
Racing Romeo, A *27* Sam Wood
Racing Sayings Illustrated *05* Harold Jeapes
Racing Scene, The *70* Andy Sidaris
Racing Strain *19* Emmett J. Flynn
Racing Strain, The *33* Jerome Storm
Racing with the Moon *84* Richard Benjamin
Racing Youth *32* Vin Moore
Rack, The *56* Arnold Laven
Racket, The *28* Lewis Milestone
Racket, The *51* John Cromwell, Nicholas Ray
Racket Busters *38* Lloyd Bacon
Racket Cheers *30* Mack Sennett
Racket Man, The *44* D. Ross Lederman
Racketeer, The *29* Howard Higgin
Racketeer Rabbit *46* Friz Freleng
Racketeer Round-Up *34* Robert Hoyt
Racketeers in Exile *37* Erle C. Kenton
Racketeers of the Range *39* D. Ross Lederman
Rackety Rax *32* Alfred L. Werker
Racquet *79* David Winters
Rad *86* Hal Needham
Rád Bízom a Feleségem *39* János Vaszary
Radan *56* Inoshiro Honda
Radar Men from the Moon *52* Fred C. Brannon
Radar Patrol *50* Sam Newfield
Radar Patrol vs. Spy King *50* Fred C. Brannon
Radar Secret Service *50* Sam Newfield
Radiance of a Thousand Suns, The *64* Pierre Kast
Radio Bar *37* Manuel Romero
Radio Bikini *87* Robert Stone
Radio Bug, The *26* Stephen Roberts
Radio Bugs *44* Cy Endfield
Radio Cab Murder *54* Vernon Sewell
Radio City Revels *38* Ben Stoloff
Radio Corbeau *88* Yves Boisset
Radio Days *86* Woody Allen
Radio Dynamics *42* Oskar Fischinger
Radio Flyer, The *24* Harry Hoyt
Radio Folla, La *86* Francesc Bellmunt
Radio Follies *34* Arthur Woods
Radio Hams *39* Felix E. Feist
Radio King, The *22* Robert F. Hill
Radio Kino-Pravda *25* Dziga Vertov
Radio Lover *36* Paul Capon, Austin Melford
Radio-Mania *23* Roy William Neill
Radio Murder Mystery, The *37* Nick Grindé

Radio Nights *39* Horace Shepherd
Radio Now! *24* S. Grunberg, Sergei Yutkevich
Radio On *79* Christopher Petit
Radio Parade *33* Richard Beville, Archie De Bear
Radio Parade of 1935 *34* Arthur Woods
Radio Patrol *32* Edward L. Cahn
Radio Patrol *37* Ford Beebe, Clifford Smith
Radio Pirates *35* Ivar Campbell
Radio Ranch *34* Otto Brower, B. Reeves Eason
Radio Revels of 1942 *41* Harold Young
Radio Rhythm *29* Joseph Santley
Radio Rhythm *31* Walter Lantz
Radio Riot *30* Dave Fleischer
Radio Runaround *43* Lambert Hillyer
Radio Star, The *34* Joseph Santley
Radio Stars on Parade *45* Leslie Goodwins
Radio Wonderful *72* Richard Loncraine
Radioactive Dreams *86* Albert Pyun
Radiobarred *36* Leslie Goodwins
Radiografia d'un Colpo d'Oro *68* Antonio Isamendi
Radishes and Carrots *64* Minoru Shibuya
Radium City *87* Carole Langer
Radon *56* Inoshiro Honda
Radon the Flying Monster *56* Inoshiro Honda
Radosti Srednego Vozrasta *88* Lembit Oulfsak
Raduga *43* Mark Donskoi
Rafaga de Plomo *86* Pedro Galindo III
Rafale, La *20* Jacques De Baroncelli
Rafferty and the Gold Dust Twins *75* Dick Richards
Rafferty and the Highway Hustlers *75* Dick Richards
Rafferty's Rise *18* Fred O'Donovan
Raffica di Coltelli *65* Mario Bava
Raffles *30* Harry D'Abbadie D'Arrast, George Fitzmaurice
Raffles *39* Sam Wood, William Wyler
Raffles the Amateur Cracksman *05* J. Stuart Blackton
Raffles the Amateur Cracksman *17* George Irving
Raffles, the Amateur Cracksman *25* King Baggot
Raffles, the American Cracksman *05* Gilbert M. Anderson
Raffles the Dog *05* Edwin S. Porter
Rafle de Chiens *04* Alice Guy-Blaché
Rafles sur la Ville *58* Pierre Chénal
Rafter Romance *33* William A. Seiter
Rag. Arturo de Fanti Bancario Precario *80* Luciano Salce
Rag Doll *61* Lance Comfort
Rag Man, The *24* Edward F. Cline
Rag-Picker, The *1896* Georges Méliès
Raga and the Emotions *71* Shyam Benegal
Ragamuffin, The *16* William DeMille
Ragamuffin, The *19* Sidney Franklin
Ragan *67* José Briz
Ragan in Ruins *25* Fred Paul
Ragazza a Saint Tropez, Una *66* Jean Girault
Ragazza Che Sapeva Troppo, La *62* Mario Bava

Ragazza con la Pistola, La *67* Mario Monicelli
Ragazza con la Valigia, La *60* Valerio Zurlini
Ragazza dei Lilla, La *86* Flavio Mogherini
Ragazza del Bersagliere, La *66* Alessandro Blasetti
Ragazza del Metro, La *89* Romano Scandariato
Ragazza del Palio, La *57* Luigi Zampa
Ragazza del Vagone Letto, La *79* Ferdinando Baldi
Ragazza di Bube, La *63* Luigi Comencini
Ragazza di Latta, La *70* Marcello Aliprandi
Ragazza di Mille Mesi, La *61* Steno
Ragazza di Passaggio, La *73* Marguerite Duras
Ragazza e il Generale, La *66* Pasquale Festa Campanile
Ragazza in Prestito, La *66* Alfredo Giannetti
Ragazza in Vetrina, La *60* Luciano Emmer
Ragazza per l'Estate, Una *59* Édouard Molinaro
Ragazza Piuttosto Complicata, Una *69* Damiano Damiani
Ragazze da Marito *52* Eduardo De Filippo
Ragazze di Piazza di Spagna, Le *52* Luciano Emmer
Ragazze di San Frediano, Le *54* Valerio Zurlini
Ragazze d'Oggi *55* Luigi Zampa
Ragazze in Bianco *49* Michelangelo Antonioni
Ragazzi del Juke-Box, I *59* Lucio Fulci
Ragazzi della Marina *58* Francesco De Robertis
Ragazzi della Via Paal, I *35* Alberto Mondadori, Mario Monicelli
Ragazzo Come Tanti, Un *86* Gianni Minello
Ragazzo dal Kimono d'Oro, Il *88* Fabrizio De Angelis, David Parker, Jr.
Ragazzo del Pony Express, Il *86* Franco Amurri
Ragazzo di Calabria, Un *87* Luigi Comencini
Ragazzo di Ebalus, Il *87* Giuseppe Schito
Rage, The *63* Myron J. Gold
Rage *66* Gilberto Gazcón
Rage *72* George C. Scott
Rage *76* David Cronenberg
Rage *86* Tonino Ricci
Rage and Glory *85* Avi Nesher
Rage at Dawn *55* Tim Whelan
Rage de Dents, Une *00* Alice Guy-Blaché
Rage in Heaven *41* W. S. Van Dyke
Rage of Honor *86* Gordon Hessler
Rage of Paris, The *21* Jack Conway
Rage of Paris, The *38* Henry Koster
Rage of the Buccaneers, The *61* Mario Costa
Rage to Kill *88* David Winters
Rage to Live, A *65* Walter Grauman
Rage Within, The *63* Myron J. Gold
Ragged Angels *39* Stuart Heisler, Archie Mayo
Ragged Earl, The *14* Lloyd B. Carleton
Ragged Edge, The *23* F. Harmon Weight

Ragged Flag, A *74* Kozaburo Yoshimura
Ragged Heiress, The *22* Harry Beaumont
Ragged Messenger, The *17* Frank Wilson
Ragged Prince, The *13* Charles H. Weston
Ragged Princess, The *16* John G. Adolfi
Ragged Robin *24* Frank S. Mattison
Raggedy Ann and Andy *41* Dave Fleischer
Raggedy Ann and Andy *77* Richard Williams
Raggedy Ann and Raggedy Andy *41* Dave Fleischer
Raggedy Man *81* Jack Fisk
Raggedy Queen, The *17* Theodore Marston
Raggedy Rawney, The *88* Bob Hoskins
Raggedy Rug *64* Joseph Barbera, William Hanna
Raggen, Det Är Jag Det *36* S. Bauman
Raging Bull *80* Martin Scorsese
Raging Moon, The *70* Bryan Forbes
Raging Tide, The *51* George Sherman
Raging Vendetta *86* Efren C. Piñon
Raging Waters *49* William D. Russell
Ragione per Vivere e Una per Morire, Una *72* Tonino Valerii
Ragman's Daughter, The *72* Harold Becker
Rags *15* James Kirkwood
Rags and the Girl *15* Van Dyke Brooke
Rags to Riches *21* Wallace Worsley
Rags to Riches *41* Joseph Kane
Ragtime *27* Scott Pembroke
Ragtime *81* Miloš Forman
Ragtime Bear, The *49* John Hubley
Ragtime Cowboy Joe *40* Ray Taylor
Ragtime Cowboy Pimple *15* Fred Evans, Joe Evans
Ragtime Mad *13* Hay Plumb
Ragtime Romeo *31* Ubbe Iwerks
Ragtime Summer *77* Alan Bridges
Rah! Rah! Heidelberg! *26* Lewis Seiler
Rah! Rah! Rah! *28* Norman Taurog
Rahba *45* Niazi Mustafa
Rai *86* Said Ali Fettar
Raíces *55* Benito Alazraki
Raíces de Sangre *77* Jesús Treviño
Raid, The *17* George Marshall
Raid, The *54* Hugo Fregonese
Raid of 1915, The *14* Fred W. Durrant
Raid of the Armoured Motor, The *06* Arthur Cooper
Raid on a Canteen, A *05* Alf Collins
Raid on a Coiner's Den *04* Alf Collins
Raid on Entebbe *76* Irvin Kershner
Raid on Rommel *70* Henry Hathaway, Arthur Hiller
Raid Paris-Monte Carlo en Deux Heures, Le *04* Georges Méliès
Raid Paris-New York en Automobile, Le *08* Georges Méliès
Raider, The *44* Pat Jackson
Raider Emden, The *28* Louis Ralph
Raiders, The *16* Charles Swickard
Raiders, The *21* Nate Watt
Raiders, The *52* Lesley Selander
Raiders, The *63* Herschel Daugherty
Raiders from Beneath the Sea *64* Maury Dexter
Raiders of Ghost City *44* Lewis D. Collins, Ray Taylor

Raiders of Leyte Gulf, The *63* Eddie Romero
Raiders of Old California *57* Albert C. Gannaway
Raiders of Red Gap *43* Sam Newfield
Raiders of Red Rock *43* Sam Newfield
Raiders of San Joaquin *43* Lewis D. Collins
Raiders of Sunset Pass *43* John English
Raiders of the Border *44* John P. McCarthy
Raiders of the Desert *41* John Rawlins
Raiders of the Golden Cobra, The *82* Antonio Margheriti
Raiders of the Lost Ark *81* Steven Spielberg
Raiders of the Lost Triangle *85* Tom Saichur
Raiders of the Range *42* John English
Raiders of the River *56* John Haggarty
Raiders of the Seven Seas *53* Sidney Salkow
Raiders of the South *46* Lambert Hillyer
Raiders of the West *42* Sam Newfield
Raiders of Tomahawk Creek *50* Fred F. Sears
Rail, The *59* Jerzy Hoffman
Rail Rider, The *16* Maurice Tourneur
Rail Rode *27* Manny Gould, Ben Harrison
Railroad Man, The *55* Pietro Germi
Railroad Man's Word, A *53* Andrzej Munk
Railroad Pickpocket, The *00* Georges Méliès
Railroad Raiders, The *17* John P. McGowan
Railroad Rhythm *36* Albert Hopkins
Railroad Rhythm *37* Manny Gould, Ben Harrison
Railroad Workers *47* Arne Mattsson
Railroad Wretch *32* Dick Huemer
Railroaded *23* Edmund Mortimer
Railroaded! *47* Anthony Mann
Railroaders, The *19* Colin Campbell
Railroaders *57* István Gaál
Railroading *22* Earl Hurd
Rails *29* Mario Camerini
Rails Into Laramie *54* Jesse Hibbs
Railway Children, The *70* Lionel Jeffries
Railway Collision, A *00* Walter R. Booth
Railway Junction *61* Kazimierz Karabasz
Railway Pickpocket, The *00* Georges Méliès
Railway Smash-Up *04* Edwin S. Porter
Railway Workers, The *47* Arne Mattsson
Railwayman's Word, A *53* Andrzej Munk
Railwaymen *63* Evald Schorm
Rain *28* Raoul Walsh
Rain *29* Mannus Franken, Joris Ivens
Rain *32* Lewis Milestone
Rain Dropper, The *28* Manny Gould, Ben Harrison
Rain for a Dusty Summer *71* Arthur Lubin
Rain Man *88* Barry Levinson
Rain Only When at Night, The *79* Choi-su Park
Rain or Shine *30* Frank Capra
Rain or Shine *60* Herbert Rappaport
Rain People, The *69* Francis Ford Coppola
Rain Yesterday, The *74* Chang-ho Lee

Rainbow, The *17* Ralph Dean
Rainbow *21* Edward José
Rainbow, The *29* Reginald Barker
Rainbow, The *43* Mark Donskoi
Rainbow, The *89* Ken Russell
Rainbow After the Storm, A *78* Santiago Álvarez
Rainbow Boys, The *73* Gerald Potterton
Rainbow Bridge *72* Chuck Wein
Rainbow Brite and the Star Stealer *85* Bernard Deyries, Kimio Yabuki
Rainbow Chasers, The *19* Geoffrey H. Malins
Rainbow Dance *36* Len Lye
Rainbow Girl, The *17* Rollin Sturgeon
Rainbow Island *44* Ralph Murphy
Rainbow Jacket, The *54* Basil Dearden, Michael Relph
Rainbow Man, The *29* Fred Newmeyer
Rainbow of This Sky, The *58* Keisuke Kinoshita
Rainbow on the River *36* Kurt Neumann
Rainbow Over Broadway *33* Richard Thorpe
Rainbow Over Texas *46* Frank McDonald
Rainbow Over the Range *40* Albert Herman
Rainbow Over the Rockies *47* Oliver Drake
Rainbow Pass, The *37* Jacques Tourneur
Rainbow Princess, The *16* J. Searle Dawley
Rainbow Professional, The *86* Fabrizio De Angelis
Rainbow Ranch *33* Harry Fraser
Rainbow Rangers *24* Forrest K. Sheldon
Rainbow Rhythm *43* Reginald LeBorg
Rainbow Riley *26* Charles Hines
Rainbow 'Round My Shoulder *52* Richard Quine
Rainbow Round the Corner *44* Victor M. Gover
Rainbow Trail, The *18* Frank Lloyd
Rainbow Trail, The *25* Lynn Reynolds
Rainbow Trail, The *32* David Howard
Rainbow Valley *35* Robert North Bradbury
Rainbow's End *35* Norman Spencer
Raindrops *62* Kokan Rakonjac
Raining in the Mountains *77* King Hu
Raining on the Mountain *77* King Hu
Rainis *49* Yuli Raizman
Rainmaker, The *26* Clarence Badger
Rainmaker, The *56* Joseph Anthony
Rainmakers, The *35* Fred Guiol
Rainmakers *51* Roger Rosfelder, Jean Rouch
Rains Came, The *39* Clarence Brown
Rains of Ranchipur, The *55* Jean Negulesco
Raintree County *57* Edward Dmytryk
Rainy Day Friends *85* Gary Kent
Rainy July, A *58* Leonard Buczkowski
Raise Ravens *75* Carlos Saura
Raise the Roof *30* Walter Summers
Raise the Titanic! *80* Jerry Jameson
Raised from the Ranks *08* Jack Chart
Raised from the Ranks *13* Dave Aylott
Raisin in the Sun, A *61* Daniel Petrie
Raisin in the Sun, A *89* Bill Duke
Raising a Riot *55* Wendy Toye
Raising Arizona *87* Joel Coen

Raising Cain *24* Charles Lamont
Raising the Roof *29* Joseph Santley
Raising the Roof *71* Michael Forlong
Raising the Wind *25* Leslie Hiscott
Raising the Wind *33* Fred Newmeyer
Raising the Wind *61* Gerald Thomas
Raisins de la Mort, Les *78* Jean Rollin
Raison Avant la Passion, La *69* Joyce Wieland
Raison d'État, La *78* André Cayatte
Raison du Plus Fou, La *72* François Reichenbach*
Raison du Plus Fou Est Toujours le Meilleure, La *72* François Reichenbach*
Rajah Harishandra *12* D. G. Phalke
Rajah's Amulet, The *17* Edward J. LeSaint
Rajah's Dream, or The Bewitched Wood, The *00* Georges Méliès
Rajah's Revenge, The *12* Dave Aylott
Rajah's Tiara, The *14* H. Oceano Martinek
Rajol fi Hayati *61* Youssef Chahine
Rajtunk is Múlik *60* Márta Mészáros
Rajul fi Hayati *61* Youssef Chahine
Rak *71* Charles Belmont
Rake's Progress, The *45* Sidney Gilliat
Rake's Romance, A *10* A. E. Coleby
Rakhee *88* R. Chandrasekhar Reddy
Rakkii-San *52* Kon Ichikawa
Rákóczi Hadnagya *53* Frigyes Bán
Rákóczi Induló *33* Gustav Fröhlich, Steve Sekely
Rákóczi Marsch *33* Gustav Fröhlich, Steve Sekely
Rákóczi's Lieutenant *53* Frigyes Bán
Rakshasa Samharam *88* Raghav
Raktha Tilakam *88* B. Gopal
Rakudai wa Shita Keredo *30* Yasujiro Ozu
Rakugai Kokuban *59* Kaneto Shindo
Rakvičkárna *66* Jan Švankmajer
Rallare *47* Arne Mattsson
Rally *71* Risto Jarva
Rally *82* Harry Hurwitz
Rally 'Round the Flag, The *09* Sidney Olcott
Rally 'Round the Flag, Boys! *58* Leo McCarey
Ralph McGill and His Times *88* Kathleen Dowdey
Ram Lakhan *89* Subhash Ghai
Ramar of the Jungle *53* Wallace Fox
Ramble Through Provincetown, A *21* Hy Mayer
Rambles Through Hopland *13* George Pearson
Ramblin' Galoot, The *26* Fred Bain
Ramblin' Kid, The *23* Edward Sedgwick
Rambling Ranger, The *27* Del Henderson
Rambo: First Blood Part II *85* George Pan Cosmatos
Rambo: First Blood, Part Three *88* Peter MacDonald
Rambo III *88* Peter MacDonald
Rameau's Nephew by Diderot (Thanx to Dennis Young) by Wilma Schoen *74* Michael Snow
Rami og Julie *88* Erik Clausen
Ramón il Messicano *66* Maurizio Pradeaux
Ramón the Mexican *66* Maurizio Pradeaux
Ramona *10* D. W. Griffith
Ramona *16* Donald Crisp

Ramona 28 Edwin Carewe
Ramona 36 Henry King
Ramoneur Malgré Lui 12 Émile Cohl
Rampage! 62 Henry Hathaway, Phil Karlson
Rampage 87 William Friedkin
Rampage at Apache Wells 65 Harald Philipp
Rampant Age, The 30 Phil Rosen
Ramparts of Clay 70 Jean-Louis Bertucelli
Ramparts We Watch, The 40 Louis De Rochemont III
Ramrod 47 André De Toth
Ramrodder, The 69 Van Guylder
Ramrodders 69 Van Guylder
Rams and Mammoths 86 Filip Robar-Dorin
Ramsbottom Rides Again 56 John Baxter
Ramshackle House 24 F. Harmon Weight
Ramuntcho 19 Jacques De Baroncelli
Ramuntcho 53 René Barberis
Ramuntcho 58 Pierre Schöndörffer
Ramūra 33 Heinosuke Gosho
Ramuz, Passage d'un Poète 61 Alain Tanner
Ran 85 Akira Kurosawa
Ran Salu 67 Lester James Peries
Ranch Chicken, The 11 Allan Dwan
Ranch degli Spietati, Il 65 Robert M. White
Ranch Girl, The 11 Allan Dwan
Ranch Girl's Rustler, The 11 Allan Dwan
Ranch Life on the Range 12 Allan Dwan
Ranch of the Rustlers 65 Robert M. White
Ranch Owner's Daughter, The 09 Lewin Fitzhamon
Ranch Tenor, The 11 Allan Dwan
Ranchero's Revenge, The 12 Christy Cabanne, D. W. Griffith
Ranchman's Marathon, The 12 Allan Dwan
Ranchman's Nerve, The 11 Allan Dwan
Rancho de los Implacables, El 64 Alfonso Balcazar
Rancho Deluxe 74 Frank Perry
Rancho Grande 38 Fernando De Fuentes
Rancho Grande 40 Frank McDonald
Rancho Notorious 51 Fritz Lang
Rancid Ransom 62 Joseph Barbera, William Hanna
Rancune, La 64 Bernhard Wicki
Randheera 88 Ravichandran
Randolph Family, The 43 Harold French
Random Flakes 25 Geoffrey Barkas
Random Harvest 42 Mervyn LeRoy
Randy Rides Alone 34 Harry Fraser
Randy Strikes Oil 33 Armand Schaefer
Rang és Mód 18 Béla Balázs
Range Beyond the Blue 47 Ray Taylor
Range Blood 24 Francis Ford
Range Boss, The 17 W. S. Van Dyke
Range Busters, The 40 S. Roy Luby
Range Buzzards 25 Tom Gibson
Range Courage 27 Ernst Laemmle
Range Defenders 37 Mack V. Wright
Range Detective, The 12 Allan Dwan
Range Feud 31 D. Ross Lederman
Range Girl and the Cowboy, The 15 Tom Mix
Range Justice 25 Ward Hayes

Range Justice 48 Ray Taylor
Range Land 49 Lambert Hillyer
Range Law 31 Phil Rosen
Range Law 44 Lambert Hillyer
Range Patrol, The 23 Harry G. Moody
Range Pirate, The 21 Leonard Franchon
Range Raiders, The 27 Paul Hurst
Range Renegades 48 Lambert Hillyer
Range Riders 27 William Wyler
Range Riders, The 27 Ben F. Wilson
Range Riders 34 Victor Adamson
Range Squatter, The 11 Allan Dwan
Range Terror, The 25 William James Craft
Range War 39 Lesley Selander
Range Warfare 35 S. Roy Luby
Rangeland 22 Neal Hart
Rangeland Empire 50 Thomas Carr
Ranger and the Lady, The 40 Joseph Kane
Ranger and the Law, The 21 Robert Kelly
Ranger Courage 36 Spencer G. Bennet
Ranger of Cherokee Strip 49 Philip Ford
Ranger of the Big Pines 25 W. S. Van Dyke
Ranger of the North 27 Jerome Storm
Ranger's Code, The 33 Robert North Bradbury
Ranger's Oath 28 Robert J. Horner
Rangers of Cherokee Strip 49 Philip Ford
Rangers of Fortune 40 Sam Wood
Rangers Ride, The 48 Derwin Abrahams
Ranger's Romance, The 14 Tom Mix
Ranger's Roundup, The 38 Sam Newfield
Rangers Step In, The 37 Spencer G. Bennet
Rangers Take Over, The 42 Albert Herman
Rangi's Catch 73 Michael Forlong
Rangle River 36 Clarence Badger
Rango 31 Ernest B. Schoedsack
Rani Radovi 69 Želimir Žilnik
Ranjau Sepanjang Jalan 85 Jamil Sulong
Rank Outsider, A 20 Richard Garrick
Ranks and People 29 Mikhail Doller, Yakov Protazanov
Ranru no Hata 74 Kozaburo Yoshimura
Ransacked Shop, The 33 Martin Frič
Ransom, The 16 Edmund Lawrence
Ransom 28 George B. Seitz
Ransom 55 Alex Segal
Ransom, The 62 Akira Kurosawa
Ransom 75 Caspar Wrede
Ransom 77 Richard Compton
Ransom, The 87 Alexander Gordon
Ransom in Sardinia 68 Gianfranco Mingozzi
Ranson of the Mounted 46 B. Reeves Eason
Ranson's Folly 15 Richard Ridgely
Ranson's Folly 26 Sidney Olcott
Rantzau, Les 24 Gaston Roudes
Rao Saheb 86 Vijaya Mehta
Raoul Wallenberg: Buried Alive 84 David Harel
Rapace, Le 68 José Giovanni
Rapaces Diurnes et Nocturnes, Les 13 Léonce-Henri Burel
Rapacité 30 André Berthomieu
Rapariga no Verão, Uma 86 Vitor Goncalves
Rape, The 65 Dinos Dimopoulos

Rape, The 67 Jacques Doniol-Valcroze
Rape 69 John Lennon, Yoko Ono
Rape, The 73 Fons Rademakers
Rape Killer, The 76 Costas Carayiannis
Rape of a Country 48 Herman van den Horst
Rape of Aphrodite, The 85 Andreas Pantzis
Rape of Cyprus, The 75 Michael Cacoyannis
Rape of Czechoslovakia, The 39 Jiří Weiss
Rape of Innocence 75 Yves Boisset
Rape of Love 77 Yannick Bellon
Rape of Malaya, The 56 Jack Lee
Rape of the Sabines, The 62 Alberto Gout
Rape of the Vampire, The 67 Jean Rollin
Rape on the Front Page 72 Marco Bellocchio
Rape on the Moor 57 Hans Koenig
Rape Squad 74 Robert Kelljan
Raphaël le Tatoué 38 Christian-Jaque
Raphaël ou Le Débauché 70 Michel Deville
Rapid Fire Romance 26 Harry Joe Brown
Rapid Stream, A 26 Heinosuke Gosho
Rappel Immédiat 39 Léon Mathot
Rappin' 85 Joel Silberg
Rappresaglia 73 George Pan Cosmatos
Rapsodía Mexicana 38 Miguel Zacarías
Rapt 33 Dmitri Kirsanov
Rapt d'Enfant par les Romanichels 04 Alice Guy-Blaché
Rapto, El 53 Emilio Fernández
Rapto de las Sabinas, El 62 Alberto Gout
Rapture 50 Goffredo Alessandrini
Rapture 65 John Guillermin
Raptus 62 Riccardo Freda
Raq lo B'Shabbat 65 Alex Joffé
Raquetteurs, Les 58 Michel Brault, Gilles Groulx
Rare Animals 21 Charles Urban
Rare Bird, A 21 Raoul Barré, Charles Bowers
Rare Book Murder, The 38 Edward Buzzell
Rare Breed, The 65 Andrew V. McLaglen
Rare Breed, A 81 David Nelson
Rare Specimen, A 10 Dave Aylott
Rarin' Romeo, A 25 Archie Mayo
Rarin' to Go 24 Richard Thorpe
Ras del Quartiere, Il 83 Carlo Vanzina
Rascal 69 Norman Tokar
Rascals 38 H. Bruce Humberstone
Rashomon 50 Akira Kurosawa
Raskenstam 83 Gunnar Hellström
Raskolnikoff 23 Robert Wiene
Raskolnikov 23 Robert Wiene
Raskolnikow 23 Robert Wiene
Rasp, The 31 Michael Powell
Raspberry Romance, The 25 Lloyd Bacon
Raspoutine 54 Georges Combret
Rasputin 29 Nikolai Larin
Rasputin 29 Max Neufeld
Rasputin 30 Martin Berger
Rasputin 32 Richard Boleslawski, Charles Brabin
Rasputin 32 Adolf Trotz
Rasputin 38 Marcel L'Herbier
Rasputin 77 Elem Klimov
Rasputin and the Empress 32 Richard Boleslawski, Charles Brabin

Rasputin the Black Monk *17* Arthur Ashley
Rasputin the Holy Devil *30* Martin Berger
Rasputin the Holy Sinner *29* Max Neufeld
Rasputin—The Mad Monk *32* Richard Boleslawski, Charles Brabin
Rasputin—The Mad Monk *65* Don Sharp
Rasskaz ob Umare Hapsoko *32* Yuli Raizman
Rasskazi o Leninye *57* Sergei Yutkevich
Rasslin' Round *34* Ubbe Iwerks
Rastaquouère Rodriquez y Papanaguaz, Le *06* Georges Méliès
Rastro de la Muerte *83* Arturo Ripstein
Rastus Runs Amuck *17* Harry S. Palmer
Rat, The *25* Graham Cutts
Rat, The *37* Jack Raymond
Rat *60* Veljko Bulajić
Rat Among the Cats *63* Minoru Shibuya
Rat d'Amérique, Le *62* Jean-Gabriel Albicocco
Rat Fink *65* James Landis
Rat Life and Diet in North America *68* Joyce Wieland
Rat Pfink and Boo-Boo *64* Ray Dennis Steckler
Rat Race, The *60* Robert Mulligan
Rat Saviour, The *77* Krsto Papić
Rat-Trap *81* Adoor Gopalakrishnan
Ratanapoum House, The *56* Mahoun Tien Nioun
Ratas, Las *63* Luis Saslavsky
Ratas de la Ciudad *87* Valentín Trujillo
Ratas No Duermen de Noche, Las *74* Juan Fortuny
Ratataa *56* Hasse Ekman
Ratataplan *79* Maurizio Nichetti
Ratboy *86* Sondra Locke
Ratcatcher, The *17* Rochus Gliese, Paul Wegener
Rated at $10,000,000 *15* Joseph Smiley
Ratelrat, De *87* Wim Verstappen
Rating Notman *82* Carlo Gebler
Rationing *43* Willis Goldbeck
Rations *18* Edwin J. Collins
Ratna Deep *47* Debaki Kumar Bose
Raton Pass *50* Edwin L. Marin
Rats, The *55* Robert Siodmak
Rats, The *82* Robert Clouse
Rats Are Coming, The *72* Andy Milligan
Rats Are Coming, the Werewolves Are Here, The *72* Andy Milligan
Rats in His Garret *27* Hugh Shields
Rats of Tobruk, The *45* Charles Chauvel
Rats Wake Up, The *67* Živojin Pavlović
Rätsel des Silbernen Halbmonds, Das *72* Umberto Lenzi
Rätsel von Bangalor, Das *17* Alexander Antalffy, Paul Leni
Rätselhafte Inserat, Das *16* Karl Gerhardt, Joe May
Ratskin *29* Manny Gould, Ben Harrison
Ratten, Die *55* Robert Siodmak
Rattenfänger von Hameln, Der *17* Rochus Gliese, Paul Wegener
Rattis *86* Lennart Gustafsson
Rattle of a Simple Man *64* Muriel Box
Rattled Rooster, The *48* Art Davis
Rattler, The *25* Paul Hurst
Rattler Kid *68* Leon Klimovsky

Rattlerat, The *87* Wim Verstappen
Rattlers *76* John McCauley
Rattler's Hiss, The *20* B. Reeves Eason
Rattlesnakes and Gunpowder *11* Allan Dwan
Ratto delle Sabine, Il *45* Mario Bonnard
Råttornas Vinter *88* Thomas Hellberg
Ratty *86* Lennart Gustafsson
Raub der Mona Lisa, Der *31* Géza von Bolváry
Raub der Sabinerinnen, Der *37* Robert A. Stemmle
Räuberbraut, Die *16* Robert Wiene
Raubfischer in Hellas *60* Horst Haechler
Raumschiff Venus Antwortet Nicht *60* Kurt Mätzig
Rausch *19* Ernst Lubitsch
Rauschgift *32* Kurt Gerron
Rautha Skikkjan *67* Gabriel Axel
Ravager, The *70* Charles Nizet
Ravagers, The *65* Eddie Romero
Ravagers, The *79* Richard Compton
Raven, The *15* Charles Brabin
Raven, The *35* Lew Landers
Raven, The *42* Dave Fleischer
Raven, The *43* Henri-Georges Clouzot
Raven, The *62* Roger Corman
Räven *86* Claes Lindberg
Raven's Dance *80* Markku Lehmuskallio
Raven's End *62* Bo Widerberg
Ravin Sans Fond, Le *17* Raymond Bernard, Jacques Feyder
Ravine, The *69* Paolo Cavara
Ravishing Idiot, A *63* Édouard Molinaro
Ravissante *61* Robert Lamoureux
Ravissante Idiote, Une *63* Édouard Molinaro
Raw Courage *84* Robert L. Rosen
Raw Deal *48* Anthony Mann
Raw Deal *77* Russell Hagg
Raw Deal *86* John Irvin
Raw Edge *56* John Sherwood
Raw Force *82* Edward Murphy
Raw Meat *72* Gary Sherman
Raw! Raw! Rooster *56* Robert McKimson
Raw Recruit, The *28* Hugh Croise
Raw Terror *85* Percival Rubens
Raw Timber *37* Ray Taylor
Raw Tunes *86* Gary Levy, Dan Lewk
Raw Weekend *64* Sidney Niehoff
Raw Wind in Eden *58* Richard Wilson
Rawhead Rex *86* George Pavlou
Rawhide *26* Richard Thorpe
Rawhide *38* Ray Taylor
Rawhide *50* Henry Hathaway
Rawhide Halo, The *62* Roger Kay
Rawhide Kid, The *28* Del Andrews
Rawhide Mail *34* Bernard B. Ray
Rawhide Rangers *41* Ray Taylor
Rawhide Romance *34* Victor Adamson
Rawhide Terror, The *34* Bruce Mitchell
Rawhide Trail, The *58* Robert Gordon
Rawhide Years, The *56* Rudolph Maté
Rawney, The *88* Bob Hoskins
Ray, A *28* Tomu Uchida
Ray Ellington and His Quartet *60* Robert Henryson
Ray Master l'Inafferrabine *67* Vittorio Sala
Ray of Sunshine, A *33* Pál Fejős
Ray of Sunshine, A *50* Horace Shepherd

Raya and Sekina *53* Salah Abu Saif
Raymie *60* Frank McDonald
Rayo, El *35* Julián González
Rayo Disintegrador, El *65* Pascual Cervera
Rayon des Amours, Le *32* Edmond T. Gréville
Rayon Invisible, Le *23* René Clair
Rayon Vert, Le *85* Eric Rohmer
Rayons Röntgen, Les *1897* Georges Méliès
Rayons X, Les *1897* Georges Méliès
Rays of Light *85* Enzo G. Castellari
Rays That Erase *16* Edwin J. Collins
Raz, Dwa, Trzy *67* Lindsay Anderson
Raza Nunca Pierde—Huele a Gas, La *87* Víctor Manuel Castro
Razbitaya Vaza *13* Yakov Protazanov
Razmakh Kryliev *87* Gennady Glagolev
Razorback *84* Russell Mulcahy
Razored in Old Kentucky *30* Mark Sandrich
Razor's Edge, The *46* Edmund Goulding
Razor's Edge, The *84* John Byrum
Razumov *36* Marc Allégret
Razzia *48* Werner Klingler
Razzia *54* Henri Decoin
Razziá sur la Chnouf *54* Henri Decoin
Razzle Dazzle *03* Edwin S. Porter
Re-Animator *85* Stuart Gordon
Re-Blazing the '49 Trail in a Motor Car Train *19* Paul M. Felton
Re Burlone, Il *35* Enrico Guazzoni
Re-Creation of Brian Kent, The *25* Sam Wood
Re dei Criminali, Il *68* Paolo Bianchini
Re dei Faisari, Il *61* Gilles Grangier
Re dei Sette Mari, Il *61* Riccardo Freda, Rudolph Maté, Primo Zeglio
Re di Denari *36* Enrico Guazzoni
Re Fantasma, Il *14* Ugo Falena
Re Ferito, Il *88* Damiano Damiani
Re-Inforcer, The *49* Jerry Lewis
Re: Lucky Luciano *73* Francesco Rosi
Re Si Diverte, Il *41* Mario Bonnard
Reach for Glory *61* Philip Leacock
Reach for the Sky *56* Lewis Gilbert
Reaching for the Moon *17* John Emerson
Reaching for the Moon *31* Edmund Goulding
Reaching for the Moon *33* Dave Fleischer
Reaching for the Stars *58* Carl Heinz Schroth
Reaching for the Sun *41* William A. Wellman
Reaching Out *73* Pat Russell
Réactions Nutritives d'Haliotis: Réactions d'Haliotis de Clamys et de Différents Échinodermes à la Présence de Certains Stellérides *56* Jean Painlevé
Reader, The *88* Michel Deville
Readin"Ritin"Rithmetic *26* Robert Eddy
Ready for Love *34* Marion Gering
Ready Money *14* Oscar Apfel
Ready, Set, Zoom! *55* Chuck Jones
Ready, Willing and Able *37* Ray Enright
Ready Woolen and Able *60* Chuck Jones
Real Adventure, The *21* King Vidor
Real Bloke, A *35* John Baxter
Real Bullets *90* Lance Lindsay
Real Danish Lunch, A *35* Anders Wilhelm Sandberg

Real End of the Great War, The 57 Jerzy Kawalerowicz
Real Estate Fraud, The 12 Allan Dwan
Real Folks 18 Walter Edwards
Real Genius 85 Martha Coolidge
Real Girl, A 29 Ralph Ince
Real Glory, The 39 Henry Hathaway
Real Gone Girls, The 70 James Hill
Real Life 78 Albert Brooks
Real Life 83 Francis Megahy
Real Life in the Forest 50 Alexander Zguridi
Real Live Teddy Bear, A 10 Frank Wilson
Real Men 87 Dennis Feldman
Real Presence, The 83 Raúl Ruiz
Real Sword Fight 69 Tomu Uchida
Real Thing, The 13 Hay Plumb
Real Thing at Last, The 16 L. C. MacBean
Real Woman, A 54 Alberto Cavalcanti
Reali di Francia, I 59 Mario Costa
Realismo Socialista, El 73 Raúl Ruiz
Realities 30 Bernerd Mainwaring
Realization, The 11 Edwin S. Porter
Really Scent 59 Chuck Jones, Abe Levitow
Realm Between the Living and the Dead 89 Ziniu Wu
Realm of Fortune, The 86 Arturo Ripstein
Realm of the Senses, The 76 Nagisa Oshima
Reap the Wild Wind 42 Cecil B. DeMille
Reapers, The 16 Burton L. King
Reaping, The 15 Elisha H. Calvert
Rear Guard 54 David Butler
Rear-Guard 87 András Kovács
Rear Gunner, The 43 Ray Enright
Rear Ravens 75 Carlos Saura
Rear Window 54 Alfred Hitchcock
Reason and Emotion 62 Jiří Brdečka
Reason, Debate and a Tale 74 Ritwik Ghatak
Reason Over Passion 69 Joyce Wieland
Reason to Live, a Reason to Die, A 72 Tonino Valerii
Reason Why, The 18 Robert Vignola
Reasonable Doubt 36 George King
Reasons of State 75 Miguel Littin
Reasons of State 78 André Cayatte
Reazione a Catena 71 Mario Bava
Rebecca 40 Alfred Hitchcock
Rebecca of Sunnybrook Farm 17 Marshall Neilan
Rebecca of Sunnybrook Farm 32 Alfred Santell
Rebecca of Sunnybrook Farm 38 Allan Dwan
Rebecca the Jewess 13 Leedham Bantock
Rebel, The 32 Edwin H. Knopf, Luis Trenker
Rebel, The 51 Rod Amateau
Rebel, The 56 Emilio Fernández
Rebel, The 60 Robert Day
Rebel, The 62 Nagisa Oshima
Rebel 85 Michael Jenkins
Rebel Angel 62 Lamont Douglas
Rebel Breed, The 78 Ted V. Mikels
Rebel City 53 Thomas Carr
Rebel Flight to Cuba 59 Gottfried Reinhardt
Rebel Gladiators, The 63 Domenico Paolella

Rebel in Town 56 Alfred L. Werker
Rebel Love 84 Milton Bagby, Jr.
Rebel Nun, The 74 Gianfranco Mingozzi
Rebel Rabbit 49 Robert McKimson
Rebel Rousers 67 Martin B. Cohen
Rebel Set, The 59 Gene Fowler, Jr.
Rebel Son, The 38 Adrian Brunel, Albert De Courville, Alexis Granowsky
Rebel Souls 37 Alejandro Galindo
Rebel with a Cause 62 Tony Richardson
Rebel Without a Cause 55 Nicholas Ray
Rebel Without Claws 61 Friz Freleng
Rebeldía 52 José Antonio Nieves Conde
Rebelión de las Muertas, La 72 Leon Klimovsky
Rebelión de los Colgados, La 54 Alfredo B. Crevenna, Emilio Fernández
Rebelión de los Colgados, La 87 Juan Buñuel
Rebelión de los Esclavos, La 61 Nunzio Malasomma
Rebelión de los Fantasmas, La 46 Adolfo Fernández Bustamante
Rebell, Der 32 Kurt Bernhardt, Luis Trenker
Rebelle, Le 80 Gérard Blain
Rebellion 36 Lynn Shores
Rebellion, Die 62 Wolfgang Staudte
Rebellion 67 Masaki Kobayashi
Rebellion 79 Lester James Peries
Rebellion in Cuba 61 Albert C. Gannaway
Rebellion in Japan 67 Heinosuke Gosho
Rebellion in Patagonia 74 Héctor Olivera
Rebellion of Kitty Belle, The 14 Christy Cabanne
Rebellion of the Dead Women, The 72 Leon Klimovsky
Rebellion of the Hanged, The 54 Alfredo B. Crevenna, Emilio Fernández
Rebellious Bride, The 19 Lynn Reynolds
Rebellious Daughters 38 Jean Yarbrough
Rebellious One, The 64 Brian G. Hutton
Rebellious Schoolgirls 07 Lewin Fitzhamon
Rebels Against the Light 64 Alexander Ramati
Rebels Die Young 62 Raymond A. Phelan
Rebirth of a Nation 65 Mario Ruspoli
Reborn 82 Bigas Luna
Rebound 31 Edward H. Griffith
Rebozo de Soledad, El 53 Roberto Gavaldón
Rebuilding an Old Japanese House 81 Richard Leacock
Rebus 89 Massimo Guglielmi
Recalling of John Grey, The 15 Frank Wilson
Recaptured Love 30 John G. Adolfi
Ręce do Góry 67 Jerzy Skolimowski
Received Payment 22 Charles Maigne
Receiver's Doom, The 09 A. E. Coleby
Recess 67 Rule Royce Johnson
Recht auf Liebe, Das 40 Joe Stöckel
Recipe for a Crime 67 Martin Frič
Récit du Colonel, Le 08 Louis Feuillade
Recitation by James Welch 13 Walter R. Booth
Reckless 35 Victor Fleming
Reckless 84 James Foley
Reckless Age, The 24 Harry A. Pollard
Reckless Age 44 Felix E. Feist

Reckless Age, The 58 David Bradley
Reckless Buckaroo, The 35 Harry Fraser
Reckless Chances 22 John P. McGowan
Reckless Courage 25 Tom Gibson
Reckless Gamble, A 28 Widgey R. Newman
Reckless Hour, The 31 John Francis Dillon
Reckless Living 31 Cyril Gardner
Reckless Living 38 Frank McDonald
Reckless Moment, The 49 Max Ophüls
Reckless Ranger, The 37 Spencer G. Bennet
Reckless Rider, The 32 Armand Schaefer
Reckless Riding Bill 24 Frank Morrow
Reckless Roads 35 Burt Lynwood
Reckless Romance 24 Scott Sidney
Reckless Romeo, A 16 Roscoe Arbuckle
Reckless Romeos 34 Vin Moore
Reckless Rosie 28 Mervyn LeRoy
Reckless Sex, The 20 Al Christie
Reckless Sex, The 25 Alvin J. Neitz
Reckless Speed 24 William James Craft
Reckless Years, The 58 Helmut Käutner
Reckless Youth 22 Ralph Ince
Reckoning, The 08 D. W. Griffith
Reckoning, The 32 Harry Fraser
Reckoning, The 69 Jack Gold
Reckoning Day, The 18 Harry A. Pollard
Reclaimed 18 Harry McRae Webster
Reclamation, The 16 Edward Sloman
Reclamation of Snarky, The 11 Bert Haldane
Recluse 81 Bob Bentley
Recognition, The 12 Allan Dwan
Recoil, The 17 George Fitzmaurice
Recoil, The 21 Milburn Morante
Recoil, The 22 Geoffrey H. Malins
Recoil, The 24 T. Hayes Hunter
Recoil 53 John Gilling
Recoil 62 Paul Wendkos
Recollections of Boyhood 54 Willard Van Dyke
Recollections of Boyhood—An Interview with Joseph Welch 54 Willard Van Dyke
Recommendation for Mercy 75 Murray Markowitz
Recompense 25 Harry Beaumont
Reconciliation, The 08 James A. Williamson
Reconstitution 70 Theodoros Angelopoulos
Reconstruction 70 Theodoros Angelopoulos
Reconstruction of a Crime 70 Theodoros Angelopoulos
Record, The 88 Daniel Helfer
Record City 77 Dennis Steinmetz
Record 413 36 Richard Pottier
Record of a Living Being 55 Akira Kurosawa
Record of a Tenement Gentleman, The 47 Yasujiro Ozu
Record of Love 61 Heinosuke Gosho
Record of Love and Desire 30 Heinosuke Gosho
Record of Newlyweds 30 Mikio Naruse
Record of Shameless Newlyweds, A 30 Mikio Naruse
Record of Youth, A 50 Keisuke Kinoshita

Record Sneeze, The *05* Alf Collins
Recours en Grâce *60* Laslo Benedek
Recreation *14* Charles Chaplin
Récréation, La *61* Fabien Collin, François Moreuil
Récréation à La Martinière *1895* Louis Lumière
Recreation I *57* Robert Breer
Recreation II *57* Robert Breer
Recruits *86* Rafal Zielinski
Recuerdos del Porvenir, Los *68* Arturo Ripstein
Recuperanti, I *69* Ermanno Olmi
Recurso del Método, El *75* Miguel Littin
Red, La *53* Emilio Fernández
Red *70* Gilles Carle
Red *76* Astrid Frank
Red Aces *29* Edgar Wallace
Red and Black *86* Miroslav Mukiljan
Red and Blue *67* Tony Richardson
Red and the Black, The *53* Claude Autant-Lara
Red and the White, The *67* Miklós Jancsó
Red and White *32* Yuri Zhelyabuzhsky
Red Angel, The *50* Jacques Daniel-Norman
Red Angel, The *66* Yasuzo Masumura
Red Ants *87* Vassilis Buduris
Red Apple, The *75* Tolomush Okeyev
Red Army Days *35* Josef Heifits, Mikhail Shapiro, Alexander Zarkhi
Red Arrow, The *87* Iskander Khamrayev, Igor Sheshukov
Red Badge of Courage, The *51* John Huston
Red Ball Express *52* Budd Boetticher
Red Balloon, The *55* Albert Lamorisse
Red Balloons, The *13* Émile Cohl
Red Baron, The *70* Roger Corman
Red Barry *38* Ford Beebe, Alvin J. Neitz
Red Beard *16* Abel Gance
Red Beard *65* Akira Kurosawa
Red Bells: I've Seen the Birth of a New World *83* Sergei Bondarchuk
Red Bells: Mexico in Flames *82* Sergei Bondarchuk
Red Beret, The *53* Terence Young
Red Berry *74* Vasili Shuksin
Red Blood *26* John P. McGowan
Red Blood and Blue *25* James C. Hutchinson
Red Blood of Courage, The *35* John English
Red Bull der Letzte Apache *20* Piel Jutzi
Red Canyon *49* George Sherman
Red Circle, The *22* George Ridgwell
Red Circle, The *60* Jürgen Roland
Red Circle, The *70* Jean-Pierre Melville
Red Clay *27* Ernst Laemmle
Red Cloak, The *55* Giuseppe M. Scotese
Red Cloak, The *58* Teinosuke Kinugasa
Red Countess, The *85* András Kovács
Red Courage *21* B. Reeves Eason
Red Crescent, The *87* Henri Safran
Red Cross Pluck *14* Ethyle Batley
Red Culottes, The *62* Alex Joffé
Red Dance, The *28* Raoul Walsh
Red Dancer of Moscow, The *28* Raoul Walsh
Red Danube, The *49* George Sidney

Red Dawn *84* John Milius
Red Desert *49* Ford Beebe
Red Desert, The *64* Michelangelo Antonioni
Red Desert Penitentiary *87* George Sluizer
Red Detachment of Women, The *60* Jin Xie
Red Dice *26* William K. Howard
Red Dragon, The *45* Phil Rosen
Red Dragon *65* Ernst Hofbauer
Red Dragon *86* Michael Mann
Red Dress, The *54* Lawrence Huntington, Charles Saunders
Red Dust *32* Victor Fleming
Red Dust *90* Ho Yim
Red Earth, The *45* Bodil Ipsen, Lau Lauritzen, Jr.
Red Ensign *33* Michael Powell
Red Flyer, The *41* Mikhail Kalatozov
Red Foam *20* Ralph Ince
Red Fork Range *31* Alvin J. Neitz
Red Fury, The *85* Lyman Dayton
Red Garters *54* George Marshall
Red Girl, The *08* D. W. Griffith
Red Glove, The *19* John P. McGowan
Red Ground, The *53* Thorold Dickinson
Red Guards in Hong Kong *87* Johnny Mak
Red Hair *28* Clarence Badger
Red-Haired Alibi *32* Christy Cabanne
Red-Haired Cupid, A *18* Clifford Smith
Red Hand, The *60* Kurt Meisel
Red Hangman, The *65* Massimo Pupillo
Red-Headed League, The *21* Maurice Elvey
Red-Headed Stranger *84* William D. Wittliff
Red-Headed Woman *32* Jack Conway
Red Heat *84* Robert Collector
Red Heat *88* Walter Hill
Red Heels *25* Michael Curtiz
Red Hornet, The *47* William Beaudine
Red, Hot and Blue *49* John Farrow
Red Hot Bullets *27* Stephen Roberts
Red Hot Dollars *19* Jerome Storm
Red Hot Hoofs *26* Robert De Lacey
Red Hot Leather *26* Albert S. Rogell
Red Hot Mama *34* Dave Fleischer
Red Hot Rangers *47* Tex Avery
Red Hot Rhythm *29* Leo McCarey
Red Hot Riding Hood *43* Tex Avery
Red Hot Romance, A *13* Mack Sennett
Red Hot Romance *22* Victor Fleming
Red Hot Speed *29* Joseph E. Henabery
Red Hot Tires *25* Erle C. Kenton
Red Hot Tires *35* D. Ross Lederman
Red Hot Wheels *50* Clarence Brown
Red House, The *47* Delmer Daves
Red Imps *23* Ivan Perestiani
Red Inn, The *23* Jean Epstein
Red Inn, The *51* Claude Autant-Lara
Red Kimono *25* Walter Lang
Red Kiss *85* Vera Belmont
Red Lane, The *20* Lynn Reynolds
Red Lantern, The *19* Albert Capellani
Red Lanterns *65* Vassilis Georgiades
Red Light, The *10* August Blom
Red Light, The *13* Warwick Buckland
Red Light *49* Roy Del Ruth
Red Light District *56* Kenji Mizoguchi

Red Lights *23* Clarence Badger
Red Lights Ahead *37* Roland Reed
Red Lily, The *23* Fred Niblo
Red Line 7000 *65* Howard Hawks
Red Lion *69* Kihachi Okamoto
Red Lips *25* Edwin Greenwood, Will P. Kellino
Red Lips *28* Melville Brown
Red Lips *60* Damiano Damiani
Red Lips *64* Giuseppe Bennati
Red Lips *67* Jesús Franco
Red Lips, The *70* Harry Kümel
Red Love *25* Edgar Lewis
Red Majesty *29* Harold Noice
Red Mantle, The *67* Gabriel Axel
Red Margaret, Moonshiner *13* Allan Dwan
Red Mark, The *28* James Cruze
Red May *68* Miklós Jancsó
Red Meadows *45* Bodil Ipsen, Lau Lauritzen, Jr.
Red Meadows *66* Emil Lotyanu
Red Men Tell No Tales *31* Edward Buzzell
Red Menace, The *49* R. G. Springsteen
Red Mill, The *26* Roscoe Arbuckle
Red Monarch *83* Jack Gold
Red Morning *34* Wallace Fox
Red Mountain *50* William Dieterle, John Farrow
Red Neck County *75* Richard Robinson
Red Nights *73* Georges Franju
Red Nights *87* Izhak Hanooka
Red Ocean *84* Lamberto Bava
Red on Red *83* Rose Marie Turko
Red Over Red *67* Marshall Stone
Red Pastures *63* Alfredo Antonini
Red Peacock, The *20* Paul Stein
Red Pearls *30* Walter Forde
Red Piers *59* Teruo Ishii
Red Planet Mars *52* Harry Horner
Red Pomegranate *68* Sergei Paradzhanov
Red Pony, The *49* Lewis Milestone
Red Poppies of Issyk-Kul, The *71* Bolotbek Shamshiev
Red Pottage *18* Meyrick Milton
Red Presnya *26* Abram Room, L. Sheffer
Red Psalm *72* Miklós Jancsó
Red Purse *38* Béla Pásztor
Red Queen Kills Seven Times, The *72* Emilio Miraglia
Red Raiders, The *27* Albert S. Rogell
Red Red Heart, The *18* Wilfred Lucas
Red Rider, The *25* Clifford Smith
Red Rider, The *34* Lew Landers
Red Riders of Canada *28* Robert De Lacey
Red Riding Hood *87* Adam Brooks
Red Riding Hood Rides Again *41* Sid Marcus
Red Riding Hoodwinked *55* Friz Freleng
Red River *47* Howard Hawks
Red River Range *38* George Sherman
Red River Renegades *46* Thomas Carr
Red River Robin Hood *42* Lesley Selander
Red River Shore *53* Harry Keller
Red River Valley *36* B. Reeves Eason
Red River Valley *41* Joseph Kane
Red Rock Outlaw *50* Elmer Clifton
Red Rope, The *37* S. Roy Luby
Red Roses *39* Giuseppe Amato, Vittorio De Sica
Red Roses for the Führer *69* Fernando Di Leo

Red Roses of Passion 66 Joe Sarno
Red Runs the River 63 Katherine Sten-
holm
Red Salute 35 Sidney Lanfield
Red Samson, The 17 Michael Curtiz
Red Saunders Plays Cupid 17 Fred A. Kel-
sey
Red Scorpion 88 Joseph Zito
Red Serpent, The 37 Ernesto Caparros
Red Shadow, The 32 Kurt Neumann
Red Sheik, The 62 Fernando Cerchio
Red Shirts 51 Goffredo Alessandrini, Fran-
cesco Rosi, Franco Rossi
Red Shoes, The 48 Michael Powell,
Emeric Pressburger
Red Sign of Madness, The 69 Mario Bava
Red Signals 27 John P. McGowan
Red Skies of Montana 52 Henry Hath-
away, Joseph M. Newman
Red Skirt, The 87 Geneviève Lefèbvre
Red Sky at Morning 70 James Goldstone
Red Snow 52 Harry S. Franklin, Boris
Petroff, Ewing Scott
Red Snowball Tree, The 74 Vasili Shuksin
Red Song 72 Miklós Jancsó
Red Sonja 85 Richard Fleischer
Red Sorghum 87 Yimou Zhang
Red Square 70 Vassily Ordynski
Red Stain, The 63 Zdenek Miler
Red Stallion, The 47 Lesley Selander
Red Stallion in the Rockies 49 Ralph
Murphy
Red Star Hidden by the Moon, The 60
Ritwik Ghatak
Red Sun 71 Terence Young
Red Sundown 55 Jack Arnold
Red Surf 90 H. Gordon Boos
Red Sword, The 29 Robert Vignola
Red Tanks 42 Z. Drapkin, R. Maiman
Red Tent, The 69 Mikhail Kalatozov
Red Tide, The 80 Richard Jeffries
Red Tomahawk 67 R. G. Springsteen
Red Tower, The 14 Mauritz Stiller
Red Train, The 73 Peter Ammann
Red Vase, The 61 Atıf Yılmaz
Red Viper, The 19 Jacques Tyrol
Red Virgin, The 15 Leon D. Kent
Red Wagon 33 Paul Stein
Red Warning, The 23 Robert North
Bradbury
Red Water 63 Satsuo Yamamoto
Red Wedding 73 Claude Chabrol
Red, White and Black, The 70 John
Cardos
Red, White and Blue 70 Allen Baron
Red, White and Blue Blood 17 Charles
Brabin
Red, White and Blue Line, The 55 John
Ford
Red, White and Busted 70 Allen Baron
Red, White and Zero 67 Peter Brook*
Red Wine 28 Raymond Cannon
Red Woman, The 17 E. Mason Hopper
Red Zone 86 Robert Enrico
Redding 29 Mannus Franken
Redeemed 15 Lawrence Trimble
Redeemer, The 65 Joseph Breen
Redeemer, The 76 Constantine S. Gochis
Redeemer, The 77 Krsto Papić
Redeemer...Son of Satan, The 76 Con-

stantine S. Gochis
Redeeming Love 16 William Desmond
Taylor
Redeeming Sin, The 24 J. Stuart Blackton
Redeeming Sin, The 29 Howard Brether-
ton
Rédemption 11 Victorin Jasset
Redemption 17 Joseph A. Golden, Julius
Steger
Redemption 17 Raymond B. West
Redemption 30 Fred Niblo
Redemption of Dave Darcey, The 16 Paul
Scardon
Redemption of His Name, The 18 Percy
Moran
Redenzione 15 Carmine Gallone
Redes 34 Emilio Gómez Muriel, Fred Zin-
nemann
Redhead 19 Charles Maigne
Redhead, The 25 Julien Duvivier
Redhead, The 32 Julien Duvivier
Redhead 34 Melville Brown
Redhead 41 Edward L. Cahn
Redhead, The 62 Helmut Käutner
Redhead and the Cowboy, The 50 Leslie
Fenton
Redhead from Manhattan 43 Lew Landers
Redhead from Wyoming, The 52 Lee
Sholem
Redheads on Parade 35 Norman Z. Mc-
Leod
Redheads Preferred 26 Allan Dale
Redl Ezredes 84 István Szabó
Redman and the Child, The 08 D. W.
Griffith
Redman's View, The 09 D. W. Griffith
Redneck 72 Silvio Narizzano
Redneck Miller 77 John Clayton
Redondela 87 Pedro Costa Muste
Redondo 86 Raúl Busteros
Reds 81 Warren Beatty
Redskin 29 Victor Schertzinger
Redskin's Offer, The 09 Lewin Fitzhamon
Reduced Weights 29 Manny Gould, Ben
Harrison
Reducing 30 Charles Reisner
Reducing Creme 34 Ubbe Iwerks
Redwing 08 Arthur Gilbert
Redwood Forest Trail 50 Philip Ford
Redwood Sap 51 Walter Lantz
Reed Case, The 17 Allen Holubar
Reed Dolls 81 Jillali Ferhati
Reed: Insurgent Mexico 70 Paul Leduc
Reed: México Insurgente 70 Paul Leduc
Reeds at the Foot of the Mountain 84 Jin
Xie
Reefer and the Model 88 Joe Comerford
Reefer Madness 36 Louis Gasnier
Reelem Moving Picture Co., The 15 Harry
S. Palmer
Reet, Petite and Gone 47 William Forest
Crouch
Referee, The 22 Ralph Ince
Reflecting Skin, The 90 Philip Ridley
Reflection of Fear, A 71 William A. Fraker
Reflections 65 Evald Schorm
Reflections 84 Kevin Billington
Reflections from a Brass Bed 76 Richard
Clausen
Reflections in a Golden Eye 67 John Hus-

ton
Reflections on Black 55 Stan Brakhage
Reflet de Claude Merccœur, Le 23 Julien
Duvivier
Reflexfilm 47 Jørgen Roos
Reform 28 Robert F. Hill
Reform Candidate, The 15 Frank Lloyd
Reform Girl 33 Sam Newfield
Reform School 39 Leo C. Popkin
Reform School Girl 57 Edward Bernds
Reform School Girls 86 Tom DeSimone
Reformation, The 14 August Blom
Reformation of Sierra Smith, The 12 Allan
Dwan
Reformatory 38 Lewis D. Collins
Reformer and the Redhead, The 49 Mel-
vin Frank, Norman Panama
Reformers, or The Lost Art of Minding
One's Business, The 13 D. W. Griffith
Refrigerator 54 Henning Carlsen
Refuge 23 Victor Schertzinger
Refuge 81 Huck Fairman
Refugee, The 18 Cecil M. Hepworth
Refugee, The 40 Bernard Vorhaus
Refugees from the Death Cave 83 San-
tiago Álvarez
Refugiados de la Cueva del Muerto, Los 83
Santiago Álvarez
Refusal, The 72 Axel Corti
Regain 37 Marcel Pagnol
Regaining the Wind 26 Frank Miller
Regal Cavalcade 35 Thomas Bentley,
Herbert Brenon, Will P. Kellino, Nor-
man Lee, Walter Summers, Marcel
Varnel
Regalo di Natale 86 Pupi Avati
Regard Picasso, Le 66 Nelly Kaplan
Regards sur la Belgique Ancienne 36
Henri Storck
Regards sur la Folie 62 Mario Ruspoli
Regards sur le Pakistan 59 Pierre Kast
Regards to Pirates 88 Koichi Goto
Régates de San Francisco, Les 59 Claude
Autant-Lara
Regen 29 Mannus Franken, Joris Ivens
Regenbogen-1, ein Formspiel 27 Oskar
Fischinger
Regenerates, The 17 E. Mason Hopper
Regenerating Love, The 15 George Ter-
williger
Regeneration 14 Wallace Reid
Regeneration, The 15 Raoul Walsh
Regeneration 88 Russel Stephens
Regeneration of Dan, The 13 Stuart
Kinder
Regeneration of Margaret, The 16 Charles
Brabin
Regent's Park Mystery, The 24 Hugh
Croise
Reggae Sunsplash 79 Stefan Paul
Reggie Mixes In 16 Christy Cabanne
Reggimento Royal Cravate, Il 22 Carmine
Gallone
Régime Sans Pain 84 Raúl Ruiz
Régiment, Le 1896 Georges Méliès
Régiment Moderne, Le 06 Alice Guy-
Blaché
Regiment of Frocks and Frills 07 Arthur
Gilbert
Regiment of Two, A 13 Ralph Ince

Return from Witch Mountain 78 John Hough

Return Home 48 Martin Frič

Return of a Citizen 86 Mohamed Khan

Return of a Man Called Horse, The 76 Irvin Kershner

Return of a Stranger 37 Joseph Losey

Return of a Stranger 61 Max Varnel

Return of a Woman in White 66 Claude Autant-Lara

Return of Batman, The 49 Spencer G. Bennet

Return of Billy Jack, The 86 Tom Laughlin

Return of Boston Blackie, The 27 Harry Hoyt

Return of Bulldog Drummond, The 34 Walter Summers

Return of Captain Invincible, The 82 Philippe Mora

Return of Carol Deane, The 38 Arthur Woods

Return of Casey Jones, The 33 John P. McCarthy

Return of Chandu, The 34 Ray Taylor

Return of Count Yorga, The 71 Robert Kelljan

Return of Daniel Boone, The 41 Lambert Hillyer

Return of Dr. Fu Manchu, The 30 Rowland V. Lee

Return of Dr. Mabuse, The 61 Harald Reinl

Return of Dr. X, The 39 Vincent Sherman

Return of Don Camillo, The 53 Julien Duvivier

Return of Dracula, The 58 Paul Landres

Return of "Draw" Egan, The 16 William S. Hart

Return of Eighteen Bronzemen 84 Joseph Kuo

Return of Eve, The 16 Arthur Berthelet

Return of Frank James, The 40 Fritz Lang

Return of Giant Majin 66 Yoshiyuki Kuroda, Kenji Misumi

Return of Godzilla, The 59 Hugo Grimaldi, Motoyoshi Odo

Return of Jack Slade, The 55 Harold Schuster

Return of Jack the Ripper, The 58 Robert S. Baker, Monty Berman

Return of Jesse James, The 50 Arthur Hilton

Return of Jimmy Valentine, The 36 Lewis D. Collins

Return of Josey Wales, The 86 Michael Parks, R. O. Taylor

Return of Majin, The 66 Yoshiyuki Kuroda, Kenji Misumi

Return of Majin, The 66 Issei Mori

Return of Martin Guerre, The 82 Daniel Vigne

Return of Mary, The 18 Wilfred Lucas

Return of Maurice Donnelly, The 15 William Humphrey

Return of Maxim, The 37 Grigori Kozintsev, Leonid Trauberg

Return of Maxwell Smart, The 79 Clive Donner

Return of Mr. H, The 63 David Bradley

Return of Mr. Moto, The 65 Ernest Morris

Return of Monte Cristo, The 46 Henry Levin

Return of Nathan Becker, The 33 R. M. Milman, B. V. Shpias

Return of October, The 48 Joseph H. Lewis

Return of Old Mother Riley, The 37 Oswald Mitchell

Return of Peter Grimm, The 26 Victor Schertzinger

Return of Peter Grimm, The 35 George Nicholls, Jr.

Return of Raffles, The 32 Mansfield Markham

Return of Rin Tin Tin, The 47 Max Nosseck

Return of Ringo, The 65 Duccio Tessari

Return of Rusty, The 46 William Castle

Return of Sabata, The 71 Gianfranco Parolini

Return of She, The 67 Cliff Owen

Return of Sherlock Holmes, The 29 Basil Dean

Return of Sophie Lang, The 36 George Archainbaud

Return of Superfly, The 90 Sig Shore

Return of Swamp Thing, The 89 Jim Wynorski

Return of Tarzan, The 20 Harry Revier

Return of the Ape Man 44 Phil Rosen

Return of the Badmen 48 Ray Enright

Return of the Black Eagle 49 Riccardo Freda

Return of the Boomerang 69 Philip Leacock

Return of the Cisco Kid, The 39 Herbert I. Leeds

Return of the Corsican Brothers, The 53 Ray Nazarro

Return of the Dragon 73 Bruce Lee

Return of the Durango Kid, The 45 Derwin Abrahams

Return of the Evil Dead, The 73 Amando De Ossorio

Return of the Five Fifteen, The 20 Vernon Stallings

Return of the Fly, The 59 Edward Bernds

Return of the Frog, The 38 Maurice Elvey

Return of the Frontiersman 50 Richard L. Bare

Return of the Giant Majin, The 66 Yoshiyuki Kuroda, Kenji Misumi

Return of the Giant Monsters 67 Noriyaki Yuasa

Return of the Golem, The 51 Martin Frič

Return of the Gunfighter 66 James Neilson

Return of the Hero 37 James Whale

Return of the James Boys 50 Arthur Hilton

Return of the Jedi 83 Richard Marquand

Return of the Killer Tomatoes! 88 John De Bello

Return of the Lash 47 Ray Taylor

Return of the Living Dead 72 Willard Huyck

Return of the Living Dead, The 85 Dan O'Bannon

Return of the Living Dead Part II 88 Ken Wiederhorn

Return of the Lone Wolf, The 26 Ralph Ince

Return of the Lost Son 66 Evald Schorm

Return of the Magnificent Seven 66 Burt Kennedy

Return of the Missus, The 06 Tom Green

Return of the Mohicans 32 Ford Beebe, B. Reeves Eason

Return of the Musketeers, The 89 Richard Lester

Return of the Pink Panther, The 74 Blake Edwards

Return of the Prodigal, The 23 A. E. Coleby

Return of the Prodigal Son, The 66 Evald Schorm

Return of the Prodigal Son 75 Youssef Chahine

Return of the Rangers 43 Elmer Clifton

Return of the Rat, The 29 Graham Cutts

Return of the Scarlet Pimpernel, The 37 Hans Schwarz*

Return of the Secaucus Seven 79 John Sayles

Return of the Seven 66 Burt Kennedy

Return of the Soldier, The 81 Alan Bridges

Return of the Spirit, The 69 Salah Abu Saif

Return of the Tall Blond Man with One Black Shoe, The 74 Yves Robert

Return of the Terror, The 34 Howard Bretherton

Return of the Texan 52 Delmer Daves

Return of the Tiger 79 Jimmy Shaw

Return of the Vampire, The 43 Lew Landers, Kurt Neumann

Return of the Vigilantes, The 47 Ray Taylor

Return of the Vikings 44 Charles Frend

Return of the Whistler 48 D. Ross Lederman

Return of the Wolfman, The 80 Jacinto Molina

Return of Vassily Bortnikov, The 53 Vsevolod I. Pudovkin

Return of Walpurgis, The 73 Carlos Aured

Return of Wild Bill, The 40 Joseph H. Lewis

Return of Wildfire, The 48 Ray Taylor

Return Ticket to Madrid 67 Bert Haanstra

Return to Boggy Creek 77 Tom Moore

Return to Campus 75 Harold Cornsweet

Return to Earth 87 Roumyana Petrova

Return to Glennascaul 51 Hilton Edwards

Return to Heaven 30 Tomu Uchida

Return to Horror High 87 Bill Froehlich

Return to Life 37 Henri Cartier-Bresson, Herbert Kline

Return to Life 49 André Cayatte, Henri-Georges Clouzot, Jean Dréville, Georges Lampin

Return to Life 78 Sergei Paradzhanov

Return to Macon County 75 Richard Compton

Return to Oestgeest 87 Theo van Gogh

Return to Oz 85 Walter Murch

Return to Paradise *53* Mark Robson
Return to Peyton Place *61* José Ferrer
Return to Salem's Lot, A *87* Larry Cohen
Return to Sender *63* Gordon Hales
Return to Snowy River *88* Geoff Burrowes
Return to the Barracks *1896* Georges Méliès
Return to the Edge of the World *78* Michael Powell
Return to the Horrors of Blood Island *70* Eddie Romero
Return to the Land *38* Jacques Tati
Return to the Land of Oz *71* Boris Kolar
Return to the Right Path *86* Huy Thanh
Return to the River Kwai *89* Andrew V. McLaglen
Return to Treasure Island *54* E. A. Dupont
Return to Warbow *57* Ray Nazarro
Return to Waterloo *85* Ray Davies
Return to Yesterday *39* Robert Stevenson
Return with Me *41* Benjamin Christensen
Returned Engagement, A *35* Leigh Jason
Returning, The *83* Joel Bender
Reuben, Reuben *82* Robert Ellis Miller
Reub's Little Girl *13* H. Oceano Martinek
Reunion *22* Dave Fleischer
Reunion *32* Ivar Campbell
Reunion *34* Frank R. Strayer
Reunion *36* Norman Taurog
Reunion *42* Jules Dassin
Reunion, The *63* Damiano Damiani
Reunion, The *77* Mike Talbot
Reunion *87* Park-huen Kwan
Reunion *89* Jerry Schatzberg
Réunion d'Officiers *1896* Georges Méliès
Reunion in France *42* Jules Dassin
Reunion in Paris *42* Jules Dassin
Reunion in Reno *51* Kurt Neumann
Reunion in Rhythm *36* Gordon Douglas
Reunion in Vienna *33* Sidney Franklin
Revak — Lo Schiavo di Cartagine *59* Rudolph Maté
Revak the Rebel *59* Rudolph Maté
Revanche de Roger-la-Honte, La *46* André Cayatte
Revanche du Maudit, La *29* René Leprince
Rêve, Le *21* Jacques De Baroncelli
Rêve à la Lune *05* Ferdinand Zecca
Rêve Brumes, Le *31* Jacques De Baroncelli
Rêve dans la Lune, Le *05* Ferdinand Zecca
Rêve d'Artiste *1898* Georges Méliès
Rêve de l'Horloger *04* Georges Méliès
Rêve de Noël, Le *00* Georges Méliès
Rêve de Singe *78* Marco Ferreri
Rêve d'Horloger, Le *04* Georges Méliès
Rêve du Chasseur, Le *04* Alice Guy-Blaché
Rêve du Garçon de Café, Le *10* Émile Cohl
Rêve du Maître de Ballet, Le *03* Georges Méliès
Rêve du Paria, Le *01* Georges Méliès
Rêve du Pauvre *1899* Georges Méliès
Rêve du Rajah ou La Forêt Enchantée, Le *00* Georges Méliès
Rêve d'un Fumeur d'Opium *06* Victorin Jasset
Rêve d'un Fumeur d'Opium, Le *07* Georges Méliès
Rêve et Réalité *01* Ferdinand Zecca

Rêve Interdit, Le *15* Albert Capellani
Réveil, Le *25* Jacques De Baroncelli
Réveil de Maddalone, Le *24* Henri Étiévant
Réveil du Jardinier, Le *04* Alice Guy-Blaché
Réveil d'un Monsieur Pressé, Le *01* Georges Méliès
Reveille *24* George Pearson
Réveille-Toi et Meurs *66* Carlo Lizzani
Reveille with Beverly *43* Charles Barton
Revelation *24* George D. Baker
Revelations *16* Arthur Maude
Revelry *14* Charles Chaplin
Revenant, Le *03* Georges Méliès
Revenant, Le *13* Louis Feuillade
Revenant, Un *46* Christian-Jaque
Revenant, Le *51* Michel Drach
Revenge *04* Alf Collins
Revenge *06* Viggo Larsen
Revenge *18* Tod Browning
Revenge *28* Edwin Carewe
Revenge! *36* Erle C. Kenton
Revenge *47* Max Neufeld
Revenge *64* Tadashi Imai
Revenge *68* Jiří Brdečka, Evald Schorm
Revenge *71* Sidney Hayers
Revenge *79* Lina Wertmuller
Revenge *86* Christopher Lewis
Revenge *90* Tony Scott
Revenge at El Paso *68* Giuseppe Colizzi
Revenge at Monte Carlo *33* B. Reeves Eason
Revenge by the Volcano *32* Yu Sun
Revenge Champion, The *31* Tomu Uchida
Revenge for Justice *86* Manuel Cinco
Revenge in El Paso *68* Giuseppe Colizzi
Revenge Is My Destiny *71* Joseph Adler
Revenge Is Sweet *13* Edwin J. Collins
Revenge Is Sweet *17* Raoul Barré, Charles Bowers
Revenge Is Sweet *34* Gus Meins, Charles Rogers
Revenge of Asia *83* Sogo Ishii
Revenge of Black Eagle, The *64* Riccardo Freda
Revenge of Dr. Death, The *72* Jim Clark
Revenge of Dracula *65* Terence Fisher
Revenge of Frankenstein, The *58* Terence Fisher
Revenge of General Ling, The *37* Ladislas Vajda
Revenge of Ivanhoe, The *65* Tanio Boccia
Revenge of King Kong, The *67* Inoshiro Honda, Arthur Rankin, Jr.
Revenge of Milady, The *73* Richard Lester
Revenge of Mr. Thomas Atkins, The *14* George Loane Tucker
Revenge of Scotland Yard, The *38* Lawrence Huntington
Revenge of Tarzan, The *20* Harry Revier
Revenge of the Barbarians *61* Giuseppe Vari
Revenge of the Black Eagle *51* Riccardo Freda
Revenge of the Black Sisters, The *73* Joe Sarno
Revenge of the Blood Beast, The *65* Michael Reeves
Revenge of the Boogeyman *82* Ulli Lom-

mel, Bruce Starr
Revenge of the Cheerleaders *76* Richard Lerner
Revenge of the Conquered *62* Luigi Capuano
Revenge of the Creature *55* Jack Arnold
Revenge of the Dead *59* Edward D. Wood, Jr.
Revenge of the Dead *75* Evan Lee
Revenge of the Ghost *81* Yoo Sub Lee
Revenge of the Gladiators *62* Luigi Capuano
Revenge of the Gladiators *65* Michele Lupo
Revenge of the Innocents *85* William Szarka
Revenge of the Living Dead *66* Domenico De Felice, Elio Scardamaglia
Revenge of the Musketeers *62* Fulvio Tulvi
Revenge of the Nerds *84* Jeff Kanew
Revenge of the Nerds II *87* Joe Roth
Revenge of the Nerds II: Nerds in Paradise *87* Joe Roth
Revenge of the Ninja *83* Sam Firstenberg
Revenge of the Pink Panther *78* Blake Edwards
Revenge of the Pirates *51* Primo Zeglio
Revenge of the Screaming Dead *72* Willard Huyck
Revenge of the Serpents *86* Şerif Gören
Revenge of the Shogun Women *82* Mei Chung Chang
Revenge of the Stolen Stars *85* Ulli Lommel
Revenge of the Teenage Vixens from Outer Space, The *86* Jeff Farrell
Revenge of the Vampire *60* Mario Bava
Revenge of the Zombies *43* Steve Sekely
Revenge of Ukeno-Jo, The *63* Kon Ichikawa
Revenge of Ursus *61* Luigi Capuano
Revenge of Yukinojo, The *35* Teinosuke Kinugasa
Revenge of Yukinojo, The *63* Kon Ichikawa
Revenge Rider, The *35* David Selman
Revenge Squad *82* Charles Braverman
Revengeful Ghost, The *72* Im Won Sik
Revengeful Spirit of Eros, The *30* Yasujiro Ozu
Revenger, The *15* Mauritz Stiller
Revenger, The *58* Dušan Vukotić
Revengers, The *72* Daniel Mann
Revenue Agent *50* Lew Landers
Revenue Man and the Girl, The *11* D. W. Griffith
Rêver ou Envol *71* François Reichenbach
Reverberation *69* Ernie Gehr
Reverendo Colt *70* Leon Klimovsky
Rêverie pour Claude Debussy *51* Jean Mitry
Reversal of Fortune *90* Barbet Schroeder
Reverse Angle *82* Wim Wenders
Reverse Be My Lot, The *38* Raymond Stross
Reverse of the Medal, The *23* George A. Cooper
Reversed Enemy *82* Hyuk Soo Lee
Reversible Divers, The *01* Edwin S. Porter
Reversing a Shave *05* Tom Green

Rêves de Printemps 29 William Dieterle
Rêves Enfantins 10 Émile Cohl
Revêtement des Routes, Le 23 Jean Grémillon
Revêtements Routiers 38 Roger Leenhardt
Revisor 33 Martin Frič
Revived 20 Pál Fejős
Reviviscence d'un Chien 29 Jean Painlevé
Revizor 52 Vladimir Petrov
Revolt, The 16 Barry O'Neil
Revolt at Fort Laramie 57 Lesley Selander
Revolt in the Big House 58 R. G. Springsteen
Revolt in the Desert 32 Nikolai Tikhonov
Revolt in the Jungle 37 Zoltán Korda
Revolt of Job, The 83 Imre Gyöngyössy, Barna Kabay
Revolt of Mamie Stover, The 55 Raoul Walsh
Revolt of the Boyars, The 46 Sergei Eisenstein
Revolt of the Dead Ones 72 Leon Klimovsky
Revolt of the Fishermen, The 34 Erwin Piscator
Revolt of the Ghosts, The 46 Adolfo Fernández Bustamante
Revolt of the Gladiators, The 58 Vittorio Cottafavi
Revolt of the Hanged 54 Alfredo B. Crevenna, Emilio Fernández
Revolt of the Mamalukes 63 Atif Salim
Revolt of the Mercenaries 62 Piero Costa
Revolt of the Praetorians 65 Alfonso Brescia
Revolt of the Robots 24 Yakov Protazanov
Revolt of the Slaves, The 61 Nunzio Malasomma
Revolt of the Tartars 56 Carmine Gallone
Revolt of the Toys 47 Hermina Tyrlova
Revolt of the Zombies 36 Victor Halperin
Revolt on the Volga 58 William Dieterle
Révolté, Le 38 Léon Mathot
Revolte, Die 69 Reinhard Hauff
Révolte dans la Prison 30 Pál Fejős
Révolte des Gueux, La 12 Alfred Machin
Révolte des Indiens Apaches, La 63 Harald Reinl
Révolte des Vivants, La 39 Richard Pottier
Révolte sur la Volga 58 William Dieterle
Révoltée, La 47 Marcel L'Herbier
Révoltées de l'Albatros, Les 62 Silvio Amadio
Révoltés, Les 55 Giuseppe M. Scotese
Revolución 63 Jorge Sanjinés
Revolución de las Flores, La 68 Álvaro Covacevich
Revolución de Mayo 10 Mario Gallo
Revolución Justicialista, La 71 Octavio Getino, Fernando Solanas
Revolution 14 Ernest G. Batley
Revolution 63 Jorge Sanjinés
Revolution 67 Peter Greenaway
Revolution 68 Jack O'Connell
Revolution 85 Hugh Hudson
Révolution d'Octobre, La 67 Frédéric Rossif
Révolution Industrielle 70 Arthur Lamothe
Revolution Marriage, A 14 August Blom

Revolution of the Sexes 26 Julian Ollendorff
Revolutionary, The 17 Yevgeni Bauer
Revolutionary, The 62 Nagisa Oshima
Revolutionary, The 65 Jean-Pierre Lefèbvre
Revolutionary, The 70 Paul Williams
Revolutionary Romance, A 11 Alice Guy-Blaché
Revolutionist, The 14 Ernest G. Batley
Revolutionist 17 Yevgeni Bauer
Revolutionists 36 Vera Stroyeva
Révolutionnaire, Le 65 Jean-Pierre Lefèbvre
Revolutions Per Minute 70 Stanley Kramer
Revolutionsbryllup 14 August Blom
Revolutionsbryllup 28 Anders Wilhelm Sandberg
Revolutsioner 17 Yevgeni Bauer
Revolver, The 75 Sergio Sollima
Revolving Doors, The 87 Francis Mankiewicz
Revolving Table, The 03 Percy Stow
Revue Montmartroise 32 Alberto Cavalcanti
Revue Navale à Cherbourg 1896 Georges Méliès
Revue Parade 38 R. A. Hopwood
Reward, The 15 Reginald Barker
Reward, The 65 Serge Bourguignon
Reward of Courage, The 13 Allan Dwan
Reward of Faith 29 M. Simon
Reward of Patience, The 16 Robert Vignola
Reward of Perseverance, The 12 Bert Haldane
Reward of the Faithless, The 17 Rex Ingram
Reward of Valor, The 12 Allan Dwan
Rewards of Virtue, The 83 Maurice Hatton
Rey de Africa 67 Sandy Howard
Rey de los Gitanos, El 33 Frank R. Strayer
Rey Se Divierte, El 44 Fernando De Fuentes
Rezerva la Start 88 Anghel Mora
Rezhou 86 Benzheng Yu
Rezzou, Le 34 Roger Leenhardt, René Zuber
Rhapsodie der Liebe 29 Steve Sekely
Rhapsodie in Blei 59 Alvin Rakoff
Rhapsody 53 Charles Vidor
Rhapsody in Blue 45 Irving Rapper
Rhapsody in Rivets 41 Friz Freleng
Rhapsody in Wood 47 George Pal
Rhapsody Rabbit 46 Friz Freleng
Rheumatics 18 Gregory La Cava
Rhin, Fleuve International, Le 52 Serge Bourguignon, André Zwoboda
Rhinestone 84 Bob Clark
Rhino! 64 Ivan Tors
Rhinoceros, The 63 Jan Lenica
Rhinoceros 74 Tom O'Horgan
Rhode Island Red 68 Yvonne Rainer
Rhodes 36 Geoffrey Barkas, Berthold Viertel
Rhodes of Africa 36 Geoffrey Barkas, Berthold Viertel
Rhosyn a Rhith 86 Stephen Bayly
Rhoudiacéta 69 Chris Marker

Rhubarb 51 Arthur Lubin
Rhubarb 69 Eric Sykes
Rhubarb and Rascals 14 Hay Plumb
Rhumba Rhythms 42 Reginald LeBorg
Rhyme of Vengeance, A 77 Kon Ichikawa
Rhyme That Went Wrong, The 20 Vernon Stallings
Rhythm 53 Len Lye
Rhythm and Song 35 Alex Brown
Rhythm Barbarian, The 63 Santiago Álvarez
Rhythm Hits the Ice 42 Bernard Vorhaus
Rhythm in the Air 36 Arthur Woods
Rhythm in the Bow 35 Ben Hardaway
Rhythm in the Clouds 37 John H. Auer
Rhythm in the Ranks 41 George Pal
Rhythm Inn 51 Paul Landres
Rhythm 'n' Greens 64 Christopher Miles
Rhythm of a City 47 Arne Sucksdorff
Rhythm of the Islands 43 Roy William Neill
Rhythm of the Rio Grande 40 Albert Herman
Rhythm of the Saddle 38 George Sherman
Rhythm on the Rampage 37 Jean Yarbrough
Rhythm on the Ranch 37 Mack V. Wright
Rhythm on the Range 36 Norman Taurog
Rhythm on the Reservation 39 Dave Fleischer
Rhythm on the River 36 William McGann
Rhythm on the River 40 Victor Schertzinger
Rhythm Parade 42 Howard Bretherton, Dave Gould
Rhythm Racketeer 37 James Seymour
Rhythm Romance 39 George Archainbaud
Rhythm Round-Up 45 Vernon Keays
Rhythm Serenade 43 Gordon Wellesley
Rhythm 21 21 Hans Richter
Rhythmetic 56 Evelyn Lambert, Norman McLaren
Rhythmus 21 21 Hans Richter
Rhythmus 23 23 Hans Richter
Rhythmus 25 25 Hans Richter
Riachuelo 34 Moglia Barth
Riavanti...Marsch! 80 Luciano Salce
Ribalta, La 12 Mario Caserini
Ric e Gian alla Conquista del West 67 Osvaldo Civirani
Ricchezza Senza Domani 39 Ferdinando Maria Poggioli
Rice 57 Tadashi Imai
Rice 64 Wheaton Galentine, Willard Van Dyke
Rice and Old Shoes 22 Malcolm St. Clair
Rice Girl 63 Raffaello Matarazzo
Rich and Famous 81 George Cukor
Rich and Famous 87 Wong Tai Lo
Rich and Strange 32 Alfred Hitchcock
Rich Are Always With Us, The 32 Alfred E. Green
Rich Bride, The 38 Ivan Pyriev
Rich But Honest 27 Albert Ray
Rich, Full Life, The 47 Robert Z. Leonard
Rich Girl, Poor Girl 21 Harry B. Harris
Rich Kids 79 Robert M. Young
Rich Man, Poor Girl 38 Reinhold Schünzel
Rich Man, Poor Man 18 J. Searle Dawley

Rich Man's Daughter, A 18 Edgar Jones
Rich Man's Folly 31 John Cromwell
Rich Man's Plaything, A 17 Carl Harbaugh
Rich Men's Sons 27 Ralph Graves
Rich Men's Wives 22 Louis Gasnier
Rich People 29 Edward H. Griffith
Rich Revenge, A 10 D. W. Griffith
Rich Slave, The 21 Romaine Fielding
Rich Vein 64 Vassily Ordynski
Rich, Young and Deadly 60 Charles Haas
Rich, Young and Pretty 51 Norman Taurog
Richard 72 Harry Hurwitz, Lorees Yerby
Richard Himber and His Orchestra 42 Jean Negulesco
Richard Mortensens Bevægelige Maleri 44 Jørgen Roos
Richard Pryor Here and Now 83 Richard Pryor
Richard Pryor Is Back Live in Concert 79 Jeff Margolis
Richard Pryor Live in Concert 79 Jeff Margolis
Richard Pryor Live on the Sunset Strip 82 Joe Layton
Richard Tauber Story, The 53 Ernst Marischka
Richard the Brazen 17 Perry N. Vekroff
Richard, the Lion-Hearted 23 Chester Withey
Richard III 13 Frederick Warde
Richard III 55 Anthony Bushell, Laurence Olivier
Richard III 84 Raúl Ruiz
Richard Wagner 13 Carl Fröhlich
Richard's Things 80 Anthony Harvey
Richelieu 09 D. W. Griffith, Frank Powell
Richelieu 14 Allan Dwan
Richelieu 35 Rowland V. Lee
Richelieu, or The Cardinal's Conspiracy 09 D. W. Griffith, Frank Powell
Richer Than the Earth 51 Robert Siodmak
Riches and Rogues 13 Charles H. Weston
Riches and Romance 36 Alfred Zeisler
Richesse et Misère ou La Cigale et la Fourmi 1899 Georges Méliès
Richest Girl, The 18 Albert Capellani
Richest Girl in the World, The 34 William A. Seiter
Richest Girl in the World, The 60 Lau Lauritzen, Jr.
Richest Man in the World, The 30 Sam Wood
Richest Man in Town, The 41 Charles Barton
Richiamo della Foresta, Il 72 Ken Annakin
Richter und Sein Henker, Der 75 Maximilian Schell
Richter von Zalamea, Der 20 Ludwig Berger
Richthofen 29 Peter Joseph, D. Kortesz
Richthofen, The Red Knight of the Air 29 Peter Joseph, D. Kortesz
Richy Guitar 85 Michael Laux
Rickety Gin 27 Walt Disney
Rickshaw 60 Allan King
Rickshaw Man, The 58 Hiroshi Inagaki
Ricky 1 83 William T. Naud

Ricochet 63 John Llewellyn Moxey
Ricochet Romance 54 Charles Lamont
Ricochets 86 Eli Cohen
Rid i Natt 42 Gustaf Molander
Riddance 73 Márta Mészáros
Riddle Gawne 18 William S. Hart, Lambert Hillyer
Riddle of Lumen, The 72 Stan Brakhage
Riddle of the Sands, The 79 Tony Maylam
Riddle Ranch 36 Charles Hutchinson
Riddle, Woman, The 20 Edward José
Riddles of the Sphinx 76 Peter Wollen
Ride a Crooked Mile 38 Alfred E. Green
Ride a Crooked Mile 58 Jesse Hibbs
Ride a Crooked Trail 58 Jesse Hibbs
Ride a Northbound Horse 69 Robert Totten
Ride a Reckless Mile 49 Joseph M. Newman
Ride a Violent Mile 57 Charles Marquis Warren
Ride a Wild Pony 76 Don Chaffey
Ride and Kill 63 José Luis Borau
Ride Back, The 57 Allen H. Miner
Ride Bene Chi Spara Ultimo 67 Luigi Vanzi
Ride Beyond Vengeance 66 Bernard McEveety
Ride Clear of Diablo 54 Jesse Hibbs
Ride 'Em Bosko 32 Friz Freleng, Hugh Harman
Ride 'Em Cowboy 36 Lesley Selander
Ride 'Em Cowboy 42 Arthur Lubin
Ride 'Em Cowgirl 38 Samuel Diege
Ride 'Em High 27 Richard Thorpe
Ride 'Em Plowboy! 28 Walt Disney
Ride for a Bride, A 11 Charles Raymond
Ride for Your Life 24 Edward Sedgwick
Ride Him, Bosko 32 Friz Freleng, Hugh Harman
Ride Him Cowboy 32 Fred Allen
Ride in a Pink Car 74 Robert J. Emery
Ride in the Whirlwind 65 Monte Hellman
Ride, Kelly, Ride 41 Norman Foster
Ride Lonesome 59 Budd Boetticher
Ride of the Valkyries, The 07 Harold Jeapes
Ride On Vaquero 41 Herbert I. Leeds
Ride Out for Revenge 57 Bernard Girard
Ride, Ranger, Ride 36 Joseph Kane
Ride, Ryder, Ride 49 Lewis D. Collins
Ride, Tenderfoot, Ride 40 Frank McDonald
Ride the High Country 61 Sam Peckinpah
Ride the High Iron 56 Don Weis
Ride the High Wind 65 David Millin
Ride the Man Down 52 Joseph Kane
Ride the Pink Horse 47 Robert Montgomery
Ride the Tiger 71 George Montgomery
Ride the Whirlwind 65 Monte Hellman
Ride the Wild Surf 64 Art Napoleon, Don Taylor
Ride the Wind 66 William Witney
Ride to Glory 70 Burt Kennedy
Ride to Hangman's Tree, The 67 Alan Rafkin
Ride Tonight! 42 Gustaf Molander
Ride, Vaquero! 52 John Farrow
Ride with Uncle Joe, A 43 Ken Annakin

Rideau Cramoisi, Le 52 Alexandre Astruc
Rideaux Blancs, Les 65 Georges Franju
Rider from Nowhere 40 Raymond K. Johnson
Rider from Tucson 50 Lesley Selander
Rider in Blue 59 Arne Mattsson
Rider in the Night, The 68 Jan Perold
Rider of Death Valley 32 Albert S. Rogell
Rider of the King Log, The 21 Harry Hoyt
Rider of the Law, The 19 John Ford
Rider of the Law 27 Paul Hurst
Rider of the Law, The 35 Robert North Bradbury
Rider of the Plains 26 W. S. Van Dyke
Rider of the Plains 31 John P. McCarthy
Rider of the White Horse, The 35 Hans Deppe, Kurt Örtel
Rider on a Dead Horse 62 Herbert L. Strock
Rider on the Rain 69 René Clément
Riders 39 Igor Savchenko
Riders from Nowhere 40 Raymond K. Johnson
Riders from the Dusk 49 Lambert Hillyer
Riders in the Sky 49 John English
Riders of Black Hills 38 George Sherman
Riders of Black Mountain 40 Sam Newfield
Riders of Black River 39 Norman Deming
Riders of Death Valley 32 Albert S. Rogell
Riders of Death Valley 41 Ford Beebe, Ray Taylor
Riders of Destiny 33 Robert North Bradbury
Riders of Mystery 25 Robert North Bradbury
Riders of Pasco Basin 40 Ray Taylor
Riders of Rio 31 Robert E. Tansey
Riders of the Badlands 41 Howard Bretherton
Riders of the Black Hills 38 George Sherman
Riders of the Cactus 31 David Kirkland
Riders of the Dark 27 Nick Grindé
Riders of the Dawn 18 Jack Conway
Riders of the Dawn 37 Robert North Bradbury
Riders of the Dawn 45 Oliver Drake
Riders of the Deadline 43 Lesley Selander
Riders of the Desert 32 Robert North Bradbury
Riders of the Dusk 49 Lambert Hillyer
Riders of the Frontier 39 Spencer G. Bennet
Riders of the Golden Gulch 32 Clifford Smith
Riders of the Law 22 Robert North Bradbury
Riders of the Lone Star 47 Derwin Abrahams
Riders of the New Forest 46 Philip Leacock
Riders of the Night 18 John H. Collins
Riders of the North 31 John P. McGowan
Riders of the Northland 42 William Berke
Riders of the Northwest Mounted 43 William Berke
Riders of the Pasco Basin 40 Ray Taylor
Riders of the Pony Express 49 Michael Salle

Riders of the Purple Sage, The *18* Frank Lloyd
Riders of the Purple Sage *25* Lynn Reynolds
Riders of the Purple Sage *31* Hamilton MacFadden
Riders of the Purple Sage *41* James Tinling
Riders of the Range *23* Otis B. Thayer
Riders of the Range *49* Lesley Selander
Riders of the Rio *31* Robert E. Tansey
Riders of the Rio Grande *29* John P. McGowan
Riders of the Rio Grande *39* Spencer G. Bennet
Riders of the Rio Grande *43* Howard Bretherton
Riders of the Rockies *37* Robert North Bradbury
Riders of the Sage *39* Harry S. Webb
Riders of the Santa Fe *44* Wallace Fox
Riders of the Storm *29* John P. McGowan
Riders of the Storm *86* Maurice Phillips
Riders of the Timberline *41* Lesley Selander
Riders of the West *27* Ben F. Wilson
Riders of the West *42* Howard Bretherton
Riders of the Whistling Pines *49* John English
Riders of the Whistling Skull *37* Mack V. Wright
Riders of Vengeance *19* John Ford
Riders of Vengeance *28* Robert J. Horner
Riders of Vengeance *52* Lesley Selander
Riders to the Sea *35* Brian Desmond Hurst
Riders to the Stars *54* Richard Carlson
Riders Up *24* Irving Cummings
Rides on an Old Car *87* Pyotr Fomenko
Ridgeway of Montana *24* Clifford Smith
Ridicule and Tears *12* Victor Sjöström
Ridin' Comet *25* Ben F. Wilson
Ridin' Demon, The *29* Ray Taylor
Ridin' Double *24* Leo D. Maloney
Ridin' Down the Canyon *42* Joseph Kane
Ridin' Down the Trail *47* Howard Bretherton
Ridin' Easy *25* Ward Hayes
Ridin' Fool, The *31* John P. McCarthy
Ridin' for Justice *32* D. Ross Lederman
Ridin' for Love *26* William Wyler
Ridin' Gent, A *26* Bennett Cohn
Ridin' Kid from Powder River, The *24* Edward Sedgwick
Ridin' Law *30* Harry S. Webb
Ridin' Luck *27* Edward R. Gordon
Ridin' Mad *24* Jacques Jaccard
Ridin' On *36* Bernard B. Ray
Ridin' on a Rainbow *41* Lew Landers
Ridin' Pretty *25* Arthur Rosson
Ridin' Pretty *25* Clifford Smith
Ridin' Rascal, The *26* Clifford Smith
Ridin' Romeo, A *20* George Marshall
Ridin' Rowdy, The *27* Richard Thorpe
Ridin' Streak, The *25* Del Andrews
Ridin' the Cherokee Trail *41* Spencer G. Bennet
Ridin' the Lone Trail *37* Sam Newfield
Ridin' the Outlaw Trail *51* Fred F. Sears
Ridin' the Trail *40* Raymond K. Johnson

Ridin' the Wind *25* Del Andrews, Alfred L. Werker
Ridin' Through *25* Arthur Rosson
Ridin' Thru *35* Harry S. Webb
Ridin' Thunder *25* Clifford Smith
Ridin' West *24* Harry S. Webb
Ridin' Wild *22* Nat Ross
Ridin' Wild *25* Leon De la Mothe
Riding Avenger, The *36* Harry Fraser
Riding Bareback Through History *82* Santiago Álvarez
Riding Demon *29* Ray Taylor
Riding Double *24* Leo D. Maloney
Riding Fool *24* Horace B. Carpenter
Riding for a King *26* Walter West
Riding for Fame *28* B. Reeves Eason
Riding for Life *26* John P. McGowan
Riding High *37* David MacDonald
Riding High *43* George Marshall
Riding High *49* Frank Capra
Riding High *81* Derek Ford
Riding On *37* Harry S. Webb
Riding on Air *37* Edward Sedgwick
Riding on Top of a Car *07* John Morland
Riding Renegade, The *28* Wallace Fox
Riding Rivals *26* Richard Thorpe
Riding Romance *26* John P. McGowan
Riding Shotgun *54* André De Toth
Riding Speed *34* Jay Wilsey
Riding Tall *71* Patrick J. Murphy
Riding the California Trail *47* William Nigh
Riding the Goat *22* Raoul Barré, Charles Bowers
Riding the Rails *38* Dave Fleischer
Riding the Sunset Trail *41* Robert E. Tansey
Riding the Wind *42* Edward Killy
Riding Through Nevada *42* William Berke
Riding Thunder *25* Clifford Smith
Riding to Fame *27* A. B. Barringer
Riding to Win *30* Richard Thorpe
Riding Tornado, The *32* D. Ross Lederman
Riding West *43* William Berke
Riding Wild *35* David Selman
Riding with Buffalo Bill *54* Spencer G. Bennet
Riding with Death *21* Jacques Jaccard
Riel *79* George Bloomfield
Rien N'Est Impossible à l'Homme *10* Émile Cohl
Rien Que les Heures *25* Alberto Cavalcanti
Riesenrad, Das *61* Géza von Radványi
Riff-Raff *59* Carlos Saura
Riff Raff Girls *59* Alex Joffé
Riff Raffy Daffy *48* Art Davis
Riff '65 *66* Eric Camiel
Riffraff *35* J. Walter Ruben
Riffraff *47* Ted Tetzlaff
Riffraff *61* Jean Valère
Rififi *54* Jules Dassin
Rififi à Tokyo *61* Jacques Deray
Rififi for Girls *59* Alex Joffé
Rififi fra le Donne *59* Alex Joffé
Rififi in Amsterdam *66* Sergio Grieco
Rififi in Paris *66* Denys De la Patellière
Rififi in Tokyo *61* Jacques Deray
Rififi Internazionale *66* Denys De la

Patellière
Rifle Bill *08* Victorin Jasset
Rifle Bill — Le Roi de la Prairie *08* Victorin Jasset
Riflemen, The *63* Jean-Luc Godard
Rift, The *56* Gillo Pontecorvo
Rigged *85* C. M. Cutry
Right After Brown *19* Alfred E. Green
Right Age to Marry, The *35* Maclean Rogers
Right and the Wrong of It, The *13* Ralph Ince
Right Approach, The *60* David Butler
Right Cross *50* John Sturges
Right Direction, The *16* E. Mason Hopper
Right Element, The *19* Rex Wilson
Right Hand Man, The *87* Di Drew
Right Hand of the Devil *63* Aram Katcher
Right Is Might *11* Bert Haldane
Right Man, The *25* John Harvey
Right Man, The *40* Edward Dmytryk
Right Man, The *59* György Révész
Right Man for a Delicate Job, The *85* János Kovácsi
Right of Fathers, The *31* Vera Stroyeva
Right of Man, The *60* Claude Lelouch
Right of the Strongest, The *24* Edgar Lewis
Right of Way *11* Frank Wilson
Right of Way, The *14* Van Dyke Brooke
Right of Way, The *15* John W. Noble
Right of Way, The *20* John Francis Dillon
Right of Way, The *31* Frank Lloyd
Right-of-Way Casey *17* George Marshall
Right of Youth, The *11* August Blom
Right Off the Bat *15* Hugh Reticker
Right On! *70* Herbert Danska
Right Out of History: The Making of Judy Chicago's Dinner Party *80* Johanna Demetrakas
Right Person, The *55* Peter Cotes
Right Stuff, The *83* Philip Kaufman
Right That Failed, The *22* Bayard Veiller
Right to Be Born, The *66* Aleksander Ford
Right to Be Happy, The *16* Rupert Julian
Right to Happiness, The *19* Allen Holubar
Right to Lie, The *19* Edwin Carewe
Right to Live, The *16* Abel Gance
Right to Live, The *21* A. E. Coleby
Right to Live, The *33* Albert Parker
Right to Live, The *35* William Keighley
Right to Live, The *45* William Nigh
Right to Love, The *20* George Fitzmaurice
Right to Love, The *30* Richard Wallace
Right to Love, The *40* Joe Stöckel
Right to Romance, The *33* Alfred Santell
Right to Strike, The *23* Fred Paul
Right to the Heart *42* Eugene Forde
Right Way, The *21* Sidney Olcott
Rights of Man, The *15* John H. Pratt
Rights of Youth, The *11* August Blom
Rigolboche *36* Christian-Jaque
Rigoletto *10* Ugo Falena
Rigoletto *22* George Wynn
Rigoletto *27* H. B. Parkinson
Rigoletto *46* Carmine Gallone
Rigor del Destino, El *86* Gerardo Vallejo
Rigor Mortis *81* Dick Maas
Rih Essed *86* Nouri Bouzid
Riisuminen *86* Lauri Törhönen

Rising in the World 27 Tomu Uchida
Rising of the Moon, The 57 John Ford
Rising Sea, The 53 László Ranódy*
Rising Stock 87 Bo Hermansson
Rising Sun Is Shining, The 29 Seichi Ina, Kenji Mizoguchi
Rising Sun Shines, The 29 Seichi Ina, Kenji Mizoguchi
Rising Target 76 Barbara Frank
Rising Tide, The 33 Paul Rotha
Rising to Fame 31 Robert Z. Leonard
Risk, The 60 John Boulting, Roy Boulting
Risky Business 20 Harry B. Harris
Risky Business 26 Alan Hale
Risky Business 39 Arthur Lubin
Risky Business 83 Paul Brickman
Risky Road, The 18 Ida May Park
Riso Amaro 48 Giuseppe De Santis
Risques du Métier, Les 67 André Cayatte
Risveglio di Paul, Il 85 Michele Saponaro
Risveglio di una Città 33 Luigi Zampa
Rita 60 Alberto Lattuada
Rita, Sue and Bob, Too! 86 Alan Clarke
Rite, The 69 Ingmar Bergman
Riten 69 Ingmar Bergman
Rites of Summer 85 Jeff Bleckner
Riti Magie Nere e Segrete Orge del Trecento 73 Renato Polselli
Ritmi di New York 38 Vittorio Sala
Ritorno di Casanova, Il 78 Pasquale Festa Campanile
Ritorno di Don Camillo, Il 53 Julien Duvivier
Ritorno di Ringo, Il 65 Duccio Tessari
Ritorno di Zanna Bianca, Il 74 Lucio Fulci
Ritos Sexuales del Diablo, Los 81 José Ramón Larraz
Ritratto di Borghesia in Nero 79 Tonino Cervi
Ritratto di Pina 66 Gian Vittorio Baldi
Ritt in die Freiheit 37 Karl Hartl
Ritual, The 69 Ingmar Bergman
Ritual dos Sádicos, O 70 José Mojica Marins
Ritual in Transfigured Time 46 Maya Deren
Ritual of Love 57 Luciano Emmer, Robert Enrico
Rituals 78 Peter Carter
Ritz, The 76 Richard Lester
Ritzy 27 Richard Rosson
Ritzy Hotel 32 Manny Gould, Ben Harrison
Riusciranno i Nostri Eroi a Ritrovare l'Amico Misteriosamente Scomparso in Africa? 68 Ettore Scola
Riusciranno i Nostri Eroi a Trovare il Loro Amico Misteriosamente Scomparso in Africa? 68 Ettore Scola
Riva dei Bruti, La 30 Mario Camerini
Rivak the Barbarian 59 Rudolph Maté
Rival, The 70 Satyajit Ray
Rival Anarchists, The 14 Langford Reed
Rival Barbers 05 James A. Williamson
Rival Captains, The 16 Ethyle Batley
Rival Cyclists, The 08 James A. Williamson
Rival Mashers, The 14 Charles Chaplin
Rival Mesmerist, The 09 Lewin Fitzhamon
Rival Music Hall Artistes, The 03 Georges Méliès
Rival Musicians, The 13 Will P. Kellino
Rival Painters, The 05 William Haggar
Rival Reflections 14 Harry Furniss
Rival Romeos 28 Walt Disney
Rival Sportsmen, The 05 Lewin Fitzhamon
Rival Suitors, The 14 Charles Chaplin, Mack Sennett
Rival World, The 54 Bert Haanstra
Rivale dell'Imperatrice, La 49 Jacopo Comin, Sidney Salkow
Rivalen der Luft 34 Frank Wisbar
Rivalen der Manège 61 Harald Philipp
Rivalen im Weltrekord 32 Ernö Metzner
Rivalité d'Amour 08 Georges Méliès
Rivalité de Max, Le 13 Max Linder
Rivals, The 03 Alf Collins
Rivals, The 06 Lewin Fitzhamon
Rivals, The 07 J. Searle Dawley, Edwin S. Porter
Rivals, The 09 Lewin Fitzhamon
Rivals, The 12 Mack Sennett
Rivals, The 15 Chester M. Franklin, Sidney Franklin
Rivals 33 A. Dmitriev
Rivals, The 63 Max Varnel
Rivals 72 Krishna Shah
Rivals 79 Lyman Dayton
Rivals 87 Victor Sadovsky
Rive Gauche 31 Alexander Korda
River, The 28 Frank Borzage
River, The 33 Josef Rovenský
River, The 37 Pare Lorentz
River, The 50 Jean Renoir
River, The 60 Nikos Koundouros
River, The 61 Rajen Tarafder
River, The 84 Mark Rydell
River and Death, The 54 Luis Buñuel
River Beat 54 Guy Green
River Boy, The 67 Noel Black
River Called Titash, A 73 Ritwik Ghatak
River Changes, The 56 Owen Crump
River Flows East in the Spring, The 47 Tsou-sen Tsai, Junli Zheng
River Fuefuki, The 60 Keisuke Kinoshita
River Gang 45 Charles David
River Gray and the River Green, The 19 Robert C. Bruce
River House Ghost, The 32 Frank Richardson
River House Mystery, The 26 A. E. Coleby
River House Mystery, The 35 Fraser Foulsham
River Lady 48 George Sherman
River Music 61 Alexander Hammid
River Niger, The 75 Krishna Shah
River of Blood, The 52 Hugo Del Carril
River of Death 89 Steve Carver
River of Dollars, A 66 Carlo Lizzani
River of Evil 64 Helmuth M. Backhaus, Franz Eichhorn
River of Fireflies 87 Eizo Sugawa
River of Forever 67 Shiro Toyoda
River of Gold, The 86 Jaime Chavarri
River of Life and Death, The 40 Elmar Klos
River of Light, The 21 Dave Aylott
River of Missing Men, The 37 Lewis D. Collins
River of No Return 54 Otto Preminger
River of Poison 49 Ray Nazarro
River of Romance, The 16 Henry Otto
River of Romance 29 Richard Wallace
River of Stars, The 21 F. Martin Thornton
River of Three Junks, The 57 André Pergament
River of Unrest 36 Brian Desmond Hurst, Walter Summers
River Patrol 48 Ben R. Hart
River Pirate, The 28 William K. Howard
River Rat 84 Tom Rickman
River Ribber 45 Paul Sommer
River Rivals 67 Harry Booth
River 70 70 Jesús Franco
River Solo Flows 51 Kon Ichikawa
River Without a Bridge 69 Tadashi Imai
River Wolves, The 33 George Pearson
River Woman, The 28 Joseph E. Henabery
Riverbed, The 85 Rachel Reichman
Riverbend 90 Sam Firstenberg
Riverboat Rhythm 46 Leslie Goodwins
Riverrun 68 John Korty
Rivers and Landscapes 34 Oskar Fischinger
River's Edge, The 57 Allan Dwan
River's Edge 86 Tim Hunter
River's End, The 20 Marshall Neilan
River's End 30 Michael Curtiz
River's End 40 Ray Enright
Riverside Murder, The 35 Albert Parker
Riverside Romance, A 13 Stuart Kinder
Riviera: Today's Eden, The 58 Agnès Varda
Rivière du Hibou, La 61 Robert Enrico
Rivolta degli Schiavi, La 61 Nunzio Malasomma
Rivolta dei Mercenari, La 62 Piero Costa
Rivolta del Gladiatori, La 58 Vittorio Cottafavi
Riyū Naki Bōkō-Gendai Seihanzua Zekkyōhen 69 Koji Wakamatsu
Road, The 54 Federico Fellini
Road, The 55 Alexander Stolper
Road a Year Long, The 57 Giuseppe De Santis
Road Agent 26 John P. McGowan
Road Agent 41 Charles Lamont
Road Agent 52 Lesley Selander
Road Back, The 37 James Whale
Road Between, The 17 Joseph Levering
Road Builder, The 71 Alastair Reid
Road Called Straight, The 19 Ira M. Lowry
Road Demon, The 21 Lynn Reynolds
Road Demon 38 Otto Brower
Road for Youth, The 36 Aleksander Ford
Road Games 81 Richard Franklin
Road Gang 36 Louis King
Road Gangs: Adventures in the Creep Zone 82 Lamont Johnson
Road Home, The 46 Alexander Ivanov
Road Home, The 88 Jerzy Kaszubowski
Road House 28 Richard Rosson
Road House 34 Maurice Elvey
Road House 48 Jean Negulesco
Road House 89 Rowdy Herrington
Road House Girl 53 Francis Searle
Road Hustlers, The 68 Larry Jackson
Road I Travel with You, The 36 Mikio Naruse

Road Is Fine, The *29* Robert Florey
Road Movie *73* Joseph Strick
Road North, The *32* A. Kamarof
Road o' Strife *15* Howell Hansel, John Ince
Road of Ambition, The *20* William P. S. Earle
Road of Death *77* René Martínez, Jr.
Road of Life *80* Nelson Pereira Dos Santos
Road Rebels *63* Reno Calarco
Road Show *29* Charles Reisner
Road Show *41* Gordon Douglas, Hal Roach, Hal Roach, Jr.
Road Through the Dark, The *18* Edmund Mortimer
Road to Alcatraz *45* Nick Grindé
Road to Andalay, The *64* Friz Freleng
Road to Arcady, The *22* Burton L. King
Road to Bali *52* Hal Walker
Road to Broadway, The *26* Howard Mitchell
Road to Calais, The *14* Charles H. Weston
Road to Corinth, The *67* Claude Chabrol
Road to Denver, The *55* Joseph Kane
Road to Divorce, The *20* Phil Rosen
Road to Ernoa, The *20* Louis Delluc
Road to Eternity, The *59* Masaki Kobayashi
Road to Fort Alamo, The *64* Mario Bava
Road to Fortune, The *30* Arthur Varney-Serrao
Road to France, The *18* Del Henderson
Road to Frisco, The *40* Raoul Walsh
Road to Glory, The *26* Howard Hawks
Road to Glory, The *36* Howard Hawks
Road to God, The *28* Heinosuke Gosho
Road to Happiness, The *16* Forest Holger-Madsen
Road to Happiness, The *26* Michael Curtiz
Road to Happiness *41* Phil Rosen
Road to Heaven, The *22* Challis Sanderson
Road to Heaven, The *42* Alf Sjöberg
Road to Hong Kong *62* Norman Panama
Road to Hope, The *50* Pietro Germi
Road to Katmandu, The *69* André Cayatte
Road to Life, The *30* Nikolai Ekk, R. Yanushkevich
Road to Life, The *56* A. Maslyukov, A. Mayevsky
Road to London, The *21* Eugene Mullen
Road to Love, The *16* Scott Sidney
Road to Love, or Romance of a Yankee Engineer in Central America, A *09* Edwin S. Porter
Road to Mandalay, The *26* Tod Browning
Road to Morocco *42* David Butler
Road to Nashville *67* Robert Patrick
Road to Paradise *30* William Beaudine
Road to Peace, The *17* Michael Curtiz
Road to Reno, The *31* Richard Wallace
Road to Reno *38* S. Sylvan Simon
Road to Rio *47* Norman Z. McLeod
Road to Romance, The *27* John S. Robertson
Road to Ruin, The *11* Bert Haldane
Road to Ruin, The *13* Allan Dwan
Road to Ruin, The *13* George Gray, Bert Haldane
Road to Ruin, The *28* Norton Parker
Road to Ruin, The *34* Dorothy Davenport, Melville Shyer
Road to St. Tropez *66* Michael Sarne
Road to Salina, The *70* Georges Lautner
Road to Shame, The *58* Édouard Molinaro
Road to Singapore *31* Alfred E. Green
Road to Singapore *40* Victor Schertzinger
Road to Success, The *13* Allan Dwan
Road to the Big House *47* Walter Colmes
Road to the Heart, The *09* D. W. Griffith
Road to the Stars *58* Pavel Klushantsev
Road to Utopia *44* Hal Walker
Road to Yesterday, The *25* Cecil B. DeMille
Road to Zanzibar *41* Victor Schertzinger
Road Trip *84* Steve Carver
Road Warrior, The *81* George Miller
Road West, The *68* Vincent McEveety
Roadblock *51* Harold Daniels
Roadhouse Girl *53* Wolf Rilla
Roadhouse Murder *32* J. Walter Ruben
Roadhouse Nights *30* Hobart Henley
Roadhouse 66 *84* Mark Robinson
Roadie *80* Alan Rudolph
Roadracers, The *59* Arthur Swerdloff
Roads Across Britain *39* Sidney Cole, Paul Rotha
Roads of Destiny *21* Frank Lloyd
Roads of Exile, The *78* Claude Goretta
Roads of the South, The *78* Joseph Losey
Roads to Katmandu, The *69* André Cayatte
Roads to the South, The *78* Joseph Losey
Roadside Impresario, A *17* Donald Crisp
Roadside Inn, A *06* Georges Méliès
Roamin' Holiday *37* Gordon Douglas
Roamin' Vandals *34* Leigh Jason
Roamin' Wild *36* Bernard B. Ray
Roaming Cowboy, The *37* Robert F. Hill
Roaming in the Gloaming *31* George Pearson
Roaming Lady *36* Albert S. Rogell
Roar *81* Noel Marshall
Roar of the Crowd *53* William Beaudine
Roar of the Dragon *32* Wesley Ruggles
Roar of the Iron Horse *50* Spencer G. Bennet, Thomas Carr
Roar of the Press *41* Phil Rosen
Roarin' Broncs *26* Richard Thorpe
Roarin' Guns *36* Sam Newfield
Roarin' Lead *36* Sam Newfield, Mack V. Wright
Roaring Adventure, A *25* Clifford Smith
Roaring Bill Atwood *26* Bennett Cohn
Roaring City *51* William Berke
Roaring Fires *27* W. T. Lackey
Roaring Forties, The *24* Russell Allen
Roaring Frontiers *41* Lambert Hillyer
Roaring Guns *44* Jean Negulesco
Roaring Lion, The *23* Erle C. Kenton
Roaring Rails *24* Tom Forman
Roaring Ranch *30* Arthur Rosson
Roaring Rangers *46* Ray Nazarro
Roaring Rider, The *26* Richard Thorpe
Roaring Road, The *19* James Cruze
Roaring Road *26* Paul Hurst
Roaring Six Guns *37* John P. McGowan
Roaring Timber *36* Howard Hawks, Richard Rosson, William Wyler
Roaring Timber *37* Phil Rosen
Roaring Twenties, The *39* Anatole Litvak, Raoul Walsh
Roaring West, The *35* Ray Taylor
Roaring Westward *49* Oliver Drake
Roaring Years *62* Luigi Zampa
Rob Roy *11* Arthur Vivian
Rob Roy *22* Will P. Kellino
Rob Roy *53* Harold French
Rob Roy the Highland Rogue *53* Harold French
Roba da Ricchi *87* Sergio Corbucci
Robachicos *87* Alberto Bojorquez
Robart's Adventure in the Great War *20* Frank Griffin
Robber and the Jew, The *08* Jack Smith
Robber of Women, The *36* Abel Gance
Robber Spider, The *15* August Blom
Robber Symphony, The *36* Friedrich Feher
Robbers, The *70* Wolfgang Staudte
Robbers and Thieves *17* Gregory La Cava, Vernon Stallings
Robbers of the Range *41* Edward Killy
Robbers' Roost *33* Louis King
Robbers' Roost *55* Sidney Salkow
Robber's Ruse, or Foiled by Fido, The *09* A. E. Coleby
Robbery *67* Peter Yates
Robbery at Old Burnside Bank *12* Frank Wilson
Robbery of the Mail Coach *03* Frank Mottershaw
Robbery, Roman Style *65* Adriano Celentano
Robbery Under Arms *57* Jack Lee
Robbery Under Arms *85* Donald Crombie, Ken Hannam
Robbery with Violence *05* Alf Collins
Robbery with Violence *58* George Ivan Barnett
Robbing Cleopatra's Tomb *1899* Georges Méliès
Robbing H.M. Mails *06* Arthur Cooper
Robbing the Widowed and Fatherless *09* Theo Bouwmeester
Robbo *64* Gordon Douglas
Robby *68* Ralph C. Bluemke
Robe, The *53* Henry Koster
Robert et Robert *78* Claude Lelouch
Robert Frost: A Love Letter to the World *63* Shirley Clarke
Robert Frost: A Lover's Quarrel with the World *63* Shirley Clarke
Robert Koch *39* Hans Steinhoff
Robert Koch der Bekämpfer des Todes *39* Hans Steinhoff
Robert Macaire and Bertrand *07* Georges Méliès
Robert Macaire et Bertrand *04* Alice Guy-Blaché
Robert Macaire et Bertrand *07* Georges Méliès
Roberta *35* William A. Seiter
Robert's Lost Supper *12* Bert Haldane
Robes of Sin *24* Russell Allen
Robin *79* Hank Aldrich
Robin and Marian *76* Richard Lester
Robin and the Seven Hoods *64* Gordon Douglas

Robin Hood *13* Theodore Marston

Robin Hood *22* Allan Dwan

Robin Hood *38* Michael Curtiz, William Keighley

Robin Hood *52* Ken Annakin, Alex Bryce

Robin Hood *73* Wolfgang Reitherman

Robin Hood and His Merry Men *08* Percy Stow

Robin Hood and the Pirates *61* Giorgio C. Simonelli

Robin Hood Daffy *58* Chuck Jones

Robin Hood, Jr. *23* Clarence Brown

Robin Hood, Jr. *34* Ubbe Iwerks

Robin Hood Junior *75* John Black, Matt McCarthy

Robin Hood Makes Good *39* Chuck Jones

Robin Hood of El Dorado *36* William A. Wellman

Robin Hood of Monterey *47* Christy Cabanne

Robin Hood of Texas *47* Lesley Selander

Robin Hood of the Pecos *41* Joseph Kane

Robin Hood of the Range *43* William Berke

Robin Hood Outlawed *12* Charles Raymond

Robin Hoodlum *48* John Hubley

Robin Hoodwinked *56* Joseph Barbera, William Hanna

Robinson, Ein *40* Arnold Fanck

Robinson *68* George Moorse

Robinson Charley *47* Joy Batchelor, John Halas

Robinson Crusoe *02* Georges Méliès

Robinson Crusoe *10* August Blom

Robinson Crusoe *16* George F. Marion

Robinson Crusoe *25* Walter Lantz

Robinson Crusoe *27* M. A. Wetherell

Robinson Crusoe *52* Luis Buñuel

Robinson Crusoe *87* Sherry Sneller

Robinson Crusoe and the Tiger *69* René Cardona, Jr.

Robinson Crusoe en Vingt-Cinq Tableaux *02* Georges Méliès

Robinson Crusoe Isle *35* Walter Lantz

Robinson Crusoe, Jr. *41* Norm McCabe

Robinson Crusoe of Clipper Island *36* Ray Taylor, Mack V. Wright

Robinson Crusoe of Mystery Island *36* Ray Taylor, Mack V. Wright

Robinson Crusoe on Mars *64* Byron Haskin

Robinson Crusoe Returns on Friday *23* W. E. Stark

Robinson Crusoeland *50* John Berry, Léo Joannon

Robinson Girl *74* Karel Kachyňa

Robinson Junior *29* Alfred Machin

Robinson no Niwa *87* Masashi Yamamoto

Robinson Soll Nicht Sterben *57* Josef von Baky

Robinsoniad, or My English Grandfather *86* Nana Dschordschadse

Robinsoniada anu Chemi Ingliseli Papa *86* Nana Dschordschadse

Robinsonka *74* Karel Kachyňa

Robinson's Garden *87* Masashi Yamamoto

Robo de Diamantes *67* Bernard Glasser

Robo Man *73* Jack Gold

Robō no Ishi *60* Seiji Hisamatsu

Robocop *87* Paul Verhoeven

Robocop 2 *90* Irvin Kershner

Robojox *87* Stuart Gordon

Robot, The *32* Dave Fleischer

Robot Asesino, El *69* René Cardona

Robot Carnival *87* Atsuko Fukushima, Hiroyuki Kitakubo, Kiroyuki Kitazume, Mao Lamdo, Kouji Morimoto, Takashi Nakamura, Hidetoshi Ohmori, Katsuhiro Otomo, Yasuomi Umetsu

Robot Holocaust *87* Tim Kincaid

Robot Humano, El *57* Rafael Portillo

Robot Jox *87* Stuart Gordon

Robot Monster *53* Phil Tucker

Robot Rabbit *53* Friz Freleng

Robot vs. the Aztec Mummy, The *57* Rafael Portillo

Rocambole *23* Charles De Marsan, Charles Maudru

Rocambole *47* Jacques De Baroncelli

Rocambole *62* Bernard Borderie

Rocco and His Brothers *60* Luchino Visconti

Rocco — Der Einzelgänger von Alamo *67* Alfio Caltabiano

Rocco e i Suoi Fratelli *60* Luchino Visconti

Rocco et Ses Frères *60* Luchino Visconti

Rocco Papaleo *71* Ettore Scola

Rocinante *86* Ann Guedes, Eduardo Guedes

Rock All Night *56* Roger Corman

Rock Around the Clock *56* Fred F. Sears

Rock Around the World *57* Gerard Bryant

Rock Baby, Rock It *57* Murray Douglas Sporup

Rock City *81* Peter Clifton

Rock Hound Magoo *57* Pete Burness

Rock Island Trail *50* Joseph Kane

Rock 'n' Roll High School *79* Allan Arkush

Rock 'n' Roll Nightmare *87* John Fasano

Rock 'n' Rule *83* Clive A. Smith

Rock of Ages *02* Edwin S. Porter

Rock of Ages *18* Bertram Phillips

Rock of Ages *28* J. Steven Edwards, H. B. Parkinson

Rock of Friendship, The *28* W. S. Van Dyke

Rock of Riches, The *16* Lois Weber

Rock, Pretty Baby *56* Richard Bartlett

Rock River Renegades *42* S. Roy Luby

Rock, Rock, Rock! *56* Will Price

Rock You Sinners *57* Denis Kavanagh

Rockabilly Baby *57* William F. Claxton

Rockabye *32* George Cukor

Rock-a-Bye Baby *58* Frank Tashlin

Rock-a-Bye Bear *52* Tex Avery

Rock-a-Bye Cowboy *33* George Stevens

Rock-a-Bye Legend, The *55* Tex Avery

Rockefeller *13* Émile Cohl

Rockers *78* Theodoros Bafaloukos

Rocket Attack, U.S.A. *59* Barry Mahon

Rocket Bye Baby *56* Chuck Jones

Rocket from Calabuch, The *56* Luis García Berlanga

Rocket Gibraltar *88* Daniel Petrie

Rocket Man, The *54* Oscar Rudolph

Rocket Ship *36* Frederick Stephani

Rocket Squad *56* Chuck Jones

Rocket to Nowhere *62* Jindřich Polák

Rocket to the Moon *53* Arthur Hilton

Rockets Galore! *57* Michael Relph

Rockets in the Dunes *60* William C. Hammond

Rocketship Expedition Moon *50* Kurt Neumann

Rocketship X-M *50* Kurt Neumann

Rockin' in the Rockies *45* Vernon Keays

Rockin' Road Trip *85* William Olsen

Rockin' the Blues *55* Arthur Rosenblum

Rocking Horse Winner, The *49* Anthony Pelissier

Rocking Horse Winner, The *83* Robert Bierman

Rocking Moon *26* George Melford

Rockinghorse *78* Yaky Yosha

Rocks and Socks *28* Hugh Harman

Rocks of Valpré, The *19* Maurice Elvey

Rocks of Valpré, The *35* Henry Edwards

Rockula *90* Luca Bercovici

Rocky *48* Phil Karlson

Rocky *76* John G. Avildsen

Rocky II *79* Sylvester Stallone

Rocky III *82* Sylvester Stallone

Rocky IV *85* Sylvester Stallone

Rocky V *90* John G. Avildsen

Rocky Horror Picture Show, The *75* Jim Sharman

Rocky Mountain *50* William Keighley

Rocky Mountain Mystery *35* Charles Barton

Rocky Mountain Rangers *40* George Sherman

Rocky Rhodes *34* Alfred Raboch

Rocky Road, The *09* D. W. Griffith

Rocky Road to Ruin, The *43* Paul Sommer

Rocky VI *86* Aki Kaurismäki

Rocky X *86* Chris Hegedus, D. A. Pennebaker

Röda Dagen *32* Gustaf Edgren

Røda Kappan, Den *67* Gabriel Axel

Röda Tornet, Det *14* Mauritz Stiller

Rodan *56* Inoshiro Honda

Røde Enge, De *45* Bodil Ipsen, Lau Lauritzen, Jr.

Røde Enke, Den *15* August Blom

Røde Kappe, Den *67* Gabriel Axel

Røde Rubin, Den *70* Annelise Meineche

Rodelkavalier, Der *18* Ernst Lubitsch

Rodent to Stardom *67* Alex Lovy

Rodeo *51* William Beaudine

Rodeo Dough *31* Manny Gould, Ben Harrison

Rodeo King and the Señorita *51* Philip Ford

Rodeo Mixup, A *24* Francis Ford

Rodeo Rhythm *41* Fred Newmeyer

Rodney Fails to Qualify *24* Andrew P. Wilson

Rodney Steps In *31* Guy Newall

Rodney Stone *20* Percy Nash

Rodnik dlia Zhazhdushchikh *65* Yuri Ilyenko

Rodnya *81* Nikita Mikhalkov

Rodolphe Bresdin 1825-1885 *61* Nelly Kaplan

Rodrigo D: No Future *90* Víctor Gaviria

Rødtotterne og Tyrannos *88* Svend Johansen

Roei no Uta *38* Kenji Mizoguchi*

Roger and Me 89 Michael Moore
Roger Corman: Hollywood's Wild Angel 78 Christian Blackwood
Roger Corman's Frankenstein Unbound 90 Roger Corman
Roger-la-Honte 22 Jacques De Baroncelli
Roger-la-Honte 45 André Cayatte
Roger la Honte 66 Riccardo Freda
Roger the Stoolie 72 John G. Avildsen, George Silano
Roger Touhy, Gangster 43 Robert Florey
RoGoPaG 62 Jean-Luc Godard, Ugo Gregoretti, Pier Paolo Pasolini, Roberto Rossellini
Rogue, The 76 Gregory Simpson
Rogue Cop 54 Roy Rowland
Rogue in Love, A 16 Bannister Merwin
Rogue in Love, A 22 Albert Brouett
Rogue of the Range 36 S. Roy Luby
Rogue of the Rio Grande 30 Spencer G. Bennet
Rogue River 50 John Rawlins
Rogue Song, The 29 Lionel Barrymore, Hal Roach
Rogue Unmasked, The 20 Charles Raymond
Rogues, The 87 Mario Monicelli
Rogues and Romance 20 George B. Seitz
Rogues' Gallery, The 13 Wilfred Lucas
Rogues' Gallery 42 Lambert Hillyer
Rogues' Gallery 44 Albert Herman
Rogues' Gallery 68 Leonard Horn
Rogue's March 52 Allan Davis
Rogues of London, The 15 Bert Haldane
Rogues of Paris 13 Alice Guy-Blaché
Rogues of Sherwood Forest 50 Gordon Douglas
Rogues of the Turf 23 Wilfred Noy
Rogues' Regiment 48 Robert Florey
Rogue's Romance, A 19 James Young
Rogues' Tavern, The 36 Robert F. Hill
Rogue's Tricks 07 Georges Méliès
Rogue's Wife, A 15 Percy Nash
Rogue's Yarn 56 Vernon Sewell
Roi, Le 50 Marc-Gilbert Sauvajon
Roi de Camargue, Le 21 André Hugon
Roi de Cœur, Le 66 Philippe de Broca
Roi de la Chine, Le 85 Fabrice Cazeneuve
Roi de la Mer, Le 17 Jacques De Baroncelli
Roi de la Montagne, Le 14 Léonce Perret
Roi de la Vitesse, Le 23 Henri Diamant-Berger
Roi de l'Air, Le 13 René Leprince, Ferdinand Zecca
Roi de Thulé, Le 10 Louis Feuillade
Roi des Bricoleurs, Le 77 Jean-Pierre Mocky
Roi des Camelots, Le 51 André Berthomieu
Roi des Champs Elysées, Le 34 Max Nosseck
Roi des Médiums, Le 10 Georges Méliès
Roi des Palaces, Le 32 Carmine Gallone
Roi des Resquilleurs, Le 32 Pierre Colombier
Roi des Tireurs, Le 05 Georges Méliès
Roi du Cirque, Le 24 Max Linder, Édouard E. Violet
Roi du Maquillage, Le 04 Georges Méliès
Roi du Village, Le 62 Henri Gruel

Roi et l'Oiseau, Le 67 Paul Grimault
Roi Lear au Village, Le 11 Louis Feuillade
Roi Pele, Le 76 François Reichenbach
Roi Sans Divertissement, Un 63 François Leterrier
Rois du Gag, Les 85 Claude Zidi
Rojet e Mjegulles 88 Isa Qosja
Rojo, El 66 Leo Colman
Rok Spokojnego Słońca 84 Krzysztof Zanussi
Rokonok 54 Félix Máriássy
Rokumeikan 86 Kon Ichikawa
Rokumeikan, High Society of Meiji 86 Kon Ichikawa
Roland the Mighty 58 Pietro Francisci
Role, The 77 Shyam Benegal
Roll Along, Cowboy 37 Gus Meins
Roll On 42 William Berke
Roll On Texas Moon 46 William Witney
Roll, Thunder, Roll 49 Lewis D. Collins
Roll, Wagons, Roll 39 Albert Herman
Roll Your Own 20 Gregory La Cava
Rolled Stockings 27 Richard Rosson
Rollende Kugel, Die 19 Henryk Galeen
Rollende Rad, Das 34 Lotte Reiniger
Roller and the Violin, The 60 Andrei Tarkovsky
Roller Boogie 79 Mark L. Lester
Roller Skate 63 Andy Warhol
Roller-Skating Groupie, The 71 George McIndoe
Rollerbabies 76 Carter Stevens
Rollerball 75 Norman Jewison
Rollerblade 85 Donald G. Jackson
Rollerblade Warriors 88 Donald G. Jackson
Rollercoaster 77 James Goldstone
Rollin' Home to Texas 40 Albert Herman
Rollin' Plains 38 Albert Herman
Rollin' Westward 39 Albert Herman
Rolling Around 21 Wallace A. Carlson
Rolling Caravans 38 Joseph Levering
Rolling Down the Great Divide 42 Sam Newfield
Rolling Home 26 William A. Seiter
Rolling Home 35 Ralph Ince
Rolling Home 46 William Berke
Rolling in Money 34 Albert Parker
Rolling in the Aisles 87 Andrew J. Kuehn
Rolling Road, The 27 Graham Cutts
Rolling Sea 51 Arne Mattsson
Rolling Stones 16 Del Henderson
Rolling Thunder 77 John Flynn
Rolling Vengeance 87 Steven Hilliard Stern
Rollover 81 Alan J. Pakula
Roma 72 Federico Fellini
Roma Bene 71 Carlo Lizzani
Roma, Città Aperta 45 Roberto Rossellini
Roma, Città Libera 46 Marcello Pagliero
Roma Contra Roma 63 Giuseppe Vari
Roma-Montevideo 48 Michelangelo Antonioni
Roma, Ora Undici 51 Giuseppe De Santis
Roma Rivuole Cesare 73 Miklós Jancsó
Romaine Kalbris 21 Georges Monca
Roman aus den Bergen, Ein 21 E. A. Dupont
Roman Behemshechim 85 Oded Kotler
Roman d'Amour 05 Ferdinand Zecca

Roman d'Amour et d'Aventures, Un 18 René Hervil, Louis Mercanton
Roman de Max, Le 12 Max Linder
Roman de Renard, Le 39 Władysław Starewicz
Roman de Sœur Louise, Le 08 Louis Feuillade
Roman de Werther, Le 38 Max Ophüls
Roman der Christine von Herre, Der 21 Ludwig Berger
Roman d'un Jeune Homme Pauvre, Le 27 Gaston Ravel
Roman d'un Jeune Homme Pauvre, Le 35 Abel Gance
Roman d'un Spahi, Le 17 Henri Pouctal
Roman d'un Tricheur, Le 36 Sacha Guitry
Roman einer Ehe 51 Kurt Mätzig
Roman einer Jungen Ehe 51 Kurt Mätzig
Roman einer Nacht 33 Carl Boese
Roman eines Dienstmädchens, Der 21 Reinhold Schünzel
Roman Holiday 53 William Wyler
Roman Legion-Hare 55 Friz Freleng
Roman Numeral Series 81 Stan Brakhage
Román s Basou 49 Jiří Trnka
Roman Scandal, A 26 Charles Bowers
Roman Scandals 33 Ralph Ceder, Frank Tuttle
Roman Signorina 55 Luigi Comencini
Roman Spring of Mrs. Stone, The 61 José Quintero
Romana, La 54 Luigi Zampa
Romance, The 13 Allan Dwan
Romance 20 Chester Withey
Romance 30 Clarence Brown
Romance 40 Åke Öhberg
Romance 40 Otakar Vávra
Romance 86 Massimo Mazzucco
Romance 88 Sergio Bianchi
Romance à la Carte 38 Maclean Rogers
Romance and Arabella 19 Walter Edwards
Romance and Bright Lights 28 Irving Cummings
Romance and Reality 21 Harry Lambart
Romance and Rheumatism 20 Frank Moser
Romance and Rhythm 38 Lloyd Bacon
Romance and Riches 36 Alfred Zeisler
Romance and Rustlers 25 Ben F. Wilson
Romance at the Studio: Guidance to Love 32 Heinosuke Gosho
Romance da Empregada 88 Bruno Barreto
Romance de Luxe 30 Stephen Roberts
Romance de Paris 41 Jean Boyer
Romance del Palmar, El 39 Ramón Peón
Romance for Lovers 74 Andrei Mikhalkov-Konchalovsky
Romance for Three 37 Edward Buzzell
Romance for Trumpet 66 Otakar Vávra
Romance in a Minor Key 43 Helmut Käutner
Romance in Budapest 33 Géza von Bolváry, Steve Sekely
Romance in Flanders, A 37 Maurice Elvey
Romance in Manhattan 34 Stephen Roberts
Romance in Paris, A 87 Merzak Allouache
Romance in Rhythm 34 Lawrence Huntington
Romance in the Dark 38 H. C. Potter

Romance in the Rain *34* Stuart Walker
Romance Is Sacred *37* Mervyn LeRoy
Romance Land *23* Edward Sedgwick
Romance of a Horse Thief *71* Abraham Polonsky
Romance of a Jewess, The *08* D. W. Griffith
Romance of a Million Dollars, The *26* Tom Terriss
Romance of a Movie Star, The *20* Richard Garrick
Romance of a Queen, The *24* Alan Crosland
Romance of a Rogue *28* King Baggot
Romance of a Royalist Maid, The *12* F. Martin Thornton
Romance of a Russian Ballerina *13* A. Bistritzky, Georg Jacoby
Romance of a War Nurse *08* Edwin S. Porter
Romance of a Will, The *14* Forest Holger-Madsen
Romance of an Umbrella, The *09* J. Stuart Blackton
Romance of Annie Laurie, The *20* Gerald Somers
Romance of Billy Goat Hill, A *16* Lynn Reynolds
Romance of Book and Sword, The *87* Ann Hui
Romance of Broadcasting, The *25* Widgey R. Newman, Challis Sanderson
Romance of Dancing, The *38* Herbert R. Parsons
Romance of Digestion, The *37* Felix E. Feist
Romance of Elaine, The *15* Joseph A. Golden, George B. Seitz, Leopold Wharton, Theodore Wharton
Romance of Happy Valley, A *18* D. W. Griffith
Romance of Lady Hamilton, The *19* Bert Haldane
Romance of Life, The *23* J. A. Norling
Romance of Lovers, The *74* Andrei Mikhalkov-Konchalovsky
Romance of Mayfair, A *25* Thomas Bentley
Romance of Old Bagdad, A *22* Kenelm Foss
Romance of Old Erin, A *10* Sidney Olcott
Romance of Postal Telegraphy, The *23* Charles C. Calvert
Romance of Puck Fair, A *16* Joseph M. Kerrigan
Romance of Radium *37* Jacques Tourneur
Romance of Riches, A *25* Sinclair Hill
Romance of Rio Grande *29* Alfred Santell
Romance of Rosy Ridge, The *47* Roy Rowland
Romance of '76, A *20* Gregory La Cava
Romance of Seville, A *29* Norman Walker
Romance of Tarzan *18* Wilfred Lucas
Romance of the Air, A *19* Harry Revier
Romance of the Forest Reserve *14* William Duncan
Romance of the Limberlost *38* William Nigh
Romance of the Mayfair, A *25* Thomas Bentley

Romance of the Rail, A *03* Edwin S. Porter
Romance of the Range *42* Joseph Kane
Romance of the Redwoods, A *17* Cecil B. DeMille
Romance of the Redwoods *39* Charles Vidor
Romance of the Rio Grande *29* Alfred Santell
Romance of the Rio Grande *41* Herbert I. Leeds
Romance of the Rockies *37* Robert North Bradbury
Romance of the Sea, A *13* Thomas Ince
Romance of the Underworld, A *18* James Kirkwood
Romance of the Underworld *28* Irving Cummings
Romance of the West *46* Robert E. Tansey
Romance of the Western Hills, A *10* D. W. Griffith
Romance of Toyland, A *16* Horace Taylor
Romance of Transportation in Canada, The *52* Wolf Koenig, Colin Low, Robert Verrall
Romance of Wastdale, A *21* Maurice Elvey
Romance of Yushima, The *55* Teinosuke Kinugasa
Romance on the Beach *64* José Benazeraf
Romance on the High Seas *48* Michael Curtiz
Romance on the Range *42* Joseph Kane
Romance on the Run *38* Gus Meins
Romance on the Western Front *37* Maurice Elvey
Romance pro Křídlovku *66* Otakar Vávra
Romance Promoters, The *20* Chester Bennett
Romance Ranch *24* Howard Mitchell
Romance Rides the Range *36* Harry Fraser
Romance Road *25* Fred Windermere
Romance Sentimentale *30* Grigori Alexandrov, Sergei Eisenstein
Romance Tropical *34* Juan E. Viguie
Romance with a Double Bass *75* Robert M. Young
Romancero Marroquín *36* Carlos Velo
Romancing Along *38* Leslie Goodwins
Romancing the Stone *84* Robert Zemeckis
Romanian People's Republic, The *53* Leonid Varmalov
Romanoff and Juliet *61* Peter Ustinov
Romans o Vljublennych *74* Andrei Mikhalkov-Konchalovsky
Romantic Adventuress, A *20* Harley Knoles
Romantic Age, The *27* Robert Florey
Romantic Age, The *34* David Burton
Romantic Age, The *48* Edmond T. Gréville
Romantic Comedy *83* Arthur Hiller
Romantic England *29* H. B. Parkinson
Romantic Englishwoman, The *75* Joseph Losey
Romantic Journey, The *16* George Fitzmaurice
Romantic Melodies *32* Dave Fleischer
Romantic Rogue *27* Harry Joe Brown
Romantic Story *86* Mladen Nikolov
Romantica Avventura, Una *40* Mario

Camerini
Romantichna-Istorija *86* Mladen Nikolov
Romantici a Venezia *48* Luciano Emmer, Enrico Gras
Romanticismo *13* Mario Caserini
Romantics, The *41* Mark Donskoi
Romantics in Venice *48* Luciano Emmer, Enrico Gras
Romantiki *41* Mark Donskoi
Romany, The *23* F. Martin Thornton
Romany Lass, A *18* F. Martin Thornton
Romany Love *31* Fred Paul
Romany Rye, The *15* Percy Nash
Romany Rye *19* Maurice Tourneur
Romany Tragedy, A *11* D. W. Griffith
Romany's Revenge, The *07* Frank Mottershaw
Romanza Final *87* José María Forqué
Romanze in der Nacht *24* Walter Ruttmann
Romanze in Moll *43* Helmut Käutner
Romanzo, Il *13* Nino Martoglio
Romanzo di una Vespa, Il *19* Mario Caserini
Romanzo di un'Epoca *41* Luciano Emmer, Enrico Gras, Tatiana Grauding
Romanzo Popolare *74* Mario Monicelli
Rome Adventure *62* Delmer Daves
Rome, Eleven o'Clock *51* Giuseppe De Santis
Rome Express *32* Walter Forde
Rome 1585 *63* Mario Bonnard
Rome Like Chicago *67* Alberto De Martino
Rome, Open City *45* Roberto Rossellini
Rome-Paris-Rome *51* Luigi Zampa
Rome — The Image of a City *83* Carlo Lizzani
Rome Wants Another Caesar *73* Miklós Jancsó
Romeo and Juliet *08* J. Stuart Blackton
Romeo and Juliet *08* Mario Caserini
Romeo and Juliet *15* Will P. Kellino
Romeo and Juliet *16* Francis X. Bushman, John W. Noble
Romeo and Juliet *16* J. Gordon Edwards
Romeo and Juliet *36* George Cukor
Romeo and Juliet *44* Miguel Delgado
Romeo and Juliet *44* Kamel Salim
Romeo and Juliet *54* Renato Castellani
Romeo and Juliet *55* Lev Arnshtam, Leonid Lavrovsky
Romeo and Juliet *64* Riccardo Freda
Romeo and Juliet *65* Paul Czinner
Romeo and Juliet *68* Franco Zeffirelli
Romeo and Juliet in the Snow *20* Ernst Lubitsch
Romeo and Juliet, 1971 — A Gentle Tale of Sex, Violence, Corruption and Murder *71* Bill Bain
Romeo e Giulietta *08* Mario Caserini
Romeo in Pyjamas *31* Edward Sedgwick
Romeo, Julie a Tma *59* Jiří Weiss
Romeo, Juliet and Darkness *59* Jiří Weiss
Roméo Pris au Piège *05* Alice Guy-Blaché
Romeo und Julia im Schnee *20* Ernst Lubitsch
Romeo und Juliet im Schnee *20* Ernst Lubitsch
Romeow and Juliecat *47* George Pal

Romero 89 John Duigan
Rommel—Desert Fox 51 Henry Hathaway
Rommel's Treasure 58 Romolo Marcellini
Romola 24 Henry King
Romolo e Remo 61 Sergio Corbucci
Romuald et Juliette 88 Coline Serreau
Romulus and the Sabines 61 Richard Pottier
Romy: Anatomie eines Gesichts 65 Hans-Jürgen Syberberg
Romy: Anatomy of a Face 65 Hans-Jürgen Syberberg
Rona Jaffe's Mazes and Monsters 82 Steven Hilliard Stern
Ronda Española 51 Ladislas Vajda
Ronde, La 50 Max Ophüls
Ronde, La 64 Roger Vadim
Ronde des Heures, La 32 Alexandre Ryder
Ronde Infernale, La 13 Alfred Machin
Ronde Infernale, La 27 Luitz-Morat
Rondo 66 Zvonimir Berković
Ronny 31 Reinhold Schünzel
Roof, The 33 George A. Cooper
Roof, The 55 Vittorio De Sica
Roof Garden, The 62 Leopoldo Torre-Nilsson
Roof Needs Mowing 71 Gillian Armstrong
Roof of the Whale, The 81 Raúl Ruiz
Roof Tree, The 21 John Francis Dillon
Roofs at Dawn 86 János Domolky
Rooftops 89 Robert Wise
Rooftops of Budapest 61 András Kovács
Rooftree 66 Jörn Donner
Roogie's Bump 54 Harold Young
Rook, The 70 Harold Prince
Rookery Nook 30 Byron Haskin, Tom Walls
Rookie, The 32 Edward F. Cline
Rookie, The 59 George O'Hanlon
Rookie, The 90 Clint Eastwood
Rookie Cop, The 39 David Howard
Rookie Fireman 50 Seymour Friedman
Rookie Revue, The 41 Friz Freleng
Rookies 27 Sam Wood
Rookies 40 Arthur Lubin
Rookies Come Home 47 Charles Barton
Rookies in Burma 43 Leslie Goodwins
Rookies on Parade 41 Joseph Santley
Rookie's Return, The 21 Jack Nelson
Room, The 67 Yoji Kuri
Room, The 72 Chantal Akerman
Room and Bird 51 Friz Freleng
Room and Board 21 Alan Crosland
Room and Bored 43 Bob Wickersham
Room at the Top 58 Jack Clayton
Room for a Stranger 66 Ted Leversuch
Room for One More 51 Norman Taurog
Room for Two 40 Maurice Elvey
Room 43 59 Alvin Rakoff
Room in the House 55 Maurice Elvey
Room in Town, A 82 Jacques Demy
Room Mates 33 George Stevens
Room Runners 32 Ubbe Iwerks
Room Service 38 William A. Seiter
Room 666 82 Wim Wenders
Room 13 64 Harald Reinl
Room to Let 49 Godfrey Grayson
Room 23 17 Edward F. Cline
Room 23 23 Edward F. Cline
Room Upstairs, The 46 Georges Lacombe

Room with a View, A 85 James Ivory
Room with Thick Walls 53 Masaki Kobayashi
Roommate, The 85 Nell Cox
Roommates 61 Gerald Thomas
Roommates 69 Jack Baran
Roommates, The 73 Arthur Marks
Roommates 82 Chuck Vincent
Rooney 57 George Pollock
Rooster, The 81 Lasse Hallström
Rooster Cogburn 75 Stuart Millar
Root of All Evil, The 46 Brock Williams
Root of Evil, The 11 D. W. Griffith
Root of Evil, The 19 George Ridgwell
Rootin' Tootin' Rhythm 37 Mack V. Wright
Roots, The 55 Benito Alazraki
Roots of Heaven, The 58 John Huston
Rooty Toot Toot 51 John Hubley
Rope 48 Alfred Hitchcock
Rope 65 Russ Meyer
Rope Around the Neck 64 Joseph Lisbona
Rope of Flesh 65 Russ Meyer
Rope of Sand 49 William Dieterle
Roped 19 John Ford
Roped In 17 George Marshall
Ropin' Fool, The 22 Clarence Badger
Roquevillard, Les 22 Julien Duvivier
Rorret 88 Fulvio Wetzl
Rory Gallagher's Irish Tour 75 Tony Palmer
Rory O'Moore 11 Sidney Olcott
Rosa Blanca, La 53 Emilio Fernández
Rosa Blanca, La 72 Roberto Gavaldón
Rosa Blanca, La 88 Francesca Romana Leonardi
Rosa de Francia 35 Gordon Wiles
Rosa de la Frontera 87 Hernando Name
Rosa de los Vientos, La 81 Patricio Guzmán
Rosa de Xochimilco 39 Carlos Villareal
Rosa di Bagdad, La 67 Anton Gino Domeneghini
Rosa di Granada, La 16 Emilio Ghione
Rosa la Rose, Fille Publique 85 Paul Vecchiali
Rosa Luxembourg 85 Margarethe von Trotta
Rosa Luxemburg 85 Margarethe von Trotta
Rosa per Tutti, Una 65 Franco Rossi
Rosal Bendito, El 37 Juan Bustillo Oro
Rosaleen Dhu 20 William Powers
Rosalie 37 W. S. Van Dyke
Rosalie 66 Walerian Borowczyk
Rosalie Goes Shopping 89 Percy Adlon
Rosanna 53 Emilio Fernández
Rosario 36 Miguel Zacarías
Rosary, The 15 Colin Campbell
Rosary, The 22 Jerome Storm
Rosary, The 28 J. Steven Edwards, H. B. Parkinson
Rosary, The 31 Guy Newall
Rosary Murders, The 87 Fred Walton
Rose 36 Raymond Rouleau
Rose, The 78 Mark Rydell
Rose 86 Yonfan Manshi
Rose and the Dagger, The 11 Edwin S. Porter
Rose and the Gold, The 63 Manuel

Summers
Rose and the Mignonette, The 45 André Michel
Rose and the Ring, The 79 Lotte Reiniger
Rose and the Ring, The 87 Jerzy Gruza
Rose Bernd 56 Wolfgang Staudte
Rose Blanche, La 13 Louis Feuillade
Rose Bowl 36 Charles Barton
Rose Bowl Story, The 52 William Beaudine
Rose by Any Other Name, A 20 Raoul Barré, Charles Bowers
Rose de Fer, La 72 Jean Rollin
Rose de la Mer, La 46 Jacques De Baroncelli
Rose Escorchée, La 69 Claude Mulot
Rose et Landry 62 J. Godbout, Jean Rouch
Rose et le Radis, La 55 Henri Gruel
Rose et le Réséda, La 45 André Michel
Rose for Everyone, A 65 Franco Rossi
Rose-France 18 Marcel L'Herbier
Rose Garden, The 89 Fons Rademakers
Rose in the Mud, The 60 Akira Kurosawa
Rose King, The 86 Werner Schroeter
Rose Marie 27 Lucien Hubbard
Rose Marie 36 W. S. Van Dyke
Rose Marie 53 Mervyn LeRoy
Rose o' Paradise 18 James Young
Rose o' Salem Town 10 D. W. Griffith
Rose o' Salem Town: A Story of Puritan Witchcraft 10 D. W. Griffith
Rose o' the River 12 Warwick Buckland
Rose o' the River 19 Robert Thornby
Rose o' the Sea 22 Fred Niblo
Rose of Blood, The 17 J. Gordon Edwards
Rose of Cimarron 52 Harry Keller
Rose of France 35 Gordon Wiles
Rose of Kentucky, The 11 D. W. Griffith
Rose of Kildare, The 27 Dallas M. Fitzgerald
Rose of Nome 20 Edward J. LeSaint
Rose of Old Mexico, A 13 Allan Dwan, Wallace Reid
Rose of Paris, The 24 Irving Cummings
Rose of Santa Rosa 47 Ray Nazarro
Rose of Surrey 13 Lawrence Trimble
Rose of the Alley 16 William Dowlan, Charles T. Horan
Rose of the Border 87 Hernando Name
Rose of the Bowery 27 Bertram Bracken
Rose of the Circus 11 Alice Guy-Blaché
Rose of the Desert 89 Mohamed Rachid Benhadj
Rose of the Golden West 27 George Fitzmaurice
Rose of the Rancho 14 Cecil B. DeMille
Rose of the Rancho 35 Robert Florey, Marion Gering
Rose of the Rio Grande 31 John P. McCarthy
Rose of the Rio Grande 38 William Nigh
Rose of the River 19 Robert Thornby
Rose of the Sea 45 Teinosuke Kinugasa
Rose of the South 16 Paul Scardon
Rose of the Tenements 26 Phil Rosen
Rose of the West 19 Harry Millarde
Rose of the Winds 81 Patricio Guzmán
Rose of the World 18 Maurice Tourneur
Rose of the World 25 Harry Beaumont

Rose of the Yukon 49 George Blair

Rose of Thistle Island, The 15 Victor Sjöström

Rose of Tralee 37 Oswald Mitchell

Rose of Tralee 42 Germain Burger

Rose of Washington Square 39 Gregory Ratoff

Rose on His Arm, The 56 Keisuke Kinoshita

Rose, Pierrot et la Luce, La 82 Claude Gagnon

Rose Rosse per Angelica 66 Steno

Rose Rouge, La 14 Henri Pouctal

Rose Rouge, La 51 Marcello Pagliero

Rose Scarlatte 39 Giuseppe Amato, Vittorio De Sica

Rose Scarlatte, Mélodie Éterne 39 Giuseppe Amato, Vittorio De Sica

Rose Tattoo, The 55 Daniel Mann

Roseanna McCoy 49 Nicholas Ray, Irving Reis

Rosebud 75 Otto Preminger

Rosebud Beach Hotel, The 84 Harry Hurwitz

Roseland 77 James Ivory

Roselyne and the Lions 89 Jean-Jacques Beineix

Roselyne et les Lions 89 Jean-Jacques Beineix

Rosemarie 58 Rolf Thiele

Rosemary 15 Fred J. Balshofer, William J. Bowman

Rosemary 38 Ladislas Vajda

Rosemary 58 Rolf Thiele

Rosemary Climbs the Heights 18 Lloyd Ingraham

Rosemary's Baby 68 Roman Polanski

Rosemary's Killer 81 Joseph Zito

Rosen aus dem Süden 26 Carl Fröhlich

Rosen aus dem Süden 35 Walter Janssen

Rosen für Bettina 56 G. W. Pabst

Rosen für den Staatsanwalt 59 Wolfgang Staudte

Rosen på Tistelön 15 Victor Sjöström

Rosenbergs Must Not Die, The 81 Stellio Lorenzi

Rosencrantz and Guildenstern Are Dead 90 Tom Stoppard

Rosenkavalier, Der 25 Robert Wiene

Rosenkavalier, Der 61 Paul Czinner

Rosenkönig, Der 86 Werner Schroeter

Rosenmontag 30 Hans Steinhoff

Rosentopf Case, The 18 Ernst Lubitsch

Roses and Thorns 17 Gregory La Cava, Vernon Stallings

Roses Are Red 47 James Tinling

Roses Bloom Twice 77 David Stevens

Roses for the Prosecutor 59 Wolfgang Staudte

Roses from the South 35 Walter Janssen

Rose's House 77 Clay Borris

Roses in December 86 Anna Carrigan

Roses in the Dust 21 Charles C. Calvert

Roses of Picardy 27 Maurice Elvey

Rose's Story, The 11 Joseph Smiley, George Loane Tucker

Rosie! 67 David Lowell Rich

Rosie Dixon, Night Nurse 78 Justin Cartwright

Rosie the Riveter 44 Joseph Santley

Rosie the Riveter 80 Connie Field

Rosier de Madame Husson, Le 32 Dominique Bernard-Deschamps

Rosier de Madame Husson, Le 50 Jean Boyer

Rosier Miraculeux, Le 04 Georges Méliès

Rosière de Pessac, La 68 Jean Eustache

Rosière de Pessac 79, La 79 Jean Eustache

Rosina the Foundling 45 Otakar Vávra

Rosita 23 Ernst Lubitsch

Rosmunda e Alboino 61 Carlo Campogalliani

Rosolino Paterno — Soldato 70 Nanni Loy

Rossa del Bar, La 86 Ventura Pons

Rossetto, Il 60 Damiano Damiani

Rossini 41 Mario Bonnard

Rossiter Case, The 50 Francis Searle

Rossiya Nikolaya II i Lev Tolstoy 28 Esther Shub

Rosso 85 Mika Kaurismäki

Rosso Segno della Follia, Il 69 Mario Bava

Rosso Veneziano 89 Étienne Périer

Rosy la Bourrasque 79 Mario Monicelli

Rosy Rapture, Scene Six 15 Percy Nash

Rötägg 46 Arne Mattsson

Rotaie 29 Mario Camerini

Rotation 49 Wolfgang Staudte

Rote, Die 62 Helmut Käutner

Rote Hexe, Die 20 Friedrich Feher

Rote Lippen 67 Jesús Franco

Rote Mühle, Die 21 Carl Boese

Rote Streifen, Der 16 Urban Gad

Rothausgasse, Die 28 Richard Oswald

Rothenburger, Die 18 Lupu Pick

Rothschild 38 Marco De Gastyne

Roti 36 Ramjankhan Mehboobkhan

Rotisserie Brothers, The 20 Grim Natwick

Rötmånad 71 Jan Halldoff

Rotten Apple, The 63 John Hayes

Rotten Fate 87 Sylvain Madigan

Rotten to the Core 65 John Boulting

Rotten to the Corps 65 John Boulting

Rotterdam-Europoort 66 Joris Ivens

Rotters, The 21 A. V. Bramble

Rotweiler: Dogs of Hell 84 Worth Keeter

Rouble à Deux Faces, Le 68 Étienne Périer

Roue, La 21 Abel Gance

Roue de la Fortune, La 38 Henri Storck

Roué's Heart, The 09 D. W. Griffith

Rouge 87 Stanley Kwan

Rouge and Riches 20 Harry Franklin

Rouge aux Lèvres, Le 70 Harry Kümel

Rouge Baiser 85 Vera Belmont

Rouge Est Mis, Le 52 René Clair

Rouge Est Mis, Le 56 Gilles Grangier

Rouge et le Blanc, Le 71 Claude Autant-Lara

Rouge et le Noir, Le 53 Claude Autant-Lara

Rouge et Noir 53 Claude Autant-Lara

Rouge Gorge 85 Pierre Zucca

Rouge Midi 85 Robert Guediguian

Rouge of the North 89 Fred Tan

Rouged Lips 23 Harold M. Shaw

Rough and Ready 18 Richard Stanton

Rough and Ready 24 Norman Taurog

Rough and Ready 27 Albert S. Rogell

Rough and the Smooth, The 59 Robert Siodmak

Rough Company 54 Rudolph Maté

Rough Cut 80 Don Siegel

Rough Diamond, A 12 Wilfred Noy

Rough Diamond, The 21 Edward Sedgwick

Rough Diamond 32 Humberto Mauro

Rough Going 25 Wally Van

Rough House, The 17 Roscoe Arbuckle

Rough House Rosie 27 Frank R. Strayer

Rough Idea of Love 30 Mack Sennett

Rough Landing 87 Mukhtar Aga-Mirzayev

Rough Lover, The 18 Joseph De Grasse

Rough Necking 34 George Stevens

Rough Night in Jericho 67 Arnold Laven

Rough Party, A 25 Charles Lamont

Rough Ride with Nitroglycerine, A 12 William Duncan

Rough Riders, The 27 Victor Fleming

Rough Riders 41 Spencer G. Bennet

Rough Riders of Cheyenne 45 Thomas Carr

Rough Riders of Durango 51 Fred C. Brannon

Rough Riders' Round-Up 39 Joseph Kane

Rough Ridin' 24 Richard Thorpe

Rough Ridin' Justice 45 Derwin Abrahams

Rough Ridin' Red 28 Louis King

Rough Ridin' Rhythm 37 John P. McGowan

Rough Riding Ranger 35 Elmer Clifton

Rough Riding Rhythm 37 John P. McGowan

Rough Riding Romance 19 Arthur Rosson

Rough Riding Romeo 32 Arthur Rosson

Rough Romance 30 A. F. Erickson

Rough Seas 31 James Parrott

Rough Shod 22 B. Reeves Eason

Rough Shoot 53 Robert Parrish

Rough Stuff 25 Del Henderson

Rough Time for the Broker, A 04 Lewin Fitzhamon

Rough Touch 86 Joe Comerford

Rough, Tough and Ready 45 Del Lord

Rough, Tough West, The 52 Ray Nazarro

Rough Toughs and Roof Tops 17 Larry Semon

Rough Treatment 78 Andrzej Wajda

Rough Waters 30 John Daumery

Roughly Speaking 45 Michael Curtiz

Roughly Squeaking 46 Chuck Jones

Roughneck, The 15 William S. Hart, Clifford Smith

Roughneck, The 19 Oscar Apfel

Roughneck, The 24 Jack Conway

Roughshod 48 Mark Robson

Roulement à Bille, Le 24 Jean Grémillon

Rouletabille 22 Henri Fescourt

Rouletabille I — Le Mystère de la Chambre Jaune 13 Émile Chautard, Maurice Tourneur

Rouletabille II: La Dernière Incarnation de Larsan 14 Maurice Tourneur

Roulette 24 Stanner E. V. Taylor

Rouli-Roulant 66 Claude Jutra

Round and Round Again 16 Gregory La Cava

Round Midnight 86 Bertrand Tavernier

'Round Rainbow Corner 50 Frank Neall

'Round the Bend 66 Olive Negus

Round Trip 67 Pierre-Dominique Gaisseau

Round-Up, The *20* George Melford
Round-Up, The *65* Miklós Jancsó
Round-Up Time in Texas *37* Joseph Kane
Rounders, The *14* Charles Chaplin
Rounders, The *64* Burt Kennedy
Rounding Up the Law *22* Charles R. Seeling
Roundup, The *41* Lesley Selander
Roundup, The *85* Stanislav Strnad
Roustabout, The *14* Charles Chaplin
Roustabout *64* John Rich
Route au Soleil, La *70* Philippe de Broca
Route de Corinthe, La *67* Claude Chabrol
Route de Devoir, La *18* Georges Monca
Route de Saint-Tropez, La *66* Michael Sarne
Route de Salina, La *70* Georges Lautner
Route des Cimes, La *57* Jean-Jacques Languepin
Route Est Belle, La *29* Robert Florey
Route Heureuse, La *36* Georges Lacombe
Route Impériale, La *35* Marcel L'Herbier
Route Inconnue, La *47* Léon Poirier
Route Napoléon, La *53* Jean Delannoy
Routes du Sud, Les *78* Joseph Losey
Routes of Rhythm, with Harry Belafonte *90* Les Blank*
Rovedderkoppen *15* August Blom
Rover, The *67* Terence Young
Rover and Me *49* Frank Chisnell
Rover Makes Good *53* John Dooley
Rover Takes a Call *05* Lewin Fitzhamon
Rover the Peacemaker *11* Lewin Fitzhamon
Rover's Rival *37* Robert Clampett
Rovesnik Veka *60* Samson Samsonov
Rovin' Tumbleweeds *39* George Sherman
Roving Rogue, A *45* Ray Nazarro
Row and Joy About Künnemann *37* Paul Wegener
Row in a Laundry, A *03* Alf Collins
Row, Row, Row *30* Dave Fleischer
Rowdy, The *21* David Kirkland
Rowdy Police *87* Movli
Rowdyman, The *71* Peter Carter
Rowing to Win *22* H. B. Parkinson
Rowing with the Wind *88* Gonzalo Suárez
Roxanne *87* Fred Schepisi
Roxie Hart *42* William A. Wellman
Roy Colt and Winchester Jack *70* Mario Bava
Roy Colt e Winchester Jack *70* Mario Bava
Royal Affair, A *50* Marc-Gilbert Sauvajon
Royal Affairs in Versailles *53* Sacha Guitry
Royal African Rifles, The *53* Lesley Selander
Royal American, The *27* Harry Joe Brown
Royal Ballet, The *59* Paul Czinner
Royal Ballet Girl, The *28* Max Neufeld
Royal Bed, The *30* Lowell Sherman
Royal Bluff, The *31* Stephen Roberts
Royal Box, The *14* Oscar Eagle
Royal Box, The *29* Bryan Foy
Royal Cat Nap *57* Joseph Barbera, William Hanna
Royal Cavalcade *35* Thomas Bentley, Herbert Brenon, Will P. Kellino, Norman Lee, Walter Summers, Marcel Varnel
Royal Demand, A *33* Gustave Minzenty
Royal Democrat *18* Jack Conway

Royal Divorce, A *23* Alexander Butler
Royal Divorce, A *38* Jack Raymond
Royal Eagle *36* George A. Cooper, Arnold Ridley
Royal England—A Story of an Empire's Throne *11* A. E. Coleby, Leo Stormont
Royal Family, A *15* William Nigh
Royal Family, The *30* George Cukor, Cyril Gardner
Royal Family of Broadway, The *30* George Cukor, Cyril Gardner
Royal Flash *75* Richard Lester
Royal Flush *46* David Butler
Royal Four Flusher, The *30* Edward Buzzell
Royal Game, The *60* Gerd Oswald
Royal Hunt, The *43* Alf Sjöberg
Royal Hunt, The *76* Mrinal Sen
Royal Hunt of the Sun, The *68* Irving Lerner
Royal Journey *52* David Bairstow
Royal Love *15* Percy Nash
Royal Mounted Patrol, The *41* Lambert Hillyer
Royal Mounted Rides Again, The *45* Lewis D. Collins, Ray Taylor
Royal Oak, The *23* Maurice Elvey
Royal Pauper, The *17* Ben Turbett
Royal Rabble, The *45* Hasse Ekman
Royal Razz, The *24* Leo McCarey
Royal Remembrances *29* Cecil M. Hepworth
Royal Rider, The *29* Harry Joe Brown
Royal Romance, A *17* James Vincent
Royal Romance, A *30* Erle C. Kenton
Royal Scandal, A *29* Hans Behrendt
Royal Scandal, A *45* Ernst Lubitsch, Otto Preminger
Royal Standard, The *07* Arthur Gilbert
Royal Track, The *68* Gunnar Höglund
Royal Waltz, The *35* Herbert Maisch
Royal Warriors *86* David Chung
Royal Wedding *50* Stanley Donen
Royale Goumbé, La *58* Jean Rouch
Royalist's Wife, The *09* Charles Raymond
Royaume des Fées, Le *03* Georges Méliès
Royaume Vous Attend, Un *76* Pierre Perrault
Rozbijemy Zabawę *57* Roman Polanski
Rozina Sebranec *45* Otakar Vávra
Rozmaring *38* Ladislas Vajda
Rozmarné Léto *68* Jiří Menzel
Rozstanie *61* Wojciech Has
Roztomilý Člověk *41* Martin Frič
Rozum a Cit *62* Jiří Brdečka
Rozwodów Nie Będzie *63* Jerzy Stefan Stawiński
Ruan Ling Yu *90* Stanley Kwan
Rub-a-Dud-Dud *18* Gregory La Cava
Ruba al Prossimo Tuo *68* Francesco Maselli
Rubacuori *32* Guido Brignone
Rubber Cement *75* Robert Breer
Rubber Gun, The *77* Allan Moyle
Rubber Heels *27* Victor Heerman
Rubber Racketeers *42* Harold Young
Rubber Tires *27* Alan Hale
Rubber Twice *40* Alexander Hammid
Rubbing It In *19* Gregory La Cava
Rube and Mandy at Coney Island *03*

Edwin S. Porter
Rube and the Baron, The *13* Mack Sennett
Rube Couple at the County Fair, A *04* Edwin S. Porter
Rubens *47* Paul Haesaerts, Henri Storck
Rubes in the Theatre *01* Edwin S. Porter
Rübezahls Hochzeit *16* Paul Wegener*
Rubia del Bar, La *86* Ventura Pons
Rubia Servios *78* Lino Brocka
Rubicon *31* Vladimir Weinstock
Rubicon *87* Leidulv Risan
Rublo de las Caras *68* Étienne Périer
Rublo de las Dos Caras, El *68* Étienne Périer
Rublyov *65* Andrei Tarkovsky
Ruby *71* Richard H. Bartlett
Ruby *77* Curtis Harrington, Stephanie Rothman
Ruby Gentry *52* King Vidor
Ruby Lips *28* James Parrott
Ruby Virgin, The *54* Phil Karlson
Rücehr, Die *78* Vojtěch Jasný
Ruckus *81* Max Kleven
Ruddigore *64* Joy Batchelor
Rude Awakening *08* Georges Méliès
Rude Awakening *89* David Greenwalt, Aaron Russo
Rude Boy *80* Jack Hazan, David Mingay
Rude Hostess, A *09* D. W. Griffith
Rude Journée pour la Reine *73* René Allio
Rudiments of Flying, The *18* J. D. Leventhal
Rudolph, the Red-Nosed Reindeer *48* Max Fleischer
Rudra Veena *88* K. Balachander
Rudrabeena *487* Pinaki Mukherjee
Rudy Vallee and His Connecticut Yankees *29* Joseph Santley
Rudy Vallee Melodies *32* Dave Fleischer
Rudyard Kipling's Jungle Book *42* André De Toth, Zoltán Korda
Rue Cases Nègres, La *83* Euzhan Palcy
Rue de Départ *86* Tony Gatlif
Rue de la Paix *27* Henri Diamant-Berger
Rue de l'Estrapade *53* Jacques Becker
Rue de Paris *59* Denys De la Patellière
Rue des Amours Faciles, La *59* Mario Camerini
Rue des Prairies *59* Denys De la Patellière
Rue du Pavé d'Amour, La *23* André Hugon
Rue Lepic Slow Race, The *68* Christopher Miles
Rue Sans Nom, La *33* Pierre Chénal
Ruée des Vikings, La *61* Mario Bava
Ruf, Der *49* Josef von Baky
Ruf aus dem Äther *53* Georg C. Klaren
Ruffians, The *60* Maurice Labro
Rugantino *73* Pasquale Festa Campanile
Rugged Bear *53* Jack Hannah
Rugged Island, The *34* Jenny Brown
Rugged O'Riordans, The *49* Charles Chauvel
Rugged Path, The *18* Arthur H. Rooke
Rugged Water *25* Irvin Willat
Ruggles of Red Gap *18* Lawrence C. Windom
Ruggles of Red Gap *23* James Cruze

Ruggles of Red Gap *34* Leo McCarey
Ruined Life, A *11* A. E. Coleby
Ruined Shopkeeper, The *33* Martin Frič
Ruins, The *83* Mrinal Sen
Ruisseau, Le *37* Claude Autant-Lara, Maurice Lehmann
Ruiter in die Nag *68* Jan Perold
Ruka *64* Jiří Trnka
Ruler, The *37* Veidt Harlan
Ruler of the Road *18* Ernest C. Warde
Ruler of the World *33* Harry Piel
Rulers of the Sea *39* Frank Lloyd
Rules of the Game, The *39* Jean Renoir
Ruletera, La *87* Víctor Manuel Castro
Ruling Class, The *72* Peter Medak
Ruling Passion, The *11* D. W. Griffith
Ruling Passion, The *16* Herbert Brenon
Ruling Passion, The *17* Rex Ingram
Ruling Passion, The *22* F. Harmon Weight
Ruling Voice, The *31* Rowland V. Lee
Rum Runner *71* Robert Enrico
Rum Runners, The *20* Raoul Barré, Charles Bowers
Rumba *31* W. S. Van Dyke
Rumba *35* Marion Gering
Rumba *39* Norman McLaren
Rumba, La *87* Roger Hanin
Rumble Fish *83* Francis Ford Coppola
Rumble on the Docks *56* Fred F. Sears
Rumbo al Cairo *40* Benito Perojo
Rumiantsev Case, The *55* Josef Heifits
Rummelplatz der Liebe *54* Kurt Neumann
Rummy, The *16* Paul Powell
Rumors *49* Jacques Daroy
Rumpelstiltskin *15* Reginald Barker, Raymond B. West
Rumpelstiltskin *65* Herbert B. Fredersdorf
Rumpelstiltskin *86* David Irving
Rumpelstilzchen *65* Herbert B. Fredersdorf
Rumsey Statues *86* Marc Silverman
Run *90* Geoff Burrowes
Run Across the River *59* Everett Chambers
Run, Angel, Run *69* Jack Starrett
Run, Appaloosa, Run *66* Larry Lansburgh
Run, Cougar, Run *72* Jerome Courtland
Run for Cover *54* Nicholas Ray
Run for the Hills *53* Lew Landers
Run for the Roses *77* Henry Levin
Run for the Sun *56* Roy Boulting
Run for Your Life Lola *86* Michel Drach
Run for Your Money, A *49* Charles Frend
Run for Your Wife *65* Gian Luigi Polidoro
Run, Hero, Run *67* Joseph Sargent
Run Home Slow *65* Tim Sullivan
Run Like a Thief *64* Richard Long, Palmer Thompson
Run Like a Thief *67* Bernard Glasser
Run, Man, Run *68* Sergio Sollima
Run of the Arrow *56* Samuel Fuller
Run on Gold, A *69* Alf Kjellin
Run, Rebel, Run *68* James Clavell
Run! Run! *20* Will P. Kellino
Run Run Sweet Roadrunner *65* Rudy Larriva
Run, Shadow, Run *70* Noel Black
Run Silent, Run Deep *58* Robert Wise
Run, Stranger, Run *73* Darren McGavin

Run to Earth by Boy Scouts *11* Dave Aylott
Run Wild, Run Free *69* Richard C. Sarafian
Run with the Devil *59* Mario Camerini
Run with the Wind *66* Lindsay Shonteff
Runaround, The *31* William James Craft
Runaround, The *46* Charles Lamont
Runaway, The *17* Del Henderson
Runaway, The *24* Dave Fleischer
Runaway, The *26* William DeMille
Runaway, The *59* Ritwik Ghatak
Runaway, The *64* Anthony Young
Runaway, The *66* Tapan Sinha
Runaway *71* Bickford Otis Webber
Runaway! *73* David Lowell Rich
Runaway *84* Michael Crichton
Runaway Bride, The *30* Donald Crisp
Runaway Bus, The *54* Val Guest
Runaway Daughter *35* Sidney Lanfield
Runaway Daughters *56* Edward L. Cahn
Runaway Express, The *26* Edward Sedgwick
Runaway Girl *66* Hamil Petroff
Runaway Girls *28* Mark Sandrich
Runaway Holiday, A *29* Bobby Harman
Runaway Horse, A *86* Peter Beauvais
Runaway Kids, The *08* Lewin Fitzhamon
Runaway Knock, The *1898* George Albert Smith
Runaway Ladies *35* Jean De Limur
Runaway Match, The *03* Alf Collins
Runaway Princess, The *28* Anthony Asquith, Frederick Wendhausen
Runaway Queen *34* Herbert Wilcox
Runaway Railway *65* Jan Darnley-Smith
Runaway Romany *17* George W. Lederer
Runaway, Runaway *71* Bickford Otis Webber
Runaway Train, The *73* David Lowell Rich
Runaway Train *85* Andrei Mikhalkov-Konchalovsky
Runaway Van, The *06* Percy Stow
Runaways, The *15* Chester M. Franklin, Sidney Franklin
Runaways, The *85* William Szarka
Runaways of St. Agil *38* Christian-Jaque
Runner, The *62* Don Owen
Runner, The *85* Amir Naderi
Runner Stumbles, The *79* Stanley Kramer
Runners *83* Charles Sturridge
Running *79* Steven Hilliard Stern
Running Away Backwards *64* Allan King
Running Brave *83* Donald Shebib
Running Fence *77* Albert Maysles, David Maysles, Charlotte Zwerin
Running from the Guns *87* John Dixon
Running Hollywood *32* Charles Lamont
Running Hot *84* Mark Griffiths
Running, Jumping and Standing Still Film, The *59* Richard Lester
Running Man, The *63* Carol Reed
Running Man, The *87* Paul Michael Glaser
Running on Empty *88* Sidney Lumet
Running Out of Luck *85* Julien Temple
Running Scared *66* Alan Rafkin
Running Scared *72* David Hemmings
Running Scared *80* Paul Glicker
Running Scared *86* Peter Hyams

Running Target *56* Marvin Weinstein
Running Water *22* Maurice Elvey
Running Wild *27* Gregory La Cava
Running Wild *55* Abner Biberman
Running Wild *73* Robert McCahon
Runt, The *15* Colin Campbell
Runt Page, The *32* Ray Nazarro
Ruota del Vizio, La *20* Augusto Genina
Rupert of Hentzau *15* George Loane Tucker
Rupert of Hentzau *23* Victor Heerman
Rupimono *22* Kenji Mizoguchi
Rupture *61* Jean-Claude Carrière, Pierre Etaix
Rupture, La *70* Claude Chabrol
Rupture *82* Mohamed Chouikh
Ruptures de Fibres *31* Jean Painlevé
Rural Chivalry *39* Alfredo De Diestro
Rural Community *50* Jerzy Kawalerowicz, Kazimierz Sumerski
Rural Demon, A *14* Henry Lehrman
Rural Elopement, A *08* D. W. Griffith
Rural Happiness *40* Carl Boese
Rural Institute *46* Mark Donskoi
Rural School *40* George Pearson
Rural Third Degree, A *13* Mack Sennett
Rurales de Texas, Los *64* Primo Zeglio
Rus Iznachalna *87* Gennady Vasiliev
Rusa, La *87* Mario Camus
Ruscello di Ripasottile, Il *40* Roberto Rossellini
Ruse, The *15* William S. Hart, Clifford Smith
Ruse, La *22* Édouard E. Violet
Ruse de Max, La *13* Max Linder
Ruse of the Rattler, The *21* John P. McGowan
Rush *84* Tonino Ricci
Rush Hour, The *27* E. Mason Hopper
Rush Hour *40* Anthony Asquith
Rush to Judgement *66* Emile De Antonio
Rushin' Ballet *37* Gordon Douglas
Rushing Business *27* Sam Newfield
Rushing Roulette *65* Robert McKimson
Rushing the Gold Rush *26* Luis Seel
Ruslan i Ludmila *14* Władysław Starewicz
Russ Meyer's Up! *76* Russ Meyer
Russ Meyer's Vixen! *68* Russ Meyer
Russia *29* Mario Bonnard
Russia *72* Theodore Holcomb
Russia House, The *90* Fred Schepisi
Russia, Land of Tomorrow *19* Maurice Sandground
Russia of Nicholas II and Leo Tolstoy, The *28* Esther Shub
Russia on Parade *46* Vasily Belyaev, I. M. Poselsky, Ivan Venzher
Russia — The Land of Oppression *10* Edwin S. Porter
Russian, The *87* Mario Camus
Russian Ballerina *47* Alexander Ivanovsky
Russian Dressing *33* Manny Gould, Ben Harrison
Russian Dressing *38* Jean Yarbrough
Russian Forest, The *63* Vladimir Petrov
Russian Lullaby *31* Dave Fleischer
Russian Miracle, The *63* Andrew Thorndike, Annelie Thorndike
Russian Question, The *47* Mikhail Romm
Russian Rhapsody *44* Robert Clampett

Russian Roulette *75* Lou Lombardo
Russian Souvenir *60* Grigori Alexandrov
Russians Are Coming! The Russians Are Coming!, The *66* Norman Jewison
Russicum *88* Pasquale Squitieri
Russicum i Giorni del Diavolo *88* Pasquale Squitieri
Russische Wunder, Das *63* Andrew Thorndike, Annelie Thorndike
Russkies *87* Richard Rosenthal
Russkii Suvenir *60* Grigori Alexandrov
Russkii Vopros *47* Mikhail Romm
Rust Never Sleeps *79* Neil Young
Rustic Chivalry *38* Florian Rey
Rustle of Silk, The *23* Herbert Brenon
Rustler Sheriff, The *11* Allan Dwan
Rustlers, The *19* John Ford
Rustlers *49* Lesley Selander
Rustlers' Hideout *44* Sam Newfield
Rustler's Hideout *46* Wallace Fox
Rustlers of Devil's Canyon *47* R. G. Springsteen
Rustlers of Red Dog *35* Lew Landers
Rustlers of the Badlands *45* Derwin Abrahams
Rustlers of the Night *21* Leonard Franchon
Rustlers on Horseback *50* Fred C. Brannon
Rustler's Paradise *35* Harry Fraser
Rustlers' Ranch *26* Clifford Smith
Rustler's Rhapsody *85* Hugh Wilson
Rustlers' Roundup *33* Henry MacRae
Rustler's Roundup *46* Wallace Fox
Rustlers' Valley *37* Nate Watt
Rustling a Bride *19* Irvin Willat
Rustling for Cupid *26* Irving Cummings
Rusty Leads the Way *48* Will Jason
Rusty Rides Alone *33* D. Ross Lederman
Rusty Saves a Life *49* Seymour Friedman
Rusty's Birthday *49* Seymour Friedman
Ruth *12* Frank Wilson
Ruth Etting *29* Joseph Santley
Ruth Halbfass *71* Volker Schlöndorff
Ruth of the Range *22* W. S. Van Dyke, Ernest C. Warde
Ruth of the Rockies *19* George Marshall
Ruthless *48* Edgar G. Ulmer
Ruthless Four, The *68* Giorgio Capitani
Ruthless People *86* Jim Abrahams, David Zucker, Jerry Zucker
Ruthless Romance *85* Eldar Ryazanov
Ruts *28* Abram Room
Rutting Ground, The *87* Grzegorz Skurski
Ruusujen Aika *69* Risto Jarva, Titta Karakorpi
Ruy Blas *48* Pierre Billon
Růžena Nasková *60* Martin Frič
Ry Cooder and the Moula Banda Rhythm Aces *88* Les Blank
Ryan's Daughter *70* David Lean
Rybář a Zlatá Rybka *51* Jiří Trnka
Ryder, P.I. *86* Karl Hosch, Chuck Walker
Rykowisko *87* Grzegorz Skurski
Rymdinvasion i Lappland *60* Virgil Vogel, Jerry Warren
Rynox *31* Michael Powell
Ryōjū *61* Heinosuke Gosho
Ryoma o Kitta Otoko *87* Kosaku Yamashita
Rys Vozvrashaetsia *88* Agasi Babayan
Rysopis *64* Jerzy Skolimowski

Rythme de Travail *76* Jean Rouch
Ryttare i Blått *59* Arne Mattsson
Ryūri no Kishi *56* Kaneto Shindo
SA Mann Brand *34* Franz Seitz
S.A.S. à San Salvador *82* Raoul Coutard
"S" As in... *84* Jean-Pierre Lefèbvre
S-Bahn Pictures *82* Alfred Behrens
S.I. *13* Urban Gad
S Lyubov i Nezhnost *78* Rangel Vulchanov
S.O.B. *80* Blake Edwards
S.O.S. *14* Ethyle Batley
S.O.S. *27* Carmine Gallone
S.O.S. *28* Leslie Hiscott
S.O.S. *39* John Eldridge
S.O.S. Coast Guard *37* Alvin J. Neitz, William Witney
S.O.S. — Die Insel der Tränen *23* Lothar Mendes
S.O.S. Eisberg *32* Arnold Fanck, Andrew Marton
S.O.S. — En Segel Sällskapsresan *88* Lasse Åberg
S.O.S. Hélicoptère *59* Claude Lelouch
S.O.S. Iceberg *32* Arnold Fanck, Andrew Marton
S.O.S. Iceberg *33* Arnold Fanck, Tay Garnett
S.O.S. Kindtand *43* Astrid Henning-Jensen, Bjarne Henning-Jensen
S.O.S. Mediterranean *37* Léo Joannon
S.O.S. Molars *43* Astrid Henning-Jensen, Bjarne Henning-Jensen
S.O.S. Noronha *57* Georges Rouquier
S.O.S. Pacific *59* Guy Green
S.O.S. Perils of the Sea *25* James P. Hogan
S.O.S. Radio Service *34* Alberto Cavalcanti
S.O.S. Sahara *38* Jacques De Baroncelli
S.O.S. Submarine *41* Francesco De Robertis
S.O.S. Tidal Wave *39* John H. Auer
S*P*Y*S *74* Irvin Kershner
S.S. Ionian *38* Humphrey Jennings
S.T.A.B. *76* Chalong Pakdivijit
S.V.D. *27* Grigori Kozintsev, Leonid Trauberg
S Vyloučením Veřejnosti *33* Martin Frič
S.W.A.L.K. *71* Andrew Birkin, Waris Hussein
S-a Furat o Bombă *61* Ion Popescu-Gopo
Sa Gosse *19* Henri Desfontaines
Sa Tête *29* Jean Epstein
Să Zîmbească Toți Copiii *57* Márta Mészáros
Saadia *53* Albert Lewin
Saat Hindustani *70* Khwaja Ahmad Abbas
Saat Saal Baad *88* S. V. Saiyed
Saba *29* Mikhail Chiaureli
Sabaka *53* Frank Ferrin
Sabaleros *68* Armando Bo
Sabata *69* Gianfranco Parolini
Sabato, Domenica e Lunedi *90* Lina Wertmuller
Sabbat of the Black Cat, The *71* Ralph Lawrence Marsden
Sabina, La *79* José Luis Borau
Sabina, The *79* José Luis Borau
Sabine und die 100 Männer *60* Wilhelm Thiele

Sabishiki Mura *24* Teinosuke Kinugasa
Sabishiki Ranbōmono *27* Heinosuke Gosho
Sable Blessing, The *16* George L. Sargent
Sable Cicada *39* Richard Poh
Sable Lorcha, The *15* Lloyd Ingraham
Sables *27* Dmitri Kirsanov
Sables of Death *25* Edwin Greenwood, Will P. Kellino
Sabor de la Venganza, El *63* Joaquín Luis Romero Marchent
Sabor de la Venganza, El *70* Alberto Mariscal
Sabotage *34* Adrian Brunel
Sabotage *36* Alfred Hitchcock
Sabotage *39* Harold Young
Sabotage at Sea *42* Leslie Hiscott
Sabotage Squad *42* Lew Landers
Saboteur *42* Alfred Hitchcock
Saboteur, The *65* Bernhard Wicki
Saboteur — Code Name Morituri, The *65* Bernhard Wicki
Saboteurs *74* Percival Rubens
Sabotier du Val de Loire, Le *55* Jacques Demy
Sabra *33* Aleksander Ford
Sabra *70* Denys De la Patellière
Sabre and the Arrow, The *52* André De Toth
Sabre Jet *53* Louis King
Sabre Tooth Tiger, The *75* Dario Argento
Sabrina *54* Billy Wilder
Sabrina Fair *54* Billy Wilder
Sabu and the Magic Ring *57* George Blair
Sac au Dos *1896* Georges Méliès
Sac de Nœuds *85* Josiane Balasko
Sacco and Vanzetti *71* Giuliano Montaldo
Sacco Bello, Un *80* Carlo Verdone
Sacco di Roma, Il *09* Enrico Guazzoni
Sacco di Roma, Il *14* Filoteo Alberini
Sacco di Roma e Clemento VII, Il *20* Enrico Guazzoni
Sacco e Vanzetti *71* Giuliano Montaldo
Sack Race *1895* Louis Lumière
Sackcloth and Scarlet *25* Henry King
Sacking of Rome, The *14* Filoteo Alberini
Sacks Up! *1896* Georges Méliès
Sacrament of Confirmation, The *24* John M. Payne
Sacre d'Édouard VII, Le *02* Georges Méliès, George Albert Smith, Charles Urban
Sacré Léonce *35* Christian-Jaque
Sacred and Profane Love *21* William Desmond Taylor
Sacred (?) Elephant, The *11* H. Oceano Martinek
Sacred Flame, The *19* Abraham S. Schomer
Sacred Flame, The *29* Archie Mayo
Sacred Flame, The *35* William Keighley
Sacred Fountain, The *01* Georges Méliès
Sacred Ground *83* Charles B. Pierce
Sacred Hearts *84* Barbara Rennie
Sacred Knives of Vengeance, The *73* Yuan Chu
Sacred Lie, The *25* Forest Holger-Madsen
Sacred Order, The *23* A. E. Coleby
Sacred Protector, The *37* Teinosuke Kinugasa

Sacred Ruby, The 20 Glenn Waite
Sacred Silence 19 Harry Millarde
Sacred Snake Worshippers, The 20 Charles Raymond
Sacred Turquoise of the Zuni, The 10 Sidney Olcott
Sacrée Jeunesse 58 André Berthomieu
Sacrificatio 86 Andrei Tarkovsky
Sacrifice, The 09 D. W. Griffith
Sacrifice 17 Frank Reicher
Sacrifice 29 Victor Peers
Sacrifice, The 86 Andrei Tarkovsky
Sacrifice 88 David Keith
Sacrifice d'Honneur 35 Marcel L'Herbier
Sacrifice for Work, A 07 Arthur Cooper
Sacrifice of Honor 35 Marcel L'Herbier
Sacrifice of Youth 86 Luanxin Zhang
Sacrifice Surhumain 13 Camille De Morlhon
Sacrilegious Hero, The 55 Kenji Mizoguchi
Sad Horse, The 59 James B. Clark
Sad Idiot, The 24 Kenji Mizoguchi
Sad Little Guinea Pigs 38 Manny Gould, Ben Harrison
Sad Sack, The 57 George Marshall
Sad Sack, The 61 Claude De Givray, François Truffaut
Sad Song of the Defeated 22 Kenji Mizoguchi
Sad Story of a Barmaid 30 Heinosuke Gosho
Sad Zhlani 88 Ali Khamrayev
Sada el Rigal, El 86 Rafaat El Mihi
Saddle Aces 35 Harry Fraser
Saddle Buster, The 32 Fred Allen
Saddle Cyclone, The 25 Richard Thorpe
Saddle Hawk, The 25 Edward Sedgwick
Saddle Jumpers 27 Ben F. Wilson
Saddle King, The 29 Ben F. Wilson
Saddle Leather Law 44 Benjamin Kline
Saddle Legion 51 Lesley Selander
Saddle Mates 28 Richard Thorpe
Saddle Mountain Roundup 41 S. Roy Luby
Saddle Pals 47 Lesley Selander
Saddle Serenade 45 Oliver Drake
Saddle Silly 41 Chuck Jones
Saddle the Wind 58 Robert Parrish
Saddle Tramp 50 Hugo Fregonese
Saddled with Five Girls 66 Evald Schorm
Saddlemates 41 Les Orlebeck
Saddles and Sagebrush 43 William Berke
Sadgati 81 Satyajit Ray
Sádico de Notre Dame, El 79 Jesús Franco
Sadie Goes to Heaven 17 W. S. Van Dyke
Sadie Hawkins Day 44 Bob Wickersham
Sadie Love 19 John S. Robertson
Sadie McKee 34 Clarence Brown
Sadie Thompson 28 Raoul Walsh
Sadique de Notre Dame, La 79 Jesús Franco
Sadist, The 63 James Landis
Sadist, The 66 Lars-Magnus Lindgren
Sadisterótica 67 Jesús Franco
Sadko 53 James Landis, Alexander Ptushko
Sado no Kuni Ondeko-Za 76 Masahiro Shinoda
Sado no Tamago 66 Yoji Kuri

Sadomania 80 Jesús Franco
Sado's Ondeko-Za 76 Masahiro Shinoda
Sadovnik 88 Viktor Buturlin
Sælfangst i Nordgrønland, En 55 Bjarne Henning-Jensen
Saetta: Principe per un Giorno 25 Mario Camerini
Safari 40 Edward H. Griffith
Safari 56 Terence Young
Safari Diamants 65 Michel Drach
Safari Drums 53 Ford Beebe
Safari 3000 82 Harry Hurwitz
Safari ya Gari 61 Albert Maysles, David Maysles
Safe, The 30 Dave Aylott
Safe Affair, A 31 Bert Wynne
Safe at Home 41 Ethan Allen
Safe at Home! 62 Walter Doniger
Safe for Democracy 18 J. Stuart Blackton
Safe in Hell 31 William A. Wellman
Safe in Jail 13 Mack Sennett
Safe Place, A 71 Henry Jaglom
Safe Proposition, A 32 Leslie Hiscott
Safecracker, The 57 Ray Milland
Safecracker, The 73 Jaromil Jireš
Safety Curtain, The 18 Sidney Franklin
Safety First 26 Fred Paul
Safety First 28 Hugh Croise
Safety in Numbers 30 Victor Schertzinger
Safety in Numbers 38 Malcolm St. Clair
Safety Last 23 Fred Newmeyer, Sam Taylor
Safety Not Last 26 Luis Seel
Safety Pin, The 13 Émile Cohl
Safety Second 50 Joseph Barbera, William Hanna
Safety Spin 53 Pete Burness
Safety Suit for Skaters, The 08 Lewin Fitzhamon
Saffi 85 Attila Dargay
Saffo, Venere di Lesbo 60 Pietro Francisci
S'Affranchir 13 Louis Feuillade
Safir Gehannam 44 Youssef Wahby
Safo 64 Luis Alcoriza
Saftest of the Family, The 31 George Pearson
Saga, En 38 George Schneevoigt
Saga de los Drácula, La 72 Leon Klimovsky
Saga of Anatahan, The 52 Josef von Sternberg
Saga of Death Valley 39 Joseph Kane
Saga of Dracula, The 72 Leon Klimovsky
Saga of Gösta Berling, The 23 Mauritz Stiller
Saga of Hemp Brown, The 58 Richard Carlson
Saga of Singoalla, The 49 Christian-Jaque
Saga of the Draculas, The 72 Leon Klimovsky
Saga of the Flying Hostesses, The 62 Steno
Saga of the Great Buddha 52 Teinosuke Kinugasa
Saga of the Road, The 55 Satyajit Ray
Saga of the Taira Clan 55 Kenji Mizoguchi
Saga of the Vagabonds 64 Toshio Sugie
Saga of the Viking Women and Their Voyage to the Waters of the Great Sea Serpent, The 57 Roger Corman

Sagacity vs. Crime 13 H. Oceano Martinek
Säge des Todes, Die 81 Jesús Franco
Sage-Femme de Première Classe 1896 Alice Guy-Blaché
Sage from the Sea, The 77 Shyam Benegal
Sage Hen, The 21 Edgar Lewis
Sage vom Hund von Baskerville, Die 15 Richard Oswald
Sagebrush Family Trails West, The 40 Sam Newfield
Sagebrush Gospel 24 Richard Hatton
Sagebrush Hamlet, A 19 Joseph Franz
Sagebrush Heroes 45 Benjamin Kline
Sagebrush Lady, The 25 Horace B. Carpenter, Horace Davey
Sagebrush Law 43 Sam Nelson
Sagebrush League, The 19 Harry A. Gant
Sagebrush Phrenologist, The 11 Allan Dwan
Sagebrush Politics 30 Victor Adamson
Sagebrush Sadie 28 Walt Disney
Sagebrush Trail, The 22 Robert Thornby
Sagebrush Trail, The 33 Armand Schaefer
Sagebrush Troubador, The 35 Joseph Kane
Sagebrusher, The 20 Edward Sloman
Saggakh 38 Pál Fejős, Gunnar Skoglund
Saginaw Trail 53 George Archainbaud
Sagolandet 86 Jan Troell
Sagrario 34 Ramón Peón
Sahara 19 Arthur Rosson
Sahara 43 Zoltán Korda
Sahara 83 Andrew V. McLaglen
Sahara Hare 55 Friz Freleng
Sahara Love 26 Sinclair Hill
Said Effendi 59 Kameran Husni
Said O'Reilly to McNab 37 William Beaudine
Saïda a Enlevé Manneken-Pis 13 Alfred Machin
Saiehaien Bolan de Bad 78 Bahman Farmanara
Saigon 48 Leslie Fenton
Saigon Commandos 87 Clark Henderson
Saigon—Year of the Cat 83 Stephen Frears
Saikaku Ichidai Onna 52 Kenji Mizoguchi
Sail a Crooked Ship 61 Irving S. Brecher
Sail Into Danger 57 Kenneth Hume
Sailboat 67 Joyce Wieland
Sailing Along 24 Charles Lamont
Sailing Along 38 Sonnie Hale
Sailing and Village Sand 58 Lew Keller
Sailing, Sailing 25 Dave Fleischer
Sailing, Sailing Over the Bounding Main 25 Dave Fleischer
Sailor and the Devil, The 67 Errol Le Cain, Richard Williams
Sailor Be Good 33 James Cruze
Sailor Beware 51 Hal Walker
Sailor Beware! 56 Gordon Parry
Sailor from Gibraltar, The 66 Tony Richardson
Sailor from the Aurora, The 26 Grigori Kozintsev, Leonid Trauberg
Sailor from the Comet, The 59 I. Annensky
Sailor George 28 Sam Newfield
Sailor Izzy Murphy 27 Henry Lehrman
Sailor Jack's Reformation 11 Sidney Olcott

Sailor-Made Man, A *21* Fred Newmeyer
Sailor Maid *37* Charles Lamont
Sailor of the King *51* Roy Boulting
Sailor Takes a Wife, The *45* Richard Whorf
Sailor Tramp, A *22* F. Martin Thornton
Sailor Who Fell from Grace with the Sea, The *75* Lewis John Carlino
Sailor's Bride, A *11* Wilfred Noy
Sailor's Consolation *51* John Halas
Sailor's Courtship, A *06* Alf Collins
Sailors Do Care *44* Lewis Gilbert
Sailors Don't Care *28* Will P. Kellino
Sailors Don't Care *40* Oswald Mitchell
Sailor's Heart, A *12* Wilfred Lucas
Sailors' Holiday *29* Fred Newmeyer
Sailor's Holiday *44* William Berke
Sailor's Lady *40* Allan Dwan
Sailor's Lass, A *07* Lewin Fitzhamon
Sailor's Lass, A *10* Lewin Fitzhamon
Sailor's Luck *33* Raoul Walsh
Sailors of the Seven Seas *20* Harry Revier
Sailors on Leave *41* Albert S. Rogell
Sailor's Return, The *07* J. H. Martin
Sailor's Return, The *78* Jack Gold
Sailor's Sacrifice, A *10* Theo Bouwmeester
Sailor's Song *13* Walter R. Booth
Sailor's Sweetheart, A *27* Lloyd Bacon
Sailors Three *40* Walter Forde
Sailor's Three Crowns, The *82* Raúl Ruiz
Sailor's Wedding, The *05* Percy Stow
Sailors' Wives *28* Joseph E. Henabery
Saimaa-Ilmiö *82* Aki Kaurismäki
Saint, Le *66* Christian-Jaque
Saint and Her Fool, The *28* William Dieterle
Saint and Her Fool, The *35* Hans Deppe
Saint and the Brave Goose, The *81* Cyril Frankel
St. Benny the Dip *51* Edgar G. Ulmer
Saint, Devil and Woman *16* Frederick Sullivan
St. Elmo *23* Jerome Storm
St. Elmo *23* Rex Wilson
St. Elmo's Fire *85* Joel Schumacher
Saint-Exupéry *57* Jean-Jacques Languepin
St. Francis of Assisi *47* Alberto Gout
St. Francis of Assisi *89* Liliana Cavani
St. George and the Seven Curses *62* Bert I. Gordon
St. Helens *81* Ernest Pintoff
Saint in London, The *39* John Paddy Carstairs
Saint in New York, The *38* Ben Holmes
Saint in Palm Springs, The *41* Jack Hively
St. Ives *76* J. Lee-Thompson
Saint Jack *79* Peter Bogdanovich
Saint Joan *27* Widgey R. Newman
Saint Joan *57* Otto Preminger
St. John's Fire *40* Arthur Maria Rabenalt
St. Lazare Railroad Station *1896* Georges Méliès
St. Louis Blues *38* Raoul Walsh
St. Louis Blues *58* Allen Reisner
St. Louis Kid, The *34* Ray Enright
St. Louis Woman *35* Albert Ray
St. Martin's Lane *38* Tim Whelan
St. Matthew Passion *52* Ernst Marischka
Saint Meets the Tiger, The *41* Paul Stein
St. Michael Had a Rooster *71* Paolo Taviani, Vittorio Taviani

St. Peter's Umbrella *17* Alexander Korda
Saint Prend l'Affût, Le *66* Christian-Jaque
Saint Strikes Back, The *39* John Farrow
Saint Takes Over, The *40* Jack Hively
Saint-Tropez Blues *60* Marcel Moussy
St. Valentine's Day Massacre, The *66* Roger Corman
Saint Versus..., The *66* Christian-Jaque
Sainte et le Fou, La *28* William Dieterle
Sainted Devil, A *24* Joseph E. Henabery
Sainted Sisters, The *48* William D. Russell
Saintly Sinner, The *16* Raymond Wells
Saintly Sinners *62* Jean Yarbrough
Saint's Adventure, The *17* Arthur Berthelet
Saints and Sinners *11* Edwin S. Porter
Saints and Sinners *16* James Kirkwood
Saints and Sinners *48* Leslie Arliss
Saint's Double Trouble, The *40* Jack Hively
Saint's Girl Friday, The *53* Seymour Friedman
Saint's Return, The *53* Seymour Friedman
Saint's Vacation, The *41* Leslie Fenton
Saison in Kairo *33* Reinhold Schünzel
Saisons du Plaisir, Les *87* Jean-Pierre Mocky
Sait-On Jamais? *57* Roger Vadim
Saiyu-Ki *60* Taiji Yabushita
Sajenko the Soviet *29* Erich Waschneck
Sakasu Gonin-Gumi *35* Mikio Naruse
Sake to Onna to Yari *60* Tomu Uchida
Sakebu Azia *33* Tomu Uchida
Saki, Woman and a Lance *60* Tomu Uchida
Sakima and the Masked Marvel *43* Spencer G. Bennet
Sakpata *58* Jean Rouch, Gilbert Rouget
Sakr, El *50* Salah Abu Saif
Sakura Dance *34* Heinosuke Gosho
Sakura Killers *87* Dusty Nelson, Richard Ward
Sakura no Mori no Mankai no Shita *75* Masahiro Shinoda
Sakura Ondō *34* Heinosuke Gosho
Sal Gorda *83* Fernando Trueba
Sal Grogan's Face *22* Edwin J. Collins
Sal of Singapore *29* Howard Higgin
Sál Ztracených Kroků *60* Jaromil Jireš
Salaam Bombay! *88* Mira Nair
Saladin *62* Youssef Chahine
Saladin and the Great Crusades *62* Youssef Chahine
Saladin the Victorious *62* Youssef Chahine
Salaire de la Peur, Le *52* Henri-Georges Clouzot
Salaire du Péché, Le *56* Denys De la Patellière
Salamander, The *15* Arthur Donaldson
Salamander, The *28* Grigori Roshal
Salamander, The *71* Alain Tanner
Salamander, The *81* Peter Zinner
Salamandra *28* Grigori Roshal
Salamandre, La *71* Alain Tanner
Salambo *62* Sergio Grieco
Salammbô *25* Pierre Marodon
Salammbô *62* Sergio Grieco
Salario para Matar *68* Sergio Corbucci
Salary, 200 a Month *36* Béla Balázs

Salauds Vont en Enfer, Les *55* Robert Hossein
Salavat Yulayev *41* Yakov Protazanov
Salé Destin *87* Sylvain Madigan
Salé Histoire, Une *77* Jean Eustache
Sale of a Heart, The *13* Maurice Costello
Salem's Lot: The Movie *79* Tobe Hooper
Salerno Beachhead *45* Lewis Milestone
Saleslady, The *16* Frederick Thompson
Saleslady *38* Arthur Greville Collins
Salesman, The *23* Al St. John
Salesman *68* Albert Maysles, David Maysles, Charlotte Zwerin
Saliut Marya *70* Josef Heifits
Salka Valka *54* Arne Mattsson
Sallah *63* Ephraim Kishon
Sallah Shabati *63* Ephraim Kishon
Salle à Manger Fantastique *1898* Georges Méliès
Sällskapsresan II — Snow Roller *85* Lasse Åberg
Sally *25* Alfred E. Green
Sally *29* John Francis Dillon
Sally and Saint Anne *52* Rudolph Maté
Sally Bishop *16* George Pearson
Sally Bishop *23* Maurice Elvey
Sally Bishop *32* T. Hayes Hunter
Sally Castleton, Southerner *15* Langdon West
Sally Fieldgood & Co. *75* Boon Collins
Sally in a Hurry *17* Wilfred North
Sally in Our Alley *13* Warwick Buckland
Sally in Our Alley *16* Lawrence Trimble
Sally in Our Alley *16* Travers Vale
Sally in Our Alley *21* Walter C. Rowden
Sally in Our Alley *27* Walter Lang
Sally in Our Alley *31* Maurice Elvey
Sally, Irene and Mary *25* Edmund Goulding
Sally, Irene and Mary *38* William A. Seiter
Sally och Friheten *81* Gunnel Lindblom
Sally of the Sawdust *25* D. W. Griffith
Sally of the Scandals *28* Lynn Shores
Sally of the Subway *32* George B. Seitz
Sally Shows the Way *17* James Kirkwood
Sally Swing *38* Dave Fleischer
Sally's Hounds *68* Robert Edelstein
Sally's Irish Rogue *58* George Pollock
Sally's Shoulders *28* Lynn Shores
Salmon Poachers — A Midnight Melee, The *05* William Haggar
Salò o Le Centoventi Giornate di Sodoma *75* Pier Paolo Pasolini
Salo, or The 120 Days of Sodom *75* Pier Paolo Pasolini
Salo — The 120 Days of Sodom *75* Pier Paolo Pasolini
Salome *02* Oskar Messter
Salome *08* J. Stuart Blackton
Salome *18* J. Gordon Edwards
Salome *22* Charles Bryant
Salome *22* Ludwig Kozma, Ernö Metzner
Salome *22* Robert Wiene
Salome *23* Malcolm Strauss
Salome *53* William Dieterle
Salomé *78* Pedro Almodóvar
Salome *80* Stan Brakhage
Salome *86* Claude D'Anna
Salome and Delilah *63* Andy Warhol

Salome Mad *09* Theo Bouwmeester

Salome Mad *09* A. E. Coleby

Salome of the Tenements *25* Sidney Olcott

Salome vs. Shenandoah *19* Erle C. Kenton*

Salome, Where She Danced *45* Erle C. Kenton, Charles Lamont

Salome's First Night *88* Ken Russell

Salome's Last Dance *88* Ken Russell

Salomy Jane *14* Alex E. Beyfuss, J. Searle Dawley

Salomy Jane *23* George Melford

Salomy Jane *32* Raoul Walsh

Salon de Coiffure *07* Georges Méliès

Salon Dora Green *33* Henryk Galeen

Salón México *48* Emilio Fernández

Salon Nautique *54* Philippe de Broca

Salonique Nid d'Espions *36* G. W. Pabst

Saloon Bar *40* Walter Forde

Salsa *76* Leon Gast, Jerry Masucci

Salsa *88* Boaz Davidson

Salt and Pepper *68* Richard Donner

Salt and the Devil *49* Edward Dmytryk

Salt for Svanetia *30* Mikhail Kalatozov

Salt Lake Raiders *50* Fred C. Brannon

Salt of Svanetia, The *30* Mikhail Kalatozov

Salt of the Black Country *69* Kazimierz Kutz

Salt of the Earth *17* Saul Harrison

Salt of the Earth *53* Herbert J. Biberman

Salt of the Sea *55* Grigori Roshal

Salt to the Devil *49* Edward Dmytryk

Salt Water Daffy *41* Walter Lantz

Salt Water Tabby *47* Joseph Barbera, William Hanna

Saltimancii *85* Elisabeta Bostan

Salto *65* Tadeusz Konwicki

Salto, O *67* Christian De Chalonge

Salto Mortale *31* E. A. Dupont

Salto Mortale *53* Victor Tourjansky

Salto nel Vuoto *79* Marco Bellocchio

Salty *73* Ricou Browning

Salty O'Rourke *45* Raoul Walsh

Salty Saunders *23* Neal Hart

Salty Sweets *85* Eva Stefankovičova

Saludos Amigos *43* Norman Ferguson, Wilfred Jackson, Jack Kinney, Hamilton Luske, Bill Roberts

Salue l'Artiste *73* Yves Robert

Salut à France *44* Garson Kanin, Jean Renoir

Salut à la France *44* Garson Kanin, Jean Renoir

Salut de Dranem, Le *01* Ferdinand Zecca*

Salut l'Artiste *73* Yves Robert

Salut les Cubains *63* Agnès Varda

Salut Malencontreux d'un Déserteur *1896* Georges Méliès

Saluta e Malato o I Poveri Muoriono Prima, La *71* Bernardo Bertolucci

Salutary Lesson, A *10* D. W. Griffith

Salute *29* David Butler, John Ford

Salute for Three *43* Ralph Murphy

Salute John Citizen *42* Maurice Elvey

Salute Maria *70* Josef Heifits

Salute of the Jugger *90* David Peoples

Salute the Toff *52* Maclean Rogers

Salute to a Great Nation *54* Vojtěch Jasný, Karel Kachyňa

Salute to a Rebel *69* Franklin J. Schaffner

Salute to Courage *41* Jules Dassin

Salute to France *44* Garson Kanin, Jean Renoir

Salute to Romance *37* Christy Cabanne

Salute to the Farmers *41* Montgomery Tully

Salute to the Marines *43* S. Sylvan Simon

Salute to the Spanish Pioneers *36* Roman Karmen

Salvador *86* Oliver Stone

Salvador Dali: A Soft Self-Portrait *69* Salvador Dali

Salvage *19* E. R. Bashame

Salvage *20* James Cruze

Salvage *21* Henry King

Salvage Gang, The *58* John Krish

Salvage with a Smile *40* Adrian Brunel

Salvare la Faccia *69* Rossano Brazzi

Salvate Mia Figlia *51* Sergio Corbucci

Salvation! *87* Beth B

Salvation Army Lass, The *09* D. W. Griffith

Salvation! Have You Said Your Prayers Today? *87* Beth B

Salvation Hunters, The *25* Josef von Sternberg

Salvation Jane *27* Phil Rosen

Salvation Joan *16* Wilfred North

Salvation Nell *21* Kenneth Webb

Salvation Nell *31* James Cruze

Salvation of Kathleen, The *14* Van Dyke Brooke

Salvation of Nancy O'Shaughnessy, The *14* Colin Campbell

Salvatore Giuliano *61* Francesco Rosi

Salviamo, la Montagna Muore *52* Piero Nelli

Salwa *72* Youssef Chahine

Salwa, or The Little Girl Who Talks to the Cows *72* Youssef Chahine

Salzburg Connection, The *72* Lee H. Katzin

Salzburg Pilgrimage *56* Paul Czinner

Sam *59* Vladimir Pogačić

Sam Cooper's Gold *68* Giorgio Capitani

Sam Marlowe, Private Eye *80* Robert Day

Sam Pepys Joins the Navy *41* Francis Searle

Sam Pośród Swoich *85* Wojciech Wójcik

Sam Small Leaves Town *37* Alfred Goulding

Sam the Pirate *46* Friz Freleng

Sam Whiskey *69* Arnold Laven

Sama *88* Nadjia Ben Mabrouk

Samanishvili's Stepmother *74* Eldar Shengelaya

Samantha *63* Melville Shavelson

Samar *62* George Montgomery

Samarang *33* Ward Wing

Samaritan, The *15* August Blom

Samaritan, The *31* Frank R. Strayer

Samaya Obayatelnaya i Privlekatelnaya *87* Gerald Bezhanov

Sambhavami Yuge Yuge *88* Siddalingaiah

Sambo *02* James A. Williamson

Same Old Tale, The *05* Tom Green

Same Player Shoots Again *67* Wim Wenders

Same Time, Next Year *78* Robert Mulligan

Same to You *87* Helmut Berger, Anja Franke, Dani Levy

Samidare Zōshi *24* Kenji Mizoguchi

Samma no Aji *62* Yasujiro Ozu

Sammie Johnsin and His Wonderful Lamp *16* Pat Sullivan

Sammie Johnsin at the Seaside *16* Pat Sullivan

Sammie Johnsin Gets a Job *16* Pat Sullivan

Sammie Johnsin, Hunter *16* Pat Sullivan

Sammie Johnsin in Mexico *16* Pat Sullivan

Sammie Johnsin, Magician *16* Pat Sullivan

Sammie Johnsin Minds the Baby *16* Pat Sullivan

Sammie Johnsin Slumbers Not *16* Pat Sullivan

Sammie Johnsin, Strong Man *16* Pat Sullivan

Sammie Johnsin's Love Affair *16* Pat Sullivan

Sammy and Rosie Get Laid *87* Stephen Frears

Sammy Going South *62* Alexander Mackendrick

Sammy Orpheus *12* Colin Campbell

Sammy Somebody *76* Joseph Adler

Sammy Stops the World *78* Mel Shapiro

Sammy the Way-Out Seal *62* Norman Tokar

Sammy's Revenge *12* Fred Rains

Sammy's Sucker *07* Walter R. Booth

Sammy's Super T-Shirt *78* Jeremy Summers

Samo Jednom Se Ljubi *80* Rajko Grlić

Samourai, Le *67* Jean-Pierre Melville

Sampo *58* Holger Harrivirta, Alexander Ptushko

Sampson-Schley Controversy *01* Edwin S. Porter

Samrat *88* V. Madhusudan Rao

Sam's Boy *22* H. Manning Haynes

Sam's Son *84* Michael Landon

Sam's Song *69* John Broderick, John Shade

Samsaram *88* Relangi Narasimah Rao

Samsaram Oka Chadarangam *87* S. P. Mutteraman

Samson *14* Gilbert P. Hamilton, Lorimer Johnston

Samson *15* Edgar Lewis

Samson *36* Maurice Tourneur

Samson *60* Gianfranco Parolini

Samson *61* Andrzej Wajda

Samson Against the Sheik *62* Domenico Paolella

Samson and Delilah *22* Edwin J. Collins

Samson and Delilah *22* Alexander Korda

Samson and Delilah *27* H. B. Parkinson

Samson and Delilah *48* Cecil B. DeMille

Samson and Delilah *85* Mark Peloe

Samson and the Sea Beasts *63* Tanio Boccia

Samson and the Seven Miracles of the World *61* Riccardo Freda

Samson and the Slave Queen *63* Umberto Lenzi

Sans Peur et Sans Reproche 88 Gérard Jugnot
Sans Soleil 82 Chris Marker
Sans Tambour ni Trompette 59 Helmut Käutner
Sans Toit Ni Loi 85 Agnès Varda
Sanshiro at Ginza 50 Kon Ichikawa
Sanshiro of Ginza 50 Kon Ichikawa
Sanshiro Sugata 43 Akira Kurosawa
Sanshiro Sugata II 45 Akira Kurosawa
Sansho Dayu 54 Kenji Mizoguchi
Sansho the Bailiff 54 Kenji Mizoguchi
Sansone 60 Gianfranco Parolini
Sånt Händer Inte Här 50 Ingmar Bergman
Sant Tukaram 37 Rajaram Vanakudre Shantaram
Santa 32 Antonio Moreno
Santa 43 Norman Foster
Santa and the Three Bears 70 Tony Benedict
Santa Catalina 11 Allan Dwan
Santa Catalina—Magic Isle of the Pacific 11 Allan Dwan
Santa Chikita 59 Alekos Sakelarios
Santa Claus 1898 George Albert Smith
Santa Claus 12 Walter R. Booth, R. H. Callum, F. Martin Thornton
Santa Claus 26 George A. Cooper
Santa Claus 60 René Cardona
Santa Claus 85 Jeannot Szwarc
Santa Claus Conquers the Martians 64 Nicholas Webster
Santa Claus' Mistake 05 Alf Collins
Santa Claus: The Movie 85 Jeannot Szwarc
Santa Claus Visits the Land of Mother Goose 67 Herschell Gordon Lewis
Sánta Dervis, A 87 Valeri Akhadov, József Kiss
Santa Fe 51 Irving Pichel
Santa Fe 85 Axel Corti
Santa Fe Bound 36 Harry S. Webb
Santa Fe Marshal 40 Lesley Selander
Santa Fe Passage 55 William Witney
Santa Fe Pete 25 Harry S. Webb
Santa Fe Rides 37 Bernard B. Ray
Santa Fe Saddlemates 45 Thomas Carr
Santa Fe Satan 74 Patrick McGoohan
Santa Fe Scouts 43 Howard Bretherton
Santa Fe Stampede 38 George Sherman
Santa Fe Trail, The 30 Otto Brower, Edwin H. Knopf
Santa Fe Trail, The 40 Michael Curtiz
Santa Fe Uprising 46 R. G. Springsteen
Santa Lucia Luntana 51 Aldo Vergano
Santa Notte 47 Mario Bava
Santa Sangre 89 Alejandro Jodorowsky
(Santa Visits) The Magic Land of Mother Goose 67 Herschell Gordon Lewis
Santarellina 11 Mario Caserini
Santa's Christmas Circus 66 Frank Wiziarde
Santa's Christmas Elf 69 Barry Mahon
Sante Est Malade ou Les Pauvres Meurent les Premiers, La 71 Bernardo Bertolucci
Santee 72 Gary Nelson
Santiago 56 Gordon Douglas
Santiago 70 Lino Brocka
Santo and Dracula's Treasure 68 René Cardona
Santo and the Blue Demon vs. the

Monsters 68 Gilberto Martínez Solares
Santo Ataca las Brujas 65 José Díaz Morales
Santo Attacks the Witches 65 José Díaz Morales
Santo Contra Blue Demon en la Atlántida 68 Julián Soler
Santo Contra Drácula 68 René Cardona
Santo Contra el Cerebro Diabólico 62 Federico Curiel
Santo Contra el Doctor Muerte 73 Rafael Romero Marchent
Santo Contra la Hija de Frankenstein 71 Miguel Delgado
Santo Contra la Invasión de los Marcianos 66 Alfredo B. Crevenna
Santo Contra los Jinetes del Terror 72 René Cardona
Santo Contra los Monstruos de Frankenstein 68 Gilberto Martínez Solares
Santo de la Espada, El 69 Leopoldo Torre-Nilsson
Santo en El Museo de Cera 63 Alfonso Corona Blake
Santo en El Tesoro de Drácula 68 René Cardona
Santo en La Casa de las Brujas 65 José Díaz Morales
Santo en La Venganza de las Mujeres Vampiro 69 Federico Curiel
Santo Guerreiro Contra o Dragão da Maldade, O 69 Glauber Rocha
Santo in the Wax Museum 63 Alfonso Corona Blake
Santo Oficio, El 74 Arturo Ripstein
Santo vs. Frankenstein's Daughter 71 Miguel Delgado
Santo vs. la Hija de Frankenstein 71 Miguel Delgado
Santo vs. the Martian Invasion 66 Alfredo B. Crevenna
Santo y Blue Demon Contra Drácula y el Hombre Lobo 71 Miguel Delgado
Santo y Blue Demon Contra los Monstruos 68 Gilberto Martínez Solares
Santo y el Tesoro de Drácula 68 René Cardona
Santos Inocentes, Los 84 Mario Camus
Santuário 52 Lima Barreto
São Bernardo 70 Leon Hirszman
São Paulo: Sinfonía de una Metrópoli 29 Adalbert Kememy
Sap, The 26 Erle C. Kenton
Sap, The 29 Archie Mayo
Sap from Abroad, The 30 A. Edward Sutherland
Sap from Syracuse, The 30 A. Edward Sutherland
Sapato de Cetim, O 85 Manoel De Oliveira
Saphead, The 20 Herbert Blaché
Sapho 13 Christy Cabanne
Sapho 60 Pietro Francisci
Sapirhurin 86 Alexander Rekhviashvili
Saplings, The 72 Revaz Chkeidze
Sapore del Grano 86 Gianni Da Campo
Sapore della Vendetta, Il 68 Julio Coll
Sapore di Mare 82 Carlo Vanzina
Sapphire 59 Basil Dearden
Sappho 13 Christy Cabanne

Sappho 17 Émile Chautard
Sappho 17 Hugh Ford
Sappho 21 Dmitri Buchowetzki
Sappho 34 Léonce Perret
Sapporo Orimpikku 72 Masahiro Shinoda
Sapporo Story 87 Wong Wah Kay
Sapporo Winter Olympic Games 72 Masahiro Shinoda
Sapporo Winter Olympics 72 Masahiro Shinoda
Saps at Sea 40 Gordon Douglas
Saps in Chaps 42 Friz Freleng
Saqueadores del Domingo, Los 65 Jacques Deray
Sara Lär Sig Folkvett 37 Gustaf Molander
Sara Learns Manners 37 Gustaf Molander
Saraba Itoshiki Hito Yo 87 Masato Harada
Saraba Mosukuwa Gūrentai 68 Hiromichi Horikawa
Saraband 48 Basil Dearden, Michael Relph
Saraband for Dead Lovers 48 Basil Dearden, Michael Relph
Saracen Blade, The 54 William Castle
Saracens, The 60 Roberto Mauri
Saragossa Manuscript, The 64 Wojciech Has
Sarah and Son 30 Dorothy Arzner
Sarah Lawrence 40 Willard Van Dyke
Sarah's Hero 11 Percy Stow
Sarajevo 40 Max Ophüls
Sarajevo 55 Fritz Kortner
Saranda 70 A. Mollica
Sarati-le-Terrible 23 René Hervil, Louis Mercanton
Saratoga 37 Jack Conway
Saratoga Trunk 43 Sam Wood
Sardinia: Ransom 68 Gianfranco Mingozzi
Sardonicus 61 William Castle
Sárga Csikó 36 Béla Pásztor
Sarge Goes to College 47 Will Jason
Sarikat Sayfeya 88 Yousry Nasrallah
Sarıpınar 1914 86 Atıf Yılmaz
Sarja 88 Raj Datta
Sarkari Prasad 26 Pendharkar Babu Rao
Sarong Girl 43 Arthur Dreifuss
Sarraounia 86 Med Hondo
Sartana 67 Alberto Cardone
Sartana—Bete um Deinen Tod 69 Gianfranco Parolini
Sartana nella Valle degli Avvoltoi 70 Roberto Mauri
Sartana Non Perdona 68 Alfonso Balcazar
Sartre par Lui-Même 72 Alexandre Astruc, Michel Contat
Sarumba 50 Marion Gering
Sarutobi 65 Masahiro Shinoda
Sarvtid 42 Arne Sucksdorff
Sasaki Kojiro 51 Hiroshi Inagaki
Sasaki Kojiro 67 Hiroshi Inagaki
Sasameyuki 83 Kon Ichikawa
Sasayashi no Joe 69 Koichi Saito
Šašek a Královna 88 Věra Chytilová
Sashshennyi Fonar 83 Agassi Aivasian
Saskatchewan 54 Raoul Walsh
Såsom i en Spegel 61 Ingmar Bergman
Sasquatch 78 Ed Ragozzini
Sasquatch—The Legend of Bigfoot 78 Ed Ragozzini
Sassy Cats 33 Dick Huemer

Sasuke Against the Wind 73 Masahiro Shinoda
Satah se Uthata Aadmi 80 Mani Kaul
Satan 69 Michael Armstrong
Satan and the Woman 28 Burton L. King
Satan Bug, The 64 John Sturges
Satan en Prison 07 Georges Méliès
Satan in High Heels 62 Jerald Intrator
Satan in Prison 07 Georges Méliès
Satan in Sables 25 James Flood
Satan Junior 19 Herbert Blaché
Satan Met a Lady 36 William Dieterle
Satan Never Sleeps 61 Leo McCarey
Satan Sanderson 15 John W. Noble
Satan Town 26 Edmund Mortimer
Satan Triumphant 17 Yakov Protazanov
Satana 12 Luigi Maggi
Satana Contra Dr. Exortio 72 Jesús Franco
Satana Likuyushchii 17 Yakov Protazanov
Satanas 16 Louis Feuillade
Satanas 19 F. W. Murnau
Satanic 68 Piero Vivarelli
Satanic Rites of Dracula, The 73 Alan Gibson
Satanist, The 68 Zoltan G. Spencer
Satan's Amazon 15 A. E. Coleby
Satan's Bed 65 Marshall Smith
Satan's Brew 76 Rainer Werner Fassbinder
Satan's Cheerleaders 77 Greydon Clark
Satan's Children 75 Joe Wiezycki
Satan's Claw 70 Piers Haggard
Satan's Cradle 49 Ford Beebe
Satan's Empire 86 Salah Abu Saif
Satan's Five Warnings 39 I. Socias
Satan's Harvest 70 George Montgomery
Satan's Mistress 80 James Polakoff
Satan's Private Door 17 J. Charles Haydon
Satan's Sadist 69 Al Adamson
Satan's Sadists 69 Al Adamson
Satan's Satellites 52 Fred C. Brannon
Satan's Sister 25 George Pearson
Satan's Sister 65 Michael Reeves
Satan's Skin 70 Piers Haggard
Satan's Slave 76 Norman J. Warren
Satan's Slave 82 Sisworo Gautama Putra
Satan's Waitin' 54 Friz Freleng
Satansbraten 76 Rainer Werner Fassbinder
Satchmo the Great 57 Fred W. Friendly, Edward R. Murrow
Satdee Night 73 Gillian Armstrong
Satellite de Vénus, Le 77 Nelly Kaplan
Satellite in the Sky 56 Paul Dickson
Satellite of Blood 58 Robert Day
Sati Manahanda 23 D. G. Phalke
Satin Girl, The 23 Arthur Rosson
Satin Mushroom, The 69 Don Brown
Satin Slipper, The 85 Manoel De Oliveira
Satin Vengeance 86 Cirio Santiago
Satin Woman, The 27 Walter Lang
Satisfaction 88 Joan Freeman
Satisfaction 88 Chuck Vincent
Satōgashi ga Kowareru Toki 67 Tadashi Imai
Satsueijō Romansu: Ren-Ai Annai 32 Heinosuke Gosho
Satsujinkyō Shidai 66 Yoji Kuri
Satsujinsha no Kao 49 Teinosuke Kinugasa
Saturday Afternoon 26 Harry Edwards
Saturday Angel 54 Kajiro Yamamoto

Saturday Evening 57 Vladimir Pogačić
Saturday Evening Puss 50 Joseph Barbera, William Hanna
Saturday Island 52 Stuart Heisler
Saturday, July 27, 1963 63 Márta Mészáros
Saturday Morning 71 Kent Mackenzie
Saturday Night 21 Cecil B. DeMille
Saturday Night and Sunday Morning 60 Karel Reisz
Saturday Night at the Baths 75 David Buckley
Saturday Night at the Palace 87 Robert Davies
Saturday Night Bath in Apple Valley 65 John Myhers
Saturday Night Fever 77 John Badham
Saturday Night in Apple Valley 65 John Myhers
Saturday Night Kid, The 29 A. Edward Sutherland
Saturday Night Out 63 Robert Hartford-Davis
Saturday Night Revue 37 Norman Lee
Saturday Shopping 03 Cecil M. Hepworth
Saturday, Sunday and Monday 90 Lina Wertmuller
Saturday the Fourteenth 81 Howard R. Cohen
Saturday the Fourteenth Strikes Back 88 Howard R. Cohen
Saturday Train, The 63 Vittorio Sala
Saturday's Children 29 Gregory La Cava
Saturday's Children 40 Vincent Sherman
Saturday's Hero 51 David Miller
Saturday's Heroes 37 Edward Killy
Saturday's Millions 33 Edward Sedgwick
Saturday's Shopping 03 Cecil M. Hepworth
Saturday's Wages 05 Percy Stow
Saturn 3 79 John Berry, Stanley Donen
Saturnin ou Le Bon Allumeur 21 Louis Feuillade
Satyagraham 88 K. S. R. Das
Satyajit Ray, Film Maker 82 Shyam Benegal
Satyam Shivam Sundaram 78 Raj Kapoor
Satyricon 69 Federico Fellini
Sauce for the Goose 18 Walter Edwards
Sauce for the Goose 19 Vernon Stallings
Saucepan Journey 50 Arne Mattsson
Saucy Madeline 18 F. Richard Jones
Saucy Sausages 29 Walter Lantz
Saudade 36 Carlos Velo
Sauf Votre Respect 89 Guy Hamilton
Saugus Series 74 Pat O'Neill
Saul and David 09 J. Stuart Blackton
Saul and David 68 Marcello Baldi
Saul e David 68 Marcello Baldi
Saúl y David 68 Marcello Baldi
Saumon Atlantique, Le 55 Georges Franju
Sausages 05 James A. Williamson
Saut, Le 67 Christian De Chalonge
Saut à la Couverture 1895 Louis Lumière
Saut de l'Ange, Le 71 Yves Boisset
Saut Humidifié de M. Plick 00 Alice Guy-Blaché
Saute Ma Ville 68 Chantal Akerman
Saute Moi Dessus 77 Jean Rollin
Sauterelle 66 Georges Lautner
Sauvage, Le 75 Jean-Paul Rappeneau

Sauvage et Beau 84 Frédéric Rossif
Sauve Qui Peut (La Vie) 79 Jean-Luc Godard
Sauve-Toi Lola 86 Michel Drach
Sauvetage en Rivière 1896 Georges Méliès
Sauveur d'Épaves 54 Edmond T. Gréville
Savage, The 17 Rupert Julian
Savage, The 26 Fred Newmeyer
Savage, The 52 George Marshall
Savage 62 Arthur A. Jones
Savage, The 75 Jean-Paul Rappeneau
Savage Abduction 75 John Lawrence
Savage American, The 66 John Carr
Savage Apocalypse 80 Antonio Margheriti
Savage Attraction 83 Frank Shields
Savage Beach 90 Andy Sidaris
Savage Beasts 82 Lewis E. Cianelli, Franco Prosperi
Savage Brigade 38 Jean Dréville, Marcel L'Herbier
Savage Creatures in Heat 87 Gilberto De Anda
Savage Dawn 84 Simon Nuchtern
Savage Drums 51 William Berke
Savage Eye, The 59 Ben Maddow, Sidney Meyers, Joseph Strick
Savage Frontier 53 Harry Keller
Savage Girl, The 32 Harry Fraser
Savage Gringo 65 Antonio Roman
Savage Guns, The 61 Michael Carreras
Savage Harvest 81 Robert Collins
Savage Horde, The 50 Joseph Kane
Savage Hordes, The 61 Remigio Del Grosso
Savage Hunger, A 84 Sparky Greene
Savage Innocents, The 59 Baccio Bandini, Nicholas Ray
Savage Is Loose, The 74 George C. Scott
Savage Island 85 Nicholas Beardsley, Eduardo Mulargia
Savage Islands 83 Ferdinand Fairfax
Savage Land 81 Zi Ling
Savage Love 24 Al Christie
Savage/Love 81 Shirley Clarke
Savage Messiah 72 Ken Russell
Savage Mutiny 53 Spencer G. Bennet
Savage Pampas 43 Lucas Demare, Hugo Fregonese
Savage Pampas 66 Hugo Fregonese
Savage Princess 52 Ramjankhan Meh-boobkhan
Savage Red—Outlaw White 74 Paul Hunt
Savage Sam 63 Norman Tokar
Savage Seven, The 68 Richard Rush
Savage Sisters 74 Eddie Romero
Savage State 78 Françoise Giroud
Savage Streets 84 Danny Steinmann
Savage Triangle 51 Jean Delannoy
Savage Weekend 76 David Paulsen
Savage Wild, The 70 Gordon Eastman
Savage Wilderness 55 Anthony Mann
Savage Woman, The 18 Edmund Mortimer
Savage Women 87 Gabriel Retes
Savages 72 James Ivory
Savages from Hell 68 Joseph Prieto
Savages of the Sea 25 Bruce Mitchell
Savannah (La Ballade) 88 Marco Pico
Savannah Smiles 82 Pierre De Moro
Savant et le Chimpanzé, Le 01 Georges Méliès

Savate, La *38* David Miller
Save a Little Sunshine *38* Norman Lee
Save the Children *73* Stan Lathan
Save the City *77* Jan Łomnicki
Save the Tiger *73* John G. Avildsen
Saved by a Burglar *09* Walter R. Booth
Saved by a Child *11* A. E. Coleby
Saved by a Dream *09* James A. Williamson
Saved by a Dream *14* Ethyle Batley
Saved by a Lie *06* Percy Stow
Saved by a Pillar Box *06* Alf Collins
Saved by a Sailor *07* J. H. Martin
Saved by Carlo *09* A. E. Coleby
Saved by Fire *12* Sidney Northcote
Saved by His Sweetheart *10* Lewin Fitzhamon
Saved by Love *08* Edwin S. Porter
Saved by Radio *22* William James Craft
Saved by the Belle *39* Charlie Chase
Saved by the Flag *10* Lawrence Trimble
Saved by the Sun *14* Charles C. Calvert
Saved by the Telegraph *09* Lewin Fitzhamon
Saved by the Telegraph Code *08* Percy Stow
Saved from Himself *10* Edwin S. Porter
Saved from Himself *11* D. W. Griffith
Saved from the Burning Wreck *07* A. E. Coleby
Saved from the Harem *15* Wilbert Melville
Saved from the Sea *09* Lewin Fitzhamon
Saved from the Sea *20* Will P. Kellino
Savetier et le Financier, Le *09* Louis Feuillade
Saving Grace, The *14* Christy Cabanne
Saving Grace *86* Robert M. Young
Saving Mabel's Dad *13* Mack Sennett
Saving of Bill Blewitt, The *37* Harry Watt
Saving Raffles *17* Fred Evans, Joe Evans
Saving Song, The *41* Maclean Rogers
Saving the Colours *14* Charles H. Weston
Saving the Family Name *16* Phillips Smalley, Lois Weber
Saving the Royal Mail *12* Lewin Fitzhamon
Savitri *14* D. G. Phalke
Savva *19* Cheslav Sabinsky
Sawdust *23* Jack Conway
Sawdust and Salome *14* Van Dyke Brooke
Sawdust and Tinsel *53* Ingmar Bergman
Sawdust Doll, The *19* William Bertram
Sawdust Paradise, The *28* Luther Reed
Sawdust Ring, The *17* Christy Cabanne, Charles Miller, Paul Powell
Sawdust Trail, The *19* Gregory La Cava
Sawdust Trail, The *24* Edward Sedgwick
Sawmill, The *21* Larry Semon, Norman Taurog
Sawmill Four, The *24* Earl Hurd
Sawwa Sher *88* Sachin
Saxo *88* Ariel Zeitoun
Saxon Charm, The *48* Claude Binyon
Say Abracadabra *52* Harold Baim
Say Ah, Jasper *44* George Pal
Say Amen, Somebody *82* George T. Nierenberg
Say Amen, Someone *82* George T. Nierenberg
Say Anything... *89* Cameron Crowe
Say Hello to Yesterday *70* Alvin Rakoff

Say It Again *26* Gregory La Cava
Say It in French *38* Andrew L. Stone
Say It with Diamonds *23* Carter DeHaven
Say It with Diamonds *27* Jack Nelson
Say It with Diamonds *35* Redd Davis
Say It with Flowers *34* John Baxter
Say It with Music *32* Jack Raymond
Say It with Sables *28* Frank Capra
Say It with Songs *29* Lloyd Bacon
Say One for Me *59* Frank Tashlin
Say That You Love Me *39* Robert Snody
Say Yes *86* Larry Yust
Say, Young Fellow *18* Joseph E. Henabery
Sayat Nova *68* Sergei Paradzhanov
Sayidat al Kitar *51* Youssef Chahine
Sayonara *57* Joshua Logan
Sayōnara, Konnichiwa *59* Kon Ichikawa
Sayon's Bell *43* Hiroshi Shimizu
Says O'Reilly to McNab *37* William Beaudine
Sbaglio di Essere Vivo, Lo *45* Carlo Ludovico Bragaglia
Sbandati, Gli *55* Francesco Maselli
Sbarco di Anzio, Lo *67* Edward Dmytryk
Sbatti il Mostro in Prima Pagina *72* Marco Bellocchio
Scacco alla Regina *70* Pasquale Festa Campanile
Scala di Giacobbe, La *20* Ugo Falena
Scalawag *73* Kirk Douglas
Scaldino, Lo *19* Augusto Genina
Scales of Justice, The *14* Thomas Heffron
Scales of Justice, The *14* Alfred Lord
Scaling the Alps *28* Mannie Davis
Scallawag, The *14* Lewin Fitzhamon
Scallywag, The *21* Challis Sanderson
Scalp *85* Gilles Carle
Scalp Merchant, The *77* Howard Rubie
Scalp Treatment *52* Walter Lantz
Scalp Trouble *39* Robert Clampett
Scalpel *76* John Grissmer
Scalpel, Please! *85* Jiří Svoboda
Scalphunters, The *68* Sydney Pollack
Scalps *83* Fred Olen Ray
Scalps *86* Werner Knox
Scamp, The *57* Wolf Rilla
Scampolo *28* Augusto Genina
Scampolo *59* Alfred Weidenmann
Scampolo—Ein Kind der Strasse *32* Hans Steinhoff
Scandal *15* Phillips Smalley, Lois Weber
Scandal *17* Charles Giblyn
Scandal, The *23* Arthur H. Rooke
Scandal *29* Wesley Ruggles
Scandal? *29* Ivan Perestiani
Scandal *50* Akira Kurosawa
Scandal *89* Michael Caton-Jones
Scandal at Scourie *52* Jean Negulesco
Scandal for Sale *32* Russell Mack
Scandal in Bohemia, A *21* Maurice Elvey
Scandal in Denmark *70* Peer Guldbrandsen
Scandal in Paris, A *28* Robert Wiene
Scandal in Paris *46* Douglas Sirk
Scandal in Sorrento *55* Dino Risi
Scandal, Inc. *56* Santos Alcocer
Scandal Mongers *18* Phillips Smalley, Lois Weber
Scandal Over the Teacups *00* George Albert Smith

Scandal Proof *25* Edmund Mortimer
Scandal Sheet *31* John Cromwell
Scandal Sheet *39* Nick Grindé
Scandal Sheet *51* Phil Karlson
Scandal '64 *64* Robert Spafford
Scandal Street *25* Whitman Bennett
Scandal Street *37* James P. Hogan
Scandale, Le *18* Jacques De Baroncelli
Scandale, Le *34* Marcel L'Herbier
Scandale, Le *66* Claude Chabrol
Scandale *82* George Mihalka
Scandale au Village, Un *13* Louis Feuillade
Scandalo Segreto *89* Monica Vitti
Scandalosa Gilda *85* Gabriele Lavia
Scandalous! *84* Rob Cohen
Scandalous Adventures of Buraikan, The *70* Masahiro Shinoda
Scandalous Boys and the Fire Chute, The *08* Percy Stow
Scandalous Eva *30* G. W. Pabst
Scandalous John *71* Robert Butler
Scandalous Tongues *22* Victor Schertzinger
Scandals *34* Thornton Freeland, Harry Lachman, George White
Scandals of Clochemerle, The *47* Pierre Chénal
Scandals of Paris *34* Joseph Losey, John Stafford
Scanian Guerilla *42* Åke Öhberg
Scanners *80* David Cronenberg
Scansati...A Trinità Arriva Eldorado *73* Dick Spitfire
Scapegoat, The *58* Robert Hamer
Scapegoat, The *63* Duccio Tessari
Scapegrace, The *13* Edwin J. Collins
Scapolo, Lo *55* Antonio Pietrangeli
Scappamento Aperto *64* Jean Becker
Scar, The *19* Frank Crane
Scar, The *48* Steve Sekely
Scar Hanan *25* Ben F. Wilson
Scar of Shame, The *27* Frank Peregini
Scarab *82* Steven Charles Jaffe
Scarab Murder Case, The *36* Michael Hankinson
Scarab Ring, The *21* Edward José
Scarabea *68* Hans-Jürgen Syberberg
Scarabea: How Much Land Does a Man Need? *68* Hans-Jürgen Syberberg
Scarabea: Wieviel Erde Braucht der Mensch? *68* Hans-Jürgen Syberberg
Scaramouche *23* Rex Ingram
Scaramouche *52* George Sidney
Scaramouche *64* Antonio Isamendi
Scaramouche *75* Enzo G. Castellari
Scaramouches, The *10* Lewin Fitzhamon
Scarecrow, The *11* Frank Wilson
Scarecrow, The *16* Cecil Birch
Scarecrow, The *20* Edward F. Cline, Buster Keaton
Scarecrow *58* Rolan Bykov
Scarecrow *73* Jerry Schatzberg
Scarecrow, The *81* Sam Pillsbury
Scarecrow in a Garden of Cucumbers *72* Robert J. Kaplan
Scarecrow Pump *04* Edwin S. Porter
Scarecrows *88* William Wesley
Scared! *32* Elliott Nugent
Scared Crows, The *39* Dave Fleischer
Scared Silly *27* Charles Lamont

Scared Stiff *45* Frank McDonald
Scared Stiff *52* George Marshall
Scared to Death *47* Christy Cabanne
Scared to Death *80* William Malone
Scaredy Cat *48* Chuck Jones
Scareheads *31* Noel Mason Smith
Scaremaker, The *84* Robert Deubel
Scaremongers, The *40* Graham Cutts
Scarf, The *50* E. A. Dupont
Scarf of Mist, Thigh of Satin *66* Joe Sarno
Scarface *32* Howard Hawks
Scarface *83* Brian DePalma
Scarface Mob, The *59* Phil Karlson
Scarface, Shame of a Nation *32* Howard Hawks
Scarface, the Shame of a Nation *32* Howard Hawks
Scarlatine, La *83* Gabriel Aghion
Scarlet and Black *53* Claude Autant-Lara
Scarlet and Gold *25* Francis J. Grandon
Scarlet Angel, The *52* Sidney Salkow
Scarlet Baroness, The *62* Rudolf Jügert
Scarlet Bat, The *51* Teinosuke Kinugasa
Scarlet Blade, The *63* John Gilling
Scarlet Brand, The *32* John P. McGowan
Scarlet Buccaneer, The *76* James Goldstone
Scarlet Camellia, The *65* Yoshitaro Nomura
Scarlet Car, The *17* Joseph De Grasse
Scarlet Car, The *23* Stuart Paton
Scarlet Claw, The *44* Roy William Neill
Scarlet Clue, The *45* Phil Rosen
Scarlet Coat, The *55* John Sturges
Scarlet Crystal, The *17* Charles Swickard
Scarlet Daredevil, The *28* T. Hayes Hunter
Scarlet Dawn *32* William Dieterle
Scarlet Days *19* D. W. Griffith
Scarlet Dove, The *28* Arthur Gregor
Scarlet Drop, The *18* John Ford
Scarlet Empress, The *34* Josef von Sternberg
Scarlet Eye, The *63* Gerd Oswald, Giovanni Roccardi
Scarlet Fever *24* Friedrich Ermler
Scarlet Fever *83* Gabriel Aghion
Scarlet Hangman, The *65* Massimo Pupillo
Scarlet Honeymoon, The *25* Alan Hale
Scarlet Horseman, The *46* Lewis D. Collins, Ray Taylor
Scarlet Hour, The *55* Michael Curtiz
Scarlet Kiss, The *20* Fred Goodwins
Scarlet Lady, The *22* Walter West
Scarlet Lady, The *28* Alan Crosland
Scarlet Letter, The *07* Sidney Olcott
Scarlet Letter, The *17* Carl Harbaugh
Scarlet Letter, The *22* Challis Sanderson
Scarlet Letter, The *26* Victor Sjöström
Scarlet Letter, The *34* Robert Vignola
Scarlet Letter, The *72* Wim Wenders
Scarlet Lily, The *23* Victor Schertzinger
Scarlet Oath, The *16* Frank Powell, Travers Vale
Scarlet Pages *30* Ray Enright
Scarlet Pimpernel, The *17* Richard Stanton
Scarlet Pimpernel, The *28* Herbert Wilcox
Scarlet Pimpernel, The *34* Rowland Brown, Alexander Korda, Harold Young

Scarlet Pumpernickel, The *50* Chuck Jones
Scarlet River *33* Otto Brower
Scarlet Road, The *16* Bruno Lessing, Clarkson Miller
Scarlet Road, The *18* Edward J. LeSaint
Scarlet Saint *25* George Archainbaud
Scarlet Seas *29* John Francis Dillon
Scarlet Shadow, The *19* Robert Z. Leonard
Scarlet Sin, The *15* Hobart Bosworth, Otis Turner
Scarlet Spear, The *54* George Breakston, Ray Stahl
Scarlet Streak, The *26* Henry MacRae
Scarlet Street *45* Fritz Lang
Scarlet Thread *50* Lewis Gilbert
Scarlet Trail, The *18* John S. Lawrence
Scarlet Web, The *54* Charles Saunders
Scarlet Weekend, A *32* George Melford
Scarlet West, The *25* John G. Adolfi
Scarlet Woman, The *16* Edmund Lawrence
Scarlet Woman, The *28* Alan Crosland
Scarlet Woman, The *69* Jean Valère
Scarlet Wooing, The *20* Sidney Morgan
Scarlet Youth *28* William Hughes Curran
Scarred *51* Mario Mattòli
Scarred *83* Rose Marie Turko
Scarred Face, The *28* Fred Paul
Scarred Hands *23* Clifford Smith
Scars of Dracula *70* Roy Ward Baker
Scars of Hate *23* Harry G. Moody
Scars of Jealousy *23* Lambert Hillyer
Scary Time, A *60* Shirley Clarke
Scat Burglars, The *37* Leslie Rowson
Scat Cats *56* Joseph Barbera, William Hanna
Scatenato, Lo *67* Franco Indovina
Scatterbrain *40* Gus Meins
Scattered Body and the World Upside Down, The *75* Raúl Ruiz
Scattered Clouds *67* Mikio Naruse
Scattergood Baines *41* Christy Cabanne
Scattergood Meets Broadway *41* Christy Cabanne
Scattergood Pulls the Strings *41* Christy Cabanne
Scattergood Rides High *42* Christy Cabanne
Scattergood Survives a Murder *42* Christy Cabanne
Scattergood Swings It *42* Christy Cabanne
Scavenger Hunt *79* Michael Schultz
Scavengers, The *59* John Cromwell
Scavengers, The *69* R. Lee Frost
Scavengers, The *69* Ermanno Olmi
Scavengers *88* Duncan McLachlan
Sceicco Bianco, Lo *51* Federico Fellini
Sceicco Rosso, Lo *62* Fernando Cerchio
Scélérats, Les *59* Robert Hossein
Scemo di Guerra *85* Dino Risi
Scenario *85* Dinos Mavroidis
Scène d'Escamotage *1898* Alice Guy-Blaché
Scène en Cabinet Particulier Vue à Travers le Trou de la Serrure, Une *02* Alice Guy-Blaché
Scene Nun, Take One *64* Maurice Hatton
Scene of the Crime *49* Roy Rowland
Scene of the Crime *86* André Téchiné
Scener ur ett Äktenskap *73* Ingmar Bergman

Scenes and Incidents, Russo-Japanese Peace Conference, Portsmouth, New Hampshire *05* Edwin S. Porter
Scenes Between Two Well Known Comedians *00* Jack Smith
Scènes de la Vie de Café *62* François Reichenbach
Scènes de Ménage *54* André Berthomieu
Scènes Directoire *04* Alice Guy-Blaché
Scenes from a Marriage *73* Ingmar Bergman
Scenes from a Murder *72* Alberto De Martino
Scenes from Country Life *17* J. Stuart Blackton
Scenes from the Class Struggle in Beverly Hills *89* Paul Bartel
Scenes from the Goldmine *86* Marc Rocco
Scenes from the Portuguese Class Struggle *77* Robert Kramer*
Scenes from Under Childhood *70* Stan Brakhage
Scenes in an Infant Orphan Asylum *03* Edwin S. Porter
Scenes in an Orphans' Asylum *03* Edwin S. Porter
Scenes in the Zoo *21* Hy Mayer
Scenes of True Life *08* J. Stuart Blackton
Scenic Route, The *78* Mark Rappaport
Scent of a Woman *74* Dino Risi
Scent of Death *87* Ismael Rodríguez, Jr.
Scent of Incense, The *64* Keisuke Kinoshita
Scent of Mystery *60* Jack Cardiff
Scent of the Matterhorn, A *61* Chuck Jones
Scent of Violets, The *85* Maria Gavala
Scent Spray, The *05* Alf Collins
Scented Envelopes, The *23* A. E. Coleby
Scent-imental Over You *46* Chuck Jones
Scent-imental Romeo *51* Chuck Jones
Scentralizowana Kontrola Przebiegu Produkcji *51* Wojciech Has
Scents and Nonsense *26* William C. Nolan
Sceny Dziecięce z Życia Prowincji *86* Tomasz Żygaldo
Sceriffo di Rockspring, Lo *71* A. Green
Sceriffo Tutto d'Oro, Uno *66* Osvaldo Civirani
Schaatsenrijden *29* Joris Ivens
Schabernack *37* E. W. Emo
Schachnovelle *60* Gerd Oswald
Schakel met het Verleden *59* Bert Haanstra
Scharlachrote Buchstabe, Der *72* Wim Wenders
Scharlatan, Der *23* Michael Curtiz
Schaste *34* Alexander Medvedkin
Schatjes *84* Ruud van Hemert
Schatten, Der *18* E. A. Dupont
Schatten *22* Arthur Robison
Schatten der Unterwelt *31* Harry Piel
Schatten der Vergangenheit *17* Richard Oswald
Schatten der Vergangenheit *40* Werner Hochbaum
Schatten des Meeres, Der *12* Curt A. Stark
Schatten Über Tiran — Kommando Sinai *68* Raphael Nussbaum

Schatten Werden Länger, Die *61* Ladislas Vajda

Schatz, Der *23* G. W. Pabst

Schatz der Azteken, Der *64* Robert Siodmak

Schatz im Silbersee, Der *62* Harald Reinl

Schaukel, Die *83* Percy Adlon

Schauplätze *67* Wim Wenders

Schauspielerin, Die *88* Siegfried Kühn

Schedroye Lito *51* Boris Barnet

Scheherazade *63* Jacques Bourdon, Pierre Gaspard-Huit

Scheide des Todes, Die *21* Lothar Mendes

Scheidungsgrund: Liebe *60* Cyril Frankel

Scheintote Chinese, Der *28* Lotte Reiniger

Scheiterhaufen, Der *45* Günther Rittau

Schéma d'une Identification *46* Alain Resnais

Schemer, The *47* Derwin Abrahams

Schemer, The *56* Gilles Grangier

Schemers, The *14* Frank Wilson

Schemers, or The Jewels of Hate, The *14* Frank Wilson

Scheming Gamblers' Paradise, The *05* Georges Méliès

Scherben *21* Lupu Pick

Scherzo *39* Norman McLaren

Scherzo del Destino in Agguato Dietro l'Angolo Come un Brigante *83* Lina Wertmuller

Scherzo del Destino in Agguato Dietro l'Angolo Come un Brigante di Strada *83* Lina Wertmuller

Schetika me ton Vassili *86* Stavros Tsiolis

Scheusal, Das *59* Zoltán Fábri

Schiava di Bagdad, La *63* Jacques Bourdon, Pierre Gaspard-Huit

Schiave Bianche, Violenza in Amazzonia *86* Mario Gariazzo

Schiave Esistono Ancora, Le *63* Roberto Malenotti, Folco Quilici

Schiavi Più Forti del Mondo, Gli *65* Michele Lupo

Schicksal am Lenkard *53* Aldo Vergano

Schicksal aus Zweiter Hand *49* Wolfgang Staudte

Schicksal der Renate Langen, Das *33* Rudolf Walther-Fein

Schicksal einer Oper *58* Edgar Reitz

Schielende Glück, Das *59* Andrzej Munk

Schiff der Verlorene Menschen, Das *27* Maurice Tourneur

Schiff in Not *36* Walter Ruttmann

Schimanski—Zahn um Zahn *85* Hajo Gies

Schimbul de Mîine *59* Márta Mészáros

Schimmelkrieg von Holledau, Der *38* A. I. Littl

Schimmelreiter, Der *35* Hans Deppe, Kurt Örtel

Schinderhannes *27* Kurt Bernhardt

Schinderhannes, Der *58* Helmut Käutner

Schizo *67* Frank Warren

Schizo *76* Peter Walker

Schizoid *64* Freddie Francis

Schizoid *71* Lucio Fulci

Schizoid *80* David Paulsen

Schlacht von Bademunde, Die *31* Philipp L. Mayring

Schlaflöse Nächte *88* Marcel Gisler

Schlagende Wetter *23* Karl Grüne

Schlager-Parade *53* Eric Ode

Schlangenei, Das *77* Ingmar Bergman

Schlangengrube und das Pendel, Die *67* Harald Reinl

Schlaraffenland *86* Doris Dörrie

Schlemiel, Der *31* Max Nosseck

Schlemihl *15* Richard Oswald

Schleppzug M-17 *33* Heinrich George

Schleuse 17 *86* Sebastian Lentz

Schlock *71* John Landis

Schloss, Das *68* Rudolf Noelte

Schloss & Siegel *87* Heidi Ulmke

Schloss Hubertus *35* Hans Deppe

Schloss im Flandern, Das *37* Géza von Bolváry

Schloss im Süden, Das *33* Géza von Bolváry

Schloss in Tirol, Das *58* Géza von Radványi

Schloss Königswald *88* Peter Schamoni

Schloss & Siegel *87* Heidi Ulmke

Schloss Vogelöd *21* F. W. Murnau

Schloss Vogelöd *36* Max Obal

Schlosser und Katen *57* Kurt Mätzig

Schlossherr von Hohenstein, Der *17* Richard Oswald

Schlussakkord *36* Douglas Sirk

Schmuck des Rajah, Der *18* Urban Gad

Schmutz *86* Paulus Manker

Schneemann, Der *85* Peter F. Bringmann

Schneeweisschen und Rosenrot *55* Erich Kobler

Schneewittchen und die Sieben Zwerge *56* Erich Kobler

Schneider von Ulm, Der *78* Edgar Reitz

Schneider's Anti-Noise Crusade *09* D. W. Griffith

Schnook, The *62* Charles Barton

Schodami w Górę, Schodami w Dół *88* Andrzej Domalik

Schön Ist die Manöverzeit *32* Erich Schönfelder

Schön Ist Es Verliebt zu Sein *36* Walter Janssen

Schön War die Zeit *89* Klaus Gietinger, Leo Hiemer

Schöne Abenteuer, Das *32* Reinhold Schünzel

Schöne Sünderin, Die *15* Richard Oswald

Schöner Gigolo—Armer Gigolo *78* David Hemmings

Schönste Geschenk, Das *16* Ernst Lubitsch

School *58* Walerian Borowczyk

School at Rincón Santo *63* James Blue

School Days *20* Norman Taurog*

School Days *21* Harry D. Leonard

School Days *21* William Nigh

School Days *32* Dave Fleischer

School Days *32* Ubbe Iwerks

School Daze *27* Manny Gould, Ben Harrison

School Daze *87* Spike Lee

School for Brides *51* John Guillermin

School for Danger *47* Edward Baird

School for Deafmutes *67* Patricio Guzmán

School for Girls *35* William Nigh

School for Husbands, A *17* George Melford

School for Husbands *37* Andrew Marton

School for Love *54* Marc Allégret

School for Postmen, The *47* Jacques Tati

School for Randle *49* John E. Blakeley

School for Scandal, The *14* Kenean Buel

School for Scandal, The *23* Edwin Greenwood

School for Scandal, The *23* Bertram Phillips

School for Scandal, The *30* Maurice Elvey

School for Scandal *52* Abram Room

School for Scoundrels *59* Robert Hamer

School for Scoundrels, or How to Win Without Actually Cheating *59* Robert Hamer

School for Secrets *46* Peter Ustinov

School for Sex *66* Ryo Kinoshita

School for Sex *68* Peter Walker

School for Sons-in-Law, The *1897* Georges Méliès

School for Spies *66* Yasuzo Masumura

School for Stars *35* Donovan Pedelty

School for Thieves *86* Neri Parenti

School for Thieves II *87* Neri Parenti

School for Unclaimed Girls *68* Robert Hartford-Davis

School for Vandals *86* Colin Finbow

School for Violence *58* Edward Bernds

School for Wives *25* Victor Halperin

School Ma'am of Snake, The *11* Allan Dwan

School of Courage *57* Vladimir Basov

School of Echoes *52* Tadashi Imai

School of Freedom, The *51* Kozaburo Yoshimura

School of Love *66* Ryo Kinoshita

School Pals *23* Lewis Seiler, Ben Stoloff

School Spirit *85* Allan Holleb

School Teacher and the Waif, The *11* D. W. Griffith

School That Ate My Brain, The *87* Ron Link

School—The Basis of Life *38* Martin Frič

School—The Beginning of Life *38* Martin Frič

School—Where Life Begins *38* Martin Frič

Schoolboy Dreams *40* Art Davis, Sid Marcus

Schoolboy Penitentiary *36* Charles Lamont

Schoolboys' Pranks *07* Tom Green

Schoolboys' Revolt, The *08* Lewin Fitzhamon

Schooldays *62* André Delvaux

Schoolgirl Diary *47* Mario Mattòli

Schoolgirl Rebels *15* Frank Wilson

Schoolhouse Scandal, A *18* Edward F. Cline

Schoolmarm's Ride for Life, A *10* Edwin S. Porter

Schoolmaster, The *35* Lewis D. Collins

Schooner Gang, The *37* W. Devenport Hackney

Schooner the Better, The *46* Howard Swift

Schot Is te Board, Het *52* Herman van den Horst

Schpountz, Le *38* Marcel Pagnol

Schrecken *20* F. W. Murnau

Schrecken der Garnison, Der *31* Carl Boese

Schrecken vom Heidekrug, Der *34* Carl Boese

Schrei der Schwarzen Wölfe, Der *72* Harald Reinl

Scrappy's Theme Song 34 Art Davis, Sid Marcus

Scrappy's Toy Shop 34 Art Davis, Sid Marcus

Scrappy's Trailer 35 Art Davis, Sid Marcus

Scrappy's Trip to Mars 38 Art Davis, Sid Marcus

Scratch As Catch Can 31 Mark Sandrich

Scratch As Scratch Can 09 Dave Aylott

Scratch Harry 69 Alex Matter

Scratch My Back 20 Sidney Olcott

Scream 73 Lee Madden

Scream 81 Byron Quisenberry

Scream and Die 73 José Ramón Larraz

Scream and Scream Again 69 Gordon Hessler

Scream, Baby, Scream 69 Joseph Adler

Scream, Blacula, Scream! 73 Robert Kelljan

Scream Bloody Murder 72 Robert J. Emery

Scream Bloody Murder 73 Marc B. Ray

Scream for Help 84 Michael Winner

Scream Free 69 Bill Brame

Scream from Silence, A 79 Anne Claire Poirier

Scream in the Dark, A 43 George Sherman

Scream in the Night, A 19 Leander De Cordova, Burton L. King

Scream in the Night 43 Fred Newmeyer

Scream of Fear 60 Seth Holt

Scream of the Butterfly 65 Ebar Lobato

Screamer 69 Gordon Hessler

Screamers 78 Sergio Martino, Dan T. Miller

Screaming Eagles 55 Charles Haas

Screaming Head, The 59 Victor Trivas

Screaming Mimi 58 Gerd Oswald

Screaming Shadow, The 20 Duke Worne

Screaming Skull, The 58 Alex Nicol

Screaming Starts, The 73 Roy Ward Baker

Screamplay 86 Rufus Butler Seder

Screams from the Second Floor 31 Mikio Naruse

Screams of a Winter Night 79 James L. Wilson

Screamtime 83 Al Beresford

Screen — Entrance Exit 74 Malcolm Le Grice

Screen Follies No. 1 20 F. A. Dahme, Luis Seel

Screen Follies No. 2 20 F. A. Dahme, Luis Seel

Screen of Death, The 60 Atıf Yılmaz

Screen Struck 16 Will P. Kellino

Screen Struck 37 Lawrence Huntington

Screen Test 83 Sam Auster

Screen Test #1 65 Andy Warhol

Screen Test #2 65 Andy Warhol

Screen Tests 77 Agnieszka Holland

Screw Loose 84 Leslie George

Screwball Football 39 Tex Avery

Screwball Hotel 88 Rafal Zielinski

Screwball Squirrel 44 Tex Avery

Screwballs 83 Rafal Zielinski

Screwdriver, The 41 Walter Lantz

Screwface 90 Dwight H. Little

Screwy Squirrel 44 Tex Avery

Screwy Truant, The 45 Tex Avery

Scroggins and the Fly Pest 11 Dave Aylott

Scroggins and the Waltz Dream 11 Dave Aylott

Scroggins Gets the Socialist Craze 11 Dave Aylott

Scroggins Goes In for Chemistry and Discovers a Marvellous Powder 11 A. E. Coleby

Scroggins Has His Fortune Told 11 A. E. Coleby

Scroggins Plays Golf 11 A. E. Coleby

Scroggins Puts Up for Blankshire 10 A. E. Coleby

Scroggins Takes the Census 11 Dave Aylott

Scroggins Visits a Palmist 11 A. E. Coleby

Scroggins Wins the Fiddle-Faddle Prize 11 A. E. Coleby

Scrooge 01 Walter R. Booth

Scrooge 13 Leedham Bantock

Scrooge 22 George Wynn

Scrooge 23 Edwin Greenwood

Scrooge 28 Hugh Croise

Scrooge 35 Henry Edwards

Scrooge 51 Brian Desmond Hurst

Scrooge 70 Ronald Neame

Scrooge, or Marley's Ghost 01 Walter R. Booth

Scrooged 88 Richard Donner

Scrub Me Mama with a Boogie Beat 41 Walter Lantz

Scrubbers 82 Mai Zetterling

Scruffy 38 Randall Faye

Scudda Hoo! Scudda Hay! 48 F. Hugh Herbert

Scullion's Joke on the Chef 00 Georges Méliès

Sculpteur Moderne 09 Segundo De Chomón

Sculptor's Dream, The 10 A. E. Coleby

Sculptor's Welsh Rabbit Dream, A 08 Edwin S. Porter

Scum 79 Alan Clarke

Scum of the Earth 63 Herschell Gordon Lewis

Scum of the Earth 76 S. F. Brownrigg

Scuola dei Timidi, La 42 Carlo Ludovico Bragaglia

Scuola d'Eroi 13 Enrico Guazzoni

Scuola di Ladri 86 Neri Parenti

Scuola di Ladri II 87 Neri Parenti

Scuola Elementare 54 Alberto Lattuada

Scusi, Facciamo l'Amore 68 Vittorio Caprioli

Scusi, Lei È Favorevole o Contrario? 66 Alberto Sordi

Scuttlers, The 20 J. Gordon Edwards

Sdelka 87 Mikhail Vedyshev

Se Abre el Abismo 45 Pierre Chénal

Se Ha Fugado un Preso 35 Benito Perojo

Se Incontri, Sartana Prega per la Tua Morte 68 Gianfranco Parolini

Se Infiel y No Mires con Quien 85 Fernando Trueba

Se Io Fossi Onesto 42 Carlo Ludovico Bragaglia

Se Ki, Se Be 18 Alexander Korda

Se lo Scopre Gargiulo 88 Elvio Porta

Se Permettete Parliamo di Donne 64 Ettore Scola

Se Permuta 85 Juan Carlos Tabio

Se Sufre Pero Se Goza 86 Julio Ruiz

Llaneza

Se Ti Incontrato T'Ammazzo 71 G. Crea

Se Vende un Palacio 43 Ladislas Vajda

Se Vuoi Vivere...Spara 68 Sergio Garrone

Sea, The 62 Giuseppe Patroni Griffi

Sea and Poison, The 87 Kei Kumai

Sea Around Us, The 51 Irwin Allen

Sea Bat, The 30 Wesley Ruggles

Sea Bathing 1896 Georges Méliès

Sea Beast, The 26 Millard Webb

Sea Breaking on the Rocks 1896 Georges Méliès

Sea Chase, The 55 John Farrow

Sea Children, The 73 David Andrews

Sea Devil 37 Pál Fejős

Sea Devils 31 Joseph Levering

Sea Devils 37 Ben Stoloff

Sea Devils 53 Raoul Walsh

Sea Dog, The 87 Maurizio Lucidi

Sea Eagle 15 Victor Sjöström

Sea Fever 27 Alberto Cavalcanti

Sea Fighting in Greece 1897 Georges Méliès

Sea Flower, The 18 Colin Campbell

Sea Fury 29 George Melford

Sea Fury 58 Cy Endfield

Sea Ghost, The 31 William Nigh

Sea God, The 30 George Abbott

Sea Gull, The 26 Charles Chaplin, Josef von Sternberg

Sea Gull, The 68 Sidney Lumet

Sea Gypsies, The 78 Stewart Raffill

Sea Hawk, The 24 Frank Lloyd

Sea Hawk, The 40 Michael Curtiz

Sea Hornet, The 51 Joseph Kane

Sea Horses 26 Allan Dwan

Sea Hound, The 47 Walter B. Eason, Mack V. Wright

Sea Killer 79 Frank C. Clark

Sea Legs 30 Victor Heerman

Sea Lion, The 21 Rowland V. Lee

Sea-Loving Son Sails Away, The 29 Tomu Uchida

Sea Master, The 17 Edward Sloman

Sea Nymphs, The 14 Roscoe Arbuckle

Sea Nymphs 63 Marion Gering

Sea of Fireworks 51 Keisuke Kinoshita

Sea of Grass, The 46 Elia Kazan

Sea of Lost Ships 53 Joseph Kane

Sea of Love 89 Harold Becker

Sea of Ravens, The 30 Jean Epstein

Sea of Sand 58 Guy Green

Sea Panther, The 18 Thomas Heffron

Sea Pirate, The 67 Sergio Bergonzelli, Roy Rowland

Sea Prowlers 28 John G. Adolfi

Sea Racketeers 37 Hamilton MacFadden

Sea Raiders 22 Edward H. Griffith

Sea Raiders 41 Ford Beebe, John Rawlins

Sea Rider, The 20 Edwin L. Hollywood

Sea Route, A 63 Revaz Chkeidze

Sea Scamps 26 Charles Lamont

Sea Serpent, The 84 Gregory Greens

Sea Shall Not Have Them, The 54 Lewis Gilbert

Sea Spoilers 36 Frank R. Strayer

Sea Sword 28 Manny Gould, Ben Harrison

Sea Tiger, The 27 John Francis Dillon

Sea Tiger 52 Frank McDonald

Sea Urchin, The 26 Graham Cutts

Sea Vulture *15* Victor Sjöström
Sea Waif, The *18* Frank Reicher
Sea Wall, The *47* Ray Nazarro
Sea Wall, The *57* René Clément
Sea Waves at Dover *1895* Birt Acres
Sea Wife *57* Bob McNaught
Sea Wolf, The *13* Hobart Bosworth
Sea Wolf, The *20* George Melford
Sea Wolf, The *25* Ralph Ince
Sea Wolf, The *30* Alfred Santell
Sea Wolf, The *41* Michael Curtiz
Sea Wolf, The *73* Wolfgang Staudte
Sea Wolves, The *80* Andrew V. McLaglen
Sea Women, The *25* Edwin Carewe
Sea Wyf and Biscuit *57* Bob McNaught
Seabo *78* Jimmy Huston
Seadogs of Good Queen Bess *22* Edwin Greenwood
Seafarers, The *52* Stanley Kubrick
Seafighters, The *63* Anthony Carras
Seagull, The *71* Yuli Karasik
Seagulls Over Sorrento *53* John Boulting, Roy Boulting
Seal, The *55* Dušan Makavejev
Seal Island *77* Ronald Spencer
Seal of Silence, The *13* Thomas Ince
Seal of Silence, The *18* Thomas R. Mills
Sealed Cargo *51* Alfred L. Werker
Sealed Envelope, The *19* Douglas Gerrard
Sealed Hearts *19* Ralph Ince
Sealed Lips *06* Alice Guy-Blaché
Sealed Lips *15* John Ince
Sealed Lips *25* Antonio Gaudio
Sealed Lips *27* Gustaf Molander
Sealed Lips *31* Kurt Neumann
Sealed Lips *33* George Archainbaud
Sealed Lips *41* George Waggner
Sealed Room, The *09* D. W. Griffith
Sealed Soil, The *78* Marva Nabili
Sealed Valley, The *15* Lawrence McGill
Sealed Verdict *48* Lewis Allen
Sealing Whacks *27* Manny Gould, Ben Harrison
Seamstress, The *36* Martin Frič
Séance de Prestidigitation *1896* Georges Méliès
Séance on a Wet Afternoon *63* Bryan Forbes
Search, The *47* Fred Zinnemann
Search, The *87* Juan Carlos De Sanzo
Search and Destroy *79* William Fruet
Search for Beauty, The *34* Erle C. Kenton
Search for Bridey Murphy, The *56* Noel Langley
Search for Danger *49* Jack Bernhard
Search for Oil, The *53* Bert Haanstra
Search for Paradise *57* Otto Lang
Search for the Evil One *67* Joseph Kane
Search for the Mother Lode *82* Joe Canutt, Charlton Heston
Search for the Mother Lode: The Last Great Treasure *82* Joe Canutt, Charlton Heston
Search for the Will, The *20* Charles Raymond
Search Into Darkness *61* Willard Van Dyke
Searchers, The *56* John Ford
Searchers of the Voodoo Mountain *87* Bobby A. Suarez

Searching Eye, The *63* Saul Bass
Searching the Hearts of Students *39* Martin Frič
Searching Wind, The *46* William Dieterle
Seas Beneath, The *31* John Ford
Sea's Shadow, The *12* Curt A. Stark
Seashell and the Clergyman, The *27* Germaine Dulac
Seashore Frolics *03* Edwin S. Porter
Seaside Comedy, A *11* Theo Bouwmeester
Seaside Episode, A *09* A. E. Coleby
Seaside Flirtation, A *06* Georges Méliès
Seaside Girl, A *07* Lewin Fitzhamon
Seaside Introduction, A *11* Lewin Fitzhamon
Seaside Lodgings *06* J. H. Martin
Seaside Swingers *64* James Hill
Seaside Views *06* Tom Green
Season for Love, The *60* Pierre Kast
Season of Dreams *87* Martin Rosen
Season of Fear *89* Doug Campbell
Season of Miracles *87* Georgy Ungwald-Khilkevich
Season of Monsters *87* Miklós Jancsó
Season of Our Return, The *87* Leonardo Kocking
Season of Passion *59* Leslie Norman
Season of the Witch *72* George Romero
Seasons *70* Ivan Ivanov-Vano
Season's Greetinks *33* Dave Fleischer
Seasons of Meiji *68* Heinosuke Gosho
Seasons of Our Love *66* Florestano Vancini
Seasons of the Meiji Period *68* Heinosuke Gosho
Seasons We Walked Together, The *62* Keisuke Kinoshita
Seated at His Right *67* Valerio Zurlini
Seated Figures *88* Michael Snow
Seats of the Mighty, The *14* T. Hayes Hunter
Seaweed Children, The *73* Henry Herbert
Sebastian *67* David Greene
Sebastian and the Sparrow *88* Scott Hicks
Sebastiane *76* Paul Humfress, Derek Jarman
Sebevrah *84* Vojtěch Jasný
Secangkir Kopi Pahit *86* Teguh Karya
Sécheresse *63* Nelson Pereira Dos Santos
Sécheresse à Simiri *73* Jean Rouch
Sechs Tage Krieg, Der *68* Raphael Nussbaum
Seclusion Near a Forest *76* Jiří Menzel
Second Awakening of Christa Klages, The *77* Volker Schlöndorff, Margarethe von Trotta
Second Best Bed *37* Tom Walls
Second Best Secret Agent in the Whole Wide World, The *65* Lindsay Shonteff
Second Breath *65* Jean-Pierre Melville
Second Bureau *35* Pierre Billon
Second Bureau *36* Joseph Losey
Second Chance *47* James Tinling
Second Chance *50* William Beaudine
Second Chance *53* Rudolph Maté
Second Chance *76* Claude Lelouch
Second Chances *32* Richard Thorpe
Second Choice *30* Howard Bretherton
Second Chorus *40* H. C. Potter
Second Coming, The *72* Willard Huyck
Second Coming of Suzanne, The *74*

Michael Barry
Second Declaration of Havana *65* Santiago Álvarez
Second Face, The *50* Jack Bernhard
Second Face, The *82* Dominik Graf
Second Fiddle *23* Frank Tuttle
Second Fiddle *39* Sidney Lanfield
Second Fiddle *57* Maurice Elvey
Second Fiddle to a Steel Guitar *65* Victor Duncan
Second Floor Mystery, The *30* Roy Del Ruth
Second Greatest Sex, The *55* George Marshall
Second-Hand Hearts *78* Hal Ashby
Second Hand Kisses *31* Lewis R. Foster
Second Hand Love *23* William A. Wellman
Second-Hand Rose *22* Lloyd Ingraham
Second Hand Wife *33* Hamilton MacFadden
Second Honeymoon *30* Phil Rosen
Second Honeymoon *37* Walter Lang
Second House from the Left *78* Evans Isle
Second in Command, The *15* William J. Bowman
Second Lawyer *40* Martin Frič
Second Lieutenant, The *15* Dave Aylott
Second Life, A *48* Hideo Sekigawa
Second Mate, The *29* J. Steven Edwards
Second Mate, The *50* John Baxter
Second Mr. Bush, The *39* John Paddy Carstairs
Second Mrs. Roebuck, The *14* Christy Cabanne*
Second Mrs. Tanqueray, The *16* Fred Paul
Second Mrs. Tanqueray, The *52* Dallas Bower
Second Night, The *86* Nino Bizzarri
Second Penalty, The *14* F. Martin Thornton
Second Shift *40* Martin Frič
Second Shot, The *43* Martin Frič
Second Sight *38* S. W. Dormand
Second Sight *82* Dominik Graf
Second Sight *89* Joel Zwick
Second Souffle, Le *59* Yannick Bellon
Second Souffle, Un *78* Gérard Blain
Second Spring *75* Ulli Lommel
Second Stain, The *22* George Ridgwell
Second Story Murder, The *30* Roy Del Ruth
Second String, The *15* Frank Wilson
Second Thoughts *38* Albert Parker
Second Thoughts *82* Lawrence Turman
Second Time Around, The *61* Vincent Sherman
Second Time Lucky *84* Michael Anderson
Second to None *26* Jack Raymond
Second Tour *40* Martin Frič
Second Trial of Arthur London, The *69* Chris Marker
Second Victory, The *86* Gerald Thomas
Second Wife *30* Russell Mack
Second Wife *36* Edward Killy
Second Wife, The *67* Salah Abu Saif
Second Wind *65* Jean-Pierre Melville
Second Wind *76* Donald Shebib
Second Wind, A *78* Gérard Blain
Second Wind *86* Gerrard Verhage

Second Woman, The *50* James V. Kern
Second Youth *24* Albert Parker
Seconda B *34* Goffredo Alessandrini
Seconda Notte, La *86* Nino Bizzarri
Seconde Vérité, La *66* Christian-Jaque
Secondo Ponzio Pilato *88* Luigi Magni
Secondo Tragico Fantozzi, Il *76* Luciano Salce
Seconds *66* John Frankenheimer
Seconds Make a Hero *87* Om Ghil Sen, Eldor Urazbayev
Seconds to Live *77* Gordon Douglas
Secours aux Naufragés *04* Alice Guy-Blaché
Secret, The *18* Henry Edwards
Secret, The *55* Cy Endfield
Secret, Le *74* Robert Enrico
Secret, The *74* Robert Enrico
Secret, The *79* Ann Hui
Secret Admirer *85* David Greenwalt
Secret Agent *33* Arthur Woods
Secret Agent *36* Alfred Hitchcock
Secret Agent *47* Boris Barnet
Secret Agent, The *84* Jackie Ochs
Secret Agent Fireball *65* Mario Donen
Secret Agent of Japan *42* Irving Pichel
Secret Agent OO *67* Alberto De Martino
Secret Agent Super Dragon *66* Giorgio Ferroni
Secret Agent X-9 *37* Ford Beebe, Clifford Smith
Secret Agent X-9 *45* Lewis D. Collins, Ray Taylor
Secret Agents, The *65* Christian-Jaque, Werner Klingler, Carlo Lizzani, Terence Young
Secret Allies *39* Jiří Weiss
Secret Beyond the Door, The *48* Fritz Lang
Secret Beyond the Door, The *82* Liliana Cavani
Secret Bride, The *34* William Dieterle
Secret Brigade *51* Alexander Feinzimmer, Vladimir Korsh-Sablin
Secret Call, The *31* Stuart Walker
Secret Cave, The *53* John Durst
Secret Ceremony *68* Joseph Losey
Secret Cinema, The *67* Paul Bartel
Secret Code, The *18* Albert Parker
Secret Code, The *42* Spencer G. Bennet
Secret Command *44* A. Edward Sutherland
Secret Conclave, The *53* Umberto Scarpelli
Secret de Cargo, Le *29* Maurice Mariaud
Secret de D'Artagnan, Le *62* Siro Marcellini
Secret de Mayerling, Le *49* Jean Delannoy
Secret de Polichinelle, Le *23* René Hervil
Secret de Polichinelle, Le *36* André Berthomieu
Secret de Rosette Lambert, Le *20* Raymond Bernard
Secret de Sœur Angèle, Le *55* Léo Joannon
Secret de Woronzeff, Le *34* Arthur Robison
Secret des Hommes Bleus, Le *60* Edmon Agabra, Marco Ferreri
Secret d'Hélène Marimon, Le *54* Henri Calef

Secret Diary of Sigmund Freud, The *84* Danford B. Greene
Secret Document, Vienna *54* André Haguet
Secret Documents, The *28* Teinosuke Kinugasa
Secret Door, The *61* José Briz
Secret Dreams of Mona Q, The *77* Charles Kaufman
Secret du Chevalier d'Eon, Le *60* Jacqueline Audry
Secret du Forçat, Le *13* Louis Feuillade
Secret du Lone Star, Le *20* Jacques De Baroncelli
Secret du Médécin, Le *09* Georges Méliès
Secret Enemies *42* Ben Stoloff
Secret Enemy *40* Lew Landers
Secret Evidence *41* William Nigh
Secret File *55* Arthur Dreifuss
Secret File: Hollywood *62* Ralph Cushman
Secret File of Hollywood *62* Ralph Cushman
Secret Flight *46* Peter Ustinov
Secret Four, The *39* Walter Forde
Secret Four, The *52* Phil Karlson
Secret Fury, The *50* Mel Ferrer
Secret Game, The *17* William DeMille
Secret Game, The *51* René Clément
Secret Games *51* René Clément
Secret Garden, The *19* G. Butler Clonebaugh
Secret Garden, The *49* Fred M. Wilcox
Secret Garden, The *85* Carlos Suárez
Secret Gift, The *20* Harry Franklin
Secret Heart, The *46* Robert Z. Leonard
Secret Honor *84* Robert Altman
Secret Honor: A Political Myth *84* Robert Altman
Secret Honor: The Last Testament of Richard M. Nixon *84* Robert Altman
Secret Hour, The *28* Rowland V. Lee
Secret Ingredient *88* Slobodan Šijan
Secret Interlude *36* Roy Del Ruth
Secret Interlude *55* Philip Dunne
Secret Invasion, The *63* Roger Corman
Secret Journey *39* John Baxter
Secret Kingdom, The *17* Charles Brabin, Theodore Marston
Secret Kingdom, The *25* Sinclair Hill
Secret Life, A *14* Wilfred Noy
Secret Life of an American Wife, The *68* George Axelrod
Secret Life of Ian Fleming, The *90* Ferdinand Fairfax
Secret Life of Plants, The *78* Walon Green
Secret Life of Walter Mitty, The *47* Norman Z. McLeod
Secret Lives *37* Edmond T. Gréville
Secret Love *16* Robert Z. Leonard
Secret Love *87* Gottfried Junker
Secret Man, The *17* John Ford
Secret Man, The *58* Ronald Kinnoch
Secret Mark of D'Artagnan, The *62* Siro Marcellini
Secret Marriage, A *12* Victor Sjöström
Secret Meeting *58* Julien Duvivier
Secret Menace *31* Richard Kahn
Secret Mission *23* Thomas Bentley
Secret Mission *42* Harold French

Secret Mission *49* Mikhail Romm
Secret Motive *42* George Sherman
Secret of a Wife *24* Teinosuke Kinugasa
Secret of Abby X, The *27* William Dieterle
Secret of Black Canyon, The *25* Ward Hayes
Secret of Black Mountain, The *17* Otto Hoffman
Secret of Blood, The *53* Martin Frič
Secret of Blood Island, The *64* Quentin Lawrence
Secret of Convict Lake, The *51* Michael Gordon
Secret of Deep Harbor *61* Edward L. Cahn
Secret of Dr. Alucard, The *67* Herschell Gordon Lewis
Secret of Dr. Hichcock, The *62* Riccardo Freda
Secret of Dr. Kildare, The *39* Harold S. Bucquet
Secret of Dr. Mabuse, The *60* Fritz Lang
Secret of Dr. Orloff, The *64* Jesús Franco
Secret of Dorian Gray, The *70* Massimo Dallamano
Secret of Eve, The *17* Perry N. Vekroff
Secret of Linda Hamilton *46* Lew Landers
Secret of Madame Blanche, The *33* Charles Brabin
Secret of Magic Island, The *64* Jean Tourane
Secret of Mayerling, The *49* Jean Delannoy
Secret of Monte Cristo, The *60* Robert S. Baker, Monty Berman
Secret of My Success, The *65* Andrew L. Stone
Secret of My Success, The *87* Herbert Ross
Secret of Navajo Cave *76* James T. Flocker
Secret of Nikola Tesla, The *80* Krsto Papić
Secret of NIMH, The *82* Don Bluth
Secret of Outer Space Island *64* Jean Tourane
Secret of Outlaw Flats *53* Frank McDonald
Secret of Professor Insarov's Portrait, The *13* Yevgeni Bauer
Secret of St. Ives, The *49* Phil Rosen
Secret of St. Job Forest, The *17* Michael Curtiz
Secret of Santa Vittoria, The *69* Stanley Kramer
Secret of Seagull Island, The *81* Nestore Ungaro
Secret of Stamboul, The *36* Andrew Marton
Secret of the Air, The *13* Herbert Brenon
Secret of the America Dock, The *17* E. A. Dupont
Secret of the Black Trunk, The *62* Werner Klingler
Secret of the Black Widow, The *63* Franz-Josef Gottlieb
Secret of the Blue Room, The *33* Kurt Neumann
Secret of the Château *34* Richard Thorpe
Secret of the Chinese Carnation, The *65* Rudolf Zehetgruber
Secret of the Forest, The *55* D'Arcy Conyers
Secret of the Hills, The *21* Chester Bennett

Secret of the Incas, The *54* Jerry Hopper
Secret of the Loch, The *34* Milton Rosmer
Secret of the Monastery, The *19* Victor Sjöström
Secret of the Moor, The *19* Lewis Willoughby
Secret of the Pueblo, The *23* Neal Hart
Secret of the Purple Reef, The *60* William Witney
Secret of the Red Orchid, The *62* Helmuth Ashley
Secret of the Sacred Forest, The *70* Michael Du Pont
Secret of the Safe, The *21* Fred Paul
Secret of the Sahara *53* E. A. Dupont
Secret of the Sphinx *64* Duccio Tessari
Secret of the Sphynx, The *15* Robert Dinesen
Secret of the Storm Country, The *17* Charles Miller
Secret of the Swamp *16* Lynn Reynolds
Secret of the Sword, The *85* Ed Friedman, Lou Kachivas, Marsh Lamore, Bill Reed, Gwen Wetzler
Secret of the Telegian, The *60* Jun Fukuda
Secret of the Three Sword Points, The *52* Carlo Ludovico Bragaglia
Secret of the Whistler, The *46* George Sherman
Secret of Treasure Island, The *38* Elmer Clifton
Secret of Treasure Mountain, The *56* Seymour Friedman
Secret of Wings, The *44* Humberto Mauro
Secret Orchard, The *15* Frank Reicher
Secret Orders *26* Chester Withey
Secret Paris *63* Claude Lelouch
Secret Partner, The *60* Basil Dearden
Secret Passion, The *62* John Huston
Secret Passions of Salvador Dali, The *61* Jonas Mekas
Secret Patrol *36* David Selman
Secret People *52* Thorold Dickinson
Secret Place, The *56* Clive Donner
Secret Places *84* Zelda Barron
Secret Policeman's Ball, The *80* John Cleese, Roger Graef
Secret Policeman's Other Ball, The *81* Roger Graef, Julien Temple
Secret Rendezvous, A *59* Ko Nakahira
Secret Rites *72* Derek Ford
Secret Room, The *15* Tom Moore
Secret Scandal *89* Monica Vitti
Secret Scrolls (Part One) *57* Hiroshi Inagaki
Secret Scrolls (Part Two) *58* Hiroshi Inagaki
Secret Servants *17* William Beaudine
Secret Service *13* Charles C. Calvert
Secret Service *19* Hugh Ford
Secret Service *31* J. Walter Ruben
Secret Service in Darkest Africa *43* Spencer G. Bennet
Secret Service Investigator *48* R. G. Springsteen
Secret Service of the Air *39* Noel Mason Smith
Secret Seven, The *13* Charles C. Calvert
Secret Seven, The *40* James Moore

Secret Seven, The *66* Alberto De Martino
Secret Sin, The *15* Frank Reicher
Secret Sinners *33* Wesley Ford
Secret Six, The *31* George W. Hill
Secret Stranger, The *35* Elmer Clifton
Secret Strings *18* John Ince
Secret Studio, The *27* Victor Schertzinger
Secret Tent, The *56* Don Chaffey
Secret Treaty, The *12* August Blom
Secret Tunnel, The *47* William C. Hammond
Secret Valley *37* Howard Bretherton
Secret Venture *55* R. G. Springsteen
Secret Voice, The *36* George Pearson
Secret Walk *87* Valery Mikhailovsky
Secret War, The *65* Christian-Jaque, Werner Klingler, Carlo Lizzani, Terence Young
Secret War of Harry Frigg, The *67* Jack Smight
Secret Ways, The *61* Phil Karlson, Richard Widmark
Secret Weapon, The *42* Roy William Neill
Secret Wife, The *86* Sebastien Grall
Secret Witness, The *31* Thornton Freeland
Secret Witness *42* Joseph H. Lewis
Secret Woman, The *18* A. E. Coleby
Secret World *69* Paul Feyder, Robert Freeman
Secret Yearnings *79* Marvin Chomsky
Secretary of Frivolous Affairs, The *15* Thomas Ricketts
Secretary of the District Committee *42* Ivan Pyriev
Secretary's Crime, The *09* A. E. Coleby
Secreto de los Hombres Azules, El *60* Edmon Agabra, Marco Ferreri
Secreto del Dr. Orloff, El *64* Jesús Franco
Secrets *24* Frank Borzage
Secrets *33* Frank Borzage, Marshall Neilan
Secrets *41* Edward Dmytryk
Secrets *43* Pierre Blanchar
Secrets *68* Wolfgang Staudte
Secrets *71* Philip Saville
Secrets *83* Gavin Millar
Secrets d'Alcôve *53* Henri Decoin, Jean Delannoy, Gianni Franciolini, Ralph Habib
Secrets de la Prestidigitation Dévoilés, Les *04* Alice Guy-Blaché
Secrets of a Co-Ed *42* Joseph H. Lewis
Secrets of a Door-to-Door Salesman *73* Wolf Rilla
Secrets of a Model *40* Sam Newfield
Secrets of a Nurse *38* Arthur Lubin
Secrets of a Secretary *31* George Abbott
Secrets of a Sorority Girl *46* Lew Landers
Secrets of a Soul *25* G. W. Pabst
Secrets of a Soul *50* Kurt Hoffmann
Secrets of a Soul *62* Albert Zugsmith
Secrets of a Superstud *76* Morton M. Lewis
Secrets of a Windmill Girl *66* Arnold Louis Miller
Secrets of a Woman's Temple *69* Tokuzo Tanaka
Secrets of an Actress *38* William Keighley
Secrets of Chinatown *35* Fred Newmeyer
Secrets of F.P. 1 *32* Karl Hartl
Secrets of G32 *42* Robert Siodmak

Secrets of Hollywood *33* George Merrick, Holbrook Todd
Secrets of Life *56* James Algar
Secrets of Monte Carlo *51* George Blair
Secrets of Paris, The *22* Kenneth Webb
Secrets of Scotland Yard *44* George Blair
Secrets of Sex *70* Antony Balch
Secrets of Sin *39* Herbert Brenon
Secrets of the City *55* Fritz Kortner
Secrets of the Confession *06* Ricardo De Baños
Secrets of the French Police *32* A. Edward Sutherland
Secrets of the Gods *76* William Sachs
Secrets of the Lone Wolf *41* Edward Dmytryk
Secrets of the Marie Celeste *35* Denison Clift
Secrets of the Nazi Criminals *62* Tore Sjöberg
Secrets of the Night *25* Herbert Blaché
Secrets of the Orient *32* Alexander Volkov
Secrets of the Range *28* Robert J. Horner
Secrets of the Reef *56* Murray Lerner, Lloyd Ritter, Robert M. Young
Secrets of the Underground *43* William Morgan
Secrets of the Wasteland *41* Derwin Abrahams
Secrets of Women *52* Ingmar Bergman
Secrets of Wu Sin, The *32* Richard Thorpe
Secrets Secrets *85* Giuseppe Bertolucci
Secta Siniestra *82* Steve McCoy
Section Anderson *66* Pierre Schöndörffer
Section des Disparus *56* Pierre Chénal
Section Spéciale *75* Costa-Gavras
Sector 13 *82* Robert Stone Jordan
Secuestrador, El *58* Leopoldo Torre-Nilsson
Secuestro de Camarena, El *86* Alfredo B. Crevenna
Secuestro de Lola—Lola la Trailera II, El *86* Raúl Fernández
Securing Evidence *11* Edwin S. Porter
Security Risk *54* Harold Schuster
Secvenţe *86* Alexandru Tatos
Seddok—L'Erede di Satana *60* Richard McNamara, Anton Giulio Majano
Seddok—Son of Satan *60* Richard McNamara, Anton Giulio Majano
Sedm Hladových *88* Karel Smyczek
Sedme Nebe *88* Otakar Kosek
Sedmi Kontinent *66* Joseph Medved, Dušan Vukotić
Sedmiklassniki *38* G. Levkoyer, Yakov Protazanov
Sedmikrásky *66* Věra Chytilová
Sedmoi Sputnik *68* Grigori Aronov, Alexei Gherman
Sedmý Den, Osmá Noc *69* Evald Schorm
Sedotta e Abbandonata *63* Pietro Germi
Sedovchy *40* Roman Karmen
Sedovites, The *40* Roman Karmen
Sedov's Expedition *40* Roman Karmen
Seducción, La *83* Arturo Ripstein
Seduce and Destroy *73* Ted V. Mikels
Seduced and Abandoned *63* Pietro Germi
Seducer, The *57* Pietro Germi
Seducers, The *62* Graeme Ferguson
Seducers, The *74* Peter S. Traynor

Seduction *29* Gustav Machatý
Seduction *48* Kozaburo Yoshimura
Seduction, The *81* David Schmoeller
Seduction by the Sea *63* Jovan Živanović
Seduction in the South *61* Mario Camerini
Seduction of Joe Tynan, The *79* Jerry Schatzberg
Seduction of Julia, The *62* Alfred Weidenmann
Seduction of Mimi, The *72* Lina Wertmuller
Seduction: The Cruel Woman *85* Elfi Mikesch, Monika Treut
Seductress, The *74* Hikmet Avedis
Séduite et Abandonnée *63* Pietro Germi
Seduta Spiritica *49* Dino Risi
Seduto alla Sua Destra *67* Valerio Zurlini
Seduttore, Il *54* Franco Rossi
Seduzidas pelo Demônio *75* Raffaele Rossi
See America Thirst *30* William James Craft
See Here My Love *78* Hugo Santiago
See Here, Private Hargrove *43* Tay Garnett, Wesley Ruggles
See How They Run *55* Leslie Arliss
See How They Run *64* David Lowell Rich
See My Lawyer *21* Al Christie
See My Lawyer *45* Edward F. Cline
See Naples and Die *51* Riccardo Freda
See No Evil *71* Richard Fleischer
See No Evil, Hear No Evil *89* Arthur Hiller
See Saw Seems *67* Stan Vanderbeek
See You After School *86* Carlos Palau
See You at Mao *68* Jean-Luc Godard, Jean-Pierre Gorin
See You in Hell Darling *66* Robert Gist
See You in Jail *27* Joseph E. Henabery
See You in the Morning *89* Alan J. Pakula
See You Later Gladiator *68* Alex Lovy
See You Tomorrow *60* Janusz Morgenstern
See You Tonight *34* William Beaudine
Seed *31* John M. Stahl
Seed of Innocence *80* Boaz Davidson
Seed of Man, The *69* Marco Ferreri
Seed of Terror *72* John Hayes
Seedling, The *74* Shyam Benegal
Seeds of Destruction *52* Frank R. Strayer
Seeds of Evil *72* James H. Kay III
Seeds of Freedom *27* Grigori Roshal
Seeds of Freedom *43* Hans Burger
Seeds of Vengeance *20* Oliver L. Sellers
Seefahrt Die Ist Lustig, Eine *38* Alwin Elling
Seein' Things *09* Georges Méliès
Seeing Ceylon *17* Hy Mayer
Seeing Ceylon with Hy Mayer *17* Hy Mayer
Seeing Double *20* James Reardon
Seeing Greenwich Village *21* Julian Ollendorff
Seeing Is Believing *34* Redd Davis
Seeing It Through *20* Claude H. Mitchell
Seeing It Through *34* Fred Newmeyer
Seeing London in One Day *10* Walter R. Booth
Seeing Nellie Home *24* Leo McCarey
Seeing New York *17* Hy Mayer
Seeing New York with Hy Mayer *17* Hy Mayer

Seeing Red—Stories of American Communists *83* James Klein, Julia Reichert
Seeing Stars *27* Stephen Roberts
Seeing Stars *32* Manny Gould, Ben Harrison
Seeing Stars *38* Roy Boulting
Seeing Things *19* Raoul Barré, Charles Bowers
Seeing Things *19* Alfred Santell
Seeing's Believing *22* Harry Beaumont
Seek and Thou Shalt Find *07* Georges Méliès
Seekers, The *16* Otis Turner
Seekers, The *54* Ken Annakin
Seelenverkäufer, Der *19* Lupu Pick
Seelische Konstruktionen *27* Oskar Fischinger
Seemabaddha *71* Satyajit Ray
Seems Like Old Times *80* Jay Sandrich
Seen at the Chiropodist's *07* Arthur Cooper
Seer of Bond Street, The *13* Charles Raymond
Seer Was Here *78* Claude Jutra
Seeschlacht, Die *17* Richard Oswald
Seeta *33* Debaki Kumar Bose
Segel im Sturm *53* Mikhail Romm
Segítség Örököltem *37* Steve Sekely
Segno del Coyote, Il *63* Mario Caiano
Segno di Venere, Il *55* Dino Risi
Segno di Zorro, Il *51* Mario Soldati
Segno di Zorro, Il *62* Mario Caiano
Segno di Zorro, Il *75* Mariano Laurenti
Segodnya *24* Dziga Vertov
Segodnya *30* Esther Shub
Segodnya Otpuska Nye Budyet *59* Andrei Tarkovsky
Segredo da Múmia, O *82* Ivan Cardozo
Segredo das Asas, O *44* Humberto Mauro
Segretaria Privata, La *31* Goffredo Alessandrini
Segreti Che Scottano *67* Christian-Jaque
Segreti Segreti *85* Giuseppe Bertolucci
Segreto del Castello di Monroe, Il *14* Augusto Genina
Segreto del Sahara, Il *88* Alberto Negrin
Segreto della Grotta Azzurra, Il *22* Carmine Gallone
Segreto delle Tre Punte, Il *52* Carlo Ludovico Bragaglia
Segua, La *85* Antonio Iglesias
Segunda Declaración de la Habana *65* Santiago Álvarez
Sehnsucht *20* F. W. Murnau
Sehnsucht der Veronika Voss, Die *81* Rainer Werner Fassbinder
Sei Donne per l'Assassino *64* Mario Bava
Sei Già Cadavere Amigo...Ti Cera Garringo *71* Ignacio F. Iquino
Sei Iellato Amico...Hai Incontrato Sacramento *72* Giorgio Cristallini
Sei Moglie di Barbablù, Le *50* Carlo Ludovico Bragaglia
Sei no Kigen *67* Kaneto Shindo
Sei per Otto, Quarantotto *45* Riccardo Freda
Sei Sei Vivo, Spara! *67* Giulio Questi
Sei Tu l'Amore *30* Alfredo Sabato
Sei una Carogna...e T'Ammazzo *72*

M. Esteba
Seifenblasen *29* Slatan Dudow
Seigneurs de la Forêt, Les *58* Henry Brandt, Heinz Seilmann, Henri Storck
Seikatsu to Mizu *52* Susumu Hani*
Seimei no Kanmuri *36* Tomu Uchida
Sein Bester Freund *18* Joe May
Sein Bester Freund *38* Harry Piel
Sein Bester Freund *62* Luis Trenker
Sein Einziger Patient *15* Ernst Lubitsch
Sein Grösster Bluff *27* Henryk Galeen, Harry Piel
Sein Liebeslied *31* Géza von Bolváry
Sein Scheidungsgrund *32* Alfred Zeisler
Sein Schwierigster Fall *15* Joe May
Seine à Rencontre Paris, La *57* Joris Ivens
Seine Frau die Unbekannte *23* Benjamin Christensen
Seine Letzte Maske *16* Richard Oswald
Seine Majestät das Bettelkind *20* Alexander Korda
Seine Meets Paris, The *57* Joris Ivens
Seine Neue Nase *16* Ernst Lubitsch
Seine Tochter Ist der Peter *38* Heinz Helbig
Seine Tochter Ist der Peter *55* Gustav Fröhlich
Seins de Glace, Les *74* Georges Lautner
Seisaku's Wife *24* Minoru Murata
Seishun *25* Heinosuke Gosho
Seishun *68* Kon Ichikawa
Seishun Kaidan *55* Kon Ichikawa
Seishun Monogatari *60* Nagisa Oshima
Seishun no Yume Ima Izuko *32* Yasujiro Ozu
Seishun no Yumeji *22* Kenji Mizoguchi
Seishun Zankoku Monogatari *60* Nagisa Oshima
Seishun Zenigata Heiji *53* Kon Ichikawa
Seitensprünge *30* Steve Sekely
Seize the Day *86* Fielder Cook
Seizure *73* Oliver Stone
Sekai Daisensō *62* Shue Matsubayashi
Sekishun-Chō *59* Keisuke Kinoshita
Sekretär der Königin, Der *16* Robert Wiene
Sekretar Raikon *42* Ivan Pyriev
Sekretnaya Missiya *49* Mikhail Romm
6-Dagesløbet *58* Jørgen Roos
Seks-Dagesløbet *58* Jørgen Roos
Seksmisja *84* Juliusz Machulski
Sekunda na Podvig *87* Om Ghil Sen, Eldor Urazbayev
Sel de la Terre, Le *50* Georges Rouquier
Selbstmörderklub, Der *20* Richard Oswald
Self-Accused *14* Charles H. Weston
Self Defence *13* Charles Raymond
Self Defense *32* Phil Rosen
Self Defense *40* A. Giacalone
Self-Defense *83* Paul Donovan, Maura O'Connell
Self-Made Failure, A *24* William Beaudine
Self-Made Lady *32* George King
Self Made Man, A *22* Rowland V. Lee
Self Made Widow *17* Travers Vale
Self-Made Wife, The *23* John Francis Dillon
Self-Portrait *73* Maurice McEndree, James Mobley

Self Starter, The *26* Harry Joe Brown
Selfish Woman, The *16* E. Mason Hopper
Selfish Yates *18* William S. Hart
Selige Exzellenz, Die *27* Wilhelm Thiele
Selige Exzellenz, Die *37* Hans Zerlett
Selina *89* Carlo Lizzani
Selina of the Weeklies *15* Dave Aylott
Selina-ella *15* Dave Aylott
Selina's Flight for Freedom *14* Edwin J. Collins
Selinunte *51* Fernando Birri
Sell 'Em Cowboy *24* Ward Hayes
Sella d'Argento *78* Lucio Fulci
Sellers of Girls *57* Maurice Cloche
Selling of America, The *85* Patrick Kelly
Sellout, The *51* Gerald Mayer
Sellout, The *75* Peter Collinson
Selskaya Uchitelnitsa *46* Mark Donskoi
Selski Vrach *51* Sergei Gerasimov
Seltsame Geschichte des Barons Torelli, Die *18* Richard Oswald
Seltsame Geschichte des Brandner Kaspar, Die *49* Josef von Baky
Seltsame Gräfin, Die *61* Josef von Baky
Seltsame Nacht, Die *26* Forest Holger-Madsen
Seltsame Nacht der Helga Wansen, Die *28* Forest Holger-Madsen
Seltsamen Abenteuer des Herrn Fridolin B, Die *48* Wolfgang Staudte
Seltsamer Fall, Ein *14* Max Mack
Seltsamer Gast, Ein *36* Gerhard Lamprecht
Selva de Fuego, La *45* Fernando De Fuentes
Selvaggia Geometra Prinetti del Vaggiamenteosvaldo, La *78* Ferdinando Baldi
Semaine de Vacances, Une *80* Bertrand Tavernier
Semana de Felicidad, Una *34* Max Nosseck
Semana del Asesino, La *72* Eloy De la Iglesia
Sembazuru *69* Yasuzo Masumura
Sembra Morto...Ma È Solo Svenuto *86* Felice Farina
Seme dell'Uomo, Il *69* Marco Ferreri
Semero Smelykh *36* Sergei Gerasimov
Semi-Tough *77* Michael Ritchie
Seminary Scandal *16* Al Christie
Semino Morte...lo Chiamavano Castigo di Dio *72* Roberto Mauri
Seminole *53* Budd Boetticher
Seminole Halfbreed, The *10* Sidney Olcott
Seminole Uprising *55* Earl Bellamy
Seminole's Vengeance, The *11* Sidney Olcott
Semiramis *55* Carlo Ludovico Bragaglia
Semmelweis *52* Frigyes Bán
Semmelweiss *38* André De Toth
Semya Openheim *38* Grigori Roshal
Semya Tarassa *45* Mark Donskoi
Sen Noci... *85* Vladimír Sís
Sen Noci Svatojánské *59* Howard Sackler, Jiří Trnka
Sen Türkülerini Söyle *86* Şerif Gören
Sen Yan's Devotion *24* A. E. Coleby
Senator, The *15* Joseph A. Golden
Senator, Der *44* Günther Rittau
Senator, The *79* Jerry Schatzberg

Senator Was Indiscreet, The *47* George S. Kaufman
Senbazuru *53* Kozaburo Yoshimura
Send a Gorilla *88* Melanie Read
Send 'Em Back Half Dead *33* Redd Davis
Send for Paul Temple *46* John Argyle
Send Home No. 7 *39* Gideon Wahlberg
Send Me No Flowers *64* Norman Jewison
Senda Ignorada *46* José Antonio Nieves Conde
Sender, The *82* Roger Christian
Sénéchal le Magnifique *57* Jean Boyer
Senechal the Magnificent *57* Jean Boyer
Sengoku Gunto-Den *64* Toshio Sugie
Sengoku Jietai *81* Kosei Saito
Sengoku Yaro *63* Kihachi Okamoto
Seni Kaybederesem *61* Atıf Yılmaz
Senilità *61* Mauro Bolognini
Senior Prom *58* David Lowell Rich
Senior Week *88* Stuart Goldman
Seniors, The *78* Rod Amateau
Senjō ni Nagareru Uta *66* Zenzo Matsuyama
Senjō no Merii Kurisumasu *82* Nagisa Oshima
Senka no Hate *50* Kozaburo Yoshimura
Senka the African *27* Ivan Ivanov-Vano
Senki Fia, A *17* Michael Curtiz
Señor Alcalde, El *39* Gilberto Martínez Solares
Señor Americano *29* Harry Joe Brown
Señor Daredevil *26* Albert S. Rogell
Señor de Osanto, El *72* Jaime Humberto Hermosillo
Señor Droopy *49* Tex Avery
Señor Jim *36* Jacques Jaccard
Señor Muy Viejo con Unas Alas Enormes, Un *88* Fernando Birri
Señora, La *87* Jordi Cadena
Señora Casada Necesita Marido *35* James Tinling
Señora de Nadie *82* María Luisa Bemberg
Señora Muerte, La *68* Jaime Salvador
Señorella and the Glass Hurache *64* Friz Freleng
Señorita *21* John Gliddon
Señorita *27* Clarence Badger
Señorita from the West *45* Frank R. Strayer
Señorita's Repentance, The *13* William Duncan
Senryo Jishin *58* Tomu Uchida
Sens de la Mort, Le *22* Yakov Protazanov
Sensacional y Extraño Caso del Hombre y la Bestia, El *51* Mario Soffici
Sensation *22* Pál Fejös
Sensation *36* Brian Desmond Hurst
Sensation Hunters *33* Charles Vidor
Sensation Hunters *45* Christy Cabanne
Sensation Seekers *27* Lois Weber
Sensations *44* Andrew L. Stone
Sensations *77* David Grant
Sensations *88* Chuck Vincent
Sensations of 1945 *44* Andrew L. Stone
Sense and Sensibility *86* Rodney Bennett
Sense of Freedom, A *85* John Mackenzie
Sense of Loss, A *72* Marcel Ophüls
Senseless *62* Ron Rice
Sensi *86* Gabriele Lavia
Sensitiva, La *70* Gianfranco Mingozzi

Senso *53* Luchino Visconti
Sensō to Heiwa *45* Fumio Kamei, Satsuo Yamamoto
Sensualita *52* Clemente Fracassi
Sensuous Nurse, The *76* Nelo Rossati
Sensuous Vampires *78* Cirio Santiago
Sentence, La *59* Jean Valère
Sentence Is Death, The *14* Dalton Somers
Sentence of Death, The *13* George Pearson
Sentence of Death, The *27* Miles Mander
Sentence Suspended *50* D. Ross Lederman
Sentenced for Life *60* Max Varnel
Sentenza di Morte *67* Mario Lanfranchi
Sentieri dell'Odio, I *64* Marino Girolami
Sentiment and Song *45* Ray Nazarro
Sentimental Journey, The *43* Peter Brook
Sentimental Journey *46* Walter Lang
Sentimental Journey *79* Michel Deville
Sentimental Lady, The *15* Sidney Olcott
Sentimental Tommy *15* Toby Cooper
Sentimental Tommy *21* John S. Robertson
Sentimental Trip to a Farm, A *87* Dmitri Dolinin
Sentimentalnoe Puteshestvie na Kartoshku *87* Dmitri Dolinin
Sentimientos: Mirta de Liniers a Estambul *87* Jorge Coscia, Guillermo Saura
Sentinel, The *76* Michael Winner
Sentinelle Endormie, La *66* Jean Dréville
Sentinels of Silence *72* Robert Amram
Sentivano...uno Strano, Eccitante, Pericoloso Puzzo di Dollari *73* Italo Alfaro
Sentry's Stratagem, The *1899* Georges Méliès
Senza Colpa *15* Carmine Gallone
Senza Famiglia Nullatenenti Cercano Affetto *72* Vittorio Gassman
Senza Famiglie *72* Vittorio Gassman
Senza Pietà *47* Alberto Lattuada
Senza Ragione *72* Silvio Narizzano
Senza Sapere Niente di Lei *69* Luigi Comencini
Senza Sapere Nulla di Lei *69* Luigi Comencini
Senza Scrupoli *86* Tonino Valerii
Senza Veli *52* Carmine Gallone
Separate Beds *63* Arthur Hiller
Separate Peace, A *72* Larry Peerce
Separate Rooms *84* Bertrand Blier
Separate Tables *58* Delbert Mann
Separate Vacations *86* Michael Anderson
Separate Ways *81* Hikmet Avedis
Separated at Home *86* Riccardo Pazzaglia
Separati in Casa *86* Riccardo Pazzaglia
Separation *68* Jack Bond
Séparation des Races, La *33* Dmitri Kirsanov
Sepia Cinderella *47* Arthur Leonard
Sepolcro dei Re, Il *60* Fernando Cerchio, Richard McNamara
Sepolta Viva, La *51* Guido Brignone
Seppan *87* Agneta Fagerström-Olsson
Seppuku *62* Masaki Kobayashi
Sept Barres d'Or, Les *10* Georges Méliès
Sept Châteaux du Diable, Les *01* Ferdinand Zecca
Sept Fois Femmes *67* Vittorio De Sica
Sept Hommes en Or *65* Marco Vicario
Sept Jours Ailleurs *67* Marin Karmitz

7 p., cuis., s. de b. *84* Agnès Varda

Sept Péchés Capitaux, Les *00* Georges Méliès

Sept Péchés Capitaux, Les *10* Louis Feuillade

Sept Péchés Capitaux, Les *51* Yves Allégret, Claude Autant-Lara, Carlo-Rim, Eduardo De Filippo, Jean Dréville, Georges Lacombe, Roberto Rossellini

Sept Péchés Capitaux, Les *61* Philippe de Broca, Claude Chabrol, Jacques Demy, Sylvaine Dhomme, Max Douy, Jean-Luc Godard, Eugene Ionesco, Édouard Molinaro, Roger Vadim

September *87* Woody Allen

September Affair *50* William Dieterle

September 56 *56* Jerzy Bossak*

September Heroes, The *52* Zahari Zhandov

September in the Rain *37* Friz Freleng

September Nights *57* Vojtěch Jasný

September Sixteenth *60* Roman Karmen

September Storm *60* Byron Haskin

September 30, 1955 *77* James Bridges

Septemberliebe *61* Kurt Mätzig

Septembrists *52* Zahari Zhandov

Septemvriisti *52* Zahari Zhandov

Septième Ciel, Le *58* Raymond Bernard

Septième Commandement, Le *57* Raymond Bernard

Septième Juré, Le *62* Georges Lautner

Séptima Página *50* Ladislas Vajda

Sequel to The Diamond from the Sky *16* Edward Sloman

Sequences *86* Alexandru Tatos

Sequestrati di Altona, I *62* Vittorio De Sica

Séquestrée, La *08* Émile Cohl

Sequestro di Persona *68* Gianfranco Mingozzi

Sequoia *34* Chester M. Franklin

Ser, El *82* Sebastián D'Arbo

Seraa fil Mina *55* Youssef Chahine

Seraa fil Wadi *52* Youssef Chahine

Serafino *68* Pietro Germi, Lee Kresel

Serafino ou L'Amour aux Champs *68* Pietro Germi, Lee Kresel

Seraglio, The *58* Lotte Reiniger

Serail *76* Eduardo De Gregorio

Séraphin ou Les Jambes Nues *21* Louis Feuillade

Seraphita's Diary *82* Frederick Wiseman

Serbia's Card *14* Émile Cohl

Serdtsi i Dollari *23* Anatole Litvak

Serdtse Betsya Vnov *56* Abram Room

Serdtse Materi *66* Mark Donskoi

Serdtse Solomona *32* Sergei Gerasimov, M. Kressin

Serdtze Materi *66* Mark Donskoi

Seré Cualquier Cosa Pero Te Quiero *86* Carlos Galettini

Serebristaya Pyl *53* Abram Room

Serebryanaya Pryazha Karoliny *87* Helle Murdmaa

Serena *62* Peter Maxwell

Serenade, The *04* Charles Raymond

Serenade *21* Raoul Walsh

Serenade *27* Harry D'Abbadie D'Arrast

Serenade *37* Willi Forst

Serenade *39* Robert Z. Leonard

Sérénade *40* Jean Boyer

Serenade *55* Anthony Mann

Sérénade au Texas *58* Richard Pottier

Sérénade aux Nuages *45* André Cayatte

Serenade einer Grossen Liebe *58* Rudolph Maté

Serenade for Two Spies *66* Michael Pfleghar

Serenade from "Faust" *06* Arthur Gilbert

Serenade für Zwei Spione *66* Michael Pfleghar

Serenade of the West *37* Joseph Kane

Serenade of the West *42* William Morgan

Serenaders, The *45* Jean Negulesco

Serenal *59* Norman McLaren

Serenata da un Soldo *52* Valerio Zurlini

Serenata Macabra *68* Jack Hill, Juan Ibáñez

Serene Velocity *70* Ernie Gehr

Serengeti *59* Bernhard Grzimek, Michael Grzimek

Serenity *61* Gregory Markopoulos

Sergantini il Pittore della Montagna *48* Dino Risi

Serge Ordjonikidze *37* Yakov Bliokh, Dziga Vertov

Serge Panin *22* Charles De Marsan, Charles Maudru

Sergeant, The *68* John Flynn

Sergeant Berry *38* Herbert Selpin

Sergeant Deadhead *65* Norman Taurog

Sergeant Deadhead the Astronaut *65* Norman Taurog

Sergeant Deadhead the Astronut *65* Norman Taurog

Sergeant Jim *56* France Štiglić

Sergeant Lightning and the Gorgonzola Gang *15* James Read

Sergeant Madden *39* Josef von Sternberg

Sergeant Mike *44* Henry Levin

Sergeant Murphy *37* B. Reeves Eason

Sgt. Pepper's Lonely Hearts Club Band *78* Michael Schultz

Sgt. Rahn *74* Ulli Lommel

Sergeant Rutledge *60* John Ford

Sergeant Ryker *63* Buzz Kulik

Sergeant Steiner *78* Andrew V. McLaglen

Sergeant Was a Lady, The *61* Bernard Glasser

Sergeant X of the Foreign Legion *60* Ludmilla Goulian

Sergeant York *41* Howard Hawks

Sergeant's Daughter, The *11* Wilfred Noy

Sergeants 3 *62* John Sturges

Sergei Kirov *35* Yakov Bliokh

Sergei Ordzhonikidze *37* Yakov Bliokh, Dziga Vertov

Sergo Kirov *35* Yakov Bliokh

Sergo Ordzhonikidzye *37* Yakov Bliokh, Dziga Vertov

Serial *80* Bill Persky

Serious Charge *59* Terence Young

Serious Sixteen *10* D. W. Griffith

Serment, Le *34* Abel Gance

Serments *31* Henri Fescourt

Serp i Molot *21* Vladimir Gardin, Vsevolod I. Pudovkin

Serpent, The *16* Raoul Walsh

Serpent, The *18* John M. Stahl

Serpent, The *66* Hans Abramson

Serpent, Le *72* Henri Verneuil

Serpent, The *72* Henri Verneuil

Serpent and the Rainbow, The *87* Wes Craven

Serpent de la Rue de la Lune, Le *08* Georges Méliès

Serpent God, The *70* Piero Vivarelli

Serpent Island *54* Bert I. Gordon

Serpent of the Nile *53* William Castle

Serpent Princess, The *38* Teinosuke Kinugasa

Serpente a Sonagli, Il *36* Raffaello Matarazzo

Serpentin à Engagé Bouboule *20* Alfred Machin

Serpentin au Harem *19* Jean Durand

Serpentine Dance, A *1896* Georges Méliès

Serpentine Dancer *02* Alf Collins

Serpent's Egg, The *77* Ingmar Bergman

Serpents of the Pirate Moon, The *73* Jean-Louis Jorge

Serpent's Tooth, The *08* Lewin Fitzhamon

Serpent's Tooth, The *17* Rollin Sturgeon

Serpent's Way, The *86* Bo Widerberg

Serpent's Way Up the Naked Rock, The *86* Bo Widerberg

Serpico *73* Sidney Lumet

Serpiente Roja, La *37* Ernesto Caparros

Sertanejo, O *54* Lima Barreto

Sérum du Docteur Hormet, Le *25* Jean Painlevé

Servant, The *27* Daisuke Ito

Servant, The *63* Joseph Losey

Servant in the House *20* Jack Conway

Servant Question, The *14* William Duncan

Servant Question, The *20* Del Henderson

Servants All *36* Alex Bryce

Servant's Dream, The *70* Santiago Álvarez

Servants' Entrance *34* Frank Lloyd

Servant's Neck, The *55* Daisuke Ito

Servants Superceded *11* Percy Stow

Servian Tragedy, The *03* Dicky Winslow

Service *33* Clarence Brown

Service de Luxe *38* Rowland V. Lee

Service de Sauvetage sur la Côte Belge, Le *30* Henri Storck

Service for Ladies *27* Harry D'Abbadie D'Arrast

Service for Ladies *31* Alexander Korda

Service Précipité *03* Alice Guy-Blaché

Service Star, The *18* Charles Miller

Service with a Smile *37* Dave Fleischer

Service with the Colors *40* B. Reeves Eason

Serving a Summons *07* A. E. Coleby

Serving the Writ *07* Lewin Fitzhamon

Seryozha *60* Georgy Danelia, Igor Talankin

Ses *86* Zeki Ökten

Ses Ancêtres *14* Émile Cohl

Sesame Street Presents: Follow That Bird *85* Ken Kwapis

60 Minutos con el Primer Mundial de Boxeo Amateur *74* Santiago Álvarez

Sesión Continua *84* José Luis García Agraz

Session with the Committee *68* Peter Sykes

Session with the Committee, A *68* Del Jack

Sesso degli Angeli, Il *68* Ugo Liberatore
Sesso della Strega, Il *73* Elo Pannaccio
Sesso e Volentieri *82* Dino Risi
Sesso Matto *73* Dino Risi
Sesto Continento *54* Leonardo Bonzi, Mario Craveri, Enrico Gras, Giorgio Moser, Folco Quilici
Sestra Angelika *32* Martin Frič
Sestri I *57* Grigori Roshal
Sestri II *59* Grigori Roshal
Sestri III *60* Grigori Roshal
Sestřičky *83* Karel Kachyňa
Set, The *70* Frank Brittain
Set 'Em Up *39* Felix E. Feist
Set Free *18* Tod Browning
Set Free *27* Arthur Rosson
Set Up, The *26* Clifford Smith
Set-Up, The *49* Robert Wise
Set-Up, The *63* Gerard Glaister
Sete Vampiras, As *86* Ivan Cardozo
Setenta Veces Siete *62* Leopoldo Torre-Nilsson
79 Primaveras *69* Santiago Álvarez
Seth's Temptation *10* Sidney Olcott
Setkání v Červenci *77* Karel Kachyňa
Setouchi Shōnen Yakyūdan *84* Masahiro Shinoda
Sette Canne e un Vestito *50* Michelangelo Antonioni
Sette Chili in Sette Giorni *86* Luca Verdone
Sette Contadini, I *57* Elio Petri
Sette Contro la Morte *64* Edgar G. Ulmer
Sette Dollari del Rosso *66* Alberto Cardone
Sette Donne per i MacGregor *67* Franco Giraldi
Sette Fatiche di Ali Baba, Le *63* Emimmo Salvi
Sette Fratelli, I *66* Carlo Lizzani
Sette Gladiatori, I *64* Pedro Lazaga Sabater
Sette Magnifiche Pistole, Le *66* Rod Gilbert
Sette Nani alla Riscossa, I *65* Paolo W. Tamburella
Sette Notte in Nero *77* Lucio Fulci
Sette Ore di Fuoco *64* Joaquín Luis Romero Marchent
Sette Peccati Capitali, I *51* Yves Allégret, Claude Autant-Lara, Carlo-Rim, Eduardo De Filippo, Jean Dréville, Georges Lacombe, Roberto Rossellini
Sette Peccati Capitali, I *61* Philippe de Broca, Claude Chabrol, Jacques Demy, Sylvaine Dhomme, Max Douy, Jean-Luc Godard, Eugene Ionesco, Édouard Molinaro, Roger Vadim
Sette Pistole per El Gringo *67* Juan Xiol Marchal
Sette Pistole per i MacGregor *65* Franco Giraldi
Sette Scialli di Seta Gialla *72* Sergio Pastore
Sette Spade del Vendicatore, Le *62* Riccardo Freda
Sette Spade per il Re *62* Riccardo Freda
Sette Uomini d'Oro *65* Marco Vicario
Sette Vergini per il Diavolo *68* Antonio Margheriti

Sette Volte Donna *67* Vittorio De Sica
Sette Winchester per un Massacro *67* Enzo G. Castellari
Setting Out *66* Jerzy Skolimowski
Setting Out in a Carriage *1895* Louis Lumière
Setting Son, The *30* Lewis R. Foster
Settled in Full *20* Geoffrey H. Malins
Settled Out of Court *25* George A. Cooper
Settlers, The *71* Jan Troell
Setu Bandhan *27* D. G. Phalke
Seul Amour, Un *43* Pierre Blanchar
Seul dans Paris *52* Hervé Bromberger
Seul ou avec d'Autres *62* Denys Arcand, Denis Héroux, Stephane Venne
Sève de la Terre, La *55* Alexander Alexeïeff, Claire Parker
Seven *79* Andy Sidaris
Seven Against the Sun *68* David Millin
Seven Ages *05* Edwin S. Porter
Seven Ages of Man, The *14* Charles Vernon
Seven Alone *75* Earl Bellamy
Seven Angry Men *55* Charles Marquis Warren
Seven Bad Men *55* Tim Whelan
Seven Bastards, The *70* İrfan Atasoy, Yılmaz Güney
Seven Beauties *75* Lina Wertmuller
Seven Brave Men *36* Sergei Gerasimov
Seven Brides for Seven Brothers *54* Stanley Donen
Seven Brothers Meet Dracula, The *73* Roy Ward Baker
Seven Capital Sins, The *00* Georges Méliès
Seven Capital Sins *61* Philippe de Broca, Claude Chabrol, Jacques Demy, Sylvaine Dhomme, Max Douy, Jean-Luc Godard, Eugene Ionesco, Édouard Molinaro, Roger Vadim
Seven Chances *25* Buster Keaton
Seven Cities of Gold *55* Robert D. Webb
Seven Cities to Atlantis *78* Kevin Connor
Seven Cutey Pups *17* Vincent Colby
Seven Daring Girls *60* Otto Meyer
Seven Days *25* Scott Sidney
Seven Days Ashore *44* John H. Auer
Seven Days in January *79* Juan Antonio Bardem
Seven Days in May *63* John Frankenheimer
Seven Days' Leave *29* John Cromwell, Richard Wallace
Seven Days' Leave *42* Tim Whelan
Seven Days, Seven Nights *60* Peter Brook
Seven Days to Noon *50* John Boulting
Seven Dead in the Cat's Eyes *73* Antonio Margheriti
Seven Deadly Sins, The *00* Georges Méliès
Seven Deadly Sins, The *51* Yves Allégret, Claude Autant-Lara, Carlo-Rim, Eduardo De Filippo, Jean Dréville, Georges Lacombe, Roberto Rossellini
Seven Deadly Sins, The *61* Philippe de Broca, Claude Chabrol, Jacques Demy, Sylvaine Dhomme, Max Douy, Jean-Luc Godard, Eugene Ionesco, Édouard Molinaro, Roger Vadim
Seven Different Ways *63* William Dieterle

Seven Doors of Death, The *80* Lucio Fulci
Seven Doors to Death *44* Elmer Clifton
Seven Dwarfs to the Rescue, The *65* Paolo W. Tamburella
711 Ocean Drive *50* Joseph M. Newman
Seven Faces *29* Berthold Viertel
7 Faces of Dr. Lao, The *63* George Pal
Seven Female Vampires, The *86* Ivan Cardozo
Seven Footprints to Satan *29* Benjamin Christensen
Seven from Texas *64* Joaquín Luis Romero Marchent
Seven Golden Men *65* Marco Vicario
Seven Golden Men Strike Again *66* Marco Vicario
Seven Graves for Rogan *83* Matt Cimber
Seven Guns for Gringo *67* Juan Xiol Marchal
Seven Guns for the MacGregors *65* Franco Giraldi
Seven Guns to Mesa *58* Edward Dein
Seven Hills of Rome, The *57* Roy Rowland
Seven Hours of Gunfire *64* Joaquín Luis Romero Marchent
Seven Hours to Judgment *88* Beau Bridges
Seven Hours Under Fire *64* Joaquín Luis Romero Marchent
Seven in the Sun *60* Sergio Bergonzelli
Seven Journeys *47* Helmut Käutner
Seven Keys *62* Pat Jackson
Seven Keys to Baldpate *17* Hugh Ford
Seven Keys to Baldpate *25* Fred Newmeyer
Seven Keys to Baldpate *30* Reginald Barker
Seven Keys to Baldpate *35* William Hamilton, Edward Killy
Seven Keys to Baldpate *47* Lew Landers
Seven Kilos in Seven Days *86* Luca Verdone
Seven Kinds of Trouble *69* Mahinur Ergün
7. Kontinent, Der *89* Michael Haneke
Seven Little Foys, The *55* Melville Shavelson
Seven Lively Arts *59* John Hubley
Seven Madmen, The *73* Leopoldo Torre-Nilsson
Seven Men at Daybreak *75* Lewis Gilbert
Seven Men from Now *56* Budd Boetticher
Seven Miles from Alcatraz *42* Edward Dmytryk
Seven Minutes, The *71* Russ Meyer
Seven Minutes *89* Klaus Maria Brandauer
Seven Minutes in Heaven *86* Linda Feferman
Seven Nights in Japan *76* Lewis Gilbert
7-9-13 *34* Anders Wilhelm Sandberg
Seven No-Goods, The *70* İrfan Atasoy, Yılmaz Güney
Seven of Clubs *16* Michael Curtiz
7 p., cuis., s. de b. *84* Agnès Varda
Seven Pearls, The *18* Louis Gasnier
Seven Percent Solution, The *76* Herbert Ross
Seven Revenges, The *67* Primo Zeglio
7 rms, kitch, bath *84* Agnès Varda
Seven Samurai *54* Akira Kurosawa

Seven Seas to Calais *61* Riccardo Freda, Rudolph Maté, Primo Zeglio
Seven Secrets of Su-Maru, The *70* Jesús Franco
Seven, Seventeen and Seventy *10* Lewin Fitzhamon
Seven Sinners *25* Lewis Milestone
Seven Sinners *36* Albert De Courville
Seven Sinners *40* Tay Garnett
Seven Sisters, The *15* Sidney Olcott
Seven Sisters *82* Mark Rosman
Seven Slaps *38* Paul Martin
Seven Slaves Against the World *65* Michele Lupo
Seven Swans, The *17* J. Searle Dawley
Seven Sweethearts *42* Frank Borzage
Seven Tasks of Ali Baba, The *63* Emimmo Salvi
07 Taxi *43* Marcello Pagliero
Seven Thieves *59* Henry Hathaway
Seven Thunders *57* Hugo Fregonese
Seven Till Five *33* Norman McLaren
Seven Times Seven *69* Michele Lupo
7254 *71* John Stember
Seven-Ups, The *73* Philip D'Antoni
Seven Waves Away *57* Richard Sale
Seven Ways from Sundown *60* Harry Keller
Seven Were Saved *47* William Pine
Seven Winds *62* Stanislav Rostotsky
Seven Women *65* John Ford
Seven Women *89* Rudolph Thome
Seven Women for the MacGregors *67* Franco Giraldi
Seven Women from Hell *61* Robert D. Webb
Seven Women, Seven Sins *87* Chantal Akerman, Bette Gordon
Seven Wonders of the World *56* Tay Garnett, Andrew Marton, Ted Tetzlaff, Walter Thompson
Seven Year Itch, The *55* Billy Wilder
Seven Years Bad Luck *21* Max Linder
Seven Years Itch *87* Johnny To
Seventeen *16* Robert Vignola
Seventeen *40* Louis King
Seventeen *65* Annelise Meineche
Seventeen *84* Joel De Mott, Jeff Kreines
Seventeen and Anxious *70* Zbyněk Brynych
17 Minutter Grønland *67* Jørgen Roos
1776 *09* D. W. Griffith
1776 *72* Peter H. Hunt
1776, or The Hessian Renegades *09* D. W. Griffith
Seventeen Years Old *57* Alf Kjellin
Seventeenth Parallel, The *68* Joris Ivens, Marceline Loridan
Seventeenth Parallel: Vietnam in War *68* Joris Ivens, Marceline Loridan
Seventh Anniversary of the Red Army, The *25* Dziga Vertov
Seventh Bandit, The *26* Scott R. Dunlap
7th Cavalry *56* Joseph H. Lewis
Seventh Commandment, The *61* Irvin Berwick
Seventh Continent, The *66* Joseph Medved, Dušan Vukotić
Seventh Continent, The *89* Michael Haneke

Seventh Cross, The *44* Fred Zinnemann
7th Dawn, The *63* Lewis Gilbert
Seventh Day, The *09* D. W. Griffith
Seventh Day, The *14* Charles H. Weston
Seventh Day, The *22* Henry King
Seventh Day, Eighth Night *69* Evald Schorm
Seventh Day, the Eighth Night, The *69* Evald Schorm
Seventh Grade *38* G. Levkoyer, Yakov Protazanov
Seventh Heaven *27* Frank Borzage
Seventh Heaven *37* Henry King
Seventh Heaven, The *56* Hasse Ekman
Seventh Juror, The *62* Georges Lautner
Seventh Person *19* George Walsh
Seventh Seal, The *56* Ingmar Bergman
Seventh Sheriff, The *23* Richard Hatton
Seventh Sign, The *88* Carl Schultz
Seventh Sin, The *17* Theodore Marston
Seventh Sin, The *57* Vincente Minnelli, Ronald Neame
Seventh Son, The *12* James Hallek Reid
Seventh Survivor, The *41* Leslie Hiscott
Seventh Sword, The *62* Riccardo Freda
Seventh Veil, The *45* Compton Bennett
Seventh Victim, The *43* Mark Robson
7th Voyage of Sinbad, The *58* Nathan Juran
Seventh Word, The *15* Wilfred Noy
Seventies People, The *75* Peter Watkins
70 *70* Robert Breer
Seventy Deadly Pills *64* Pat Jackson
Seventy-Five Mile Gun, The *18* Raoul Barré, Charles Bowers
79 A.D. *63* Gianfranco Parolini
79 Primaveras *69* Santiago Álvarez
79 Springtimes *69* Santiago Álvarez
79 Springtimes of Ho Chi Minh *69* Santiago Álvarez
77 *77* Robert Breer
77 Park Lane *31* Albert De Courville
70-Talets Människor *75* Peter Watkins
70,000 Witnesses *32* Ralph Murphy
Seventy Times Seven *62* Leopoldo Torre-Nilsson
Several Days in the Life of I. I. Oblomov *79* Nikita Mikhalkov
Several Interviews on Personal Matters *79* Lana Gogoberidze
Severance *88* David Max Steinberg
Severed Arm, The *73* Thomas S. Alderman
Severed Head, A *70* Dick Clement
Severed Heads *70* Glauber Rocha
Severny Anekdot *65* Alexander Alov, Vladimir Naumov
Severo Torelli *14* Louis Feuillade
Sevillana, La *30* Ramón Navarro
Sevres Porcelain *09* Émile Cohl
Sewer, The *12* Alice Guy-Blaché
Sewers of Gold *81* Francis Megahy
Sex *20* Fred Niblo
Sex Agent *63* Ernst R. von Theumer
Sex and the Other Woman *73* Stanley Long
Sex and the Single Girl *64* Richard Quine
Sex and the Teenager *71* Buzz Kulik
Sex and the Vampire *70* Jean Rollin
Sex and Violence *82* Dino Risi

Sex Appeal *86* Chuck Vincent
Sex at Night *61* Pierre Mère
Sex-Business: Made in Passing *69* Hans-Jürgen Syberberg
Sex Charge *73* Hans Sternbeck
Sex Check, The *68* Yasuzo Masumura
Sex Crime of the Century *72* Wes Craven
Sex Cycle, The *66* Joe Sarno
Sex Demons, The *72* Jesús Franco
Sex du Jour *76* Beau Buchanan
Sex Express *75* Derek Ford
Sex Farm *74* Arnold Louis Miller
Sex Games *73* Derek Ford
Sex Hygiene *41* John Ford
Sex in Chains *28* William Dieterle
Sex in Fetters *28* William Dieterle
Sex in the Afternoon *64* Mario Monicelli, Elio Petri, Franco Rossi, Luciano Salce
Sex Is a Woman *65* Frederic Goode
Sex Kittens Go to College *60* Albert Zugsmith
sex, lies, and videotape *89* Steven Soderbergh
Sex Life in a Convent *77* Walerian Borowczyk
Sex Life of a Female Private Eye, The *73* Lindsay Shonteff
Sex, Love and Marriage *71* Terry Gould
Sex Lure, The *16* Ivan Abramson
Sex Mission *84* Juliusz Machulski
Sex Monster *69* René Cardona
Sex O'Clock News, The *86* Romano Vanderbes
Sex O'Clock U.S.A. *76* François Reichenbach
Sex of Angels, The *68* Ugo Liberatore
Sex on the Groove Tube *73* Sean S. Cunningham, Brad Talbot
Sex on the Rocks *81* Siggi Götz
Sex on the Run *76* Franz Antel
Sex Party *63* Jean Josipovici, Ambroglio Molteni
Sex Play *74* Jack Arnold
Sex Quartet *66* Mauro Bolognini, Mario Monicelli, Antonio Pietrangeli, Luciano Salce
Sex Racketeers, The *70* Peter Walker
Sex Shop *72* Claude Berri
Sex Shop, Le *72* Claude Berri
Sex Symbol, The *74* David Lowell Rich
Sex Thief, The *73* Martin Campbell
Sex Through a Window *72* Jeannot Szwarc
Sex Vampires *71* Jean Rollin
Sex Victims, The *73* Derek Robbins
Sex with a Smile *76* Sergio Martino
Sex with the Stars *80* Anwar Kawadri
Sexe des Anges, Le *63* Pasquale Festa Campanile, Massimo Franciosa
Sexe Faible, Le *32* Robert Siodmak
Sexes Enchaînes, Les *28* William Dieterle
Sexier Than Sex *72* Jörn Donner
Sexo Sangriento *81* Manuel Esteba Gallego
Sexo Va *77* Pedro Almodóvar
Sexorcist, The *74* Mario Gariazzo
Sexplorer, The *75* Derek Ford
Sexpot *88* Chuck Vincent
Sextänerin, Die *38* S. Innemann
Sexte Sinn, Der *86* Dagmar Beiersdorf, Lothar Lambert
Sextet *76* Derek Robbins

Shadows of the Orient *37* Burt Lynwood
Shadows of the Past *14* Ralph Ince
Shadows of the Past *19* Ralph Ince
Shadows of the Past *28* Walter Lang
Shadows of the Past *40* Werner Hochbaum
Shadows of the Peacock *86* Phillip Noyce
Shadows of the Sea *22* Alan Crosland
Shadows of the Underworld *39* David MacDonald
Shadows of the West *21* Paul Hurst
Shadows of the West *49* Ray Taylor
Shadows of the Yoshiwara, The *28* Teinosuke Kinugasa
Shadows of Tombstone *53* William Witney
Shadows of Yoshiwara, The *28* Teinosuke Kinugasa
Shadows on the Range *46* Lambert Hillyer
Shadows on the Sage *42* Les Orlebeck
Shadows on the Snow *45* Arne Sucksdorff
Shadows on the Stairs *41* D. Ross Lederman
Shadows Over Chinatown *46* Terry Morse
Shadows Over Shanghai *38* Charles Lamont
Shadows Over the Snow *45* Arne Sucksdorff
Shadows Over Yoshiwara *28* Teinosuke Kinugasa
Shadows Run Black *81* Howard Heard
Shadowzone *90* J. S. Cardone
Shady Lady, The *29* Edward H. Griffith
Shady Lady *45* George Waggner
Shaft *71* Gordon Parks
Shaft in Africa *73* John Guillermin
Shaft's Big Score! *72* Gordon Parks
Shag *88* Zelda Barron
Shag *88* Alexander Mitta
Shag: The Movie *88* Zelda Barron
Shagai, Soviet! *26* Dziga Vertov
Shaggy *48* Robert E. Tansey
Shaggy D.A., The *76* Robert Stevenson
Shaggy Dog, The *59* Charles Barton
Shahenshah *88* Tinnu Anand
Shaitan el Sahara *54* Youssef Chahine
Shake Hands with Murder *44* Albert Herman
Shake Hands with the Devil *59* Michael Anderson
Shake (Otis Redding) *86* D. A. Pennebaker
Shake, Rattle and Rock *56* Edward L. Cahn
Shake Your Powder Puff *34* Friz Freleng
Shakedown, The *28* William Wyler
Shakedown *34* John Francis Dillon
Shakedown *36* David Selman
Shakedown *50* Joseph Pevney
Shakedown, The *59* John Lemont
Shakedown *88* James Glickenhaus
Shaker Run *85* Bruce Morrison
Shakespeare Écrivant "Jules César" *07* Georges Méliès
Shakespeare: La Mort de Jules César *07* Georges Méliès
Shakespeare og Kronborg *50* Jørgen Roos
Shakespeare Wallah *65* James Ivory
Shakespeare — With Tin Ears *33* Leslie Goodwins
Shakespeare Writing "Julius Caesar" *07* Georges Méliès

Shakespearian Spinach *40* Dave Fleischer
Shakhmatnaya Goryachka *25* Vsevolod I. Pudovkin, Nikolai Shpikovsky
Shakhtery *34* Sergei Yutkevich
Shakiest Gun in the West, The *67* Alan Rafkin
Shaking the Shimmy *20* Raoul Barré, Charles Bowers
Shakti *88* Prabhakar
Shakuntala *43* Rajaram Vanakudre Shantaram
Shalako *68* Edward Dmytryk
Shalimar *78* Krishna Shah
Shall the Children Pay? *33* Willard Mack
Shall We Dance? *37* Mark Sandrich
Shall We Forgive Her? *17* Arthur Ashley
Shallow Box Trick, The *03* Georges Méliès
Shallow Grave *87* Richard Styles
Shalom *73* Yaky Yosha
Sham *21* Thomas Heffron
Sham Rock 'n' Roll *69* Robert McKimson
Sham Sword Swallower, The *06* James A. Williamson
Shaman Psalm *81* James Broughton
Shame *18* John W. Noble
Shame *21* Emmett J. Flynn
Shame *32* Friedrich Ermler, Sergei Yutkevich
Shame *61* Roger Corman
Shame *68* Ingmar Bergman
Shame, The *68* Ingmar Bergman
Shame *88* Steve Jodrell
Shame of a Nation, The *32* Howard Hawks
Shame of Mary Boyle, The *30* Alfred Hitchcock
Shame of Patty Smith, The *62* Leo Handel
Shame of the Jungle *75* Jean-Marc Picha, Boris Szulzinger
Shame of the Sabine Women, The *62* Alberto Gout
Shame, Shame, Everybody Knows Her Name *69* Joseph Jacoby
Shamed *49* Giovanni Paolucci
Shameful Behavior? *26* Albert Kelley
Shameful Dream *27* Heinosuke Gosho
Shameless...But Honorable *87* Rafael Villaseñor Kuri
Shameless Old Lady, The *64* René Allio
Shaming, The *79* Marvin Chomsky
Shaming of the True, The *30* Walter Creighton
Shamisen and Motorcycle *61* Masahiro Shinoda
Shamisen to Ōtobai *61* Masahiro Shinoda
Shampoo *75* Hal Ashby
Shamrock Alley *27* Charles Lamont
Shamrock and the Rose, The *27* Jack Nelson
Shamrock Handicap, The *26* John Ford
Shamrock Hill *49* Arthur Dreifuss
Shams of Society *21* Thomas B. Walsh
Shamus *59* Eric Marquis
Shamus *72* Buzz Kulik
Shamus O'Brien, or Saved from the Scaffold *05* Tom Green
Shan Chung Ch'uan-Ch'i *78* King Hu
Shan-Ko Lien *65* Chen Lo

Shane *53* George Stevens
Shanghai *35* James Flood
Shanghai *38* Fumio Kamei
Shanghai Blues *84* Hark Tsui
Shanghai Bound *27* Luther Reed
Shanghai Chest, The *48* William Beaudine
Shanghai Cobra, The *45* Phil Karlson
Shanghai Document *28* Yakov Bliokh
Shanghai Drama, The *37* G. W. Pabst
Shanghai Express *32* Josef von Sternberg
Shanghai Gesture, The *41* Josef von Sternberg
Shanghai Lady *29* John S. Robertson
Shanghai Madness *33* John G. Blystone
Shanghai Moon *41* Mikio Naruse
Shanghai Rose *29* Scott Pembroke
Shanghai Story, The *54* Frank Lloyd
Shanghai Surprise *86* Jim Goddard
Shanghai Vance King *84* Kinji Fukasaku
Shanghaied *10* Edwin S. Porter
Shanghaied *15* Charles Chaplin
Shanghaied *27* Ralph Ince
Shanghaied Love *31* George B. Seitz
Shanghaied Lovers *24* Roy Del Ruth
Shanghaied Shipmates *36* Jack King
Shangoo la Pistola Infallibile *70* Eduardo Mulargia
Shanhai no Tsuki *41* Mikio Naruse
Shanks *74* William Castle
Shannon of the Sixth *14* George Melford
Shannons of Broadway, The *29* Emmett J. Flynn
Shanthinivasa *88* Bhargava
Shanty Tramp *67* Joseph Prieto
Shanty Where Santy Claus Lives, The *33* Rudolf Ising
Shantytown *43* Joseph Santley
Shaolin Drunkard *85* Wo Ping Yuen
Shape of Films to Come *68* Willard Van Dyke
Shape of the Land, The *84* Junya Sato
Shape of Things to Come *68* Willard Van Dyke
Shape of Things to Come, The *79* George McCowan
Sharad of Atlantis *36* B. Reeves Eason, Joseph Kane
Sharadama *88* Kranti Kumar
Sharashandri *21* Pendharkar Babu Rao
Shards *81* István Gaál
Share and Share Alike *25* Whitman Bennett
Share Cropper *80* Shyam Benegal
Share Out, The *62* Gerard Glaister
Shared Room *60* Wojciech Has
Shariah el Bahlawane *49* Salah Abu Saif
Shark, The *20* Del Henderson
Shark! *67* Samuel Fuller
Shark *81* Enzo G. Castellari
Shark Boy of Bora Bora *79* Frank C. Clark
Shark God, The *49* Leon Leonard
Shark Kill *76* William A. Graham
Shark Master, The *21* Fred LeRoy Granville
Shark Monroe *18* William S. Hart
Shark Reef *58* Roger Corman
Shark River *53* John Rawlins
Shark Rosso nell'Oceano *84* Lamberto Bava

Shark That Knew Too Much, The *89* Claes Eriksson
Shark Woman, The *41* Ward Wing
Sharkfighters, The *56* Jerry Hopper
Sharks Is Sharks *17* Gregory La Cava
Shark's Treasure *74* Cornel Wilde
Sharky's Machine *81* Burt Reynolds
Sharma and Beyond *84* Brian Gilbert
Sharon's Baby *75* Peter Sasdy
Sharp Practice *12* Wilfred Noy
Sharp Shooters *28* John G. Blystone
Sharp-Witted Thief, The *10* Lewin Fitzhamon
Sharps and Flats *15* Cecil Birch
Sharps and Flats *27* William C. Nolan
Sharpshooters *38* James Tinling
Shatranj ke Khilari *77* Satyajit Ray
Shatter *74* Michael Carreras, Monte Hellman, Gordon Hessler, Seth Holt
Shattered *21* Lupu Pick
Shattered *71* Alastair Reid
Shattered *76* Serge Leroy
Shattered Dreams *22* Paul Scardon
Shattered Faith *23* Jesse J. Ormont
Shattered Idols *22* Edward Sloman
Shattered Idyll, A *16* Dave Aylott
Shattered Lives *25* Henry McCarthy
Shattered Memories *15* Robert Z. Leonard
Shattered Vase, The *13* Yakov Protazanov
Shatterhand *64* Hugo Fregonese
Shaughraun, The *12* Sidney Olcott
Shave by Instalments on the Uneasy System, A *05* J. H. Martin
Shaved Heads *87* Dimitris Makris
Shawly Not *14* Dave Aylott
Shaytan al Sahara *54* Youssef Chahine
Shchors *39* Alexander Dovzhenko, Yulia Solntseva
She *08* Edwin S. Porter
She *16* Will Barker, H. Lisle Lucoque
She *17* Kenean Buel
She *25* Leander De Cordova
She *26* Heinosuke Gosho
She *35* Lansing Holden, Irving Pichel
She *65* Robert Day
She *82* Avi Nesher
She Always Gets Their Man *62* Godfrey Grayson
She and He *63* Susumu Hani
She and He *69* Mauro Bolognini
She and the Three *22* E. A. Dupont
She and the Three *38* Viktor Jansen
She Asked for It *37* Erle C. Kenton
She Asked for Trouble *12* Hay Plumb
She-Beast, The *65* Michael Reeves
She Bumps *37* George Pal
She Came Like a Wind *52* Erik Faustman
She Came to the Valley *79* Alfredo Antonini
She Conquered *15* Victor Sjöström
She Couldn't Help It *21* Maurice Campbell
She Couldn't Say No *30* Lloyd Bacon
She Couldn't Say No *39* Graham Cutts
She Couldn't Say No *41* William Clemens
She Couldn't Say No *52* Lloyd Bacon
She Couldn't Take It *35* Tay Garnett
She-Creature, The *56* Edward L. Cahn
She Dances Alone *81* Robert Dornhelm
She Defends Her Country *43* Friedrich Ermler

She-Demons *58* Richard Cunha
She-Devil, The *18* J. Gordon Edwards
She-Devil *34* Arthur Hoerl
She-Devil *57* Kurt Neumann
She-Devil *89* Susan Seidelman
She-Devil Island *36* Raphael J. Sevilla
She-Devils on Wheels *68* Herschell Gordon Lewis
She Didn't Say No! *58* Cyril Frankel
She Didn't Want to Do It *15* Toby Cooper
She Done Him Right *33* Walter Lantz
She Done Him Right *40* William Beaudine
She Done Him Wrong *33* Lowell Sherman
She Dreamt of Onions *11* A. E. Coleby
She Drives Me Crazy *89* Stephen Withrow
She-Freak *66* Byron Mabe
She Gets Her Man *35* William Nigh
She Gets Her Man *44* Erle C. Kenton
She Gods of Shark Reef *58* Roger Corman
She Goes to War *29* Henry King
She Got Her Man *42* Roy Del Ruth
She Got What She Asked For *63* Vittorio De Sica
She Got What She Wanted *30* James Cruze
She Had to Choose *34* Ralph Ceder
She Had to Eat *37* Malcolm St. Clair
She Had to Say Yes *33* George Amy, Busby Berkeley
She Had to Say Yes *52* Lloyd Bacon
She Has Lived Her Destiny *24* Teinosuke Kinugasa
She Has What It Takes *43* Charles Barton
She Hired a Husband *18* John Francis Dillon
She Is Ma Daisy *31* George Pearson
She Is My Daisy *07* Arthur Gilbert
She Is My Daisy *31* George Pearson
She Knew All the Answers *41* Richard Wallace
She Knew What She Wanted *36* Thomas Bentley
She Knows Y'Know! *62* Montgomery Tully
She Learned About Sailors *34* George Marshall
She Left Without Her Trunks *16* Tefft Johnson
She Let Him Continue *68* Noel Black
She Likes Me *87* Anvar Turayev
She Loved a Fireman *37* John Farrow
She Loves and Lies *20* Chester Withey
She Loves Me Not *34* Elliott Nugent
She Made Her Bed *34* Ralph Murphy
She-Man, The *67* Bob Clark
She Married a Cop *39* Sidney Salkow
She Married an Artist *38* Marion Gering
She Married Her Boss *35* Gregory La Cava
She-Monster of the Night *58* Richard Cunha
She Must Be Seeing Things *87* Sheila McLaughlin
She Must Have Swallowed It *12* Percy Stow
She Played with Fire *56* Sidney Gilliat
She Reminds Me of You *34* Dave Fleischer

She Returned at Dawn *38* Henri Decoin
She Served Him Right *31* Edward Buzzell
She Shall Have Murder *50* Daniel Birt
She Shall Have Music *35* Leslie Hiscott
She Should'a Said No *49* Sam Newfield
She Sighed by the Seaside *21* Erle C. Kenton
She Steps Out *30* Hamilton MacFadden
She Stoops to Conquer *14* George Loane Tucker
She Stoops to Conquer *23* Edwin Greenwood
She Stoops to Conquer *71* Michael Elliott
She, the Only One *26* Gustaf Molander
She Too Smoked Cigars *86* Alessandro Di Robiland
She Triumphs *15* Victor Sjöström
She Walketh Alone *15* B. Reeves Eason
She Wanted a Millionaire *32* John G. Blystone
She Was a Hippy Vampire *66* Jerry Warren
She Was a Lady *34* Hamilton MacFadden
She Was an Acrobat's Daughter *37* Friz Freleng
She Was Like a Daisy *55* Keisuke Kinoshita
She Was Like a Wild Chrysanthemum *55* Keisuke Kinoshita
She Was Only a Village Maiden *33* Arthur Maude
She Was Victorious *15* Victor Sjöström
She Went to the Races *45* Willis Goldbeck
She Who Dares *43* Henry S. Kesler, Fedor Ozep
She-Wolf, The *19* Clifford Smith
She-Wolf *31* James Flood
She-Wolf, The *53* Alberto Lattuada
She-Wolf, The *63* Alex Muratova, Kira Muratova
She-Wolf, The *64* Rafael Baledón
She-Wolf, The *65* Rangel Vulchanov
She-Wolf of Devil's Moor, The *78* Helmut Pfandler
She-Wolf of London *46* Jean Yarbrough
She-Wolf of Wall Street, The *31* James Flood
She-Wolves *25* Maurice Elvey
She-Wolves, The *57* Luis Saslavsky
She Wore a Yellow Ribbon *49* John Ford
She Would Be a Suffragette *08* James A. Williamson
She Would Be Wed, or Leap Year Proposals *08* A. E. Coleby
She Would Talk *11* Dave Aylott
She Wouldn't Say Yes *45* Alexander Hall
She Wronged Him Right *34* Dave Fleischer
She Wrote the Book *46* Charles Lamont
Sheba *19* Cecil M. Hepworth
Sheba *73* Don Chaffey
Sheba Baby *75* William Girdler
Shed No Tears *48* Jean Yarbrough
Shedding the Profiteer *20* Gregory La Cava
Sheela *87* Deepak Balraj
Sheena *84* John Guillermin
Sheena, Queen of the Jungle *84* John Guillermin
Sheep Ahoy *54* Chuck Jones

Sheep Has Five Legs, The *54* Henri Verneuil

Sheep in the Deep, A *62* Chuck Jones

Sheep Skinned *29* Manny Gould, Ben Harrison

Sheep Stealers Anonymous *63* Joseph Barbera, William Hanna

Sheep Trail *26* Harry Fraser

Sheepdog of the Hills *41* Germain Burger

Sheepish Wolf, The *42* Friz Freleng

Sheepman, The *58* George Marshall

Sheepman's Daughter, The *11* Allan Dwan

Sheepskin Trousers, or Not in These *12* Percy Stow

Sheer Bluff *21* Frank Richardson

Sheer Madness *82* Margarethe von Trotta

Sheer Trickery *22* Adrian Brunel

Sheere Sanggy *87* Massoud Jafari Jozani

Sheffield Blade, A *18* Joseph J. Bamberger, Harry Roberts

Shehar aur Sapna *63* Khwaja Ahmad Abbas

Shéhérazade *63* Jacques Bourdon, Pierre Gaspard-Huit

Shéhérazade *90* Philippe de Broca

Sheik, The *21* George Melford

Sheik, The *22* George Wynn

Sheik of Araby, The *26* Miles Mander

Sheik Steps Out, The *37* Irving Pichel

Sheik's Wife, The *21* Henri Roussel

Sheila Levine Is Dead and Living in New York *74* Sidney J. Furie

She'll Be Wearing Pink Pajamas *85* John Goldschmidt

She'll Be Wearing Pink Pyjamas *85* John Goldschmidt

She'll Follow You Anywhere *71* David C. Rea

Shell Forty-Three *16* Reginald Barker

Shell Game, The *18* George D. Baker

Shell Game, The *19* Raoul Barré, Charles Bowers

She'll Have to Go *61* Robert Asher

Shell Shock *64* John Hayes

Shell Shock *88* Yoel Sharon

Shell Shocked Egg, The *48* Robert McKimson

Shell Shocked Sammy *23* Frank S. Mattison

Shelley *87* Christian Bruyere

Shells, More Shells *15* Joe Evans

Sheltered Daughters *21* Edward Dillon

Sheltering Sky, The *90* Bernardo Bertolucci

Shenandoah *65* Andrew V. McLaglen

Shenanigans *77* Joseph Jacoby

Shep Comes Home *48* Ford Beebe

Shepherd, The *66* Bolotbek Shamshiev

Shepherd Girl, The *65* Chen Lo

Shepherd King, The *23* J. Gordon Edwards

Shepherd Lassie of Argyle *14* Lawrence Trimble

Shepherd of Souls, The *15* Frank Wilson

Shepherd of the Hills, The *20* Harold Bell Wright

Shepherd of the Hills, The *28* Albert S. Rogell

Shepherd of the Hills *41* Henry Hathaway

Shepherd of the Hills, The *64* Ben Parker

Shepherd of the Ozarks *42* Frank McDonald

Shepherd—Psalm 23, The *27* Charles Barnett

Shepherdess and the Chimney Sweep, The *52* Paul Grimault

Shepherd's Daughter, The *56* D. Dadaras

Shepherd's Dog, The *09* Lewin Fitzhamon

Shepherds of Confusion, The *67* Nikos Papatakis

Shepper-Newfounder, The *30* Leo McCarey

Sher Shivaji *88* Ram Gabale

Sheriff, The *14* Chester M. Franklin, Sidney Franklin

Sheriff, The *18* Roscoe Arbuckle

Sheriff, The *21* Harry D. Leonard

Sheriff del O.K. Corral, El *64* Tulio Demicheli

Sheriff Nell's Comeback *20* Edward F. Cline

Sheriff of Cimarron *45* Yakima Canutt

Sheriff of Fractured Jaw, The *58* Raoul Walsh

Sheriff of Hope Eternal, The *21* Ben F. Wilson

Sheriff of Las Vegas *44* Lesley Selander

Sheriff of Medicine Bow, The *48* Lambert Hillyer

Sheriff of Redwood Valley *46* R. G. Springsteen

Sheriff of Sage Valley *42* Sam Newfield

Sheriff of Sun-Dog, The *22* Ben F. Wilson

Sheriff of Sundown *44* Lesley Selander

Sheriff of Tombstone *41* Joseph Kane

Sheriff of Wichita *49* R. G. Springsteen

Sheriff Was a Lady, The *64* Hugo Fregonese

Sheriff with the Gold, The *66* Osvaldo Civirani

Sheriff's Baby, The *13* D. W. Griffith

Sheriff's Daughter, The *10* Lewin Fitzhamon

Sheriff's Girl *26* Ben F. Wilson

Sheriff's Lash, The *29* Cliff Lyons

Sheriff's Lone Hand, The *24* Alvin J. Neitz

Sheriff's Oath, The *20* Phil Rosen

Sheriff's Secret, The *31* James P. Hogan

Sheriff's Sisters, The *11* Allan Dwan

Sheriff's Son, The *19* Victor Schertzinger

Sheriff's Strange Son, The *86* Fernando Durán

Sherlock and Me *88* Thom Eberhardt

Sherlock Brown *21* Bayard Veiller

Sherlock Hawkshaw and Co. *20* Raoul Barré, Charles Bowers

Sherlock Holmes *05* J. Stuart Blackton

Sherlock Holmes *16* Arthur Berthelet

Sherlock Holmes *22* Albert Parker

Sherlock Holmes *32* William K. Howard

Sherlock Holmes *39* Alfred L. Werker

Sherlock Holmes *62* Terence Fisher, Frank Winterstein

Sherlock Holmes and Saucy Jack *78* Bob Clark

Sherlock Holmes and the Deadly Necklace *62* Terence Fisher, Frank Winterstein

Sherlock Holmes and the Missing Rembrandt *32* Leslie Hiscott

Sherlock Holmes and the Scarlet Claw *44* Roy William Neill

Sherlock Holmes and the Secret Code *46* Roy William Neill

Sherlock Holmes and the Secret Weapon *42* Roy William Neill

Sherlock Holmes and the Spider Woman *43* Roy William Neill

Sherlock Holmes and the Voice of Terror *42* John Rawlins

Sherlock Holmes and the Woman in Green *45* Roy William Neill

Sherlock Holmes Faces Death *43* Roy William Neill

Sherlock Holmes' Fatal Hour *31* Leslie Hiscott

Sherlock Holmes Grösster Fall *65* James Hill

Sherlock Holmes in Washington *43* Roy William Neill

Sherlock Holmes, Jr. *11* Edwin S. Porter

Sherlock Holmes: Murder by Decree *78* Bob Clark

Sherlock Holmes und das Halsband des Todes *62* Terence Fisher, Frank Winterstein

Sherlock, Jr. *24* Buster Keaton

Sherman Said It *33* Charlie Chase

Sherman's March *86* Ross McElwee

Sherry *20* Edgar Lewis

She's a Boy *27* Charles Lamont

She's a He *30* Sam Newfield

She's a Sheik *27* Clarence Badger

She's a Soldier Too *44* William Castle

She's a Sweetheart *44* Del Lord

She's Back *88* Tim Kincaid

She's Back on Broadway *53* Gordon Douglas

She's Dangerous *37* Milton Carruth, Lewis R. Foster

She's for Me *43* Reginald LeBorg

She's Got Everything *37* Joseph Santley

She's Gotta Have It *86* Spike Lee

She's Having a Baby *87* John Hughes

She's in the Army *42* Jean Yarbrough

She's My Baby *27* Fred Windermere

She's My Girl! *28* Sam Newfield

She's My Lovely *42* Charles Lamont

She's My Weakness *30* Melville Brown

She's No Lady *37* Charles Vidor

She's Out of Control *89* Stan Dragoti

She's Proud and She's Beautiful *08* Arthur Gilbert

She's the Only One *26* Gustaf Molander

She's Working Her Way Through College *52* H. Bruce Humberstone

Shestaya Chast Mira *26* Dziga Vertov

Shestoe Iulya *68* Yuli Karasik

Sh-h-h-h! *55* Tex Avery

Shi Yao *81* Zhihong Gui

Shibaido *44* Mikio Naruse

Shibil *68* Zahari Zhandov

Shichimenchō no Yukue *24* Kenji Mizoguchi

Shichinin no Samurai *54* Akira Kurosawa

Shield for Murder *54* Howard W. Koch, Edmond O'Brien

Shield of Faith, The *56* Norman Walker

Shield of Honor, The *27* Emory Johnson

Shield of Silence, The *25* Leo D. Maloney

Shielding Shadow, The 16 Louis Gasnier, Donald Mackenzie
Shifrovanny Dokument 28 Alexander Ptushko
Shift 74 Ernie Gehr
Shifting Sands 18 Albert Parker
Shifting Sands 22 Fred LeRoy Granville
Shiga Naoya 58 Susumu Hani
Shiiku 61 Nagisa Oshima
Shikamo Karera wa Yuku 31 Kenji Mizoguchi
Shilling Short of His Wages, A 07 Alf Collins
Shillingbury Blowers, The 80 Val Guest
Shima no Ratai Jiken 31 Heinosuke Gosho
Shimmie Shivers 20 Gregory La Cava
Shimmy Lagano Tarantelle e Vino 78 Lina Wertmuller
Shimmy Sheik, The 23 Adrian Brunel
Shimpu Group, The 33 Kenji Mizoguchi
Shimpu-Ren 33 Kenji Mizoguchi
Shin Heike Monogatari 55 Kenji Mizoguchi
Shin Josei no Kagami 28 Heinosuke Gosho
Shin Joseikan 28 Heinosuke Gosho
Shin no Shikōtei 65 Shigeo Tanaka
Shin Ōnō Ga Tsumi 26 Kenji Mizoguchi
Shin Yorokobi mo Kanashimi mo Ikutoshitsuki 86 Keisuke Kinoshita
Shina Ningyō 81 Shuji Terayama
Shinano Fudok 41 Fumio Kamei
shinbone alley 71 David Detiege, John D. Wilson
Shindig, The 30 Burton Gillett
Shindo 36 Heinosuke Gosho
Shine Bright My Star 69 Alexander Mitta
Shine Girl, The 16 William Parke
Shine On Harvest Moon 32 Dave Fleischer
Shine On, Harvest Moon 38 Joseph Kane
Shine On, Harvest Moon 44 David Butler
Shinel 26 Grigori Kozintsev, Leonid Trauberg
Shinel 59 Alexei Batalov
Shining, The 79 Stanley Kubrick
Shining Adventure, The 25 Hugo Ballin
Shining Arc, The 89 Jun Zhao Zhang
Shining Hour, The 38 Frank Borzage
Shining in the Red Sunset 25 Kenji Mizoguchi*
Shining Ray, The 11 Joris Ivens
Shining Star 75 Sig Shore
Shining Sun Becomes Clouded 26 Teinosuke Kinugasa
Shining Victory 41 Irving Rapper
Shinjō Ten no Amijima 69 Masahiro Shinoda
Shinju Yoimachigusa 25 Teinosuke Kinugasa
Shinjuku Dorobō Nikki 68 Nagisa Oshima
Shinken Shōbei 69 Tomu Uchida
Shinkin Stones 54 Teinosuke Kinugasa
Shinkonki 30 Mikio Naruse
Shinku Chitai 52 Satsuo Yamamoto
Shinobi no Mono I 62 Satsuo Yamamoto
Shinobi no Mono II 63 Satsuo Yamamoto
Shinran: Path to Purity 87 Rentaro Mikuni
Shinran: Shiro Michi 87 Rentaro Mikuni
Shinsengumi 70 Tadashi Sawajima

Shinsetsu 42 Heinosuke Gosho
Shinshaku Yotsuya Kaidan 49 Keisuke Kinoshita
Ship, The 26 Teinosuke Kinugasa
Ship, The 61 Jan Troell
Ship Ahoy! 19 Charlie Chase
Ship Ahoy 20 Wallace A. Carlson
Ship Ahoy 42 Edward Buzzell
Ship and the Stars, The 75 Bjarne Henning-Jensen
Ship Bound for India, A 47 Ingmar Bergman
Ship Cafe 35 Robert Florey
Ship Comes In, A 28 William K. Howard
Ship from Shanghai, The 29 Charles Brabin
Ship Is Born, A 42 Jean Negulesco
Ship Is Born, A 61 Jan Łomnicki
Ship of Aliens, The 87 Sergei Nikonenko
Ship of Condemned Women, The 63 Raffaello Matarazzo
Ship of Doom, The 17 Whyndham Gittens
Ship of Fools 65 Stanley Kramer
Ship of Lost Men, The 27 Maurice Tourneur
Ship of Souls 25 Charles Miller
Ship of the Ether, The 38 George Pal
Ship of Wanted Men 33 Lewis D. Collins
Ship Safety 43 Alberto Cavalcanti
Ship That Died, The 38 Jacques Tourneur
Ship That Died of Shame, The 55 Basil Dearden, Michael Relph
Ship to India, A 47 Ingmar Bergman
Ship Was Loaded, The 57 Val Guest
Shipbuilders, The 43 John Baxter
Shipmates 09 H. Oceano Martinek
Shipmates 26 Hugh Croise
Shipmates 31 Harry A. Pollard
Shipmates Forever 35 Frank Borzage
Shipmates o' Mine 36 Oswald Mitchell
Ships Attack the Fortifications, The 53 Mikhail Romm
Ships Attacking Forts 53 Mikhail Romm
Ship's Concert 37 Leslie Hiscott
Ships of Hate 31 John P. McCarthy
Ships of the Night 28 Duke Worne
Ships Storm the Bastions, The 53 Mikhail Romm
Ships That Meet 15 Victor Sjöström
Ships That Pass in the Night 21 Percy Nash
Ships with Wings 41 Sergei Nolbandov
Shipwreck 78 Stewart Raffill
Shipwreck Island 62 Emilio Gómez Muriel
Shipwrecked 26 Joseph E. Henabery
Shipwrecked 31 Walter Lantz
Shipyard 33 Paul Rotha
Shipyard Sally 39 Monty Banks
Shir Hashirim 35 Henry Lynn
Shiralee, The 57 Leslie Norman
Shirasagi 57 Teinosuke Kinugasa
Shirayuri wa Nageku 25 Kenji Mizoguchi
Shiraz 28 Franz Osten, Victor Peers
Shirikurae Magoichi 70 Kenji Misumi
Shirins Hochzeit 76 Helma Sanders-Brahms
Shirin's Wedding 76 Helma Sanders-Brahms
Shirker's Nightmare, The 14 Walter R.

Booth
Shirley 22 A. V. Bramble
Shirley Kaye 17 Émile Chautard
Shirley of the Circus 22 Rowland V. Lee
Shirley Thompson vs. the Aliens 68 Jim Sharman
Shirley Valentine 89 Lewis Gilbert
Shiro Amakusa from Tokisada 62 Nagisa Oshima
Shiro Amakusa the Christian Rebel 62 Nagisa Oshima
Shiro to Kuro 61 Hiromichi Horikawa
Shirogane Shinju 55 Kaneto Shindo
Shiroi Gake 60 Tadashi Imai
Shiroi Kiba 60 Heinosuke Gosho
Shiroi Yajū 49 Mikio Naruse
Shirt, The 89 Bilge Olgac
Shirts 14 Kelly Storrie
Shishkabugs 62 Friz Freleng
Shito no Densetsu 63 Keisuke Kinoshita
Shitto 49 Kozaburo Yoshimura
Shiva und die Galgenblume 45 Hans Steinhoff
Shiver Me Timbers! 34 Dave Fleischer
Shivers 34 Arthur Ripley
Shivers 74 David Cronenberg
Shivers 80 Wojciech Marczewski
Shivers in Summer 63 Luigi Zampa
Shizukanaru Kettō 48 Akira Kurosawa
Shkola Zlosloviya 52 Abram Room
Shli Soldati 57 Leonid Trauberg
Shlosha Yamin ve' Yeled 67 Uri Zohar
Shnei Kuni Lemel 66 Israel Becker
Shoah 85 Claude Lanzmann
Shock, The 23 Lambert Hillyer
Shock 34 Roy Pomeroy
Shock 46 Alfred L. Werker
Shock 72 Alain Jessua
Shock 74 William Castle
Shock 76 Lamberto Bava, Mario Bava
Shock Corridor 63 Samuel Fuller
Shock Patrol 56 Claude Bernard-Aubert
Shock Punch, The 25 Paul Sloane
Shock to the System, A 90 Jan Egleson
Shock (Transfer Suspense Hypnos) 76 Lamberto Bava, Mario Bava
Shock Treatment 64 Denis Sanders
Shock Treatment 72 Alain Jessua
Shock Treatment 81 Jim Sharman
Shock Troops 66 Costa-Gavras
Shock Troops 67 Alain Robbe-Grillet
Shock Waves 70 Ken Wiederhorn
Shocker 60 Gottfried Reinhardt
Shocker 89 Wes Craven
Shocking 70 Brunello Rondi
Shocking Accident, A 83 James Scott
Shocking Bad Form 14 Dave Aylott
Shock-ing Complaint, A 12 Dave Aylott
Shocking Idea, A 21 Raoul Barré, Charles Bowers
Shocking Job, A 13 Dave Aylott
Shocking Miss Pilgrim, The 46 George Seaton
Shocking Night, A 21 Eddie Lyons, Lee Moran
Shockproof 49 Douglas Sirk
Shocks and Shorts 13 Dave Aylott
Shod with Fire 20 Emmett J. Flynn
Shōdō Satsujin, Musukoyo 79 Keisuke Kinoshita

Shoe Salon Pinkus 16 Ernst Lubitsch
Shoe Shine Jasper 46 George Pal
Shoeblack at Work in a London Street 1895 Birt Acres
Shoeblack of Piccadilly, The 20 L. Stuart Greening
Shoein' Hosses 34 Dave Fleischer
Shoemaker and the Elves, The 67 Erich Kobler
Shoemaker and the Hatter, The 49 Joy Batchelor, John Halas
Shoes 16 Lois Weber
Shoes, The 61 Ernest Pintoff
Shoes of the Fisherman, The 68 Michael Anderson
Shoes That Danced 18 Frank Borzage
Shoeshine 46 Vittorio De Sica
Shoestore Pinkus 16 Ernst Lubitsch
Shogun 81 Jerry London
Shogun Assassin 72 Kenji Misumi
Shogun Assassin 80 Robert Houston
Shogun Island 82 Edward Murphy
Shogun's Samurai, The 79 Kinji Fukasaku
Shōhin—Shūsoku 24 Teinosuke Kinugasa
Shōhin—Shūto 24 Teinosuke Kinugasa
Shojo no Shi 27 Heinosuke Gosho
Shojo Nyūyō 30 Heinosuke Gosho
Shojo Yō Sayōnara 33 Heinosuke Gosho
Shokei no Heya 56 Kon Ichikawa
Shokei no Shima 66 Masahiro Shinoda
Shokkaku 69 Kaneto Shindo
Shokutaku no Nai Ie 85 Masaki Kobayashi
Shonben Raidaa 85 Shinji Somai
Shōnen 69 Nagisa Oshima
Shōnen Ki 50 Keisuke Kinoshita
Shōnen Sarutobi Sasuke 60 Akira Daikubara, Sanae Yamamoto
Shōnin no Isu 64 Satsuo Yamamoto
Shoot, The 64 Robert Siodmak
Shoot 76 Harvey Hart
Shoot First 53 Robert Parrish
Shoot First, Laugh Last 67 Luigi Vanzi
Shoot for the Sun 86 Ian Knox
Shoot It: Black, Shoot It: Blue 74 Dennis McGuire
Shoot Loud, Louder...I Don't Understand 66 Eduardo De Filippo
Shoot Out at Big Sag 62 Roger Kay
Shoot the Moon 81 Alan Parker
Shoot the Nets 52 Herman van den Horst
Shoot the Pianist 60 François Truffaut
Shoot the Piano Player 60 François Truffaut
Shoot the Sun Down 76 David Leeds
Shoot the Works 34 Wesley Ruggles
Shoot to Kill 47 William Berke
Shoot to Kill 60 Michael Winner
Shoot to Kill 88 Roger Spottiswoode
Shootin' Fish 21 Earl Hurd
Shootin' for Love 23 Edward Sedgwick
Shootin' Irons 27 Richard Rosson
Shootin' Irons 43 Oliver Drake
Shootin' Mad 18 Gilbert M. Anderson
Shooting, The 66 Monte Hellman
Shooting a Boer Spy 1899 Robert Ashe
Shooting at the Karash Pass 68 Bolotbek Shamshiev
Shooting High 40 Alfred E. Green
Shooting in the Back-Country 87 Vladimir Khotinenko

Shooting of Dan McGoo, The 45 Tex Avery
Shooting of Dan McGrew, The 15 Herbert Blaché
Shooting of Dan McGrew, The 24 Clarence Badger
Shooting Party, The 78 Emil Lotyanu
Shooting Party, The 84 Alan Bridges
Shooting Stars 27 Anthony Asquith, A. V. Bramble
Shooting Stars 37 Eric Humphris
Shooting Straight 27 William Wyler
Shooting Straight 30 George Archainbaud
Shooting the Chutes 1898 Georges Méliès
Shooting Wild 27 Mark Sandrich
Shootist, The 76 Don Siegel
Shootout 71 Henry Hathaway
Shootout at Medicine Bend 57 Richard L. Bare
Shop Angel 32 E. Mason Hopper
Shop Around the Corner, The 39 Ernst Lubitsch
Shop at Sly Corner, The 46 George King
Shop Girl, The 16 George D. Baker
Shop in the High Street 64 Ján Kadár, Elmar Klos
Shop, Look and Listen 40 Friz Freleng
Shop on High Street, The 64 Ján Kadár, Elmar Klos
Shop on Main Street, The 64 Ján Kadár, Elmar Klos
Shop on the High Street, A 64 Ján Kadár, Elmar Klos
Shopgirls 14 Lawrence Trimble
Shopgirls of Paris 43 André Cayatte
Shopgirls, or The Great Question 14 Lawrence Trimble
Shoplifter, The 05 Frank Mottershaw
Shoplifter, The 65 Andy Warhol
Shopping Mall 85 Michael Barnard
Shopsoiled Girl, The 15 Leedham Bantock
Shopworn 32 Nick Grindé
Shopworn Angel 28 Richard Wallace
Shopworn Angel 38 H. C. Potter
Shore Acres 14 John H. Pratt
Shore Acres 20 Rex Ingram
Shore Enough 26 William C. Nolan
Shore Leave 25 John S. Robertson
Shores of Phos: A Fable, The 72 Stan Brakhage
Shōri no Hi Made 45 Mikio Naruse
Shors 39 Alexander Dovzhenko, Yulia Solntseva
Short and Curlies, The 87 Mike Leigh
Short and Suite 59 Evelyn Lambert, Norman McLaren
Short Change 24 Archie Mayo
Short Changed 85 George Ogilvie
Short Circuit 86 John Badham
Short Circuit 2 88 Kenneth Johnson
Short Cut 80 Jiří Menzel
Short Cut to Hell 57 James Cagney
Short Cuts 80 Jiří Menzel
Short Encounters 67 Kira Muratova
Short Eyes 77 Robert M. Young
Short Film About Killing, A 88 Krzysztof Kieślowski
Short Film About Love, A 88 Krzysztof Kieślowski
Short Films, 1975 75 Stan Brakhage

Short Films, 1976 76 Stan Brakhage
Short Fuse 86 Blaine Novak
Short Grass 50 Lesley Selander
Short Is the Summer 62 Bjarne Henning-Jensen
Short Meetings 67 Kira Muratova
Short Shave 65 Michael Snow
Short-Sighted Errand Boy, The 10 Lewin Fitzhamon
Short-Sighted Jane 07 Alf Collins
Short-Sighted Sammy 05 J. H. Martin
Short Skirts 21 Harry B. Harris
Short Skirts 28 Erle C. Kenton
Short Snorts on Sports 48 Alex Lovy
Short Stories of Terror 60 Enrique Carreras
Short Tall Story 70 John Halas
Short Time 90 Gregg Champion
Shortcut 89 Giuliano Montaldo
Shortest Day, The 63 Sergio Corbucci
Shot, The 14 Mauritz Stiller
Shot and Bothered 66 Rudy Larriva
Shot at Dawn, A 34 Alfred Zeisler
Shot from the Heart, A 86 Kristian Levring
Shot in the Dark, A 33 George Pearson
Shot in the Dark, A 35 Charles Lamont
Shot in the Dark, The 41 William McGann
Shot in the Dark, A 64 Blake Edwards
Shot in the Head 68 Péter Bacsó
Shot in the Heart, A 65 Jean-Daniel Pollet
Shotgun 55 Lesley Selander
Shotgun Pass 31 John P. McGowan
Shotgun Wedding, The 63 Boris Petroff
Shotguns That Kick 14 Roscoe Arbuckle
Shots Ring Out 63 Augustin Navarro
Shōchū Nikki 24 Daisuke Ito
Should a Doctor Tell? 23 Alexander Butler
Should a Doctor Tell? 30 H. Manning Haynes
Should a Girl Marry? 29 Scott Pembroke
Should a Girl Marry? 39 Lambert Hillyer
Should a Husband Forgive? 19 Raoul Walsh
Should a Mother Tell? 15 J. Gordon Edwards
Should a Mother Tell? 25 Alexander Butler
Should a Wife Work? 22 Horace G. Plympton
Should a Woman Divorce? 14 Ivan Abramson
Should a Woman Forgive? 15 Henry King
Should a Woman Tell? 19 John Ince
Should Crooners Marry? 33 George Stevens
Should Dummies Wed? 20 Roy Del Ruth
Should Husbands Be Watched? 25 Leo McCarey
Should Husbands Work? 39 Gus Meins
Should Ladies Behave? 33 Harry Beaumont
Should Married Men Go Home? 28 Leo McCarey, James Parrott
Should Parents Tell? 48 Erle C. Kenton
Should She Obey? 17 George Siegmann
Should Wives Work? 37 Leslie Goodwins
Should Women Drive? 28 Leo McCarey

Side Show *31* Roy Del Ruth
Side Street *29* Malcolm St. Clair
Side Street *49* Anthony Mann
Side Street Angel *37* Ralph Ince
Side Street Story *50* Eduardo De Filippo
Side Streets *33* Ivar Campbell
Side Streets *34* Alfred E. Green
Sidecar Racers *75* Earl Bellamy
Sidehackers, The *69* Gus Trikonis
Sidelong Glances of a Pigeon Kicker, The *70* John Dexter
Sideshow, The *28* Erle C. Kenton
Sideshow *50* Jean Yarbrough
Sideshow of Life, The *24* Herbert Brenon
Sideshow Wrestlers *08* Georges Méliès
Sidewalk Stories *89* Charles Lane
Sidewalks of London *38* Tim Whelan
Sidewalks of New York *23* Lester Park
Sidewalks of New York, The *29* Dave Fleischer
Sidewalks of New York, The *31* Zion Myers, Jules White
Sidewinder One *77* Earl Bellamy
Sidney Sheldon's Bloodline *79* Terence Young
Sidney's Joujoux *00* Alice Guy-Blaché
Sid's Long Count *30* Sam Newfield
Sidste Akt *87* Edward Fleming
Sidste Vinter, Den *60* Jørgen Roos
Sie *54* Rolf Thiele
Sie Nannten Ihn Gringo *64* Roy Rowland
Sie Sind Frei, Doktor Korczak! *73* Aleksander Ford
Sie Tötete in Extase *70* Jesús Franco
Sie und die Drei *22* E. A. Dupont
Sie und die Drei *38* Viktor Jansen
Sieben Frauen *89* Rudolph Thome
Sieben Männer der Su-Maru, Die *70* Jesús Franco
Sieben Ohrfeigen *38* Paul Martin
Sieben vom Rhein *54* Andrew Thorndike, Annelie Thorndike
Siebente Gebot, Das *20* Richard Oswald
7. Kontinent, Der *89* Michael Haneke
Siedma Pevnina *66* Joseph Medved, Dušan Vukotić
Sieg des Glaubens *33* Leni Riefenstahl
Siege *25* Svend Gade
Siege, The *50* Juan De Orduna
Siege *83* Paul Donovan, Maura O'Connell
Siege at Red River, The *54* Rudolph Maté
Siège de Syracuse, Le *62* Pietro Francisci
Siège des Trois, Le *18* Jacques De Baroncelli
Siege of Fort Bismarck, The *63* Kengo Furusawa
Siege of Hell Street, The *60* Robert S. Baker, Monty Berman
Siege of Liege, The *15* Harry S. Palmer
Siege of Pinchgut, The *59* Harry Watt
Siege of Red River, The *54* Rudolph Maté
Siege of Sidney Street, The *60* Robert S. Baker, Monty Berman
Siege of Syracuse, The *62* Pietro Francisci
Siege of the Saxons, The *63* Nathan Juran
Sieger, Der *22* Walter Ruttmann
Siegfried *12* Mario Caserini
Siegfried *23* Fritz Lang
Siegfried *87* Andrzej Domalik
Siegfried's Death *23* Fritz Lang

Siegfrieds Tod *23* Fritz Lang
Siekierezada *87* Witold Leszczyński
Siempre Tuya *50* Emilio Fernández
Siero della Verità, Il *49* Dino Risi
Sierra *50* Alfred E. Green
Sierra Baron *58* James B. Clark
Sierra de Teruel *39* André Malraux
Sierra Jim's Reformation *14* Raoul Walsh
Sierra Leone *87* Uwe Schrader
Sierra Passage *51* Frank McDonald
Sierra Stranger *57* Lee Sholem
Sierra Sue *41* William Morgan
Siesta *87* Mary Lambert
Siesta Samba *76* Vilgot Sjöman
Šiesta Veta *86* Stefan Uher
Siete Días de Enero *79* Juan Antonio Bardem
Siete Espartanos, Los *64* Pedro Lazaga Sabater
Siete Hombres de Oro *65* Marco Vicario
Siete Locos, Los *73* Leopoldo Torre-Nilsson
Siete Magníficas, Las *66* Rudolf Zehetgruber
Siete Mujeres para los MacGregors *67* Franco Giraldi
Siete Pistolas para los MacGregors *65* Franco Giraldi
Sight-Seeing Through Whiskey *07* Georges Méliès
Sight Unseen, A *14* Stanner E. V. Taylor
Sigillo de Pechino, Il *66* Bill Catching, James Hill
Sigma III *66* Albert Whiteman
Sign Invisible, The *18* Edgar Lewis
Sign o' the Times *87* Prince
Sign of Aquarius *70* Robert J. Emery
Sign of Disaster *86* Mikhail Ptashuk
Sign of Four, The *23* Maurice Elvey
Sign of Four, The *32* Graham Cutts, Rowland V. Lee
Sign of Four *83* Desmond Davis
Sign of Leo, The *56* Eric Rohmer
Sign of the Cactus, The *25* Clifford Smith
Sign of the Claw, The *26* B. Reeves Eason
Sign of the Cross, The *1899* Georges Méliès
Sign of the Cross, The *04* William Haggar
Sign of the Cross, The *32* Cecil B. DeMille
Sign of the Dagger *48* Ray Nazarro
Sign of the Gladiator *58* Michelangelo Antonioni, Riccardo Freda
Sign of the Lion *56* Eric Rohmer
Sign of the Pagan *54* Douglas Sirk
Sign of the Poppy, The *16* Charles Swickard
Sign of the Ram, The *48* John Sturges
Sign of the Rose, The *15* Thomas Ince
Sign of the Rose, The *22* Harry Garson
Sign of the Spade, The *16* Murdock MacQuarrie
Sign of the Vampire, The *70* Jesús Franco
Sign of the Virgin *69* Zbyněk Brynych
Sign of the Wolf, The *31* Forrest K. Sheldon, Harry S. Webb
Sign of the Wolf *41* Howard Bretherton
Sign of Venus, The *55* Dino Risi
Sign of Zorro, The *60* Lewis R. Foster, Norman Foster

Sign on the Door, The *21* Herbert Brenon
Sign Please *33* John Rawlins
Sign Writer, The *1897* George Albert Smith
Signal Fires of Shanghai *44* Hiroshi Inagaki
Signal 7 *83* Rob Nilsson
Signal Through the Flames *84* Maxine Harris, Sheldon Rochlin
Signal Tower, The *24* Clarence Brown
Signale — Ein Weltraumabenteuer *70* Gottfried Kolditz
Signals — An Adventure in Space *70* Gottfried Kolditz
Signals in the Night *13* H. Oceano Martinek
Signé Arsène Lupin *59* Yves Robert
Signé Charlotte *86* Caroline Huppert
Signe du Lion, Le *56* Eric Rohmer
Signé Renart *85* Michel Soutter
Signed Arsène Lupin *59* Yves Robert
Signed Judgment *44* Benjamin Kline
Signed: Lino Brocka *87* Christian Blackwood
Signo del Vampiro, El *70* Jesús Franco
Signor Bruschino, Il *68* Vittorio Sala
Signor Max, Il *37* Mario Camerini
Signor Potti's Love Affair *11* A. E. Coleby
Signor Robinson, Monstruosa Storia d'Amore e d'Avventure, Il *76* Sergio Corbucci
Signora Arlecchino, La *18* Mario Caserini
Signora Ciclone, La *16* Augusto Genina
Signora degli Orrori, La *77* Mauro Bolognini
Signora della Notte, La *86* Piero Schivazappa
Signora delle Camelie, La *09* Ugo Falena
Signora delle Camelie, La *15* Baldassare Negroni
Signora delle Camelie, La *47* Carmine Gallone
Signora dell'Ovest, Una *42* Carlo Koch
Signora di Montecarlo, La *38* Mario Soldati
Signora di Tutti, La *34* Max Ophüls
Signora Fortuna *37* Gennaro Righelli
Signora Paradiso *34* Enrico Guazzoni
Signora Senza Camelie, La *53* Michelangelo Antonioni
Signore e Signori *65* Pietro Germi
Signore e Signori, Buonanotte *76* Leonardo Benvenuti, Luigi Comencini, Piero De Bernardi, Nanni Loy, Ruggero Maccari, Luigi Magni, Mario Monicelli, Ugo Pirro, Ettore Scola
Signori e Signore *65* Pietro Germi
Signori in Carrozza! *51* Luigi Zampa
Signorina Madre di Famiglia, La *24* Carmine Gallone
Signorinette *42* Luigi Zampa
Signpost to Murder *64* George Englund
Signs of Life *67* Werner Herzog
Signs of Life *89* John David Coles
Signs of Spring *16* Harry S. Palmer
Sigui Année Zéro *66* Germaine Dieterlen, Jean Rouch
Sigui: L'Enclume de Yougo *67* Jean Rouch
Sigui 1968: Les Danseurs de Tyogou *68* Germaine Dieterlen, Jean Rouch

Sigui 1969: La Caverne de Bongo *69* Germaine Dieterlen, Jean Rouch

Sigui 1970: Les Clameurs d'Amani *70* Germaine Dieterlen, Jean Rouch

Sigui 1971: La Dune d'Idyeli *71* Germaine Dieterlen, Jean Rouch

Sigui 1972: Les Pagnes de Iame *72* Germaine Dieterlen, Jean Rouch

Sigui 1973: L'Auvent de la Circoncision *73* Jean Rouch

Sikat Safar *86* Bashir El Deek

Sikkim, 1971 *71* Satyajit Ray

Sikkim, Terre Secrète *56* Serge Bourguignon

Sila *88* B. R. Ishara

Silas at the Seaside *16* Joe Evans

Silas Marner *16* Ernest C. Warde

Silas Marner *22* Frank P. Donovan

Silas Marner *85* Giles Foster

Silberne Kugel, Die *15* Richard Oswald

Silence *20* Louis Delluc

Silence, Le *20* Louis Delluc

Silence *26* Hugh Brooke, John Greenidge

Silence *26* Rupert Julian

Silence *31* Louis Gasnier, Max Marcin

Silence, The *39* Norman Walker

Silence *63* Kazimierz Kutz

Silence, The *63* Ingmar Bergman

Silence *71* Masahiro Shinoda

Silence *74* John Korty

Silence and Cry *67* Miklós Jancsó

Silence at Bethany, The *88* Joel Oliansky

Silence dans la Forêt, Le *29* William Dieterle

Silence de la Mer, Le *47* Jean-Pierre Melville

Silence = Death *90* Rosa von Praunheim

Silence Est d'Or, Le *47* René Clair

Silence Has No Wings *71* Kazuo Kuroki

Silence Is Golden *47* René Clair

Silence of Dean Maitland, The *34* Ken Hall

Silence of Dr. Evans, The *73* Budimir Metalnikov

Silence of Jasper Holt, The *15* Edwin J. Collins

Silence of Martha, The *15* Chester M. Franklin, Sidney Franklin

Silence of Richard Wilton, The *13* Warwick Buckland

Silence of the Forest, The *29* William Dieterle

Silence of the Forest, The *37* Hans Deppe

Silence of the Heart *68* Lester James Peries

Silence of the North *81* Allan King

Silence Sellers, The *17* Burton L. King

Silencers, The *65* Phil Karlson

Silencieux, Le *73* Claude Pinoteau

Silencio Sublime *37* Ramón Peón

Silent Accuser, The *23* Richard Thomas

Silent Accuser, The *24* Chester M. Franklin

Silent Assassins *88* Doo-yong Lee, Scott Thomas

Silent Avenger, The *20* William Duncan

Silent Avenger, The *27* James P. Hogan

Silent Barricade, The *49* Otakar Vávra

Silent Barrier, The *20* William Worthington

Silent Barriers *37* Geoffrey Barkas, Milton Rosmer

Silent Battle, The *16* Jack Conway

Silent Battle, The *39* Herbert Mason

Silent Call, The *21* Lawrence Trimble

Silent Call, The *61* John Bushelman

Silent Code, The *35* Stuart Paton

Silent Command, The *15* Robert Z. Leonard

Silent Command, The *23* J. Gordon Edwards

Silent Conflict *48* George Archainbaud

Silent Cry *82* Márta Mészáros

Silent Death *57* Reginald LeBorg

Silent Duel, A *48* Akira Kurosawa

Silent Dust *49* Lance Comfort

Silent Enemy, The *30* H. P. Carver

Silent Enemy, The *58* William Fairchild

Silent Evidence *22* Charles C. Calvert

Silent Flute, The *78* Richard Moore

Silent Guardian, The *26* William Bletcher

Silent Hero, The *27* Duke Worne

Silent House, The *29* Walter Forde

Silent Invasion, The *62* Max Varnel

Silent Journey *55* Jonas Mekas

Silent Joy *85* Dušan Hanák

Silent Lady, The *17* Elsie Jane Wilson

Silent Lie, The *17* Raoul Walsh

Silent Love *86* David Chiang

Silent Lover, The *26* George Archainbaud

Silent Madness *84* Simon Nuchtern

Silent Man, The *17* William S. Hart, Lambert Hillyer

Silent Man of Timber Gulch, The *16* Robert Z. Leonard

Silent Master, The *17* Léonce Perret

Silent Member, The *16* Robert Z. Leonard

Silent Men *33* D. Ross Lederman

Silent Message, The *10* Gilbert M. Anderson

Silent Movie *76* Mel Brooks

Silent Murder, The *59* Hideo Sekigawa

Silent Mystery, The *19* Francis Ford

Silent Night *88* Monica Teuber

Silent Night, Bloody Night *72* Theodore Gershuny

Silent Night, Deadly Night *84* Charles E. Sellier

Silent Night, Deadly Night Part II *87* Lee Harry

Silent Night, Deadly Night III: Better Watch Out! *89* Monte Hellman

Silent Night, Evil Night *74* Bob Clark

Silent One, The *73* Claude Pinoteau

Silent One, The *84* Yvonne Mackay

Silent Pal *25* Henry McCarthy

Silent Partner, The *17* Marshall Neilan

Silent Partner, The *23* Charles Maigne

Silent Partner, The *27* William Wyler

Silent Partner *44* George Blair

Silent Partner, The *78* Daryl Duke

Silent Passenger, The *35* Reginald Denham

Silent Pioneers, The *84* Lucy Winer

Silent Playground, The *63* Stanley Goulder

Silent Power, The *26* Frank O'Connor

Silent Rage *82* Michael Miller

Silent Raid, The *62* Paul Rotha

Silent Raiders *54* Richard Bartlett

Silent Rider *18* Clifford Smith

Silent Rider, The *27* Lynn Reynolds

Silent Running *71* Douglas Trumbull

Silent Sanderson *25* Scott R. Dunlap

Silent Scream *80* Denny Harris

Silent Sentence *83* Larry Spangler

Silent Sentinel *29* Alvin J. Neitz

Silent Shelby *16* Frank Borzage

Silent Sheldon *25* Harry S. Webb

Silent Signal, The *11* Alice Guy-Blaché

Silent Sound Sense Stars Subotnik and Sender *62* Stan Brakhage

Silent Star *60* Kurt Mätzig

Silent Stranger, The *24* Albert S. Rogell

Silent Stranger, The *58* Harry Keller

Silent Stranger, The *66* Luigi Vanzi

Silent Strength *19* Paul Scardon

Silent Trail *28* John P. McGowan

Silent Tweetment *46* Bob Wickersham

Silent Valley *35* Bernard B. Ray

Silent Village, The *43* Humphrey Jennings

Silent Voice, The *15* Fred J. Balshofer, William J. Bowman

Silent Voice, The *22* F. Harmon Weight

Silent Voice, The *32* John G. Adolfi

Silent Voice, The *52* Rudolph Maté

Silent Vow, The *22* William Duncan

Silent Watcher, The *24* Frank Lloyd

Silent Weapon, The *61* Peter Duffell

Silent Witness, A *13* Frank Wilson

Silent Witness, The *17* Gerald F. Bacon, Harry Lambart

Silent Witness, The *32* R. Lee Hough, Marcel Varnel

Silent Witness *42* Joseph H. Lewis

Silent Witness *42* Jean Yarbrough

Silent Witness, The *54* Montgomery Tully

Silent Witness, The *62* Ken Kennedy

Silent Witness, The *78* David W. Rolfe

Silent Witnesses *14* Yevgeni Bauer

Silent Woman, The *18* Herbert Blaché

Silent World, The *55* Jacques-Yves Cousteau, Louis Malle

Silent Years *21* Louis Gasnier

Silhouette des Teufels, Die *17* Joe May

Silhouettes *82* Giuseppe Murolo

Silicates, The *66* Terence Fisher

Silip *85* Elwood Perez

Silk *86* Cirio Santiago

Silk, Blood and Sun *43* Fernando Rivero

Silk Express, The *33* Ray Enright

Silk Hat Kid *35* H. Bruce Humberstone

Silk Hosiery *20* Fred Niblo

Silk Husbands and Calico Wives *20* Alfred E. Green

Silk Legs *27* Arthur Rosson

Silk-Lined Burglar, The *19* John Francis Dillon

Silk Noose, The *48* Edmond T. Gréville

Silk Stocking Girl *24* Tod Browning

Silk Stocking Sal *24* Tod Browning

Silk Stockings *27* Wesley Ruggles

Silk Stockings *57* Rouben Mamoulian

Silken Affair, The *56* Roy Kellino

Silken Shackles *26* Walter Morosco

Silken Skin *62* François Truffaut

Silken Spider, The *16* Frank Borzage

Silken Threads *28* Leslie Eveleigh

Silken Trap, The *68* Francis D. Lyon

Silks and Saddles *29* Robert F. Hill

Silks and Saddles *38* Robert F. Hill

Silks and Satins *16* J. Searle Dawley
Silkwood *83* Mike Nichols
Silliettes *23* Herbert M. Dawley
Silly Billies *36* Fred Guiol
Silly Hoots *20* Henry D. Bailey
Silly Sammy *11* Percy Stow
Silly Scandals *31* Dave Fleischer
Silly Younger Brother and Clever Elder
    Brother *31* Heinosuke Gosho
Silnice Zpívá *37* Alexander Hammid
Silt *31* Daniel Birt
Siluramento dell'Oceania, Il *17* Augusto
    Genina
Silver Bandit, The *50* Elmer Clifton
Silver Bears *77* Ivan Passer
Silver Blaze *12* Georges Treville
Silver Blaze *23* George Ridgwell
Silver Blaze *37* Thomas Bentley
Silver Bridge, The *20* Dallas Cairns
Silver Buddha, The *23* A. E. Coleby
Silver Bullet, The *35* Bernard B. Ray
Silver Bullet, The *42* Joseph H. Lewis
Silver Bullet *85* Daniel Attias
Silver Canyon *51* John English
Silver Car, The *21* David Smith
Silver Chains *51* Ray Nazarro
Silver Chalice, The *54* Victor Saville
Silver City *47* Ray Enright
Silver City *51* Byron Haskin
Silver City *68* Wim Wenders
Silver City *84* Sophia Turkiewicz
Silver City Bonanza *51* George Blair
Silver City Kid *44* John English
Silver City Raiders *43* William Berke
Silver Comes Through *27* Lloyd Ingraham
Silver Comes Thru *27* Lloyd Ingraham
Silver Cord, The *33* John Cromwell
Silver Darlings, The *47* Clarence Elder,
    Clifford Evans
Silver Devil *31* Sidney Algier, Richard
    Thorpe
Silver Dollar, The *11* Thomas Ince
Silver Dollar *32* Alfred E. Green
Silver Double Suicide *55* Kaneto Shindo
Silver Dream Racer *80* David Wickes
Silver Dust *53* Abram Room
Silver Fingers *26* John P. McGowan
Silver Fleet, The *42* Michael Powell, Vernon Sewell, Gordon Wellesley
Silver Girl, The *19* Eliot Howe, Frank
    Keenan
Silver Goat, The *16* Michael Curtiz
Silver Greyhound, The *19* Bannister
    Merwin
Silver Greyhound, The *32* William
    McGann
Silver Grindstone, The *13* William
    Duncan
Silver Horde, The *20* Frank Lloyd
Silver Horde, The *30* George Archainbaud
Silver Key, The *44* William Berke
Silver King, The *19* George Irving
Silver King, The *29* T. Hayes Hunter
Silver King Comes Thru *27* Lloyd Ingraham
Silver Lining, The *11* Bert Haldane
Silver Lining, The *15* B. Reeves Eason
Silver Lining, The *19* A. E. Coleby
Silver Lining, The *21* Roland West
Silver Lining, The *27* Thomas Bentley

Silver Lining, The *31* Alan Crosland
Silver Lode *54* Allan Dwan
Silver on the Sage *39* Lesley Selander
Silver-Plated Gun, The *13* Allan Dwan
Silver Queen *42* Lloyd Bacon
Silver Raiders *50* Wallace Fox
Silver Range *46* Lambert Hillyer
Silver River *48* Raoul Walsh
Silver Skates *42* Leslie Goodwins
Silver Slave, The *27* Howard Bretherton
Silver Spoon, The *34* George King
Silver Spurs *22* Henry McCarthy
Silver Spurs *36* Ray Taylor
Silver Spurs *43* Joseph Kane
Silver Stallion *41* Edward Finney
Silver Star, The *55* Richard Bartlett
Silver Streak, The *34* Thomas Atkins
Silver Streak *76* Arthur Hiller
Silver Tenor, or The Song That Failed,
    The *04* Alf Collins
Silver Threads Among the Gold *15* Pierce
    Kingsley
Silver Threads Among the Gold *21* Walter
    C. Rowden
Silver Top *37* George King
Silver Trail, The *37* Bernard B. Ray
Silver Trails *48* Christy Cabanne
Silver Treasure, The *26* Rowland V. Lee
Silver Valley *27* Ben Stoloff
Silver Whip, The *53* Harmon Jones
Silver Wings *22* Edwin Carewe, John Ford
Silverado *85* Lawrence Kasdan
Simabaddha *71* Satyajit Ray
Simão o Caolho *52* Alberto Cavalcanti
Simba *54* Brian Desmond Hurst
Simba the King of Beasts *27* Martin E.
    Johnson
Simchon Family, The *69* Joel Silberg
Similitudes de Longueurs et des Vitesses
    38 Jean Painlevé
Simion of Maldeniye *87* D. B. Nihalsingha
Simiri Siddo Kuma *78* Jean Rouch
Simon *80* Marshall Brickman
Simon and Laura *55* Muriel Box
Simón Bolívar *41* Miguel Torres Contreras
Simon Bolivar *68* Alessandro Blasetti
Simón del Desierto *63* Luis Buñuel
Simon, King of Witches *71* Bruce Kessler
Simon Menyhért Születése *54* Károly
    Makk
Simon of the Desert *63* Luis Buñuel
Simon, Simon *70* Graham Stark
Simon the Jester *15* Edward José
Simon the Jester *25* George Melford
Simon the One-Eyed *52* Alberto Cavalcanti
Simon the Swiss *70* Claude Lelouch
Simone *18* Camille De Morlhon
Simone *26* Donatien
Simone Evrard, or Deathless Devotion *23*
    Edwin Greenwood
Simparele *74* Humberto Solás
Simpkins' Dream of a Holiday *11* Walter
    R. Booth, Theo Bouwmeester
Simpkins Gets the War Scare *14* Frank
    Wilson
Simpkins' Little Swindle *14* Hay Plumb
Simpkins' Saturday Off *07* Lewin Fitzhamon

Simpkins, Special Constable *14* Hay
    Plumb
Simpkins' Sunday Dinner *14* Hay Plumb
Simple Case, A *30* Mikhail Doller, Vsevolod I. Pudovkin
Simple Case of Money, A *50* André
    Hunebelle
Simple Charity *10* D. W. Griffith
Simple Histoire, Une *58* Marcel Hanoun
Simple Life, The *19* Larry Semon
Simple Life, The *26* H. B. Parkinson
"Simple Life" Cure, The *14* Hay Plumb
Simple Love, The *12* Allan Dwan
Simple Love, A *59* Félix Máriássy
Simple Melody, A *74* Kjell Grede
Simple People *45* Grigori Kozintsev,
    Leonid Trauberg
Simple Simon *22* Henry Edwards
Simple Simon *35* Ubbe Iwerks
Simple Simon at the Races *09* S. Wormald
Simple Simon's Surprise Party *04* Georges
    Méliès
Simple Siren *45* Paul Sommer
Simple Sis *27* Herman Raymaker
Simple Souls *20* Robert Thornby
Simple Story, A *30* Alexander Stolper
Simple Story, A *78* Claude Sautet
Simple Tailor, The *34* Vladimir Vilner
Simplet *42* Carlo-Rim, Fernandel
Simplette *19* René Hervil
Simply Irresistible *83* Edwin Brown
Simply Killing *31* Norman Taurog
Simply Terrific *38* Roy William Neill
Sin *15* Herbert Brenon
Sin *16* Georgy Azagarov, Yakov Protazanov
Sin *28* Gustaf Molander
Sin, The *61* Kon Ichikawa
Sin, The *71* Alberto Lattuada
Sin, The *79* Marvin Chomsky
Sin Cargo *26* Louis Gasnier
Sin Flood, The *21* Frank Lloyd
Sin Flood *30* Frank Lloyd
Sin in the Suburbs *62* Joe Sarno
Sin Now...Pay Later *66* Don Rolos
Sin Now...Pay Later *66* Gianni Vernuccio
Sin of Abbé Mouret, The *70* Georges
    Franju
Sin of Adam and Eve, The *72* Miguel
    Zacarías
Sin of Father Mouret, The *70* Georges
    Franju
Sin of Harold Diddlebock, The *46* Preston
    Sturges
Sin of Jesus *61* Robert Frank
Sin of Lena Rivers, The *32* Phil Rosen
Sin of Madelon Claudet, The *31* Edgar
    Selwyn
Sin of Martha Queed, The *21* Allan Dwan
Sin of Mona Kent, The *61* Charles Hundt
Sin of Nora Moran, The *33* Phil Goldstone
Sin of the Parent *16* Frank Lloyd
Sin on the Beach *64* José Benazeraf
Sin Ship, The *31* Lynn Shores, Louis Wolheim
Sin Sister *29* Charles Klein
Sin, Suffer and Repent *65* Herschell Gordon Lewis*

Sin Takes a Holiday *30* Paul Stein
Sin That Was His, The *20* Hobart Henley
Sin Town *29* J. Gordon Cooper
Sin Town *42* Ray Enright
Sin Uniforme *48* Ladislas Vajda
Sin-Ventura, La *22* Donatien
Sin Ye Do, The *16* Walter Edwards
Sin You Sinners *63* Joe Sarno
Sinai Commandos *68* Raphael Nussbaum
Sinai Commandos: The Story of the Six Day War *68* Raphael Nussbaum
Sinai Field Mission *77* Frederick Wiseman
Sinatra: A Man and His Music *67* Michael Pfleghar
Sinaya Tetrad *63* Lev Kulidzhanov
Sinbad *71* Zoltán Huszárik
Sinbad and the Eye of the Tiger *77* Sam Wanamaker
Sinbad the Sailor *35* Ubbe Iwerks
Sinbad the Sailor *47* Richard Wallace
Since You Went Away *44* John Cromwell, André De Toth
Sincere Heart *53* Masaki Kobayashi
Sincerely Charlotte *86* Caroline Huppert
Sincerely Yours *55* Gordon Douglas
Sincerity *39* Mikio Naruse
Sincerity *53* Masaki Kobayashi
Sincerity *73* Stan Brakhage
Sincerity II *75* Stan Brakhage
Sincerity III *78* Stan Brakhage
Sincerity IV *80* Stan Brakhage
Sincerity V *80* Stan Brakhage
Sindbad *71* Zoltán Huszárik
Sinews of Steel *27* Frank O'Connor
Sinfin, Death Is No Solution *87* Cristián Pauls
Sinfin, la Muerta No Es Ninguna Solución *87* Cristián Pauls
Sinfonía del Más Allá *66* Federico Curiel
Sinfonia per Due Spie *66* Michael Pfleghar
Sinfonia per un Massacro *63* Jacques Deray
Sinful Davey *68* John Huston
Sinful Life, A *89* William Schreiner
Sing *89* Richard Baskin
Sing a Jingle *43* Edward Lilley
Sing a Song *32* Dave Fleischer
Sing a Song for Heaven's Sake *60* Ulf Van Court
Sing a Song of Sex *67* Nagisa Oshima
Sing-Along, Dance-Along, Do-Along *88* Jim Henson
Sing Along with Me *52* Peter Graham Scott
Sing and Be Happy *37* James Tinling
Sing and Like It *34* William A. Seiter
Sing and Swing *63* Lance Comfort
Sing Another Chorus *41* Charles Lamont
Sing As We Go *34* Rowland Brown, Basil Dean
Sing As You Swing *37* Redd Davis
Sing, Babies, Sing *33* Dave Fleischer
Sing, Baby, Sing *36* Sidney Lanfield
Sing, Boy, Sing *58* Henry Ephron
Sing, Cowboy, Sing *37* Robert North Bradbury
Sing, Dance, Plenty Hot *40* Lew Landers
Sing for Your Supper *41* Charles Barton
Sing Me a Love Song *35* Stuart Walker
Sing Me a Love Song *36* Ray Enright

Sing Me a Song of Texas *45* Vernon Keays
Sing, Neighbor, Sing *44* Frank McDonald
Sing-Sing *71* Barbet Schroeder
Sing Sing *83* Sergio Corbucci
Sing Sing Nights *34* Lewis D. Collins
Sing Sing Thanksgiving *74* David Hoffman, Harry Wiland
Sing, Sinner, Sing *33* Howard Christy
Sing, Sister, Sing *35* James Parrott
Sing, Sisters, Sing! *33* Dave Fleischer
Sing While You Dance *46* D. Ross Lederman
Sing While You're Able *36* Marshall Neilan
Sing, You Dancers *30* Norman Taurog
Sing, You Sinners *38* Wesley Ruggles
Sing, Young People *63* Keisuke Kinoshita
Sing Your Songs *86* Şerif Gören
Sing Your Way Home *45* Anthony Mann
Sing Your Worries Away *42* A. Edward Sutherland
Singapore *47* John Brahm
Singapore Mutiny, The *28* Ralph Ince
Singapore, Singapore *68* Bernard Toublanc-Michel
Singapore Story, The *52* B. Reeves Eason
Singapore Woman *41* Jean Negulesco
Singaree *10* August Blom
Singe en Hiver, Un *62* Henri Verneuil
Singed *27* John Griffith Wray
Singed Wings *15* Yevgeni Bauer
Singed Wings *22* Penrhyn Stanlaws
Singende Stadt, Die *30* Carmine Gallone
Singer and the Champ, The *85* Nini Grassia
Singer and the Dancer, The *76* Gillian Armstrong
Singer from Seville, The *30* Charles Brabin
Singer Jim McKee *24* Clifford Smith
Singer Midget's Scandal *21* Edward F. Cline
Singer Midget's Side Show *21* Edward F. Cline
Singer Not the Song, The *60* Roy Ward Baker
Singer of Naples, The *34* Howard Bretherton
Singer of Seville, The *30* Ramón Navarro
Singeries Humaines *10* Émile Cohl
Singin' in the Corn *46* Del Lord
Singin' in the Rain *51* Stanley Donen, Gene Kelly
Singing Angels *52* Gustav Ucicky
Singing Blacksmith, The *38* Edgar G. Ulmer
Singing Buckaroo, The *37* Tom Gibson
Singing Cop, The *38* Arthur Woods
Singing Cowboy, The *36* Mack V. Wright
Singing Cowgirl, The *39* Samuel Diege
Singing Fool, The *28* Lloyd Bacon
Singing Guns *50* R. G. Springsteen
Singing Hill, The *41* Lew Landers
Singing Hills, The *41* Lew Landers
Singing in the Air *37* Jean Yarbrough
Singing in the Dark *56* Max Nosseck
Singing Kid, The *36* William Keighley
Singing Lesson, The *67* Lindsay Anderson
Singing Makes Life Beautiful *50* Márton Keleti

Singing Marine, The *37* Ray Enright
Singing Musketeer, The *38* Allan Dwan
Singing Nun, The *65* Henry Koster
Singing on the Trail *46* Ray Nazarro
Singing on the Treadmill *74* Gyula Gazdag
Singing Outlaw, The *37* Joseph H. Lewis
Singing Princess, The *67* Anton Gino Domeneghini
Singing River *21* Charles Giblyn
Singing Sap, The *30* Walter Lantz
Singing Sheriff, The *44* Leslie Goodwins
Singing Spurs *48* Ray Nazarro
Singing Taxi Driver *50* Carmine Gallone
Singing the Blues in Red *86* Kenneth Loach
Singing Through *35* Max Mack
Singing Vagabond, The *35* Carl Pierson
Single and Married *14* Anders Wilhelm Sandberg
Single Code, The *17* Thomas Ricketts
Single Girls, The *73* Beverly Sebastian, Ferd Sebastian
Single Handed *23* Edward Sedgwick
Single-Handed *51* Roy Boulting
Single-Handed Sanders *32* Lloyd Nosler
Single Life *21* Edwin J. Collins
Single Man, The *19* A. V. Bramble
Single Man, A *28* Harry Beaumont
Single Parent *72* Krishna Shah
Single Room, Furnished *68* Matt Cimber
Single Shot Parker *17* E. A. Martin
Single Sin, The *31* William Nigh
Single Standard, The *14* D. W. Griffith
Single Standard, The *29* John S. Robertson
Single Track, The *21* Webster Campbell
Single Wives *24* George Archainbaud
Singleton's Pluck *84* Richard Eyre
Singoalla *49* Christian-Jaque
Sinhalese Dance, A *50* Lester James Peries
Sinhasta, or The Path to Immortality *68* Shyam Benegal
Siniestro Dr. Orloff, El *82* Jesús Franco
Sininen Imettäjä *86* Markku Lehmuskallio
Sinister Dr. Orloff, The *82* Jesús Franco
Sinister Hands *32* Armand Schaefer
Sinister House *48* Bernard Carr
Sinister Invasion *71* Jack Hill, Juan Ibáñez
Sinister Journey *48* George Archainbaud
Sinister Man, The *61* Clive Donner
Sinister Street *22* George A. Beranger
Sinister Urge, The *61* Edward D. Wood, Jr.
Sink or Swim *38* S. W. Dormand
Sink the Bismarck! *60* Lewis Gilbert
Sinkin' in the Bathtub *30* Hugh Harman, Rudolf Ising
Sinking of the Lusitania, The *18* Winsor McCay
Sinless Sinner, A *19* Herbert Brenon
Sinless Sinner, A *19* James McKay
Sinner, The *50* Willi Forst
Sinner, The *59* Steve Sekely
Sinner, The *68* Jacques Deray
Sinner, The *75* James Frawley
Sinner in Paradise, A *68* Nagisa Oshima
Sinner or Saint *23* Lawrence C. Windom
Sinner Take All *36* Errol Taggart
Sinners *20* Kenneth Webb

Sinners, The 49 Julien Duvivier
Sinners, The 61 Wolfgang Glück
Sinners Go to Hell 62 Tad Danielewski
Sinner's Holiday 30 John G. Adolfi
Sinners' Holiday 47 Edwin L. Marin
Sinners in Heaven 24 Alan Crosland
Sinners in Love 28 George Melford
Sinners in Paradise 37 James Whale
Sinners in Silk 24 Hobart Henley
Sinners in the Sun 32 Alexander Hall
Sinners of Paris 58 Pierre Chénal
Sinner's Parade 28 John G. Adolfi
Sinner's Repentance, A 09 Theo Bouw-
     meester
Sinners to Hell, The 60 Nobuo Nakagawa
Sinnui Yauman II 87 Hark Tsui
Sino'ng Kapiling, Sino'ng Kasiping? 77
     Eddie Romero
Sins of a Father, The 23 Edwin Green-
     wood
Sins of Babylon 63 Michele Lupo
Sins of Casanova 54 Steno
Sins of Dorian Gray 82 Tony Maylam
Sins of Her Parents 16 Frank Lloyd
Sins of Jezebel 53 Reginald LeBorg
Sins of Lola Montes, The 55 Max Ophüls
Sins of Man 36 Otto Brower, Gregory
     Ratoff
Sins of Men 16 James Vincent
Sins of Mona Kent, The 61 Charles Hundt
Sins of Paris 54 Henri Lepage
Sins of Rachel, The 75 Richard Fontaine
Sins of Rachel Cade, The 60 Gordon
     Douglas
Sins of Rome 52 Riccardo Freda
Sins of Rose Bernd, The 56 Wolfgang
     Staudte
Sins of Rozanne, The 20 Tom Forman
Sins of St. Anthony, The 20 James Cruze
Sins of Society 15 Oscar Eagle
Sins of the Borgias 52 Christian-Jaque
Sins of the Children 11 Urban Gad
Sins of the Children, The 16 Forest
     Holger-Madsen
Sins of the Children 18 John S. Lopez
Sins of the Children 30 Sam Wood
Sins of the Fathers 28 Ludwig Berger
Sins of the Fathers 48 Richard Jarvis, Phil
     Rosen
Sins of the Fathers 82 Harry Hook
Sins of the Fleshapoids 65 Mike Kuchar
Sins of the Mothers, The 15 Ralph Ince
Sins of the Parents 21 Allan Dwan
Sins of Youth, The 19 Ernest G. Batley
Sins of Youth 41 Maurice Tourneur
Sins of Youth 60 Louis Duchesne
Sin's Pay Day 32 George B. Seitz
Sins Ye Do, The 24 Fred LeRoy Granville
Sintflut, Die 17 Richard Oswald
Sinthia the Devil's Doll 68 Ray Dennis
     Steckler
Sinverguenza...Pero Honrado 87 Rafael
     Villaseñor Kuri
Sioux Blood 29 John Waters
Sioux City Sue 46 Frank McDonald
Sioux Me 39 Cal Dalton, Ben Hardaway
Sir Arne's Treasure 19 Mauritz Stiller
Sir Arne's Treasure 54 Gustaf Molander
Sir Gawain and the Green Knight 72
     Stephen Weeks

Sir Henry at Rawlinson End 80 Steve
     Roberts
Sir James Mortimer's Wager 16 Leslie
     Seldon-Truss
Sir John Greift Ein 30 Alfred Hitchcock
Sir Lumberjack 26 Harry Garson
Sir or Madam 28 Carl Boese
Sir Rupert's Wife 22 Challis Sanderson
Sir Sidney 19 Raoul Barré, Charles Bowers
Sir Thomas Lipton Out West 13 Mack
     Sennett
Sir, You Are a Widower 71 Václav
     Vorlíček
Sira fi'l Mina 55 Youssef Chahine
Sira fi'l Wadi 52 Youssef Chahine
Sire le Roy N'A Plus Rien Dit 64 Georges
     Rouquier
Siren, The 14 Wallace Reid
Siren, The 17 Roland West
Siren, The 27 Byron Haskin
Siren Call, The 22 Irvin Willat
Siren of Atlantis 48 John Brahm, Arthur
     Ripley, Douglas Sirk, Gregg Tallas
Siren of Bagdad 53 Richard Quine
Siren of Impulse, A 12 D. W. Griffith
Siren of Seville, The 24 Jerome Storm,
     Hunt Stromberg
Siren of the South Seas 37 Arthur Greville
     Collins
Siréna 47 Karel Steklý
Sirène, La 04 Georges Méliès
Sirène, La 07 Louis Feuillade
Sirène de Pierre, La 22 Roger Lion
Sirène des Tropiques, La 28 Henri
     Étiévant
Sirène du Mississippi, La 68 François
     Truffaut
Sirens of the Sea 17 Allen Holubar
Siren's Song, The 19 J. Gordon Edwards
Sirius Remembered 59 Stan Brakhage
Sirkus Fandango 54 Arne Skouen
Sirocco 31 Jacques Severac
Sirocco 38 Pierre Chénal
Sirocco 51 Kurt Bernhardt
Sirocco d'Hiver 69 Miklós Jancsó
Sirokkó 69 Miklós Jancsó
Sis 89 Ömer Zülfü Livaneli
Sis Hopkins 19 Clarence Badger
Sis Hopkins 41 Joseph Santley
Sisimilut 66 Jørgen Roos
Siska 62 Alf Kjellin
Sissi 32 Lotte Reiniger
Sissi 55 Ernst Marischka
Sissi—Die Junge Kaiserin 55 Ernst
     Marischka
Sissi—Schicksalsjahre einer Kaiserin 55
     Ernst Marischka
Sissignora 42 Ferdinando Maria Poggioli
Sissignore 68 Ugo Tognazzi
Sista Paret Ut 55 Alf Sjöberg
Sista Stegen, De 60 John Cromwell
Sistemo l'America È Torno 73 Nanni Loy
Sister, The 11 Sidney Olcott
Sister Against Sister 17 James Vincent
Sister Against Sister 20 Herbert Brenon
Sister Angela's Secret 55 Léo Joannon
Sister Angelica 32 Martin Frič
Sister Cecilia 15 Forest Holger-Madsen
Sister-in-Law, The 74 Joseph Ruben
Sister Kenny 46 Dudley Nichols

Sister Mary Jane's Top Note 07 Lewin
     Fitzhamon
Sister of Love 86 Amos Guttman
Sister of Six, A 16 Chester M. Franklin,
     Sidney Franklin
Sister, Sister 87 William Condon
Sister Susie's Sewing Shirts for Soldiers 15
     Harry Buss
Sister Susie's Sewing Shirts for Soldiers 17
     Wilfred Noy
Sister to Assist 'Er, A 13 Walter R. Booth
Sister to Assist 'Er, A 22 George Dewhurst
Sister to Assist 'Er, A 27 George Dewhurst
Sister to Assist 'Er, A 30 George Dewhurst
Sister to Assist 'Er, A 38 George Dew-
     hurst, Widgey R. Newman
Sister to Assist 'Er, A 47 George Dewhurst
Sister to Judas 33 E. Mason Hopper
Sister to Salome, A 20 Edward J. LeSaint
Sisterhood, The 88 Cirio Santiago
Sisters 11 Thomas Ince
Sisters, The 11 Wilfred Noy
Sisters, The 14 Christy Cabanne
Sisters 15 Percy Nash
Sisters 22 Albert Capellani
Sisters 30 James Flood
Sisters, The 38 Anatole Litvak
Sisters, The 69 Errikos Andreou
Sisters 72 Brian DePalma
Sisters All 13 Lawrence Trimble
Sister's Burden, A 15 Robert Vignola
Sisters in Arms 18 Walter West
Sister's Love, A 11 D. W. Griffith
Sisters of Corruption 72 Juan Antonio
     Bardem
Sisters of Death 76 Joseph Mazzuca
Sisters of Eve 28 Scott Pembroke
Sisters of Gion 36 Kenji Mizoguchi
Sisters of Nishijin, The 52 Kozaburo
     Yoshimura
Sisters of the Gion 36 Kenji Mizoguchi
Sisters I 57 Grigori Roshal
Sisters II 59 Grigori Roshal
Sisters III 60 Grigori Roshal
Sisters, or The Balance of Happiness 79
     Margarethe von Trotta
Sisters Under the Skin 34 David Burton
Sit Tight 31 Lloyd Bacon
Sittin' on a Backyard Fence 33 Earl Duvall
Sittin' Pretty 24 Leo McCarey
Sitting Bull 54 Sidney Salkow
Sitting Bull at the Spirit Lake Massacre 27
     Robert North Bradbury
Sitting Ducks 79 Henry Jaglom
Sitting in Limbo 86 John Smith
Sitting on the Moon 36 Ralph Staub
Sitting Pretty 33 Harry Joe Brown
Sitting Pretty 47 Walter Lang
Sitting Target 71 Douglas Hickox
Situation Hopeless But Not Serious 65
     Gottfried Reinhardt
Situation Normal All Fouled Up 70 Nanni
     Loy
Situation of Marriage, The 40 Tadashi
     Imai
Situation of the Human World, The 28
     Heinosuke Gosho
Siva l'Invisible 04 Georges Méliès
Siva Mechida Kannappa 88 Vijay
Sivude Shankarudu 88 Babu Surendra

Ski Troop Attack *60* Roger Corman
Skiachtra, I *85* Manoussos Manoussakis
Skicka Hem Nr. 7 *39* Gideon Wahlberg
Skid Kids *53* Don Chaffey
Skid Proof *23* Scott R. Dunlap
Skid Row *56* Allan King
Skidoo! *68* Otto Preminger
Skies Above *64* Yves Ciampi
Skilsmissens Børn *39* Benjamin Christensen
Skimpy in the Navy *49* Stafford Dickens
Skin *86* Vibeke Løkkeberg
Skin Deep *22* Lambert Hillyer
Skin Deep *29* Ray Enright
Skin Deep *78* Geoff Steven
Skin Deep *87* Gianluca Fumagalli
Skin Deep *89* Blake Edwards
Skin Deep in Love *66* Joe Sarno
Skin Game, The *20* B. E. Doxat-Pratt
Skin Game, The *31* Alfred Hitchcock
Skin Game, The *62* Arnold Louis Miller
Skin Game *71* Paul Bogart, Gordon Douglas
Skin Games *62* Arnold Louis Miller
Skin Skin *67* Mikko Niskanen
Skinheads — The Second Coming of Hate *90* Greydon Clark
Skinner Steps Out *29* William James Craft
Skinner's Baby *17* Harry Beaumont
Skinner's Big Idea *28* Lynn Shores
Skinner's Bubble *17* Harry Beaumont
Skinner's Dress Suit *17* Harry Beaumont
Skinner's Dress Suit *26* William A. Seiter
Skinning Skinners *21* William Nigh
Skinny *27* Manny Gould, Ben Harrison
Skinny Ennis and His Orchestra *41* Jean Negulesco
Skinny's Finish *08* Edwin S. Porter
Skip the Maloo! *31* James Parrott
Skip Tracer *77* Zale Dalen
Skip Tracer *86* Roger Young
Skipalong Rosenbloom *51* Sam Newfield
Skipper *71* Barry Shear
Skipper & Co. *74* Bjarne Henning-Jensen
Skipper Next to God *50* Louis Daquin
Skipper of the Osprey, The *16* Frank Miller
Skipper of the Osprey *33* Norman Walker
Skipper Surprised His Wife, The *50* Elliott Nugent
Skipper's Wooing, The *22* H. Manning Haynes
Skipping Cheeses, The *07* Georges Méliès
Skipping the Pen *21* R. E. Donahue, J. J. McManus
Skippy *31* Norman Taurog
Skirl of the Pibroch, The *08* Dave Aylott
Skirmish Between Russian and Japanese Advance Guards *04* Edwin S. Porter
Skirt Shy *21* James Cruze
Skirts *21* Hampton Del Ruth
Skirts *28* Wheeler Dryden, Jess Robbins
Skirts Ahoy! *52* Sidney Lanfield
Skis de France *47* Marcel Ichac
Sklaven der Liebe *24* Carl Boese
Sklaven Roms, Die *61* Nunzio Malasomma
Sklavenkönigin, Die *24* Michael Curtiz
Skleníková Venuša *85* Martin Tapak
Skogsdotterns Hemlighet *13* Victor Sjöström

Škola — Základ Života *38* Martin Frič
Skomakare Bliv vid Din Läst *15* Victor Sjöström
Skønheden og Udyret *83* Nils Malmros
Skönhetsvård i Djungeln *37* Pál Fejős
Skopje 1963 *64* Veljko Bulajić
Skorbnoe Beschuvstvie *87* Alexander Sokurov
Skorpió, A *18* Michael Curtiz
Skotinins, The *26* Grigori Roshal
Skottet *14* Mauritz Stiller
Skovens Børn *17* Forest Holger-Madsen
Skřivánci na Nítích *69* Jiří Menzel
Skud fra Hjertet, Et *86* Kristian Levring
Skud i Mørket, Et *14* August Blom
Skuggor Över Snön *45* Arne Sucksdorff
Skull, The *65* Freddie Francis
Skull and Crown *35* Elmer Clifton
Skullduggery *60* Stan Vanderbeek
Skullduggery *70* Gordon Douglas, Richard Wilson
Skupa Moya, Skupi Moy *86* Eduard Zahariev
Skupljači Perja *67* Aleksandar Petrović
Skvenei Anekdot *65* Alexander Alov, Vladimir Naumov
Sky Above Heaven *64* Yves Ciampi
Sky Above, the Mud Below, The *61* Pierre-Dominique Gaisseau
Sky Bandits, The *40* Ralph Staub
Sky Bandits *86* Zoran Perisic
Sky Beyond Heaven *64* Yves Ciampi
Sky Bike, The *67* Charles Frend
Sky Bound *26* Stephen Roberts
Sky Boy *29* Leo McCarey
Sky Bride *31* Stephen Roberts
Sky Calls, The *59* Mikhail Karyukov, Alexander Kozyr
Sky Commando *53* Fred F. Sears
Sky Devils *32* A. Edward Sutherland
Sky Dragon, The *49* Lesley Selander
Sky-Eye *20* Aubrey M. Kennedy
Sky Full of Moon *52* Norman Foster
Sky Giant *38* Lew Landers
Sky Hawk, The *29* John G. Blystone
Sky High *22* Lynn Reynolds
Sky High *51* Sam Newfield
Sky High *75* Robert Amram
Sky High Corral *26* Clifford Smith
Sky High Saunders *27* Bruce Mitchell
Sky Is Clear, The *25* Heinosuke Gosho
Sky Is Falling, The *75* Silvio Narizzano
Sky Is Red, The *52* Claudio Gora
Sky Is Yours, The *43* Jean Grémillon
Sky Jumper, The *25* George Marshall
Sky Larks, The *34* Walter Lantz
Sky Liner *49* William Berke
Sky Murder *40* George B. Seitz
Sky of Our Childhood, The *67* Tolomush Okeyev
Sky Parade, The *36* Otho Lovering
Sky Patrol *39* Howard Bretherton
Sky Pilot, The *21* King Vidor
Sky Pilot *24* Walter Lantz
Sky Pilot *39* George Waggner
Sky Pilot's Intemperance, The *11* Allan Dwan
Sky Pirate, The *14* Roscoe Arbuckle, Edward Dillon
Sky Pirate, The *70* Andrew Meyer

Sky Pirates *37* George Pal
Sky Pirates *77* C. M. Pennington-Richards
Sky Pirates *86* Colin Eggleston
Sky Princess, The *42* George Pal
Sky Raider, The *25* T. Hayes Hunter
Sky Raiders *31* Christy Cabanne
Sky Raiders, The *38* Fraser Foulsham
Sky Raiders *41* Ford Beebe, Ray Taylor
Sky Ranger, The *21* George B. Seitz
Sky Ranger, The *28* Harry Joe Brown
Sky Rider, The *28* Alvin J. Neitz
Sky Riders *76* Douglas Hickox
Sky Scraper *69* Hideo Sekigawa
Sky Scraper Caper *68* Alex Lovy
Sky Scraping *30* Dave Fleischer
Sky Scrappers *28* Walt Disney
Sky Shines, The *25* Heinosuke Gosho
Sky Ship, The *17* Forest Holger-Madsen
Sky Skidder, The *29* Bruce Mitchell
Sky Spider, The *31* Richard Thorpe
Sky Splitter, The *22* J. A. Norling
Sky Terror *72* John Guillermin
Sky, the Earth, The *65* Joris Ivens
Sky West and Crooked *65* John Mills
Sky Without Stars *55* Helmut Käutner
Skybound *35* Raymond K. Johnson
Skydivers, The *63* Coleman Francis
Skyggen af Emma *88* Søren Kragh-Jacobsen
Skyhigh *85* Nico Mastorakis
Skyjacked *72* John Guillermin
Skylark *41* Mark Sandrich
Skylark *64* László Ranódy
Skylark Growing Up *55* Heinosuke Gosho
Skylarks *36* Thornton Freeland
Skylarks on a String *69* Jiří Menzel
Skyldig — Ikke Skyldig *53* Jørgen Roos
Skylight Room, The *17* Martin Justice
Skyline *31* Sam Taylor
Skyline *83* Fernando Colomo
Skyrider *76* John Halas
Skyrocket, The *26* Marshall Neilan
Sky's the Limit *25* I. W. Irving
Sky's the Limit, The *37* Jack Buchanan, Lee Garmes
Sky's the Limit, The *43* Edward H. Griffith
Skyscraper *28* Howard Higgin
Skyscraper *58* Shirley Clarke, Irving Jacoby, Willard Van Dyke
Skyscraper Souls *32* Edgar Selwyn
Skyscraper Story, The *69* Hideo Sekigawa
Skyscraper Symphony *28* Robert Florey
Skyscraper Wilderness *37* Frank Borzage
Skytturnar *87* Fridrik Thor Fridriksson
Skywatch *60* Lewis Gilbert
Skyway *33* Lewis D. Collins
Skywayman, The *20* James P. Hogan
Skywayman, The *28* Harry Joe Brown
Slå Først, Frede! *67* Erik Balling
Slacker, The *17* Christy Cabanne
Slade *53* Harold Schuster
Sladke Starosti *86* Juraj Herz
Slædepatruljen Sirius *80* Jørgen Roos
Slag's Place *65* Gwyneth Furdivall, David Naden
Slalom *36* Max Obal
Slalom *65* Luciano Salce
Slam Bang Jim *17* Edward Sloman
Slam Dunk *87* Jim Brown

Slamdance 87 Wayne Wang
Slammer 77 Robert M. Young
Slammer Girls 85 Chuck Vincent
Slams, The 73 Jonathan Kaplan
Slander 16 Will S. Davis
Slander 56 Roy Rowland
Slander House 38 Charles Lamont
Slander the Woman 23 Allen Holubar
Slanderers, The 24 Nat Ross
Slané Cukríky 85 Eva Stefankovičova
Slant 58 George Romero
Slantseto i Syankata 62 Rangel Vulchanov
Slap Happy Lion 47 Tex Avery
Slap Happy Pappy 40 Robert Clampett
Slap-Hoppy Mouse 56 Robert McKimson
Slap in the Face 75 Rolf Thiele
Slap in the Face, A 80 Genrikh Malyan
Slap Shot 77 George Roy Hill
Slapstick 82 Steven Paul
Slapstick (Of Another Kind) 82 Steven Paul
Slash Dance 89 James Shyman
Slasher, The 52 Lewis Gilbert
Slasher, The 75 Roberto Bianchi Montero
Slate, Wyn & Me 87 Don McLennan
Slattery's Hurricane 49 André De Toth
Slaughter, The 13 Avrom Yitskhok Kaminsky
Slaughter 72 Jack Starrett
Slaughter, The 74 Michael Findlay, Roberta Findlay
Slaughter 76 Burt Brinckerhoff
Slaughter High 86 George Dugdale, Mark Ezra, Peter Litten
Slaughter Hotel 71 Fernando Di Leo
Slaughter in Matamoros 86 José Luis Urquieta
Slaughter in San Francisco 73 William Lowe
Slaughter of the Vampires 61 Roberto Mauri
Slaughter on Tenth Avenue 57 Arnold Laven
Slaughter Trail 51 Irving Allen
Slaughterday 81 Peter Patzak
Slaughterers, The 80 Antonio Margheriti
Slaughterhouse 88 Rick Roessler
Slaughterhouse Five 71 George Roy Hill
Slaughterhouse Rock 88 Dimitri Logothetis
Slaughter's Big Rip-Off 73 Gordon Douglas
Slava Sovetskim Geroinyam 38 Dziga Vertov
Slave, The 09 D. W. Griffith
Slave, The 17 William Nigh
Slave, The 18 Arrigo Bocchi
Slave, The 62 Sergio Corbucci
Slave, The 71 Al Freeman, Jr.
Slave Coast 87 Werner Herzog
Slave Girl, The 15 Tod Browning
Slave Girl 47 Charles Lamont
Slave Girl, The 54 Lew Landers
Slave Girls 66 Michael Carreras
Slave Girls from Beyond Infinity 87 Ken Dixon
Slave Girls of Sheba 64 Giacomo Gentilomo, Guido Zurli
Slave Market, The 16 Hugh Ford
Slave of Desire 23 George D. Baker

Slave of Fashion, A 25 Hobart Henley
Slave of Love, A 76 Nikita Mikhalkov
Slave of Passion, Slave of Vice 14 M. Martov
Slave of the Cannibal God 78 Sergio Martino
Slave of Vanity, A 20 Henry Otto
Slave Queen of Babylon 62 Primo Zeglio
Slave Ship 37 Tay Garnett
Slave Trade in the World Today 63 Roberto Malenotti, Folco Quilici
Slave Trading in a Harem 1897 Georges Méliès
Slave Woman, The 55 Carlo Ludovico Bragaglia
Slaver, The 27 Harry Revier
Slavers 77 Jürgen Goslar
Slavers of the Thames 15 Percy Moran
Slavery Days—The New Master 06 Harold Hough
Slaves 68 Herbert J. Biberman
Slaves 73 Russ Meyer
Slaves of Babylon 53 William Castle
Slaves of Beauty 27 John G. Blystone
Slaves of Destiny 24 Maurice Elvey
Slaves of New York 89 James Ivory
Slaves of Pride 20 George Terwilliger
Slaves of the Invisible Monster 50 Fred C. Brannon
Slaves of the Night 14 Michael Curtiz
Slavey Student, The 15 John H. Collins
Slavey's Dream, The 04 Lewin Fitzhamon
Slavey's Legacy, The 16 Bert Haldane
Slavica 47 Vjekoslav Afrić
Slavnosti Sněženek 82 Jiří Menzel
Slay It with Flowers 43 Bob Wickersham
Slayer, The 82 J. S. Cardone
Slayground 83 Terry Bedford
Slaying of the Serpent, The 19 D. G. Phalke
Sledge 70 Vic Morrow
Sledy Oborotnya 87 Almantas Grikyavicus
Sleep 63 Andy Warhol
Sleep Breakers, The 10 Alf Collins
Sleep, My Love 48 Douglas Sirk
Sleep of Death, The 81 Calvin Floyd
Sleep Walker, The 22 Edward J. LeSaint
Sleep Well, My Love 87 Arne Mattsson
Sleepaway Camp 83 Robert Hiltzik
Sleepaway Camp 2: Unhappy Campers 88 Michael A. Simpson
Sleepaway Camp 3: Teenage Wasteland 89 Michael A. Simpson
Sleeper 73 Woody Allen
Sleepers East 34 Kenneth MacKenna
Sleepers West 41 Eugene Forde
Sleeping Beauty 08 Segundo De Chomón
Sleeping Beauty, The 12 Elwin Neame
Sleeping Beauty 17 Paul Leni
Sleeping Beauty 24 Herbert M. Dawley
Sleeping Beauty 29 Georgy Vasiliev, Sergei Vasiliev
Sleeping Beauty 42 Luigi Chiarini
Sleeping Beauty, The 54 Lotte Reiniger
Sleeping Beauty 59 Les Clark, Clyde Geronimi, Eric Larson, Wolfgang Reitherman
Sleeping Beauty 65 Fritz Genschow
Sleeping Beauty, The 66 Apollinari Dudko, Konstantin Sergeyev

Sleeping Beauty 68 Kozaburo Yoshimura
Sleeping Beauty 86 David Irving
Sleeping Car 33 Anatole Litvak
Sleeping Car, The 90 Douglas Curtis
Sleeping Car Murder, The 64 Costa-Gavras
Sleeping Car to Trieste 48 John Paddy Carstairs
Sleeping Cardinal, The 31 Leslie Hiscott
Sleeping City, The 50 George Sherman
Sleeping Cutie, The 30 Lewis R. Foster
Sleeping Dogs 77 Roger Donaldson
Sleeping Embers 28 Humberto Mauro
Sleeping Fires 17 Hugh Ford
Sleeping Lion, The 19 Rupert Julian
Sleeping Lovers, The 1899 James A. Williamson
Sleeping Memory, A 17 George D. Baker
Sleeping Partners 30 Seymour Hicks
Sleeping Tiger, The 54 Joseph Losey
Sleeping with a Long Sword 32 Sadao Yamanaka
Sleeping Words of the Bride 33 Heinosuke Gosho
Sleeping Words of the Bridegroom 34 Heinosuke Gosho
Sleepless Nights 32 Thomas Bentley
Sleepless Years, The 59 Félix Máriássy
Sleepwalk 86 Sara Driver
Sleepwalker, The 03 Alf Collins
Sleepwalker, The 09 Theo Bouwmeester
Sleepwalker, The 15 Anders Wilhelm Sandberg
Sleepwalker, The 25 Lewis Seiler
Sleepwalkers of the Pont de l'Alma, The 83 Raúl Ruiz
Sleepy Holler 29 Manny Gould, Ben Harrison
Sleepy Lagoon 43 Joseph Santley
Sleepy Sam's Awakening 10 A. E. Coleby
Sleepy Time Down South 32 Dave Fleischer
Sleepy Time Possum 51 Robert McKimson
Sleepy Time Tom 51 Joseph Barbera, William Hanna
Sleepytime Gal 42 Albert S. Rogell
Sleigh Bells, The 07 Sidney Olcott
Sleigh Bells 28 Walt Disney
Sleighing in Central Park, New York 04 Edwin S. Porter
Slender Thread, The 65 Sydney Pollack
Slepaya 30 Mikhail Kalatozov
Slepoy Muzikant 62 Tatiana Lukashevich
Sleuth, The 22 Larry Semon, Norman Taurog
Sleuth 72 Joseph L. Mankiewicz
Sleuth Slayer, The 84 Jimmy Huston
Sleuths 18 F. Richard Jones
Sleuths at the Floral Parade, The 13 Mack Sennett
Sleuth's Last Stand, The 13 Mack Sennett
Slezi 14 Yevgeni Bauer
Slice of Life 53 Alessandro Blasetti
Slick and Tricky 16 Lee Connor
Slick Chick, The 62 Robert McKimson
Slick Hare 47 Friz Freleng
Slick Sleuths 26 Charles Bowers
Slick Tartan 49 Frank Chisnell
Slicked-Up Pup 51 Joseph Barbera, William Hanna

Slicker, The *21* Al St. John
Slide, Kelly, Slide *27* Edward Sedgwick
Slides *19* Dave Fleischer
Sliding Down Ice Mound at Niagara Falls *04* Edwin S. Porter
Slight Case of Larceny, A *53* Don Weis
Slight Case of Murder, A *38* Lloyd Bacon
Slightly Daffy *44* Robert Clampett
Slightly Dangerous *43* Wesley Ruggles
Slightly French *49* Douglas Sirk
Slightly Honorable *39* Tay Garnett
Slightly Married *32* Richard Thorpe
Slightly Pregnant Man, A *73* Jacques Demy
Slightly Scandalous *46* Will Jason
Slightly Scarlet *30* Louis Gasnier, Edwin H. Knopf
Slightly Scarlet *56* Allan Dwan
Slightly Tempted *40* Lew Landers
Slightly Terrific *44* Edward F. Cline
Slightly Used *27* Archie Mayo
Slikovnica Pčelara *58* Dušan Makavejev
Slim *37* Ray Enright
Slim Carter *57* Richard Bartlett
Slim Fingers *29* Josef Levigard
Slim Princess, The *15* Elisha H. Calvert
Slim Princess, The *20* Victor Schertzinger
Slim Shoulders *22* Alan Crosland
Slime City *88* Gregory Lamberson
Slime People, The *63* Robert Hutton
Slinger, The *60* Karel Kachyňa
Slingrevalsen *81* Esben Høilund Carlsen
Slingshot Kid, The *27* Louis King
Slingshot 6⅞ *51* Walter Lantz
Slinky the Yegg *16* Lee Connor
Slip at the Switch, A *32* Mark Sandrich
Slip Slide Adventures *78* Lionel Jeffries
Slip-Up, The *72* Jan Łomnicki
Slipper and the Rose, The *76* Bryan Forbes
Slipper and the Rose—The Story of Cinderella, The *76* Bryan Forbes
Slipper Episode, The *35* Jean De Limur
Slippery Burglar, The *1899* Georges Méliès
Slippery Jim the Burglar *06* Tom Green
Slippery McGee *22* Wesley Ruggles
Slippery Pimple *13* Fred Evans, Joe Evans
Slippery Road *28* Norman Taurog
Slippery Slippers *62* Joseph Barbera, William Hanna
Slippery Visitor, A *06* Arthur Cooper
Slipping Into Darkness *89* Eleanor Gaver
Slippy McGee *22* Wesley Ruggles
Slippy McGee *48* Albert Kelley
Slips and Slops *15* Dave Aylott
Slipstream *73* David Acomba
Slipstream *89* Steven Lisberger
Slither *73* Howard Zieff
Slithis *78* Stephen Traxler
Sloane *86* Richard Belding, Daniel Rosenthal
Slocum Harriers, The *19* Maurice Sandground
Slogan *70* Pierre Grimblat
Sloper's New Hat *11* Stuart Kinder
Sloper's Visit to Brighton *1898* James A. Williamson
Sloppy Bill of the Rollicking R *11* Allan Dwan
Sloppy Jalopy *52* Pete Burness

Sloshton Quartette, The *08* Alf Collins
Slot i et Slot, Et *54* Carl Theodor Dreyer, Jørgen Roos
Sloth *17* Theodore Marston
Slow As Lightning *23* Grover Jones
Slow Attack *80* Reinhard Hauff
Slow Beau *30* Manny Gould, Ben Harrison
Slow Dancing in the Big City *78* John G. Avildsen
Slow Dynamite *25* Frank S. Mattison
Slow Motion *79* Jean-Luc Godard
Slow Moves *83* Jon Jost
Slow Run *68* Larry Kardish
Slowce M *63* Jiří Brdečka
Śluby Ułańskie *35* Mieczysław Krawicz
Slučaj Harms *88* Slobodan D. Pešić
Sluchai na Stadione *29* Alexander Ptushko
Sluchai v Vulkanye *41* Lev Kuleshov*
Sluchaynye Passazhiry *87* Mikhail Ordovsky
Slug in the Heater, A *58* Michel Deville, Charles Gérard
Sluggard's Surprise, The *00* Cecil M. Hepworth
Slugger's Wife, The *84* Hal Ashby
Slugs *88* Juan Piquer Simon
Sluice *78* Stan Brakhage
Slum *52* Jørgen Roos
Slumber Party *77* William A. Levey
Slumber Party '57 *77* William A. Levey
Slumber Party in a Haunted House *66* Don Weis
Slumber Party in Horror House *66* Don Weis
Slumber Party Massacre *82* Amy Jones, Aaron Lipstadt
Slumber Party Massacre II *87* Deborah Brock
Slumberland Express *36* Walter Lantz
Slump Is Over, The *34* Robert Siodmak
Slums of Berlin *25* Gerhard Lamprecht
Slums of Tokyo *30* Teinosuke Kinugasa
Slunce, Seno a Pár Faček *89* Zdeněk Troska
Slutshai na Telegrafe *41* Grigori Kozintsev
Smaak van Water, De *82* Orlow Seunke
Smala, La *84* Jean-Loup Hubert
Small Adventure *64* Nagisa Oshima
Small Bachelor, The *27* William A. Seiter
Small Back Room, The *48* Michael Powell, Emeric Pressburger
Small Change *75* François Truffaut
Small Child's First Adventure, A *64* Nagisa Oshima
Small Circle of Friends, A *80* Rob Cohen
Small Fry *39* Dave Fleischer
Small Hotel *57* David MacDonald
Small Hours, The *62* Norman C. Chaitin
Small Man, The *35* John Baxter
Small Miracle, The *51* Maurice Cloche, Ralph Smart
Small Space *64* Yoji Kuri
Small Stranger, The *62* Georges M. Nasser
Small Town Boy *37* Glenn Tryon
Small Town Deb *41* Harold Schuster
Small Town Girl, The *14* Allan Dwan
Small Town Girl *17* John G. Adolfi
Small Town Girl *36* William A. Wellman
Small Town Girl *52* Leslie Kardos

Small Town Guy, The *17* Lawrence C. Windom
Small Town Idol, A *21* Erle C. Kenton
Small Town in Texas, A *76* Jack Starrett
Small Town Lawyer *39* Dudley Murphy
Small Town Sinners *28* Bruno Rahn
Small Town Story *53* Montgomery Tully
Small Voice, The *48* Fergus McDonnell
Small World in the Dark, A *38* Hans Richter
Small World of Sammy Lee, The *62* Ken Hughes
Smallest Show on Earth, The *57* Basil Dearden
Smallest Worm, The *15* Frank Wilson
Smania Andosso, La *63* Marcello Andrei
Smart Alec *51* John Guillermin
Smart Alec *86* James L. Wilson
Smart Alecks *42* Wallace Fox
Smart Blonde *36* Frank McDonald
Smart Capture, A *04* Alf Collins
Smart Capture, A *07* Lewin Fitzhamon
Smart Girl *35* Aubrey H. Scotto
Smart Girls Don't Talk *48* Richard L. Bare
Smart Guy *43* Lambert Hillyer
Smart Money *31* Alfred E. Green
Smart Money *88* John Hanson
Smart Politics *48* Will Jason
Smart Set, A *19* A. V. Bramble
Smart Set, The *28* Jack Conway
Smart Sex, The *21* Fred LeRoy Granville
Smart Steppers *29* Stephen Roberts
Smart Woman *31* Gregory La Cava
Smart Woman *48* Edward A. Blatt
Smart Work *31* Roscoe Arbuckle
Smarter Than the Teacher *1896* Georges Méliès
Smartest Girl in Town *36* Joseph Santley
Smarty *33* Robert Florey
Smash and Grab *36* Tim Whelan
Smash Palace *81* Roger Donaldson
Smash-Up Alley *73* Edward J. Lakso
Smash-Up in China, A *19* Gregory La Cava
Smash-Up, the Story of a Woman *47* Stuart Heisler
Smashing Barriers *19* William Duncan
Smashing Bird I Used to Know, The *68* Robert Hartford-Davis
Smashing the Crime Syndicate *70* Al Adamson
Smashing the Money Ring *39* Terry Morse
Smashing the Rackets *38* Lew Landers
Smashing the Spy Ring *38* Christy Cabanne
Smashing Through *18* Elmer Clifton
Smashing Through *28* Will P. Kellino
Smashing Through *32* Armand Schaefer
Smashing Time *67* Desmond Davis
S'Matter, Pete? *27* Walter Lantz
Smeder på Luffen *49* Erik Faustman
Smell of Honey, The *66* B. Ron Elliott
Smell of Honey, a Swallow of Brine, A *66* B. Ron Elliott
Smemorato, Lo *40* Gennaro Righelli
Smešný Pán *69* Karel Kachyňa
Smic, Smac, Smoc *71* Claude Lelouch
Smích Se Lepí na Paty *86* Hynek Bočan
Śmierć Prezydenta *77* Jerzy Kawalerowicz
Śmierć Prowincjala *66* Krzysztof Zanussi

Smil 16 Forest Holger-Madsen
Smile 74 Michael Ritchie
Smile, Brother, Smile 27 John Francis Dillon
Smile in the Dark, A 90 Ulli Lommel
Smile of a Child, A 11 D. W. Griffith
Smile of Our Earth 25 Kenji Mizoguchi
Smile of the Lamb, The 86 Shimon Dotan
Smile Orange 76 Trevor Rhone
Smile 61 61 Dušan Makavejev
Smiler Has Stage Fever 11 A. E. Coleby
Smiles 19 Arvid E. Gillstrom
Smiles 29 Dave Fleischer
Smiles 64 John G. Avildsen
Smiles and Tears 12 Victor Sjöström
Smiles Are Trumps 22 George Marshall
Smiles of a Summer Night 55 Ingmar Bergman
Smiley 56 Anthony Kimmins
Smiley Gets a Gun 58 Anthony Kimmins
Smilin' Along 32 John Argyle
Smilin' at Trouble 25 Harry Garson
Smilin' Guns 29 Henry MacRae
Smilin' On 23 William James Craft
Smilin' Through 22 Sidney Franklin
Smilin' Through 32 Sidney Franklin
Smilin' Through 41 Frank Borzage
Smiling Again 54 Márta Mészáros
Smiling All the Way 21 Fred J. Butler
Smiling Along 38 Monty Banks
Smiling Billy 27 Duke Worne
Smiling Character, A 30 Heinosuke Gosho
Smiling Earth, The 25 Kenji Mizoguchi
Smiling Ghost, The 41 Lewis Seiler
Smiling Irish Eyes 29 William A. Seiter
Smiling Jim 22 Joseph Franz
Smiling Lieutenant, The 31 Ernst Lubitsch
Smiling Life, A 30 Heinosuke Gosho
Smiling Madame Beudet, The 22 Germaine Dulac
Smiling Terror, The 29 Josef Levigard
Smith 17 Maurice Elvey
Smith 39 Michael Powell
Smith! 69 Michael O'Herlihy
Smith and Machinery at Work 1895 Birt Acres
Smith of Minnesota 42 Lew Landers
Smithereens 82 Susan Seidelman
Smith's Baby 26 Edward F. Cline
Smith's Burglar 28 Frank Capra
Smith's Customer 27 Lloyd Bacon
Smith's New Home 27 Lloyd Bacon
Smith's Surprise 27 Lloyd Bacon
Smith's Vacation 26 Edward F. Cline
Smith's Wives 35 H. Manning Haynes
Smithsonian Institution, The 65 Charles Eames, Ray Eames
Smithsonian Newsreel, The 65 Charles Eames, Ray Eames
Smithy 33 George King
Smithy 45 Ken Hall
Smitten Kitten 52 Joseph Barbera, William Hanna
Smog 62 Franco Rossi
Smoke 25 Daisuke Ito
Smoke 70 Miklós Jancsó
Smoke Bellew 29 Scott R. Dunlap
Smoke Eater, The 25 William C. Nolan
Smoke Eaters, The 26 Charles J. Hunt
Smoke in the Wind 71 Joseph Kane

Smoke Jumpers 52 Henry Hathaway, Joseph M. Newman
Smoke Lightning 33 David Howard
Smoke of the 45, The 11 Allan Dwan
Smoke Signal 55 Jerry Hopper
Smoke Tree Range 37 Lesley Selander
Smoked Husband, A 08 D. W. Griffith
Smoker, The 10 D. W. Griffith
Smoker's Joke, The 07 Arthur Cooper
Smokes and Lollies 75 Gillian Armstrong
Smokescreen 64 James O'Connolly
Smokey and the Bandit 77 Hal Needham
Smokey and the Bandit II 80 Hal Needham
Smokey and the Bandit Ride Again 80 Hal Needham
Smokey and the Bandit 3 83 Dick Lowry
Smokey and the Goodtime Outlaws 78 Alexander Grasshoff
Smokey and the Hotwire Gang 80 Anthony Cardoza
Smokey Bites the Dust 81 Charles B. Griffith
Smokey Joe's Revenge 74 Ronald Spencer
Smokey Smith 35 Robert North Bradbury
Smokey Smokes 20 Gregory La Cava
Smoking Guns 34 Alvin J. Neitz
Smoking Guns 42 Sam Newfield
Smoking Lamp, The 09 Émile Cohl
Smoking Trail, The 24 William Bertram
Smoky 33 Eugene Forde
Smoky 46 Louis King
Smoky 66 George Sherman
Smoky Canyon 51 Fred F. Sears
Smoky Mountain Melody 48 Ray Nazarro
Smoky River Serenade 47 Derwin Abrahams
Smoky Story, A 12 Charles C. Calvert
Smoky Trails 39 Bernard B. Ray
Smooth As Satin 25 Ralph Ince
Smooth As Silk 46 Charles Barton
Smooth Moves 84 Charles E. Sellier
Smooth Talk 85 Joyce Chopra
Smorgasbord 60 Barry Mahon
Smorgasbord 82 Jerry Lewis
Smouldering Embers 20 Frank Keenan
Smouldering Fires 24 Clarence Brown
Smouldering Flame, The 16 Colin Campbell
Smrt Krásných Srncû 86 Karel Kachyňa
Smrt Mouchy 75 Karel Kachyňa
Smrt Si Říká Engelchen 62 Ján Kadár, Elmar Klos
Smudge 22 Charles Ray
Smudge the Great Detective 13 Charles C. Calvert
Smugglarens Dotter 15 Victor Sjöström
Smugglarkungen 85 Sune Lund-Sørensen
Smuggled Cargo 39 John H. Auer
Smuggler and the Girl, The 11 Allan Dwan
Smugglers, The 04 Charles Raymond
Smugglers, The 13 Victor Sjöström, Mauritz Stiller
Smugglers, The 15 Fred Evans
Smugglers, The 16 Sidney Olcott
Smugglers, The 47 Bernard Knowles
Smugglers 58 Félix Máriássy
Smugglers, The 69 Luc Moullet
Smugglers' Cave, The 14 J. Wallett Waller

Smuggler's Cave, The 15 B. Reeves Eason
Smugglers' Cove 48 William Beaudine
Smuggler's Daughter, The 12 Gilbert M. Anderson
Smuggler's Daughter, The 13 Edwin J. Collins
Smuggler's Daughter of Anglesea, The 12 Sidney Northcote
Smuggler's Gold 51 William Berke
Smugglers' Harvest 38 John R. Phipps
Smuggler's Island 51 Edward Ludwig
Smugglers of Death 59 Karel Kachyňa
Smugglers of Sligo, The 14 Christy Cabanne
Smuggler's Stepdaughter, The 11 Lewin Fitzhamon
Smultronstället 57 Ingmar Bergman
Smurfs and the Magic Flute, The 84 José Dutillieu, John Rust
Snack Bar Budapest 88 Tinto Brass
Snafu 45 Jack Moss
Snake Bite 78 Ray Townsend
Snake God, The 70 Piero Vivarelli
Snake People, The 68 Jack Hill, Juan Ibáñez
Snake Pit, The 48 Anatole Litvak
Snake Pit, The 67 Harald Reinl
Snake Pit and the Pendulum, The 67 Harald Reinl
Snake Princess, The 38 Teinosuke Kinugasa
Snake River Desperadoes 51 Fred F. Sears
Snake Woman, The 60 Sidney J. Furie
Snakes and Ladders 60 John Halas*
Snakes and Ladders 79 Raúl Ruiz
Snap 86 Deb Ellis
Snap and the Beanstalk 60 John Halas*
Snap Goes East 60 John Halas*
Snap Happy Traps 46 Bob Wickersham
Snap Judgement 20 Burton Gillett
Snap Judgment 17 Edward Sloman
Snap Shot 76 Allan Eastman
Snapping the Whip 29 Henry D. Bailey
Snappy Cheese 19 Gregory La Cava
Snappy Salesman 30 Walter Lantz
Snap's Rocket 60 John Halas*
Snapshot 79 Simon Wincer
Snapshots of the City 61 Stan Vanderbeek
Snapshotting an Audience 00 George Albert Smith
Snare, The 18 Frank Wilson
Snare, The 29 Leslie Eveleigh
Snare of Fate, The 13 William Humphrey
Snares 39 Robert Siodmak
Snares of Paris 19 Howard Mitchell
Snarl, The 17 Raymond B. West
Snarl of Hate, The 27 Noel Mason Smith
Snatched from a Terrible Death 08 Lewin Fitzhamon
Snatched from Death 13 Charles C. Calvert
Snatchers 34 Alexander Medvedkin
Snaypery 87 Bolotbek Shamshiev
Sneak, The 19 Edward J. LeSaint
Sneak, Snoop and Snitch 40 Dave Fleischer
Sneak, Snoop and Snitch in Triple Trouble 41 Dave Fleischer
Sneaking 34 Kozaburo Yoshimura
Sneeze, The 14 Hay Plumb

Sneezing 09 Frank Danvers Yates
Sneezing Weasel, The 37 Tex Avery
Sněhová Královna 78 Evald Schorm
Snezhnaya Skazka 59 A. Sakharov, Eldar Shengelaya
Sniffkins, Detective and the Missing Cigarette Cards 14 Edwin J. Collins
Sniffles Bells the Cat 40 Chuck Jones
Sniffles Takes a Trip 40 Chuck Jones
Sniffles the Bookworm 39 Chuck Jones
Sniper 32 Semen Timoshenko
Sniper, The 52 Edward Dmytryk
Snipers 87 Bolotbek Shamshiev
Sniper's Ridge 61 John Bushelman
Snitching Hour, The 22 Alan Crosland
Sno-Line 84 Douglas F. O'Neons
Snob, The 20 Sam Wood
Snob, The 24 Monta Bell
Snob Buster, The 25 Albert S. Rogell
Snobs 14 Lawrence Trimble
Snobs 15 Oscar Apfel
Snobs! 61 Jean-Pierre Mocky
Snobs, Les 61 Jean-Pierre Mocky
Snooks As a Fireman 14 Will P. Kellino
Snookums' Portrait 13 Émile Cohl
Snoopy Come Home 72 Bill Melendez
Snoopy Loopy 60 Joseph Barbera, William Hanna
Snorkel, The 57 Guy Green
Snout, The 63 Ken Annakin
Snow 81 Juliet Berto, Jean-Henri Roger
Snow Balling 84 Charles E. Sellier
Snow Bride, The 23 Henry Kolker
Snow Business 53 Friz Freleng
Snow Country 57 Shiro Toyoda
Snow Country 65 Hideo Oba
Snow Creature, The 54 W. Lee Wilder
Snow Demons 65 Antonio Margheriti
Snow Devils 65 Antonio Margheriti
Snow Dog 50 Frank McDonald
Snow Excuse 66 Robert McKimson
Snow Fairy Tale 59 A. Sakharov, Eldar Shengelaya
Snow Festival 52 Susumu Hani
Snow Flurry 59 Keisuke Kinoshita
Snow Ghost 68 Tokuzo Tanaka
Snow in the Desert 19 Walter West
Snow in the South Seas 63 Seiji Hisamatsu
Snow Job 72 George Englund
Snow Maiden, The 14 Władysław Starewicz
Snow Maiden, The 52 Ivan Ivanov-Vano
Snow Man, The 1899 Georges Méliès
Snow Man 65 Antonio Margheriti
Snow Man's Land 39 Chuck Jones
Snow Queen, The 59 Phil Patton
Snow Queen, The 78 Evald Schorm
Snow Queen, The 86 Päivi Hartzell
Snow Time for Comedy 41 Chuck Jones
Snow Treasure 68 Irving Jacoby
Snow Was Black, The 52 Luis Saslavsky
Snow White 16 J. Searle Dawley
Snow White 33 Dave Fleischer
Snow White 56 Erich Kobler
Snow White 87 Michael Berz
Snow White and Rose Red 53 Lotte Reiniger
Snow White and Rose Red 55 Erich Kobler

Snow White and the Seven Dwarfs 37 William Cottrell, David Hand, Wilfred Jackson, Larry Morey, Perce Pearce, Ben Sharpsteen
Snow White and the Three Clowns 61 Walter Lang
Snow White and the Three Stooges 61 Walter Lang
Snowball 60 Pat Jackson
Snowball and His Pal 12 Jack Conway
Snowball Express 72 Norman Tokar
Snowballing 04 William Haggar
Snowbird 16 Edwin Carewe
Snowblind 21 Reginald Barker
Snowblind 68 Hollis Frampton
Snowbody Loves Me 64 Chuck Jones
Snowbound 27 Phil Goldstone
Snowbound 48 David MacDonald
Snowdon Aviary, The 66 Jack Gold
Snowdrift 23 Scott R. Dunlap
Snowdrop, A 86 Kichitaro Negishi
Snowdrop Feast 82 Jiří Menzel
Snowdrop Festival 82 Jiří Menzel
Snowed In 26 Spencer G. Bennet
Snowed Under 36 Ray Enright
Snowfall 74 Ferenc Kósa
Snowfire 58 Dorrell McGowan, Stuart McGowan
Snowman, The 08 Wallace McCutcheon
Snowman, The 66 Hermina Tyrlova
Snowman 75 Kent Bateman
Snowman's Romance, A 28 Karl Freund
Snows of Destiny 19 Mauritz Stiller
Snows of Kilimanjaro, The 52 Henry King
Snowshoe Trail, The 22 Chester Bennett
Snowshoers, The 58 Michel Brault, Gilles Groulx
Snowstorm 44 Åke Öhberg
Snowy Fairy Tale, A 59 A. Sakharov, Eldar Shengelaya
Snowy Heron, The 57 Teinosuke Kinugasa
Snubbed by a Snob 40 Dave Fleischer
Snuff 74 Michael Findlay, Roberta Findlay
Snuff Bottle 88 Han-hsiang Li
Snuffy Smith 42 Edward F. Cline
Snuffy Smith, the Yard Bird 42 Edward F. Cline
Snuffy Smith, Yard Bird 42 Edward F. Cline
Snuffy Stuff, Snuff 14 Edwin J. Collins
So Alone 58 John Ford
So and Sew 36 Jean Yarbrough
So Big 24 Charles Brabin
So Big 32 William A. Wellman
So Big 53 Robert Wise
So Bright the Flame 52 John Sturges
So-Called Cariatids, The 84 Agnès Varda
So Close to Life 57 Ingmar Bergman
So Dark the Night 46 Joseph H. Lewis
So Dear to My Heart 48 Hamilton Luske, Harold Schuster
So Does an Automobile 39 Dave Fleischer
So ein Mädel 20 Urban Gad
So ein Mädel Vergisst Man Nicht 32 Fritz Kortner
So Ends Our Night 41 John Cromwell
So Evil My Love 48 Lewis Allen
So Evil My Sister 72 Reginald LeBorg
So Evil, So Young 61 Godfrey Grayson
So Far from India 82 Mira Nair

So Fine 81 Andrew Bergman
So Goes My Love 46 Frank Ryan
So Goes the Day 68 Márta Mészáros
So Is This 82 Michael Snow
So It's Sunday 32 Edward I. Luddy
So Like a Woman 30 E. Mason Hopper
So Like Him 19 James Reardon
So Little Time 51 Compton Bennett
So Long at the Fair 50 Anthony Darnborough, Terence Fisher
So Long Blue Boy 73 Gerald Gordon
So Long, Letty 20 Al Christie
So Long Letty 29 Lloyd Bacon
So Long Philippine 61 Jacques Rozier
So Lovely, So Deadly 57 Will Kohler
So Many Dreams 87 Heiner Carow
So Much for So Little 49 Friz Freleng, Chuck Jones
So Much Good in the Worst of Us 14 Frank Wilson
So Near, Yet So Far 12 D. W. Griffith
So Proudly We Hail! 43 Mark Sandrich
So Red the Rose 35 King Vidor
So Runs the Way 13 Christy Cabanne
So Sad About Gloria 73 Harry Thomason
So Sind die Menschen 30 Robert Siodmak
So That Men Are Free 62 Willard Van Dyke
So This Is Africa 33 Edward F. Cline
So This Is Arizona 22 Francis Ford
So This Is College 29 Sam Wood
So This Is Hamlet? 23 Gregory La Cava
So This Is Harris 32 Mark Sandrich
So This Is Hollywood 24 Alfred E. Green
So This Is Jollygood 25 Adrian Brunel
So This Is London 30 John G. Blystone
So This Is London 34 Edgar Anstey, John Grierson
So This Is London 39 Thornton Freeland
So This Is Love 28 Frank Capra
So This Is Love 53 Gordon Douglas
So This Is Marriage 24 Hobart Henley
So This Is New York 48 Richard Fleischer
So This Is Paris 26 Ernst Lubitsch
So This Is Paris 26 Richard Wallace
So This Is Paris 54 Richard Quine
So This Is Washington 43 Ray McCarey
So This Was Paris 41 John Harlow
So Viele Träume 87 Heiner Carow
So Well Remembered 47 Edward Dmytryk
So What? 87 Helmut Berger, Anja Franke, Dani Levy
So You Don't Know Korff Yet? 39 Fritz Holl
So You Won't Talk? 35 Monty Banks
So You Won't Talk? 40 Edward Sedgwick
So Young, So Bad 50 Bernard Vorhaus
Soak the Old 40 Sammy Lee
Soak the Poor 37 Harold S. Bucquet
Soak the Rich 36 Ben Hecht, Charles MacArthur
Soap Bubbles 06 Georges Méliès
Soap Bubbles 29 Slatan Dudow
Soap Girl, The 18 Martin Justice
Soap Opera 64 Andy Warhol*
Soap vs. Blacking 02 Walter R. Booth
Soapbox Derby 58 D'Arcy Conyers
Soapsuds Lady, The 25 Edward F. Cline
Soapy Soup 07 Arthur Cooper
Sob Sister 31 Alfred Santell

Soldier Old Man *32* Manny Gould, Ben Harrison

Soldier on Duty *58* Carlo Ludovico Bragaglia

Soldier, Policeman and Cook *1899* Arthur Cooper

Soldier, Sailor *44* Alexander Shaw

Soldier Who Declared Peace, The *70* Joseph Sargent

Soldiers, The *63* Jean-Luc Godard

Soldiers and Other Cosmic Objects *77* Stan Brakhage

Soldiers and Women *30* Edward Sloman

Soldiers Aren't Born *68* Alexander Stolper

Soldiers at War *40* Fumio Kamei

Soldiers' Bride *39* Risto Orko

Soldier's Courtship, The *1896* Alfred Moul

Soldier's Duties, A *47* Erik Faustman

Soldier's Duty, A *12* Charles Brabin

Soldier's Father, A *65* Revaz Chkeidze

Soldier's French Leave, A *1898* Georges Méliès

Soldier's Honor, The *13* Thomas Ince

Soldier's Honour, A *11* H. Oceano Martinek

Soldier's Honour, A *14* Charles C. Calvert

Soldiers in White *41* B. Reeves Eason

Soldier's Jealousy, A *07* Lewin Fitzhamon

Soldiers March, The *57* Leonid Trauberg

Soldiers Marched On, The *57* Leonid Trauberg

Soldier's Oath, A *15* Oscar Apfel

Soldiers of Chance *17* Paul Scardon

Soldiers of Fortune *14* Augustus Thomas

Soldiers of Fortune *19* Allan Dwan

Soldiers of Fortune *32* Paul Sloane

Soldiers of Freedom, The *76* S. Kurganov, Yuri Ozerov

Soldiers of Pancho Villa, The *59* Ismael Rodríguez

Soldiers of the Air *42* William A. Wellman

Soldiers of the King *33* Maurice Elvey

Soldiers of the Storm *33* D. Ross Lederman

Soldier's Pay, A *30* Michael Curtiz

Soldier's Plaything, A *30* Michael Curtiz

Soldier's Prayer, A *61* Masaki Kobayashi

Soldier's Return, The *02* James A. Williamson

Soldier's Revenge *84* David Worth

Soldier's Romance, A *04* Frank Mottershaw

Soldier's Sons *16* Wilbert Melville

Soldier's Story, A *84* Norman Jewison

Soldier's Sweetheart, A *11* Dave Aylott

Soldier's Tale, The *64* Michael Birkett

Soldier's Tale, A *88* Larry Parr

Soldier's Tedious Duty, A *1898* Georges Méliès

Soldiers Three *51* Tay Garnett

Soldiers Three *62* John Sturges

Soldiers: 365 Days Till Dawn *87* Marco Risi

Soldier's Unlucky Salutation, A *1896* Georges Méliès

Soldier's Wedding, A *07* Percy Stow

Soldiers Were Marching *57* Leonid Trauberg

Sole *28* Alessandro Blasetti

Sole Anche di Notte, Il *90* Paolo Taviani, Vittorio Taviani

Sole Buio, Il *90* Damiano Damiani

Sole Mates *29* Manny Gould, Ben Harrison

Sole negli Occhi, Il *53* Antonio Pietrangeli

Sole Sorge Ancora, Il *46* Aldo Vergano

Sole Sotta Terra, Il *71* Aldo Florio

Sole Support *29* Charles Lamont

Sole Survivor *84* Thom Eberhardt

Soledad *58* Mario Craveri

Soledad *66* Jacqueline Audry

Soleil des Voyous, Le *66* Jean Delannoy

Soleil Noir *66* Denys De la Patellière

Soleil Ô *70* Med Hondo

Soleil Rouge *71* Terence Young

Soleils de l'Île de Pâques, Les *72* Pierre Kast

Solid Explanation, A *51* Peter Bradford

Solid Gold *26* Stephen Roberts

Solid Gold Cadillac, The *56* Richard Quine

Solid Serenade *46* Joseph Barbera, William Hanna

Solid Tin Coyote, The *66* Rudy Larriva

Solidaridad, Cuba y Vietnam *65* Santiago Álvarez

Solidarity *73* Joyce Wieland

Solidarity, Cuba and Vietnam *65* Santiago Álvarez

Soliloques du Pauvre, Les *51* Michel Drach

Soliloquy *49* Lester James Peries

Solimano il Conquistare *61* Vatroslav Mimica, Mario Tota

Solimano il Conquistatore *61* Vatroslav Mimica, Mario Tota

Solitaire, Le *87* Jacques Deray

Solitaire Man, The *33* Jack Conway

Solitary Child, The *58* Gerald Thomas

Solitary Cyclist, The *21* Maurice Elvey

Solitary Sin, The *19* Frederick Sullivan

Soliti Ignoti, I *56* Mario Monicelli

Soliti Ignoti Vent'Anni Dopo, I *85* Amanzio Todini

Solitude *28* Pál Fejős

Solitude *61* Walerian Borowczyk, Jan Lenica

Solitude du Chanteur de Fond, La *74* Chris Marker

Solntse Svetit Vsem *61* Konstantin Voinov

Solo *69* Jean-Pierre Mocky

Solo *78* Tony Williams

Solo *84* Lyman Dayton

Solo Contro Roma *61* Riccardo Freda, Luciano Ricci, Marco Vicario

Solo Contro Tutti *65* Antonio Del Amo

Solo for Sparrow *62* Gordon Flemyng

Solo per Danne *39* A. Giacalone

Solo per Te *38* Carmine Gallone

Solo per Te, Lucia *52* Franco Rossi

Solo Sunny *79* Wolfgang Kohlhaase, Konrad Wolf

Sólo un Ataúd *66* Santos Alcocer

Solomennie Kolokoka *88* Yuri Ilyenko

Solomon and Sheba *59* King Vidor

Solomon in Society *22* Lawrence C. Windom

Solomon King *74* Jack Bomay, Sal Watts

Solomon's Heart *32* Sergei Gerasimov, M. Kressin

Solomon's Twins *16* Alfonse Frenguelli, Lewis Gilbert

Solos en la Madrugada *77* José Luis García Ágraz

Solstik *53* Astrid Henning-Jensen, Bjarne Henning-Jensen

Solution by Phone *54* Alfred Travers

Solution of the Mystery, The *15* B. Reeves Eason

Solutions Françaises *39* Jean Painlevé

Solutions Françaises *48* Jean Painlevé

Sølv *56* Jørgen Roos

Solving the Puzzle *10* Émile Cohl

Solyaris *71* Andrei Tarkovsky

Solzhenitsyn's Children...Are Making a Lot of Noise in Paris *79* Michael Rubbo

Som Folk Är Mest *44* Hasse Ekman

Som Natt och Dag *69* Jonas Cornell

Sombra de Pancho Villa, La *32* Miguel Torres Contreras

Sombra del Murciélago, La *66* Federico Curiel

Sombra the Spider Woman *46* Spencer G. Bennet, Fred C. Brannon

Sombras de Gloria *29* Andrew L. Stone

Sombre Dimanche *48* Jacqueline Audry

Sombrero *52* Norman Foster

Sombrero de Tres Picos, El *34* Harry D'Abbadie D'Arrast, Ricardo Soriano

Sombrero Kid, The *42* George Sherman

Some Actors *15* Will P. Kellino

Some Artist *19* Rex Wilson

Some Barrier *17* Paul Terry

Some Blondes Are Dangerous *37* Milton Carruth

Some Boy *17* Otis Turner

Some Bride *19* Henry Otto

Some Call It Loving *73* James B. Harris

Some Came Running *58* Vincente Minnelli

Some Chickweed for the Little Birds *62* Marcel Carné

Some Dancer *17* Fred Evans, Joe Evans

Some Day *35* Michael Powell

Some Detectives *16* Bert Haldane

Some Fish! *14* Dave Aylott

Some Fish *16* Harry Buss

Some Fun *15* Fred Evans, Joe Evans

Some Girls *88* Michael Hoffman

Some Girls Do *68* Ralph Thomas

Some Impressions on the Subject of Thrift *24* Paul M. Felton

Some Job *18* Alfred Santell

Some Kind of a Nut *52* Maclean Rogers

Some Kind of a Nut *69* Garson Kanin

Some Kind of Hero *72* Marvin Lichtner

Some Kind of Hero *82* Michael Pressman

Some Kind of Wonderful *87* Howard Deutch

Some Liar *19* Henry King

Some Like It Cold *60* Steno

Some Like It Cool *61* Michael Winner

Some Like It Cool *76* Franz Antel

Some Like It Hot *39* George Archainbaud

Some Like It Hot *59* Billy Wilder

Some Like It Not *55* Tex Avery

Some Like It Sexy *69* Donovan Winter

Some Little Things Our Tommies Leave Behind Them *14* Arrigo Bocchi

Son of Dr. Jekyll, The *51* Seymour Friedman
Son of Dracula *43* Robert Siodmak
Son of Dracula *74* Freddie Francis
Son of Erin, A *16* Julia Ivers
Son of Fate, The *15* Mauritz Stiller
Son of Flubber *63* Robert Stevenson
Son of France, A *14* George Pearson
Son of Frankenstein *39* Rowland V. Lee
Son of Fury *42* John Cromwell
Son of Geronimo *52* Spencer G. Bennet
Son of God's Country *48* R. G. Springsteen
Son of Godzilla *67* Jun Fukuda
Son of Greetings *70* Brian DePalma
Son of Hercules in the Land of Fire *63* Giorgio C. Simonelli
Son of His Father, The *17* Victor Schertzinger
Son of His Father, A *25* Victor Fleming
Son of India *31* Jacques Feyder
Son of India *60* Ramjankhan Mehboobkhan
Son of Ingagi *40* Richard Kahn
Son of Japan, A *13* Charles H. Weston
Son of Kissing Cup *22* Walter West
Son of Kong *33* Ernest B. Schoedsack
Son of Lassie *45* S. Sylvan Simon
Son of Lifeboat *49* Jerry Lewis
Son of Mars, A *12* Dave Aylott
Son of Mine *32* Louis King
Son of Mongolia *36* R. Suslovich, Ilya Trauberg
Son of Monte Cristo, The *40* Rowland V. Lee
Son of Oklahoma *32* Robert North Bradbury
Son of Paleface *52* Frank Tashlin
Son of Pedro Navajas, The *87* Alfonso Rosas Priego
Son of Roaring Dan *40* Ford Beebe
Son of Robin Hood *58* George Sherman
Son of Rusty, The *47* Lew Landers
Son of Samson *60* Carlo Campogalliani
Son of Satan *24* Oscar Micheaux
Son of Satan *63* Mario Bava
Son of Sinbad *55* Ted Tetzlaff
Son of Sontag, The *25* Paul Hurst
Son of Spartacus *62* Sergio Corbucci
Son of Spellbound *49* Jerry Lewis
Son of Tarzan, The *20* Arthur J. Flaven, Harry Revier
Son of the Blob *71* Larry Hagman
Son of the Border *33* Lloyd Nosler
Son of the Desert, A *28* William Merrill McCormick
Son of the Gods *30* Frank Lloyd
Son of the Golden West *28* Eugene Forde
Son of the Guardsman *46* Derwin Abrahams
Son of the Hills, A *17* Harry Davenport
Son of the Immortals, A *16* Otis Turner
Son of the Land, A *31* Edward Ioganson
Son of the Navy *40* William Nigh
Son of the Nile, The *51* Youssef Chahine
Son of the Plains *31* Robert North Bradbury
Son of the Red Corsair *60* Primo Zeglio
Son of the Regiment *48* Vassili M. Pronin
Son of the Renegade *53* Reginald Brown

Son of the Sahara, A *24* Edwin Carewe
Son of the Sahara *67* Frederic Goode
Son of the Sea, A *15* Ernest G. Batley
Son of the Sheik *26* George Fitzmaurice
Son of the Star *53* Leopoldo Torre-Nilsson, Leopoldo Torres Ríos
Son of the Wolf, The *22* Norman Dawn
Son of Wallingford, The *21* George Randolph Chester
Son of Zorro *47* Spencer G. Bennet, Fred C. Brannon
Son Tornata per Te *52* Luigi Comencini
Son Urfalı *87* Ömer Uğur
Son v Ruku, ili Chemodon *87* Earnest Yasan
Sonad Oskuld *14* Victor Sjöström
Soñadores de la Gloria *38* Miguel Torres Contreras
Sonámbulos *77* Manuel Gutiérrez Aragón
Sonar Killa *74* Satyajit Ray
Sonáta Kreutzerova *26* Gustav Machatý
Sonatas *59* Juan Antonio Bardem
Sonate à Kreutzer, La *56* Eric Rohmer
Söndag i September, En *63* Jörn Donner
Sondeurs d'Abîme *43* Marcel Ichac
Song a Day, A *36* Dave Fleischer
Song About Flowers, The *59* Otar Ioseliani
Song About Happiness *34* Mark Donskoi, Vladimir Legoshin
Song and Dance Concert *52* Alexander Ivanovsky, Herbert Rappaport
Song and Dance Man, The *26* Herbert Brenon
Song and Dance Man, The *36* Allan Dwan
Song and Dance Over the Vistula *56* Boris Ivanov, I. M. Poselsky
Song and the Silence, The *69* Nathan Cohen
Song at Eventide *34* Harry Hughes
Song Birds, The *20* Raoul Barré, Charles Bowers
Song Birds *33* John Harlow
Song for Miss Julie, A *45* William Rowland
Song for Tomorrow, A *48* Terence Fisher
Song from My Heart, The *70* Noboru Nakamura
Song in Soho *37* R. A. Hopwood
Song Is Born, A *47* Howard Hawks
Song Lantern, The *43* Mikio Naruse
Song o' My Heart *30* Frank Borzage
Song of a Flower Basket *37* Heinosuke Gosho
Song of a Sad Country *37* Jiří Weiss
Song of Abaya *45* E. Aron, Grigori Roshal
Song of Arizona *46* Frank McDonald
Song of Bernadette, The *43* Henry King
Song of Bwana Toshi, The *65* Susumu Hani
Song of Bygone Days *87* Albert Mkrtchyan
Song of Ceylon *34* Basil Wright
Song of China *36* Ming-yau Lo
Song of Conscience, The *09* D. W. Griffith
Song of Dolores *49* Benito Perojo
Song of Failure, The *22* Kenji Mizoguchi
Song of Freedom *36* J. Elder Wills

Song of Fukagawa, The *60* So Yamamura
Song of Happiness, The *33* Carl Boese
Song of Happiness, The *34* Mark Donskoi, Vladimir Legoshin
Song of Hate, The *15* J. Gordon Edwards
Song of Heroes *32* Joris Ivens
Song of Home, The *25* Kenji Mizoguchi
Song of Idaho *48* Ray Nazarro
Song of India *49* Albert S. Rogell
Song of Kentucky *29* Lewis Seiler
Song of Life, The *21* John M. Stahl
Song of Life, The *31* Alexis Granowsky
Song of Love, The *23* Chester M. Franklin, Frances Marion
Song of Love, The *29* Erle C. Kenton
Song of Love *47* Clarence Brown
Song of Love, A *64* Jiří Brdečka
Song of Love *67* Yoji Yamada
Song of Mexico *45* James A. Fitzpatrick
Song of Mutsuko *86* Hiromichi Horikawa
Song of My Heart *47* Benjamin Glazer
Song of Nevada *44* Joseph Kane
Song of New Life *30* Alexander Dovzhenko
Song of Norway *55* Maclean Rogers
Song of Norway *70* Andrew L. Stone
Song of Old Wyoming *45* Robert E. Tansey
Song of Paris *52* John Guillermin
Song of Paris, The *54* Marcel Carné
Song of Remembrance *36* Douglas Sirk
Song of Revolt *37* Roy Rowland
Song of Russia *43* Gregory Ratoff
Song of Sadness, The *52* Humberto Mauro
Song of Scheherazade *47* Walter Reisch
Song of Sister Maria, The *52* Rafael Gil
Song of Sixpence, A *17* Ralph Dean
Song of Soho *30* Harry Lachman
Song of Songs, The *18* Joseph Kaufman
Song of Songs *33* Rouben Mamoulian
Song of Songs *35* Henry Lynn
Song of Steel, A *28* V. Granatman, Josef Heifits, Mikhail Shapiro, Alexander Zarkhi
Song of Surrender *49* Mitchell Leisen
Song of Texas *43* Joseph Kane
Song of the Balalaika *71* Henri Diamant-Berger
Song of the Birds, The *35* Dave Fleischer
Song of the Buckaroo *38* Albert Herman
Song of the Caballero *30* Harry Joe Brown
Song of the Camp, The *38* Kenji Mizoguchi*
Song of the Cart, The *59* Satsuo Yamamoto
Song of the City *37* Errol Taggart
Song of the Cossack Gloota, The *37* Igor Savchenko
Song of the Damned *35* Albert S. Rogell
Song of the Drifter *47* Lambert Hillyer
Song of the Eagle *33* Ralph Murphy
Song of the Exile *90* Ann Hui
Song of the Fisherman *34* Tsou-sen Tsai
Song of the Flame *30* Alan Crosland
Song of the Flower Basket *37* Heinosuke Gosho
Song of the Forest *63* Viktor Ivchenko
Song of the Forge *37* Henry Edwards
Song of the Godbody *77* James Broughton

Song of the Gringo *36* John P. McCarthy
Song of the Islands *42* Walter Lang
Song of the Land *53* Ed N. Harrison, Henry S. Kesler, Frances Roberts
Song of the Lantern *43* Mikio Naruse
Song of the Lark *37* S. Innemann
Song of the Little Road *55* Satyajit Ray
Song of the Loon *70* Andrew Herbert
Song of the Meet *49* Jiří Weiss
Song of the Merchant Kalashnikov *09* Vasili M. Goncharov*
Song of the Mountain Pass, The *23* Kenji Mizoguchi
Song of the Native Country *25* Kenji Mizoguchi
Song of the Open Road *44* S. Sylvan Simon
Song of the Partisans, The *38* Seto Wai-mon
Song of the Plough *33* John Baxter
Song of the Prairie *45* Ray Nazarro
Song of the Prairie *49* Jiří Trnka
Song of the Range *44* Wallace Fox
Song of the Red Ruby, The *70* Annelise Meineche
Song of the Rivers *54* Joris Ivens
Song of the Road *36* Alex Bryce
Song of the Road *37* John Baxter
Song of the Road *55* Satyajit Ray
Song of the Saddle *36* Louis King
Song of the Sarong *45* Harold Young
Song of the Scarlet Flower *18* Mauritz Stiller
Song of the Scarlet Flower, The *56* Gustaf Molander
Song of the Sea, The *52* Alberto Caval-canti
Song of the Sephardi *80* David Raphael
Song of the Shirt, The *08* D. W. Griffith
Song of the Sierras *46* Oliver Drake
Song of the Sierras *47* William Witney
Song of the Siren *46* Norman Foster
Song of the Soul, The *18* Tom Terriss
Song of the Soul, The *20* John W. Noble
Song of the Soul *38* Chano Urueta
Song of the South *46* Harve Foster, Wil-fred Jackson
Song of the Street *33* Victor Trivas
Song of the Thin Man *47* Edward Buzzell
Song of the Trail *36* Russell Hopton
Song of the Wage Slave, The *15* Herbert Blaché
Song of the Wasteland *47* Thomas Carr
Song of the West *30* Ray Enright
Song of the Wildwood Flute, The *10* D. W. Griffith
Song of Tomorrow *48* Terence Fisher
Song of Triumphant Love *15* Yevgeni Bauer
Song of Two Human Beings *27* F. W. Murnau
Song of Two Humans, A *27* F. W. Murnau
Song of Victory *42* Bob Wickersham
Song of Victory *45* Kenji Mizoguchi*
Song of Yearning, The *52* Humberto Mauro
Song or Two, A *29* R. E. Jeffrey
Song Over Moscow *63* Herbert Rappaport
Song Remains the Same, The *76* Peter

Clifton, Joe Massot
Song Service *30* Norman Taurog
Song Shopping *33* Dave Fleischer
Song to Her, The *35* Ivar Johansson
Song to Remember, A *44* Charles Vidor
Song Which Grandmother Sang, The *12* August Blom
Song Without End *59* George Cukor, Charles Vidor
Song You Gave Me, The *33* Paul Stein
Song-copation *29* R. E. Jeffrey
Songe d'Or de l'Avare, Le *00* Georges Méliès
Songe d'un Garçon de Café, Le *10* Émile Cohl
Songhay Empire, The *63* Ousmane Sembène
Songhays *63* Ousmane Sembène
Songlines *89* Godfrey Reggio
Songs *69* Stan Brakhage
Songs and Bullets *38* Sam Newfield
Songs and Saddles *38* Harry Fraser
Songs My Mother Sang *26* Hugh Croise
Songs of England *25* James A. Fitzpatrick
Songs of Ireland *25* James A. Fitzpatrick
Songs of Scotland *25* James A. Fitzpatrick
Songs of Scotland *66* Laurence Henson, Edward McConnell
Songs of Siberia *47* Ivan Pyriev
Songs of the British Isles *25* James A. Fitzpatrick
Songs of the Organ *37* Widgey R. Newman
Songs of the Vistula *56* Jerzy Bossak
Songs of the West Countree *26* Hugh Croise
Songs 1-14 *80* Stan Brakhage
Songs Over the Dnieper *58* G. Svetlanov
Songwriter *84* Alan Rudolph
Sonho de Vampiros, Um *69* Ibere Cavalcanti
Sonho Sem Fim *86* Lauro Escorel Filho
Sonhos de Menina Moça *88* Tereza Trautman
Sonia *21* Denison Clift
Sonia *28* Hector V. Sarno
Sonido de la Muerte, El *64* José Antonio Nieves Conde
Sonido Prehistórico, El *64* José Antonio Nieves Conde
Sonja *43* Erik Faustman
Sonnambula, La *52* Cesare Barlacchi
Sonne Geht Auf, Die *35* Willy Reiber
Sønnen *14* August Blom
Sonnenstrahl *33* Pál Fejös
Sonnensucher, Die *58* Konrad Wolf
Sonnette d'Alarme, La *35* Christian-Jaque
Sonntagmorgen in Warschau, Ein *55* An-drzej Munk
Sonntags...Nie *59* Jules Dassin
Sonny *22* Henry King
Sonny and Jed *73* Sergio Corbucci
Sonny Boy *29* Archie Mayo
Sonny Boy *88* Robert Martin Carroll
Sono Fotogenico *80* Dino Risi
Sono Sartana, il Vostro Becchino *69* Giu-liano Carmineo
Sono Stato Io *40* Raffaello Matarazzo
Sono Stato Io *72* Alberto Lattuada
Sono un Fenomeno Paranormale *85* Sergio

Corbucci
Sono Yo no Tsuma *30* Yasujiro Ozu
Sono Yo wa Wasurenai *62* Kozaburo Yoshimura
Sonora Kid, The *27* Robert De Lacey
Sonora Stagecoach *44* Robert E. Tansey
Sonrisa de la Vírgen, La *61* Roberto Rod-ríguez, Ken Smith
Sons, The *46* Alexander Ivanov
Sons and Daughters of the Good Earth *64* King Hu
Sons and Lovers *60* Jack Cardiff
Sons and Mothers *66* Mark Donskoi
Sons Anglais *68* Jean-Luc Godard, Jean-Pierre Gorin
Sons o' Guns *36* Lloyd Bacon
Sons of Adventure *48* Yakima Canutt
Sons of Darkness, The *81* Chang-ho Lee
Sons of Good Earth *64* King Hu
Sons of Great Bear, The *65* Josef Mach
Sons of Ingmar, The *18* Victor Sjöström
Sons of Katie Elder, The *65* Henry Hathaway
Sons of Liberty *39* Michael Curtiz
Sons of Martha *07* Charles Raymond
Sons of Matthew *49* Charles Chauvel
Sons of New Mexico *49* John English
Sons of Satan, The *15* George Loane Tucker
Sons of Satan *68* Duccio Tessari
Sons of Steel *35* Charles Lamont
Sons of Steel *88* Gary L. Keady
Sons of the Desert *33* William A. Seiter
Sons of the Finest *40* Sam Newfield
Sons of the Good Earth *64* King Hu
Sons of the Legion *33* William A. Seiter
Sons of the Legion *38* James P. Hogan
Sons of the Musketeers *49* Lewis Allen
Sons of the Pioneers *42* Joseph Kane
Sons of the Saddle *30* Harry Joe Brown
Sons of the Sea *25* H. Bruce Woolfe
Sons of the Sea *26* James Cruze
Sons of the Sea *39* Maurice Elvey
Sons of the Sea *41* Walter Forde
Sons of Thunder *61* Duccio Tessari
Son's Return, The *09* D. W. Griffith
Sooky *31* Norman Taurog
Sooner or Later *20* Wesley Ruggles
Sooty Sketches *09* Walter R. Booth
Sopernitsy *87* Victor Sadovsky
Sophia *87* Alejandro Doria
Sophie et le Crime *58* Pierre Gaspard-Huit
Sophie Lang *34* Ralph Murphy
Sophie Lang Goes West *37* Charles Reisner
Sophienlund *43* Heinz Rühmann
Sophie's Choice *82* Alan J. Pakula
Sophie's Place *69* James O'Connolly
Sophie's Ways *70* Moshe Mizrahi
Sophomore, The *29* Leo McCarey
Soppy Green Loses a Legacy *12* A. E. Coleby
Sopraluoghi in Palestina *63* Pier Paolo Pasolini
Sopravvissuti della Città Morta, I *84* Antonio Margheriti
Sopravvissuto, Il *16* Augusto Genina
Sor Juana Inés de la Cruz *36* Ramón Peón
Sora wa Haretari *25* Heinosuke Gosho

Sorcellerie Culinaire *04* Georges Méliès
Sorcerer, The *44* Christian-Jaque
Sorcerer, The *63* Teinosuke Kinugasa
Sorcerer *77* William Friedkin
Sorcerer, the Prince and the Good Fairy, The *00* Georges Méliès
Sorcerers, The *67* Michael Reeves
Sorcerer's Apprentice, The *55* Michael Powell
Sorcerer's Revenge, The *03* Georges Méliès
Sorcerer's Scissors, The *07* Walter R. Booth
Sorcerers' Village *58* Hassoldt Davis
Sorceress, The *55* André Michel
Sorceress *82* Brian Stuart
Sorceress *87* Suzanne Schiffman
Sorcier, Le *03* Georges Méliès
Sorcier, le Prince et le Bon Génie, Le *00* Georges Méliès
Sorcière, La *55* André Michel
Sorcières, Les *66* Mauro Bolognini, Vittorio De Sica, Pier Paolo Pasolini, Franco Rossi, Luchino Visconti
Sorcières de Salem, Les *57* Raymond Rouleau
Sorcières du Bord du Lac, Les *71* Tonino Cervi
Sordid Affair, A *57* Pietro Germi
Sorekara *86* Yoshimitsu Morita
Sorella *20* Mario Caserini
Sorella Contro Sorella *20* Herbert Brenon
Sorella di Satana, La *65* Michael Reeves
Sorelle Materassi, Le *43* Ferdinando Maria Poggioli
Soria-Moria *47* Arne Sucksdorff
Sorobanzuku *87* Yoshimitsu Morita
Sorochinskaya Yamarka *39* Nikolai Ekk
Sorochinski Fair, The *39* Nikolai Ekk
49 Dney *64* Gennady Gabay
Sorok Pervyi *26* Yakov Protazanov
Sorok Pervyi *56* Grigori Chukhrai
Sorok Serdets *31* Lev Kuleshov
Sorority Babes in the Slimeball Bowl-O-Rama *87* David DeCoteau
Sorority Girl *57* Roger Corman
Sorority House *39* John Farrow
Sorority House Massacre *86* Carol Frank
Sorority Sisters *87* David DeCoteau
Sorpasso, Il *62* Dino Risi
Sorprese dell'Amore, Le *59* Luigi Comencini
Sorrell and Son *27* Herbert Brenon
Sorrell and Son *33* Jack Raymond
Sorrida Prego *49* Valerio Zurlini
Sorriso del Grande Tentatore, Il *72* Damiano Damiani
Sorrow and the Pity, The *69* Marcel Ophüls
Sorrow and the Shame, The *69* Marcel Ophüls
Sorrow Is Only for Women *58* Kaneto Shindo
Sorrowful Example, The *11* D. W. Griffith
Sorrowful Jones *49* Sidney Lanfield
Sorrowful Shore, The *13* Christy Cabanne, D. W. Griffith
Sorrowing Mother, The *17* Abel Gance
Sorrows Moment *69* Gregory Markopoulos
Sorrows of a Chaperone, The *09* Lewin Fitzhamon

Sorrows of Happiness *16* Joseph Kaufman
Sorrows of Love, The *16* Charles Giblyn
Sorrows of Satan, The *17* Alexander Butler
Sorrows of Satan, The *26* D. W. Griffith
Sorrows of Selina, The *14* Dave Aylott
Sorrows of the Unfaithful, The *10* D. W. Griffith
Sorry, Can't Stop *09* Dave Aylott
Sorry, I'll Make It My Way *86* Lui Farias
Sorry, Wrong Number *48* Anatole Litvak
Sorry You've Been Troubled *32* Jack Raymond
Sort-of-Girl Who Came from Heaven, The *15* Ralph Ince
Sorta Drøm, Den *11* Urban Gad
Sorte Kansler, Den *12* August Blom
Sortie des Ateliers Vibert *1896* Georges Méliès
Sortie des Usines, La *1895* Louis Lumière
Sortie des Usines Lumière, La *1895* Louis Lumière
Sortie du Port, La *1895* Louis Lumière
Sortie du "Rubis," Une *50* Jacques-Yves Cousteau
Sortie Sans Permission *1898* Georges Méliès
Sortilèges *44* Christian-Jaque
Sorting Office *35* Harry Watt
Sorting Refuse at Incinerating Plant, New York City *03* Edwin S. Porter
Sortűz egy Fekete Bivalyért *85* László Szabó
Sōryū Hiken *58* Hiroshi Inagaki
So's Your Aunt Emma! *42* Jean Yarbrough
So's Your Old Man *26* Gregory La Cava
So's Your Uncle! *43* Jean Yarbrough
Soseiji Gakkyū *56* Susumu Hani
Sōshun *56* Yasujiro Ozu
Sosie, Le *15* Louis Feuillade
Sospetto, Il *75* Francesco Maselli
Søster Ceciles Offer *15* Forest Holger-Madsen
Sōteio *27* Tomu Uchida
Sotelo *76* Raúl Ruiz
Sotto a Chi Tocca *72* Gianfranco Parolini
Sotto gli Occhi dell'Assassino *82* Dario Argento
Sotto il Cielo Stellato *66* Renato Castellani
Sotto il Ristorante Cinese *87* Bruno Bozzetto
Sotto il Segno dello Scorpione *68* Paolo Taviani, Vittorio Taviani
Sotto il Sole di Roma *47* Renato Castellani
Sotto il Tallone *65* Pierre Granier-Deferre
Sotto il Vestito Niente *85* Carlo Vanzina
Sotto il Vestito Niente II *88* Dario Piana
Sotto...Sotto *84* Lina Wertmuller
Sottozero *87* Gian Luigi Polidoro
Soubrette's Troubles on a Fifth Avenue Stage *01* Edwin S. Porter
Souchastniki *87* Ina Tumanyan
Souffle au Cœur, Le *71* Louis Malle
Soufrière, La *76* Werner Herzog
Souhvězdí Panny *69* Zbyněk Brynych
Soul *86* Kei Shu
Soul Adrift, A *18* Alice Guy-Blaché, Léonce Perret
Soul and Body *21* Frank Beal
Soul Enslaved, A *16* Cleo Madison

Soul Fire *25* John S. Robertson
Soul for Sale, A *15* Thomas Bentley
Soul for Sale, A *18* Allen Holubar
Soul Harvest, The *23* William H. Clifford
Soul Herder, The *17* John Ford
Soul in Bondage, A *13* Van Dyke Brooke
Soul in Trust, A *18* Gilbert P. Hamilton
Soul Kiss, The *30* Sidney Franklin
Soul Man *86* Steve Miner
Soul Market, The *16* Francis J. Grandon
Soul Master, The *17* Marguerite Bertsch
Soul Mates *16* William Russell
Soul Mates *25* Jack Conway
Soul of a Beautiful Girl *59* Han-hsiang Li
Soul of a Child, The *16* John Gorman
Soul of a Man, The *21* William Nigh
Soul of a Monster, The *44* Will Jason
Soul of a Thief, The *13* Allan Dwan
Soul of a Woman, The *15* Edwin Carewe
Soul of an Artist *25* Germaine Dulac
Soul of Broadway, The *15* Herbert Brenon
Soul of Buddha, The *18* J. Gordon Edwards
Soul of France, The *28* A. Duges, Alexandre Ryder
Soul of Guilda Lois, The *19* Frank Wilson
Soul of Honor, The *14* James Kirkwood
Soul of Kura San, The *16* Edward J. LeSaint
Soul of Magdalene, The *17* Burton L. King
Soul of Man, The *21* William Nigh
Soul of Mexico *32* David Kirkland
Soul of Nigger Charley, The *73* Larry Spangler
Soul of Satan, The *17* Otis Turner
Soul of the Accordion, The *40* Mario Soffici
Soul of the Beast *23* John Griffith Wray
Soul of the Slums *31* Frank R. Strayer
Soul of Youth, The *20* William Desmond Taylor
Soul Soldier *70* John Cardos
Soul Soldiers *70* John Cardos
Soul to Devils, A *71* Ko Nakahira
Soul to Soul *71* Denis Sanders
Soul Triumphant *17* Christy Cabanne
Soul Violin, The *20* Raoul Barré, Charles Bowers
Soul Without Windows, A *18* Travers Vale
Soulier de Satin, Le *85* Manoel De Oliveira
Souls Adrift *17* Harley Knoles
Souls Aflame *28* Raymond Wells
Souls at Sea *37* Henry Hathaway
Soul's Awakening, A *22* Will P. Kellino
Soul's Crucifixion, A *19* Frank Wilson
Soul's Cycle, The *16* Ulysses Davis
Souls for Sables *25* James McKay
Souls for Sables *32* Robert F. Hill
Souls for Sale *23* Rupert Hughes
Souls for Sale *62* Albert Zugsmith
Souls in Bondage *16* Edgar Lewis
Souls in Bondage *23* William H. Clifford
Souls in Conflict *55* Leonard Reeve, Dick Ross
Souls in Pawn *17* Henry King
Souls in Pawn *30* George B. Samuelson
Souls of Children, The *28* Jean Benoît-Lévy, Marie Epstein

Souls of Sin *49* Powell Lindsay
Souls of Sin *61* Carlos Rinaldi
Souls on the Road *21* Minoru Murata, Kaoru Osanai
Souls Triumphant *15* John B. O'Brien
Souna Kouma *75* Jean Rouch
Sound and Fury *88* Jean-Claude Brisseau
Sound and the Fury, The *58* Martin Ritt
Sound Barrier, The *52* David Lean, Anthony Squire
Sound Eroticism *85* Péter Tímár
Sound from a Million Years Ago *64* José Antonio Nieves Conde
Sound of Fury, The *50* Cy Endfield
Sound of Her Voice, The *14* Maurice Elvey
Sound of Horror, The *64* José Antonio Nieves Conde
Sound of Laughter, The *63* John O' Shaughnessy
Sound of Life, The *62* Tatiana Lukashevich
Sound of Music, The *64* Robert Wise
Sound of the City: London 1964-1973 *81* Peter Clifton
Sound of the Mountain *54* Mikio Naruse
Sound of the Violin, The *15* Forest Holger-Madsen
Sound of Trumpets, The *61* Ermanno Olmi
Sound of Youth *57* Hideo Sekigawa
Sound Off *52* Richard Quine
Sound Sleeper, A *09* D. W. Griffith
Sound Your "A" *19* Raoul Barré, Charles Bowers
Sounder *71* Martin Ritt
Sounder, Part Two *76* William A. Graham
Soundies, The *86* Don McGlynn
Sounding Wave *21* Walter Ruttmann
Sounds from the Mountains *54* Mikio Naruse
Soup for One *82* Jonathan Kaufer
Soup Song, The *31* Ubbe Iwerks
Soup to Nuts *30* Ben Stoloff
Soup to Nuts *82* Michael Herz, Lloyd Kaufman
Soupçon *79* Jean-Charles Tacchella
Soupe aux Poulets, La *63* Philippe Agostini
Soupirant, Le *62* Pierre Etaix
Sour Grapes *85* John De Bello
Sour Puss, The *40* Robert Clampett
Source, La *00* Alice Guy-Blaché
Source, The *18* Donald Crisp, George Melford
Source de Beauté, La *15* Abel Gance
Source of Happiness, The *15* Frank Lloyd
Sourd dans la Ville, Le *87* Mireille Dansereau
Sourdough *77* Martin J. Spinelli
Souriante Madame Beudet, La *22* Germaine Dulac
Souricière, La *50* Henri Calef
Sourire, Le *60* Serge Bourguignon
Sourire aux Lèvres *55* Claude Sautet
Sourire d'Or, Le *35* Pál Fejős
Sourires de la Destinée, Les *63* Pierre Kast
Souris Blanche, La *11* Louis Feuillade
Souris la Semaine Prochaine, Une *67* Pierre Hébert

Soursweet *88* Mike Newell
Sous la Griffe *35* Christian-Jaque
Sous la Lune du Maroc *31* Julien Duvivier
Sous la Menace *16* André Hugon
Sous le Ciel de Paris *50* Julien Duvivier
Sous le Ciel de Paris Coule la Seine *50* Julien Duvivier
Sous le Joug *11* Louis Feuillade
Sous le Signe de Monte-Cristo *69* André Hunebelle
Sous le Signe du Taureau *69* Gilles Grangier
Sous le Soleil de Satan *87* Maurice Pialat
Sous les Toits de Paris *29* René Clair
Sous les Yeux d'Occident *36* Marc Allégret
Sous l'Uniforme *14* Camille De Morlhon
Sous-Marin de Cristal, Le *28* Marcel Vandal
Sous un Autre Soleil *55* Philippe de Broca
Sousto *59* Jan Němec
South, The *83* Victor Erice
South *87* Fernando Solanas
South American George *41* Marcel Varnel
South American Sway *44* Jean Negulesco
South American Swing *44* Jean Negulesco
South Bronx Heroes *85* William Szarka
South of Algiers *52* Jack Lee
South of Arizona *38* Sam Nelson
South of Caliente *51* William Witney
South of Death Valley *49* Ray Nazarro
South of Dixie *44* Jean Yarbrough
South of Hell Mountain *71* Louis Lehman, William Sachs
South of Monterey *46* William Nigh
South of Northern Lights *22* Neal Hart
South of Pago-Pago *40* Alfred E. Green
South of Panama *41* Jean Yarbrough
South of Reno *87* Mark Rezyka
South of Rio *49* Philip Ford
South of St. Louis *49* Ray Enright
South of Santa Fe *32* Bert Glennon
South of Santa Fe *42* Joseph Kane
South of Suez *40* Lewis Seiler
South of Suva *22* Frank Urson
South of Tahiti *41* George Waggner
South of Tana River *64* Bent Christensen, Sven Methling, Jr.
South of the Border *39* George Sherman
South of the Chisholm Trail *47* Derwin Abrahams
South of the Equator *24* William James Craft
South of the Rio Grande *32* Lambert Hillyer
South of the Rio Grande *45* Lambert Hillyer
South Pacific *57* Joshua Logan
South Pacific 1942 *80* Paul Donovan
South Pacific Trail *52* William Witney
South Pole Flight, The *28* Ben Clopton, Hugh Harman
South Riding *37* Victor Saville
South Sea Bubble, A *28* T. Hayes Hunter
South Sea Love *23* David Soloman
South Sea Love *27* Ralph Ince
South Sea Rose *29* Allan Dwan
South Sea Sickness *35* Arthur Ripley
South Sea Sinner *49* H. Bruce Humberstone
South Sea Sweetheart *38* George Pal

South Sea Woman *53* Arthur Lubin
South Seas Adventure *58* Carl Dudley, Richard Goldstone, Francis D. Lyon, Walter Thompson, Basil Wrangell
South Seas Fury *54* Phil Karlson
South to Karanga *40* Harold Schuster
South Wind *39* Minoru Shibuya
South Wind *42* Kozaburo Yoshimura
South Wind, Sequel *42* Kozaburo Yoshimura
Southern Blood *14* Wilfred Noy
Southern Comfort *81* Walter Hill
Southern Cross *82* Peter Maxwell
Southern Double Cross *73* Don Edmonds
Southern Exposure *34* Manny Gould, Ben Harrison
Southern Exposure *36* Charlie Chase
Southern Fried Rabbit *53* Friz Freleng
Southern Justice *17* Lynn Reynolds
Southern Love *24* Herbert Wilcox
Southern Maid, A *33* Harry Hughes
Southern Pride *17* Henry King
Southern Rhodesia *45* Basil Wright
Southern Roses *36* Fred Zelnik
Southern Spring *32* Tsou-sen Tsai
Southern Star, The *69* Sidney Hayers
Southern Teheran *59* Farrokh Ghaffary
Southern Yankee, A *48* Edward Sedgwick
Southerner, The *31* Harry A. Pollard
Southerner, The *45* Jean Renoir
Southside 1-1000 *50* Boris Ingster
Southward Ho! *39* Joseph Kane
Southwest Passage *54* Ray Nazarro
Southwest to Sonora *66* Sidney J. Furie
Souvenir *48* Jean Delannoy
Souvenir *88* Geoffrey Reeve
Souvenir d'Italie *57* Antonio Pietrangeli
Souvenir from Calvary, A *58* Jerzy Hoffman
Souvenir of Paradise *40* Elmar Klos
Souvenirs *20* Will P. Kellino
Souvenirs *38* George Pearson
Souvenirs de Paris *28* Marcel Duhamel, Pierre Prévert
Souvenirs d'en France *74* André Téchiné
Souvenirs from Sweden *60* Henning Carlsen
Souvenirs Perdus *49* Christian-Jaque
Sovetskoi Igrushki *24* Dziga Vertov
Sovetskoi Iskusstvo *44* Dziga Vertov
Soviet Art *44* Dziga Vertov
Soviet Border *38* Alexander Ivanov
Soviet Frontiers on the Danube *41* Ilya Kopalin, I. M. Poselsky
Soviet Georgia *51* Roman Karmen
Soviet Mordovia *51* Josef Heifits
Soviet Playthings *24* Dziga Vertov
Soviet Russia Today *35* Edward Tissé
Soviet Toys *24* Dziga Vertov
Soviet Turkmenistan *50* Roman Karmen
Soviet Village *44* Paul Rotha
Soviets Greet New Turkey, The *34* Lev Arnshtam, Sergei Yutkevich
Soviets on Parade *33* I. M. Poselsky
Søvngængersken *14* Forest Holger-Madsen
Sovversivi, I *67* Paolo Taviani, Vittorio Taviani
Sowers, The *16* William DeMille
Sowers and Reapers *17* George D. Baker
Soweto *87* Michael Raeburn

Sowing the Wind *16* Cecil M. Hepworth

Sowing the Wind *20* John M. Stahl

Soy Chato Pero las Huelo *39* Miguel Zacarías

Soy-Kuba *62* Mikhail Kalatozov

Soy México *67* C. Fuentes, François Reichenbach

Soy Puro Mexicano *42* Emilio Fernández

Soylent Green *72* Richard Fleischer

Soyons Doncs Sportifs *09* Émile Cohl

Soyuz Velikovo Dela *27* Grigori Kozintsev, Leonid Trauberg

Space *65* Andy Warhol

Space Amoeba, The *70* Inoshiro Honda

Space Angels *85* Ted V. Mikels

Space Children, The *58* Jack Arnold

Space Cruiser *77* Yoshinobu Nishizaki

Space Cruiser Yamato *77* Yoshinobu Nishizaki

Space Devils *65* Antonio Margheriti

Space Firebird 2772 *79* Suguru Sugiyama, Osamu Tezuku

Space Invasion from Lapland *60* Virgil Vogel, Jerry Warren

Space Invasion of Lapland *60* Virgil Vogel, Jerry Warren

Space-Men *60* Antonio Margheriti

Space Men Appear in Tokyo *56* Koji Shima

Space Mission of the Lost Planet *70* Al Adamson, George Joseph

Space Monster *65* Leonard Katzman

Space Monster Dogora *64* Inoshiro Honda

Space Movie, The *80* Tony Palmer

Space Rage *85* Peter McCarthy, Conrad E. Palmisano

Space Raiders *83* Howard R. Cohen

Space Riders *84* Joe Massot

Space Ship, The *35* Vasili Zhuravlev

Space Soldiers *36* Frederick Stephani

Space Station X *65* Hugo Grimaldi

Space Station X-14 *65* Hugo Grimaldi

Space 2074 *88* Philip Cook

Space Works, The *81* Joseph Strick

Spaceballs *87* Mel Brooks

SpaceCamp *86* Harry Winer

Spaced Invaders *90* Patrick Read Johnson

Spaced Out *79* Norman J. Warren

Spaceflight IC-1 *65* Bernard Knowles

Spacehunter: Adventures in the Forbidden Zone *82* Lamont Johnson

Spaceman and King Arthur, The *79* Russ Mayberry

Spaceman in King Arthur's Court, A *79* Russ Mayberry

Spacemaster X-7 *58* Edward Bernds

Spacemen Saturday Night *57* Edward L. Cahn

Spacerek Staromiejski *58* Andrzej Munk

Spaceship *62* Maury Dexter

Spaceship *81* Bruce Kimmel

Spaceship to the Unknown *36* Frederick Stephani

Spaceship to Venus *60* Kurt Mätzig

Spaceways *53* Terence Fisher

Spada del Cid, La *62* Miguel Iglesias Bonns

Spada e la Croce, La *58* Carlo Ludovico Bragaglia

Spada Imbattibile, La *57* Hugo Fregonese

Spadaccino di Siena, Lo *61* Baccio Bandini, Étienne Périer

Spædbarnet *53* Jørgen Roos

Spaghetti for Two *21* Harry D. Leonard

Spaghetti in the Desert *61* Carlo Ludovico Bragaglia

Spain *37* Roman Karmen, Esther Shub

Spain Loyal in Arms *37* Luis Buñuel

Spain '37 *37* Luis Buñuel

Špaliček *47* Jiří Trnka

Span of Life, The *14* Edward Mackey

Spangles *26* Frank O'Connor

Spangles *28* George J. Banfield

Spaniard, The *25* Raoul Walsh

Spaniard's Curse, The *58* Ralph Kemplen

Spanish A.B.C. *38* Sidney Cole, Thorold Dickinson

Spanish Affair *57* Don Siegel

Spanish Cape Mystery, The *35* Lewis D. Collins

Spanish Dancer, The *23* Herbert Brenon

Spanish Dances *00* Louis Lumière

Spanish Dilemma, A *12* Mack Sennett

Spanish Earth, The *37* Joris Ivens

Spanish Eyes *30* George B. Samuelson

Spanish Fiesta, The *19* Germaine Dulac

Spanish Fiesta *42* Jean Negulesco

Spanish Fly *75* Bob Kellett

Spanish Gardener, The *56* Philip Leacock

Spanish Girl, The *09* Gilbert M. Anderson

Spanish Gypsy, The *11* D. W. Griffith

Spanish Inquisition, The *1899* Georges Méliès

Spanish Jade, The *15* Wilfred Lucas

Spanish Jade *22* Tom Geraghty, John S. Robertson

Spanish Love *25* Raoul Walsh

Spanish Main, The *45* Frank Borzage

Spanish Romeo, A *25* George Marshall

Spanish Shotgun, The *78* Luis García Berlanga

Spanish Sword, The *62* Ernest Morris

Spanking Breezes *26* Edward F. Cline

Spara Forte, Più Forte...Non Capisco *66* Eduardo De Filippo

Spara, Gringo, Spara *68* Bruno Corbucci

Spara Joe...e Così Sia *72* Emilio Miraglia

Spare a Copper *40* John Paddy Carstairs

Spare Life, The *86* Piero Vida

Spare Man *53* Lewis Gilbert

Spare Room, The *32* Redd Davis

Spare the Child *55* Abe Liss

Spare the Rod *61* Leslie Norman

Spare Time *39* Humphrey Jennings

Spare Tyres, The *67* Michael J. Lane

Spark *22* Teinosuke Kinugasa

Spark *56* Teinosuke Kinugasa

Spark Divine, The *19* Tom Terriss

Sparkle *76* Sam O'Steen

Sparkling Winds *68* Miklós Jancsó

Sparks of Flint *21* Roy Clements

Sparring Partner *24* Dave Fleischer

Sparrow, The *13* Maurice Tourneur

Sparrow, The *73* Youssef Chahine

Sparrow of Pigalle, The *74* Guy Casaril

Sparrows *26* William Beaudine

Sparrows Can't Sing *62* Joan Littlewood

Sparrow's Fluttering, The *89* Gianfranco Mingozzi

Spartaco *11* Ernesto Maria Pasquali

Spartaco *52* Riccardo Freda

Spartacus *52* Riccardo Freda

Spartacus *59* Stanley Kubrick, Anthony Mann

Spartacus and the Ten Gladiators *65* Nick Nostro

Spartacus the Gladiator *52* Riccardo Freda

Spartakiada *29* I. M. Poselsky, V. Rotov

Spartakiáda *60* Ján Kadár, Elmar Klos

Spårvagn till Havet *87* Håkan Alexandersson

Sparviero del Nilo, Lo *49* Goffredo Alessandrini

Spasmo *76* Umberto Lenzi

Spasms *81* William Fruet

Špatně Namalovaná Slepice *63* Jiří Brdečka

Spats to Spurs *39* Edwin L. Marin

Spawn of the Desert *23* Ben F. Wilson

Spawn of the North *38* Henry Hathaway

Spawn of the Slithis *78* Stephen Traxler

Spaziale K.1 *65* Hugo Grimaldi

Speak Easily *32* Edward Sedgwick

Speakeasy, The *19* F. Richard Jones

Speakeasy *29* Ben Stoloff

Speaking About Glass *57* Bert Haanstra

Speaking Directly *73* Jon Jost

Speaking Directly: Some American Notes *73* Jon Jost

Speaking from America *38* Humphrey Jennings

Speaking of Animals Down on the Farm *41* Tex Avery

Speaking of Animals in a Pet Shop *41* Tex Avery

Speaking of Animals in the Zoo *41* Tex Avery

Speaking of Glass *57* Bert Haanstra

Speaking of Murder *56* Gilles Grangier

Speaking of the Weather *37* Frank Tashlin

Speaking Parts *89* Atom Egoyan

Spear, The *87* Cirio Santiago

Special Agent *35* William Keighley

Special Agent *49* William C. Thomas

Special Agent K-7 *37* Raymond K. Johnson

Special Boy-Soldiers of the Navy *72* Tadashi Imai

Special Constable, The *14* Ernest G. Batley

Special Day, A *77* Ettore Scola

Special Delivery *27* Roscoe Arbuckle

Special Delivery *55* John Brahm

Special Delivery *76* Paul Wendkos

Special Duty *40* Sam Nelson

Special Edition *38* Redd Davis

Special Effects *84* Larry Cohen

Special Inspector *39* Leon Barsha

Special Investigator *36* Louis King

Special License, The *09* Theo Bouwmeester

Special Police *85* Michael Vianey

Special Section *75* Costa-Gavras

Special Treatment *80* Goran Paskaljević

Specialist, The *66* James Hill

Specialist, The *75* Hikmet Avedis

Spécialiste, Le *69* Sergio Corbucci

Spécialistes, Les *85* Patrice Leconte

Specialisti, Gli *69* Sergio Corbucci

Speckled Band, The *12* Georges Treville
Speckled Band, The *23* George Ridgwell
Speckled Band, The *31* Jack Raymond
Spectacle Maker, The *34* John Farrow
Specter of the Rose *46* Ben Hecht
Specters *87* Marcello Avallone
Spectre, Le *1899* Georges Méliès
Spectre, Le *16* Louis Feuillade
Spectre, The *63* Riccardo Freda
Spectre Haunts Europe, A *23* Vladimir Gardin
Spectre of Edgar Allan Poe, The *73* Mohy Quandour
Spectre of Freedom, The *74* Luis Buñuel
Spectre of Suspicion, The *17* Henry King
Spectre of the Rose *46* Ben Hecht
Spectre of War, The *88* Ramiro Lacayo-Deshon
Spectre Vert, Le *30* Jacques Feyder
Speed *20* Al St. John
Speed *22* George B. Seitz
Speed *25* Edward J. LeSaint
Speed *31* Mack Sennett
Speed *36* Edwin L. Marin
Speed Brent Wins *33* Robert North Bradbury
Speed Classic, The *28* Bruce Mitchell
Speed Cop *26* Duke Worne
Speed Crazed *26* Duke Worne
Speed Crazy *59* William Hole, Jr.
Speed Demon, The *12* Mack Sennett
Speed Demon, The *25* Robert North Bradbury
Speed Demon *32* D. Ross Lederman
Speed Devils *35* Ralph Henabery
Speed Girl, The *21* Maurice Campbell
Speed King *23* Grover Jones
Speed Kings, The *13* Mack Sennett
Speed Limit, The *26* Frank O'Connor
Speed Limit 65 *72* Yaphet Kotto
Speed Limited *40* Albert Herman
Speed Lovers *68* William McGaha
Speed Mad *25* Jay Marchant
Speed Madness *25* Bruce Mitchell
Speed Madness *32* George Crone
Speed Maniac, The *19* Edward J. LeSaint
Speed Queen, The *13* Mack Sennett
Speed Reporter, The *31* Noel Mason Smith
Speed Reporter *36* Bernard B. Ray
Speed Spook, The *24* Charles Hines
Speed to Burn *38* Otto Brower
Speed to Spare *37* Lambert Hillyer
Speed to Spare *48* William Berke
Speed Wild *25* Harry Garson
Speed Wings *34* Otto Brower
Speed Zone! *89* James R. Drake
Speeding Hoofs *27* Louis Chaudet
Speeding Into Trouble *24* Lee Morrison
Speeding Through *26* Bertram Bracken
Speeding Venus, The *26* Robert Thornby
Speedtrap *77* Earl Bellamy
Speedway *29* Harry Beaumont
Speedway *68* Norman Taurog
Speedy *28* Ted Wilde
Speedy Ghost to Town *67* Alex Lovy
Speedy Gonzales *55* Friz Freleng
Speedy Meade *19* Ira M. Lowry
Speedy Smith *27* Duke Worne
Speedy Spurs *26* Richard Thorpe

Speedy the Telegraph Boy *11* Percy Stow
Spejbl na Stopě *55* Břetislav Pojar
Spejbl on the Train *55* Břetislav Pojar
Spell of Amy Nugent, The *40* John Harlow
Spell of Ireland, The *54* Harry Dugan
Spell of the Ball, The *62* Márta Mészáros
Spell of the Circus *31* Robert F. Hill
Spell of the Hypnotist *56* W. Lee Wilder
Spell of the Poppy, The *15* Tod Browning
Spell of the Yukon, The *16* Burton L. King
Spell II, The *86* Raúl Araiza
Spellbinder, The *28* Tay Garnett
Spellbinder, The *39* Jack Hively
Spellbinder *88* Janet Greek
Spellbound *16* H. D. Horkheimer, H. M. Horkheimer
Spellbound *40* John Harlow
Spellbound *45* Alfred Hitchcock, William Cameron Menzies
Spellbound Hound *50* John Hubley
Spellcaster *87* Rafal Zielinski
Spelnione Marzenia *39* N. Brazybulski
Spencer's Mountain *63* Delmer Daves
Spend It All *71* Les Blank
Spender, The *19* Charles Swickard
Spender, or The Fortunes of Peter, The *15* Donald Mackenzie
Spenders, The *21* Jack Conway
Spending Money *75* François Truffaut
Spendthrift, The *15* Walter Edwin
Spendthrift *36* Raoul Walsh
Sperduta di Allah, La *28* Enrico Guazzoni
Sperduti nel Buio *14* Nino Martoglio
Spergiura *09* Luigi Maggi
Speriamo Che Sia Femmina *85* Mario Monicelli
Spermula *76* Charles Matton
Spessart Inn, The *61* Kurt Hoffmann
Spettacolo di Pupi, Uno *53* Francesco Maselli
Spetters *80* Paul Verhoeven
Spettri *87* Marcello Avallone
Spettro, Lo *63* Riccardo Freda
Sphères *69* Norman McLaren
Spheres *69* Norman McLaren
Spherical Space No. 1 *67* Stan Vanderbeek
Sphinx, The *16* John G. Adolfi
Sphinx, The *33* Phil Rosen
Sphinx *80* Franklin J. Schaffner
Sphynx *18* Béla Balázs
Spiaggia, La *53* Alberto Lattuada
Spice of Life, The *48* Jean Dréville, Noël-Noël
Spice of Wickedness, The *84* Elka Tupiak
Spices *86* Ketan Mehta
Spicy Rice *87* Jan Schütte
Spider, The *16* Robert Vignola
Spider, The *31* Kenneth MacKenna, William Cameron Menzies
Spider, The *39* Maurice Elvey
Spider, The *42* Ilya Trauberg, I. Zemgano
Spider, The *45* Robert D. Webb
Spider, The *58* Bert I. Gordon
Spider and Her Web, The *14* Phillips Smalley
Spider and the Fly, The *16* J. Gordon Edwards
Spider and the Fly, The *31* Wilfred Jack-

son
Spider and the Fly, The *49* Robert Hamer
Spider and the Rose, The *23* John McDermott
Spider Baby *64* Jack Hill
Spider Baby, or The Maddest Story Ever Told *64* Jack Hill
Spider Girl *66* Yasuzo Masumura
Spider-Man Strikes Back *78* Ron Satlof
Spider Returns, The *41* James W. Horne
Spider Webs *27* Wilfred Noy
Spider Woman, The *43* Roy William Neill
Spider Woman Strikes Back, The *46* Arthur Lubin
Spiderman *77* E. W. Swackhamer
Spiders à Go-Go *68* Ko Nakahira
Spider's Lair, The *28* Mannie Davis
Spider's Nest, The *89* Gianfranco Giagni
Spiders—Part I: Der Goldene See, The *19* Fritz Lang
Spiders, Part Two, The *20* Fritz Lang
Spider's Strategem, The *69* Bernardo Bertolucci
Spider's Strategy, The *69* Bernardo Bertolucci
Spider's Web *24* B. Reeves Eason
Spider's Web, The *27* Oscar Micheaux
Spider's Web, The *38* James W. Horne, Ray Taylor
Spider's Web, The *59* Fritz Böttger
Spider's Web, The *60* Godfrey Grayson
Spider's Web, The *87* Bernhard Wicki
Spie Uccidono a Beirut, Le *65* Mario Donen
Spie Vengono dal Semifreddo, Le *66* Mario Bava
Spiegel des Lebens, Der *40* Géza von Bolváry
Spiegel van Holland *50* Bert Haanstra
Spiel der Königin, Das *23* Ludwig Berger
Spiel der Wellen *21* Walter Ruttmann
Spiel im Sand *64* Werner Herzog
Spiel in Farben, Ein *34* Oskar Fischinger
Spiel in Sommerwind *39* Roger von Norman
Spiel mit dem Feuer, Das *21* Georg Kroll, Robert Wiene
Spiel mit dem Feuer *34* Ralph A. Roberts
Spiel ums Leben, Ein *24* Michael Curtiz
Spiel von Liebe und Tod, Das *19* Urban Gad
Spieler, The *28* Tay Garnett
Spieler, Der *38* Gerhard Lamprecht
Spieler aus Leidenschaft *22* Fritz Lang
Spielerin, Die *20* Richard Oswald
Spielzeug von Paris, Das *25* Michael Curtiz
Spies *15* Frank Wilson
Spies *27* Fritz Lang
Spies, The *57* Henri-Georges Clouzot
Spies à Go-Go *64* James Landis
Spies and Spills *18* Larry Semon
Spies at Work *39* Harold Young
Spies from Salonika *36* G. W. Pabst
Spies in the Air *39* David MacDonald
Spies Like Us *85* John Landis
Spies of the Air *39* David MacDonald
Spietate Colt del Gringo, La *66* José Luis Madrid
Spike Jones Story, The *88* Don McGlynn

Spike of Bensonhurst *88* Paul Morrissey
Spiker *86* Roger Tilton
Spikes Gang, The *74* Richard Fleischer
Spild Er Penge *42* Ole Palsbo
Spin a Dark Web *56* Vernon Sewell
Spin of a Coin *61* Joseph M. Newman
Spina Dorsale del Diavolo, La *70* Burt Kennedy
Spina nel Cuore, Una *85* Alberto Lattuada
Spinach Face *87* José Sacristán
Spinach Overture, The *35* Dave Fleischer
Spinach Roadster, The *36* Dave Fleischer
Spinal Tap *84* Rob Reiner
Spindle of Life, The *17* George Cochrane
Spinnen, Die *19* Fritz Lang
Spinnen Part II: Das Brillantenschiff, Die *20* Fritz Lang
Spinnennetz, Das *87* Bernhard Wicki
Spinner o' Dreams *18* Wilfred Noy
Spinning Earth *28* Tomotaka Tasaka, Tomu Uchida
Spinning Plates *1895* Louis Lumière
Spinning Wheel *83* Doo-yong Lee
Spinout *66* Norman Taurog
Spinster, The *61* Charles Walters
Spinsters, The *54* Leopoldo Torre-Nilsson
Spione, Die *19* E. A. Dupont
Spione *27* Fritz Lang
Spione am Werk *33* Gerhard Lamprecht
Spione Unter Sich *65* Christian-Jaque, Werner Klingler, Carlo Lizzani, Terence Young
Spionen fra Tokio *10* August Blom
Spiral, The *78* Krzysztof Zanussi
Spiral *87* Christopher Frank
Spiral Bureau, The *74* Ian Coughlan
Spiral Road, The *62* Robert Mulligan
Spiral Staircase, The *45* Robert Siodmak
Spiral Staircase, The *75* Peter Collinson
Spirala *78* Krzysztof Zanussi
Spirale, La *75* Chris Marker*
Spirale *78* Krzysztof Zanussi
Spirale *87* Christopher Frank
Spirals *25* Oskar Fischinger
Spirit and the Flesh, The *40* Mario Camerini
Spirit and the Flesh, The *48* Valentino Brosio
Spirit Awakened, The *11* D. W. Griffith
Spirit Is Willing, The *66* William Castle
Spirit of Adventure, The *15* B. Reeves Eason
Spirit of Annapolis, The *42* Jean Negulesco
Spirit of Culver *39* Joseph Santley
Spirit of Good, The *20* Paul Cazeneuve
Spirit of Notre Dame, The *31* Russell Mack
Spirit of Romance, The *17* E. Mason Hopper
Spirit of St. Louis, The *57* Billy Wilder
Spirit of '17, The *17* William Desmond Taylor
Spirit of '76, The *17* George Siegmann
Spirit of 1776, The *35* Leigh Jason
Spirit of Stanford, The *42* Charles Barton
Spirit of the Beehive, The *73* Victor Erice
Spirit of the Dead *68* Vernon Sewell
Spirit of the Dead *72* Peter Newbrook
Spirit of the Flag, The *13* Allan Dwan

Spirit of the Light, The *11* J. Stuart Blackton
Spirit of the People *40* John Cromwell
Spirit of the Pond, The *23* Teinosuke Kinugasa
Spirit of the U.S.A., The *24* Emory Johnson
Spirit of the West *32* Otto Brower
Spirit of the Wilderness *37* Hiroshi Inagaki
Spirit of the Wind *79* Ralph Liddle
Spirit of Variety *37* Hal Wilson
Spirit of West Point, The *42* Jean Negulesco
Spirit of West Point, The *47* Ralph Murphy
Spirit of Youth, The *29* Walter Lang
Spirit of Youth *37* Harry Fraser
Spiritism *61* Benito Alazraki
Spiritisme Abracadabrant *00* Georges Méliès
Spiritisten *14* Forest Holger-Madsen
Spirits, The *14* Forest Holger-Madsen
Spirits *18* Gregory La Cava
Spirits *29* Hugh Croise
Spirits of the Air *86* Alexander Proyas
Spirits of the Dead *67* Federico Fellini, Louis Malle, Roger Vadim
Spiritual Boxer, Part Two *79* Jialiang Liu
Spiritual Constructions *27* Oskar Fischinger
Spiritualism Exposed *13* Charles Raymond
Spiritualism Exposed *26* A. E. Coleby
Spiritualist, The *14* Forest Holger-Madsen
Spiritualist, The *48* Bernard Vorhaus
Spiritualist Photographer, A *03* Georges Méliès
Spiritualistic Meeting, A *06* Georges Méliès
Spiritualistic Photographer, A *03* Georges Méliès
Spiste Horisonter *50* W. Freddie, Jørgen Roos
Spite Bride, The *19* Charles Giblyn
Spite Fright *33* Ubbe Iwerks
Spite Marriage *29* Edward Sedgwick
Spitfire, The *24* Christy Cabanne
Spitfire *34* John Cromwell
Spitfire *42* Leslie Howard
Spitfire of Seville, The *19* George Siegmann
Spittin' Image *83* Russell S. Kern
Spitting Image, The *63* Fons Rademakers
Spitzen *26* Forest Holger-Madsen
Spivs *53* Federico Fellini
Splash! *84* Ron Howard
Splash Me Nicely *17* Will P. Kellino
Splatter University *84* Richard W. Haines
Splendid Coward, The *18* F. Martin Thornton
Splendid Crime, The *25* William DeMille
Splendid Days, The *60* Georgy Danelia, Igor Talankin
Splendid Fellows *34* Beaumont Smith
Splendid Folly *19* Arrigo Bocchi
Splendid Hazard, A *20* Arthur Rosson
Splendid Lie, The *22* Charles T. Horan
Splendid Road, The *25* Frank Lloyd
Splendid Romance, The *18* Edward José
Splendid Sin, The *19* Howard Mitchell

Splendid Sinner, The *18* Edwin Carewe
Splendor *35* Elliott Nugent
Splendor *89* Ettore Scola
Splendor in the Grass *61* Elia Kazan
Splendorie e Miserie di Madame Royale *70* Vittorio Caprioli
Splintered *79* Claude Chabrol
Splinters *29* Jack Raymond
Splinters in the Air *37* Alfred Goulding
Splinters in the Navy *31* Walter Forde
Split, The *62* George Breakston, Kenneth Crane
Split, The *68* Gordon Flemyng
Split Decisions *88* David Drury
Split Image *81* Ted Kotcheff
Split of the Spirit *87* Fred Tan
Split Second *52* Dick Powell
Splitface *45* William Berke
Splitting Hairs *22* Erle C. Kenton
Splitting the Breeze *27* Robert De Lacey
Splitting Up *81* Herman van Veen
Splitz *84* Domonic Paris
Spøgelset i Gravkælderen *10* August Blom
Spoiled Children *77* Bertrand Tavernier
Spoiled Rotten *68* Yannis Dalianidis
Spoilers, The *14* Colin Campbell
Spoilers, The *23* Lambert Hillyer
Spoilers, The *30* David Burton, Edwin Carewe
Spoilers, The *42* Ray Enright
Spoilers, The *55* Jesse Hibbs
Spoilers of the Forest *57* Joseph Kane
Spoilers of the North *47* Richard Sale
Spoilers of the Plains *51* William Witney
Spoilers of the Range *39* C. C. Coleman, Jr.
Spoilers of the Sea *57* Roberto Gavaldón
Spoilers of the West *27* W. S. Van Dyke
Spoils *34* George B. Samuelson
Spoils of the Night *69* Shinji Murayama
Spoilt Child, The *04* Lewin Fitzhamon
Spoilt Child, The *09* Lewin Fitzhamon
Spoilt Child of Fortune, A *10* Lewin Fitzhamon
Spokoinyi Den v Kontse Voiny *70* Nikita Mikhalkov
Spokój *76* Krzysztof Kieslowski
Społem *36* Aleksander Ford
Spoleto: Festival of Two Worlds *67* Christian Blackwood
Spomenicima Ne Treba Verovati *58* Dušan Makavejev
Sponge Man, The *20* Gregory La Cava
Spontaneous Combustion *89* Tobe Hooper
Spoof *15* Will P. Kellino
Spoof for Oof *15* Edwin J. Collins
Spook Busters *46* William Beaudine
Spook Castle of Spessart, The *60* Kurt Hoffmann
Spook Chasers *57* George Blair
Spook Easy *30* Manny Gould, Ben Harrison
Spook Ranch *25* Edward Laemmle
Spook Sport *40* Mary Ellen Bute, Norman McLaren
Spook Town *44* Elmer Clifton
Spook Warfare *68* Yoshiyuki Kuroda
Spook Who Sat by the Door, The *73* Ivan Dixon
Spookies *86* Thomas Doran, Brendan Faulkner, Eugenie Joseph

Spooks *15* Marshall Neilan
Spooks *30* Walter Lantz
Spooks *31* Ubbe Iwerks
Spooks and Spasms *17* Larry Semon
Spooks Run Wild *41* Phil Rosen
Spooky Bunch, The *80* Ann Hui
Spooky Encounters *80* Samo Hung
Spooky Hooky *36* Gordon Douglas
Spooky Movie Show, The *61* Julian Roffman
Spooning *06* J. H. Martin
Spoorloos *88* George Sluizer
Sporck'schen Jäger, Die *26* Forest Holger-Madsen
Sporck'schen Jäger, Die *37* Rolf Randolf
Sport Chumpions *41* Friz Freleng
Sport et Parapluie *47* André Michel
Sport Minore *51* Francesco Maselli
Sport of a Nation *32* Russell Mack
Sport of Fate, The *13* Edwin J. Collins
Sport of Kings, The *21* Arthur H. Rooke
Sport of Kings, The *30* Victor Saville
Sport of Kings *47* Robert Gordon
Sport of the Gods, The *21* Henry J. Vernot
Sport Parade, The *32* Dudley Murphy
Sport, Sport, Sport *70* Elem Klimov
Sporting Age, The *28* Erle C. Kenton
Sporting Blood *16* Bertram Bracken
Sporting Blood *31* Charles Brabin
Sporting Blood *40* S. Sylvan Simon
Sporting Chance, A *13* Edwin J. Collins
Sporting Chance, A *19* Henry King
Sporting Chance, A *19* George Melford
Sporting Chance *25* Oscar Apfel
Sporting Chance *31* Albert Herman
Sporting Chance, A *45* George Blair
Sporting Club, The *71* Larry Peerce
Sporting Double, A *22* Arthur H. Rooke
Sporting Duchess, The *15* Barry O'Neil
Sporting Duchess, The *20* George Terwilliger
Sporting Fame *50* Mark Donskoi
Sporting Goods *28* Malcolm St. Clair
Sporting Honor *51* Vladimir Petrov
Sporting Instinct, The *22* Arthur H. Rooke
Sporting Life *18* Maurice Tourneur
Sporting Life *25* Maurice Tourneur
Sporting Life *29* Malcolm St. Clair
Sporting Love *36* J. Elder Wills
Sporting Lover, The *26* Alan Hale
Sporting Mice, The *09* Charles Armstrong
Sporting Offer, A *11* Wilfred Noy
Sporting Scenes *22* Hy Mayer
Sporting Venus *25* Marshall Neilan
Sporting Widow, The *32* Harry Wagstaff Gribble, Alexander Hall
Sporting Youth *24* Harry A. Pollard
Sportive Navvies, The *03* Alf Collins
Sportive Puppet, A *09* Émile Cohl
Sportivnaya Chest *51* Vladimir Petrov
Sportivnaya Slava *50* Mark Donskoi
Sportloto—82 *87* Leonid Gaidai
Sports in Toyland *14* Stuart Kinder
Sports Lottery—82 *87* Leonid Gaidai
Sportsman, The *20* Larry Semon, Norman Taurog
Sportsman's Wife, A *21* Walter West
Sportszerelem *38* Zoltán Farkas, Leslie

Kardos
Sposa Americana, La *86* Giovanni Soldati
Sposa Bella, La *60* Nunnally Johnson
Sposa della Morte, La *15* Emilio Ghione
Sposa Era Bellissima, La *86* Pál Gábor
Sposero Simon le Bon *86* Carlo Cotti
Spot *74* Jeffrey Bloom
Spot As Cupid *12* Stuart Kinder
Spot Filming of Windsor Hotel Fire in New York *1899* J. Stuart Blackton
Spot in the Shade, A *49* Jerry Lewis
Spot Light *25* Norman Taurog
Spot of Bother, A *38* David MacDonald
Spot the Microdot *70* Malcolm Le Grice
Spotkania z Warszawą *65* Jan Łomnicki
Spotkanie na Atlantyku *79* Jerzy Kawalerowicz
Spotkanie w Mroku *60* Wanda Jakubowska
Spotlight, The *27* Frank Tuttle
Spotlight *38* R. A. Hopwood
Spotlight on Murder *60* Georges Franju
Spotlight on Scandal *43* William Beaudine
Spotlight on the Killer *60* Georges Franju
Spotlight Revue *43* William Beaudine
Spotlight Sadie *19* Lawrence Trimble
Spotlight Scandals *43* William Beaudine
Spots *25* Leslie Hiscott
Spots on My Leopard, The *74* Tim Spring
Spotted Lily, The *17* Harry Solter
Sprained Ankle, A *11* Lewin Fitzhamon
Správca Skanzenu *88* Stefan Uher
Spread Eagle *50* Lewis R. Foster
Spreadin' the Jam *45* Charles Walters
Spreading Cloud *51* Heinosuke Gosho
Spreading Dawn, The *17* Lawrence Trimble
Spreading Evil, The *19* James Keane
Spree! *63* Walon Green, Mitchell Leisen
Spring *29* Mikhail Kaufman
Spring *47* Grigori Alexandrov
Spring, The *56* Masaki Kobayashi
Spring Affair *60* Bernard B. Ray
Spring and a Girl *32* Tomotaka Tasaka
Spring and Port Wine *70* Peter Hammond
Spring and Saganaki *58* Lew Keller
Spring and Winter *51* John Halas
Spring Awakening *47* Mikio Naruse
Spring Awakens *47* Mikio Naruse
Spring Ball *86* Koreyoshi Kurahara
Spring Banquet, A *58* Teinosuke Kinugasa
Spring Break *83* Sean S. Cunningham
Spring Cleaning *03* James A. Williamson
Spring Cleaning *22* Bernard Dudley
Spring Cleaning in the House of Scroggins *11* Dave Aylott
Spring Comes from the Ladies *32* Yasujiro Ozu
Spring Comes with the Ladies *32* Yasujiro Ozu
Spring Dreams *60* Keisuke Kinoshita
Spring Fever *14* Charles Chaplin
Spring Fever *20* Gregory La Cava
Spring Fever *23* Archie Mayo
Spring Fever *27* Edward Sedgwick
Spring Fever *83* Joseph L. Scanlan
Spring Flirtation *49* Kajiro Yamamoto
Spring for the Thirsty, A *65* Yuri Ilyenko

Spring Handicap *37* Herbert Brenon
Spring Hats *21* Hy Mayer
Spring in Budapest *55* Félix Máriássy
Spring in Moscow *53* Josef Heifits, N. Kosheverova
Spring in Park Lane *47* Herbert Wilcox
Spring in Southern Islands *25* Heinosuke Gosho
Spring in the Air *34* Norman Lee, Joseph Losey
Spring in the Meadows of Dalby *62* Jan Troell
Spring in the Park *34* Walter Lantz
Spring in the Pastures of Dalby *62* Jan Troell
Spring in Wintertime *17* Michael Curtiz
Spring Into Summer *73* Pascal Thomas
Spring Is Here *30* John Francis Dillon
Spring Madness *38* S. Sylvan Simon
Spring Meeting *40* Walter C. Mycroft
Spring Night, Summer Night *67* J. L. Anderson
Spring of a Nineteen-Year-Old *33* Heinosuke Gosho
Spring of Life *57* Arne Mattsson
Spring of Southern Island *25* Heinosuke Gosho
Spring Offensive *40* Humphrey Jennings
Spring on Lepers' Island *40* Shiro Toyoda
Spring on Zarechnaya Street *56* Marlen Khutsiev, F. Mironer
Spring Parade *40* Henry Koster
Spring Reunion *57* Robert Pirosh
Spring River Flows East *47* Tsou-sen Tsai, Junli Zheng
Spring Shower *32* Pál Fejös
Spring Snow *50* Kozaburo Yoshimura
Spring Song *42* Alexander Ivanovsky
Spring Song *46* Montgomery Tully
Spring Song *60* John Halas*
Spring Symphony *83* Peter Schamoni
Spring Tonic *35* Clyde Bruckman
Spring Voices *55* S. Gurov, Eldar Ryazanov
Spring Wind *30* Tomotaka Tasaka
Springen *86* Jean-Pierre De Decker
Springer and S.S. Men, The *45* Jiří Brdečka, Jiří Trnka
Springfield Rifle *52* André De Toth
Springtime *15* Edward M. Roskam
Springtime *29* Ubbe Iwerks
Springtime *46* Montgomery Tully
Springtime for Henry *34* Frank Tuttle
Springtime for Thomas *46* Joseph Barbera, William Hanna
Springtime in Budapest *55* Félix Máriássy
Springtime in Italy *49* Renato Castellani
Springtime in Texas *45* Oliver Drake
Springtime in the Rock Age *40* Dave Fleischer
Springtime in the Rockies *37* Joseph Kane
Springtime in the Rockies *42* Irving Cummings
Springtime in the Sierras *47* William Witney
Springtime on the Volga *61* Veniamin Dorman, Genrikh Oganisyan
Springtime Serenade *35* Walter Lantz
Sprinkled, The *1895* Louis Lumière
Sprout Wings and Fly *83* Les Blank

Sprung ins Glück 27 Augusto Genina
Spud Murphy's Redemption 13 Charles C. Calvert
Spuds 27 Larry Semon
Spuk im Hause des Professors, Der 14 Joe May
Spukschloss im Spessart, Das 60 Kurt Hoffmann
Spur des Falken 68 Gottfried Kolditz
Spurs 30 B. Reeves Eason
Spurs and Saddles 27 Clifford Smith
Spurs of Sybil, The 18 Travers Vale
Sputnik 58 Jean Dréville
Sputnik Speaking 59 Sergei Gerasimov*
Sputnik Speaks, The 59 Sergei Gerasimov*
Spy, The 09 Lewin Fitzhamon
Spy, The 14 Otis Turner
Spy, The 17 Richard Stanton
Spy, The 27 Fritz Lang
Spy, The 31 Berthold Viertel
Spy, The 65 Satsuo Yamamoto
Spy Busters 68 Robert Butler
Spy Catchers 14 Will P. Kellino
Spy Chasers 55 Edward Bernds
Spy Fever 11 Dave Aylott
Spy for a Day 39 Mario Zampi
Spy Games 87 Jack M. Sell
Spy Has Not Yet Died, The 42 Kozaburo Yoshimura
Spy Hunt 50 George Sherman
Spy I Love, The 64 Maurice Labro
Spy in Black, The 39 Michael Powell
Spy in the Green Hat, The 66 Joseph Sargent
Spy in the Pantry 39 Tim Whelan
Spy in the Sky 58 W. Lee Wilder
Spy in White, The 36 Andrew Marton
Spy in Your Eye 65 Vittorio Sala
Spy Isn't Dead Yet, The 42 Kozaburo Yoshimura
Spy Mania, The 12 Dave Aylott
Spy of Madame Pompadour 28 Karl Grüne
Spy of Napoleon 36 Maurice Elvey
Spy Ring, The 38 Joseph H. Lewis
Spy 77 33 Arthur Woods
Spy Ship 42 B. Reeves Eason
Spy Smasher 42 William Witney
Spy Smasher Returns 42 William Witney
Spy Squad 61 Will Zens
Spy Story 76 Lindsay Shonteff
Spy Swatter 67 Rudy Larriva
Spy 13 33 Richard Boleslawski
Spy Train 43 Harold Young
Spy Who Came in from the Cold, The 65 Martin Ritt
Spy Who Loved Me, The 77 Lewis Gilbert
Spy with a Cold Nose, The 66 Daniel Petrie
Spy with My Face, The 65 John Newland
Spyashchaya Krasavitsa 29 Georgy Vasiliev, Sergei Vasiliev
Spyashchaya Krasavitsa 66 Apollinari Dudko, Konstantin Sergeyev
Spylarks 65 Robert Asher
Spymaker 90 Ferdinand Fairfax
Spy's Wife, The 72 Gerry O'Hara
Squad Car 60 Ed Leftwich
Squadra Selvaggia 86 Umberto Lenzi

Squadron Leader X 42 Lance Comfort
Squadron 992 39 Harry Watt
Squadron No. 5 39 Abram Room
Squadron of Honor 38 C. C. Coleman, Jr.
Squadrone Bianco, Lo 36 Augusto Genina
Squall, The 29 Alexander Korda
Squamish Five, The 88 Paul Donovan
Squandered Lives 20 Franklin Dyall
Squarcia 56 Gillo Pontecorvo
Square, A 71 István Szabó
Square Crooks 28 Lewis Seiler
Square Dance 86 Daniel Petrie
Square Dance Jubilee 49 Paul Landres
Square Dance Katy 50 Jean Yarbrough
Square Deal, A 17 Harley Knoles
Square Deal, A 18 Lloyd Ingraham
Square Deal Man, The 17 William S. Hart
Square Deal Sanderson 19 William S. Hart, Lambert Hillyer
Square Deceiver, The 17 Fred J. Balshofer
Square Jungle, The 55 Jerry Hopper
Square Mile Murder, The 61 Allan Davis
Square of Violence 61 Leonardo Bercovici
Square Peg, The 58 John Paddy Carstairs
Square Ring, The 53 Basil Dearden, Michael Relph
Square Root of Zero, The 64 William Cannon
Square Shooter 20 Paul Cazeneuve
Square Shooter 27 William Wyler
Square Shooter 35 David Selman
Square Shooter, The 51 Sam Newfield
Square Shoulders 29 E. Mason Hopper
Squared Circle, The 50 Reginald LeBorg
Squarehead, The 14 Charles Chaplin, Mabel Normand
Squares 34 Oskar Fischinger
Squares 71 Patrick J. Murphy
Squaring the Account 09 Dave Aylott
Squaring the Circle 83 Michael Hodges
Squartatore di New York, Lo 81 Lucio Fulci
Squatter's Daughter, The 06 Lewin Fitzhamon
Squatter's Daughter 33 Ken Hall
Squatter's Rights, The 12 Edwin S. Porter
Squaw Man, The 13 Oscar Apfel, Cecil B. DeMille
Squaw Man, The 18 Cecil B. DeMille
Squaw Man, The 31 Cecil B. DeMille
Squaw Man's Son, The 17 Edward J. LeSaint
Squawkin' Hawk, The 42 Chuck Jones
Squaw's Love, The 11 D. W. Griffith
Squeaker, The 30 Edgar Wallace
Squeaker, The 37 William K. Howard
Squeaker, The 64 Alfred Vohrer
Squealer, The 30 Harry Joe Brown
Squeek in the Deep, A 66 Robert McKimson
Squeeze, The 76 Antonio Margheriti
Squeeze, The 77 Michael Apted
Squeeze, The 86 Roger Young
Squeeze a Flower 69 Marc Daniels
Squeeze Play 80 Michael Herz, Lloyd Kaufman
Squibs 21 George Pearson
Squibs 35 Henry Edwards
Squibs' Honeymoon 23 George Pearson

Squibs MP 23 George Pearson
Squibs Wins the Calcutta Sweep 22 George Pearson
Squinting Luck 59 Andrzej Munk
Squire of Long Hadley, The 25 Sinclair Hill
Squire Phin 21 Leopold Wharton
Squire's Daughter, The 05 William Haggar
Squire's Romance, The 10 A. E. Coleby
Squirm 76 Jeff Lieberman
Squizzy Taylor 82 Kevin Dobson
Srećna Nova '49 86 Štole Popov
Sredi Sreyrk Kamney 83 Kira Muratova
Sredni Vashtar 81 Andrew Birkin
Sreo Sam Čak i Srećne Cigane 67 Aleksandar Petrović
Sri Lanka no Ai to Wakare 76 Keisuke Kinoshita
Srinivasa Kalyanam 88 Kodi Ramakrishna
Srpnová Neděle 60 Otakar Vávra
Srub 65 Jaromil Jireš
Sruthi 88 Mohan
Sruti and Graces of Indian Music 71 Shyam Benegal
Ssaki 62 Roman Polanski
SSSSnake! 73 Bernard Kowalski
SSSSSSSS 73 Bernard Kowalski
Stab of Disgrace, The 12 Bert Haldane
Stabilizer, The 87 Arizal
Stable Companions 22 Albert Ward
Stable Rivals 53 Leonard Reeve
Stablemates 38 Sam Wood
Stacey 73 Andy Sidaris
Stacey and Her Gangbusters 73 Andy Sidaris
Stachka 24 Sergei Eisenstein
Stacked Cards 26 Robert Eddy
Stacking 87 Martin Rosen
Stacy's Knights 83 James L. Wilson
Stad 58 Jan Troell
Stade Zero 64 Yves Ciampi
Stadio 34 Carlo Campogalliani
Stadium Murders, The 38 David Howard
Stadt Anatol 36 Victor Tourjansky
Stadt der Tausend Freuden, Die 27 Carmine Gallone
Stadt der Verheissung 35 Walter Ruttmann
Stadt der Verlorenen Seelen 83 Rosa von Praunheim
Stadt in Sicht 23 Henryk Galeen
Stadt Ist Voller Geheimnisse, Die 55 Fritz Kortner
Stadt Ohne Mitleid 60 Gottfried Reinhardt
Stadt Steht Kopf, Eine 32 Gustaf Gründgens
Stadtrand 87 Volker Führer
Stadtstreicher, Der 65 Rainer Werner Fassbinder
Staféta 70 András Kovács
Staffs 27 Oskar Fischinger
Stag Party 64 Wolfgang Staudte
Stage, The 87 Alexander Rekhviashvili
Stage Coach Hold-Up in the Days of '49 01 Edwin S. Porter
Stage Coached 28 Manny Gould, Ben Harrison
Stage Door 37 Gregory La Cava

Stage Door Canteen *43* Frank Borzage
Stage Door Cartoon *44* Friz Freleng
Stage Door Magoo *55* Pete Burness
Stage Fright *28* Stephen Roberts
Stage Fright *40* Chuck Jones
Stage Fright *50* Alfred Hitchcock
Stage Fright *81* Jon Jost
Stage Frights *47* Harry Hughes
Stage from Blue River *51* Lewis D. Collins
Stage Hand, The *20* Larry Semon, Norman Taurog
Stage Hoax *52* Walter Lantz
Stage Kisses *27* Albert Kelley
Stage Krazy *33* Manny Gould, Ben Harrison
Stage Madness *27* Victor Schertzinger
Stage Memories of an Old Theatrical Trunk *08* Edwin S. Porter
Stage Mother *33* Charles Brabin
Stage Robbers of San Juan, The *11* Allan Dwan
Stage Romance, A *22* Herbert Brenon
Stage Rustler, The *08* Wallace McCutcheon
Stage Struck *07* J. Searle Dawley, Edwin S. Porter
Stage Struck *17* Edward Morrissey
Stage Struck *25* Allan Dwan
Stage Struck *36* Busby Berkeley
Stage Struck *48* William Nigh
Stage Struck *58* Sidney Lumet
Stage-Struck Carpenter, The *11* Percy Stow
Stage-Struck Tora-San *78* Yoji Yamada
Stage Stunt *29* Walter Lantz
Stage to Blue River *51* Lewis D. Collins
Stage to Chino *40* Edward Killy
Stage to Mesa City *47* Ray Taylor
Stage to Thunder Rock *64* William F. Claxton
Stage to Tucson *50* Ralph Murphy
Stage Whispers *31* Richard Thorpe
Stagecoach *39* John Ford
Stagecoach *66* Gordon Douglas
Stagecoach Buckaroo *42* Ray Taylor
Stagecoach Days *38* Joseph Levering
Stagecoach Driver *51* Lewis D. Collins
Stagecoach Express *42* George Sherman
Stagecoach Kid *49* Lew Landers
Stagecoach Line *44* Lewis D. Collins
Stagecoach Outlaws *45* Sam Newfield
Stagecoach to Dancer's Rock *62* Earl Bellamy
Stagecoach to Denver *46* R. G. Springsteen
Stagecoach to Fury *56* William F. Claxton
Stagecoach to Hell *64* William F. Claxton
Stagecoach to Monterey *44* Lesley Selander
Stagecoach War *40* Lesley Selander
Stagioni del Nostro Amore, Le *66* Florestano Vancini
Stahl *32* Walter Ruttmann
Stain, The *14* Frank Powell
Stain in the Blood, The *16* Murdock MacQuarrie
Stain on His Conscience, A *68* Dušan Vukotić
Stained Glass at Fairford, The *55* Basil Wright
Stainless Barrier, The *17* Thomas Heffron
Staircase *68* Stanley Donen

Stairs, The *53* Ben Maddow
Stairs of Sand *29* Otto Brower
Stairway to Heaven *46* Michael Powell, Emeric Pressburger
Stake Out, The *73* William A. Graham
Stakeout *62* James Landis
Stakeout *87* John Badham
Stakeout on Dope Street *58* Irvin Kershner
Stal *59* Jan Łomnicki
Stalag 17 *53* Billy Wilder
Stalingrad *43* Leonid Varmalov
Stalingrad *69* Grigori Chukhrai
Stalingradskaya Bitva *69* Grigori Chukhrai
Stalingradskaya Bitva I *49* Vladimir Petrov
Stalingradskaya Bitva II *50* Vladimir Petrov
Stalin's Kids *87* Nadav Levitan
Stalker *79* Andrei Tarkovsky
Stalking Moon, The *68* Robert Mulligan
Stålkongens Vilje *13* Forest Holger-Madsen
Stallion Canyon *49* Harry Fraser
Stallion Road *47* James V. Kern, Raoul Walsh
Stamboul *31* Dmitri Buchowetzki
Stamboul Quest *34* Sam Wood
Stammen Lever An *37* Pál Fejős
Stammheim *86* Reinhard Hauff
Stamp Fantasia *59* Yoji Kuri
Stampede, The *11* Alice Guy-Blaché
Stampede, The *21* Raoul Barré, Charles Bowers
Stampede, The *21* Francis Ford
Stampede *30* Major C. Court Treatt
Stampede *36* Ford Beebe
Stampede *49* Lesley Selander
Stampede *60* Robert D. Webb
Stampede, The *71* Santiago Álvarez
Stampede Thunder *25* Tom Gibson
Stampeded! *57* Gordon Douglas
Stampedin' Trouble *25* Forrest K. Sheldon
Stan Posiadania *89* Krzysztof Zanussi
Stances à Sophie, Les *70* Moshe Mizrahi
Stand Alone *85* Alan Beattie
Stand and Deliver *28* Donald Crisp
Stand and Deliver *41* Wallace Fox
Stand and Deliver *87* Ramón Menéndez
Stand at Apache River, The *53* Lee Sholem
Stand by All Networks *42* Lew Landers
Stand by for Action! *42* Robert Z. Leonard
Stand by Me *86* Rob Reiner
Stand der Dinge, Der *82* Wim Wenders
Stand Easy *52* Maclean Rogers
Stand-In *37* Tay Garnett
Stand-In, The *85* Robert N. Zagone
Stand-In, The *87* Jianxin Huang
Stand Up and Be Counted *71* Jackie Cooper
Stand Up and Cheer *34* Hamilton MacFadden
Stand Up and Fight *38* W. S. Van Dyke
Stand Up Virgin Soldiers *77* Norman Cohen
Standard Time *67* Michael Snow
Standby Moves In, The *87* Earnest Yasan
Standhafte Benjamin, Der *17* Robert Wiene
Standing in the Shadows of Love *84*

William Crain
Standing Room Only *44* Sidney Lanfield
Standschütze Bruggler *37* Werner Klingler
Stanislaw and Anna *87* Kazimierz Konrad, Piotr Stefaniak
Stanisław i Anna *87* Kazimierz Konrad, Piotr Stefaniak
Stanley *25* M. A. Wetherell
Stanley *72* William Grefé
Stanley and Iris *90* Martin Ritt
Stanley and Livingstone *39* Henry King
Stanno Tutti Bene *90* Giuseppe Tornatore
Stanza del Vescovo, La *77* Dino Risi
Staphylokok-Faren *60* Jørgen Roos
Star, The *52* Stuart Heisler
Star, The *53* Alexander Ivanov
Star! *68* Robert Wise
Star *89* Peter Del Monte
Star and Lyra *73* Grigori Alexandrov
Star Called Wormwood, A *64* Martin Frič
Star Chamber, The *83* Peter Hyams
Star Child *83* Howard R. Cohen
Star Crystal *86* Lance Lindsay
Star Disappears, A *35* Robert Villers
Star Dust *21* Hobart Henley
Star Dust *40* Walter Lang
Star 80 *83* Bob Fosse
Star Fell from Heaven, A *36* Paul Merzbach
Star for a Night *36* Lewis Seiler
Star Garden *74* Stan Brakhage
Star Globe-Trotter, The *08* Walter R. Booth
Star Impersonations *30* Harry Hughes
Star in the Dust *55* Charles Haas
Star in the Night *45* Don Siegel
Star in the West *61* Vincent Sherman
Star Inspector, The *80* Mark Kovalyov, Vladimir Polin
Star Is Bored, A *56* Friz Freleng
Star Is Born, A *37* William A. Wellman
Star Is Born, A *54* George Cukor
Star Is Born, A *76* Frank Pierson
Star Is Hatched, A *38* Friz Freleng
Star Knight *86* Fernando Colomo
Star Maker, The *39* Roy Del Ruth
Star Named Wormwood, A *64* Martin Frič
Star of Bethlehem, The *12* Lawrence Marston
Star of Bethlehem, The *56* Lotte Reiniger
Star of Damascus, The *19* Michael Curtiz
Star of Hong Kong *62* Yasuke Chiba
Star of India, The *13* Herbert Blaché, Alice Guy-Blaché
Star of India *53* Arthur Lubin
Star of Married Couples *26* Teinosuke Kinugasa
Star of Midnight *35* Stephen Roberts
Star of My Night *54* Paul Dickson
Star of Texas, The *53* Thomas Carr
Star of the Circus *38* Albert De Courville
Star of the Sea *40* Corrado D'Enrico
Star Packer, The *34* Robert North Bradbury
Star Pilot *66* Pietro Francisci
Star Prince, The *59* Eijiro Wakabayashi
Star Quest *87* Yoshiyuki Sadamoto
Star Quest: Beyond the Rising Moon *88* Philip Cook
Star Reporter, The *21* Duke Worne

Star Reporter *39* Howard Bretherton
Star-Rock *80* Menahem Golan
Star Rover, The *20* Edward Sloman
Star Said No!, The *51* Melvin Frank, Norman Panama
Star Sex *79* Willy Roe
Star Shall Rise, A *52* John Brahm
Star Slammer *86* Fred Olen Ray
Star Slammer: The Escape *88* Fred Olen Ray
Star-Spangled Banner, The *17* Edward H. Griffith
Star Spangled Girl *71* Jerry Paris
Star Spangled Rhythm *42* George Marshall
Star Squadron *30* Leonard Buczkowski
Star Studded Ride *54* William Cameron Menzies
Star Trek — The Motion Picture *79* Robert Wise
Star Trek II: The Wrath of Khan *82* Nicholas Meyer
Star Trek III: The Search for Spock *84* Leonard Nimoy
Star Trek IV: The Voyage Home *86* Leonard Nimoy
Star Trek V: The Final Frontier *89* William Shatner
Star Wars *77* George Lucas
Star Without Light *47* Marcel Blistène
Star Witness *31* William A. Wellman
Stará Čínská Opera *54* Vojtěch Jasný, Karel Kachyňa
Staraya Azbuka *87* Victor Prokhorov
Starbird and Sweet William *75* Jack Hively
Starblack *66* Giovanni Grimaldi
Starchaser: The Legend of Orin *85* Steven Hahn, John Sparey
Starcrash *79* Luigi Cozzi
Stardoom *71* Lino Brocka
Stardust *37* Melville Brown
Stardust *74* Michael Apted
Stardust Memories *80* Woody Allen
Stardust on the Sage *42* William Morgan
Stardust Trail *25* Edmund Mortimer
Staré Pověsti České *53* Jiří Trnka
Starfighters, The *64* Will Zens
Starfish, The *50* Alan Cooke, John Schlesinger
Starflight One *82* Jerry Jameson
Starhops *78* Barbara Peeters
Stark Fear *63* Ned Hockman
Stark Love *27* Karl Brown
Stark Mad *29* Lloyd Bacon
Stark Nature *30* Arthur Woods
Stark Raving Mad *83* George F. Hood
Starkaste, Den *29* Axel Lindholm, Alf Sjöberg
Starke Ferdinand, Der *75* Alexander Kluge
Stärker Als die Liebe *39* Joe Stöckel
Stärker Als die Nacht *54* Slatan Dudow
Stärkste Trieb, Der *22* Karl Grüne
Starlet *39* René Cardona
Starlift *51* Roy Del Ruth
Starlight *86* Orin Wachsberg
Starlight Hotel *87* Sam Pillsbury
Starlight Over Texas *38* Albert Herman
Starlight Parade *37* Eric Humphris
Starlight Serenade *44* Denis Kavanagh
Starlight Slaughter *76* Tobe Hooper

Starlight the Untamed *25* Harry S. Webb
Starlight's Revenge *26* Harry S. Webb
Starlit Garden, The *23* Guy Newall
Starman *84* John Carpenter
Staroye i Novoye *29* Grigori Alexandrov, Sergei Eisenstein
Starry Is the Night *89* Ann Hui
Stars *50* László Ranódy
Stars *58* Konrad Wolf
Stars and Bars *17* Ford Sterling
Stars and Bars *88* Pat O'Connor
Stars and Stripes *39* Norman McLaren
Stars and Stripes Forever *52* Henry Koster
Stars Are Beautiful, The *74* Stan Brakhage
Stars Are Singing, The *53* Norman Taurog
Stars by Day *66* Igor Talankin
Stars' Home *74* Chang-ho Lee
Stars in May, The *59* Stanislav Rostotsky
Stars in My Crown *49* Jacques Tourneur
Stars in the Back Yard *57* Hugo Haas
Stars in Uniform *44* Lew Landers
Stars in Your Backyard *57* Hugo Haas
Stars in Your Eyes *56* Maurice Elvey
Stars Look Down, The *39* Carol Reed
Stars Must Shine, The *54* Witold Lesiewicz, Andrzej Munk
Stars of a Summer Night *59* Gerard Bryant
Stars of the Russian Ballet *54* Herbert Rappaport
Stars of the Ukraine *53* Alexander Rou
Stars on Parade *35* Oswald Mitchell, Challis Sanderson
Stars on Parade *44* Lew Landers
Stars Over Arizona *37* Robert North Bradbury
Stars Over Broadway *35* William Keighley
Stars Over Texas *46* Robert E. Tansey
Stars Shine, The *38* Hans Zerlett
Stars Who Made the Cinema *52* Karel Reisz
Starship *85* Roger Christian
Starship Invasions *77* Ed Hunt
Starstruck *82* Gillian Armstrong
Start Cheering *37* Albert S. Rogell
Start of Ocean Race for Kaiser's Cup *05* Edwin S. Porter
Start the Music *39* Jean Yarbrough
Start the Revolution Without Me *69* Bud Yorkin
Starting Over *79* Alan J. Pakula
Starting Point, The *19* Edwin J. Collins
Startling Announcement, A *14* Harcourt Brown
Starve a Fever *16* Cecil Birch
Staryi Nayezhdnik *40* Boris Barnet
Stasera Sciopero *51* Mario Bonnard
Šťastnou Cestu *43* Otakar Vávra
Šťastný Konec *66* Oldřich Lipský
State Department — File 649 *48* Sam Newfield
State Department Store *22* Dziga Vertov
State Fair *33* Henry King
State Fair *45* Walter Lang
State Fair *62* José Ferrer
State of Emergency, A *86* Richard Bennett
State of Grace *86* Jacques Rouffio
State of Grace *90* Phil Joanou
State of Siege *72* Costa-Gavras
State of Siege, A *77* Vincent Ward

State of Survival *86* Mario Azzopardi
State of the Union *48* Frank Capra
State of Things, The *82* Wim Wenders
State Official *30* Ivan Pyriev
State Park *87* Rafal Zielinski
State Penitentiary *50* Lew Landers
State Police *38* John Rawlins
State Police *48* Vernon Keays
State Secret *50* Sidney Gilliat
State Street Sadie *28* Archie Mayo
State Trooper *33* D. Ross Lederman
Stateless *62* Tad Danielewski
Stateless Man, The *55* Paul Gherzo
Stateline Motel *75* Maurizio Lucidi
States *67* Hollis Frampton
State's Attorney *32* George Archainbaud
State's Warning *12* Edwin S. Porter
Static *85* Mark Romanek
Static in the Attic *39* Charlie Chase
Station Content *18* Arthur Hoyt
Station for Two, A *83* Eldar Ryazanov
Station Master, The *28* Ivan Mozhukhin, Yuri Zhelyabuzhsky
Station Master's Wife, The *77* Rainer Werner Fassbinder
Station Six — Sahara *62* Seth Holt
Station 307 *54* Louis Malle
Station to Heaven *85* Masanobu Deme
Station West *48* Sidney Lanfield
Statue, La *05* Alice Guy-Blaché
Statue, The *70* Rod Amateau
Statue Animée, La *03* Georges Méliès
Statue de Neige, La *1899* Georges Méliès
Statue of Liberty, The *35* Seto Waimon
Statue Parade *37* Paul Rotha
Statues Meurent Aussi, Les *53* Chris Marker, Alain Resnais
Status Quo at Wembley *75* Tony Palmer
Statutory Affair, The *69* Richard Donner
Stavisky *73* Alain Resnais
Stay As You Are *78* Alberto Lattuada
Stay Away, Joe *68* Peter Tewksbury
Stay Home *22* George D. Baker
Stay Hungry *75* Bob Rafelson
Staying Alive *83* Sylvester Stallone
Staying the Same *89* Lee Grant
Staying Together *89* Lee Grant
Stazione, La *52* Valerio Zurlini
Stazione Termini *53* Vittorio De Sica
Steadfast Heart, The *23* Sheridan Hall
Steady Company *32* Edward Ludwig
Steady Now *53* Herman van den Horst
Steagle, The *71* Paul Sylbert
Steal Wool *57* Chuck Jones
Stealers, The *20* Christy Cabanne
Stealin' Ain't Honest *40* Dave Fleischer
Stealing Heaven *88* Clive Donner
Stealing Home *88* Will Aldis, Steven Kampmann
Steam Heat *63* Russ Meyer
Steam Scow "Cinderella" and Ferryboat "Cincinnati" *03* Edwin S. Porter
Steam Threshing-Machines *1896* Georges Méliès
Steamboat Bill, Jr. *28* Charles Reisner
Steamboat 'Round the Bend *35* John Ford
Steamboat Willie *28* Walt Disney, Ubbe Iwerks
Steamboats on River Seine *1896* Georges Méliès

Steamer Entering the Harbour of Jersey 1899 Georges Méliès
Steaming 84 Joseph Losey
Steamroller and the Violin, The 60 Andrei Tarkovsky
Steckbrief Z 48 32 Friedrich Feher
Steel 32 Walter Ruttmann
Steel 35 Paul Rotha
Steel 40 Per Lindberg
Steel 59 Jan Łomnicki
Steel 69 Lester James Peries
Steel 80 Steve Carver
Steel: A Whole New Way of Life 71 Shyam Benegal
Steel Against the Sky 41 A. Edward Sutherland
Steel and Lace 90 Ernest Farino
Steel Arena 73 Mark L. Lester
Steel Bayonet 57 Michael Carreras
Steel Cage, The 54 Walter Doniger
Steel Claw, The 61 George Montgomery
Steel Dawn 87 Lance Hool
Steel Fist, The 52 Wesley Barry
Steel Helmet, The 50 Samuel Fuller
Steel Highway, The 31 William A. Wellman
Steel Jungle, The 55 Walter Doniger
Steel Key, The 53 Robert S. Baker
Steel King, The 19 Oscar Apfel
Steel King's Last Wish, The 13 Forest Holger-Madsen
Steel Lady, The 53 E. A. Dupont
Steel Magnolias 89 Herbert Ross
Steel Preferred 25 James P. Hogan
Steel Town 43 Willard Van Dyke
Steel Town 50 Martin Frič
Steel Town 52 George Sherman
Steel Trail, The 23 William Duncan
Steel Trap, The 52 Andrew L. Stone
Steel Workers 37 Walter Lantz
Steele Justice 87 Robert Boris
Steele of the Royal Mounted 25 David Smith
Steelheart 21 William Duncan
Steeltown 43 Willard Van Dyke
Steelyard Blues 73 Alan Myerson
Steeplejacks, The 14 Percy Nash
Stefania 68 Yannis Dalianidis
Stefanie 58 Josef von Baky
Stefanie in Rio 60 Kurt Bernhardt
Stein Song, The 30 Dave Fleischer
Steiner — Das Eiserne Kreuz 2. Teil 78 Andrew V. McLaglen
Steinreicher Mann, Ein 32 Steve Sekely
Stella 21 Edwin J. Collins
Stella 50 Claude Binyon
Stella 54 Michael Cacoyannis
Stella 90 John Erman
Stella Dallas 25 Henry King
Stella Dallas 37 King Vidor
Stella del Mare 40 Corrado D'Enrico
Stella Maris 18 Marshall Neilan
Stella Maris 25 Charles Brabin
Stella Parish 35 Mervyn LeRoy
Stella Star 79 Luigi Cozzi
Stem van het Water, De 65 Bert Haanstra
Stemning i April 47 Astrid Henning-Jensen, Bjarne Henning-Jensen
Step 77 Sergei Bondarchuk
Step, The 86 Alexander Rekhviashvili

Step Away 79 Marcos Zurinaga
Step by Step 46 Phil Rosen
Step Down to Terror 58 Harry Keller
Step Lightly 25 Norman Taurog
Step Lively 44 Tim Whelan
Step Lively Jeeves! 37 Eugene Forde
Step on It! 22 Jack Conway
Step on It 31 Dave Fleischer
Step Out of Your Mind 65 Joe Sarno
Stepan Khalturin 25 Alexander Ivanovsky
Stepan Razin 39 Olga Preobrazhenskaya
Stepchild 32 Mikio Naruse
Stepchild 47 James Flood
Stepchildren 58 Tenghiz Abuladze, Revas Djaparidze
Stepfather 81 Bertrand Blier
Stepfather, The 86 Joseph Ruben
Stepfather II 89 Jeff Burr
Stepfather 2: Make Room for Daddy 89 Jeff Burr
Stepford Wives, The 74 Bryan Forbes
Stephane Grappelli and His Quintet 48 Horace Shepherd
Stephania 68 Yannis Dalianidis
Stephanie in Rio 60 Kurt Bernhardt
Stephen King's Cat's Eye 85 Lewis Teague
Stephen King's Graveyard Shift 90 Ralph S. Singleton
Stephen King's Silver Bullet 85 Daniel Attias
Stephen Steps Out 23 Joseph E. Henaberry
Stepmother, The 12 Allan Dwan
Stepmother, The 14 Avrom Yitskhok Kaminsky
Stepmother, The 71 Hikmet Avedis
Steppa, La 61 Alberto Lattuada
Steppe, La 61 Alberto Lattuada
Steppe, The 61 Alberto Lattuada
Steppe, The 77 Sergei Bondarchuk
Steppenwolf 74 Fred Haines
Steppes, The 77 Sergei Bondarchuk
Steppin' in Society 45 Alexander Esway
Steppin' Out 25 Frank R. Strayer
Steppin' Out 79 Lyndall Hobbs
Stepping Along 26 Charles Hines
Stepping Fast 23 Joseph Franz
Stepping High 28 Bert Glennon
Stepping Into Society 36 Lewis D. Collins
Stepping Lively 24 James W. Horne
Stepping Out 19 Fred Niblo
Stepping Out 31 Charles Reisner
Stepping Out 81 Esben Høilund Carlsen
Stepping Sisters 32 Seymour Felix
Stepping Stone, The 16 Reginald Barker
Stepping Stones 31 Geoffrey Benstead
Stepping Stones 32 Dick Huemer
Stepping Toes 38 John Baxter
Steps of Age, The 51 Ben Maddow
Steps to the Moon 63 Ion Popescu-Gopo
Steptoe and Son 72 Cliff Owen
Steptoe and Son Ride Again 73 Peter Sykes
Sterbende Modell, Das 18 Urban Gad
Stereo 69 David Cronenberg
Sterile Cuckoo, The 69 Alan J. Pakula
Stern von Bethlehem, Der 21 Lotte Reiniger
Stern von Damaskus, Der 19 Michael Curtiz
Stern von Valencia, Der 34 Alfred Zeisler

Stern Young Man, A 36 Abram Room
Sterne 58 Konrad Wolf
Sterne Über Colombo 53 Veidt Harlan
Stet Priklyuchenni 29 Alexander Ptushko
Stevedores, The 37 Walter Lantz
Stevie 78 Robert Enders
Stevie, Samson and Delilah 75 Steven Hawkes
Stewardess School 86 Ken Blancato
Stewed, Fried and Boiled 29 James Parrott
Stewed Missionary 04 Alf Collins
Sti Skia tou Fovou 88 Giorgos Karipidis
Stick 85 Burt Reynolds
Stick, The 87 Darrell Roodt
Stick 'Em Up 50 John E. Blakeley
Stick to Your Guns 41 Lesley Selander
Stick to Your Last, Shoemaker 15 Victor Sjöström
Stick to Your Story 26 Harry Joe Brown
Stick-Up, The 77 Jeffrey Bloom
Stickphast 11 Frank Wilson
Stickpin, The 33 Leslie Hiscott
Sticks 17 Sherwood MacDonald
Sticky Affair, A 13 Frank Wilson
Sticky Bicycle, The 07 Lewin Fitzhamon
Sticky Fingers 88 Catlin Adams
Stier von Olivera, Der 21 Dmitri Buchowetzki, Erich Schönfelder
Stiffs 86 Ralph Rosenblum
Stigma 72 David Durston
Stigma 81 José Ramón Larraz
Stigma 83 Uri Barbash
Stigmate, Le 24 Maurice Champreux, Louis Feuillade
Stigmatized One, The 21 Carl Theodor Dreyer
Stiletto 69 Bernard Kowalski
Still 71 Ernie Gehr
Still Alarm, The 03 Edwin S. Porter
Still Alarm, The 18 Colin Campbell
Still Alarm, The 26 Edward Laemmle
Still Life 66 Bruce Baillie
Still Life 69 Jan Lenica
Still Life 85 Marie-Louise de Geer Bergenstrahle
Still of the Night 82 Robert Benton
Still Point, The 86 Barbara Boyd-Anderson
Still Room in Hell 63 Ernst R. von Theumer
Still Smokin' 83 Thomas Chong
Still Waters 15 J. Searle Dawley
Still Waters 28 Manny Gould, Ben Harrison
Still Waters Run Deep 16 Fred Paul
Still We Live 51 Tadashi Imai
Still Worthy of the Name 08 Jack Chart
Stilla Flirt, En 33 Gustaf Molander
Stilleben 69 Jan Lenica
Stilleben 85 Marie-Louise de Geer Bergenstrahle
Stillness 64 Vladimir Basov
Stilte Rond Christine M., De 82 Marleen Gorris
Stilts 84 Carlos Saura
Stimme der Liebe, Die 36 Viktor Jansen
Stimme des Blutes 37 Carmine Gallone
Stimulantia 65 Ingmar Bergman, Jörn Donner, Gustaf Molander, Vilgot Sjöman

Stín Kapradiny 85 František Vláčil
Sting, The 73 George Roy Hill
Sting II, The 83 Jeremy Paul Kagan
Sting of Death, The 21 Fred Paul
Sting of Death 66 William Grefé
Sting of Stings, The 29 James Parrott
Sting of the Lash, The 21 Henry King
Sting of the Scorpion, The 23 Richard Hatton
Sting of Victory, The 16 J. Charles Haydon
Stingaree 16 James W. Horne
Stingaree 34 William A. Wellman
Stingray 78 Richard Taylor
Stinker 25 Yasujiro Shimazu
Stips 51 Carl Fröhlich
Stir 80 Stephen Wallace
Stir Crazy 80 Sidney Poitier
Stir Patra 74 Purnendu Pattrea
Stirring the Pool 70 Peter Weir
Stirrup Cup Sensation, The 24 Walter West
Stitch in Time, A 08 Alf Collins
Stitch in Time, A 19 Ralph Ince
Stitch in Time, A 24 Dave Fleischer
Stitch in Time, A 25 Alexander Butler
Stitch in Time, A 63 Robert Asher
Stitches 85 Rod Holcomb
Stjælne Ansigt, Det 14 Forest Holger-Madsen
Sto Govorit MOC? 24 Abram Room
Što Je Radnički Savjet? 59 Dušan Makavejev
150 na Godzinę 71 Wanda Jakubowska
Stock Car 55 Wolf Rilla
Stock Exchange, The 39 Hans Richter
Stock Is As Good As Money 13 H. Oceano Martinek
Stockbroker, The 13 Mauritz Stiller
Stockbroker's Clerk, The 22 George Ridgwell
Stocks and Blondes 28 Dudley Murphy
Stoggles' Christmas Dinner 13 Will P. Kellino
Støj 65 Jørgen Roos
Stoker, The 32 Chester M. Franklin
Stoker, The 35 Leslie Pearce
Stolen Affections 47 Marcel L'Herbier
Stolen Airliner, The 55 Don Sharp
Stolen Airship, The 66 Karel Zeman
Stolen Airship Plans, The 12 Stuart Kinder
Stolen Assignment 55 Terence Fisher
Stolen Birthright, The 14 Louis Gasnier
Stolen Bride, The 06 Percy Stow
Stolen Bride, The 16 A. E. Coleby
Stolen Bride, The 27 Alexander Korda
Stolen Bridle, The 07 Lewin Fitzhamon
Stolen by Gypsies 05 Edwin S. Porter
Stolen Clothes, The 09 Frank Wilson
Stolen Desire 58 Shohei Imamura
Stolen Dirigible, The 66 Karel Zeman
Stolen Drink, The 1898 Cecil M. Hepworth
Stolen Duck, The 08 Frank Mottershaw
Stolen Face, The 51 Terence Fisher
Stolen Favourite, The 09 Percy Stow
Stolen Favourite, The 26 Walter West
Stolen Frontier, The 47 Jiří Weiss
Stolen Fruit 06 Harold Jeapes

Stolen Glory 12 Mack Sennett
Stolen Goods 15 George Melford
Stolen Goods 24 Leo McCarey
Stolen Guy, The 05 Lewin Fitzhamon
Stolen Harmony 35 Alfred L. Werker
Stolen Heart, The 34 Lotte Reiniger
Stolen Heaven 31 George Abbott
Stolen Heaven 37 Andrew L. Stone
Stolen Heir, The 10 A. E. Coleby
Stolen Heirlooms, The 15 Charles Raymond
Stolen Holiday 36 Michael Curtiz
Stolen Honor 18 Richard Stanton
Stolen Honours 14 Joe Evans
Stolen Hours 18 Travers Vale
Stolen Hours 63 Daniel Petrie
Stolen Identity 53 Günther von Fritsch
Stolen Jewels, The 08 D. W. Griffith
Stolen Jewels, The 21 Edward R. Gordon
Stolen Keyhole, The 18 Alfred Santell
Stolen Kiss 20 Kenneth Webb
Stolen Kisses 29 Ray Enright
Stolen Kisses 68 François Truffaut
Stolen Letters, The 11 Lewin Fitzhamon
Stolen Life, A 39 Paul Czinner
Stolen Life, A 46 Kurt Bernhardt
Stolen Love 28 Lynn Shores
Stolen Love 51 Kon Ichikawa
Stolen Magic 15 Mack Sennett
Stolen Masterpiece, The 14 H. Oceano Martinek
Stolen Moments 20 James Vincent
Stolen Necklace, The 12 Fred Rains
Stolen Necklace, The 33 Leslie Hiscott
Stolen Orders 18 George Kelson, Harley Knoles
Stolen Papers, The 12 Georges Treville
Stolen Paradise, The 17 Harley Knoles
Stolen Paradise 41 Louis Gasnier
Stolen Picture, The 12 Frank Wilson
Stolen Pig, The 04 Percy Stow
Stolen Plans, The 14 Charles Brabin
Stolen Plans, The 52 James Hill
Stolen Play, The 17 Harry Harvey
Stolen Pleasure 62 Yasuzo Masumura
Stolen Pleasures 26 Phil Rosen
Stolen Puppy, The 04 Lewin Fitzhamon
Stolen Pups, The 11 Frank Wilson
Stolen Purse, The 05 Percy Stow
Stolen Purse, The 13 Mack Sennett
Stolen Ranch, The 26 William Wyler
Stolen Ruby, The 15 Robert Vignola
Stolen Sacrifice, The 16 Sidney Morgan
Stolen Secrets 23 Irving Cummings
Stolen Snooze, The 22 Raoul Barré, Charles Bowers
Stolen Sweets 34 Richard Thorpe
Stolen Time 45 Derwin Abrahams
Stolen Time 55 Charles Deane
Stolen Treaty, The 17 Paul Scardon
Stolen Triumph, The 16 David Thompson
Stolen Violin, The 12 Edwin J. Collins
Stolen Wealth 40 Joseph H. Lewis
Stolz der 3 Kompagnie, Der 32 Fred Sauer
Stomach Trouble 27 William C. Nolan
Stone 74 Sandy Harbutt
Stone Age, The 22 Charlie Chase
Stone Age, The 31 Walter Lantz
Stone Age Roost Robber, The 16 L. M.

Glackens
Stone Boy, The 84 Christopher Cain
Stone Boy 86 J. Erastheo Navoa
Stone Cold Dead 79 George Mendeluk
Stone Flower, The 46 Alexander Ptushko
Stone Into Steel 61 Paul Dickson
Stone Killer, The 73 Michael Winner
Stone of Mazarin, The 23 George Ridgwell
Stone of Silver Creek 34 Nick Grindé
Stone Rider, The 23 Fritz Wendhausen
Stone, Time, Song 60 Emil Lotyanu
Stone Upon Stone 70 Santiago Álvarez
Stone Wedding 73 Dan Piţa, Mircea Veroiu
Stone Years 85 Pantelis Voulgaris
Stoning, The 15 Charles Brabin
Stony Island 78 Andrew Davis
Stony Lion 87 Massoud Jafari Jozani
Stooge, The 52 Norman Taurog
Stooge for a Mouse 50 Friz Freleng
Stoogemania 85 Chuck Workman
Stooges Go West 51 Edward Bernds
Stool Pigeon, The 15 Lon Chaney
Stool Pigeon 28 Renaud Hoffman
Stool Pigeon, The 28 Leigh Jason
Stoolie, The 62 Jean-Pierre Melville
Stoolie, The 72 John G. Avildsen, George Silano
Stoopnocracy 33 Dave Fleischer
Stop 68 Mark Petersen
STOP 70 Bill Gunn
Stop at Nothing 24 Charles R. Seeling
Stop, Cease, Hesitate! 19 Alfred Santell
Stop Flirting 25 Scott Sidney
Stop, Look and Hasten! 54 Chuck Jones
Stop, Look and Listen 26 Larry Semon
Stop, Look and Love 39 Otto Brower
Stop Making Sense 84 Jonathan Demme
Stop Me Before I Kill! 61 Val Guest
Stop Press Girl 49 Michael Barry
Stop That Bus! 03 Percy Stow
Stop That Cab 51 Eugenio De Liguoro
Stop That Man 28 Nat Ross
Stop That Noise 35 Dave Fleischer
Stop the Fight 11 Fred Evans
Stop the Old Fox 59 Teinosuke Kinugasa
Stop the World—I Want to Get Off 66 Philip Saville
Stop the World, I Want to Get Off 78 Mel Shapiro
Stop Thief! 01 James A. Williamson
Stop Thief! 13 Charles C. Calvert
Stop Thief! 15 George Fitzmaurice
Stop Thief! 20 Harry Beaumont
Stop Train 349 64 Rolf Haedrich
Stop Tyven 45 Ole Palsbo
Stop Your Tickling, Jock 07 Arthur Gilbert
Stop, You're Killing Me 52 Roy Del Ruth
Stopover Forever 64 Frederic Goode
Stopover Tokyo 57 Richard L. Breen
Stopping the Show 32 Dave Fleischer
Stopy 60 Jaromil Jireš
Stora Amatören, Den 58 Hasse Ekman
Stora Äventyret, Det 53 Arne Sucksdorff
Stora Löftet, Det 87 Bengt Danneborn
Storch Hat Uns Getraut, Der 33 Henry Koster
Storch Streikt, Der 32 E. W. Emo

Strained Pearl, The *16* Henry King
Strait-Jacket *63* William Castle
Straitjacket *63* Samuel Fuller
Straits of Love and Hate, The *37* Kenji Mizoguchi
Straka v Hrsti *88* Juraj Herz
Strakh *87* Gunar Tselinsky
Strakoff the Adventurer *15* Forest Holger-Madsen
Strana la Vita *88* Giuseppe Bertolucci
Strana Orchidea con Cinque Goccie di Sangue, Una *72* Sergio Martino
Strana Rodnaya *42* Alexander Dovzhenko, Esther Shub
Strana Sovietov *37* Esther Shub
Stranded *16* Lloyd Ingraham
Stranded *27* Phil Rosen
Stranded *35* Frank Borzage
Stranded *65* Juleen Compton
Stranded *67* Josef Leytes
Stranded *87* Tex Fuller
Stranded in Arcady *17* Frank Crane
Stranded in Paris *26* Arthur Rosson
Stranded in Paris *38* Mitchell Leisen
Strandhugg *49* Arne Sucksdorff
Strange Adventure *32* Hampton Del Ruth, Phil Whitman
Strange Adventure, A *56* William Witney
Strange Adventure of Allan Gray, The *31* Carl Theodor Dreyer
Strange Adventure of David Gray, The *31* Carl Theodor Dreyer
Strange Adventures of Mr. Smith, The *37* Maclean Rogers
Strange Affair *44* Alfred E. Green
Strange Affair, The *68* David Greene
Strange Affair of Uncle Harry, The *45* Robert Siodmak
Strange Affection *57* Wolf Rilla
Strange Affinity *69* Kaneto Shindo
Strange Alibi *41* D. Ross Lederman
Strange Alibi *46* Ray McCarey
Strange Awakening, The *58* Montgomery Tully
Strange Bargain *49* Will Price
Strange Bedfellows *64* Melvin Frank
Strange Behavior *81* Michael Laughlin
Strange Behaviour *80* Anthony Penrose
Strange Boarder, The *20* Clarence Badger
Strange Boarders *38* Herbert Mason
Strange Brew *83* Rick Moranis, Dave Thomas
Strange Cargo *29* Benjamin Glazer, Arthur Gregor
Strange Cargo *36* Lawrence Huntington
Strange Cargo *40* Frank Borzage
Strange Case of Blondie, The *54* Ken Hughes
Strange Case of Captain Ramper, The *28* Max Reichmann
Strange Case of Clara Deane, The *32* Louis Gasnier, Max Marcin
Strange Case of District Attorney M., The *30* Rudolf Meinert
Strange Case of Dr. Jekyll and Mr. Hyde, The *87* Alexander Orlov
Strange Case of Dr. Jekyll and Mrs. Osbourne, The *81* Walerian Borowczyk
Strange Case of Dr. Manning, The *58* Arthur Crabtree

Strange Case of Dr. Meade, The *38* Lewis D. Collins
Strange Case of Dr. Rx, The *42* William Nigh
Strange Case of Madeleine, The *50* David Lean
Strange Case of Mr. Todmorden, The *35* Fraser Foulsham, A. B. Imeson
Strange Case of Philip Kent, The *16* Fred W. Durrant
Strange Case of the Cosmic Rays, The *57* Frank Capra
Strange Case of the Man and the Beast, The *51* Mario Soffici
Strange Confession *43* Julien Duvivier
Strange Confession *45* John Hoffman
Strange Conquest *46* John Rawlins
Strange Conspiracy, The *34* William A. Wellman
Strange Countess, The *61* Josef von Baky
Strange Dead Bodies *81* Kang Bum Koo
Strange Death of Adolf Hitler, The *43* James P. Hogan
Strange Deception *48* William Dieterle
Strange Deception *50* Curzio Malaparte
Strange Door, The *51* Joseph Pevney
Strange Encounters *82* Benzheng Yu
Strange Evidence *32* Robert Milton
Strange Experiment *37* Albert Parker
Strange Faces *38* Errol Taggart
Strange Fascination *52* Hugo Haas
Strange Fetishes, The *67* Enrico Blancocello
Strange Fetishes of the Go-Go Girls, The *67* Enrico Blancocello
Strange Gamble *48* George Archainbaud
Strange Glory *38* Jacques Tourneur
Strange Holiday *45* Arch Oboler
Strange Holiday *69* Mende Brown
Strange Idols *22* Bernard J. Durning
Strange Illusion *45* Edgar G. Ulmer
Strange Impersonation *45* Anthony Mann
Strange Incident *42* William A. Wellman
Strange Inn of Pleasures, The *76* Marcelo Motta
Strange Interlude *32* Robert Z. Leonard
Strange Interval *32* Robert Z. Leonard
Strange Intruder *56* Irving Rapper
Strange Invaders *83* Michael Laughlin
Strange Journey *46* James Tinling
Strange Journey *53* Don Chaffey
Strange Journey *66* Richard Fleischer
Strange Justice *32* Victor Schertzinger
Strange Lady in Town *54* Mervyn LeRoy
Strange Laws *37* Noel Mason Smith
Strange Love of Martha Ivers, The *46* Lewis Milestone
Strange Love of Molly Louvain, The *32* Michael Curtiz
Strange Lovers *63* Robert Stambler
Strange Masquerade *77* Pál Sándor
Strange Meeting, A *09* D. W. Griffith
Strange Mr. Bartleby, The *53* John Guillermin
Strange Mr. Gregory, The *45* Phil Rosen
Strange Mr. Victor, The *38* Jean Grémillon
Strange Mrs. Crane, The *48* Sam Newfield
Strange Mrs. X, The *50* Jean Grémillon
Strange Obsession, The *66* Damiano

Damiani
Strange One, The *57* Jack Garfein
Strange Ones, The *49* Jean-Pierre Melville
Strange People *33* Richard Thorpe
Strange People *70* Vasili Shuksin
Strange Rider, The *25* Ward Hayes
Strange Roads *32* Albert Herman
Strange Shadows in an Empty Room *76* Alberto De Martino
Strange Skirts *41* Robert Z. Leonard
Strange Stories *53* John Guillermin
Strange Tales *69* John Dooley
Strange to Relate *43* Widgey R. Newman
Strange to the Sudeten Country *38* H. Wassermann
Strange Transgressor, A *17* Reginald Barker
Strange Triangle *46* Ray McCarey
Strange Vengeance of Rosalie, The *72* Jack Starrett
Strange Victory *48* Leo T. Hurwitz
Strange Voyage *45* Irving Allen
Strange Wives *35* Richard Thorpe
Strange Woman, The *18* Edward J. LeSaint
Strange Woman *29* Ivan Pyriev
Strange Woman, The *46* Edgar G. Ulmer
Strange Woman, A *77* Yuli Raizman
Strange World *50* Franz Eichhorn
Strange World, The *57* Gilbert Gunn
Strange World of Planet X, The *57* Gilbert Gunn
Strange World of Zé do Caixão, The *68* José Mojica Marins
Strange Years *52* Vojtěch Jasný, Karel Kachyňa
Stranger, The *10* Sidney Olcott
Stranger, The *13* Nahum Lipovsky
Stranger, The *24* Joseph E. Henabery
Stranger, The *39* Sam Nelson
Stranger, The *46* Orson Welles
Stranger, The *61* Roger Corman
Stranger, The *67* Luchino Visconti
Stranger, The *87* Adolfo Aristarain
Stranger, The *87* Ryszard Ber
Stranger and the Fog, The *74* Bahram Beizai
Stranger and the Gunfighter, The *74* Antonio Margheriti
Stranger at Coyote, The *12* Allan Dwan
Stranger at My Door *50* Desmond Leslie, Brendan Stafford
Stranger at My Door *56* William Witney
Stranger at Sacramento *65* Sergio Bergonzelli
Stranger Came Home, The *53* Terence Fisher
Stranger from Arizona, The *38* Elmer Clifton
Stranger from Cruz del Sur Street, The *86* Jordi Grau
Stranger from Hong Kong *64* Jacques Poitrenaud
Stranger from Pecos, The *43* Lambert Hillyer
Stranger from Ponca City, The *47* Derwin Abrahams
Stranger from Santa Fe *45* Lambert Hillyer
Stranger from Somewhere, A *16* William Worthington

Stranger from Texas, The *39* Sam Nelson
Stranger from Venus *54* Burt Balaban
Stranger in Between, The *51* Charles Crichton
Stranger in Canyon Valley, The *21* Clifford Smith
Stranger in Hollywood *68* Rodion Slipyj
Stranger in My Arms, A *58* Helmut Käutner
Stranger in the Family *45* Albert Herman
Stranger in the House *67* Pierre Rouve
Stranger in the House *74* Bob Clark
Stranger in Town *32* Erle C. Kenton
Stranger in Town, A *43* Roy Rowland
Stranger in Town *56* George Pollock
Stranger in Town, A *66* Luigi Vanzi
Stranger Is Watching, A *82* Sean S. Cunningham
Stranger Knocks, A *63* Johan Jacobsen
Stranger Left No Card, The *52* Wendy Toye
Stranger of the Hills, The *22* Bruce Mitchell
Stranger on Horseback *54* Jacques Tourneur
Stranger on the Prowl *51* Joseph Losey
Stranger on the Third Floor *40* Boris Ingster
Stranger—Psalm 119, The *27* Charles Barnett
Stranger Returns, The *67* Luigi Vanzi
Stranger Than Fiction *21* John A. Barry
Stranger Than Love *63* Robert Stambler
Stranger Than Paradise *84* Jim Jarmusch
Stranger Walked In, A *47* Richard Whorf
Stranger Within a Woman, The *65* Mikio Naruse
Stranger Wore a Gun, The *53* André De Toth
Strangers, The *11* Edwin S. Porter
Strangers *53* Roberto Rossellini
Strangers *70* Gilbert Cates
Strangers All *34* Charles Vidor
Strangers at Sunrise *69* Percival Rubens
Stranger's Banquet, The *22* Marshall Neilan
Strangers Came, The *49* Alfred Travers
Stranger's Gundown, The *69* Sergio Garrone
Stranger's Hand, The *53* Mario Soldati
Strangers' Honeymoon *36* Albert De Courville
Strangers in Love *32* Lothar Mendes
Strangers in Paradise *83* Lino Brocka
Strangers in Paradise *84* Ulli Lommel
Strangers in the City *62* Rick Carrier
Strangers in the House *41* Henri Decoin
Strangers in the Night *44* Anthony Mann
Strangers Kiss *84* Matthew Chapman
Strangers May Kiss *31* George Fitzmaurice
Strangers' Meeting *57* Robert Day
Strangers of the Evening *32* H. Bruce Humberstone
Strangers of the Night *23* Fred Niblo
Strangers on a Honeymoon *36* Albert De Courville
Strangers on a Train *51* Alfred Hitchcock
Stranger's Return, The *33* King Vidor
Strangers Upstairs, The *61* Yoji Yamada
Strangers When We Meet *59* Richard

Quine
Strangest Case, The *43* Eugene Forde
Strangled Eggs *61* Robert McKimson
Stranglehold *31* Henry Edwards
Stranglehold *62* Lawrence Huntington
Strangler, The *32* Norman Lee
Strangler, The *40* Harold Huth
Strangler, The *64* Burt Topper
Strangler of Bengal, The *59* Terence Fisher
Strangler of Blackmoor Castle, The *63* Harald Reinl
Strangler of the Swamp *45* Frank Wisbar
Strangler of Vienna, The *71* Guido Zurli
Strangler vs. Strangler *86* Slobodan Šijan
Strangler's Morgue *36* George King, Paul White
Stranglers of Bombay, The *59* Terence Fisher
Strangler's Web *65* John Llewellyn Moxey
Strangling Threads *22* Cecil M. Hepworth
Strangolatore di Vienna, Il *71* Guido Zurli
Straniero, Lo *67* Luchino Visconti
Straniero a Paso Bravo, Uno *68* Salvatore Rosso
Straniero a Sacramento, Uno *65* Sergio Bergonzelli
Straniero Fatti il Segno della Croce *68* D. Fidani
Stranitsy Zhizn *48* Boris Barnet, Alexander Macharet
Strannaya Zhenshchina *77* Yuli Raizman
Strannayar Istoriyar Doktora Dzhekila i Mistera Khaida *87* Alexander Orlov
Strannye Lyudi *70* Vasili Shuksin
Strano Tipo, Uno *63* Lucio Fulci
Strano Vizio della Signora Ward, Lo *71* Sergio Martino
Strapless *89* David Hare
Strashnaya Mest *13* Władysław Starewicz
Strašidla z Vikýře *88* Radim Cvrček
Strass and Co. *15* Abel Gance
Strass et Cie *15* Abel Gance
Strasse, Die *23* Karl Grüne
Strategia del Ragno, La *69* Bernardo Bertolucci
Strategic Air Command *55* Anthony Mann
Strategija Svrake *87* Zlatko Lavanić
Strategy *15* Harold Weston
Strategy of Terror *64* Jack Smight
Stratford Adventure, The *54* Morten Parker
Stratos-Fear *33* Ubbe Iwerks
Stratton Story, The *49* Sam Wood
Strauss' Great Waltz *33* Alfred Hitchcock
Strauss' Salome *23* Malcolm Strauss
Strauss the Waltz King *29* Conrad Wiene
Stravinsky *65* Wolf Koenig, Roman Kroitor
Stravinsky Portrait, A *64* Richard Leacock*
Straw Dogs *71* Sam Peckinpah
Straw Man, The *15* Chester M. Franklin, Sidney Franklin
Straw Man, The *53* Donald Taylor
Strawberries Need Rain *70* Larry Buchanan
Strawberry Blonde, The *41* Raoul Walsh
Strawberry Fields *88* Al Brodax
Strawberry Roan *33* Alvin J. Neitz
Strawberry Roan *44* Maurice Elvey

Strawberry Roan, The *48* John English
Strawberry Statement, The *70* Stuart Hagmann
Strawfire *71* Volker Schlöndorff
Straws in the Wind *24* Bertram Phillips
Stray Days *87* Filippo Ottoni
Stray Dog *49* Akira Kurosawa
Stray Lamb *36* Tsou-sen Tsai
Straziami Ma di Baci Saziami *68* Dino Risi
Streak of Luck, A *25* Richard Thorpe
Stream, The *63* István Gaál
Stream of Life, The *19* Horace G. Plympton
Stream of Youth, The *59* Tomotaka Tasaka
Streamers *83* Robert Altman
Streamline Express *35* Leonard Fields
Streamlined Donkey, The *41* Sid Marcus
Streamlined Greta Green *37* Friz Freleng
Streamlined Swing *38* Buster Keaton
Stree *62* Rajaram Vanakudre Shantaram
Street, The *23* Karl Grüne
Street, The *39* Satsuo Yamamoto
Street, The *49* Gösta Werner
Street Angel *28* Frank Borzage
Street Angel *37* Muzhi Yuan
Street Arab, A *09* Lewin Fitzhamon
Street Asylum *90* Gregory Brown
Street Bandits *51* R. G. Springsteen
Street Called Straight, The *20* Wallace Worsley
Street Car Chivalry *03* Edwin S. Porter
Street Cat Named Sylvester, A *53* Friz Freleng
Street Corner *48* Albert Kelley
Street Corner *53* Muriel Box
Street Corner Frauds *26* F. W. Engholm
Street Corners *29* Russell Birdwell
Street Fight *74* Ralph Bakshi
Street Fighter *59* A. N. White
Street Fleet *83* Joel Schumacher
Street Gang *82* William Lustig
Street Girl *29* Wesley Ruggles
Street Girls *75* Michael Miller
Street Is My Beat, The *66* Irvin Berwick
Street Juggler, The *25* Minoru Murata
Street Justice *88* Richard C. Sarafian
Street Legal *89* John Mackenzie
Street Legion, The *32* Aleksander Ford
Street Love *83* Rose Marie Turko
Street Music *81* Jenny Bowen
Street of Adventure, The *21* Kenelm Foss
Street of Chance *30* John Cromwell
Street of Chance *42* Jack Hively
Street of Darkness *58* Robert Walker
Street of Departures *86* Tony Gatlif
Street of Desires, The *85* Haruhiko Mimura
Street of Forgotten Men, The *25* Herbert Brenon
Street of Hope, The *86* Şerif Gören
Street of Illusion, The *28* Erle C. Kenton
Street of Love *28* Tomotaka Tasaka
Street of Love and Hope, A *59* Nagisa Oshima
Street of Memories *40* Shepard Traube
Street of Missing Men *39* Sidney Salkow
Street of Missing Women *40* Sidney Salkow
Street of My Childhood *86* Astrid Henning-Jensen

Street of Seven Stars, The 18 John B. O'Brien

Street of Shadows 36 G. W. Pabst

Street of Shadows 53 Richard Vernon

Street of Shame 56 Kenji Mizoguchi

Street of Sin, The 28 Josef von Sternberg, Mauritz Stiller

Street of Sinners 57 William Berke

Street of Sorrow, The 25 G. W. Pabst

Street of Tears, The 24 Travers Vale

Street of the Puppet Show 49 Salah Abu Saif

Street of the Young 36 Aleksander Ford

Street of Violence, The 50 Satsuo Yamamoto

Street of Women 32 Archie Mayo

Street Partner, The 60 Basil Dearden

Street People 76 Maurizio Lucidi

Street Scene 31 King Vidor

Street Scenes 25 Kenji Mizoguchi*

Street Scenes 70 Jonathan Kaplan, Martin Scorsese, Oliver Stone

Street Singer, The 37 Jean De Marguenat

Street Sketches 25 Kenji Mizoguchi*

Street Smart 87 Jerry Schatzberg

Street Song 35 Bernard Vorhaus

Street Story 88 Joseph B. Vasquez

Street to Die, A 85 Bill Bennett

Street Trash 87 Jim Muro

Street Tumblers, The 22 George Wynn

Street Under the Snow, A 78 Henning Carlsen

Street Watchman's Story, The 14 Charles Vernon

Street with No Name, The 48 William Keighley

Street Without End 34 Mikio Naruse

Street Without Sun, The 53 Satsuo Yamamoto

Streetcar Named Desire, A 51 Elia Kazan

Streetfighter, The 75 Walter Hill

Streets 90 Katt Shea Ruben

Streets of Fire 83 Walter Hill

Streets of Ghost Town 50 Ray Nazarro

Streets of Gold 86 Joe Roth

Streets of Hong Kong 79 Hilton Alexander

Streets of Illusion, The 17 William Parke

Streets of Laredo 49 Leslie Fenton

Streets of London, The 28 Norman Lee

Streets of New York, The 22 Burton L. King

Streets of New York 39 William Nigh

Streets of Night 58 Shohei Imamura

Streets of Paris 59 Denys De la Patellière

Streets of San Francisco 49 George Blair

Streets of Shanghai 27 Louis Gasnier

Streets of Sin 49 Elmer Clifton, Ida Lupino

Streets of Sinners 57 William Berke

Streets of Sorrow 52 Giorgio Pastina

Streetwalker, The 76 Walerian Borowczyk

Streetwalkin' 84 Joan Freeman

Streetwise 84 Martin Bell

Strega in Amore, La 66 Damiano Damiani

Stregati 87 Francesco Nuti

Streghe, Le 66 Mauro Bolognini, Vittorio De Sica, Pier Paolo Pasolini, Franco Rossi, Luchino Visconti

Streit Um den Knaben Jo 38 Erich Waschneck

Strejda 59 Jaromil Jireš

Strejken 13 Victor Sjöström

Strelle nel Fosso, Le 78 Pupi Avati

Strength of a Mustache, The 31 Mikio Naruse

Strength of Donald McKenzie, The 16 William Russell

Strength of Love 30 Mikio Naruse

Strength of the Hungarian Soil, The 16 Michael Curtiz

Strength of the Pines 22 Edgar Lewis

Strength of the Weak, The 16 Lucius Henderson

Strength That Failed, The 14 Dave Aylott

Strenuous Life, or Anti-race Suicide, The 04 Edwin S. Porter

Strenuous Ride, A 14 Vincent Whitman

Stress and Emotions 84 Robin Spry

Stress Es Tres, Tres 68 Carlos Saura

Stress Is Three, Three 68 Carlos Saura

Stress of Circumstance, The 14 Warwick Buckland

Stress of Youth 61 Karel Kachyňa

Stretch Hunter 80 Horace Ove

Striations 70 Norman McLaren

Strich Durch die Rechnung 34 Alfred Zeisler

Stricken Home, The 10 Theo Bouwmeester

Strictly Business 32 Mary Field, Jacqueline Logan

Strictly Confidential 19 Clarence Badger

Strictly Confidential 34 Frank Capra

Strictly Confidential 59 Charles Saunders

Strictly Dishonorable 31 John M. Stahl

Strictly Dishonorable 51 Melvin Frank, Norman Panama

Strictly Dynamite 34 Elliott Nugent

Strictly for Cash 84 Gerry O'Hara

Strictly for Pleasure 58 Blake Edwards

Strictly for the Birds 63 Vernon Sewell

Strictly Fresh Yeggs 34 George Stevens

Strictly Illegal 35 Ralph Ceder

Strictly in Confidence 33 Clyde Cook

Strictly in the Groove 42 Vernon Keays

Strictly Modern 22 William Beaudine

Strictly Modern 30 William A. Seiter

Strictly Personal 33 Ralph Murphy

Strictly Secret Previews 67 Martin Frič

Strictly Unconventional 30 David Burton

Strictly Unreliable 32 George Marshall

Stride, Soviet! 26 Dziga Vertov

Striden Går Vidare 41 Gustaf Molander

Strife Eternal, The 15 Bert Haldane, F. Martin Thornton

Strife of the Party, The 31 Mark Sandrich

Strife Over the Boy Jo 38 Erich Waschneck

Strife with Father 50 Robert McKimson

Strijd der Geuzen, De 12 Alfred Machin

Strijd Zonder Einden 54 Bert Haanstra

Strike, The 09 Edwin S. Porter

Strike! 13 Victor Sjöström

Strike 24 Sergei Eisenstein

Strike! 33 Michael Powell

Strike, The 47 Karel Steklý

Strike Commando 87 Bruno Mattei

Strike Fever 20 Frank Miller

Strike It Rich 33 Leslie Hiscott

Strike It Rich 48 Lesley Selander

Strike It Rich 88 James Scott

Strike Leader, The 11 Wilfred Noy

Strike Me Deadly 63 Ted V. Mikels

Strike Me Deadly 63 Herbert L. Strock

Strike Me Pink 35 Robert Alton, Norman Taurog

Strike the Monster on Page One 72 Marco Bellocchio

Strike Up the Band 30 Dave Fleischer

Strike Up the Band 40 Busby Berkeley

Strikebound 83 Richard Lowenstein

Striker 85 Don Edmonds

Strikers, The 63 Mario Monicelli

Strikes and Spares 34 Felix E. Feist

Striking Back 79 William Fruet

String Beans 18 Victor Schertzinger

String of Pearls, A 11 D. W. Griffith

String of Pearls, A 16 Will Page

Stringent Prediction at the Early Hermaphroditic Stage, A 61 George Landow

Strip, The 51 Leslie Kardos

Strip Poker 68 Peter Walker

Strip, Strip, Hooray! 32 Norman Lee

Strip-Tease 65 Jacques Poitrenaud

Strip Tease Murder 61 Ernest Morris

Striped Stocking Gang, The 15 Fred W. Durrant

Stripes 81 Ivan Reitman

Stripes and Stars 29 Walter Lantz

Stripped for a Million 19 L. De la Parelle

Stripped to Kill 87 Katt Shea Ruben

Stripped to Kill II: Live Girls 89 Katt Shea Ruben

Stripper, The 62 Franklin J. Schaffner

Stripper 85 Jerome Gary

Striptease 57 Walerian Borowczyk, Jan Lenica

Striptease Lady 43 William A. Wellman

Strit og Stumme 87 Jannik Hastrup

Striving for Fortune 26 Nat Ross

Stroboscopes, Les 63 Walerian Borowczyk

Strogi Yunosha 36 Abram Room

Strohfeuer 71 Volker Schlöndorff

Stroke of Midnight, The 20 Victor Sjöström

Stroke of Phoebus Eight, The 13 Charles Brabin

Stroke the Cat's Ears 85 Josef Pinkava

Stroker Ace 83 Hal Needham

Stroll on the Sands, A 04 Alf Collins

Strollers, The 52 Emil E. Reinert

Strolling Home with Angelina 06 Arthur Gilbert

Strom, Der 42 Günther Rittau

Stromboli 49 Roberto Rossellini

Stromboli, Terra di Dio 49 Roberto Rossellini

Strømlinede Gris, Den 52 Jørgen Roos

Stromy a Lidé 62 Evald Schorm

Strong Argument, A 15 Percy Nash

Strong Boy 29 John Ford

Strong for Love 25 Lewis Seiler

Strong Is the Female 24 Kenji Mizoguchi

Strong Man, The 17 Vsevolod Meyerhold

Strong Man, The 26 Frank Capra

Strong Man's Love, A 13 Wilfred Noy

Strong Man's Weakness, A 17 A. E. Coleby

Strong Meat 86 André Klotzel
Strong Medicine 79 Richard Foreman
Strong Revenge, A 13 Mack Sennett
Strong to the Finich 34 Dave Fleischer
Strong Way, The 18 George Kelson
Strong Woman and Weak Man 68 Kaneto Shindo
Stronger, The 76 Lee Grant
Stronger Get Hooked, The 89 Jingqin Hu
Stronger Love, The 16 Frank Lloyd
Stronger Love, The 28 Erle C. Kenton
Stronger Man, The 11 Allan Dwan
Stronger Passion, The 22 Herbert Brenon
Stronger Sex, The 31 V. Gareth Gundrey
Stronger Than Death 20 Herbert Blaché, Charles Bryant
Stronger Than Desire 39 Leslie Fenton
Stronger Than Fear 50 Mark Robson, Charles Vidor
Stronger Than Love 39 Joe Stöckel
Stronger Than the Night 54 Slatan Dudow
Stronger Than the Rule 37 Jürgen von Alten
Stronger Than the Sun 77 Michael Apted
Stronger Vow, The 19 Reginald Barker
Stronger Will, The 28 Bernard F. McEveety
Strongest, The 19 Raoul Walsh
Strongest, The 29 Axel Lindholm, Alf Sjöberg
Strongest Man in the World, The 75 Vincent McEveety
Strongest One, The 29 Axel Lindholm, Alf Sjöberg
Strongheart 14 James Kirkwood
Stronghold 51 Steve Sekely
Stronghold 85 Bobby Eerhart
Strongman Ferdinand 75 Alexander Kluge
Strongroom 62 Vernon Sewell
Strop 62 Věra Chytilová
Stroszek 77 Werner Herzog
Structure of Crystals, The 69 Krzysztof Zanussi
Struggle, The 13 George Melford
Struggle, The 16 John R. Bray
Struggle, The 16 John Ince
Struggle, The 21 Otto Lederer
Struggle, The 31 D. W. Griffith
Struggle Against Cancer, The 47 Carl Theodor Dreyer
Struggle Continues, The 71 Robert Van Lieropl
Struggle Everlasting, The 18 James Kirkwood
Struggle for His Heart, The 16 Mauritz Stiller
Struggle for Love 70 Jean-Pierre Lefèbvre
Struggle for Moscow, The 85 Yuri Ozerov
Struggle in Italy 69 Jean-Luc Godard, Jean-Pierre Gorin
Struggle in the Port 55 Youssef Chahine
Struggle in the Valley 52 Youssef Chahine
Struggle on the Pier 55 Youssef Chahine
Struggling Author, A 11 Bert Haldane
Struggling Hearts 16 Alexander Korda
Struggling Hearts 20 Fritz Lang
Struktura Kryształu 69 Krzysztof Zanussi
Strul 88 Jonas Frick
Stryke and Hyde 82 Don Siegel

Stryker 83 Cirio Santiago
Stryker's Progress 54 William Beaudine
Stubborn Moke, The 08 Lewin Fitzhamon
Stubbornness of Geraldine, The 15 Gaston Mervale
Stubbs' New Servants 11 Mack Sennett
Stubby 73 Bo Widerberg
Stuck in the Mud 22 Raoul Barré, Charles Bowers
Stuck on You 83 Michael Herz, Lloyd Kaufman
Stuckey's Last Stand 80 Lawrence G. Goldfarb
Stud, The 69 Jean-Pierre Mocky
Stud, The 75 Billy White
Stud, The 78 Quentin Masters
Stud Brown 75 Al Adamson
Stud Farm, The 78 András Kovács
Student Affairs 86 Chuck Vincent
Student and the Housemaid, The 04 James A. Williamson
Student Bodies 81 Mickey Rose
Student Body, The 76 Gus Trikonis
Student Confidential 87 Richard Horian
Student Connection, The 75 Rafael Romero Marchent
Student Games at La Martinière 1895 Louis Lumière
Student Nurse 44 Francis Searle
Student Nurses, The 70 Stephanie Rothman
Student of Prague, The 13 Stellan Rye
Student of Prague, The 26 Henryk Galeen
Student of Prague, The 35 Arthur Robison
Student Prince, The 27 Ernst Lubitsch
Student Prince, The 54 Richard Thorpe
Student Prince in Old Heidelberg, The 27 Ernst Lubitsch
Student Romance 35 Otto Kanturek
Student Sein 31 Heinz Paul
Student Teachers, The 73 Jonathan Kaplan
Student Tour 34 Charles Reisner
Student von Prag, Der 13 Stellan Rye
Student von Prag, Der 26 Henryk Galeen
Student von Prag, Der 35 Arthur Robison
Students 16 Aleksander Hertz
Students' Night Out, The 14 Will P. Kellino
Student's Romance, The 35 Otto Kanturek
Studie I 52 Peter Weiss
Studie II 52 Peter Weiss
Studie III 53 Peter Weiss
Studie IV 54 Peter Weiss
Studie V 55 Peter Weiss
Studies and Sketches 65 George Landow
Studies in Clay 15 Vincent Whitman
Studies in Movement 28 Joris Ivens
Studio Girl, The 18 Émile Chautard, Charles Giblyn
Studio Murder Mystery, The 29 Frank Tuttle
Studio of Dr. Faustus, The 56 Peter Weiss
Studio Pests 29 Stephen Roberts
Studio Romance, A 32 Heinosuke Gosho
Studio Romance 37 William Clemens
Studs Lonigan 60 Irving Lerner
Study in Choreography for Camera, A 45

Maya Deren
Study in Crayon, A 13 Hy Mayer
Study in Feet, A 01 George Albert Smith
Study in Scarlet, A 14 George Pearson
Study in Scarlet, A 32 Edwin L. Marin
Study in Skarlit, A 15 Fred Evans, Joe Evans
Study in Terror, A 65 James Hill
Study No. 1 29 Oskar Fischinger
Study No. 2 30 Oskar Fischinger
Study No. 3 30 Oskar Fischinger
Study No. 4 30 Oskar Fischinger
Study No. 5 30 Oskar Fischinger
Study No. 6 30 Oskar Fischinger
Study No. 7 31 Oskar Fischinger
Study No. 8 31 Oskar Fischinger
Study No. 9 31 Oskar Fischinger
Study No. 10 32 Oskar Fischinger
Study No. 11 32 Oskar Fischinger
Study No. 12 32 Oskar Fischinger
Study No. 13 33 Oskar Fischinger
Study No. 14 33 Oskar Fischinger
Stuff, The 85 Larry Cohen
Stuff Heroes Are Made Of, The 11 D. W. Griffith
Stuff Stephanie in the Incinerator 90 Don Nardo
Stuffed Lions 21 Charles Reisner
Stuffie 40 Fred Zinnemann
Stump Run 60 Edward Dew
Stump Speech 05 Alf Collins
Stunde der Versuchung, Die 36 Paul Wegener
Stunde Null 76 Edgar Reitz
Stung 17 Leighton Budd
Stung by a Woman 23 Bertram Phillips
Stunt Man 68 Marcello Baldi
Stunt Man, The 78 Richard Rush
Stunt Pilot 39 George Waggner
Stunt Rock 78 Brian Trenchard-Smith
Stunts 77 Mark L. Lester
Stupen 87 Alexander Rekhviashvili
Stupid Bom 53 Nils Poppe
Stupid But Brave 24 Al St. John
Stupid Cupid, The 44 Frank Tashlin
Stupid Young Brother and Wise Old Brother 31 Heinosuke Gosho
Stupně Poražených 88 Julius Matula
Stupor Duck 56 Robert McKimson
Stupor Salesman, The 48 Art Davis
Sturm im Wasserglas 31 Georg Jacoby
Sturm im Wasserglas 60 Josef von Baky
Sturm Über la Sarraz 29 Sergei Eisenstein, Ivor Montagu, Hans Richter
Stürme der Leidenschaft 31 Robert Siodmak
Stürme Über dem Montblanc 30 Arnold Fanck
Stuttgart 35 Walter Ruttmann
Stuttgart: Die Großstadt Zwischen Wald und Reben 35 Walter Ruttmann
Stützen der Gesellschaft 35 Douglas Sirk
Styrene Song, The 58 Alain Resnais
Štyridsat-Štyri 57 Pal'o Bielek
Su Da Yanar 87 Ali Özgentürk
Su Gran Aventura 38 Fernando De Fuentes
Su le Mani...Cadaverei Sei in Arresto 71 Leon Klimovsky
Su Última Canción 34 John H. Auer

Suddenly, One Day *88* Mrinal Sen
Suds *20* John Francis Dillon
Sue Me *85* Steno
Sue of the South *19* W. Eugene Moore
Sue Ultime 12 Ore, Le *50* Luigi Zampa
Sued for Libel *39* Leslie Goodwins
Suéltate el Pelo *88* Manuel Summers
Sueño, El *75* Pedro Almodóvar
Sueño de Amor *36* José Bohr
Sueño de Juan Bassín, El *53* Tomás Gutiérrez Alea
Sueño de Noche de Verano *84* Celestino Coronado
Sueño del Pongo, El *70* Santiago Álvarez
Sueños y Realidades *62* Jorge Sanjinés
Suez *38* Allan Dwan
Suez Canal, The *62* Leonid Varmalov
Suffer Mammon *87* Manuel Summers
Sufferin' Cats *43* Joseph Barbera, William Hanna
Suffering Ones, The *75* Yılmaz Güney, Atıf Yılmaz
Sufficiency *19* Vernon Stallings
Suffragette, Die *13* Urban Gad
Suffragette, The *13* William Duncan
Suffragette, The *13* Mauritz Stiller
Suffragette Battle of Nuttyville, The *14* Christy Cabanne
Suffragette in Spite of Himself, A *12* Ashley Miller
Suffragette Minstrels, The *13* Christy Cabanne
Suffragetten, Den *13* Mauritz Stiller
Suffragettes and the Hobble Skirt, The *10* Theo Bouwmeester
Suffragettes' Downfall, or Who Said "Rats"?, The *11* Fred Rains
Suffragettes in the Bud *13* Percy Stow
Sufre Mamón *87* Manuel Summers
Sugar *43* Bjarne Henning-Jensen
Sugar and Spice *15* Ernst Lubitsch, F. Matray
Sugar and Spies *66* Robert McKimson
Sugar Cane Alley *83* Euzhan Palcy
Sugar Colt *66* Franco Giraldi
Sugar Cookies *77* Theodore Gershuny
Sugar Cottage *80* Karel Kachyňa
Sugar Daddy *39* Fernando De Fuentes
Sugar Hill *74* Paul Maslansky
Sugar Manufacture *14* King Vidor
Sugar Plum Papa *30* Mack Sennett
Sugarbaby *84* Percy Adlon
Sugarfoot *51* Edwin L. Marin
Sugarland Express, The *73* Steven Spielberg
Sugata Sanshiro *43* Akira Kurosawa
Sugata Sanshiro *65* Seiichiro Uchikawa
Sugata Sanshiro II *45* Akira Kurosawa
Sugata Sanshiro Zoku *45* Akira Kurosawa
Suicide, The *50* Hasse Ekman
Suicide *65* Andy Warhol
Suicide, The *84* Vojtěch Jasný
Suicide Attack *51* Irving Lerner
Suicide Battalion *58* Edward L. Cahn
Suicide Club, The *09* D. W. Griffith
Suicide Club, The *14* Maurice Elvey
Suicide Club, The *20* Richard Oswald
Suicide Club, The *36* J. Walter Ruben
Suicide Club, The *87* James Bruce
Suicide Commando *69* Camillo Bazzoni

Suicide Fleet *31* Albert S. Rogell
Suicide Legion *37* Norman Walker
Suicide Mission *56* Michael Forlong
Suicide Run *69* Robert Aldrich
Suicide Squadron *41* Brian Desmond Hurst
Suicide Troops of the Watch Tower, The *42* Tadashi Imai
Suit That Didn't Suit, The *12* Percy Stow
Suita Polska *62* Jan Łomnicki
Suited to a T. *31* Dave Fleischer
Suitor, The *20* Larry Semon, Norman Taurog
Suitor, The *62* Pierre Etaix
Suivez Cet Homme! *53* Georges Lampin
Suivez Mon Regard *86* Jean Curtelin
Suizo — Un Amour en Espagne, El *86* Richard Dindo
Sujata *59* Bimal Roy
Sukeban Deka — Kazama Sanshimai no Gyakushū *88* Hideo Tanaka
Suki Nareba Koso *28* Heinosuke Gosho
Sukker *42* Bjarne Henning-Jensen
Suleiman the Conqueror *61* Vatroslav Mimica, Mario Tota
Sulfatara *55* Vittorio De Seta
Sulla Cupola di San Pietro *45* Alessandro Blasetti
Sulla Via di Damasco *47* Luciano Emmer, Enrico Gras
Sulle Rome di Verdi *48* Luciano Emmer, Enrico Gras
Sullivans, The *44* Lloyd Bacon
Sullivan's Empire *67* Thomas Carr, Harvey Hart
Sullivan's Pavilion *87* Fred G. Sullivan
Sullivan's Travels *41* Preston Sturges
Sult *66* Henning Carlsen
Sultana of the Desert, A *15* Tom Santschi
Sultane de l'Amour, La *19* Charles Burguet, René Le Somptier
Sultans, Les *65* Jean Delannoy
Sultan's Daughter, The *43* Arthur Dreifuss
Sultan's Wife, The *17* Clarence Badger
Sumka Dipkuryera *27* Alexander Dovzhenko
Summer *29* Ubbe Iwerks
Summer *85* Eric Rohmer
Summer *87* Philip Groning
Summer Affair, A *77* Claude Berri
Summer and Sinners *60* Arne Mattsson
Summer and Smoke *61* Peter Glenville
Summer at Grandpa's, A *84* Hsiao-hsien Hou
Summer Bachelors *26* Allan Dwan
Summer Battle of Osaka, The *37* Teinosuke Kinugasa
Summer Camp *79* Chuck Vincent
Summer Camp Nightmare *87* Bert L. Dragin
Summer Caricatures *13* Hy Mayer
Summer Carnival *66* Jan Němec
Summer City *76* Christopher Fraser
Summer Clouds *57* Zoltán Fábri
Summer Clouds *58* Mikio Naruse
Summer Day, A *60* Jan Troell
Summer Fires *65* Tony Richardson
Summer Flight *63* Daniel Petrie

Summer Games *85* Bruno Cortini
Summer Girl, The *16* Edwin August
Summer Girls, The *18* Edward F. Cline
Summer Heat *82* Jack Starrett
Summer Heat *87* Michie Gleason
Summer Holiday *46* Rouben Mamoulian
Summer Holiday *62* Herbert Ross, Peter Yates
Summer Holidays *85* Nini Grassia
Summer Idyll, A *10* D. W. Griffith
Summer in the City *68* Christian Blackwood
Summer in the City *70* Wim Wenders
Summer in the City (Dedicated to the Kinks) *70* Wim Wenders
Summer in the Country, The *76* Otar Ioseliani
Summer Interlude *49* Arne Sucksdorff
Summer Interlude *50* Ingmar Bergman
Summer Is Nearly Over, The *87* Bruno Cortini
Summer Light *42* Jean Grémillon
Summer Lightning *33* Maclean Rogers
Summer Lightning *48* F. Hugh Herbert
Summer Lightning *71* Volker Schlöndorff
Summer Love *57* Charles Haas
Summer Lovers *82* Randal Kleiser
Summer Madness *55* David Lean
Summer Magic *62* James Neilson
Summer Maneuvers *55* René Clair
Summer Night Is Sweet, The *61* Arne Mattsson
Summer Night with a Grecian Profile, Almond Eyes and the Scent of Basil *86* Lina Wertmuller
Summer Night with Greek Profile, Almond Eyes and Scent of Basil *86* Lina Wertmuller
Summer Nights *87* Gunnel Lindblom
Summer of Fear *78* Wes Craven
Summer of '42 *71* Robert Mulligan
Summer of Innocence *78* John Milius
Summer of Miss Forbes, The *88* Jaime Humberto Hermosillo
Summer of Secrets *76* Jim Sharman
Summer of '64 *65* William Witney
Summer of the Samurai *86* Hans-Christof Blumenberg
Summer of the Seventeenth Doll *59* Leslie Norman
Summer on a Soft Slope *87* Gérard Krawczyk
Summer on the Hill *67* Péter Bacsó
Summer Paradise *77* Gunnel Lindblom
Summer Place, A *59* Delmer Daves
Summer Place Is Wanted, A *57* Hasse Ekman
Summer Rain, A *60* András Kovács
Summer Rain, A *77* Carlos Diegués
Summer Rental *85* Carl Reiner
Summer Run *74* Leon Capetanos
Summer Scenes *21* Hy Mayer
Summer School *87* Carl Reiner
Summer School Teachers *75* Barbara Peeters
Summer Showers *77* Carlos Diegués
Summer Sister *72* Nagisa Oshima
Summer Skin *61* Leopoldo Torre-Nilsson
Summer Soldiers *71* Hiroshi Teshigahara
Summer Stock *50* Charles Walters

Sunset Serenade *42* Joseph Kane
Sunset Sprague *20* Paul Cazeneuve, Thomas Heffron
Sunset Strip *85* William Webb
Sunset Strip Case, The *38* Louis Gasnier
Sunset Trail, The *17* George Melford
Sunset Trail, The *24* Whyndham Gittens
Sunset Trail, The *32* B. Reeves Eason
Sunset Trail *38* Lesley Selander
Sunshine *16* Edward F. Cline
Sunshine *73* Joseph Sargent
Sunshine After Storm *08* James A. Williamson
Sunshine Ahead *36* Wallace Orton
Sunshine Alley *17* John W. Noble
Sunshine and Clouds of Paradise Alley, The *15* Frank Stather
Sunshine and Gold *17* Henry King
Sunshine and Shadows *14* Van Dyke Brooke
Sunshine Boys, The *75* Herbert Ross
Sunshine Dad *16* Edward Dillon
Sunshine Follows Rain *46* Gustaf Edgren
Sunshine Girl, The *63* Yoji Yamada
Sunshine Harbor *22* Edward L. Hemmer
Sunshine in Attica *52* John Argyle
Sunshine Molly *15* Phillips Smalley, Lois Weber
Sunshine Nan *18* Charles Giblyn
Sunshine of Paradise Alley *26* Jack Nelson
Sunshine Part II *75* Daniel Haller
Sunshine Run *79* Chris Robinson
Sunshine Sue *10* D. W. Griffith
Sunshine Susie *31* Victor Saville
Sunshine Through the Dark *11* D. W. Griffith
Sunshine Trail, The *23* James W. Horne
Sunstroke *84* Yaky Yosha
Sunstruck *72* James Gilbert
Sunus Palaidunas *86* Marijonas Giedrys
Suo Destino, Il *38* Enrico Guazzoni
Suo Modo di Fari, Il *68* Franco Brusati
Suo Nome Era Pot...Ma...lo Chiamavano Allegria, Il *71* Dennis Ford
Suo Nome Gridava Vendetta, Il *68* Mario Caiano
Suola Romana, La *60* Francesco Maselli
Suona Player, The *86* Daw-ming Lee
Suor Letizia *56* Mario Camerini
Suor Omicidi *78* Giulio Berruti
Suor Teresa *16* Ugo Falena
Super, El *79* León Ichaso, Orlando Jiménez-Leal
Super Citizen *85* Jen Wan
Super Cool *69* Ray Dennis Steckler
Super Cops, The *73* Gordon Parks
Super Dick *70* John G. Avildsen
Super Dragon *66* Giorgio Ferroni
Super Fight, The *69* Murray Voroner
Super Fool *81* Po-chih Leong
Super Fuzz *81* Sergio Corbucci
Super-Imposition *65* Stan Vanderbeek
Super Inframan, The *75* Hua-Shan
Super-Jocks, The *80* Emil Nofal, Ray Sergeant
Super Rabbit *43* Chuck Jones
Super Seal *76* Michael Dugan
Super Secret Service, The *53* Charles W. Green
Super-Sex, The *22* Lambert Hillyer

Super Shylock, A *16* Forest Holger-Madsen
Super Sleuth *37* Ben Stoloff
Super Snooper, The *52* Robert McKimson
Super Speed *25* Albert S. Rogell
Super Spook *75* Anthony Major
Super Stupid *34* Leigh Jason
Superargo *68* Paolo Bianchini
Superargo Contra Diabolicus: Superargo el Hombre Enmascarado *66* Nick Nostro
Superargo Contro Diabolikus *66* Nick Nostro
Superargo e i Giganti Senza Volto *68* Paolo Bianchini
Superargo el Gigante *68* Paolo Bianchini
Superargo el Hombre Enmascarado *66* Nick Nostro
Superargo the Giant *68* Paolo Bianchini
Superargo vs. Diabolicus *66* Nick Nostro
Superbeasts *72* George Schenck
Superbitch *73* Massimo Dallamano
Superbug, Super Agent *76* Rudolf Zehetgruber
Superbug, the Wild One *77* David Mark
Superchick *73* Ed Forsyth
Supercock *75* Gus Trikonis
Supercross *86* Fritz Kiersch
Superdad *72* Vincent McEveety
Superdiabolici, I *65* Steno
Superdude *73* Henry Hathaway
Superfantagenio *87* Bruno Corbucci
Superfantozzi *87* Neri Parenti
Superflaco, El *67* Miguel Delgado
Superflaco, Il *67* Miguel Delgado
Superfluous People *26* Alexander Rasumny
Superfly *72* Gordon Parks, Jr.
Superfly T.N.T. *73* Ron O'Neal
Supergiant *56* Teruo Ishii
Supergiant Against the Satellites *58* Teruo Ishii
Supergiant II *57* Koreyoshi Akasaka, Teruo Ishii, Akira Mitsuwa
Supergirl *83* Jeannot Szwarc
Supergrass, The *85* Peter Richardson
Superhuman *79* Riccardo Freda
Superintendent Is a Good Sort, The *34* Jacques Becker, Pierre Prévert
Superintendent Sansho, The *54* Kenji Mizoguchi
Superintendents *18* Raoul Barré, Charles Bowers
Superman *41* Dave Fleischer
Superman *48* Spencer G. Bennet, Thomas Carr
Superman *77* Richard Donner
Superman II *80* Richard Donner, Richard Lester
Superman III *83* Richard Lester
Superman IV: The Quest for Peace *87* Sidney J. Furie
Superman and the Mole Men *51* Lee Sholem
Superman and the Strange People *51* Lee Sholem
Superman in Billion Dollar Limited *42* Dave Fleischer
Superman in Electric Earthquake *42* Dave Fleischer
Superman in Terror on the Midway *42* Dave Fleischer

Superman in The Arctic Giant *42* Dave Fleischer
Superman in The Bulleteers *42* Dave Fleischer
Superman in The Magnetic Telescope *42* Dave Fleischer
Superman in The Mechanical Monsters *41* Dave Fleischer
Superman in Volcano *42* Dave Fleischer
Superman—The Movie *77* Richard Donner
Supernatural *33* Victor Halperin
Supernatural *80* Eugenio Martin
Supernaturals, The *85* Armand Mastroianni
Supersabio, El *48* Miguel Delgado
Supersnooper *81* Sergio Corbucci
Supersonic Man *79* Juan Piquer Simon
Supersonic Saucer *56* S. G. Ferguson
Superspeed *35* Lambert Hillyer
Superstars in Film Concert *71* Peter Clifton
Superstition *17* Allan Dwan
Superstition *85* James Roberson
Superstition of the Black Cat, The *34* Ray Nazarro
Superstition of the Rabbit's Foot, The *35* Ray Nazarro
Superstition of Three on a Match, The *34* Ray Nazarro
Superstition of Walking Under a Ladder, The *34* Ray Nazarro
Superstitious Man, The *83* Gregory Dark
Superstizione *48* Michelangelo Antonioni
Supervan *77* Lamar Card
Supervixens *74* Russ Meyer
Superzan and the Space Boy *72* Rafael Lanuza
Superzan y el Niño del Espacio *72* Rafael Lanuza
Supplication *67* Tenghiz Abuladze
Supplice de Tantale, Le *01* Ferdinand Zecca
Support Your Local Gunfighter *70* Burt Kennedy
Support Your Local Sheriff! *68* Burt Kennedy
Suppose They Gave a War and Nobody Came? *70* Hy Averback
Suppressed Duck *65* Robert McKimson
Suprema Ley *38* R. Portas
Suprême Épopée, La *19* Henri Desfontaines
Supreme Kid, The *76* Peter Bryant
Supreme Law *38* R. Portas
Supreme Passion, The *21* Samuel Bradley
Supreme Sacrifice *13* Alfred Machin
Supreme Sacrifice, The *16* Lionel Belmore, Harley Knoles
Supreme Sacrifice *38* Chano Urueta
Supreme Secret, The *57* Norman Walker
Supreme Temptation, The *16* Harry Davenport
Supreme Test, The *15* Edward J. LeSaint
Supreme Test, The *23* Walter P. MacNamara
Supremo Sacrificio *38* Chano Urueta
Sur, El *83* Victor Erice
Sur *87* Fernando Solanas
Sur la Barricade *07* Alice Guy-Blaché

Sur la Route de Salina 70 Georges Lautner
Sur le Pont d'Avignon 56 Georges Franju
Sur les Bords de la Caméra 32 Henri Storck
Sur les Routes de l'Été 36 Henri Storck
Sur les Toits 1897 Georges Méliès
Sur un Air de Charleston 26 Jean Renoir
Suraag 82 Jag Mohan Mundhra
Surabaya Conspiracy 75 Roy Davis
Surcos 51 José Antonio Nieves Conde
Surcouf—Le Dernier Corsaire 67 Sergio Bergonzelli, Roy Rowland
Surcouf—Le Tigre des Sept Mers 67 Sergio Bergonzelli, Roy Rowland
Surcouf—L'Eroe dei Sette Mari 67 Sergio Bergonzelli, Roy Rowland
Sure Cure, The 20 William A. Seiter
Sure Cure 27 Stephen Roberts
Sure Cure for Indigestion 02 Georges Méliès
Sure Death 85 Hokyu Sadanaga
Sure Death IV 87 Kinji Fukasaku
Sure Fire 21 John Ford
Sure Fire 90 Jon Jost
Sure Fire Flint 22 Del Henderson
Sure Thing, The 85 Rob Reiner
Surely You'll Insure 15 Dave Aylott
Surf, The 35 Ivar Johansson
Surf 77 Don Chaffey
Surf and Seaweed 31 Ralph Steiner
Surf Girl, The 16 Mack Sennett
Surf Nazis Must Die 87 Peter George
Surf Party 63 Maury Dexter
Surf Terror 65 Jon Hall
Surf II 83 Randall Badat
Surf II—The End of the Trilogy 83 Randall Badat
Surface Tension 68 Hollis Frampton
Surfacemen 57 István Gaál
Surfacing 78 Claude Jutra
Surfari 67 Milton Blair
Surfer, The 87 Frank Shields
Surfing Movie 68 Andy Warhol
Surftide 77 62 R. Lee Frost
Surftide 777 62 R. Lee Frost
Surgeon's Child, The 12 Harry Thurston Harris
Surgeon's Knife, The 57 Gordon Parry
Surging Seas 24 James Chapin
Suri Lanka no Ai to Wakare 76 Keisuke Kinoshita
Surmenés, Les 58 Jacques Doniol-Valcroze
Surogat 61 Dušan Vukotić
Surprise 23 Dave Fleischer
Surprise Broadcast 41 Andrew Buchanan
Surprise du Chef, La 76 Pascal Thomas
Surprise Package 60 Stanley Donen
Surprise Packet, The 13 Charles C. Calvert
Surprise Packet, A 14 August Blom
Surprise Party 82 Roger Vadim
Surprises de l'Affichage, Les 04 Alice Guy-Blaché
Surprises of an Empty Hotel, The 16 Theodore Marston
Surprising a Picket 1899 Robert Ashe
Surprising Encounter, A 13 Percy Stow
Surprising Hunt, The 60 Boris Dolin
Surrender 27 Edward Sloman
Surrender 31 William K. Howard
Surrender 50 Allan Dwan

Surrender 87 Jerry Belson
Surrender—Hell! 59 John Barnwell
Surrender of Tournavos, The 1897 Georges Méliès
Surrey Garden, A 1896 Birt Acres
Surrogate, The 84 Don Carmody
Surrogate Woman 86 Kwon-taek Im
Surrounded 60 Arne Skouen
Surrounded by Women 37 George B. Seitz
Surrounded House, The 22 Victor Sjöström
Sürü 78 Zeki Ökten
Survival 30 Manfred Noa
Survival 62 Ray Milland
Survival 65 Tad Danielewski
Survival 76 Michael Campus
Survival Game 87 Herb Freed
Survival 1967 67 Jules Dassin
Survival Quest 86 Don Coscarelli
Survival Run 74 Jack Smight
Survival Run 79 Larry Spiegel
Survival '67 67 Jules Dassin
Survival Zone 81 Percival Rubens
Survivalist, The 86 Sig Shore
Survivants de la Préhistoire 55 Pierre-Dominique Gaisseau
Survive! 76 René Cardona, Jr.
Surviving in New York 90 Rosa von Praunheim
Surviving Shinsengumi, The 32 Teinosuke Kinugasa
Survivor, The 80 David Hemmings
Survivor 88 Michael Shackleton
Survivors, The 79 Tomás Gutiérrez Alea
Survivors, The 83 Michael Ritchie
Surya 88 Baraguru Ramachandrappa
Susan and God 39 George Cukor
Susan Dances 79 Edgar Reitz
Susan Lenox 31 Robert Z. Leonard
Susan Lenox (Her Fall and Rise) 31 Robert Z. Leonard
Susan Rocks the Boat 16 Paul Powell
Susan Slade 61 Delmer Daves
Susan Slept Here 54 Frank Tashlin
Susan Starr 62 Richard Leacock, D. A. Pennebaker
Susana 50 Luis Buñuel
Susana Tiene un Secreto 35 Benito Perojo
Susanna 42 Frank McDonald
Susanna in the Bath 37 Jürgen von Alten
Susanna Pass 49 William Witney
Susanna Tutta Panna 57 Steno
Susannah of the Mounties 39 William A. Seiter
Susanne im Bade 37 Jürgen von Alten
Susanne Tanzt 79 Edgar Reitz
Susan's Gentleman 17 Edwin Stevens
Susan's Revenge 10 Fred Rains
Susceptible, The 52 George Tzavellas
Susie 45 Arne Mattsson
Susie Snowflake 16 James Kirkwood
Susie Steps Out 46 Reginald LeBorg
Susman 86 Shyam Benegal
Suspect, The 16 Sidney Rankin Drew
Suspect, The 44 Robert Siodmak
Suspect 60 John Boulting, Roy Boulting
Suspect 87 Peter Yates
Suspected 50 Ray Nazarro
Suspected Alibi 56 Alfred Shaughnessy

Suspected, or The Mysterious Lodger 09 Jack Smith
Suspected Person 42 Lawrence Huntington
Suspects, Les 57 Jean Dréville
Suspended 87 Waldemar Krzystek
Suspended Alibi 56 Alfred Shaughnessy
Suspended Forth 69 James Horwitz
Suspended Sentence 13 Allan Dwan
Suspended Vocation, The 77 Raúl Ruiz
Suspense 18 Frank Reicher
Suspense 30 Walter Summers
Suspense 46 Frank Tuttle
Suspense 61 Jack Clayton
Suspense 76 Lamberto Bava, Mario Bava
Suspicion 18 John M. Stahl
Suspicion 41 Alfred Hitchcock
Suspicious Mr. Brown 13 Bert Haldane
Suspicious Wives 21 John M. Stahl
Suspiria 76 Dario Argento
Sussi 88 Gonzalo Justiniano
Sussurri nel Buio 76 Marcello Aliprandi
Sussurro nel Buio, Un 76 Marcello Aliprandi
Susume Dokuritsuki 43 Teinosuke Kinugasa
Susuz Yaz 64 David Durston, Erkan Metin, Ismail Metin
Süt a Nap 39 László Kalmár
Sutradhar 87 Chandrakant Joshi
Sutrapat 88 Mridul Gupta
Sutter's Gold 36 James Cruze
Sutyi a Szerencsegyerek 38 Béla Balázs
Sutyi the Lucky Child 38 Béla Balázs
Suuri Illusioni 86 Tuija-Maija Niskanen
Suvorov 40 Mikhail Doller, Vsevolod I. Pudovkin
Suwanee River 25 Dave Fleischer
Suzanna 22 F. Richard Jones
Suzanne 16 René Hervil, Louis Mercanton
Suzanne 32 Léo Joannon, Raymond Rouleau
Suzanne 74 Michael Barry
Suzanne 80 Robin Spry
Suzanne au Bain 30 Henri Storck
Suzanne et les Brigands 48 Yves Ciampi
Suzanne Simonin, la Religieuse de Denis Diderot 65 Jacques Rivette
Suzanne Simonin, la Religieuse de Diderot 65 Jacques Rivette
Suzanne's Profession 63 Eric Rohmer
Suzy 36 George Fitzmaurice
Suzy Saxophone 29 Karel Lamač
Švadlenka 36 Martin Frič
Sværta Horisonter 36 Pál Fejős
Svält 66 Henning Carlsen
Svänger på Slottet, Det 59 Alf Kjellin
Svart Gryning 87 Carlos Lemos
Svarta Maskerna, De 12 Mauritz Stiller
Svarta Palmkronor 67 Lars-Magnus Lindgren
Svarta Rosor 32 Gustaf Molander
Svegliati e Uccidi 66 Carlo Lizzani
Švejk v Civilu 27 Gustav Machatý
Svengali 31 Archie Mayo
Svengali 54 Noel Langley
Svengarlic 31 Manny Gould, Ben Harrison
Svesas Kaislibas 86 Ianas Streitch
Svět Alfonse Muchy 80 Jaromil Jireš
Svet na Kozarju 52 France Štiglic

Svet Nad Rossiei 47 Sergei Yutkevich
Svět Patří Nám 37 Martin Frič
Světlo Proniká Tmou 31 Otakar Vávra
Svetlyi Put 40 Grigori Alexandrov
Svev Dalekoi Zvesdy 65 Ivan Pyriev
Svidanie na Mlechnom Puti 87 Ianas Streitch
Svindlande Affärer 85 Janne Carlsson, Peter Schildt
Svinyarka i Pastukh 41 Ivan Pyriev
Sviračut 68 Mende Brown
Svitato, Lo 56 Carlo Lizzani
Svobodnoe Padenie 88 Mikhail Tumanishvili
Svoi Sredi Chuzhikh, Chuzhoi Sredi Svoikh 74 Nikita Mikhalkov
Swab Your Choppers 47 Stephen Bosustow
Swain 50 Gregory Markopoulos
Swajara Doran 30 Pendharkar Babu Rao
Swallow, The 38 Miguel Torres Contreras
Swallow Storm, The 86 Attila Candimir
Swallow the Leader 49 Robert McKimson
Swallows and Amazons 74 Claude Whatham
Swamp, The 21 Colin Campbell
Swamp Country 66 Robert Patrick
Swamp Diamonds 55 Roger Corman
Swamp Fire 46 William Pine
Swamp Lady 41 Elmer Clifton
Swamp of the Lost Monsters, The 65 Rafael Baledón
Swamp Thing 82 Wes Craven
Swamp Water 41 Jean Renoir
Swamp Woman 41 Elmer Clifton
Swamp Woman 55 Roger Corman
Swamp Women 55 Roger Corman
Swan, The 25 Dmitri Buchowetzki
Swan, The 56 Charles Vidor
Swan Lake 57 Serge Tulubyeva
Swan Lake 67 Truck Branss
Swan Lake 80 Norman Morrice
Swan Song 86 Zeming Zhang
Swanee River 31 Raymond Cannon
Swanee River 39 Sidney Lanfield
Swanker and the Witch's Curse 14 Edwin J. Collins
Swanker Meets His Girl 14 Edwin J. Collins
Swann in Love 83 Volker Schlöndorff
Swap, The 69 John Broderick, John Shade
Swap 77 Gyula Gazdag
Swap and How They Make It, The 65 Joe Sarno
Swap Meet 79 Brice Mack
Swappers, The 70 Derek Ford
Swarm, The 78 Irwin Allen
Swash Buckled 62 Joseph Barbera, William Hanna
Swashbuckler 76 James Goldstone
Swastika 74 Philippe Mora
Swastika Savages 70 Al Adamson
Swat the Fly 18 Gregory La Cava
Swat the Fly 35 Dave Fleischer
Swat the Spy 18 Arvid E. Gillstrom
Sweat 29 Tomu Uchida
Sweater, The 15 Frank Wilson
Sweater Girl 42 William Clemens
Sweater Girls 78 Don Jones
Sweden 60 Willard Van Dyke

Swedenhielms 35 Gustaf Molander
Swedish Fly Girls 71 Jack O'Connell
Swedish Mistress, The 62 Vilgot Sjöman
Swedish Tiger, A 48 Gustaf Edgren
Swedish Wedding Night 64 Åke Falck
Sweeney! 76 David Wickes
Sweeney Todd 26 George Dewhurst
Sweeney Todd 28 Walter West
Sweeney Todd 35 George King
Sweeney Todd, the Demon Barber of Fleet Street 35 George King
Sweeney 2 78 Tom Clegg
Sweep, The 04 Alf Collins
Sweep 20 Will P. Kellino
Sweep, The 22 Bernard Dudley
Sweep! Sweep! Sweep! 13 Percy Stow
Sweepings 33 John Cromwell
Sweepstake Annie 35 William Nigh
Sweepstake Racketeers 39 Howard Bretherton
Sweepstakes 31 Albert S. Rogell
Sweepstakes Winner 39 William McGann
Sweet Absence 87 Claudio Sestieri
Sweet Adeline 26 Dave Fleischer
Sweet Adeline 26 Jerome Storm
Sweet Adeline 29 Frank Moser
Sweet Adeline 34 Mervyn LeRoy
Sweet Aloes 36 Archie Mayo
Sweet Alyssum 15 Colin Campbell
Sweet and Low Down 44 Archie Mayo
Sweet and Sexy 70 Anthony Sloman
Sweet and Sour 63 Jacques Baratier
Sweet and the Bitter, The 62 James Clavell
Sweet and Twenty 09 D. W. Griffith
Sweet and Twenty 19 Sidney Morgan
Sweet Beat 59 Ronnie Albert
Sweet Bird of Youth 61 Richard Brooks
Sweet Body, The 67 Romolo Guerrieri
Sweet Body of Deborah, The 67 Romolo Guerrieri
Sweet Charity 68 Bob Fosse
Sweet Cookie 33 George Marshall
Sweet Country 86 Michael Cacoyannis
Sweet Creek County War, The 79 J. Frank James
Sweet Daddies 26 Alfred Santell
Sweet Daddy 24 Leo McCarey
Sweet Deception 71 Édouard Molinaro
Sweet Devil 37 René Guissart
Sweet Dirty Tony 80 Chuck Workman
Sweet Dreamers 81 Tom Cowan
Sweet Dreams 68 John G. Avildsen
Sweet Dreams 85 Karel Reisz
Sweet Ecstasy 62 Max Pecas
Sweet Genevieve 47 Arthur Dreifuss
Sweet Ginger Brown 84 Garry Marshall
Sweet Heart's Dance 88 Robert Greenwald
Sweet Hours 81 Carlos Saura
Sweet Hunters 69 Ruy Guerra
Sweet Inniscarra 34 Emmett Moore
Sweet Jenny Lee 32 Dave Fleischer
Sweet Jesus, Preacher Man 73 Henning Schellerup
Sweet Kill 70 Curtis Hanson
Sweet Kitty Bellairs 16 James Young
Sweet Kitty Bellairs 30 Alfred E. Green
Sweet Lavender 15 Cecil M. Hepworth
Sweet Lavender 20 Paul Powell
Sweet Liberty 08 Alf Collins

Sweet Liberty 86 Alan Alda
Sweet Lies 86 Nathalie Delon
Sweet Life, The 59 Federico Fellini
Sweet Light in a Dark Room 59 Jiří Weiss
Sweet Light in the Dark Window 59 Jiří Weiss
Sweet Lorraine 86 Steve Gomer
Sweet Love, Bitter 67 Herbert Danska
Sweet Mama 30 Edward F. Cline
Sweet Memories 11 Thomas Ince
Sweet Movie 74 Dušan Makavejev
Sweet Music 34 Alfred E. Green
Sweet November 67 Robert Ellis Miller
Sweet Papa 19 Raoul Barré, Charles Bowers
Sweet Pickle, A 19 Gregory La Cava
Sweet Pickle, A 25 Edward F. Cline
Sweet Revenge 09 D. W. Griffith
Sweet Revenge 38 János Vaszary
Sweet Revenge 76 Jerry Schatzberg
Sweet Revenge 86 Mark S. Sobel
Sweet Ride, The 68 Harvey Hart
Sweet Rosie O'Grady 26 Frank R. Strayer
Sweet Rosie O'Grady 43 Irving Cummings
Sweet Savior 71 Bob Roberts
Sweet Secret 71 Kozaburo Yoshimura
Sweet Sioux 37 Friz Freleng
Sweet Sixteen 28 Scott Pembroke
Sweet Sixteen 46 Arthur Dreifuss
Sweet Sixteen 54 Marc Allégret
Sweet 16 81 Jim Sotos
Sweet Skin 65 Jacques Poitrenaud
Sweet Smell of Love 66 Edward Dein
Sweet Smell of Success 57 Alexander Mackendrick
Sweet Soul Music 77 Peter Clifton
Sweet Sound of Death 65 Javier Seto
Sweet Sounds 76 James Ivory
Sweet Stepmother 35 Béla Balázs
Sweet Substitute 64 Laurence L. Kent
Sweet Suffragettes 06 Tom Green
Sweet Sugar 72 Michel Levesque
Sweet Surrender 35 Monte Brice
Sweet Suzy! 73 Russ Meyer
Sweet Sweat 64 Shiro Toyoda
Sweet Sweetback's Baadasssss Song 71 Melvin Van Peebles
Sweet Talker 90 Michael Jenkins
Sweet Toronto 70 D. A. Pennebaker
Sweet Trash 70 John Hayes
Sweet Violence 62 Max Pecas
Sweet Violent Tony 80 Chuck Workman
Sweet Virgin 73 James Kenelm Clarke
Sweet William 80 Claude Whatham
Sweet Worries 86 Juraj Herz
Sweeter Song, A 76 Allan Eastman
Sweetheart, The 51 Kon Ichikawa
Sweetheart Days 21 Malcolm St. Clair
Sweetheart of Sigma Chi, The 33 Edwin L. Marin
Sweetheart of Sigma Chi 46 Jack Bernhard
Sweetheart of the Campus 41 Edward Dmytryk
Sweetheart of the Doomed 17 Reginald Barker
Sweetheart of the Fleet 42 Charles Barton
Sweetheart of the Gods 60 Gottfried Reinhardt
Sweetheart of the Navy 37 Duncan Mansfield

Sweetheart Serenade 43 Jean Negulesco
Sweethearts 19 Rex Wilson
Sweethearts 38 W. S. Van Dyke
Sweethearts and Wives 30 Clarence Badger
Sweethearts Forever 45 Frank Richardson
Sweethearts of the U.S.A. 44 Lewis D. Collins
Sweethearts on Parade 30 Marshall Neilan
Sweethearts on Parade 44 Lewis D. Collins
Sweethearts on Parade 53 Allan Dwan
Sweetie 29 Frank Tuttle
Sweetie 89 Jane Campion
Sweets from a Stranger 87 Franco Ferrini
Sweetwater 88 Lasse Glom
Swell Guy 46 Frank Tuttle
Swell-Head, The 27 Ralph Graves
Swell-Head 35 Ben Stoloff
Swelled Head, A 01 Georges Méliès
Swellhead, The 30 James Flood
Swept Away 74 Lina Wertmuller
Swept Away...by a Strange Destiny in a Blue August Sea 74 Lina Wertmuller
Swept Away...by a Strange Destiny on an Azure August Sea 74 Lina Wertmuller
Swept Away...by an Unusual Destiny in the Blue Sea of August 74 Lina Wertmuller
Swift Justice 40 Sam Newfield
Swift Shadow, The 27 Jerome Storm
Swift Vengeance 39 David Howard
Swift Water 52 Tony Thompson
Swifty 35 Alvin J. Neitz
Swim, Girl, Swim 27 Clarence Badger
Swim or Sink 32 Dave Fleischer
Swim Princess, The 28 Frank Capra
Swim Team 79 James Polakoff
Swimmer, The 67 Frank Perry, Sydney Pollack
Swimmer, The 81 Irakli Kvirikadze
Swimming Pool, The 68 Jacques Deray
Swimming to Cambodia 87 Jonathan Demme
Swindle, The 55 Federico Fellini
Swindler, The 19 Maurice Elvey
Swindler Meets Swindler 67 Kajiro Yamamoto
Swindlers, The 46 Charles Barton
Swindlers, The 55 Federico Fellini
Swineherd and Shepherd 41 Ivan Pyriev
Swing 36 Oscar Micheaux
Swing 38 R. A. Hopwood
Swing, The 83 Percy Adlon
Swing and Sway 44 Lew Landers
Swing Banditry 36 Reginald LeBorg
Swing Cleaning 41 Dave Fleischer
Swing, Cowboy, Swing 44 Elmer Clifton
Swing Ding Amigo 66 Robert McKimson
Swing Fever 37 Jean Yarbrough
Swing Fever 43 Tim Whelan
Swing Frolic 43 Reginald LeBorg
Swing High 30 Joseph Santley
Swing High 43 Edgar G. Ulmer
Swing High, Swing Low 37 Mitchell Leisen
Swing Hostess 44 Sam Newfield
Swing in the Saddle 44 Lew Landers
Swing It! 36 Leslie Goodwins
Swing It, Buddy 37 Marshall Neilan
Swing It Miss! 56 Stig Olin

Swing It, Professor 37 Marshall Neilan
Swing It, Sailor 37 Raymond Cannon
Swing It Soldier 41 Harold Young
Swing Out, Sister 45 Edward Lilley
Swing Out the Blues 43 Malcolm St. Clair
Swing Parade of 1946 46 Phil Karlson
Swing School 38 Dave Fleischer
Swing Shift 83 Jonathan Demme
Swing Shift Cinderella 45 Tex Avery
Swing Shift Maisie 43 Norman Z. McLeod
Swing, Sister, Swing 38 Joseph Santley
Swing Social 40 Joseph Barbera, William Hanna
Swing Song from "Véronique" 06 Arthur Gilbert
Swing, Teacher, Swing 38 Raoul Walsh
Swing Tease 40 Denis Kavanagh
Swing That Cheer 38 Harold Schuster
Swing: The Story of Mandy 36 Oscar Micheaux
Swing the Western Way 47 Derwin Abrahams
Swing Time 36 George Stevens
Swing Vacation 39 Jean Yarbrough
Swing, You Sinners 30 Dave Fleischer
Swing Your Lady 37 Ray Enright
Swing Your Partner 43 Frank McDonald
Swinger, The 66 George Sidney
Swinger's Paradise 63 Sidney J. Furie
Swingin' Affair, A 63 Jay Lawrence
Swingin' Along 62 Charles Barton
Swingin' in the Groove 60 Barry Shear
Swingin' Maiden, The 62 Gerald Thomas
Swingin' on a Rainbow 45 William Beaudine
Swingin' Set, The 64 Sidney Miller
Swingin' Summer, A 65 Robert Sparr
Swinging Affair, A 63 Jay Lawrence
Swinging at the Castle 59 Alf Kjellin
Swinging Barmaids, The 75 Gus Trikonis
Swinging Cheerleaders, The 74 Jack Hill
Swinging Coeds, The 76 Ross Meyers
Swinging Fink, The 65 James Landis
Swinging His Vacation 20 Gregory La Cava
Swinging Pearl Mystery, The 36 Ben Holmes
Swinging Set 64 Sidney Miller
Swinging Teacher 74 Michael Montgomery
Swinging the Lambeth Walk 39 Len Lye
Swinging the Lead 34 David MacKane
Swinging U.K. 64 Frank Gilpin
Swingonometry 43 Horace Shepherd
Swingtime Johnny 44 Edward F. Cline
Swirl of Glory 51 Edwin L. Marin
Swiss—A Love in Spain, The 86 Richard Dindo
Swiss Army Knife with Rats and Pigeons 81 Robert Breer
Swiss Conspiracy, The 75 Jack Arnold
Swiss Family Robinson 40 Edward Ludwig
Swiss Family Robinson, The 60 Ken Annakin
Swiss Honeymoon 47 Henry C. James, Jan Sikorsky
Swiss Made 68 Fritz Mäder, Fredi M. Murer, Yves Yersin
Swiss Miss 38 John G. Blystone, Hal Roach
Swiss Movements 31 Manny Gould, Ben

Harrison
Swiss Tease 47 Sid Marcus
Swiss Tour 49 Leopold Lindtberg
Swiss Trip 34 Oskar Fischinger
Swissmakers, The 78 Rolf Lyssy
Switch, The 63 Peter Maxwell
Switch, The 74 Joe Sarno
Switch in Time, A 87 Paul Donovan
Switchblade Sisters 75 Jack Hill
Switchboard Operator, The 66 Dušan Makavejev
Switching Channels 88 Ted Kotcheff
Swooner Crooner, The 44 Frank Tashlin
Sword, The 45 Kenji Mizoguchi
Sword and Dice 59 Imre Fehér
Sword and the Balance, The 62 André Cayatte
Sword and the Cross, The 58 Carlo Ludovico Bragaglia
Sword and the Dragon, The 56 Alexander Ptushko
Sword and the Flute, The 59 James Ivory
Sword and the Rose, The 53 Ken Annakin
Sword and the Sorcerer, The 82 Albert Pyun
Sword and the Sumo Ring, A 31 Hiroshi Inagaki
Sword and the Sumo Ring, The 34 Teinosuke Kinugasa
Sword for Hire 52 Hiroshi Inagaki
Sword in the Desert 49 George Sherman
Sword in the Stone, The 63 Wolfgang Reitherman
Sword of Ali Baba, The 65 Arthur Lubin, Virgil Vogel
Sword of Damascus 62 Mario Amendola
Sword of Damocles, The 20 George Ridgwell
Sword of D'Artagnan, The 51 Budd Boetticher
Sword of Doom, The 66 Kihachi Okamoto
Sword of El Cid, The 62 Miguel Iglesias Bonns
Sword of Fate, The 21 Frances E. Grant
Sword of Granada 53 Edward Dein, Carlos Vejar
Sword of Heaven 85 Byron Meyers
Sword of Honour 38 Maurice Elvey
Sword of Islam, The 62 Andrew Marton
Sword of Justice, Part Two 75 Yasuzo Masumura
Sword of Lancelot 62 Cornel Wilde
Sword of Monte Cristo, The 51 Maurice Geraghty
Sword of Penitence 27 Yasujiro Ozu
Sword of Sherwood Forest 60 Terence Fisher
Sword of the Avenger 48 Sidney Salkow
Sword of the Conqueror 61 Carlo Campogalliani
Sword of the Empire 63 Sergio Grieco
Sword of the Valiant 82 Stephen Weeks
Sword of Valor, The 24 Duke Worne
Sword of Vengeance 72 Kenji Misumi
Sword of Venus 52 Harold Daniels
Sword Points 28 Mark Sandrich
Sword Without a Country 61 Carlo Veo
Swordkill 84 J. Larry Carroll
Swords and Hearts 11 D. W. Griffith

Swords and the Woman *23* Henry Kolker
Swords of Blood *61* Philippe de Broca
Swords of Death *69* Tomu Uchida
Swordsman, The *38* Daisuke Ito
Swordsman, The *42* Kenji Mizoguchi
Swordsman, The *47* Joseph H. Lewis
Swordsman, The *76* Lindsay Shonteff
Swordsman, The *90* Ann Hui, Hark Tsui
Swordsman of Siena, The *61* Baccio Bandini, Étienne Périer
Swordsmen Three *63* Riccardo Blasco
Sworn Brothers *87* David Lai
Sworn Enemy *36* Edwin L. Marin
Sybil *21* Jack Denton
Sybil *76* Daniel Petrie
Sylva *45* Alexander Ivanovsky
Sylvester *23* Lupu Pick
Sylvester *85* Tim Hunter
Sylvia *65* Gordon Douglas
Sylvia *85* Michael Firth
Sylvia and the Ghost *44* Claude Autant-Lara
Sylvia and the Phantom *44* Claude Autant-Lara
Sylvia Gray *14* Charles L. Gaskill
Sylvia of the Secret Service *17* George Fitzmaurice
Sylvia on a Spree *18* Harry Franklin
Sylvia Scarlett *35* George Cukor
Sylvie and the Phantom *44* Claude Autant-Lara
Sylvie Destin *26* Dmitri Kirsanov
Sylvie et le Fantôme *44* Claude Autant-Lara
Symbol of Decadence *46* Curtis Harrington
Symbol of the Unconquered *21* Oscar Micheaux
Symmetricks *72* Stan Vanderbeek
Symmetry *67* Philip Stapp
Sympathy for the Devil *68* Jean-Luc Godard
Symphonie d'Amour *46* Robert Siodmak
Symphonie Fantastique, La *41* Christian-Jaque
Symphonie Industrielle *31* Joris Ivens
Symphonie Mécanique *55* Jean Mitry
Symphonie Pastorale, La *38* Satsuo Yamamoto
Symphonie Pastorale, La *46* Jean Delannoy
Symphonie Pathétique, La *29* Henri Étiévant
Symphonie Paysanne *44* Henri Storck*
Symphonie pour un Massacre *63* Jacques Deray
Symphonie van den Arbeid *31* Joris Ivens
Symphony, The *28* F. Harmon Weight
Symphony for a Massacre *63* Jacques Deray
Symphony in Slang *51* Tex Avery
Symphony in Two Flats *30* V. Gareth Gundrey
Symphony Nr 3 in Es-Dur, Opus 55: "Eroica" von Ludwig van Beethoven *67* Henri Colpi
Symphony of a City *47* Arne Sucksdorff
Symphony of Life *47* Ivan Pyriev
Symphony of Living *35* Frank R. Strayer
Symphony of Love *32* Gustav Machatý

Symphony of Love *58* Teinosuke Kinugasa
Symphony of Love and Death *14* Victor Tourjansky
Symphony of Six Million *32* Gregory La Cava
Symphony of the Don Basin *30* Dziga Vertov
Symphony of the Metropolis *29* Kenji Mizoguchi
Symphony of the Tropics *60* Herman van den Horst
Symptoms *74* José Ramón Larraz
Syn Mongolyi *36* R. Suslovich, Ilya Trauberg
Synanon *65* Richard Quine
Synchromy *71* Norman McLaren
Syncopated Sioux *40* Walter Lantz
Syncopating Sue *26* Richard Wallace
Syncopation *29* Bert Glennon
Syncopation *42* William Dieterle
Synd *28* Gustaf Molander
Syndens Datter *15* August Blom
Syndicate, The *68* Frederic Goode
Syndig Kærlighed *15* August Blom
Synnöve Solbakken *19* John W. Brunius
Synthetic Sound Experiments *32* Oskar Fischinger
Synthetic Wife *29* William A. Seiter
Syskonbädd 1782 *66* Vilgot Sjöman
System, The *53* Lewis Seiler
System, The *64* Michael Winner
System, The *81* Peter Yung
System of Dr. Tarr and Professor Feather, The *72* Juan López Moctezuma
System of Doctor Tarr and Professor Fether, The *12* Maurice Tourneur
Système du Docteur Goudron et du Professeur Plume, Le *12* Maurice Tourneur
Système du Docteur Sonflamort, Le *05* Georges Méliès
Sytten *65* Annelise Meineche
17 Minutter Grønland *67* Jørgen Roos
Sytten Minutter Grønland *67* Jørgen Roos
Syuzhet dlya Nebolshovo Rasskaza *68* Sergei Yutkevich
Syv Dager før Elisabeth *27* Leif Sinding
7-9-13 *34* Anders Wilhelm Sandberg
Szabad Lélegzet *73* Márta Mészáros
Szabó Anna *49* Félix Máriássy
Szabóné *49* Félix Máriássy
Szakadék *55* László Ranódy
Szamárbör *18* Michael Curtiz
Szamárköhögés *87* Péter Gardos
Szár és a Gyökér Fejlödése, A *61* Márta Mészáros
Szárnyas Ügynök, A *88* Sándor Soth
Szegény Gazdagok *59* Frigyes Bán
Szegénylegények *65* Miklós Jancsó
Szegénylegények Nehézéletüek *65* Miklós Jancsó
Szeleburdi Vakáció *88* György Palásthy
Szent Péter Esernyöje *17* Alexander Korda
Szent Péter Esernyöje *36* Géza von Cziffra
Szentendre—Town of Painters *64* Márta Mészáros
Szentjóbi Erdö Titka, A *17* Michael Curtiz
Szenzáció *22* Pál Fejös
Szenzáció *36* Steve Sekely, Ladislas Vajda
Szép Lányok, Ne Sírjatok *70* Márta Mészáros

Szerelem *71* Károly Makk
Szerelem Elsö Vérig *85* György Dobray, Péter Horváth
Szerelem Három Éjszakája, Egy *67* György Révész
Szerelem Második Vérig *88* György Dobray
Szerelemböl Nösültem *37* Steve Sekely
Szerelmem, Elektra *74* Miklós Jancsó
Szerelmesfilm *70* István Szabó
Szerelmi Álmodik *37* Heinz Hille
Szerencsés Dániel *83* Pál Sándor
Szeretet *63* Márta Mészáros
Szeretök *83* András Kovács
Szerkezettervezés *60* Miklós Jancsó
Sziget a Szárazföldön *68* Judit Elek
Szindbád *71* Zoltán Huszárik
Színfoltok Kínából *57* Miklós Jancsó
Szivdobogás *61* Márta Mészáros
Szívet Szívért *38* Steve Sekely
Szkoła *58* Walerian Borowczyk
Szörnyek Évadja *87* Miklós Jancsó
Szovjet Mezögazdasági Küldöttségek Tanításai, A *51* István György, Miklós Jancsó
Sztandar Młodych *57* Walerian Borowczyk, Jan Lenica
Sztuka Młodych *49* Andrzej Munk
Szyfry *66* Wojciech Has
T.A.G. The Assassination Game *82* Nick Castle
T.A.M.I. Show, The *64* Steve Binder
T-Bird Gang *59* Richard Harbinger
T. Dan Smith *87* Vivienne Dawson, Elaine Drainville, Dave Eadington, Richard Grassick, Ellin Hare, Sirkka-Liisa Konttinen, Pat McCarthy, Murray Martin, Jane Neatrour, Lorna Powell, Peter Roberts, Ray Stubbs, Judith Tomlinson, Steve Trafford
T.G. — Psychic Rally in Heaven *81* Derek Jarman
THX-1138 *70* George Lucas
THX-1138: 4 EB *65* George Lucas
T-Men *47* Anthony Mann
T.N.P., Le *56* Georges Franju
T.N.T. Jackson *74* Cirio Santiago
T.P.A. *67* Theodore J. Flicker
T.R. Baskin *71* Herbert Ross
'T Sal Waarachtig Wel Gaen *39* Mannus Franken
T.V. Interview *67* Stan Vanderbeek
T.V. of Tomorrow *53* Tex Avery
TV's First Music Videos *88* Don McGlynn
'T Was Een April *35* Jacques van Pol, Douglas Sirk
TZ *79* Robert Breer
'T Zal Waarachtig Wel Gaan *39* Mannus Franken
Ta Chi *64* Feng Yueh
Ta' Hvad Du Vil Ha' *47* Ole Palsbo
Ta Luan-Hui *83* King Hu, Han-hsiang Li, Ching-jui Pai
Ta-Ra-Ra-Boom-De-A *25* Dave Fleischer
Ta-Ra-Ra-Boom-Dee-Aye *25* Dave Fleischer
Ta-Ta, Come Again *11* Charles Armstrong
Ta-Ti Erh-Nu *64* King Hu
Ta-Ti Nu-Erh *64* King Hu
Ta Tsui Hsia *65* King Hu

Taken by Surprise *67* Rudi Dorn
Taken for a Ride *31* Manny Gould, Ben Harrison
Takeoff at 18:00 *69* Santiago Álvarez
Takers, The *59* Laslo Benedek
Taketori Monogatari *87* Kon Ichikawa
Taki no Shiraito *33* Kenji Mizoguchi
Takiji Kobayashi *74* Tadashi Imai
Taking a Chance *28* Norman Z. McLeod
Taking a Film *15* Percy Nash
Taking Care of Business *90* Arthur Hiller
Taking Chances *22* Grover Jones
Taking Father's Dinner *12* Frank Wilson
Taking His Medicine *11* Mack Sennett
Taking Mood, The *69* Derek Williams
Taking of Luke McVane, The *15* William S. Hart, Clifford Smith
Taking of Pelham 1-2-3, The *74* Joseph Sargent
Taking Off *70* Miloš Forman
Taking Sides *50* Fred F. Sears
Taking the Blame *35* Dave Fleischer
Taking Tiger Mountain *83* Tom Huckabee, Kent Smith
Taking Uncle for a Ride *11* Frank Wilson
Taking Ways *33* John Baxter
Taková Láska *59* Jiří Weiss
Tal der Tanzenden Witwen, Das *74* Volker Vogeler
Tal Farlow *80* Len Lye
Tala—Indian Love Song *07* Arthur Gilbert
Tale of a Black Eye, The *13* Mack Sennett
Tale of a Carpenter *65* Shiro Toyoda
Tale of a Cat, The *11* Edwin S. Porter
Tale of a City *48* Michael Fisher
Tale of a Coat, The *05* Alf Collins
Tale of a Dog *44* Cy Endfield
Tale of a Fish, The *17* Gregory La Cava
Tale of a Link, The *48* Boris Dolin
Tale of a Monkey, The *17* Gregory La Cava
Tale of a Mouse, The *07* J. H. Martin
Tale of a Pig, The *18* Raoul Barré, Charles Bowers
Tale of a Shirt, The *05* Harold Jeapes
Tale of a Shirt, The *16* Will P. Kellino
Tale of a Shirt, The *19* Gregory La Cava
Tale of a Turk, The *16* William Beaudine
Tale of a Wag, The *20* Gregory La Cava, Vernon Stallings
Tale of a Whale, The *16* Harry S. Palmer
Tale of a Wolf *60* Joseph Barbera, William Hanna
Tale of Africa, A *81* Susumu Hani*
Tale of Archery at the Sanjusangendo, A *45* Mikio Naruse
Tale of Beautiful Aisulu, The *87* Victor Chugunov, Rustem Tazhbayev
Tale of Czar Saltan, The *66* Alexander Ptushko
Tale of Five Cities, A *51* Géza von Cziffra, Romolo Marcellini, Emil E. Reinert, Wolfgang Staudte, Montgomery Tully
Tale of Five Women, A *51* Géza von Cziffra, Romolo Marcellini, Emil E. Reinert, Wolfgang Staudte, Montgomery Tully
Tale of Genji, A *51* Kozaburo Yoshimura
Tale of How Tsar Peter Married Off His Moor, The *76* Alexander Mitta

Tale of John and Mary, The *80* Karel Zeman
Tale of Lost Time *64* Alexander Ptushko
Tale of Peonies and Lanterns, A *68* Satsuo Yamamoto
Tale of Priest Pankrati *18* Alexander Arkatov, Olga Preobrazhenskaya
Tale of Ruby Rose, The *87* Roger Scholes
Tale of Springtime, A *89* Eric Rohmer
Tale of Tails, A *12* Percy Stow
Tale of Tails, A *33* Horace Shepherd
Tale of the Ark, The *09* Arthur Cooper
Tale of the Cock *66* John Derek, David Nelson
Tale of the Fjords *47* Arne Sucksdorff
Tale of the Foothills, A *12* Thomas Ince
Tale of the Monk, The *26* David Hand, Walter Lantz
Tale of the Sea, A *06* Edwin S. Porter
Tale of the Tsar Sultan, The *66* Alexander Ptushko
Tale of the West, A *09* Gilbert M. Anderson
Tale of the Wilderness, A *11* D. W. Griffith
Tale of Three Women, A *54* Thelma Connell, Paul Dickson
Tale of Tiffany Lust, The *81* Radley Metzger
Tale of Two Cities, A *11* William Humphrey
Tale of Two Cities, A *17* Frank Lloyd
Tale of Two Cities, A *22* Walter C. Rowden
Tale of Two Cities, A *35* Jack Conway, W. S. Van Dyke
Tale of Two Cities, A *58* Ralph Thomas
Tale of Two Kitties, A *42* Robert Clampett
Tale of Two Mice, A *45* Frank Tashlin
Tale of Two Tables, A *13* Edwin J. Collins
Tale of Two Worlds, A *21* Frank Lloyd
Tale of Umar Khaptsoko, The *32* Yuli Raizman
Tale of Ursus, The *52* Andrzej Munk
Tale of Wishes, A *84* Yuli Raizman
Tale on the Twelve Points *56* Károly Makk
Tale-Teller Phone, The *28* Bertram Phillips
Tale That Is Not, A *16* Gregory La Cava, Vernon Stallings
Tale the Autumn Leaves Told *08* Edwin S. Porter
Tale the Camera Told, The *10* Edwin S. Porter
Talent Competition *63* Miloš Forman
Talent for Loving, A *68* Richard Quine
Talent Scout *37* William Clemens
Tales *70* Cassandra Gerstein
Tales After the Rain *53* Kenji Mizoguchi
Tales by Capek *47* Martin Frič
Tales for All (Part 5) *86* Vojtěch Jasný
Tales from a Country by the Sea *28* Teinosuke Kinugasa
Tales from Beyond the Grave *73* Kevin Connor
Tales from Capek *47* Martin Frič
Tales from the Beyond *73* Kevin Connor
Tales from the Crypt *71* Freddie Francis
Tales from the Crypt, Part II *72* Roy

Ward Baker
Tales from the Darkside: The Movie *90* John Harrison
Tales from the Gimli Hospital *88* Guy Maddin
Tales from the Magino Village *87* Shinsuke Ogawa
Tales from the Vienna Woods *35* Georg Jacoby
Tales from the Vienna Woods *78* Maximilian Schell
Tales of a Salesman *65* Don Russell
Tales of a Traveling Salesman *65* Don Russell
Tales of Beatrix Potter *71* Reginald Mills
Tales of Budapest *38* Béla Gaál
Tales of Budapest *76* István Szabó
Tales of Ensign Steel, The *26* John W. Brunius
Tales of Hoffman, The *51* Michael Powell, Emeric Pressburger
Tales of Hoffmann *11* Jakob Fleck, Anton Kolm, Luise Kolm, Claudius Valtee
Tales of Hoffmann *15* Richard Oswald
Tales of Hoffmann *23* Max Neufeld
Tales of Horror *19* Richard Oswald
Tales of Manhattan *42* Julien Duvivier
Tales of Mystery *67* Federico Fellini, Louis Malle, Roger Vadim
Tales of 1001 Nights *21* Victor Tourjansky
Tales of Ordinary Madness *81* Marco Ferreri
Tales of Paris *62* Marc Allégret, Claude Barma, Michel Boisrond, Jacques Poitrenaud
Tales of Robin Hood *51* James Tinling
Tales of Terror *61* Roger Corman
Tales of the Crypt, Part II *72* Roy Ward Baker
Tales of the Floating Weeds *59* Yasujiro Ozu
Tales of the Ninja *67* Nagisa Oshima
Tales of the Pale and Silvery Moon After the Rain *53* Kenji Mizoguchi
Tales of the Siberian Land *47* Ivan Pyriev
Tales of the Taira Clan *55* Kenji Mizoguchi
Tales of the Third Dimension *85* Todd Durham, Worth Keeter, Thom McIntyre
Tales of the Trashcan Kid *70* Edgar Reitz, Ula Stöckl
Tales of the Typewriter *16* Alexander Korda
Tales of the Uncanny *19* Richard Oswald
Tales of the Uncanny *31* Richard Oswald
Tales That Witness Madness *73* Freddie Francis
Tales the Searchlight Told *08* Edwin S. Porter
Talion *66* Michael Moore
Talíře Nad Velkým Malíkovem *77* Jaromil Jireš
Talisman, The *11* Charles Magnusson
Talisman, The *66* John Carr
Talison, Le *21* Charles De Marsan, Charles Maudru
Talk About a Lady *46* George Sherman
Talk About a Stranger *52* David Bradley
Talk About Jacqueline *42* Harold French
Talk of a Million *51* John Paddy Carstairs

Talk of Hollywood, The 29 Mark Sandrich
Talk of the Devil 36 Carol Reed
Talk of the Devil 67 Francis Searle
Talk of the Town, The 18 Allen Holubar
Talk of the Town 41 Per Lindberg
Talk of the Town, The 42 George Stevens
Talk-of-the-Town Tora-San 78 Yoji Yamada
Talk Radio 88 Oliver Stone
Talker, The 25 Alfred E. Green
Talkies, The 29 Stephen Roberts
Talking Bear, The 60 Edmond Séchan
Talking Feet 37 John Baxter
Talking Hands 36 Ivar Campbell
Talking Pictures 86 Caetano Veloso
Talking Through My Heart 36 Dave Fleischer
Talking to Strangers 88 Rob Tregenza
Talking Turkey 30 Mark Sandrich
Talking Walls 82 Stephen Verona
Tall Blond Man with One Black Shoe, The 72 Yves Robert
Tall, Dark and Handsome 41 H. Bruce Humberstone
Tall Guy, The 89 Mel Smith
Tall Headlines 52 Terence Young
Tall in the Saddle 44 Edwin L. Marin
Tall Lie, The 51 Paul Henreid
Tall Man Riding 55 Lesley Selander
Tall Men, The 55 Raoul Walsh
Tall Shadows of the Wind 78 Bahman Farmanara
Tall Story 59 Joshua Logan
Tall Stranger, The 57 Thomas Carr
Tall T, The 57 Budd Boetticher
Tall Tales 41 Willard Van Dyke
Tall, Tan and Terrific 46 Bud Pollard
Tall Target, The 51 Anthony Mann
Tall Texan, The 52 Elmo Williams
Tall Timber 28 Walt Disney
Tall Timber 50 Jean Yarbrough
Tall Timbers 37 Ken Hall
Tall Trouble, The 57 Paul Landres
Tall Women, The 66 Rudolf Zehetgruber
Talla 67 Malcolm Le Grice
Tally Brown, N.Y. 79 Rosa von Praunheim
Tally Ho! 01 Frank Parker
Tally Ho! Pimple 15 Fred Evans, Joe Evans
Tallyman, The 28 Maurice Sandground
Talmae and Pomdari 87 Yun Ryong Gyu
Talmae wa Pomdari 87 Yun Ryong Gyu
Talpalatnyi Föld 48 Frigyes Bán
Talvisota 89 Pekka Parikka
Tam-Lin 70 Roddy McDowall
Tam na Konečné 56 Ján Kadár, Elmar Klos
Tam o' Shanter 30 R. E. Jeffrey
Tamacha 88 Ramesh Ahuja
Tamahine 62 Philip Leacock
Tamale Vendor, The 31 Roscoe Arbuckle
Tamango 57 John Berry
Tamaño Natural 73 Philippe Agostini, Luis García Berlanga
Tamar, Wife of Er 69 Riccardo Freda
Tamara la Complaisante 37 Jean Delannoy, Félix Gandéra
Tamarind Seed, The 74 Blake Edwards
Tamas 87 Govind Nihalani
Tambora 37 Pál Fejös

Tambour Battant 33 Arthur Robison
Tambour des Dogons, Le 66 Jean Rouch, Gilbert Rouget
Tambourin Fantastique, Le 07 Georges Méliès
Tambourine Dancing Quartette 02 George Albert Smith
Tambours de Pierre 66 Jean Rouch, Gilbert Rouget
Tame Cat, A 12 Percy Stow
Tame Cat, The 21 William Bradley
T'Amerò Sempre 32 Mario Camerini
T'Amerò Sempre 43 Mario Camerini
Taming a Husband 10 D. W. Griffith
Taming Liza 16 Joe Evans
Taming Mrs. Shrew 12 Edwin S. Porter
Taming of Big Ben, The 12 Will P. Kellino
Taming of Dorothy, The 50 Mario Soldati
Taming of Texas Pete, The 13 William Duncan
Taming of the Dragon, The 53 Hermina Tyrlova
Taming of the Shrew, The 08 D. W. Griffith
Taming of the Shrew, The 14 Forest Holger-Madsen
Taming of the Shrew, The 15 Arthur Backner
Taming of the Shrew, The 23 Edwin J. Collins
Taming of the Shrew, The 29 Sam Taylor
Taming of the Shrew, The 66 Franco Zeffirelli
Taming of the West, The 25 Arthur Rosson
Taming of the West, The 39 Norman Deming
Taming Sutton's Gal 57 Lesley Selander
Taming the Mekong 65 Willard Van Dyke
Taming the Wild 37 Robert F. Hill
Taming Tony 17 Harry S. Palmer
T'Ammazzo, Raccomandati a Dio 68 Osvaldo Civirani
Tammy 57 Joseph Pevney
Tammy and the Bachelor 57 Joseph Pevney
Tammy and the Doctor 63 Harry Keller
Tammy and the Millionaire 67 Leslie Goodwins, Sidney Miller, Ezra Stone
Tammy Tell Me True 61 Harry Keller
Tampico 33 Irving Cummings
Tampico 44 Lothar Mendes
Tampico 47 Luis Buñuel
Tampopo 86 Juzo Itami
Tanah Sabrang 38 Mannus Franken
Tanda Singui 72 Jean Rouch
Tandem 85 Mária Soós
Tandem 87 Patrice Leconte
Tanga Tika 53 Dwight Long
Tanganyika 54 André De Toth
Tange Sazen 33 Daisuke Ito
Tangier 46 George Waggner
Tangier Assignment 54 Ted Leversuch
Tangier Incident 53 Lew Landers
Tangle, The 14 Harry Lambart
Tangle of Fates, A 11 H. Oceano Martinek
Tangled Affair, A 13 Mack Sennett
Tangled Angler, The 41 Frank Tashlin
Tangled Destinies 32 Frank R. Strayer

Tangled Evidence 34 George A. Cooper
Tangled Fates 16 Travers Vale
Tangled Fortunes 32 John P. McGowan
Tangled Hearts 16 Joseph De Grasse
Tangled Hearts 20 William Humphrey
Tangled Herds 26 William Bertram
Tangled Lives 11 Sidney Olcott
Tangled Lives 17 J. Gordon Edwards
Tangled Lives 18 Paul Scardon
Tangled Television 40 Sid Marcus
Tangled Threads 19 William A. Seiter
Tangled Trails 21 Charles E. Bartlett
Tangled Travels 44 Alec Geiss
Tangled Web, A 12 Edwin S. Porter
Tango, The 13 Frank Wilson
Tango 36 Phil Rosen
Tango & Cash 89 Andrei Mikhalkov-Konchalovsky
Tango-Bar 35 John Reinhardt
Tango Bar 88 Marcos Zurinaga
Tango Blu 88 Alberto Bevilacqua
Tango Cavalier 23 Charles R. Seeling
Tango Dancers, The 20 Raoul Barré, Charles Bowers
Tango de la Muerte, El 17 José A. Ferreyra
Tango en Broadway, El 34 Louis Gasnier
Tango Mad 14 Hay Plumb
Tango Tangles 14 Mack Sennett
Tangos 85 Fernando Solanas
Tangos—L'Exil de Gardel 85 Fernando Solanas
Tangos—The Exile of Gardel 85 Fernando Solanas
Tangram, The 14 Walter R. Booth
Tanin no Kao 65 Hiroshi Teshigahara
Tanítványok, A 85 Géza Beremenyi
Tank 84 Marvin Chomsky
Tank Battalion 58 Sherman Rose
Tank Cartoons 16 Walter R. Booth
Tank Commando 59 Burt Topper
Tank Commandos 59 Burt Topper
Tank Force 57 Terence Young
Tank Patrol 44 John Eldridge
Tankless Job, A 17 Gregory La Cava, Vernon Stallings
Tanks 16 Walter R. Booth
Tanks, The 17 Gregory La Cava
Tanks a Million 41 Fred Guiol
Tanks Are Coming, The 41 B. Reeves Eason
Tanks Are Coming, The 51 D. Ross Lederman, Lewis Seiler
Tanned Legs 29 Marshall Neilan
Tannenberg 34 Heinz Paul
Tanoshiki Kana Jinsei 44 Mikio Naruse
Tansy 21 Cecil M. Hepworth
Tant d'Amour Perdu 58 Léo Joannon
Tant Que Vous Serez Heureux 11 Louis Feuillade
Tant Qu'Il y Aura des Femmes 55 Edmond T. Gréville
Tant Qu'Il y Aura des Femmes 87 Didier Kaminka
Tant Qu'On A la Santé 65 Pierre Etaix
Tantalizing Fly 19 Dave Fleischer
Tante Esther 56 Jean Dewever
Tante Gusti Kommandiert 34 Karl Heinz Wolff
Tante Zita 67 Robert Enrico
Tantsploshchadka 87 Samson Samsonov

Tanú, A *68* Péter Bacsó

Tanya *40* Grigori Alexandrov

Tanya *76* Nate Rogers

Tanya's Island *80* Alfred Sole

Tanz auf dem Vulkan *38* Hans Steinhoff

Tanz Geht Weiter, Der *30* William Dieterle

Tanz ins Glück, Der *30* Max Nosseck

Tanzende Herz, Das *58* Wolfgang Liebeneiner

Tänzer Meiner Frau, Der *25* Alexander Korda

Tänzerin Marion, Die *20* Friedrich Feher

Tanzhusar, Der *33* Fred Sauer

Tanzmusik *36* J. A. Hübler-Kahla

Tap *89* Nick Castle

Tap Roots *48* George Marshall

Tapage Nocturne *79* Catherine Breillat

Tapdancin' *80* Christian Blackwood

Tapeheads *88* Bill Fishman

Tapis de Moyse, Le *31* Edmond T. Gréville

Tapis Moquette, Le *35* Roger Leenhardt

Taps *81* Harold Becker

Taqdeer *43* Ramjankhan Mehboobkhan

Tar Heel Warrior *17* E. Mason Hopper

Tarahumara *64* Luis Alcoriza

Tarakanova *29* Raymond Bernard

Tarakanova *37* Fedor Ozep

Taranta, La *62* Gianfranco Mingozzi

Tarantella Napoletana *54* Camillo Mastrocinque

Tarantelle, La *00* Alice Guy-Blaché

Tarantola dal Ventre Nero, La *71* Paolo Cavara

Tarantos, Los *63* Rovira-Beleta

Tarantula *16* George D. Baker

Tarantula *55* Jack Arnold

Taras Bulba *27* Joseph N. Ermolieff

Taras Bulba *38* Adrian Brunel, Albert De Courville, Alexis Granowsky

Taras Bulba *62* J. Lee-Thompson

Taras Family, The *45* Mark Donskoi

Taras Shevchenko *51* Alexander Alov, Vladimir Naumov, Igor Savchenko

Tarawa Beachhead *58* Paul Wendkos

Tarde de Domingo, Una *57* Carlos Saura

Tarde de Toros *55* Ladislas Vajda

Tarde del Domingo, La *57* Carlos Saura

Tare, La *11* Louis Feuillade

Tarentule au Ventre Noir, La *71* Paolo Cavara

Tares *18* Cecil M. Hepworth

Target, The *16* Norval MacGregor

Target *52* Stuart Gilmore

Target *85* Arthur Penn

Target Eagle *84* José Antonio De la Loma

Target Earth *54* Sherman Rose

Target for Killing, A *66* Manfred Kohler

Target for Scandal *52* Robert Pirosh

Target for Today *44* William Keighley

Target for Tonight *41* Harry Watt

Target: Harry *68* Roger Corman

Target—Hong Kong *52* Fred F. Sears

Target in the Sun *75* Robert Arkless

Target of an Assassin *76* Peter Collinson

Target Practice *06* Arthur Cooper

Target, Sea of China *54* Franklin Adreon

Target Unknown *51* George Sherman

Target Zero *55* Harmon Jones

Targets *67* Peter Bogdanovich

Tarik el Masdud, El *58* Salah Abu Saif

Taris *31* Jean Vigo

Taris, Champion de Natation *31* Jean Vigo

Taris: Roi de l'Eau *31* Jean Vigo

Tarka the Otter *79* David Cobham

Tarnish *24* George Fitzmaurice

Tarnished *50* Harry Keller

Tarnished Angel *38* Leslie Goodwins

Tarnished Angels, The *57* Douglas Sirk

Tarnished Heroes *61* Ernest Morris

Tarnished Lady *31* George Cukor

Tarnished Lady: A Story of a New York Lady *31* George Cukor

Tarnished Reputations *18* Alice Guy-Blaché, Léonce Perret

Taro's Youth *67* Ko Nakahira

Tarot *86* Rudolph Thome

Tarps Elin *57* Kenne Fant

Tars and Spars *45* Alfred E. Green

Tars and Stripes *35* Charles Lamont

Tartar Invasion *62* Remigio Del Grosso

Tartari, I *60* Ferdinando Baldi, Richard Thorpe

Tartarin de Tarascon *08* Georges Méliès

Tartarin de Tarascon *34* Raymond Bernard

Tartarin de Tarascon *62* Francis Blanche

Tartarin de Tarascon ou Une Chasse à l'Ours *08* Georges Méliès

Tartars, The *60* Ferdinando Baldi, Richard Thorpe

Tartassati, I *59* Steno

Tartu *43* Harold S. Bucquet

Tartüff *25* F. W. Murnau

Tartuffe *25* F. W. Murnau

Tartuffe, Le *84* Gérard Depardieu

Tarzan and His Mate *34* Jack Conway, Cedric Gibbons

Tarzan and Jane Regained...Sort Of *63* Andy Warhol*

Tarzan and the Amazons *45* Kurt Neumann

Tarzan and the Golden Lion *26* John P. McGowan

Tarzan and the Great River *67* Robert Day

Tarzan and the Green Goddess *35* Edward Kull, Wilbur F. McGaugh

Tarzan and the Huntress *47* Kurt Neumann

Tarzan and the Jungle Boy *68* Robert Gordon

Tarzan and the Jungle Goddess *51* Phil Brandon, Byron Haskin

Tarzan and the Jungle Queen *50* Lee Sholem

Tarzan and the Jungle Queen *51* Phil Brandon, Byron Haskin

Tarzan and the Leopard Woman *46* Kurt Neumann

Tarzan and the Lost Safari *56* H. Bruce Humberstone, Victor Stoloff

Tarzan and the Mermaids *47* Robert Florey

Tarzan and the She-Devil *53* Kurt Neumann

Tarzan and the Slave Girl *50* Lee Sholem

Tarzan and the Trappers *58* Charles Haas, Sandy Howard

Tarzan and the Valley of Gold *65* Robert Day

Tarzan Escapes! *36* Richard Thorpe, William A. Wellman

Tarzan Finds a Son! *39* Richard Thorpe

Tarzan Goes to India *62* John Guillermin

Tarzan No. 22 *68* Robert Gordon

Tarzan of the Apes *18* Scott Sidney

Tarzan '65 *65* Robert Day

Tarzan '66 *65* Robert Day

Tarzan, the Ape Man *31* W. S. Van Dyke

Tarzan the Ape Man *59* Joseph M. Newman

Tarzan, the Ape Man *81* John Derek

Tarzan the Fearless *33* Robert F. Hill

Tarzan the Magnificent *60* Robert Day

Tarzan the Mighty *28* Jack Nelson, Ray Taylor

Tarzan the Tiger *29* Henry MacRae

Tarzan Triumphs *43* Wilhelm Thiele

Tarzan vs. IBM *65* Jean-Luc Godard

Tarzana *79* Steve De Jarnatt

Tarzanova Smrt *68* Jaroslav Balík

Tarzan's Deadly Silence *70* Lawrence Dobkin, Robert L. Friend

Tarzan's Desert Mystery *43* Wilhelm Thiele

Tarzan's Fight for Life *58* H. Bruce Humberstone

Tarzan's Greatest Adventure *59* John Guillermin

Tarzan's Hidden Jungle *55* Harold Schuster

Tarzan's Jungle Rebellion *70* William Witney

Tarzan's Magic Fountain *49* Lee Sholem

Tarzan's New Adventure *35* Edward Kull, Wilbur F. McGaugh

Tarzan's New York Adventure *42* Richard Thorpe

Tarzan's Peril *51* Phil Brandon, Byron Haskin

Tarzan's Revenge *38* D. Ross Lederman

Tarzan's Savage Fury *52* Cy Endfield

Tarzan's Secret Treasure *41* Richard Thorpe

Tarzan's Three Challenges *63* Robert Day

Tarzoon—Shame of the Jungle *75* Jean-Marc Picha, Boris Szulzinger

Task Force *49* Delmer Daves

Tasogare Sakaba *55* Tomu Uchida

Tassels in the Air *38* Charlie Chase

Tassinaro, Il *82* Alberto Sordi

Tassinaro a New York, Un *87* Alberto Sordi

Taste for Killing, A *66* Tonino Valerii

Taste for Women, A *64* Jean Léon

Taste of Blood, A *67* Herschell Gordon Lewis

Taste of Catnip, A *66* Robert McKimson

Taste of Corn, A *86* Gianni Da Campo

Taste of Excitement *68* Don Sharp

Taste of Fear *60* Seth Holt

Taste of Flesh, A *67* Doris Wishman

Taste of Hell, A *73* Basil Bradbury, Neil Yarema

Taste of Honey, A *61* Tony Richardson

Taste of Honey, a Swallow of Brine, A *66* B. Ron Elliott

Taste of Hot Lead, A *51* Stuart Gilmore

Taste of Life *19* John Francis Dillon

Taste of Mackerel, The *62* Yasujiro Ozu
Taste of Money, A *60* Max Varnel
Taste of Sin, A *83* Ulli Lommel
Taste of the Savage, The *70* Alberto Mariscal
Taste of Water, The *82* Orlow Seunke
Taste the Blood of Dracula *69* Peter Sasdy
Tasveer Apni *84* Mrinal Sen
Tat der Gräfin Worms, Die *16* Karl Gerhardt, Joe May
Tatakai Heitai *40* Fumio Kamei
Tatárjárás *17* Michael Curtiz
Tateshina no Shiki *66* Kaneto Shindo
Tathapil *50* Bimal Roy
Tatiana *23* Anatole Litvak
Tatiana *84* David Hamilton
Tatjana *23* Robert Dinesen
Tatlo, Dalawa, Isa *74* Lino Brocka
Tatoué, Le *68* Denys De la Patellière
Tatras Zauber *33* Adolf Trotz
Tatsu *62* Hiroshi Inagaki
Tattercoats *24* Herbert M. Dawley
Tattered Dress, The *57* Jack Arnold
Tatterly *16* H. Lisle Lucoque
Tatters, a Tale of the Slums *11* A. E. Coleby
Tattlers, The *20* Howard Mitchell
Tattoo *80* Bob Brooks
Tattooed Arm, The *13* Wallace Reid
Tattooed Stranger, The *50* Edward Montagne
Tattooed Swordswoman *70* Teruo Ishii
Tattooed Temptress, The *68* Hideo Sekigawa
Tattooed Will, The *14* Ernest G. Batley
Tatuaje *76* Bigas Luna
Taugenichts, Der *22* Carl Fröhlich
Tauq wal Iswira, Al *86* Khairy Bishara
Taur the Mighty *63* Antonio Leonviola
Tausend Augen des Dr. Mabuse, Die *60* Fritz Lang
Tausend für Eine Nacht *34* Max Mack
Tauw *70* Ousmane Sembène
Tauwetter *78* Markus Imhoof
Tavasz a Télben *17* Michael Curtiz
Tavaszi Zápor *32* Pál Fejős
Tavern Keeper's Daughter, The *08* D. W. Griffith
Tavern Knight, The *20* Maurice Elvey
Tavern of Tragedy, The *14* Donald Crisp
Tavola dei Poveri, La *32* Alessandro Blasetti
Tawny Pipit *44* Bernard Miles, Charles Saunders
Tax from the Rear, A *20* Vernon Stallings
Tax Season *90* Tom Law
Taxes *22* Milt Gross
Taxi *19* Lawrence C. Windom
Taxi! *31* Roy Del Ruth
Taxi *53* Gregory Ratoff
Taxi Blues *90* Pavel Lounguine
Taxi Boy *86* Alain Paige
Taxi Dancer, The *26* Harry Millarde
Taxi di Notte *50* Carmine Gallone
Taxi Driver, The *53* George Tzavellas
Taxi Driver *75* Martin Scorsese
Taxi Driver in New York, A *87* Alberto Sordi
Taxi for Tobruk *61* Denys De la Patellière
Taxi for Two *29* Denison Clift, Alexander Esway

Taxi Mauve, Un *77* Yves Boisset
Taxi Mister! *43* Kurt Neumann
Taxi Mystery, The *26* Fred Windermere
Taxi nach Kairo *87* Frank Ripploh
Taxi nach Tobruk *61* Denys De la Patellière
Taxi para Tobruk, Un *61* Denys De la Patellière
Taxi pour Tobruk, Un *61* Denys De la Patellière
Taxi Roulotte et Corrida *58* André Hunebelle
Taxi...Signore? *57* Sergio Leone
Taxi, Taxi *27* Melville Brown
Taxi 13 *28* Marshall Neilan
Taxi to Cairo *87* Frank Ripploh
Taxi to Heaven *43* Herbert Rappaport
Taxi to Paradise *33* Adrian Brunel
Taxi 313 x 7, Le *22* Pierre Colombier
Taxi zum Klo *81* Frank Ripploh
Taxidi sta Kithira *84* Theodoros Angelopoulos
Taxidi stin Kythera *84* Theodoros Angelopoulos
Taximeter Cab, The *09* Frank Danvers Yates
Taxing Woman, A *87* Juzo Itami
Taxing Woman II, A *88* Juzo Itami
Taxing Woman Returns, A *88* Juzo Itami
Taxing Woman's Return, A *88* Juzo Itami
Taylor Mead Dances *63* Paul Morrissey
Taylor Mead's Ass *64* Andy Warhol
Taynaya Progulka *87* Valery Mikhailovsky
Taynoe Puteshestvie Emira *87* Fardi Davletshin
Tayny Madam Vong *87* Stepan Puchinyan
Taza, Son of Cochise *54* Douglas Sirk
Tchaikovsky *70* Igor Talankin, Dmitri Tiomkin
Tchao Pantin *83* Claude Berri
Tche Sen *25* Pan Liu
Tchin-Chao the Chinese Conjurer *04* Georges Méliès
Te *63* István Szabó
Te Amo *86* Eduardo Calcagno
Te Csak Pipálj Ladányi *38* Márton Keleti
Te Deum *73* Enzo G. Castellari
Te o Tsunagu Kora *48* Hiroshi Inagaki
Te o Tsunagu Kora *62* Susumu Hani
Te Quiero con Locura *35* John Boland
Te Quiero para Mí *44* Ladislas Vajda
Tea and Rice *52* Yasujiro Ozu
Tea and Sympathy *56* Vincente Minnelli
Tea for Three *27* Robert Z. Leonard
Tea for Two *50* David Butler
Tea in the Garden *58* Joyce Wieland*
Tea in the Harem *85* Mehdi Charef
Tea in the Harem of Archimedes *85* Mehdi Charef
Tea Leaves in the Wind *38* Ward Wing
Tea with a Kick *23* Erle C. Kenton
Teacher, The *39* Sergei Gerasimov
Teacher, The *74* Hikmet Avedis
Teacher and the Miracle, The *58* Aldo Fabrizi, Carol Riethof, Peter Riethof
Teacher Teacher *26* Norman Taurog
Teachers *84* Arthur Hiller
Teachers in Transformation *63* Alexander Kluge, Karen Kluge

Teacher's Pest *31* Dave Fleischer
Teacher's Pests, The *32* Walter Lantz
Teacher's Pet *58* George Seaton
Teaching a Husband a Lesson *09* Theo Bouwmeester
Teaching Dad to Like Her *11* D. W. Griffith
Teachings of a Soviet Agricultural Delegation, The *51* István György, Miklós Jancsó
Teahouse of the August Moon, The *56* Daniel Mann
Team, The *41* Leslie Arliss
Teammates *78* Steven Jacobson
Tear Gas Squad *40* Terry Morse
Tear Me But Satiate Me with Your Kisses *68* Dino Risi
Tearaway *86* Bruce Morrison
Tearin' Into Trouble *27* Richard Thorpe
Tearin' Loose *25* Richard Thorpe
Tearing Down the Spanish Flag *1898* J. Stuart Blackton, Albert E. Smith
Tearing Through *25* Arthur Rosson
Tears *14* Yevgeni Bauer
Tears and Smiles *17* William Bertram
Tears Are Not Enough *85* John Zaritsky
Tears for Simon *55* Guy Green
Tears of an Onion, The *38* Dave Fleischer
Tears of Blood *52* Guido Brignone
Tears of Happiness *74* Sarky Mouradian
Tears on the Lion's Mane *62* Masahiro Shinoda
Tease for Two *65* Robert McKimson
Teaser, The *25* William A. Seiter
Teasers, The *77* George Lancer
Teasing Grandpa *01* James A. Williamson
Tebe, Front: Kazakhstan Front *43* Dziga Vertov
Tebye Front *43* Dziga Vertov
Technique d'un Meurtre *67* Franco Prosperi
Techniques Minières *70* Arthur Lamothe
Techno-Cracked *33* Ubbe Iwerks
Techno-Crazy *33* Charles Lamont
Technoracket *33* Dick Huemer
Techo de la Ballena *81* Raúl Ruiz
Teckman Mystery, The *54* Wendy Toye
Tecnica di un Omicidio *67* Franco Prosperi
Tecnica e il Rito, La *71* Miklós Jancsó
Técnicas de Duelo *88* Sergio Cabrera
Ted Heath and His Music *61* Robert Henryson
Teddy and the Angel Cake *16* Earl Hurd
Teddy at the Throttle *16* Clarence Badger
Teddy Bear, The *68* Arne Mattsson
Teddy Bears, The *07* Edwin S. Porter
Teddy By Kovril *19* Gustav Machatý
Teddy Laughs Last *21* Milton Elmore
Teddy, the Rough Rider *40* Ray Enright
Teddy Wants to Smoke *19* Gustav Machatý
Tee for Two *25* Edward F. Cline
Tee for Two *45* Joseph Barbera, William Hanna
Teen Age *44* Dick L'Estrange
Teen-Age Crime Wave *55* Fred F. Sears
Teen Kanya *61* Satyajit Ray
Teen Mothers *80* Boaz Davidson

Teen Witch 89 Dorian Walker
Teen Wolf 85 Rod Daniel
Teen Wolf Too 87 Christopher Leitch
Teenage Bad Girl 56 Herbert Wilcox
Teenage Caveman 58 Roger Corman
Teenage Delinquents 57 David Lowell
  Rich
Teenage Devil Dolls 52 Bamlet L. Price,
  Jr.
Teenage Doll 57 Roger Corman
Teenage Father 78 Taylor Hackford
Teenage Frankenstein 57 Herbert L.
  Strock
Teenage Gang Debs 66 Sande Johnsen
Teenage Graffiti 77 Christopher Casler
Teenage Hitchhikers 75 Gerri Sedley
Teenage Lovers 60 Richard Rush
Teenage Millionaire 61 Lawrence Doheny
Teenage Monster 57 Jacques Marquette
Teenage Mother 67 Jerry Gross
Teenage Mutant Ninja Turtles 90 Steve
  Barron
Teenage Psycho Meets Bloody Mary,
  The 62 Ray Dennis Steckler
Teenage Rebel 56 Edmund Goulding
Teenage Rebellion 67 Jörn Donner, Nor-
  man Herbert, Richard Lester
Teenage Slasher Sluts 88 Gorman Bechard
Teenage Strangler 64 Bill Posner
Teenage Tease 83 Richard Erdman
Teenage Teasers 82 Jack Angel
Teenage Thunder 57 Paul Helmick
Teenage Tramp 63 Gerry O'Hara
Teenage Wolf Pack 56 Georg Tressler
Teenage Zombies 57 Jerry Warren
Teenager 62 Leonard Buczkowski
Teenager 74 Gerald Seth Sindell
Teenagers, The 86 Nicolae Corjos
Teenagers from Outer Space 59 Tom
  Graeff
Teenagers in Space 75 Richard Viktorov
Teeth 24 John G. Blystone
Teeth of the Tiger, The 19 Chester
  Withey
Tegnap 59 Márton Keleti
Teheran 47 William Freshman, Giacomo
  Gentilomo
Teilnehmer Antwortet Nicht 32 Rudolf
  Katscher, Marc Sorkin
Tejano, El 66 Lesley Selander
Teka Dypkuryera 27 Alexander Dov-
  zhenko
Tekka Bugyō 54 Teinosuke Kinugasa
Tekki Kūshu 43 Kozaburo Yoshimura
Tel Aviv—Berlin 87 Tzipi Trope
Tel Aviv—Los Angeles 88 Shmuel Im-
  berman
Tel Aviv Taxi 56 Larry Frisch
Tel Est Pris Qui Croyait Prendre 01 Alice
  Guy-Blaché
Télécouture Sans Fil, La 10 Émile Cohl
Telefilm 28 Dave Fleischer
Telefon 77 Don Siegel
Telefoni Bianchi 75 Dino Risi
Telefootlers 40 John Paddy Carstairs
Telefteo Psemma, To 57 Michael Cacoyan-
  nis
Telefteo Stichima 87 Costas Zirinis
Telegian, The 60 Jun Fukuda
Telegraph Trail, The 33 Tenny Wright

Telephone, The 88 Rip Torn
Telephone Book, The 71 Nelson Lyon
Telephone Call, The 10 Lewin Fitzhamon
Telephone Calls, The 86 Mohammad-Reza
  Honarmand
Telephone Girl, The 24 Malcolm St. Clair
Telephone Girl, The 27 Herbert Brenon
Telephone Girl and the Lady, The 12 D.
  W. Griffith
Telephone Operator 37 Scott Pembroke
Telephone Rings in the Evening, A 59
  Kozaburo Yoshimura
Téléphone Rose, Le 75 Édouard Molinaro
Telephone Ship 33 Stuart Legg
Téléphone Sonne Toujours Deux Fois, Le
  85 Jean-Pierre Vergne
Telephone Tangle, A 12 A. E. Coleby
Telephone Workers 33 Stuart Legg
Teletests 80 Raúl Ruiz
Television Fan, The 61 Jiří Brdečka
Television Follies, The 33 Geoffrey Ben-
  stead
Television Spy 39 Edward Dmytryk
Television Talent 37 Robert Edmunds
Téli Sirokkó 69 Miklós Jancsó
Téli Sirokkó Lék 69 Miklós Jancsó
Teljes Gözzel 51 Félix Máriássy
Teljes Nap, Egy 88 Ferenc Grunwalsky
Tell 'Em Nothing 26 Leo McCarey
Tell England 30 Anthony Asquith,
  Geoffrey Barkas
Tell It to a Star 45 Frank McDonald
Tell It to Sweeney 27 Gregory La Cava
Tell It to the Judge 28 Leo McCarey
Tell It to the Judge 49 Norman Foster
Tell It to the Marines 18 Arvid E. Gill-
  strom
Tell It to the Marines 26 George W. Hill
Tell It to the Marines 52 William Beau-
  dine
Tell Me 80 Chantal Akerman
Tell Me a Riddle 80 Lee Grant
Tell Me If It Hurts 34 Richard Massing-
  ham
Tell Me in the Sunlight 67 Steve Cochran
Tell Me Lies 67 Peter Brook
Tell Me That You Love Me 83 Tzipi
  Trope
Tell Me That You Love Me, Junie Moon
  69 Otto Preminger
Tell Me Tonight 32 Anatole Litvak
Tell No Tales 38 Leslie Fenton
Tell-Tale Globe, The 15 Cecil Birch
Tell-Tale Heart, The 34 Brian Desmond
  Hurst
Tell-Tale Heart, The 41 Jules Dassin
Tell-Tale Heart, The 53 J. B. Williams
Tell-Tale Heart, The 54 Ted Parmelee
Tell-Tale Heart, The 60 Ernest Morris
Tell-Tale Kinematograph, The 08 Lewin
  Fitzhamon
Tell-Tale Shells, The 12 Allan Dwan
Tell-Tale Taps, The 45 Paul Barralet
Tell-Tale Telephone, The 06 Tom Green
Tell-Tale Umbrella, The 12 Bert Haldane
Tell Tale Wire, The 19 B. Reeves Eason
Tell Tales 30 R. E. Jeffrey
Tell Them Willie Boy Is Here 69 Abra-
  ham Polonsky
Tell Your Children 22 Donald Crisp

Tell Your Children 36 Louis Gasnier
Telling the Tale 14 Dave Aylott
Telling the Tale 16 Cecil Birch
Telling the World 28 Sam Wood
Telltale Light, The 13 Mack Sennett
Tema 79 Gleb Panfilov
Tembo 52 Howard Hill
Témoin, Le 12 Louis Feuillade
Témoin, Le 78 Jean-Pierre Mocky
Témoin dans la Ville, Un 58 Édouard
  Molinaro
Témoin de Minuit, Le 52 Dmitri Kirsanov
Tempeldanserindens Elskov 14 Forest
  Holger-Madsen
Temperamental Husband, A 12 Mack
  Sennett
Temperamental Wife, A 19 David
  Kirkland
Temperance Fete, The 31 Graham Cutts
Temperance Lecture, The 13 Ernest Lepard
Tempered Steel 18 Ralph Ince
Tempered Steel 50 Martin Frič
Tempered with Mercy 10 Lewin Fitzhamon
Tempest, The 08 Percy Stow
Tempest 28 Sam Taylor, Victor Tourjan-
  sky
Tempest 31 Robert Siodmak
Tempest 58 Michelangelo Antonioni,
  Alberto Lattuada
Tempest, The 74 Michael Powell
Tempest, The 79 Derek Jarman
Tempest 82 Paul Mazursky
Tempest 86 Allen Fong
Tempest and Sunshine 16 Carlton S. King
Tempest in a Paint Pot, A 16 Gregory La
  Cava, Vernon Stallings
Tempest in the Flesh 57 Ralph Habib
Tempesta, La 58 Michelangelo Antonioni,
  Alberto Lattuada
Tempesta Su Ceylon 63 Gerd Oswald,
  Giovanni Roccardi
Tempestaire, Le 47 Jean Epstein
Tempestuous Love 57 Falk Harnack
Tempête dans une Chambre à Coucher
  01 Ferdinand Zecca
Tempête sur la Jetée du Tréport 1896
  Georges Méliès
Tempête sur l'Asie 38 Richard Oswald
Tempête sur les Alpes 45 Marcel Ichac
Tempêtes 22 Robert Boudrioz
Tempi Duri per i Vampiri 59 Steno
Tempi Nostri 53 Alessandro Blasetti
Temple de la Magie, Le 01 Georges Méliès
Temple Drake 33 Stephen Roberts
Temple of Dusk 18 James Young
Temple of the Sun, The 01 Georges
  Méliès
Temple of the Swinging Doll 61 Paul
  Wendkos
Temple of the White Elephants 63 Um-
  berto Lenzi
Temple of Venus, The 23 Henry Otto
Temple Tower 30 Donald Gallagher
Tempo degli Avvoltoi, Il 67 Nando Cicero
Tempo di Massacro 66 Lucio Fulci, Terry
  Van Tell
Tempo di Roma 63 Denys De la Patellière
Tempo dos Leopardos, O 85 Zdravko
  Velimirović
Tempo Massimo 36 Mario Mattòli

Tempo Si È Fermato, Il *59* Ermanno Olmi
Temporale Rosy *79* Mario Monicelli
Temporarily Broke *39* József Kanizsay
Temporary Gentleman, A *20* Fred W. Durrant
Temporary Lady, The *21* Adrian Brunel
Temporary Marriage *23* Lambert Hillyer
Temporary Paradise *81* András Kovács
Temporary Sheriff *26* Richard Hatton
Temporary Truce, A *11* D. W. Griffith
Temporary Vagabond, A *20* Henry Edwards
Temporary Widow, The *30* Gustav Ucicky
Tempos Difíceis *88* João Botelho
Temps de Mourir, Le *69* André Farwagi
Temps des Amants, Le *68* Vittorio De Sica
Temps des Assassins, Le *55* Julien Duvivier
Temps des Cerises, Le *38* Jean-Paul Le Chanois
Temps des Écoliers, Le *62* André Delvaux
Temps des Loups *70* Sergio Gobbi
Temps des Œufs Durs, Le *58* Norbert Carbonneaux
Temps du Ghetto, Le *61* Frédéric Rossif
Temps d'un Instant, Le *85* Pierre Jallaud
Temps d'une Chasse, Le *73* Francis Mankiewicz
Temps Perdue, Le *64* Michel Brault
Temptation *14* Charles C. Calvert
Temptation *15* Cecil B. DeMille
Temptation *23* Edward J. LeSaint
Temptation *30* E. Mason Hopper
Temptation *34* Max Neufeld
Temptation *36* Oscar Micheaux
Temptation *46* Irving Pichel
Temptation *48* Kozaburo Yoshimura
Temptation *57* Karel Kachyňa
Temptation *57* Ko Nakahira
Temptation *58* Edmond T. Gréville
Temptation *87* Sergio Bergonzelli
Temptation and Forgiveness *10* A. E. Coleby
Temptation and the Man *16* Robert F. Hill
Temptation Harbour *46* Lance Comfort
Temptation Island *58* Edmond T. Gréville
Temptation of Adam, The *16* Alfred E. Green
Temptation of Carlton Earle, The *23* Wilfred Noy
Temptation of Don Juan, The *87* Grigori Koltunov, Vasily Levin
Temptation of Edwin Swayne, The *15* Frank Lloyd
Temptation of Joseph, The *14* Langford Reed
Temptation of Mr. Prokouk, The *47* Karel Zeman
Temptation of St. Anthony, The *1898* Georges Méliès
Temptation of the Big Cities *15* Forest Holger-Madsen
Temptation's Hour *16* Sidney Morgan
Temptations of a Great City *10* August Blom
Temptations of a Shop Girl *27* Tom Terriss
Temptations of Satan, The *13* Herbert Blaché
Temptations of the Devil *86* Gyula Maar
Tempter, The *13* R. H. Callum, F. Martin Thornton
Tempter, The *74* Damiano Damiani
Tempter, The *74* Alberto De Martino
Tempting of Mrs. Chestney, The *15* Forest Holger-Madsen
Temptress, The *20* George Edwardes Hall
Temptress, The *26* Fred Niblo, Mauritz Stiller
Temptress, The *49* Oswald Mitchell
Temptress, The *63* Eisuke Takizawa
Temptress and the Monk, The *63* Eisuke Takizawa
Tempu di li Pisci Spata, Lu *54* Vittorio De Seta
10 *79* Blake Edwards
Ten Black Women *61* Kon Ichikawa
Ten Cent Adventure, A *14* Chester M. Franklin, Sidney Franklin
Ten Cents a Dance *31* Lionel Barrymore
Ten Cents a Dance *45* Will Jason
Ten Commandments, The *23* Cecil B. DeMille
Ten Commandments, The *54* Cecil B. DeMille
Ten Condemned *32* Richard Ordynski
Ten Dark Women *61* Kon Ichikawa
Ten Days *25* Duke Worne
Ten Days in Paris *39* Tim Whelan
Ten Days That Shook the World *27* Grigori Alexandrov, Sergei Eisenstein
Ten Days to Die *55* G. W. Pabst
Ten Days to Tulara *58* George Sherman
Ten Days' Wonder *70* Claude Chabrol
Ten Dollar Raise, The *21* Edward Sloman
Ten Dollar Raise *35* George Marshall
Ten for Survival *79* John Halas
Ten from Your Show of Shows *73* Max Liebman
Ten Gentlemen from West Point *42* Henry Hathaway
Ten Gladiators, The *64* Gianfranco Parolini
Ten Ladies in an Umbrella *03* Georges Méliès
Ten Ladies in One Umbrella *03* Georges Méliès
Ten Ladies Under One Umbrella *03* Georges Méliès
Ten Laps to Go *38* Elmer Clifton
Ten Little Indians *45* René Clair
Ten Little Indians *65* George Pollock
Ten Little Indians *74* Peter Collinson
Ten Little Indians *89* Alan Birkinshaw
Ten Little Nigger Boys *12* Arthur Cooper
Ten Little Niggers *45* René Clair
Ten Minute Alibi *35* Bernard Vorhaus
Ten Minutes Egg, A *24* Leo McCarey
Ten Minutes to Live *32* Oscar Micheaux
Ten Modern Commandments *27* Dorothy Arzner
Ten Nights in a Bar Room *21* Oscar Apfel
Ten Nights in a Barroom *31* William A. O'Connor
Ten Nights Without a Barroom *20* Edward F. Cline
Ten North Frederick *58* Philip Dunne
Ten O'Clock Mystery, The *14* Abel Gance
Ten of Diamonds *17* Raymond B. West
Ten Pickaninnies *08* Edwin S. Porter
10 Rillington Place *70* Richard Fleischer
Ten Second Film *65* Bruce Conner
Ten Seconds to Hell *58* Robert Aldrich
Ten Tall Men *51* Willis Goldbeck
10:30 P.M. Summer *66* Jules Dassin
Ten Thousand Bedrooms *56* Richard Thorpe
10,000 Dollari per un Massacro *66* Romolo Guerrieri
10,000 Dollars *15* Frank Lloyd
10,000 Dollars Blood Money *66* Romolo Guerrieri
$10,000 Under a Pillow *21* Frank Moser
Ten Thousand Suns, The *67* Ferenc Kósa
10 to Midnight *82* J. Lee-Thompson
Ten Violent Women *82* Ted V. Mikels
Ten Wanted Men *54* H. Bruce Humberstone
Ten Weeks with a Circus *60* Charles Barton
Ten Who Dared *60* William Beaudine
Ten Year Lunch: The Wit and Legend of the Algonquin Round Table, The *87* Aviva Slesin
Ten Year Plan, The *45* Lewis Gilbert
Tenant, The *76* Roman Polanski
Tenchū *70* Hideo Gosha
Tenda da Milagres *75* Nelson Pereira Dos Santos
Tenda Rossa, La *69* Mikhail Kalatozov
Tender Age, The *68* Bernard Toublanc-Michel
Tender Comrade *43* Edward Dmytryk
Tender Cousins *80* David Hamilton
Tender Dracula, or Confessions of a Blood Drinker *74* Alain Robbe-Grillet
Tender Enemy, The *36* Max Ophüls
Tender Feet *25* Archie Mayo
Tender Flesh *73* Laurence Harvey
Tender Folly, A *86* Nini Grassia
Tender Game *58* Faith Hubley, John Hubley
Tender-Hearted Boy, The *12* D. W. Griffith
Tender Hearts *09* D. W. Griffith
Tender Hearts *55* Hugo Haas
Tender Hooks *88* Mary Callaghan
Tender Hour, The *27* George Fitzmaurice
Tender Is the Night *61* Henry King
Tender Loving Care *74* Don Edmonds
Tender Mercies *82* Bruce Beresford
Tender Moment, The *68* Michel Boisrond
Tender Scoundrel *66* Jean Becker
Tender Sharks *66* Michel Deville
Tender Trap, The *55* Charles Walters
Tender Warrior, The *71* Stewart Raffill
Tender Years, The *47* Harold Schuster
Tenderfoot, The *17* William Duncan
Tenderfoot, The *31* Ray Enright
Tenderfoot Courage *27* William Wyler
Tenderfoot Goes West, A *37* Maurice G. O'Neil
Tenderfoot's Triumph, The *10* D. W. Griffith
Tenderloin *28* Michael Curtiz
Tenderly *68* Franco Brusati
Tenderness *30* Richard Loewenbein
Tenderness *66* Elior Ishmukhamedov

Tenderness 72 Jörn Donner
Tenderness of the Wolves 73 Ulli Lommel
Tenderness of Wolves, The 73 Ulli Lommel
Tendre Cousines 80 David Hamilton
Tendre Ennemie, La 36 Max Ophüls
Tendre et Violente Élisabeth 60 Henri Decoin
Tendre Poulet 77 Philippe de Broca
Tendre Voyou 66 Jean Becker
Tendres Chasseurs 69 Ruy Guerra
Tendres Requins 66 Michel Deville
Tendron d'Achille, Le 32 Christian-Jaque
Tenebrae 82 Dario Argento
Tenement 86 Roberta Findlay
Tenente dei Carabinieri, Il 86 Maurizio Ponzi
Tenera Follia, Una 86 Nini Grassia
Tenerezza 87 Enzo Millioni
Ténériffe 32 Yves Allégret
Tengo Fe en Tí 79 Santiago Álvarez
Tengoku ni Musube Koi 32 Heinosuke Gosho
Tengoku Sonohi-Gaeri 30 Tomu Uchida
Tengoku to Jigoku 62 Akira Kurosawa
Teni Zabytykh Predkov 64 Sergei Paradzhanov
Tenichibo and Iganosuke 26 Teinosuke Kinugasa
Tenichibo and Iganosuke 33 Teinosuke Kinugasa
Tenichibo to Iganosuke 26 Teinosuke Kinugasa
Tenichibo to Iganosuke 33 Teinosuke Kinugasa
Tenka Taiheiki 28 Hiroshi Inagaki
Tenkosai 85 Nobuhiko Obayashi
Tenkrát o Vánocích 58 Karel Kachyňa
Tenkū no Shiro Laputa 87 Hayao Miyazaki
Tennessee Beat, The 66 Richard Brill
Tennessee Champ 54 Fred M. Wilcox
Tennessee Johnson 42 William Dieterle
Tennessee Stallion 82 Don Hulette
Tennessee's Pardner 16 George Melford
Tennessee's Partner 55 Allan Dwan
Tennis Chumps 49 Joseph Barbera, William Hanna
Tennis Tactics 37 David Miller
Tenor, Inc. 16 Ernst Lubitsch
Tenore per Forza 48 Riccardo Freda
Tense Alignment 77 Malcolm Le Grice
Tension 49 John Berry
Tension at Table Rock 56 Charles Marquis Warren
Tent of Miracles, The 75 Nelson Pereira Dos Santos
Tentacles 69 Kaneto Shindo
Tentacles 77 Ovidio Assonitis
Tentacles of the North 26 Louis Chaudet
Tentation, La 29 Jacques De Baroncelli
Tentation de Saint-Antoine, La 1898 Georges Méliès
Tentation d'Isabelle, La 85 Jacques Doillon
Tentations 64 José Antonio De la Loma, Louis Duchesne, Radley Metzger
Tentative d'Assassinat en Chemin de Fer 04 Alice Guy-Blaché
Tentative de Films Abstraits 30 Henri

Storck
Tentativo Sentimentale, Un 63 Pasquale Festa Campanile, Massimo Franciosa
Tentazione 87 Sergio Bergonzelli
Tenth Avenue 28 William DeMille
Tenth Avenue Angel 48 Roy Rowland
Tenth Avenue Kid 38 Bernard Vorhaus
Tenth Case, The 17 George Kelson
Tenth Man, The 36 Brian Desmond Hurst
Tenth October Anniversary, The 28 Dziga Vertov
Tenth of a Second 87 Darrell Roodt
Tenth One in Hiding, The 89 Lina Wertmuller
Tenth Symphony, The 17 Abel Gance
Tenth Victim, The 65 Elio Petri
Tenth Woman, The 24 James Flood
Tenting Tonight on the Old Campground 43 Lewis D. Collins
Tents of Allah, The 23 Charles Logue
Tenue de Soirée 86 Bertrand Blier
Teo el Pelirrojo 86 Paco Lucio
Teo the Redhead 86 Paco Lucio
Teodora 27 Luigi Maggi
Teodora, Imperatrice di Bisanzio 09 Ernesto Maria Pasquali
Teodora, Imperatrice di Bisanzio 53 Riccardo Freda
Teodoro e Socio 24 Mario Bonnard
Teorema 68 Pier Paolo Pasolini
Tequila Mockingbird 64 Friz Freleng
Tequila Sunrise 88 Robert Towne
Tequiman 87 Jorge Vivanco
Tér 71 István Szabó
Tercentenary of the Romanov Dynasty's Accession to the Throne 13 Nikolai Larin, A. Uralsky
Tere Bina Kya Jina 89 P. P. Ghosh
Teresa 50 Fred Zinnemann
Teresa 87 Dino Risi
Teresa la Ladra 73 Carlo Di Palma
Teresa Raquin 15 Nino Martoglio
Teresa the Thief 73 Carlo Di Palma
Teresa Venerdì 41 Vittorio De Sica
Terirem 87 Apostolos C. Doxiadis
Terje Vigen 16 Victor Sjöström
Term of Trial 62 Peter Glenville
Termina Siempre Así 40 Enrique T. Susini
Terminal Choice 85 Sheldon Larry
Terminal Entry 87 John Kincade
Terminal Island 73 Stephanie Rothman
Terminal Man, The 74 Michael Hodges
Terminal Station 53 Vittorio De Sica
Terminal Station Indiscretion 53 Vittorio De Sica
Termination 66 Bruce Baillie
Terminator, The 84 James Cameron
Terminus 60 John Schlesinger
Terminus 86 Pierre-William Glenn
Terminus Love 57 Georg Tressler
Terminus Station 53 Vittorio De Sica
Terms of Endearment 83 James L. Brooks
Ternosecco 86 Giancarlo Giannini
Terra del Melodramma, La 47 Luciano Emmer, Enrico Gras
Terra di Nessuno 40 Mario Baffico
Terra em Transe 66 Glauber Rocha
Terra Incognita 59 Walerian Borowczyk
Terra Ladina 49 Dino Risi
Terra Madre 31 Alessandro Blasetti

Terra Senza Donne 29 Carmine Gallone
Terra Trema, La 47 Luchino Visconti
Terra Trema: Episodio del Mare, La 47 Luchino Visconti
Terrace, The 62 Leopoldo Torre-Nilsson
Terrace, The 80 Ettore Scola
Terraco Augusta 33 Fernando Mantilla, Carlos Velo
Terrain Vague 60 Marcel Carné
Terraza, La 62 Leopoldo Torre-Nilsson
Terrazza, La 80 Ettore Scola
Terre, La 21 André Antoine
Terre de Feu 38 Marcel L'Herbier
Terre de Flandre 38 Henri Storck
Terre des Taureaux, La 25 Musidora
Terre des Toros, La 25 Musidora
Terre du Diable, La 21 Luitz-Morat
Terre Promise, La 25 Henri Roussel
Terre Sans Pain 32 Luis Buñuel
Terres Brulées 34 Charles Dekeukeleire
Terres d'Or, Les 25 René Le Somptier
Terreur 24 Edward José
Terreur des Batignolles, La 31 Henri-Georges Clouzot
Terreur des Mers, La 61 Lee Kresel, Domenico Paolella
Terreur sur la Savane 62 Yves Allégret
Terrible Beauty, A 60 Tay Garnett
Terrible Bourreau Turc, Le 04 Georges Méliès
Terrible Bout de Papier, Le 14 Émile Cohl
Terrible Discovery, A 11 D. W. Griffith
Terrible Eruption of Mount Pelee and Destruction of St. Pierre, Martinique, The 02 Georges Méliès
Terrible Flirt, A 05 Lewin Fitzhamon
Terrible Kids, The 06 Edwin S. Porter
Terrible Lesson, A 12 Alice Guy-Blaché
Terrible Night, A 1896 Georges Méliès
Terrible Night, A 12 Alice Guy-Blaché
Terrible One, The 15 Wilbert Melville
Terrible Ordeal, A 15 Forest Holger-Madsen
Terrible People, The 28 Spencer G. Bennet
Terrible People, The 60 Harald Reinl
Terrible Plant, A 13 Lewin Fitzhamon
Terrible Revenge, A 13 Władysław Starewicz
Terrible Scrap of Paper, The 14 Émile Cohl
Terrible Secret of Dr. Hichcock, The 62 Riccardo Freda
Terrible 'Tec, The 16 Will P. Kellino
Terrible Teddy the Grizzly King 01 Edwin S. Porter
Terrible Time, A 21 Wallace A. Carlson
Terrible Toreador, El 29 Walt Disney, Ubbe Iwerks
Terrible Troubador, The 33 Walter Lantz
Terrible Turkish Executioner, The 04 Georges Méliès
Terrible Turkish Executioner, or It Served Him Right, The 04 Georges Méliès
Terrible Twins, The 14 Elwin Neame
Terrible Two, The 14 Joe Evans
Terrible Two, The 14 Hay Plumb
Terrible Two—A.B.S., The 15 James Read
Terrible Two Abroad, The 15 James Read
Terrible Two Had, The 15 James Read

Terrible Two in Luck, The *14* James Read

Terrible Two Join the Police Force, The *14* Hay Plumb

Terrible Two, Kidnappers, The *14* James Read

Terrible Two on the Mash, The *14* Joe Evans

Terrible Two on the Stage, The *14* Joe Evans

Terrible Two on the Twist, The *14* Joe Evans

Terrible Two on the Wait, The *14* James Read

Terrible Two on the Wangle, The *14* James Read

Terrible Two on the Warpath, The *14* Joe Evans

Terribly Talented *48* Willard Van Dyke

Terrier Stricken *52* Chuck Jones

Terrificante Notte del Demonio, La *71* Jean Brismée

Terrified! *62* Lew Landers

Territoire, Le *81* Raúl Ruiz

Territory, The *81* Raúl Ruiz

Terror, The *17* Frank Myton, Raymond Wells

Terror, The *20* Jacques Jaccard

Terror, The *26* Clifford Smith

Terror *28* Louis King

Terror, The *28* Roy Del Ruth

Terror, The *37* Richard Bird

Terror, The *62* Francis Ford Coppola, Roger Corman, Monte Hellman, Jack Hill, Dennis Jacob, Jack Nicholson

Terror *73* Robert H. Oliver

Terror *78* Norman J. Warren

Terror Aboard *33* Paul Sloane

Terror After Midnight *62* Jürgen Goslar

Terror and Black Lace *86* Luis Alcoriza

Terror and the Terrier, The *10* A. E. Coleby

Terror at Black Falls *62* Richard C. Sarafian

Terror at Halfday *65* Herschell Gordon Lewis

Terror at Midnight *56* Franklin Adreon

Terror at Red Wolf Inn *72* Bud Townsend

Terror Beneath the Sea *66* Hajime Sato

Terror by Night *31* Thornton Freeland

Terror by Night *46* Roy William Neill

Terror Camping Site *87* Ruggero Deodato

Terror Caníbal *81* Julio Pérez Tabernero

Terror Castle *63* Richard McNamara, Antonio Margheriti

Terror Castle *73* Robert H. Oliver

Terror Circus *73* Alan Rudolph

Terror Creatures from the Grave *66* Massimo Pupillo

Terror en el Espacio *65* Mario Bava

Terror Eyes *80* Ken Hughes

Terror Faces Magoo *59* Chris Ishii

Terror Factor, The *80* William Malone

Terror from 5000 A.D. *58* Robert Gurney, Jr.

Terror from the Sun *59* Thomas Bontross, Gianbatista Cassarino, Robert Clarke

Terror from the Unknown *83* Donald M. Dohler

Terror from the Year 5000 *58* Robert Gurney, Jr.

Terror from Under the House *71* Sidney Hayers

Terror House *42* Leslie Arliss

Terror House *72* Bud Townsend

Terror in a Texas Town *58* Joseph H. Lewis

Terror in Space *65* Mario Bava

Terror in the Aisles *84* Andrew J. Kuehn

Terror in the City *64* Allen Baron

Terror in the Crypt *63* Camillo Mastrocinque

Terror in the Forest *83* Don Jones

Terror in the Haunted House *58* Harold Daniels

Terror in the Jungle *68* Tom DeSimone, Alexander Grattan, Andy Janzack

Terror in the Midnight Sun *60* Virgil Vogel, Jerry Warren

Terror in the Wax Museum *73* Georg Fenady

Terror in Toyland *80* Lewis Jackson

Terror Is a Man *59* Gerry De Leon, Eddie Romero

Terror Island *20* James Cruze

Terror Mountain *28* Louis King

Terror of Bar X, The *27* Scott Pembroke

Terror of Dr. Chaney, The *75* Michael Pataki

Terror of Dr. Hichcock, The *62* Riccardo Freda

Terror of Dr. Mabuse, The *60* Werner Klingler

Terror of Dracula *21* F. W. Murnau

Terror of Frankenstein *75* Calvin Floyd

Terror of Godzilla *75* Inoshiro Honda

Terror of Mechagodzilla *75* Inoshiro Honda

Terror of Rome Against the Son of Hercules, The *64* Mario Caiano

Terror of Sheba, The *73* Don Chaffey

Terror of the Air, The *14* Frank Wilson

Terror of the Black Mask *60* Umberto Lenzi

Terror of the Bloodhunters *62* Jerry Warren

Terror of the Hatchet Men *60* Anthony Bushell

Terror of the House, The *05* Alf Collins

Terror of the Mad Doctor, The *60* Werner Klingler

Terror of the Mummy *59* Terence Fisher

Terror of the Neighbourhood, The *05* Charles Raymond

Terror of the Plains *34* Harry S. Webb

Terror of the Red Mask *60* Piero Pierotti

Terror of the Snake Woman, The *60* Sidney J. Furie

Terror of the Steppe *64* Tanio Boccia

Terror of the Tongs, The *60* Anthony Bushell

Terror of the Vampires, The *70* Jean Rollin

Terror of Tiny Town, The *38* Sam Newfield

Terror on a Train *53* Ted Tetzlaff

Terror on Blood Island *68* Gerry De Leon, Eddie Romero

Terror on the Midway *42* Dave Fleischer

Terror on Tiptoe *36* Louis Renoir

Terror on Tour *80* Don Edmonds

Terror Ship *54* Vernon Sewell

Terror Squad *88* Peter Maris

Terror Street *53* Montgomery Tully

Terror Strikes, The *58* Bert I. Gordon

Terror Trail *33* Armand Schaefer

Terror Trail *46* Ray Nazarro

Terror Train *79* Roger Spottiswoode

Terror Within, The *88* Thierry Notz

Terror y Encajes Negro *86* Luis Alcoriza

Terrore *63* Sergio Corbucci, Antonio Margheriti

Terrore con gli Occhi Storti, Il *72* Steno

Terrore dei Barbari, Il *59* Carlo Campogalliani

Terrore dei Mare, Il *61* Lee Kresel, Domenico Paolella

Terrore dell'Oklahoma, Il *60* Mario Amendola

Terrore nello Spazio *65* Mario Bava

Terrorista, Il *63* Gianfranco De Bosio

Terrorists, The *75* Caspar Wrede

Terrorizer *86* Edward Yang

Terrorizers, The *86* Edward Yang

Terrornauts, The *67* Montgomery Tully

Terrors *30* Erle O. Smith

Terrors on Horseback *46* Sam Newfield

Terrorvision *86* Ted Nicolaou

Terry and the Pirates *40* James W. Horne

Terry of the Times *30* Henry MacRae

Terry on the Fence *85* Frank Godwin

Teru hi Kumoru hi *26* Teinosuke Kinugasa

Terug naar Oestgeest *87* Theo van Gogh

Terza Liceo *53* Luciano Emmer

Teseo Contro il Minotauro *61* Silvio Amadio

Tesha *27* Edwin Greenwood, Victor Saville

Tesla *80* Krsto Papić

Tesoro *88* Diego De la Texera

Tesoro de Drácula, El *68* René Cardona

Tesoro de la Diosa Blanca, El *83* Jesús Franco

Tesoro de las Cuatro Coronas, El *82* Ferdinando Baldi

Tesoro de Makuba, El *66* José María Elorrieta

Tesoro de Pancho Villa, El *36* Arcady Boytler

Tesoro del Amazonas, El *83* René Cardona, Jr.

Tesoro di Rommel, Il *58* Romolo Marcellini

Tesouro Perdido *27* Humberto Mauro

Tess *79* Roman Polanski

Tess of the D'Urbervilles *13* J. Searle Dawley, Edwin S. Porter

Tess of the D'Urbervilles *24* Marshall Neilan

Tess of the Storm Country *14* Edwin S. Porter

Tess of the Storm Country *22* John S. Robertson

Tess of the Storm Country *32* Alfred Santell

Tess of the Storm Country *60* Paul Guilfoyle

Tessie *25* Dallas M. Fitzgerald

Test, The *09* D. W. Griffith

Test, The *11* Allan Dwan

Test, The *13* Bert Haldane

Test, The *14* Wallace Reid
Test, The *15* James W. Castle
Test, The *15* George Fitzmaurice
Test, The *16* Charles C. Calvert
Test, The *23* Edwin Greenwood
Test, The *26* William J. Elliott
Test, The *87* Ann Zacharias
Test for Love, A *37* Vernon Sewell
Test of Affection, A *11* Percy Stow
Test of Donald Norton, The *26* B. Reeves Eason
Test of Fidelity *54* Ivan Pyriev
Test of Friendship, The *08* D. W. Griffith
Test of Honor, The *19* John S. Robertson
Test of Love, A *84* Gil Brealey
Test of Pilot Pirx, The *78* Marek Piestrak
Test Pilot *38* Victor Fleming
Test Pilot Pirx *78* Marek Piestrak
Test Trip *60* Félix Máriássy
Testa o Croce *69* Piero Pierotti
Testa or Croce *82* Nanni Loy
Testa T'Ammazzo, Croce Sei Morto...Mi Chiamano Alleluja *71* Giuliano Carmineo
Testament *74* James Broughton
Testament, Le *74* André Cayatte
Testamentet *83* Lynne Littman
Testament *88* John Akomfrah
Testament de Moyse, Le *31* Edmond T. Gréville
Testament de Pierrot, Le *04* Alice Guy-Blaché
Testament des Dr. Mabuse, Das *32* Fritz Lang
Testament des Dr. Mabuse, Das *60* Werner Klingler
Testament d'Orphée, Le *59* Jean Cocteau
Testament du Dr. Cordelier, Le *59* Jean Renoir
Testament du Dr. Mabuse, Le *32* Fritz Lang
Testament d'un Poète Juif Assassine *87* Franck Cassenti
Testament of a Murdered Jewish Poet *87* Franck Cassenti
Testament of Dr. Cordelier, The *59* Jean Renoir
Testament of Dr. Mabuse, The *32* Fritz Lang
Testament of Dr. Mabuse, The *60* Werner Klingler
Testament of Orpheus, The *59* Jean Cocteau
Testament of Professor Wilczur, The *39* Leonard Buczkowski
Testamentet *14* Forest Holger-Madsen
Testamentets Hemmelighed *14* Forest Holger-Madsen
Testamento de Madigan, El *67* Dan Ash, Giorgio Gentili, L. Lelli
Testamento del Virrey, El *44* Ladislas Vajda
Testet *87* Ann Zacharias
Testigo Azul *88* Francisco Rodríguez
Testigo para un Crimen *66* Emilio Vieyra
Testimone, Il *45* Pietro Germi
Testimonies of Her *63* Jörn Donner
Testimony *20* Guy Newall
Testimony *73* Kwon-taek Im
Testimony *87* Tony Palmer
Testing Block, The *20* Lambert Hillyer

Testing of Mildred Vane, The *18* Wilfred Lucas
Teta—Behavy Max a Strašidla *88* Juraj Jakubisko
Tête Contre les Murs, La *58* Georges Franju
Tête Coupée, La *15* Louis Feuillade
Tête dans le Sac, La *84* Gérard Lauzier
Tête de Normande St. Onge, La *75* Gilles Carle
Tête de Turc *35* Jacques Becker
Tête d'un Homme, La *32* Julien Duvivier
Tête la Première, La *65* Claude Sautet
Tête Qui Rapporte, Une *35* Jacques Becker
Têtes de Femmes, Femmes de Tête *16* Jacques Feyder
Tetička *41* Martin Frič
Tętno Polskiego Manchesteru *28* Aleksander Ford
Tettes Ismeretlen, A *57* László Ranódy
Tetto, Il *55* Vittorio De Sica
Teufel, Der *18* E. A. Dupont
Teufel der Liebe, Der *19* Paul Stein
Teufel in Seide *68* Rolf Hansen
Teufelskerl, Ein *38* Georg Jacoby
Teuflischen Schwestern, Die *77* Jesús Franco
Tevya *39* Maurice Schwartz
Tevya the Milkman *39* Maurice Schwartz
Tevye *39* Maurice Schwartz
Tevye and His Seven Daughters *68* Menahem Golan
Tex *26* Tom Gibson
Tex *82* Tim Hunter
Tex e il Signore degli Abissi *85* Duccio Tessari
Tex Granger *48* Derwin Abrahams
Tex Rides with the Boy Scouts *37* Ray Taylor
Tex Takes a Holiday *32* Alvin J. Neitz
Tex Willer and the Lord of the Deep *85* Duccio Tessari
Texaco Hour, The *85* Eduardo Barberena
Texan, The *20* Lynn Reynolds
Texan, The *30* John Cromwell
Texan, The *32* Clifford Smith
Texan Meets Calamity Jane, The *50* Ande Lamb
Texans, The *38* James P. Hogan
Texans Never Cry *51* Frank McDonald
Texas *22* William Bertram
Texas *41* George Marshall
Texas Across the River *66* Michael Gordon
Texas Addio *66* Ferdinando Baldi
Texas Bad Man, The *32* Edward Laemmle
Texas Bad Man *53* Lewis D. Collins
Texas Bearcat, The *25* B. Reeves Eason
Texas, Brooklyn and Heaven *48* William Castle
Texas Buddies *32* Robert North Bradbury
Texas Carnival *51* Charles Walters
Texas Chainsaw Massacre, The *74* Tobe Hooper
Texas Chainsaw Massacre 2, The *86* Tobe Hooper
Texas City *52* Lewis D. Collins
Texas Cyclone *32* D. Ross Lederman
Texas Desperadoes *36* Otho Lovering
Texas Detour *78* Hikmet Avedis

Texas Dynamo *50* Ray Nazarro
Texas Flash *28* Robert J. Horner
Texas Gun Fighter *32* Phil Rosen
Texas in 1999 *31* Dave Fleischer
Texas Jack *35* Bernard B. Ray
Texas John Slaughter *58* Harry Keller
Texas Justice *42* Sam Newfield
Texas Kid, The *20* B. Reeves Eason
Texas Kid, The *43* Lambert Hillyer
Texas Kid, The *66* Lesley Selander
Texas Kid—Outlaw *49* Kurt Neumann
Texas Lady *55* Tim Whelan
Texas Lawman *51* Lewis D. Collins
Texas Legend, A *82* Jack Starrett
Texas Lightning *81* Gary Graver
Texas Man Hunt *42* Sam Newfield
Texas Marshal, The *41* Sam Newfield
Texas Masquerade *44* George Archainbaud
Texas Panhandle *45* Ray Nazarro
Texas Pioneers *32* Harry Fraser
Texas Rambler, The *35* Robert F. Hill
Texas Ranger, The *31* D. Ross Lederman
Texas Rangers, The *36* King Vidor
Texas Rangers, The *51* Phil Karlson
Texas Rangers Ride Again, The *40* James P. Hogan
Texas Renegades *40* Sam Newfield
Texas Road Agent *41* Charles Lamont
Texas Romance—1909, A *64* Robert Benton
Texas Rose *55* Harold Schuster
Texas Serenade *36* Joseph Kane
Texas Serial Killings, The *86* John Dwyer
Texas Stagecoach *40* Joseph H. Lewis
Texas Stampede *39* Sam Nelson
Texas Steer, A *15* Giles Warren
Texas Steer, A *27* Richard Wallace
Texas Streak, The *26* Lynn Reynolds
Texas Terror *35* Robert North Bradbury
Texas Terrors *40* George Sherman
Texas to Bataan *42* Robert E. Tansey
Texas to Tokyo *43* John Rawlins
Texas Tom *50* Joseph Barbera, William Hanna
Texas Tommy *28* John P. McGowan
Texas Tornado, The *28* Frank Howard Clark
Texas Tornado *32* Oliver Drake
Texas Trail, The *25* Scott R. Dunlap
Texas Trail *37* David Selman
Texas Trouble Shooters *42* S. Roy Luby
Texas Wildcats *39* Sam Newfield
Texasville *90* Peter Bogdanovich
Texican, The *66* Lesley Selander
Text of Light, The *74* Stan Brakhage
Textiles and Ornamental Arts of India *55* Charles Eames, Ray Eames
Teyzem *86* Halit Refik
Těžký Život Dobrodruha *41* Martin Frič
Thaal and Rhythm *71* Shyam Benegal
Thaïs *14* Constance Crawley, Arthur Maude
Thaïs *17* Hugo Ballin, Frank Crane
Thames, The *48* David Hand
Thanatopsis *62* Ed Emshwiller
Thanatos *86* Cristián González
Thank Evans *38* Roy William Neill
Thank God It's Friday *78* Robert Klane
Thank Heaven for Small Favors *63* Jean-Pierre Mocky

Thank You 25 John Ford
Thank You All Very Much 69 Waris Hussein
Thank You, Aunt 67 Salvatore Samperi
Thank You, Jeeves 36 Arthur Greville Collins
Thank You Jesus for the Eternal Present: 1 73 George Landow
Thank You Jesus for the Eternal Present: 2 — A Film of Their 1973 Spring Tour Commissioned by Christian World Liberation Front of Berkeley, California 74 George Landow
Thank You Madame 35 Carmine Gallone
Thank You, Mr. Jeeves 36 Arthur Greville Collins
Thank You, Mr. Moto 38 Norman Foster
Thank You Mr. Robertson 86 Pierre Levie
Thank You, Santiago 84 Santiago Álvarez
Thank Your Lucky Stars 43 David Butler
Thank Your Stars 34 Wesley Ruggles
Thanking the Audience 00 Georges Méliès
Thanks a Million 35 Roy Del Ruth
Thanks for Everything 38 William A. Seiter
Thanks for Listening 37 Marshall Neilan
Thanks for the Boat Ride 26 Charles Lamont
Thanks for the Buggy Ride 27 William A. Seiter
Thanks for the Memory 38 George Archainbaud
Thanks for the Memory 38 Dave Fleischer
Thanos and Despina 67 Nikos Papatakis
Thark 32 Tom Walls
Thassios, O 75 Theodoros Angelopoulos
That Awful Baby 05 Alf Collins
That Awful Cigar 02 George Albert Smith
That Awful Pipe 09 Walter R. Booth
That Awful Pipe 13 Bert Haldane
That Boy from the "B" End 87 Romano Scandariato
That Brennan Girl 46 Alfred Santell
That Brute Simmons 28 Hugh Croise
That Busy Bee 04 Alf Collins
That Cat 63 Vojtěch Jasný
That Certain Age 38 Edward Ludwig
That Certain Feeling 56 Melvin Frank, Norman Panama
That Certain Something 41 Clarence Badger
That Certain Thing 28 Frank Capra
That Certain Woman 37 Edmund Goulding
That Championship Season 82 Jason Miller
That Chink at Golden Gulch 10 D. W. Griffith
That Christmas 58 Karel Kachyňa
That Cold Day in the Park 69 Robert Altman
That Dangerous Age 49 Gregory Ratoff
That Dare Devil 11 Mack Sennett
That Darn Cat! 65 Robert Stevenson
That Day, at the Beach 83 Edward Yang
That Day of Rest 48 Kenneth Fairbairn
That Day on the Beach 83 Edward Yang
That Devil Bateese 18 William Wolbert
That Devil Quemado 25 Del Andrews
That Dirty Story of the West 68 Enzo G.

Castellari
That Dreadful Donkey 04 Frank Mottershaw
That Eternal Ping-Pong 02 Percy Stow
That Fatal Sneeze 07 Lewin Fitzhamon
That Female Scent 74 Dino Risi
That Fine Day 63 France Štiglić
That Forsyte Woman 49 Compton Bennett
That French Lady 24 Edmund Mortimer
That Funny Feeling 65 Richard Thorpe
That Gal of Burke's 16 Frank Borzage
That Gang of Mine 40 Joseph H. Lewis
That Girl from Beverly Hills 65 Michael Pfleghar
That Girl from College 39 John Farrow
That Girl from Paris 36 Leigh Jason
That Girl Is a Tramp 74 Jack Guy
That Girl Montana 21 Robert Thornby
That Girl of Burke's 16 Frank Borzage
That Golf Game 48 Kenneth Fairbairn
That Gosh Darn Mortgage 26 Edward F. Cline
That Hagen Girl 47 Peter Godfrey
That Hamilton Woman 41 Alexander Korda
That Happy Couple 51 Juan Antonio Bardem, Luis García Berlanga
That Happy Pair 51 Juan Antonio Bardem, Luis García Berlanga
That House in the Outskirts 80 Eugenio Martin
That House on the Outskirts 80 Eugenio Martin
That I May Live 37 Allan Dwan
That Is the Port Light 61 Tadashi Imai
That Jane from Maine 59 Richard Quine
That Joyous Eve 60 Fons Rademakers
That Kind of Girl 51 Reginald LeBorg
That Kind of Girl 63 Gerry O'Hara
That Kind of Love 59 Jiří Weiss
That Kind of Woman 59 Sidney Lumet
That Lady 54 Terence Young
That Lady from Peking 70 Eddie Davis
That Lady in Ermine 48 Ernst Lubitsch, Otto Preminger
That Lass of Chandler's 29 W. J. Sargent
That Letter from Teddy 10 Edwin S. Porter
That Little Band of Gold 15 Roscoe Arbuckle
That Little Big Fellow 27 Dave Fleischer
That Little Difference 69 Duccio Tessari
That Love Might Last 21 Fred Paul
That Lucky Stiff 81 Chuck Vincent
That Lucky Touch 75 Christopher Miles
That Mad Mad Hospital 86 Julio Ruiz Llaneza
That Mad Mr. Jones 48 S. Sylvan Simon
That Man Bolt 72 Henry Levin, David Lowell Rich
That Man Flintstone 66 Joseph Barbera, William Hanna
That Man from Rio 63 Philippe de Broca
That Man from Tangier 53 Robert Elwyn
That Man George! 65 Jacques Deray
That Man in Istanbul 66 Antonio Isamendi
That Man Jack 25 William James Craft
That Man Mr. Jones 48 S. Sylvan Simon

That Man of Mine 47 William Alexander
That Man Samson 37 Leslie Goodwins
That Man's Here Again 37 Louis King
That Marvellous Gramophone 09 Lewin Fitzhamon
That Midnight Kiss 49 Norman Taurog
That Minstrel Man 14 Roscoe Arbuckle
That Model from Paris 26 Robert Florey, Louis Gasnier
That Mothers Might Live 38 Fred Zinnemann
That Murder in Berlin 29 Friedrich Feher
That Mysterious Fez 14 Hay Plumb
That Nasty Sticky Stuff 08 Frank Mottershaw
That Naughty Girl 03 Alf Collins
That Navy Spirit 37 Kurt Neumann
That Nazty Nuisance 43 Glenn Tryon
That Night 17 Edward F. Cline
That Night 28 Leo McCarey
That Night 57 John Newland
That Night in London 32 Rowland V. Lee
That Night in Rio 41 Irving Cummings
That Night with You 45 William A. Seiter
That Night's Wife 30 Yasujiro Ozu
That Obscure Object of Desire 77 Luis Buñuel
That Old Gang of Mine 25 May Tully
That Old Gang of Mine 31 Dave Fleischer
That Other Girl 13 Phillips Smalley
That Other Woman 42 Ray McCarey
That Others May Live 48 Aleksander Ford
That Party in Person 29 Joseph Santley
That Pesky Pup 17 Joseph Harwitz
That Ragtime Band 13 Mack Sennett
That Reminds Me 19 Gregory La Cava
That Rhythm, Those Blues 89 George T. Nierenberg
That Riviera Touch 66 Cliff Owen
That Royle Girl 25 D. W. Griffith
That Sharp Note 13 Allan Dwan
That Silly Ass 15 H. Oceano Martinek
That Sinking Feeling 79 Bill Forsyth
That Skating Carnival 10 Percy Stow
That Something 21 Lawrence Underwood, Margery Wilson
That Son of Sheik 22 Al Christie
That Sort 16 Charles Brabin
That Sort of Girl 16 Charles Brabin
That Splendid November 68 Mauro Bolognini
That Springtime Feeling 15 Del Henderson
That Summer 79 Harley Cokliss
That Sweet Word "Freedom" 73 Vytautas Zalakevicius
That Tender Age 64 Gian Vittorio Baldi, Michel Brault, Jean Rouch, Hiroshi Teshigahara
That Tender Touch 69 Russ Vincent
That Tennessee Beat 66 Richard Brill
That Terrible Dog 06 Frank Mottershaw
That Terrible Pest 11 Dave Aylott
That Texas Jamboree 46 Ray Nazarro
That They May Live 37 Abel Gance
That Too Will Pass 86 Nenad Dizdarević
That Touch of Mink 62 Delbert Mann
That Uncertain Feeling 41 Ernst Lubitsch
That Was Then...This Is Now 85 Christopher Cain

That Way with Women 47 Frederick De Cordova
That Wild West 24 Alvin J. Neitz
That Woman 22 Harry Hoyt
That Woman 68 Will Tremper
That Woman Opposite 57 Compton Bennett
That Wonderful Urge 48 Robert B. Sinclair
That'll Be the Day 74 Claude Whatham
That's a Good Girl 33 Jack Buchanan, Herbert Wilcox
That's Adequate 86 Harry Hurwitz
That's All American 17 Christy Cabanne
That's All That Matters 31 Joe May
That's an Order 55 John Irwin
That's Called the Dawn 55 Luis Buñuel
That's Carry On! 77 Gerald Thomas
That's Dancing! 85 Jack Haley, Jr.
That's Done It 15 Cecil Birch
That's Entertainment! 74 Jack Haley, Jr.
That's Entertainment, Part 2 75 Jack Haley, Jr., Gene Kelly
That's Entertainment, Too! 75 Jack Haley, Jr., Gene Kelly
That's Good 19 Harry Franklin
That's Gratitude 34 Frank Craven
That's His Weakness 30 John Argyle
That's How It Is 72 Vasili Shuksin
That's It 66 Jorge Sanjinés
That's Life! 86 Blake Edwards
That's My Baby 26 William Beaudine
That's My Baby 44 William Berke
That's My Baby 85 John Bradshaw, Edie Yolles
That's My Boy 32 Roy William Neill
That's My Boy 51 Hal Walker
That's My Daddy 27 Fred Newmeyer
That's My Gal 47 George Blair
That's My Man 46 Frank Borzage
That's My Pup 53 Joseph Barbera, William Hanna
That's My Story 37 Sidney Salkow
That's My Uncle 35 George Pearson
That's My Wife 29 Lloyd French
That's My Wife 33 Leslie Hiscott
That's Not Right—Watch Me 07 Percy Stow
That's Right, You're Wrong 39 David Butler
That's That 23 Richard Thorpe
That's the Spirit 45 Charles Lamont
That's the Stuff 85 Larry Cohen
That's the Ticket 40 Redd Davis
That's the Way It Is 70 Denis Sanders
That's the Way of the World 75 Sig Shore
That's the Way to Do It 82 Stanley Long
That's Torn It! 14 Percy Stow
That's Us 87 Sultan Khodjikov
That's Your Funeral 72 John Robins
Thau le Pêcheur 57 Pierre Schöndörffer
Thaumatopoea 60 Robert Enrico
Thaumaturge Chinois, Le 04 Georges Méliès
Thaviya Aase 88 Raj Kishore
Thaw, The 31 Boris Barnet
Thaw 86 Chang Bom Rim, Ko Hak Rim
Thaw and the Lasso 13 Émile Cohl
Thaw and the Spider 13 Émile Cohl
Thayi Karulu 88 N. S. Dhananjaya

Thayikotta Thali 88 Ravindranath
Thé au Harem d'Archimèdes, Le 85 Mehdi Charef
Thé chez la Concierge, Le 07 Louis Feuillade
The F.J. Holden 77 Michael Thornhill
Thea Roland 32 Henry Koster
Theater 44 Mikio Naruse
Theater of Life 36 Tomu Uchida
Theaternächte von Berlin 32 Willi Wolff
Théâtre de Monsieur et Madame Kabal, Le 67 Walerian Borowczyk
Théâtre des Matières, Le 78 Jean-Claude Biette
Théâtre National Populaire, Le 56 Georges Franju
Theatre of Blood 73 Douglas Hickox
Theatre of Death 66 Samuel Gallu
Theatre Royal 30 George Cukor, Cyril Gardner
Theatre Royal 43 John Baxter
Theatrical Chimney Sweep, The 09 Jack Smith
Thee and Me 48 Terry Bishop
Theft, The 24 Teinosuke Kinugasa
Theft of the Mona Lisa, The 31 Géza von Bolváry
Their Big Moment 34 James Cruze
Their Compact 17 Edwin Carewe
Their Dark Secret 16 William Beaudine
Their Fates Sealed 11 Mack Sennett
Their First Acquaintance 14 Donald Crisp
Their First Arrest 16 William Beaudine
Their First Cigar 07 Tom Green
Their First Divorce 11 Mack Sennett
Their First Divorce Case 11 Mack Sennett
Their First Kidnapping Case 12 Mack Sennett
Their First Mistake 32 George Marshall
Their First Misunderstanding 11 Thomas Ince, George Loane Tucker
Their First Trip to Tokyo 53 Yasujiro Ozu
Their First Vacation 22 Malcolm St. Clair
Their Golden Wedding 15 Frank Lloyd
Their Hero Son 12 Allan Dwan
Their Hour 28 Alfred Raboch
Their Husbands 13 Henry Lehrman
Their Last Night 53 Georges Lacombe
Their Legacy 62 Kozaburo Yoshimura
Their Love Growed Cold 23 Earl Hurd
Their Mad Moment 31 Hamilton MacFadden, Chandler Sprague
Their Masterpiece 13 Allan Dwan
Their Mutual Child 20 George L. Cox
Their Night Out 33 Harry Hughes
Their Only Chance 78 J. David Siddon
Their Only Son 14 Bert Haldane
Their Own Desire 29 E. Mason Hopper
Their Own World 59 Tomu Uchida
Their Purple Moment 28 James Parrott
Their Secret Affair 56 H. C. Potter
Their Wives' Vacation 30 Stephen Roberts
Theirs Is the Glory 45 Brian Desmond Hurst
Thelema Abbey 55 Kenneth Anger
Thelma 18 A. E. Coleby, Arthur H. Rooke
Thelma 22 Chester Bennett
Thelma Jordan 49 Robert Siodmak
Thelma, or Saved from the Sea 14

B. Harold Brett
Thelonious Monk: Straight, No Chaser 88 Charlotte Zwerin
Them! 54 Gordon Douglas
Them Nice Americans 58 Anthony Young
Them Thar Hills 34 Charles Rogers
Them Were the Happy Days 17 Otto Messmer
Thema Amore 61 Alexander Kluge
Theme, The 79 Gleb Panfilov
Theme for a Short Story 68 Sergei Yutkevich
Themes and Variations 28 Germaine Dulac
Thèmes et Variations 28 Germaine Dulac
Themroc 72 Claude Faraldo
Then Came Bronson 69 William A. Graham
Then Came the Pawn 30 Edward Buzzell
Then Came the Woman 26 David M. Hartford
Then He Did Laugh, But... 12 Frank Wilson
Then He Juggled 13 Frank Wilson
Then I'll Come Back to You 16 George Irving
Then Nothing Was the Same Anymore 87 Gerd Roman Forsch
Then There Were Three 61 Alex Nicol
Then You'll Remember Me 18 Edward Waltyre
Theodor Hierneis oder Wie Man Ehem. Hofkoch Wird 72 Hans-Jürgen Syberg
Theodor Körner 32 Carl Boese
Theodor Pištěk 58 Martin Frič
Theodora 21 Arturo Ambrosio
Theodora Goes Wild 36 Richard Boleslawski
Theodora, Slave Empress 53 Riccardo Freda
Theofilos 87 Lakis Papastathis
Theorem 68 Pier Paolo Pasolini
Theory of the Hand Grenade 19 E. Dean Parmelee
Theory of the Long Range Shell 19 E. Dean Parmelee
There Ain't No Justice 39 Pen Tennyson
There Are Feet on the Ceiling 12 Abel Gance
There Are Girls Wanted Here 13 Percy Stow
There Are No Villains 21 Bayard Veiller
There Are Some Guys Downstairs 85 Emilio Alfaro, Rafael Filipelli
There Auto Be a Law 53 Robert McKimson
There Burned a Flame 43 Gustaf Molander
There Came Two Men 58 Arne Mattsson
There Goes Barder 54 John Berry
There Goes Kelly 44 Phil Karlson
There Goes My Girl 37 Ben Holmes
There Goes My Heart 38 Norman Z. McLeod
There Goes Susie 34 Joseph Losey, John Stafford
There Goes the Bride 32 Albert De Courville
There Goes the Bride 79 Ray Cooney

They Made Her a Spy *39* Jack Hively
They Made Me a Criminal *39* Busby Berkeley
They Made Me a Criminal *47* Alberto Cavalcanti
They Made Me a Fugitive *47* Alberto Cavalcanti
They Made Me a Killer *46* William C. Thomas
They Meet Again *41* Erle C. Kenton
They Met at Midnight *46* Herbert Wilcox
They Met in a Taxi *36* Alfred E. Green
They Met in Argentina *41* Leslie Goodwins, Jack Hively
They Met in Bombay *41* Clarence Brown
They Met in Havana *61* Jerzy Hoffman
They Met in Moscow *41* Ivan Pyriev
They Met in the Dark *43* Karel Lamač, Basil Sydney
They Met on Skis *40* Henri Sokal
They Might Be Giants *71* Anthony Harvey
They Never Come Back *32* Fred Newmeyer
They Never Learn *56* Denis Kavanagh
They Only Kill Their Masters *72* James Goldstone
They Passed This Way *48* Alfred E. Green
They Raid by Night *42* Spencer G. Bennet
They Raid by Night: A Story of the Commandos *42* Spencer G. Bennet
They Ran for Their Lives *68* John Payne
They Rode West *54* Phil Karlson
They Saved Hitler's Brain *63* David Bradley
They Say—Let Them Say *14* Warwick Buckland
They Say Pigs Is Pigs *17* Harry S. Palmer
They Serve Abroad *42* Roy Boulting
They Shall Have Faith *45* William Nigh
They Shall Have Music *39* Stuart Heisler, Archie Mayo
They Shall Not Die *59* Bernhard Grzimek, Michael Grzimek
They Shall Pay *21* Martin Justice
They Shoot Horses, Don't They? *69* Sydney Pollack
They Staked Their Lives *39* Alf Sjöberg
They Still Call Me Bruce *86* James Orr, Johnny Yune
They Tell You About Brazil *69* Chris Marker
They Wanted Peace *38* Mikhail Chiaureli
They Wanted to Marry *37* Lew Landers
They Went That-a-Way and That-a-Way *78* Stuart McGowan, Edward Montagne, Eric Weston
They Went to Vostok *64* Giuseppe De Santis
They Were Expendable *45* John Ford, Robert Montgomery
They Were Five *35* Julien Duvivier
They Were Four *17* George Marshall
They Were Not Divided *50* Terence Young
They Were Sisters *45* Arthur Crabtree
They Were So Young *55* Kurt Neumann
They Were So Young and So in Danger *55* Kurt Neumann
They Were Ten *61* Baruch Dienar

They Who Dare *53* Lewis Milestone
They Who Step on the Tiger's Tail *45* Akira Kurosawa
They Who Tread on the Tiger's Tail *45* Akira Kurosawa
They Won't Believe Me *47* Irving Pichel
They Won't Forget *37* Mervyn LeRoy
They Would Be Acrobats *09* Charles Raymond
They Would Elope *09* D. W. Griffith
They Would Play Cards *07* Jack Smith
They Wouldn't Believe Me *25* Alexander Butler
They're a Weird Mob *66* Michael Powell
They're All After Flo *15* Frank Wilson
They're Always Caught *38* Harold S. Bucquet
They're Coming to Get You *70* Al Adamson
They're Coming to Get You *72* Sergio Martino
They're Off *17* Roy William Neill
They're Off *22* Francis Ford
They're Off! *33* John Rawlins
They're Off *38* David Butler
They're Playing with Fire *84* Hikmet Avedis
They've Changed Faces *71* Corrado Farina
Thick and Thin of It, The *14* Walter West
Thick-Walled Room, The *53* Masaki Kobayashi
Thicker Than Water *24* James W. Horne
Thief, The *12* Edwin J. Collins
Thief, The *15* Edgar Lewis
Thief *16* M. Bonch-Tomashevsky
Thief, The *20* Charles Giblyn
Thief, The *22* George A. Cooper
Thief, The *52* Russell Rouse
Thief, The *66* Louis Malle
Thief *81* Michael Mann
Thief and the Girl, The *11* D. W. Griffith
Thief at the Casino, The *08* Lewin Fitzhamon
Thief Catcher, A *14* Charles Chaplin, Mabel Normand
Thief in Paradise, A *25* George Fitzmaurice
Thief in the Dark *28* Albert Ray
Thief Is Shogun's Kin, The *58* Tomu Uchida
Thief of Bagdad, The *24* Raoul Walsh
Thief of Bagdad, The *40* Ludwig Berger, Alexander Korda, Zoltán Korda, William Cameron Menzies, Michael Powell, Tim Whelan
Thief of Bagdad, The *60* Arthur Lubin
Thief of Bagdad, The *78* Clive Donner
Thief of Damascus, The *52* Will Jason
Thief of Hearts *43* Albert Mertz, Jørgen Roos
Thief of Hearts *84* Douglas Day Stewart
Thief of Paris, The *66* Louis Malle
Thief of Venice, The *50* John Brahm
Thief on Holiday *58* Salah Abu Saif
Thief on the Run *65* Kajiro Yamamoto
Thief Who Came to Dinner, The *72* Bud Yorkin
Thief's Wife, The *12* Allan Dwan
Thiella, I *29* Dimitrios Gaziadis
Thieves *19* Frank Beal

Thieves *77* John Berry, Al Viola
Thieves After Dark *83* Samuel Fuller
Thieves' Decoy, The *10* Bert Haldane
Thieves Fall Out *41* Ray Enright
Thieves' Gold *18* John Ford
Thieves' Highway *49* Jules Dassin
Thieves' Holiday *46* Douglas Sirk
Thieves in the Night *83* Samuel Fuller
Thieves Like Us *74* Robert Altman
Thigh Line Lyre Triangular *61* Stan Brakhage
Thikana *88* Mahesh Bhatt
Thili Jhai Heli Bahu *88* Bijay Bhaskar
Thimble Thimble *20* Edward H. Griffith
Thin Air *69* Gerry Levy
Thin Blue Line, The *87* Errol Morris
Thin Ice *19* Thomas R. Mills
Thin Ice *37* Sidney Lanfield
Thin Ice *60* John Halas*
Thin Ice *61* Lamont Johnson
Thin Line, The *65* Mikio Naruse
Thin Line, The *80* Michal Bat-Adam
Thin Line, The *87* Andreas O. Loucka
Thin Man, The *34* W. S. Van Dyke
Thin Man Goes Home, The *44* Richard Thorpe
Thin Red Line, The *64* Andrew Marton
Thing, The *51* Howard Hawks, Christian Nyby
Thing, The *82* John Carpenter
Thing (From Another World), The *51* Howard Hawks, Christian Nyby
Thing in the Attic, The *74* Freddie Francis
Thing That Came from Another World, The *51* Howard Hawks, Christian Nyby
Thing That Couldn't Die, The *58* Will Cowan
Thing with Two Heads, The *72* R. Lee Frost
Thing Without a Face, A *64* Julio Coll
Things Are Looking Up *34* Albert De Courville
Things Are Tough All Over *82* Thomas K. Avildsen
Things Change *88* David Mamet
Things Happen at Night *48* Francis Searle
Things Men Do *21* Robert North Bradbury
Things of Life, The *69* Claude Sautet
Things to Come *36* William Cameron Menzies
Things We Love, The *18* Lou Tellegen
Things We Want to Know *15* Hay Plumb
Things Wives Tell *26* Hugh Dierker
Think *65* Charles Eames, Ray Eames
Think Dirty *70* Jim Clark, Richard Williams
Think Fast, Mr. Moto *37* Norman Foster
Think First *39* Roy Rowland
Think It Over *17* Herbert Blaché
Think It Over *38* Jacques Tourneur
Think of a Number *68* Palle Kjærulff-Schmidt
Think 20th *67* Richard Fleischer
Thinkin' Big *85* S. F. Brownrigg
Third Alarm, The *22* Emory Johnson
Third Alarm, The *30* Emory Johnson
Third Alibi, The *61* Montgomery Tully
Third Blow, The *48* Igor Savchenko
Third-Class Love *59* Félix Máriássy
Third Clue, The *34* Albert Parker

Third Day, The *65* Jack Smight
Third Degree, The *14* Barry O'Neil
Third Degree, The *19* Tom Terriss
Third Degree, The *26* Michael Curtiz
Third Dimensional Murder *40* George Sidney
Third Dragon, The *85* Peter Hledik
Third Eye, The *20* James W. Horne
Third Eye, The *28* Maclean Rogers
Third Eye, The *89* Orhan Oğuz
Third Finger, Left Hand *40* Robert Z. Leonard
Third Generation, The *15* Harold M. Shaw
Third Generation, The *20* Henry Kolker
Third Generation, The *79* Rainer Werner Fassbinder
Third God, The *14* Stuart Kinder
Third Gun, The *29* Geoffrey Barkas
Third Key, The *56* Charles Frend
Third Kiss, The *19* Robert Vignola
Third Liberty Loan Bomb, The *18* Leighton Budd
Third Lover, The *61* Claude Chabrol
Third Man, The *49* Carol Reed
Third Man on the Mountain *59* Ken Annakin
Third Meshchanskaya *26* Abram Room, Sergei Yutkevich
Third of a Man *62* Robert Lewin
Third Party Risk *54* Daniel Birt
Third Party Risk *56* Nathan Juran
Third Party Speculation *79* Malcolm Le Grice
Third Road, The *63* Lewis Gilbert
Third Secret, The *64* Charles Crichton
Third Sex, The *57* Veidt Harlan
Third Solution, The *88* Pasquale Squitieri
Third String, The *14* George Loane Tucker
Third String, The *32* George Pearson
Third Time Lucky *31* Walter Forde
Third Time Lucky *48* Gordon Parry
Third Visitor, The *51* Maurice Elvey
Third Voice, The *59* Hubert Cornfield
Third Walker, The *78* Teri McLuhan
Third Wish, The *57* Ján Kadár, Elmar Klos
Third Witness, The *17* A. E. Coleby
Third Woman, The *20* Charles Swickard
Thirst *29* William Nigh
Thirst *49* Ingmar Bergman
Thirst *79* Rod Hardy
Thirst for Love, The *66* Koreyoshi Kurahara
Thirst of Baron Blood, The *72* Mario Bava
Thirst of Men, The *52* Serge De Poligny
Thirsty Dead, The *75* Terry Becker
Thirteen, The *37* Mikhail Romm
Thirteen *66* Michael Anderson, Sidney J. Furie, Arthur Hiller, J. Lee-Thompson
Thirteen *70* Nicolas Gessner
Thirteen Chairs, The *70* Nicolas Gessner
Thirteen Days in France *68* Claude Lelouch, François Reichenbach
Thirteen Days of Love *42* Louis Valray
13 East Street *52* Robert S. Baker
13 Fighting Men *60* Harry Gerstad
13 Frightened Girls *63* William Castle
13 Ghosts *60* William Castle
Thirteen Hours by Air *36* Mitchell Leisen

Thirteen Lead Soldiers *48* Frank McDonald
Thirteen Men and a Girl *30* Kurt Bernhardt
Thirteen Men and a Gun *38* Mario Zampi
Thirteen Most Beautiful Boys, The *65* Andy Warhol
Thirteen Most Beautiful Women, The *64* Andy Warhol
Thirteen O'Clock *88* Larry Leahy, Frank Mazzola
13. Revír *45* Martin Frič
13 Rue Madeleine *46* Henry Hathaway
Thirteen Steps to Death *60* Roy Del Ruth
13 Washington Square *28* Melville Brown
13 West Street *61* Philip Leacock
Thirteen Women *32* George Archainbaud
Thirteenth Bride of the Prince, The *87* Ivanka Grubcheva
Thirteenth Candle, The *33* John Daumery
Thirteenth Chair, The *19* Léonce Perret
Thirteenth Chair, The *29* Tod Browning
Thirteenth Chair, The *36* George B. Seitz
Thirteenth Chamber, The *68* Otakar Vávra
Thirteenth Commandment, The *20* Robert Vignola
Thirteenth Guest, The *32* Albert Ray
Thirteenth Hour, The *27* Chester M. Franklin
13th Hour, The *47* William Clemens
Thirteenth Instant, The *40* Ronald Haines
Thirteenth Juror, The *27* Edward Laemmle
Thirteenth Letter, The *50* Otto Preminger
Thirteenth Man, The *37* William Nigh
Thirteenth Room, The *68* Otakar Vávra
Thirtham *87* Mohan
Thirtieth Piece of Silver, The *20* George L. Cox
-30- *59* Jack Webb
Thirty a Week *18* Harry Beaumont
30 Below Zero *26* Lambert Hillyer, Robert T. Kerr
Thirty Day Princess *34* Marion Gering
Thirty Days *22* James Cruze
Thirty Days *31* Alan Crosland
'38 *86* Wolfgang Glück
35 Boulevard General Koenig *71* Gregory Markopoulos
30 Foot Bride of Candy Rock, The *59* Sidney Miller
30 Is a Dangerous Age, Cynthia *67* Joseph McGrath
Thirty Million Rush, The *87* Karl Maka
39 East *20* John S. Robertson
Thirty-Nine Steps, The *35* Alfred Hitchcock
39 Steps, The *59* Ralph Thomas
Thirty-Nine Steps, The *78* Don Sharp
39-es Dandár, A *59* Károly Makk
Thirty Seconds Over Tokyo *44* Mervyn LeRoy
37.2 Degrés le Matin *86* Jean-Jacques Beineix
37°2 le Matin *86* Jean-Jacques Beineix
36 Chowringhee Lane *82* Aparna Sen
36 Fillette *88* Catherine Breillat
36 Hours *53* Montgomery Tully
36 Hours *64* George Seaton

Thirty-Six Hours to Kill *36* Eugene Forde
Thirty-Six Hours to Live *36* Eugene Forde
$30,000 *20* Ernest C. Warde
33.333 *24* Gustaf Molander
Thirty Times Your Money *65* Bo Widerberg
32 Dicembre *88* Luciano De Crescenzo
32 Rue de Montmartre *39* Georges Lacombe, Yves Mirande
Thirty Winchesters for El Diablo *65* Gianfranco Baldanello
Thirty Years Later *28* Oscar Micheaux
Thirty Years of Experiments *51* Hans Richter*
Thirumathi Oru Vegumathi *87* Visu
This Above All *42* Anatole Litvak
This Acting Business *33* John Daumery
This Angry Age *57* René Clément
This Can't Happen Here *50* Ingmar Bergman
This Changing World—Broken Treaties *41* Paul Fennell
This Changing World—How War Came *41* Paul Fennell
This Changing World—The Carpenters *41* Paul Fennell
This Charming Couple *49* Willard Van Dyke
This Could Be the Night *57* Robert Wise
This Crazy Urge *62* Luciano Salce
This Day and Age *32* Cecil B. DeMille
This Doesn't Happen Here *50* Ingmar Bergman
This Dusty World *24* Kenji Mizoguchi
This Earth Is Mine *59* Henry King
This England *40* David MacDonald
This Freedom *23* Denison Clift
This Green Hell *36* Randall Faye
This Gun for Hire *42* Frank Tuttle
This Happy Breed *43* David Lean
This Happy Couple *51* Juan Antonio Bardem, Luis García Berlanga
This Happy Feeling *58* Blake Edwards
This Happy Life *44* Mikio Naruse
This Hero Stuff *19* Henry King
This House Surrounded *22* Victor Sjöström
This Immoral Age *64* William Cannon
This Instant *69* Emil Lotyanu
This Is a Hijack *73* Barry Pollack
This Is a Life? *55* Friz Freleng
This Is America *43* Richard Fleischer
This Is Barbara Barondess: One Life Is Not Enough *85* John A. Gallagher
This Is Cinerama *52* Ernest B. Schoedsack*
This Is Dynamite! *52* William Dieterle
This Is Elvis *81* Malcolm Leo, Andrew Solt
This Is England *41* Humphrey Jennings
This Is Heaven *29* Alfred Santell
This Is How It Began *54* Lev Kulidzhanov, Yakov Segel
This Is It *71* James Broughton
This Is Korea! *51* John Ford
This Is My Affair *37* William A. Seiter
This Is My Affair *51* Michael Gordon
This Is My Body *59* Russ Meyer
This Is My Ducky Day *61* Joseph Barbera, William Hanna
This Is My Love *54* Stuart Heisler

Those Nuisances 46 Ken Hughes
Those of the Railroad 42 René Clément
Those People Next Door 52 John Harlow
Those Redheads from Seattle 53 Lewis R. Foster
Those Three French Girls 30 Harry Beaumont
Those Troublesome Boys 02 James A. Williamson
Those Two Boys 29 Stephen Roberts
Those We Love 32 Robert Florey
Those Were the Days 34 Thomas Bentley
Those Were the Days 35 Josef Heifits, Mikhail Shapiro, Alexander Zarkhi
Those Were the Days 38 Manuel Romero
Those Were the Days 40 Theodore Reed
Those Were the Days 46 James M. Anderson
Those Were the Happy Times 68 Robert Wise
Those Were Wonderful Days 34 Bernard Brown
Those Who Dance 24 Lambert Hillyer
Those Who Dance 30 William Beaudine
Those Who Dare 24 John B. O'Brien
Those Who Dwell in Darkness 14 Charles Raymond
Those Who Judge 24 Burton L. King
Those Who Live in Glass Houses 25 Alexander Butler
Those Who Love 29 H. Manning Haynes
Those Who Make Tomorrow 46 Akira Kurosawa, Hideo Sekigawa, Kajiro Yamamoto
Those Who Pay 18 Raymond B. West
Those Who Toil 16 Edgar Lewis
Those Who Tread on the Tiger's Tail 45 Akira Kurosawa
Those Without Sin 17 Marshall Neilan
Those Wonderful Men with a Crank 78 Jiří Menzel
Those Wonderful Movie Cranks 78 Jiří Menzel
Thot Fal'n 78 Stan Brakhage
Thou Art My Joy 40 Karl Heinz Martin
Thou Art the Man 15 Sidney Rankin Drew
Thou Art the Man 20 Thomas Heffron
Thou Fool 26 Fred Paul
Thou Old, Thou Free 39 Gunnar Olsson
Thou Shalt Honor Thy Wife 25 Carl Theodor Dreyer
Thou Shalt Not 10 D. W. Griffith
Thou Shalt Not 14 Will S. Davis
Thou Shalt Not 19 Charles Brabin
Thou Shalt Not 28 Jacques Feyder
Thou Shalt Not Bear False Witness 88 Krzysztof Kieslowski
Thou Shalt Not Commit Adultery 88 Krzysztof Kieslowski
Thou Shalt Not Covet 16 Colin Campbell
Thou Shalt Not Covet Thy Neighbor's Goods 88 Krzysztof Kieslowski
Thou Shalt Not Covet Thy Neighbor's Wife 88 Krzysztof Kieslowski
Thou Shalt Not Kill 13 James Hallek Reid
Thou Shalt Not Kill 14 D. W. Griffith
Thou Shalt Not Kill 39 John H. Auer
Thou Shalt Not Kill 61 Claude Autant-Lara
Thou Shalt Not Kill 88 Krzysztof Kieslowski

Thou Shalt Not Kill...Except 85 Josh Becker
Thou Shalt Not Pass 25 Charles Bowers
Thou Shalt Not Steal 14 Warwick Buckland
Thou Shalt Not Steal 17 William Nigh
Thou Shalt Not Steal 29 Viktor Jansen
Thou Shalt Not Steal 88 Krzysztof Kieslowski
Thou Shalt Not Take the Name of the Lord Thy God in Vain 88 Krzysztof Kieslowski
Thought 16 Vladimir Gardin*
Thoughtless Beauty, A 08 Lewin Fitzhamon
Thoughtless Giovanni 86 Marco Colli
Thoughtless Women 20 Daniel Carson Goodman
Thousand and One Nights, A 05 Georges Méliès
Thousand and One Nights, A 45 Alfred E. Green
Thousand and One Nights, A 47 Kon Ichikawa*
Thousand and One Nights, A 68 José María Elorrieta
Thousand and One Nights, A 74 Pier Paolo Pasolini
Thousand and One Nights, A 74 Karel Zeman
Thousand and One Nights in Tokyo, A 38 Tomu Uchida
Thousand and One Wives 89 Michal Bat-Adam
Thousand Clowns, A 65 Fred Coe
Thousand Cranes, A 53 Kozaburo Yoshimura
Thousand Cranes, A 69 Yasuzo Masumura
Thousand Cries Has the Night, A 81 Juan Piquer Simon
Thousand Dollar Bill, The 37 Glenn Tryon
Thousand Dollar Husband, The 16 James Young
Thousand Eyes of Dr. Mabuse, The 60 Fritz Lang
Thousand Pound Spook, The 07 Walter R. Booth
Thousand to One, A 20 Rowland V. Lee
Thousand Wives of Naftali, The 89 Michal Bat-Adam
Thousands Cheer 43 Vincente Minnelli, George Sidney
Thrashin' 86 David Winters
Thread o' Scarlet 30 Peter Godfrey
Thread of Destiny, The 10 D. W. Griffith
Thread of Life, The 12 Allan Dwan
Threads 32 George B. Samuelson
Threads 84 Mick Jackson
Threads of Destiny 14 Joseph Smiley
Threads of Fate 17 Eugene Nowland
Threat, The 47 Derwin Abrahams
Threat, The 49 Felix E. Feist
Threat, The 60 Charles R. Rondeau
Threatening Sky, The 65 Joris Ivens
Three 65 Aleksandar Petrović
Three 69 James Salter
Three After Christine, The 40 Hans Deppe

Three Ages, The 23 Edward F. Cline, Buster Keaton
Three American Beauties 06 Edwin S. Porter
Three American Beauties No. 2 07 J. Searle Dawley, Edwin S. Porter
Three American LPs 69 Wim Wenders
¡Three Amigos! 86 John Landis
Three and a Day 39 Jean Negulesco
Three-and-a-Half Musketeers 57 Gilberto Martínez Solares
Three Avengers, The 64 Gianfranco Parolini
Three Bacchants, The 00 Georges Méliès
Three Bad Men 26 John Ford
Three Bad Men and a Girl 15 Francis Ford
Three Bad Men in a Hidden Fortress 58 Akira Kurosawa
Three Bad Men in the Hidden Fortress 58 Akira Kurosawa
Three Bad Sisters 56 José Briz
Three Bags Full 48 John Baxter
Three Bases East 25 Wesley Ruggles
Three Bears, The 25 Walter Lantz
Three Bears, The 35 Ubbe Iwerks
Three Bewildered People in the Night 87 Gregg Araki
Three Bites of the Apple 66 Alvin Ganzer
Three Blind Mice 38 William A. Seiter
Three Blind Mice 45 George Dunning
Three Blondes in His Life 60 Leon Chooluck
Three Boys and a Baby 11 Frank Wilson
Three Brave Men 56 Philip Dunne
Three Broadway Girls 32 Lowell Sherman
Three Brothers, The 29 Malcolm St. Clair
Three Brothers 80 Francesco Rosi
Three Buckaroos, The 22 Fred J. Balshofer
Three Bullets for a Long Gun 73 Peter Henkel
Three Burlesque Dancers 1896 Birt Acres
Three Caballeros, The 44 Norman Ferguson, Clyde Geronimi, Jack Kinney, Bill Roberts, Harold Young
Three Cadets 45 Ken Annakin
Three Came Home 50 Jean Negulesco
Three Came to Kill 60 Edward L. Cahn
Three Card Monte 77 Les Rose
Three Cases of Murder 54 David Eady, George More O'Ferrall, Wendy Toye
Three Cheers for Little Märta 45 Hasse Ekman
Three Cheers for Love 36 Ray McCarey
Three Cheers for the Irish 40 Lloyd Bacon
Three Christmasses 15 Alfonse Frenguelli
Three Cockeyed Sailors 40 Walter Forde
Three Coins in the Fountain 54 Jean Negulesco
Three Comrades, The 12 August Blom
Three Comrades 38 Frank Borzage
Three-Cornered Fate 54 David MacDonald
Three-Cornered Hat, The 34 Mario Camerini
Three-Cornered Hat, The 34 Harry D'Abbadie D'Arrast, Ricardo Soriano
Three-Cornered Moon 33 Elliott Nugent
Three Crazy Legionnaires 36 Hamilton MacFadden
Three Crooked Men 58 Ernest Morris
Three Crowns of the Sailor 82 Raúl Ruiz

Thrill of a Romance *45* Richard Thorpe
Thrill of Brazil, The *46* S. Sylvan Simon
Thrill of It All, The *63* Norman Jewison
Thrill of Youth, The *32* Richard Thorpe
Thrill Seekers, The *27* Harry Revier
Thrill Seekers *63* Robert Hartford-Davis
Thrilled to Death *81* William Asher
Thrilled to Death *88* Chuck Vincent
Thriller *83* John Landis
Thrilling *65* Carlo Lizzani, Gian Luigi
Polidoro, Ettore Scola
Thrilling Drill, A *20* Vernon Stallings
Thrilling Story, A *10* Dave Aylott
Thrilling Youth *26* Grover Jones
Thrillkill *84* Anthony D'Andrea, Anthony
Kramreither
Thrills and Chills *38* Dave Fleischer
Throat—12 Years After *84* Gerard Damiano
Throne of Blood *57* Akira Kurosawa
Throne of Fire, The *86* Franco Prosperi
Throne of the Blood Monster *69* Jesús
Franco
Through a Glass Darkly *61* Ingmar
Bergman
Through a Glass Window *22* Maurice
Campbell
Through a Higher Power *12* Edwin S.
Porter
Through a Lens Brightly *66* Gregory
Markopoulos
Through Darkened Vales *11* D. W.
Griffith
Through Days and Months *69* Noboru
Nakamura
Through Death's Valley *12* Sidney Northcote
Through Different Eyes *42* Thomas Z.
Loring
Through Dumb Luck *11* Mack Sennett
Through Fire and Water *23* Thomas Bentley
Through Fire to Fortune *11* Theo Bouwmeester
Through Fire to Fortune, or The Sunken
Village *14* Lloyd B. Carleton
Through Hell to Glory *58* Edward L.
Cahn
Through His Wife's Picture *11* Mack
Sennett
Through India *52* Leonid Varmalov
Through Solid Walls *16* Walter Murton
Through Stormy Seas *14* B. Harold Brett
Through Stormy Waters *20* Frederick
Goddard
Through the Ages *14* Dave Aylott
Through the Back Door *21* Alfred E.
Green, Jack Pickford
Through the Breakers *09* D. W. Griffith
Through the Breakers *28* Joseph C. Boyle
Through the Clouds *13* Charles H.
Weston
Through the Dark *24* George W. Hill
Through the Firing Line *14* Charles H.
Weston
Through the Flames *12* Ethyle Batley
Through the Keyhole *13* Charles C.
Calvert
Through the Keyhole *20* Roy Del Ruth
Through the Looking Glass *71* Stephanie

Rothman
Through the Storm *22* Horace G. Plympton
Through the Storm *40* Sam Nelson
Through the Toils *19* Harry Hoyt
Through the Valley of Shadows *14* Lawrence Trimble
Through the Wall *16* Rollin Sturgeon
Through the Wire *90* Nina Rosenblum
Through the Wrong Door *19* Clarence
Badger
Through Thick and Thin *27* B. Reeves
Eason, Jack Nelson
Through Trials to Victory *11* Urban Gad
Through Turbulent Waters *15* Duncan
Macrae
Throw a Saddle on a Star *46* Ray Nazarro
Throw Momma from the Train *87* Danny
DeVito
Throw of Dice, A *29* Alan Campbell,
Franz Osten
Throw of the Dice, A *13* Frank Wilson
Throw of the Dice, A *29* Alan Campbell,
Franz Osten
Throwback, The *35* Ray Taylor
Throwing a Party *40* Ray Enright
Throwing Lead *28* Robert J. Horner
Throwing the Ball *18* Raoul Barré, Charles
Bowers
Throwing the Bull *17* Gregory La Cava,
Vernon Stallings
Throwing the Sixteen Pound Hammer *03*
Edwin S. Porter
Thrown Out of Joint *33* Leslie Goodwins*
Thrown to the Lions *16* Lucius Henderson
Thru Different Eyes *29* John G. Blystone
Thru Different Eyes *42* Thomas Z. Loring
Thru the Eyes of Men *20* Charles Taylor
Thru the Flames *23* Jack Nelson
Thru Thin and Thicket, or Who's Zoo in
Africa *33* Mark Sandrich
Thugs with Dirty Mugs *39* Fred Allen,
Tex Avery
Thumb Fun *52* Robert McKimson
Thumb Tripping *72* Quentin Masters
Thumbelina *24* Herbert M. Dawley
Thumbelina *55* Lotte Reiniger
Thumbelina *70* Barry Mahon
Thumbs Down *27* Phil Rosen
Thumbs Up *14* Dave Aylott
Thumbs Up *43* Joseph Santley
Thunder *20* Louis Delluc
Thunder *29* William Nigh
Thunder *83* Fabrizio De Angelis
Thunder Across the Pacific *51* Allan Dwan
Thunder Afloat *39* George B. Seitz
Thunder Alley *67* Richard Rush
Thunder Alley *85* J. S. Cardone
Thunder and Lightning *77* Corey Allen
Thunder at the Border *66* Alfred Vohrer
Thunder Bay *53* Anthony Mann
Thunder Below *32* Richard Wallace
Thunder Birds *42* William A. Wellman
Thunder in Carolina *60* Paul Helmick
Thunder in Dixie *65* William T. Naud
Thunder in God's Country *51* George
Blair
Thunder in the Blood *62* André Haguet,
Jean-Paul Sassy
Thunder in the City *37* Marion Gering

Thunder in the Desert *38* Sam Newfield
Thunder in the Dust *50* George Templeton
Thunder in the East *34* Nicolas Farkas
Thunder in the East *52* Charles Vidor
Thunder in the Hills *47* Vaclav Kubasek
Thunder in the Night *35* George Archainbaud
Thunder in the Pines *48* Robert Edwards
Thunder in the Sun *58* Russell Rouse
Thunder in the Valley *47* Louis King
Thunder Island *21* Norman Dawn
Thunder Island *63* Jack Leewood
Thunder, Lightning and Sunshine *36* Erich
Engel
Thunder Mountain *25* Victor Schertzinger
Thunder Mountain *35* David Howard
Thunder Mountain *47* Lew Landers
Thunder Mountain *64* Ben Parker
Thunder of Drums, A *61* Joseph M.
Newman
Thunder of the Gods *66* Ann Todd
Thunder of the Kings *67* Ann Todd
Thunder on the Hill *51* Douglas Sirk
Thunder on the Trail *51* Ron Ormond
Thunder Over Arizona *56* Joseph Kane
Thunder Over Hawaii *56* Roger Corman
Thunder Over Paris *39* Léon Mathot
Thunder Over Sangoland *55* Sam Newfield
Thunder Over Tangier *57* Lance Comfort
Thunder Over Texas *34* Edgar G. Ulmer
Thunder Over the Plains *52* André De
Toth
Thunder Over the Prairie *41* Lambert
Hillyer
Thunder Pass *37* Charles Barton
Thunder Pass *54* Frank McDonald
Thunder Riders *27* William Wyler
Thunder River Feud *42* S. Roy Luby
Thunder Road *58* Arthur Ripley
Thunder Rock *42* Roy Boulting
Thunder Run *85* Gary Hudson
Thunder Town *46* Harry Fraser
Thunder Trail *37* Charles Barton
Thunder Warrior *83* Fabrizio De Angelis
Thunder Warrior II *87* Fabrizio De
Angelis
Thunderball *65* Terence Young
Thunderbird 6 *68* David Lane
Thunderbirds *52* John H. Auer
Thunderbirds Are Go *66* David Lane
Thunderbolt *19* Colin Campbell
Thunderbolt *29* Josef von Sternberg
Thunderbolt *35* Stuart Paton
Thunderbolt *45* John Sturges, William
Wyler
Thunderbolt *72* Henry Levin, David
Lowell Rich
Thunderbolt and Lightfoot *74* Michael
Cimino
Thunderbolts of Fate *19* Edward Warren
Thunderbolt's Tracks *27* John P. McGowan
Thunderclap *21* Richard Stanton
Thundercloud, The *19* Alexander Butler
Thundercloud *50* Edwin L. Marin
Thundergap Outlaws *43* Albert Herman
Thundergate *23* Joseph De Grasse
Thundergod *28* Charles J. Hunt

Thunderhead—Son of Flicka 45 Louis King
Thunderhoof 48 Phil Karlson
Thundering Caravans 52 Harry Keller
Thundering Dawn 23 Harry Garson
Thundering Frontier 40 D. Ross Lederman
Thundering Gun Slingers 44 Sam Newfield
Thundering Herd, The 25 William K. Howard
Thundering Herd, The 33 Henry Hathaway
Thundering Hoofs 22 Francis Ford
Thundering Hoofs 24 Albert S. Rogell
Thundering Hoofs 41 Lesley Selander
Thundering Jets 58 Helmut Dantine
Thundering Romance 24 Richard Thorpe
Thundering Speed 26 Alvin J. Neitz
Thundering Thompson 29 Ben F. Wilson
Thundering Through 25 Fred Bain
Thundering Trail, The 51 Ron Ormond
Thundering Trails 43 John English
Thundering West, The 39 Sam Nelson
Thundering Wheels 65 William T. Naud
Thunderstorm 34 Vladimir Petrov
Thunderstorm 55 John Guillermin
Thursday 62 Dino Risi
Thursday Morning Murders, The 76 Michael Nahay
Thursday the Twelfth 82 Alfred Sole
Thursday's Child 42 Rodney Ackland
Thursday's Children 53 Lindsay Anderson, Guy Brenton
Thursdays, Miracle 57 Luis García Berlanga
Thus Another Day 59 Keisuke Kinoshita
Thus It Turned Love 24 Teinosuke Kinugasa
Thus Spake Theodor Herzl 67 Alberto Cavalcanti
Thy Kingdom Come...Thy Will Be Done 88 Antony Thomas
Thy Name Is Woman 24 Fred Niblo
Thy Neighbor's Wife 53 Hugo Haas
Thy Neighbor's Wife 89 José Fonseca e Costa
Thy Soul Shall Bear Witness 20 Victor Sjöström
Ti Conosco Mascherina! 43 Eduardo De Filippo
Ti-Cul Tougas 77 Jean-Guy Noël
Ti Ho Sposato per Allegria 67 Luciano Salce
Ti-Koyo e il Suo Pescecane 62 Folco Quilici
Ti-Koyo et Son Requin 62 Folco Quilici
Ti Presento un'Amica 88 Francesco Massaro
Tía Alexandra, La 80 Arturo Ripstein
Tía de las Muchachas, La 39 Juan Bustillo Oro
Tianxia Diyi Quan 72 Cheng Chang Ho
Tião Medonho 62 Roberto Farias
Tiara Tahiti 62 Ted Kotcheff
Tibet Proibito 49 Francesco Maselli
Tiburón 34 Ramón Peón
Tiburoneros 62 Luis Alcoriza
Tic, Un 08 Louis Feuillade
Tichá Radost 85 Dušan Hanák
Tichtown Tumblers, The 15 Ernest G. Batley

Tichý Společník 89 Zdeněk Flídr
Tichý Týden v Domě 69 Jan Švankmajer
...tick...tick...tick... 69 Ralph Nelson
Tick Tock Tuckered 44 Robert Clampett
Ticket 86 Kwon-taek Im
Ticket for the Theater, A 11 Percy Stow
Ticket for Two, A 08 Lewin Fitzhamon
Ticket Mania 06 Charles Raymond
Ticket o' Leave 22 Edwin J. Collins
Ticket of Leave 36 Michael Hankinson
Ticket-of-Leave Man, The 18 Bert Haldane
Ticket of Leave Man, The 37 George King
Ticket to a Crime 34 Lewis D. Collins
Ticket to Crime 34 Lewis D. Collins
Ticket to Heaven 81 Ralph L. Thomas
Ticket to Paradise 36 Aubrey H. Scotto
Ticket to Paradise 60 Francis Searle
Ticket to Paradise 62 Arne Mattsson
Ticket to Tomahawk, A 50 Richard Sale
Tickle Me 65 Norman Taurog
Tickled Pink 61 Bob Wehling
Ticklish Affair, A 63 George Sidney
Ticklish Business 29 Stephen Roberts
Tidal Wave, The 18 William Stoermer
Tidal Wave, The 20 Sinclair Hill
Tidal Wave 39 John H. Auer
Tidal Wave 48 William Dieterle
Tidal Wave 73 Andrew Meyer, Shiro Moritani
Tide of Empire 29 Allan Dwan
Tide of Fortune, The 11 Theo Bouwmeester
Tide Rising Over the Breakwater 1896 Georges Méliès
Tides of Barnegat, The 17 Marshall Neilan
Tides of Fate 17 George Cowl
Tides of Passion 22 Graham Cutts
Tides of Passion 25 J. Stuart Blackton
Tides of Sorrow, The 14 J. Farrell MacDonald
Tie Me Up! Tie Me Down! 90 Pedro Almodóvar
Tie That Binds, The 23 Joseph Levering
Tiefland 54 Leni Riefenstahl
Tiempo de Lobos 82 Alberto Isaac
Tiempo de Morir 65 Arturo Ripstein
Tiempo de Morir 85 Jorge Ali Triana
Tiempo de Revancha 81 Adolfo Aristarain
Tiempo de Silencio 86 Vicente Aranda
Tiempo Es el Viento, El 76 Santiago Álvarez
Tiempo Libre a La Roca 81 Santiago Álvarez
T'ien-Hsia Ti-Yi 83 King Hu
Tiens, Vous Êtes à Poitiers? 16 Jacques Feyder
Tierra, Amor y Dolor 35 Ramón Peón
Tierra Baja 11 Mario Gallo
Tierra Brava 38 René Cardona
Tierra Brutal 61 Michael Carreras
Tierra Caliente 54 Carlos Velo
Tierra de Fuego 65 Jesús Jaime Balcazar, Mark Stevens
Tierra de los Alvargonzález, La 69 Miguel Picazo
Tierra de Pasiones 44 José Benavides
Tierra de Valientes 87 Luis Quintanilla Rico
Tierra del Fuego Se Apaga, La 55 Emilio Fernández

Tierra del Mariachi, La 38 Raúl De Anda
Tierra Prometida, La 72 Miguel Littin
Tierra Prometida, La 86 Roberto G. Rivera
Tierra Sin Pan 32 Luis Buñuel
Tierra y el Cielo, La 77 Manuel Octavio Gómez
Tierras Blancas, Las 59 Hugo Del Carril
Ties 77 István Gaál
Tiff and What Became of It, The 15 Toby Cooper
Tiffany Jones 73 Peter Walker
Tiffany Memorandum 66 Sergio Grieco
Tifusari 63 Vatroslav Mimica
Tiger Among Us, The 61 Philip Leacock
Tiger and the Flame, The 55 Sohrab M. Modi
Tiger and the Pussycat, The 67 Dino Risi
Tiger Bay 33 J. Elder Wills
Tiger Bay 59 J. Lee-Thompson
Tiger by the Tail 55 John Gilling
Tiger by the Tail 68 R. G. Springsteen
Tiger Fangs 43 Sam Newfield
Tiger Flight 65 Kengo Furusawa
Tiger Girl 55 Alexander Ivanovsky, N. Kosheverova
Tiger Has Leaped and Killed, But It Will Die...It Will Die, The 73 Santiago Álvarez
Tiger Hunt in Assam 58 Willard Van Dyke
Tiger in the Sky 55 Gordon Douglas
Tiger in the Smoke 56 Roy Ward Baker
Tiger Likes Fresh Blood, The 64 Claude Chabrol
Tiger Lily, The 19 George L. Cox
Tiger Lily, The 76 Paul Bernard
Tiger Love 24 George Melford
Tiger Makes Out, The 67 Arthur Hiller
Tiger Man, The 18 William S. Hart
Tiger Man, The 44 William Beaudine
Tiger of Bengal 58 Fritz Lang
Tiger of Eschnapur, The 58 Fritz Lang
Tiger of San Pedro, The 21 Maurice Elvey
Tiger of the Sea 64 Tan Ida
Tiger of the Seven Seas 62 Luigi Capuano
Tiger Rose 23 Sidney Franklin
Tiger Rose 29 George Fitzmaurice
Tiger Shark 32 Howard Hawks
Tiger the 'Tec 11 Lewin Fitzhamon
Tiger Thompson 23 B. Reeves Eason
Tiger True 21 John P. McGowan
Tiger von Berlin, Der 30 Johannes Meyer
Tiger von Eschnapur, Der 58 Fritz Lang
Tiger Walks, A 63 Norman Tokar
Tiger Warsaw 87 Amin Q. Chaudhri
Tiger Woman, The 17 J. Gordon Edwards
Tiger Woman, The 44 Spencer G. Bennet, Wallace A. Grissell
Tiger Woman, The 45 Philip Ford
Tiger's Claw, The 23 Joseph E. Henabery
Tiger's Coat, The 20 Roy Clements
Tiger's Cub, The 20 Charles Giblyn
Tigers Don't Cry 76 Peter Collinson
Tigers in Lipstick 79 Luigi Zampa
Tiger's Shadow, The 28 Spencer G. Bennet
Tiger's Son 28 David Butler
Tiger's Tale, A 87 Peter Douglas
Tiger's Trail, The 19 Louis Gasnier

Toby's Bow *19* Harry Beaumont
Toccata *67* Herman van den Horst
Toccata for Toy Trains *57* Charles Eames, Ray Eames
Tochter *37* Lotte Reiniger
Tochter der Landstrasse, Die *14* Urban Gad
Tochter des Regiments, Die *33* Karel Lamač
Tochter des Samurai, Die *37* Arnold Fanck
Töchter Ihrer Exzellenz, Die *34* Reinhold Schünzel
Tochūken Kumoemon *36* Mikio Naruse
Tocsin, Le *20* Pierre Marodon
Tocsin, The *87* Arkady Kordon
Tod der Maria Malibran, Der *71* Werner Schroeter
Tod des Andern, Der *19* Richard Oswald
Tod des Empedokles, Der *86* Danièle Huillet, Jean-Marie Straub
Tod des Weissen Pferdes, Der *85* Christian Ziewer
Tod im November *78* Helmut Pfandler
Tod in Sevilla, Der *13* Urban Gad
Tod Ritt Dienstags, Der *67* Tonino Valerii
Tod Über Schanghai *33* Rolf Randolf
Toda Brothers and Sisters, The *41* Yasujiro Ozu
Toda-Ke no Kyōdai *41* Yasujiro Ozu
Toda la Vida *87* Víctor Manuel Castro
Toda Nudez Será Castigada *73* Arnaldo Jabor
Toda una Vida *33* Adelqui Millar
Today *17* Ralph Ince
Today *24* Dziga Vertov
Today *30* William Nigh
Today *30* Esther Shub
Today and Tomorrow *12* Michael Curtiz
Today for the Last Time *58* Martin Frič
Today I Hang *42* Oliver Drake, George Merrick
Today It's Me...Tomorrow You! *68* Tonino Cervi
Today Mexico, Tomorrow the World *70* Peter Shillingford
Today or Tomorrow *65* András Kovács
Today We Kill, Tommorow We Die *72* Tonino Servi
Today We Live *33* Howard Hawks
Today We Live *62* René Clément
Todd Killings, The *71* Barry Shear
Todd of the Times *19* Eliot Howe
Toddles, Scout *11* Lewin Fitzhamon
Toddlin' Along *28* Karl Freund
Todeskuss des Dr. Fu Manchu, Der *68* Jesús Franco
Todessmaragd, Der *19* F. W. Murnau
Todesstrahlen des Dr. Mabuse, Die *64* Hugo Fregonese
Todo Modo *76* Elio Petri
Todo un Hombre *36* Ramón Peón
Todo un Hombre *43* Pierre Chénal
Todos los Colores de la Oscuridad *72* Sergio Martino
Todos Somos Necesarios *56* José Antonio Nieves Conde
To'È Morta la Nonna! *69* Mario Monicelli
Tōge no Uta *23* Kenji Mizoguchi
Together *18* Oscar A. C. Lund

Together *55* Lorenza Mazzetti
Together *71* Sean S. Cunningham
Together *76* James Broughton
Together? *79* Armenia Balducci
Together *87* Rafael Rosales Durán
Together Again *44* Charles Vidor
Together at Last *87* Kari Kyrönseppä
Together Brothers *74* William A. Graham
Together for Days *72* Michael Schultz
Together in Paris *63* Richard Quine
Together in the Weather *45* George Pal
Together We Live *35* Willard Mack
Togetherness *70* Arthur Marks
Togger *37* Jürgen von Alten
Tōhō Senichiya *47* Kon Ichikawa*
Tōhoku no Zunmutachi *57* Kon Ichikawa
Tōi Kumo *55* Keisuke Kinoshita
Toi le Venin *58* Robert Hossein
Toile d'Araignée Merveilleuse, La *08* Georges Méliès
Toiler, The *32* Gustavo Sereno
Toilers, The *19* Tom Watts
Toilers, The *28* Reginald Barker
Toilers of the Sea *23* Roy William Neill
Toilers of the Sea *36* Ted Fox, Selwyn Jepson
Toit de la Baleine, Le *81* Raúl Ruiz
Tojin Okichi *30* Kenji Mizoguchi
Tojin Okichi *31* Teinosuke Kinugasa
Tokai Kōkyōgaku *29* Kenji Mizoguchi
Tokaido Yotsuya Kaidan *59* Nobuo Nakagawa
Tokaji Rapszódia *38* János Vaszary
Toki no Ujigami *32* Kenji Mizoguchi
Tokimeki ni Shisu *86* Yoshimitsu Morita
Tokkan *75* Kihachi Okamoto
Tokkan Kozō *29* Yasujiro Ozu
Tokugawa Ieyasu *65* Daisuke Ito
Tokugawa Onna Keibatsushi *68* Teruo Ishii
Tokyo After Dark *59* Norman Herman
Tokyo Blackout *87* Toshio Masuda
Tokyo Bordello *86* Hideo Gosha
Tōkyō Boshoku *57* Yasujiro Ozu
Tokyo Chorus *31* Yasujiro Ozu
Tokyo File 212 *51* Dorrell McGowan, Stuart McGowan
Tokyo-Ga *84* Wim Wenders
Tokyo Joe *49* Stuart Heisler
Tokyo Jokio *43* Norm McCabe
Tōkyō Kōshinkyoku *29* Kenji Mizoguchi
Tokyo March *29* Kenji Mizoguchi
Tōkyō Monogatari *53* Yasujiro Ozu
Tokyo 1958 *58* Susumu Hani, Hiroshi Teshigahara
Tōkyō no Gasshō *31* Yasujiro Ozu
Tōkyō no Onna *33* Yasujiro Ozu
Tōkyō no Yado *35* Yasujiro Ozu
Tokyo Olympiad *65* Kon Ichikawa
Tōkyō Ōrimpikku *65* Kon Ichikawa
Tokyo Pop *87* Fran Rubel Kazui
Tokyo Rose *45* Lew Landers
Tōkyō Saiban *83* Masaki Kobayashi
Tōkyō Senichiya *38* Tomu Uchida
Tōkyō Sensō Sengo Hiwa *70* Nagisa Oshima
Tokyo Siren, A *20* Norman Dawn
Tokyo Story *53* Yasujiro Ozu
Tokyo Trial, The *83* Masaki Kobayashi
Tokyo Trials, The *83* Masaki Kobayashi

Tokyo Twilight *57* Yasujiro Ozu
Tokyo Woman, A *33* Yasujiro Ozu
Tōkyō Yawa *61* Shiro Toyoda
Tōkyō Yoi Toko *35* Yasujiro Ozu
Tokyo's a Nice Place *35* Yasujiro Ozu
Tol'able David *21* Henry King
Tol'able David *30* John G. Blystone
Told at Twilight *17* Henry King
Told in the Hills *19* George Melford
Tolerance *87* Pál Erdöss
Tolken *68* André Delvaux
Toll Bridge Troubles *42* Bob Wickersham
Toll Gate, The *20* Lambert Hillyer
Toll of Mamon *14* Harry Handworth
Toll of the Desert *35* William Berke
Toll of the Sea, The *22* Chester M. Franklin
Toll of the Youth, The *15* Frank Lloyd
Toll of Youth, The *15* Frank Lloyd
Tolle Bomberg, Der *35* Georg Asagaroff
Tolle Heirat von Laló, Die *18* Lupu Pick
Tolle Nacht, Eine *26* Richard Oswald
Toller Einfall, Ein *34* Kurt Gerron
Toller Hecht auf Krümmer Tour *62* Ákos von Ráthonyi
Tolonc, A *14* Michael Curtiz
Tom *73* Greydon Clark
Tom and His Pals *26* Robert De Lacey
Tom and Jerry in the Hollywood Bowl *50* Joseph Barbera, William Hanna
Tom Brown of Culver *32* William Wyler
Tom Brown's School Days *40* Robert Stevenson
Tom Brown's Schooldays *16* Rex Wilson
Tom Brown's Schooldays *51* Gordon Parry
Tom Cringle in Jamaica *13* Charles Raymond
Tom, Dick and Harry *41* Garson Kanin
Tom Horn *79* William Wiard
Tom Jones *17* Edwin J. Collins
Tom Jones *63* Tony Richardson
Tom Merry, Lightning Cartoonist *1895* Birt Acres
Tom Old Boot *1897* Georges Méliès
Tom Old Boot, a Grotesque Dwarf *1897* Georges Méliès
Tom Sawyer *17* William Desmond Taylor
Tom Sawyer *30* John Cromwell
Tom Sawyer *38* Norman Taurog
Tom Sawyer *73* Don Taylor
Tom Sawyer—Detective *38* Louis King
Tom Thumb *34* Manny Gould, Ben Harrison
Tom Thumb *36* Ubbe Iwerks
Tom Thumb *58* René Cardona
tom thumb *58* George Pal
Tom Thumb *72* Michel Boisrond
Tom Thumb in Trouble *40* Chuck Jones
Tom Thumb's Brother *41* Sid Marcus
Tom Tight et Dum Dum *03* Georges Méliès
Tom-Tom Tomcat *53* Friz Freleng
Tom Turk and Daffy *44* Chuck Jones
Tom Whisky ou L'Illusioniste Toqué *1899* Georges Méliès
Tomahawk *50* George Sherman
Tomahawk and the Cross, The *56* George Marshall
Tomahawk Trail, The *50* Phil Karlson
Tomahawk Trail *56* Lesley Selander

Tomb, The *85* Fred Olen Ray
Tomb of Ligeia, The *64* Roger Corman
Tomb of the Cat *64* Roger Corman
Tomb of the Living Dead *68* Gerry De Leon, Eddie Romero
Tomb of the Undead *72* John Hayes
Tomb of Torture *66* Antonio Boccacci
Tombeau Sous l'Arc de Triomphe, Le *27* Robert Wiene
Tombolo *49* Giorgio Ferroni
Tomboy, The *09* Sidney Olcott
Tomboy, The *21* Carl Harbaugh
Tomboy, The *24* David Kirkland
Tomboy *40* Robert McGowan
Tomboy *85* Herb Freed
Tomboy and the Champ *61* Francis D. Lyon
Tomboy Bessie *12* Mack Sennett
Tombs of Horror *63* Sergio Corbucci, Antonio Margheriti
Tombs of Horror, The *66* Massimo Pupillo
Tombs of Our Ancestors *37* Pál Fejős
Tombs of the Blind Dead *71* Amando De Ossorio
Tombstone *42* William McGann
Tombstone Canyon *32* Alvin J. Neitz
Tombstone Terror *35* Robert North Bradbury
Tombstone (The Town Too Tough to Die) *42* William McGann
Tomcat, The *67* Georges Robin
Tomcats *77* Harry Kerwin
Tomfoolery *70* John Halas
Tom-ic Energy *65* Chuck Jones
Tomkins Buys a Donkey *08* Lewin Fitzhamon
Tommaso Blu *86* Florian Furtwängler
Tommi *31* Yakov Protazanov
Tommy *31* Yakov Protazanov
Tommy *37* Béla Balázs
Tommy *74* Ken Russell
Tommy and the Mouse in the Art School *01* George Albert Smith
Tommy and the Policeman's Whistle *08* Alf Collins
Tommy and the Sticktite *08* A. E. Coleby
Tommy and the Whooping Cough *12* Frank Wilson
Tommy Atkins *15* Bert Haldane
Tommy Atkins *28* Norman Walker
Tommy Atkins and His Harriet on a Bank Holiday *02* George Albert Smith
Tommy Atkins' Dream *03* Alf Collins
Tommy on a Visit to His Aunt *08* Arthur Cooper
Tommy Steele Story, The *57* Gerard Bryant
Tommy the Tinpot Hero *07* Alf Collins
Tommy the Toreador *59* John Paddy Carstairs
Tommy Tricker and the Stamp Traveler *88* Michael Rubbo
Tommy Tucker's Tooth *22* Walt Disney
Tommy's Box of Tools *07* Harold Hough
Tommy's Experiments in Photography *05* Alf Collins
Tommy's Freezing Spray *15* Cecil Birch
Tommy's Initiation *18* Walter R. Booth
Tommy's Locomotive *10* Percy Stow
Tommy's Money Scheme *14* Frank Wilson

Tomorrow *72* Joseph Anthony
Tomorrow *86* Juha Rosma
Tomorrow *89* Kazuo Kuroki
Tomorrow and Tomorrow *32* Richard Wallace
Tomorrow at Midnight *39* Albert S. Rogell
Tomorrow at Seven *33* Ray Enright
Tomorrow at Ten *62* Lance Comfort
Tomorrow Begins Today: Industrial Research *76* Shyam Benegal
Tomorrow I'll Wake Up and Scald Myself with Tea *77* Jindřich Polák
Tomorrow Is Another Day *51* Felix E. Feist
Tomorrow Is Forever *45* Irving Pichel
Tomorrow Is My Turn *60* André Cayatte
Tomorrow Is the Final Day *71* Yılmaz Güney
Tomorrow Is the Last Day *71* Yılmaz Güney
Tomorrow Is Too Late *49* Léonide Moguy
Tomorrow Man, The *79* Tibor Takacs
Tomorrow Never Comes *77* Peter Collinson
Tomorrow the World *44* Leslie Fenton
Tomorrow There Came War *87* Yuri Kara
Tomorrow We Live *36* H. Manning Haynes
Tomorrow We Live *42* George King
Tomorrow We Live *42* Edgar G. Ulmer
Tomorrow Will Be Friday *01* James A. Williamson
Tomorrow's a Killer *87* George Kaczender
Tomorrow's a Wonderful Day *49* Siegfried Lehmann
Tomorrow's Children *34* Crane Wilbur
Tomorrow's Dancers *39* Kozaburo Yoshimura
Tomorrow's Island *68* Charles Crichton
Tomorrow's Love *25* Paul Bern
Tomorrow's Warrior *81* Michael Papas
Tomorrow's Youth *34* Charles Lamont
Tom's Gang *27* Robert De Lacey
Tom's Photo Finish *55* Joseph Barbera, William Hanna
Tom's Ride *44* Darrell Catling
Tom's Vacation *28* Louis King
Ton Kero tou Ellinon *81* Lakis Papastathis
Ton Ombre Est la Mienne *61* André Michel
Tonari no Yane no Shita *31* Mikio Naruse
Tonari no Yarō *65* Yoji Kuri
Tondeur de Chiens, Le *00* Alice Guy-Blaché
Tonelli *43* Victor Tourjansky
Tönende Welle, Die *21* Walter Ruttmann
Tong Man, The *19* William Worthington
Tong Nien Wang Shi *85* Hsiao-hsien Hou
Tong Sandwich, The *21* Raoul Barré, Charles Bowers
Tong Tied *28* Manny Gould, Ben Harrison
Tongnian Wangshi *85* Hsiao-hsien Hou
Tongs — A Chinatown Story *86* Philip Chan
Tongues *83* Shirley Clarke
Tongues of Flame *18* Colin Campbell
Tongues of Flame *24* Joseph E. Henabery
Tongues of Men, The *16* Frank Lloyd

Tongues of Scandal *27* Roy Clements
Toni *28* Arthur Maude
Toni *34* Jean Renoir
Tonic, The *28* Ivor Montagu
Tonight a Town Dies *61* Jan Rybkowski
Tonight and Every Night *44* Victor Saville
Tonight at 8:30 *52* Anthony Pelissier
Tonight at Twelve *29* Harry A. Pollard
Tonight for Sure *61* Francis Ford Coppola
Tonight I Will Make Your Corpse Turn Red *66* José Mojica Marins
Tonight I Will Paint in Flesh Color *66* José Mojica Marins
Tonight Is Ours *32* Mitchell Leisen, Stuart Walker
Tonight or Never *31* Mervyn LeRoy
Tonight or Never *41* Gustaf Molander
Tonight or Never *60* Michel Deville
Tonight Pancho Dines Out (Bachelor Party) *87* Víctor Manuel Castro
Tonight the Skirts Fly *56* Dmitri Kirsanov
Tonight We Raid Calais *43* John Brahm
Tonight We Sing *53* Mitchell Leisen
Tonight's the Night *32* Monty Banks
Tonight's the Night *54* Mario Zampi
Tonight's the Night, Pass It On *32* Monty Banks
Tonio Kröger *64* Rolf Thiele
Tonio, Son of the Sierras *25* Ben F. Wilson
Tonka *58* Lewis R. Foster
Tonneau des Naïades, Le *00* Georges Méliès
Tonnelier, Le *00* Alice Guy-Blaché
Tonnelier, Le *42* Georges Rouquier
Tonnerre, Le *20* Louis Delluc
Tonnerre de Dieu, Le *65* Denys De la Patellière
Tonnerre de Jupiter, Le *03* Georges Méliès
Tons of Money *24* Frank Crane
Tons of Money *30* Tom Walls
Tons of Trouble *55* Leslie Hiscott
Tonsorial Artists *18* Raoul Barré, Charles Bowers
Tonsorial Slot Machine, A *18* Leighton Budd
Tonto Basin Outlaws *41* S. Roy Luby
Tonto Kid, The *35* Harry Fraser
Tontons Flingueurs, Les *63* Georges Lautner
Tony America *18* Thomas Heffron
Tony Arzenta *72* Duccio Tessari
Tony Draws a Horse *50* John Paddy Carstairs
Tony Kinsey Quartet, The *61* Robert Henryson
Tony Rome *67* Gordon Douglas
Tony Runs Wild *26* Thomas Buckingham
Too Bad She's Bad *54* Alessandro Blasetti
Too Beautiful for You *89* Bertrand Blier
Too Big Gig *87* Ere Kokkonen
Too Busy to Work *32* John G. Blystone
Too Busy to Work *39* Otto Brower
Too Clever for Once *10* Frank Wilson
Too Dangerous to Live *39* Anthony Hankey, Leslie Norman
Too Dangerous to Love *50* Bretaigne Windust
Too-Devoted Wife, A *07* Lewin Fitzhamon

Too Early, Too Late *81* Danièle Huillet, Jean-Marie Straub
Too Fat to Fight *18* Hobart Henley
Too Hop to Handle *56* Robert McKimson
Too Hot to Handle *30* Lewis R. Foster
Too Hot to Handle *38* Jack Conway
Too Hot to Handle *60* Terence Young
Too Hot to Handle *76* Don Schain
Too Keen a Sense of Humour *11* Frank Wilson
Too Late Blues *61* John Cassavetes
Too Late for Tears *49* Byron Haskin
Too Late the Hero *69* Robert Aldrich
Too Late to Love *58* Henri Decoin
Too Many Admirers *10* A. E. Coleby
Too Many Blondes *41* Thornton Freeland
Too Many Burglars *11* Mack Sennett
Too Many Chefs *78* Ted Kotcheff
Too Many Cooks *18* Gregory La Cava
Too Many Crooks *19* Ralph Ince
Too Many Crooks *21* Adrian Brunel
Too Many Crooks *27* Fred Newmeyer
Too Many Crooks *30* George King
Too Many Crooks *31* William A. Seiter
Too Many Crooks *58* Mario Zampi
Too Many Detectives *53* Oscar Burn, John Wall
Too Many Girls *10* Edwin S. Porter
Too Many Girls *40* George Abbott
Too Many Highballs *33* Clyde Bruckman
Too Many Husbands *38* Ivar Campbell
Too Many Husbands *40* Wesley Ruggles
Too Many Kisses *25* Paul Sloane
Too Many Lovers *57* Henri Decoin
Too Many Mamas *24* Leo McCarey
Too Many Millions *18* James Cruze
Too Many Millions *34* Harold Young
Too Many Parents *36* Robert McGowan
Too Many Thieves *66* Abner Biberman
Too Many Too Soon *61* Lester James Peries
Too Many Winners *47* William Beaudine
Too Many Wives *33* George King
Too Many Wives *37* Ben Holmes
Too Many Women *29* Sam Newfield
Too Many Women *31* Michael Curtiz
Too Many Women *42* Bernard B. Ray
Too Much *87* Eric Rochant
Too Much Beef *36* Robert F. Hill
Too Much Business *22* Jess Robbins
Too Much for One Man *66* Pietro Germi
Too Much Harmony *33* A. Edward Sutherland
Too Much Johnson *19* Donald Crisp
Too Much Johnson *38* Orson Welles
Too Much Lobster *09* Lewin Fitzhamon
Too Much Married *21* Scott R. Dunlap
Too Much Money *26* John Francis Dillon
Too Much of a Good Thing *02* George Albert Smith
Too Much Pep *21* Jack King
Too Much Sausage *16* Walter R. Booth
Too Much Soap *22* Raoul Barré, Charles Bowers
Too Much Speed *21* Frank Urson
Too Much Talk *59* Yasujiro Ozu
Too Much to Carry *59* Evald Schorm
Too Much, Too Soon *58* Art Napoleon
Too Much Wife *22* Thomas Heffron
Too Much Youth *25* Duke Worne
Too Outrageous! *87* Richard Benner

Too Scared to Scream *82* Tony Lo Bianco
Too Soon to Die *66* Carlo Lizzani
Too Soon to Love *60* Richard Rush
Too Strong *85* Sergio Leone, Carlo Verdone
Too Tough to Kill *35* D. Ross Lederman
Too Wise Wives *21* Lois Weber
Too Young to Kiss *51* Robert Z. Leonard
Too Young to Know *45* Frederick De Cordova
Too Young to Love *59* Muriel Box
Too Young to Marry *30* Mervyn LeRoy
Too Young, Too Immoral *62* Raymond A. Phelan
Toolbox Murders, The *77* Dennis Donnelly
Toolbox Murders II, The *87* Richard L. Bare
Toomorrow *70* Val Guest
Toot! Toot! *26* Dave Fleischer
Tooth or Consequences *47* Howard Swift
Tooth Will Out *33* Frank Cadman
Tootles Buys a Gun *12* Dave Aylott
Tootsie *82* Sydney Pollack
Top, The *62* Věra Chytilová
Top Banana *54* Alfred E. Green
Top Dog, The *18* Arrigo Bocchi
Top Dog *78* Feliks Falk
Top Dogs *60* John Halas*
Top Floor Girl *59* Max Varnel
Top Gun *55* Ray Nazarro
Top Gun *86* Tony Scott
Top Hat *35* Mark Sandrich
Top Job *68* Giuliano Montaldo
Top Man *43* Charles Lamont
Top Model *88* Aristide Massaccesi
Top o' the Morning, The *22* Edward Laemmle
Top o' the Morning *48* David Miller
Top of New York, The *22* William Desmond Taylor
Top of the Bill *31* Melville Brown
Top of the Bill *71* Arnold Louis Miller
Top of the Form *53* John Paddy Carstairs
Top of the Heap *72* Christopher St. John
Top of the Town *37* Ralph Murphy
Top of the Whale, The *81* Raúl Ruiz
Top of the World, The *25* George Melford
Top of the World *55* Lewis R. Foster
Top Secret *52* Mario Zampi
Top Secret! *84* Jim Abrahams, David Zucker, Jerry Zucker
Top Secret Affair *56* H. C. Potter
Top Sergeant *42* Christy Cabanne
Top Sergeant Mulligan *28* James P. Hogan
Top Sergeant Mulligan *41* Jean Yarbrough
Top Speed *29* Charles Lamont
Top Speed *30* Mervyn LeRoy
Topa Topa *38* Charles Hutchinson, Vin Moore
Topaz *69* Alfred Hitchcock
Topaze *32* Louis Gasnier
Topaze *33* Harry D'Abbadie D'Arrast
Topaze *36* Marcel Pagnol
Topaze *50* Marcel Pagnol
Topeka *53* Thomas Carr
Topeka Terror, The *45* Howard Bretherton
Topi Grigi, I *18* Emilio Ghione

Topical Topics *14* Hy Mayer
Topical Tricks *05* Walter R. Booth
Topical War Cartoons *14* Hy Mayer
Topical War Cartoons No. 2 *14* Hy Mayer
Topio stin Omichli *88* Theodoros Angelopoulos
Topkapi *63* Jules Dassin
Topo, El *71* Alejandro Jodorowsky
Topo Galileo *88* Francesco Laudadio
Topo Gigio e i Sei Ladri *67* Kon Ichikawa
Topo Gigio e la Guerra del Missile *67* Kon Ichikawa
Topos *85* Antoinetta Angelidi
Topper *37* Norman Z. McLeod
Topper Returns *41* Roy Del Ruth
Topper Takes a Trip *38* Norman Z. McLeod
Topper Triumphant *14* Hay Plumb
Toppo Gigio and the Missile War *67* Kon Ichikawa
Toppo Jijo no Botan Sensō *67* Kon Ichikawa
Toprini Nász *38* André De Toth
Tops *69* Charles Eames, Ray Eames
Tops Is the Limit *36* Lewis Milestone
Tops with Pops *56* Joseph Barbera, William Hanna
Topsey Turvey *27* George A. Cooper
Topsy and Eva *27* D. W. Griffith, Del Lord
Topsy Turkey *48* Sid Marcus
Topsy Turvy *27* Manny Gould, Ben Harrison
Topsy-Turvy *53* Minoru Shibuya
Topsy-Turvy Dance by Three Quaker Maidens *02* George Albert Smith
Topsy-Turvy Journey *70* Shoji Segawa
Topsy Turvy Villa *00* Cecil M. Hepworth
Topsy's Dream of Toyland *11* A. E. Coleby
Tora no O *45* Akira Kurosawa
Tora no O o Fuma Otokotachi *45* Akira Kurosawa
Tora-San, from Shibamata, with Love *86* Yoji Yamada
Tora-San Goes North *87* Yoji Yamada
Tora-San Goes Religious? *83* Yoji Yamada
Tora-San Goes to Vienna *89* Yoji Yamada
Tora-San Loves an Artist *73* Yoji Yamada
Tora-San Meets His Lordship *77* Yoji Yamada
Tora-San Meets the Songstress Again *75* Yoji Yamada
Tora-San, Our Lovable Tramp *69* Yoji Yamada
Tora-San, Part Two *69* Yoji Yamada
Tora-San Plays Cupid *77* Yoji Yamada
Tora-San Plays Daddy *87* Yoji Yamada
Tora-San, the Expert *82* Yoji Yamada
Tora-San, the Go-Between *85* Yoji Yamada
Tora-San: The Good Samaritan *71* Yoji Yamada
Tora-San, the Intellectual *75* Yoji Yamada
Tora-San, the Matchmaker *79* Yoji Yamada
Tora-San's Bluebird Fantasy *86* Yoji Yamada
Tora-San's Cherished Mother *69* Yoji Yamada

Towers Open Fire 63 Antony Balch
Towing 78 Maura Smith
Towing a Boat on the River 1896 Georges Méliès
Town, The 43 Josef von Sternberg
Town and Its Drains, The 53 Susumu Hani
Town Bloody Hall 79 Chris Hegedus, D. A. Pennebaker
Town Called Bastard, A 71 Robert Parrish
Town Called Hell, A 71 Robert Parrish
Town in the Awkward Age, A 62 Márta Mészáros
Town Like Alice, A 56 Jack Lee
Town Mouse and Country Mouse 12 Hay Plumb
Town of Anger 49 Mikio Naruse
Town of Crooked Ways, The 20 Bert Wynne
Town of Fire 22 Kenji Mizoguchi
Town of Love and Hope, A 59 Nagisa Oshima
Town of Yun, The 89 U Son Kim
Town on Trial, A 52 Luigi Zampa
Town on Trial! 56 John Guillermin
Town People 26 Heinosuke Gosho
Town Scandal, The 23 King Baggot
Town Tamer 65 Lesley Selander
Town That Cried Terror, The 77 Richard Compton
Town That Dreaded Sundown, The 77 Charles B. Pierce
Town That God Forgot, The 22 Harry Millarde
Town Went Wild, The 44 Ralph Murphy
Town Will Die Tonight, A 61 Jan Rybkowski
Town Without Pity 60 Gottfried Reinhardt
Towne Hall Follies 35 Walter Lantz
Towns and Years 73 Alexander Zarkhi
Toxi 52 Robert A. Stemmle
Toxic Avenger, The 84 Michael Herz, Lloyd Kaufman
Toxic Avenger, Part II, The 89 Michael Herz, Lloyd Kaufman
Toxic Avenger Part III — The Last Temptation of Toxie, The 89 Michael Herz, Lloyd Kaufman
Toxic Zombies 79 Chuck McCrann
Toy, The 76 Francis Veber
Toy, The 82 Richard Donner
Toy Box, The 71 Ron Garcia
Toy Grabbers, The 68 Don Joslyn
Toy Makers, The 20 Raoul Barré, Charles Bowers
Toy Shoppe, The 34 Walter Lantz
Toy Soldiers 83 David Fisher
Toy Tiger 56 Jerry Hopper
Toy Trouble 41 Chuck Jones
Toy Wife, The 38 Richard Thorpe
Toyland 08 Georges Méliès
Toyland 30 Alexander Oumansky
Toyland Mystery, A 16 Horace Taylor
Toyland Paper Chase, The 16 C. Allen Gilbert
Toyland Premiere 34 Walter Lantz
Toyland Robbery, A 16 Horace Taylor
Toyland Villain, The 16 Horace Taylor
Toymaker, the Doll and the Devil, The 10 Edwin S. Porter
Toymaker's Dream, The 10 Arthur Cooper
Tōyō Bukyōden 27 Tomu Uchida
Toys Are Not for Children 72 Stanley H. Brasloff
Toys in the Attic 63 George Roy Hill
Toys of Fate 09 Edwin S. Porter
Toys of Fate 18 George D. Baker
Toytown Hall 36 Friz Freleng
Tra i Gorghi 16 Carmine Gallone
Tra Moglie e Marito 77 Luigi Comencini
Tracassin ou Les Plaisirs de la Ville, Le 61 Alex Joffé
Tracco di Veleno in una Coppa di Champagne 75 Gordon Hessler
Trace of a Turkey, The 24 Kenji Mizoguchi
Trachoma 64 Lars Braw, Jan Troell
Track of the Cat 54 William A. Wellman
Track of the Falcon 68 Gottfried Kolditz
Track of the Moon Beast 76 Richard Ashe
Track of the Vampire 66 Jack Hill, Stephanie Rothman
Track of Thunder 67 Joseph Kane
Track the Man Down 54 R. G. Springsteen
Track 29 87 Nicolas Roeg
Trackdown 76 Richard T. Heffron
Tracked 28 Jerome Storm
Tracked by the Police 27 Ray Enright
Tracked by Tiger 11 Lewin Fitzhamon
Tracked in the Snow Country 25 Herman Raymaker
Tracked to Earth 22 William Worthington
Trackers 85 Peter McCarthy, Conrad E. Palmisano
Tracking a Treacle Tin 10 Frank Wilson
Tracking the Baby 13 Arthur Charrington
Tracking the Sleeping Death 38 Fred Zinnemann
Tracks 22 Joseph Franz
Tracks 76 Henry Jaglom
Tracks in the Snow 85 Orlow Seunke
Tractor Drivers 39 Ivan Pyriev
Tracy Rides 35 Harry S. Webb
Tracy the Outlaw 28 Otis B. Thayer
Trade Tattoo 37 Len Lye
Trade Winds 38 Tay Garnett
Trader Ginsburg 30 Mark Sandrich
Trader Horn 30 W. S. Van Dyke
Trader Horn 73 Reza Badiyi
Trader Hornee 70 Tsanusdi
Trader Tom of the China Seas 54 Franklin Adreon
Trädgårdsmästaren 12 Victor Sjöström
Tradimento, Il 51 Riccardo Freda
Trading Hearts 88 Neil Leifer
Trading Places 83 John Landis
Tradition 21 Paul Otto
Traffic 15 Charles Raymond
Traffic 70 Bert Haanstra, Jacques Tati
Traffic Cop, The 16 Howard Mitchell
Traffic Cop, The 26 Harry Garson
Traffic in Babes 14 Frank Lloyd
Traffic in Crime 46 Lesley Selander
Traffic in Hearts 24 Scott R. Dunlap
Traffic in Souls 13 George Loane Tucker
Traffic in Souls 37 Robert Siodmak
Traffic Jam 79 Luigi Comencini
Traffic Troubles 31 Burton Gillett

Trafic 70 Bert Haanstra, Jacques Tati
Trafiquant, Le 11 Louis Feuillade
Träfracken 66 Lars-Magnus Lindgren
Tragedia di un Uomo Ridicolo, La 81 Bernardo Bertolucci
Tragedia Senza Lacrime 19 Mario Caserini
Tragédie de Carmen, La 83 Peter Brook
Tragédie de la Mine, La 31 G. W. Pabst
Tragédie de Lourdes, La 23 Julien Duvivier
Tragédie d'un Homme Ridicule, La 81 Bernardo Bertolucci
Tragédie Impériale, La 38 Marcel L'Herbier
Tragedies of the Crystal Globe, The 15 Richard Ridgely
Tragedija Službenice P.T.T. 66 Dušan Makavejev
Tragedy at Holly Cottage 16 Ernest G. Batley
Tragedy at Midnight, A 42 Joseph Santley
Tragedy in One Line, A 21 Jean Gic
Tragedy in Pimple's Life, A 13 Fred Evans, Joe Evans
Tragedy in Spain, A 08 Georges Méliès
Tragedy in the Alps, A 13 Charles H. Weston
Tragedy in the House of Hapsburg 24 Alexander Korda
Tragedy of a Comic Song, The 21 Maurice Elvey
Tragedy of a Dress Suit, The 11 Mack Sennett
Tragedy of a Ridiculous Man, The 81 Bernardo Bertolucci
Tragedy of a Switchboard Operator, The 66 Dušan Makavejev
Tragedy of Ambition, The 14 Colin Campbell
Tragedy of Barnsdale Manor, The 24 Hugh Croise
Tragedy of Basil Grieve, The 14 Frank Wilson
Tragedy of Lourdes, The 23 Julien Duvivier
Tragedy of Love 23 Joe May
Tragedy of the Afghan, The 86 Zmarai Kasi, Mark M. Rissi
Tragedy of the Cornish Coast, A 12 Sidney Northcote
Tragedy of the Desert 12 Sidney Olcott
Tragedy of the Ice, A 07 J. H. Martin
Tragedy of the Olden Times, A 11 Theo Bouwmeester
Tragedy of the Sawmills, A 06 Lewin Fitzhamon
Tragedy of the Truth, A 09 T. J. Gobbett
Tragedy of Whispering Creek 14 Allan Dwan
Tragedy of Youth, The 28 George Archainbaud
Tragic Circus, The 39 Manuel R. Ojeda
Tragic Earthquake in Mexico 87 Francisco Guerrero
Tragic Festival, The 39 Charles Lamont
Tragic Hunt 47 Giuseppe De Santis
Tragic Love 09 D. W. Griffith
Tragic Mistake, A 15 Ethyle Batley
Tragic Pursuit, The 47 Giuseppe De Santis

Tragic Ship, The 22 Victor Sjöström
Tragica Notte 41 Mario Soldati
Tragical Tale of a Belated Letter, The 03 Percy Stow
Tragico Fantozzi 75 Luciano Salce
Trágico Terremoto en México 87 Francisco Guerrero
Tragikomödie 22 Robert Wiene
Tragique Amour de Mona Lisa, Le 14 Albert Capellani
Tragödie 25 Carl Fröhlich
Tragödie der Liebe 23 Joe May
Tragödie eines Kindes, Die 20 Richard Oswald
Tragödie eines Verlorenen, Die 26 Hans Steinhoff
Tragödie eines Verschollenen Fürstensohnes, Die 22 Alexander Korda
Tragödie im Hause Hapsburg 24 Alexander Korda
Tragoedia 76 Stan Brakhage
Traidor, El 38 José Bohr
Traidores de San Ángel, Los 66 Leopoldo Torre-Nilsson
Traigo...Muertas, Las 87 Rafael Baledón
Trail, The 10 Ernest G. Batley
Trail 40 Moglia Barth
Trail, The 83 Ronnie Yu
Trail Beyond, The 34 Robert North Bradbury
Trail Blazers, The 40 George Sherman
Trail Blazers 53 Wesley Barry
Trail Drive 33 Alvin J. Neitz
Trail Dust 24 Gordon Hines
Trail Dust 36 Nate Watt
Trail Guide 52 Lesley Selander
Trail of Books, The 11 D. W. Griffith
Trail of Courage, The 28 Wallace Fox
Trail of Hate, The 17 Francis Ford, John Ford
Trail of Hate 22 William Hughes Curran
Trail of Kit Carson 45 Lesley Selander
Trail of '98, The 28 Clarence Brown
Trail of Robin Hood 50 William Witney
Trail of Sand, The 11 Bert Haldane
Trail of Terror 35 Robert North Bradbury
Trail of Terror 43 Oliver Drake
Trail of the Arrow 52 Thomas Carr
Trail of the Axe, The 22 Ernest C. Warde
Trail of the Books, The 11 D. W. Griffith
Trail of the Cigarette, The 20 Tom Collins
Trail of the Eucalyptus, The 11 Allan Dwan
Trail of the Fatal Ruby, The 12 Bert Haldane
Trail of the Hawk 35 Edward Dmytryk
Trail of the Horse Thieves, The 29 Robert De Lacey
Trail of the Law 24 Oscar Apfel
Trail of the Lonesome, The 23 Charles Maigne
Trail of the Lonesome Pine, The 14 Frank L. Dear
Trail of the Lonesome Pine, The 15 Cecil B. DeMille
Trail of the Lonesome Pine 26 Dave Fleischer
Trail of the Lonesome Pine, The 36 Henry Hathaway

Trail of the Mounties 47 Howard Bretherton
Trail of the Pink Panther 82 Blake Edwards
Trail of the Rustlers 50 Ray Nazarro
Trail of the Shadow, The 17 Edwin Carewe
Trail of the Silver Spurs 41 S. Roy Luby
Trail of the Vigilantes 40 Allan Dwan
Trail of the Yukon 49 William Beaudine
Trail of Vengeance, The 24 Al Ferguson
Trail of Vengeance 37 Sam Newfield
Trail Ride, The 73 William Byron Hillman
Trail Rider, The 25 W. S. Van Dyke
Trail Riders 28 John P. McGowan
Trail Riders 42 Robert E. Tansey
Trail Street 47 Ray Enright
Trail to Gunsight 44 Vernon Keays
Trail to Laredo 48 Ray Nazarro
Trail to Mexico 46 Oliver Drake
Trail to Red Dog, The 21 Leonard Franchon
Trail to San Antone 47 John English
Trail to Vengeance 45 Wallace Fox
Trail to Yesterday, The 18 Edwin Carewe
Trailblazer Magoo 56 Pete Burness
Trailer 59 Robert Breer
Trailer Thrills 37 Walter Lantz
Trailin' 21 Lynn Reynolds
Trailin' Back 28 John P. McGowan
Trailin' Double Trouble 40 S. Roy Luby
Trailin' North 33 John P. McCarthy
Trailin' Trouble 30 Arthur Rosson
Trailin' Trouble 37 Arthur Rosson
Trailin' West 36 Noel Mason Smith
Trailing African Wild Animals 23 Martin E. Johnson
Trailing Along 37 Jean Yarbrough
Trailing Big Game in Africa 23 Martin E. Johnson
Trailing Danger 47 Lambert Hillyer
Trailing Double Trouble 40 S. Roy Luby
Trailing North 33 John P. McCarthy
Trailing the Counterfeit 11 Mack Sennett
Trailing the Killer 32 Herman Raymaker
Trailing Trouble 30 Arthur Rosson
Trailing Trouble 37 Arthur Rosson
Trail's End 22 Francis Ford
Trail's End 35 Albert Herman
Trail's End 49 Lambert Hillyer
Trails of Adventure 35 Jay Wilsey
Trails of Danger 30 Alvin J. Neitz
Trails of Peril 30 Alvin J. Neitz
Trails of the Golden West 31 Leander De Cordova
Trails of the Wild 35 Sam Newfield
Trails of Treachery 28 Robert J. Horner
Train, The 20 Dziga Vertov
Train, The 48 Gösta Werner
Train, Le 64 John Frankenheimer, Arthur Penn
Train, The 64 John Frankenheimer, Arthur Penn
Train 66 Peter Greenaway
Train, Le 73 Pierre Granier-Deferre
Train, The 86 Ahmed Fouad
Train de Berlin Est Arrêté, Le 64 Rolf Haedrich
Train de la Victoire, Le 64 Joris Ivens

Train de Labrador, Le 67 Arthur Lamothe
Train de Plaisir 35 Léo Joannon
Train d'Enfer 65 Gilles Grangier
Train des Suicidés, Le 31 Edmond T. Gréville
Train en Marche, Le 71 Chris Marker
Train for the Stars, A 87 Carlos Diegues
Train Goes East, The 47 Yuli Raizman
Train Goes to Kiev, The 61 Alexei Mishurin
Train of Dreams 87 John Smith
Train of Events 49 Sidney Cole, Charles Crichton, Basil Dearden
Train of Gold, The 87 Bohdan Poręba
Train of Terror 79 Roger Spottiswoode
Train of the Central Committee 20 Dziga Vertov
Train of the Pioneers, The 86 Leonel Gallego
Train Ride to Hollywood 75 Charles R. Rondeau
Train Robber, The 20 Vernon Stallings
Train Robbers, The 71 Andrew V. McLaglen
Train Robbers, The 73 Burt Kennedy
Train Robbery Confidential 62 Roberto Farias
Train Rolls On, The 71 Chris Marker
Train Sans Yeux, Le 25 Alberto Cavalcanti
Train to Alcatraz 48 Philip Ford
Train to Durango 67 Mario Caiano
Train to Heaven 72 Karel Kachyňa
Train to Hollywood 87 Radysław Piwowarski
Train to Tombstone 50 William Berke
Train Trouble 40 Joy Batchelor, John Halas
Train 2419 33 John P. McCarthy
Train Without a Timetable 58 Veljko Bulajić
Train Wreckers, The 05 Edwin S. Porter
Train Wreckers, The 25 John P. McGowan
Trained Dogs 02 Alf Collins
Trained Hoofs 35 David Miller
Trained Horse, The 20 Vernon Stallings
Trained Nurse at Bar Z, The 11 Allan Dwan
Trained to Kill 73 Daniel J. Vance
Trained to Kill 82 Samuel Fuller
Trainer and Temptress 25 Walter West
Trainer's Daughter, The 07 J. Searle Dawley, Edwin S. Porter
Training for Husbands 18 Edward F. Cline
Training Pigeons 36 Dave Fleischer
Training Woodpeckers 21 Raoul Barré, Charles Bowers
Trains de Plaisir 30 Henri Storck
Trait d'Union, Le 08 Georges Méliès
Traite des Blanches, La 67 Georges Combret
Traitement de Choc 72 Alain Jessua
Traitement du Hoquet, Le 18 Raymond Bernard
Traitement 706, Le 10 Georges Méliès
Traitor 14 Lois Weber
Traitor, The 15 Cecil M. Hepworth
Traitor 26 Abram Room, L. Sheffer
Traitor, The 36 Sam Newfield
Traitor, The 57 Michael McCarthy
Traitor, The 63 Kokan Rakonjac

Traitor—Psalm 25, The 27 Charles Barnett
Traitor Spy 40 Walter Summers
Traitor to His King, A 08 A. E. Coleby
Traitor Within, The 42 Frank McDonald
Traitors 57 Sadatsugu Matsuda
Traitors, The 62 Robert Tronson
Traitor's Gate 64 Freddie Francis
Traitors of San Angel 66 Leopoldo Torre-Nilsson
Traitor's Reward 15 Victor Sjöström
Traitress of Parton's Court, The 12 Hay Plumb
Traja 69 Pal'o Bielek
Trakom 64 Lars Braw, Jan Troell
Trakoristi 39 Ivan Pyriev
Tram to the Sea, A 87 Håkan Alexandersson
Tramel S'en Fiche 27 Julien Duvivier
Tramp, The 08 Jack Smith
Tramp, The 15 Charles Chaplin
Tramp, The 86 Werner Masten
Tramp and the Baby's Bottle, The 03 William Haggar
Tramp and the Lady, The 14 Dalton Somers
Tramp and the Mattress Makers, The 06 Georges Méliès
Tramp and the Nursing Bottle, The 01 Edwin S. Porter
Tramp and the Typewriter, The 05 J. H. Martin
Tramp and the Washerwoman, The 03 William Haggar
Tramp at the Door 86 Allan Kroeker
Tramp Chef, The 16 William Beaudine
Tramp in Killarney, A 39 Nigel Byass
Tramp, the Boys Are Marching 26 Dave Fleischer
Tramp Tramp Tramp 18 Gregory La Cava
Tramp, Tramp, Tramp 26 Frank Capra, Harry Edwards
Tramp Tramp Tramp 26 Dave Fleischer
Tramp Tramp Tramp 35 Charles Lamont
Tramp, Tramp, Tramp 42 Charles Barton
Tramp, Tramp, Tramp the Boys Are Marching 26 Dave Fleischer
Tramp Trouble 37 Leslie Goodwins
Tramping Tramps 30 Walter Lantz
Tramplers, The 66 Alfredo Antonini, Mario Sequi
Tramps and the Purse, The 08 Lewin Fitzhamon
Tramps and the Washerwoman, The 04 Frank Mottershaw
Tramp's Cycling Mania, The 08 Walter R. Booth
Tramp's Dream, The 01 Edwin S. Porter
Tramp's Dream, The 06 Lewin Fitzhamon
Tramp's Dream of Wealth, A 07 Lewin Fitzhamon
Tramp's Duck Hunt, The 04 Frank Mottershaw
Tramp's Gratitude, The 12 Allan Dwan
Tramp's Miraculous Escape, The 01 Edwin S. Porter
Tramp's Paradise, The 15 James Read
Tramp's Revenge, The 04 James A. Williamson
Tramp's Revenge, The 07 Lewin Fitzhamon

Tramp's Strategy That Failed 01 Edwin S. Porter
Tramp's Surprise, The 02 Alf Collins
Tramp's Toilet, The 04 Alf Collins
Tramp's Unexpected Skate, The 01 Edwin S. Porter
Tramwaj do Nieba 58 Wincenty Ronisz, Krzysztof Zanussi
Trancers 84 Charles Band
Trances 81 Ahmed El Maanouni
Tranches de Vie 85 François Leterrier
Tränen Die Ich Dir Geweint 29 William Dieterle
Tranquil Father, The 46 René Clément
Tranquillo Posto di Campagna, Un 68 Elio Petri
Trans 79 Shirley Clarke
Trans-Europ-Express 66 Alain Robbe-Grillet
Transatlantic 31 William K. Howard
Transatlantic 61 Ernest Morris
Transatlantic Flight 19 Gregory La Cava
Transatlantic Merry-Go-Round 34 Ben Stoloff
Transatlantic Night Express, The 20 Harry D. Leonard
Transatlantic Trouble 37 William Beaudine
Transatlantic Tunnel 35 Maurice Elvey
Transatlantiques, Les 28 Pierre Colombier
Transcontinent Express 50 Joseph Kane
Transcontinental Limited 26 Nat Ross
Transes 81 Ahmed El Maanouni
Transfigurations, Les 09 Émile Cohl
Transfo Transforme l'Énergie du Pyrium 47 Alain Resnais
Transformation 59 Ed Emshwiller
Transformation Élastique 08 Segundo De Chomón
Transformation of Mike, The 11 D. W. Griffith
Transformation of the Land 50 Ilya Kopalin
Transformations 00 Alice Guy-Blaché
Transformations 04 Alice Guy-Blaché
Transformations 14 F. Percy Smith
Transformations 88 Jay Kamen
Transformations with Hats 1895 Louis Lumière
Transformers—The Movie, The 86 Kozo Morishita, Nelson Shin
Transforms 70 Stan Vanderbeek
Transfuge, Le 85 Philippe Lefèbvre
Transgression 17 Paul Scardon
Transgression 31 Herbert Brenon
Transgression, The 87 Fabrizio Rampelli
Transgression of Manuel, The 13 Allan Dwan
Transgressor, The 18 Joseph Levering
Transient Lady 35 Edward Buzzell
Transit 66 Bernhard Wicki
Transit 79 Daniel Wachsmann
Transit Dreams 86 Hartmut Jahn, Peter Wensierski
Transit of Venus, The 12 Hay Plumb
Transitträume 86 Hartmut Jahn, Peter Wensierski
Transmission, The 68 Theodoros Angelopoulos

Transmissions Hydrauliques, Les 55 Roger Leenhardt
Transmutations 88 Clive Barker
Transmutations Imperceptibles, Les 04 Georges Méliès
Transparency 69 Ernie Gehr
Transport from Paradise 67 Zbyněk Brynych
Transport of Fire 29 Alexander Ivanov
Transport z Ráje 67 Zbyněk Brynych
Transvestite, The 53 Edward D. Wood, Jr.
Transylvania 6-5000 63 Chuck Jones
Transylvania 6-5000 85 Rudy De Luca
Trap, The 18 George Archainbaud
Trap, The 18 Frank Reicher
Trap, The 22 Robert Thornby
Trap, The 46 Howard Bretherton
Trap, The 50 Martin Frič
Trap, The 58 Norman Panama
Trap, The 65 Yoji Yamada
Trap, The 66 Sidney Hayers
Trap, The 75 Peter Watkins
Trap Door, The 80 Beth B, Scott B
Trap for Cinderella, A 65 André Cayatte
Trap for Santa Claus, A 09 D. W. Griffith
Trap for the Assassin 66 Riccardo Freda
Trap Happy 46 Joseph Barbera, William Hanna
Trap Happy Porky 45 Chuck Jones
Trap on Cougar Mountain 72 Keith Larsen
Trap Them and Kill Them 77 Aristide Massaccesi
Trápení 61 Karel Kachyňa
Trapeze 31 E. A. Dupont
Trapeze 56 Carol Reed
Trapeze Artist, The 34 Manny Gould, Ben Harrison
Trapeze Disrobing Act 01 Edwin S. Porter
Trapianto, Il 69 Steno
Trapp-Familie, Die 56 Wolfgang Liebeneiner
Trapp Family, The 56 Wolfgang Liebeneiner
Trapped 23 Dave Fleischer
Trapped 31 Bruce Mitchell
Trapped 31 Kurt Neumann
Trapped 37 Leon Barsha
Trapped 49 Richard Fleischer
Trapped 82 William Fruet
Trapped by Boston Blackie 48 Seymour Friedman
Trapped by Fear 69 Jacques Dupont
Trapped by G-Men 37 Lewis D. Collins
Trapped by Television 36 Del Lord
Trapped by the London Sharks 16 L. C. MacBean
Trapped by the Mormons 22 H. B. Parkinson
Trapped by the Terror 49 Cecil Musk
Trapped by Wireless 36 Albert S. Rogell
Trapped in a Submarine 31 Walter Summers
Trapped in Tangiers 57 Riccardo Freda
Trapped in the Air 22 Henry McCarthy
Trapped in the Sky 39 Lewis D. Collins
Traqué, Le 50 Frank Tuttle
Traquenards 69 Jean-François Davy
Traquenards Érotiques 69 Jean-François Davy

Tras el Cristal *86* Agustín Villaronga
Tras la Reja *37* Jorge M. Dada
Trasgressione, La *87* Fabrizio Rampelli
Trash *70* Paul Morrissey
Trastienda, La *75* Jorge Grau
Tratta delle Bianche, La *52* Luigi Comencini
Tratta delle Bianche, La *67* Georges Combret
Trattato Scomparso, Il *33* Mario Bonnard
Traum vom Elch, Der *87* Siegfried Kühn
Traum vom Glück, Ein *24* Paul Stein
Traum vom Rhein, Der *35* Herbert Selpin
Traum von Lieschen Müller, Der *61* Helmut Käutner
Traum von Schönbrunn *33* Johannes Meyer
Trauma *62* Robert M. Young
Trauma *75* James Kenelm Clarke
Träumende Mund, Der *32* Paul Czinner
Träumende Mund, Der *52* Josef von Baky
Traumstadt *73* Johannes Schaaf
Traumulus *36* Carl Fröhlich
Travail *19* Henri Pouctal
Travailleurs de la Mer, Les *18* André Antoine
Travaux du Tunnel Sous l'Escaut *32* Henri Storck
Travel Notebook *60* Joris Ivens
Travel Path, The *86* Bashir El Deek
Travelaugh *21* Hy Mayer
Traveler, The *66* Mani Kaul
Travelin' On *21* Lambert Hillyer
Traveling Actors *40* Mikio Naruse
Traveling Artists *88* Dodo Abashidze, Sergei Paradzhanov
Traveling Boy *50* Charles Eames, Ray Eames
Traveling Executioner, The *70* Jack Smight
Traveling Forts *17* J. D. Leventhal
Traveling Hopefully *82* John G. Avildsen
Traveling Husbands *31* Paul Sloane
Traveling Lady *64* Robert Mulligan
Traveling Saleslady, The *35* Ray Enright
Traveling Salesman, The *16* Joseph Kaufman
Traveling Salesman, The *21* Joseph E. Henabery
Traveling Saleswoman, The *50* Charles Reisner
Traveling Stiltwalkers, The *10* Alf Collins
Traveller, The *57* Khwaja Ahmad Abbas, Vassili M. Pronin
Traveller *81* Joe Comerford
Travellers, The *57* Richard L. Bare
Traveller's Joy *49* Ralph Thomas
Travelling Avant *87* Jean-Charles Tacchella
Travelling North *86* Carl Schultz
Travelling Players, The *75* Theodoros Angelopoulos
Travels Under the Blue Sky *32* Hiroshi Inagaki
Travels with Anita *78* Lee Kresel, Mario Monicelli
Travels with My Aunt *72* George Cukor
Traversée de la France, La *61* Sidney Jézéquel, Roger Leenhardt
Traversée de Paris, La *56* Claude Autant-Lara

Traverseur d'Atlantique, Le *36* Léo Joannon
Travestie, La *88* Yves Boisset
Traviata, La *22* Challis Sanderson
Traviata, La *27* H. B. Parkinson
Traviata, La *47* Carmine Gallone
Traviata, La *66* Mario Lanfranchi
Traviata, La *82* Franco Zeffirelli
Traviata '53 *53* Vittorio Cottafavi
Traviesa Molinera, La *34* Harry D'Abbadie D'Arrast, Ricardo Soriano
Travolti da un Insolito Destino nell'Azzurro Mare d'Agosto *74* Lina Wertmuller
Traxx *88* Jerome Gary
Tray Full of Trouble, A *20* William Campbell
Trayler para Amantes de lo Prohibido *85* Pedro Almodóvar
Tre Anni Senza Donne *37* Guido Brignone
Tre Avventurieri, I *67* Robert Enrico
Tre Che Sconvolsero il West, I *68* Enzo G. Castellari
Tre Colpi di Winchester per Ringo *66* Emimmo Salvi
Tre Corsari, I *52* Mario Soldati
Tre Croci per Non Morire *68* Sergio Garrone
Tre del Colorado, I *65* Amando De Ossorio
Tre Dollari di Piombo *64* Joseph Trader
Tre Fili Fino a Milano *58* Ermanno Olmi
Tre Fratelli, I *80* Francesco Rosi
Tre Implacabili, I *63* Joaquín Luis Romero Marchent
Tre Innamorati, I *37* Nunzio Malasomma
Tre Kammerater, De *12* August Blom
Tre Meno Due *20* Augusto Genina
Tre Notti d'Amore *64* Renato Castellani, Luigi Comencini, Franco Rossi
Tre Notti Violente *66* Nick Nostro
Tre Passi nel Delirio *67* Federico Fellini, Louis Malle, Roger Vadim
Tre Piger i Paris *59* Gabriel Axel
Tre Pistole Contro Cesare *66* Enzo Peri
Tre Ragazzi d'Oro *66* Enzo Peri
Tre Scener med Ingmar Bergman *75* Jörn Donner
Tre Sentimentali, I *20* Augusto Genina
Tre Spietati, I *63* Joaquín Luis Romero Marchent
Tre Storie Proibite *52* Augusto Genina
Tre Supermen a Santo Domingo *86* Italo Martinenghi
Tre Tigri Contro Tre Tigri *77* Sergio Corbucci, Steno
Tre Uomini in Frak *32* Mario Bonnard
Tre Volti, I *64* Michelangelo Antonioni, Mauro Bolognini
Tre Volti della Paura, I *63* Mario Bava
Treacherous Policeman, The *09* Theo Bouwmeester
Treachery on the High Seas *36* Emil E. Reinert
Treachery Rides the Range *36* Frank McDonald
Tread *72* Richard Leacock
Tread Softly *52* David MacDonald

Tread Softly Stranger *58* Gordon Parry
Treason *17* Allen Holubar
Treason *18* Burton L. King
Treason *33* George B. Seitz
Treason *37* Irvin Willat
Treason *49* Felix E. Feist
Treasure *18* Frank Reicher
Treasure, The *23* G. W. Pabst
Treasure *49* Leonard Buczkowski
Treasure, The *51* Marian Leonard
Treasure, The *61* Revaz Chkeidze
Treasure, The *70* Lester James Peries
Treasure, The *74* Cornel Wilde
Treasure at the Mill *57* Max Anderson
Treasure Blues *35* James Parrott
Treasure Girl *30* Richard Boleslawski
Treasure Hunt *32* Dick Huemer
Treasure Hunt *52* John Paddy Carstairs
Treasure in Malta *63* Derek Williams
Treasure Island *12* J. Searle Dawley
Treasure Island *17* Chester M. Franklin, Sidney Franklin
Treasure Island *20* Maurice Tourneur
Treasure Island *34* Victor Fleming
Treasure Island *50* Byron Haskin
Treasure Island *72* John Hough
Treasure Island *85* Raúl Ruiz
Treasure Jest *45* Howard Swift
Treasure Mountain *29* Yasujiro Ozu
Treasure of Arne, The *19* Mauritz Stiller
Treasure of Bird Island, The *52* Karel Zeman
Treasure of Desert Isle, The *13* Ralph Ince
Treasure of Fear *45* Frank McDonald
Treasure of Heaven, The *16* A. E. Coleby
Treasure of Ice Cake Island *60* John Halas*
Treasure of Jamaica Reef, The *74* Virginia Stone
Treasure of Kalifa, The *53* E. A. Dupont
Treasure of Lost Canyon, The *51* Ted Tetzlaff
Treasure of Makuba, The *66* José María Elorrieta
Treasure of Matecumbe *76* Vincent McEveety
Treasure of Monte Cristo *49* William Berke
Treasure of Monte Cristo, The *60* Robert S. Baker, Monty Berman
Treasure of Pancho Villa, The *55* George Sherman
Treasure of Ruby Hills *55* Frank McDonald
Treasure of San Gennaro, The *65* Dino Risi
Treasure of San Teresa *59* Alvin Rakoff
Treasure of Silver Lake, The *62* Harald Reinl
Treasure of Tayopa *74* Bob Cawley
Treasure of the Amazon, The *83* René Cardona, Jr.
Treasure of the Four Crowns *82* Ferdinando Baldi
Treasure of the Golden Condor *53* Delmer Daves
Treasure of the Living Dead, The *82* Jesús Franco
Treasure of the Moon Goddess *85* José Luis García Agraz, Eric Weston

Treasure of the Piranha 78 Antonio Margheriti, Herbert V. Theiss
Treasure of the Sea, The 18 Frank Reicher
Treasure of the Sierra Madre, The 48 John Huston
Treasure of the White Goddess, The 83 Jesús Franco
Treasure of the Yankee Zephyr 81 David Hemmings
Treasure Seekers 77 Henry Levin
Treasure Trove 22 Frank Miller
Treasured Earth 48 Frigyes Bán
Treasures of Satan, The 02 Georges Méliès
Treat 'Em Rough 19 Lynn Reynolds
Treat 'Em Rough 42 Ray Taylor
Treating 'Em Rough 19 Pat Sullivan
Treatise on Japanese Bawdy Song, A 67 Nagisa Oshima
Treatment, The 61 Val Guest
Trechi Mynydd y Teigr 83 Tom Huckabee, Kent Smith
Tredie Magt, Den 12 August Blom
Tree 66 Peter Greenaway
Tree, The 69 Robert Guenette
Tree Cornered Tweety 56 Friz Freleng
Tree for Two 43 Bob Wickersham
Tree for Two 52 Friz Freleng
Tree Grows in Brooklyn, A 45 Elia Kazan
Tree of Hands, The 90 Giles Foster
Tree of Knowledge, The 20 William DeMille
Tree of Liberty, The 40 Frank Lloyd
Tree of the Wooden Clogs, The 78 Ermanno Olmi
Tree of Wishes, The 76 Tenghiz Abuladze
Tree of Wooden Clogs, The 78 Ermanno Olmi
Tree Saps 31 Dave Fleischer
Tree We Hurt, The 86 Demos Avdeliodis
Tree We Were Hurting, The 86 Demos Avdeliodis
Trees and Jamaica Daddy 58 Lew Keller
Trees and People 62 Evald Schorm
Treffen in Travers 89 Michael Gwisdek
Treffpunkt Leipzig 85 Jürgen Klauss
Tregova 49 Zahari Zhandov
Treibhaus, Das 87 Peter Gödel
Treichville 56 Jean Rouch
Treichville Story 87 Claude Cadiou
Treize à Table 56 André Hunebelle
Treize Jours en France 68 Claude Lelouch, François Reichenbach
Trek of Life, The 81 Şerif Gören
Trek to Mashomba 50 Vernon Sewell
Trekschuit, De 32 Mannus Franken
Trelawney of the Wells 16 Cecil M. Hepworth
Trelawney of the Wells 28 Sidney Franklin
Treloar and Miss Marshall, Prize Winners at the Physical Culture Show in Madison Square Garden 04 Edwin S. Porter
Trem para as Estrelas, Um 87 Carlos Dieguês
Tremarne Case, The 24 Hugh Croise
Trembling Hour, The 19 George Siegmann
Tremendously Rich Man, A 32 Steve Sekely
Tremors 90 Ron Underwood
Tren de la Victoria, El 64 Joris Ivens

Tren de los Pioneros, El 86 Leonel Gallego
Trena di Panna 88 Andrea De Carlo
Trenchcoat 83 Michael Tuchner
Trenck 34 Heinz Paul
Treno, Il 64 John Frankenheimer, Arthur Penn
Treno degli Spettri, Il 13 Mario Caserini
Treno del Sabato, Il 63 Vittorio Sala
Treno È Fermo a Berlino, Un 64 Rolf Haedrich
Treno per Durango, Un 67 Mario Caiano
32 Dicembre 88 Luciano De Crescenzo
Trenta Secondi D'Amore 36 Mario Bonnard
Trente Ans de la Vie d'un Skieur 72 Marcel Ichac
Trente Ans ou La Vie d'un Joueur 03 Ferdinand Zecca
32 Rue de Montmartre 39 Georges Lacombe, Yves Mirande
36 Fillette 88 Catherine Breillat
37.2 Degrés le Matin 86 Jean-Jacques Beineix
37°2 le Matin 86 Jean-Jacques Beineix
Trent's Last Case 20 Richard Garrick
Trent's Last Case 29 Howard Hawks
Trent's Last Case 52 Herbert Wilcox
Tres Amores 34 Moe Sackin
Tres Cantos 49 Luis García Berlanga
Tres Citas con el Destino 53 Fernando De Fuentes
Tres de Copas, El 87 Felipe Cazals
Tres Espadas del Zorro, Las 63 Riccardo Blasco
Tres Espejos 47 Ladislas Vajda
Tres Hombres Buenos 63 Joaquín Luis Romero Marchent
Três Menos Eu 88 João Canijo
Tres Noches Violentas 66 Nick Nostro
Tres Tristes Tigres 68 Raúl Ruiz
Tresa 15 Emilio Ghione
Trésor, Le 11 Louis Feuillade
Trésor de Cantenac, Le 49 Sacha Guitry
Trésor des Montagnes Bleues, Le 64 Harald Reinl
Trésor des Morts Vivants, Le 82 Jesús Franco
Trésor d'Ostende, Le 55 Henri Storck
Trésor du Lac d'Argent, Le 62 Harald Reinl
Trésors de Satan, Les 02 Georges Méliès
Trespasser, The 29 Edmund Goulding
Trespasser, The 46 Henry Levin
Trespasser, The 47 George Blair
Trespassers, The 76 John Duigan
Trespasses 83 Loren Bivens, Adam Roarke
Třetí Přání 57 Ján Kadár, Elmar Klos
Třetí Sarkan 85 Peter Hledik
Tretia Mecht Chanskaya 26 Abram Room, Sergei Yutkevich
33.333 24 Gustaf Molander
Tretya Meshchanskaya 26 Abram Room, Sergei Yutkevich
Tretyakov Gallery, The 56 Mikhail Kaufman
Tretyi Taym 64 Y. Karelov
Trêve, La 68 Claude Guillemot
Trevico-Torino...Viaggio nel Fiat Nam 73 Ettore Scola

Trevozhnaya Molodost 54 Alexander Alov, Vladimir Naumov
Trewey: Under the Hat 1895 Louis Lumière
Trey of Hearts 14 Wilfred Lucas, Henry MacRae
Tri 65 Aleksandar Petrović
Tri Geroini 38 Dziga Vertov
Tri Pesni o Leninye 34 Dziga Vertov
Tři Přání 57 Ján Kadár, Elmar Klos
Tri Sestry 64 Samson Samsonov
Tri Tolstyaka 66 Alexei Batalov, Josef Shapiro
Tři Vejce do Skla 37 Martin Frič
Tri Vstrechi 15 Richard Boleslawski
Tri Vstrechi 48 Alexander Ptushko, Vsevolod I. Pudovkin, Sergei Yutkevich
Tři Zlaté Vlasy Děda Vševěda 63 Martin Frič
Tria Tula, La 64 Miguel Picazo
Triad 38 Hans Hinrich
Trial, The 47 G. W. Pabst
Trial 55 Mark Robson
Trial, The 62 Orson Welles
Trial and Error 62 James Hill
Trial Balloons 82 Robert Breer
Trial by Combat 76 Kevin Connor
Trial in Smolensk, The 46 Esther Shub
Trial Marriage 28 William Hughes Curran
Trial Marriage 29 Erle C. Kenton
Trial of Billy Jack, The 74 Tom Laughlin
Trial of Joan of Arc, The 61 Robert Bresson
Trial of Lee Harvey Oswald, The 64 Larry Buchanan
Trial of Madame X, The 48 Paul England
Trial of Mary Dugan, The 29 Bayard Veiller
Trial of Mary Dugan, The 40 Norman Z. McLeod
Trial of Mironov, The 19 Dziga Vertov
Trial of Mr. Wolf, The 41 Friz Freleng
Trial of Portia Merriman, The 37 George Nicholls, Jr.
Trial of Sergeant Rutledge, The 60 John Ford
Trial of the Catonsville Nine, The 72 Gordon Davidson
Trial of the Social Revolutionaries, The 22 Dziga Vertov
Trial of the Three Millions, The 26 Yakov Protazanov
Trial of the Witches, The 69 Jesús Franco
Trial of Vivienne Ware, The 32 William K. Howard
Trial on the Road 71 Alexei Gherman
Trial Run 84 Melanie Read
Trial Without Jury 50 Philip Ford
Trials and Tribulations 18 Alfred E. Green
Trials of a Gypsy Gentleman, The 08 Lewin Fitzhamon
Trials of a Merry Widow, The 12 Charles C. Calvert
Trials of a Movie Cartoonist, The 16 Pat Sullivan
Trials of a Schoolmaster, The 01 Georges Méliès
Trials of Alger Hiss, The 80 John Lowenthal
Trials of Celebrity 19 Forest Holger-Madsen

Triumph of Hercules, The *64* Alberto De Martino
Triumph of Love *29* William Dieterle
Triumph of Michael Strogoff, The *61* Victor Tourjansky
Triumph of Robin Hood *62* Giancarlo Romitelli
Triumph of Sherlock Holmes, The *35* Leslie Hiscott
Triumph of the Heart *29* Gustaf Molander
Triumph of the Just *87* Josef Bierbichler
Triumph of the Rat, The *26* Graham Cutts
Triumph of the Scarlet Pimpernel, The *28* T. Hayes Hunter
Triumph of the Son of Hercules *63* Tanio Boccia
Triumph of the Spirit *89* Robert M. Young
Triumph of the Ten Gladiators *64* Nick Nostro
Triumph of the Weak, The *18* Tom Terriss
Triumph of the Will *34* Leni Riefenstahl
Triumph of Venus, The *18* Edwin Bower Hesser
Triumph Over Violence *64* Mikhail Romm
Triumphal March *75* Marco Bellocchio
Triumphs of a Man Called Horse *82* John Hough
Triumphs Without Drums *41* Joseph M. Newman
Trixie from Broadway *19* Roy William Neill
Tro, Håb og Kærlighed *84* Bille August
Trocadero *44* William Nigh
Trofei d'Africa *54* Folco Quilici
Trog *70* Freddie Francis
Troika *69* Frederic Hobbs, Gordon Mueller
Trois Bacchantes, Les *00* Georges Méliès
317ᵉᵐᵉ Section, La *65* Pierre Schöndörffer
Trois Chambres à Manhattan *65* Marcel Carné
Trois Chansons de la Résistance *44* Alberto Cavalcanti
Trois Chants pour la France *44* Alberto Cavalcanti
Trois Couronnes Danois de Matelots, Les *82* Raúl Ruiz
Trois Couronnes du Matelot, Les *82* Raúl Ruiz
Trois Enfants dans le Désordre *66* Léo Joannon
Trois Femmes *51* André Michel
Trois Femmes, Trois Âmes *51* André Michel
Trois Font la Paire, Les *57* Clément Duhour, Sacha Guitry
Trois Gants de la Dames en Noir, Les *20* Pierre Marodon
Trois Hommes à Abattre *80* Jacques Deray
Trois Hommes et un Couffin *85* Coline Serreau
Trois Jeunes Filles *28* Robert Boudrioz
Trois Jours à Vivre *56* Gilles Grangier
Trois Masques, Les *21* Henry Krauss
Trois-Mâts, Le *35* Henri Storck
Trois Mousquetaires, Les *12* André Calmettes, Henri Pouctal

Trois Mousquetaires, Les *21* Henri Diamant-Berger
Trois Mousquetaires, Les *32* Henri Diamant-Berger
Trois Mousquetaires, Les *53* André Hunebelle
Trois Passions, Les *28* Rex Ingram
Trois Places pour le 26 *88* Jacques Demy
Trois-Six-Neuf *37* Raymond Rouleau
Trois Télégrammes *50* Henri Decoin
Trois Thèmes *79* Alexander Alexeïeff, Claire Parker
Trois Vérités *63* François Villiers
Trois Vies Une Corde *33* Henri Storck
Troisième Jeunesse *65* Jean Dréville
Trojan Brothers, The *46* Maclean Rogers
Trojan Horse, The *62* Giorgio Ferroni
Trojan War, The *62* Giorgio Ferroni
Trojan Women, The *71* Michael Cacoyannis
Trold Kan Tæmmes *14* Forest Holger-Madsen
Troll *71* Vilgot Sjöman
Troll *86* John Buechler
Trollenberg Terror, The *58* Quentin Lawrence
Trolley Troubles *27* Walt Disney
Trollflöjten *74* Ingmar Bergman
Troløs *13* August Blom
Troma's War *87* Michael Herz, Lloyd Kaufman
Tromba *52* Helmut Weiss
Tromba, the Tiger Man *52* Helmut Weiss
Trombone from Heaven *43* Jean Yarbrough
Tromboner's Strong Note, The *14* Will P. Kellino
Trompé Mais Content *02* Alice Guy-Blaché
Trompette Anti-Neurasthénique, La *14* Émile Cohl
Tron *82* Steven Lisberger
Trône de France, Le *36* Alexander Alexeïeff, Claire Parker
Trono di Fuoco, Il *69* Jesús Franco
Trono e la Seggiola, Il *18* Augusto Genina
Troop Beverly Hills *89* Jeff Kanew
Troop Train, The *19* Edgar Lewis
Trooper, The *34* Ray Taylor
Trooper 44 *17* Roy Gahris
Trooper Hook *57* Charles Marquis Warren
Trooper O'Neill *22* Scott R. Dunlap, William K. Howard, C. R. Wallace
Troopers Three *29* B. Reeves Eason, Norman Taurog
Troopship *37* Tim Whelan
Trop Belle pour Toi *89* Bertrand Blier
Trop Tôt, Trop Tard *81* Danièle Huillet, Jean-Marie Straub
Trop Vieux! *08* Georges Méliès
Tropic Fury *39* Christy Cabanne
Tropic Holiday *38* Theodore Reed
Tropic Madness *28* Robert Vignola
Tropic of Cancer *69* Joseph Strick
Tropic of Ice *87* Lauri Törhönen
Tropic Zone *52* Lewis R. Foster
Tropical Eggs-pedition, A *19* Raoul Barré, Charles Bowers
Tropical Flower *83* Chang-ho Bae
Tropical Fury *44* Harold Young

Tropical Heat Wave *52* R. G. Springsteen
Tropical Love *21* Ralph Ince
Tropical Nights *28* Elmer Clifton
Tropical Trouble *36* Harry Hughes
Tropicana *43* Gregory Ratoff
Tropici *68* Gianni Amico
Tropics *68* Gianni Amico
Tropisk Kærlighed *11* August Blom
Troppo Bella *41* Carmine Gallone
Troppo Forte *85* Sergio Leone, Carlo Verdone
Trots *52* Gustaf Molander
Trötte Teodor *32* Gustaf Edgren
Trotter on the Trot *20* Tom Aitken
Trottie True *49* Brian Desmond Hurst
Trottoirs de Saturne, Les *85* Hugo Santiago
Trou, Le *59* Jacques Becker
Trou Normand, Le *52* Jean Boyer
Troubadour, The *49* Carmine Gallone
Troubadour's Triumph, The *12* Lois Weber
Trouble *22* Albert Austin
Trouble *33* Maclean Rogers
Trouble Ahead *34* Monty Banks
Trouble Along the Way *53* Michael Curtiz
Trouble at Melody Mesa *49* W. Merle Connell
Trouble at Midnight *37* Ford Beebe
Trouble at 16 *60* Charles Haas
Trouble at Townsend *46* Darrell Catling
Trouble Back Stairs *35* Veidt Harlan
Trouble Below Stairs *05* J. H. Martin
Trouble Brewing *24* James Davis, Larry Semon
Trouble Brewing *39* Anthony Kimmins
Trouble Bruin *64* Joseph Barbera, William Hanna
Trouble Buster, The *17* Frank Reicher
Trouble Buster, The *25* Leo D. Maloney
Trouble Busters *33* Lewis D. Collins
Trouble Chaser *40* Albert S. Rogell
Trouble Chasers *45* Lew Landers
Trouble-Fête *64* Pierre Patry
Trouble for Father *58* Alekos Sakelarios
Trouble for Juno *57* Barbara Woodhouse
Trouble for Nothing *16* Maurice Elvey
Trouble for Two *36* J. Walter Ruben
Trouble for Two *39* Walter Tennyson
Trouble in Mind *85* Alan Rudolph
Trouble in Molopolis *72* Philippe Mora
Trouble in Morocco *37* Ernest B. Schoedsack
Trouble in Panama *38* William Clemens
Trouble in Paradise *32* Ernst Lubitsch
Trouble in Store *34* Clyde Cook
Trouble in Store *53* John Paddy Carstairs
Trouble in Sundown *39* David Howard
Trouble in Texas *37* Robert North Bradbury
Trouble in the Air *48* Charles Saunders
Trouble in the Glen *53* Herbert Wilcox
Trouble in the Morning *52* Heinosuke Gosho
Trouble in the Sky *60* Charles Frend
Trouble Indemnity *50* Pete Burness
Trouble Makers *17* Kenean Buel
Trouble Makers *48* Reginald LeBorg
Trouble Man *72* Ivan Dixon
Trouble on the Trail *54* Frank McDonald

Try and Get Me 50 Cy Endfield
Trygon Factor, The 67 Cyril Frankel
Trying to Catch an Early Train 01 Edwin S. Porter
Trying to Fool Uncle 12 Mack Sennett
Trying to Get Arrested 09 D. W. Griffith
Tryst, The 29 Sidney Gilliat*
Tryst 81 Allen Ross
Tryton, A 17 Alfréd Deesy
Trzy Stopy Nad Ziemią 85 Janusz Kidawa
Tsar Ivan Vasilyevich Grozny 15 Alexander Ivanov-Gai
Tsar Nikolai II 17 A. Ivonin, Boris Mikhin
Tsar's Bride, The 66 Vladimir Gorikker
Tsarskaya Nevesta 66 Vladimir Gorikker
Tschaikovsky 70 Igor Talankin, Dmitri Tiomkin
Tschetan der Indianerjunge 73 Hark Böhm
Tsena Cheloveka 28 Mikhail Averbakh, Mark Donskoi
Tsubaki Sanjuro 62 Akira Kurosawa
Tsubasa no Gaika 42 Satsuo Yamamoto
Tsuchi 39 Tomu Uchida
Tsuki no Wataridōri 51 Teinosuke Kinugasa
Tsukigata Hanpeita 25 Teinosuke Kinugasa
Tsukigata Hanpeita 56 Teinosuke Kinugasa
Tsuma 53 Mikio Naruse
Tsuma no Himitsu 24 Teinosuke Kinugasa
Tsuma no Kokoro 55 Mikio Naruse
Tsuma to Onna no Aida 76 Kon Ichikawa, Shiro Toyoda
Tsuma-Toshite, Onna-Toshite 61 Mikio Naruse
Tsuma Yo Bara no Yo Ni 35 Mikio Naruse
Tsuruhachi and Tsurujiro 38 Mikio Naruse
Tsuruhachi Tsurujiro 38 Mikio Naruse
Tsuyomushi Onna to Yowamushi Otoko 68 Kaneto Shindo
Tsvet Granata 68 Sergei Paradzhanov
Tsvetok na Kamne 62 Sergei Paradzhanov
Tu Empêches Tout le Monde de Dormir 82 Gérard Lauzier
Tu Es Danse et Vertige 67 Raoul Coutard
Tu Es Pierre 58 Philippe Agostini
Tu Hijo 34 José Bohr
Tu M'Appartiens 29 Maurice Gleize
Tu M'As Sauvé la Vie 50 Sacha Guitry
Tu Mi Turbi 82 Roberto Benigni
Tu Ne Tueras Point 61 Claude Autant-Lara
Tu N'Épouseras Jamais un Avocat 14 Louis Feuillade
Tú Perdonas...Yo No 67 Giuseppe Colizzi
Tu Seras Duchesse 32 René Guissart
Tu Seras Terriblement Gentille 69 Dirk Sanders
Tú y el Mar 51 Emilio Fernández
Tua Prima Volta, La 85 Arduino Sacco
Tubby and the Clutching Hand 16 Frank Wilson
Tubby the Tuba 47 George Pal
Tubby's Bungle-Oh! 16 Frank Wilson
Tubby's Dugout Comedies 16 Frank Wilson

Tubby's Good Work 16 Frank Wilson
Tubby's Rest Cure 16 Frank Wilson
Tubby's River Trip 16 Frank Wilson
Tubby's Spanish Girls 16 Frank Wilson
Tubby's Tip 16 Frank Wilson
Tubby's Typewriter 16 Frank Wilson
Tubby's Uncle 16 Frank Wilson
Tube of Death, The 13 Alexander Butler
Tubog sa Ginto 70 Lino Brocka
Tuborgfilm 30 Anders Wilhelm Sandberg
Tuck Everlasting 80 Frederick King Keller
Tucker 88 Francis Ford Coppola
Tucker: The Man and His Dream 88 Francis Ford Coppola
Tucson 49 William F. Claxton
Tucson Raiders 44 Spencer G. Bennet
Tudor Rose 36 Robert Stevenson
Tue Mani sul Mio Corpo, Le 70 Brunello Rondi
Tuesday in November 45 John Berry
Tuesday Wednesday 87 John Pedersen
Tueur Aime les Bonbons, Le 68 Maurice Cloche, Richard Owens
Tueur de Chicago 59 Phil Karlson
Tuff Turf 85 Fritz Kiersch
Tugboat Annie 33 Mervyn LeRoy
Tugboat Annie Sails Again 40 Lewis Seiler
Tugboat Granny 56 Friz Freleng
Tugboat Princess 36 David Selman
Tugthusfange No. 97 14 August Blom
Tugthusfangerne Nr. 10 og 13 11 August Blom
Tükör, Egy 71 István Szabó
Túl a Kálvin Téren 55 Márta Mészáros
Tulipa 67 Manuel Octavio Gómez
Tulipää 80 Pirjo Honkasalo, Pekka Lehto
Tulipani di Harlem, I 70 Franco Brusati
Tulipe d'Or, La 14 Alfred Machin
Tulipe Noire, La 63 Christian-Jaque
Tulips 81 Rex Bromfield, Mark Warren, Al Waxman
Tulips Shall Grow 42 George Pal
Tulitikkutehtaan Tyttö 90 Aki Kaurismäki
Tullivapaa Avioliitto 80 János Zsombolyai
Tulsa 49 Stuart Heisler
Tulsa Kid, The 40 George Sherman
Tumannost Andromedy 68 Yevgeny Sherstobitov
Tumba de la Isla Maldita, La 72 Ray Danton, Julio Salvador
Tumba de los Muertos Vivientes, La 82 Jesús Franco
Tumbledown Ranch in Arizona 41 S. Roy Luby
Tumbleweed 53 Nathan Juran
Tumbleweed Trail 42 Sam Newfield
Tumbleweed Trail 46 Robert E. Tansey
Tumbleweeds 25 King Baggot, William S. Hart
Tumbling River 27 Lewis Seiler
Tumbling Tumbleweeds 35 Joseph Kane
Tumult in Damascus 39 Gustav Ucicky
Tumult in Toy Town 19 Milt Gross
Tumultuous Elopement, A 09 Georges Méliès
Tuna Clipper 49 William Beaudine
Tunda Baida 87 Govind Tej
Tundra 36 Norman Dawn
Tune in Tomorrow... 90 Jon Amiel
Tune Time 42 Reginald LeBorg

Tune Up and Sing 34 Dave Fleischer
Tune Up the Uke 28 Karl Freund
Túnel, El 88 Antonio Drove
Tunes of Glory 60 Ronald Neame
Tunes of the Times 39 Horace Shepherd
Tung 66 Bruce Baillie
Tung-Nien Wang-Shih 85 Hsiao-hsien Hou
Tung-Tung-Te-Chia-Ch'i 84 Hsiao-hsien Hou
Tuning His Ivories 14 Charles Chaplin
Tunisian Victory 43 Roy Boulting, Frank Capra
Tunnel, Der 33 Kurt Bernhardt
Tunnel, Le 33 Kurt Bernhardt
Tunnel, The 33 Kurt Bernhardt
Tunnel, The 35 Maurice Elvey
Tunnel, Il 79 Gillo Pontecorvo
Tunnel, The 79 Gillo Pontecorvo
Tunnel of Love, The 58 Gene Kelly
Tunnel Sous la Manche, Le 07 Georges Méliès
Tunnel Sous la Manche ou Le Cauchemar Franco-Anglais, Le 07 Georges Méliès
Tunnel to the Sun 68 Kei Kumai
Tunnel 28 62 Robert Siodmak
Tunneling the English Channel 07 Georges Méliès
Tunnelvision 76 Neal Israel, Brad Swirnoff
Tuntematon Sotilas 55 Edvin Laine
Tuntematon Sotilas 85 Rauni Mollberg
Tuo Vizio È una Stanza Chiusa e Solo Io Ne Ho la Chiave, Il 72 Sergio Martino
Tür Geht Auf, Ein 33 Alfred Zeisler
Turbina 41 Otakar Vávra
Turbine, The 41 Otakar Vávra
Turbine d'Odio 14 Carmine Gallone
Turbulent Years, The 61 Yulia Solntseva
Turbulent Youth 54 Alexander Alov, Vladimir Naumov
Turf Conspiracy, A 18 Frank Wilson
Turf Sensation, The 24 B. Reeves Eason
Turista 61 Evald Schorm
Turistas Interplanetarios 60 Miguel Zacarías
Turk 182! 85 Bob Clark
Turkey Dinner 36 Walter Lantz
Turkey Shoot 81 Brian Trenchard-Smith
Turkey Time 33 Tom Walls
Turkeys in a Row 24 Kenji Mizoguchi
Turkeys, Whereabouts Unknown 24 Kenji Mizoguchi
Türkischen Gurken, Die 63 Rolf Olsen
Turkish Bath, The 21 Raoul Barré, Charles Bowers
Turkish Cucumber, The 63 Rolf Olsen
Turkish Delight 19 Pat Sullivan
Turkish Delight 27 Paul Sloane
Turkish Delight 73 Paul Verhoeven
Turks Fruit 73 Paul Verhoeven
Turksib 29 Victor Turin
Turlis Abenteuer 69 Ron Merk
Turmoil, The 16 Edgar Jones
Turmoil, The 24 Hobart Henley
Turn Back the Clock 33 Edgar Selwyn
Turn Back the Hours 28 Howard Bretherton
Turn in the Road, The 18 King Vidor
Turn It Out 47 Ken Annakin
Turn of the Card, The 18 Oscar Apfel

Unternehmen Michael *38* Karl Ritter
Unternehmen Teutonenschwert *58* Andrew Thorndike, Annelie Thorndike
Untertan, Der *49* Wolfgang Staudte
Until Hell Is Frozen *60* Leopold Lahola
Until I Die *40* Ben Hecht, Charles MacArthur
Until September *84* Richard Marquand
Until the Day We Meet Again *32* Yasujiro Ozu
Until the Day We Meet Again *50* Tadashi Imai
Until They Get Me *17* Frank Borzage
Until They Sail *57* Robert Wise
Until Victory Day *45* Mikio Naruse
Until We Meet Again *50* Tadashi Imai
Untimely Man, The *73* Abram Room
Unto a Good Land *71* Jan Troell
Unto Each Other *29* A. E. Coleby
Unto Those Who Sin *16* Colin Campbell
Untouchables, The *59* Phil Karlson
Untouchables, The *87* Brian DePalma
Untypical Story, An *77* Grigori Chukhrai
Unusual Case, An *34* Ilya Trauberg
Unusual Exhibition, An *68* Eldar Shengelaya
Unusual Years *52* Vojtěch Jasný, Karel Kachyňa
Unutulan Sır *47* Lütfü Akat
Unvanquished, The *45* Mark Donskoi
Unvanquished, The *56* Satyajit Ray
Unveiling, The *11* D. W. Griffith
Unveiling Hand, The *19* Frank Crane
Unwanted, The *24* Walter Summers
Unwanted Bride, The *22* Edwin Greenwood
Unwed Mother *58* Walter Doniger
Unwelcome Chaperone, The *09* Dave Aylott
Unwelcome Guest, The *12* D. W. Griffith
Unwelcome Mother, The *16* James Vincent
Unwelcome Mrs. Hatch, The *14* Allan Dwan
Unwelcome Saint, An *11* Edwin S. Porter
Unwelcome Stranger *35* Phil Rosen
Unwelcome Visitors *39* Joseph Levering
Unwelcome Wife, The *15* Ivan Abramson
Unwiderst Ehliche, Der *37* Géza von Bolváry
Unwilling Agent *59* Franz Peter Wirth
Unwilling Hero, An *21* Clarence Badger
Unwilling Sinner, The *15* Forest Holger-Madsen
Unwritten Code, The *19* Bernard J. Durning
Unwritten Code, The *44* Herman Rotsten
Unwritten Law, The *25* Edward J. LeSaint
Unwritten Law, The *29* Sinclair Hill
Unwritten Law, The *32* Christy Cabanne
Unwritten Law, The *85* Ng See Yuen
Uomini, Che Mascalzoni, Gli *32* Mario Camerini
Uomini Contro *70* Francesco Rosi
Uomini dal Passo Pesante, Gli *66* Alfredo Antonini, Mario Sequi
Uomini del Marmo *55* Gillo Pontecorvo
Uomini Duri *87* Maurizio Ponzi
Uomini e Cieli *43* Francesco De Robertis
Uomini e i Tori, Gli *59* Gianfranco Mingozzi

Uomini e Lupi *56* Giuseppe De Santis
Uomini H *58* Inoshiro Honda
Uomini Merce *76* Carlo Lizzani
Uomini-Ombra *55* Francesco De Robertis
Uomini Si Nasce Poliziotti Si Muore *76* Ruggero Deodato
Uomini sul Fondo *41* Francesco De Robertis
Uomini Vogliono Vivere, Gli *62* Léonide Moguy
Uomo a Metà, Un *65* Vittorio De Seta
Uomo Che Ride, L' *66* Sergio Corbucci
Uomo Che Sorr'de, L' *37* Mario Mattòli
Uomo Che Viene da Canyon City, L' *65* Alfonso Balcazar
Uomo Chiamata Apocalisse Joe, Un *70* Leopoldo Savona
Uomo da Bruciare, Un *62* Valentino Orsini, Paolo Taviani, Vittorio Taviani
Uomo da Rispettare, Un *73* Michele Lupo
Uomo dai Cinque Palloni, L' *65* Marco Ferreri
Uomo dai Palloncini, L' *65* Marco Ferreri
Uomo dal Lungo Facice, L' *69* Harald Reinl
Uomo dalla Pelle Dura, Un *71* Franco Prosperi
Uomo dalle Due Ombre, L' *70* Terence Young
Uomo del Romanzo, L' *40* Mario Bonnard
Uomo della Croce, L' *42* Roberto Rossellini
Uomo della Mancha, L' *72* Arthur Hiller
Uomo della Pistola d'Oro, L' *67* Alfonso Balcazar
Uomo della Valle Maledetta, L' *64* Primo Zeglio
Uomo di Hong Kong, L' *65* Philippe de Broca
Uomo di Paglia, L' *57* Pietro Germi
Uomo di Rio, L' *63* Philippe de Broca
Uomo e una Colt, Un *67* Tulio Demicheli
Uomo in Ginocchio, Un *79* Damiano Damiani
Uomo, la Bestia e la Virtù, L' *53* Steno
Uomo Mezzo Ammazzato...Parola di Spirito Santo *72* Giuliano Carmineo
Uomo Senza Domenica, L' *57* Giuseppe De Santis
Uomo, un Cavallo, una Pistola, Un *67* Luigi Vanzi
Up! *76* Russ Meyer
Up a Tree *10* D. W. Griffith
Up a Tree *30* Roscoe Arbuckle
Up and At 'Em *22* William A. Seiter
Up and Going *22* Lynn Reynolds
Up for Murder *31* Monta Bell
Up for the Cup *31* Jack Raymond
Up for the Cup *50* Jack Raymond
Up for the Derby *33* Maclean Rogers
Up Frankenstein *73* Antonio Margheriti, Paul Morrissey
Up from the Beach *65* Robert Parrish
Up from the Depths *79* Charles B. Griffith
Up Front *51* Alexander Hall
Up Goes Maisie *45* Harry Beaumont
Up in Arms *27* Norman Taurog
Up in Arms *44* Elliott Nugent
Up in Central Park *48* William A. Seiter

Up in Mabel's Room *26* E. Mason Hopper
Up in Mabel's Room *44* Allan Dwan
Up in Mary's Attick *20* William Watson
Up in Smoke *57* William Beaudine
Up in Smoke *78* Lou Adler
Up in the Air *18* Gregory La Cava
Up in the Air *40* Howard Bretherton
Up in the Air *69* Jan Darnley-Smith
Up in the Cellar *70* Theodore J. Flicker
Up in the Clouds *65* Mrinal Sen
Up in the World *56* John Paddy Carstairs
Up Jumped a Swagman *65* Christopher Miles
Up Jumped the Devil *39* William Beaudine
Up 'n' Atom *47* Sid Marcus
Up on the Farm *24* Lewis Seiler
Up or Down *17* Lynn Reynolds
Up Periscope! *58* Gordon Douglas
Up Pompeii *71* Bob Kellett
Up Pops the Devil *31* A. Edward Sutherland
Up Pops the Duke *31* Roscoe Arbuckle
Up, Right and Wrong *47* George Dunning, Colin Low
Up Romance Road *18* Henry King
Up She Goes *20* Wallace A. Carlson
Up She Goes *45* Harry Beaumont
Up the Academy *80* Robert Downey
Up the Chastity Belt *71* Bob Kellett
Up the Creek *58* Val Guest
Up the Creek *83* Robert Butler
Up the Down Staircase *66* Robert Mulligan
Up the Front *72* Bob Kellett
Up the Junction *67* Peter Collinson
Up the Ladder *25* Edward Sloman
Up the MacGregors *67* Franco Giraldi
Up the Naked Rock *86* Bo Widerberg
Up the Pole *09* Walter R. Booth
Up the Poll *29* R. E. Jeffrey
Up the River *30* William Collier, John Ford
Up the River *38* Alfred L. Werker
Up the Road with Sallie *18* William Desmond Taylor
Up the Sandbox *72* Irvin Kershner
Up the Thames to Westminster *10* Sidney Olcott
Up to a Certain Point *83* Tomás Gutiérrez Alea
Up to a Point *83* Tomás Gutiérrez Alea
Up-to-Date Clothes Cleaning *08* Georges Méliès
Up-to-Date Conjurer, An *1899* Georges Méliès
Up-to-Date Dentist, An *1897* Georges Méliès
Up-to-Date Pickpockets *10* Fred Rains
Up-to-Date Spiritualism *00* Georges Méliès
Up-to-Date Studio, An *04* Percy Stow
Up-to-Date Surgery *02* Georges Méliès
Up to His Ears *65* Philippe de Broca
Up to His Neck *54* John Paddy Carstairs
Up to Mars *30* Dave Fleischer
Up to the Neck *33* Jack Raymond
Up with the Lark *43* Phil Brandon
Up Your Alley *75* Art Lieberman
Up Your Alley *89* Bob Logan

Vernon Howe Bailey's Sketchbook of Washington 16 Vernon Howe Bailey
Vernost Materi 66 Mark Donskoi
Verona Trial, The 62 Carlo Lizzani
Veronica Voss 81 Rainer Werner Fassbinder
Verónico Cruz 88 Miguel Pereira
Veronika 85 Otakar Vávra
Veronika Voss 81 Rainer Werner Fassbinder
Véronique 49 Robert Vernay
Véronique et Son Cancre 58 Eric Rohmer
Veronique's Long Night 66 Gianni Vernuccio
Verrat an Deutschland 54 Veidt Harlan
Verräter 37 Karl Ritter
Verräterin, Die 11 Urban Gad
Verrätertor, Das 64 Freddie Francis
Verrohrung des Franz Blums, Die 74 Reinhard Hauff
Verrückteste Auto der Welt, Das 74 Rudolf Zehetgruber
Verrufenen, Die 25 Gerhard Lamprecht
Vers Abécher la Mystérieuse 24 Henri Desfontaines
Vers l'Extase 60 René Wheeler
Versailles 53 Sacha Guitry
Versailles 66 Albert Lamorisse
Verschleierte Bild von Gross Kleindorf 13 Joe May
Verschleierte Dame, Die 15 Richard Oswald
Verschlossene Tür, Die 17 Urban Gad
Verschwörung zu Genua, Die 20 Paul Leni
Verse and Worse 21 Ray Enright
Verso la Vita 46 Dino Risi
Verspätung in Marienborn 64 Rolf Haedrich
Versteckte Liebe 87 Gottfried Junker
Versuchen Sie Meine Schwester 30 Karel Lamač
Versunkene Welt, Eine 22 Alexander Korda
Vertical Features Remake 78 Peter Greenaway
Vertige, Le 17 André Hugon
Vertige, Le 26 Marcel L'Herbier
Vertige d'un Soir 36 Victor Tourjansky
Vertiges 85 Christine Laurent
Vertigine 19 Baldassare Negroni
Vertigo 58 Alfred Hitchcock
Vertigo 62 Karel Kachyňa
Vertu de Lucette, La 12 Louis Feuillade
Veruntreute Himmel, Der 59 Ernst Marischka
Verwehte Spuren 38 Veidt Harlan
Verweigerung, Die 72 Axel Corti
Verwirrung der Liebe 58 Slatan Dudow
Very Big Withdrawal, A 79 Noel Black
Very Busy Day, A 20 Gregory La Cava
Very Close Encounters of the Fourth Kind 79 Mario Gariazzo
Very Close Quarters 83 Vladimir Rif
Very Confidential 27 James Tinling
Very Curious Girl, A 69 Nelly Kaplan
Very Edge, The 63 Cyril Frankel
Very Eye of Night, The 58 Maya Deren
Very Friendly Neighbors, The 69 Albert Zugsmith

Very Good Young Man, A 19 Donald Crisp
Very Handy Man, A 63 Alessandro Blasetti
Very Happy Alexander 67 Yves Robert
Very Happy Alexandre 67 Yves Robert
Very Honorable Guy, A 34 Lloyd Bacon
Very Honourable Man, A 34 Lloyd Bacon
Very Idea, The 20 Lawrence C. Windom
Very Idea, The 29 Frank Craven, William Le Baron, Richard Rosson
Very Important Person, A 61 Ken Annakin
Very Late Afternoon of a Faun, The 84 Věra Chytilová
Very Like a Whale 81 Alan Bridges
Very Moral Night, A 77 Károly Makk
Very Natural Thing, A 74 Christopher Larkin
Very Old Man with Enormous Wings, A 88 Fernando Birri
Very Petit Bourgeois, A 77 Mario Monicelli
Very Powerful Voice, A 11 Lewin Fitzhamon
Very Private Affair, A 61 Louis Malle
Very Private Affair, A 69 Nelly Kaplan
Very Special Favor, A 65 Michael Gordon
Very Thought of You, The 44 Delmer Daves
Very Truly Yours 22 Harry Beaumont
Very Young Lady, A 41 Harold Schuster
Ves v Pohraničí 48 Jiří Weiss
Veselaia Kanaraika 29 Lev Kuleshov
Veselaya Kanareika 29 Lev Kuleshov
Veselé Vánoce Přejí Chobotnice 86 Jindřich Polák
Veselý Cirkus 50 Jiří Trnka
Vesna 47 Grigori Alexandrov
Vesna v Moskve 53 Josef Heifits, N. Kosheverova
Vesničko Má Středisková 85 Jiří Menzel
Vesnoy 29 Mikhail Kaufman
Vessel of Wrath 38 Erich Pommer
Vesta Victoria Singing "Poor John" 07 Edwin S. Porter
Vesta Victoria Singing "Waiting at the Church" 07 Edwin S. Porter
Vestale du Gange, La 27 André Hugon
Vester Vov Vov 27 Forest Holger-Madsen
Vesterhavsdrenge 50 Astrid Henning-Jensen, Bjarne Henning-Jensen
Vestido Cor de Fogo, O 86 Lauro Antonio
Vestige, A 48 Heinosuke Gosho
Vestire gli Ignudi 54 Marcello Pagliero
Vesyolye Musikanty 37 Alexander Ptushko
Vesyolye Rebyata 34 Grigori Alexandrov
Veszprém—Town of Bells 66 Márta Mészáros
Vet in the Doghouse 61 D'Arcy Conyers
Vêtements Sigrand, Les 37 Alexander Alexeïeff, Claire Parker
Veter 58 Alexander Alov, Vladimir Naumov
Veter s Vostoka 41 Abram Room
Veter v Litso 29 Josef Heifits, Alexander Zarkhi
Veteran, The 26 Hugh Croise
Veteran, The 72 Bob Clark
Veteran of Waterloo, The 33 A. V.

Bramble
Veteran's Pension, The 11 Frank Wilson
Vettä 57 Jörn Donner
Vetter aus Dingsda, Der 36 Georg Zoch
Veuve Couderc, La 71 Pierre Granier-Deferre
Veuve en Or, Une 69 Michel Audiard
Veuves de Quinze Ans, Les 64 Jean Rouch
Vi Arme Syndere 52 Ole Palsbo
Vi Behöver Varann 44 Erik Faustman
Vi Bringer en Advarsel 44 Ole Palsbo
Vi Hænger i en Tråd 62 Jørgen Roos
Vi Har Många Namn 75 Mai Zetterling
Vi of Smith's Alley 21 Walter West
Vi på Solgläntan 40 Gunnar Olsson
Vi Som Går Köksvägen 32 Gustaf Molander
Vi Tre Debutera 53 Hasse Ekman
Vi Två 30 John W. Brunius
Vi Två 39 S. Bauman
Via Cabaret 13 Wallace Reid
Via Crucis 18 August Blom
Via de Oro, La 32 Edino Cominetti
Via dei Cessati Spiriti 59 Gian Vittorio Baldi
Via dei Piopponi 61 Gianfranco Mingozzi
Via del Petrolio, La 66 Bernardo Bertolucci
Via delle Cinque Lune 42 Luigi Chiarini
Via Emilia Km 147 49 Carlo Lizzani
Via Fast Freight 21 James Cruze
Via Lattea, La 68 Luis Buñuel
Vía Libre a la Zafra del '64 64 Santiago Álvarez
Via Mala 45 Josef von Baky
Via Margretha 59 Mario Camerini
Via Margutta 59 Mario Camerini
Via Montenapoleone 87 Carlo Vanzina
Via Più Lunga, La 17 Mario Caserini
Via Pony Express 33 Lewis D. Collins
Via Wireless 15 George Fitzmaurice
Viaccia, La 60 Mauro Bolognini
Viaggiatori della Sera, I 79 Ugo Tognazzi
Viaggio, Il 73 Vittorio De Sica
Viaggio al Sud 49 Carlo Lizzani
Viaggio con Anita 78 Lee Kresel, Mario Monicelli
Viaggio di Capitan Fracassa, Il 90 Ettore Scola
Viaggio in Italia 53 Roberto Rossellini
Viaje a Ninguna Parte 86 Fernando Fernán Gómez
Viaje al Centro de la Tierra 76 Juan Piquer Simon
Viaje al Más Allá 80 Sebastián D'Arbo
Viaje al Paraíso 87 Ignacio Retes
Viaje Sin Regreso, El 46 Pierre Chénal
Viale della Speranza, Il 53 Dino Risi
Viasmos tis Aphrodites, O 85 Andreas Pantzis
Vibes 88 Ken Kwapis
Vibration 69 Torbjörn Axelman
Vibrations 67 Joe Sarno
Vibrations Sensuelles 76 Jean Rollin
Vic Dyson Pays 25 Jacques Jaccard
Vicar of Bray, The 37 Henry Edwards
Vicar of Vejlby, The 20 August Blom
Vicar of Wakefield, The 12 Frank Powell
Vicar of Wakefield, The 13 John Douglas
Vicar of Wakefield, The 13 Frank Wilson

Vie Platinée, La 87 Claude Cadiou
Vie Pôle Nord 54 Marcel Ichac
Vie Privée, La 61 Louis Malle
Vie Sans Joie, Une 24 Albert Dieudonné
Vieil Homme et l'Enfant, Le 66 Claude Berri
Vieille Dame Indigne, La 64 René Allio
Vieille Fille, La 72 Jean-Pierre Blanc
Vieilles Estampes 04 Alice Guy-Blaché
Vieilles Femmes de l'Hospice, Les 17 Jacques Feyder
Vieja Música, La 85 Mario Camus
Viejecito, El 59 Manuel Summers
Viejo Amor, Un 40 Luis Lezama
Viejo Doctor, El 40 Mario Soffici
Vienna Burgtheater 36 Willi Forst
Vienna—City of Songs 30 Richard Oswald
Vienna Strangler, The 71 Guido Zurli
Vienna Tales 40 Géza von Bolváry
Vienna Waltzes 51 Emil E. Reinert
Viennese Nights 30 Alan Crosland
Viento Negro 65 Servando González
Viento Norte 37 Mario Soffici
Vier Gesellen, Die 38 Carl Fröhlich
Vier im Jeep, Die 51 Leopold Lindtberg
Vier Musketiere, Die 35 Heinz Paul
Vier um die Frau 20 Fritz Lang
Vier und Zwanzig Stunden im Leben einer Frau 68 Dominique Delouche
Vier von der Infanterie 30 G. W. Pabst
Vierde Man, Die 82 Paul Verhoeven
Vieren Maar 54 Herman van den Horst
Vierge d'Argos, La 11 Louis Feuillade
Vierge du Rhin, La 53 Gilles Grangier
Vierge Folle, La 29 Luitz-Morat
Vierge Folle, La 38 Henri Diamant-Berger
Vierge pour le Prince, Une 65 Pasquale Festa Campanile
Vierges, Les 62 Jean-Pierre Mocky
Vierges et Vampires 71 Jean Rollin
Viernes de la Eternidad, Los 81 Héctor Olivera
Vierte Gebot, Das 20 Richard Oswald
Viertelstunde Großstadtstatistik, Eine 33 Oskar Fischinger
Vierzehn Menschenleben 54 Zoltán Fábri
Vierzig M Deutschland 86 Tevfik Baser
Vietnam 54 Roman Karmen
Viêt-nam! 65 Joris Ivens
Vietnam—An American Journey 78 Robert Richter
Vieux Chaland, Le 32 Jean Epstein
Vieux de la Vieille, Les 60 Gilles Grangier
Vieux Fusil, Le 75 Robert Enrico
Vieux Garçon, Un 31 Jacques Tourneur
Vieux Pays Où Rimbaud Est Mort, Le 77 Jean-Pierre Lefèbvre
View from Pompey's Head, The 55 Philip Dunne
View from the Bridge, A 61 Sidney Lumet
View from the People Wall 65 Charles Eames, Ray Eames
View from the Satellite 71 Bruce Beresford
View of the Wreck of the Maine, A 1898 Georges Méliès
View to a Kill, A 85 John Glen
Víg Özvegy, A 18 Michael Curtiz
Vigil, The 35 Marcel L'Herbier
Vigil 83 Vincent Ward
Vigil in the Night 40 George Stevens

Vigilante, The 47 Wallace Fox
Vigilante 82 William Lustig
Vigilante Force 76 George Armitage
Vigilante Hideout 50 Fred C. Brannon
Vigilante Terror 53 Lewis D. Collins
Vigilantes Are Coming, The 36 Ray Taylor, Mack V. Wright
Vigilantes of Boomtown 47 R. G. Springsteen
Vigilantes of Dodge City 44 Wallace A. Grissell
Vigilantes Return, The 47 Ray Taylor
Vigilantes Ride, The 44 William Berke
Vigile, Il 60 Luigi Zampa
Vigilia di Mezza Estate, La 59 Gian Vittorio Baldi
Vigliacchi Non Pregano, I 68 Marion Sirko
Vignes du Seigneur, Les 58 Jean Boyer
Vigour of Youth 31 Russell Mack
Vihar 52 Zoltán Fábri
Vijay 88 Jayanthi
Vikhri Vrazhdebnye 56 Mikhail Kalatozov
Viki 37 Márton Keleti
Viking, The 28 Roy William Neill
Viking, The 31 George Melford
Viking Queen, The 66 Don Chaffey
Viking Women 57 Roger Corman
Viking Women and the Sea Serpent, The 57 Roger Corman
Viking Women vs. the Sea Serpent 57 Roger Corman
Vikings, The 58 Richard Fleischer
Viking's Bride, The 07 Lewin Fitzhamon
Viking's Daughter, The 08 J. Stuart Blackton
Viktor und Viktoria 33 Reinhold Schünzel
Viktoria 34 Karl Hoffmann
Viktoria und Ihr Husar 31 Richard Oswald
Vilaine Histoire 34 Christian-Jaque
Vilambaram 87 Balachandra Menon
Vild Fågel, En 21 John W. Brunius
Vildfåglar 54 Alf Sjöberg
Vildledt Elskov 11 August Blom
Villa! 58 James B. Clark
Villa dei Mostri, La 50 Michelangelo Antonioni
Villa delle Anime Maledette, La 83 Carlo Ausino
Villa Destin 20 Marcel L'Herbier
Villa Dévalisée 05 Alice Guy-Blaché
Villa Falconieri 28 Richard Oswald
Villa in the Suburbs 59 Věra Chytilová
Villa Miranda 72 Lino Brocka
Villa of the Movies 17 Edward F. Cline
Villa Rides! 68 Buzz Kulik
Villa Santo-Sospir, La 51 Jean Cocteau
Village, The 53 Leopold Lindtberg
Village, The 75 Yoji Yamada
Village Barber, The 30 Ubbe Iwerks
Village Barn Dance 40 Frank McDonald
Village Blacksmith, The 1898 Arthur Cooper
Village Blacksmith, The 05 Percy Stow
Village Blacksmith, The 08 A. E. Coleby
Village Blacksmith, The 17 A. E. Coleby, Arthur H. Rooke
Village Blacksmith, The 20 Ben Sharpsteen
Village Blacksmith, The 22 John Ford
Village Blacksmith, The 37 Henry Edwards

Village Bride, The 27 Heinosuke Gosho
Village Choir, The 00 George Albert Smith
Village Cutups, The 21 Raoul Barré, Charles Bowers
Village Doctor, The 51 Sergei Gerasimov
Village Feud, The 51 Henri Verneuil
Village Fire Brigade, The 07 James A. Williamson
Village Hero, The 11 Mack Sennett
Village Homestead, The 15 Joseph Byron Totten
Village in Crisis 20 Cheslav Sabinsky
Village in the Jungle 80 Lester James Peries
Village in the Mist 82 Kwon-taek Im
Village Love Story, A 10 Bert Haldane
Village Magique, Le 53 Jean-Paul Le Chanois
Village Mill, The 50 Jerzy Kawalerowicz, Kazimierz Sumerski
Village Near the Pleasant Fountain, The 38 Pál Fejös
Village of Daughters 61 George Pollock
Village of Sin, The 27 Olga Preobrazhenskaya
Village of Tajinko, The 40 Tadashi Imai
Village of the Damned 60 Wolf Rilla
Village of the Giants 65 Bert I. Gordon
Village on the Frontier, The 48 Jiří Weiss
Village on the River 58 Fons Rademakers
Village Rogue, The 37 Béla Pásztor
Village Scandal, A 11 Fred Rains
Village Scandal, A 12 Lewin Fitzhamon
Village Scandal, A 13 Bert Haldane
Village Scandal, The 15 Roscoe Arbuckle
Village School Teacher, The 46 Mark Donskoi
Village Sheik, The 22 Al St. John
Village Sleuth 20 Jerome Storm
Village Smithie, The 31 Ubbe Iwerks
Village Smithy, The 36 Tex Avery
Village Specialist, The 31 Ubbe Iwerks
Village Squire, The 35 Reginald Denham
Village Tale 35 John Cromwell
Village Tattooed Man, The 35 Sadao Yamanaka
Village Teacher, A 25 Yasujiro Shimazu
Village Teacher 46 Mark Donskoi
Village Wife 58 Heinosuke Gosho
Villages d'Enfants 69 Maurice Pialat
Villain 71 Michael Tuchner
Villain, The 79 Hal Needham
Villain Foiled, The 11 Mack Sennett
Villain Still Pursued Her, The 13 Charles C. Calvert
Villain Still Pursued Her, The 40 Edward F. Cline
Villainous Villain, A 16 Larry Semon
Villain's Downfall, The 09 Lewin Fitzhamon
Villain's Wooing, The 05 Lewin Fitzhamon
Villanelle des Rubans, La 32 Jean Epstein
Ville à Chandigarh, Une 66 Alain Tanner
Ville Comme les Autres, Une 55 Claude Lelouch
Ville des Pirates, La 83 Raúl Ruiz
Ville Étrangère 88 Didier Goldschmidt

Virgins and Vampires *71* Jean Rollin
Virgins of Rome, The *60* Carlo Ludovico Bragaglia, Vittorio Cottafavi
Virgin's Sacrifice, A *22* Webster Campbell
Viridiana *61* Luis Buñuel
Virilidad a la Española *75* Francisco Lara Polop
Virtue *32* Edward Buzzell
Virtue's Revolt *24* James Chapin
Virtuous Bigamist, The *57* Mario Soldati
Virtuous Dames of Pardubicke, The *44* Martin Frič
Virtuous Husband *31* Vin Moore
Virtuous Liars *24* Whitman Bennett
Virtuous Men *19* Ralph Ince
Virtuous Model, The *19* Albert Capellani
Virtuous Outcast, The *16* James Kirkwood
Virtuous Scoundrel, The *52* Sacha Guitry
Virtuous Sin, The *30* George Cukor, Louis Gasnier
Virtuous Sinners *19* Emmett J. Flynn
Virtuous Thief, The *19* Fred Niblo
Virtuous Tramps, The *33* Hal Roach, Charles Rogers
Virtuous Vamp, A *19* David Kirkland
Virtuous Wife, The *31* George B. Seitz
Virtuous Wives *18* George Loane Tucker
Virus *79* Kinji Fukasaku
Virus *80* Antonio Margheriti
Virus Cannibale *81* Bruno Mattei
Virus Has No Morals, A *86* Rosa von Praunheim
Virus Kennt Keine Moral, Ein *86* Rosa von Praunheim
Virus Knows No Morals, A *86* Rosa von Praunheim
Virus — L'Inferno dei Morti Viventi *81* Bruno Mattei
Visa to Canton *60* Michael Carreras
Visa U.S.A. *86* Lisandro Duque Naranjo
Visage Pale *85* Claude Gagnon
Visages de France *36* Dmitri Kirsanov
Visages de Paris *55* François Reichenbach
Visages d'Enfants *23* Jacques Feyder, Françoise Rosay
Visages Voiles...Âmes Closes *21* Henri Roussel
Viscount, The *67* Maurice Cloche
Vishvamitra *52* Pendharkar Babu Rao
Visible Manifestations *63* George Dunning
Vision d'Ivrogne *1897* Georges Méliès
Vision of the Shepherd, The *15* Colin Campbell
Vision Quest *85* Harold Becker
Visionari, I *69* Maurizio Ponzi
Visione del Sabba, La *87* Marco Bellocchio
Visioniii *58* Stan Vanderbeek
Visions *77* Chuck Vincent
Visions of an Opium Smoker, The *05* J. H. Martin
Visions of Eight *72* Miloš Forman, Kon Ichikawa, Claude Lelouch, Yuri Ozerov, Arthur Penn, Michael Pfleghar, John Schlesinger, Mai Zetterling
Visions of Sugar-Plums *84* Todd Durham
Visions of the Deep *83* Al Giddings
Visit, A *54* François Truffaut
Visit, The *59* Jack Gold
Visit, The *63* Antonio Pietrangeli
Visit, The *64* Bernhard Wicki

Visit at Twilight *66* Jan Rybkowski
Visit of Santa Claus, The *1898* George Albert Smith
Visit to a Chief's Son *74* Lamont Johnson
Visit to a Foreign Country *62* Michel Brault, Claude Jutra
Visit to a Small Planet *60* Norman Taurog
Visit to a Spiritualist, A *06* Arthur Cooper
Visit to India *56* Roman Karmen
Visit to Monica, A *74* Richard Leacock
Visit to Norman *75* Richard Leacock
Visit to the Seaside, A *08* George Albert Smith
Visit to the Spiritualist, A *1899* J. Stuart Blackton
Visit to the Zoo, A *15* Wallace A. Carlson
Visit to Uncle Dudley's Farm, A *15* Wallace A. Carlson
Visit Vezhlivosti *73* Yuli Raizman
Visit with Picasso *49* Paul Haesaerts
Visit Zakopane *63* Jerzy Hoffman
Visita, La *63* Antonio Pietrangeli
Visitaciones del Diablo, Las *71* Alberto Isaac
Visitatore, Il *79* Giulio Paradisi
Visite, Une *54* François Truffaut
Visite à César Domela *47* Alain Resnais
Visite à Félix Labisse *47* Alain Resnais
Visite à Hans Hartung *47* Alain Resnais
Visite à Lucien Coutaud *47* Alain Resnais
Visite à Max Ernst *47* Alain Resnais
Visite à Oscar Dominguez *47* Alain Resnais
Visite au Haras *51* Henri Decaë
Visite de l'Épave du Maine *1898* Georges Méliès
Visite Sous-Marin du Maine *1898* Georges Méliès
Visiteur, Le *46* Jean Dréville
Visiteurs du Soir, Les *42* Marcel Carné
Visiting Hours *81* Jean-Claude Lord
Visitor, The *73* John Wright
Visitor, The *79* Giulio Paradisi
Visitors, The *71* Elia Kazan
Visitors from the Galaxy *81* Dušan Vukotić
Viskningar och Rop *72* Ingmar Bergman
Vispa Teresa, La *39* Roberto Rossellini
Vissi d'Arte, Vissi d'Amore *52* Carmine Gallone
Visszaesök *83* Zsolt Kézdi-Kovács
Visszaszámlálás *85* Pál Erdöss
Vistula People, The *37* Helena Boguszewska, Aleksander Ford, J. Kornacki, J. Zarzycki
Vita, a Volte, e Molto Dura, Vero "Providenza," La *72* Giulio Petroni
Vita Agra, La *64* Carlo Lizzani
Vita Avventurosa di Milady, La *52* Vittorio Cottafavi
Vita Col Figlio *66* Luigi Comencini
Vita da Cani *50* Mario Monicelli, Steno
Vita di Scorta, La *86* Piero Vida
Vita Difficile, Una *61* Dino Risi
Vita È Bella, La *44* Carlo Ludovico Bragaglia
Vita È Bella, La *82* Grigori Chukhrai
Vita e Morte *16* Mario Caserini
Vita Frun *62* Arne Mattsson
Vita Katten, Den *50* Hasse Ekman

Vita Privata *61* Louis Malle
Vita Ricomincia, La *47* Mario Mattòli
Vita Sporten, Den *68* Bo Widerberg*
Vita Violenta, Una *62* Paolo Heusch, Brunello Rondi
Vital Question, The *16* Sidney Rankin Drew
Vital Signs *90* Marisa Silver
Vital Victuals *34* Nick Grindé
Vitamin G-Man, The *43* John Hubley, Paul Sommer
Vitamin Hay *41* Dave Fleischer
Vite Perdute *61* Adelchi Bianchi, Roberto Mauri
Vite Semplice, La *45* Francesco De Robertis
Vitelius *11* Henri Pouctal
Vitelloni, I *53* Federico Fellini
Vitesse Est à Vous, La *61* Jean-Jacques Languepin
Vítimas do Prazer — Snuff *74* Claúdio Cunha
Vitrail Diabolique, Le *10* Georges Méliès
Vittel *26* Claude Autant-Lara
Vittima dell'Amore, La *16* Mario Caserini
Vittnesbörd om Henne *63* Jörn Donner
Viuda de Montiel, La *79* Miguel Littin
Viva Buddy *34* Jack King
Viva Cisco Kid *40* Norman Foster
Viva el Presidente *75* Miguel Littin
Viva Gringo *66* Georg Marischka
Viva il Primo Maggio Rosso *69* Marco Bellocchio*
Viva Italia *77* Mario Monicelli, Dino Risi, Ettore Scola
Viva Knievel! *77* Gordon Douglas
Viva la Muerte *71* Fernando Arrabal
Viva la Muerte...Tua! *71* Duccio Tessari
¡Viva la Soldera! *58* Miguel Torres Contreras
Viva Las Vegas! *55* Roy Rowland
Viva Las Vegas! *64* George Sidney
Viva l'Italia *60* Roberto Rossellini
Viva Maria! *65* Louis Malle
Viva Max! *69* Jerry Paris
Viva Portugal *75* Christiane Gerhards, Serge July, Peer Oliphant, Malte Rauch, Samuel Schirmbeck
Viva Revolución *56* Roberto Gavaldón
Viva Villa! *34* Jack Conway, Howard Hawks
Viva Willie *34* Ubbe Iwerks
Viva Zapata! *52* Elia Kazan
Vivacious Lady *38* George Stevens
¡Vivan los Novios! *69* Luis García Berlanga
Vivante Épingle, La *21* Jacques Robert
Vive Henri IV...Vive l'Amour! *61* Claude Autant-Lara
Vive la France! *18* Roy William Neill
Vive la France *73* Michel Audiard
Vive la Vie *37* Jean Epstein
Vive la Vie! *84* Claude Lelouch
Vive le Sabotage *07* Louis Feuillade
Vive le Tour! *61* Louis Malle
Vive les Femmes! *85* Claude Confortes
Vive l'Italie *77* Mario Monicelli, Dino Risi, Ettore Scola
Vivement Dimanche! *82* François Truffaut
Vivere *38* Guido Brignone
Vivere in Pace *46* Luigi Zampa

Volga-Volga *28* Victor Tourjansky
Volga-Volga *38* Grigori Alexandrov
Volk Will Leben, Ein *39* Robert A. Stemmle
Volkfest Kannstadt *35* Walter Ruttmann
Volksfeind, Ein *37* Hans Steinhoff
Volkskrankheit Krebs *41* Walter Ruttmann
Volkskrankheit Krebs/Jeder Achte *41* Walter Ruttmann
Volley for a Black Buffalo *85* László Szabó
Volleyball *67* Yvonne Rainer
Volnaya Ptitsa *13* Yevgeni Bauer
Volnitsa *55* Grigori Roshal
Volnyi Umirayut na Beregu *87* Tynchylyk Razzakov
Volnyi Veter *61* A. Tontichkin, Leonid Trauberg
Volochayevsk Days *37* Georgy Vasiliev, Sergei Vasiliev
Volochayevskiye Dni *37* Georgy Vasiliev, Sergei Vasiliev
Volonté *17* Henri Pouctal
Volpone *39* Maurice Tourneur
Volpone, Il *88* Maurizio Ponzi
Voltaire *33* John G. Adolfi
Voltati Eugenio *79* Luigi Comencini
Voltati...Ti Uccido *67* Alfonso Brescia
Voltera, Comune Medievale *55* Valentino Orsini, Paolo Taviani, Vittorio Taviani
Volti dell'Amore, I *23* Carmine Gallone
Voltige, La *1895* Louis Lumière
Voluntad del Muerto, La *30* George Melford
Volunteer, The *18* Harley Knoles
Volunteer, The *43* Michael Powell, Emeric Pressburger
Volunteer Jam *76* Stanley Dorfman
Volunteers *85* Nicholas Meyer
Volunteers *86* Predrag Golubović
Volver a Empezar *81* José Luis García Agraz
Vom Blitz zum Fernsehbild *36* Hans Richter
Vom Himmel Gefallen *55* John Brahm
Vom Teufel Gejagt *50* Victor Tourjansky
Von der Liebe Besiegt *56* Luis Trenker
Von Loon's Non-Capturable Aeroplane *18* L. M. Glackens
Von Loon's 25,000 Mile Gun *18* L. M. Glackens
Von Richthofen and Brown *70* Roger Corman
Von Rosa von Praunheim *67* Rosa von Praunheim
Von Ryan's Express *65* Mark Robson
Voodoo Blood Bath *64* Del Tenney
Voodoo Blood Death *64* Lindsay Shonteff
Voodoo Girl *74* Paul Maslansky
Voodoo Heartbeat *72* Charles Nizet
Voodoo Island *57* Reginald LeBorg
Voodoo Man *44* William Beaudine
Voodoo Tiger *52* Spencer G. Bennet
Voodoo Woman *57* Edward L. Cahn
Voor Recht en Vrijheid te Kortrijk *39* Henri Storck
Vor Fælles Ven *20* Anders Wilhelm Sandberg
Vor Sonnenuntergang *56* Gottfried Reinhardt
Vor Uns Liegt das Leben *48* Günther Rittau

Vorderhaus und Hinterhaus *25* Richard Oswald*
Vordertreppe und Hintertreppe *14* Urban Gad
Vorgluten des Balkanbrandes *12* Joe May
Vörös Grófnő *85* András Kovács
Vörös Május *68* Miklós Jancsó
Vörös Sámson, A *17* Michael Curtiz
Vortex, The *18* Gilbert P. Hamilton
Vortex, The *27* Adrian Brunel
Vortex *78* John Cardos
Vortex *82* Beth B, Scott B
Voruntersuchung *31* Robert Siodmak
Vory v Zakone *88* Yuri Kara
18-28 *28* Nutsa Gogoberidze, Mikhail Kalatozov
Voskhozhdenie *76* Larissa Shepitko
Voskresniye *63* Mikhail Shveytser
Voskresniye Papa *88* Naum Birman
Vostaniye Rybakov *34* Erwin Piscator
Vot Moya Derevnya *87* Viktor Tregubovich
Vote for Huggett *48* Ken Annakin
Voter's Guide, The *06* Lewin Fitzhamon
Votes for Women, A Caricature *09* Charles Armstrong
Voto, Il *51* Mario Bonnard
Voulez-Vous Danser avec Moi? *59* Michel Boisrond
Vous Intéressez-Vous à la Chose? *74* Jacques Baratier
Vous N'Aurez Pas l'Alsace et la Lorraine *77* Coluche
Vous N'Avez Rien à Déclarer? *36* Yves Allégret, Léo Joannon
Vous Verrez la Semaine Prochaine *29* Alberto Cavalcanti
Vow, The *15* Stanner E. V. Taylor
Vow, The *38* Henryk Szaro
Vow, The *46* Mikhail Chiaureli
Vow of Vengeance, The *23* Harry G. Moody
Voyage *04* Georges Méliès
Voyage, The *73* Vittorio De Sica
Voyage à Biarritz, Le *62* Gilles Grangier
Voyage à la Planète Jupiter *07* Segundo De Chomón
Voyage à Paimpol, Le *85* John Berry
Voyage à Travers l'Impossible, Le *04* Georges Méliès
Voyage Across the Impossible *04* Georges Méliès
Voyage au Bout du Monde, Le *76* Jacques-Yves Cousteau, Philippe Cousteau
Voyage au Centre de la Terre *09* Segundo De Chomón
Voyage au Congo *26* Marc Allégret*
Voyage au Pays de Rimbaud *83* Dariush Mehrjui
Voyage Autour d'une Étoile *06* Gaston Velle
Voyage Autour d'une Main *83* Raúl Ruiz
Voyage Beyond the Sun *65* Leonard Katzman
Voyage by Night *86* Kitty Kino
Voyage d'Agrément *35* Christian-Jaque
Voyage dans la Lune, Le *02* Georges Méliès
Voyage dans la Lune *09* Segundo De Cho-

món
Voyage dans le Ciel *36* A. P. Dufour, Jean Painlevé
Voyage de Badabou, Le *55* Henri Gruel
Voyage de Brigitte Bardot aux U.S.A *66* François Reichenbach
Voyage de Gulliver à Lilliput et chez les Géants, Le *02* Georges Méliès
Voyage de la Famille Bourrichon, Le *10* Georges Méliès
Voyage de Monsieur Perrichon, Le *34* Marcel Pagnol
Voyage de Noces, Le *76* Nadine Trintignant
Voyage de Noces en Ballon *08* Georges Méliès
Voyage de Noces en Espagne *12* Max Linder
Voyage du Père, Le *66* Denys De la Patellière
Voyage en Algérie *50* Sacha Vierny
Voyage en Amérique, Le *51* Henri Lavorel
Voyage en Ballon, Le *60* Albert Lamorisse
Voyage en Douce *79* Michel Deville
Voyage en Espagne *06* Alice Guy-Blaché
Voyage en Grande Tartarie *73* Jean-Charles Tacchella
Voyage Home: Star Trek IV, The *86* Leonard Nimoy
Voyage Imaginaire, Le *25* René Clair
Voyage in a Balloon *60* Albert Lamorisse
Voyage in Italy *53* Roberto Rossellini
Voyage of Peter Joe, The *46* Harry Hughes
Voyage of Silence *67* Christian De Chalonge
Voyage of "The Arctic," The *03* Walter R. Booth
Voyage of the Damned *76* Stuart Rosenberg
Voyage of the Rock Aliens *84* James Fargo
Voyage of the Viking Women to the Waters of the Great Sea Serpent, The *57* Roger Corman
Voyage Sans Espoir *43* Christian-Jaque
Voyage Surprise *46* Pierre Prévert
Voyage to a Prehistoric Planet *65* Peter Bogdanovich, Pavel Klushantsev
Voyage to America *51* Henri Lavorel
Voyage to Cythera *84* Theodoros Angelopoulos
Voyage to Danger *62* Wolfgang Schleif
Voyage to Grand Tartarie *73* Jean-Charles Tacchella
Voyage to Italy *53* Roberto Rossellini
Voyage to Melonia *87* Per Ahlin
Voyage to Next *74* John Hubley
Voyage to Nowhere *86* Fernando Fernán Gómez
Voyage to Prehistory *54* Karel Zeman
Voyage to the Bottom of the Sea *61* Irwin Allen
Voyage to the Edge of the World *76* Jacques-Yves Cousteau, Philippe Cousteau
Voyage to the End of the Universe *63* Jindřich Polák
Voyage to the Planet of Prehistoric Women *65* Peter Bogdanovich, Pavel Klushantsev

Wähle das Leben *62* Erwin Leiser

Wahnsinn *19* Conrad Veidt

Wahre Jakob, Der *31* Hans Steinhoff

Wahre Liebe, Die *19* Joe May

Wahsh, El *54* Salah Abu Saif

Waif, The *15* William L. Roubert

Waif and the Statue, The *07* Walter R. Booth

Waif and the Wizard, The *01* Walter R. Booth

Waif and the Wizard, or The Home Made Happy, The *01* Walter R. Booth

Waifs, The *15* Percy Nash

Waifs, The *16* Scott Sidney

Waifs *18* Albert Parker

Waikiki Wedding *37* Frank Tuttle

Waise von Lowood, Die *26* Kurt Bernhardt

Wait *68* Ernie Gehr

Wait and See *10* Alf Collins

Wait and See *28* Walter Forde

Wait for Me! *43* Boris Ivanov, Alexander Stolper

Wait for Me in Heaven *88* Antonio Mercero

Wait for the Dawn *60* Roberto Rossellini

Wait for Us at Dawn *63* Emil Lotyanu

Wait 'Til the Sun Shines, Nellie *52* Henry King

Wait Till I Catch You *10* Percy Stow

Wait Till Jack Comes Home *03* James A. Williamson

Wait Till the Sun Shines, Nellie *32* Dave Fleischer

Wait Till the Work Comes 'Round *07* Arthur Gilbert

Wait Until Dark *67* Terence Young

Wait Until Spring, Bandini *89* Dominique Deruddere

Waiter, The *14* Charles Chaplin, Mabel Normand

Waiter from the Ritz, The *26* James Cruze

Waiter No. 5 *10* D. W. Griffith

Waiter No. 5: A Story of Russian Despotism *10* D. W. Griffith

Waiters, The *69* Jan Darnley-Smith

Waiter's Ball, The *16* Roscoe Arbuckle

Waiter's Picnic, The *13* Mack Sennett

Waiting *25* Stephen Roberts

Waiting at the Church *06* Edwin S. Porter

Waiting at the Church *31* William James Craft

Waiting for Caroline *67* Ron Kelly

Waiting for Darkness *86* Pauli Pentti

Waiting for Him Tonight *07* John Morland

Waiting for Salazar *89* Jim Kouf

Waiting for the Bride *31* William James Craft

Waiting for the Moon *87* Jill Godmilow

Waiting for the Rain *78* Karel Kachyňa

Waiting for the Robert E. Lee *27* Dave Fleischer

Waiting for Waiting for Godot *82* Derek Jarman

Waiting in the Wings *87* Edward Fleming

Waiting Room, The *77* Bob Kellett

Waiting Soul, The *17* Burton L. King

Waiting Women *52* Ingmar Bergman

Waitress! *82* Michael Herz, Lloyd Kaufman

Wajan *38* Gdeh Ray, Walter Spies

Wak-Wak, ein Märchenzauber *26* Lotte Reiniger

Wakai Hito *52* Kon Ichikawa

Wakai Hitotachi *54* Kozaburo Yoshimura

Wakaki Hi *29* Yasujiro Ozu

Wakaki Hi no Chuji *25* Teinosuke Kinugasa

Wakaki Hi no Kangeki *31* Heinosuke Gosho

Wakamba *55* Edgar M. Queeny

Wakamono Tachi *70* Tokihisa Morikawa

Wakare *69* Hideo Oba

Wakare-Gumo *51* Heinosuke Gosho

Wakarete Ikiru Toki Mo *61* Hiromichi Horikawa

Wake in Fright *70* Ted Kotcheff

Wake Island *42* John Farrow

Wake Me When It's Over *60* Mervyn LeRoy

Wake of the Red Witch *48* Edward Ludwig

Wake Up! *14* Lawrence Cowen

Wake Up and Die *66* Carlo Lizzani

Wake Up and Dream *34* Kurt Neumann

Wake Up and Dream *42* Edward F. Cline

Wake Up and Dream *46* Lloyd Bacon

Wake Up and Kill *66* Carlo Lizzani

Wake Up and Live *37* Sidney Lanfield

Wake Up Famous *37* Gene Gerrard

Wake Up! or A Dream of Tomorrow *14* Lawrence Cowen

Wake Up the Gypsy in Me *33* Rudolf Ising

Wakefield Case, The *21* George Irving

Wakefield Express *52* Lindsay Anderson

Waking Hour, The *71* Stephanie Rothman

Waking Up the Town *25* James Cruze

Wakodo no Yume *28* Yasujiro Ozu

Walden *68* Jonas Mekas

Waldwinter *36* Fritz Peter Buch

Wales *49* David Hand

Walk a Crooked Mile *48* Gordon Douglas

Walk a Crooked Path *69* John Brason

Walk a Tightrope *63* Frank Nesbitt

Walk by the Sea *63* George Nader

Walk Cheerfully *30* Yasujiro Ozu

Walk, Don't Run *66* Charles Walters

Walk East on Beacon *52* Alfred L. Werker

Walk in the Night, The *20* F. W. Murnau

Walk in the Old City of Warsaw, A *58* Andrzej Munk

Walk in the Old Town, A *58* Andrzej Munk

Walk in the Shadow *62* Basil Dearden

Walk in the Spring Rain, A *69* Guy Green

Walk in the Sun, A *45* Lewis Milestone

Walk Into Hell *57* Lee Robinson

Walk Into Paradise *56* Marcello Pagliero

Walk Like a Dragon *60* James Clavell

Walk Like a Man *86* Melvin Frank

Walk-Offs, The *20* Herbert Blaché

Walk on the Moon, A *85* Raphael D. Silver

Walk on the Wild Side *62* Edward Dmytryk

Walk Proud *79* Robert Collins

Walk Softly, Stranger *50* Robert Stevenson

Walk Tall *60* Maury Dexter

Walk the Angry Beach *61* John Hayes

Walk the Dark Street *56* Wyott Ordung

Walk the Proud Land *56* Jesse Hibbs

Walk the Walk *70* Jac Zacha

Walk Through H, A *78* Peter Greenaway

Walk with Love and Death, A *69* John Huston

Walkabout *70* Nicolas Roeg

Walker *87* Alex Cox

Walkers on the Tiger's Tail *45* Akira Kurosawa

Walking After Midnight *88* Jonathon Kay

Walking Back *28* Rupert Julian

Walking Back Home *33* George Stevens

Walking Dead, The *36* Michael Curtiz

Walking Down Broadway *33* Erich von Stroheim, Raoul Walsh, Alfred L. Werker

Walking Down Broadway *38* Norman Foster

Walking Hills, The *49* John Sturges

Walking My Baby Back Home *53* Lloyd Bacon

Walking on Air *36* Joseph Santley

Walking on Air *46* Aveling Ginever

Walking Stick, The *70* Eric Till

Walking Tall *73* Phil Karlson

Walking Tall, Part 2 *75* Earl Bellamy

Walking Target, The *60* Edward L. Cahn

Walking the Edge *85* Norbert Meisel

Walking the Streets of Moscow *63* Georgy Danelia

Walking to Heaven *59* Imre Fehér

Walking, Walking *83* Ermanno Olmi

Walking Woman Work, A *64* Michael Snow

Walkman Blues *86* Alfred Behrens

Walkover *65* Jerzy Skolimowski

Walkower *65* Jerzy Skolimowski

Walky Talky Hawky *46* Robert McKimson

Wall, The *47* Leopoldo Torre-Nilsson

Wall, The *82* Yılmaz Güney

Wall, The *82* Alan Parker

Wall Between, The *16* John W. Noble

Wall Driller, The *85* György Szomjas

Wall Flower, The *22* Rupert Hughes

Wall for San Sebastian *67* Henri Verneuil

Wall in Jerusalem, A *68* Albert Knobler, Frédéric Rossif

Wall of Death *51* Lewis Gilbert

Wall of Death *56* Montgomery Tully

Wall of Flesh *67* Joe Sarno

Wall of Fury *62* Luis Trenker

Wall of Money, The *13* Allan Dwan

Wall of Noise *63* Richard Wilson

Wall Street *16* Charles Bowers

Wall Street *29* Roy William Neill

Wall Street *87* Oliver Stone

Wall Street Cowboy *39* Joseph Kane

Wall Street Mystery, The *20* Tom Collins

Wall Street Tragedy, A *16* Lawrence Marston

Wall Street Whiz, The *25* Jack Nelson

Wall Walls *80* Agnès Varda

Wallaby Jim of the Islands *37* Charles Lamont

Wallers Last Trip *89* Christian Wagner

Wallers Letzter Gang *89* Christian Wagner

Wallet, The *52* Morton M. Lewis

Walleyed Nippon *63* Hideo Suzuki
Wallflower *48* Frederick De Cordova
Wallflowers *28* James Leo Meehan
Wallingford *31* Sam Wood
Wallop, The *21* John Ford
Walloping Kid *26* Robert J. Horner
Walloping Wallace *24* Richard Thorpe
Walls *68* András Kovács
Walls *85* Tom Shandel
Walls Came Tumbling Down, The *46* Lothar Mendes
Walls of Fear *62* Raoul André
Walls of Fire *74* Herbert Kline
Walls of Glass *85* Scott Goldstein
Walls of Gold *33* Kenneth MacKenna
Walls of Hell, The *64* Gerry De Leon, Eddie Romero
Walls of Jericho, The *14* James K. Hackett
Walls of Jericho, The *48* John M. Stahl
Walls of Malapaga, The *49* René Clément
Walls of Prejudice *20* Charles C. Calvert
Walls of Sana, The *70* Pier Paolo Pasolini
Wally, La *39* Guido Brignone
Walpurgis Night *35* Gustaf Edgren
Walrus Gang, The *17* Dave Aylott
Walter & Carlo: Op på Fars Hat *85* Per Holst
Walter Finds a Father *21* Joseph J. Bamberger
Walter Makes a Move *22* Walter Forde, Tom Seymour
Walter Tells the Tale *26* James B. Sloan
Walter the Prodigal *26* James B. Sloan
Walter the Sleuth *26* James B. Sloan
Walter Wants Work *22* Walter Forde, Tom Seymour
Walter Wins a Wager *22* Walter Forde, Tom Seymour
Walter's Day Out *26* James B. Sloan
Walter's Paying Policy *26* James B. Sloan
Walter's Trying Frolic *22* Walter Forde, Tom Seymour
Walter's Winning Ways *21* William J. Bowman
Walter's Worries *26* James B. Sloan
Waltz Across Texas *82* Ernest Day
Waltz at Noon *49* Kozaburo Yoshimura
Waltz Dream, A *25* Ludwig Berger
Waltz King, The *63* Steve Previn
Waltz Me Around Again Willie *08* Arthur Gilbert
Waltz Melodies *38* Karel Lamač
Waltz Must Change to a March, The *06* Arthur Gilbert
Waltz of the Toreadors *62* John Guillermin
Waltz Time *33* Wilhelm Thiele
Waltz Time *45* Paul Stein
Waltz Time in Vienna *33* Ludwig Berger
Waltzes from Vienna *33* Alfred Hitchcock
Walzer für Dich, Ein *36* Georg Zoch
Walzer vom Strauss, Ein *32* Conrad Wiene
Walzerkönig, Der *29* Conrad Wiene
Walzerkönig, Der *32* Manfred Noa
Walzerkrieg *33* Ludwig Berger
Walzerlange *38* Karel Lamač
Walzerparadies *33* Fred Zelnik
Walzertraum, Ein *25* Ludwig Berger
Wam Bam Thank You Spaceman *75* William A. Levey

Wan Zhong *89* Ziniu Wu
Wanda *71* Barbara Loden
Wanda Nevada *79* Peter Fonda
Wander Love Story *70* Fletcher Fist
Wanderer, The *12* Allan Dwan
Wanderer, The *13* D. W. Griffith
Wanderer, The *25* Raoul Walsh
Wanderer, The *67* Jean-Gabriel Albicocco
Wanderer and the Whozitt, The *18* Robert C. Bruce
Wanderer Beyond the Grave *15* Victor Tourjansky
Wanderer of the Wasteland, The *24* Irvin Willat
Wanderer of the Wasteland *35* Otho Lovering
Wanderer of the Wasteland *45* Wallace A. Grissell, Edward Killy
Wanderer of the West *27* Robin E. Williamson, Joseph E. Zivelli
Wanderer Returns, The *14* Cecil Birch
Wanderers, The *37* Jacques Feyder
Wanderers, The *73* Kon Ichikawa
Wanderers, The *79* Philip Kaufman
Wanderer's Notebook, A *62* Mikio Naruse
Wanderers of the West *41* Robert F. Hill
Wanderer's Return, or Many Years After, The *09* Dave Aylott
Wand-erful Will *16* Toby Cooper
Wandering *67* Jan Curik, Antonin Masa
Wandering Bill *15* Carl Francis Lederer
Wandering Bird *38* R. O'Quigley
Wandering Daughters *23* James Young
Wandering Fires *26* Maurice Campbell
Wandering Footsteps *25* Phil Rosen
Wandering Gambler, The *28* Hiroshi Inagaki
Wandering Girls *27* Ralph Ince
Wandering Gypsy, The *12* Allan Dwan
Wandering Husbands *24* William Beaudine
Wandering Image, The *20* Fritz Lang
Wandering Jew, The *04* Georges Méliès
Wandering Jew, The *23* Maurice Elvey
Wandering Jew, The *33* Maurice Elvey
Wandering Jew, The *33* George Roland
Wandering Jew, The *47* Goffredo Alessandrini
Wandering Minstrel, The *1899* Georges Méliès
Wandering Minstrel, A *07* John Morland
Wandering Minstrel, The *28* Henry D. Bailey
Wandering on Highways *56* Márta Mészáros
Wandering Stars *27* G. Gricher-Cherikover
Wandering with the Moon *45* Hasse Ekman
Wanderlove *70* Fletcher Fist
Wanderlust *35* William Keighley
Wandernde Bild, Das *20* Fritz Lang
Wandernde Licht, Das *16* Robert Wiene
Wang Lao Wou *38* Tsou-sen Tsai
Wang Ma Gwi *67* Hyuk-jin Kwon
Wangsibri Street *76* Kwon-taek Im
Waning Sex, The *26* Robert Z. Leonard
Wann—Wenn Nicht Jetzt? *88* Michael Juncker
Wannsee Conference, The *84* Heinz

Schirk
Wannseekonferenz *84* Heinz Schirk
Wanpaku Ogi no Orochitaiji *63* Yugo Serikawa
Want a Ride Little Girl? *74* William Grefé
Wanta Make a Dollar? *17* William Beaudine
Wanted *29* Howard Higgin
Wanted *33* Phil Whitman
Wanted *37* George King
Wanted *68* Giorgio Ferroni
Wanted, a Bath Chair Attendant *10* H. Oceano Martinek
Wanted, a Boy *24* Thomas Bentley
Wanted, a Brother *18* Robert Ensminger
Wanted: A Child *09* D. W. Griffith
Wanted, a Coward *27* Roy Clements
Wanted: A Film Actress *17* Mauritz Stiller
Wanted—A Home *16* Phillips Smalley, Lois Weber
Wanted, a Housekeeper *12* Wilfred Noy
Wanted, a Husband *06* Alf Collins
Wanted, a Husband *13* Arthur Charrington
Wanted: A Husband *16* Al Christie
Wanted—A Husband *19* Lawrence C. Windom
Wanted: A Leading Lady *15* Al Christie
Wanted—A Mother *18* Harley Knoles
Wanted, a Mummy *10* A. E. Coleby
Wanted, a Nice Young Man *08* Dave Aylott
Wanted, a Stronghand *13* Van Dyke Brooke
Wanted a Wife *18* Percy Nash
Wanted: An Actress *17* Mauritz Stiller
Wanted: An Athletic Instructor *10* Edwin S. Porter
Wanted at Headquarters *20* Stuart Paton
Wanted: Babysitter *75* René Clément
Wanted by Scotland Yard *37* Norman Lee
Wanted by the Law *24* Robert North Bradbury
Wanted by the Police *38* Howard Bretherton
Wanted: Dead or Alive *51* Thomas Carr
Wanted: Dead or Alive *86* Gary Sherman
Wanted, Field Marshals for the Gorgonzola Army *11* H. Oceano Martinek
Wanted for Murder *19* Frank Crane
Wanted for Murder *39* Sam Newfield
Wanted for Murder *46* Lawrence Huntington
Wanted for Murder, or Bride of Hate *17* Walter Edwards
Wanted: Jane Turner *36* Edward Killy
Wanted Johnny Texas *67* Emimmo Salvi
Wanted Men *30* Albert De Courville
Wanted Men *31* Bennett Cohn, Forrest K. Sheldon
Wanted Men *36* Clifford Pember
Wanted: Perfect Mother *70* Lino Brocka
Wanted Sabata *70* Roberto Mauri
Wanted Women *75* Al Adamson
Wanters, The *23* John M. Stahl
Wanting Weight, The *71* Bernhard Wicki
Wanton, The *49* Yves Allégret
Wanton Contessa, The *53* Luchino Visconti

Wanton Countess, The *53* Luchino Visconti

Wanzerbé *68* Jean Rouch

Wanzerbé, Capitale de la Magie *48* Marcel Griaule, Jean Rouch

War *60* Veljko Bulajić

WAR *86* Raphael Nussbaum

War *87* Michael Herz, Lloyd Kaufman

War Against Mrs. Hadley, The *42* Harold S. Bucquet

War and Love *85* Moshe Mizrahi

War and Peace *15* Vladimir Gardin, Yakov Protazanov

War and Peace *45* Fumio Kamei, Satsuo Yamamoto

War and Peace *55* Mario Soldati, King Vidor

War and Peace *67* Sergei Bondarchuk

War and Peace *82* Axel Ängstfeld, Stefan Aust, Heinrich Böll, Alexander Kluge, Volker Schlöndorff

War and Piece *69* Paul Hunt

War and Pieces *64* Chuck Jones

War and the Woman *17* Ernest C. Warde

War and Woman Teacher *66* Kwon-taek Im

War Arrow *53* George Sherman

War at Wallaroo Mansions, The *22* Kenneth Graeme

War Babies *32* Charles Lamont

War Baby, The *14* Charles H. Weston

War Between Men and Women, The *72* Melville Shavelson

War Between the Planets *65* Antonio Margheriti

War Birds *89* Ulli Lommel

War Boy, The *84* Allan Eastman

War Bride, The *28* Henry D. Bailey

War Brides *16* Herbert Brenon

War Bride's Secret, The *16* Kenean Buel

War Cartoons by Hy Mayer *14* Hy Mayer

War Cloud, The *15* Harold Weston

War Comes to America *44* Frank Capra, Anatole Litvak

War Correspondent *32* Paul Sloane

War Correspondent *45* William A. Wellman

War Cry *51* Ray Nazarro

War Dogs *42* S. Roy Luby

War Dogs *43* Joseph Barbera, William Hanna

War Drums *57* Reginald LeBorg

War Episodes *1897* Georges Méliès

War Es die Grosse Liebe? *53* Vincente Minnelli, Gottfried Reinhardt

War Game, The *61* Mai Zetterling

War Game, The *65* Peter Watkins

War Games *70* Hy Averback

War Gardens *18* Gregory La Cava

War God, The *29* Yefim Dzigan

War Goddess *73* Terence Young

War Gods of Babylon *62* Silvio Amadio

War Gods of the Deep *65* Jacques Tourneur

War Head *61* Cyril Frankel

War Hero *63* Burt Topper

War Horse, The *27* Lambert Hillyer

War Hunt *61* Denis Sanders

War in Space *77* Jun Fukuda

War in Turkey *13* Émile Cohl

War Is a Racket *34* Samuel Cummings, Jacques Koerpel

War Is Hell *15* Ethyle Batley

War Is Hell *63* Burt Topper

War Is Over, The *66* Alain Resnais

War, Italian Style *67* Luigi Scattini

War Jester *85* Dino Risi

War Lord *34* John Farrow

War Lord *37* John Farrow

War Lord, The *65* Franklin J. Schaffner

War Lover, The *62* Philip Leacock

War Madness *63* Burt Topper

War Mamas *31* Marshall Neilan

War! Nakdong River *76* Kwon-taek Im

War Nurse *30* Edgar Selwyn

War O'Dreams, The *15* E. A. Martin

War of 600 Million People, The *58* Joris Ivens

War of the Aliens *77* Ed Hunt

War of the Buttons, The *62* Yves Robert

War of the Colossal Beast *58* Bert I. Gordon

War of the Gardens, The *82* Raúl Ruiz

War of the Gargantuas, The *66* Inoshiro Honda

War of the Madmen, The *87* Manolo Matji

War of the Monsters *66* Shigeo Tanaka

War of the Monsters *72* Jun Fukuda

War of the Planets *65* Antonio Margheriti

War of the Planets *77* Alfonso Brescia

War of the Planets *77* Jun Fukuda

War of the Range *33* John P. McGowan

War of the Roses, The *89* Danny DeVito

War of the Satellites *57* Roger Corman

War of the Waltzes *33* Ludwig Berger

War of the Wildcats *43* Albert S. Rogell

War of the Wizards *83* Sadamasa Arikawa, Richard Caan

War of the Worlds *52* Byron Haskin

War of the Worlds—Next Century, The *81* Piotr Szulkin

War of the Zombies *63* Giuseppe Vari

War on the Plains *12* Thomas Ince

War Paint *26* W. S. Van Dyke

War Paint *53* Lesley Selander

War Party *64* Lesley Selander

War Party *88* Franc Roddam

War Requiem *88* Derek Jarman

War Shock *56* Paul Henreid

War Story, A *81* Anne Wheeler

War Trilogy *67* Puriša Djordjević

War Wagon, The *67* Burt Kennedy

War Without End *36* Francis Searle

War Zone *87* Nathaniel Gutman

Warai no Ningen *60* Yoji Kuri

Ward No. 9 *55* Károly Makk

Ward 13 *81* Boaz Davidson

Wardcare of Psychotic Patients *41* Harold F. Kress

Warden's Daughter, The *41* William Beaudine

Wardogs *87* Bjorn Carlstrom, Daniel Hubenbecker

Wardrobe, The *59* George Dunning

Ware Case, The *17* Walter West

Ware Case, The *28* H. Manning Haynes

Ware Case, The *38* Robert Stevenson

Warehouse *73* Yasuzo Masumura

Warera ga Kyōkan *39* Tadashi Imai

Warfare of the Flesh, The *17* Edward Warren

WarGames *83* John Badham

Warhead *74* John O'Connor

Warhol's Frankenstein *73* Antonio Margheriti, Paul Morrissey

Warkill *67* Ferde Grofé, Jr.

Warlock *59* Edward Dmytryk

Warlock Moon *73* Bill Herbert

Warlord, The *37* John Farrow

Warlord of Crete *61* Silvio Amadio

Warlords of Atlantis *78* Kevin Connor

Warlords of the Deep *65* Jacques Tourneur

Warlords of the 21st Century *81* Harley Cokliss

Warm-Blooded Spy, The *63* Édouard Molinaro

Warm Body, The *62* André Haguet, Jean-Paul Sassy

Warm Corner, A *30* Victor Saville

Warm Current *39* Kozaburo Yoshimura

Warm December, A *72* Sidney Poitier

Warm in the Bud *70* Rudolph Caringi

Warm It Was That Winter *84* Chang-ho Bae

Warm Nights and Hot Pleasures *64* Joe Sarno

Warm Nights, Hot Pleasures *81* Hubert Frank

Warm Nights on a Slow Moving Train *87* Bob Ellis

Warm Reception, A *14* Toby Cooper

Warm Reception, A *14* H. Oceano Martinek

Warm Reception, A *20* Gregory La Cava, Vernon Stallings

Warming Up *28* Fred Newmeyer

Warn London! *34* T. Hayes Hunter

Warn That Man *43* Lawrence Huntington

Warned Off *28* Walter West

Warning, The *14* Donald Crisp

Warning, The *15* Edmund Lawrence

Warning, The *27* George B. Seitz

Warning, The *28* Reginald Fogwell

Warning, The *39* Alberto Cavalcanti

Warning! *47* Martin Frič

Warning, The *82* Juan Antonio Bardem

Warning, Bandits *86* Claude Lelouch

Warning from Space *56* Koji Shima

Warning of a Holy Whore *70* Rainer Werner Fassbinder

Warning Shadows *22* Arthur Robison

Warning Shot *66* Buzz Kulik

Warning Shot *77* Péter Bacsó

Warning Sign *85* Hal Barwood

Warning Signal, The *26* Charles J. Hunt

Warning to Wantons *48* Donald B. Wilson

Warnung vor einer Heiligen Nutte *70* Rainer Werner Fassbinder

Warpath *51* Byron Haskin

Warra' el Setar *37* Kamel Salim

Warren Case, The *34* Walter Summers

Warrendale *66* Allan King

Warrens of Virginia, The *14* Cecil B. De-Mille

Warrens of Virginia, The *24* Elmer Clifton

Warring Clans *63* Kihachi Okamoto

Warrior and the Slave Girl, The *58* Vittorio Cottafavi

Warrior and the Sorceress, The 84 John Broderick

Warrior Empress, The 60 Pietro Francisci

Warrior Gap 25 Alvin J. Neitz

Warrior of the Lost World 85 David Worth

Warrior Queen 86 Chuck Vincent

Warrior Strain, The 19 F. Martin Thornton

Warrior Women, The 60 Carlo Ludovico Bragaglia, Vittorio Cottafavi

Warriors, The 55 Henry Levin

Warriors, The 70 Brian G. Hutton

Warriors, The 79 Walter Hill

Warriors Five 62 Leopoldo Savona

Warrior's Husband, The 33 Walter Lang

Warriors of the Apocalypse 87 Bobby A. Suarez

Warriors of the Wasteland 82 Enzo G. Castellari

Warriors of the Wind 84 Kazuo Komatsubara

Warrior's Rest 62 Roger Vadim

War's Grim Reality 14 Dave Aylott

Wars of Mice and Men, The 21 Frank Moser

Wars of the Primal Tribes 13 D. W. Griffith

Warsaw Debut, The 51 Jan Rybkowski

Warsaw 56 54 Jerzy Bossak

Warsaw World Youth Meeting I-III 55 Miklós Jancsó

Wartime Romance 85 Pyotr Todorovsky

Warty Wooing, The 13 Dave Aylott

Warui Yatsu Hodo Yoku Nemuru 60 Akira Kurosawa

Warui Yatsu Yoku Nemuru 60 Akira Kurosawa

Warum Läuft Herr R. Amok? 69 Rainer Werner Fassbinder, Michael Fengler

Warum Sind Sie Gegen Uns? 58 Bernhard Wicki

Was Bin Ich Ohne Dich? 35 Arthur Maria Rabenalt

Was Frauen Traumen 33 Géza von Bolváry

Was He a Coward? 11 D. W. Griffith

Was He a Coward? 13 Bert Haldane

Was He a Gentleman? 14 Arthur Finn

Was He a German Spy? 12 Hay Plumb

Was He Justified? 12 Bert Haldane

Was Ist Los mit Nanette? 28 Forest Holger-Madsen

Was It a Dream? 56 Olive Negus

Was It a Serpent's Bite? 09 Dave Aylott

Was It Bigamy? 25 Charles Hutchinson

Was It He? 14 G. Fletcher Hewitt

Was Justice Served? 09 D. W. Griffith

Was Pimple (W)right? 15 Fred Evans, Joe Evans

Was She Guilty? 22 George A. Beranger

Was She Justified? 22 Walter West

Wasei Kenka Tomodachi 29 Yasujiro Ozu

Wash, The 88 Michael Toshiyuki Uno

Wash Day 29 Mannie Davis

Wash on der Line, Der 19 Gregory La Cava

Washee Ironee 34 James Parrott

Washerwomen, The 1896 Georges Méliès

Washing Day 08 Alf Collins

Washing the Sweep 1898 James A. Williamson

Washington Affair, The 77 Victor Stoloff

Washington at Valley Forge 08 Sidney Olcott

Washington at Valley Forge 14 Grace Cunard, Francis Ford

Washington, B.C. 73 Fred Levinson

Washington Cowboy 39 George Sherman

Washington Masquerade 32 Charles Brabin

Washington Melodrama 41 S. Sylvan Simon

Washington Merry-Go-Round 32 James Cruze

Washington Story 52 Robert Pirosh

Wasn't That a Time! 82 Jim Brown

Wasp, The 15 B. Reeves Eason

Wasp, The 18 Lionel Belmore

Wasp, The 86 Gilles Carle

Wasp Woman, The 59 Roger Corman

Wasp's Nest, The 88 Horea Popescu

Wasser für Canitoga 39 Herbert Selpin

Wasted Lives 23 Clarence Geldert

Wasted Lives 25 John Gorman

Wasted Lives 82 Pál Gábor

Wasted Love 29 Richard Eichberg

Wasteland 60 Marcel Carné

Wastrel, The 60 Michael Cacoyannis, Giovanni Paolucci

Wastrels, The 53 Federico Fellini

Wasurerareta Kora 49 Hiroshi Inagaki

Wat Zien Ik 71 Paul Verhoeven

Watakushi-Tachi no Kekkon 62 Masahiro Shinoda

Watan 36 Ramjankhan Mehboobkhan

Watashi Ga Suteta Onna 70 Kiriro Urayama

Watashi no Subete o 54 Kon Ichikawa

Watashi o Ski ni Tsuretette 87 Yasuo Baba

Watashi wa Bellett 64 Nagisa Oshima

Watashi wa Nisai 62 Kon Ichikawa

Watch, The 49 Tso-lin Wang

Watch Beverly 32 Arthur Maude

Watch, George! 27 Sam Newfield

Watch Him Step 22 Jack Nelson

Watch It, Sailor! 61 Wolf Rilla

Watch on the Lime 49 Jerry Lewis

Watch on the Rhine 43 Herman Shumlin

Watch Out 53 Don Chaffey

Watch Out for the Automobile 66 Eldar Ryazanov

Watch Out, We're Mad 74 Marcello Fondato

Watch the Birdie 28 Sam Newfield

Watch the Birdie 50 Jack Donohue

Watch the Birdie! 56 Martin Frič

Watch-Tower in the Carpathians 14 Alexander Korda*

Watch Your House 20 Robert McCay, Winsor McCay

Watch Your Step 20 Geoffrey H. Malins

Watch Your Step 22 William Beaudine

Watch Your Step 26 Julian Ollendorff

Watch Your Stern 60 Gerald Thomas

Watch Your Watch 15 Edwin J. Collins

Watch Your Wife 26 Svend Gade

Watcha Watchin'? 63 Joseph Barbera, William Hanna

Watched! 72 John Parsons

Watched Pot, A 18 Santry

Watcher in the Woods, The 80 John Hough, Vincent McEveety

Watchers 88 Jon Hess

Watchers 2 90 Thierry Notz

Watchful Waiting 16 John R. Bray

Watchful Waiting 16 Harry S. Palmer

Watching Eyes 21 Geoffrey H. Malins

Watchmaker of St. Paul, The 73 Bertrand Tavernier

Water 52 Susumu Hani*

Water 57 Jörn Donner

Water 75 Peter Greenaway

Water 84 Dick Clement

Water Also Burns 87 Ali Özgentürk

Water and Power 89 Pat O'Neill

Water Babies, The 78 Lionel Jeffries

Water Babies, or The Little Chimney Sweep, The 07 Percy Stow

Water Circle, The 75 James Broughton

Water Clue, The 15 Rupert Julian

Water Cyborgs 66 Hajime Sato

Water for Canitoga 39 Herbert Selpin

Water for Fire Fighting 48 John Halas*

Water from the Land 46 Carl Theodor Dreyer

Water Gipsies, The 31 Maurice Elvey

Water Girl, The 24 Jean Renoir

Water Gypsies, The 31 Maurice Elvey

Water Hole, The 28 F. Richard Jones

Water in Our Life 52 Susumu Hani*

Water in the Ground 35 Eusebio Ardavin

Water Lily, The 19 George Ridgwell

Water Magician, The 33 Kenji Mizoguchi

Water Nymph, The 12 Mack Sennett

Water Rats of London, The 14 James Youngdeer

Water Rustlers 39 Samuel Diege

Water Stuff 21 Hy Mayer

Water War, The 11 Allan Dwan

Water, Water Every Hare 52 Chuck Jones

Water, Water, Everywhere 19 Clarence Badger

Water Water Everywhere 20 Vernon Stallings

Water Wrackets 75 Peter Greenaway

Waterfront 28 William A. Seiter

Waterfront 39 Terry Morse

Waterfront 44 Steve Sekely

Waterfront 50 Michael Anderson

Waterfront at Midnight 48 William Berke

Waterfront Lady 35 Joseph Santley

Waterfront Wolves 24 Tom Gibson

Waterfront Women 50 Michael Anderson

Waterhole No. 3 67 William A. Graham

Waterhole 3 67 William A. Graham

Watering the Elephants 21 Raoul Barré, Charles Bowers

Watering the Flowers 1896 Georges Méliès

Watering the Gardner 1895 Louis Lumière

Waterless Summer 64 David Durston, Erkan Metin, Ismail Metin

Waterloo 28 Karl Grüne

Waterloo 70 Sergei Bondarchuk

Waterloo Bridge 31 James Whale

Waterloo Bridge 40 Mervyn LeRoy

Waterloo Bridge Handicap, The 78 Ross Cramer

Waterloo Road 44 Sidney Gilliat

Watermelon Man 70 Melvin Van Peebles
Watermelon Patch, The 05 Edwin S. Porter
Waterpower 78 Gerard Damiano
Waterproof Willie 08 Walter R. Booth
Waters of Time 50 Bill Launder, Basil Wright
Watersark 65 Joyce Wieland
Watership Down 78 Martin Rosen
Watertight 43 Alberto Cavalcanti
Watery Gravey 26 William C. Nolan
Watery Romance, A 15 James Read
Watery Romance, A 20 S. Vanderlyn
Watts Monster, The 76 William Crain
Wattstax 73 Mel Stuart
Watusi 59 Kurt Neumann
Watusi à Go-Go 64 Sidney Miller
Wave, The 34 Emilio Gómez Muriel, Fred Zinnemann
Wave, a WAC and a Marine, A 44 Phil Karlson
Wave, Coral and Rock 64 Ebrahim Golestan
Wave of Unrest, A 54 Jin Xie
Waveband 83 Bill Leeson
Wavelength 67 Michael Snow
Wavelength 83 Mike Gray
Waverly Steps 48 John Eldridge
Waves and Spray 1898 George Albert Smith
Waves Die on the Shore 87 Tynchylyk Razzakov
Wawel Concert 60 Jan Łomnicki
Wax Model, The 17 E. Mason Hopper
Wax Works, The 34 Walter Lantz
Waxwork 88 Anthony Hickox
Waxworks 24 Paul Leni
Way, The 81 Şerif Gören
Way Ahead, The 44 Carol Reed
Way and the Body, The 63 Mario Bava
Way Back, The 15 Carlton S. King
Way Back Home 31 William A. Seiter
Way Back When a Nag Was Only a Horse 40 Dave Fleischer
Way Back When a Nightclub Was a Stick 40 Dave Fleischer
Way Back When a Razzberry Was a Fruit 40 Dave Fleischer
Way Back When a Triangle Had Its Points 40 Dave Fleischer
Way Back When Women Had Their Weigh 40 Dave Fleischer
Way Down East 20 D. W. Griffith
Way Down East 35 Henry King
Way Down South 39 Bernard Vorhaus
Way Down Yonder in the Corn 43 Bob Wickersham
Way for a Sailor 30 Sam Wood
Way Home, The 81 Alexander Rekhviashvili
Way in the Wilderness, A 40 Fred Zinnemann
Way It Is, The 86 Eric Mitchell
Way Men Love, The 24 Roy William Neill
Way of a Gaucho 52 Jacques Tourneur
Way of a Girl, The 25 Robert Vignola
Way of a Maid, The 21 William P. S. Earle
Way of a Man, The 21 Charles C. Calvert
Way of a Man 24 George B. Seitz
Way of a Man with a Maid, The 18 Donald Crisp

Way of a Mother, The 15 Jack Conway
Way of a Woman, The 14 Wallace Reid
Way of a Woman, The 19 Robert Z. Leonard
Way of a Woman, The 25 Geoffrey H. Malins
Way of All Fish, The 31 Mark Sandrich
Way of All Flesh, The 27 Victor Fleming
Way of All Flesh, The 40 Louis King
Way of All Men, The 30 Frank Lloyd
Way of All Pants, The 27 James Parrott
Way of All Pests 41 Art Davis
Way of an Eagle, The 18 George B. Samuelson
Way of Drama, The 44 Mikio Naruse
Way of Learning, A 67 Tobe Hooper
Way of Life, The 32 Thornton Freeland
Way of Lost Souls, The 29 Paul Czinner
Way of Man, The 09 D. W. Griffith
Way of the Cross, The 09 J. Stuart Blackton
Way of the Enthusiast 30 Nikolai Pavlovich Okhlopkov
Way of the Lotus, The 87 Tissa Abeysekara
Way of the Strong 19 Edwin Carewe
Way of the Strong, The 28 Frank Capra
Way of the Transgressor, The 23 William James Craft
Way of the West, The 11 Allan Dwan
Way of the West, The 34 Robert E. Tansey
Way of the Wicked 58 Luis Saslavsky
Way of the World, The 10 D. W. Griffith
Way of the World, The 16 Lloyd B. Carleton
Way of the World, The 20 A. E. Coleby
Way of the World, The 47 James Komisarjevsky
Way of Youth, The 34 Norman Walker
Way of Youth, The 59 Michel Boisrond
Way Out, The 18 George Kelson
Way Out, The 55 Montgomery Tully
Way Out 66 Irvin S. Yeaworth, Jr.
Way Out Love 67 Julian Marsh
Way Out, Way In 70 Michihiko Obimori
Way Out West 30 Fred Niblo
Way Out West 36 James W. Horne
Way They Were, The 87 Andrés Linares
Way to Bresson, The 84 Leo de Boer, Jurrien Rood
Way to Love, The 33 Norman Taurog
Way to Shadow Garden, The 54 Stan Brakhage
Way to the God, The 28 Heinosuke Gosho
Way to the Gold, The 57 Robert D. Webb
Way to the Harbour, The 62 Georgy Danelia
Way to the Neighbor, The 63 Dušan Vukotić
Way to the Skies, The 58 Wincenty Ronisz, Krzysztof Zanussi
Way to the Stars, The 45 Anthony Asquith
Way Up Thar 35 Mack Sennett
Way Up Yonder 20 Leonard S. Sugden
Way...Way Out 66 Gordon Douglas

Way We Live, The 46 Jill Craigie
Way We Live Now, The 70 Barry Brown
Way We Were, The 73 Sydney Pollack
Way West, The 67 Andrew V. McLaglen
Way Women Love, The 20 Marcel Perez
Waylaid Women 58 Erwin Marno
Wayne Murder Case, The 32 Hampton Del Ruth, Phil Whitman
Ways in the Night 79 Krzysztof Zanussi
Ways of Fate, The 13 Allan Dwan, Wallace Reid
Ways of Life 23 Teinosuke Kinugasa
Ways of Love 33 Marcel Pagnol
Ways of Love 48 Marcel Pagnol, Jean Renoir, Roberto Rossellini
Ways of the Lord Are Finite, The 87 Massimo Troisi
Ways of the World, The 15 L. C. MacBean
Wayside Pebble, The 60 Seiji Hisamatsu
Wayward 32 Edward Sloman
Wayward Bus, The 57 Henry Hathaway, Victor Vicas
Wayward Girl, The 57 Lesley Selander
Wayward Girl, The 59 Edith Carlmar
Wayward Wife, The 52 Mario Soldati
Wayward Youth 27 Christy Cabanne
We Accomplished 62 Santiago Álvarez
We Accuse 37 Abel Gance
We Accuse 87 Timofei Levchuk
We Aim to Please 34 Dave Fleischer
We All Loved Each Other So Much 74 Ettore Scola
We All Walked Into the Shop 06 Arthur Gilbert
We All Walked Into the Shop 07 John Morland
We Americans 28 Edward Sloman
We Are All Demons 69 Henning Carlsen
We Are All for Peace 51 Joris Ivens, Ivan Pyriev
We Are All Murderers 52 André Cayatte
We Are All Naked 70 Claude Pierson
We Are Arab Jews in Israel 79 Igaal Niddam
We Are Building 29 Joris Ivens
We Are But Little Children Weak 13 Warwick Buckland
We Are for Peace 51 Joris Ivens, Ivan Pyriev
We Are from Kronstadt 36 Yefim Dzigan
We Are from the Urals 44 Lev Kuleshov*
We Are Going to Eat You 80 Hark Tsui
We Are in the Navy Now 62 Wendy Toye
We Are Living 51 Tadashi Imai
We Are Not Alone 39 Edmund Goulding
We Are the Lambeth Boys 58 Karel Reisz
We Are the Marines 42 Louis De Rochemont III
We Are the Women 53 Roberto Rossellini, Luchino Visconti, Luigi Zampa
We Are Young 67 Alexander Hammid, Francis Thompson
We at Solglantan 40 Gunnar Olsson
We Can't Go Home Again 73 Nicholas Ray
We Can't Have Everything 18 Cecil B. DeMille
We Close at Two on Thursday 08 Arthur Gilbert

We Did It 36 Dave Fleischer
We Die Alone 57 Arne Skouen
We Dine at Seven 31 Frank Richardson
We Dive at Dawn 43 Anthony Asquith
We Do Believe in Ghosts 47 Walter West
We Don't Think 14 Hay Plumb
We Expect Victory There 41 Alexander Medvedkin, Ilya Trauberg
We Faw Down 27 Leo McCarey
We French 16 Rupert Julian
We from Kronstadt 36 Yefim Dzigan
We from the Urals 44 Lev Kuleshov*
We Go Fast 41 William McGann
We Go Through the Kitchen 32 Gustaf Molander
We Have Been the Guests of China 57 Miklós Jancsó
We Have Come for Your Daughters 70 François Reichenbach
We Have Many Faces 75 Mai Zetterling
We Have Many Names 75 Mai Zetterling
We Have Only One Life 58 George Tzavellas
We Have Our Moments 37 Alfred L. Werker
We Humans 31 Frank Borzage
We Humans 42 Louis King
We Joined the Navy 62 Wendy Toye
We Live Again 34 Rouben Mamoulian
We Live in Prague 34 Otakar Vávra
We Live in Two Worlds 37 Alberto Cavalcanti
We Lived Through Buchenwald 47 E. G. DeMyest
We May Eat of the Fruit of the Trees of the Garden 69 Věra Chytilová
We Moderns 25 John Francis Dillon
We Must Undo the House 87 José Luis García Sánchez
We Need Each Other 44 Erik Faustman
We Need No Money 31 Carl Boese
We Need Virgins 30 Heinosuke Gosho
We of the Never Never 82 Igor Auzins
We of the Urals 44 Lev Kuleshov*
We Only Live Once 58 George Tzavellas
We Parted on the Shore 07 Arthur Gilbert
We Sail at Midnight 43 John Ford
We Shall Return 63 Philip Goodman
We Shall See 64 Quentin Lawrence
We Should Worry 18 Kenean Buel
We Slip Up 27 Leo McCarey
We Still Kill the Old Way 66 Elio Petri
We Take Off Our Hats 30 Harry Hughes
We, the Animals Squeak 41 Robert Clampett
We the Living 42 Goffredo Alessandrini
We the Women 53 Roberto Rossellini, Luchino Visconti, Luigi Zampa
We Think the World of You 88 Colin Gregg
We Three 31 John G. Adolfi
We Three 39 Ramjankhan Mehboobkhan
We Three 84 Pupi Avati
We Three Are Making Our Debut 53 Hasse Ekman
We Took Over the Cause of Peace 50 Miklós Jancsó*
We Two 39 S. Bauman
We Visit Moscow 54 Kenneth Wright

We Want a Child 54 Lau Lauritzen, Jr., Alice O'Fredericks
We Want the Colonels 72 Mario Monicelli
We Want to Live Alone 63 Peter Graham Scott
We Went to College 36 Joseph Santley
We Were Dancing 41 Robert Z. Leonard
We Were One Man 78 Philippe Vallois
We Were Seven Sisters 39 Nunzio Malasomma
We Were Seven Widows 40 Mario Mattòli
We Were Strangers 49 John Huston
We Who Are About to Die 36 Christy Cabanne
We Who Are Young 40 Harold S. Bucquet
We Will All Meet in Paradise 77 Yves Robert
We Will Come Back 42 Ivan Pyriev
We Will Not Grow Old Together 72 Maurice Pialat
We Will Remember 66 Zenzo Matsuyama
We Will Rock You 83 Saul Swimmer
We Women 25 Will P. Kellino
We Won't Grow Old Together 72 Maurice Pialat
We Work for You 32 Ilya Trauberg
Weak and the Wicked, The 53 J. Lee-Thompson
Weak But Willing 26 Archie Mayo
Weaker Brother, The 12 Allan Dwan
Weaker Sex, The 17 Raymond B. West
Weaker Sex, The 48 Roy Ward Baker
Weaker Vessel, The 19 Paul Powell
Weakly Reporter, The 44 Chuck Jones
Weakness of Man, The 16 Barry O'Neil
Weakness of Men, The 25 Edwin Greenwood, Will P. Kellino
Weakness of Strength, The 16 Harry Revier
Wealth 21 William Desmond Taylor
Wealthy Brother John 11 Bert Haldane
Weapon, The 13 Maurice Costello
Weapon, The 56 Val Guest
Weapons of Destruction 57 Karel Zeman
Wearing of the Grin, The 51 Chuck Jones
Wearing the Grin 51 Chuck Jones
Weary Death 21 Fritz Lang
Weary River 29 Frank Lloyd
Weary Willie 1897 George Albert Smith
Weary Willie and the Gardener 01 Edwin S. Porter
Weary Willie and Tired Tim Turn Barbers 03 William Haggar
Weary Willie Kidnaps the Child 04 Alfred C. Abadie, Edwin S. Porter
Weary Willie Steals a Fish 08 Lewin Fitzhamon
Weary Willies 29 Walter Lantz
Weary's Dog Dream 16 Harry S. Palmer
Weasel Stop 56 Robert McKimson
Weasel While You Work 58 Robert McKimson
Weather in the Streets, The 83 Gavin Millar
Weather Wizards 38 Fred Zinnemann
Weaver of Dreams 18 John H. Collins
Weavers, The 29 Fred Zelnik
Weavers, The 59 Francesco Rosi
Weavers of Fortune 22 Arthur H. Rooke

Weavers of Life 17 Edward Warren
Weavers: Wasn't That a Time!, The 82 Jim Brown
Web, The 47 Michael Gordon
Web, The 56 Peter Watkins
Web Feet 27 Manny Gould, Ben Harrison
Web of Chance, The 19 Alfred E. Green
Web of Danger, The 47 Philip Ford
Web of Deceit, The 20 Edwin Carewe
Web of Desire, The 17 Émile Chautard
Web of Evidence 59 Jack Cardiff
Web of Fate, The 16 Lewis Gilbert
Web of Fate 27 Dallas M. Fitzgerald
Web of Fear 63 François Villiers
Web of Passion 59 Claude Chabrol
Web of Suspicion 59 Max Varnel
Web of the Law, The 23 Tom Gibson
Web of the Spider 70 Antonio Margheriti
Web of Violence 66 Nick Nostro
Webs of Steel 25 John P. McGowan
Webster Boy, The 61 Don Chaffey
Wedaa ya Bonaparte, Al 84 Youssef Chahine
Wedding, The 72 Andrzej Wajda
Wedding, A 78 Robert Altman
Wedding, A 80 Allen Ross
Wedding Band 90 Daniel Raskov
Wedding Bells 21 Chester Withey
Wedding Bells 27 Eric Reaton
Wedding Bells 33 Manny Gould, Ben Harrison
Wedding Bells 50 Stanley Donen
Wedding Bells Out of Tune 21 Malcolm St. Clair
Wedding Bells, Wedding Belles 80 Ho Yim
Wedding Belts 40 Dave Fleischer
Wedding Bill$ 27 Erle C. Kenton
Wedding Blues 20 Al Christie
Wedding Breakfast 56 Richard Brooks
Wedding by Correspondence, A 04 Georges Méliès
Wedding Day 60 Kenne Fant
Wedding Day, The 60 Mrinal Sen
Wedding Dress, The 12 Allan Dwan
Wedding Dress of the Ghost 81 Yoon Kyo Park
Wedding Eve 35 Charles Barnett
Wedding Group 36 Alex Bryce, Campbell Gullan
Wedding in Blood 73 Claude Chabrol
Wedding in Galilee, A 87 Michel Khleifi
Wedding in Toprin 38 André De Toth
Wedding in White 72 William Fruet
Wedding Journey, The 39 Karl Ritter
Wedding March, The 12 Edwin S. Porter
Wedding March, The 27 Erich von Stroheim
Wedding March 51 Kon Ichikawa
Wedding Night, The 35 King Vidor
Wedding Night 69 Piers Haggard
Wedding of Ian Knuck, The 35 Alexander Ivanov
Wedding of Lilli Marlene, The 53 Arthur Crabtree
Wedding of Sandy McNab, The 07 Arthur Gilbert
Wedding Party, The 64 Brian DePalma, Wilford Leach, Cynthia Munroe
Wedding Party Is Accused, A 87 Alexander Itygilov

Wedding Present *36* Richard Wallace
Wedding Present *63* Rolf Olsen
Wedding Rehearsal *32* Alexander Korda
Wedding Ring, The *44* Martin Frič
Wedding Rings *29* William Beaudine
Wedding Song, The *25* Alan Hale
Wedding—Swedish Style *64* Åke Falck
Wedding That Didn't Come Off, The *08* Joe Rosenthal
Wedding That Didn't Come Off, The *10* Theo Bouwmeester
Wedding Yells *27* Charles Lamont
Weddings and Babies *58* Morris Engel
Weddings Are Wonderful *38* Maclean Rogers
Wedlock *18* Wallace Worsley
Wedlock House: An Intercourse *59* Stan Brakhage
Wednesday Children, The *73* Robert D. West
Wednesday's Child *34* John S. Robertson
Wednesday's Child *71* Kenneth Loach
Wednesday's Luck *36* George Pearson
Wedtime Story, A *36* Leslie Goodwins
Wee Bit o' Scotch, A *19* Gregory La Cava
Wee Geordie *55* Frank Launder
Wee Hoose Amang the Heather *31* George Pearson
Wee Lady Betty *17* Frank Borzage, Charles Miller
Wee MacGregor's Sweetheart, The *22* George Pearson
Wee Sandy *62* Lotte Reiniger
Wee Willie Winkie *37* John Ford
Weed of Crime, The *63* Jun Fukuda
Weeds *73* Kwon-taek Im
Weeds *87* John Hancock
Week-End, The *20* George L. Cox
Weekend *28* Walter Ruttmann
Weekend *62* Palle Kjærulff-Schmidt
Weekend *67* Jean-Luc Godard
Week-End, Le *67* Jean-Luc Godard
Weekend *87* Igor Talankin
Week-End à Zuydcoote *64* Henri Verneuil
Weekend at Bernie's *89* Ted Kotcheff
Weekend at Dunkirk *64* Henri Verneuil
Week-End at the Waldorf *45* Robert Z. Leonard
Weekend Babysitter *69* Don Henderson
Weekend en Mer *62* François Reichenbach
Week-End for Three *41* Irving Reis
Week-End Husbands *24* Edward H. Griffith
Weekend im Paradies *32* Robert Land
Week-End in Havana *41* Walter Lang
Weekend in Paris *61* Clive Donner
Weekend, Italian Style *65* Dino Risi
Weekend Lives *32* Thornton Freeland
Weekend Lover *69* Dwayne Avery
Weekend Madness *36* Charles Lamont
Weekend Marriage *32* Thornton Freeland
Weekend Millionaire *36* Arthur Woods
Weekend Murders *72* Michele Lupo
Weekend of Fear *66* Joe Danford
Weekend of Shadows *78* Tom Jeffrey
Weekend Pass *44* Jean Yarbrough
Weekend Pass *84* Lawrence Bassoff
Weekend Warriors *86* Bert Convy
Weekend with Father *51* Douglas Sirk
Weekend with Lulu, A *61* John Paddy Carstairs
Weekend with the Babysitter *69* Don Henderson
Weekend Wives *28* Harry Lachman
Weekend Wives *65* Dino Risi
Week-Ends Only *32* Alan Crosland
Week's Holiday, A *80* Bertrand Tavernier
Week's Vacation, A *80* Bertrand Tavernier
Weenie Roast, The *31* Manny Gould, Ben Harrison
Weeping Blue Sky *31* Mikio Naruse
Weeping for a Bandit *64* Carlos Saura
Weg Durch die Nacht, Der *29* Robert Dinesen
Weg ins Freie, Der *18* Richard Oswald
Weg naar Bresson, De *84* Leo de Boer, Jurrien Rood
Weg nach Oben, Der *50* Andrew Thorndike
Weg nach Shanghai, Der *36* Paul Wegener
Weg zum Nachbarn *63* Dušan Vukotić
Wege des Schreckens *20* Michael Curtiz
Wege im Zwielicht *48* Gustav Fröhlich
Wege in der Nacht *79* Krzysztof Zanussi
Weib des Pharao, Das *21* Ernst Lubitsch
Weib im Dschungel *30* Dmitri Buchowetzki
Weiberregiment *36* Karl Ritter
Weibsteufel, Der *66* Georg Tressler
Weight for Me *55* John Halas*
Weight of a Feather, The *12* Edwin S. Porter
Weir-Falcon Saga, The *69* Stan Brakhage
Weird Love-Makers, The *63* Koreyoshi Kurahara
Weird Ones, The *62* Pat Boyette
Weird Science *85* John Hughes
Weird Tales *64* Masaki Kobayashi
Weird Woman *44* Reginald LeBorg
Weisse Dämon, Der *32* Kurt Gerron
Weisse Hölle vom Piz Palü, Die *29* Arnold Fanck, G. W. Pabst
Weisse Majestät, Die *39* Anton Kutter
Weisse Pfau, Der *20* E. A. Dupont
Weisse Rausch, Der *31* Arnold Fanck
Weisse Rosen *14* Urban Gad
Weisse Schatten *51* Helmut Käutner
Weisse Sklaven *37* Karl Anton
Weisse Sklavin, Die *27* Augusto Genina
Weisse Spinne, Die *27* Carl Boese
Welcome Burglar, A *08* D. W. Griffith
Welcome, Children *21* Harry C. Mathews
Welcome Danger *29* Clyde Bruckman, Malcolm St. Clair
Welcome Granger *25* Wesley Ruggles
Welcome Home *12* Hay Plumb
Welcome Home *25* James Cruze
Welcome Home *35* James Tinling
Welcome Home *45* Jack Moss
Welcome Home *89* Franklin J. Schaffner
Welcome Home Brother Charles *75* Jamaa Fanaka
Welcome Home, Roxy Carmichael *90* Jim Abrahams
Welcome Home Soldier Boys *72* Richard Compton
Welcome in Vienna *86* Axel Corti
Welcome Intruder, A *13* D. W. Griffith
Welcome Kostya! *65* Ilya Klimov
Welcome Maria *87* Juan López Moctezuma
Welcome, Mr. Beddoes *66* Ronald Neame, Cliff Owen
Welcome, Mr. Marshall! *52* Luis García Berlanga
Welcome Mr. Washington *44* Leslie Hiscott
Welcome, or No Entry for Unauthorized Persons *64* Elem Klimov
Welcome Stranger *24* James Young
Welcome Stranger *41* D. Ross Lederman
Welcome Stranger *47* Elliott Nugent
Welcome to Arrow Beach *73* Laurence Harvey
Welcome to Blood City *77* Peter Sasdy
Welcome to Britain *43* Anthony Asquith, Burgess Meredith
Welcome to 18 *86* Terry Carr
Welcome to Germany *88* Thomas Brasch
Welcome to Hard Times *66* Burt Kennedy
Welcome to L.A. *76* Alan Rudolph
Welcome to L.A. the City of One Night Stands *76* Alan Rudolph
Welcome to My Nightmare *76* David Winters
Welcome to Our City *22* Robert H. Townley
Welcome to the Club *70* Walter Shenson
Welcome to the Parade *86* Stuart Clarfield
Welcome to Vendsyssel *54* Henning Carlsen
Welfare *75* Frederick Wiseman
Welfare of the Workers *40* Pat Jackson, Humphrey Jennings
Well, The *13* Christy Cabanne
Well, The *51* Leo C. Popkin, Russell Rouse
We'll Blow 3 x 27 Billion Dollars on a Destroyer *71* Alexander Kluge
We'll Bury You *62* Jack W. Thomas
We'll Call Him Andrew *72* Vittorio De Sica
Well-Digger's Daughter, The *40* Marcel Pagnol
Well Done, Henry *36* Wilfred Noy
Well Done, Scouts *11* Dave Aylott
Well-Filled Day, A *73* Jean-Louis Trintignant
We'll Get by Till Monday *68* Stanislav Rostotsky
Well Groomed Bride, The *46* Sidney Lanfield
We'll Grow Thin Together *79* Michel Vocoret
Well I'm... *15* Edwin J. Collins
Well Made Marriage, The *81* Eric Rohmer
We'll Meet Again *42* Phil Brandon
Well Paid Stroll, A *65* Miloš Forman
Well Planned West End Jewel Robbery, A *19* Frank Carlton
We'll Say They Do *19* Milt Gross
We'll Smile Again *42* John Baxter
Well Spent Life, A *71* Les Blank
Well Worn Daffy *65* Robert McKimson
Well, Young Man? *63* György Révész
Wellington Mystery, The *18* Michael Curtiz
Wellingtoni Rejtély, A *18* Michael Curtiz
Wells Fargo *37* Frank Lloyd

Wells Fargo Gunmaster *51* Philip Ford
Welsh Singer, A *15* Henry Edwards
Welshed, A Derby Day Incident *03* Alf Collins
Welt am Draht *73* Rainer Werner Fassbinder
Welt Ohne Maske, Die *34* Harry Piel
Welt Ohne Waffen *18* Paul Wegener
Weltbrand *20* Urban Gad
Weltspiegel, Der *18* Lupu Pick
Weltstrasse See *38* Walter Ruttmann
Weltstrasse See — Welthafen Hamburg *38* Walter Ruttmann
Wen Kümmert's... *60* Volker Schlöndorff
Wench, The *48* Henri Calef
Wend Kuuni *82* Gaston J. M. Kaboré
Wenn am Sonntagabend die Dorfmusik Spielt *35* Charles Klein
Wenn der Hahn Kräht *36* Carl Fröhlich
Wenn die Geigen Klingen *31* Friedrich Feher
Wenn die Liebe Mode Macht *33* Franz Wenzler
Wenn die Liebe Nicht Wär! *25* Robert Dinesen
Wenn die Maske Fällt *12* Urban Gad
Wenn die Musik Nicht Wär *35* Carmine Gallone
Wenn Du eine Schwiegermutter Hast *38* Joe Stöckel
Wenn Frauen Schweigen *37* Fritz Kirchhoff
Wenn Herzen Sich Finden *34* Erich Engel
Wenn Männer Schwindeln *50* Carl Boese
Wenn Vier Dasselbe Machen *17* Ernst Lubitsch
Wenn Vier Dasselbe Tun *17* Ernst Lubitsch
Wenn Wir Alle Engel Wären *36* Carl Fröhlich
Went the Day Well? *42* Alberto Cavalcanti
Wer Kennt Johnny R? *65* José Luis Madrid
Wer Nimmt die Liebe Ernst? *31* Erich Engel
Werdegang, Ein *20* Richard Oswald
We're All Gamblers *27* James Cruze
We're Going to Be Rich *38* Monty Banks
We're Going to Eat You *80* Hark Tsui
We're Going to Play House *75* Edgar Reitz
Were I Thy Bride *07* John Morland
We're in the Army Now *39* H. Bruce Humberstone
We're in the Legion Now *36* Crane Wilbur
We're in the Money *33* Rudolf Ising
We're in the Money *35* Ray Enright
We're in the Navy Now *26* A. Edward Sutherland
We're No Angels *55* Michael Curtiz
We're No Angels *89* Neil Jordan
We're Not Dressing *34* Norman Taurog
We're Not Made of Stone *68* Manuel Summers
We're Not Married *52* Edmund Goulding
We're Not the Jet Set *75* Robert Duvall
We're on the Jury *37* Ben Holmes
We're Only Human *35* James Flood

We're Rich Again *34* William A. Seiter
Were You Not to Koko Plighted? *07* John Morland
Werewolf, The *13* Henry MacRae
Werewolf, The *56* Fred F. Sears
Werewolf, The *71* Raffaele Rossi
Werewolf and the Yeti, The *75* Miguel Iglesias Bonns
Werewolf in a Girl's Dormitory *61* Paolo Heusch
Werewolf of London, The *35* Stuart Walker
Werewolf of Washington, The *73* Milton Moses Ginsberg
Werewolf Tom *87* Eric Latsis
Werewolf vs. the Vampire Woman, The *70* Leon Klimovsky
Werewolf Woman *76* Salvatore Di Silvestro
Werewolf's Shadow, The *70* Leon Klimovsky
Werewolf's Tracks, The *87* Almantas Grikyavicus
Werewolves Are Here, The *72* Andy Milligan
Werewolves on Wheels *71* Michel Levesque
Werft zum Grauen Hecht, Die *35* Frank Wisbar
Werner Herzog Eats His Shoe *80* Les Blank
Wert Thou Not to Koko Plighted *06* Arthur Gilbert
Werther *10* André Calmettes
Werther *22* Germaine Dulac
Werther *38* Max Ophüls
Werther *86* Pilar Miró
Werwolf von W., Der *88* Manfred Müller
Weryfikacja *87* Mirosław Gronowski
Wesele *72* Andrzej Wajda
Wessada el Khalia, El *57* Salah Abu Saif
West and Soda *65* Bruno Bozzetto
West Case, The *23* A. E. Coleby
West 11 *63* Michael Winner
West End Frolics *37* R. A. Hopwood
West End Nights *38* Ronald Haines
West End Pals *16* Joe Evans
West Indies *79* Med Hondo
West Is Best *20* Phil Rosen
West Is East *19* Raoul Barré, Charles Bowers
West Is East *22* Marcel Perez
West Is Still Wild, The *77* Don von Mizener
West Is West *20* Val Paul
West Is West *22* George Marshall
West Is West *88* David Rathod
West of Abilene *40* Ralph Ceder
West of Arizona *25* Tom Gibson
West of Broadway *26* Robert Thornby
West of Broadway *31* Harry Beaumont
West of Carson City *40* Ray Taylor
West of Cheyenne *31* Harry S. Webb
West of Cheyenne *38* Sam Nelson
West of Chicago *22* Scott R. Dunlap, C. R. Wallace
West of Cimarron *41* Les Orlebeck
West of Dodge City *47* Ray Nazarro
West of Eldorado *49* Ray Taylor
West of Kerry *38* Richard Bird

West of Montana *63* Burt Kennedy
West of Nevada *36* Robert F. Hill
West of Pesos *60* Friz Freleng
West of Pinto Basin *40* S. Roy Luby
West of Rainbow's End *38* Alvin J. Neitz
West of Santa Fe *28* John P. McGowan
West of Santa Fe *38* Sam Nelson
West of Shanghai *37* John Farrow
West of Singapore *33* Albert Ray
West of Sonora *48* Ray Nazarro
West of Suez *57* Arthur Crabtree
West of Texas *43* Oliver Drake
West of the Alamo *46* Oliver Drake
West of the Badlands *40* Joseph Kane
West of the Brazos *50* Thomas Carr
West of the Divide *34* Robert North Bradbury
West of the Law *26* Ben F. Wilson
West of the Law *42* Howard Bretherton
West of the Mojave *25* Harry Fraser
West of the Pecos *22* Neal Hart
West of the Pecos *34* Phil Rosen
West of the Pecos *45* Edward Killy
West of the Rainbow's End *26* Bennett Cohn
West of the Rio Grande *21* Robert H. Townley
West of the Rio Grande *44* Lambert Hillyer
West of the Rockies *29* Horace B. Carpenter
West of the Suez *57* Arthur Crabtree
West of the Water Tower *23* Rollin Sturgeon
West of Tombstone *42* Howard Bretherton
West of Wyoming *50* Wallace Fox
West of Zanzibar *28* Tod Browning
West of Zanzibar *53* Harry Watt
West on Parade *34* Bernard B. Ray
West Point *27* Edward Sedgwick
West Point of the Air *35* Richard Rosson
West Point Story, The *50* Roy Del Ruth
West Point Widow *41* Robert Siodmak
West Riding, The *46* Ken Annakin
West Side Kid, The *43* George Sherman
West Side Story *61* Jerome Robbins, Robert Wise
West Texas *73* Alan Gadney
West Ti Va Stretto, Amico... È Arrivato Alleluja, Il *72* Giuliano Carmineo
West to Glory *47* Ray Taylor
West vs. East *22* Marcel Perez
West Wind *42* Arne Sucksdorff
Westbound *58* Budd Boetticher
Westbound Limited, The *23* Emory Johnson
Westbound Limited *37* Ford Beebe
Westbound Mail *37* Folmer Blangsted
Westbound Stage *39* Spencer G. Bennet
Western Approaches *44* Pat Jackson
Western Blood *18* Lynn Reynolds
Western Blood *23* Robert Hunter
Western Caravans *39* Sam Nelson
Western Chivalry *10* Gilbert M. Anderson
Western Code, The *32* John P. McCarthy
Western Courage *27* Ben F. Wilson
Western Courage *35* Spencer G. Bennet
Western Cyclone *43* Sam Newfield
Western Daze *41* George Pal

Western Demon, A 22 Robert McKenzie

Western Doctor's Peril, The 11 Allan Dwan

Western Dreamer, A 11 Allan Dwan

Western Engagement, A 25 Paul Hurst

Western Fate 24 George Holt

Western Feuds 24 Francis Ford

Western Firebrands 21 Charles R. Seeling

Western Front, 1918, The 30 G. W. Pabst

Western Frontier 35 Albert Herman

Western Gold 37 Howard Bretherton

Western Governor's Humanity, A 15 Romaine Fielding

Western Grit 24 Ad Cook

Western Hearts 21 Clifford Smith

Western Heritage 48 Wallace A. Grissell

Western History 71 Stan Brakhage

Western Honor 30 John P. McGowan

Western Isles 42 Terry Bishop

Western Jamboree 38 Ralph Staub

Western Justice 07 Gilbert M. Anderson

Western Justice 23 Fred Caldwell

Western Justice 35 Robert North Bradbury

Western Knights 30 Stephen Roberts

Western Limited, The 32 Christy Cabanne

Western Love 13 Alice Guy-Blaché

Western Luck 24 George A. Beranger

Western Mail 42 Robert E. Tansey

Western Musketeer, The 22 William Bertram

Western Pacific Agent 50 Sam Newfield

Western Pluck 26 Travers Vale

Western Racketeers 35 Robert J. Horner

Western Renegades 49 Wallace Fox

Western Rover, The 27 Albert S. Rogell

Western Speed 22 Scott R. Dunlap, C. R. Wallace, William Wallace

Western Trails 26 Horace B. Carpenter

Western Trails 37 George Waggner

Western Union 41 Fritz Lang

Western Vengeance 24 John P. McGowan

Western Waif, A 11 Allan Dwan

Western Wallop, The 24 Clifford Smith

Western Ways 22 Clyde E. Elliott

Western Welcome, A 38 Leslie Goodwins

Western Whirlwind, The 27 Albert S. Rogell

Western Yesterdays 24 Francis Ford

Westerner, The 34 David Selman

Westerner, The 40 Lewis Milestone, William Wyler

Westerners, The 19 Edward Sloman

Westfront 1918 30 G. W. Pabst

Westinghouse ABC 65 Charles Eames, Ray Eames

Westland Case, The 37 Christy Cabanne

Westler 86 Wieland Speck

Westminster Passion Play—Behold the Man, The 51 Walter Rilla

Westward Bound 31 Harry S. Webb

Westward Bound 44 Robert E. Tansey

Westward Desperado 61 Kihachi Okamoto

Westward Ho! 19 Percy Nash

Westward Ho 20 Wallace A. Carlson

Westward Ho! 35 Robert North Bradbury

Westward Ho! 40 Thorold Dickinson

Westward Ho! 42 John English

Westward Ho the Wagons! 56 William Beaudine

Westward Passage 32 Robert Milton

Westward the Women 51 William A. Wellman

Westward Trail, The 48 Ray Taylor

Westward Whoa 24 Lewis Seiler

Westward Whoa 26 Charles Bowers

Westward Whoa! 36 Jack King

Westworld 73 Michael Crichton

Wet Asphalt 58 Frank Wisbar

Wet Day, A 07 Percy Stow

Wet Dreams 74 Dušan Makavejev

Wet Gold 21 Ralph Ince

Wet Hare 62 Robert McKimson

Wet Knight, A 32 Walter Lantz

Wet Night, A 26 Harry Hughes

Wet Paint 26 Arthur Rosson

Wet Parade, The 32 Victor Fleming

Wetbacks 56 Hank McCune

Wetherby 85 David Hare

Wetterleuchten Um Maria 57 Luis Trenker

We've Got to Have Love 35 Patrick Brunner

We've Never Been Licked 43 John Rawlins

Whacks Museum 33 Manny Gould, Ben Harrison

Whale, The 27 Naburo Ofugi

Whale, The 52 Naburo Ofugi

Whale Hunter 84 Chang-ho Bae

Whale Hunter II 85 Chang-ho Bae

Whale of a Story, A 23 W. E. Stark

Whale of a Tale, A 77 Ewing M. Brown

Whalers 39 Anders Henrikson

Whales of August, The 87 Lindsay Anderson

Whale's Roof, The 81 Raúl Ruiz

Wharf 68 Malcolm Le Grice

Wharf Angel 34 William Cameron Menzies, George Somnes

Wharf Rat, The 16 Chester Withey

What! 63 Mario Bava

What? 73 Roman Polanski

What a Blonde! 45 Leslie Goodwins

What a Bounder 15 Will P. Kellino

What a Bozo! 31 James Parrott

What a Carry On 49 John E. Blakeley

What a Carve Up! 61 Pat Jackson

What a Chassis! 61 Robert Dhéry

What a Crazy World 63 Michael Carreras

What a Day 29 Stephen Roberts

What a Find 15 Cecil Birch

What a Holiday! 13 Charles C. Calvert

What a Husband! 52 Donald Taylor

What a Kiss Will Do 14 Arthur Finn

What a Knight 32 Manny Gould, Ben Harrison

What a Life! 18 James Reardon

What a Life! 32 Ubbe Iwerks

What a Life! 39 Theodore Reed

What a Life! 48 Michael Law

What a Lion 38 William Hanna

What a Man! 30 George Crone

What a Man! 37 Edmond T. Gréville

What a Man! 41 Edward F. Cline

What a Man! 43 William Beaudine

What a Night! 14 Charles H. Weston

What a Night 24 Norman Taurog

What a Night! 28 A. Edward Sutherland

What a Night! 31 Monty Banks

What a Night! 58 György Révész

What a Picnic 15 Cecil Birch

What a Pretty Girl Can Do 10 Percy Stow

What a Sell! 14 Hay Plumb

What a Way to Go! 64 J. Lee-Thompson

What a Whopper! 61 Gilbert Gunn

What a Widow! 30 Allan Dwan

What a Wife Learned 23 John Griffith Wray

What a Woman! 38 Alexander Hall

What a Woman! 43 Irving Cummings

What a Woman! 45 Charles Barton

What a Woman Will Do 14 Charles H. Weston

What Am I Bid? 19 Robert Z. Leonard

What Am I Bid? 67 Gene Nash

What an Excuse 27 Sam Newfield

What Became of Jack and Jill? 71 Bill Bain

What Becomes of the Children? 18 Walter Richard Stahl

What Befell the Inventor's Visitor 02 Georges Méliès

What Changed Charley Farthing 74 Sidney Hayers

What Color Is the Wind? 84 Frank Zuniga

What Comes Around 86 Jerry Reed

What Could Be Sweeter? 20 Carter DeHaven

What Could the Doctor Do? 11 Percy Stow

What Could the Poor Man Do? 13 Percy Stow

What Demoralized the Barber Shop 01 Edwin S. Porter

What Did the Lady Forget? 37 Yasujiro Ozu

What Did William Tell? 23 W. E. Stark

What Did You Do in the War, Daddy? 66 Blake Edwards

What Do I Tell the Boys at the Station? 72 Simon Nuchtern

What Do Men Want? 21 Lois Weber

What Do We Do Now? 45 Charles Hawtrey

What Do You Say to a Naked Lady? 70 Allen Funt

What Do You Say to a Naked Woman? 70 Allen Funt

What Do You Think? 37 Felix E. Feist, Jacques Tourneur

What Do You Think? 67 Yoji Kuri

What Drink Did 09 D. W. Griffith

What D'Yer Want to Talk About It For? 07 John Morland

What Ever Happened to Aunt Alice? 69 Lee H. Katzin

What Ever Happened to Baby Jane? 62 Robert Aldrich

What Every Girl Should Know 27 Charles Reisner

What Every Woman Knows 17 Fred W. Durrant

What Every Woman Knows 21 William DeMille

What Every Woman Knows 34 Gregory La Cava

What Every Woman Learns 19 Fred Niblo

What Every Woman Wants 19 Jesse D. Hampton

What Every Woman Wants 54 Maurice Elvey

What's Home Without a Dog *16* Harry S. Palmer
What's in a Name? *15* Cecil Birch
What's in a Name? *34* Ralph Ince
What's in It for Harry? *68* Roger Corman
What's My Lion? *61* Friz Freleng
What's New, Pussycat? *65* Clive Donner
What's Next? *74* Peter Smith
What's Opera, Doc? *57* Chuck Jones
What's Past Is Dead *87* Ine Schenkkan
What's So Bad About Feeling Good? *68* George Seaton
What's the Joke? *12* Dave Aylott
What's the Limit? *21* Julian Ollendorff
What's the Matter with Helen? *71* Curtis Harrington
What's the Time, Mr. Clock? *85* Péter Bacsó
What's the Use of Grumbling? *18* Henry Edwards
What's Up Doc? *50* Robert McKimson
What's Up, Doc? *72* Peter Bogdanovich
What's Up Front *64* Bob Wehling
What's Up Nurse? *77* Derek Ford
What's Up Superdoc? *78* Derek Ford
What's Up Tiger Lily? *66* Woody Allen, Senkichi Taniguchi
What's Worthwhile? *21* Lois Weber
What's Wrong with the Women? *22* Roy William Neill
What's Wrong with This Picture? *72* George Landow
What's Your Daughter Doing? *24* Rollin Sturgeon
What's Your Hurry? *09* D. W. Griffith
What's Your Hurry? *20* Sam Wood
What's Your Hurry? *26* Sam Newfield
What's Your Husband Doing? *19* Lloyd Ingraham
What's Your I.Q.? *40* George Sidney
What's Your Racket? *34* Fred Guiol
What's Your Reputation Worth? *21* Webster Campbell
What's Yours Is Mine *15* Frank Wilson
Wheat Ripens, The *39* Béla Gaál
Wheatmeal Bread *41* Len Lye
Wheeeeels No. 1 *58* Stan Vanderbeek
Wheeeeels No. 2 *59* Stan Vanderbeek
Wheel, The *21* Abel Gance
Wheel, The *25* Victor Schertzinger
Wheel, The *83* Doo-yong Lee
Wheel of Ashes *70* Peter Goldman
Wheel of Chance *28* Alfred Santell
Wheel of Death, The *16* A. E. Coleby
Wheel of Destiny, The *27* Duke Worne
Wheel of Fate, The *35* Nitin Bose
Wheel of Fate *53* Francis Searle
Wheel of Fortune *41* John H. Auer
Wheel of Life, The *14* Wallace Reid
Wheel of Life, The *29* Victor Schertzinger
Wheel of Life, The *83* King Hu, Hanhsiang Li, Ching-jui Pai
Wheel of the Law, The *16* George D. Baker
Wheelchair, The *59* Marco Ferreri
Wheeler Dealers, The *63* Arthur Hiller
Wheels of Chance, The *22* Harold M. Shaw
Wheels of Destiny *34* Alvin J. Neitz
Wheels of Fate *22* Challis Sanderson

Wheels of Fire *85* Cirio Santiago
Wheels of Justice *15* Theodore Marston
Wheels of Terror *87* Gordon Hessler
Wheels of Time, The *60* Miklós Jancsó
Wheels on Meals *84* Samo Hung
When a Dog Loves *27* John P. McGowan
When a Feller Needs a Friend *32* Harry A. Pollard
When a Fellow Needs a Friend *32* Harry A. Pollard
When a Girl Loves *18* Phillips Smalley, Lois Weber
When a Girl Loves *24* Victor Halperin
When a Girl's Beautiful *47* Frank McDonald
When a Man Loves *10* D. W. Griffith
When a Man Loves *20* Chester Bennett
When a Man Loves *26* Alan Crosland
When a Man Rides Alone *18* Henry King
When a Man Rides Alone *33* John P. McGowan
When a Man Sees Red *17* Frank Lloyd
When a Man Sees Red *34* Alvin J. Neitz
When a Man's a Man *24* Edward F. Cline
When a Man's a Man *35* Edward F. Cline
When a Man's a Prince *26* Edward F. Cline
When a Man's Single *16* Kelly Storrie
When a Stranger Calls *79* Fred Walton
When a Woman Ascends the Stairs *60* Mikio Naruse
When a Woman Is in Love *76* Roger Vadim
When a Woman Loves *59* Heinosuke Gosho
When a Woman Saddles a Horse *74* Khodzhakuli Narliev
When a Woman Sins *18* J. Gordon Edwards
When a Woman Strikes *19* Roy Clements
When a Woman Won't *13* Allan Dwan
When Angels Don't Fly *56* Mario Camerini
When Angels Fall *59* Roman Polanski
When Artists Love *14* Mauritz Stiller
When Baby Forgot *17* W. Eugene Moore
When Bearcat Went Dry *19* Oliver L. Sellers
When Blonde Meets Blonde *31* Frank R. Strayer
When Boys Are Forbidden to Smoke *08* Frank Mottershaw
When Boys Leave Home *27* Alfred Hitchcock
When Broadway Was a Trail *14* Oscar A. C. Lund
When Carnival Comes *72* Carlos Diegués
When Clubs Were Clubs *15* Dave Aylott
When Cripples Meet *06* Alf Collins
When Daddy Comes Home *02* Percy Stow
When Damon Fell for Pythias *16* William Beaudine
When Danger Calls *27* Charles Hutchinson
When Danger Smiles *22* William Duncan
When Darkness Falls *60* Arne Mattsson
When Dawn Came *20* Colin Campbell
When Destiny Wills *21* R. C. Baker
When Dinosaurs Ruled the Earth *69* Val Guest

When Do We Eat? *18* Fred Niblo
When Doctors Disagree *19* Victor Schertzinger
When Does a Hen Lay? *17* Charles E. Howell
When Dreams Come True *13* Mack Sennett
When Dreams Come True *29* Duke Worne
When East Comes West *11* Allan Dwan
When East Comes West *22* B. Reeves Eason
When East Meets West *15* Wilfred Noy
When Eight Bells Toll *71* Étienne Périer, Paul Stader
When Every Man's a Soldier *14* Percy Stow
When Extremes Meet *05* Alf Collins
When False Tongues Speak *17* Carl Harbaugh
When Fate Decides *19* Harry Millarde
When Fate Leads Trump *14* Harry Handworth
When Father Buys the Beer *10* Percy Stow
When Father Eloped with Cook *06* Lewin Fitzhamon
When Father Fetched the Doctor *12* Dave Aylott
When Father Got a Holiday *06* Percy Stow
When Father Laid the Carpet on the Stairs *05* Frank Mottershaw
When Father Laid the Carpet on the Stairs *05* Percy Stow
When Father Learnt to Bike *13* Edwin J. Collins
When Father Makes a Pudding *04* Alf Collins
When Father Put Up the Bedstead *11* Frank Wilson
When Father Was Away on Business *85* Emir Kusturica
When Father Wears Stays *09* Percy Stow
When Flirting Didn't Pay *16* Will Page
When Four Do the Same *17* Ernst Lubitsch
When G-Men Step In *38* C. C. Coleman, Jr.
When Gangland Strikes *56* R. G. Springsteen
When George Hops *27* Sam Newfield
When Giants Fought *26* Geoffrey H. Malins, H. B. Parkinson
When Girls Leave Home *36* Phil Rosen
When Gold Is Dross *12* Bert Haldane
When Greek Meets Greek *22* Walter West
When Harry Met Sally *89* Rob Reiner
When He Wants a Dog He Wants a Dog *13* Émile Cohl
When Hell Broke Loose *58* Kenneth Crane
When Hell Froze Over *26* Charles Bowers
When Hubby Wasn't Well *11* Frank Wilson
When Husbands Deceive *22* Wallace Worsley
When Husbands Flirt *25* William A. Wellman
When I Grow Up *51* Michael Kanin
When I Was Dead *16* Ernst Lubitsch
When I Yoo-Hoo *36* Friz Freleng

When the Mummy Cried for Help *15* Al Christie
When the New Director Arrives at His Post *56* Pan Liu
When the North Wind Blows *74* Stewart Raffill
When the Pie Was Opened *39* Len Lye
When the Poppies Bloom Again *37* David MacDonald
When the Poppies Bloom Again *75* Bert Haanstra
When the Rain Begins to Fall *84* James Fargo
When the Raven Flies *85* Hrafn Gunnlaugsson
When the Red Red Robin Comes Bob Bob Bobbin' Along *32* Dave Fleischer
When the Redskins Rode *51* Lew Landers
When the Road Parts *14* William Desmond Taylor
When the Screaming Stops *72* Amando De Ossorio
When the Sleeper Wakes *04* Lewin Fitzhamon
When the Snow Bled *81* Jack Arnold
When the Spider Tore Loose *15* Frank Lloyd
When the Strings of the Heart Sound *14* Boris Suskevich
When the Tocsin Calls *12* Mauritz Stiller
When the Trees Were Big *61* Lev Kulidzhanov
When the Trees Were Tall *61* Lev Kulidzhanov
When the Whales Came *89* Clive Rees
When the Wife's Away *05* J. H. Martin
When the Wife's Away *26* Frank R. Strayer
When the Wind Blows *37* Leo McCarey
When the Wind Blows *86* Jimmy T. Murakami
When They Fall in Love *54* Erik Blomberg
When They Were 21 *15* Carl Francis Lederer
When Thief Meets Thief *37* Raoul Walsh
When Thieves Fall Out *09* Theo Bouwmeester
When Tilly's Uncle Flirted *11* Lewin Fitzhamon
When Time Ran Out... *79* James Goldstone
When Tomorrow Comes *39* John M. Stahl
When Tomorrow Dies *66* Laurence L. Kent
When Uncle Took Clarence for a Walk *10* Frank Wilson
When We Are Married *42* Lance Comfort
When We Called the Plumber In *10* Percy Stow
When We Look Back *35* Arthur Lubin
When We Were in Our Teens *10* D. W. Griffith
When We Were Twenty-One *15* Hugh Ford, Edwin S. Porter
When We Were Twenty-One *20* Henry King
When We Were Young *85* Mikhail Belikov
When Were You Born? *38* William McGann

When Wifey Holds the Purse Strings *11* Mack Sennett
When Will We Dead Awaken? *18* I. M. Poselsky
When Willie Comes Marching Home *50* John Ford
When Winter Went *25* Reginald Morris
When Wolves Cry *69* Terence Young
When Woman Hates *16* Albert Ward
When Women Go on the Warpath *13* Wilfred North, James Young
When Women Had Tails *70* Pasquale Festa Campanile
When Women Join the Force *10* H. Oceano Martinek
When Women Keep Silent *37* Fritz Kirchhoff
When Women Lie *63* Teinosuke Kinugasa, Kozaburo Yoshimura
When Women Lost Their Tails *72* Pasquale Festa Campanile
When Women Rule *08* Lewin Fitzhamon
When Women Rule *15* Joe Evans
When Words Fail *46* Hugo Fregonese
When Worlds Collide *51* Rudolph Maté
When You and I Were Young *17* Alice Guy-Blaché
When You Can't Believe Anyone *68* Tadashi Imai
When You Come Home *47* John Baxter
When You Comin' Back Red Ryder? *79* Milton Katselas
When You Have a Mother-in-Law *38* Joe Stöckel
When You're in Love *37* Robert Riskin
When You're Married *14* Charles Chaplin, Mabel Normand
When You're Smiling *50* Joseph Santley
When Youth Conspires *40* Robert McGowan
When Yuba Plays the Rumba on the Tuba *33* Dave Fleischer
When's Your Birthday? *37* Harry Beaumont, Robert Clampett
Where Am I? *25* Charles Bowers
Where Ambition Leads *19* Billy Asher
Where Angels Go...Trouble Follows! *67* James Neilson
Where Are My Children? *16* Phillips Smalley, Lois Weber
Where Are the Children? *86* Bruce Malmuth
Where Are the Dreams of Youth? *32* Yasujiro Ozu
Where Are the Papers? *18* Gregory La Cava
Where Are You Going? *86* Rangel Vulchanov
Where Are Your Children? *43* William Nigh
Where Bonds Are Loosed *19* David G. Fischer
Where Breakers Roar *08* D. W. Griffith
Where Broadway Meets the Mountains *12* Allan Dwan
Where Charity Begins *13* Phillips Smalley
Where Chimneys Are Seen *53* Heinosuke Gosho
Where Danger Lives *50* John Farrow
Where Destiny Guides *13* Allan Dwan

Where Did You Get It? *00* George Albert Smith
Where Did You Get That Girl? *41* Arthur Lubin
Where Do We Go from Here? *45* Gregory Ratoff
Where Do We Go from Here? *88* Rangel Vulchanov
Where Do You Go? *61* Kazimierz Karabasz
Where Does It Hurt? *72* Rod Amateau
Where Eagles Dare *68* Yakima Canutt, Brian G. Hutton
Where East Is East *29* Tod Browning
Where Has My Little Coal Bin? *19* Gregory La Cava
Where Has Poor Mickey Gone? *64* Gerry Levy
Where History Has Been Written *13* George Pearson
Where Is My Father? *16* Joseph Adelman
Where Is My Treasure? *16* Ernst Lubitsch
Where Is My Wandering Boy Tonight? *22* James P. Hogan, Millard Webb
Where Is Parsifal? *84* Henri Helman
Where Is This Girl? *32* Joseph Losey, Ladislas Vajda
Where Is This Lady? *32* Joseph Losey, Ladislas Vajda
Where Is This West? *23* George Marshall
Where Is Your Love? *79* Julien Temple
Where It's At *69* Garson Kanin
Where Lights Are Low *21* Colin Campbell
Where Love Has Gone *61* Aleksandar Petrović
Where Love Has Gone *64* Edward Dmytryk
Where Love Is, God Is *37* Donald Carter
Where Love Leads *16* Frank Griffin
Where Men Are Men *21* William Duncan
Where Mountains Float *55* Bjarne Henning-Jensen
Where No Vultures Fly *51* Harry Watt
Where Now Are the Dreams of Youth? *32* Yasujiro Ozu
Where Oh Where Has My Little Dog Gone? *07* John Morland
Where Romance Rides *25* Ward Hayes
Where Sinners Meet *34* J. Walter Ruben
Where Spring Comes Late *70* Yoji Yamada
Where the Blood Flows *63* Richard McNamara, Antonio Margheriti
Where the Boys Are *60* Henry Levin
Where the Boys Are *84* Hy Averback
Where the Boys Are '84 *84* Hy Averback
Where the Breakers Roar *08* D. W. Griffith
Where the Buffalo Roam *38* Albert Herman
Where the Buffalo Roam *80* Art Linson
Where the Bullets Fly *66* John Gilling
Where the Eagle Flies *72* John Florea
Where the Ganges Flows *61* Raj Kapoor
Where the Green Ants Dream *84* Werner Herzog
Where the Heart Is *89* John Boorman
Where the Hot Wind Blows *58* Jules Dassin
Where the Lilies Bloom *73* William A. Graham

Where the North Begins 23 Chester M. Franklin
Where the North Begins 47 Howard Bretherton
Where the North Holds Sway 27 Bennett Cohn
Where the Padma Flows 71 Ritwik Ghatak
Where the Pavement Ends 22 Rex Ingram
Where the Rainbow Ends 21 H. Lisle Lucoque
Where the Red Fern Grows 74 Norman Tokar
Where the River Bends 52 Anthony Mann
Where the River Runs Black 86 Christopher Cain
Where the Shamrock Grows 11 Edwin S. Porter
Where the Sidewalk Ends 50 Otto Preminger
Where the Spies Are 65 Val Guest
Where the Summer Wind Blows 53 Åke Öhberg
Where the Trail Divides 14 James Neill
Where the Truth Lies 61 Henri Decoin
Where the West Begins 19 Henry King
Where the West Begins 28 Robert J. Horner
Where the West Begins 38 John P. McGowan
Where the Winds Lead 48 Åke Öhberg
Where the Worst Begins 25 John McDermott
Where There's a Heart 12 Allan Dwan
Where There's a Swill There's a Spray 13 Charles C. Calvert
Where There's a Swill There's a Sway 13 Frank Wilson
Where There's a Will 36 William Beaudine
Where There's a Will 37 Marcel Varnel
Where There's a Will 55 Vernon Sewell
Where There's a Will There's a Way 06 James A. Williamson
Where There's a Will There's a Way 12 F. Martin Thornton
Where There's Life 47 Sidney Lanfield
Where There's Smoke 72 André Cayatte
Where Time Began 76 Juan Piquer Simon
Where Trails Begin 27 Noel Mason Smith
Where Trails Divide 37 Robert North Bradbury
Where Trails End 42 Robert E. Tansey
Where Was I? 25 William A. Seiter
Where Were You When the Lights Went Out? 68 Hy Averback
Where Will They Go? 58 Allan King
Where Words Fail 46 Hugo Fregonese
Where's Baby? 12 Percy Stow
Where's Charley? 52 David Butler
Where's George? 35 Jack Raymond
Where's Jack? 68 James Clavell
Where's Johnny? 74 David Eady
Where's Picone? 84 Nanni Loy
Where's Poppa? 70 Carl Reiner
Where's Sally? 36 Arthur Woods
Where's That Fire? 39 Marcel Varnel
Where's the Key? 18 James Reardon
Where's Watling? 18 F. Martin Thornton
Where's Willie? 78 John Florea
Wherever She Goes 51 Michael Gordon

Wherever You Are 88 Krzysztof Zanussi
Which Is Which? 16 Forest Holger-Madsen
Which Is Which? 26 Sam Newfield
Which Is Witch? 15 Edwin J. Collins
Which Is Witch? 49 Friz Freleng
Which Is Witch? 55 John Halas*
Which of the Two 12 Percy Stow
Which Shall It Be? 24 Renaud Hoffman
Which Switch? 24 Gaston Quiribet
Which Way Is Up? 77 Michael Schultz
Which Way to the Front? 70 Jerry Lewis
Which Will You Have? 49 Donald Taylor
Which Woman? 18 Tod Browning
Whiff of Onion, A 13 Theo Bouwmeester
Whiffs 75 Ted Post
While America Sleeps 39 Fred Zinnemann
While I Live 47 John Harlow
While Justice Waits 22 Bernard J. Durning
While London Sleeps 22 Graham Cutts
While London Sleeps 26 Howard Bretherton
While London Sleeps 34 Adrian Brunel
While Mexico Sleeps 38 Alejandro Galindo
While Nero Fiddled 44 Harry Watt
While New York Sleeps 20 Charles Brabin
While New York Sleeps 38 H. Bruce Humberstone
While Parents Sleep 35 Adrian Brunel
While Paris Sleeps 20 Maurice Tourneur
While Paris Sleeps 32 Allan Dwan
While Plucking the Daisy 56 Marc Allégret
While Satan Sleeps 22 Joseph E. Henabery
While Shepherds Watched 13 Lewin Fitzhamon
While the Attorney Is Asleep 45 Johan Jacobsen
While the Cat's Away 71 Chuck Vincent
While the City Sleeps 28 Jack Conway
While the City Sleeps 55 Fritz Lang
While the Cook Slept 12 A. E. Coleby
While the Devil Laughs 21 George W. Hill
While the Household Sleeps 05 J. H. Martin
While the Patient Slept 35 Ray Enright
While the Sun Shines 46 Anthony Asquith
While There Is Light 87 Felipe Vega
While Under a Hypnotist's Influence 1897 Georges Méliès
While You Sleep 50 Andrzej Wajda
While You're Asleep 50 Andrzej Wajda
Whims of Society, The 18 Travers Vale
Whims of the Gods 22 Rowland V. Lee
Whimsical Illusions 09 Georges Méliès
Whimsicalities by Hy Mayer 13 Hy Mayer
Whine of the Rhine, The 18 Pat Sullivan
Whip, The 17 Maurice Tourneur
Whip, The 28 Charles Brabin
Whip, The 39 José Bohr
Whip and the Body, The 63 Mario Bava
Whip Hand, The 51 William Cameron Menzies
Whip Law 50 Howard Bretherton
Whip Woman, The 28 Joseph C. Boyle

Wherever You Are 88 Krzysztof Zanussi
Whiplash 48 Lewis Seiler
Whipped, The 50 Cy Endfield
Whipping Boss, The 24 John P. McGowan
Whip's Women 68 Jerry Denby
Whipsaw 35 Sam Wood
Whirl of Life, The 15 Oliver D. Bailey
Whirl of Life, The 29 Richard Eichberg
Whirligig of Time, The 13 Edwin J. Collins
Whirling the Worlds 04 Georges Méliès
Whirlpool, The 18 Alan Crosland
Whirlpool 33 Edmond T. Gréville
Whirlpool 34 Roy William Neill
Whirlpool 49 Otto Preminger
Whirlpool 59 Lewis Allen
Whirlpool 69 José Ramón Larraz
Whirlpool of Destiny, The 16 Otis Turner
Whirlpool of Fate, The 24 Jean Renoir
Whirlpool of Flesh 64 Ko Nakahira
Whirlpool of Women 64 Ko Nakahira
Whirls and Girls 29 Mack Sennett
Whirlwind, The 33 D. Ross Lederman
Whirlwind 51 John English
Whirlwind 64 Hiroshi Inagaki
Whirlwind Horseman 38 Robert F. Hill
Whirlwind Kids, The 14 Lewin Fitzhamon
Whirlwind of Paris 46 Henri Diamant-Berger
Whirlwind of Youth, The 27 Rowland V. Lee
Whirlwind Raiders 48 Vernon Keays
Whirlwind Ranger, The 24 Richard Hatton
Whirlwind Rider, The 35 Robert J. Horner
Whirr of the Spinning Wheel, The 14 Frank Wilson
Whiskey and Sofa 63 Günther Gräwert
Whiskey Mountain 77 William Grefé
Whiskey vs. Bullets 01 George Albert Smith
Whisky e Fantasmi 74 Antonio Margheriti
Whisky Galore! 48 Alexander Mackendrick
Whisper in the Dark, A 76 Marcello Aliprandi
Whisper Market, The 20 George L. Sargent
Whisper of Spring 52 Shiro Toyoda
Whispered Name, The 24 King Baggot
Whisperers, The 66 Bryan Forbes
Whispering Canyon 26 Tom Forman
Whispering Chorus, The 17 Cecil B. DeMille
Whispering City 47 Fedor Ozep
Whispering Death 78 Jürgen Goslar
Whispering Devils 20 Harry Garson
Whispering Enemies 39 Lewis D. Collins
Whispering Footsteps 43 Howard Bretherton
Whispering Gables 27 Edwin Greenwood
Whispering Ghosts 42 Alfred L. Werker
Whispering Joe 69 Koichi Saito
Whispering Sage 27 Scott R. Dunlap
Whispering Shadows 22 Émile Chautard
Whispering Shadows 33 Colbert Clark, Albert Herman
Whispering Skull, The 44 Elmer Clifton
Whispering Smith 16 John P. McGowan

Whispering Smith *26* George Melford
Whispering Smith *48* Leslie Fenton
Whispering Smith Hits London *51* Francis Searle
Whispering Smith Rides *27* Ray Taylor
Whispering Smith Speaks *35* David Howard
Whispering Smith vs. Scotland Yard *51* Francis Searle
Whispering Tongues *34* George Pearson
Whispering Winds *29* James Flood
Whispering Wires *26* Albert Ray
Whispering Women *21* James Keane
Whispers *20* William P. S. Earle
Whispers *90* Douglas Jackson
Whispers in the Dark *37* Dave Fleischer
Whispers of Fear *74* Harry Bromley Davenport
Whist! Here Comes the Picture Man *12* Hay Plumb
Whistle, The *21* Lambert Hillyer
Whistle at Eaton Falls, The *51* Robert Siodmak
Whistle Blower, The *86* Simon Langton
Whistle Down the Wind *61* Bryan Forbes
Whistle in My Heart, A *59* Mikio Naruse
Whistle Stop *45* Léonide Moguy
Whistle Stop *63* Boris Barnet
Whistler, The *26* Miles Mander
Whistler, The *44* William Castle
Whistler, The *49* Jerry Lewis
Whistlin' Dan *32* Phil Rosen
Whistling Bet, The *12* Will P. Kellino
Whistling Bullets *37* John English
Whistling Cobblestone, The *71* Gyula Gazdag
Whistling Hills *51* Derwin Abrahams
Whistling in Brooklyn *43* S. Sylvan Simon
Whistling in Dixie *42* S. Sylvan Simon
Whistling in Kotan *59* Mikio Naruse
Whistling in the Dark *32* Elliott Nugent
Whistling in the Dark *41* S. Sylvan Simon
Whistling Jim *25* Wilbur F. McGaugh
Whistling William *13* Frank Wilson
Whitchurch Down *72* Malcolm Le Grice
White and Black *19* Alexander Rasumny
White and Unmarried *21* Tom Forman
White Angel, The *36* William Dieterle
White Apache *86* Bruno Mattei
White Banners *38* Edmund Goulding
White Beast *49* Mikio Naruse
White Bim the Black Ear *77* Stanislav Rostotsky
White Bird Marked with Black, The *70* Yuri Ilyenko
White Bird with Black Marking, A *70* Yuri Ilyenko
White Black Sheep, The *26* Sidney Olcott
White Blood *52* Ken Annakin
White Bondage *37* Nick Grindé
White Boys, The *16* Frank Wilson
White Buffalo, The *77* J. Lee-Thompson
White Bus, The *66* Lindsay Anderson
White Caps, The *04* Edwin S. Porter
White Captive *43* Arthur Lubin
White Caravan, The *64* A. Sakharov, Eldar Shengelaya
White Cargo *29* Arthur W. Barnes, J. B. Williams
White Cargo *42* Richard Thorpe

White Cargo *74* Ray Selfe
White Cat, The *23* Herbert Blaché
White Cat, The *50* Hasse Ekman
White Christmas *54* Michael Curtiz
White Circle, The *20* Maurice Tourneur
White Cliff *60* Tadashi Imai
White Cliffs Mystery, The *57* Montgomery Tully
White Cliffs of Dover, The *44* Clarence Brown
White Cockatoo, The *35* Alan Crosland
White Comanche *67* José Briz
White Corridors *51* Pat Jackson
White Cradle Inn *47* Harold French
White Dawn, The *74* Philip Kaufman
White Death *36* Edward Bowen
White Demon, The *32* Kurt Gerron
White Desert, The *25* Reginald Barker
White Devil, The *15* Forest Holger-Madsen
White Devil, The *31* Alexander Volkov
White Devil, The *48* Nunzio Malasomma
White Disease, The *36* Hugo Haas
White Dog *82* Samuel Fuller
White Dove, The *20* Henry King
White Dove, The *86* Sergei Soloviev
White Dragon *86* Jerzy Domaradzki
White Dwarf, The *86* Timo Humaloja
White Eagle *21* Fred Jackman, W. S. Van Dyke
White Eagle, The *28* Yakov Protazanov
White Eagle *32* Lambert Hillyer
White Eagle *41* James W. Horne
White Ecstasy, The *31* Arnold Fanck
White Elephant, A *28* Hugh Shields
White Elephant *84* Werner Grusch
White Ensign *34* John Hunt
White Face *32* T. Hayes Hunter
White Fang *25* Lawrence Trimble
White Fang *36* David Butler
White Fang *46* Alexander Zguridi
White Fang *72* Ken Annakin
White Fang *72* Lucio Fulci
White Fangs *60* Heinosuke Gosho
White Feather, The *14* Maurice Elvey
White Feather *55* Robert D. Webb
White Field Duration *72* Malcolm Le Grice
White Fire *53* John Gilling
White Fire *88* Eddie Romero
White Flannels *27* Lloyd Bacon
White Flood *40* Sidney Meyers*
White Flower, The *23* Julia Ivers
White Flowers for the Dead *78* Lester James Peries
White Frenzy, The *31* Arnold Fanck
White Game, The *68* Bo Widerberg*
White Ghost, The *13* Forest Holger-Madsen
White Ghost *88* B. J. Davis
White Girl, The *87* Tony Brown
White Goddess, The *53* Wallace Fox
White Gold *27* William K. Howard
White Gorilla *47* Harry Fraser
White Gypsy, The *19* Ricardo De Baños
White-Haired Girl, The *70* Sang Hu
White Hand, The *15* Cecil Birch
White Hands *22* Lambert Hillyer
White Heat *26* Thomas Bentley
White Heat *34* Lois Weber

White Heat *49* Raoul Walsh
White Heather, The *19* Maurice Tourneur
White Hell *22* Bernard Feikel
White Hell of Pitz Palu, The *29* Arnold Fanck, G. W. Pabst
White Hen, The *21* Frank Richardson
White Heron, The *57* Teinosuke Kinugasa
White Hood, The *35* Hiroshi Inagaki
White Hope, The *15* Frank Wilson
White Hope, The *17* Gregory La Cava
White Hope, The *22* Frank Wilson
White Horse Inn, The *52* Willi Forst
White Hot *87* Robby Benson
White House Madness *75* Mark L. Lester
White Hunter *36* Irving Cummings
White Hunter *65* George Michael
White Hunter, Black Heart *90* Clint Eastwood
White Huntress *54* George Breakston
White Laager, The *78* Peter Davis
White Legion, The *36* Karl Brown
White Lie, The *25* Harcourt Templeman
White Lies *20* Edward J. LeSaint
White Lies *35* Leo Bulgakov
White Lightnin' Road *67* Ron Ormond
White Lightning *53* Edward Bernds
White Lightning *73* Joseph Sargent
White Lilac *35* Albert Parker
White Lily Laments, The *25* Kenji Mizoguchi
White Line, The *50* Luigi Zampa
White Line Fever *75* Jonathan Kaplan
White Lions, The *79* Mel Stuart
White Little Dove *73* Raúl Ruiz
White Majesty *39* Anton Kutter
White Man, The *13* Oscar Apfel, Cecil B. DeMille
White Man, The *18* Cecil B. DeMille
White Man *24* Louis Gasnier
White Man, The *31* Cecil B. DeMille
White Mane *52* Albert Lamorisse
White Man's Law *18* James Young
White Man's Throne, The *35* Tomu Uchida
White Man's Way, A *12* F. Martin Thornton
White Masks, The *21* George Holt
White Mice *26* Edward H. Griffith
White Mischief *87* Michael Radford
White Moll *20* Harry Millarde
White Monkey, The *25* Phil Rosen
White Moor *65* Ion Popescu-Gopo
White Moth, The *24* Maurice Tourneur
White Negro, The *12* Abel Gance, Jean Joulout
White Nights *16* Alexander Korda
White Nights *57* Luchino Visconti
White Nights *59* Ivan Pyriev
White Nights *85* Taylor Hackford
White Oak *21* Lambert Hillyer
White of the Eye *86* Donald Cammell
White Orchid, The *54* Reginald LeBorg
White Outlaw, The *25* Clifford Smith
White Outlaw, The *29* Robert J. Horner
White Palace *90* Luis Mandoki
White Panther, The *24* Alvin J. Neitz
White Pants Willie *27* Charles Hines
White Parade, The *34* Irving Cummings
White Paws *48* Jean Grémillon
White Peacock, The *20* E. A. Dupont

White Pebbles 27 Richard Thorpe
White Phantom 87 Dusty Nelson
White Pongo 45 Sam Newfield
White Rat, The 22 George A. Cooper
White Rat 72 Steve Mullen
White Raven, The 17 George D. Baker
White Raven, The 41 Sergei Yutkevich
White Red Man, The 11 Edwin S. Porter
White, Red, Yellow and Pink 66 Massimo
  Mida
White, Red, Yellow, Pink 66 Massimo
  Mida
White Reindeer, The 52 Erik Blomberg
White Renegade 31 Jack Irwin
White Rider, The 20 William James Craft
White Rock 77 Tony Maylam
White Rocker, The 49 Sidney Peterson
White Room, The 90 Patricia Rozema
White Rose 19 Alexander Korda
White Rose, The 23 D. W. Griffith
White Rose, The 67 Bruce Conner
White Rose, The 81 Si-hyun Kim
White Rose, The 82 Michael Verhoeven
White Rose of Hong Kong 65 Jun Fukuda
White Rose of the Wilds, The 11 D. W.
  Griffith
White Roses 10 D. W. Griffith
White Rosette, The 16 Donald Mac-
  Donald
White Savage 41 George Waggner
White Savage 43 Arthur Lubin
White Scar, The 15 Hobart Bosworth
White Sea of Yushima 55 Teinosuke
  Kinugasa
White Shadow, The 24 Graham Cutts
White Shadows 24 Graham Cutts
White Shadows in the South Seas 28 Rob-
  ert Flaherty, W. S. Van Dyke
White Sheep, The 24 Hal Roach
White Sheik, The 28 Harley Knoles
White Sheik, The 51 Federico Fellini
White Ship, The 41 Roberto Rossellini
White Ship, The 75 Bolotbek Shamshiev
White Shoulders 22 Tom Forman
White Shoulders 31 Melville Brown
White Sickness, The 36 Hugo Haas
White Sin, The 24 William A. Seiter
White Sister, The 15 Fred E. Wright
White Sister, The 23 Henry King
White Sister, The 33 Victor Fleming
White Sister 71 Alberto Lattuada
White Slave, The 10 August Blom
White Slave 86 Mario Gariazzo
White Slave Racket 53 Barry Mahon
White Slave Ship 62 Silvio Amadio
White Slave Trade 52 Luigi Comencini
White Slide, The 60 Martin Frič
White Slippers 24 Sinclair Hill
White Snows of Fuji 35 Hiroshi Inagaki
White Spider, The 63 Harald Reinl
White Squadron, The 36 Augusto Genina
White Squaw, The 56 Ray Nazarro
White Stallion 44 Robert E. Tansey
White Stallion, The 54 Fred F. Sears
White Star 15 Bertram Phillips
White Star S.S. "Baltic" Leaving Pier on
  First Eastern Voyage 04 Edwin S. Porter
White Stocking, The 14 Will P. Kellino
White Sun of the Desert, The 72 V.
  Motyl

White Telephones 75 Dino Risi
White Terror, The 15 Stuart Paton
White Threads of the Cascades 33 Kenji
  Mizoguchi
White Threads of the Waterfall, The 33
  Kenji Mizoguchi
White Thunder 25 Ben F. Wilson
White Tie and Tails 46 Charles Barton
White Tiger, The 23 Tod Browning
White to Black 09 S. Wormald
White Tower, The 50 Ted Tetzlaff
White Trap, The 59 Sidney Hayers
White Trash on Moonshine Mountain 64
  Herschell Gordon Lewis
White Treachery 12 Allan Dwan
White Unicorn, The 47 Bernard Knowles
White Voices 63 Pasquale Festa Cam-
  panile, Massimo Franciosa
White Wall, The 75 Stig Björkman
White Warrior, The 58 Riccardo Freda
White Water Men 25 Geoffrey Barkas
White Water Summer 85 Jeff Bleckner
White Whales 87 Friđrik Thor Friđriksson
White White Boy, A 74 Andrei Tarkovsky
White Widow, The 15 August Blom
White Wilderness 57 James Algar
White Witch, The 13 Hubert von Herko-
  mer
White Witch Doctor 53 Henry Hathaway
White Woman, The 13 Forest Holger-
  Madsen
White Woman 33 Stuart Walker
White, Yellow, Black 75 Sergio Corbucci
White Youth 20 Norman Dawn
White Zombie 32 Victor Halperin
Whitechapel 20 E. A. Dupont
Whitewashers, The 14 Fred Evans, Joe
  Evans
Whitewashing the Ceiling 14 Will Day
Whitewashing the Policeman 04 William
  Haggar
Whither? 56 Georges M. Nasser
Whither Germany? 32 Slatan Dudow
Whither Now? 88 Rangel Vulchanov
Whither Thou Goest 17 Raymond B.
  West
Whity 70 Rainer Werner Fassbinder
Who? 73 Jack Gold
Who? 74 Sonia Assonitis, Roberto d'Et-
  tore Piazzoli
Who Am I? 21 Henry Kolker
Who Are My Parents? 22 J. Searle Dawley
Who Are the De Bolts? ... And Where
  Did They Get 19 Kids? 77 John Korty
Who Are You Mr. Sorge? 60 Yves Ciampi
Who Are You Polly Maggoo? 66 William
  Klein
Who Can Kill a Child? 75 Narciso Ibáñez
  Serrador
Who Cares? 19 Walter Edwards
Who Cares? 24 David Kirkland
Who Cares... 60 Volker Schlöndorff
Who Dares Wins 82 Ian Sharp
Who Does She Think She Is? 74 Patricia
  Lewis Jaffe, Gaby Rodgers
Who Done It? 17 William Beaudine
Who Done It? 42 Erle C. Kenton
Who Done It? 55 Basil Dearden, Michael
  Relph
Who Fears the Devil 72 John Newland

Who Fell Asleep? 80 Scott Mansfield
Who Framed Roger Rabbit? 87 Richard
  Williams, Robert Zemeckis
Who Goes Next? 38 Maurice Elvey
Who Goes There? 17 William P. S. Earle
Who Goes There? 52 Anthony Kimmins
Who Got Stung? 14 Charles Chaplin
Who Got the Reward? 12 Mack Sennett
Who Has Been Rocking My Dream Boat?
  41 Kenneth Anger
Who Has Seen the Wind 77 Allan King
Who Hit Me? 26 Stephen Roberts
Who Ho Ray No. 1 72 Stan Vanderbeek
Who Is Beta? 72 Nelson Pereira Dos
  Santos
Who Is Guilty? 39 Fred Zelnik
Who Is Happier Than I? 40 Guido Brig-
  none
Who Is Harry Kellerman, and Why Is He
  Saying Those Terrible Things About
  Me? 71 Ulu Grosbard
Who Is Hope Schuyler? 42 Thomas Z.
  Loring
Who Is Killing the Great Chefs of Europe?
  78 Ted Kotcheff
Who Is Killing the Stuntmen? 77 Mark L.
  Lester
Who Is That Man? 85 Ewa Petelska,
  Czesław Petelski
Who Is the Boss? 21 Albert Brouett
Who Is the Bride? 60 Farrokh Ghaffary
Who Is the Man? 24 Walter Summers
Who Is to Blame? 18 Frank Borzage
Who Killed Aunt Maggie? 40 Arthur
  Lubin
Who Killed Barno O'Neal? 16 Forest
  Holger-Madsen
Who Killed Doc Robbin? 48 Bernard Carr
Who Killed Doc Robin? 30 Will P. Kel-
  lino
Who Killed Fen Markham? 37 Thomas
  Bentley
Who Killed Gail Preston? 38 Leon Barsha
Who Killed Jessie? 65 Václav Vorlíček
Who Killed Joe Merrion? 15 Tefft Johnson
Who Killed John Savage? 37 Maurice
  Elvey
Who Killed Mary What's'ername? 71
  Ernest Pintoff
Who Killed Santa Claus? 40 Christian-
  Jaque
Who Killed Teddy Bear? 65 Joseph Cates
Who Killed the Cat? 66 Montgomery
  Tully
Who Killed Van Loon? 48 Gordon Kyle,
  Lionel Tomlinson
Who Killed Walton? 18 Thomas Heffron
Who Killed Waring? 45 Vernon Keays
Who Killed Who? 43 Tex Avery
Who Kissed Her? 15 Will P. Kellino
Who Laughs Last 20 James Youngdeer
Who Looks for Gold 74 Jiří Menzel
Who Looks, Pays! 06 Georges Méliès
Who Loved Him Best? 18 Del Henderson
Who, Me? 32 George Stevens
Who Pays? 15 Henry King
Who Rides with Kane 68 Burt Kennedy
Who Saw Him Die? 67 Jan Troell
Who Says I Can't Ride a Rainbow? 71 San-
  tos Alcocer

Who Scent You? *60* Chuck Jones

Who Seeks a Handful of Gold *74* Jiří Menzel

Who Seeks the Gold Bottom *74* Jiří Menzel

Who Shall Live and Who Shall Die? *81* Laurence Jarvik

Who Shall Take My Life? *18* Colin Campbell

Who Slew Auntie Roo? *71* Curtis Harrington

Who So Loveth His Father's Honor *15* Forest Holger-Madsen

Who Stole My Wheels? *78* Maura Smith

Who Stole Pa's Purse? *15* Frank Wilson

Who Stole the Beer? *06* Percy Stow

Who Stole the Body? *62* Jean Girault

Who Takes Love Seriously? *31* Erich Engel

Who Wants to Kill Jessie? *65* Václav Vorlíček

Who Was Maddox? *64* Geoffrey Nethercott

Who Was That Lady? *59* George Sidney

Who Was the Other Man? *17* Francis Ford

Who Was to Blame? *14* Will P. Kellino

Who Were You With Last Night? *15* Cecil Birch

Who Will Marry Martha? *14* Joe Evans

Who Will Marry Me? *19* Paul Powell

Who Winked at the Soldier? *07* Harold Jeapes

Who Would Kill a Child? *75* Narciso Ibáñez Serrador

Who Would Kill Jessie? *65* Václav Vorlíček

Who Writes to Switzerland *37* Alberto Cavalcanti

Whoa, Be Gone! *58* Chuck Jones

Whoever Is Here, Is Here *87* Piero Natoli

Whoever Looks for Gold *74* Jiří Menzel

Whoever Says the Truth Shall Die *81* Philo Bergstein

Whoever Slew Auntie Roo? *71* Curtis Harrington

Whole Dam Family and the Dam Dog, The *05* Edwin S. Porter

Whole Family Works, The *39* Mikio Naruse

Whole Shootin' Match, The *78* Eagle Pennell

Whole Town's Talking, The *26* Edward Laemmle

Whole Town's Talking, The *34* John Ford

Whole Truth, The *57* John Guillermin

Who'll Stop the Rain? *78* Karel Reisz

Wholly Moses! *80* Gary Weis

Wholly Smoke *38* Frank Tashlin

Whom the Gods Destroy *16* Herbert Brenon

Whom the Gods Destroy *19* Frank Borzage

Whom the Gods Destroy *34* Walter Lang

Whom the Gods Love *36* Basil Dean

Whom the Gods Wish to Destroy *66* Harald Reinl

Whom the Gods Would Destroy *15* Joseph Smiley

Whom the Gods Would Destroy *16* Herbert Brenon

Whom the Gods Would Destroy *19* Frank

Borzage

Whoopee! *30* Thornton Freeland

Whoopee Boys *29* Stephen Roberts

Whoopee Boys, The *86* John Byrum

Whooping Cough *87* Péter Gardos

Whoops Apocalypse *86* Tom Bussmann

Whoops! I'm a Cowboy *37* Dave Fleischer

Who's Afraid? *27* Charles Lamont

Who's Afraid of the Avant-Garde? *68* Richard Leacock*

Who's Afraid of Virginia Woolf? *66* Mike Nichols

Who's Been Sleeping in My Bed? *63* Daniel Mann

Who's Cheating? *24* Joseph Levering

Who's Crazy *65* Tom White, Allan Zion

Who's Got My Hat? *10* Lewin Fitzhamon

Who's Got the Action? *62* Daniel Mann

Who's Got the Black Box? *67* Claude Chabrol

Who's Guilty? *45* Howard Bretherton, Wallace A. Grissell

Who's Harry Crumb? *89* Paul Flaherty

Who's Kitten Who? *52* Robert McKimson

Who's Looney Now? *17* Al Christie

Who's Looney Now? *36* Leslie Goodwins

Who's Lyin'? *28* Stephen Roberts

Who's Minding the Mint? *67* Howard Morris

Who's Minding the Store? *63* Frank Tashlin

Who's My Wife? *26* Stephen Roberts

Who's Singing Over There? *80* Slobodan Šijan

Who's That A-Calling? *05* Alf Collins

Who's That Girl? *87* James Foley

Who's That Knocking at My Door? *67* Martin Scorsese

Who's That Singing Over There? *80* Slobodan Šijan

Who's to Blame? *05* Arthur Cooper

Who's Which? *14* Cecil Birch

Who's Who in Society *15* George Fitzmaurice

Who's Who in the Zoo *42* Norm McCabe

Who's Your Brother? *19* John G. Adolfi

Who's Your Father? *18* Henry Lehrman

Who's Your Father? *35* Henry W. George

Who's Your Friend? *16* Frank Wilson

Who's Your Friend? *25* Forrest K. Sheldon

Who's Your Lady Friend? *37* Carol Reed

Who's Your Neighbor? *17* Sidney Rankin Drew

Who's Zoo in Hollywood *41* Art Davis

Whose Baby? *14* Edwin J. Collins

Whose Baby? *17* Clarence Badger

Whose Baby? *17* William Beaudine

Whose Child Am I? *76* Lawrence Britten

Whose Life Is It Anyway? *81* John Badham

Whose Little Wife Are You? *18* Edward F. Cline

Whose Who? *21* Edward F. Cline

Whose Wife? *17* Rollin Sturgeon

Whoso Diggeth a Pit *15* Ralph Dewsbury

Whoso Findeth a Wife *16* Frank Crane

Whoso Is Without Sin *16* Fred Paul

Whoso Taketh a Wife *16* Frank Crane

Whosoever Shall Offend *19* Arrigo Bocchi

Whozit Weekly No. 115, The *19* Leslie Elton

Whozit Weekly No. 123, The *19* Leslie Elton

Whozit Weekly No. 124, The *19* Leslie Elton

Whozit Weekly No. 126, The *19* Leslie Elton

Whozit Weekly No. 129, The *19* Leslie Elton

Whozit Weekly No. 131, The *19* Leslie Elton

Whozit Weekly No. 134, The *19* Leslie Elton

Whozit Weekly No. 137, The *19* Leslie Elton

Whozit Weekly No. 143, The *19* Leslie Elton

Whozit Weekly No. 144, The *19* Leslie Elton

Whozit Weekly No. 164, The *20* Leslie Elton

Why? *16* John R. Bray

Why? *64* Evald Schorm

Why *70* Ritwik Ghatak

Why? *71* Nanni Loy

Why Am I Here? *13* Ralph Ince

Why America Will Win *18* Richard Stanton

Why Anna? *70* Nelo Risi

Why Announce Your Marriage? *22* Alan Crosland

Why Be Good? *29* William A. Seiter

Why Blame Me? *18* Frank Beal

Why Bother to Knock? *61* Cyril Frankel

Why Brigit Stopped Drinking *01* Edwin S. Porter

Why Bring That Up? *29* George Abbott

Why Change Your Husband? *20* Jack King

Why Change Your Husband? *31* Lloyd Bacon

Why Change Your Wife? *19* Cecil B. DeMille

Why Cry at Parting? *30* Richard Eichberg

Why Did Bodhi-Djarma Go East? *89* Yong-kyun Bae

Why Do I Dream Those Dreams? *34* Friz Freleng

Why Do You Smile Mona Lisa? *66* Jiří Brdečka

Why Does Herr R. Run Amok? *69* Rainer Werner Fassbinder, Michael Fengler

Why Does Your Husband Leave You? *68* Manuel Summers

Why Father Grew a Beard *09* Walter R. Booth

Why Father Learned to Ride *09* Lewin Fitzhamon

Why, George! *26* Charles Lamont

Why Germany Must Pay *19* Charles Miller

Why Girls Go Back Home *26* James Flood

Why Girls Leave Home *21* William Nigh

Why Girls Leave Home *45* William Berke

Why Go Home? *20* Charlie Chase

Why He Gave Up *11* Mack Sennett

Why Hesitate? *25* Archie Mayo

Why Husbands Go Mad *24* Leo McCarey

Why I Should Not Marry *18* Richard Stanton

Wife Trap, The *22* Robert Wullner
Wife vs. Secretary *36* Clarence Brown
Wife Wanted, A *13* Mack Sennett
Wife Wanted *14* Ralph Ince
Wife Wanted *46* Phil Karlson
Wife Who Wasn't Wanted, The *25* James Flood
Wife Whom God Forgot, The *20* William Humphrey
Wifemistress *77* Marco Vicario
Wife's Awakening, A *21* Louis Gasnier
Wife's Confession *61* Yasuzo Masumura
Wife's Family, The *31* Monty Banks
Wife's Forgiveness, A *06* Charles Raymond
Wife's Heart, A *55* Mikio Naruse
Wife's Relations, The *28* Maurice Marshall
Wife's Romance, A *23* Thomas Heffron
Wife's Sacrifice, A *16* J. Gordon Edwards
Wife's Strategy *08* Edwin S. Porter
Wifey's Mistake *04* Edwin S. Porter
Wig and Buttons *05* Alf Collins
Wigwam, De *11* Joris Ivens
Wigwam, The *11* Joris Ivens
Wij Bouwen *29* Joris Ivens
Wilbur and the Lion *47* George Pal
Wilby Conspiracy, The *74* Ralph Nelson
Wild About Hurry *59* Chuck Jones
Wild Affair, The *63* John Krish
Wild and the Brave, The *74* Eugene S. Jones
Wild and the Innocent, The *59* Jack Sher
Wild and the Sweet, The *73* Sidney Lumet
Wild and the Willing, The *62* Ralph Thomas
Wild and Wicked *23* Gregory La Cava
Wild and Willing *65* James Landis
Wild and Wonderful *63* Michael Anderson
Wild and Woolfy *45* Tex Avery
Wild and Woolly *17* John Emerson
Wild and Woolly *32* Walter Lantz
Wild and Woolly *37* Alfred L. Werker
Wild and Woolly Hare *59* Friz Freleng
Wild and Woolly West, The *16* A. D. Reed
Wild and Woozy West *42* Allen Rose
Wild Angels, The *66* Roger Corman
Wild Arctic *70* Gordon Eastman
Wild at Heart *90* David Lynch
Wild Beasts *48* Jiří Weiss
Wild Beasts *82* Lewis E. Cianelli, Franco Prosperi
Wild Beauty *27* Henry MacRae
Wild Beauty *46* Wallace Fox
Wild Beds *79* Luigi Zampa
Wild Bill Hickok *23* William S. Hart, Clifford Smith
Wild Bill Hickok Rides *41* Ray Enright
Wild Bill's Defeat *10* Edwin S. Porter
Wild Bird, A *21* John W. Brunius
Wild Birds *54* Alf Sjöberg
Wild Blood *29* Henry MacRae
Wild Blue Yonder, The *51* Allan Dwan
Wild Born *27* Edward R. Gordon
Wild Boy *34* Albert De Courville
Wild Boy *51* Jean Delannoy
Wild Boys of the Road *33* William A. Wellman

Wild Brian Kent *36* Howard Bretherton
Wild Bull's Lair, The *25* Del Andrews
Wild Bunch, The *69* Sam Peckinpah
Wild Cargo *34* Armand Denis
Wild Cargo *62* Silvio Amadio
Wild Cats on the Beach *59* Vittorio Sala
Wild Chase, The *65* Hawley Pratt
Wild Cherry Trees *63* Herbert Rappaport
Wild Child, The *69* François Truffaut
Wild Clown, The *86* Josef Rödl
Wild Company *30* Leo McCarey
Wild Country *47* Ray Taylor
Wild Country, The *70* Robert Totten
Wild Country *88* Percival Rubens
Wild Crazy and the Lunatics, The *86* Naftali Alter
Wild Dakotas, The *56* Sam Newfield
Wild Dog, The *82* Choi-su Park
Wild Dog *86* Daniel Díaz Torres
Wild Drifter *74* Monte Hellman
Wild Duck, The *76* Hans W. Geissendörfer
Wild Duck, The *83* Henri Safran
Wild Elephinks *33* Dave Fleischer
Wild Eye, The *68* Paolo Cavara
Wild Flowers *81* Jean-Pierre Lefèbvre
Wild for Kicks *59* Edmond T. Gréville
Wild Force *87* Ruben De Guzman
Wild, Free and Hungry *70* H. P. Edwards
Wild Frontier, The *47* Philip Ford
Wild Game *72* Rainer Werner Fassbinder
Wild Geese *27* Phil Goldstone
Wild Geese *53* Shiro Toyoda
Wild Geese, The *78* Andrew V. McLaglen
Wild Geese Calling *41* John Brahm
Wild Geese II *85* Peter R. Hunt
Wild Girl, The *17* Howard Estabrook
Wild Girl, The *25* William Bletcher
Wild Girl *32* Raoul Walsh
Wild Girl of the Sierras, A *16* Paul Powell
Wild Gold *34* George Marshall
Wild Goose, The *21* Albert Capellani
Wild Goose Chase, A *08* Percy Stow
Wild Goose Chase, The *15* Cecil B. De-Mille
Wild Goose Chase *19* Harry Beaumont
Wild Goose Chase, The *75* Claude Zidi
Wild Goose Chaser, The *24* Lloyd Bacon
Wild Guitar *62* Ray Dennis Steckler
Wild Gypsies *69* Marc B. Ray
Wild Hare, A *40* Tex Avery
Wild Harvest *47* Tay Garnett
Wild Harvest *62* Jerry Baerwitz
Wild Heart, The *50* Rouben Mamoulian, Michael Powell, Emeric Pressburger
Wild Heather *21* Cecil M. Hepworth
Wild Herd, The *39* Albert Herman
Wild Heritage *58* Charles Haas
Wild Honey *19* Francis J. Grandon
Wild Honey *22* Wesley Ruggles
Wild Horse *31* Sidney Algier, Richard Thorpe
Wild Horse Ambush *52* Fred C. Brannon
Wild Horse Canyon *38* Robert F. Hill
Wild Horse Hank *79* Eric Till
Wild Horse Mesa *25* George B. Seitz
Wild Horse Mesa *32* Henry Hathaway
Wild Horse Mesa *47* Wallace A. Grissell
Wild Horse Phantom *44* Sam Newfield
Wild Horse Range *40* Raymond K. John-

son
Wild Horse Rodeo *37* George Sherman
Wild Horse Round-Up *37* Alvin J. Neitz
Wild Horse Rustlers *43* Sam Newfield
Wild Horse Stampede, The *26* Albert S. Rogell
Wild Horse Stampede *43* Alvin J. Neitz
Wild Horse Valley *40* Ira Webb
Wild Horses *62* Kazimierz Kutz
Wild Horses *73* John Sturges
Wild Horses *84* Derek Morton
Wild in the Country *61* Philip Dunne
Wild in the Sky *71* William T. Naud
Wild in the Streets *68* Barry Shear
Wild Innocence *37* Ken Hall
Wild Is My Love *63* Richard Hilliard
Wild Is the Wind *57* George Cukor
Wild Jungle Captive *45* Harold Young
Wild Justice *25* Chester M. Franklin
Wild Life *18* Henry Otto
Wild Life, The *84* Art Linson
Wild Love *55* Mauro Bolognini
Wild Love-Makers *63* Koreyoshi Kurahara
Wild Man of Borneo, The *02* William Haggar
Wild Man of Borneo, The *41* Robert B. Sinclair
Wild McCullochs, The *75* Max Baer
Wild Men of Africa *20* Leonard J. Vandenberg
Wild Money *37* Louis King
Wild Mustang *35* Harry Fraser
Wild Night, A *15* Toby Cooper
Wild Night, A *20* Alfred Santell
Wild 90 *68* Norman Mailer
Wild North, The *51* Andrew Marton
Wild Oat, The *52* Henri Verneuil
Wild Oats *15* Harold Weston
Wild Oats *19* C. Jay Williams
Wild Oats Lane *26* Marshall Neilan
Wild on the Beach *65* Maury Dexter
Wild One, The *53* Laslo Benedek
Wild Ones on Wheels *61* Ray Dennis Steckler
Wild Oranges *24* King Vidor
Wild Orchid *90* Zalman King
Wild Orchids *28* Sidney Franklin
Wild Over You *53* Chuck Jones
Wild Pack, The *71* Hall Bartlett
Wild Pair, The *87* Beau Bridges
Wild Party, The *23* Herbert Blaché
Wild Party, The *29* Dorothy Arzner
Wild Party, The *56* Harry Horner
Wild Party, The *74* James Ivory
Wild Primrose *18* Frederick Thompson
Wild Racers, The *68* Daniel Haller
Wild Rebels, The *67* William Grefé
Wild Ride, A *13* Colin Campbell
Wild Ride, The *60* Harvey Berman
Wild Riders *71* Richard Kanter
Wild Rivals *27* William C. Nolan
Wild River *60* Elia Kazan
Wild Rose *40* Béla Balázs
Wild Rovers *71* Blake Edwards
Wild Scene, The *70* William Rowland
Wild Season *68* Emil Nofal
Wild Seed, The *64* Brian G. Hutton
Wild Shadows *68* Kokan Rakonjac
Wild Side, The *83* Penelope Spheeris
Wild Stallion *52* Lewis D. Collins

Wild Stallion *52* Albert Lamorisse
Wild Stampede *59* Raúl De Anda
Wild Strain, The *18* William Wolbert
Wild Strawberries *57* Ingmar Bergman
Wild Style *82* Charlie Ahearn
Wild Sumac *17* William V. Mong
Wild Team *86* Umberto Lenzi
Wild Thing *87* Max Reid
Wild to Go *26* Robert De Lacey
Wild Waves *25* Stephen Roberts
Wild Waves *29* Burton Gillett
Wild Waves and Angry Women *19* Raoul
  Barré, Charles Bowers
Wild Weed *49* Sam Newfield
Wild West, The *25* Robert F. Hill
Wild West *46* Robert E. Tansey
Wild West Days *37* Ford Beebe, Clifford
  Smith
Wild West Days *39* B. Reeves Eason
Wild West Romance *28* R. Lee Hough
Wild West Show, The *28* Del Andrews
Wild West Whoopee *31* Robert J. Horner
Wild Westerners, The *62* Oscar Rudolph
Wild Wheels *69* Kent Osborne
Wild Wife *54* Robert McKimson
Wild, Wild Planet *65* Antonio Margheriti
Wild, Wild Susan *25* A. Edward
  Sutherland
Wild, Wild Westers, The *11* H. Oceano
  Martinek
Wild, Wild Winter *66* Lennie Weinrib
Wild Wild Women, The *58* Renato
  Castellani
Wild Wild World *60* Robert McKimson
Wild Wind, The *86* Aleksandar Petković
Wild Winship's Widow *17* Charles Miller
Wild Women *18* John Ford
Wild Women of Wongo *59* James L.
  Wolcott
Wild World of Batwoman, The *66* Jerry
  Warren
Wild Youth *18* George Melford
Wild Youth *59* John Schreyer
Wildcat, The *17* Sherwood MacDonald
Wildcat, The *21* Ernst Lubitsch
Wildcat, The *26* Harry Fraser
Wildcat *42* Frank McDonald
Wildcat, The *53* Bert Haanstra
Wildcat *76* Don Taylor
Wildcat Bus *40* Frank Woodruff
Wildcat Jordan *22* Alfred Santell
Wildcat of Paris, The *18* Joseph De Grasse
Wildcat of Tucson, The *40* Lambert
  Hillyer
Wildcat Saunders *36* Harry Fraser
Wildcat Trooper *36* Elmer Clifton
Wildcat Valley *28* Charles Lamont
Wildcats *86* Michael Ritchie
Wildcats of St. Trinian's, The *80* Frank
  Launder
Wildcatter, The *37* Lewis D. Collins
Wilde Clown, Der *86* Josef Rödl
Wilde Mann, Der *88* Matthias Zschokke
Wilde Seison *68* Emil Nofal
Wildente, Die *76* Hans W. Geissendörfer
Wilderness, The *89* Ferenc András
Wilderness Family, Part 2 *78* Frank
  Zuniga
Wilderness Mail, The *14* Colin Campbell
Wilderness Mail *35* Forrest K. Sheldon

Wilderness Trail, The *19* Edward J. Le-
  Saint
Wilderness Woman, The *26* Howard
  Higgin
Wildest Dreams *87* Chuck Vincent
Wildfire *15* Edwin Middleton
Wildfire *25* T. Hayes Hunter
Wildfire *45* Robert E. Tansey
Wildfire *87* Zalman King
Wildfire: The Story of a Horse *45* Robert
  E. Tansey
Wildflower *14* Warwick Buckland
Wildflower *14* Allan Dwan
Wildflower of Gyimes *39* Ákos von
  Ráthonyi
Wildlife in Danger *64* Seth Holt
Wildness of Youth *22* Ivan Abramson
Wildrose *84* John Hanson
Wildschut *85* Bobby Eerhart
Wildwechsel *72* Rainer Werner Fassbinder
Wilfredo Lam *78* Humberto Solás
Wilful Maid, A *11* Lewin Fitzhamon
Wilful Peggy *10* D. W. Griffith
Wilful Youth *27* Dallas M. Fitzgerald
Wilhelm Pieck—Das Leben Unseres
  Präsidenten *51* Andrew Thorndike
Will, The *21* A. V. Bramble
Will, The *40* Kamel Salim
Will *68* Stan Vanderbeek
Will and a Way, A *22* H. Manning
  Haynes
Will Any Gentleman . . . ? *53* Michael
  Anderson
Will Evans Harnessing a Horse *13* Frank
  Wilson
Will Evans: On the Doorstep—
  Novelette—The Jockey *07* Arthur
  Gilbert
Will He Do It? *13* Edwin J. Collins
Will James' Sand *49* Louis King
Will o' the Wisp *63* Louis Malle
Will of Her Own, A *15* Maurice Elvey
Will of His Grace, The *19* Victor Sjöström
Will of James Waldron, The *12* Allan
  Dwan
Will of the People, The *17* A. E. Coleby
Will Penny *67* Tom Gries
Will Power *36* Arthur Ripley
Will Success Spoil Rock Hunter? *57* Frank
  Tashlin
Will the Express Overtake Them? *03* Joe
  Rosenthal
Will Tomorrow Ever Come? *46* Frank
  Borzage
Will You Be Staying for Supper? *19* Ken-
  neth Webb
Willard *70* Daniel Mann
Willi Tobler and the Decline of the 6th
  Fleet *70* Alexander Kluge
Willi Tobler und der Untergang der 6.
  Flotte *70* Alexander Kluge
William at the Circus *48* Val Guest
William Comes to Town *48* Val Guest
William Drake, Thief *12* Charles C.
  Calvert
William Fox Movietone Follies of 1929
  29 David Butler, Marcel Silver
William Hohenzollern Sausage Maker *19*
  Raoul Barré, Charles Bowers
William Tell *25* Emil Harder

William Tell *34* Walter Lantz
William Tell and the Clown *1898* Georges
  Méliès
William Webb Ellis Are You Mad? *71*
  Richard Taylor
Williamsburg: The Story of a Patriot *57*
  George Seaton
Willie and Joe Back at the Front *52*
  George Sherman
Willie and Joe in Tokyo *52* George
  Sherman
Willie and Phil *79* Paul Mazursky
Willie and Scratch *75* Robert J. Emery
Willie and the Mouse *41* George Sidney
Willie and Tim Get a Surprise *06* Alf
  Collins
Willie and Tim in the Motor Car *05* Percy
  Stow
Willie Becomes an Artist *12* Mack Sennett
Willie Dynamite *73* Gilbert Moses
Willie Goodchild Visits His Auntie *07*
  Walter R. Booth
Willie Minds the Dog *13* Mack Sennett
Willie the Kid *52* Robert Cannon
Willie's Disguise *14* Phillips Smalley
Willie's Dream *07* Frank Mottershaw
Willie's Dream of Mick Squinter *13* Dave
  Aylott
Willie's Great Scheme *13* Phillips Smalley
Willie's Magic Wand *07* Walter R. Booth
Willoughby's Magic Hat *43* Bob Wicker-
  sham
Willow *88* Ron Howard
Willow Tree, The *20* Henry Otto
Willow Tree in the Ginza, A *32* Heino-
  suke Gosho
Willows of Ginza *32* Heinosuke Gosho
Wills and Burke *85* Bob Weis
Willy *63* Allan A. Buckhantz
Willy McBean and His Magic Machine *65*
  Arthur Rankin, Jr.
Willy/Milly *85* Paul Schneider
Willy Reilly and His Colleen Bawn *18*
  John McDonagh
Willy Tobler and the Wreck of the 6th
  Fleet *70* Alexander Kluge
Willy Tobler und der Untergang der 6.
  Flotte *70* Alexander Kluge
Willy Wonka and the Chocolate Factory
  71 Mel Stuart
Willy Would A-Wooing Go *13* Charles C.
  Calvert
Wilmar 8, The *80* Lee Grant
Wilson *44* Henry King
Wilson and the Broom *13* Émile Cohl
Wilson and the Hats *13* Émile Cohl
Wilson and the Tariffs *13* Émile Cohl
Wilson or the Kaiser? *18* Charles Miller
Wilson Surrenders *15* W. C. Morris
Wilson's Row Row *13* Émile Cohl
Wilt *89* Michael Tuchner
Wilton's Zoo *39* Douglas Sirk
Wily Fiddler, The *07* Arthur Cooper
Wily Jap, The *15* Flohri
Wily Weasel, The *37* Walter Lantz
Wily William's Washing *13* Dave Aylott
Wim and Wigor *20* Wallace A. Carlson
Wimmin Hadn't Oughta Drive *40* Dave
  Fleischer
Wimmin Is a Myskery *40* Dave Fleischer

Wimps *86* Chuck Vincent
Win, Lose or Draw *25* Leo D. Maloney
Win, Place and Show *51* William Beaudine
Win, Place or Steal *75* Richard Bailey
Win That Girl *27* David Butler
Winchester '73 *50* Anthony Mann
Winchester Woman, The *19* Wesley Ruggles
Wind, The *27* Victor Sjöström
Wind, The *58* Alexander Alov, Vladimir Naumov
Wind, The *82* Souleymane Cissé
Wind, The *86* Nico Mastorakis
Wind Across the Everglades *58* Nicholas Ray
Wind and the Lion, The *75* John Milius
Wind and the River, The *51* Arne Sucksdorff
Wind Bloweth Where It Listeth, The *56* Robert Bresson
Wind Cannot Read, The *58* Ralph Thomas
Wind from the East *41* Abram Room
Wind from the East *69* Daniel Cohn-Bendit, Jean-Luc Godard, Jean-Pierre Gorin
Wind from the West, The *42* Arne Sucksdorff
Wind in the Face *29* Josef Heifits, Alexander Zarkhi
Wind Is My Lover, The *49* Christian-Jaque
Wind of Change, The *61* Vernon Sewell
Wind of Hate *58* M. Tsiforos
Wind of Honor *49* Kajiro Yamamoto
Wind of This World *28* Tomu Uchida
Windbag the Sailor *36* William Beaudine
Windblown Hare, The *49* Robert McKimson
Windbreaker, The *83* Pasquale Festa Campanile
Windfall *35* George King
Windfall *55* Henry Cass
Windfall in Athens *53* Michael Cacoyannis
Windflowers *67* Adolfas Mekas
Windflowers: The Story of a Draft Dodger *67* Adolfas Mekas
Winding Road, The *20* Bert Haldane, Frank Wilson
Winding Stair, The *25* John Griffith Wray
Winding Trail, The *18* John H. Collins
Winding Trail, The *21* George Martin
Windjammer, The *26* Harry Joe Brown
Windjammer, The *30* John Orton
Windjammer *37* Ewing Scott
Windjammer *58* Bill Colleran, Louis De Rochemont III
Windmill, The *37* Arthur Woods
Windmill in Barbados *30* Basil Wright
Windmill Revels *37* R. A. Hopwood
Windmills *40* Arthur Sánchez
Windmobile *77* James Broughton
Windom's Way *57* Ronald Neame
Window, The *49* Ted Tetzlaff
Window, The *65* Yoji Kuri
Window *76* Stan Brakhage
Window Cleaner, The *32* Anthony Asquith
Window Cleaner, The *69* Mike Leigh

Window Cleaners, The *19* Raoul Barré, Charles Bowers
Window Dummy, The *25* Lloyd Bacon
Window in London, A *39* Herbert Mason
Window in Piccadilly, A *28* Sidney Morgan
Window of America, The *52* Shih Hueh, Tso-lin Wang
Window Shopping *38* Sid Marcus
Window Shopping *88* Chantal Akerman
Window to Let, A *10* Percy Stow
Window to the Sky, A *74* Larry Peerce
Window Water Baby Moving *59* Stan Brakhage
Windows *75* Peter Greenaway
Windows *79* Gordon Willis
Windows of Time, The *69* Tamás Fejér
Windrider *86* Vincent Monton
Windrose, Die *56* Yannick Bellon, Alberto Cavalcanti, Sergei Gerasimov, Gillo Pontecorvo
Windrose, The *56* Yannick Bellon, Alberto Cavalcanti, Sergei Gerasimov, Gillo Pontecorvo
Winds of Autumn, The *76* Charles B. Pierce
Winds of Chance *25* Frank Lloyd
Winds of Change *78* Takashi
Winds of Fogo, The *70* Colin Low
Winds of the Pampas *27* Arthur Varney-Serrao
Winds of the Wasteland *36* Mack V. Wright
Windschaduw *86* Frans van de Staak
Windshade *86* Frans van de Staak
Windsor Castle *26* Maurice Elvey
Windsplitter, The *71* Julius D. Feigelson
Windstärke 9 *24* Reinhold Schünzel
Windwalker *80* Kieth Merrill
Windy *35* Harold S. Bucquet
Windy City *84* Armyan Bernstein
Windy Day *67* Faith Hubley, John Hubley
Windy Riley Goes to Hollywood *31* Roscoe Arbuckle
Wine *24* Louis Gasnier
Wine and the Music, The *70* Daniel Haller
Wine Cellar Burglars *02* Georges Méliès
Wine Girl, The *18* Harvey Gates, Stuart Paton
Wine of Life, The *24* Arthur H. Rooke
Wine of Youth *24* King Vidor
Wine, Women and Horses *37* Louis King
Wine, Women and Song *33* Herbert Brenon
Wine, Women, But No Song *31* Edward Buzzell
Wing and a Prayer *44* Henry Hathaway
Wing Beats in the Night *53* Kenne Fant
Wing to Wing *51* Cyril Frankel
Wing Toy *21* Howard Mitchell
Winged Devils *33* Roy William Neill
Winged Devils *70* Duccio Tessari
Winged Horse, The *32* Walter Lantz
Winged Horseman, The *29* B. Reeves Eason, Arthur Rosson
Winged Idol, The *15* Walter Edwards
Winged Mystery, The *17* Joseph De Grasse
Winged Serpent *77* Ed Hunt

Winged Serpent, The *82* Larry Cohen
Winged Victory *44* George Cukor
Wings, The *16* Mauritz Stiller
Wings *27* William A. Wellman
Wings *66* Larissa Shepitko
Wings and the Woman *42* Herbert Wilcox
Wings for the Eagle *42* Lloyd Bacon
Wings in the Dark *35* James Flood
Wings of a Serf *26* Leonid Leonidov, Yuri Tarich
Wings of Adventure *30* Richard Thorpe
Wings of Chance *61* Edward Dew
Wings of Danger *52* Terence Fisher
Wings of Death *61* Allan Davis
Wings of Death *85* Nicholas Bruce, Michael Coulson
Wings of Desire *87* Wim Wenders
Wings of Eagles, The *56* John Ford
Wings of Honneamise — Royal Space Force, The *87* Yoshiyuki Sadamoto
Wings of Mystery *62* Gilbert Gunn
Wings of Steel *41* B. Reeves Eason
Wings of the Apache *90* David Green
Wings of the Hawk *53* Budd Boetticher
Wings of the Morning *19* J. Gordon Edwards
Wings of the Morning *37* Harold Schuster
Wings of the Navy *38* Lloyd Bacon
Wings of the Storm *26* John G. Blystone
Wings of Victory *41* Mikhail Kalatozov
Wings of Youth *25* Emmett J. Flynn
Wings Over Africa *36* Ladislas Vajda
Wings Over Honolulu *37* H. C. Potter
Wings Over the Chaco *39* Christy Cabanne
Wings Over the Pacific *43* Phil Rosen
Wings Over Wyoming *37* Ewing Scott
Wingspan *87* Gennady Glagolev
Winifred the Shop Girl *16* George D. Baker
Winifred Wagner *75* Hans-Jürgen Syberberg
Winifred Wagner und die Geschichte des Hauses Wahnfried von 1914-1975 *75* Hans-Jürgen Syberberg
Wink of an Eye *58* Winston Jones
Winking Idol, The *26* Francis Ford
Win(k)some Widow, The *14* James Young
Winky Accused of an 'Orrible Crime *14* Cecil Birch
Winky and the Ants *14* Cecil Birch
Winky and the Cannibal Chief *14* Cecil Birch
Winky and the Gorgonzola Cheese *14* Cecil Birch
Winky and the Leopard *14* Cecil Birch
Winky As a Suffragette *14* Cecil Birch
Winky at the Front *14* Cecil Birch
Winky Becomes a Family Man *14* Cecil Birch
Winky, Bigamist *14* Cecil Birch
Winky Causes a Smallpox Panic *14* Cecil Birch
Winky Diddles the Hawker *14* Cecil Birch
Winky Dons the Petticoats *14* Cecil Birch
Winky Gets Puffed Up *14* Cecil Birch
Winky Gets Spotted *14* Cecil Birch
Winky Goes Camping *14* Cecil Birch
Winky Goes Spy Catching *14* Cecil Birch

Wise Old Elephant, A *13* Colin Campbell
Wise Owl *40* Ubbe Iwerks
Wise Quackers *49* Friz Freleng
Wise Quacking Duck, The *43* Robert Clampett
Wise Quacks *39* Robert Clampett
Wise Son, A *23* Phil Rosen
Wise Virgin, The *24* Lloyd Ingraham
Wise Wife, The *27* E. Mason Hopper
Wise Wimmin *29* Stephen Roberts
Wiser Age, The *62* Mikio Naruse
Wiser Sex, The *32* Berthold Viertel
Wish-Fulfillment, The *70* Mrinal Sen
Wish You Were Here *87* David Leland
Wishbone, The *33* Arthur Maude
Wishbone Cutter *78* Earl E. Smith
Wishes *34* Will P. Kellino
Wishing Duck, The *22* Raoul Barré, Charles Bowers
Wishing Machine *67* Josef Pinkava
Wishing Ring, The *14* Maurice Tourneur
Wishing Ring Man, The *19* David Smith
Wishing Seat, The *13* Allan Dwan
Wishing Tree, The *76* Tenghiz Abuladze
Wishing Well *54* Maurice Elvey
Wishwamitra *52* Pendharkar Babu Rao
Wisp o' the Woods *19* Lewis Willoughby
Wisselwachter, De *86* Jos Stelling
Wistful Widow, The *47* Charles Barton
Wistful Widow of Wagon Gap, The *47* Charles Barton
Wit Wins *20* Burton L. King
Witch, The *06* Georges Méliès
Witch, The *16* Frank Powell
Witch, The *52* Roland Af Hällström
Witch, The *54* Chano Urueta
Witch, The *66* Damiano Damiani
Witch, The *85* James Roberson
Witch and Warlock *64* Don Sharp
Witch Beneath the Sea, The *62* Zygmunt Sulistrowski
Witch Doctor *46* Thorold Dickinson
Witch Hunt, The *81* Anja Breien
Witch Hunt *87* Barbara A. Chobocky
Witch in Love, The *66* Damiano Damiani
Witch of Leányvár *39* Victor Gertler
Witch of Salem, The *13* Raymond B. West
Witch of the Range, The *11* Allan Dwan
Witch of the Welsh Mountains, The *12* Sidney Northcote
Witch Returns to Life, The *52* Roland Af Hällström
Witch Who Came from the Sea, The *76* Matt Cimber
Witch Without a Broom, A *67* José María Elorrieta
Witch Woman, The *18* Travers Vale
Witch Woman, The *20* Carl Theodor Dreyer
Witchboard *85* Kevin S. Tenney
Witchcraft *16* Frank Reicher
Witchcraft *59* William Hole, Jr.
Witchcraft *64* Don Sharp
Witchcraft Through the Ages *21* Benjamin Christensen
Witchery *89* Fabrizio Laurenti
Witches, The *66* Mauro Bolognini, Vittorio De Sica, Pier Paolo Pasolini, Franco Rossi, Luchino Visconti

Witches, The *66* Cyril Frankel
Witches, The *90* Nicolas Roeg
Witches' Brew *80* Richard Shorr, Herbert L. Strock
Witches' Mountain *70* Raúl Artigot
Witches of Eastwick, The *87* George Miller
Witches of Salem, The *57* Raymond Rouleau
Witches' Trial, The *69* Jesús Franco
Witches: Violated and Tortured to Death *72* Adrian Hoven
Witchfinder General *68* Michael Reeves
Witchfire *86* Vincent J. Privitera
Witchhammer *69* Otakar Vávra
Witching, The *72* Bert I. Gordon
Witching Hour, The *16* George Irving
Witching Hour, The *21* William Desmond Taylor
Witching Hour, The *34* Henry Hathaway
Witching Hour, The *85* Jaime De Armiñán
Witchkiller of Blackmoor, The *69* Jesús Franco
Witchmaker, The *69* William O. Brown
Witch's Cradle, The *61* Maya Deren
Witch's Curse, The *62* Riccardo Freda
Witch's Mirror, The *60* Chano Urueta
Witch's Revenge, The *03* Georges Méliès
Witch's Tangled Hare, A *59* Abe Levitow
With a Kodak *12* Mack Sennett
With a Smile *36* Maurice Tourneur
With a Song in My Heart *52* Walter Lang
With All Force *24* August Blom
With All Her Heart *20* Frank Wilson
With Beauty and Sorrow *65* Masahiro Shinoda
With Bridges Burned *15* Ashley Miller
With Broken Wings *40* Orestes Caviglia
With Davy Crockett at the Fall of the Alamo *26* Robert North Bradbury
With Dieric Bouts *75* André Delvaux
With Faith in God *34* Mihailo-Mika Popović
With Father's Help *22* Peggy Hyland
With Fire and Sword *61* Fernando Cerchio
With General Custer at Little Big Horn *26* Harry Fraser
With Gunilla Monday Evening and Tuesday *67* Lars Görling
With Her Card *09* D. W. Griffith
With Hercules to the Center of the Earth *61* Mario Bava
With Hoops of Steel *18* Eliot Howe
With Human Instinct *13* H. Oceano Martinek
With Joyous Heart *67* Serge Bourguignon
With Kit Carson Over the Great Divide *25* Frank S. Mattison
With Lee in Virginia *12* Thomas Ince
With Love and Kisses *36* Leslie Goodwins
With Love and Tenderness *78* Rangel Vulchanov
With Love from Truman *66* Albert Maysles, David Maysles
With Love from Truman: A Visit with Truman Capote *66* Albert Maysles, David Maysles
With Love in Mind *70* Robin Cecil-Wright

With Love to the Person Next to Me *87* Brian McKenzie
With Neatness and Dispatch *18* Will S. Davis
With Poopdeck Pappy *40* Dave Fleischer
With Sitting Bull at the Spirit Lake Massacre *27* Robert North Bradbury
With Six You Get Eggroll *68* Howard Morris
With the Aid of a Rogue *27* J. H. Payne
With the Best Intentions *11* Stuart Kinder
With the Enemy's Help *12* D. W. Griffith
With the French Army in Vosges *16* Geoffrey H. Malins
With the Halo Askew *57* Hasse Ekman
With These Hands *50* Jack Arnold
With These Hands *71* Don Chaffey
With This Ring *25* Fred Windermere
With Williamson Beneath the Sea *32* J. Ernest Williamson
With You in My Arms *40* Hasse Ekman
Within an Ace *09* Theo Bouwmeester
Within Memory *81* Claude Lelouch
Within Our Gates *20* Oscar Micheaux
Within Prison Walls *21* Sidney Olcott
Within the Cup *18* Raymond B. West
Within the Law *17* William P. S. Earle
Within the Law *23* Frank Lloyd
Within the Law *30* Sam Wood
Within the Law *39* Gustav Machatý
Within These Walls *45* H. Bruce Humberstone
Withnail & I *87* Bruce Robinson
Without a Clue *88* Thom Eberhardt
Without a Country *14* Forest Holger-Madsen
Without a Home *39* Alexander Marten
Without a Soul *14* James Young
Without a Trace *68* Péter Bacsó
Without a Trace *83* Stanley Jaffe
Without Anesthesia *78* Andrzej Wajda
Without Anesthetic *78* Andrzej Wajda
Without Anesthetics *78* Andrzej Wajda
Without Apparent Motive *71* Philippe Labro
Without Benefit of Clergy *21* James Young
Without Children *36* William Nigh
Without Coal *20* Vernon Stallings
Without Compromise *22* Emmett J. Flynn
Without Dowry *36* Yakov Protazanov
Without Each Other *62* Saul Swimmer
Without Fear *22* Kenneth Webb
Without Fear or Reproach *63* Alexander Mitta
Without Her Father's Consent *10* Lewin Fitzhamon
Without Honor *17* E. Mason Hopper
Without Honor *49* Irving Pichel
Without Honors *32* William Nigh
Without Hope *14* Fred Mace
Without Limit *21* George D. Baker
Without Love *45* Harold S. Bucquet
Without Mercy *25* George Melford
Without Orders *26* Leo D. Maloney
Without Orders *36* Lew Landers
Without Pity *47* Alberto Lattuada
Without Regret *35* Harold Young
Without Reservations *46* Mervyn LeRoy
Without Return *87* Vasily Brescanu

Without Risk *51* Fred F. Sears
Without Scruples *86* Tonino Valerii
Without the Option *26* Charles Barnett
Without Warning *24* Irvin Willat
Without Warning *52* Arnold Laven
Without Warning *80* Greydon Clark
Without Witnesses *83* Nikita Mikhalkov
Without You *34* John Daumery
Without You *87* Franz-Josef Gottlieb
Without You, I'm Nothing *90* John Boskovich
Witness, The *45* Pietro Germi
Witness, The *59* Geoffrey Muller
Witness, The *68* Péter Bacsó
Witness *85* Peter Weir
Witness Chair, The *36* George Nicholls, Jr.
Witness for the Defense, The *19* George Fitzmaurice
Witness for the Prosecution *57* Billy Wilder
Witness in the City *58* Édouard Molinaro
Witness in the Dark *59* Wolf Rilla
Witness Out of Hell *67* Zita Mitrović
Witness Seat, The *64* Satsuo Yamamoto
Witness to a Killing *87* Chandran Rutnam
Witness to Murder *54* Roy Rowland
Witness Vanishes, The *39* Otis Garrett
Witnesses, The *61* Frédéric Rossif
Witnesses *88* Martyn Burke
Wit's End *71* Joel M. Reed
Wits vs. Wits *20* Harry Grossman
Wives *75* Anja Breien
Wives and Lovers *63* John Rich
Wives and Other Wives *18* Lloyd Ingraham
Wives at Auction *26* Elmer Clifton
Wives Beware *32* Fred Niblo
Wives Never Know *36* Elliott Nugent
Wives of Jamestown, The *13* Sidney Olcott
Wives of Men *18* John M. Stahl
Wives of the Prophet, The *26* J. A. Fitzgerald
Wives—Ten Years After *85* Anja Breien
Wives Under Suspicion *38* James Whale
Wives Won't Weaken *28* Stephen Roberts
Wiz, The *78* Sidney Lumet
Wizard, The *27* Richard Rosson
Wizard, The *64* Alfred Vohrer
Wizard, The *89* Todd Holland
Wizard and the Brigands, The *11* Walter R. Booth, Theo Bouwmeester
Wizard of Ants, The *41* Dave Fleischer
Wizard of Bagdad, The *60* George Sherman
Wizard of Gore, The *68* Herschell Gordon Lewis
Wizard of Loneliness, The *88* Jenny Bowen
Wizard of Mars *64* David L. Hewitt
Wizard of Oz, The *25* Larry Semon
Wizard of Oz, The *38* Victor Fleming, King Vidor
Wizard of Speed and Time, The *88* Mike Jittlov
Wizard of the Saddle *27* Frank Howard Clark
Wizard, the Prince and the Good Fairy, The *00* Georges Méliès

Wizards *77* Ralph Bakshi
Wizards of the Lost Kingdom *85* Héctor Olivera
Wizard's Walking Stick, The *09* Walter R. Booth
Wo Che-Yang Kuo-Le Yi-Sheng *86* Yi Zhang
Wo die Grünen Ameisen Träumen *84* Werner Herzog
Wo Erh Han-Sheng *86* Yi Zhang
Wo Ist Mein Schatz? *16* Ernst Lubitsch
Wo-Te Ai *88* Yi Zhang
Wochenende *28* Walter Ruttmann
Woe Oh Ho No *71* Ed Emshwiller
Woes of a Married Man, The *07* Arthur Cooper
Woes of Roller Skates, The *08* Georges Méliès
Wogen des Schicksals *18* Joe May
Wohin? *88* Herbert Achternbusch
Wohin mit Willfried? *86* Dieter Koster
Wojna Światów—Nastepne Stulecie *81* Piotr Szulkin
Wold-Shadow, The *72* Stan Brakhage
Wolf, The *14* Barry O'Neil
Wolf, The *16* Michael Curtiz
Wolf, The *19* James Young
Wolf and His Mate, The *17* Edward J. LeSaint
Wolf and the Waif, The *12* Fred Rains
Wolf, Are You There? *83* Eric Rohmer
Wolf at the Door, The *32* Dick Huemer
Wolf at the Door, The *86* Henning Carlsen
Wolf Blood *25* George Chesebro
Wolf Call *39* George Waggner
Wolf Chalet *86* Věra Chytilová
Wolf Chases Pig *42* Frank Tashlin
Wolf Cubs *83* Joe Sarno
Wolf Dog, The *33* Colbert Clark, Harry Fraser
Wolf Dog *58* Sam Newfield
Wolf Fangs *27* Lewis Seiler
Wolf Forest, The *68* Pedro Olea
Wolf Hounded *59* Joseph Barbera, William Hanna
Wolf Hunters, The *26* Stuart Paton
Wolf Hunters, The *49* Budd Boetticher
Wolf in Cheap Clothing, The *32* Edward Buzzell
Wolf in Sheep Dog's Clothing *63* Joseph Barbera, William Hanna
Wolf Lake *78* Burt Kennedy
Wolf Larsen *58* Harmon Jones
Wolf Larsen *74* Giuseppe Vari
Wolf Law *22* Stuart Paton
Wolf Lowry *17* William S. Hart
Wolf Man, The *24* Edmund Mortimer
Wolf Man, The *41* George Waggner
Wolf Man, The *76* Salvatore Di Silvestro
Wolf of Debt, The *15* John Harvey
Wolf of New York *40* William McGann
Wolf of Wall Street, The *29* Rowland V. Lee
Wolf Pack *22* William James Craft
Wolf Riders *35* Harry S. Webb
Wolf Song *29* Victor Fleming
Wolf Trap *57* Jiří Weiss
Wolf! Wolf! *34* Walter Lantz
Wolf Woman, The *16* Walter Edwards,

Raymond B. West, Irvin Willat
Wolfe, or The Conquest of Quebec *14* Sidney Olcott
Wolfen *81* Michael Wadleigh
Wölfin von Teufelsmoor, Die *78* Helmut Pfandler
Wolfman, The *61* Terence Fisher
Wolfman *79* Worth Keeter
Wolfman of Count Dracula, The *67* Enrique L. Equiluz
Wolfman of Galicia, The *68* Pedro Olea
Wolfpack *56* Georg Tressler
Wolfpack *70* Lamont Johnson
Wolfpen Principle, The *74* Jack Darcus
Wolf's Chalet *86* Věra Chytilová
Wolf's Clothing *27* Roy Del Ruth
Wolf's Clothing *36* Andrew Marton
Wolf's Fangs, The *22* Oscar Apfel
Wolf's Fangs, The *27* Lewis Seiler
Wolf's Forest, The *68* Pedro Olea
Wolf's Hole *86* Věra Chytilová
Wolf's Lair *86* Věra Chytilová
Wolf's Trail *27* Francis Ford
Wolfshead—The Legend of Robin Hood *69* John Hough
Wolga-Wolga *28* Victor Tourjansky
Wolnyoui Han *80* In Soo Kim
Wolo Czarwienko *16* Mauritz Stiller
Wolo, Wolo *16* Mauritz Stiller
Wolverine, The *21* William Bertram
Wolves *30* Albert De Courville
Wolves *55* Kaneto Shindo
Wolves, The *72* Hideo Gosha
Wolves of Society *15* Frank Lloyd
Wolves of the Air *27* Francis Ford
Wolves of the Border *18* Clifford Smith
Wolves of the Border *23* Alvin J. Neitz
Wolves of the City *29* Leigh Jason
Wolves of the Deep *59* Silvio Amadio
Wolves of the Desert *26* Ben F. Wilson
Wolves of the Night *19* J. Gordon Edwards
Wolves of the North *21* Norman Dawn
Wolves of the North *24* William Duncan
Wolves of the Rail *18* William S. Hart
Wolves of the Range *43* Sam Newfield
Wolves of the Road *25* Ward Hayes
Wolves of the Sea *38* Elmer Clifton
Wolves of the Street *20* Otis B. Thayer
Wolves of the Underworld *33* George A. Cooper
Woman, A *15* Charles Chaplin
Woman, The *15* George Melford
Woman *18* Maurice Tourneur
Woman *39* Ramjankhan Mehboobkhan
Woman *43* Marcello Pagliero, Roberto Rossellini
Woman *48* Keisuke Kinoshita
Woman *48* Marcel Pagnol, Jean Renoir, Roberto Rossellini
Woman *62* Rajaram Vanakudre Shantaram
Woman, a Man, a City, A *78* Manuel Octavio Gómez
Woman Accused *33* Paul Sloane
Woman Against the World, A *28* George Archainbaud
Woman Against the World *38* David Selman
Woman Against Woman *14* Travers Vale

Woman Against Woman *38* Robert B. Sinclair

Woman Alone, A *17* Harry Davenport

Woman Alone, A *36* Eugene Frenke

Woman Alone, A *36* Alfred Hitchcock

Woman Always Pays, The *11* Urban Gad

Woman and Bean Soup *68* Heinosuke Gosho

Woman and Officer 26, The *20* Bert Haldane, Harry Lorraine

Woman and the Beast, The *17* Ernest C. Warde

Woman and the Hunter, The *57* George Breakston

Woman and the Law, The *18* Raoul Walsh

Woman and the Pirates, The *59* Daisuke Ito

Woman and the Puppet, The *20* Reginald Barker

Woman and the Puppet, The *58* Julien Duvivier

Woman and Wife *18* Edward José

Woman and Wine *15* Arthur Shirley

Woman at Her Window, A *76* Pierre Granier-Deferre

Woman at the Helm *62* Imre Fehér

Woman Bait *57* Jean Delannoy

Woman Barber *1898* George Albert Smith

Woman Basketball Player No. 5 *57* Jin Xie

Woman Behind Everything *51* Erik Faustman

Woman Beneath, The *17* Travers Vale

Woman Between, The *31* Miles Mander

Woman Between, The *31* Victor Schertzinger

Woman Between, The *37* Anatole Litvak

Woman Between Friends, The *18* Tom Terriss

Woman Chases Man *37* John G. Blystone

Woman Commands, A *32* Paul Stein

Woman Condemned *34* Dorothy Davenport

Woman Conquers, The *22* Tom Forman

Woman Decides, The *31* Miles Mander

Woman Demon Human *90* Shuquin Huang

Woman Destroyed, A *47* Stuart Heisler

Woman Disappeared, A *39* Jacques Feyder

Woman Disputed, The *28* Henry King, Sam Taylor

Woman Doctor *39* Sidney Salkow

Woman Don't Make Your Name Dirty *30* Heinosuke Gosho

Woman Eater, The *57* Charles Saunders

Woman Eternal, The *18* Ralph Ince

Woman Flambée, A *82* Robert Van Ackeren

Woman for All Men, A *75* Arthur Marks

Woman for Charley, A *70* Anton Leader

Woman for Joe, The *55* George More O'Ferrall

Woman from China, The *30* Edward Dryhurst

Woman from Headquarters *50* George Blair

Woman from Hell, The *29* A. F. Erickson

Woman from Mellon's, The *09* D. W. Griffith

Woman from Monte Carlo, The *31* Michael Curtiz

Woman from Moscow, The *28* Ludwig Berger

Woman from Nowhere, The *22* Louis Delluc

Woman from Tangier, The *48* Harold Daniels

Woman from the Mountain, The *43* Renato Castellani

Woman from the Property-Owning Middle Class, Born 1908, A *72* Alexander Kluge

Woman from the Provinces, The *85* Andrzej Baranski

Woman from Warren's, The *15* Tod Browning

Woman from Warsaw, The *56* Mikhail Kalatozov

Woman Game, The *20* William P. S. Earle

Woman Gives, The *20* Roy William Neill

Woman God Changed, The *21* Robert Vignola

Woman God Forgot, The *17* Cecil B. DeMille

Woman God Sent, The *20* Lawrence Trimble

Woman Hater, The *20* Sidney Goldin

Woman Hater, The *25* James Flood

Woman Hater *48* Terence Young

Woman Haters, The *13* Henry Lehrman

Woman He Chose, The *17* Victor Sjöström

Woman He Loved, The *22* Edward Sloman

Woman He Married, The *22* Fred Niblo

Woman He Scorned, The *29* Paul Czinner

Woman Hungry *31* Clarence Badger

Woman Hunt *49* Julien Duvivier

Woman Hunt *72* Eddie Romero

Woman I Love, The *29* George Melford

Woman I Love, The *37* Anatole Litvak

Woman I Stole, The *33* Irving Cummings

Woman in a Dressing Gown *57* J. Lee-Thompson

Woman in a Twilight Garden *79* André Delvaux

Woman in Black, The *12* Christy Cabanne

Woman in Black, The *14* Lawrence Marston

Woman in Black *58* Arne Mattsson

Woman in Bondage *32* Basil Dean

Woman in Brown, The *48* W. Lee Wilder

Woman in Chains, The *23* William P. Burt

Woman in Chains *32* Basil Dean

Woman in Chains *68* Henri-Georges Clouzot

Woman in Command, The *33* Maurice Elvey

Woman in Distress *37* Lynn Shores

Woman in Flames, A *82* Robert Van Ackeren

Woman in 47, The *16* George Irving

Woman in Green, The *45* Roy William Neill

Woman in Her Thirties, A *34* Alfred E. Green

Woman in Hiding *49* Michael Gordon

Woman in Hiding *53* Terence Fisher

Woman in His House, The *20* John M. Stahl

Woman in His House, The *32* George Cukor, Edward H. Griffith

Woman in July, A *62* Franklin J. Schaffner

Woman in Pawn, A *27* Edwin Greenwood, Victor Saville

Woman in Politics, The *16* W. Eugene Moore

Woman in Question, The *50* Anthony Asquith

Woman in Red, The *34* Robert Florey

Woman in Red, The *84* Gene Wilder

Woman in Room 13, The *20* Frank Lloyd

Woman in Room 13, The *32* Henry King

Woman in the Case, A *11* A. E. Coleby

Woman in the Case, A *16* Hugh Ford

Woman in the Case, The *35* William Nigh

Woman in the Case *45* William Nigh

Woman in the Dark *34* Phil Rosen

Woman in the Dark *52* George Blair

Woman in the Dunes *63* Hiroshi Teshigahara

Woman in the Hall, The *47* Jack Lee

Woman in the Moon, The *28* Fritz Lang

Woman in the Night, A *27* Edwin Greenwood, Victor Saville

Woman in the Night *48* William Rowland

Woman in the Painting, The *55* Franco Rossi

Woman in the Rain *76* Paul Hunt

Woman in the Rumor, The *54* Kenji Mizoguchi

Woman in the Suitcase, The *19* Fred Niblo

Woman in the Ultimate, A *13* D. W. Griffith

Woman in the Window, The *44* Fritz Lang

Woman in the Window *60* Luciano Emmer

Woman in White, The *17* Ernest C. Warde

Woman in White, The *29* Herbert Wilcox

Woman in White, The *48* Peter Godfrey

Woman in White *49* Arne Mattsson

Woman in White, A *65* Claude Autant-Lara

Woman Inside, The *81* Joseph Van Winkle

Woman Is a Flower *65* Jan Lenica

Woman Is a Woman, A *60* Jean-Luc Godard

Woman Is the Judge, A *39* Nick Grindé

Woman Juror, The *26* Milton Rosmer

Woman Like Satan, A *58* Julien Duvivier

Woman Michael Married, The *19* Henry Kolker

Woman Misunderstood, A *21* Fred Paul, Jack Raymond

Woman Must Be Afraid of Man, A *65* George Tzavellas

Woman Named En, A *71* Tadashi Imai

Woman Next Door, The *19* Robert Vignola

Woman Next Door, The *81* François Truffaut

Woman Obsessed *59* Henry Hathaway
Woman Obsessed, A *89* Larry Vincent
Woman of a Misty Moonlight, A *36* Heinosuke Gosho
Woman of a Pale Night *36* Heinosuke Gosho
Woman of Affairs, A *28* Clarence Brown
Woman of Antwerp *47* Yves Allégret
Woman of Atlantis *21* Jacques Feyder
Woman of Bronze, The *23* King Vidor
Woman of Darkness *66* Arne Mattsson
Woman of Distinction, A *50* Edward Buzzell
Woman of Dolwyn *49* Emlyn Williams
Woman of Experience, A *31* Harry Joe Brown
Woman of His Dream, The *21* Harold M. Shaw
Woman of Impulse, A *18* Edward José
Woman of Lies *19* Gilbert P. Hamilton
Woman of Marvels, The *85* Alberto Bevilacqua
Woman of Mona Diggins, The *15* Robert Z. Leonard
Woman of Musashino *51* Kenji Mizoguchi
Woman of My Life, The *86* Régis Wargnier
Woman of Mystery, The *14* Alice Guy-Blaché
Woman of Mystery, A *57* Ernest Morris
Woman of Naniwa *40* Kenji Mizoguchi
Woman of No Importance, A *21* Denison Clift
Woman of Osaka *40* Kenji Mizoguchi
Woman of Osaka, A *58* Teinosuke Kinugasa
Woman of Pale Night *36* Heinosuke Gosho
Woman of Paris, A *23* Charles Chaplin
Woman of Pleasure, A *19* Wallace Worsley
Woman of Pleasure *24* Kenji Mizoguchi
Woman of Redemption, A *18* Travers Vale
Woman of Rome *54* Luigi Zampa
Woman of Rumour, A *54* Kenji Mizoguchi
Woman of Sin *61* Guy Lefranc
Woman of Straw *63* Basil Dearden
Woman of Summer *62* Franklin J. Schaffner
Woman of the Dunes *63* Hiroshi Teshigahara
Woman of the Ganges *73* Marguerite Duras
Woman of the Index, The *19* Hobart Henley
Woman of the Iron Bracelets, The *20* Sidney Morgan
Woman of the Lake *66* Yoshishige Yoshida
Woman of the Mist *36* Heinosuke Gosho
Woman of the North Country *52* Joseph Kane
Woman of the Osore Mountains, A *64* Heinosuke Gosho
Woman of the River *54* Mario Soldati
Woman of the Rumor, The *54* Kenji Mizoguchi
Woman of the Sea, A *26* Charles Chap-

lin, Josef von Sternberg
Woman of the Sleeping Forest, The *29* Georgy Vasiliev, Sergei Vasiliev
Woman of the Snow *68* Tokuzo Tanaka
Woman of the Town, The *43* George Archainbaud
Woman of the World, A *25* Malcolm St. Clair
Woman of the World, A *34* Robert Z. Leonard
Woman of the Year *41* George Stevens
Woman of Tokyo *33* Yasujiro Ozu
Woman of Tomorrow *14* Pyotr Chardynin
Woman on Fire, A *70* Fernando Di Leo
Woman on Her Own *81* Agnieszka Holland
Woman on Pier 13, The *49* Robert Stevenson
Woman on the Beach, The *46* Jean Renoir
Woman on the Jury, The *24* Harry Hoyt
Woman on the Moon, The *28* Fritz Lang
Woman on the Run *50* Norman Foster
Woman on Trial, The *27* Mauritz Stiller
Woman or Two, A *85* Daniel Vigne
Woman Pays, The *15* Ethyle Batley
Woman Pays, The *15* Edgar Jones
Woman Possessed, A *58* Max Varnel
Woman-Proof *23* Alfred E. Green
Woman Pursued *31* Richard Boleslawski
Woman Racket, The *29* Albert Kelley, Robert Ober
Woman Racket *37* Robert Siodmak
Woman Rebels, A *36* Mark Sandrich
Woman Redeemed, A *27* Sinclair Hill
Woman Scorned, A *10* Lewin Fitzhamon
Woman Scorned, A *11* D. W. Griffith
Woman Supreme *06* Harold Jeapes
Woman Supreme *06* J. H. Martin
Woman Tamer *35* Tay Garnett
Woman Tempted, The *26* Maurice Elvey
Woman Tempted Me, The *15* Forest Holger-Madsen
Woman That Night, The *34* Yasujiro Shimazu
Woman the Flower *65* Jan Lenica
Woman the Germans Shot, The *18* John G. Adolfi
Woman There Was, A *19* J. Gordon Edwards
Woman They Almost Lynched, The *53* Allan Dwan
Woman Thou Gavest Me, The *19* Hugh Ford
Woman Times Seven *67* Vittorio De Sica
Woman to Be Hanged, A *86* Başar Sabuncu
Woman to Discover, A *87* Riccardo Sesani
Woman to Woman *23* Graham Cutts
Woman to Woman *29* Victor Saville
Woman to Woman *46* Maclean Rogers
Woman to Woman *87* Mauricio Walerstein
Woman Trap *29* William A. Wellman
Woman Trap *36* Harold Young
Woman Trouble *48* Mario Camerini
Woman Unafraid *34* William Cowen
Woman Under Cover, The *19* George Siegmann
Woman Under Oath *19* John M. Stahl
Woman Under the Influence, A *74* John

Cassavetes
Woman Untamed, The *20* John H. Pratt
Woman Upstairs, The *21* Fred Paul
Woman Vampire, The *59* Nobuo Nakagawa
Woman vs. Woman *10* Bert Haldane
Woman, Wake Up! *21* Marcus Harrison, King Vidor
Woman Walks the Earth Alone, A *53* Fumio Kamei
Woman Wanted *35* George B. Seitz
Woman Who Believed, The *22* John Harvey
Woman Who Came Back, The *45* Walter Colmes
Woman Who Dared, The *15* Thomas Bentley
Woman Who Dared, The *16* George E. Middleton
Woman Who Dared, The *43* Jean Grémillon
Woman Who Did, The *15* Walter West
Woman Who Did, The *24* Benjamin Christensen
Woman Who Did Not Care, The *27* Phil Rosen
Woman Who Followed Me, The *16* Robert Z. Leonard
Woman Who Fooled Herself, The *22* Robert Ellis, Charles Logue
Woman Who Gave, The *18* Kenean Buel
Woman Who Invented Love, The *18* Vyacheslav Viskovsky
Woman Who Killed a Vulture, The *21* E. A. Dupont
Woman Who Obeyed, The *23* Sidney Morgan
Woman Who Sinned, A *25* Finis Fox
Woman Who Touched Legs, The *52* Kon Ichikawa
Woman Who Touched the Legs, The *26* Yutaka Abe
Woman Who Touched the Legs, The *52* Kon Ichikawa
Woman Who Understood, A *20* William Parke
Woman Who Walked Alone, The *22* George Melford
Woman Who Was Forgotten, The *30* Richard Thomas
Woman Who Was Nothing, The *17* Maurice Elvey
Woman Who Wasn't, The *08* Alf Collins
Woman Who Wouldn't Die, The *64* Gordon Hessler
Woman Who Wouldn't Marry, A *87* Hideo Gosha
Woman Wins, The *18* Frank Wilson
Woman Wise *28* Albert Ray
Woman-Wise *37* Allan Dwan
Woman with a Dagger *16* Yakov Protazanov
Woman with a Whip *57* Samuel Fuller
Woman with Four Faces, The *23* Herbert Brenon
Woman with No Name, The *50* George More O'Ferrall, Ladislas Vajda
Woman with Red Boots, The *74* Juan Buñuel
Woman with the Fan, The *21* René Plaissetty

Woman Without a Face *47* Gustaf Molander

Woman Without a Face *65* Delbert Mann

Woman Without a Soul, The *15* Charles H. Weston

Woman Without Camellias, The *53* Michelangelo Antonioni

Woman Without Love, A *51* Luis Buñuel

Woman Without Name, A *86* Luigi Russo

Woman, Woman *19* Kenean Buel

Womaneater *57* Charles Saunders

Womanhandled *25* Gregory La Cava

Womanhood *17* J. Stuart Blackton, William P. S. Earle

Womanhood *34* Harry Hughes

Womanhunt *61* Maury Dexter

Womanlight *79* Costa-Gavras

Womanpower *26* Harry Beaumont

Woman's Angle, The *52* Leslie Arliss

Woman's Awakening, A *17* Chester Withey

Woman's Business, A *20* B. A. Rolfe

Woman's Daring, A *16* Edward Sloman

Woman's Day *87* Branko Baletić

Woman's Decision, A *74* Krzysztof Zanussi

Woman's Decoration *60* Kozaburo Yoshimura

Woman's Descent *60* Kozaburo Yoshimura

Woman's Destiny, A *52* Slatan Dudow

Woman's Devotion, A *56* Paul Henreid

Woman's Experience, A *18* Perry N. Vekroff

Woman's Eyes, A *16* George Marshall*

Woman's Face, A *37* Gustaf Molander

Woman's Face, A *41* George Cukor

Woman's Face, A *49* Tadashi Imai

Woman's Faith, A *25* Edward Laemmle

Woman's Fight, A *16* Herbert Blaché

Woman's Folly, A *10* Theo Bouwmeester

Woman's Folly, A *10* Wilfred Noy

Woman's Fool, A *18* John Ford

Woman's Hate, A *13* Ernest G. Batley

Woman's Heart, A *26* Phil Rosen

Woman's Heresy, A *24* Teinosuke Kinugasa

Woman's Honor *13* Allan Dwan

Woman's Honor, A *16* Roland West

Woman's Law, The *16* Lawrence McGill

Woman's Law *27* Dallas M. Fitzgerald

Woman's Life, A *49* Fumio Kamei

Woman's Life, A *53* Kaneto Shindo

Woman's Life, A *63* Mikio Naruse

Woman's Love, A *53* Jean Grémillon

Woman's Man *20* Warren Gordon

Woman's Man, A *34* Edward Ludwig

Woman's Pale Blue Handwriting, A *84* Axel Corti

Woman's Paradise *39* Arthur Maria Rabenalt

Woman's Past, A *15* Frank Powell

Woman's Past, A *15* Anders Wilhelm Sandberg

Woman's Place *21* Victor Fleming

Woman's Place, A *62* Mikio Naruse

Woman's Power, A *16* Robert Thornby

Woman's Privilege, A *62* Anthony Bushell

Woman's Privilege in Leap Year *12* Dave Aylott

Woman's Resurrection, A *15* J. Gordon Edwards

Woman's Revenge, A *39* Sam Nelson

Woman's Sacrifice, A *06* Tom Green

Woman's Sacrifice, A *22* Webster Campbell

Woman's Secret, A *22* Graham Cutts

Woman's Secret, A *24* Herbert Wilcox

Woman's Secret, A *48* Nicholas Ray

Woman's Side, The *22* John A. Barry

Woman's Sorrows, A *37* Mikio Naruse

Woman's Status *62* Mikio Naruse

Woman's Story, A *63* Mikio Naruse

Woman's Temptation, A *59* Godfrey Grayson

Woman's Testament, A *59* Kon Ichikawa, Yasuzo Masumura, Kozaburo Yoshimura

Woman's Treachery, A *10* Theo Bouwmeester

Woman's Triumph, A *14* J. Searle Dawley

Woman's Vanity, A *09* Theo Bouwmeester

Woman's Vengeance, A *39* Sam Nelson

Woman's Vengeance, A *47* Zoltán Korda

Woman's Way, A *08* D. W. Griffith

Woman's Way, A *16* Barry O'Neil

Woman's Way, A *28* Edmund Mortimer

Woman's Weal, Woman's Woe *31* Grigori Alexandrov

Woman's Weapons *18* Robert Vignola

Woman's Wit, A *12* Warwick Buckland

Woman's Wit *16* Joseph M. Kerrigan

Woman's Woman, A *22* Charles Giblyn

Woman's World *32* Yefim Dzigan

Woman's World *54* Jean Negulesco

Woman's Youth, A *56* Salah Abu Saif

Womantrap *37* Lynn Shores

Wombling Free *77* Lionel Jeffries

Women, The *39* George Cukor

Women, The *69* Harvey Cort

Women, The *73* Stan Brakhage

Women *76* Márta Mészáros

Women *85* Stanley Kwan

Women and Bloody Terror *70* Joy Houck, Jr.

Women and Diamonds *24* F. Martin Thornton

Women and Gold *24* James P. Hogan

Women and Miso Soup *68* Heinosuke Gosho

Women and Roses *14* Wallace Reid

Women and War *13* Allan Dwan

Women and War *61* Georges Lautner

Women Are Dangerous *33* Richard Thorpe

Women Are Like That *38* Stanley Logan

Women Are Like That *60* Bernard Borderie

Women Are Strong *24* Kenji Mizoguchi

Women Are Trouble *36* Errol Taggart

Women Are Weak *59* Michel Boisrond

Women Aren't Angels *42* Lawrence Huntington

Women at War *43* Len Lye, Jean Negulesco

Women Defend the Home! *39* Kozaburo Yoshimura

Women Do Not Shame Your Names *30* Heinosuke Gosho

Women Everywhere *30* Alexander Korda

Women First *24* B. Reeves Eason

Women for Sale *75* Ernest Farmer

Women from Headquarters *50* George Blair

Women Go On Forever *31* Walter Lang

Women in Bondage *43* Steve Sekely

Women in Cages *72* Gerry De Leon, Cirio Santiago

Women in Cell Block 7 *77* Salvatore Di Silvestro

Women in Chains, The *23* William P. Burt

Women in Hiding *40* Joseph M. Newman

Women in His Life, The *33* George B. Seitz

Women in Limbo *72* Mark Robson

Women in Love *69* Ken Russell

Women in New York *77* Rainer Werner Fassbinder

Women in Prison *33* Howard Bretherton, William Keighley

Women in Prison *37* Lambert Hillyer

Women in Prison *43* Olof Molander

Women in Prison *57* Seiji Hisamatsu

Women in Revolt *71* Paul Morrissey, Andy Warhol

Women in the Night *48* William Rowland

Women in the Spinnery *71* Márta Mészáros

Women in the Wind *39* John Farrow

Women in Twilight *79* André Delvaux

Women in War *40* John H. Auer

Women in War *61* Georges Lautner

Women Left Alone *13* Allan Dwan

Women Love Diamonds *27* Edmund Goulding

Women Love Once *31* Edward Goodman

Women Men Forget *20* John M. Stahl

Women Men Love *21* Samuel Bradley

Women Men Marry *22* Edward Dillon

Women Men Marry *31* Charles Hutchinson

Women Men Marry, The *37* Errol Taggart

Women Must Dress *35* Reginald Barker

Women of All Nations *31* Raoul Walsh

Women of Bloody Terror *70* Joy Houck, Jr.

Women of Desire *68* Vincent L. Sinclair

Women of Devil's Island *61* Domenico Paolella

Women of Doom *71* Rafael Moreno Alba

Women of Fire, The *03* Georges Méliès

Women of Glamour *37* Gordon Wiles

Women of Kyoto *60* Kozaburo Yoshimura

Women of Nazi Germany *61* Stuart Heisler

Women of Niskavuori *38* Valentin Vaala

Women of Paris *27* Gustaf Molander

Women of Pitcairn Island, The *56* Jean Yarbrough

Women of Ryazan *27* Olga Preobrazhenskaya

Women of the Frontier *87* Iván Argüello

Women of the Ginza *55* Kozaburo Yoshimura

Women of the Night *48* Kenji Mizoguchi

Women of the North Country *52* Joseph Kane

Women of the Prehistoric Planet *66* Arthur C. Pierce

Women of the World *62* Paolo Cavara, Gualtiero Jacopetti, Franco Prosperi
Women of Twilight *52* Gordon Parry
Women on the Firing Line *33* Yasujiro Ozu
Women on the Roof, The *89* Carl-Gustaf Nykvist
Women on the Verge of a Nervous Breakdown *88* Pedro Almodóvar
Women Should Stay at Home *39* Kozaburo Yoshimura
Women: So We Are Made *71* Dino Risi
Women They Talk About *28* Lloyd Bacon
Women Who Dare *28* Burton L. King
Women Who Give *24* Reginald Barker
Women Who Play *32* Arthur Rosson
Women Who Wait *21* Philip Van Loan
Women Who Win *19* Fred W. Durrant, Percy Nash
Women Who Work *40* Manuel Romero
Women Without Men *52* Youssef Chahine
Women Without Men *56* Elmo Williams
Women Without Names *39* Robert Florey
Women Without Names *49* Géza von Radványi
Women Won't Tell *32* Richard Thorpe
Women's Club, The *87* Sandra Weintraub
Women's Crusade *31* Grigori Alexandrov
Women's Penitentiary I *71* Jack Hill
Women's Penitentiary II *72* Jack Hill
Women's Penitentiary III *72* Gerry De Leon, Cirio Santiago
Women's Penitentiary IV *84* Bruno Mattei
Women's Prison *55* Lewis Seiler
Women's Prison *67* Akira Inoue
Women's Prison Massacre *86* Gilbert Roussel
Women's Street *40* Tadashi Imai
Women's Town *40* Tadashi Imai
Women's Victory *46* Kenji Mizoguchi
Women's Wares *27* Arthur Gregor
Women's Weapons *18* Robert Vignola
Won by a Child *13* Edwin J. Collins
Won by a Fish *12* Mack Sennett
Won by a Fluke *15* Cecil Birch
Won by a Head *20* Percy Nash
Won by a Neck *30* Roscoe Arbuckle
Won by a Snapshot *12* Bert Haldane
Won by Grit *17* George Marshall
Won by Losing *16* Bertram Phillips
Won by Strategy *04* Lewin Fitzhamon
Won by Warr *22* Edwin J. Collins
Won in a Closet *14* Mabel Normand
Won in the Clouds *28* Bruce Mitchell
Won: One Flivver *21* Charles Reisner
Won Through a Medium *11* Mack Sennett
Won Ton Ton, the Dog Who Saved Hollywood *75* Michael Winner
Wonder Bar *34* Lloyd Bacon
Wonder Boy *51* Karl Hartl
Wonder Child *51* Karl Hartl
Wonder Gloves *51* Robert Cannon
Wonder Kid, The *51* Karl Hartl
Wonder Man, The *20* John G. Adolfi
Wonder Man *45* H. Bruce Humberstone
Wonder of Women, The *29* Clarence Brown
Wonder of Wool *60* John Halas
Wonder Plane *39* Richard Harlan

Wonder Ring, The *55* Stan Brakhage, Joseph Cornell
Wonder Women *73* Robert Vincent O'Neil
Wonder Women *87* Kwok-leung Kam
Wonderful Adventure, The *15* Frederick Thompson
Wonderful Adventures of Herr Münchhausen, The *10* Émile Cohl
Wonderful Adventures of Nils, The *62* Kenne Fant
Wonderful Chance, The *20* George Archainbaud
Wonderful Charm *08* Georges Méliès
Wonderful Country, The *59* Robert Parrish
Wonderful Crook, The *74* Claude Goretta
Wonderful Day *65* Kenneth Hume
Wonderful Electric Belt, The *07* Romeo Rosetti
Wonderful Eye, The *11* Mack Sennett
Wonderful Land of Oz, The *68* Barry Mahon
Wonderful Lies of Nova Petrova, The *30* Hans Schwarz
Wonderful Life, A *51* William Beaudine
Wonderful Life *63* Sidney J. Furie
Wonderful Living Fan, The *04* Georges Méliès
Wonderful Nights with Peter Kinema *14* George Pearson
Wonderful Rose Tree, The *04* Georges Méliès
Wonderful Story, The *22* Graham Cutts
Wonderful Story, The *32* Reginald Fogwell
Wonderful Sunday *47* Akira Kurosawa
Wonderful Thing, The *21* Herbert Brenon
Wonderful Things! *58* Herbert Wilcox
Wonderful to Be Young *61* Sidney J. Furie
Wonderful Visit, The *74* Marcel Carné
Wonderful Wife, A *22* Paul Scardon
Wonderful Wooing, The *25* Geoffrey H. Malins
Wonderful World of the Brothers Grimm, The *62* Henry Levin, George Pal
Wonderful Year, The *21* Kenelm Foss
Wonderful Years, The *58* Helmut Käutner
Wonderland *31* Walter Lantz
Wonderland *88* Philip Saville
Wonders of Aladdin, The *61* Mario Bava, Henry Levin
Wonders of the Congo *31* Martin E. Johnson
Wonders of the Deep *03* Georges Méliès
Wonders of the Sea *22* J. Ernest Williamson
Wonderwall *68* Joe Massot
Wonkey's Wager *12* Frank Wilson
Won't You Throw Me a Kiss? *07* Arthur Gilbert
Woo Woo Blues *51* Richard Quine
Woo Woo Kid, The *87* Phil Alden Robinson
Wood and Stone *40* Heinosuke Gosho
Wood Nymph, The *16* Paul Powell
Woodcroft Castle *26* Walter West
Woodcutter's Daughter, The *13* Ernest G.

Batley
Woodcutters of the Deep South *73* Lionel Rogosin
Woodcutter's Romance, The *11* Theo Bouwmeester
Wooden Crosses *32* Raymond Bernard
Wooden Crosses *36* Howard Hawks
Wooden Head *40* Heinosuke Gosho
Wooden Horse, The *50* Jack Lee
Wooden Leg, The *09* D. W. Griffith
Wooden Money *29* John Foster
Wooden Shoes *17* Raymond B. West
Wooden Shoes *33* Manny Gould, Ben Harrison
Wooden Soldiers *34* Gus Meins, Charles Rogers
Woodland Tragedy, A *07* Harold Jeapes
Woodman Spare That Tree *42* Bob Wickersham
Woodpecker in the Rough *52* Walter Lantz
Woodpigeon Patrol, The *30* F. R. Lucas, Ralph Smart
Woods, The *31* Sergei Gerasimov
Woods Are Full of Cuckoos, The *37* Frank Tashlin
Woodstock *70* Michael Wadleigh
Woody Woodpecker *41* Walter Lantz
Woody Woodpecker Polka *51* Walter Lantz
Wooers of Mountain Kate, The *12* Allan Dwan
Wooing Auntie *13* Edwin J. Collins
Wooing of Miles Standish, The *08* Sidney Olcott
Wooing of Princess Pat, The *18* William P. S. Earle
Wooing of Widow Wilkins, The *12* Dave Aylott
Wooing of Winifred, The *11* J. Stuart Blackton
Woolen Under Where *63* Chuck Jones
Woolly Tale, The *64* Hermina Tyrlova
Wooruzhyon i Ochen Opasen *77* Vladimir Vainstok
Word, The *43* Gustaf Molander
Word, The *54* Carl Theodor Dreyer
Wordless Message, The *12* Allan Dwan
Words and Music *19* Scott R. Dunlap
Words and Music *29* James Tinling
Words and Music *48* Norman Taurog
Words and Music *84* Elie Chouraqui
Words and Music by . . . *19* Scott R. Dunlap
Words for Battle *41* Humphrey Jennings*
Wordsmith, The *78* Claude Jutra
Work *15* Charles Chaplin
Work Is a Four Letter Word *67* Peter Hall
Work Made Easy *07* J. Stuart Blackton
Work of the First Aid Nursing Yeomanry Corps, The *09* Frank E. Butcher
Work or Profession? *63* Márta Mészáros
Work Party *41* Len Lye
Worker, The *43* Ahmad Kamel Morsi
Workers and Jobs *35* Arthur Elton
Worker's Diary, A *67* Risto Jarva
Workers '80 *82* Andrzej Chodakowski, Andrzej Zajączkowski
Workers Leaving the Factory *1895* Louis Lumière

Worse You Are the Better You Sleep, The 60 Akira Kurosawa

Worst of Farm Disasters 41 Joris Ivens

Worst Secret Agents 64 Lucio Fulci

Worst Woman in Paris, The 33 Monta Bell

Worth Winning 89 Will Mackenzie

Worthless, The 82 Mika Kaurismäki

Worthless Duel, The 63 Tomu Uchida

Worthy Deceivers 33 Reginald Denny

Wot Dot 70 Joy Batchelor

Wot, No Gangsters? 46 E. W. White

Wotan's Wake 62 Brian DePalma

Wotta Nitemare 39 Dave Fleischer

Would-Be Gentleman, The 60 Jean Meyer

Would-Be Heir, The 12 Allan Dwan

Would-Be Hero, A 09 Joe Rosenthal

Would-Be Shriner, The 12 Mack Sennett

Would You Believe It! 29 Walter Forde

Would You Forgive? 20 Scott R. Dunlap

Would You Kill a Child? 75 Narciso Ibáñez Serrador

Wounded Bird, The 56 Ernest Pintoff

Wounded by the Beauty 19 Wallace A. Carlson

Wow! 69 Claude Jutra

Wow You're a Cartoonist! 88 Jim Henson

Woyseck 78 Werner Herzog

Woyzeck 78 Werner Herzog

Wozzeck 62 Georg C. Klaren

Wozzeck 78 Werner Herzog

Wraith, The 86 Mike Marvin

Wraith of the Tomb, The 15 Charles C. Calvert

Wrangler's Roost 41 S. Roy Luby

Wrath 17 Theodore Marston

Wrath of Dionysus, The 14 Yakov Protazanov

Wrath of God, The 68 Alberto Cardone

Wrath of God, The 72 Ralph Nelson

Wrath of Jealousy 36 Alex Bryce, Campbell Gullan

Wrath of Love 17 James Vincent

Wrath of the Gods, The 14 Reginald Barker, Thomas Ince

Wrath of the Gods, or The Destruction of Sakura Jima, The 14 Reginald Barker, Thomas Ince

Wrath of the Seas, The 29 Manfred Noa

Wreath for the Bandits, A 68 Sergio Pastore

Wreath in Time, A 08 D. W. Griffith

Wreath of Orange Blossoms, A 10 D. W. Griffith

Wreck, The 13 Ralph Ince

Wreck, The 19 Ralph Ince

Wreck, The 27 William James Craft

Wreck and Ruin 14 Wilfred Noy

Wreck of the Hesperus, The 26 Frank Tilley

Wreck of the Hesperus, The 27 Elmer Clifton

Wreck of the Hesperus, The 48 John Hoffman

Wreck of the Mary Deare, The 59 Michael Anderson

Wreck of the Mary Jane, The 07 Percy Stow

Wreck of the Singapore, The 28 Ralph Ince

Wreck Raisers 72 Harold Orton

Wreckage 25 Scott R. Dunlap

Wrecker, The 28 Géza von Bolváry

Wrecker, The 33 Albert S. Rogell

Wrecker of Lives, The 14 Charles C. Calvert

Wreckers, The 60 John Gilling

Wrecking an Armoured Train 1899 Robert Ashe

Wrecking Crew 42 Frank McDonald

Wrecking Crew, The 68 Phil Karlson

Wrecking Yard, The 63 John Hayes

Wreckless Lady, The 26 Howard Higgin

Wrested from the Sea 49 Herman van den Horst

Wrestler, The 74 Jim Westman

Wrestler and the Clown, The 57 Boris Barnet, Konstantin Yudin

Wrestlers, The 20 Raoul Barré, Charles Bowers

Wrestling 61 Michel Brault, Marcel Carrière, Claude Fournier, Claude Jutra

Wrestling Sextette, The 00 Georges Méliès

Wrestling Women vs. the Aztec Mummy, The 64 René Cardona

Wrestling Women vs. the Murdering Robot 69 René Cardona

Wright Idea, The 28 Charles Hines

Wringing Good Joke, A 00 Edwin S. Porter

Writing on the Wall, The 1897 Walter D. Welford

Writing on the Wall, The 16 Tefft Johnson

Written in the Sand 66 René Clément

Written Law, The 31 Reginald Fogwell

Written on the Sand 68 André De Toth

Written on the Wind 56 Douglas Sirk

Wrong Again 29 Leo McCarey

Wrong Arm of the Law, The 62 Cliff Owen

Wrong Bet 90 Sheldon Lettich

Wrong Box, The 66 Bryan Forbes

Wrong Cab, The 09 Lewin Fitzhamon

Wrong Chimney, The 03 James A. Williamson

Wrong Chimney, The 07 Tom Green

Wrong Coat, The 09 Theo Bouwmeester

Wrong Couples, The 87 John Chiang

Wrong Damn Film, The 75 Carson Davidson

Wrong Doers, The 25 Hugh Dierker

Wrong Door, The 16 Carter DeHaven

Wrong Envelopes, The 12 Lewin Fitzhamon

Wrong Guys, The 88 Danny Bilson

Wrong House, The 15 Will P. Kellino

Wrong Is Right 82 Richard Brooks

Wrong Kind of Girl, The 56 Joshua Logan

Wrong Man, The 56 Alfred Hitchcock

Wrong Medicine, The 08 Lewin Fitzhamon

Wrong Miss Right, The 37 Charles Lamont

Wrong Mr. Perkins, The 31 Arthur Varney-Serrao

Wrong Mr. Wright, The 27 Scott Sidney

Wrong Move, The 74 Wim Wenders

Wrong Movement 74 Wim Wenders

Wrong Number 48 Ray Nazarro

Wrong Number 59 Vernon Sewell

Wrong Poison, The 03 James A. Williamson

Wrong Queue, The 26 William C. Nolan

Wrong Road, The 37 James Cruze

Wrong Romanie 37 Leslie Goodwins

Wrong Track, The 20 Gregory La Cava, Vernon Stallings

Wrong Way Out, The 38 Gustav Machatý

Wrong Woman, The 15 Richard Ridgely

Wrong Woman, The 20 Ivan Abramson

Wrong World 86 Ian Pringle

Wrongdoers, The 71 Yılmaz Güney

Wrongly Accused 42 William Berke

Wrzos 38 Jerzy Starczewski

Wspólny Pokój 60 Wojciech Has

Wstretscha s Maksimom 41 Sergei Gerasimov

Wszystko na Sprzedaż 67 Andrzej Wajda

Wu-Hou 65 Han-hsiang Li

Wu Li Chang 30 Nick Grindé

Wunder, Das 85 Eckhart Schmidt

Wunder des Malachias, Das 61 Bernhard Wicki

Wunder des Schneeschuhs, Das 20 Arnold Fanck*

Wunderbarer Sommer, Ein 58 Georg Tressler

Würger der Welt, Die 19 E. A. Dupont

Würger Kommt auf Leisen Socken, Der 71 Guido Zurli

Wutai Jiemei 64 Jin Xie

Wuthering Heights 20 A. V. Bramble

Wuthering Heights 39 William Wyler

Wuthering Heights 52 Luis Buñuel

Wuthering Heights 70 Robert Fuest

Wuthering Heights 85 Jacques Rivette

Wuya yu Maque 49 Junli Zheng

Wylie 69 David Lowell Rich

Wynona's Vengeance 13 Francis Ford

Wyoming 28 W. S. Van Dyke

Wyoming 40 Richard Thorpe

Wyoming 47 Joseph Kane

Wyoming Bandit, The 49 Philip Ford

Wyoming Hurricane 44 William Berke

Wyoming Kid, The 47 Raoul Walsh

Wyoming Mail 50 Reginald LeBorg

Wyoming Outlaw 39 George Sherman

Wyoming Renegades 55 Fred F. Sears

Wyoming Roundup 52 Thomas Carr

Wyoming Whirlwind 32 Armand Schaefer

Wyoming Wildcat, The 25 Robert De Lacey

Wyoming Wildcat 41 George Sherman

Wyrok Śmierci 81 Witold Orzechowski

Wyścig Pokoju Warszawa-Berlina-Praga 52 Joris Ivens

X 63 Roger Corman

X 86 Odvar Einarson

X-15 61 Richard Donner

X-15 Pilot 60 Robert Drew, Richard Leacock

X from Outer Space, The 64 Kazui Nihonmatsu

X Marks the Spot 31 Erle C. Kenton

X Marks the Spot 42 George Sherman

X-Paroni 64 Risto Jarva, Jaakko Pakkasvirta, Spede Pasasen

X-Pilot 60 Robert Drew, Richard Leacock

X-Ray *81* Boaz Davidson

X-Ray Fiend, The *1897* George Albert Smith

X-Ray Glasses *09* Émile Cohl

X-Ray Mirror, The *1899* Wallace Mc-Cutcheon

X-Ray of a Killer *63* Jean Maley

X-Rays *1897* George Albert Smith

X: The Man with the X-Ray Eyes *63* Roger Corman

X the Unknown *56* Joseph Losey, Leslie Norman

X, Y & Zee *71* Brian G. Hutton

XYZ Murders, The *85* Sam Raimi

Xala *74* Ousmane Sembène

Xanadu *80* Robert Greenwald

Xaver *88* Werner Possardt

Xero *88* Maggie Greenwald

Xi Xuefu *62* Tie Li

Xiangnu Xiaoxiao *86* Lan Niao, Fei Xie

Xiaosheng Papa *82* Kar-wing Lau

Xiaozi Bei *80* Luo Tai, Jiayi Wang

Xica *75* Carlos Dieguês

Xica da Silva *75* Carlos Dieguês

Xie *80* Zhihong Gui

Xiong Bang *81* Dennis Yu

Xmas Greeting Film *11* Walter Speer

Xochimilco *42* Emilio Fernández

Xtro *82* Harry Bromley Davenport

Y el Cielo Fué Tomado por Asalto *73* Santiago Álvarez

Y el Demonio Creó a los Hombres *70* Armando Bo, Jack Curtis

Y la Noche Se Hizo Arcoiris *78* Santiago Álvarez

Y Seguían Robándose el Milión de Dólares *71* Eugenio Martin

Y Tenemos Sabor *67* Sara Gómez

Ya, Babushka, Illiko & Illarion *63* Tenghiz Abuladze

Y'à Bon les Blancs *87* Marco Ferreri

Ya Cuba *62* Mikhail Kalatozov

Ya-Kuba *62* Mikhail Kalatozov

Ya Kupil Papu *64* Ilya Frez

Ya Lyubil Vac Bolshe Zhizni *87* Rasim Izmailov

Ya Lyublyu *36* Leonid Lukov

Y'à Pas le Feu *85* Richard Balducci

Ya Shagayu po Moskve *66* Georgy Danelia

Ya Tebya Pomnyu *85* Ali Khamrayev

Ya Yey Nravlyus *87* Anvar Turayev

Yaaba *89* Idrissa Ouedraogo

Yabu no Naka no Kuroneko *67* Kaneto Shindo

Yabunirami Nippon *63* Hideo Suzuki

Yabure Daiko *49* Keisuke Kinoshita

Yabure Taiko *49* Keisuke Kinoshita

Yacht Race, The *20* Raoul Barré, Charles Bowers

Yacula *73* Jesús Franco

Yagodki Lyubvi *26* Alexander Dovzhenko

Yagua *41* Pál Fejös

Yaguar *87* Sebastián Alarcón

Yagyu Bugeichō *57* Hiroshi Inagaki

Yagyu Secret Scrolls *57* Hiroshi Inagaki

Yahidka Kokhannya *26* Alexander Dovzhenko

Yahudi *58* Bimal Roy

Yako—Cazador de Malditos *86* Rubén Galindo, Jr.

Yako—Hunter of the Damned *86* Rubén Galindo, Jr.

Yakov Bogomolov *70* Abram Room

Yakov Sverdlov *40* Sergei Yutkevich

Yakuza, The *74* Sydney Pollack

Yakuza Papers, The *73* Kinji Fukasaku

Yaldei Stalin *87* Nadav Levitan

Yam Daabo *87* Idrissa Ouedraogo

Yama no Oto *54* Mikio Naruse

Yama no Sanka: Moyuru Wakamono-Tachi *62* Masahiro Shinoda

Yamabiko Gakkō *52* Tadashi Imai

Yamashita Shōnen Monogatari *86* Shukei Matsubayashi

Yamata *19* Alexander Korda

Yambao *57* Alfredo B. Crevenna

Yanapanacuna *70* Santiago Álvarez

Yanco *60* Servando González

Yang Kwei Fei *55* Kenji Mizoguchi

Yang Kwei Fei *64* Han-hsiang Li

Yangtse Incident *56* Michael Anderson

Yanık Kaval *46* Baha Gelenbevi

Yank at Eton, A *42* Norman Taurog

Yank at Oxford, A *37* Jack Conway

Yank in Dutch, A *42* Richard Wallace

Yank in Ermine, A *55* Gordon Parry

Yank in Indo-China, A *52* Wallace A. Grissell

Yank in Korea, A *51* Lew Landers

Yank in Libya, A *42* Albert Herman

Yank in London, A *45* Herbert Wilcox

Yank in Rome, A *45* Luigi Zampa

Yank in the R.A.F., A *41* Henry King

Yank in Vietnam, A *64* Marshall Thompson

Yank on the Burma Road, A *41* George B. Seitz

Yankee *66* Tinto Brass

Yankee, The *70* Lars Forsberg

Yankee at King Arthur's Court, The *31* David Butler

Yankee Buccaneer *52* Frederick De Cordova

Yankee Clipper, The *27* Rupert Julian

Yankee Consul, The *24* James W. Horne

Yankee Don *31* Noel Mason Smith

Yankee Dood It *56* Friz Freleng

Yankee Doodle Boy *29* Dave Fleischer

Yankee Doodle Bugs *54* Friz Freleng

Yankee Doodle Daffy *43* Friz Freleng

Yankee Doodle Dandy *42* Michael Curtiz

Yankee Doodle Duke, A *26* Charles Lamont

Yankee Doodle Goes to Town *39* Jacques Tourneur

Yankee Doodle Home *39* Arthur Dreifuss

Yankee Doodle in Berlin *19* F. Richard Jones

Yankee Doodle, Jr. *22* John H. Pratt

Yankee Doodle Mouse *43* Joseph Barbera, William Hanna

Yankee Fakir *47* W. Lee Wilder

Yankee from the West, A *15* George Siegmann

Yankee Girl, The *15* Phillips Smalley

Yankee Go-Getter, A *21* Duke Worne

Yankee in King Arthur's Court, A *48* Tay Garnett

Yankee Madness *24* Charles R. Seeling

Yankee Man-o-Warman's Fight for Love —

An Incident During the Pacific Cruise of the American Fleet, A *08* Edwin S. Porter

Yankee No! *60* Richard Leacock*

Yankee Pasha *54* Joseph Pevney

Yankee Pluck *17* George Archainbaud

Yankee Princess, A *19* David Smith

Yankee Señor, The *26* Emmett J. Flynn

Yankee Speed *24* Robert North Bradbury

Yankee Way, The *17* Richard Stanton

Yankel dem Schmidt *38* Edgar G. Ulmer

Yanki No! *60* Richard Leacock*

Yanks *79* John Schlesinger

Yanks Ahoy! *43* Kurt Neumann

Yanks Are Coming, The *42* Alexis Thurn-Taxis

Yanky Clippers *28* Walter Lantz, Tom Palmer

Yanqui No! *60* Richard Leacock*

Yanzhi Kou *87* Stanley Kwan

Yaqui, The *16* Lloyd B. Carleton

Yaqui Cur, The *13* D. W. Griffith

Yaqui Drums *56* Jean Yarbrough

Yari no Gonza *85* Masahiro Shinoda

Yarın Son Gündür *71* Yılmaz Güney

Yasemin *88* Hark Böhm

Yasha *85* Yasuo Furuhata

Yashaga Ike *79* Masahiro Shinoda

Yasmina *26* André Hugon

Yasmina *61* Mohammed Lakhdar Amina, Jamal Chanderli

Yataro-Gasa *32* Hiroshi Inagaki

Yataro's Sedge Hat *32* Hiroshi Inagaki

Y'A-t-Il un Français dans la Salle? *82* Jean-Pierre Mocky

Yatō Kaze no Naka o Hashiru *61* Hiroshi Inagaki

Yatrik *66* Mani Kaul

Yawar Mallku *69* Jorge Sanjinés

Yawara Sempū Dotō no Taiketsu *66* Masateru Nishiyama

Ye Bang Ge Sheng *61* Quifeng Yuan

Ye Banks and Braes *19* Tom Watts

Ye Happy Pilgrims *34* Walter Lantz

Ye Jinghum *82* Po-chih Leong

Ye Olde Melodies *29* Dave Fleischer

Ye Olde Saw Mill *35* Mack Sennett

Ye Olde Swap Shop *40* Ubbe Iwerks

Ye Olde Waxworks by the Terrible Two *15* James Read

Ye Shan *86* Xueshu Yan

Ye Wooing of Peggy *17* Bertram Phillips

Yeah! Yeah! Yeah! *64* Albert Maysles, David Maysles, Charlotte Zwerin

Yeah! Yeah! Yeah! New York Meets the Beatles *64* Albert Maysles, David Maysles, Charlotte Zwerin

Year in Frank's Life, A *67* Kazimierz Karabasz*

Year My Voice Broke, The *87* John Duigan

Year 1919, The *38* Ilya Trauberg

Year of Awakening, The *86* Fernando Trueba

Year of Living Dangerously, The *82* Peter Weir

Year of the Cannibals, The *69* Liliana Cavani

Year of the Cricket *68* Steve Sekely

Year of the Dragon *85* Michael Cimino

Year of the Horse, The 66 Irving Sunasky

Year of the Horse 68 Larry Lansburgh, Norman Tokar

Year of the Jellyfish, The 84 Christopher Frank

Year of the Mouse 65 Chuck Jones

Year of the Peaceful Sun, The 84 Krzysztof Zanussi

Year of the Quiet Sun, The 84 Krzysztof Zanussi

Year of the Rabbit, The 87 Fernando Ayala

Year of the Tiger 64 Marshall Thompson

Year of the Turtle, The 89 Ute Wieland

Year of the Yahoo! 71 Herschell Gordon Lewis

Year One 74 Roberto Rossellini

Year 2889 66 Larry Buchanan

Yearling, The 46 Clarence Brown

Yearning 35 Heinosuke Gosho

Yearning 64 Mikio Naruse

Years Are So Long, The 37 Leo McCarey

Years Between, The 46 Compton Bennett

Years of Change 50 Willard Van Dyke

Years of the Locust, The 16 George Melford

Years of Trial 25 Alexander Rasumny

Years of Youth 41 Igor Savchenko

Years Without Days 40 Anatole Litvak

Yedi Belalılar 70 İrfan Atasoy, Yılmaz Güney

Yedinozhdy Solgar 88 Vladimir Bortko

Yeelen 87 Souleymane Cissé

Yeh Kyon 70 Ritwik Ghatak

Yehoshua—Yehoshua 87 Avi Cohen

Yehudi Menuhin—Chemin de la Lumière 70 Bernard Gavoty, François Reichenbach

Yehudi Menuhin—Road of Light 70 Bernard Gavoty, François Reichenbach

Yehudi Menuhin Story 70 Bernard Gavoty, François Reichenbach

Yekaterina Ivanovna 15 A. Uralsky

Yell of a Night, A 32 Gustave Minzenty

Yellow Back, The 26 Del Andrews

Yellow Balloon, The 52 J. Lee-Thompson

Yellow Boy 36 Béla Pásztor

Yellow Bullet, The 17 Harry Harvey

Yellow Cab Man, The 49 Jack Donohue

Yellow Caesar 40 Alberto Cavalcanti

Yellow Cameo, The 28 Spencer G. Bennet

Yellow Canary, The 43 Herbert Wilcox

Yellow Canary, The 63 Buzz Kulik

Yellow Car, The 63 Arne Mattsson

Yellow Cargo 36 Crane Wilbur

Yellow Claw, The 20 René Plaissetty

Yellow Contraband 28 Leo D. Maloney

Yellow Crow 57 Heinosuke Gosho

Yellow Cruise, The 36 André Sauvage

Yellow Dog, The 18 Colin Campbell

Yellow Dog 73 Terence Donovan

Yellow Dust 36 Wallace Fox

Yellow Earth 84 Kaige Chen

Yellow Face 21 Maurice Elvey

Yellow Fin 51 Frank McDonald

Yellow Fingers 26 Emmett J. Flynn

Yellow Flame, The 13 Thomas Ince

Yellow Flowers Through a Rainy Day 37 Seto Waimon

Yellow Golliwog, The 63 Robert Hartford-Davis

Yellow Hair and the Fortress of Gold 84 Matt Cimber

Yellow-Haired Kid, The 52 Frank McDonald

Yellow Handkerchief, The 77 Yoji Yamada

Yellow Hat, The 66 Honoria Plesch

Yellow Horse 65 Bruce Baillie

Yellow Jack 38 George B. Seitz

Yellow Lily, The 28 Alexander Korda

Yellow Mask, The 30 Harry Lachman

Yellow Men and Gold 22 Irvin Willat

Yellow Menace 42 William Nigh

Yellow Mountain, The 54 Jesse Hibbs

Yellow Pages 85 James Kenelm Clarke

Yellow Pass, The 28 Fedor Ozep

Yellow Passport, The 16 Edwin August

Yellow Passport, The 31 Raoul Walsh

Yellow Pawn, The 16 George Melford

Yellow Peril 00 Walter R. Booth

Yellow Robe, The 54 David MacDonald

Yellow Robe, The 67 Lester James Peries

Yellow Rolls-Royce, The 64 Anthony Asquith

Yellow Rose of Texas, The 44 Joseph Kane

Yellow Sands 38 Herbert Brenon

Yellow Sky 48 William A. Wellman

Yellow Slippers, The 61 Sylwester Checinski

Yellow Squadron, The 54 Stig Olin

Yellow Stain, The 22 John Francis Dillon

Yellow Stockings 28 Theodor Komisarjevsky

Yellow Streak, A 15 William Nigh

Yellow Streak, A 27 Ben F. Wilson

Yellow Streak, The 45 Derwin Abrahams

Yellow Submarine 68 George Dunning

Yellow Taifun, The 20 Edward José

Yellow Teddybears, The 63 Robert Hartford-Davis

Yellow the Sun 71 Marguerite Duras

Yellow Ticket, The 18 William Parke

Yellow Ticket, The 28 Fedor Ozep

Yellow Ticket, The 31 Raoul Walsh

Yellow Tickets 18 William DeMille

Yellow Tomahawk, The 54 Lesley Selander

Yellow Traffic, The 14 Alice Guy-Blaché

Yellow Typhoon 20 Edward José

Yellow Winton Flyer, The 69 Mark Rydell

Yellowback, The 29 Jerome Storm

Yellowbeard 83 Mel Damski

Yellowneck 55 R. John Hugh

Yellowstone 36 Arthur Lubin

Yellowstone Kelly 59 Gordon Douglas

Yelp Wanted 31 Dick Huemer

Yen Family 88 Yojiro Takita

Yenan and the Eighth Army on the Road 39 Mou-che Yen

Yenendi 51 Roger Rosfelder, Jean Rouch

Yenendi de Boukoki 72 Jean Rouch

Yenendi de Ganghel 68 Jean Rouch

Yenendi de Simiri 71 Jean Rouch

Yenendi de Yantalla 70 Jean Rouch

Yenendi: Les Hommes Qui Font la Pluie 51 Roger Rosfelder, Jean Rouch

Yenethlia Poli 87 Takis Papayannidis

Yentl 83 Barbra Streisand

Yeojaeui Banran 86 Hyeong-myeong Kim

Yer Demir, Gök Bakır 87 Ömer Zülfü Livaneli

Yerba Sangrienta 87 Ismael Rodríguez, Jr.

Yerma 62 Alberto Cavalcanti

Yes 64 György Révész

Yes Dear 20 Grim Natwick

Yes, Det Er Far! 86 John Hilbard

Yes, Giorgio 82 Franklin J. Schaffner

Yes Girls, The 72 Lindsay Shonteff

Yes, He's Been with Me 63 Arne Mattsson

Yes, It's Your Dad! 86 John Hilbard

Yes, Madam 33 Leslie Hiscott

Yes Madam? 38 Norman Lee

Yes, Mr. Brown 33 Jack Buchanan, Herbert Wilcox

Yes, My Darling Daughter 39 William Keighley

Yes, No, Maybe, Maybenot 67 Malcolm Le Grice

Yes or No? 15 B. Reeves Eason

Yes or No 20 Roy William Neill

Yes Sir, Mr. Bones 51 Ron Ormond

Yes Sir, That's My Baby 49 George Sherman

Yes Times Have Changed 20 L. M. Glackens

Yes We Have No... 23 Adrian Brunel

Yes! We Have No Bananas 30 Dave Fleischer

Yessongs 73 Peter Neal

Yesterday 59 Márton Keleti

Yesterday 74 Brian Jackson

Yesterday 80 Laurence L. Kent

Yesterday and Today 53 Abner J. Greshler

Yesterday Girl 66 Alexander Kluge

Yesterday Goes On Forever 60 Alexander Kluge, Peter Schamoni

Yesterday Is Over Your Shoulder 40 Thorold Dickinson

Yesterday, Today and Tomorrow 63 Vittorio De Sica

Yesterday's Enemy 59 Val Guest

Yesterday's Hero 37 William Nigh

Yesterday's Hero 79 Neil Leifer

Yesterday's Heroes 40 Herbert I. Leeds

Yesterday's Tomorrow 78 Wolfgang Staudte

Yesterday's Wife 23 Edward J. LeSaint

Yesterday's Witness: A Tribute to the American Newsreel 74 Christian Blackwood

Yet Spies Haven't Died 42 Kozaburo Yoshimura

Yeti 77 Gianfranco Parolini

Yeux Cernés, Les 64 Robert Hossein

Yeux de l'Aime, Les 22 Roger Lion

Yeux de l'Amour, Les 60 Denys De la Patellière

Yeux Fermes, Les 72 Joel Santoni

Yeux Fertiles, Les 77 Marco Bellocchio

Yeux, la Bouche, Les 82 Marco Bellocchio

Yeux Ne Peuvent Pas en Tout Temps Se Fermer ou Peut-Être Qu'un Jour Rome Se Permettra de Choisir à Son Tour, Les 69 Danièle Huillet, Jean-Marie Straub

Yeux Ne Veulent Pas en Tout Temps Se Fermer ou Peut-Être Qu'un Jour Rome

Se Permettra de Choisir à Son Tour, Les 69 Danièle Huillet, Jean-Marie Straub
Yeux Noirs, Les 35 Victor Tourjansky
Yeux Ouverts, Les 13 Louis Feuillade
Yeux Qui Fascinent, Les 16 Louis Feuillade
Yeux Qui Meurent, Les 12 Louis Feuillade
Yeux Rouges ou Les Vérités Accidentelles, Les 82 Yves Simoneau
Yeux Sans Visage, Les 59 Georges Franju
Yevgeni Onegin 11 Vasili M. Goncharov
Yevo Prevosoditielstvo 27 Grigori Roshal
Yevo Prizyv 25 Yakov Protazanov
Yevo Zovut Robert 67 Ilya Olshvanger
Yevo Zovut Sukhe-Bator 42 Josef Heifits, Alexander Zarkhi
Yhdeksan Tapaa Lähestyä Helsinkiä 82 Jörn Donner
Yi Ge Si Zhe Dul Sheng Zhe De Fang Wen 88 Jianxin Huang
Yi Lou Yi 87 Park-huen Kwan
Yiddish Connection 86 Paul Boujenah
Yiddisher Cowboy, The 11 Allan Dwan
Yiddle and His Fiddle 12 H. Oceano Martinek
Yiddle on My Fiddle 12 Will P. Kellino
Yiddle with His Fiddle 36 Joseph Green, Jan Nowina-Przybylski
Yidl Mitn Fidl 36 Joseph Green, Jan Nowina-Przybylski
Yield to the Night 56 J. Lee-Thompson
Yijiang Chunshui Xiang Dong Liu 47 Tsou-sen Tsai, Junli Zheng
Yılanların Öcü 86 Şerif Gören
Yin and Yang of Dr. Go, The 72 Burgess Meredith
Yin Ji 82 Zhao Li
Yin-Yang Chieh 74 Shan-hsi Ting
Yineka Pou Evlepe ta Onira, I 88 Nikos Panayotopoulos
Ying-Ch'un ko Chih Feng-Po 72 King Hu
Yingxiong Bense 85 John Woo
Yingyang Jie 89 Ziniu Wu
Yip, Yip, Yippy 39 Dave Fleischer
Yngsjömordet 66 Arne Mattsson
Yo 80 Young-hyo Kim
Yo el Ejecutor 87 Valentín Trujillo
Yo...Tu...y...Ella 33 John Reinhardt
Yö vai Päivä 62 Risto Jarva, Jaakko Pakkasvirta
Yoake Mae 53 Kozaburo Yoshimura
Yob, The 88 Ian Emes
Yoba 76 Tadashi Imai
Yodelin' Kid from Pine Ridge 37 Joseph Kane
Yog—Monster from Space 70 Inoshiro Honda
Yoghi, Der 16 Rochus Gliese, Paul Wegener
Yogi, The 16 Rochus Gliese, Paul Wegener
Yogoto no Yume 33 Mikio Naruse
Yoicks 32 Lloyd Brinder
Yoidōri Tenshi 48 Akira Kurosawa
Yōjimbō 61 Akira Kurosawa
Yōkai Daisensō 68 Yoshiyuki Kuroda
Yōkai Hyaku Monogatari 68 Kimiyoshi Yasuda
Yoke, The 15 James Warry Vickers
Yoke of Gold, The 16 Lloyd B. Carleton

Yokel, The 26 William A. Wellman
Yokel Boy 42 Joseph Santley
Yokel Boy Makes Good 38 Walter Lantz
Yōki no Uramachi 39 Kozaburo Yoshimura
Yokihi 55 Kenji Mizoguchi
Yokiro 84 Hideo Gosha
Yoku 58 Heinosuke Gosho
Yokubō 53 Kozaburo Yoshimura
Yol 81 Şerif Gören
Yolanda 24 Robert Vignola
Yolanda 42 Dudley Murphy, Manuel Reachi
Yolanda and the Thief 45 Vincente Minnelli
Yolanda—The Daughter of the Black Pirate 52 Mario Soldati
Yolanta 64 Vladimir Gorikker
Yom el Sades, El 86 Youssef Chahine
Yongkari—Monster from the Deep 67 Kiduck Kim
Yonjū Ichi Jikan no Kyōfu 60 Shigeaki Hidaka
Yonjūhassai no Teikō 56 Kozaburo Yoshimura
Yonkers, Hanging Out 73 Chantal Akerman
Yoom Helw. Yoom Mor 88 Khairy Bishara
Yor 83 Antonio Margheriti
Yor—The Hunter from the Future 83 Antonio Margheriti
Yorck 32 Gustav Ucicky
York Mystery, The 24 Hugh Croise
York State Folks 15 Harry Jackson
Yorkshire Ditty, A 49 David Hand
Yorktown: Le Sens d'un Bataille 82 Marcel Ophüls
Yorokobi mo Kanashimi mo Ikutoshitsuki 57 Keisuke Kinoshita
Yoru 23 Kenji Mizoguchi
Yoru Hiraku 31 Heinosuke Gosho
Yoru no Chō 57 Kozaburo Yoshimura
Yoru no Kawa 56 Kozaburo Yoshimura
Yoru no Meneko 28 Heinosuke Gosho
Yoru no Mesuneko 28 Heinosuke Gosho
Yoru no Nagare 60 Yuzo Kawashima, Mikio Naruse
Yoru no Onnatachi 48 Kenji Mizoguchi
Yoru no Sugao 58 Kozaburo Yoshimura
Yoru no Tsuzumi 58 Tadashi Imai
Yosakoi Journey 70 Shoji Segawa
Yosakoi Ryokō 70 Shoji Segawa
Yōsei Gorasu 62 Inoshiro Honda
Yōsei Gorath 62 Inoshiro Honda
Yosemite Trail, The 22 Bernard J. Durning
Yoshinaka o Meguru Sannin no Onna 56 Teinosuke Kinugasa
Yoshiwara 37 Max Ophüls
Yoshiwara Enjo 86 Hideo Gosha
Yoso 63 Teinosuke Kinugasa
Yotsuya Ghost Story, The 49 Keisuke Kinoshita
Yotsuya Kaidan 49 Keisuke Kinoshita
Yotsuya Kaidan 65 Shiro Toyoda
Yotsuya Kaidan—Ōiwa no Bōrei 69 Issei Mori
Yottsu no Koi no Monogatari 47 Teinosuke Kinugasa, Mikio Naruse

You 16 Harold M. Shaw
You 63 István Szabó
You and I 17 Victor Sjöström
You and I 41 Tomotaka Tasaka
You and I 71 Larissa Shepitko
You and Me 38 Fritz Lang
You and Me 72 David Carradine
You Are Guilty 23 Edgar Lewis
You Are in Danger 23 W. S. Van Dyke
You Are My Adventure 58 Stig Olin
You Are My Love 56 Youssef Chahine
You Are Not Alone 78 Ernst Johansen, Lasse Nielsen
You Are Stupid 32 Heinosuke Gosho
You Are the World for Me 53 Ernst Marischka
You Are Weighed in the Balance But Are Found Lacking 74 Lino Brocka
You Are Weighed in the Balance But Are Found Wanting 74 Lino Brocka
You Are What You Eat 68 Barry Feinstein
You Belong to Me 34 Alfred L. Werker
You Belong to Me 41 Wesley Ruggles
You Belong to My Heart 51 Don Hartman
You Betcha My Life 41 Jean Yarbrough
You Better Watch Out 80 Lewis Jackson
You Came Along 45 John Farrow
You Came to My Rescue 37 Dave Fleischer
You Came Too Late 62 D. Kapsakis
You Can Be Had 35 Sam Newfield
You Can Change the World 51 Leo McCarey
You Can't Beat Love 37 Christy Cabanne
You Can't Beat the Irish 51 John Paddy Carstairs
You Can't Beat the Law 28 Charles J. Hunt
You Can't Beat the Law 43 Lambert Hillyer
You Can't Beat the Law 43 Phil Rosen
You Can't Believe Everything 18 Jack Conway
You Can't Buy Everything 34 Charles Reisner
You Can't Buy Luck 37 Lew Landers
You Can't Cheat an Honest Man 38 Edward F. Cline, George Marshall
You Can't Do That to Me 44 Harry Beaumont
You Can't Do Without Love 44 Walter Forde
You Can't Escape 55 Wilfred Eades
You Can't Escape Forever 42 Jo Graham
You Can't Fool an Irishman 49 Alfred Travers
You Can't Fool Your Wife 23 George Melford
You Can't Fool Your Wife 40 Ray McCarey
You Can't Get Away with It 23 Rowland V. Lee
You Can't Get Away with Murder 39 Lewis Seiler
You Can't Go Home Again 73 Nicholas Ray
You Can't Have Everything 18 Cecil B. DeMille
You Can't Have Everything 37 Norman Taurog

You Can't Have Everything *70* Martin Zweiback

You Can't Hide the Sun with Your Finger *76* Santiago Álvarez

You Can't Hurry Love *88* Richard Martini

You Can't Ration Love *44* Lester Fuller

You Can't Run Away from It *56* Dick Powell

You Can't Run Far *61* Edward L. Cahn

You Can't See 'Round Corners *69* David Cahill

You Can't Shoe a Horsefly *40* Dave Fleischer

You Can't Sleep Here *49* Howard Hawks

You Can't Steal Love *74* Marvin Chomsky

You Can't Take It with You *38* Frank Capra

You Can't Take Money *37* Alfred Santell

You Can't Win 'Em All *69* Robert Sparr

You Can't Win 'Em All *70* Peter Collinson

You Can't Win Them All *70* Peter Collinson

You Do, I Do, We Do *72* Stan Vanderbeek

You Don't Need Pajamas at Rosie's *68* James Neilson

You Don't Need Pyjamas at Rosie's *68* James Neilson

You Find It Everywhere *21* Charles T. Horan

You for Me *52* Don Weis

You Gotta Be a Football Hero *35* Dave Fleischer

You Gotta Stay Happy *48* H. C. Potter

You Have to Run Fast *61* Edward L. Cahn

You Just Kill Me *66* Ken Hughes

You Killed Elizabeth *55* David Eady

You Know What Sailors Are *28* Maurice Elvey

You Know What Sailors Are *54* Ken Annakin

You Leave Me Breathless *38* Dave Fleischer

You Light Up My Life *77* Joseph Brooks

You Live and Learn *37* Arthur Woods

You Lucky People *55* Maurice Elvey

You Made Me Love You *33* Monty Banks

You May Be Next! *36* Albert S. Rogell

You Must Be Joking! *65* Michael Winner

You Must Get Married *36* Leslie Pearce

You Must Marry *62* Heinosuke Gosho

You Never Can Tell *20* Chester M. Franklin

You Never Can Tell *51* Lou Breslow

You Never Know *22* Robert Ensminger

You Never Know *51* Lou Breslow

You Never Know Women *26* William A. Wellman

You Never Know Your Luck *19* Frank Powell

You Never Saw Such a Girl *19* Robert Vignola

You Only Live Once *37* Fritz Lang

You Only Live Once *69* Dirk Sanders

You Only Live Twice *67* Lewis Gilbert, Bob Simmons

You Only Love Once *80* Rajko Grlić

You Oughta Be in Pictures *40* Friz Freleng

You Pay Your Money *56* Maclean Rogers

You Remember Ellen? *11* Sidney Olcott

You Said a Hatful *34* Charlie Chase

You Said a Mouthful *32* Lloyd Bacon

You Should Know Hadimrska *31* Martin Frič, Karel Lamač

You Talkin' to Me? *87* Charles Winkler

You the People *40* Roy Rowland

You Took the Words Right Out of My Heart *38* Dave Fleischer

You Try Somebody Else *32* Dave Fleischer

You Were Like a Wild Chrysanthemum *55* Keisuke Kinoshita

You Were Meant for Me *48* Lloyd Bacon

You Were Never Duckier *48* Chuck Jones

You Were Never Lovelier *42* William A. Seiter

You Who Are About to Enter *45* Arne Mattsson

You Will Be My Husband *38* Béla Gaál

You Will Die at Midnight *86* Lamberto Bava

You Will Remember *40* Jack Raymond

You'd Be Surprised *26* Arthur Rosson

You'd Be Surprised! *30* Walter Forde

You'll Find Out *40* David Butler

You'll Like My Mother *72* Lamont Johnson

You'll Never Get Rich *41* Sidney Lanfield

You'll Remember Me *06* Arthur Gilbert

Young America *18* Arthur Berthelet

Young America *31* Frank Borzage

Young America *42* Louis King

Young America Flies *40* B. Reeves Eason

Young Americans *67* Alexander Grasshoff

Young and Beautiful *34* Joseph Santley

Young and Dangerous *57* William F. Claxton

Young and Dumb *23* Al St. John

Young and Eager *61* Gordon Douglas

Young and Evil *57* Alfredo B. Crevenna

Young and Healthy *33* Rudolf Ising

Young and Immoral, The *61* Edward D. Wood, Jr.

Young and in Love *50* Åke Öhberg

Young and Innocent *37* Alfred Hitchcock

Young and the Brave, The *63* Francis D. Lyon

Young and the Cool, The *61* William Hole, Jr.

Young and the Damned, The *50* Luis Buñuel

Young and the Guilty, The *58* Peter Cotes

Young and the Immoral, The *61* Edward D. Wood, Jr.

Young and the Passionate, The *53* Federico Fellini

Young and the Willing, The *62* Ralph Thomas

Young and Wild *58* William Witney

Young and Wild *75* Dwayne Avery

Young and Willing *43* Edward H. Griffith

Young and Willing *53* J. Lee-Thompson

Young and Willing *62* Ralph Thomas

Young Animals, The *68* Maury Dexter

Young Aphrodites *62* Nikos Koundouros

Young April *26* Donald Crisp

Young As You Feel *31* Frank Borzage

Young As You Feel *40* Malcolm St. Clair

Young at Heart *54* Gordon Douglas

Young Bess *53* George Sidney

Young Bill Hickok *40* Joseph Kane

Young Billy Young *68* Burt Kennedy

Young Blood *32* Phil Rosen

Young Bride *32* William A. Seiter

Young Briton Foils the Enemy *14* F. Martin Thornton

Young Buffalo Bill *40* Joseph Kane

Young Captives, The *58* Irvin Kershner

Young Caruso, The *53* Giacomo Gentilomo

Young Cassidy *64* Jack Cardiff, John Ford

Young Chopin *52* Aleksander Ford

Young Composer's Odyssey, A *86* Georgy Shengelaya

Young Couple, The *69* René Gainville

Young Cycle Girls, The *79* Peter Perry

Young Daniel Boone *50* Reginald LeBorg

Young Days *55* Ján Kadár, Elmar Klos

Young Desire *30* Lewis D. Collins

Young Detectives, The *63* Gilbert Gunn

Young Diana, The *22* Albert Capellani, Robert Vignola

Young Dillinger *65* Terry Morse

Young Dr. Kildare *38* Harold S. Bucquet

Young Doctors, The *61* Phil Karlson

Young Doctors in Love *82* Garry Marshall

Young Donovan's Kid *31* Fred Niblo

Young Don't Cry, The *57* Alfred L. Werker

Young Dracula *73* Antonio Margheriti, Paul Morrissey

Young Dracula *74* Freddie Francis

Young Dynamite *37* Leslie Goodwins

Young Eagles *30* William A. Wellman

Young Eagles *34* Spencer G. Bennet

Young Einstein *86* Yahoo Serious

Young Emmanuelle, A *76* Nelly Kaplan

Young Erotic Fanny Hill, The *70* Joe Sarno

Young Farmers *42* John Eldridge

Young Figure *43* Shiro Toyoda

Young Forest, The *34* Josef Leytes

Young Frankenstein *74* Mel Brooks

Young Fugitives *38* John Rawlins

Young Fury *65* Christian Nyby

Young Generation, The *52* Kon Ichikawa

Young Giants *83* Terrell Tannen

Young Girls Beware *57* Yves Allégret

Young Girls of Good Families *63* Pierre Montazel

Young Girls of Okinawa, The *53* Tadashi Imai

Young Girls of Rochefort, The *66* Jacques Demy

Young Girls of Wilko, The *78* Andrzej Wajda

Young Go Wild, The *62* Alfred Vohrer

Young Graduates, The *71* Robert Anderson

Young Guard, The *47* Sergei Gerasimov

Young Guns, The *56* Alfredo Antonini

Young Guns *88* Christopher Cain

Young Guns II *90* Geoff Murphy

Young Guns of Texas *62* Maury Dexter

Young Guy Graduates *69* Jun Fukuda

Young Guy on Mt. Cook *69* Jun Fukuda

Young Hannah, Queen of the Vampires *72* Ray Danton, Julio Salvador

Young Have No Morals, The *59* Jean-Pierre Mocky
Young Have No Time, The *59* Johannes Allen
Young Hearts *87* Michael Hoffman
Young Hellions *58* Jack Arnold
Young Hollywood *27* Robert Thornby
Young Husbands *57* Mauro Bolognini
Young Ideas *24* Robert F. Hill
Young Ideas *43* Jules Dassin
Young in Heart, The *38* Richard Wallace
Young in Heart, The *43* George Archainbaud
Young Invaders, The *57* William A. Wellman
Young Ironsides *32* James Parrott
Young Jacobites, The *59* John Reeve
Young Jesse James *60* William F. Claxton
Young Ladies' Dormitory, The *05* Alf Collins
Young Ladies of Wilko, The *78* Andrzej Wajda
Young Lady Chatterley *77* Alan Roberts
Young Lady of Björneborg, The *22* Gustaf Edgren
Young Land, The *57* Ted Tetzlaff
Young Lions, The *58* Edward Dmytryk
Young Lochinvar *23* Will P. Kellino
Young Lord, The *70* Gustav R. Sellner
Young Love *33* Josef Rovenský
Young Love *83* Michal Bat-Adam
Young Lover, The *61* Roman Polanski
Young Lovers, The *49* Ida Lupino
Young Lovers, The *54* Anthony Asquith
Young Lovers, The *64* Samuel Goldwyn, Jr.
Young Lust *82* Gary Weis
Young Magician, The *87* Waldemar Dziki
Young Man and Moby Dick, The *78* Jaromil Jireš
Young Man and the White Whale, The *78* Jaromil Jireš
Young Man I Think You're Dying *70* James Kelly
Young Man of Manhattan *30* Monta Bell
Young Man of Music *50* Michael Curtiz
Young Man with a Horn *50* Michael Curtiz
Young Man with Ideas *52* Mitchell Leisen
Young Man's Bride, The *68* George Gunter
Young Man's Fancy *20* Malcolm St. Clair
Young Man's Fancy *39* Robert Stevenson
Young Master *80* Jackie Chan
Young Medardus *23* Michael Curtiz
Young Miss *30* Yasujiro Ozu
Young Miss *37* Satsuo Yamamoto
Young Mr. Lincoln *39* John Ford
Young Mr. Pitt, The *41* Carol Reed
Young Monk, The *78* Herbert Achternbusch
Young Mother Hubbard *17* Arthur Berthelet
Young Mrs. Winthrop *20* Walter Edwards
Young Nick at the Picnic *15* Edwin J. Collins
Young Nick Carter Detectiff *17* Will Anderson
Young Nobleman, The *24* Rune Carlsten
Young Nowheres *29* Frank Lloyd
Young Nurses, The *73* Clinton Kimbrough

Young Nurses in Love *86* Chuck Vincent
Young Oldfield *24* Leo McCarey
Young One, The *60* Luis Buñuel
Young Ones, The *60* Luis Alcoriza
Young Ones, The *61* Sidney J. Furie
Young Painter, The *22* Herbert Blaché
Young Partisans, The *42* Lev Kuleshov
Young Paul Baroni *52* Harold Schuster
Young People *37* Shiro Toyoda
Young People *40* Allan Dwan
Young People *52* Kon Ichikawa
Young People *54* Kozaburo Yoshimura
Young People *65* Henning Carlsen
Young People, Remember! *55* Miklós Jancsó
Young Philadelphians, The *59* Vincent Sherman
Young Pimple and His Little Sister *14* Fred Evans, Joe Evans
Young Pimple's Frolics *14* Fred Evans, Joe Evans
Young Playthings *72* Joe Sarno
Young Pushkin *37* Arcady Naroditsky
Young Racers, The *62* Francis Ford Coppola, Roger Corman
Young Rajah, The *22* Phil Rosen
Young Rebel *67* Vincent Sherman
Young Rebels, The *57* Roger Corman
Young Recruit, The *40* William Nigh
Young Redskins, The *09* Dave Aylott
Young Romance *15* George Melford
Young Runaways, The *68* Arthur Dreifuss
Young Savages, The *61* John Frankenheimer
Young Scamps *07* Lewin Fitzhamon
Young Scarface *47* John Boulting
Young Seducers, The *74* Michael Thomas
Young Sherlock Holmes *85* Barry Levinson
Young Sherlock Holmes and the Pyramid of Fear *85* Barry Levinson
Young Sinner, The *61* Tom Laughlin
Young Sinners *31* John G. Blystone
Young Stranger, The *56* John Frankenheimer
Young Summer *54* Kenne Fant
Young Swingers, The *63* Maury Dexter
Young Swordsman *63* Hiroshi Inagaki
Young, the Evil and the Savage, The *68* Antonio Margheriti
Young Tom Edison *39* Norman Taurog
Young Törless *66* Volker Schlöndorff
Young Toscanini *88* Franco Zeffirelli
Young Veterans *41* Alberto Cavalcanti, Charles Crichton
Young Virgin, The *34* Yasujiro Ozu
Young Warriors, The *67* John Peyser
Young Warriors *83* Lawrence Foldes
Young Whirlwind *28* Louis King
Young Widow *46* Edwin L. Marin
Young, Willing and Eager *61* Lance Comfort
Young Wine *86* Václav Vorlíček
Young Winston *71* Richard Attenborough
Young Wives' Tale *51* Henry Cass
Young Wolves, The *67* Marcel Carné
Young Woodley *29* Thomas Bentley
Young Woodley *30* Thomas Bentley
Young World, A *65* Vittorio De Sica
Young Years of Our Country *45* I. M.

Poselsky, Ivan Venzher, Sergei Yutkevich
Youngblood *78* Noel Nosseck
Youngblood *86* Peter Markle
Youngblood Hawke *64* Delmer Daves
Younger Brother *60* Kon Ichikawa
Younger Brothers, The *49* Edwin L. Marin
Younger Generation, The *29* Frank Capra
Younger Sister, The *13* Lawrence Trimble
Youngest Profession, The *43* Edward Buzzell
Youngest Spy, The *62* Andrei Tarkovsky
Younita *13* Bert Haldane
Younita, from Gutter to Footlights *13* Bert Haldane
Your Acquaintance *27* Lev Kuleshov
Your Beer *54* Susumu Hani
Your Best Friend *21* William Nigh
Your Cheatin' Heart *64* Gene Nelson
Your Contemporary *67* Yuli Raizman
Your Country Needs You *14* Bert Haldane
Your Daddy Like This? *71* Doo-yong Lee
Your Day Will Come *51* Salah Abu Saif
Your Destiny *28* Oskar Fischinger
Your Dog Ate My Lunch Mum *08* Walter R. Booth
Your First Time *85* Arduino Sacco
Your Friend and Mine *23* Clarence Badger
Your Girl and Mine *14* Giles Warren
Your Highness *40* Tadashi Imai
Your Job in Germany *45* Frank Capra
Your Last Act *41* Fred Zinnemann
Your Lips One *70* Malcolm Le Grice
Your Lips Three *71* Malcolm Le Grice
Your Money or Your Life *65* Jean-Pierre Mocky
Your Money or Your Life *81* Henning Carlsen
Your Money or Your Wife *59* Anthony Simmons
Your Name Brown? *14* Arthur Finn
Your Neighbor's Wife *89* José Fonseca e Costa
Your Number's Up *31* John Francis Dillon
Your Obedient Servant *17* Edward H. Griffith
Your Own Land *40* Arne Sucksdorff
Your Past Is Showing! *57* Mario Zampi
Your Peaceful Sky *87* Vladimir Gorpenko, Isaac Shmaruk
Your Presence *70* István Szabó
Your Red Wagon *47* Nicholas Ray
Your Shadow Is Mine *61* André Michel
Your Son and Brother *66* Vasili Shuksin
Your Teeth Are in My Neck *67* Roman Polanski
Your Three Minutes Are Up *73* Douglas Schwartz
Your Ticket Is No Longer Valid *79* George Kaczender
Your Turn Darling *63* Bernard Borderie
Your Turn, My Turn *78* François Leterrier
Your Uncle Dudley *35* Eugene Forde, James Tinling
Your Vice Is a Closed Room and Only I Have the Key *72* Sergio Martino
Your Wife and Mine *27* Frank O'Connor
Your Witness *50* Robert Montgomery
You're a Big Boy Now *66* Francis Ford Coppola

Za Ścianą *71* Krzysztof Zanussi
Za Sreću Je Potrebno Troje *86* Rajko Grlić
Za Vitrinoi Univermaga *55* Samson Samsonov
Za Winy Niepopelnione *39* Eugene Bodo
Za Život Radostný *51* Vojtěch Jasný, Karel Kachyňa
Zaa le Petit Chameau Blanc *60* Yannick Bellon
Zaak M.P., De *60* Bert Haanstra
Zaat *82* Don Barton
Zabaglione *66* Georges Robin
Zabavy Molodykh *88* Yevgeni Gerasimov
Zabicie Ciotki *85* Grzegorz Królikiewicz
Zabij Mnie, Glino *89* Jacek Bromski
Zabil Jsem Einsteina, Pánové *69* Oldřich Lipský
Zaboravljeni *88* Darko Bajić
Zabou *87* Hajo Gies
Zabravote Tozi Slochai *86* Krassimir Spassov
Zabriskie Point *69* Michelangelo Antonioni
Zabudnite na Mozarta *85* Miloslav Luther
Žaby a Ine Ryby *86* Julius Jarabek
Začarani Dvorac u Dudincima *51* Dušan Vukotić
Zachariah *70* George Englund
Zacharovannaya Desna *64* Yulia Solntseva
Zaczęło Się w Hiszpanii *50* Andrzej Munk
Zaduszki *61* Tadeusz Konwicki
Zafra, La *58* Lucas Demare
Zagavor Obrechyonnikh *50* Mikhail Kalatozov
Zagranichnii Pokhod Sudov Baltiiskogo Flota Kreisere "Aurora" i Uchebnogo Sudna "Komsomolts" August 8, 1925 *25* Dziga Vertov
Zahn um Zahn *85* Hajo Gies
Zahrada *68* Jan Švankmajer
Zaida — Die Tragödie eines Modells *23* Forest Holger-Madsen
Zakázané Uvolnenie *86* Juraj Libosit
Zaklyatie Doliny Zmei *88* Marek Piestrak
Zakon Velikoi Lyubvi *45* Boris Dolin
Zakonny Brak *86* Albert Mkrtchyan
Zakonye Bolshoi Zemli *48* Mark Donskoi
Zakroishchik iz Torzhka *25* Yakov Protazanov
Žalm *66* Evald Schorm
Zamach *58* Jerzy Passendorfer
Zamba *49* William Berke
Zamba the Gorilla *49* William Berke
Zamboanga *38* Eduardo De Castro
Zamri Oumi Voskresni *90* Vitaly Kanevski
Zan Boko *88* Gaston J. M. Kaboré
Zancos, Los *84* Carlos Saura
Zander the Great *25* George W. Hill
Zandra Rhodes *81* Peter Greenaway
Zandunga, La *37* Fernando De Fuentes
Zandy's Bride *74* Jan Troell
Zange no Yaiba *27* Yasujiro Ozu
Zangiku Monogatari *39* Kenji Mizoguchi
Zangir *86* Pervaiz Malik
Zanguezour *38* Amo Bek-Nazarov
Zanjin Zamba Ken *29* Daisuke Ito
Zanna Bianca *72* Lucio Fulci
Zanzibar *40* Harold Schuster
Zanzibar *89* Christine Pascal
Zaostřit, Prosím *56* Martin Frič

Zapatas Bande *14* Urban Gad
Zápor *60* András Kovács
Zaporosch sa Dunayem *39* Edgar G. Ulmer
Zaporozh za Dunayem *39* Edgar G. Ulmer
Zaporozhetz za Dunayem *39* Edgar G. Ulmer
Zappa *83* Bille August
Zappatore *32* Gustavo Sereno
Zapped! *82* Robert J. Rosenthal
Zapretnaya Zona *88* Nikolai Gubenko
Zaproszenie do Wnętrza *78* Andrzej Wajda
Zarak *56* Yakima Canutt, John Gilling, Terence Young
Zardoz *73* John Boorman
Zare *27* Amo Bek-Nazarov
Zářijové Noci *57* Vojtěch Jasný
Zarte Haut in Schwarzer Seide *62* Max Pecas
Zärtliche Chaoten *87* Franz-Josef Gottlieb
Zärtliche Chaoten 2 *88* Holm Dressler, Thomas Gottschalk
Zärtlichen Verwandten, Die *30* Richard Oswald
Zärtlichkeit der Wölfe *73* Ulli Lommel
Zasadil Dědek Řepu *45* Jiří Trnka
Zastihla Ma Noc *85* Juraj Herz
Zátah *85* Stanislav Strnad
Zatoichi *68* Kimiyoshi Yasuda
Zatoichi and the Scoundrels *68* Kimiyoshi Yasuda
Zatoichi Challenged *70* Kenji Misumi
Zatōichi Chikemuri Kaidō *70* Kenji Misumi
Zatoichi Enters Again *63* Tokuzo Tanaka
Zatōichi Jigokutabi *68* Kenji Misumi
Zatōichi Kenkatabi *68* Kimiyoshi Yasuda
Zatoichi Meets Yojimbo *70* Kihachi Okamoto
Zatoichi on the Road *68* Kimiyoshi Yasuda
Zatōichi Rō-Yaburi *67* Satsuo Yamamoto
Zatōichi to Yōjimbō *70* Kihachi Okamoto
Zatoichi's Conspiracy *74* Kimiyoshi Yasuda
Zauberberg, Der *81* Hans W. Geissendörfer
Závada Není na Vašem Přijímači *61* Jiří Brdečka
Zavallılar *75* Yılmaz Güney, Atıf Yılmaz
Závrať *62* Karel Kachyňa
Zavtra Bila Voina *87* Yuri Kara
Zawga el Sania, El *67* Salah Abu Saif
Zawgat Ragol Mohim *87* Mohamed Khan
Zaza *09* Ernesto Maria Pasquali
Zaza *15* Hugh Ford, Edwin S. Porter
Zaza *23* Allan Dwan
Zaza *38* George Cukor
Zaza *42* Renato Castellani
Zaza the Dancer *13* Bert Haldane
Zazie *60* Louis Malle
Zazie dans le Métro *60* Louis Malle
Zazie in the Subway *60* Louis Malle
Zazie in the Underground *60* Louis Malle
Zazzennyj Fonar *83* Agassi Aivasian
Zbabělec *61* Jiří Weiss
Zbehovia a Poutníci *68* Juraj Jakubisko
Zdjęcia Próbne *77* Agnieszka Holland

Zdravstvui Moskva! *45* Sergei Yutkevich
Zdravstvuitye Deti *62* Mark Donskoi
Ze American Girl *20* Jean Gic
Ze Soboty na Neděli *31* Gustav Machatý
Zebra Force *77* Giuseppe Tornatore
Zebra in the Kitchen *65* Ivan Tors
Zebra Killer, The *74* William Girdler
Zed and Two Noughts, A *85* Peter Greenaway
Zeder *83* Pupi Avati
Zeder — Voices from the Beyond *83* Pupi Avati
Zee & Co. *71* Brian G. Hutton
Zeebrugge *24* A. V. Bramble, H. Bruce Woolfe
Zeedijk Film Study *27* Joris Ivens
Zeedijk-Filmstudie *27* Joris Ivens
Zegen *87* Shohei Imamura
Zehn Minuten Mozart *30* Lotte Reiniger
Zeisters *83* John Golden
Zejal Sumro *88* Sharad Palekar
Zelena Letá *85* Milan Muchna
Železničáři *63* Evald Schorm
Zelig *83* Woody Allen
Zelly and Me *88* Bettina Rathborne
Země Zemi *62* Evald Schorm
Zemlya *30* Alexander Dovzhenko
Zemlya *57* Zahari Zhandov
Zemlya i Zoloto *87* Armen Manaryan, Henry Markaryan
Zemlya v Plenu *28* Fedor Ozep
Zemlya Zhazhdyot *30* Yuli Raizman
Zemma *50* Keisuke Kinoshita
Zenabel *69* Ruggero Deodato
Zengin Mutfağı *89* Başar Sabuncu
Zeni no Odori *64* Kon Ichikawa
Zenobia *39* Gordon Douglas
Ženu Ani Květinou Neuhodíš *66* Zdeněk Podskalský
Zeppelin *71* Étienne Périer
Zeppelin and Love, The *47* Jiří Brdečka
Zeppelin's Last Raid, The *17* Irvin Willat
Zeppelins of London *16* Cecil Birch
Zerbrochene Krug, Der *38* Gustav Ucicky
Zerkalo *74* Andrei Tarkovsky
Zerkalo dlya Geroya *88* Vladimir Khotinenko
Zero *28* Jack Raymond
Zero *60* Anthony Asquith
Zero Boys, The *85* Nico Mastorakis
Zero City *89* Karen Shakhnazarov
Zéro de Conduite *33* Jean Vigo
Zéro de Conduite, Jeunes Diables au Collège *33* Jean Vigo
08/15 *54* Paul Ostermayer
08/15 in der Heimat *55* Paul Ostermayer
08/15, II Teil *55* Paul Ostermayer
0-18, or A Message from the Sky *14* George Loane Tucker
Zero for Conduct *33* Jean Vigo
Zero Hour, The *18* Travers Vale
Zero Hour *36* Howard Hawks
Zero Hour *39* Sidney Salkow
Zero Hour! *57* Hall Bartlett
Zero Hour *76* Edgar Reitz
Zero in the Universe *65* George Moorse
Zero Murder Case, The *45* Robert Siodmak
Zero no Hakken *63* Yoji Kuri
Zero Population Growth *71* Michael Campus

07 Taxi *43* Marcello Pagliero
Zero, the Hound *41* Dave Fleischer
Zero to Sixty *78* Don Weis
002 Agenti Segretissimi *64* Lucio Fulci
00-2 Most Secret Agents *64* Lucio Fulci
002 Operazione Luna *66* Lucio Fulci
Žert *68* Jaromil Jireš
Zestos Menas Augoustos, O *69* Sokrates Kapsakis
Zeta One *69* Michael Cort
Zeugin Aus der Hölle *67* Zita Mitrović
Zex *57* Montgomery Tully
Zezowate Szczęście *59* Andrzej Munk
Zheleznoe Pole *87* Yaropolk Lapshin
Zhen Nu *88* Jianxin Huang
Zhenitba Balzaminova *66* Konstantin Voinov
Zhenshchina s Kinzhalom *16* Yakov Protazanov
Zhenshchina Zakhochet, Chorta Obmoro-chit *14* Yakov Protazanov
Zhi Mo Nu *68* Weng Jin, Yixiu Lin
Zhilibyli Starik so Starukhoi *64* Grigori Chukhrai
Zhitel Nyeobitayemovo Ostrova *15* Władysław Starewicz
Zhivoi Lenin *48* Mikhail Romm, Mia Slavenska
Zhivoi Trup *28* Fedor Ozep
Zhivyot Takoi Paren *64* Vasili Shuksin
Zhizn *27* Mikhail Averbakh, Mark Donskoi
Zhizn v Smerti *14* Yevgeni Bauer
Zhizn za Zhizn *16* Yevgeni Bauer
Zhonghua Nuer *49* Zhifeng Ling, Jiang Zhai
Zhukovsky *50* Vsevolod I. Pudovkin, Dmitri Vasiliev
Zhumoreski *24* Dziga Vertov
Zhurnalist *66* Sergei Gerasimov
Zhurnalista *27* Lev Kuleshov
Zia Smemorata, La *41* Ladislas Vajda
Zidore ou Les Métamorphoses *21* Louis Feuillade
Ziegfeld Follies *45* Lemuel Ayres, Roy Del Ruth, Robert Lewis, Vincente Minnelli, George Sidney, Charles Walters
Ziegfeld Girl *41* Robert Z. Leonard
Ziel den Wolken *39* Wolfgang Liebe-neiner
Zielarze z Kamiennej Doliny *52* Wojciech Has
Ziemia Czeka *54* Jan Łomnicki
Ziemia Obiecana *74* Andrzej Wajda
Zig-Zag *75* László Szabó
Zigano der Brigant vom Monte Diavolo *25* Harry Piel
Zigeunerbaron *35* Karl Hartl
Zigeunerbaron, Der *54* Arthur Maria Rabenalt
Zigeunerblut *11* Urban Gad
Zigeunerblut *35* Charles Klein
Zigeunerweisen *40* Géza von Bolváry
Ziggy Stardust and the Spiders from Mars *73* D. A. Pennebaker
Zigomar *10* Victorin Jasset
Zigomar Contre Nick Carter *12* Victorin Jasset
Zigomar Peau d'Anguille *12* Victorin Jasset

Zigomar, Roi des Voleurs *10* Victorin Jasset
Zigzag *70* Richard A. Colla
Zigzag of Success, The *68* Eldar Ryazanov
Žijeme v Praze *34* Otakar Vávra
Žil Zpívající Drozd *72* Otar Ioseliani
Zillah, A Gipsy Romance *11* A. E. Coleby
Zimatar *87* Ric Santiago, José F. Sibal
Zimmer 36 *88* Markus Fischer
Zimni Vecher v Gagrakh *86* Karen Shakhnazarov
Zina *85* Ken McMullen
Zina-Zinulya *87* Pavel Chukhrai
Zindigi *39* Pramatesh Chandra Barua
Zinker, Der *31* Martin Frič, Karel Lamač
Zio d'America, Lo *39* A. Benedetti
Zio Indegno, Lo *89* Franco Brusati
Zio Tom *72* Gualtiero Jacopetti, Franco Prosperi
Zip 'n' Snort *61* Chuck Jones
Zipp the Dodger *14* Roscoe Arbuckle
Zipping Along *53* Chuck Jones
Zippy Buys a Pet Pup *16* Charles E. Howell
Zippy in a Sanatorium *16* Charles E. Howell
Zippy's Insurance *16* H. M. Freck
Zirkus Leben *32* Heinz Paul
Zirkus Renz *43* Arthur Maria Rabenalt
Zirkusblut *16* Richard Oswald
Zirkuskönig, Der *24* Max Linder, Édouard E. Violet
Zis Boom Bah *41* William Nigh
Zischke *87* Martin Theo Krieger
Ziska la Danseuse Espionne *22* Henri An-dréani
Žít Svůj Život *63* Evald Schorm
Zita *67* Robert Enrico
Zítra Vstanu a Opařím Se Čajem *77* Jin-dřich Polák
Zivatar a Pusztán *37* István György
Ziveli!: Medicine for the Heart *87* Les Blank
Zivile Knete *85* Detlef Gumm, Hans-Georg Ullrich
Život Je Pes *33* Martin Frič
Život Radnika *87* Miroslav Mandić
Život Sa Stricem *88* Krsto Papić
Zizanie, La *78* Claude Zidi
Zjoek *87* Eric van Zuylen
Zkrocení Zlého Muže *86* Marie Poled-ňáková
Zlatá Reneta *65* Otakar Vávra
Zlaté Kapradí *63* Jiří Weiss
Zlatye Gori *31* Sergei Yutkevich
Zločin v Dívčí Škole *65* Jiří Menzel*
Zločin v Šantánu *68* Jiří Menzel
Złoto *62* Wojciech Has
Złoty Mahmudia *87* Kazimierz Tarnas
Złoty Pociąg *87* Bohdan Poręba
Zły Chłopiec *50* Andrzej Wajda
Zmítaná *69* Ján Kadár, Elmar Klos
Znachor *38* Michael Waszyński
Znaju Tolko Ia *88* Karen Gevorkyan
Znak Bedy *86* Mikhail Ptashuk
Znay Nashikh *87* Sultan Khodjikov
Znoi *63* Larissa Shepitko
Zō o Kutta Renchū *47* Kozaburo Yoshi-mura
Zoárd Mester *17* Michael Curtiz

Zocelení *50* Martin Frič
Zocker-Express *88* Klaus Lemke
Zodiac Couples, The *70* Alan Roberts, Bob Stein
Zoeken naar Eileen *87* Rudolf van den Berg
Zoku Minami no Kaze *42* Kozaburo Yoshimura
Zoku Miyamoto Musashi *67* Hiroshi Inagaki
Zoku Ningen no Jōken *59* Masaki Kobayashi
Zoku Otoko wa Tsuraiyō *69* Yoji Yamada
Zoku Sugata Sanshiro *45* Akira Kurosawa
Zöld Ár *65* István Gaál
Zollenstein *17* Edgar Jones
Żołnierz Zwycięstwa *53* Wanda Jaku-bowska
Zolotaya Baba *87* Viktor Kobzev
Zolotoi Klyuchik *39* Alexander Ptushko
Zolotoi Med *28* N. Bersenev, Vladimir Petrov
Zolotye Vorota *69* Yulia Solntseva
Zoltan, Hound of Dracula *77* Alfredo An-tonini
Zombi 2 *79* Lucio Fulci
Zombie *64* Del Tenney
Zombie, The *65* John Gilling
Zombie *79* Lucio Fulci
Zombie 2 *79* Lucio Fulci
Zombie III *80* Andrea Bianchi
Zombie Brigade *88* Carmelo Musca, Barrie Pattison
Zombie Child *77* Robert Voskanian
Zombie Creeping Flesh *81* Bruno Mattei
Zombie Flesh Eaters *79* Lucio Fulci
Zombie High *87* Ron Link
Zombie Holocaust *79* Marino Girolami
Zombie Horror *80* Andrea Bianchi
Zombie Island Massacre *84* John N. Carter
Zombie Nightmare *86* Jack Bravman
Zombies *64* Del Tenney
Zombies, The *65* John Gilling
Zombies *77* George Romero
Zombies—Dawn of the Dead *77* George Romero
Zombies of Mora-Tau *57* Edward L. Cahn
Zombies of Sugar Hill, The *74* Paul Maslansky
Zombies of the Stratosphere *52* Fred C. Brannon
Zombies on Broadway *45* Gordon Douglas
Zon *20* Robert Boudrioz
Zona Pericolosa *51* Francesco Maselli
Zona Roja *75* Emilio Fernández
Zone, La *27* Georges Lacombe
Zone de la Mort, La *16* Abel Gance
Zone Moment *56* Stan Brakhage
Zone of Death, The *28* Fred Paul
Zone Rouge *86* Robert Enrico
Zone Troopers *86* Danny Bilson
Zongar *18* Bernard MacFadden
Zoning *86* Ulrich Krenkler
Zontar, the Thing from Venus *66* Larry Buchanan
Zontik dlya Novobrachnykh *87* Rodion Nakhapetov
Zoo, The *20* Hy Mayer
Zoo, The *33* Walter Lantz
Zoo *62* Bert Haanstra